EPHESIANS 6:12

For we don't wrestle against flesh and blood, but against the rulers, against the authorities, against the cosmic powers over this present darkness, against the spiritual forces of <u>evil</u> in the heavenly places,...

; you and I prayed down, as I said, that evil against Anthony that time, and now you have a new family; never forget our family, our real fight!

Know <u>your</u> enemy

Sword of Spirit — God's Word

<u>our</u> fight

Gospel Transformation Bible

Presented to

Big Sis Lisa

Take this spirit sword and fight the evil that has hunted us, since WV!

Ephesians 6:13 (p. 1594)

by

Jon

on

4/18/14

"Good Friday"

Marriages

Husband

Wife

Place Date

Husband

Wife

Place Date

Husband

Wife

Place Date

Husband

Wife

Place Date

Husband

Wife

Place Date

Husband

Wife

Place Date

English
Standard
Version

Christ
in all of
Scripture.

Gospel Transformation Bible

Grace
for all of
Life.

CROSSWAY Wheaton, Illinois www.esvbible.org

ESV Text Edition: 2011

All italics in quotations of Scripture have been added by the authors.

Library of Congress Catalog Card Number 2013006494

Printed in the United States of America
Published by Crossway
Wheaton, Illinois 60187, U.S.A.
www.crossway.org

Crossway is a not-for-profit publishing ministry that exists solely for the purpose of publishing the Good News of the Gospel and the Truth of God's Word, the Bible. A portion of the purchase price of every ESV Bible is donated to help support Bible distribution ministry around the world.

The ESV Bible is free online and on mobile devices everywhere worldwide, including a selection of free Bible study resources, at www.esvbible.org.

RRDC 22 21 20 19 18 17 16 15 14 13
13 12 11 10 9 8 7 6 5 4 3 2 1

Table of Contents

The Books of the Bible

in Alphabetical Order

Introduction

to the ESV Gospel Transformation Bible

The goal of the *Gospel Transformation Bible* is twofold: (1) to enable readers to understand that the whole Bible is a unified message of the gospel of God's grace culminating in Christ Jesus, and (2) to help believers apply this good news to their everyday lives in a heart-transforming way. Our hope is that, as Christians throughout the world learn to see the message of salvation by grace unfolding throughout Scripture, they will respond to God with greater love, faithfulness, and power.

This is not a new way of studying the Bible. Rather, this approach honors our Lord's own instruction to see the gospel in all of Scripture, so that his love empowers the transformation of our lives from the inside out.

THE GOSPEL IN ALL OF SCRIPTURE

Christ's grace does not wait until the last chapters of Matthew to make its first appearance, but rather is the dawning light increasing throughout Scripture toward the day the Savior came. Jesus himself made this clear when he spoke to the religious leaders of his day, saying, "You search the Scriptures because you think that in them you have eternal life; and it is they that bear witness about me" (John 5:39; see also 1:45). After his resurrection, he spoke similarly to the disciples on the road to Emmaus. Luke records Jesus' conversation this way: "And beginning with Moses and all the Prophets, he interpreted to them in all the Scriptures the things concerning himself" (Luke 24:27; see also v. 44).

Jesus says repeatedly that all the Scriptures bear witness of him. But of course, a key question remaining for us is, how do all the Scriptures do this? Jesus cannot be contending that all portions of Scripture make direct mention of him. Most verses and most accounts in the Bible make no explicit reference to Jesus.

We will understand what Jesus meant about all of Scripture bearing witness to him as we remember the big picture of the Bible. An old cliché says, "Biblical history is 'his-story.'" But how is this story of Jesus unfolding across the past and future millennia the Bible describes? A standard way of thinking about the whole picture of God's dealing with humanity begins with a good creation, spoiled by Adam's fall, redeemed by Christ's provision, and perfected in the consummation of Christ's rule over all things. This creation-fall-redemption-consummation perspective helps us map all the events of Scripture. All have a place in this great unfolding plan of "his-story."

In addition to seeing the overall plan of "his-story," it is important to remember that the "redemption" component of biblical history begins unfolding long before the crucifixion narrative in the Gospels. The Bible reveals the dawning light of redemption near the very beginning. Immediately after Adam's and Eve's sin, God says to the one who tempted them, "I will put enmity between you and the woman, and between your offspring and her offspring; he shall bruise your head, and you shall bruise his heel" (Gen. 3:15). Bible scholars refer to this verse as the "first gospel." It is God's first promise to redeem his world and people—broken by Adam's sin—by the divine provision of One who would come through a human source to defeat Satan while also suffering an awful attack from him.

This early verse in Genesis sets the stage for all that follows in the Bible. The rest of human history will be played out on this stage. Thus, every piece of Scripture that follows has a redemptive context. Our goal as Bible readers who are interpreting as Christ intends is not to try to make Jesus magically appear in every text, but to show where every text properly stands on this redemptive stage. Jesus is the chief and culminating figure on this stage. The stage is set for him; all that transpires on the stage relates to him; and we do not fully understand anything on the stage until we have identified its relation to him.

It should be emphasized that placing every text in its redemptive context does not mean that every text mentions Jesus. Rather, every text relates some aspect of God's redeeming grace that finds its fullest expression in Christ. Ultimately, we understand who he is and what he does by how he "fleshes out" the message of redemption that unfolds throughout the Bible.

This unfolding gospel perspective may be communicated in a variety of ways in the commentary portions of this *Gospel Transformation Bible*. Many texts specifically describe, prophesy, or typify (set a pattern for) the ministry of Jesus. Straightforward identification of obvious gospel truths is sufficient for understanding these texts. There are many more texts, however, that prepare for or reflect upon Christ's ministry by disclosing aspects of the grace of God that find their completed expression in Jesus. These "gospel windows" revealing God's gracious nature and provision may be identified and/or described through a variety of means—for example, locating a text in its redemptive-historical context, identifying a literary motif typifying God's redemptive work that carries through the Old and New Testaments, describing doctrinal developments that are foundational to gospel understanding, or simply showing how God's divine care for his people evidences the grace necessary for our redemption.

Our goal will be to identify gospel themes through methods readers can identify and repeat in their own study of Scripture. We want to distinguish such interpretation from speculative approaches that have sometimes cast doubt upon the gospel focus or veracity of Scripture. In the past, some interpreters have understood Christ's statements about all the Scriptures speaking of him to justify fanciful references to Jesus in Old Testament passages with little biblical support. Such "allegorical" interpretations may, for example, claim that because Noah's ark was made of wood, and the cross was made of wood, therefore the ark represents the cross. Of course, someone else could say that the wood of Noah's ark represents the wood of the ark of the covenant, or the wood panels of the temple of Israel, or the wood of the boat from which Christ stilled the storm. The trouble with such allegorical interpretations is that they are more a reflection of human imagination than biblical revelation.

If the New Testament does not indicate that a specific object or account is about Jesus, it is best not to force an interpretation that logic cannot prove. At the same time, we should be very willing to learn principles of redemptive interpretation that the New Testament writers employed and exemplified. From these principles we learn that the more common approach to understanding the redemptive nature of all biblical texts is to identify how God's Word *predicts*, *prepares for*, *reflects*, or *results from* the person and/or work of Christ. These four categories of gospel explanation are not meant to be exhaustive or kept rigidly separate, but they do help us explain how all of Scripture bears witness to who Christ is and/or what he must do.

1. Some passages—such as the prophecies and the messianic Psalms—clearly *predict* who Christ is and what he will do. Isaiah wrote of the Messiah, that "his name shall be called Wonderful Counselor, Mighty God, Everlasting Father, Prince of Peace. Of the increase of his government and of peace there will be no end" (Isa. 9:6–7). This is a clear prediction of Jesus' person and work, and there are many more such predictions in the prophetic portions of Scripture.

2. Other passages *prepare* God's people to understand the grace that God must provide to redeem his people. When God uses his servant David to show mercy to King Saul's lame grandson (a royal descendant who would be David's blood-rival for Israel's throne), we understand something about God's ways of forgiving enemies and showing mercy toward the helpless.

   Not only do many Old Testament passages prepare God's people to understand the grace of *his provision*, they also prepare the people to understand *their need*. When Paul writes in Galatians 3:24 that the law was our schoolmaster or guardian helping lead us to Christ, we understand that the high and holy standards of the law ultimately prepare us to seek God's provision of mercy rather than to depend on the quality of our performance to make us acceptable to him. The sacrifice system further prepares us to understand that without the shedding of blood there is no atonement for our failures to keep the law (Heb. 9:22). And because Abraham's faith was counted to him as righteousness, we are prepared to understand that our standing before God depends upon our faith in the provision of another (Rom. 4:23–24).

   Grace does not spring up like a surprise jack-in-the-box in the New Testament. God's people have been prepared for millennia to understand and receive the grace of Christ on their behalf.

3. Because grace is the key to understanding the purposes of God throughout the whole Bible, culminating in Christ, aspects of the gospel are *reflected* throughout Scripture. When a text neither plainly predicts nor prepares for Christ's person or work, the redemptive truths reflected in the text can always be discerned by asking two questions that are fair to ask of any text:

   What does this text reflect about the nature of God
   who provides redemption?
   and/or
   What does this text reflect about the nature of humanity
   that requires redemption?

These simple questions are the lenses to the reading glasses through which we can look at any text to see what the Bible is reflecting of God's nature and/or human nature. Inevitably these lenses enable us see that God is holy and we are not, or that God is sovereign and we are vulnerable, or that God is merciful and we require his mercy. Such reading glasses always make us aware of our need of God's grace to compensate for our sin and inability. Christ may not be specifically mentioned in the text, but the reflection of God's nature and ours makes the necessity of his grace apparent.

Using these reading glasses throughout the Old and New Testament will enable us to see the gracious nature of God who provides redemption as he gives strength to the weak, rest to the weary, deliverance to the disobedient, faithfulness to the unfaithful, food to the hungry, and salvation to sinners. We also learn something about the human nature that requires redemption when heroes fail, patriarchs lie, kings fall, prophets cower, disciples doubt, and covenant people become idolaters. These lenses prevent us from setting up characters in the Bible *only* as moral heroes to emulate, rather than as flawed men and women who themselves needed the grace of God.

Every text, seen in its redemptive context, is reflecting an aspect of humanity's fallen condition that requires the grace of God. Focus upon this fallen condition will inevitably cause readers to consider the divine solution characteristic of the grace that culminates in the provision of the Savior.

4. Finally, we understand how God's redemptive message appears in Scripture by those texts that are a *result* of Christ's work in our behalf. We are justified and sanctified as a result of Christ's atoning work and spiritual indwelling. Our prayers are heard as a result of his priestly intercession for us. Our wills are transformed as result of our union with him. We worship as a result of God's gracious provision for every aspect of our salvation.

   Ultimately, the reason to read Scripture with an eye to understanding how our actions and status are a result of grace is to keep straight the order of Scripture's imperatives and indicatives. The imperatives (what we are to do) are always a *consequence* of the indicatives (who we are by God's gracious provision); what we do is never a *cause* of who we are with respect to our eternal status in God's kingdom and family. We obey as a *result* of being God's beloved, not to cause God to love us. His grace toward us precedes, enables, and motivates our efforts toward holiness.

   A key example of imperatives flowing from indicatives occurs when God gives the Ten Commandments to his people. He does not make their obedience a condition of his love. He first declares, "I am the LORD your God, who brought you out of the land of Egypt, out of the house of slavery" (Deut. 5:6), and then he gives the commandments. He rescued his people before they obeyed. Their obedience was expected as a consequence of receiving God's deliverance, not as a condition for obtaining it. By understanding this consistent redemptive pattern in Scripture, we not only have a tool for understanding the Bible's structure, we have a way of seeing the grace of the gospel even in passages dominated by God's commands.

The indicative/imperative pattern of Scripture leads us next to consider why it is so important to see the grace message pervading Scripture and culminating in Christ. So far we have only considered *how* we can excavate grace from all of Scripture, but we have not discussed *why* this is so important. The reason is that grace not only underlies God's imperatives, it is also the ultimate power that enables us to live these standards, as we are transformed from the inside out.

EMPOWERED APPLICATION

A second major goal of the *Gospel Transformation Bible* is therefore to help readers apply gospel truths to their everyday lives. Faithful application typically answers four questions: 1) What to do? 2) Where to do it? 3) Why to do it? and 4) How to do it? Previous application-focused study Bibles have emphasized the first two of these questions. The *Gospel Transformation Bible*, while not ignoring the first two questions, seeks to be a primary resource for the latter two. Contributors' notes indicate how the unfolding gospel truths in any given passage of Scripture motivate and enable believers to honor their Savior from the heart—in short, how grace *transforms* them.

Our goal is to make plain the imperatives of God's Word, while undermining the human reflex to base God's affection on human performance. Contributors have therefore indicated how the indicatives of the gospel (i.e., the status and privileges believers have by virtue of God's grace alone) provide motivation and power for God's people to honor him from the heart.

The Motivation of Grace

The Bible recognizes no definition of grace that encourages moral license. Instead, feasting on grace fuels love for God that enables us to fulfill the commandment that is foundational to all others: "you shall love the Lord your God with all your heart and with all your soul and with all your mind and with all your strength" (Mark 12:30). When we love him rightly, we delight to walk with him in every dimension of our lives. Only the grace of God ultimately displayed in the provision of Christ for sinners can stimulate such loving obedience.

Warnings and rewards are also clearly given in Scripture to motivate believers through identification of the consequences of disobedience and the blessings of obedience. But in themselves, these motivations do not create an obedience that is a product of loving God with all our heart, soul, mind, and strength. In fact, if we only or primarily obey God to avoid consequences and/or to gain rewards, then selfish love motivates us more than love for God. For the believer, biblical warnings must be understood as expressions of care from a loving Father, and blessings must be received as benevolent responses to inadequate performance. Without this perspective the warnings and blessings accomplish the opposite of their biblical purpose—creating fear and pride rather than love and thanksgiving.

Relishing the gracious provision God has made for us despite our sin and inability stimulates true humility, gratitude, sacrifice, obedience, and praise. We live to honor God in response to the love he has shown us, more than living for the sake of earthly priorities. Heaven's priorities become our own because expressing love for the One who first loved us becomes our greatest delight and deepest satisfaction. We pursue holiness in loving response to the heavenly Father who has been so gracious to us, not to bribe a divine ogre in the sky to be favorable toward us.

Since God's love for us is the soil in which love for God grows, identifying his grace in all the Scriptures is not simply an interpretive scheme. It is supremely practical. For regular exaltation of the gospel is what ignites love for God in the hearts of believers. We identify the grace pervading Scripture in order to fan into flame our zeal for the Savior. Our goal is not merely good interpretation but stimulation of a profound love for God that bears holy fruit, as pleasing the One we love above all brings our most profound and compelling joy.

The Power of Grace

Grace pervades Scripture not only to motivate godliness, but also to empower it. In order to discern how grace empowers, we need to consider the sources of power for the Christian life.

Knowledge is power. One source of spiritual power is knowledge. We need to know what to do and believe in order to apply God's Word to our lives. If we do not *know* what to believe, then we cannot honor the truths about God; and, if we do not *know* what to do, then we cannot truly please God. Among other things, this means that consistently uncovering the grace of God in Scripture does not render superfluous the law of God. The law reflects the character and care of God (Ps. 19:7–10). By the direction of his commands, God gives us a safe path for our lives and, in doing so, he reveals that he is good.

The law is *un*gracious when it is presented as a means of meriting God's favor or acceptance, but Jesus taught us that the law itself is good—and that not one iota of it would pass away until heaven and earth did (Matt. 5:17–18). As counterintuitive as it may seem, we are *not* being gracious when we minimize the moral standards of God, because by doing so we rob others of the knowledge of the safe path that God's Word provides *and* of the knowledge of the good God who laid that path.

Yet, as important as it is to know what to believe and what to do, such knowledge is still insufficient for living the Christian life. If we have no will or ability to act on the knowledge we have, we cannot please God. That's why uncovering the message of grace in all of Scripture is so important. The love for God that the gospel of grace stimulates in us provides power for Christian living that knowledge alone cannot.

Love is power. To help us grasp the full power of love for God, we must consider a critical question: What is the primary reason that sin gains power over believers? Sin's power has already been defeated; we are no longer its slaves (Rom. 6:14–17). By virtue of their renewed minds and the indwelling power of the Holy Spirit, sin no more has dominion over those united to Christ (Rom. 12:1–2; Gal. 2:20; 1 John 4:4). So why do we yield to sin? The answer is, because we love it. Consider this: If sin did not attract us, it would have no power over us. We turn from God because we are drawn to sin's temporary pleasures and false promises (Heb. 11:25; James 1:14–15).

The understanding that sin takes control of our lives through our love of it leads to another critical question: What will drive our love for sin from our hearts? First, understanding that the pleasures of sin are temporary and that its consequences are ruinous will help turn us from sin. The warnings in Scripture confirm the importance of this understanding. But what will cut off love for sin at its source, so that it does not even have the opportunity to gain control of our heart? The answer is: a surpassing, transforming love.

Our love for sin, which grants it present power in our lives, is overcome when displaced by a greater love. Thomas Chalmers's famous sermon two hundred years ago on "The Expulsive Power of a New Affection" still rings true. When love for Christ exceeds all other loves, we want to please him above all other pleasures. This is why Jesus said, "If you love me, you will keep my commandments" (John 14:15).

Understanding the power of a surpassing love leads to a final critical question: If a surpassing love for God makes his priorities our own, then what fills our hearts with such love for him? The answer is, in the words of John Newton's famous hymn, "amazing grace . . . that saved a wretch like me." He loved me before I knew him. He died for me while I was yet his enemy. He keeps me when I fall. He holds me when I fail. He remains faithful though I am faithless. He forgives me when I am wrong, and loves me still. Such grace is intended to fill our hearts with a surpassing love for God that empowers genuine Christian living. The power of grace to stimulate an all-conquering love for God is the ultimate reason we must identify the heart of the gospel in all of Scripture. Interpretation marked by consistent adulation of God's mercy continually fills the Christian heart with more cause to love him. This love becomes the primary force for Christian obedience as hearts in which the Spirit dwells respond with love for their Savior. This is why the apostle Paul could say, "the love of Christ controls us" (2 Cor. 5:14), and that "the grace of God" is "training us to renounce ungodliness and worldly passions, and to live self-controlled, upright, and godly lives" (Titus 2:11–12). Grace leads to godliness.

In the *Gospel Transformation Bible*, we will consistently excavate the gospel truths that pervade Scripture so that the hearts of believers might be filled with love for God that drives out love for the world. Without love for the world, its temptations have no power. We are not tempted to do what we have no desire to do. Instead, a preeminent love for God makes doing his will the believer's greatest joy, and this joy is our strength (Neh. 8:10).

By showing how grace motivates and empowers the Christian life, the heart-application that the *Gospel Transformation Bible* commentators provide is not a legalistic add-on to Bible exposition. These reflections on how we can apply the Bible to our lives in a grace-centered way are rather the spiritual unfolding of the implications of the gospel in the life of the believer. Because grace finds its ultimate expression in Christ's love for us, we love him. As a consequence, we delight to love what and whom he loves. Our delight in his delight is not only the power behind personal holiness but the stimulus to love the unlovely, provide for the needy, and care for all that Christ loves.

Bryan Chapell
General Editor

Contributors

EDITORS

Bryan Chapell
General Editor
Senior Pastor, Grace Presbyterian Church, Peoria, Illinois;
President Emeritus, Covenant Theological Seminary

Dane Ortlund
Managing Editor
Vice President for Bible Publishing, Crossway

STUDY NOTE CONTRIBUTORS

Under the oversight of the editors, the following people contributed content for the *ESV Gospel Transformation Bible* study notes.

Genesis
Willem VanGemeren
Professor of Old Testament and Semitic Languages, Trinity Evangelical Divinity School

Exodus
Sean Michael Lucas
Senior Minister, First Presbyterian Church, Hattiesburg, Mississippi

Leviticus
Jay Sklar
Professor of Old Testament, Covenant Theological Seminary

Numbers
L. Michael Morales
Provost and Professor of Old Testament, Reformation Bible College

Deuteronomy
Mark D. Futato
Robert L. Maclellan Professor of Old Testament, Reformed Theological Seminary

Joshua
Michael Horton
J. Gresham Machen Professor of Systematic Theology and Apologetics, Westminster Seminary California

Judges
W. Brian Aucker
Assistant Professor of Old Testament, Covenant Theological Seminary

Ruth
Mary Beth McGreevy
Speaker and Author

1–2 Samuel
V. Philips Long
Professor of Old Testament, Regent College

1–2 Kings, 1–2 Chronicles
Miles Van Pelt
Alan Belcher Professor of Old Testament and Biblical Languages, Reformed Theological Seminary

Ezra, Nehemiah
Kathleen Nielson
Director of Women's Initiatives, The Gospel Coalition

Esther
Elyse Fitzpatrick
Speaker and Author

Job
Paul F. M. Zahl
Dean/President Emeritus, Trinity Episcopal School for Ministry

Psalms 1–100
George Robertson
Senior Pastor, First Presbyterian Church, Augusta, Georgia

Psalms 101–150
Bruce A. Ware
Professor of Christian Theology, The Southern Baptist Theological Seminary

Proverbs
Raymond C. Ortlund Jr.
Lead Pastor, Immanuel Church, Nashville, Tennessee

Ecclesiastes, Song of Solomon
Doug O'Donnell
Lecturer in Biblical Studies, Queensland Theological College

Isaiah
Kelly M. Kapic
Professor of Theological Studies, Covenant College

Jeremiah, Lamentations
Graeme Goldsworthy
Former Lecturer in Old Testament and Biblical Theology, Moore Theological College

Ezekiel
Greg Gilbert
Senior Pastor, Third Avenue Baptist Church, Louisville, Kentucky

Daniel
Bryan Chapell
Senior Pastor, Grace Presbyterian Church, Peoria, Illinois; President Emeritus, Covenant Theological Seminary

Hosea
James M. Hamilton Jr.
Associate Professor of Biblical Theology, The Southern Baptist Theological Seminary

Joel
Timothy Z. Witmer
Professor of Practical Theology, Westminster Theological Seminary

Amos
David Helm
Lead Pastor, Holy Trinity Church, Chicago, Illinois; Chairman, The Charles Simeon Trust

Obadiah
Michael J. Glodo
Associate Professor of Biblical Studies, Reformed Theological Seminary

Jonah
Colin Smith
Senior Pastor, The Orchard Evangelical Free Church, Arlington Heights, Illinois

Micah
Nancy Guthrie
Bible Teacher and Author

Nahum
Michael J. Glodo
Associate Professor of Biblical Studies, Reformed Theological Seminary

Habakkuk
Julius J. Kim
Dean of Students and Associate Professor of Practical Theology, Westminster Seminary California

Zephaniah
Darrin Patrick
Lead Pastor, The Journey, St. Louis, Missouri

Haggai, Zechariah, Malachi
Iain Duguid
Professor of Old Testament, Grove City College

Matthew
Frank Thielman
Presbyterian Professor of Divinity, Beeson Divinity School

Mark
Hans F. Bayer
Professor of New Testament, Covenant Theological Seminary

Luke
Jonathan Pennington
Associate Professor of New Testament Interpretation, The Southern Baptist Theological Seminary

John
Scotty Smith
Founding Pastor, Christ Community Church, Franklin, Tennessee

Acts
Justin S. Holcomb
Adjunct Professor of Theology and Philosophy, Reformed Theological Seminary

Romans
Robert W. Yarbrough
Professor of New Testament, Covenant Theological Seminary

1 Corinthians
C. D. (Jimmy) Agan III
Professor of New Testament, Covenant Theological Seminary

2 Corinthians
Stephen T. Um
Senior Minister, Citylife Presbyterian Church, Boston, Massachusetts

Galatians
Ian Smith
Principal, Presbyterian Theological Centre, Sydney, Australia

Ephesians
Kevin DeYoung
Senior Pastor, University Reformed Church, East Lansing, Michigan

Philippians
Jon Dennis
Senior Pastor, Holy Trinity Church, Chicago, Illinois

Colossians
Julius J. Kim
Dean of Students and Associate Professor of Practical Theology, Westminster Seminary California

1–2 Thessalonians
Burk Parsons
Co-pastor, Saint Andrew's Chapel, Sanford, Florida; Editor, *Tabletalk*

1–2 Timothy
R. Kent Hughes
Pastor Emeritus, College Church, Wheaton, Illinois

Titus
J. D. Greear
Lead Pastor, The Summit Church, Raleigh-Durham, North Carolina

Philemon
Julius J. Kim
Dean of Students and Associate Professor of Practical Theology, Westminster Seminary California

Hebrews
Robert A. Peterson
Professor of Systematic Theology, Covenant Theological Seminary

James
Daniel M. Doriani
Vice President of Strategic Academic Projects and Professor of Theology, Covenant Theological Seminary

1–2 Peter
Jared C. Wilson
Pastor, Middletown Springs Community Church, Middletown Springs, Vermont

1–3 John
Mike Bullmore
Senior Pastor, CrossWay Community Church, Bristol, Wisconsin

Jude
Jared C. Wilson
Pastor, Middletown Springs Community Church, Middletown Springs, Vermont

Revelation
James M. Hamilton Jr.
Associate Professor of Biblical Theology, The Southern Baptist Theological Seminary

Preface

to the English Standard Version

The Bible

"This Book [is] the most valuable thing that this world affords. Here is Wisdom; this is the royal Law; these are the lively Oracles of God." With these words the Moderator of the Church of Scotland hands a Bible to the new monarch in Britain's coronation service. These words echo the King James Bible translators, who wrote in 1611: "God's sacred Word . . . is that inestimable treasure that excelleth all the riches of the earth." This assessment of the Bible is the motivating force behind the publication of the English Standard Version.

Translation Legacy

The English Standard Version (ESV) stands in the classic mainstream of English Bible translations over the past half-millennium. The fountainhead of that stream was William Tyndale's New Testament of 1526; marking its course were the King James Version of 1611 (KJV), the English Revised Version of 1885 (RV), the American Standard Version of 1901 (ASV), and the Revised Standard Version of 1952 and 1971 (RSV). In that stream, faithfulness to the text and vigorous pursuit of accuracy were combined with simplicity, beauty, and dignity of expression. Our goal has been to carry forward this legacy for a new century.

To this end each word and phrase in the ESV has been carefully weighed against the original Hebrew, Aramaic, and Greek, to ensure the fullest accuracy and clarity and to avoid under-translating or overlooking any nuance of the original text. The words and phrases themselves grow out of the Tyndale–King James legacy, and most recently out of the RSV, with the 1971 RSV text providing the starting point for our work. Archaic language has been brought to current usage and significant corrections have been made in the translation of key texts. But throughout, our goal has been to retain the depth of meaning and enduring language that have made their indelible mark on the English-speaking world and have defined the life and doctrine of the church over the last four centuries.

Translation Philosophy

The ESV is an "essentially literal" translation that seeks as far as possible to capture the precise wording of the original text and the personal style of each Bible writer. As such, its emphasis is on "word-for-word" correspondence, at the same time taking into account differences of grammar, syntax, and idiom between current literary English and the original languages. Thus it seeks to be transparent to the original text, letting the reader see as directly as possible the structure and meaning of the original.

In contrast to the ESV, some Bible versions have followed a "thought-for-thought" rather than "word-for-word" translation philosophy, emphasizing "dynamic equivalence" rather than the "essentially literal" meaning of the original. A "thought-for-thought" translation is of necessity more inclined to reflect the interpretive opinions of the translator and the influences of contemporary culture.

Every translation is at many points a trade-off between literal precision and readability, between "formal equivalence" in expression and "functional equivalence" in communication, and the ESV is no exception. Within this framework we have sought to be "as literal as possible" while maintaining clarity of expression and literary excellence. Therefore, to the extent that plain English permits and the meaning in each case allows, we have sought to use the same English word for important recurring words in the original; and, as far as grammar and syntax allow, we have rendered Old Testament passages cited in the New in ways that show their correspondence. Thus in each of these areas, as well as throughout the Bible as a whole, we have sought to capture the echoes and overtones of meaning that are so abundantly present in the original texts.

As an essentially literal translation, then, the ESV seeks to carry over every possible nuance of meaning in the original words of Scripture into our own language. As such, the ESV is ideally suited for in-depth study of the Bible. Indeed, with its emphasis on literary excellence, the ESV is equally suited for public reading and preaching, for private reading and reflection, for both academic and devotional study, and for Scripture memorization.

Translation Principles and Style

The ESV also carries forward classic translation principles in its literary style. Accordingly it retains theological terminology—words such as grace, faith, justification, sanctification, redemption, regeneration, reconciliation, propitiation—because of their central importance for Christian doctrine and also because the underlying Greek words were already becoming key words and technical terms in New Testament times.

The ESV lets the stylistic variety of the biblical writers fully express itself—from the exalted prose that opens Genesis, to the flowing narratives of the historical books, to the rich metaphors and dramatic imagery of the poetic books, to the ringing rhetorical indictments in the prophetic books, to the smooth elegance of Luke, to the profound simplicities of John, and the closely reasoned logic of Paul.

In punctuating, paragraphing, dividing long sentences, and rendering connectives, the ESV follows the path that seems to make the ongoing flow of thought clearest in English. The biblical languages regularly connect sentences by frequent repetition of words such as "and," "but," and "for," in a way that goes beyond the conventions of literary English. Effective translation, however, requires that these links in the original be reproduced so that the flow of the argument will be transparent to the reader. We have therefore normally translated these connectives, though occasionally we have varied the rendering by using alternatives (such as "also," "however," "now," "so," "then," or "thus") when they better capture the sense in specific instances.

In the area of gender language, the goal of the ESV is to render literally what is in the original. For example, "anyone" replaces "any man" where there is no word corresponding to "man" in the original languages, and "people" rather than "men" is regularly used where the original languages refer to both men and women. But the words "man" and "men" are retained where a male meaning component is part of the original Greek or Hebrew. Likewise, the word "man" has been retained where the original text intends to convey a clear contrast between "God" on the one hand and "man" on the other hand, with "man" being used in the collective sense of the whole human race (see Luke 2:52). Similarly, the English word "brothers" (translating the Greek word *adelphoi*) is retained as an important familial form of address between fellow-Jews and fellow-Christians in the first century. A recurring note is included to indicate that the term "brothers" (*adelphoi*) was often used in Greek to refer to both men and women, and to indicate the specific instances in the text where this is the case. In addition, the English word "sons" (translating the Greek word *huioi*) is retained in specific instances because the underlying Greek term usually includes a male meaning component and it was used as a legal term in the adoption and inheritance laws of first-century Rome. As used by the apostle Paul, this term refers to the status of all Christians, both men and women, who, having been adopted into God's family, now enjoy all the privileges, obligations, and inheritance rights of God's children.

The inclusive use of the generic "he" has also regularly been retained, because this is consistent with similar usage in the original languages and because an essentially literal translation would be impossible without it.

In each case the objective has been transparency to the original text, allowing the reader to understand the original on its own terms rather than on the terms of our present-day culture.

The Translation of Specialized Terms

In the translation of biblical terms referring to God, the ESV takes great care to convey the specific nuances of meaning of the original Hebrew and Greek terms. First, concerning terms that refer to God in the Old Testament: God, the Maker of heaven and earth, introduced himself to the people of Israel with a special personal name, the consonants for which are YHWH (see Exodus 3:14–15). Scholars call this the "Tetragrammaton," a Greek term referring to the four Hebrew letters YHWH. The exact pronunciation of YHWH is uncertain, because the Jewish people considered the personal name of God to be so holy that it should never be spoken aloud. Instead of reading the word YHWH, they would normally read the Hebrew word *'adonay* ("Lord"), and the ancient translations into Greek, Syriac, and Aramaic also followed this practice. When the vowels of the word *'adonay* are placed with the consonants of YHWH, this results in the familiar word *Jehovah* that was used in some earlier English Bible translations. As is common among English translations today, the ESV usually renders the personal name of God (YHWH) with the word LORD (printed in small capitals). An exception to this is when the Hebrew word *'adonay* appears together with YHWH, in which case the two words are rendered together as "the Lord [in lower case] GOD [in small capitals]." In contrast to the personal name for God (YHWH), the more general name for God in Old Testament Hebrew is *'elohim* and its related forms of *'el* or *'eloah*, all of which are normally translated "God" (in lower case letters). The use of these different ways to translate the Hebrew words for God is especially beneficial to the English reader, enabling the reader to see and understand the different ways that the *personal* name and the *general* name for God are both used to refer to the *One True God* of the Old Testament.

Second, in the New Testament, the Greek word *Christos* has been translated consistently as "Christ." Although the term originally meant "anointed," among Jews in New Testament times the term came to designate the Messiah, the great Savior that God had promised to raise up.

In other New Testament contexts, however, especially among Gentiles, *Christos* ("Christ") was on its way to becoming a proper name. It is important, therefore, to keep the context in mind in understanding the various ways that *Christos* ("Christ") is used in the New Testament. At the same time, in accord with its "essentially literal" translation philosophy, the ESV has retained consistency and concordance in the translation of *Christos* ("Christ") throughout the New Testament.

Third, a particular difficulty is presented when words in biblical Hebrew and Greek refer to ancient practices and institutions that do not correspond directly to those in the modern world. Such is the case in the translation of *'ebed* (Hebrew) and *doulos* (Greek), terms which are often rendered "slave." These terms, however, actually cover a range of relationships that require a range of renderings—either "slave," "bondservant," or "servant"—depending on the context. Further, the word "slave" currently carries associations with the often brutal and dehumanizing institution of slavery in nineteenth-century America. For this reason, the ESV translation of the words *'ebed* and *doulos* has been undertaken with particular attention to their meaning in each specific context. Thus in Old Testament times, one might enter slavery either voluntarily (e.g., to escape poverty or to pay off a debt) or involuntarily (e.g., by birth, by being captured in battle, or by judicial sentence). Protection for all in servitude in ancient Israel was provided by the Mosaic Law. In New Testament times, a *doulos* is often best described as a "bondservant"—that is, as someone bound to serve his master for a specific (usually lengthy) period of time, but also as someone who might nevertheless own property, achieve social advancement, and even be released or purchase his freedom. The ESV usage thus seeks to express the nuance of meaning in each context. Where absolute ownership by a master is in view (as in Romans 6), "slave" is used; where a more limited form of servitude is in view, "bondservant" is used (as in 1 Corinthians 7:21–24); where the context indicates a wide range of freedom (as in John 4:51), "servant" is preferred. Footnotes are generally provided to identify the Hebrew or Greek and the range of meaning that these terms may carry in each case.

Fourth, it is sometimes suggested that Bible translations should capitalize pronouns referring to deity. It has seemed best not to capitalize deity pronouns in the ESV, however, for the following reasons: first, there is nothing in the original Hebrew and Greek manuscripts that corresponds to such capitalization; second, the practice of capitalizing deity pronouns in English Bible translations is a recent innovation, which began only in the mid-twentieth century; and, third, such capitalization is absent from the KJV Bible and the whole stream of Bible translations that the ESV seeks to carry forward.

A fifth specialized term, the word "behold," usually has been retained as the most common translation for the Hebrew word *hinneh* and the Greek word *idou*. Both of these words mean something like "Pay careful attention to what follows! This is important!" Other than the word "behold," there is no single word in English that fits well in most contexts. Although "Look!" and "See!" and "Listen!" would be workable in some contexts, in many others these words lack sufficient weight and dignity. Given the principles of "essentially literal" translation, it is important not to leave *hinneh* and *idou* completely untranslated, and so to lose the intended emphasis in the original languages. The older and more formal word "behold" has usually been retained, therefore, as the best available option for conveying the original sense of meaning.

Textual Basis and Resources

The ESV is based on the Masoretic text of the Hebrew Bible as found in *Biblia Hebraica Stuttgartensia* (2nd ed., 1983), and on the Greek text in the 1993 editions of the *Greek New Testament* (4th corrected ed.), published by the United Bible Societies (UBS), and *Novum Testamentum Graece* (27th ed.), edited by Nestle and Aland. The currently renewed respect among Old Testament scholars for the Masoretic text is reflected in the ESV's attempt, wherever possible, to translate difficult Hebrew passages as they stand in the Masoretic text rather than resorting to emendations or to finding an alternative reading in the ancient versions. In exceptional, difficult cases, the Dead Sea Scrolls, the Septuagint, the Samaritan Pentateuch, the Syriac Peshitta, the Latin Vulgate, and other sources were consulted to shed possible light on the text, or, if necessary, to support a divergence from the Masoretic text. Similarly, in a few difficult cases in the New Testament, the ESV has followed a Greek text different from the text given preference in the UBS/Nestle-Aland 27th edition. Throughout, the translation team has benefited greatly from the massive textual resources that have become readily available recently, from new insights into biblical laws and culture, and from current advances in Hebrew and Greek lexicography and grammatical understanding.

Textual Footnotes

The footnotes that accompany the ESV text are an integral part of the ESV translation, informing the reader of textual variations and difficulties and showing how these have been resolved by the ESV translation team. In addition to this, the footnotes indicate significant alternative readings and occasionally provide an explanation for technical terms or for a difficult reading in the text.

Publishing Team

The ESV publishing team includes more than a hundred people. The fourteen-member Translation Oversight Committee has benefited from the work of more than fifty biblical experts serving as Translation Review Scholars and from the comments of the more than fifty members of the Advisory Council, all of which has been carried out under the auspices of the Crossway Board of Directors. This hundred-plus-member team shares a common commitment to the truth of God's Word and to historic Christian orthodoxy and is international in scope, including leaders in many denominations.

To God's Honor and Praise

We know that no Bible translation is perfect or final; but we also know that God uses imperfect and inadequate things to his honor and praise. So to our triune God and to his people we offer what we have done, with our prayers that it may prove useful, with gratitude for much help given, and with ongoing wonder that our God should ever have entrusted to us so momentous a task.

Soli Deo Gloria!—To God alone be the glory!

*The Translation Oversight Committee**

*A complete list of the Translation Oversight Committee, the Translation Review Scholars, and the Advisory Council, is available upon request from Crossway.

Explanation of

Features

Included in This Edition

The *ESV Gospel Transformation Bible* includes a number of valuable features to encourage the reading and study of the Bible. Following is a brief description of these features.

SPECIAL FEATURES OF THE *ESV GOSPEL TRANSFORMATION BIBLE*

In accordance with the goals stated in the "Introduction to the ESV Gospel Transformation Bible" (pages vii–xiii), this edition of the ESV Bible features study notes for the entire Bible that show readers, passage by passage, how each particular book carries forward God's redemptive purposes in history, culminating in Christ. These notes enable readers to see how the gospel of grace is the overarching message of the Bible, and how it transforms the human heart. Introductions to each book of the Bible are also provided, which include a section called "The Gospel in [Book]." This section orients readers to the big picture of how that book develops the story line of God's redemptive plan.

In addition, there is a full index (pages 1755–1785) to help readers see the unity of Scripture and how various themes course through the Bible from beginning to end. By looking up various biblical themes—such as temple, idolatry, feasting, or marriage—readers can appreciate the way the Bible picks up and develops various motifs in a coherent, unified, and progressive way.

STANDARD FEATURES OF THE ESV BIBLE

Cross-Reference System

The *ESV Gospel Transformation Bible* includes one of the most extensive and useful cross-reference systems available. It is based on a comprehensive system developed more than a hundred years ago by a team of Bible scholars from Oxford and Cambridge Universities. It was first used in the English Revised Version (RV) and has been highly regarded around the world for its effectiveness in showing the internal interrelationship of the text throughout the Bible. The cross-reference system as it appears in the this edition has been adapted from the RV system for use with the ESV. In some cases, therefore, the specific wording of the reference passage may differ, although the underlying meaning and relationship to the referenced text is normally the same.

Using the ESV Cross-Reference System

If there is a cross-reference for a portion of Bible text, this is indicated by a *letter* superscript. These always *precede* the text to which they apply. *Number* superscripts, which always *follow* the words to which they apply, indicate textual footnotes. For example, in the phrase "[a]from faith for faith[1]" the superscripted letter "a" preceding the phrase refers to a cross-reference while the superscripted number "1" at the end refers to a footnote.

Types of Cross-References

The ESV cross-reference system includes several types of cross-references.

1. *References to Specific Words or Phrases.* References to *words and phrases* within the same chapter appear as, e.g., "ver. 7"; within the same book, as, e.g., "ch. 9:6"; in other books of the Bible, as, e.g., "Heb. 4:2."
2. *Comparative References.* These references direct the reader to passages with the *same theme* and are indicated by square brackets, e.g., "[ch. 9:6; 2 Tim. 2:13]."
3. *Less Direct References.* These references generally provide additional information or insight about a specific theme and are introduced with the word "See," e.g., "See John 8:26."
4. *Quoted References.* These references indicate the source for verses or phrases quoted from other places in the Bible, e.g., "Cited from Ps. 51:4."

The notations "(Heb.)" and "(Gk.)" indicate that the reference is clearer in Hebrew or Greek than in English. "(Gk.)" in New Testament citations of the Old Testament indicates that the reference is most clear in the Septuagint, a Greek translation of the Old Testament.

Textual Footnotes

Several kinds of footnotes related to the ESV text are provided throughout this Bible. These footnotes appear at the bottom of the page and are indicated in the ESV text by a superscript *number* that *follows* the word or phrase to which the footnote applies (e.g., "Isaac[2]"). Superscript *letters* that *precede* a word indicate cross-references. The footnotes included in the ESV Bible are an integral part of the text and provide important information concerning the understanding and translation of the text. The footnotes fall mainly into four categories:

Types of Textual Footnotes

1. *Alternative Translations.* Footnotes of this kind provide alternative translations for specific words or phrases when there is a strong possibility that such words or phrases could be translated in another way, such as: "Or *keep awake*" (see Matt. 26:38); and "Or *down payment*" (see Eph. 1:14). In such cases, the translation deemed to have the stronger support is in the text while other possible renderings are given in the note.
2. *Explanation of Greek and Hebrew Terms.* Notes of this kind relate primarily to the meaning of specific Greek or Hebrew terms, as illustrated by the following examples:

a. Notes about the meaning of names in the original languages, such as: "*Isaac* means *he laughs*" (see Gen. 17:19); and "*Simeon* sounds like the Hebrew for *heard*" (see Gen. 29:33).
b. Notes that give the literal translation of a Greek or Hebrew word or phrase deemed too awkward to be used in the English text, such as: "Greek *girding up the loins of your mind*" (see 1 Pet. 1:13).
c. Notes indicating that absolute certainty of the meaning of a word or phrase is not possible given our best understanding of the original language (e.g., Hebrew words occurring so infrequently in the Old Testament that their meaning cannot be determined with certainty). Such words are identified with a note stating that "The meaning of the Hebrew is uncertain" (see, e.g., Josh. 17:11).
d. Notes that indicate the specialized use of a Greek word, such as: "brothers," translating the Greek word *adelphoi* (see, e.g., the extended note on Rom. 1:13, corresponding to the first occurrence of *adelphoi* in any New Testament book, and the abbreviated note, e.g., on Rom. 7:1, corresponding to subsequent occurrences of *adelphoi* in any New Testament book); and "sons," translating the Greek word *huioi* (see, e.g., Rom. 8:14). See also the discussion of *adelphoi* and *huioi* in the Preface.

3. *Other Explanatory Notes.* Footnotes of this kind provide clarifying information as illustrated by the following examples:
    a. Notes clarifying additional meanings that may not otherwise be apparent in the text, such as: "*Leprosy* was a term for several skin diseases; see Leviticus 13."
    b. Notes clarifying important grammatical points that would not otherwise be apparent in English, such as: "In Hebrew *you* is plural in verses 1–5" (see Gen. 3:1).
    c. Notes clarifying when the referent for a pronoun has been supplied in the English text, such as: "Greek *he*" (see, e.g., Mark 1:43).
    d. Notes giving English equivalents for weights, measures, and monetary values.
4. *Technical Translation Notes.* Footnotes of this kind indicate how decisions have been made in the translation of difficult Hebrew and Greek passages. Such notes occasionally include technical terms. For an explanation of these terms the reader is referred to standard Bible study reference works. See further the section in the Preface on "Textual Basis and Resources" for an explanation of the original-language texts used in the translation of the ESV Bible and how the translation of difficult passages has been resolved.

Maps

A set of color maps is provided at the end of the *ESV Gospel Transformation Bible*. These include maps describing the biblical world and key historical periods in the life of ancient Israel and in New Testament times. Also included are maps showing Jerusalem in the time of Jesus and the missionary journeys of the apostle Paul.

The Old Testament

Introduction to Genesis

Author and Date

The book of Genesis is the first book of the Pentateuch (Genesis–Deuteronomy). It gives the foundation stories of God's relation to the world, to the patriarchs, and to Israel. The name of Moses has been closely associated with the Pentateuch. He led Israel out of Egypt and was God's faithful servant. His ministry has been variously dated from 1500 to 1300 B.C.

Audience

Genesis narrates for Israel the story of people who walked with the Lord (Enoch, Noah, Abraham, Isaac, Jacob, and Joseph) to encourage their descendants to break away from their resistant and recurring hardness of heart. The author intends the reader of the Pentateuch to connect the foundation stories (exile from Eden, human wickedness, and God's unfolding promises of grace) with Israel's new opportunity (of entering the land, despite Israel's rebelliousness, and through God's unfailing faithfulness to his promises). Genesis identifies the promises and path to life that must be understood and followed in order for the people of God to fulfill their calling as it is described and prescribed in Moses' later books (e.g., Deut. 30:19–20) and, indeed, the rest of Scripture.

The Gospel in Genesis

The foundation stories of Genesis set the stage of the drama of Scripture in many ways. First, the Creator is the King over all of his creation. He has made everything well and has chosen humans to be his image-bearers on earth. They were created to live in glad relationship with their heavenly Father.

Second, sin entered the world and took away human freedom—through the consequences and dominion of evil. Sin, alienation, and death now mark human existence.

Third, in contrast to the continual disobedience of humanity, God reveals the depth of his grace and love. Though all human beings bear the scars of the sin of Adam and Eve, the Lord continues in his everlasting grace to work out his purposes. He is the heavenly Father who does not give up on his earthly children. In the wake of the flood that came to punish pervasive evil and destroyed almost all life, God promised to maintain his grace to all created life, both animal and human.

Fourth, God called frail humans to represent him: Noah, Abraham, Isaac, Jacob, and Joseph. Each of these men was profoundly flawed, a point to which the Bible gives ample testimony. Yet God gave them grace upon grace, keeping his promise, at whatever cost, to bless them and through them to bless all humanity.

Fifth, these giants of faith learned to love God more than the goods of this life. They served God, and despite their flawed humanity God made them lights in their dark generations. They walked with God by his grace and learned wisdom from him. Through these stories Moses taught Israel that there are one of two paths people must choose: folly and death, or wisdom and life.

Sixth, Genesis reveals that the riches of God's grace render people without excuse. People at the time of Enosh, Noah, Abraham, Isaac, Jacob, and Joseph received God's grace and walked with him. Others received messages of grace and spurned them—with evident consequences (e.g., Cain, the generation of the flood, and Esau).

Seventh, the Lord of the universe committed himself by oath to one man, Abraham. Then, God promised to extend his grace to all humanity through that one man's "offspring." Though Israel was numbered among Abraham's offspring, the sad stories of that nation evidence her lack of faith, her inability to accomplish what God required, and her need of God's provision. That provision was ultimately made through the eventual coming of Jesus Christ from the lineage of Israel. Only in him do we learn how the promises of God are made true (2 Cor. 1:20). He is the true and final Good News in which all of God's promises find decisive fulfillment. He is the promised "offspring" of Abraham who will accomplish God's covenant purposes (Gen. 3:15; 12:7; Gal. 3:16). Beginning with his first coming and to be completed at his second coming, Jesus opens the doors to the new creation and the new humanity—to a world without the sin, death, and evil that found their entry as first described in Genesis. The final triumph of Jesus over all evil is first described in this Bible book as well (Gen. 3:15).

Outline

I. The Creator Is Sovereign King of the Whole World (1:1–2:3)

II. The Creation of the Garden of Eden and the First Human Family: Adam and Eve, Their Sin, Expulsion from Eden, and Life to the East of Eden (2:4–4:26)

III. The Family of Adam: From Adam to Noah (5:1–6:8)

IV. The Story of Noah: His Walk with God, the Flood, the Ark, and God's Covenant (6:9–9:29)

V. The Family of Noah: The Nations and the Tower of Babel (10:1–11:9)

VI. The Family of Shem: From Shem to Terah (11:10–26)

VII. The Family of Terah: Abraham, Isaac, and Ishmael and God's Covenant with Abraham to the Exclusion of Ishmael (11:27–25:11)

VIII. The Family of Ishmael (25:12–18)

IX. The Family of Isaac: God's Promises to Isaac and Jacob and the Exclusion of Esau (25:19–35:29)

X. The Family of Esau (36:1–43)

XI. The Family of Jacob: The Twelve Tribes (37:1–50:26)

Genesis

The Creation of the World

1 In the [a]beginning, God created the heavens
and the earth. 2 The earth was [b]without
form and void, and darkness was over the face
of the deep. And the Spirit of God was hovering over the face of the waters.

3 And God said, [c]"Let there be light," and
there was light. 4 And God saw that the light
was good. And God separated the light from
the darkness. 5 God called the light Day, and
the darkness he called Night. And there was
evening and there was morning, the first day.

1:1–11:26 The first part of Genesis presents God as the Creator (1:1–2:3) and righteous overseer of humanity (2:4–11:26). The story develops a drama beginning with the creation of the world and with the creation of human beings as the climactic act. They alone are made in the divine image.

The communion with the Lord enabled by humans' divine image-bearing, however, is shattered by their rebelliousness: (1) the rebellion of Adam and Eve in the garden of Eden and of their descendants outside of the garden; (2) the evil of humanity before the flood (6:9–9:29); and (3) the arrogance of humanity at Babel (11:1–9).

This final episode of turning from dependence upon God introduces the reader to the ancestors and relatives of Abraham (11:10–26), through whose descendants, and supremely through Jesus Christ, God would redeem the world for all who choose to depend upon him. Indeed, at each stage in the history of Genesis there is the hope of redemption in the midst of humanity's failures: (1) Enoch walked with the Lord and was taken up to heaven; (2) Noah, a second Adam through whom humanity would get a second start, walked with God and was instrumental in saving humanity, being appropriately named God's "comforter" despite his and his family's sin; and (3) Abraham, despite his flaws, acted in faith and became the father of the faithful.

1:1–2:3 The Creator is the sovereign King of the whole world. The Pentateuch (the first five books of the Bible) taught Israel to embrace the uniqueness of God (instead of polytheism), the power of God's word in creation and redemption, and God's gracious election of humans to serve him in his priestly kingdom. From the beginning to the very end of the Bible (Revelation 21–22), the Creator is the Redeemer of the world. The triune God is the Maker of heaven and earth: the Father speaks creation into being through the Son and by the operation of the Holy Spirit (see Gen. 1:1–2; Ps. 33:6; 104:30; John 1:1–3; 4:34; Col. 1:16; Heb. 1:2; 11:3).

1:1–2 The drama of redemption begins "in the beginning." Genesis is more concerned with God the Creator than with the time or details of creation. He is the sovereign King whose kingdom was orderly and good, but which is in need of redemption because of the tragedy of human sin. In the New Testament, John 1:1 associates the Word of the Creator with Jesus Christ. The early church confessed readily that the Father, the Son, and the Spirit were all involved in the work of creation, reinforcing early Christian beliefs about the Trinity.

Indeed, Jesus is the one without whom nothing exists (Col. 1:16). He is "the firstborn" of creation by his resurrection (Col. 1:15, 18). Darkness, water, and the deep (Gen. 1:2) suggest an uninhabitable world, which in the Old Testament is associated with opposition, battle, and even demonic presence. Thus, there are consistent images in the Bible of the sea being subdued as signs of God's bringing a new and redeemed order to his world (see 1:2; 7–9; Ex. 14:19–30; Jonah 1:12–15; Mark 4:37–39;

Chapter 1

1[a] Job 38:4-7; Ps. 33:6; 136:5; Isa. 42:5; 45:18; John 1:1-3; Acts 14:15; 17:24; Col. 1:16, 17; Heb. 1:10; 11:3; Rev. 4:11
2[b] Jer. 4:23
3[c] 2 Cor. 4:6

6 And God said, [d]"Let there be an expanse[1] in the midst of the waters, and let it separate the waters from the waters." 7 And God made[2] the expanse and [e]separated the waters that were under the expanse from the waters that were [f]above the expanse. And it was so. 8 And God called the expanse Heaven.[3] And there was evening and there was morning, the second day.

9 And God said, [g]"Let the waters under the heavens be gathered together into one place, and let the dry land appear." And it was so. 10 God called the dry land Earth,[4] and the waters that were gathered together he called Seas. And God saw that it was good.

11 And God said, [h]"Let the earth sprout vegetation, plants[5] yielding seed, and fruit trees bearing fruit in which is their seed, each according to its kind, on the earth." And it was so. 12 The earth brought forth vegetation, plants yielding seed according to their own kinds, and trees bearing fruit in which is their seed, each according to its kind. And God saw that it was good. 13 And there was evening and there was morning, the third day.

14 And God said, "Let there be lights in the expanse of the heavens to separate the day from the night. And let them be for [i]signs and for [j]seasons,[6] and for days and years, 15 and let

[1] Or *a canopy*; also verses 7, 8, 14, 15, 17, 20 [2] Or *fashioned*; also verse 16 [3] Or *Sky*; also verses 9, 14, 15, 17, 20, 26, 28, 30; 2:1 [4] Or *Land*; also verses 11, 12, 22, 24, 25, 26, 28, 30; 2:1 [5] Or *small plants*; also verses 12, 29 [6] Or *appointed times*

6[d] Job 37:18; Ps. 136:5; Jer. 10:12; 51:15
7[e] Prov. 8:27-29 [f] Ps. 148:4
9[g] Job 38:8-11; Ps. 33:7; 136:6; Jer. 5:22; 2 Pet. 3:5
11[h] Ps. 104:14
14[i] Jer. 10:2; Ezek. 32:7, 8; Joel 2:30, 31; 3:15; Matt. 24:29; Luke 21:25 [j] Ps. 104:19

Rev. 21:1). God's Spirit consequently demonstrates his redeeming presence from the very beginning (Gen. 1:2). There are no aspects of creation, including those of disorder and malevolence, over which God is not ultimately bringing a redemptive order. Matthew's mention of the dove in the account of Jesus' baptism (Matt. 3:13–17) may also echo back to the Spirit hovering over the face of the waters. The verb "hover" suggests the movement of a bird. Such an appearance of the Spirit over God's Son indicates that Jesus has come with God's power and prerogative to renew creation.

1:3–31 The six days of creation are connected by the repetition of key words and phrases. The tendency to read them only sequentially is challenged by various literary features, including the account of the fourth day repeating the vocabulary of the first three days and the seventh day marking the completion of all of God's creative acts but lacking phrases such as "God said" or "it was evening and morning." God forms the various realms of the world (days 1–3) and then fills each with appropriate entities and diverse life forms (days 4–6).

In all this we see God's gracious delight in his created world. For every created thing, God provides a natural and hospitable environment. This is supremely the case for humanity made in his image.

1:3–13 Three days reveal the formation of creation. God separates light from darkness (days 1 and 4). He also separates the water into sky above and water below, and separates the land from the water (days 2 and 3; cf. 2 Pet. 3:5). God's word establishes order, revealing his will to make the earth his kingdom and to prepare it for human rule. At every stage, God is *for* his creation.

The repetition of "God said" connects God, the creation of the world, and God's word. The tenfold repetition in Genesis 1 confirms that all is made by his word (Psalm 33; cf. Heb. 11:3; 2 Pet. 3:5; John 1:1). The prominence of light on days 1 and 4, together with the repetition of "evening and morning" and "day," highlights the temporal dimension of God's creation. In his kind condescension, God establishes time. Throughout history and particularly at the incarnation of the Lord Jesus Christ, God himself enters time. He is the Lord of time and of the Sabbath (see Gen. 2:1–3). In the new creation, the light of the sun will be nothing compared to the radiance of God's presence (Isa. 60:19; Zech. 14:6–7; Rev. 21:23). Darkness and water, though a part of God's world, have negative associations with chaos—yet God is in absolute control. Jesus' calming of the storm demonstrates his own divine identity, manifesting not only his power but also his gentle concern for his followers (Matt. 8:26–27).

All creation, in short, reflects God's goodness: darkness and light, sun and moon, the earth with its vegetation, the animal world, and supremely humanity. God's goodness is also found in marriage (Gen. 2:24) and in food and drink (2:16). These benefits are to be received with thanksgiving (1 Tim. 4:4). And all of these wonderful blessings are an echo of the supreme goodness of God ultimately manifested in

them be lights in the expanse of the heavens to give light upon the earth." And it was so. 16 And God [k]made the two great lights—the greater light to rule the day and the lesser light to rule the night—and the stars. 17 And God set them in the expanse of the heavens to give light on the earth, 18 to [l]rule over the day and over the night, and to separate the light from the darkness. And God saw that it was good. 19 And there was evening and there was morning, the fourth day.

20 And God said, "Let the waters swarm with swarms of living creatures, and let birds[1] fly above the earth across the expanse of the heavens." 21 So [m]God created the great sea creatures and every living creature that moves, with which the waters swarm, according to their kinds, and every winged bird according to its kind. And God saw that it was good. 22 And God blessed them, saying, [n]"Be fruitful and multiply and fill the waters in the seas, and let birds multiply on the earth." 23 And there was evening and there was morning, the fifth day.

24 And God said, "Let the earth bring forth living creatures according to their kinds—livestock and creeping things and beasts of the earth according to their kinds." And it was so. 25 And God made the beasts of the earth according to their kinds and the livestock according to their kinds, and everything that creeps on the ground according to its kind. And God saw that it was good.

26 Then God said, [o]"Let us make man[2] in our image, [p]after our likeness. And [q]let them have dominion over the fish of the sea and over the birds of the heavens and over the livestock and over all the earth and over every creeping thing that creeps on the earth."

[1] Or *flying things*; see Leviticus 11:19–20 [2] The Hebrew word for *man* (*adam*) is the generic term for mankind and becomes the proper name *Adam*

Jesus Christ—the Light of the World (John 8:12), our great Bridegroom (Mark 2:19; Eph. 5:32), and the Bread of Life (John 6:35).

1:14–31 Three days reveal the filling of creation with the potentiality of life. The sun, moon, and constellations are created. They are not objects of worship but function to maintain God's order and to provide light for the world, above all for humanity. Light on planet Earth is distinctive as it enables vegetation to grow, and through vegetation all life forms, from the smallest to the largest, have the potential of vitality. Light also marks the rhythms of nature and the cycles of time. Nature has its own calendar apart from humans. The order of nature (days 1–3) regulates the potentiality of life for animals and humans. By creating all this, God demonstrates his fatherly care for his creation.

God's creation of animals and humans in days 5 and 6 reveals the vibrant, delightful diversity of creation. God's blessing of vitality rests on them. This blessing is God's expression of empowerment and of development from generation to generation. He graciously wills his creatures to live in enjoyment of his rich abundance, to reproduce, and to multiply. God takes delight in all of his creatures—the great sea creatures, the wild animals great and small, the birds, the creeping things. All are his creatures in which he delights and over which he exercises his wise governance.

1:26–28 The pinnacle of creation is humanity. Humans (both male and female) are made in the image of God (cf. 1:26 and 5:1–2). They therefore have life that is sacred (cf. 9:6), and they are to resemble God in character, speech, and actions so that they might have relationships of fellowship and worship with him and with one another. Their calling was, in short, to be fruitful so that the glory and goodness of God would multiply through them (1:28). That is, they were to be agents of God's dominion on earth, and the blessing of fruitfulness would enable them to fill the earth with God's image-bearers. As God's kingdom extends to the whole world, so his rule was to extend to every corner of the earth by his direct influence and by his image-bearers—which we are privileged to be.

People failed by their sin (ch. 3), corruption (6:5–6), and rebelliousness to fulfill their image-bearing responsibilities (11:1–9; cf. Ps. 2:1–2). Yet the Lord renewed the mandate of fruitful multiplication to Noah (Gen. 9:1, 7) and to Abraham (12:2; 17:2, 6, 8). He similarly blessed Israel (Ex. 1:7) and promised to bless her as she humbly obeyed (Lev. 26:9). Yet, again and again, Israel failed.

Jesus Christ, however, as the second Adam, fulfills God's image-bearing purposes and enables God's people to do the same. The apostle Paul speaks of "the light of the

16 [k]Deut. 4:19; Ps. 136:7-9
18 [l]Jer. 31:35
21 [m]Ps. 104:25, 26
22 [n]ch. 8:17; 9:1
26 [o]ch. 3:22; 11:7; Isa. 6:8 [p]ch. 5:1; 9:6; 1 Cor. 11:7; Eph. 4:24; Col. 3:10; James 3:9 [q]ch. 9:2; Ps. 8:6-8; James 3:7

27 So God created man in his own image,
in the image of God he created him;
[r]male and female he created them.

28 And God blessed them. And God said
to them, [s]"Be fruitful and multiply and fill
the earth and subdue it, and have dominion
over the fish of the sea and over the birds of
the heavens and over every living thing that
moves on the earth." 29 And God said, "Behold,
I have given every plant yielding seed that
is on the face of all the earth, and every tree
with seed in its fruit. [t]You shall have them
for food. 30 And [u]to every beast of the earth
and to every bird of the heavens and to everything that creeps on the earth, everything that
has the breath of life, I have given every green
plant for food." And it was so. 31 [v]And God saw
everything that he had made, and behold, it
was very good. And there was evening and
there was morning, the sixth day.

The Seventh Day, God Rests

2 Thus the heavens and the earth were finished, and [w]all the host of them. 2 And [x]on
the seventh day God finished his work that

27[r] ch. 2:18, 21-23; 5:2; Mal. 2:15; Matt. 19:4; Mark 10:6
28[s] ch. 9:1, 7
29[t] ch. 9:3; Ps. 104:14, 15; 145:15, 16
30[u] Ps. 147:9
31[v] Eccles. 7:29; 1 Tim. 4:4

Chapter 2
1[w] Deut. 4:19; Ps. 33:6
2[x] Ex. 20:8-11; 31:17; Deut. 5:12-14; Heb. 4:4

gospel of the glory of Christ, *who is the image of God*" (2 Cor. 4:4; cf. Col. 1:15). Jesus is the image of God that we were intended to be. And as we are united to him by faith, God sees us as his children, clothed in the righteousness of his Son, to whom we are conformed (Rom. 8:29) in righteousness and holiness (Eph. 4:24). Through his living a perfect life and suffering the penalty for our sin as the perfect God-man, Jesus provided for humans to be renewed in the image of God through faith in him (2 Cor. 3:18; Phil. 2:6–7; Col. 3:10). Thus, those united to Christ again become God's image-bearing participants in his rule over the earth, fulfilling the original mandate to multiply and make manifest God's goodness and glory in all the places that his people dwell (Col. 1:13–20).

In short, God's original goal of spreading his righteous rule throughout the earth is being realized by the proclamation of the gospel of grace throughout the world (see Col. 1:6, 10). Just as Adam and Eve were to reproduce and multiply, so the early church is spoken of as reproducing and multiplying (Acts 6:7; 12:24; 19:20; Col. 1:8–15).

2:1–3 The Sabbath (day 7) marks the consecration of a holy time. It is the climax of the temporal aspects of creation that are the focus of days 1 and 4 with their sequence of day and night, seasons, and years. The focus of the Sabbath is on celebrating the completion of creation. The pattern of work and rest revealed to Israel is grounded in the creation order. The rhythm of time pauses every seven days for a time of refreshment, blessing, and consecration. God's provision of a Sabbath rest is indicative of his willingness to provide for his people when their labors are not providing for their needs—an aspect of grace in all times. As such, the Sabbath was God's "wedding present" to Israel (Ex. 31:13–17) and anticipated the presence and provision of God for his people in the Promised Land.

Yet, despite this chapter's indication of the origins of Israel's Sabbath, because of unbelief Moses and Joshua were unable to bring Israel into God's promised rest (cf. Ps. 95:7–11; Heb. 3:7–4:11). By these observations, biblical writers inform us that the rest that God provides is not simply a weekly cessation from labor, or the provision of land in which God's people were able to rest from slave labor. The rest is not only about a day or the inheritance of a piece of geography. The Sabbath rest is ultimately a spiritual rest in which sinners may find peace with God and enjoy his presence (Matt. 11:28–30). This rest is also an end-time reality (e.g., Isa. 14:3, 7; Rev. 21:1–4). We learn further in Scripture that the privilege of enjoying and anticipating this final rest is the gracious result of Christ's high priestly ministry and atonement (Heb. 4:1–16).

The threefold observation that God's work was finished in making and blessing the earth as a kind of divine sanctuary (Gen. 2:1–3; cf. 2:4–25) anticipates the completion and consecration of the tabernacle at the time of Moses (Ex. 40:9–11, 33). The tabernacle was a type of the heavenly temple (Heb. 8:5) and was destroyed, but the heavenly reality was never at risk. The book of Hebrews argues for the superiority of Jesus to Moses in terms of this sanctuary motif. Both were faithful, but Jesus' ministry alone assures the godly that he has not only satisfied the Father but will complete the mission leading to his people's rest (Heb. 8:5–9). As Moses is associated with the exodus that was needed to take God's people to the Promised Land of rest from slavery, so is Jesus' ministry at the cross as the "Passover lamb" (1 Cor. 5:7; 1 Pet. 1:19)

he had done, and he rested on the seventh
day from all his work that he had done. 3 So
God blessed the seventh day and made it holy,
because on it God rested from all his work that
he had done in creation.

The Creation of Man and Woman

4 [y]These are the generations
of the heavens and the earth when they
were created,
in the day that the LORD God made the
earth and the heavens.

5 When no [z]bush of the field[1] was yet in the
land[2] and no small plant of the field had yet
sprung up—for the LORD God had not caused
it to rain on the land, and there was no man
[a]to work the ground, 6 and a mist[3] was going
up from the land and was watering the whole
face of the ground— 7 then the LORD God
formed the man of [b]dust from the ground
and [c]breathed into his [d]nostrils the breath of
life, and [e]the man became a living creature.
8 And the LORD God planted a [f]garden in Eden,
in the east, and there he put the man whom
he had formed. 9 And out of the ground the
LORD God made to spring up every tree that

[1] Or *open country* [2] Or *earth*; also verse 6 [3] Or *spring*

4 [y] ch. 1:1
5 [z] [ch. 1:11, 12] [a] ch. 3:23
7 [b] ch. 3:19, 23; 18:27; Ps. 103:14; Eccles. 12:7; 1 Cor. 15:47 [c] ch. 7:22; Job 33:4; Isa. 2:22 [d] Job 27:3 [e] Cited 1 Cor. 15:45
8 [f] ver. 15; ch. 13:10; Isa. 51:3; Ezek. 28:13; 31:8; Joel 2:3

associated with the new exodus (Heb. 4:8–10). All the beneficiaries of Christ's ministry will enter his rest, because they have received the new covenant in his blood (Heb. 8:6–13). Jesus completed the work he came to do and rested on the seventh day.

The *blessing* and *consecration* of the Sabbath rest are established at creation (Gen. 2:3), but the blessings were not entered into by God's people until God consecrated Israel (Ex. 31:13–18), ultimately anticipating the spiritual rest we enter upon consecration by Christ. *Blessing* is associated with God's gift of potentiality and vitality. *Consecration* is the act of setting the Sabbath apart for the Lord and for all whom he invites to rest with him. Thus, Sabbath observance is a form of trusting and honoring God, consecrating time to him while also experiencing his blessing; i.e., God can do more with our six days than we can do with all seven. So we can and should rest in him.

It is remarkable that the word "holy," attributed to the Sabbath (Gen. 2:3), occurs only here in Genesis, though it is a key word in the Pentateuch. By using the word "holy" to designate the *rest* that *God provides*, we are helped to understand that the sanctity of the Sabbath is intended to be a gracious expression of God's concern for his people, rather than a legalistic burden to be carried out by human effort (Mark 2:27). Observance of the Sabbath is to be a conscientious and joyful celebration of the rest from labor that God provides. Christ has opened the way to the anticipated and greater spiritual rest through his ministry as High Priest and as the sacrificial lamb. The new rest he provides is celebrated in the new covenant sign and seal of the Lord's Supper—a reflection of the Passover meal that was the provision and preparation for Israel's escape from slavery and entry into the Promised Land of rest from their labors (cf. Heb. 10:19–25).

2:4–50:26 The gracious story of creation unfolds in ten stages. Each of the ten accounts begins with the phrase "these are the generations of," marking off a focus on ten key individuals or families crucial to redemptive recovery from chaotic times or events.

The first five stages take the reader from creation (2:4) to Terah, the father of Abraham (11:32). The central focus of the story is God's presence in the garden of Eden followed by the alienation, guilt, condemnation, and widespread degeneration of the human race away from the garden (2:4–6:8). God's judgment brought the flood, but Noah was chosen as an agent of the renewal of God's grace toward humanity. The story then broadens to include the descendants of Noah and their rebellion against the Creator-King (11:1–9) before focusing on the family of Shem and Terah (11:10–32).

The second five stages focus on the transmission of God's blessing (12:1–50:26). They illuminate the way God's covenant blessings pass from Abraham to Isaac, Jacob, and Joseph, bypassing Ishmael and Esau.

2:4–4:26 This block of Genesis narrates the garden of Eden, the entrance of sin, the expulsion from Eden, and life outside of Eden. Eden is described as a place associated with rivers, precious metals and stones, vegetation, and animals. The focus of the story, however, is on the family of the first Adam.

is pleasant to the sight and good for food. [g]The tree of life was in the midst of the garden, [h]and the tree of the knowledge of good and evil.

10 A river flowed out of Eden to water the garden, and there it divided and became four rivers. 11 The name of the first is the Pishon. It is the one that flowed around the whole land of [i]Havilah, where there is gold. 12 And the gold of that land is good; bdellium and onyx stone are there. 13 The name of the second river is the Gihon. It is the one that flowed around the whole land of Cush. 14 And the name of the third river is the [j]Tigris, which flows east of Assyria. And the fourth river is the Euphrates.

15 The LORD God took the man [k]and put him in the garden of Eden to work it and keep it. 16 And the LORD God commanded the man, saying, "You may surely eat of every tree of the garden, 17 but of the tree of the knowledge of good and evil [l]you shall not eat, for in the day that you eat[1] of it you [m]shall surely die."

18 Then the LORD God said, "It is not good that the man should be alone; [n]I will make him a helper fit for[2] him." 19 [o]Now out of the ground the LORD God had formed[3] every beast of the field and every bird of the heavens and [p]brought them to the man to see what he would call them. And whatever the man called every living creature, that was its name. 20 The man gave names to all livestock and to the birds of the heavens and to every beast of the field. But for Adam[4] there was not found a helper fit for him. 21 So the LORD God caused a [q]deep sleep to fall upon the man, and while he slept took one of his ribs and closed up its place with flesh. 22 And the rib that the LORD God had taken from the man he made[5] into a woman and brought her to the man. 23 Then the man said,

"This at last is [r]bone of my bones
and flesh of my flesh;
she shall be called Woman,
because she was [s]taken out of Man."[6]

24 [t]Therefore a man shall leave his father and his mother and hold fast to his wife, and they shall become one flesh. 25 And the man and his wife were both naked and were not ashamed.

The Fall

3 Now [u]the serpent was more crafty than any other beast of the field that the LORD God had made.

He said to the woman, "Did God actually say, 'You[7] shall not eat of any tree in the garden'?" 2 And the woman said to the serpent, "We may eat of the fruit of the trees in the garden, 3 but God said, [v]'You shall not eat of the fruit of the

[1] Or *when you eat* [2] Or *corresponding to*; also verse 20 [3] Or *And out of the ground the LORD God formed* [4] Or *the man* [5] Hebrew *built* [6] The Hebrew words for *woman* (*ishshah*) and *man* (*ish*) sound alike [7] In Hebrew *you* is plural in verses 1–5

9[g] ch. 3:22; Rev. 2:7; 22:2, 14 [h] ver. 17
11[i] ch. 10:7, 29; 25:18; 1 Sam. 15:7
14[j] Dan. 10:4
15[k] ver. 8
17[l] ch. 3:1-3, 11, 17 [m] Rom. 6:23; James 1:15
18[n] 1 Cor. 11:9; 1 Tim. 2:13
19[o] ch. 1:20, 24 [p] Ps. 8:6
21[q] ch. 15:12; 1 Sam. 26:12
23[r] ch. 29:14; Judg. 9:2; 2 Sam. 5:1; 19:13; [Eph. 5:28-30] [s] 1 Cor. 11:8
24[t] Cited Matt. 19:5; Mark 10:7; 1 Cor. 6:16; Eph. 5:31; [Ps. 45:10; 1 Cor. 7:10, 11]
Chapter 3
1[u] Matt. 10:16; 2 Cor. 11:3; Rev. 12:9; 20:2
3[v] ch. 2:17

Adam and Eve were set apart by God's special creation (2:7, 21–22) and by marriage (2:24). They alone had been endowed with God's image. Adam was called to serve the Lord in the garden (2:15). He was permitted to eat from any vegetation except for the tree of the knowledge of good and evil (2:16–17). Along with this tree, however, was the tree of life, which symbolized God's grace of wisdom and of life (Prov. 3:18; Rev. 2:7; 22:2, 14). Grace is on display in several ways at this point in the narrative: the man and woman have being and breath through no ability of their own (Gen. 2:7); they have the provision of sustenance and purpose through no power of their own (2:15; cf. the "cultural mandate" of 1:28–30); they have a warning of the consequences of sin (if God did not love, he would not warn; 2:16–17); they have the opportunity for intimacy with God through contact and conversation; and, in their marriage relationship, they each have fellowship with another person made in the image of God (2:18).

The shrewdness of the serpent (cf. Isa. 27:1; cf. Rev. 20:2) may explain the deception of Adam and Eve (Gen. 3:1). Nevertheless, they were accountable for their defiance of God. Instead of receiving spiritual insight and wisdom, they demonstrated folly and brought upon themselves and their descendants alienation and death. Through Adam and Eve, sin entered into the world with its promised punishment/consequence: death, both physical and spiritual. Adam and Eve are plunged into alienation both from God and from one another. They are driven out of the garden, away from God's presence. Even this act of punishment includes aspects of grace as exclusion from the garden provides Adam, Eve, and their descendants protection from eternity in corruption—since they are now denied access to the tree of life (3:24; until it reappears for our noncorrupted state in glory; see Rev. 22:2).

tree that is in the midst of the garden, neither
shall you touch it, lest you die.'" 4 [w]But the serpent said to the woman, "You will not surely
die. 5 For God knows that when you eat of it
your eyes will be opened, and you will be like
God, knowing good and evil." 6 So when the
woman saw that the tree was good for food,
and that it was a delight to the eyes, and that
the tree was to be desired to make one wise,[1]
she took of its fruit [x]and ate, and she also gave
some to her husband who was with her, [y]and
he ate. 7 [z]Then the eyes of both were opened,
[a]and they knew that they were naked. And
they sewed fig leaves together and made themselves loincloths.

8 And they heard the sound of the LORD God
walking in the garden in the cool[2] of the day,
and the man and his wife [b]hid themselves
from the presence of the LORD God among
the trees of the garden. 9 But the LORD God
called to the man and said to him, "Where are
you?"[3] 10 And he said, "I heard the sound of you
in the garden, and I was afraid, [c]because I was
naked, and I hid myself." 11 He said, "Who told
you that you were naked? Have you eaten of
the tree of which I commanded you not to
eat?" 12 The man said, [d]"The woman whom you
gave to be with me, she gave me fruit of the
tree, and I ate." 13 Then the LORD God said to
the woman, "What is this that you have done?"
The woman said, [e]"The serpent deceived me,
and I ate."

14 The LORD God said to the serpent,

"Because you have done this,
cursed are you above all livestock
and above all beasts of the field;
on your belly you shall go,
and [f]dust you shall eat
all the days of your life.
15 I will put enmity between you and the woman,
and between your offspring[4] and [g]her offspring;
[h]he shall bruise your head,
and you shall bruise his heel."

16 To the woman he said,

"I will surely multiply your pain in childbearing;
[i]in pain you shall bring forth children.
[j]Your desire shall be for[5] your husband,
and he shall [k]rule over you."

17 And to Adam he said,

[1] Or *to give insight* [2] Hebrew *wind* [3] In Hebrew *you* is singular in verses 9 and 11 [4] Hebrew *seed*; so throughout Genesis [5] Or *against*

4 [w] ver. 13; John 8:44; [2 Cor. 11:3]
6 [x] 1 Tim. 2:14 [y] ver. 12, 17; Hos. 6:7
7 [z] ver. 5 [a] ch. 2:25
8 [b] [Ps. 139:1-12; Jer. 23:23, 24]
10 [c] ver. 7; ch. 2:25
12 [d] ch. 2:18; Job 31:33
13 [e] ver. 4; 2 Cor. 11:3; 1 Tim. 2:14
14 [f] Isa. 65:25; Mic. 7:17
15 [g] Isa. 7:14; Mic. 5:3; Matt. 1:23, 25; Luke 1:34, 35; Gal. 4:4; 1 Tim. 2:15 [h] Rom. 16:20; Heb. 2:14; Rev. 20:1-3, 10
16 [i] [John 16:21] [j] ch. 4:7; Song 7:10 [k] 1 Cor. 11:3; 14:34; Eph. 5:22-24; Col. 3:18; 1 Tim. 2:11, 12; Titus 2:5; 1 Pet. 3:1, 5, 6

There is no humanly generated way out of this horrible predicament of sin and alienation from the Paradise of God's provision. Indeed, all those descended from Adam and Eve are not only guilty of sin but they love to sin; and they cannot do otherwise, having inherited Adam's fallen nature (Rom. 5:12–14). While we retain God's image, it and creation have been deeply marred by the sinful actions of our representative (or "federal") head, i.e., Adam (Rom. 8:20–22). We need *saving*. This God promises to do with the very first announcement of his redemptive design for a messianic deliverer, a descendant (an "offspring" or "seed") of the woman whom Satan has deceived—a Seed who will ultimately overcome Satan and his influence (Gen. 3:15). This gracious promise becomes an organizing theme for the rest of Scripture and the rest of human history, as every character and event find their place in relation to the great battle that now unfolds between the conquering Seed of the woman and the resistance of Satan.

In his confounding defiance of what we deserve, God himself undertakes to save his people. He does this in Jesus Christ, the second Adam (Rom. 5:12–19). Jesus was fully obedient to the Father, is the source of life, and triumphs over Satan and death (Heb. 2:14–15). His rule will end all opposition to God's kingdom (1 Cor. 15:25; 1 John 3:8). Through him believers have access to the presence of God, his wisdom, and eternal life. They are united to Christ, the second Adam, and become truly human again as originally designed, as God's image is renewed in them once more (Col. 3:10).

Though the corruptions of sin quickly infect humanity, grace is displayed for Adam's and Eve's descendants ("offspring" or "seed"): there is a seed despite Adam's and Eve's sin (Gen. 4:1); there is a means to relate to God despite sin (4:3); there is protection for a murderer despite sin (4:15); there is warning of the corruption of sin (through Cain's line; 4:17–19) and at the same time indication of the faithfulness of God to provide the "Seed" for sinners (through Seth, i.e., Abel's replacement; 4:25–26).

"Because you have listened to the voice of
your wife
and have eaten of the tree
[l]of which I commanded you,
'You shall not eat of it,'
[m]cursed is the ground because of you;
[n]in pain you shall eat of it all the days
of your life;
18 thorns and thistles it shall bring forth
for you;
and you shall eat the plants of the
field.
19 By the sweat of your face
you shall eat bread,
till you return to the ground,
for out of it you were taken;
[o]for you are dust,
and [p]to dust you shall return."

20 The man called his wife's name Eve,
because she was the mother of all living.[1]
21 And the LORD God made for Adam and for
his wife garments of skins and clothed them.
22 Then the LORD God said, [q]"Behold, the
man has become like one of us in knowing
good and evil. Now, lest he reach out his hand
[r]and take also of the tree of life and eat, and
live forever—" 23 therefore the LORD God sent
him out from the garden of Eden [s]to work the
ground from which he was taken. 24 He drove
out the man, and at the east of the garden of
Eden he placed the [t]cherubim and a flaming
sword that turned every way to guard the way
to the tree of life.

Cain and Abel

4 Now Adam knew Eve his wife, and she
conceived and bore Cain, saying, "I have
gotten[2] a man with the help of the LORD."
2 And again, she bore his brother Abel. Now
Abel was a keeper of sheep, and Cain a worker
of the ground. 3 In the course of time Cain
brought to the LORD an offering of [u]the fruit
of the ground, 4 and Abel also brought of [v]the
firstborn of his flock and of their fat portions.
And the LORD [w]had regard for Abel and his
offering, 5 but [x]for Cain and his offering he
had no regard. So Cain was very angry, and his
face fell. 6 The LORD said to Cain, "Why are you
angry, and why has your face fallen? 7 [y]If you do
well, will you not be accepted?[3] And if you do
not do well, sin is crouching at the door. [z]Its
desire is for[4] you, but you must rule over it."
8 Cain spoke to Abel his brother.[5] And when
they were in the field, Cain rose up against his
brother Abel and [a]killed him. 9 Then the LORD
said to Cain, "Where is Abel your brother?"
He said, [b]"I do not know; am I my brother's
keeper?" 10 And the LORD said, "What have
you done? The voice of your brother's blood
[c]is crying to me from the ground. 11 And now
[d]you are cursed from the ground, which has
opened its mouth to receive your brother's
blood from your hand. 12 When you work the
ground, it shall no longer yield to you its
strength. You shall be a fugitive and a wanderer on the earth." 13 Cain said to the LORD,
"My [e]punishment is greater than I can bear.[6]
14 Behold, [f]you have driven me today away
from the ground, and [g]from your face I shall
be hidden. I shall be a fugitive and a wanderer
on the earth, [h]and whoever finds me will kill
me." 15 Then the LORD said to him, "Not so! If
anyone kills Cain, vengeance shall be taken on
him [i]sevenfold." And the LORD [j]put a mark on
Cain, lest any who found him should attack
him. 16 Then Cain went away from the pres-

[1] *Eve* sounds like the Hebrew for *life-giver* and resembles the word for *living* [2] *Cain* sounds like the Hebrew for *gotten* [3] Hebrew *will there not be a lifting up* [of your face]? [4] Or *against* [5] Hebrew; Samaritan, Septuagint, Syriac, Vulgate add *Let us go out to the field* [6] Or *My guilt is too great to bear*

4:17–5:32 In the genealogies of Cain and Seth are hidden gems of God's continuing grace to sinful humanity: Cain's lineage is traced through six generations (4:17–24). The line of Seth (through whom "people began to call upon the name of the LORD"; 4:26) is traced through ten generations. The seventh from Adam through Seth was Enoch, who was godly (5:24); the seventh from Adam through Cain was the first polygamist (4:19) and a killer (4:23–24), named Lamech. In each genealogy (Cain's line in ch. 4 and Seth's line in ch. 5), the words of only two individuals are recorded, and both are named Lamech. Cain's Lamech threatens revenge by his own hand (4:24); Seth's Lamech trusts in God's provision of rest and rescue through Noah (5:29). The distinction of the lines is important because Noah's son, Shem, becomes the father of the Semites—that is, the Jews, through whom Jesus, the promised Seed of deliverance, would come.

17 [l] ch. 2:17 [m] ch. 5:29; [Rom. 8:20-22] [n] Eccles. 2:22, 23
19 [o] ch. 2:7; Ps. 103:14 [p] Job 34:15; Ps. 104:29; Eccles. 3:20; 12:7; Rom. 5:12
22 [q] ver. 5 [r] ch. 2:9
23 [s] ch. 2:5
24 [t] Ps. 18:10; 104:4; Heb. 1:7; [Ex. 25:18-22; Ezek. 28:11-16]

Chapter 4
3 [u] Lev. 2:12; Num. 18:12
4 [v] Ex. 13:12; Num. 18:17; Prov. 3:9 [w] Heb. 11:4
5 [x] [Prov. 21:27]
7 [y] Eccles. 8:12, 13; Isa. 3:10, 11; Rom. 2:6-11 [z] ch. 3:16

8 [a] Matt. 23:35; Heb. 12:24; 1 John 3:12; Jude 11 **9** [b] John 8:44 **10** [c] Heb. 12:24; [Rev. 6:10] **11** [d] Deut. 27:24; [Num. 35:33] **13** [e] ch. 19:15 **14** [f] Job 15:20-24 [g] 2 Kgs. 24:20; Ps. 51:11; 143:7; Jer. 52:3 [h] ch. 9:6; Num. 35:19 **15** [i] Ps. 79:12 [j] [Ezek. 9:4, 6; Rev. 14:9, 11]

ence of the LORD and settled in the land of
Nod,[1] east of Eden.
17 Cain knew his wife, and she conceived and
bore Enoch. When he built a city, he called
the name of the city after the name of his son,
Enoch. 18 To Enoch was born Irad, and Irad
fathered Mehujael, and Mehujael fathered
Methushael, and Methushael fathered
Lamech. 19 And Lamech took two wives. The
name of the one was Adah, and the name of
the other Zillah. 20 Adah bore Jabal; he was the
father of those who dwell in tents and have
livestock. 21 His brother's name was Jubal; he
was the father of all those who play the lyre
and pipe. 22 Zillah also bore Tubal-cain; he was
the forger of all instruments of bronze and
iron. The sister of Tubal-cain was Naamah.
23 Lamech said to his wives:

"Adah and Zillah, hear my voice;
you wives of Lamech, listen to what
I say:
I have killed a man for wounding me,
a young man for striking me.
24 [k]If Cain's revenge is sevenfold,
then Lamech's is seventy-sevenfold."

25 And Adam knew his wife again, and she
bore a son and called his name Seth, for she
said, "God has appointed[2] for me another offspring instead of Abel, for Cain killed him."
26 To [l]Seth also a son was born, and he called
his name [m]Enosh. At that time people began
[n]to call upon the name of the LORD.

Adam's Descendants to Noah

5 This is the book of the generations of
Adam. When God created man, [o]he made
him in the likeness of God. 2 Male and female
he created them, and he blessed them and
named them Man[3] when they were created.
3 When Adam had lived 130 years, he fathered
a son in his own likeness, after his image, and
[p]named him Seth. 4 [q]The days of Adam after
he fathered Seth were 800 years; and he had
other sons and daughters. 5 Thus all the days
that Adam lived were 930 years, [r]and he died.
6 When Seth had lived 105 years, [s]he fathered
Enosh. 7 Seth lived after he fathered Enosh
807 years and had other sons and daughters.
8 Thus all the days of Seth were 912 years, and
he died.
9 When Enosh had lived 90 years, he fathered

[1] *Nod* means *wandering* [2] *Seth* sounds like the Hebrew for *he appointed* [3] Hebrew *adam*

5:1–6:8 The genealogy of Adam serves to connect Adam with Noah and with humanity as a whole. The human race as a whole was marked with the image of God (5:3) but it was also marked by death. The only exception was Enoch. He walked with God and did not die (5:24; cf. Heb. 11:5; Jude 14). The genealogy ends with four comments.

First, an explanation of Noah's name is given. He is God's comforter (i.e., relief), in a world that is groaning for redemption (Gen. 5:29), for all generations after the flood. As such, he is a "second Adam" and thus prefigures Christ, giving humanity a second start with a clean slate after the contagion of sin (6:5). Important parallels of Noah and Adam occur in the narrative. Their "worlds" are created out of a watery chaos. Both Adam and Noah are said to be in the "image of God," the only occurrences of the phrase in Genesis (1:27; 5:1; 9:6). Both "walked with God" (3:8; 6:9). Both exercise dominion over animals (Adam by naming; Noah by preserving). God's commands to be fruitful, to multiply, and to rule are given to both Adam and Noah (1:28–30; 9:1–7). Both work the ground (3:17–19; 9:20). Both sin in connection with food: Adam by eating (3:6); Noah by drinking (9:21). The sins of both result in shame and the need for clothing (3:7, 21; 9:21, 23). Both have three sons (4:1–2, 25; 6:10). Their sons represent contrasting paths for humanity, with Seth and Shem being the path of hope, and Cain and Ham the path of judgment—showing that the promised Seed of the woman is the path of life and the seed of the serpent that of death. Both of these "starts" of humanity also indicate the need of God's grace to finish humanity's purpose with his blessing.

Second, there is the episode of the sons of God and the daughters of men (6:1–3). The narrator leaves out too many details to know the identity of these "sons of God," but it seems that Moses is indicating that corruption is spreading through humanity—probably as the godly line of Seth (i.e., sons of God) intermarries with the ungodly line of Cain (daughters of men). Whatever happened, God gradually restricted the span of human life to 120 years, as the corruptions of the fall increasingly touched every aspect of human existence.

24 [k] ver. 15
26 [l] 1 Chr. 1:1; Luke 3:38 [m] ch. 5:6 [n] Ps. 116:17; Zeph. 3:9; Zech. 13:9

Chapter 5
1 [o] See ch. 1:26, 27
3 [p] ch. 4:25
4 [q] For ver. 4-32, see 1 Chr. 1:1-4; Luke 3:36-38
5 [r] ch. 3:19
6 [s] ch. 4:26

Kenan. 10 Enosh lived after he fathered Kenan 815 years and had other sons and daughters. 11 Thus all the days of Enosh were 905 years, and he died.

12 When Kenan had lived 70 years, he fathered Mahalalel. 13 Kenan lived after he fathered Mahalalel 840 years and had other sons and daughters. 14 Thus all the days of Kenan were 910 years, and he died.

15 When Mahalalel had lived 65 years, he fathered Jared. 16 Mahalalel lived after he fathered Jared 830 years and had other sons and daughters. 17 Thus all the days of Mahalalel were 895 years, and he died.

18 When Jared had lived 162 years he fathered [t]Enoch. 19 Jared lived after he fathered Enoch 800 years and had other sons and daughters. 20 Thus all the days of Jared were 962 years, and he died.

21 When Enoch had lived 65 years, he fathered Methuselah. 22 Enoch [u]walked with God[1] after he fathered Methuselah 300 years and had other sons and daughters. 23 Thus all the days of Enoch were 365 years. 24 Enoch [u]walked with God, and he was not,[2] [v]for God took him.

25 When Methuselah had lived 187 years, he fathered Lamech. 26 Methuselah lived after he fathered Lamech 782 years and had other sons and daughters. 27 Thus all the days of Methuselah were 969 years, and he died.

28 When Lamech had lived 182 years, he fathered a son 29 and called his name Noah, saying, "Out of the ground [w]that the LORD has cursed, this one shall bring us relief[3] from our work and from the painful toil of our hands." 30 Lamech lived after he fathered Noah 595 years and had other sons and daughters. 31 Thus all the days of Lamech were 777 years, and he died.

32 After Noah was 500 years old, Noah fathered [x]Shem, Ham, and [y]Japheth.

Increasing Corruption on Earth

6 When man began to multiply on the face of the land and daughters were born to them, 2 the sons of God saw that the daughters of man were attractive. And they took as their wives any they chose. 3 Then the LORD said, [z]"My Spirit shall not abide in[4] man forever, [a]for he is flesh: his days shall be 120 years." 4 The Nephilim[5] were on the earth in those days, and also afterward, when the sons of God came in to the daughters of man and they bore children to them. These were the mighty men who were of old, the men of renown.

5 [b]The LORD saw that the wickedness of man was great in the earth, and that every [c]intention of the thoughts of his heart was only evil continually. 6 And [d]the LORD regretted that he had made man on the earth, and it [e]grieved him to his heart. 7 So the LORD said, "I will blot out man whom I have created from the face of the land, man and animals and creeping things and birds of the heavens, for I am sorry that I have made them." 8 But Noah [f]found favor in the eyes of the LORD.

Noah and the Flood

9 These are the generations of Noah. [g]Noah was a righteous man, [h]blameless in his generation. Noah [i]walked with God. 10 And Noah had three sons, Shem, Ham, and Japheth.

11 Now the earth was corrupt in God's sight,

[1] Septuagint *pleased God* [2] Septuagint *was not found* [3] *Noah* sounds like the Hebrew for *rest* [4] Or *My Spirit shall not contend with* [5] Or *giants*

18 [t] Jude 14
22 [u] ver. 24; ch. 6:9; [Mic. 6:8; Mal. 2:6]
24 [u] [See ver. 22 above] [v] Heb. 11:5; [2 Kgs. 2:11]
29 [w] ch. 3:17
32 [x] ch. 6:10 [y] ch. 10:21

Chapter 6

3 [z] 1 Pet. 3:19, 20; [Neh. 9:30; Gal. 5:16, 17] [a] Ps. 78:39
5 [b] Ps. 14:2, 3 [c] ch. 8:21; Job 14:4; 15:14; Ps. 51:5; Jer. 17:9; Matt. 15:19; Rom. 3:23
6 [d] 1 Sam. 15:11; 2 Sam. 24:16; Joel 2:13; [Num. 23:19; 1 Sam. 15:29] [e] Isa. 63:10; Eph. 4:30
8 [f] ch. 19:19; Ex. 33:12, 13, 16, 17
9 [g] ch. 7:1; Ezek. 14:14, 20; 2 Pet. 2:5 [h] Job 1:1, 8; Luke 1:6 [i] ch. 5:22, 24; [Heb. 11:7]

Third, the occasion of the Nephilim ("fallen ones") is a reminder of the fallen condition of humanity eroding into increasing perversion and violence (6:4, 13).

Fourth, the fallenness of humanity occasions God's judgment. Humanity is now thoroughly degenerate (6:5). The flood would bring an end to that generation (6:7)—an end to all except the family of Noah.

6:9–9:29 Prior to the flood, Noah walked with the Lord, trusting in him at all cost. Divine grace kept Noah close to the Lord, so he walked with God and lived a life of wisdom (6:9). Noah is thus one of the great examples of what it means to live by faith (Heb. 11:7). Noah executed the mission of building the ark with integrity (cf. Matt. 24:37–42).

When the flood wiped out the rest of humanity, Noah became a second Adam figure, bringing comfort to humanity by being an instrument of the renewal of God's blessing (Gen. 9:1, 7). Noah also echoed Adam's role as recipient of a covenant that God made with him, his descendants, and with all of life (9:8–17). Jesus compared the day of his second coming to the days of Noah: people lived their lives apart from God, foolishly unaware of his gracious offer of life (Luke 17:26). Peter drew a lesson

and the earth was filled with violence. 12 And
God [j]saw the earth, and behold, it was corrupt, [k]for all flesh had corrupted their way
on the earth. 13 And God said to Noah, [l]"I have
determined to make an end of all flesh,[1] for
the earth is filled with violence through them.
Behold, I will destroy them with the earth.
14 Make yourself an ark of gopher wood.[2] Make
rooms in the ark, and cover it inside and out
with pitch. 15 This is how you are to make it:
the length of the ark 300 cubits,[3] its breadth
50 cubits, and its height 30 cubits. 16 Make a
roof[4] for the ark, and finish it to a cubit above,
and set the door of the ark in its side. Make it
with lower, second, and third decks. 17 [m]For
behold, I will bring a flood of waters upon the
earth to destroy all flesh in which is the breath
of life under heaven. Everything that is on the
earth shall die. 18 But [n]I will establish my covenant with you, and you shall come into the
ark, you, your sons, your wife, and your sons'
wives with you. 19 And of every living thing of
all flesh, you shall bring two of every sort into
the ark to keep them alive with you. They shall
be male and female. 20 Of the birds according
to their kinds, and of the animals according
to their kinds, of every creeping thing of the
ground, according to its kind, two of every
sort shall come in to you to keep them alive.
21 Also take with you every sort of food that is
eaten, and store it up. It shall serve as food for
you and for them." 22 [o]Noah did this; he did all
that God commanded him.

7 Then the LORD said to Noah, [p]"Go into the
ark, you and all your household, for I have
seen that [q]you are righteous before me in this
generation. 2 Take with you seven pairs of all
[r]clean animals,[5] the male and his mate, and
a pair of the animals that are not clean, the
male and his mate, 3 and seven pairs[6] of the
birds of the heavens also, male and female,
to keep their offspring alive on the face of all
the earth. 4 For in seven days [s]I will send rain
on the earth forty days and forty nights, [t]and
every living thing[7] that I have made I will blot
out from the face of the ground." 5 [u]And Noah
did all that the LORD had commanded him.

6 Noah was six hundred years old when the
flood of waters came upon the earth. 7 And
Noah and his sons and his wife and his sons'
wives with him went into the ark to escape the
waters of the flood. 8 Of clean animals, and of
animals that are not clean, and of birds, and
of everything that creeps on the ground, 9 two
and two, male and female, went into the ark
with Noah, as God had commanded Noah.
10 And after seven days the waters of the flood
came upon the earth.

11 In the six hundredth year of Noah's life, in
the second month, on the seventeenth day of
the month, on that day all the [v]fountains of the
great deep burst forth, and [w]the windows of
the heavens were opened. 12 And rain fell upon
the earth forty days and forty nights. 13 On the
very same day Noah and his sons, Shem and
Ham and Japheth, and Noah's wife and the
three wives of his sons with them entered the
ark, 14 they and every beast, according to its
kind, and all the livestock according to their
kinds, and every creeping thing that creeps on
the earth, according to its kind, and every bird,
according to its kind, every winged creature.

[1] Hebrew *The end of all flesh has come before me* [2] An unknown kind of tree; transliterated from Hebrew [3] A *cubit* was about 18 inches or 45 centimeters [4] Or *skylight* [5] Or *seven of each kind of clean animal* [6] Or *seven of each kind* [7] Hebrew *all existence*; also verse 23

of God's ultimate justice with parallels regarding his deliverance of Noah from the ancient world that perished (2 Pet. 2:5).

The story of the flood is a sober reminder that God's final judgment will echo the events surrounding Noah. This time, however, the earth will not be cleansed by water but will be purified as by fire (2 Pet. 3:6–7; cf. Matt. 24:37–42). Peter employs the analogy of the water of the flood to represent salvation from any further judgment (1 Pet. 3:21–22). God showed his favor to Noah by calling him to be his instrument of salvation. In full obedience to the Lord (Gen. 6:22; 7:5, 9, 16), Noah constructed an ark and led his family and the clean and unclean animals into it. He received the promise of preservation through covenant (6:18), waited patiently for the flood to be over, and upon leaving the ark he sacrificed an offering of thanksgiving (8:20).

The Noahic covenant is God's gracious commitment to preserve creation till the final judgment. Amid the flood of judgment God preserved humans and animals, but all this did not change the nature of humans. Noah took his sin nature with him into the ark, and he and his sons passed that sin nature on to their descendants, just as they had received it from Adam (see 9:20–25).

12 [j] Ps. 14:2, 3; 53:2, 3 [k] Job 22:15-17
13 [l] Ezek. 7:2, 3, 6
17 [m] ch. 7:4; 2 Pet. 2:5
18 [n] ch. 9:9, 11
22 [o] Heb. 11:7; [Ex. 40:16]

Chapter 7
1 [p] Matt. 24:38, 39; Luke 17:26, 27; Heb. 11:7; 1 Pet. 3:20; 2 Pet. 2:5 [q] ch. 6:9
2 [r] ch. 8:20; [Lev. 11]
4 [s] ver. 12, 17; [Job 37:11-13] [t] ch. 6:17
5 [u] ch. 6:22
11 [v] ch. 8:2; Prov. 8:28; [Amos 9:6] [w] ch. 8:2; 2 Kgs. 7:19; Isa. 24:18; Mal. 3:10; [Ps. 78:23]

15 They [x]went into the ark with Noah, two and two of all flesh in which there was the breath of life. 16 And those that entered, male and female of all flesh, went in [y]as God had commanded him. And the LORD shut him in.

17 The flood [z]continued forty days on the earth. The waters increased and bore up the ark, and it rose high above the earth. 18 The waters prevailed and increased greatly on the earth, and the ark floated on the face of the waters. 19 And the waters prevailed so mightily on the earth that all the high mountains under the whole heaven were covered. 20 The waters prevailed above the mountains, covering them fifteen cubits[1] deep. 21 And [a]all flesh died that moved on the earth, birds, livestock, beasts, all swarming creatures that swarm on the earth, and all mankind. 22 Everything on the dry land [b]in whose nostrils was the breath of life died. 23 He blotted out every living thing that was on the face of the ground, man and animals and creeping things and birds of the heavens. They were blotted out from the earth. Only [c]Noah was left, and those who were with him in the ark. 24 And the waters prevailed on the earth 150 days.

The Flood Subsides

8 But God [d]remembered Noah and all the beasts and all the livestock that were with him in the ark. And [e]God made a wind blow over the earth, and the waters subsided. 2 [f]The fountains of the deep and [f]the windows of the heavens were closed, the rain from the heavens was restrained, 3 and the waters receded from the earth continually. At the end [g]of 150 days the waters had abated, 4 and in the seventh month, on the seventeenth day of the month, the ark came to rest on the mountains of [h]Ararat. 5 And the waters continued to abate until the tenth month; in the tenth month, on the first day of the month, the tops of the mountains were seen.

6 At the end of forty days Noah opened the window of the ark that he had made 7 and sent forth a raven. It went to and fro until the waters were dried up from the earth. 8 Then he sent forth a dove from him, to see if the waters had subsided from the face of the ground. 9 But the dove found no place to set her foot, and she returned to him to the ark, for the waters were still on the face of the whole earth. So he put out his hand and took her and brought her into the ark with him. 10 He waited another seven days, and again he sent forth the dove out of the ark. 11 And the dove came back to him in the evening, and behold, in her mouth was a freshly plucked olive leaf. So Noah knew that the waters had subsided from the earth. 12 Then he waited another seven days and sent forth the dove, and she did not return to him anymore.

13 In the six hundred and first year, in the first month, the first day of the month, the waters were dried from off the earth. And Noah removed the covering of the ark and looked, and behold, the face of the ground was dry. 14 In the second month, on the twenty-seventh day of the month, the earth had dried out. 15 Then God said to Noah, 16 "Go out from the ark, [i]you and your wife,

[1] A *cubit* was about 18 inches or 45 centimeters

15 [x]ch. 6:20
16 [y]ver. 2, 3
17 [z]ver. 4, 12
21 [a]ver. 4; ch. 6:13, 17; 2 Pet. 3:6
22 [b]ch. 2:7
23 [c]2 Pet. 2:5
Chapter 8
1 [d]ch. 19:29; 30:22; Ex. 2:24; 1 Sam. 1:19 [e]Ex. 14:21
2 [f]ch. 7:11
3 [g]ch. 7:24
4 [h]2 Kgs. 19:37; Isa. 37:38; Jer. 51:27
16 [i]ch. 7:13

Nevertheless, God used this judgment as a gracious blessing for all humanity by restating the blessing of life and offspring originally given to Adam and Eve (9:1, 7). He formally expanded the dietary restrictions by allowing the consumption of animal meat (9:3–4). He also upheld the sanctity of life by reminding humans that they are created in the divine image (9:6). All of life, human and animal, belongs to God (cf. Lev. 17:11). Disregard for human life provokes divine judgment and demands human judgment as well (Gen. 9:5).

The Bible describes both God's common grace and his special covenant grace (9:9, 11; etc.). God's common grace is the grace that he as King gives to his human creatures, whether they are regenerate or not. They receive his blessings of general sustenance and restraint of the full potential of evil for their earthly existence. God's special covenant grace is his gift solely to his spiritual children, as he commits himself to be present with them in provision and in protection for their eternal welfare (see 12:1–3). The sign of the covenant with Noah is the rainbow. Every rainbow is a reminder of God's ongoing common-grace mercy, down through the generations since Noah, indicating that he will never flood the earth again (9:13–15). The rainbow should also remind us that God was providing special grace through Noah, preserving through him the promised Seed of eternal deliverance for sinful people.

and your sons and your sons' wives with you.
17 Bring out with you every living thing that
is with you of all flesh—birds and animals
and every creeping thing that creeps on the
earth—that they may swarm on the earth,
and [j]be fruitful and multiply on the earth."
18 So Noah went out, and his sons and his wife
and his sons' wives with him. 19 Every beast,
every creeping thing, and every bird, everything that moves on the earth, went out by
families from the ark.

God's Covenant with Noah

20 Then Noah built an altar to the LORD and
took some of every clean animal and some of
every clean bird and offered burnt offerings on
the altar. 21 And when the LORD smelled [k]the
pleasing aroma, the LORD said in his heart, "I
will never again [l]curse[1] the ground because
of man, for [m]the intention of man's heart is
evil from his youth. [n]Neither will I ever again
strike down every living creature as I have
done. 22 [o]While the earth remains, seedtime
and harvest, cold and heat, summer and winter, [p]day and night, shall not cease."

9 And God blessed Noah and his sons and
said to them, [q]"Be fruitful and multiply
and fill the earth. 2 [r]The fear of you and the
dread of you shall be upon every beast of the
earth and upon every bird of the heavens,
upon everything that creeps on the ground
and all the fish of the sea. Into your hand
they are delivered. 3 [s]Every moving thing that
lives shall be food for you. And [t]as I gave you
the green plants, I give you everything. 4 But
you shall not eat flesh with its [u]life, that is, its
blood. 5 And for your lifeblood I will require
a reckoning: [v]from every beast I will require
it and [w]from man. From his fellow man I will
require a reckoning for the life of man.

6 [x]"Whoever sheds the blood of man,
by man shall his blood be shed,
[y]for God made man in his own image.

7 And you,[2] be fruitful and multiply, increase
greatly on the earth and multiply in it."
8 Then God said to Noah and to his sons
with him, 9 "Behold, [z]I establish my covenant with you and your offspring after you,
10 and with every living creature that is with
you, the birds, the livestock, and every beast of
the earth with you, as many as came out of the
ark; it is for every beast of the earth. 11 [a]I establish my covenant with you, that never again
shall all flesh be cut off by the waters of the
flood, and never again shall there be a flood to
destroy the earth." 12 And God said, [b]"This is the
sign of the covenant that I make between me
and you and every living creature that is with
you, for all future generations: 13 I have set [c]my
bow in the cloud, and it shall be a sign of the
covenant between me and the earth. 14 When
I bring clouds over the earth and the bow is
seen in the clouds, 15 [d]I will remember my covenant that is between me and you and every
living creature of all flesh. And the waters shall
never again become a flood to destroy all flesh.
16 When the bow is in the clouds, I will see it and
remember [e]the everlasting covenant between
God and every living creature of all flesh that
is on the earth." 17 God said to Noah, "This is
the sign of the covenant that I have established
between me and all flesh that is on the earth."

Noah's Descendants

18 The sons of Noah who went forth from the
ark were [f]Shem, Ham, and Japheth. (Ham was
the father of Canaan.) 19 These three were the
sons of Noah, and [g]from these the people of
the whole earth were dispersed.[3]
20 Noah began to be a man of the soil, and he
planted a vineyard.[4] 21 He drank of the wine

[1] Or *dishonor* [2] In Hebrew *you* is plural [3] Or *from these the whole earth was populated* [4] Or *Noah, a man of the soil, was the first to plant a vineyard*

9:20–29 The need of God's special grace is evident in that even Noah remained corrupted by sin his entire life. The account of Noah ends on a strange note, as he winds up drunk and naked in his tent (vv. 20–21), with an immoral (cf. v. 22 and Lev. 18:6–18; 20:17) and dysfunctional family being divided by cursing and blessings (Gen. 9:22–27). Even a man as great as Noah required mercy from God. In Jesus, the Seed descendant of Noah over whom the floods of divine judgment passed, this mercy was secured at the climax of all of human history (Eph. 1:10). It is available to all, then or today, who by faith call on the name of Lord and look to Christ.

17 [j]ch. 1:22, 28; 9:1
21 [k]Ex. 29:18, 25, 41; Lev. 1:9, 13, 17; See Ezek. 16:19; 20:41; 2 Cor. 2:15; Eph. 5:2; Phil. 4:18 [l]ch. 3:17; 6:17 [m]ch. 6:5; Ps. 58:3; Rom. 1:21; [Matt. 15:19] [n]ch. 9:11, 15; Isa. 54:9
22 [o]Jer. 5:24 [p]Jer. 33:20, 25
Chapter 9
1 [q]ch. 1:22, 28; 8:17

2 [r][Ps. 8:6-8; James 3:7] **3** [s]Deut. 12:15; 1 Tim. 4:3, 4 [t]ch. 1:29 **4** [u]Lev. 17:10, 11, 14; Deut. 12:16, 23; 1 Sam. 14:33; Acts 15:20, 29 **5** [v]Ex. 21:28 [w]ch. 4:10, 11 **6** [x]Ex. 21:12, 14; Lev. 24:17; Num. 35:31, 33; [Matt. 26:52; Rev. 13:10] [y]ch. 1:27; 5:1; James 3:9 **9** [z]ch. 6:18; 8:20-22 **11** [a]Isa. 54:9, 10 **12** [b]ch. 17:11 **13** [c]Ezek. 1:28; [Rev. 4:3; 10:1] **15** [d][Lev. 26:42, 45; 1 Kgs. 8:23; Ezek. 16:60] **16** [e]ch. 17:7, 13, 19 **18** [f]ch. 5:32; 10:1 **19** [g]ch. 10:32

and became drunk and lay uncovered in his
tent. 22 And Ham, the father of Canaan, saw
the nakedness of his father and told his two
brothers outside. 23 Then Shem and Japheth
took a garment, laid it on both their shoulders, and walked backward and covered the
nakedness of their father. Their faces were
turned backward, and they did not see their
father's nakedness. 24 When Noah awoke from
his wine [h]and knew what his youngest son had
done to him, 25 he said,

> [i]"Cursed be Canaan;
> [j]a servant of servants shall he be to his brothers."

26 He also said,

> "Blessed be the LORD, the God of Shem;
> and let Canaan be his servant.
> 27 May God enlarge Japheth,[1]
> and let him dwell in the tents of Shem,
> and let Canaan be his servant."

28 After the flood Noah lived 350 years. 29 All
the days of Noah were 950 years, and he died.

Nations Descended from Noah

10 These are the generations of the sons of
Noah, Shem, Ham, and Japheth. Sons
were born to them after the flood.
2 [k]The sons of Japheth: Gomer, Magog,
Madai, Javan, Tubal, Meshech, and Tiras.
3 The sons of Gomer: Ashkenaz, Riphath,
and Togarmah. 4 The sons of Javan: Elishah,
[l]Tarshish, [m]Kittim, and Dodanim. 5 From these
[n]the coastland peoples spread in their lands,
each with his own language, by their clans, in
their nations.
6 [o]The sons of Ham: Cush, Egypt, Put, and
Canaan. 7 The sons of Cush: Seba, Havilah,
Sabtah, Raamah, and Sabteca. The sons of
Raamah: Sheba and Dedan. 8 Cush fathered
Nimrod; he was the first on earth to be a
mighty man.[2] 9 He was a mighty hunter before
the LORD. Therefore it is said, "Like Nimrod a
mighty hunter before the LORD." 10 The beginning of his kingdom was [p]Babel, Erech, Accad,
and Calneh, in [q]the land of Shinar. 11 From that
land he went into Assyria and built Nineveh,
Rehoboth-Ir, Calah, and 12 Resen between
Nineveh and Calah; that is the great city.

[1] *Japheth* sounds like the Hebrew for *enlarge* [2] Or *he began to be a mighty man on the earth*

24[h] [Hab. 2:15]
25[i] Deut. 27:16 [j] Josh. 9:23; Judg. 1:28; 1 Kgs. 9:20, 21
Chapter 10
2[k] For ver. 1-5, see 1 Chr. 1:5-7; Ezek. 38:1-6
4[l] Ps. 72:10; Ezek. 38:13 [m] Num. 24:24; Isa. 23:1, 12; Dan. 11:30
5[n] Isa. 11:11; Jer. 2:10; 25:22; Ezek. 27:6; Zeph. 2:11
6[o] For ver. 6-8, see 1 Chr. 1:8-10
10[p] ch. 11:9 [q] ch. 11:2

10:1–32 The brief note on the dispersion of the nations (9:19) leads to two further explanations: the nations associated with the descendants of Noah (10:1–32) and the occasion of the dispersion (11:1–9). The genealogies of Noah's descendants are arranged by language, ethnicity, location, and political arena.

The "table of nations" of chapter 10 affirms the continuation of the "seed" or "offspring" (as promised in 3:15) and the gracious repopulation of the earth through the establishment of nations. In reviewing these genealogies we are reminded of the determined covenant mercies of God to one day bring restoration of Eden through Jesus Christ (Rev. 21:1–22:5). For it is through a human mediator, Jesus Christ, descended from Adam (Luke 3:38), that this gracious restoration will finally come about.

The list of Noah's descendants begins with Japheth and continues with Ham and on to Shem, whose genealogy is further detailed in Genesis 11:10–26. Prominent in Israel's history are the African nations (Cush, Egypt), Canaan, and the territories of Assyria and Babylon (10:6–14). The account of the Ethiopian eunuch (Acts 8:26–40) may explain how the gospel reaches the descendants of Ham. Greater details are given of Canaan, because of Israel's entry into that land. Genealogical connections helped Israel to know the people groups that had come under God's judgment (Deut. 7:1–2; 20:16–17). The cities of "Sodom . . . Zeboiim" had already been destroyed by the time Israel entered Canaan (Genesis 19). The mention of the diversity of languages and clans supports the biblical teaching that the Lord willed and graciously forced the dispersion from Babel both to keep humanity from vain pursuit and to allow his purposes to unfold throughout the world (see Deut. 32:8; Acts 17:26).

In summary, God intended that his redemption would reach all nations. The gospel reveals God's equanimity. He called Israel to be set apart from the world *for the sake of* the world. God's gracious welcome is as wide as the entire human race, for those who repent and trust in Christ.

13 [r]Egypt fathered Ludim, Anamim, Lehabim,
Naphtuhim, 14 Pathrusim, Casluhim (from
whom[1] the Philistines came), and [s]Caphtorim.
15 [t]Canaan fathered Sidon his firstborn and
Heth, 16 and the Jebusites, the Amorites, the
Girgashites, 17 the Hivites, the Arkites, the
Sinites, 18 the Arvadites, the Zemarites, and
the Hamathites. Afterward the clans of the
Canaanites dispersed. 19 And the territory of
the Canaanites extended from Sidon in the
direction of Gerar as far as Gaza, and in the
direction of Sodom, Gomorrah, Admah, and
Zeboiim, as far as Lasha. 20 These are the sons
of Ham, by their clans, their languages, their
lands, and their nations.
21 To Shem also, the father of all the children
of Eber, the elder brother of Japheth, children were born. 22 The [u]sons of Shem: Elam,
Asshur, Arpachshad, Lud, and Aram. 23 The
sons of Aram: Uz, Hul, Gether, and Mash.
24 Arpachshad fathered [v]Shelah; and Shelah
fathered Eber. 25 [w]To Eber were born two sons:
the name of the one was Peleg,[2] for in his
days the earth was divided, and his brother's
name was Joktan. 26 Joktan fathered Almodad,
Sheleph, Hazarmaveth, Jerah, 27 Hadoram,
Uzal, Diklah, 28 Obal, Abimael, Sheba, 29 [x]Ophir,
Havilah, and Jobab; all these were the sons of
Joktan. 30 The territory in which they lived
extended from Mesha in the direction of
Sephar to the hill country of the east. 31 These
are the sons of Shem, by their clans, their languages, their lands, and their nations.
32 These are the clans of the sons of Noah,
according to their genealogies, in their
nations, [y]and from these the nations spread
abroad on the earth after the flood.

The Tower of Babel

11 Now the whole earth had one language
and the same words. 2 And as people
migrated from the east, they found a plain
in [z]the land of Shinar and settled there. 3 And
they said to one another, "Come, let us make
bricks, and burn them thoroughly." And they
had brick for stone, [a]and bitumen for mortar.
4 Then they said, "Come, let us build ourselves
a city and a tower [b]with its top in the heavens,
and let us make a name for ourselves, lest we
be dispersed over the face of the whole earth."
5 And [c]the LORD came down to see the city and
the tower, which the children of man had built.
6 And the LORD said, "Behold, they are one people, and they have all one language, and this is

[1] Or *from where* [2] *Peleg* means *division*

11:1–9 The spread of humanity was God's will from the beginning (1:28), but the effects of sin (including mankind's forced exile from Eden) meant that this dispersion occurred in ways that God did not intend. In the account of the Tower of Babel, we see once more what it looks like for sin, rather than obedience, to fuel the spreading of humanity.

In Genesis 11 humanity becomes wickedly united in its defiance of the Creator. God decreed to make humans in his image, saying "let us make . . ." (1:26). At Babel, however, humans use the same expression ("let us make . . ."; 11:3) to seek to displace God's glory with their own glory. The three episodes of human fallenness in Genesis 2–11 are: Adam and Eve in Eden, the generation of the flood, and the generation of Babel. This third episode is the most violent, as fallen humans here seek to determine their own destiny (11:4). In each case God's judgment is not final, and his judgment reveals his gracious purposes for and patience with humanity. Each episode is not catastrophic but instead opens up new possibilities. God gave Adam and Eve the promise of a coming deliverer (3:15). With Noah, God confirms his commitment to his created order. The story of Babel leads to the story of Abraham, which reveals God's commitment to all the families of the earth (12:3).

In the story of Babel there is obvious warning of the inability of human effort to reach God. It thus becomes an early doctrinal signpost of the nature of redemption. God actively intervenes, through the confusion of languages, to stop this human striving toward him. However, these language differences are reversed by the Holy Spirit in Acts 2 at Pentecost, and they are made to be fully harmonious in the great song of the Great Day of heavenly gathering "from every tribe and language and people and nation" (Rev. 5:9). God's grace enables his people not only to reach him but to do so in unity and not by mere human capacity.

The Babel account also repeats the narrative pattern of a return to chaos (see the note on Gen. 5:1–6:8) prior to the focus on God's redemptive provision through another family—this time the family of Abraham.

13[r] For ver. 13-18, see 1 Chr. 1:11-16
14[s] Deut. 2:23; Jer. 47:4; Amos 9:7
15[t] [ch. 15:18-21]
22[u] For ver. 22-29, see 1 Chr. 1:17-25
24[v] ch. 11:12; Luke 3:35, 36
25[w] 1 Chr. 1:19
29[x] 1 Kgs. 9:28; 10:11
32[y] ver. 1; ch. 9:19
Chapter 11
2[z] ch. 10:10; 14:1, 9; Isa. 11:11; Dan. 1:2; Zech. 5:11
3[a] ch. 14:10; Ex. 2:3
4[b] Deut. 1:28
5[c] ch. 18:21

only the beginning of what they will do. And
nothing that they propose to do will now be
impossible for them. 7 Come, [d]let us go down
and there confuse their language, so that they
may not understand one another's speech." 8 So
[e]the LORD dispersed them from there over the
face of all the earth, and they left off building
the city. 9 Therefore its name was called [f]Babel,
because there the LORD confused[1] the language
of all the earth. And from there the LORD dispersed them over the face of all the earth.

Shem's Descendants

10 [g]These are the generations of Shem.
When Shem was 100 years old, he fathered
Arpachshad two years after the flood. 11 And
Shem lived after he fathered Arpachshad 500
years and had other sons and daughters.
12 When Arpachshad had lived 35 years, he
fathered Shelah. 13 And Arpachshad lived after
he fathered Shelah 403 years and had other
sons and daughters.
14 When Shelah had lived 30 years, he
fathered Eber. 15 And Shelah lived after he
fathered Eber 403 years and had other sons
and daughters.
16 When Eber had lived 34 years, he fathered
Peleg. 17 And Eber lived after he fathered Peleg
430 years and had other sons and daughters.
18 When Peleg had lived 30 years, he fathered
Reu. 19 And Peleg lived after he fathered Reu
209 years and had other sons and daughters.
20 When Reu had lived 32 years, he fathered
Serug. 21 And Reu lived after he fathered Serug
207 years and had other sons and daughters.
22 When Serug had lived 30 years, he fathered
Nahor. 23 And Serug lived after he fathered
Nahor 200 years and had other sons and
daughters.
24 When [h]Nahor had lived 29 years, he
fathered Terah. 25 And Nahor lived after he
fathered Terah 119 years and had other sons
and daughters.
26 When [h]Terah had lived 70 years, he
fathered Abram, Nahor, and Haran.

Terah's Descendants

27 Now these are the generations of Terah.
Terah fathered Abram, Nahor, and Haran;
and Haran fathered Lot. 28 Haran died in the
presence of his father Terah in the land of his
kindred, in Ur of the Chaldeans. 29 And Abram
and Nahor took wives. The name of Abram's
wife was [i]Sarai, and the name of Nahor's wife,
[j]Milcah, the daughter of Haran the father of
Milcah and Iscah. 30 Now Sarai was barren; she
had no child.
31 Terah [k]took Abram his son and Lot the son

[1] *Babel* sounds like the Hebrew for *confused*

7[d] ch. 1:26; [Ps. 2:4]
8[e] ch. 10:25, 32; Luke 1:51
9[f] ch. 10:10
10[g] [ch. 10:22]; For ver. 10-26, see 1 Chr. 1:17-27
24[h] Josh. 24:2
26[h] [See ver. 24 above]
29[i] ch. 17:15 [j] ch. 22:20
31[k] ch. 12:1

11:27–50:26 The second part of Genesis orients Israel to her own national roots (Abraham, Isaac, Jacob) and to her relationship with other nations such as the Moabites, the Ammonites, the Ishmaelites, and the Edomites. Throughout all these accounts we are brought to marvel at the goodness of God in working his redemptive purposes into our space-and-time history, to bring to pass his unstoppable goal of restoring the world to the way it was supposed to be.

11:27–25:11 The descendants of Terah were Abraham, Lot, and Laban. The three sons of Terah (Abram, Nahor, and Haran) find their parallel with the three sons of Noah (Shem, Ham, and Japheth). In each case one son (first Shem; then Abram [later called Abraham]) becomes the primary carrier of the lineage from Noah to Israel. God continues to oversee all that happens in world history to bring about the redemption of his people and of the entire cosmos.

The story of Abraham is the story of all of God's true children, because Abraham is their spiritual father (Gal. 3:7–9). In a dispute with the Jews (John 7:1–8:59), Jesus argued that they were not Abraham's children for they did not respond to Jesus the way Abraham would have responded (John 8:39; see Gen. 18:1–8). Abraham would have rejoiced at Jesus' coming (John 8:56) as the source of all blessing. For Jesus, Abraham's descendant, is more than just that (Gal. 3:16); he is the great "I am" (John 8:58). Jesus is God incarnate.

11:30 Sarai's barrenness introduces a theme that travels through the whole Bible: the barren woman who becomes an agent of redemption. Sarai (Sarah), Rebekah, and Rachel were all barren; so were Hannah (1 Samuel 1–2) and Elizabeth (Luke 1). God had blessed Adam and Eve and told them to multiply and spread across the earth: barrenness, therefore, represented the painful antithesis of God's good blessing.

of Haran, his grandson, and Sarai his daughter-in-law, his son Abram's wife, and they went
forth together [l]from Ur of the Chaldeans to go
into the land of Canaan, but when they came
to Haran, they settled there. 32 The days of
Terah were 205 years, and Terah died in Haran.

The Call of Abram

12 Now [m]the LORD said[1] to Abram, "Go
from your country[2] and your kindred
and your father's house to the land that I will
show you. 2 [n]And I will make of you a great
nation, and I will bless you and make your
name great, so that you will be a blessing. 3 [o]I
will bless those who bless you, and him who
dishonors you I will curse, and [p]in you all the
families of the earth shall be blessed."[3]
4 So Abram went, as the LORD had told him,
and Lot went with him. Abram was seventy-
five years old when he departed from [q]Haran.
5 And Abram took Sarai his wife, and Lot his
brother's son, and all their possessions that

[1] Or *had said* [2] Or *land* [3] Or *by you all the families of the earth shall bless themselves*

31 [l]ch. 15:7; Josh. 24:2; Neh. 9:7; Acts 7:2, 4

Chapter 12
1 [m]Acts 7:3; Heb. 11:8
2 [n]ch. 17:6; 18:18; [Gal. 3:14]
3 [o]ch. 27:29; Num. 24:9 [p]ch. 18:18; 22:18; 26:4; 28:14; Jer. 4:2; Acts 3:25; Gal. 3:16; Cited Gal. 3:8
4 [q]ch. 11:31

Yet in a strange twist, though one that is indicative of the way God works in the world, it is precisely the barren woman who comes to represent the one on whom God's true blessing rests (cf. Isa. 49:20–21; 54:1). They are agents of redemption (cf. 1 Tim. 2:15). God delights to work out his redemptive purposes through those whom the world deems weak and helpless, unable to contribute meaningfully to society. Such people are often the only ones humble and destitute enough to be open to God and his mighty purposes of grace.

12:1–3 Abraham is also a kind of second Adam. As Adam is the father of all humans, Abraham is the father of all believers, that is, of all who are united to God by the kind of faith Abraham demonstrated (Gen. 12:3; Gal. 3:29).

The Lord had blessed Adam and Noah (Gen. 1:28; 9:1). Now he promised to bless Abraham and his "seed" (or "offspring"; 12:7). The particulars of God's promise are the multiplication of Abram's progeny (a great nation), the magnificence of his reputation (name), and the blessing of God's protection (God's presence) in order to bless others (God's purpose). In short, because Abraham was blessed (his indicative status), he was to be a blessing (his imperative calling, enabled by God) to all the families of the earth (see 10:1–11:9).

The repetition of the particulars of this ancient covenantal promise throughout Genesis—to Abraham (18:18; 22:18), Isaac (26:4), and Jacob (28:14), as well as in the Prophets (Jer. 4:2) and the Wisdom Literature (Ps. 72:5–17)—raises the hope that God's kingdom will be universal and that one day corruption will cease on earth. The blessing of Abraham sets the stage for the story of Israel but also for the story of Christ and his church (see Luke's many references to Abraham in Luke 1–2). Peter confirms that all nations will be blessed in Abraham (Acts 3:25). Jesus is the true "offspring" of Abraham (Gal. 3:16). Paul argues that God's promise to Abraham extends equal citizenship to all in God's kingdom. Any Jew or Gentile who believes in the Lord Jesus is a child of God and of Abraham (Gal. 3:7–9).

God's gracious provision of secure salvation in Christ is not offered to a privileged few. It is for the entire world. It is for "all nations" (Matt. 28:19).

12:4–9 Upon receiving the promise of the land (v. 7), Abram constructs an altar, even as Noah had done after the flood (8:20). The building of an altar is connected with the hope in God's blessing of the earth. The altar is placed centrally in Canaanite territory, proclaiming Yahweh's superior claim upon the land. It is placed where Joshua will later bring the Israelites to worship when they are released from Egypt to take possession of the land in fulfillment of the promise to their forefather Abraham (Abram). Abram also called on the name of the Lord, an expression of true worship (12:8). At the time of Paul, to "call on the Lord" expressed commitment to the Lord Jesus Christ (Rom. 10:12–13). Though Abraham knew little about the true God, he responded to the limited revelation he had received.

In the fullness of time, the world would see the true and ultimate son of Abraham enter human history, bringing decisive clarity to what it means to call on the name of the Lord—namely, to repent and turn in faith to Jesus Christ. For he bore the ultimate punishment in our place by being sacrificed not on an altar but on a cross.

they had gathered, and the people that they
had acquired in Haran, and they set out to
go to the land of Canaan. When they came to
the land of Canaan, 6 Abram [r]passed through
the land to the place at Shechem, to [s]the
oak[1] of [t]Moreh. At that time [u]the Canaanites
were in the land. 7 Then the LORD appeared
to Abram and said, [v]"To your offspring I will
give this land." So he built there an altar to
the LORD, who had appeared to him. 8 From
there he moved to the hill country on the east
of [w]Bethel and pitched his tent, with Bethel on
the west and Ai on the east. And there he built
an altar to the LORD and called upon the name
of the LORD. 9 And Abram journeyed on, still
going toward the Negeb.

Abram and Sarai in Egypt

10 Now [x]there was a famine in the land. So
Abram went down to Egypt to sojourn there,
for the famine was severe in the land. 11 When
he was about to enter Egypt, he said to Sarai his
wife, "I know that you are a woman beautiful
in appearance, 12 and when the Egyptians see
you, they will say, 'This is his wife.' Then they
[y]will kill me, but they will let you live. 13 Say
you are my sister, that it may go well with me
because of you, and that my life may be spared
for your sake." 14 When Abram entered Egypt,
the Egyptians saw that the woman was very
beautiful. 15 And when the princes of Pharaoh
saw her, they praised her to Pharaoh. And the
woman was taken into Pharaoh's house. 16 And
for her sake he dealt well with Abram; and he
had sheep, oxen, male donkeys, male servants,
female servants, female donkeys, and camels.
17 But the LORD [z]afflicted Pharaoh and his
house with great plagues because of Sarai,
Abram's wife. 18 So Pharaoh called Abram and
said, "What is this you have done to me? Why
did you not tell me that she was your wife?
19 Why did you say, 'She is my sister,' so that
I took her for my wife? Now then, here is your
wife; take her, and go." 20 And Pharaoh gave
men orders concerning him, and they sent
him away with his wife and all that he had.

Abram and Lot Separate

13 So Abram went up from Egypt, he and
his wife and all that he had, and Lot
with him, [a]into the Negeb.
2 [b]Now Abram was very rich in livestock, in
silver, and in gold. 3 And he journeyed on from
the Negeb as far as Bethel to the place where
his tent had been at the beginning, between
Bethel and Ai, 4 to [c]the place where he had
made an altar at the first. And there Abram
called upon the name of the LORD. 5 And Lot,

[1] Or *terebinth*

6 [r][Heb. 11:9] [s]ch. 13:18 [t]Deut. 11:30; Judg. 7:1 [u]ch. 13:7
7 [v]ch. 13:15; 17:8; Ex. 33:1; Ps. 105:9-12; [Num. 32:11]; Gal. 3:16
8 [w]ch. 28:19
10 [x]ch. 26:1; 43:1
12 [y]See ch. 20:1-18; 26:6-11
17 [z]1 Chr. 16:21; Ps. 105:14
Chapter 13
1 [a]ch. 12:9
2 [b]ch. 24:35; [Ps. 112:1-3; Prov. 10:22]
4 [c]ch. 12:7, 8

12:10 Abraham had no child but was promised a family. He had no soil to cultivate but was promised a land. He was promised blessing, but he experienced famine in the land. He lived with promise but experienced only toil upon the earth the Lord had cursed (5:29). In short, Abraham was forced into dependent trust in the Lord. Then as now, it is in the crucible of life, when all hope seems to have fled, that the path is cleared for God to work supernaturally. It is precisely at the moment when we despair and think we have nothing to offer the Lord, that he can truly get to work on our hearts and through our lives.

12:11–20 God was with Abram in Egypt. When Abram anticipated trouble in Egypt because of his wife, he planned a deceptive scheme to deal with the situation. Sarai was his half sister, so there was some truth in what Abram said. But he failed to trust in the Lord, and he put his own interests ahead of his wife's. Abram increased his wealth, but he nearly lost his marriage—and with it the covenant promise of many descendants. In the end, the Lord protected his servant by afflicting Pharaoh's household. God's protection, Abram's despoiling the Egyptians (vv. 16, 20), and Pharaoh's order to have Abram expelled foreshadow what would happen with the Israelites in Egypt many centuries later (Ex. 3:22; 12:36).

Above all, we are reminded that our foibles and failures, grievous and tragic though they be, do not define our usefulness to God. Indeed, God seems to be specially drawn toward the weak and sinful. For it is precisely such people who are most open to his saving and empowering grace.

13:1–18 Abram journeyed from Egypt to the Negeb, and back to the area of Bethel and Ai. He constructed another altar (vv. 1–4; see 12:8). The relationship between the shepherds of Lot and of Abram portrays another effect of human sinfulness.

who went with Abram, also had flocks and
herds and tents, 6 so that [d]the land could not
support both of them dwelling together; for
their possessions were so great that they could
not dwell together, 7 [e]and there was strife
between the herdsmen of Abram's livestock
and the herdsmen of Lot's livestock. At that
time [f]the Canaanites and the Perizzites were
dwelling in the land.
8 Then Abram said to Lot, [g]"Let there be
no strife between you and me, and between
your herdsmen and my herdsmen, [h]for we are
kinsmen.[1] 9 [i]Is not the whole land before you?
Separate yourself from me. If you take the left
hand, then I will go to the right, or if you take
the right hand, then I will go to the left." 10 And
Lot lifted up his eyes and saw that the [j]Jordan
Valley was well watered everywhere like [k]the
garden of the LORD, like the land of Egypt,
in the direction of [l]Zoar. (This was before the
LORD [m]destroyed Sodom and Gomorrah.) 11 So
Lot chose for himself all the Jordan Valley, and
Lot journeyed east. Thus they separated from
each other. 12 Abram settled in the land of
Canaan, while Lot settled among the cities of
the valley and moved his tent as far as Sodom.
13 Now the men of Sodom [n]were wicked, great
sinners against the LORD.
14 The LORD said to Abram, after Lot had
separated from him, "Lift up your eyes and
look from the place where you are, [o]northward
and southward and eastward and westward,
15 for all the land that you see I will give [p]to
you and [q]to your offspring forever. 16 [r]I will
make your offspring as the dust of the earth,
so that if one can count the dust of the earth,
your offspring also can be counted. 17 Arise,
walk through the length and the breadth of
the land, for I will give it to you." 18 So Abram
moved his tent and came and [s]settled by the
[t]oaks[2] of Mamre, which [u]are at Hebron, and
there he built an altar to the LORD.

Abram Rescues Lot

14 In the days of Amraphel king of
[v]Shinar, Arioch king of Ellasar, Chedorlaomer king of [w]Elam, and Tidal king of
Goiim, 2 these kings made war with [x]Bera
king of Sodom, Birsha king of Gomorrah,
Shinab king of [y]Admah, Shemeber king of
[y]Zeboiim, and the king of Bela (that is, Zoar).
3 And all these joined forces in the Valley of
Siddim ([z]that is, the Salt Sea). 4 Twelve years
they had served Chedorlaomer, but in the
thirteenth year they rebelled. 5 In the fourteenth year Chedorlaomer and the kings
who were with him came and defeated the
[a]Rephaim in [b]Ashteroth-karnaim, the [c]Zuzim
in Ham, the [d]Emim in Shaveh-kiriathaim,
6 and the [e]Horites in their hill country of
Seir as far as [f]El-paran on the border of the
wilderness. 7 Then they turned back and
came to En-mishpat (that is, [g]Kadesh) and
defeated all the country of the Amalekites,

[1] Hebrew *we are men, brothers* [2] Or *terebinths*

Lot chose to dwell in the area of the Jordan Valley where Sodom and Gomorrah were located. It was renowned for its fertility. It was also known for its moral corruption, representative of the Canaanite culture (13:7, 13; see chs. 14; 18; 19).

Abram, however, trusts the Lord to take care of him—and he will not be disappointed. The Lord confirms to him the promise of countless descendants and of land (13:14–17). What the boundaries of that land will be, however, remains less distinct; it is subject to the fulfillment of God's promise that Abram's offspring will become as numerous as the dust of the earth (v. 16) and will be a blessing to all the families of the earth (12:3). Abram's freedom of movement (13:17) symbolizes the extent of the Promised Land but does not restrict it. As God blesses his people, they will eventually inherit the entire world (cf. 22:17–18).

14:1–16 Abram's character has been tested by obedience to God's call, by the severe famine, and by a family dispute. Now he is tested by the capture of Lot, when Sodom and Gomorrah are captured and plundered by a group of collaborating kings from the east. The kings of Sodom and Gomorrah flee the battle; Abram, on the other hand, proactively takes his men and sets out to rescue the captives.

This account highlights Abram's trust in the Lord as Abram leaves the Promised Land to rescue Lot. It also highlights God's protection of Abram as the one through whose descendants the covenant promises will be fulfilled.

6[d] ch. 36:6, 7
7[e] ch. 26:20 [f] ch. 12:6
8[g] [1 Cor. 6:1-8] [h] [Acts 7:26]
9[i] ch. 20:15; 34:10
10[j] ch. 19:17, 25, 28; Deut. 34:3; 1 Kgs. 7:46; [Matt. 3:5] [k] ch. 2:8; Isa. 51:3; Ezek. 28:13; Joel 2:3 [l] ch. 14:2, 8; 19:22 [m] ch. 19:24, 25
13[n] ch. 18:20; Ezek. 16:49; 2 Pet. 2:7, 8
14[o] ch. 28:14
15[p] ch. 17:8; 28:13; 35:12; Acts 7:5 [q] ch. 12:7; 15:18; 24:7; 26:4; Deut. 34:4; 2 Chr. 20:7
16[r] ch. 22:17; 28:14; 32:12; Num. 23:10; [1 Kgs. 3:8]; See ch. 15:5
18[s] ch. 14:13 [t] ch. 12:6 [u] ch. 35:27

Chapter 14
1[v] ch. 10:10; 11:2 [w] ch. 10:22; Isa. 11:11; Acts 2:9
2[x] ver. 8; ch. 13:10; 19:22 [y] Deut. 29:23
3[z] Num. 34:12; Deut. 3:17; Josh. 3:16
5[a] ch. 15:20; Deut. 2:11; 3:11 [b] Deut. 1:4 [c] [Deut. 2:20] [d] Deut. 2:10, 11

6[e] Deut. 2:12, 22 [f] [ch. 21:21; Num. 12:16; 13:3] **7**[g] ch. 16:14; 20:1; Num. 13:26

and also the Amorites who were dwelling [h]in
Hazazon-tamar.
8 Then the king of Sodom, the king of
Gomorrah, the king of Admah, the king of
Zeboiim, and the king of Bela (that is, Zoar)
went out, and they joined battle in the Valley
of Siddim 9 with Chedorlaomer king of Elam,
Tidal king of Goiim, Amraphel king of Shinar,
and Arioch king of Ellasar, four kings against
five. 10 Now the Valley of Siddim was full of
[i]bitumen pits, and as the kings of Sodom and
Gomorrah fled, some fell into them, and the
rest fled [j]to the hill country. 11 So the enemy took
[k]all the possessions of Sodom and Gomorrah,
and all their provisions, and went their way.
12 They also took Lot, [l]the son of Abram's
brother, [m]who was dwelling in Sodom, and
his possessions, and went their way.
13 Then one who had escaped came and
told Abram the Hebrew, [n]who was living by
the [o]oaks[1] of Mamre the Amorite, brother of
Eshcol and of Aner. These were allies of Abram.
14 When Abram heard that his kinsman had
been taken captive, he led forth his trained
men, [p]born in his house, 318 of them, and went
in pursuit as far as [q]Dan. 15 And he divided his
forces against them by night, he and his servants, and defeated them and pursued them to
Hobah, north of Damascus. 16 Then he brought
back all the possessions, and also brought back
his kinsman Lot [r]with his possessions, and the
women and the people.

Abram Blessed by Melchizedek

17 After his return from the defeat of Chedorlaomer and the kings who were with him,
the king of Sodom went out to meet him
at the Valley of Shaveh (that is, the [s]King's
Valley). 18 And [t]Melchizedek king of Salem
brought out bread and wine. (He was [u]priest
of [v]God Most High.) 19 And he blessed him
and said,

[w]"Blessed be Abram by God Most High,
[x]Possessor[2] of heaven and earth;
20 and blessed be God Most High,
who has delivered your enemies into
your hand!"

And Abram gave him [y]a tenth of everything.
21 And the king of Sodom said to Abram, "Give
me the persons, but take the goods for yourself." 22 But Abram said to the king of Sodom,
[z]"I have lifted my hand[3] to the LORD, God Most
High, Possessor of heaven and earth, 23 that [a]I
would not take a thread or a sandal strap or
anything that is yours, lest you should say, 'I
have made Abram rich.' 24 I will take nothing

[1] Or *terebinths* [2] Or *Creator*; also verse 22 [3] Or *I have taken a solemn oath*

7 [h] 2 Chr. 20:2
10 [i] ch. 11:3; Ex. 2:3 [j] ch. 19:17, 30
11 [k] ver. 16, 21
12 [l] ch. 12:5 [m] ch. 13:12
13 [n] ch. 13:18 [o] ch. 12:6
14 [p] ch. 15:3; 17:12, 13, 23, 27; Eccles. 2:7 [q] Judg. 18:29
16 [r] ver. 11, 12
17 [s] 2 Sam. 18:18
18 [t] Heb. 7:1 [u] Ps. 110:4; Heb. 5:6, 10; 7:1, 11, 17 [v] Ps. 57:2; Acts 16:17
19 [w] Heb. 7:6, 7 [x] Matt. 11:25
20 [y] Heb. 7:4; [ch. 28:22]
22 [z] Ex. 6:8; Num. 14:30; Deut. 32:40; Ezek. 20:5, 6, 15, 23, 28; Dan. 12:7; Rev. 10:5, 6
23 [a] [Esth. 9:15, 16]

14:17–24 After every test, Abram receives assurances of God's presence with him: (1) Pharaoh sent him from Egypt with great possessions (ch. 12); (2) the Lord confirmed the promise of the seed and land (ch. 13); and now (3) Melchizedek will bless Abram (ch. 14).

The mysterious character Melchizedek is mentioned several times in Scripture (Ps. 110:4; Heb. 5:6, 10; 7:1, 11, 17). We do not know his earthly lineage, origin, or end (Heb. 7:3). What we do know is that he was the priest-king of Jerusalem, a worshiper of God Most High (*El Elyon*), was hospitable to Abram, and pronounced a blessing over him. In turn Abram gave him a tenth of his battle spoils. After the institution of the Aaronic priesthood and its corruption, a hope arose for a priestly king according to the order of Melchizedek. The significance of the names Salem ("peace") and Melchizedek ("king of righteousness") with the absence of earthly origins subtly anticipates the final bringer of peace and king of righteousness (cf. Heb. 7:2). Psalm 110 confers this privilege on a Davidic king who is seated at God's right hand and would rule "forever" over the nations "in holy garments" (Ps. 110:1–4). Hebrews confirms that Jesus is this unique kind of royal priest (Heb. 6:20) and adds that Jesus was made perfect through suffering (Heb. 5:7–9), unlike the Aaronic priests. His ministry is far superior to the Old Testament priesthood. He lives forever (Heb. 7:16). Moreover, his ministry was grounded on God's promise, and it inaugurated the new covenant (Heb. 7:20–22).

The refusal of Melchizedek's offer of gifts (Gen. 14:21–24) confirms powerfully that Abram is trusting in God's provision above all. Similarly we too today are free to resist all that the world tantalizingly holds before us and instead receive the offer of "another priest [who arose] after the order of Melchizedek" (Heb. 7:11). This priest-

but what the young men have eaten, and the
share of the men who went with me. Let [b]Aner,
Eshcol, and Mamre take their share."

God's Covenant with Abram

15 After these things the word of the LORD
came to Abram in a vision: [c]"Fear not,
Abram, I am [d]your shield; your reward shall
be very great." 2 But Abram said, "O Lord GOD,
what will you give me, for I continue[1] childless, and the heir of my house is Eliezer of
Damascus?" 3 And Abram said, "Behold, you
have given me no offspring, and [e]a member of
my household will be my heir." 4 And behold,
the word of the LORD came to him: "This
man shall not be your heir; [f]your very own
son[2] shall be your heir." 5 And he brought him
outside and said, "Look toward heaven, and
[g]number the stars, if you are able to number
them." Then he said to him, [h]"So shall your
offspring be." 6 And [i]he believed the LORD, and
[j]he counted it to him as righteousness.

7 And he said to him, "I am the LORD who
[k]brought you out from Ur of the Chaldeans
[l]to give you this land to possess." 8 But he said,
"O Lord GOD, [m]how am I to know that I shall

[1] Or *I shall die* [2] Hebrew *what will come out of your own loins*

king, Jesus Christ, offers us no material guarantee but the promise of eternal life itself, restoration to God—he offers us the only thing that truly satisfies.

15:1–21 God addresses Abram's anxiety over prolonged childlessness with one of the Bible's most powerful affirmations of the goodness of God toward his people. God himself is Abram's shield (v. 1), so Abram must not fear. God confirms his promise to Abram of offspring and land (cf. 13:14–16).

15:6 Abraham's trusting faith in God and his promise is the pattern for all who walk with the Lord. The apostle Paul quotes this verse as he insists on the primacy of faith in God's promise as the basis of salvation (Rom. 4:1–8; Gal. 3:1–7). This promise to Abraham was given many years before the giving of the law (Gal. 3:15–18). Divine promise is therefore the prior and larger category within which human law-keeping is subsumed (Gal. 3:17). Faith in God's promise, not human obedience, defines the fate of all who seek his salvation.

The key issue here, as Paul makes clear, is nothing less than justification: how is a sinner put right with a holy and righteous God? God justifies Abraham and all who come to him by faith (Gal. 3:6–9). The law witnesses against us that we are sinners and that all who break the law are under God's curse (Gal. 3:13). The law could not give righteousness or life because no one could perfectly keep its standards before a holy God (Gal. 2:14–16), but Christ has carried the penalty (the curse) of the law in order to redeem us (Gal. 3:13; see Deut. 21:23). Those who trust in Christ for their justification are ushered into the family of God and become the happy beneficiaries of God's fatherly favor.

The circumstances of life frequently tempt us to doubt God's goodness. Like Abram in his childlessness, our lives often seem to be spinning out of control. Relationships, work, sickness, anxiety—there is much that threatens to overwhelm us. Above all, our own sin burdens our consciences and weighs us down. Through it all, the Christian gospel is a message of hope founded on our faith in what God alone can provide: the invincible rock of Christ's atoning work. Leaving our moral resumes at home, we are invited into God's shining favor if we will bring nothing to him but our need, with trust in his ultimate care. It is Christ-trusting sinners, not the self-trusting "righteous," who are the children of Abraham and are entitled to all the promises God made to Abraham (Mark 2:17; Luke 19:10; Gal. 3:26–29).

15:7 The land promise is signed with God's name. The self-identification "I am the LORD who brought you out from Ur of the Chaldeans" is reminiscent of the introduction to the Ten Commandments, where God identifies himself as the One who brought Israel out of Egyptian slavery (Ex. 20:2). The God of Israel is the God of Abraham. God's very identity is the One who redeems. This is who God *is*. When God shows mercy to stumbling sinners, he is not acting out of accord with his nature—he is rather displaying his very heart. He is, as the apostle Peter would say, "the God of all grace" (1 Pet. 5:10).

24[b] ver. 13

Chapter 15

1[c] ch. 26:24; Dan. 10:12; Luke 1:13, 30 [d] Ps. 3:3; 18:2; 84:11; 119:114
3[e] ch. 14:14
4[f] ch. 17:16
5[g] Ps. 147:4 [h] ch. 22:17; 26:4; Ex. 32:13; Deut. 1:10; 10:22; 1 Chr. 27:23; Heb. 11:12; Cited Rom. 4:18
6[i] Rom. 4:9, 22; Gal. 3:6; James 2:23 [j] Cited Rom. 4:3; [Ps. 106:31]
7[k] ch. 11:31; 12:1; Neh. 9:7, 8; Acts 7:2-4 [l] Ps. 105:42, 44
8[m] [Judg. 6:17; 2 Kgs. 20:8; Ps. 86:17; Isa. 7:11-13; Luke 1:18]

possess it?" 9 He said to him, "Bring me a heifer three years old, a female goat three years old, a ram three years old, a turtledove, and a young pigeon." 10 And he brought him all these, [n]cut them in half, and laid each half over against the other. But [o]he did not cut the birds in half. 11 And when birds of prey came down on the carcasses, Abram drove them away.

12 As the sun was going down, a [p]deep sleep fell on Abram. And behold, dreadful and great darkness fell upon him. 13 Then the LORD said to Abram, "Know for certain [q]that your offspring will be sojourners in a land that is not theirs and will be servants there, and [r]they will be afflicted for [s]four hundred years. 14 But [t]I will bring judgment on the nation that they serve, and afterward [u]they shall come out with great possessions. 15 As for you, you shall go to your fathers in peace; [v]you shall be buried in a good old age. 16 And they shall come back here in the fourth generation, for [w]the iniquity of the Amorites [x]is not yet complete."

17 When the sun had gone down and it was dark, behold, a smoking fire pot and a flaming torch passed between these pieces. 18 On that day the LORD made a covenant with Abram, saying, [y]"To your offspring I give[1] this land, from [z]the river of Egypt to the great river, the river Euphrates, 19 the land of the Kenites, the Kenizzites, the Kadmonites, 20 the Hittites, the Perizzites, the Rephaim, 21 the Amorites, the Canaanites, the Girgashites and the Jebusites."

Sarai and Hagar

16 [a]Now Sarai, Abram's wife, had borne him no children. She had a female Egyptian servant whose name was [b]Hagar. 2 And Sarai said to Abram, "Behold now, the LORD has prevented me from bearing chil-

[1] Or *have given*

10[n] Jer. 34:18, 19 [o] Lev. 1:17
12[p] ch. 2:21
13[q] Acts 7:6, 7 [r] Ex. 1:11, 12; 3:7 [s] Acts 7:6; [Ex. 12:40, 41; Gal. 3:17]
14[t] Ex. 6:6 [u] Ex. 12:36; Ps. 105:37
15[v] ch. 25:8
16[w] 1 Kgs. 21:26; Amos 2:9 [x] [Dan. 8:23; Matt. 23:32; 1 Thess. 2:16]
18[y] ch. 12:7; 13:15; 24:7; 26:4; Num. 34:2; Deut. 34:4; Neh. 9:8 [z] Ex. 23:31; Deut. 1:7; Josh. 1:4

Chapter 16
1[a] ch. 15:2, 3 [b] ch. 21:9; Gal. 4:24

15:8–17 The Abrahamic covenant is the basis for the expectation that God's promises will be fulfilled. God is free to choose when and how he will fulfill his promises, but he is faithful, and so his true children live by faith.

This truth is sealed by the ritual covenant action in verses 9–11. The slaughter and division of the animals was part of an ancient rite (cf. Jer. 34:18–21) according to which a sovereign makes a solemn commitment to fulfill certain promises. The ceremony amounts to a legally recognized "self-curse"; that is, God promises that if he forsakes his covenant, the fate of the dead animals—being cut in two—will be borne by God. The covenant is initiated by God, sovereignly administered by him, and kept by him independent of the actions of the party to whom he swears his commitment.

God also tells Abram of Israel's future bondage, of their eventual exodus from bondage, and of how God will provide for them at that time (Gen. 15:13–14). These prophetic words would be especially important to the nation during its Egyptian travail, and to later generations during their wilderness wanderings—times when they would surely wonder if God had remembered his covenant and would be faithful to it.

In the generations that follow these events, God did keep his word (Rom. 9:6). It is we, the human covenant partner, who have failed. And yet at the pinnacle of human history God resolved nevertheless to undergo the curses of the covenant himself (Gal. 3:13). He sent his Son to bear the punishment of our sin. This mercy startles us into quiet worship. This is a God worthy of all our trust and adoration.

16:1–16 Sarai's proposal that Abram have a child with Hagar was in accordance with custom, but the rivalry that ensues after Hagar's pregnancy with Ishmael reveals the effects of any deviation from God's plan (cf. 2:24). God movingly comes to the aid of Hagar after she is expelled by Sarai. She receives a blessing, is instructed to name her child Ishmael ("God hears"), and names the place of the revelation Beer-lahai-roi ("well of the Living One who sees me").

The story is a poignant reminder of the strong temptation to take matters into our own hands when God's promises seem to be beyond fulfillment. Sarai's desire for children to fulfill God's promise bypassed her calling to trust the Lord and his own timing. Yet even in the midst of Sarai's failure God showed mercy not only to Hagar but also to Sarai, who eventually did bear a son—a birth that truly fulfilled God's promise to Abraham and that would ultimately result in the birth of Christ. God's people are called to trust him no matter how hopeless his promises may seem.

dren. Go in to my servant; it may be that I shall
obtain children[1] by her." And Abram listened
to the voice of Sarai. 3 So, after Abram [c]had
lived ten years in the land of Canaan, Sarai,
Abram's wife, took Hagar the Egyptian, her
servant, and gave her to Abram her husband
as a wife. 4 And he went in to Hagar, and she
conceived. And when she saw that she had
conceived, [d]she looked with contempt on her
mistress.[2] 5 And Sarai said to Abram, "May
the wrong done to me be on you! I gave my
servant to your embrace, and when she saw
that she had conceived, she looked on me with
contempt. May [e]the LORD judge between you
and me!" 6 But Abram said to Sarai, "Behold,
your servant is in your power; do to her as you
please." Then Sarai dealt harshly with her, and
she fled from her.

7 The angel of the LORD found her by a spring
of water in the wilderness, the spring on the
way to [f]Shur. 8 And he said, "Hagar, servant of
Sarai, where have you come from and where
are you going?" She said, "I am fleeing from
my mistress Sarai." 9 The angel of the LORD
said to her, "Return to your mistress and submit to her." 10 The angel of the LORD also said
to her, [g]"I will surely multiply your offspring
so that they cannot be numbered for multitude." 11 And the angel of the LORD said to her,

"Behold, you are pregnant
and shall bear a son.
You shall call his name Ishmael,[3]
[h]because the LORD has listened to your
affliction.
12 He shall be [i]a wild donkey of a man,
his hand against everyone
and everyone's hand against him,
and he shall dwell [j]over against all his
kinsmen."

13 So she called the name of the LORD who spoke
to her, "You are a God of seeing,"[4] for she said,
[k]"Truly here I have seen him who looks after
me."[5] 14 Therefore the well was called [l]Beer-
lahai-roi;[6] it lies between [m]Kadesh and Bered.

15 And Hagar bore Abram a son, and Abram
called the name of his son, whom Hagar bore,
Ishmael. 16 Abram was eighty-six years old
when Hagar bore Ishmael to Abram.

Abraham and the Covenant of Circumcision

17 When Abram was ninety-nine years old
the LORD appeared to Abram and said
to him, "I am God Almighty;[7] walk before me,
and be [n]blameless, 2 that I may make my covenant between me and you, and [o]may multiply
you greatly." 3 Then Abram [p]fell on his face.
And God said to him, 4 "Behold, my covenant
is with you, and you shall be [q]the father of a

[1] Hebrew *be built up*, which sounds like the Hebrew for *children* [2] Hebrew *her mistress was dishonorable in her eyes*; similarly in verse 5 [3] *Ishmael* means *God hears* [4] Or *You are a God who sees me* [5] Hebrew *Have I really seen him here who sees me?* or *Would I have looked here for the one who sees me?* [6] *Beer-lahai-roi* means *the well of the Living One who sees me* [7] Hebrew *El Shaddai*

3[c] ch. 12:5
4[d] [1 Sam. 1:6, 7]
5[e] ch. 31:53; 1 Sam. 24:12
7[f] ch. 25:18; Ex. 15:22
10[g] ch. 17:20; 21:18; See ch. 25:12-18
11[h] [ch. 29:32]
12[i] Job 39:5-8; [ch. 21:20] [j] ch. 25:18
13[k] [ch. 32:30; Ex. 19:21; 33:20; Judg. 13:22]
14[l] ch. 24:62; 25:11 [m] ch. 14:7; 20:1; Num. 13:26

Chapter 17
1[n] ch. 6:9; Deut. 18:13; Job 1:1; Ps. 119:1; Matt. 5:48
2[o] ch. 12:2; 13:16; 22:17
3[p] ver. 17
4[q] Rom. 4:11, 12, 16

The supreme example of God fulfilling his promises amid what appears to be his utter absence is the cross of Christ. Here, if ever, it seemed that Satan was winning. Yet it was precisely here that God was at work to decisively fulfill his promises to his people.

17:1–8 God appeared to Abraham as *El Shaddai*. The origin of this name is unclear, but it is associated with the idea that God keeps his promises. By this time Abraham was 99 years old and had walked with God for a long time without seeing the fulfillment of the covenant promises. Now, the Lord confirms the promise of the multiplication of his offspring. Abram will be the father of a multitude of nations.

To this end God changes Abram's name, which means "exalted father," to Abraham, "father of a multitude." The promise of nations and kings is also given to Sarah and later to Jacob (v. 16; 35:11; cf. 48:19). It is associated with the promise of "population explosion" given to Adam (1:28) and Noah (9:1). God purposes to fill the earth with people, but this time he clarifies that godly people will fill the earth and that the earth is the Lord's (cf. Rom. 4:13). The promise of the land expands exponentially as the promise of the offspring explodes. The essence of the promise is God's commitment to his people.

The expression "to be God to you and to your offspring after you" (Gen. 17:7) is the ground of the believer's confidence and echoes throughout the Old Testament (26:24; 28:13; Jer. 7:23; 24:7; 30:22; 31:1; 31:33; Ezek. 11:20). It lies at the heart of both the Abrahamic covenant and the new covenant (2 Cor. 6:16; Heb. 8:10). The Lord commits himself to a people, frail as they are. He has bound himself to us. In Christ, this bond cannot be broken. It is secure.

multitude of nations. [5]No longer shall your
name be called Abram,[1] but [r]your name shall
be Abraham,[2] [s]for I have made you the father
of a multitude of nations. [6]I will make you
exceedingly fruitful, and I will make [t]you into
nations, and [u]kings shall come from you. [7]And
I will [v]establish my covenant between me and
you and your offspring after you throughout
their generations for an everlasting covenant,
[w]to be God to you and to your offspring after
you. [8]And [x]I will give to you and to your offspring after you the land of your sojournings,
all the land of Canaan, for an everlasting possession, and [y]I will be their God."
[9]And God said to Abraham, "As for you, you
shall keep my covenant, you and your offspring after you throughout their generations.
[10]This is my covenant, which you shall keep,
between me and you and your offspring after
you: Every male among you shall be circumcised. [11]You shall be circumcised in the flesh
of your foreskins, and it shall be a [z]sign of the
covenant between me and you. [12]He who is
[a]eight days old among you shall be circumcised. Every male throughout your generations, whether born in your house or [b]bought
with your money from any foreigner who is
not of your offspring, [13]both he who is born
in your house and he who is bought with your
money, shall surely be circumcised. So shall
my covenant be in your flesh an everlasting
covenant. [14]Any uncircumcised male who is
not circumcised in the flesh of his foreskin
shall be cut off from his people; he has broken
my covenant."

Isaac's Birth Promised

[15]And God said to Abraham, "As for Sarai
your wife, you shall not call her name Sarai,
but Sarah[3] shall be her name. [16]I will bless
her, and moreover, I will [c]give[4] you a son by
her. I will bless her, and [d]she shall become
nations; kings of peoples shall come from
her." [17]Then Abraham [e]fell on his face [f]and
laughed and said to himself, "Shall a child
be born to a man who is a hundred years old?
Shall Sarah, who is ninety years old, bear a
child?" [18]And Abraham said to God, "Oh that
Ishmael might live before you!" [19]God said,
"No, but [g]Sarah your wife shall bear you a
son, and you shall call his name [h]Isaac.[5] I will
establish my covenant with him as an everlasting covenant for his offspring after him.
[20]As for Ishmael, I have heard you; behold,
I have blessed him and will make him fruitful and [i]multiply him greatly. He [j]shall father

[1] *Abram* means *exalted father* [2] *Abraham* means *father of a multitude* [3] *Sarai* and *Sarah* mean *princess* [4] Hebrew *have given* [5] *Isaac* means *he laughs*

5 [r]Neh. 9:7 [s]Cited Rom. 4:17
6 [t]ch. 35:11 [u]ver. 16
7 [v]Gal. 3:17 [w]Heb. 11:16; [ch. 26:24; 28:13]
8 [x]ch. 12:7; 13:15; Ps. 105:11 [y]Ex. 6:7; Lev. 26:12
11 [z]Acts 7:8; Rom. 4:11
12 [a]Lev. 12:3; Luke 1:59; 2:21; Phil. 3:5 [b][Ex. 12:48, 49]
16 [c]ch. 18:10 [d]ch. 35:11
17 [e]ver. 3 [f]ch. 21:6; Rom. 4:19; [John 8:56]
19 [g]ch. 18:10; 21:2; Gal. 4:23, 28 [h]ch. 21:3
20 [i]ch. 16:10 [j]See ch. 25:12-16

17:9–14 The command to have every male circumcised sets the male descendants of Abraham apart from other nations physically. As a sign of a holy covenant, the circumcision of the head of each family designates that family as belonging to the Lord. In Hebrew, to make a covenant was actually "to cut a covenant" (*karat berith*). Typically an animal was cut off from life as a ritual sign of the covenant relationship being consecrated and of the judgment deserved for violation of the covenant. In circumcision, the foreskin was cut off to save the whole person from being cut off in God's judgment. Consequently, the family produced from that individual was also the product of this consecration and was identified with the covenant sign. Conversely, uncircumcised males (and their families) are "cut off" from God's covenant (v. 14).

Circumcision would become more than a merely external sign, however. Moses later charged Israel with duplicity, as they wanted to have the benefits of the covenant even while they were resistant to the God of the covenant. He spoke of an inner circumcision of the heart (Deut. 10:16; 30:6). Jeremiah, too, spoke of this spiritual circumcision as a vital ingredient of the new covenant (Jer. 31:33; cf. 4:4).

Indeed, the New Testament speaks of the futility of physical circumcision if it is not accompanied by internal, spiritual circumcision. Paul testified that his own circumcision on the eighth day was worthless in comparison to his being in Christ (Phil. 3:4–7). Every believer is circumcised spiritually in Christ through the renewal that comes from Christ's resurrection (Col. 2:11–13).

17:15–18:15 Sarai's name, like her husband's, undergoes a change—from Sarai to Sarah. Both names signify "princess," but the Lord adds another layer of meaning. She will be a princess over the multitudes that she will "mother," including nations and kings. The Lord promises that Sarah will give birth to a son. This son will be the natural son of Abraham and Sarah, but he will also be the son of God's promise (Gal. 4:21–31).

twelve princes, and [k]I will make him into a
great nation. 21 But [l]I will establish my covenant with Isaac, [m]whom Sarah shall bear to
you at this time next year."
22 When he had finished talking with
him, [n]God went up from Abraham. 23 Then
Abraham took Ishmael his son and all those
born in his house or bought with his money,
every male among the men of Abraham's
house, and he circumcised the flesh of their
foreskins that very day, as God had said to him.
24 Abraham was ninety-nine years old when he
was circumcised in the flesh of his foreskin.
25 And Ishmael his son was thirteen years old
when he was circumcised in the flesh of his
foreskin. 26 That very day Abraham and his
son Ishmael were circumcised. 27 And all the
men of his house, those born in the house and
those bought with money from a foreigner,
were circumcised with him.

18 And the LORD appeared to him by the
[o]oaks[1] of Mamre, as he sat at the door
of his tent in the heat of the day. 2 He lifted up
his eyes and looked, and behold, three men
were standing in front of him. [p]When he saw
them, he ran from the tent door to meet them
and bowed himself to the earth 3 and said, "O
Lord,[2] if I have found favor in your sight, do
not pass by your servant. 4 Let a [q]little water
be brought, and wash your feet, and rest yourselves under the tree, 5 while I bring a morsel
of bread, that [r]you may refresh yourselves,
and after that you may pass on—[s]since you
have come to your servant." So they said, "Do
as you have said." 6 And Abraham went quickly
into the tent to Sarah and said, "Quick! Three
seahs[3] of fine flour! Knead it, and make cakes."
7 And Abraham ran to the herd and took a calf,
tender and good, and gave it to a young man,
who prepared it quickly. 8 Then he took curds
and milk and the calf that he had prepared,
and set it before them. And he stood by them
under the tree while they ate.
9 They said to him, "Where is Sarah your
wife?" And he said, "She is [t]in the tent." 10 The
LORD said, "I will surely return to you [u]about
this time next year, and [v]Sarah your wife shall
have a son." And Sarah was listening at the
tent door behind him. 11 Now [w]Abraham and
Sarah were old, advanced in years. The way
of women had ceased to be with Sarah. 12 [x]So
Sarah laughed to herself, saying, [y]"After I am
worn out, and [z]my lord is old, shall I have
pleasure?" 13 The LORD said to Abraham, "Why
did Sarah laugh and say, 'Shall I indeed bear
a child, now that I am old?' 14 [a]Is anything too
hard[4] for the LORD? [b]At the appointed time
I will return to you, about this time next year,
and Sarah shall have a son." 15 But Sarah denied
it,[5] saying, "I did not laugh," for she was afraid.
He said, "No, but you did laugh."
16 Then the men set out from there, and they
looked down toward Sodom. And Abraham
went with them to set them on their way. 17 The

[1] Or *terebinths* [2] Or *My lord* [3] A *seah* was about 7 quarts or 7.3 liters [4] Or *wonderful* [5] Or *acted falsely*

Throughout this passage we continue to marvel at the insistence of divine grace. Against all odds, and in spite of Abraham's and Sarah's laughter, God remains determined to bless Sarah (Gen. 17:16) and Isaac (17:21) beyond anything they deserve.

God's purposes of grace are not held captive by human sin or adverse circumstances. He is the God who works out his purposes through weak and ordinary human beings such as Abraham and Sarah. It is God's grace, not human merit, that determines the course, and the blessing, of our lives.

This theme is picked up in the next chapter of Genesis, where the Lord appears to Abraham and once more reiterates that Abraham and Sarah will have a son. In fact, the Lord says that this will happen within one year (18:10). Sarah laughs at this, but the Lord responds, "Is anything too hard for the LORD?" (18:14). The walk of faith involves looking our difficult circumstances in the face and, with the promises of God, defying the discouragements, disappointments, and frustrations that tempt us to abandon hope in God. Nothing is too hard for God. Indeed, he has already done the hardest thing, in becoming one of us and dying for us (Rom. 5:9–10; 8:32); shall he fail to care for us in a thousand lesser ways?

18:16–33 God treated Abraham as a friend, especially since he had chosen him to extend divine blessing to many nations (v. 18). God thus revealed to Abraham his intention to destroy Sodom and Gomorrah. Upon revealing the destruction of these cities, the Lord entertains Abraham's petition on behalf of the righteous that may be found in the cities (vv. 25–32). The interaction between God and Abraham, whereby

20 [k]ch. 21:13, 18
21 [l]ch. 26:2-5 [m]ch. 21:2
22 [n]ch. 35:13
Chapter 18
1 [o]ch. 13:18; 14:13
2 [p]ch. 19:1; [Heb. 13:2]
4 [q]ch. 19:2; 24:32; 43:24; [Luke 7:44; John 13:14]
5 [r]Judg. 19:5; [Ps. 104:15] [s]ch. 19:8; 33:10
9 [t]ch. 24:67
10 [u]ver. 14; 2 Kgs. 4:16 [v]ch. 17:19, 21; 21:2; Cited Rom. 9:9
11 [w]ch. 17:17; Rom. 4:19; Heb. 11:11, 12
12 [x][ch. 17:17] [y][Luke 1:18] [z]1 Pet. 3:6
14 [a]Job 42:2; Jer. 32:17, 27; Zech. 8:6; Matt. 19:26; Luke 1:37 [b]ver. 10

LORD said, [c]"Shall I hide from Abraham what I am about to do, 18 seeing that Abraham shall surely become a great and mighty nation, and all the nations of the earth shall be [d]blessed in him? 19 For I have [e]chosen[1] him, that he may command his children and his household after him to keep the way of the LORD by doing righteousness and justice, so that the LORD may bring to Abraham what he has promised him." 20 Then the LORD said, "Because [f]the outcry against Sodom and Gomorrah is great and their sin is very grave, 21 [g]I will go down to see whether they have done altogether[2] according to the outcry that has come to me. And if not, [h]I will know."

Abraham Intercedes for Sodom

22 [i]So the men turned from there and went toward Sodom, but Abraham [j]still stood before the LORD. 23 Then Abraham drew near and said, [k]"Will you indeed sweep away the righteous with the wicked? 24 Suppose there are fifty righteous within the city. Will you then sweep away the place and not spare it for the fifty righteous who are in it? 25 Far be it from you to do such a thing, to put the righteous to death with the wicked, [l]so that the righteous fare as the wicked! Far be that from you! [m]Shall not the Judge of all the earth do what is just?" 26 And the LORD said, [n]"If I find at Sodom fifty righteous in the city, I will spare the whole place for their sake."

27 Abraham answered and said, [o]"Behold, I have undertaken to speak to the Lord, I who am but dust and ashes. 28 Suppose five of the fifty righteous are lacking. Will you destroy the whole city for lack of five?" And he said, "I will not destroy it if I find forty-five there." 29 Again he spoke to him and said, "Suppose forty are found there." He answered, "For the sake of forty I will not do it." 30 Then he said, "Oh let not the Lord be angry, and I will speak. Suppose thirty are found there." He answered, "I will not do it, if I find thirty there." 31 He said, "Behold, I have undertaken to speak to the Lord. Suppose twenty are found there." He answered, "For the sake of twenty I will not destroy it." 32 Then he said, [p]"Oh let not the Lord be angry, and I will speak again but this once. Suppose ten are found there." He answered, "For the sake of ten I will not destroy it." 33 And the LORD went his way, when he had finished speaking to Abraham, and Abraham returned to his place.

God Rescues Lot

19 The [q]two angels came to Sodom in the evening, and Lot was sitting in the gate of Sodom. When Lot saw them, he rose to meet them and bowed himself with his face to the earth 2 and said, "My lords, [r]please turn aside to your servant's house and spend the night [s]and wash your feet. Then you may rise up early and go on your way." They said, [t]"No; we will spend the night in the town square." 3 But he pressed them strongly; so they turned aside to him and entered his house. And he made them a feast and baked unleavened bread, and they ate.

4 But before they lay down, the men of the city, the men of Sodom, both young and old, all the people to the last man, surrounded the house. 5 [u]And they called to Lot, "Where are the men who came to you tonight? [v]Bring them out to us, that we [w]may know them." 6 Lot went out to the men at the entrance, shut the door after him, 7 and said, "I beg you, my brothers, do not act so wickedly. 8 [x]Behold, I have two daughters who have not known any man. Let me bring them out to you, and do to them as you please.

[1] Hebrew *known* [2] Or *they deserve destruction*; Hebrew *they have made a complete end*

the hypothetical number of righteous people in the city is whittled down from 50 to 10, underscores that God will not destroy the righteous along with the wicked. This indeed proves to be the case, as only Lot and his family escape from Sodom while the rest of Sodom and the other cities of the plain are destroyed.

Today, as then, God's justice will only punish the guilty. The trouble, of course, is that before God's eyes none are truly righteous (Rom. 3:9–18). Yet Jesus Christ underwent the punishment deserved by fallen people by becoming guilty in their place (2 Cor. 5:21). Because of Christ's work on the cross, all who believe in him have been declared righteous. And they can be assured of God's mercy, for to punish God's children would be to punish the righteous. "There is therefore now no condemnation for those who are in Christ Jesus" (Rom. 8:1).

17 [c][Ps. 25:14; Amos 3:7; John 15:15]
18 [d]ch. 12:3; 22:18; 26:4; Acts 3:25; Gal. 3:8
19 [e][Amos 3:2]
20 [f]ch. 4:10; 19:13; [Isa. 3:9; Ezek. 16:49, 50; James 5:4]
21 [g]ch. 11:5, 7; Ex. 3:8 [h]Josh. 22:22
22 [i]ver. 16; ch. 19:1 [j]ver. 1; [Ps. 106:23; Jer. 18:20]
23 [k]ch. 20:4; Num. 16:22; 2 Sam. 24:17
25 [l][Job 8:20] [m]Deut. 32:4; Job 8:3; 34:10; Rom. 3:5, 6
26 [n]Jer. 5:1; Ezek. 22:30; [Isa. 65:8]

27 [o][Luke 18:1] **32** [p]Judg. 6:39 **Chapter 19** **1** [q]ch. 18:22 **2** [r]Heb. 13:2; [Judg. 4:18] [s]See ch. 18:4 [t][Luke 24:28] **5** [u]Isa. 3:9; [ch. 13:13] [v]Judg. 19:22 [w]Rom. 1:24, 27; Jude 7 **8** [x][Judg. 19:24]

Only do nothing to these men, for they have come under the shelter of my roof." 9 But they said, "Stand back!" And they said, "This fellow [y]came to sojourn, and [z]he has become the judge! Now we will deal worse with you than with them." Then they pressed hard against the man Lot, and drew near to break the door down. 10 But the men reached out their hands and brought Lot into the house with them and shut the door. 11 And they struck with [a]blindness the men who were at the entrance of the house, both small and great, so that they wore themselves out groping for the door.

12 Then the men said to Lot, "Have you anyone else here? Sons-in-law, sons, daughters, or anyone you have in the city, [b]bring them out of the place. 13 For we are about to destroy this place, [c]because the outcry against its people has become great before the LORD, and the LORD has sent us to destroy it." 14 So Lot went out and said to his sons-in-law, who were to marry his daughters, [d]"Up! Get out of this place, for the LORD is about to destroy the city." But he seemed to his sons-in-law to be jesting.

15 As morning dawned, the angels urged Lot, saying, "Up! Take your wife and your two daughters who are here, lest you be swept away in the punishment of the city." 16 But he lingered. So the men seized him and his wife and his two daughters by the hand, [e]the LORD being merciful to him, and they brought him out and set him outside the city. 17 And as they brought them out, one said, "Escape for your life. [f]Do not look back or stop anywhere in the [g]valley. Escape to the hills, lest you be swept away." 18 And Lot said to them, "Oh, no, my lords. 19 Behold, your servant has found favor in your sight, and you have shown me great kindness in saving my life. But I cannot escape to the hills, lest the disaster overtake me and I die. 20 Behold, this city is near enough to flee to, and it is a little one. Let me escape there—is it not a little one?—and my life will be saved!" 21 He said to him, "Behold, I grant you this favor also, that I will not overthrow the city of which you have spoken. 22 Escape there quickly, for I can do nothing till you arrive there." Therefore the name of the city was called [h]Zoar.[1]

God Destroys Sodom

23 The sun had risen on the earth when Lot came to Zoar. 24 Then [i]the LORD rained on Sodom and Gomorrah sulfur and fire from the LORD out of heaven. 25 And he overthrew those cities, and all the valley, and all the inhabitants of the cities, and what grew on the ground. 26 But Lot's wife, behind him, looked back, and she became [j]a pillar of salt.

27 And Abraham went early in the morning to the place where he had [k]stood before the LORD. 28 And he looked down toward Sodom and Gomorrah and toward all the land of the valley, and he looked and, behold, the smoke of the land went up like the smoke of a furnace.

29 So it was that, when God destroyed the cities of the valley, God [l]remembered Abraham and sent Lot out of the midst of the overthrow when he overthrew the cities in which Lot had lived.

[1] *Zoar* means *little*

19:1–29 In contrast to Abraham, Lot is a tragic character. He had gained much prestige, but in the end he loses everything. Like Abraham, Lot hosts the "angelic" visitors. But unlike the generous and warm hospitality they experience in Abraham's tent, the visitors are threatened with rape by the men of Sodom. The Lord marvelously protects Lot (v. 11), but the sons-in-law reject Lot's pleading to leave the city (vv. 12–15).

Jesus compared the day of his second coming to the days of Noah and Lot, as people give themselves to the pursuit of happiness (Luke 17:26–30). Even Lot lingered and barely escaped (Gen. 19:15–16). Like Abraham, he petitioned God's mercy, and God spared Zoar for Lot's convenience (vv. 18–22). The Lord remembered his commitment to Abraham as the ground of the deliverance of Lot's family (v. 29). Lot's wife, however, will always be remembered for her lack of faith (Luke 17:32). And Sodom and the cities of the plain will always be remembered for both the mercy and the severity of God's judgment (Matt. 10:15; 11:23–24; Jude 7; cf. Isa. 1:9).

The key statement in this horrifying account is in Genesis 19:16—"the LORD being merciful to him . . ." This is a story of mercy: mercy to Lot, mercy to Lot's family, mercy to Abraham in sparing his nephew. And ultimately, this is a story of mercy to us—we who have been similarly rescued from the impending judgment of condemnation and hell.

9 [y] ch. 13:12 [z] Ex. 2:14
11 [a] [2 Kgs. 6:18; Acts 13:11]
12 [b] 2 Pet. 2:7, 9; [Rev. 18:4, 5]
13 [c] ch. 18:20
14 [d] Num. 16:21, 26, 45; Jer. 51:6
16 [e] [Ps. 34:22]
17 [f] ver. 26; [Matt. 24:16-18] [g] ch. 13:10
22 [h] ch. 14:2
24 [i] Deut. 29:23; Jer. 20:16; 50:40; Lam. 4:6; Amos 4:11; Zeph. 2:9; Luke 17:29; 2 Pet. 2:6
26 [j] Luke 17:32
27 [k] ch. 18:22
29 [l] See ch. 8:1

Lot and His Daughters

30 Now Lot went up out of Zoar and [m]lived in the hills with his two daughters, for he was afraid to live in Zoar. So he lived in a cave with his two daughters. 31 And the firstborn said to the younger, "Our father is old, and there is not a man on earth to come in to us after the manner of all the earth. 32 Come, let us make our father drink wine, and we will lie with him, that we may preserve offspring from our father." 33 So they made their father drink wine that night. And the firstborn went in and lay with her father. He did not know when she lay down or when she arose.

34 The next day, the firstborn said to the younger, "Behold, I lay last night with my father. Let us make him drink wine tonight also. Then you go in and lie with him, that we may preserve offspring from our father." 35 So they made their father drink wine that night also. And the younger arose and lay with him, and he did not know when she lay down or when she arose. 36 Thus both the daughters of Lot became pregnant by their father. 37 The firstborn bore a son and called his name Moab.[1] [n]He is the father of the Moabites to this day. 38 The younger also bore a son and called his name Ben-ammi.[2] [o]He is the father of the Ammonites to this day.

Abraham and Abimelech

20 From there Abraham journeyed toward the territory of the Negeb and lived between [p]Kadesh and Shur; and he [q]sojourned in [r]Gerar. 2 And Abraham said of Sarah his wife, [s]"She is my sister." And Abimelech king of Gerar sent and took Sarah. 3 [t]But God came to Abimelech [u]in a dream by night and said to him, "Behold, you are a dead man because of the woman whom you have taken, for she is a man's wife." 4 Now Abimelech had not approached her. So he said, [v]"Lord, will you kill an innocent people? 5 Did he not himself say to me, 'She is my sister'? And she herself said, 'He is my brother.' In the integrity of my heart and the innocence of my hands I have done this." 6 Then God said to him in the dream, "Yes, I know that you have done this in the integrity of your heart, and it was I who kept you from sinning [w]against me. Therefore I did not let you touch her. 7 Now then, return the man's wife, [x]for he is a prophet, so that he will pray for you, and you shall live. But if you do not return her, know that you shall surely die, you [y]and all who are yours."

8 So Abimelech rose early in the morning and called all his servants and told them all these things. And the men were very much afraid. 9 Then Abimelech called Abraham and said to him, "What have you done to us? And how have I sinned against you, that you have brought on me and my kingdom a great sin? You have done to me things that ought not to be done." 10 And Abimelech said to Abraham, "What did you see, that you did this thing?" 11 Abraham said, "I did it because I thought, [z]'There is no fear of God at all in this place, and [a]they will kill me because of my wife.' 12 Besides, [b]she is indeed my sister, the daughter of my father though not the daughter of my mother, and she became my wife. 13 And when [c]God caused me to wander from my father's house, I said to her, 'This is the kindness you must do me: at every place to which we come, [d]say of me, "He is my brother."'"

14 Then Abimelech [e]took sheep and oxen, and male servants and female servants, and gave them to Abraham, and returned Sarah his wife to him. 15 And Abimelech said, "Behold, [f]my land is before you; dwell where it pleases you." 16 To Sarah he said, "Behold, I have given [g]your brother a thousand pieces of silver. It is [h]a sign of your innocence in the eyes of all[3] who are with you, and before everyone you are vindicated." 17 Then [i]Abraham prayed to God,

[1] *Moab* sounds like the Hebrew for *from father* [2] *Ben-ammi* means *son of my people* [3] Hebrew *It is a covering of eyes for all*

20:1–18 This story bears similarities with the experience of Abram in Egypt (12:10–20) and of Isaac at Gerar many years later (26:1–11). In each case the husband deceptively says that his wife is his sister, and each time God intervenes miraculously with undeserved grace and deliverance.

We are starkly reminded that God's purposes for his people are not tethered to their performance. The family sins that are passed down from one generation to the next do not determine God's presence and redemptive action in their lives. The Lord has mercy on whom he will have mercy (Rom. 9:15).

30 [m] ver. 17, 19
37 [n] Deut. 2:9
38 [o] Deut. 2:19

Chapter 20
1 [p] ch. 16:7, 14 [q] ch. 26:3 [r] ch. 26:6
2 [s] See ch. 12:13-20; 26:7-11
3 [t] Ps. 105:14 [u] Job 33:15, 16; Matt. 1:20; 2:12
4 [v] ch. 18:23; [1 Chr. 21:17]
6 [w] ch. 39:9; Ps. 51:4
7 [x] 1 Sam. 7:5; Job 42:8 [y] [Num. 16:32, 33]
11 [z] Prov. 16:6 [a] ch. 12:12; 26:7
12 [b] [ch. 11:29]
13 [c] ch. 12:1 [d] ch. 12:13
14 [e] ch. 12:16
15 [f] ch. 13:9; 34:10
16 [g] [ver. 5] [h] [ch. 24:65]
17 [i] [James 5:16]

and God healed Abimelech, and also healed
his wife and female slaves so that they bore
children. 18 For the LORD [j]had closed all the
wombs of the house of Abimelech because of
Sarah, Abraham's wife.

The Birth of Isaac

21 The LORD [k]visited Sarah as he had said,
and the LORD did to Sarah [l]as he had
promised. 2 And Sarah [m]conceived and bore
Abraham a son in his old age [n]at the time of
which God had spoken to him. 3 Abraham
called the name of his son who was born to
him, whom Sarah bore him, [o]Isaac.[1] 4 And
Abraham [p]circumcised his son Isaac when he
was eight days old, [q]as God had commanded
him. 5 [r]Abraham was a hundred years old when
his son Isaac was born to him. 6 And Sarah said,
[s]"God has made laughter for me; everyone
who hears will laugh over me." 7 And she said,
"Who would have said to Abraham that Sarah
would nurse children? [t]Yet I have borne him a
son in his old age."

God Protects Hagar and Ishmael

8 And the child grew and was weaned. And
Abraham made a great feast on the day that
Isaac was weaned. 9 But Sarah [u]saw the son
of Hagar the Egyptian, whom she had borne
to Abraham, [v]laughing.[2] 10 So she said to
Abraham, [w]"Cast out this slave woman with
her son, for the son of this slave woman shall
not be heir with my son Isaac." 11 And the thing
was very displeasing to Abraham on account
of his son. 12 But God said to Abraham, "Be not
displeased because of the boy and because of
your slave woman. Whatever Sarah says to you,
do as she tells you, for [x]through Isaac shall
your offspring be named. 13 And I will make
[y]a nation of the son of the slave woman also,
because he is your offspring." 14 So Abraham
rose early in the morning and took bread and
a skin of water and gave it to Hagar, putting
it on her shoulder, along with the child, and
sent her away. And she departed and wandered
in the wilderness of [z]Beersheba.

15 When the water in the skin was gone, she
put the child under one of the bushes. 16 Then
she went and sat down opposite him a good
way off, about the distance of a bowshot, for
she said, "Let me not look on the death of the
child." And as she sat opposite him, she lifted
up her voice and wept. 17 And God heard the
voice of the boy, and the angel of God called
to Hagar from heaven and said to her, "What
troubles you, Hagar? Fear not, for God has
heard the voice of the boy where he is. 18 Up!
Lift up the boy, and hold him fast with your
hand, for I will make him into a great nation."
19 Then [a]God opened her eyes, and she saw a
well of water. And she went and filled the skin
with water and gave the boy a drink. 20 And
God was with the boy, and he grew up. He

[1] *Isaac* means *he laughs* [2] Possibly *laughing in mockery*

21:1–21 After all the promises raising Abraham's expectations of a large family, the fulfillment of God's word is singularly brief: "The LORD visited Sarah as he had said, and the LORD did to Sarah as he had promised" (v. 1). Isaac is born, and he undergoes the covenant ritual of circumcision (v. 4; cf. Acts 7:8).

The promise of offspring (Genesis 12–20) is being fulfilled, but Abraham's joy is cut short by four troubling incidents: (1) the rivalry between Ishmael and Isaac; (2) the rivalry and distrust from Abimelech; (3) the command to sacrifice Isaac; and (4) the death of Sarah. All his life Abraham awaited the birth of his child, but the laughter (17:17; 18:12–15) soon turned to pain. Abraham's experience prepared God's people for the birth of the Messiah, who came to save his people from their sins (Matt. 1:21) but whose birth and life were also associated with pain and suffering.

Such is the way God works out his promises in the lives of his people. Pain is normally the channel through which divine blessing and favor flows. For it is pain that brings us to truly trust in the Lord. It is adversity that convinces us of the emptiness of the things the world runs after. Suffering is God's fatherly way of drawing us to himself.

Indeed it was pain, supreme pain, that achieved the fulfillment of God's promise to his people to bless them and be with them, to be their God as they were his people, to multiply them and give them long life in the land. For all the promises of God were achieved not through a victorious military campaign or sufficient human obedience or any other humanly generated strategy but through a cross (1 Cor. 1:22–25; 2 Cor. 1:20).

18 [j] [ch. 12:17]
Chapter 21
1 [k] 1 Sam. 2:21 [l] ch. 17:19; 18:10, 14
2 [m] Heb. 11:11; [Gal. 4:22] [n] ch. 17:21
3 [o] ch. 17:19
4 [p] Acts 7:8 [q] ch. 17:10, 12
5 [r] ch. 17:1, 17; Rom. 4:19
6 [s] [Isa. 54:1; Gal. 4:27]
7 [t] ch. 18:11, 12
9 [u] ch. 16:1, 15 [v] [Gal. 4:29]
10 [w] Cited Gal. 4:30
12 [x] Cited Rom. 9:7; Heb. 11:18
13 [y] ver. 18; ch. 16:10; 17:20
14 [z] ver. 31
19 [a] Num. 22:31; 2 Kgs. 6:17, 18, 20; [Luke 24:16, 31]

lived in the wilderness [b]and became an expert with the bow. 21 He lived in the wilderness of Paran, and his mother took a wife for him from the land of Egypt.

A Treaty with Abimelech

22 At that time [c]Abimelech and Phicol the commander of his army said to Abraham, [d]"God is with you in all that you do. 23 Now therefore swear to me here by God that you will not deal falsely with me or with my descendants or with my posterity, but [e]as I have dealt kindly with you, so you will deal with me and with the land where you have sojourned." 24 And Abraham said, "I will swear."

25 When Abraham reproved Abimelech about a well of water that Abimelech's servants [f]had seized, 26 Abimelech said, "I do not know who has done this thing; you did not tell me, and I have not heard of it until today." 27 So Abraham took sheep and oxen and gave them to Abimelech, and the two men [g]made a covenant. 28 Abraham set seven ewe lambs of the flock apart. 29 And Abimelech said to Abraham, "What is the meaning of these seven ewe lambs that you have set apart?" 30 He said, "These seven ewe lambs you will take from my hand, that this[1] may be a witness for me that I dug this well." 31 Therefore [h]that place was called Beersheba,[2] because there both of them swore an oath. 32 So they made a covenant at Beersheba. Then Abimelech and Phicol the commander of his army rose up and returned to the land of the Philistines. 33 Abraham planted a tamarisk tree in Beersheba and [i]called there on the name of the LORD, [j]the Everlasting God. 34 And Abraham sojourned many days in the land of the Philistines.

The Sacrifice of Isaac

22 After these things [k]God tested Abraham and said to him, "Abraham!" And he said, "Here I am." 2 He said, "Take your son, your only son Isaac, whom you love, and go to [l]the land of Moriah, and offer him there as a burnt offering on one of the mountains of which I shall tell you." 3 So Abraham rose early in the morning, saddled his donkey, and took two of his young men with him, and his son Isaac. And he cut the wood for the burnt offering and arose and went to the place of which God had told him. 4 On the third day Abraham lifted up his eyes and saw the place from afar. 5 Then Abraham said to his young men, "Stay here with the donkey; I and the boy[3] will go over there and worship and come again to you." 6 And Abraham took the wood of the burnt offering and [m]laid it on Isaac his son. And he took in his hand the fire and the knife. So they went both of them together. 7 And Isaac said to his father Abraham, "My father!" And he said, "Here I am, my son." He said, "Behold, the fire and the wood, but where is the lamb for a burnt offering?" 8 Abraham said, [n]"God will provide for himself the lamb

[1] Or *you* [2] *Beersheba* means *well of seven* or *well of the oath* [3] Or *young man*; also verse 12

20[b] ch. 16:12
22[c] ch. 20:2; [ch. 26:1, 26] [d] [ch. 26:28]
23[e] ch. 20:14
25[f] [ch. 26:15, 18, 20-22]
27[g] ch. 26:31
31[h] ch. 26:33
33[i] ch. 4:26; 12:8 [j] Isa. 40:28; [Ps. 90:2]
Chapter 22
1[k] 1 Cor. 10:13; Heb. 11:17; James 1:12, 13; 1 Pet. 1:6, 7
2[l] 2 Chr. 3:1
6[m] [John 19:17]
8[n] [John 1:29, 36; 1 Pet. 1:19; Rev. 5:12]

22:1–19 Abraham's whole life anticipated what God would do to Israel: forced exile from Egypt (12:20); dependence on God for food and drink; and the test of the firstborn son (Ex. 12:12–13). We are even told later in the Bible that God tested Israel for the same reason Abraham was put to the test (Deut. 8:2; cf. Gen. 22:12). His faith was tested and confirmed.

The Lord called on Abraham to journey to Moriah to sacrifice his son. The choice of Mount Moriah as the place of Isaac's sacrifice providentially anticipates the location of the temple (2 Chron. 3:1) and the area of Jesus' crucifixion. The mountain of the Lord would later on evoke the image of Zion, the special place of God's dwelling (Ps. 24:3; Isa. 2:3). The journey toward his son's death took Abraham three days, and on the third day he experienced the reversal from death to life. He believed that the Lord would provide (Gen. 22:8), probably through somehow bringing Isaac back to life (cf. Heb. 11:19). Trusting the Lord at great personal cost, Abraham bound his son to the wood of the altar. Everything was at stake—the long-anticipated covenant promise to Abraham of many descendants, finally at long last fulfilled in Isaac, seemed to be slipping away. Yet at the last moment the Lord himself provides a ram, which is sacrificed as a substitute in Isaac's place.

We cannot avoid difficult questions about God testing Abraham (and instructing us) through the shocking instructions to sacrifice Isaac, but the ultimate purposes revealed on Mount Moriah help us navigate those difficulties: (1) we learn that it was

for a burnt offering, my son." So they went both of them together.

9 When they came to the place of which God had told him, Abraham built the altar there and laid the wood in order and bound Isaac his son and [o]laid him on the altar, on top of the wood. 10 Then Abraham reached out his hand and took the knife to slaughter his son. 11 But the angel of the LORD called to him from heaven and said, "Abraham, Abraham!" And he said, "Here I am." 12 He said, [p]"Do not lay your hand on the boy or do anything to him, for [q]now I know that you fear God, seeing you have not withheld your son, your only son, from me." 13 And Abraham lifted up his eyes and looked, and behold, behind him was a ram, caught in a thicket by his horns. And Abraham went and took the ram and offered it up as a burnt offering instead of his son. 14 So Abraham called the name of that place, [r]"The LORD will provide";[1] as it is said to this day, "On the mount of the LORD it shall be provided."[2]

15 And the angel of the LORD called to Abraham a second time from heaven 16 and said, [s]"By myself I have sworn, declares the LORD, because you have done this and have not withheld your son, your only son, 17 I will surely bless you, and I will surely multiply your offspring [t]as the stars of heaven and [u]as the sand that is on the seashore. And your offspring shall possess [v]the gate of his[3] enemies, 18 and [w]in your offspring shall all the nations of the earth be blessed, [x]because you have obeyed my voice." 19 So Abraham returned to his young men, and they arose and went together to [y]Beersheba. And Abraham lived at [y]Beersheba.

20 Now after these things it was told to Abraham, "Behold, [z]Milcah also has borne children to your brother Nahor: 21 [a]Uz his firstborn, [b]Buz his brother, Kemuel the father of Aram, 22 Chesed, Hazo, Pildash, Jidlaph, and Bethuel." 23 ([c]Bethuel fathered Rebekah.) These eight Milcah bore to Nahor, Abraham's brother. 24 Moreover, his concubine, whose name was Reumah, bore Tebah, Gaham, Tahash, and Maacah.

Sarah's Death and Burial

23 Sarah lived 127 years; these were the years of the life of Sarah. 2 And Sarah died at [d]Kiriath-arba (that is, [e]Hebron) in the land of Canaan, and Abraham went in to mourn for Sarah and to weep for her. 3 And Abraham rose up from before his dead and said to the Hittites,[4] 4 [f]"I am a sojourner and foreigner among you; [g]give me property among you for a burying place, that I may bury my dead out of my sight." 5 The Hittites answered Abraham, 6 "Hear us, my lord; you are a prince of God[5] among us. Bury your dead in the choicest of our tombs. None of us will withhold from you his tomb to hinder you from burying your dead." 7 Abraham rose and bowed to the Hittites, the people of the land. 8 And he said to them, "If you are willing that I should bury my dead out of my sight, hear me and entreat for me Ephron the son of Zohar, 9 that he may give me the cave of Machpelah, which he owns; it is at the end of

[1] Or *will see* [2] Or *he will be seen* [3] Or *their* [4] Hebrew *sons of Heth*; also verses 5, 7, 10, 16, 18, 20 [5] Or *a mighty prince*

never God's intention to sacrifice Isaac; (2) we learn that it is God's nature to provide what he requires (even a gracious sacrifice); and (3), far from approving human sacrifice, God's stopping the hand of Abraham in a culture where human sacrifice was common clearly indicates that God did not approve worship that sought to appease him with human suffering or effort.

Not only is this a marvelous account of the mercy of God in keeping his promises to his people, it is also a striking foreshadowing of another substitutionary death centuries later. Abraham was called to sacrifice his one and only son, but was spared from finally going through with this horrific act. God himself, however, sacrificed his one and only Son (John 1:14; 3:16) without sparing him. Christ himself is the substitute sacrifice for all who would renounce their own moral record and look in trusting faith to him.

23:1–20 At the death of Sarah, Abraham negotiates the purchase of a field with a cave suitable for multiple burials. The patriarchs and matriarchs were all buried in that cave. Abraham's purchase of the land, in this place where he was still a wandering outsider (v. 4; cf. Heb. 11:9, 13), showed his faith in God's promise that this land of Canaan would someday be his. His faith was also shown in the negotiations for the burial site, as he paid much more than the full value of the land (Gen. 23:7–17).

9 [o]Heb. 11:17; James 2:21
12 [p][Mic. 6:7, 8] [q][ch. 26:5]
14 [r]ver. 8
16 [s]Ps. 105:9; Luke 1:73; Heb. 6:13
17 [t]Jer. 33:22; See ch. 15:5 [u]See ch. 13:16 [v]ch. 24:60; Ps. 127:5
18 [w]ch. 12:3; 18:18; 26:4; Gal. 3:8; Cited Acts 3:25 [x]ver. 3; ch. 26:5
19 [y]ch. 21:31
20 [z]ch. 11:29
21 [a]Job 1:1 [b]Jer. 25:23
23 [c]ch. 24:15

Chapter 23
2 [d]ch. 35:27; Josh. 14:15; Judg. 1:10 [e]ver. 19
4 [f]ch. 17:8; 1 Chr. 29:15; Ps. 105:12; Heb. 11:9, 13 [g]Acts 7:5

his field. For the full price let him give it to me in your presence as property for a burying place."

10 Now Ephron was sitting among the Hittites, and Ephron the Hittite answered Abraham in the hearing of the Hittites, of all who [h]went in at the gate of his city, 11 "No, my lord, hear me: I give you the field, and I give you the cave that is in it. In the sight of the sons of my people I give it to you. Bury your dead." 12 Then Abraham bowed down before the people of the land. 13 And he said to Ephron in the hearing of the people of the land, "But if you will, hear me: I give the price of the field. Accept it from me, that I may bury my dead there." 14 Ephron answered Abraham, 15 "My lord, listen to me: a piece of land worth four hundred [i]shekels[1] of silver, what is that between you and me? Bury your dead." 16 Abraham listened to Ephron, and Abraham [j]weighed out for Ephron the silver that he had named in the hearing of the Hittites, four hundred shekels of silver, according to the weights current among the merchants.

17 So [k]the field of Ephron in Machpelah, which was to the east of Mamre, the field with the cave that was in it and all the trees that were in the field, throughout its whole area, was made over 18 to Abraham as a possession in the presence of the Hittites, before all who went in at the gate of his city. 19 After this, Abraham buried Sarah his wife in the cave of the field of Machpelah east of Mamre (that is, Hebron) in the land of Canaan. 20 The field and the cave that is in it [l]were made over to Abraham as property for a burying place by the Hittites.

Isaac and Rebekah

24 Now Abraham was old, well advanced in years. And the LORD [m]had blessed Abraham in all things. 2 And Abraham said to his servant, [n]the oldest of his household, who had charge of all that he had, [o]"Put your hand under my thigh, 3 that I may make you swear by the LORD, the God of heaven and God of the earth, that [p]you will not take a wife for my son from the daughters of the Canaanites, among whom I dwell, 4 [q]but will go to my country and to my kindred, and take a wife for my son Isaac." 5 The servant said to him, "Perhaps the woman may not be willing to follow me to this land. Must I then take your son back to the land from which you came?" 6 Abraham said to him, "See to it that you do not take my son back there. 7 The LORD, the God of heaven, [r]who took me from my father's house and from the land of my kindred, and who spoke to me and swore to me, [s]'To your offspring I will give this land,' [t]he will send his angel before you, and you shall take a wife for my son from there. 8 But if the woman is not willing to follow you, then [u]you will be free from this oath of mine; only you must not take my son back there." 9 So the servant [v]put his hand under the thigh of Abraham his master and swore to him concerning this matter.

10 Then the servant took ten of his master's camels and departed, taking all sorts of choice gifts from his master; and he arose and went to [w]Mesopotamia[2] to the city of Nahor. 11 And he

[1] A *shekel* was about 2/5 ounce or 11 grams [2] Hebrew *Aram-naharaim*

10[h] ch. 34:20, 24; Ruth 4:1
15[i] Ex. 30:13; Ezek. 45:12
16[j] 1 Chr. 21:25; Jer. 32:9; Zech. 11:12
17[k] ch. 25:9; 49:29-32; 50:13
20[l] [Ruth 4:7-10; Jer. 32:10-14]
Chapter 24
1[m] ver. 35; ch. 13:2
2[n] [ch. 15:2] [o] ver. 9; ch. 47:29
3[p] ch. 26:34, 35; 27:46; Deut. 7:3; [2 Cor. 6:14]
4[q] [ch. 28:2]
7[r] ch. 12:1 [s] See ch. 12:7 [t] Ex. 23:20, 23; 33:2; [Heb. 1:14]
8[u] See Josh. 2:17-20
9[v] ver. 2
10[w] Deut. 23:4; Judg. 3:8

Several centuries later, the entire Israelite nation would become sojourners as they were exiled from the Land of Promise by the Assyrians and then by the Babylonians, before their later restoration to the land. The New Testament then picks up the language of sojourning and exile to describe what it means to live as a disciple of Christ before our own final restoration. "Beloved," writes Peter, "I urge you as sojourners and exiles to abstain from the passions of the flesh, which wage war against your soul" (1 Pet. 2:11; cf. 1:1). "Our citizenship is in heaven," says Paul (Phil. 3:20). This fallen world will one day be fully cleansed and redeemed; until then, we are out of step with the world and its godless influences (cf. Eph. 2:2).

24:1–9 At an advanced age, Abraham sends his trusted servant to the area around Haran where his relatives live, to find a wife for Isaac. Abraham makes the servant solemnly swear that he will choose the wife from among Abraham's relatives and not from among the Canaanites (vv. 2–3, 9). Abraham also insists that the woman must be willing to return with the servant to Canaan (vv. 6–8), lest the covenant promises God has made to Abraham fail to be fulfilled, for these promises include the very specific land promise of Canaan. Abraham's confidence lies in the God who called him away from his family (v. 7) and with whom he had walked all these years (v. 40).

made the camels kneel down outside the city by the well of water at the time of evening, the time when [x]women go out to draw water. [12] And he said, "O LORD, [y]God of my master Abraham, [z]please grant me success today and show steadfast love to my master Abraham. [13] Behold, [a]I am standing by the spring of water, and the daughters of the men of the city are coming out to draw water. [14] Let the young woman to whom I shall say, 'Please let down your jar that I may drink,' and who shall say, 'Drink, and I will water your camels'—let her be the one whom you have appointed for your servant Isaac. [b]By this[1] I shall know that you have shown steadfast love to my master."

[15] Before he had finished speaking, behold, Rebekah, who was born to Bethuel the son of [c]Milcah, the wife of Nahor, Abraham's brother, came out with her water jar on her shoulder. [16] The young woman [d]was very attractive in appearance, a maiden[2] whom no man had known. She went down to the spring and filled her jar and came up. [17] Then the servant ran to meet her and said, "Please give me a little water to drink from your jar." [18] She said, "Drink, my lord." And she quickly let down her jar upon her hand and gave him a drink. [19] When she had finished giving him a drink, she said, "I will draw water for your camels also, until they have finished drinking." [20] So she quickly emptied her jar into the trough and ran again to the well to draw water, and she drew for all his camels. [21] The man gazed at her in silence to learn whether the LORD had prospered his journey or not.

[22] When the camels had finished drinking, the man took a gold ring weighing a half shekel,[3] and two bracelets for her arms weighing ten gold shekels, [23] and said, "Please tell me whose daughter you are. Is there room in your father's house for us to spend the night?" [24] She said to him, [e]"I am the daughter of Bethuel the son of Milcah, whom she bore to Nahor." [25] She added, "We have plenty of both straw and fodder, and room to spend the night." [26] [f]The man bowed his head and worshiped the LORD [27] and said, "Blessed be the LORD, [g]the God of my master Abraham, who has not forsaken [h]his steadfast love and his faithfulness toward my master. As for me, the LORD [i]has led me in the way to the house of my master's kinsmen." [28] Then the young woman ran and told her mother's household about these things.

[29] Rebekah had a brother whose name was [j]Laban. Laban ran out toward the man, to the spring. [30] As soon as he saw the ring and the bracelets on his sister's arms, and heard the words of Rebekah his sister, "Thus the man spoke to me," he went to the man. And behold, he was standing by the camels at the spring. [31] He said, "Come in, [k]O blessed of the LORD. Why do you stand outside? For I have prepared the house and a place for the camels." [32] So the man came to the house and unharnessed the camels, and gave [l]straw and fodder to the camels, and there was [m]water to wash his feet and the feet of the men who were with him. [33] Then food was set before him to eat. But he said, "I will not eat until I have said what I have to say." He said, "Speak on."

[34] So he said, "I am Abraham's servant. [35] The LORD [n]has greatly blessed my master, and he has become great. He has given him flocks

[1] Or *By her* [2] Or *a woman of marriageable age* [3] A *shekel* was about 2/5 ounce or 11 grams

24:10–67 Providentially, the servant met Rebekah (v. 15; cf. 22:23). He had arranged for a test to see which maiden would give him water and drink for his camels (24:12–14). He gave her precious jewelry (v. 22) and discovered that she was from Abraham's family (v. 24). He knew then that God had arranged these circumstances (v. 27). Rebekah's brother Laban was enticed by the precious gifts his sister had received. He brought Abraham's servant to his home (vv. 29–33), where the servant revealed his mission and reported on God's providential care (vv. 34–49). The family agreed that the Lord was in the circumstances and gave Rebekah permission to marry Isaac (vv. 50–51). The servant hastily departed the next day to speed his journey home. Upon leaving, Rebekah received a blessing from her family, in words reminiscent of the angelic blessing at Mount Moriah (v. 60; cf. 22:17). The story ends with the providential meeting and marriage of Rebekah and Isaac (24:62–67).

Throughout this account, the hand of God is not explicitly mentioned. Yet God's divine governance of all that transpires here—to bring a wife to Isaac and continue the covenant line—is unmistakable. God was seeing to the fulfillment of the promises he had made to Abraham.

11 [x]1 Sam. 9:11; John 4:7
12 [y]ver. 27, 42, 48 [z]ch. 27:20
13 [a]ver. 43
14 [b]See ch. 15:8
15 [c]ch. 11:29; 22:23
16 [d]ch. 26:7
24 [e]ver. 15; ch. 22:23
26 [f]ver. 48, 52; Ex. 4:31
27 [g]ver. 12, 42, 48 [h]ch. 32:10; Ps. 98:3 [i]ver. 48
29 [j]ch. 25:20; 28:2; 29:5
31 [k][ch. 26:29; Judg. 17:2; Ruth 3:10]
32 [l]ch. 43:24; Judg. 19:21 [m]See ch. 18:4
35 [n]ver. 1

and herds, silver and gold, male servants and female servants, camels and donkeys. 36 And Sarah my master's wife [o]bore a son to my master when she was old, and [p]to him he has given all that he has. 37 [q]My master made me swear, saying, 'You shall not take a wife for my son from the daughters of the Canaanites, in whose land I dwell, 38 but you shall go to my father's house and to my clan and take a wife for my son.' 39 I said to my master, 'Perhaps the woman will not follow me.' 40 But he said to me, 'The LORD, [r]before whom I have walked, will send his angel with you and [s]prosper your way. You shall take a wife for my son from my clan and from my father's house. 41 Then you will be free from my oath, when you come to my clan. And if they will not give her to you, you will be free from my oath.'

42 "I came today to the spring and said, [t]'O LORD, the God of my master Abraham, if now you [s]are prospering the way that I go, 43 behold, I am standing [u]by the spring of water. Let the virgin who comes out to draw water, to whom I shall say, "Please give me a little water from your jar to drink," 44 [v]and who will say to me, "Drink, and I will draw for your camels also," let her be the woman whom the LORD has appointed for my master's son.'

45 "Before I had finished [w]speaking in my heart, behold, Rebekah came out with her water jar on her shoulder, and she went down to the spring and drew water. I said to her, 'Please let me drink.' 46 She quickly let down her jar from her shoulder and said, 'Drink, and I will give your camels drink also.' So I drank, and she gave the camels drink also. 47 Then I asked her, 'Whose daughter are you?' She said, 'The daughter of Bethuel, Nahor's son, whom Milcah bore to him.' [x]So I put the ring on her nose and the bracelets on her arms. 48 [y]Then I bowed my head and worshiped the LORD and blessed the LORD, [t]the God of my master Abraham, who had led me by the right way[1] to take [z]the daughter of my master's kinsman for his son. 49 Now then, if you are going to [a]show steadfast love and faithfulness to my master, tell me; and if not, tell me, that I may turn to the right hand or to the left."

50 Then Laban and Bethuel answered and said, "The thing has come from the LORD; we cannot [b]speak to you bad or good. 51 Behold, Rebekah is before you; take her and go, and let her be the wife of your master's son, [c]as the LORD has spoken."

52 When Abraham's servant heard their words, [y]he bowed himself to the earth before the LORD. 53 And the servant brought out jewelry of silver and of gold, and garments, and gave them to Rebekah. He also gave to her brother and to her mother costly ornaments. 54 And he and the men who were with him ate and drank, and they spent the night there. When they arose in the morning, he said, [d]"Send me away to my master." 55 Her brother and her mother said, "Let the young woman remain with us a while, at least ten days; after that she may go." 56 But he said to them, "Do not delay me, since the LORD has prospered my way. Send me away that I may go to my master." 57 They said, "Let us call the young woman and ask her." 58 And they called Rebekah and said to her, "Will you go with this man?" She said, "I will go." 59 So they sent away Rebekah their sister and [e]her nurse, and Abraham's servant and his men. 60 And they blessed Rebekah and said to her,

"Our sister, may you [f]become
 thousands of ten thousands,
and [g]may your offspring possess
 the gate of those who hate him!"[2]

61 Then Rebekah and her young women arose and rode on the camels and followed the man. Thus the servant took Rebekah and went his way.

62 Now Isaac had returned from [h]Beer-lahai-roi and was dwelling in the Negeb. 63 And Isaac went out [i]to meditate in the field toward evening. And he lifted up his eyes and saw, and behold, there were camels coming. 64 And Rebekah lifted up her eyes, and when she saw Isaac, she dismounted from the camel 65 and said to the servant, "Who is that man, walking in the field to meet us?" The servant said, "It is my master." So she took her veil and covered herself. 66 And the servant told Isaac all the things that he had done. 67 Then Isaac brought her into the tent of Sarah his mother and took Rebekah, and she became his wife, and he loved her. So Isaac was [j]comforted after his mother's [k]death.

[1] Or *faithfully* [2] Or *hate them*

36 [o]ch. 21:2 [p]ch. 25:5 **37** [q]ver. 3-8 **40** [r]ch. 17:1 [s]ver. 21 **42** [t]ver. 12, 27 [s][See ver. 40 above] **43** [u]ver. 13 **44** [v]ver. 14, 18 **45** [w]1 Sam. 1:13 **47** [x][Ezek. 16:11, 12] **48** [y]ver. 26, 52 [t][See ver. 42 above] [z][ch. 22:23] **49** [a]ch. 47:29; Josh. 2:14 **50** [b]ch. 31:24; 2 Sam. 13:22 **51** [c]See ver. 13-15, 42-46 **52** [y][See ver. 48 above] **54** [d]ver. 56, 59 **59** [e]ch. 35:8 **60** [f]ch. 17:16 [g]ch. 22:17 **62** [h]ch. 16:14; 25:11 **63** [i]Ps. 77:12; 143:5 **67** [j]ch. 37:35; 38:12 [k]ch. 23:2

Abraham's Death and His Descendants

25 Abraham took another wife, whose
name was Keturah. 2 [l]She bore him
Zimran, Jokshan, Medan, Midian, Ishbak, and
Shuah. 3 Jokshan fathered Sheba and Dedan.
The sons of Dedan were Asshurim, Letushim,
and Leummim. 4 The sons of Midian were
Ephah, Epher, Hanoch, Abida, and Eldaah.
All these were the children of Keturah. 5 [m]Abra-
ham gave all he had to Isaac. 6 But to the sons of
his concubines Abraham gave gifts, and while
he was still living he [n]sent them away from his
son Isaac, eastward [o]to the east country.

7 These are the days of the years of Abraham's
life, 175 years. 8 Abraham [p]breathed his last
and [q]died in a good old age, an old man and
full of years, and was gathered to his people.
9 Isaac and Ishmael [r]his sons buried him in the
cave of Machpelah, in the field of Ephron
the son of Zohar the Hittite, east of Mamre,
10 the field [s]that Abraham purchased from the
Hittites. [t]There Abraham was buried, with
Sarah his wife. 11 After the death of Abraham,
God blessed Isaac his son. And Isaac settled at
[u]Beer-lahai-roi.

12 These are the generations of Ishmael,
Abraham's son, [v]whom Hagar the Egyptian,
Sarah's servant, bore to Abraham. 13 [w]These are
the names of the sons of Ishmael, named in
the order of their birth: [x]Nebaioth, the firstborn of Ishmael; and [x]Kedar, Adbeel, Mibsam,
14 Mishma, Dumah, Massa, 15 Hadad, [y]Tema,
[z]Jetur, [z]Naphish, and Kedemah. 16 These are
the sons of Ishmael and these are their names,
by their villages and by their encampments,
[a]twelve princes according to their tribes.
17 (These are the years of the life of Ishmael:
137 years. He [b]breathed his last and died, and
was gathered to his people.) 18 [c]They settled
from Havilah to [d]Shur, which is opposite
Egypt in the direction of Assyria. He settled[1]
over against all his kinsmen.

The Birth of Esau and Jacob

19 These are the generations of Isaac, Abraham's son: [e]Abraham fathered Isaac, 20 and
Isaac was forty years old when he took Rebekah, [f]the daughter of Bethuel the Aramean
of [g]Paddan-aram, [h]the sister of Laban the
Aramean, to be his wife. 21 And Isaac prayed
to the LORD for his wife, because she was barren. And [i]the LORD granted his prayer, and
Rebekah his wife conceived. 22 The children
struggled together within her, and she said,
"If it is thus, why is this happening to me?"[2]
So she went [j]to inquire of the LORD. 23 And the
LORD said to her,

[1] Hebrew *fell* [2] Or *why do I live?*

25:1–6 Abraham also had children with Keturah (vv. 1–4), but he "gave all he had to Isaac" (v. 5). The inheritance was not distributed equally among all of Abraham's children. While this may at first glance seem like favoritism, from another perspective we see once more that God was sovereignly overseeing events to ensure the well-being of the patriarchal line, through whose seed the entire world would be blessed.

25:7–11 Abraham died and was buried in the presence of Ishmael and Isaac in the cave of Machpelah. This is recorded as a way of underscoring the ongoing fulfillment of the land promise to Abraham (cf. 12:7). The final fulfillment of the covenant land promises to Abraham is not simply a plot of land in the Middle East but rather the entire world (cf. 12:3; 17:4–5). The apostle Paul speaks of "the promise to Abraham and his offspring that he would be heir *of the world*" (Rom. 4:13).

25:19–35:29 The story of Isaac moves quickly on to focus on Jacob. The narrator views Isaac as a link between the stories of Abraham (11:27–25:18) and of Jacob (27:1–35:29). He virtually bypasses Isaac in favor of Jacob, the father of the 12 tribes. Like Abraham, Isaac is subject to divine testing—including barrenness of his wife, famine, tense relations with Abimelech, and sibling rivalry among his children—all of which demonstrates that God's covenant is not thwarted by the deficiencies and difficulties of his people.

25:19–34 Isaac, son of Abraham, married Rebekah. Like Sarah, she was barren. Yet the Lord responded to Isaac's prayer. After twenty years of marriage, Rebekah conceived twin boys, and the Lord forewarned her of the rivalry and destiny of the two. The older (Esau) would serve the younger (Jacob). Their rivalry, like that of Ishmael and Isaac, would lead to estrangement.

Chapter 25
2 [l]1 Chr. 1:32, 33
5 [m]ch. 24:36
6 [n]ch. 21:14 [o][Judg. 6:3]
8 [p]ver. 17; ch. 35:29; 49:33 [q]ch. 15:15
9 [r]ch. 35:29
10 [s]ch. 23:16; 50:13 [t]ch. 49:30, 31
11 [u]ch. 16:14; 24:62
12 [v]ch. 16:15
13 [w]1 Chr. 1:29-31 [x]Isa. 60:7
15 [y]Job 6:19; Isa. 21:14 [z]1 Chr. 5:19
16 [a]ch. 17:20
17 [b]ver. 8
18 [c]1 Sam. 15:7 [d]ch. 16:7; 20:1; Ex. 15:22
19 [e]Matt. 1:2
20 [f]ch. 22:23 [g]See ch. 28:2 [h]ch. 24:29
21 [i]2 Sam. 21:14; 24:25; 1 Chr. 5:20; 2 Chr. 33:13; Ezra 8:23
22 [j][1 Sam. 9:9]

[k]"Two nations are in your womb,
and two peoples from within you[1]
shall be divided;
[l]the one shall be stronger than the other,
[m]the older shall serve the younger."

24 When her days to give birth were completed, behold, there were twins in her womb.
25 The first came out red, [n]all his body like a
hairy cloak, so they called his name Esau.
26 Afterward his brother came out with [o]his
hand holding Esau's heel, so [p]his name was
called Jacob.[2] Isaac was sixty years old when
she bore them.

27 When the boys grew up, Esau was [q]a skillful hunter, a man of the field, while Jacob was
a quiet man, [r]dwelling in tents. 28 Isaac loved
Esau because [s]he ate of his game, but Rebekah
loved Jacob.

Esau Sells His Birthright

29 Once when Jacob was cooking stew, Esau
came in from the field, and he was exhausted.
30 And Esau said to Jacob, "Let me eat some of
that red stew, for I am exhausted!" (Therefore
his name was called Edom.[3]) 31 Jacob said, "Sell
me your birthright now." 32 Esau said, "I am
about to die; of what use is a birthright to
me?" 33 Jacob said, "Swear to me now." So he
swore to him and [t]sold his birthright to Jacob.
34 Then Jacob gave Esau bread and lentil stew,
and he ate and drank and rose and went his
way. Thus Esau despised his birthright.

God's Promise to Isaac

26 Now there was a famine in the land,
besides [u]the former famine that was in
the days of Abraham. And Isaac went to Gerar
to [v]Abimelech king of the [w]Philistines. 2 And
the LORD appeared to him and said, "Do not
go down to Egypt; dwell [x]in the land of which
I shall tell you. 3 [y]Sojourn in this land, and [z]I
will be with you and will bless you, for [a]to you
and to your offspring I will give all these lands,
and I will establish [b]the oath that I swore to
Abraham your father. 4 [c]I will multiply your
offspring as the stars of heaven and will give
to your offspring all these lands. And [d]in your
offspring all the nations of the earth shall be
blessed, 5 because [e]Abraham obeyed my voice
and kept my charge, my commandments, my
statutes, and my laws."

Isaac and Abimelech

6 So Isaac settled in Gerar. 7 When the men of
the place asked him about his wife, [f]he said,
"She is my sister," for [g]he feared to say, "My
wife," thinking, "lest the men of the place

[1] Or *from birth* [2] *Jacob* means *He takes by the heel*, or *He cheats* [3] *Edom* sounds like the Hebrew for *red*

23 [k]ch. 17:16; 24:60 [l][2 Sam. 8:14]; See Obad. 18-21 [m]ch. 27:29, 40; Cited Rom. 9:12
25 [n]ch. 27:11, 16, 23
26 [o]Hos. 12:3 [p]ch. 27:36
27 [q]ch. 27:3, 5 [r]Heb. 11:9
28 [s]ch. 27:4, 7, 9
33 [t]Heb. 12:16
Chapter 26
1 [u]ch. 12:10 [v]ch. 20:2 [w]ch. 21:34
2 [x]ch. 12:1
3 [y]ch. 20:1; Heb. 11:9 [z]ch. 28:15 [a]See ch. 13:15 [b][Mic. 7:20]; See ch. 22:16-18
4 [c]Cited Ex. 32:13; See ch. 15:5 [d]See ch. 12:3
5 [e]ch. 22:18
7 [f]ch. 12:13; 20:2, 13 [g][Prov. 29:25]

Yet through all the family dysfunction God's purposes continued to unfold. In Romans, Paul reflects on these Genesis accounts— the Lord's election of Isaac instead of Ishmael and of Jacob instead of Esau—as examples of God's sovereign grace (Rom. 9:6–13; cf. Mal. 1:2–3). God is free from human expectations as to how he will show his compassion (cf. Ex. 33:19). His choosing the younger son rather than the older demonstrates God's sovereign freedom and works subversively against the way human society naturally assesses significance and worth.

The birth of the boys explains their nature and destiny. Esau is reddish and hairy. The words for red (*'adom*) and hairy (*se'ar*) in Hebrew connect with the destiny of his descendants, the Edomites (see Gen. 25:30), who lived in the region of Seir. Esau lived by hunting, was an outdoorsman, and loved life (v. 27). Jacob's holding on to his brother's heel (*'aqeb*) suggests a play on the name Jacob. In his dealings with people, he was a conniver. Jacob loved to be indoors and was more tender than Esau. Their lifestyles separated them (vv. 27, 29–30) and divided the love of their parents for them (v. 27). Jacob forced the issue of the birthright by bargaining with Esau's weakness. When Esau was exhausted and hungry, Jacob "sold" food to him in exchange for his birthright (vv. 29–34). All Esau wanted was to satisfy his appetite, not giving much thought to the seriousness of Jacob's trickery. The author of Hebrews mentions this incident as an example of despising God's grace (Heb. 12:16).

What is striking in all this is that Jacob was not morally superior to Esau. Both were rascals. Yet God chose to set his love on the younger rather than the older brother. God's love does not seek out those who are intrinsically worthy of it. Indeed, no one is intrinsically worthy of God's love. This is what it means for grace to be grace. "But if it is by grace, it is no longer on the basis of works; otherwise grace would no longer be grace" (Rom. 11:6).

should kill me because of Rebekah," because
[h]she was attractive in appearance. 8 When he
had been there a long time, Abimelech king
of the Philistines looked out of a window and
saw Isaac laughing with[1] Rebekah his wife. 9 So
Abimelech called Isaac and said, "Behold, she
is your wife. How then could you say, 'She is my
sister'?" Isaac said to him, "Because I thought,
'Lest I die because of her.'" 10 Abimelech said,
"What is this you have done to us? One of the
people might easily have lain with your wife,
and [i]you would have brought guilt upon us."
11 So Abimelech warned all the people, saying,
"Whoever touches this man or his wife shall
surely be put to death."

12 And Isaac sowed in that land and reaped
in the same year a hundredfold. The LORD
[j]blessed him, 13 and the man became rich,
and gained more and more until he became
very wealthy. 14 He had possessions of flocks
and herds and many servants, so that the
Philistines [k]envied him. 15 (Now the Philistines
had stopped and filled with earth all the wells
[l]that his father's servants had dug in the days
of Abraham his father.) 16 And Abimelech said
to Isaac, "Go away from us, for you are much
mightier than we."

17 So Isaac departed from there and encamped
in the Valley of Gerar and settled there. 18 And
Isaac dug again the wells of water that had
been dug in the days of Abraham his father,
which the Philistines had stopped after the
death of Abraham. And [m]he gave them the
names that his father had given them. 19 But
when Isaac's servants dug in the valley and
found there a well of spring water, 20 the
herdsmen of Gerar [n]quarreled with Isaac's
herdsmen, saying, "The water is ours." So he
called the name of the well Esek,[2] because
they contended with him. 21 Then they dug
another well, and they quarreled over that
also, so he called its name Sitnah.[3] 22 And he
moved from there and dug another well, and
they did not quarrel over it. So he called its
name Rehoboth,[4] saying, "For now the LORD
has made room for us, and we shall be fruitful
in the land."

23 From there he went up to Beersheba.
24 And the LORD appeared to him the same
night and said, [o]"I am the God of Abraham
your father. [p]Fear not, for [q]I am with you and
will bless you and multiply your offspring for
my servant Abraham's sake." 25 So he [r]built an
altar there and called upon the name of the
LORD and pitched his tent there. And there
Isaac's servants dug a well.

26 When Abimelech went to him from Gerar
with Ahuzzath his adviser and [s]Phicol the
commander of his army, 27 Isaac said to them,
"Why have you come to me, seeing that you
hate me and [t]have sent me away from you?"
28 They said, "We see plainly that the LORD has
been with you. So we said, let there be a sworn
pact between us, between you and us, and let
us make a covenant with you, 29 that you will
do us no harm, just as we have not touched
you and have done to you nothing but good
and have sent you away in peace. [u]You are
now the blessed of the LORD." 30 So he made
them a feast, and they ate and drank. 31 In
the morning they rose early and [v]exchanged
oaths. And Isaac sent them on their way, and
they departed from him in peace. 32 That same
day Isaac's servants came and told him about

[1] Hebrew may suggest an intimate relationship [2] *Esek* means *contention* [3] *Sitnah* means *enmity* [4] *Rehoboth* means *broad places*, or *room*

26:1–33 The theme of this chapter is divine provision and promise in the midst of adversity. Amid famine (v. 1), fear for his own life (v. 7), and contention over sources of water (vv. 19–21), Isaac receives reaffirmation of God's covenant promises (vv. 3–5, 24). And through the adversity Isaac faces, he is blessed—his possessions multiply (vv. 12–13), and it is obvious to all that Isaac is "the blessed of the LORD" (v. 29). The supreme blessing in Isaac's life was not material possessions, however, but the Lord himself. "I am with you," God said to Isaac (v. 24). Moreover, the covenant promises continue to unfold and Isaac recognizes this as he declares, "we shall be fruitful in the land" (v. 22). God is fulfilling not only his promise to Abraham of many descendants (12:1–3, 7) but also the original mandate of 1:28, to be fruitful and fill the earth.

Once more we see that it is through weak, even cowardly men that God works out his redemptive purposes in the world. Putting his own well-being before that of his wife, as his father had before him (ch. 20), Isaac capitulates to fear and lies about Rebekah's identity (26:7). Yet this is the great patriarch through whom God is keeping his promises to redeem the world. This is amazing grace—to Isaac and to us.

7[h] ch. 24:16
10[i] ch. 20:9
12[j] ver. 3; ch. 24:1, 35
14[k] [Eccles. 4:4]
15[l] ch. 21:30
18[m] ch. 21:31
20[n] ch. 21:25
24[o] ch. 17:7; 24:12; 28:13; Ex. 3:6 [p] ch. 15:1; See Ps. 27:1-3 [q] ch. 28:15; 31:3; [ch. 21:22, 23]
25[r] ch. 12:7; 13:18
26[s] ch. 21:22
27[t] ver. 16
29[u] ch. 24:31
31[v] ch. 21:31

the well that they had dug and said to him, "We have found water." 33 He called it Shibah;[1] therefore the name of the city is [w]Beersheba to this day.

34 When Esau was forty years old, he took [x]Judith the daughter of Beeri the Hittite to be his wife, and Basemath the daughter of Elon the Hittite, 35 and [y]they made life bitter[2] for Isaac and Rebekah.

Isaac Blesses Jacob

27 When Isaac was old and [z]his eyes were dim so that he could not see, he called Esau his older son and said to him, "My son"; and he answered, "Here I am." 2 He said, "Behold, I am old; I do not know the day of my death. 3 [a]Now then, take your weapons, your quiver and your bow, and go out to the field and hunt game for me, 4 and prepare for me delicious food, such as I love, and bring it to me so that I may eat, that my soul [b]may bless you before I die."

5 Now Rebekah was listening when Isaac spoke to his son Esau. So when Esau went to the field to hunt for game and bring it, 6 Rebekah said to her son Jacob, "I heard your father speak to your brother Esau, 7 'Bring me game and prepare for me delicious food, that I may eat it and bless you before the LORD before I die.' 8 Now therefore, my son, [c]obey my voice as I command you. 9 Go to the flock and bring me two good young goats, so that I may prepare from them delicious food for your father, such as he loves. 10 And you shall bring it to your father to eat, [d]so that he may bless you before he dies." 11 But Jacob said to Rebekah his mother, "Behold, [e]my brother Esau is a hairy man, and I am a smooth man. 12 Perhaps my father [f]will feel me, and I shall seem to be mocking him and bring [g]a curse upon myself and not a blessing." 13 His mother said to him, [h]"Let your curse be on me, my son; only obey my voice, and go, bring them to me."

14 So he went and took them and brought them to his mother, and his mother prepared delicious food, such as his father loved. 15 Then Rebekah took the [i]best garments of Esau her older son, which were with her in the house, and put them on Jacob her younger son. 16 And the skins of the young goats she put on his hands and on the smooth part of his neck. 17 And she put the delicious food and the bread, which she had prepared, into the hand of her son Jacob.

18 So he went in to his father and said, "My father." And he said, "Here I am. Who are you, my son?" 19 Jacob said to his father, "I am Esau your firstborn. I have done as you told me; now sit up and eat of my game, that your soul may bless me." 20 But Isaac said to his son, "How is it that you have found it so quickly, my son?" He answered, "Because the LORD your God granted me success." 21 Then Isaac said to Jacob, "Please come near, that I [j]may feel you, my son, to know whether you are really my son Esau or not." 22 So Jacob went near to Isaac his father, who felt him and said, "The voice is Jacob's voice, but the hands are the hands of Esau." 23 And he did not recognize him, because [k]his hands were hairy like his brother Esau's hands. [l]So he blessed him. 24 He said, "Are you really my son Esau?" He answered, "I am." 25 Then he said, "Bring it near to me, [m]that I may eat of my son's game and bless you." So he brought it near to him, and he ate; and he brought him wine, and he drank.

26 Then his father Isaac said to him, "Come near and kiss me, my son." 27 So he came near

[1] *Shibah* sounds like the Hebrew for *oath* [2] Hebrew *they were bitterness of spirit*

33 [w] ch. 21:31; 22:19
34 [x] [ch. 28:9; 36:2, 3]
35 [y] ch. 27:46
Chapter 27
1 [z] ch. 48:10; 1 Sam. 3:2
3 [a] ch. 25:27, 28
4 [b] ch. 10:25; 48:9, 15; 49:28; Deut. 33:1
8 [c] ver. 13
10 [d] ver. 4
11 [e] ch. 25:25
12 [f] ver. 21, 22 [g] [Deut. 27:18]
13 [h] [1 Sam. 25:24; 2 Sam. 14:9; Matt. 27:25]
15 [i] ver. 27
21 [j] ver. 12
23 [k] ver. 16 [l] Heb. 11:20
25 [m] ver. 10

27:1–29 The story of Rebekah and Jacob's deception of Isaac and the vindictive response of Esau has many intriguing angles. Through it all we see God working out his purposes that "the older shall serve the younger" (25:23). Isaac is deceived and blesses Jacob with a variation of the Abrahamic promises (27:27–29; cf. 12:3; see Heb. 11:20). God providentially uses all kinds of human actions—good, bad, and mixed—to carry out his promised purposes.

The supreme instance of God working through the mixed actions of various people to bring about his promised purposes is the cross of Christ. Jesus is wrongly condemned and killed. Yet note Peter's commentary on this event: "there were gathered together against your holy servant Jesus, whom you anointed, both Herod and Pontius Pilate, along with the Gentiles and the peoples of Israel, to do whatever your hand and your plan had predestined to take place" (Acts 4:27–28; cf. 2:23). All that takes place in our world is under the wise and fatherly hand of God.

and kissed him. And Isaac smelled the smell
of his garments [l]and blessed him and said,

"See, [n]the smell of my son
is as the smell of a field that the LORD
has blessed!
28 May God give you of [o]the dew of heaven
and of the fatness of the earth
and [p]plenty of grain and wine.
29 Let peoples serve you,
and nations [q]bow down to you.
[r]Be lord over your brothers,
and may your mother's sons bow
down to you.
[s]Cursed be everyone who curses you,
and blessed be everyone who blesses
you!"

30 As soon as Isaac had finished blessing
Jacob, when Jacob had scarcely gone out
from the presence of Isaac his father, Esau
his brother came in from his hunting. 31 He
also prepared delicious food and brought it
to his father. And he said to his father, "Let
my father arise and eat of his son's game, that
you may bless me." 32 His father Isaac said
to him, "Who are you?" He answered, "I am
your son, your firstborn, Esau." 33 Then Isaac
trembled very violently and said, "Who was
it then that hunted game and brought it to
me, and I ate it all before you came, and I have
blessed him? Yes, and he shall be blessed." 34 As
soon as Esau heard the words of his father, [t]he
cried out with an exceedingly great and bitter cry and said to his father, "Bless me, even
me also, O my father!" 35 But he said, "Your
brother came deceitfully, and he has taken
away your blessing." 36 Esau said, [u]"Is he not
rightly named Jacob?[1] For he has cheated me
these two times. [v]He took away my birthright,
and behold, now he has taken away my blessing." Then he said, "Have you not reserved a
blessing for me?" 37 Isaac answered and said
to Esau, "Behold, [w]I have made him lord over
you, and all his brothers I have given to him
for servants, and [x]with grain and wine I have
sustained him. What then can I do for you,
my son?" 38 Esau said to his father, "Have you
but one blessing, my father? Bless me, even
me also, O my father." And [t]Esau lifted up his
voice and wept.
39 Then Isaac his father answered and said
to him:

"Behold, [y]away from[2] the fatness of the
earth shall your dwelling be,
and away from[3] the dew of heaven on
high.
40 By your sword you shall live,
and you [z]shall serve your brother;
but when you grow restless
[a]you shall break his yoke from your
neck."

41 Now Esau [b]hated Jacob because of the
blessing with which his father had blessed
him, and Esau said to himself, [c]"The days of
mourning for my father are approaching;
[d]then I will kill my brother Jacob." 42 But
the words of Esau her older son were told
to Rebekah. So she sent and called Jacob her
younger son and said to him, "Behold, your
brother Esau comforts himself about you by
planning to kill you. 43 Now therefore, my son,
obey my voice. Arise, flee to Laban my brother
in Haran 44 and stay with him a while, until
your brother's fury turns away— 45 until your
brother's anger turns away from you, and he
forgets what you have done to him. Then I will
send and bring you from there. Why should
I be bereft of you both in one day?"
46 Then Rebekah said to Isaac, [e]"I loathe my
life because of the Hittite women.[4] [f]If Jacob
marries one of the Hittite women like these,
one of the women of the land, what good will
my life be to me?"

[1] *Jacob* means *He takes by the heel*, or *He cheats* [2] Or *Behold, of* [3] Or *and of* [4] Hebrew *daughters of Heth*

27:42–28:5 Rebekah schemed to save her favorite son from being murdered, but she knew that she could not keep him safe forever. She sent Jacob to the ancestral family home and would never see him again. Her life was virtually over, because of the wretched family relations with her daughters-in-law (27:46). She experienced the anguish and sorrow resulting from God's judgment (3:16), but she failed to experience the joy of victory over evil (3:15). She was a participant in the wicked schemes she hatched. And yet in a strange twist of divine grace she was also a participant in God's plan. She and Isaac charged Jacob to marry one of the daughters of Rebekah's brother Laban (28:2). They sent him away with Isaac's blessing (28:3–4), praying that "God Almighty" (*El Shaddai*; 28:3; cf. 17:1) would bestow the Abrahamic blessing on Jacob.

27[l] [See ver. 23 above] [n] [Hos. 14:6]
28[o] Deut. 33:13; Zech. 8:12; [ch. 49:25; 2 Sam. 1:21] [p] Deut. 7:13; 33:28; Joel 2:19
29[q] [ch. 49:8] [r] [2 Sam. 8:14] [s] ch. 12:3; Num. 24:9
34[t] Heb. 12:17
36[u] ch. 25:26 [v] ch. 25:33
37[w] ver. 29; [2 Sam. 8:14] [x] ver. 28
38[t] [See ver. 34 above]
39[y] ver. 28; ch. 36:6, 7
40[z] ch. 25:23; [2 Sam. 8:14]; See Obad. 18-21

[a] [2 Kgs. 8:20-22] **41**[b] [ch. 37:4] [c] ch. 50:3, 4, 10 [d] [Amos 1:11; Obad. 10] **46**[e] ch. 26:34, 35; 28:8 [f] ch. 24:3

Jacob Sent to Laban

28 Then Isaac called Jacob [g]and blessed
him and directed him, [f]"You must
not take a wife from the Canaanite women.
2 [h]Arise, go to Paddan-aram to the house of
[i]Bethuel your mother's father, and take as your
wife from there one of the daughters of Laban
your mother's brother. 3 [j]God Almighty[1] bless
you and make you fruitful and multiply you,
that you may become a company of peoples.
4 May he give [k]the blessing of Abraham to you
and to your offspring with you, that you may
take possession of [l]the land of your sojournings that God gave to Abraham!" 5 Thus Isaac
sent Jacob away. And he went to Paddan-aram,
to Laban, the son of Bethuel the Aramean, the
brother of Rebekah, Jacob's and Esau's mother.

Esau Marries an Ishmaelite

6 Now Esau saw that Isaac had blessed Jacob
and sent him away to Paddan-aram to take a
wife from there, and that as he blessed him he
directed him, "You must not take a wife from
the Canaanite women," 7 and that Jacob had
obeyed his father and his mother and gone to
Paddan-aram. 8 So when Esau saw [m]that the
Canaanite women did not please Isaac his
father, 9 Esau went to Ishmael and took as his
wife, besides the wives he had, [n]Mahalath the
daughter of Ishmael, Abraham's son, the sister
of [o]Nebaioth.

Jacob's Dream

10 Jacob left [p]Beersheba and went toward
[q]Haran. 11 And he came to a certain place and
stayed there that night, because the sun had
set. Taking one of the stones of the place, he
put it under his head and lay down in that
place to sleep. 12 And he [r]dreamed, and behold,
there was a ladder[2] set up on the earth, and the
top of it reached to heaven. And behold, [s]the
angels of God were ascending and descending
on it! 13 And behold, [t]the LORD stood above it[3]
and said, [u]"I am the LORD, the God of Abraham
your father and the God of Isaac. [v]The land on
which you lie I will give to you and to your offspring. 14 Your offspring shall be like [w]the dust
of the earth, and you shall spread abroad to
the west and to the east and to the north and
to the south, and in you and [x]your offspring
shall all the families of the earth be blessed.
15 Behold, [y]I am with you and will keep you
wherever you go, and [z]will bring you back to
this land. For I will [a]not leave you until I have
done what I have promised you." 16 Then Jacob
awoke from his sleep and said, "Surely the
LORD is [b]in this place, and I did not know it."
17 And he was afraid and said, "How awesome
is this place! This is none other than the house
of God, and this is the gate of heaven."

18 So early in the morning Jacob took the
stone that he had put under his head and set
it up [c]for a pillar [d]and poured oil on the top of
it. 19 He called the name of that place [e]Bethel,[4]
but the name of the city was Luz at the first.
20 Then Jacob [f]made a vow, saying, "If God will
be with me and will keep me in this way that
I go, and will give me bread to eat and clothing
to wear, 21 [g]so that I come again to my father's
house in peace, [h]then the LORD shall be my
God, 22 and this stone, which I have set up for

[1] Hebrew *El Shaddai* [2] Or *a flight of steps* [3] Or *beside him* [4] *Bethel* means *the house of God*

Chapter 28
1 [g] ver. 6 [f] [See ch. 27:46 above]
2 [h] Hos. 12:12 [i] ch. 22:23
3 [j] See ch. 17:1
4 [k] See ch. 12:2, 3 [l] ch. 17:8; 36:7; 37:1
8 [m] ch. 24:3; 26:35
9 [n] [ch. 36:3] [o] ch. 25:13; 36:3
10 [p] ch. 21:31; 26:33 [q] [Acts 7:2]
12 [r] [Num. 12:6; Job 33:15, 16] [s] [John 1:51]
13 [t] [ch. 35:1; 48:3] [u] ch. 26:24 [v] ch. 35:12; See ch. 13:14-16
14 [w] See ch. 13:16 [x] See ch. 12:3
15 [y] ch. 26:24; 31:3 [z] ch. 35:6 [a] 1 Kgs. 8:57
16 [b] Ex. 3:5; Josh. 5:15
18 [c] ch. 31:13, 45; 35:14; [1 Sam. 7:12; 2 Sam. 18:18] [d] [Lev. 8:10, 11; Num. 7:1]
19 [e] ch. 35:7; Judg. 1:23, 26
20 [f] ch. 31:13
21 [g] [Judg. 11:31; 2 Sam. 15:7-9] [h] Deut. 26:17

28:10–22 On Jacob's way to Paddan-aram, and again on his way back (35:1–15), the Lord appeared to him at Bethel. God revealed himself to Jacob as the God of Abraham and of Isaac (28:13). Jacob saw a ladder with angels ascending and descending (v. 12). With this divinely provided link between heaven and earth, God committed himself to keep his promise to Jacob, and to be present with him during his journey (vv. 12–15). Jacob called the name of the place Bethel, saying "This is . . . the house [or temple] of God," and "this is the gate of heaven" (vv. 17, 19). He set up the stone on which he had slept as a sacred stone (v. 18).

Centuries later, at the height of human history, we read of Jesus Christ telling Nathanael, "Truly, truly, I say to you, you will see heaven opened, and the angels of God ascending and descending on the Son of Man" (John 1:51). Here the angels go from heaven to earth not on a ladder but on Jesus himself—Jesus, in other words, *is* the ladder. In him, sinners on earth are restored to God in heaven. Jesus is the final "Bethel" or house of God, the true end-time temple. For in him, as in the temple of old, mankind is restored to God. In him, unclean sinners are made clean. Reflecting on such grace, our hearts are moved with fresh worship of the Lord of mercy who undertook to draw near to us sinners in our weakness and filth (Luke 19:10; Rom. 5:8).

a pillar, [i]shall be God's house. And [j]of all that
you give me I will give a full tenth to you."

Jacob Marries Leah and Rachel

29 Then Jacob went on his journey and
came to [k]the land of the people of the
east. 2 As he looked, he saw a well in the field,
and behold, three flocks of sheep lying beside
it, for out of that well the flocks were watered.
The stone on the well's mouth was large, 3 and
when all the flocks were gathered there, the
shepherds would roll the stone from the
mouth of the well and water the sheep, and
put the stone back in its place over the mouth
of the well.
4 Jacob said to them, "My brothers, where
do you come from?" They said, [l]"We are from
Haran." 5 He said to them, "Do you know Laban
the son of Nahor?" They said, "We know him."
6 He said to them, "Is it well with him?" They
said, "It is well; and see, Rachel his daughter is
coming with the sheep!" 7 He said, "Behold, it
is still high day; it is not time for the livestock
to be gathered together. Water the sheep and
go, pasture them." 8 But they said, "We cannot
until all the flocks are gathered together and
the stone is rolled from the mouth of the well;
then we water the sheep."
9 While he was still speaking with them,
[m]Rachel came with her father's sheep, for she
was a shepherdess. 10 Now as soon as Jacob saw
Rachel the daughter of Laban his mother's
brother, and the sheep of Laban his mother's
brother, Jacob came near and rolled the stone
from the well's mouth and watered the flock
of Laban his mother's brother. 11 Then Jacob
kissed Rachel and wept aloud. 12 And Jacob
told Rachel that he was [n]her father's kinsman,
and that he was Rebekah's son, [o]and she ran
and told her father.
13 As soon as Laban heard the news about
Jacob, his sister's son, [o]he ran to meet him and
embraced him and kissed him and brought
him to his house. Jacob told Laban all these
things, 14 and Laban said to him, [p]"Surely you
are my bone and my flesh!" And he stayed with
him a month.
15 Then Laban said to Jacob, "Because you are
my kinsman, should you therefore serve me
for nothing? Tell me, what shall your wages
be?" 16 Now Laban had two daughters. The
name of the older was Leah, and the name
of the younger was Rachel. 17 Leah's eyes were
weak,[1] but Rachel was beautiful in form and
appearance. 18 Jacob loved Rachel. And he said,
[q]"I will serve you seven years for your younger
daughter Rachel." 19 Laban said, "It is better
that I give her to you than that I should give
her to any other man; stay with me." 20 So
Jacob [q]served seven years for Rachel, and they
seemed to him but a few days because of the
love he had for her.
21 Then Jacob said to Laban, "Give me my wife
that I may go in to her, for my time is completed." 22 So Laban gathered together all the
people of the place and [r]made a feast. 23 But
in the evening he took his daughter Leah and
brought her to Jacob, and he went in to her.
24 (Laban gave[2] [s]his female servant Zilpah to
his daughter Leah to be her servant.) 25 And in
the morning, behold, it was Leah! And Jacob
said to Laban, "What is this you have done
to me? Did I not serve with you for Rachel?
Why then have you deceived me?" 26 Laban
said, "It is not so done in our country, to give
the younger before the firstborn. 27 [t]Complete
the week of this one, and we will give you the
other also in return for serving me another
seven years." 28 Jacob did so, and completed
her week. Then Laban gave him his daughter

[1] Or *soft* [2] Or *had given*; also verse 29

29:1–30 Jacob, the deceiver, is deceived. Laban tricks him into another seven years of service by deceiving Jacob into marrying Leah instead of Rachel. Jacob's extraordinary physical prowess is demonstrated in his rolling away the stone (v. 10) that normally required a group of shepherds to move it (v. 3). Yet this same man is made weak by deceitfulness such as he himself had utilized against his own family—stealing first Esau's birthright and then his blessing.

Yet Laban's deceitfulness toward Jacob is not some kind of divine "payback." Rather this painful experience in Jacob's life is part of God's ongoing purposes of mercy to mold Jacob into a man submissive to and humble before God, one whose physical strength does not impede God's grace entering his life. Later on, God will even take from Jacob his physical strength (32:24–28), for it is often only through pain and weakness that God can get through to fallen human beings.

22[i] ch. 35:7, 14 [j] ch. 14:20; Lev. 27:30-33

Chapter 29

1[k] Num. 23:7; Judg. 6:3
4[l] ch. 27:43
9[m] Ex. 2:16, 17
12[n] ch. 13:8; 14:14, 16 [o] [ch. 24:28, 29]
13[o] [See ver. 12 above]
14[p] ch. 2:23; 37:27; Judg. 9:2; 2 Sam. 5:1; 19:12, 13; 1 Chr. 11:1
18[q] ch. 30:26; 31:41; [Hos. 12:12]
20[q] [See ver. 18 above]
22[r] Judg. 14:10; [John 2:1, 2]
24[s] See ch. 30:9-12
27[t] [Judg. 14:12]

Rachel to be his wife. 29 (Laban gave [u]his female
servant Bilhah to his daughter Rachel to be her
servant.) 30 So Jacob went in to Rachel also, and
he loved Rachel more than Leah, and served
Laban [v]for another seven years.

Jacob's Children

31 When the LORD saw that Leah was [w]hated,
[x]he opened her womb, but Rachel was barren.
32 And Leah conceived and bore a son, and she
called his name Reuben,[1] for she said, "Because
the LORD [y]has looked upon my affliction; for
now my husband will love me." 33 She conceived again and bore a son, and said, "Because
the LORD has heard that I am hated, he has
given me this son also." And she called his
name Simeon.[2] 34 Again she conceived and
bore a son, and said, "Now this time my husband will be [z]attached to me, because I have
borne him three sons." Therefore his name was
called Levi.[3] 35 And she conceived again and
bore a son, and said, "This time I will praise
the LORD." Therefore she called his name
[a]Judah.[4] Then she ceased bearing.

30 When Rachel saw that [b]she bore Jacob
no children, she envied her sister. She
said to Jacob, "Give me children, or I shall die!"
2 Jacob's anger was kindled against Rachel, and
he said, "Am I in the place of God, [c]who has
withheld from you the fruit of the womb?"
3 Then she said, "Here is my servant [d]Bilhah;
go in to her, so that she may give birth [e]on
my behalf,[5] that even I may have children[6]
through her." 4 So she gave him her servant
Bilhah as a wife, and Jacob went in to her.
5 And Bilhah conceived and bore Jacob a son.
6 Then Rachel said, "God has [f]judged me, and
has also heard my voice and given me a son."
Therefore she called his name Dan.[7] 7 Rachel's
servant Bilhah conceived again and bore Jacob
a second son. 8 Then Rachel said, "With mighty
wrestlings[8] I have wrestled with my sister
and have prevailed." So she called his name
[g]Naphtali.[9]

9 When Leah saw that she had ceased bearing children, she took her servant Zilpah and
[h]gave her to Jacob as a wife. 10 Then Leah's
servant Zilpah bore Jacob a son. 11 And Leah
said, [i]"Good fortune has come!" so she called
his name [i]Gad.[10] 12 Leah's servant Zilpah bore
Jacob a second son. 13 And Leah said, "Happy
am I! For women [j]have called me happy." So
she called his name Asher.[11]

14 In the days of wheat harvest Reuben
went and found [k]mandrakes in the field
and brought them to his mother Leah. Then
Rachel said to Leah, "Please give me some of
your son's mandrakes." 15 But she said to her,
"Is it a small matter that you have taken away
my husband? Would you take away my son's
mandrakes also?" Rachel said, "Then he may
lie with you tonight in exchange for your son's
mandrakes." 16 When Jacob came from the field
in the evening, Leah went out to meet him
and said, "You must come in to me, for I have
hired you with my son's mandrakes." So he
lay with her that night. 17 And God listened to
Leah, and she conceived and bore Jacob a fifth

[1] *Reuben* means *See, a son* [2] *Simeon* sounds like the Hebrew for *heard* [3] *Levi* sounds like the Hebrew for *attached* [4] *Judah* sounds like the Hebrew for *praise* [5] Hebrew *on my knees* [6] Hebrew *be built up*, which sounds like the Hebrew for *children* [7] *Dan* sounds like the Hebrew for *judged* [8] Hebrew *With wrestlings of God* [9] *Naphtali* sounds like the Hebrew for *wrestling* [10] *Gad* sounds like the Hebrew for *good fortune* [11] *Asher* sounds like the Hebrew for *happy*

29[u] See ch. 30:3-7
30[v] ver. 20; ch. 31:41
31[w] Deut. 21:15 [x] [ch. 30:22]
32[y] ch. 31:42; Ex. 3:7; 4:31; Deut. 26:7
34[z] [Num. 18:2, 4]
35[a] Matt. 1:2; [ch. 49:8]
Chapter 30
1[b] ch. 29:31
2[c] [ch. 16:2; 1 Sam. 1:5]
3[d] ch. 29:29 [e] ch. 50:23
6[f] [ch. 49:16]
8[g] [Matt. 4:13]
9[h] ver. 4; ch. 29:24
11[i] [ch. 49:19]
13[j] [Luke 1:48]
14[k] Song 7:13

29:31–30:24 As the Lord is teaching Jacob the deceiver what it is like to be deceived, Leah, it seems, suffers the painful fate of being passed over by Jacob for her more beautiful sister, Rachel. Yet in an intriguing paragraph that draws forth once more the whole-Bible theme of blessing despite barrenness (see note on 11:30), the Lord makes Rachel barren and Leah fruitful. Amid much sisterly dysfunction (30:14–18), Leah, the unloved one, is enabled to carry out the divine mandate to be fruitful and multiply and fill the earth (1:28). Rachel is unable to participate in this mandate until the very end of the episode (30:22), and only after she, like Jacob, wrestles and prevails (30:8).

Yet Leah, too, must learn that it is only through the Lord that her identity can be truly established. As she bears Jacob one son after another, she seeks to use her childbearing as a way to get Jacob to love her—"Now this time," she says, "my husband will be attached to me, because I have borne him three sons" (29:34). She is building her identity on her husband's love for her instead of on the Lord's love for her. With the fourth son, however, divine grace breaks through: "This time I will praise the LORD" (29:35). Her fundamental affection has been redirected. And the name of the fourth son? Judah—the one through whom the covenant promises will finally be fulfilled (Heb. 7:14; Rev. 5:5).

son. 18 Leah said, "God has given me my wages
because I gave my servant to my husband." So
she called his name Issachar.[1]
19 And Leah conceived again, and she bore
Jacob a sixth son. 20 Then Leah said, "God has
endowed me with a good endowment; now
my husband will honor me, because I have
borne him six sons." So she called his name
[l]Zebulun.[2] 21 Afterward she bore a daughter
and called her name Dinah.
22 Then God [m]remembered Rachel, and God
listened to her and [n]opened her womb. 23 She
conceived and bore a son and said, "God has
taken away [o]my reproach." 24 And she called
his name Joseph,[3] saying, [p]"May the LORD add
to me another son!"

Jacob's Prosperity

25 As soon as Rachel had borne Joseph, Jacob
said to Laban, "Send me away, that I may go to
my own home and country. 26 Give me my wives
and my children [q]for whom I have served you,
that I may go, for you know the service that
I have given you." 27 But Laban said to him, "If
I have found favor in your sight, I have learned
by divination that[4] the LORD has blessed me
because of you. 28 [r]Name your wages, and
I will give it." 29 Jacob said to him, [s]"You yourself know how I have served you, and how
your livestock has fared with me. 30 For you
had little before I came, [t]and it has increased
abundantly, and the LORD has blessed you
wherever I turned. But now when shall I [u]pro-
vide for my own household also?" 31 He said,
"What shall I give you?" Jacob said, "You shall
not give me anything. If you will do this for
me, I will again pasture your flock and keep
it: 32 let me pass through all your flock today,
removing from it every speckled and spotted
sheep and every black lamb, and the spotted
and speckled among the goats, and [v]they shall
be my wages. 33 So my honesty will answer for
me later, when you come to look into my wages
with you. Every one that is not speckled and
spotted among the goats and black among the
lambs, if found with me, shall be counted stolen." 34 Laban said, "Good! Let it be as you have
said." 35 But that day Laban removed the male
goats that were striped and spotted, and all the
female goats that were speckled and spotted,
every one that had white on it, and every lamb
that was black, and put them in the charge of
his sons. 36 And he set a distance of three days'
journey between himself and Jacob, and Jacob
pastured the rest of Laban's flock.
37 Then [w]Jacob took fresh sticks of poplar and almond and plane trees, and peeled
white streaks in them, exposing the white
of the sticks. 38 He set the sticks that he had
peeled in front of the flocks in the troughs,
that is, the [x]watering places, where the flocks
came to drink. And since they bred when they
came to drink, 39 the flocks bred in front of the
sticks and so the flocks brought forth striped,
speckled, and spotted. 40 And Jacob separated
the lambs and set the faces of the flocks toward
the striped and all the black in the flock of
Laban. He put his own droves apart and did
not put them with Laban's flock. 41 Whenever
the stronger of the flock were breeding, Jacob

[1] *Issachar* sounds like the Hebrew for *wages*, or *hire* [2] *Zebulun* sounds like the Hebrew for *honor* [3] *Joseph* means *May he add*, and sounds like the Hebrew for *taken away* [4] Or *have become rich and*

30:25–31:24 More trickery and deceit abounds in the sordid account of Jacob's clever prosperity, sneaking away from Laban, being overtaken by Laban, and the two finally coming to terms with each other. Through an anxiety-riddled encounter with Laban in chapter 31 and another one with Esau in the next, Jacob continues to learn what it means to trust the Lord.

The key verse in Genesis 31 is Jacob's statement in verse 42: "If the God of my father, the God of Abraham and the Fear of Isaac, had not been on my side, surely now you would have sent me away empty-handed." Just the opposite, of course, has been the case—Jacob has magnificently prospered, to the point that his wealth has become a source of friction between him and Laban (31:1–3). Yet this is not because of Jacob's cleverness (there really is no scientific explanation for his herd's increase) but because of the Lord's providential goodness. In short, as the Lord himself told Jacob at the beginning of this chapter, "I will be with you." God was on Jacob's side. God was with Jacob. This, and no other reason, is the explanation for Jacob's continued prosperity despite his own sins and relational adversity. Rachel's theft of her father's household gods (31:19), whether as a claim upon his property (such idols were sometimes valuable in themselves or associated with land deeds) or as a superstitious hope, were not the cause of her family's deliverance (31:29, 42, 53).

20 [l][Matt. 4:13]
22 [m]See ch. 8:1 [n]ch. 29:31; [Ps. 127:3]
23 [o]Luke 1:25; [1 Sam. 1:6; Isa. 4:1]
24 [p]ch. 35:17
26 [q]ch. 29:20, 30
28 [r]ch. 29:15
29 [s]ch. 31:6, 38-40
30 [t]ver. 43 [u][1 Tim. 5:8]
32 [v]ch. 31:8
37 [w]See ch. 31:8-12
38 [x][Ex. 2:16]

would lay the sticks in the troughs before the eyes of the flock, that they might breed among the sticks, 42 but for the feebler of the flock he would not lay them there. So the feebler would be Laban's, and the stronger Jacob's. 43 Thus the man [y]increased greatly and [z]had large flocks, female servants and male servants, and camels and donkeys.

Jacob Flees from Laban

31 Now Jacob heard that the sons of Laban were saying, "Jacob has taken all that was our father's, and from what was our father's he has gained all this wealth." 2 And Jacob saw [a]that Laban did not regard him with favor as before. 3 Then the LORD said to Jacob, [b]"Return to the land of your fathers and to your kindred, and I will be with you."

4 So Jacob sent and called Rachel and Leah into the field where his flock was 5 and said to them, [c]"I see that your father does not regard me with favor as he did before. But the God of my father [d]has been with me. 6 [e]You know that I have served your father with all my strength, 7 yet your father has cheated me and changed my wages [f]ten times. But God did not permit him to harm me. 8 If he said, [g]'The spotted shall be your wages,' then all the flock bore spotted; and if he said, 'The striped shall be your wages,' then all the flock bore striped. 9 Thus God has [h]taken away the livestock of your father and given them to me. 10 In the breeding season of the flock I lifted up my eyes and saw in a dream that the goats that mated with the flock were striped, spotted, and mottled. 11 Then the angel of God said to me in the dream, 'Jacob,' and I said, 'Here I am!' 12 And he said, 'Lift up your eyes and see, all the goats that mate with the flock are striped, spotted, and mottled, for [i]I have seen all that Laban is doing to you. 13 I am the God of Bethel, [j]where you anointed a pillar and made a vow to me. Now [k]arise, go out from this land and return to the land of your kindred.'" 14 Then Rachel and Leah answered and said to him, "Is there [l]any portion or inheritance left to us in our father's house? 15 Are we not regarded by him as foreigners? For [m]he has sold us, and he has indeed devoured our money. 16 All the wealth that God has taken away from our father belongs to us and to our children. Now then, whatever God has said to you, do."

17 So Jacob arose and set his sons and his wives on camels. 18 He drove away all his livestock, all his property that he had gained, the livestock in his possession that he had acquired in [n]Paddan-aram, to go to the land of Canaan to his father Isaac. 19 Laban had gone to shear his sheep, and Rachel stole her father's [o]household gods. 20 And Jacob tricked[1] Laban the Aramean, by not telling him that he intended to flee. 21 He fled with all that he had and arose and crossed the [p]Euphrates,[2] and [q]set his face toward the hill country of Gilead.

22 When it was told Laban on the third day that Jacob had fled, 23 he took his kinsmen with him and pursued him for seven days and followed close after him into the hill country of Gilead. 24 But God came to Laban the Aramean [r]in a dream by night and said to him, "Be careful not to say anything to Jacob, [s]either good or bad."

25 And Laban overtook Jacob. Now Jacob had pitched his tent in the hill country, and Laban with his kinsmen pitched tents in the hill country of Gilead. 26 And Laban said to Jacob, "What have you done, that you have [t]tricked me and driven away my daughters like captives of the sword? 27 Why did you flee secretly [t]and trick me, and did not tell me, so that I might have sent you away with mirth and songs, with tambourine and lyre? 28 And why did you not permit me [u]to kiss my sons and my daughters

[1] Hebrew *stole the heart of*; also verses 26, 27 [2] Hebrew *the River*

43[y] ver. 30 [z] ch. 24:35; 26:13, 14
Chapter 31
2[a] ch. 4:5
3[b] ver. 13; ch. 28:15; 32:9
5[c] ver. 2 [d] ver. 3
6[e] ver. 38-40; ch. 30:29
7[f] ver. 41; [Num. 14:22; Neh. 4:12; Job 19:3; Zech. 8:23]
8[g] ch. 30:32
9[h] ver. 1
12[i] [Ex. 3:7]
13[j] See ch. 28:18-22 [k] ver. 3; ch. 32:9

As with Jacob, unless the God of such grace is with us and on our side, our hopes and future are empty. But this covenant-keeping God is with us through the ministry of the ultimate Son of Jacob, the Lord Jesus Christ. Indeed, we can know far more clearly and confidently that these things are true for believers today. For we see Jesus Christ, God come to earth as a man, to be with us, to take our punishment, and to dwell within us by his Spirit in order to restore us to God. God has come to be with us indeed—this is the doctrine of the incarnation. And God is now on our side—this is the doctrine of the atonement. Praise God. All has been taken care of not by our cleverness or strength but by the God of Jacob.

14[l] [2 Sam. 20:1; 1 Kgs. 12:16] **15**[m] ch. 30:26; See ch. 29:15-20, 27 **18**[n] ch. 25:20; 28:2, 6, 7 **19**[o] ver. 30, 34; [Judg. 17:5; 1 Sam. 15:23; 19:13; Ezek. 21:21; Hos. 3:4; Zech. 10:2] **21**[p] Ex. 23:31; Ps. 72:8 [q] 2 Kgs. 12:17; Luke 9:51 **24**[r] See ch. 20:3 [s] ch. 24:50; Num. 24:13; 2 Sam. 13:22 **26**[t] ver. 20 **27**[t] [See ver. 26 above] **28**[u] ver. 55; Ruth 1:9, 14; 1 Kgs. 19:20; Acts 20:37

farewell? Now you have done foolishly. 29 It is [v]in my power to do you harm. But the [w]God of your[1] father spoke to me last night, saying, 'Be careful not to say anything to Jacob, [x]either good or bad.' 30 And now you have gone away because you longed greatly for your father's house, but why did you [y]steal my gods?" 31 Jacob answered and said to Laban, "Because I was afraid, for I thought that you would take your daughters from me by force. 32 [z]Anyone with whom you find your gods shall not live. In the presence of our kinsmen point out what I have that is yours, and take it." Now Jacob did not know that Rachel had stolen them.

33 So Laban went into Jacob's tent and into Leah's tent and into the tent of the two female servants, but he did not find them. And he went out of Leah's tent and entered Rachel's. 34 Now Rachel had taken the household gods and put them in the camel's saddle and sat on them. Laban felt all about the tent, but did not find them. 35 And she said to her father, "Let not my lord be angry that I cannot [a]rise before you, for the way of women is upon me." So he searched but did not find the household gods.

36 Then Jacob became angry and berated Laban. Jacob said to Laban, "What is my offense? What is my sin, that you have hotly pursued me? 37 For you have felt through all my goods; what have you found of all your household goods? Set it here before my kinsmen and [b]your kinsmen, that they may decide between us two. 38 These twenty years I have been with you. Your ewes and your female goats have not miscarried, and I have not eaten the rams of your flocks. 39 What was torn by wild beasts I did not bring to you. I bore the loss of it myself. [c]From my hand you required it, whether stolen by day or stolen by night. 40 There I was: by day the heat consumed me, and the cold by night, and my sleep fled from my eyes. 41 These twenty years I have been in your house. [d]I served you fourteen years for your two daughters, and six years for your flock, and [e]you have changed my wages ten times. 42 [f]If the God of my father, the God of Abraham and the [g]Fear of Isaac, had not been on my side, surely now you would have sent me away empty-handed. [h]God saw my affliction and the labor of my hands and [i]rebuked you last night."

43 Then Laban answered and said to Jacob, "The daughters are my daughters, the children are my children, the flocks are my flocks, and all that you see is mine. But what can I do this day for these my daughters or for their children whom they have borne? 44 Come now, [j]let us make a covenant, you and I. [k]And let it be a witness between you and me." 45 So Jacob [l]took a stone and set it up as a pillar. 46 And Jacob said to his kinsmen, "Gather stones." And they took stones and made a heap, and they ate there by the heap. 47 Laban called it Jegar-sahadutha,[2] but Jacob called it Galeed.[3] 48 Laban said, [m]"This heap is a witness between you and me today." Therefore he named it Galeed, 49 [n]and Mizpah,[4] for he said, "The LORD watch between you and me, when we are out of one another's sight. 50 If you oppress my daughters, or if you take wives besides my daughters, although no one is with us, see, [o]God is witness between you and me."

51 Then Laban said to Jacob, "See this heap and the pillar, which I have set between you and me. 52 [p]This heap is a witness, and the pillar is a witness, that I will not pass over this heap to you, and you will not pass over this heap and this pillar to me, to do harm. 53 The God of Abraham and the God of Nahor, the God of their father, judge between us." So Jacob swore by the [q]Fear of his father Isaac, 54 and Jacob offered a sacrifice in the hill country and called [r]his kinsmen to eat bread. They ate bread and spent the night in the hill country.

55 [5] Early in the morning Laban arose and kissed [s]his grandchildren and his daughters and blessed them. Then Laban departed and returned home.

Jacob Fears Esau

32 Jacob went on his way, and the angels of God met him. 2 And when Jacob saw them he said, "This is God's [t]camp!" So he called the name of that place [u]Mahanaim.[6]

[1] The Hebrew for *your* is plural here [2] Aramaic *the heap of witness* [3] Hebrew *the heap of witness* [4] *Mizpah* means *watchpost* [5] Ch 32:1 in Hebrew [6] *Mahanaim* means *two camps*

32:1–33:20 For the second time in Genesis we hear of "the angels of God" (32:1)—and once more they are seen by Jacob and become a source of encouragement that God is with him (32:2). This is important, for Jacob is on the doorstep of the greatest trial

29 [v]Deut. 28:32; Neh. 5:5 (Heb.); Prov. 3:27; Mic. 2:1 [w]ver. 42, 53; ch. 28:13 [x]ver. 24

30 [y]ver. 19; Judg. 18:24 **32** [z][ch. 44:9] **35** [a][Lev. 19:32] **37** [b]ver. 54 **39** [c][Ex. 22:12] **41** [d]ch. 29:27, 28 [e]ver. 7 **42** [f]Ps. 124:1, 2 [g]ver. 53 [h]See ch. 29:32 [i]ver. 29 **44** [j]ch. 26:28 [k]Josh. 24:27 **45** [l]ch. 28:18 **48** [m]ver. 44 **49** [n]Judg. 11:29, 34 **50** [o]Judg. 11:10; 1 Sam. 12:5; Jer. 42:5; Mic. 1:2; [Job 16:19] **52** [p]ver. 43, 44 **53** [q]ver. 42 **54** [r]ver. 37 **55** [s]ver. 28, 43 **Chapter 32** **2** [t][Josh. 5:14; Luke 2:13] [u]Josh. 21:38; 2 Sam. 2:8; 17:24, 27; 1 Kgs. 2:8

3 And Jacob sent[1] messengers before him to
Esau his brother in the land of [v]Seir, the country of Edom, 4 instructing them, "Thus you
shall say to my lord Esau: Thus says your servant Jacob, 'I have sojourned with Laban and
stayed until now. 5 I have oxen, donkeys, flocks,
male servants, and female servants. I have sent
to tell my lord, in order that [w]I may find favor
in your sight.'"
6 And the messengers returned to Jacob,
saying, "We came to your brother Esau, and
[x]he is coming to meet you, and there are four
hundred men with him." 7 Then Jacob was
[y]greatly afraid and distressed. He divided the
people who were with him, and the flocks and
herds and camels, into two camps, 8 thinking,
"If Esau comes to the one camp and attacks it,
then the camp that is left will escape."
9 And Jacob said, [z]"O God of my father
Abraham and God of my father Isaac, O LORD
who [a]said to me, 'Return to your country and
to your kindred, that I may do you good,' 10 [b]I
am not worthy of the least of all the deeds
of steadfast love and all the faithfulness that
you have shown to your servant, for with only
my staff I crossed this Jordan, and now I have
become two camps. 11 Please deliver me from
the hand of my brother, from the hand of
Esau, for [c]I fear him, that he may come and
attack me, the mothers with the children.
12 But [d]you said, 'I will surely do you good, and
make your offspring as the sand of the sea,
which cannot be numbered for multitude.'"
13 So he stayed there that night, and from
what he had with him he took [e]a present
for his brother Esau, 14 two hundred female
goats and twenty male goats, two hundred
ewes and twenty rams, 15 thirty milking camels and their calves, forty cows and ten bulls,
twenty female donkeys and ten male donkeys.
16 These he handed over to his servants, every
drove by itself, and said to his servants, "Pass
on ahead of me and put a space between drove
and drove." 17 He instructed the first, "When
Esau my brother meets you and asks you, 'To
whom do you belong? Where are you going?
And whose are these ahead of you?' 18 then you
shall say, 'They belong to your servant Jacob.
They are a present sent to my lord Esau. And
moreover, he is behind us.'" 19 He likewise
instructed the second and the third and all
who followed the droves, "You shall say the
same thing to Esau when you find him, 20 and
you shall say, 'Moreover, your servant Jacob is
behind us.'" For he thought, "I may appease
him[2] with the present that goes ahead of me,
and afterward I shall see his face. Perhaps he
will accept me."[3] 21 So the present passed on
ahead of him, and he himself stayed that night
in the camp.

[1] Or *had sent* [2] Hebrew *appease his face* [3] Hebrew *he will lift my face*

3 [v] ch. 36:8, 9; Deut. 2:5; Josh. 24:4
5 [w] ch. 33:8, 15
6 [x] ch. 33:1
7 [y] ch. 35:3
9 [z] ch. 28:13; 31:42, 53 [a] ch. 31:3, 13
10 [b] [2 Sam. 7:18]
11 [c] [Prov. 18:19]
12 [d] ch. 28:13-15
13 [e] ch. 43:11; [Prov. 17:8; 18:16; 19:6; 21:14]

of his life. He is about to meet his estranged brother Esau, who has every right to hate his younger, swindling brother. The situation is truly dire: Jacob has an angry brother ahead of him, an angry father-in-law behind him, and all his family and accumulated wealth at stake. His conniving has cornered him into imminent disaster. He has no hope except divine deliverance, but that does not stop him from trying once again to make his own cleverness his salvation.

Throughout this account we are given glimpses into what is truly driving Jacob. Sending messengers and gifts ahead to Esau, Jacob says that he is doing this "in order that I may find favor [or "grace"] in your sight" (32:5). Later on we are given another window into Jacob's mind as he sends these lavish gifts on ahead: "For he thought, 'I may appease him with the present that goes ahead of me. . . . Perhaps he will accept me'" (32:20). Jacob is desperate to appease the brother whose birthright he stole by trickery, but he knows the effort has little chance of success.

In the tense anxiety of that night of waiting for Esau's response, Jacob wrestles with God—the One whose help he should have sought long before. The man of physical prowess, Jacob, is made weak through the wrestling—a match that ends with God ironically declaring that Jacob has "prevailed" (32:28), despite showing his divine power by crippling Jacob with a touch (32:25, 31). Thus, we understand that Jacob prevailed not by strength but by declaring his dependence upon the blessing of God (32:26)—a vital lesson in grace. So, despite "prevailing," Jacob lives the rest of his life with a limp (32:31)—another lesson in what it means to be a conduit of God's grace. Later, when he meets Esau, Jacob and his family are too weak to keep up with him (33:12–14). This new weakness is a strange, upside-down blessing to a man of great strength, but it is precisely this that is the answer to Jacob's insistence

Jacob Wrestles with God

22 The same night he arose and took his two
wives, his two female servants, and his eleven
children,[1] and crossed the ford of the [f]Jabbok.
23 He took them and sent them across the
stream, and everything else that he had. 24 And
Jacob was left alone. And [g]a man wrestled with
him until the breaking of the day. 25 When
the man saw that he did not prevail against
Jacob, he touched his hip socket, and Jacob's
hip was put out of joint as he wrestled with
him. 26 Then he said, "Let me go, for the day
has broken." But Jacob said, [h]"I will not let you
go unless you bless me." 27 And he said to him,
"What is your name?" And he said, "Jacob."
28 Then he said, [i]"Your name shall no longer be
called Jacob, but Israel,[2] for [j]you have striven
with God and [k]with men, and have prevailed."
29 Then Jacob asked him, "Please tell me your
name." But he said, [l]"Why is it that you ask my
name?" And there he blessed him. 30 So Jacob
called the name of the place Peniel,[3] saying,
"For [m]I have seen God face to face, and yet my
life has been delivered." 31 The sun rose upon
him as he passed [n]Penuel, limping because of
his hip. 32 Therefore to this day the people of
Israel do not eat the sinew of the thigh that
is on the hip socket, because he touched the
socket of Jacob's hip on the sinew of the thigh.

Jacob Meets Esau

33 And Jacob lifted up his eyes and looked,
and behold, [o]Esau was coming, and
four hundred men with him. So he divided
the children among Leah and Rachel and the
two female servants. 2 And he put the servants
with their children in front, then Leah with
her children, and Rachel and Joseph last of all.
3 He himself went on before them, [p]bowing
himself to the ground seven times, until he
came near to his brother.
4 [q]But Esau ran to meet him and embraced
him [r]and fell on his neck and kissed him, and
they wept. 5 And when Esau lifted up his eyes
and saw the women and children, he said,
"Who are these with you?" Jacob said, [s]"The
children whom God has graciously given your
servant." 6 Then the servants drew near, they
and their children, and bowed down. 7 Leah
likewise and her children drew near and
bowed down. And last Joseph and Rachel drew
near, and they bowed down. 8 Esau said, "What
do you mean by [t]all this company[4] that I met?"
Jacob answered, [u]"To find favor in the sight

[1] Or *sons* [2] *Israel* means *He strives with God*, or *God strives* [3] *Peniel* means *the face of God* [4] Hebrew *camp*

that he be blessed. Down through history, it has been God's strange and beautiful pattern to pour out his grace through weakness in order to comfort his people in adversity and affliction (2 Cor. 1:3–5).

In Genesis 32:20 Jacob had expressed a hope that he would appease Esau, and the text literally reads "appease his face." Jacob then reiterates a hope that Esau would "accept me"—again, literally, "lift my face." In wrestling with God, however, Jacob is brought to see that it is not the face of Esau with which he is to be most concerned, but the face of God. This is precisely the significance Jacob himself attaches to his wrestling match, calling the place "Peniel," which means "face of God," and saying "For I have seen God face to face, and yet my life has been delivered" (32:30). *This* was the approval Jacob most truly needed. *This* was the vertical acceptance which, once granted, renders all horizontal, human acceptance so much less important.

The next day, then, when Jacob does finally meet Esau, he can do so without the profound existential anxiety that had made him the deceiver he had been all his life. He had seen God's face and had been delivered. Nothing could really hurt him now. Perhaps this is why Jacob "himself went on before [his wives and children]" (33:3). His own welfare and acceptance was no longer uppermost in his mind. His own identity had been settled. Strong in body and weak in soul before wrestling with God, Jacob was now weak in body and strong in soul. When Jacob meets Esau, Jacob insists that Esau keep the gifts, "because God has dealt graciously with me" (33:11).

All human beings know the desire buried deep within them to be accepted, approved, welcomed in. We desire this in our relationships with other humans, but most deeply we desire this with God. The glory of the gospel is that we need not make ourselves acceptable to God in order to be welcomed in. Jesus Christ, in his life, death, and resurrection, has secured all that we need to be restored to God. In Jesus we can say, with Jacob, "I have seen God face to face, and yet my life has been delivered" (32:30).

22 [f] Deut. 2:37; 3:16; Josh. 12:2
24 [g] Hos. 12:3, 4
26 [h] [Luke 18:1]; See Matt. 15:21-28
28 [i] ch. 35:10; 2 Kgs. 17:34 [j] Hos. 12:3, 4 [k] ch. 33:4
29 [l] Judg. 13:18
30 [m] ch. 16:13; Ex. 24:10, 11; Deut. 5:24; Judg. 6:22; 13:22; [Ex. 33:20; Isa. 6:5]
31 [n] Judg. 8:8, 17; 1 Kgs. 12:25
Chapter 33
1 [o] ch. 32:6
3 [p] ch. 18:2; 42:6; 43:26
4 [q] ch. 32:28 [r] ch. 45:14
5 [s] ch. 48:9; Ps. 127:3; Isa. 8:18
8 [t] ch. 32:16 [u] ver. 15; ch. 32:5

of my lord." 9 But Esau said, "I have enough, my brother; keep what you have for yourself." 10 Jacob said, "No, please, if I have found favor in your sight, then accept my present from my hand. [v]For I have seen your face, which is like seeing the face of God, and you have accepted me. 11 Please accept my [w]blessing that is brought to you, because God has dealt graciously with me, and because I have enough." Thus he [x]urged him, and he took it.

12 Then Esau said, "Let us journey on our way, and I will go ahead of[1] you." 13 But Jacob said to him, "My lord knows that the children are frail, and that the nursing flocks and herds are a care to me. If they are driven hard for one day, all the flocks will die. 14 Let my lord pass on ahead of his servant, and I will lead on slowly, at the pace of the livestock that are ahead of me and at the pace of the children, until I come to my lord [y]in Seir."

15 So Esau said, "Let me leave with you some of the people who are with me." But he said, "What need is there? [z]Let me find favor in the sight of my lord." 16 So Esau returned that day on his way to [a]Seir. 17 But Jacob journeyed to [b]Succoth, and built himself a house and made booths for his livestock. Therefore the name of the place is called Succoth.[2]

18 And Jacob came safely[3] to the city of [c]Shechem, which is in the land of Canaan, on his way from Paddan-aram, and he camped before the city. 19 And from the sons of [d]Hamor, Shechem's father, [e]he bought for a hundred pieces of money[4] the piece of land on which he had pitched his tent. 20 There he erected an altar and called it El-Elohe-Israel.[5]

The Defiling of Dinah

34 Now [f]Dinah the daughter of Leah, whom she had borne to Jacob, went out to see the women of the land. 2 And when Shechem the son of [g]Hamor the Hivite, the prince of the land, saw her, he seized her and lay with her and humiliated her. 3 And his soul was drawn to Dinah the daughter of Jacob. He loved the young woman and spoke tenderly to her. 4 So Shechem [h]spoke to his father Hamor, saying, "Get me this girl for my wife."

5 Now Jacob heard that he had defiled his daughter Dinah. But his sons were with his livestock in the field, so Jacob held his peace until they came. 6 And Hamor the father of Shechem went out to Jacob to speak with him. 7 The sons of Jacob had come in from the field as soon as they heard of it, and the men were indignant and [i]very angry, because he [j]had done an outrageous thing in Israel by lying with Jacob's daughter, [k]for such a thing must not be done.

8 But Hamor spoke with them, saying, "The soul of my son Shechem longs for your[6] daughter. Please give her to him to be his wife. 9 Make marriages with us. Give your daughters to us, and take our daughters for yourselves. 10 You shall dwell with us, and [l]the land shall be open to you. Dwell and [m]trade in it, and [n]get property in it." 11 Shechem also said to her father and to her brothers, [o]"Let me find favor in your eyes, and whatever you say to me I will give. 12 Ask me for as great a [p]bride price[7] and gift as you will, and I will give whatever you say to me. Only give me the young woman to be my wife."

[1] Or *along with* [2] *Succoth* means *booths* [3] Or *peacefully* [4] Hebrew *a hundred qesitah*; a unit of money of unknown value [5] *El-Elohe-Israel* means *God, the God of Israel* [6] The Hebrew for *your* is plural here [7] Or *engagement present*

10[v] ch. 18:1; 19:1
11[w] 2 Kgs. 5:15 [x] [2 Sam. 13:25, 27; 2 Kgs. 5:23]
14[y] ch. 32:3
15[z] ver. 8; ch. 34:11; 47:25; Ruth 2:13
16[a] ch. 32:3
17[b] Josh. 13:27; Judg. 8:5; Ps. 60:6
18[c] Josh. 24:1; Judg. 9:1; Ps. 60:6; Acts 7:16
19[d] Acts 7:16 [e] Josh. 24:32; John 4:5
Chapter 34
1[f] ch. 30:21
2[g] Acts 7:16
4[h] [Judg. 14:2]
7[i] ch. 49:7 [j] Josh. 7:15; Judg. 20:6 [k] ver. 31; ch. 20:9; 2 Sam. 13:12
10[l] ch. 13:9; 20:15 [m] ver. 21; ch. 42:34 [n] ch. 47:27
11[o] See ch. 33:15 **12**[p] Ex. 22:16, 17; 1 Sam. 18:25; [Deut. 22:29]

34:1–31 God had come through marvelously for Jacob—restoring his relationship to his estranged brother and restoring him to the land of Canaan (33:18–20). But as soon as he found himself settling in, disaster hit. Jacob's daughter Dinah was raped by Shechem, a Canaanite whose father (Hamor) had sold this piece of land to Jacob. Simeon and Levi, with a punishment that far exceeded the crime, killed all the males of Shechem—and they did so by utilizing the repeated family sin of deceitfulness (34:13).

What is at stake in this account is nothing less than the covenant promise of God. Jacob tells his rash sons that if the surrounding peoples unite against Jacob, he and all his family will be wiped out. Even if Jacob survives, the land he has just bought from Shechem is certainly at risk in light of Simeon and Levi's rashness. The promise of descendants as numerous as the sand, then, and also the promise of the land of Canaan are both suddenly precariously endangered.

Jacob was the appeaser; he simply wanted no trouble. His passivity throughout Genesis 34 is in stark contrast to his sons' unchecked fury, who forcefully and mur-

13 The sons of Jacob answered Shechem and his father Hamor deceitfully, because he had defiled their sister Dinah. 14 They said to them, "We cannot do this thing, to give our sister to one who is uncircumcised, for [q]that would be a disgrace to us. 15 Only on this condition will we agree with you—that you will become as we are by every male among you being circumcised. 16 Then we will give our daughters to you, and we will take your daughters to ourselves, and we will dwell with you and become one people. 17 But if you will not listen to us and be circumcised, then we will take our daughter, and we will be gone."

18 Their words pleased Hamor and Hamor's son Shechem. 19 And the young man did not delay to do the thing, because he delighted in Jacob's daughter. Now [r]he was the most honored of all his father's house. 20 So Hamor and his son Shechem [s]came to the gate of their city and spoke to the men of their city, saying, 21 "These men are at peace with us; let them dwell in the land and [t]trade in it, for behold, the land is large enough for them. Let us take their daughters as wives, and let us give them our daughters. 22 Only on this condition will the men agree to dwell with us to become one people—when every male among us is circumcised as they are circumcised. 23 Will not their livestock, their property and all their beasts be ours? Only let us agree with them, and they will dwell with us." 24 And all who went out of the gate of his city listened to Hamor and his son Shechem, and every male was circumcised, all who [u]went out of the gate of his city.

25 On the third day, when they were sore, two of the sons of Jacob, [v]Simeon and Levi, [w]Dinah's brothers, took their swords and came against the city while it felt secure and killed all the males. 26 They killed Hamor and his son Shechem with the sword and took Dinah out of Shechem's house and went away. 27 The sons of Jacob came upon the slain and plundered the city, because they had defiled their sister. 28 They took their flocks and their herds, their donkeys, and whatever was in the city and in the field. 29 All their wealth, all their little ones and their wives, all that was in the houses, they captured and plundered.

30 Then Jacob said to Simeon and Levi, [x]"You have brought trouble on me [y]by making me stink to the inhabitants of the land, [z]the Canaanites and the Perizzites. [a]My numbers are few, and if they gather themselves against me and attack me, I shall be destroyed, both I and my household." 31 But they said, "Should he treat our sister like a prostitute?"

God Blesses and Renames Jacob

35 God said to Jacob, "Arise, go up to [b]Bethel and dwell there. Make an altar there to the God who appeared to you [c]when you fled from your brother Esau." 2 So Jacob said to his [d]household and to all who were with him, "Put away [e]the foreign gods that are

derously avenged their sister. Neither course of action is a gospel way of living. The gospel grants courage to those of us tempted to appease through passivity, for if God has been appeased through Jesus, we need not be concerned with appeasing others. Yet the gospel also grants calm sanity to our outbursts of anger, for God's own righteous anger and fury toward us has been calmed in the cross of Christ. The gospel deflates both our desire to appease and our need to avenge. Neither Jacob's nor his sons' way is the ultimate means of their covenant preservation. We see in the next chapter (35:5) that God himself intervenes to protect his covenant promise and people—as is ever the case.

35:1–15 God tells Jacob to return to the crucial location of Bethel, "House of God," where Jacob had seen the angels of God ascending and descending. This was sacred ground for Jacob, and God protects him on the journey to this place of promise (v. 5). Here the Lord confirms to Jacob the lavish covenant promises that have been traveling down through the patriarchs, all by God's free grace. Jacob will inherit the land, and he will have many descendants—indeed, "nations" and "kings" shall come from Jacob. We also hear a striking reiteration of the mandate of 1:28 to "be fruitful and multiply" (35:11). Through Jacob and his family, then, God is continuing to restore the world and carry out his original mandate for his people to spread throughout the earth and rule over it. In reiterating the name change from Jacob to Israel (v. 10; cf. 32:28), God underscores the radical change in Jacob's identity that has taken place as he limps along—dependent upon God's strength—to Bethel.

14 [q]Josh. 5:9
19 [r][1 Chr. 4:9]
20 [s]See Ruth 4:1
21 [t]ver. 10; ch. 42:34
24 [u][ch. 23:10]
25 [v]See ch. 49:5-7 [w]ch. 29:33, 34; 30:21
30 [x]Josh. 7:25 [y]Ex. 5:21; 1 Sam. 13:4; 27:12; 2 Sam. 10:6; 16:21; 1 Chr. 19:6 (Heb.) [z]ch. 13:7; 15:20, 21 [a]1 Chr. 16:19; Ps. 105:12

Chapter 35
1 [b]ch. 28:19 [c]ch. 27:43
2 [d]ch. 18:19; Josh. 24:15 [e][ch. 31:19; Josh. 24:23; 1 Sam. 7:3]

among you and [f]purify yourselves and change your garments. 3 Then let us arise and go up to Bethel, so that I may make there an altar to the God [g]who answers me in the day of my distress and [h]has been with me wherever I have gone." 4 So they gave to Jacob all the foreign gods that they had, and the rings that were in their ears. Jacob hid them under [i]the terebinth tree that was near Shechem.

5 And as they journeyed, a terror from God fell upon the cities that were around them, so that they did not pursue the sons of Jacob. 6 And Jacob came to [j]Luz (that is, Bethel), which is in the land of Canaan, he and all the people who were with him, 7 and there he built an altar and called the place El-bethel,[1] because [k]there God had revealed himself to him when he fled from his brother. 8 And [l]Deborah, Rebekah's nurse, died, and she was buried under an oak below Bethel. So he called its name Allon-bacuth.[2]

9 God appeared[3] to Jacob again, when he came from Paddan-aram, and blessed him. 10 And God said to him, "Your name is Jacob; [m]no longer shall your name be called Jacob, but [n]Israel shall be your name." So he called his name Israel. 11 And God said to him, [o]"I am God Almighty:[4] be [p]fruitful and multiply. [q]A nation and a company of nations shall come from you, and kings shall come from your own body.[5] 12 [r]The land that I gave to Abraham and Isaac I will give to you, and I will give the land to your offspring after you." 13 Then God [s]went up from him in the place where he had spoken with him. 14 And Jacob [t]set up a pillar in the place where he had spoken with him, a pillar of stone. He poured out a drink offering on it and poured oil on it. 15 So Jacob called the name of the place where God had spoken with him [u]Bethel.

The Deaths of Rachel and Isaac

16 Then they journeyed from Bethel. When they were still some distance[6] from Ephrath, Rachel went into labor, and she had hard labor. 17 And when her labor was at its hardest, the midwife said to her, "Do not fear, for [v]you have another son." 18 And as her soul was departing (for she was dying), she called his name Ben-oni;[7] [w]but his father called him Benjamin.[8] 19 So [x]Rachel died, and she was buried on the way to [y]Ephrath (that is, Bethlehem), 20 and Jacob set up a pillar over her tomb. It is [z]the pillar of Rachel's tomb, which is there to this day. 21 Israel journeyed on and pitched his tent beyond the tower of Eder.

[1] *El-bethel* means *God of Bethel* [2] *Allon-bacuth* means *oak of weeping* [3] Or *had appeared* [4] Hebrew *El Shaddai* [5] Hebrew *from your loins* [6] Or *about two hours' distance* [7] *Ben-oni* could mean *son of my sorrow*, or *son of my strength* [8] *Benjamin* means *son of the right hand*

2[f] Ex. 19:10
3[g] ch. 32:7, 24 [h] ch. 28:20; 31:3
4[i] Josh. 24:26; Judg. 9:6
6[j] ch. 28:19
7[k] ver. 1
8[l] ch. 24:59
10[m] [ch. 17:5, 15] [n] ch. 32:28
11[o] See ch. 17:1 [p] ch. 28:3; 48:4 [q] ch. 17:5, 6, 16; 26:4
12[r] ch. 12:7; 13:15; 17:8; 26:3; 28:13
13[s] ch. 17:22
14[t] ch. 28:18; 31:45
15[u] ch. 28:19
17[v] ch. 30:24
18[w] [Luke 1:59, 60]
19[x] ch. 48:7 [y] Ruth 1:2; 4:11; Mic. 5:2; Matt. 2:6, 16-18
20[z] 1 Sam. 10:2; [2 Sam. 18:18]

35:16–29 The fresh reiteration of the covenant promises is surrounded by two deaths. Rebekah's nurse from Paddan-aram passes away (v. 8) and Rachel dies in childbirth (vv. 16–21).

The reality of death is a stark reminder of the preciousness of God's promises that speak of a new creation filled with God's blessing. We look forward to such, much as the ancient Jews looked forward to the blessings of God's Promised Land. The change in name from *Ben-oni* ("son of my sorrow") to Benjamin (*Ben-yamini*, "son of my right hand") similarly symbolizes the transformation from the old to the new. Benjamin is the only son born to Jacob in Canaan.

The reiteration of covenant promise is also wedged in between two horrendous acts: Simeon and Levi arranged the murder of the men at Shechem to avenge the rape of their sister Dinah (34:5–29); and, Reuben, Jacob's firstborn and son of Leah, had sexual relations with his father's concubine (Bilhah; 35:22). From the beginning to the end of Genesis, the reality of sin is never blunted but is regularly placed in contrasting juxtaposition with the hope of God's promise. The listing of Jacob's 12 sons also gives hope (vv. 22b–26) but is followed by a contrasting notice of the death and burial of Isaac (vv. 27–29).

Life and death is thus a major theme in Genesis. God gave life, and Adam and Eve chose death. Throughout Genesis the reality of death is painfully hammered home again and again. Only in Jesus Christ is the awful and unavoidable reality of death defanged. For Christ is himself "the Author of life" (Acts 3:15) who conquered death with his bodily resurrection on the third day (1 Cor. 15:3–4). All who are united to him, by faith, likewise share in both his death and his resurrection (Rom. 6:3–5; Eph. 2:6; Col. 3:1).

22 While Israel lived in that land, Reuben
went and [a]lay with Bilhah his father's concubine. And Israel heard of it.

Now the sons of Jacob were twelve. 23 The
sons of Leah: [b]Reuben (Jacob's firstborn),
Simeon, Levi, Judah, Issachar, and Zebulun.
24 The sons of Rachel: Joseph and Benjamin.
25 The sons of Bilhah, Rachel's servant: Dan
and Naphtali. 26 The sons of Zilpah, Leah's servant: Gad and Asher. These were the sons of
Jacob who were born to him in Paddan-aram.

27 And Jacob came to his father Isaac at
[c]Mamre, or [d]Kiriath-arba (that is, Hebron),
where Abraham and Isaac had sojourned.
28 Now the days of Isaac were 180 years. 29 And
Isaac breathed his last, and he died [e]and was
gathered to his people, old and full of days.
And [f]his sons Esau and Jacob buried him.

Esau's Descendants

36 These are the generations of Esau (that
is, [g]Edom). 2 Esau [h]took his wives from
the Canaanites: Adah the daughter of Elon the
Hittite, [i]Oholibamah the daughter of Anah
the daughter[1] of Zibeon the Hivite, 3 and
[j]Basemath, Ishmael's daughter, the sister of
Nebaioth. 4 And Adah bore to Esau, [k]Eliphaz;
Basemath bore Reuel; 5 and Oholibamah bore
Jeush, Jalam, and Korah. These are the sons
of Esau who were born to him in the land of
Canaan.

6 Then Esau took his wives, his sons, his
daughters, and all the members of his household, his livestock, all his beasts, and all his
property that he had acquired in the land of
Canaan. He went into a land away from his
brother Jacob. 7 [l]For their possessions were too
great for them to dwell together. [m]The land
of their sojournings could not support them
because of their livestock. 8 So Esau settled in
[n]the hill country of Seir. ([o]Esau is Edom.)

9 These are the generations of Esau the father
of [p]the Edomites in the hill country of Seir.
10 These are the names of Esau's sons: [q]Eliphaz
the son of Adah the wife of Esau, Reuel the
son of Basemath the wife of Esau. 11 The
sons of Eliphaz were Teman, Omar, Zepho,
Gatam, and Kenaz. 12 (Timna was a concubine
of Eliphaz, Esau's son; she bore [r]Amalek to
Eliphaz.) These are the sons of Adah, Esau's
wife. 13 These are the sons of Reuel: Nahath,
Zerah, Shammah, and Mizzah. These are the
sons of Basemath, Esau's wife. 14 These are the
sons of [s]Oholibamah the daughter of Anah
the daughter of Zibeon, Esau's wife: she bore
to Esau Jeush, Jalam, and Korah.

15 These are [t]the chiefs of the sons of
Esau. [u]The sons of Eliphaz the firstborn of
Esau: the chiefs Teman, Omar, Zepho, Kenaz,
16 Korah, Gatam, and Amalek; these are the
chiefs of Eliphaz in the land of Edom; these
are the sons of Adah. 17 These are the sons of
[v]Reuel, Esau's son: the chiefs Nahath, Zerah,
Shammah, and Mizzah; these are the chiefs
of Reuel in the land of Edom; these are the
sons of Basemath, Esau's wife. 18 These are the
sons of [w]Oholibamah, Esau's wife: the chiefs
Jeush, Jalam, and Korah; these are the chiefs
born of Oholibamah the daughter of Anah,
Esau's wife. 19 These are the sons of Esau ([x]that
is, Edom), and these are their chiefs.

20 [y]These are the sons of [z]Seir the Horite,
the inhabitants of the land: Lotan, Shobal,
Zibeon, Anah, 21 Dishon, Ezer, and Dishan;
these are the chiefs of the Horites, the sons
of Seir in the land of Edom. 22 The sons of
Lotan were Hori and Hemam; and Lotan's
sister was Timna. 23 These are the sons of
Shobal: Alvan, Manahath, Ebal, Shepho, and
Onam. 24 These are the sons of Zibeon: Aiah
and Anah; he is the Anah who found the hot
springs in the wilderness, as he pastured the
donkeys of Zibeon his father. 25 These are the
children of Anah: Dishon and [a]Oholibamah

[1] Hebrew; Samaritan, Septuagint, Syriac *son*; also verse 14

36:1–43 The "two-sons" theme of Genesis (Cain and Abel; Ishmael and Isaac; Jacob and Esau; etc.), marking out separate human destinies, continues here. Esau's family is outlined in detail, beginning with the wives he took from the Canaanites (v. 2)—something the patriarchs throughout Genesis have been adamant about avoiding (e.g., 24:2–4). Esau's tragic rejection by God is not the final word in Genesis, however. Before moving on to recount the life of Joseph as the final part of this book, chapter 36 recounts in great detail the many descendants of Esau. Even as an outsider to the privileged covenant promises of God, Esau has been granted life and family (cf. Ishmael in 17:20).

22[a] ch. 49:4; 1 Chr. 5:1; [2 Sam. 16:22; 20:3; 1 Cor. 5:1]
23[b] For ver. 23-26, see ch. 46:8-27; Ex. 1:2-4
27[c] ch. 13:18; 23:19 [d] ch. 23:2; Josh. 14:15; 15:13
29[e] ch. 15:15; 25:8 [f] ch. 25:9; 49:31

Chapter 36
1[g] ch. 25:30
2[h] ch. 26:34 [i] ver. 14, 18, 25
3[j] [ch. 28:9]
4[k] ver. 10; 1 Chr. 1:35

7[l] ch. 13:6 [m] ch. 17:8; 23:4; 28:4; 37:1; Heb. 11:9 **8**[n] See ch. 32:3 [o] ver. 1, 19 **9**[p] ver. 43 **10**[q] ver. 4 **12**[r] Num. 24:20; 1 Sam. 15:2, 3 **14**[s] ver. 2 **15**[t] Ex. 15:15 [u] ver. 11, 12 **17**[v] ver. 13 **18**[w] ver. 14 **19**[x] ver. 1, 8 **20**[y] For ver. 20-28, see 1 Chr. 1:38-42 [z] ch. 14:6; Deut. 2:12, 22 **25**[a] ver. 2

the daughter of Anah. 26 These are the sons of Dishon: Hemdan, Eshban, Ithran, and Cheran. 27 These are the sons of Ezer: Bilhan, Zaavan, and Akan. 28 These are the sons of Dishan: Uz and Aran. 29 These are the chiefs of the Horites: the [b]chiefs Lotan, Shobal, Zibeon, Anah, 30 Dishon, Ezer, and Dishan; these are the chiefs of the Horites, chief by chief in the land of Seir.

31 [c]These are the kings who reigned in the land of Edom, before any king reigned over the Israelites. 32 Bela the son of Beor reigned in Edom, the name of his city being Dinhabah. 33 Bela died, and Jobab the son of Zerah of Bozrah reigned in his place. 34 Jobab died, and Husham of the land of the Temanites reigned in his place. 35 Husham died, and Hadad the son of Bedad, who defeated Midian in the country of Moab, reigned in his place, the name of his city being Avith. 36 Hadad died, and Samlah of Masrekah reigned in his place. 37 Samlah died, and Shaul of [d]Rehoboth on the Euphrates[1] reigned in his place. 38 Shaul died, and Baal-hanan the son of Achbor reigned in his place. 39 Baal-hanan the son of Achbor died, and Hadar reigned in his place, the name of his city being Pau; his wife's name was Mehetabel, the daughter of Matred, daughter of Mezahab.

40 These are the names of the chiefs of Esau, according to their clans and their dwelling places, by their names: the chiefs Timna, Alvah, Jetheth, 41 Oholibamah, Elah, [e]Pinon, 42 Kenaz, Teman, Mibzar, 43 Magdiel, and Iram; these are the chiefs of Edom (that is, Esau, the father of [f]Edom), according to their dwelling places in the land of their possession.

Joseph's Dreams

37 Jacob lived in [g]the land of his father's sojournings, in the land of Canaan.

2 These are the generations of Jacob.

Joseph, being seventeen years old, was pasturing the flock with his brothers. He was a boy with the sons of Bilhah and Zilpah, his father's wives. And Joseph brought [h]a bad report of them to their father. 3 Now Israel loved Joseph more than any other of his sons, because he was [i]the son of his old age. And he made him [j]a robe of many colors.[2] 4 But when his brothers saw that their father loved him more than all his brothers, they hated him and could not speak peacefully to him.

5 Now Joseph had a dream, and when he told it to his brothers they hated him even more. 6 He said to them, "Hear this dream that I have dreamed: 7 Behold, we were binding sheaves in the field, and behold, [k]my sheaf arose and stood upright. And behold, your sheaves gathered around it and [l]bowed down to my sheaf." 8 His brothers said to him, "Are you indeed to reign over us? Or are you indeed to rule over us?" So they hated him even more for his dreams and for his words.

9 Then he dreamed another dream and told it to his brothers and said, "Behold, I have dreamed another dream. Behold, the sun, the

[1] Hebrew *the River* [2] See Septuagint, Vulgate; or (with Syriac) *a robe with long sleeves*. The meaning of the Hebrew is uncertain; also verses 23, 32

29[b] ver. 20
31[c] For ver. 31-43, see 1 Chr. 1:43-54
37[d] [ch. 26:22]
41[e] [Num. 33:42]
43[f] ver. 9
Chapter 37
1[g] See ch. 36:7
2[h] [1 Sam. 2:23, 24]
3[i] ch. 44:20 [j] ver. 23, 32
7[k] ch. 42:6, 9 [l] ch. 43:26; 44:14

37:1–11 The rest of Genesis now turns its attention to Joseph and the ups and downs of his life, providentially ordered by the Lord for the ultimate good of his people and the fulfillment of God's covenant promises. These fourteen closing chapters of Genesis teach not only divine providence but also the pattern throughout the Bible of God's chosen deliverers being rejected, with even the rejection playing a crucial part in the process of deliverance. Christ himself is the ultimate example of this motif (Acts 4:27–28).

Genesis 37 opens with a statement about Joseph being uniquely favored over his brothers. This theme of special love resting on one brother among others is a major motif of Genesis. And once more we see that the one on whom God's favor rests is not ethically superior to others: here, Joseph foolishly flaunts his dreams before his brothers, eliciting the frustration even of his doting father (v. 10). Believers are reminded that the divine choice of Isaac over Ishmael and Jacob over Esau are not rooted in anything inherent in Isaac or Jacob, for they were just as fallen as their older brothers. Rather, their election is all of grace. Paul drives this home powerfully in Romans 9 in making the argument that salvation is all of grace. God fixed his favor on Jacob over Isaac even when "they were not yet born and had done nothing either good or bad" (Rom. 9:11). Such depths of divine mercy draw our hearts up to God in quiet worship and wonder at his kindness to us.

moon, and eleven stars were bowing down to
me." 10 But when he told it to his father and
to his brothers, his father rebuked him and
said to him, "What is this dream that you have
dreamed? Shall I and [m]your mother and your
brothers indeed come [n]to bow ourselves to
the ground before you?" 11 And [o]his brothers
were jealous of him, [p]but his father kept the
saying in mind.

Joseph Sold by His Brothers

12 Now his brothers went to pasture their
father's flock near [q]Shechem. 13 And Israel said
to Joseph, "Are not your brothers pasturing
the flock at Shechem? Come, I will send you to
them." And he said to him, "Here I am." 14 So
he said to him, "Go now, see if it is well with
your brothers and with the flock, and bring
me word." So he sent him from the Valley of
[r]Hebron, and he came to Shechem. 15 And a
man found him wandering in the fields. And
the man asked him, "What are you seeking?"
16 "I am seeking my brothers," he said. "Tell me,
please, where they are pasturing the flock."
17 And the man said, "They have gone away,
for I heard them say, 'Let us go to [s]Dothan.'"
So Joseph went after his brothers and found
them at [s]Dothan.

18 They saw him from afar, and before he
came near to them [t]they conspired against him
to kill him. 19 They said to one another, "Here
comes this dreamer. 20 Come now, [u]let us kill
him and throw him into one of the pits.[1] Then
we will say that a fierce animal has devoured
him, and we will see what will become of his
dreams." 21 But when [v]Reuben heard it, he rescued him out of their hands, saying, "Let us
not take his life." 22 And Reuben said to them,
"Shed no blood; throw him into this pit here
in the wilderness, but do not lay a hand on
him"—[w]that he might rescue him out of their
hand to restore him to his father. 23 So when
Joseph came to his brothers, they stripped him
of his robe, [x]the robe of many colors that he
wore. 24 And they took him and [y]threw him
into a pit. The pit was empty; there was no
water in it.

25 Then they sat down to eat. And looking
up they saw a [z]caravan of [a]Ishmaelites coming from Gilead, with their camels bearing
[b]gum, balm, and myrrh, on their way to carry
it down to Egypt. 26 Then Judah said to his
brothers, "What profit is it [c]if we kill our
brother and conceal his blood? 27 Come, let us
sell him to the Ishmaelites, and [d]let not our
hand be upon him, for he is our brother, our
own flesh." And his brothers listened to him.
28 Then [e]Midianite traders passed by. And they
drew Joseph up and lifted him out of the pit,
and [f]sold him to the Ishmaelites for twenty
shekels[2] of silver. They took Joseph to Egypt.

29 When Reuben returned to the pit and
saw that Joseph was not in the pit, he [g]tore
his clothes 30 and returned to his brothers
and said, "The boy [h]is gone, and I, where
shall I go?" 31 Then they took [i]Joseph's robe
and slaughtered a goat and dipped the robe in
the blood. 32 And they sent the robe of many
colors and brought it to their father and said,
"This we have found; please identify whether
it is your son's robe or not." 33 And he identified it and said, "It is my son's robe. [j]A fierce
animal has devoured him. Joseph is without
doubt torn to pieces." 34 Then Jacob tore his

[1] Or *cisterns*; also verses 22, 24 [2] A *shekel* was about 2/5 ounce or 11 grams

37:12–17 Joseph's brothers heartlessly sell their younger brother into slavery. Here and throughout this account, however, the reader is being trained to see that the *apparent hiddenness* of God does not indicate the *uncaring absence* of God.

One small reminder of this is that at Dothan Joseph finds his brothers and is betrayed by them—uncared for, it would seem, by the Lord. Yet it was also at Dothan, years later, that Elisha was encircled by the intimidating Syrian army. While Elisha's servant, perhaps like Joseph, failed to see the presence of God, Elisha saw the surrounding countryside filled with horses and chariots of fire, the very army of God. Indeed, at the very moment when, above all others, God seemed absent—at the cross of his own Son—God was himself quite present, working to redeem and restore (Acts 2:22–24).

37:31 The sin of deceit passes on down through the generations. Jacob deceived his father with the skin of a goat (27:9, 16). Now, he is himself deceived by his sons with the blood of a goat. Yet even this is part of God's plan to work out the ancient promises to Abraham.

10[m] [ch. 35:18] [n] ver. 7, 9
11[o] Acts 7:9 [p] [Luke 2:19, 51]
12[q] See ch. 33:18
14[r] ch. 13:18; 35:27
17[s] 2 Kgs. 6:13
18[t] [Ps. 37:12, 32]
20[u] ver. 26
21[v] ch. 42:22
22[w] ver. 29, 30
23[x] ver. 3
24[y] [Jer. 38:6; Lam. 3:53]
25[z] Job 6:19; Isa. 21:13 [a] [ver. 28, 36; ch. 39:1] [b] ch. 43:11; Jer. 8:22; 46:11
26[c] ver. 20
27[d] [1 Sam. 18:17]
28[e] ver. 36; Judg. 8:22, 24 [f] ch. 45:4; Ps. 105:17; Acts 7:9
29[g] ch. 44:13; Num. 14:6; 2 Sam. 1:11; 3:31; Job 1:20
30[h] ch. 42:13, 32, 36; 44:31; Jer. 31:15; Lam. 5:7
31[i] ver. 23
33[j] ver. 20; ch. 44:28

garments and put sackcloth on his loins and
mourned for his son many days. 35 All his sons
and all his daughters [k]rose up to comfort him,
but he refused to be comforted and said, "No, [l]I
shall go down to Sheol to my son, mourning."
Thus his father wept for him. 36 Meanwhile
[m]the Midianites had sold him in Egypt to
Potiphar, an officer of Pharaoh, [n]the captain
of the guard.

Judah and Tamar

38 It happened at that time that Judah
went down from his brothers and
[o]turned aside to a certain [p]Adullamite, whose
name was Hirah. 2 There Judah saw the daughter of a certain Canaanite whose name was
[q]Shua. He took her and went in to her, 3 and
she conceived and bore a son, and he called his
name [r]Er. 4 She conceived again and bore a son,
and she called his name [r]Onan. 5 Yet again she
bore a son, and she called his name [r]Shelah.
Judah[1] was in Chezib when she bore him.
6 And Judah took a wife for Er his firstborn,
and her name was Tamar. 7 But Er, Judah's
firstborn, [s]was wicked in the sight of the
LORD, and the LORD put him to death. 8 Then
Judah said to Onan, "Go in to [t]your brother's
wife and [u]perform the duty of a brother-in-law
to her, and raise up offspring for your brother."
9 But Onan knew that the offspring would not
be his. So whenever he went in to his brother's
wife he would waste the semen on the ground,
so as not to give offspring to his brother. 10 And
what he did was wicked in the sight of the
LORD, and he put him to death also. 11 Then
Judah said to Tamar his daughter-in-law,
[v]"Remain a widow in your father's house, till
Shelah my son grows up"—for he feared that
he would die, like his brothers. So Tamar went
and remained [w]in her father's house.
12 In the course of time the wife of Judah,
Shua's daughter, died. When Judah [x]was
comforted, he went up to [y]Timnah to his
sheepshearers, he and his friend Hirah the
Adullamite. 13 And when Tamar was told,
"Your father-in-law is going up to Timnah to
shear his sheep," 14 she took off her widow's
garments [z]and covered herself with a veil,
wrapping herself up, and sat at the entrance
to [a]Enaim, which is on the road to Timnah.
For she saw that Shelah was grown up, [b]and
she had not been given to him in marriage.

[1] Hebrew *He*

35 [k][2 Sam. 12:17] [l]ch. 42:38; 44:29, 31
36 [m]ver. 28; [ver. 25; ch. 39:1] [n]ch. 40:3, 4; 41:10, 12
Chapter 38
1 [o]ver. 16; ch. 19:3; 2 Kgs. 4:8 [p]1 Sam. 22:1; 2 Sam. 23:13; 1 Chr. 11:15; Mic. 1:15
2 [q][1 Chr. 2:3]
3 [r]ch. 46:12; Num. 26:19, 20
4 [r][See ver. 3 above]
5 [r][See ver. 3 above]
7 [s]1 Chr. 2:3
8 [t]Matt. 22:24; Mark 12:19; Luke 20:28 [u]See Deut. 25:5-10
11 [v][Ruth 1:12, 13] [w]Lev. 22:13
12 [x]ch. 24:67; 37:35; 2 Sam. 13:39 [y]Judg. 14:1
14 [z][ver. 19; ch. 24:65] [a]ver. 21 [b]ver. 26

38:1–30 The trickery continues, this time involving sordid sexual sin. Here, Judah represents his brothers in their lifestyle of deception. And yet the unsavory account of Judah's illicit relationship with Tamar, which interrupts the ongoing story of Joseph's time in Egypt, plays an important role in Genesis. For this chapter focuses on the continuation of Judah's family line, and concludes with a birth account in which a firstborn son is pushed aside by his younger brother (vv. 27–30). It is especially striking that the ugly actions of Genesis 38 are committed by Judah, the one through whom the Messiah would ultimately be born. This continues the whole-Bible theme of God using the most unlikely subjects for working out his redemptive purposes in the world (1 Cor. 1:26–29).

The unlikeliness of the path of grace is even more striking as the details of this account unfold across generations. First, note that the Judah story continues the narrative pattern of "blessed" and "unblessed" sons (Abel and Cain; Jacob and Esau; Isaac and Ishmael; Joseph and Judah). But note also through whom the blessing flows in this account: it flows through Judah, the predecessor of Jesus (see Gen. 49:8–12 [Jacob's blessing]; and 2 Sam. 7:16).

We learn much, in this story, that would make Judah undeserving of such a distinction. He takes a Canaanite wife and has three sons by her. The first son is so wicked that God puts him to death; the second, Onan, refuses to fulfill his levirate marriage obligation (cf. Deut. 25:5–6) of impregnating Tamar, his dead brother's wife—probably because he doesn't want to diminish his sons' inheritance by greater division among more heirs. Onan is thus put to death by God. Some time later Judah, having lost his wife, mistakenly thinks his daughter-in-law Tamar is a prostitute, impregnates her, and orders her death when he discovers she is pregnant. He then discovers the pregnancy is his own responsibility, and Tamar goes on to bear twin sons. The firstborn of the illegitimate twins is Perez, from whom will come Boaz, who marries Ruth, a Moabite. Boaz and Ruth will be the ancestors of David, from whose line will come Jesus the Messiah! (Cf. Ruth 4:18–22; Matt. 1:5.)

15 When Judah saw her, he thought she was a
prostitute, for she had covered her face. 16 He
turned to her at the roadside and said, "Come,
let me come in to you," for he did not know
that she was his daughter-in-law. She said,
"What will you give me, that you may come
in to me?" 17 He answered, "I will send you a
young goat from the flock." And she said, "If
you give me a pledge, until you send it—"
18 He said, "What pledge shall I give you?" She
replied, [c]"Your signet and your cord and your
staff that is in your hand." So he gave them
to her and went in to her, and she conceived
by him. 19 Then she arose and went away, and
taking off [d]her veil she put on the garments
of her widowhood.
20 When Judah sent the young goat by his
friend the Adullamite to take back the pledge
from the woman's hand, he did not find her.
21 And he asked the men of the place, "Where
is the cult prostitute[1] who was at [e]Enaim at the
roadside?" And they said, "No cult prostitute
has been here." 22 So he returned to Judah and
said, "I have not found her. Also, the men of
the place said, 'No cult prostitute has been
here.'" 23 And Judah replied, "Let her keep the
things as her own, or we shall be laughed at.
You see, I sent this young goat, and you did
not find her."
24 About three months later Judah was
told, "Tamar your daughter-in-law [f]has
been immoral.[2] Moreover, she is pregnant by
immorality."[3] And Judah said, "Bring her out,
and [g]let her be burned." 25 As she was being
brought out, she sent word to her father-
in-law, "By the man to whom these belong,
I am pregnant." And she said, "Please identify
whose these are, [h]the signet and the cord and
the staff." 26 Then Judah identified them and
said, [i]"She is more righteous than I, since [j]I did
not give her to my son Shelah." And he did not
know her again.
27 When the time of her labor came, there
were twins in her womb. 28 And when she was
in labor, one put out a hand, and the midwife
took and tied a scarlet thread on his hand, saying, "This one came out first." 29 But as he drew
back his hand, behold, his brother came out.
And she said, "What a breach you have made
for yourself!" Therefore his name was called
[k]Perez.[4] 30 Afterward his brother came out with
the scarlet thread on his hand, and his name
was called [k]Zerah.

Joseph and Potiphar's Wife

39 Now Joseph had been brought down
to Egypt, and [l]Potiphar, an officer of Pharaoh, the captain of the guard,
an Egyptian, [m]had bought him from the
[n]Ishmaelites who had brought him down
there. 2 [o]The LORD was with Joseph, and he
became a successful man, and he was in the
house of his Egyptian master. 3 His master
saw that the LORD was with him and that the
LORD [p]caused all that he did to succeed in his
hands. 4 So Joseph [q]found favor in his sight
and attended him, and he made him overseer
of his house [r]and put him in charge of all that
he had. 5 From the time that he made him
overseer in his house and over all that he had,
the LORD blessed the Egyptian's house [s]for
Joseph's sake; the blessing of the LORD was on
all that he had, in house and field. 6 So he left
all that he had in Joseph's charge, and because
of him he had no concern about anything but
the food he ate.

[1] Hebrew *sacred woman*; a woman who served a pagan deity by prostitution; also verse 22 [2] Or *has committed prostitution* [3] Or *by prostitution* [4] *Perez* means *a breach*

39:1–23 Unlike his brothers and his family history, Joseph is not given to trickery and deception. He is a man of integrity, is tested, and demonstrates the maturity borne of wisdom. The Lord was evidently with Joseph, despite his earlier immaturity (cf. v. 2 and 37:10). He became a source of blessing (39:2–3) and rose to be responsible over his master's household (vv. 4–6). He did not give in to the enticements of his master's wife (vv. 6–14). He was entrapped by her and escaped (vv. 11–13), but she accused him falsely and he was imprisoned (vv. 14–20).

Throughout this tumultuous chapter, the key point hammered home repeatedly is God's presence with Joseph. This was the secret to Joseph's endurance under trial. "The LORD was with Joseph" (v. 2). "His master saw that the LORD was with him" (v. 3). "But the LORD was with Joseph and showed him steadfast love" (v. 21). "The LORD was with him" (v. 23). Success over Potiphar's house (vv. 1–6), success in temptation (vv. 7–12), and success in overseeing the prison (vv. 21–23) all shared a single source: God's favoring presence.

18 [c]ver. 25
19 [d]ver. 14
21 [e]ver. 14
24 [f]Judg. 19:2 [g]Lev. 21:9; [Deut. 22:21; John 8:5]
25 [h]ver. 18
26 [i]1 Sam. 24:17 [j]ver. 14
29 [k]ch. 46:12; Num. 26:20; 1 Chr. 2:4; Matt. 1:3
30 [k][See ver. 29 above]

Chapter 39
1 [l]ch. 37:36 [m]ch. 37:28 [n]ch. 37:25
2 [o]ver. 21; Acts 7:9; [ch. 21:22; 26:24, 28; 28:15; 1 Sam. 16:18; 18:14, 28]
3 [p]2 Chr. 26:5; Ps. 1:3
4 [q]ver. 21; ch. 19:19; 33:10 [r]ver. 8
5 [s][ch. 30:27]

Now Joseph was [t]handsome in form and appearance. 7 And after a time his master's wife cast her eyes on Joseph and said, "Lie with me." 8 But he refused and said to his master's wife, "Behold, because of me my master has no concern about anything in the house, and [u]he has put everything that he has in my charge. 9 He is not greater in this house than I am, nor has he kept back anything from me except you, because you are his wife. How then can I do this great wickedness and [v]sin against God?" 10 And as she spoke to Joseph day after day, he [w]would not listen to her, to lie beside her or to be with her.

11 But one day, when he went into the house to do his work and none of the men of the house was there in the house, 12 [x]she caught him by his garment, saying, "Lie with me." But he left his garment in her hand and fled and got out of the house. 13 And as soon as she saw that he had left his garment in her hand and had fled out of the house, 14 she called to the men of her household and said to them, "See, he has brought among us a Hebrew to laugh at us. He came in to me to lie with me, and I cried out with a loud voice. 15 And as soon as he heard that I lifted up my voice and cried out, he left his garment beside me and fled and got out of the house." 16 Then she laid up his garment by her until his master came home, 17 and she told him the same story, saying, "The Hebrew servant, whom you have brought among us, came in to me to laugh at me. 18 But as soon as I lifted up my voice and cried, he left his garment beside me and fled out of the house."

19 As soon as his master heard the words that his wife spoke to him, "This is the way your servant treated me," his anger was kindled. 20 And Joseph's master took him and [y]put him into the [z]prison, the place where the king's prisoners were confined, and he was there in prison. 21 But [a]the LORD was with Joseph and showed him steadfast love [b]and gave him favor in the sight of the keeper of the prison. 22 And the keeper of the prison [c]put Joseph in charge of all the prisoners who were in the prison. Whatever was done there, he was the one who did it. 23 The keeper of the prison paid no attention to anything that was in Joseph's charge, because [d]the LORD was with him. And whatever he did, the LORD made it succeed.

Joseph Interprets Two Prisoners' Dreams

40 Some time after this, the [e]cupbearer of the king of Egypt and his baker committed an offense against their lord the king of Egypt. 2 And Pharaoh was angry with his two officers, the chief cupbearer and the chief baker, 3 [f]and he put them in custody in the house of the captain of the guard, in the prison where Joseph was confined. 4 The captain of the guard appointed Joseph to be with them, and he attended them. They continued for some time in custody.

5 And one night they both dreamed—the cupbearer and the baker of the king of Egypt, who were confined in the prison—each his own dream, and each dream with its own interpretation. 6 When Joseph came to them in the morning, he saw that they were troubled. 7 So he asked Pharaoh's officers who were with him in custody in his master's house, [g]"Why are your faces downcast today?" 8 They said to him, [h]"We have had dreams, and there is no one to interpret them." And Joseph said to them, [i]"Do not interpretations belong to God? Please tell them to me."

9 So the chief cupbearer told his dream to Joseph and said to him, "In my dream there was a vine before me, 10 and on the vine there were three branches. As soon as it budded, its blossoms shot forth, and the clusters ripened into grapes. 11 Pharaoh's cup was in my hand, and I took the grapes and pressed them into Pharaoh's cup and placed the cup in Pharaoh's hand." 12 Then Joseph said to him, [j]"This is its interpretation: [k]the three branches are three

6 [t] [ch. 29:17; 1 Sam. 16:12]
8 [u] ver. 4
9 [v] 2 Sam. 12:13; Ps. 51:4
10 [w] [Prov. 1:10]
12 [x] [Prov. 7:13, 18]
20 [y] Ps. 105:18 [z] ch. 40:3, 5; [ch. 40:15; 41:14]
21 [a] ver. 2; Acts 7:9, 10 [b] Ex. 3:21; 11:3; 12:36
22 [c] ch. 40:4
23 [d] ver. 2, 3

Christians today can take heart in reading Genesis 39. Like Joseph, most of us will experience great highs and great lows in life. Through all the ups and downs, those who are in Christ can always draw comfort from the presence of God, even when it is unfelt or unseen (Heb. 13:5). Indeed, the coming of Jesus Christ in the incarnation is the very proof that God has drawn near. The Savior's very name, Immanuel (Matt. 1:21–23), means "God with us." Having ascended to heaven, Jesus then left his presence with us even more profoundly through his Spirit (John 14:16–17).

Felt or unfelt, seen or unseen, in sin or success, God is with us.

Chapter 40 1 [e] Neh. 1:11 3 [f] [ch. 39:20] 7 [g] [Neh. 2:2] 8 [h] ch. 41:15 [i] ch. 41:16; Dan. 2:28, 47 12 [j] ver. 18; ch. 41:12; [Dan. 2:36] [k] [ch. 41:26, 27]

days. 13 In three days Pharaoh will [l]lift up your
head and restore you to your office, and you
shall place Pharaoh's cup in his hand as formerly, when you were his cupbearer. 14 Only
remember me, when it is well with you, and
please do me the kindness to mention me to
Pharaoh, and so get me out of this house. 15 For
[m]I was indeed stolen out of the land of the
Hebrews, and [n]here also I have done nothing
that they should put me into the pit."

16 When the chief baker saw that the interpretation was favorable, he said to Joseph, "I also
had a dream: there were three cake baskets on
my head, 17 and in the uppermost basket there
were all sorts of baked food for Pharaoh, but
the birds were eating it out of the basket on
my head." 18 And Joseph answered and said,
[o]"This is its interpretation: the three baskets
are three days. 19 [p]In three days Pharaoh will
lift up your head—from you!—and [q]hang
you on a tree. And the birds will eat the flesh
from you."

20 On the third day, which was Pharaoh's
[r]birthday, he made a feast for all his servants
and [s]lifted up the head of the chief cupbearer
and the head of the chief baker among his
servants. 21 [t]He restored the chief cupbearer
to his position, and [u]he placed the cup in
Pharaoh's hand. 22 But he [v]hanged the chief
baker, as Joseph had interpreted to them. 23 Yet
the chief cupbearer did not remember Joseph,
but forgot him.

Joseph Interprets Pharaoh's Dreams

41 After two whole years, Pharaoh
dreamed that he was standing by the
Nile, 2 and behold, there came up out of the
Nile seven cows attractive and plump, and
they fed in the reed grass. 3 And behold, seven
other cows, ugly and thin, came up out of the
Nile after them, and stood by the other cows
on the bank of the Nile. 4 And the ugly, thin
cows ate up the seven attractive, plump cows.
And Pharaoh awoke. 5 And he fell asleep and
dreamed a second time. And behold, seven
ears of grain, plump and good, were growing on one stalk. 6 And behold, after them
sprouted seven ears, thin and [w]blighted by
the east wind. 7 And the thin ears swallowed
up the seven plump, full ears. And Pharaoh
awoke, and behold, it was a dream. 8 So in
the morning [x]his spirit was troubled, and he
sent and called for all the [y]magicians of Egypt
and all its wise men. Pharaoh told them his
dreams, but there was none who could interpret them to Pharaoh.

9 Then the chief cupbearer said to Pharaoh,
"I remember my offenses today. 10 When
Pharaoh was [z]angry with his servants [a]and
put me and the chief baker in custody in
the house of the captain of the guard, 11 [b]we
dreamed on the same night, he and I, each
having a dream with its own interpretation.
12 A young Hebrew was there with us, a servant
of the captain of the guard. When we told him,
[c]he interpreted our dreams to us, giving an
interpretation to each man according to his
dream. 13 And [d]as he interpreted to us, so it
came about. I was restored to my office, and
the baker was hanged."

14 [e]Then Pharaoh sent and called Joseph,
and they [f]quickly brought him [g]out of
the pit. And when he had shaved himself
and changed his clothes, he came in before
Pharaoh. 15 And Pharaoh said to Joseph, "I
have had a dream, and there is no one who

40:1–41:57 As chapter 39 closes, Joseph is on the rise even while being imprisoned; two chapters later, he is second in power in Egypt only to Pharaoh himself. As in chapter 39, it is clear that God continues to be with Joseph, working sovereignly for the ultimate fulfillment of his covenant promises to the patriarchs. After thirteen years of humiliation and testing, Joseph was exalted according to a divinely sovereign timing that must have challenged Joseph's faith as the years rolled by—a frequent theme of Genesis and all of Scripture (cf. 41:46; Ps. 27:14; Gal. 6:9; James 5:11). He was married in Egypt and became father of two sons. He named them Manasseh ("forgetting") and Ephraim ("increasing"), recognizing that God's goodness had helped him forget his troubles and had given him the joy of offspring (Gen. 41:51–52). God's promises to Abraham of many descendants (12:1–3, 7) were being carried forward.

Throughout this account it becomes increasingly clear that human prosperity is not self-generated—rather, as Jeremiah puts it, "the way of man is not in himself . . . it is not in man who walks to direct his steps" (Jer. 10:23). The Lord of heaven oversees every event in the lives of his people down to every last detail. And he does this all with fatherly concern.

13 [l] 2 Kgs. 25:27; Jer. 52:31; [ver. 19, 20, 22; Ps. 3:3]
15 [m] ch. 37:28 [n] ch. 39:20
18 [o] See ver. 12
19 [p] ver. 13 [q] ver. 22
20 [r] Matt. 14:6; Mark 6:21 [s] ver. 13, 19
21 [t] ver. 13 [u] Neh. 2:1
22 [v] ver. 19

Chapter 41

6 [w] [Ezek. 17:10; 19:12]; Hos. 13:15
8 [x] Ps. 77:4; Dan. 2:1, 3 [y] ver. 24; Ex. 7:11, 22; [Dan. 1:20; 2:2; 4:7; Matt. 2:1]
10 [z] ch. 40:2, 3 [a] [ch. 39:20]
11 [b] ch. 40:5
12 [c] See ch. 40:12-19
13 [d] ch. 40:21, 22
14 [e] Ps. 105:20 [f] [Dan. 2:25] [g] [1 Sam. 2:8; Ps. 113:7, 8]

can interpret it. [h]I have heard it said of you that when you hear a dream you can interpret it." 16 Joseph answered Pharaoh, [i]"It is not in me; [j]God will give Pharaoh a favorable answer."[1] 17 Then Pharaoh said to Joseph, "Behold, [k]in my dream I was standing on the banks of the Nile. 18 Seven cows, plump and attractive, came up out of the Nile and fed in the reed grass. 19 Seven other cows came up after them, poor and very ugly and thin, such as I had never seen in all the land of Egypt. 20 And the thin, ugly cows ate up the first seven plump cows, 21 but when they had eaten them no one would have known that they had eaten them, for they were still as ugly as at the beginning. Then I awoke. 22 I also saw in my dream seven ears growing on one stalk, full and good. 23 Seven ears, withered, thin, and blighted by the east wind, sprouted after them, 24 and the thin ears swallowed up the seven good ears. And [l]I told it to the magicians, but there was no one who could explain it to me."

25 Then Joseph said to Pharaoh, "The dreams of Pharaoh are one; [m]God has revealed to Pharaoh what he is about to do. 26 The seven good cows are seven years, and the seven good ears are seven years; the dreams are one. 27 The seven lean and ugly cows that came up after them are seven years, and the seven empty ears blighted by the east wind are also [n]seven years of famine. 28 It is as I told Pharaoh; [o]God has shown to Pharaoh what he is about to do. 29 There will come [p]seven years of great plenty throughout all the land of Egypt, 30 but after them there will arise [q]seven years of famine, and all the plenty will be forgotten in the land of Egypt. [r]The famine will consume the land, 31 and the plenty will be unknown in the land by reason of the famine that will follow, for it will be very severe. 32 And the doubling of Pharaoh's dream means that the [s]thing is fixed by God, and God will shortly bring it about. 33 Now therefore let Pharaoh select a discerning and wise man, and set him over the land of Egypt. 34 Let Pharaoh proceed to appoint overseers over the land and take one-fifth of the produce of the land[2] of Egypt during the seven plentiful years. 35 And [t]let them gather all the food of these good years that are coming and store up grain under the authority of Pharaoh for food in the cities, and let them keep it. 36 That food shall be a reserve for the land against the seven years of famine that are to occur in the land of Egypt, so that the land may not perish through the famine."

Joseph Rises to Power

37 This proposal pleased Pharaoh and all his servants. 38 And Pharaoh said to his servants, "Can we find a man like this, [u]in whom is the Spirit of God?"[3] 39 Then Pharaoh said to Joseph, "Since God has shown you all this, there is none so discerning and wise as you are. 40 [v]You shall be over my house, and all my people shall order themselves as you command.[4] Only as regards the throne will I be greater than you." 41 And Pharaoh said to Joseph, "See, [w]I have set you over all the land of

[1] Or (compare Samaritan, Septuagint) *Without God it is not possible to give Pharaoh an answer about his welfare* [2] Or *over the land and organize the land* [3] Or *of the gods* [4] Hebrew *and according to your command all my people shall kiss the ground*

15[h] ver. 12; Dan. 5:16
16[i] Dan. 2:30 [j] ch. 40:8; Dan. 2:22, 28, 47
17[k] See ver. 1-7
24[l] ver. 8; [Dan. 4:7]
25[m] [Dan. 2:28, 29, 45; Rev. 4:1]
27[n] [2 Kgs. 8:1]
28[o] ver. 25
29[p] ver. 47
30[q] ver. 54; ch. 45:6 [r] ch. 47:13
32[s] Num. 23:19; Isa. 14:24; 46:10, 11
35[t] ver. 48
38[u] Num. 27:18; Dan. 4:8, 18; 5:11, 14
40[v] Ps. 105:21; Acts 7:10
41[w] ch. 42:6

Joseph himself acknowledges God as sovereign when brought before Pharaoh. Responding to Pharaoh's comment that he has heard that Joseph can interpret dreams, Joseph immediately responds, "It is not in me; God will give Pharaoh a favorable answer" (Gen. 41:16). The Hebrew text emphasizes "God" in underscoring that it is not Joseph but the Lord who lies behind Joseph's remarkable ability to interpret dreams. Indeed, throughout this chapter, Joseph ascribes all credit to God: "God has revealed to Pharaoh what he is about to do" (41:25); "God has shown to Pharaoh what he is about to do" (41:28); "the thing is fixed by God" (41:32). Finally, Pharaoh himself acknowledges God: "Since God has shown you all this . . ." (41:39)—an acknowledgment that stands in stark contrast to the unwillingness of a later Pharaoh to bow the knee to God throughout the early chapters of Exodus.

Key to living a life "worthy of the gospel of Christ" (Phil. 1:27) is the ascribing of all glory to God for all fruit borne in our lives. Jesus himself did this, honoring his Father (John 12:28). In the upside-down framework of the gospel, it is precisely through glorifying God that humans regain their true dignity and their own derivative glory (Rom. 2:7, 10; 3:23; 8:30; 2 Cor. 3:18). Or as Jesus said, "Whoever would be great among you must be your servant" (Matt. 20:26)—a servanthood-unto-greatness that Jesus himself supremely exemplified in his great love for us (John 13:1–20).

Egypt." 42 Then Pharaoh [x]took his signet ring from his hand and put it on Joseph's hand, and [y]clothed him in garments of fine linen [z]and put a gold chain about his neck. 43 And he made him ride in his second chariot. [a]And they called out before him, "Bow the knee!"[1] Thus he set him [b]over all the land of Egypt. 44 Moreover, Pharaoh said to Joseph, "I am Pharaoh, and [c]without your consent no one shall lift up hand or foot in all the land of Egypt." 45 And Pharaoh called Joseph's name Zaphenath-paneah. And he gave him in marriage Asenath, the daughter of Potiphera priest of On. So Joseph went out over the land of Egypt.

46 Joseph was thirty years old when he [d]entered the service of Pharaoh king of Egypt. And Joseph went out from the presence of Pharaoh and went through all the land of Egypt. 47 During the seven plentiful years the earth produced abundantly, 48 and he gathered up all the food of these seven years, which occurred in the land of Egypt, and put the food in the cities. He put in every city the food from the fields around it. 49 And Joseph stored up grain in great abundance, [e]like the sand of the sea, until he ceased to measure it, for it could not be measured.

50 Before the year of famine came, [f]two sons were born to Joseph. Asenath, the daughter of Potiphera priest of On, bore them to him. 51 Joseph called the name of the firstborn Manasseh. "For," he said, "God has made me forget all my hardship and all my father's house."[2] 52 The name of the second he called Ephraim, "For God has [g]made me fruitful in the land of my affliction."[3]

53 The seven years of plenty that occurred in the land of Egypt came to an end, 54 and [h]the seven years of famine began to come, [i]as Joseph had said. There was famine in all lands, but in all the land of Egypt there was bread. 55 When all the land of Egypt was famished, the people cried to Pharaoh for bread. Pharaoh said to all the Egyptians, "Go to Joseph. What he says to you, do."

56 So when the famine had spread over all the land, Joseph opened all the storehouses[4] and [j]sold to the Egyptians, for the famine was severe in the land of Egypt. 57 Moreover, all the earth came to Egypt to Joseph to buy grain, because the famine was severe [k]over all the earth.

Joseph's Brothers Go to Egypt

42 When [l]Jacob learned that there was grain for sale in Egypt, he said to his sons, "Why do you look at one another?" 2 And he said, "Behold, I have heard that there is grain for sale in Egypt. Go down and buy grain for us there, that we may [m]live and not die." 3 So ten of Joseph's brothers went down to buy grain in Egypt. 4 But Jacob did not send Benjamin, [n]Joseph's brother, with his brothers, for [o]he feared that harm might happen to him. 5 Thus the sons of Israel came to buy among the others who came, for the famine was in the land of Canaan.

6 Now Joseph was governor [p]over the land. He was the one who sold to all the people of the land. And Joseph's brothers came and [q]bowed themselves before him with their faces to the ground. 7 Joseph saw his brothers and recognized them, but he treated them like strangers and [r]spoke roughly to them. "Where do you come from?" he said. They said, "From the land of Canaan, to buy food." 8 And Joseph recognized his brothers, but they did not recognize him. 9 And Joseph [s]remembered the dreams that he had dreamed of them. [t]And he said to them, "You are spies; you have come to see the

[1] *Abrek*, probably an Egyptian word, similar in sound to the Hebrew word meaning *to kneel* [2] *Manasseh* sounds like the Hebrew for *making to forget* [3] *Ephraim* sounds like the Hebrew for *making fruitful* [4] Hebrew *all that was in them*

In John 2:5, Jesus' mother tells some servants to do whatever Jesus tells them to do, just as Pharaoh had said to his servants concerning Joseph (Gen. 41:55). In recording these words, perhaps John wanted us to see that the abundance of blessing brought to the world through Joseph is now supremely filled out in the abundance of blessing brought to the world through Jesus.

42:1–43:34 In a strange twist of fortune in these chapters, Joseph the betrayed and imprisoned becomes the master of the fate of his own starving brothers. Through a series of strategic conversations and events, Joseph works out in his brothers' lives the same hard lesson he had himself learned from God—namely, that it is the adversity of life that softens us sufficiently to make us open to the Lord's grace.

42 [x] Esth. 3:10; 8:2, 8, 10 [y] [Esth. 8:15] [z] Ezek. 16:11; [Dan. 5:7, 29]
43 [a] [Esth. 6:9] [b] ver. 40; ch. 42:6; 45:8, 9, 26
44 [c] [Ps. 105:21, 22]
46 [d] 1 Sam. 16:21; 1 Kgs. 12:6, 8; Dan. 1:19
49 [e] ch. 22:17; Judg. 7:12; 1 Sam. 13:5; Ps. 78:27
50 [f] ch. 46:20; 48:5
52 [g] [ch. 49:22; Hos. 13:15]
54 [h] Ps. 105:16; Acts 7:11 [i] ver. 30
56 [j] ch. 42:6; [ch. 47:14, 20, 24]
57 [k] ver. 54, 56

Chapter 42 **1** [l] Acts 7:12 **2** [m] ch. 43:8 **4** [n] ch. 35:18 [o] ver. 38 **6** [p] ch. 41:41 [q] ch. 37:7, 9, 10 **7** [r] ver. 30 **9** [s] ch. 37:5, 9 [t] ver. 7, 30

nakedness of the land.” 10 They said to him, “No, my lord, your servants have come to buy food. 11 We are all sons of one man. We are honest men. Your servants have never been spies.”

12 He said to them, “No, it is the nakedness of the land that you have come to see.” 13 And they said, “We, your servants, are twelve brothers, the sons of one man in the land of Canaan, and behold, the youngest is this day with our father, and one [u]is no more.” 14 But Joseph said to them, “It is as I said to you. You are spies. 15 By this you shall be tested: by the life of Pharaoh, you shall not go from this place unless your youngest brother comes here. 16 Send one of you, and let him bring your brother, while you remain confined, that your words may be tested, whether there is truth in you. Or else, by the life of Pharaoh, surely you are spies.” 17 And he put them all together in custody for three days.

18 On the third day Joseph said to them, “Do this and you will live, [v]for I fear God: 19 if you are honest men, let one of your brothers remain confined where you are in custody, and let the rest go and carry [w]grain for the famine of your households, 20 and [x]bring your youngest brother to me. So your words will be verified, and you shall not die.” And they did so. 21 Then they said to one another, [y]“In truth we are guilty concerning our brother, in that we saw the distress of his soul, when he begged us and we did not listen. That is why this distress has come upon us.” 22 And Reuben answered them, [z]“Did I not tell you not to sin against the boy? But you did not listen. So now [a]there comes a reckoning for his blood.” 23 They did not know that Joseph understood them, for there was an interpreter between them. 24 Then he turned away from them and [b]wept. And he returned to them and spoke to them. And he took Simeon from them and bound him before their eyes. 25 [c]And Joseph gave orders to fill their bags with grain, and to replace every man’s money in his sack, and to give them provisions for the journey. This was done for them.

26 Then they loaded their donkeys with their grain and departed. 27 And as [d]one of them opened his sack to give his donkey fodder at [e]the lodging place, he saw his money in the mouth of his sack. 28 He said to his brothers, “My money has been put back; here it is in the mouth of my sack!” At this their hearts failed them, and they turned trembling to one another, saying, “What is this that God has done to us?”

29 When they came to Jacob their father in the land of Canaan, they told him all that had happened to them, saying, 30 “The man, the lord of the land, [f]spoke roughly to us and took us to be spies of the land. 31 But we said to him, ‘We are honest men; we have never been spies. 32 We are twelve brothers, sons of our father. One [g]is no more, and the youngest is this day with our father in the land of Canaan.’ 33 Then the man, the lord of the land, said to us, [h]‘By this I shall know that you are honest men: leave one of your brothers with me, and take [i]grain for the famine of your households, and go your way. 34 Bring your youngest brother to me. Then I shall know that you are not spies but honest men, and I will deliver your brother to you, and you shall [j]trade in the land.’ ”

35 [k]As they emptied their sacks, behold, every man’s bundle of money was in his sack. And when they and their father saw their bundles of money, they were afraid. 36 And Jacob their father said to them, “You have [l]bereaved me of my children: Joseph is no more, and Simeon is no more, and now you would take Benjamin. All this has come against me.” 37 Then Reuben

13[u] ver. 32; See ch. 37:30
18[v] Lev. 25:43; Neh. 5:15
19[w] ver. 33
20[x] ver. 34; ch. 43:5; 44:23
21[y] [Job 36:8, 9]; See ch. 37:23-28
22[z] ch. 37:21 [a] ch. 9:5; 2 Chr. 24:22; [1 Kgs. 2:32; Ps. 9:12; Luke 11:50, 51]
24[b] ch. 43:30
25[c] ch. 44:1
27[d] ver. 35; ch. 43:21 [e] Ex. 4:24; Jer. 9:2
30[f] ver. 7, 9
32[g] ver. 13
33[h] ver. 15, 19, 20 [i] ver. 19
34[j] ch. 34:10, 21
35[k] ver. 27; ch. 43:21
36[l] ch. 43:14

Joseph’s own softening before God is clear from the numerous times he breaks down and weeps in the presence of his brothers (42:24; 43:30; 45:2, 14, 15; 46:29). And in the emerging new gentleness among his brothers, the discerning reader perceives God’s transforming grace reaching their hearts through their once-hated younger brother. When Joseph insists that Benjamin be brought to Egypt, for example, Judah pacifies Jacob’s objections by pledging his own life for Benjamin (43:8–9). Reuben had movingly proposed something similar (42:37). These brothers who once betrayed a younger brother now place their own lives as pledges for the life of another younger brother. They also begin to see, as Joseph has, the hand of God in the events of their lives: “What is this that *God* has done to us?” they ask (42:28). Their hearts are slowly being trained to leave behind the steely bitterness that caused them to sell Joseph into slavery.

said to his father, "Kill [m] my two sons if I do not
bring him back to you. Put him in my hands,
and I will bring him back to you." 38 But he
said, "My son shall not go down with you, for
[n] his brother is dead, and he is the only one left.
[o] If harm should happen to him on the journey
that you are to make, [p] you would bring down
my gray hairs with sorrow to Sheol."

Joseph's Brothers Return to Egypt

43 Now the famine was [q] severe in the
land. 2 And when they had eaten the
grain that they had brought from Egypt, their
father said to them, "Go again, buy us a little
food." 3 But Judah said to him, "The man solemnly warned us, saying, 'You shall not see my
face unless your [r] brother is with you.' 4 If you
will send our brother with us, we will go down
and buy you food. 5 But if you will not send
him, we will not go down, for the man said
to us, 'You shall not see my face, unless your
brother is with you.'" 6 Israel said, "Why did
you treat me so badly as to tell the man that
you had another brother?" 7 They replied, "The
man questioned us carefully about ourselves
and our kindred, saying, 'Is your father still
alive? Do you have another brother?' What
we told him was in answer to these questions.
Could we in any way know that he would say,
'Bring your brother down'?" 8 And Judah said
to Israel his father, "Send the boy with me,
and we will arise and go, that we may [s] live and
not die, both we and you and also our little
ones. 9 I will be a pledge of his safety. From my
hand you shall require him. [t] If I do not bring
him back to you and set him before you, then
let me bear the blame forever. 10 If we had not
delayed, we would now have returned twice."

11 Then their father Israel said to them, "If
it must be so, then do this: take some of the
choice fruits of the land in your bags, and carry
a present down to the man, a little [u] balm and
a little honey, gum, myrrh, pistachio nuts,
and almonds. 12 Take double the money with
you. Carry back with you the money [v] that was
returned in the mouth of your sacks. Perhaps
it was an oversight. 13 Take also your brother,
and arise, go again to the man. 14 May [w] God
Almighty [1] [x] grant you mercy before the man,
and may he send back your other brother and
Benjamin. And as for me, [y] if I am bereaved of
my children, I am bereaved."

15 So the men took this present, and they took
double the money with them, and Benjamin.
They arose and went down to Egypt and stood
before Joseph.

16 When Joseph saw Benjamin with them, he
said to the [z] steward of his house, "Bring the
men into the house, and slaughter an animal
and make ready, for the men are to dine with
me at noon." 17 The man did as Joseph told him
and brought the men to Joseph's house. 18 And
the men were afraid because they were brought
to Joseph's house, and they said, "It is because
of the money, which was replaced in our sacks
the first time, that we are brought in, so that
he may assault us and fall upon us to make us
servants and seize our donkeys." 19 So they went
up to the steward of Joseph's house and spoke
with him at the door of the house, 20 and said,
[a] "Oh, my lord, [b] we came down the first time
to buy food. 21 And [c] when we came to the lodging place we opened our sacks, and there was
each man's money in the mouth of his sack,
our money in full weight. So we have brought
it again with us, 22 and we have brought other
money down with us to buy food. We do not
know who put our money in our sacks." 23 He
replied, "Peace to you, do not be afraid. Your
God and the God of your father has put treasure in your sacks for you. I received your
money." Then he brought Simeon out to them.
24 And when the man had brought the men
into Joseph's house and [d] given them water, and
they had washed their feet, and when he had
given their donkeys fodder, 25 they prepared
[e] the present for Joseph's coming at noon, for
they heard that they should eat bread there.

26 When Joseph came home, they brought
into the house to him the present that they
had with them and [f] bowed down to him to
the ground. 27 And he inquired about their
welfare and said, "Is your father well, the old
man [g] of whom you spoke? Is he still alive?"
28 They said, "Your servant our father is well;
he is still alive." And they [h] bowed their heads
and prostrated themselves. 29 And he lifted up
his eyes and saw his brother Benjamin, [i] his
mother's son, and said, "Is this your youngest
brother, [g] of whom you spoke to me? God be

[1] Hebrew *El Shaddai*

37 [m] [ch. 46:9] **38** [n] ver. 13, 32, 36; ch. 37:33; 44:28 [o] ver. 4; ch. 44:29 [p] ch. 37:35; 44:31 **Chapter 43** **1** [q] ch. 41:54, 57 **3** [r] ch. 42:20; 44:23 **8** [s] ch. 42:2 **9** [t] ch. 42:37; 44:32 **11** [u] See ch. 37:25 **12** [v] ch. 42:25, 27, 35 **14** [w] See ch. 17:1 [x] [Neh. 1:11] [y] ch. 42:36 **16** [z] ver. 19; ch. 44:1, 4; [ch. 24:2; 39:4] **20** [a] ch. 44:18 [b] ch. 42:3, 10 **21** [c] ch. 42:27 **24** [d] See ch. 18:4 **25** [e] ver. 11 **26** [f] ch. 42:6; See ch. 37:5-11 **27** [g] ch. 42:11, 13 **28** [h] ver. 26 **29** [i] ch. 35:18 [g] [See ver. 27 above]

gracious to you, my son!" 30 Then Joseph hurried out, for [j]his compassion grew warm for
his brother, and he sought a place to weep.
And he entered his chamber and [k]wept there.
31 Then he washed his face and came out. And
[l]controlling himself he said, "Serve the food."
32 They served him by himself, and them by
themselves, and the Egyptians who ate with
him by themselves, because the Egyptians
could not eat with the Hebrews, for that is
[m]an abomination to the Egyptians. 33 And they
sat before him, the firstborn according to his
birthright and the youngest according to his
youth. And the men looked at one another in
amazement. 34 [n]Portions were taken to them
from Joseph's table, but Benjamin's portion
was [o]five times as much as any of theirs. And
they drank and were merry[1] with him.

Joseph Tests His Brothers

44 Then he commanded [p]the steward of
his house, [q]"Fill the men's sacks with
food, as much as they can carry, and put each
man's money in the mouth of his sack, 2 and
put my cup, the silver cup, in the mouth of the
sack of the youngest, with his money for the
grain." And he did as Joseph told him.

3 As soon as the morning was light, the men
were sent away with their donkeys. 4 They had
gone only a short distance from the city. Now
Joseph said to his [r]steward, "Up, follow after
the men, and when you overtake them, say to
them, 'Why have you repaid evil for good?[2]
5 Is it not from this that my lord drinks, and
[s]by this that he practices divination? You have
done evil in doing this.' "

6 When he overtook them, he spoke to them
these words. 7 They said to him, "Why does my
lord speak such words as these? Far be it from
your servants to do such a thing! 8 Behold, [t]the
money that we found in the mouths of our
sacks we brought back to you from the land of
Canaan. How then could we steal silver or gold
from your lord's house? 9 [u]Whichever of your
servants is found with it shall die, and we also
will be [v]my lord's servants." 10 He said, "Let it be
as you say: he who is found with it shall be my
servant, and the rest of you shall be innocent."
11 Then each man quickly lowered his sack to
the ground, and each man opened his sack.
12 And he searched, beginning with the eldest
and ending with the youngest. And the cup
was found in Benjamin's sack. 13 Then they
[w]tore their clothes, and every man loaded his
donkey, and they returned to the city.

14 When Judah and his brothers came to
Joseph's house, he was still there. They [x]fell
before him to the ground. 15 Joseph said to
them, "What deed is this that you have done?
Do you not know that a man like me [y]can
indeed practice divination?" 16 And Judah said,
"What shall we say to my lord? What shall we
speak? Or how can we clear ourselves? God has
found out [z]the guilt of your servants; behold,
we are [a]my lord's servants, both we and he also
in whose hand the cup has been found." 17 But
he said, "Far be it from me that I should do
so! Only the man in whose hand the cup was
found shall be my servant. But as for you, go
up in peace to your father."

18 Then Judah went up to him and said, [b]"Oh,
my lord, please let your servant speak a word
in my lord's ears, and [c]let not your anger burn
against your servant, for [d]you are like Pharaoh
himself. 19 My lord asked his servants, saying, 'Have you a father, or a brother?' 20 And
we said to my lord, 'We have a father, an old
man, [e]and a young brother, [f]the child of his
old age. His brother is dead, and he alone is
left of his mother's children, and his father
loves him.' 21 Then you said to your servants,
[g]'Bring him down to me, that I may set my

[1] Hebrew *and became intoxicated* [2] Septuagint (compare Vulgate) adds *Why have you stolen my silver cup?*

30[j] 1 Kgs. 3:26; [Jer. 31:20] [k] ch. 42:24
31[l] ch. 45:1
32[m] ch. 46:34; Ex. 8:26
34[n] [2 Sam. 11:8] [o] [ch. 45:22]
Chapter 44
1[p] ver. 4; See ch. 43:16 [q] ch. 42:25
4[r] ver. 1
5[s] ver. 15; ch. 30:27; [2 Kgs. 21:6; 2 Chr. 33:6]
8[t] ch. 43:21
9[u] [ch. 31:32] [v] ver. 16
13[w] ch. 37:29

44:1–45:28 Once more Judah intercedes poignantly for the sake of his family. He asks Joseph to keep him captive in Egypt instead of the young boy Benjamin.

This is the moment that finally breaks Joseph down (45:1) and brings him to reveal himself to his brothers. For here the final step in his brothers' heart-transformation has occurred. Judah is now willing to sacrifice himself for the sake of a younger brother in danger—the very thing he and his brothers were unwilling to do for the sake of their other younger brother, Joseph, years before. Remembering that this is the same Judah who was guilty of such terrible sin in earlier chapters (see Genesis 37–38), we grow to understand that God's grace does not keep a record of wrongs but matures us in God's ways and heart.

14[x] ch. 37:7, 9, 10; 42:6; 43:26, 28 **15**[y] ver. 5 **16**[z] ch. 37:18; [Num. 32:23] [a] ver. 9 **18**[b] ch. 43:20 [c] Ex. 32:22 [d] ch. 41:40 **20**[e] ver. 30; [ch. 43:8] [f] [ch. 37:3] **21**[g] ch. 42:15, 20; 43:3, 5

eyes on him.' 22 We said to my lord, 'The boy cannot leave his father, for if he should leave his father, [h]his father would die.' 23 Then you said to your servants, [i]'Unless your youngest brother comes down with you, you shall not see my face again.'

24 "When we went back to your servant my father, we told him the words of my lord. 25 And when [j]our father said, 'Go again, buy us a little food,' 26 we said, 'We cannot go down. If our youngest brother goes with us, then we will go down. For we cannot see the man's face unless our youngest brother is with us.' 27 Then your servant my father said to us, 'You know that my wife bore me [k]two sons. 28 One left me, and I said, [l]"Surely he has been torn to pieces," and I have never seen him since. 29 If you [m]take this one also from me, [n]and harm happens to him, you will bring down my gray hairs in evil to Sheol.'

30 "Now therefore, as soon as I come to your servant my father, and the boy is not with us, then, as his life is bound up in the boy's life, 31 as soon as he sees that the boy is not with us, he will die, and your servants will bring down the gray hairs of your servant our father with sorrow to Sheol. 32 For your servant became a pledge of safety for the boy to my father, saying, [o]'If I do not bring him back to you, then I shall bear the blame before my father all my life.' 33 Now therefore, please let your servant remain instead of the boy as a servant to my lord, and let the boy go back with his brothers. 34 For how can I go back to my father if the boy is not with me? I fear to see the evil that would find my father."

Joseph Provides for His Brothers and Family

45 Then Joseph could not [p]control himself before all those who stood by him. He cried, "Make everyone go out from me." So no one stayed with him when Joseph made himself known to his brothers. 2 And he wept aloud, so that the Egyptians heard it, and the household of Pharaoh heard it. 3 And Joseph said to his brothers, [q]"I am Joseph! Is my father still alive?" But his brothers could not answer him, for they were dismayed at his presence.

4 So Joseph said to his brothers, "Come near to me, please." And they came near. And he said, "I am your brother, Joseph, [r]whom you sold into Egypt. 5 And now do not be distressed or angry with yourselves because you sold me here, [s]for God sent me before you to preserve life. 6 For the famine has been in the land these two years, and there are [t]yet five years in which there will be neither [u]plowing nor harvest. 7 And God sent me before you to preserve for you a remnant on earth, and to keep alive for you many survivors. 8 So it was not you who sent me here, but God. He has made me a father to Pharaoh, and lord of all his house and [v]ruler over all the land of Egypt. 9 Hurry and go up to my father and say to him, 'Thus says your son Joseph, God has made me lord of all Egypt. Come down to me; do not tarry. 10 [w]You shall dwell in the land of Goshen, and you shall be near me, you and your children and your children's children, and your flocks, your herds, and all that you have. 11 [x]There I will provide for you, for there are yet five years of famine to come, so that you and your household, and all that you have, do not come to poverty.' 12 And now your eyes see, and the eyes of my brother Benjamin see, that it is [y]my mouth that speaks to you. 13 You must tell my father of all my honor in Egypt, and of all that you have seen. Hurry and [z]bring my father down here." 14 Then he fell upon his brother Benjamin's neck and wept, and Benjamin wept upon his neck. 15 And he kissed all his brothers and wept upon them. After that his brothers talked with him.

16 When the report was heard in Pharaoh's house, "Joseph's brothers have come," it pleased Pharaoh and his servants. 17 And Pharaoh said to Joseph, "Say to your brothers, 'Do this: load your beasts and go back to the

Jesus said, "Greater love has no one than this, that someone lay down his life for his friends" (John 15:13). Judah exemplifies in Genesis 44 this greatest act of love. In doing so he was preparing the way and foreshadowing the character of his great descendant, Jesus himself, who would substitute himself not for one man but for all those who put their faith in him. What Judah said to Joseph, Jesus said to the Father: "I shall bear the blame" (44:32). The most magnificent substitution of human history occurred on an obscure hill outside Jerusalem, where Jesus pledged his own life for our sake (2 Cor. 5:21).

22 [h] [ver. 31]
23 [i] ch. 43:3
25 [j] ch. 43:2
27 [k] ch. 46:19
28 [l] ch. 37:33
29 [m] ch. 42:36, 38 [n] ch. 42:4, 38
32 [o] ch. 43:9

Chapter 45
1 [p] ch. 43:31; [Esth. 5:10]
3 [q] Acts 7:13
4 [r] ch. 37:28

5 [s] ch. 50:20; Ps. 105:16, 17 **6** [t] ch. 41:30 [u] Ex. 34:21; Deut. 21:4; 1 Sam. 8:12; [Isa. 30:24] **8** [v] ver. 26; ch. 41:43 **10** [w] ch. 46:34; 47:1, 4, 6, 27; 50:8; Ex. 8:22; [ch. 47:11; Josh. 10:41] **11** [x] ch. 47:12; 50:21 **12** [y] [ch. 42:23] **13** [z] Acts 7:14

land of Canaan, 18 and take your father and
your households, and come to me, and [a]I will
give you the best of the land of Egypt, and
you shall eat the fat of the land.' 19 And you,
Joseph, are commanded to say, 'Do this: take
[b]wagons from the land of Egypt for your little
ones and for your wives, and bring your father,
and come. 20 Have no concern for[1] your goods,
for the best of all the land of Egypt is yours.'"

21 The sons of Israel did so: and Joseph gave
them [b]wagons, according to the command of
Pharaoh, and gave them provisions for the
journey. 22 To each and all of them he gave [c]a
change of clothes, but to Benjamin he gave
three hundred shekels[2] of silver and [d]five
changes of clothes. 23 To his father he sent as
follows: ten donkeys loaded with the good
things of Egypt, and ten female donkeys
loaded with grain, bread, and provision for
his father on the journey. 24 Then he sent his
brothers away, and as they departed, he said to
them, [e]"Do not quarrel on the way."

25 So they went up out of Egypt and came to
the land of Canaan to their father Jacob. 26 And
they told him, "Joseph is still alive, and he is
ruler over all the land of Egypt." And his heart
became numb, for he did not believe them.
27 But when they told him all the words of
Joseph, which he had said to them, and when
he saw [f]the wagons that Joseph had sent to carry
him, the spirit of their father Jacob revived.
28 And Israel said, "It is enough; Joseph my son
is still alive. I will go and see him before I die."

Joseph Brings His Family to Egypt

46 So Israel took his journey with all that
he had and came to [g]Beersheba, and
offered sacrifices [h]to the God of his father
Isaac. 2 And God spoke to Israel [i]in visions
of the night and said, "Jacob, Jacob." And he
said, "Here I am." 3 Then he said, "I am God,
[j]the God of your father. Do not be afraid to go
down to Egypt, for there I will [k]make you into
a great nation. 4 I myself will go down with you
to Egypt, and I will also [l]bring you up again,
and [m]Joseph's hand shall close your eyes."

5 Then Jacob set out from Beersheba. The
sons of Israel carried Jacob their father, their
little ones, and their wives, in the wagons [n]that
Pharaoh had sent to carry him. 6 They also took
their livestock and their goods, which they
had gained in the land of Canaan, and [o]came
into Egypt, Jacob and all his offspring with
him, 7 his sons, and his sons' sons with him,
his daughters, and his sons' daughters. All his
offspring he brought with him into Egypt.

8 [p]Now [q]these are the names of the descendants of Israel, who came into Egypt, Jacob
and his sons. [r]Reuben, Jacob's firstborn, 9 and
the sons of Reuben: Hanoch, Pallu, Hezron,
and Carmi. 10 The sons of Simeon: Jemuel,
Jamin, Ohad, Jachin, Zohar, and Shaul, the
son of a Canaanite woman. 11 The sons of [s]Levi:
Gershon, Kohath, and Merari. 12 The sons of
[t]Judah: Er, Onan, Shelah, Perez, and Zerah
(but [u]Er and Onan died in the land of Canaan);
and the sons of [v]Perez were Hezron and
Hamul. 13 [w]The sons of Issachar: Tola, Puvah,
Yob, and Shimron. 14 The sons of Zebulun:
Sered, Elon, and Jahleel. 15 These are the sons
of Leah, [x]whom she bore to Jacob in Paddan-
aram, together with his daughter Dinah; altogether his sons and his daughters numbered
thirty-three.

16 The sons of Gad: Ziphion, Haggi, Shuni,
Ezbon, Eri, Arodi, and Areli. 17 [y]The sons of
Asher: Imnah, Ishvah, Ishvi, Beriah, with Serah
their sister. And the sons of Beriah: Heber
and Malchiel. 18 [z]These are the sons of Zilpah,
[a]whom Laban gave to Leah his daughter; and
these she bore to Jacob—sixteen persons.
19 The sons of Rachel, Jacob's wife: Joseph

[1] Hebrew *Let your eye not pity* [2] A *shekel* was about 2/5 ounce or 11 grams

46:1–47:31 Reading the Joseph narrative against the backdrop of the promise to Abraham that "in you all the families of the earth shall be blessed" (12:3) clarifies for us the divine purpose in Joseph's shrewd administrative leadership: namely, fulfillment of this promise. Through Joseph the people were greatly blessed, as God had promised Abraham would be true of his descendants. Indeed, it is striking to note the concluding statement of 47:27 that Joseph's family, having settled in Egypt, "were fruitful and multiplied greatly." This goes back not merely to Genesis 12 but to Genesis 1: "Be fruitful and multiply and fill the earth and subdue it" (1:28). It is the mandate given to Adam and Eve. Through Joseph, God is recovering and restoring the original charge given to humanity.

18 [a]ch. 47:6
19 [b]ch. 46:5
21 [b][See ver. 19 above]
22 [c][2 Kgs. 5:5, 22, 23] [d][ch. 43:34]
24 [e][ch. 42:22]
27 [f]ver. 19, 21; ch. 46:5

Chapter 46

1 [g]ch. 21:31, 33; 26:33; 28:10 [h]ch. 26:24, 25; 28:13; 31:42
2 [i]ch. 15:1; Job 33:14, 15
3 [j]ch. 28:13 [k]ch. 35:11; [ch. 12:2; Ex. 1:7, 9; Deut. 26:5]
4 [l]ch. 15:16; 28:15; 48:21; 50:24; Ex. 3:8 [m]ch. 50:1 **5** [n]ch. 45:19, 21, 27 **6** [o]Josh. 24:4; Ps. 105:23; Isa. 52:4; Acts 7:14, 15 **8** [p]For ver. 8-11, see Ex. 6:14-16 [q]Ex. 1:1-5 [r]Num. 26:5; 1 Chr. 5:1-3 **11** [s]1 Chr. 6:1 **12** [t]1 Chr. 2:3; 4:21 [u]ch. 38:3, 7, 10 [v]ch. 38:29; 1 Chr. 2:5 **13** [w]1 Chr. 7:1 **15** [x]See ch. 29:32-35; 30:1-21 **17** [y]1 Chr. 7:30 **18** [z]See ch. 30:10-13 [a]ch. 29:24

and Benjamin. 20 And [b]to Joseph in the land
of Egypt were born Manasseh and Ephraim,
whom Asenath, the daughter of Potiphera
the priest of [c]On, bore to him. 21 And [d]the
sons of Benjamin: Bela, Becher, Ashbel, Gera,
Naaman, Ehi, Rosh, Muppim, Huppim, and
Ard. 22 These are the sons of Rachel, who were
born to Jacob—fourteen persons in all.
23 The son[1] of Dan: Hushim. 24 [e]The sons of
Naphtali: Jahzeel, Guni, Jezer, and Shillem.
25 [f]These are the sons of Bilhah, [g]whom Laban
gave to Rachel his daughter, and these she
bore to Jacob—seven persons in all.
26 All the persons belonging to Jacob who
came into Egypt, who were his own descendants, not including Jacob's sons' wives, were
sixty-six persons in all. 27 And the sons of
Joseph, who were born to him in Egypt, were
two. [h]All the persons of the house of Jacob who
came into Egypt were seventy.

Jacob and Joseph Reunited

28 He had sent Judah ahead of him to Joseph
to show the way before him in Goshen, and
they came [i]into the land of Goshen. 29 Then
Joseph prepared his chariot and went up to
meet Israel his father in Goshen. He presented
himself to him and [j]fell on his neck and wept
on his neck a good while. 30 Israel said to
Joseph, [k]"Now let me die, since I have seen
your face and know that you are still alive."
31 Joseph said to his brothers and to his father's
household, [l]"I will go up and tell Pharaoh and
will say to him, 'My brothers and my father's
household, who were in the land of Canaan,
have come to me. 32 [m]And the men are shepherds, for they have been keepers of livestock,
and they have brought their flocks and their
herds and all that they have.' 33 When Pharaoh
calls you and says, [m]'What is your occupation?'
34 you shall say, [m]'Your servants have been
keepers of livestock [n]from our youth even
until now, both we and our fathers,' in order
that you may dwell [o]in the land of Goshen,
for every shepherd is [p]an abomination to the
Egyptians."

Jacob's Family Settles in Goshen

47 So Joseph [q]went in and told Pharaoh,
"My father and my brothers, with their
flocks and herds and all that they possess, have
come from the land of Canaan. They are now
in [r]the land of Goshen." 2 And from among
his brothers he took five men and [s]presented
them to Pharaoh. 3 Pharaoh said to his brothers, [t]"What is your occupation?" And they said
to Pharaoh, [u]"Your servants are shepherds,
as our fathers were." 4 They said to Pharaoh,
[v]"We have come to sojourn in the land, for
there is no pasture for your servants' flocks,
for the famine is severe in the land of Canaan.
And now, please let your servants dwell [w]in
the land of Goshen." 5 Then Pharaoh said to
Joseph, "Your father and your brothers have
come to you. 6 The land of Egypt is before
you. Settle your father and your brothers [x]in
the best of the land. [y]Let them settle in the
land of Goshen, and if you know any [z]able
men among them, put them in charge of my
livestock."
7 Then Joseph brought in Jacob his father
and stood him before Pharaoh, [a]and Jacob
blessed Pharaoh. 8 And Pharaoh said to Jacob,
"How many are the days of the years of your
life?" 9 And Jacob said to Pharaoh, "The days of
the years of my [b]sojourning are 130 years. [c]Few
and evil have been the days of the years of my
life, and [d]they have not attained to the days of
the years of the life of my fathers in the days
of their [b]sojourning." 10 And Jacob [e]blessed

[1] Hebrew *sons*

Yet while the chosen line is multiplying fruitfully, it is not subduing the earth. Rather, as Genesis closes and Exodus opens, Joseph's family winds up *being* subdued. Yet the paradox of fruitfulness through affliction, already observed in Joseph's life and then heightened in Exodus (Ex. 1:7, 12), is ratcheted up even more in the New Testament. It is through affliction rather than prosperity that God's people bear fruit (2 Cor. 6:10; 12:9–10; Heb. 12:11).

In Jesus above all we see this strange principle at work. "For he was crucified in *weakness*, but lives by the *power* of God" (2 Cor. 13:4). Jesus himself is the paradigmatic grain of wheat from his own teaching: "I say to you, unless a grain of wheat falls into the earth and dies, it remains alone; but if it dies, it bears much fruit" (John 12:24). His atoning death and resurrection bear the fruit of our salvation, all of grace.

20 [b] ch. 41:50-52 [c] ch. 41:45
21 [d] See Num. 26:38-40; 1 Chr. 7:6-12; 8:1
24 [e] 1 Chr. 7:13
25 [f] See ch. 30:5-8 [g] ch. 29:29
27 [h] Ex. 1:5; Deut. 10:22; [Acts 7:14]
28 [i] See ch. 45:10
29 [j] [ch. 45:14]
30 [k] [Luke 2:29, 30]
31 [l] ch. 47:1
32 [m] ch. 47:3
33 [m] [See ver. 32 above]
34 [m] [See ver. 32 above] [n] ch. 37:12 [o] ver. 28 [p] ch. 43:32; Ex. 8:26

Chapter 47 **1** [q] ch. 46:31 [r] See ch. 45:10 **2** [s] Acts 7:13 **3** [t] ch. 46:33 [u] ch. 46:32, 34 **4** [v] ch. 15:13; Deut. 26:5 [w] ch. 46:34 **6** [x] ch. 45:18 [y] ver. 4 [z] Ex. 18:21, 25 **7** [a] ver. 10 **9** [b] 1 Chr. 29:15; Ps. 39:12; 119:19, 54; Heb. 11:9, 13 [c] Job 14:1; [Ps. 39:4, 5; James 4:14] [d] ch. 11:32; 25:7; 35:28 **10** [e] ver. 7

Pharaoh and went out from the presence of Pharaoh. 11 Then Joseph settled his father and his brothers and gave them a possession in the land of Egypt, in the best of the land, in the land of [f]Rameses, [g]as Pharaoh had commanded. 12 And Joseph [h]provided his father, his brothers, and all his father's household with food, according to the number of their dependents.

Joseph and the Famine

13 Now there was no food in all the land, for the famine was very severe, so that the land of Egypt and the land of Canaan languished by reason of the famine. 14 [i]And Joseph gathered up all the money that was found in the land of Egypt and in the land of Canaan, in exchange for the grain that they bought. And Joseph brought the money into Pharaoh's house. 15 And when the money was all spent in the land of Egypt and in the land of Canaan, all the Egyptians came to Joseph and said, "Give us food. [j]Why should we die before your eyes? For our money is gone." 16 And Joseph answered, "Give your livestock, and I will give you food in exchange for your livestock, if your money is gone." 17 So they brought their livestock to Joseph, and Joseph gave them food in exchange for the horses, the flocks, the herds, and the donkeys. He supplied them with food in exchange for all their livestock that year. 18 And when that year was ended, they came to him the following year and said to him, "We will not hide from my lord that our money is all spent. The herds of livestock are my lord's. There is nothing left in the sight of my lord but our bodies and our land. 19 Why should we die before your eyes, both we and our land? [k]Buy us and our land for food, and we with our land will be servants to Pharaoh. And give us seed that we may live and not die, and that the land may not be desolate."

20 So Joseph bought all the land of Egypt for Pharaoh, for all the Egyptians sold their fields, because the famine was severe on them. The land became Pharaoh's. 21 As for the people, he made servants of them[1] from one end of Egypt to the other. 22 [l]Only the land of the priests he did not buy, for the priests had a fixed allowance from Pharaoh and lived on the allowance that Pharaoh gave them; therefore they did not sell their land.

23 Then Joseph said to the people, "Behold, I have this day bought you and your land for Pharaoh. Now here is seed for you, and you shall sow the land. 24 And at the harvests you shall give a [m]fifth to Pharaoh, and four fifths shall be your own, as seed for the field and as food for yourselves and your households, and as food for your little ones." 25 And they said, "You have saved our lives; [n]may it please my lord, we will be servants to Pharaoh." 26 So Joseph made it a statute concerning the land of Egypt, and it stands to this day, that Pharaoh should have the fifth; [o]the land of the priests alone did not become Pharaoh's.

27 Thus Israel settled in the land of Egypt, [p]in the land of Goshen. [q]And they gained possessions in it, and were fruitful and multiplied greatly. 28 And Jacob lived in the land of Egypt seventeen years. [r]So the days of Jacob, the years of his life, were 147 years.

29 And [s]when the time drew near that Israel must die, he called his son Joseph and said to him, "If now [t]I have found favor in your sight, [u]put your hand under my thigh and [v]promise to deal kindly and truly with me. [w]Do not bury me in Egypt, 30 but let me lie with my fathers. Carry me out of Egypt and [x]bury me in their burying place." He answered, "I will do as you have said." 31 And he said, "Swear to me"; and he swore to him. Then [y]Israel bowed himself upon the head of his bed.[2]

Jacob Blesses Ephraim and Manasseh

48 After this, Joseph was told, "Behold, your father is ill." So he took with him his two sons, Manasseh and Ephraim. 2 And it was told to Jacob, "Your son Joseph has come to you." Then Israel summoned his strength and sat up in bed. 3 And Jacob said to Joseph, [z]"God Almighty[3] appeared to me at [a]Luz in the land of Canaan and blessed me, 4 and said to

[1] Samaritan, Septuagint, Vulgate; Hebrew *he removed them to the cities* [2] Hebrew; Septuagint *staff* [3] Hebrew *El Shaddai*

11[f] Ex. 1:11; 12:37; [ch. 45:10] [g] ver. 6
12[h] ch. 45:11; 50:21
14[i] ch. 41:56
15[j] ver. 19
19[k] [Neh. 5:2, 3]

48:1–22 Once more it is the younger son who receives the blessing (see note on 25:19–34). Ephraim receives from Jacob the blessing of the firstborn, indicating that the special line traced throughout Genesis will continue through his descendants, ultimately reaching culmination in Jesus Christ.

22[l] [Ezra 7:24] **24**[m] ch. 41:34 **25**[n] See ch. 33:15 **26**[o] ver. 22 **27**[p] See ch. 45:10 [q] ch. 46:3 **28**[r] [ver. 9] **29**[s] Deut. 31:14; 1 Kgs. 2:1 [t] See ch. 33:15 [u] ch. 24:2 [v] ch. 24:49 [w] [ch. 50:25] **30**[x] ch. 49:29; 50:5, 13 **31**[y] ch. 48:2; 1 Kgs. 1:47; [Heb. 11:21] **Chapter 48** **3**[z] See ch. 17:1 [a] ch. 28:13, 19; 35:6, 9

me, 'Behold, I will make you fruitful and multiply you, and I will make of you a company
of peoples and will give this land to your offspring after you [b]for an everlasting possession.'
5 And now your [c]two sons, who were born to
you in the land of Egypt before I came to you
in Egypt, [d]are mine; Ephraim and Manasseh
shall be mine, as Reuben and Simeon are.
6 And the children that you fathered after
them shall be yours. They shall be called by the
name of their brothers in their inheritance.
7 As for me, when I came from Paddan, to my
sorrow [e]Rachel died in the land of Canaan on
the way, when there was still some distance[1] to
go to Ephrath, and I buried her there on the
way to Ephrath (that is, Bethlehem)."
8 When Israel saw Joseph's sons, he said,
"Who are these?" 9 Joseph said to his father,
[f]"They are my sons, whom God has given me
here." And he said, "Bring them to me, please,
that [g]I may bless them." 10 Now [h]the eyes of
Israel were dim with age, so that he could not
see. So Joseph brought them near him, [i]and
he kissed them and embraced them. 11 And
Israel said to Joseph, [j]"I never expected to see
your face; and behold, God has let me see your
offspring also." 12 Then Joseph removed them
from his knees, and he bowed himself with his
face to the earth. 13 And Joseph took them both,
Ephraim in his right hand toward Israel's left
hand, and Manasseh in his left hand toward
Israel's right hand, and brought them near
him. 14 [k]And Israel stretched out his right hand
and laid it on the head of Ephraim, who was
the younger, and his left hand on the head of
Manasseh, [l]crossing his hands (for Manasseh
was the firstborn). 15 And he blessed Joseph
and said,

"The God [m]before whom my fathers
Abraham and Isaac walked,
the God who has been my shepherd
all my life long to this day,
16 [n]the angel who has [o]redeemed me from
all evil, bless the boys;
and in them let [p]my name be carried
on, and the name of my fathers
Abraham and Isaac;
and let them [q]grow into a multitude[2]
in the midst of the earth."

17 When Joseph saw that his father [r]laid his
right hand on the head of Ephraim, it displeased him, and he took his father's hand to
move it from Ephraim's head to Manasseh's
head. 18 And Joseph said to his father, "Not
this way, my father; since this one is the firstborn, put your right hand on his head." 19 But
his father refused and said, [r]"I know, my son,
I know. He also shall become a people, and he
also shall be great. Nevertheless, [s]his younger
brother shall be greater than he, and his offspring shall become a multitude[3] of nations."
20 So he blessed them that day, saying,

"By you Israel will pronounce blessings,
saying,
[t]'God make you as Ephraim and as
Manasseh.'"

Thus he put Ephraim before Manasseh. 21 Then
Israel said to Joseph, "Behold, I am about
to die, but [u]God will be with you and will
bring you again to the land of your fathers.
22 Moreover, I have given to [v]you rather than to
your brothers one mountain slope[4] that I took
from the hand of the Amorites with my sword
and with my bow."

[1] Or *about two hours' distance* [2] Or *let them be like fish for multitude* [3] Hebrew *fullness* [4] Or *one portion of the land*; Hebrew *shekem*, which sounds like the town and district called *Shechem*

The covenant promises are put front and center in this chapter in Jacob's opening words, from his deathbed: "God Almighty appeared to me . . . and blessed me, and said to me, 'Behold, I will make you fruitful and multiply you, and I will make of you a company of peoples and will give this land to your offspring after you for an everlasting possession'" (48:3–4). Here the three specific promises from 12:1–3, 7 are reiterated: land, descendants, and divine blessing. We also see once more, as we have seen throughout Genesis, a reiteration of 1:28, the mandate to be fruitful and multiply. Yet throughout Genesis this divine mandate, originally given to Adam and Eve, gradually becomes transferred to the Lord himself—it is God who will cause his people to be fruitful and multiply. The grace of this catches us off guard—what God has called his people to do, he undertakes to fulfill himself. What he demands of us, he does for us.

Such is the way, of course, that God's gospel works. All that he demands of us—not only multiplying but the entire keeping of the law—he himself undertakes for us in his Son.

4 [b] ch. 17:8
5 [c] ch. 41:50-52; 46:20 [d] Josh. 13:7; 14:4; 17:17
7 [e] See ch. 35:9-19
9 [f] [ch. 33:5] [g] ch. 49:25, 26; Heb. 11:21; [ch. 27:4]
10 [h] [ch. 27:1] [i] ch. 27:27
11 [j] [ch. 37:33; 45:26]
14 [k] ver. 17 [l] ver. 19
15 [m] ch. 17:1; 24:40
16 [n] ch. 28:15; 31:11, 13, 24; Ex. 23:20 [o] Isa. 44:22, 23; 49:7; 63:9; [2 Sam. 4:9; Ps. 34:22; 121:7] [p] Amos 9:12; Acts 15:17 [q] [Num. 26:34, 37]
17 [r] ver. 14
19 [r] [See ver. 17 above] [s] Num. 1:33, 35; 2:19, 21; Deut. 33:17
20 [t] [Ruth 4:11, 12]
21 [u] ch. 46:4; 50:24
22 [v] Josh. 24:32; John 4:5

Jacob Blesses His Sons

49 [w]Then Jacob called his sons and said, "Gather yourselves together, that I may tell you what shall happen to you [x]in days to come.

2 "Assemble and listen, O sons of Jacob,
listen to Israel your father.

3 "Reuben, you are [y]my firstborn,
my might, and the [z]firstfruits of my strength,
preeminent in dignity and preeminent in power.
4 Unstable as water, you shall not have preeminence,
because you [a]went up to your father's bed;
then you defiled it—he went up to my couch!

5 [b]"Simeon and Levi are brothers;
weapons [c]of violence are their swords.
6 Let my soul come not into their council;
[d]O my glory, [e]be not joined to their company.
For in their anger they killed men,
and in their willfulness they [f]hamstrung oxen.
7 Cursed be their anger, for it is fierce,
and their wrath, for it is cruel!
I will [g]divide them in Jacob
and scatter them in Israel.

8 "Judah, [h]your brothers shall praise you;
[i]your hand shall be on the neck of your enemies;
[j]your father's sons shall bow down before you.
9 Judah is [k]a lion's cub;
from the prey, my son, you have gone up.
[l]He stooped down; he crouched as a lion
and as a lioness; who dares rouse him?
10 The [m]scepter shall not depart from Judah,
nor the ruler's staff [n]from between his feet,
until tribute comes to him;[1]
and to him shall be the obedience of the peoples.
11 Binding his foal to the vine
and his donkey's colt to the choice vine,
he has washed his garments in wine
and his vesture in the blood of grapes.
12 His [o]eyes are darker than wine,
and his teeth whiter than milk.

13 [p]"Zebulun shall dwell at the [q]shore of the sea;
he shall become a haven for ships,
and his border shall be at Sidon.

14 [r]"Issachar is a strong donkey,
crouching between the sheepfolds.[2]
15 He saw that a resting place was good,
and that the land was pleasant,
so he bowed his shoulder to bear,
and [s]became a servant at forced labor.

16 [t]"Dan shall [u]judge his people
as one of the tribes of Israel.
17 Dan [v]shall be a serpent in the way,
a viper by the path,
that bites the horse's heels
so that his rider falls backward.
18 I [w]wait for your salvation, O LORD.

19 [x]"Raiders shall raid [y]Gad,[3]
but he shall raid at their heels.

20 [z]"Asher's food shall be rich,
and he shall yield royal delicacies.

[1] By a slight revocalization; a slight emendation yields (compare Septuagint, Syriac, Targum) *until he comes to whom it belongs*; Hebrew *until Shiloh comes*, or *until he comes to Shiloh* [2] Or *between its saddlebags* [3] *Gad* sounds like the Hebrew for *raiders* and *raid*

Chapter 49
1 [w]For ver. 1-27, see Deut. 33:6-25 [x]Num. 24:14; Deut. 4:30; 31:29; Isa. 2:2; Jer. 23:20; Dan. 2:28; 10:14; Hos. 3:5
3 [y]ch. 29:32 [z]Deut. 21:17
4 [a]ch. 35:22; 1 Chr. 5:1
5 [b]ch. 29:33, 34 [c]ch. 34:25, 26
6 [d][Ps. 16:9; 57:8] [e][Ps. 26:9] [f]Josh. 11:6, 9; 2 Sam. 8:4

49:1–27 After focusing in chapter 48 on Joseph's two sons, Ephraim and Manasseh, chapter 49 focuses on the other sons of Jacob. Some sons are given a curse, others a blessing.

The most striking is Judah, about whom Jacob says (1) he will be praised by others; (2) he will prove triumphant over his enemies; (3) he is like a lion; and (4) he will rule eternally as (5) the nations of the earth submit to him (vv. 8–10). Intriguingly, all five of these marks come to be true of Jesus the Messiah, the anointed Son of David, who comes from this very line of Judah (see notes on 38:1–30 and 44:1–45:28).

7 [g]See Num. 3:5-13; Josh. 19:1-9; 1 Chr. 4:24-39 **8** [h]ch. 29:35; [ch. 27:29] [i][Job 16:12] [j]1 Chr. 5:2 **9** [k]Rev. 5:5; [Deut. 33:22; Hos. 5:14] [l][Num. 23:24; 24:9] **10** [m]Num. 24:17; Zech. 10:11 [n]Deut. 28:57 **12** [o]Prov. 23:29 **13** [p][Deut. 33:18, 19]; Josh. 19:10, 11 [q][Deut. 1:7; Josh. 9:1; Judg. 5:17] **14** [r]Judg. 5:16; [1 Chr. 12:32] **15** [s]Josh. 16:10 **16** [t][Deut. 33:22] [u]ch. 30:6 **17** [v]Judg. 18:27 **18** [w]Ps. 25:5; 119:166, 174; Isa. 25:9; Mic. 7:7; [Luke 2:25] **19** [x][Deut. 33:20] [y]See 1 Chr. 5:18-22 **20** [z][Deut. 33:24]

21 [a]"Naphtali is a doe let loose
that bears beautiful fawns.[1]

22 "Joseph is [b]a fruitful bough,
a fruitful bough by a spring;
his branches run over the wall.[2]
23 The archers [c]bitterly attacked him,
shot at him, and harassed him
severely,
24 yet [d]his bow remained unmoved;
his arms[3] were made agile
by the hands of the [e]Mighty One of
Jacob
(from there is [f]the Shepherd,[4] [g]the
Stone of Israel),
25 [h]by the God of your father who will help
you,
by [i]the Almighty[5] [j]who will bless you
with blessings of heaven above,
blessings of the deep that crouches
beneath,
blessings of the breasts and of the
womb.
26 The blessings of your father
are mighty beyond the blessings of
my parents,
up to the bounties [k]of the everlasting
hills.[6]
May they be [l]on the head of Joseph,
and on the brow of him who was set
apart from his brothers.

27 [m]"Benjamin is a ravenous wolf,
in the morning devouring the prey
and at evening [n]dividing the spoil."

Jacob's Death and Burial

28 All these are the twelve tribes of Israel. This
is what their father said to them as he blessed
them, blessing each with the blessing suitable
to him. 29 Then he commanded them and said
to them, "I am to be [o]gathered to my people;
[p]bury me with my fathers [q]in the cave that
is in the field of Ephron the Hittite, 30 in the
cave that is in the field at Machpelah, to the
east of Mamre, in the land of Canaan, [r]which
Abraham bought with the field from Ephron
the Hittite to possess as a burying place.
31 [s]There they buried Abraham and Sarah his
wife. There [t]they buried Isaac and Rebekah
his wife, and there I buried Leah— 32 the field
and the cave that is in it were bought from the
Hittites." 33 When Jacob finished commanding his sons, he drew up his feet into the bed
and breathed his last and [u]was gathered to
his people.

50 Then Joseph [v]fell on his father's face
and wept over him and kissed him.
2 And Joseph commanded his servants the
physicians to [w]embalm his father. So the
physicians embalmed Israel. 3 Forty days
were required for it, for that is how many are
required for embalming. And the Egyptians
[x]wept for him seventy days.

4 And when the days of weeping for him
were past, Joseph spoke to the household of
Pharaoh, saying, [y]"If now I have found favor in
your eyes, please speak in the ears of Pharaoh,
saying, 5 'My father made me swear, saying, "I
am about to die: in my tomb [z]that I hewed out
for myself in the land of Canaan, there shall
you bury me." Now therefore, let me please go
up and bury my father. Then I will return.'"
6 And Pharaoh answered, "Go up, and bury
your father, as he made you swear." 7 So Joseph
went up to bury his father. With him went up
all the servants of Pharaoh, the elders of his
household, and all the elders of the land of
Egypt, 8 as well as all the household of Joseph,
his brothers, and his father's household. Only
their children, their flocks, and their herds

[1] Or *he gives beautiful words*, or *that bears fawns of the fold* [2] Or *Joseph is a wild donkey, a wild donkey beside a spring, his wild colts beside the wall* [3] Hebrew *the arms of his hands* [4] Or *by the name of the Shepherd* [5] Hebrew *Shaddai* [6] A slight emendation yields (compare Septuagint) *the blessings of the eternal mountains, the bounties of the everlasting hills*

49:28–50:14 The purpose of this section of the conclusion to Genesis is to underscore the ongoing fulfillment of the land promise to Abraham (see 12:1–3, 7). Jacob's final wish was to be buried in the ancestral burial plot at Machpelah, in Canaan, on the very plot of land Abraham bought from the original inhabitants of the land (49:29–30; cf. 23:1–20). This wish is honored, despite the great inconvenience and traveling that is required to fulfill it. The reader is reminded that God's future for his people lies in Canaan, the Promised Land, not in Egypt. This is reinforced in the very closing words of Genesis, as a dying Joseph tells his sons that he too will eventually be brought up to Canaan (50:22–26).

21[a] [Deut. 33:23]
22[b] ch. 41:52; Josh. 17:14, 18
23[c] [ch. 37:24, 28; 39:20]
24[d] Job 29:20 [e] Ps. 132:2, 5; Isa. 1:24 [f] Ps. 23:1; 80:1 [g] Isa. 28:16; Eph. 2:20; 1 Pet. 2:4; [Deut. 32:4]
25[h] ch. 35:3; 50:17 [i] ch. 17:1; 35:11 [j] Deut. 33:13
26[k] Deut. 33:15; Hab. 3:6 [l] Deut. 33:16
27[m] [Judg. 20:21, 25; Ezek. 22:27] [n] Zech. 14:1; [Ezek. 39:10] **29**[o] ver. 33; ch. 25:8 [p] ch. 47:30 [q] ch. 50:13; [ch. 23:9] **30**[r] See ch. 23:16-18 **31**[s] ch. 23:19; 25:9 [t] ch. 35:29 **33**[u] ver. 29 **Chapter 50** **1**[v] ch. 46:4 **2**[w] ver. 26; [2 Chr. 16:14; Mark 16:1; Luke 23:56; John 19:39, 40] **3**[x] [ver. 10; Num. 20:29; Deut. 34:8; 1 Sam. 31:13; Job 2:13] **4**[y] ch. 47:29; See ch. 33:15 **5**[z] 2 Chr. 16:14; Isa. 22:16; Matt. 27:60

were left [a]in the land of Goshen. 9 And there
went up with him both chariots and horsemen. It was a very great company. 10 When they
came to the threshing floor of Atad, which
is beyond the Jordan, [b]they lamented there
with a very great and grievous lamentation,
and he [c]made a mourning for his father seven
days. 11 When the inhabitants of the land, the
Canaanites, saw the mourning on the threshing floor of Atad, they said, "This is a grievous
mourning by the Egyptians." Therefore the
place was named Abel-mizraim;[1] it is beyond
the Jordan. 12 Thus his sons did for him as he
had commanded them, 13 for [d]his sons carried
him to the land of Canaan and buried him in
the cave of the field at Machpelah, to the east of
Mamre, which Abraham [e]bought with the field
from Ephron the Hittite to possess as a burying
place. 14 After he had buried his father, Joseph
returned to Egypt with his brothers and all
who had gone up with him to bury his father.

God's Good Purposes

15 When Joseph's brothers saw that their
father was dead, they said, "It may be that
Joseph will hate us and pay us back for all
the evil that we did to him." 16 So they sent a
message to Joseph, saying, "Your father gave
this command before he died: 17 'Say to Joseph,
"Please forgive the transgression of your
brothers and their sin, because they did evil to
you."' And now, please forgive the transgression of the servants of [f]the God of your father."
Joseph wept when they spoke to him. 18 His
brothers also came and [g]fell down before him
and said, "Behold, we are your servants." 19 But
Joseph said to them, "Do not fear, for [h]am I in
the place of God? 20 As for you, you meant
evil against me, but [i]God meant it for good,
to bring it about that many people[2] should be
kept alive, as they are today. 21 So do not fear; [j]I
will provide for you and your little ones." Thus
he comforted them and spoke kindly to them.

The Death of Joseph

22 So Joseph remained in Egypt, he and
his father's house. Joseph lived 110 years.
23 And Joseph saw Ephraim's children [k]of
the third generation. The [l]children also of
Machir the son of Manasseh were [m]counted
as Joseph's own.[3] 24 And Joseph said to his
brothers, "I am about to die, but [n]God will
visit you and bring you up out of this land to
the land [o]that he swore to Abraham, to Isaac,
and to Jacob." 25 Then [p]Joseph made the sons
of Israel swear, saying, "God will surely visit
you, and you shall carry up my bones from
here." 26 So Joseph died, being 110 years old.
They [q]embalmed him, and he was put in a
coffin in Egypt.

[1] *Abel-mizraim* means *mourning* (or *meadow*) *of Egypt* [2] Or *a numerous people* [3] Hebrew *were born on Joseph's knees*

8 [a] See ch. 45:10
10 [b] [2 Sam. 1:17; Acts 8:2] [c] [ver. 3]
13 [d] ch. 49:29, 30; [Acts 7:16] [e] ch. 23:16
17 [f] ch. 49:25
18 [g] [ch. 37:7, 10]
19 [h] ch. 30:2; [2 Kgs. 5:7]
20 [i] ch. 45:5, 7
21 [j] ch. 45:11; 47:12
23 [k] [Job 42:16; Ps. 128:6] [l] Num. 32:39; 1 Chr. 7:14, 15 [m] [ch. 30:3]
24 [n] ch. 15:14; 46:4; 48:21; Ex. 3:16, 17; [Heb. 11:22] [o] ch. 15:18; 26:3; 28:13; 35:12; 46:4
25 [p] Ex. 13:19; Josh. 24:32
26 [q] See ver. 2

50:15–21 When he first revealed himself to his brothers, Joseph said three times that it was most ultimately *God* who had sent him on to Egypt, not his brothers (45:5, 7, 8). Now Joseph returns to this truth and articulates explicitly what has been implicit all through the Joseph narrative and indeed all through Genesis: all things, including the evil actions of godless men, are under the wise, governing hand of a gracious God who intends final good for his people (50:20).

The historical climax of this profound truth is the cross of Christ—here, if anywhere, is an act of evil: the crucifixion of the one person who ever lived a life undeserving of punishment of any kind. Yet even this, the book of Acts tells us, was under God's good hand. Jesus was "delivered up according to the definite plan and foreknowledge of God" (Acts 2:23; cf. 4:27–28). This does not exonerate the wicked actions that carry out such evil, but it does give us the broadest vision for what is happening at any given point of history, even when evil seems to triumph most horrifically. God is there. He is with his people. He is working out his redemptive purposes.

In these closing words of Joseph and of Genesis, we are reminded once more of the heart of the gospel. Responding to his brothers' fear that Joseph will punish them now that their father Jacob has died, Joseph responds, "Do not fear, for am I in the place of God?" (Gen. 50:19). The answer to that question had to be no, for Joseph knew that he, a man, could not rule or judge in the place of God. To seek to do so remains the supreme folly. We dare not seek to share in judgment that belongs only to a holy God. Yet at the culmination of redemptive history God became a man and put himself under judgment in the place of sinful man. This is supreme mercy. He dared to share in what only, to that point, had belonged to sinful man—yet he did so without sinning—to provide everlasting good from what we humans intended for evil.

Introduction to Exodus

Author and Date

Exodus (meaning exit) was probably written by Moses, like the rest of the Pentateuch. There is no agreement among scholars as to the date when the events of the exodus took place. A common view is that the exodus occurred in c. 1446 B.C., though some scholars believe it took place around 1260 B.C.

The Gospel in Exodus

Exodus offers the greatest paradigmatic redemption event in the Bible prior to Christ's incarnation. As such, it is profoundly good news to captives, to those who labor in bondage to sin and misery. In addition, it shapes Christians' continued understanding of and hope for redemption. In the redemption gained through the life, death, burial, resurrection, ascension, and continued ministry of Jesus, we have a new exodus, a fulfillment of what Exodus pictured for the people of God.

Exodus tells us that redemption begins with God remembering his covenant promises offered in Genesis: the promise of the death blow to our ancient Enemy through the offspring of the woman (Gen. 3:15); the promise to Abraham of an offspring through whom all the families of the earth will be blessed (Gen. 12:1–3); and the promise that Abraham's offspring will be in captivity for a time, but will return to the Promised Land (Gen. 15:13–14). Exodus opens with God remembering his covenant with Abraham (Ex. 2:23–25) and coming down to redeem his people through his chosen mediator, Moses (chs. 3–4).

Through Moses, God goes forward to redeem his people "out of the land of Egypt, out of the house of slavery" (20:2). Central to this redemption is judgment and salvation: judgment on the gods of Egypt and especially on their representative, Pharaoh, through the plagues; salvation amid the death of the firstborn of Egypt, of both humans and beasts, through the substitutionary death of spotless lambs for Israel (chs. 7–13). In the final contest between God and Pharaoh, God as the true King of the world crushes his enemy in the floods of the Red Sea and delivers his people through the waters of salvation. No wonder Moses' song ends, "The LORD will reign forever and ever" (15:18).

Having redeemed his people, God then guides them through the wilderness and brings them to Mount Sinai to instruct them in his ways. That is always the order of the Bible: redemption, then response; grace, then law. However, the Mosaic covenant could not deliver people from their sins; it was not meant to do so—rather, it served to point beyond itself to One who would come to fulfill all the foreshadowings in the tabernacle and all the requirements of the law's "rules" (21:1).

This Old Testament paradigm of redemption in Exodus, then, helps Christians see more clearly the ultimate redemption that God works out through Jesus, his Mediator between God and mankind (1 Tim. 2:5). In Jesus the Messiah, God acts because he remembers his covenant. His earliest promises to Adam and Eve and to Abraham find their fulfillment in Jesus (Gal. 3:7–18). And so, in Jesus, God himself comes down to deliver his people (John 1:14–18). Jesus is the Lamb of God whose blood serves as the redemption-price to deliver his people from God's wrath and the Enemy's captivity (John 1:29; Rom. 3:24–26; 1 Cor. 5:7; Eph. 1:7; 2:1–10). Those who trust in him are delivered from death itself—displayed in baptism—and brought to new life in Christ through his power (Rom. 6:1–11; 1 Cor. 10:1–4). That is why New Testament saints sing Moses' song as well (Rev. 15:3): Jesus has thrown the Evil One into the sea of God's wrath.

Moreover, as God's redeemed people, we live our lives in the wilderness as we make our way to the Promised Land, looking for a permanent city built by God (Heb. 11:10–16; 13:14). As we go through this world, God's Word and Spirit guide us as God's people under the oversight of elders (cf. Exodus 18 with Acts 15; 1 Timothy 3; Titus 1). We know God's presence. We are instructed in God's ways: his law no longer condemns us, but serves as a guide for our lives as we pursue holiness (Heb. 12:14; 1 Pet. 1:16) as those already viewed as holy to the Lord (1 Cor. 6:11).

Thus, Exodus offers a paradigm for God's redemption gained for us in Jesus Christ. As we read and meditate on this book, we are drawn into the drama of God's working that helps us to see and delight in the work of Jesus, with the result that we love even more the One who first loved us.

Outline

I. God Hears, and Remembers His Covenant (1:1–2:25)

II. God Comes Down and Calls His Deliverer (3:1–4:17)

III. God Redeems His People (4:18–15:21)

- A. God redeems his people through his promise (4:18–7:7)
- B. God redeems his people through his plagues (7:8–10:29)
- C. God redeems his people through his Passover (11:1–13:16)
- D. God redeems his people through his power (13:17–15:21)

IV. God Leads His People (15:22–18:27)

V. God Instructs His People (19:1–40:38)

- A. God instructs his people through the commandments (19:1–20:17)
- B. God instructs his people through the covenant (20:18–24:11)
- C. God instructs his people through the tabernacle (24:12–40:38)

Exodus

Israel Increases Greatly in Egypt

1 [a]These are the names of the sons of Israel
who came to Egypt with Jacob, each with
his household: 2 Reuben, Simeon, Levi, and
Judah, 3 Issachar, Zebulun, and Benjamin,
4 Dan and Naphtali, Gad and Asher. 5 All the
descendants of Jacob were [b]seventy persons;
Joseph was already in Egypt. 6 Then [c]Joseph
died, and all his brothers and all that generation. 7 [d]But the people of Israel were fruitful
and increased greatly; they multiplied and
grew exceedingly strong, so that the land was
filled with them.

Pharaoh Oppresses Israel

8 Now there arose a new king over Egypt,
[e]who did not know Joseph. 9 And he said to his
people, "Behold, [f]the people of Israel are too
many and too mighty for us. 10 [g]Come, [h]let us
deal shrewdly with them, lest they multiply,
and, if war breaks out, they join our enemies
and fight against us and escape from the land."
11 Therefore they set taskmasters over them [i]to
afflict them with heavy [j]burdens. They built
for Pharaoh [k]store cities, Pithom and [l]Raamses.
12 But the more they were oppressed, the more
they multiplied and the more they spread
abroad. And the Egyptians were in dread of
the people of Israel. 13 So they ruthlessly made
the people of Israel [m]work as slaves 14 and
[n]made their lives bitter with hard service, in
mortar and brick, and in all kinds of work
in the field. In all their work they ruthlessly
made them work as slaves.

15 Then the king of Egypt said to the Hebrew
midwives, one of whom was named Shiphrah
and the other Puah, 16 "When you serve as midwife to the Hebrew women and see them on
the birthstool, if it is a son, you shall kill him,
but if it is a daughter, she shall live." 17 But the
midwives [o]feared God and did not do as the
king of Egypt commanded them, but let
the male children live. 18 So the king of Egypt
called the midwives and said to them, "Why
have you done this, and let the male children live?" 19 The midwives said to Pharaoh,
"Because the Hebrew women are not like the

1:1–7 The sons of Israel are listed in the same order here as in Genesis 35:23–26; only Joseph is excepted because he was already in Egypt. This list recalls the connections between Genesis and Exodus: specifically, Genesis 46:1–4, where God directs Jacob/Israel to go to Egypt. God promises to make Israel a great nation, but more, he promises, "I myself will go down with you to Egypt, and I will also bring you up again" (Gen. 46:4). Israel's God is not localized to Palestine; his reach extends to Egypt as well. We must remember that we serve the God to whom the earth belongs; his reach extends to the nations; and he will gain their service for his praise (Ps. 24:1; 67:4).

1:13–14 Where was God in all of his people's suffering? Here is God's mysterious wisdom at work. He had told Abraham that his posterity would be "sojourners in a land that is not theirs and will be servants there, and they will be afflicted for four hundred years" (Gen. 15:13). And yet, the suffering of God's people would be used to bring judgment upon Egypt and blessing to Israel (Gen. 15:14). Even so, our sufferings work together for God's salvation purposes because they are part of his eternal plan.

1:15–21 God's blessing of the midwives was not due to their apparent shading of the truth. Rather, he blessed them because they feared God more than Pharaoh (1:21; cf. Acts 4:19). They did not follow the command to kill the sons; rather, they allowed them to live. The ironic result is that Israel continued to multiply. God's gracious blessing continued to be with his people despite the horrific circumstances they encountered.

Chapter 1

1 [a]For ver. 1-4, see Gen. 35:23-26; 46:8-26
5 [b]Gen. 46:27; Deut. 10:22
6 [c]Gen. 50:26
7 [d]Deut. 26:5; Acts 7:17; [Gen. 46:3]
8 [e]Cited Acts 7:18
9 [f]Ps. 105:24
10 [g]Ps. 83:3, 4 [h]Ps. 105:25; Acts 7:19
11 [i]ch. 3:7; Gen. 15:13; Deut. 26:6 [j]ch. 2:11; 5:4, 5; 6:6, 7; Ps. 81:6 [k][2 Chr. 16:4] [l][ch. 12:37; Gen. 47:11]
13 [m]See ch. 5:7-19
14 [n][ch. 2:23; 6:9; Num. 20:15; Acts 7:19, 34]
17 [o]Prov. 16:6; [Dan. 3:16-18; 6:13; Acts 5:29]

Egyptian women, for they are vigorous and give birth before the midwife comes to them." 20 [p]So God dealt well with the midwives. And the people multiplied and grew very strong. 21 And because the midwives feared God, [q]he gave them families. 22 Then Pharaoh commanded all his people, [r]"Every son that is born to the Hebrews[1] you shall cast into [s]the Nile, but you shall let every daughter live."

The Birth of Moses

2 Now a [t]man from the house of Levi went and took as his wife a Levite woman. 2 The woman conceived and bore a son, and [u]when she saw that he was a fine child, she hid him three months. 3 When she could hide him no longer, she took for him a basket made of bulrushes[2] and daubed it with bitumen and pitch. She put the child in it and placed it among the [v]reeds by the river bank. 4 And [w]his sister stood at a distance to know what would be done to him. 5 Now the daughter of Pharaoh came down to bathe at the river, while her young women walked beside the river. She saw the basket among the reeds and sent her servant woman, and she took it. 6 When she opened it, she saw the child, and behold, the baby was crying. She took pity on him and said, "This is one of the Hebrews' children." 7 Then his sister said to Pharaoh's daughter, "Shall I go and call you a nurse from the Hebrew women to nurse the child for you?" 8 And Pharaoh's daughter said to her, "Go." So the girl went and called the child's mother. 9 And Pharaoh's daughter said to her, "Take this child away and nurse him for me, and I will give you your wages." So the woman took the child and nursed him. 10 When the child grew older, she brought him to Pharaoh's daughter, and he became [x]her son. She named him Moses, "Because," she said, "I [y]drew him out of the water."[3]

Moses Flees to Midian

11 One day, [z]when Moses had grown up, he went out to his people and looked on their [a]burdens, and he saw an Egyptian beating a Hebrew, one of his people.[4] 12 He looked this way and that, and seeing no one, he [b]struck down the Egyptian and hid him in the sand. 13 When [c]he went out the next day, behold, two Hebrews were struggling together. And he said to the man in the wrong, "Why do you strike your companion?" 14 He answered, [d]"Who made you a prince and a judge over us? Do you mean to kill me as you killed the Egyptian?" Then Moses was afraid, and thought, "Surely the thing is known." 15 When Pharaoh heard of it, he sought to kill Moses. But [e]Moses fled from Pharaoh and stayed in the land of Midian. And he sat down by [f]a well.

[1] Samaritan, Septuagint, Targum; Hebrew lacks *to the Hebrews* [2] Hebrew *papyrus reeds* [3] *Moses* sounds like the Hebrew for *draw out* [4] Hebrew *brothers*

20[p] [Eccles. 8:12]
21[q] [1 Sam. 2:35; 2 Sam. 7:11, 27; 1 Kgs. 2:24; 11:38; Ps. 127:1]
22[r] Acts 7:19 [s] Gen. 41:1
Chapter 2
1[t] ch. 6:20; Num. 26:59; 1 Chr. 23:14
2[u] Acts 7:20; Heb. 11:23
3[v] ver. 5; Isa. 19:6
4[w] ch. 15:20; Num. 26:59
10[x] Acts 7:21; [Heb. 11:24] [y] 2 Sam. 22:17; Ps. 18:16
11[z] Acts 7:23; Heb. 11:24-26 [a] See ch. 1:11
12[b] Acts 7:24
13[c] Acts 7:23-28
14[d] [Luke 12:14]
15[e] Acts 7:29; Heb. 11:27 [f] Gen. 24:11; 29:2

2:1–10 Moses is introduced and will serve as the deliverer of his people. His special birth casts the mind back to another child of promise, Isaac, and forward to other cared-for children of promise, especially Samson (Judg. 13:1–25), Samuel (1 Sam. 1:1–20) and, later, Jesus (Matt. 1:18–25). God's protection of his appointed deliverer occurs as Moses is himself delivered from Pharaoh's decree of death. This calls to mind how Jesus, God's appointed deliverer of his people, was delivered from Herod's decree of death (Matt. 2:13–23).

2:3 In the same way that God delivered Noah from judgment by having him build an ark that floated upon the waters (Gen. 6:11–14), so God delivered Moses from Pharaoh's judgment by having his mother build an ark that floated upon the waters. God rescued Moses through the faith of his parents, who not only hid him but also entrusted him to God's care and deliverance (Heb. 11:23). Faith trusts the unseen God, knowing that he has delivered in times past and will deliver his people in future days as well. God uses and honors the faith of parents today as he keeps his promises to them and their children (Gen. 17:1–14; Acts 2:38–39).

2:10–11 Moses lived in Pharaoh's household 40 years. During that time, he was "instructed in all the wisdom of the Egyptians" (Acts 7:22). Like Daniel, who also excelled amid such "pagan" instruction (Dan. 1:17–20), Moses was prepared with the best that his culture offered. God's purpose for Moses—leading a nation of millions through the wilderness—required such preparation.

Are we patient in similar periods of training? Do we see the value of our educations in areas of "general revelation" or "secular" topics? God uses these times to shape our minds for future usefulness. It is a mark of his great love for us.

[16] Now the [g]priest of Midian had seven
daughters, and [h]they came and drew water
and filled the troughs to water their father's
flock. [17] The shepherds came and drove them
away, but Moses stood up and saved them,
and [i]watered their flock. [18] When they came
home to their father [j]Reuel, he said, "How is
it that you have come home so soon today?"
[19] They said, "An Egyptian delivered us out
of the hand of the shepherds and even drew
water for us and [i]watered the flock." [20] He said
to his daughters, "Then where is he? Why have
you left the man? Call him, that he may [k]eat
bread." [21] And Moses was content to dwell with
the man, and he gave Moses his daughter
[l]Zipporah. [22] She gave birth to a son, and he
called his name [m]Gershom, for he said, "I have
been a [n]sojourner[1] in a foreign land."

God Hears Israel's Groaning

[23] [o]During those many days the king of Egypt
died, and the people of Israel [p]groaned because
of their slavery and cried out for help. [q]Their
cry for rescue from slavery came up to God.
[24] And [r]God heard their groaning, and God
[s]remembered his covenant with [t]Abraham,
with Isaac, and with Jacob. [25] God [u]saw the
people of Israel—and God [v]knew.

The Burning Bush

3 Now Moses was keeping the flock of his
father-in-law, Jethro, the priest of Midian,
and he led his flock to the west side of the wilderness and came to Horeb, the [w]mountain of
God. [2] [x]And [y]the angel of the LORD appeared
to him in a flame of fire out of the midst of a
bush. He looked, and behold, the bush was
burning, yet it was not consumed. [3] And Moses
said, "I will turn aside to see this great sight,
why the bush is not burned." [4] When the LORD
saw that he turned aside to see, [z]God called to
him [a]out of the bush, "Moses, Moses!" And
he said, "Here I am." [5] Then he said, "Do not
come near; [b]take your sandals off your feet,

[1] *Gershom* sounds like the Hebrew for *sojourner*

2:23–25 These verses frame the section that began at 1:1. There, the list of the 12 tribes of Israel and God's blessing with fruitfulness recalled God's covenant promise to Abraham. Here, the text explicitly says, "God remembered his covenant with Abraham." In the exodus event, God specifically acts to save Israel because of his covenant promises to Abraham in Genesis 15:14. Often, we become impatient for God to remember his promise to make the world new; but God is not slow in keeping his promise (cf. 2 Pet. 3:1–9). He is the faithful, covenant-making, covenant-keeping God.

3:1–4:17 Because God remembered his covenant, he chose Moses as a deliverer for his people. This section demonstrates both the inadequacy of Moses as a deliverer and the adequacy of the God who calls him (cf. 2 Cor. 3:4–6). In response to every question or objection that Moses offers, God patiently shows how his presence, limitless sufficiency, and power will be with him. And that's the point: God is the true deliverer of his people in and through Moses, his chosen servant. Moses' call was to trust the Lord in obedient faith, believing that God's power would be displayed in Moses' weakness (cf. 2 Cor. 12:9–10).

3:2 The angel of the Lord frequently appears in the Old Testament as the Lord's messenger, a distinct being who is yet so identified with Yahweh that to see him is to see God (Genesis 16; 18; 22:11–18; Numbers 22; Judges 6; 13). In Exodus, the angel is identified with the pillar of cloud and fire (Ex. 14:19) and is the means of God's leading Israel to the Promised Land (23:20, 23; 32:34; 33:2). While many identify the angel's appearances in the Old Testament as those of the preincarnate Son of God (but see Matt. 1:20, 24; 2:13, 19; where the angel of the Lord appears after Jesus has already been conceived), it can at least be said that he serves to foreshadow the way that Jesus reveals God to his people as one sent from and yet identified with God.

3:2–4 In the Bible, fire often accompanies the self-revelation of God (Gen. 15:17; Ex. 13:21–22; 14:24; 19:18; 24:17; 40:38; Deut. 4:24; 9:3; Heb. 12:29). It generally stands for God's glory, holiness, and purity (Ex. 3:5). As a glorious and pure being, God cannot tolerate impurity (1 John 1:5), but must judge and consume it. The wonder of the burning bush—what made it a "great sight"—was that the fire did *not* consume the bush. Hence, what was a picture of God's sovereign power over creation and his holy presence with his people was also a picture of his mercy and grace—that the fiery holiness of God would not destroy or consume the object of his revelation.

16 [g]ch. 3:1 [h]Gen. 24:11; 29:10; 1 Sam. 9:11
17 [i][Gen. 29:10]
18 [j]Num. 10:29; [ch. 3:1; 4:18; 18:1, 5, 9, 12]
19 [i][See ver. 17 above]
20 [k]Gen. 31:54; 43:25
21 [l]ch. 4:25; 18:2
22 [m]ch. 18:3 [n]Acts 7:29; [Heb. 11:13, 14]
23 [o][ch. 7:7]; Acts 7:23, 30 [p][Deut. 26:7] [q]ch. 3:9; Gen. 18:20, 21; James 5:4
24 [r]ch. 6:5 [s]Ps. 105:8, 42; 106:45 [t]Gen. 15:14; 46:4
25 [u]ch. 3:7; 4:31; [Luke 1:25] [v][ch. 3:16]

Chapter 3
1 [w]ch. 4:27; 18:5; 24:13; Num. 10:33; 1 Kgs. 19:8
2 [x]For ver. 2-10, see Acts 7:30-35 [y]Isa. 63:9
4 [z]ch. 19:3 [a]Deut. 33:16
5 [b]Josh. 5:15; [ch. 19:12; Eccles. 5:1]

for the place on which you are standing is holy
ground." 6 And he said, [c]"I am the God of your
father, the God of Abraham, the God of Isaac,
and the God of Jacob." And Moses hid his face,
for [d]he was afraid to look at God.
7 Then the LORD said, [e]"I have surely seen
the affliction of my people who are in Egypt
and have heard their cry because of their
[f]taskmasters. I know their sufferings, 8 and
[g]I have come down to deliver them out of the
hand of the Egyptians and [h]to bring them
up out of that land to a [i]good and broad
land, a land [j]flowing with milk and honey,
to the place of [k]the Canaanites, the Hittites,
the Amorites, the Perizzites, the Hivites, and
the Jebusites. 9 And now, behold, [l]the cry
of the people of Israel has come to me, and
I have also seen the [m]oppression with which
the Egyptians oppress them. 10 [n]Come, I will
send you to Pharaoh that you may bring my
people, the children of Israel, out of Egypt."
11 But Moses said to God, [o]"Who am I that
I should go to Pharaoh and bring the children of Israel out of Egypt?" 12 He said, [p]"But
I will be with you, and this shall be the sign
for you, that I have sent you: when you have
brought the people out of Egypt, [q]you shall
serve God on this mountain."
13 Then Moses said to God, "If I come to the
people of Israel and say to them, 'The God
of your fathers has sent me to you,' and they
ask me, 'What is his name?' what shall I say
to them?" 14 God said to Moses, "I AM WHO
I AM."[1] And he said, "Say this to the people
of Israel, [r]'I AM has sent me to you.'" 15 God
also said to Moses, "Say this to the people of
Israel, 'The LORD,[2] the [s]God of your fathers,
the God of Abraham, the God of Isaac, and the
God of Jacob, has sent me to you.' This is [t]my
name forever, and thus I am to be remembered
throughout all generations. 16 Go and [u]gather
the elders of Israel together and say to them,
'The LORD, the God of your fathers, the God of
Abraham, of Isaac, and of Jacob, has appeared
to me, saying, [v]"I have observed you and what
has been done to you in Egypt, 17 and I promise that [w]I will bring you up out of the affliction of Egypt to the land of the Canaanites,
the Hittites, the Amorites, the Perizzites, the
Hivites, and the Jebusites, a land [w]flowing
with milk and honey."' 18 And [x]they will listen to your voice, and you and the elders of
Israel [y]shall go to the king of Egypt and say
to him, 'The LORD, the God of the Hebrews,
has [z]met with us; and now, please let us go a
three days' journey into the wilderness, that

[1] Or *I AM WHAT I AM*, or *I WILL BE WHAT I WILL BE* [2] The word *LORD*, when spelled with capital letters, stands for the divine name, *YHWH*, which is here connected with the verb *hayah*, "to be" in verse 14

6 [c] ch. 4:5; Gen. 28:13; 1 Kgs. 18:36; Cited Matt. 22:32; Mark 12:26; [Luke 20:37] [d] [1 Kgs. 19:13; Isa. 6:1, 2, 5]
7 [e] ch. 2:23-25; Neh. 9:9; Ps. 106:44 [f] ch. 5:13, 14
8 [g] Gen. 11:5, 7; 18:21 [h] ch. 6:6; 12:51; [Gen. 50:24] [i] Deut. 1:25; 8:7, 8, 9 [j] ch. 13:5; 33:3; Lev. 20:24; Num. 13:27; Deut. 26:9, 15; Jer. 11:5; 32:22; Ezek. 20:6 [k] Gen. 15:18-21
9 [l] ch. 2:23 [m] ch. 1:11-14, 22
10 [n] [Ps. 105:26; Mic. 6:4]
11 [o] ch. 6:12; [1 Sam. 18:18; Isa. 6:5, 8; Jer. 1:6]
12 [p] ch. 4:12, 15; Deut. 31:8, 23; Josh. 1:5 [q] See ch. 19
14 [r] ch. 6:3; Ps. 68:4; John 8:58; Heb. 13:8; Rev. 1:4; 4:8
15 [s] ver. 6 [t] Hos. 12:5; [Ps. 135:13]
16 [u] ch. 4:29 [v] ch. 4:31; Gen. 50:24; [Luke 1:68]
17 [w] ver. 8
18 [x] ch. 4:31 [y] ch. 5:1 [z] Num. 23:3, 4, 15, 16

3:11–12 God's answer to Moses' first objection should have been sufficient for all the rest: "But I will be with you." This is far more than God's omnipresence. Rather, this is God's active, powerful presence with his people to deliver (cf. 33:14). Remember that God said, "I have come down to deliver them. . . . Come, I will send you" (3:8, 10). God is present in and through Moses to deliver his people. The blessing that Jesus, God incarnate, gave to his disciples offers us this same confidence: "Behold, I am with you always, to the end of the age" (Matt. 28:20). Our God, through the Spirit of Jesus, is powerfully present with us to guide, comfort, and deliver. We can take comfort, confidence, and courage in this reality.

3:13–16 Naming has great importance in the Bible. In the garden of Eden, the giving of names demonstrates lordship over the creation (Gen. 1:26–27; 2:19, 23; 3:20) and can often relate to hopes (Gen. 4:1), memories (Gen. 35:18), or prophecies (Isa. 7:14; Matt. 1:21). In naming, one's character is revealed.

Moses' question is therefore supremely important: what is the name, the character, of this God of whom I will speak? God's response seems enigmatic. But notice how the revelation of God's name builds: "I AM WHO I AM" (Ex. 3:14a); "Say this . . . , 'I AM has sent me to you'" (3:14b); "Say this . . . , 'The LORD [I AM], the God of your fathers'" (3:15, 16). In other words, this living, personal God who revealed himself to Abraham and made covenant with him is the God who is moving to deliver his people now.

All of this makes Jesus' own use of this divine name significant as well, not only in the seven "I am" statements in the Gospel of John (John 6:35; 8:12; 10:9, 11; 11:25; 14:6; 15:1), but especially his declaration to the Pharisees that "before Abraham was, I am" (John 8:58). In saying this, Jesus was claiming to be the same living, personal God who made covenant with Abraham, the same God who revealed himself to Moses, and the one who was now moving to deliver his people.

we may sacrifice to the LORD our God.’ 19But
I know that the king of Egypt [a]will not let you
go unless compelled [b]by a mighty hand.[1] 20So
[c]I will stretch out my hand and strike Egypt
with [d]all the wonders that I will do in it; [e]after
that he will let you go. 21And [f]I will give this
people favor in the sight of the Egyptians; and
when you go, you shall not go empty, 22but
each woman shall ask of her neighbor, and
any woman who lives in her house, for [g]silver
and gold jewelry, and for clothing. You shall
put them on your sons and on your daughters.
So [h]you shall plunder the Egyptians.”

Moses Given Powerful Signs

4 Then Moses answered, “But behold, they
will not believe me or listen to my voice,
for they will say, ‘The LORD did not appear to
you.’ ” 2The LORD said to him, “What is that
in your hand?” He said, [i]“A staff.” 3And he
said, “Throw it on the ground.” So he threw
it on the ground, and it became a serpent,
and Moses ran from it. 4But the LORD said to
Moses, “Put out your hand and catch it by the
tail”—so he put out his hand and caught it,
and it became a staff in his hand— 5“that they
may [j]believe that the LORD, [k]the God of their
fathers, the God of Abraham, the God of Isaac,
and the God of Jacob, has appeared to you.”
6Again, the LORD said to him, “Put your hand
inside your cloak.”[2] And he put his hand inside
his cloak, and when he took it out, behold, his
hand was [l]leprous[3] like snow. 7Then God said,
“Put your hand back inside your cloak.” So he
put his hand back inside his cloak, and when
he took it out, behold, [m]it was restored like
the rest of his flesh. 8“If they will not believe
you,” God said, “or listen to the first sign, they
may believe the latter sign. 9If they will not
believe even these two signs or listen to your
voice, you shall take some water from the Nile
and pour it on the dry ground, and the water
that you shall take from the Nile [n]will become
blood on the dry ground.”

10But Moses said to the LORD, “Oh, my Lord,
I am not eloquent, either in the past or since
you have spoken to your servant, but [o]I am slow
of speech and of tongue.” 11Then the LORD said
to him, “Who has made man’s mouth? Who
makes him mute, or deaf, or seeing, or blind?
Is it not I, the LORD? 12Now therefore go, and
[p]I will be with your mouth and teach you what
you shall speak.” 13But he said, “Oh, my Lord,
please send someone else.” 14Then the anger
of the LORD was kindled against Moses and
he said, “Is there not Aaron, your brother, the
Levite? I know that he can speak well. Behold,
[q]he is coming out to meet you, and when he
sees you, he will be glad in his heart. 15[r]You
shall speak to him and [s]put the words in his
mouth, and [p]I will be with your mouth and
with his mouth and will teach you both what
to do. 16[t]He shall speak for you to the people,
and he shall be your mouth, and [u]you shall be
as God to him. 17And take in your hand [v]this
staff, with which you shall do the signs.”

Moses Returns to Egypt

18Moses went back to [w]Jethro his father-in-law
and said to him, “Please let me go back to my

[1] Septuagint, Vulgate; Hebrew *go, not by a mighty hand* [2] Hebrew *into your bosom*; also verse 7 [3] *Leprosy* was a term for several skin diseases; see Leviticus 13

3:19–20 God tells Moses, “I know that the king of Egypt will not let you go.” But this is not mere foreknowledge; rather, this foreknowledge is related to God’s overarching purpose—“I will stretch out my hand . . . ; after that he will let you go.” Even more, God’s purpose is not simply to defeat Pharaoh, but to “plunder the Egyptians” (v. 22; 12:36). What confidence Moses should have known because God already had told him what would happen! Likewise, what confidence we should have because we know that our God is the Lord of history. He knows “the end from the beginning” because his sovereign purpose rules and overrules all (Isa. 46:7–10)!

4:1–9 In response to Moses’ objection that Israel “will not believe me or listen to my voice” (v. 1), God gives him signs (vv. 8, 9). These serve as confirmations of God’s word and pictures of God’s power. As *confirmations*, they were meant to persuade Israel to “believe that the LORD . . . has appeared to you” (v. 5). As *pictures*, they demonstrate how God will act as Israel trusts him: as sovereign King he will seize the tail of Egyptian power (in the serpent). As the Redeemer he will purify his unclean nation (in the leprous hand). God condescended to Israel’s weak capacities in giving these signs to strengthen their hearts.

He continues to do the same for us today in his signs of baptism and the Lord’s Supper, signs that confirm his promises and picture his good news for us.

19[a] ch. 5:2; 7:4 [b] ch. 6:1; 13:3
20[c] Deut. 6:22; Neh. 9:10; Jer. 32:20; Acts 7:36; See ch. 7–12 [d] ch. 4:21 [e] ch. 12:31
21[f] ch. 11:2, 3; 12:35, 36; [Gen. 15:14]
22[g] [ch. 33:6] [h] [Ezek. 39:10]

Chapter 4
2[i] ver. 17, 20
5[j] ch. 19:9 [k] See ch. 3:6
6[l] Num. 12:10; 2 Kgs. 5:27
7[m] [2 Kgs. 5:14]
9[n] ch. 7:19
10[o] [ch. 6:12; Jer. 1:6]
12[p] [ch. 3:12; Isa. 50:4; Jer. 1:9; Ezek. 33:22; Matt. 10:19, 20; Mark 13:11; Luke 12:11, 12; 21:15]
14[q] ver. 27
15[r] ch. 7:1, 2 [s] Num. 22:38; 23:5, 12, 16; Deut. 18:18; 2 Sam. 14:3, 19; Isa. 51:16 [p] [See ver. 12 above]
16[t] ver. 30 [u] [ch. 7:1; 18:19]
17[v] ver. 2; ch. 7:15
18[w] [ch. 2:18]

brothers in Egypt to see whether they are still alive." And Jethro said to Moses, "Go in peace." 19 And the LORD said to Moses in Midian, "Go back to Egypt, for [x]all the men who were seeking your life are dead." 20 So Moses took [y]his wife and his sons and had them ride on a donkey, and went back to the land of Egypt. And Moses took [z]the staff of God in his hand.

21 And the LORD said to Moses, "When you go back to Egypt, see that you do before Pharaoh all the [a]miracles that I have put in your power. But [b]I will harden his heart, so that he will not let the people go. 22 Then you shall say to Pharaoh, 'Thus says the LORD, [c]Israel is my [d]firstborn son, 23 and I say to you, "Let my son go that he may serve me." If you refuse to let him go, behold, I [e]will kill your firstborn son.' "

24 At a lodging place on the way [f]the LORD met him and [g]sought to put him to death. 25 Then [h]Zipporah took a [i]flint and cut off her son's foreskin and touched Moses'[1] feet with it and said, "Surely you are a bridegroom of blood to me!" 26 So he let him alone. It was then that she said, "A bridegroom of blood," because of the circumcision.

27 The LORD said to Aaron, "Go into the wilderness [j]to meet Moses." So he went and met him at the [k]mountain of God and kissed him. 28 And Moses [l]told Aaron all the words of the LORD with which he had sent him to speak, and all [m]the signs that he had commanded him to do. 29 Then Moses and Aaron [n]went and gathered together all the elders of the people of Israel. 30 [o]Aaron spoke all the words that the LORD had spoken to Moses and did the signs in the sight of the people. 31 And the people [p]believed; and when they heard that the LORD had [q]visited the people of Israel and that he had [r]seen their affliction, [s]they bowed their heads and worshiped.

Making Bricks Without Straw

5 Afterward Moses and Aaron went and said to Pharaoh, "Thus says the LORD, the God of Israel, 'Let my people go, that they may hold [t]a feast to me in the wilderness.' " 2 But Pharaoh said, [u]"Who is the LORD, that I should obey his voice and let Israel go? I do not know the LORD, and moreover, [v]I will not let Israel go." 3 Then they said, "The [w]God of the Hebrews has met with us. Please let us go a three days' journey into the wilderness that we may sacrifice to the LORD our God, lest he fall upon us with pestilence or with the sword." 4 But the king of Egypt said to them, "Moses and Aaron, why do you take the people away from their work? Get back to your [x]burdens." 5 And Pharaoh said, "Behold, [y]the people of the land are now many,[2] and you make them rest from their burdens!" 6 The same day Pharaoh commanded the [z]taskmasters of the people and their [a]foremen, 7 "You shall no longer give the people straw to make bricks, as in the past; let them go and gather straw for themselves. 8 But the number of bricks that they made in the past you shall impose on them, you shall by no means reduce it, for they are idle. Therefore they cry, 'Let us go and offer sacrifice to our God.' 9 Let heavier work be laid on the men that they may labor at it and pay no regard to lying words."

10 So the [b]taskmasters and the foremen of the people went out and said to the people, "Thus says Pharaoh, 'I will not give you straw. 11 Go and get your straw yourselves wherever you can find it, but your work will not be reduced in the least.' " 12 So the people were scattered throughout all the land of Egypt to gather stubble for straw. 13 The [c]taskmasters were urgent, saying, "Complete your work, your daily task each day, as when there was straw." 14 And the foremen of the people of

[1] Hebrew *his* [2] Samaritan *they are now more numerous than the people of the land*

19[x] ch. 2:15, 23; [Matt. 2:20]
20[y] ch. 18:2-4 [z] ch. 17:9; Num. 20:8, 9
21[a] ch. 3:20 [b] ch. 7:13, 22; 8:15, 32; 9:12, 35; 10:1; 14:8; Rom. 9:17, 18; [Deut. 2:30; Josh. 11:20; Isa. 63:17]
22[c] Hos. 11:1 [d] Jer. 31:9
23[e] ch. 11:5; 12:29
24[f] [Num. 22:22; 1 Chr. 21:16] [g] [Gen. 17:14]
25[h] ch. 2:21 [i] Josh. 5:2, 3
27[j] ver. 14 [k] See ch. 3:1
28[l] ver. 15, 16 [m] See ver. 3-9
29[n] ch. 3:16

5:5–21 Not only does Moses' appeal to Pharaoh that he let Israel go fail, it produces a disastrous result: the intensification of Israel's hardship and affliction. Underlying this increased affliction is a larger battle: a battle between the Lord, the God of Israel, and Pharaoh, representing the gods of Egypt. Whereas Moses came with "thus says the LORD" (v. 1), Pharaoh speaks to Israel with "thus says Pharaoh" (v. 10). As God will tell Moses, this was exactly the point: this confrontation was so that "the Egyptians shall know that I am the LORD" (7:5).

This is what we pray for in the Lord's Prayer: "Hallowed be your name" is the request that God will vindicate himself and show himself to be the true Lord of this world.

30[o] ver. 16 **31**[p] ver. 8, 9; ch. 3:18 [q] See ch. 3:16 [r] ch. 2:25; 3:7 [s] ch. 12:27; Gen. 24:26; 1 Chr. 29:20 **Chapter 5** **1**[t] ch. 10:9 **2**[u] [2 Kgs. 18:35; Job 21:15] [v] ch. 3:19 **3**[w] ch. 3:18; 7:16; 9:1, 13 **4**[x] ch. 1:11 **5**[y] ch. 1:7, 9 **6**[z] ch. 3:7 [a] ver. 14, 15, 19 **10**[b] ch. 3:7 **13**[c] ch. 3:7

Israel, whom Pharaoh's [c]taskmasters had set over them, were beaten and were asked, "Why have you not done all your task of making bricks today and yesterday, as in the past?"

15 Then the foremen of the people of Israel came and cried to Pharaoh, "Why do you treat your servants like this? 16 No straw is given to your servants, yet they say to us, 'Make bricks!' And behold, your servants are beaten; but the fault is in your own people." 17 But he said, "You are idle, you are idle; that is why you say, 'Let us go and sacrifice to the LORD.' 18 Go now and work. No straw will be given you, but you must still deliver the same number of bricks." 19 The foremen of the people of Israel saw that they were in trouble when they said, "You shall by no means reduce your number of bricks, your daily task each day." 20 They met Moses and Aaron, who were waiting for them, as they came out from Pharaoh; 21 and [d]they said to them, "The LORD look on you and judge, because you have made us stink in the sight of Pharaoh and his servants, and have put a sword in their hand to kill us."

22 Then Moses turned to the LORD and said, "O Lord, why have you done evil to this people? Why did you ever send me? 23 For since I came to Pharaoh to speak in your name, he has done evil to this people, and you have not delivered your people at all."

God Promises Deliverance

6 But the LORD said to Moses, "Now you shall see what I will do to Pharaoh; for with a strong hand he will send them out, and with [e]a strong hand he will [f]drive them out of his land."

2 God spoke to Moses and said to him, [g]"I am the LORD. 3 I appeared to Abraham, to Isaac, and to Jacob, as [h]God Almighty,[1] but by my name the [i]LORD I did not make myself known to them. 4 [j]I also established my covenant with them [k]to give them the land of Canaan, the land in which they lived as sojourners. 5 Moreover, [l]I have heard the groaning of the people of Israel whom the Egyptians hold as slaves, and I have remembered my covenant. 6 Say therefore to the people of Israel, [m]'I am the LORD, and [n]I will bring you out from under the burdens of the Egyptians, and I will deliver you from slavery to them, and [o]I will redeem you with an outstretched arm and with great acts of judgment. 7 I [p]will take you to be my people, and [q]I will be your God,

[1] Hebrew *El Shaddai*

5:21–23 The discouragement of Israel in general and Moses in particular is palpable. Israel's leaders rebuke Moses for making Israel "stink in the sight of Pharaoh" and for putting "a sword in their hand to kill us"; Moses cries out, "O Lord, why have you done evil to this people?" But Israel and Moses should have remembered God's word—he had already said that Pharaoh would not let them go unless "compelled by a mighty hand" (3:19).

Our discouragement in the face of difficulty and affliction often comes from forgetting what God has already said in his Word. Remembering that God's purposes are being worked out in our lives gives us courage when evil happens to us. Supremely, the gospel itself—what God has done in Jesus Christ for our sake—must be held before our eyes each day in remembrance (1 Cor. 15:1–2).

6:1–9 Before God delivers his people through mighty signs and wonders (chs. 4–15), he returns to his covenant promises. God's word is prior to his deeds and interprets his deeds; his promises ground his salvific actions. The Lord reminds his people of his past faithfulness in establishing his covenant with the patriarchs (6:2–4). He notes that he has now remembered that covenant (6:5). The Lord also declares what he will now do as a result: redemption (6:6), relationship (6:7), rest in the Promised Land (6:8).

It is God's covenant that sustains us when our sin and our circumstances threaten to overwhelm us. Have we taken our hearts to God's covenant promises in the midst of our struggle with sin? If we have been united to Christ, his work of grace in our life is assured (redemption). Christ has secured the eternal love of the heavenly Father for us (relationship). We *will* be brought to heaven, in spite of all our sin and failure (rest).

6:7 "I will take you to be my people, and I will be your God." This is the central promise of the Bible: God's promise to claim a people for himself and to enter into communion with them. Here election and covenant meet: God chooses Israel to be his own people (Deut. 7:6; 14:2; 26:18; cf. 1 Pet. 2:9) and he binds himself to them in

14 [c] [See ver. 13 above]
21 [d] ch. 6:9

Chapter 6
1 [e] ch. 3:19; 13:3 [f] ch. 11:1; 12:33, 39
2 [g] [Isa. 42:8; Mal. 3:6]
3 [h] Gen. 17:1 [i] Ps. 68:4; 83:18; [John 8:58; Rev. 1:4, 8]
4 [j] Gen. 15:18; 17:4, 7 [k] Gen. 17:8; 28:4
5 [l] ch. 2:24
6 [m] [Isa. 42:8; Mal. 3:6] [n] ch. 7:4; Deut. 26:8; Ps. 136:11, 12; [ch. 3:17] [o] ch. 15:13; Deut. 7:8; 2 Kgs. 17:36; 1 Chr. 17:21; Neh. 1:10
7 [p] Deut. 4:20; 7:6; 14:2; 26:18; 2 Sam. 7:24; [1 Pet. 2:9] [q] ch. 29:45, 46; Gen. 17:8; Lev. 22:33; Deut. 29:13; [Rev. 21:7]

and you shall know that [m]I am the LORD your God, who has brought you out [n]from under the burdens of the Egyptians. 8 I will bring you into [r]the land that I [s]swore to give to Abraham, to Isaac, and to Jacob. I will give it to you for a possession. [m]I am the LORD.'" 9 Moses spoke thus to the people of Israel, but they [t]did not listen to Moses, because of their broken spirit and harsh slavery.

10 So the LORD said to Moses, 11 "Go in, tell Pharaoh king of Egypt to let the people of Israel go out of his land." 12 But Moses said to the LORD, "Behold, the people of Israel have [t]not listened to me. How then shall Pharaoh listen to me, for [u]I am of uncircumcised lips?" 13 But the LORD spoke to Moses and Aaron and gave them a charge about the people of Israel and about Pharaoh king of Egypt: to bring the people of Israel out of the land of Egypt.

The Genealogy of Moses and Aaron

14 These are the heads of their fathers' houses: the [v]sons of Reuben, the firstborn of Israel: Hanoch, Pallu, Hezron, and Carmi; these are the clans of Reuben. 15 The [w]sons of Simeon: Jemuel, Jamin, Ohad, Jachin, Zohar, and Shaul, the son of a Canaanite woman; these are the clans of Simeon. 16 These are the names of the [x]sons of Levi according to their generations: Gershon, Kohath, and Merari, the years of the life of Levi being 137 years. 17 The [y]sons of Gershon: Libni and Shimei, by their clans. 18 The [z]sons of Kohath: Amram, Izhar, Hebron, and Uzziel, the years of the life of Kohath being 133 years. 19 The [a]sons of Merari: Mahli and Mushi. These are the clans of the Levites according to their generations. 20 [b]Amram took as his wife Jochebed his father's sister, and she bore him Aaron and Moses, the years of the life of Amram being 137 years. 21 [c]The sons of Izhar: Korah, Nepheg, and Zichri. 22 The [d]sons of Uzziel: Mishael, Elzaphan, and Sithri. 23 Aaron took as his wife Elisheba, the daughter of [e]Amminadab and the sister of [f]Nahshon, and she bore him [g]Nadab, Abihu, Eleazar, and Ithamar. 24 The [h]sons of Korah: Assir, Elkanah, and Abiasaph; these are the clans of the Korahites. 25 Eleazar, Aaron's son, took as his wife one of the daughters of Putiel, and [i]she bore him Phinehas. These are the heads of the fathers' houses of the Levites by their clans.

26 These are the Aaron and Moses [j]to whom the LORD said: "Bring out the people of Israel from the land of Egypt [k]by their hosts." 27 It was they who spoke to Pharaoh king of Egypt about bringing out the people of Israel from Egypt, this Moses and this Aaron.

28 On the day when the LORD spoke to Moses in the land of Egypt, 29 the LORD said to Moses, [l]"I am the LORD; [m]tell Pharaoh king of Egypt all that I say to you." 30 But Moses said to the LORD, "Behold, [n]I am of uncircumcised lips. How will Pharaoh listen to me?"

Moses and Aaron Before Pharaoh

7 And the LORD said to Moses, "See, I have made you like [o]God to Pharaoh, and your brother Aaron shall be your [p]prophet. 2 [q]You shall speak all that I command you, and your brother Aaron shall tell Pharaoh to let the people of Israel go out of his land. 3 But [r]I will harden Pharaoh's heart, and though

7[m] [See ver. 6 above] [n] [See ver. 6 above]
8[r] ch. 32:13; Gen. 15:18; 26:3; 28:13; 35:12; Ezek. 20:6, 42 [s] [Gen. 14:22; Deut. 32:40; Ezek. 20:5, 6; 47:14] [m] [See ver. 6 above]
9[t] ch. 5:21; [Acts 7:25]
12[t] [See ver. 9 above] [u] ver. 30; ch. 4:10; Jer. 1:6; [Jer. 6:10; Ezek. 44:7]
14[v] Gen. 46:9; 1 Chr. 5:3
15[w] Gen. 46:10; 1 Chr. 4:24
16[x] Gen. 46:11; Num. 3:17; 1 Chr. 6:1, 16
17[y] Num. 3:18; 1 Chr. 6:17; 23:7
18[z] Num. 3:19; 26:57; 1 Chr. 6:2, 18
19[a] Num. 3:20; 1 Chr. 6:19; 23:21
20[b] See ch. 2:1
21[c] Num. 16:1; 1 Chr. 6:37, 38
22[d] Lev. 10:4; Num. 3:30
23[e] Ruth 4:19, 20; 1 Chr. 2:10; Matt. 1:4; Luke 3:33

covenant relationship (Jer. 7:23, 11:4, 30:22; Ezek. 36:28). We are the Lord's. We belong to him. This is our new identity.

6:10–7:7 This section represents a recommissioning of Moses. As in 3:1–4:17, so here: Moses argues that his failure as a deliverer is the result of "uncircumcised lips" (6:12, 30); God reiterates that he will be with his lips as he speaks "all that I command" (7:2) and reminds him that Aaron has been given to him as "your prophet" (7:1). How patient God is with us: even through our failure and our repeated excuses, he sends us back to our work with his promise that he is with us.

7:3–5 Once again (cf. 4:21), God reminds Moses that there is a larger reason why Pharaoh will not let the people go: namely, God's own purposes of judgment upon Pharaoh (7:4) and glorification of himself (v. 5). Here is divine mystery: that God would harden people's hearts so that he might be glorified even in judgment (Rom. 9:14–23). Such judgment of Pharaoh magnifies God's grace to a greater degree—for surely Israel did not "deserve" mercy and deliverance. They too deserved judgment. What made them different from the Egyptians? God's electing decree and covenant promise.

[f] Num. 1:7; 2:3; 7:12, 17; 10:14; Matt. 1:4; Luke 3:32 [g] Lev. 10:1; Num. 3:2; 26:60; 1 Chr. 6:3; 24:1 **24**[h] 1 Chr. 6:22, 23, 37 **25**[i] Num. 25:7, 11; Josh. 24:33; Ps. 106:30 **26**[j] ver. 13 [k] ch. 7:4; 12:17, 51; Num. 33:1 **29**[l] See ver. 2 [m] ver. 11; [ch. 7:2] **30**[n] [Isa. 6:5]; See ver. 12 **Chapter 7** **1**[o] ch. 4:16 [p] Gen. 20:7; [1 Sam. 9:9] **2**[q] [ch. 4:15; 6:29] **3**[r] See ch. 4:21

I [s]multiply my signs and wonders in the
land of Egypt, 4 Pharaoh will not listen to
you. Then I will lay my hand on Egypt and
bring my hosts, my people the children of
Israel, out of the land of Egypt by great acts
of judgment. 5 The Egyptians [t]shall know that
I am the LORD, when I stretch out my hand
against Egypt and bring out the people of
Israel from among them." 6 Moses and Aaron
did so; they did just as the LORD commanded
them. 7 Now Moses was [u]eighty years old, and
Aaron eighty-three years old, when they spoke
to Pharaoh.

8 Then the LORD said to Moses and Aaron,
9 "When Pharaoh says to you, [v]'Prove yourselves by working a miracle,' then you shall
say to Aaron, 'Take your staff and cast it down
before Pharaoh, that it may become a serpent.'" 10 So Moses and Aaron went to Pharaoh
and did just as the LORD commanded. Aaron
cast down his staff before Pharaoh and his servants, and it became a serpent. 11 Then Pharaoh
summoned the wise men and the sorcerers,
and they, the [w]magicians of Egypt, also [x]did the
same by their secret arts. 12 For each man cast
down his staff, and they became serpents. But
Aaron's staff swallowed up their staffs. 13 Still
[r]Pharaoh's heart was hardened, and he would
not listen to them, [r]as the LORD had said.

The First Plague: Water Turned to Blood

14 Then the LORD said to Moses, "Pharaoh's
heart is hardened; he refuses to let the people
go. 15 [y]Go to Pharaoh in the morning, as he is
going out to the water. Stand on the bank of
the Nile to meet him, and take in your hand
[z]the staff that turned into a [a]serpent. 16 And you
shall say to him, 'The [b]LORD, the God of the
Hebrews, sent me to you, saying, "Let my people go, [c]that they may serve me in the wilderness." But so far, you have not obeyed. 17 Thus
says the LORD, "By this [d]you shall know that
I am the LORD: behold, with the staff that is in
my hand I will strike the water that is in the
Nile, and [e]it shall turn into blood. 18 The fish
in the Nile shall die, and the Nile will stink,
and the Egyptians will [f]grow weary of drinking water from the Nile."'" 19 And the LORD
said to Moses, "Say to Aaron, 'Take your staff
and [g]stretch out your hand over the waters of

So it is for us as well: we deserve God's judgment and wrath because of our sin. The only thing that makes us different from those who receive God's judgment is his sovereign grace. In Christ, we could not be more secure.

7:10–13 This combat of the staffs transforming into serpents serves as a prologue to the plagues in this sense: "Aaron's staff swallowed up their staffs" signifies the power of Israel's God which will overcome Egypt's gods. Until the final plague, the rest of the plagues use "natural" elements for a "supernatural" purpose: to demonstrate to Egypt through his rule over all creation "that I am the LORD" (v. 5). The God of redemption is also the God of creation. Israel's God is the true King over all the earth (cf. Ps. 24:1).

7:14–10:29 Some see these nine plagues in terms of three triads of related disasters: the first group including blood, frogs, and gnats (7:14–8:19); the second with flies, livestock death, and boils (8:20–9:12); and the third with hail, locusts, and darkness (9:13–10:29). In addition, in the first triad, the Egyptian magicians will no longer be able to replicate the plagues, admitting that they represent "the finger of God" (8:19); in the second, Israel is distinguished from Egypt as God protects his people from judgment (8:22; 9:4); and in the third, Pharaoh struggles against the relentless judgment of God (9:27; 10:7–8, 24).

All of this is for God's purpose to show Pharaoh "my power, so that my name may be proclaimed in all the earth" (9:16). God will show his power to his enemies for the purpose of proclaiming his name. As we preach and speak the gospel today, God delights to show himself mighty so that the nations might know him.

7:14–25 The first plague, water turned into blood, serves as a pattern for many of the rest: "the LORD said to Moses" is followed by a description of the plague; the plague happens; Moses interacts with Pharaoh; and we are given commentary on the state of Pharaoh's heart. So here: the Lord speaks to Moses (v. 14); the plague is described (vv. 15–19); the plague happens (vv. 20–21); there is interaction with Pharaoh (v. 22a); and commentary on Pharaoh's heart follows (vv. 22b–24). Note again God's purpose in these plagues: "By this you shall know that I am the LORD" (v. 17). God gains a name for himself as the sovereign King glorified in judgment and salvation.

3 [s] ch. 11:9; Ps. 135:9; See Ps. 78:43-51; 105:26-36
5 [t] ver. 17; ch. 8:10, 22; 14:4, 18
7 [u] [Deut. 29:5; 31:2; 34:7; Acts 7:23, 30]
9 [v] [Isa. 7:11; John 2:18; 4:48; 6:30]
11 [w] Gen. 41:8 [x] ver. 12, 22; ch. 8:7, 18; 9:11; 2 Tim. 3:8
13 [r] [See ver. 3 above]
15 [y] ch. 8:20; 9:13 [z] ch. 4:2, 17; 17:5 [a] ch. 4:3
16 [b] ch. 3:18; 5:3; 9:1, 13 [c] ch. 3:12, 18; 5:1, 3
17 [d] ver. 5 [e] ch. 4:9; [Rev. 16:4]
18 [f] ver. 21, 24
19 [g] ch. 8:5, 6, 16, 17; 9:22; 10:12, 21; 14:16, 21, 26

Egypt, over their rivers, their canals, and their
ponds, and all their pools of water, so that they
may become blood, and there shall be blood
throughout all the land of Egypt, even in vessels of wood and in vessels of stone.' "
20 Moses and Aaron did as the LORD commanded. In the sight of Pharaoh and in the
sight of his servants he [h]lifted up the staff
and struck the water in the Nile, and all the
[i]water in the Nile turned into blood. 21 And
the fish in the Nile died, and the Nile stank,
so that the Egyptians [j]could not drink water
from the Nile. There was blood throughout
all the land of Egypt. 22 But [k]the magicians
of Egypt did the same by their secret arts. So
[l]Pharaoh's heart remained hardened, and he
would not listen to them, as [m]the LORD had
said. 23 Pharaoh turned and went into his
house, and he did not take even this to heart.
24 And all the Egyptians dug along the Nile
for water to drink, for they could not drink
the water of the Nile.
25 Seven full days passed after the LORD had
struck the Nile.

The Second Plague: Frogs

8 [1] Then the LORD said to Moses, "Go in to
Pharaoh and say to him, 'Thus says the
LORD, "Let my people go, that [n]they may serve
me. 2 But if you [o]refuse to let them go, behold,
I will plague all your country with [p]frogs. 3 The
Nile shall swarm with frogs that shall come
up into your house and into [q]your bedroom
and on your bed and into the houses of your
servants and your people,[2] and into your ovens
and your kneading bowls. 4 The frogs shall
come up on you and on your people and on
all your servants." ' " 5 [3] And the LORD said to
Moses, "Say to Aaron, [r]'Stretch out your hand
with your staff over the rivers, over the canals
and over the pools, and make frogs come up
on the land of Egypt!' " 6 So Aaron stretched
out his hand over the waters of Egypt, and
[s]the frogs came up and covered the land of
Egypt. 7 But [t]the magicians did the same by
their secret arts and made frogs come up on
the land of Egypt.
8 Then Pharaoh called Moses and Aaron and
said, [u]"Plead with the LORD to take away the
frogs from me and from my people, and [v]I will
let the people go to sacrifice to the LORD."
9 Moses said to Pharaoh, "Be pleased to command me when [u]I am to plead for you and
for your servants and for your people, that
the frogs be cut off from you and your houses
and be left only in the Nile." 10 And he said,
"Tomorrow." Moses said, "Be it as you say, so
[w]that you may know that [x]there is no one like
the LORD our God. 11 The frogs shall go away
from you and your houses and your servants
and your people. They shall be left only in the
Nile." 12 So Moses and Aaron went out from
Pharaoh, and Moses cried to the LORD about
the frogs, as he had agreed with Pharaoh.[4]
13 And the LORD did according to the word of
Moses. The frogs died out in the houses, the
courtyards, and the fields. 14 And they gathered
them together in heaps, and the land stank.
15 But when Pharaoh saw that there was a
[y]respite, he [z]hardened his heart and would
not listen to them, as the LORD had said.

The Third Plague: Gnats

16 Then the LORD said to Moses, "Say to
Aaron, [a]'Stretch out your staff and strike the
dust of the earth, so that it may become gnats
in all the land of Egypt.' " 17 And they did so.
Aaron stretched out his hand with his staff
and struck the dust of the earth, and [b]there
were gnats on man and beast. All the dust
of the earth became gnats in all the land of
Egypt. 18 The [c]magicians tried by their secret
arts to produce gnats, but they could not. So
there were gnats on man and beast. 19 Then the
magicians said to Pharaoh, "This is [d]the finger
of God." But Pharaoh's heart was hardened,
and he would not listen to them, as the LORD
had said.

[1] Ch 7:26 in Hebrew [2] Or *among your people* [3] Ch 8:1 in Hebrew [4] Or *which he had brought upon Pharaoh*

20[h] ch. 17:9 [i] Ps. 78:44; 105:29
21[j] ver. 18, 24
22[k] ver. 11 [l] ver. 13 [m] ver. 3, 4
Chapter 8
1[n] ver. 20; ch. 3:12, 18
2[o] ch. 7:14; 9:2 [p] [Rev. 16:13]
3[q] Ps. 105:30
5[r] See ch. 7:19
6[s] Ps. 78:45; 105:30

8:15 Here we see the mysterious interaction between God's sovereign purpose and human beings' free agency. Who was responsible for hardening Pharaoh's heart: God or Pharaoh? The answer is *both*. Pharaoh had determined to maintain Hebrew slavery and not to bow to Moses' (and the Lord's) demands, and so he hardened his heart and suppressed the truth that he heard. Yet the reason why he never softened was God's purpose of judgment. God gave Pharaoh over to what his heart wanted and withheld his mercy (cf. Rom. 1:18–32). In the end, Pharaoh's hardness would serve God's glory (Ex. 9:16).

7[t] See ch. 7:11 **8**[u] ver. 28, 30; ch. 9:28; 10:17, 18; [Num. 21:7; 1 Kgs. 13:6; Acts 8:24] [v] ver. 25-28; ch. 10:8, 24; 12:31, 32 **9**[u] [See ver. 8 above] **10**[w] ver. 22; ch. 7:17 [x] ch. 9:14; Deut. 33:26; 2 Sam. 7:22; 1 Chr. 17:20; Ps. 86:8; Isa. 46:9; Jer. 10:6, 7 **15**[y] [Eccles. 8:11] [z] ver. 32; ch. 7:14; 9:7, 34; 10:1 **16**[a] See ch. 7:19 **17**[b] Ps. 105:31 **18**[c] See ch. 7:11 **19**[d] ch. 31:18; Ps. 8:3; Luke 11:20

The Fourth Plague: Flies

20 Then the LORD said to Moses, [e]"Rise up
early in the morning and present yourself to
Pharaoh, as he goes out to the water, and say
to him, 'Thus says the LORD, [f]"Let my people
go, that they may serve me. 21 Or else, if you
will not let my people go, behold, I will send
swarms of flies on you and your servants and
your people, and into your houses. And the
houses of the Egyptians shall be filled with
swarms of flies, and also the ground on which
they stand. 22 But on that day [g]I will set apart
the land of Goshen, where my people dwell, so
that no swarms of flies shall be there, [h]that you
may know that I am the LORD in the midst of
the earth.[1] 23 Thus I will put a division[2] between
my people and your people. Tomorrow this
sign shall happen."'" 24 And the LORD did
so. [i]There came great swarms of flies into the
house of Pharaoh and into his servants' houses.
Throughout all the land of Egypt the land was
ruined by the swarms of flies.

25 Then Pharaoh called Moses and Aaron
and said, "Go, sacrifice to your God within
the land." 26 But Moses said, "It would not be
right to do so, for the offerings we shall sacrifice to the LORD our God are an [j]abomina-
tion to the Egyptians. If we sacrifice offerings
[j]abominable to the Egyptians before their eyes,
will they not stone us? 27 We must go [k]three
days' journey into the wilderness and sacrifice to the LORD our God [l]as he tells us." 28 So
Pharaoh said, "I will let you go to sacrifice to
the LORD your God in the wilderness; only
you must not go very far away. [m]Plead for me."
29 Then Moses said, "Behold, I am going out
from you and I will plead with the LORD that
the swarms of flies may depart from Pharaoh,
from his servants, and from his people, tomorrow. Only let not Pharaoh [n]cheat again by
not letting the people go to sacrifice to the
LORD." 30 So Moses went out from Pharaoh
and prayed to the LORD. 31 And the LORD did as
Moses asked, and removed the swarms of flies
from Pharaoh, from his servants, and from
his people; not one remained. 32 But Pharaoh
[o]hardened his heart this time also, and did not
let the people go.

The Fifth Plague: Egyptian Livestock Die

9 Then the LORD said to Moses, [p]"Go in to
Pharaoh and say to him, 'Thus says [q]the
LORD, the God of the Hebrews, "Let my people
go, that they may serve me. 2 For if you refuse
to let them go and still hold them, 3 behold,
[r]the hand of the LORD will fall with a very
severe plague upon your livestock that are in
the field, the horses, the donkeys, the camels,
the herds, and the flocks. 4 [s]But the LORD will
make a distinction between the livestock of
Israel and the livestock of Egypt, so that nothing of all that belongs to the people of Israel
shall die."'" 5 And the LORD set a time, saying,
"Tomorrow the LORD will do this thing in the
land." 6 And the next day the LORD did this
thing. [t]All the livestock of the Egyptians died,
but not one of the livestock of the people of
Israel died. 7 And Pharaoh sent, and behold,
not one of the livestock of Israel was dead. But
[u]the heart of Pharaoh was hardened, and he
did not let the people go.

The Sixth Plague: Boils

8 And the LORD said to Moses and Aaron,
"Take handfuls of soot from the kiln, and let
Moses throw them in the air in the sight of
Pharaoh. 9 It shall become fine dust over all
the land of Egypt, and become [v]boils breaking out in sores on man and beast throughout all the land of Egypt." 10 So they took
soot from the kiln and stood before Pharaoh.
And Moses threw it in the air, and it became
boils breaking out in sores on man and beast.
11 And [w]the magicians could not stand before
Moses because of the boils, for the boils
came upon the magicians and upon all the
Egyptians. 12 [x]But the LORD hardened the heart
of Pharaoh, and he did not listen to them, as
[y]the LORD had spoken to Moses.

The Seventh Plague: Hail

13 Then the LORD said to Moses, [z]"Rise up
early in the morning and present yourself

[1] Or *that I the LORD am in the land* [2] Septuagint, Vulgate; Hebrew *set redemption*

9:13–16 With this seventh plague, God begins the last triad of plagues, which in turn will lead to the final, promised judgment, the death of Egypt's firstborn. "I will send all my plagues on you yourself" (v. 14) has the idea of sending the full force of God's judgment and wrath against Egypt. Once again, God reiterates his purpose: "That you may know that there is none like me in all the earth. . . . That my name may be

20[e] ch. 7:15; 9:13 [f] ver. 1
22[g] ch. 9:4; 11:7; [Mal. 3:18] [h] ver. 10; ch. 7:17
24[i] Ps. 78:45; 105:31; [Isa. 7:18]
26[j] [Gen. 43:32; 46:34]
27[k] ch. 3:18 [l] ch. 3:12
28[m] See ver. 8

29[n] ver. 15; [Jer. 42:20, 21] **32**[o] ver. 15 **Chapter 9** **1**[p] ch. 8:1, 2 [q] See ch. 7:16 **3**[r] ch. 7:4 **4**[s] ch. 8:22; 11:7 **6**[t] [ver. 19] **7**[u] ch. 7:14 **9**[v] Lev. 13:18; Deut. 28:27; 2 Kgs. 20:7; Job 2:7; Isa. 38:21; Rev. 16:2 **11**[w] See ch. 7:11; 2 Tim. 3:9 **12**[x] See ch. 4:21 [y] ch. 4:21 **13**[z] ch. 7:15; 8:20

before Pharaoh and say to him, 'Thus says the LORD, the God of the Hebrews, "Let my people go, that they may serve me. 14 For this time I will send all my plagues on you yourself,[1] and on your servants and your people, so [a]that you may know that there is none like me in all the earth. 15 For by now I could have put out my hand and struck you and your people with pestilence, and you would have been cut off from the earth. 16 [b]But for this purpose I have raised you up, to show you my power, so [c]that my name may be proclaimed in all the earth. 17 [d]You are still exalting yourself against my people and will not let them go. 18 Behold, about this time tomorrow I will cause very heavy hail to fall, such as never has been in Egypt from the day it was founded until now. 19 Now therefore send, [e]get your livestock and all that you have in the field into safe shelter, for every man and beast that is in the field and is not brought home will die when the hail falls on them."'" 20 Then whoever feared the word of the LORD among the servants of Pharaoh hurried his slaves and his livestock into the houses, 21 but whoever did not pay attention to the word of the LORD left his slaves and his livestock in the field.

22 Then the LORD said to Moses, "Stretch out your hand toward heaven, so that there may be [f]hail in all the land of Egypt, on man and beast and every plant of the field, in the land of Egypt." 23 Then Moses stretched out his staff toward heaven, and the [g]LORD sent thunder and hail, and fire ran down to the earth. And the LORD rained hail upon the land of Egypt. 24 There was hail and fire flashing continually in the midst of the hail, very heavy hail, such as had never been in all the land of Egypt since it became a nation. 25 The hail struck down everything that was in the field in all the land of Egypt, both man and beast. And the hail [h]struck down every plant of the field and broke every tree of the field. 26 [i]Only in the land of Goshen, where the people of Israel were, was there no hail.

27 Then Pharaoh sent and called Moses and Aaron and said to them, "This time [j]I have sinned; the [k]LORD is in the right, and I and my people are in the wrong. 28 [l]Plead with the LORD, for there has been enough of God's thunder and hail. I will let you go, and you shall stay no longer." 29 Moses said to him, "As soon as I have gone out of the city, [m]I will stretch out my hands to the LORD. The thunder will cease, and there will be no more hail, so that you may know that [n]the earth is the LORD's. 30 But as for you and your servants, [o]I know that you do not yet fear the LORD God." 31 (The flax and the barley were struck down, for the barley was in the ear and the flax was in bud. 32 But the wheat and the emmer[2] were not struck down, for they are late in coming up.) 33 So Moses went out of the city from Pharaoh and [m]stretched out his hands to the LORD, and the thunder and the hail ceased, and the rain no longer poured upon the earth. 34 But when Pharaoh saw that the rain and the hail and the thunder had ceased, he sinned yet again and [p]hardened his heart, [q]he and his servants. 35 So [r]the heart of Pharaoh was hardened, and he did not let the people of Israel go, just as the LORD had spoken through Moses.

The Eighth Plague: Locusts

10 Then the LORD said to Moses, "Go in to Pharaoh, for I have hardened his heart and the heart of his servants, that I may show

[1] Hebrew *on your heart* [2] A type of wheat

14[a] ch. 8:10
16[b] Cited Rom. 9:17; [ch. 10:1, 2; 11:9; 14:17; Prov. 16:4] [c] [Ps. 83:18]; Isa. 63:12
17[d] [Neh. 9:10]
19[e] [ver. 4]
22[f] Rev. 16:21
23[g] Ps. 78:47, 48; 105:32; [Josh. 10:11; 1 Sam. 12:17; Ps. 18:13; 148:8; Isa. 30:30; Ezek. 38:22; Rev. 8:7]
25[h] Ps. 78:47; 105:33
26[i] ver. 4, 6; ch. 8:22; 10:23; 11:7; 12:13; [Isa. 32:18]
27[j] ch. 10:16 [k] 2 Chr. 12:6; Ps. 129:4; 145:17; Lam. 1:18; Dan. 9:14
28[l] See ch. 8:8
29[m] 1 Kgs. 8:22, 38; Ps. 143:6; Isa. 1:15 [n] Ps. 24:1; 1 Cor. 10:26; [Deut. 10:14]
30[o] Isa. 26:10
33[m] [See ver. 29 above]
34[p] See ch. 7:14 [q] 1 Sam. 6:6
35[r] See ch. 4:21

proclaimed in all the earth" (vv. 14, 16). Far from being a tribal deity localized in a particular location, the Lord is the King who rules over the nations and who will gain glory from his creation (v. 29).

9:27 Several times to this point, Pharaoh has appeared repentant (8:8, 25, 28) only to change his mind and further harden his heart. Here he even admits that "I have sinned; the LORD is in the right, and I and my people are in the wrong" (see also 10:17–18). Is this real repentance? No: once "the rain and the hail and the thunder had ceased, he sinned yet again and hardened his heart" (9:34).

Many times people will confess that they have sinned without being truly repentant, especially when they experience difficulty, affliction, sickness, and hardship (cf. Matt. 13:20–21). The test of genuine repentance is those fruits produced by the Spirit in our lives: godly sorrow leading to mortification of sin and increasing holiness of life (Luke 3:8; Rom. 8:12–13; 2 Cor. 7:9–10; Col. 3:1–17).

these signs of mine among them, 2 and [s]that
you may tell in the hearing of your son and
of your grandson how I have dealt harshly
with the Egyptians and what signs I have done
among them, [t]that you may know that I am
the LORD."
3 So Moses and Aaron went in to Pharaoh
and said to him, "Thus says the LORD, the God
of the Hebrews, 'How long will you refuse to
[u]humble yourself before me? Let my people
go, that they may serve me. 4 For if you refuse
to let my people go, behold, tomorrow I will
bring [v]locusts into your country, 5 and they
shall cover the face of the land, so that no one
can see the land. And they shall [w]eat what is
left to you after the hail, and they shall eat
every tree of yours that grows in the field, 6 and
they shall fill [x]your houses and the houses of
all your servants and of all the Egyptians, as
neither your fathers nor your grandfathers
have seen, from the day they came on earth
to this day.'" Then he turned and went out
from Pharaoh.
7 Then Pharaoh's servants said to him, "How
long shall this man be a snare to us? Let the
men go, that they may serve the LORD their
God. Do you not yet understand that Egypt is
ruined?" 8 So Moses and Aaron were brought
back to Pharaoh. And he said to them, [y]"Go,
serve the LORD your God. But which ones
are to go?" 9 Moses said, "We will go with our
young and our old. We will go with our sons
and daughters and with our flocks and herds,
for [z]we must hold a feast to the LORD." 10 But
he said to them, "The LORD be with you, if ever
I let you and your [a]little ones go! Look, you
have some evil purpose in mind.[1] 11 No! Go, the
men among you, and serve the LORD, for that
is what you are asking." And they were driven
out from Pharaoh's presence.
12 Then the LORD said to Moses, [b]"Stretch
out your hand over the land of Egypt for the
locusts, so that they may come upon the land
of Egypt and [c]eat every plant in the land, all
that the hail has left." 13 So Moses stretched out
his staff over the land of Egypt, and the LORD
brought an east wind upon the land all that
day and all that night. When it was morning,
the east wind had brought the locusts. 14 [d]The
locusts came up over all the land of Egypt and
settled on the whole country of Egypt, [e]such
a dense swarm of locusts as had never been
before, nor ever will be again. 15 They covered
the face of the whole land, so that the land
was darkened, and [f]they ate all the plants in
the land and all the fruit of the trees that the
hail had left. Not a green thing remained, neither tree nor plant of the field, through all the
land of Egypt. 16 Then Pharaoh hastily called
Moses and Aaron and said, [g]"I have sinned
against the LORD your God, and against you.
17 Now therefore, forgive my sin, please, only
this once, and [h]plead with the LORD your God
only to remove this death from me." 18 So [i]he
went out from Pharaoh and pleaded with
the LORD. 19 And the LORD turned the wind
into a very strong west wind, which lifted the
locusts and drove them[j]into the Red Sea. Not
a single locust was left in all the country of
Egypt. 20 But the LORD [k]hardened Pharaoh's
heart, and he did not let the people of Israel go.

The Ninth Plague: Darkness

21 Then the LORD said to Moses, [l]"Stretch out
your hand toward heaven, that there may be
[m]darkness over the land of Egypt, a darkness
to be felt." 22 So Moses stretched out his hand

[1] Hebrew *before your face*

10:2 God gives Moses a new purpose for these plagues: not only for gaining glory through the judgment upon Egypt, but also for teaching future Israelite generations "that I am the LORD." This divine purpose of teaching will show up elsewhere in Exodus (12:26–27; 13:14) as well as later in Scripture (Deut. 4:9; 6:20–22; Ps. 78:5–7).

God not only secures the salvation of individuals, but also delights to work through his people's generations, granting saving mercy to households who trust in him (see Gen. 17:1–14; Ex. 20:6; Josh. 24:15; Isa. 49:25; 54:13; 60:9). This pattern of working in and through households is consistent throughout Scripture, in the New Testament as well as the Old Testament (Acts 2:38–39; 16:11–15, 25–34; 1 Cor. 7:14; Eph. 6:1–3).

10:21 This penultimate plague is significant: "darkness over the land of Egypt, a darkness to be felt." Here is a direct demonstration of God's power over Egypt: he humiliates Egypt's main deity, Ra, the sun god; he distinguishes Egypt from Israel by granting his people light (v. 23); and he shadows forth what will next happen in darkness, the death of the firstborn (11:4–10).

Chapter 10
2 [s][ch. 13:8, 14; Deut. 4:9; 6:20-22; Ps. 78:5-7; Joel 1:3] [t]ch. 7:17
3 [u]1 Kgs. 21:29
4 [v]Lev. 11:22; Prov. 30:27; Joel 1:4; 2:25; Rev. 9:3
5 [w]ch. 9:32
6 [x][ch. 8:3, 21; Joel 2:9]
8 [y]ver. 24
9 [z]ch. 5:1; [ch. 3:18]
10 [a]ver. 24
12 [b]See ch. 7:19 [c]ver. 4, 5
14 [d]Ps. 78:46; 105:34 [e]Joel 2:2
15 [f]Ps. 105:35
16 [g]ch. 9:27
17 [h]See ch. 8:8
18 [i]ch. 8:30; 9:33
19 [j][Joel 2:20]
20 [k]See ch. 4:21
21 [l]ver. 12 [m]Ps. 105:28

toward heaven, and there was pitch darkness
in all the land of Egypt three days. 23 They did
not see one another, nor did anyone rise from
his place for three days, but [n]all the people
of Israel had light where they lived. 24 Then
Pharaoh called Moses and said, [o]"Go, serve the
LORD; [p]your little ones also may go with you;
only let your flocks and your herds remain
behind." 25 But Moses said, "You must also let
us have sacrifices and burnt offerings, that we
may sacrifice to the LORD our God. 26 Our livestock also must go with us; not a hoof shall be
left behind, for we must take of them to serve
the LORD our God, and we do not know with
what we must serve the LORD until we arrive
there." 27 But the LORD [q]hardened Pharaoh's
heart, and he would not let them go. 28 Then
Pharaoh said to him, "Get away from me; take
care never to see my face again, for on the day
you see my face you shall die." 29 Moses said,
"As you say! [r]I will not see your face again."

A Final Plague Threatened

11 The LORD said to Moses, "Yet [s]one
plague more I will bring upon Pharaoh
and upon Egypt. Afterward he will let you
go from here. [t]When he lets you go, he will
drive you away completely. 2 Speak now in the
hearing of the people, that [u]they ask, every
man of his neighbor and every woman of her
neighbor, for silver and gold jewelry." 3 [v]And
the LORD gave the people favor in the sight of
the Egyptians. Moreover, the man Moses was
very great in the land of Egypt, in the sight
of Pharaoh's servants and in the sight of the
people.
4 So Moses said, "Thus says the LORD: [w]'About
midnight I will go out in the midst of Egypt,
5 and every firstborn in the land of Egypt shall
die, from the firstborn of Pharaoh who sits
on his throne, even to the firstborn of the
slave girl who is [x]behind the handmill, and
all the firstborn of the cattle. 6 [y]There shall be
a great cry throughout all the land of Egypt,
such as there has never been, nor ever will be
again. 7 But not a dog shall growl [z]against any
of the people of Israel, either man or beast,
that you may know that the LORD [a]makes a
distinction between Egypt and Israel.' 8 And
[b]all these your servants shall come down to me
and bow down to me, saying, 'Get out, you and
all the people who follow you.' And after that
I will go out." And he went out from Pharaoh
in hot anger. 9 Then the LORD said to Moses,
[c]"Pharaoh will not listen to you, that [d]my wonders may be multiplied in the land of Egypt."
10 Moses and Aaron did all these wonders
before Pharaoh, and the LORD [e]hardened
Pharaoh's heart, and he did not let the people
of Israel go out of his land.

The Passover

12 The LORD said to Moses and Aaron in
the land of Egypt, 2 [f]"This month shall
be for you the beginning of months. It shall
be the first month of the year for you. 3 Tell

23[n] [ch. 8:22; 9:4, 6]
24[o] ver. 8 [p] ver. 10
27[q] ver. 20
29[r] [Heb. 11:27]
Chapter 11
1[s] [ch. 4:23] [t] ch. 12:31, 33, 39
2[u] ch. 3:22; 12:35
3[v] ch. 3:21; 12:36
4[w] ch. 12:29; [Job 34:20; Amos 4:10]
5[x] Matt. 24:41; Luke 17:35
6[y] ch. 12:30; [Amos 5:16, 17]
7[z] [ch. 8:22; 9:4] [a] ch. 9:4
8[b] ch. 12:33
9[c] ch. 3:19; 7:4; 10:1 [d] ch. 7:3
10[e] See ch. 4:21
Chapter 12
2[f] ch. 13:4; 23:15; 34:18; Deut. 16:1

Not only does Israel's God rule the darkness, he sees through the darkness; in fact, "the darkness is not dark to you; . . . for darkness is as light with you" (Ps. 139:12). He is light in the darkness for his people; God and his Word serve as a lamp, ensuring their safety and security (Ps. 18:28; 119:105). When we experience darkness, we must remember that we serve a God who is light itself and who offers light in his Word. This is seen supremely in Jesus Christ, "the light of the world" (John 8:12).

11:1–8 All of the previous nine plagues were preparatory for this final one (cf. 4:21–23; 7:3–4). All along, God's purpose was to gain glory for himself so that both Israel (6:7) and Egypt (7:5) would know that he is the Lord. It was in judgment and salvation—through the death of the firstborn in the Passover—that God would be known.

So it was at the cross. In the death of his one and only Son, in the judgment and salvation that occurred at the cross, God gained glory for himself as the Lord. In the first Passover, God spared Israel's firstborn sons. Yet in the cross of Christ, God did not spare his own Son (Rom. 8:32). Christ himself is "our Passover lamb" (1 Cor. 5:7).

12:1–28 The redemption of Israel from "the house of slavery" (13:3) is rooted in the Passover event, which is then later remembered in the Passover festival. The significance of God's redemptive action is seen in several ways: (1) *New era.* God commands that Israel reorient their calendars around this new era that has begun with the Passover; this event creates a new year, a new way of telling time (12:2–3). (2) *Particular substitution.* The substitution of the lamb is given for particular people: "a lamb for a household" (vv. 3–4). The sacrificial lamb was not given for everyone, but for those families identifying

all the congregation of Israel that on the tenth
day of this month every man shall take a lamb
[g]according to their fathers' houses, a lamb for a
household. 4 And if the household is too small
for a lamb, then he and his nearest neighbor
shall take according to the number of persons;
according to what each can eat you shall make
your count for the lamb. 5 Your lamb shall be
[h]without blemish, a male a year old. You may
take it from the sheep or from the goats, 6 and
you shall keep it until the [i]fourteenth day of
this month, when the whole assembly of the
congregation of Israel shall kill their lambs
at twilight.[1]

7 "Then they shall take some of the blood and
put it on the [j]two doorposts and the lintel of
the houses in which they eat it. 8 They shall
eat the flesh that night, roasted on the fire;
with [k]unleavened bread and bitter herbs they
shall eat it. 9 Do not eat any of it raw or boiled
in water, but [l]roasted, its head with its legs
and its inner parts. 10 And [m]you shall let none
of it remain until the morning; anything that
remains until the morning you shall burn.
11 In this manner you shall eat it: with [n]your
belt fastened, your sandals on your feet, and
your staff in your hand. And you shall eat it in
haste. [o]It is the LORD's Passover. 12 For [p]I will
pass through the land of Egypt that night,
and I will strike all the firstborn in the land
of Egypt, both man and beast; and on [q]all the
gods of Egypt I will execute judgments: [r]I am
the LORD. 13 [s]The blood shall be a sign for you,
on the houses where you are. And when I see
the blood, I will pass over you, and no plague
will befall you to destroy you, when I strike
the land of Egypt.

14 "This day shall be [t]for you a memorial day,
and you shall keep it as a feast to the LORD;
throughout your generations, as a [u]statute
forever, you shall keep it as a feast. 15 [v]Seven
days you shall eat unleavened bread. On the
first day you shall remove leaven out of your
houses, for if anyone eats what is leavened,
from the first day until the seventh day, [w]that
person shall be cut off from Israel. 16 On the
first day you shall hold a [x]holy assembly, and
on the seventh day a holy assembly. No work

[1] Hebrew *between the two evenings*

themselves as God's people. Thus, this substitution was particular and definite; that is, specific people were really delivered through the death of a spotless lamb. (3) *Judgment and salvation.* The Passover focuses on provision of both salvation and judgment—Egypt is punished and the lamb's blood is shed (judgment); the lamb's blood is applied to the doorposts of God's people (the provision of v. 7); God himself will pass over those identified with the blood of the lamb (the salvation of vv. 13, 23). (4) *New festival.* Strictly speaking, there was only one Passover day, only one day of judgment and salvation. However, the Passover festival was to serve as "a memorial day" in which God's people would remember the day of the Lord, in which salvation and judgment happened (v. 14). Surrounding this remembrance is the week-long Feast of Unleavened Bread, a festival that would serve purposes of remembrance and instruction (vv. 15–20; 13:3–10).

All of these things find their fulfillment in the New Testament era through the redemptive action secured through the death of Jesus, "the Passover lamb" (1 Cor. 5:7; cf. John 1:29, 36). In Jesus' death, *a new era* was inaugurated and realized (2 Cor. 5:17). His substitutionary death was *particular* and definite: he laid down his life and shed his blood for his people (John 10:11, 15; Acts 20:28). His death was the day of the Lord in which *salvation and judgment* was brought about (1 Cor. 1:18). Jesus' death was the "once-for-all" sacrifice that delivered his people from judgment and death (Heb. 10:10–14). And a *new festival* was established as a means of remembrance and instruction—the Lord's Supper which proclaims the Lord's death until he comes (1 Cor. 11:23–26; Luke 22:14–20).

12:5 Just as the Passover lamb was to be "without blemish," so the New Testament notes that Jesus, our "Passover lamb," was without blemish (representative of purity from sin) as well (1 Cor. 5:7; Heb. 10:14; 1 Pet. 1:18). Further, the New Testament teaches us that Jesus desires to present believers as those without blemish (Eph. 5:27; Phil. 2:15; 2 Pet. 3:14). As those united to the perfect Lamb of God, we know Jesus' own purity and righteousness as our own (2 Cor. 5:21). We seek to purify ourselves even as he is pure (1 John 3:1–3). Yet we do so in the confidence that we are cleansed from all our guilty stains and presented blameless before God's throne by virtue of Christ's work alone (Jude 24).

3 [g]ver. 21
5 [h]Lev. 22:19-21; Deut. 17:1; Mal. 1:8, 14; Heb. 9:14
6 [i]ver. 18; Lev. 23:5; Num. 9:3; 28:16; Josh. 5:10; Ezra 6:19
7 [j]ver. 22
8 [k]ch. 23:18; 34:25; Num. 9:11; Deut. 16:3; 1 Cor. 5:8
9 [l]Deut. 16:7; 2 Chr. 35:13
10 [m]ch. 23:18; 29:34; 34:25; Deut. 16:4; [Lev. 7:15]
11 [n][Luke 12:35; Eph. 6:14; 1 Pet. 1:13] [o]ver. 27; Lev. 23:5; Deut. 16:5; [1 Cor. 5:7]
12 [p]ver. 23; ch. 11:4, 5 [q]Num. 33:4 [r]ch. 6:2; Isa. 43:11
13 [s][Heb. 11:28]
14 [t]ch. 13:9 [u]ver. 17, 24, 43; ch. 13:10; 2 Kgs. 23:21
15 [v]ch. 13:6, 7; 23:15; 34:18, 25; Lev. 23:6; Num. 28:17; Deut. 16:3, 8; [1 Cor. 5:7, 8] [w][Gen. 17:14; Num. 9:13]
16 [x]Lev. 23:7, 8; Num. 28:18, 25

shall be done on those days. But what everyone needs to eat, that alone may be prepared by you. 17 And you shall observe the Feast of Unleavened Bread, for [y]on this very day I brought your [z]hosts out of the land of Egypt. Therefore you shall observe this day, throughout your generations, as a statute forever. 18 [a]In the first month, from the fourteenth day of the month at evening, you shall eat unleavened bread until the twenty-first day of the month at evening. 19 [b]For seven days no leaven is to be found in your houses. If anyone eats what is leavened, [b]that person will be cut off from the congregation of Israel, [c]whether he is a sojourner or a native of the land. 20 You shall eat nothing leavened; in all your dwelling places you shall eat unleavened bread."

21 Then Moses called all the elders of Israel and said to them, "Go and select lambs for yourselves [d]according to your clans, and kill the Passover lamb. 22 Take a bunch of [e]hyssop and [f]dip it in the blood that is in the basin, and touch [g]the lintel and the two doorposts with the blood that is in the basin. [h]None of you shall go out of the door of his house until the morning. 23 [i]For the LORD will pass through to strike the Egyptians, and when he sees the blood on [g]the lintel and on the two doorposts, the LORD will pass over the door and [j]will not allow the destroyer to enter your houses to strike you. 24 You shall observe this rite as a statute for you and for your sons forever. 25 And when you come to the land that the LORD will give you, [k]as he has promised, you shall keep this service. 26 And [l]when your children say to you, 'What do you mean by this service?' 27 you shall say, [m]'It is the sacrifice of the LORD's Passover, for he passed over the houses of the people of Israel in Egypt, when he struck the Egyptians but spared our houses.'" And the people [n]bowed their heads and worshiped.

28 Then the people of Israel went and did so; as the LORD had commanded Moses and Aaron, so they did.

The Tenth Plague: Death of the Firstborn

29 [o]At midnight the [p]LORD struck down all the firstborn in the land of Egypt, [q]from the firstborn of Pharaoh who sat on his throne to the firstborn of the captive who was in the dungeon, and all the firstborn of the livestock. 30 And Pharaoh rose up in the night, he and all his servants and all the Egyptians. And there was [r]a great cry in Egypt, for there was not a house where someone was not dead. 31 Then he summoned Moses and Aaron by night and said, "Up, go out from among my people, [s]both you and the people of Israel; and go, serve the LORD, as you have said. 32 [t]Take your flocks and your herds, as you have said, and be gone, and bless me also!"

The Exodus

33 [u]The Egyptians were urgent with the people to send them out of the land in haste. For they said, "We shall all be dead." 34 So the people took their dough before it was leavened, their kneading bowls being bound up in their cloaks on their shoulders. 35 The people of Israel had also done as Moses told them, for they had [v]asked the Egyptians for silver and gold jewelry and for clothing. 36 [w]And the LORD had given the people favor in the sight of the Egyptians, so that [x]they let them have what they asked. Thus they plundered the Egyptians.

37 And the [y]people of Israel journeyed from [z]Rameses to Succoth, [a]about six hundred thousand men on foot, besides women and children. 38 A [b]mixed multitude also went up with them, and very much livestock, both flocks and herds. 39 And they baked unleavened cakes of the dough that they had brought out of Egypt, for it was not leavened, because [u]they were thrust out of Egypt and [c]could not wait, nor had they prepared any provisions for themselves.

40 The time that the people of Israel lived in Egypt was 430 years. 41 At the end of [d]430 years, on that very day, all the hosts of the LORD went out from the land of Egypt. 42 It was a night of watching by the LORD, to bring them out of the land of Egypt; so this same night is a [e]night of watching kept to the LORD by all the people of Israel throughout their generations.

Institution of the Passover

43 And the LORD said to Moses and Aaron, "This is the statute of the Passover: no foreigner shall eat of it, 44 but every slave[1] that is

[1] Or *servant*; the Hebrew term *'ebed* designates a range of social and economic roles (see Preface)

17 [y] ch. 13:3 [z] ver. 51; ch. 7:4 **18** [a] Lev. 23:5; Num. 28:16 **19** [b] ver. 15 [c] ver. 48, 49 **21** [d] ver. 3 **22** [e] Lev. 14:6; Num. 19:18; Ps. 51:7; Heb. 9:19 [f] Heb. 11:28 [g] ver. 7 [h] [Isa. 26:20] **23** [i] ver. 12, 13 [g] [See ver. 22 above] [j] Heb. 11:28; [Ezek. 9:6; Rev. 7:3; 9:4] **25** [k] ch. 3:8, 17 **26** [l] ch. 13:8, 14; Deut. 6:20; 32:7; Josh. 4:6, 21; Ps. 78:3-6 **27** [m] ver. 11, 21 [n] ch. 4:31 **29** [o] ch. 11:4 [p] Num. 8:17; 33:4; Ps. 78:51; 105:36; 135:8; 136:10 [q] ch. 4:23; 11:5 **30** [r] ch. 11:6; [Amos 5:16, 17] **31** [s] [ch. 10:9-11] **32** [t] [ch. 10:24-26] **33** [u] ch. 6:1; 11:1, 8; Ps. 105:38 **35** [v] ch. 3:22; 11:2 **36** [w] ch. 3:21; 11:3 [x] Gen. 15:14; Ps. 105:37 **37** [y] Num. 33:3, 5 [z] Gen. 47:11; [ch. 1:11] [a] [ch. 38:26; Num. 1:46; 2:32; 11:21; 26:51] **38** [b] Lev. 24:10, 11; Num. 11:4; [Neh. 13:3] **39** [u] [See ver. 33 above] [c] [Deut. 16:3] **41** [d] Gal. 3:17; [Gen. 15:13; Acts 7:6] **42** [e] See Deut. 16:1-6

[f]bought for money may eat of it after you have circumcised him. 45 [g]No foreigner or hired worker may eat of it. 46 It shall be eaten in one house; you shall not take any of the flesh outside the house, and [h]you shall not break any of its bones. 47 [i]All the congregation of Israel shall keep it. 48 [j]If a stranger shall sojourn with you and would keep the Passover to the LORD, let all his males be circumcised. Then he may come near and keep it; he [k]shall be as a native of the land. But no uncircumcised person shall eat of it. 49 There shall be [l]one law for the native and for the [j]stranger who sojourns among you."

50 All the people of Israel did just as the LORD commanded Moses and Aaron. 51 And on that very day the [m]LORD brought the people of Israel out of the land of Egypt by their [n]hosts.

Consecration of the Firstborn

13 The LORD said to Moses, 2 [o]"Consecrate to me all the firstborn. Whatever is the first to open the womb among the people of Israel, both of man and of beast, is mine."

The Feast of Unleavened Bread

3 Then Moses said to the people, [p]"Remember this day in which you came out from Egypt, out of the house of slavery, [q]for by a strong hand the LORD brought you out from this place. [r]No leavened bread shall be eaten. 4 Today, in the month of [s]Abib, you are going out. 5 And when the LORD brings you into [t]the land of the Canaanites, the Hittites, the Amorites, the Hivites, and the Jebusites, which [u]he swore to your fathers to give you, a land [v]flowing with milk and honey, [w]you shall keep this service in this month. 6 [x]Seven days you shall eat unleavened bread, and on the seventh day there shall be a feast to the LORD. 7 Unleavened bread shall be eaten for seven days; no leavened bread shall be seen with you, and no leaven shall be seen with you in all your territory. 8 [y]You shall tell your son on that day, 'It is because of what the LORD did for me when I came out of Egypt.' 9 And it shall [z]be to you as a sign on your hand and as [a]a memorial [z]between your eyes, that the law of the LORD may be in your mouth. For with a strong hand the LORD has brought you out of Egypt. 10 [b]You shall therefore keep this statute at its appointed time from year to year.

11 "When the LORD brings you into the land of the Canaanites, [c]as he swore to you and your fathers, and shall give it to you, 12 [d]you shall set apart to the LORD all that first opens the womb. All the firstborn of your animals that are males shall be the LORD's. 13 [e]Every firstborn of a donkey you shall redeem with a lamb, or if you will not redeem it you shall break its neck. Every [f]firstborn of man among your sons you shall redeem. 14 [g]And when in time to come your son asks you, 'What does this mean?' you shall say to him, [h]'By a strong hand the LORD brought us out of Egypt, from the house of [i]slavery. 15 For when Pharaoh stubbornly refused to let us go, the [j]LORD killed all the firstborn in the land of Egypt, both the firstborn of man and the firstborn of animals. Therefore I sacrifice to the LORD all the males that first open the womb, but [k]all the firstborn of my sons I redeem.' 16 [l]It shall be as a mark on your hand or frontlets between your eyes, for [m]by a strong hand the LORD brought us out of Egypt."

Pillars of Cloud and Fire

17 When Pharaoh let the people go, God did [n]not lead them by way of the land of the Philistines, although that was near. For God said, "Lest the people [o]change their minds when they see war and return to Egypt." 18 But God [p]led the people around by the way of the wilderness toward the Red Sea. And the people of Israel went up out of the land of Egypt equipped for battle. 19 Moses took the bones

13:1–16 The Lord had claimed Israel as his firstborn (4:22–23). He had delivered Israel by means of the death of Pharaoh's firstborn as well as the particular substitute of lambs for Israel's firstborn (12:1–28). Now, he claims all of Israel's firstborn—both "of man and of beast"—as his own (13:1–2). These firstborn must be redeemed with a lamb (v. 13).

Once again, the lesson was clear: redemption came through the death of the firstborn (v. 15). It would prepare people for a greater truth: ultimate redemption for God's people would come through the sacrificial, particular death of God's "firstborn" Son (John 3:16; Col. 1:15–20).

44 [f][Gen. 17:12, 13]
45 [g]Lev. 22:10
46 [h]Num. 9:12; Cited John 19:36
47 [i]ver. 6
48 [j]Num. 9:14 [k]ver. 19
49 [l]Num. 9:14; 15:15, 16 [j][See ver. 48 above]
51 [m]ver. 41; Acts 13:17 [n]ver. 17
Chapter 13
2 [o]ver. 12, 13, 15; ch. 22:29, 30; 34:19; Lev. 27:26; Num. 3:13; 8:16, 17; 18:15; Deut. 15:19; Cited Luke 2:23 **3** [p]ch. 12:42; Deut. 16:3 [q]ch. 3:19; 6:1 [r]See ch. 12:8 **4** [s]ch. 23:15; 34:18; Deut. 16:1 **5** [t]ch. 3:8; 23:23; 33:2; 34:11; Josh. 12:8; 24:11 [u]ch. 6:8 [v]See ch. 3:8 [w]ch. 12:25, 26 **6** [x]ch. 12:15, 16 **8** [y]See ch. 12:26 **9** [z]Deut. 6:8; 11:18; [Num. 15:39; Matt. 23:5] [a]ch. 12:14, 24 **10** [b][ch. 12:14, 17, 24, 43] **11** [c]ver. 5 **12** [d]ver. 2 **13** [e]ch. 34:20 [f]Num. 3:46, 47; 18:15, 16 **14** [g]See ch. 12:26 [h]ver. 3, 16 [i]ver. 3 **15** [j]ch. 12:29 [k]ver. 13 **16** [l]ver. 9 [m]ver. 14 **17** [n][Ps. 107:7] [o]ch. 14:11, 12; [Neh. 9:17]; See Num. 14:1-4 **18** [p]ch. 14:2; [Deut. 32:10]; See Num. 33:6-49

of Joseph with him, for Joseph[1] had made the
sons of Israel solemnly swear, saying, [q]"God
will surely visit you, and you shall carry up my
bones with you from here." 20 And [r]they moved
on from Succoth and encamped at Etham, on
the edge of the wilderness. 21 And [s]the LORD
went before them by day in a pillar of cloud
to lead them along the way, and by night in
a pillar of fire to give them light, that they
might travel by day and by night. 22 The pillar
of cloud by day and the pillar of fire by night
did not depart from before the people.

Crossing the Red Sea

14 Then the LORD said to Moses, 2 "Tell
the people of Israel to [t]turn back and
encamp in front of Pi-hahiroth, between
[u]Migdol and the sea, in front of Baal-zephon;
you shall encamp facing it, by the sea. 3 For
Pharaoh will say of the people of Israel, 'They
are wandering in the land; the wilderness has
shut them in.' 4 And [v]I will harden Pharaoh's
heart, and he will pursue them, and I will [w]get
glory over Pharaoh and all his host, [x]and the
Egyptians shall know that I am the LORD."
And they did so.

5 When the king of Egypt was told that the
people had fled, the [y]mind of Pharaoh and his
servants was changed toward the people, and
they said, "What is this we have done, that
we have let Israel go from serving us?" 6 So
he made ready his chariot and took his army
with him, 7 and took [z]six hundred chosen
chariots and all the other chariots of Egypt
with officers over all of them. 8 And [v]the LORD
hardened the heart of Pharaoh king of Egypt,
and he pursued the people of Israel while [a]the
people of Israel were going out defiantly. 9 The
[b]Egyptians pursued them, all Pharaoh's horses
and chariots and his horsemen and his army,
and overtook them [c]encamped at the sea, by
Pi-hahiroth, in front of Baal-zephon.

10 When Pharaoh drew near, the people of
Israel lifted up their eyes, and behold, the
Egyptians were marching after them, and they
feared greatly. And the people of Israel [d]cried
out to the LORD. 11 They [e]said to Moses, "Is it
because there are no graves in Egypt that you
have taken us away to die in the wilderness?
What have you done to us in bringing us out
of Egypt? 12 Is not this what [f]we said to you in
Egypt: 'Leave us alone that we may serve the
Egyptians'? For it would have been better for
us to serve the Egyptians than to die in the
wilderness." 13 And Moses said to the people,
[g]"Fear not, stand firm, and see the salvation of

[1] Samaritan, Septuagint; Hebrew *he*

19[q] Gen. 50:25; Josh. 24:32; Heb. 11:22; [Acts 7:16]
20[r] ch. 12:37; Num. 33:6
21[s] ch. 14:19, 24; 40:38; Num. 10:34; 14:14; Deut. 1:33; Neh. 9:12, 19; Ps. 78:14; 99:7; 105:39; 1 Cor. 10:1; [Isa. 4:5]; See Num. 9:15-23
Chapter 14
2[t] ch. 13:18, 20; Num. 33:7, 8 [u] Jer. 44:1
4[v] See ch. 4:21 [w] Rom. 9:17, 22, 23; See ch. 9:16 [x] ch. 7:5
5[y] Ps. 105:25
7[z] ch. 15:4; [Isa. 31:1]
8[v] [See ver. 4 above] [a] ch. 6:1; 13:3, 9, 16; Num. 33:3; Deut. 26:8; Acts 13:17; [ch. 3:19]
9[b] ch. 15:9; Josh. 24:6 [c] ver. 2
10[d] Josh. 24:7; Neh. 9:9
11[e] Ps. 106:7; [ch. 13:17]
12[f] ch. 5:21; 6:9
13[g] 2 Chr. 20:15, 17; Isa. 41:10, 13, 14

14:1–31 This scene would prove significant in the memories of Israel as they recalled God's mighty acts of salvation (Ps. 77:16–20; 78:13; 136:13–16). This was the final contest between the Lord and Pharaoh: did Pharaoh have power over Israel as their ruler or did the Lord have that power? The Lord tells Moses in advance what would happen ("Pharaoh will say of the people of Israel" [Ex. 14:3]; "he will pursue them" [v. 4]) and for what purpose ("I will get glory over Pharaoh and all his host, and the Egyptians shall know that I am the LORD" [v. 4]). All of this signals that God is in control, ruling over events for his greater glory. He is the true King of Israel.

Here is a profound foreshadowing of the effect of the cross and resurrection of Jesus. For at the climax of human history God redeems his people through the substitutionary death of Jesus and the shedding of his blood. God takes Jesus through the depths of the grave and raises him from the dead as a confirmation of that redemption. For those who have been united to Jesus, who have been "baptized into him," never again will we be brought back into slavery to sin, Satan, or death. God in Jesus has delivered us completely (Acts 2:22–36; Eph. 1:7–10; Rom. 1:1–5; 6:1–11; 1 Cor. 10:1–4).

14:13–15 Here is a contrast: on the one hand, Israel was to "fear not, stand firm, and see the salvation of the LORD." The salvation of Israel was completely dependent upon God's working on their behalf. On the other hand, they were to "go forward" and cross the Red Sea. In fact, God says, "Why do you cry to me?" There are some matters that do not require anxious crying out to God but rather call for trusting obedience based on his promises (cf. Heb. 11:29).

Do we hesitate to do what we know the Lord has commanded? We should instead go forward in the confidence that the Lord has worked out salvation for us and is continuing to work it out as we obey him (cf. Phil. 2:1–12). If he has united us to his Son, he will most assuredly see us through to full and final restoration (Phil. 1:6; Rom. 5:9–10; 8:32).

the LORD, which he will work for you today.
For [h]the Egyptians whom you see today, you
shall never see again. 14 [i]The LORD will fight for
you, and you have only [j]to be silent."
15 The LORD said to Moses, "Why do you
cry to me? Tell the people of Israel to go forward. 16 [k]Lift up your staff, and [k]stretch out
your hand over the sea and divide it, that the
people of Israel may go through the sea on dry
ground. 17 And [l]I will harden the hearts of the
Egyptians so that they shall go in after them,
and [m]I will get glory over Pharaoh and all his
host, his chariots, and his horsemen. 18 And
the Egyptians [n]shall know that I am the LORD,
[m]when I have gotten glory over Pharaoh, his
chariots, and his horsemen."
19 [o]Then the angel of God who was going
before the host of Israel moved and went
behind them, and the pillar of cloud moved
from before them and stood behind them,
20 coming between the host of Egypt and the
host of Israel. And there was the cloud and the
darkness. And it lit up the night[1] without one
coming near the other all night.
21 Then Moses [k]stretched out his hand over
the sea, and the LORD drove the sea back by [p]a
strong east wind all night and [q]made the sea
dry land, and the waters were [r]divided. 22 And
[s]the people of Israel went into the midst of the
sea on dry ground, the waters being [t]a wall
to them on their right hand and on their left.
23 The Egyptians pursued and went in after
them into the midst of the sea, all Pharaoh's
horses, his chariots, and his horsemen. 24 And
in the morning watch the LORD in the pillar of
fire and of cloud looked down on the Egyptian
forces and threw the Egyptian forces into a
panic, 25 clogging[2] their chariot wheels so that
they drove heavily. And the Egyptians said,
"Let us flee from before Israel, for the [u]LORD
fights for them against the Egyptians."
26 Then the LORD said to Moses, [v]"Stretch out
your hand over the sea, that the water may
come back upon the Egyptians, upon their
chariots, and upon their horsemen." 27 [w]So
Moses stretched out his hand over the sea, and
the sea [x]returned to its normal course when the
morning appeared. And as the Egyptians fled
into it, the LORD [y]threw[3] the Egyptians into
the midst of the sea. 28 The [z]waters returned
and covered the chariots and the horsemen; of
all the host of Pharaoh that had followed them
into the sea, [a]not one of them remained. 29 But
the [b]people of Israel walked on dry ground
through the sea, the waters being a wall to
them on their right hand and on their left.
30 Thus the LORD [c]saved Israel that day from
the hand of the Egyptians, and Israel saw the
Egyptians dead on the seashore. 31 [d]Israel saw
the great power that the LORD used against
the Egyptians, so the people feared the LORD,
and they [e]believed in the LORD and in his servant Moses.

The Song of Moses

15 Then Moses and the people of Israel
[f]sang this song to the LORD, saying,

[g]"I will sing to the LORD, for he has triumphed gloriously;
the horse and his rider[4] he has thrown
into the sea.

[1] Septuagint *and the night passed* [2] Or *binding* (compare Samaritan, Septuagint, Syriac); Hebrew *removing* [3] Hebrew *shook off* [4] Or *its chariot*; also verse 21

14:21–31 The Lord's actions dominate this scene: "the LORD drove the sea back" (v. 21); "the LORD . . . looked down on the Egyptian forces and threw the Egyptian forces into a panic" (v. 24); "the LORD threw the Egyptians into the midst of the sea" (v. 27); "the LORD saved Israel that day" (v. 30).

All of this had a purpose: not only that God might gain glory over the Egyptians. And not only that Egypt might know "I am the LORD" (v. 18), but also that Israel would respond with faith: "the people feared the LORD, and they believed in the LORD" (v. 31). The proper response to God's mighty acts of salvation is faithful reverence and reverent faith.

15:1–21 The victory of God should inspire praise of God. Here God's people sing God's praises because "he has triumphed gloriously" (v. 1). What is notable is how theological and personal this praise is. *Glorious theology* is here: God's covenant (v. 2); God's character (vv. 3, 11, 13); God's name (v. 4); God's work (vv. 6–7, 12, 16); God's purpose (vv. 17–18). And yet, *how personal*: "The LORD is *my* strength and *my* song, and he has become *my* salvation; this is *my* God, and *I* will praise him, *my* father's God and *I* will exalt him" (v. 2). At its best, all of our praise contains such rich theology made personal.

13 [h][ver. 30]
14 [i]ver. 25; Deut. 1:30; 3:22; 20:4; Josh. 10:14, 42; 23:3; 2 Chr. 20:15, 29; Neh. 4:20 [j][Isa. 30:15]
16 [k]See ch. 7:19
17 [l][ver. 4, 8] [m]ver. 4
18 [n]ch. 7:5 [m][See ver. 17 above]
19 [o]ch. 23:20; 32:34; Num. 20:16; Isa. 63:9; [ch. 13:21]
21 [k][See ver. 16 above] [p]ch. 15:10 [q]Ps. 66:6 [r]ch. 15:8; Neh. 9:11; Ps. 74:13; 78:13; 106:9; 114:3; Isa. 51:10; 63:12; [Josh. 3:16; 4:23; Isa. 10:26; 11:15, 16]
22 [s]ver. 29; ch. 15:19; Num. 33:8; Ps. 66:6; Isa. 63:13; 1 Cor. 10:1; Heb. 11:29; [Ps. 77:19] [t]Ps. 78:13; [Hab. 3:10]
25 [u]ver. 14
26 [v]ver. 16, 21

27 [w]ver. 21 [x][Josh. 4:18] [y]ch. 15:1, 7; Deut. 11:4; Ps. 78:53; Heb. 11:29 **28** [z][Hab. 3:8-13] [a]Ps. 106:11 **29** [b]See ver. 22 **30** [c]Ps. 106:8, 10 **31** [d]Ps. 92:9-11; [ver. 13] [e]Ps. 106:12; [John 2:11; 11:45] **Chapter 15** **1** [f]Ps. 106:12; [Judg. 5:1; 2 Sam. 22:1] [g]ver. 21

2 [h]The LORD is my strength and my [i]song,
and he has become [j]my salvation;
this is my God, and I will praise him,
[k]my father's God, and [l]I will exalt him.
3 The LORD is [m]a man of war;
[n]the LORD is his name.

4 [o]"Pharaoh's chariots and his host he cast
into the sea,
and his chosen [p]officers were sunk in
the Red Sea.
5 The [q]floods covered them;
they [r]went down into the depths like
a stone.
6 [s]Your right hand, O LORD, glorious in
power,
your right hand, O LORD, [t]shatters the
enemy.
7 In the [u]greatness of your majesty you
overthrow your adversaries;
you send out your fury; it [v]consumes
them like stubble.
8 At the [w]blast of your nostrils the waters
piled up;
the [x]floods stood up in a heap;
the deeps congealed in the heart of
the sea.
9 The enemy said, [y]'I will pursue, I will
overtake,
I [z]will divide the spoil, my desire shall
have its fill of them.
I will draw my sword; my hand shall
destroy them.'
10 You [a]blew with your wind; the [b]sea covered them;
they sank like lead in the mighty
waters.

11 [c]"Who is like you, O LORD, among the
gods?
Who is like you, majestic in holiness,
awesome in [d]glorious deeds, [e]doing
wonders?
12 You stretched out [f]your right hand;
the earth swallowed them.

13 "You have [g]led in your steadfast love the
people whom [h]you have
redeemed;
you have [i]guided them by your
strength to your holy abode.
14 [j]The peoples have heard; they tremble;
pangs have seized the inhabitants of
Philistia.
15 Now are the chiefs of Edom [k]dismayed;
trembling seizes the leaders of [l]Moab;
[m]all the inhabitants of Canaan have
melted away.
16 Terror and [n]dread fall upon them;
because of the greatness of your arm,
they are still [o]as a stone,
till your people, O LORD, pass by,
till the people pass by whom [p]you
have purchased.
17 You will bring them in and [q]plant them
on your own mountain,
the place, O LORD, which you have
made for your abode,
[r]the sanctuary, O Lord, which your
hands have established.
18 [s]The LORD will reign forever and ever."

19 For when [t]the horses of Pharaoh with his
chariots and his horsemen went into the sea,
[u]the LORD brought back the waters of the sea
upon them, but the people of Israel walked
on dry ground in the midst of the sea. 20 Then
[v]Miriam [w]the prophetess, the [x]sister of Aaron,
took a tambourine in her hand, and [y]all the
women went out after her with tambourines
and dancing. 21 And Miriam sang to them:

[z]"Sing to the LORD, for he has triumphed
gloriously;
the horse and his rider he has thrown
into the sea."

2 [h]Ps. 18:1, 2; 59:17; 118:14; 140:7; Isa. 12:2 [i]Deut. 10:21; Ps. 109:1 [j]Ps. 18:46; Hab. 3:18 [k]ch. 3:6, 15, 16 [l]2 Sam. 22:47; Ps. 34:3; 99:5, 9; 118:28; 145:1; Isa. 25:1
3 [m]Ps. 24:8; Rev. 19:11 [n]ch. 3:15; 6:3; Ps. 83:18; Isa. 42:8; Mal. 3:6
4 [o]ch. 14:28 [p]ch. 14:7
5 [q]ver. 10; ch. 14:28 [r]Neh. 9:11

And this song was not simply for Old Testament Israel—rather, this is a song for all the people of God throughout redemptive history. In Revelation 15:2–3, "those who had conquered the beast" are those who "sing the song of Moses, the servant of God, and the song of the Lamb." The reason Moses' song is fitting for all redemptive history is because God has triumphed gloriously over all his enemies—not only Pharaoh and his armies, but Satan and his more terrifying weapons, including death itself. Indeed, Exodus 15:18 is the note of praise for God's people throughout all ages: "the LORD will reign forever and ever" (cf. Rev. 11:15).

6 [s]ver. 12; Ps. 118:15, 16; Isa. 51:9 [t]Ps. 2:9; Rev. 2:27 **7** [u]Deut. 33:26 [v][Isa. 5:24; 47:14; Mal. 4:1] **8** [w]ch. 14:21, 22; 2 Sam. 22:16; Job 4:9; Ps. 18:15; [2 Thess. 2:8] [x]Ps. 78:13; [Josh. 3:16; Hab. 3:10] **9** [y]ch. 14:9 [z]Gen. 49:27; Judg. 5:30; Isa. 53:12; Luke 11:22 **10** [a]ch. 14:21; [Isa. 11:15; 40:24] [b]ver. 5; ch. 14:28 **11** [c]Deut. 3:24; 1 Sam. 2:2; 2 Sam. 7:22; 1 Kgs. 8:23; 2 Chr. 6:14; Jer. 10:6 [d][Isa. 6:3; Rev. 4:8] [e]Ps. 77:14 **12** [f]ver. 6 **13** [g]Ps. 77:20 [h]Ps. 77:15 [i]Ps. 78:54 **14** [j]Num. 14:14; Deut. 2:25; Josh. 2:9, 10; 9:24 **15** [k][Deut. 2:4] [l]Num. 22:3 [m]Josh. 2:9, 11, 24; 5:1 **16** [n]Deut. 2:25; 11:25 [o]1 Sam. 25:37 [p]Ps. 74:2; [1 Pet. 2:9] **17** [q]Ps. 44:2; 80:8; [Jer. 32:41] [r]Ps. 78:54; 132:13, 14 **18** [s]Ps. 10:16; 29:10; 45:6; 146:10; Rev. 11:15 **19** [t]ch. 14:23 [u]ch. 14:28, 29 **20** [v]Mic. 6:4 [w][Judg. 4:4; 2 Kgs. 22:14; Neh. 6:14; Luke 2:36] [x]ch. 2:4; Num. 26:59 [y]Judg. 11:34; 1 Sam. 18:6; Ps. 68:25; 149:3; 150:4 **21** [z]ver. 1

Bitter Water Made Sweet

22 Then Moses made Israel set out from the
Red Sea, and they went into the wilderness
of [a]Shur. They went three days in the wilderness and found no water. 23 When they came
to [b]Marah, they could not drink the water of
Marah because it was bitter; therefore it was
named Marah.[1] 24 And the people [c]grumbled
against Moses, saying, "What shall we drink?"
25 And he [d]cried to the LORD, and the LORD
showed him a log,[2] and he [e]threw it into the
water, and the water became sweet.

There the LORD[3] made for them a statute and
a rule, and there he [f]tested them, 26 saying, [g]"If
you will diligently listen to the voice of the
LORD your God, and do that which is right in
his eyes, and give ear to his commandments
and keep all his statutes, I will put none of the
[h]diseases on you that I put on the Egyptians,
for I am the LORD, [i]your healer."

27 Then [j]they came to Elim, where there were
twelve springs of water and seventy palm
trees, and they encamped there by the water.

Bread from Heaven

16 They [k]set out from Elim, and all the
congregation of the people of Israel
came to the wilderness of Sin, which is
between Elim and Sinai, on the fifteenth day
of the second month after they had departed
from the land of Egypt. 2 And the whole congregation of the people of Israel [l]grumbled
against Moses and Aaron in the wilderness, 3 and the people of Israel said to them,
[m]"Would that we had died by the hand of the
LORD in the land of Egypt, [n]when we sat by
the meat pots and ate bread to the full, for you
have brought us out into this wilderness to
kill this whole assembly with hunger."

4 Then the LORD said to Moses, "Behold, I am
about to rain [o]bread from heaven for you, and
the people shall go out and gather a day's portion every day, that I may [p]test them, whether
they will walk in my law or not. 5 On the sixth
day, when they prepare what they bring in,
[q]it will be twice as much as they gather daily."
6 So Moses and Aaron said to all the people of

[1] *Marah* means *bitterness* [2] Or *tree* [3] Hebrew *he*

15:22–17:7 Having been delivered from God's enemies, God's people now move toward a different set of trials: the lack of food and water. Each scene—at Marah (water), in the wilderness of Sin (food), and at Rephidim (water)—involved testing (15:25; 16:4; 17:2). In the first two scenes, God tested his people to see whether they would trust and obey him during their pilgrimage; in the third scene, God's people tested God, questioning whether the God who provided at Marah and Elim and in the wilderness could provide again.

God often moves us from times of triumph and victory to places of trial and testing. He does so, so that we might learn that "man does not live by bread alone, but man lives by every word that comes from the mouth of the LORD" (Deut. 8:3; cf. Matt. 4:4; Luke 4:4). The provision is not dependent upon our obedience (see, e.g., Ex. 16:27–30). Rather, the provision is rooted in God's steadfast love for his people. The testing fosters greater dependence on and love for God.

15:22–27 God's people have just sung about God's deliverance. But after three days' journey into the wilderness, they worried about water. And they came to Marah—the word means "bitterness." The people felt, as Naomi would feel many years later, that "the Almighty [had] dealt very bitterly" with them (Ruth 1:20) by bringing them to a place where there was no water. But God brought them to that place to "test" them and to teach them obedience to God's Word (Ex. 15:25–26). And he woos them to obedience by reminding them that "I am the LORD, your healer" (v. 26).

God our healer purifies and transforms our hearts so that we are purified and empowered to listen diligently to the Lord's voice and obey him. He does this pre-eminently through the gospel of grace (Rom. 12:1–2; Titus 2:11–12).

16:1–36 Once again, the Lord tests his people to see "whether they will walk in my law or not" (v. 4). In this instance, would Israel trust in him to provide for them by raining bread and birds from heaven? Each day, "morning by morning" (v. 21), they were required to trust God for "daily bread" (Matt. 6:11). Likewise, their faith and obedience were tried by whether they would gather on the sixth day enough to sustain them as they rested on the seventh (Ex. 16:5, 22–30).

Ultimately, this daily dependence upon God's provision pointed to a resting in and receiving of Jesus, "the bread of God" who came from heaven (John 6:31–35).

22[a] Gen. 16:7; 25:18; 1 Sam. 15:7
23[b] [Ruth 1:20]
24[c] ch. 16:2; 17:3
25[d] ch. 14:10; 17:4 [e] [2 Kgs. 2:21; 4:41] [f] ch. 16:4; Deut. 8:2, 16; Judg. 2:22; 3:1, 4; Ps. 66:10
26[g] See Lev. 26:3-13; Deut. 7:12-15 [h] Deut. 28:27, 60 [i] ch. 23:25; Ps. 103:3; 147:3; Hos. 6:1
27[j] Num. 33:9

Chapter 16
1[k] Num. 33:10, 11
2[l] ch. 15:24; 17:3; 1 Cor. 10:10
3[m] [Num. 20:3-5] [n] Num. 11:4, 5
4[o] Neh. 9:15; Ps. 78:24, 25; 105:40; John 6:31, 32; 1 Cor. 10:3 [p] See ch. 15:25
5[q] ver. 22

Israel, [r]"At evening [s]you shall know that it was
the LORD who brought you out of the land of
Egypt, 7 and in the morning you shall see the
[t]glory of the LORD, because he has heard your
grumbling against the LORD. For [u]what are
we, that you grumble against us?" 8 And Moses
said, "When the LORD gives you in the evening
meat to eat and in the morning bread to the
full, because the LORD has heard your grumbling that you grumble against him—[v]what
are we? Your grumbling is not [w]against us but
against the LORD."

9 Then Moses [x]said to Aaron, "Say to the
whole congregation of the people of Israel,
[y]'Come near before the LORD, for he has heard
your grumbling.'" 10 And as soon as Aaron
spoke to the whole congregation of the people
of Israel, they looked toward the wilderness,
and behold, the [t]glory of the LORD appeared
in the cloud. 11 And the LORD said to Moses,
12 "I [z]have heard the grumbling of the people
of Israel. Say to them, 'At [a]twilight you shall eat
meat, and [b]in the morning you shall be filled
with bread. Then you shall know that I am the
LORD your God.'"

13 In the evening [c]quail came up and covered the camp, and in the morning [d]dew lay
around the camp. 14 And when the dew had
gone up, there was on the face of the wilderness a fine, flake-like thing, fine as frost on
the ground. 15 When the people of Israel saw
it, they said to one another, [e]"What is it?"[1] For
they [f]did not know what it was. And Moses
said to them, [g]"It is the bread that the LORD
has given you to eat. 16 This is what the LORD
has commanded: 'Gather of it, each one of you,
as much as he can eat. You shall each take an
[h]omer,[2] according to the number of the persons
that each of you has in his tent.'" 17 And the
people of Israel did so. They gathered, some
more, some less. 18 But when they measured
it with an omer, [i]whoever gathered much had
nothing left over, and whoever gathered little
had no lack. Each of them gathered as much as
he could eat. 19 And Moses said to them, "Let
no one leave any of it over till the morning."
20 But they did not listen to Moses. Some left
part of it till the morning, and [j]it bred worms
and stank. And Moses was angry with them.
21 Morning by morning they gathered it, each
as much as he could eat; but when the sun
grew hot, it melted.

22 On [k]the sixth day they gathered twice as
much bread, two omers each. And when all
the leaders of the congregation came and told
Moses, 23 he said to them, "This is what the
LORD has commanded: 'Tomorrow is a day of
[l]solemn rest, a holy Sabbath to the LORD; bake
what you will bake and boil what you will boil,
and all that is left over lay aside to be kept till
the morning.'" 24 So they laid it aside till the
morning, as Moses commanded them, and
[m]it did not stink, and there were no worms
in it. 25 Moses said, "Eat it today, for [l]today is a
Sabbath to the LORD; today you will not find it
in the field. 26 Six days you shall gather it, but
on the seventh day, which is a Sabbath, there
will be none."

27 On the seventh day some of the people
went out to gather, but they found none.
28 And the LORD said to Moses, [n]"How long
will you refuse to keep my commandments
and my laws? 29 See! The LORD has given you
the Sabbath; therefore on the sixth day he
gives you bread for two days. Remain each of
you in his place; let no one go out of his place
on the seventh day." 30 So the people [o]rested
on the seventh day.

31 Now the house of Israel called its name
[p]manna. It was [q]like coriander seed, white, and

[1] Or *"It is manna."* Hebrew *man hu* [2] An *omer* was about 2 quarts or 2 liters

6[r] ver. 12, 13 [s] ch. 6:7; [Num. 16:28-30]
7[t] ch. 40:34; Num. 16:19; 1 Kgs. 8:10, 11; [ch. 13:21; 14:24] [u] Num. 16:11
8[v] ver. 7 [w] [Num. 14:27; 1 Sam. 8:7; Luke 10:16; Rom. 13:2]
9[x] [ch. 4:14-16] [y] Num. 16:16
10[t] [See ver. 7 above]
12[z] ver. 8 [a] ver. 6 [b] ver. 7
13[c] Num. 11:31; Ps. 78:27, 28; 105:40 [d] Num. 11:9
15[e] ver. 31 [f] Deut. 8:3 [g] Deut. 8:3; See ver. 4
16[h] ver. 36
18[i] Cited 2 Cor. 8:15

16:22–30 It is not clear whether God's people were regularly observing Sabbath rest to this point. If not, then this process of gathering for six days and resting on the seventh began to teach them the rhythm of "six days you shall labor" and the seventh shall be "a Sabbath to the LORD your God" (20:8–10). God, the Lord of the Sabbath, established this pattern in creation (Gen. 1:1–2:4), renewed it in the wilderness (Ex. 16:22–30), commanded it in his law (20:8–11), clarified its purpose in Christ (Luke 6:1–11), and will consummate it in the age to come (Heb. 4:9–11).

This pattern of work and rest remains a gracious gift for us today, given to us by the Lord of the Sabbath (Mark 2:28). And we it do all in the glad knowledge that the supreme rest—rest from working for our salvation—has been secured in the work of Jesus (Heb. 4:9–10).

20[j] [ver. 24] **22**[k] ver. 5 **23**[l] ch. 35:2, 3; Gen. 2:3; Lev. 23:3; See ch. 20:8-11; 31:14-17 **24**[m] [ver. 20] **25**[l] [See ver. 23 above] **28**[n] [Ps. 78:10; Ezek. 20:13]
30[o] Luke 23:56 **31**[p] ver. 15 [q] Num. 11:7, 8

the taste of it was like wafers made with honey.
32 Moses said, "This is what the LORD has commanded: 'Let an omer of it be kept throughout your generations, so that they may see the
bread with which I fed you in the wilderness,
when I brought you out of the land of Egypt.'"
33 And Moses said to Aaron, "Take a [r]jar, and
put an omer of manna in it, and place it before
the LORD to be kept throughout your generations." 34 As the LORD commanded Moses, so
Aaron placed it before [s]the testimony to be
kept. 35 The people of Israel [t]ate the manna
forty years, till they came to a habitable land.
They ate the manna till [u]they came to the border of the land of Canaan. 36 (An omer is [v]the
tenth part of an ephah.)[1]

Water from the Rock

17 [w]All the congregation of the people of
Israel moved on from the wilderness of
Sin by stages, according to the commandment
of the LORD, and camped at Rephidim, but
there was no water for the people to drink.
2 [x]Therefore the people quarreled with Moses
and said, "Give us water to drink." And Moses
said to them, "Why do you quarrel with me?
Why do you [y]test the LORD?" 3 But the people thirsted there for water, and [z]the people
grumbled against Moses and said, "Why did
you bring us up out of Egypt, to kill us and
our children and our livestock with thirst?"
4 So Moses cried to the LORD, "What shall I do
with this people? They are almost ready [a]to
stone me." 5 And the LORD said to Moses, "Pass
on before the people, taking with you some of
the elders of Israel, and take in your hand the
staff with [b]which you struck the Nile, and go.
6 [c]Behold, I will stand before you there on the
rock at Horeb, and you shall strike the rock,
and water shall come out of it, and the people
will drink." And Moses did so, in the sight of
the elders of Israel. 7 And he called the name
of the place [d]Massah[2] and [e]Meribah,[3] because
of the quarreling of the people of Israel, and
because they tested the LORD by saying, "Is the
LORD among us or not?"

Israel Defeats Amalek

8 [f]Then Amalek came and fought with Israel
at Rephidim. 9 So Moses said to [g]Joshua,
"Choose for us men, and go out and fight
with Amalek. Tomorrow I will stand on the
top of the hill with [h]the staff of God in my
hand." 10 So [g]Joshua did as Moses told him, and

[1] An *ephah* was about 3/5 bushel or 22 liters [2] *Massah* means *testing* [3] *Meribah* means *quarreling*

17:1–7 For a third time, God's people grumble against Moses and the Lord about water or food. This time, rather than God testing his people, God's people "test the LORD" (vv. 2, 7). But God did not respond by judging his people. Instead, astoundingly, he responded by being judged for his people. He tells Moses, "I will stand before you there on the rock at Horeb, and you shall strike the rock, and water shall come out of it, and the people will drink" (v. 6). God stands before Horeb/Sinai, the place of the law; he is struck for the failure of God's people to trust and obey him; and he provides rivers of living water from which God's people drink (cf. John 7:38; Rev. 22:1).

We are told in 1 Corinthians 10:4 that "the Rock was Christ." For those who questioned, "Is the LORD among us or not?" the answer was clear that he was—Christ himself was present to sustain, save, bless, and be judged.

17:8–18:27 In both of these scenes, we discover that Moses is unable to do his ministry alone. In the battle against the Amalekites, when Moses' posture of supplication was so necessary for Israel's success, he needed others to provide a stone to sit on, to hold up his hands (17:12), and actually to fight the battle (17:13). In the later scene with Jethro, Moses was told that "you are not able to do it alone" (18:18); rather, the work of judging and inquiring of God required many hands, with the result that "God will direct you, you will be able to endure, and all this people also will go to their place in peace" (18:23).

This provision of grace through the aid of believing leaders would continue to be God's pattern for life and ministry. And so, in the New Testament, Jesus gathers groups of disciples with different levels of access and responsibility—three, twelve, seventy-two (Matt. 10:1–4; 17:1; Luke 10:1). The apostles appoint deacons to serve tables while they preach and pray (Acts 6:1–7). Paul and Barnabas appoint elders in every city in which they labor (Acts 14:23; Titus 1:5) and they take along ministerial assistants on their journeys (Acts 15:23–16:5). How should this shape our understanding of ministry? How does this text critique a "go-it-alone" approach to the Christian life?

33 [r]Heb. 9:4
34 [s]ch. 25:16, 21; 26:33, 34; 27:21; 30:6, 26, 36; 40:21
35 [t]Deut. 8:2, 3; Neh. 9:20, 21 [u]Josh. 5:12
36 [v]Lev. 5:11; 6:20

Chapter 17
1 [w]ch. 16:1; Num. 33:12, 14
2 [x]Num. 20:3, 4 [y]Deut. 6:16; Ps. 78:18, 41; 95:8, 9; Isa. 7:12; Matt. 4:7; 1 Cor. 10:9; Heb. 3:8, 9
3 [z]ch. 15:24; 16:2
4 [a]Num. 14:10; 1 Sam. 30:6; 2 Chr. 24:21; Matt. 23:37; Luke 13:34; John 8:59; 10:31-33; 11:8; Acts 7:58; 14:5, 19; 2 Cor. 11:25; Heb. 11:37; [Josh. 9:25; 1 Kgs. 21:13]
5 [b]ch. 7:20
6 [c]Num. 20:8-11; Deut. 8:15; Neh. 9:15; Ps. 78:15, 16, 20; 105:41; 114:8; Isa. 43:20; 48:21; 1 Cor. 10:4
7 [d]Ps. 95:8 [e]Num. 20:13; Ps. 81:7; 95:8
8 [f]Deut. 25:17; 1 Sam. 15:2
9 [g]ch. 24:13; 32:17; 33:11 [h]ch. 4:20
10 [g][See ver. 9 above]

fought with Amalek, while Moses, Aaron, and [i]Hur went up to the top of the hill. 11 Whenever Moses [j]held up his hand, Israel prevailed, and whenever he lowered his hand, Amalek prevailed. 12 But Moses' hands grew weary, so they took a stone and put it under him, and he sat on it, while Aaron and [i]Hur held up his hands, one on one side, and the other on the other side. So his hands were steady until the going down of the sun. 13 And [g]Joshua overwhelmed Amalek and his people with the sword.

14 Then the LORD said to Moses, "Write this as a memorial in a book and recite it in the ears of [g]Joshua, that [k]I will utterly blot out the memory of Amalek from under heaven." 15 And Moses [l]built an altar and called the name of it, The LORD Is My Banner, 16 saying, "A hand upon the throne[1] of the LORD! [k]The LORD will have war with Amalek from generation to generation."

Jethro's Advice

18 [m]Jethro, [n]the priest of Midian, Moses' father-in-law, heard of all that God had done for Moses and for Israel his people, how the LORD had brought Israel out of Egypt. 2 Now Jethro, Moses' father-in-law, had taken Zipporah, Moses' wife, after he had sent her home, 3 along with her [o]two sons. The name of the one was Gershom ([p]for he said, [q]"I have been a sojourner[2] in a foreign land"), 4 and the name of the other, Eliezer[3] (for he said, "The God of my father was my help, and delivered me from the sword of Pharaoh"). 5 Jethro, Moses' father-in-law, came with his sons and his wife to Moses in the wilderness where he was encamped at the [r]mountain of God. 6 And when he sent word to Moses, "I,[4] your father-in-law Jethro, am coming to you with your wife and her two sons with her," 7 Moses [s]went out to meet his father-in-law and bowed down and [t]kissed him. And they asked each other of their welfare and went into the tent. 8 Then Moses told his father-in-law [u]all that the LORD had done to Pharaoh and to the Egyptians for Israel's sake, all the hardship that had come upon them in the way, and how the LORD had delivered them. 9 And Jethro rejoiced for all the good that the LORD had done to Israel, in that he had delivered them out of the hand of the Egyptians.

10 Jethro said, [v]"Blessed be the LORD, who has delivered you out of the hand of the Egyptians and out of the hand of Pharaoh and has delivered the people from under the hand of the Egyptians. 11 Now I know that [w]the LORD is greater than all gods, because in this affair they [x]dealt arrogantly with the people."[5] 12 And Jethro, Moses' father-in-law, brought a burnt offering and sacrifices to God; and Aaron came with all the elders of Israel to eat bread with Moses' father-in-law [y]before God.

13 The next day Moses sat to judge the people, and the people stood around Moses from morning till evening. 14 When Moses' father-in-law saw all that he was doing for the people, he said, "What is this that you are doing for the

[1] A slight change would yield *upon the banner* [2] *Gershom* sounds like the Hebrew word for *sojourner* [3] *Eliezer* means *My God is help* [4] Hebrew; Samaritan, Septuagint, Syriac *behold* [5] Hebrew *with them*

10 [i] ch. 24:14; 31:2
11 [j] [1 Tim. 2:8]
12 [i] [See ver. 10 above]
13 [g] [See ver. 9 above]
14 [g] [See ver. 9 above] [k] Num. 24:20; Deut. 25:19; 1 Sam. 15:3, 7; 30:1, 17; 2 Sam. 8:12
15 [l] [Judg. 6:24]
16 [k] [See ver. 14 above]
Chapter 18
1 [m] [ch. 2:18] [n] ver. 12; ch. 2:16
3 [o] ch. 4:20; Acts 7:29 [p] ch. 2:22 [q] Ps. 39:12; Heb. 11:13
5 [r] See ch. 3:1
7 [s] Gen. 14:17; 18:2; 19:1; 1 Kgs. 2:19 [t] [Gen. 29:13; 33:4]; 2 Sam. 19:39
8 [u] See Neh. 9:9-15; Ps. 78:12-28, 42-53; 106:7-12
10 [v] Gen. 14:20; 2 Sam. 18:28; Luke 1:68
11 [w] 1 Chr. 16:25; 2 Chr. 2:5; Ps. 95:3; 97:9; 135:5 [x] Neh. 9:10; [Ps. 119:21; Dan. 4:37; Luke 1:51]
12 [y] Deut. 12:7; 14:26; 1 Chr. 29:22; [ch. 24:11; Gen. 31:54]

17:11–13 Here we discover an important lesson: sustained prayer was the unseen basis for successful battle. Moses stands in the position of prayer, holding up his hands (cf. 1 Tim. 2:8). When he "prayed" in a posture of godly dependence, Israel prevailed. When he ceased, Israel faltered.

So it was for Jesus in the garden of Gethsemane (Matt. 26:36–46). Prior to the battle with the forces of darkness at the cross, he spent the hours watching and praying. The encouragement for believers is that Jesus continues in the position of intercession for his people (Heb. 7:25; Rom. 8:34). His prayers, coupled with our own, sustain us in the day of spiritual battle (Eph. 6:18).

18:1–12 Moses and Israel have arrived at "the mountain of God" (v. 5). Jethro, his father-in-law, "the priest of Midian" (v. 1), returns Moses' family to him. He also hears about "all that the LORD had done to Pharaoh and to the Egyptians for Israel's sake" (v. 8). Jethro "rejoices" and blesses the Lord: "Now I know that the LORD is greater than all gods" (v. 11). Here Jethro echoes God's stated purpose for the plagues and the exodus: that all would know that "I am the LORD" (6:7; 7:5).

Our testimony of God's power, wisdom, and goodness serves our family in just this way. Through us, they come to know that the Lord is God. Through us, they come to hear of the supreme instance of God's power, wisdom, and goodness: Jesus Christ (1 Cor. 1:24).

people? Why do you sit alone, and all the people stand around you from morning till evening?" 15 And Moses said to his father-in-law,
"Because [z]the people come to me to inquire of
God; 16 [a]when they have a dispute, they come
to me and I decide between one person and
another, and I [b]make them know the statutes
of God and his laws." 17 Moses' father-in-law
said to him, "What you are doing is not good.
18 You and the people with you will certainly
wear yourselves out, for the thing is too heavy
for you. [c]You are not able to do it alone. 19 Now
obey my voice; I will give you advice, and God
be with you! You shall [d]represent the people
before God and [e]bring their cases to God,
20 and you shall warn them about the statutes
and the laws, and make them know [f]the way
in which they must walk and [g]what they must
do. 21 Moreover, look for [h]able men from all the
people, men who fear God, who are trustworthy and hate a bribe, and place such men over
the people as chiefs of thousands, of hundreds,
of fifties, and of tens. 22 And [i]let them judge the
people at all times. [j]Every great matter they
shall bring to you, but any small matter they
shall decide themselves. So it will be easier for
you, and they will [k]bear the burden with you.
23 If you do this, God will direct you, you will
be [l]able to endure, and all this people also will
go to their place in peace."
24 So Moses listened to the voice of his father-
in-law and did all that he had said. 25 [m]Moses
chose able men out of all Israel and made them
heads over the people, chiefs of thousands, of
hundreds, of fifties, and of tens. 26 And [n]they
judged the people at all times. Any hard case
they brought to Moses, but any small matter
they decided themselves. 27 Then Moses let his
father-in-law depart, and [o]he went away to his
own country.

Israel at Mount Sinai

19 On the third new moon after the
people of Israel had gone out of the
land of Egypt, on that day they [p]came into
the wilderness of Sinai. 2 They set out from
[q]Rephidim and came into the wilderness of
Sinai, and they encamped in the wilderness.
There Israel encamped before [r]the mountain,
3 while [s]Moses went up to God. [t]The LORD
called to him out of the mountain, saying,
"Thus you shall say to the house of Jacob, and
tell the people of Israel: 4 [u]You yourselves have
seen what I did to the Egyptians, and how
[v]I bore you on eagles' wings and brought you
to myself. 5 Now therefore, if you will indeed
obey my voice and keep my covenant, you
shall be [w]my treasured possession among all
peoples, for [x]all the earth is mine; 6 and you
shall be to me a [y]kingdom of priests and [z]a
holy nation. These are the words that you shall
speak to the people of Israel."
7 So Moses came and called the elders of the
people and set before them all these words
that the LORD had commanded him. 8 [a]All
the people answered together and said, "All
that the LORD has spoken we will do." And
Moses reported the words of the people to the

19:4–6 God articulates here the movements of grace: redemption (v. 4), requirement (v. 5), reward (v. 6).

The Lord redeemed his people, delivering them from the Egyptians, bearing them through their journey, bringing them to himself. All of this was rooted in God's gracious covenant. He remembered his covenant with Abraham (2:23–25). He claimed Israel as his "firstborn" (4:22). He took Israel as his own people and gave them glorious covenant promises (6:6–7). Therefore he redeemed them out of Egypt, out of the house of slavery (i.e., life maintained by human work).

Now, the Lord will give his redeemed people his requirements (20:1ff), essentially saying, "This is what it looks like to live in a blessed relationship with the God who has redeemed you." And he will give the promise of redemption's (not work's) reward: they will be God's treasured possession and they will be to God a kingdom of priests and a holy nation.

This movement of God's grace is the same for God's people today. God redeems us through Jesus Christ because of his gracious covenant; he gives us the requirements of his Word, picturing the life of grateful obedience; and he declares redemption's reward, that we would be his inheritance (Eph. 1:18), his treasured possession, a kingdom of priests, and a holy nation (1 Pet. 2:9; Rev. 1:6).

15 [z][Lev. 24:12; Num. 15:34]
16 [a]ch. 24:14; Deut. 17:8; [2 Sam. 15:2, 3; 1 Cor. 6:1] [b]Deut. 4:5; 5:1
18 [c]Num. 11:14, 17; Deut. 1:9, 12
19 [d]ch. 4:16; [ch. 20:19; Deut. 5:5] [e]Num. 27:5
20 [f]Ps. 143:8 [g]Deut. 1:18
21 [h]Deut. 1:15; 16:18; See 2 Chr. 19:5-10; [Acts 6:3]
22 [i]ver. 26 [j]Lev. 24:11; Num. 15:33; 27:2; 36:1; Deut. 1:17; 17:8 [k]Num. 11:17
23 [l]ver. 18
25 [m]Deut. 1:15
26 [n]ver. 22
27 [o][Num. 10:29, 30]
Chapter 19
1 [p]Num. 33:15
2 [q]ch. 17:1, 8 [r]See ch. 3:1
3 [s]ch. 20:21; [Acts 7:38] [t]ch. 3:4
4 [u]Deut. 29:2 [v]Deut. 32:11, 12; Isa. 63:9; Rev. 12:14
5 [w]Deut. 7:6; 14:2; 26:18; Ps. 135:4; Mal. 3:17; Titus 2:14 [x]ch. 9:29; Deut. 10:14; Job 41:11; Ps. 24:1; 50:12; 1 Cor. 10:26

6 [y]1 Pet. 2:5, 9; Rev. 1:6; 5:10; 20:6 [z]Lev. 20:26; Deut. 7:6; 14:21; 26:19; 28:9; Isa. 62:12; 1 Pet. 2:9 **8** [a]ch. 24:3, 7; Deut. 5:27; 26:17

LORD. 9 And the LORD said to Moses, "Behold,
I am coming to you [b]in a thick cloud, that [c]the
people may hear when I speak with you, and
may also [d]believe you forever."

When Moses told the words of the people to
the LORD, 10 the LORD said to Moses, "Go to the
people and [e]consecrate them today and tomorrow, and let them [f]wash their garments 11 and
be ready for the third day. For on the third day
[g]the LORD will come down on Mount Sinai in
the sight of all the people. 12 And you shall set
limits for the people all around, saying, 'Take
care not to go up into the mountain or touch
the edge of it. [h]Whoever touches the mountain
shall be put to death. 13 No hand shall touch
him, but he shall be stoned or shot;[1] whether
beast or man, he shall not live.' When [i]the
trumpet sounds a long blast, they shall come
up to the mountain." 14 So Moses [j]went down
from the mountain to the people and [e]conse-
crated the people; [f]and they washed their garments. 15 And he said to the people, "Be ready
for the [k]third day; [l]do not go near a woman."

16 On the morning of the [k]third day there
were [m]thunders and lightnings and [n]a thick
cloud on the mountain and a very loud [o]trum-
pet blast, so that all the people in the camp
[p]trembled. 17 Then [q]Moses brought the people out of the camp to meet God, and they
took their stand at the foot of the mountain.
18 Now [r]Mount Sinai was wrapped in smoke
because the LORD had descended on it in fire.
The smoke of it went up like the smoke of
a kiln, and [s]the whole mountain trembled
greatly. 19 And as the [o]sound of the trumpet
grew louder and louder, Moses spoke, and
[t]God answered him in thunder. 20 The LORD
came down on Mount Sinai, to the top of the
mountain. And the LORD called Moses to the
top of the mountain, and Moses went up.

21 And the LORD said to Moses, "Go down and
warn the people, lest they break through to
the LORD [u]to look and many of them perish.
22 Also let the priests who come near to the
LORD [v]consecrate themselves, lest the LORD
[w]break out against them." 23 And Moses said
to the LORD, "The people cannot come up
to Mount Sinai, for you yourself warned us,
saying, [x]'Set limits around the mountain and
consecrate it.'" 24 And the LORD said to him,
"Go down, and come up bringing Aaron with
you. But do not let the priests and the people
[y]break through to come up to the LORD, lest
he break out against them." 25 So Moses went
down to the people and told them.

The Ten Commandments

20 [z]And [a]God spoke all these words,
saying,

2 [b]"I am the LORD your God, who brought
you out of the land of Egypt, out of the house
of slavery.

3 [c]"You shall have no other gods before[2] me.

4 [d]"You shall not make for yourself a carved
image, or any likeness of anything that is in
heaven above, or that is in the earth beneath,

[1] That is, shot with an arrow [2] Or *besides*

9 [b] ch. 20:21; 24:16; Deut. 4:11; Ps. 18:11; 97:2; [Matt. 17:5] [c] Deut. 4:12, 36; [John 12:28, 29] [d] ch. 14:31
10 [e] Lev. 11:44, 45; [Josh. 3:5] [f] [Gen. 35:2; Lev. 15:5]
11 [g] ch. 34:5; [Deut. 33:2]
12 [h] Cited Heb. 12:20
13 [i] ver. 16, 19
14 [j] ver. 3 [e] [See ver. 10 above] [f] [See ver. 10 above]
15 [k] ver. 11 [l] [1 Sam. 21:4, 5; 1 Cor. 7:5]
16 [k] [See ver. 15 above] [m] Ps. 77:18; Heb. 12:18; Rev. 4:5; 8:5; 11:19 [n] ver. 9 [o] ver. 13 [p] Heb. 12:21
17 [q] Deut. 4:10
18 [r] ch. 24:17; Judg. 5:5; [Ps. 144:5; Isa. 6:4; Rev. 15:8] [s] Ps. 68:8; Heb. 12:26
19 [o] [See ver. 16 above] [t] Neh. 9:13; Ps. 81:7
21 [u] [ch. 3:6; 1 Sam. 6:19]
22 [v] Lev. 10:3 [w] 2 Sam. 6:8; 1 Chr. 13:11
23 [x] ver. 12; [Josh. 3:4]
24 [y] 2 Sam. 6:8; 1 Chr. 13:11

19:16–20 The picture of God given here is one of awesome glory and stark holiness. When the Lord came down on Mount Sinai, it was accompanied by thunder and lightning, fire and smoke, trumpets blasting louder and louder. And the result was that God's people trembled (v. 16) and the whole mountain trembled greatly (v. 18).

Though God's glory and holiness have not changed—he still remains "a consuming fire" (Heb. 12:29)—he has made a way to come into his presence without fear. For through Jesus, we do not come to Mount Sinai, but to Mount Zion. We do not come to gloom and tempest but to "festal gathering." We do not come to a voice, but to Jesus himself through his sprinkled blood (Heb. 12:18–24). Is it any wonder that Hebrews warns us not to refuse Jesus and his great salvation? He himself has made a way into God's presence for us (Heb. 10:19–25)!

20:1–2 Notice that the gracious relationship that God had established with his people was prior to the holy requirements that God gave. God identified himself in royal and personal terms—"I am the LORD your God." He speaks of what he has done in redemption—"who brought you out of the land of Egypt, out of the house of slavery." He speaks of whom his people belonged to in the past (slaves to Pharaoh) and speaks of whose they are now (by implication, belonging to God). God's grace, then, grounds his law.

Chapter 20 **1** [z] For ver. 1-17, see Deut. 5:6-21 [a] Deut. 5:22 **2** [b] Lev. 26:13; Ps. 81:10; Hos. 13:4 **3** [c] 2 Kgs. 17:35; Jer. 25:6; 35:15 **4** [d] Lev. 26:1; Deut. 27:15; Ps. 97:7; [Acts 17:29]

or that is in the water under the earth. 5 [e]You
shall not bow down to them or serve them, for
I the LORD your God am [f]a jealous God, [g]visit-
ing the iniquity of the fathers on the children
to the third and the fourth generation of those
who hate me, 6 but showing steadfast love to
thousands[1] of those who love me and keep my
commandments.

7 [h]"You shall not take the name of the LORD
your God in vain, for the LORD will not hold
him guiltless who takes his name in vain.

8 [i]"Remember the Sabbath day, to keep it holy.
9 [j]Six days you shall labor, and do all your work,
10 but the [k]seventh day is a Sabbath to the LORD
your God. On it you shall not do any work, you,
or your son, or your daughter, your male servant, or your female servant, or your livestock,
or the [l]sojourner who is within your gates. 11 For
[m]in six days the LORD made heaven and earth,
the sea, and all that is in them, and rested
on the seventh day. Therefore the LORD blessed
the Sabbath day and made it holy.

[1] Or *to the thousandth generation*

5 [e] ch. 23:24; Josh. 23:7 [f] ch. 34:14; Deut. 4:24; 6:15; Josh. 24:19; Nah. 1:2 [g] ch. 34:7; Num. 14:18; [Ps. 79:8; 109:14; Isa. 65:6, 7; Jer. 32:18]
7 [h] Lev. 19:12; [Matt. 5:34, 35; James 5:12]
8 [i] Lev. 19:3, 30; 26:2; See ch. 31:13-17
9 [j] ch. 23:12; 34:21; 35:2; Lev. 23:3; Luke 13:14
10 [k] ch. 16:26; 31:15; Gen. 2:2, 3; Ezek. 20:12; See Num. 15:32-36 [l] See Neh. 13:16-19
11 [m] See Gen. 1:1–2:3

Yet it is also true that his law leads us back to God and his grace. Shortly after Israel hears these words from God's own voice, they fall into idolatry and sensuality, violating nearly the entire moral law (32:1–6). Israel's failure represents the need we all have for gracious forgiveness (pictured in Israel through the sacrificial system) and also for God to write his law on our hearts (Jer. 31:31–34).

This is what God through Christ by his Spirit does in the new covenant—Christ's sacrificial death secures God's gracious forgiveness once-for-all, and Christ's Spirit accomplishes in the hearts of God's people all that Jeremiah had prophesied (Heb. 7:11–9:28). Christians have God's law written on our hearts and God's Spirit dwelling within us, offering a greater possibility of obedience grounded in our gracious relationship with God established through Jesus. And so it is that grace grounds law, and law leads us back to grace.

20:3 To have a god, according to the sixteenth-century reformer Martin Luther, is "to trust and believe in that one with your whole heart. . . . You lay hold of God when your heart grasps him and clings to him." And so, this first command tells us that, because God is our redeemer and because we are in relationship with him, we should grasp and cling to no one else besides the Lord. No other love should take priority over him; no other love should be placed alongside or substituted for him. No other love should be set in confrontation with the Lord in a test or trial. Because we are in relationship with God through his redeeming work, we are called to an exclusive devotion to and a thorough delight in him.

20:4–6 Because we are in relationship with God through his redeeming work, we are called to worship God in the way he details. And central to this is that we not make "a carved image, or any likeness" for the purpose of bowing down or serving. For those whom God has redeemed, we are not to domesticate him through images that might be manipulated for our own purposes. Rather, we are to listen to his voice, to his word, for our worship and service (Deut. 4:12). And this is because the Lord is a jealous God—his love for us is a passionate, exclusive love; for those who respond to his love, he maintains steadfast love "to the thousandth generation" (see ESV footnote).

20:7 To "take" God's name is to invoke God's own presence and character. When God's name is spoken, God is there in his glory (34:5–7). He is present to judge and save, to speak and teach (Isa. 52:5–6). This commandment therefore means: because God has redeemed us, he prohibits futile, purposeless naming of God whether in our daily speech, in our lifestyles, or in our worship (Lev. 19:12; Amos 2:7; Mal. 1:6–7). Instead, because we belong to God, we are to honor and vindicate the Lord as our God by living our lives in every respect in the light of his presence (1 John 1:5–6).

20:8–11 Already in 16:22–26, God reminded his people of the pattern of six days for work and one day for rest. Now, he tells us that because he has delivered us from slavery, he has freed us to "remember the Sabbath day, to keep it holy." As the Lord of the Sabbath, and for our good, God sets apart one day for his worship and our rest.

God grounds this command in creation—just as God created (labored) in six days and rested on the seventh, so God's people ought to do. In Deuteronomy 5:12–15, God grounds the Sabbath command in redemption—just as God delivered his people

12[n]"Honor your father and your mother, [o]that
your days may be long in the land that the
LORD your God is giving you.
13[p]"You shall not murder.[1]
14[q]"You shall not commit adultery.
15[r]"You shall not steal.
16[s]"You shall not bear false witness against
your neighbor.
17[t]"You shall not covet [u]your neighbor's
house; [v]you shall not covet your neighbor's
wife, or his male servant, or his female servant,
or his ox, or his donkey, or anything that is
your neighbor's."
18 Now when all the people saw [w]the thunder
and the flashes of lightning and the sound of
the trumpet and the mountain smoking, the
people were afraid[2] and trembled, and they
stood far off 19 and said to Moses, [x]"You speak
to us, and we will listen; but do not let God
speak to us, lest we die." 20[y]Moses said to the
people, "Do not fear, for God has come to [z]test
you, that the fear of him may be before you,

[1] The Hebrew word also covers causing human death through carelessness or negligence [2] Samaritan, Septuagint, Syriac, Vulgate; Masoretic Text *the people saw*

12[n] Lev. 19:3; Cited Matt. 15:4; 19:19; Mark 7:10; 10:19; Luke 18:20; Eph. 6:2; [Jer. 35:18, 19] [o] Eph. 6:3
13[p] Cited Matt. 5:21; 19:18; Rom. 13:9; [Gen. 9:5, 6; 1 John 3:15]
14[q] Lev. 18:20; Deut. 22:22; Prov. 6:32; 1 Cor. 6:9; Heb. 13:4; Cited Matt. 5:27; Rom. 13:9
15[r] Lev. 19:11; Eph. 4:28; Cited Matt. 19:18; Rom. 13:9
16[s] ch. 23:1; Prov. 19:5, 9; 21:28; 24:28; 25:18; Cited Matt. 19:18; See Deut. 19:16-20
17[t] Luke 12:15; Eph. 5:3, 5; Cited Rom. 7:7; 13:9; [Col. 3:5; Heb. 13:5] [u] Mic. 2:2 [v] Jer. 5:8; Matt. 5:28
18[w] Heb. 12:18
19[x] Deut. 5:25, 27; 18:16; Gal. 3:19, 20; Heb. 12:19
20[y] [1 Sam. 12:20] [z] [Gen. 22:1]; Deut. 13:3

from slavery with the result that they no longer have to work every day, so God's people are now freed to "keep the Sabbath day"—that is, trusting in his provision where their labors end.

20:12 God tells his people that, because he is the Lord their God, they should honor their parents—to attach value to them, care for them, provide for them (1 Tim. 5:8), to bless them and listen to them.

The Lord speaks to his people in this way because they are his covenant people; this is the same reason that the apostle Paul quotes this commandment in Ephesians 6:1–3. The blessing promised is that God will sustain our generations and our generations will sustain us in this world (cf. Psalms 127–128).

20:13 Underlying the issues of intentional and unintentional killing prohibited in this command (cf. Num. 35:11, 15) are the deeper issues of the heart. For underneath every murder is a deeper hatred—from Cain's time on, anger and hatred are expressed in murderous action (see Gen. 4:7–8; 2 Sam. 13:23–33; Matt. 5:21–22; 15:18–20a; 1 John 3:15).

As a result, because we belong to God, redeemed by him, we are called to set aside hatred and malice in order to preserve the lives of others through forgiveness and mercy (cf. Eph. 4:29–32; Col. 3:8, 12–14). The same forgiveness and mercy that has been lavished upon us in Christ is to be reflected in the way we treat others.

20:14 As with the sixth commandment, so with the seventh: not only is adultery prohibited (negatively), but God is (positively) calling upon us to direct our desires toward our spouses in marriage. Because he is our God and because he has redeemed us, we now are to live with our desires directed rightly—toward our spouses and ultimately toward God (Eph. 5:29–31). And so, adultery is prohibited, but so is lust (cf. Matt. 5:27–28) as well as other sexual sins, such as incest, fornication, and homosexuality (Rom. 1:24–25; 1 Cor. 5:1–13; 6:9–11).

20:15 Because we belong to the Lord our God, we recognize that all things belong to him and that he has assigned stewardships to each of us. As a result, we do not steal what is not ours, but rather we labor so that we might benefit our earthly and heavenly masters and so that we might have something to share with others (Eph. 4:28; 6:5–9; Col. 3:22–4:1).

20:16 Those who tell lies and bear false witness are like the Devil himself (John 8:44). The problem is that our own hearts lie to us; they are deceitful and are hardened by the deceitfulness of sin (Jer. 17:9; Heb. 3:12–13). For those who have been delivered from slavery to sin and who belong to God, we are now freed to tell the truth to and about our brothers and sisters in Christ (Eph. 4:25).

20:17 When God prohibits coveting, he once again is dealing with our hearts. To covet is to crave or yearn for that which is not ours. While this commandment connects to the seventh commandment, it is broader: for we can covet our neighbor's place (Mic. 2:2), people (Ex. 20:14), or property (Josh. 7:20–21).

that you may not sin." 21 The people stood far
off, while Moses drew near to the [a]thick darkness where God was.

Laws About Altars

22 And the LORD said to Moses, "Thus you
shall say to the people of Israel: 'You have
seen for yourselves that I have [b]talked with
you from heaven. 23 [c]You shall not make gods
of silver to be with me, nor shall you make for
yourselves gods of gold. 24 An altar of earth
you shall make for me and sacrifice on it your
burnt offerings and your peace offerings, your
sheep and your oxen. [d]In every place where
I cause my name to be remembered I will
come to you and [e]bless you. 25 [f]If you make
me an altar of stone, [g]you shall not build it of
hewn stones, for if you wield your tool on it
you profane it. 26 And you shall not go up by
steps to my altar, that your nakedness be not
exposed on it.'

Laws About Slaves

21 "Now these are the [h]rules that you
shall set before them. 2 [i]When you buy
a Hebrew slave,[1] he shall serve six years, and in
the seventh he shall go out free, for nothing.
3 If he comes in single, he shall go out single; if
he comes in married, then his wife shall go out
with him. 4 If his master gives him a wife and

[1] Or *servant*; the Hebrew term *'ebed* designates a range of social and economic roles; also verses 5, 6, 7, 20, 21, 26, 27, 32 (see Preface)

According to the apostle Paul, covetousness is a powerful desire that cannot be rooted out simply by outward obedience (Rom. 7:12–17). Further, Paul equates covetousness to idolatry (Eph. 5:5; Col. 3:5). All of this means that we have come full circle to the first commandment—because the Lord our God has redeemed us, we must desire nothing more than him.

20:22–23:19 God's redeemed people have heard him speak as he gave them the Ten Commandments. Now Moses returns up the mountain in order to receive more specific application of the moral law in the detailed legislation that would guide Israel's life. We must remember that God's gracious redemption of his people preceded the regulation of their lives: God's people would not secure salvation by keeping the law; rather, because they were already God's people, they were to obey him. And as they lived in this way, order, civility, and charity would be the character of their life together.

The question for Christians is whether and how these "rules" (21:1) are still applicable today. Clearly, there are some that are not: the laws about altars (20:22–26) and Sabbath festivals (23:10–19) have been fulfilled in Christ's sacrifice (Rom. 10:4). Likewise, some of the sentences proposed—namely, the death sentence—seem far harsher than anything we can imagine (see, e.g., Ex. 21:15, 17; 22:18–20). In addition, systems of slavery—whether ancient or modern—are now held to be unacceptable, making directions concerning slaves irrelevant to our situation (21:1–11).

Instruction in the letters of Paul and, particularly, in the book of Hebrews guides us in distinguishing the civil and ceremonial laws of Old Testament Israel from the moral law applicable to believers in all ages. In addition, there are principles of general equity for the care of neighbor (e.g., Matt. 22:39). These serve not only to illustrate the Ten Commandments themselves but also to provide mercy, justice, and restitution. All this guides Christians in determining what the obedience of faith looks like in our contexts. Above all, we gain a picture of how seriously God takes sin and how much we need a Savior who was a perfect law-keeper, fulfilling the intent and detail of God's law.

21:1–11 After worship (20:22–26), the first thing that God regulates is how Israel deals with their slaves. The reason would be stated repeatedly in Deuteronomy: Israel was to remember that they had been slaves in Egypt. Consequently, they needed to treat their own slaves differently (Deut. 5:15; 15:15; 16:12; 24:18, 22; cf. Ex. 22:21; 23:9). Most importantly, slaves were to be treated as human beings; male slaves were to be released after six years; and lifetime service was the slave's, not the master's, choice.

While these laws do not advocate for it directly, the overarching direction of the biblical story is freedom, spiritual freedom in Christ (Gal. 5:1, 13; Eph. 6:5; Col. 3:22–25) as well as human liberation (1 Cor. 7:21; Philem. 18–19). As those who have come to know genuine liberty in Christ (2 Cor. 3:17), Christians today are rightly involved in seeking spiritual and physical liberation for people around the world.

21 [a] Deut. 4:11; 2 Sam. 22:10; 1 Kgs. 8:12; Ps. 18:9; 97:2
22 [b] Deut. 4:36; Neh. 9:13; Heb. 12:25
23 [c] [ch. 32:31; 2 Kgs. 17:33; Ezek. 20:39; Zeph. 1:5]
24 [d] Deut. 12:5, 11; 14:23; 16:6, 11; 26:2; 1 Kgs. 8:29; 9:3; 2 Chr. 6:6; 7:16; 12:13; Ezra 6:12; Neh. 1:9; Ps. 74:7; Jer. 7:10, 12 [e] Deut. 7:13
25 [f] Deut. 27:5; Josh. 8:31 [g] [1 Kgs. 5:17; 1 Chr. 22:2]

Chapter 21

1 [h] ch. 24:3; Deut. 4:14; 6:1
2 [i] Deut. 15:12; Jer. 34:14; See Lev. 25:39-41

she bears him sons or daughters, the wife and
her children shall be her master's, and he shall
go out alone. 5 But [j]if the slave plainly says,
'I love my master, my wife, and my children;
I will not go out free,' 6 then his master shall
bring him to [k]God, and he shall bring him to
the door or the doorpost. And his master shall
bore his ear through with an awl, and he shall
be his slave forever.
7 "When a man [l]sells his daughter as a slave,
she shall not go out as the male slaves do. 8 If
she does not please her master, who has designated her[1] for himself, then he shall let her
be redeemed. He shall have no right to sell
her to a foreign people, since he has broken
faith with her. 9 If he designates her for his
son, he shall deal with her as with a daughter.
10 If he takes another wife to himself, he shall
not diminish her food, her clothing, or [m]her
marital rights. 11 And if he does not do these
three things for her, she shall go out for nothing, without payment of money.
12 [n]"Whoever strikes a man so that he dies
shall be put to death. 13 [o]But if he did not lie
in wait for him, but God let him fall into his
hand, then [p]I will appoint for you a place to
which he may flee. 14 But if a man willfully
attacks another to kill him by cunning, [q]you
shall take him from my altar, that he may die.
15 "Whoever strikes his father or his mother
shall be put to death.
16 [r]"Whoever steals a man and sells him, and
anyone found [s]in possession of him, shall be
put to death.
17 [t]"Whoever curses[2] his father or his mother
shall be put to death.
18 "When men quarrel and one strikes the
other with a stone or with his fist and the man
does not die but takes to his bed, 19 then if the
man rises again and walks outdoors with his
staff, he who struck him shall be clear; only
he shall pay for the loss of his time, and shall
have him thoroughly healed.
20 "When a man strikes his slave, male or
female, with a rod and the slave dies under
his hand, he shall be avenged. 21 But if the slave
survives a day or two, he is not to be avenged,
for the [u]slave is his money.
22 "When men strive together and hit a pregnant woman, so that her children come out,
but there is no harm, the one who hit her shall
surely be fined, as the woman's husband shall
impose on him, and [v]he shall pay as the [w]judges
determine. 23 But if there is harm,[3] then you
shall pay [x]life for life, 24 [y]eye for eye, tooth for
tooth, hand for hand, foot for foot, 25 burn for
burn, wound for wound, stripe for stripe.
26 "When a man strikes the eye of his slave,
male or female, and destroys it, he shall let the
slave go free because of his eye. 27 If he knocks
out the tooth of his slave, male or female, he
shall let the slave go free because of his tooth.
28 "When an ox gores a man or a woman to
death, the [z]ox shall be stoned, and its flesh
shall not be eaten, but the owner of the ox
shall not be liable. 29 But if the ox has been
accustomed to gore in the past, and its owner
has been warned but has not kept it in, and it
kills a man or a woman, the ox shall be stoned,
and its owner also shall be put to death. 30 If
[a]a ransom is imposed on him, then [v]he shall
give for the redemption of his life whatever
is imposed on him. 31 If it gores a man's son
or daughter, he shall be dealt with according
to this same rule. 32 If the ox gores a slave,
male or female, the owner shall give to their
master [b]thirty shekels[4] of silver, and [z]the ox
shall be stoned.

[1] Or *so that he has not designated her* [2] Or *dishonors*; Septuagint *reviles* [3] Or *so that her children come out and it is clear who was to blame, he shall be fined as the woman's husband shall impose on him, and he alone shall pay. If it is unclear who was to blame . . .*
[4] A *shekel* was about 2/5 ounce or 11 grams

5 [j]Deut. 15:16, 17
6 [k][Ps. 82:6; John 10:34, 35]
7 [l]Neh. 5:5
10 [m]1 Cor. 7:5
12 [n]Gen. 9:6; Lev. 24:17; Num. 35:30, 31; [Matt. 26:52]
13 [o]Deut. 19:4, 5; See Num. 35:22-25 [p]Num. 35:11; Deut. 4:41-43; 19:2, 3; See Josh. 20:2-9
14 [q]See 1 Kgs. 2:28-34
16 [r]Deut. 24:7; 1 Tim. 1:10 [s]ch. 22:4
17 [t]Lev. 20:9; Deut. 27:16; Cited Matt. 15:4; Mark 7:10; [Prov. 20:20; 30:11]

21:12–32 Underlying many of these laws was the *lex talionis*, the law of "eye for an eye" (vv. 23–24). Strictly speaking, this teaching was not simply prescriptive, as though you *must* take an eye for an eye, but restrictive, limiting the nature of retribution. As such, it was an application of the sixth commandment and was meant to break the reality of blood feuds and escalating retaliation (cf. Lev. 24:19–20; Deut. 19:21).

When Jesus speaks of this in Matthew 5:38–48, not only does he urge non-retaliation, but he speaks of overcoming evil with good (cf. Rom. 12:19–21). And that is possible only because we are "sons of your Father who is in heaven" (Matt. 5:45); we belong to a heavenly Father who has overcome our evil with his good. As we live out of the rich resources of the gospel, we recognize that God does not repay us as our sins deserve but continues to shower us with mercy and compassion (cf. Ps. 103:8–12).

21 [u][Lev. 25:45, 46] **22** [v][Deut. 22:18, 19] [w][Job 31:11] **23** [x]Deut. 19:21 **24** [y]Lev. 24:20; Deut. 19:21; Cited Matt. 5:38 **28** [z]Gen. 9:5 **30** [a]ch. 30:12; Num. 35:31, 32 [v][See ver. 22 above] **32** [b][Zech. 11:12, 13; Matt. 26:15] [z][See ver. 28 above]

Laws About Restitution

33 “When a man opens a pit, or when a man digs a pit and does not cover it, and an ox or a donkey falls into it, 34 the owner of the pit shall make restoration. He shall give money to its owner, and the dead beast shall be his.

35 “When one man’s ox butts another’s, so that it dies, then they shall sell the live ox and share its price, and the dead beast also they shall share. 36 Or if it is known that the ox has been accustomed to gore in the past, and its owner has not kept it in, he shall repay ox for ox, and the dead beast shall be his.

22 [1] “If a man steals an ox or a sheep, and kills it or sells it, he shall repay five oxen for an ox, and [c]four sheep for a sheep. 2 [2] If a thief is found [d]breaking in and is struck so that he dies, there shall be no bloodguilt for him, 3 but if the sun has risen on him, there shall be bloodguilt for him. He shall surely pay. If he has nothing, then [e]he shall be sold for his theft. 4 If the stolen beast [f]is found alive in his possession, whether it is an ox or a donkey or a sheep, [g]he shall pay double.

5 “If a man causes a field or vineyard to be grazed over, or lets his beast loose and it feeds in another man’s field, he shall make restitution from the best in his own field and in his own vineyard.

6 “If fire breaks out and catches in thorns so that the stacked grain or the standing grain or the field is consumed, he who started the fire shall make full restitution.

7 “If a man gives to his neighbor money or goods to keep safe, and it is stolen from the man’s house, then, if the thief is found, [g]he shall pay double. 8 If the thief is not found, the owner of the house shall come near to God to show whether or not he has put his hand to his neighbor’s property. 9 For every breach of trust, whether it is for an ox, for a donkey, for a sheep, for a cloak, or for any kind of lost thing, of which one says, ‘This is it,’ the case of both parties shall come before God. The one whom God condemns shall pay double to his neighbor.

10 “If a man gives to his neighbor a donkey or an ox or a sheep or any beast to keep safe, and it dies or is injured or is driven away, without anyone seeing it, 11 [h]an oath by the LORD shall be between them both to see whether or not he has put his hand to his neighbor’s property. The owner shall accept the oath, and he shall not make restitution. 12 But if [i]it is stolen from him, he shall make restitution to its owner. 13 If it is torn by beasts, let him bring it as evidence. He shall not make restitution for what has been torn.

14 “If a man borrows anything of his neighbor, and it is injured or dies, the owner not being with it, he shall make full restitution. 15 If the owner was with it, he shall not make restitution; if it was hired, it came for its hiring fee.[3]

Laws About Social Justice

16 [j]“If a man seduces a virgin[4] who is not betrothed and lies with her, he shall give the bride-price[5] for her and make her his wife. 17 If her father utterly refuses to give her to him, [j]he shall pay money equal to the [k]bride-price for virgins.

18 [l]“You shall not permit a sorceress to live.

19 [m]“Whoever lies with an animal shall be put to death.

20 [n]“Whoever sacrifices to any god, other than the LORD alone, shall be devoted to destruction.[6]

21 [o]“You shall not wrong a sojourner or oppress him, for you were sojourners in the land of Egypt. 22 [p]You shall not mistreat any widow or fatherless child. 23 If you do mistreat them, and they [q]cry out to me, I will surely [r]hear their cry, 24 and my wrath will burn, and I will kill you with the sword, and [s]your wives shall become widows and your children fatherless.

[1] Ch 21:37 in Hebrew [2] Ch 22:1 in Hebrew [3] Or *it is reckoned in* (Hebrew *comes into*) *its hiring fee* [4] Or *a girl of marriageable age*; also verse 17 [5] Or *engagement present*; also verse 17 [6] That is, set apart (devoted) as an offering to the Lord (for destruction)

21:33–22:15 The laws about restitution seek again to honor life and property—illustrating the eighth commandment—but also to limit and regulate the retribution that others might exact. Yet the New Testament pictures the redeemed heart as willing to make restitution in just these terms: as Zaccheus came to faith in Jesus, he willingly declared, “If I have defrauded anyone of anything, I restore it fourfold” (Luke 19:8), echoing Exodus 22:1. A heart that is unwilling to make restitution has not come to understand sin and redemption, faith and repentance.

Chapter 22
1 [c] 2 Sam. 12:6; [Prov. 6:31; Luke 19:8]
2 [d] Matt. 24:43
3 [e] [ch. 21:2]
4 [f] ch. 21:16 [g] [ver. 1]
7 [g] [See ver. 4 above]
11 [h] Heb. 6:16
12 [i] Gen. 31:39
16 [j] Deut. 22:28, 29

17 [j] [See ver. 16 above] [k] Gen. 34:12; 1 Sam. 18:25 **18** [l] Lev. 19:26, 31; 20:27; Deut. 18:10, 11; 1 Sam. 28:3, 9 **19** [m] Lev. 18:23; 20:15; Deut. 27:21 **20** [n] [Num. 25:2, 7, 8; Josh. 23:16]; See Deut. 13:1-15; 17:2-5 **21** [o] ch. 23:9; Lev. 19:33; Deut. 10:18, 19; Jer. 7:6; Zech. 7:10; Mal. 3:5 **22** [p] Deut. 24:17; 27:19; Ps. 94:6; Isa. 1:17, 23; 10:2; Ezek. 22:7; Zech. 7:10; James 1:27 **23** [q] Job 34:28; Luke 18:7 [r] Ps. 18:6; 145:19; [James 5:4] **24** [s] Ps. 109:9; Lam. 5:3

25 [t]"If you lend money to any of my people
with you who is poor, you shall not be like a
moneylender to him, and you shall not exact
interest from him. 26 [u]If ever you take your
neighbor's cloak in pledge, you shall return
it to him before the sun goes down, 27 for that
is his only covering, and it is his cloak for his
body; in what else shall he sleep? And if he
[q]cries to me, I will hear, for I am [v]compassionate.
28 [w]"You shall not revile God, nor [w]curse a
ruler of your people.
29 "You shall not delay to offer from the fullness of your harvest and from the outflow of
your presses. [x]The firstborn of your sons you
shall give to me. 30 [y]You shall do the same with
your oxen and with your sheep: [z]seven days
it shall be with its mother; on the eighth day
you shall give it to me.
31 [a]"You shall be consecrated to me. Therefore
[b]you shall not eat any flesh that is torn by beasts
in the field; [c]you shall throw it to the dogs.
23 [d]"You shall not spread a false report.
You shall not join hands with a wicked
man to be a [e]malicious witness. 2 You shall
not fall in with the many to do evil, nor shall
you bear witness in a lawsuit, siding with the
many, so as to pervert justice, 3 [f]nor shall you
be partial to a poor man in his lawsuit.
4 [g]"If you meet your enemy's ox or his donkey
going astray, you shall bring it back to him.
5 If you see the donkey of one who hates you
lying down under its burden, you shall refrain
from leaving him with it; you shall rescue it
with him.
6 [h]"You shall not pervert the justice due to
your poor in his lawsuit. 7 [d]Keep far from a
false charge, and [i]do not kill the innocent and
righteous, for [j]I will not acquit the wicked.
8 [k]And you shall take no bribe, for a bribe
blinds the clear-sighted and subverts the cause
of those who are in the right.
9 [l]"You shall not oppress a sojourner. You
know the heart of a sojourner, for you were
sojourners in the land of Egypt.

Laws About the Sabbath and Festivals

10 [m]"For six years you shall sow your land and
gather in its yield, 11 but the seventh year you
shall let it rest and lie fallow, that the poor
of your people may eat; and what they leave
the beasts of the field may eat. You shall do
likewise with your vineyard, and with your
olive orchard.
12 [n]"Six days you shall do your work, but on
the seventh day you shall rest; that your ox
and your donkey may have rest, and the son
of your servant woman, and the alien, may
be refreshed.
13 [o]"Pay attention to all that I have said to you,
and make no mention of the names of other
gods, nor let it be heard on your lips.
14 [p]"Three times in the year you shall keep
a feast to me. 15 [q]You shall keep the Feast of
Unleavened Bread. As I commanded you, you
shall eat unleavened bread for seven days at
the appointed time in the month of [r]Abib,
for in it you came out of Egypt. [s]None shall
appear before me empty-handed. 16 You shall
keep [t]the Feast of Harvest, of the firstfruits
of your labor, of what you sow in the field.
You shall keep the [u]Feast of Ingathering at
the end of the year, when you gather in from
the field the fruit of your labor. 17 [p]Three times
in the year shall all your males appear before
the Lord GOD.
18 [v]"You shall not offer the blood of my sacrifice with anything leavened, or let the fat of
my feast remain until the morning.
19 "The best of the [w]firstfruits of your ground
you shall bring into the house of the LORD
your God.
[x]"You shall not boil a young goat in its mother's milk.

23:20–24:11 This section closes with two lines of encouragement for Israel. First, God promises that the angel of the Lord will go before his people in order to deliver them into the Promised Land (cf. 3:2; Josh. 5:13–15). God's own name and authority is "in" the angel (Ex. 23:21); he is the visible representative of God himself.

Second, God calls Moses and Israel's representatives up the mountain in order to confirm his covenant through sacrifice and a meal. It was through "the blood of the covenant" that Israel became God's people (24:8) and through that same blood that God's people might see the God of Israel and feast in his presence.

25 [t] Lev. 25:35-37; Deut. 23:19, 20; Neh. 5:7; Ps. 15:5; Prov. 28:8; Ezek. 18:8, 13, 17; 22:12
26 [u] Deut. 24:13, 17; Prov. 20:16; Ezek. 18:7, 16; Amos 2:8; [Prov. 22:27]
27 [q] [See ver. 23 above] [v] ch. 34:6; 2 Chr. 30:9; Neh. 9:17
28 [w] Cited Acts 23:5; [2 Sam. 19:21; Eccles. 10:20; Jude 8]
29 [x] See ch. 13:2
30 [y] Deut. 15:19 [z] Lev. 22:27

31 [a] ch. 19:6; Lev. 11:44, 45 [b] Lev. 22:8; Ezek. 4:14; 44:31 [c] [Matt. 7:6] **Chapter 23** **1** [d] [Lev. 19:11; Ps. 15:3; 101:5] [e] Deut. 19:16-18; Ps. 35:11; [1 Kgs. 21:10, 13; Matt. 26:59-61; Acts 6:11, 13] **3** [f] Lev. 19:15; [Deut. 1:17] **4** [g] [Deut. 22:1, 4; Prov. 25:21; Matt. 5:44; Rom. 12:20; 1 Thess. 5:15] **6** [h] Deut. 27:19; Eccles. 5:8; Isa. 10:1, 2; Jer. 5:28, 29; Mal. 3:5 **7** [d] [See ver. 1 above] [i] Deut. 27:25; [Prov. 17:26] [j] ch. 34:7 **8** [k] Deut. 16:19; [1 Sam. 8:3; 2 Chr. 19:7; Ps. 26:10; Prov. 17:23; Isa. 1:23; 5:23; 33:15] **9** [l] See ch. 22:21 **10** [m] Lev. 25:3, 4 **12** [n] See ch. 20:9 **13** [o] Deut. 4:9; Josh. 22:5; 23:7; Hos. 2:17; Zech. 13:2 **14** [p] ver. 17; ch. 34:23; Deut. 16:16 **15** [q] See ch. 12:15 [r] ch. 13:4 [s] ch. 34:20; Deut. 16:16 **16** [t] ch. 34:22; See Lev. 23:9-21 [u] Deut. 16:13; See Lev. 23:34-44 **17** [p] [See ver. 14 above] **18** [v] ch. 12:8; 34:25; Lev. 2:11 **19** [w] ch. 34:26; Lev. 2:12; 23:10, 17; Num. 18:12, 13; Deut. 26:2, 10; Neh. 10:35; Ezek. 44:30 [x] ch. 34:26; Deut. 14:21

Conquest of Canaan Promised

20 [y]"Behold, I send an angel before you to
guard you on the way and to bring you to
the place that I have prepared. 21 Pay careful
attention to him and obey his voice; [z]do not
rebel against him, [a]for he will not pardon your
transgression, for my name is in him.

22 "But if you carefully obey his voice and do
all that I say, then [b]I will be an enemy to your
enemies and an adversary to your adversaries.

23 [y]"When my angel goes before you and brings
you [c]to the Amorites and the Hittites and the
Perizzites and the Canaanites, the Hivites and
the Jebusites, and I blot them out, 24 you shall
[d]not bow down to their gods nor serve them,
[e]nor do as they do, but [f]you shall utterly overthrow them and break their [g]pillars in pieces.
25 You [h]shall serve the LORD your God, and [i]he[1]
will bless your bread and your water, and [j]I will
take sickness away from among you. 26 [k]None
shall miscarry or be barren in your land; I will
fulfill the [l]number of your days. 27 I will send
[m]my terror before you and will throw into
[n]confusion all the people against whom you
shall come, and I will make all your enemies
turn their backs to you. 28 And [o]I will send
hornets[2] before you, which shall drive out the
Hivites, the Canaanites, and the Hittites from
before you. 29 [p]I will not drive them out from
before you in one year, lest the land become
desolate and the wild beasts multiply against
you. 30 Little by little I will drive them out from
before you, until you have increased and possess the land. 31 [q]And I will set your border from
the Red Sea to the Sea of the Philistines, and
from the wilderness to the Euphrates,[3] for [r]I will
give the inhabitants of the land into your hand,
and you shall drive them out before you. 32 [s]You
shall make no covenant with them and their
gods. 33 They shall not dwell in your land, lest
they make you sin against me; for if you serve
their gods, [t]it will surely be a snare to you."

The Covenant Confirmed

24 Then he said to Moses, "Come up to
the LORD, you and Aaron, [u]Nadab, and
Abihu, and [v]seventy of the elders of Israel, and
worship from afar. 2 Moses [w]alone shall come
near to the LORD, but the others shall not
come near, and the people shall not come up
with him."

3 Moses came and told the people all the
words of the LORD and [x]all the rules.[4] And
all the people answered with one voice and
said, [y]"All the words that the LORD has spoken we will do." 4 And [z]Moses wrote down
all the words of the LORD. He rose early in
the morning and built an altar at the foot of
the mountain, and twelve [a]pillars, according
to the twelve tribes of Israel. 5 And he sent
young men of the people of Israel, who offered
burnt offerings and sacrificed peace offerings
of oxen to the LORD. 6 And [b]Moses took half of
the blood and put it in basins, and half of the
blood he threw against the altar. 7 Then he took
the Book of the Covenant and read it in the
hearing of the people. And they said, [x]"All that
the LORD has spoken we will do, and we will
be obedient." 8 [c]And Moses took the blood and
threw it on the people and said, "Behold the
blood of the covenant that the LORD has made
with you in accordance with all these words."

9 Then Moses and Aaron, Nadab, and Abihu,
and [d]seventy of the elders of Israel [e]went up,
10 and they [f]saw the God of Israel. There was
under his feet as it were a pavement of [g]sap-
phire stone, like the very heaven for clearness.
11 And he did not lay his hand on the chief men
of the people of Israel; they beheld God, and
[h]ate and drank.

12 The LORD said to Moses, [i]"Come up to me
on the mountain and wait there, that I may
give you the [j]tablets of stone, with the law and
the commandment, which I have written for
their instruction." 13 So Moses rose with his

[1] Septuagint, Vulgate / [2] Or *the hornet* [3] Hebrew *the River* [4] Or *all the just decrees*

Likewise, not only do believers today have the continued promise of God's presence through the Spirit of Jesus (Matt. 28:20; John 14:16–17, 25–26; Eph. 1:11–14), but we continue to participate in a meal that promises Jesus' presence and power through the "blood of the [new] covenant" (Matt. 26:26–29; Luke 22:19–20; 1 Cor. 11:23–26). We too then have encouragement for our continued journey through this wilderness to the City of God (Heb. 11:13–16).

20 [y] ch. 14:19; 33:2, 14; Josh. 5:13, 14; 6:2; Isa. 63:9
21 [z] Ps. 78:40, 56 [a] [ch. 32:34; 34:7; Num. 14:35; Josh. 24:19]
22 [b] Gen. 12:3; Deut. 30:7; Jer. 30:20
23 [y] [See ver. 20 above]

[c] See ch. 13:5 **24** [d] ch. 20:5 [e] Lev. 18:3; Deut. 12:30, 31 [f] ch. 34:13; Num. 33:52; Deut. 7:5, 25; 12:3 [g] See Deut. 16:22 **25** [h] Deut. 6:13; 10:12, 20; 11:13; 13:4; Josh. 22:5; Matt. 4:10 [i] Deut. 7:13; 28:5, 8 [j] ch. 15:26; Deut. 7:15 **26** [k] Deut. 7:14 [l] [Job 5:26; Ps. 55:23] **27** [m] Deut. 2:25; Josh. 2:9 [n] Deut. 7:23 **28** [o] Deut. 7:20; Josh. 24:12 **29** [p] Deut. 7:22 **31** [q] Gen. 15:18; Num. 34:3; Deut. 11:24; Josh. 1:4; [1 Kgs. 4:21, 24; Ps. 72:8] [r] Josh. 21:44; Judg. 1:4; 11:21 **32** [s] ch. 34:12, 15; Deut. 7:2 **33** [t] ch. 34:12; Deut. 7:16; Josh. 23:13; Judg. 2:3; Ps. 106:36 **Chapter 24** **1** [u] ch. 28:1; See ch. 6:23 [v] Num. 11:16 **2** [w] ver. 13, 15, 18 **3** [x] ch. 21:1 [y] ch. 19:8; Deut. 5:27 **4** [z] Deut. 31:9 [a] Gen. 28:18; 31:45; [ch. 23:24] **6** [b] Heb. 9:18, 19 **7** [x] [See ver. 3 above] **8** [c] Cited Heb. 9:19, 20; [Heb. 13:20; 1 Pet. 1:2] **9** [d] Num. 11:16 [e] [ver. 1] **10** [f] Gen. 32:30; Judg. 13:22; Isa. 6:1, 5; [ch. 33:20, 23; John 1:18; 1 Tim. 6:16; 1 John 4:12, 20] [g] Ezek. 1:26; 10:1 **11** [h] [ch. 18:12; Gen. 31:54] **12** [i] ver. 2, 15, 18 [j] ch. 31:18; 32:15, 16; Deut. 5:22

assistant [k]Joshua, and Moses went up [l]into the mountain of God. 14 And he said to the elders, "Wait here for us until we return to you. And behold, Aaron and [m]Hur are with you. Whoever has a dispute, let him go to them."

15 Then Moses went up on the mountain, and [n]the cloud covered the mountain. 16 [o]The glory of the LORD dwelt on Mount Sinai, and the cloud covered it six days. And on the seventh day he called to Moses out of the midst of the cloud. 17 Now the appearance of the glory of the LORD was like a [p]devouring fire on the top of the mountain in the sight of the people of Israel. 18 Moses entered the cloud and went up on the mountain. And Moses [q]was on the mountain forty days and forty nights.

Contributions for the Sanctuary

25 The LORD said to Moses, 2 [r]"Speak to the people of Israel, that they take for me a contribution. From [s]every man whose heart moves him you shall receive the contribution for me. 3 And this is the contribution that you shall receive from them: gold, silver, and bronze, 4 [t]blue and purple and scarlet yarns and fine twined linen, goats' hair, 5 tanned [u]rams' skins, goatskins,[1] acacia wood, 6 [v]oil for the lamps, [w]spices for the anointing oil and for the fragrant incense, 7 onyx stones, and stones for setting, for the [x]ephod and for the breastpiece. 8 And let them make me a [y]sanctuary, that [z]I may dwell in their midst. 9 [a]Exactly as I show you concerning the pattern of the [b]tabernacle, and of all its furniture, so you shall make it.

The Ark of the Covenant

10 [c]"They shall make an ark of acacia wood. Two cubits[2] and a half shall be its length, a cubit and a half its breadth, and a cubit and a half its height. 11 You shall overlay it with [d]pure gold, inside and outside shall you overlay it, and you shall make on it a molding of gold around it. 12 You shall cast four rings of

[1] Uncertain; possibly *dolphin skins*, or *dugong skins*; compare 26:14 [2] A *cubit* was about 18 inches or 45 centimeters

13[k] ch. 33:11; [ch. 17:9, 10]
[l] See ch. 3:1
14[m] ch. 17:10, 12; 31:2
15[n] ch. 19:9, 16; [Matt. 17:5]
16[o] ch. 16:10; Lev. 9:23; Num. 14:10; 16:42
17[p] ch. 3:2; 19:18; Deut. 4:36; Heb. 12:18, 29
18[q] ch. 34:28; Deut. 9:9, 18, 25; 10:10
Chapter 25
2[r] For ver. 1-7, see ch. 35:4-9 [s] ch. 35:5, 21, 29; 36:2; Judg. 5:2; 1 Chr. 29:5; [Ezra 1:6; 2:68; 3:5; 7:16]; Neh. 11:2; [2 Cor. 8:12; 9:7]
4[t] ch. 26:1, 31, 36
5[u] ch. 26:14
6[v] ch. 27:20 [w] ch. 30:7, 23, 34; 31:11
7[x] ch. 28:4, 15
8[y] Heb. 9:1, 2; See ch. 36:1-4 [z] ch. 29:45; 1 Kgs. 6:13; 2 Cor. 6:16; Rev. 21:3
9[a] ver. 40 [b] ch. 26:1
10[c] ch. 37:1-3; Deut. 10:3; Heb. 9:4
11[d] ver. 24, 25; ch. 30:3, 4; 37:2

25:1–31:17 Having redeemed his people and declared his will for them, the Lord God declares his desire to dwell in the midst of his people: "let them make me a sanctuary, that I may dwell in their midst" (25:8; cf. 29:45). This theme—the dwelling of God in the midst of his people—is a significant biblical theme. In the garden of Eden, God walked in the midst of the garden in the cool of the day (Gen. 3:8). Creation itself was the "sanctuary" in which God dwelt with Adam and Eve (Ps. 104:1–3, 13).

Now, after the exodus, God makes provision to dwell in the midst of his redeemed people. This tabernacle served as a copy and shadow of the heavenly tabernacle in which God dwelt (Heb. 8:5). Eventually, the tabernacle would be replaced with the temple (2 Sam. 7:4–17; 1 Kings 5:3; 6:1–38; 7:13–9:9). As God declares, "I will dwell among the children of Israel and will not forsake my people Israel" (1 Kings 6:13). After God's people forsake him, however, he forsakes the temple. The temple's destruction by the Babylonians was the end of an era. The second temple, built under the oversight and encouragement of Haggai and Zechariah also knew the promise of God's presence (Hag. 2:7–9).

And yet, the tabernacle and temples pointed to a greater reality: with the coming of Jesus, God had come to dwell—to "tabernacle"—among us (John 1:14). Jesus' own body was the temple that would be destroyed and raised (John 2:19). And because Jesus is the resurrected temple, he is the foundation (1 Cor. 3:10–11) or cornerstone (Eph. 2:19–20; 1 Pet. 2:6) of a new temple, the New Testament people of God, who in turn serve as the "dwelling place for God by the Spirit" (Eph. 2:21–22; cf. 1 Cor. 3:16–17; 1 Pet. 2:4–5). In the new earth, the new Jerusalem will descend and God's throne shall be on earth. God will be the temple—we will have our dwelling in him (Rev. 21:22).

25:9 It is significant that Moses does not devise the plan for creating a sanctuary for God; rather, the Lord provides a detailed "pattern of the tabernacle and of all its furniture" and demands that Moses produce it "exactly as I show you" (v. 9). At the end of Exodus, the testimony is that "according to all that the LORD commanded him, so he did" (40:16). As an extension of the second commandment (20:4–6), God shows Israel that his worship occurs according to his pattern. As a holy God, he was not to be approached according to the best Israelite ideas or the whims of the culture, but according to his Word.

This continues to be the pattern for approaching God today: not according to our ideas or cultural whims, but according to the divine mandate.

gold for it and put them on its [e]four feet, two
rings on the one side of it, and two rings on
the other side of it. 13 You shall make poles
of acacia wood and overlay them with gold.
14 And you shall put the poles into the rings on
the sides of the ark to carry the ark by them.
15 The [f]poles shall remain in the rings of the
ark; they shall not be taken from it. 16 [g]And
you shall put into the ark the [h]testimony that
I shall give you.

17 [i]"You shall make a mercy seat[1] of pure gold.
Two cubits and a half shall be its length, and
a cubit and a half its breadth. 18 And you shall
make two cherubim of gold; of [j]hammered
work shall you make them, on the two ends
of the mercy seat. 19 Make one cherub on the
one end, and one cherub on the other end. [k]Of
one piece with the mercy seat shall you make
the cherubim on its two ends. 20 [l]The cherubim
shall spread out their wings above, overshadowing the mercy seat with their wings, their
faces one to another; toward the mercy seat
shall the faces of the cherubim be. 21 And you
shall put the mercy seat on the top of the ark,
and in the ark you shall put the testimony that
I shall give you. 22 [m]There I will meet with you,
and from above the mercy seat, from [n]between
the two cherubim that are on the ark of the
testimony, I will speak with you about all
that I will give you in commandment for the
people of Israel.

The Table for Bread

23 [o]"You shall make a table of acacia wood.
Two cubits shall be its length, a cubit its
breadth, and a cubit and a half its height.
24 You shall overlay it with [p]pure gold and
make a molding of gold around it. 25 And you
shall make a rim around it a handbreadth[2]
wide, and a molding of gold around the rim.
26 And you shall make for it four rings of gold,
and fasten the rings to the four corners at its
four legs. 27 Close to the frame the rings shall
lie, as [q]holders for the poles to carry the table.
28 You shall make the poles of acacia wood, and
overlay them with gold, and the table shall be
carried with these. 29 And you shall make its
plates and [r]dishes for incense, and its flagons
and bowls with which to pour drink offerings;
you shall make them of pure gold. 30 And you
shall set the [s]bread of the Presence on the table
before me regularly.

The Golden Lampstand

31 [t]"You shall make a lampstand of pure gold.
The lampstand shall be made of hammered
work: its base, its stem, its cups, its calyxes,

[1] Or *cover* [2] A *handbreadth* was about 3 inches or 7.5 centimeters

25:16–22 The ark contained the "testimony," the Ten Commandments, as the summary of the moral law. It was a witness against God's people, condemning them for their failure to keep God's law. However, the "mercy seat" (or "cover"; see ESV footnote) was the solid golden lid for the ark; it was the place where the blood of atonement was applied (Lev. 16:14). As the blood was applied to the cover of the ark, it pictured the covering of the law—broken by God's people—with blood; Israel's sin was atoned for through the blood of substitutionary sacrifice, and God's wrath was propitiated. In this way, the cover became a place or a "seat" of mercy.

All of this pointed forward to Jesus the High Priest, who entered the heavenly tabernacle "by means of his own blood, thus securing an eternal redemption" (Heb. 9:11–14). Jesus' blood covered and atoned for all our lawbreaking; God's wrath was propitiated (turned away); and we are set free to "serve the living God" (Heb. 9:14). No wonder we rejoice to flee to the mercy seat!

25:23–30 God did not need to be "fed." Rather, these 12 loaves were "from" the people to represent the 12 tribes in God's presence (Lev. 24:5–9). God then gave the bread to the priests to sustain them. Jesus is the true Israel. He is also the true bread that comes from God's presence in heaven. He came to offer his body as bread to save and sustain his people (John 6:51–58). As God's people dwell in his presence, he provides for and sustains them.

God continues to provide "daily bread" for his people in response to our prayers (Matt. 6:11). All of this takes place because of the gospel, through which free access to God is fully opened up to us (Heb. 4:14–16).

25:31–40 The lampstand has a basic purpose: to provide light in the tabernacle for the priests' work (27:20–21). However, it is very ornate: the lampstand's branches were modeled after a flowering almond tree; it had seven arms with cups and calyxes; and

12 [e] ch. 37:3
15 [f] 1 Kgs. 8:8
16 [g] [Deut. 31:26; 1 Kgs. 8:9] [h] See ch. 16:34
17 [i] ch. 37:6; Heb. 9:5
18 [j] ver. 31; ch. 37:7, 17, 22; Num. 8:4; 10:2
19 [k] ch. 37:8
20 [l] 1 Kgs. 8:7; 1 Chr. 28:18; Heb. 9:5
22 [m] ch. 29:42, 43; 30:6, 36; Lev. 16:2; Num. 17:4 [n] Num. 7:89
23 [o] For ver. 23-29, see ch. 37:10-16; [1 Kgs. 7:48; 2 Chr. 4:8; Heb. 9:2]
24 [p] ver. 11
27 [q] ch. 26:29; 30:4; 36:34; 37:14, 27; 38:5
29 [r] ch. 37:16; Num. 4:7
30 [s] Lev. 24:5, 6
31 [t] For ver. 31-39, see ch. 37:17-24; [1 Kgs. 7:49; Zech. 4:2; Heb. 9:2; Rev. 1:12]

and its flowers shall be of one piece with it. 32 And there shall be six branches going out of its sides, three branches of the lampstand out of one side of it and three branches of the lampstand out of the other side of it; 33 three cups made like almond blossoms, each with calyx and flower, on one branch, and three cups made like almond blossoms, each with calyx and flower, on the other branch—so for the six branches going out of the lampstand. 34 And on the lampstand itself there shall be four cups made like almond blossoms, with their calyxes and flowers, 35 and a calyx of one piece with it under each pair of the six branches going out from the lampstand. 36 Their calyxes and their branches shall be of one piece with it, the whole of it a single piece of hammered work of pure gold. 37 You shall make seven lamps for it. And the lamps [u]shall be set up so as [v]to give light on the space in front of it. 38 Its tongs and their trays shall be of pure gold. 39 It shall be made, with all these utensils, out of a talent[1] of pure gold. 40 And [w]see that you make them after the pattern for them, which is being shown you on the mountain.

The Tabernacle

26 "Moreover, [x]you shall make the [y]tabernacle with ten curtains of [z]fine twined linen and blue and purple and scarlet yarns; you shall make them with cherubim [z]skillfully worked into them. 2 The length of each curtain shall be twenty-eight cubits,[2] and the breadth of each curtain four cubits; all the curtains shall be the same size. 3 Five curtains shall be coupled to one another, and the other five curtains shall be coupled to one another. 4 And you shall make loops of blue on the edge of the outermost curtain in the first set. Likewise you shall make loops on the edge of the outermost curtain in the second set. 5 Fifty loops you shall make on the one curtain, and fifty loops you shall make on the edge of the curtain that is in the second set; the loops shall be opposite one another. 6 And you shall make fifty clasps of gold, and couple the curtains one to the other with the clasps, so that the tabernacle may be a single whole.

7 "You shall also make [a]curtains of goats' hair for a tent over the tabernacle; eleven curtains shall you make. 8 The length of each curtain shall be thirty cubits, and the breadth of each curtain four cubits. The eleven curtains shall be the same size. 9 You shall couple five curtains by themselves, and six curtains by themselves, and the sixth curtain you shall double over at the front of the tent. 10 You shall make fifty loops on the edge of the curtain that is outermost in one set, and fifty loops on the edge of the curtain that is outermost in the second set.

11 "You shall make fifty clasps of bronze, and put the clasps into the loops, and couple the tent together that it may be a single whole. 12 And the part that remains of the curtains of the tent, the half curtain that remains, shall hang over the back of the tabernacle. 13 And the extra that remains in the length of the curtains, the cubit on the one side, and the cubit on the other side, shall hang over the sides of the tabernacle, on this side and that side, to cover it. 14 [b]And you shall make for the tent a covering of tanned [c]rams' skins and a covering of goatskins on top.

15 "You shall make upright frames for the tabernacle of acacia wood. 16 Ten cubits shall be the length of a frame, and a cubit and a half the breadth of each frame. 17 There shall be two tenons in each frame, for fitting together. So shall you do for all the frames of the tabernacle. 18 You shall make the frames for the tabernacle: twenty frames for the south side; 19 and forty bases of silver you shall make under the twenty frames, two bases under one frame for its two tenons, and two bases under the next frame for its two tenons; 20 and for the second side of the tabernacle, on the north side twenty frames, 21 and their forty bases of silver, two bases under one frame, and two bases under the next frame. 22 And

[1] A *talent* was about 75 pounds or 34 kilograms [2] A *cubit* was about 18 inches or 45 centimeters

37[u] Lev. 24:2-4; 2 Chr. 13:11 [v] Num. 8:2
40[w] ver. 9; ch. 26:30; 27:8; Num. 8:4; Acts 7:44; Cited Heb. 8:5; [1 Chr. 28:11, 19]
Chapter 26
1[x] For ver. 1-37, see ch. 36:8-38 [y] ch. 25:9 [z] ver. 31, 36; ch. 28:6, 15; 36:8, 35; 39:3, 8
7[a] ch. 36:14
14[b] ch. 36:19 [c] ch. 25:5

it stood in the midst of the tabernacle, the place of God's presence. As a result, it looked back to God's creation of the garden of Eden and the tree of life.

But it also looked forward to that day when Jesus would come to be "the light" (John 1:5; 8:12). Indeed, Jesus' face reflects the light of the glory of God (2 Cor. 4:6). And as we embrace Christ our light, we individually (Matt. 5:14–16; 2 Cor. 3:18) and corporately (Rev. 1:20) reflect his light in the world by his Spirit (as probably represented in Rev. 4:5).

for the rear of the tabernacle westward you
shall make six frames. 23 And you shall make
two frames for corners of the tabernacle in
the rear; 24 they shall be separate beneath, but
joined at the top, at the first ring. Thus shall
it be with both of them; they shall form the
two corners. 25 And there shall be eight frames,
with their bases of silver, sixteen bases; two
bases under one frame, and two bases under
another frame.

26 "You shall make bars of acacia wood, five
for the frames of the one side of the tabernacle, 27 and five bars for the frames of the
other side of the tabernacle, and five bars for
the frames of the side of the tabernacle at the
rear westward. 28 The middle bar, halfway up
the frames, shall run from end to end. 29 You
shall overlay the frames with gold and shall
make their rings of gold for [d]holders for the
bars, and you shall overlay the bars with gold.
30 Then you shall erect the tabernacle [e]accord-
ing to the plan for it that you were shown on
the mountain.

31 [f]"And you shall make a veil of blue and purple and scarlet yarns and [g]fine twined linen.
It shall be made with cherubim [g]skillfully
worked into it. 32 And you shall hang it on four
pillars of acacia overlaid with gold, with hooks
of gold, on four bases of silver. 33 And you shall
hang [f]the veil from the clasps, and bring [h]the
ark of the testimony in there within the veil.
And the veil shall separate for you the Holy
Place from the Most Holy. 34 [i]You shall put the
mercy seat on the ark of the testimony in the
Most Holy Place. 35 And [j]you shall set the table
outside the veil, and the [k]lampstand on the
south side of the tabernacle opposite the table,
and you shall put the table on the north side.

36 "You shall make a [l]screen for the entrance
of the tent, of [m]blue and purple and scarlet
yarns and [g]fine twined linen, embroidered
with needlework. 37 And you shall make for the
screen five pillars of acacia, and overlay them
with gold. Their hooks shall be of gold, and
you shall cast five bases of bronze for them.

The Bronze Altar

27 "You shall make the [n]altar of acacia
wood, five cubits[1] long and five cubits
broad. The altar shall be square, and its height
shall be three cubits. 2 And you shall make
[o]horns for it on its four corners; its horns shall
be of one piece with it, and [p]you shall overlay it with bronze. 3 You shall make pots for
it to receive its ashes, and shovels and basins
and [q]forks and fire pans. You shall make all its
utensils of bronze. 4 You shall also make for it
a grating, a network of bronze, and on the net
you shall make four bronze rings at its four
corners. 5 And you shall set it under the ledge
of the altar so that the net extends halfway
down the altar. 6 And you shall make poles
for the altar, poles of acacia wood, and overlay
them with bronze. 7 And the poles shall be put
through the rings, so that the poles are on the
two sides of the altar when it is carried. 8 You
shall make it hollow, with boards. [r]As it has
been shown you on the mountain, so shall it
be made.

The Court of the Tabernacle

9 [s]"You shall make the court of the tabernacle. On the south side the court shall have
hangings of fine twined linen a hundred
cubits long for one side. 10 Its twenty pillars
and their twenty bases shall be of bronze, but
the hooks of the pillars and their fillets shall
be of silver. 11 And likewise for its length on the
north side there shall be hangings a hundred
cubits long, its pillars twenty and their bases
twenty, of bronze, but the hooks of the pillars
and their fillets shall be of silver. 12 And for the
breadth of the court on the west side there
shall be hangings for fifty cubits, with ten pillars and ten bases. 13 The breadth of the court

[1] A *cubit* was about 18 inches or 45 centimeters

27:1–8 The bronze altar was the place at which most of the sacrifices were made. Positioned in the midst of the court of the tabernacle (38:1), it reminded God's people that they could approach God only by means of a bloody sacrifice (Leviticus 1; 4). As the priests offered sacrifices of bulls and goats repeatedly, it should have become clear that the blood of animals could not truly atone for human sin.

What was needed was a once-for-all sacrifice: Jesus, the sinless one, who offered himself as a "single sacrifice for sins" (Heb. 10:11–14). It is Jesus' blood that cleanses us from "all sin" (1 John 1:7; cf. Heb. 9:14; 10:19–22; 1 Pet. 1:18). Nothing more is needed.

29 [d]See ch. 25:27
30 [e]See ch. 25:40
31 [f]ch. 36:35; [Lev. 16:2; 2 Chr. 3:14; Matt. 27:51; Heb. 9:3] [g]ver. 1
33 [f][See ver. 31 above] [h]See ch. 16:34
34 [i]ch. 25:21; 40:20
35 [j]ch. 40:22; Heb. 9:2 [k]ch. 40:24
36 [l]ch. 27:16; 36:37 [m]ver. 1, 31; ch. 25:4 [g][See ver. 31 above]

Chapter 27 **1** [n]For ver. 1-8, see ch. 38:1-7; [Ezek. 43:13] **2** [o]ch. 29:12; 30:2; [Lev. 4:7, 30; 1 Kgs. 1:50; Ps. 118:27] [p][Num. 16:38] **3** [q][1 Sam. 2:13] **8** [r]See ch. 25:40 **9** [s]For ver. 9-19, see ch. 38:9-20

on the front to the east shall be fifty cubits. 14 The hangings for the one side of the gate shall be fifteen cubits, with their three pillars and three bases. 15 On the other side the hangings shall be fifteen cubits, with their three pillars and three bases. 16 For the gate of the court there shall be [t]a screen twenty cubits long, of blue and purple and scarlet yarns and fine twined linen, embroidered with needlework. It shall have four pillars and with them four bases. 17 All the pillars around the court shall be filleted with silver. Their hooks shall be of silver, and their bases of bronze. 18 The length of the court shall be a hundred cubits, the breadth fifty, and the height five cubits, with hangings of fine twined linen and bases of bronze. 19 All the utensils of the tabernacle for every use, and all its pegs and all the pegs of the court, shall be of bronze.

Oil for the Lamp

20 [u]"You shall command the people of Israel that they bring to you pure beaten olive oil for the light, that a lamp may regularly be set up to burn. 21 [v]In the tent of meeting, [w]outside the veil that is before the testimony, Aaron and his sons shall tend it from evening to morning before the LORD. It shall be a statute forever to be observed throughout their generations by the people of Israel.

The Priests' Garments

28 "Then bring near to you [x]Aaron your brother, and his sons with him, from among the people of Israel, to serve me as priests—Aaron and Aaron's sons, [y]Nadab and Abihu, Eleazar and Ithamar. 2 [z]And you shall make holy garments for Aaron your brother, for glory and for beauty. 3 You shall speak to all the [a]skillful, whom I have filled with a spirit of skill, that they make Aaron's garments to consecrate him for my priesthood. 4 These are the garments that they shall make: a [b]breastpiece, an [c]ephod, [d]a robe, [e]a coat of checker work, [e]a turban, and [e]a sash. They shall make holy garments for Aaron your brother and his sons to serve me as priests. 5 They shall receive [f]gold, blue and purple and scarlet yarns, and fine twined linen.

6 [g]"And they shall make the ephod of gold, of blue and purple and scarlet yarns, and of fine twined linen, skillfully worked. 7 It shall have two shoulder pieces attached to its two edges, so that it may be joined together. 8 And the [h]skillfully woven band on it shall be made like it and be of one piece with it, of gold, blue and purple and scarlet yarns, and fine twined linen. 9 You shall take two onyx stones, and engrave on them the names of the sons of Israel, 10 six of their names on the one stone, and the names of the remaining six on the other stone, in the order of their birth. 11 As a jeweler engraves signets, so shall you engrave the two stones with the names of the sons of Israel. You shall enclose them in settings of gold filigree. 12 And you shall set the two stones on the shoulder pieces of the ephod, as stones of remembrance for the sons of Israel. And [i]Aaron shall bear their names before the LORD on his two shoulders [j]for remembrance. 13 You shall make settings of gold filigree, 14 and two chains of pure gold, twisted like cords; and you shall attach the corded chains to the settings.

15 [k]"You shall make a breastpiece of judgment, in skilled work. In the style of the ephod you shall make it—of gold, blue and purple and scarlet yarns, and fine twined linen shall you make it. 16 It shall be square and doubled, a span[1] its length and a span its breadth. 17 [l]You

[1] A *span* was about 9 inches or 22 centimeters

16 [t]ch. 26:36
20 [u]Lev. 24:1-4
21 [v]ch. 25:22; 29:42; 30:36 [w]See ch. 26:31
Chapter 28
1 [x]Num. 18:7; Heb. 5:4 [y]See ch. 6:23
2 [z]ver. 40; ch. 29:29; 31:10; 39:1, 2; Lev. 8:7, 30; Num. 20:26, 28; See ch. 29:5-9
3 [a]ch. 31:6; 35:10, 25; 36:1
4 [b]ver. 15 [c]ver. 6 [d]ver. 31 [e]ver. 39; [Lev. 8:7]
5 [f]ch. 25:3
6 [g]For ver. 6-12, see ch. 39:2-7
8 [h]ver. 27, 28; ch. 29:5; 39:5; Lev. 8:7 **12** [i]ver. 29, 30 [j][Num. 16:40; Josh. 4:7; Zech. 6:14] **15** [k]For ver. 15-28, see ch. 39:8-21 **17** [l][Ezek. 28:13; Rev. 21:19, 20]

28:1–43 Although God's people had heard God's voice (20:19–21), and although they were to be "a kingdom of priests" (19:6), God established a priesthood to mediate between himself and his people (28:1–2). He chose Aaron and his sons "from among the people of Israel" (v. 1) to serve in this way, identified with their fellow human beings as representatives and in weakness (Heb. 5:1–4). God dressed Aaron in "holy garments" that would serve to cover his sinfulness and make him fit to stand in God's presence (Ex. 28:4). These garments shared the same kind of fabrics as the tabernacle, showing that the priest's ministry was a heavenly one. In addition, the breastpiece of judgment also had 12 stones on which the names of the tribes of Israel were engraved; this breastpiece was positioned so that the tribes were "on his heart" (vv. 14–30). There was a plate on his head that said "Holy to the LORD" (v. 36).

shall set in it four rows of stones. A row of
sardius,[1] topaz, and carbuncle shall be the
first row; 18 and the second row an emerald, a
sapphire, and a diamond; 19 and the third row
a jacinth, an agate, and an amethyst; 20 and
the fourth row a beryl, an onyx, and a jasper.
They shall be set in gold filigree. 21 There shall
be twelve stones with their names according
to the names of the sons of Israel. They shall
be like signets, each engraved with its name,
for the twelve tribes. 22 You shall make for the
breastpiece twisted chains like cords, of pure
gold. 23 And you shall make for the breastpiece
two rings of gold, and put the two rings on the
two edges of the breastpiece. 24 And you shall
put the two cords of gold in the two rings at
the edges of the breastpiece. 25 The two ends
of the two cords you shall attach to the two
settings of filigree, and so attach it in front to
the shoulder pieces of the ephod. 26 You shall
make two rings of gold, and put them at the
two ends of the breastpiece, on its inside edge
next to the ephod. 27 And you shall make two
rings of gold, and attach them in front to the
lower part of the two shoulder pieces of the
ephod, at its seam above the [m]skillfully woven
band of the ephod. 28 And they shall bind the
breastpiece by its rings to the rings of the
ephod with a lace of blue, so that it may lie
on the skillfully woven band of the ephod, so
that the breastpiece shall not come loose from
the ephod. 29 [n]So Aaron shall bear the names
of the sons of Israel in the breastpiece of judgment on his heart, when he goes into the Holy
Place, to bring them to regular [o]remembrance
before the LORD. 30 And in the breastpiece of
judgment [p]you shall put the Urim and the
Thummim, and they shall be on Aaron's heart,
when he goes in before the LORD. Thus Aaron
shall bear the judgment of the people of Israel
on his heart before the LORD regularly.

31 [q]"You shall make the robe of the ephod
all of blue. 32 It shall have an opening for the
head in the middle of it, with a woven binding around the opening, like the opening in
a garment,[2] so that it may not tear. 33 On its
hem you shall make pomegranates of blue
and purple and scarlet yarns, around its hem,
with bells of gold between them, 34 a golden
bell and a pomegranate, a golden bell and a
pomegranate, around the hem of the robe.
35 And it shall be on Aaron when he ministers,
and its sound shall be heard when he goes into
the Holy Place before the LORD, and when he
comes out, so that he does not die.

36 "You shall make [r]a plate of pure gold and
engrave on it, like the engraving of a signet,
[s]'Holy to the LORD.' 37 And you shall fasten it
on the turban by a cord of blue. It shall be on
the front of the turban. 38 It shall be on Aaron's
forehead, and Aaron shall [t]bear any guilt from
the holy things that the people of Israel consecrate as their holy gifts. It shall regularly be
on his forehead, that they may be accepted
before the LORD.

39 "You shall weave the coat in checker work
of fine linen, and you shall make a turban of
fine linen, and you shall make a sash embroidered with needlework.

40 [u]"For Aaron's sons you shall make coats
and sashes and caps. You shall make them [v]for
glory and beauty. 41 And you shall put them
on Aaron your brother, and on his sons with
him, and shall [w]anoint them and ordain them
and [x]consecrate them, that they may serve me
as priests. 42 You shall make for them [y]linen
undergarments to cover their naked flesh.
They shall reach from the hips to the thighs;
43 and they shall be on Aaron and on his sons
when they go into the tent of meeting or when
they come near the altar to minister in the
Holy Place, lest they [z]bear guilt and die. [a]This
shall be a statute forever for him and for his
offspring after him.

[1] The identity of some of these stones is uncertain [2] The meaning of the Hebrew word is uncertain; possibly *coat of mail*

Jesus, our Great High Priest, was chosen by God to serve as priest; he identified with human beings in our suffering and obedience so that he might be sympathetic to our weaknesses (Heb. 2:17–18; 5:5–10). He did not require holy garments to cover his sin; for he was the sinless one (Heb. 4:14–15) who was "holy, innocent, unstained, separated from sinners, and exalted above the heavens" (Heb. 7:26). He bore his people upon his heart as he made intercession for them, and he continues to do so (Heb. 7:25). And he clothes us with his righteousness so that we, as those who participate in his priesthood (1 Pet. 2:9; Rev. 1:5), have our sins covered and are "holy to the LORD."

27 [m] ver. 8
29 [n] ver. 12, 30 [o] See ver. 12
30 [p] Lev. 8:8; Num. 27:21; Deut. 33:8; 1 Sam. 28:6; Ezra 2:63; Neh. 7:65; [1 Sam. 23:9; 30:7, 8]
31 [q] For ver. 31-37, see ch. 39:22-31
36 [r] Lev. 8:9 [s] Zech. 14:20
38 [t] Lev. 10:17; Num. 18:1; [Isa. 53:11; Ezek. 4:4-6; John 1:29; Heb. 9:28; 1 Pet. 2:24]

40 [u] ch. 39:27-29, 41; [Ezek. 44:17, 18] [v] ver. 2 **41** [w] ch. 29:7; 30:30; 40:13, 15; Lev. 10:7 [x] ch. 29:9; Heb. 7:28; [Lev. 21:10] **42** [y] Lev. 6:10; 16:4; [Ezek. 44:18]
43 [z] Lev. 5:1, 17; 20:19 [a] ch. 27:21

Consecration of the Priests

29 "Now this is what you shall do to
them to consecrate them, that they
may serve me as priests. [b]Take one bull of the
herd and two rams without blemish, 2 [c]and
unleavened bread, unleavened cakes mixed
with oil, and unleavened wafers smeared with
oil. You shall make them of fine wheat flour.
3 You shall put them in one basket and bring
them in the basket, and bring the bull and
the two rams. 4 You shall bring Aaron and his
sons to the entrance of the tent of meeting
and [d]wash them with water. 5 Then [e]you shall
take the garments, and put on Aaron the coat
and the robe of the ephod, and the ephod,
and the breastpiece, and gird him with the
[f]skillfully woven band of the ephod. 6 [g]And
you shall set the turban on his head and put
the holy crown on the turban. 7 You shall take
[h]the anointing oil and pour it on his head and
anoint him. 8 Then you [i]shall bring his sons
and put coats on them, 9 and you shall gird
Aaron and his sons with [j]sashes and bind caps
on them. And [k]the priesthood shall be theirs
by a statute forever. Thus you shall [l]ordain
Aaron and his sons.
10 "Then you shall bring the bull before the
tent of meeting. [m]Aaron and his sons shall lay
their hands on the head of the bull. 11 Then
you shall kill the bull before the LORD at the
entrance of the tent of meeting, 12 and [n]shall
take part of the blood of the bull and put it on
the [o]horns of the altar with your finger, and
the rest of[1] the blood you shall pour out at the
base of the altar. 13 And you shall take all [p]the
fat that covers the entrails, and the long lobe of
the liver, and the two kidneys with the fat that
is on them, and burn them on the altar. 14 But
the flesh of the bull and its skin and its dung
you shall burn with fire [q]outside the camp; [r]it
is a sin offering.
15 "Then [s]you shall take one of the rams, and
[t]Aaron and his sons shall lay their hands on the
head of the ram, 16 and you shall kill the ram
and shall take its blood and throw it against
the sides of the altar. 17 Then you shall [u]cut the
ram into pieces, and wash its entrails and its
legs, and put them with its pieces and its head,
18 and burn the whole ram on the altar. It is a
burnt offering to the LORD. It is a [v]pleasing
aroma, a food offering[2] to the LORD.
19 [w]"You shall take the other ram, [t]and Aaron
and his sons shall lay their hands on the head
of the ram, 20 and you shall kill the ram and
take part of its blood and put it on the tip
of the right ear of Aaron and on the tips of
the right ears of his sons, and on the thumbs
of their right hands and on the great toes
of their right feet, and throw the rest of the
blood against the sides of the altar. 21 Then you
shall take part of the blood that is on the altar,
and of the [x]anointing oil, and sprinkle it on
Aaron and his garments, and on his sons and
his sons' garments with him. He and his garments shall be holy, and his sons and his sons'
garments with him.
22 "You shall also take the fat from the ram
and the fat tail and the [y]fat that covers the
entrails, and the long lobe of the liver and the
two kidneys with the fat that is on them, and
the right thigh (for it is a ram of [z]ordination),
23 and [a]one loaf of bread and one cake of bread
made with oil, and one wafer out of the basket
of unleavened bread that is before the LORD.
24 You shall put all these on the palms of Aaron
and on the palms of his sons, and [b]wave them
for a wave offering before the LORD. 25 Then
[c]you shall take them from their hands and

[1] Hebrew *all* [2] Or *an offering by fire*; also verses 25, 41

Chapter 29
1 [b]Lev. 8:2
2 [c]Lev. 2:4; See Lev. 6:20-22
4 [d]ch. 40:12; Lev. 8:6; [Heb. 10:22]
5 [e]ch. 28:2-4 [f]ch. 28:8
6 [g]ch. 28:36, 37; Lev. 8:9; [Num. 6:7]
7 [h]ver. 21; ch. 28:41; 30:25; Lev. 8:12, 30; 10:7; 21:10; Num. 35:25
8 [i]Lev. 8:13
9 [j]ch. 28:4, 39 [k]ch. 27:21; Num. 18:7 [l]ver. 29, 33; Lev. 8:33; 16:32; See ch. 28:41
10 [m]ver. 15, 19; Lev. 1:4; 8:14
12 [n]Lev. 8:15 [o]See ch. 27:2
13 [p]Lev. 3:3, 4

29:1–46 Aaron's consecration involved washing (v. 4), vesting (vv. 5–6), anointing (v. 7), and sacrifice (vv. 10–28). The washing, vesting, and anointing is all ultimately fulfilled in the priesthood of the sinless Jesus: he was already clean, clothed, and Spirit-empowered for his work as priest. And these three actions all came before the sacrifices, which were offered, not for Aaron and his sons as persons, but as priests (Heb. 5:3). The blood of the sacrifice was applied to ear, hand, and toe to speak of the total consecration of the priest: he would hear, act, and walk only for God's holy purpose.

And yet, only Jesus could manifest such complete consecration, all the way to offering himself as both priest and sacrifice (Heb. 10:5–10). As those who participate in Jesus' bloody sacrifice by faith, we are washed clean (John 13:10; Heb. 10:22), clothed (Isa. 61:10; Rev. 19:8), and anointed (1 John 2:20) to serve in his name, consecrated to him, a kingdom of priests (1 Pet. 2:9).

14 [q]Lev. 4:11, 12, 21; Num. 19:3, 5; Heb. 13:11 [r]ver. 36; ch. 30:10 15 [s]ver. 1; Lev. 8:18 [t]ver. 19; Lev. 1:4; 8:14 17 [u]Lev. 8:20 18 [v]ver. 25, 41; See Gen. 8:21 19 [w]ver. 1; Lev. 8:22 [t][See ver. 15 above] 21 [x]ver. 7 22 [y]ver. 13 [z]Lev. 7:37; 8:28, 31, 33 23 [a]ver. 2, 3; Lev. 8:26 24 [b]Lev. 7:30; 8:27, 29; Num. 5:25; 6:20 25 [c]Lev. 6:22; 8:28

burn them on the altar on top of the burnt offering, as a [d]pleasing aroma before the LORD. It is a food offering to the LORD.

26 "You shall take the [e]breast of the ram of Aaron's [f]ordination and [g]wave it for a wave offering before the LORD, and it shall be your portion. 27 And you shall consecrate the [h]breast of the wave offering that is waved and the [i]thigh of the priests' portion that is contributed from the ram of [f]ordination, from what was Aaron's and his sons'. 28 It shall be for Aaron and his sons as a [j]perpetual due from the people of Israel, for it is a [g]contribution. It shall be a [g]contribution from the people of Israel from their peace offerings, their contribution to the LORD.

29 "The holy garments of Aaron [k]shall be for his sons after him; they shall [l]be anointed in them and ordained in them. 30 The son who succeeds him as priest, who comes into the tent of meeting to minister in the Holy Place, shall wear them [m]seven days.

31 "You shall take the ram of ordination and [n]boil its flesh in a holy place. 32 And Aaron and his sons shall eat the flesh of the ram and the [o]bread that is in the basket in the entrance of the tent of meeting. 33 [p]They shall eat those things with which atonement was made at their ordination and consecration, but an [q]outsider shall not eat of them, because they are holy. 34 And if any of the flesh for the ordination or of the bread remain until the morning, then you shall [r]burn the remainder with fire. It shall not be eaten, because it is holy.

35 "Thus you shall do to Aaron and to his sons, according to all that I have commanded you. Through [s]seven days shall you ordain them, 36 and every day you shall offer a [t]bull as a sin offering for atonement. Also you shall purify the altar, when you make atonement for it, and shall [u]anoint it to consecrate it. 37 Seven days you shall make atonement for the altar and consecrate it, and the [v]altar shall be most holy. [w]Whatever touches the altar shall become holy.

38 "Now this is what you shall offer on the altar: [x]two lambs a year old [y]day by day regularly. 39 One lamb you shall offer [z]in the morning, and the other lamb you shall offer [a]at twilight. 40 And with the first lamb a tenth measure[1] of fine flour mingled with a fourth of a hin[2] of beaten oil, and a fourth of a hin of wine for a drink offering. 41 The other lamb you shall offer [a]at twilight, and shall offer with it a grain offering and its drink offering, as [b]in the morning, for a [c]pleasing aroma, a food offering to the LORD. 42 It shall be a [d]regular burnt offering throughout your generations at the entrance of the tent of meeting before the LORD, [e]where I will meet with you, to speak to you there. 43 There I will meet with the people of Israel, and it shall be [f]sanctified by my glory. 44 I will consecrate the tent of meeting and the altar. [g]Aaron also and his sons I will consecrate to serve me as priests. 45 [h]I will dwell among the people of Israel and will be their God. 46 And they shall know that [i]I am the LORD their God, who brought them out of the land of Egypt that I might dwell among them. I am the LORD their God.

The Altar of Incense

30 [j]"You shall make [k]an altar on which to burn incense; you shall make it of acacia wood. 2 A cubit[3] shall be its length, and a cubit its breadth. It shall be square, and two cubits shall be its height. [l]Its horns shall be of one piece with it. 3 You shall [m]overlay it with pure gold, its top and around its sides and its horns. And you shall make a molding of gold around it. 4 And you shall make two golden rings for it. Under its molding on two opposite sides of it you shall make them, and they shall be [n]holders for poles with which to carry it. 5 You shall make the poles of acacia wood and overlay them with gold. 6 And you shall

[1] Possibly an ephah (about 3/5 bushel or 22 liters) [2] A *hin* was about 4 quarts or 3.5 liters [3] A *cubit* was about 18 inches or 45 centimeters

30:1–10 It appears that the altar of incense represented the prayers of God's people coming before him (Ps. 141:2; Luke 1:9–10; Rev. 5:8; 8:3–4). The incense was to be burned both morning and evening, signifying the continued praying of God's people (1 Thess. 5:17). But above all, it anticipated the continued intercession of our Lord Jesus Christ, who "always lives to make intercession" for us (Heb. 7:25; cf. Rom. 8:34).

25 [d] ver. 18, 41
26 [e] Lev. 8:29 [f] ver. 22 [g] ver. 24
27 [h] Lev. 7:31, 34; 10:14, 15; Num. 18:11, 18 [i] Lev. 7:32, 34; 10:15; Num. 18:11 [f] [See ver. 26 above]
28 [j] Lev. 10:15 [g] [See ver. 26 above]

29 [k] Num. 18:8; [Num. 20:26, 28] [l] ver. 9 **30** [m] Lev. 8:33, 35 **31** [n] Lev. 8:31 **32** [o] [Matt. 12:4] **33** [p] Lev. 10:14, 15, 17 [q] Lev. 22:10 **34** [r] Lev. 8:32 **35** [s] Lev. 8:33-35 **36** [t] ver. 14; ch. 30:10 [u] ch. 30:26, 28, 29; 40:10 **37** [v] ch. 40:10 [w] ch. 30:29; [Matt. 23:19] **38** [x] Num. 28:3; 1 Chr. 16:40; 2 Chr. 2:4; 13:11; 31:3; Ezra 3:3 [y] [Dan. 8:11-13; 9:27; 12:11]; Heb. 10:11 **39** [z] 2 Kgs. 16:15; Ezek. 46:13-15 [a] 1 Kgs. 18:29, 36; Ezra 9:4, 5; Ps. 141:2; Dan. 9:21 **41** [a] [See ver. 39 above] [b] ch. 30:9; 40:29 [c] ver. 18, 25 **42** [d] Num. 28:6 [e] See ch. 25:22 **43** [f] ch. 40:34; [1 Kgs. 8:11; 2 Chr. 5:14; 7:1-3; Ezek. 43:5; Hag. 2:7, 9; Mal. 3:1] **44** [g] Lev. 21:15; 22:9, 16 **45** [h] ch. 25:8; Lev. 26:12; Zech. 2:10; 2 Cor. 6:16; Rev. 21:3 **46** [i] ch. 20:2 **Chapter 30** **1** [j] For ver. 1-5, see ch. 37:25-28 [k] ch. 40:5; Lev. 4:7; Rev. 8:3 **2** [l] See ch. 27:2 **3** [m] ch. 39:38; 40:5, 26; Num. 4:11 **4** [n] See ch. 25:27

put it in front of the veil that is above the ark
of the testimony, in front of the [o]mercy seat
that is above the testimony, where I will meet
with you. 7 And Aaron shall [p]burn fragrant
incense on it. Every morning when he [q]dresses
the lamps he shall burn it, 8 and when Aaron
sets up the lamps at twilight, he shall burn
it, a regular incense offering before the LORD
throughout your generations. 9 You shall not
offer [r]unauthorized incense on it, or a burnt
offering, or a grain offering, and you shall
not pour a drink offering on it. 10 [s]Aaron shall
make atonement on its horns once a year. With
the blood of the [t]sin offering of atonement he
shall make atonement for it once in the year
throughout your generations. It is most holy
to the LORD."

The Census Tax

11 The LORD said to Moses, 12 [u]"When you take
the census of the people of Israel, then each
shall give [v]a ransom for his life to the LORD
when you number them, that there be no
plague among them when you number them.
13 Each one who is numbered in the census shall
give this: half a shekel[1] according to the [w]shekel
of the sanctuary (the [x]shekel is twenty gerahs),[2]
[y]half a shekel as an offering to the LORD.
14 Everyone who is numbered in the census,
from twenty years old and upward, shall give
the LORD's offering. 15 The rich shall not give
more, and the poor shall not give less, than [y]the
half shekel, when you give the LORD's offering
to make atonement for your lives. 16 You shall
take the atonement money from the people
of Israel and shall [z]give it for the service of the
tent of meeting, that it may bring the people
of Israel to [a]remembrance before the LORD, so
as to make atonement for your lives."

The Bronze Basin

17 The LORD said to Moses, 18 "You shall also
make a [b]basin of bronze, with its stand of
bronze, for washing. [b]You shall put it between
the tent of meeting and the altar, and you shall
put water in it, 19 with which Aaron and his
sons [c]shall wash their hands and their feet.
20 When they go into the tent of meeting, or
when they come near the altar to minister, to
burn a food offering[3] to the LORD, they shall
wash with water, so that they may not die.
21 They shall wash their hands and their feet,
so that they may not die. It shall [d]be a statute
forever to them, even to him and to his offspring throughout their generations."

The Anointing Oil and Incense

22 The LORD said to Moses, 23 "Take the [e]fin-
est spices: of liquid myrrh 500 shekels, and of
sweet-smelling cinnamon half as much, that
is, 250, and 250 of [f]aromatic cane, 24 and 500 of
cassia, according to the shekel of the sanctuary,
and a [g]hin[4] of olive oil. 25 And you shall make
of these a sacred anointing oil blended as by
the [h]perfumer; it shall be a [i]holy anointing oil.
26 [j]With it you shall anoint the tent of meeting
and the ark of the testimony, 27 and the table
and all its utensils, and the lampstand and its
utensils, and the altar of incense, 28 and the
altar of burnt offering with all its utensils and
the [k]basin and its stand. 29 You shall consecrate
them, that they may be most holy. [l]Whatever
touches them will become holy. 30 [m]You shall
anoint Aaron and his sons, and consecrate
them, that they may serve me as priests. 31 And
you shall say to the people of Israel, 'This shall
be my holy anointing oil throughout your generations. 32 It shall not be poured on the body
of an ordinary person, and you shall make no
other like it in composition. [n]It is holy, and it
shall be holy to you. 33 [o]Whoever compounds
any like it or whoever puts any of it on an outsider shall be cut off from his people.'"

34 The LORD said to Moses, [p]"Take sweet
spices, stacte, and onycha, and galbanum,
sweet spices with pure frankincense (of each
shall there be an equal part), 35 and make an
[q]incense blended as by the [r]perfumer, [s]sea-
soned with salt, pure and holy. 36 You shall beat
some of it very small, and put part of it before
the testimony in the tent of meeting [t]where
I shall meet with you. [u]It shall be most holy
for you. 37 And the incense that you shall make
[v]according to its composition, you shall not
make for yourselves. It shall be for you holy to
the LORD. 38 [w]Whoever makes any like it to use
as perfume shall be cut off from his people."

[1] A *shekel* was about 2/5 ounce or 11 grams [2] A *gerah* was about 1/50 ounce or 0.6 gram [3] Or *an offering by fire* [4] A *hin* was about 4 quarts or 3.5 liters

6 [o]ch. 25:21, 22 **7** [p]ver. 34; ch. 31:11; 37:29; 40:27; 1 Sam. 2:28; 1 Chr. 23:13; 2 Chr. 2:4; 29:11; Luke 1:9 [q]See ch. 27:20, 21 **9** [r]Lev. 10:1 **10** [s]Lev. 16:18; 23:27 [t]ch. 29:36 **12** [u]Num. 1:2-4; 26:2; 2 Sam. 24:2 [v]ch. 21:30; Num. 31:50; [Ps. 49:7] **13** [w]ch. 38:24; Lev. 5:15; 27:3, 25 [x]Lev. 27:25; Num. 3:47; 18:16; Ezek. 45:12 [y]ch. 38:26; Matt. 17:24; [Gen. 24:22] **15** [y][See ver. 13 above] **16** [z]See ch. 38:25-31 [a][ch. 28:12; 39:7; Num. 16:40] **18** [b]ch. 40:7, 30; [1 Kgs. 7:38] **19** [c]ch. 40:31, 32; Ps. 26:6; [Isa. 52:11; Heb. 10:22] **21** [d]See ch. 27:21 **23** [e]Song 4:14; Ezek. 27:22 [f]Ezek. 27:19 **24** [g]ch. 29:40 **25** [h]ch. 37:29 [i]ch. 37:29; Num. 35:25; Ps. 89:20; 133:2 **26** [j]ch. 40:9; Lev. 8:10; Num. 7:1 **28** [k]ch. 40:11 **29** [l]ch. 29:37 **30** [m]See ch. 29:7 **32** [n]ver. 25, 37 **33** [o]ver. 38 **34** [p]ver. 7; ch. 25:6; 37:29 **35** [q]ver. 25 [r]See ver. 25 [s][Lev. 2:13] **36** [t]See ch. 25:22 [u][ch. 40:10] **37** [v]ver. 32 **38** [w]ver. 33

Oholiab and Bezalel

31 The LORD said to Moses, 2 "See, I have called by name [x]Bezalel the son of Uri, son of [y]Hur, of the tribe of Judah, 3 and I have [z]filled him with the Spirit of God, with ability and intelligence, with knowledge and all craftsmanship, 4 to devise artistic designs, to work in gold, silver, and bronze, 5 in cutting stones for setting, and in carving wood, to work in every craft. 6 And behold, I have appointed with him [a]Oholiab, the son of Ahisamach, of the tribe of Dan. And I have given to all able men [b]ability, that they may make all that I have commanded you: 7 [c]the tent of meeting, and [d]the ark of the testimony, and [e]the mercy seat that is on it, and all the furnishings of the tent, 8 [f]the table and its utensils, and [g]the pure lampstand with all its utensils, and [h]the altar of incense, 9 and [i]the altar of burnt offering with all its utensils, and [j]the basin and its stand, 10 and [k]the finely worked garments,[1] the holy garments for Aaron the priest and the garments of his sons, for their service as priests, 11 and [l]the anointing oil and the fragrant [m]incense for the Holy Place. According to all that I have commanded you, they shall do."

The Sabbath

12 And the LORD said to Moses, 13 "You are to speak to the people of Israel and say, 'Above all you shall keep my Sabbaths, for this is a sign between me and you throughout your generations, that you may know that I, the LORD, sanctify you. 14 You shall keep the Sabbath, because it is holy for you. Everyone who profanes it shall be put to death. [n]Whoever does any work on it, that soul shall be cut off from among his people. 15 [o]Six days shall work be done, but [p]the seventh day is a Sabbath of solemn rest, holy to the LORD. [n]Whoever does any work on the Sabbath day shall be put to death. 16 Therefore the people of Israel shall keep the Sabbath, observing the Sabbath throughout their generations, as a covenant forever. 17 [q]It is a sign forever between me and the people of Israel that [r]in six days the LORD made heaven and earth, and [s]on the seventh day he rested and was refreshed.'"

18 And he gave to Moses, when he had finished speaking with him on Mount Sinai, the [t]two tablets of the testimony, tablets of stone, written with [u]the finger of God.

The Golden Calf

32 When the people saw that Moses [v]delayed to come down from the mountain, the people gathered themselves together to Aaron and said to him, [w]"Up, make us gods who shall [x]go before us. As for this Moses, the man who brought us up out of the land of Egypt, we do not know what has become of him." 2 So Aaron said to them, "Take off the [y]rings of gold that are in the ears of your wives, your sons, and your daughters, and bring them to me." 3 So all the people took off the rings of gold that were in their ears and brought them to Aaron. 4 [z]And he received the gold from their hand and fashioned it with a graving tool and made a golden[2] calf. And they said, [a]"These are your gods, O Israel, who brought you up out of the land of Egypt!" 5 When Aaron saw this, he built an altar before it. And Aaron [b]made a proclamation and said, "Tomorrow shall be a feast to the LORD." 6 And they rose up early the next day and offered burnt offerings and brought peace offerings. And [c]the people sat down to eat and drink and rose up [d]to play.

[1] Or *garments for worship* [2] Hebrew *cast metal*; also verse 8

32:1–34:35 Up to this point in Exodus, Israel has grumbled, quarreled, and tested the Lord (15:24; 16:2; 17:2, 7), even refusing to keep his commandments (16:28). And yet Israel had not rebelled in such a way that they drew God's wrath—until now. What makes this scene so shocking is that Israel had heard God's voice (19:19) and twice pledged themselves to obey him (19:8; 24:7). Though they had said they would obey, when Moses "delayed" in coming down the mountain (32:1), they proceeded to break many of the Ten Commandments. The problem was not with the law; the problem was with the people's hearts.

One of the blessings of the new covenant is that God promises to write the law on our hearts and empower us to keep his ways (Heb. 8:8–13). Yet still we falter and fail, sometimes in the massive ways represented in this scene. That is why we must resiliently take comfort in Jesus, the One who did make atonement for us (cf. Ex.

Chapter 31
2 [x]ch. 35:30; 36:1; 1 Chr. 2:20 [y]ch. 17:10, 12; 24:14
3 [z]ch. 35:31; [1 Kgs. 7:14]
6 [a]ch. 35:34 [b]ch. 28:3; 35:10, 35; 36:1
7 [c]See ch. 36:8-38 [d]See ch. 37:1-5 [e]See ch. 37:6-9
8 [f]See ch. 37:10-16 [g]See ch. 37:17-24 [h]See ch. 37:25-28
9 [i]See ch. 38:1-7 [j]ch. 38:8
10 [k]ch. 35:19; 39:1, 41
11 [l]ch. 30:25, 31; 37:29 [m]ch. 30:7, 34
14 [n]ch. 35:2; [Jer. 17:27]; See Num. 15:32-36
15 [o]See ch. 20:9 [p]ch. 16:23; 20:10; Gen. 2:2

[n][See ver. 14 above] **17** [q]ver. 13 [r]Gen. 1:31 [s]Gen. 2:2; Heb. 4:4, 10 **18** [t]ch. 24:12; 32:15, 16; Deut. 4:13; 5:22; 9:10, 11; [2 Cor. 3:3] [u]See ch. 8:19 **Chapter 32** **1** [v]ch. 24:18; Deut. 9:9 [w]ver. 23; Cited Acts 7:40 [x]ch. 13:21 **2** [y][ch. 12:35, 36]; See Judg. 8:24-27 **4** [z]Deut. 9:16; Neh. 9:18; Ps. 106:19; Acts 7:41; [Judg. 17:3, 4] [a]1 Kgs. 12:28 **5** [b][2 Kgs. 10:20] **6** [c]Cited 1 Cor. 10:7 [d]Gen. 26:8; [Judg. 21:21]

7 And the LORD said to Moses, [e]"Go down,
for your people, whom you brought up out
of the land of Egypt, have [f]corrupted themselves. 8 They have turned aside quickly out
of the way that [g]I commanded them. They
have made for themselves a golden calf and
have worshiped it and sacrificed to it and said,
'These are your gods, O Israel, who brought
you up out of the land of Egypt!'" 9 And the
LORD said to Moses, "I have seen this people,
and behold, [h]it is a stiff-necked people. 10 Now
therefore [i]let me alone, that [j]my wrath may
burn hot against them and [k]I may consume
them, in order that [l]I may make a great nation
of you."

11 But [m]Moses implored the LORD his God
and said, "O LORD, why does your wrath
burn hot against your people, whom you
have brought out of the land of Egypt with
great power and with a mighty hand? 12 [n]Why
should the Egyptians say, 'With evil intent
did he bring them out, to kill them in the
mountains and to consume them from the
face of the earth'? Turn from your burning
anger and [o]relent from this disaster against
your people. 13 Remember Abraham, Isaac,
and Israel, your servants, to whom you [p]swore
by your own self, and said to them, [q]'I will
multiply your offspring as the stars of heaven,
and all this land that I have promised I will
give to your offspring, and they shall inherit
it forever.'" 14 And the LORD [r]relented from
the disaster that he had spoken of bringing
on his people.

15 Then [s]Moses turned and went down from
the mountain with the [t]two tablets of the testimony in his hand, tablets that were written on
both sides; on the front and on the back they
were written. 16 [u]The tablets were the work of
God, and the writing was the writing of God,
engraved on the tablets. 17 When [v]Joshua heard
the noise of the people as they shouted, he said
to Moses, "There is a noise of war in the camp."
18 But he said, "It is not the sound of [w]shouting
for victory, or the sound of the cry of defeat,
but the sound of singing that I hear." 19 And as
soon as he came near the camp and [x]saw the
calf and the dancing, Moses' anger burned hot,
and he threw the tablets out of his hands and
broke them at the foot of the mountain. 20 He
took the calf that they had made and burned
it with fire and ground it to powder and scattered it on the water and made the people of
Israel drink it.

21 And Moses said to Aaron, [y]"What did this
people do to you that you have brought such a
great sin upon them?" 22 And Aaron said, "Let
not the anger of my lord burn hot. [z]You know
the people, that they are set on evil. 23 For [a]they
said to me, 'Make us gods who shall go before
us. As for this Moses, the man who brought us
up out of the land of Egypt, we do not know
what has become of him.' 24 So [b]I said to them,
'Let any who have gold take it off.' So they gave
it to me, and I threw it into the fire, and out
came this calf."

25 And when Moses saw that the people had
broken loose (for Aaron had let them break
loose, [c]to the derision of their enemies), 26 then
Moses stood in the gate of the camp and said,
"Who is on the LORD's side? Come to me."
And all the sons of Levi gathered around him.
27 And he said to them, "Thus says the LORD
God of Israel, 'Put your sword on your side
each of you, and go to and fro from gate to
gate throughout the camp, and each of you
[d]kill his brother and his companion and his
neighbor.'" 28 And the sons of Levi did according to the word of Moses. And that day about
three thousand men of the people fell. 29 And

32:30), who promises never to leave us or forsake us (cf. 33:3, 14–17), and whose name is mercy and grace and compassion (see 33:19).

32:7–14 Moses' intercession is remarkable. In response to God's pronouncement of judgment for the sin of his people, Moses pleads for mercy toward them based on three things: (1) *God's past work of redemption* (v. 11). God has just redeemed his people out of the land of slavery with "great power" and a "mighty hand"; would he undo that redemption by destroying Israel? (2) *God's reputation among the nations* (v. 12). All that God had done was so that the nations, especially Egypt, would know that he is the Lord (7:5, 17; 8:10, 22; 9:29; 14:4); but if he destroys Israel, what would Egypt say? (3) *God's prior covenant promises to Abraham* (32:13). All of this was to fulfill God's prior promise to Abraham about a great nation and a messianic seed (2:23–25); how could the Lord fulfill that promise if he destroyed Israel?

7 [e] Deut. 9:12 [f] Judg. 2:19; [Hos. 9:9]
8 [g] ch. 20:3, 4, 23; Deut. 9:16
9 [h] ch. 33:3, 5; 34:9; Deut. 9:6, 13; 31:27; 2 Chr. 30:8; Acts 7:51; [Isa. 48:4]
10 [i] Deut. 9:14 [j] ch. 22:24 [k] ch. 33:3 [l] Num. 14:12
11 [m] Deut. 9:18, 26-29; Ps. 106:23; [Ps. 74:1, 2]
12 [n] [Deut. 32:27]; See Num. 14:13-16 [o] See ver. 14
13 [p] Gen. 22:16; Heb. 6:13 [q] Gen. 12:7; 13:15; 15:7, 18; 26:4; 28:13; 35:11, 12; 48:16
14 [r] Ps. 106:45; [1 Chr. 21:15; Jer. 18:8; 26:13, 15, 19; Amos 7:3, 6; Jonah 3:10; 4:2]
15 [s] Deut. 9:15 [t] ch. 34:29

16 [u] ch. 31:18 **17** [v] ch. 17:9, 10; 24:13; 33:11 **18** [w] Jer. 51:14 **19** [x] Deut. 9:16, 17, 21 **21** [y] [Gen. 20:9] **22** [z] [ch. 14:11; 15:24; 16:2, 20; 17:2, 4; 1 Sam. 15:24] **23** [a] ver. 1 **24** [b] ver. 2-4 **25** [c] [ver. 12] **27** [d] [Num. 25:5; Deut. 33:9]

Moses said, "Today you have been [e]ordained
for the service of the LORD, each one at the cost
of his son and of his brother, so that he might
bestow a blessing upon you this day."
30 The next day Moses said to the people,
[f]"You have sinned a great sin. And now I will
go up to the LORD; [g]perhaps I can make atonement for your sin." 31 So Moses returned to the
LORD and said, "Alas, [f]this people has sinned
a great sin. They have [h]made for themselves
gods of gold. 32 But now, if [i]you will forgive
their sin—but if not, please [j]blot me out of
[k]your book that you have written." 33 But the
LORD said to Moses, [l]"Whoever has sinned
against me, I will blot out of my book. 34 [m]But
now go, lead the people to the place about
which I have spoken to you; [n]behold, my angel
shall go before you. Nevertheless, in the day
when I visit, I will visit their sin upon them."
35 Then the LORD sent a plague on the people, because they made the calf, the one that
Aaron made.

The Command to Leave Sinai

33 The LORD said to Moses, "Depart; go up
from here, you [o]and the people whom
you have brought up out of the land of Egypt,
to the land of which I swore to Abraham, Isaac,
and Jacob, saying, 'To [p]your offspring I will
give it.' 2 I will send an [q]angel before you, [r]and
I will drive out the Canaanites, the Amorites,
the Hittites, the Perizzites, the Hivites, and
the Jebusites. 3 [s]Go up to a land flowing with
milk and honey; [t]but I will not go up among
you, [u]lest I consume you on the way, for you
are a [v]stiff-necked people."
4 When the people heard this disastrous
word, they [w]mourned, and [x]no one put on his
ornaments. 5 For the LORD had said to Moses,
"Say to the people of Israel, 'You are a [v]stiff-
necked people; if for a single moment I should
go up among you, I would [y]consume you. So
now [x]take off your ornaments, that I may
know what to do with you.'" 6 Therefore the
people of Israel stripped themselves of their
ornaments, from Mount Horeb onward.

The Tent of Meeting

7 Now Moses used to take the tent and pitch
it outside the camp, far off from the camp, and
[z]he called it the tent of meeting. And everyone
who [a]sought the LORD would go out to the
tent of meeting, which was outside the camp.
8 Whenever Moses went out to the tent, all the
people would rise up, and [b]each would stand
at his tent door, and watch Moses until he had
gone into the tent. 9 When Moses entered the
tent, the [c]pillar of cloud would descend and
stand at the entrance of the tent, and the
LORD[1] would speak with Moses. 10 And when
all the people saw the pillar of cloud standing at the entrance of the tent, all the people
would rise up and worship, each at his tent
door. 11 Thus [d]the LORD used to speak to Moses
face to face, as a man speaks to his friend.
When Moses turned again into the camp, his
[e]assistant Joshua the son of Nun, a young man,
would not depart from the tent.

[1] Hebrew *he*

32:30–32 Israel had sinned "a great sin." Not only had they engaged in idolatry, but worse, they had turned from the voice of God (proclaimed by Moses and thundered on the mountain) to an image of God in direct contradiction to the Word of God (20:4–6). Essentially, Israel committed Adam and Eve's sin: rather than abiding by God's Word, they determined that they knew better than God himself and ascribed God's character, presence, and redemptive action to the bull calf (Gen. 3:1–8).

But Moses' thought that "perhaps I can make atonement for your sin" was equally mistaken (Ex. 32:30). He thought that he could offer himself in the place of the people: "Please forgive their sins; if not, then please let me die in their place." Moses was offering his life in place of his people. And God rejected his offer, because at this point, "sinners" should die, not the one who was "guiltless."

Yet there was another reason why Moses' atonement was not accepted: he was not actually guiltless. As will come clear in the return visit to Meribah (Num. 20:1–13), he too was a sinner, unfit to make atonement. All the instruction about the tabernacle, its priesthood, and its sacrifices had pointed forward to a spotless lamb that would bear sin. And when John the Baptist pointed out Jesus, he declared: "Behold, the Lamb of God, who takes away the sin of the world" (John 1:29). Only Jesus could make atonement and intercession for us on the basis of his blood that takes away our very great sin (Heb. 7:25; 9:11–14; 1 John 1:7).

29 [e] [Zech. 13:3; Matt. 10:37; Luke 14:26]; See Num. 25:11-13; Deut. 13:6-10
30 [f] See ver. 21; [1 Sam. 12:20] [g] 2 Sam. 16:12; Amos 5:15
31 [f] [See ver. 30 above] [h] ch. 20:23
32 [i] [Num. 14:19] [j] [Rom. 9:3] [k] Ps. 56:8; 69:28; 139:16; Dan. 12:1; Phil. 4:3
33 [l] Ezek. 18:4, 20
34 [m] ch. 33:12 [n] See ch. 14:19

Chapter 33

1 [o] ch. 32:7 [p] ch. 32:13; See Gen. 12:7
2 [q] See ch. 14:19 [r] See ch. 13:5
3 [s] See ch. 3:8 [t] [ver. 15-17] [u] ch. 32:10; Num. 16:21, 45 [v] See ch. 32:9
4 [w] Num. 14:39 [x] [Ezek. 24:17, 23; 26:16]
5 [v] [See ver. 3 above] [y] ch. 32:12 [x] [See ver. 4 above]
7 [z] ch. 29:42, 43 [a] Deut. 4:29; 2 Sam. 21:1; 1 Chr. 16:10, 11; Ps. 40:16
8 [b] [Num. 16:27]
9 [c] See ch. 13:21
11 [d] Num. 12:8; Deut. 34:10; See Gen. 32:30 [e] ch. 17:9, 10; 24:13; 32:17

Moses' Intercession

12 Moses said to the LORD, "See, [f]you say to
me, 'Bring up this people,' but you have not
let me know whom you will send with me.
Yet you have said, [g]'I know you by name, and
you have also found favor in my sight.' 13 Now
therefore, if I have found favor in your sight,
please [h]show me now your ways, that I may
know you in order to find favor in your sight.
Consider too that this nation is [i]your people."
14 And he said, [j]"My presence will go with you,
and [k]I will give you rest." 15 And he said to him,
[l]"If your presence will not go with me, do not
bring us up from here. 16 For how shall it be
known that I have found favor in your sight,
I and your people? [m]Is it not in your going
with us, [n]so that we are distinct, I and your
people, from every other people on the face
of the earth?"

17 And the LORD said to Moses, "This very
thing that you have spoken I will do, [o]for you
have found favor in my sight, and I know you
by name." 18 Moses said, "Please [p]show me your
glory." 19 And he said, [q]"I will make all my
goodness pass before you and will proclaim
before you my name 'The LORD.' And [r]I will
be gracious to whom I will be gracious, and
will show mercy on whom I will show mercy.
20 But," he said, "you cannot see my face, for
[s]man shall not see me and live." 21 And the
LORD said, "Behold, there is a place by me
where you shall stand on the rock, 22 and while
my glory passes by I will put you in a [t]cleft of
the rock, and I will [u]cover you with my hand
until I have passed by. 23 Then I will take away
my hand, and you shall see my back, but my
face shall [v]not be seen."

Moses Makes New Tablets

34 The LORD said to Moses, [w]"Cut for
yourself two tablets of stone like
the first, [x]and I will write on the tablets the
words that were on the first tablets, [y]which
you broke. 2 Be ready by the morning, and
come up in the morning to Mount Sinai, and
present yourself there to me [z]on the top of
the mountain. 3 No [a]one shall come up with
you, and let no one be seen throughout all
the mountain. Let no flocks or herds graze
opposite that mountain." 4 So Moses cut two
tablets of stone like the first. And he rose early
in the morning and went up on Mount Sinai,
as the LORD had commanded him, and took
in his hand two tablets of stone. 5 The LORD
[b]descended in the cloud and stood with him
there, and [c]proclaimed the name of the LORD.
6 The LORD passed before him and proclaimed,
[d]"The LORD, the LORD, a God merciful and
[e]gracious, slow to anger, and abounding in
steadfast [f]love and faithfulness, 7 [g]keeping
steadfast love for thousands,[1] [h]forgiving iniquity and transgression and sin, but [i]who will

[1] Or *to the thousandth generation*

12[f] ch. 32:34 [g] ver. 17
13[h] Ps. 25:4; [Ps. 103:7] [i] Deut. 9:29; [Joel 2:17]
14[j] Josh. 1:5; Isa. 63:9; See ch. 40:34-38 [k] Deut. 3:20; Josh. 21:44; 22:4; 23:1; [Ps. 95:11]
15[l] [ver. 1-3]
16[m] Num. 14:14 [n] ch. 19:5, 6; 1 Kgs. 8:53
17[o] ver. 12, 13
18[p] [ver. 20; 1 Tim. 6:16]
19[q] Ps. 31:19; Jer. 31:14; [ch. 34:5-7] [r] Cited Rom. 9:15
20[s] Gen. 32:30; Deut. 5:24; Judg. 6:22, 23; 13:22; Isa. 6:5; Rev. 1:17; [ch. 24:10, 11]
22[t] Isa. 2:21 [u] Ps. 91:1, 4
23[v] ver. 20; John 1:18; 1 Tim. 6:16; 1 John 4:12

Chapter 34
1[w] Deut. 10:1 [x] ver. 28; Deut. 10:2, 4 [y] ch. 32:19
2[z] ch. 19:20
3[a] ch. 19:12, 13, 21
5[b] Num. 11:25; [1 Kgs. 8:10, 11] [c] ch. 33:19
6[d] Num. 14:18; 2 Chr. 30:9; Neh. 9:17; Ps. 86:15; 103:8; 111:4; 112:4; 116:5; 145:8; Joel 2:13 [e] ch. 22:27 [f] Ps. 57:10; 108:4
7[g] ch. 20:5, 6; Deut. 5:10; Jer. 32:18; Dan. 9:4

33:12–23 Moses asks God for three things in his continued intercession for Israel.

1) *Moses asks God to "show me . . . your ways"* (v. 13). He wants to know God's mind, to stay in constant communion with God, to experience the reality of his presence.

2) *Moses asks God to go with Israel on the journey* (vv. 14–17). Earlier God had indicated that he would not go with his people (vv. 1–6) lest he destroy them. But for Moses, that was not good enough; he would rather not go to the Promised Land if God did not go with them. In response, God reaffirms that he would go with them and he would grant them favor.

3) *Moses asks God to show his glory to him* (v. 18). One would think that Moses has already seen the glory of the Lord at the burning bush, through the plagues, at the Red Sea, and in many other ways. But Moses is looking for a confirming sign like in 24:9–11, when God ate a covenant meal as a confirmation of the Book of the Covenant. The confirming sign God gives is for his "goodness" (33:19) to pass by and for his name to be proclaimed. In his mercy, God grants all of these requests. He delights to give his children good things, especially the best thing of all: himself (cf. Ps. 37:4).

34:1–28 God renews his covenant with his sinful people. And it is striking that God does not lower his standards in the light of his people's failure. Rather, the law remains the law, and the holy character of God that it represents remains the same. Its permanence is signified not only in being reiterated, but also in being carved again in tablets of stone (31:18; 32:16; 34:1, 28).

[h] Ps. 103:3; 130:4; Dan. 9:9; 1 John 1:9 [i] ch. 23:21; Josh. 24:19; Job 10:14; Nah. 1:3

by no means clear the guilty, [j]visiting the iniquity of the fathers on the children and the children's children, to the third and the fourth
generation." 8 And Moses quickly [k]bowed his
head toward the earth and worshiped. 9 And
he said, "If now I have found favor in your
sight, O Lord, please [l]let the Lord go in the
midst of us, for [m]it is a stiff-necked people, and
pardon our iniquity and our sin, and take us
for [n]your inheritance."

The Covenant Renewed

10 And he said, "Behold, [o]I am making a covenant. Before all your people [p]I will do mar-
vels, such as have not been created in all the
earth or in any nation. And all the people
among whom you are shall see the work of the
LORD, for it is an [q]awesome thing that I will
do with you.
11 "Observe what I command you this day.
Behold, [r]I will drive out before you the
Amorites, the Canaanites, the Hittites, the
Perizzites, the Hivites, and the Jebusites.
12 [s]Take care, lest you make a covenant with the
inhabitants of the land to which you go, lest
it become a [t]snare in your midst. 13 You shall
[u]tear down their altars and [v]break their pillars
and cut down their [w]Asherim 14 (for [x]you shall
worship no other god, for the LORD, whose
name is Jealous, is a jealous God), 15 [s]lest you
make a covenant with the inhabitants of the
land, and when they [y]whore after their gods
and sacrifice to their gods and [z]you are invited,
you eat of his sacrifice, 16 and you take of [a]their
daughters for your sons, and their daughters
[y]whore after their gods and make your sons
whore after their gods.
17 [b]"You shall not make for yourself any gods
of cast metal.
18 [c]"You shall keep the Feast of Unleavened
Bread. Seven days you shall eat unleavened
bread, as I commanded you, at the time
appointed in [d]the month Abib, for in the
month Abib you came out from Egypt. 19 [e]All
that open the womb are mine, all your male[1]
livestock, the firstborn of cow and sheep.
20 The [f]firstborn of a donkey you shall redeem
with a lamb, or if you will not redeem it you
shall break its neck. All the firstborn of your
sons you shall redeem. And [g]none shall appear
before me empty-handed.
21 [h]"Six days you shall work, but on the seventh day you shall rest. In plowing time and
in harvest you shall rest. 22 [i]You shall observe
the Feast of Weeks, the firstfruits of wheat harvest, and the Feast of Ingathering at the year's
end. 23 [j]Three times in the year shall all your
males appear before the LORD God, the God of
Israel. 24 For I will [k]cast out nations before you
and [l]enlarge your borders; [m]no one shall covet
your land, when you go up to appear before
the LORD your God three times in the year.
25 [n]"You shall not offer the blood of my sacrifice with anything leavened, [o]or let the sacrifice of the Feast of the Passover remain until
the morning. 26 [p]The best of the firstfruits of
your ground you shall bring to the house
of the LORD your God. [q]You shall not boil a
young goat in its mother's milk."
27 And the LORD said to Moses, "Write these
words, for in accordance with these words [r]I
have made a covenant with you and with Israel."
28 [s]So he was there with the LORD forty days and
forty nights. He neither ate bread nor drank
water. And he [t]wrote on the tablets the words of
the covenant, the Ten Commandments.[2]

The Shining Face of Moses

29 When Moses came down from Mount
Sinai, with [u]the two tablets of the testimony
in his hand as he came down from the mountain, Moses did not know that the skin of his

[1] Septuagint, Theodotion, Vulgate, Targum; the meaning of the Hebrew is uncertain [2] Hebrew *the ten words*

The special emphasis in the additional words of verses 10–28 focused on the necessity of not turning to idols and the religious practices of the Canaanites—an obvious concern in light of the incident with the golden bull calf. But the law continues to hold out a constant standard. It is a standard that can be met only by One who was perfectly righteous and holy, our Savior, Jesus.

34:29–35 Moses' face shone with the reflected glory of God; having heard his glory and seen his glory, Moses reflected God's glory. And yet, Paul tells us that the ministry

7 [j]Deut. 5:9
8 [k]ch. 4:31; 12:27
9 [l]ch. 33:15, 16 [m]See ch. 32:9 [n]Deut. 32:9; Ps. 28:9; 33:12; 78:62; 94:14; Jer. 10:16; Zech. 2:12
10 [o]ver. 27; Deut. 5:2; 29:1 [p]Deut. 4:32-35; Josh. 6:20; 10:12, 13; 2 Sam. 7:23; Ps. 77:14; 78:12 [q]Deut. 10:21; Ps. 145:6; [Isa. 64:3]

11 [r]See ch. 13:5 **12** [s]ch. 23:32; Deut. 7:2; Josh. 23:12, 13; Judg. 2:2 [t]See ch. 23:33 **13** [u]Deut. 7:5; 12:3; Judg. 2:2; 6:25; 2 Chr. 34:3, 4 [v]ch. 23:24; 2 Kgs. 18:4; 23:14; 2 Chr. 31:1 [w]See Deut. 16:21 **14** [x]ch. 20:3, 5 **15** [s][See ver. 12 above] [y]Lev. 17:7; 20:5; Deut. 31:16; Judg. 2:17; Jer. 3:9; Ezek. 6:9 [z]Num. 25:2; Ps. 106:28; [1 Cor. 8:4, 7, 10; 10:27] **16** [a]Deut. 7:3, 4; 1 Kgs. 11:2; Ezra 9:2; Neh. 13:25 [y][See ver. 15 above] **17** [b]Lev. 19:4; Deut. 27:15; [ch. 32:4, 8] **18** [c]See ch. 12:15 [d]ch. 13:4 **19** [e]See ch. 13:2 **20** [f]ch. 13:13; Num. 18:15 [g]ch. 23:15; Deut. 16:16 **21** [h]See ch. 20:9 **22** [i]ch. 23:16; Deut. 16:10, 13 **23** [j]ch. 23:14, 17; Deut. 16:16 **24** [k]ch. 33:2; Deut. 7:1; Ps. 78:55; 80:8; See ch. 23:27-31 [l]Deut. 12:20; 19:8 [m][Prov. 16:7] **25** [n]See ch. 12:8 [o]See ch. 12:10 **26** [p]See ch. 23:19 [q]Deut. 14:21 **27** [r]ver. 10 **28** [s]See ch. 24:18 [t][ver. 1; ch. 31:18; 32:16; Deut. 4:13; 10:2, 4] **29** [u]ch. 32:15

face [v]shone because he had been talking with God.[1] 30 Aaron and all the people of Israel saw Moses, and behold, the skin of his face [w]shone, and they were afraid to come near him. 31 But Moses called to them, and Aaron and all the leaders of the congregation returned to him, and Moses talked with them. 32 Afterward all the people of Israel came near, and he [x]commanded them all that the LORD had spoken with him in Mount Sinai. 33 And when Moses had finished speaking with them, he put a [y]veil over his face.

34 Whenever Moses [z]went in before the LORD to speak with him, he would remove the veil, until he came out. And when he came out and told the people of Israel what he was commanded, 35 the people of Israel would see the face of Moses, that the skin of Moses' face was [a]shining. And Moses would put the veil over his face again, until he went in to speak with him.

Sabbath Regulations

35 Moses assembled all the congregation of the people of Israel and said to them, [b]"These are the things that the LORD has commanded you to do. 2 [c]Six days work shall be done, but on the seventh day you shall have a Sabbath of solemn rest, holy to the LORD. Whoever does any work on it shall be put to death. 3 [d]You shall kindle no fire in all your dwelling places on the Sabbath day."

Contributions for the Tabernacle

4 Moses said to all the congregation of the people of Israel, "This is the thing that the LORD has commanded. 5 [e]Take from among you a contribution to the LORD. [f]Whoever is of a generous heart, let him bring the LORD's contribution: gold, silver, and bronze; 6 blue and purple and scarlet yarns and fine twined linen; goats' hair, 7 tanned rams' skins, and goatskins;[2] acacia wood, 8 oil for the light, spices for the anointing oil and for the fragrant incense, 9 and onyx stones and stones for setting, for the ephod and for the breastpiece.

10 "Let [g]every skillful craftsman among you come and make all that the LORD has commanded: 11 [h]the tabernacle, its tent and its covering, its hooks and its frames, its bars, its pillars, and its bases; 12 [i]the ark with its poles, the mercy seat, and the [j]veil of the screen; 13 [k]the table with its poles and all its utensils, and the [l]bread of the Presence; 14 [m]the lampstand also for the light, with its utensils and its lamps, and the [n]oil for the light; 15 [o]and the altar of incense, with its poles, [p]and the anointing oil and the [q]fragrant incense, and [r]the screen for the door, at the door of the tabernacle; 16 [s]the altar of burnt offering, with its grating of bronze, its poles, and all its utensils, the [t]basin and its stand; 17 [u]the hangings of the court, its pillars and its bases, and the screen for the gate of the court; 18 [v]the pegs of the tabernacle and the pegs of the court, and their [w]cords; 19 the [x]finely worked garments for ministering[3] in the Holy Place, the holy garments for Aaron the priest, and the garments of his sons, for their service as priests."

20 Then all the congregation of the people of Israel departed from the presence of Moses. 21 And they came, [y]everyone whose heart stirred him, and everyone whose spirit moved him, [z]and brought the LORD's contribution to be used for the tent of meeting, and for all its service, and for the holy garments. 22 So they came, both men and women. All who were of a willing heart brought brooches and earrings and signet rings and armlets, all sorts of gold objects, every man dedicating an offering of gold to the LORD. 23 And [a]every one who possessed [b]blue or purple or scarlet yarns or fine linen or

[1] Hebrew *him* [2] The meaning of the Hebrew word is uncertain; also verse 23; compare 25:5 [3] Or *garments for worship*; see 31:10

29[v] 2 Cor. 3:7; [Matt. 17:2]
30[w] ver. 29
32[x] ch. 24:3
33[y] 2 Cor. 3:13
34[z] 2 Cor. 3:16
35[a] ver. 29
Chapter 35
1[b] ch. 34:32
2[c] ch. 31:15; See ch. 20:9
3[d] ch. 16:23
5[e] For ver. 5-9, see ch. 25:2-7 [f] See ch. 25:2
10[g] ver. 25; ch. 28:3; 31:6; 36:1, 2
11[h] See ch. 26:1-30

of the new covenant is superior to Moses' own because it is a ministry of the Spirit, of the gospel, and of a permanent administration (2 Cor. 3:7–11). The wonder of the gospel is that we behold the glory of the Lord, mediated by the Spirit of Jesus through his Word (2 Cor. 4:6), so that we are being transformed from glory to glory (2 Cor. 3:16–18).

35:4–29 In order to proceed to build the tabernacle, the people needed to make appropriate preparations for it. Here the people gave free will offerings (v. 29) to build this meeting place with God. As with the collections that Paul would encourage in 2 Corinthians 9:6–15, so here: the need was made known; people's hearts were "stirred" and "moved"; and they came with "the LORD's contribution" for this effort (Ex. 35:21). As we give in response to God's grace, joy is the result.

12[i] See ch. 25:10-16 [j] ch. 26:31, 33; 39:34; 40:3, 21; Num. 4:5 **13**[k] See ch. 25:23-29 [l] ch. 25:30 **14**[m] See ch. 25:31-39 [n] ch. 27:20 **15**[o] See ch. 30:1-10 [p] See ch. 30:23-33 [q] See ch. 30:34-38 [r] ch. 26:36 **16**[s] See ch. 27:1-8 [t] See ch. 30:18-21 **17**[u] See ch. 27:9-17 **18**[v] ch. 27:19 [w] ch. 39:40 **19**[x] ch. 31:10 **21**[y] See ch. 25:2 [z] ch. 36:3 **23**[a] [1 Chr. 29:8] [b] ver. 6, 7; ch. 25:4, 5

goats' hair or tanned rams' skins or goatskins
brought them. 24 [c]Everyone who could make a
contribution of silver or bronze brought it as
the LORD's contribution. And every one who
possessed acacia wood of any use in the work
brought it. 25 And every [d]skillful woman spun
with her hands, and they all brought what they
had spun in blue and purple and scarlet yarns
and fine twined linen. 26 All the women [y]whose
hearts stirred them to use their skill spun the
goats' hair. 27 And the [e]leaders brought onyx
stones and stones to be set, for the ephod and
for the breastpiece, 28 and spices and oil for the
light, and for the anointing oil, and for the fragrant incense. 29 [f]All the men and women, the
people of Israel, whose heart moved them to
bring anything for the work that the LORD had
commanded by Moses to be done brought it as
a freewill offering to the LORD.

Construction of the Tabernacle

30 [g]Then Moses said to the people of Israel,
"See, the LORD has called by name Bezalel the
son of Uri, son of Hur, of the tribe of Judah;
31 and he has filled him with the Spirit of God,
with [h]skill, with intelligence, with knowledge,
and with all craftsmanship, 32 to devise artistic
designs, to work in gold and silver and bronze,
33 in cutting stones for setting, and in carving
wood, for work in every skilled craft. 34 And
he has inspired him to teach, both him and
Oholiab the son of Ahisamach of the tribe of
Dan. 35 He has [h]filled them with skill to do
every sort of work done by an engraver or by
a designer or by an embroiderer in blue and
purple and scarlet yarns and fine twined linen,
or by a weaver—by any sort of workman or
skilled designer.

36 "Bezalel and Oholiab and [i]every craftsman in whom the LORD has put skill
and intelligence to know how to do any work
in the construction of the sanctuary shall
work in accordance with all that the LORD
has commanded."

2 And Moses called Bezalel and Oholiab and
every craftsman in whose mind the LORD
had put skill, everyone [j]whose heart stirred
him up to come to do the work. 3 And they
received from Moses all the [k]contribution that
the people of Israel had brought for doing the
work on the sanctuary. They still kept bringing him [l]freewill offerings every morning, 4 so
that all the craftsmen who were doing every
sort of task on the sanctuary came, each from
the task that he was doing, 5 and said to Moses,
[m]"The people bring much more than enough
for doing the work that the LORD has commanded us to do." 6 So Moses gave command,
and word was proclaimed throughout the
camp, "Let no man or woman do anything
more for the [n]contribution for the sanctuary."
So the people were restrained from bringing,
7 for the material they had was sufficient to do
all the work, and more.

8 [o]And all the craftsmen among the workmen made the tabernacle with ten curtains.
They were made of fine twined linen and blue
and purple and scarlet yarns, with cherubim
skillfully worked. 9 The length of each curtain
was twenty-eight cubits,[1] and the breadth of
each curtain four cubits. All the curtains were
the same size.

10 He[2] coupled five curtains to one another,
and the other five curtains he coupled to
one another. 11 He made loops of blue on the
edge of the outermost curtain of the first set.
Likewise he made them on the edge of the outermost curtain of the second set. 12 He made
fifty loops on the one curtain, and he made
fifty loops on the edge of the curtain that was
in the second set. The loops were opposite one
another. 13 And he made fifty clasps of gold,
and coupled the curtains one to the other with
clasps. So the tabernacle was a single whole.

[1] A *cubit* was about 18 inches or 45 centimeters [2] Probably Bezalel (compare 35:30; 37:1)

35:30–39:43 As a testimony, Moses made sure that all that was done in building the tabernacle, its furniture, and the priestly garments was according to the specifications that God had given in chapters 25–31. The final words of the section acknowledge the faithful commitment of both Moses and the people: "According to all that the LORD had commanded Moses, so the people of Israel had done all the work" (39:42). Having learned from the failure to obey in chapters 32–34, God's people make sure that they follow God's Word exactly at this point.

Often it is our past failures and the experience of God's grace in forgiveness that equip us with greater determination to say no to sin and yes to godliness. Since we have known the mercies of God, we present ourselves to God in holy obedience according to his Word (cf. Rom. 12:1–2).

24 [c] ch. 36:3, 6
25 [d] ver. 10
26 [y] [See ver. 21 above]
27 [e] [1 Chr. 29:6-8; Ezra 2:68]
29 [f] ch. 36:3
30 [g] For ver. 30-34, see ch. 31:1-6
31 [h] [1 Kgs. 7:14; 2 Chr. 2:14]
35 [h] [See ver. 31 above]

Chapter 36
1 [i] ch. 28:3; 31:6; 35:10, 25
2 [j] See ch. 25:2
3 [k] ch. 35:24 [l] See ch. 35:29
5 [m] [2 Chr. 31:10; 2 Cor. 8:2, 3]
6 [n] ver. 3
8 [o] For ver. 8-19, see ch. 26:1-14

14 He also made curtains of goats' hair for a
tent over the tabernacle. He made eleven curtains. 15 The length of each curtain was thirty
cubits, and the breadth of each curtain four
cubits. The eleven curtains were the same size.
16 He coupled five curtains by themselves, and
six curtains by themselves. 17 And he made fifty
loops on the edge of the outermost curtain of
the one set, and fifty loops on the edge of the
other connecting curtain. 18 And he made fifty
clasps of bronze to couple the tent together
that it might be a single whole. 19 And he made
for the tent a covering of tanned rams' skins
and goatskins.

20 [p]Then he made the upright frames for the
tabernacle of [q]acacia wood. 21 Ten cubits was
the length of a frame, and a cubit and a half the
breadth of each frame. 22 Each frame had two
tenons for fitting together. He did this for all
the frames of the tabernacle. 23 The frames for
the tabernacle he made thus: twenty frames
for the south side. 24 And he made forty bases
of silver under the twenty frames, two bases
under one frame for its two tenons, and two
bases under the next frame for its two tenons.
25 For the second side of the tabernacle, on the
north side, he made twenty frames 26 and their
forty bases of silver, two bases under one frame
and two bases under the next frame. 27 For the
rear of the tabernacle westward he made six
frames. 28 He made two frames for corners of
the tabernacle in the rear. 29 And they were
separate beneath but joined at the top, at the
first ring. He made two of them this way for
the two corners. 30 There were eight frames
with their bases of silver: sixteen bases, under
every frame two bases.

31 He made bars of acacia wood, five for the
frames of the one side of the tabernacle, 32 and
five bars for the frames of the other side of
the tabernacle, and five bars for the frames of
the tabernacle at the rear westward. 33 And he
made the middle bar to run from end to end
halfway up the frames. 34 And he overlaid the
frames with gold, and made their rings of gold
for holders for the bars, and overlaid the bars
with gold.

35 [r]He made the veil of blue and purple and
scarlet yarns and fine twined linen; with
cherubim skillfully worked into it he made it.
36 And for it he made four pillars of acacia and
overlaid them with gold. Their hooks were of
gold, and he cast for them four bases of silver.
37 He also made a screen for the entrance of
the tent, of blue and purple and scarlet yarns
and fine twined linen, embroidered with
needlework, 38 and its five pillars with their
hooks. He overlaid their capitals, and their
fillets were of gold, but their five bases were
of bronze.

Making the Ark

37 [s]Bezalel made the ark of acacia wood.
Two cubits[1] and a half was its length, a
cubit and a half its breadth, and a cubit and a
half its height. 2 And he overlaid it with pure
gold inside and outside, and made a molding
of gold around it. 3 And he cast for it four rings
of gold for its [t]four feet, two rings on its one
side and two rings on its other side. 4 And he
made poles of acacia wood and overlaid them
with gold 5 and put the poles into the rings on
the sides of the ark to carry the ark. 6 And he
made a mercy seat of pure gold. Two cubits
and a half was its length, and a cubit and a
half its breadth. 7 And he made two cherubim
of gold. He made them of hammered work on
the two ends of the mercy seat, 8 one cherub
on the one end, and one cherub on the other
end. Of one piece with the mercy seat he made
the cherubim on its two ends. 9 The cherubim
spread out their wings above, overshadowing
the mercy seat with their wings, with their
faces one to another; toward the mercy seat
were the faces of the cherubim.

Making the Table

10 [u]He also made the table of acacia wood.
Two cubits was its length, a cubit its breadth,
and a cubit and a half its height. 11 And he overlaid it with pure gold, and made a molding of
gold around it. 12 And he made a rim around it
a handbreadth[2] wide, and made a molding of
gold around the rim. 13 He cast for it four rings
of gold and fastened the rings to the four corners at its four legs. 14 Close to the frame were
the rings, as holders for the poles to carry the
table. 15 He made the poles of acacia wood to
carry the table, and overlaid them with gold.
16 And he made the vessels of pure gold that
were to be on the table, its plates and dishes
for incense, and its bowls and flagons with
which to pour drink offerings.

[1] A *cubit* was about 18 inches or 45 centimeters [2] A *handbreadth* was about 3 inches or 7.5 centimeters

20[p] For ver. 20-34, see ch. 26:15-29 [q] ch. 25:5, 28; 30:5 **35**[r] For ver. 35-38, see ch. 26:31-37 **Chapter 37** **1**[s] For ver. 1-9, see ch. 25:10-20 **3**[t] ch. 25:12
10[u] For ver. 10-16, see ch. 25:23-29

Making the Lampstand

17 [v]He also made the lampstand of pure gold. He made the lampstand of hammered work. Its base, its stem, its cups, its calyxes, and its flowers were of one piece with it. 18 And there were six branches going out of its sides, three branches of the lampstand out of one side of it and three branches of the lampstand out of the other side of it; 19 three cups made like almond blossoms, each with calyx and flower, on one branch, and three cups made like almond blossoms, each with calyx and flower, on the other branch—so for the six branches going out of the lampstand. 20 And on the lampstand itself were four cups made like almond blossoms, with their calyxes and flowers, 21 and a calyx of one piece with it under each pair of the six branches going out of it. 22 Their calyxes and their branches were of one piece with it. The whole of it was a single piece of hammered work of pure gold. 23 And he made its seven lamps and its tongs and its trays of pure gold. 24 He made it and all its utensils out of a talent[1] of pure gold.

Making the Altar of Incense

25 [w]He made the altar of incense of acacia wood. Its length was a cubit, and its breadth was a cubit. It was square, and two cubits was its height. Its horns were of one piece with it. 26 He overlaid it with pure gold, its top and around its sides and its horns. And he made a molding of gold around it, 27 and made two rings of gold on it under its molding, on two opposite sides of it, as holders for the poles with which to carry it. 28 And he made the poles of acacia wood and overlaid them with gold.

29 [x]He made the holy anointing oil also, and the [y]pure fragrant incense, blended as by the perfumer.

Making the Altar of Burnt Offering

38 [z]He made the altar of burnt offering of acacia wood. Five cubits[2] was its length, and five cubits its breadth. It was square, and three cubits was its height. 2 He made horns for it on its four corners. Its horns were of one piece with it, and he overlaid it with bronze. 3 And he made all the utensils of the altar, the pots, the shovels, the basins, the forks, and the fire pans. He made all its utensils of bronze. 4 And he made for the altar a grating, a network of bronze, under its ledge, extending halfway down. 5 He cast four rings on the four corners of the bronze grating as holders for the poles. 6 He made the poles of acacia wood and overlaid them with bronze. 7 And he put the poles through the rings on the sides of the altar to carry it with them. He made it hollow, with boards.

Making the Bronze Basin

8 [a]He made the basin of bronze and its stand of bronze, from the mirrors of the [b]ministering women who ministered in the entrance of the tent of meeting.

Making the Court

9 [c]And he made the court. For the south side the hangings of the court were of fine twined linen, a hundred cubits; 10 their twenty pillars and their twenty bases were of bronze, but the hooks of the pillars and their fillets were of silver. 11 And for the north side there were hangings of a hundred cubits, their twenty pillars, their twenty bases were of bronze, but the hooks of the pillars and their fillets were of silver. 12 And for the west side were hangings of fifty cubits, their ten pillars, and their ten bases; the hooks of the pillars and their fillets were of silver. 13 And for the front to the east, fifty cubits. 14 The hangings for one side of the gate were fifteen cubits, with their three pillars and three bases. 15 And so for the other side. On both sides of the gate of the court were hangings of fifteen cubits, with their three pillars and their three bases. 16 All the hangings around the court were of fine twined linen. 17 And the bases for the pillars were of bronze, but the hooks of the pillars and their fillets were of silver. The overlaying of their capitals was also of silver, and all the pillars of the court were filleted with silver. 18 And the screen for the gate of the court was embroidered with needlework in blue and purple and scarlet yarns and fine twined linen. It was twenty cubits long and five cubits high in its breadth, corresponding to the hangings of the court. 19 And their pillars were four in number. Their four bases were of bronze, their hooks of silver, and the overlaying of their capitals and their fillets of silver. 20 And all the pegs for the tabernacle and for the court all around were of bronze.

[1] A *talent* was about 75 pounds or 34 kilograms [2] A *cubit* was about 18 inches or 45 centimeters

17[v] For ver. 17-24, see ch. 25:31-39 **25**[w] For ver. 25-28, see ch. 30:1-5 **29**[x] ch. 30:23, 24, 34, 35 [y] ch. 30:7 **Chapter 38** **1**[z] For ver. 1-7, see ch. 27:1-8 **8**[a] ch. 30:18 [b] 1 Sam. 2:22; [Num. 4:23; 8:24] **9**[c] For ver. 9-20, see ch. 27:9-19

Materials for the Tabernacle

21 These are the records of the tabernacle,
[d]the tabernacle of the testimony, as they were
recorded at the commandment of Moses, the
responsibility of the Levites [e]under the direction of Ithamar the son of Aaron the priest.
22 [f]Bezalel the son of Uri, son of Hur, of the
tribe of Judah, made all that the LORD commanded Moses; 23 and with him was [f]Oholiab
the son of Ahisamach, of the tribe of Dan,
an engraver and designer and embroiderer
in blue and purple and scarlet yarns and fine
twined linen.
24 All the gold that was used for the work, in
all the construction of the sanctuary, the gold
from the offering, was twenty-nine talents and
730 shekels,[1] by [g]the shekel of the sanctuary.
25 The silver from those of the congregation
who were recorded was a hundred talents and
1,775 shekels, by the shekel of the sanctuary:
26 a [g]beka[2] a head (that is, half a shekel, by the
shekel of the sanctuary), for everyone who was
listed in the records, from twenty years old
and upward, for [h]603,550 men. 27 The hundred
talents of silver were for casting the [i]bases of
the sanctuary and the bases of the veil; a hundred bases for the hundred talents, a talent
a base. 28 And of the 1,775 shekels he made
hooks for the pillars and overlaid their capitals and made fillets for them. 29 The bronze
that was offered was seventy talents and 2,400
shekels; 30 with it he made the [j]bases for the
entrance of the tent of meeting, [k]the bronze
altar and the bronze grating for it and all the
utensils of the altar, 31 the [l]bases around the
court, and the [m]bases of the gate of the court,
all the [n]pegs of the tabernacle, and all the pegs
around the court.

Making the Priestly Garments

39 From the [o]blue and purple and scarlet yarns they made [p]finely woven
garments,[3] for ministering in the Holy Place.
They made the holy garments for Aaron, [q]as
the LORD had commanded Moses.
2 [r]He made the ephod of gold, blue and purple and scarlet yarns, and fine twined linen.
3 And they hammered out gold leaf, and he
cut it into threads to work into the blue and
purple and the scarlet yarns, and into the fine
twined linen, in skilled design. 4 They made
for the ephod attaching shoulder pieces,
joined to it at its two edges. 5 And the skillfully woven band on it was of one piece with
it and made like it, of gold, blue and purple
and scarlet yarns, and fine twined linen, as the
LORD had commanded Moses.
6 They made the onyx stones, enclosed in settings of gold filigree, and engraved like the
engravings of a signet, according to the names
of the sons of Israel. 7 And he set them on the
shoulder pieces of the ephod to be stones of
remembrance for the sons of Israel, as the
LORD had commanded Moses.
8 [s]He made the breastpiece, in skilled work,
in the style of the ephod, of gold, blue and
purple and scarlet yarns, and fine twined
linen. 9 It was square. They made the breastpiece doubled, a span[4] its length and a span
its breadth when doubled. 10 And they set in
it four rows of stones. A row of sardius, topaz,
and carbuncle was the first row; 11 and the second row, an emerald, a sapphire, and a diamond; 12 and the third row, a jacinth, an agate,
and an amethyst; 13 and the fourth row, a beryl,
an onyx, and a jasper. They were enclosed in
settings of gold filigree. 14 There were twelve
stones with their names according to the
names of the sons of Israel. They were like
signets, each engraved with its name, for the
twelve tribes. 15 And they made on the breastpiece twisted chains like cords, of pure gold.
16 And they made two settings of gold filigree
and two gold rings, and put the two rings on
the two edges of the breastpiece. 17 And they
put the two cords of gold in the two rings at
the edges of the breastpiece. 18 They attached
the two ends of the two cords to the two settings of filigree. Thus they attached it in front
to the shoulder pieces of the ephod. 19 Then
they made two rings of gold, and put them at
the two ends of the breastpiece, on its inside
edge next to the ephod. 20 And they made two
rings of gold, and attached them in front to
the lower part of the two shoulder pieces of
the ephod, at its seam above the skillfully
woven band of the ephod. 21 And they bound
the breastpiece by its rings to the rings of the
ephod with a lace of blue, so that it should lie
on the skillfully woven band of the ephod,

[1] A *talent* was about 75 pounds or 34 kilograms; a *shekel* was about 2/5 ounce or 11 grams [2] A *beka* was about 1/5 ounce or 5.5 grams
[3] Or *garments for worship* [4] A *span* was about 9 inches or 22 centimeters

21 [d]Num. 1:50, 53; 9:15; 10:11; 17:7, 8; 18:2; 2 Chr. 24:6; Acts 7:44; [ch. 16:34] [e]ch. 6:23; 28:1; Num. 4:28, 33 **22** [f]ch. 31:2, 6 **23** [f][See ver. 22 above]
24 [g]See ch. 30:13 **26** [g][See ver. 24 above] [h]Num. 1:46 **27** [i]ch. 26:19, 21, 25, 32 **30** [j]ch. 26:37 [k]ch. 27:2-4 **31** [l]ch. 27:10-12 [m]ch. 27:16, 17 [n]ch. 27:19
Chapter 39 **1** [o]ch. 35:23, 25 [p]ver. 41; ch. 31:10; 35:19 [q]ch. 28:2-4 **2** [r]For ver. 2-7, see ch. 28:6-12 **8** [s]For ver. 8-21, see ch. 28:15-28

and that the breastpiece should not come
loose from the ephod, as the LORD had commanded Moses.
22 [t]He also made the robe of the ephod woven
all of blue, 23 and the opening of the robe in
it was like the opening in a garment, with a
binding around the opening, so that it might
not tear. 24 On the hem of the robe they made
pomegranates of blue and purple and scarlet
yarns and fine twined linen. 25 They also made
bells of pure gold, and put the bells between
the pomegranates all around the hem of the
robe, between the pomegranates— 26 a bell
and a pomegranate, a bell and a pomegranate
around the hem of the robe for ministering, as
the LORD had commanded Moses.
27 [u]They also made the coats, woven of fine
[v]linen, for Aaron and his sons, 28 and the [v]tur-
ban of fine linen, and the caps of fine linen,
and the linen undergarments of fine twined
linen, 29 and the sash of fine twined linen and
of blue and purple and scarlet yarns, embroidered with needlework, as the LORD had commanded Moses.
30 [w]They made the plate of the holy crown
of pure gold, and wrote on it an inscription,
like the engraving of a signet, "Holy to the
LORD." 31 And they tied to it a cord of blue to
fasten it on the turban above, as the LORD had
commanded Moses.
32 Thus all the work of the tabernacle of the
tent of meeting was finished, and the people
of Israel did [x]according to all that the LORD
had commanded Moses; so they did. 33 Then
they brought the tabernacle to Moses, the tent
and all its utensils, its hooks, its frames, its
bars, its pillars, and its bases; 34 the covering of
tanned rams' skins and goatskins, and the [y]veil
of the screen; 35 the ark of the testimony with
its poles and the mercy seat; 36 the table with
all its utensils, and the bread of the Presence;
37 [z]the lampstand of pure gold and its lamps
with the lamps set and all its utensils, and
the oil for the light; 38 [a]the golden altar, the
anointing oil and the fragrant incense, and
[b]the screen for the entrance of the tent; 39 the
bronze altar, and its grating of bronze, its
poles, and all its utensils; the basin and its
stand; 40 [c]the hangings of the court, its pillars, and its bases, and the [d]screen for the gate
of the court, its [e]cords, and its pegs; and all
the utensils for the service of the tabernacle,
for the tent of meeting; 41 the finely worked
garments for ministering in the Holy Place,
the holy garments for Aaron the priest, and
the garments of his sons for their service as
priests. 42 [f]According to all that the LORD had
commanded Moses, so the people of Israel
had done all the work. 43 And Moses saw all
the work, and behold, they had done it; as the
LORD had commanded, so had they done it.
Then Moses [g]blessed them.

The Tabernacle Erected

40 The LORD spoke to Moses, saying, 2 "On
the [h]first day of the first month you
shall [i]erect the tabernacle of the tent of meeting. 3 And you shall put in it the ark of the
testimony, and you shall [j]screen the ark with
the veil. 4 And [k]you shall bring in the table
and arrange it, and [l]you shall bring in the
lampstand and set up its lamps. 5 [m]And you
shall put the golden altar for incense before
the ark of the testimony, and set up the screen
for the door of the tabernacle. 6 [n]You shall set
the altar of burnt offering before the door of
the tabernacle of the tent of meeting, 7 [o]and
place the basin between the tent of meeting
and the altar, and put water in it. 8 And you
shall set up the court all around, and hang up
the screen for the gate of the court.
9 "Then you shall take the [p]anointing oil
and anoint the tabernacle and all that is in
it, and consecrate it and all its furniture, so
that it may become holy. 10 You shall also
anoint [q]the altar of burnt offering and all
its utensils, and consecrate the altar, [r]so that
the altar may become most holy. 11 You shall
also anoint the basin and its stand, and consecrate it. 12 [s]Then you shall bring Aaron and
his sons to the entrance of the tent of meeting
and shall wash them with water 13 and put on
Aaron the holy garments. And you shall anoint
him and consecrate him, that he may serve
me as priest. 14 You shall bring his sons also
and put coats on them, 15 [t]and anoint them, as
you anointed their father, that they may serve
me as priests. And their anointing shall admit
them to a [u]perpetual priesthood throughout
their generations."
16 This Moses did; according to all that the

22[t] For ver. 22-26, see ch. 28:31-34 **27**[u] ch. 28:39, 40, 42 [v] Ezek. 44:18 **28**[v] [See ver. 27 above] **30**[w] ch. 28:36, 37; 29:6 **32**[x] ver. 42, 43; ch. 25:40 **34**[y] ch. 35:12 **37**[z] [ch. 25:31] **38**[a] ch. 30:3; 37:26; 40:5, 26 [b] ch. 26:36; 36:37 **40**[c] See ch. 27:9-15; 38:9-17 [d] ch. 27:16; 38:18 [e] ch. 35:18 **42**[f] ch. 35:10 **43**[g] Lev. 9:22, 23; Josh. 22:6; 2 Sam. 6:18; 1 Kgs. 8:14; 2 Chr. 6:3; 30:27; See Num. 6:23-27 **Chapter 40** **2**[h] [ch. 12:2; 13:4] [i] ver. 17; ch. 26:30 **3**[j] ver. 21; [ch. 35:12] **4**[k] ver. 22; ch. 26:35 [l] ver. 24, 25 **5**[m] ver. 26; [ch. 39:38] **6**[n] ver. 29 **7**[o] ver. 30; ch. 30:18 **9**[p] ch. 30:26 **10**[q] ch. 30:28 [r] ch. 29:37 **12**[s] See Lev. 8:1-13 **15**[t] ch. 28:41; 29:7 [u] Num. 25:13

LORD commanded him, so he did. 17 In the first month in the second year, on the first day of the month, [v]the tabernacle was erected. 18 Moses erected the tabernacle. He laid its bases, and set up its frames, and put in its poles, and raised up its pillars. 19 And he spread the tent over the tabernacle and put the covering of the tent over it, as the LORD had commanded Moses. 20 He [w]took the testimony and put it into the ark, and put the poles on the ark and set the mercy seat above on the ark. 21 And he brought the ark into the tabernacle and [x]set up the veil of the screen, and screened [y]the ark of the testimony, as the LORD had commanded Moses. 22 [z]He put the table in the tent of meeting, on the north side of the tabernacle, outside the veil, 23 and arranged the bread on it before the LORD, as the LORD had commanded Moses. 24 [a]He put the lampstand in the tent of meeting, opposite the table on the south side of the tabernacle, 25 [b]and set up the lamps before the LORD, as the LORD had commanded Moses. 26 [c]He put the golden altar in the tent of meeting before the veil, 27 and burned fragrant incense on it, as the LORD had commanded Moses. 28 [d]He put in place the screen for the door of the tabernacle. 29 [e]And he set the altar of burnt offering at the entrance of the tabernacle of the tent of meeting, and offered on it the burnt offering and the [f]grain offering, as the LORD had commanded Moses. 30 [g]He set the basin between the tent of meeting and the altar, and put water in it for washing, 31 with which Moses and [h]Aaron and his sons [i]washed their hands and their feet. 32 When they went into the tent of meeting, and when they approached the altar, they washed, as the LORD commanded Moses. 33 [j]And he erected the court around the tabernacle and the altar, and set up the screen of the gate of the court. So [k]Moses finished the work.

The Glory of the LORD

34 Then [l]the cloud covered the tent of meeting, and [m]the glory of the LORD filled the tabernacle. 35 And Moses was not able to enter the tent of meeting because the cloud settled on it, and the glory of the LORD filled the tabernacle. 36 Throughout all their journeys, [n]whenever the cloud was taken up from over the tabernacle, the people of Israel would set out. 37 But [o]if the cloud was not taken up, then they did not set out till the day that it was taken up. 38 For the cloud of the LORD was on the tabernacle by day, and fire was in it by night, in the sight of all the house of Israel throughout all their journeys.

17 [v] ver. 2; Num. 7:1
20 [w] ch. 25:16; See ch. 16:34
21 [x] ver. 3; See ch. 35:12 [y] ver. 3, 20
22 [z] ver. 4; ch. 26:35
24 [a] ch. 26:35
25 [b] ver. 4; ch. 25:37
26 [c] ver. 5; ch. 30:6, 7
28 [d] ver. 5; ch. 26:36
29 [e] ver. 6 [f] ch. 29:41; 30:9

40:34–38 Once the tabernacle was complete, the glory of the Lord filled it. It was a sign that God accepted all that his people had done. God in his sovereign mercy was delighted to have his presence in the tabernacle and to fill it with his glory (cf. 1 Kings 8:10–11). The glory cloud was present by day and the pillar of fire by night to guide God's people. And God continued to be present with his people as they set out from Sinai toward the Promised Land, chasing them with goodness and mercy on their way home (Ps. 23:6).

30 [g] ver. 7 **31** [h] ch. 30:19, 20 [i] ch. 30:21 **33** [j] ver. 8; ch. 27:9, 16 [k] [Heb. 3:2, 5] **34** [l] See ch. 13:21 [m] ch. 29:43; Lev. 16:2; Num. 9:15; [1 Kgs. 8:10, 11; 2 Chr. 5:13, 14; 7:2; Isa. 6:4; Hag. 2:7, 9; Rev. 15:8] **36** [n] Num. 9:17; 10:11; [Neh. 9:19] **37** [o] See Num. 9:19-22

Introduction to Leviticus

Author

As with the other books of the Pentateuch, Moses was probably the author of Leviticus. In Leviticus, Moses continues the story of Exodus.

The Gospel in Leviticus

On the one hand, it is very natural to think of Leviticus in terms of the grace of the gospel. This is because of the many ways it speaks of ideas and concepts that find their ultimate fulfillment in the person and work of Jesus—sacrificial atonement, for example, or the priesthood. The book of Hebrews makes much of these connections, emphasizing again and again that Jesus is the Great High Priest (Heb. 4:14; 10:21), the one without any sin (Heb. 9:14; cf. 9:7), who offers himself as the ultimate sacrifice that cleanses all our sin (Heb. 1:3; 7:26–27; 9:12, 14, 26, 28; 10:10, 12, 14; 13:11–12) and therefore gives us confidence to draw near to God (10:19–22).

On the other hand, it is sometimes difficult to think of Leviticus in terms of the grace seen in the gospel. This is because Leviticus is primarily a collection of laws, and it is common to view these laws as being disconnected from grace. This is tremendously unfortunate and a very different view of the law than the Israelites held. For example, the longest psalm in the Bible—Psalm 119—is a celebration of the Lord's law, something the psalmist longs for (Ps. 119:20, 40, 131) and delights in (Ps. 119:16, 24, 35, 47, 70, 77, 143, 174). Significantly, the "law" he is speaking of included Leviticus!

The psalmist's love of the law should not surprise us. The law was given by the Lord to the Israelites in order to guide them in how to live as the "kingdom of priests and . . . holy nation" he had called them to be (Ex. 19:5–6). This in itself was actually an act of grace. In his kindness, the Lord gave his people these laws in order that they might know how to live properly in relationship with him, with one another, and with his world. No wonder the psalmist sings over it with joy! What is more, the law was given by the Lord *after* he had redeemed the Israelites, not before (cf. Exodus 1–19 with Exodus 20–24). As a result, they were not to follow these laws in order to earn salvation from the Lord, but as the appropriate response of reverential love and worship to the Lord who had already redeemed them. This should sound very familiar to Christians, who are exhorted to live lives of wholehearted obedience as the only appropriate response to the amazing mercies of God found in Jesus (cf. Rom. 12:1 with Romans 9–11).

In order to read Leviticus well we must therefore remember these two things: (1) the many ways that Jesus has become the far greater priest who intercedes for us on the basis of his perfect and far greater atoning sacrifice; and (2) that obedience to God's law is not meant to earn his salvation but to be an appropriate response to the salvation he has so richly provided.

Where is the gospel in Leviticus? On every page.

Outline

I. Five Major Offerings (1:1–6:7)

II. Handling of the Offerings (6:8–7:38)

III. The Establishment of the Priesthood (8:1–10:20)

IV. The Laws on Cleanness and Uncleanness (11:1–15:33)

V. The Day of Atonement Ritual (16:1–34)

VI. The Handling and Meaning of Blood (17:1–16)

VII. The Call to Holiness (18:1–22:33)

VIII. Holy Times (23:1–25:55)

IX. Blessings and Curses (26:1–46)

X. Vows and Dedication (27:1–34)

Leviticus

Laws for Burnt Offerings

1 [a]The LORD called Moses and spoke to him [b]from the tent of meeting, saying, 2 “Speak to the people of Israel and say to them, [c]When any one of you brings an offering to the LORD, you shall bring your offering of livestock from the herd or from the flock.

3 “If his offering is a burnt offering from the herd, he shall offer [d]a male without blemish. He shall bring it to the entrance of the tent of meeting, that he may be accepted before the LORD. 4 [e]He shall lay his hand on the head of the burnt offering, and it shall be [f]accepted for him [g]to make atonement for him. 5 Then he shall kill the bull before the LORD, and Aaron’s sons the priests shall bring the blood [h]and throw the blood against the sides of the altar that is at the entrance of the tent of meeting. 6 Then he shall flay the burnt offering and cut it into pieces, 7 and the sons of Aaron the priest shall put fire on the altar and [i]arrange wood on the fire. 8 And Aaron’s sons the priests shall arrange the pieces, the head, and the fat, on the wood that is on the fire on the altar; 9 but its entrails and its legs he shall wash with water. And the priest shall burn all of it on the altar, as [j]a burnt offering, a food offering[1] with a [k]pleasing aroma to the LORD.

10 “If his gift for a burnt offering is from the flock, from the sheep or goats, he shall bring a male without blemish, 11 [l]and he shall kill it on the north side of the altar before the LORD, and Aaron’s sons the priests shall throw its blood against the sides of the altar. 12 And he shall cut it into pieces, with its head and its fat, and the priest shall arrange them on the wood that is on the fire on the altar, 13 but the entrails and the legs he shall wash with water. And the priest shall offer all of it and burn it on the altar; it is [j]a burnt offering, a food offering with [k]a pleasing aroma to the LORD.

14 “If his offering to the LORD is a burnt offering of birds, then he shall bring his offering of [m]turtledoves or pigeons. 15 And the priest shall bring it to the altar and wring off its head and burn it on the altar. Its blood shall be drained out on the side of the altar. 16 He shall remove its crop with its contents[2] and cast it [n]beside the altar on the east side, in the place for ashes. 17 He shall tear it open by its wings, but [o]shall

[1] Or *an offering by fire*; so throughout Leviticus [2] Or *feathers*

1:4–5 By laying a hand on the head of the blameless sacrifice, the offerer established a relationship with the animal such that it was accepted on the offerer’s behalf. This meant that the offerer received the benefits of the sacrifice, such as atonement.

In general, the word *atonement* communicates two ideas: (1) ransoming, and (2) purifying. On the one hand, sin or impurity puts people at risk of the Lord’s judgment, from which they need to be ransomed. On the other hand, sin and impurity are defiling, as a result of which people need to be purified. The word atonement has both of these in view: it is a “ransom-purification” taking place by means of the animal’s lifeblood.

Jesus was the ultimate blameless sacrifice presented on our behalf (1 Pet. 1:19), and those who put their trust in him receive all the benefits of his sacrifice, including forgiveness of sin and adoption into God’s family (Rom. 4:25–5:2; Gal. 4:4–5; 1 John 1:7). Because Jesus’ sacrifice is atoning, it is sometimes described as that which ransoms us (Matt. 20:28) and at other times as that which purifies us (Titus 2:14). In either case, we can receive this atonement because Jesus has given his lifeblood in place of our own (Rom. 5:8; 1 Pet. 3:18). This is such a precious gift, given at such a great cost, it fills us with thankful reverence and a desire to live lives worthy of our Savior (1 Cor. 6:18–20; 1 Pet. 1:17–19).

Chapter 1
1 [a]Ex. 19:3 [b]Ex. 40:34, 35
2 [c]ch. 22:18, 19
3 [d]See Ex. 12:5
4 [e]ch. 3:2, 8, 13; 4:4, 15, 24, 29, 33; 8:14, 18, 22; 16:21; Ex. 29:10, 15, 19 [f]ch. 22:21, 27; [Isa. 56:7; Rom. 12:1; Phil. 4:18] [g]ch. 4:20, 26, 31, 35; Num. 15:25; 2 Chr. 29:23, 24; [ch. 9:7; 16:24]
5 [h]ch. 3:8; 2 Chr. 35:11; Heb. 12:24; 1 Pet. 1:2
7 [i][Gen. 22:9]
9 [j]ch. 2:3, 9, 10, 11, 16; 3:5, 9, 11, 14, 16; 4:35; Ex. 29:18, 25, 41 [k]See Gen. 8:21
11 [l]ver. 5
13 [j][See ver. 9 above] [k][See ver. 9 above]
14 [m]ch. 5:7; 12:8; [Luke 2:24]
16 [n]ch. 6:10
17 [o][Gen. 15:10]

not sever it completely. And the priest shall burn it on the altar, on the wood that is on the fire. It is a burnt offering, a food offering with a pleasing aroma to the LORD.

Laws for Grain Offerings

2 "When anyone brings a [p]grain offering as an offering to the LORD, his offering shall be of fine flour. [q]He shall pour oil on it and put frankincense on it 2 and bring it to Aaron's sons the priests. And he shall take from it a handful of the fine flour and oil, with all of its frankincense, and the priest shall burn this as its [r]memorial portion on the altar, a food [s]offering with a pleasing aroma to the LORD. 3 But the [t]rest of the grain offering shall be for Aaron and his sons; [u]it is a most holy part of the LORD's food offerings.

4 "When you bring a grain offering baked in the oven as an offering, it shall be [v]unleavened loaves of fine flour mixed with oil or unleavened wafers smeared with oil. 5 And if your offering is a grain offering [w]baked on a griddle, it shall be of fine flour unleavened, mixed with oil. 6 You shall break it in pieces and pour oil on it; it is a grain offering. 7 And if your offering is a grain offering cooked in a pan, it shall be made of fine flour with oil. 8 And you shall bring the grain offering that is made of these things to the LORD, and when it is presented to the priest, he shall bring it to the altar. 9 And the priest shall take from the grain offering its memorial portion and burn this on the altar, a food [x]offering with a [y]pleasing aroma to the LORD. 10 But the [z]rest of the grain offering shall be for Aaron and his sons; [z]it is a most holy part of the LORD's food offerings.

11 "No grain offering that you bring to the LORD shall be made with [a]leaven, for you shall burn no leaven nor any honey as a food offering to the LORD. 12 [b]As an offering of firstfruits you may bring them to the LORD, but they shall not be offered on the altar for a pleasing aroma. 13 You [c]shall season all your grain offerings with salt. You shall not let the [d]salt of the covenant with your God be missing from your grain offering; [e]with all your offerings you shall offer salt.

14 "If you offer a grain offering of firstfruits to the LORD, you shall offer for the grain offering of your firstfruits fresh [f]ears, roasted with fire, crushed new grain. 15 And [g]you shall put oil on it and lay frankincense on it; it is a grain offering. 16 And the priest shall burn as its [h]memorial portion some of the crushed grain and some of the oil with all of its frankincense; it is a food offering to the LORD.

Laws for Peace Offerings

3 "If his offering is [i]a sacrifice of peace offering, if he offers an animal from the herd, male or female, [j]he shall offer it [k]without blemish before the LORD. 2 And [l]he shall lay his hand on the head of his offering and kill it at the entrance of the tent of meeting, and Aaron's sons the priests shall throw the blood against the sides of the altar. 3 And from the sacrifice of the peace offering, as a food offering to the LORD, he shall offer [m]the fat covering the entrails and all the fat that is on the entrails, 4 [n]and the two kidneys with the fat that is on them at the loins, and the long lobe of the liver that he shall remove with the kidneys. 5 Then Aaron's sons [o]shall burn it on the

2:2 As its name implies, the purpose of the memorial portion was to bring the offerer to the Lord's remembrance. This does not mean the Lord had forgotten the offerer. Rather, Israelites used such language to describe the Lord's favor toward his people and his care over them (Num. 10:9; Ps. 8:4; Isa. 38:3). By having this portion presented on their behalf, the Israelites were thanking God for his remembrance of them and acknowledging their need of the Lord's favor and grace. The thief on the cross recognized this need clearly when he said, "Jesus, remember me when you come into your kingdom" (Luke 23:42). It is a prayer Jesus gladly answers: "Truly, I say to you, today you will be with me in Paradise" (Luke 23:43). The Lord delights to "remember" those who acknowledge their need of his favor and grace.

3:1–17 Most of the meat of a peace offering was shared between offerer and priest (7:15–21, 31–34). All of the fat, however, was burned as an offering to the Lord (3:3–4). This was because the fat was considered the best part of the meat (to this day, fat is added to food to make it taste better). By giving it to the Lord, the Israelites were acknowledging that he was their sovereign King who was worthy of their honor and praise.

Chapter 2
1 [p]ch. 6:14; 9:17; Num. 15:4 [q]ver. 15
2 [r]ver. 9, 16; ch. 5:12; 6:15; 24:7; [Acts 10:4] [s]See ch. 1:9
3 [t]ch. 7:9; 10:12, 13 [u][Ex. 40:10]
4 [v]Ex. 29:2
5 [w]ch. 6:21; 7:9; [1 Chr. 23:29; Ezek. 4:3]
9 [x]See ch. 1:9 [y][Phil. 4:18]
10 [z]ver. 3
11 [a]ch. 6:17; [Matt. 16:12; Mark 8:15; Luke 12:1; 1 Cor. 5:8; Gal. 5:9]
12 [b]See Ex. 23:19
13 [c]Col. 4:6 [d]Num. 18:19; [2 Chr. 13:5] [e]Ezek. 43:24
14 [f]ch. 23:14; [Josh. 5:11]
15 [g]ver. 1
16 [h]See ver. 2
Chapter 3
1 [i]ch. 17:5; 22:21; 23:19; Amos 5:22; See ch. 7:11-21, 29-34 [j]ver. 7, 12 [k]See Ex. 12:5 **2** [l]See ch. 1:4 **3** [m]ch. 4:8, 9; Ex. 29:13, 22 **4** [n]ver. 10 **5** [o]ch. 6:12

altar on top of the burnt offering, which is on
the wood on the fire; it is a food offering with
a pleasing aroma to the LORD.
6 "If his offering for a sacrifice of peace offering to the LORD is an animal from the flock,
male or female, he shall offer it [k]without blemish. 7 If he offers a lamb for his offering, then
he shall offer it before the LORD, 8 lay his hand
on the head of his offering, and kill it in front
of the tent of meeting; and Aaron's sons shall
throw its blood against the sides of the altar.
9 Then from the sacrifice of the peace offering
he shall offer as a food offering to the LORD
its fat; he shall remove the whole [p]fat tail, cut
off close to the backbone, and the fat that covers the entrails and all the fat that is on the
entrails 10 and the two kidneys with the fat
that is on them at the loins and the long lobe
of the liver that he shall remove [q]with the kidneys. 11 And the priest shall burn it on the altar
as [r]a food offering to the LORD.
12 "If his offering is a goat, then he shall offer
it before the LORD 13 and lay his hand on its
head and kill it in front of the tent of meeting,
and the sons of Aaron shall throw its blood
against the sides of the altar. 14 Then he shall
offer from it, as his offering for a food offering to the LORD, the fat covering the entrails
and all the fat that is on the entrails 15 and the
two kidneys with the fat that is on them at
the loins and the long lobe of the liver that
he shall remove [q]with the kidneys. 16 And the
priest shall burn them on the altar as a [r]food
offering with a pleasing aroma. [s]All fat is the
LORD's. 17 It shall be a statute forever throughout your generations, in all your dwelling
places, that you eat neither [s]fat nor [t]blood."

Laws for Sin Offerings

4 And the LORD spoke to Moses, saying,
2 "Speak to the people of Israel, saying,
[u]If anyone sins unintentionally[1] in any of the
LORD's commandments [v]about things not to
be done, and does any one of them, 3 if it is the
anointed priest who [w]sins, thus bringing guilt
on the people, then he shall offer for the sin
that he has committed [x]a bull from the herd
without blemish to the LORD for a sin offering. 4 He shall bring the bull to the [y]entrance
of the tent of meeting before the LORD and
lay his hand on the head of the bull and kill
the bull before the LORD. 5 And the anointed
priest [z]shall take some of the blood of the bull
and bring it into the tent of meeting, 6 and
the priest shall dip his finger in the blood and
[z]sprinkle part of the blood seven times before
the LORD in front of the veil of the sanctuary.
7 And the priest [a]shall put some of the blood
on the horns of the altar of fragrant incense
before the LORD that is in the tent of meeting,
and [b]all the rest of the blood of the bull he
shall pour out at the base of the altar of burnt
offering that is at the entrance of the tent of
meeting. 8 And all the fat of the bull of the sin
offering he shall remove from it, [c]the fat that
covers the entrails and all the fat that is on
the entrails 9 [d]and the two kidneys with the
fat that is on them at the loins and the long
lobe of the liver that he shall remove with the
kidneys 10 (just as these arc taken from the ox

[1] Or *by mistake*; so throughout Leviticus

The fat is described as a "food offering" (vv. 5, 11) to emphasize that the entire sacrifice functions like a meal. In particular, people in ancient Israel often ate together to confirm a covenant relationship (Gen. 26:28–30; 31:44–46, 53–54; Ex. 24:9–11). The peace offering functioned in this way, enabling the Israelites to reaffirm their covenant relationship to one another and to the sovereign God who had rescued them. Jesus uses the concept of a covenant meal when he establishes the Lord's Supper (cf. Luke 22:20 with Ex. 24:8). It is a time for believers to reaffirm their covenant commitment to one another and to the covenant Lord who has so graciously redeemed them (1 Cor. 10:17; 11:23–26). Remembering the Lord's sovereignty and redemption is the spring from which a life of wholehearted faithfulness gratefully flows.

4:1–5:13 The Bible often uses the metaphor of impurity to describe sin (16:30; 20:3; Ezek. 36:17). It is a metaphor we can identify with: sin often makes us feel dirty (cf. Ps. 51:2). For the Israelites, their sin defiled both themselves and the Lord's holy dwelling place in their midst (Lev. 15:31). Because of his great purity, the Lord could not allow such defilement to remain in his holy camp. But because of his great mercy, he provided a way for the Israelites to remove this impurity: the sin offering, in which the lifeblood of an animal without blemish ransomed sinners from the Lord's just punishment and cleansed the defilement of their sin (cf. at 1:4–5).

6 [k] [See ver. 1 above]
9 [p] ch. 9:19; Ex. 29:22
10 [q] ver. 4
11 [r] ch. 21:6, 8, 17, 21, 22; 22:7, 25; Num. 28:2; Ezek. 44:7; Mal. 1:7
15 [q] [See ver. 10 above]
16 [r] [See ver. 11 above] [s] ch. 7:23-25; 1 Sam. 2:15; Ezek. 44:7, 15
17 [s] [See ver. 16 above] [t] ch. 7:26; 17:10, 14; 19:26; Gen. 9:4; Deut. 12:16, 23; 15:23; 1 Sam. 14:33; Acts 15:20, 29

Chapter 4
2 [u] ch. 5:15, 18; [Ps. 19:12]; See Num. 15:22-29 [v] ver. 13, 22, 27; ch. 5:17
3 [w] [Heb. 7:27, 28] [x] ch. 9:2
4 [y] ch. 1:3, 4
5 [z] ver. 16, 17; ch. 5:9; 16:14; Num. 19:4; [Isa. 52:15]
6 [z] [See ver. 5 above]
7 [a] ch. 8:15; 9:9; 16:18; [Ex. 39:38] [b] ch. 5:9; 8:15; 9:9; Ex. 29:12
8 [c] ch. 3:3
9 [d] ch. 3:4

of the sacrifice of the peace offerings); and the priest shall burn them on the altar of burnt offering. [11] But [e]the skin of the bull and all its flesh, with its head, its legs, its entrails, and its dung— [12] all the rest of the bull—he shall carry [f]outside the camp to a clean place, to the ash heap, and shall [g]burn it up on a fire of wood. On the ash heap it shall be burned up.

[13] [h]"If the whole congregation of Israel sins unintentionally[1] and [i]the thing is hidden from the eyes of the assembly, and they do any one of the things that by the LORD's commandments ought not to be done, and they realize their guilt,[2] [14] [j]when the sin which they have committed becomes known, the assembly shall offer a bull from the herd for a sin offering and bring it in front of the tent of meeting. [15] And the elders of the congregation [k]shall lay their hands on the head of the bull before the LORD, and the bull shall be killed before the LORD. [16] Then [l]the anointed priest shall bring some of the blood of the bull into the tent of meeting, [17] and the priest shall dip his finger in the blood and sprinkle it seven times before the LORD in front of the veil. [18] And he shall put some of the blood on the horns of the altar that is in the tent of meeting before the LORD, and the rest of the blood he shall pour out at the base of the altar of burnt offering that is at the entrance of the tent of meeting. [19] And all its fat he shall take from it and burn on the altar. [20] Thus shall he do with the bull. As he did [m]with the bull of the sin offering, so shall he do with this. [n]And the priest shall make atonement for them, and they shall be forgiven. [21] And he shall carry the bull [f]outside the camp and burn it up as he burned the first bull; it is the sin offering for the assembly.

[22] "When a leader sins, [o]doing unintentionally any one of all the things that by the commandments of the LORD his God ought not to be done, and realizes his guilt, [23] or [p]the sin which he has committed is made known to him, he shall bring as his offering a goat, a male without blemish, [24] and [q]shall lay his hand on the head of the goat and kill it in the place where they kill the burnt offering before the LORD; it is a sin offering. [25] [r]Then the priest shall take some of the blood of the sin offering with his finger and put it on the horns of the altar of burnt offering and pour out the rest of its blood at the base of the altar of burnt offering. [26] And all its fat he shall burn on the altar, like [s]the fat of the sacrifice of peace offerings. So [t]the priest shall make atonement for him for his sin, and he shall be forgiven.

[27] "If [u]anyone of the common people sins unintentionally in doing any one of the things that by the LORD's commandments ought not to be done, and realizes his guilt, [28] [v]or the sin which he has committed is made known to him, he shall bring for his offering a goat, a female without blemish, for his sin which he has committed. [29] [w]And he shall lay his hand on the head of the sin offering and kill the sin offering in the place of burnt offering. [30] And the priest shall take some of its blood with his finger and put it on the horns of the altar of burnt offering and pour out all the rest of its blood at the base of the altar. [31] And [x]all its fat he shall remove, [y]as the fat is removed from the peace offerings, and the priest shall burn it on the altar for a [z]pleasing aroma to the LORD. [a]And the priest shall make atonement for him, and he shall be forgiven.

[32] "If he brings a lamb as his offering for a sin offering, he shall bring [b]a female without blemish [33] [w]and lay his hand on the head of the sin offering and kill it for a sin offering in the place where they kill the burnt offering. [34] Then the priest shall take some of the blood of the sin offering with his finger and put it on the horns of the altar of burnt offering and pour out all the rest of its blood at the base of the altar. [35] And all its fat he shall remove [c]as the fat of the lamb is removed from the sacrifice of peace offerings, and the priest shall burn it on the altar, on top of the LORD's food

[1] Or *makes a mistake* [2] Or *suffer for their guilt*, or *are guilty*; also verses 22, 27, and chapter 5

11 [e] ch. 9:11; Ex. 29:14; Num. 19:5
12 [f] ch. 6:11; 10:4, 5; 14:3; 16:27; 24:14, 23; Ex. 29:14; 33:7 [g] Heb. 13:11
13 [h] Num. 15:24-26 [i] ch. 5:2-4
14 [j] ver. 23
15 [k] See ch. 1:4

The sin offering prefigured for God's people the mercy we see in a far greater way in Jesus' sacrificial death. This was the ultimate sin offering (Rom. 8:3; Heb. 1:3; 13:11–12), and it was great enough to cleanse all our sins (Heb. 9:28; 10:10, 12, 14; 1 John 1:9). Because of this, we can boldly draw near to God, knowing that because of Jesus' sacrifice we are fully cleansed of all sin and impurity and therefore fully accepted by the Father (Heb. 10:19–22).

16 [l] See ver. 5-12 **20** [m] ver. 3 [n] Num. 15:25, 28 **21** [f] [See ver. 12 above] **22** [o] ver. 2, 13, 27 **23** [p] ver. 14 **24** [q] See ch. 1:4 **25** [r] ver. 7, 18, 30, 34 **26** [s] ver. 31; ch. 3:3, 5 [t] ver. 20, 31, 35; ch. 5:10, 13, 16, 18; 6:7; 14:18; 15:15 **27** [u] ver. 2; Num. 15:27 **28** [v] ver. 14, 23 **29** [w] ver. 4, 15, 24; See ch. 1:4 **31** [x] ch. 3:14 [y] ver. 10, 26; ch. 3:3 [z] ch. 1:9; See Gen. 8:21 [a] ver. 20, 26, 35 **32** [b] ver. 28 **33** [w] [See ver. 29 above] **35** [c] ch. 3:3, 9

offerings. [d]And the priest shall make atonement for him for the sin which he has committed, and he shall be forgiven.

5 “If anyone sins in that he hears a public
[e]adjuration to testify, and though he is a
witness, whether he has seen or come to know
the matter, yet does not speak, he shall [f]bear
his iniquity; 2 or [g]if anyone touches an unclean
thing, whether a carcass of an unclean wild
animal or a carcass of unclean livestock or a
carcass of unclean swarming things, and it is
hidden from him and he has become unclean,
and he realizes his guilt; 3 or if he touches
[h]human uncleanness, of whatever sort the
uncleanness may be with which one becomes
unclean, and it is hidden from him, when he
comes to know it, and realizes his guilt; 4 or if
anyone utters with his lips a [i]rash oath to do
evil or to do good, any sort of rash oath that
people [j]swear, and it is hidden from him, when
he comes to know it, and he realizes his guilt
in any of these; 5 when he realizes his guilt
in any of these and [k]confesses the sin he has
committed, 6 he shall bring to the LORD as his
compensation[1] for the sin that he has committed, a female from the flock, a lamb or a goat,
for a sin offering. And the priest shall make
atonement for him for his sin.

7 “But [l]if he cannot afford a lamb, then he
shall bring to the LORD as his compensation
for the sin that he has committed two [m]turtle-
doves or two pigeons,[2] one for a sin offering
and the other for a burnt offering. 8 He shall
bring them to the priest, who shall offer first
the one for the sin offering. He shall [n]wring
its head from its neck [n]but shall not sever it
completely, 9 and he shall sprinkle some of the
blood of the sin offering on the side of the altar,
while [o]the rest of the blood shall be drained
out [p]at the base of the altar; it is a sin offering.
10 Then he shall offer the second for a burnt
offering according to the rule. [q]And the priest
shall make atonement for him for the sin that
he has committed, and he shall be forgiven.

11 “But if he cannot afford two turtledoves
or two pigeons, then he shall bring as his
offering for the sin that he has committed a
[r]tenth of an ephah[3] of fine flour for a sin offering. He [r]shall put no oil on it and shall put
no frankincense on it, for it is a sin offering.
12 And he shall bring it to [s]the priest, and the
priest shall take a handful of it as its memorial portion and [t]burn this on the altar, on
the LORD's food offerings; it is a sin offering.
13 Thus [q]the priest shall make atonement for
him for the sin which he has committed in any
one of these things, and he shall be forgiven.
And the remainder[4] shall be for the priest, as
in the grain offering.”

Laws for Guilt Offerings

14 The LORD spoke to Moses, saying, 15 [u]“If
anyone commits a breach of faith and sins
unintentionally in any of the holy things of
the LORD, [v]he shall bring to the LORD as his
compensation, a ram without blemish out of
the flock, valued[5] in silver shekels,[6] according to the [w]shekel of the sanctuary, for a guilt
offering. 16 He shall also make restitution for
what he has done amiss in the holy thing and
[x]shall add a fifth to it and give it to the priest.
[q]And the priest shall make atonement for him
with the ram of the guilt offering, and he shall
be forgiven.

17 [y]“If anyone sins, doing any of the things
that by the LORD's commandments ought not

[1] Hebrew *his guilt penalty*; so throughout Leviticus [2] Septuagint *two young pigeons*; also verse 11 [3] An *ephah* was about 3/5 bushel or 22 liters [4] Septuagint; Hebrew *it* [5] Or *flock, or its equivalent* [6] A *shekel* was about 2/5 ounce or 11 grams

5:14–6:7 A guilt offering was brought when Israelites sinned by defiling something belonging to the Lord. Such possessions included holy food items (5:14–16; cf. 22:10–16; Num. 18:8–13) or even the Lord's own holy name (Lev. 6:1–7; v. 3 assumes a false oath in the Lord's name). This offering was to be brought even when people *suspected* they might have committed such an offense (5:17–19). In either case (of actual or suspected sin), to sin against what belonged to the holy King was to show disrespect to the King himself, while to show respect to what was his was to respect him.

Paul applies this principle to believers when he exhorts us to be sexually pure, in this way acknowledging that we belong to the Lord and have been bought at a great price: Jesus' lifeblood (1 Cor. 6:18–20; cf. Eph. 1:7). When we revere God's holiness and the greatness of the redemption he has accomplished for us, we are spurred to live holy lives as an act of reverential worship before our holy and redeeming King.

35 [d]ver. 20, 26, 31

Chapter 5

1 [e]1 Kgs. 8:31; Prov. 29:24; [1 Sam. 14:24, 26; Matt. 26:63] [f]ver. 17; ch. 7:18; 10:17; 17:16; 19:8; 20:17, 19; Num. 5:31; [Num. 9:13]
2 [g]ch. 11:24, 28, 31, 39; Num. 19:11, 13, 16
3 [h]See ch. 12; ch. 13; ch. 15
4 [i][Judg. 11:30, 31; 1 Sam. 14:24; 25:22; Mark 6:23; Acts 23:12] [j]Eccles. 5:2
5 [k]ch. 16:21; 26:40; Num. 5:7; Ezra 10:1; [Josh. 7:19]
7 [l]ch. 12:8; 14:21 [m]See ch. 1:14
8 [n]ch. 1:15, 17
9 [o]ch. 1:15 [p]ch. 4:7, 18, 30, 34
10 [q]See ch. 4:20, 26, 31, 35

11 [r]Num. 5:15 **12** [s]ch. 2:2 [t]ch. 4:35 **13** [q][See ver. 10 above] **15** [u]ch. 22:14; [Ezra 10:2] [v][Ezra 10:19] [w]See Ex. 30:13 **16** [x]ch. 6:5; 22:14; 27:13, 15, 27, 31; Num. 5:7 [q][See ver. 10 above] **17** [y]ch. 4:2

to be done, [z]though he did not know it, then
realizes his guilt, he shall bear his iniquity.
18 [a]He shall bring to the priest a ram without
blemish out of the flock, or its equivalent for
a guilt offering, and [q]the priest shall make
atonement for him for the mistake that he
made unintentionally, and he shall be forgiven. 19 It is a guilt offering; he has indeed
incurred guilt before[1] the LORD."

6 [2] The LORD spoke to Moses, saying, 2 "If
anyone sins and [b]commits a breach
of faith against the LORD by [c]deceiving his
neighbor in [d]a matter of deposit or security,
or through robbery, or [e]if he has oppressed his
neighbor 3 or [f]has found something lost and
lied about it, [g]swearing falsely—in any of all
the things that people do and sin thereby—
4 if he has sinned and has realized his guilt
and will restore [e]what he took by robbery or
what he got by oppression or the deposit that
was committed to him or the lost thing that he
found 5 or anything about which he has sworn
falsely, he shall [h]restore it in full and shall
add a fifth to it, and give it to him to whom it
belongs on the day he realizes his guilt. 6 And
he shall bring to the priest as his compensation to the LORD [i]a ram without blemish out of
the flock, or its equivalent for a guilt offering.
7 [j]And the priest shall make atonement for him
before the LORD, and he shall be forgiven for
any of the things that one may do and thereby
become guilty."

The Priests and the Offerings

8 [3] The LORD spoke to Moses, saying, 9 "Command Aaron and his sons, saying, This is the
law of the burnt offering. The burnt offering
shall be on the hearth on the altar all night
until the morning, and the fire of the altar
shall be kept burning on it. 10 And [k]the priest
shall put on his linen garment and put his
linen undergarment on his body, and he shall
take up the ashes to which the fire has reduced
the burnt offering on the altar and put them
[l]beside the altar. 11 Then [m]he shall take off his
garments and put on other garments and
carry the ashes [n]outside the camp to a clean
place. 12 The fire on the altar shall be kept burning on it; it shall not go out. The priest shall
burn wood on it every morning, and he shall
arrange the burnt offering on it and shall burn
on it [o]the fat of the peace offerings. 13 Fire shall
be kept burning on the altar continually; it
shall not go out.

14 "And this is the law of [p]the grain offering.
The sons of Aaron shall offer it before the
LORD in front of the altar. 15 And one shall
take from it a handful of the fine flour of the
grain offering and its oil and all the frankincense that is on the grain offering and burn
this as its [q]memorial portion on the altar, a
pleasing aroma to the LORD. 16 And [r]the rest
of it Aaron and his sons shall eat. It shall be
eaten unleavened [s]in a holy place. In the court
of the tent of meeting they shall eat it. 17 [t]It
shall not be baked with leaven. [u]I have given
it as their portion of my food offerings. [v]It is a
thing most holy, like the sin offering and the
guilt offering. 18 Every male among the children of Aaron may eat of it, as decreed forever
throughout your generations, from the LORD's
food offerings. Whatever touches them shall
become holy."

19 The LORD spoke to Moses, saying, 20 [w]"This
is the offering that Aaron and his sons shall
offer to the LORD on the day when he is
anointed: a [x]tenth of an ephah[4] of fine flour
as a regular grain offering, half of it in the
morning and half in the evening. 21 It shall be
made with oil [y]on a griddle. You shall bring
it [z]well mixed, in baked[5] pieces like a grain
offering, and offer it for a pleasing aroma to

[1] Or *he has paid full compensation to* [2] Ch 5:20 in Hebrew [3] Ch 6:1 in Hebrew [4] An *ephah* was about 3/5 bushel or 22 liters [5] The meaning of the Hebrew is uncertain

6:8–7:38 This section explains laws on the five major offerings introduced in 1:1–6:7. It differs from the earlier section in that it focuses on the proper handling of the various offering portions, such as the ritual state necessary for touching or eating the offerings (6:25, 27, 29; 7:6, 19–21), how to distribute offering portions among the priests (6:16, 18, 26; 7:6–10), and how to dispose of any remains (6:10–11, 22–23). In doing so, it emphasizes two themes. First, these offerings had to be treated properly because they were the Lord's holy property (cf. at 5:14–6:7). Second, it was important to provide for the priests' practical needs so they could focus on leading the Lord's people in worship and teaching them his laws (cf. Neh. 13:10–11).

17 [z] Num. 15:29; [Luke 12:48]
18 [a] ver. 15 [q] [See ver. 10 above]

Chapter 6
2 [b] Num. 5:6 [c] ch. 19:11 [d] Ex. 22:7, 10 [e] ch. 19:13; Mic. 2:2
3 [f] Ex. 23:4; Deut. 22:1-3 [g] ch. 19:12; Ex. 22:11
4 [e] [See ver. 2 above]
5 [h] Num. 5:7; [ch. 5:16; 2 Sam. 12:6; Luke 19:8]
6 [i] ch. 5:15, 18
7 [j] See ch. 4:26

10 [k] ch. 16:4; Ezek. 44:18; See Ex. 28:39-43 [l] ch. 1:16 **11** [m] ch. 16:23; Ezek. 42:14; 44:19 [n] See ch. 4:12 **12** [o] ch. 3:3, 9, 14 **14** [p] ch. 2:1; Num. 15:4 **15** [q] ch. 2:2, 9 **16** [r] ch. 2:3, 10; Ezek. 44:29; [1 Cor. 9:13] [s] ver. 26; ch. 10:12, 13 **17** [t] ch. 2:11 [u] Num. 18:9 [v] ver. 25, 29; ch. 2:3; 7:1 **20** [w] Ex. 29:1, 2 [x] ch. 5:11; Ex. 16:36 **21** [y] ch. 2:5; 7:9 [z] ch. 7:12

the LORD. 22 The priest from among Aaron's sons, who is anointed to succeed him, shall offer it to the LORD as decreed forever. [a]The whole of it shall be burned. 23 Every grain offering of a priest shall be wholly burned. It shall not be eaten."

24 The LORD spoke to Moses, saying, 25 "Speak to Aaron and his sons, saying, [b]This is the law of the sin offering. [c]In the place where the burnt offering is killed shall the sin offering be killed before the LORD; [d]it is most holy. 26 [e]The priest who offers it for sin shall eat it. [f]In a holy place it shall be eaten, in the court of the tent of meeting. 27 Whatever touches its flesh shall be holy, and when any of its blood is splashed on a garment, you shall wash that on which it was splashed in a holy place. 28 And [g]the earthenware vessel in which it is boiled [h]shall be broken. But if it is boiled in a bronze vessel, that shall be scoured and rinsed in water. 29 Every male among the priests may eat of it; [d]it is most holy. 30 [i]But no sin offering shall be eaten from which any blood is brought into the tent of meeting to make atonement in the Holy Place; it shall be burned up with fire.

7 [j]"This is the law of the [k]guilt offering. [l]It is most holy. 2 [m]In the place where they kill the burnt offering they shall kill the guilt offering, and its blood shall be thrown against the sides of the altar. 3 And [n]all its fat shall be offered, the fat tail, the fat that covers the entrails, 4 the two kidneys with the fat that is on them at the loins, and the long lobe of the liver that he shall remove [o]with the kidneys. 5 The priest shall burn them on the altar as a food offering to the LORD; it is a guilt offering. 6 [p]Every male among the priests may eat of it. It shall be eaten in a holy place. [q]It is most holy. 7 The [r]guilt offering is just like the sin offering; there is one law for them. The priest who makes atonement with it shall have it. 8 And the priest who offers any man's burnt offering shall have for himself the skin of the burnt offering that he has offered. 9 And [s]every grain offering baked [t]in the oven and all that is prepared [u]on a pan or a griddle shall belong to the priest who offers it. 10 And every grain offering, mixed with oil or dry, shall be shared equally among all the sons of Aaron.

11 "And this is the law of the sacrifice of peace offerings that one may offer to the LORD. 12 If he offers it for a thanksgiving, then he shall offer with the thanksgiving sacrifice [v]unleavened loaves mixed with oil, unleavened wafers smeared with oil, and loaves of fine flour [w]well mixed with oil. 13 [x]With the sacrifice of his peace offerings for thanksgiving he shall bring his offering with loaves of leavened bread. 14 And from it he shall offer one loaf from each offering, as a [y]gift to the LORD. [z]It shall belong to the priest who throws the blood of the peace offerings. 15 And the flesh of the sacrifice of his peace offerings [a]for thanksgiving shall be eaten on the day of his offering. He shall not leave any of it until the morning. 16 But [b]if the sacrifice of his offering is a vow offering or a freewill offering, it shall be eaten on the day that he offers his sacrifice, and on the next day what remains of it shall be eaten. 17 But what remains of the flesh of the sacrifice on the third day shall be burned up with fire. 18 If any of the flesh of the sacrifice of his peace offering is eaten on the third day, he who offers it shall not be accepted, neither shall it be credited to him. It is [c]tainted, and he who eats of it shall bear his iniquity.

19 "Flesh that touches any unclean thing shall not be eaten. It shall be burned up with fire. All who are clean may eat flesh, 20 but the person who eats of the flesh of the sacrifice of the LORD's peace offerings [d]while an uncleanness is on him, that person shall be cut off from his people. 21 And if anyone touches an unclean thing, whether [e]human uncleanness or an [f]unclean beast or any [g]unclean detestable creature, and then eats some flesh from the sacrifice of the LORD's peace offerings, that person shall be cut off from his people."

22 The LORD spoke to Moses, saying, 23 "Speak

This principle of providing for the leaders of the Lord's people is carried on by the New Testament as well (1 Cor. 9:13–14; Gal. 6:6). We do so in obedience to the Lord, who is our Good Shepherd and has provided us with leaders to shepherd us in his holy ways and to extend his care to us (John 21:15–17; Acts 20:28).

22 [a] Ex. 29:25 **25** [b] See ch. 4 [c] ch. 1:3, 5, 11; 4:24, 29, 33; [ch. 7:2] [d] ver. 17, 29 **26** [e] ch. 10:17, 18; Num. 18:9, 19; Ezek. 44:27-29 [f] ver. 16 **28** [g] ch. 11:32, 33; 15:12 [h] [ch. 11:33; 15:12] **29** [d] [See ver. 25 above] **30** [i] ch. 4:7, 11, 12, 18, 21; 16:27; Heb. 13:11; [ver. 26, 29; ch. 10:18] **Chapter 7** **1** [j] See ch. 5:1–6:7 [k] ver. 37 [l] ch. 6:17, 25 **2** [m] ch. 6:25 **3** [n] ch. 3:3, 4, 9, 10, 14-16; 4:8, 9; Ex. 29:13, 22 **4** [o] ch. 3:4 **6** [p] ch. 6:18, 29 [q] ver. 1 **7** [r] ch. 6:25, 26; 14:13 **9** [s] ch. 2:3, 10; Num. 18:9; Ezek. 44:29 [t] ch. 2:7 [u] ch. 2:5; 6:21 **12** [v] ch. 2:4; Num. 6:15 [w] ch. 6:21 **13** [x] Amos 4:5 **14** [y] Ex. 29:27, 28 [z] Num. 18:8, 11, 19 **15** [a] ch. 22:29, 30 **16** [b] ch. 19:6-8; 22:21 **18** [c] ch. 19:7 **20** [d] ch. 15:3; 22:3 **21** [e] See ch. 12; ch. 13; ch. 15 [f] See ch. 11:24-28 [g] See ch. 11:10-23

to the people of Israel, saying, [h]You shall eat no fat, of ox or sheep or goat. 24 The fat of an animal [i]that dies of itself and the fat of one that is torn by beasts may be put to any other use, but on no account shall you eat it. 25 For every person who eats of the fat of an animal of which a food offering may be made to the LORD shall be cut off from his people. 26 Moreover, [j]you shall eat no blood whatever, whether of fowl or of animal, in any of your dwelling places. 27 Whoever eats any blood, that person shall be cut off from his people."

28 The LORD spoke to Moses, saying, 29 "Speak to the people of Israel, saying, [k]Whoever offers the sacrifice of his peace offerings to the LORD shall bring his offering to the LORD from the sacrifice of his peace offerings. 30 [l]His own hands shall bring the LORD's food offerings. He shall bring the fat with [m]the breast, that the breast may be waved as a wave offering before the LORD. 31 [n]The priest shall burn the fat on the altar, but [o]the breast shall be for Aaron and his sons. 32 And [o]the right thigh you shall give to the priest as a contribution from the sacrifice of your peace offerings. 33 Whoever among the sons of Aaron offers the blood of the peace offerings and the fat shall have the right thigh for a portion. 34 For the breast that is [o]waved and the thigh that is [o]contributed I have taken from the people of Israel, out of the sacrifices of their peace offerings, and [p]have given them to Aaron the priest and to his sons, as a perpetual due from the people of Israel. 35 This is the portion of Aaron and of his sons from the LORD's food offerings, from the day they were presented to serve as priests of the LORD. 36 The LORD commanded this to be given them by the people of Israel, [q]from the day that he anointed them. It is a perpetual due throughout their generations."

37 This is the law [r]of the burnt offering, of the grain offering, of the sin offering, [s]of the guilt offering, [t]of the ordination offering, and [u]of the peace offering, 38 which the LORD commanded Moses on Mount Sinai, on the day that he commanded the people of Israel [v]to bring their offerings to the LORD, in the wilderness of Sinai.

Consecration of Aaron and His Sons

8 [w]The LORD spoke to Moses, saying, 2 "Take Aaron and his sons with him, and [x]the garments and [y]the anointing oil and the bull of the sin offering and the two rams and the basket of unleavened bread. 3 And assemble all the congregation at the entrance of the tent of meeting." 4 And Moses did as the LORD commanded him, and the congregation was assembled at the entrance of the tent of meeting.

5 And Moses said to the congregation, [z]"This is the thing that the LORD has commanded to be done." 6 And Moses brought Aaron and his sons and washed them with water. 7 And he put [a]the coat on him and tied the sash around his waist and clothed him with the robe and put the ephod on him and tied the skillfully woven band of the ephod around him, binding it to him with the band.[1] 8 And he placed the breastpiece on him, and [b]in the breastpiece he put the Urim and the Thummim. 9 And he set [a]the turban on his head, and [c]on the turban, in front, he set the golden plate, the holy crown, as the LORD commanded Moses.

10 [d]Then Moses took the anointing oil and anointed the tabernacle and all that was in it, and consecrated them. 11 And he sprinkled some of it on the altar seven times, and anointed the altar and all its utensils and the basin and its stand, to consecrate them. 12 And [e]he poured some of the anointing oil on Aaron's head and anointed him to consecrate him. 13 And Moses brought Aaron's sons

[1] Hebrew *with it*

23[h] ch. 3:16, 17
24[i] ch. 17:15; 22:8; Ex. 22:31; Deut. 14:21; Ezek. 4:14; 44:31
26[j] See ch. 3:17
29[k] ch. 3:1
30[l] ch. 3:3, 4, 9, 14 [m] See Ex. 29:24
31[n] ch. 3:5, 11, 16 [o] [ch. 9:21; Num. 6:20]
32[o] [See ver. 31 above]
34[o] [See ver. 31 above]

8:1–36 This chapter describes the ordination ceremony for priests. It emphasizes two themes. The first is the Israelites' need of holy priestly mediators before the Lord, mediators who could atone for the Israelites' sins and present their offerings to the Lord. That the Lord provided such mediators was a clear demonstration of his desire for the Israelites to enjoy close covenant fellowship with him. His provision of Jesus Christ—the ultimate holy priestly Mediator—demonstrates the same. The Lord desires to save us and bring us into covenant fellowship with himself (1 Tim. 2:4–5; Heb. 7:25; 10:19–22; 1 John 2:1).

[p] Ex. 29:28; Num. 18:18, 19 **36**[q] ch. 8:12, 30; Ex. 40:13-15 **37**[r] ch. 6:9, 14, 25 [s] ver. 1 [t] ch. 6:20; Ex. 29:1 [u] ver. 11 **38**[v] ch. 1:2 **Chapter 8** **1**[w] See Ex. 29 **2**[x] See Ex. 28:2-4 [y] See Ex. 30:23-25 **5**[z] Ex. 29:4 **7**[a] Ex. 28:4 **8**[b] See Ex. 28:30 **9**[a] [See ver. 7 above] [c] ch. 21:12; Ex. 28:36, 37 **10**[d] See Ex. 30:26-29 **12**[e] ch. 21:10, 12; Ex. 30:30; Ps. 133:2

and clothed them with coats and tied sashes around their waists and bound caps on them, as the LORD commanded Moses.

14 Then he brought [f]the bull of the sin offering, and Aaron and his sons [g]laid their hands on the head of the bull of the sin offering. 15 And he[1] killed it, and [h]Moses took the blood, and with his finger put it on the horns of the altar around it and purified the altar and poured out the blood at the base of the altar and consecrated it to make atonement for it. 16 [i]And he took all the fat that was on the entrails and the long lobe of the liver and the two kidneys with their fat, and Moses burned them on the altar. 17 But [j]the bull and its skin and its flesh and its dung he burned up with fire outside the camp, as the LORD commanded Moses.

18 [k]Then he presented the ram of the burnt offering, and Aaron and his sons laid their hands on the head of the ram. 19 And he killed it, and Moses threw the blood against the sides of the altar. 20 He cut the ram into pieces, and Moses burned [l]the head and the pieces and the fat. 21 He washed the entrails and the legs with water, and Moses burned the whole ram on the altar. It was a burnt offering with a pleasing aroma, a food offering for the LORD, as the LORD commanded Moses.

22 Then [m]he presented the other ram, the ram of ordination, and Aaron and his sons laid their hands on the head of the ram. 23 And he killed it, and Moses took some of its blood and [n]put it on the lobe of Aaron's right ear and on the thumb of his right hand and on the big toe of his right foot. 24 Then he presented Aaron's sons, and Moses put some of the blood on the lobes of their right ears and on the thumbs of their right hands and on the big toes of their right feet. And Moses threw the blood against the sides of the altar. 25 Then he took the fat and the fat tail and all the fat that was on the entrails and the long lobe of the liver and the two kidneys with their fat and the right thigh, 26 and out of the basket of unleavened bread that was before the LORD he took one unleavened loaf and one loaf of bread with oil and one wafer and placed them on the pieces of fat and on the right thigh. 27 And he put all these in the hands of Aaron and in the hands of his sons and waved them as a wave offering before the LORD. 28 Then Moses took them from their hands and burned them on the altar with the burnt offering. This was an ordination offering with a pleasing aroma, a food offering to the LORD. 29 And Moses took the breast and waved it for a wave offering before the LORD. It was Moses' portion of the ram of ordination, as the LORD commanded Moses.

30 Then [o]Moses took some of the anointing oil and of the blood that was on the altar and sprinkled it on Aaron and his garments, and also on his sons and his sons' garments. So he consecrated Aaron and his garments, and his sons and his sons' garments with him.

31 And Moses said to Aaron and his sons, "Boil the flesh at the entrance of the tent of meeting, and there eat it and the bread that is in the basket of ordination offerings, as I commanded, saying, 'Aaron and his sons shall eat it.' 32 And what remains of the flesh and the bread you shall burn up with fire. 33 And you shall not go outside the entrance of the tent of meeting for seven days, until the days of your ordination are completed, for it [p]will take seven days to ordain you. 34 As has been done today, the LORD has commanded to be done to make atonement for you. 35 At the entrance of the tent of meeting you shall remain day and night for seven days, performing what the LORD has [q]charged, so that you do not die, for so I have been commanded." 36 And Aaron and his sons did all the things that the LORD commanded by Moses.

[1] Probably Aaron or his representative; possibly Moses; also verses 16–23

The second theme is that the priests were not holy in and of themselves. They were just as sinful and impure as the other Israelites, and therefore they needed a series of elaborate rites in order to bring themselves into a state of ritual holiness. In strong contrast to this, Jesus Christ, the Great High Priest (Heb. 4:14; 10:21), never sinned and therefore never needed atonement. Instead, he made perfect atonement by his holy life and offered himself as the ultimate atoning sacrifice for sinners (Heb. 7:26–27; 9:12, 14, 26; 1 Pet. 3:18). Those who understand these things look to him alone for their salvation, "For there is one God, and there is one mediator between God and men, the man Christ Jesus" (1 Tim. 2:5).

14 [f]Ezek. 43:19 [g]ch. 4:4
15 [h]ch. 4:7; Ezek. 43:20, 26; [Heb. 9:22]
16 [i]ch. 3:4; 4:8
17 [j]ch. 4:11, 12
18 [k]ver. 2
20 [l]ch. 1:8
22 [m]ver. 2
23 [n]See ch. 14:14-17
30 [o]Ex. 30:30; Num. 3:3
33 [p]Ezek. 43:25, 26
35 [q]Num. 3:7; 9:19; Deut. 11:1; 1 Kgs. 2:3; Zech. 3:7

The LORD Accepts Aaron's Offering

9 [r]On the eighth day Moses called Aaron and
his sons and the elders of Israel, 2 and he
said to Aaron, [s]"Take for yourself a bull calf
for a sin offering and [t]a ram for a burnt offering, both without blemish, and offer them
before the LORD. 3 And say to the people of
Israel, [u]'Take a male goat for a sin offering,
and a calf and a lamb, both a year old without
blemish, for a burnt offering, 4 and an ox and
a ram for peace offerings, to sacrifice before
the LORD, and [v]a grain offering mixed with
oil, for [w]today the LORD will appear to you.'"
5 And they brought what Moses commanded
in front of the tent of meeting, and all the
congregation drew near and stood before the
LORD. 6 And Moses said, "This is the thing
that the LORD commanded you to do, that the
glory of the LORD may appear to you." 7 Then
Moses said to Aaron, "Draw near to the altar
and [x]offer your sin offering and your burnt
offering and [y]make atonement for yourself
and for the people, and bring the offering of
the people and make atonement for them, as
the LORD has commanded."
8 So Aaron drew near to the altar and killed
the calf of the sin offering, which was for
himself. 9 [z]And the sons of Aaron presented
the blood to him, and he dipped his finger in
the blood and [a]put it on the horns of the altar
and poured out the blood at the base of the
altar. 10 [b]But the fat and the kidneys and the
long lobe of the liver from the sin offering he
burned on the altar, [c]as the LORD commanded
Moses. 11 [d]The flesh and the skin he burned up
with fire outside the camp.
12 Then he killed the burnt offering, and
Aaron's sons handed him the blood, and he
[e]threw it against the sides of the altar. 13 [f]And
they handed the burnt offering to him, piece
by piece, and the head, and he burned them on
the altar. 14 [g]And he washed the entrails and the
legs and burned them with the burnt offering
on the altar.
15 [h]Then he presented the people's offering
and took the goat of the sin offering that
was for the people and killed it and [i]offered
it as a sin offering, [j]like the first one. 16 And
he presented the burnt offering and offered
it [k]according to the [l]rule. 17 And he presented
the [m]grain offering, took a handful of it, and
burned it on the altar, [n]besides the burnt offering of the morning.
18 Then he killed the ox and the ram, [o]the
sacrifice of peace offerings for the people. And
Aaron's sons handed him the blood, and he
threw it against the sides of the altar. 19 But
the fat pieces of the ox and of the ram, the fat
tail and that which covers [p]the entrails and
the kidneys and the long lobe of the liver—
20 they put the fat pieces on the breasts, [q]and
he burned the fat pieces on the altar, 21 but the
breasts and the right thigh Aaron waved [r]for
a wave offering before the LORD, as Moses
commanded.
22 Then Aaron [s]lifted up his hands toward
the people and [t]blessed them, and he came
down from offering the sin offering and the
burnt offering and the peace offerings. 23 And
Moses and Aaron went into the tent of meeting, and when they came out they blessed the
people, and [u]the glory of the LORD appeared
to all the people. 24 And [v]fire came out from
before the LORD and consumed the burnt
offering and the pieces of fat on the altar, and
when all the people saw it, [w]they shouted and
[x]fell on their faces.

The Death of Nadab and Abihu

10 Now [y]Nadab and Abihu, the sons of
Aaron, [z]each took his censer and put
fire in it and laid incense on it and offered
[a]unauthorized[1] fire before the LORD, which
he had not commanded them. 2 And fire [b]came
out from before the LORD and consumed
them, and they died before the LORD. 3 Then
Moses said to Aaron, "This is what the LORD
has said: 'Among [c]those who are near me [d]I will

[1] Or *strange*

Chapter 9
1 [r]Ezek. 43:27
2 [s]ch. 4:3; 8:14; Ex. 29:1 [t]ch. 8:18
3 [u]ch. 4:23; [Ezra 6:17]
4 [v]ver. 17; ch. 2:4 [w]ver. 6, 23; Ex. 29:43

9:1–24 In this chapter, the public worship of the Lord at the tabernacle begins. In response to the Israelites' sacrifices, the Lord gives an awesome display of his glory and might (vv. 23–24). He does this so his people might know that he was now dwelling among them as their covenant King and receiving their worship and praise (cf. Ex. 29:45–46).

7 [x]ch. 4:3; Heb. 5:1-3; 7:27; 9:7 [y]ch. 4:16, 20 **9** [z]ch. 4:6; 8:15 [a]See ch. 4:7 **10** [b]ch. 8:16 [c]ch. 4:8 **11** [d]ch. 4:11, 12; 8:17 **12** [e]ch. 1:5; 8:19 **13** [f]ch. 8:20 **14** [g]ch. 8:21 **15** [h]ver. 3, 7; Heb. 2:17; 5:3 [i]See ch. 6:26 [j]ver. 8 **16** [k]ch. 1:3, 10 [l]ch. 5:10 **17** [m]ver. 4; ch. 2:1, 2 [n]Ex. 29:38, 39 **18** [o]ch. 3:1, 12, 16 **19** [p]ch. 3:3, 9, 14; 4:8; 7:3 **20** [q]ch. 3:5, 16 **21** [r]Ex. 29:24, 26; See ch. 7:30-34 **22** [s][Luke 24:50] [t]Deut. 21:5; See Num. 6:23-27 **23** [u]ver. 4, 6 **24** [v][Judg. 6:21; 13:19, 20; 1 Kgs. 18:38; 1 Chr. 21:26; 2 Chr. 7:1] [w][Ezra 3:11] [x][1 Kgs. 18:39; 2 Chr. 7:3] **Chapter 10** **1** [y]ch. 16:1; Ex. 6:23; 28:1; Num. 3:4; 26:61; 1 Chr. 24:2 [z][Num. 16:18] [a]Ex. 30:9 **2** [b]ch. 9:24; Num. 16:35; [2 Sam. 6:7] **3** [c]ch. 21:17, 21 [d]Ezek. 28:22

be sanctified, and before all the people I will be
glorified.'" [e]And Aaron held his peace.
4 And Moses called Mishael and Elzaphan,
the sons of [f]Uzziel the uncle of Aaron, and
said to them, "Come near; carry your brothers away from the front of the sanctuary and
out of the camp." 5 So they came near and carried them in their coats out of the camp, as
Moses had said. 6 And Moses said to Aaron
and to Eleazar and Ithamar his sons, [g]"Do not
let the hair of your heads hang loose, and do
not tear your clothes, lest you die, and [h]wrath
come upon all the congregation; but let your
brothers, the whole house of Israel, bewail
the burning that the LORD has kindled. 7 [i]And
do not go outside the entrance of the tent of
meeting, lest you die, [j]for the anointing oil of
the LORD is upon you." And they did according to the word of Moses.
8 And the LORD spoke to Aaron, saying,
9 [k]"Drink no wine or strong drink, you or your
sons with you, when you go into the tent of
meeting, lest you die. It shall be a statute forever throughout your generations. 10 You are
to [l]distinguish between the holy and the common, and between the unclean and the clean,
11 and [m]you are to teach the people of Israel
all the statutes that the LORD has spoken to
them by Moses."
12 Moses spoke to Aaron and to Eleazar and
Ithamar, his surviving sons: "Take the [n]grain
offering that is left of the LORD's food offerings, and eat it unleavened beside the altar,
for [o]it is most holy. 13 You shall eat it in a holy
place, because it is your due and your sons'
due, from the LORD's food offerings, for [p]so
I am commanded. 14 But the [q]breast that is
waved and the thigh that is contributed you
shall eat in a clean place, you and your sons
and your daughters with you, for they are
given as your due and your sons' due from
the sacrifices of the peace offerings of the
people of Israel. 15 [r]The thigh that is contributed and the breast that is waved they
shall bring with the food offerings of the fat
pieces to wave for a wave offering before the
LORD, and it shall be yours and your sons'
with you as a due forever, as the LORD has
commanded."
16 Now Moses diligently inquired about [s]the
goat of the sin offering, and behold, it was
burned up! And he was angry with Eleazar
and Ithamar, the surviving sons of Aaron,
saying, 17 [t]"Why have you not eaten the sin
offering in the place of the sanctuary, since
[o]it is a thing most holy and has been given
to you that you may bear the iniquity of the
congregation, to make atonement for them
before the LORD? 18 Behold, [u]its blood was not
brought into the inner part of the sanctuary.
You certainly ought to have eaten it in the
sanctuary, [v]as I commanded." 19 And Aaron
said to Moses, "Behold, [w]today they have
offered their sin offering and their burnt
offering before the LORD, and yet such things
as these have happened to me! If I had eaten
the sin offering today, [x]would the LORD have
approved?" 20 And when Moses heard that,
he approved.

The ultimate demonstration of God's presence with us comes when he sends Jesus Christ to dwell in our midst, revealing to us afresh the glory of God (John 1:14; 2:11; 2 Cor. 4:6)—that is, those things that are so wonderful about God that we cannot help but fall before him and give him glory (cf. Lev. 9:24).

10:1–20 This chapter contrasts obedient priests (v. 7) with priests who were disobedient and experienced the Lord's judgment (vv. 1–3). In so doing, it emphasizes how important it was for priests to carry out their duties faithfully so they could lead the Lord's people in his ways and teach them how to live godly lives (vv. 10–11). If the captain of the ship is not faithful, all the passengers are at risk of danger.

As applied today, this chapter emphasizes that the leaders of the Lord's people are held to higher account (cf. James 3:1). Pastors and preachers in particular are to be diligent in their duties and faithful in their lives (1 Tim. 4:12–16). But they do not do this alone. They cry out for help and strength to Jesus, the Great High Priest who understands and can help. "For we do not have a high priest who is unable to sympathize with our weaknesses, but one who in every respect has been tempted as we are, yet without sin. Let us then with confidence draw near to the throne of grace, that we may receive mercy and find grace to help in time of need" (Heb. 4:15–16).

3 [e] [Ps. 39:9]
4 [f] Ex. 6:18, 22; Num. 3:19, 30
6 [g] ch. 13:45; 21:10; Ezek. 24:16, 17 [h] Num. 1:53; 16:22, 46; 18:5; Josh. 7:1; 22:18, 20
7 [i] ch. 21:12 [j] ch. 8:30
9 [k] Ezek. 44:21; [Num. 6:3, 20; Luke 1:15; 1 Tim. 3:3, 8]
10 [l] ch. 11:47; 20:25; Ezek. 22:26; 44:23
11 [m] ch. 14:57; Deut. 24:8; Neh. 8:2, 8, 9; [Jer. 18:18; Mal. 2:7]
12 [n] ch. 6:16; Num. 18:9, 10 [o] See ch. 6:17
13 [p] ch. 2:3; 6:16
14 [q] ch. 7:31, 34; Ex. 29:24, 26, 27; Num. 18:11
15 [r] ch. 7:31, 34
16 [s] ch. 9:3, 15
17 [t] ch. 6:26, 29 [o] [See ver. 12 above]
18 [u] ch. 6:30 [v] ch. 6:26
19 [w] ch. 9:8, 12 [x] Jer. 6:20; 14:12; Hos. 9:4; Mal. 1:10, 13; 2:13

Clean and Unclean Animals

11 And the LORD spoke to Moses and
Aaron, saying to them, 2 “Speak to the
people of Israel, saying, [y]These are the living
things that you may eat among all the animals that are on the earth. 3 Whatever parts
the hoof and is cloven-footed and chews
the cud, among the animals, you may eat.
4 Nevertheless, among those that chew the cud
or part the hoof, you shall not eat these: The
camel, because it chews the cud but does not
part the hoof, is unclean to you. 5 And the [z]rock
badger, because it chews the cud but does not
part the hoof, is unclean to you. 6 And the hare,
because it chews the cud but does not part the
hoof, is unclean to you. 7 And the pig, because
it parts the hoof and is cloven-footed but does
not chew the cud, [a]is unclean to you. 8 You shall
not eat any of their flesh, and you shall not
touch their carcasses; they are unclean to you.
9 “These you may eat, of all that are in the
waters. Everything in the waters that has fins
and scales, whether in the seas or in the rivers,
you may eat. 10 But anything in the seas or the
rivers that does not have fins and scales, of
the swarming creatures in the waters and of
the living creatures that are in the waters, is
[b]detestable to you. 11 You shall regard them
as detestable; you shall not eat any of their
flesh, and you shall detest their carcasses.
12 Everything in the waters that does not have
fins and scales is detestable to you.
13 “And these you shall detest among the
birds;[1] they shall not be eaten; they are [b]detest-
able: [c]the eagle,[2] the bearded vulture, the black
vulture, 14 the kite, [d]the falcon of any kind,
15 every raven of any kind, 16 the ostrich, the
nighthawk, the sea gull, the [e]hawk of any
kind, 17 the [f]little owl, the cormorant, the
[g]short-eared owl, 18 the barn owl, the [h]tawny
owl, the carrion vulture, 19 the stork, the heron
of any kind, the hoopoe, and [i]the bat.
20 “All winged insects that go on all fours are
detestable to you. 21 Yet among the winged
insects that go on all fours you may eat those
that have jointed legs above their feet, with
which to hop on the ground. 22 Of them you
may eat: [j]the locust of any kind, the bald locust
of any kind, the cricket of any kind, and the
grasshopper of any kind. 23 But all other
winged insects that have four feet are detestable to you.
24 “And by these you shall become unclean.
Whoever touches their carcass shall be unclean
until the evening, 25 and whoever carries any
part of their carcass [k]shall wash his clothes and
be unclean until the evening. 26 Every animal
that parts the hoof but is not cloven-footed
or does not chew the cud is unclean to you.
Everyone who touches them shall be unclean.
27 And all that walk on their paws, among the
animals that go on all fours, are unclean to
you. Whoever touches their carcass shall be
unclean until the evening, 28 and he who car-

[1] Or *things that fly*; compare Genesis 1:20 [2] The identity of many of these birds is uncertain

Chapter 11
2 [y] For ver. 1-47, see Deut. 14:3-20; [Matt. 15:11; Mark 7:15, 18; Acts 10:12-15; 11:6-9; Rom. 14:14; 1 Cor. 8:8; Col. 2:16, 21; Heb. 9:10]
5 [z] Ps. 104:18; Prov. 30:26
7 [a] [Isa. 65:4; 66:3, 17]
10 [b] ch. 7:21
13 [b] [See ver. 10 above] [c] Job 39:26, 30
14 [d] Job 28:7
16 [e] Job 39:26
17 [f] Ps. 102:6 [g] Isa. 34:11
18 [h] Ps. 102:6; Isa. 34:11; Zeph. 2:14
19 [i] Isa. 2:20
22 [j] Ex. 10:4; Joel 1:4; [Matt. 3:4; Mark 1:6]
25 [k] ch. 13:6, 34; 14:8, 9, 47; 15:5; 16:26, 28; 17:15; Num. 19:10; 31:24

11:1–15:31 Since the holy Lord was now dwelling in the Israelites' midst (Exodus 40; Leviticus 9), the Israelites had to make sure they did not defile his holy place with their ritual impurities. These chapters therefore describe how to deal with these impurities properly. Significantly, the language of *ritual* purity and impurity is often used to describe the *moral* purity the Israelites are to have and the moral impurity they are to avoid (cf. Ps. 24:2–3; Isa. 1:16; Jer. 4:14; etc.). The laws of these chapters would therefore serve as a constant reminder: just as you seek *ritual* purity in all of life, so do likewise in terms of *moral* purity.

The reason for such obedience is given near the end of chapter 11: “For I am the LORD who brought you up out of the land of Egypt to be your God. You shall therefore be holy, for I am holy.” The Lord had redeemed them (Ex. 20:2; Lev. 11:45), and set them apart to be his people (Ex. 19:4–6; Lev. 11:45; 20:24; 22:32b–33), so that he might dwell among them and be their God (Ex. 29:46). It was the Israelites' privilege to respond to this redemption by living lives of reverential worship before him and reflecting his holiness to the watching world.

Under the new covenant in Jesus, the concepts of ritual purity and impurity are no longer in force (cf. Mark 7:19; Acts 15:1–35; Rom. 14:14; Hebrews 8–10). Nonetheless, the New Testament still emphasizes that believers must seek moral purity, and avoid moral impurity, in every aspect of life. As with the Israelites, believers today do this as a response of reverential worship to their redeeming Lord (Eph. 1:3–4; cf. 1 Pet. 1:3–12 with 1 Pet. 1:13–16) and as a means of reflecting the Lord's holiness to a watching world (2 Cor. 6:16–7:1; 1 Pet. 1:14–16).

ries their carcass [k]shall wash his clothes and
be unclean until the evening; they are unclean
to you.
29 "And these are unclean to you among the
swarming things that swarm on the ground:
the mole rat, [l]the mouse, the great lizard of
any kind, 30 the gecko, the monitor lizard, the
lizard, the sand lizard, and the chameleon.
31 These are unclean to you among all that
swarm. Whoever touches them when they
are dead shall be unclean until the evening.
32 And anything on which any of them falls
when they are dead shall be unclean, whether
it is an article of wood or a garment or a skin
or a sack, any article that is used for any purpose. [m]It must be put into water, and it shall
be unclean until the evening; then it shall be
clean. 33 And if any of them falls into any earthenware vessel, all that is in it shall be unclean,
and you [n]shall break it. 34 Any food in it that
could be eaten, on which water comes, shall
be unclean. And all drink that could be drunk
from every such vessel shall be unclean. 35 And
everything on which any part of their carcass
falls shall be unclean. Whether oven or stove, it
shall be broken in pieces. They are unclean and
shall remain unclean for you. 36 Nevertheless,
a spring or a cistern holding water shall be
clean, but whoever touches a carcass in them
shall be unclean. 37 And if any part of their
carcass falls upon any seed grain that is to be
sown, it is clean, 38 but if water is put on the
seed and any part of their carcass falls on it, it
is unclean to you.
39 "And if any animal which you may eat dies,
whoever touches its carcass shall be unclean
until the evening, 40 and [o]whoever eats of its
carcass shall wash his clothes and be unclean
until the evening. And whoever carries the
carcass shall wash his clothes and be unclean
until the evening.
41 [p]"Every swarming thing that swarms on
the ground is detestable; it shall not be eaten.
42 Whatever goes on its belly, and whatever
goes on all fours, or whatever has many feet,
any swarming thing that swarms on the
ground, you shall not eat, for they are detestable. 43 [q]You shall not make yourselves detestable with any swarming thing that swarms,
and you shall not defile yourselves with them,
and become unclean through them. 44 For I am
the LORD your God. Consecrate yourselves
therefore, and [r]be holy, for I am holy. [q]You
shall not defile yourselves with any swarming
thing that crawls on the ground. 45 [s]For I am
the LORD who brought you up out of the land
of Egypt to be your God. [r]You shall therefore
be holy, for I am holy."
46 This is the law about beast and bird and
every living creature that moves through the
waters and every creature that swarms on
the ground, 47 [t]to make a distinction between
the unclean and the clean and between the living creature that may be eaten and the living
creature that may not be eaten.

Purification After Childbirth

12 The LORD spoke to Moses, saying,
2 "Speak to the people of Israel, saying,
If a woman conceives and bears a male child,
then [u]she shall be unclean seven days. [v]As at
the time of her menstruation, she shall be
unclean. 3 And on the [w]eighth day thc flesh
of his foreskin shall be circumcised. 4 Then
she shall continue for thirty-three days in the
blood of her purifying. She shall not touch

11:1–47 By following these dietary laws, the Israelites would set themselves apart from the nations as the Lord's holy people. The reason for such obedience has been commented on above (see note on 11:1–15:31). What may be noted here is that in Israel, all of life became an opportunity to show loyalty to the Lord, even in terms of what they ate. The Lord had redeemed their lives entirely, and they were to gratefully acknowledge his sovereign redemption with their entire lives.

Paul picks up on the same thought when he exhorts Christians, "I appeal to you therefore, brothers, by the mercies of God, to present your bodies as a living sacrifice, holy and acceptable to God, which is your spiritual worship" (Rom. 12:1). Obedience to God in all aspects of life (Rom. 12:1) is the proper response to the wonders of his sovereign mercies in Jesus (Romans 9–11).

12:1–8 For reasons that are not clear to us, losing large amounts of blood was considered to be ritually defiling in ancient Israel. This explains why childbirth resulted in the mother becoming ritually impure (cf. v. 2b). As a result of her impurity, she could not draw near to the Lord's holy dwelling or partake in holy sacrificial meals (v. 4).

28[k] [See ver. 25 above]
29[l] Isa. 66:17
32[m] ch. 15:12
33[n] ch. 6:28; 15:12
40[o] ch. 17:15; 22:8; Deut. 14:21; Ezek. 4:14; 44:31
41[p] [ver. 29]
43[q] ch. 20:25
44[r] ch. 19:2; 20:7, 26; 21:8; Ex. 19:6; Cited 1 Pet. 1:16; [1 Thess. 4:7] [q] [See ver. 43 above]
45[s] Ex. 6:7 [r] [See ver. 44 above]
47[t] ch. 10:10; 20:25

Chapter 12
2[u] [Luke 2:22] [v] ch. 15:19
3[w] Gen. 17:12; Luke 1:59; 2:21; John 7:22, 23

anything holy, nor come into the sanctuary, until the days of her purifying are completed. 5 But if she bears a female child, then she shall be unclean two weeks, as in her menstruation. And she shall continue in the blood of her purifying for sixty-six days.

6 [u]"And when the days of her purifying are completed, whether for a son or for a daughter, she shall bring to the priest at the entrance of the tent of meeting a lamb a year old for a burnt offering, and a pigeon or a turtledove for a sin offering, 7 and he shall offer it before the LORD and make atonement for her. Then she shall be clean from the flow of her blood. This is the law for her who bears a child, either male or female. 8 And if she cannot afford a lamb, then she shall take [x]two turtledoves or two pigeons,[1] [y]one for a burnt offering and the other for a sin offering. [z]And the priest shall make atonement for her, and she shall be clean."

Laws About Leprosy

13 The LORD spoke to Moses and Aaron, saying, 2 "When a person has on the skin of his body a [a]swelling or an eruption or a spot, and it turns into a case of leprous[2] disease on the skin of his body, [b]then he shall be brought to Aaron the priest or to one of his sons the priests, 3 and the priest shall examine the diseased area on the skin of his body. And if the hair in the diseased area has turned white and the disease appears to be deeper than the skin of his body, it is a case of leprous disease. When the priest has examined him, he shall pronounce him unclean. 4 But if the spot is white in the skin of his body and appears no deeper than the skin, and the hair in it has not turned white, [c]the priest shall shut up the diseased person for seven days. 5 And the priest shall examine him on the seventh day, and if in his eyes the disease is checked and the disease has not spread in the skin, then the [c]priest shall shut him up for another seven days. 6 And the priest shall examine him again on the seventh day, and if the diseased area has faded and the disease has not spread in the skin, then the priest shall pronounce him clean; it is only an eruption. And [d]he shall wash his clothes and be clean. 7 But if the eruption spreads in the skin, after he has shown himself to the priest for his cleansing, he shall appear again before the priest. 8 And the priest shall look, and if the eruption has spread in the skin, then the priest shall pronounce him unclean; it is a leprous disease.

9 "When a man is afflicted with a leprous disease, he shall be brought to the priest, 10 and the priest shall look. And if there is a [e]white swelling in the skin that has turned the hair white, and there is raw flesh in the swelling, 11 it is a chronic leprous disease in the skin of his body, and the priest shall pronounce him unclean. [f]He shall not shut him up, for he is unclean. 12 And if the leprous disease breaks out in the skin, so that the leprous disease covers all the skin of the diseased person from head to foot, so far as the priest can see, 13 then the priest shall look, and if the leprous disease has covered all his body, he shall pronounce him clean of the disease; it has all turned white, and he is clean. 14 But when raw flesh appears on him, he shall be unclean. 15 And the priest shall examine the raw flesh and pronounce him unclean. Raw flesh is unclean, for it is a leprous disease. 16 But if the raw flesh recovers and turns white again, then he shall come to the priest, 17 and the priest shall examine him, and if the disease has turned white,

[1] Septuagint *two young pigeons* [2] *Leprosy* was a term for several skin diseases

6 [u] [See ver. 2 above]
8 [x] ch. 1:14; 5:7; Cited Luke 2:24 [y] ver. 6 [z] ch. 4:26
Chapter 13
2 [a] ch. 14:56 [b] Deut. 24:8
4 [c] [ver. 11]
5 [c] [See ver. 4 above]
6 [d] See ch. 11:25
10 [e] [Num. 12:10, 12; 2 Kgs. 5:27; 15:5; 2 Chr. 26:20, 21]
11 [f] [ver. 4, 5]

Significantly, the Lord does not leave her in this state, but mercifully provides directions on how to become ritually pure so she can once again participate fully in Israel's covenant worship. This is always the Lord's desire for his people: the ability to worship him and to enjoy fellowship with their covenant brothers and sisters. He shows this desire most clearly by sending Jesus, who came to bring about this same worship and fellowship among his followers (John 14:2–6; 17:20–21). To engage in both activities is to acknowledge that this is what we have been created and redeemed to do.

13:1–14:57 These chapters explain how to address ritually defiling skin diseases on people (13:1–46; 14:1–32) and ritually defiling infestations in garments (13:47–59) or in houses (14:33–53). As in the previous two chapters, the ritual impurity had to be addressed because the holy Lord lived in the Israelites' midst. And in those earlier chapters, the Lord mercifully provides instructions on how to address the impurity so that the Israelites could maintain covenant fellowship with him.

then the priest shall pronounce the diseased
person clean; he is clean.
18 “If there is in the skin of one’s body a [g]boil
and it heals, 19 and in the place of the boil there
comes a white swelling or a [h]reddish-white
spot, then it shall be shown to the priest.
20 And the priest shall look, and if it appears
deeper than the skin and its hair has turned
white, then the priest shall pronounce him
unclean. It is a case of leprous disease that has
broken out in the boil. 21 But if the priest examines it and there is no white hair in it and it is
not deeper than the skin, but has faded, then
the priest shall shut him up seven days. 22 And
if it spreads in the skin, then the priest shall
pronounce him unclean; it is a disease. 23 But
[i]if the spot remains in one place and does not
spread, it is the scar of the boil, and the priest
shall pronounce him clean.
24 “Or, when the body has a burn on its
skin and the raw flesh of the burn becomes
a spot, [j]reddish-white or white, 25 the priest
shall examine it, and if the hair in the spot has
turned white and it appears deeper than the
skin, then it is a leprous disease. It has broken
out in the burn, and the priest shall pronounce
him unclean; it is a case of leprous disease.
26 But if the priest examines it and there is no
white hair in the spot and it is no deeper than
the skin, but has faded, the priest shall shut
him up seven days, 27 and the priest shall examine him the seventh day. If it is spreading in
the skin, then the priest shall pronounce him
unclean; it is a case of leprous disease. 28 But
if the spot remains [k]in one place and does not
spread in the skin, but has faded, it is a swelling
from the burn, and the priest shall pronounce
him clean, for it is the scar of the burn.
29 “When a man or woman has a disease on
the head or the beard, 30 the priest shall examine the disease. And if it appears deeper than
the skin, and the hair in it is yellow and thin,
then the priest shall pronounce him unclean.
It is an itch, a leprous disease of the head or
the beard. 31 And if the priest examines the
itching disease and it appears no deeper than
the skin and there is no black hair in it, then
the priest shall shut up the person with the
itching disease for seven days, 32 and on the
seventh day the priest shall examine the disease. If the itch has not spread, and there is in
it no yellow hair, and the itch appears to be
no deeper than the skin, 33 then he shall shave
himself, but the itch he shall not shave; and
the priest shall shut up the person with the
itching disease for another seven days. 34 And
on the seventh day the priest shall examine
the itch, and if the itch has not spread in the
skin and it appears to be no deeper than the
skin, then the priest shall pronounce him
clean. And [l]he shall wash his clothes and be
clean. 35 But if the itch spreads in the skin after
his cleansing, 36 then the priest shall examine
him, and if the itch has spread in the skin,
the priest need not seek for the yellow hair;
he is unclean. 37 But if in his eyes the itch is
unchanged and black hair has grown in it, the
itch is healed and he is clean, and the priest
shall pronounce him clean.
38 “When a man or a woman has spots on the
skin of the body, white spots, 39 the priest shall
look, and if the spots on the skin of the body
are of a dull white, it is leukoderma that has
broken out in the skin; he is clean.
40 “If a man’s hair falls out from his head, he
is bald; he is clean. 41 And if a man’s hair falls
out from his forehead, he has baldness of the
forehead; he is clean. 42 But if there is on the
bald head or the bald forehead a reddish-white
diseased area, it is a leprous disease breaking
out on his bald head or his bald forehead.
43 Then the priest shall examine him, and if
the diseased swelling is reddish-white on his
bald head or on his bald forehead, like the
appearance of leprous disease in the skin of
the body, 44 he is a leprous man, he is unclean.
The priest must pronounce him unclean; his
disease is on his head.
45 “The leprous person who has the disease
shall wear torn clothes and [m]let the hair of his
head hang loose, and he shall [n]cover his upper
lip[1] and cry out, [o]‘Unclean, unclean.’ 46 He shall

[1] Or *mustache*

When Jesus came, he addressed this ritual impurity in the most radical way: with a simple touch of his hand, he removed a ritually defiling disease from a man and made him clean (Mark 1:40–42). It was a sign of the much deeper cleansing he would accomplish for our sins (1 John 1:7, 9). If those who experienced cleansing of the body fell in worshipful thankfulness before the Lord (Luke 17:15–16), how much more those of us who have experienced his cleansing of our soul.

18 [g] See Ex. 9:9
19 [h] ver. 24
23 [i] ver. 28
24 [j] ver. 19
28 [k] ver. 23
34 [l] ver. 6
45 [m] ch. 10:6 [n] Ezek. 24:17, 22; Mic. 3:7 [o] [Lam. 4:15]

remain unclean as long as he has the disease.
He is unclean. He shall live alone. His dwelling
shall be [p]outside the camp.
47 "When there is a case of leprous disease
in a [q]garment, whether a woolen or a linen
garment, 48 in warp or woof of linen or wool,
or in a skin or in anything made of skin, 49 if
the disease is greenish or reddish in the garment, or in the skin or in the warp or the woof
or in any article made of skin, it is a case of
leprous disease, and it shall be shown to the
priest. 50 And the priest shall examine the
disease and shut up that which has the disease for seven days. 51 Then he shall examine
the disease on the seventh day. If the disease
has spread in the garment, in the warp or the
woof, or in the skin, whatever be the use of
the skin, the disease is a [r]persistent leprous
disease; it is unclean. 52 And he shall burn the
garment, or the warp or the woof, the wool or
the linen, or any article made of skin that is
diseased, for it is a persistent leprous disease.
It shall be burned in the fire.
53 "And if the priest examines, and if the
disease has not spread in the garment, in the
warp or the woof or in any article made of
skin, 54 then the priest shall command that
they wash the thing in which is the disease,
and he shall shut it up for another seven
days. 55 And the priest shall examine the diseased thing after it has been washed. And if
the appearance of the diseased area has not
changed, though the disease has not spread,
it is unclean. You shall burn it in the fire,
whether the rot is on the back or on the front.
56 "But if the priest examines, and if the diseased area has faded after it has been washed,
he shall tear it out of the garment or the skin
or the warp or the woof. 57 Then if it appears
again in the garment, in the warp or the woof,
or in any article made of skin, it is spreading.
You shall burn with fire whatever has the disease. 58 But the garment, or the warp or the
woof, or any article made of skin from which
the disease departs when you have washed
it, shall then be washed a second time, and
be clean."
59 This is the law for a case of leprous disease
in a garment of wool or linen, either in the
warp or the woof, or in any article made of skin,
to determine whether it is clean or unclean.

Laws for Cleansing Lepers

14 The LORD spoke to Moses, saying,
2 "This shall be the law of the leprous
person for the day of his cleansing. [s]He shall
be brought to the priest, 3 and the priest shall
go [t]out of the camp, and the priest shall look.
Then, if the case of leprous disease is healed
in the leprous person, 4 the priest shall command them to take for him who is to be
cleansed two live[1] clean birds and [u]cedarwood
and [v]scarlet yarn and [w]hyssop. 5 And the priest
shall command them to kill one of the birds in
an earthenware vessel over fresh[2] water. 6 He
shall take the live bird with the cedarwood and
the scarlet yarn and the hyssop, and dip them
and the live bird in the blood of the bird that
was killed over the fresh water. 7 And he shall
[x]sprinkle it [y]seven times on him who is to be
cleansed of the leprous disease. Then he shall
pronounce him clean and shall [z]let the living
bird go [a]into the open field. 8 And he who is to
be cleansed [b]shall wash his clothes and shave
off all his hair and bathe himself in water, and
he shall be clean. And after that he may come
into the camp, but [c]live outside his tent seven
days. 9 And [d]on the seventh day he shall shave
off all his hair from his head, his beard, and his
eyebrows. He shall shave off all his hair, and
then he [b]shall wash his clothes and bathe his
body in water, and he shall be clean.
10 "And on the eighth day he [e]shall take two
male lambs without blemish, and one ewe
lamb a year old without blemish, and a [f]grain
offering of three tenths of an ephah[3] of fine
flour mixed with oil, and one log[4] of oil. 11 And
the priest who cleanses him shall set the man
who is to be cleansed and these things before
the LORD, at the entrance of the tent of meeting. 12 And the priest shall take one of the male
lambs and [g]offer it for a guilt offering, along
with the log of oil, and [h]wave them for a wave
offering before the LORD. 13 And he shall kill
the lamb [i]in the place where they kill the sin
offering and the burnt offering, in the place of
the sanctuary. For [j]the guilt offering, like the
sin offering, belongs to the priest; [k]it is most

[1] Or *wild* [2] Or *running*; Hebrew *living*; also verses 6, 50, 51, 52 [3] An *ephah* was about 3/5 bushel or 22 liters [4] A *log* was about 1/3 quart or 0.3 liter

46[p] Num. 5:2; 12:14, 15; [2 Kgs. 7:3; 15:5; 2 Chr. 26:21; Luke 17:12] **47**[q] [Jude 23; Rev. 3:4] **51**[r] ch. 14:44 **Chapter 14** **2**[s] Matt. 8:2, 4; Mark 1:40, 44; Luke 5:12, 14; 17:14 **3**[t] [2 Kgs. 7:10; Luke 17:12] **4**[u] Num. 19:6 [v] Heb. 9:19 [w] See Ex. 12:22 **7**[x] Heb. 9:13 [y] [2 Kgs. 5:10, 14] [z] [ch. 16:22] [a] ver. 53; [ch. 17:5] **8**[b] ver. 47; See ch. 11:25 [c] Num. 12:15 **9**[d] [Num. 31:19] [b] [See ver. 8 above] **10**[e] [Matt. 8:4]; Mark 1:44; Luke 5:14 [f] Num. 15:4; See ch. 2 **12**[g] ch. 5:18; 6:6, 7 [h] See Ex. 29:24 **13**[i] ch. 1:5, 11; 4:4, 24 [j] ch. 7:7 [k] ch. 2:3; 7:6

holy. 14 The priest shall take some of the blood of the guilt offering, and the priest shall put it [l]on the lobe of the right ear of him who is to be cleansed and on the thumb of his right hand and on the big toe of his right foot. 15 Then the priest shall take some of the log of oil and pour it into the palm of his own left hand 16 and dip his right finger in the oil that is in his left hand and sprinkle some oil with his finger seven times before the LORD. 17 And some of the oil that remains in his hand the priest shall put on the lobe of the right ear of him who is to be cleansed and on the thumb of his right hand and on the big toe of his right foot, on top of the blood of the guilt offering. 18 And the rest of the oil that is in the priest's hand he shall put on the head of him who is to be cleansed. [m]Then the priest shall make atonement for him before the LORD. 19 The priest shall offer the sin offering, to make atonement for him who is to be cleansed from his uncleanness. And afterward he shall kill the burnt offering. 20 And the priest shall offer the burnt offering and the [f]grain offering on the altar. [m]Thus the priest shall make atonement for him, and he shall be clean.

21 "But [n]if he is poor and cannot afford so much, then he shall take one male lamb for a guilt offering [h]to be waved, to make atonement for him, and a tenth of an ephah of fine flour mixed with oil for a grain offering, and a log of oil; 22 [o]also two turtledoves or two pigeons, whichever he can afford. The one shall be a sin offering and the other a burnt offering. 23 [p]And on the eighth day he shall bring them for his cleansing to the priest, to the entrance of the tent of meeting, before the LORD. 24 [q]And the priest shall take the lamb of the guilt offering and the log of oil, and the priest shall wave them for a wave offering before the LORD. 25 And he shall kill the lamb of the guilt offering. [r]And the priest shall take some of the blood of the guilt offering and put it on the lobe of the right ear of him who is to be cleansed, and on the thumb of his right hand and on the big toe of his right foot. 26 And the priest shall pour some of the oil into the palm of his own left hand, 27 and shall sprinkle with his right finger some of the oil that is in his left hand seven times before the LORD. 28 And the priest shall put some of the oil that is in his hand on the lobe of the right ear of him who is to be cleansed and on the thumb of his right hand and on the big toe of his right foot, in the place where the blood of the guilt offering was put. 29 And the rest of the oil that is in the priest's hand he shall put on the head of him who is to be cleansed, to make atonement for him before the LORD. 30 And he shall offer, of the [s]turtledoves or pigeons, whichever he can afford, 31 one[1] for a sin offering and the other for a burnt offering, along with a grain offering. [m]And the priest shall make atonement before the LORD for him who is being cleansed. 32 This is the law for him in whom is a case of leprous disease, who cannot afford [t]the offerings for his cleansing."

Laws for Cleansing Houses

33 The LORD spoke to Moses and Aaron, saying, 34 "When you come into the land of Canaan, which I give you [u]for a possession, and I put a case of leprous disease in a house in the land of your possession, 35 then he who owns the house shall come and tell the priest, 'There seems to me to be some case of [v]disease in my house.' 36 Then the priest shall command that they empty the house before the priest goes to examine the disease, lest all that is in the house be declared unclean. And afterward the priest shall go in to see the house. 37 And he shall examine the disease. And if the disease is in the walls of the house with greenish or reddish spots, and if it appears to be deeper than the surface, 38 then the priest shall go out of the house to the door of the house and shut up the house seven days. 39 And the priest shall come again on the seventh day, and look. If the disease has spread in the walls of the house, 40 then the priest shall command that they take out the stones in which is the disease and throw them into an unclean place outside the city. 41 And he shall have the inside of the house scraped all around, and the plaster that they scrape off they shall pour out in an unclean place outside the city. 42 Then they shall take other stones and put them in the place of those stones, and he shall take other plaster and plaster the house.

43 "If the disease breaks out again in the house, after he has taken out the stones and

[1] Septuagint, Syriac; Hebrew *afford, 31 such as he can afford, one*

14[l] [ch. 8:23; Ex. 29:20] **18**[m] See ch. 4:26 **20**[f] [See ver. 10 above] [m] [See ver. 18 above] **21**[n] ch. 5:7, 11; 12:8 [h] [See ver. 12 above] **22**[o] See ch. 12:8 **23**[p] ver. 10, 11 **24**[q] ver. 12 **25**[r] For ver. 25-29, see ver. 14-18 **30**[s] ver. 22; ch. 15:15 **31**[m] [See ver. 18 above] **32**[t] ver. 10 **34**[u] Gen. 17:8; Num. 32:22; Deut. 32:49 **35**[v] [Ps. 91:10; Zech. 5:4]

scraped the house and plastered it, 44 then the
priest shall go and look. And if the disease has
spread in the house, it is a [w]persistent leprous
disease in the house; it is unclean. 45 And he
shall break down the house, its stones and
timber and all the plaster of the house, and he
shall carry them out of the city to an unclean
place. 46 Moreover, whoever enters the house
while it is shut up shall be unclean until the
evening, 47 and whoever sleeps in the house
[x]shall wash his clothes, and whoever eats in
the house shall wash his clothes.

48 "But if the priest comes and looks, and if
the disease has not spread in the house after
the house was plastered, then the priest shall
pronounce the house clean, for the disease is
healed. 49 And for the [y]cleansing of the house
he shall take [z]two small birds, with cedarwood
and scarlet yarn and hyssop, 50 and shall kill
one of the birds in an earthenware vessel over
fresh water 51 and shall take the cedarwood and
the hyssop and the scarlet yarn, along with
the live bird, and dip them in the blood of the
bird that was killed and in the fresh water and
sprinkle the house seven times. 52 Thus he shall
cleanse the house with the blood of the bird
and with the fresh water and with the live
bird and with the cedarwood and hyssop and
scarlet yarn. 53 And he shall let the live bird go
out of the city [a]into the open country. So he
shall [b]make atonement for the house, and it
shall be clean."

54 This is the law for any case of leprous disease: for [c]an itch, 55 for [d]leprous disease in a
garment or in [e]a house, 56 and [f]for a swelling
or an eruption or a spot, 57 to [g]show when it is
unclean and when it is clean. This is the law
for leprous disease.

Laws About Bodily Discharges

15 The LORD spoke to Moses and Aaron,
saying, 2 "Speak to the people of Israel
and say to them, [h]When any man has a discharge from his body,[1] his discharge is unclean.
3 And this is the law of his uncleanness for
a discharge: whether his body runs with his
discharge, or his body is blocked up by his
discharge, it is his uncleanness. 4 Every bed
on which the one with the discharge lies
shall be unclean, and everything on which
he sits shall be unclean. 5 And anyone who
touches his bed [i]shall wash his clothes and
[j]bathe himself in water and be unclean until
the evening. 6 And whoever sits on anything
on which the one with the discharge has sat
shall wash his clothes and bathe himself in
water and be unclean until the evening. 7 And
whoever touches the body of the one with
the discharge shall wash his clothes and bathe
himself in water and be unclean until the
evening. 8 And if the one with the discharge
spits on someone who is clean, then he shall
wash his clothes and bathe himself in water
and be unclean until the evening. 9 And any
saddle on which the one with the discharge
rides shall be unclean. 10 And whoever touches
anything that was under him shall be unclean
until the evening. And whoever carries such
things shall wash his clothes and bathe himself in water and be unclean until the evening.
11 Anyone whom the one with the discharge
touches without having rinsed his hands in
water shall wash his clothes and bathe himself
in water and be unclean until the evening.
12 And an [k]earthenware vessel that the one with
the discharge touches shall be broken, and
every vessel of wood shall be rinsed in water.

13 "And when the one with a discharge is
cleansed of his discharge, then [l]he shall count
for himself seven days for his cleansing, and
wash his clothes. And he shall bathe his body
in fresh water and shall be clean. 14 And on the
eighth day he shall take two [m]turtledoves or
two pigeons and come before the LORD to the
entrance of the tent of meeting and give them
to the priest. 15 And the priest shall use them,
[n]one for a sin offering and the other for a burnt

[1] Hebrew *flesh*; also verse 3

44[w] ch. 13:51, 52
47[x] See ch. 11:25
49[y] ver. 52 [z] [ver. 4-6]
53[a] See ver. 7 [b] ver. 19, 20
54[c] ch. 13:30
55[d] ch. 13:47 [e] ver. 34
56[f] ch. 13:2
57[g] See ch. 10:10, 11
Chapter 15
2[h] ch. 22:4; Num. 5:2; 2 Sam. 3:29

15:1–33 This chapter describes the ritual impurity that comes from genital discharges that are both normal (vv. 18–24) and abnormal (vv. 2–15, 25–30). Like Leviticus chapters 12–14, it explains how the Israelites are to address these impurities so that the Lord may continue to live among them (cf. comments at 12:1–8 and 13:1–14:57). As noted earlier, these commands to seek *ritual* purity would have served as reminders to seek *moral* purity as well (see note on 11:1–15:31). And since the impurities here result from genital discharges, this chapter would have especially reminded the Israelites of the importance of sexual purity.

5[i] See ch. 11:25 [j] ch. 16:26; 17:15 12[k] ch. 6:28; 11:32, 33 13[l] ver. 28; [ch. 14:8] 14[m] See ch. 12:8 15[n] ch. 14:30, 31

offering. [o]And the priest shall make atonement for him before the LORD for his discharge.

16 [p]"If a man has an emission of semen, he shall bathe his whole body in water and be unclean until the evening. 17 And every garment and every skin on which the semen comes shall be washed with water and be unclean until the evening. 18 If a man lies with a woman and has an emission of semen, both of them shall bathe themselves in water and [q]be unclean until the evening.

19 "When a woman has a discharge, and the discharge in her body is blood, she shall be in her menstrual impurity for seven days, and whoever touches her shall be unclean until the evening. 20 [r]And everything on which she lies during her menstrual impurity shall be unclean. Everything also on which she sits shall be unclean. 21 And whoever touches her bed shall wash his clothes and bathe himself in water and be unclean until the evening. 22 And whoever touches anything on which she sits shall wash his clothes and bathe himself in water and be unclean until the evening. 23 Whether it is the bed or anything on which she sits, when he touches it he shall be unclean until the evening. 24 And [s]if any man lies with her and her menstrual impurity comes upon him, he shall be unclean seven days, and every bed on which he lies shall be unclean.

25 "If [t]a woman has a discharge of blood for many days, not at the time of her menstrual impurity, or if she has a discharge beyond the time of her impurity, all the days of the discharge she shall continue in uncleanness. As in the days of her impurity, she shall be unclean. 26 Every bed on which she lies, all the days of her discharge, shall be to her as the bed of her impurity. And everything on which she sits shall be unclean, as in the uncleanness of her menstrual impurity. 27 And whoever touches these things shall be unclean, and shall wash his clothes and bathe himself in water and be unclean until the evening. 28 But [u]if she is cleansed of her discharge, she shall count for herself seven days, and after that she shall be clean. 29 And on the eighth day she shall take two [v]turtledoves or two pigeons and bring them to the priest, to the entrance of the tent of meeting. 30 And the priest shall use one for a sin offering and the other for a burnt offering. And the priest shall make atonement for her before the LORD for her unclean discharge.

31 "Thus you shall keep the people of Israel separate from their uncleanness, lest they die in their uncleanness by [w]defiling my tabernacle that is in their midst."

32 This is the law [x]for him who has a discharge and [y]for him who has an emission of semen, becoming unclean thereby; 33 [z]also for her who is unwell with her menstrual impurity, that is, for anyone, [x]male or [a]female, who has a discharge, and for the [b]man who lies with a woman who is unclean.

The Day of Atonement

16 The LORD spoke to Moses after [c]the death of the two sons of Aaron, when they drew near before the LORD and died, 2 and the LORD said to Moses, "Tell Aaron your brother not to [d]come at any time into the Holy Place inside the veil, before the mercy seat that is on the ark, so that he may not die. For [e]I will appear in the cloud over the mercy seat. 3 But in this way Aaron shall come into the Holy Place: [f]with a bull from the herd for a sin offering and [g]a ram for a burnt offering. 4 He shall put on [h]the holy linen coat and shall have the linen undergarment on his body, and he shall tie the linen sash around his waist, and wear the linen turban; these are the holy garments. [i]He shall bathe his body in water and then put them on. 5 And he shall take from

The New Testament picks up on this theme when it exhorts believers to live lives of moral purity in response to the presence of the holy God who dwells not only among them (cf. Ex. 40:34–38), but, because of Jesus, within them (1 Cor. 6:13–20). We do so knowing the Lord will give us the strength to obey and honor him (1 Cor. 10:13).

16:1–34 While Leviticus 4–5 explains how to deal with various sins, and Leviticus 11–15 explains how to deal with various ritual impurities, it remains the case that not every Israelite would have addressed these things properly. As a result, sins and impurities remained and defiled the camp and the Lord's holy dwelling. He therefore provides this ceremony, the Day of Atonement, to cleanse the tabernacle and the camp of these sins and impurities so he can remain among his people.

15 [o]ver. 30; See ch. 4:26
16 [p]ch. 22:4; Deut. 23:10
18 [q][1 Sam. 21:4]
20 [r]See ver. 4-10
24 [s]ch. 18:19; [ch. 20:18]
25 [t]Matt. 9:20; Mark 5:25; Luke 8:43
28 [u]For ver. 28-30, see ver. 13-15
29 [v]See ch. 12:8
31 [w]Num. 5:3; 19:13, 20; Ezek. 5:11; 23:38
32 [x]ver. 2 [y]ver. 16
33 [z]ver. 19 [x][See ver. 32 above] [a]ver. 25 [b]ver. 24

Chapter 16 **1** [c]ch. 10:1, 2 **2** [d][Ex. 30:10; Heb. 9:7, 12, 24, 25; 10:19-22] [e]Ex. 25:22; 40:34, 35; [1 Kgs. 8:10-12] **3** [f]ch. 4:3 [g]ch. 1:10; 8:18 **4** [h]ch. 6:10; 8:7; Ezek. 44:17, 18; See Ex. 28:39-43 [i]ch. 8:6, 7; Ex. 30:20

[j]the congregation of the people of Israel two male goats for a sin offering, and one ram for a burnt offering.

6 "Aaron shall [k]offer the bull as a sin offering for himself and shall [l]make atonement for himself and for his house. 7 Then he shall take the two goats and set them before the LORD at the entrance of the tent of meeting. 8 And Aaron shall cast lots over the two goats, one lot for the LORD and the other lot for [m]Azazel.[1] 9 And Aaron shall present the goat on which the lot fell for the LORD and use it as a sin offering, 10 but the goat on which the lot fell for [m]Azazel shall be presented alive before the LORD to make atonement over it, that it may be sent away into the wilderness to [m]Azazel.

11 "Aaron shall present [k]the bull as a sin offering for himself, and shall make atonement for himself and for his house. He shall kill the bull as a sin offering for himself. 12 And he shall take [n]a censer full of coals of fire from the altar before the LORD, and two handfuls of sweet incense beaten small, and he shall bring it inside the veil 13 [o]and put the incense on the fire before the LORD, that the cloud of the incense may cover [p]the mercy seat that is over the testimony, so that he does not die. 14 And [q]he shall take some of the blood of the bull and sprinkle it with his finger on the front of the mercy seat on the east side, and in front of the mercy seat he shall sprinkle some of the blood with his finger seven times.

15 [r]"Then he shall kill the goat of the sin offering that is for the people and bring its blood [s]inside the veil and do with its blood as he did with the blood of the bull, sprinkling it over the mercy seat and in front of the mercy seat. 16 Thus he shall [t]make atonement for the Holy Place, because of the uncleannesses of the people of Israel and because of their transgressions, all their sins. And so he shall do for the tent of meeting, which dwells with them in the midst of their uncleannesses. 17 [u]No one may be in the tent of meeting from the time he enters to make atonement in the Holy Place until he comes out and has made atonement for himself and for his house and for all the assembly of Israel. 18 Then he shall go out to the altar that is [v]before the LORD and [w]make atonement for it, and shall take some of the blood of the bull and some of the blood of the goat, and put it on the horns of the altar all around. 19 And he shall sprinkle some of the blood on it with his finger seven times, and cleanse it and consecrate it from the uncleannesses of the people of Israel.

20 "And when he has made an end of [x]atoning for the Holy Place and the tent of meeting and the altar, he shall present the live goat. 21 And Aaron shall lay both his hands on the head of the live goat, and confess over it all the iniquities of the people of Israel, and all their transgressions, all their sins. And he shall [y]put them on the head of the goat and send it away into the wilderness by the hand of a man who is in readiness. 22 The goat shall [z]bear all their iniquities on itself to a remote area, and [a]he shall let the goat go free in the wilderness.

23 "Then Aaron shall come into the tent of meeting and [b]shall take off the linen garments that he put on when he went into the Holy Place and shall leave them there. 24 And he shall bathe his body in water in a holy place and put on his garments and come out and [c]offer his burnt offering and the burnt offering of the people and make atonement for him-

[1] The meaning of *Azazel* is uncertain; possibly the name of a place or a demon, traditionally a scapegoat; also verses 10, 26

The heart of the ceremony consisted of three rites: purification offerings to cleanse the tabernacle (16:11–19), the scapegoat to bear the Israelites' sins out of the camp (vv. 20–22), and burnt offerings to emphasize the atonement made that day (vv. 23–24). For these rites to be effective, it was important that the Israelites had repentant hearts (vv. 29, 31).

Jesus' crucifixion was the ultimate Day of Atonement. In reflection and fulfillment of the purification offerings, he cleansed our sin by means of his own blood (Heb. 9:12, 14, 24). In reflection and completion of the sign of the scapegoat, he bore our sins away (Heb. 9:28; cf. Isa. 53:11–12). In reflection and fulfillment of the burnt offerings, he made atonement for us. We therefore look to him with hearts that not only mourn and repent of our sin but that also rejoice that his sacrifice cleanses us so completely that we can draw near to God with the full assurance that he accepts us completely (Heb. 10:19–22).

5 [j]ch. 4:14; Num. 29:11; 2 Chr. 29:21; Ezra 6:17
6 [k]Ezek. 45:22 [l]ver. 17, 24; ch. 9:7; Heb. 7:27, 28; 9:7
8 [m]ver. 26
10 [m][See ver. 8 above]
11 [k][See ver. 6 above]
12 [n]ch. 10:1; Num. 16:46; Rev. 8:3-5
13 [o]Ex. 30:1, 7, 8 [p]Ex. 25:21
14 [q]Heb. 9:13, 25; 10:4; See ch. 4:5, 6
15 [r]Heb. 2:17; 5:1; 9:7 [s]ver. 2; Heb. 6:19; 9:3, 7
16 [t]ver. 18; [Ex. 29:36; Ezek. 45:18; Heb. 9:22, 23]
17 [u][Luke 1:10, 21]
18 [v]ch. 1:5; 4:24 [w]ver. 16; ch. 4:7, 18; Ex. 30:6, 10
20 [x]ver. 16, 18; Ezek. 43:20; 45:20 **21** [y][Isa. 53:6; 2 Cor. 5:21] **22** [z][Isa. 53:11, 12; John 1:29; Heb. 9:28; 1 Pet. 2:24] [a][ch. 14:7] **23** [b]See ch. 6:11 **24** [c]ver. 3, 5

self and for the people. 25 And [d]the fat of the sin offering he shall burn on the altar. 26 And he who lets the goat go to [e]Azazel shall wash his clothes and [f]bathe his body in water, and afterward he may come into the camp. 27 [g]And the bull for the sin offering and the goat for the sin offering, whose blood was brought in to make atonement in the Holy Place, shall be carried outside the camp. Their skin and their flesh and their dung shall be burned up with fire. 28 And he who burns them shall wash his clothes and bathe his body in water, and afterward he may come into the camp.

29 "And it shall be a statute to you forever that [h]in the seventh month, on the tenth day of the month, you shall [i]afflict yourselves[1] and shall do no work, either [j]the native or the stranger who sojourns among you. 30 For on this day shall atonement be made for you [k]to cleanse you. You shall be clean before the LORD from all your sins. 31 [l]It is a Sabbath of solemn rest to you, and you shall [i]afflict yourselves; it is a statute forever. 32 [m]And the priest who is anointed and [n]consecrated as priest in his father's place [o]shall make atonement, wearing the holy linen garments. 33 He shall make atonement for [p]the holy sanctuary, and he shall make atonement for the tent of meeting and for [q]the altar, and he shall make atonement for [r]the priests and for [s]all the people of the assembly. 34 And this shall be a statute forever for you, that atonement may be made for the people of Israel [t]once in the year because of all their sins." And Aaron[2] did as the LORD commanded Moses.

The Place of Sacrifice

17 And the LORD spoke to Moses, saying, 2 "Speak to Aaron and his sons and to all the people of Israel and say to them, This is the thing that the LORD has commanded. 3 If any one of the house of Israel [u]kills an ox or a lamb or a goat in the camp, or kills it outside the camp, 4 and [v]does not bring it to the entrance of the tent of meeting to offer it as a gift to the LORD in front of the tabernacle of the LORD, bloodguilt shall be imputed to that man. He has shed blood, and that man [w]shall be cut off from among his people. 5 This is to the end that the people of Israel may bring their sacrifices that they sacrifice [x]in the open field, that they may bring them to the LORD, to the priest at the entrance of the tent of meeting, and sacrifice them [y]as sacrifices of peace offerings to the LORD. 6 And the priest shall [y]throw the blood on the altar of the LORD at the entrance of the tent of meeting and burn the fat [z]for a pleasing aroma to the LORD. 7 So they shall no more sacrifice their sacrifices to goat demons, after whom they [a]whore. This shall be a statute forever for them throughout their generations.

8 "And you shall say to them, Any one of the house of Israel, or of the strangers who sojourn among them, who [b]offers a burnt offering or sacrifice 9 and [c]does not bring it to the entrance of the tent of meeting to offer it to the LORD, [w]that man shall be cut off from his people.

Laws Against Eating Blood

10 "If any one of the house of Israel or of the strangers who sojourn among them [d]eats any blood, I will [e]set my face against that person who eats blood and will cut him off from among his people. 11 [f]For the life of the flesh is in the blood, and I have given it for you on the altar [g]to make atonement for your souls, [h]for it is the blood that makes atonement by the life. 12 Therefore I have said to the people of Israel, No person among you shall eat blood, neither

[1] Or *shall fast*; also verse 31 [2] Hebrew *he*

17:10–12 These verses prohibit the Israelites from eating meat that still has the blood in it (cf. Gen. 9:4; Deut. 12:23). The blood represented the animal's life (Lev. 17:11a), and all life belongs to the Lord. The Israelites were not free to use it as they wished. But the Lord did allow them to use it for a specific purpose: "I have given it for you on the altar to make atonement for your souls" (v. 11).

Atonement is the Lord's gracious gift, one he grants to sinful people. Indeed, while we usually think of sacrifice as that which the Israelites gave to God, here he turns this idea on its head: sacrificial atonement is something he mercifully and lovingly grants to them, allowing the lifeblood of the sacrifice to ransom the lifeblood of the guilty person.

25 [d]ch. 4:8-10; Ex. 29:13
26 [e]ver. 8, 10 [f][ch. 15:5; 17:15]
27 [g]ch. 4:11, 12, 21; 6:30; Heb. 13:11, 12
29 [h]ch. 23:27; Num. 29:7 [i]ch. 23:32; Ps. 35:13; Isa. 58:3, 5; Dan. 10:12 [j]ch. 17:15; 18:26; 19:34; [Ex. 12:49]
30 [k]Ps. 51:2; Jer. 33:8; Heb. 10:1, 2; 1 John 1:7, 9
31 [l]ch. 23:32 [i][See ver. 29 above]
32 [m][ch. 21:10] [n]Ex. 29:29, 30; [Num. 20:28] [o]ver. 4
33 [p]ver. 16 [q]ver. 18 [r]ver. 6

[s]ver. 24 **34** [t]Ex. 30:10; Heb. 9:7, 25 **Chapter 17** **3** [u][Deut. 12:5, 6, 13-15, 21] **4** [v]ver. 9 [w][Ex. 30:33] **5** [x]ch. 14:7, 53 [y]ch. 1:5 **6** [y][See ver. 5 above] [z]See Gen. 8:21 **7** [a]See Ex. 34:15 **8** [b]ch. 1:2, 3 **9** [c]ver. 4 [w][See ver. 4 above] **10** [d]See ch. 3:17 [e]ch. 20:3, 6; 26:17; Jer. 44:11; Ezek. 14:8; 15:7; [Ps. 34:16] **11** [f]ver. 14 [g][Matt. 26:28; Mark 14:24; Rom. 3:25; 5:9; Eph. 1:7; Col. 1:14, 20; Heb. 13:12; 1 John 1:7; Rev. 1:5] [h]Heb. 9:22

shall any stranger who sojourns among you eat blood.

13 "Any one also of the people of Israel, or of the strangers who sojourn among them, who takes in hunting any beast or bird that may be eaten shall [i]pour out its blood and [j]cover it with earth. 14 For the life of every creature[1] is its [k]blood: its blood is its life.[2] Therefore I have said to the people of Israel, You shall not eat the blood of any creature, for the life of every creature is its blood. Whoever eats it shall be cut off. 15 [l]And every person who eats what dies of itself or what is torn by beasts, [m]whether he is a native or a sojourner, [n]shall wash his clothes and [o]bathe himself in water and be unclean until the evening; then he shall be clean. 16 But if he does not wash them or bathe his flesh, [p]he shall bear his iniquity."

Unlawful Sexual Relations

18 And the LORD spoke to Moses, saying, 2 "Speak to the people of Israel and say to them, [q]I am the LORD your God. 3 [r]You shall not do as they do in the land of Egypt, where you lived, and [s]you shall not do as they do in the land of Canaan, to which I am bringing you. You shall not walk in their statutes. 4 [t]You shall follow my rules[3] and keep my statutes and walk in them. [q]I am the LORD your God. 5 [t]You shall therefore keep my statutes and my rules; [u]if a person does them, he shall live by them: I am the LORD.

6 "None of you shall approach any one of his close relatives to uncover nakedness. I am the LORD. 7 [v]You shall not uncover the nakedness of your father, which is the nakedness of your mother; she is your mother, you shall not uncover her nakedness. 8 [w]You shall not uncover the nakedness of your father's wife; it is your father's nakedness. 9 [x]You shall not uncover the nakedness of your sister, your father's daughter or your mother's daughter, whether brought up in the family or in another home. 10 You shall not uncover the nakedness of your son's daughter or of your daughter's daughter, for their nakedness is your own nakedness. 11 You shall not uncover the nakedness of your father's wife's daughter, brought up in your father's family, since she is your sister. 12 You shall not uncover the nakedness of your father's sister; she is your father's relative. 13 You shall not uncover the nakedness of your mother's sister, for she is your mother's relative. 14 You shall not uncover the nakedness of your father's brother, that is, you shall not approach his wife; she is your aunt. 15 [y]You shall not uncover the nakedness of your daughter-in-law; she is your son's wife, you shall not uncover her nakedness. 16 [z]You shall not uncover the nakedness of your brother's wife; it is your brother's nakedness. 17 You shall not uncover the nakedness of a woman and of her daughter, and you shall not take her son's daughter or her daughter's daughter to uncover her nakedness; they are relatives; it is depravity. 18 And you shall not take a woman

[1] Hebrew *all flesh* [2] Hebrew *it is in its life* [3] Or *my just decrees*; also verse 5

13 [i]Deut. 12:16, 24; 15:23 [j]Ezek. 24:7
14 [k]ver. 11; See Gen. 9:4
15 [l]See ch. 22:8 [m]See ch. 16:29 [n]See ch. 11:25 [o]ch. 15:5
16 [p][Num. 19:20]; See ch. 5:1
Chapter 18
2 [q]ch. 11:44; 19:4; 20:7; Ex. 6:6, 7
3 [r]Ezek. 20:7, 8; 23:8 [s]Ex. 23:24; Deut. 12:30, 31
4 [t]ver. 26; ch. 19:19, 37; 20:8, 22; 25:18; Deut. 4:1, 6; 5:1; 6:1; 12:1; Ezek. 20:19 [q][See ver. 2 above]
5 [t][See ver. 4 above] [u]Ezek. 20:11, 13, 21; Cited Rom. 10:5; Gal. 3:12; [Luke 10:28]
7 [v]For ver. 7-16, see ch. 20:11-21
8 [w]Deut. 22:30; 27:20; 1 Cor. 5:1; [Gen. 49:4; Amos 2:7]
9 [x][2 Sam. 13:12; Ezek. 22:11]
15 [y][Gen. 38:26; Ezek. 22:11]
16 [z][Gen. 38:8; Deut. 25:5; Matt. 22:24; Mark 12:19; Luke 20:28]

This same mercy and love is demonstrated supremely in the sacrificial death of Jesus, the ultimate ransom for the guilty (Mark 10:45), whom God himself sends to rescue a sinful people: "But God shows his love for us in that while we were still sinners, Christ died for us" (Rom. 5:8). We therefore trust in Jesus alone to rescue us from the justice that our sins deserve, and then we follow him in grateful obedience and praise (Rom. 5:11; 6:1–14).

18:1–30 The Israelites must avoid the unholy practices of the land's inhabitants, especially sexual immorality (vv. 6–20, 22–23) and illicit worship (v. 21). These things were contrary to the Lord's purpose for his creation and were met with his justice (vv. 24–29). This was especially tragic because the Lord had created humanity to experience his favor and blessing (Gen. 1:26–28). It is for this reason that he exhorts them to follow his laws (Lev. 18:1–5, 24–30), in this way staying within the sphere of his favor and experiencing life according to the blessings he intends (v. 5). Such obedience was not meant to merit relationship with God, but to acknowledge that they already belonged, body and soul, to the holy Lord who had redeemed them and provided the ways best for them.

Christians today acknowledge the same by means of their wholehearted obedience to the Lord Jesus, whose redemption is so tremendous it causes us to flee things such as sexual immorality and idolatrous loves because of our reverential fear of the Lord and our wonder at what he provides for us (1 Cor. 6:15–20; Phil. 3:4–11; 1 Tim. 6:11–12).

as a [a]rival wife to her sister, uncovering her nakedness [b]while her sister is still alive.

19 [c]"You shall not approach a woman to uncover her nakedness while she is in her menstrual uncleanness. 20 [d]And you shall not lie sexually with your neighbor's wife and so make yourself unclean with her. 21 You shall not give any of your children to [e]offer them[1] to [f]Molech, and so [g]profane the name of your God: I am the LORD. 22 [h]You shall not lie with a male as with a woman; it is an abomination. 23 [i]And you shall not lie with any animal and so make yourself unclean with it, neither shall any woman give herself to an animal to lie with it: it is [j]perversion.

24 [k]"Do not make yourselves unclean by any of these things, [l]for by all these the nations I am driving out before you have become unclean, 25 and the [m]land became unclean, so that I punished its iniquity, and the land [n]vomited out its inhabitants. 26 But [o]you shall keep my statutes and my rules and do none of these abominations, either the [p]native or the stranger who sojourns among you 27 (for the people of the land, who were before you, did all of these abominations, so that the land became unclean), 28 lest the land vomit you out when you make it unclean, as it vomited out the nation that was before you. 29 For everyone who does any of these abominations, the persons who do them shall be cut off from among their people. 30 [q]So keep my charge never to practice [r]any of these abominable customs that were practiced before you, and never to make yourselves unclean by them: [s]I am the LORD your God."

The LORD Is Holy

19 And the LORD spoke to Moses, saying, 2 "Speak to all the congregation of the people of Israel and say to them, [t]'You shall be holy, for I the LORD your God am holy. 3 [u]Every one of you shall revere his mother and his father, and [v]you shall keep my Sabbaths: I am the LORD your God. 4 [w]Do not turn to idols [x]or make for yourselves any gods of cast metal: I am the LORD your God.

5 [y]"When you offer a sacrifice of peace offerings to the LORD, you shall offer it so [z]that you may be accepted. 6 It shall be eaten the same day you offer it or on the day after, and anything left over until the third day shall be burned up with fire. 7 If it is eaten at all on the third day, it is [a]tainted; it will not be accepted, 8 and everyone who eats it shall [b]bear his iniquity, because [c]he has profaned what is holy to the LORD, and that person shall be cut off from his people.

Love Your Neighbor as Yourself

9 [d]"When you reap the harvest of your land, you shall not reap your field right up to its edge, neither shall you gather the gleanings after your harvest. 10 And you shall not strip your vineyard bare, neither shall you gather the fallen grapes of your vineyard. You shall leave them for the poor and for the sojourner: I am the LORD your God.

11 [e]"You shall not steal; [f]you shall not deal falsely; you shall not lie to one another. 12 [g]You shall not swear by my name falsely, and so [h]profane the name of your God: I am the LORD.

13 [i]"You shall not oppress your neighbor or

[1] Hebrew *to make them pass through* [the fire]

19:1–37 This chapter contains a long list of unholy practices the Israelites must avoid and holy practices they must perform. Significantly, the Lord continually grounds these commands with the phrase "I am the LORD (your God)" (vv. 2–4, 10, 12, 14, 16, 18, 25, 28, 30–32, 34, 36–37). This was a shorthand way of reminding them that he had redeemed them (Ex. 20:2; Lev. 11:45) and set them apart to be his (Ex. 19:4–6; Lev. 11:45; 20:24; 22:32b–33), so that he might dwell among them and be their God (Ex. 29:46). This makes clear that their obedience was to be a response of loving and reverential worship to their redeeming King, a response that would enable them to embody his holy kingdom in the world. Significantly, many of these commands for holy living relate to the way in which we are to love others. These can be summarized in the words of Lev. 19:18: "You shall love your neighbor as yourself."

Jesus showed this love in the ultimate way (John 15:13) and calls those who know him to show that same love to others (Matt. 7:12, 22:37–39; John 13:34–35; 15:12; cf. Eph. 5:2).

18 [a][1 Sam. 1:6] [b][Gen. 31:50]
19 [c][ch. 15:24; 20:18; Ezek. 18:6; 22:10]
20 [d]See Ex. 20:14
21 [e]ch. 20:2-5; Deut. 18:10 [f][1 Kgs. 11:7, 33; Acts 7:43] [g]ch. 19:12; 20:3; 21:6; 22:2, 32; Ezek. 36:20, 22; Mal. 1:12
22 [h]ch. 20:13; [Gen. 19:5; Judg. 19:22; Rom. 1:27; 1 Cor. 6:9, 10; 1 Tim. 1:9, 10]
23 [i]ch. 20:15, 16; Ex. 22:19 [j]ch. 20:12
24 [k]ver. 30; [Matt. 15:19, 20; Mark 7:21-23] [l]ch. 20:23; [Deut. 18:12]
25 [m]Num. 35:34; Jer. 2:7; Ezek. 36:17 [n]ch. 20:22
26 [o]See ver. 4, 5 [p]See ch. 16:29
30 [q]ch. 22:9 [r]ver. 3, 26; ch. 20:23; Deut. 18:9 [s]See ver. 2

Chapter 19 **2** [t]See ch. 11:44, 45 **3** [u]See Ex. 20:12 [v]See Ex. 20:8 **4** [w]ch. 26:1; 1 John 5:21; See Ex. 20:3-5 [x]Ex. 34:17; [Deut. 27:15] **5** [y]See ch. 7:15-18 [z]ch. 1:3; 22:19 **7** [a]ch. 7:18 **8** [b]See ch. 5:1 [c]ch. 22:15 **9** [d]ch. 23:22; Deut. 24:19-21; [Ruth 2:15, 16] **11** [e]See Ex. 20:15 [f][ch. 6:2, 3; Eph. 4:15, 25; Col. 3:9] **12** [g]See Ex. 20:7 [h]See ch. 18:21 **13** [i]ch. 6:2, 3

rob him. [j]The wages of a hired worker shall not remain with you all night until the morning. 14 [k]You shall not curse the deaf or put a stumbling block before the blind, but you shall [l]fear your God: I am the LORD.

15 [m]"You shall do no injustice in court. You shall not be partial to the poor or defer to the great, but in righteousness shall you judge your neighbor. 16 [n]You shall not go around as a slanderer among your people, and you shall not [o]stand up against the life[1] of your neighbor: I am the LORD.

17 [p]"You shall not hate your brother in your heart, but [q]you shall reason frankly with your neighbor, lest you [r]incur sin because of him. 18 [s]You shall not take vengeance or bear a grudge against the sons of your own people, but [t]you shall love your neighbor as yourself: I am the LORD.

You Shall Keep My Statutes

19 [u]"You shall keep my statutes. You shall not let your cattle breed with a different kind. [v]You shall not sow your field with two kinds of seed, nor shall you wear a garment of cloth made of two kinds of material.

20 "If a man lies sexually with a woman who is a slave, assigned to another man and not yet ransomed or given her freedom, a distinction shall be made. They shall not be put to death, because she was not free; 21 but [w]he shall bring his compensation to the LORD, to the entrance of the tent of meeting, a ram for a guilt offering. 22 And the priest shall make atonement for him with the ram of the guilt offering before the LORD for his sin that he has committed, and he shall be forgiven for the sin that he has committed.

23 "When you come into the land and plant any kind of tree for food, then you shall regard its fruit as forbidden.[2] Three years it shall be forbidden to you; it must not be eaten. 24 And in the fourth year all its fruit shall be holy, an offering of praise to the LORD. 25 But in the fifth year you may eat of its fruit, to increase its yield for you: I am the LORD your God.

26 [x]"You shall not eat any flesh with the blood in it. [y]You shall not interpret omens or [z]tell fortunes. 27 [a]You shall not round off the hair on your temples or mar the edges of your beard. 28 You shall not make any [b]cuts on your body for the dead or tattoo yourselves: I am the LORD.

29 [c]"Do not profane your daughter by making her a prostitute, lest the land fall into prostitution and the land become full of depravity. 30 [d]You shall keep my Sabbaths and [e]reverence my sanctuary: I am the LORD.

31 [f]"Do not turn to mediums or necromancers; do not seek them out, and so make yourselves unclean by them: I am the LORD your God.

32 [g]"You shall stand up before the gray head and honor the face of an old man, and you shall [h]fear your God: I am the LORD.

33 [i]"When a stranger sojourns with you in your land, you shall not do him wrong. 34 [j]You shall treat the stranger who sojourns with you as the native among you, and [k]you shall love him as yourself, for you were strangers in the land of Egypt: I am the LORD your God.

35 [l]"You shall do no wrong in judgment, in measures of length or weight or quantity. 36 [m]You shall have just balances, just weights, a just ephah, and a just hin:[3] I am the LORD your God, who brought you out of the land of Egypt. 37 And [n]you shall observe all my statutes and all my rules, and do them: I am the LORD."

Punishment for Child Sacrifice

20 The LORD spoke to Moses, saying, 2 "Say to the people of Israel, [o]Any one of the people of Israel or of the strangers who sojourn in Israel who gives any of his children

[1] Hebrew *blood* [2] Hebrew *as its uncircumcision* [3] An *ephah* was about 3/5 bushel or 22 liters; a *hin* was about 4 quarts or 3.5 liters

13 [j]Deut. 24:14, 15; Mal. 3:5; [James 5:4]
14 [k]Deut. 27:18 [l]ver. 32; ch. 25:17; Eccles. 5:7; 12:13; 1 Pet. 2:17
15 [m]Ex. 23:2, 3; Deut. 1:17; 16:19; 27:19; Ps. 82:2; Prov. 24:23; James 2:9; [2 Chr. 19:6, 7]
16 [n]Prov. 11:13; 20:19

20:1–27 Leviticus 18 listed unholy practices the Israelites were to avoid in the realms of sexual immorality and illicit worship. This chapter now describes the penalties that come from engaging in those practices. These penalties emphasize the seriousness of sin, the importance of addressing it among the Lord's people, and the reality of the Lord's justice for those who persist in it (cf. Acts 5:1–11; Gal. 6:7). But grace is not absent. The penalties serve as warnings of sin's consequences and of the pain of distance from fellowship with God. If God did not love his people, he would not so warn them.

[o]Ex. 23:1, 7; [Matt. 26:60, 61]; See 1 Kgs. 21:10-13; Acts 6:11-13 **17** [p]1 John 2:9, 11; 3:15 [q]Prov. 27:5, 6; Matt. 18:15; Luke 17:3; Gal. 6:1; Eph. 5:11 [r][ch. 22:16; Rom. 1:32; 1 Tim. 5:22; 2 John 11] **18** [s]Prov. 20:22; Rom. 12:17, 19; Heb. 10:30 [t]Matt. 5:43; Cited Matt. 19:19; 22:39; Mark 12:31; Luke 10:27; Rom. 13:9; Gal. 5:14; James 2:8 **19** [u]See ch. 18:4, 5 [v]Deut. 22:9-11 **21** [w]ch. 5:15; 6:6, 7 **26** [x]See ch. 3:17 [y]Deut. 18:10; 2 Kgs. 17:17 [z]2 Kgs. 21:6; 2 Chr. 33:6 **27** [a]ch. 21:5; [Isa. 15:2; Jer. 9:26; 48:37] **28** [b]ch. 21:1, 4, 5; Deut. 14:1; 1 Kgs. 18:28; Jer. 16:6; 41:5; 47:5; 48:37 **29** [c][Deut. 23:17] **30** [d]ver. 3; ch. 26:2; See Ex. 20:8 [e]Eccles. 5:1; [Matt. 21:12, 13; Mark 11:15-17; Luke 19:45, 46; John 2:14-16] **31** [f]ch. 20:6, 27; Deut. 18:11; Isa. 8:19; [Ex. 22:18; 1 Sam. 28:3, 7, 9; 1 Chr. 10:13; Acts 16:16] **32** [g]Prov. 20:29; [Lam. 5:12] [h]See ver. 14 **33** [i]Ex. 22:21; 23:9; Mal. 3:5 **34** [j]See ch. 16:29 [k]Deut. 10:19; See ver. 18 **35** [l]See ver. 15 **36** [m]Deut. 25:13, 15; Prov. 11:1; 16:11; 20:10; Ezek. 45:10; [Amos 8:5; Mic. 6:11] **37** [n]See ch. 18:4, 5 **Chapter 20** **2** [o]See ch. 18:21

to Molech shall surely be put to death. The
people of the land shall stone him with stones.
3 [p]I myself will set my face against that man
and will cut him off from among his people,
because he has given one of his children to
Molech, to make my sanctuary [q]unclean and
[r]to profane my holy name. 4 And if the people
of the land do at all close their eyes to that man
when he gives one of his children to Molech,
and do not [s]put him to death, 5 then I will set
my face against that man and against his clan
and will cut them off from among their people, him and all who follow him in [t]whoring
after Molech.
6 "If [u]a person turns to mediums and necromancers, whoring after them, [v]I will set my
face against that person and will cut him off
from among his people. 7 [w]Consecrate yourselves, therefore, and be holy, for I am the
LORD your God. 8 [x]Keep my statutes and do
them; [y]I am the LORD who sanctifies you. 9 For
[z]anyone who curses his father or his mother
shall surely be put to death; he has cursed his
father or his mother; [a]his blood is upon him.

Punishments for Sexual Immorality

10 "If a [b]man commits adultery with the wife
of[1] his neighbor, both the adulterer and the
adulteress shall surely be put to death. 11 [c]If a
man lies with his father's wife, he has uncovered his father's nakedness; both of them shall
surely be put to death; their blood is upon
them. 12 [d]If a man lies with his daughter-in-law,
both of them shall surely be put to death; they
have committed [e]perversion; their blood is
upon them. 13 [f]If a man lies with a male as with
a woman, both of them have committed an
abomination; they shall surely be put to death;
their blood is upon them. 14 [g]If a man takes a
woman and her mother also, it is depravity; he
and they shall be burned with fire, that there
may be no depravity among you. 15 [h]If a man
lies with an animal, he shall surely be put to
death, and you shall kill the animal. 16 [h]If a
woman approaches any animal and lies with
it, you shall kill the woman and the animal;
they shall surely be put to death; their blood
is upon them.
17 [i]"If a man takes his sister, a daughter of his
father or a daughter of his mother, and sees
her nakedness, and she sees his nakedness, it
is a disgrace, and they shall be cut off in the
sight of the children of their people. He has
uncovered his sister's nakedness, and he shall
bear his iniquity. 18 [j]If a man lies with a woman
during her menstrual period and uncovers
her nakedness, he has made naked her fountain, and she has uncovered the fountain of
her blood. Both of them shall be cut off from
among their people. 19 [k]You shall not uncover
the nakedness of your mother's sister or of
your father's sister, for that is to make naked
[l]one's relative; they shall bear their iniquity.
20 [m]If a man lies with his uncle's wife, he has
uncovered his uncle's nakedness; they shall
bear their sin; they shall die childless. 21 [n]If a
man takes his brother's wife, it is impurity.[2] He
has uncovered his brother's nakedness; they
shall be childless.

You Shall Be Holy

22 [o]"You shall therefore keep all my statutes
and all my rules and do them, that the land
where I am bringing you to live may not
[p]vomit you out. 23 [q]And you shall not walk in
the customs of the nation that I am driving
out before you, for they did all these things,
and therefore I detested them. 24 But [r]I have
said to you, 'You shall inherit their land, and
I will give it to you to possess, a land [s]flow-
ing with milk and honey.' I am the LORD your
God, [t]who has separated you from the peoples. 25 [u]You shall therefore separate the clean
beast from the unclean, and the unclean bird
from the clean. You shall not make yourselves
detestable by beast or by bird or by anything
with which the ground crawls, which I have
set apart for you to hold unclean. 26 [v]You shall

[1] Hebrew repeats *if a man commits adultery with the wife of* [2] Literally *menstrual impurity*

The chapter also emphasizes that experiencing these penalties was not the Lord's intent for humanity. His desire is that people experience his blessing and good pleasure as they walk in close fellowship with him in his ways (Lev. 20:22–26; see note on 18:1–30). It is this same desire that prompts Jesus to call us to take his yoke upon us, learning from him how to walk in God's ways, in this way finding rest for our souls (Matt. 11:28–30).

3 [p] See ch. 17:10 [q] ch. 19:30; Ezek. 5:11; 23:38, 39 [r] See ch. 18:21
4 [s] Deut. 17:2, 3, 5
5 [t] See Ex. 34:15
6 [u] See ch. 19:31 [v] See ch. 17:10
7 [w] See ch. 11:44

8 [x] See ch. 18:4 [y] ch. 21:8, 15, 23; 22:32; Ex. 31:13; Ezek. 37:28 **9** [z] See Ex. 21:17 [a] ver. 11, 12, 13, 16, 27; [2 Sam. 1:16; 1 Kgs. 2:32, 33, 37] **10** [b] ch. 18:20; Deut. 22:22; John 8:4, 5 **11** [c] See ch. 18:8 **12** [d] ch. 18:15 [e] ch. 18:23 **13** [f] See ch. 18:22 **14** [g] ch. 18:17; Deut. 27:23 **15** [h] ch. 18:23; Ex. 22:19; Deut. 27:21 **16** [h] [See ver. 15 above] **17** [i] ch. 18:9; Deut. 27:22 **18** [j] ch. 18:19; [ch. 15:24] **19** [k] ch. 18:12, 13 [l] ch. 18:6 **20** [m] ch. 18:14 **21** [n] ch. 18:16 **22** [o] See ch. 18:4 [p] ch. 18:25, 28 **23** [q] ch. 18:3, 24, 30; Deut. 9:5 **24** [r] Ex. 3:17; 6:8 [s] See Ex. 3:8 [t] Ex. 33:16; 1 Kgs. 8:53; [Ex. 19:5; Deut. 7:6; 14:2; 1 Kgs. 8:53] **25** [u] See ch. 11:2-47; Deut. 14:4-20 **26** [v] Ex. 19:6

be holy to me, [w]for I the LORD am holy and
have separated you from the peoples, that you
should be mine.
27 [x]"A man or a woman who is a medium or a
necromancer shall surely be put to death. They
shall be [y]stoned with stones; [z]their blood shall
be upon them."

Holiness and the Priests

21 And the LORD said to Moses, "Speak to
the priests, the sons of Aaron, and say
to them, [a]No one shall make himself unclean
for the dead among his people, 2 except for
his closest relatives, his mother, his father,
his son, his daughter, his brother, 3 or his virgin sister (who is near to him because she has
had no husband; for her he may make himself
unclean). 4 He shall not make himself unclean
as a husband among his people and so profane
himself. 5 [b]They shall not make bald patches
on their heads, nor shave off the edges of their
beards, nor make any cuts on their body. 6 They
shall be holy to their God and [c]not profane the
name of their God. For they offer the LORD's
food offerings, [d]the bread of their God; therefore they shall be holy. 7 [e]They shall not marry
a prostitute or a woman who has been defiled,
neither shall they marry a woman [f]divorced
from her husband, for the priest is holy to his
God. 8 You shall sanctify him, for he offers the
bread of your God. He shall be holy to you, for
[g]I, the LORD, who sanctify you, [h]am holy. 9 And
the daughter of any priest, if she profanes herself by whoring, profanes her father; [i]she shall
be burned with fire.
10 [j]"The priest who is chief among his brothers, on whose head the anointing oil is poured
and who has been consecrated to wear the
garments, [k]shall not let the hair of his head
hang loose nor tear his clothes. 11 He shall not
[l]go in to any dead bodies nor make himself
unclean, even for his father or for his mother.
12 [m]He shall not go out of the sanctuary, lest
he [n]profane the sanctuary of his God, for
the [o]consecration of the anointing oil of his
God is on him: I am the LORD. 13 And he shall
take a wife in her virginity.[1] 14 A widow, [p]or a
divorced woman, or a woman who has been
defiled, or a prostitute, these he shall not
marry. But he shall take as his wife a virgin[2]
of his own people, 15 that he may not profane
his offspring among his people, for [q]I am the
LORD who sanctifies him."
16 And the LORD spoke to Moses, saying,
17 "Speak to Aaron, saying, None of your offspring throughout their generations who has
a blemish may [q]approach to offer the bread of
his God. 18 For no one who has a blemish shall
draw near, a man [r]blind or lame, or one who
has a mutilated face [s]or a limb too long, 19 or
a man who has an injured foot or an injured
hand, 20 or a hunchback or a dwarf or a man
with a [r]defect in his sight or an itching disease or scabs or [t]crushed testicles. 21 No man
of the offspring of Aaron the priest who has a
blemish shall come near to [u]offer the LORD's
food offerings; since he has a blemish, he shall
not come near to offer the bread of his God.
22 He may eat the bread of his God, both of
[v]the most holy and of the [w]holy things, 23 but
he shall not go through the veil or approach
the altar, because he has a blemish, that he
may not [x]profane my sanctuaries, [y]for I am
the LORD who sanctifies them." 24 So Moses
spoke to Aaron and to his sons and to all the
people of Israel.

22 And the LORD spoke to Moses, saying, 2 "Speak to Aaron and his sons so
that they [z]abstain from the holy things of the
people of Israel, which they [a]dedicate to me,
so that they do not [b]profane my holy name:
I am the LORD. 3 Say to them, 'If any one of all
your offspring throughout your generations
approaches the holy things that the people of
Israel dedicate to the LORD, while [c]he has an
uncleanness, that person shall be cut off from
my presence: I am the LORD. 4 None of the offspring of Aaron who has a leprous disease or

[1] Or *a young wife* [2] Hebrew *young woman*

26[w] ver. 7; See ch. 11:44
27[x] See ch. 19:31 [y] ver. 2 [z] ver. 9
Chapter 21
1[a] Ezek. 44:25
5[b] Ezek. 44:20; [ch. 19:27, 28; Deut. 14:1]

21:1–22:16 This section emphasizes that priests are held to higher standards than other Israelites. This is no surprise. The priests served in the holy place of the holy Lord and therefore had to show extra care in terms of their ritual purity (so as not to defile the Lord's holy precincts). What is more, as the Israelites' spiritual leaders, the priests were to be models of moral purity and show Israel how to be a holy people.

6[c] See ch. 18:21 [d] See ch. 3:11 **7**[e] ver. 13, 14; Ezek. 44:22 [f] See Deut. 24:1-4 **8**[g] ch. 22:9, 16 [h] See ch. 11:44 **9**[i] [Gen. 38:24] **10**[j] ch. 8:12; 16:32; Ex. 29:29, 30; Num. 35:25 [k] ch. 10:6 **11**[l] Num. 19:14; [ver. 1, 2] **12**[m] ch. 10:7 [n] ver. 23 [o] [ch. 8:9, 12, 30] **14**[p] ver. 7; Ezek. 44:22 **15**[g] [See ver. 8 above] **17**[q] ch. 10:3; [Num. 16:5; Ps. 65:4] **18**[r] ch. 22:22 [s] [ch. 22:23] **20**[r] [See ver. 18 above] [t] [Deut. 23:1] **21**[u] ver. 6 **22**[v] ch. 2:3, 10; 6:17, 25; 7:1; 10:12, 17; 14:13; 24:9; Num. 18:9 [w] ch. 22:10, 12 **23**[x] ver. 12 [y] ch. 22:9, 16 **Chapter 22** **2**[z] [Num. 6:3] [a] ver. 3; Ex. 28:38; Deut. 15:19 [b] [Num. 18:32]; See ch. 18:21 **3**[c] ch. 7:20

a [d]discharge may eat of the holy things [e]until he is clean. [f]Whoever touches anything that is unclean through contact with the dead or [g]a man who has had an emission of semen, 5 and [h]whoever touches a swarming thing by which he may be made unclean or [i]a person from whom he may take uncleanness, whatever his uncleanness may be— 6 the person who touches such a thing shall be unclean until the evening and shall not eat of the holy things unless he has [j]bathed his body in water. 7 When the sun goes down he shall be clean, and afterward he may eat of the holy things, because [k]they are his food. 8 [l]He shall not eat what dies of itself or is torn by beasts, and so make himself unclean by it: I am the LORD.' 9 They shall therefore keep my charge, [m]lest they bear sin for it and die thereby when they profane it: [n]I am the LORD who sanctifies them.

10 [o]"A lay person shall not eat of a holy thing; no foreign guest of the priest or hired worker shall eat of a holy thing, 11 but if a priest buys a slave[1] as his property for money, the slave[2] may eat of it, and [p]anyone born in his house may eat of his food. 12 If a priest's daughter marries a layman, she shall not eat of the contribution of the holy things. 13 But if a priest's daughter is widowed or divorced and has no child and [q]returns to her father's house, [r]as in her youth, she may eat of her father's food; yet no lay person shall eat of it. 14 [s]And if anyone eats of a holy thing unintentionally, he shall add [t]the fifth of its value to it and give the holy thing to the priest. 15 They [u]shall not profane the holy things of the people of Israel, which they contribute to the LORD, 16 and so cause them [m]to bear iniquity and guilt, by eating their holy things: [n]for I am the LORD who sanctifies them."

Acceptable Offerings

17 And the LORD spoke to Moses, saying, 18 "Speak to Aaron and his sons and all the people of Israel and say to them, [v]When any one of the house of Israel or of the sojourners in Israel presents a burnt offering as his offering, for any of their vows or freewill offerings that they offer to the LORD, 19 if it is to be accepted for you it shall be a [w]male without blemish, of the bulls or the sheep or the goats. 20 [x]You shall not offer anything that has a blemish, for it will not be acceptable for you. 21 And when anyone [y]offers a sacrifice of peace offerings to the LORD [z]to fulfill a vow or as a freewill offering from the herd or from the flock, to be accepted it must be perfect; there shall be no blemish in it. 22 Animals [a]blind or disabled or mutilated or having a discharge or [b]an itch or scabs you shall not offer to the LORD or give them to the LORD as a food [c]offering on the altar. 23 You may present a bull or a lamb that has a part [d]too long or too short for a freewill offering, but for a vow offering it cannot be accepted. 24 Any animal that has its testicles bruised or crushed or torn or cut you shall not offer to the LORD; you shall not do it within your land, 25 neither shall you offer as [e]the bread of your God any such animals gotten from a foreigner. Since there is a [f]blemish in them, because of their mutilation, they will not be accepted for you."

[1] Or *servant*; twice in this verse [2] Hebrew *he*

The New Testament also emphasizes that the spiritual leaders of the Lord's people are held to higher standards (1 Tim. 3:1–7; Titus 1:6–9; James 3:1). They must undertake their duties with special reverence (1 Tim. 4:7–8, 12–16). They do so, however, in the glad and liberating knowledge that Jesus provides them the model to follow (1 Cor. 11:1) and the strength that they so desperately need (Phil. 4:13).

22:17–33 These verses focus on offering the proper animals (vv. 17–25) in the proper way (vv. 26–30) in order for them to be accepted (vv. 19–21, 23, 25, 27, 29), that is, for the Lord to respond with favor and pleasure to the offering and therefore the offerer. By following God's sacrificial laws, the Israelites acknowledged he was their holy and redeeming King (vv. 31–33; cf. at 19:1–37) and were assured he would accept them with favor.

The New Testament describes Jesus as the ultimate unblemished sacrifice (Heb. 9:14; 1 Pet. 1:19). It is through his sacrifice alone that we are accepted by God, and indeed, cleansed so deeply that we are considered to be holy and without blemish (John 14:6; Eph. 5:25–27). This fills us with confidence to draw near to him, knowing that because of Jesus we can be sure of God's favor (Heb. 10:19–22).

4[d] ch. 15:2 [e] ch. 14:2; 15:13 [f] Num. 19:11 [g] ch. 15:16
5[h] ch. 11:24, 43, 44 [i] ch. 15:7, 19
6[j] [Heb. 10:22]; See ch. 15:5-11
7[k] ch. 21:22; [Num. 18:11, 13]; See ch. 3:11
8[l] See ch. 7:24
9[m] [Ex. 28:43]; See ch. 19:17 [n] ch. 21:8, 15, 23
10[o] ch. 24:9; [1 Sam. 21:6; Matt. 12:4; Mark 2:26; Luke 6:4]
11[p] Num. 18:11, 13
13[q] [Gen. 38:11; Ruth 1:8] [r] ch. 10:14; Num. 18:11, 19
14[s] ch. 4:2; 5:15, 16, 18 [t] ch. 27:13, 15, 19
15[u] ch. 19:8; Num. 18:32
16[m] [See ver. 9 above] [n] [See ver. 9 above]
18[v] ch. 1:2, 3, 10; Num. 15:14
19[w] ch. 1:3, 10
20[x] Deut. 15:21; 17:1; Mal. 1:8, 14; [Heb. 9:14; 1 Pet. 1:19]
21[y] ch. 3:1, 6 [z] ch. 7:16; Num. 15:3, 8; Deut. 23:21, 23; Ps. 61:8; 65:1; Eccles. 5:4, 5 **22**[a] ver. 20; ch. 21:18; Mal. 1:8 [b] ch. 21:20 [c] ch. 1:9, 13; 3:3, 5 **23**[d] ch. 21:18 **25**[e] See ch. 3:11 [f] Mal. 1:14

26 And the LORD spoke to Moses, saying,
27 [g]"When an ox or sheep or goat is born, it
shall remain seven days with its mother, and
from the eighth day on it shall be acceptable
as a food offering to the LORD. 28 But you shall
not kill an ox or a sheep [h]and her young in one
day. 29 And when you sacrifice a [i]sacrifice of
thanksgiving to the LORD, you shall sacrifice
it so that you may be accepted. 30 It shall be
eaten on the same day; [j]you shall leave none
of it until morning: I am the LORD.

31 [k]"So you shall keep my commandments
and do them: I am the LORD. 32 [l]And you shall
not profane my holy name, that [m]I may be
sanctified among the people of Israel. [n]I am
the LORD who sanctifies you, 33 who brought
you out of the land of Egypt [o]to be your God:
I am the LORD."

Feasts of the LORD

23 The LORD spoke to Moses, saying,
2 "Speak to the people of Israel and say
to them, [p]These are the appointed feasts of the
LORD that you shall [q]proclaim as [r]holy convocations; they are my appointed feasts.

The Sabbath

3 [s]"Six days shall work be done, but on the seventh day is a Sabbath of solemn rest, a holy convocation. You shall do no work. It is a Sabbath
to the LORD in all your dwelling places.

The Passover

4 [p]"These are the appointed feasts of the
LORD, the [t]holy convocations, which you shall
proclaim at the time appointed for them. 5 [u]In
the first month, on the fourteenth day of the
month at twilight,[1] is the LORD's Passover.
6 And on the fifteenth day of the same month
is the Feast of Unleavened Bread to the LORD;
for seven days you shall eat unleavened bread.
7 [v]On the first day you shall have a holy convocation; you shall not do any ordinary work.
8 But you shall present a food offering to the
LORD for seven days. On the seventh day is a
holy convocation; you shall not do any ordinary work."

The Feast of Firstfruits

9 And the LORD spoke to Moses, saying,
10 "Speak to the people of Israel and say to them,
[w]When you come into the land that I give you
and reap its harvest, you shall bring the sheaf
of [x]the firstfruits of your harvest to the priest,
11 and he shall [y]wave the sheaf before the LORD,
so that you may be accepted. On the day after
the Sabbath the priest shall wave it. 12 And on
the day when you [y]wave the sheaf, you shall
offer a [z]male lamb a year old without blemish as a burnt offering to the LORD. 13 [a]And the
grain offering with it shall be two tenths of
an ephah[2] of fine flour mixed with oil, a food
offering to the LORD with a pleasing aroma,
[b]and the drink offering with it shall be of wine,
a fourth of a hin.[3] 14 And you shall eat neither
bread nor grain [c]parched or [c]fresh until this
same day, until you have brought the offering
of your God: it is a statute forever throughout
your generations in all your dwellings.

The Feast of Weeks

15 [d]"You shall count seven full weeks from the
day after the Sabbath, from the day that you
brought the sheaf of the [y]wave offering. 16 You
shall count [e]fifty days to the day after the seventh Sabbath. Then you shall present a grain
offering of [f]new grain to the LORD. 17 You shall
bring from your dwelling places two loaves
of bread to be waved, made of two tenths of
an ephah. They shall be of fine flour, and they
shall be baked with leaven, as [g]firstfruits to the
LORD. 18 And you shall present with the bread
seven lambs a year old without blemish, and
one bull from the herd and two rams. They
shall be a burnt offering to the LORD, with

[1] Hebrew *between the two evenings* [2] An *ephah* was about 3/5 bushel or 22 liters [3] A *hin* was about 4 quarts or 3.5 liters

27 [g] Ex. 22:30
28 [h] [Deut. 22:6]
29 [i] ch. 7:12; Ps. 107:22; 116:17; Amos 4:5
30 [j] ch. 7:15
31 [k] ch. 19:37; Num. 15:40; Deut. 4:40
32 [l] See ch. 18:21 [m] ch. 10:3 [n] See ch. 20:8
33 [o] See Ex. 6:7

23:1–44 This chapter focuses on the Lord's holy times. Each such occasion provided a reminder to the Israelites of who the Lord is or what he had done on their behalf. The weekly Sabbath reminded them he was their covenant King, the Lord of creation (v. 3; cf. Ex. 20:8–11; 31:12–17), while the annual festivals reminded them of his redemption and provision (Lev. 23:4–43). These reminders were meant to strengthen them in faithful obedience to the Lord (cf. Deut. 8:11–14) and in their covenant love to one another (cf. Deut. 16:9–12).

Chapter 23 **2** [p] ver. 4, 37; Num. 29:39; See Ex. 23:14-17 [q] Num. 10:10; Ps. 81:3; Joel 2:15 [r] Ex. 12:16 **3** [s] ch. 19:3; Ex. 23:12; 31:15; 34:21; Luke 13:14; See Ex. 20:8-11; Deut. 5:12-15 **4** [p] [See ver. 2 above] [t] Ex. 12:16 **5** [u] Ex. 13:3, 10; 23:15; 34:18; Num. 9:2, 3; 28:16, 17; Josh. 5:10; 2 Kgs. 23:21; Ezra 6:19; [Num. 9:10, 11; 2 Chr. 30:2, 13, 15]; See Ex. 12:2-14; Deut. 16:1-8 **7** [v] Ex. 12:16; Num. 28:18, 25 **10** [w] Ex. 23:19; 34:26; Num. 15:18, 19; 28:26; Deut. 26:1, 2 [x] ver. 17 **11** [y] ver. 15, 20; Ex. 29:24 **12** [y] [See ver. 11 above] [z] ch. 1:10 **13** [a] ch. 2:14-16 [b] Ex. 29:40 **14** [c] [ch. 2:14] **15** [d] Ex. 34:22; Deut. 16:9 [y] [See ver. 11 above] **16** [e] Acts 2:1 (Gk.) [f] Num. 28:26 **17** [g] See ver. 10

their grain offering and their drink offerings,
a food offering with a pleasing aroma to the
LORD. 19 And you shall offer one [h]male goat
for a sin offering, and two male lambs a year
old as a sacrifice of [i]peace offerings. 20 And the
priest shall [y]wave them with the bread of the
firstfruits as a wave offering before the LORD,
with the two lambs. [j]They shall be holy to the
LORD for the priest. 21 And you shall make a
proclamation on the same day. You shall hold
a holy convocation. You shall not do any ordinary work. It is a statute forever in all your
dwelling places throughout your generations.
22 "And [k]when you reap the harvest of your
land, you shall not reap your field right up to
its edge, nor shall you gather the gleanings
after your harvest. You shall leave them for
the poor and for the sojourner: I am the LORD
your God."

The Feast of Trumpets

23 And the LORD spoke to Moses, saying,
24 "Speak to the people of Israel, saying, In
[l]the seventh month, on the first day of the
month, you shall observe a day of solemn
rest, [m]a memorial proclaimed with blast of
trumpets, a holy convocation. 25 You shall not
do any ordinary work, and you shall present
a food offering to the LORD."

The Day of Atonement

26 And the LORD spoke to Moses, saying,
27 "Now [n]on the tenth day of this seventh
month is the Day of Atonement. It shall be for
you a time of holy convocation, and you shall
afflict yourselves[1] and present a food offering
to the LORD. 28 And you shall not do any work
on that very day, for it is a Day of Atonement,
to make atonement for you before the LORD
your God. 29 For whoever is not afflicted on
that very day [o]shall be cut off from his people.
30 And whoever does any work on that very
day, that person I will destroy from among
his people. 31 You shall not do any work. It is a
statute forever throughout your generations
in all your dwelling places. 32 It shall be to you
a Sabbath of solemn rest, and you shall afflict
yourselves. On the ninth day of the month
beginning at evening, from evening to evening shall you keep your Sabbath."

The Feast of Booths

33 And the LORD spoke to Moses, saying,
34 "Speak to the people of Israel, saying, [p]On
the fifteenth day of this seventh month and
for seven days is the Feast of Booths[2] to the
LORD. 35 On the first day shall be a holy convocation; you shall not do any ordinary work.
36 For seven days you shall present food offerings to the LORD. [q]On the eighth day you shall
hold a holy convocation and present a food
offering to the LORD. It is a [r]solemn assembly;
you shall not do any ordinary work.
37 [s]"These are the appointed feasts of the
LORD, which you shall proclaim as times of
holy convocation, for presenting to the LORD
food offerings, burnt offerings and grain offerings, sacrifices and drink offerings, each on its
proper day, 38 [t]besides the LORD's Sabbaths and
besides your gifts and besides all your vow
offerings and besides all your freewill offerings, which you give to the LORD.
39 "On the fifteenth day of the seventh
month, when you have [u]gathered in the produce of the land, you shall celebrate the feast
of the LORD seven days. On the first day shall
be a solemn rest, and on the eighth day shall
be a solemn rest. 40 And [v]you shall take on the
first day the fruit of splendid trees, branches of
palm trees and boughs of leafy trees and willows of the brook, and [w]you shall rejoice before
the LORD your God seven days. 41 [x]You shall
celebrate it as a feast to the LORD for seven
days in the year. It is a statute forever throughout your generations; you shall celebrate it
in the seventh month. 42 [y]You shall dwell in
booths for seven days. All native Israelites shall
dwell in booths, 43 that [z]your generations may
know that I made the people of Israel dwell in
booths when I brought them out of the land
of Egypt: I am the LORD your God."

[1] Or *shall fast*; also verse 32 [2] Or *tabernacles*

The Lord's Supper is to function in the same way for believers today. It is done in remembrance of Jesus, as a regular proclamation that he is our redeeming King (Luke 22:19–20; 1 Cor. 11:23–26). In this way it serves as a meal that strengthens our faith in him with the good news of the gospel and propels us to love our covenant brothers and sisters for whom he died (1 Cor. 10:16–17).

19 [h] ch. 4:23, 28; Num. 28:30 [i] See ch. 3:1
20 [y] [See ver. 11 above] [j] Num. 18:12; Deut. 18:4
22 [k] ch. 19:9, 10; Deut. 24:19; [Ruth 2:2, 3]
24 [l] Num. 29:1 [m] ch. 25:9

27 [n] ch. 16:29, 30; Num. 29:7 **29** [o] See Ex. 30:33 **34** [p] Num. 29:12; Deut. 16:13; Ezra 3:4; Neh. 8:14; Ezek. 45:25; Hos. 12:9; Zech. 14:16; John 7:2 **36** [q] Num. 29:35; Neh. 8:18; John 7:37 [r] Num. 29:35; Deut. 16:8; 2 Kgs. 10:20; 2 Chr. 7:9; Neh. 8:18; Isa. 1:13; Joel 1:14; 2:15; Amos 5:21 **37** [s] ver. 2, 4 **38** [t] Num. 29:39 **39** [u] Ex. 23:16; Deut. 16:13 **40** [v] See Neh. 8:14-18 [w] Deut. 16:14, 15 **41** [x] See Num. 29:12-38 **42** [y] See Neh. 8:14-18 **43** [z] See Deut. 31:10-13

44 Thus Moses [a]declared to the people of Israel the appointed feasts of the LORD.

The Lamps

24 [b]The LORD spoke to Moses, saying, 2 "Command the people of Israel to bring you pure oil from beaten olives for the lamp, that a light may be kept burning regularly. 3 Outside the veil of the testimony, in the tent of meeting, Aaron shall arrange it from evening to morning before the LORD regularly. It shall be a statute forever throughout your generations. 4 He shall arrange the lamps on the [c]lampstand of pure gold[1] before the LORD regularly.

Bread for the Tabernacle

5 "You shall take fine flour and bake twelve [d]loaves from it; two tenths of an ephah[2] shall be in each loaf. 6 And you shall set them in two piles, six in a pile, [e]on the table of pure gold[3] before the LORD. 7 And you shall put pure frankincense on each pile, that it may go with the bread as a memorial portion as a food offering to the LORD. 8 [f]Every Sabbath day Aaron shall arrange it before the LORD regularly; it is from the people of Israel as a covenant forever. 9 And [g]it shall be for Aaron and his sons, and [h]they shall eat it in a holy place, since it is for him a most holy portion out of the LORD's food offerings, a perpetual due."

Punishment for Blasphemy

10 Now an Israelite woman's son, whose father was an Egyptian, went out among the people of Israel. And the Israelite woman's son and a man of Israel fought in the camp, 11 and the Israelite woman's son [i]blasphemed the [j]Name, and cursed. Then they [k]brought him to Moses. His mother's name was Shelomith, the daughter of Dibri, of the tribe of Dan. 12 And [l]they put him in custody, [m]till the will of the LORD should be clear to them.

13 Then the LORD spoke to Moses, saying, 14 [n]"Bring out of the camp the one who cursed, and let all who heard him [o]lay their hands on his head, and let all the congregation stone him. 15 And speak to the people of Israel, saying, Whoever curses his God shall [p]bear his sin. 16 Whoever [q]blasphemes the name of the LORD shall surely be put to death. All the congregation shall stone him. The sojourner as well as the native, when he blasphemes the Name, shall be put to death.

An Eye for an Eye

17 [r]"Whoever takes a human life shall surely be put to death. 18 [s]Whoever takes an animal's life shall make it good, life for life. 19 If anyone injures his neighbor, [t]as he has done it shall be done to him, 20 fracture for fracture, eye for eye, tooth for tooth; whatever injury he has given a person shall be given to him. 21 [s]Whoever kills an animal shall make it good, [r]and whoever kills a person shall be put to death. 22 You shall have the [u]same rule for the sojourner and for the native, for I am the LORD your God." 23 So Moses spoke to the people of Israel, and [v]they brought out of the camp the one who had cursed and stoned him with stones. Thus the people of Israel did as the LORD commanded Moses.

The Sabbath Year

25 [w]The LORD spoke to Moses on Mount Sinai, saying, 2 "Speak to the people of Israel and say to them, When you come

[1] Hebrew *the pure lampstand* [2] An *ephah* was about 3/5 bushel or 22 liters [3] Hebrew *the pure table*

44[a] ver. 2
Chapter 24
1[b] Ex. 27:20, 21
4[c] Ex. 31:8; 39:37
5[d] Ex. 25:30
6[e] Ex. 25:23, 24; 1 Kgs. 7:48; 2 Chr. 4:19; 13:11; Heb. 9:2
8[f] 1 Chr. 9:32; [Num. 4:7; 2 Chr. 2:4]
9[g] 1 Sam. 21:6; Matt. 12:4; Mark 2:26; Luke 6:4 [h] [ch. 6:16; 8:31; 21:22; Ex. 29:33]
11[i] See ver. 16 [j] [Ex. 3:14, 15; Phil. 2:9] [k] Ex. 18:22, 26
12[l] [Num. 15:34] [m] [Ex. 18:15, 16; Num. 27:5; 36:5, 6]
14[n] [ver. 23] [o] [Deut. 13:9; 17:7]
15[p] ch. 5:1; 20:17, 20; 22:9; Num. 9:13; [Ex. 20:7]

24:10–23 This section uses a story about a blasphemer (vv. 10–16, 23) to introduce principles of public justice (vv. 17–22). The basic principle is expressed with the well-known phrase "an eye for an eye, a tooth for a tooth" (cf. v. 20). Israelites understood that this was not to be applied in a vengeful or mechanical way, but was a guiding principle for the public courts, emphasizing the importance of justice: the punishment must fit the crime (cf. Ex. 21:26–27).

In Jesus' day, it appears that some were misusing this principle by applying it in the context of personal relationships and using it to excuse acts of revenge. Jesus corrects this misinterpretation and teaches instead that our personal relationships are to be guided by the law of love and forgiveness (Matt. 5:38–42; cf. Lev. 19:18). In doing so, we will be showing to others the same patient love we ourselves have received, and continue to receive, from Jesus himself (Eph. 5:2; cf. Matt. 18:21–35).

16[q] ver. 11; 1 Kgs. 21:10, 13; Matt. 26:65, 66; Mark 14:63, 64; John 10:33 17[r] Gen. 9:5, 6; Ex. 21:12; Num. 35:31; Deut. 19:11, 12 18[s] Ex. 21:33, 34 19[t] Ex. 21:23-25; Deut. 19:21; Matt. 5:38; 7:2 21[s] [See ver. 18 above] [r] [See ver. 17 above] 22[u] ch. 19:34; Ex. 12:49; Num. 15:16 23[v] [ver. 14] **Chapter 25**
1[w] ch. 26:46

into [x]the land that I give you, the land shall keep a Sabbath to the LORD. 3 For six years you shall sow your field, and for six years you shall prune your vineyard and gather in its fruits, 4 but in the seventh year there shall be a Sabbath of solemn rest for the land, a Sabbath to the LORD. You shall not sow your field or prune your vineyard. 5 [y]You shall not reap what grows of itself in your harvest, or gather the grapes of your undressed vine. It shall be a year of solemn rest for the land. 6 The Sabbath of the land[1] shall provide food for you, for yourself and for your male and female slaves[2] and for your hired worker and the sojourner who lives with you, 7 and for your cattle and for the wild animals that are in your land: [z]all its yield shall be for food.

The Year of Jubilee

8 "You shall count seven weeks[3] of years, seven times seven years, so that the time of the seven weeks of years shall give you forty-nine years. 9 Then you shall sound [a]the loud trumpet on the tenth day of the seventh month. [b]On the Day of Atonement you shall sound the trumpet throughout all your land. 10 And you shall consecrate the fiftieth year, and [c]proclaim liberty throughout the land to all its inhabitants. It shall be a jubilee for you, when each of you shall return to his property and each of [d]you shall return to his clan. 11 That fiftieth year shall be a jubilee for you; in it [e]you shall neither sow nor reap [y]what grows of itself nor gather the grapes from the undressed vines. 12 For it is a jubilee. It shall be holy to you. [f]You may eat the produce of the field.[4]

13 [d]"In this year of jubilee each of you shall return to his property. 14 And if you make a sale to your neighbor or buy from your neighbor, [g]you shall not wrong one another. 15 [h]You shall pay your neighbor according to the number of years after the jubilee, and he shall sell to you according to the number of years for crops. 16 If the years are many, you shall increase the price, and if the years are few, you shall reduce the price, for it is the number of the crops that he is selling to you. 17 [i]You shall not wrong one another, but you shall fear your God, for I am the LORD your God.

18 [j]"Therefore you shall do my statutes and keep my rules and perform them, and then [k]you will dwell in the land securely. 19 [l]The land will yield its fruit, and [m]you will eat your fill [k]and dwell in it securely. 20 And if you say, [n]'What shall we eat in the seventh year, if [o]we may not sow or gather in our crop?' 21 I will [p]command my blessing on you in the sixth year, so that it will produce a crop sufficient for three years. 22 [q]When you sow in the eighth year, you will be eating some of [r]the old crop; you shall eat the old until the ninth year, when its crop arrives.

Redemption of Property

23 "The land shall not be sold in perpetuity, for [s]the land is mine. For you are strangers and sojourners with me. 24 And in all the country you possess, you shall allow a redemption of the land.

25 "If your brother becomes poor and sells part of his property, [t]then his nearest redeemer shall come and redeem what his brother has

[1] That is, the Sabbath produce of the land [2] Or *servants* [3] Or *Sabbaths* [4] Or *countryside*

25:1–55 This section gives laws for the seventh year rest (vv. 1–7), the Year of Jubilee (vv. 8–17), and laws that apply redemption and the jubilee to those who become poor (vv. 23–55). These laws help the Israelites to depend upon God's provision and to know how to usher in a society in which the justice, harmony, love, and mercy the Lord intended for humanity could be lived out in practice. Socially, families would be reunited and strengthened, while economically, there would be equity and opportunity.

Jesus explains that his mission was to put these principles into reality (see Luke 4:18–19, quoting Isa. 61:1–2, a passage rich in the language of Leviticus 25). This not only involved helping those who were economically distressed (Luke 14:13; cf. 16:19–31), but it went much further, with Jesus redeeming people from sickness (Luke 7:22) and spiritual oppression (Luke 4:31–37; 8:1–2). Most of all, he redeemed them from the debt of their sins (Luke 7:36–50; 19:1–10), making a way for them to become members of God's family (Luke 15:11–32). He now calls those who know his redemption to extend it in all its forms to those around them (Matt. 28:18–20).

2 [x] Ex. 23:10, 11; [ch. 26:34, 35; 2 Chr. 36:21]
5 [y] [2 Kgs. 19:29]; Isa. 37:30
7 [z] ver. 12
9 [a] [ch. 23:24; Isa. 27:13] [b] ch. 23:24, 27
10 [c] Isa. 61:1; Jer. 34:8, 13, 15, 17; Ezek. 46:17; [Isa. 61:2; 63:4; Luke 4:19] [d] ch. 27:24; Num. 36:4
11 [e] ver. 4, 5 [y] [See ver. 5 above]
12 [f] ver. 6, 7
13 [d] [See ver. 10 above]
14 [g] [ch. 19:33]
15 [h] ch. 27:18, 23
17 [i] ver. 36, 43; ch. 19:14, 32
18 [j] See ch. 18:4, 5 [k] ch. 26:5, 6; Deut. 12:10; [Prov. 1:33; Jer. 23:6; Ezek. 34:25, 28]
19 [l] Ps. 85:12; Ezek. 34:26, 27 [m] ch. 26:5; Deut. 11:15; [Joel 2:19, 26] [k] [See ver. 18 above]

20 [n] [Matt. 6:25, 31; Luke 12:22, 29] [o] ver. 4, 5 **21** [p] Deut. 28:8 **22** [q] [2 Kgs. 19:29] [r] ch. 26:10 **23** [s] Deut. 32:43; 2 Chr. 7:20; Ps. 85:1; Hos. 9:3; Joel 2:18; 3:2
25 [t] Ruth 2:20; 3:9, 12; 4:4, 6; Jer. 32:7, 8

sold. 26 If a man has no one to redeem it and
then himself becomes prosperous and finds
sufficient means to redeem it, 27 let [u]him calculate the years since he sold it and pay back
the balance to the man to whom he sold it, and
then return to his property. 28 But if he does
not have sufficient means to recover it, then
what he sold shall remain in the hand of the
buyer until the year of jubilee. In the jubilee
it shall [v]be released, and [w]he shall return to
his property.

29 "If a man sells a dwelling house in a
walled city, he may redeem it within a year
of its sale. For a full year he shall have the
right of redemption. 30 If it is not redeemed
within a full year, then the house in the walled
city shall belong in perpetuity to the buyer,
throughout his generations; [v]it shall not be
released in the jubilee. 31 But the houses of the
villages that have no wall around them shall
be classified with the fields of the land. They
may be redeemed, and [v]they shall be released
in the jubilee. 32 As for [x]the cities of the Levites,
the Levites may redeem at any time the houses
in the cities they possess. 33 And if one of the
Levites exercises his right of redemption, then
the house that was sold in a city they possess
shall be released in the jubilee. For the houses
in the cities of the Levites are their possession
among the people of Israel. 34 But the fields [y]of
pastureland belonging to their cities may not
be sold, for that is their possession forever.

Kindness for Poor Brothers

35 "If your brother becomes poor and cannot
maintain himself with you, [z]you shall support him as though he were a stranger and a
sojourner, and he shall live with you. 36 [a]Take
no interest from him or profit, but [b]fear your
God, that your brother may live beside you.
37 [a]You shall not lend him your money at interest, nor give him your food for profit. 38 [c]I am
the LORD your God, who brought you out
of the land of Egypt to give you the land of
Canaan, and to be your God.

39 [d]"If your brother becomes poor beside you
and sells himself to you, you shall not make
him serve as a slave: 40 he shall be with you as a
hired worker and as a sojourner. He shall serve
with you until the year of the jubilee. 41 [v]Then
he shall go out from you, [e]he and his children
with him, and go back to his own clan and
return [f]to the possession of his fathers. 42 For
they are [g]my servants,[1] whom I brought out
of the land of Egypt; they shall not be sold as
slaves. 43 [h]You shall not rule over him [i]ruthlessly
but [j]shall fear your God. 44 As for your male and
female slaves whom you may have: you may
buy male and female slaves from among the
nations that are around you. 45 [k]You may also
buy from among the strangers who sojourn
with you and their clans that are with you, who
have been born in your land, and they may be
your property. 46 You may bequeath them to
your sons after you to inherit as a possession
forever. You may make slaves of them, but over
your brothers the people of Israel [l]you shall not
rule, one over another ruthlessly.

Redeeming a Poor Man

47 "If a stranger or sojourner with you
becomes rich, and [m]your brother beside him
becomes poor and sells himself to the stranger
or sojourner with you or to a member of the
stranger's clan, 48 then after he is sold he
may be redeemed. One of his brothers may
redeem him, 49 or his uncle or his cousin may
[n]redeem him, or a close relative from his clan
may redeem him. Or if he [o]grows rich he may
redeem himself. 50 He shall calculate with his
buyer from the year when he sold himself to
him until the year of jubilee, and the price of
his sale shall vary with the number of years.
The time he was with his owner shall be [p]rated
as the time of a hired worker. 51 If there are still
many years left, he shall pay proportionately
for his redemption some of his sale price. 52 If
there remain but a few years until the year
of jubilee, he shall calculate and pay for his
redemption in proportion to his years of service. 53 He shall treat him as a worker hired year
by year. [l]He shall not rule ruthlessly over him in
your sight. 54 And if he is not redeemed by these
means, then [q]he and his children with him
shall be released in the year of jubilee. 55 For it
is [r]to me that the people of Israel are servants.[2]
They are my servants whom I brought out of
the land of Egypt: I am the LORD your God.

[1] Hebrew *slaves* [2] Or *slaves*

27[u] See ver. 50-52 **28**[v] ch. 27:21 [w] ver. 13, 41 **30**[v] [See ver. 28 above] **31**[v] [See ver. 28 above] **32**[x] [Num. 35:2]; See Josh. 21:2-40 **34**[y] Num. 35:2; 1 Chr. 13:2; [Acts 4:36, 37]; See Josh. 21:11-42; 1 Chr. 6:55-81 **35**[z] Deut. 15:7, 8; [Ps. 41:1; 112:5, 9; Prov. 14:31; Acts 11:29; 1 John 3:17] **36**[a] See Ex. 22:25 [b] ver. 17, 43; Neh. 5:9; [Mal. 3:5] **37**[a] [See ver. 36 above] **38**[c] ver. 42, 55; ch. 22:32, 33; 26:13 **39**[d] Ex. 21:2; Deut. 15:12; 1 Kgs. 9:22; 2 Kgs. 4:1; Neh. 5:5 **41**[v] [See ver. 28 above] [e] [Ex. 21:3] [f] ver. 13, 28 **42**[g] ver. 55; [Rom. 6:22; 1 Cor. 7:23] **43**[h] [Eph. 6:9; Col. 4:1] [i] Ex. 1:13, 14; Ezek. 34:4 [j] ver. 17, 36 **45**[k] Isa. 14:1, 2; 56:3, 6 **46**[l] Ex. 1:13, 14; Ezek. 34:4 **47**[m] ver. 25, 35, 39 **49**[n] See Neh. 5:1-5 [o] ver. 26, 47 **50**[p] Job 7:1; Isa. 16:14; 21:16 **53**[l] [See ver. 46 above] **54**[q] ver. 41; Ex. 21:2, 3 **55**[r] ver. 42

Blessings for Obedience

26 "You shall not make [s]idols for yourselves or erect an [t]image or [u]pillar, and
you shall not set up a [v]figured stone in your
land to bow down to it, for I am the LORD your
God. 2 [w]You shall keep my Sabbaths and reverence my sanctuary: I am the LORD.
3 [x]"If you walk in my statutes and observe my
commandments and do them, 4 then [y]I will
give you your rains in their season, and the
land shall yield its increase, and the trees of
the field shall yield their fruit. 5 [z]Your threshing shall last to the time of the grape harvest,
and the grape harvest shall last to the time
for sowing. And [a]you shall eat your bread to
the full and [b]dwell in your land securely. 6 [c]I
will give peace in the land, and [d]you shall lie
down, and none shall make you afraid. And
[e]I will remove harmful beasts from the land,
[f]and the sword shall not go through your
land. 7 You shall chase your enemies, and they
shall fall before you by the sword. 8 [g]Five of
you shall chase a hundred, and a hundred of
you shall chase ten thousand, and your enemies shall fall before you by the sword. 9 [h]I will
turn to you and [i]make you fruitful and multiply you and will confirm my covenant with
you. 10 You shall eat [j]old store long kept, and
you shall clear out the old to make way for
the new. 11 [k]I will make my dwelling[1] among
you, and my soul shall not abhor you. 12 [l]And
I [m]will walk among you and will be your God,
and you shall be my people. 13 [n]I am the LORD
your God, who brought you out of the land
of Egypt, that you should not be their slaves.
[o]And I have broken the bars of your yoke and
made you walk erect.

Punishment for Disobedience

14 [p]"But if you will not listen to me and will
not do all these commandments, 15 if you spurn
my statutes, and if your soul abhors my rules,
so that you will not do all my commandments,
but [q]break my covenant, 16 then I will do this to
you: I will visit you with panic, with [r]wasting
disease and fever that consume the eyes and
make the heart ache. And [s]you shall sow your
seed in vain, for your enemies shall eat it. 17 I
will [t]set my face against you, and [u]you shall be
struck down before your enemies. [v]Those who
hate you shall rule over you, and [w]you shall
flee when none pursues you. 18 And if in spite
of this you will not listen to me, then I will
discipline you again [x]sevenfold for your sins,
19 and I will break [y]the pride of your power, and
I [z]will make your heavens like iron and your
earth like bronze. 20 And [a]your strength shall
be spent in vain, for [b]your land shall not yield
its increase, and the trees of the land shall not
yield their fruit.
21 [c]"Then if you walk contrary to me and
will not listen to me, I will continue striking
you, sevenfold for your sins. 22 And [d]I will let
loose the wild beasts against you, which shall
bereave you of your children and destroy your
livestock and make you few in number, so that
[e]your roads shall be deserted.
23 "And [f]if by this discipline you are not
turned to me [c]but walk contrary to me,
24 [g]then I also will walk contrary to you, and
I myself will strike you sevenfold for your

[1] Hebrew *tabernacle*

26:1–46 In the ancient Near East, covenant documents often had blessings and curses near the end. Their presence here emphasizes that the laws of Leviticus were considered part of the covenant between Israel and the Lord.

The Lord's desire is that his people experience his blessing (cf. Gen. 1:28; 12:1–3), which they did by obeying his laws, thereby staying within the bounds of his kingdom. Such obedience was not to earn relationship with him, but was the proper response to their redeeming covenant King (see note on Lev. 18:1–30). The blessings begin by addressing the Israelites' physical needs (26:4–10) and culminate by addressing their spiritual needs: relationship with the Lord (vv. 11–12). The cursings primarily relate to the people's difficulties in and with the land (vv. 14–26), and their subsequent ejection from it after persistent disobedience (vv. 27–39). But even the worst of discipline identified in the cursings was not intended as a final rejection (vv. 44–45) but as a means of turning God's children back to him (vv. 23, 40–42).

Chapter 26

1 [s]See ch. 19:4 [t]See Ex. 20:4, 5 [u]Ex. 23:24 [v]Num. 33:52; [Ezek. 8:10]
2 [w]ch. 19:30; See Ex. 20:8
3 [x]Deut. 11:13-15; 28:1-14; See ch. 18:4
4 [y]Ps. 67:6; 85:12; Ezek. 34:26, 27; 36:30; Joel 2:23, 24; Zech. 8:12; [ver. 20; Deut. 11:17]
5 [z][Amos 9:13] [a]See ch. 25:19 [b]See ch. 25:18
6 [c][1 Kgs. 4:25; 1 Chr. 22:9] [d]Job 11:19; Jer. 30:10; Zeph. 3:13 [e]Ezek. 34:25; [2 Kgs. 17:25; Isa. 35:9; Ezek. 5:17; 14:15] [f][Ezek. 14:17]
8 [g][Deut. 32:30; Josh. 23:10; Isa. 30:17]

9 [h]2 Kgs. 13:23 [i]Neh. 9:23 **10** [j]ch. 25:22 **11** [k]Ezek. 37:26-28; [Rev. 21:3] **12** [l]Ex. 29:45; Cited 2 Cor. 6:16 [m]Jer. 7:23; 11:4; 24:7; 30:22; Ezek. 11:20; 14:11; 36:28; 37:27; See Ex. 6:7 **13** [n]See ch. 25:38 [o]Ezek. 34:27; [Jer. 27:2; 28:10, 13] **14** [p][Lam. 2:17; Mal. 2:2]; See Deut. 28:15-68 **15** [q]ver. 44; Deut. 31:20 **16** [r]Deut. 28:21 [s]Deut. 28:33, 51; Job 31:8; Jer. 5:17; Mic. 6:15 **17** [t]See ch. 17:10 [u]Deut. 28:25; Judg. 2:14; Jer. 19:7 [v]Ps. 106:41 [w]Prov. 28:1; [ver. 36; Ps. 53:5] **18** [x]ver. 21, 24, 28; 1 Sam. 2:5; Ps. 119:164; Prov. 24:16 **19** [y]Ezek. 30:6; [Jer. 13:9] [z]Deut. 28:23 **20** [a][Ps. 127:1; Isa. 49:4] [b][Hag. 1:10]; See ver. 4 **21** [c]ver. 27 **22** [d]Deut. 32:24; See ver. 6 [e]Judg. 5:6; Isa. 33:8; Lam. 1:4; Zech. 7:14 **23** [f]Jer. 2:30; 5:3; See Amos 4:6-12 [c][See ver. 21 above] **24** [g]2 Sam. 22:27; Ps. 18:26

sins. 25 And [h]I will bring a sword upon you,
that shall execute vengeance for the covenant.
And if you gather within your cities, [i]I will
send pestilence among you, and you shall be
delivered into the hand of the enemy. 26 [j]When
I break your supply[1] of bread, ten women shall
bake your bread in a single oven and shall
dole out your bread again by weight, and [k]you
shall eat and not be satisfied.
27 "But [l]if in spite of this you will not listen
to me, but walk contrary to me, 28 then I will
walk contrary to you [m]in fury, and I myself will
discipline you [x]sevenfold for your sins. 29 [n]You
shall eat the flesh of your sons, and you shall
eat the flesh of your daughters. 30 And [o]I will
destroy your high places and cut down your
incense altars and [p]cast your dead bodies upon
the dead bodies of your idols, and my soul will
abhor you. 31 And I will [q]lay your cities waste
and will [r]make your sanctuaries desolate, and
[s]I will not smell your pleasing aromas. 32 And
[t]I myself will devastate the land, so that your
enemies who settle in it shall be [u]appalled at
it. 33 And [v]I will scatter you among the nations,
and I will unsheathe the sword after you, and
your land shall be a desolation, and your cities
shall be a waste.
34 [w]"Then the land shall enjoy[2] its Sabbaths
as long as it lies desolate, while you are in your
enemies' land; then the land shall rest, and
enjoy its Sabbaths. 35 As long as it lies desolate
it shall have rest, the rest that it did not have
on your Sabbaths when you were dwelling in
it. 36 And as for those of you who are left, [x]I will
send faintness into their hearts in the lands
of their enemies. The [y]sound of a [z]driven leaf
shall put them to flight, and they shall flee as
one flees from the sword, and they shall fall
when none pursues. 37 They shall stumble over
one another, as if to escape a sword, though
none pursues. And [a]you shall have no power
to stand before your enemies. 38 And you shall
perish among the nations, and the land of
your enemies shall eat you up. 39 And those
of you who are left shall [b]rot away in your
enemies' lands because of their iniquity, and
also because of the iniquities of their fathers
they shall rot away like them.
40 "But if [c]they confess their iniquity and the
iniquity of their fathers in their treachery that
they [d]committed against me, and also in walking contrary to me, 41 so that I walked contrary
to them and brought them into the land of
their enemies—if then their [e]uncircumcised
heart is [f]humbled and they make amends
for their iniquity, 42 then I will [g]remember
my covenant with Jacob, and I will remember my covenant with Isaac and my covenant
with Abraham, and I will [h]remember the land.
43 But [w]the land shall be abandoned by them
and enjoy its Sabbaths while it lies desolate
without them, and they shall make amends
for their iniquity, because they spurned my
rules and their soul abhorred my statutes.
44 Yet for all that, when they are in the land of
their enemies, [i]I will not spurn them, neither
will I abhor them so as to destroy them utterly
and [j]break my covenant with them, for I am
the LORD their God. 45 But I will for their sake
remember the covenant with their forefathers,
[k]whom I brought out of the land of Egypt [l]in
the sight of the nations, that I might be their
God: I am the LORD."
46 [m]These are the statutes and rules and laws
that the LORD made between himself and the
people of Israel through Moses [n]on Mount
Sinai.

Laws About Vows

27 The LORD spoke to Moses, saying,
2 "Speak to the people of Israel and say
to them, If anyone [o]makes a special vow to

[1] Hebrew *staff* [2] Or *pay for*; twice in this verse; also verse 43

In the new covenant, Jesus takes on himself the curses that our rebellion deserves, thereby making a way for us to experience forever the blessing of knowing and abiding with the Lord (Gal. 3:8–14). Jesus also exhorts us to keep our relationship with God at the center of our lives, trusting that our heavenly Father will meet our physical needs (Matt. 6:19–34) as well our eternal ones. This we can do, by knowing and remembering that the Lord loves his children and will care for them, body and soul.

25 [h]Deut. 32:25; Jer. 14:12; 24:10; 29:17, 18; Ezek. 5:17; 6:3; 14:17; 29:8; 33:2 [i]Num. 14:12; Deut. 28:21
26 [j]Ps. 105:16; Isa. 3:1; Ezek. 4:16; 5:16; 14:13 [k]Isa. 9:20; Mic. 6:14; Hag. 1:6
27 [l]ver. 21, 24
28 [m]Isa. 59:18; 63:3; 66:15; Jer. 21:5; Ezek. 5:13, 15; 8:18

[x][See ver. 18 above] **29** [n]Deut. 28:53; Ezek. 5:10; [2 Kgs. 6:29; Lam. 4:10] **30** [o]2 Chr. 14:5; 34:3, 4, 7; See Ezek. 6:3-6 [p][2 Kgs. 23:20; 2 Chr. 34:5; Ezek. 6:5] **31** [q]Neh. 2:3; Jer. 4:7; See 2 Kgs. 25:4-10 [r]Ps. 74:7; Lam. 1:10; Ezek. 9:6; 21:2 [s]Jer. 6:20; See Isa. 1:11-15; Amos 5:21-23 **32** [t]Jer. 9:11; 25:11, 18 [u]Deut. 28:37; 1 Kgs. 9:8; Jer. 18:16; 19:8; Ezek. 5:15 **33** [v]Deut. 4:27; 28:64; Neh. 1:8; Ps. 44:11; Jer. 9:16; Ezek. 12:15; 20:23; 22:15; Zech. 7:14; [Luke 21:24] **34** [w]2 Chr. 36:21; See ch. 25:2 **36** [x]Ezek. 21:7 [y]ver. 17 [z]Job 13:25 **37** [a]Josh. 7:12, 13; Judg. 2:14 **39** [b]Deut. 28:65; Ezek. 4:17; 24:23; 33:10; [Ezek. 6:9] **40** [c][Neh. 9:2; Prov. 28:13; 1 John 1:9]; See 1 Kgs. 8:33-36; Dan. 9:4-19 [d]ch. 6:2; Num. 5:6 **41** [e]See Ex. 6:12 [f][1 Kgs. 21:29; 2 Chr. 12:6, 7; 32:26; 33:12, 13] **42** [g]Ex. 2:24; 6:5; Ps. 106:45; Ezek. 16:60 [h][Ps. 85:1] **43** [w][See ver. 34 above] **44** [i][Deut. 4:31; 2 Kgs. 13:23; Neh. 9:31; Rom. 11:2] [j]ver. 15 **45** [k]ch. 22:33 [l]Ps. 98:2; Ezek. 20:9, 22 **46** [m]ch. 27:34; Deut. 6:1; 12:1 [n]ch. 25:1 **Chapter 27** **2** [o][Judg. 11:30, 31, 39; 1 Sam. 1:11, 28; See Num. 30]

the LORD involving the valuation of persons, 3 then the valuation of a male from twenty years old up to sixty years old shall be fifty shekels[1] of silver, according to the [p]shekel of the sanctuary. 4 If the person is a female, the valuation shall be thirty shekels. 5 If the person is from five years old up to twenty years old, the valuation shall be for a male twenty shekels, and for a female ten shekels. 6 If the person is from a month old up to five years old, the valuation shall be for a male five shekels of silver, and for a female the valuation shall be three shekels of silver. 7 And if the person is sixty years old or over, then the valuation for a male shall be fifteen shekels, and for a female ten shekels. 8 And if someone is too poor to pay the valuation, then he shall be made to stand before the priest, and the priest shall value him; the priest shall value him according to what the vower can afford.

9 "If the vow[2] is an animal that may be offered as an offering to the LORD, all of it that he gives to the LORD is holy. 10 [q]He shall not exchange it or make a substitute for it, good for bad, or bad for good; and if he does in fact substitute one animal for another, then both it and the substitute shall be holy. 11 And if it is any unclean animal that may not be offered as an offering to the LORD, then he shall stand the animal before the priest, 12 and the priest shall value it as either good or bad; as the priest values it, so it shall be. 13 [r]But if he wishes to redeem it, he shall add a [s]fifth to the valuation.

14 "When a man dedicates his house as a holy gift to the LORD, the priest shall value it as either good or bad; as the priest values it, so it shall stand. 15 [t]And if the donor wishes to redeem his house, he shall add a [s]fifth to the valuation price, and it shall be his.

16 "If a man dedicates to the LORD part of the land that is his possession, then the valuation shall be in proportion to its seed. A homer[3] of barley seed shall be valued at fifty shekels of silver. 17 If he dedicates his field from the year of jubilee, the valuation shall stand, 18 but if he dedicates his field after the jubilee, then the priest shall [u]calculate the price according to the years that remain until the year of jubilee, and a deduction shall be made from the valuation. 19 [v]And if he who dedicates the field wishes to redeem it, then he shall add a [s]fifth to its valuation price, and it shall remain his. 20 But if he does not wish to redeem the field, or if he has sold the field to another man, it shall not be redeemed anymore. 21 But the field, [w]when it is released in the jubilee, shall be a holy gift to the LORD, like a field that has been [x]devoted. The priest shall be in [y]possession of it. 22 If he dedicates to the LORD a field that he has bought, [z]which is not a part of his possession, 23 [a]then the priest shall calculate the amount of the valuation for it up to the year of jubilee, and the man shall give the valuation on that day as a holy gift to the LORD. 24 [b]In the year of jubilee the field shall return to him from whom it was bought, to whom the land belongs as a possession. 25 Every valuation shall be according to [c]the shekel of the sanctuary: [d]twenty gerahs[4] shall make a shekel.

26 "But a [e]firstborn of animals, which as a firstborn belongs to the LORD, no man may dedicate; whether ox or sheep, it is the LORD's. 27 And if it is an unclean animal, then he shall buy it back at the valuation, [f]and add a fifth to it; or, if it is not redeemed, it shall be sold at the valuation.

28 "But [g]no devoted thing that a man devotes

[1] A *shekel* was about 2/5 ounce or 11 grams [2] Hebrew *it* [3] A *homer* was about 6 bushels or 220 liters [4] A *gerah* was about 1/50 ounce or 0.6 gram

27:1–34 This chapter contains further laws relating to the jubilee year and to redemption (cf. Leviticus 25). It deals with voluntary gifts (27:1–25) as well as required gifts (vv. 26–33). People often promised voluntary gifts to ensure that they thanked the Lord appropriately for answering prayer or providing a blessing (Ps. 66:13, 16; cf. 1 Sam. 1:24–2:10). They were also to give required gifts, such as the tithe (Lev. 27:30–33), to thank the Lord for his provision as well as to acknowledge that he was a King worthy of their tribute.

In either case, this chapter emphasizes that people must honor their commitments to the Lord. This is true with regard to discipleship in general: following Jesus is to be a wholehearted and lifelong commitment (Luke 9:61–62; 14:25–33). Such a commitment is not only an appropriate expression of thanksgiving for his amazing provision of salvation; it is also an acknowledgment of him as the redeeming King worthy of any tribute we can bring (Phil. 2:9–11; 3:7–11).

3 [p] ver. 25; See Ex. 30:13
10 [q] ver. 33
13 [r] ver. 15, 19 [s] ch. 22:14
15 [t] ver. 13 [s] [See ver. 13 above]
18 [u] ver. 23; ch. 25:15, 16
19 [v] ver. 13 [s] [See ver. 13 above]
21 [w] ch. 25:28, 30, 31, 33, 41 [x] ver. 28 [y] Num. 18:14; Ezek. 44:29
22 [z] ch. 25:10, 25
23 [a] ver. 18
24 [b] ch. 25:28
25 [c] ver. 3 [d] See Ex. 30:13
26 [e] See Ex. 13:2
27 [f] ver. 11-13
28 [g] ver. 21; Josh. 6:17-19; 1 Sam. 15:21

to the LORD, of anything that he has, whether
man or beast, or of his inherited field, shall
be sold or redeemed; every devoted thing is
most holy to the LORD. 29 [h]No one devoted,
who is to be devoted for destruction[1] from
mankind, shall be ransomed; he shall surely
be put to death.

30 [i]"Every tithe of the land, whether of the
seed of the land or of the fruit of the trees, is
the LORD's; it is holy to the LORD. 31 If a man
wishes to redeem some of his tithe, he shall
add a fifth to it. 32 And every tithe of herds
and flocks, every tenth animal of all that [j]pass
under the herdsman's staff, shall be holy to the
LORD. 33 One shall not differentiate between
good or bad, [k]neither shall he make a substitute
for it; and if he does substitute for it, then
both it and the substitute shall be holy; it shall
not be redeemed."

34 [l]These are the commandments that the
LORD commanded Moses for the people of
Israel [m]on Mount Sinai.

[1] That is, set apart (devoted) as an offering to the Lord (for destruction)

29[h] [Num. 21:2; Judg. 11:35] **30**[i] Gen. 14:20; 28:22; Num. 18:21, 24; Deut. 14:28; 2 Chr. 31:5, 6, 12; Neh. 13:12; Mal. 3:8, 10 **32**[j] Ezek. 20:37; [Jer. 33:13] **33**[k] ver. 10 **34**[l] ch. 26:46 [m] ch. 25:1; 26:46

Introduction to Numbers

Author

Moses is the author of the book of Numbers, which is the fourth of five volumes in the Pentateuch. Its English name comes from the censuses in chapters 1–4 and 26. Numbers tells of Israel's journey from Mount Sinai to the borders of the Promised Land, summarizing some 40 years of the nation's history.

The Gospel in Numbers

The book of Numbers narrates the wilderness journey of Israel on the way to the Promised Land. Its application, then, is especially relevant for life "in the wilderness." With the oppression of Egypt behind and the bountiful land of Canaan before, the wilderness is a place of transition and testing. It is therefore a time when the people of God must exercise faith, trusting daily in his guidance and provision.

Though an arduous journey, fraught with trials and failures, every step of the trek testifies to God's faithfulness. First, that the people of God found themselves in the wilderness at all is evidence of God's saving grace, for with mighty signs and wonders he had delivered them out of slavery in Egypt and brought them through the waters of the sea. Second, this journey through the wilderness to Canaan was itself a part of God's fulfilling the gracious promises he swore to Abraham, Isaac, and Jacob (Gen. 12:1, 7; 26:2–4; 35:12).

Third, because of these promises, God's people in the wilderness could truly say, "The LORD is my Shepherd" (Ps. 23:1), for he provided them with a supply of water from the rock, and with manna and quail. He protected them from enemies. He sustained them so that neither their clothes nor their sandals wore out for forty years (Deut. 29:5). Fourth, to be among the people of God in the wilderness meant, above all, to have the Lord God dwelling in their midst—his tabernacle was pitched at the heart of the Israelite encampment, a sure sign of his desire to be with his people, to atone for their sins, and to guide them into the land flowing with milk and honey.

Because the New Testament consistently describes the church's life in the present age as being "in the wilderness," there is much application in Numbers for us to glean. The Christian is one who has been delivered out of the bondage of sin and brought through the waters of baptism into the pilgrim life of the church, journeying to the promised new heavens and earth. With this comparison in mind, the author of Hebrews warns the church that many in the wilderness never entered into God's rest due to the disobedience of unbelief (Heb. 3:7–4:13). The apostle Paul similarly explains that the wilderness generation serves as an example to us, noting how the Israelites had been baptized in the sea and had eaten spiritual food, and how, remarkably, the spiritual Rock from which they drank was

Christ himself (1 Cor. 10:1–11). Ultimately, then, those who did not enter the Promised Land failed to do so because they neglected God's gracious provision for the wilderness journey—namely, Christ. As believers in the wilderness, plagued by the deceptions and enticements of the world, we should avail ourselves of the "means of grace" God has provided for sustaining us throughout this journey. Through the ministry of the Word and sacraments, Christ feeds and nourishes our souls with himself, supplying us with grace to press onward in joyful hope.

Finally, any mention of the wilderness generation almost immediately conjures up the dysfunction and sinfulness of God's people, expressed repeatedly as "murmuring" (or grumbling) against the Lord. Yet while many of the Israelites were consequently judged for their rebellion, the overriding message of Numbers is that, because of God's longsuffering love for them, there is nothing better than to be identified with the people of God. For, to the praise of his grace, his people will indeed enter the land since he has determined to bless them and not curse (Num. 22:12; 23:20). In the additional light the New Testament places upon such grace, the church more clearly perceives that God is able to bless his people through their struggles with sin and circumstances only because of the work of Jesus Christ. By his righteous obedience in the wilderness (Matt. 4:1–11), and by his atoning death on the cross for our sins, God's people will assuredly enter the eternal splendors of the new creation. So, through all the church's storms down through the centuries, the people of God are still worthy of Balaam's inspired acknowledgment, "How lovely are your tents, O Jacob, your encampments, O Israel!" (Num. 24:5).

Outline

I. Israel Prepares to Enter the Land (1:1–10:10)

II. Marching from Sinai to Kadesh (10:11–12:16)

III. Forty Years near Kadesh (13:1–19:22)

IV. Marching from Kadesh to the Plains of Moab (20:1–21:35)

V. Israel in the Plains of Moab (22:1–36:13)

Numbers

A Census of Israel's Warriors

1 The LORD spoke to Moses [a]in the wilderness of Sinai, [b]in the tent of meeting, on
the first day of the second month, in the second year after they had come out of the land
of Egypt, saying, 2 [c]"Take a census of all the
congregation of the people of Israel, by clans,
[d]by fathers' houses, according to the number
of names, every male, head by head. 3 [e]From
twenty years old and upward, all in Israel who
are able to go to war, you and Aaron shall list
them, [f]company by company. 4 And there shall
be with you a man from each tribe, each man
being the head of the house of his fathers.
5 And these are the names of the men who shall
assist you. From Reuben, [g]Elizur the son of
Shedeur; 6 from Simeon, [h]Shelumiel the son
of Zurishaddai; 7 from Judah, [i]Nahshon the
son of Amminadab; 8 from Issachar, [j]Nethanel
the son of Zuar; 9 from Zebulun, [k]Eliab the
son of Helon; 10 from the sons of Joseph, from
Ephraim, [l]Elishama the son of Ammihud,
and from Manasseh, [m]Gamaliel the son of
Pedahzur; 11 from Benjamin, [n]Abidan the son
of Gideoni; 12 from Dan, [o]Ahiezer the son of
Ammishaddai; 13 from Asher, [p]Pagiel the son
of Ochran; 14 from Gad, Eliasaph the son of
[q]Deuel; 15 from Naphtali, [r]Ahira the son of
Enan." 16 These were the ones [s]chosen from
the congregation, [t]the chiefs of their ancestral
tribes, the heads of the clans of Israel.

17 Moses and Aaron took these men [u]who
had been named, 18 and on the first day of
the second month, they assembled the whole
congregation together, who registered themselves by clans, by fathers' houses, according
to the number of names from twenty years
old and upward, head by head, 19 as the LORD
commanded Moses. So he listed them in the
wilderness of Sinai.

20 The people of [v]Reuben, Israel's firstborn,
their generations, by their clans, by their
fathers' houses, according to the number of
names, head by head, every male from twenty
years old and upward, all who were able to go
to war: 21 those listed of the tribe of Reuben
were [w]46,500.

22 Of the people of Simeon, their generations,
by their clans, by their fathers' houses, those of
them who were listed, according to the number of names, head by head, every male from
twenty years old and upward, all who were
able to go to war: 23 those listed of the tribe of
Simeon were [x]59,300.

24 Of the people of Gad, their generations, by
their clans, by their fathers' houses, according

1:1–46 Numbers begins with the Lord revealing his will to his people by speaking to Moses. God's people always need a mediator, and Moses fills that office supremely in the Old Testament, speaking to God as with a friend (12:8; Ex. 33:11). Yet with the advent of Jesus Christ, the Word of God itself became flesh and tabernacled among us (John 1:14). Because no one knows God more intimately than his Son, it is Christ, the long-awaited new and greater Moses (Deut. 18:15; John 1:17), who has made God known most fully (John 1:18).

Having delivered the Israelites out of Egypt, God now shows his ongoing grace as he prepares them to conquer the land. The census reminds the people that God has already been faithful to fulfill one part of his gracious promise to Abraham, to make him into a great nation, so that the enumeration of those "able to go to war" should now bolster confidence that God will also fulfill the land promise (Gen. 12:1–3).

Chapter 1

1 [a] ch. 10:11, 12; Ex. 19:1 [b] Ex. 25:22
2 [c] Ex. 30:12; 38:26; 2 Sam. 24:2; 1 Chr. 21:2; See ch. 26:2-51 [d] ver. 18, 20, 22; ch. 3:47; 1 Chr. 23:3, 24
3 [e] ch. 14:29; Ex. 30:14 [f] Ex. 12:51
5 [g] ch. 7:30
6 [h] ch. 7:36
7 [i] See Ex. 6:23
8 [j] ch. 7:18
9 [k] ch. 7:24
10 [l] ch. 7:48; 1 Chr. 7:26 [m] ch. 7:54
11 [n] ch. 7:60
12 [o] ch. 7:66
13 [p] ch. 7:72

14 [q] ch. 7:42 **15** [r] ch. 7:78 **16** [s] ch. 26:9 [t] ch. 7:2; [Ex. 18:21, 25]; See 1 Chr. 27:16-22 **17** [u] 1 Chr. 12:31; 16:41; 2 Chr. 28:15; 31:19; Ezra 8:20 **20** [v] For ver. 20-46, see ch. 2:3-32 **21** [w] [ch. 26:7] **23** [x] [ch. 26:14]

to the number of the names, from twenty years
old and upward, all who were able to go to war:
25 those listed of the tribe of Gad were [y]45,650.
26 Of the people of Judah, their generations,
by their clans, by their fathers' houses, according to the number of names, from twenty
years old and upward, every man able to go
to war: 27 those listed of the tribe of Judah were
[z]74,600.
28 Of the people of Issachar, their generations, by their clans, by their fathers' houses,
according to the number of names, from
twenty years old and upward, every man
able to go to war: 29 those listed of the tribe of
Issachar were [a]54,400.
30 Of the people of Zebulun, their generations, by their clans, by their fathers' houses,
according to the number of names, from
twenty years old and upward, every man
able to go to war: 31 those listed of the tribe of
Zebulun were [b]57,400.
32 Of the people of Joseph, namely, of the
people of Ephraim, their generations, by their
clans, by their fathers' houses, according to the
number of names, from twenty years old and
upward, every man able to go to war: 33 those
listed of the tribe of Ephraim were [c]40,500.
34 Of the people of Manasseh, their generations, by their clans, by their fathers' houses,
according to the number of names, from
twenty years old and upward, every man
able to go to war: 35 those listed of the tribe of
Manasseh were [d]32,200.
36 Of the people of Benjamin, their generations, by their clans, by their fathers' houses,
according to the number of names, from
twenty years old and upward, every man
able to go to war: 37 those listed of the tribe of
Benjamin were [e]35,400.
38 Of the people of Dan, their generations, by
their clans, by their fathers' houses, according
to the number of names, from twenty years
old and upward, every man able to go to war:
39 those listed of the tribe of Dan were [f]62,700.
40 Of the people of Asher, their generations,
by their clans, by their fathers' houses, according to the number of names, from twenty years
old and upward, every man able to go to war:
41 those listed of the tribe of Asher were [g]41,500.
42 Of the people of Naphtali, their generations, by their clans, by their fathers' houses,
according to the number of names, from
twenty years old and upward, every man able
to go to war: 43 those listed of the tribe of
Naphtali were [h]53,400.
44 [i]These are those who were listed, whom
Moses and Aaron listed with the help of the
chiefs of Israel, twelve men, each representing his fathers' house. 45 So all those listed of
the people of Israel, by their fathers' houses,
from twenty years old and upward, every man
able to go to war in Israel— 46 all those listed
were [j]603,550.

Levites Exempted

47 But [k]the Levites were not listed along with
them by their ancestral tribe. 48 For the LORD
spoke to Moses, saying, 49 "Only the tribe of
Levi you shall not list, and you shall not take
a census of them among the people of Israel.
50 [l]But appoint the Levites over the tabernacle
of the testimony, and over all its furnishings,
and over all that belongs to it. They are to carry
the tabernacle and all its furnishings, and they
shall take care of it [m]and shall camp around
the tabernacle. 51 [n]When the tabernacle is to set
out, the Levites shall take it down, and when
the tabernacle is to be pitched, the Levites
shall set it up. [o]And if any outsider comes
near, he shall be put to death. 52 The people
of Israel shall pitch their tents by their companies, each man in his own camp and [p]each
man by his own standard. 53 But the Levites
shall camp around the tabernacle of the testimony, so that there may be no [q]wrath on the
congregation of the people of Israel. [r]And the
Levites shall keep guard over the tabernacle
of the testimony." 54 Thus did the people of
Israel; they did according to all that the LORD
commanded Moses.

We too, having been delivered out of sin and death through the new exodus of Christ's suffering and glory, are called upon to engage in battle spiritually. We do this by putting to death the deeds of our sinful nature and resisting temptation (Col. 3:5; Eph. 6:10–18). In all of our spiritual struggles, our confidence is in God's gracious purpose demonstrated in the cross of Christ. Having died to reconcile us to God, Christ now lives to bring us into glory (Rom. 5:8–10; 8:32; Heb. 7:25).

25 [y] [ch. 26:18]
27 [z] [ch. 26:22; 2 Sam. 24:9]
29 [a] [ch. 26:25]
31 [b] [ch. 26:27]
33 [c] [ch. 26:37]
35 [d] [ch. 26:34]
37 [e] [ch. 26:41]
39 [f] [ch. 26:43]
41 [g] [ch. 26:47]

43 [h] [ch. 26:50] **44** [i] ch. 26:64 **46** [j] Ex. 38:26; [ch. 11:21; 26:51; Ex. 12:37] **47** [k] ch. 2:33; [ch. 26:57, 58, 62]; See ch. 3; ch. 4; 1 Chr. 6 **50** [l] ch. 3:7, 8; Ex. 38:21; See ch. 4:15-33 [m] See ch. 3:23-38 **51** [n] ch. 10:17, 21 [o] ch. 3:10, 38; 18:22; [1 Sam. 6:19; 2 Sam. 6:6, 7; 1 Chr. 13:10] **52** [p] ch. 2:2, 34 **53** [q] ch. 8:19; 16:46; 18:5 [r] ch. 3:7, 8, 38; 8:26; 9:19, 23; 18:3-5; 31:30, 47; 1 Chr. 23:32; [2 Chr. 13:11]

Arrangement of the Camp

2 The Lord spoke to Moses and Aaron,
saying, 2 [s]"The people of Israel shall camp
each by his own standard, with the banners
of their fathers' houses. They shall camp facing the tent of meeting on every side. 3 Those
to camp on the east side toward the sunrise
shall be of the standard of the camp of Judah
by their companies, the chief of the people of
Judah being [t]Nahshon the son of Amminadab,
4 his company as listed being 74,600. 5 Those
to camp next to him shall be the tribe of
Issachar, the chief of the people of Issachar
being Nethanel the son of Zuar, 6 his company as listed being 54,400. 7 Then the tribe
of Zebulun, the chief of the people of Zebulun
being Eliab the son of Helon, 8 his company
as listed being 57,400. 9 All those listed of
the camp of Judah, by their companies, were
186,400. [u]They shall set out first on the march.

10 "On the south side shall be the standard of
the camp of Reuben by their companies, the
chief of the people of Reuben being Elizur
the son of Shedeur, 11 his company as listed
being 46,500. 12 And those to camp next to him
shall be the tribe of Simeon, the chief of the
people of Simeon being Shelumiel the son of
Zurishaddai, 13 his company as listed being
59,300. 14 Then the tribe of Gad, the chief of
the people of Gad being Eliasaph the son of
[v]Reuel, 15 his company as listed being 45,650.
16 All those listed of the camp of Reuben, by
their companies, were 151,450. [w]They shall
set out second.

17 [x]"Then the tent of meeting shall set out,
with the camp of the Levites in the midst of
the camps; as they camp, so shall they set out,
each in position, standard by standard.

18 "On the west side shall be the standard of
the camp of Ephraim by their companies, the
chief of the people of Ephraim being Elishama
the son of Ammihud, 19 his company as listed
being 40,500. 20 And next to him shall be the
tribe of Manasseh, the chief of the people of
Manasseh being Gamaliel the son of Pedahzur,
21 his company as listed being 32,200. 22 Then
the tribe of Benjamin, the chief of the people
of Benjamin being Abidan the son of Gideoni,
23 his company as listed being 35,400. 24 All
those listed of the camp of Ephraim, by their
companies, were 108,100. [y]They shall set out
third on the march.

25 "On the north side shall be the standard
of the camp of Dan by their companies, the
chief of the people of Dan being Ahiezer the
son of Ammishaddai, 26 his company as listed
being 62,700. 27 And those to camp next to
him shall be the tribe of Asher, the chief of
the people of Asher being Pagiel the son of
Ochran, 28 his company as listed being 41,500.
29 Then the tribe of Naphtali, the chief of the
people of Naphtali being Ahira the son of
Enan, 30 his company as listed being 53,400.
31 All those listed of the camp of Dan were
157,600. [z]They shall set out last, standard
by standard."

32 These are the people of Israel as listed by
their fathers' houses. All those listed in the
camps by their companies were [a]603,550. 33 But
[b]the Levites were not listed among the people
of Israel, as the Lord commanded Moses.

34 Thus did the people of Israel. According
to all that the Lord commanded Moses, [c]so
they camped by their standards, and so they
set out, each one in his clan, according to his
fathers' house.

2:1–34 Israel's encampment is now organized for a military campaign, prepared for warfare. With the tabernacle as his royal tent pitched at the center of the camp, God is portrayed as the campaigner with the companies of Israel as his hosts—the battle belongs to the Lord, indeed. Here the representations of grace are not of stereotypical gentleness. Rather, the descriptions remind God's people that he provides all that is necessary to overcome the enemies that threaten us and his purposes. Though we often forget, the nature of the church on earth is that of the "church militant," marching onward to the Promised Land. Our battle, however, is not against flesh and blood, but against the spiritual forces of evil (Eph. 6:10–18), and our assurance of victory comes from knowing that the Lord dwells in our midst, guiding the church heavenward.

Preeminence is given to the camp of Judah, stationed east of the tabernacle just beyond the priests (who entered the tabernacle from the east). This pride of place reflects God's promise that from Judah's line, the Ruler would come to deliver his people from their enemies (Gen. 49:8–12). Partially realized through David (2 Sam. 3:18), the promise was fulfilled ultimately through the Greater Son of David (Matt. 1:1), Jesus Christ, who leads us in salvation (Matt. 1:1; Heb. 2:10).

Chapter 2
2 [s] ch. 1:52
3 [t] See Ex. 6:23
9 [u] ch. 10:14-16
14 [v] [ch. 7:42, 47; 10:20]
16 [w] ch. 10:18-20
17 [x] ch. 10:17, 21
24 [y] ch. 10:22-24; [Ps. 80:2]
31 [z] ch. 10:25-27
32 [a] See ch. 1:46
33 [b] See ch. 1:47
34 [c] [ch. 24:2, 5, 6]

The Sons of Aaron

3 These are the generations of Aaron and Moses at the time when the LORD spoke with Moses on Mount Sinai. 2 These are the names of the sons of Aaron: [d]Nadab the firstborn, and Abihu, Eleazar, and Ithamar. 3 These are the names of the sons of Aaron, [e]the anointed priests, [f]whom he ordained to serve as priests. 4 [g]But Nadab and Abihu died before the LORD when they offered unauthorized fire before the LORD in the wilderness of Sinai, and they had no children. So Eleazar and Ithamar served as priests in the lifetime of Aaron their father.

Duties of the Levites

5 And the LORD spoke to Moses, saying, 6 [h]"Bring the tribe of Levi near, and set them before Aaron the priest, that they may minister to him. 7 They shall keep guard over him and over the whole congregation before the tent of meeting, [i]as they minister at the tabernacle. 8 They shall guard all the furnishings of the tent of meeting, and keep guard over the people of Israel as they minister at the tabernacle. 9 And [j]you shall give the Levites to Aaron and his sons; they are [k]wholly given to him from among the people of Israel. 10 And you shall appoint Aaron and his sons, and [l]they shall guard their priesthood. But if [m]any outsider comes near, he shall be put to death."

11 And the LORD spoke to Moses, saying, 12 "Behold, [n]I have taken the Levites from among the people of Israel instead of every firstborn who opens the womb among the people of Israel. The Levites shall be mine, 13 for [o]all the firstborn are mine. [p]On the day that I struck down all the firstborn in the land of Egypt, I consecrated for my own all the firstborn in Israel, both of man and of beast. They shall be mine: I am the LORD."

14 And the LORD spoke to Moses in the wilderness of Sinai, saying, 15 "List the sons of Levi, by fathers' houses and by clans; [q]every male from a month old and upward you shall list." 16 So Moses listed them according to the word of the LORD, as he was commanded. 17 [r]And these were the sons of Levi by their names: Gershon and Kohath and Merari. 18 And these are the names of the sons of Gershon by their clans: [s]Libni and Shimei. 19 And the sons of Kohath by their clans: [t]Amram, Izhar, Hebron, and Uzziel. 20 And the sons of Merari by their clans: [u]Mahli and Mushi. These are the clans of the Levites, by their fathers' houses.

21 To Gershon belonged the clan of the Libnites and the clan of the Shimeites; these were the clans of the Gershonites. 22 Their listing according to the number of all the males from a month old and upward was[1] 7,500. 23 [v]The clans of the Gershonites were to camp behind the tabernacle on the west, 24 with Eliasaph, the son of Lael as chief of the fathers' house of the Gershonites. 25 And the [w]guard duty of the sons of Gershon in the tent of meeting involved [x]the tabernacle, [y]the tent with [z]its covering, [a]the screen for the entrance of the tent of meeting, 26 [b]the hangings of the court, [c]the screen for the door of the court that is around the tabernacle and the altar, and [d]its cords—all the service connected with these.

27 To Kohath belonged the clan of the [e]Amramites and the clan of the Izharites and the clan of the Hebronites and the clan of the Uzzielites; these are the clans of the Kohathites. 28 According to the number of all the males, from a month old and upward, there were 8,600, keeping guard over the sanctuary. 29 The clans of the sons of Kohath were to camp on the south side of the tabernacle, 30 with [f]Elizaphan the son of Uzziel as chief of the fathers' house of the clans of the Kohathites. 31 And their guard duty involved [g]the ark, [h]the table, [i]the lampstand, [j]the altars,

[1] Hebrew *their listing was*

Chapter 3
2 [d]See Ex. 6:23
3 [e]See Lev. 8 [f]See Ex. 28:41
4 [g]ch. 26:61; Lev. 10:1, 2; 1 Chr. 24:2
6 [h]ch. 1:50; 8:6; 18:2
7 [i]ch. 8:11, 15, 24, 26
9 [j]ch. 8:19; 18:6 [k]ch. 8:16
10 [l]ch. 18:7; [Rom. 12:7] [m]ver. 38; See ch. 1:51
12 [n]ver. 41; ch. 8:16; 18:6
13 [o]See Ex. 13:2 [p]ch. 8:17; Ex. 13:12, 15 **15** [q]ver. 39; ch. 26:62; [ch. 1:47] **17** [r]ch. 26:57; Gen. 46:11; Ex. 6:16; 1 Chr. 6:1, 16; 23:6 **18** [s]Ex. 6:17; 1 Chr. 6:17; 23:7 **19** [t]Ex. 6:18; 1 Chr. 6:2, 18; 23:12 **20** [u]Ex. 6:19; 1 Chr. 6:19; 23:21 **23** [v]ch. 1:53 **25** [w]ch. 4:24-26 [x]Ex. 25:9 [y]Ex. 26:7; 36:14 [z]Ex. 26:14 [a]Ex. 26:36 **26** [b]Ex. 27:9 [c]Ex. 27:16 [d]ver. 37; Ex. 35:18; 39:40 **27** [e]1 Chr. 26:23 **30** [f][Ex. 6:22; Lev. 10:4] **31** [g]Ex. 25:10 [h]Ex. 25:23 [i]Ex. 25:31 [j]Ex. 27:1; 30:1

3:1–4:49 The Levites were exempted from the census for war, as their duties lay primarily in setting up and taking down the tabernacle and its furnishings, along with guarding its premises so that God's wrath would not come upon trespassers (1:47–54). In Numbers 3 God commands a census for them since, in their service to the Lord, they were substitutes for the firstborn sons of the other tribes of Israel (8:18). Another census of the Levites is commanded in Numbers 4 with the purpose of distributing the tabernacle work. As servants completely dedicated to the things of God, the Levites did not inherit land—the Lord himself was their inheritance.

the vessels of the sanctuary with which the priests minister, and [k]the screen; all the service connected with these. 32 And Eleazar the son of Aaron the priest was to be chief over the chiefs of the Levites, and to have oversight of those who kept guard over the sanctuary.

33 To Merari belonged the clan of the Mahlites and the clan of the Mushites: these are the clans of Merari. 34 Their listing according to the number of all the males from a month old and upward was 6,200. 35 And the chief of the fathers' house of the clans of Merari was Zuriel the son of Abihail. They were to camp on the north side of the tabernacle. 36 [l]And the appointed guard duty of the sons of Merari involved the [m]frames of the tabernacle, [n]the bars, [o]the pillars, the bases, and all their accessories; all the service connected with these; 37 also [p]the pillars around the court, with their bases and [q]pegs and [r]cords.

38 Those who were to camp before the tabernacle on the east, before the tent of meeting toward the sunrise, were Moses and Aaron and his sons, [s]guarding the sanctuary itself, to protect[1] the people of Israel. And any outsider who came near was to be put to death. 39 All those listed among the Levites, whom Moses and Aaron listed at the commandment of the LORD, by clans, all the males from a month old and upward, were [t]22,000.

Redemption of the Firstborn

40 And the LORD said to Moses, "List all the firstborn males of the people of Israel, from a month old and upward, taking the number of their names. 41 [u]And you shall take the Levites for me—I am the LORD—instead of all the firstborn among the people of Israel, and the cattle of the Levites instead of all the firstborn among the cattle of the people of Israel." 42 So Moses listed all the firstborn among the people of Israel, as the LORD commanded him. 43 And all the firstborn males, according to the number of names, from a month old and upward as listed were 22,273.

44 And the LORD spoke to Moses, saying, 45 [v]"Take the Levites instead of all the firstborn among the people of Israel, and the cattle of the Levites instead of their cattle. The Levites shall be mine: I am the LORD. 46 And [w]as the redemption price for the 273 of the firstborn of the people of Israel, over and above the number of the male Levites, 47 you shall take [x]five shekels[2] per head; you shall take them according to [y]the shekel of the sanctuary (the shekel of twenty gerahs[3]), 48 and give the money to Aaron and his sons as the redemption price for those who are over." 49 So Moses took the redemption money from those who were over and above those redeemed by the Levites. 50 From the firstborn of the people of Israel he took the money, [z]1,365 shekels, by the shekel of the sanctuary. 51 And Moses [a]gave the redemption money to Aaron and his sons, according to the word of the LORD, as the LORD commanded Moses.

Duties of the Kohathites

4 The LORD spoke to Moses and Aaron, saying, 2 "Take a census of the sons of Kohath from among the sons of Levi, by their clans and their fathers' houses, 3 [b]from thirty years old up to fifty years old, all who can come on duty, to do the work in the tent of meeting. 4 This is the service of the sons of Kohath in the tent of meeting: [c]the most holy things. 5 When the camp is to set out, Aaron and his sons shall go in and take down [d]the veil of the screen and cover [e]the ark of the testimony with it. 6 Then they shall put on it a covering of goatskin[4] and spread on top of that a cloth all of blue, and shall put in its [f]poles. 7 And over the [g]table of the bread of the Presence they shall spread a cloth of blue and put on it the plates, the dishes for incense, the bowls, and the flagons for the drink offering; [h]the regular showbread

[1] Hebrew *guard* [2] A *shekel* was about 2/5 ounce or 11 grams [3] A *gerah* was about 1/50 ounce or 0.6 gram [4] The meaning of the Hebrew word is uncertain; compare Exodus 25:5

The Levites' high and holy calling was accomplished profoundly by Christ, who came to serve (Mark 10:45), and whose food was to do the will of the Father (John 4:34). In his service to God, Christ is our substitute, fulfilling righteous obedience to the law and becoming the atoning sacrifice for our sins on the cross. Gratefully looking to Christ, moreover, we too are enabled to live as "Levites" on earth, desiring rather to inherit God himself in the heavenly city he has prepared for us (Heb. 11:13–16; 12:1–2).

31 [k]Ex. 26:36
36 [l]ch. 4:31, 32 [m]Ex. 26:15 [n]Ex. 26:26 [o]Ex. 26:32, 37
37 [p]Ex. 27:10 [q]Ex. 27:19 [r]ver. 26
38 [s]See ch. 1:53
39 [t][ver. 22, 28, 34; See ver. 46-49]
41 [u]ver. 12, 45
45 [v]ver. 12, 41

46 [w]ch. 18:15, 16; Ex. 13:13 **47** [x]ch. 18:16; Lev. 27:6 [y]See Ex. 30:13 **50** [z]ver. 46, 47 **51** [a]ver. 48 **Chapter 4** **3** [b]ver. 23, 30, 35, 39, 43, 47; [ch. 8:24; 1 Chr. 23:3, 24, 27] **4** [c]ver. 19 **5** [d]See Ex. 26:31 [e]Ex. 25:10, 16 **6** [f]Ex. 25:13 **7** [g]Ex. 25:23, 29, 30; 37:16; Lev. 24:6, 8 [h]2 Chr. 2:4

also shall be on it. 8 Then they shall spread over them a cloth of scarlet and cover the same with a covering of goatskin, and shall [i]put in its poles. 9 And they shall take a cloth of blue and cover [j]the lampstand for the light, with its lamps, its tongs, its trays, and all the vessels for oil with which it is supplied. 10 And they shall put it with all its utensils in a covering of goatskin and put it on the carrying frame. 11 And over [k]the golden altar they shall spread a cloth of blue and cover it with a covering of goatskin, and shall put in its poles. 12 And they shall take all [l]the vessels of the service that are used in the sanctuary and put them in a cloth of blue and cover them with a covering of goatskin and put them on the carrying frame. 13 And they shall take away the ashes from the altar and spread a purple cloth over it. 14 And they shall put on it all the utensils of the altar, which are used for the service there, the fire pans, the forks, the shovels, and the basins, all the utensils of the altar; and they shall spread on it a covering of goatskin, and shall put in its poles. 15 And when Aaron and his sons have finished covering the sanctuary and all the furnishings of the sanctuary, as the camp sets out, after that [m]the sons of Kohath shall come to carry these, [n]but they must not touch the holy things, lest they die. These are the things of the tent of meeting that the sons of Kohath are to carry.

16 "And Eleazar the son of Aaron the priest shall have charge of [o]the oil for the light, the [p]fragrant incense, [q]the regular grain offering, and [r]the anointing oil, with the oversight of the whole tabernacle and all that is in it, of the sanctuary and its vessels."

17 The LORD spoke to Moses and Aaron, saying, 18 "Let not the tribe of the clans of the Kohathites be destroyed from among the Levites, 19 but deal thus with them, that they may live and not die when they come near to [s]the most holy things: Aaron and his sons shall go in and appoint them each to his task and to his burden, 20 [t]but they shall not go in to look on the holy things even for a moment, lest they die."

21 The LORD spoke to Moses, saying, 22 "Take a census of the sons of Gershon also, by their fathers' houses and by their clans. 23 [u]From thirty years old up to fifty years old, you shall list them, all who can [v]come to do duty, to do service in the tent of meeting. 24 This is the service of the clans of the Gershonites, in serving and bearing burdens: 25 [w]they shall carry [x]the curtains of the tabernacle and the tent of meeting with [y]its covering and the covering of goatskin that is on top of it and the screen for the entrance of the tent of meeting 26 and the hangings of the court and the screen for the entrance of the gate of the court that is around the tabernacle and the altar, and their cords and all the equipment for their service. And they shall do all that needs to be done with regard to them. 27 All the service of the sons of the Gershonites shall be at the command of Aaron and his sons, in all that they are to carry and in all that they have to do. And you shall assign to their charge all that they are to carry. 28 This is the service of the clans of the sons of the Gershonites in the tent of meeting, and their guard duty is to be [z]under the direction of Ithamar the son of Aaron the priest.

29 "As for the sons of Merari, you shall list them by their clans and their fathers' houses. 30 [u]From thirty years old up to fifty years old, you shall list them, everyone who can come on duty, to do the service of the tent of meeting. 31 And [a]this is what they are charged to carry, as the whole of their service in the tent of meeting: the frames of the tabernacle, with its bars, pillars, and bases, 32 and the pillars around the court with their bases, pegs, and cords, with all their equipment and all their accessories. And you shall [b]list by name the objects that they are required to carry. 33 This is the service of the clans of the sons of Merari, the whole of their service in the tent of meeting, [c]under the direction of Ithamar the son of Aaron the priest."

34 And Moses and Aaron and the chiefs of the congregation listed the sons of the Kohathites, by their clans and their fathers' houses, 35 [u]from thirty years old up to fifty years old, everyone who could come on duty, for service in the tent of meeting; 36 and those listed by clans were 2,750. 37 [d]This was the list of the clans of the Kohathites, all who served in the tent of meeting, whom Moses and Aaron listed according to the commandment of the LORD by Moses.

8 [i] [Ex. 25:15, 28] **9** [j] See Ex. 25:31-39 **11** [k] Ex. 30:1, 3 **12** [l] [1 Chr. 9:28, 29] **15** [m] ch. 7:9; 10:21; Deut. 31:9 [n] 2 Sam. 6:6, 7; 1 Chr. 13:9, 10 **16** [o] Ex. 25:6; 27:20; Lev. 24:2 [p] Ex. 25:6; 31:11 [q] Ex. 29:40, 41 [r] Ex. 31:11; See Ex. 30:23-33 **19** [s] ver. 4 **20** [t] [Ex. 19:21; 1 Sam. 6:19] **23** [u] ver. 3 [v] ch. 8:24; [Ex. 38:8; 1 Sam. 2:22] **25** [w] [ch. 3:25, 26] [x] See Ex. 26:1-6; 36:8-13 [y] Ex. 36:14, 19 **28** [z] ver. 33 **30** [u] [See ver. 23 above] **31** [a] ch. 3:36, 37 **32** [b] Ex. 38:21 **33** [c] ver. 28 **35** [u] [See ver. 23 above] **37** [d] ver. 2

38 Those listed of the sons of Gershon, by their clans and their fathers' houses, 39 [u]from thirty years old up to fifty years old, everyone who could come on duty for service in the tent of meeting— 40 those listed by their clans and their fathers' houses were 2,630. 41 [e]This was the list of the clans of the sons of Gershon, all who served in the tent of meeting, whom Moses and Aaron listed according to the commandment of the LORD.

42 Those listed of the clans of the sons of Merari, by their clans and their fathers' houses, 43 [u]from thirty years old up to fifty years old, everyone who could come on duty, for service in the tent of meeting— 44 those listed by clans were 3,200. 45 [f]This was the list of the clans of the sons of Merari, whom Moses and Aaron listed according to the commandment of the LORD by Moses.

46 All those who were listed of the Levites, whom Moses and Aaron and the chiefs of Israel listed, by their clans and their fathers' houses, 47 [u]from thirty years old up to fifty years old, everyone who could come to do the service of ministry and the service of bearing burdens in the tent of meeting, 48 those listed were 8,580. 49 According to the commandment of the LORD through Moses they were listed, [g]each one with his task of serving or carrying. Thus they were listed by him, [h]as the LORD commanded Moses.

Unclean People

5 The LORD spoke to Moses, saying, 2 "Command the people of Israel that they [i]put out of the camp everyone who is leprous[1] or has [j]a discharge and everyone who is [k]unclean through contact with the dead. 3 You shall put out both male and female, putting them outside the camp, that they may not defile their camp, [l]in the midst of which I dwell." 4 And the people of Israel did so, and put them outside the camp; as the LORD said to Moses, so the people of Israel did.

Confession and Restitution

5 And the LORD spoke to Moses, saying, 6 "Speak to the people of Israel, [m]When a man or woman commits any of the sins that people commit by breaking faith with the LORD, and that person realizes his guilt, 7 [n]he shall confess his sin that he has committed.[2] [o]And he shall make full restitution for his wrong, adding a fifth to it and giving it to him to whom he did the wrong. 8 But if the man has no next of kin to whom restitution may be made for the wrong, the restitution for wrong shall go to the LORD for the priest, in addition to [p]the ram of atonement with which atonement is made for him. 9 And [q]every contribution, all the holy donations of the people of Israel, which they bring to the priest, shall be his. 10 Each one shall keep his holy donations: whatever anyone gives to the priest shall be his."

A Test for Adultery

11 And the LORD spoke to Moses, saying, 12 "Speak to the people of Israel, If any man's wife goes astray and breaks faith with him, 13 if a man [r]lies with her sexually, and it is hidden from the eyes of her husband, and she is undetected though she has defiled herself, and there is no witness against her, [s]since she was not taken in the act, 14 and if the spirit of jealousy comes over him and he is jealous of his wife who has defiled herself, or if the spirit of jealousy comes over him and he is jealous of his wife, though she has not defiled herself, 15 then the man shall bring his wife to the priest and bring the offering required of her, a tenth of an ephah[3] of barley flour. [t]He shall pour no oil on it and put no frankincense on it, for it is a grain offering of jealousy, a grain offering of remembrance, [u]bringing iniquity to remembrance.

16 "And the priest shall bring her near and set her before the LORD. 17 And the priest shall take holy water in an earthenware vessel and take some of the dust that is on the floor of the

[1] *Leprosy* was a term for several skin diseases; see Leviticus 13 [2] Hebrew *they shall confess their sin that they have committed* [3] An *ephah* was about 3/5 bushel or 22 liters

5:1–6:21 Because a holy God was dwelling among the Israelites, their camp required purification. Therefore, Numbers 5 and 6 deal with the handling of various actual or potential issues of uncleanness. To be unclean was to be unfit for the presence of God, such that a person would have to be removed from the camp out into the wilderness. Otherwise, God would have to abandon his people (to keep from destroying them).

39 [u] [See ver. 23 above]
41 [e] ver. 22
43 [u] [See ver. 23 above]
45 [f] ver. 29
47 [u] [See ver. 23 above]
49 [g] ver. 15, 24, 31 [h] ver. 1, 21, 29

Chapter 5 **2** [i] ch. 12:14; Lev. 13:46 [j] Lev. 15:2 [k] ch. 9:6, 10; 19:11, 13; 31:19; Lev. 21:1; [Hag. 2:13] **3** [l] See Lev. 26:11, 12 **6** [m] Lev. 6:2, 3 **7** [n] Lev. 5:5; 26:40; [Josh. 7:19] [o] Lev. 6:5 **8** [p] Lev. 6:6, 7 **9** [q] ch. 18:19; Ex. 29:28; Lev. 6:17, 18; 7:6, 7, 9, 10, 14; Deut. 18:3, 4 **13** [r] Lev. 18:20 [s] John 8:4 **15** [t] [Lev. 2:1, 15; 5:11] [u] 1 Kgs. 17:18; Ezek. 29:16

tabernacle and put it into the water. 18 And the
priest shall set the woman before the LORD
and [v]unbind the hair of the woman's head
and place in her hands the grain offering of
remembrance, which is the grain offering
of jealousy. And in his hand the priest shall
have the water of bitterness that brings the
curse. 19 Then the priest shall make her take
an oath, saying, 'If no man has lain with you,
and if you have not turned aside to uncleanness while you were under your husband's
authority, be free from this water of bitterness
that brings the curse. 20 But if you have gone
astray, though you are under your husband's
authority, and if you have defiled yourself,
and some man other than your husband has
lain with you, 21 then' (let the priest make the
woman take the oath of the curse, and say
to the woman) [w]'the LORD make you a curse
and an oath among your people, when the
LORD makes your thigh fall away and your
body swell. 22 May this water that brings the
curse [x]pass into your bowels and make your
womb swell and your thigh fall away.' And the
woman shall say, [y]'Amen, Amen.'
23 "Then the priest shall write these curses
in a book and wash them off into the water
of bitterness. 24 And he shall make the woman
drink the water of bitterness that brings the
curse, and the water that brings the curse
shall enter into her and cause bitter pain.
25 And the priest shall take the grain offering
of jealousy out of the woman's hand [z]and shall
wave the grain offering before the LORD and
bring it to the altar. 26 And the priest [a]shall
take a handful of the grain offering, as its
memorial portion, and burn it on the altar,
and afterward shall make the woman drink
the water. 27 And when he has made her drink
the water, then, if she has defiled herself and
has broken faith with her husband, the water
that brings the curse shall enter into her and
cause bitter pain, and her womb shall swell,
and her thigh shall fall away, and the woman
[b]shall become a curse among her people. 28 But
if the woman has not defiled herself and is
clean, then she shall be free and shall conceive
children.
29 "This is the law in cases of jealousy, when
a wife, [c]though under her husband's authority, goes astray and defiles herself, 30 or when
the spirit of jealousy comes over a man and
he is jealous of his wife. Then he shall set the
woman before the LORD, and the priest shall
carry out for her all this law. 31 The man shall be
free from iniquity, but the woman [d]shall bear
her iniquity."

The Nazirite Vow

6 And the LORD spoke to Moses, saying,
2 "Speak to the people of Israel and say to
them, When either a man or a woman makes
a special vow, the vow of [e]a Nazirite,[1] [f]to separate himself to the LORD, 3 he [g]shall separate
himself from wine and strong drink. He shall
drink no vinegar made from wine or strong
drink and shall not drink any juice of grapes
or eat grapes, fresh or dried. 4 All the days of
his separation[2] he shall eat nothing that is produced by the grapevine, not even the seeds or
the skins.
5 "All the days of his vow of separation, no
[h]razor shall touch his head. Until the time is
completed for which he separates himself to
the LORD, he shall be holy. [i]He shall let the
locks of hair of his head grow long.
6 "All the days that he separates himself to
the LORD [j]he shall not go near a dead body.
7 [k]Not even for his father or for his mother,
for brother or sister, if they die, shall he make
himself unclean, because his separation to
God is on his head. 8 All the days of his separation he is holy to the LORD.
9 "And if any man dies very suddenly beside
him and he defiles his consecrated head,
then [l]he shall shave his head on the day of his

[1] *Nazirite* means *one separated*, or *one consecrated* [2] Or *Naziriteship*

18[v] [1 Cor. 11:5-7]
21[w] [Jer. 29:22]
22[x] Ps. 109:18 [y] See Deut. 27:15-26
25[z] [Lev. 8:27]
26[a] Lev. 2:2, 9; 5:12
27[b] Deut. 28:37; Jer. 24:9; 29:18, 22; 42:18; 44:12; Zech. 8:13
29[c] ver. 19, 20
31[d] Lev. 20:17, 19, 20

As the church is called to be holy, sometimes her members must be disciplined, even to the extent of excommunication for someone in hardened unrepentance (1 Cor. 5:1–13), as a reminder that "nothing unclean will ever enter" the new Jerusalem (Rev. 21:27). Even this process, however, is a means of grace from God designed to purify his people and to encourage all (including the disciplined individual) to cling more tightly to Christ since our clean state is found in him alone. We enter the new Jerusalem not having purified ourselves by our efforts but having been washed in the blood of the Lamb (Rev. 1:5), so that our names are written in his book of life (Rev. 21:27).

Chapter 6 **2**[e] Judg. 13:5; [Acts 21:23] [f] [Rom. 1:1] **3**[g] Amos 2:12; Luke 1:15 **5**[h] Judg. 13:5; 16:17; 1 Sam. 1:11 [i] Ezek. 44:20; [1 Cor. 11:14] **6**[j] ch. 19:11, 16; Lev. 21:11 **7**[k] Lev. 21:1, 2, 11 **9**[l] Acts 18:18; 21:24

cleansing; on the seventh day he shall shave
it. 10 [m]On the eighth day he shall bring two
turtledoves or two pigeons to the priest to
the entrance of the tent of meeting, 11 and the
priest shall offer one for a sin offering and the
other for a burnt offering, and make atonement for him, because he sinned by reason
of the dead body. And he shall consecrate his
head that same day 12 and separate himself to
the LORD for the days of his separation and
bring a male lamb a year old [n]for a guilt offering. But the previous period shall be void,
because his separation was defiled.

13 "And this is the law for the Nazirite, [o]when
the time of his separation has been completed:
he shall be brought to the entrance of the tent
of meeting, 14 and he shall bring his gift to the
LORD, one male lamb a year old without blemish for a burnt offering, and one ewe lamb a
year old without blemish [p]as a sin offering, and
one ram without blemish [q]as a peace offering,
15 and a basket of unleavened bread, [r]loaves
of fine flour mixed with oil, and unleavened
wafers smeared with oil, and their [s]grain
offering and their [t]drink offerings. 16 And the
priest shall bring them before the LORD and
offer [u]his sin offering and his burnt offering,
17 and he shall offer the ram as a sacrifice of
peace offering to the LORD, with the basket of
unleavened bread. The priest shall offer also
its grain offering and its drink offering. 18 And
the Nazirite [v]shall shave his consecrated head
at the entrance of the tent of meeting and shall
take the hair from his consecrated head and
put it on the fire that is under the sacrifice of
the peace offering. 19 And the priest shall take
the [w]shoulder of the ram, when it is boiled,
and one unleavened loaf out of the basket and
one unleavened wafer, and [x]shall put them on
the hands of the Nazirite, after he has shaved
the hair of his consecration, 20 and the priest
shall wave them for a wave offering before the
LORD. [y]They are a holy portion for the priest,
together with the breast that is waved and the
thigh that is contributed. And after that the
Nazirite may drink wine.

21 "This is the law of the Nazirite. But if
he vows an offering to the LORD above his
Nazirite vow, as he can afford, in exact accordance with the vow that he takes, then he shall
do in addition to the law of the Nazirite."

Aaron's Blessing

22 The LORD spoke to Moses, saying, 23 "Speak
to Aaron and his sons, saying, Thus [z]you shall
bless the people of Israel: you shall say to them,

24 The LORD [a]bless you and [b]keep you;
25 the LORD [c]make his face to shine upon
you and be gracious to you;
26 the LORD [d]lift up his countenance[1] upon
you and give you peace.

27 [e]"So shall they put my name upon the
people of Israel, and I will bless them."

Offerings at the Tabernacle's Consecration

7 On the day when Moses had finished [f]set-
ting up the tabernacle and had anointed
and [g]consecrated it with all its furnishings
and had anointed and consecrated the altar
with all its utensils, 2 [h]the chiefs of Israel, heads
of their fathers' houses, who were the chiefs

[1] Or *face*

6:22–27 This beloved Aaronic benediction is placed as an encouragement after the strict guidelines on cleansing the camp of Israel. The ritual state of cleanness, along with the sacrificial system, has as its goal to bring the people near to God, the fountain of abundant life and profound peace (see, e.g., 2 Sam. 6:11). That the Creator dwells among them thus makes Israel's lot, even in the wilderness, enviable among the nations (Num. 24:5). God's desire to bless his people, despite their sinfulness, is one of the major themes of Numbers, climactically reaffirmed in the Balaam narratives (chs. 22–24).

The ultimate expression of God's desire to bless us is found in the giving of his Son to bear the curse of God's wrath upon our sin (Gal. 3:13–14). In reconciling us with God and bringing us near to him, Jesus himself is our peace (Eph. 2:14–22).

7:1–89 The lengthy, repetitive description of the offerings of the 12 tribes throughout 12 days for the dedication of the altar serves to underscore two points. First, the altar was the focus of worship, where God was encountered through the blood of sacrifice. Second, every tribe of Israel had a vested interest in the worship of God and was responsible to support the ministry. Even these gifts, however, were out of God's gracious provision, as he enabled the Israelites to "plunder Egypt" upon their deliverance (Ex. 12:35–36).

10 [m]Lev. 5:7; 14:22; 15:14, 29
12 [n]Lev. 5:6
13 [o]Acts 21:26
14 [p]Lev. 4:32 [q]Lev. 3:6
15 [r]Ex. 29:2; Lev. 2:4 [s]See Ex. 29:41 [t]ch. 15:5, 7, 10
16 [u]ver. 14
18 [v]Acts 18:18; 21:24
19 [w]1 Sam. 2:15 [x]Ex. 29:23, 24
20 [y][ch. 5:25; Ex. 29:27, 28]
23 [z]Lev. 9:22; Deut. 21:5; 1 Chr. 23:13
24 [a]Ps. 134:3 [b]See Ps. 121:3-8
25 [c]Ps. 31:16; 67:1; 80:3, 7, 19; 119:135; [Dan. 9:17]
26 [d]Ps. 4:6
27 [e]Deut. 28:10; 2 Chr. 7:14; Dan. 9:18, 19

Chapter 7
1 [f]Ex. 40:17, 18 [g]Lev. 8:10, 11
2 [h]ch. 1:4

of the tribes, who were over those who were listed, approached 3 and brought their offerings before the LORD, six wagons and twelve oxen, a wagon for every two of the chiefs, and for each one an ox. They brought them before the tabernacle. 4 Then the LORD said to Moses, 5 "Accept these from them, that they may be used in the service of the tent of meeting, and give them to the Levites, to each man according to his service." 6 So Moses took the wagons and the oxen and gave them to the Levites. 7 Two wagons and four oxen [i]he gave to the sons of Gershon, according to their service. 8 And four wagons and eight oxen [j]he gave to the sons of Merari, according to their service, under the direction of Ithamar the son of Aaron the priest. 9 But to the sons of Kohath he gave none, because they were charged with [k]the service of the holy things that [l]had to be carried on the shoulder. 10 And the chiefs offered offerings for the [m]dedication of the altar on the day it was anointed; and the chiefs offered their offering before the altar. 11 And the LORD said to Moses, "They shall offer their offerings, one chief each day, for the dedication of the altar."

12 He who offered his offering the first day was [n]Nahshon the son of Amminadab, of the tribe of Judah. 13 And his offering was one silver plate whose weight was 130 shekels,[1] one silver basin of 70 shekels, according to [o]the shekel of the sanctuary, both of them full of fine flour mixed with oil for a [p]grain offering; 14 one golden dish of 10 shekels, full of [q]incense; 15 [r]one bull from the herd, one ram, one male lamb a year old, for a burnt offering; 16 one male goat for a [s]sin offering; 17 and for [t]the sacrifice of peace offerings, two oxen, five rams, five male goats, and five male lambs a year old. This was the offering of Nahshon the son of Amminadab.

18 On the second day [u]Nethanel the son of Zuar, the chief of Issachar, made an offering. 19 He offered for his offering one silver plate whose weight was 130 shekels, one silver basin of 70 shekels, according to the shekel of the sanctuary, both of them full of fine flour mixed with oil for a grain offering; 20 one golden dish of 10 shekels, full of incense; 21 one bull from the herd, one ram, one male lamb a year old, for a burnt offering; 22 one male goat for a sin offering; 23 and for the sacrifice of peace offerings, two oxen, five rams, five male goats, and five male lambs a year old. This was the offering of Nethanel the son of Zuar.

24 On the third day [v]Eliab the son of Helon, the chief of the people of Zebulun: 25 his offering was one silver plate whose weight was 130 shekels, one silver basin of 70 shekels, according to the shekel of the sanctuary, both of them full of fine flour mixed with oil for a grain offering; 26 one golden dish of 10 shekels, full of incense; 27 one bull from the herd, one ram, one male lamb a year old, for a burnt offering; 28 one male goat for a sin offering; 29 and for the sacrifice of peace offerings, two oxen, five rams, five male goats, and five male lambs a year old. This was the offering of Eliab the son of Helon.

30 On the fourth day [w]Elizur the son of Shedeur, the chief of the people of Reuben: 31 his offering was one silver plate whose weight was 130 shekels, one silver basin of 70 shekels, according to the shekel of the sanctuary, both of them full of fine flour mixed with oil for a grain offering; 32 one golden dish of 10 shekels, full of incense; 33 one bull from the herd, one ram, one male lamb a year old, for a burnt offering; 34 one male goat for a sin offering; 35 and for the sacrifice of peace offerings, two oxen, five rams, five male goats, and five male lambs a year old. This was the offering of Elizur the son of Shedeur.

36 On the fifth day [x]Shelumiel the son of Zurishaddai, the chief of the people of Simeon: 37 his offering was one silver plate whose weight was 130 shekels, one silver basin of 70 shekels, according to the shekel of the sanctuary, both of them full of fine flour mixed with oil for a grain offering; 38 one golden dish of 10 shekels, full of incense; 39 one bull from the

[1] A *shekel* was about 2/5 ounce or 11 grams

7 [i]ch. 4:25, 28
8 [j]ch. 4:29, 31, 33
9 [k]ch. 3:31; See ch. 4:4-15 [l][2 Sam. 6:13; 1 Chr. 15:5, 15]
10 [m]Deut. 20:5; 1 Kgs. 8:63; 2 Chr. 7:5, 9; Ezra 6:16; Neh. 12:27

The grace signified by the altar has been fulfilled by the cross as the heart of the church's worship (Heb. 10:19–22), spread through the church's proclamation (1 Cor. 1:18–25), and reiterated by the church's sacraments (Rom. 6:3; 1 Cor. 11:26). Out of God's gracious provision in Christ, we all the more gladly support the ministry of the church (1 Cor. 9:13–14; 2 Corinthians 9).

12 [n]See Ex. 6:23 **13** [o]See Ex. 30:13 [p]ch. 8:8; See Ex. 29:41 **14** [q]Ex. 30:34, 35 **15** [r]Lev. 1:2, 3 **16** [s]Lev. 4:23, 24 **17** [t]Lev. 3:1 **18** [u]ch. 1:8 **24** [v]ch. 1:9 **30** [w]ch. 1:5 **36** [x]ch. 1:6

herd, one ram, one male lamb a year old, for a
burnt offering; 40 one male goat for a sin offering; 41 and for the sacrifice of peace offerings,
two oxen, five rams, five male goats, and five
male lambs a year old. This was the offering of
Shelumiel the son of Zurishaddai.

42 On the sixth day [y]Eliasaph the son of
Deuel, the chief of the people of Gad: 43 his
offering was one silver plate whose weight
was 130 shekels, one silver basin of 70 shekels, according to the shekel of the sanctuary,
both of them full of fine flour mixed with oil
for a grain offering; 44 one golden dish of 10
shekels, full of incense; 45 one bull from the
herd, one ram, one male lamb a year old, for a
burnt offering; 46 one male goat for a sin offering; 47 and for the sacrifice of peace offerings,
two oxen, five rams, five male goats, and five
male lambs a year old. This was the offering
of Eliasaph the son of Deuel.

48 On the seventh day [z]Elishama the son of
Ammihud, the chief of the people of Ephraim:
49 his offering was one silver plate whose
weight was 130 shekels, one silver basin of 70
shekels, according to the shekel of the sanctuary, both of them full of fine flour mixed with
oil for a grain offering; 50 one golden dish of
10 shekels, full of incense; 51 one bull from the
herd, one ram, one male lamb a year old, for a
burnt offering; 52 one male goat for a sin offering; 53 and for the sacrifice of peace offerings,
two oxen, five rams, five male goats, and five
male lambs a year old. This was the offering
of Elishama the son of Ammihud.

54 On the eighth day [a]Gamaliel the son of
Pedahzur, the chief of the people of Manasseh:
55 his offering was one silver plate whose
weight was 130 shekels, one silver basin of 70
shekels, according to the shekel of the sanctuary, both of them full of fine flour mixed with
oil for a grain offering; 56 one golden dish of
10 shekels, full of incense; 57 one bull from the
herd, one ram, one male lamb a year old, for a
burnt offering; 58 one male goat for a sin offering; 59 and for the sacrifice of peace offerings,
two oxen, five rams, five male goats, and five
male lambs a year old. This was the offering
of Gamaliel the son of Pedahzur.

60 On the ninth day [b]Abidan the son of
Gideoni, the chief of the people of Benjamin:
61 his offering was one silver plate whose
weight was 130 shekels, one silver basin of 70
shekels, according to the shekel of the sanctuary, both of them full of fine flour mixed with
oil for a grain offering; 62 one golden dish of
10 shekels, full of incense; 63 one bull from the
herd, one ram, one male lamb a year old, for a
burnt offering; 64 one male goat for a sin offering; 65 and for the sacrifice of peace offerings,
two oxen, five rams, five male goats, and five
male lambs a year old. This was the offering
of Abidan the son of Gideoni.

66 On the tenth day [c]Ahiezer the son of
Ammishaddai, the chief of the people of
Dan: 67 his offering was one silver plate whose
weight was 130 shekels, one silver basin of 70
shekels, according to the shekel of the sanctuary, both of them full of fine flour mixed with
oil for a grain offering; 68 one golden dish of
10 shekels, full of incense; 69 one bull from the
herd, one ram, one male lamb a year old, for a
burnt offering; 70 one male goat for a sin offering; 71 and for the sacrifice of peace offerings,
two oxen, five rams, five male goats, and five
male lambs a year old. This was the offering of
Ahiezer the son of Ammishaddai.

72 On the eleventh day [d]Pagiel the son of
Ochran, the chief of the people of Asher: 73 his
offering was one silver plate whose weight
was 130 shekels, one silver basin of 70 shekels, according to the shekel of the sanctuary,
both of them full of fine flour mixed with oil
for a grain offering; 74 one golden dish of 10
shekels, full of incense; 75 one bull from the
herd, one ram, one male lamb a year old, for a
burnt offering; 76 one male goat for a sin offering; 77 and for the sacrifice of peace offerings,
two oxen, five rams, five male goats, and five
male lambs a year old. This was the offering
of Pagiel the son of Ochran.

78 On the twelfth day [e]Ahira the son of Enan,
the chief of the people of Naphtali: 79 his offering was one silver plate whose weight was
130 shekels, one silver basin of 70 shekels,
according to the shekel of the sanctuary, both
of them full of fine flour mixed with oil for a
grain offering; 80 one golden dish of 10 shekels, full of incense; 81 one bull from the herd,
one ram, one male lamb a year old, for a burnt
offering; 82 one male goat for a sin offering;
83 and for the sacrifice of peace offerings, two
oxen, five rams, five male goats, and five male
lambs a year old. This was the offering of Ahira
the son of Enan.

42[y] ch. 1:14; [ch. 2:14] **48**[z] ch. 1:10 **54**[a] ch. 1:10 **60**[b] ch. 1:11 **66**[c] ch. 1:12 **72**[d] ch. 1:13 **78**[e] ch. 1:15

84 This was the dedication offering for the altar on the day when it was anointed, from the chiefs of Israel: twelve silver plates, twelve silver basins, twelve golden dishes, 85 each silver plate weighing 130 shekels and each basin 70, all the silver of the vessels 2,400 shekels according to the shekel of the sanctuary, 86 the twelve golden dishes, full of incense, weighing 10 shekels apiece according to the shekel of the sanctuary, all the gold of the dishes being 120 shekels; 87 all the cattle for the burnt offering twelve bulls, twelve rams, twelve male lambs a year old, with their grain offering; and twelve male goats for a sin offering; 88 and all the cattle for the sacrifice of peace offerings twenty-four bulls, the rams sixty, the male goats sixty, the male lambs a year old sixty. This was the dedication offering for the altar after it [f]was anointed.

89 And when Moses went into the tent of meeting [g]to speak with the LORD, he heard [h]the voice speaking to him from above the mercy seat that was on the ark of the testimony, from between the two cherubim; and it spoke to him.

The Seven Lamps

8 Now the LORD spoke to Moses, saying, 2 "Speak to Aaron and say to him, When you set up the lamps, the seven lamps shall give light in front of the lampstand." 3 And Aaron did so: he set up its lamps in front of the lampstand, as the LORD commanded Moses. 4 And [i]this was the workmanship of the lampstand, hammered work of gold. From its base to its flowers, it was hammered work; according to the pattern that the LORD had shown Moses, so he made the lampstand.

Cleansing of the Levites

5 And the LORD spoke to Moses, saying, 6 "Take the Levites from among the people of Israel and cleanse them. 7 Thus you shall do to them to cleanse them: sprinkle the [j]water of purification upon them, and [k]let them go with a razor over all their body, and wash their clothes and cleanse themselves. 8 Then let them take a bull from the herd and [l]its grain offering of fine flour mixed with oil, [m]and you shall take another bull from the herd for a sin offering. 9 [n]And you shall bring the Levites before the tent of meeting [o]and assemble the whole congregation of the people of Israel. 10 When you bring the Levites before the LORD, the people of Israel [p]shall lay their hands on the Levites, 11 and Aaron shall offer the Levites before the LORD as a wave offering from the people of Israel, that they may do the service of the LORD. 12 Then the Levites [q]shall lay their hands on the heads of the bulls, and you shall offer [r]the one for a sin offering and the other for a burnt offering to the LORD to make atonement for the Levites. 13 And you shall set the Levites before Aaron and his sons, and shall offer them as [s]a wave offering to the LORD.

14 "Thus you shall separate the Levites from among the people of Israel, and [t]the Levites shall be mine. 15 And after that the Levites shall go in to serve at the tent of meeting, when you have cleansed them and offered them as a [s]wave offering. 16 For they are [u]wholly given to me from among the people of Israel. [v]Instead of all who open the womb, the firstborn of all the people of Israel, I have taken them for myself. 17 [w]For all the firstborn among the people of Israel are mine, both of man and of beast. On the day that I struck down all the firstborn in the land of Egypt I consecrated them for myself, 18 and I have taken the Levites instead of all the firstborn among the people of Israel. 19 [u]And I have given the Levites as a gift to Aaron and his sons from among the people of Israel, to do the service for the people of Israel at the tent of meeting and [x]to make atonement

88 [f]ver. 1, 10
89 [g]ch. 12:8; See Ex. 33:9-11 [h]See Ex. 25:22
Chapter 8
4 [i]Ex. 25:31
7 [j]ch. 19:9, 17; [Lev. 8:6] [k][Lev. 14:8, 9]
8 [l]Lev. 2:1; See Ex. 29:41 [m]ver. 12
9 [n][Ex. 29:4; 40:12] [o][Lev. 8:3]
10 [p][Lev. 1:4]
12 [q][Ex. 29:10] [r]ver. 8
13 [s]ver. 11, 21

8:1–4 The essence of the Aaronic benediction (6:22–27) is here portrayed, as the lamps of the lampstand are positioned so as to shine the divine light upon the 12 loaves of bread, symbolic of Israel's 12 tribes. This blessed reality is fully realized in the church's relationship to Christ, who is "the light of the world" (John 8:12).

8:5–26 This section is linked with Numbers 7, as the Levites themselves were part of the offerings given for the tabernacle service (8:21) that were first provided by God (vv. 15–19). Their ministry directs our gaze upon God's provision of Christ as the worship leader of the church (Heb. 8:1–2) who, out of the plunder of his victorious exodus from the grave, provides all the gifts for holy life and ministry (Eph. 4:7–16).

14 [t]ch. 3:45; [ch. 16:9] 15 [s][See ver. 13 above] 16 [u]ch. 3:9 [v]ch. 3:12, 45 17 [w]See Ex. 13:2 19 [u][See ver. 16 above] [x]ch. 25:11, 13

for the people of Israel, [y]that there may be no
plague among the people of Israel when the
people of Israel come near the sanctuary."
20 Thus did Moses and Aaron and all the congregation of the people of Israel to the Levites.
According to all that the LORD commanded
Moses concerning the Levites, the people of
Israel did to them. 21 And [z]the Levites purified
themselves from sin and washed their clothes,
and [a]Aaron offered them as a wave offering
before the LORD, and Aaron made atonement
for them to cleanse them. 22 And after that the
Levites went in to do their service in the tent
of meeting before Aaron and his sons; as the
LORD had commanded Moses concerning the
Levites, so they did to them.

Retirement of the Levites

23 And the LORD spoke to Moses, saying,
24 "This applies to the Levites: [b]from twenty-
five years old and upward they[1] shall come to
do duty in the service of the tent of meeting.
25 And from the age of fifty years they shall
withdraw from the duty of the service and
serve no more. 26 They minister[2] to their brothers in the tent of meeting [c]by keeping guard,
but they shall do no service. Thus shall you do
to the Levites in assigning their duties."

The Passover Celebrated

9 And the LORD spoke to Moses in the wilderness of Sinai, [d]in the first month of the
second year after they had come out of the land
of Egypt, saying, 2 "Let the people of Israel keep
the Passover at its appointed time. 3 [e]On the
fourteenth day of this month, at twilight, you
shall keep it at its appointed time; according to
all its statutes and all its rules you shall keep
it." 4 So Moses told the people of Israel that they
should keep the Passover. 5 And they kept the
Passover in the first month, on the fourteenth
day of the month, at twilight, in the wilderness of Sinai; according to all that the LORD
commanded Moses, so the people of Israel
did. 6 And there were certain men who were
[f]unclean through touching a dead body, so that
they could not keep the Passover on that day,
and [g]they came before Moses and Aaron on
that day. 7 And those men said to him, "We are
unclean through touching a dead body. Why
are we kept from bringing the LORD's [h]offer-
ing at its appointed time among the people
of Israel?" 8 And Moses said to them, "Wait,
that [i]I may hear what the LORD will command
concerning you."
9 The LORD spoke to Moses, saying, 10 "Speak
to the people of Israel, saying, If any one of
you or of your descendants is unclean through
touching a dead body, or is on a long journey,
he shall still keep the Passover to the LORD.
11 [j]In the second month on the fourteenth day
at twilight they shall keep it. [k]They shall eat
it with unleavened bread and bitter herbs.
12 [l]They shall leave none of it until the morning, [m]nor break any of its bones; [n]according
to all the statute for the Passover they shall
keep it. 13 But if anyone who is clean and is
not on a journey fails to keep the Passover,
[o]that person shall be cut off from his people
because he did not bring the LORD's [p]offering
at its appointed time; that man shall bear his
sin. 14 And if a stranger sojourns among you
and would keep the Passover to the LORD,
according to the statute of the Passover and
according to its rule, so shall he do. [q]You shall
have one statute, both for the sojourner and
for the native."

The Cloud Covering the Tabernacle

15 [r]On the day that the tabernacle was set up,
the cloud covered the tabernacle, the tent of
the testimony. And [s]at evening it was over the
tabernacle like the appearance of fire until
morning. 16 So it was always: the cloud covered

[1] Hebrew *he*; also verses 25, 26 [2] Hebrew *He ministers*

9:1–23 Keeping the Passover before setting out from Sinai serves to situate afresh the wilderness march within the gracious context of the exodus deliverance out of Egypt, which the Passover, along with the Feast of Unleavened Bread, commemorates. As something of a continuation of the exodus journey, the Lord once more guides his people with a cloud by day and fire by night.

In the New Testament, the apostles continually remind us that our journey in sanctification through the wilderness of this age is by the ongoing grace of God—the same grace that first delivered us through the new exodus from the slavery of sin (Rom. 6:6–7; Gal. 3:3; 1 Cor. 10:1–2, 11; 15:10; Phil. 1:6; Col. 1:29).

19 [y]See ch. 1:53
21 [z]ver. 7 [a]ver. 11, 12, 13, 15
24 [b][ch. 4:3; 1 Chr. 23:3, 24, 27]
26 [c]See ch. 1:53
Chapter 9
1 [d][ch. 1:1]
3 [e]See Lev. 23:5
6 [f]ch. 5:2; 19:11, 16; [John 18:28] [g]ch. 27:2; Ex. 18:15, 19, 26
7 [h]ver. 13
8 [i]ch. 27:5
11 [j]See Ex. 12:6; 2 Chr. 30:2-15
[k]Ex. 12:8; [Deut. 16:3] **12** [l]Ex. 12:10 [m]Ex. 12:46; Cited John 19:36 [n]Ex. 12:43, 49 **13** [o]Ex. 12:15; [Gen. 17:14] [p]ver. 7 **14** [q]Ex. 12:48, 49 **15** [r]Ex. 40:17, 34 [s]See Ex. 13:21

it by day[1] and the appearance of fire by night.
17 And whenever the cloud [t]lifted from over
the tent, after that the people of Israel set
out, and in the place where the cloud settled
down, there the people of Israel camped. 18 At
the command of the LORD the people of Israel
set out, and at the command of the LORD they
camped. [u]As long as the cloud rested over the
tabernacle, they remained in camp. 19 Even
when the cloud continued over the tabernacle many days, the people of Israel [v]kept
the charge of the LORD and did not set out.
20 Sometimes the cloud was a few days over the
tabernacle, and according to the command of
the LORD they remained in camp; then according to the command of the LORD they set out.
21 And sometimes the cloud remained from
evening until morning. And when the cloud
lifted in the morning, they set out, or if it continued for a day and a night, when the cloud
lifted they set out. 22 Whether it was two days,
or a month, or a longer time, that the cloud
continued over the tabernacle, abiding there,
the people of Israel [w]remained in camp and
did not set out, but when it lifted they set out.
23 At the command of the LORD they camped,
and at the command of the LORD they set out.
[v]They kept the charge of the LORD, at the command of the LORD by Moses.

The Silver Trumpets

10 The LORD spoke to Moses, saying,
2 "Make two silver trumpets. Of hammered work you shall make them, and you
shall use them for [x]summoning the congregation and for breaking camp. 3 And when [y]both
are blown, all the congregation shall gather
themselves to you at the entrance of the tent of
meeting. 4 But if they blow only one, then [z]the
chiefs, the heads of the tribes of Israel, shall
gather themselves to you. 5 When you blow an
alarm, [a]the camps that are on the east side shall
set out. 6 And when you blow an alarm the second time, [b]the camps that are on the south side
shall set out. An alarm is to be blown whenever
they are to set out. 7 But when the assembly is
to be gathered together, [c]you shall blow a long
blast, but you shall not [d]sound an alarm. 8 [e]And
the sons of Aaron, the priests, shall blow the
trumpets. The trumpets shall be to you for
a perpetual statute throughout your generations. 9 And [f]when you go to war in your land
against the adversary who [g]oppresses you,
then you shall [d]sound an alarm with the trumpets, that you may be [h]remembered before the
LORD your God, and you shall be saved from
your enemies. 10 [i]On the day of your gladness
also, and at your appointed feasts and [j]at the
beginnings of your months, you shall blow
the trumpets over your burnt offerings and
over the sacrifices of your peace offerings. They
shall be [k]a reminder of you before your God:
I am the LORD your God."

Israel Leaves Sinai

11 In the second year, in the second month,
on the twentieth day of the month, [l]the cloud
lifted from over the tabernacle of the testimony, 12 and the people of Israel [m]set out by
stages from the [n]wilderness of Sinai. And the
cloud settled down in the [o]wilderness of Paran.
13 They set out for the first time [p]at the command of the LORD by Moses. 14 The standard of
the camp of the people of Judah set out [q]first
by their companies, and over their company
was [r]Nahshon the son of Amminadab. 15 And
over the company of the tribe of the people of
Issachar was Nethanel the son of Zuar. 16 And
over the company of the tribe of the people of
Zebulun was Eliab the son of Helon.

[1] Septuagint, Syriac, Vulgate; Hebrew lacks *by day*

17[t] ch. 10:11, 33, 34; Ex. 40:36
18[u] [1 Cor. 10:1]
19[v] See ch. 1:53
22[w] Ex. 40:36, 37
23[v] [See ver. 19 above]
Chapter 10
2[x] Isa. 1:13; Joel 1:14; [Ps. 81:3]
3[y] Jer. 4:5; Joel 2:15
4[z] ch. 1:16; 7:2; Ex. 18:21
5[a] ver. 14; See ch. 2:3-9
6[b] ver. 18; See ch. 2:10-16
7[c] ver. 3 [d] Joel 2:1
8[e] 1 Chr. 15:24; 2 Chr. 13:12
9[f] ch. 31:6; 2 Chr. 13:14; [Josh. 6:5] [g] Judg. 2:18; 4:3; 10:8, 12; 1 Sam. 10:18 [d] [See ver. 7 above] [h] See Gen. 8:1

10:1–36 The trumpet blasts for both worship and war, along with the battle order of the tribes, once more portray the people of God in the wilderness as an army marching out for warfare. While their enemies are strong, it is the Lord himself, symbolized by the ark, who goes before Israel, scattering his and their enemies (vv. 35–36). God provides whatever victory comes.

For the church's gospel marching orders, we too have the promise of Christ's triumphant presence (Matt. 28:16–20) along with the assurance that he will subdue all of his and our enemies (Rom. 16:20; 1 Cor. 15:25). Thankfully, the primary way Christ subdues his enemies is by his saving grace (Rom. 5:10; Eph. 2:1–10). For when we were his enemies he suffered to win us back (Rom. 5:6–11). Those who remain his enemies, however, will suffer their defeat eternally in hell (2 Thess. 1:5–10).

10[i] ch. 29:1; 1 Chr. 15:24; 2 Chr. 5:12, 13; 7:6; 29:26-28; Ezra 3:10; Neh. 12:35 [j] Ps. 81:3; See ch. 28:11 [k] ver. 9 **11**[l] ch. 9:17 **12**[m] [Ex. 40:36] [n] ch. 1:1; 9:5; Ex. 19:1, 2 [o] ch. 12:16; 13:3, 26; Gen. 21:21; Deut. 1:1 **13**[p] ver. 5, 6; ch. 2:34 **14**[q] See ch. 2:3-9 [r] For ver. 14-16, see ch. 1:7-9

17 And when [s]the tabernacle was taken down,
the sons of Gershon and the sons of Merari,
[t]who carried the tabernacle, set out. 18 And
[u]the standard of the camp of Reuben set out
by their companies, and over their company
was [v]Elizur the son of Shedeur. 19 And over the
company of the tribe of the people of Simeon
was [w]Shelumiel the son of Zurishaddai. 20 And
over the company of the tribe of the people of
Gad was [x]Eliasaph the son of [y]Deuel.

21 Then the Kohathites set out, [z]carrying the
holy things, and [a]the tabernacle was set up
before their arrival. 22 And [b]the standard of
the camp of the people of Ephraim set out by
their companies, and over their company was
[c]Elishama the son of Ammihud. 23 And over the
company of the tribe of the people of Manasseh
was [c]Gamaliel the son of Pedahzur. 24 And
over the company of the tribe of the people
of Benjamin was [d]Abidan the son of Gideoni.

25 Then [e]the standard of the camp of the
people of Dan, acting as the [f]rear guard of all
the camps, set out by their companies, and
over their company was [g]Ahiezer the son of
Ammishaddai. 26 And over the company of
the tribe of the people of Asher was [h]Pagiel
the son of Ochran. 27 And over the company
of the tribe of the people of Naphtali was
[i]Ahira the son of Enan. 28 [j]This was the order
of march of the people of Israel by their companies, when they set out.

29 And Moses said to Hobab the son of [k]Reuel
the Midianite, Moses' father-in-law, "We are
setting out for the place of which the LORD
said, 'I will give it to you.' Come with us, and we
will do good to you, for [m]the LORD has promised good to Israel." 30 But he said to him, "I will
not go. I will depart to my own land and to my
kindred." 31 And he said, "Please do not leave
us, for you know where we should camp in the
wilderness, and you will serve [n]as eyes for us.
32 And if you do go with us, [o]whatever good the
LORD will do to us, the same will we do to you."

33 So they set out from [p]the mount of the
LORD three days' journey. And the ark of the
covenant of the LORD went before them three
days' journey, to seek out [q]a resting place for
them. 34 [r]And the cloud of the LORD was over
them by day, whenever they set out from the
camp.

35 And whenever the ark set out, Moses said,
[s]"Arise, O LORD, and let your enemies be scattered, and let those who hate you flee before
you." 36 And when it rested, he said, "Return,
O LORD, to the ten thousand thousands of
Israel."

The People Complain

11 And [t]the people complained in the
hearing of the LORD about their misfor-
tunes, and when the LORD heard it, [u]his anger
was kindled, and [v]the fire of the LORD burned
among them and consumed some outlying
parts of the camp. 2 Then [w]the people cried
out to Moses, [x]and Moses prayed to the LORD,
and the fire died down. 3 So the name of that
place was called [y]Taberah,[1] because the fire of
the LORD burned among them.

4 Now the [z]rabble that was among them had
a strong craving. And the people of Israel also
[a]wept again and said, [b]"Oh that we had meat
to eat! 5 [c]We remember the fish we ate in Egypt
that cost nothing, the cucumbers, the melons,
the leeks, the onions, and the garlic. 6 But now

[1] *Taberah* means *burning*

11:1 Sharply contrasting the repeated reports of their obedience in preparing to set out (in chs. 1–10), Numbers 11 opens with Israel complaining as soon as the march begins. This negative view of the "wilderness generation" comprises the central bulk of Numbers (chs. 11–25), and offers several gospel lessons.

First, we are reminded that God's people are sinners saved by grace—the Israelites were neither delivered from Egypt nor brought into the Promised Land because of their own righteousness (Deut. 9:6). Second, the fearful reality that some Israelites were destroyed in the wilderness for their rebellion serves as a sanctifying example for us to persevere by God's grace, laying hold of Christ by faith (1 Cor. 10:1–11; Heb. 3:7–4:13). Third, the people's sinfulness stresses our dire need of a mediator to intercede on our behalf. Apart from Moses' intercessory prayers, Israel would have been consumed by God's wrath on various occasions. Our assurance of eternal life rests in knowing that we have the perfect Mediator, Jesus Christ, who ever lives to make intercession for us (Rom. 8:34; Heb. 7:24–25; 8:6).

17 [s]ch. 1:51 [t]See ch. 4:24-33; 7:6-8
18 [u]See ch. 2:10-16 [v]ch. 1:5
19 [w]ch. 1:6
20 [x]ch. 1:14 [y][ch. 2:14]
21 [z]ch. 7:9; See ch. 4:4-15 [a][ver. 17]
22 [b]See ch. 2:18-24 [c]ch. 1:10
23 [c][See ver. 22 above]
24 [d]ch. 1:11
25 [e]See ch. 2:25-31 [f][Josh. 6:9] [g]ch. 1:12
26 [h]ch. 1:13
27 [i]ch. 1:15
28 [j]ch. 2:34
29 [k]See Ex. 2:18 [l]Gen. 12:7 [m]Gen. 32:12; Ex. 3:8; 6:7, 8
31 [n][Job 29:15]
32 [o]ver. 29; [Judg. 1:16; 4:11]
33 [p]See Ex. 3:1 [q]Ps. 132:8; Jer. 31:2
34 [r]See Ex. 13:21

35 [s]Ps. 68:1, 2 **Chapter 11** **1** [t]Deut. 9:22 [u]Ps. 78:21 [v][ch. 16:35; Lev. 10:2; 2 Kgs. 1:12; Ps. 106:18; Rev. 13:13] **2** [w][ch. 21:7] [x][James 5:16]; See ch. 16:45-48
3 [y]Deut. 9:22 **4** [z]See Ex. 12:38 [a]ch. 14:1 [b]Ps. 78:18; 106:14; 1 Cor. 10:6 **5** [c][ch. 21:5; Ex. 16:3; Acts 7:39]

our strength is dried up, and there is nothing
at all but this manna to look at."
7 Now [d]the manna was like coriander seed,
and its appearance like that of bdellium. 8 [e]The
people went about and gathered it and ground
it in handmills or beat it in mortars and boiled
it in pots and made cakes of it. [f]And the taste
of it was like the taste of cakes baked with oil.
9 [g]When the dew fell upon the camp in the
night, the manna fell with it.
10 Moses heard the people [h]weeping throughout their clans, everyone at the door of his
tent. And the anger of the LORD blazed hotly,
and Moses was displeased. 11 [i]Moses said to
the LORD, "Why have you dealt ill with your
servant? And why have I not found favor in
your sight, that you lay the burden of all this
people on me? 12 Did I conceive all this people?
Did I give them birth, that you should say to
me, [j]'Carry them in your bosom, as a [k]nurse
carries a nursing child,' to the land [l]that you
swore to give their fathers? 13 [m]Where am I to
get meat to give to all this people? For they
weep before me and say, 'Give us meat, that
we may eat.' 14 [n]I am not able to carry all this
people alone; the burden is too heavy for me.
15 If you will treat me like this, kill me at once,
if I find favor in your sight, that I may not see
my wretchedness."

Elders Appointed to Aid Moses

16 Then the LORD said to Moses, "Gather for
me [o]seventy men of the elders of Israel, whom
you know to be the elders of the people and
[p]officers over them, and bring them to the tent
of meeting, and let them take their stand there
with you. 17 [q]And I will come down and talk
with you there. And [r]I will take some of the
Spirit that is on you and put it on them, and
[s]they shall bear the burden of the people with
you, so that you may not bear it yourself alone.
18 And say to the people, [t]'Consecrate yourselves
for tomorrow, and you shall eat meat, for you
have wept in the hearing of the LORD, saying,
"Who will give us meat to eat? [u]For it was better for us in Egypt." Therefore the LORD will
give you meat, and you shall eat. 19 You shall
not eat just one day, or two days, or five days,
or ten days, or twenty days, 20 but a whole
month, [v]until it comes out at your nostrils and
becomes loathsome to you, because you have
rejected the LORD who is among you and have
wept before him, saying, [w]"Why did we come
out of Egypt?"'" 21 But Moses said, [x]"The people among whom I am number six hundred
thousand on foot, and you have said, 'I will give
them meat, that they may eat a whole month!'
22 [y]Shall flocks and herds be slaughtered for
them, and be enough for them? Or shall all the
fish of the sea be gathered together for them,
and be enough for them?" 23 And the LORD said
to Moses, [z]"Is the LORD's hand shortened? Now
you shall see whether [a]my word will come true
for you or not."
24 So Moses went out and told the people the
words of the LORD. [b]And he gathered seventy
men of the elders of the people and placed
them around the tent. 25 Then [c]the LORD came
down in the cloud and spoke to him, and took
some of the Spirit that was on him and put it
on the seventy elders. And as soon as the Spirit
rested on them, they prophesied. But they did
not continue doing it.
26 Now two men remained in the camp, one
named Eldad, and the other named Medad,
and the Spirit rested on them. They were
among those registered, but they [d]had not
gone out to the tent, and so they prophesied
in the camp. 27 And a young man ran and told
Moses, "Eldad and Medad are prophesying in
the camp." 28 And [e]Joshua the son of Nun, the
assistant of Moses from his youth, said, "My
lord Moses, [f]stop them." 29 But Moses said to
him, "Are you jealous for my sake? [g]Would
that all the LORD's people were prophets,
that the LORD would put his Spirit on them!"
30 And Moses and the elders of Israel returned
to the camp.

Quail and a Plague

31 Then a [h]wind from the LORD sprang up,
and it brought quail from the sea and let them
fall beside the camp, about a day's journey on
this side and a day's journey on the other side,
around the camp, and about two cubits[1] above
the ground. 32 And the people rose all that day
and all night and all the next day, and gathered
the quail. Those who gathered least gathered

[1] A *cubit* was about 18 inches or 45 centimeters

7 [d] Ex. 16:14, 31 **8** [e] Ex. 16:16-18 [f] [Ex. 16:31] **9** [g] Ex. 16:13, 14 **10** [h] [Zech. 12:12-14] **11** [i] [1 Kgs. 19:4; Jonah 4:1-4, 9] **12** [j] Isa. 40:11; [Deut. 1:31] [k] [Isa. 49:23; 1 Thess. 2:7] [l] Gen. 50:24; Ex. 13:5 **13** [m] [2 Kgs. 7:2; Matt. 15:33; Mark 8:4; John 6:7, 9] **14** [n] Ex. 18:18; Deut. 1:9, 12 **16** [o] [Ex. 24:1, 9] [p] Deut. 1:15; 16:18 **17** [q] ver. 25; ch. 12:5; Gen. 11:5; 18:21; Ex. 19:20 [r] [2 Kgs. 2:9, 15; Neh. 9:20] [s] Ex. 18:22 **18** [t] Ex. 19:10 [u] See ver. 5 **20** [v] [Ps. 78:29; 106:15] [w] ch. 21:5 **21** [x] Ex. 12:37; [ch. 1:46; Ex. 38:26] **22** [y] [ver. 13] **23** [z] Isa. 50:2; 59:1 [a] ch. 23:19; Ezek. 12:25; 24:14 **24** [b] ver. 16 **25** [c] ver. 17 **26** [d] [1 Sam. 20:26; Jer. 36:5] **28** [e] ch. 26:65; Ex. 24:13; [ch. 13:8]; See ch. 13:16 [f] [Mark 9:38; Luke 9:49] **29** [g] [1 Cor. 14:5] **31** [h] Ex. 16:13; Ps. 78:26-28; 105:40

ten [i]homers.[1] And they spread them out for themselves all around the camp. 33 [j]While the meat was yet between their teeth, before it was consumed, the anger of the LORD was kindled against the people, and [k]the LORD struck down the people with a very great plague. 34 Therefore the name of that place was called [l]Kibroth-hattaavah,[2] because there they buried the people who had the craving. 35 [m]From Kibroth-hattaavah the people journeyed to [n]Hazeroth, and they remained at [n]Hazeroth.

Miriam and Aaron Oppose Moses

12 Miriam and Aaron spoke against Moses because of the Cushite woman whom he had married, for he had married a Cushite woman. 2 And they said, "Has the LORD indeed spoken only through Moses? [o]Has he not spoken through us also?" And [p]the LORD heard it. 3 Now the man Moses was very meek, more than all people who were on the face of the earth. 4 And suddenly the LORD said to Moses and to Aaron and Miriam, "Come out, you three, to the tent of meeting." And the three of them came out. 5 And [q]the LORD came down in a pillar of cloud and stood at the entrance of the tent and called Aaron and Miriam, and they both came forward. 6 And he said, "Hear my words: If there is a prophet among you, I the LORD make myself known to him [r]in a vision; I speak with him [s]in a dream. 7 Not so with [t]my servant Moses. [u]He is faithful in all my house. 8 With him I speak [v]mouth to mouth, clearly, and not in [w]riddles, and he beholds [x]the form of the LORD. Why then were you not afraid to speak against my servant Moses?" 9 And the anger of the LORD was kindled against them, and he departed.

10 When the cloud removed from over the tent, behold, [y]Miriam was [z]leprous,[3] like snow. And Aaron turned toward Miriam, and behold, she was leprous. 11 And Aaron said to Moses, "Oh, my lord, [a]do not punish us[4] because we have done foolishly and have sinned. 12 Let her not be as one dead, whose flesh is half eaten away when he comes out of his mother's womb." 13 And Moses cried to the LORD, "O God, please heal her—please." 14 But the LORD said to Moses, "If her father had but [b]spit in her face, should she not be shamed seven days? Let her be [c]shut outside the camp seven days, and after that she may be brought in again." 15 So Miriam [d]was shut outside the camp seven days, and the people did not set out on the march till Miriam was brought in again. 16 After that the people set out from [e]Hazeroth, and camped in [f]the wilderness of Paran.

Spies Sent into Canaan

13 The LORD spoke to Moses, saying, 2 [g]"Send men to spy out the land of Canaan, which I am giving to the people of

[1] A *homer* was about 6 bushels or 220 liters [2] *Kibroth-hattaavah* means *graves of craving* [3] *Leprosy* was a term for several skin diseases; see Leviticus 13 [4] Hebrew *do not lay sin upon us*

11:29 Moses' longing that all the Lord's people would receive his Spirit is echoed as a divine promise by the prophet Joel (2:28–32) and proclaimed by Peter as accomplished through Christ on the day of Pentecost (Acts 2). Jesus Christ, by his righteous obedience and atoning death, has earned all authority in heaven and on earth to fulfill God's promise. Being raised from the dead and exalted to the right hand of God, he accordingly received the promise from the Father and poured out the Holy Spirit upon his people (Acts 2:33). There is no way to overestimate the precious gift of the Holy Spirit through whom we are adopted into God's household, and by whom we cry out, "Abba! Father!" to God (Rom. 8:12–17).

12:1–16 This challenge by Miriam and Aaron as to Moses' role as mediator between God and his people is met with an admonishing reaffirmation of the unique status of Moses as the prophet with whom God speaks "mouth to mouth" (v. 8). The New Testament both upholds Moses' distinctive place within the old covenant and attests to the superiority of Christ's within the new covenant (Heb. 3:2–6).

No other prophet of earthly origin had been as intimate with God as Moses. But the Son, who came from the Father's side as our ultimate Prophet, has most fully made him known (Luke 7:16; John 1:17–18; Acts 3:22). We therefore look happily to Christ alone for grace and truth.

13:1–14:45 Demonstrating the trustworthiness of God's word that the land was indeed bountiful, the cluster of grapes (13:23) should have encouraged the Israelites to claim God's promise and enter the Promised Land. Tragically, however, the people desired to reverse the exodus and go back to Egypt instead (14:1–4). This faithlessness,

32 [i] Ex. 16:36; [Ezek. 45:11]
33 [j] Ps. 78:30, 31 [k] [ch. 16:49]
34 [l] Deut. 9:22
35 [m] ch. 33:17 [n] ch. 12:16; 33:17, 18

Chapter 12
2 [o] Mic. 6:4 [p] ch. 11:1; 2 Kgs. 19:4; Isa. 37:4; Ezek. 35:12, 13; [Mal. 3:16]
5 [q] ch. 11:25; 16:19
6 [r] Gen. 46:2; Ezek. 1:1; Dan. 8:2; 10:8, 16; Luke 1:11, 22; Acts 10:11; 22:17, 18 [s] Gen. 20:6; 31:10, 11; 1 Kgs. 3:5; Job 33:15; Matt. 1:20; 27:19
7 [t] Ps. 105:26 [u] Heb. 3:2, 5
8 [v] ch. 7:89; [Ex. 33:11; Deut. 34:10; 1 Cor. 13:12] [w] Ps. 49:4; 78:2; Prov. 1:6 [x] [Ex. 33:20, 23]
10 [y] Deut. 24:9 [z] See Lev. 13:10
11 [a] [2 Sam. 19:19; 24:10; Prov. 30:32]
14 [b] Deut. 25:9; Job 30:10 [c] See Lev. 13:46
15 [d] [2 Kgs. 15:5; 2 Chr. 26:20, 21; Luke 17:12]
16 [e] ch. 11:35; [ch. 33:18] [f] See ch. 10:12

Chapter 13
2 [g] ch. 32:8; See Deut. 1:22-25

Israel. From each tribe of their fathers you shall send a man, every one a chief among them.” 3 So Moses sent them from [h]the wilderness of Paran, according to the command of the LORD, all of them men who were heads of the people of Israel. 4 And these were their names: From the tribe of Reuben, Shammua the son of Zaccur; 5 from the tribe of Simeon, Shaphat the son of Hori; 6 [i]from the tribe of Judah, [j]Caleb the son of Jephunneh; 7 from the tribe of Issachar, Igal the son of Joseph; 8 from the tribe of Ephraim, [k]Hoshea the son of Nun; 9 from the tribe of Benjamin, Palti the son of Raphu; 10 from the tribe of Zebulun, Gaddiel the son of Sodi; 11 from the tribe of Joseph (that is, from the tribe of Manasseh), Gaddi the son of Susi; 12 from the tribe of Dan, Ammiel the son of Gemalli; 13 from the tribe of Asher, Sethur the son of Michael; 14 from the tribe of Naphtali, Nahbi the son of Vophsi; 15 from the tribe of Gad, Geuel the son of Machi. 16 These were the names of the men whom Moses sent to spy out the land. And Moses called [k]Hoshea the son of Nun Joshua.

17 Moses sent them to spy out the land of Canaan and said to them, “Go up into [l]the Negeb and go up into [m]the hill country, 18 and see what the land is, and whether the people who dwell in it are strong or weak, whether they are few or many, 19 and whether the land that they dwell in is good or bad, and whether the cities that they dwell in are camps or strongholds, 20 and whether the land is [n]rich or poor, and whether there are trees in it or not. [o]Be of good courage and bring some of the fruit of the land.” Now the time was the season of the first ripe grapes.

21 So they went up and spied out the land [p]from the wilderness of Zin to Rehob, [q]near Lebo-hamath. 22 They went up into [m]the Negeb and came to [r]Hebron. [s]Ahiman, Sheshai, and Talmai, the [t]descendants of Anak, were there. ([u]Hebron was built seven years before [u]Zoan in Egypt.) 23 And [v]they came to the Valley of Eshcol and cut down from there a branch with a single cluster of grapes, and they carried it on a pole between two of them; they also brought some pomegranates and figs. 24 That place was called the Valley of Eshcol,[1] because of the cluster that the people of Israel cut down from there.

Report of the Spies

25 At the end of forty days they returned from spying out the land. 26 And they came to Moses and Aaron and to all the congregation of the people of Israel in the wilderness of Paran, at [w]Kadesh. They brought back word to them and to all the congregation, and showed them the fruit of the land. 27 And they told him, “We came to the land to which you sent us. It [x]flows with milk and honey, [y]and this is its fruit. 28 [z]However, the people who dwell in the land are strong, and the cities are fortified and very large. And besides, we saw the descendants of Anak there. 29 [a]The Amalekites dwell in the land of the Negeb. The Hittites, the Jebusites, and the Amorites dwell in the hill country. [b]And the Canaanites dwell by the sea, and along the Jordan.”

30 But [c]Caleb quieted the people before Moses and said, “Let us go up at once and occupy it, for we are well able to overcome it.” 31 [d]Then the men who had gone up with him said, “We are not able to go up against the people,

[1] *Eshcol* means *cluster*

denying the purpose of the exodus at the very cusp of its fulfillment, brings on the most severe crisis since the golden calf idolatry, as God once more suggests annihilating the whole lot and starting over with Moses (14:12; Ex. 32:10), as he once did with Noah and the world (Genesis 6–9). Yet, according to the Lord's steadfast love, Moses' mediation preserves the promise of the land for the next generation of Israelites (Num. 14:13–20).

Life in the wilderness, full of trials and hardships, exposes our hearts—are they hardened by difficulties so that we want to turn back, or purged by them so that we long all the more to press onward into the heavenly land held out before us? When by faith we look to Christ, who in the wilderness lived on God's word (Matt. 4:4), who died and lives as our Mediator to assure us of God's steadfast love to us, and who by the Eucharist (the celebration of the Lord's Supper) feeds us with the powers of the age to come, we are strengthened to endure the journey of faith marked out before us (Heb. 12:1–2).

3 [h]ver. 26; ch. 12:16; 32:8; Deut. 1:19; 9:23
6 [i]ch. 34:19; 1 Chr. 4:15 [j]ver. 30; ch. 14:6, 30; 26:65; 32:12; Deut. 1:36; See Josh. 14:6-15; 15:13-18; Judg. 1:12-15
8 [k]ver. 16; ch. 11:28; 14:6, 30, 38; Ex. 24:13; Deut. 32:44; [Neh. 8:17]
16 [k][See ver. 8 above]
17 [l]ver. 22, 29; ch. 21:1; Josh. 15:19; Judg. 1:15 [m]ver. 29; Judg. 1:9, 19
20 [n]Neh. 9:25, 35; Ezek. 34:14 [o]Deut. 31:6, 7, 23
21 [p]ch. 20:1; 33:36; 34:3; Josh. 15:1 [q]ch. 34:8
22 [m][See ver. 17 above] [r]See Josh. 14:15 [s]Josh. 15:14; Judg. 1:10 [t]ver. 33; Deut. 1:28; 2:10; 9:2; Josh. 11:21, 22 [u]Ps. 78:12, 43; Isa. 19:11, 13; 30:4; Ezek. 30:14 **23** [v]ch. 32:9; Deut. 1:24, 25 **26** [w]ch. 20:1, 16; 32:8; 33:36; Deut. 1:19; Josh. 14:6, 7 **27** [x]See Ex. 3:8 [y]Deut. 1:25 **28** [z]Deut. 1:28; 9:1, 2 **29** [a]ch. 14:43; Ex. 17:8 [b][ch. 14:25] **30** [c][ch. 14:6, 24] **31** [d]ch. 32:9; Deut. 1:28; Josh. 14:8

for they are stronger than we are." 32 So [e]they brought to the people of Israel a bad report of the land that they had spied out, saying, "The land, through which we have gone to spy it out, is a land that devours its inhabitants, and [f]all the people that we saw in it are of great height. 33 And there we saw the [g]Nephilim (the sons of Anak, who come from the [g]Nephilim), and we seemed to ourselves [h]like grasshoppers, and so we seemed to them."

The People Rebel

14 Then all the congregation raised a loud cry, and the people [i]wept that night. 2 And all the people of Israel [j]grumbled against Moses and Aaron. The whole congregation said to them, "Would that we had died in the land of Egypt! Or [k]would that we had died in this wilderness! 3 Why is the LORD bringing us into this land, to fall by the sword? [l]Our wives and our little ones will become a prey. Would it not be better for us to go back to Egypt?" 4 And they said to one another, [m]"Let us choose a leader and [n]go back to Egypt."

5 Then [o]Moses and Aaron fell on their faces before all the assembly of the congregation of the people of Israel. 6 [p]And Joshua the son of Nun and Caleb the son of Jephunneh, who were among those who had spied out the land, tore their clothes 7 and said to all the congregation of the people of Israel, [q]"The land, which we passed through to spy it out, is an exceedingly good land. 8 If [r]the LORD delights in us, he will bring us into this land and give it to us, [s]a land that flows with milk and honey. 9 Only [t]do not rebel against the LORD. And [u]do not fear the people of the land, for [v]they are bread for us. Their protection is removed from them, and the LORD is with us; do not fear them." 10 [w]Then all the congregation said to stone them with stones. But [x]the glory of the LORD appeared at the tent of meeting to all the people of Israel.

11 And the LORD said to Moses, "How long will this people [y]despise me? And how long will they not [z]believe in me, in spite of all the signs that I have done among them? 12 I will strike them with the pestilence and disinherit them, and I [a]will make of you a nation greater and mightier than they."

Moses Intercedes for the People

13 But [b]Moses said to the LORD, "Then the Egyptians will hear of it, for you brought up this people in your might from among them, 14 and they will tell the inhabitants of this land. [c]They have heard that you, O LORD, are in the midst of this people. For you, O LORD, are seen face to face, and [d]your cloud stands over them and you go before them, in a pillar of cloud by day and in a pillar of fire by night. 15 Now if you kill this people as one man, then the nations who have heard your fame will say, 16 'It is because the LORD [e]was not able to bring this people into the land that he swore to give to them that he has killed them in the wilderness.' 17 And now, please let the power of the Lord be great as you have promised, saying, 18 [f]'The LORD is slow to anger and abounding in steadfast love, forgiving iniquity and transgression, but he will by no means clear the guilty, [g]visiting the iniquity of the fathers on the children, to the third and the fourth generation.' 19 Please [h]pardon the iniquity of this people, according to the greatness of your steadfast love, just [i]as you have forgiven this people, from Egypt until now."

God Promises Judgment

20 Then the LORD said, "I have pardoned, [j]according to your word. 21 But truly, as I live, and as all [k]the earth shall be filled with the glory of the LORD, 22 [l]none of the men who have seen my glory and my signs that I did in Egypt and in the wilderness, and yet have put me to the test these [m]ten times and have not obeyed my voice, 23 [n]shall see the land that I swore to give to their fathers. And none of those who despised me shall see it. 24 But my servant [o]Caleb, because he has a different spirit and has [p]followed me fully, I will bring into the land into which he went, and his descendants shall possess it. 25 [q]Now, since the Amalekites and the Canaanites dwell in the valleys, [r]turn tomorrow and set out for the wilderness by the way to the Red Sea."

26 And the LORD spoke to Moses and to

32 [e]ch. 14:36, 37 [f][Amos 2:9] **33** [g]Gen. 6:4 [h]Isa. 40:22 **Chapter 14** **1** [i]ch. 11:4 **2** [j]ver. 27, 29, 33; ch. 16:41; Ex. 15:24; 16:2; 17:3; Ps. 106:25; [Josh. 9:18] [k][ver. 27-29] **3** [l]ver. 31 **4** [m]Neh. 9:17 [n][Deut. 17:16; Acts 7:39] **5** [o]ch. 16:4, 22; 20:6 **6** [p]ver. 30; ch. 13:6, 8 **7** [q]ch. 13:27; Deut. 1:25 **8** [r]Deut. 10:15; 2 Sam. 22:20; 1 Kgs. 10:9; Ps. 18:19; 22:8; Isa. 62:4 [s]See Ex. 3:8 **9** [t]Josh. 22:16, 18, 19, 29 [u]Deut. 7:18; 20:3 [v]ch. 24:8; [Ps. 14:4; 74:14] **10** [w]Ex. 17:4 [x]See Lev. 9:23 **11** [y]ver. 23; ch. 16:30 [z]Deut. 1:32; 9:23; Ps. 78:22, 32; 106:24; Heb. 3:18; [John 12:37] **12** [a]Ex. 32:10 **13** [b]Ex. 32:12; [Deut. 9:28; 32:27; Ps. 106:23; Ezek. 20:9, 14] **14** [c]Ex. 15:14; Josh. 2:9, 10; 5:1 [d]See Ex. 13:21 **16** [e]Deut. 9:28; [Josh. 7:9] **18** [f]See Ex. 34:6, 7 [g]See Ex. 20:5 **19** [h]Ex. 34:9 [i]Ps. 78:38; 106:45 **20** [j]Ps. 106:23; [James 5:16]; See 1 John 5:14-16 **21** [k]Ps. 72:19; Hab. 2:14 **22** [l]Deut. 1:35; Ps. 95:11; 106:26; Heb. 3:17, 18 [m][Gen. 31:7; Job 19:3] **23** [n]ch. 32:11; Ezek. 20:15; [ch. 26:64] **24** [o]ver. 6; ch. 13:6 [p]ch. 32:12; Josh. 14:8, 9 **25** [q]ver. 43, 45; See ch. 13:29 [r]Deut. 1:40

Aaron, saying, 27 "How long shall [s]this wicked congregation grumble against me? [t]I have heard the grumblings of the people of Israel, which they grumble against me. 28 Say to them, [u]'As I live, declares the LORD, [v]what you have said in my hearing I will do to you: 29 [w]your dead bodies shall fall in this wilderness, and [x]of all your number, listed in the census [y]from twenty years old and upward, who have grumbled against me, 30 not one shall come into the land where I [z]swore that I would make you dwell, [a]except Caleb the son of Jephunneh and Joshua the son of Nun. 31 [b]But your little ones, who you said would become a prey, I will bring in, and they shall know the land that [c]you have rejected. 32 But as for you, [w]your dead bodies shall fall in this wilderness. 33 And your children [d]shall be shepherds in the wilderness [e]forty years and shall [f]suffer for your faithlessness, until the last of your dead bodies lies in the wilderness. 34 [g]According to the number of the days in which you spied out the land, [h]forty days, a year for each day, you shall bear your iniquity forty years, and you shall know my displeasure.' 35 [i]I, the LORD, have spoken. Surely this will I do to all [j]this wicked congregation who are gathered together against me: in this wilderness they shall come to a full end, and there they shall die."

36 [k]And the men whom Moses sent to spy out the land, who returned and made all the congregation grumble against him by bringing up a bad report about the land— 37 the men who brought up a bad report of the land— [l]died by plague before the LORD. 38 Of those men who went to spy out the land, [m]only Joshua the son of Nun and Caleb the son of Jephunneh remained alive.

Israel Defeated in Battle

39 When Moses told these words to all the people of Israel, the people [n]mourned greatly. 40 And they rose early in the morning and went up to the heights of the hill country, saying, [o]"Here we are. We will go up to the place that the LORD has promised, for we have sinned." 41 [p]But Moses said, "Why now are you transgressing the command of the LORD, when that will not succeed? 42 [q]Do not go up, [r]for the Lord is not among you, lest you be struck down before your enemies. 43 For there [s]the Amalekites and the Canaanites are facing you, and you shall fall by the sword. Because you have turned back from following the LORD, the LORD will not be with you." 44 [t]But they presumed to go up to the heights of the hill country, although neither [u]the ark of the covenant of the LORD nor Moses departed out of the camp. 45 Then [v]the Amalekites and the Canaanites who lived in that hill country came down and defeated them and pursued them, even to [w]Hormah.

Laws About Sacrifices

15 The LORD spoke to Moses, saying, 2 "Speak to the people of Israel and say to them, [x]When you come into the land you are to inhabit, which I am giving you, 3 and [y]you offer to the LORD from the herd or from the flock a food offering[1] or a burnt offering or a sacrifice, [z]to fulfill a vow or as a freewill offering or [a]at your appointed feasts, to make a [b]pleasing aroma to the LORD, 4 then [c]he who brings his offering shall offer to the LORD [d]a grain offering of a tenth of an ephah[2] of fine flour, [e]mixed with a quarter of a hin[3] of oil; 5 and you shall offer with the burnt offering, or for the sacrifice, a quarter of a hin of [f]wine

[1] Or *an offering by fire*; so throughout Numbers [2] An *ephah* was about 3/5 bushel or 22 liters [3] A *hin* was about 4 quarts or 3.5 liters

27 [s]ver. 35 [t]Ex. 16:7, 12
28 [u]ver. 21, 23; ch. 26:65 [v][ver. 2]
29 [w]1 Cor. 10:5; Heb. 3:17 [x]ch. 1:45; 26:64; Deut. 1:35 [y]ch. 1:3; Ex. 30:14
30 [z]See Gen. 14:22 [a]ver. 6, 38; See ch. 13:6
31 [b]ver. 3; Deut. 1:39 [c]Ps. 106:24
32 [w][See ver. 29 above]
33 [d]ch. 32:13; [Ps. 107:40] [e]Ps. 95:10; [Deut. 2:14] [f]Ezek. 23:35
34 [g]ch. 13:25 [h][Ezek. 4:6]
35 [i]ch. 23:19 [j]ver. 27
36 [k]ch. 13:32

15:2 After the dismal events of the previous two chapters, including rebellion, judgment, and defeat at the hands of the Canaanites, the Lord commands Moses to speak a bold word of grace to Israel, reasserting his promise without qualification: "*When* you come into the land . . ." There is no "maybe" here but rather the assurance that God will fulfill his covenant promise to the patriarchs of Israel.

The gospel, too, comes to us as a bold word of grace, that one day we will finish our journey and find ourselves in the new earth with no more striving against sin or sorrow (Revelation 21). What is more, in the face of difficult circumstances challenging our faith in God's promise, we possess the indwelling Holy Spirit to guarantee that life to come (2 Cor. 5:2), and we are further assured in that the humanity of Jesus Christ has already been resurrected and glorified (Heb. 2:9–10; 1 Cor. 15:20).

37 [l]1 Cor. 10:10; Heb. 3:17; Jude 5 **38** [m]ch. 26:65; See ch. 13:16 **39** [n]Ex. 33:4 **40** [o]Deut. 1:41 **41** [p][2 Chr. 24:20] **42** [q]Deut. 1:42 [r][Deut. 31:17] **43** [s]ver. 25, 45; See ch. 13:29 **44** [t]Deut. 1:43 [u][1 Sam. 4:3] **45** [v]ver. 43; [Deut. 1:44] [w]ch. 21:3; Judg. 1:17 **Chapter 15** **2** [x]ver. 18; Lev. 23:10; Deut. 26:1 **3** [y]Lev. 1:2, 3 [z]Lev. 22:21; 27:2 [a]ch. 28:19, 27; Lev. 23:8, 12, 36; Deut. 16:10 [b]Ex. 29:18; Lev. 4:31; See Gen. 8:21 **4** [c]Lev. 2:1; 6:14 [d]Ex. 29:40; Lev. 23:13 [e]ch. 28:5; Lev. 14:10 **5** [f]ch. 28:7, 14

for the drink offering for each lamb. 6 [g]Or for a ram, you shall offer for a grain offering two tenths of an ephah of fine flour mixed with a third of a hin of oil. 7 And for the drink offering you shall offer a third of a hin of wine, a [b]pleasing aroma to the LORD. 8 And when you offer a bull as a burnt offering or sacrifice, to [z]fulfill a vow or for [h]peace offerings to the LORD, 9 then one shall offer [i]with the bull a grain offering of three tenths of an ephah of fine flour, mixed with half a hin of oil. 10 And you shall offer for the drink offering half a hin of wine, as a food offering, a pleasing aroma to the LORD.

11 [j]"Thus it shall be done for each bull or ram, or for each lamb or young goat. 12 As many as you offer, so shall you do with each one, as many as there are. 13 Every native Israelite shall do these things in this way, in offering a food offering, with a pleasing aroma to the LORD. 14 And if a stranger is sojourning with you, or anyone is living permanently among you, and he wishes to offer a food offering, with a pleasing aroma to the LORD, he shall do as you do. 15 For the assembly, [k]there shall be one statute for you and for the stranger who sojourns with you, a statute forever throughout your generations. You and the sojourner shall be alike before the LORD. 16 One law and one rule shall be for you and for the stranger who sojourns with you."

17 The LORD spoke to Moses, saying, 18 [l]"Speak to the people of Israel and say to them, When you come into the land to which I bring you 19 and when you eat of [m]the bread of the land, you shall present a contribution to the LORD. 20 [n]Of the first of your dough you shall present a loaf as a contribution; like a [o]contribution from the threshing floor, so shall you present it. 21 [n]Some of the first of your dough you shall give to the LORD as a contribution throughout your generations.

Laws About Unintentional Sins

22 [p]"But if you sin unintentionally,[1] and do not observe all these commandments that the LORD has spoken to Moses, 23 all that the LORD has commanded you by Moses, from the day that the LORD gave commandment, and onward throughout your generations, 24 then if it was done unintentionally [q]without the knowledge of the congregation, all the congregation shall offer one bull from the herd for a burnt offering, a pleasing aroma to the LORD, [r]with its grain offering and its drink offering, according to the rule, and [s]one male goat for a sin offering. 25 [t]And the priest shall make atonement for all the congregation of the people of Israel, and they shall be forgiven, because it was a mistake, and they have brought their offering, a food offering to the LORD, and their sin offering before the LORD for their mistake. 26 And all the congregation of the people of Israel shall be forgiven, and the stranger who sojourns among them, because the whole population was involved in the mistake.

27 [u]"If one person sins unintentionally, he shall offer a female goat a year old for a sin offering. 28 [v]And the priest shall make atonement before the LORD for the person who makes a mistake, when he sins unintentionally, to make atonement for him, and he shall be forgiven. 29 [w]You shall have one law for him who does anything unintentionally, for him who is native among the people of Israel and for the stranger who sojourns among them. 30 [x]But the person who does anything with a high hand, whether he is native or a sojourner, reviles the LORD, and that person shall be cut off from among his people. 31 Because he has [y]despised the word of the LORD and has broken his commandment, that person shall be utterly cut off; his iniquity shall be on him."

A Sabbathbreaker Executed

32 While the people of Israel were in the wilderness, they found a man [z]gathering sticks on the Sabbath day. 33 And those who found him gathering sticks brought him to Moses and Aaron and to all the congregation. 34 [a]They put him in custody, because it had not been made clear what should be done to him. 35 And the LORD said to Moses, [b]"The man shall be put to death; all the congregation shall [c]stone him with stones outside the camp." 36 And all the congregation brought him outside the camp and stoned him to death with stones, as the LORD commanded Moses.

[1] Or *by mistake*; also verses 24, 27, 28, 29

6 [g] ch. 28:12, 14 **7** [b] [See ver. 3 above] **8** [z] [See ver. 3 above] [h] Lev. 7:11 **9** [i] ch. 28:12, 14; See Lev. 6:14-17 **11** [j] See ch. 28 **15** [k] ver. 29, 30; ch. 9:14; Ex. 12:49 **18** [l] ver. 2 **19** [m] [Josh. 5:11, 12] **20** [n] Deut. 26:2, 10; Neh. 10:37; Ezek. 44:30 [o] Lev. 2:14; See Lev. 23:10-17 **21** [n] [See ver. 20 above] **22** [p] [Lev. 4:2] **24** [q] [Lev. 4:13] [r] ver. 8-10 [s] ch. 28:15; Lev. 4:23 **25** [t] Lev. 4:20 **27** [u] Lev. 4:27, 28 **28** [v] Lev. 4:35 **29** [w] See ver. 15 **30** [x] [Deut. 17:12; Ps. 19:13; Heb. 10:26] **31** [y] 2 Sam. 12:9; 2 Chr. 36:16; Prov. 13:13 **32** [z] Ex. 35:3; See Ex. 20:8, 9 **34** [a] Lev. 24:12 **35** [b] Ex. 31:14, 15 [c] Lev. 24:14-16; Josh. 7:25; 1 Kgs. 21:13; Acts 7:58

Tassels on Garments

37 The LORD said to Moses, 38 "Speak to the people of Israel, and tell them to [d]make tassels on the corners of their garments throughout their generations, and to put a cord of blue on the tassel of each corner. 39 And it shall be a tassel for you to look at and remember all the commandments of the LORD, to do them, [e]not to follow[1] after your own heart and your own eyes, which you are inclined [f]to whore after. 40 So you shall remember and do all my commandments, and be [g]holy to your God. 41 [h]I am the LORD your God, who brought you out of the land of Egypt to be your God: I am the LORD your God."

Korah's Rebellion

16 Now [i]Korah the son of Izhar, son of Kohath, son of Levi, and [j]Dathan and Abiram the sons of Eliab, and On the son of Peleth, sons of Reuben, took men. 2 And they rose up before Moses, with a number of the people of Israel, 250 chiefs of the congregation, chosen from the assembly, well-known men. 3 [k]They assembled themselves together against Moses and against Aaron and said to them, [l]"You have gone too far! For [m]all in the congregation are holy, every one of them, and the LORD is among them. Why then do you exalt yourselves above the assembly of the LORD?" 4 When Moses heard it, [n]he fell on his face, 5 and he said to Korah and all his company, "In the morning the LORD will show [o]who is his,[2] and who is [p]holy, and will bring him near to him. The one [q]whom he chooses he will [r]bring near to him. 6 Do this: take [s]censers, Korah and all his company; 7 put fire in them and put incense on them before the LORD tomorrow, and the man whom the LORD chooses shall be the holy one. [t]You have gone too far, sons of Levi!" 8 And Moses said to Korah, "Hear now, you sons of Levi: 9 is it [u]too small a thing for you that the God of Israel has [v]separated you from the congregation of Israel, to bring you near to himself, to do service in the tabernacle of the LORD and to stand before the congregation to minister to them, 10 and that he has brought you near him, and all your brothers the sons of Levi with you? And would you seek the priesthood also? 11 Therefore it is against the LORD that you and all your company have gathered together. What is [w]Aaron that you grumble against him?"

12 And Moses sent to call Dathan and Abiram the sons of Eliab, and they said, "We will not come up. 13 Is it [x]a small thing that you have brought us up out of [y]a land flowing with milk and honey, to kill us in the wilderness, that you must also [z]make yourself a prince over us? 14 Moreover, you have not brought us into a land flowing with milk and honey, nor given us inheritance of fields and vineyards. Will you put out the eyes of these men? We will not come up." 15 And Moses was very angry and said to the LORD, [a]"Do not respect their offering. [b]I have not taken one donkey from them, and I have not harmed one of them."

16 And Moses said to Korah, "Be present, you and all your company, [c]before the LORD, you and they, and Aaron, tomorrow. 17 And [d]let every one of you take his censer and put incense on it, and every one of you bring before the LORD his censer, [e]250 censers; you also, and Aaron, each his censer." 18 So every man took his censer and put fire in them and laid incense on them and stood at the entrance

[1] Hebrew *to spy out* [2] Septuagint *The LORD knows those who are his*

38[d] Deut. 22:12; [Matt. 23:5]
39[e] [Job 31:7; Eccles. 11:9; Ezek. 6:9] [f] Ps. 73:27; 106:39; [Ezek. 6:9]
40[g] See Lev. 11:44
41[h] Lev. 22:33; See Lev. 20:8

Chapter 16
1[i] ch. 27:3; Ex. 6:16, 18, 21; Jude 11 [j] ch. 26:9
3[k] Ps. 106:16-18 [l] ver. 7 [m] See Ex. 19:6
4[n] ch. 14:5; 20:6
5[o] [2 Tim. 2:19] [p] ver. 3 [q] ch. 17:5; 1 Sam. 2:28; Ps. 105:26; [Ex. 28:1] [r] ch. 3:10; Lev. 10:3; Ps. 65:4; Ezek. 40:46; 44:15, 16
6[s] Lev. 10:1
7[t] ver. 3

16:1–17:13 This section is the literary center and theological heart of Numbers, as God's people challenge Aaron's prerogative as high priest three times (16:1–40, 41–50; 17:1–13). Their having been too fearful to enter Canaan is now revealed as having been due to their not fearing the Lord enough, for they were *all too eager* to enter the Most Holy Place—a privilege reserved for the high priest. The last rebellion is resolved when, out of the 12 staffs (representing each of the tribes of Israel) that were deposited by the ark, Aaron's staff alone budded with blossoms and ripe almonds, while the others remained dry wood. This life out of death symbol served as God's justification of Aaron as the designated mediator. Significantly, then, in the Pentateuch "messiah" refers exclusively to Aaron the high priest (cf. "anointed"; Lev. 4:3, 5, 16; 6:22)—he is the one anointed with oil, whose mediation allows God's people to draw near in worship. Drawing near to God through Aaron would lead to life. Doing so apart from this messiah would lead to death (Num. 17:12).

9[u] ver. 13; 1 Sam. 18:23; Isa. 7:13; [Ezek. 16:20] [v] ch. 8:14; Deut. 10:8 **11**[w] Ex. 16:8; [1 Cor. 3:5] **13**[x] ver. 9 [y] See Ex. 3:8 [z] Ex. 2:14; Acts 7:27, 35 **15**[a] [Gen. 4:4, 5] [b] 1 Sam. 12:3; [Acts 20:33; 2 Cor. 7:2] **16**[c] Ex. 16:9; 1 Sam. 12:3, 7 **17**[d] ver. 6, 7 [e] ver. 35

of the tent of meeting with Moses and Aaron.
19 Then Korah assembled all the congregation
against them at the entrance of the tent of
meeting. [f]And the glory of the LORD appeared
to all the congregation.
20 And the LORD spoke to Moses and to
Aaron, saying, 21 [g]"Separate yourselves from
among this congregation, that I may consume
them [h]in a moment." 22 And they [i]fell on their
faces and said, "O God, [j]the God of the spirits
of all flesh, [k]shall one man sin, and will you be
angry with all the congregation?" 23 And the
LORD spoke to Moses, saying, 24 "Say to the
congregation, Get away from the dwelling of
Korah, Dathan, and Abiram."
25 Then Moses rose and went to Dathan and
Abiram, and the elders of Israel followed him.
26 And he spoke to the congregation, saying, [l]"Depart, please, from the tents of these
wicked men, and touch nothing of theirs, lest
you be swept away with all their sins." 27 So
they got away from the dwelling of Korah,
Dathan, and Abiram. And Dathan and Abiram
came out and stood [m]at the door of their tents,
together with their wives, their sons, and their
little ones. 28 And Moses said, "Hereby you
shall know that the LORD has sent me to do
all these works, and that it has not been [n]of
my own accord. 29 If these men die as all men
die, or if they are visited by the fate of all mankind, [o]then the LORD has not sent me. 30 But
if the LORD creates something new, and [p]the
ground opens its mouth and swallows them
up with all that belongs to them, and they [q]go
down alive into Sheol, then you shall know
that these men have despised the LORD."
31 [r]And as soon as he had finished speaking
all these words, the ground under them split
apart. 32 And the earth opened its mouth and
swallowed them up, with their households
and [s]all the people who belonged to Korah
and all their goods. 33 So they and all that
belonged to them went down alive into Sheol,
and the earth closed over them, and [t]they perished from the midst of the assembly. 34 And
all Israel who were around them fled at their
cry, for they said, "Lest the earth swallow us
up!" 35 And [u]fire came out from the LORD and
consumed [v]the 250 men offering the incense.
36 [1] Then the LORD spoke to Moses, saying,
37 "Tell Eleazar the son of Aaron the priest to
take up the censers out of the blaze. Then scatter the fire far and wide, for they have become
holy. 38 As for the censers of [w]these men who
have sinned at the cost of their lives, let them
be made into hammered plates as a covering
for the altar, for they offered them before the
LORD, and they became holy. [x]Thus they shall
be a sign to the people of Israel." 39 So Eleazar
the priest took the bronze censers, which those
who were burned had offered, and they were
hammered out as a covering for the altar, 40 to
be a reminder to the people of Israel, so [y]that
no outsider, who is not of the descendants
of Aaron, should draw near to burn incense
before the LORD, lest he become like Korah
and his company—as the LORD said to him
through Moses.
41 But on the next day all the congregation of
the people of Israel [z]grumbled against Moses
and against Aaron, saying, "You have killed
the people of the LORD." 42 And when the
congregation had assembled against Moses
and against Aaron, they turned toward the
tent of meeting. And behold, [a]the cloud covered it, and [b]the glory of the LORD appeared.
43 And Moses and Aaron came to the front of
the tent of meeting, 44 and the LORD spoke to
Moses, saying, 45 [c]"Get away from the midst of
this congregation, that I may consume them
in a moment." [d]And they fell on their faces.
46 And Moses said to Aaron, "Take your censer, and put fire on it from off the altar and
lay incense on it and carry it quickly to the
congregation and make atonement for them,
for [e]wrath has gone out from the LORD; the

[1] Ch 17:1 in Hebrew

With the coming of Jesus Christ, the symbolic worship of the tabernacle has given way to the reality: we draw near to God through the torn flesh and shed blood of *the* Messiah (Heb. 10:19–25). Christ's life-out-of-death resurrection is God's justification of his mediatorial work (Acts 17:31). Indeed, having such a High Priest—one who sacrificed himself to endure the wrath of God for our sins—we are compelled to draw near to God through him alone, worshiping our triune God with assurance, joy, reverence, and awe.

19 [f]See Lev. 9:23
21 [g]ver. 45; [Gen. 19:17, 22; Jer. 51:6; Rev. 18:4] [h]Ex. 33:5; Ps. 73:19
22 [i]ver. 45; ch. 14:5; 20:6 [j]ch. 27:16; Job 12:10; Eccles. 12:7; Isa. 57:16; Zech. 12:1 [k][Gen. 18:23-25; 2 Sam. 24:17]
26 [l][Gen. 19:12-14; Isa. 52:11; 2 Cor. 6:17; Rev. 18:4]

27 [m][Ex. 33:8] **28** [n][Jer. 23:16; Ezek. 13:2, 17] **29** [o][1 Kgs. 22:28] **30** [p][Gen. 4:11] [q]ver. 33; Ps. 55:15 **31** [r]ch. 26:10; 27:3; Deut. 11:6; Ps. 106:17 **32** [s][ch. 26:11; 1 Chr. 6:22, 27] **33** [t]Jude 11 **35** [u][ch. 11:1]; Lev. 10:2; Ps. 106:18 [v]ver. 17 **38** [w]Prov. 20:2; Hab. 2:10; [1 Kgs. 2:23] [x]ch. 17:10; 26:10 **40** [y]ch. 3:10; 2 Chr. 26:18 **41** [z]See ch. 14:2 **42** [a]Ex. 40:34 [b]ver. 19; See Lev. 9:23 **45** [c]ver. 21, 24 [d]ver. 22 **46** [e]ch. 8:19; 11:33; Lev. 10:6; 1 Chr. 27:24

plague has begun." 47 So Aaron took it as Moses said and ran into the midst of the assembly. And behold, the plague had already begun among the people. And he put on the incense and made atonement for the people. 48 And he stood between the dead and the living, and [f]the plague was stopped. 49 Now those who died in the plague were 14,700, [g]besides those who died in the affair of Korah. 50 And Aaron returned to Moses at the entrance of the tent of meeting, when the plague was stopped.

Aaron's Staff Buds

17 [1] The LORD spoke to Moses, saying, 2 [h]"Speak to the people of Israel, and get from them staffs, one for each fathers' house, from all their chiefs according to their fathers' houses, twelve staffs. Write each man's name on his staff, 3 and write Aaron's name on the staff of Levi. For there shall be one staff for the head of each fathers' house. 4 Then you shall deposit them in the tent of meeting before the testimony, [i]where I meet with you. 5 And the staff of the man [j]whom I choose shall sprout. Thus I will make to cease from me [k]the grumblings of the people of Israel, which they grumble against you." 6 Moses spoke to the people of Israel. And all their chiefs gave him staffs, one for each chief, according to their fathers' houses, twelve staffs. And the staff of Aaron was among their staffs. 7 And Moses deposited the staffs before the LORD in [l]the tent of the testimony.

8 On the next day Moses went into the tent of the testimony, and behold, the staff of Aaron for the house of Levi had sprouted and put forth buds and produced blossoms, and it bore ripe almonds. 9 Then Moses brought out all the staffs from before the LORD to all the people of Israel. And they looked, and each man took his staff. 10 And the LORD said to Moses, "Put back [m]the staff of Aaron before the testimony, to be kept [n]as a sign for the rebels, [o]that you may make an end of their grumblings against me, lest they die." 11 Thus did Moses; as the LORD commanded him, so he did.

12 And the people of Israel said to Moses, "Behold, we perish, we are undone, we are all undone. 13 [p]Everyone who comes near, who comes near to the tabernacle of the LORD, shall die. Are we all to perish?"

Duties of Priests and Levites

18 So the LORD said to Aaron, "You and your sons and your father's house with you shall [q]bear iniquity connected with the sanctuary, [r]and you and your sons with you shall bear iniquity connected with your priesthood. 2 And with you bring your brothers also, the tribe of Levi, the tribe of your father, that they may [s]join you and [t]minister to you while you and your sons with you are before the tent of the testimony. 3 They shall keep guard over you and [u]over the whole tent, [v]but shall not come near to the vessels of the sanctuary or to the altar [w]lest they, and you, die. 4 They shall join you and keep guard over the tent of meeting for all the service of the tent, [x]and no outsider shall come near you. 5 And you shall [y]keep guard over the sanctuary and over the altar, [z]that there may never again be wrath on the people of Israel. 6 [a]And behold, I have taken your brothers the Levites from among the people of Israel. [b]They are a gift to you, given to the LORD, to do the service of the tent of meeting. 7 And [c]you and your sons with you shall guard your priesthood for all that concerns the altar and [d]that is within the veil; and you shall serve. I give your priesthood as a gift,[2] and [e]any outsider who comes near shall be put to death."

8 Then the LORD spoke to Aaron, "Behold, [f]I have given you charge of the contributions made to me, all the consecrated things of the people of Israel. I have given them to you [g]as a portion and to your sons as a perpetual due.

[1] Ch 17:16 in Hebrew [2] Hebrew *service of gift*

48[f] ver. 50; ch. 25:8; 2 Sam. 24:25; Ps. 106:30
49[g] ch. 27:3
Chapter 17
2[h] [Ezek. 37:16]
4[i] See Ex. 25:22
5[j] ch. 16:5 [k] ch. 16:11
7[l] ch. 18:2; Ex. 38:21; 2 Chr. 24:6; Acts 7:44
10[m] Heb. 9:4 [n] ch. 16:38 [o] ver. 5
13[p] See ch. 1:51

18:1–32 The last section's reassertion of priestly rights flows naturally into this chapter's delineation of the duties of priests and Levites, along with the support they are due by way of tithes and offerings. It is also our delight in the new covenant to materially support our ministers through whom God has blessed us spiritually (1 Cor. 9:3–12; 16:2; 1 Tim. 5:17–18). Paul rejoiced in the generosity of the Philippian church because it was the manifest fruit of the grace of God in their lives—a fragrant sacrifice to the very God who promises to supply all of our needs according to his riches in Christ Jesus (Phil. 4:10–20).

Chapter 18 1[q] ver. 23; See Ex. 28:38 [r] ver. 23 2[s] [Gen. 29:34] [t] See ch. 3:6-10 3[u] ch. 3:25, 31, 36 [v] ch. 16:40 [w] ch. 4:15 4[x] See ch. 17:13 5[y] ch. 3:38; Ex. 27:21; 30:7; Lev. 24:3 [z] See Lev. 10:6 6[a] ch. 3:12, 45 [b] ch. 3:9; 8:19 7[c] ch. 3:10 [d] Heb. 9:3, 6 [e] See ch. 1:51 8[f] ch. 5:9; Lev. 7:32 [g] Ex. 29:29; 40:13, 15

9 This shall be yours of the most holy things,
reserved from the fire: every offering of theirs,
every grain offering of theirs and every [h]sin
offering of theirs and every [i]guilt offering of
theirs, which they render to me, shall be most
holy to you and to your sons. 10 In a most holy
place shall you eat it. Every male may eat it; it
is holy to you. 11 This also is yours: the contribution of their gift, all the [j]wave offerings of
the people of Israel. I have given them to [k]you,
and to your sons and daughters with you, as a
perpetual due. [l]Everyone who is clean in your
house may eat it. 12 [m]All the best of the oil and
all the best of the wine and of the grain, [n]the
firstfruits of what they give to the LORD, I give
to you. 13 The first ripe fruits of all that is in
their land, [o]which they bring to the LORD,
shall be yours. [l]Everyone who is clean in your
house may eat it. 14 [p]Every devoted thing in
Israel shall be yours. 15 [q]Everything that opens
the womb of all flesh, whether man or beast,
which they offer to the LORD, shall be yours.
Nevertheless, [r]the firstborn of man you shall
redeem, and the firstborn of unclean animals
you shall redeem. 16 And their redemption
price [s](at a month old you shall redeem them)
you shall fix at five shekels[1] in silver, according to the shekel of the sanctuary, [t]which is
twenty gerahs. 17 [u]But the firstborn of a cow,
or the firstborn of a sheep, or the firstborn of
a goat, you shall not redeem; they are holy.
You shall sprinkle their blood on the altar and
shall burn their fat as a food offering, with a
pleasing aroma to the LORD. 18 But their flesh
shall be yours, as [v]the breast that is waved and
as the right thigh are yours. 19 [w]All the holy
contributions that the people of Israel present
to the LORD I give to you, and to your sons and
daughters with you, as a perpetual due. [x]It is
a covenant of salt forever before the LORD for
you and for your offspring with you." 20 And
the LORD said to Aaron, "You shall have no
inheritance in their land, neither shall you
have any portion among them. [y]I am your portion and your inheritance among the people
of Israel.

21 [z]"To the Levites I have given every tithe in
Israel for an inheritance, in return for their
service that they do, their service in the tent
of meeting, 22 [a]so that the people of Israel do
not come near the tent of meeting, [b]lest they
bear sin and die. 23 But [c]the Levites shall do
the service of the tent of meeting, [d]and they
shall bear their iniquity. It shall be a perpetual statute throughout your generations, and
among the people of Israel they shall have no
inheritance. 24 For the tithe of the people of
Israel, which [e]they present as a contribution
to the LORD, I have given to the Levites for
an inheritance. Therefore I have said of them
that they shall have no inheritance [f]among the
people of Israel."

25 And the LORD spoke to Moses, saying,
26 "Moreover, you shall speak and say to the
Levites, 'When you take from the people of
Israel the tithe that I have given you from
them for your inheritance, then you shall
present a contribution from it to the LORD,
[g]a tithe of the tithe. 27 [h]And your contribution
shall be counted to you as though it were the
grain of the threshing floor, and as the fullness of the winepress. 28 So you shall also present a contribution to the LORD from all your
tithes, which you receive from the people of
Israel. And from it you shall give the LORD's
contribution to Aaron the priest. 29 Out of all
the gifts to you, you shall present every contribution due to the LORD; from each its best
part is to be dedicated.' 30 Therefore you shall
say to them, 'When you have offered from it
the best of it, [i]then the rest shall be counted to
the Levites as produce of the threshing floor,
and as produce of the winepress. 31 And you
may eat it in any place, you and your households, for it is [j]your reward in return for your
service in the tent of meeting. 32 And you shall
[k]bear no sin by reason of it, when you have
contributed the best of it. But you shall not
[l]profane the holy things of the people of Israel,
lest you die.'"

Laws for Purification

19 Now the LORD spoke to Moses and to
Aaron, saying, 2 "This is the statute of
the law that the LORD has commanded: Tell
the people of Israel to bring you a red heifer
without defect, in which there is no blemish, [m]and on which a yoke has never come.

[1] A *shekel* was about 2/5 ounce or 11 grams

9 [h] Lev. 4:22, 27; 6:25, 26 [i] Lev. 7:7; 14:13 **11** [j] Ex. 29:27, 28; Lev. 7:30, 34 [k] Lev. 10:14; [Deut. 18:3] [l] [Lev. 22:2, 3, 11-13] **12** [m] Deut. 18:4 [n] Ex. 23:19; 34:26; Neh. 10:35, 36 **13** [o] Ex. 22:29; Lev. 2:14; Deut. 26:2 [l] [See ver. 11 above] **14** [p] Lev. 27:28 **15** [q] See Ex. 13:2 [r] Ex. 13:13; 34:20 **16** [s] ch. 3:47; Lev. 27:2, 6 [t] See Ex. 30:13 **17** [u] Deut. 15:19 **18** [v] Ex. 29:26, 28; Lev. 7:31, 32, 34 **19** [w] ver. 11 [x] Lev. 2:13; 2 Chr. 13:5 **20** [y] ver. 23, 24; Deut. 10:9; 12:12; 14:27; 18:1, 2; Josh. 13:33; 14:3; 18:7; Ezek. 44:28 **21** [z] ver. 24, 26; Lev. 27:30, 32; Deut. 14:22; Neh. 10:37; 12:44; Heb. 7:5, 8, 9; [Gen. 14:20; 28:22] **22** [a] See ch. 1:51 [b] Lev. 22:9 **23** [c] ch. 3:7 [d] ver. 1 **24** [e] ver. 19, 26, 29 [f] ver. 20, 21, 26 **26** [g] Neh. 10:38 **27** [h] ver. 30 **30** [i] ver. 27 **31** [j] [Matt. 10:10; Luke 10:7; 1 Tim. 5:17, 18]; See 1 Cor. 9:4-14 **32** [k] Lev. 19:8; 22:16 [l] Lev. 22:2, 15 **Chapter 19** **2** [m] Deut. 21:3; 1 Sam. 6:7

3 And you shall give it to Eleazar the priest, and [n]it shall be taken outside the camp and slaughtered before him. 4 And Eleazar the priest shall take some of its blood with his finger, and [o]sprinkle some of its blood toward the front of the tent of meeting seven times. 5 And the heifer shall be burned in his sight. [p]Its skin, its flesh, and its blood, with its dung, shall be burned. 6 And the priest shall take [q]cedarwood and hyssop and scarlet yarn, and throw them into the fire burning the heifer. 7 Then the priest [r]shall wash his clothes and bathe his body in water, and afterward he may come into the camp. But the priest shall be unclean until evening. 8 [s]The one who burns the heifer [r]shall wash his clothes in water and bathe his body in water and shall be unclean until evening. 9 And a man who is clean shall gather up [t]the ashes of the heifer and deposit them outside the camp in a [u]clean place. And they shall be kept for the water for [v]impurity for the congregation of the people of Israel; it is a sin offering. 10 And the one who gathers the ashes of the heifer [r]shall wash his clothes and be unclean until evening. And this shall be a perpetual statute for the people of Israel, and for the stranger who sojourns among them.

11 [w]"Whoever touches the dead body of any person shall be unclean seven days. 12 He [x]shall cleanse himself with the water on the third day and on the seventh day, and so be clean. But if he does not cleanse himself on the third day and on the seventh day, he will not become clean. 13 Whoever touches a dead person, the body of anyone who has died, and does not cleanse himself, [y]defiles the tabernacle of the LORD, [z]and that person shall be cut off from Israel; because the water for impurity was not thrown on him, he shall be unclean. His uncleanness is still on him.

14 "This is the law when someone dies in a tent: everyone who comes into the tent and everyone who is in the tent shall be unclean seven days. 15 And every [a]open vessel that has no cover fastened on it is unclean. 16 [b]Whoever in the open field touches someone who was killed with a sword or who died naturally, or touches a human bone or a [c]grave, shall be unclean seven days. 17 For the unclean they shall take [d]some ashes of the burnt sin offering, and fresh[1] water shall be added in a vessel. 18 Then a clean person shall take [e]hyssop and dip it in the water and sprinkle it on the tent and on all the furnishings and on the persons who were there and on whoever touched the bone, or the slain or the dead or the grave. 19 And the clean person shall sprinkle it on the unclean [f]on the third day and on the seventh day. [g]Thus on the seventh day he shall cleanse him, and he shall [h]wash his clothes and bathe himself in water, and at evening he shall be clean.

20 "If the man who is unclean does not cleanse himself, [i]that person shall be cut off from the midst of the assembly, since he has defiled the sanctuary of the LORD. Because the water for impurity has not been thrown on him, he is unclean. 21 And it shall be a statute forever for them. The one who sprinkles the water for impurity shall wash his clothes, and the one who touches the water for impurity shall be unclean until evening. 22 And [j]whatever the unclean person touches shall be unclean, and anyone who touches it shall be unclean until evening."

The Death of Miriam

20 And the people of Israel, the whole congregation, came [k]into the wilderness of Zin in the first month, and the people stayed in Kadesh. And [l]Miriam died there and was buried there.

The Waters of Meribah

2 [m]Now there was no water for the congregation. [n]And they assembled themselves

[1] Hebrew *living*

3[n] Lev. 4:12; [Heb. 13:11]
4[o] [Lev. 4:6, 17; 16:14, 19]; Heb. 9:13
5[p] Ex. 29:14; Lev. 4:11, 12
6[q] See Lev. 14:4, 6, 49
7[r] See Lev. 11:25
8[s] ver. 5 [r] [See ver. 7 above]
9[t] Heb. 9:13 [u] Lev. 4:12; 6:11; 10:14 [v] ver. 13, 20, 21; ch. 31:23

20:1–29 This somewhat stark chapter begins with the death of Miriam, ends with the death of Aaron, and recounts in the middle the judgment of Moses and Aaron, who would not be allowed to bring the people into the land since they did not uphold the Lord "as holy" in the eyes of Israel (v. 12). The nature of Moses' sin appears to be in his not following precisely God's command to "tell" the rock to yield its water (v. 8), striking it instead (v. 11). Considering that it was likely struck with Aaron's budded staff (v. 9) and that this rock represented Christ who supplies us with a spring

10[r] [See ver. 7 above] **11**[w] ver. 16; See ch. 5:2; 9:6, 10; 31:19 **12**[x] ch. 31:19 **13**[y] ver. 20; Lev. 15:31 [z] See Ex. 30:33 **15**[a] ch. 31:20; Lev. 11:32 **16**[b] ver. 11 [c] [Matt. 23:27; Luke 11:44] **17**[d] Heb. 9:13 **18**[e] See Ex. 12:22 **19**[f] ver. 12 [g] [Lev. 14:9] [h] See Lev. 11:25 **20**[i] See Ex. 30:33 **22**[j] [ver. 11; Hag. 2:13]
Chapter 20 **1**[k] See ch. 13:21 [l] ch. 12:1; 26:59; Ex. 15:20 **2**[m] [Ex. 17:1] [n] ch. 16:19, 42

together against Moses and against Aaron.
3 And the people [o]quarreled with Moses and
said, "Would that we had perished [p]when our
brothers perished before the LORD! 4 Why have
you brought the assembly of the LORD into
this wilderness, that we should die here, both
we and our cattle? 5 And [q]why have you made
us come up out of Egypt to bring us to this evil
place? It is no place for grain or figs or vines or
pomegranates, and there is no water to drink."
6 Then Moses and Aaron went from the presence of the assembly to the entrance of the
tent of meeting and [r]fell on their faces. [s]And
the glory of the LORD appeared to them, 7 and
the LORD spoke to Moses, saying, 8 [t]"Take the
staff, and assemble the congregation, you and
Aaron your brother, and tell the rock before
their eyes to yield its water. So [u]you shall bring
water out of the rock for them and give drink
to the congregation and their cattle." 9 And
Moses took the staff [v]from before the LORD,
as he commanded him.

Moses Strikes the Rock

10 Then Moses and Aaron gathered the
assembly together before the rock, and he
said to them, [w]"Hear now, you rebels: shall
we bring water for you out of this rock?" 11 And
Moses lifted up his hand and struck the rock
with his staff twice, [u]and water came out abundantly, and the congregation drank, and their
livestock. 12 And the LORD said to Moses and
Aaron, "Because [x]you did not believe in me,
[y]to uphold me as holy in the eyes of the people
of Israel, therefore you shall not bring this
assembly into the land that I have given them."
13 [z]These are the waters of Meribah,[1] where the
people of Israel quarreled with the LORD, and
through them he showed himself holy.

Edom Refuses Passage

14 [a]Moses sent messengers from Kadesh to
[b]the king of Edom: "Thus says [c]your brother
Israel: You know all the hardship that we
have met: 15 [d]how our fathers went down to
Egypt, [e]and we lived in Egypt a long time. [f]And
the Egyptians dealt harshly with us and our
fathers. 16 And [g]when we cried to the LORD,
he heard our voice and [h]sent an angel and
brought us out of Egypt. And here we are in
Kadesh, a city on the edge of your territory.
17 [i]Please let us pass through your land. We
will not pass through field or vineyard, [j]or
drink water from a well. We will go along the
King's Highway. We will not turn aside to the
right hand or to the left until we have passed
through your territory." 18 But Edom said to
him, "You shall not pass through, lest I come
out with the sword against you." 19 And the
people of Israel said to him, "We will go up by
the highway, [k]and if we drink of your water,
I and my livestock, [l]then I will pay for it. Let
me only pass through on foot, nothing more."
20 But he said, [m]"You shall not pass through."
And Edom came out against them with a large
army and with a strong force. 21 Thus Edom
[n]refused to give Israel passage through his territory, so Israel [o]turned away from him.

The Death of Aaron

22 And they journeyed from [p]Kadesh, and
the people of Israel, the whole congregation,
came to [q]Mount Hor. 23 And the LORD said to
Moses and Aaron at Mount Hor, on the border
of the land of Edom, 24 [r]"Let Aaron be gathered to his people, for he shall not enter the
land that I have given to the people of Israel,
because [s]you rebelled against my command
at the waters of Meribah. 25 Take Aaron and

[1] *Meribah* means *quarreling*

of water welling up to eternal life (John 4:13–14; cf. 7:37–38; 1 Cor. 10:4), Moses' sin was especially grievous. By saying and doing what he was not instructed in order to provide for God's people, Moses was giving himself the status of Israel's mediator and lord. Yet we see God's grace here in that he nevertheless supplied the water to his quarreling people, and he was faithful to raise up a new leader, Joshua, to bring his people into the land (Num. 27:18–23; Josh. 1:1–18). (See additional notes related to this event at Ex. 17:1–7, the contrasting example; and Deut. 3:23–29, the later account.)

Inasmuch as Moses is identified with the law, we understand that the law cannot bring us into the heavenly land—for this we need Jesus, the Greek form of "Joshua," who was struck so that living waters of salvation might flow (Rom. 8:3–4; John 1:17; 7:37–39).

3 [o] ch. 14:2; [Ex. 17:2] [p] ch. 11:1, 33; 14:37; 16:32, 33, 35, 49
5 [q] [Ex. 17:3]
6 [r] ch. 14:5; 16:4, 22, 45 [s] See Lev. 9:23
8 [t] [Ex. 17:5] [u] See Ex. 17:6
9 [v] ch. 17:10
10 [w] Ps. 106:32, 33
11 [u] [See ver. 8 above]
12 [x] ch. 27:14; Deut. 1:37; 3:26; 32:51 [y] Ezek. 20:41; 36:23; 38:16
13 [z] ch. 27:14; Ex. 17:7; Deut. 32:51; 33:8; Ps. 81:7; 95:8; 106:32
14 [a] Judg. 11:16, 17 [b] See Gen. 36:31-39 [c] Deut. 2:4, 8; 23:7; Obad. 10, 12 **15** [d] Gen. 46:6; Acts 7:15 [e] See Ex. 12:40 [f] Ex. 1:11; Deut. 26:6 **16** [g] Ex. 2:23; 3:7 [h] Ex. 3:2; 14:19; 23:20; 33:2 **17** [i] [ch. 21:22; Deut. 2:27] [j] [ver. 19] **19** [k] [ver. 17] [l] Deut. 2:6, 28 **20** [m] [Judg. 11:17; Amos 1:11] **21** [n] [Deut. 2:29] [o] [ch. 21:4; Deut. 2:8; Judg. 11:18] **22** [p] ch. 33:37 [q] ch. 21:4; 33:37 **24** [r] ch. 27:13; Deut. 32:50; [ch. 31:2; Gen. 25:8] [s] ver. 12

Eleazar his son and bring them up to Mount Hor. 26 And strip Aaron of his garments and put them on Eleazar his son. And Aaron [r]shall be gathered to his people and shall die there." 27 Moses did as the LORD commanded. And they went up Mount Hor in the sight of all the congregation. 28 [t]And Moses stripped Aaron of his garments and put them on Eleazar his son. And Aaron died there [u]on the top of the mountain. Then Moses and Eleazar came down from the mountain. 29 And when all the congregation saw that Aaron had perished, [v]all the house of Israel wept for Aaron thirty days.

Arad Destroyed

21 When [w]the Canaanite, the king of Arad, who lived in [x]the Negeb, heard that Israel was coming by the way of Atharim, he fought against Israel, and took some of them captive. 2 [y]And Israel vowed a vow to the LORD and said, "If you will indeed give this people into my hand, then I will devote their cities to destruction."[1] 3 And the LORD heeded the voice of Israel and gave over the Canaanites, and they devoted them and their cities to destruction. So the name of the place was called [z]Hormah.[2]

The Bronze Serpent

4 From Mount Hor [a]they set out by the way to the Red Sea, [b]to go around the land of Edom. And the people became impatient on the way. 5 And the people [c]spoke against God and against Moses, [d]"Why have you brought us up out of Egypt to die in the wilderness? For there is no food and no water, and [e]we loathe this worthless food." 6 [f]Then the LORD sent fiery serpents among the people, and [g]they bit the people, so that many people of Israel died. 7 [h]And the people came to Moses and said, "We have sinned, for we have spoken against the LORD and against you. [i]Pray to the LORD, that he take away the serpents from us." So Moses prayed for the people. 8 And the LORD said to Moses, "Make a fiery serpent and set it on a pole, and everyone who is bitten, when he sees it, shall live." 9 So [j]Moses made a bronze[3] serpent and set it on a pole. And if a serpent bit anyone, he would look at the bronze serpent and live.

The Song of the Well

10 And the people of Israel set out and [k]camped in Oboth. 11 [k]And they set out from Oboth and [k]camped at Iye-abarim, in the wilderness that is opposite Moab, toward the sunrise. 12 From there they set out and camped in [l]the Valley of Zered. 13 From there they set out and camped on the other side of the Arnon, which is in the wilderness that extends from the border of the Amorites, for the [m]Arnon is the border of Moab, between Moab and the Amorites. 14 Therefore it is said in the Book of the Wars of the LORD,

"Waheb in Suphah, and the valleys of the
Arnon,
15 and the slope of the valleys
that extends to the seat of [n]Ar,
and leans to the border of Moab."

16 And from there they continued [o]to Beer;[4] that is the well of which the LORD said to

[1] That is, set apart (devote) as an offering to the Lord (for destruction); also verse 3 [2] *Hormah* means *destruction* [3] Or *copper*
[4] *Beer* means *well*

26 [r][See ver. 24 above]
28 [t]Ex. 29:29, 30 [u]ch. 33:38; Deut. 32:50; [Deut. 10:6]
29 [v]Deut. 34:8
Chapter 21
1 [w]ch. 33:40; [Judg. 1:16] [x]See ch. 13:17
2 [y][Gen. 28:20; Judg. 11:30]
3 [z]ch. 14:45; Deut. 1:44; Josh. 19:4; Judg. 1:17
4 [a]ch. 20:22; 33:41 [b]Judg. 11:18
5 [c]Ps. 78:19 [d]Ex. 16:3; 17:3 [e][ch. 11:6]
6 [f]Deut. 8:15; 1 Cor. 10:9; [Isa. 14:29; 30:6] [g]Jer. 8:17
7 [h]Ps. 78:34; [ch. 11:2] [i][Ex. 8:8, 28; 1 Sam. 12:19; 1 Kgs. 13:6; Acts 8:24]
9 [j]John 3:14, 15; [2 Kgs. 18:4]
10 [k]ch. 33:43, 44
11 [k][See ver. 10 above]
12 [l]Deut. 2:13
13 [m]ch. 22:36; Judg. 11:18
15 [n]ver. 28; Deut. 2:9, 18, 29; Isa. 15:1
16 [o][2 Sam. 20:14]

21:1–3 Nearly 40 years earlier at the same site of Hormah, the people of Israel had been driven back from entering the land (14:45). Now they achieve their first battle victory here, something of a pledge and guarantee that God will be faithful to his promise to bring them in. For believers in the new covenant, God often provides opportunities to right our wrongs, but the indwelling Holy Spirit himself—the sign of God's presence and a seal of Christ's victory on the cross—is the guarantee of our inheritance (Eph. 1:13–14).

21:4–9 Amid the fiery serpents we see God's mercy in that this judgment led his people to repentance (v. 7). Sometimes the affliction in our lives is but the merciful chastening of our loving Father (Prov. 3:12; Heb. 12:3–11). We also see once more the blessing of a mediator as Moses prays effectively on their behalf, then, according to God's instruction, fashions the bronze serpent and sets it on a pole so the Israelites might look upon it and live. The serpent is probably emblematic of the venom coming from the complaining lips of the people and/or of the Serpent roots of all our sin, but unquestionably its presence upon the pole required the people to face their sin and God's instruction of healing as they looked to it in order to live.

Moses, "Gather the people together, so that [p]I may give them water." 17 Then Israel sang this song:

"Spring up, O well!—Sing to it!—
18 the well that the princes made,
that the nobles of the people dug,
with [q]the scepter and with their staffs."

And from the wilderness they went on to
Mattanah, 19 and from Mattanah to Nahaliel,
and from Nahaliel to Bamoth, 20 and from
Bamoth to the valley lying in the region of Moab by the top of Pisgah [r]that looks down on the desert.[1]

King Sihon Defeated

21 Then [s]Israel sent messengers to Sihon
king of the Amorites, saying, 22 [t]"Let me pass
through your land. We will not turn aside into field or vineyard. We will not drink the water of a well. We will go by the King's Highway until we have passed through your territory."
23 [u]But Sihon would not allow Israel to pass
through his territory. He gathered all his people together and went out against Israel to the wilderness and [v]came to Jahaz and fought
against Israel. 24 [w]And Israel defeated him with
the edge of the sword and took possession of his land from the Arnon to the [x]Jabbok, as far as to the Ammonites, for the border of the
Ammonites was strong. 25 And Israel took all
these cities, and Israel settled in all the cities of the Amorites, in Heshbon, and in all its
villages. 26 For Heshbon was the city of Sihon
the king of the Amorites, who had fought against the former king of Moab and taken all his land out of his hand, as far as the Arnon.
27 Therefore the [y]ballad singers say,

"Come to [z]Heshbon, let it be built;
let the city of Sihon be established.
28 For [a]fire came out from [z]Heshbon,
flame from the city of Sihon.
It devoured [n]Ar of Moab,
and swallowed[2] the heights of the Arnon.
29 [a]Woe to you, O Moab!
You are undone, O people of [b]Chemosh!
He has made his sons fugitives,
and his daughters captives,
to an Amorite king, Sihon.
30 So we overthrew them;
Heshbon, as far as [c]Dibon, perished;
and we laid waste as far as Nophah;
fire spread as far as [d]Medeba."[3]

King Og Defeated

31 Thus Israel lived in the land of the
Amorites. 32 And Moses sent to spy out [e]Jazer,
and they captured its villages and dispossessed the Amorites who were there. 33 Then they
turned and went up by the way to Bashan. And Og the king of Bashan came out against them, he and all his people, to battle [f]at Edrei. 34 [g]But
the LORD said to Moses, "Do not fear him, for I have given him into your hand, and all his people, and his land. And [h]you shall do to him as you did to Sihon king of the Amorites, who lived at Heshbon." 35 So they defeated him and
his sons and all his people, until he had no survivor left. And they possessed his land.

Balak Summons Balaam

22 Then [i]the people of Israel set out and camped in the plains of Moab beyond
the Jordan at Jericho. 2 And [j]Balak the son of
Zippor saw all that Israel had done to the
Amorites. 3 And [k]Moab was in great dread of
the people, because they were many. Moab was overcome with fear of the people of Israel.
4 And Moab said to [l]the elders of Midian, "This

[1] Or *Jeshimon* [2] Septuagint; Hebrew *the lords of* [3] Compare Samaritan and Septuagint; Hebrew *and we laid waste as far as Nophah, which is as far as Medeba*

Jesus Christ not only prays on our behalf, but he became a curse for us on the cross so that we might look to him and live. Like the serpent set upon a pole, so Christ crucified is the means God himself has provided for us to look upon our sin and be saved from his own righteous judgment (John 3:14–15). This is because, for believers, their end-time judgment has already taken place—at the cross of Christ, the punishment we deserve was poured out on Another in our place.

22:1–24:25 On the verge of realizing God's promise, Israel faces a new threat from Balak the king of Moab, who secures Balaam, a renowned pagan diviner, to curse God's people. As the following stories will demonstrate, however, God's determined

16[p] [ch. 20:8; Ex. 17:6]
18[q] See Gen. 49:10
20[r] [ch. 23:28]
21[s] Deut. 2:26, 27; Judg. 11:19
22[t] [ch. 20:17]
23[u] Deut. 29:7 [v] Deut. 2:32; Judg. 11:20
24[w] Deut. 2:33; Josh. 12:1, 2; 24:8; Neh. 9:22; Ps. 135:11; 136:19, 20; Amos 2:9 [x] See Gen. 32:22
27[y] See ch. 23:7 [z] See ch. 32:37
28[a] Jer. 48:45, 46 [z] [See ver. 27 above]

[n] [See ver. 15 above] **29**[a] [See ver. 28 above] [b] Judg. 11:24; 1 Kgs. 11:7; 2 Kgs. 23:13; Jer. 48:7 **30**[c] ch. 32:3; Josh. 13:17; Isa. 15:2; Jer. 48:18; [ch. 33:45, 46] [d] 1 Chr. 19:7; Isa. 15:2 **32**[e] ch. 32:1; Josh. 13:25; 2 Sam. 24:5; Jer. 48:32 **33**[f] Deut. 1:4; 3:1; Josh. 13:12 **34**[g] Deut. 3:2 [h] See ver. 24 **Chapter 22** **1**[i] ch. 26:3, 63; 31:12; 33:48, 50; 35:1; 36:13 **2**[j] Judg. 11:25 **3**[k] Ex. 15:15 **4**[l] ch. 31:8; Josh. 13:21

horde will now lick up all that is around us, as
the ox licks up the grass of the field." So Balak
the son of Zippor, who was king of Moab at
that time, 5 [m]sent messengers to Balaam the
son of Beor [n]at Pethor, which is near the River
in the land of the people of Amaw,[1] to call
him, saying, "Behold, a people has come out
of Egypt. They cover the face of the earth,
and they are dwelling opposite me. 6 [o]Come
now, curse this people for me, since they are
too mighty for me. Perhaps I shall be able to
defeat them and drive them from the land, for
I know that he whom you bless is blessed, and
he whom you curse is cursed."

7 So the elders of Moab and [l]the elders of
Midian departed with [p]the fees for divination in their hand. And they came to Balaam
and gave him Balak's message. 8 And he said
to them, "Lodge here tonight, and I will bring
back word to you, as the LORD speaks to me."
So the princes of Moab stayed with Balaam.
9 [q]And God came to Balaam and said, "Who are
these men with you?" 10 And Balaam said to
God, "Balak the son of Zippor, king of Moab,
has sent to me, saying, 11 'Behold, a people
has come out of Egypt, and it covers the face
of the earth. Now come, curse them for me.
Perhaps I shall be able to fight against them
and drive them out.'" 12 God said to Balaam,
"You shall not go with them. You shall not
curse the people, for [r]they are blessed." 13 So
Balaam rose in the morning and said to the
princes of Balak, "Go to your own land, for the
LORD has refused to let me go with you." 14 So
the princes of Moab rose and went to Balak
and said, "Balaam refuses to come with us."

15 Once again Balak sent princes, more in
number and more honorable than these.
16 And they came to Balaam and said to him,
"Thus says Balak the son of Zippor: 'Let nothing hinder you from coming to me, 17 [s]for I will
surely do you great honor, and whatever you
say to me I will do. [t]Come, curse this people for
me.'" 18 But Balaam answered and said to the
servants of Balak, [u]"Though Balak were to give
me his house full of silver and gold, [v]I could
not go beyond the command of the LORD my
God to do less or more. 19 So you, too, [w]please
stay here tonight, that I may know what more
the LORD will say to me." 20 [q]And God came to
Balaam at night and said to him, "If the men
have come to call you, rise, go with them; [x]but
only do what I tell you." 21 So Balaam rose in
the morning and saddled his donkey and went
with the princes of Moab.

Balaam's Donkey and the Angel

22 But God's anger was kindled because he
went, [y]and the angel of the LORD took his stand
in the way [z]as his adversary. Now he was riding on the donkey, and his two servants were
with him. 23 And the donkey saw the angel of
the LORD standing in the road, with a drawn
sword in his hand. And the donkey turned
aside out of the road and went into the field.
And Balaam struck the donkey, to turn her into
the road. 24 Then the angel of the LORD stood
in a narrow path between the vineyards, with
a wall on either side. 25 And when the donkey
saw the angel of the LORD, she pushed against
the wall and pressed Balaam's foot against the
wall. So he struck her again. 26 Then the angel
of the LORD went ahead and stood in a narrow
place, where there was no way to turn either
to the right or to the left. 27 When the donkey
saw the angel of the LORD, she lay down under
Balaam. And Balaam's anger was kindled, and
he struck the donkey with his staff. 28 Then the
LORD [a]opened the mouth of the donkey, and
she said to Balaam, "What have I done to you,
that you have struck me these three times?"
29 And Balaam said to the donkey, "Because you
have made a fool of me. I wish I had a sword in
my hand, for then I would kill you." 30 And the
donkey said to Balaam, "Am I not your donkey,
on which you have ridden all your life long to
this day? Is it my habit to treat you this way?"
And he said, "No."

[1] Or *the people of his kindred*

5[m] Deut. 23:4; Josh. 24:9; Neh. 13:2; Mic. 6:5; 2 Pet. 2:15; Jude 11; Rev. 2:14 [n] Deut. 23:4; [ch. 23:7]
6[o] ch. 23:7
7[l] [See ver. 4 above] [p] [1 Sam. 9:7, 8; Mic. 3:11]
9[q] [Gen. 20:3; Job 33:15, 16]
12[r] See ch. 23:20
17[s] ver. 37; ch. 24:11 [t] ver. 11
18[u] ch. 24:13 [v] ver. 38; ch. 23:26; [1 Kgs. 22:14; 2 Chr. 18:13] **19**[w] ver. 8 **20**[q] [See ver. 9 above] [x] ver. 35; ch. 23:12, 26; 24:13 **22**[y] [Ex. 4:24; 1 Chr. 21:16] [z] ver. 32 **28**[a] 2 Pet. 2:16

purpose is to bless his people despite their sin (22:22; 6:23–27). While Christians may be persecuted and reviled by the world, our security and joy comes in knowing that every promise of God has been secured for us by Christ (2 Cor. 1:20; Eph. 1:3)—thus, no powers can separate us from the love of God in Christ Jesus (Num. 23:23; Rom. 8:31–39).

22:22–41 This memorable incident with Balaam's donkey serves to display God's sovereign ability to bless his people. If he can speak common sense through a donkey, how much more can he speak a word of blessing through this pagan prophet Balaam!

31 Then the LORD [b]opened the eyes of Balaam,
and he saw the angel of the LORD standing in
the way, with his drawn sword in his hand.
And he bowed down and fell on his face. 32 And
the angel of the LORD said to him, "Why have
you struck your donkey these three times?
Behold, I have come out [c]to oppose you
because your way is perverse[1] before me. 33 The
donkey saw me and turned aside before me
these three times. If she had not turned aside
from me, surely just now I would have killed
you and let her live." 34 Then Balaam said to
the angel of the LORD, [d]"I have sinned, for I did
not know that you stood in the road against
me. Now therefore, if it is evil in your sight,
I will turn back." 35 And the angel of the LORD
said to Balaam, "Go with the men, [e]but speak
only the word that I tell you." So Balaam went
on with the princes of Balak.

36 When Balak heard that Balaam had come,
he went out to meet him at the city of Moab,
[f]on the border formed by the Arnon, at the
extremity of the border. 37 And Balak said to
Balaam, "Did I not send to you to call you?
Why did you not come to me? Am I not able to
[g]honor you?" 38 Balaam said to Balak, "Behold,
I have come to you! Have I now any power of
my own to speak anything? [h]The word that
God puts in my mouth, that must I speak."
39 Then Balaam went with Balak, and they
came to Kiriath-huzoth. 40 And Balak sacrificed oxen and sheep, and sent for Balaam and
for the princes who were with him.

41 And in the morning Balak took Balaam
and brought him up to Bamoth-baal, and
from there he saw a fraction of the people.

Balaam's First Oracle

23 And Balaam said to Balak, [i]"Build for
me here seven altars, and prepare for
me here seven bulls and seven rams." 2 Balak
did as Balaam had said. And Balak and
Balaam [j]offered on each altar a bull and a ram.
3 And Balaam said to Balak, [k]"Stand beside
your burnt offering, and I will go. Perhaps the
LORD will come [l]to meet me, and whatever
he shows me I will tell you." And he went
to a bare height, 4 [m]and God met Balaam.
And Balaam said to him, "I have arranged
the seven altars and I have offered on each
altar a bull and a ram." 5 And the LORD [n]put
a word in Balaam's mouth and said, "Return
to Balak, and thus you shall speak." 6 And he
returned to him, and behold, he and all the
princes of Moab were standing beside his
burnt offering. 7 And Balaam [o]took up his
discourse and said,

"From [p]Aram Balak has brought me,
the king of Moab [q]from the eastern
mountains:
'Come, [r]curse Jacob for me,
and come, denounce Israel!'
8 How can I curse whom God has not
cursed?
How can I denounce whom the LORD
has not denounced?
9 For from the top of the crags [s]I see him,
from the hills I behold him;
behold, [t]a people dwelling alone,
and [u]not counting itself among the
nations!
10 [v]Who can count the dust of Jacob
or number the fourth part[2] of Israel?
Let me die [w]the death of the upright,
and let my end be like his!"

11 And Balak said to Balaam, "What have you
done to me? [x]I took you to curse my enemies,
and behold, you have done nothing but bless
them." 12 And he answered and said, [y]"Must
I not take care to speak what the LORD puts
in my mouth?"

[1] Or *reckless* [2] Or *dust clouds*

23:1–24:25 Far from cursing Israel, God—through the rascal Balaam—marvelously expands upon his promises to Abraham (Gen. 12:1–3). Balaam's first oracle confirms the Abrahamic promise of numerous descendants (Num. 23:10); his second oracle confirms the promise of blessing and security (23:21–23); his third oracle confirms the promise of land and blessing to the nations (24:5–7, 18–24), expressly through the reign of a messianic ruler (24:16–17). Now, as Jesus Christ reigns in exaltation, we have a more sure confidence that all things will work together for the good of God's people (Rom. 8:28–30). For if God was able to speak a word of blessing through Balaam, how much more so through the blood of Christ, which has secured our salvation (Heb. 12:24).

31[b] [Gen. 21:19; 2 Kgs. 6:17; Luke 24:16, 31]
32[c] ver. 22
34[d] [1 Sam. 15:24; 26:21; 2 Sam. 12:13; Job 34:31, 32]
35[e] ver. 20
36[f] ch. 21:13
37[g] ver. 17; ch. 24:11
38[h] ver. 18
Chapter 23
1[i] ver. 29
2[j] ver. 14, 30
3[k] ver. 15 [l] [ch. 24:1]
4[m] ver. 16

5[n] ver. 12, 16; ch. 22:38; Deut. 18:18; Isa. 51:16; 59:21; Jer. 1:9 **7**[o] ver. 18; ch. 24:3, 15, 20, 21, 23; Job 27:1; 29:1; Ps. 49:4; 78:2; Isa. 14:4; Mic. 2:4; [ch. 21:27] [p] [ch. 22:5] [q] [Gen. 29:1] [r] ch. 22:6 **9**[s] [ch. 24:17] [t] Deut. 32:28 [u] Ex. 33:16; [Ezra 9:2; Esth. 3:8; Eph. 2:14] **10**[v] See Gen. 13:16 [w] Ps. 37:37; 116:15; Rev. 14:13 **11**[x] ch. 22:11; 24:10; Deut. 23:5; Neh. 13:2 **12**[y] See ver. 5

Balaam's Second Oracle

13 And Balak said to him, "Please come with
me to another place, from which you may see
them. You shall see only a fraction of them
and shall not see them all. Then curse them
for me from there." 14 And he took him to
the field of Zophim, to the top of Pisgah,
[z]and built seven altars and offered a bull and
a ram on each altar. 15 Balaam said to Balak,
[a]"Stand here beside your burnt offering, while
I meet the LORD over there." 16 And the LORD
met Balaam and [b]put a word in his mouth
and said, "Return to Balak, and thus shall you
speak." 17 And he came to him, and behold, he
was standing beside his burnt offering, and
the princes of Moab with him. And Balak said
to him, "What has the LORD spoken?" 18 And
Balaam took up his discourse and said,

"Rise, Balak, and hear;
give ear to me, O son of Zippor:
19 [c]God is not man, that he should lie,
or a son of man, that he should change his mind.
Has he said, and will he not do it?
Or has he spoken, and will he not fulfill it?
20 Behold, I received a command to bless:
[d]he has blessed, and [e]I cannot revoke it.
21 [f]He has not beheld misfortune in Jacob,
nor has he seen trouble in Israel.
The LORD their God is with them,
and the shout of a king is among them.
22 [g]God brings them out of Egypt
and is for them like [h]the horns of the wild ox.
23 For there is no enchantment against Jacob,
no [i]divination against Israel;
now it shall be said of Jacob and Israel,
[j]'What has God wrought!'
24 Behold, a people! [k]As a lioness it rises up
and as a lion it lifts itself;
[l]it does not lie down until it has devoured the prey
and drunk the blood of the slain."

25 And Balak said to Balaam, "Do not curse
them at all, and do not bless them at all."
26 But Balaam answered Balak, "Did I not
tell you, [m]'All that the LORD says, that I must
do'?" 27 And Balak said to Balaam, [n]"Come
now, I will take you to another place. Perhaps
it will please God that you may curse them
for me from there." 28 So Balak took Balaam
to the top of [o]Peor, which overlooks [p]the desert.[1] 29 And Balaam said to Balak, [q]"Build for
me here seven altars and prepare for me here
seven bulls and seven rams." 30 [r]And Balak did
as Balaam had said, and offered a bull and a
ram on each altar.

Balaam's Third Oracle

24 When Balaam saw that it pleased the
LORD to bless Israel, he did not go, as
at [s]other times, to look for omens, but set
his face toward the wilderness. 2 And Balaam
lifted up his eyes and saw Israel [t]camping
tribe by tribe. And [u]the Spirit of God came
upon him, 3 and he [v]took up his discourse
and said,

"The oracle of Balaam the son of Beor,
the oracle of the man whose eye is opened,[2]
4 the oracle of him who hears the words of God,
who sees the vision of the Almighty,
[w]falling down with his eyes uncovered:
5 How lovely are your tents, O Jacob,
your encampments, O Israel!
6 Like palm groves[3] that stretch afar,
like gardens beside a river,

[1] Or *Jeshimon* [2] Or *closed*, or *perfect*; also verse 15 [3] Or *valleys*

14[z] ver. 1, 2
15[a] ver. 3
16[b] ver. 5, 12
19[c] 1 Sam. 15:29; Mal. 3:6; Rom. 11:29; Titus 1:2; Heb. 6:18; James 1:17
20[d] ch. 22:12; Gen. 12:2; 22:17 [e] ch. 22:18
21[f] [Jer. 50:20]
22[g] ch. 24:8 [h] Deut. 33:17; Job 39:9-12; Ps. 22:21; 92:10
23[i] ch. 22:7 [j] Ps. 44:1

24:5–7 Though God's people have endured the wilderness for nearly forty years, when Balaam gazes upon them, he describes them as the well-watered garden of Eden. Through the Spirit of God upon him, Balaam is able to discern the loveliness of Israel, expressing a desire to be among the encampments of the covenant community. So, too, having God's blessed promises before us and the presence of Christ among us by his Spirit, we are able—however the world derides or pities—to sing of the joys and glories of being counted among God's people, members of the heavenly Zion (Psalm 87; Gal. 4:26; Rev. 21:2).

24[k] Gen. 49:9 [l] Gen. 49:27 **26**[m] See ch. 22:18 **27**[n] ver. 13 **28**[o] ch. 25:18; 31:16; Josh. 22:17; Ps. 106:28, 29; Hos. 9:10; [ch. 25:3, 5] [p] See ch. 21:20 **29**[q] ver. 1 **30**[r] ver. 2 **Chapter 24** **1**[s] ch. 23:3, 15 **2**[t] See ch. 2:22-31 [u] Judg. 3:10; 1 Sam. 19:20, 23; 2 Chr. 15:1; 20:14 **3**[v] See ch. 23:7 **4**[w] [Ezek. 1:28; 3:23; Rev. 1:10, 17]

[x]like aloes [y]that the LORD has planted,
like cedar trees beside the waters.
7 Water shall flow from his buckets,
and his seed shall be [z]in many waters;
his king shall be higher than [a]Agag,
and [b]his kingdom shall be exalted.
8 God brings him out of Egypt
and is for him like the [c]horns of the wild ox;
he shall [d]eat up the nations, his adversaries,
and shall [e]break their bones in pieces
and [f]pierce them through with his arrows.
9 He crouched, he lay down like a lion
and [g]like a lioness; who will rouse him up?
[h]Blessed are those who bless you,
and cursed are those who curse you."

10 And Balak's anger was kindled against
Balaam, and he [i]struck his hands together. And
Balak said to Balaam, [j]"I called you to curse my
enemies, and behold, you have blessed them
these three times. 11 Therefore now flee to your
own place. I said, [k]'I will certainly honor you,'
but the LORD has held you back from honor."
12 And Balaam said to Balak, "Did I not tell
your messengers whom you sent to me, 13 [l]'If
Balak should give me his house full of silver
and gold, I would not be able to go beyond
the word of the LORD, to do either good or
bad [m]of my own will. What the LORD speaks,
that will I speak'? 14 And now, behold, I am
going to my people. Come, [n]I will let you know
what this people will do to your people [o]in the
latter days."

Balaam's Final Oracle

15 [p]And he took up his discourse and said,

"The oracle of Balaam the son of Beor,
the oracle of the man whose eye is opened,
16 the oracle of him who hears the words of God,
and knows the knowledge of [q]the Most High,
who sees the vision of the Almighty,
[r]falling down with his eyes uncovered:
17 [s]I see him, but not now;
I behold him, but not near:
[t]a star shall come out of Jacob,
and [u]a scepter shall rise out of Israel;
it shall [v]crush the forehead[1] of Moab
and break down all the sons of Sheth.
18 [w]Edom shall be dispossessed;
[x]Seir also, his enemies, shall be dispossessed.
Israel is doing valiantly.
19 And one from Jacob shall exercise dominion
and destroy the survivors of cities!"

20 Then he looked on Amalek and [y]took up
his discourse and said,

"Amalek was the first among the nations,
[z]but its end is utter destruction."

21 And he looked on the Kenite, and took up
his discourse and said,

"Enduring is your dwelling place,
and your nest is set in the rock.
22 Nevertheless, Kain shall be burned
when Asshur takes you away captive."

23 And he took up his discourse and said,

"Alas, who shall live when God does this?
24 But ships shall come from [a]Kittim
and shall afflict Asshur and [b]Eber;
and he too [c]shall come to utter destruction."

25 Then Balaam rose and [d]went back to his
place. And Balak also went his way.

[1] Hebrew *corners* [of the head]

24:17–19 The glad tidings of the New Testament, preannounced here by Balaam, proclaim that in Jesus, the Son of David, *the* Messiah has come (Acts 2:36), fulfilling this and all messianic prophecies. When the magi saw his star in the east, they inquired as to where the king had been born so they might worship him (Matt. 2:2; Rev. 22:16). Jesus is the victorious ruler who through his reign (i.e., his scepter) will defeat God's enemies and establish eternal peace among the nations in the new creation (Psalm 2; 110; 1 Cor. 15:25; Rev. 11:15).

6 [x][Ps. 1:3; Jer. 17:8] [y]Ps. 104:16; Isa. 61:3 **7** [z][Jer. 51:13; Rev. 17:1] [a]1 Sam. 15:8 [b]2 Sam. 5:12; 1 Chr. 14:2 **8** [c]See ch. 23:22 [d][ch. 14:9; 23:24] [e]Isa. 38:13; Jer. 50:17 [f]Ps. 45:5; Jer. 50:9 **9** [g]ch. 23:24; Gen. 49:9 [h]Gen. 12:3; 27:29 **10** [i][Job 27:23; Lam. 2:15; Ezek. 21:14, 17; 22:13] [j]See ch. 23:11 **11** [k]ch. 22:17, 37 **13** [l]ch. 22:18 [m]See ch. 16:28 **14** [n][Mic. 6:5; Rev. 2:14] [o]See Gen. 49:1 **15** [p][ch. 21:27]; See ch. 23:7 **16** [q]Acts 7:48 [r]See ver. 4 **17** [s][ch. 23:9] [t]Matt. 2:2; Rev. 22:16 [u]Gen. 49:10 [v]Jer. 48:45; [2 Sam. 8:2] **18** [w][2 Sam. 8:14; Ps. 60:8, 9; Amos 9:12] [x]Gen. 32:3; 36:8 **20** [y]See ch. 23:7 [z][Ex. 17:14; 1 Sam. 15:3, 8] **24** [a]Gen. 10:4; Dan. 11:30 [b]Gen. 10:21, 25 [c]ver. 20 **25** [d][ch. 31:8]

Baal Worship at Peor

25 While Israel lived in [e]Shittim, [f]the people began to whore with the daughters of Moab. 2 [g]These invited the people to the sacrifices of their gods, and the people ate and bowed down to their gods. 3 So Israel yoked himself to Baal of Peor. And the anger of the LORD was kindled against Israel. 4 And the LORD said to Moses, [h]"Take all the chiefs of the people and [i]hang[1] them in the sun before the LORD, [j]that the fierce anger of the LORD may turn away from Israel." 5 And Moses said to [k]the judges of Israel, [l]"Each of you kill those of his men who have yoked themselves to Baal of Peor."

6 And behold, one of the people of Israel came and brought a Midianite woman to his family, in the sight of Moses and in the sight of the whole congregation of the people of Israel, while they were [m]weeping in the entrance of the tent of meeting. 7 [n]When Phinehas [o]the son of Eleazar, son of Aaron the priest, saw it, he rose and left the congregation and took a spear in his hand 8 and went after the man of Israel into the chamber and pierced both of them, the man of Israel and the woman through her belly. Thus the plague on the people of Israel was stopped. 9 Nevertheless, [p]those who died by the plague were twenty-four thousand.

The Zeal of Phinehas

10 And the LORD said to Moses, 11 "Phinehas the son of Eleazar, son of Aaron the priest, has turned back my wrath from the people of Israel, in that he [q]was jealous with my jealousy among them, so that I did not consume the people of Israel in [r]my jealousy. 12 Therefore say, [s]'Behold, I give to him my covenant of peace, 13 and it shall be to him and to [t]his descendants after him the covenant of [u]a perpetual priesthood, because he was jealous for his God and made atonement for the people of Israel.'"

14 The name of the slain man of Israel, who was killed with the Midianite woman, was Zimri the son of Salu, chief of a father's house belonging to the Simeonites. 15 And the name of the Midianite woman who was killed was Cozbi the daughter of [v]Zur, who was the tribal head of a father's house in Midian.

16 And the LORD spoke to Moses, saying, 17 [w]"Harass the Midianites and strike them down, 18 for they have harassed you with their [x]wiles, with which they beguiled you in the matter of [y]Peor, and in the matter of Cozbi, the daughter of the chief of Midian, their sister, who was killed on the day of the plague on account of Peor."

Census of the New Generation

26 [z]After the plague, the LORD said to Moses and to Eleazar the son of Aaron, the priest, 2 [a]"Take a census of all the congregation of the people of Israel, from twenty years old and upward, by their fathers' houses, all in Israel who are able to go to war." 3 And Moses and Eleazar the priest spoke with them [b]in the plains of Moab by the Jordan at Jericho,

[1] Or *impale*

Chapter 25
1 [e]ch. 33:49; Josh. 2:1; 3:1; Mic. 6:5 [f][ch. 31:16]
2 [g]Ex. 34:15, 16; Josh. 22:17; Ps. 106:28; Hos. 9:10; [1 Cor. 10:20]
4 [h]See Deut. 4:3 [i][Deut. 21:23; 2 Sam. 21:6; Gal. 3:13] [j]ver. 11; Deut. 13:17
5 [k][ch. 11:16; Ex. 18:21, 25] [l][Ex. 32:27]
6 [m]Joel 2:17
7 [n]Ps. 106:30 [o]Ex. 6:25
9 [p]Deut. 4:3; [1 Cor. 10:8]
11 [q][2 Cor. 11:2] [r]Deut. 32:16, 21; 1 Kgs. 14:22; Ps. 78:58; Zeph. 1:18; 3:8; 1 Cor. 10:22; [Ex. 20:5]
12 [s]Mal. 2:4, 5
13 [t]See 1 Chr. 6:4-15 [u]Ex. 40:15
15 [v]ch. 31:8; Josh. 13:21
17 [w]ch. 31:2, 7
18 [x]ch. 31:16; Rev. 2:14 [y]See ch. 23:28

Chapter 26
1 [z]ch. 25:9
2 [a]ch. 1:2, 3; Ex. 30:12; 38:25, 26
3 [b]ver. 63; See ch. 22:1

25:1–18 Much like when Israel worshiped the golden calf while God was delivering them the Decalogue through Moses atop Sinai (Exodus 32), so here Israel engaged in sexual immorality with Moabite women while God was delivering them blessings through Balaam atop Peor (Num. 23:28). Yet while Aaron the high priest had played a leading role in the former idolatry, his grandson Phinehas, zealous for the Lord's honor, turns back God's wrath by putting an end to the apostasy, making atonement for the people.

Phinehas first reminds us of the grace that our walk with God is not predetermined by family background or sinful contexts. Even more, we are reminded of the indispensable blessing of priestly mediation that our High Priest Jesus Christ, zealous for God and the things of God (Ps. 69:9; John 2:17), has made by his atonement—allowing his own body to be pierced for our sake.

Though a sad contrast to God's gracious dealings only moments earlier, the people's sin in the face of divine blessing is a pattern repeated throughout Scripture and in our own lives. It is precisely because of the human propensity to sin that the gospel comes to us as truly good news—we are saved by the obedience of Christ on our behalf, utterly by grace through faith alone (Rom. 3:21–24; 5:19–21)! Because of Christ's atoning death and righteous fulfillment of the law, our failures in the ongoing battle with sin are not able to thwart God's resolve to bless his people any more than the schemes of Balak were.

saying, 4 “Take a census of the people,[1] from
twenty years old and upward,” as the LORD
[c]commanded Moses. The people of Israel who
came out of the land of Egypt were:

5 [d]Reuben, the firstborn of Israel; the sons of
Reuben: of Hanoch, the clan of the Hanochites;
of Pallu, the clan of the Palluites; 6 of Hezron,
the clan of the Hezronites; of Carmi, the clan
of the Carmites. 7 These are the clans of the
Reubenites, and those listed were [e]43,730.
8 And the sons of Pallu: Eliab. 9 The sons of
Eliab: Nemuel, Dathan, and Abiram. These
are the Dathan and Abiram, [f]chosen from the
congregation, who contended against Moses
and Aaron in the company of Korah, when
they contended against the LORD 10 and [g]the
earth opened its mouth and swallowed them
up together with Korah, when that company
died, when the fire devoured 250 men, and
[h]they became a warning. 11 But [i]the sons of
Korah did not die.

12 The sons of [j]Simeon according to their
clans: of Nemuel, the clan of the Nemuelites;
of Jamin, the clan of the Jaminites; of Jachin,
the clan of the Jachinites; 13 of Zerah, the
clan of the Zerahites; of Shaul, the clan of
the Shaulites. 14 These are the clans of the
Simeonites, [k]22,200.

15 The sons of [l]Gad according to their clans:
of Zephon, the clan of the Zephonites; of
Haggi, the clan of the Haggites; of Shuni, the
clan of the Shunites; 16 of Ozni, the clan of the
Oznites; of Eri, the clan of the Erites; 17 of Arod,
the clan of the Arodites; of Areli, the clan of
the Arelites. 18 These are the clans of the sons
of Gad as they were listed, [m]40,500.

19 The sons of [n]Judah were Er and Onan; and
Er and Onan died in the land of Canaan. 20 And
the sons of Judah according to their clans
were: of Shelah, the clan of the Shelanites; of
Perez, the clan of the Perezites; of Zerah, the
clan of the Zerahites. 21 And the sons of Perez
were: of Hezron, the clan of the Hezronites; of
Hamul, the clan of the Hamulites. 22 These are
the clans of Judah as they were listed, [o]76,500.

23 The sons of [p]Issachar according to their
clans: of Tola, the clan of the Tolaites; of
Puvah, the clan of the Punites; 24 of Jashub,
the clan of the Jashubites; of Shimron, the clan
of the Shimronites. 25 These are the clans of
Issachar as they were listed, [q]64,300.

26 The sons of [r]Zebulun, according to their
clans: of Sered, the clan of the Seredites; of
Elon, the clan of the Elonites; of Jahleel, the
clan of the Jahleelites. 27 These are the clans of
the Zebulunites as they were listed, [s]60,500.

28 The sons of [t]Joseph according to their
clans: Manasseh and Ephraim. 29 [u]The sons of
Manasseh: of [v]Machir, the clan of the Machirites;
and Machir was the father of Gilead; [w]of Gilead,
the clan of the Gileadites. 30 These are the sons
of Gilead: of Iezer, the clan of the Iezerites; of
Helek, the clan of the Helekites; 31 and of Asriel,
the clan of the Asrielites; and of Shechem, the
clan of the Shechemites; 32 and of Shemida, the
clan of the Shemidaites; and of Hepher, the clan
of the Hepherites. 33 Now [x]Zelophehad the son
of Hepher had no sons, but daughters. And the
names of the daughters of Zelophehad were
Mahlah, Noah, Hoglah, Milcah, and Tirzah.
34 These are the clans of Manasseh, and those
listed were [y]52,700.

[1] *Take a census of the people* is implied (compare verse 2)

26:1–65 The second census, while also numbering those “able to go to war” (v. 2), is not conducted primarily for the purpose of battle, but rather for the sake of the land inheritance (vv. 52–56). The hope is so sure that the conquest is already assumed. This census also reveals that, while the first wilderness generation had died off in judgment, God was faithful to raise up a new generation, with most of the tribes showing an increase in their numbers. Even in the wilderness of their rebellion, as when under Egyptian oppression, God’s people had experienced his blessing of fruitfulness (Gen. 1:28; Ex. 1:7–20).

Because of the emphasis upon God’s sure promise evidenced in this land distribution, we naturally think here of the blessedness of inheriting the new earth (Matt. 5:5; Rev. 21:1–4) and the joys of being numbered among the people of God (Luke 10:20; Phil. 4:3; Heb. 12:23; Rev. 3:5; 13:8; 17:8; 20:12, 15). Knowing that our names are registered in heaven only through the saving death of Christ (Rev. 21:27), our hearts are filled with gratitude for the grace of God and we yearn to love and serve him more faithfully.

4 [c] ch. 1:1
5 [d] Gen. 46:8, 9; Ex. 6:14; 1 Chr. 5:1-3
7 [e] [ch. 1:21]
9 [f] ch. 1:16; 16:2
10 [g] See ch. 16:31-35 [h] ch. 16:38; [1 Cor. 10:6; 2 Pet. 2:6]
11 [i] Ex. 6:24; 1 Chr. 6:22; [ch. 16:32]
12 [j] Gen. 46:10; Ex. 6:15; 1 Chr. 4:24
14 [k] [ch. 1:23]
15 [l] Gen. 46:16
18 [m] [ch. 1:25]
19 [n] Gen. 46:12; 1 Chr. 2:3-5; See Gen. 38:3-10
22 [o] [ch. 1:27]
23 [p] Gen. 46:13; 1 Chr. 7:1
25 [q] [ch. 1:29]
26 [r] Gen. 46:14
27 [s] [ch. 1:31]
28 [t] Gen. 46:20
29 [u] For ver. 29-37, see 1 Chr. 7:14-20 [v] Josh. 17:1 [w] ch. 36:1 **33** [x] ch. 27:1; 36:11; Josh. 17:3 **34** [y] [ch. 1:35]

35 These are the sons of Ephraim according to their clans: of Shuthelah, the clan of
the Shuthelahites; of Becher, the clan of the
Becherites; of Tahan, the clan of the Tahanites.
36 And these are the sons of Shuthelah: of Eran,
the clan of the Eranites. 37 These are the clans
of the sons of Ephraim as they were listed,
[z]32,500. These are the sons of Joseph according to their clans.

38 The sons of [a]Benjamin according to their
clans: of Bela, the clan of the Belaites; of
Ashbel, the clan of the Ashbelites; of Ahiram,
the clan of the Ahiramites; 39 of Shephupham,
the clan of the Shuphamites; of Hupham, the
clan of the Huphamites. 40 And the sons of
Bela were Ard and Naaman: of Ard, the clan
of the Ardites; of Naaman, the clan of the
Naamites. 41 These are the sons of Benjamin
according to their clans, and those listed were
[b]45,600.

42 These are the sons of [c]Dan according
to their clans: of Shuham, the clan of the
Shuhamites. These are the clans of Dan
according to their clans. 43 All the clans of the
Shuhamites, as they were listed, were [d]64,400.

44 The sons of [e]Asher according to their
clans: of Imnah, the clan of the Imnites; of
Ishvi, the clan of the Ishvites; of Beriah, the
clan of the Beriites. 45 Of the sons of Beriah: of
Heber, the clan of the Heberites; of Malchiel,
the clan of the Malchielites. 46 And the name
of the daughter of Asher was Serah. 47 These
are the clans of the sons of Asher as they were
listed, [f]53,400.

48 The sons of [g]Naphtali according to their
clans: of Jahzeel, the clan of the Jahzeelites; of
Guni, the clan of the Gunites; 49 of Jezer, the
clan of the Jezerites; of Shillem, the clan of the
Shillemites. 50 These are the clans of Naphtali
according to their clans, and those listed were
[h]45,400.

51 This was the list of the people of Israel,
[i]601,730.

52 The LORD spoke to Moses, saying,
53 [j]"Among these the land shall be divided
for inheritance according to the number of
names. 54 [k]To a large tribe you shall give a large
inheritance, and to a small tribe you shall give
a small inheritance; every tribe shall be given
its inheritance in proportion to its list. 55 But
the land shall be [l]divided by lot. According to
the names of the tribes of their fathers they
shall inherit. 56 Their inheritance shall be
divided according to lot between the larger
and the smaller."

57 [m]This was the list of the Levites according to their clans: of Gershon, the clan of
the Gershonites; of Kohath, the clan of the
Kohathites; of Merari, the clan of the Merarites.
58 These are the clans of Levi: the clan of the
Libnites, the clan of the Hebronites, the clan
of the Mahlites, the clan of the Mushites, the
clan of the Korahites. And Kohath was the
father of Amram. 59 The name of Amram's
wife was [n]Jochebed the daughter of Levi, who
was born to Levi in Egypt. And she bore to
Amram Aaron and Moses and Miriam their
sister. 60 [o]And to Aaron were born Nadab,
Abihu, Eleazar, and Ithamar. 61 [p]But Nadab
and Abihu died when they offered unauthorized fire before the LORD. 62 And those listed
were [q]23,000, every male from a month old
and upward. For [r]they were not listed among
the people of Israel, because [s]there was no
inheritance given to them among the people
of Israel.

63 These were those listed by Moses and
Eleazar the priest, who listed the people of
Israel [t]in the plains of Moab by the Jordan at
Jericho. 64 [u]But among these there was not one
of those listed by Moses and Aaron the priest,
who had listed the people of Israel in the wilderness of Sinai. 65 For the LORD had said of
them, [v]"They shall die in the wilderness." Not
one of them was left, [w]except Caleb the son of
Jephunneh and Joshua the son of Nun.

The Daughters of Zelophehad

27 Then drew near the daughters of
[x]Zelophehad the son of Hepher, son of
Gilead, son of Machir, son of Manasseh, from
the clans of Manasseh the son of Joseph. The
names of his daughters were: Mahlah, Noah,
Hoglah, Milcah, and Tirzah. 2 And they stood
before Moses and before Eleazar the priest and
before the chiefs and all the congregation, at
the entrance of the tent of meeting, saying,
3 "Our father [y]died in the wilderness. He was
not among the company of those who gathered themselves together against the LORD

37[z] [ch. 1:33] **38**[a] Gen. 46:21; 1 Chr. 7:6; See 1 Chr. 8:1-5 **41**[b] [ch. 1:37] **42**[c] Gen. 46:23 **43**[d] [ch. 1:39] **44**[e] Gen. 46:17; 1 Chr. 7:30, 31 **47**[f] [ch. 1:41] **48**[g] Gen. 46:24; 1 Chr. 7:13 **50**[h] [ch. 1:43] **51**[i] [ch. 1:46] **53**[j] Josh. 11:23; 14:1, 2; Ps. 105:44 **54**[k] ch. 33:54; 35:8 **55**[l] ch. 33:54; 34:13; Josh. 11:23; 14:2 **57**[m] Gen. 46:11; See Ex. 6:16-19; 1 Chr. 6:1, 16-30 **59**[n] Ex. 2:1, 2, 4; 6:20 **60**[o] ch. 3:2; 1 Chr. 24:1 **61**[p] ch. 3:4; Lev. 10:1, 2; 1 Chr. 24:2 **62**[q] [ch. 3:39] [r] ch. 1:49 [s] See ch. 18:20 **63**[t] ver. 3; See ch. 22:1 **64**[u] [ch. 1:44; Deut. 2:14, 15] **65**[v] ch. 14:28, 29; 1 Cor. 10:5 [w] See ch. 13:6 **Chapter 27** **1**[x] ch. 26:33; 36:11; Josh. 17:3 **3**[y] ch. 14:35; 26:64, 65

[z]in the company of Korah, but [a]died for his own sin. And he had no sons. 4 Why should the name of our father be taken away from his clan because he had no son? [b]Give to us a possession among our father's brothers."

5 Moses [c]brought their case before the LORD. 6 And the LORD said to Moses, 7 "The daughters of Zelophehad [d]are right. [e]You shall give them possession of an inheritance among their father's brothers and transfer the inheritance of their father to them. 8 And you shall speak to the people of Israel, saying, 'If a man dies and has no son, then you shall transfer his inheritance to his daughter. 9 And if he has no daughter, then you shall give his inheritance to his brothers. 10 And if he has no brothers, then you shall give his inheritance to his father's brothers. 11 And if his father has no brothers, then you shall give his inheritance to the nearest [f]kinsman of his clan, and he shall possess it. And it shall be for the people of Israel [g]a statute and rule, as the LORD commanded Moses.'"

Joshua to Succeed Moses

12 The LORD said to Moses, "Go up into [h]this mountain of Abarim and see the land that I have given to the people of Israel. 13 When you have seen it, you also [i]shall be gathered to your people, as your brother Aaron was, 14 [j]because you rebelled against my word in the wilderness of Zin when the congregation quarreled, failing [k]to uphold me as holy at the waters before their eyes." (These are [l]the waters of Meribah of Kadesh in the wilderness of Zin.) 15 Moses spoke to the LORD, saying, 16 "Let the LORD, [m]the God of the spirits of all flesh, appoint a man over the congregation 17 who [n]shall go out before them and come in before them, who shall lead them out and bring them in, that the congregation of the LORD may not be [o]as sheep that have no shepherd." 18 So the LORD said to Moses, "Take [p]Joshua the son of Nun, a man [q]in whom is the Spirit, and [r]lay your hand on him. 19 Make him stand before Eleazar the priest and all the congregation, and you shall [s]commission him in their sight. 20 You shall invest him with some of your authority, [t]that all the congregation of the people of Israel may obey. 21 And he shall stand before Eleazar the priest, who shall inquire for him [u]by the judgment of the Urim before the LORD. At his word they shall go out, and at his word they shall come in, both he and all the people of Israel with him, the whole congregation." 22 And Moses did as the LORD commanded him. He took Joshua and made him stand before Eleazar the priest and the whole congregation, 23 and he laid his hands on him and [s]commissioned him as the LORD directed through Moses.

Daily Offerings

28 The LORD spoke to Moses, saying, 2 "Command the people of Israel and say to them, 'My offering, [v]my food for my food offerings, my [w]pleasing aroma, you shall be careful to offer to me at its appointed time.' 3 [x]And you shall say to them, This is the food offering that you shall offer to the LORD: two male lambs a year old without blemish, day by day, as a regular offering. 4 The one lamb you shall offer in the morning, and the other lamb you shall offer at twilight; 5 also [y]a tenth

27:12–23 Reminded of his impending death, Moses' compassionate and selfless plea is for the Lord to provide another leader so that the people would not be left "as sheep that have no shepherd" (v. 17). Though having immediate reference to Joshua, this prayer was answered ultimately in Jesus Christ, who was moved with compassion when God's people were harassed and helpless as sheep without a shepherd (Matt. 9:36). As the Good Shepherd, Jesus even gave his life to save the flock of God (John 10:11).

28:1–29:40 As with the other narratives in the last third of Numbers (chs. 26–36), this section on festivals is founded upon the people's anticipation of possessing the land, delineating the proper response of worship once settled within it and thus reaffirming God's promise to bring them in. Moreover, the large number of sacrifices called for presupposes that the land is indeed flowing with milk and honey, and that God's people will experience his abundant blessings. In addition, then, to focusing the purpose of land entry upon the fellowship with God to be enjoyed in worship, these regulations serve as something of a pledge that he will provide for them abundantly—since God supplies all that his people need for a life of godliness. This promise is affirmed in the New Testament by Christ himself (Matt. 6:33).

3 [z]ch. 16:1, 2 [a][Ezek. 18:4]
4 [b]Josh. 17:4
5 [c]Ex. 18:19
7 [d]ch. 36:5 [e]ch. 36:2
11 [f]See Ruth 4:3-6; Jer. 32:6-9 [g]ch. 35:29
12 [h]ch. 21:11; 33:44, 47; Deut. 32:49; [Deut. 3:27; 34:1]
13 [i]See ch. 20:24
14 [j]ch. 20:12, 24 [k]ch. 20:12, 13 [l]ch. 20:13; Deut. 32:51; [Ex. 17:7]
16 [m]See ch. 16:22
17 [n]Deut. 31:2; 1 Sam. 8:20; 18:13; 1 Kgs. 3:7; 2 Chr. 1:10; [Josh. 14:11] [o]1 Kgs. 22:17; Ezek. 34:5; Zech. 10:2; Matt. 9:36; Mark 6:34
18 [p]ch. 32:28 [q]Gen. 41:38; See Judg. 3:10 [r]Deut. 34:9
19 [s]Deut. 3:28; 31:7, 8
20 [t]See Josh. 1:16-18
21 [u]See Ex. 28:30
23 [s][See ver. 19 above]

Chapter 28 **2** [v]See Lev. 3:11 [w]See Gen. 8:21 **3** [x]For ver. 3-8, see Ex. 29:38-42 **5** [y]ch. 15:4; Ex. 16:36

of an ephah[1] of fine flour for [z]a grain offering, mixed [a]with a quarter of a hin[2] of beaten oil. 6 It is a [b]regular burnt offering, which was ordained at Mount Sinai for a pleasing aroma, a food offering to the LORD. 7 Its drink offering shall be a quarter of a hin for each lamb. In the Holy Place you shall pour out a drink offering of strong drink to the LORD. 8 The other lamb you shall offer at twilight. Like the grain offering of the morning, and like its drink offering, you shall offer it as a food offering, with a pleasing aroma to the LORD.

Sabbath Offerings

9 "On the Sabbath day, two male lambs a year old without blemish, and two tenths of an ephah of fine flour for a grain offering, mixed with oil, and its drink offering: 10 this is [c]the burnt offering of every Sabbath, besides the regular burnt offering and its drink offering.

Monthly Offerings

11 [d]"At the beginnings of your months, you shall offer a burnt offering to the LORD: two bulls from the herd, one ram, seven male lambs a year old without blemish; 12 also [e]three tenths of an ephah of fine flour for a grain offering, mixed with oil, for each bull, and two tenths of fine flour for a grain offering, mixed with oil, for the one ram; 13 and a tenth of fine flour mixed with oil as a grain offering for every lamb; for a burnt offering with a pleasing aroma, a food offering to the LORD. 14 Their drink offerings shall be half a hin of wine for a bull, a third of a hin for a ram, and a quarter of a hin for a lamb. This is the burnt offering of each month throughout the months of the year. 15 Also [f]one male goat for a sin offering to the LORD; it shall be offered besides the regular burnt offering and its drink offering.

Passover Offerings

16 [g]"On the fourteenth day of the first month is the LORD's Passover, 17 [h]and on the fifteenth day of this month is a feast. Seven days shall unleavened bread be eaten. 18 [i]On the first day there shall be a holy convocation. You shall not do any ordinary work, 19 but offer a food offering, a burnt offering to the LORD: two bulls from the herd, one ram, and seven male lambs a year old; [j]see that they are without blemish; 20 also their grain offering of fine flour mixed with oil; three tenths of an ephah shall you offer for a bull, and two tenths for a ram; 21 a tenth shall you offer for each of the seven lambs; 22 also [k]one male goat for a sin offering, to make atonement for you. 23 You shall offer these besides the burnt offering of the morning, which is for a regular burnt offering. 24 In the same way you shall offer daily, for seven days, the food of a food offering, with a pleasing aroma to the LORD. It shall be offered besides the regular burnt offering and its drink offering. 25 And [l]on the seventh day you shall have a holy convocation. You shall not do any ordinary work.

Offerings for the Feast of Weeks

26 "On [m]the day of the firstfruits, when you offer a grain offering of new grain to the LORD at your Feast of Weeks, you shall have a holy convocation. You shall not do any ordinary work, 27 but offer a burnt offering, with a pleasing aroma to the LORD: [n]two bulls from the herd, one ram, seven male lambs a year old; 28 also their grain offering of fine flour mixed with oil, three tenths of an ephah for each bull, two tenths for one ram, 29 a tenth for each of the seven lambs; 30 with [o]one male goat, to make atonement for you. 31 Besides the regular burnt offering and its grain offering, you shall offer them and their drink offering. [p]See that they are without blemish.

Offerings for the Feast of Trumpets

29 "On the first day of the seventh month you shall have a holy convocation. You shall not do any ordinary work. [q]It is a day for

[1] An *ephah* was about 3/5 bushel or 22 liters [2] A *hin* was about 4 quarts or 3.5 liters

5[z] Lev. 2:1 [a] Ex. 29:40
6[b] Ex. 29:42; [Amos 5:25]
10[c] [Ezek. 46:4, 5]
11[d] ch. 10:10; 1 Sam. 20:5; 1 Chr. 23:31; 2 Chr. 2:4; Ezra 3:5; Isa. 1:13, 14; Ezek. 45:17; 46:6; Hos. 2:11; Col. 2:16
12[e] For ver. 12-14, see ch. 15:4-12
15[f] ver. 22, 30; ch. 15:24;

Through the apostle John, we are given a similar glimpse of life in the coming age, a vision that sanctifies us now as we more eagerly anticipate the glorious reality of entering the new creation (Rev. 21:1–4). What's more, the sacrifices discussed in this section of Numbers direct our gaze to Christ, who in being sacrificed once for all fulfills all the sacrifices, ushering us into the presence of God in worship so that we are able to taste the future glory and sweetness of divine fellowship even now, as we journey through the wilderness (Heb. 12:22–24).

29:11, 16, 19, 25 **16**[g] Deut. 16:1; Ezek. 45:21; See Ex. 12:6 **17**[h] Lev. 23:6; [Ex. 12:18] **18**[i] Ex. 12:16; Lev. 23:7 **19**[j] ver. 31; ch. 29:8, 13; Lev. 22:20; Deut. 15:21; 17:1 **22**[k] ver. 15, 30; ch. 29:22, 28, 31, 34, 38 **25**[l] Ex. 12:16; 13:6; Lev. 23:8 **26**[m] Ex. 23:16; 34:22; Lev. 23:10, 15; Deut. 16:10; [Acts 2:1] **27**[n] [Lev. 23:18, 19] **30**[o] ver. 15, 22 **31**[p] ver. 19 **Chapter 29** **1**[q] Lev. 23:24; See ch. 10:1-10

you to blow the trumpets, 2 and you shall offer
a burnt offering, for a pleasing aroma to the
LORD: one bull from the herd, one ram, seven
male lambs a year old without blemish; 3 also
their grain offering of fine flour mixed with
oil, three tenths of an ephah[1] for the bull, two
tenths for the ram, 4 and one tenth for each of
the seven lambs; 5 with [o]one male goat for a sin
offering, to make atonement for you; 6 besides
[r]the burnt offering of the new moon, and its
grain offering, and [s]the regular burnt offering
and its grain offering, and their drink offering,
according to the rule for them, for a pleasing
aroma, a food offering to the LORD.

Offerings for the Day of Atonement

7 [t]"On the tenth day of this seventh month
you shall have a holy convocation and [u]afflict
yourselves.[2] You shall do no work, 8 but you
shall offer a burnt offering to the LORD, a
pleasing aroma: one bull from the herd, one
ram, seven male lambs a year old: [v]see that
they are without blemish. 9 And their grain
offering shall be of fine flour mixed with oil,
three tenths of an ephah for the bull, two
tenths for the one ram, 10 a tenth for each of
the seven lambs: 11 also [w]one male goat for a
sin offering, besides [x]the sin offering of atonement, and the regular burnt offering and its
grain offering, and their drink offerings.

Offerings for the Feast of Booths

12 [y]"On the fifteenth day of the seventh
month you shall have a holy convocation. You
shall not do any ordinary work, and you shall
keep a feast to the LORD seven days. 13 And [z]you
shall offer a burnt offering, a food offering,
with a pleasing aroma to the LORD, thirteen
bulls from the herd, two rams, fourteen male
lambs a year old; they shall be without blemish; 14 and their grain offering of fine flour
mixed with oil, three tenths of an ephah for
each of the thirteen bulls, two tenths for each
of the two rams, 15 and a tenth for each of the
fourteen lambs; 16 also one male goat for a sin
offering, besides the regular burnt offering, its
grain offering and its drink offering.

17 "On the second day twelve bulls from the
herd, two rams, fourteen male lambs a year
old without blemish, 18 with the grain offering and the drink offerings for the bulls, for
the rams, and for the lambs, [a]in the prescribed
quantities; 19 also one male goat for a sin offering, besides the regular burnt offering and its
grain offering, and their drink offerings.

20 "On the third day eleven bulls, two rams,
fourteen male lambs a year old without blemish, 21 with the grain offering and the drink
offerings for the bulls, for the rams, and for
the lambs, in the prescribed quantities; 22 also
one male goat for a sin offering, besides the
regular burnt offering and its grain offering
and its drink offering.

23 "On the fourth day ten bulls, two rams,
fourteen male lambs a year old without blemish, 24 with the grain offering and the drink
offerings for the bulls, for the rams, and for
the lambs, in the prescribed quantities; 25 also
one male goat for a sin offering, besides the
regular burnt offering, its grain offering and
its drink offering.

26 "On the fifth day nine bulls, two rams,
fourteen male lambs a year old without blemish, 27 with the grain offering and the drink
offerings for the bulls, for the rams, and for
the lambs, in the prescribed quantities; 28 also
one male goat for a sin offering; besides the
regular burnt offering and its grain offering
and its drink offering.

29 "On the sixth day eight bulls, two rams,
fourteen male lambs a year old without blemish, 30 with the grain offering and the drink
offerings for the bulls, for the rams, and for
the lambs, in the prescribed quantities; 31 also
one male goat for a sin offering; besides the
regular burnt offering, its grain offering, and
its drink offerings.

32 "On the seventh day seven bulls, two rams,
fourteen male lambs a year old without blemish, 33 with the grain offering and the drink
offerings for the bulls, for the rams, and for
the lambs, in the prescribed quantities; 34 also
one male goat for a sin offering; besides the
regular burnt offering, its grain offering, and
its drink offering.

35 [b]"On the eighth day you shall have a [c]sol-
emn assembly. You shall not do any ordinary
work, 36 but you shall offer a burnt offering,
a food offering, with a pleasing aroma to the
LORD: one bull, one ram, seven male lambs
a year old without blemish, 37 and the grain

[1] An *ephah* was about 3/5 bushel or 22 liters [2] Or *and fast*

5[o] [See ch. 28:30 above] **6**[r] See ch. 28:11-15 [s] See ch. 28:3-8 **7**[t] Lev. 16:29; 23:27 [u] ch. 30:13; Ps. 35:13; Isa. 58:5 **8**[v] ver. 13, 17, 20, 23, 26, 29, 32, 36; See ch. 28:19 **11**[w] See ch. 28:15 [x] Lev. 16:3, 5 **12**[y] See Lev. 23:34 **13**[z] Ezra 3:4 **18**[a] ver. 21, 24, 27, 30, 33, 37; ch. 15:12; 28:7, 14 **35**[b] [John 7:37] [c] See Lev. 23:36

offering and the drink offerings for the bull, for the ram, and for the lambs, in the prescribed quantities; [38]also one male goat for a sin offering; besides the regular burnt offering and its grain offering and its drink offering.

[39]"These you shall offer to the LORD at your [d]appointed feasts, in addition to your [e]vow offerings and your freewill offerings, for your burnt offerings, and for your grain offerings, and for your drink offerings, and for your peace offerings."

[40][1] So Moses told the people of Israel everything just as the LORD had commanded Moses.

Men and Vows

30 Moses spoke to [f]the heads of the tribes of the people of Israel, saying, "This is what the LORD has commanded. [2][g]If a man vows a vow to the LORD, or [h]swears an oath to bind himself by a pledge, he shall not break his word. [i]He shall do according to all that proceeds out of his mouth.

Women and Vows

[3]"If a woman vows a vow to the LORD and binds herself by a pledge, while within her father's house in her youth, [4]and her father hears of her vow and of her pledge by which she has bound herself and says nothing to her, then all her vows shall stand, and every pledge by which she has bound herself shall stand. [5]But if her father opposes her on the day that he hears of it, no vow of hers, no pledge by which she has bound herself shall stand. And the LORD will forgive her, because her father opposed her.

[6]"If she marries a husband, while under her [j]vows or any thoughtless utterance of her lips by which she has bound herself, [7]and her husband hears of it and says nothing to her on the day that he hears, then her vows shall stand, and her pledges by which she has bound herself shall stand. [8]But if, on the day that her husband comes to hear of it, he opposes her, then he makes void her [j]vow that was on her, and the thoughtless utterance of her lips by which she bound herself. [k]And the LORD will forgive her. [9](But any vow of a widow or of a divorced woman, anything by which she has bound herself, shall stand against her.) [10]And if she vowed in her husband's house or bound herself by a pledge with an oath, [11]and her husband heard of it and said nothing to her and did not oppose her, then all her vows shall stand, and every pledge by which she bound herself shall stand. [12]But if her husband makes them null and void on the day that he hears them, then whatever proceeds out of her lips concerning her vows or concerning her pledge of herself shall not stand. Her husband has made them void, and [l]the LORD will forgive her. [13]Any vow and any binding oath to afflict herself,[2] her husband may establish,[3] or her husband may make void. [14]But if her husband says nothing to her from day to day, then he establishes all her vows or all her pledges that are upon her. He has established them, because he said nothing to her on the day that he heard of them. [15]But if he makes them null and void after he has heard of them, then [m]he shall bear her iniquity."

[16]These are the statutes that the LORD commanded Moses about a man and his wife and about a father and his daughter while she is in her youth within her father's house.

Vengeance on Midian

31 The LORD spoke to Moses, saying, [2][n]"Avenge the people of Israel on the Midianites. Afterward you shall [o]be gathered to your people." [3]So Moses spoke to the peo-

[1] Ch 30:1 in Hebrew [2] Or *to fast* [3] Or *may allow to stand*

39[d] Lev. 23:2, 4; 1 Chr. 23:31; 2 Chr. 31:3; Ezra 3:5; Neh. 10:33; [Isa. 1:14] [e] Lev. 7:11, 16; 22:21, 23
Chapter 30
1[f] ch. 1:4, 16; 7:2
2[g] Deut. 23:21; Eccles. 5:4; See Lev. 27:2 [h] See Lev. 5:4 [i] Job 22:27; Ps. 22:25; 50:14; 66:13, 14; 116:14, 18; Nah. 1:15
6[j] Ps. 56:12
8[j] [See ver. 6 above] [k] ver. 12
12[l] ver. 8
15[m] See Lev. 5:1
Chapter 31
2[n] ch. 25:17 [o] See ch. 20:24

30:1–16 As sacrifices were often used for the payment of vows (Lev. 7:16; Ps. 50:14), this chapter flows naturally out of the previous two. Yet we should keep in view the presupposed entry into the Promised Land as the gracious context for these injunctions: because God fulfilled his vow to Abraham to bring his people into the Promised Land, so the Israelites out of gratitude should now dutifully keep their vows as well.

In this way, we see that God's grace lavished upon us does not lead to increasing sinfulness, but rather lovingly compels us to honor him in all our ways (Rom. 12:1–2; Eph. 5:1–2).

31:1–32:42 The war on the Midianites is referred to as "the LORD's vengeance" (v. 3) since this would be their punishment for having seduced the Israelites to be unfaithful to the Lord (25:1–13). More importantly, this battle stands as a foretaste of the conquest of Canaan: not one Israelite was lost (31:39), and the tribes of Reuben and Gad were

ple, saying, "Arm men from among you for the
war, that they may go against Midian to execute the LORD's vengeance on Midian. 4 You
shall send a thousand from each of the tribes
of Israel to the war." 5 So there were provided,
out of the thousands of Israel, a thousand
from each tribe, twelve thousand [p]armed for
war. 6 And Moses sent them to the war, a thousand from each tribe, together with Phinehas
the son of Eleazar the priest, with the vessels of the sanctuary and [q]the trumpets for
the alarm in his hand. 7 They warred against
Midian, as the LORD commanded Moses, and
[r]killed every male. 8 They killed the kings
of Midian with the rest of their slain, [s]Evi,
Rekem, [t]Zur, Hur, and Reba, the five kings of
Midian. And they also killed [u]Balaam the son
of Beor with the sword. 9 And the people of
Israel took captive the women of Midian and
their little ones, and they took as plunder all
their cattle, their flocks, and all their goods.
10 All their cities in the places where they lived,
and all their [v]encampments, they burned with
fire, 11 [w]and took all the spoil and all the plunder, both of man and of beast. 12 Then they
brought the captives and the plunder and the
spoil to Moses, and to Eleazar the priest, and
to the congregation of the people of Israel, at
the camp on [x]the plains of Moab by the Jordan
at Jericho.

13 Moses and Eleazar the priest and all the
chiefs of the congregation went to meet them
outside the camp. 14 And Moses was angry with
[y]the officers of the army, the commanders of
thousands and the commanders of hundreds,
who had come from service in the war. 15 Moses
said to them, "Have you [z]let all the women
live? 16 Behold, [a]these, [b]on Balaam's advice,
caused the people of Israel to act treacherously
against the LORD in the incident of [c]Peor, and
so [d]the plague came among the congregation of the LORD. 17 Now therefore, [e]kill every
male among the little ones, and kill every
woman who has known man by lying with
him. 18 But all the young girls who have not
known man by lying with him [f]keep alive for
yourselves. 19 [g]Encamp outside the camp seven
days. Whoever of you has killed any person
and [h]whoever has touched any slain, purify
yourselves and your captives on the third day
and on the seventh day. 20 You shall purify
every garment, every article of skin, all work
of goats' hair, and every article of wood."

21 Then Eleazar the priest said to the men
in the army who had gone to battle: "This is
the statute of the law that the LORD has commanded Moses: 22 only the gold, the silver,
the bronze, the iron, the tin, and the lead,
23 everything that can stand the fire, you shall
pass through the fire, and it shall be clean.
Nevertheless, it shall also be purified [i]with
the water for impurity. And whatever cannot stand the fire, you shall pass through the
water. 24 You must [j]wash your clothes on the
seventh day, and you shall be clean. And afterward you may come into the camp."

25 The LORD said to Moses, 26 "Take the count
of the plunder that was taken, both of man
and of beast, you and Eleazar the priest and
the heads of the fathers' houses of the congregation, 27 and [k]divide the plunder into two
parts between the warriors who went out to
battle and all the congregation. 28 And levy
for the LORD a tribute from the men of war
who went out to battle, [l]one out of five hundred, of the people and of the oxen and of the
donkeys and of the flocks. 29 Take it from their
half and give it to Eleazar the priest as a contribution to the LORD. 30 And from the people
of Israel's half you shall take [m]one drawn out
of every fifty, of the people, of the oxen, of the
donkeys, and of the flocks, of all the cattle,
and give them to the Levites [n]who keep guard
over the tabernacle of the LORD." 31 And Moses
and Eleazar the priest did as the LORD commanded Moses.

32 Now the plunder remaining of the spoil
that the army took was 675,000 sheep,
33 72,000 cattle, 34 61,000 donkeys, 35 and
32,000 persons in all, women who had not

allocated land (ch. 32). When facing armies within the land and tempted to fear, the Israelites could look to this past faithfulness of God—his giving them complete victory along with land even outside Canaan—and renew their trust in him.

As Christians, we look to the cross of Christ to renew our trust in God's faithfulness. As the apostle Paul put it, "He who did not spare his own Son but gave him up for us all, how will he not also with him graciously give us all things?" (Rom. 8:32).

5[p] ch. 32:27; Josh. 4:13
6[q] ch. 10:6, 9; Lev. 23:24
7[r] [Deut. 20:13; Judg. 21:11; 1 Sam. 27:9; 1 Kgs. 11:15, 16]
8[s] Josh. 13:21 [t] ch. 25:15 [u] Josh. 13:22
10[v] Gen. 25:16
11[w] [Deut. 20:14; Josh. 8:2]
12[x] See ch. 22:1

14[y] ver. 48 15[z] [1 Sam. 15:3] 16[a] ch. 25:2 [b] ch. 24:14; 2 Pet. 2:15; Rev. 2:14 [c] See ch. 23:28 [d] ch. 25:9 17[e] Judg. 21:11, 12 18[f] See Deut. 21:10-14 19[g] ch. 5:2 [h] See ch. 19:12, 22 23[i] ch. 19:9 24[j] See Lev. 11:25 27[k] Josh. 22:8; 1 Sam. 30:24 28[l] [ch. 18:26]; See ver. 30-41, 47 30[m] See ver. 42-47 [n] See ch. 1:53

known man by lying with him. 36 And the half, the portion of those who had gone out in the army, numbered 337,500 sheep, 37 and [o]the LORD's tribute of sheep was 675. 38 The cattle were 36,000, of which the LORD's tribute was 72. 39 The donkeys were 30,500, of which the LORD's tribute was 61. 40 The persons were 16,000, of which the LORD's tribute was 32 persons. 41 And Moses gave the tribute, which was the contribution for the LORD, to Eleazar the priest, [p]as the LORD commanded Moses.

42 From the people of Israel's half, which Moses separated from that of the men who had served in the army— 43 now the congregation's half was 337,500 sheep, 44 36,000 cattle, 45 and 30,500 donkeys, 46 and 16,000 persons— 47 [q]from the people of Israel's half Moses took one of every 50, both of persons and of beasts, and gave them to the Levites who kept guard over the tabernacle of the LORD, as the LORD commanded Moses.

48 Then [r]the officers who were over the thousands of the army, the commanders of thousands and the commanders of hundreds, came near to Moses 49 and said to Moses, "Your servants have counted the men of war who are under our command, and there is not a man missing from us. 50 And we have brought the LORD's offering, what each man found, articles of gold, armlets and bracelets, signet rings, earrings, and beads, [s]to make atonement for ourselves before the LORD." 51 And Moses and Eleazar the priest received from them the gold, all crafted articles. 52 And all the gold of the contribution that they presented to the LORD, from the commanders of thousands and the commanders of hundreds, was 16,750 shekels.[1] 53 [t](The men in the army had each taken plunder for himself.) 54 And Moses and Eleazar the priest received the gold from the commanders of thousands and of hundreds, and brought it into the tent of meeting, [u]as a memorial for the people of Israel before the LORD.

Reuben and Gad Settle in Gilead

32 Now the people of Reuben and the people of Gad had a very great number of livestock. And they saw the land of [v]Jazer and the land of Gilead, and behold, the place was a place for livestock. 2 So the people of Gad and the people of Reuben came and said to Moses and to Eleazar the priest and to the chiefs of the congregation, 3 [w]"Ataroth, [x]Dibon, Jazer, Nimrah, Heshbon, Elealeh, Sebam, [y]Nebo, and Beon, 4 the land [z]that the LORD struck down before the congregation of Israel, is a land for livestock, and your servants have livestock." 5 And they said, "If we have found favor in your sight, let this land be given to your servants for a possession. Do not take us across the Jordan."

6 But Moses said to the people of Gad and to the people of Reuben, "Shall your brothers go to the war while you sit here? 7 Why will you discourage the heart of the people of Israel from going over into the land that the LORD has given them? 8 Your fathers did this, [a]when I sent them from Kadesh-barnea to see the land. 9 For when they went up to the Valley of Eshcol and saw the land, they discouraged the heart of the people of Israel from going into the land that the LORD had given them. 10 [b]And the LORD's anger was kindled on that day, and he swore, saying, 11 'Surely none of the men who came up out of Egypt, [c]from twenty years old and upward, shall see the land that I swore to give [d]to Abraham, to Isaac, and to Jacob, because they have not wholly followed me, 12 none except Caleb the son of Jephunneh the [e]Kenizzite and Joshua the son of Nun, for [f]they have wholly followed the LORD.' 13 And the LORD's anger was kindled against Israel, and he made them [g]wander in the wilderness forty years, until [h]all the generation that had done evil in the sight of the LORD was gone. 14 And behold, you have risen in your fathers' place, a brood of sinful men, to increase still more the fierce anger of the LORD against Israel! 15 For if you [i]turn away from following him, he will again abandon them in the wilderness, and you will destroy all this people."

16 Then they came near to him and said, [j]"We will build sheepfolds here for our livestock, and cities for our little ones, 17 but [k]we will take up arms, ready to go before the people of Israel, until we have brought them to their place. And our little ones shall live in the fortified cities because of the inhabitants of the land. 18 [l]We will not return to our homes until each of the people of Israel has gained his inheritance. 19 For we will not inherit with

[1] A *shekel* was about 2/5 ounce or 11 grams

37[o] ver. 28 **41**[p] [ch. 18:8, 19] **47**[q] ver. 30 **48**[r] ver. 14 **50**[s] See Ex. 30:12 **53**[t] ver. 32; Deut. 20:14 **54**[u] Ex. 30:16 **Chapter 32** **1**[v] ver. 3, 35; See ch. 21:32 **3**[w] ver. 34 [x] ver. 34; See ch. 21:30 [y] ver. 38; ch. 33:47; Deut. 32:49; 1 Chr. 5:8; Isa. 15:2; 46:1; Jer. 48:1, 22 **4**[z] ch. 21:24, 34; [ver. 33] **8**[a] See ch. 13:3, 21-33; Deut. 1:22-28 **10**[b] For ver. 10-12, see Deut. 1:34-36 **11**[c] ch. 14:29 [d] See Gen. 50:24 **12**[e] Josh. 14:6; 15:17 [f] ch. 14:24; Deut. 1:36; Josh. 14:8, 9 **13**[g] See ch. 14:33-35 [h] ch. 26:64, 65 **15**[i] [Deut. 30:17; Josh. 22:16, 18; 2 Chr. 7:19, 20; 15:2] **16**[j] ver. 24 **17**[k] Josh. 4:12, 13 **18**[l] Josh. 22:4

them on the other side of the Jordan and
beyond, [m]because our inheritance has come
to us on this side of the Jordan to the east."
20 So [n]Moses said to them, "If you will do this,
if you will take up arms to go before the LORD
for the war, 21 and every armed man of you will
pass over the Jordan before the LORD, until he
has [o]driven out his enemies from before him
22 and the land is subdued before the LORD;
then after that you shall return and be free of
obligation to the LORD and to Israel, and [p]this
land shall be your possession before the LORD.
23 But if you will not do so, behold, you have
sinned against the LORD, and [q]be sure your
sin will find you out. 24 [r]Build cities for your
little ones and folds for your sheep, and do
what you have promised." 25 And the people of
Gad and the people of Reuben said to Moses,
"Your servants will do as my lord commands.
26 [s]Our little ones, our wives, our livestock, and
all our cattle shall remain there in the cities
of Gilead, 27 [t]but your servants will pass over,
every man who is [u]armed for war, before the
LORD to battle, as my lord orders."

28 So [v]Moses gave command concerning
them to Eleazar the priest and to [w]Joshua the
son of Nun and to the heads of the fathers'
houses of the tribes of the people of Israel.
29 And Moses said to them, "If the people of
Gad and the people of Reuben, every man
who is armed to battle before the LORD, will
pass with you over the Jordan and the land
shall be subdued before you, then you shall
give them the land of Gilead for a possession.
30 However, if they will not pass over with
you armed, they shall have possessions among
you in the land of Canaan." 31 And the people
of Gad and the people of Reuben answered,
"What the LORD has said to your servants, we
will do. 32 We will pass over armed before the
LORD into the land of Canaan, and the possession of our inheritance shall remain with
us beyond the Jordan."

33 And [x]Moses gave to them, to the people of
Gad and to the people of Reuben and to the
half-tribe of Manasseh the son of Joseph, the
kingdom of Sihon king of the Amorites and
the kingdom of Og king of Bashan, the land
and its cities with their territories, the cities
of the land throughout the country. 34 And
the people of Gad built [y]Dibon, [z]Ataroth,
[a]Aroer, 35 Atroth-shophan, [b]Jazer, Jogbehah,
36 [c]Beth-nimrah and Beth-haran, [d]fortified cities, and folds for sheep. 37 And the people of
Reuben built [e]Heshbon, [y]Elealeh, Kiriathaim,
38 [f]Nebo, and [g]Baal-meon ([h]their names were
changed), and [c]Sibmah. And they gave other
names to the cities that they built. 39 And the
sons of [i]Machir the son of Manasseh went to
Gilead and captured it, and dispossessed the
Amorites who were in it. 40 And Moses [j]gave
Gilead to Machir the son of Manasseh, and he
settled in it. 41 And [k]Jair the son of Manasseh
went and captured their villages, and called
them Havvoth-jair.[1] 42 And Nobah went and
captured Kenath and its villages, and called
it Nobah, after his own name.

Recounting Israel's Journey

33 These are the stages of the people
of Israel, when they went out of the
land of Egypt by their companies under
the leadership of Moses and Aaron. 2 Moses
wrote down their starting places, [l]stage by
stage, by command of the LORD, and these
are their stages according to their starting
places. 3 They [m]set out from Rameses in [n]the
first month, on the fifteenth day of the first
month. On the day after the Passover, the
people of Israel went out [o]triumphantly in
the sight of all the Egyptians, 4 while the
Egyptians were burying all their firstborn,
[p]whom the LORD had struck down among

[1] *Havvoth-jair* means *the villages of Jair*

33:1–49 Recounting the journey functions as Israel's testimony to the faithfulness of God, who led them as their Shepherd throughout the wilderness era—a fitting acknowledgment on the brink of entering the Promised Land. This backward glance at God's dealings in history served to bolster Israel's embrace of what God was about to do. Similarly, Matthew's Gospel begins with a genealogy summarizing the history of Israel as it culminated in Jesus Christ (Matt. 1:1–17). The church, including every Christian within her, continues the record of God's faithful providence, as he shepherds us by the hand of Christ to himself in eternal glory.

19 [m]ver. 33; Josh. 12:1; 13:8
20 [n]Deut. 3:18; Josh. 1:13, 14; 4:12, 13
21 [o]ch. 33:52
22 [p]Deut. 3:12, 15, 16, 18; Josh. 1:15; 13:8, 32; 22:4, 9
23 [q][Gen. 44:16; Isa. 59:12]
24 [r]ver. 16; See ver. 34-38
26 [s]Josh. 1:14
27 [t]Josh. 4:12, 13 [u]ch. 31:5
28 [v]Josh. 1:13 [w]ch. 27:18
33 [x]Deut. 29:8; Josh. 12:6; 13:8; 22:4; See Deut. 3:12-17 **34** [y]ver. 3 [z]ver. 3 [a]See Deut. 2:36 **35** [b]ver. 1; See ch. 21:32 **36** [c][ver. 3] [d]ver. 17 **37** [e]ver. 3; ch. 21:27 [y][See ver. 34 above]
38 [f]See ver. 3 [g][ver. 3; Josh. 13:17; Jer. 48:23] [h][Ex. 23:13; Josh. 23:7] [c][See ver. 36 above] **39** [i]Gen. 50:23; 1 Chr. 7:14, 15 **40** [j]Deut. 3:13, 15; Josh. 13:31; 17:1
41 [k]Deut. 3:14; See 1 Chr. 2:21-23 **Chapter 33** **2** [l]See ch. 9:17-23 **3** [m]Ex. 12:37 [n]Ex. 12:2; 13:4 [o]Ex. 14:8 **4** [p]Ex. 12:29

them. [q]On their gods also the LORD executed judgments.

5 So the people of Israel set out from Rameses and camped at [r]Succoth. 6 And they set out from Succoth and camped at [s]Etham, which is on the edge of the wilderness. 7 And they set out from Etham and turned back to [t]Pi-hahiroth, which is east of Baal-zephon, and they camped before Migdol. 8 And they set out from before Hahiroth[1] and [u]passed through the midst of the sea into the wilderness, and they [v]went a three days' journey in the wilderness of Etham and camped at Marah. 9 And they set out from Marah and came to [w]Elim; at Elim there were twelve springs of water and seventy palm trees, and they camped there. 10 And they set out from Elim and camped by the Red Sea. 11 And they set out from the Red Sea and camped in [x]the wilderness of Sin. 12 And they set out from the wilderness of Sin and camped at Dophkah. 13 And they set out from Dophkah and camped at Alush. 14 And they set out from Alush and camped at [y]Rephidim, where there was no water for the people to drink. 15 And they set out from Rephidim and camped in the [z]wilderness of Sinai. 16 And they set out from the wilderness of Sinai and camped at [a]Kibroth-hattaavah. 17 And they set out from Kibroth-hattaavah and camped at [b]Hazeroth. 18 And they [c]set out from Hazeroth and camped at Rithmah. 19 And they set out from Rithmah and camped at Rimmon-perez. 20 And they set out from Rimmon-perez and camped at Libnah. 21 And they set out from Libnah and camped at Rissah. 22 And they set out from Rissah and camped at Kehelathah. 23 And they set out from Kehelathah and camped at Mount Shepher. 24 And they set out from Mount Shepher and camped at Haradah. 25 And they set out from Haradah and camped at Makheloth. 26 And they set out from Makheloth and camped at Tahath. 27 And they set out from Tahath and camped at Terah. 28 And they set out from Terah and camped at Mithkah. 29 And they set out from Mithkah and camped at Hashmonah. 30 And they set out from Hashmonah and camped at Moseroth. 31 And they set out from Moseroth and camped at [d]Bene-jaakan. 32 And they set out from Bene-jaakan and camped at [e]Hor-haggidgad. 33 And they set out from Hor-haggidgad and camped at [e]Jotbathah. 34 And they set out from Jotbathah and camped at Abronah. 35 And they set out from Abronah and camped at [f]Ezion-geber. 36 And they set out from Ezion-geber and camped in the [g]wilderness of Zin (that is, Kadesh). 37 And they set out from [h]Kadesh and camped at [i]Mount Hor, on the edge of the land of Edom.

38 And Aaron the priest went up [j]Mount Hor at the command of the LORD and died there, in the fortieth year after the people of Israel had come out of the land of Egypt, on the first day of the fifth month. 39 And Aaron was [k]123 years old when he died on Mount Hor.

40 And [l]the Canaanite, the king of Arad, who lived in the Negeb in the land of Canaan, heard of the coming of the people of Israel.

41 And they set out from Mount Hor and camped at Zalmonah. 42 And they set out from Zalmonah and camped at Punon. 43 And they set out from Punon and camped at [m]Oboth. 44 And they set out from Oboth and camped at [n]Iye-abarim, in the territory of Moab. 45 And they set out from Iyim and camped at [o]Dibon-gad. 46 And they set out from Dibon-gad and camped at Almon-diblathaim. 47 And they set out from Almon-diblathaim [p]and camped in the mountains of Abarim, before Nebo. 48 And they set out from the mountains of Abarim and camped in [q]the plains of Moab by the Jordan at Jericho; 49 they camped by the Jordan from Beth-jeshimoth as far as [r]Abel-shittim in the plains of Moab.

Drive Out the Inhabitants

50 And the LORD spoke to Moses in the plains of Moab by the Jordan at Jericho, saying, 51 "Speak to the people of Israel and say to them, [s]When you pass over the Jordan into the land of Canaan, 52 then [t]you shall drive out [u]all the

[1] Some manuscripts and versions *Pi-hahiroth*

4[q] Ex. 12:12; [Isa. 19:1]
5[r] Ex. 12:37
6[s] Ex. 13:20
7[t] Ex. 14:2, 9
8[u] Ex. 14:22 [v] Ex. 15:22, 23
9[w] Ex. 15:27

33:50–34:29 In his amazing love, God gives his people something of a literary tour of the Promised Land (34:1–12), cleared of all wickedness and profanation (33:50–56), visually "tangible" features by which to stir their hearts for life beyond the wilderness. In much the same way, God gives us a symbolic survey of the measurements of the

11[x] Ex. 16:1 **14**[y] Ex. 17:1 **15**[z] Ex. 19:1, 2 **16**[a] ch. 11:34 **17**[b] ch. 11:35; 12:16 **18**[c] ch. 12:16 **31**[d] [Deut. 10:6] **32**[e] Deut. 10:7 **33**[e] [See ver. 32 above] **35**[f] Deut. 2:8; 1 Kgs. 9:26; 22:48; 2 Chr. 8:17 **36**[g] ch. 20:1; 27:14 **37**[h] ch. 20:1, 14, 22 [i] ch. 20:23; 21:4; 34:7, 8 **38**[j] ch. 20:25-28; Deut. 32:50; [Deut. 10:6] **39**[k] [Ex. 7:7] **40**[l] ch. 21:1 **43**[m] ch. 21:10 **44**[n] ch. 21:11 **45**[o] ch. 21:30; [ch. 32:34] **47**[p] Deut. 32:49 **48**[q] ch. 22:1 **49**[r] See ch. 25:1 **51**[s] Deut. 9:1; [Josh. 3:17] **52**[t] ch. 32:21 [u] Ex. 23:24, 33; 34:13; Deut. 7:2, 5; 12:3

inhabitants of the land from before you and destroy all their [v]figured stones and destroy all their metal images and demolish all their high places. 53 And you shall take possession of the land and settle in it, for I have given the land to you to possess it. 54 [w]You shall inherit the land by lot according to your clans. [x]To a large tribe you shall give a large inheritance, and to a small tribe you shall give a small inheritance. Wherever the lot falls for anyone, that shall be his. According to the tribes of your fathers you shall inherit. 55 But if you do not drive out the inhabitants of the land from before you, then those of them whom you let remain shall be as [y]barbs in your eyes and thorns in your sides, and they shall trouble you in the land where you dwell. 56 And I will do to you [z]as I thought to do to them."

Boundaries of the Land

34 The LORD spoke to Moses, saying, 2 "Command the people of Israel, and say to them, When you enter [a]the land of Canaan [b](this is the land that shall fall to you for an inheritance, the land of Canaan as defined by its borders), 3 [c]your south side shall be from the wilderness of Zin alongside Edom, and your southern border shall run from the end of [d]the Salt Sea on the east. 4 And your border shall turn south of [e]the ascent of Akrabbim, and cross to Zin, and its limit shall be south of Kadesh-barnea. Then it shall go on to [e]Hazar-addar, and pass along to Azmon. 5 And the border shall turn [f]from Azmon to [g]the Brook of Egypt, and its limit shall be at the sea.

6 "For the western border, you shall have the Great Sea and its[1] coast. This shall be your western border.

7 "This shall be your northern border: from the Great Sea you shall draw a line to [h]Mount Hor. 8 From Mount Hor you shall draw a line [i]to Lebo-hamath, and the limit of the border shall be at [j]Zedad. 9 Then the border shall extend to Ziphron, and its limit shall be at [k]Hazar-enan. This shall be your northern border.

10 "You shall draw a line for your eastern border from Hazar-enan to Shepham. 11 And the border shall go down from Shepham to [l]Riblah on the east side of Ain. And the border shall go down and reach to the shoulder of [m]the Sea of Chinnereth on the east. 12 And the border shall go down to the Jordan, and its limit shall be at [n]the Salt Sea. This shall be your land as defined by its borders all around."

13 Moses commanded the people of Israel, saying, [o]"This is the land that you shall inherit by lot, which the LORD has commanded to give to the nine tribes and to the half-tribe. 14 [p]For the tribe of the people of Reuben by fathers' houses and the tribe of the people of Gad by their fathers' houses have received their inheritance, and also the half-tribe of Manasseh. 15 The two tribes and the half-tribe have received their inheritance beyond the Jordan east of Jericho, toward the sunrise."

List of Tribal Chiefs

16 The LORD spoke to Moses, saying, 17 "These are the names of the men who shall divide the land to you for inheritance: [q]Eleazar the priest and Joshua the son of Nun. 18 You shall take one [r]chief from every tribe to divide the land for inheritance. 19 These are the names of the men: Of the tribe of Judah, Caleb the son of Jephunneh. 20 Of the tribe of the people of Simeon, Shemuel the son of Ammihud. 21 Of the tribe of Benjamin, Elidad the son of Chislon. 22 Of the tribe of the people of Dan a chief, Bukki the son of Jogli. 23 Of the people of Joseph: of the tribe of the people of Manasseh a chief, Hanniel the son of Ephod. 24 And of the tribe of the people of Ephraim a chief, Kemuel the son of Shiphtan. 25 Of the tribe of the people of Zebulun a chief, Elizaphan the son of Parnach. 26 Of the tribe of the people of Issachar a chief, Paltiel the son of Azzan. 27 And of the tribe of the people of Asher a chief, Ahihud the son of Shelomi. 28 Of the tribe of the people of Naphtali a chief, Pedahel the son of Ammihud. 29 These are the men whom the

[1] Syriac; Hebrew lacks *its*

new Jerusalem (Rev. 21:9–22:5), cleared of all wickedness and profanation (Rev. 21:8). This glimpse of the new heaven and earth stirs our hearts to seek those things above, where Christ is (Col. 3:1), as we persevere through this wilderness age. Indeed, our citizenship is in the heavenly Jerusalem (Phil. 3:20).

52 [v] Lev. 26:1
54 [w] ch. 26:53, 55 [x] ch. 26:54; 35:8
55 [y] Josh. 23:13; Judg. 2:3; Ps. 106:34, 36
56 [z] [Deut. 28:63]

Chapter 34 **2** [a] Gen. 17:8; Ex. 3:8; Ps. 105:11 [b] ver. 13 **3** [c] Josh. 15:1; See Gen. 15:18-21; Ezek. 47:13-21 [d] ver. 12; Gen. 14:3; Josh. 15:2 **4** [e] Josh. 15:3 **5** [f] Josh. 15:4 [g] Gen. 15:18; Josh. 15:4, 47; 1 Kgs. 8:65; 2 Kgs. 24:7; 1 Chr. 13:5; 2 Chr. 7:8; Isa. 27:12 **7** [h] ch. 33:37 **8** [i] ch. 13:21; 2 Kgs. 14:25; Ezek. 48:1 [j] Ezek. 47:15 **9** [k] Ezek. 47:17 **11** [l] 2 Kgs. 23:33; Jer. 39:5 [m] Deut. 3:17; Josh. 11:2; 12:3; 19:35; Matt. 4:18; Luke 5:1 **12** [n] ver. 3 **13** [o] ver. 2; Josh. 14:1, 2 **14** [p] ch. 32:33; Josh. 14:3 **17** [q] Josh. 14:1; 19:51 **18** [r] ch. 1:4, 16

LORD commanded to divide the inheritance for the people of Israel in the land of Canaan."

Cities for the Levites

35 The LORD spoke to Moses in [s]the plains of Moab by the Jordan at Jericho, saying, 2 [t]"Command the people of Israel to give to the Levites some of the inheritance of their possession as cities for them to dwell in. And you shall give to the Levites pasturelands around the cities. 3 The cities shall be theirs to dwell in, and their pasturelands shall be for their cattle and for their livestock and for all their beasts. 4 The pasturelands of the cities, which you shall give to the Levites, shall reach from the wall of the city outward a thousand cubits[1] all around. 5 And you shall measure, outside the city, on the east side two thousand cubits, and on the south side two thousand cubits, and on the west side two thousand cubits, and on the north side two thousand cubits, the city being in the middle. This shall belong to them as pastureland for their cities.

6 "The cities that you give to the Levites shall be [u]the six cities of refuge, where you shall permit the manslayer to flee, and in addition to them you shall give forty-two cities. 7 All the cities that you give to the Levites shall be [v]forty-eight, with their pasturelands. 8 And as for the cities that you shall give [w]from the possession of the people of Israel, [x]from the larger tribes you shall take many, and from the smaller tribes you shall take few; each, in proportion to the inheritance that it inherits, shall give of its cities to the Levites."

Cities of Refuge

9 And the LORD spoke to Moses, saying, 10 "Speak to the people of Israel and say to them, [y]When you cross the Jordan into the land of Canaan, 11 [z]then you shall select cities to be cities of refuge for you, that the manslayer who kills any person without intent may flee there. 12 The cities shall be for you a refuge from the avenger, that the manslayer may not die until he stands before the congregation for judgment. 13 And the cities that you give shall be your [a]six cities of refuge. 14 [b]You shall give three cities beyond the Jordan, and three cities in the land of Canaan, to be cities of refuge. 15 These six cities shall be for refuge for the people of Israel, and [c]for the stranger and for the sojourner among them, that anyone who kills any person without intent may flee there.

16 [d]"But if he struck him down with an iron object, so that he died, he is a murderer. The murderer shall be put to death. 17 And if he struck him down with a stone tool that could cause death, and he died, he is a murderer. The murderer shall be put to death. 18 Or if he struck him down with a wooden tool that could cause death, and he died, he is a murderer. The murderer shall be put to death. 19 [e]The avenger of blood shall himself put the murderer to death; when he meets him, he shall put him to death. 20 And if he pushed him out of hatred or hurled something at him, [f]lying in wait, so that he died, 21 or in enmity struck him down with his hand, so that he died, then he who struck the blow shall be put to death. He is a murderer. [e]The avenger of blood shall put the murderer to death when he meets him.

22 "But if he pushed him suddenly without enmity, or hurled anything on him [g]without lying in wait 23 or used a stone that could cause death, and without seeing him dropped it on him, so that he died, though he was not his enemy and did not seek his harm, 24 then [h]the congregation shall judge between the manslayer and [e]the avenger of blood, in accordance

[1] A *cubit* was about 18 inches or 45 centimeters

Chapter 35
1 [s]See ch. 22:1
2 [t]Josh. 14:3, 4; 21:2; See Ezek. 45:1-5; 48:8-14
6 [u]ver. 13; Deut. 4:41, 42; Josh. 20:2, 7, 8; 21:3, 13, 21, 27, 32, 36, 38
7 [v]Josh. 21:41
8 [w]Josh. 21:3 [x]ch. 26:54; 33:54
10 [y]For ver. 10-12, see Deut. 19:2-4; Josh. 20:2-6
11 [z]Ex. 21:13
13 [a]See ver. 6
14 [b]Deut. 4:41; Josh. 20:8
15 [c]ch. 15:16

35:1–34 The Levites received no land inheritance, as the Lord himself was their inheritance. Therefore, every tribe was to allot cities within their various territories for the Levites (vv. 1–8), some of which were also to be designated as cities of refuge for those guilty of unpremeditated murder (vv. 9–34). Like salt, the Levites were thus sprinkled about the Promised Land as a reminder to the rest of God's people of their high and holy calling, that the Lord was their refuge, and that, ultimately, all land belonged to the Lord who dwelled in their midst (v. 34).

Knowing that, through Christ, God himself is our inheritance, we, like the Levites of old, live *in* this world without being *of* it. We are looking rather for the city of God to come in the new creation (Hebrews 11). There the Lord God himself will dwell in our midst (Rev. 21:22–22:5).

16 [d]Ex. 21:12, 14; Lev. 24:17; Deut. 19:11, 12 **19** [e]Deut. 19:6, 12; Josh. 20:3, 5 **20** [f]Ex. 21:14; Deut. 19:11 **21** [e][See ver. 19 above] **22** [g]Ex. 21:13 **24** [h]ver. 12; Josh. 20:6 [e][See ver. 19 above]

with these rules. 25 And the congregation shall
rescue the manslayer from the hand of the
avenger of blood, and the congregation shall
restore him to his city of refuge to which he
had fled, and he shall live in it [i]until the death
of the high priest [j]who was anointed with the
holy oil. 26 But if the manslayer shall at any
time go beyond the boundaries of his city of
refuge to which he fled, 27 and [e]the avenger of
blood finds him outside the boundaries of his
city of refuge, and the avenger of blood kills
the manslayer, he shall not be guilty of blood.
28 For he must remain in his city of refuge
[i]until the death of the high priest, but after
the death of the high priest the manslayer may
return to the land of his possession. 29 And
these things shall be for [k]a statute and rule for
you throughout your generations in all your
dwelling places.

30 "If anyone kills a person, the murderer
shall be put to death on the [l]evidence of witnesses. But no person shall be put to death on
the testimony of one witness. 31 Moreover, you
shall accept no ransom for the life of a murderer, who is guilty of death, but he shall be
put to death. 32 And you shall accept no ransom for him who has fled to his city of refuge,
that he may return to dwell in the land before
the death of the high priest. 33 You shall not
[m]pollute the land in which you live, for blood
[m]pollutes the land, and no atonement can be
made for the land for the blood that is shed in
it, except [n]by the blood of the one who shed it.
34 [o]You shall not defile the land in which you
live, in the midst of which I dwell, [p]for I the
LORD dwell in the midst of the people of Israel."

Marriage of Female Heirs

36 The heads of the fathers' houses of the
clan of the [q]people of Gilead the son of
Machir, son of Manasseh, from the clans of the
people of Joseph, came near and spoke before
Moses and before the chiefs, the heads of the
fathers' houses of the people of Israel. 2 They
said, [r]"The LORD commanded my lord to give
the land for inheritance by lot to the people of
Israel, and [s]my lord was commanded by the
LORD to give the inheritance of Zelophehad
our brother to his daughters. 3 But if they are
married to any of the sons of the other tribes
of the people of Israel, then their inheritance
will be taken from the inheritance of our
fathers and added to the inheritance of the
tribe into which they marry. So it will be taken
away from the lot of our inheritance. 4 And
when [t]the jubilee of the people of Israel comes,
then their inheritance will be added to the
inheritance of the tribe into which they marry,
and their inheritance will be taken from the
inheritance of the tribe of our fathers."

5 And Moses commanded the people of Israel
according to the word of the LORD, saying,
"The tribe of the people of Joseph [u]is right.
6 This is what the LORD commands concerning
the daughters of Zelophehad: 'Let them marry
whom they think best, [v]only they shall marry
within the clan of the tribe of their father. 7 The
inheritance of the people of Israel shall not be
transferred from one tribe to another, for every
one of the people of Israel [w]shall hold on to the
inheritance of the tribe of his fathers. 8 And
[x]every daughter who possesses an inheritance
in any tribe of the people of Israel shall be wife

35:25 The high priest's last act of atonement was his own death, bearing the bloodguilt of accidental manslaughter away so that the one who killed without intent was finally freed to leave the city of refuge and return home. This law is significant inasmuch as Moses' death appears to reflect something of this pattern in Deuteronomy: God's people cannot enter the Promised Land until after he dies (Deut. 3:25–28; 34:1–5). Even more meaningful for us, Jesus Christ the Mediator and High Priest of the new covenant ushers us into the heavenly presence of God, ultimately in the new creation, through his atoning death on the cross (Heb. 10:19–22). Every moment of our lives in the land of glory will be but the fruit of the shed blood of Christ's death on our behalf, and so will be lived in praise of him (Rev. 5:11–14; 21:27).

36:1–13 This is the second episode with the daughters of Zelophehad, bracketing the final major section of Numbers (27:1–10; 36:1–13). This passage functions not only as another assurance that entry into the Promised Land is imminent; it functions primarily to underscore that this land inheritance will be a lasting inheritance for the people of God—not to be transferred (v. 9). This is a fitting note with which to conclude a book about life in the wilderness. When finally we exit the wilderness of this age and enter into the joys of the Promised Land, those joys amid the presence of God, his angels, and his people will last forever and ever (Rom. 6:23; John 3:16; Rev. 22:17).

25 [i] Josh. 20:6 [j] Ex. 29:7; Lev. 4:3; 21:10
27 [e] [See ver. 19 above]
28 [i] [See ver. 25 above]
29 [k] ch. 27:11
30 [l] Deut. 17:6; 19:15; Heb. 10:28; [Matt. 18:16; John 8:17; 2 Cor. 13:1; 1 Tim. 5:19]
33 [m] Ps. 106:38; Jer. 3:1, 2, 9; [Mic. 4:11] [n] See Gen. 9:6
34 [o] Lev. 18:25; Deut. 21:23 [p] See Ex. 29:45

Chapter 36
1 [q] ch. 26:29
2 [r] ch. 26:55; 33:54 [s] ch. 27:1, 7; Josh. 17:3, 4
4 [t] Lev. 25:10
5 [u] [ch. 27:7]
6 [v] ver. 12
7 [w] [1 Kgs. 21:3]
8 [x] 1 Chr. 23:22

to one of the clan of the tribe of her father,
so that every one of the people of Israel may
possess the inheritance of his fathers. 9 So no
inheritance shall be transferred from one tribe
to another, for each of the tribes of the people
of Israel shall hold on to its own inheritance.'"
10 The daughters of Zelophehad did as the
LORD commanded Moses, 11 [y]for Mahlah,
Tirzah, Hoglah, Milcah, and Noah, the daughters of Zelophehad, were married to sons of
their father's brothers. 12 They were married
into the clans of the people of Manasseh the
son of Joseph, and their inheritance remained
in the tribe of their father's clan.

13 These are the commandments and the
rules that the LORD commanded through
Moses to the people of Israel [z]in the plains of
Moab by the Jordan at Jericho.

11[y] ch. 27:1; Josh. 17:3 **13**[z] See ch. 22:1

Introduction to Deuteronomy

Author

Deuteronomy, the final book in the Pentateuch, contains Moses' last three sermons and two prophetic poems about Israel's future.

The Gospel in Deuteronomy

Deuteronomy is clearly one of the most important books in the Old Testament. First, Jesus quoted the book of Deuteronomy more than any other book in the Old Testament. Second, Jesus used the book of Deuteronomy in his own life more than any other book in the Old Testament. For example, Jesus answered all three of his temptations in the wilderness with quotations from the book of Deuteronomy (Luke 4:1–13). Since the person of Jesus is at the very heart of the gospel and Deuteronomy was so important in his life, it should therefore not be hard to find the gospel in this last book of Moses' Pentateuch.

We can see the gospel in the overall structure of the book of Deuteronomy. While it is true that the majority of the book and the center of the book are occupied with laws (chs. 5–26) and the consequences of keeping or breaking those laws (chs. 27–30), this "law" section is surrounded by grace. The first four chapters are in effect an account of how gracious God has been to Israel in the past. So, God's grace in the past serves as the context and motivation for Israel's keeping the law. Likewise, the last four chapters are in effect an account of how gracious God will be to Israel in the future. So also, God's grace in the future serves as the context and motivation for Israel's keeping the law. Thus, in the book of Deuteronomy, the law is surrounded by grace, and keeping the law is a response to grace received and anticipated.

We can also see the gospel within the central section of the book of Deuteronomy. The notes that follow will repeatedly show how keeping the law in the book of Deuteronomy is a response to God's grace and not a means to earn God's favor. This truth is articulated nowhere more clearly than in the Ten Commandments (Deuteronomy 5), where all of the commandments are rooted in God's gracious redemption.

The apostle Paul certainly saw the gospel in the book of Deuteronomy. In his letter to the Romans, for example, Paul drew on Deuteronomy to teach that the law reveals sin (Rom. 7:7), that righteousness is by faith (Rom. 10:6–8, 19 [Deut. 30:12–14]), that a circumcision of the heart is necessary for true obedience (Rom. 2:29 [Deut. 30:6]), that keeping the law is the way to love one's neighbor (Rom. 13:9 [Deut. 5:17–19, 21]), that we should not seek personal revenge (Rom. 12:19 [Deut. 32:35]), and that we should expect Gentiles to be added to an originally all-Jewish people of God (Rom. 15:10 [Deut. 32:43]).

Finally, Jesus saw the gospel in the book of Deuteronomy. This is revealed not only in that he quoted extensively from Deuteronomy and used it in his own life, but also in that he reflected theologically on Deuteronomy. When asked, "Which commandment is the most important of all?" (Mark 12:28), Jesus answered by including a quote from Deuteronomy 6:4–5: "The most important is, 'Hear, O Israel: The Lord our God, the Lord is one. And you shall love the Lord your God with all your heart and with all your soul and with all your mind and with all your strength'" (Mark 12:30). Jesus taught that we love God because of who he is, "the Lord our God." We love him by keeping his commandments because he is our God; he is not our God because we love him by keeping his commandments. That is grace. It is gospel. And because we have received this grace, we keep the second greatest commandment, "you shall love your neighbor as yourself" (Mark 12:31). We love because he loved (1 John 4:19). We extend grace because he extended grace.

Outline

I. Prologue (1:1–5)

II. Moses' First Speech: Historical Prologue (1:6–4:43)

III. Moses' Second Speech: General Covenant Stipulations (4:44–11:32)

IV. Moses' Second Speech: Specific Covenant Stipulations (12:1–26:19)

V. Moses' Third Speech: Blessings and Curses (27:1–28:68)

VI. Moses' Third Speech: Final Exhortation (29:1–30:20)

VII. Succession of Leadership (31:1–34:12)

Deuteronomy

The Command to Leave Horeb

1 These are the words that Moses spoke to all
Israel beyond the Jordan in the wilderness,
in [a]the Arabah opposite [b]Suph, between [c]Paran
and Tophel, Laban, Hazeroth, and Dizahab.
2 It is eleven days' journey from Horeb by the
way of Mount Seir to [d]Kadesh-barnea. 3 [e]In the
fortieth year, on the first day of the eleventh
month, Moses spoke to the people of Israel
according to all that the LORD had given him
in commandment to them, 4 after [f]he had
defeated Sihon the king of the Amorites, who
lived in Heshbon, and [g]Og the king of Bashan,
who lived in Ashtaroth and in [h]Edrei. 5 Beyond
the Jordan, [i]in the land of Moab, Moses undertook to explain this law, saying, 6 "The LORD
our God said to us in Horeb, [j]'You have stayed
long enough at this mountain. 7 Turn and take
your journey, and go to [k]the hill country of the
Amorites and to all their neighbors in [a]the
Arabah, [l]in the hill country and in the lowland
and in the Negeb and [l]by the seacoast, the land
of the Canaanites, and Lebanon, as far as the
great river, the river Euphrates. 8 See, I have
set the land before you. Go in and take possession of the land that the LORD swore to your
fathers, [m]to Abraham, to Isaac, and to Jacob, to
give to them and to their offspring after them.'

Leaders Appointed

9 "At that time [n]I said to you, 'I am not able to
bear you by myself. 10 The LORD your God has
multiplied you, and behold, [o]you are today as
numerous as the stars of heaven. 11 [p]May the
LORD, the God of your fathers, make you a
thousand times as many as you are and bless
you, [q]as he has promised you! 12 [r]How can
I bear by myself the weight and burden of
you and your strife? 13 [s]Choose for your tribes
wise, understanding, and experienced men,
and I will appoint them as your heads.' 14 And
you answered me, 'The thing that you have
spoken is good for us to do.' 15 So I took the
heads of your tribes, wise and experienced
men, [t]and set them as heads over you, commanders of thousands, commanders of hundreds, commanders of fifties, commanders
of tens, and officers, throughout your tribes.
16 And I charged your judges at that time, 'Hear
the cases between your brothers, and [u]judge
righteously between a man and his brother or
the alien who is with him. 17 [v]You shall not be

1:1–8 In Jewish (Hebrew) tradition Deuteronomy is called "Words." The name "Deuteronomy" comes from the later Greek title, meaning "second law," since the book contains a repeat of much that Moses revealed earlier in the Pentateuch. Deuteronomy opens with a reference to the "words that Moses spoke" (v. 1), the words "that the LORD had given him" (v. 3), and the words that "Moses undertook to explain" (v. 5). From the beginning, God graciously spoke redemptive words to fallen humanity (Gen. 3:15). Those words included God's promise to bless humanity through Abraham and his descendants (Gen. 12:1–3). Some 400 years later God fulfilled the word spoken to Abraham when Moses said, "Go in and take possession of the land that the LORD swore to your fathers" (Deut. 1:8).

Some 1,400 years after that, God spoke the ultimate redemptive word "by his Son," who is "heir of all things," as the One who "upholds the universe by the word of his power" and has made "purification for sins" (Heb. 1:1–4).

Since God has spoken this ultimate word of redemptive grace "by his Son," let us "pay much closer attention to what we have heard," so that we do not neglect God's "great salvation" (Heb. 2:1–3).

Chapter 1
1 [a]ch. 3:17 [b][Num. 21:14] [c]1 Sam. 25:1
2 [d]ch. 2:14; 9:23; Num. 13:26; 32:8; 34:4
3 [e][Num. 33:38]
4 [f]See Num. 21:21-32 [g]See Num. 21:33-35 [h]ch. 3:1, 10; Josh. 12:4; 13:12
5 [i]ch. 29:1
6 [j]ch. 2:3; [Ex. 19:1; Num. 10:11]
7 [k][Num. 13:29] [a][See ver. 1 above] [l]Josh. 9:1
8 [m]Gen. 12:7; 13:14, 15; 15:18; 17:7, 8; 26:3, 4; 28:13, 14; 50:24
9 [n]Num. 11:14; [Ex. 18:18]
10 [o][ch. 10:22; 28:62]; See Gen. 15:5
11 [p][2 Sam. 24:3] [q]Gen. 12:2; 22:17; 26:3, 24
12 [r][1 Kgs. 3:8, 9]
13 [s][Ex. 18:21; Num. 11:16, 17]

15 [t]Ex. 18:25 **16** [u]ch. 16:18; John 7:24 **17** [v]ch. 16:19; Ex. 23:2, 3; Lev. 19:15; 2 Chr. 19:7; Prov. 24:23; 28:21; Mal. 2:9; James 2:1, 9

partial in judgment. You shall hear the small
and the great alike. You shall not be intimidated by anyone, for [w]the judgment is God's.
And the case that is too hard for you, you shall
[x]bring to me, and I will hear it.' 18 And I commanded you at that time all the things that
you should do.

Israel's Refusal to Enter the Land

19 "Then we set out from Horeb and [y]went
through all that great and terrifying wilderness that you saw, on the way to the hill
country of the Amorites, as the LORD our God
commanded us. And [z]we came to Kadesh-
barnea. 20 And I said to you, 'You have come
to the hill country of the Amorites, which the
LORD our God is giving us. 21 See, the LORD
your God has set the land before you. Go up,
take possession, as the LORD, the God of your
fathers, has told you. [a]Do not fear or be dismayed.' 22 Then all of you came near me and
said, 'Let us send men before us, that they
may explore the land for us and bring us
word again of the way by which we must go
up and the cities into which we shall come.'
23 The thing seemed good to me, and [b]I took
twelve men from you, one man from each
tribe. 24 And [c]they turned and went up into
the hill country, and came to the Valley of
Eshcol and spied it out. 25 And they took in
their hands some of the fruit of the land and
brought it down to us, and brought us word
again and said, 'It is a good land that the LORD
our God is giving us.'

26 "Yet you would not go up, but rebelled
against the command of the LORD your God.
27 And [d]you murmured in your tents and said,
'Because the LORD [e]hated us he has brought
us out of the land of Egypt, [f]to give us into the
hand of the Amorites, to destroy us. 28 Where
are we going up? [g]Our brothers have made our
hearts melt, saying, [h]"The people are greater
and taller than we. The cities are great and fortified up to heaven. And besides, we have seen
[i]the sons of the Anakim there."' 29 Then I said
to you, 'Do not be in dread or afraid of them.
30 The LORD your God who goes before you
[j]will himself fight for you, just as he did for
you in Egypt before your eyes, 31 and in the wilderness, where you have seen how the LORD
your God [k]carried you, as a man carries his
son, all the way that you went until you came
to this place.' 32 Yet in spite of this word [l]you
did not believe the LORD your God, 33 [m]who
went before you in the way [n]to seek you out a
place to pitch your tents, in fire by night and
in the cloud by day, to show you by what way
you should go.

The Penalty for Israel's Rebellion

34 "And the LORD heard your words and
was angered, and he swore, 35 [o]'Not one of
these men of this evil generation shall see the
good land that I swore to give to your fathers,
36 [p]except Caleb the son of Jephunneh. He shall
see it, and to him and to his children I will give
the land on which he has trodden, because he
has wholly followed the LORD!' 37 Even with
me [q]the LORD was angry on your account and
said, 'You also shall not go in there. 38 [r]Joshua
the son of Nun, [r]who stands before you, he
shall enter. [s]Encourage him, for he shall cause
Israel to inherit it. 39 And as for [t]your little
ones, who you said would become a prey, and
your children, who today [u]have no knowledge
of good or evil, they shall go in there. And to
them I will give it, and they shall possess it.
40 But as for you, [v]turn, and journey into the
wilderness in the direction of the Red Sea.'
41 "Then you answered me, [w]'We have sinned

17[w] 2 Chr. 19:6; [Ex. 21:6] [x] Ex. 18:22, 26
19[y] ch. 8:15; 32:10; Jer. 2:6; [Num. 10:12] [z] See ver. 2
21[a] ch. 31:8; Josh. 1:9
23[b] Num. 13:3
24[c] See Num. 13:22-27
27[d] Ps. 106:25; See Num. 14:1-4 [e] ch. 9:28 [f] [Josh. 7:7]
28[g] Josh. 14:8 [h] ch. 9:1, 2; See Num. 13:28-33 [i] See Num. 13:22
30[j] ch. 3:22; Ex. 14:14, 25; Josh. 10:14, 42; 23:3, 10; [Neh. 4:20]
31[k] ch. 32:11, 12; Ex. 19:4; Isa. 46:3, 4; 63:9; Hos. 11:3
32[l] Ps. 106:24; Jude 5

1:19–46 Israel knew that God was bringing them into a "good land" (v. 25), that God had graciously cared for them in the wilderness (v. 31), and that he had promised to fight for them against the Canaanites just as he had fought against the Egyptians (v. 30). Yet they did not respond to God's grace with faith (v. 32). Their unbelief led them to conclude that God hated them and was intent on destroying them (v. 27), and this resulted in their failure to enter the "good land" (v. 35).

But all was not lost. There was one, Caleb, who "wholly followed the LORD" (v. 36; see Num. 14:24 and Josh. 14:14). Had God's people believed God's word and followed this devoted leader, they would have inherited the promise. Here the Holy Spirit instructs us to know the testimony of God's grace recorded in his Word, to embrace that grace by faith, and to follow our devoted Leader into our eternal inheritance (Heb. 12:1–3).

33[m] See Ex. 13:21 [n] Num. 10:33 **35**[o] See ch. 2:15; Num. 14:20-30 **36**[p] Num. 14:30; Josh. 14:9 **37**[q] ch. 4:21; 32:51; 34:4; Num. 20:12; 27:13, 14; [Ps. 106:32]
38[r] ch. 31:3, 7; Ex. 24:13; [1 Sam. 16:22] [s] ch. 31:7, 23; Num. 27:18-20 **39**[t] Num. 14:3, 31 [u] Isa. 7:15, 16 **40**[v] ch. 2:1; Num. 14:25 **41**[w] Num. 14:40

against the LORD. We ourselves will go up and
fight, just as the LORD our God commanded
us.' And every one of you fastened on his weapons of war and thought it easy to go up into
the hill country. 42 And the LORD said to me,
[x]'Say to them, Do not go up or fight, [y]for I am
not in your midst, lest you be defeated before
your enemies.' 43 So I spoke to you, and you
would not listen; but you rebelled against the
command of the LORD and [z]presumptuously
went up into the hill country. 44 [a]Then the
Amorites who lived in that hill country came
out against you and chased you [b]as bees do and
beat you down in Seir as far as [c]Hormah. 45 And
you returned and wept before the LORD, but
the LORD did not listen to your voice or give
ear to you. 46 So [d]you remained at Kadesh many
days, the days that you remained there.

The Wilderness Years

2 "Then we turned and journeyed into the
wilderness in the direction of the Red Sea,
[e]as the LORD told me. And for many days we
traveled around Mount Seir. 2 Then the LORD
said to me, 3 'You have been traveling around
this mountain country [f]long enough. Turn
northward 4 and command the people, "You
are about to pass through the territory of
[g]your brothers, the people of Esau, [h]who live
in Seir; and [i]they will be afraid of you. So be
very careful. 5 Do not contend with them, for
I will not give you any of their land, no, not
so much as for the sole of the foot to tread on,
because [h]I have given Mount Seir to Esau as
a possession. 6 [j]You shall purchase food from
them with money, that you may eat, and you
shall also buy water from them with money,
that you may drink. 7 For the LORD your
God has blessed you in all the work of your
hands. [k]He knows your going through this
great wilderness. [l]These forty years the LORD
your God has been with you. You have lacked
nothing."' 8 So [m]we went on, away from our
brothers, the people of Esau, who live in Seir,
away from [n]the Arabah road from [o]Elath and
[p]Ezion-geber.

"And we turned and went in the direction
of the wilderness of Moab. 9 And the LORD
said to me, [q]'Do not harass Moab or contend
with them in battle, for I will not give you any
of their land for a possession, because I have
given [r]Ar to [s]the people of Lot for a possession.'
10 ([t]The Emim formerly lived there, [u]a people
great and many, and tall [v]as the Anakim.
11 Like the Anakim they are also counted as
[w]Rephaim, but the Moabites call them Emim.
12 [x]The Horites also lived in Seir formerly, but
the people of Esau dispossessed them and
destroyed them from before them and settled
in their place, [y]as Israel did to the land of their
possession, which the LORD gave to them.)
13 'Now rise up and go over [z]the brook Zered.'
So we went over [z]the brook Zered. 14 And the
time from our leaving [a]Kadesh-barnea until
we crossed [b]the brook Zered was thirty-eight
years, [c]until the entire generation, that is, the
men of war, had perished from the camp, as
the LORD had sworn to them. 15 For indeed the
hand of the LORD was against them, to destroy
them from the camp, until they had perished.

16 "So as soon as all the men of war had perished and were dead from among the people,
17 the LORD said to me, 18 'Today you are to
cross the border of Moab at Ar. 19 And when
you approach the territory of the people of
Ammon, [d]do not harass them or contend
with them, for I will not give you any of the
land of the people of Ammon as a possession,
because I have given it to [e]the sons of Lot for

2:1–25 The recitation of covenant history in Deuteronomy 1–4 is a means to an end. The end is motivation to live by the teachings found in Deuteronomy 5–26. The means is reminding the covenant people of the grace that God had granted them in the past by his promises, provision, and deliverance. Deuteronomy 2:1–25 exemplifies such motivational history, as it reminds the covenant people how God had blessed them in the wilderness—so that they lacked nothing (v. 7)—and how God had begun to grant them their inheritance in the Promised Land (vv. 24–25).

As in the old covenant, so in the new covenant, obedience to God's teachings is always to be motivated by what God has graciously done for us in the past, whether that is in redemptive history or in our own personal history. Ultimately, Jesus and his work on our behalf is the supreme instance and ultimate portrait of the gracious nature of God revealed in these opening sections of Deuteronomy (Eph. 5:1–2).

42[x] Num. 14:42 [y] [ch. 31:17]
43[z] Num. 14:44
44[a] Num. 14:45 [b] [Ps. 118:12; Isa. 7:18] [c] See Num. 21:3
46[d] Num. 20:1, 22; Judg. 11:17

Chapter 2
1[e] ch. 1:40; Num. 14:25
3[f] ch. 1:6
4[g] ch. 23:7; Amos 1:11; Obad. 10, 12 [h] See Gen. 32:3 [i] See Num. 20:18-21
5[h] [See ver. 4 above]
6[j] ver. 28
7[k] [Job 23:10] [l] See ch. 8:2-4
8[m] Judg. 11:18 [n] See ch. 1:1 [o] 1 Kgs. 9:26; [2 Kgs. 14:22; 16:6; 2 Chr. 26:2] [p] See Num. 33:35

9[q] ver. 19, 29 [r] ver. 18; Num. 21:15; Isa. 15:1 [s] ver. 19; Gen. 19:36, 37 **10**[t] Gen. 14:5 [u] [ver. 21] [v] See Num. 13:22 **11**[w] See Gen. 14:5 **12**[x] ver. 22; Gen. 14:6; See Gen. 36:20-30 [y] Num. 21:24, 31, 35 **13**[z] [Num. 21:12] **14**[a] See ch. 1:2, 19 [b] [Num. 21:12] [c] Num. 14:33, 35; 26:64; Ps. 78:33; 95:11; 106:26; Ezek. 20:15; [1 Cor. 10:5; Heb. 3:17]; See ch. 1:35 **19**[d] [ver. 9] [e] Gen. 19:36, 38

a possession.' 20 (It is also counted as a land of
[f]Rephaim. Rephaim formerly lived there—
but the Ammonites call them Zamzummim—
21 [g]a people great and many, and tall as the
Anakim; but the LORD destroyed them before
the Ammonites,[1] and they dispossessed them
and settled in their place, 22 as he did for the
people of Esau, who live in Seir, when he
destroyed [h]the Horites before them and they
dispossessed them and settled in their place
even to this day. 23 As for [i]the Avvim, who lived
in villages as far as [j]Gaza, [k]the Caphtorim, who
came from Caphtor, destroyed them and settled in their place.) 24 'Rise up, set out on your
journey and [l]go over the Valley of the Arnon.
Behold, I have given into your hand Sihon
the Amorite, king of [m]Heshbon, and his land.
Begin to take possession, and [n]contend with
him in battle. 25 This day I will begin to put
[o]the dread and fear of you on the peoples who
are under the whole heaven, who shall hear
the report of you and shall tremble and be in
anguish because of you.'

The Defeat of King Sihon

26 "So I sent messengers from the wilderness
of [p]Kedemoth to Sihon the king of [m]Heshbon,
[q]with words of peace, saying, 27 [r]'Let me pass
through your land. I will go only by the road;
I will turn aside neither to the right nor to the
left. 28 [s]You shall sell me food for money, that
I may eat, and give me water for money, that
I may drink. Only let me pass through on foot,
29 [t]as the sons of Esau who live in Seir and the
Moabites who live in Ar did for me, until I go
over the Jordan into the land that the LORD
our God is giving to us.' 30 But [u]Sihon the king
of [m]Heshbon would not let us pass by him, for
the LORD your God [v]hardened his spirit and
made his heart obstinate, that he might give
him into your hand, as he is this day. 31 And
the LORD said to me, 'Behold, I have begun to
give Sihon and his land over to you. Begin to
take possession, that you may occupy his land.'
32 Then [w]Sihon came out against us, he and
all his people, to battle at Jahaz. 33 And [x]the
LORD our God gave him over to us, and [y]we
defeated him and his sons and all his people.
34 And we captured all his cities at that time
and devoted to destruction[2] every [z]city, men,
women, and children. We left no survivors.
35 Only the livestock we took as spoil for ourselves, with the plunder of the cities that we
captured. 36 [a]From Aroer, which is on the edge
of the Valley of the Arnon, and from [b]the city
that is in the valley, as far as Gilead, there was
not a city too high for us. [c]The LORD our God
gave all into our hands. 37 Only to the land of
the sons of Ammon you did not draw near,
that is, to all the banks of the river [d]Jabbok
and the cities of the hill country, whatever the
LORD our God had forbidden us.

The Defeat of King Og

3 "Then we turned and went up the way to
Bashan. And [e]Og the king of Bashan came
out against us, he and all his people, to battle
at [f]Edrei. 2 But the LORD said to me, 'Do not
fear him, for I have given him and all his people and his land into your hand. And you shall
do to him as you did to [g]Sihon the king of the
Amorites, who lived at Heshbon.' 3 So the LORD
our God gave into our hand Og also, the king
of Bashan, and all his people, [h]and we struck
him down until he had no survivor left. 4 And
we took all his cities at that time—there was
not a city that we did not take from them—
sixty cities, [i]the whole region of Argob, the
kingdom of Og in Bashan. 5 All these were cities fortified with high walls, gates, and bars,
besides very many unwalled villages. 6 And
[j]we devoted them to destruction,[3] as we did
to Sihon the king of Heshbon, devoting to
destruction every [k]city, men, women, and children. 7 But all the livestock and the spoil of
the cities we took as our plunder. 8 So we took
the land at that time out of the hand of the
two kings of the Amorites who were beyond
the Jordan, from the Valley of the Arnon to
Mount Hermon 9 (the Sidonians call [l]Hermon
[m]Sirion, while the Amorites call it [n]Senir), 10 all
the cities of the [o]tableland and all Gilead and
all Bashan, as far as [p]Salecah and Edrei, cities
of the kingdom of Og in Bashan. 11 (For [q]only
Og the king of Bashan was left of the remnant
of [r]the Rephaim. Behold, his bed was a bed of

[1] Hebrew *them* [2] That is, set apart (devoted) as an offering to the Lord (for destruction) [3] That is, set apart (devoted) as an offering to the Lord (for destruction); twice in this verse

20 [f]See Gen. 14:5 **21** [g][ver. 10] **22** [h]Gen. 14:6; See Gen. 36:20-30 **23** [i]Josh. 13:3, 4 [j]Gen. 10:19; Jer. 25:20 [k]See Gen. 10:14 **24** [l]Num. 21:13, 14; Judg. 11:18, 21 [m]Num. 21:27, 28, 30 [n][ver. 9] **25** [o]ch. 11:25; 28:10; See Ex. 15:14-16; Josh. 2:9-11 **26** [p]Josh. 13:18; 1 Chr. 6:79 [m][See ver. 24 above] [q][ch. 20:10] **27** [r]Num. 21:21, 22; Judg. 11:19 **28** [s]ver. 6; Num. 20:19 **29** [t]ver. 5, 9; [ch. 23:3, 4; Num. 20:18; Judg. 11:17, 18] **30** [u]Num. 21:23 [m][See ver. 24 above] [v]See Ex. 4:21 **32** [w]See Num. 21:23-30 **33** [x][ch. 7:2] [y]ch. 29:7 **34** [z]ch. 3:6 **36** [a]ch. 3:12; 4:48; Josh. 12:2; 13:9, 16; 2 Kgs. 10:33 [b]Josh. 13:9, 16; 2 Sam. 24:5 [c]Ps. 44:3 **37** [d]ch. 3:16; Gen. 32:22; Num. 21:24; Josh. 12:2; Judg. 11:22 **Chapter 3** **1** [e]ch. 29:7; Num. 21:33, 35 [f]See ch. 1:4 **2** [g]See Num. 21:23-26, 34 **3** [h]Num. 21:35 **4** [i]1 Kgs. 4:13 **6** [j]See ch. 7:2; Ps. 135:10-12 [k]ch. 2:34 **9** [l]ch. 4:48; Josh. 11:3, 17; 12:5 [m]Ps. 29:6; [ch. 4:48] [n]1 Chr. 5:23; Song 4:8; Ezek. 27:5 **10** [o]ch. 4:43; Josh. 13:9, 16, 17, 21; Jer. 48:8, 21 [p]Josh. 12:5; 13:11; 1 Chr. 5:11 **11** [q]ch. 2:11, 20 [r]See Gen. 14:5

iron. Is it not in [s]Rabbah of the Ammonites?
Nine cubits[1] was its length, and four cubits
its breadth, according to the [t]common cubit.[2])
[12]“When we took possession of this land at
that time, I gave to the Reubenites and the
Gadites the territory beginning [u]at Aroer,
which is on the edge of the Valley of the
Arnon, and half the hill country of Gilead with
[v]its cities. [13][w]The rest of Gilead, and all Bashan,
the kingdom of Og, that is, [x]all the region of
Argob, I gave to the half-tribe of Manasseh.
(All that portion of Bashan is called the land
of [r]Rephaim. [14][y]Jair the Manassite took all the
region of Argob, that is, Bashan, as far as the
border of [z]the Geshurites and the Maacathites,
and called the villages [a]after his own name,
Havvoth-jair, as it is to this day.) [15]To Machir [b]I
gave Gilead, [16]and to the Reubenites [c]and the
Gadites I gave the territory from Gilead as far
as the Valley of the Arnon, with the middle of
the valley as a border, as far over as the river
Jabbok, [d]the border of the Ammonites; [17]the
Arabah also, with the Jordan as the border,
from [e]Chinnereth as far as [f]the Sea of the
Arabah, [g]the Salt Sea, under [h]the slopes of
Pisgah on the east.
[18]“And I commanded you at that time, saying, ‘The LORD your God has given you this
land to possess. [i]All your men of valor shall
cross over armed before your brothers, the
people of Israel. [19]Only your wives, your little
ones, and your livestock [j](I know that you
have much livestock) shall remain in the cities that I have given you, [20][k]until the LORD
gives rest to your brothers, as to you, and they
also occupy the land that the LORD your God
gives them beyond the Jordan. Then each of
you may return to his possession which I have
given you.’ [21]And I commanded [l]Joshua at that
time, ‘Your eyes have seen all that the LORD
your God has done to these two kings. So will
the LORD do to all the kingdoms into which
you are crossing. [22]You shall not fear them, for
it is [m]the LORD your God who fights for you.’

Moses Forbidden to Enter the Land

[23]“And I pleaded with the LORD at that time,
saying, [24]‘O Lord GOD, you have only begun
to show your servant [n]your greatness and your
mighty hand. For [o]what god is there in heaven
or on earth who can do such works and mighty
acts as yours? [25]Please let me go over and see
[p]the good land beyond the Jordan, that good
hill country and [q]Lebanon.’ [26]But [r]the LORD

[1] A *cubit* was about 18 inches or 45 centimeters [2] Hebrew *cubit of a man*

3:21–22 There is a pattern repeated throughout Deuteronomy: hope for the future is rooted in the past. What God did to Sihon and Og should encourage Joshua and the covenant people with regard to what God would do to the kingdoms in the land of Canaan (v. 21). The ultimate expression of this pattern is the hope for our future resurrection, rooted in the past resurrection of Jesus Christ (1 Cor. 15:20–23).

Related to this pattern is the repeated principal that “it is the LORD your God who fights for you” (Deut. 3:22; Ex. 14:14; Deut. 1:30; 20:4; Josh. 23:10). As Israel's entrance into and life in the Promised Land was guaranteed by what God did for them rather than what they did for God, so too, our entrance into and life in God's eternal kingdom is guaranteed by what God has done for us in Christ rather than by what we do for God.

3:23–29 Though the consequences of Moses' sin are severe, grace is not absent. The nature of Moses' sin at the waters of Meribah (see Num. 20:2–13) was that he did not “uphold [God] as holy” (Num. 20:12) but instead portrayed himself as having divine status and prerogatives (saying and doing what God had not instructed in order to provide for the people). For God to allow Moses to take Israel into the Promised Land, as though a human were their deity, would not have been gracious to the nation or to Moses. Instead, God protects his people's relationship with himself by denying Moses entry.

But God is also gracious to Moses, allowing his humbled leadership to continue for a time, letting him see the Promised Land, giving him the privilege of charging his successor with faithfulness. In this way God grants Moses the honor of completing the testimony of God's faithfulness (i.e., the Pentateuch) that will better lead God's people in all future generations—and, providing for Moses ultimately to arrive in the Promised Land by virtue of Christ's transfiguration (see Matt. 17:1–13). (See also notes related to these events at Ex. 17:1–7, the contrasting example; and Num. 20:1–29, the previous account.)

11[s] 2 Sam. 11:1; 12:26; Jer. 49:2; Ezek. 21:20; 25:5; Amos 1:14 [t] [Rev. 21:17]
12[u] See ch. 2:36 [v] See Num. 32:32-38; Josh. 13:8-13
13[w] See Num. 32:39-42; Josh. 13:29-31 [x] 1 Kgs. 4:13 [r] [See ver. 11 above]
14[y] Num. 32:41; [1 Chr. 2:22, 23] [z] Josh. 12:5; 13:11, 13; 2 Sam. 3:3; 10:6; 13:37, 38 [a] Num. 32:41
15[b] Num. 32:39
16[c] [2 Sam. 24:5] [d] Num. 21:24; Josh. 12:2
17[e] See Num. 34:11 [f] ch. 4:49; Josh. 3:16; 12:3; 2 Kgs. 14:25 [g] See Gen. 14:3 [h] [Num. 21:15]
18[i] Num. 32:20, 21; Josh. 1:14; 4:12
19[j] Num. 32:1, 4
20[k] Josh. 22:4
21[l] [Num. 27:18]
22[m] See Ex. 14:14
24[n] ch. 5:24; 11:2; 32:3; 1 Chr. 29:11 [o] See Ex. 15:11
25[p] ch. 4:22; Ex. 3:8 [q] [Josh. 1:4]
26[r] See ch. 1:37

was angry with me because of you and would not listen to me. And the LORD said to me, [s]'Enough from you; do not speak to me of this matter again. 27 [t]Go up to the top of Pisgah and lift up your eyes westward and northward and southward and eastward, and look at it with your eyes, for you shall not go over this Jordan. 28 But [u]charge Joshua, and encourage and strengthen him, for he shall go over at the head of this people, and he shall put them in possession of the land that you shall see.' 29 So we remained in [v]the valley opposite Beth-peor.

Moses Commands Obedience

4 "And now, O Israel, listen to [w]the statutes and the rules[1] that I am teaching you, and do them, [x]that you may live, and go in and take possession of the land that the LORD, the God of your fathers, is giving you. 2 [y]You shall not add to the word that I command you, nor take from it, that you may keep the commandments of the LORD your God that I command you. 3 Your eyes have seen what the LORD did [z]at Baal-peor, for the LORD your God destroyed from among you all the men who followed the Baal of Peor. 4 But you who held fast to the LORD your God are all alive today. 5 See, I have taught you statutes and rules, as the LORD my God commanded me, that you should do them in the land that you are entering to take possession of it. 6 [a]Keep them and do them, for [b]that will be your wisdom and your understanding in the sight of the peoples, who, when they hear all these statutes, will say, 'Surely this great nation is a wise and understanding people.' 7 For [c]what great nation is there that has [d]a god so near to it as the LORD our God is to us, whenever we call upon him? 8 And what great nation is there, that has statutes and rules so [e]righteous as all this law that I set before you today?

9 [f]"Only take care, and [g]keep your soul diligently, lest you forget the things that your eyes have seen, and lest they depart from your heart all the days of your life. [h]Make them known to your children and your children's children— 10 how on [i]the day that you stood before the LORD your God at Horeb, the LORD said to me, [j]'Gather the people to me, that I may let them hear my words, [k]so that they may learn to fear [l]me all the days that they live on the earth, and that they may teach their children so.' 11 And [m]you came near and stood at the foot of the mountain, while [n]the mountain burned with fire to the heart of heaven, wrapped in darkness, cloud, and gloom. 12 Then [o]the LORD spoke to you out of the midst of the fire. You heard the sound of words, [p]but saw no form; [q]there was only a voice. 13 [r]And he declared to you his covenant, which he commanded you to perform, that is, [s]the Ten Commandments,[2] [t]and he wrote them on two tablets of stone. 14 And [u]the LORD commanded me at that time to teach you statutes and rules, that you might do them in the land that you are going over to possess.

Idolatry Forbidden

15 [v]"Therefore watch yourselves very carefully. Since [w]you saw no form on the day that the LORD spoke to you at Horeb out of the midst of the fire, 16 beware [x]lest you act corruptly [y]by

[1] Or *just decrees*; also verses 5, 8, 14, 45 [2] Hebrew *words*

26 [s][2 Cor. 12:9]
27 [t]Num. 27:12, 13
28 [u]ch. 1:38; 31:3, 7; Num. 27:23
29 [v]ch. 4:46; 34:6
Chapter 4
1 [w]See Lev. 18:4 [x]ch. 6:24; 8:1
2 [y]ch. 12:32; [Josh. 1:7; Prov. 30:6; Rev. 22:18, 19]
3 [z]See Num. 23:28; 25:3-9
6 [a]ch. 29:9 [b]Job 28:28; Ps. 111:10; Prov. 1:7; 9:10
7 [c]2 Sam. 7:23 [d]Ps. 34:18; 46:1; 145:18; 148:14; [James 4:8]
8 [e]Rom. 7:12
9 [f]ver. 23 [g][Prov. 4:23] [h]ch. 6:7; 11:19; 32:46; Gen. 18:19; See Ps. 78:4-6
10 [i]Ex. 19:9, 16; Heb. 12:18, 19 [j]ch. 31:12 [k]ch. 14:23; 17:19 [l]ch. 12:1; 31:13; 1 Kgs. 8:40
11 [m]Ex. 19:17 [n]ch. 5:22, 23; Ex. 19:18; 20:18, 21; [Ex. 24:16, 17]
12 [o]ver. 33, 36; ch. 5:4, 22; Ex. 20:1, 19 [p]ver. 15 [q]Ex. 20:22; [1 Kgs. 19:12; Job 4:16]
13 [r]ch. 9:9, 11 [s]Ex. 34:28 [t]See Ex. 24:12
14 [u]See Ex. 21–23
15 [v]Josh. 23:11 [w]ver. 12
16 [x]ver. 25 [y]ver. 23; ch. 5:8; Ex. 20:4; [Acts 17:29]

4:1–14 This section on God's "statutes and rules" starts and stops on the same note: "do them" (vv. 1, 14). With regard to God's teachings, Moses exhorts the people to "listen" and "do them" (v. 1). Listening is not enough; doing must follow. This principle is likewise taught in the New Testament (James 1:22).

You "do them, that you may live" (Deut. 4:1) and to demonstrate "your wisdom" (v. 6). "Live" coupled with "wisdom" refers not to earning eternal life by obedience but to experiencing abundant/blessed life by living in keeping with the principles that God has established for life in the world he has made—recognizing that the blessings are always from the joy of fulfilling God's eternal purposes, not necessarily in knowing earthly ease or gain (Prov. 3:1–2).

Salvation is by grace alone through faith alone in Christ alone, who has perfectly obeyed the law in our place. For those who are saved, the law now functions as a guide to meaningful, joy-filled life in God's world.

4:15–31 Covenant relationship in Deuteronomy, as in the ancient Near East, requires exclusive loyalty. That God is "a jealous God" (v. 24) simply means that he tolerates

making a carved image for yourselves, in the
form of any figure, [z]the likeness of male or
female, 17 the likeness of any animal that is
on the earth, the likeness of any winged bird
that flies in the air, 18 the likeness of anything
that creeps on the ground, the likeness of any
fish that is in the water under the earth. 19 And
beware lest you raise your eyes to heaven, and
when you see [a]the sun and the moon and the
stars, [b]all the host of heaven, you be drawn
away and bow down to them and serve them,
things that the LORD your God has allotted to
all the peoples under the whole heaven. 20 But
the LORD has taken you and [c]brought you
out of the iron furnace, out of Egypt, [d]to be a
people of his own inheritance, as you are this
day. 21 Furthermore, [e]the LORD was angry with
me because of you, and he swore that I should
not cross the Jordan, and that I should not
enter the good land that the LORD your God
is giving you for an inheritance. 22 For I must
die in this land; [f]I must not go over the Jordan.
But you shall go over and take possession of
[g]that good land. 23 [h]Take care, lest you forget
the covenant of the LORD your God, which he
made with you, and [i]make a carved image, the
form of anything that the LORD your God has
forbidden you. 24 For [j]the LORD your God is a
consuming fire, [k]a jealous God.

25 "When you father children and children's
children, and have grown old in the land, [l]if
you act corruptly by making a carved image
in the form of anything, and [m]by doing what
is evil in the sight of the LORD your God, so
as to provoke him to anger, 26 I [n]call heaven
and earth to witness against you today, that
you will soon utterly perish from the land
that you are going over the Jordan to possess.
You will not live long in it, but will be utterly
destroyed. 27 And the LORD [o]will scatter you
among the peoples, [p]and you will be left few
in number among the nations where the LORD
will drive you. 28 And [q]there you will serve gods
of wood and stone, the work of human hands,
[r]that neither see, nor hear, nor eat, nor smell.
29 [s]But from there you will seek the LORD your
God and you will find him, if you search after
him with all your heart and with all your soul.
30 When you are in tribulation, and all these
things come upon you [t]in the latter days, you
will return to the LORD your God and obey his
voice. 31 For the LORD your God is [u]a merciful
God. [v]He will not leave you or destroy you or
forget the covenant with your fathers that he
swore to them.

The LORD Alone Is God

32 "For [w]ask now of the days that are past,
which were before you, since the day that God
created man on the earth, and ask from one
end of heaven to the other, whether such a
great thing as this has ever happened or was
ever heard of. 33 [x]Did any people ever hear
the voice of a god speaking out of the midst
of the fire, as you have heard, and still live?
34 Or has any god ever attempted to go and
take a nation for himself from the midst of
another nation, by trials, [y]by signs, by wonders, and [z]by war, [a]by a mighty hand and [b]an
outstretched arm, and by great deeds of terror, all of which the LORD your God did for
you in Egypt before your eyes? 35 To you it was

no rivals in his relationship with his covenant people. Idols ("carved image," v. 16; "gods," v. 28) are anyone or anything that we make ultimate in our lives in place of the true and living God. When we are "drawn away and bow down to them and serve them" (v. 19), God disciplines us (vv. 25–28), but he does not abandon us. He always receives us when we return to him (vv. 28–30), because he "is a merciful God" (v. 31). His mercy to Israel in the old covenant was rooted in the abiding promises made to Abraham, Isaac, and Jacob—not in the transient obedience of Israel (v. 31). His mercy to us in the new covenant is rooted in the eternal promises made to his Son—not in our frequently faltering obedience (John 6:39).

4:32–40 The God of Israel is not just the only God whom we should worship (vv. 15–31). He is also the only God. "The LORD is God; there is no other besides him" (v. 35). "The LORD is God in heaven above and on the earth beneath; there is no other" (v. 39). It is in keeping with this truth that Jesus said, "No one comes to the Father except through me" (John 14:6). There is one way to the one true God, and Jesus is that way. The reason for this truth is that Jesus is himself the one true God (John 1:1).

16 [z]Rom. 1:23
19 [a]ch. 17:3; Job 31:26-28 [b]2 Kgs. 17:16; 21:3; [Gen. 2:1]
20 [c]1 Kgs. 8:51; Jer. 11:4 [d]ch. 9:29; 32:9
21 [e]See ch. 1:37
22 [f]ch. 3:27 [g]ch. 3:25
23 [h]ver. 9 [i]ch. 5:8; Ex. 20:4; [Acts 17:29]
24 [j]Ex. 24:17; Cited Heb. 12:29; [ch. 9:3; Isa. 10:16-18; 29:6; 30:27, 30; Zeph. 1:18] [k][Isa. 42:8]; See Ex. 20:5
25 [l]ver. 16 [m]ch. 9:18; 2 Kgs. 17:17
26 [n]ch. 30:18, 19; 31:28; 32:1; Isa. 1:2; Jer. 2:12; 6:19; Mic. 6:2
27 [o]See Lev. 26:33 [p]ch. 28:62
28 [q]ch. 28:36, 64; Jer. 16:13 [r]Ps. 115:4-7; 135:15-17; Isa. 44:9; 46:7
29 [s]ch. 30:2, 3; Lev. 26:40-42; 2 Chr. 15:4; Neh. 1:9; Isa. 55:6, 7; Jer. 29:13, 14 **30** [t]See Gen. 49:1 **31** [u]Ex. 34:6; 2 Chr. 30:9; Neh. 9:31; Jonah 4:2 [v]ch. 31:6, 8; Josh. 1:5; 1 Chr. 28:20
32 [w]Job 8:8 **33** [x]ver. 12; ch. 5:24, 26; Ex. 3:6; 19:21; [Gen. 32:30; Ex. 24:11; 33:20, 23; Judg. 6:22, 23; 13:22] **34** [y]ch. 26:8; Ex. 7:3; Jer. 32:21 [z]See Ex. 15:3-10 [a]ch. 7:8; 11:2; 26:8; 34:12 [b]Ex. 6:6; Jer. 32:21

shown, [c]that you might know that the LORD is God; [d]there is no other besides him. 36 [e]Out of heaven he let you hear his voice, that he might discipline you. And on earth he let you see his great fire, and [x]you heard his words out of the midst of the fire. 37 And because [f]he loved your fathers and chose their offspring after them[1] and brought you out of Egypt [g]with his own presence, by his great power, 38 [h]driving out before you nations greater and mightier than you, to bring you in, to give you their land for an inheritance, as it is this day, 39 know therefore today, and lay it to your heart, that [i]the LORD is God in heaven above and on the earth beneath; [j]there is no other. 40 [k]Therefore you shall keep his statutes and his commandments, which I command you today, [l]that it may go well with you and with your children after you, and that you may prolong your days in the land that the LORD your God is giving you for all time."

Cities of Refuge

41 Then Moses [m]set apart three cities in the east beyond the Jordan, 42 that [n]the manslayer might flee there, anyone who kills his neighbor unintentionally, without being at enmity with him in time past; he may flee to one of these cities and save his life: 43 [o]Bezer in the wilderness on the [p]tableland for the Reubenites, Ramoth in Gilead for the Gadites, and Golan in Bashan for the Manassites.

Introduction to the Law

44 This is the law that Moses set before the people of Israel. 45 These are the testimonies, the statutes, and the rules, which Moses spoke to the people of Israel when they came out of Egypt, 46 beyond the Jordan [q]in the valley opposite Beth-peor, in the land of Sihon the king of the Amorites, who lived at Heshbon, [r]whom Moses and the people of Israel defeated when they came out of Egypt. 47 And they took possession of his land and the land [s]of Og, the king of Bashan, the two kings of the Amorites, who lived to the east beyond the Jordan; 48 [t]from Aroer, which is on the edge of the Valley of the Arnon, as far as Mount [u]Sirion[2] (that is, [v]Hermon), 49 together with all the Arabah on the east side of the Jordan as far as [w]the Sea of the Arabah, under the slopes of Pisgah.

The Ten Commandments

5 And Moses summoned all Israel and said to them, "Hear, O Israel, the statutes and the rules that I speak in your hearing today, and you shall learn them and be careful to do them. 2 [x]The LORD our God made a covenant with us in Horeb. 3 [y]Not with our fathers did the LORD make this covenant, but with us, who are all of us here alive today. 4 The LORD spoke with you [z]face to face at the mountain, out of the midst of the fire, 5 [a]while I stood between the LORD and you at that time, to declare to you the word of the LORD. For [b]you were afraid because of the fire, and you did not go up into the mountain. He said:

6 [c]" 'I am the LORD your God, who brought you out of the land of Egypt, out of the house of slavery.

7 " 'You shall have no other gods before[3] me.

8 " 'You shall not make for yourself a carved image, or any likeness of anything that is in heaven above, or that is on the earth beneath, or that is in the water under the earth. 9 You shall not bow down to them or serve them; for I the LORD your God am a jealous God, visiting the iniquity of the fathers on the children to the third and fourth generation of those who hate me, 10 but showing steadfast love to

[1] Hebrew *his offspring after him* [2] Syriac; Hebrew *Sion* [3] Or *besides*

35 [c][Ex. 10:2] [d]ver. 39; 1 Sam. 2:2; 2 Sam. 22:32; Isa. 45:5, 18, 22; 46:9; Cited Mark 12:32
36 [e]Ex. 19:9, 19; Neh. 9:13 [x][See ver. 33 above]
37 [f]ch. 10:15 [g]Ex. 33:14; [Isa. 63:9]
38 [h]ch. 7:1; 11:23; Ex. 23:27, 28; 34:24; See ch. 9:1-5
39 [i]Josh. 2:11; 1 Kgs. 8:23; 2 Chr. 20:6; Eccles. 5:2 [j]1 Sam. 2:2; 2 Sam. 22:32; Isa. 45:5, 18, 22; 46:9; Cited Mark 12:32

Since the God of Israel is the only God, it is his teaching that we must follow as the path to abundant life in his world (Deut. 4:40). Not to do so would be to deny ourselves the grace for life that he alone offers. Since Jesus is the only God, he can also tell us to make disciples, "teaching them to observe all that I have commanded" (Matt. 28:20). We obey our God because of who he is: the only God, our Redeemer.

5:1–21 Deuteronomy 5–26 contains the laws that Israel was to keep in the land they were about to enter. The Ten Commandments stand at the beginning of all other laws, and at the beginning of the Ten Commandments we read, "I am the LORD your God, who brought you out of the land of Egypt, out of the house of slavery" (5:6).

40 [k]Lev. 22:31 [l]ch. 5:16; 6:2, 3; 11:9; 12:25, 28; 22:7; [Prov. 3:1, 2; 10:27] **41** [m]Num. 35:6, 14 **42** [n]ch. 19:4 **43** [o]Josh. 20:8; 21:36; 1 Chr. 6:78 [p]See ch. 3:10 **46** [q]ch. 3:29 [r]ch. 1:4; Num. 21:24 **47** [s]ch. 3:3, 4; Num. 21:33, 35 **48** [t]See ch. 2:36 [u][ch. 3:9] [v]See ch. 3:9 **49** [w]See ch. 3:17 **Chapter 5** **2** [x]ch. 4:23; Ex. 19:5 **3** [y][Heb. 8:9] **4** [z][ch. 34:10; Ex. 33:11; Num. 14:14; Judg. 6:22] **5** [a]Ex. 20:21; [Gal. 3:19] [b]Ex. 19:16; 20:18; 24:2 **6** [c]For ver. 6-21, see Ex. 20:2-17

[d]thousands[1] of those who love me and keep
my commandments.
11 " 'You shall not take the name of the LORD
your God in vain, for the LORD will not hold
him guiltless who takes his name in vain.
12 " 'Observe the Sabbath day, to keep it holy,
as the LORD your God commanded you. 13 Six
days you shall labor and do all your work,
14 but [e]the seventh day is a Sabbath to the LORD
your God. On it you shall not do any work, you
or your son or your daughter or your male
servant or your female servant, or your ox or
your donkey or any of your livestock, or the
sojourner who is within your gates, [f]that your
male servant and your female servant may rest
as well as you. 15 [g]You shall remember that you
were a slave[2] in the land of Egypt, and the
LORD your God brought you out from there
[h]with a mighty hand and an outstretched arm.
Therefore the LORD your God commanded
you to keep the Sabbath day.
16 " 'Honor your father and your mother, as
the LORD your God commanded you, [i]that
your days may be long, and that it may go well
with you in the land that the LORD your God
is giving you.
17 [j]" 'You shall not murder.[3]
18 [j]" 'And you shall not commit adultery.
19 " 'And you shall not steal.
20 " 'And you shall not bear false witness
against your neighbor.
21 " 'And you shall not covet your neighbor's
wife. And you shall not desire your neighbor's house, his field, or his male servant, or
his female servant, his ox, or his donkey, or
anything that is your neighbor's.'
22 "These words the LORD spoke to all your
assembly [k]at the mountain out of the midst
of the fire, the cloud, and the thick darkness,
with a loud voice; and he added no more.
And [l]he wrote them on two tablets of stone
and gave them to me. 23 And [m]as soon as you
heard the voice out of the midst of the darkness, while the mountain was burning with
fire, you came near to me, all the heads of
your tribes, and your elders. 24 And you said,
'Behold, the LORD our God has shown us his
glory and [n]greatness, and [o]we have heard his
voice out of the midst of the fire. This day we
have seen God speak with man, and man [p]still
live. 25 Now therefore why should we die? For
this great fire will consume us. [q]If we hear the
voice of the LORD our God any more, we shall
die. 26 [p]For who is there of all flesh, that has
heard the voice of the living God speaking out
of the midst of fire as we have, and has still
lived? 27 Go near and hear all that the LORD
our God will say, and [r]speak to us all that the
LORD our God will speak to you, and we will
hear and do it.'
28 "And the LORD heard your words, when
you spoke to me. And the LORD said to me, 'I
have heard the words of this people, which
they have spoken to you. [s]They are right in
all that they have spoken. 29 [t]Oh that they had
such a heart as this always, to fear me and to
keep all my commandments, [u]that it might
go well with them and with their descendants[4] forever! 30 Go and say to them, "Return
to your tents." 31 But you, stand here by me,
and [v]I will tell you the whole commandment
and the statutes and the rules that you shall
teach them, that they may do them in the
land that I am giving them to possess.' 32 You
shall be careful therefore to do as the LORD
your God has commanded you. [w]You shall
not turn aside to the right hand or to the left.
33 [x]You shall walk in all the way that the LORD
your God has commanded you, that you may
live, and [y]that it may go well with you, and
that you may live long in the land that you
shall possess.

[1] Or *to the thousandth generation* [2] Or *servant* [3] The Hebrew word also covers causing human death through carelessness or negligence
[4] Or *sons*

Law follows grace. God saved Israel before he gave them his law to follow. God rescued Israel not because of their obedience to the law but because of his promise to Abraham, Isaac, and Jacob (Ex. 3:15–16). Israel's deliverance was therefore not because of their obedience to the law but because God saw their affliction and cared enough to deliver them from their suffering to an abundant life (Ex. 3:7–8). This truth provides the context in which to read the whole of Deuteronomy 5–26. Indeed, this gospel rhythm provides the context in which we carry out our obedience to God. Law follows grace. We obey from, not for, God's favor.

10 [d]Ex. 20:6; Jer. 32:18
14 [e]Ex. 16:29, 30; Heb. 4:4 [f][Ex. 23:12]
15 [g]ch. 15:15; 16:12; 24:18, 22 [h]See ch. 4:34
16 [i]See ch. 4:40
17 [j]Matt. 5:21, 27; Luke 18:20; James 2:11
18 [j][See ver. 17 above]
22 [k]See ch. 4:11 [l]ch. 9:10, 11; Ex. 24:12
23 [m]See ch. 4:12

24 [n]See ch. 3:24 [o]Ex. 19:19 [p]See ch. 4:33 **25** [q]ch. 18:16 **26** [p][See ver. 24 above] **27** [r]See Ex. 20:19 **28** [s]ch. 18:17 **29** [t]ch. 32:29; Ps. 81:13; Isa. 48:18; [Matt. 23:37; Luke 19:42] [u]See ch. 4:40 **31** [v]Gal. 3:19 **32** [w]ch. 17:20; 28:14; Josh. 1:7; 23:6; 2 Kgs. 22:2; Prov. 4:27 **33** [x]ch. 10:12; 30:16; Jer. 7:23; [Luke 1:6] [y]See ch. 4:40

The Greatest Commandment

6 “Now this is [z]the commandment—the statutes and the rules[1]—that the LORD your God commanded me to teach you, that you may do them in the land to which you are going over, to possess it, 2 that [a]you may fear the LORD your God, you and your son and your son's son, by keeping all his statutes and his commandments, which I command you, all the days of your life, and [b]that your days may be long. 3 Hear therefore, O Israel, and be careful to do them, that it may go well with you, and that you may multiply greatly, [c]as the LORD, the God of your fathers, has promised you, in a land flowing with milk and honey.

4 “Hear, O Israel: [d]The LORD our God, the LORD is one.[2] 5 You [e]shall love the LORD your God with all your heart and with all your soul and with all your might. 6 And [f]these words that I command you today shall be on your heart. 7 [g]You shall teach them diligently to your children, and shall talk of them when you sit in your house, and when you walk by the way, and when you lie down, and when you rise. 8 [h]You shall bind them as a sign on your hand, and they shall be as frontlets between your eyes. 9 [i]You shall write them on the doorposts of your house and on your gates.

10 “And when the LORD your God brings you into the land that he swore to your fathers, to Abraham, to Isaac, and to Jacob, to give you—with great and good cities [j]that you did not build, 11 and houses full of all good things that you did not fill, and cisterns that you did not dig, and vineyards and olive trees that you did not plant—and when you eat and are full, 12 [k]then take care lest you forget the LORD, who brought you out of the land of Egypt, out of the house of slavery. 13 It is [l]the LORD your God you shall fear. Him you shall serve and [m]by his name you shall swear. 14 You shall not [n]go after other gods, [o]the gods of the peoples who are around you— 15 for [p]the LORD your God in your midst [q]is a jealous God—[r]lest the anger of the LORD your God be kindled against you, and he destroy you from off the face of the earth.

16 [s]“You shall not put the LORD your God to the test, [t]as you tested him at Massah. 17 You shall [u]diligently keep the commandments of the LORD your God, and his testimonies and his statutes, which he has commanded you. 18 [v]And you shall do what is right and good in the sight of the LORD, that it may go well with you, and that you may go in and take possession of the good land that the LORD swore to give to your fathers 19 [w]by thrusting out all your enemies from before you, as the LORD has promised.

20 [x]“When your son asks you in time to come, ‘What is the meaning of the testimonies and the statutes and the rules that the LORD our

[1] Or *just decrees*; also verse 20 [2] Or *The LORD our God is one LORD*; or *The LORD is our God, the LORD is one*; or *The LORD is our God, the LORD alone*

Chapter 6
1 [z] ch. 4:1; 5:31; 12:1
2 [a] ch. 5:29; 10:12, 20; 13:4; Ps. 128:1; Eccles. 12:13 [b] See ch. 4:40
3 [c] Gen. 15:5; 22:17; 26:4; 28:14; Ex. 32:13
4 [d] Cited Mark 12:29; [Isa. 42:8; Zech. 14:9; John 17:3; 1 Cor. 8:4, 6]
5 [e] Cited Matt. 22:37; Mark 12:30; Luke 10:27; [2 Kgs. 23:25]
6 [f] ch. 11:18; 32:46; Ps. 37:31; Isa. 51:7; Jer. 31:33
7 [g] See ch. 4:9
8 [h] ch. 11:18; Prov. 3:3; 6:21; 7:3; See Ex. 13:9
9 [i] ch. 11:20; [Isa. 57:8]
10 [j] Josh. 24:13; [Josh. 11:13; Neh. 9:25; Ps. 105:44]
12 [k] [Prov. 30:8, 9]
13 [l] Cited Matt. 4:10; Luke 4:8 [m] ch. 10:20; Josh. 2:12; Ps. 63:11; Isa. 45:23; 65:16; Jer. 12:16
14 [n] ch. 8:19; 11:16, 28; 13:2, 3; 28:14; Jer. 25:6 [o] ch. 13:7
15 [p] ch. 7:21 [q] See Ex. 20:5 [r] ch. 7:4; 11:17

6:4–5 This great declaration of the nature of the redeeming, covenant-keeping God of Israel (“our God,” following the reminders of his faithfulness and intentions in vv. 1–3), provides the motivation for the whole-person engagement with God commanded here and later commended by Jesus (e.g., Matt. 22:37–40). But it must be noted in each case that God covenants, redeems, and rescues *before* such obedience is possible. One day a lawyer would ask Jesus, “Teacher, what shall I do to inherit eternal life?” (Luke 10:25). Implied in the question is the idea that eternal life can be earned by what we do, and it can (Luke 10:28), if we keep the law perfectly. The problem is we cannot keep this law, which requires submission of every aspect of our being in order to earn eternal life (see Luke 18:18–30; James 2:10). But Jesus has kept the law perfectly in our place, and he died on the cross to pay the penalty for our lawbreaking.

Loving God with all that we are and all that we have is now the supreme goal of those who have been saved by grace alone through faith alone in Christ alone. And one of the key ways that we love God is by loving our neighbor, as stated here and reiterated in the New Testament (Luke 10:29–37; 1 John 4:20). We do this not to earn eternal life but to show God our gratitude for the gracious gift of life in his Son.

6:20–25 “What is the meaning of” keeping God's commandments (v. 20)? One: remembering that the commandments have been given to those already redeemed from slavery (vv. 21–22). Two: acknowledging that the commandments have been given

16 [s] Cited Matt. 4:7; Luke 4:12 [t] ch. 9:22; 33:8; Ps. 95:8; [1 Cor. 10:9]; See Ex. 17:2-7 17 [u] ch. 11:22; Ps. 119:4 18 [v] See ch. 12:25 19 [w] Ex. 23:28-30; Num. 33:52, 53 20 [x] Ex. 12:26; 13:14

God has commanded you?' 21 then you shall
say to your son, [y]'We were Pharaoh's slaves in
Egypt. And the LORD brought us out of Egypt
with a mighty hand. 22 And [z]the LORD showed
signs and wonders, great and grievous, against
Egypt and against Pharaoh and all his household, before our eyes. 23 And he brought us
out from there, that he might bring us in and
give us the land that he swore to give to our
fathers. 24 And the LORD commanded us to do
all these statutes, [a]to fear the LORD our God,
[b]for our good always, that [c]he might preserve
us alive, as we are this day. 25 And [d]it will be
righteousness for us, if we are careful to do all
this commandment before the LORD our God,
as he has commanded us.'

A Chosen People

7 "When the [e]LORD your God brings you
into the land that you are entering to take
possession of it, and clears away many nations
before you, [f]the Hittites, the Girgashites, the
Amorites, the Canaanites, the Perizzites, the
Hivites, and the Jebusites, seven nations [g]more
numerous and mightier than you, 2 [h]and when
the LORD your God gives them over to you,
and you defeat them, then you must [i]devote
them to complete destruction.[1] [j]You shall
make no covenant with them and show no
mercy to them. 3 [k]You shall not intermarry
with them, giving your daughters to their
sons or taking their daughters for your sons,
4 for they would turn away your sons from
following me, to serve other gods. [l]Then the
anger of the LORD would be kindled against
you, and he would destroy you [m]quickly. 5 But
thus shall you deal with them: [n]you shall break
down their altars and dash in pieces their [n]pil-
lars and chop down their [n]Asherim and [o]burn
their carved images with fire.

6 "For [p]you are a people holy to the LORD your
God. The LORD your God has chosen you to
be [p]a people for his treasured possession, out
of all the peoples who are on the face of the
earth. 7 It was not because you were more in
number than any other people that the LORD
set his love on you and chose you, for you were
the fewest of all peoples, 8 but [q]it is because
the LORD loves you and is keeping [r]the oath
that he swore to your fathers, that the LORD
has brought you out with a mighty hand and
redeemed you from the house of slavery, from
the hand of Pharaoh king of Egypt. 9 Know
therefore that the LORD your God is God, [s]the
faithful God [t]who keeps covenant and steadfast love with those who love him and keep his
commandments, to a thousand generations,
10 and [u]repays to their face those who hate him,
by destroying them. [v]He will not be slack with
one who hates him. He will repay him to his
face. 11 [w]You shall therefore be careful to do the
commandment and the statutes and the rules
that I command you today.

12 [x]"And because you listen to these rules and
keep and do them, the LORD your God will
keep with you [y]the covenant and the steadfast

[1] That is, set apart (devote) as an offering to the Lord (for destruction)

to those whom God intends to bless with abundant life in the world that he has made, because living in keeping with God's law generally results in the "good life" God intends for us (vv. 23–24; cf. note on 4:1–14; also Proverbs 3). Three: keeping the commandments with the understanding that they are "righteousness for us" (Deut. 6:25), not in the sense that we are justified by keeping the commandments but in the sense that those who are justified by grace are counted among "the righteous" who draw near and follow after God according to his standards (e.g., Ps. 1:5; 5:12; 7:9; 11:3, 5, 7; etc.).

7:6–11 Why did God choose Israel to be "a people for his treasured possession" (v. 6)? It was not because of any good quality inherent in them (v. 7), but because of his love for them and his faithfulness to the promise made to Abraham, Isaac, and Jacob (v. 8). Since God so loved Israel, Israel was to respond by loving God and keeping his commandments (vv. 9–11).

Similarly, the apostle Paul says, "In love [God] predestined us for adoption as sons through Jesus Christ" (Eph. 1:4–5). Like Israel, we were chosen because of God's love for us that was expressed before we could try to claim anything inherent in us or accomplished by us. So, as the undistinguished people of Israel were to respond in obedience to God's inexplicable "treasuring" of them, we too respond by loving God and keeping his commandments (1 John 4:19; John 14:15).

21 [y] [Ex. 20:2]
22 [z] Ps. 135:9; See ch. 4:34
24 [a] ver. 2, 13 [b] ch. 10:13; Jer. 32:39 [c] ch. 4:1; 8:1; [Lev. 18:5; Ps. 41:2]
25 [d] ch. 24:13

Chapter 7

1 [e] ch. 31:3; Ps. 44:2, 3 [f] See Ex. 23:23 [g] ch. 4:38; 9:1; 11:23
2 [h] ver. 23; ch. 23:14 [i] ch. 20:17; Ex. 22:20; Lev. 27:29; Num. 21:2, 3 [j] Ex. 23:32; 34:12; Judg. 2:2; [ch. 20:10; Josh. 2:14; 9:18; Judg. 1:24]
3 [k] Ex. 34:16; Josh. 23:12, 13; 1 Kgs. 11:2; [Ezra 9:2]
4 [l] ch. 6:15 [m] [ch. 4:26; 28:20]
5 [n] See Ex. 34:13 [o] ver. 25
6 [p] ch. 14:2; 26:19; 28:9; Ex. 19:6; 22:31; Jer. 2:3; Amos 3:2; 1 Pet. 2:9; See Ex. 19:5
8 [q] ch. 10:15; Isa. 43:4; 63:9; Jer. 31:3; Hos. 11:1; Mal. 1:2 [r] Ex. 32:13; Ps. 105:9-11; Luke 1:72, 73
9 [s] Isa. 49:7; 1 Cor. 1:9; 10:13; 2 Cor. 1:18; 1 Thess. 5:24; 2 Thess. 3:3; 2 Tim. 2:13; Heb. 10:23; 1 John 1:9 [t] ch. 5:10; Ex. 20:6; 2 Chr. 6:14; Neh. 1:5; 9:32; Dan. 9:4
10 [u] Job 34:11; Isa. 59:18; Nah. 1:2, 3 [v] [2 Pet. 3:9]
11 [w] ch. 10:13
12 [x] For ver. 12-16, see ch. 28:1-14; Lev. 26:3-13 [y] Ps. 105:8; Luke 1:55, 72

love that he swore to your fathers. 13 He will [z]love you, bless you, and multiply you. [a]He will also bless the fruit of your womb and the fruit of your ground, your grain and your wine and your oil, the increase of your herds and the young of your flock, in the land that he swore to your fathers to give you. 14 You shall be blessed above all peoples. [b]There shall not be male or female barren among you or among your livestock. 15 And the LORD will take away from you all sickness, and none of the evil [c]diseases of Egypt, which you knew, will he inflict on you, but he will lay them on all who hate you. 16 And [d]you shall consume all the peoples that the LORD your God will give over to you. [e]Your eye shall not pity them, neither shall you serve their gods, for that would be [f]a snare to you.

17 "If you say in your heart, 'These nations are greater than I. How can I dispossess them?' 18 [g]you shall not be afraid of them but you shall [h]remember what the LORD your God did to Pharaoh and to all Egypt, 19 the great trials that your eyes saw, [i]the signs, the wonders, the mighty hand, and the outstretched arm, by which the LORD your God brought you out. So will the LORD your God do to all the peoples of whom you are afraid. 20 Moreover, [j]the LORD your God will send hornets among them, until those who are left and hide themselves from you are destroyed. 21 You shall not be in dread of them, for the LORD your God is [k]in your midst, [l]a great and awesome God. 22 [m]The LORD your God will clear away these nations before you little by little. You may not make an end of them at once,[1] lest the wild beasts grow too numerous for you. 23 [n]But the LORD your God will give them over to you and throw them into great confusion, until they are destroyed. 24 And [o]he will give their kings into your hand, and you shall [p]make their name perish from under heaven. [q]No one shall be able to stand against you until you have destroyed them. 25 The carved images of their gods [r]you shall burn with fire. You [s]shall not covet the silver or the gold that is on them or take it for yourselves, lest you be [t]ensnared by it, for it is an abomination to the LORD your God. 26 And you shall not bring an abominable thing into your house and become devoted to destruction[2] like it. You shall utterly detest and abhor it, [u]for it is devoted to destruction.

Remember the LORD Your God

8 "The whole commandment that I command you today [v]you shall be careful to do, that you may live and multiply, and go in and possess the land that the LORD swore to give to your fathers. 2 And you shall remember the whole way that the LORD your God has led you [w]these forty years in the wilderness, that he might humble you, [x]testing you [y]to know what was in your heart, [z]whether you would keep his commandments or not. 3 And he humbled you and [a]let you hunger and [b]fed you with manna, which you did not know, nor did your fathers know, that he might make you know that [c]man does not live by bread alone, but man lives by every word[3] that comes from the mouth of the LORD. 4 [d]Your clothing did not wear out on you and your foot did not swell these forty years. 5 Know then in your heart that, [e]as a man disciplines his son, the LORD your God disciplines you. 6 So you shall keep the commandments of the LORD your God by walking in his ways and by fearing him. 7 For the LORD your God is bringing you into a good land, [f]a land of brooks of water,

[1] Or *quickly* [2] That is, set apart (devoted) as an offering to the Lord (for destruction); twice in this verse [3] Hebrew *by all*

13[z] [John 14:21] [a] ch. 30:9
14[b] Ex. 23:26
15[c] ch. 28:27, 60; Ex. 9:14; 15:26
16[d] ver. 2 [e] ch. 13:8; 19:13, 21; 25:12 [f] ver. 25; ch. 12:30; Judg. 8:27; See Ex. 23:33
18[g] ch. 1:29; 31:6 [h] Ps. 77:11; 105:5
19[i] ch. 6:22; 11:3
20[j] Ex. 23:28; Josh. 24:12
21[k] ch. 6:15; Num. 11:20; 14:14; Josh. 3:10 [l] ch. 10:17; Neh. 1:5; 4:14; 9:32; [ch. 28:58]
22[m] Ex. 23:29, 30
23[n] ver. 2

8:1–20 In the wilderness God humbled Israel, so that the people would learn to depend on him and walk in his ways (vv. 1–6), and so that it would go well with them in the end (v. 16). In the Promised Land God blessed Israel with an abundance (vv. 7–10), so that they would learn to depend on him, not saying it was "my power" but rather knowing that it was the Lord who empowered them for abundant life (vv. 17–18). Israel was not to forget God (v. 11) but was instead to remember him continually (v. 18).

Jesus taught us this same principle of dependence, using the figure of a vine and branches (John 15:5). As a branch depends on the main stock, so we depend on Jesus to live a truly fruitful life. Depending on Jesus is one aspect of "abiding" in him (John 15:4–6), and abiding in him certainly requires that we remember him continually, as Israel was to remember the Lord continually.

24[o] Josh. 10:24, 42; 11:12; See Josh. 12:1 [p] See ch. 9:14 [q] ch. 11:25; Josh. 1:5; 10:8; 23:9 **25**[r] ver. 5; ch. 12:3; [Ex. 32:20; 1 Chr. 14:12] [s] [Josh. 7:1, 21] [t] See ver. 16 **26**[u] ch. 13:17; Lev. 27:28; Josh. 6:17, 18; 7:1; [Mic. 4:13] **Chapter 8** **1**[v] ch. 4:1; 5:32, 33; 6:1-3 **2**[w] ch. 1:3; 2:7; 29:5; Amos 2:10 [x] ver. 16; Ex. 15:25 [y] [2 Chr. 32:31] [z] [Ex. 16:4; Judg. 3:4] **3**[a] Ex. 16:2, 3 [b] Ex. 16:12, 14, 15, 35; [Num. 11:6-9; 21:5] [c] Cited Matt. 4:4; Luke 4:4; [John 6:49-51] **4**[d] ch. 29:5; Neh. 9:21 **5**[e] Prov. 3:12; Heb. 12:5, 6; [2 Sam. 7:14; Prov. 29:17; Hos. 10:10; Rev. 3:19] **7**[f] ch. 11:10-12

of fountains and springs, flowing out in the
valleys and hills, 8 a land of wheat and barley,
[g]of vines and fig trees and pomegranates, a
land of olive trees and honey, 9 a land in which
you will eat bread without scarcity, in which
you will lack nothing, a land whose stones are
iron, and out of whose hills you can dig copper. 10 And you shall eat and be full, and you
shall bless the LORD your God for the good
land he has given you.

11 "Take care lest you forget the LORD your
God by not keeping his commandments
and his rules and his statutes, which I command you today, 12 [h]lest, when you have eaten
and are full and have built good houses and
live in them, 13 and when your herds and flocks
multiply and your silver and gold is multiplied
and all that you have is multiplied, 14 [i]then your
heart be lifted up, and you [j]forget the LORD
your God, who brought you out of the land
of Egypt, out of the house of slavery, 15 who
[k]led you through the great and terrifying wilderness, [l]with its fiery serpents and scorpions
[m]and thirsty ground where there was no water,
[n]who brought you water out of the flinty rock,
16 who fed you in the wilderness with [o]manna
that your fathers did not know, that he might
humble you and test you, [p]to do you good in
the end. 17 Beware [q]lest you say in your heart,
'My power and the might of my hand have
gotten me this wealth.' 18 You shall remember
the LORD your God, for [r]it is he who gives you
power to get wealth, [s]that he may confirm his
covenant that he swore to your fathers, as it
is this day. 19 And if you forget the LORD your
God and go after other gods and serve them
and worship them, [t]I solemnly warn you today
that you shall surely perish. 20 Like the nations
that the LORD makes to perish before you, [u]so
shall you perish, because you would not obey
the voice of the LORD your God.

Not Because of Righteousness

9 "Hear, O Israel: you are [v]to cross over the
Jordan today, to go in to dispossess nations
[w]greater and mightier than you, cities great
and fortified up to heaven, 2 a people great
and tall, [x]the sons of the Anakim, [y]whom you
know, and of whom you have heard it said,
'Who can stand before the sons of Anak?'
3 Know therefore today that he who [z]goes over
before you [a]as a consuming fire is the LORD
your God. He will destroy them and subdue
them before you. [b]So you shall drive them out
and make them perish quickly, as the LORD
has promised you.

4 [c]"Do not say in your heart, after the LORD
your God has thrust them out before you,
'It is because of my righteousness that the
LORD has brought me in to possess this land,'
whereas it is [d]because of the wickedness of
these nations that the LORD is driving them
out before you. 5 [e]Not because of your righteousness or the uprightness of your heart are
you going in to possess their land, but because
of the wickedness of these nations the LORD
your God is driving them out from before you,
and that he may confirm [f]the word that the
LORD swore to your fathers, to Abraham, to
Isaac, and to Jacob.

6 "Know, therefore, that the LORD your God
is not giving you this good land to possess
because of your righteousness, for you are
[g]a stubborn people. 7 Remember and do not

9:1–12 No text in Deuteronomy besides these verses makes it more clear that Israel's inheritance of the Promised Land was based on grace and not law. "Do not say in your heart . . . 'It is because of my righteousness'" (v. 4). "Not because of your righteousness" (v. 5). "Not because of your righteousness" (v. 6). Verses 7–24 then recount Israel's repeated rebellion against God in the wilderness.

Two explicit reasons are given for Israel's inheritance of the Promised Land: (1) the wickedness of the Canaanites (vv. 4, 5) and (2) the promise made to Abraham, Isaac, and Jacob (v. 5; see 7:8). God's unconditional promise to the patriarchs continues to surface in the book of Deuteronomy (see 1:8; 4:31; 7:8).

A third reason is implicit: the mediation of Moses (9:25–29). Had there been no mediator to stand in the gap between the holy God and sinful Israel, they would never have inherited the land. In the mediatorial work of Moses we have an anticipation of the mediatorial work of Christ (1 Tim. 2:5; Heb. 8:6; 12:24). Not because of our righteousness but because "he is the mediator of a new covenant," we "may receive the promised eternal inheritance" (Heb. 9:15).

As we reflect on the merciful work of our perfect Mediator, our hearts are transformed to love and serve him with joy.

8 [g] [Num. 20:5]
12 [h] ch. 6:11, 12; 28:47; 32:15; Prov. 30:9; Hos. 13:6
14 [i] [1 Cor. 4:7] [j] Ps. 78:11; 106:21
15 [k] See ch. 1:19 [l] Num. 21:6; Isa. 30:6 [m] Hos. 13:5 [n] Ex. 17:6; Num. 20:11; Ps. 78:15; 114:8; [ch. 32:13]
16 [o] ver. 3; Ex. 16:15 [p] [Jer. 24:5-7; Heb. 12:11]
17 [q] [ch. 9:4]
18 [r] [Prov. 10:22; Hos. 2:8] [s] ch. 7:8, 12
19 [t] [ch. 4:26; 30:18]
20 [u] [Dan. 9:11, 12]
Chapter 9
1 [v] ch. 11:31; 12:10; Josh. 1:11 [w] See ch. 4:38
2 [x] See Num. 13:22 [y] ch. 1:28
3 [z] ch. 31:3; [Josh. 3:11] [a] See ch. 4:24 [b] ch. 7:24; Ex. 23:29-31
4 [c] [ch. 8:17] [d] ch. 18:12; Lev. 18:24, 25; 20:23; [ch. 20:18]
5 [e] [Titus 3:5] [f] See Gen. 50:24
6 [g] ch. 10:16

forget how you provoked the LORD your God to wrath in the wilderness. [h]From the day you came out of the land of Egypt until you came to this place, you have been rebellious against the LORD. 8 Even [i]at Horeb you provoked the LORD to wrath, and the LORD was so angry with you that he was ready to destroy you. 9 [j]When I went up the mountain to receive the tablets of stone, the tablets of the covenant that the LORD made with you, I remained on the mountain [k]forty days and forty nights. I neither ate bread nor drank water. 10 And [l]the LORD gave me the two tablets of stone written with the finger of God, and on them were all the words that the LORD had spoken with you on the mountain out of the midst of the fire [m]on the day of the assembly. 11 And at the end of forty days and forty nights the LORD gave me the two tablets of stone, the tablets of the covenant. 12 Then the LORD said to me, [n]'Arise, go down quickly from here, for your people whom you have brought from Egypt have acted corruptly. They have [o]turned aside quickly out of the way that I commanded them; they have made themselves a metal image.'

The Golden Calf

13 [p]"Furthermore, the LORD said to me, 'I have seen this people, and behold, it is [q]a stubborn people. 14 [q]Let me alone, that I may destroy them and [r]blot out their name from under heaven. And [s]I will make of you a nation mightier and greater than they.' 15 [t]So I turned and came down from the mountain, and [u]the mountain was burning with fire. And the two tablets of the covenant were in my two hands. 16 And [v]I looked, and behold, you had sinned against the LORD your God. You had made yourselves a golden[1] calf. [w]You had turned aside quickly from the way that the LORD had commanded you. 17 So I took hold of the two tablets and threw them out of my two hands and broke them before your eyes. 18 Then I [x]lay prostrate before the LORD [y]as before, forty days and forty nights. I neither ate bread nor drank water, because of all the sin that you had committed, [z]in doing what was evil in the sight of the LORD to provoke him to anger. 19 For I was afraid of the anger and hot displeasure that the LORD bore against you, so that he was ready to destroy you. [a]But the LORD listened to me that time also. 20 And the LORD was so angry with Aaron that he was ready to destroy him. And I prayed for Aaron also at the same time. 21 Then [b]I took the sinful thing, the calf that you had made, and burned it with fire and crushed it, grinding it very small, until it was as fine as dust. And I threw the dust of it into the brook that ran down from the mountain.

22 "At [c]Taberah also, and at [d]Massah and at [e]Kibroth-hattaavah you provoked the LORD to wrath. 23 And [f]when the LORD sent you from Kadesh-barnea, saying, 'Go up and take possession of the land that I have given you,' then you rebelled against the commandment of the LORD your God and [g]did not believe him or obey his voice. 24 [h]You have been rebellious against the LORD from the day that I knew you.

25 [x]"So I lay prostrate before the LORD for these forty days and forty nights, because the LORD had said he would destroy you. 26 [i]And I prayed to the LORD, 'O Lord GOD, do not destroy your people and your heritage, whom you have redeemed through your greatness, whom you have brought out of Egypt with a mighty hand. 27 Remember your servants, Abraham, Isaac, and Jacob. Do not regard the stubbornness of this people, or their wickedness or their sin, 28 lest the land from which you brought us say, [j]"Because the LORD was not able to bring them into the land that he promised them, and because he hated them, he has brought them out to put them to death in the wilderness." 29 [k]For they are your people and your heritage, whom you brought out by your great power and by your outstretched arm.'

New Tablets of Stone

10 "At that time the LORD said to me, [l]'Cut for yourself two tablets of stone like the first, and come up to me on the mountain and [m]make an ark of wood. 2 And I will write on the tablets the words that were on the first tablets that you broke, and [n]you shall put them in the ark.' 3 So I made an ark [o]of acacia

[1] Hebrew *cast metal*

7[h] ver. 24; ch. 31:27; [Ex. 14:11; 15:24; 16:2; 17:2; Num. 11:4; 14:2, 11, 41; 20:2; 21:5; 25:2] 8[i] Ex. 32:4; Ps. 106:19 9[j] Ex. 24:12, 15 [k] Ex. 24:18; 34:28; [1 Kgs. 19:8; Matt. 4:2; Luke 4:1, 2] 10[l] Ex. 31:18 [m] ch. 4:10; 10:4; 18:16; Ex. 19:17 12[n] Ex. 32:7, 8 [o] [ch. 31:29; Judg. 2:17] 13[p] Ex. 32:9 [q] [See ver. 6 above] 14[q] Ex. 32:10 [r] ch. 7:24; 25:19; 29:20; Ex. 17:14 [s] Num. 14:12 15[t] Ex. 32:15 [u] ch. 4:11; 5:23; Ex. 19:18 16[v] Ex. 32:19 [w] [ch. 31:29; Judg. 2:17] 18[x] Ex. 34:28; [Ps. 106:23] [y] ver. 9; ch. 10:10 [z] ch. 4:25 19[a] ch. 10:10; Ex. 32:14; 33:17 21[b] Ex. 32:20 22[c] Num. 11:1-3 [d] Ex. 17:7 [e] Num. 11:34 23[f] Num. 13:3; 14:1-4 [g] Ps. 106:24, 25 24[h] ver. 7; ch. 31:27 25[x] [See ver. 18 above] 26[i] See Ex. 32:11-13 28[j] Num. 14:16 29[k] ch. 4:20; 1 Kgs. 8:51; Neh. 1:10; [Ps. 95:7]
Chapter 10 1[l] Ex. 34:1, 2 [m] Ex. 25:10 2[n] Ex. 25:16, 21 3[o] Ex. 25:10; 37:1

wood, and [p]cut two tablets of stone like the
first, and went up the mountain with the two
tablets in my hand. 4 And [q]he wrote on the
tablets, in the same writing as before, the Ten
Commandments[1] [r]that the LORD had spoken
to you on the mountain out of the midst of
the fire [s]on the day of the assembly. And the
LORD gave them to me. 5 Then I turned and
[t]came down from the mountain and [u]put the
tablets in the ark that I had made. [v]And there
they are, as the LORD commanded me."

6 (The people of Israel [w]journeyed from
Beeroth Bene-jaakan[2] to Moserah. [x]There
Aaron died, and there he was buried. And his
son Eleazar ministered as priest in his place.
7 [y]From there they journeyed to Gudgodah,
and from Gudgodah to Jotbathah, a land with
brooks of water. 8 At that time [z]the LORD set
apart the tribe of Levi [a]to carry the ark of the
covenant of the LORD [b]to stand before the
LORD to minister to him and [c]to bless in his
name, to this day. 9 [d]Therefore Levi has no
portion or inheritance with his brothers. The
LORD is his inheritance, as the LORD your God
said to him.)

10 [e]"I myself stayed on the mountain, as at the
first time, forty days and forty nights, [f]and the
LORD listened to me that time also. The LORD
was unwilling to destroy you. 11 [g]And the LORD
said to me, 'Arise, go on your journey at the
head of the people, so that they may go in and
possess the land, which I swore to their fathers
to give them.'

Circumcise Your Heart

12 "And now, Israel, [h]what does the LORD
your God require of you, but [i]to fear the
LORD your God, [j]to walk in all his ways, [k]to
love him, to serve the LORD your God with
all your heart and with all your soul, 13 and
[l]to keep the commandments and statutes of
the LORD, which I am commanding you today
[m]for your good? 14 Behold, [n]to the LORD your
God belong heaven and the heaven of heav-
ens, [o]the earth with all that is in it. 15 Yet [p]the
LORD set his heart in love on your fathers and
chose their offspring after them, you above
all peoples, as you are this day. 16 Circumcise
therefore [q]the foreskin of your heart, and be
no longer [r]stubborn. 17 For the LORD your God
is [s]God of gods and [t]Lord of lords, [u]the great,
the mighty, and the awesome God, who is [v]not
partial and takes no bribe. 18 [w]He executes justice for the fatherless and the widow, and loves
the sojourner, giving him food and clothing.
19 [x]Love the sojourner, therefore, for you were
sojourners in the land of Egypt. 20 [i]You shall
fear the LORD your God. You shall serve him
and [y]hold fast to him, and [z]by his name you
shall swear. 21 [a]He is your praise. He is your
God, [b]who has done for you these great and
terrifying things that your eyes have seen.
22 Your fathers went down to Egypt [c]seventy
persons, and now the LORD your God has
made you [d]as numerous as the stars of heaven.

Love and Serve the LORD

11 [e]"You shall therefore love the LORD your
God and [f]keep his charge, his statutes,
his rules, and his commandments always.
2 And consider today (since I am not speaking
to [g]your children who have not known or seen
it), consider the discipline[3] of the LORD your
God, [h]his greatness, [i]his mighty hand and his
outstretched arm, 3 [j]his signs and his deeds
that he did in Egypt to Pharaoh the king of
Egypt and to all his land, 4 and what he did
to the army of Egypt, to their horses and to
their chariots, [k]how he made the water of the
Red Sea flow over them as they pursued after
you, and how the LORD has destroyed them
to this day, 5 and [l]what he did to you in the

[1] Hebrew *words* [2] Or *the wells of the Bene-jaakan* [3] Or *instruction*

10:12–22 "And now, Israel, what does the LORD your God require of you" (v. 12). Or, how should we respond to God's gracious salvation? By loving God (v. 12) and by loving the sojourner/those in need/neighbor (v. 19). If we truly love God, then we will love what and whom he loves. Our response to God's gracious salvation is in keeping with who God is, for he loves those in need (v. 18); and this is in keeping with an understanding of who *we* used to be, for we used to be those in need (v. 19) before God saved us by his grace.

3 [p]Ex. 34:4
4 [q]Ex. 34:28 [r]Ex. 20:1 [s]See ch. 9:10
5 [t]Ex. 34:29 [u]Ex. 40:20 [v]1 Kgs. 8:9
6 [w]Num. 33:30, 31 [x][Num. 20:28; 33:38]
7 [y]Num. 33:32, 33
8 [z]Num. 3:6; 8:14; 16:9; [1 Chr. 23:13] [a]Num. 4:5, 15

[b]ch. 17:12; 18:5, 7 [c]ch. 21:5; Lev. 9:22; See Num. 6:23-26 **9** [d]See Num. 18:20 **10** [e]ch. 9:18, 25 [f]ch. 9:19 **11** [g]Ex. 32:34; 33:1 **12** [h][Mic. 6:8] [i]See ch. 6:2, 13 [j]See ch. 5:33 [k]See ch. 6:5 **13** [l]ch. 7:11 [m]ch. 6:24 **14** [n]1 Kgs. 8:27; 2 Chr. 6:18; Neh. 9:6; Ps. 115:16; Isa. 66:1 [o]Ex. 19:5; Ps. 24:1 **15** [p]ch. 4:37; [ch. 7:7] **16** [q]ch. 30:6; Jer. 4:4; [Acts 7:51] [r]See ch. 9:6 **17** [s]Josh. 22:22; Ps. 136:2; Dan. 2:47; 11:36 [t]Rev. 17:14; 19:16 [u]Neh. 9:32; See ch. 7:21 [v]2 Chr. 19:7; Job 34:19; Acts 10:34; Rom. 2:11; Gal. 2:6; Eph. 6:9; Col. 3:25; 1 Pet. 1:17 **18** [w]Ps. 68:5; 146:9; [ch. 24:17; Ex. 22:22] **19** [x]Ex. 22:21; 23:9; Lev. 19:33, 34 **20** [i][See ver. 12 above] [y]ch. 11:22; 13:4; 30:20 [z]See ch. 6:13 **21** [a]Ps. 22:3; 109:1; Jer. 17:14 [b]2 Sam. 7:23; Ps. 106:21, 22 **22** [c]Gen. 46:27; Ex. 1:5; [Acts 7:14] [d]ch. 28:62; Neh. 9:23; See Gen. 15:5 **Chapter 11** **1** [e]See ch. 6:5 [f][Ezek. 44:16]; See Lev. 8:35 **2** [g]ch. 31:13 [h]ch. 3:24; 5:24 [i]See ch. 4:34 **3** [j]ch. 6:22; 7:19 **4** [k]Ex. 14:27, 28; 15:9, 10; Ps. 106:11 **5** [l]See Ps. 78:14-40

wilderness, until you came to this place, 6 and
[m]what he did to Dathan and Abiram the sons
of Eliab, son of Reuben, how the earth opened
its mouth and swallowed them up, with their
households, their tents, and every living thing
that followed them, in the midst of all Israel.
7 For your eyes have seen [n]all the great work of
the LORD that he did.
8 "You shall therefore keep the whole commandment that I command you today, that
you may [o]be strong, and go in and take possession of the land that you are going over to possess,
9 and [p]that you may live long in the land
[q]that the LORD swore to your fathers to give
to them and to their offspring, [r]a land flowing
with milk and honey.
10 For the land that you
are entering to take possession of it is not like
the land of Egypt, from which you have come,
where you sowed your seed and irrigated it,[1]
like a garden of vegetables.
11 [s]But the land that
you are going over to possess is a land of hills
and valleys, which drinks water by the rain
from heaven,
12 a land that the LORD your God
cares for. [t]The eyes of the LORD your God are
always upon it, from the beginning of the year
to the end of the year.
13 "And if you will indeed obey my commandments that I command you today, [u]to love the
LORD your God, and to serve him with all your
heart and with all your soul,
14 [v]he[2] will give
the rain for your land in its season, [w]the early
rain and the later rain, that you may gather in
your grain and your wine and your oil.
15 [x]And
he will give grass in your fields for your livestock, and [y]you shall eat and be full.
16 Take
care [z]lest your heart be deceived, and you turn
aside and [a]serve other gods and worship them;
17 then [b]the anger of the LORD will be kindled
against you, and he [c]will shut up the heavens,
so that there will be no rain, and the land will
yield no fruit, and [d]you will perish quickly off
the good land that the LORD is giving you.
18 [e]"You shall therefore lay up these words
of mine in your heart and in your soul, and
[f]you shall bind them as a sign on your hand,
and they shall be as frontlets between your
eyes.
19 You shall teach them to your children,
talking of them when you are sitting in your
house, and when you are walking by the way,
and when you lie down, and when you rise.
20 [g]You shall write them on the doorposts of
your house and on your gates,
21 [h]that your
days and the days of your children may be
multiplied in the land that the LORD swore
to your fathers to give them, [i]as long as the
heavens are above the earth.
22 For if [j]you will
be careful to do all this commandment that
I command you to do, loving the LORD your
God, walking in all his ways, and [k]holding
fast to him,
23 then the LORD [l]will drive out
all these nations before you, and you will
[m]dispossess nations greater and mightier
than you.
24 [n]Every place on which the sole of
your foot treads shall be yours. Your territory
shall be [o]from the wilderness to[3] the Lebanon
and from the River, the river Euphrates, to the
western sea.
25 [p]No one shall be able to stand
against you. The LORD your God will lay [q]the
fear of you and the dread of you on all the
land that you shall tread, [r]as he promised you.
26 [s]"See, I am setting before you today a blessing and a curse:
27 [t]the blessing, if you obey the
commandments of the LORD your God, which
I command you today,
28 and [u]the curse, if you
do not obey the commandments of the LORD
your God, but turn aside from the way that
I am commanding you today, [v]to go after other
gods that you have not known.
29 And when

[1] Hebrew *watered it with your feet* [2] Samaritan, Septuagint, Vulgate; Hebrew *I*; also verse 15 [3] Hebrew *and*

11:13–28 God gave Israel two alternatives: a blessing for keeping the commandments, or a curse for breaking them (vv. 26–28). The blessing would be abundant life in the land (vv. 13–15), while the curse would be expulsion from the land (vv. 16–17). These were in effect the same alternatives given to Adam and Eve in the garden. And just as Adam and Eve broke the commands and were expelled from the garden, eventually Israel broke the commands and was expelled from the land.

Jesus came as the second Adam (Rom. 5:12–21; 1 Cor. 15:22, 45) and as the new Israel (cf. Ex. 4:22–23; Matt. 1:1; 2:15; 3:13–4:2). But Jesus perfectly kept the commands and therefore merited the blessing of eternal life in the presence of God. We are therefore to take God's word to heart (Deut. 11:18), pass it on to the next generation (v. 19), and have it govern our domestic and public life (v. 20). In this way we enjoy abundant life in the world that God has made (v. 21; Eph. 6:1–3).

6 [m] Num. 16:1, 31; 27:3; Ps. 106:17
7 [n] Judg. 2:7
8 [o] ch. 31:6, 7; Josh. 1:6, 7, 9, 18
9 [p] See ch. 4:40 [q] See Gen. 50:24 [r] Ex. 3:8
11 [s] ch. 8:7
12 [t] [1 Kgs. 9:3; Jer. 24:6]
13 [u] See ch. 6:5
14 [v] ch. 28:12; Lev. 26:4 [w] [Job 29:23; Jer. 5:24; Hos. 6:3; Joel 2:23; James 5:7]
15 [x] Ps. 104:14 [y] ch. 6:11; [Joel 2:19]
16 [z] [Job 31:27] [a] ver. 28; See ch. 6:14
17 [b] ch. 6:15 [c] 1 Kgs. 8:35; 2 Chr. 6:26; 7:13; [ch. 28:23, 24; Lev. 26:19, 20; Amos 4:7; Zech. 14:17; Rev. 11:6] [d] ch. 4:26; 30:18; Josh. 23:15, 16 **18** [e] See ch. 6:6 [f] See ch. 6:8 **20** [g] ch. 6:9 **21** [h] See ch. 4:40 [i] Ps. 89:29 **22** [j] ch. 6:17 [k] See ch. 10:20 **23** [l] See ch. 4:38 [m] ch. 9:1 **24** [n] Josh. 1:3; [Josh. 14:9] [o] See Ex. 23:31 **25** [p] See ch. 7:24 [q] ch. 2:25 [r] Ex. 23:27 **26** [s] ch. 30:1, 15, 19 **27** [t] See ch. 28:2-14 **28** [u] See ch. 28:15-45 [v] See ch. 6:14

the LORD your God brings you into the land
that you are entering to take possession of it,
you shall set [w]the blessing on Mount Gerizim
and the curse on Mount Ebal. 30 Are they not
beyond the Jordan, west of the road, toward
the going down of the sun, in the land of the
Canaanites who live in the [x]Arabah, opposite
Gilgal, beside [y]the oak[1] of Moreh? 31 For you are
[z]to cross over the Jordan to go in to take possession of the land that the LORD your God is giving you. And when you possess it and live in it,
32 you shall be careful [a]to do all the statutes and
the rules that I am setting before you today.

The LORD's Chosen Place of Worship

12 [b]"These are the statutes and rules that
you shall be careful to do in the land
that the LORD, the God of your fathers, has
given you to possess, [c]all the days that you
live on the earth. 2 [d]You shall surely destroy
all the places where the nations whom you
shall dispossess served their gods, [e]on the high
mountains and on the hills and under every
green tree. 3 You shall tear down their altars
and dash in pieces [f]their pillars and burn their
[g]Asherim with fire. You shall chop down the
carved images of their gods and [h]destroy their
name out of that place. 4 [i]You shall not worship
the LORD your God in that way. 5 But you shall
seek [j]the place that the LORD your God will
choose out of all your tribes to put his name
and make his habitation[2] there. There you
shall go, 6 and there you shall bring your burnt
offerings and your sacrifices, [k]your tithes and
the contribution that you present, your vow
offerings, your freewill offerings, and the
[l]firstborn of your herd and of your flock. 7 And
[m]there you shall eat before the LORD your God,
and [n]you shall rejoice, you and your households, in all that you undertake, in which the
LORD your God has blessed you.

8 "You shall not do according to all that we
are doing here today, [o]everyone doing whatever is right in his own eyes, 9 for you have not
as yet come to [p]the rest and to the inheritance
that the LORD your God is giving you. 10 But
when [q]you go over the Jordan and live in the
land that the LORD your God is giving you to
inherit, [r]and when he gives you rest from all
your enemies around, so that you live in safety,
11 then to [j]the place that the LORD your God
will choose, to make his name dwell there,
there you shall bring all that I command you:
your burnt offerings and your sacrifices, [k]your
tithes and the contribution that you present,
and all your finest vow offerings that you vow
to the LORD. 12 And [n]you shall rejoice before
the LORD your God, you and your sons and
your daughters, your male servants and your
female servants, and the Levite that is within
your towns, since [s]he has no portion or inheritance with you. 13 [t]Take care that you do not
offer your burnt offerings at any place that
you see, 14 but at [j]the place that the LORD will
choose in one of your tribes, there you shall
offer your burnt offerings, and there you shall
do all that I am commanding you.

15 "However, you may slaughter and eat
meat within any of your towns, as much
as you desire, [u]according to the blessing of
the LORD your God that he has given you.
[v]The unclean and the clean may eat of it, as
of the gazelle and as of the deer. 16 [w]Only you
shall not eat the blood; you shall pour it out
on the earth like water. 17 You may not eat
within your towns [k]the tithe of your grain or
of your wine or of your oil, or the firstborn of
your herd or of your flock, or any of your vow
offerings that you vow, or your freewill offerings or the contribution that you present,
18 but [m]you shall eat them before the LORD

[1] Septuagint, Syriac; see Genesis 12:6. Hebrew *oaks*, or *terebinths* [2] Or *name as its habitation*

12:1–28 Under the old covenant the public worship of God had to take place at the temple in Jerusalem, because that was where the special presence of God was manifested (vv. 5–7, 11, 17–18, 21, 26). In the new covenant the special presence of God is manifested in Jesus Christ, the true and final temple (John 2:19–22; Eph. 2:19–22) who "tabernacled" among us (John 1:14) and now dwells within his people—both individually and corporately (e.g., 1 Cor. 3:16–17; Gal. 2:20; Eph. 2:21–22; Heb. 8:1–2; 9:11–12). As a result, our worship of God is not restricted to any one locale. In Christ we are not required to worship God in any particular place. Rather we are required to worship God "in spirit and truth" (John 4:23).

29 [w] ch. 27:12, 13; Josh. 8:33
30 [x] See ch. 1:1 [y] Judg. 7:1
31 [z] ch. 9:1; 12:10; Josh. 1:11
32 [a] ch. 5:32; 12:32

Chapter 12
1 [b] ch. 6:1 [c] ch. 4:10
2 [d] ch. 7:5; Ex. 34:13 [e] 1 Kgs. 14:23; 2 Kgs. 16:4; 17:10; Jer. 3:6
3 [f] See ch. 16:22 [g] See ch. 16:21 [h] [Zeph. 1:4; Zech. 13:2]
4 [i] ver. 31
5 [j] ch. 16:2; 26:2; 1 Kgs. 8:29; 2 Chr. 7:12; [Josh. 18:1]

6 [k] ch. 14:22, 23; 15:19, 20 [l] ch. 14:23 **7** [m] ch. 14:23, 26; 15:20 [n] ch. 14:26; 16:11, 14, 15; 26:11; 27:7; 28:8; Lev. 23:40 **8** [o] Judg. 17:6; 21:25 **9** [p] 1 Kgs. 8:56; Ps. 95:11; [Heb. 4:8] **10** [q] See ch. 11:31 [r] ch. 25:19; Josh. 23:1; [2 Sam. 7:1; 1 Kgs. 5:4] **11** [j] [See ver. 5 above] [k] [See ver. 6 above] **12** [n] [See ver. 7 above] [s] See Num. 18:20 **13** [t] Lev. 17:3, 4; [1 Kgs. 12:28, 33] **14** [j] [See ver. 5 above] **15** [u] ch. 16:17 [v] ch. 14:5; 15:22 **16** [w] See Lev. 3:17 **17** [k] [See ver. 6 above] **18** [m] [See ver. 7 above]

your God in [j]the place that the LORD your
God will choose, you and your son and your
daughter, your male servant and your female
servant, and the Levite who is within your
towns. And [n]you shall rejoice before the LORD
your God in all that you undertake. 19 [x]Take
care that you do not neglect the Levite as long
as you live in your land.
20 "When the LORD your God [y]enlarges your
territory, [z]as he has promised you, and you say,
'I will eat meat,' because you crave meat, you
may eat meat whenever you desire. 21 If [a]the
place that the LORD your God will choose to
put his name there is too far from you, [b]then
you may kill any of your herd or your flock,
which the LORD has given you, as I have commanded you, and you may eat within your
towns whenever you desire. 22 Just [c]as the
gazelle or the deer is eaten, so you may eat of
it. [c]The unclean and the clean alike may eat
of it. 23 [d]Only be sure that you do not eat the
blood, [e]for the blood is the life, and you shall
not eat the life with the flesh. 24 You shall not
eat it; you shall pour it out on the earth like
water. 25 You shall not eat it, [f]that all may go
well with you and with your children after
you, [g]when you do what is right in the sight
of the LORD. 26 But the [h]holy things that are
due from you, and [i]your vow offerings, you
shall take, and you shall go to [a]the place that
the LORD will choose, 27 and [j]offer your burnt
offerings, the flesh and the blood, on the altar
of the LORD your God. The blood of your sacrifices shall be poured out on the altar of the
LORD your God, but the flesh you may eat.
28 Be careful to obey all these words that I command you, [f]that it may go well with you and
with your children after you forever, when you
do what is good and right in the sight of the
LORD your God.

Warning Against Idolatry

29 "When [k]the LORD your God cuts off before
you the nations whom you go in to dispossess,
and you dispossess them and dwell in their
land, 30 take care [l]that you be not ensnared to
follow them, after they have been destroyed
before you, and that you do not inquire about
their gods, saying, 'How did these nations
serve their gods?—that I also may do the
same.' 31 [m]You shall not worship the LORD your
God in that way, for every [n]abominable thing
that the LORD hates they have done for their
gods, for [o]they even burn their sons and their
daughters in the fire to their gods.
32 [1] "Everything that I command you, you
shall be careful to do. [p]You shall not add to it
or take from it.

13 "If a prophet or [q]a dreamer of dreams
arises among you and gives you a sign
or a wonder, 2 and [r]the sign or wonder that
he tells you comes to pass, and if he says, 'Let
us go after other gods,' which you have not
known, 'and let us serve them,' 3 you shall not
listen to the words of that prophet or that
dreamer of dreams. For the LORD your God
[s]is testing you, to know whether you love the
LORD your God with all your heart and with
all your soul. 4 You shall [t]walk after the LORD
your God and fear him and keep his commandments and obey his voice, and you shall
serve him and [u]hold fast to him. 5 But [v]that
prophet or that dreamer of dreams shall be
put to death, because he has taught rebellion

[1] Ch 13:1 in Hebrew

18[j] [See ver. 5 above] [n] [See ver. 7 above]
19[x] ch. 14:27; [2 Chr. 31:4]
20[y] ch. 19:8 [z] ch. 11:24; 19:8, 9; Gen. 28:14; Ex. 34:24
21[a] See ver. 5 [b] ver. 15
22[c] ch. 14:5; 15:22
23[d] See Lev. 3:17 [e] See Gen. 9:4
25[f] ch. 4:40; [Eccles. 8:12; Isa. 3:10] [g] ch. 6:18; 13:18; Ex. 15:26; 1 Kgs. 11:38
26[h] [Num. 5:9, 10; 18:19] [i] [1 Sam. 1:21] [a] [See ver. 21 above]
27[j] Lev. 1:5, 9, 13; 17:11
28[f] [See ver. 25 above]
29[k] ch. 19:1; Josh. 23:4, 5
30[l] ch. 7:16
31[m] ver. 4; Lev. 18:3, 26, 30; [2 Kgs. 17:15] [n] ch. 7:25; 17:1; 18:12; 23:18; 25:16; 27:15 [o] 2 Kgs. 17:31; Jer. 7:31; 19:5 **32**[p] See ch. 4:2 **Chapter 13** **1**[q] Jer. 23:25, 32; 27:9; 29:8; Zech. 10:2 **2**[r] [ch. 18:22; Jer. 28:9] **3**[s] ch. 8:2 **4**[t] 2 Kgs. 23:3; 2 Chr. 34:31 [u] See ch. 10:20 **5**[v] ch. 18:20; [Jer. 2:8; 14:14, 15; Zech. 13:3]

12:29–13:18 Loyalty to God because of his grace is the theme of this section. Israel was not to "follow" other gods (12:30), "go after other gods" (13:2), or "serve other gods" (13:6, 13). Rather, they were to love God with complete loyalty (13:3). Why? Because in his great grace, God had brought them out of slavery (13:5, 10) and dispossessed the Canaanites (12:29) in fulfillment of his gracious promise to Abraham, Isaac, and Jacob (13:17). Israel was to demonstrate this loyalty based on grace by not being conformed to the ways of the Canaanites (12:30–32), but rather walking in the ways of the Lord (13:4, 18).

This same pattern is articulated in the New Testament. The apostle Paul, for example, urges believers not to be conformed to the world but to be transformed so as to live a life pleasing to God based on his mercy (Rom. 12:1–2). The practical teaching in Romans 12:3–15:13 shows believers what this loyalty looks like in daily living. As his redeemed and utterly secure children, it is our delight to yield ourselves fully to the Lord and his ways.

against the LORD your God, who brought you
out of the land of Egypt and redeemed you out
of the house of slavery, to make you leave the
way in which the LORD your God commanded
you to walk. [w]So you shall purge the evil[1] from
your midst.
6 [x]"If your brother, the son of your mother,
or your son or your daughter or [y]the wife you
embrace[2] or your friend [z]who is as your own
soul entices you secretly, saying, 'Let us go and
serve other gods,' [a]which neither you nor your
fathers have known, 7 some [b]of the gods of the
peoples who are around you, whether near
you or far off from you, from the one end of
the earth to the other, 8 you shall [c]not yield to
him or listen to him, nor [d]shall your eye pity
him, nor shall you spare him, nor shall you
conceal him. 9 But you shall kill him. [e]Your
hand shall be first against him to put him
to death, and afterward the hand of all the
people. 10 [f]You shall stone him to death with
stones, because he sought to draw you away
from the LORD your God, who brought you
out of the land of Egypt, out of the house of
slavery. 11 And [g]all Israel shall hear and fear and
never again do any such wickedness as this
among you.
12 "If you hear in one of your cities, which the
LORD your God is giving you to dwell there,
13 that certain [h]worthless fellows have gone out
among you and have drawn away the inhabitants of their city, saying, 'Let us go and serve
other gods,' which you have not known, 14 then
you shall inquire and make search and ask
[i]diligently. And behold, if it be true and certain that such an abomination has been done
among you, 15 you shall surely put the inhabitants of that city to the sword, devoting it to
destruction,[3] all who are in it and its cattle,
with the edge of the sword. 16 You shall gather
all its spoil into the midst of its open square
and [j]burn the city and all its spoil with fire, as
a whole burnt offering to the LORD your God.
It shall be a [k]heap forever. It shall not be built
again. 17 [l]None of the devoted things shall stick
to your hand, [m]that the LORD may turn from
the fierceness of his anger and show you mercy
and have compassion on you and multiply
you, [n]as he swore to your fathers, 18 if you obey
the voice of the LORD your God, [o]keeping all
his commandments that I am commanding
you today, and doing what is right in the sight
of the LORD your God.

Clean and Unclean Food

14 "You are [p]the sons of the LORD your
God. [q]You shall not cut yourselves or
make any [r]baldness on your foreheads for the
dead. 2 For [s]you are a people holy to the LORD
your God, and the LORD has chosen you to be
a people for his treasured possession, out of all
the peoples who are on the face of the earth.
3 [t]"You shall not eat any abomination.
4 [u]These are the animals you may eat: the ox,
the sheep, the goat, 5 the deer, the gazelle, the
roebuck, the wild goat, the ibex,[4] the antelope,
and the mountain sheep. 6 Every animal that
parts the hoof and has the hoof cloven in two
and chews the cud, among the animals, you
may eat. 7 Yet of those that chew the cud or
have the hoof cloven you shall not eat these:
the camel, the hare, and the [v]rock badger,
because they chew the cud but do not part
the hoof, are unclean for you. 8 And the pig,
because it parts the hoof but does not chew
the cud, is unclean for you. Their flesh you
shall not eat, and [w]their carcasses you shall
not touch.
9 "Of all that are in the waters you may eat
these: whatever has fins and scales you may

[1] Or *evil person* [2] Hebrew *the wife of your bosom* [3] That is, setting apart (devoting) as an offering to the Lord (for destruction) [4] Or *addax*

14:1–21 Israel was to observe various ceremonial laws—for example, those pertaining to clean and unclean food. To be ceremonially clean was symbolic of being morally holy. This explains why this text on clean and unclean food is bracketed by references to Israel being "a people holy to the LORD" (vv. 2, 21).

In the new covenant the requirement to observe these ceremonial laws has been abrogated, because they have served their purpose of pointing to the perfect holiness of Christ (Col. 2:16–23; Heb. 9:1–10:26). Living out the moral holiness to which these ceremonial laws pointed is, however, still the goal of those who have been united to Christ by grace through faith (2 Cor. 6:14–7:1). Believers are to "touch no unclean thing" (2 Cor. 6:17) and "bring holiness to completion in the fear of God" (2 Cor. 7:1).

5 [w]ch. 17:7; 19:19; 21:21; 22:21; 24:7; [1 Cor. 5:13]
6 [x]ch. 17:2 [y]ch. 28:54, 56; Mic. 7:5 [z][1 Sam. 18:1, 3; 20:17] [a]ch. 28:64
7 [b]ch. 6:14
8 [c]Prov. 1:10 [d]See ch. 7:16
9 [e]ch. 17:7
10 [f]ch. 17:5; See Josh. 7:25
11 [g]ch. 17:13; 19:20; 21:21
13 [h]Judg. 19:22; 20:13; 1 Sam. 2:12; 25:17; 2 Sam. 16:7; 20:1; 1 Kgs. 21:10, 13
14 [i]ch. 17:4; 19:18
16 [j]Josh. 6:24 [k]Josh. 8:28; Jer. 49:2; [Isa. 17:1; 25:2; Jer. 30:18] **17** [l]Josh. 6:18 [m]Josh. 7:26 [n]See Gen. 50:24 **18** [o]ch. 12:25, 28 **Chapter 14** **1** [p][Isa. 1:2; Hos. 1:10; John 1:12; Rom. 9:8, 26; Gal. 3:26] [q]See Lev. 19:28 [r][Isa. 15:2; 22:12; Ezek. 7:18; Amos 8:10] **2** [s]See ch. 7:6 **3** [t]Ezek. 4:14; [Acts 10:13, 14] **4** [u]For ver. 4-20, see Lev. 11:2-23 **7** [v]Lev. 11:5; [Ps. 104:18; Prov. 30:26] **8** [w][Lev. 11:26]

eat. 10 And whatever does not have fins and scales you shall not eat; it is unclean for you.

11 "You may eat all clean birds. 12 But these are the ones that you shall not eat: the eagle,[1] the bearded vulture, the black vulture, 13 the kite, the falcon of any kind; 14 every raven of any kind; 15 the ostrich, the nighthawk, the sea gull, the hawk of any kind; 16 the little owl and the short-eared owl, the barn owl 17 and the tawny owl, the carrion vulture and the cormorant, 18 the stork, the heron of any kind; the hoopoe and the bat. 19 And all winged insects are unclean for you; they shall not be eaten. 20 All clean winged things you may eat.

21 [x]"You shall not eat anything that has died naturally. You may give it to the sojourner who is within your towns, that he may eat it, or you may sell it to a foreigner. For [y]you are a people holy to the LORD your God.

[z]"You shall not boil a young goat in its mother's milk.

Tithes

22 [a]"You shall tithe all the yield of your seed that comes from the field year by year. 23 And before the LORD your God, in the place that he will choose, to make his name dwell there, [b]you shall eat the tithe of your grain, of your wine, and of your oil, [c]and the firstborn of your herd and flock, [d]that you may learn to fear the LORD your God always. 24 And if the way is too long for you, so that you are not able to carry the tithe, when the LORD your God blesses you, because [e]the place is too far from you, which the LORD your God chooses, to set his name there, 25 then you shall turn it into money and bind up the money in your hand and go to the place that the LORD your God chooses 26 and spend the money for whatever you desire—oxen or sheep or wine or strong drink, whatever your appetite craves. And [b]you shall eat there before the LORD your God and rejoice, you and your household. 27 And you shall not neglect [f]the Levite who is within your towns, for [g]he has no portion or inheritance with you.

28 [h]"At the end of every three years you shall bring out all the tithe of your produce in the same year and lay it up within your towns. 29 And the Levite, because [g]he has no portion or inheritance with you, and the sojourner, the fatherless, and the widow, who are within your towns, shall come and eat and be filled, that [i]the LORD your God may bless you in all the work of your hands that you do.

The Sabbatical Year

15 "At the end of [j]every seven years you shall grant a release. 2 And this is the manner of the release: every creditor shall release what he has lent to his neighbor. He shall not exact it of his neighbor, his brother, because the LORD's release has been proclaimed. 3 [k]Of a foreigner you may exact it, but whatever of yours is with your brother your hand shall release. 4 [l]But there will be no poor among you; [m]for the LORD will bless you in the land that the LORD your God is giving you for an inheritance to possess— 5 [n]if only you will strictly obey the voice of the LORD your God, being careful to do all this commandment that I command you today. 6 For the LORD your God will bless you, [o]as he promised you, and [p]you shall lend to many nations, but you shall not borrow, and [q]you shall rule over many nations, but they shall not rule over you.

[1] The identity of many of these birds is uncertain

21 [x] See Lev. 7:24 [y] See ch. 7:6 [z] See Ex. 23:19
22 [a] See Num. 18:21
23 [b] ch. 12:7; 15:20 [c] ch. 12:6 [d] ch. 4:10; 17:19
24 [e] ch. 12:21
26 [b] [See ver. 23 above]
27 [f] See ch. 12:19 [g] See Num. 18:20
28 [h] ch. 26:12; [Amos 4:4]
29 [g] [See ver. 27 above] [i] ch. 15:10; 24:19; Ps. 41:1; Prov. 14:21; 19:17; 22:9; Mal. 3:10
Chapter 15
1 [j] ch. 31:10; Neh. 10:31; [ver. 12; Ex. 23:10, 11; Lev. 25:2-4]
3 [k] [ch. 23:20]
4 [l] [ver. 11] [m] ch. 28:8
5 [n] ch. 28:1
6 [o] ch. 7:13; Ex. 23:25 [p] ch. 28:12, 44 [q] ch. 28:13; 1 Kgs. 4:21, 24; Ezra 4:20; [Prov. 22:7]

15:1–18 The sabbatical year illustrates the principle of generosity based on grace. There would have been times in ancient Israel when someone would have run into financial difficulties and needed a loan (vv. 7–11) or even more radically would have been sold into slavery because of financial destitution (vv. 12–18). Lending freely not grudgingly (v. 10) and providing liberally (v. 14) was to characterize God's people. Why was such generosity to be the norm? Because Israel knew what it was to be slaves in Egypt (v. 15) and to experience the generosity of God (v. 14).

Jesus taught that this same spirit of generosity is operative in the "kingdom of heaven" (Matt. 18:23–35). Out of his extravagant generosity, the divine King released us from a debt we could never have paid back on our own (Matt. 18:27), and he expects us to show this same kind of generosity to others who are in need (Matt. 18:28–35). Our generosity to others is to be motivated by God's prior grace to us (2 Cor. 8:9).

As we consider the depths of God's own love for us and the riches that he has lavished upon us in Christ (Eph. 1:7–8, 18), our hearts cannot help but be moved to give to others as a reflection of what God has given to us.

7 “If among you, one of your brothers should become poor, in any of your towns within your land that the LORD your God is giving you, [r]you shall not harden your heart or shut your hand against your poor brother, 8 but [s]you shall open your hand to him and lend him sufficient for his need, whatever it may be. 9 Take care lest there be an unworthy thought in your heart and you say, ‘The seventh year, the year of release is near,’ and your [t]eye look grudgingly[1] on your poor brother, and you give him nothing, and he [u]cry to the LORD against you, and [v]you be guilty of sin. 10 You shall give to him freely, and [w]your heart shall not be grudging when you give to him, because [x]for this the LORD your God will bless you in all your work and in all that you undertake. 11 For [y]there will never cease to be poor in the land. Therefore I command you, [s]‘You shall open wide your hand to your brother, to the needy and to the poor, in your land.’

12 [z]“If your brother, a Hebrew man or a Hebrew woman, is sold[2] to you, he shall serve you six years, and in the seventh year you shall let him go free from you. 13 And when you let him go free from you, you shall not let him go empty-handed. 14 You shall furnish him liberally out of your flock, out of your threshing floor, and out of your winepress. [a]As the LORD your God has blessed you, you shall give to him. 15 [b]You shall remember that you were a slave in the land of Egypt, and the LORD your God redeemed you; therefore I command you this today. 16 But [c]if he says to you, ‘I will not go out from you,’ because he loves you and your household, since he is well-off with you, 17 then you shall take an awl, and put it through his ear into the door, and he shall be your slave[3] forever. And to your female slave[4] you shall do the same. 18 It shall not seem hard to you when you let him go free from you, for at half the cost of a hired worker he has served you six years. So the LORD your God will bless you in all that you do.

19 [d]“All the firstborn males that are born of your herd and flock you shall dedicate to the LORD your God. You shall do no work with the firstborn of your herd, nor shear the firstborn of your flock. 20 [e]You shall eat it, you and your household, before the LORD your God year by year at the place that the LORD will choose. 21 [f]But if it has any blemish, if it is lame or blind or has any serious blemish whatever, you shall not sacrifice it to the LORD your God. 22 You shall eat it within your towns. [g]The unclean and the clean alike may eat it, as though it were a gazelle or a deer. 23 [h]Only you shall not eat its blood; you shall pour it out on the ground like water.

Passover

16 “Observe the [i]month of Abib and keep the Passover to the LORD your God, for [j]in the month of Abib the LORD your God brought you out of Egypt by night. 2 And you shall offer the Passover sacrifice to the LORD your God, from the flock or [k]the herd, [l]at the place that the LORD will choose, to make his name dwell there. 3 You shall eat no leavened bread with it. [m]Seven days you shall eat it with unleavened bread, the bread of affliction—for you came out of the land of Egypt [n]in haste—that all the days of your life you may remember the day when you came out of the land of Egypt. 4 [o]No leaven shall be seen with you in all your territory for seven days, [p]nor shall any of the flesh that you sacrifice on the evening

[1] Or *be evil*; also verse 10 [2] Or *sells himself* [3] Or *servant*; the Hebrew term *'ebed* designates a range of social and economic roles (see Preface) [4] Or *servant*

16:1–8 Passover, which celebrated Israel's exodus from Egypt (v. 1), was closely associated with the Feast of Unleavened Bread (v. 16; Lev. 23:5–6), because during this combined feast the Israelites removed all leaven from their diets (Deut. 16:3) and from their land (v. 4), as a reminder of their affliction in Egypt and the haste of their departure (v. 3).

The apostle Paul says that, “Christ, our Passover lamb, has been sacrificed” (1 Cor. 5:7). As the blood of the Passover lamb protected the Israelites from death (Ex. 12:13), so the blood of Christ, “our Passover lamb,” protects us from death (Rom. 6:23). As the ancient Israelites were to remove all leaven literally, so the church is to remove all leaven metaphorically, i.e., the church is to live without moral corruption and in “sincerity and truth” (1 Cor. 5:8). Our striving to live with moral purity (1 Cor. 5:8) is our response to God's grace granted through “our Passover lamb” (1 Cor. 5:7).

7 [r][1 John 3:17]
8 [s]Lev. 25:35; [Matt. 5:42; Luke 6:34, 35]
9 [t]ch. 28:54, 56; Prov. 23:6; 28:22; Matt. 20:15 [u]ch. 24:15 [v][Matt. 25:41, 42]
10 [w][2 Cor. 9:7] [x]Prov. 28:27; See ch. 14:29
11 [y][Matt. 26:11; Mark 14:7; John 12:8] [s][See ver. 8 above]
12 [z]Ex. 21:2; Jer. 34:14; [Lev. 25:39-41]
14 [a]ch. 8:18; 16:17
15 [b]See ch. 5:15
16 [c]Ex. 21:5, 6
19 [d]See Ex. 13:2
20 [e]ch. 12:7; 14:23, 26

21 [f]See Lev. 22:20 **22** [g]ch. 12:15 **23** [h]See Lev. 3:17 **Chapter 16** **1** [i]For ver. 1-8, see Ex. 12:2-39 [j]Ex. 13:4; 34:18 **2** [k]Num. 28:19 [l]See ch. 12:5 **3** [m]Ex. 13:6 [n]Ex. 12:11; [Isa. 52:12] **4** [o]Ex. 13:7 [p]Ex. 34:25

of the first day remain all night until morning. 5 You may not offer the Passover sacrifice within any of your towns that the LORD your God is giving you, 6 but at the place that the LORD your God will choose, to make his name dwell in it, there you shall offer the Passover sacrifice, in the evening at sunset, at the time you came out of Egypt. 7 And you shall cook it and eat it at the place that the LORD your God will choose. And in the morning you shall turn and go to your tents. 8 For [q]six days you shall eat unleavened bread, and on the seventh day there shall be [r]a solemn assembly to the LORD your God. You shall do no work on it.

The Feast of Weeks

9 [s]"You shall count seven weeks. Begin to count the seven weeks from the time the sickle is first put to the standing grain. 10 Then you shall keep [t]the Feast of Weeks to the LORD your God with [u]the tribute of a freewill offering from your hand, which you shall give [v]as the LORD your God blesses you. 11 And [w]you shall rejoice before the LORD your God, you and your son and your daughter, your male servant and your female servant, the Levite who is within your towns, the sojourner, the fatherless, and the widow who are among you, at the place that the LORD your God will choose, to make his name dwell there. 12 [x]You shall remember that you were a slave in Egypt; and you shall be careful to observe these statutes.

The Feast of Booths

13 [y]"You shall keep the Feast of Booths seven days, when you have gathered in the produce from your threshing floor and your winepress. 14 [z]You shall rejoice in your feast, you and your son and your daughter, your male servant and your female servant, the Levite, the sojourner, the fatherless, and the widow who are within your towns. 15 For [a]seven days you shall keep the feast to the LORD your God at the place that the LORD will choose, because the LORD your God will bless you in all your produce and in all the work of your hands, so that you will be altogether joyful.

16 [b]"Three times a year all your males shall appear before the LORD your God at the place that he will choose: at the Feast of Unleavened Bread, at the Feast of Weeks, and at the Feast of Booths. [c]They shall not appear before the LORD empty-handed. 17 Every man [d]shall give as he is able, [v]according to the blessing of the LORD your God that he has given you.

Justice

18 "You shall appoint [e]judges and officers in all your towns that the LORD your God is giving you, according to your tribes, and they shall judge the people with righteous judgment. 19 [f]You shall not pervert justice. [g]You shall not show partiality, [h]and you shall not accept a bribe, for a bribe blinds the eyes of the wise and subverts the cause of the righteous. 20 Justice, and only justice, you shall follow, that you may live and inherit the land that the LORD your God is giving you.

Forbidden Forms of Worship

21 "You shall not plant any tree as [i]an Asherah beside the altar of the LORD your God that you shall make. 22 And you shall not set up a pillar, which the LORD your God hates.

17 [j]"You shall not sacrifice to the LORD your God an ox or a sheep in which is a blemish, any defect whatever, for that is an abomination to the LORD your God.

2 [k]"If there is found among you, within any of your towns that the LORD your God is giving you, a man or woman who does what is evil in the sight of the LORD your God, [l]in transgressing his covenant, 3 and has gone and served other gods and worshiped them, or [m]the sun or the moon or any of the host of heaven, [n]which I have forbidden, 4 and it is told you and you hear of it, then you shall inquire [o]diligently, and if it is true and certain that such an abomination has been done in Israel, 5 then you shall bring out to your gates that man or woman who has done this evil thing, and you [p]shall stone that man or woman to death with stones. 6 [q]On the evidence of two witnesses or of three witnesses the one who is to die shall be put to death; a person shall not be put to death on the evidence of one witness. 7 [r]The hand of the witnesses shall be first against him to put him to death, and afterward the hand of all the people. So [s]you shall purge[1] the evil[2] from your midst.

[1] Septuagint *drive out*; also verse 12 [2] Or *evil person*; also verse 12

8 [q][Ex. 13:6] [r]Lev. 23:8, 36 **9** [s]Ex. 23:16; 34:22; Lev. 23:15; Num. 28:26; [Acts 2:1] **10** [t]2 Chr. 8:13 [u]See ch. 26:1-11 [v]ch. 12:15; [1 Cor. 16:2] **11** [w]ch. 12:7, 12, 18; 14:26; See Neh. 8:9-12 **12** [x]See ch. 5:15 **13** [y]Ex. 23:16; See Lev. 23:34 **14** [z]ver. 11; See Neh. 8:9-12 **15** [a]Lev. 23:39 **16** [b]ch. 31:11; Ex. 23:14, 17; 34:23 [c]Ex. 23:15 **17** [d][Ezek. 46:5, 11; 2 Cor. 8:12] [v][See ver. 10 above] **18** [e]ch. 1:16; Num. 11:16; Josh. 1:10; 1 Chr. 23:4; 26:29 **19** [f]ch. 27:19; Ex. 23:2, 6; Isa. 10:2; Amos 5:12; [Lev. 19:15]; See ch. 24:17 [g]See ch. 1:17 [h]See Ex. 23:8 **21** [i]Ex. 34:13; Judg. 6:25; 1 Kgs. 14:15; 16:33; 2 Kgs. 13:6; 17:16; 2 Chr. 33:3 **Chapter 17** **1** [j]See Lev. 22:20 **2** [k]For ver. 2-7, see ch. 13:6-14 [l]Josh. 7:11, 15; 23:16; Judg. 2:20; 2 Kgs. 18:12; Hos. 6:7; 8:1 **3** [m]See ch. 4:19 [n][Jer. 7:31; 19:5; 32:35] **4** [o]ch. 13:14; 19:18 **5** [p][Lev. 24:14, 16; Josh. 7:25] **6** [q][John 8:17]; See Num. 35:30 **7** [r]ch. 13:9; [Acts 7:58] [s]ver. 12; See ch. 13:5

Legal Decisions by Priests and Judges

8 "If any case arises requiring decision
between one kind of homicide and another,
one kind of legal right and another, or one
kind of assault and another, any case within
your towns that is too difficult for you, then
you shall arise and go up to [t]the place that the
LORD your God will choose. 9 [u]And you shall
come to the Levitical priests and to the judge
who is in office in those days, and you shall
consult them, and [v]they shall declare to you
the decision. 10 Then you shall do according to
what they declare to you from that place that
the LORD will choose. And you shall be careful to do according to all that they direct you.
11 According to the instructions that they give
you, and according to the decision which they
pronounce to you, you shall do. You shall not
turn aside from the verdict that they declare
to you, either to the right hand or to the left.
12 The man who [w]acts presumptuously by not
obeying the priest [x]who stands to minister
there before the LORD your God, or the judge,
that man shall die. So [s]you shall purge the evil
from Israel. 13 And all the people [y]shall hear
and fear and not act presumptuously again.

Laws Concerning Israel's Kings

14 "When you come to the land that the LORD
your God is giving you, and you possess it and
dwell in it and then say, [z]'I will set a king over
me, like all the nations that are around me,'
15 you may indeed set a king over you [a]whom
the LORD your God will choose. One [b]from
among your brothers you shall set as king over
you. You may not put a foreigner over you,
who is not your brother. 16 Only he must not
acquire many [c]horses for himself or cause the
people [d]to return to Egypt in order to acquire
many horses, since the LORD has said to you,
[e]'You shall never return that way again.' 17 And
he [f]shall not acquire many wives for himself,
lest his heart turn away, [g]nor shall he acquire
for himself excessive silver and gold.

18 "And when he sits on the throne of his
kingdom, [h]he shall write for himself in a book
a copy of this law, [i]approved by[1] the Levitical
priests. 19 And [j]it shall be with him, and he
shall read in it all the days of his life, [k]that he
may learn to fear the LORD his God by keeping
all the words of this law and these statutes,
and doing them, 20 that his heart may not be
lifted up above his brothers, and that he [l]may
not turn aside from the commandment, either
to the right hand or to the left, [m]so that he
may continue long in his kingdom, he and his
children, in Israel.

Provision for Priests and Levites

18 "The Levitical priests, all the tribe of
Levi, [n]shall have no portion or inheritance with Israel. They [o]shall eat the LORD's
food offerings[2] as their[3] inheritance. 2 They
shall have no inheritance among their brothers; the LORD is their inheritance, as he promised them. 3 And this shall be the priests' due
from the people, from those offering a sacrifice, whether an ox or a sheep: [p]they shall
give to the priest the shoulder and the two
cheeks and the stomach. 4 [q]The firstfruits of
your grain, of your wine and of your oil, and
the first fleece of your sheep, you shall give

[1] Hebrew *from before* [2] Or *the offerings by fire to the LORD* [3] Hebrew *his*

17:14–20 Stated negatively, Israel's king was not to acquire excessive horses, wives, or silver and gold, so that he would not turn away from trusting in the Lord by trusting in earthly resources (vv. 14–17). Stated positively, Israel's king was to trust in the Lord, demonstrated by his reading the Scriptures and putting them into practice, so as to secure the blessings of the kingdom in the present and the future (vv. 18–20). Even Israel's best kings, however, failed in this regard (2 Sam. 24:1–17; 1 Kings 11:3).

King Jesus had no earthly resources to speak of (Matt. 8:20) and relied wholeheartedly on his Father (Matt. 26:39; Luke 23:46). He knew the Scriptures and lived them perfectly (Luke 2:52; Heb. 4:15), thereby securing the blessings of the kingdom for himself and for all those who trust in him (Heb. 12:1–3). We, like Israel's ancient kings, are continually tempted to trust in our own earthly resources. As we continue "looking to Jesus," we have the ability to use all the resources that God has put at our disposal, while relying entirely on him (Heb. 12:1–3). For Jesus was the true and final King, who lived as every king before him was supposed to, yet he was put on a cross and treated like a common criminal—so that we, by nature criminals, can freely receive the benefits of the true King (Mark 10:45; 2 Cor. 5:21). One day, we will reign with him on a new earth (1 Cor. 6:2; Rev. 5:10).

8 [t]See ch. 12:5
9 [u]ch. 19:17; 21:5; 2 Chr. 19:8, 10; Ps. 122:5; Jer. 18:18; Hag. 2:11; Mal. 2:7 [v]Ezek. 44:24
12 [w][ch. 18:20, 22; Ezra 10:8] [x]ch. 10:8; 18:5, 7 [s][See ver. 7 above]
13 [y]See ch. 13:11
14 [z][1 Sam. 8:5, 19, 20]
15 [a][1 Sam. 9:15; 10:24; 16:12; 1 Chr. 22:10] [b][Jer. 30:21]
16 [c][1 Kgs. 4:26; 10:26, 28; 2 Chr. 1:16; 9:28; Isa. 2:7; 31:1] [d]Isa. 31:1; Ezek. 17:15 [e]ch. 28:68; Hos. 11:5; [Ex. 13:17; 14:13; Num. 14:3, 4]; See Jer. 42:15-19
17 [f][1 Kgs. 11:3, 4; Neh. 13:26] [g][Isa. 2:7]
18 [h][2 Kgs. 11:12] [i]ch. 31:9, 26; 2 Kgs. 22:8; 2 Chr. 34:14
19 [j]Josh. 1:8 [k]ch. 4:10; 14:23
20 [l]ch. 5:32; 1 Kgs. 15:5 [m]ch. 4:40

Chapter 18 **1** [n]See Num. 18:20 [o]Num. 18:8, 9; Josh. 13:14; 1 Sam. 2:28; [1 Cor. 9:13] **3** [p]See Lev. 7:30-34 **4** [q]Num. 18:12; 2 Chr. 31:5

him. 5 For the LORD your God has chosen him
out of all your tribes [r]to stand and minister
in the name of the LORD, him and his sons
for all time.

6 "And if a Levite comes from any of your
towns out of all Israel, [s]where he lives—and
he may come when he desires[1]—[t]to the place
that the LORD will choose, 7 and ministers in
the name of the LORD his God, [u]like all his fellow Levites who stand to minister there before
the LORD, 8 then he may have equal [v]portions
to eat, besides what he receives from the sale
of his patrimony.[2]

Abominable Practices

9 "When you come into the land that the
LORD your God is giving you, [w]you shall not
learn to follow the abominable practices of
those nations. 10 There shall not be found
among you anyone [x]who burns his son or his
daughter as an offering,[3] anyone who [y]prac-
tices divination or [z]tells fortunes or interprets omens, or [a]a sorcerer 11 or a charmer or
[b]a medium or a necromancer or [c]one who
inquires of the dead, 12 [d]for whoever does these
things is an abomination to the LORD. And
[e]because of these abominations the LORD your
God is driving them out before you. 13 You
shall be blameless before the LORD your God,
14 for these nations, which you are about to
dispossess, listen to fortune-tellers and to
diviners. But as for you, the LORD your God
has not allowed you to do this.

A New Prophet like Moses

15 [f]"The LORD your God will raise up for you
a prophet like me from among you, from your
brothers—it is to him you shall listen— 16 just
as you desired of the LORD your God at Horeb
[g]on the day of the assembly, when you said,
[h]'Let me not hear again the voice of the LORD
my God or see this great fire any more, lest
I die.' 17 And the LORD said to me, [i]'They are
right in what they have spoken. 18 [f]I will raise
up for them a prophet like you from among
their brothers. [j]And I will put my words in his
mouth, and [k]he shall speak to them all that
I command him. 19 [l]And whoever will [m]not
listen to my words that he shall speak in my
name, I myself will require it of him. 20 [n]But
the prophet who presumes to speak a word
in my name that I have not commanded him
to speak, or[4] who speaks in the name of other
gods, that same prophet shall die.' 21 And if you
say in your heart, 'How may we know the word
that the LORD has not spoken?'— 22 [o]when a
prophet speaks in the name of the LORD, if the
word does not come to pass or come true, that
is a word that the LORD has not spoken; [n]the
prophet has spoken it presumptuously. You
need not be afraid of him.

Laws Concerning Cities of Refuge

19 "When [p]the LORD your God cuts off the
nations whose land the LORD your God
is giving you, and you dispossess them and
dwell in their cities and in their houses, 2 [q]you

[1] Or *lives—if he comes enthusiastically* [2] The meaning of the Hebrew is uncertain [3] Hebrew *makes his son or his daughter pass through the fire* [4] Or *and*

5 [r]ch. 17:12
6 [s]Num. 35:2, 3; Judg. 17:7; 19:1 [t]See ch. 12:5
7 [u][1 Chr. 23:6; 2 Chr. 31:2]
8 [v]2 Chr. 31:4; Neh. 12:44, 47; 13:10
9 [w]ch. 12:29-31; See Lev. 18:26-30
10 [x]See Lev. 18:21 [y]2 Kgs. 17:17 [z]See Lev. 19:26 [a][Ex. 22:18]
11 [b]See Lev. 19:31 [c][1 Sam. 28:7]
12 [d]ch. 22:5; 25:16 [e]See ch. 9:4
15 [f]John 1:21, 25, 45; Cited Acts 3:22; 7:37
16 [g]See ch. 9:10 [h]See Ex. 20:19
17 [i]ch. 5:28
18 [f][See ver. 15 above] [j]Jer. 1:9; 5:14; [John 17:8] [k][John 4:25; 8:28; 12:49, 50]
19 [l][Acts 3:23] [m]Jer. 29:19; 35:13
20 [n]See ch. 13:5
22 [o][ch. 13:1-3; Jer. 28:9] [n][See ver. 20 above]
Chapter 19
1 [p]ch. 12:29
2 [q]Ex. 21:13; Num. 35:10, 14; Josh. 20:2, 8

18:15–22 Moses was unique among the prophets (Num. 12:6–8) and was the first in a long line of prophets (Deut. 18:15) who would be inspired by God to speak God's word to the people (v. 18). The Israelites could recognize a true prophet, because his word never failed to come to pass (vv. 21–22).

Moses promised that God would raise up "a prophet" singular. On the one hand, the singular noun refers to the single prophetic office, filled by numerous prophets, as indicated by verses 21–22, which provide instructions for distinguishing true prophets from false prophets. On the other hand, at least some ancient Jews understood this promise to pertain to a single, particular prophet, as is clear from texts like John 1:21; 6:14; and 7:40. Jesus is this expected prophet "like" Moses (Acts 3:22; 7:37). But Jesus is also the prophet "worthy of more glory than Moses" (Heb. 3:3). If it was necessary for ancient Israel to listen to Moses, who was "*faithful in* all God's house as a *servant*" (Heb. 3:5), how much more necessary is it for the church to listen to the final Prophet (Heb. 3:7–19), who was "*faithful over* God's house as a *son*" (Heb. 3:6)?

19:1–13 God's grace can be seen in his provision of "six cities of refuge" (Num. 35:6). These cities provided a safe haven for someone who accidentally took the life of another person and so did not deserve the death penalty (Deut. 19:4–6). They did not, however, provide safe haven for those guilty of murder (vv. 11–13).

shall set apart three cities for yourselves in the land that the LORD your God is giving you to possess. 3 You shall measure the distances[1] and divide into three parts the area of the land that the LORD your God gives you as a possession, so that any manslayer can flee to them.

4 "This is the provision for [r]the manslayer, who by fleeing there may save his life. If anyone kills his neighbor unintentionally without having hated him in the past— 5 as when someone goes into the forest with his neighbor to cut wood, and his hand swings the axe to cut down a tree, and the head slips from the handle and strikes his neighbor so that he dies—he may flee to one of these cities and live, 6 lest [s]the avenger of blood in hot anger pursue the manslayer and overtake him, because the way is long, and strike him fatally, though the man did not deserve to die, since he had not hated his neighbor in the past. 7 Therefore I command you, You shall set apart three cities. 8 [t]And if the LORD your God enlarges your territory, [u]as he has sworn to your fathers, and [v]gives you all the land that he promised to give to your fathers— 9 provided you are careful to keep all this commandment, which I command you today, by loving the LORD your God and by walking ever in his ways—[w]then you shall add three other cities to these three, 10 lest innocent blood be shed in your land that the LORD your God is giving you for an inheritance, and so the guilt of bloodshed be upon you.

11 "But if anyone hates his neighbor and lies in wait for him and attacks him [x]and strikes him fatally so that he dies, and he flees into one of these cities, 12 then the elders of his city shall send and take him from there, and hand him over to the avenger of blood, so that he may die. 13 [y]Your eye shall not pity him, [z]but you shall purge the guilt of innocent blood[2] from Israel, so that it may be well with you.

Property Boundaries

14 [a]"You shall not move your neighbor's landmark, which the men of old have set, in the inheritance that you will hold in the land that the LORD your God is giving you to possess.

Laws Concerning Witnesses

15 "A single witness shall not suffice against a person for any crime or for any wrong in connection with any offense that he has committed. [b]Only on the evidence of two witnesses or of three witnesses shall a charge be established. 16 If [c]a malicious witness arises to accuse a person of wrongdoing, 17 then both parties to the dispute shall appear before the LORD, [d]before the priests and the judges who are in office in those days. 18 The judges shall [e]inquire diligently, and if the witness is a false witness and has accused his brother falsely, 19 [f]then you shall do to him as he had meant to do to his brother. So you shall purge the evil[3] from your midst. 20 And the rest [g]shall hear and fear, and shall never again commit any such evil among you. 21 [y]Your eye shall not pity. [h]It shall be life for life, eye for eye, tooth for tooth, hand for hand, foot for foot.

Laws Concerning Warfare

20 "When you go out to war against your enemies, and see [i]horses and chariots and an army larger than your own, you shall not be afraid of them, for the LORD your God is [j]with you, who brought you up out of the land of Egypt. 2 And when you draw near to the battle, [k]the priest shall come forward and speak to the people 3 and shall say to them, 'Hear, O Israel, today you are drawing near for battle against your enemies: let not your heart faint. Do not fear or panic or be in dread of them, 4 for the LORD your God is he who goes with you [l]to fight for you against your enemies, to give you the victory.' 5 Then the officers shall speak to the people, saying, 'Is there any man who has built a new house and has not dedicated it? Let him go back to his house, lest he die in the battle and another man dedicate it. 6 And is there any man who has planted a vineyard and has not [m]enjoyed its fruit? Let him go back to his house, lest he die in the

[1] Hebrew *road* [2] Or *the blood of the innocent* [3] Or *evil person*

In the gospel we see an amplification of this grace principle, because in Christ God provides a safe haven for those who do deserve the death penalty (Rom. 6:23). Life in this safe haven means "that we serve in the new way of the Spirit and not in the old way of the written code" (Rom. 7:6).

4 [r] ch. 4:42; Num. 35:15; Josh. 20:3, 5
6 [s] Num. 35:12, 19, 21, 24, 25, 27
8 [t] ch. 12:20 [u] Ex. 34:24; [Ex. 23:31] [v] See Gen. 15:18-21

9 [w] ver. 2; [Josh. 20:7] **11** [x] ch. 27:24; Ex. 21:12, 14; See Num. 35:16-21 **13** [y] See ch. 7:16 [z] ch. 21:9; Num. 35:33; [1 Kgs. 2:31] **14** [a] ch. 27:17; Job 24:2; Prov. 22:28; 23:10; Hos. 5:10 **15** [b] Cited Matt. 18:16; 2 Cor. 13:1; See Num. 35:30 **16** [c] [Ex. 23:1; Ps. 35:11] **17** [d] ch. 17:8, 9; [ch. 21:5] **18** [e] ch. 13:14; 17:4 **19** [f] Prov. 19:5, 9; [Dan. 6:24] **20** [g] See ch. 13:11 **21** [y] [See ver. 13 above] [h] See Ex. 21:23, 24 **Chapter 20** **1** [i] [Josh. 17:18; Ps. 20:7; Isa. 31:1] [j] ch. 31:6, 8; 2 Chr. 13:12; 32:8 **2** [k] [Num. 10:8, 9; 31:6] **4** [l] ch. 1:30; 3:22; Josh. 23:10 **6** [m] ch. 28:30; Lev. 19:23-25; [1 Cor. 9:7]

battle and another man enjoy its fruit. 7 [n]And
is there any man who has betrothed a wife
and has not taken her? Let him go back to his
house, lest he die in the battle and another
man take her.’ 8 And the officers shall speak
further to the people, and say, [o]‘Is there any
man who is fearful and fainthearted? Let him
go back to his house, lest he make the heart of
his fellows melt like his own.’ 9 And when the
officers have finished speaking to the people,
then commanders shall be appointed at the
head of the people.
10 “When you draw near to a city to fight
against it, [p]offer terms of peace to it. 11 And if
it responds to you peaceably and it opens to
you, then all the people who are found in it
shall do forced labor for you and shall serve
you. 12 But if it makes no peace with you, but
makes war against you, then you shall besiege
it. 13 And when the LORD your God gives it
into your hand, [q]you shall put all its males
to the sword, 14 [r]but the women and the little
ones, the livestock, and everything else in the
city, all its spoil, you [s]shall take as plunder for
yourselves. And [t]you shall enjoy the spoil of
your enemies, which the LORD your God has
given you. 15 Thus you shall do to all the cities that are very far from you, which are not
cities of the nations here. 16 But [u]in the cities
of these peoples that the LORD your God is
giving you for an inheritance, you shall save
alive nothing that breathes, 17 but [v]you shall
devote them to complete destruction,[1] the
Hittites and the Amorites, the Canaanites and
the Perizzites, the Hivites and the Jebusites,
as the LORD your God has commanded, 18 that
[w]they may not teach you to do according to
all their abominable practices that they have
done for their gods, and so you [x]sin against
the LORD your God.
19 “When you besiege a city for a long time,
making war against it in order to take it, [y]you
shall not destroy its trees by wielding an axe
against them. You may eat from them, but you
shall not cut them down. Are the trees in the
field human, that they should be besieged by
you? 20 Only the trees that you know are not
trees for food you may destroy and cut down,
that you may build siegeworks against the city
that makes war with you, until it falls.

Atonement for Unsolved Murders

21 “If in the land that the LORD your
God is giving you to possess someone
is found slain, lying in the open country, and
it is not known who killed him, 2 then your
elders and your judges shall come out, and
they shall measure the distance to the surrounding cities. 3 And the elders of the city
that is nearest to the slain man shall take a
heifer [z]that has never been worked and that
has not pulled in a yoke. 4 And the elders of
that city shall bring the heifer down to a valley
with running water, which is neither plowed
nor sown, and shall break the heifer’s neck
there in the valley. 5 Then the priests, the sons
of Levi, shall come forward, for the LORD your
God has chosen [a]them to minister to him and
to bless in the name of the LORD, and [b]by their
word every dispute and every assault shall be
settled. 6 And all the elders of that city nearest
to the slain man [c]shall wash their hands over
the heifer whose neck was broken in the valley, 7 and they shall testify, ‘Our hands did not
shed this blood, nor did our eyes see it shed.
8 Accept atonement, O LORD, for your people
Israel, whom you have redeemed, and [d]do not
set the guilt of innocent blood in the midst of
your people Israel, so that their blood guilt be
atoned for.’ 9 So [e]you shall purge the guilt of
innocent blood from your midst, when you do
what is right in the sight of the LORD.

Marrying Female Captives

10 “When you go out to war against your
enemies, and the LORD your God gives them
into your hand and you take them captive,

[1] That is, set apart (devote) as an offering to the Lord (for destruction)

20:19–20 God demonstrated a balanced perspective when he gave wartime legislation. He allowed use but prohibited abuse. He allowed the chopping down of non-fruit-bearing trees to be used as siege works (v. 20). He also allowed the use of fruit for human sustenance, but prohibited the chopping down of fruit trees as abuse, since the long-term loss outweighed the short-term gain (v. 19). These trees, which Israel had not planted (6:10), were part of Israel’s inheritance and were intended for Israel’s long-term enjoyment in the kingdom.

7 [n] [ch. 24:5; 28:30]
8 [o] [Judg. 7:3]
10 [p] Judg. 21:13; [ch. 2:26; 2 Sam. 20:18, 20]
13 [q] Num. 31:7
14 [r] Num. 31:9 [s] Josh. 8:2 [t] Josh. 22:8
16 [u] ch. 7:1, 2; Num. 33:52; Josh. 11:14
17 [v] See ch. 7:2
18 [w] ch. 7:4; 12:30, 31; 18:9
[x] Ex. 23:33 **19** [y] [2 Kgs. 3:19, 25] **Chapter 21** **3** [z] [Num. 19:2] **5** [a] See ch. 10:8 [b] ch. 17:8, 9; 19:17 **6** [c] [Ps. 26:6; 73:13; Matt. 27:24] **8** [d] [Jonah 1:14]
9 [e] ch. 19:13

11 and you see among the captives a beautiful
woman, and you desire to take her to be your
wife, 12 and you bring her home to your house,
she shall shave her head and pare her nails.
13 And she shall take off the clothes in which
she was captured and shall remain in your
house and [f]lament her father and her mother a
full month. After that you may go in to her and
be her husband, and she shall be your wife.
14 But if you no longer delight in her, you shall
[g]let her go where she wants. But you shall not
sell her for money, nor shall you [h]treat her as a
slave, since you have humiliated her.

Inheritance Rights of the Firstborn

15 "If a man has two wives, [i]the one loved and
the other unloved, and both the loved and the
unloved have borne him children, and if the
firstborn son belongs to the unloved,[1] 16 then
on the day when [j]he assigns his possessions
as an inheritance to his sons, he may not treat
the son of the loved as the firstborn in preference to the son of the unloved, who is the
firstborn, 17 but he shall acknowledge the firstborn, the son of the unloved, by giving him
a double portion of all that he has, for he is
[k]the firstfruits of his strength. [l]The right of
the firstborn is his.

A Rebellious Son

18 "If a man has a stubborn and rebellious
son who will not obey the voice of his father
or the voice of his mother, and, though they
discipline him, will not listen to them, 19 then
his father and his mother shall take hold of
him and bring him out to the elders of his city
at the gate of the place where he lives, 20 and
they shall say to the elders of his city, 'This
our son is stubborn and rebellious; he will not
obey our voice; he is a glutton and a drunkard.'
21 [m]Then all the men of the city shall stone him
to death with stones. [n]So you shall purge the
evil from your midst, [o]and all Israel shall hear,
and fear.

A Man Hanged on a Tree Is Cursed

22 "And if a man has committed a crime punishable by death and he is put to death, and
you hang him on a tree, 23 [p]his body shall not
remain all night on the tree, but you shall
bury him the same day, for [q]a hanged man is
cursed by God. [r]You shall not defile your land
that the LORD your God is giving you for an
inheritance.

Various Laws

22 "You [s]shall not see your brother's ox
or his sheep going astray and ignore
them. You shall take them back to your
brother. 2 And if he does not live near you and
you do not know who he is, you shall bring
it home to your house, and it shall stay with
you until your brother seeks it. Then you shall
restore it to him. 3 And you shall do the same

[1] Or *hated*; also verses 16, 17

21:22–23 "A hanged man is cursed by God" (v. 23). Since God did not bring Israel into the land to curse them but to bless them (7:12–16), God required that the body of a cursed/hanged man be buried on the day of his death, so that the curse would not remain in the land of Israel's inheritance (21:23), the land promised to Abraham.

This principle reaches its culmination in Christ. After his crucifixion, Christ's body was taken down from the cross and buried on the same day (Mark 15:43), in compliance with Deuteronomy 21:22–23 and in contrast to what happened to Judas (Matt. 27:5; Acts 1:16–19). In the scandal of the gospel, however, Christ was cursed/hanged on a tree not because of his own sin but because of ours. He was condemned in our place as our substitute. The purpose of this was that "in Christ Jesus the blessing of Abraham might come to" us (Gal. 3:13–14). All those who trust in Christ, whatever their ethnic background, share in the eternal blessings of the gospel.

22:1–4 Fellow Israelites ("brothers") were required to act in the interest of others, so that others could experience restoration in one form or another. Why? Ultimately, because acting in the interest of others reflects who God is. The very heart of God is self-giving love. The apostle Paul taught that fellow believers were to act in the interest of others (Phil. 2:3–4) because such a life of love reflects who Christ Jesus is (Phil. 2:5–7). Following in the footsteps of our Master, we delight to give of ourselves for the sake of others. Knowing who Christ is and what he has done for us motivates us to act on behalf of others so that they can experience restoration as well. This is our true joy.

13 [f][Ps. 45:10]
14 [g][Jer. 34:16] [h]ch. 24:7
15 [i][Gen. 29:30, 33; 1 Sam. 1:4, 5]
16 [j]1 Chr. 5:1, 2; [1 Chr. 26:10; 2 Chr. 11:19, 20, 22]
17 [k]Gen. 49:3 [l]Gen. 25:31, 33; 27:36
21 [m]ch. 13:10; See Josh. 7:25 [n]See ch. 13:5 [o]ch. 13:11; 17:13; 19:20
23 [p][Josh. 8:29; 10:26, 27; John 19:31] [q]Cited Gal. 3:13 [r]Num. 35:34
Chapter 22
1 [s]Ex. 23:4

with his donkey or with his garment, or with any lost thing of your brother's, which he loses and you find; you may not ignore it. 4 [t]You shall not see your brother's donkey or his ox fallen down by the way and ignore them. You shall help him to lift them up again.

5 "A woman shall not wear a man's garment, nor shall a man put on a woman's cloak, [u]for whoever does these things is an abomination to the LORD your God.

6 "If you come across a bird's nest in any tree or on the ground, with young ones or eggs and the mother sitting on the young or on the eggs, [v]you shall not take the mother with the young. 7 You shall let the mother go, but the young you may take for yourself, [w]that it may go well with you, and that you may live long.

8 "When you build a new house, you shall make a parapet for your roof, that you may not bring the guilt of blood upon your house, if anyone should fall from it.

9 [x]"You shall not sow your vineyard with two kinds of seed, lest the whole yield be forfeited,[1] the crop that you have sown and the yield of the vineyard. 10 You shall not plow with an ox and a donkey together. 11 You shall not wear cloth of wool and linen mixed together.

12 [y]"You shall make yourself tassels on the four corners of the garment with which you cover yourself.

Laws Concerning Sexual Immorality

13 "If any man takes a wife and [z]goes in to her and then hates her 14 and accuses her of misconduct and brings a bad name upon her, saying, 'I took this woman, and when I came near her, I did not find in her evidence of virginity,' 15 then the father of the young woman and her mother shall take and bring out the evidence of her virginity to the elders of the city in the gate. 16 And the father of the young woman shall say to the elders, 'I gave my daughter to this man to marry, and he hates her; 17 and behold, he has accused her of misconduct, saying, "I did not find in your daughter evidence of virginity." And yet this is the evidence of my daughter's virginity.' And they shall spread the cloak before the elders of the city. 18 Then the elders of that city shall take the man and whip[2] him, 19 and they shall fine him a hundred shekels[3] of silver and give them to the father of the young woman, because he has brought a bad name upon a virgin[4] of Israel. And she shall be his wife. [a]He may not divorce her all his days. 20 But if the thing is true, that evidence of virginity was not found in the young woman, 21 then they shall bring out the young woman to the door of her father's house, and [b]the men of her city shall stone her to death with stones, because she has [c]done an outrageous thing in Israel by whoring in her father's house. [d]So you shall purge the evil from your midst.

22 [e]"If a man is found lying with the wife of another man, both of them shall die, the man who lay with the woman, and the woman. [d]So you shall purge the evil from Israel.

23 "If there is a [f]betrothed virgin, and a man meets her in the city and lies with her, 24 then you shall bring them both out to the gate of that city, and you shall stone them to death with stones, the young woman because she did not cry for help though she was in the city, and the man because he violated his neighbor's wife. [d]So you shall purge the evil from your midst.

25 "But if in the open country a man meets a young woman who is betrothed, and the man seizes her and lies with her, then only the man who lay with her shall die. 26 But you shall do nothing to the young woman; she has committed no offense punishable by death. For this case is like that of a man attacking and murdering his neighbor, 27 because he met her in the open country, and though the betrothed young woman cried for help there was no one to rescue her.

28 [g]"If a man meets a virgin who is not betrothed, and seizes her and lies with her, and they are found, 29 then the man who lay

[1] Hebrew *become holy* [2] Or *discipline* [3] A *shekel* was about 2/5 ounce or 11 grams [4] Or *girl of marriageable age*

Christ's ultimate act in the interest of others was his death on the cross (Phil. 2:8), which led to his restoration to exaltation (Phil. 2:9–11). This act of self-giving love is to be imitated in terms of the pattern is sets up, but it must not and cannot be imitated in its efficacy. Only the work of Christ can atone for sin, not the work of his followers. Indeed, it is awareness of this very gospel truth that propels believers forward in acts of love.

4[t] Ex. 23:5
5[u] [ch. 18:12; 25:16]
6[v] Lev. 22:28
7[w] See ch. 4:40
9[x] Lev. 19:19
12[y] Num. 15:38; [Matt. 23:5]
13[z] [2 Sam. 13:15]
19[a] [Matt. 19:8, 9; Mark 10:11; Luke 16:18] **21**[b] [ch. 21:21] [c] See Gen. 34:7 [d] See ch. 13:5 **22**[e] Lev. 20:10; [Ezek. 16:38, 40; 23:45, 47; John 8:5] [d] [See ver. 21 above] **23**[f] [Matt. 1:18, 19] **24**[d] [See ver. 21 above] **28**[g] Ex. 22:16, 17

with her shall give to the father of the young
woman fifty shekels of silver, and she shall be
his wife, because he has violated her. He may
not divorce her all his days.
30[1] [h]"A man shall not take his father's wife,
so that he does not [i]uncover his father's
nakedness.[2]

Those Excluded from the Assembly

23 "No one whose testicles are crushed or
whose male organ is cut off shall enter
the assembly of the LORD.
2 [j]"No one born of a forbidden union may
enter the assembly of the LORD. Even to the
tenth generation, none of his descendants may
enter the assembly of the LORD.
3 [k]"No Ammonite or Moabite may enter the
assembly of the LORD. Even to the tenth generation, none of them may enter the assembly of the LORD forever, 4 [l]because they did
not meet you with bread and with water on
the way, when you came out of Egypt, and
because they [m]hired against you Balaam the
son of Beor from Pethor of [n]Mesopotamia,
to curse you. 5 But the LORD your God would
not listen to Balaam; instead the LORD your
God turned [o]the curse into a blessing for you,
because the LORD your God loved you. 6 You
[p]shall not seek their peace or their prosperity
all your days forever.
7 "You shall not abhor an Edomite, for [q]he is
your brother. You shall not abhor an Egyptian,
because [r]you were a sojourner in his land.
8 Children born to them in the third generation may enter the assembly of the LORD.

Uncleanness in the Camp

9 "When you are encamped against your
enemies, then you shall keep yourself from
every evil thing.
10 "If any man among you becomes [s]unclean
because of a nocturnal emission, then he shall
go outside the camp. He shall not come inside
the camp, 11 but when evening comes, he shall
[t]bathe himself in water, and as the sun sets, he
may come inside the camp.
12 "You shall have a place outside the camp,
and you shall go out to it. 13 And you shall
have a trowel with your tools, and when you
sit down outside, you shall dig a hole with it
and turn back and cover up your excrement.
14 Because [u]the LORD your God walks in the
midst of your camp, to deliver you and to
give up your enemies before you, therefore
your camp must be holy, so that he may not
see anything indecent among you and turn
away from you.

Miscellaneous Laws

15 [v]"You shall not give up to his master a
slave[3] who has escaped from his master to you.
16 He shall dwell with you, in your midst, in
the place that he shall choose within one of
your towns, wherever it suits him. You shall
not wrong him.
17 "None of the [w]daughters of Israel shall
be a cult prostitute, and none [x]of the sons of
Israel shall be a cult prostitute. 18 You shall not
bring the fee of a prostitute or the wages of a
dog[4] into the house of the LORD your God in
payment for any vow, for both of these are an
abomination to the LORD your God.
19 [y]"You shall not charge interest on loans
to your brother, [z]interest on money, interest on food, interest on anything that is lent
for interest. 20 [a]You may charge a foreigner
interest, but you may not charge your brother
interest, [b]that the LORD your God may bless
you in all that you undertake in the land that
you are entering to take possession of it.

[1] Ch 23:1 in Hebrew [2] Hebrew *uncover his father's skirt* [3] Or *servant*; the Hebrew term *'ebed* designates a range of social and economic roles (see Preface) [4] Or *male prostitute*

23:15–16 The Israelites were instructed not to return escaped slaves but to grant them freedom in the Promised Land. The slaves in view were probably those who had escaped from another country to Israel. In the ancient Near East it was standard practice to return escaped slaves, so why were the Israelites to be different? Because the Israelites knew what it was to be liberated slaves. Repeatedly in the book of Deuteronomy, Israel's conduct was to be motivated by the fact that they had been slaves in Egypt but had escaped and found freedom in the Promised Land (5:15; 6:21; 15:15; 24:18, 22).

Similarly, believers used to be slaves to sin (Gal. 3:22; 4:5) and under obligation to keep the law as the basis of inheriting eternal life (Gal. 4:21–31), but they are now God's children, heirs based on his promise (Gal. 3:29; 4:7), called to live in freedom (Gal. 5:1). As liberated slaves, we do not use our freedom to sin but to serve in love (Gal. 5:13–14; see Rom. 8:12–17).

30 [h]See Lev. 18:8 [i]ch. 27:20; [Ruth 3:9; Ezek. 16:8]
Chapter 23
2 [j][Zech. 9:6]
3 [k]Neh. 13:1, 2
4 [l][ch. 2:29] [m]Num. 22:5, 6; [2 Pet. 2:15] [n]Acts 7:2
5 [o]Num. 23:11; 24:10
6 [p][Ezra 9:12]
7 [q]Gen. 25:24-26; Num. 20:14; Obad. 10, 12 [r]ch. 10:19; Ex. 22:21; 23:9; Lev. 19:34
10 [s]Lev. 15:16
11 [t]See Lev. 15:5
14 [u]Lev. 26:12
15 [v]1 Sam. 30:15
17 [w]Lev. 19:29 [x]1 Kgs. 14:24; 15:12; 22:46; 2 Kgs. 23:7
19 [y]See Ex. 22:25 [z][Neh. 5:10]
20 [a][ch. 15:3] [b]ch. 15:10

21 [c]"If you make a vow to the LORD your God,
you shall not delay fulfilling it, for the LORD
your God will surely require it of you, and you
will be guilty of sin. 22 But if you refrain from
vowing, you will not be guilty of sin. 23 You
shall be careful to do what has passed your
lips, for you have voluntarily vowed to the
LORD your God what you have promised with
your mouth.

24 "If you go into your neighbor's vineyard,
you may eat your fill of grapes, as many as
you wish, but you shall not put any in your
bag. 25 If you go into your neighbor's standing grain, [d]you may pluck the ears with your
hand, but you shall not put a sickle to your
neighbor's standing grain.

Laws Concerning Divorce

24 "When a man takes a wife and marries
her, if then she finds no favor in his eyes
because he has found some indecency in her,
and [e]he writes her a certificate of divorce and
puts it in her hand and sends her out of his
house, and she departs out of his house, 2 and
if she goes and becomes another man's wife,
3 and the latter man hates her and writes her
a certificate of divorce and puts it in her hand
and sends her out of his house, or if the latter
man dies, who took her to be his wife, 4 then
[f]her former husband, who sent her away, may
not take her again to be his wife, after she has
been defiled, for that is an abomination before
the LORD. And you shall not bring sin upon
the land that the LORD your God is giving you
for an inheritance.

Miscellaneous Laws

5 [g]"When a man is newly married, he shall
not go out with the army or be liable for any
other public duty. He shall be free at home
one year [h]to be happy with his wife whom he
has taken.

6 "No one shall take a mill or an upper millstone in pledge, for that would be taking a
life in pledge.

7 [i]"If a man is found stealing one of his brothers of the people of Israel, and if he [j]treats him
as a slave or sells him, then that thief shall die.
[k]So you shall purge the evil from your midst.

8 "Take care, in [l]a case of leprous[1] disease, to
be very careful to do according to all that the
Levitical priests shall direct you. As I commanded them, so you shall be careful to do.
9 Remember what the LORD your God did to
[m]Miriam [n]on the way as you came out of Egypt.

10 "When you make your neighbor a loan of
any sort, you shall not go into his house to
collect his pledge. 11 You shall stand outside,
and the man to whom you make the loan shall
bring the pledge out to you. 12 And if he is a
poor man, you shall not sleep in his pledge.
13 [o]You shall restore to him the pledge as the
sun sets, that he may sleep in his cloak and
[p]bless you. And [q]it shall be righteousness for
you before the LORD your God.

14 "You shall not [r]oppress a hired worker who
is poor and needy, whether he is one of your
brothers or one of the sojourners who are in
your land within your towns. 15 [s]You shall give
him his wages on the same day, before the sun
sets (for he is poor and counts on it), [t]lest he
cry against you to the LORD, and you be guilty
of sin.

16 [u]"Fathers shall not be put to death because
of their children, nor shall children be put to
death because of their fathers. Each one shall
be put to death for his own sin.

17 [v]"You shall not pervert the justice due to
the sojourner or to the fatherless, [w]or take a
widow's garment in pledge, 18 but [x]you shall
remember that you were a slave in Egypt and
the LORD your God redeemed you from there;
therefore I command you to do this.

[1] *Leprosy* was a term for several skin diseases; see Leviticus 13

21[c] [Ps. 66:13, 14; 76:11]; See Num. 30:2
25[d] [Matt. 12:1; Mark 2:23; Luke 6:1]
Chapter 24
1[e] Matt. 19:7; Mark 10:4; Cited Matt. 5:31; [Isa. 50:1; Jer. 3:8]
4[f] [Jer. 3:1]
5[g] [ch. 20:7] [h] Prov. 5:18
7[i] Ex. 21:16; [1 Tim. 1:10] [j] ch. 21:14 [k] See ch. 13:5
8[l] See Lev. 13–14

24:16 Normal criminal law in the Old Testament did not permit penal substitution for capital offenses. Individuals were to pay for their own sins. But normal criminal law was not the operative principle in other spheres in the Old Testament. For example, "devotion to destruction" (see 7:2; 13:15; 20:17) allowed for the death of children based on the sins of parents. A specific example was Achan's entire family being put to death for Achan's sin (Josh. 7:24–26). The treatment of Achan's family can be understood in the larger context of the Old Testament, where the one stands for the many and the many for the one. In the ancient world, family units, people groups, and even whole nations were viewed as having one collective identity and fate.

9[m] See Num. 12:10-15 [n] ch. 25:17 **13**[o] See Ex. 22:26 [p] Job 29:13; 31:20 [q] Ps. 112:9; Dan. 4:27; [ch. 6:25] **14**[r] Mal. 3:5; See Lev. 25:39-43 **15**[s] Jer. 22:13; See Lev. 19:13 [t] ch. 15:9; James 5:4 **16**[u] Cited 2 Kgs. 14:6; 2 Chr. 25:4; [Jer. 31:29, 30; Ezek. 18:20] **17**[v] Ex. 22:21, 22; 23:6; [ch. 10:18; 27:19; Isa. 1:23; Jer. 5:28]; See ch. 16:19 [w] [ver. 6, 13; Job 24:3] **18**[x] See ch. 5:15

19 [y]"When you reap your harvest in your field
and forget a sheaf in the field, you shall not
go back to get it. It shall be for the sojourner,
the fatherless, and the widow, [z]that the LORD
your God may bless you in all the work of your
hands. 20 When you beat your olive trees, you
shall not go over them again. It shall be for
the sojourner, the fatherless, and the widow.
21 When you gather the grapes of your vineyard, you shall not strip it afterward. It shall
be for the sojourner, the fatherless, and the
widow. 22 [x]You shall remember that you were
a slave in the land of Egypt; therefore I command you to do this.

25 "If there is a [a]dispute between men and
they come into court and the judges
decide between them, [b]acquitting the innocent and condemning the guilty, 2 then if the
guilty man deserves to be beaten, the judge
shall cause him to lie down and be beaten in
his presence with a number of stripes in proportion to his offense. 3 [c]Forty stripes may be
given him, but not more, lest, if one should go
on to beat him with more stripes than these,
your brother be degraded in your sight.
4 [d]"You shall not muzzle an ox when it is
treading out the grain.

Laws Concerning Levirate Marriage

5 [e]"If brothers dwell together, and one of
them dies and has no son, the wife of the
dead man shall not be married outside the
family to a stranger. Her [f]husband's brother
shall go in to her and take her as his wife and
perform the duty of a husband's brother to her.
6 And the first son whom she bears shall succeed to the name of his dead brother, that [g]his
name may not be blotted out of Israel. 7 And
if the man does not wish to take his brother's
wife, then his brother's wife shall [h]go up to
the gate to the elders and say, 'My husband's
brother refuses to perpetuate his brother's
name in Israel; he will not perform the duty
of a husband's brother to me.' 8 Then the elders
of his city shall call him and speak to him,
and if he persists, saying, [i]'I do not wish to
take her,' 9 then his brother's wife shall go up
to him in the presence of the elders and [j]pull
his sandal off his foot and [k]spit in his face. And
she shall answer and say, 'So shall it be done to
the man who does not [l]build up his brother's
house.' 10 And the name of his house[1] shall be
called in Israel, 'The house of him who had his
sandal pulled off.'

Miscellaneous Laws

11 "When men fight with one another and
the wife of the one draws near to rescue her
husband from the hand of him who is beating
him and puts out her hand and seizes him by
the private parts, 12 then you shall cut off her
hand. [m]Your eye shall have no pity.
13 "You [n]shall not have in your bag two kinds
of weights, a large and a small. 14 You shall not

[1] Hebrew *its name*

Whereas normal criminal law did not permit penal substitution, believers have been reconciled to the Father through the penal substitution of Christ, who died on the cross to pay the penalty for our sins (Rom. 3:21–26; Gal. 3:13; Eph. 2:16; Col. 1:20). By the same principle of corporate solidarity, in which the one stands for the many and the many for the one, Christ represents his people (Rom. 5:18–19; Heb. 7:27). His fate is theirs. His followers died with him, were buried with him, and were raised with him (Rom. 6:3–4; Col. 3:1–4). They are no longer in Adam but in Christ (Rom. 5:12–19; 1 Cor. 15:20–22).

25:5–10 In the Old Testament, as well as in other cultures, it was the responsibility of a brother to produce a child with a deceased brother's wife, if the deceased brother was childless. One reason for this practice was so that family land would not be lost (Ruth 4:5; see also Num. 26:33; 27:1–11; 36:1–12). But the reason given in our text is "that his name may not be blotted out of Israel" (v. 6). The desire to continue the name was a desire to continue the family line.

This desire to continue the family line was rooted in the promise made to Abraham that he would have many descendants (Gen. 17:6–8), and this promise was rooted in the promise that the seed of the woman would crush the head of the serpent (Gen. 3:15). At the heart of both of these promises was the hope of a coming Redeemer. So the responsibility of a brother to produce a child with a deceased brother's wife was an exercise of faith in the promise of God that a Redeemer would one day come, perhaps from this very family line. At the climax of all of human history, such a Redeemer did come (Gal. 4:4).

19 [y]Lev. 19:9; 23:22 [z]See ch. 14:29
22 [x][See ver. 18 above]
Chapter 25
1 [a]ch. 19:17 [b][1 Kgs. 8:32; Prov. 17:15]
3 [c][2 Cor. 11:24]
4 [d]Cited 1 Cor. 9:9; 1 Tim. 5:18
5 [e]Matt. 22:24; Mark 12:19; Luke 20:28 [f][Gen. 38:8, 9; Ruth 1:12, 13; 3:9]
6 [g]Ruth 4:10
7 [h][Ruth 4:1, 2]
8 [i][Ruth 4:6]
9 [j][Ruth 4:7] [k][Num. 12:14; Job 30:10; Isa. 50:6] [l]Ruth 4:11
12 [m]See ch. 7:16
13 [n]Lev. 19:35, 36; [Prov. 16:11; Ezek. 45:10; Amos 8:5; Mic. 6:11]

have in your house two kinds of measures,
a large and a small. 15 A full and fair[1] weight
you shall have, a full and fair measure you
shall have, [o]that your days may be long in the
land that the LORD your God is giving you.
16 For [p]all who do such things, all who act dis-
honestly, [q]are an abomination to the LORD
your God.

17 [r]"Remember what Amalek did to you [s]on
the way as you came out of Egypt, 18 how he
attacked you on the way when you were faint
and weary, and [t]cut off your tail, those who
were lagging behind you, and he did not
fear God. 19 Therefore [u]when the LORD your
God has given you rest from all your enemies
around you, in the land that the LORD your
God is giving you for an inheritance to possess, you shall [v]blot out the memory of Amalek
from under heaven; you shall not forget.

Offerings of Firstfruits and Tithes

26 "When you come into the land that
the LORD your God is giving you for
an inheritance and have taken possession of
it and live in it, 2 [w]you shall take some of the
first of all the fruit of the ground, which you
harvest from your land that the LORD your
God is giving you, and you shall put it in a
basket, and you shall [x]go to the place that the
LORD your God will choose, to make his name
to dwell there. 3 And you shall go to the priest
who is in office at that time and say to him, 'I
declare today to the LORD your God that I have
come into the land [y]that the LORD swore to our
fathers to give us.' 4 Then the priest shall take
the basket from your hand and set it down
before the altar of the LORD your God.

5 "And you shall make response before the
LORD your God, 'A [z]wandering Aramean was
my father. And he went down into Egypt and
sojourned there, [a]few in number, and there he
became a nation, great, mighty, and populous.
6 And [b]the Egyptians treated us harshly and
humiliated us and laid on us hard labor. 7 Then
[c]we cried to the LORD, the God of our fathers,
and the LORD heard our voice and saw our
affliction, our toil, and our oppression. 8 And
[d]the LORD brought us out of Egypt [e]with a
mighty hand and an outstretched arm, with
great deeds of terror,[2] with signs and wonders.
9 And he brought us into this place and gave us
this land, [f]a land flowing with milk and honey.
10 And behold, now I bring the first of the fruit
of the ground, which you, O LORD, have given
me.' And you shall set it down before the LORD
your God and worship before the LORD your
God. 11 And [g]you shall rejoice in all the good
that the LORD your God has given to you and
to your house, you, and the Levite, and the
sojourner who is among you.

12 "When you have finished paying all [h]the
tithe of your produce in the third year, which
is [i]the year of tithing, giving it to the Levite,
the sojourner, the fatherless, and the widow,
so that they may eat within your towns and
be filled, 13 then you shall say before the LORD
your God, 'I have removed the sacred portion
out of my house, and moreover, I have given it
to the Levite, the sojourner, the fatherless, and
the widow, according to all your commandment that you have commanded me. I have
not transgressed any of your commandments,
[j]nor have I forgotten them. 14 [k]I have not eaten
of the tithe while I was mourning, or removed
any of it while I was unclean, or offered any of
it [l]to the dead. I have obeyed the voice of the

[1] Or *just*, or *righteous*; twice in this verse [2] Hebrew *with great terror*

15[o] See ch. 4:40
16[p] Prov. 11:1 [q] ch. 18:12; 22:5
17[r] Ex. 17:8 [s] ch. 24:9
18[t] [Josh. 10:19]
19[u] [1 Sam. 15:2, 3] [v] See Ex. 17:8-14

Chapter 26
2[w] ch. 16:10; Ex. 23:19; 34:26; Num. 15:20; 18:13; Prov. 3:9 [x] See ch. 12:5
3[y] Ex. 13:5; See ch. 1:8
5[z] Gen. 43:1, 2 [a] [ch. 10:22; Gen. 46:27; Acts 7:14, 15]
6[b] Ex. 1:11, 14; Num. 20:15
7[c] Ex. 2:23-25; 3:9; Num. 20:16
8[d] Ex. 12:37, 51 [e] See ch. 4:34
9[f] See Ex. 3:8
11[g] See ch. 12:7
12[h] See Lev. 27:30 [i] ch. 14:28, 29; [Amos 4:4]
13[j] Ps. 119:141, 153, 176
14[k] Lev. 7:20; 21:1, 11; Hos. 9:4 [l] [Jer. 16:7]

26:1–11 The first portion of the harvest was to be given to God in response to his past grace and as a sign of trust in his continuing and future provision (vv. 1–2). The firstfruits acknowledged God's gracious promise made to Abraham, Isaac, and Jacob (vv. 3–4) and also were a recognition of God's gracious redemption, culminating in Israel's entrance into the land (vv. 5–9). This thanksgiving response was not to be onerous but joyful (vv. 10–11).

In the new covenant, believers themselves are the firstfruits (2 Thess. 2:13), as they thankfully offer their lives to God in fruitful service (James 1:18; Rev. 14:4), because they have received the "firstfruits of the Spirit" (Rom. 8:23). As the first-fruits in the old covenant were a foretaste of the full harvest, so the firstfruits of the Holy Spirit are a foretaste of the full harvest of resurrection life, guaranteed by Christ's resurrection from the dead (1 Cor. 15:20, 23). Jesus in his glorified, resurrected body is the first installment of the one great harvest in which all those who are in him will participate.

LORD my God. I have done according to all that you have commanded me. 15 [m]Look down from your holy habitation, from heaven, and bless your people Israel and the ground that you have given us, as you swore to our fathers, a land flowing with milk and honey.'

16 "This day the LORD your God commands you to do these statutes and rules. You shall therefore be careful to do them with all your heart and with all your soul. 17 [n]You have declared today that the LORD is your God, and that you will walk in his ways, and keep his statutes and his commandments and his rules, and will obey his voice. 18 And the LORD has declared today that you are [o]a people for his treasured possession, as he has promised you, and that you are to keep all his commandments, 19 and that he will set you in praise and in fame and in honor [p]high above all nations [q]that he has made, and that you shall be [r]a people holy to the LORD your God, as he promised."

The Altar on Mount Ebal

27 Now Moses and the elders of Israel commanded the people, saying, "Keep the whole commandment that I command you today. 2 And on the day [s]you cross over the Jordan to the land that the LORD your God is giving you, you shall set up large stones and plaster them with plaster. 3 [t]And you shall write on them all the words of this law, when you cross over to enter the land that the LORD your God is giving you, [u]a land flowing with milk and honey, as the LORD, the God of your fathers, has promised you. 4 And when you have crossed over the Jordan, you shall set up these stones, concerning which I command you today, [v]on Mount Ebal, and you shall plaster them with plaster. 5 And there you shall build an altar to the LORD your God, an altar of stones. [w]You shall wield no iron tool on them; 6 you shall build an altar to the LORD your God of uncut[1] stones. And you shall offer burnt offerings on it to the LORD your God, 7 and you shall sacrifice peace offerings and [x]shall eat there, and you [x]shall rejoice before the LORD your God. 8 And [y]you shall write on the stones all the words of this law very plainly."

Curses from Mount Ebal

9 Then Moses and the Levitical priests said to all Israel, "Keep silence and hear, O Israel: [z]this day you have become the people of the LORD your God. 10 You shall therefore obey the voice of the LORD your God, keeping his commandments and his statutes, which I command you today."

11 That day Moses charged the people, saying, 12 "When you have crossed over the Jordan, [a]these shall stand on Mount Gerizim to bless the people: Simeon, Levi, Judah, Issachar, Joseph, and Benjamin. 13 And these shall stand on Mount Ebal for the curse: Reuben, Gad, Asher, Zebulun, Dan, and Naphtali. 14 And [b]the

[1] Hebrew *whole*

27:9–26 This text, especially verses 15–26, have a rather "bad news" ring to them. The repetition of "cursed" 12 times as the lead word in 12 successive verses makes the topic of this section clear. The choice of 12 is probably intended to correspond to the 12 tribes of Israel assembled on Mount Gerizim and Mount Ebal (vv. 11–14). Thus, all are under obligation to either keep the law or experience its curse (v. 10). While some of these sins could have been known by others, there seems to be an emphasis in the text on the "secret" nature of the sins (vv. 15, 24). Even when no one else knows, sin brings one under the divine curse. And in case one thinks that one has kept the particulars of the first 11, the twelfth (v. 26) seems to be a catch-all.

It is important not to read these curse portions of Deuteronomy (27:9–26 and 28:15–68) in isolation from the overall and culminating message of God's desire for his people to "choose life" (30:19). While this list of curses makes it clear that the Lord's reproach may fall upon individuals for their sin and upon the nation for a time, God remains faithful to his covenant people and purpose (30:19–20), maintaining his plan to fulfill his promises (31:3–6) and fellowship again with all who repent of their sin (30:1–3). God clearly warns of the consequences of sin by these words of cursing and by the object lessons that those who experience his reproach become to others. Still, the purpose of both kinds of warning is to turn his people from paths of destruction for themselves, their families, and the larger community. Grace is never absent from God's heart or purpose even as he gives his people these dire warnings.

15[m] Isa. 63:15; Zech. 2:13
17[n] [Ex. 24:7]
18[o] ch. 7:6; 14:2; See Ex. 19:5
19[p] ch. 28:1; [ch. 32:8] [q] Ps. 86:9 [r] See ch. 7:6

Chapter 27
2[s] Josh. 4:1
3[t] Josh. 8:32 [u] See Ex. 3:8
4[v] ch. 11:29; Josh. 8:30
5[w] Ex. 20:25; Josh. 8:31
7[x] See ch. 12:7
8[y] [Hab. 2:2]
9[z] ch. 26:18
12[a] ch. 11:29; Josh. 8:33; [Judg. 9:7]
14[b] [ch. 33:10; Dan. 9:11]

Levites shall declare to all the men of Israel in
a loud voice:
15 [c]"'Cursed be the man who makes a carved
or cast metal image, an abomination to the
LORD, a thing made by the hands of a craftsman, and sets it up in secret.' [d]And all the
people shall answer and say, 'Amen.'
16 [e]"'Cursed be anyone who dishonors his
father or his mother.' And all the people shall
say, 'Amen.'
17 [f]"'Cursed be anyone who moves his neighbor's landmark.' And all the people shall say,
'Amen.'
18 [g]"'Cursed be anyone who misleads a blind
man on the road.' And all the people shall say,
'Amen.'
19 [h]"'Cursed be anyone who perverts the
justice due to the sojourner, the fatherless,
and the widow.' And all the people shall say,
'Amen.'
20 [i]"'Cursed be anyone who lies with his
father's wife, because he has [j]uncovered his
father's nakedness.'[1] And all the people shall
say, 'Amen.'
21 [k]"'Cursed be anyone who lies with any kind
of animal.' And all the people shall say, 'Amen.'
22 [l]"'Cursed be anyone who lies with his sister, whether the daughter of his father or the
daughter of his mother.' And all the people
shall say, 'Amen.'
23 [m]"'Cursed be anyone who lies with his
mother-in-law.' And all the people shall say,
'Amen.'
24 [n]"'Cursed be anyone who strikes down his
neighbor in secret.' And all the people shall
say, 'Amen.'
25 [o]"'Cursed be anyone who takes a bribe to
shed innocent blood.' And all the people shall
say, 'Amen.'
26 [p]"'Cursed be anyone who does not confirm
the words of this law by doing them.' And all
the people shall say, 'Amen.'

Blessings for Obedience

28 "And [q]if you faithfully obey the voice of
the LORD your God, being careful to do
all his commandments that I command you
today, the LORD your God will set you [r]high
above all the nations of the earth. 2 And all
these blessings shall come upon you and [s]over-
take you, if you obey the voice of the LORD
your God. 3 Blessed shall you be in the city,
and [t]blessed shall you be in the field. 4 Blessed
shall be [u]the fruit of your womb and the fruit
of your ground and the fruit of your cattle,
the increase of your herds and the young of
your flock. 5 Blessed shall be your basket and
your [v]kneading bowl. 6 Blessed shall you be
[w]when you come in, and blessed shall you be
when you go out.
7 "The LORD [x]will cause your enemies who
rise against you to be defeated before you.
They shall come out against you one way and
flee before you seven ways. 8 The LORD [y]will
command the blessing on you in your barns
and [z]in all that you undertake. [a]And he will

[1] Hebrew *uncovered his father's skirt*

15[c] See Ex. 20:4; 34:17 [d][Num. 5:22; Neh. 5:13; Ps. 106:48; Jer. 11:5; 28:6; 1 Cor. 14:16]
16[e] Ex. 20:12; 21:17; Lev. 19:3; See ch. 21:18-21
17[f] See ch. 19:14
18[g] Lev. 19:14
19[h] See Ex. 22:21, 22
20[i] See Lev. 18:8 [j] See ch. 22:30
21[k] See Lev. 18:23
22[l] Lev. 18:9; 20:17; [Ezek. 22:11]
23[m] Lev. 18:17; 20:14
24[n] ch. 19:11; Ex. 21:12, 14
25[o] ch. 16:19; Ex. 23:7, 8; Ezek. 22:12
26[p] ch. 28:15; Jer. 11:3; Cited Gal. 3:10

Chapter 28
1[q] [Ex. 15:26; 23:22; Lev. 26:3; Isa. 55:2] [r] ch. 26:19
2[s] ver. 15; Zech. 1:6
3[t] [Gen. 39:5]
4[u] ch. 7:13; 30:9; [Gen. 49:25; Ex. 23:26]
5[v] ver. 17; [Ex. 8:3; 12:34]
6[w] Ps. 121:8
7[x] Ex. 23:22, 27; Lev. 26:7, 8; [ver. 25]; See 2 Sam. 22:38-41; Ps. 18:37-40
8[y] Lev. 25:21; Ps. 133:3 [z] See ch. 12:7 [a] ch. 15:4

Were our keeping of the law our only hope, we would all be cursed along with the wayward Israelites. It is perhaps 27:26 that James has in mind when he says, "For whoever keeps the whole law but fails in one point has become accountable for all of it" (James 2:10). Since no one can keep the law without failing, all have sinned and fallen short (Rom. 3:23). The consequence of this failure is death (Rom. 6:23), the ultimate curse. But through his life, death, and resurrection, "Christ redeemed us from the curse of the law by becoming a curse for us . . . so that in Christ Jesus the blessing of Abraham might come" to us (Gal. 3:13–14). Blessing, not curse! Another was cursed in our place. This is good news!

28:1–14 Perhaps no other text in the Old Testament articulates so clearly the blessings of the covenant held out to God's people upon their obedience. (In these 14 verses, the verb "bless(ed)" occurs eight times and the noun "blessing" occurs two times.) Verse 2 promises "all these blessings," then we read in verses 3–6 "Blessed," "Blessed," "Blessed," "Blessed." Finally, verse 11 says, "the LORD will make you abound in prosperity." And perhaps no other text in the Old Testament articulates so clearly obedience as the condition for these blessings. The stress on obedience is found in the beginning (vv. 1–2), the middle (v. 9), and the end (vv. 13–14).

The problem is that we do not abide by all the things written in God's law. Left to ourselves, the result can only be curse rather than blessing (Gal. 3:10). But Christ obeyed for us (Rom. 5:19) and bore the curse for us (Gal. 3:13), so that we might

bless you in the land that the LORD your God
is giving you. 9 [b]The LORD will establish you
as a people holy to himself, as he has sworn
to you, if you keep the commandments of the
LORD your God and walk in his ways. 10 And
[c]all the peoples of the earth shall see that you
are [d]called by the name of the LORD, and they
shall be [e]afraid of you. 11 And [f]the LORD will
make you abound in prosperity, in [u]the fruit
of your womb and in the fruit of your livestock and in the fruit of your ground, within
the land that the LORD swore to your fathers
to give you. 12 The LORD will open to you his
good treasury, the heavens, [g]to give the rain
to your land in its season and [h]to bless all the
work of your hands. And [i]you shall lend to
many nations, but you shall not borrow. 13 And
the LORD will make you [j]the head and not the
tail, and you shall only go up and not down,
if you obey the commandments of the LORD
your God, which I command you today, being
careful to do them, 14 [k]and if you do not turn
aside from any of the words that I command
you today, to the right hand or to the left, to
go after other gods to serve them.

Curses for Disobedience

15 "But [l]if you will not obey the voice of the
LORD your God or be careful to do all his
commandments and his statutes that I command you today, then all these curses shall
come upon you and [m]overtake you. 16 Cursed
shall you be [n]in the city, and cursed shall you
be in the field. 17 Cursed shall be your basket
and your kneading bowl. 18 Cursed shall be
the fruit of your womb and the fruit of your
ground, the increase of your herds and the
young of your flock. 19 Cursed shall you be
when you come in, and cursed shall you be
when you go out.
20 "The LORD [o]will send on you curses, confusion, and [p]frustration in all that you undertake to do, [q]until you are destroyed and perish
quickly on account of the evil of your deeds,
because you have forsaken me. 21 The LORD
will make [r]the pestilence stick to you until he
has consumed you off the land that you are
entering to take possession of it. 22 [s]The LORD
will strike you with wasting disease and with
fever, inflammation and fiery heat, and with
drought[1] and with [t]blight and with mildew.
They shall pursue you until you perish. 23 And
[u]the heavens over your head shall be bronze,
and the earth under you shall be iron. 24 The
LORD will make the rain of your land powder.
From heaven dust shall come down on you
until you are destroyed.
25 [v]"The LORD will cause you to be defeated
before your enemies. You shall go out one
way against them and flee seven ways before
them. And you [w]shall be a horror to all the
kingdoms of the earth. 26 And [x]your dead body
shall be food for all birds of the air and for the
beasts of the earth, and [y]there shall be no one
to frighten them away. 27 The LORD will strike
you [z]with the boils of Egypt, and with tumors
and [a]scabs and itch, of which you cannot be
healed. 28 The LORD will strike you with [b]mad-
ness and blindness and confusion of mind,
29 and you shall [c]grope at noonday, as the blind
grope in darkness, and you shall not prosper
in your ways.[2] And you shall be only oppressed
and robbed continually, and there shall be no
one to help you. 30 [d]You shall betroth a wife,
but another man shall ravish her. [e]You shall
build a house, but you shall not dwell in it.
[f]You shall plant a vineyard, but you shall not
enjoy its fruit. 31 Your ox shall be slaughtered
before your eyes, but you shall not eat any of it.
Your donkey shall be seized before your face,
but shall not be restored to you. Your sheep
shall be given to your enemies, but there shall

[1] Or *sword* [2] Or *shall not succeed in finding your ways*

receive these blessings through our faith and not by our obedience (Gal. 3:14). Those who are free from the obligation to keep the law in order to merit the promised blessings (Gal. 5:1) do not use that freedom to sin (Gal. 5:13) but rather to serve in love (Gal. 5:14). As we do, we can expect to receive more of the covenant blessings in this life even as we anticipate experiencing the fullness of those blessings in the life to come.

Blessing, true blessing, real *shalom*, is ours for the asking—as long as we resist the urge to try to help pay for it.

28:15–68 On the curses for disobedience to the Lord, see note on 27:9–26.

9 [b]ch. 7:6; 26:18, 19; 29:13; See Ex. 19:5, 6
10 [c][Isa. 61:9] [d]See Num. 6:27 [e]ch. 2:25; 11:25
11 [f]ch. 30:9 [u][See ver. 4 above]
12 [g]ch. 11:14; Lev. 26:4 [h]ch. 14:29 [i]ch. 15:6; [ver. 44; Ps. 37:26]
13 [j]Isa. 9:14, 15; 19:15
14 [k]See ch. 5:32
15 [l]Lev. 26:14; Lam. 2:17; Dan. 9:11, 13; Mal. 2:2 [m]ver. 2
16 [n][ver. 3-6]

20 [o]Mal. 2:2 [p]Ps. 80:16; Isa. 30:17; 51:20; 66:15 [q]Josh. 23:16 **21** [r]See Lev. 26:25 **22** [s]Lev. 26:16 [t]1 Kgs. 8:37; 2 Chr. 6:28; Amos 4:9; Hag. 2:17 **23** [u]Lev. 26:19 **25** [v]ch. 32:30; Lev. 26:17, 37; Isa. 30:17; [ver. 7] [w]Ezek. 23:46 **26** [x][1 Sam. 17:44, 46; Ps. 79:2; Jer. 16:4; 19:7; 34:20] [y]Jer. 7:33 **27** [z][ver. 35] [a]Lev. 21:20; 22:22 **28** [b][ver. 34; Zech. 12:4] **29** [c]Job 5:14; Isa. 59:10 **30** [d]ch. 20:5-7; Jer. 8:10 [e]Amos 5:11; Zeph. 1:13 [f]ch. 20:6; Lev. 19:23-25; [Mic. 6:15]

be no one to help you. 32 [g]Your sons and your daughters shall be given to another people, while your eyes look on and fail with longing for them all day long, [h]but you shall be helpless. 33 A nation that you have not known shall eat up the fruit of your ground and of all your labors, and you shall be only oppressed and crushed continually, 34 so that you are driven mad [i]by the sights that your eyes see. 35 The LORD will strike you on the knees and on the legs [j]with grievous boils of which you cannot be healed, from the sole of your foot to the crown of your head.

36 "The LORD will [k]bring you and your king whom you set over you to a nation that neither you [l]nor your fathers have known. And [m]there you shall serve other gods of wood and stone. 37 And you shall become [n]a horror, a proverb, and a byword among all the peoples where the LORD will lead you away. 38 [o]You shall carry much seed into the field and shall gather in little, for [p]the locust shall consume it. 39 [q]You shall plant vineyards and dress them, but you shall neither drink of the wine nor gather the grapes, for the worm shall eat them. 40 You shall have olive trees throughout all your territory, but you [r]shall not anoint yourself with the oil, for your olives shall drop off. 41 You shall father sons and daughters, but they shall not be yours, for [s]they shall go into captivity. 42 [p]The cricket[1] shall possess all your trees and the fruit of your ground. 43 [t]The sojourner who is among you shall rise higher and higher above you, and you shall come down lower and lower. 44 [u]He shall lend to you, and you shall not lend to him. [t]He shall be the head, and you shall be the tail.

45 [v]"All these curses shall come upon you and pursue you and overtake you till you are destroyed, because you did not obey the voice of the LORD your God, to keep his commandments and his statutes that he commanded you. 46 They shall be [w]a sign and a wonder against you and your offspring forever. 47 [x]Because you did not serve the LORD your God with joyfulness and gladness of heart, because of the abundance of all things, 48 therefore you shall serve your enemies whom the LORD will send against you, in hunger and thirst, in nakedness, and lacking everything. And he [y]will put a yoke of iron on your neck until he has destroyed you. 49 [z]The LORD will bring a nation against you from far away, from the end of the earth, [a]swooping down like the eagle, a nation [b]whose language you do not understand, 50 a hard-faced nation [c]who shall not respect the old or show mercy to the young. 51 It shall [d]eat the offspring of your cattle and the fruit of your ground, until you are destroyed; it also shall not leave you grain, wine, or oil, the increase of your herds or the young of your flock, until they have caused you to perish.

52 "They shall [e]besiege you in all your towns, until your high and fortified walls, in which you trusted, come down throughout all your land. And they shall besiege you in all your towns throughout all your land, which the LORD your God has given you. 53 And [f]you shall eat the fruit of your womb, the flesh of your sons and daughters, whom the LORD your God has given you, [g]in the siege and in the distress with which your enemies shall distress you. 54 The man who is the most tender and refined among you will [h]begrudge food to his brother, to [i]the wife he embraces,[2] and to the last of the children whom he has left, 55 so that he will not give to any of them any of the flesh of his children whom he is eating, because he has nothing else left, [j]in the siege and in the distress with which your enemy shall distress you in all your towns. 56 [k]The most tender and refined woman among you, who would not venture to set the sole of her foot on the ground because she is so delicate and tender, will begrudge to the husband she embraces,[3] to her son and to her daughter, 57 her afterbirth that comes out from between her feet and her children whom she bears, because lacking everything she will eat them secretly, [j]in the siege and in the distress with which your enemy shall distress you in your towns.

58 "If you are not careful to do all the words of this law that are written in this book, that you may fear this glorious and awesome name, [l]the LORD your God, 59 then the LORD will bring on you and your offspring extraordinary afflictions, afflictions severe and lasting,

[1] Identity uncertain [2] Hebrew *the wife of his bosom* [3] Hebrew *the husband of her bosom*

32 [g] [2 Chr. 29:9; Joel 3:6] [h] Neh. 5:5 **34** [i] ver. 67 **35** [j] [ver. 27] **36** [k] 2 Kgs. 17:4, 6; 24:12, 14; 25:7, 11; 2 Chr. 33:11; 36:6, 20 [l] Jer. 9:16; 16:13 [m] ver. 64; ch. 4:28 **37** [n] 1 Kgs. 9:7, 8; 2 Chr. 7:20; Jer. 24:9; 25:9; [Ezek. 14:8] **38** [o] Mic. 6:15; Hag. 1:6 [p] Joel 1:4; 2:25 **39** [q] Zeph. 1:13 **40** [r] Mic. 6:15 **41** [s] Lam. 1:5 **42** [p] [See ver. 38 above] **43** [t] [ver. 13] **44** [u] [ver. 12] [t] [See ver. 43 above] **45** [v] ver. 15 **46** [w] [Isa. 8:18] **47** [x] Neh. 9:35-37 **48** [y] Jer. 28:14 **49** [z] [Jer. 5:15-17; 6:22, 23]; See Isa. 5:26-30 [a] Jer. 48:40; 49:22; Lam. 4:19; Hos. 8:1; Hab. 1:8; [Ezek. 17:3, 12] [b] Isa. 28:11; 33:19; Jer. 5:15 **50** [c] [2 Chr. 36:17; Isa. 47:6] **51** [d] ver. 33; Jer. 5:17; [Isa. 62:8, 9] **52** [e] [2 Kgs. 17:5; 25:1, 2, 4] **53** [f] ver. 57; Lev. 26:29; Jer. 19:9; Ezek. 5:10; [2 Kgs. 6:28, 29; Lam. 2:20; 4:10] [g] ver. 55, 57 **54** [h] See ch. 15:9 [i] ch. 13:6 **55** [j] ver. 53 **56** [k] ver. 54; Isa. 47:1 **57** [j] [See ver. 55 above] **58** [l] Ex. 6:3

and sicknesses grievous and lasting. 60 And
he will bring upon you again all [m]the diseases
of Egypt, of which you were afraid, and they
shall cling to you. 61 Every sickness also and
every affliction that is not recorded in the
book of this law, the LORD will bring upon
you, until you are destroyed. 62 Whereas [n]you
were as numerous [o]as the stars of heaven,
you shall be left few in number, because you
did not obey the voice of the LORD your God.
63 And as the LORD [p]took delight in doing you
good and multiplying you, so the LORD will
[q]take delight in bringing ruin upon you and
destroying you. And you shall be plucked off
the land that you are entering to take possession of it.

64 "And the LORD [r]will scatter you among
all peoples, from one end of the earth to the
other, and [s]there you shall serve other gods
[t]of wood and stone, [u]which neither you nor
your fathers have known. 65 And [v]among these
nations you shall find no respite, and there
shall be no resting place for the sole of your
foot, but [w]the LORD will give you there a trembling heart and failing eyes and [x]a languishing
soul. 66 Your life shall hang in doubt before
you. Night and day you shall be in dread and
have no assurance of your life. 67 [y]In the morning you shall say, 'If only it were evening!' and
at evening you shall say, 'If only it were morning!' because of the dread that your heart shall
feel, and [z]the sights that your eyes shall see.
68 And the LORD [a]will bring you back in ships
to Egypt, a journey that I promised that [b]you
should never make again; and there you shall
offer yourselves for sale to your enemies as
male and female slaves, but there will be no
buyer."

The Covenant Renewed in Moab

29 [1] These are the words of the covenant
that the LORD commanded Moses to
make with the people of Israel [c]in the land of
Moab, besides [d]the covenant that he had made
with them at Horeb.

2 [2] And Moses summoned all Israel and said
to them: [e]"You have seen all that the LORD
did before your eyes in the land of Egypt, to
Pharaoh and to all his servants and to all his
land, 3 the great [f]trials that your eyes saw, the
signs, and those great wonders. 4 But to this
day [g]the LORD has not given you a heart to
understand or eyes to see or ears to hear. 5 [h]I
have led you forty years in the wilderness.
Your clothes have not worn out on you, and
your sandals have not worn off your feet. 6 [i]You
have not eaten bread, and you have not drunk
wine or strong drink, that you may know that
I am the LORD your God. 7 And when you came
to this place, [j]Sihon the king of Heshbon and
Og the king of Bashan came out against us to
battle, but we defeated them. 8 We took their
land and [k]gave it for an inheritance to the
Reubenites, the Gadites, and the half-tribe of
the Manassites. 9 [l]Therefore keep the words
of this covenant and do them, that you may
prosper[3] in all that you do.

10 "You are standing today all of you before
the LORD your God: the heads of your tribes,[4]
your elders, and your officers, all the men of
Israel, 11 your little ones, your wives, and the
[m]sojourner who is in your camp, from [n]the
one who chops your wood to the one who
draws your water, 12 so that you may enter into
the [o]sworn covenant of the LORD your God,
which the LORD your God is making with you
today, 13 that he may [p]establish you today as his
people, and that [q]he may be your God, as he
promised you, and [r]as he swore to your fathers,
to Abraham, to Isaac, and to Jacob. 14 It is not
with you alone [s]that I am making this sworn
covenant, 15 but with whoever is standing here
with us today before the LORD our God, [t]and
with whoever is not here with us today.

16 "You know how we lived in the land of
Egypt, and how we came through the midst
of the nations through which you passed.
17 And you have seen their detestable things,
their idols of wood and stone, of silver and
gold, which were among them. 18 Beware lest
there be among you a man or woman or clan
or tribe whose heart is turning away today
from the LORD our God to go and serve the
gods of those nations. Beware lest there be
among you [u]a root bearing poisonous and bitter fruit, 19 one who, when he hears the words
of this sworn covenant, blesses himself in his
heart, saying, 'I shall be safe, though I walk in

[1] Ch 28:69 in Hebrew [2] Ch 29:1 in Hebrew [3] Or *deal wisely* [4] Septuagint, Syriac; Hebrew *your heads, your tribes*

60 [m] See ch. 7:15 **62** [n] ch. 4:27; [2 Kgs. 24:14; Neh. 7:4; Jer. 42:2] [o] See ch. 10:22 **63** [p] ch. 30:9; Jer. 32:41; Zeph. 3:17 [q] [Prov. 1:26; Isa. 1:24; Ezek. 5:13] **64** [r] See Lev. 26:33 [s] ver. 36 [t] ch. 4:28 [u] ch. 13:6; Jer. 19:4; 44:3 **65** [v] [Amos 9:4] [w] [Lev. 26:36] [x] Lev. 26:16 **67** [y] Job 7:3, 4 [z] ver. 34 **68** [a] Hos. 8:13; 9:3; [Jer. 43:7] [b] See ch. 17:16 **Chapter 29** **1** [c] ch. 1:5 [d] ch. 5:2, 3 **2** [e] Ex. 19:4; [Josh. 23:3] **3** [f] See ch. 4:34 **4** [g] [Isa. 6:9, 10; 63:17; John 8:43; Acts 28:26, 27; Rom. 11:8, 10] **5** [h] ch. 1:3; 8:2, 4; Amos 2:10; Acts 13:18 **6** [i] ch. 8:3; See Ex. 16:4 **7** [j] ch. 2:24, 26, 32; 3:1; See Num. 21:21-24, 33-35 **8** [k] ch. 3:12, 13; Num. 32:33 **9** [l] ch. 4:6 **11** [m] [Ex. 12:38] [n] [Josh. 9:21, 23, 27] **12** [o] Neh. 10:29 **13** [p] ch. 28:9 [q] Ex. 6:7 [r] Gen. 17:7; [Gen. 50:24] **14** [s] [Jer. 31:31-33; Heb. 8:8-10] **15** [t] [Acts 2:39] **18** [u] Heb. 12:15

the stubbornness of my heart.' This will lead
to the sweeping away of moist and dry alike.
20 The LORD will not be willing to forgive
him, but rather [v]the anger of the LORD and
[w]his jealousy will smoke against that man,
and the curses written in this book will settle
upon him, and the LORD [x]will blot out his
name from under heaven. 21 And the LORD
will single him out from all the tribes of Israel
for calamity, in accordance with all the curses
of the covenant written in this Book of the
Law. 22 And the next generation, your children
who rise up after you, and the foreigner who
comes from a far land, [y]will say, when they see
the afflictions of that land and the sicknesses
with which the LORD has made it sick— 23 the
whole land burned out with brimstone and
[z]salt, nothing sown and nothing growing,
where no plant can sprout, [a]an overthrow
like that of Sodom and Gomorrah, [b]Admah,
and Zeboiim, which the LORD overthrew
in his anger and wrath— 24 all the nations
[c]will say, [d]'Why has the LORD done thus to
this land? What caused the heat of this great
anger?' 25 Then people will say, 'It is because
they abandoned the covenant of the LORD,
the God of their fathers, which he made with
them when he brought them out of the land
of Egypt, 26 and went and served other gods
and worshiped them, gods whom they had
not known and whom he had not allotted
to them. 27 Therefore the anger of the LORD
was kindled against this land, [e]bringing upon
it all the curses written in this book, 28 and
the LORD [f]uprooted them from their land
in anger and fury and great wrath, and [g]cast
them into another land, as they are this day.'

29 "The secret things belong to the LORD our
God, but the things that are revealed belong
to us and to our children forever, that we may
do all the words of this law.

Repentance and Forgiveness

30 [h]"And [i]when all these things come
upon you, the blessing and the
curse, which I have set before you, and [j]you
call them to mind among all the nations
where the LORD your God has driven you,
2 and [k]return to the LORD your God, you and
your children, and obey his voice in all that
I command you today, with all your heart and
with all your soul, 3 then the LORD your God

20 [v]Ps. 74:1 [w]Ps. 79:5 [x]See ch. 9:14
22 [y]ver. 24
23 [z]Judg. 9:45; Jer. 17:6; Ezek. 47:11; Zeph. 2:9 [a]Gen. 19:24, 25; Jer. 20:16; 49:18; 50:40; 2 Pet. 2:6 [b]Gen. 14:2; Hos. 11:8
24 [c]ver. 22 [d]1 Kgs. 9:8, 9; Jer. 22:8, 9
27 [e]See ch. 28:15-68; Lev. 26:14-39; Dan. 9:11-14
28 [f]1 Kgs. 14:15; 2 Chr. 7:20; Jer. 12:14 [g]Jer. 22:26

Chapter 30
1 [h]ch. 11:26-28; Lev. 26:40-42 [i]See ch. 28 [j]ch. 4:29-31; See 1 Kgs. 8:47-50
2 [k]Neh. 1:9; Isa. 55:7; Lam. 3:40; Joel 2:12, 13

29:29 There are things that are hidden, things that God has chosen not to reveal. For example, why did God deeply desire that Israel have "a heart as this always, to fear me and to keep all my commandments" (5:29) but then not give Israel "a heart to understand or eyes to see or ears to hear" (29:4)? Or why did God require obedience of a people who would not obey and receive the blessing but who would disobey and be exiled from the land (vv. 27–28; 30:1)? Examples could be multiplied.

While God has not revealed everything in an absolute sense, he has revealed everything that we need to know (1 Pet. 1:3). And he has certainly revealed much more "in these last days" through "his Son" (Heb. 1:2). Since God has revealed more to us in the new covenant, "we must pay much closer attention to what we have heard, lest we drift away from it" (Heb. 2:1), relying on the grace of God that is ours through him who suffered death in our place (Heb. 2:9).

30:1–10 Here we read of repentance and restoration. That this text is about repentance is clear from the fact that returning/turning to the Lord brackets the text (vv. 2 and 10). This repentance is not just external but internal, since it is "with all your heart and with all your soul" (vv. 2 and 10). This repentance is also the result of divine grace, since it results from God circumcising the heart, "so that you will love the LORD your God with all your heart and with all your soul" (v. 6) and "again obey the voice of the LORD and keep all his commandments" (v. 8). That this text is about restoration is clear from the fact that the Lord "will restore" (v. 3) those who return/turn (vv. 2 and 10); the Hebrew word for "restore" is the same as the word for "return/turn."

This inner work of grace, this circumcision of the heart, is spoken of by the prophet Jeremiah as God putting his law within people and writing it on their hearts according to the promise of the new covenant (Jer. 31:31). This promise is fulfilled in the person and work of Christ (Hebrews 8). While the law required internalization (Deut. 6:5), the gospel brings this internalization into realization (Rom. 8:3), so that obedience from the heart is possible for those who now walk "according to the Spirit" (Rom. 8:4).

[l]will restore your fortunes and have mercy
on you, and he will [m]gather you again from
all the peoples where the LORD your God has
scattered you. 4 [n]If your outcasts are in the
uttermost parts of heaven, from there the
LORD your God will gather you, and from
there he will take you. 5 And the LORD your
God will bring you into the land that your
fathers possessed, that you may possess it.
[o]And he will make you more prosperous and
numerous than your fathers. 6 And [p]the LORD
your God will circumcise your heart and the
heart of your offspring, [q]so that you will love
the LORD your God with all your heart and
with all your soul, that you may live. 7 And
the LORD your God will put all these curses
on your foes and enemies who persecuted
you. 8 And you shall again obey the voice of
the LORD and keep all his commandments
that I command you today. 9 [r]The LORD your
God will make you abundantly prosperous
in all the work of your hand, in the fruit of
your womb and in the fruit of your cattle and
in the fruit of your ground. [s]For the LORD
will again take delight in prospering you,
as he took delight in your fathers, 10 when
you obey the voice of the LORD your God,
to keep his commandments and his statutes
that are written in this Book of the Law, when
you turn to the LORD your God with all your
heart and with all your soul.

The Choice of Life and Death

11 "For this commandment that I command
you today [t]is not too hard for you, neither
is it far off. 12 [u]It is not in heaven, that you
should say, 'Who will ascend to heaven for
us and bring it to us, that we may hear it and
do it?' 13 Neither is it beyond the sea, that you
should say, 'Who will go over the sea for us
and bring it to us, that we may hear it and
do it?' 14 But the word is very near you. It is
in your mouth and in your heart, so that you
can do it.

15 "See, [v]I have set before you today life
and good, death and evil. 16 If you obey the
commandments of the LORD your God[1] that
I command you today, [w]by loving the LORD
your God, by walking in his ways, and by
keeping his commandments and his statutes and his rules,[2] then you shall live and
multiply, and the LORD your God will bless
you in the land that you are entering to take
possession of it. 17 But if [x]your heart turns
away, and you will not hear, but are drawn
away to worship other gods and serve them,
18 [y]I declare to you today, that you shall surely
perish. You shall not live long in the land that
you are going over the Jordan to enter and
possess. 19 I call heaven and earth to witness
against you today, that I have set before you
life and death, [z]blessing and curse. Therefore
choose life, that you and your offspring may
live, 20 loving the LORD your God, obeying
his voice [a]and holding fast to him, for [b]he is
your life and length of days, that you may
dwell in [c]the land that the LORD swore to
your fathers, to Abraham, to Isaac, and to
Jacob, to give them."

[1] Septuagint; Hebrew lacks *If you obey the commandments of the LORD your God* [2] Or *his just decrees*

30:11–14 The sanctifying grace that internalizes the commandments and enables their keeping is from the same source that gives the commandments (v. 14; see note on 30:1–10). Here Moses identifies the enabling grace as "the word [that] is very near you. It is in your mouth and in your heart, so that you can do it" (vv. 13–14). God had given the word that would enable obedience, and we know from the New Testament that this must be because such a word is from the Holy Spirit, who both expresses God's truth and enables its reception and application (1 Cor. 2:14–16; Eph. 6:17).

This grace, operative by God's Word in the Old Testament (though not yet fully manifest) is like the grace that justifies and is received through faith in Christ (Rom. 10:6–8). From the perspective of the whole Bible, the commandment of God is indeed "not too hard" (Deut. 30:11) when it is done in the power of the Spirit and in the knowledge that Christ himself is the only one who has kept God's commandment perfectly. Because the righteousness of Christ's obedience has been transferred to our account (Rom. 4:3–8; 5:19), believers are indeed motivated from the inside out to keep God's commandments. "And his commandments," writes the apostle John, "are not burdensome" (1 John 5:3). This is because ultimately the commandments of God boil down to this simple call: love (1 John 5:2). Obedience is impossible apart from the gospel, but inevitable *with* it.

3 [l]Ps. 126:1, 4 [m]Jer. 32:37; Ezek. 34:13; 36:24
4 [n]ch. 28:64; Neh. 1:9
5 [o]Zeph. 3:19, 20; See ch. 28:63
6 [p][Jer. 31:33; 32:39, 40; Ezek. 11:19; 36:26, 27]; See ch. 10:16 [q]ver. 16
9 [r]ch. 28:11 [s]Zeph. 3:19, 20; See ch. 28:63
11 [t][Isa. 45:19; 48:16]
12 [u][Rom. 10:6-8]
15 [v][ch. 11:26; 32:47]
16 [w]ver. 6; See ch. 6:5
17 [x]ch. 29:18
18 [y]See ch. 4:26
19 [z]ver. 1
20 [a]See ch. 10:20 [b]Ps. 27:1; 66:9; John 11:25 [c]See ch. 1:8

Joshua to Succeed Moses

31 So Moses continued to speak these
words to all Israel. 2 And he said to
them, "I am [d]120 years old today. I am no longer able to [e]go out and come in. The LORD
has said to me, [f]'You shall not go over this
Jordan.' 3 The LORD your God [g]himself will go
over before you. He will destroy these nations
before you, so that you shall dispossess them,
and Joshua will go over at your head, [h]as the
LORD has spoken. 4 And the LORD will do to
them [i]as he did to Sihon [j]and Og, the kings
of the Amorites, and to their land, when he
destroyed them. 5 And the LORD will give them
over to you, and you shall do to them [k]accord-
ing to the whole commandment that I have
commanded you. 6 [l]Be strong and courageous.
Do not fear or be in dread of them, [m]for it is the
LORD your God who goes with you. [n]He will
not leave you or forsake you."
7 Then [o]Moses summoned Joshua and said to
him in the sight of all Israel, [l]"Be strong and
courageous, for you shall go with this people
into the land that the LORD has sworn to their
fathers to give them, and you shall put them
in possession of it. 8 It is the LORD [p]who goes
before you. He will be with you; [n]he will not
leave you or forsake you. [q]Do not fear or be
dismayed."

The Reading of the Law

9 Then Moses [r]wrote this law and gave it
to the priests, the sons of Levi, [s]who carried
the ark of the covenant of the LORD, and to
all the elders of Israel. 10 And Moses commanded them, [t]"At the end of every seven
years, at the set time in the year of release, at
[u]the Feast of Booths, 11 when all Israel comes
[v]to appear before the LORD your God at the
place that he will choose, [w]you shall read this
law before all Israel in their hearing. 12 [x]As-
semble the people, men, women, and little
ones, and the sojourner within your towns,
that they may hear and learn to fear the LORD
your God, and be careful to do all the words
of this law, 13 and that their children, [y]who
have not known it, [z]may hear and learn to
fear the LORD your God, [a]as long as you live
in the land that you are going over the Jordan
to possess."

Joshua Commissioned to Lead Israel

14 And the LORD said to Moses, [b]"Behold,
the days approach when you must die. Call
Joshua and present yourselves in the tent of
meeting, that [c]I may commission him." And
Moses and Joshua went and presented themselves in the tent of meeting. 15 And [d]the LORD
appeared in the tent in a pillar of cloud. And
the pillar of cloud stood over the entrance
of the tent.
16 And the LORD said to Moses, [b]"Behold,
you are about to lie down with your fathers.
Then this people will rise and [e]whore after
the foreign gods among them in the land
that they are entering, and they will [f]forsake
me and [g]break my covenant that I have made
with them. 17 Then my anger will be kindled
against them in that day, and [h]I will forsake
them and [i]hide my face from them, and they
will be devoured. And many evils and troubles
will come upon them, so that they will say
in that day, [j]'Have not these evils come upon
us because [k]our God is not among us?' 18 And
I will surely hide my face in that day because of
all the evil that they have done, because [l]they
have turned to other gods.
19 "Now therefore write [m]this song and
[n]teach it to the people of Israel. Put it in their
mouths, that this song may be [o]a witness for
me against the people of Israel. 20 For when
I have brought them into the land [p]flowing

Chapter 31
2 [d]ch. 34:7; [Ex. 7:7] [e]See Num. 27:17 [f]ch. 3:27; See ch. 1:37
3 [g]ch. 9:3 [h]ch. 1:38; 3:28; Num. 27:18, 21
4 [i]See ch. 2:31-35; Num. 21:21-25 [j]See ch. 3:1-7; Num. 21:33-35
5 [k]See ch. 7:2
6 [l]ver. 23; Josh. 1:6, 7; 10:25; 1 Chr. 22:13; 28:20 [m]See ch. 20:4 [n]Josh. 1:5
7 [o][ch. 3:28]

31:1–8 Israel's entrance into the Promised Land was the result of both sovereign grace and human responsibility. Israel dispossessed the nations, because the Lord went before his people (v. 3). Israel conquered the nations according to the commandments, because the Lord gave the nations to his people (v. 5). Israel could be strong and courageous in the mission against the nations, because God was always with his people (vv. 6, 7–8).

In the same way, Jesus promised to be with the church always (Matt. 28:20), so the church can be strong and courageous in carrying out the divine mandate to make disciples of the nations (Matt. 28:19).

[l][See ver. 6 above] **8** [p]See Ex. 13:21 [n][See ver. 6 above] [q]ch. 1:21; 7:18; Josh. 1:9; 8:1; 10:25 **9** [r][ch. 17:18] [s]Num. 4:15; Josh. 3:3; 8:33; 1 Chr. 15:15 **10** [t]See ch. 15:1 [u]See Lev. 23:34 **11** [v]ch. 16:16; Ex. 23:14, 17; 34:23 [w]Josh. 8:34, 35; 2 Kgs. 23:2; See Neh. 8:1-3 **12** [x]ch. 4:10 **13** [y]ch. 11:2 [z]Ps. 78:5, 6 [a]See ch. 4:10 **14** [b][ch. 34:5; Num. 27:13] [c][ver. 23; Num. 27:19] **15** [d]Ex. 33:9; Num. 12:5 **16** [b][See ver. 14 above] [e]Ex. 34:15, 16; Lev. 20:5; Num. 15:39 [f]ch. 32:15; Judg. 2:12; 10:6, 13 [g]Judg. 2:20 **17** [h]2 Chr. 12:5; 15:2; 24:20 [i]ch. 32:20; Ps. 30:7; 104:29; Isa. 8:17; 64:7; [Isa. 59:2] [j]Judg. 6:13 [k]Num. 14:42 **18** [l]ver. 20 **19** [m]See ch. 32:1-43 [n][2 Sam. 1:18] [o]ver. 21, 26 **20** [p]See Ex. 3:8

with milk and honey, which I swore to give
to their fathers, and they have eaten and are
full and [q]grown fat, [r]they will turn to other
gods and serve them, and [s]despise me and
[g]break my covenant. 21 And when many evils
and troubles have come upon them, this song
shall confront them as [t]a witness (for it will
live unforgotten in the mouths of their offspring). For [u]I know what they are inclined
to do even today, before I have brought them
into the land that I swore to give." 22 So Moses
wrote this song the same day and taught it to
the people of Israel.
23 [v]And the LORD[1] commissioned Joshua the
son of Nun and said, [w]"Be strong and courageous, for you shall bring the people of Israel
into the land that I swore to give them. [x]I will
be with you."
24 When Moses had finished [y]writing the
words of this law in a book to the very end,
25 Moses commanded [z]the Levites who carried
the ark of the covenant of the LORD, 26 "Take
this Book of the Law [a]and put it by the side of
the ark of the covenant of the LORD your God,
that it may be there for [b]a witness against
you. 27 For I know how rebellious and [c]stub-
born you are. Behold, even today while I am
yet alive with you, [d]you have been rebellious
against the LORD. How much more after
my death! 28 Assemble to me all the elders
of your tribes and your officers, that I may
speak [e]these words in their ears and [f]call
heaven and earth to witness against them.
29 For I know that after my death [g]you will
surely act corruptly and turn aside from the
way that I have commanded you. And [h]in the
days to come [i]evil will befall you, because you
will do what is evil in the sight of the LORD,
[j]provoking him to anger through the work
of your hands."

The Song of Moses

30 Then Moses spoke the words of this song
until they were finished, in the ears of all the
assembly of Israel:

32 "Give ear, [k]O heavens, and I will speak,
and let [l]the earth hear the words of my mouth.
2 May [m]my teaching drop as the rain,
my speech distill as the dew,
like gentle rain upon the tender grass,
and [n]like showers upon the herb.
3 For I will proclaim the name of the LORD;
ascribe [o]greatness to our God!

4 [p]"The Rock, [q]his work is perfect,
for [r]all his ways are justice.
A God of faithfulness and [s]without iniquity,
just and upright is he.
5 They have dealt corruptly with him;
they are no longer his children
[t]because they are blemished;
they are [u]a crooked and twisted generation.
6 Do you thus repay the LORD,
you foolish and senseless people?
Is not he [v]your father, who [w]created you,
who [x]made you and established you?
7 [y]Remember the days of old;
consider the years of many generations;
[z]ask your father, and he will show you,
your elders, and they will tell you.
8 When the Most High [a]gave to the nations their inheritance,
when he [b]divided mankind,
he fixed the borders[2] of the peoples
according to the number of the sons of God.[3]

[1] Hebrew *he* [2] Or *territories* [3] Compare Dead Sea Scroll, Septuagint; Masoretic Text *sons of Israel*

32:1–43 The Song of Moses has a predominantly negative tone. It speaks of Israel's sin (vv. 5–6, 15–17) against the backdrop of God's goodness (vv. 7–14, 18), and it speaks of God's judgment of Israel by means of the nations (vv. 19–35). But at the heart of the Song is the compassion of God that leads to the vindication of his people, when he sees that they are helpless (vv. 36–38; see Ps. 135:14). Because he is the only true God, he will vindicate his people, bring cleansing (Deut. 32:39–43), and fulfill the patriarchal promise—which will be not only for his people's sake, but also for the sake of the nations (cf. 32:43 and Rom. 15:10).

This same compassion for the helpless motivated Jesus to instruct his disciples to pray earnestly for laborers to be sent into the harvest (Matt. 9:36–38). May this compassion motivate us not only to pray but also to be the answer to that prayer.

20 [q]ch. 32:15; Neh. 9:25, 26; Jer. 5:28; Hos. 13:6 [r]ver. 18 [s]Num. 14:11, 23; 16:30 [g][See ver. 16 above]
21 [t]ver. 19, 26 [u][Hos. 5:3; 13:5]
23 [v][ver. 14] [w]See ver. 6 [x]ver. 8; Josh. 1:5; 3:7
24 [y]ver. 9
25 [z]See ver. 9
26 [a][2 Kgs. 22:8] [b]ver. 19, 21
27 [c]See ch. 9:6 [d]See ch. 9:7
28 [e]See ch. 32:1-43 [f]See ch. 4:26
29 [g]Judg. 2:19; Hos. 9:9 [h]See Gen. 49:1 [i][Jer. 44:23]

[j]ch. 4:25; 9:18; 32:16, 21; 1 Kgs. 16:7; 2 Kgs. 22:17 **Chapter 32** **1** [k]Ps. 50:4; [Josh. 24:27]; See ch. 4:26 [l]Isa. 34:1; Mic. 1:2; 6:1, 2 **2** [m]Isa. 55:10, 11; [Job 29:22, 23] [n]Ps. 72:6; Mic. 5:7 **3** [o]See ch. 3:24 **4** [p]ver. 15, 18, 30, 31, 37; Ps. 18:2, 31; Isa. 30:29; Hab. 1:12; See 2 Sam. 22:2 [q][Ps. 18:30] [r]Dan. 4:37; Rev. 15:3 [s]Job 34:10 **5** [t][2 Pet. 2:13] [u]Matt. 17:17; Luke 9:41; Phil. 2:15 **6** [v]Isa. 63:16; 64:8 [w]Ps. 74:2 [x]ver. 15; Isa. 44:2; 51:13 **7** [y][Isa. 63:11] [z]Ps. 44:1 **8** [a]Acts 17:26 [b]Gen. 11:8

9 But the LORD's portion is his people,
Jacob his allotted heritage.

10 "He found him [c]in a desert land,
and in the howling waste of the wilderness;
he [d]encircled him, he cared for him,
he [e]kept him as the apple of his eye.
11 [f]Like an eagle that stirs up its nest,
that flutters over its young,
spreading out its wings, catching them,
bearing them on its pinions,
12 [g]the LORD alone guided him,
[h]no foreign god was with him.
13 [i]He made him ride on the high places of the land,
and he ate the produce of the field,
and he suckled him with [j]honey out of the rock,
and [k]oil out of [l]the flinty rock.
14 Curds from the herd, and milk from the flock,
with fat[1] of lambs,
rams of Bashan and goats,
with the very finest[2] of the wheat—
and you drank foaming wine made from [m]the blood of the grape.

15 "But [n]Jeshurun grew fat, and [o]kicked;
[p]you grew fat, stout, and sleek;
[q]then he forsook God [r]who made him
and scoffed at [s]the Rock of his salvation.
16 [t]They stirred him to jealousy with strange gods;
with abominations they provoked him to anger.
17 [u]They sacrificed to demons that were no gods,
to gods they had never known,
to [v]new gods that had come recently,
whom your fathers had never dreaded.
18 You were unmindful of [w]the Rock that bore[3] you,
and you [x]forgot the God who gave you birth.

19 [y]"The LORD saw it and spurned them,
because of the provocation of [z]his sons and his daughters.
20 And he said, [a]'I will hide my face from them;
I will see what their end will be,
for they are a perverse generation,
children in whom is no faithfulness.
21 [b]They have made me jealous with what is no god;
they have provoked me to anger [c]with their idols.
So [d]I will make them jealous with those who are no people;
I will provoke them to anger with [e]a foolish nation.
22 For [f]a fire is kindled by my anger,
and it burns to [g]the depths of Sheol,
devours the earth and its increase,
and sets on fire the foundations of the mountains.

23 " 'And I will heap disasters upon them;
[h]I will spend my arrows on them;
24 they shall be wasted with hunger,
and devoured by plague
and poisonous pestilence;
I will send [i]the teeth of beasts against them,
with the venom of [j]things that crawl in the dust.
25 [k]Outdoors the sword shall bereave,
and indoors terror,
for young man and woman alike,
the nursing child with the man of gray hairs.
26 [l]I would have said, "I will cut them to pieces;
[m]I will wipe them from human memory,"
27 had I not feared provocation by the enemy,
lest their adversaries should misunderstand,
lest they should say, [n]"Our hand is triumphant,
it was not the LORD who did all this." '

28 "For they are a nation void of counsel,
and there is [o]no understanding in them.

[1] That is, with the best [2] Hebrew *with the kidney fat* [3] Or *fathered*

10[c] ch. 8:15; Jer. 2:6; Hos. 13:5 [d] Ps. 32:10 [e] Ps. 17:8; Prov. 7:2; Zech. 2:8 **11**[f] Ex. 19:4 **12**[g] Ps. 78:52, 53 [h] Isa. 43:12 **13**[i] Isa. 58:14; Ezek. 36:2 [j] Ps. 81:16 [k] Job 29:6 [l] ch. 8:15 **14**[m] Gen. 49:11 **15**[n] ch. 33:5, 26; Isa. 44:2 [o] [1 Sam. 2:29] [p] See ch. 31:20 [q] ch. 31:16 [r] ver. 6 [s] 2 Sam. 22:47; Ps. 89:26; 95:1 **16**[t] Ps. 78:58; See Num. 25:11 **17**[u] Ps. 106:37; [1 Cor. 10:20] [v] [Judg. 5:8] **18**[w] 2 Sam. 22:47; Ps. 89:26; 95:1 [x] Isa. 17:10; Jer. 2:27, 32; Hos. 8:14 **19**[y] [Judg. 2:14] [z] [Isa. 1:2] **20**[a] See ch. 31:17 **21**[b] Ps. 78:58; See Num. 25:11 [c] 1 Kgs. 16:13, 26; Ps. 31:6; Jonah 2:8; Acts 14:15 [d] Cited Rom. 10:19; [Hos. 1:9, 10] [e] [Ps. 74:18] **22**[f] Jer. 15:14; 17:4; Lam. 4:11 [g] Ps. 86:13 **23**[h] Job 6:4; Ps. 7:12, 13; 38:2; Lam. 3:12, 13; Ezek. 5:16 **24**[i] Lev. 26:22; Ezek. 5:17 [j] Jer. 8:17; Mic. 7:17 **25**[k] Lam. 1:20; Ezek. 7:15 **26**[l] Ezek. 20:23 [m] Job 18:17; Ps. 34:16; 109:15 **27**[n] Ps. 140:8; Isa. 10:13; [Num. 14:16] **28**[o] Isa. 27:11; Jer. 4:22

29 [p]If they were wise, they would understand this;
they would [q]discern their latter end!
30 How could [r]one have chased a thousand,
and two have put ten thousand to flight,
unless their Rock [s]had sold them,
and the LORD had given them up?
31 For [t]their rock is not as our Rock;
[u]our enemies are by themselves.
32 For their vine [v]comes from the vine of Sodom
and from the fields of Gomorrah;
their grapes are grapes of [w]poison;
their clusters are bitter;
33 their wine is the poison of [x]serpents
and the cruel venom of asps.

34 "'Is not this laid up in store with me,
[y]sealed up in my treasuries?
35 [z]Vengeance is mine, and recompense,[1]
[a]for the time when their foot shall slip;
for [b]the day of their calamity is at hand,
and their doom comes swiftly.'
36 For [c]the LORD will vindicate[2] his people
[d]and have compassion on his servants,
when he sees that their power is gone
and there is none remaining, [e]bond or free.
37 Then he will say, [f]'Where are their gods,
[g]the rock in which they took refuge,
38 who ate the fat of their sacrifices
and drank the wine of their drink offering?
Let them rise up and help you;
let them be your protection!

39 "'See now that [h]I, even I, am he,
and there is no god beside me;
[i]I kill and I make alive;
[j]I wound and I heal;
and there is none that can deliver out of my hand.
40 For [k]I lift up my hand to heaven
and swear, As I live forever,
41 if I [l]sharpen my flashing sword[3]
and my hand takes hold on judgment,
I will take vengeance on my adversaries
and will repay those who hate me.
42 I will make my arrows drunk with blood,
and [m]my sword shall devour flesh—
with the blood of the slain and the captives,
from the [n]long-haired heads of the enemy.'

43 [o]"Rejoice with him, O heavens;[4]
bow down to him, all gods,[5]
for he [p]avenges the blood of his children[6]
and takes vengeance on his adversaries.
He repays those who hate him[7]
and cleanses[8] his people's land."[9]

44 Moses came and recited all the words of
this song in the hearing of the people, he and
[q]Joshua[10] the son of Nun. 45 And when Moses
had finished speaking all these words to all
Israel, 46 he said to them, [r]"Take to heart all
the words by which I am warning you today,
[s]that you may command them to your children, that they may be careful to do all the
words of this law. 47 For it is no empty word for
you, [t]but your very life, and by this word you
shall live long in the land that you are going
over the Jordan to possess."

Moses' Death Foretold

48 That very day the LORD spoke to Moses,
49 "Go up [u]this mountain of the Abarim,
Mount Nebo, which is in the land of Moab,
opposite Jericho, and view the land of Canaan,
which I am giving to the people of Israel for a
possession. 50 And die on the mountain which
you go up, and be gathered to your people, as
[v]Aaron your brother died in Mount Hor and
was gathered to his people, 51 [w]because you
broke faith with me in the midst of the people
of Israel at the waters of Meribah-kadesh, in
the wilderness of Zin, and because you did not
treat me as holy in the midst of the people of
Israel. 52 For [x]you shall see the land before you,
but you shall not go there, into the land that
I am giving to the people of Israel."

[1] Septuagint *and I will repay* [2] Septuagint *judge* [3] Hebrew *the lightning of my sword* [4] Dead Sea Scroll, Septuagint; Masoretic Text *Rejoice his people, O nations* [5] Masoretic Text lacks *bow down to him, all gods* [6] Dead Sea Scroll, Septuagint; Masoretic Text *servants* [7] Dead Sea Scroll, Septuagint; Masoretic Text lacks *He repays those who hate him* [8] Or *atones for* [9] Septuagint, Vulgate; Hebrew *his land his people* [10] Septuagint, Syriac, Vulgate; Hebrew *Hoshea*

29[p] ch. 5:29; Ps. 81:13; Luke 19:42 [q] Isa. 47:7; Lam. 1:9 **30**[r] See Lev. 26:8 [s] See Judg. 2:14 **31**[t] 1 Sam. 2:2 [u] [1 Sam. 4:8] **32**[v] [Isa. 1:10; Jer. 23:14; Ezek. 16:46] [w] ch. 29:18 **33**[x] Job 20:14, 16; Ps. 58:4 (Heb.) **34**[y] [Job 14:17; Hos. 13:12; Rom. 2:5] **35**[z] Ps. 94:1; Isa. 1:24; 59:18; Nah. 1:2; Cited Rom. 12:19; Heb. 10:30 [a] [Ps. 94:18] [b] [2 Pet. 2:3] **36**[c] Ps. 135:14; Cited Heb. 10:30 [d] Judg. 2:18; Ps. 106:45; [Ps. 90:13] [e] 1 Kgs. 14:10; 21:21; 2 Kgs. 9:8; 14:26 **37**[f] Judg. 10:14; 1 Kgs. 18:27; Jer. 2:28 [g] [ver. 31] **39**[h] Isa. 41:4; 48:12 [i] 1 Sam. 2:6; 2 Kgs. 5:7 [j] Job 5:18; Hos. 6:1 **40**[k] See Gen. 14:22 **41**[l] Ps. 7:12; Isa. 27:1; 34:5; 66:16; Ezek. 21:9, 10 **42**[m] Jer. 46:10 [n] See Ps. 68:21 **43**[o] Cited Rom. 15:10 [p] Rev. 6:10; 19:2; [2 Kgs. 9:7; Ps. 79:10] **44**[q] Num. 13:8, 16 **46**[r] ch. 11:18; See ch. 6:6 [s] See ch. 4:9 **47**[t] [Lev. 18:5]; See ch. 30:20 **49**[u] See Num. 27:12 **50**[v] Num. 20:24, 25, 28; 33:38 **51**[w] Num. 20:11-13; 27:14 **52**[x] ch. 3:27; 34:4

Moses' Final Blessing on Israel

33 This is the blessing with which Moses [y]the man of God blessed the people of Israel before his death. 2 He said,

[z]"The LORD came from Sinai
and dawned from Seir upon us;[1]
he shone forth from Mount Paran;
he came [a]from the ten thousands of holy ones,
with flaming fire[2] at his right hand.
3 Yes, [b]he loved his people,[3]
[c]all his holy ones were in his[4] hand;
[d]so they followed[5] in your steps,
receiving direction from you,
4 when [e]Moses commanded us a law,
as a possession for the assembly of Jacob.
5 Thus the LORD[6] [f]became king in [g]Jeshurun,
when the heads of the people were gathered,
all the tribes of Israel together.

6 [h]"Let Reuben live, and not die,
but let his men be few."

7 And this he said of Judah:

"Hear, O LORD, the voice of Judah,
and bring him in to his people.
With your hands contend[7] for him,
and be a help against his adversaries."

8 And [i]of Levi he said,

"Give to Levi[8] [j]your Thummim,
and your Urim to your godly one,
[k]whom you tested at Massah,
with whom you quarreled at the waters of Meribah;
9 who said of his father and mother,
'I regard them not';
[l]he disowned his brothers
and ignored his children.
For [m]they observed your word
and kept your covenant.
10 [n]They shall teach Jacob your rules
and Israel your law;
[o]they shall put incense before you
and [p]whole burnt offerings on your altar.
11 Bless, O LORD, his substance,
and [q]accept the work of his hands;
crush the loins of his adversaries,
of those who hate him, that they rise not again."

12 [r]Of Benjamin he said,

"The beloved of the LORD dwells in safety.
The High God[9] surrounds him all day long,
and dwells between his shoulders."

13 And [s]of Joseph he said,

[t]"Blessed by the LORD be his land,
with the choicest gifts of heaven [u]above,[10]
and of the deep that crouches beneath,
14 with the choicest fruits of the sun
and the rich yield of the months,
15 with the finest produce of the ancient mountains
and the abundance of [v]the everlasting hills,
16 with the best gifts of the earth and [w]its fullness
and the favor of [x]him who dwells in the bush.
May these rest on the head of Joseph,
on the pate of him who is prince among his brothers.

[1] Septuagint, Syriac, Vulgate; Hebrew *them* [2] The meaning of the Hebrew word is uncertain [3] Septuagint; Hebrew *peoples* [4] Hebrew *your* [5] The meaning of the Hebrew word is uncertain [6] Hebrew *Thus he* [7] Probable reading; Hebrew *With his hands he contended* [8] Dead Sea Scroll, Septuagint; Masoretic Text lacks *Give to Levi* [9] Septuagint; Hebrew *dwells in safety by him. He* [10] Two Hebrew manuscripts and Targum; Hebrew *with the dew*

33:1–29 Moses' final words, recorded in the next to the last chapter of Deuteronomy, were not words of judgment but of blessing. (The words "bless/blessed/blessing" occur seven times in this passage.) Jacob's final words, in the next to the last chapter of the book of Genesis, were also not words of judgment but of blessing. Thus the first book and the last book in the Pentateuch end with blessing. The gospel ends with blessing, as Jesus' very last action before his ascension was not to judge but to bless his disciples (Luke 24:50–51). All of these final blessings are a reflex of the very first thing God did after creating the human race: he blessed them (Gen 1:28; 5:1–2).

Chapter 33
1[y] Josh. 14:6; 1 Chr. 23:14; 2 Chr. 30:16; Ezra 3:2
2[z] [Ex. 19:18, 20; Judg. 5:4, 5; Ps. 68:7, 8; Hab. 3:3] [a] [Ps. 68:17; Dan. 7:10; Acts 7:53; Gal. 3:19; Heb. 2:2; Jude 14; Rev. 5:11]
3[b] ch. 7:7, 8; 10:15; Hos. 11:1 [c] [John 10:27-29; Rom. 8:35, 38, 39] [d] [Luke 10:39; Acts 22:3]
4[e] John 1:17; 7:19
5[f] Num. 23:21; [Judg. 8:23; Isa. 33:22] [g] See ch. 32:15 **6**[h] [Gen. 49:3, 4] **8**[i] [Gen. 49:5] [j] See Ex. 28:30 [k] See Ex. 17:7; Num. 20:13 **9**[l] See Ex. 32:26-29 [m] Mal. 2:4-6 **10**[n] ch. 17:9-11; Ezek. 44:23; See Lev. 10:11 [o] Ex. 30:7, 8; 1 Sam. 2:28 [p] Ps. 51:19; Ezek. 43:27 **11**[q] Ezek. 20:40, 41; 43:27; [Amos 5:22] **12**[r] [Gen. 49:27] **13**[s] [Gen. 49:22] [t] Gen. 49:25 [u] ver. 28; Gen. 27:28 **15**[v] Gen. 49:26; Hab. 3:6; [Ps. 90:2] **16**[w] Ps. 24:1 [x] Ex. 3:2-4; Acts 7:30, 35

17 [y]A firstborn bull[1]—he has majesty,
and his horns are the horns of a [z]wild ox;
with them [a]he shall gore the peoples,
all of them, to the ends of the earth;
[b]they are the ten thousands of Ephraim,
and they are the thousands of Manasseh."

18 And of Zebulun he said,

[c]"Rejoice, Zebulun, in your going out,
and Issachar, in your tents.
19 They shall call peoples [d]to their mountain;
there they offer [e]right sacrifices;
for they draw from the abundance of the seas
and the hidden treasures of the sand."

20 And [f]of Gad he said,

"Blessed be he who enlarges Gad!
Gad crouches [g]like a lion;
he tears off arm and scalp.
21 [h]He chose the best of the land for himself,
for there a commander's portion was reserved;
and [i]he came with the heads of the people,
with Israel he executed the justice of the LORD,
and his judgments for Israel."

22 And [j]of Dan he said,

[k]"Dan is a lion's cub
[l]that leaps from Bashan."

23 And [m]of Naphtali he said,

"O Naphtali, sated with favor,
and full of the blessing of the LORD,
[n]possess the lake[2] and the south."

24 And [o]of Asher he said,

"Most blessed of sons be Asher;
let him be the favorite of his brothers,
and let him [p]dip his foot in oil.
25 Your bars shall be iron and bronze,
and as your days, so shall your strength be.

26 [q]"There is none like God, O [r]Jeshurun,
[s]who rides through the heavens to your help,
through the skies in his majesty.
27 The eternal God is your [t]dwelling place,[3]
and underneath are the everlasting arms.[4]
And he thrust out the enemy before you
and said, 'Destroy.'
28 So Israel lived in safety,
[u]Jacob lived [v]alone,[5]
in a land of grain and wine,
whose heavens drop down dew.
29 Happy are you, O Israel! [w]Who is like you,
a people [x]saved by the LORD,
[y]the shield of your help,
and the sword of your triumph!
Your enemies shall come fawning to you,
and you shall tread upon their backs."

The Death of Moses

34 Then Moses went up from the plains
of Moab [a]to Mount Nebo, to the top
of Pisgah, which is opposite Jericho. And the
LORD showed him all the land, Gilead as far
as Dan, 2 all Naphtali, the land of Ephraim and
Manasseh, all the land of Judah [b]as far as the
western sea, 3 [c]the Negeb, and [d]the Plain, that is,
the Valley of Jericho [e]the city of palm trees, as
far as [f]Zoar. 4 And the LORD said to him, [g]"This
is the land of which I swore to Abraham, to

[1] Dead Sea Scroll, Septuagint, Samaritan; Masoretic Text *His firstborn bull* [2] Or *west* [3] Or *a dwelling place* [4] Revocalization of verse 27 yields *He subdues the ancient gods, and shatters the forces of old* [5] Hebrew *the abode of Jacob was alone*

Deuteronomy 33:1–29 reflects the heart of God revealed throughout the Scriptures from beginning to end: the God of the Scriptures is a God of blessing. It is simply and profoundly true that, "There is none like God" (v. 26), and so there are none like the people of God: "Happy are you, O Israel! Who is like you, a people saved by the LORD . . . ?" (v. 29).

34:1–12 Deuteronomy ends with a record of Moses' death (vv. 1–8) and his eulogy (vv. 9–12). Moses was eulogized as unique: "there has not arisen a prophet since in Israel like Moses" (v. 10) and there was "none like him for all the signs and the wonders that the LORD sent him to do . . . and for all the mighty power and all the great deeds of terror that Moses did in the sight of all Israel" (vv. 11–12). There were truly none like Moses (see note on 18:15–22).

17 [y][1 Chr. 5:1] [z]See Num. 23:22 [a]1 Kgs. 22:11; Ps. 44:5; Dan. 8:4 [b][Gen. 48:19; Num. 1:33, 35]
18 [c][Gen. 49:13-15]
19 [d]Ex. 15:17; Isa. 2:3 [e]Ps. 4:5; 51:19
20 [f][Gen. 49:19] [g][1 Chr. 12:8]
21 [h]See Num. 32:1-5, 16-19 [i]Num. 32:31, 32; See Josh. 1:12-15; 1 Chr. 5:18-22
22 [j][Gen. 49:16] [k][Gen. 49:9] [l][Josh. 19:47; Judg. 18:27]
23 [m][Gen. 49:21] [n]See Josh. 19:32-39
24 [o][Gen. 49:20] [p][Job 29:6]
26 [q]See Ex. 15:11 [r]See ch. 32:15 [s]Ps. 68:33, 34; 104:3; Isa. 19:1; Hab. 3:8 **27** [t]Ps. 90:1; 91:9 **28** [u][Ps. 68:26; Isa. 48:1] [v]Num. 23:9 **29** [w][2 Sam. 7:23] [x]Isa. 45:17 [y]Ps. 33:20; 115:9-11
Chapter 34 **1** [a]See Num. 27:12 **2** [b]See ch. 11:24 **3** [c]ch. 1:7 [d]Gen. 13:12; 19:17, 25, 28, 29; 2 Sam. 18:23 [e]Judg. 1:16; 3:13; 2 Chr. 28:15 [f]Gen. 14:2; 19:22
4 [g]See Gen. 12:7; 50:24

Isaac, and to Jacob, 'I will give it to your offspring.' [h]I have let you see it with your eyes,
but [i]you shall not go over there." 5 So Moses
the servant of the LORD died there in the land
of Moab, according to the word of the LORD,
6 and he buried him in the valley in the land of
Moab opposite Beth-peor; but [j]no one knows
the place of his burial to this day. 7 [k]Moses
was 120 years old when he died. [l]His eye was
undimmed, and his vigor unabated. 8 And the
people of Israel [m]wept for Moses in the plains
of Moab thirty days. Then the days of weeping
and mourning for Moses were ended.

9 And Joshua the son of Nun was full of
[n]the spirit of wisdom, for [o]Moses had laid
his hands on him. So [p]the people of Israel
obeyed him and did as the LORD had commanded Moses. 10 And there has not [q]arisen
a prophet since in Israel like Moses, [r]whom
the LORD knew face to face, 11 none like him
for all [s]the signs and the wonders that the
LORD sent him to do in the land of Egypt, to
Pharaoh and to all his servants and to all his
land, 12 and for all the mighty power and all
the great deeds of terror that Moses did in
the sight of all Israel.

4 [h] ch. 3:27; 32:52 [i] See ch. 1:37
6 [j] [Jude 9]
7 [k] ch. 31:2 [l] [Gen. 27:1; 48:10; Josh. 14:10, 11; 1 Sam. 3:2; 4:15]
8 [m] Num. 20:29; [Gen. 50:3]
9 [n] Ex. 28:3; Isa. 11:2 [o] Num. 27:18, 23 [p] Josh. 1:17
10 [q] [ch. 18:15, 18] [r] ch. 5:4; See Ex. 33:11
11 [s] See ch. 4:34

Until Jesus! "For Jesus has been counted worthy of more glory than Moses . . ." (Heb. 3:3). Whereas Moses was a servant, Jesus is a son (Heb. 3:5–6). Jesus is the Son who was slain and who was raised, so that the grace of God might flow backward to Israel, qualifying them to enter the Promised Land, and might flow forward to the church, qualifying her to enter the eternal rest. Because Jesus was slain and raised, Moses together with the church throughout the ages will be raised, so that together we might enjoy the kingdom of God, to the glory of God (1 Cor. 15:20–28).

Introduction to Joshua

Author and Date

While this book mentions Joshua writing (8:32; 24:26), it does not claim that he wrote this particular book. The repeated references to something existing "to this day" (see 4:9; 5:9; 6:25; etc.) seem to suggest that there was a lapse of time between the events recorded in the book (c. 1400 B.C.) and the time when the writing of the book was completed. The final writing may have taken place in the time of the exile (after 586 B.C.), but the writing probably began much earlier.

The Gospel in Joshua

From the beginning to the end of the book of Joshua, the formula is repeated: God *gives* and Israel *inherits*. The spotlight is not on Joshua's moral example or on timeless principles of conduct but on Yahweh's fulfillment of a historical promise. Even Joshua's name ("Yahweh Saves!") points away from himself to the real hero of the story. Joshua is a story of grace.

God's gracious covenant with Abraham in Genesis 15 involved key promises, including a temporal land and nation (the "type," or beginning of a pattern) and an everlasting inheritance for all nations through his descendant—Jesus Christ (the reality to which the type pointed; see Gal. 3:16). Though *entering* land is a gracious gift (Deut. 7:6–9; 9:4–8), *remaining* God's holy nation did depend on Israel's obedience to the covenant. This echoes Adam's testing in Eden, with the consequent promise of life or death, blessing or curse, enjoyment of God or exile (Ex. 19:4–8; 24:3, 8; Deut. 11:17, 26; 28:1–68). Even after heeding the voice of the serpent, Adam and Eve received God's gracious promise of a Savior, the seed (or "offspring") of the woman, who would crush the serpent's head (Gen. 3:15). Would this seed be Israel? Was Israel the fulfillment of God's promise? In spite of much genuine faith and obedience under Joshua, already this book hints at the tragic verdict: "But like Adam they [Israel] transgressed the covenant" (Hos. 6:7). The nation of Israel was not the ultimate seed of God's promise but rather was God's instrument for providing it (that is, for providing *him*).

Jesus Christ, the true Seed of promise descending from Israel, secured the everlasting promise through an obedience and triumph not displayed in the nation of Israel. God's people remain secure from the consequences of all their transgressions and Satan's power by trust in this righteous Seed alone. Jesus is the final conqueror of Satan; he does what Adam and then Israel failed to do (Col. 2:15). This is the point of Paul's contrast in Galatians 3–4 between "two covenants"—the law and the promise, the earthly Jerusalem and the heavenly Jerusalem. It is also a familiar contrast throughout the book of Hebrews (e.g., Heb. 11:16; 12:18–24). With Christ as the faithful servant and mediator, the new covenant "is enacted on better promises" (Heb. 8:6).

Overlooking these distinctions of Christ's role in contrast to Israel, the conquest recounted in Joshua has been mistakenly invoked by Christian empires and nations to justify Christian holy war. Others, in reaction to these errors, have criticized this portion of God's Word as being incompatible with the God of peace whom we meet in Jesus Christ. How do we respond to such misunderstandings?

First, we should recognize that the accounts of Joshua are not the whole story of God's covenant purposes. There is a progression in God's plan that we can perceive only this side of the cross. In fulfillment of the Abrahamic promise of a worldwide family in Christ, the new covenant church is distinct from all geopolitical states. God is not now funneling his redemptive activity through a single nation such as was needed during the time of Old Testament Israel. God's *common grace* (not saving grace) is now more apparent in its encompassing of believers and unbelievers alike (Matt. 5:43–48), and the nation of Israel is no longer uniquely designed to exhibit the sole rule of God. Even Jesus affirms Caesar's political authority over Judea (Mark 12:17; cf. Rom. 13:1–7). In this New Testament phase of his kingdom, Christ conquers the earth (not just a small territory like Canaan) in *saving grace* by his Word and Spirit, rather than in military exploit (Eph. 6:12–17). Thus, in this era, reflecting our Savior before us, believers spread the gospel not by violence but through faithful witness that involves enduring the opposition—and perhaps even violence—of the world.

Like the spies Joshua sent into Jericho, the apostles were an advance force for the conquering purposes of God. But the means of their conquest were quite different. Jesus rebuked James and John for wanting to execute holy war on Samaritans that had rejected the gospel (Luke 9:51–56). Their mission was to preach the gospel of Christ's kingdom. Jesus similarly instructed the 72 to fulfill their mission not by force but by preaching (Luke 10–12), giving them "authority to tread on serpents" (Luke 10:19). However, it is Satan—the real Enemy behind the earthly enemies—whose head is finally being crushed (Luke 10:17–20; cf. Rom. 16:20).

Our God yet retains the physical and spiritual authority to do as he wishes for the whole world. When Christ returns, he will judge the whole earth, together with his saints (1 Cor. 6:2). His victory will be more powerful and forceful than anything that we read about in the book of Joshua; it will mark the final destruction of evil and the establishment of everlasting righteousness and peace. Through Joshua's conquest we discern the power of God's might through an incredibly flawed nation, but only in the Seed that would come through Joshua's people do we see the true purpose and end of God's conquering promises. Unlike the wars of old that led only to more bloodshed and misery, Christ's global judgment and victory when he comes again will truly be the war to end all wars (Matt. 3:11–12; 24:27–25:46; Rev. 17:1–20:15).

Outline

I. Crossing into the Land (1:1–5:15)

II. Taking the Land (6:1–12:24)

III. Dividing the Land (13:1–21:45)

IV. Serving the Lord in the Land (22:1–24:33)

Joshua

God Commissions Joshua

1 After the death of Moses the [a]servant of the LORD, the LORD said to Joshua the son of Nun, Moses' [b]assistant, 2 "Moses my servant is dead. Now therefore arise, go over this Jordan, you and all this people, into the land that I am giving to them, to the people of Israel. 3 [c]Every place that the sole of your foot will tread upon I have given to you, just as I promised to Moses. 4 [d]From the wilderness and this Lebanon as far as the great river, the river Euphrates, all the land of the Hittites to the Great Sea toward the going down of the sun shall be your territory. 5 [e]No man shall be able to stand before you all the days of your life. Just [f]as I was with Moses, so [g]I will be with you. [h]I will not leave you or forsake you. 6 [i]Be strong and courageous, for you shall cause this people to inherit the land that I swore to their fathers to give them. 7 Only be strong and [j]very courageous, being careful to do according to all the law [k]that Moses my servant commanded you. [l]Do not turn from it to the right hand or to the left, that you may have good success[1] wherever you go. 8 This Book of the Law shall not depart from your mouth, but [m]you shall meditate on it day and night, so that you may be careful to do according to all that is written in it. For then you will make your way prosperous, and then you will have good success. 9 Have I not commanded you? [n]Be strong and courageous. [o]Do not be frightened, and do not be dismayed, for the LORD your God is with you wherever you go."

Joshua Assumes Command

10 And Joshua commanded the [p]officers of the people, 11 "Pass through the midst of the camp and command the people, 'Prepare your provisions, for [q]within three days [r]you are to pass over this Jordan to go in to take possession of the land that the LORD your God is giving you to possess.' "

[1] Or *may act wisely*

1:1–18 Though he was not allowed to lead the wilderness generation into the inheritance, Moses is dignified here as "Moses the servant of the LORD" (v. 1). Joshua himself will inherit this title at the end (24:29). The same respect is accorded to Moses in the New Testament, though he must give way to the Messiah to whom his ministry pointed (Acts 3:22–24; Heb. 3:2–4). (See note on Num. 20:1–29 regarding the reasons and results of Moses' being forbidden to enter Canaan.)

The prosperity God promises (Josh. 1:5–9) must not be allegorized or generalized. It is a promise of health, wealth, and happiness, as long as Israel keeps the covenant. We have to be careful therefore not to explore such passages for modern application, as if all aspects of the covenant mediated by Moses were the same as the everlasting covenant mediated by Christ. Such conditional promises pertain to a specific era in the history of redemption.

Despite the conditional aspect of this covenant, God pledges never to abandon Joshua (v. 5). This is the eternal pledge that the New Testament applies to our everlasting inheritance in Christ (Heb. 13:5–8). And indeed, it is only with the confidence this promise supplies that Joshua can obey God's call to "be strong and courageous" (Josh. 1:6, 18). The intensity with which God calls Joshua to meditation on the Law and instruction of the people (vv. 7–9) reminds us that this conquest is a *holy* war. It is not maps and strategies that Joshua has spread out in his military tent but the Law—and God gives him the battle plans.

Chapter 1
1 [a] ver. 13, 15; Ex. 14:31; Num. 12:7; Deut. 34:5 [b] Deut. 1:38; [Ex. 24:13]
3 [c] Deut. 11:24; [ch. 14:9]
4 [d] Gen. 15:18; Ex. 23:31; See Num. 34:3-12
5 [e] Deut. 7:24 [f] ver. 17; Ex. 3:12 [g] ver. 9, 17; ch. 3:7; 6:27; Deut. 31:8, 23 [h] Gen. 28:15; Deut. 31:6, 8; 1 Chr. 28:20; Cited Heb. 13:5
6 [i] ver. 7, 9, 18; Deut. 31:6, 7
7 [j] ch. 23:6 [k] ch. 11:15 [l] Deut. 5:32; 28:14
8 [m] Ps. 1:2; 119:15
9 [n] ver. 6, 7, 18 [o] Deut. 1:29; 7:21; 20:3; 31:6, 8
10 [p] Deut. 16:18
11 [q] ch. 3:2 [r] Deut. 9:1; 11:31

12 And to the Reubenites, the Gadites, and
the half-tribe of Manasseh Joshua said,
13 "Remember the word that [s]Moses the servant of the LORD commanded you, saying,
'The LORD your God is providing you a place
of rest and will give you this land.' 14 Your
wives, your little ones, and your livestock
shall remain in the land that Moses gave you
beyond the Jordan, but all the men of valor
among you shall pass over armed before your
brothers and shall help them, 15 [t]until the
LORD gives rest to your brothers as he has to
you, and they also take possession of the land
that the LORD your God is giving them. [u]Then
you shall return to the land of your possession and shall possess it, the land that Moses
the servant of the LORD gave you beyond the
Jordan toward the sunrise."

16 And they answered Joshua, "All that you
have commanded us we will do, and wherever
you send us we will go. 17 Just as we obeyed
Moses in all things, so we will obey you. Only
may the LORD your God [v]be with you, as he
was with Moses! 18 Whoever rebels against
your commandment and disobeys your words,
whatever you command him, shall be put to
death. [w]Only be strong and courageous."

Rahab Hides the Spies

2 And Joshua the son of Nun [x]sent[1] two
men secretly from Shittim as spies, saying, "Go, view the land, especially Jericho."
And they went and came into the house of
[y]a prostitute whose name was [z]Rahab and
lodged there. 2 And it was told to the king of
Jericho, "Behold, men of Israel have come here
tonight to search out the land." 3 Then the king
of Jericho sent to Rahab, saying, "Bring out the
men who have come to you, who entered your
house, for they have come to search out all
the land." 4 But the woman had taken the two
men and hidden them. And she said, "True,
the men came to me, but I did not know where
they were from. 5 And when the gate was about
to be closed at dark, the men went out. I do
not know where the men went. Pursue them
quickly, for you will overtake them." 6 But
she had brought them up to the roof and hid
them with the stalks of flax that she had laid
in order on the roof. 7 So the men pursued after
them on the way to the Jordan [a]as far as the
fords. And the gate was shut as soon as the
pursuers had gone out.

8 Before the men[2] lay down, she came up
to them on the roof 9 and said to the men,
"I know that the LORD has given you the land,
[b]and that the fear of you has fallen upon us,
and that all the inhabitants of the land [c]melt
away before you. 10 For we have heard how the
LORD [d]dried up the water of the Red Sea before
you when you came out of Egypt, and [e]what
you did to the two kings of the Amorites who
were beyond the Jordan, to [f]Sihon and Og,
whom you devoted to destruction.[3] 11 And [g]as
soon as we heard it, [h]our hearts melted, and
there was no spirit left in any man because
of you, for [i]the LORD your God, he is God in
the heavens above and on the earth beneath.

[1] Or *had sent* [2] Hebrew *they* [3] That is, set apart (devoted) as an offering to the Lord (for destruction)

13[s] See Num. 32:20-28
15[t] Deut. 3:20 [u] ch. 22:4
17[v] ver. 5
18[w] ver. 6, 7, 9
Chapter 2
1[x] Num. 25:1 [y] Heb. 11:31; James 2:25 [z] Matt. 1:5
7[a] Judg. 3:28; 7:24
9[b] Ex. 15:16; 23:27 [c] ver. 11, 24; Ex. 15:15
10[d] ch. 4:23; Ex. 14:21 [e] See Num. 21:23-26, 33-35 [f] Ps. 135:11; 136:19, 20
11[g] Ex. 15:14, 15 [h] ver. 9; ch. 5:1; 7:5; [2 Sam. 17:10; Ps. 22:14; Isa. 13:7; Ezek. 21:7] [i] Deut. 4:39

2:1–24 Two spies are sent to check out the land—the city of Jericho in particular. The judgment of the idolatrous and violent cities in Canaan was prophesied in Genesis 15:13–16 (see Lev. 18:24–30; Deut. 9:5).

Rahab is not only a Canaanite but a prostitute. Her lie (Josh. 2:4–11) is not only deceitful but treasonous. Yet two New Testament writers commend Rahab for her *faith* (Heb. 11:31; James 2:25). Far from acting out of "fear," Rahab confesses her faith in "the LORD" (Josh. 2:9) as the true and proper King of this land that her own people have usurped and profaned. Rahab's faith drives her courageous obedience, in contrast with the earlier generation of the Israelites, who had died in the wilderness because of their lack of faith.

Like the repentant prostitutes whom Jesus welcomed into his fellowship, Rahab surrenders her former identity to become part of God's redemptive story. Her messy moral background is no impediment. In fact, she is included in Matthew's genealogy of Jesus Christ (Matt. 1:5). In hiding the spies, she joins the church in "treading on serpents" (see Luke 10:19), foreshadowing Christ's ultimate triumph over the gates of hell by the proclamation of the gospel. Rahab also anticipates the justification of Gentiles by faith (Gal. 3:6–9; Heb. 11:31; James 2:25). In short, she is a beautiful paradigm of God's purpose of grace in human history—taking the outsiders, the unqualified, and using them for his redemptive purposes.

12 Now then, please swear to me by the LORD
that, as I have dealt kindly with you, you also
will deal kindly with my father's house, and
[j]give me a sure sign 13 that you will save alive
my father and mother, my brothers and sisters,
and all who belong to them, and deliver our
lives from death." 14 And the men said to her,
"Our life for yours even to death! If you do
not tell this business of ours, then when the
LORD gives us the land [k]we will deal kindly
and faithfully with you."

15 Then she [l]let them down by a rope through
the window, for her house was built into the
city wall, so that she lived in the wall. 16 And
she said[1] to them, "Go into the hills, or the pursuers will encounter you, and hide there three
days until the pursuers have returned. Then
afterward you may go your way." 17 The men
said to her, "We will be guiltless with respect
to this oath of yours that you have made us
swear. 18 [m]Behold, when we come into the land,
you shall tie this scarlet cord in the window
through which you let us down, [n]and you
shall gather into your house your father and
mother, your brothers, and all your father's
household. 19 Then if anyone goes out of the
doors of your house into the street, [o]his blood
shall be on his own head, and we shall be guiltless. But if a hand is laid on anyone who is
with you in the house, his blood shall be on
our head. 20 But if you [p]tell this business of
ours, then we shall be guiltless with respect to
your oath that you have made us swear." 21 And
she said, "According to your words, so be it."
Then she sent them away, and they departed.
And she tied the scarlet cord in the window.

22 They departed and went into the hills and
remained there three days until the pursuers
returned, and the pursuers searched all along
the way and found nothing. 23 Then the two
men returned. They came down from the hills
and [q]passed over and came to Joshua the son of
Nun, and they told him all that had happened
to them. 24 And they said to Joshua, "Truly [r]the
LORD has given all the land into our hands.
And also, all the inhabitants of the land [s]melt
away because of us."

Israel Crosses the Jordan

3 Then Joshua rose early in the morning and
they set out [t]from Shittim. And they came
to the Jordan, he and all the people of Israel,
and lodged there before they passed over. 2 [u]At
the end of three days the officers went through
the camp 3 and commanded the people, "As
soon as you see the ark of the covenant of the
LORD your God being carried by [v]the Levitical
priests, then you shall set out from your place
and follow it. 4 [w]Yet there shall be a distance
between you and it, about 2,000 cubits[2] in

[1] Or *had said* [2] A *cubit* was about 18 inches or 45 centimeters

12 [j]ver. 18
14 [k]Judg. 1:24, 25
15 [l]1 Sam. 19:12; Acts 9:25; 2 Cor. 11:33
18 [m]ver. 12 [n]ver. 12; ch. 6:23
19 [o][Matt. 27:25]
20 [p]ver. 14
23 [q]ver. 7
24 [r]ch. 21:44; Ex. 23:31 [s]ver. 9
Chapter 3
1 [t]ch. 2:1
2 [u]ch. 1:10, 11
3 [v]ver. 8; Deut. 31:9, 25
4 [w][Ex. 19:12]

3:1–17 Israel is now preparing to pass at God's command from the *tohu wabohu* (darkness and void; see Gen. 1:2) into the Promised Land of Sabbath rest. As in God's work of creation, and the similar task given to Adam as his image-bearer, this endeavor is a transition from chaos to order and rest.

Through Rahab's faithfulness, the spies had returned with good news. After three days of rest, the Israelite vanguard is readied for crossing the Jordan in conquest. This echoes the command God gave at Mount Sinai for the people to consecrate themselves in preparation for his appearing before them *on the third day* in glory (Ex. 19:10–11). The ark of the covenant (representing God's very presence) is the banner the warriors follow. It is God's own mobile throne of conquest, indicating that the provision for Israel is not of their power (Josh. 3:3, 8). Yet God's people are warned sternly against coming too close to his presence (v. 4). This is the precise opposite of what happens when the presence of God comes to dwell among his people not in an ark but in a human body (John 1:14). In Jesus of Nazareth, the journey toward rest for God's people is more complete as God draws near and invites all to come to him (Matt. 11:28), even touching the unclean and making them clean (Matt. 8:2–3).

Joshua will not exalt himself in battle; rather, God promises to exalt Joshua "in the sight of all Israel, that they may know that, as I was with Moses, so I will be with you" (Josh. 3:7). As Joshua himself explained, "tomorrow the LORD will do wonders among you" (v. 5). It is almost as if the Israelite warriors are merely spectators of God's conquest. Joshua tells the soldiers that it is God who "will without fail drive out [the wicked] from before you" (v. 10). Echoing the exodus from Egypt 40 years earlier, the moment that the ark-bearing priests stand in the waters, the Jordan will be cut off and "shall stand in one heap" until the whole company passes through (vv. 13–17).

length. Do not come near it, in order that you
may know the way you shall go, for you have
not passed this way before." 5 Then Joshua
said to the people, [x]"Consecrate yourselves, for
tomorrow the LORD will do wonders among
you." 6 And Joshua said to the priests, [y]"Take
up the ark of the covenant and pass on before
the people." So they took up the ark of the
covenant and went before the people.

7 The LORD said to Joshua, "Today I will
begin to [z]exalt you in the sight of all Israel,
that they may know that, [a]as I was with Moses,
so I will be with you. 8 And as for you, command [b]the priests who bear the ark of the covenant, 'When you come to the brink of the
waters of the Jordan, [c]you shall stand still in
the Jordan.'" 9 And Joshua said to the people
of Israel, "Come here and listen to the words
of the LORD your God." 10 And Joshua said,
"Here is how you shall know that [d]the living
God is among you and that he will without
fail [e]drive out from before you the Canaanites,
the Hittites, the Hivites, the Perizzites, the
Girgashites, the Amorites, and the Jebusites.
11 Behold, the ark of the covenant of [f]the Lord
of all the earth[1] [g]is passing over before you
into the Jordan. 12 Now therefore [h]take twelve
men from the tribes of Israel, [i]from each tribe
a man. 13 And [j]when the soles of the feet of the
priests bearing the ark of the LORD, [f]the Lord
of all the earth, shall rest in the waters of the
Jordan, the waters of the Jordan shall be cut
off from flowing, and the waters coming down
from above shall [k]stand in one heap."

14 So when the people set out from their
tents to pass over the Jordan with the priests
bearing [l]the ark of the covenant before the
people, 15 and as soon as those bearing the ark
had come as far as the Jordan, and [m]the feet of
the priests bearing the ark were dipped in the
brink of the water (now [n]the Jordan overflows
all its banks [o]throughout the time of harvest),
16 the waters coming down from above stood
and rose up in a heap very far away, at Adam,
the city that is beside [p]Zarethan, and those
flowing down toward the Sea of [q]the Arabah,
[r]the Salt Sea, were completely cut off. And the
people passed over opposite Jericho. 17 Now
the priests bearing the ark of the covenant of
the LORD stood firmly on dry ground in the
midst of the Jordan, [s]and all Israel was passing over on dry ground until all the nation
finished passing over the Jordan.

Twelve Memorial Stones from the Jordan

4 When all the nation had finished passing [t]over the Jordan, the LORD said to
Joshua, 2 [u]"Take twelve men from the people,
from each tribe a man, 3 and command them,
saying, 'Take [v]twelve stones from here out of
the midst of the Jordan, from the very place
[w]where the priests' feet stood firmly, and bring
them over with you and lay them down in
[x]the place where you lodge tonight.'" 4 Then
Joshua called the twelve men from the people
of Israel, whom he had appointed, a man from
each tribe. 5 And Joshua said to them, "Pass on
before the ark of the LORD your God into the

[1] Hebrew *the ark of the covenant, the Lord of all the earth*

5 [x] ch. 7:13; Ex. 19:10, 14, 15; Lev. 20:7; Num. 11:18; 1 Sam. 16:5; Joel 2:16
6 [y] Num. 4:15
7 [z] ch. 4:14; 1 Chr. 29:25; 2 Chr. 1:1 [a] ch. 1:5
8 [b] ver. 3 [c] ver. 17
10 [d] Deut. 5:26; 1 Sam. 17:26 [e] Ex. 33:2; Deut. 7:1; Ps. 44:2; [Ex. 13:5]
11 [f] Mic. 4:13; Zech. 4:14; 6:5 [g] [Deut. 9:3]
12 [h] ch. 4:2, 4 [i] [Num. 13:2]
13 [j] ver. 15, 16 [f] [See ver. 11 above] [k] Ps. 114:3; [Ex. 15:8; Ps. 78:13]
14 [l] Acts 7:44, 45
15 [m] ver. 13 [n] 1 Chr. 12:15; Jer. 12:5; 49:19; 50:44 [o] [ch. 4:18; 5:10, 12]
16 [p] 1 Kgs. 4:12; 7:46 [q] See Deut. 1:1 [r] Gen. 14:3; Num. 34:3
17 [s] ch. 4:22; [Ex. 14:29]
Chapter 4
1 [t] ch. 3:17
2 [u] ch. 3:12
3 [v] Deut. 27:2; [1 Kgs. 18:31] [w] ch. 3:13, 15 [x] ver. 8, 19, 20

At the exodus from Egypt, the Lord made a way through the Red Sea; he now makes a way through the Jordan River into Canaan. All of this prepares us for the way he has made through his own Son, who himself walked on the sea as if it were dry land (Mark 6:45–52). The way to ultimate rest in God himself is made for us through Christ's death and resurrection, as he atones for the sins of fallen humans—we who invariably seek to make our way in life through our own means.

4:1–24 Twelve men were chosen to take one stone each from the Jordan, representing the 12 tribes and showing that God's provision had been and would be for every branch of his people. This symbol would be picked up in the New Testament as Jesus chose 12 men to bring the gospel to the nations (Matt. 10:1–15; 28:16–20).

As a victorious King, Yahweh commands these 12 representatives to build a monument. The army's joyful and faithful response marks a great moment in Israel's history (Josh. 4:1–14). After the priests carried the ark out of the riverbed, "the waters of the Jordan returned to their place and overflowed all its banks, as before" (v. 18). The Jordan monument would testify to future generations of Yahweh's mighty deeds for his people (vv. 20–24). While nations mark their own imperial triumphs, Israel's monuments celebrate Yahweh's victories.

The supreme victory God's people celebrate today is the mighty deed accomplished in Christ's life, death, and resurrection.

midst of the Jordan, and take up each of you
a stone upon his shoulder, according to the
number of the tribes of the people of Israel,
6 that this may be a sign among you. [y]When
your children ask in time to come, 'What do
those stones mean to you?' 7 then you shall tell
them that [z]the waters of the Jordan were cut
off before the ark of the covenant of the LORD.
When it passed over the Jordan, the waters of
the Jordan were cut off. So these stones shall
be to the people of Israel [a]a memorial forever."
8 And the people of Israel did just as Joshua
commanded and took up twelve stones out
of the midst of the Jordan, according to the
number of the tribes of the people of Israel,
just as the LORD told Joshua. And they carried them over with them to the place where
they lodged and laid them down[1] there. 9 And
Joshua set up[2] twelve stones in the midst of
the Jordan, [b]in the place where the feet of the
priests bearing the ark of the covenant had
stood; and they are there to this day. 10 For
the priests bearing the ark stood in the midst
of the Jordan until everything was finished
that the LORD commanded Joshua to tell the
people, according to all that Moses had commanded Joshua.
The people passed over in haste. 11 And when
all the people had finished passing over, the
ark of the LORD and the priests passed over
before the people. 12 The sons of Reuben and
the sons of Gad and the half-tribe of Manasseh
[c]passed over armed before the people of Israel,
as Moses had told them. 13 About 40,000 ready
for war passed over before the LORD for battle,
to the plains of Jericho. 14 On that day the LORD
[d]exalted Joshua in the sight of all Israel, and
they stood in awe of him just as they had stood
in awe of Moses, all the days of his life.
15 And the LORD said to Joshua, 16 "Command
the priests bearing [e]the ark of the testimony
to come up out of the Jordan." 17 So Joshua
commanded the priests, "Come up out of the
Jordan." 18 And when the priests bearing the
ark of the covenant of the LORD came up from
the midst of the Jordan, and the soles of the
priests' feet were lifted up on dry ground, the
waters of the Jordan returned to their place
and overflowed all its banks, [f]as before.
19 The people came up out of the Jordan on
the tenth day of the first month, and they
encamped at [g]Gilgal on the east border of
Jericho. 20 And [h]those twelve stones, which
they took out of the Jordan, Joshua set up at
Gilgal. 21 And he said to the people of Israel,
[i]"When your children ask their fathers in
times to come, 'What do these stones mean?'
22 then you shall let your children know, [j]'Israel
passed over this Jordan on dry ground.' 23 For
the LORD your God dried up the waters of the
Jordan for you until you passed over, as the
LORD your God did to the Red Sea, [k]which
he dried up for us until we passed over, 24 [l]so
that all the peoples of the earth may know that
the hand of the LORD is [m]mighty, that you may
[n]fear the LORD your God forever."[3]

The New Generation Circumcised

5 As soon as all the kings of the Amorites
who were beyond the Jordan to the west,
and all the kings of the Canaanites [o]who were
by the sea, [p]heard that the LORD had dried
up the waters of the Jordan for the people of
Israel until they had crossed over, their hearts
[q]melted and [r]there was no longer any spirit in
them because of the people of Israel.
2 At that time the LORD said to Joshua, "Make
[s]flint knives and circumcise the sons of Israel

[1] Or *to rest* [2] Or *Joshua had set up* [3] Or *all the days*

5:1–12 It is little wonder that the kings and rulers beyond the Jordan were terrified of Israel (v. 1). Even before they see the first flashing sword of Yahweh, the idolatrous usurpers of God's throne and land are under the death sentence. Everything—land, people, livestock, pots and pans—is consecrated to God now, either for destruction or for deliverance.

Before turning his sword toward the Canaanites, in this chapter God draws it toward the Israelites and even toward Joshua. The Israelites are circumcised—a cutting that consecrates them to deliverance rather than to destruction.

God instituted circumcision with Abraham (Genesis 17). In Hebrew idiom, to make a covenant was actually "to cut a covenant" (*karat berith*). An animal was cut off from life as a substitute to save a consecrated family in the Passover meal, while in circumcision the foreskin was cut off to save the whole person from being cut off by God's sword of judgment—and consequently to consecrate the family produced from that individual. Uncircumcised males (and the families so represented) are "cut

6 [y]ver. 21; [Ex. 12:26; 13:14; Deut. 6:20]
7 [z]ch. 3:16 [a]Ex. 12:14; Num. 16:40
9 [b]ver. 3
12 [c]ch. 6:7, 9, 13; Num. 32:20, 21, 27
14 [d]See ch. 3:7
16 [e]Ex. 25:16, 21, 22
18 [f]ch. 3:15
19 [g]ch. 5:9
20 [h]ver. 3, 9
21 [i]ver. 6
22 [j]ch. 3:17
23 [k]ch. 2:10; Ex. 14:21
24 [l]1 Kgs. 8:42, 43 [m]Deut. 3:24; Ps. 89:13 [n]Ex. 14:31; Deut. 6:2

Chapter 5
1 [o]Num. 13:29 [p]Ex. 15:14 [q]See ch. 2:11 [r]1 Kgs. 10:5
2 [s]Ex. 4:25

a second time." 3 So Joshua made flint knives
and circumcised the sons of Israel at Gibeath-
haaraloth.[1] 4 And this is the reason why Joshua
circumcised them: [t]all the males of the people
who came out of Egypt, all the men of war, had
died in the wilderness on the way after they
had come out of Egypt. 5 Though all the people
who came out had been circumcised, yet all
the people who were born on the way in the
wilderness after they had come out of Egypt
had not been circumcised. 6 For the people of
Israel walked [u]forty years in the wilderness,
until all the nation, the men of war who came
out of Egypt, perished, because they did not
obey the voice of the LORD; the LORD [v]swore
to them that he would not let them see the
land that the LORD had sworn to their fathers
to give to us, [w]a land flowing with milk and
honey. 7 So it was [x]their children, whom he
raised up in their place, that Joshua circumcised. For they were uncircumcised, because
they had not been circumcised on the way.

8 When the circumcising of the whole nation
was finished, they remained in their places in
the camp until they were healed. 9 And the
LORD said to Joshua, "Today I have rolled away
the [y]reproach of Egypt from you." And so the
name of that place is called [z]Gilgal[2] to this day.

First Passover in Canaan

10 While the people of Israel were encamped
at Gilgal, they kept the Passover [a]on the fourteenth day of the month in the evening on
the plains of Jericho. 11 And the day after the
Passover, on that very day, they ate of the
produce of the land, unleavened cakes and
parched grain. 12 And [b]the manna ceased the
day after they ate of the produce of the land.
And there was no longer manna for the people
of Israel, but they ate of the fruit of the land
of Canaan that year.

The Commander of the LORD's Army

13 When Joshua was by Jericho, he lifted up
his eyes and looked, and behold, [c]a man was
standing before him [d]with his drawn sword in
his hand. And Joshua went to him and said to
him, "Are you for us, or for our adversaries?"
14 And he said, "No; but I am the commander of
the army of the LORD. Now I have come." And
Joshua [e]fell on his face to the earth and worshiped and said to him, "What does my lord
say to his servant?" 15 And the commander of

[1] *Gibeath-haaraloth* means *the hill of the foreskins* [2] *Gilgal* sounds like the Hebrew for *to roll*

4[t] Num. 14:29; 26:64, 65; Deut. 2:16; Ps. 106:26; 1 Cor. 10:5; Heb. 3:17
6[u] Num. 14:33; Deut. 1:3; 2:7, 14; 8:4; Ps. 95:10 [v] Num. 14:23; Ps. 95:11; Heb. 3:11 [w] See Ex. 3:8
7[x] Num. 14:31; Deut. 1:39
9[y] Gen. 34:14 [z] ch. 4:19
10[a] Ex. 12:6; Num. 9:5
12[b] Ex. 16:35
13[c] Gen. 18:2; 32:24; Acts 1:10; [Ex. 23:20, 23] [d] Num. 22:23, 31
14[e] Gen. 17:3

off" from God's covenant (Gen. 17:14). Just before leading his people across the Red Sea, Yahweh had instituted Passover and circumcised the males to mark his people as "Mine!" (Ex. 12:43–13:2). However, the fathers in the wilderness failed even to keep this basic requirement, so "the sons of Israel" needed to be circumcised "a second time" (Josh. 5:2–7). After they healed, God sheathed his sword against Israel and even "rolled away the reproach of Egypt from you" (v. 9). It is a new chapter. The unfaithfulness of the fathers now lies discarded in the past. In the new covenant, baptism serves as a new sign of consecration analogous to circumcision but without the shedding of blood, since Christ's blood was shed once for all (Col. 2:11–12; cf. 1 Cor. 10:1–13; Heb. 10:10).

Also similar to the exodus, the circumcised then "kept the Passover" (Josh. 5:10). "And the day after the Passover, on that very day, they ate of the produce of the land" (v. 11). No longer needing "manna and quail sandwiches" along the road, they had arrived at their sumptuous destination and "they ate of the fruit of the land of Canaan that year" (v. 12). By God's promise and power, his people had entered the Promised Land. The ancient promises of God were marching toward completion.

5:13–15 This strange account is both jarring and confusing. A man draws his sword before Joshua. On guard, Joshua asks whose side he is on. Neither, he says. "But I am the commander of the army of the LORD. Now I have come" (vv. 13–14). Reportedly, when a friend assured Abraham Lincoln that, "God is on your side," he replied, "Sir, my concern is not whether God is on our side; my greatest concern is to be on God's side, for God is always right." Regardless of what one makes of Lincoln's personal faith, this is precisely the view that Israel is expected to take here. In common war, the stranger's announcement might have seemed like a threat. After all, was not Joshua the commander of the Lord's army? Yet Joshua knew he was dealing with God himself. The posture, the address (from a "servant" to a "lord"), and the question he asks indicate Joshua's recognition of a treaty or covenant relationship in which he is confronted by his own great King. The commander's demand for Joshua to remove his shoes,

the LORD's army said to Joshua, [f]"Take off your
sandals from your feet, for the place where you
are standing is holy." And Joshua did so.

The Fall of Jericho

6 Now Jericho was shut up inside and outside because of the people of Israel. None
went out, and none came in. 2 And the LORD
said to Joshua, "See, [g]I have given Jericho into
your hand, with its king and mighty men of
valor. 3 You shall march around the city, all
the men of war going around the city once.
Thus shall you do for six days. 4 Seven priests
shall bear seven [h]trumpets of [i]rams' horns
before the ark. On the seventh day you shall
march around the city seven times, and [j]the
priests shall blow the trumpets. 5 And when
they make a long blast with the ram's horn,
when you hear the sound of the trumpet,
then all the people shall shout with a great
shout, and the wall of the city will fall down
flat,[1] and the people shall go up, everyone
straight before him." 6 So Joshua the son of
Nun called the priests and said to them, "Take
up the ark of the covenant and let seven priests
bear seven trumpets of rams' horns before the
ark of the LORD." 7 And he said to the people,
"Go forward. March around the city and let
[k]the armed men pass on before the ark of the
LORD."

8 And just as Joshua had commanded the
people, the seven priests bearing the seven
trumpets of rams' horns before the LORD went
forward, blowing the trumpets, with the ark
of the covenant of the LORD following them.
9 The armed men were walking before the
priests who were blowing the trumpets, and
the [l]rear guard was walking after the ark,
while the trumpets blew continually. 10 But
Joshua commanded the people, "You shall not
shout or make your voice heard, neither shall
any word go out of your mouth, until the day
I tell you to shout. Then you shall shout." 11 So
he caused the ark of the LORD to circle the city,

[1] Hebrew *under itself*; also verse 20

15 [f]Ex. 3:5; Acts 7:33
Chapter 6
2 [g]ch. 2:9, 24; Deut. 7:24; Neh. 9:24; [ch. 8:1]
4 [h]Judg. 7:16, 22 [i]ver. 5, 6, 8, 13 [j]Num. 10:8
7 [k]ch. 4:12, 13
9 [l]ver. 13; Num. 10:25; Isa. 52:12; 58:8

identical to that given by Yahweh to Moses from the burning bush, provoked a quick response from Joshua (vv. 14–15). Only with his absolute and unconditional surrender to this commander was Joshua spared and then given the battle plan by the one who would lead his army, enthroned on the ark of the covenant.

Though we must resist flights of fancy, there are several Old Testament accounts that many theologians believe identify "the angel of the LORD" as a mysterious appearance—a "theophany"—of none other than Yahweh himself (e.g., Gen. 16:7–14; 19:1–5; 22:11–19; Num. 22:22; Zechariah 3). These appearances indicate that God has been continually providing for his people throughout history by the mediation and intervention of his Son. Jesus Christ is the divine Son installed by the Father as King (Psalm 2), the divine commander of the armies of God (Matt. 28:18; Heb. 2:14–15; Rev. 17:14; 19:11–21). Today he continues to command his forces from heaven, in human flesh at the Father's right hand, with his Spirit leading the ground campaign. From that throne he will return to earth in the final event of judgment and full deliverance.

In the meantime, we remember the gospel. Joshua asked, "Are you for us, or for our adversaries?" (Josh. 5:13). We today can pose this question in our hearts and know that the answer from heaven is, he is *for us*. For Jesus himself went to a cross and allowed the sword to be applied to himself. Jesus allowed God to be against him, so that God is always, even in our failures, for us. "There is therefore now no condemnation for those who are in Christ Jesus. . . . If God is *for us*, who can be against us?" (Rom. 8:1, 31).

6:1–27 Again the emphasis falls on Yahweh's (not Israel's) action. God informs Joshua, "See, I have given Jericho into your hand" (vv. 1–2). Even before the actual surrender, victory is already an objective fact. Not unlike a royal ceremony in more recent times, the blowing of the ram's horn in the ancient Near East announced the presence of the conquering king.

The final day of Jericho's conquest was the Sabbath (i.e., the time of rest provided by God). However, Israel is not working to *attain* but is rather *receiving* a kingdom. Yahweh fights, while Israel simply announces (with the horn) and inherits the victory. Every living thing (people and animals) must be destroyed (vv. 16–17, 21)—although once again we should recall that this command is given only with regard to Israel's dealings with the Canaanites (see Deut. 20:10–18).

going about it once. And they came into the
camp and spent the night in the camp.
[12]Then Joshua rose early in the morning,
and [m]the priests took up the ark of the LORD.
[13]And the seven priests bearing the seven
trumpets of rams' horns before the ark of the
LORD walked on, and they blew the trumpets
continually. And the armed men were walking
before them, and the rear guard was walking
after the ark of the LORD, while the trumpets
blew continually. [14]And the second day they
marched around the city once, and returned
into the camp. So they did for six days.
[15]On the seventh day they rose early, at the
dawn of day, and marched around the city in
the same manner seven times. It was only on
that day that they marched around the city
seven times. [16]And at the seventh time, when
the priests had blown the trumpets, Joshua
said to the people, "Shout, for the LORD has
given you the city. [17]And the city and all that
is within it shall be [n]devoted to the LORD for
destruction.[1] Only Rahab the prostitute and
all who are with her in her house shall live,
because she [o]hid the messengers whom we
sent. [18]But you, keep yourselves from the
things devoted to destruction, lest when
you have devoted them you take any of the
devoted things and make the camp of Israel
[p]a thing for destruction and [q]bring trouble
upon it. [19]But all silver and gold, and every vessel of bronze and iron, are holy to the LORD;
they shall go into the treasury of the LORD."
[20]So the people shouted, and the trumpets
were blown. As soon as the people heard the
sound of the trumpet, the people shouted a
great shout, and [r]the wall fell down flat, so
that the people went up into the city, every
man straight before him, and they captured
the city. [21]Then they [s]devoted all in the city
to destruction, both men and women, young
and old, oxen, sheep, and donkeys, with the
edge of the sword.
[22]But to the two men who had spied out the
land, Joshua said, "Go into the prostitute's
house and bring out from there the woman
and all who belong to her, [t]as you swore to her."
[23]So the young men who had been spies went
in and brought out Rahab and [u]her father and
mother and brothers and all who belonged to
her. And they brought all her relatives and put
them outside the camp of Israel. [24]And they
burned the city with fire, and everything in
it. [v]Only the silver and gold, and the vessels of
bronze and of iron, they put into the treasury
of the house of the LORD. [25]But Rahab the

[1] That is, set apart (devoted) as an offering to the Lord (for destruction); also verses 18, 21

12[m] See ch. 3:6
17[n] Lev. 27:28; Deut. 20:17 [o] ch. 2:4
18[p] [ch. 7:12] [q] ch. 7:25; 1 Chr. 2:7
20[r] ver. 5; Heb. 11:30
21[s] [Deut. 7:2]
22[t] ch. 2:14; Heb. 11:31
23[u] ch. 2:13
24[v] ver. 19

The acts of marching and music that God commands Joshua to perform (Josh. 6:3–5) seem almost comical for a military campaign. Yet Joshua does as he is commanded, and on the seventh day (the Sabbath) the walls of Jericho come tumbling down (vv. 9–21). As Israel fulfills its commission to rule and subdue as Yahweh's representative on earth, the people enter God's Sabbath rest.

The fall of Jericho is similar to the fall of Babylon in the book of Revelation, where the saints follow the sword-bearing Lamb in triumph. Even the conspiracy of kings (cf. Joshua 10–11 with Revelation 12) and the seven trumpets (cf. Joshua 6 with Revelation 8–11) recur in the last battle, as the rebellious empire is finally brought down forever (Revelation 17–18). Ultimately, the enemies of Yahweh and his saints (Pharaoh, the Canaanites, Babylon) are merely servants of *the* enemy, who is to be finally cast into the lake of fire (Rev. 20:7–10). The story behind all of these stories is the war between the Seed of the woman (Christ) and the Serpent (Gen. 3:15).

Joshua 6:12–27 emphasizes the total destruction of everyone and *everything*. In fact, the warriors are warned not to take any of the spoils for themselves. They are not raiders, deserving their piece of the action, but holy ministers (vv. 16–19).

Everyone and everything is destroyed *except* Rahab and her household, indicating grace toward all—even the worst—who turn to Israel's God. After Rahab and her family are taken into safekeeping, the whole city "and everything in it" is burned (v. 24). Joshua pronounces God's curse on anyone who even lays a foundation to rebuild Jericho (v. 26), a curse which is fulfilled in 1 Kings 16:34.

Just as everything belonging to the ungodly is "devoted to destruction," everyone belonging to a believer is declared holy (Josh. 6:22–23, 25; cf. Acts 2:39; 16:15, 31–33; 1 Cor. 1:16; 7:14). This corporate solidarity runs counter to the sensibilities of modern individualism and democracy. Yet it is crucial for understanding the biblical concept of covenantal identity: as goes the leader, so go the people—as goes the family head,

prostitute and her father's household and all who belonged to her, Joshua saved alive. And [w]she has lived in Israel to this day, because she hid the messengers whom Joshua sent to spy out Jericho.

26 Joshua laid an oath on them at that time, saying, [x]"Cursed before the LORD be the man who rises up and rebuilds this city, Jericho.

"At the cost of his firstborn shall he
lay its foundation,
and at the cost of his youngest son
shall he set up its gates."

27 [y]So the LORD was with Joshua, and [z]his fame was in all the land.

Israel Defeated at Ai

7 But the people of Israel broke faith in regard to the devoted things, for [a]Achan the son of Carmi, son of Zabdi, son of Zerah, of the tribe of Judah, took some of the devoted things. And the anger of the LORD burned against the people of Israel.

2 Joshua sent men from Jericho to Ai, which is near [b]Beth-aven, east of Bethel, and said to them, "Go up and spy out the land." And the men went up and spied out Ai.
3 And they returned to Joshua and said to him, "Do not have all the people go up, but let about two or three thousand men go up and attack Ai. Do not make the whole people toil up there, for they are few."
4 So about three thousand men went up there from the people. And [c]they fled before the men of Ai,
5 and the men of Ai killed about thirty-six of their men and chased them before the gate as far as Shebarim and struck them at the descent. And the hearts of the people [d]melted and became as water.

6 Then Joshua [e]tore his clothes and [f]fell to the earth on his face before the ark of the LORD until the evening, he and the elders of Israel. And they put [g]dust on their heads.
7 And Joshua said, "Alas, O Lord GOD, [h]why have you brought this people over the Jordan at all, to give us into the hands of the Amorites, to destroy us? Would that we had been content to dwell beyond the Jordan!
8 O Lord, what can I say, when Israel has turned their backs before their enemies!
9 For the Canaanites and all the inhabitants of the land will hear of it and will surround us and [i]cut off our name from the earth. And what will you do for your great name?"

The Sin of Achan

10 The LORD said to Joshua, "Get up! Why have you fallen on your face?
11 Israel has sinned; they have [j]transgressed my covenant that I commanded them; they have taken some of the [k]devoted things; they have stolen

so goes the family. The New Testament picks up this interpretive principle to explain that all those in Adam share in his fate of death, while all those in Christ share in his "fate" of eternal life. Just as Yahweh triumphs over Jericho on behalf of his people as they look on, so Jesus triumphs over Satan on our behalf as we look on.

7:1–26 The high note of the King's faithfulness is followed by the servant's fall. So far, there has actually been very little for Israel to do or to claim in Yahweh's victory. Yahweh conquers; Israel inherits. "But the people of Israel broke faith in regard to the devoted things," as Achan pocketed some of the spoils. "And the anger of the LORD burned against the people of Israel" (v. 1; see also note on 6:1–27). Meanwhile, Joshua kept moving out in conquest, toward the city of Ai. Forced to retreat, however, it was now the Israelites whose hearts "melted and became as water" (v. 5). How the tide had turned! Similar to some of Moses' complaints, Joshua tore his clothes and cried out in confusion before Yahweh, until the King informed his servant that the setback was due to sin in the camp: specifically, keeping items devoted for destruction (vv. 6–11). God's zeal for his own house consumed him (cf. John 2:17), and it would now literally consume Israel unless something was done about it.

Once more, given our individualistic assumptions, it may strike us as unjust that God would judge the whole nation for the actions of one man. In the ancient Near East, however, the individual was part of the family, the family part of the city, and the city part of the empire. The great king was the head and each person, from the greatest to the least, was part of his imperial body. This was true for Israel too. Yahweh had chosen, liberated, and called his people—not just one by one but as a whole people, and as one man they swore their oath at Mount Sinai. Later in Israel's history, the king speaks representatively for the people. As goes the king, so go the people. He is their covenant head.

25[w] [Matt. 1:5]
26[x] [1 Kgs. 16:34]
27[y] See ch. 1:5 [z] ch. 9:9

Chapter 7

1[a] ch. 22:20; [1 Chr. 2:6, 7]
2[b] ch. 18:12; 1 Sam. 13:5; 14:23; Hos. 4:15; 5:8; 10:5
4[c] Lev. 26:17; Deut. 28:25
5[d] ch. 2:9, 11
6[e] Gen. 37:29, 34; Num. 14:6; 2 Sam. 1:11; 13:31 [f] Num. 14:5 [g] 1 Sam. 4:12
7[h] Ex. 5:22; 2 Kgs. 3:10
9[i] Ps. 83:4
11[j] ver. 15 [k] ch. 6:17, 18

and lied and put them among their own belongings. 12 [l]Therefore the people of Israel cannot stand before their enemies. They [m]turn their backs before their enemies, because they have become [n]devoted for destruction.[1] I will be with you no more, unless you destroy [o]the devoted things from among you. 13 Get up! Consecrate the people and say, [p]'Consecrate yourselves for tomorrow; for thus says the LORD, God of Israel, "There are devoted things in your midst, O Israel. You cannot stand before your enemies until you take away the devoted things from among you." 14 In the morning therefore you shall be brought near [q]by your tribes. And the tribe that the LORD takes by lot shall come near by clans. And the clan that the LORD takes shall come near by households. And the household that the LORD takes shall come near man by man. 15 [r]And he who is taken with the devoted things shall be burned with fire, he and all that he has, because he has [s]transgressed the covenant of the LORD, and because he has done [t]an outrageous thing in Israel.'"

16 So Joshua rose early in the morning and brought Israel near tribe by tribe, and the tribe of Judah was taken. 17 And he brought near the clans of Judah, and the clan of the [u]Zerahites was taken. And he brought near the clan of the Zerahites man by man, and Zabdi was taken. 18 And he brought near his household man by man, and Achan the son of Carmi, son of Zabdi, son of Zerah, of the tribe of Judah, was taken. 19 Then Joshua said to Achan, "My son, [v]give glory to the LORD God of Israel and [w]give praise[2] to him. And [x]tell me now what you have done; do not hide it from me." 20 And Achan answered Joshua, "Truly [y]I have sinned against the LORD God of Israel, and this is what I did: 21 when I saw among the spoil a beautiful cloak from Shinar, and 200 shekels of silver, and a bar of gold weighing 50 shekels,[3] then I coveted them and took them. And see, they are hidden in the earth inside my tent, with the silver underneath."

22 So Joshua sent messengers, and they ran to the tent; and behold, it was hidden in his tent with the silver underneath. 23 And they took them out of the tent and brought them to Joshua and to all the people of Israel. And they laid them down before the LORD. 24 And Joshua and all Israel with him took Achan the son of Zerah, and the silver and the cloak and the bar of gold, and his sons and daughters and his oxen and donkeys and sheep and his tent and all that he had. And they brought them up to the [z]Valley of Achor. 25 And Joshua said, "Why did you [a]bring trouble on us? The LORD brings trouble on you today." And all Israel [b]stoned him with stones. [c]They

[1] That is, set apart (devoted) as an offering to the Lord (for destruction) [2] Or *and make confession* [3] A *shekel* was about 2/5 ounce or 11 grams

12 [l]Num. 14:45; Judg. 2:14 [m]ver. 8 [n]ch. 6:18 [o]ver. 11
13 [p]ch. 3:5
14 [q]1 Sam. 10:19
15 [r]1 Sam. 14:38, 39 [s]ver. 11 [t]Gen. 34:7; Judg. 20:6
17 [u]Num. 26:20
19 [v]1 Sam. 6:5; Jer. 13:16; Mal. 2:2; John 9:24 [w]Num. 5:6, 7; 2 Chr. 30:22; Ezra 10:11; Dan. 9:4 [x]1 Sam. 14:43
20 [y]2 Sam. 12:13
24 [z]ver. 26; ch. 15:7; Isa. 65:10; Hos. 2:15
25 [a]ch. 6:18; 1 Chr. 2:7 [b]Lev. 20:2; 24:14 [c]ch. 22:20

The principle of imputing (accounting) sin or obedience from the covenant head to his whole body is evident in Romans 5 in the contrast between Adam and Christ. Achan is not a head of all of Israel, but his guilt is nevertheless imputed to the whole body. With his sin there is a tear in the fabric of God's covenant relationship with his people. It must be repaired. So the whole nation appears in God's court by tribes. Then, to identify the guilty person, Yahweh will select a tribe by lot, followed by a clan, then households, then person by person. Then the perpetrator will himself be devoted to burning—"he and all that he has"—for violating the covenant (Josh. 7:15).

In striking contrast with Rahab's faith, Achan's sin had been compounded by the reliance of Israel's spies on the "thousands" of Israel's army rather than on Yahweh (vv. 3–4). With the whole assembly of Israel, Joshua brought Achan up to the Valley of Achor (Achor means "Trouble") and "all Israel stoned him with stones" (v. 25). What happened to Jericho now happens to Achan: he and his whole family, livestock and all possessions, are burned. "And they raised over him a great heap of stones that remains to this day. Then the LORD turned from his burning anger" (v. 26). With Achan's execution, Yahweh's wrath turned away from the camp of Israel.

Achan, representing the people, deserved to be killed for his sin. Jesus, representing his people, did not. "He committed no sin, neither was deceit found in his mouth" (1 Pet. 2:22). In both cases we sense both the seriousness of sin and the lengths to which God will go to preserve his people from sin's contagion and corruption. Both Achan and Jesus were executed to turn away God's wrath. But in a breathtaking act of substitution, we sinners, deserving the fate of Achan, are freely forgiven and welcomed into God's family because Jesus, our representative head, has paid for our sins.

burned them with fire and stoned them with
stones. 26 And they raised over him [d]a great
heap of stones that remains to this day. Then
[e]the LORD turned from his burning anger.
Therefore, to this day the name of that place
is called the Valley of Achor.[1]

The Fall of Ai

8 And the LORD said to Joshua, [f]"Do not fear
and do not be dismayed. Take all the fighting men with you, and arise, go up to Ai. See,
[g]I have given into your hand the king of Ai,
and his people, his city, and his land. 2 And you
shall do to Ai and its king as you did [h]to Jericho
and its king. Only [i]its spoil and its livestock
you shall take as plunder for yourselves. Lay
an ambush against the city, behind it."
3 So Joshua and all the fighting men arose to
go up to Ai. And Joshua chose 30,000 mighty
men of valor and sent them out by night. 4 And
he commanded them, "Behold, [j]you shall lie
in ambush against the city, behind it. Do not
go very far from the city, but all of you remain
ready. 5 And I and all the people who are with
me will approach the city. And when they
come out against us [k]just as before, we shall
flee before them. 6 And they will come out after
us, until we have [l]drawn them away from the
city. For they will say, 'They are fleeing from
us, just as before.' So we will flee before them.
7 Then you shall rise up from the ambush and
seize the city, for the LORD your God will give
it into your hand. 8 And as soon as you have
taken the city, you shall set the city on fire. You
shall do according to the word of the LORD.
[m]See, I have commanded you." 9 So Joshua
sent them out. And they went to the place of
ambush and lay between Bethel and Ai, to the
west of Ai, but Joshua spent that night among
the people.
10 Joshua arose early in the morning and
mustered the people and went up, he and
the elders of Israel, before the people to Ai.
11 And [n]all the fighting men who were with
him went up and drew near before the city
and encamped on the north side of Ai, with a
ravine between them and Ai. 12 He took about
5,000 men and set them in ambush between
Bethel and Ai, to the west of the city. 13 So they
stationed the forces, the main encampment
that was north of the city and its rear guard
west of the city. But Joshua spent that night in
the valley. 14 And as soon as the king of Ai saw
this, he and all his people, the men of the city,
hurried and went out early to the appointed
place[2] toward [o]the Arabah to meet Israel in
battle. [p]But he did not know that there was
an ambush against him behind the city. 15 And
Joshua and all Israel [q]pretended to be beaten
before them and fled in the direction of the
wilderness. 16 So all the people who were in
the city were called together to pursue them,
and as they pursued Joshua they [r]were drawn
away from the city. 17 Not a man was left in Ai
or Bethel who did not go out after Israel. They
left the city open and pursued Israel.

[1] *Achor* means *trouble* [2] Hebrew *appointed time*

8:1–35 Now holy war can resume, as God's people, with the sin of Achan behind them, return to trusting the Lord. God tells Joshua, "See, I have given into your hand the king of Ai, and his people, his city, and his land" (v. 1). Only now God allows the people to take the city's goods and livestock as spoils, making provision for themselves from a now consecrated victory (vv. 1–2). Ai's inhabitants "to the very last," both men and women, fall to the sword; the city is burned and the king is hanged and buried under a heap of stones (vv. 22–29).

In view of God's victory, Joshua builds an altar on Mount Ebal and renews the covenant, reading every word to the people, with sin-offerings and fellowship-offerings (vv. 31–35). This event follows closely Moses' building of the altar and threatening of the covenant curses on Mount Ebal (Deut. 27:1–26). The place is also near (if not actually where) Abraham first built an altar to God to claim Canaan for Yahweh generations previously (Gen. 12:6–7), and where Israel (i.e., Jacob) dedicated an altar to God after reentering the land of his forefather (Gen. 33:20). In other words, the people are made to see that, despite the passing of time and despite their waywardness, God has been faithful to ancient promises in providing this land of their covenant forefathers.

In Joshua 8, God's people go to battle, and once victory is secured, sacrifices are made to God. In the gospel, this very sensible order is surprisingly reversed. Jesus, our Passover Lamb, has already been sacrificed (1 Cor. 5:7). We now do battle against our real enemies—Satan, hell, and condemnation—in light of the offering that has already been made.

26 [d]ch. 8:29; 2 Sam. 18:17; [Lam. 3:53] [e]Deut. 13:17
Chapter 8
1 [f]ch. 1:9; 10:25; Deut. 1:21; 7:18; 31:8 [g]ch. 2:24; 6:2
2 [h]ch. 6:21 [i]ver. 27; Deut. 20:14
4 [j][Judg. 20:29]
5 [k]ch. 7:5
6 [l]ver. 16
8 [m]2 Sam. 13:28
11 [n]ver. 5
14 [o]See Deut. 1:1 [p]Judg. 20:34
15 [q]Judg. 20:36
16 [r]ver. 6

18 Then the LORD said to Joshua, [s]“Stretch out the javelin that is in your hand toward Ai, for I will give it into your hand.” And Joshua stretched out the javelin that was in his hand toward the city. 19 And the men in the ambush rose quickly out of their place, and as soon as he had stretched out his hand, they ran and entered the city and captured it. And they hurried to set the city on fire. 20 So when the men of Ai looked back, behold, the smoke of the city went up to heaven, and they had no power to flee this way or that, for the people who fled to the wilderness turned back against the pursuers. 21 And when Joshua and all Israel saw that the ambush had captured the city, and that the smoke of the city went up, then they turned back and struck down the men of Ai. 22 And the others came out from the city against them, so they were in the midst of Israel, some on this side, and some on that side. And Israel struck them down, until there was [t]left none that survived or escaped. 23 But the king of Ai they took alive, and brought him near to Joshua.

24 When Israel had finished killing all the inhabitants of Ai in the open wilderness where they pursued them, and all of them to the very last had fallen by the edge of the sword, all Israel returned to Ai and struck it down with the edge of the sword. 25 And all who fell that day, both men and women, were 12,000, all the people of Ai. 26 But Joshua did not draw back his hand with which he [u]stretched out the javelin until he had devoted all the inhabitants of Ai to destruction.[1] 27 Only the livestock and the spoil of that city Israel took as their plunder, according to the word of the LORD that he [v]commanded Joshua. 28 So Joshua burned Ai and made it forever a [w]heap of ruins, as it is to this day. 29 [x]And he hanged the king of Ai on a tree until evening. [y]And at sunset Joshua commanded, and they took his body down from the tree and threw it at the entrance of the gate of the city and [z]raised over it a great heap of stones, which stands there to this day.

Joshua Renews the Covenant

30 At that time Joshua built an altar to the LORD, the God of Israel, [a]on Mount Ebal, 31 just as Moses the servant of the LORD had commanded the people of Israel, as it is written in the Book of the Law of Moses, “an altar of uncut stones, upon which no man has wielded an iron tool.” And they offered on it burnt offerings to the LORD and sacrificed peace offerings. 32 And there, in the presence of the people of Israel, he wrote on [b]the stones a copy of the law of Moses, which he had written. 33 And all Israel, [c]sojourner as well as native born, with their elders and officers and their judges, stood on opposite sides of the ark before the Levitical priests [d]who carried the ark of the covenant of the LORD, half of them in front of Mount Gerizim and half of them in front of Mount Ebal, [e]just as Moses the servant of the LORD had commanded at the first, to bless the people of Israel. 34 And afterward [f]he read all the words of the law, [g]the blessing and the curse, according to all that is written in the Book of the Law. 35 There was not a word of all that Moses commanded that Joshua did not read before all the assembly of Israel, [h]and the women, and the little ones, and [i]the sojourners who lived[2] among them.

The Gibeonite Deception

9 As soon as all the kings who were beyond the Jordan [j]in the hill country and in the lowland all along the coast [k]of the Great Sea toward Lebanon, [l]the Hittites, the Amorites, the Canaanites, the Perizzites, the Hivites, and the Jebusites, heard of this, 2 they gathered together as one to fight against Joshua and Israel.

3 But when the inhabitants of [m]Gibeon heard what Joshua had done [n]to Jericho and [o]to Ai,

[1] That is, set apart (devoted) as an offering to the Lord (for destruction) [2] Or *traveled*

18[s] ver. 26
22[t] Deut. 7:2
26[u] ver. 18
27[v] ver. 2
28[w] Deut. 13:16
29[x] ch. 10:26 [y] Deut. 21:23 [z] ch. 7:26
30[a] See Ex. 20:24, 25; Deut. 27:4-6
32[b] Deut. 27:2-4
33[c] Deut. 31:12 [d] Deut. 31:9, 25 [e] Deut. 11:29; 27:11-13

9:1–27 Now even nations that had been enemies of one another form a common alliance (v. 2) against God's approaching storm of divine destruction. The very people for whom God told Abraham he was storing up his wrath (Gen. 15:16) are now on the “ready for destruction” list (Josh. 9:1–2). One of those nations, however, is spared through its act of deception (vv. 3–13) as well as through Israel's failure to consult and do the Lord's will (vv. 14–15). Although Joshua soon learned that the leaders of Gibeon had acted deceitfully, he nevertheless let them live. But he made them servants, doing menial work as woodcutters and water-carriers (vv. 16–27).

34[f] Deut. 31:11; Neh. 8:2, 3; 13:1 [g] Deut. 30:19; See Deut. 28:2-68 **35**[h] Deut. 31:12 [i] ver. 33 **Chapter 9** **1**[j] Deut. 1:7 [k] Num. 34:6 [l] ch. 3:10; 12:8 **3**[m] ch. 10:2, 10, 12; 2 Sam. 21:1, 2; 1 Kgs. 3:4, 5; 9:2 [n] ch. 6:21, 24 [o] ch. 8:26, 28

4 they on their part acted with cunning and went and made ready provisions and took worn-out sacks for their donkeys, and wineskins, worn-out and torn and mended, 5 with worn-out, patched sandals on their feet, and worn-out clothes. And all their provisions were dry and crumbly. 6 And they went to Joshua in [p]the camp at Gilgal and said to him and to the men of Israel, "We have come from a distant country, so now make a covenant with us." 7 But the men of Israel said to [q]the Hivites, "Perhaps you live among us; then [r]how can we make a covenant with you?" 8 They said to Joshua, [s]"We are your servants." And Joshua said to them, "Who are you? And where do you come from?" 9 They said to him, [t]"From a very distant country your servants have come, because of the name of the LORD your God. [u]For we have heard a report of him, and all that he did in Egypt, 10 [v]and all that he did to the two kings of the Amorites who were beyond the Jordan, to Sihon the king of Heshbon, and to Og king of Bashan, who lived in [w]Ashtaroth. 11 So our elders and all the inhabitants of our country said to us, 'Take provisions in your hand for the journey and go to meet them and say to them, "We are your servants. Come now, make a covenant with us."' 12 Here is our bread. It was still warm when we took it from our houses as our food for the journey on the day we set out to come to you, but now, behold, it is dry and crumbly. 13 These wineskins were new when we filled them, and behold, they have burst. And these garments and sandals of ours are worn out from the very long journey." 14 So the men took some of their provisions, but [x]did not ask counsel from the LORD. 15 And Joshua [y]made peace with them and made a covenant with them, to let them live, and the leaders of the congregation swore to them.

16 At the end of three days after they had made a covenant with them, they heard that they were their neighbors [z]and that they lived among them. 17 And the people of Israel set out and reached their cities on the third day. [a]Now their cities were Gibeon, Chephirah, Beeroth, and Kiriath-jearim. 18 But the people of Israel did not attack them, because the leaders of the congregation had sworn to them by the LORD, the God of Israel. Then all the congregation murmured against the leaders. 19 But all the leaders said to all the congregation, "We have sworn to them by the LORD, the God of Israel, and now we may not touch them. 20 This we will do to them: let them live, lest [b]wrath be upon us, [c]because of the oath that we swore to them." 21 And the leaders said to them, "Let them live." So they became [d]cutters of wood and drawers of water for all the congregation, just as the leaders [e]had said of them.

22 Joshua summoned them, and he said to them, "Why did you deceive us, saying, [f]'We are very far from you,' when [g]you dwell among us? 23 Now therefore you are cursed, and some of you shall never be anything but servants, [h]cutters of wood and drawers of water for the house of my God." 24 They answered Joshua, "Because it was told to your servants for a certainty that the LORD your God had [i]commanded his servant Moses to give you all the land and to destroy all the inhabitants of the land from before you—so [j]we feared greatly for our lives because of you and did this thing. 25 And now, behold, we are in your hand. Whatever seems good and right in your sight to do to us, do it." 26 So he did this to them and delivered them out of the hand of the people of Israel, and they did not kill them. 27 But Joshua made them that day [k]cutters of wood and drawers of water for the congregation and for the altar of the LORD, to this day, [l]in the place that he should choose.

Yahweh actually satisfies his purposes through this situation, as making the Gibeonites servants in his land fulfills Noah's curse on Canaan to be the slave of Shem (Gen. 9:26). Even through deception (first Rahab, now the Gibeonites), God is fulfilling his purposes. All this anticipates the day when a remnant from all nations will stream into Zion (Luke 24:47; Acts 1:8; Rev. 5:9–10).

Indeed, the sporadic inclusion of Gentiles such as Rahab or the Gibeonites in the people of God is not an anomaly; it is built into the very heart of the story of redemption that traces through the whole Bible (Rom. 15:4–13). God promised Abraham that through him all the families of the earth would be blessed (Gen. 12:3), and in the new earth we see the Lamb being praised by "a great multitude that no one could number, from every nation, from all tribes and peoples and languages, standing before the throne" (Rev. 7:9).

6 [p] ch. 5:10
7 [q] ch. 11:19 [r] Ex. 23:32; Deut. 7:2; Judg. 2:2
8 [s] ver. 11
9 [t] Deut. 20:15 [u] ch. 2:10; 6:27
10 [v] See Num. 21:21-35 [w] ch. 12:4; Deut. 1:4
14 [x] Num. 27:21
15 [y] ch. 11:19
16 [z] ver. 22
17 [a] [ch. 18:25-28; Ezra 2:25]
20 [b] [Num. 1:53] [c] 2 Sam. 21:2
21 [d] ver. 23, 27; Deut. 29:11 [e] ver. 15
22 [f] ver. 6, 9 [g] ver. 16
23 [h] ver. 21, 27
24 [i] Deut. 7:1, 2 [j] Ex. 15:14
27 [k] ver. 21, 23; [1 Chr. 9:2; Ezra 2:43; 8:20; Neh. 7:60; 11:3] [l] Deut. 12:5

The Sun Stands Still

10 As soon as Adoni-zedek, king of Jerusalem, heard how Joshua had captured
Ai and had devoted it to destruction,[1] [m]doing
to Ai and its king [n]as he had done to Jericho
and its king, and [o]how the inhabitants of
Gibeon had made peace with Israel and were
among them, 2 [p]he[2] feared greatly, because
Gibeon was a great city, like one of the royal
cities, and because it was greater than Ai, and
all its men were warriors. 3 So Adoni-zedek
king of Jerusalem sent to Hoham king of
Hebron, to Piram king of Jarmuth, to Japhia
king of Lachish, and to Debir king of Eglon,
saying, 4 "Come up to me and help me, and
let us strike Gibeon. For [q]it has made peace
with Joshua and with the people of Israel."
5 Then the five kings of the Amorites, the king
of Jerusalem, the king of Hebron, the king of
Jarmuth, the king of Lachish, and the king of
Eglon, [r]gathered their forces and went up with
all their armies and encamped against Gibeon
and made war against it.

6 And the men of Gibeon sent to Joshua
[s]at the camp in Gilgal, saying, "Do not relax
your hand from your servants. Come up to
us quickly and save us and help us, for all the
kings of the Amorites who dwell in the hill
country are gathered against us." 7 So Joshua
went up from Gilgal, he and [t]all the people of
war with him, and all the mighty men of valor.
8 And the LORD said to Joshua, [u]"Do not fear
them, for I have given them into your hands.
[v]Not a man of them shall stand before you."
9 So Joshua came upon them suddenly, having marched up all night from Gilgal. 10 [w]And
the LORD threw them into a panic before
Israel, who[3] struck them with a great blow at
Gibeon and chased them by the way of [x]the
ascent of Beth-horon and struck them as far
as Azekah and Makkedah. 11 And as they fled
before Israel, while they were [x]going down the
ascent of Beth-horon, [y]the LORD threw down
large stones from heaven on them as far as
Azekah, and they died. There were more who
died because of the hailstones than the sons
of Israel killed with the sword.

12 At that time Joshua spoke to the LORD in
the day when the LORD gave the Amorites over
to the sons of Israel, and he said in the sight
of Israel,

[z]"Sun, stand still at Gibeon,
and moon, in the Valley of Aijalon."
13 And the sun stood still, and the moon
stopped,
until the nation took vengeance on
their enemies.

Is this not written in the Book of Jashar? The
sun stopped in the midst of heaven and did
not hurry to set for about a whole day. 14 [a]There
has been no day like it before or since, when
the LORD heeded the voice of a man, for [b]the
LORD fought for Israel.

15 So [c]Joshua returned, and all Israel with
him, to the camp at Gilgal.

Five Amorite Kings Executed

16 These five kings fled and hid themselves
in the cave at [d]Makkedah. 17 And it was told to
Joshua, "The five kings have been found, hidden in the cave at Makkedah." 18 And Joshua
said, "Roll large stones against the mouth
of the cave and set men by it to guard them,
19 but do not stay there yourselves. Pursue
your enemies; [e]attack their rear guard. Do
not let them enter their cities, for the LORD

[1] That is, set apart (devoted) as an offering to the Lord (for destruction); also verses 28, 35, 37, 39, 40 [2] One Hebrew manuscript, Vulgate (compare Syriac); most Hebrew manuscripts *they* [3] Or *and he*

Chapter 10
1[m] ch. 8:22, 26-29 [n] See ch. 6:21, 24 [o] ch. 9:15
2[p] Deut. 11:25
4[q] ver. 1; ch. 9:15
5[r] ch. 9:2
6[s] ch. 5:10; 9:6
7[t] ch. 8:1, 3
8[u] ch. 11:6; Judg. 4:14 [v] ch. 1:5
10[w] Judg. 4:15; 1 Sam. 7:10; Ps. 18:14; Isa. 28:21 [x] ch. 16:3, 5; 18:13, 14; 1 Kgs. 9:17; 1 Chr. 7:24; 2 Chr. 8:5
11[x] [See ver. 10 above] [y] [Ps. 18:12-14; Isa. 30:30; Rev. 16:21]
12[z] Hab. 3:11; [Isa. 28:21]
14[a] Isa. 38:8; [2 Kgs. 20:11] [b] ver. 42; ch. 23:3, 10
15[c] ver. 43
16[d] ver. 10, 28, 29
19[e] [Deut. 25:18]

10:1–28 Like any vassal nation invoking its suzerain (king) in the face of imminent threat, Gibeon appealed to Joshua to protect them from an alliance of pagan kings (vv. 1–6). Again God promised that he would deliver the opposing alliance into Joshua's hands without a survivor (v. 8). And again it was a direct and miraculous triumph, as the enemies fled before Yahweh's army (vv. 9–11). The sources of military victory—mighty hailstones hurled down by God, and the sun standing still—underscore the point that this is a victory from heaven. It is the Lord, once more, who has fought for Israel. It is not the result of Israel's greater wit or strength (vv. 11–15).

With the five kings locked safely away in caves, the Israelites are commanded by God to attack their enemies. After the victory, Joshua tells his soldiers, "Come near; put your feet on the necks of these kings" (vv. 22–24). Again we hear the echoes of the promised Messiah who will crush the serpent's head (Gen. 3:15), and of Christ's disciples who return breathless with the news that they trample serpents (i.e., subdue the demons) in his name (Luke 10:17–19).

your God has given them into your hand."
20 When Joshua and the sons of Israel had finished striking them with a great blow [f]until
they were wiped out, and when the remnant
that remained of them had entered into the
fortified cities, 21 then all the people returned
safe to Joshua in the camp at Makkedah. [g]Not
a man moved his tongue against any of the
people of Israel.
22 Then Joshua said, "Open the mouth of the
cave and bring those five kings out to me from
the cave." 23 And they did so, and brought those
five kings out to him from the cave, the king
of Jerusalem, the king of Hebron, the king of
Jarmuth, the king of Lachish, and the king of
Eglon. 24 And when they brought those kings
out to Joshua, Joshua summoned all the men
of Israel and said to the chiefs of the men of
war who had gone with him, "Come near; put
your feet on the necks of these kings." Then
they came near and put their feet on their
necks. 25 And Joshua said to them, [h]"Do not be
afraid or dismayed; be strong and courageous.
[i]For thus the LORD will do to all your enemies
against whom you fight." 26 And afterward
Joshua struck them and put them to death,
and he hanged them on five trees. And [j]they
hung on the trees until evening. 27 But at the
time of the going down of the sun, Joshua
commanded, and [k]they took them down from
the trees and threw them into the cave where
they had hidden themselves, and they set large
stones against the mouth of the cave, which
remain to this very day.
28 As for [l]Makkedah, Joshua captured it on
that day and struck it, and its king, with the
edge of the sword. He devoted to destruction
every person in it; he left none remaining. And
he did to the king of Makkedah [m]just as he had
done to the king of Jericho.

Conquest of Southern Canaan

29 Then Joshua and all Israel with him passed
on from Makkedah to [n]Libnah and fought
against Libnah. 30 And the LORD gave it also
and its king into the hand of Israel. And he
struck it with the edge of the sword, and every
person in it; he left none remaining in it. And
he did to its king [m]as he had done to the king
of Jericho.
31 Then Joshua and all Israel with him passed
on from Libnah to [o]Lachish and laid siege to
it and fought against it. 32 And the LORD gave
Lachish into the hand of Israel, and he captured it on the second day and struck it with
the edge of the sword, and every person in it,
as he had done to Libnah.
33 Then Horam king of [p]Gezer came up to
help Lachish. And Joshua struck him and his
people, until he left none remaining.
34 Then Joshua and all Israel with him passed
on from Lachish to [q]Eglon. And they laid siege
to it and fought against it. 35 And they captured
it on that day, and struck it with the edge of the
sword. And he devoted every person in it to
destruction that day, as he had done to Lachish.
36 Then Joshua and all Israel with him went
up from Eglon to [r]Hebron. And they fought
against it 37 and captured it and struck it with
the edge of the sword, and its king and its
towns, and every person in it. He left none
remaining, as he had done to Eglon, and
devoted it to destruction and every person in it.
38 Then Joshua and all Israel with him turned
back to [s]Debir and fought against it 39 and he
captured it with its king and all its towns. And
they struck them with the edge of the sword
and devoted to destruction every person in it;
he left none remaining. Just as he had done to
Hebron and to Libnah and its king, so he did
to Debir and to its king.
40 So Joshua struck the whole land, the hill

10:29–12:24 First in the conquest of southern Canaan (10:29–43) and then also in the north (11:1–23), the now-familiar formula is repeated frequently: "And the LORD gave it also and its king into the hand of Israel," with no survivors (10:30). One by one the cities fall, as God delivers them into Israel's hands and Israel takes possession (10:21–41). "And Joshua captured all these kings and their land at one time, *because the* LORD God of Israel fought for Israel" (10:42).

Again, however, among the triumphant anthems of God's victory there are the broken notes of Israel's incomplete obedience, marked by the qualifications "But none" (11:13), "except" (11:19), and "only" (11:22). These notes highlight the point that we sin as much by omission as by commission—not only by what we have done but by what we have left undone. These omissions stand in marked contrast to the reports concerning King Yahweh that "*not one word* has failed of all the good things that the LORD your God promised concerning you" (23:14).

20 [f]ch. 8:24
21 [g]Ex. 11:7
25 [h]ch. 1:6, 9; See Deut. 31:6-8 [i]Deut. 3:21; 7:19
26 [j]ch. 8:29
27 [k]Deut. 21:22, 23
28 [l]ver. 10, 16, 17 [m]ch. 6:21
29 [n]ch. 21:13
30 [m][See ver. 28 above]
31 [o]ver. 3
33 [p]ch. 16:10; Judg. 1:29; See 1 Kgs. 9:15-17
34 [q]ver. 3
36 [r]ch. 15:13; Judg. 1:10; See ch. 14:13-15
38 [s]See ch. 15:15-17; Judg. 1:11-13

country and the Negeb and the lowland [t]and
the slopes, and all their kings. He left none
remaining, [u]but devoted to destruction all
that breathed, just as the LORD God of Israel
commanded. 41 And Joshua struck them from
[v]Kadesh-barnea as far as Gaza, and all the
country of [w]Goshen, as far as Gibeon. 42 And
Joshua captured all these kings and their land
at one time, [x]because the LORD God of Israel
fought for Israel. 43 [y]Then Joshua returned,
and all Israel with him, to the camp at Gilgal.

Conquests in Northern Canaan

11 When Jabin, king of Hazor, heard of
this, he [z]sent to Jobab king of Madon,
and to the king of Shimron, and to the king
of Achshaph, 2 and to the kings who were in
the northern hill country, and in the [a]Ara-
bah south of [b]Chinneroth, and in the lowland, and [c]in Naphoth-dor on the [d]west, 3 to
the Canaanites in the east and the west, the
Amorites, the Hittites, the Perizzites, and the
[e]Jebusites in the hill country, and the [f]Hivites
under [g]Hermon in the land of [h]Mizpah. 4 And
they came out with all their troops, a great
horde, in number [i]like the sand that is on the
seashore, with very many horses and chariots.
5 And all these kings joined their forces and
came and encamped together at the waters of
Merom to fight against Israel.

6 And the LORD said to Joshua, [j]"Do not be
afraid of them, for tomorrow at this time I will
give over all of them, slain, to Israel. You shall
[k]hamstring their horses and burn their [l]chari-
ots with fire." 7 So Joshua and all his warriors
came [m]suddenly against them by the waters
of Merom and fell upon them. 8 And the LORD
gave them into the hand of Israel, who struck
them and chased them as far as [n]Great Sidon
and [o]Misrephoth-maim, and eastward as far as
the Valley of [p]Mizpeh. And they struck them
until he left none remaining. 9 And Joshua did
to them [q]just as the LORD said to him: he hamstrung their horses and burned their chariots
with fire.

10 And Joshua turned back at that time and
captured [r]Hazor and struck its king with the
sword, for Hazor formerly was the head of
all those kingdoms. 11 And they struck with
the sword all who were in it, devoting them
to destruction;[1] [s]there was none left that
breathed. And he burned Hazor with fire.
12 And all the cities of those kings, and all
their kings, Joshua captured, and struck them
with the edge of the sword, devoting them to
destruction, [t]just as Moses the servant of the
LORD had commanded. 13 But none of the cities
that stood on mounds did Israel burn, except
Hazor alone; that Joshua burned. 14 And all
the spoil of these cities and the livestock, the
people of Israel took for their plunder. But
every person they struck with the edge of the
sword until they had destroyed them, and
they did not leave any who breathed. 15 [u]Just
as the LORD had commanded Moses his servant, [v]so Moses commanded Joshua, [w]and so
Joshua did. He left nothing undone of all that
the LORD had commanded Moses.

16 So Joshua took all that land, [x]the hill
country and all the Negeb and [y]all the land
of Goshen [z]and the lowland [z]and the Arabah
[a]and the hill country of Israel and its lowland
17 [b]from Mount Halak, which rises toward Seir,
as far as [c]Baal-gad in the Valley of Lebanon
below [d]Mount Hermon. And he captured [e]all
their kings and struck them and put them to
death. 18 Joshua made war [f]a long time with
all those kings. 19 There was not a city that
made peace with the people of Israel except
[g]the Hivites, the inhabitants of Gibeon. They
took them all in battle. 20 For it was the LORD's
doing [h]to harden their hearts that they should

[1] That is, setting apart (devoting) as an offering to the Lord (for destruction); also verses 12, 20, 21

Joshua's story of conquest is real history, just as it will be when Christ returns (Eph. 1:15–23; Rev. 5:9–10; 19:11–21; 20:7–10). Yet we are sobered in reading these accounts of the conquest of Canaan; the careful reader unavoidably observes the unfailing provision and faithfulness of God in stark contrast to the fickle faith and wavering obedience of Israel. This is a tension that cannot exist forever, given God's righteous holiness. Israel must either fulfill its covenant obligations, or die.

In Christ, the true and final Israel, all this is fulfilled. In Christ's life, death, and resurrection, God's justice and holiness are fully upheld, a faithful Israelite fulfills the covenant obligations, and guilt is punished with death. And God's people, looking to God to fight on their behalf, emerge freely and fully exonerated.

40 [t]ch. 12:8 [u]Deut. 20:16, 17
41 [v]Deut. 9:23 [w]ch. 11:16
42 [x]ver. 14
43 [y]ver. 15

Chapter 11
1 [z]ch. 10:3
2 [a]ch. 3:16; Deut. 1:1 [b]ch. 12:3; 13:27; 19:35; Num. 34:11 [c]ch. 12:23 [d]ch. 17:11; Judg. 1:27
3 [e]ch. 15:63 [f]Judg. 3:3 [g]See Deut. 3:8 [h]ver. 8; Gen. 31:49
4 [i]Gen. 22:17; 32:12; Judg. 7:12; 1 Sam. 13:5
6 [j][ch. 10:8] [k]ver. 9; 2 Sam. 8:4; 1 Chr. 18:4; [Gen. 49:6] [l]ch. 17:16-18; Deut. 20:1; Judg. 1:19; 4:3 **7** [m]ch. 10:9 **8** [n]ch. 19:28 [o]ch. 13:6 [p]ver. 3 **9** [q]ver. 6 **10** [r][Judg. 4:2] **11** [s]ch. 10:40 **12** [t]Deut. 20:16, 17 **15** [u]Ex. 34:11, 12 [v]Deut. 7:2 [w]ch. 1:7 **16** [x]ch. 12:8 [y]ch. 10:41; 15:51 [z]ver. 2 [a]ver. 21 **17** [b]ch. 12:7 [c]ch. 12:7; 13:5 [d]See ver. 3 [e]ch. 12:7; Deut. 7:24 **18** [f][ch. 14:7, 10] **19** [g]ch. 9:3, 7 **20** [h]See Ex. 4:21

come against Israel in battle, in order that they should be devoted to destruction and should receive no mercy but be destroyed, [i]just as the LORD commanded Moses.

21 And Joshua came at that time and cut off [j]the Anakim from the hill country, from Hebron, from Debir, from Anab, and from all the hill country of Judah, and from all the hill country of Israel. Joshua devoted them to destruction with their cities. 22 There was none of the Anakim left in the land of the people of Israel. Only in Gaza, [k]in Gath, and in Ashdod did some remain. 23 So Joshua took the whole land, [l]according to all that the LORD had spoken to Moses. [m]And Joshua gave it for an inheritance to Israel [n]according to their tribal allotments. And the land had rest from war.

Kings Defeated by Moses

12 Now these are the kings of the land whom the people of Israel defeated and took possession of their land beyond the Jordan toward the sunrise, from [o]the Valley of the Arnon to Mount Hermon, with all [p]the Arabah eastward: 2 [q]Sihon king of the Amorites who lived at Heshbon and ruled from Aroer, which is on the edge of the Valley of the Arnon, and [r]from the middle of the valley as far as the [s]river Jabbok, the boundary of the Ammonites, that is, half of Gilead, 3 and [p]the Arabah [t]to the Sea of Chinneroth eastward, and in the direction of Beth-jeshimoth, to the Sea of the Arabah, the Salt Sea, southward to the foot of [u]the slopes of Pisgah; 4 and [v]Og[1] king of Bashan, one of the remnant of [w]the Rephaim, [x]who lived at Ashtaroth and at Edrei 5 and ruled over [y]Mount Hermon and [z]Salecah and all Bashan [a]to the boundary of the Geshurites and the Maacathites, and over half of Gilead to the boundary of Sihon king of Heshbon. 6 [b]Moses, the servant of the LORD, and the people of Israel defeated them. And Moses the servant of the LORD [c]gave their land for a possession to the Reubenites and the Gadites and the half-tribe of Manasseh.

Kings Defeated by Joshua

7 And these are the kings of the land whom Joshua and the people of Israel defeated on the west side of the Jordan, from Baal-gad in the Valley of Lebanon to [d]Mount Halak, that rises toward Seir (and Joshua gave their land to the tribes of Israel as a possession [e]according to their allotments, 8 [f]in the hill country, in the lowland, in the Arabah, in the slopes, in the wilderness, and in the Negeb, the land of [g]the Hittites, the Amorites, the Canaanites, the Perizzites, the Hivites, and the Jebusites): 9 [h]the king of Jericho, one; [i]the king of Ai, which is beside Bethel, one; 10 [j]the king of Jerusalem, one; [j]the king of Hebron, one; 11 [j]the king of Jarmuth, one; [j]the king of Lachish, one; 12 [j]the king of Eglon, one; [k]the king of Gezer, one; 13 [l]the king of Debir, one; the king of Geder, one; 14 the king of Hormah, one; the king of Arad, one; 15 [m]the king of Libnah, one; the king of Adullam, one; 16 [n]the king of Makkedah, one; [o]the king of Bethel, one; 17 the king of Tappuah, one; the king of Hepher, one; 18 the king of Aphek, one; the king of Lasharon, one; 19 [p]the king of Madon, one; [q]the king of Hazor, one; 20 [p]the king of Shimron-meron, one; [p]the king of Achshaph, one; 21 [r]the king of Taanach, one; [r]the king of Megiddo, one; 22 the king of Kedesh, one; the king of Jokneam in Carmel, one; 23 [r]the king of Dor in [s]Naphath-dor, one; the king of Goiim in Galilee,[2] one; 24 the king of Tirzah, one: in all, thirty-one kings.

Land Still to Be Conquered

13 Now Joshua [t]was old and advanced in years, and the LORD said to him, "You are old and advanced in years, and there remains yet very much land [u]to possess. 2 [v]This is the land that yet remains: all the [w]regions of the Philistines, and all those of

[1] Septuagint; Hebrew *the boundary of Og* [2] Septuagint; Hebrew *Gilgal*

13:1–14:15 Joshua 13:8 marks a major transition from the phase of conquest to dividing the spoils. It is not a haphazard land rush, with each man for himself, looting and pillaging like the wicked. Rather, it is an orderly distribution of the inheritance that God had prescribed for each tribe (see Numbers 32–35). Inheritance of God's blessings is always according to God's plan (Eph. 1:11, 14; 2:18; 1 Pet. 1:4; 2 Pet. 3:13). And the distribution of the land is, above all, a celebration of the fulfillment of God's promises.

20 [i] Deut. 20:16, 17
21 [j] ch. 15:13, 14; Num. 13:22, 23; Deut. 1:28
22 [k] [1 Sam. 17:4]
23 [l] See Num. 34:2-12 [m] See ch. 14–19; Num. 26:52-56 [n] ch. 12:7; 18:10

Chapter 12
1 [o] Num. 21:13, 24; Deut. 3:8, 9 [p] See Deut. 1:1 **2** [q] Deut. 2:32, 33; 3:6, 16; See Num. 21:21-26 [r] Deut. 2:36 [s] Gen. 32:22 **3** [p] [See ver. 1 above] [t] ch. 11:2 [u] ch. 13:20; Deut. 3:17; 4:49 **4** [v] Deut. 3:3, 10; See Num. 21:33-35 [w] ch. 13:12; 15:8; 18:16 [x] ch. 9:10; Deut. 1:4 **5** [y] Deut. 3:8, 9 [z] ch. 13:11; Deut. 3:10 [a] Deut. 3:14 **6** [b] See Num. 21:23, 24, 33-35 [c] ch. 13:8; Num. 32:29, 33; Deut. 3:11, 12 **7** [d] ch. 11:17 [e] ch. 11:23; 18:10 **8** [f] ch. 10:40; 11:16 [g] ch. 9:1 **9** [h] [ch. 6:2] [i] ch. 8:29 **10** [j] ch. 10:23 **11** [j] [See ver. 10 above] **12** [j] [See ver. 10 above] [k] ch. 10:33 **13** [l] ch. 10:38, 39 **15** [m] ch. 10:29 **16** [n] ch. 10:28 [o] ch. 8:17; Judg. 1:22 **19** [p] ch. 11:1 [q] ch. 11:1, 10 **20** [p] [See ver. 19 above] **21** [r] ch. 17:11 **23** [r] [See ver. 21 above] [s] ch. 11:2 **Chapter 13** **1** [t] ch. 14:10; 23:1 [u] Deut. 31:3 **2** [v] Judg. 3:1 [w] Joel 3:4

the Geshurites 3 (from the [x]Shihor, which is east of Egypt, northward to the boundary of Ekron, it is counted as Canaanite; [y]there are five rulers of the Philistines, those of Gaza, Ashdod, Ashkelon, Gath, and Ekron), and those of [z]the Avvim, 4 in the south, all the land of the Canaanites, and Mearah that belongs to the Sidonians, to Aphek, to the boundary of [a]the Amorites, 5 and the land of the [b]Gebalites, and all Lebanon, toward the sunrise, from [c]Baal-gad below Mount Hermon to [d]Lebo-hamath, 6 all the inhabitants of the hill country from Lebanon to [e]Misrephoth-maim, even all the Sidonians. I myself will drive [f]them out from before the people of Israel. Only [g]allot the land to Israel [h]for an inheritance, as I have commanded you. 7 Now therefore [i]divide this land for an inheritance to the nine tribes and half the tribe of Manasseh."

The Inheritance East of the Jordan

8 With the other half of the tribe of Manasseh[1] the Reubenites and the Gadites received their inheritance, [j]which Moses gave them, beyond the Jordan eastward, as Moses the servant of the LORD gave them: 9 [k]from Aroer, which is on the edge of the Valley of the Arnon, and the city that is in the middle of the valley, and [l]all the tableland of Medeba as far as Dibon; 10 [m]and all the cities of Sihon king of the Amorites, who reigned in Heshbon, as far as the boundary of the Ammonites; 11 and Gilead, and the [n]region of the Geshurites and Maacathites, and all Mount Hermon, and [n]all Bashan to Salecah; 12 [n]all the kingdom of Og in Bashan, who reigned in Ashtaroth and in Edrei (he alone was left of [n]the remnant of the Rephaim); [o]these Moses had struck and driven out. 13 [p]Yet the people of Israel did not drive out the Geshurites or the Maacathites, but Geshur and Maacath dwell in the midst of Israel to this day.

14 [q]To the tribe of Levi alone Moses gave no inheritance. The offerings by fire to the LORD God of Israel are their inheritance, as he said to him.

15 And Moses gave an inheritance to the tribe of the people of Reuben according to their clans. 16 So their territory was from Aroer, [r]which is on the edge of the Valley of the Arnon, and the city that is in the middle of the valley, and all the tableland by [s]Medeba; 17 with Heshbon, and all its cities that are in the tableland; [s]Dibon, and Bamoth-baal, and Beth-baal-meon, 18 [t]and Jahaz, and Kedemoth, and Mephaath, 19 and [u]Kiriathaim, and [u]Sibmah, and Zereth-shahar on the hill of the valley, 20 and [v]Beth-peor, and [w]the slopes of Pisgah, and [w]Beth-jeshimoth, 21 that is, [x]all the cities of the tableland, and all the kingdom of Sihon king of the Amorites, who reigned in Heshbon, [y]whom Moses defeated with [z]the leaders of Midian, Evi and Rekem and Zur and Hur and Reba, the princes of Sihon, who lived in the land. 22 [z]Balaam also, the son of Beor, the one who practiced divination, was killed with the sword by the people of Israel among the rest of their slain. 23 And the border of the people of Reuben was the Jordan as a boundary. This was the inheritance of the people of Reuben, according to their clans with their cities and villages.

[1] Hebrew *With it*

3 [x]1 Chr. 13:5; Jer. 2:18 [y]Judg. 3:3 [z]Deut. 2:23
4 [a]See Judg. 1:34-36
5 [b]1 Kgs. 5:18; Ps. 83:7; Ezek. 27:9 [c]ch. 11:17; 12:7 [d]Num. 34:8
6 [e]ch. 11:8 [f][ch. 23:13; Judg. 2:21-23] [g]ch. 23:4 [h]ch. 23:4; Num. 34:2
7 [i]ch. 14:1, 2
8 [j]ch. 12:6; See Num. 32:33
9 [k]Deut. 2:36 [l]ver. 16; [Num. 21:30]
10 [m]Num. 21:24, 25
11 [n]Deut. 3:14
12 [n][See ver. 11 above] [o]Num. 21:24, 35
13 [p]ver. 11
14 [q]ch. 14:3, 4; See Num. 18:20-32
16 [r]ver. 9 [s][Num. 21:30]
17 [s][See ver. 16 above]
18 [t]Num. 21:23
19 [u]Num. 32:37, 38
20 [v]Deut. 4:46 [w]See ch. 12:3
21 [x]Deut. 3:10 [y]Num. 21:24 [z]Num. 31:8
22 [z][See ver. 21 above]

Just as God subdued the watery chaos and set creature-kings over each realm, he turns chaos into an ordered cosmos by placing the land of Canaan under the rule of the 12 tribes. God will continue to drive out his enemies. He does the work; Joshua is simply to receive the Lord's victory and parcel out the geographical spoils according to God's word (Josh. 13:6–7).

But all is not well. "Yet the people of Israel did not drive out the Geshurites or the Maacathites, but Geshur and Maacath dwell in the midst of Israel to this day" (13:13). The same failure is mentioned in 15:63. Such allowances of evil, like Adam allowing words of the evil serpent in the garden instead of expelling him, would eventually lead to Israel's seduction, just as God had warned (Deut. 7:4; 12:29–31).

A notable exception is Caleb. In Joshua 14:6–15, Joshua consents to Caleb's request to conquer Hebron, despite the fearsome strength of the Anakim living there and the fact that Caleb is now 85 years old. Confident in Yahweh, Caleb is given strength equal to his youth and inherits Hebron. Caleb is thus an early example of the pattern of godliness described in Hebrews as those who "do not shrink back" despite their own incapacities, and who therefore inherit God's blessing through faith (Heb. 10:39; cf. Rom. 4:13–16; Gal. 3:7, 18).

24 Moses gave an inheritance also to the tribe of Gad, to the people of Gad, according to their clans. 25 [a]Their territory was Jazer, and all the cities of Gilead, and half the land of the Ammonites, to Aroer, which is east of [b]Rabbah, 26 and from Heshbon to Ramath-mizpeh and Betonim, and from [c]Mahanaim to the territory of Debir,[1] 27 and in the valley Beth-haram, Beth-nimrah, [d]Succoth, and Zaphon, the rest of the kingdom of Sihon king of Heshbon, having the Jordan as a boundary, to the lower end of the Sea of [e]Chinnereth, eastward beyond the Jordan. 28 This is the inheritance of the people of Gad according to their clans, with their cities and villages.

29 And Moses gave an inheritance to the half-tribe of Manasseh. It was allotted to the half-tribe of the people of Manasseh according to their clans. 30 Their region extended from [f]Mahanaim, through all Bashan, the whole kingdom of Og king of Bashan, and all [g]the towns of Jair, which are in Bashan, sixty cities, 31 and half Gilead, and [h]Ashtaroth, and Edrei, the cities of the kingdom of Og in Bashan. These were allotted to the people of [i]Machir the son of Manasseh for the half of the people of Machir according to their clans.

32 These are the inheritances that Moses distributed [j]in the plains of Moab, beyond the Jordan east of Jericho. 33 [k]But to the tribe of Levi Moses gave no inheritance; the LORD God of Israel is their inheritance, [k]just as he said to them.

The Inheritance West of the Jordan

14 These are the inheritances that the people of Israel received in the land of Canaan, which [l]Eleazar the priest and Joshua the son of Nun and the heads of the fathers' houses of the tribes of the people of Israel gave them to inherit. 2 Their inheritance was [m]by lot, just as the LORD had commanded by the hand of Moses for the nine and one-half tribes. 3 [n]For Moses had given an inheritance to the two and one-half tribes beyond the Jordan, [o]but to the Levites he gave no inheritance among them. 4 For [p]the people of Joseph were two tribes, Manasseh and Ephraim. And no portion was given to the Levites in the land, but only cities to dwell in, with their pasturelands for their livestock and their substance. 5 The people of Israel did [q]as the LORD commanded Moses; they allotted the land.

Caleb's Request and Inheritance

6 Then the people of Judah came to Joshua at Gilgal. And Caleb the son of Jephunneh the [r]Kenizzite said to him, "You know [s]what the LORD said to Moses the man of God in Kadesh-barnea concerning you and me. 7 I was forty years old when Moses the servant of the LORD [t]sent me from Kadesh-barnea to spy out the land, and I brought him word again as it was in my heart. 8 But [u]my brothers who went up with me made the heart of the people melt; yet I wholly followed the LORD my God. 9 And Moses swore on that day, saying, [v]'Surely the land [w]on which your foot has trodden shall be an inheritance for you and your children forever, because you have wholly followed the LORD my God.' 10 And now, behold, the LORD has kept me alive, [x]just as he said, these [y]forty-five years since the time that the LORD spoke this word to Moses, while Israel walked in the wilderness. And now, behold, I am this day [y]eighty-five years old. 11 [z]I am still as strong today as I was in the day that Moses sent me; my strength now is as my strength was then, for war and [a]for going and coming. 12 So now give me this hill country of which the LORD spoke on that day, for you heard on that day how the [b]Anakim were there, with great fortified cities. It may be that the LORD will be with me, and I shall drive them out just as the LORD said."

13 Then Joshua [c]blessed him, and he gave

[1] Septuagint, Syriac, Vulgate; Hebrew *Lidebir*

Nevertheless, after Israel's victories, "the land had rest from war" (Josh. 14:15; see 11:23). For a brief and shining moment, there was a glimpse of God's everlasting Sabbath: rest, in a land flowing with milk and honey. This is a rest that was given in Eden, lost in the fall, regained in Christ (Matt. 11:28–30), and will one day be finally and perfectly fulfilled in the new earth (Rev. 21:1–4). As Christians today read of Joshua and the people of God entering the land and enjoying peace, our minds are brought to rest on the inheritance that is ours (Matt. 19:28–29; Rom. 4:13) and is invincibly secure, because of Christ's finished work.

25 [a]Num. 32:34-36 [b][Deut. 3:11; 2 Sam. 11:1; 12:26]
26 [c]Gen. 32:2; 2 Sam. 2:8, 12; 17:24
27 [d]Gen. 33:17 [e]See ch. 11:2
30 [f]See ver. 26 [g]Num. 32:41; 1 Chr. 2:23; [Deut. 3:14]
31 [h]ch. 12:4 [i]ch. 17:1; Num. 32:39, 40
32 [j]Num. 22:1
33 [k]ver. 14; ch. 18:7; Num. 18:20

Chapter 14 **1** [l]ch. 17:4; 21:1; Num. 34:17, 18 **2** [m]Num. 26:56; 33:54; 34:13 **3** [n]See ch. 13:8 [o]See ch. 13:33 **4** [p]Gen. 48:5; 1 Chr. 5:1, 2 **5** [q]ch. 21:2; Num. 35:1, 2 **6** [r]ver. 13, 14; Num. 32:12; [ch. 15:17] [s]Num. 14:24, 30; Deut. 1:36, 38 **7** [t]Num. 13:6, 16, 30; 14:6-9 **8** [u]Deut. 1:28; See Num. 13:31-33 **9** [v]Num. 14:24; Deut. 1:36 [w]ch. 1:3 **10** [x]Num. 14:30 [y][ver. 7] **11** [z][Deut. 34:7] [a]Deut. 31:2 **12** [b]Num. 13:28, 33 **13** [c]ch. 22:6

[d]Hebron to Caleb the son of Jephunneh for an inheritance. 14 Therefore Hebron became the inheritance of Caleb the son of Jephunneh the Kenizzite to this day, [e]because he wholly followed the LORD, the God of Israel. 15 [f]Now the name of Hebron formerly was Kiriath-arba.[1] (Arba[2] was the greatest man among the Anakim.) [g]And the land had rest from war.

The Allotment for Judah

15 The allotment for the tribe of the people of Judah according to their clans reached southward [h]to the boundary of Edom, to [i]the wilderness of Zin at the farthest south. 2 And their south boundary ran from the end of the [h]Salt Sea, from the bay that faces southward. 3 It goes out southward of [j]the ascent of Akrabbim, passes along to Zin, and goes up south of Kadesh-barnea, along by Hezron, up to Addar, turns about to Karka, 4 passes along to Azmon, goes out by [k]the Brook of Egypt, and comes to its end at the sea. This shall be your south boundary. 5 And the east boundary is the [h]Salt Sea, to the mouth of the Jordan. And the boundary on the north side runs from the bay of the sea at the mouth of the Jordan. 6 And the boundary goes up to [l]Beth-hoglah and passes along north of [m]Beth-arabah. And the boundary goes up to [n]the stone of Bohan the son of Reuben. 7 And the boundary goes up to Debir from [o]the Valley of Achor, and so northward, turning toward Gilgal, which is opposite [p]the ascent of Adummim, which is on the south side of the valley. And the boundary passes along to the waters of [p]En-shemesh and ends at [q]En-rogel. 8 Then the boundary goes up by [r]the Valley of the Son of Hinnom at the southern shoulder of the Jebusite ([s]that is, Jerusalem). And the boundary goes up to the top of the mountain that lies over against the Valley of Hinnom, on the west, at the northern end of the Valley [t]of Rephaim. 9 Then the boundary extends from the top of the mountain [u]to the spring of the waters of Nephtoah, and from there to the cities of Mount Ephron. Then the boundary bends around to Baalah ([v]that is, Kiriath-jearim). 10 And the boundary circles west of Baalah to Mount Seir, passes along to the northern shoulder of Mount Jearim (that is, Chesalon), and goes down to [w]Beth-shemesh and passes along by [x]Timnah. 11 The boundary goes out [y]to the shoulder of the hill north of Ekron, then the boundary bends around to Shikkeron and passes along to Mount [z]Baalah and goes out to Jabneel. Then the boundary comes to an end at the sea. 12 And the west boundary was [a]the Great Sea with its coastline. This is the boundary around the people of Judah according to their clans.

13 According to the commandment of the LORD to Joshua, he gave to Caleb the son of Jephunneh a portion among the people of Judah, [b]Kiriath-arba, that is, [b]Hebron (Arba was the father of Anak). 14 And Caleb drove out from there the three sons of Anak, [c]Sheshai and Ahiman and Talmai, the descendants of Anak. 15 And he went up from there against the inhabitants of Debir. [d]Now the name of Debir formerly was Kiriath-sepher. 16 And Caleb said, "Whoever strikes Kiriath-sepher and captures it, to him will I give Achsah my daughter as wife." 17 [e]And Othniel the son of Kenaz, [f]the brother of Caleb, captured it. And he gave him

[1] *Kiriath-arba* means *the city of Arba* [2] Hebrew *He*

15:1–21:45 Chapter 15 continues the measuring out of Israel's allotted inheritance in the Promised Land. The division of the inheritance concludes in chapter 18 with the report that, "Then the whole congregation of the people of Israel assembled at Shiloh and set up the tent of meeting there. The land lay subdued before them" (18:1). Just as in Genesis 1 and 2 Yahweh's word had subdued chaos and divided creation into allotted and ordered realms under various creature-kings, with man as his representative ruler over all, Canaan's moral chaos—*tohu wabohu* (darkness and void; Gen. 1:2)—has been overcome. The serpent has been at least partially driven out. Each tribe, like a creature-king, has its realm to guard and keep on Yahweh's behalf. The result, at least for now, is rest: "The land lay subdued before them."

Also anticipating both inevitable corruption in God's land as well as God's redemptive provision, six cities of refuge are assigned in chapter 20, as well as the cities of Levites in chapter 21. Both deal with the problem of sin. Yet as with the other aspects of this covenant, the new covenant will surpass the old just as the reality of Christ will be greater than its Old Testament "types."

13[d] ch. 10:36, 37; 15:13, 14; 21:11, 12; Judg. 1:20; 1 Chr. 6:55, 56
14[e] ver. 8, 9
15[f] ver. 13; Gen. 23:2; 35:27; Judg. 1:10; See ch. 10:36 [g] See ch. 11:23

Chapter 15
1[h] Num. 34:3 [i] Num. 33:36
2[h] [See ver. 1 above]
3[j] Num. 34:4; Judg. 1:36
4[k] ver. 47; Num. 34:5; [ch. 13:3]
5[h] [See ver. 1 above]
6[l] ch. 18:19, 21 [m] ch. 18:18, 22 [n] ch. 18:17
7[o] ch. 7:26 [p] ch. 18:17 [q] ch. 18:16; 2 Sam. 17:17; 1 Kgs. 1:9
8[r] ch. 18:16; 2 Kgs. 23:10 [s] ver. 63; ch. 18:28; [Judg. 19:10; 1 Chr. 11:4] [t] ch. 18:16; See ch. 12:4
9[u] ch. 18:15 [v] ver. 60; 1 Chr. 13:6 **10**[w] 1 Sam. 6:9, 12 [x] Gen. 38:12-14; Judg. 14:1 **11**[y] ch. 13:3 [z] ver. 9 **12**[a] ver. 47; ch. 23:4; Num. 34:6, 7; Ezek. 47:20
13[b] ver. 54; See ch. 14:13-15 **14**[c] Num. 13:22; Judg. 1:10, 20 **15**[d] Judg. 1:11; [ver. 49] **17**[e] See Judg. 1:13 [f] See ch. 14:6, 13

Achsah his daughter as wife. 18 When she came
to him, she urged him to ask her father for a
field. And she got off her donkey, and Caleb
said to her, "What do you want?" 19 She said
to him, "Give me a blessing. Since you have
given me the land of the Negeb, give me also
springs of water." And he gave her the upper
springs and the lower springs.

20 This is the inheritance of the tribe of
the people of Judah according to their clans.
21 The cities belonging to the tribe of the people of Judah in the extreme south, toward
the boundary of Edom, were Kabzeel, [g]Eder,
Jagur, 22 Kinah, Dimonah, Adadah, 23 Kedesh,
Hazor, Ithnan, 24 [h]Ziph, Telem, Bealoth,
25 Hazor-hadattah, Kerioth-hezron (that is,
Hazor), 26 Amam, Shema, Moladah, 27 Hazar-
gaddah, Heshmon, Beth-pelet, 28 Hazar-
shual, [i]Beersheba, Biziothiah, 29 Baalah, Iim,
Ezem, 30 Eltolad, Chesil, Hormah, 31 [j]Ziklag,
Madmannah, Sansannah, 32 Lebaoth, Shilhim,
Ain, and Rimmon: in all, twenty-nine cities
with their villages.

33 And in the lowland, [k]Eshtaol, Zorah,
Ashnah, 34 Zanoah, En-gannim, Tappuah,
Enam, 35 [l]Jarmuth, [m]Adullam, [n]Socoh, [n]Azekah,
36 Shaaraim, Adithaim, Gederah, Gederothaim:
fourteen cities with their villages.

37 Zenan, Hadashah, Migdal-gad, 38 Dilean,
Mizpeh, Joktheel, 39 [o]Lachish, Bozkath, [p]Eglon,
40 Cabbon, Lahmam, Chitlish, 41 Gederoth,
Beth-dagon, Naamah, and [q]Makkedah: sixteen cities with their villages.

42 [r]Libnah, Ether, Ashan, 43 Iphtah, Ashnah,
Nezib, 44 [s]Keilah, Achzib, and Mareshah: nine
cities with their villages.

45 [t]Ekron, with its towns and its villages;
46 from Ekron to the sea, all that were by the
side of Ashdod, with their villages.

47 [t]Ashdod, its towns and its villages; [t]Gaza,
its towns and its villages; to [u]the Brook of
Egypt, and [v]the Great Sea with its coastline.

48 And in the hill country, Shamir, Jattir,
Socoh, 49 Dannah, Kiriath-sannah ([w]that is,
Debir), 50 Anab, Eshtemoh, Anim, 51 [x]Goshen,
Holon, and [y]Giloh: eleven cities with their
villages.

52 Arab, Dumah, Eshan, 53 Janim, Beth-
tappuah, Aphekah, 54 Humtah, [z]Kiriath-arba
(that is, [z]Hebron), and Zior: nine cities with
their villages.

55 [a]Maon, [a]Carmel, [b]Ziph, Juttah, 56 Jezreel,
Jokdeam, Zanoah, 57 Kain, Gibeah, and [c]Tim-
nah: ten cities with their villages.

58 Halhul, Beth-zur, Gedor, 59 Maarath,
Beth-anoth, and Eltekon: six cities with their
villages.

60 [d]Kiriath-baal (that is, Kiriath-jearim), and
Rabbah: two cities with their villages.

61 In the wilderness, [e]Beth-arabah, Middin,
Secacah, 62 Nibshan, the City of Salt, and
[f]Engedi: six cities with their villages.

63 But the [g]Jebusites, the inhabitants of
Jerusalem, [h]the people of Judah could not
drive out, [h]so the Jebusites dwell with the
people of Judah at Jerusalem to this day.

The Allotment for Ephraim and Manasseh

16 The allotment of the people of Joseph
went from the Jordan by Jericho, east
of the waters of Jericho, [i]into the wilderness,
going up from Jericho into the hill country
to Bethel. 2 Then [j]going from Bethel to Luz,
it passes along to Ataroth, the territory of the
Archites. 3 Then it goes down westward to the

Once again underscoring the difference between Israel's story and the dreary record of empires and nations invoking religious justification for violence, the hero of the conquest of Canaan is Yahweh. Joshua is *not* the "founding father" of Israel in Canaan. Caleb is *not* celebrated for his patriotism and military prowess. "Thus *the* LORD gave to Israel all the land that he swore to give to their fathers. And they took possession of it, and they settled there" (Josh. 21:43). This is the repeated refrain we have heard throughout the book of Joshua. "And the LORD gave them rest on every side. . . . for the LORD had given all their enemies into their hands. Not one word of all the good promises that the LORD had made to the house of Israel had failed; all came to pass" (21:44–45).

Reading of God's exhaustive faithfulness to keep his word is heartening for believers today in the face of all kinds of trials. Not one promise from God to his people will fail, for Jesus Christ has secured "all the promises of God" (2 Cor. 1:20). Jesus promises rest (Matt. 11:28). He promises triumph over our enemies (Luke 10:19). And he promises to bring us home one day to him (John 14:2–3).

21[g] Gen. 35:21
24[h] 1 Sam. 23:14, 15, 19, 24; 26:1, 2
28[i] Gen. 21:31; 26:23, 33
31[j] 1 Sam. 27:6; 30:1
33[k] [Num. 13:23]
35[l] ch. 10:3 [m] 1 Sam. 22:1 [n] 1 Sam. 17:1
39[o] ch. 10:3, 31, 32 [p] ch. 10:3, 36, 37
41[q] ch. 10:10, 21
42[r] ch. 10:29, 30
44[s] 1 Sam. 23:1, 2
45[t] ch. 13:3
47[t] [See ver. 45 above] [u] See ver. 4 [v] See ver. 12
49[w] [ver. 15]
51[x] ch. 10:41; 11:16 [y] 2 Sam. 15:12
54[z] ver. 13
55[a] 1 Sam. 23:24, 25; 25:2 [b] ver. 24
57[c] ver. 10

60[d] ver. 9 **61**[e] ver. 6 **62**[f] 1 Sam. 23:29; 24:1 **63**[g] See ver. 8 [h] [Judg. 1:8, 21; 2 Sam. 5:6] **Chapter 16** **1**[i] ch. 8:15; 18:12 **2**[j] [ch. 18:13; Gen. 28:19; Judg. 1:23, 26]

territory of the Japhletites, as far as the territory of Lower [k]Beth-horon, then to [l]Gezer, and it ends at the sea.

4 [m]The people of Joseph, Manasseh and Ephraim, received their inheritance.

5 The territory of the people of Ephraim by their clans was as follows: the boundary of their inheritance on the east was [n]Atarothaddar as far as Upper Beth-horon, 6 and the boundary goes from there to the sea. On the north is [o]Michmethath. Then on the east the boundary turns around toward Taanathshiloh and passes along beyond it on the east to Janoah, 7 then it goes down from Janoah to Ataroth and [p]to Naarah, and touches Jericho, ending at the Jordan. 8 From [q]Tappuah the boundary goes westward to the brook Kanah and ends at the sea. Such is the inheritance of the tribe of the people of Ephraim by their clans, 9 together with [q]the towns that were set apart for the people of Ephraim within the inheritance of the Manassites, all those towns with their villages. 10 However, [r]they did not drive out the Canaanites who lived in Gezer, so the Canaanites have lived in the midst of Ephraim to this day but have been made [s]to do forced labor.

17 Then allotment was made to the people of Manasseh, for he was [t]the firstborn of Joseph. To [u]Machir the firstborn of Manasseh, the father of Gilead, [v]were allotted Gilead and Bashan, because he was a man of war. 2 And allotments were made [w]to the rest of the people of Manasseh by their clans, Abiezer, Helek, Asriel, Shechem, Hepher, and Shemida. These were the male descendants of Manasseh the son of Joseph, by their clans.

3 Now [x]Zelophehad the son of Hepher, son of Gilead, son of Machir, son of Manasseh, had no sons, but only daughters, and these are the names of his daughters: [x]Mahlah, Noah, Hoglah, Milcah, and Tirzah. 4 They approached [y]Eleazar the priest and Joshua the son of Nun and the leaders and said, [z]"The LORD commanded Moses to give us an inheritance along with our brothers." So according to the mouth of the LORD he gave them an inheritance among the brothers of their father. 5 Thus there fell to Manasseh ten portions, besides [a]the land of Gilead and Bashan, which is on the other side of the Jordan, 6 because the daughters of Manasseh received an inheritance along with his sons. The land of Gilead was allotted to the rest of the people of Manasseh.

7 The territory of Manasseh reached from Asher to [b]Michmethath, which is east of Shechem. Then the boundary goes along southward to the inhabitants of En-tappuah. 8 The land of [c]Tappuah belonged to Manasseh, but the town of Tappuah on the boundary of Manasseh belonged to the people of Ephraim. 9 [c]Then the boundary went down to the brook Kanah. These cities, to the south of the brook, among the cities of Manasseh, belong to Ephraim. Then the boundary of Manasseh goes on the north side of the brook and ends at the sea, 10 the land to the south being Ephraim's and that to the north being Manasseh's, with the sea forming its boundary. On the north Asher is reached, and on the east Issachar. 11 Also in Issachar and in Asher [d]Manasseh had Beth-shean and its villages, and Ibleam and its villages, and the inhabitants of [d]Dor and its villages, and the inhabitants of En-dor and its villages, and the inhabitants of [d]Taanach and its villages, and the inhabitants of [d]Megiddo and its villages; [e]the third is Naphath.[1] 12 [f]Yet the people of Manasseh could not take possession of those cities, but the Canaanites persisted in dwelling in that land. 13 Now when the people of Israel grew strong, they put the Canaanites [g]to forced labor, but did not utterly drive them out.

14 Then [h]the people of Joseph spoke to Joshua, saying, "Why have you given me but [i]one lot and one portion as an inheritance, although I am [j]a numerous people, since all along the LORD has blessed me?" 15 And Joshua said to them, "If you are a numerous people, go up by yourselves to the forest, and there clear ground for yourselves in the land of the Perizzites and [k]the Rephaim, since [l]the hill country of Ephraim is too narrow for you." 16 The people of Joseph said, "The hill country is not enough for us. Yet all the Canaanites who dwell in the plain have [m]chariots of iron, both those in Beth-shean and its villages and those in [n]the Valley of Jezreel." 17 Then Joshua

[1] The meaning of the Hebrew is uncertain

3[k] See ch. 10:10 [l] See ch. 10:33 **4**[m] [ch. 17:14] **5**[n] ch. 18:13 **6**[o] ch. 17:7 **7**[p] 1 Chr. 7:28 **8**[q] ch. 17:8, 9 **9**[q] [See ver. 8 above] **10**[r] Judg. 1:29; 1 Kgs. 9:16 [s] ch. 17:13; Gen. 49:15 **Chapter 17** **1**[t] Gen. 41:51; 46:20; 48:18 [u] Gen. 50:23; Num. 26:29; 32:39, 40; 1 Chr. 7:14 [v] Deut. 3:13, 15 **2**[w] See Num. 26:29-32 **3**[x] Num. 26:33; 27:1; 36:2, 11 **4**[y] ch. 14:1; 21:1; Num. 34:17 [z] Num. 27:6, 7; 36:2 **5**[a] ver. 1; ch. 13:30, 31 **7**[b] ch. 16:6 **8**[c] ch. 16:8, 9 **9**[c] [See ver. 8 above] **11**[d] 1 Chr. 7:29; [1 Kgs. 4:11, 12] [e] [ch. 11:2; 12:23] **12**[f] Judg. 1:27, 28 **13**[g] ch. 16:10; Gen. 49:15 **14**[h] ch. 16:4 [i] [Gen. 48:22] [j] Gen. 48:19; [Num. 26:34, 37] **15**[k] See ch. 12:4 [l] ch. 24:33; Judg. 3:27 **16**[m] See ch. 11:6 [n] Judg. 6:33

said to the house of Joseph, to Ephraim and
Manasseh, "You are a numerous people and
have great power. You shall not have one
allotment only, 18 but the hill country shall be
yours, for though it is a forest, you shall clear
it and possess it to its farthest borders. For
you shall drive out the Canaanites, [o]though
they have chariots of iron, and though they
are strong."

Allotment of the Remaining Land

18 Then the whole congregation of the
people of Israel assembled at [p]Shiloh
and set up [q]the tent of meeting there. The land
lay subdued before them.

2 There remained among the people of Israel
seven tribes whose inheritance had not yet
been apportioned. 3 So Joshua said to the people of Israel, [r]"How long will you put off going
in to take possession of the land, which the
LORD, the God of your fathers, has given you?
4 Provide three men from each tribe, and I will
send them out that they may set out and go up
and down the land. They shall write a description of it with a view to their inheritances,
and then come to me. 5 They shall divide it
into seven portions. [s]Judah shall continue in
his territory on the south, [t]and the house of
Joseph shall continue in their territory on
the north. 6 And you shall describe the land
in seven divisions and bring the description
here to me. [u]And I will cast lots for you here
before the LORD our God. 7 [v]The Levites have
no portion among you, for the priesthood
of the LORD is their heritage. [w]And Gad and
Reuben and half the tribe of Manasseh have
received their inheritance beyond the Jordan
eastward, which Moses the servant of the
LORD gave them."

8 So the men arose and went, and Joshua
charged those who went to write the description of the land, saying, "Go up and down in
the land and write a description and return
to me. And I will cast lots for you here before
the LORD in Shiloh." 9 So the men went and
passed up and down in the land and wrote in a
book a description of it by towns in seven divisions. Then they came to Joshua to the camp
at Shiloh, 10 and Joshua [x]cast lots for them in
Shiloh before the LORD. And there Joshua
apportioned the land to the people of Israel,
[y]to each his portion.

The Inheritance for Benjamin

11 The lot of the tribe of the people of
Benjamin according to its clans came up,
and the territory allotted to it fell between
the people of Judah and the people of Joseph.
12 [z]On the north side their boundary began
at the Jordan. [a]Then the boundary goes up
to the shoulder north of Jericho, then up
through the hill country westward, and it
ends at the wilderness of [b]Beth-aven. 13 From
there the boundary passes along southward
in the direction of Luz, to the shoulder of
[c]Luz (that is, Bethel), then the boundary goes
down to [d]Ataroth-addar, on the mountain
that lies south of Lower [e]Beth-horon. 14 Then
the boundary goes in another direction, turning on the [f]western side southward from
the mountain that lies to the south, opposite Beth-horon, and it ends at Kiriath-baal
([g]that is, Kiriath-jearim), a city belonging to
the people of Judah. This forms the western
side. 15 And the southern side begins at the
outskirts of Kiriath-jearim. And the boundary
goes from there to Ephron,[1] [g]to the spring of
the waters of Nephtoah. 16 Then the boundary
goes down to the border of the mountain that
overlooks [h]the Valley of the Son of Hinnom,
which is at the north end of the Valley of
[i]Rephaim. And it then goes down the [h]Valley
of Hinnom, south of the shoulder of the
Jebusites, and downward to [j]En-rogel. 17 Then
it bends in a northerly direction going on to
En-shemesh, and from there goes to Geliloth,
which is opposite the ascent of Adummim.
Then it goes down to [k]the stone of Bohan the
son of Reuben, 18 and passing on to the north
of [l]the shoulder of Beth-arabah[2] it goes down
to [l]the Arabah. 19 Then the boundary passes on
to the north of the shoulder of [k]Beth-hoglah.
And the boundary ends at the northern bay of
[m]the Salt Sea, at the south end of the Jordan:
this is the southern border. 20 The Jordan
forms its boundary on the eastern side. This
is the inheritance of the people of Benjamin,
according to their clans, boundary by boundary all around.

21 Now the cities of the tribe of the people
of Benjamin according to their clans were

[1] See 15:9; Hebrew *westward* [2] Septuagint; Hebrew *to the shoulder over against the Arabah*

18[o] Deut. 20:1; See ch. 11:6 **Chapter 18** **1**[p] ch. 19:51; 21:2; 22:9, 12 [q] ch. 19:51 **3**[r] [Judg. 18:9] **5**[s] [ch. 15:1] [t] [ch. 16:1, 4] **6**[u] ver. 10; ch. 14:2 **7**[v] See ch. 13:33 [w] See ch. 13:8 **10**[x] ver. 6 [y] ch. 11:23; 12:7 **12**[z] [ch. 16:1] [a] ver. 21 [b] See ch. 7:2 **13**[c] See ch. 16:2 [d] ch. 16:5 [e] ch. 16:3; See ch. 10:10 **14**[f] [ch. 19:11] [g] ch. 15:9 **15**[g] [See ver. 14 above] **16**[h] See ch. 15:8 [i] See ch. 12:4 [j] See ch. 15:7 **17**[k] ch. 15:6 **18**[l] ch. 11:2; 15:6 **19**[k] [See ver. 17 above] [m] ch. 15:2

[n]Jericho, Beth-hoglah, Emek-keziz, 22 Beth-arabah, Zemaraim, Bethel, 23 Avvim, Parah, Ophrah, 24 Chephar-ammoni, Ophni, Geba—twelve cities with their villages: 25 Gibeon, Ramah, Beeroth, 26 Mizpeh, Chephirah, Mozah, 27 Rekem, Irpeel, Taralah, 28 Zela, Haeleph, [o]Jebus[1] (that is, Jerusalem), Gibeah[2] and Kiriath-jearim[3]—fourteen cities with their villages. This is the inheritance of the people of Benjamin according to its clans.

The Inheritance for Simeon

19 The second lot came out for Simeon, for the tribe of the people of Simeon, according to their clans, [p]and their inheritance was in the midst of the inheritance of the people of Judah. 2 [q]And they had for their inheritance Beersheba, Sheba, Moladah, 3 Hazar-shual, Balah, Ezem, 4 Eltolad, Bethul, Hormah, 5 Ziklag, Beth-marcaboth, Hazar-susah, 6 Beth-lebaoth, and Sharuhen—thirteen cities with their villages; 7 Ain, Rimmon, Ether, and Ashan—four cities with their villages, 8 together with all the villages around these cities as far as Baalath-beer, Ramah of the Negeb. This was the inheritance of the tribe of the people of Simeon according to their clans. 9 [r]The inheritance of the people of Simeon formed part of the territory of the people of Judah. Because the portion of the people of Judah was too large for them, the people of Simeon obtained an inheritance in the midst of their inheritance.

The Inheritance for Zebulun

10 The third lot came up for the people of Zebulun, according to their clans. And the territory of their inheritance reached as far as Sarid. 11 Then their boundary goes up [s]westward and on to Mareal and touches Dabbesheth, then the brook that is east of [t]Jokneam. 12 From Sarid it goes in the other direction eastward toward the sunrise to the boundary of Chisloth-tabor. From there it goes to Daberath, then up to Japhia. 13 From there it passes along on the east toward the sunrise to Gath-hepher, to Eth-kazin, and going on to Rimmon it bends toward Neah, 14 then on the north the boundary turns about to Hannathon, and it ends at the Valley of Iphtahel; 15 and Kattath, Nahalal, [u]Shimron, Idalah, and Bethlehem—twelve cities with their villages. 16 This is the inheritance of the people of Zebulun, according to their clans—these cities with their villages.

The Inheritance for Issachar

17 The fourth lot came out for Issachar, for the people of Issachar, according to their clans. 18 Their territory included Jezreel, Chesulloth, [v]Shunem, 19 Hapharaim, Shion, Anaharath, 20 Rabbith, Kishion, Ebez, 21 Remeth, En-gannim, En-haddah, Beth-pazzez. 22 The boundary also touches Tabor, Shahazumah, and Beth-shemesh, and its boundary ends at the Jordan—sixteen cities with their villages. 23 This is the inheritance of the tribe of the people of Issachar, according to their clans—the cities with their villages.

The Inheritance for Asher

24 The fifth lot came out for the tribe of the people of Asher according to their clans. 25 Their territory included Helkath, Hali, Beten, Achshaph, 26 Allammelech, Amad, and Mishal. On the west it touches [w]Carmel and Shihor-libnath, 27 then it turns eastward, it goes to Beth-dagon, and touches Zebulun and the Valley of Iphtahel northward to Beth-emek and Neiel. Then it continues in the north to [x]Cabul, 28 Ebron, Rehob, Hammon, Kanah, as far as [y]Sidon the Great. 29 Then the boundary turns to Ramah, reaching to the fortified city of Tyre. Then the boundary turns to Hosah, and it ends at the sea; Mahalab,[4] Achzib, 30 Ummah, Aphek and Rehob—twenty-two cities with their villages. 31 This is the inheritance of the tribe of the people of Asher according to their clans—these cities with their villages.

The Inheritance for Naphtali

32 The sixth lot came out for the people of Naphtali, for the people of Naphtali, according to their clans. 33 And their boundary ran from Heleph, from [z]the oak in Zaanannim, and Adami-nekeb, and Jabneel, as far as Lakkum, and it ended at the Jordan. 34 Then the boundary turns [a]westward to Aznoth-tabor and goes from there to Hukkok, touching Zebulun at the south and Asher on the west and Judah on the east at the Jordan. 35 The fortified cities are Ziddim, Zer,

[1] Septuagint, Syriac, Vulgate; Hebrew *the Jebusite* [2] Hebrew *Gibeath* [3] Septuagint; Hebrew *Kiriath* [4] Compare Septuagint; Hebrew *Mehebel*

21[n] ver. 12 **28**[o] See ch. 15:8 **Chapter 19** **1**[p] ver. 9; [Gen. 49:7] **2**[q] For ver. 2-8, see 1 Chr. 4:28-33 **9**[r] ver. 1 **11**[s] [ch. 18:14; Gen. 49:13] [t] ch. 12:22; 21:34 **15**[u] ch. 11:1 **18**[v] 1 Sam. 28:4 **26**[w] 1 Kgs. 18:19, 20, 42; 2 Kgs. 2:25; 4:25; Song 7:5; Isa. 33:9; Jer. 50:19 **27**[x] [1 Kgs. 9:13] **28**[y] ch. 11:8; [Judg. 1:31] **33**[z] [Judg. 4:11] **34**[a] [Deut. 33:23]

Hammath, Rakkath, [b]Chinnereth, 36 Adamah,
Ramah, [c]Hazor, 37 Kedesh, Edrei, En-hazor,
38 Yiron, Migdal-el, Horem, Beth-anath, and
Beth-shemesh—nineteen cities with their
villages. 39 This is the inheritance of the tribe
of the people of Naphtali according to their
clans—the cities with their villages.

The Inheritance for Dan

40 The seventh lot came out for the tribe of
the people of Dan, according to their clans.
41 And the territory of its inheritance included
Zorah, Eshtaol, Ir-shemesh, 42 [d]Shaalabbin,
[d]Aijalon, Ithlah, 43 Elon, Timnah, Ekron,
44 Eltekeh, Gibbethon, Baalath, 45 Jehud, Bene-
berak, Gath-rimmon, 46 and Me-jarkon and
Rakkon with the territory over against [e]Joppa.
47 When [f]the territory of the people of Dan was
lost to them, the people of Dan went up and
fought against Leshem, and after capturing it
and striking it with the sword they took possession of it and settled in it, calling Leshem,
Dan, after the name of Dan their ancestor.
48 This is the inheritance of the tribe of the
people of Dan, according to their clans—these
cities with their villages.

The Inheritance for Joshua

49 When they had finished distributing
the several territories of the land as inheritances, the people of Israel gave an inheritance
among them to Joshua the son of Nun. 50 By
command of the LORD they gave him the
city that he asked, [g]Timnath-serah in the hill
country of Ephraim. And he rebuilt the city
and settled in it.

51 [h]These are the inheritances that Eleazar
the priest and Joshua the son of Nun and the
heads of the fathers' houses of the tribes of the
people of Israel distributed by lot [i]at Shiloh
before the LORD, at the entrance of the tent of
meeting. So they finished dividing the land.

The Cities of Refuge

20 Then the LORD said to Joshua, 2 "Say to
the people of Israel, [j]'Appoint the cities
of refuge, of which I spoke to you through
Moses, 3 that the manslayer who strikes any
person without intent or unknowingly may
flee there. They shall be for you a refuge from
the avenger of blood. 4 He shall flee to one of
these cities and shall stand [k]at the entrance
of the gate of the city and explain his case to
the elders of that city. Then they shall take
him into the city and give him a place, and he
shall remain with them. 5 And if the avenger of
blood pursues him, they shall not give up the
manslayer into his hand, because he struck his
neighbor unknowingly, and did not hate him
in the past. 6 And he shall remain in that city
[l]until he has stood before the congregation for
judgment, until the death of him who is high
priest at the time. Then the manslayer may
return to his own town and his own home, to
the town from which he fled.'"

7 So they set apart [m]Kedesh in Galilee in the
hill country of Naphtali, and [n]Shechem in
the hill country of Ephraim, and [o]Kiriath-
arba (that is, Hebron) [p]in the hill country of
Judah. 8 And beyond the Jordan east of Jericho,
they appointed [q]Bezer in the wilderness on
the tableland, from the tribe of Reuben, and
[r]Ramoth in Gilead, from the tribe of Gad, and
[s]Golan in Bashan, from the tribe of Manasseh.
9 These were the cities designated for all the
people of Israel and [t]for the stranger sojourning among them, that anyone who killed a
person without intent could flee there, so that
he might not die by the hand of the avenger of
blood, till he stood before the congregation.

Cities and Pasturelands Allotted to Levi

21 Then the heads of the fathers' houses
of the Levites came [u]to Eleazar the
priest and to Joshua the son of Nun and to
the heads of the fathers' houses of the tribes
of the people of Israel. 2 And they said to them
[v]at Shiloh in the land of Canaan, [w]"The LORD
commanded through Moses that we be given
cities to dwell in, along with their pasturelands for our livestock." 3 So by command
of the LORD the people of Israel gave to the
Levites the following cities and pasturelands
out of their inheritance.

4 The lot came out for the clans of the
Kohathites. So those Levites who were descendants of Aaron the priest [x]received by lot from
the tribes of Judah, Simeon, and Benjamin,
thirteen cities.

5 And the rest of the Kohathites received by
lot [y]from the clans of the tribe of Ephraim,
from the tribe of Dan and the half-tribe of
Manasseh, ten cities.

35 [b] See ch. 11:2 **36** [c] ch. 11:1 **42** [d] Judg. 1:35 **46** [e] 2 Chr. 2:16; Ezra 3:7 **47** [f] Judg. 1:34, 35; 18:1 **50** [g] ch. 24:30; Judg. 2:9 **51** [h] ch. 14:1; Num. 34:17 [i] See ch. 18:1 **Chapter 20** **2** [j] Ex. 21:13; See Num. 35:6, 11-14; Deut. 4:41-43; 19:2-9 **4** [k] [Deut. 21:19; Ruth 4:1, 2; Ps. 127:5] **6** [l] Num. 35:12, 24, 25 **7** [m] ch. 21:32; 1 Chr. 6:76 [n] ch. 21:21 [o] ch. 21:11, 13; See ch. 14:13-15 [p] ch. 21:11; Luke 1:39 **8** [q] ch. 21:36; 1 Chr. 6:78 [r] ch. 21:38; [1 Kgs. 22:3] [s] ch. 21:27; 1 Chr. 6:71 **9** [t] Num. 35:15 **Chapter 21** **1** [u] ch. 14:1; 17:4; 19:51; Num. 34:17, 18 **2** [v] See ch. 18:1 [w] Num. 35:2 **4** [x] See ver. 9-19; Ex. 6:16-19; Num. 3:17-20 **5** [y] See ver. 20-26

6 The [z]Gershonites received by lot from the
clans of the tribe of Issachar, from the tribe of
Asher, from the tribe of Naphtali, and from
the half-tribe of Manasseh in Bashan, thirteen
cities.

7 The [a]Merarites according to their clans
received from the tribe of Reuben, the tribe
of Gad, and the tribe of Zebulun, twelve cities.

8 These cities and their pasturelands the
people of Israel [b]gave by lot to the Levites, [c]as
the LORD had commanded through Moses.

9 Out of the tribe of the people of Judah and
the tribe of the people of Simeon they gave the
following cities mentioned by name, 10 which
went to [d]the descendants of Aaron, one of the
clans of the Kohathites who belonged to the
people of Levi; since the lot fell to them first.
11 [e]They gave them [f]Kiriath-arba (Arba being
the father of Anak), that is Hebron, [g]in the hill
country of Judah, along with the pasturelands
around it. 12 But the fields of the city and its
villages had been given to Caleb the son of
Jephunneh as his possession.

13 And to the descendants of Aaron the priest
they gave Hebron, [h]the city of refuge for the
manslayer, with its pasturelands, [i]Libnah with
its pasturelands, 14 Jattir with its pasturelands,
Eshtemoa with its pasturelands, 15 Holon with
its pasturelands, Debir with its pasturelands,
16 Ain with its pasturelands, Juttah with its
pasturelands, Beth-shemesh with its pasturelands—nine cities out of these two tribes;
17 then out of the tribe of Benjamin, [j]Gibeon
with its pasturelands, Geba with its pasturelands, 18 Anathoth with its pasturelands, and
Almon with its pasturelands—four cities.
19 The cities of the descendants of Aaron, the
priests, were in all thirteen cities with their
pasturelands.

20 [k]As to the rest of the Kohathites belonging to the Kohathite clans of the Levites, the
cities allotted to them were out of the tribe
of Ephraim. 21 To them were given Shechem,
[l]the city of refuge for the manslayer, with its
pasturelands in the hill country of Ephraim,
Gezer with its pasturelands, 22 Kibzaim with
its pasturelands, Beth-horon with its pasturelands—four cities; 23 and out of the tribe of
Dan, Elteke with its pasturelands, Gibbethon
with its pasturelands, 24 Aijalon with its pasturelands, Gath-rimmon with its pasturelands—four cities; 25 and out of the half-tribe
of Manasseh, Taanach with its pasturelands,
and Gath-rimmon with its pasturelands—
two cities. 26 The cities of the clans of the rest
of the Kohathites were ten in all with their
pasturelands.

27 [m]And to the Gershonites, one of the clans of
the Levites, were given out of the half-tribe of
Manasseh, Golan in Bashan with its pasturelands, [l]the city of refuge for the manslayer, and
Beeshterah with its pasturelands—two cities; 28 and out of the tribe of Issachar, Kishion
with its pasturelands, Daberath with its pasturelands, 29 Jarmuth with its pasturelands,
En-gannim with its pasturelands—four cities;
30 and out of the tribe of Asher, Mishal with its
pasturelands, Abdon with its pasturelands,
31 Helkath with its pasturelands, and Rehob
with its pasturelands—four cities; 32 and out
of the tribe of Naphtali, Kedesh in Galilee
with its pasturelands, [l]the city of refuge for
the manslayer, Hammoth-dor with its pasturelands, and Kartan with its pasturelands—
three cities. 33 The cities of the several clans of
the Gershonites were in all thirteen cities with
their pasturelands.

34 [n]And to the rest of the Levites, the Merarite
clans, were given out of the tribe of Zebulun,
Jokneam with its pasturelands, Kartah with
its pasturelands, 35 Dimnah with its pasturelands, Nahalal with its pasturelands—four
cities; 36 and out of the tribe of Reuben, [o]Bezer
with its pasturelands, Jahaz with its pasturelands, 37 Kedemoth with its pasturelands, and
Mephaath with its pasturelands—four cities; 38 and out of the tribe of Gad, [o]Ramoth in
Gilead with its pasturelands, the city of refuge
for the manslayer, [p]Mahanaim with its pasturelands, 39 [p]Heshbon with its pasturelands, Jazer
with its pasturelands—four cities in all. 40 As
for the cities of the several Merarite clans, that
is, the remainder of the clans of the Levites,
those allotted to them were in all twelve cities.

41 [q]The cities of the Levites in the midst of
the possession of the people of Israel were in
all forty-eight cities with their pasturelands.
42 These cities each had its pasturelands
around it. So it was with all these cities.

43 [r]Thus the LORD gave to Israel all the land
that he swore to give to their fathers. And they
took possession of it, and they settled there.

6[z] See ver. 27-33 **7**[a] See ver. 34-40 **8**[b] ver. 3 [c] Num. 35:2; See ch. 14:3-5 **10**[d] ver. 4 **11**[e] For ver. 11-19, see 1 Chr. 6:54-60 [f] See ch. 14:13-15 [g] ch. 20:7; Luke 1:39 **13**[h] ch. 20:7 [i] ch. 10:29 **17**[j] ch. 9:3 **20**[k] For ver. 20-26, see 1 Chr. 6:66-70 **21**[l] ch. 20:7, 8 **27**[m] For ver. 27-33, see 1 Chr. 6:71-76 [l] [See ver. 21 above] **32**[l] [See ver. 21 above] **34**[n] For ver. 34-40, see 1 Chr. 6:77-81 **36**[o] ch. 20:8 **38**[o] [See ver. 36 above] [p] See ch. 13:26 **39**[p] [See ver. 38 above] **41**[q] Num. 35:7 **43**[r] Gen. 13:15; 15:18; 26:3; 28:4, 13

44 [s]And the LORD gave them rest on every side
just as he had sworn to their fathers. [t]Not one
of all their enemies had withstood them, for
[u]the LORD had given all their enemies into
their hands. 45 [v]Not one word of all the good
promises that the LORD had made to the house
of Israel had failed; all came to pass.

The Eastern Tribes Return Home

22 At that time Joshua summoned the
Reubenites and the Gadites and the
half-tribe of Manasseh, 2 and said to them,
"You have kept [w]all that Moses the servant of
the LORD commanded you [x]and have obeyed
my voice in all that I have commanded you.
3 You have not forsaken your brothers these
many days, down to this day, but have been
careful to keep the charge of the LORD your
God. 4 [y]And now the LORD your God has given
rest to your brothers, as he promised them.
Therefore turn and go to your tents in the land
where your possession lies, [z]which Moses the
servant of the LORD gave you on the other side
of the Jordan. 5 [a]Only be very careful to observe
the commandment and the law that Moses the
servant of the LORD commanded you, [b]to love
the LORD your God, and to walk in all his ways
and to keep his commandments and to cling
to him and to serve him with all your heart
and with all your soul." 6 So Joshua [c]blessed
them and sent them away, and they went to
their tents.

7 Now to the one half of the tribe of Manasseh Moses had given a possession in Bashan,
[d]but to the other half Joshua had given a possession beside their brothers in the land west
of the Jordan. And when Joshua sent them
away to their homes and blessed them, 8 he
said to them, "Go back to your tents with
much wealth and with very much livestock,
with silver, gold, bronze, and iron, and with
much clothing. [e]Divide the spoil of your enemies with your brothers." 9 So the people of
Reuben and the people of Gad and the half-
tribe of Manasseh returned home, parting
from the people of Israel at Shiloh, which is
in the land of Canaan, to go [f]to the land of
Gilead, their own land of which they had possessed themselves by command of the LORD
through Moses.

The Eastern Tribes' Altar of Witness

10 And when they came to the region of the
Jordan that is in the land of Canaan, the people of Reuben and the people of Gad and the
half-tribe of Manasseh built there an altar by
the Jordan, an altar of imposing size. 11 And the
people of Israel [g]heard it said, "Behold, the
people of Reuben and the people of Gad and
the half-tribe of Manasseh have built the
altar at the frontier of the land of Canaan, in
the region about the Jordan, on the side that
belongs to the people of Israel." 12 And when
the people of Israel heard of it, [h]the whole

22:1–9 The tribes of Reuben and Gad and the half-tribe of Manasseh had been granted land east of the Jordan, on the condition that they would help the rest of the tribes conquer Canaan (see Numbers 32; Josh. 13:8–33). Joshua 22 records the return of the eastern tribes to their land after Joshua commends them for following God's commands—though even here, Yahweh as the true deliverer is identified as the one who "has given rest to your brothers" (v. 4). Now the eastern tribes too are to take possession of their own allotted inheritance. They are exhorted to "be very careful to observe the commandment and the law," loving God with their whole heart and soul (vv. 4–6).

This pattern of instructions following deliverance echoes the treaty structure common among kings in ancient times: a great king (here, Yahweh) has delivered; now, in glad and grateful response, here is how the lesser party (here, Israel) is to live in the land. The inheritance that Yahweh has won has been granted to Israel. The message is clear: "The land is now holy; keep it that way."

22:10–34 The eastern tribes want to celebrate Yahweh's victory at the boundary of the Jordan, and the western tribes (led by the zealous priest Phinehas, grandson of Aaron) are ready to declare holy war on their brothers for setting up what they see as a rival altar to the one God commanded at Shiloh. Phinehas accuses them of breaking the covenant and bringing God's wrath upon "the whole congregation of Israel" (v. 18). Once again, covenantal solidarity is underscored, reminiscent of the Achan episode, as Phinehas himself recalls (v. 20). However, when the eastern tribes explain their covenant-honoring motives in building the altar (vv. 21–29), the western tribes stand down.

44 [s]See ch. 11:23 [t]ch. 10:8; 23:9 [u]ch. 2:24; Deut. 7:24
45 [v]ch. 23:14, 15
Chapter 22
2 [w]See Num. 32:20-22; Deut. 3:18-20 [x]ch. 1:16, 17
4 [y]See ch. 11:23 [z]See ch. 13:8
5 [a]Deut. 6:6, 17; 11:22 [b]ch. 23:11; Deut. 6:5; 10:12; 11:1, 13, 22
6 [c]ch. 14:13
7 [d]ch. 17:5
8 [e]Num. 31:27; 1 Sam. 30:24
9 [f]Num. 32:1, 26, 29
11 [g]See Deut. 13:12-15
12 [h]Judg. 20:1

assembly of the people of Israel gathered at Shiloh to make war against them.

13 Then the people of Israel sent to the people of Reuben and the people of Gad and the half-tribe of Manasseh, in the land of Gilead, [i]Phinehas the son of Eleazar the priest, 14 and with him ten chiefs, one from each of the tribal families of Israel, [j]every one of them the head of a family among the clans of Israel. 15 And they came to the people of Reuben, the people of Gad, and the half-tribe of Manasseh, in the land of Gilead, and they said to them, 16 "Thus says the whole congregation of the LORD, 'What is this breach of faith that you have committed against the God of Israel in turning away this day from following the LORD by building yourselves an altar this day [k]in rebellion against the LORD? 17 Have we not had enough of [l]the sin at Peor from which even yet we have not cleansed ourselves, and for which there came a plague upon the congregation of the LORD, 18 that you too must turn away this day from following the LORD? And if [k]you too rebel against the LORD today then tomorrow [m]he will be angry with the whole congregation of Israel. 19 But now, if the land of your possession is unclean, pass over into the LORD's land [n]where the LORD's tabernacle stands, and take for yourselves a possession among us. [o]Only do not rebel against the LORD or make us as rebels by building for yourselves an altar other than the altar of the LORD our God. 20 [p]Did not Achan the son of Zerah break faith in the matter of the devoted things, and [m]wrath fell upon all the congregation of Israel? And he did not perish alone for his iniquity.'"

21 Then the people of Reuben, the people of Gad, and the half-tribe of Manasseh said in answer to the heads of the families of Israel, 22 "The Mighty One, [q]God, the LORD! The Mighty One, God, the LORD! [r]He knows; and let Israel itself know! If it was in rebellion or in breach of faith against the LORD, do not spare us today 23 for building an altar to turn away from following the LORD. Or if we did so to offer burnt offerings or grain offerings or peace offerings on it, may the LORD himself [s]take vengeance. 24 No, but we did it from fear that [t]in time to come your children might say to our children, 'What have you to do with the LORD, the God of Israel? 25 For the LORD has made the Jordan a boundary between us and you, you people of Reuben and people of Gad. You have no portion in the LORD.' So your children might make our children cease to worship the LORD. 26 Therefore we said, 'Let us now build an altar, not for burnt offering, nor for sacrifice, 27 but to be [u]a witness between us and you, and between our generations after us, that we [v]do perform the service of the LORD in his presence with our burnt offerings and sacrifices and peace offerings, so your children will not say to our children in time to come, "You have no portion in the LORD."' 28 And we thought, 'If this should be said to us or to our descendants in time to come, we should say, "Behold, the copy of the altar of the LORD, which our fathers made, not for burnt offerings, nor for sacrifice, but to be [u]a witness between us and you."' 29 Far be it from us that we should [w]rebel against the LORD and turn away this day from following the LORD [w]by building an altar for burnt offering, grain offering, or sacrifice, other than the altar of the LORD our God that stands before his tabernacle!"

30 When [x]Phinehas the priest and the chiefs of the congregation, the heads of the families of Israel who were with him, heard the words that the people of Reuben and the people of Gad and the people of Manasseh spoke, [y]it was good in their eyes. 31 And Phinehas the son of Eleazar the priest said to the people of Reuben and the people of Gad and the people of Manasseh, "Today we know that [z]the LORD

13[i] Ex. 6:25; Num. 25:7; Judg. 20:28
14[j] Num. 1:4
16[k] ver. 18, 19; Num. 14:9; [Lev. 17:8, 9; Deut. 12:13, 14]
17[l] Num. 25:3; Deut. 4:3; Ps. 106:28
18[k] [See ver. 16 above] [m] Num. 16:22
19[n] ch. 18:1 [o] ver. 16, 18
20[p] ch. 7:1, 5 [m] [See ver. 18 above]
22[q] Deut. 10:17 [r] 1 Kgs. 8:39
23[s] Deut. 18:19; 1 Sam. 20:16
24[t] See ch. 4:6, 21

On the one hand, this episode highlights the holy zeal of both sides. On the other hand, it highlights the tension and mutual suspicion provoked by the recognition of God's holiness and their own sinfulness. Already the Israelites are a bit edgy, eager to keep faith and avoid God's sword of judgment turning on them. The whole scene exposes the restive feeling of dwelling in the land that Yahweh had consecrated and whose presence could spell life or death. Everyone—Yahweh, Joshua, and the Israelites—seem to expect a short honeymoon. Once more the superiority of the new covenant is exhibited, with no less than God himself—the Holy Spirit—as the Altar of Witness, a permanently indwelling Gift who seals our reconciliation and a deposit guaranteeing our final redemption (2 Cor. 1:22; Eph. 1:13–14).

27[u] ver. 34; ch. 24:27; Gen. 31:48 [v] Deut. 12:5, 6, 17, 18 **28**[u] [See ver. 27 above] **29**[w] See ver. 16 **30**[x] ver. 13, 14 [y] ver. 33 **31**[z] Lev. 26:11, 12

is in our midst, because you have not committed this breach of faith against the LORD. Now you have delivered the people of Israel from the hand of the LORD."

[32] Then Phinehas the son of Eleazar the priest, and the chiefs, returned from the people of Reuben and the people of Gad [a]in the land of Gilead to the land of Canaan, to the people of Israel, and brought back word to them. [33] And the report [b]was good in the eyes of the people of Israel. And the people of Israel [c]blessed God and spoke no more of making war against them to destroy the land where the people of Reuben and the people of Gad were settled. [34] The people of Reuben and the people of Gad called the altar Witness, "For," they said, [d]"it is a witness between us that the LORD is God."

Joshua's Charge to Israel's Leaders

23 A long time afterward, when the LORD had given [e]rest to Israel from all their surrounding enemies, and Joshua [f]was old and well advanced in years, [2] Joshua [g]summoned all Israel, its elders and heads, its judges and officers, and said to them, "I am now old and well advanced in years. [3] And you have seen all that the LORD your God has done to all these nations for your sake, [h]for it is the LORD your God who has fought for you. [4] Behold, [i]I have allotted to you as an inheritance for your tribes those nations that remain, along with all the nations that I have already cut off, from the Jordan to the Great Sea in the west. [5] The LORD your God [j]will push them back before you and drive them out of your sight. And you shall possess their land, [k]just as the LORD your God promised you. [6] Therefore, [l]be very strong to keep and to do all that is written in the Book of the Law of Moses, [m]turning aside from it neither to the right hand nor to the left, [7] [n]that you may not mix with these nations remaining among you [o]or make mention of the names of their gods [p]or swear by them or serve them or bow down to them, [8] [q]but you shall cling to the LORD your God just as you have done to this day. [9] [r]For the LORD has driven out before you great and strong nations. And as for you, [s]no man has been able to stand before you to this day. [10] [t]One man of you puts to flight a thousand, since it is the LORD your God [u]who fights for you, just as he promised you. [11] [v]Be very careful, therefore, to love the LORD your God. [12] For if you turn back and cling to the remnant of these nations remaining among you [w]and make marriages with them, so that you associate with them and they with you, [13] know for certain that [x]the LORD your God will no longer drive out these nations before you, [y]but they shall be a snare and a trap for you, a whip on your sides and thorns in your eyes, until you perish from off this good ground that the LORD your God has given you.

[14] "And now [z]I am about to go the way of all the earth, and you know in your hearts and souls, all of you, that [a]not one word has failed of all the good things[1] that the LORD your God promised concerning you. All have come to pass for you; not one of them has failed. [15] But just as all the good things that the LORD your God promised concerning you have been fulfilled for you, so the LORD will bring upon you [b]all the evil things, until he has destroyed you from off this good land that the LORD your God has given you, [16] if you transgress the covenant of the LORD your God, which he commanded you, and go and serve other gods and bow down to them. Then the anger of the LORD will be kindled against you, and you shall perish quickly from off the good land that he has given to you."

[1] Or *words*; also twice in verse 15

23:1–24:33 Joshua charges Israel's leaders to obey the covenant, again on the basis of God's total faithfulness to his promise (23:1–3). Their obedience will be *in response to* God's provision rather than *earning* it. The people have received their allotted inheritance. Therefore, it is time for Israel again to swear—and keep—its oath, loyally yielding to God's commands. Otherwise, the serpent will again beguile the servant "until you perish from off this good ground that the LORD your God has given you" (23:13). God has kept every word, but if Israel does not, every one of the curses God has brought on the Canaanites will fall on their head "until he has destroyed you from off this good land that the LORD your God has given you" (23:14–16).

32 [a] ver. 10, 11, 15
33 [b] ver. 30 [c] 1 Chr. 29:20; Neh. 8:6; Dan. 2:19; Luke 2:28
34 [d] ver. 27

Chapter 23
1 [e] See ch. 11:23 [f] ch. 13:1
2 [g] ch. 24:1; [Deut. 31:28; 1 Chr. 28:1]
3 [h] ch. 10:14, 42; Ex. 14:14
4 [i] See ch. 13:2-7
5 [j] ch. 13:6; Ex. 23:30; 33:2; 34:11; Deut. 11:23 [k] Num. 33:53

6 [l] ch. 1:7 [m] ch. 1:7; Deut. 5:32; 28:14 **7** [n] Ex. 23:33; Deut. 7:2, 3 [o] Ex. 23:13; [Ps. 16:4] [p] Jer. 5:7; [Zeph. 1:5] **8** [q] ch. 22:5; Deut. 10:20; 11:22; 13:4 **9** [r] ch. 13:6; Ex. 23:30; 33:2; 34:11; Deut. 11:23 [s] ch. 1:5; 10:8; 21:44 **10** [t] [Lev. 26:8; Deut. 32:30] [u] ver. 3; Ex. 14:14; Deut. 3:22 **11** [v] ch. 22:5 **12** [w] Ex. 34:16; Deut. 7:3 **13** [x] Judg. 2:3, 21 [y] Ex. 23:33; Num. 33:55; Deut. 7:16; Judg. 2:3 **14** [z] 1 Kgs. 2:2 [a] ch. 21:45 **15** [b] See Lev. 26:14-39; Deut. 28:15-68

The Covenant Renewal at Shechem

24 Joshua gathered all the tribes of Israel [c]to Shechem and [d]summoned the elders, the heads, the judges, and the officers of Israel. And [e]they presented themselves before God. 2 And Joshua said to all the people, "Thus says the LORD, the God of Israel, 'Long ago, [f]your fathers lived beyond the Euphrates,[1] Terah, the father of Abraham and of Nahor; and [g]they served other gods. 3 [h]Then I took your father Abraham from beyond the River and [i]led him through all the land of Canaan, and made his offspring many. [j]I gave him Isaac. 4 And to Isaac I gave [k]Jacob and Esau. [l]And I gave Esau the hill country of Seir to possess, [m]but Jacob and his children went down to Egypt. 5 [n]And I sent Moses and Aaron, [o]and I plagued Egypt with what I did in the midst of it, and [p]afterward I brought you out.

6 "'Then [p]I brought your fathers out of Egypt, and [q]you came to the sea. [r]And the Egyptians pursued your fathers with chariots and horsemen to the Red Sea. 7 [s]And when they cried to the LORD, [t]he put darkness between you and the Egyptians [u]and made the sea come upon them and cover them; [v]and your eyes saw what I did in Egypt. [w]And you lived in the wilderness a long time. 8 Then I brought you to the land of the Amorites, who lived on the other side of the Jordan. [x]They fought with you, and I gave them into your hand, and you took possession of their land, and I destroyed them before you. 9 [y]Then Balak the son of Zippor, king of Moab, arose and fought against Israel. [z]And he sent and invited Balaam the son of Beor to curse you, 10 [a]but I would not listen to Balaam. [a]Indeed, he blessed you. So I delivered you out of his hand. 11 [b]And you went over the Jordan and came to Jericho, [c]and the leaders of Jericho fought against you, and also [c]the Amorites, the Perizzites, the Canaanites, the Hittites, the Girgashites, the Hivites, and the Jebusites. And I gave them into your hand. 12 And I sent [d]the hornet before you, which drove them out before you, the two kings of the Amorites; it was [e]not by your sword or by your bow. 13 I gave you a land on which you had not labored [f]and cities that you had not built, and you dwell in them. You eat the fruit of vineyards and olive orchards that you did not plant.'

Choose Whom You Will Serve

14 [g]"Now therefore fear the LORD and serve him in sincerity and in faithfulness. [h]Put away the gods that your fathers served beyond the River and in Egypt, and serve the LORD. 15 [i]And if it is evil in your eyes to serve the LORD, [j]choose this day whom you will serve, whether [h]the gods your fathers served in the region beyond the River, or [k]the gods of the Amorites in whose land you dwell. [l]But as for me and my house, we will serve the LORD."

[1] Hebrew *the River*

Chapter 24
1 [c] ver. 25, 32 [d] See ch. 23:2 [e] 1 Sam. 10:19
2 [f] See Gen. 11:27-32 [g] [Gen. 31:30; 35:2]
3 [h] See Gen. 12:1-5; Acts 7:2-4 [i] Gen. 12:6 [j] Gen. 21:2, 3
4 [k] Gen. 25:24-26 [l] Gen. 36:8; Deut. 2:5 [m] Gen. 46:1, 6; Acts 7:15
5 [n] Ex. 3:10; 4:14 [o] See Ex. 7–12 [p] Ex. 12:37, 51
6 [p] [See ver. 5 above] [q] Ex. 14:2 [r] Ex. 14:9
7 [s] Ex. 14:10 [t] Ex. 14:20 [u] Ex. 14:27, 28 [v] Deut. 4:34; 29:2 [w] See ch. 5:6
8 [x] See Num. 21:21-35
9 [y] [Judg. 11:25] [z] Num. 22:5; Deut. 23:4
10 [a] Num. 23:11, 20; 24:1, 10
11 [b] ch. 3:14, 17; 4:10-13 [c] ch. 6:1; See ch. 10:1-3; 11:1-3
12 [d] Ex. 23:28; Deut. 7:20 [e] Ps. 44:3
13 [f] Deut. 6:10, 11; [ch. 11:13]
14 [g] Deut. 10:12; 1 Sam. 12:24 [h] ver. 2, 23
15 [i] 1 Kgs. 18:21; Ezek. 20:39 [j] ver. 22 [h] [See ver. 14 above] [k] Ex. 23:24, 32, 33; 34:15; Deut. 13:7; 29:18; Judg. 6:10 [l] Gen. 18:19

Chapter 24 relates the culminating covenant renewal at Shechem. As at Mount Sinai, Israel has the speaking part in the renewal of the covenant in Shechem. In both cases, the covenant presupposes that God has already made his promises and kept them.

We are also reminded that Yahweh alone is King. This is the first of the Ten Commandments and the summary of the entire covenant (Deut. 5:7; see also Matt. 6:24; 10:34–39; John 14:6; Acts 4:12; 1 Cor. 10:21–22). Again the covenant formula appears: God has given; "Now therefore fear the LORD and serve him in sincerity and faithfulness'" (Josh. 24:13–14). The people's response shows that they understand this order in the covenant: God's deliverance and gift as the basis for their response of loving obedience to his commands. They swear to do everything in his law (24:16–18).

Joshua's response to the people's pledge in 24:19–20 hardly identifies him as a great motivational leader by modern standards. On the contrary, Joshua suspects (and Yahweh already knows) that Israel will fail to keep this law. Something similar is found in Deuteronomy, where Israel is called to circumcise its own heart (Deut. 10:16) and yet God prophesies that after Israel's failure and exile he will save his people and that "'[I] will circumcise your heart and the heart of your offspring . . .'" (Deut. 30:6). Already, even "stapled" to the old covenant, the blessings of the new covenant—blessings that defy the unfaithfulness and condemnation of the human partner—are anticipated. We see this more fully in the Prophets (Jeremiah 31 and Ezekiel 36), and this internal heart-work wrought out on God's own initiative is ultimately fulfilled in Christ by his Spirit (Rom. 2:25–29; Col. 2:11).

16 Then the people answered, "Far be it from us that we should forsake the LORD to serve other gods, 17 for it is the LORD our God who brought us and our fathers up from the land of Egypt, out of the house of slavery, and who did those great signs in our sight and preserved us in all the way that we went, and among all the peoples through whom we passed. 18 And the LORD drove out before us all the peoples, the Amorites who lived in the land. Therefore we also will serve the LORD, for he is our God."

19 But Joshua said to the people, "You are not able to serve the LORD, for he is [m]a holy God. He is [n]a jealous God; [o]he will not forgive your transgressions or your sins. 20 [p]If you forsake the LORD and serve foreign gods, then [q]he will turn and do you harm and consume you, after having done you good." 21 And the people said to Joshua, "No, but we will serve the LORD." 22 Then Joshua said to the people, "You are witnesses against yourselves that [r]you have chosen the LORD, to serve him." And they said, "We are witnesses." 23 He said, "Then [s]put away the foreign gods that are among you, and incline your heart to the LORD, the God of Israel." 24 And the people said to Joshua, "The LORD our God we will serve, and his voice we will obey." 25 So Joshua [t]made a covenant with the people that day, and put in place [u]statutes and rules for them at Shechem. 26 And Joshua [v]wrote these words in the Book of the Law of God. And [w]he took a large stone and set it up there [x]under the terebinth that was by the sanctuary of the LORD. 27 And Joshua said to all the people, "Behold, [y]this stone shall be a witness against us, for [z]it has heard all the words of the LORD that he spoke to us. Therefore it shall be a witness against you, lest you deal falsely with your God." 28 So Joshua [a]sent the people away, every man to his inheritance.

Joshua's Death and Burial

29 [b]After these things Joshua the son of Nun, the servant of the LORD, died, being 110 years old. 30 And they buried him in his own inheritance at [c]Timnath-serah, which is in the hill country of Ephraim, north of the mountain of Gaash.

31 [d]Israel served the LORD all the days of

"No, but we will serve the LORD," the people respond (Josh. 24:21). Joshua solemnly confirms their response: "'You are witnesses against yourselves that you have chosen the LORD, to serve him.' And they said, 'We are witnesses'" (24:22). The swearing ceremony is complete. Israel is married to Yahweh, a gracious and holy God who will always fulfill his promises. The only thing left to do is to deposit the covenant treaty in the archive, in this case "a large stone" near "the sanctuary of the LORD" as "a witness against" them (24:25–27). Everyone returned to his own inheritance, and Joshua went to his heavenly inheritance, at 110 years of age. Here for the first time he is called "the servant of the LORD" (24:29)—a title that to this point has been reserved for Moses, and that will one day be taken up by the Messiah himself (Isa. 52:13–53:12; Acts 3:13, 26).

With the death of Joshua comes the transition from the age of promise (Genesis 15 to the exodus and conquest) to the age of fulfillment (ruling and keeping the Promised Land). Yet, like Hamlet's play-within-a-play, this story is a parable or miniature narrative of a much deeper and wider pattern of promise and fulfillment. Israel will be exiled for unfaithfulness in the land. Yet beyond exile, the greatest promise made to Abraham will be fulfilled: namely, the gift of a Seed in whom all the families of the earth will be blessed, a greater Joshua who will conquer, subdue, and rule the world in righteousness forever, and a greater priest even than zealous Phinehas, for this priest could most truly say after cleansing the temple, "Zeal for your house will consume me" (John 2:17; quoting Ps. 69:9).

Unlike what happens in Joshua, believers do not inherit merely a plot of land in a sliver of the Middle East. Rather, they "shall inherit the earth" (Matt. 5:5). Moreover, in a scandalous twist of divine grace, our everlasting inheritance is not dependent on our faithfulness. For, like Rahab, we have heard the fame of God's mighty acts and we repent of our alliance with death and hell, embracing Christ in faith as our conquering King. Because of Christ's resurrection we have been given "an inheritance that is imperishable, undefiled, and unfading, kept in heaven for you, who by God's power are being guarded through faith for a salvation ready to be revealed in the last time" (1 Pet. 1:4).

19 [m] Lev. 19:2; 1 Sam. 6:20; Ps. 99:5, 9; Isa. 5:16 [n] Ex. 20:5; Nah. 1:2 [o] Ex. 23:21
20 [p] [1 Chr. 28:9; 2 Chr. 15:2; Ezra 8:22; Isa. 1:28; 65:11, 12; Jer. 17:13] [q] ch. 23:15; Isa. 63:10; [Acts 7:42]
22 [r] ver. 15
23 [s] ver. 14; Judg. 10:16; 1 Sam. 7:3
25 [t] 2 Kgs. 11:17; 2 Chr. 23:16; Neh. 9:38 [u] Ex. 15:25
26 [v] Deut. 31:24 [w] [ch. 4:3; Gen. 28:18] [x] Gen. 35:4; Judg. 9:6
27 [y] ch. 22:27, 28, 34; Gen. 31:48, 52; Deut. 31:19, 21, 26 [z] [Deut. 32:1]
28 [a] Judg. 2:6
29 [b] For ver. 29-31, see Judg. 2:7-9
30 [c] [ch. 19:50]
31 [d] Judg. 2:7

Joshua, and all the days of the elders who outlived Joshua [e]and had known all the work that the LORD did for Israel.

32 [f]As for the bones of Joseph, which the people of Israel brought up from Egypt, they buried them at Shechem, in the piece of land [g]that Jacob bought from the sons of Hamor the father of Shechem for a hundred pieces of money.[1] It became an inheritance of the descendants of Joseph.

33 And Eleazar the son of Aaron died, and they buried him at Gibeah, the town of [h]Phinehas his son, which had been given him in [i]the hill country of Ephraim.

[1] Hebrew *for a hundred qesitah*; a unit of money of unknown value

31 [e] Deut. 11:2; 31:13
32 [f] Gen. 50:25; Ex. 13:19 [g] Gen. 33:19
33 [h] ch. 22:13 [i] ver. 30; ch. 17:15

As great as it was to be a theocratic "kingdom of priests and a holy nation" (Ex. 19:6), the experience of that privilege depended entirely on Israel's successful oath-keeping and was limited to one people. In the new covenant, however, the whole church of Jewish and Gentile believers in Christ is crowned with these precious titles (2 Pet. 3:13; see Rev. 5:9–10). The church functions as the new Jerusalem coming down out of heaven (Rev. 21:1–2). We have not come to Mount Sinai, but to Mount Zion, "the heavenly Jerusalem" (Heb. 12:18, 22). Every kingdom—including the one established at Mount Sinai—can and will be shaken, depending as it does on the love, justice, and peace required of incapable sinners. But one day everything in creation will be shaken, so that Christ's kingdom alone is left standing. "Therefore let us be grateful for receiving a kingdom that cannot be shaken, and thus let us offer to God acceptable worship, with reverence and awe, for our God is a consuming fire" (Heb. 12:25–29).

Introduction to Judges

Author and Date

The author of Judges is unknown. The events recorded in its pages took place in the period between Joshua's death and the rise of Samuel and Saul. Most of the book was likely written by David's time (1010–970 B.C.).

The Gospel in Judges

Judges and 1–2 Samuel bridge the gap from the entrance of the people of God into the Promised Land under the faithful leadership of Joshua to their expulsion from the land due to unfaithful kings in 1–2 Kings. Judges portrays the people of God languishing without good leadership. Since the conquest of the land is not complete, the book begins with the question of who will lead in battle (Judg. 1:1) and ends with the statement, "In those days there was no king in Israel. Everyone did what was right in his own eyes" (21:25). The need for a king who will lead God's people into their full inheritance is an important theme.

A larger problem looms, however. The people of God have abandoned him for pagan gods. The Lord loves his people too much to permit this ongoing rejection of their distinctive calling to be a kingdom of priests, chosen to testify to his glory among the nations. Given over to recurring cycles of oppression by foreign nations, they constantly cry to the Lord for help, and he intervenes on their behalf. Judges tells the story of these cycles (2:16–19). Despite the people's continuous rejection of God's kingship, he is moved to compassion for them. Individual judges, described as those who "saved Israel" (2:16, 18; 3:9, 31; 6:14, 15; 8:22; 10:1; 13:5), are provided by the Lord again and again. Clearly, there is a need for a king who can break this cycle of idolatry and oppression.

The fabric of unfaithfulness is woven so deeply into human nature, and the need for a savior who can free us from oppression is so pervasive, that it is tempting to make every story of Judges end with the same result: humanity is a mess; humanity needs a savior. Broadly speaking, this is correct. It is right for us to consider how these patterns in Judges prepare us for Jesus, the final King and Judge to end all judges and all kings. He will destroy the darkness of sin and restore and enable the people of God to fulfill their original role as a kingdom of priests (Ex. 19:5–6; 1 Pet. 2:9–10). No sin, no failure, no corruption, no despair, no brokenness is beyond the reach of his compassion. In light of God's faithfulness to Israel in Judges, what can we do but worship him and live for his glory?

Yet in Judges we can drill even deeper into the area of humanity and its need for redemption. The book addresses significant issues vital to the life of God's people—issues that will be integrally tied to an understanding of the need of God's grace in other portions of Scripture. Among many such issues we note,

- the relationship of the believer to culture and the ongoing need to be united to the true Vine (John 15:1–4);
- the importance of telling the story of God's redemption to following generations (Judg. 2:10);
- the continuing struggle with cycles of sin and its oppression and the Savior who destroys sin's condemnation (Rom. 7:24–8:1);
- the subtlety of idolatry and compromise and the seriousness of drifting from the Lord (Jude 17–22);
- the tendency of human leaders to pursue their own ends rather than God's end, requiring his intervention and care for the good of his flock (Luke 22:25–27);
- the willingness and even delight of God, who is much larger, greater, and higher than our sins and shortcomings, to use fallen, unwilling, weak, and frail people—even as leaders—to advance his kingdom (1 Cor. 1:27–31);
- the grace of God made evident in his plan to use the people of his calling (i.e., the church), who are so often under-resourced (from a human standpoint), so that we trust in the One with all resources (2 Cor. 1:8–10).

The failures of both people and judges are so significant that they urge us to long for the hero who will never fail. Cut off from God's kingship, the people of God are left with only private religion and personal ambition. God is the king, however, and will not long tolerate seeing his people destroy themselves. The people of God are never beyond the reach of his grace. Israel in Judges is in bad shape, but a new day is dawning when God will provide, from the line of David, King Jesus, the king of his choosing.

Outline

I. The Roots of Israel's Unfaithfulness (1:1–3:6)

II. The Downward Spiral of Israel's Unfaithfulness (3:7–16:31)

III. The Depths of Israel's Unfaithfulness (17:1–21:25)

Judges

The Continuing Conquest of Canaan

1 After the death of Joshua, the people of
Israel [a]inquired of the LORD, [b]“Who shall
go up first for us against the Canaanites, to
fight against them?” 2 The LORD said, “Judah
shall go up; behold, I have given the land into
his hand.” 3 And Judah said to Simeon his
brother, “Come up with me into the territory
allotted to me, that we may fight against the
Canaanites. [c]And I likewise will go with you
into the territory allotted to you.” So Simeon
went with him. 4 Then Judah went up and the
LORD gave the Canaanites and the Perizzites
into their hand, and they defeated 10,000 of
them at Bezek. 5 They found Adoni-bezek at
Bezek and fought against him and defeated
the Canaanites and the Perizzites. 6 Adoni-
bezek fled, but they pursued him and caught
him and cut off his thumbs and his big toes.
7 And Adoni-bezek said, “Seventy kings with
their thumbs and their big toes cut off [d]used to
pick up scraps under my table. [e]As I have done,
so God has repaid me.” And they brought him
to Jerusalem, and he died there.

8 [f]And the men of Judah fought against
Jerusalem and captured it and struck it with
the edge of the sword and set the city on fire.
9 And afterward the men of Judah went down
to fight against the Canaanites who lived in
[g]the hill country, in the Negeb, and in [g]the lowland. 10 [h]And Judah went against the Canaanites
who lived in Hebron [i](now the name of Hebron
was formerly Kiriath-arba), and they defeated
[j]Sheshai and Ahiman and Talmai.

11 From there they went against the inhabitants of Debir. The name of Debir was formerly Kiriath-sepher. 12 And Caleb said, “He
who attacks Kiriath-sepher and captures
it, I will give him Achsah my daughter for
a wife.” 13 And Othniel the son of Kenaz,
[k]Caleb’s younger brother, captured it. And
he gave him Achsah his daughter for a wife.
14 When she came to him, she urged him to
ask her father for a field. And she dismounted
from her donkey, and Caleb said to her, “What
do you want?” 15 She said to him, “Give me a
blessing. Since you have set me in the land
of the Negeb, give me also springs of water.”
And Caleb gave her the upper springs and the
lower springs.

16 And the descendants of the [l]Kenite, Moses’
father-in-law, went up with the people of
Judah [m]from the city of palms into the wilderness of Judah, which lies in the Negeb
near [n]Arad, [o]and they went and settled with
the people. 17 [p]And Judah went with Simeon
his brother, and they defeated the Canaanites
who inhabited Zephath and devoted it to
destruction. So the name of the city was called
[q]Hormah.[1] 18 Judah also [r]captured Gaza with its
territory, and Ashkelon with its territory, and
Ekron with its territory. 19 [p]And the LORD was

[1] *Hormah* means *utter destruction*

1:1–2:10 From beginning to end, Judges establishes Israel’s need for godly saviors and the need for God to provide them. In light of Joshua’s death, the question arises: Who will lead Israel in battle against the Canaanites? (1:1). Likewise, Judges ends with the refrain that there is no king in Israel (21:25).

At this early point in Judges, God does not provide an individual savior or king but appoints the tribe of Judah to take the lead (1:2; cf. 20:18). The appointment of Judah looks forward to the kingship of David and ultimately of David’s Greater Son, the Lord Jesus Christ, both of whom arise from Judah (Gen. 49:10; 1 Sam. 17:12; 18:16; Zech. 12:7; Matt. 1:1–6; 2 Tim. 2:8).

Chapter 1
1 [a]Num. 27:21; 1 Sam. 22:10; 2 Sam. 2:1 [b]ch. 20:18
3 [c]ver. 17
7 [d][Luke 16:21] [e][Lev. 24:19; 1 Sam. 15:33]
8 [f][Josh. 15:63]
9 [g]Josh. 9:1; 11:2, 16; 12:8
10 [h]For ver. 10-15, see Josh. 15:13-19 [i]Josh. 14:15; 15:13 [j]Num. 13:22; Josh. 15:14
13 [k]ch. 3:9
16 [l]ch. 4:11, 17; 1 Sam. 15:6 [m]Deut. 34:3 [n]Num. 21:1

[o]See Num. 10:29-32 **17** [p]ver. 3 [q]Num. 21:3 **18** [r][ch. 3:3; Josh. 11:22] **19** [p][See ver. 17 above]

with Judah, and he took possession of the [s]hill
country, but he could not drive out the inhabitants of the plain because they had [t]chariots
of iron. 20 [u]And Hebron was given to Caleb,
as Moses had said. And he drove out from it
[v]the three sons of Anak. 21 But the people of
Benjamin did not drive out the Jebusites who
lived in Jerusalem, [w]so the Jebusites have lived
with the people of Benjamin in Jerusalem to
this day.

22 The house of Joseph also went up against
Bethel, [x]and the LORD was with them. 23 And
the house of Joseph scouted out Bethel.
([y]Now the name of the city was formerly Luz.)
24 And the spies saw a man coming out of the
city, and they said to him, "Please show us the
way into the city, [z]and we will deal kindly with
you." 25 And he showed them the way into the
city. And they struck the city with the edge
of the sword, but they let the man and all his
family go. 26 And the man went to [a]the land of
the Hittites and built a city and called its name
Luz. That is its name to this day.

Failure to Complete the Conquest

27 [b]Manasseh did not drive out the inhabitants of Beth-shean and its villages, or
Taanach and its villages, or the inhabitants
of Dor and its villages, or the inhabitants of
Ibleam and its villages, or the inhabitants of
Megiddo and its villages, for the Canaanites
persisted in dwelling in that land. 28 When
Israel grew strong, they put the Canaanites
to forced labor, but did not drive them out
completely.

29 [c]And Ephraim did not drive out the Canaanites who lived in Gezer, so the Canaanites
lived in Gezer among them.

30 Zebulun did not drive out the inhabitants
of Kitron, or the inhabitants of [d]Nahalol, so
the Canaanites lived among them, but became
subject to forced labor.

31 [e]Asher did not drive out the inhabitants of
Acco, or the inhabitants of Sidon or of Ahlab
or of Achzib or of Helbah or of Aphik or of
Rehob, 32 so the Asherites lived among the
Canaanites, the inhabitants of the land, for
they did not drive them out.

33 Naphtali did not drive out the inhabitants
of [f]Beth-shemesh, or the inhabitants of Beth-
anath, so they lived among the Canaanites,
the inhabitants of the land. Nevertheless, the
inhabitants of Beth-shemesh and of Beth-
anath became subject to forced labor for them.

34 [g]The Amorites pressed the people of Dan
back into the hill country, for they did not
allow them to come down to the plain. 35 The
Amorites persisted in dwelling in Mount
Heres, [h]in Aijalon, and in Shaalbim, but the
hand of the house of Joseph rested heavily on
them, and they became subject to forced labor.
36 And the border of the Amorites ran from [i]the
ascent of Akrabbim, from Sela and upward.

Israel's Disobedience

2 Now the angel of the LORD went up from
Gilgal to [j]Bochim. And he said, "I brought
you up from Egypt and brought you into
the land that I swore to give to your fathers.
I said, [k]'I will never break my covenant with
you, 2 [l]and you shall make no covenant with
the inhabitants of this land; [m]you shall break
down their altars.' But you have not obeyed
my voice. What is this you have done? 3 So now
I say, [n]I will not drive them out before you, but
they shall become [o]thorns in your sides, and
their gods shall be a snare to you." 4 As soon
as the angel of the LORD spoke these words
to all the people of Israel, the people lifted up
their voices and wept. 5 And they called the

Judah's external success (Judg. 1:4–10, 11, 17), however, conceals compromise. The ongoing refrain that Israel's tribes did not drive out the inhabitants of the land increases throughout the chapter (1:19, 21, 27, 28, 29, 30, 31). Ultimately, this failure leads to the people of God living among Canaanites. Subsequently, Israel is negatively influenced, spiritually undermined, and militarily attacked (1:30–32; cf. 3:5–6). In the case of Dan, the tribe is actually pushed out of its inheritance (1:34).

As with our forefathers in the faith, we are called to be a people separate from the world but dedicated to testifying about the Lord in the world (1 Pet. 2:9–10). Just as all have sinned and fall short of the glory of God (Rom. 3:23), so all the tribes of Israel falter in the mission God gave them at this time in redemptive history. External success may lead us to trust in our own strength and leave us unprepared for the subtle compromises that lead to divided loyalty. Initial disobedience provides the soil in which further unfaithfulness takes root.

19 [s]See ver. 9 [t]Josh. 17:16, 18
20 [u]Num. 14:24; Deut. 1:36; Josh. 14:9, 13; 15:13, 14 [v]ver. 10
21 [w][Josh. 15:63]
22 [x]ver. 19
23 [y]Gen. 28:19; 35:6; 48:3; Josh. 18:13
24 [z]Josh. 2:12, 14
26 [a]Josh. 1:4
27 [b]For ver. 27, 28, see Josh. 17:11-13
29 [c]Josh. 16:10; 1 Kgs. 9:16
30 [d][Josh. 19:15; 21:35]
31 [e]For ver. 31, 32, see Josh. 19:24-30
33 [f]For ver. 33, see Josh. 19:32-39
34 [g][Josh. 19:47, 48]
35 [h]Josh. 19:42
36 [i]Num. 34:4; Josh. 15:3 **Chapter 2** **1** [j]ver. 5 [k]Gen. 17:7; Ex. 6:4; Deut. 31:16 **2** [l]Deut. 7:2 [m]Deut. 12:3 **3** [n]ver. 21 [o]Num. 33:55; Josh. 23:13

name of that place Bochim.[1] And they sacrificed there to the LORD.

The Death of Joshua

6 When Joshua dismissed the people, the
people of Israel went each to his inheritance to
take possession of the land. 7 [p]And the people
served the LORD all the days of Joshua, and
all the days of the elders who outlived Joshua,
who had seen all the great work that the LORD
had done for Israel. 8 And Joshua the son of
Nun, the servant of the LORD, died at the age
of 110 years. 9 And they buried him within the
boundaries of [q]his inheritance in Timnath-
heres, [r]in the hill country of Ephraim, north of
the mountain of Gaash. 10 And all that generation also were gathered to their fathers. And
there arose another generation after them who
did not know the LORD or the work that he
had done for Israel.

Israel's Unfaithfulness

11 [s]And the people of Israel did what was evil
in the sight of the LORD and served the Baals.
12 [t]And they abandoned the LORD, the God of
their fathers, who had brought them out of
the land of Egypt. [u]They went after other gods,
from among the gods of the peoples who were
around them, and [v]bowed down to them. [w]And
they provoked the LORD to anger. 13 They abandoned the LORD [x]and served the Baals and the
Ashtaroth. 14 [y]So the anger of the LORD was
kindled against Israel, and he [z]gave them over
to plunderers, who plundered them. [a]And he
sold them into the hand of their surrounding
enemies, [b]so that they could no longer withstand their enemies. 15 Whenever they marched
out, the hand of the LORD was against them
for harm, as the LORD had warned, [c]and as
the LORD had sworn to them. And they were
in terrible distress.

The LORD Raises Up Judges

16 [d]Then the LORD raised up judges, [e]who
saved them out of the hand of those who
plundered them. 17 Yet they did not listen to
their judges, for [f]they whored after other gods
and bowed down to them. [g]They soon turned
aside from the way in which their fathers
had walked, who had obeyed the commandments of the LORD, and they did not do so.
18 Whenever the LORD raised up judges for
them, [h]the LORD was with the judge, and he
saved them from the hand of their enemies all
the days of the judge. [i]For the LORD was moved
to pity by [j]their groaning because of those who
afflicted and oppressed them. 19 But [k]when-
ever the judge died, they turned back and were
more corrupt than their fathers, going after
other gods, serving them and bowing down to
them. They did not drop any of their practices
or their stubborn ways. 20 [l]So the anger of the
LORD was kindled against Israel, and he said,
"Because this people [m]have transgressed my
covenant that I commanded their fathers and
have not obeyed my voice, 21 [n]I will no longer

[1] *Bochim* means *weepers*

2:11–15 The statement that Israel did what was evil in the sight of the Lord (v. 11) is further defined as abandoning the Lord and pursing other gods (vv. 12–13). This evaluation occurs at the introduction to each major judge in the book (3:7, 12; 4:1; 6:1; 10:6; 13:1), preparing us for the later evaluation of various tribes (1 Kings 14:22) and kings (1 Kings 11:6; 15:26, 34; 16:25; 22:52; 2 Kings 3:2; 8:18; etc.). It is the task of the former generation to tell the story of God's work to later generations (Judg. 2:10; Ps. 78:4–8).

For God's people today, this supremely means passing on the story of God's greatest work—the gospel (cf. 1 Cor. 15:3–4; 2 Tim. 2:1–2).

2:16–19 The Lord provides judges and saviors. These key verses equate Israel's idolatry with spiritual whoredom (v. 17). Throughout Judges, a persistent cycle of sin, subjugation, and supplication is met with the Lord's unfailing provision of salvation. Mercy keeps following failure.

Astonishingly, God's compassion for his people extends deeper than the failure of his people even when those failures are self-inflicted. The ultimate Judge and Savior, Jesus (Matt. 1:21), represents this grace in its ultimate form, interrupting the ongoing cycle of sin in the lives of his people throughout time and throughout the world. There is no sin, no failure, and no act of unfaithfulness that is beyond the reach of Christ's redemptive love. Having received from God such undeserved assurances of forgiveness and reconciliation, we are now called to respond with wholehearted obedience to him and to extend his grace to others (2 Cor. 5:18–21).

7 [p] For ver. 7-9, see Josh. 24:29-31
9 [q] Josh. 19:50 [r] Josh. 24:33
11 [s] ch. 3:7; 4:1; 6:1; 10:6; 13:1
12 [t] Deut. 31:16 [u] [Deut. 6:14] [v] ver. 17, 19; [Ex. 20:5] [w] Deut. 31:29
13 [x] ch. 3:7; 10:6; Ps. 106:36; [1 Sam. 7:4]
14 [y] ver. 20 [z] 2 Kgs. 17:20 [a] ch. 3:8; 4:2; [Deut. 32:30; 1 Sam. 12:9] [b] Lev. 26:37; Josh. 7:12, 13
15 [c] See Lev. 26:14-46; Deut. 28:15-68
16 [d] ch. 3:9, 15; 1 Sam. 12:11; Acts 13:20 [e] ch. 3:31; 10:1, 12, 13; 12:2, 3; 13:5; [ch. 3:9; Neh. 9:27]
17 [f] ch. 8:33; Ex. 34:15 [g] Deut. 9:12
18 [h] [Josh. 1:5] [i] Gen. 6:6; Deut. 32:36; Ps. 106:45; Jer. 18:8; 26:3; [Num. 23:19] [j] Ex. 2:24; 6:5
19 [k] [ch. 3:12; 4:1; 6:1; 8:33]
20 [l] ver. 14 [m] Deut. 17:2; Josh. 23:16
21 [n] ver. 3; Josh. 23:13

drive out before them any of the nations that Joshua left when he died, 22 in order [o]to test Israel by them, whether they will take care to walk in the way of the LORD as their fathers did, or not." 23 So the LORD left those nations, not driving them out quickly, and he did not give them into the hand of Joshua.

3 [p]Now these are the nations that the LORD left, to test Israel by them, that is, all in Israel who had not experienced all the wars in Canaan. 2 It was only in order that the generations of the people of Israel might know war, to teach war to those who had not known it before. 3 These are the nations: [q]the five lords of the Philistines and all the Canaanites and the Sidonians and the Hivites who lived on Mount Lebanon, from Mount Baal-hermon as far as Lebo-hamath. 4 They were for [r]the testing of Israel, to know whether Israel would obey the commandments of the LORD, which he commanded their fathers by the hand of Moses. 5 So the people of Israel lived [s]among the Canaanites, the Hittites, the Amorites, the Perizzites, the Hivites, and the Jebusites. 6 [t]And their daughters they took to themselves for wives, and their own daughters they gave to their sons, and they served their gods.

Othniel

7 [u]And the people of Israel did what was evil in the sight of the LORD. They forgot the LORD their God and served the Baals and [v]the Asheroth. 8 Therefore the anger of the LORD was kindled against Israel, [w]and he sold them into the hand of [x]Cushan-rishathaim king of Mesopotamia. And the people of Israel served Cushan-rishathaim eight years. 9 But when the people of Israel [y]cried out to the LORD, the LORD raised up a [z]deliverer for the people of Israel, who saved them, [a]Othniel the son of Kenaz, Caleb's younger brother. 10 [b]The Spirit of the LORD was upon him, and he judged Israel. He went out to war, and the LORD gave Cushan-rishathaim king of Mesopotamia into his hand. And his hand prevailed over Cushan-rishathaim. 11 [c]So the land had rest forty years. Then Othniel the son of Kenaz died.

Ehud

12 [d]And the people of Israel again did what was evil in the sight of the LORD, and the LORD strengthened Eglon [e]the king of Moab against Israel, because they had done what was evil in the sight of the LORD. 13 He gathered to himself the Ammonites and the [f]Amalekites, and went and defeated Israel. And they took possession of [g]the city of palms. 14 And the people of Israel served Eglon the king of Moab eighteen years.

15 Then the people of Israel [h]cried out to the LORD, and the LORD raised up for them [h]a deliverer, Ehud, the son of Gera, the Benjaminite, [i]a left-handed man. The people of Israel sent tribute by him to Eglon the king of Moab. 16 And Ehud made for himself a sword with two edges, a cubit[1] in length, and he bound it on his right thigh under his clothes. 17 And he presented the tribute to Eglon king of Moab. Now Eglon was a very fat man. 18 And when Ehud had finished presenting the tribute, he sent away the people who carried the tribute. 19 But he himself turned back [j]at the idols near Gilgal and said, "I have a secret message for you, O king." And

[1] A *cubit* was about 18 inches or 45 centimeters

22[o] ch. 3:1, 4; Ex. 15:25; [Deut. 8:2, 16; 13:3]
Chapter 3
1[p] ver. 4; ch. 2:21, 22
3[q] See Josh. 13:2-6
4[r] ver. 1
5[s] Ex. 3:8; Ps. 106:35
6[t] [Ex. 34:16; Deut. 7:3; Ezra 9:12]
7[u] ch. 2:11-13 [v] ch. 6:25; Ex. 34:13
8[w] ch. 2:14 [x] Hab. 3:7
9[y] ver. 15; ch. 4:3; 6:7; 10:10 [z] ver. 15; ch. 2:16; Neh. 9:27 [a] ch. 1:13
10[b] ch. 6:34; 11:29; 13:25; 14:6, 19; 15:14
11[c] [ver. 30; ch. 5:31; 8:28; Josh. 11:23]
12[d] ch. 2:19 [e] 1 Sam. 12:9
13[f] ch. 6:33; Ps. 83:7 [g] ch. 1:16; Deut. 34:3
15[h] See ver. 9 [i] ch. 20:16; [1 Chr. 12:2] **19**[j] ver. 26; [Josh. 4:20]

3:7–11 Othniel provides a "lived illustration" of the cycles of oppression and salvation (2:11–19). God's people are not left to chance. It is the Lord who directs their corporate life. Just as Judah was the first tribe to lead (1:2), so the first judge is from Judah. The people are handed over to a foreign oppressor (3:8) and then the oppressor is given into the hand of Caleb's nephew, Othniel (v. 10; cf. 1:12–14). This exchange of power happens because the Spirit of the Lord comes upon Othniel. The Spirit's actions increase throughout the book as evidence and display of God's power and faithfulness on behalf of a weak and errant people (e.g., 6:34; 11:29; 13:25; 14:6, 19; 15:14).

The apostle James states that "we all stumble in many ways" (James 3:2). It is tempting to think that difficulty and oppression in the believer's life always follow disobedience as punishment. However, consider the desperate situation in Judges. The people abandon and forget God repeatedly and as a way of life, but he does not abandon them. While consequences of their sin are used to instruct, so too is unmerited mercy. God graciously rescues and patiently teaches his people that genuine life and lasting peace are found only in service to their true King.

he commanded, "Silence." And all his attendants went out from his presence. 20 And
Ehud came to him as he was sitting alone
in his [k]cool roof chamber. [l]And Ehud said,
"I have a message from God for you." And he
arose from his seat. 21 And Ehud reached with
his left hand, took the sword from his right
thigh, and thrust it into his belly. 22 And the
hilt also went in after the blade, and the fat
closed over the blade, for he did not pull the
sword out of his belly; and the dung came out.
23 Then Ehud went out into the porch[1] and
closed the doors of the roof chamber behind
him [m]and locked them.

24 When he had gone, the servants came,
and when they saw that the doors of the roof
chamber were locked, they thought, [n]"Surely
he is relieving himself in the closet of the cool
chamber." 25 And they waited till they were
embarrassed. But when he still did not open
the doors of the roof chamber, they took the
key and opened them, and there lay their lord
dead on the floor.

26 Ehud escaped while they delayed, and
he passed beyond [o]the idols and escaped to
Seirah. 27 When he arrived, [p]he sounded the
trumpet in [q]the hill country of Ephraim.
Then the people of Israel went down with
him from the hill country, and he was their
leader. 28 And he said to them, "Follow after
me, [r]for the LORD has given your enemies the
Moabites into your hand." So they went down
after him and seized [s]the fords of the Jordan
against the Moabites and did not allow anyone
to pass over. 29 And they killed at that time
about 10,000 of the Moabites, all strong, able-
bodied men; not a man escaped. 30 So Moab
was subdued that day under the hand of Israel.
[t]And the land had rest for eighty years.

Shamgar

31 After him was [u]Shamgar the son of Anath,
who killed 600 of the Philistines [v]with an
oxgoad, and he also [w]saved Israel.

Deborah and Barak

4 [x]And the people of Israel again did what
was evil in the sight of the LORD after
Ehud died. 2 And the LORD [y]sold them into the
hand of [z]Jabin king of Canaan, who reigned
in [z]Hazor. The commander of his army was
[a]Sisera, who lived in [b]Harosheth-hagoyim.
3 Then the people of Israel [c]cried out to the
LORD for help, for he had [d]900 chariots of iron
and he oppressed the people of Israel cruelly
for twenty years.

4 Now Deborah, a prophetess, the wife of
Lappidoth, was judging Israel at that time.
5 She used to sit under the palm of Deborah
between Ramah and Bethel in [e]the hill country of Ephraim, and the people of Israel
came up to her for judgment. 6 She sent and
summoned [f]Barak the son of Abinoam from
[g]Kedesh-naphtali and said to him, "Has not
the LORD, the God of Israel, commanded you,
'Go, gather your men at Mount [h]Tabor, taking 10,000 from the people of Naphtali and
the people of Zebulun. 7 And I will draw out
Sisera, the general of Jabin's army, to meet you
by [i]the river Kishon with his chariots and his
troops, [j]and I will give him into your hand'?"
8 Barak said to her, "If you will go with me,
I will go, but if you will not go with me, I will
not go." 9 And she said, "I will surely go with
you. Nevertheless, the road on which you are

[1] The meaning of the Hebrew word is uncertain

3:12–30 As Judah and Benjamin act first in the book (1:18–21), so the first judges arise from Judah (Othniel) and Benjamin (Ehud) and they are given the explicit title "deliverer" (3:9, 15). This prepares us for the final conflict in the book, led by the tribe of Judah against Benjamin (20:18). From these tribes will arise the first monarchs of Israel and the conflict between Saul the Benjaminite and David the Judahite. This trajectory reverberates into the New Testament as the great Davidic king, Jesus, from the tribe of Judah, overcomes (and redeems!) the persecutor Saul (Paul), the Benjaminite (Acts 9:3–9; cf. Rom. 11:1).

Rejoice that God uses us in his mission to the world. Judges constantly recounts unexpected persons and their actions delivering God's people in unexpected ways. Ehud, a left-handed Benjaminite ("son of the right hand") straps his sword to his right thigh (Judg. 3:16). This "doubled-edged" sword is God's "message" delivered to the oppressor (vv. 20–21; cf. Heb. 4:12). Like the gospel, this message from Ehud delivers God's people in a surprising way.

20 [k]Amos 3:15 [l][2 Sam. 20:9, 10]
23 [m][2 Sam. 13:17, 18]
24 [n]1 Sam. 24:3
26 [o]ver. 19
27 [p]ch. 6:34; 1 Sam. 13:3 [q]See Josh. 24:33
28 [r]ch. 4:7, 14; 7:9, 15; 1 Sam. 17:47; 2 Chr. 16:8; [1 Kgs. 22:12, 15] [s]ch. 12:5; Josh. 2:7; [ch. 7:24]
30 [t]ver. 11
31 [u]ch. 5:6 [v][ch. 5:8; 1 Sam. 13:19, 22] [w]See ch. 2:16

Chapter 4
1 [x]See ch. 2:19
2 [y]ch. 2:14 [z][Josh. 11:1, 10] [a]1 Sam. 12:9; Ps. 83:9 [b]ver. 13, 16
3 [c]See ch. 3:9 [d]ver. 13; [ch. 1:19]

5 [e]See Josh. 24:33 **6** [f]Heb. 11:32 [g]Josh. 19:37 [h]ch. 8:18 **7** [i]ver. 13; ch. 5:21; 1 Kgs. 18:40; Ps. 83:9 [j]See ch. 3:28

going will not lead to your glory, for the LORD will [k]sell Sisera into the hand of a woman." Then Deborah arose and went with Barak to Kedesh. 10 And Barak called out [l]Zebulun and Naphtali to Kedesh. And 10,000 men went up at his heels, and Deborah went up with him.

11 Now Heber [m]the Kenite had separated from the Kenites, the descendants of [n]Hobab the father-in-law of Moses, and had pitched his tent as far away as the oak in [o]Zaanannim, which is near Kedesh.

12 When Sisera was told that Barak the son of Abinoam had gone up to Mount Tabor, 13 Sisera called out all his chariots, [p]900 chariots of iron, and all the men who were with him, from Harosheth-hagoyim to the river Kishon. 14 And Deborah said to Barak, "Up! For this is the day in which [q]the LORD has given Sisera into your hand. [r]Does not the LORD go out before you?" So Barak went down from Mount Tabor with 10,000 men following him. 15 [s]And the LORD routed Sisera and all his chariots and all his army before Barak by the edge of the sword. And Sisera got down from his chariot and fled away on foot. 16 And Barak pursued the chariots and the army to Harosheth-hagoyim, and all the army of Sisera fell by the edge of the sword; not a man was left.

17 But Sisera fled away on foot to the tent of Jael, the wife of Heber the Kenite, for there was peace between Jabin the king of Hazor and the house of Heber the Kenite. 18 And Jael came out to meet Sisera and said to him, "Turn aside, my lord; turn aside to me; do not be afraid." So he turned aside to her into the tent, and she covered him with a rug. 19 And he said to her, "Please give me a little water to drink, for I am thirsty." So she opened [t]a skin of milk and gave him a drink and covered him. 20 And he said to her, "Stand at the opening of the tent, and if any man comes and asks you, 'Is anyone here?' say, 'No.'" 21 But Jael the wife of Heber took a tent peg, and took a hammer in her hand. Then she went softly to him and drove the peg into his temple until it went down into the ground while he was lying fast asleep from weariness. So he died. 22 And behold, as Barak was pursuing Sisera, Jael went out to meet him and said to him, "Come, and I will show you the man whom you are seeking." So he went in to her tent, and there lay Sisera dead, with the tent peg in his temple.

23 [u]So on that day God subdued Jabin the king of Canaan before the people of Israel. 24 And the hand of the people of Israel pressed harder and harder against Jabin the king of Canaan, until they destroyed Jabin king of Canaan.

The Song of Deborah and Barak

5 [v]Then sang Deborah and Barak the son of Abinoam on that day:

2 "That the leaders took the lead in Israel,
that [w]the people offered themselves
willingly,
bless the LORD!

3 "Hear, O kings; give ear, O princes;
to the LORD I will sing;
I will make melody to the LORD, the
God of Israel.

9 [k]See ch. 2:14
10 [l]ch. 5:18
11 [m]ch. 1:16 [n]Num. 10:29 [o]Josh. 19:33
13 [p]ver. 3
14 [q]ver. 7 [r]Deut. 9:3; 2 Sam. 5:24; Ps. 68:7; Isa. 52:12
15 [s]ver. 23; Ps. 83:9; [Josh. 10:10]
19 [t]ch. 5:25
23 [u]ver. 15
Chapter 5
1 [v][Ex. 15:1]
2 [w]ver. 9; [2 Chr. 17:16]

4:12–16 Deborah's gender marks her out as unique among the judges. Like the final judge Samuel, she also combines the roles of prophet and judge. Rather than leading in battle, her ministry as judge entails judicial decisions among the Israelites (vv. 4–5). As prophetess, Deborah delivers a word from God to Barak that he should lead in battle (vv. 6–7). Barak's reluctance to trust God's promise of victory (v. 8) results in glory being given not to Barak or Deborah but to Jael—again, God effects rescue from a surprising source (vv. 9, 17–22). God provides in ways that are not in accord with normal human strengths or expectations.

The literary structure of chapter 4 highlights the central section of verses 12–16, and the focus of this central section is found at verse 14, which bears the gospel implication for the passage: God fights for his people. Failure to trust in God's defense was one of Israel's abiding public sins (cf. 1 Sam. 8:4–8). The profound question of the pious Deborah is addressed not simply to Barak but to believers in all ages: "Does not the LORD go out before you?" (Judg. 4:14). We remember that this grace of God providing what is needed for his people's rescue is similarly displayed through Jesus Christ, our ultimate deliverer (Rev. 19:11–16). He has gone out before us.

5:1–31 Israel sings praise to God for his deliverance (vv. 1, 3, 10–11) but also blesses the Lord for providing leaders who "offered themselves willingly" (vv. 2, 9) and for entire tribes who risk their lives for the sake of God's people (v. 18). We sing since God is

4 “LORD, [x]when you went out from Seir,
when you marched from the region of Edom,
[y]the earth trembled
and the heavens dropped,
yes, the clouds dropped water.
5 The mountains [z]quaked before the LORD,
[a]even Sinai before the LORD, the God of Israel.

6 “In the days of [b]Shamgar, son of Anath,
in the days of [c]Jael, [d]the highways were abandoned,
and travelers kept to the byways.
7 The villagers ceased in Israel;
they ceased to be until I arose;
I, Deborah, arose as a mother in Israel.
8 [e]When new gods were chosen,
then war was in the gates.
[f]Was shield or spear to be seen
among forty thousand in Israel?
9 My heart goes out to the commanders of Israel
who [g]offered themselves willingly among the people.
Bless the LORD.

10 “Tell of it, [h]you who ride on white donkeys,
you who sit on rich carpets[1]
and you who walk by the way.
11 To the sound of musicians[2] at the watering places,
there they repeat the righteous triumphs of the LORD,
the righteous triumphs of his villagers in Israel.

“Then down to the gates marched the people of the LORD.

12 [i]“Awake, awake, Deborah!
Awake, awake, break out in a song!
Arise, Barak, [j]lead away your captives,
O son of Abinoam.
13 Then down marched the remnant of the noble;
the people of the LORD marched down for me against the mighty.
14 From [k]Ephraim their root [l]they marched down into the valley,[3]
following you, Benjamin, with your kinsmen;
from [m]Machir marched down the commanders,
and from Zebulun those who bear the lieutenant's[4] staff;
15 the princes of Issachar came with Deborah,
and Issachar faithful to [n]Barak;
into the valley they rushed at his heels.
Among the clans of Reuben
there were great searchings of heart.
16 Why did you sit still [o]among the sheepfolds,
to hear the whistling for the flocks?
Among the clans of Reuben
there were great searchings of heart.
17 [p]Gilead stayed beyond the Jordan;
[q]and Dan, why did he stay with the ships?
[r]Asher sat still [s]at the coast of the sea,
staying by his landings.
18 [t]Zebulun is a people who risked their lives to the death;
[t]Naphtali, too, on the heights of the field.

19 “The kings came, they fought;
then fought the kings of Canaan,

[1] The meaning of the Hebrew word is uncertain; it may connote *saddle blankets* [2] Or *archers*; the meaning of the Hebrew word is uncertain [3] Septuagint; Hebrew *in Amalek* [4] Hebrew *commander's*

our warrior, but we are not mere observers of the conflict. God chooses to make us participants in his righteous triumphs in the world (v. 11), even when circumstances are most grim (vv. 6–8).

Final rejoicing is reserved for the heroine Jael, who exemplifies God's use of weakness to defeat strength (vv. 24–27). The crushing of Sisera's head reveals the destiny of all the forces of evil arrayed against God's people (vv. 28, 31; cf. Gen. 3:15). This culminates in the ministry of Jesus Christ, who offered his life willingly and, in the weakness of the cross, defeated the great deceiver (Rom. 16:20; 1 Cor. 1:26–31; Col. 2:15). Following a crucified Savior, we too are heartened even in our weaknesses. For we know that our weaknesses are the catalyst for and not an obstacle to the Lord's strength and grace (2 Cor. 6:10; 12:9–10; 13:4).

4[x] Deut. 33:2; [Ps. 68:7] [y] 2 Sam. 22:8; Ps. 18:7; 68:8; 77:18; Nah. 1:5; Hab. 3:10
5[z] Isa. 64:1, 3 [a] [Ex. 19:18; Deut. 4:11]
6[b] ch. 3:31 [c] ch. 4:17 [d] Lev. 26:22; Isa. 33:8; Lam. 1:4
8[e] ch. 2:12, 17; Deut. 32:16 [f] [1 Sam. 13:19, 22]
9[g] ver. 2
10[h] [ch. 10:4; 12:14; Zech. 9:9]
12[i] Ps. 57:8 [j] Ps. 68:18; Eph. 4:8
14[k] ch. 3:27; 12:15 [l] [ch. 12:15] [m] Num. 32:39, 40
15[n] ch. 4:14
16[o] Gen. 49:14; Ps. 68:13; [Num. 32:1]
17[p] See Josh. 13:24-28 [q] [Josh. 19:46] [r] [Josh. 19:29, 31] [s] Gen. 49:13 **18**[t] ch. 4:10

at [u]Taanach, by the waters of [v]Megiddo;
[w]they got no spoils of silver.
20 [x]From heaven the stars fought,
from their courses they fought
against Sisera.
21 [y]The torrent Kishon swept them away,
the ancient torrent, the torrent
Kishon.
March on, my soul, with might!

22 "Then loud beat the horses' hoofs
with the galloping, galloping of his
steeds.

23 "Curse Meroz, says the angel of the LORD,
curse its inhabitants thoroughly,
[z]because they did not come to the help of
the LORD,
to the help of the LORD against the
mighty.

24 "Most blessed of women be [a]Jael,
the wife of Heber the Kenite,
of tent-dwelling women most
blessed.
25 [b]He asked for water and she gave him
milk;
she brought him curds in a noble's
bowl.
26 [c]She sent her hand to the tent peg
and her right hand to the workmen's
mallet;
she struck Sisera;
she crushed his head;
she shattered and pierced his temple.
27 Between her feet
he sank, he fell, he lay still;
between her feet
he sank, he fell;
where he sank,
there he fell—dead.

28 [d]"Out of the window she peered,
the mother of Sisera wailed through
[e]the lattice:
'Why is his chariot so long in coming?
Why tarry the hoofbeats of his chariots?'
29 Her wisest princesses answer,
indeed, she answers herself,
30 'Have they not found and [f]divided the
spoil?—
A womb or two for every man;
spoil of dyed materials for Sisera,
spoil of dyed materials embroidered,
two pieces of dyed work embroidered
for the neck as spoil?'

31 [g]"So may all your enemies perish, O LORD!
But your friends be [h]like the sun [i]as he
rises in his might."

[j]And the land had rest for forty years.

Midian Oppresses Israel

6 [k]The people of Israel did what was evil
in the sight of the LORD, and the LORD
gave them into the hand of [l]Midian seven
years. 2 And the hand of Midian overpowered
Israel, and because of Midian the people of
Israel made for themselves the dens that are in
the mountains and [m]the caves and the strongholds. 3 For whenever the Israelites planted
crops, the Midianites and [n]the Amalekites and
[o]the people of the East would come up against
them. 4 They would encamp against them
[p]and devour the produce of the land, as far as
Gaza, and leave no sustenance in Israel and no
sheep or ox or donkey. 5 For they would come
up with their livestock and their tents; they
would come [q]like locusts in number—both
they and their camels could not be counted—
so that they laid waste the land as they came
in. 6 And Israel was brought very low because
of Midian. And the people of Israel [r]cried out
for help to the LORD.
7 When the people of Israel cried out to the
LORD on account of the Midianites, 8 the LORD
sent a prophet to the people of Israel. And he
said to them, "Thus says the LORD, the God of
Israel: [s]I led you up from Egypt and brought
you out of the house of slavery. 9 And I delivered you from the hand of the Egyptians and
from the hand of all who oppressed you, and
[t]drove them out before you and gave you
their land. 10 And I said to you, 'I am the LORD
your God; [u]you shall not fear the gods of the
Amorites in whose land you dwell.' But you
have not obeyed my voice."

The Call of Gideon

11 Now the angel of the LORD came and
sat under the terebinth at Ophrah, which
belonged to Joash [v]the Abiezrite, while his son
[w]Gideon was beating out wheat in the wine-

19 [u]ch. 1:27; Josh. 17:11; 1 Kgs. 4:12 [v]2 Kgs. 9:27; 23:29, 30; 2 Chr. 35:22 [w][ver. 30] **20** [x]Josh. 10:11 **21** [y]ch. 4:7 **23** [z][ch. 21:9, 10] **24** [a]ch. 4:17 **25** [b]ch. 4:19 **26** [c]ch. 4:21 **28** [d][2 Sam. 6:16] [e][Prov. 7:6] **30** [f]Ex. 15:9 **31** [g][Ps. 83:9, 10] [h][2 Sam. 23:4; Dan. 12:3; Matt. 13:43] [i]Ps. 19:5; 37:6 [j]See ch. 3:11
Chapter 6 **1** [k]See ch. 2:19 [l]Gen. 25:2; Num. 25:17, 18; Hab. 3:7 **2** [m]1 Sam. 13:6; Heb. 11:38 **3** [n]ch. 3:13 [o]ver. 33; ch. 7:12; 8:10; Gen. 29:1; 1 Kgs. 4:30; Job 1:3 **4** [p][Lev. 26:16]; See Deut. 28:30-33, 51; Mic. 6:15 **5** [q]ch. 7:12 **6** [r]See ch. 3:9 **8** [s]1 Sam. 10:18 **9** [t]Ps. 44:2, 3 **10** [u]Josh. 24:15; See 2 Kgs. 17:35-38 **11** [v]ch. 8:2; Josh. 17:2 [w]Heb. 11:32

press to hide it from the Midianites. 12 And [x]the angel of the LORD appeared to him and said to him, [y]"The LORD is with you, O mighty man of valor." 13 And Gideon said to him, "Please, sir,[1] if the LORD is with us, why then has all this happened to us? And where are [z]all his wonderful deeds [a]that our fathers recounted to us, saying, 'Did not the LORD bring us up from Egypt?' But now the LORD has forsaken us and given us into the hand of Midian." 14 And the LORD[2] turned to him and said, "Go in this might of yours and save Israel from the hand of Midian; [b]do not I send you?" 15 And he said to him, [c]"Please, Lord, how can I save Israel? Behold, [d]my clan is the weakest in Manasseh, and I am the least in my father's house." 16 And the LORD said to him, [e]"But I will be with you, and you shall strike the Midianites as one man." 17 And he said to him, [f]"If now I have found favor in your eyes, then [g]show me a sign that it is you who speak with me. 18 Please [h]do not depart from here until I come to you and bring out my present and set it before you." And he said, "I will stay till you return."

19 So Gideon went into his house [i]and prepared a young goat and unleavened cakes from an ephah[3] of flour. The meat he put in a basket, and the broth he put in a pot, and brought them to him under the terebinth and presented them. 20 And the angel of God said to him, "Take the meat and the unleavened cakes, and put them [j]on this rock, and [k]pour the broth over them." And he did so. 21 Then the angel of the LORD reached out the tip of the staff that was in his hand and touched the meat and the unleavened cakes. [l]And fire sprang up from the rock and consumed the meat and the unleavened cakes. And the angel of the LORD vanished from his sight. 22 Then Gideon perceived that he was the angel of the LORD. And Gideon said, [m]"Alas, O Lord GOD! For now I have seen the angel of the LORD face to face." 23 But the LORD said to him, [n]"Peace be to you. Do not fear; you shall not die." 24 Then Gideon built an altar there to the LORD and called it, [o]The LORD Is Peace. To this day it still stands at [p]Ophrah, which belongs to the Abiezrites.

25 That night the LORD said to him, "Take your father's bull, and the second bull seven years old, and pull down the altar of Baal that your father has, and cut down [q]the Asherah that is beside it 26 and build an altar to the LORD your God on the top of the [r]stronghold here, with stones laid in due order. Then take the second bull and offer it as a burnt offering with the wood of the Asherah that you shall cut down." 27 So Gideon took ten men of his servants and did as the LORD had told him. But because he was too afraid of his family and the men of the town to do it by day, he did it by night.

Gideon Destroys the Altar of Baal

28 When the men of the town rose early in the morning, behold, the altar of Baal was broken down, and the Asherah beside it was cut down, and the second bull was offered on the altar that had been built. 29 And they said to one another, "Who has done this thing?" And after they had searched and inquired, they said, "Gideon the son of Joash has done this thing." 30 Then the men of the town said to Joash, "Bring out your son, that he may die, for he has broken down the altar of Baal and cut down the Asherah beside it." 31 But Joash said to all who stood against him, "Will you contend for Baal? Or will you save him? Whoever contends for him shall be put to death by morning. If he is a god, let him contend for himself, because his altar has been broken down." 32 Therefore on that day Gideon[4] was called [s]Jerubbaal, that is to say, "Let Baal contend against him," because he broke down his altar.

[1] Or *Please, my Lord* [2] Septuagint *the angel of the LORD*; also verse 16 [3] An *ephah* was about 3/5 bushel or 22 liters [4] Hebrew *he*

6:11–27 Those whom God designates "savior" know his presence. Nowhere is that clearer than in Gideon's request for a sign (v. 17), when God himself meets Gideon in the person of the angel of the Lord (vv. 22–23). This is the first of three confirmatory signs given to encourage the uncertain leader. Later, Gideon "sets out the fleece" (vv. 36–40), not as a method to determine God's will but as specific confirmation of what is already promised, namely, that God is with him and will save Israel through him (v. 37; cf. v. 14). Our God willingly condescends to meet his servants because he understands our fear and frailty—qualities much more evident in Gideon than his heroism (vv. 11, 15, 27; Ps. 103:13–14).

12 [x] ch. 13:3; Luke 1:11; [Acts 10:3] [y] Josh. 1:5
13 [z] Ps. 89:49; Isa. 63:15 [a] Ps. 44:1
14 [b] 1 Sam. 12:11; [Josh. 1:9]
15 [c] [Ex. 3:11] [d] 1 Sam. 9:21; 18:18
16 [e] Ex. 3:12; Josh. 1:5
17 [f] Ex. 33:13 [g] 2 Kgs. 20:8, 9; Isa. 7:11; [ver. 36, 37]; See Ex. 4:1-8
18 [h] ch. 13:15; Gen. 18:3-5
19 [i] Gen. 18:6-8

20 [j] ch. 13:19 [k] [1 Kgs. 18:33, 34] **21** [l] Lev. 9:24; 1 Kgs. 18:38; 2 Chr. 7:1 **22** [m] ch. 13:21, 22; [Gen. 32:30; Ex. 33:20; Deut. 5:26] **23** [n] Dan. 10:19 **24** [o] [Gen. 22:14; Ex. 17:15; Ezek. 48:35] [p] ver. 11; ch. 8:27, 32 **25** [q] ch. 3:7 **26** [r] Dan. 11:7, 10, 31 (Heb.) **32** [s] ch. 7:1; 1 Sam. 12:11; [2 Sam. 11:21]

33 Now [t]all the Midianites and the Amalekites
and the people of the East came together, and
they crossed the Jordan and encamped in [u]the
Valley of Jezreel. 34 But [v]the Spirit of the LORD
clothed Gideon, [w]and he sounded the trumpet,
and the Abiezrites were called out to follow
him. 35 [x]And he sent messengers throughout
all Manasseh, and they too were called out to
follow him. [x]And he sent messengers to Asher,
Zebulun, and Naphtali, and they went up to
meet them.

The Sign of the Fleece

36 [y]Then Gideon said to God, "If you will save
Israel by my hand, as you have said, 37 behold,
I am laying a fleece of wool on the threshing
floor. If there is dew on the fleece alone, and it
is dry on all the ground, then I shall know that
you will save Israel by my hand, as you have
said." 38 And it was so. When he rose early next
morning and squeezed the fleece, he wrung
enough dew from the fleece to fill a bowl with
water. 39 Then Gideon said to God, [z]"Let not
your anger burn against me; let me speak just
once more. Please let me test just once more
with the fleece. Please let it be dry on the fleece
only, and on all the ground let there be dew."
40 And God did so that night; and it was dry
on the fleece only, and on all the ground there
was dew.

Gideon's Three Hundred Men

7 Then [a]Jerubbaal (that is, Gideon) and all
the people who were with him rose early
and encamped beside [b]the spring of Harod.
And the camp of Midian was north of them,
[c]by the hill of Moreh, in the valley.

2 The LORD said to Gideon, "The people with
you are too many for me to give the Midianites
into their hand, [d]lest Israel boast over me,
saying, 'My own hand has saved me.' 3 Now
therefore proclaim in the ears of the people,
saying, [e]'Whoever is fearful and trembling, let
him return home and hurry away from Mount
Gilead.'" Then 22,000 of the people returned,
and 10,000 remained.

4 And the LORD said to Gideon, "The people
are still too many. Take them down to the
water, and I will test them for you there, and
anyone of whom I say to you, 'This one shall
go with you,' shall go with you, and anyone
of whom I say to you, 'This one shall not go
with you,' shall not go." 5 So he brought the
people down to the water. And the LORD said
to Gideon, "Every one who laps the water with
his tongue, as a dog laps, you shall set by himself. Likewise, every one who kneels down to
drink." 6 And the number of those who lapped,
putting their hands to their mouths, was 300
men, but all the rest of the people knelt down
to drink water. 7 And the LORD said to Gideon,
[f]"With the 300 men who lapped I will save you
and give the Midianites into your hand, and
let all the others go every man to his home."
8 So the people took provisions in their hands,
and their trumpets. And he sent all the rest of
Israel every man to his tent, but retained the
300 men. And the camp of Midian was below
him [g]in the valley.

9 That same [h]night the LORD said to him,
"Arise, go down against the camp, [i]for I have
given it into your hand. 10 But if you are afraid
to go down, go down to the camp with Purah
your servant. 11 [j]And you shall hear what
they say, and afterward your hands shall be
strengthened to go down against the camp."
[k]Then he went down with Purah his servant
to the outposts of the armed men who were
in the camp. 12 And the Midianites and the
Amalekites and [l]all the people of the East lay
along the valley like locusts in abundance,
and their camels were without number, [m]as
the sand that is on the seashore in abundance.
13 When Gideon came, behold, a man was
telling a dream to his comrade. And he said,
"Behold, I dreamed a dream, and behold, a
cake of barley bread tumbled into the camp of
Midian and came to the tent and struck it so

33 [t]ver. 3 [u]Josh. 17:16
34 [v]See ch. 3:10 [w]ch. 3:27
35 [x]ch. 7:24
36 [y]For ver. 36-40, see Ex. 4:1-7
39 [z]Gen. 18:32
Chapter 7
1 [a]ch. 6:32 [b][1 Sam. 29:1] [c]Gen. 12:6; Deut. 11:30
2 [d]Deut. 8:17; [Isa. 10:13]
3 [e]Deut. 20:8
7 [f][1 Sam. 14:6; 2 Chr. 14:11]
8 [g]ver. 1

It is confirmation of God's presence that enables Gideon to pull down idols (Judg. 6:22, 25–27). In the incarnation of Jesus Christ, the Word made flesh (John 1:14), God promises to be with us forever (Matt. 1:23; 28:20). It is only through Jesus' work on our behalf that we are able to destroy the strongholds of idolatry (2 Cor. 10:3–5).

In spite of Gideon's objections, neither the presence of difficult circumstances nor the absence of God's dramatic work should be taken as evidence that God has forsaken us (Judg. 6:13). Neither does a flawed or weak family background impede our usefulness in advancing the kingdom of God (v. 15; 1 Sam 16:10–12; 2 Sam. 7:18; 1 Cor. 15:9–10).

9 [h]Gen. 46:2, 3; 1 Kgs. 3:5 [i]See ch. 3:28 11 [j]See ver. 13-15 [k][1 Sam. 14:9, 10] 12 [l]See ch. 6:3 [m]Josh. 11:4

that it fell and turned it upside down, so that the tent lay flat." 14 And his comrade answered, "This is no other than the sword of Gideon the son of Joash, a man of Israel; God has given into his hand Midian and all the camp."

15 As soon as Gideon heard the telling of the dream and its interpretation, he worshiped. And he returned to the camp of Israel and said, "Arise, for the LORD has given the host of Midian into your hand." 16 And he divided the 300 men into three companies and put trumpets into the hands of all of them and empty jars, with [n]torches inside the jars. 17 And he said to them, "Look at me, and do likewise. When I come to the outskirts of the camp, do as I do. 18 When I blow the trumpet, I and all who are with me, then blow the trumpets also on every side of all the camp and shout, [o]'For the LORD and for Gideon.'"

Gideon Defeats Midian

19 So Gideon and the hundred men who were with him came to the outskirts of the camp at the beginning of the middle watch, when they had just set the watch. And they blew the trumpets and smashed the jars that were in their hands. 20 Then the three companies blew the trumpets and broke the jars. They held in their left hands the torches, and in their right hands the trumpets to blow. [o]And they cried out, "A sword for the LORD and for Gideon!" 21 Every man stood in his place around the camp, [p]and all the army ran. They cried out and fled. 22 [q]When they blew the 300 trumpets, [r]the LORD set [s]every man's sword against his comrade and against all the army. And the army fled as far as Beth-shittah toward Zererah,[1] as far as the border of Abel-meholah, by Tabbath. 23 And the men of Israel were called out from Naphtali and from Asher and from all Manasseh, and they pursued after Midian.

24 [t]Gideon sent messengers throughout [u]all the hill country of Ephraim, saying, "Come down against the Midianites and capture the waters against them, as far as [v]Beth-barah, and also the Jordan." So all the men of Ephraim were called out, and they captured the waters as far as Beth-barah, and also the Jordan. 25 And they captured [w]the two princes of Midian, Oreb and Zeeb. They killed Oreb [x]at the rock of Oreb, and Zeeb they killed at the winepress of Zeeb. Then they pursued Midian, and they brought the heads of Oreb and Zeeb to Gideon [y]across the Jordan.

Gideon Defeats Zebah and Zalmunna

8 [z]Then the men of Ephraim said to him, "What is this that you have done to us, not to call us when you went to fight against Midian?" And they accused him fiercely. 2 And he said to them, "What have I done now in comparison with you? Is not [a]the gleaning of the grapes of Ephraim better than the grape harvest of Abiezer? 3 [b]God has given into your hands the princes of Midian, Oreb and Zeeb. What have I been able to do in comparison with you?" [c]Then their anger[2] against him subsided when he said this.

4 And Gideon came to the Jordan and crossed over, he and [d]the 300 men who were with him, exhausted yet pursuing. 5 So he said to the men of [e]Succoth, "Please give loaves of bread to the

[1] Some Hebrew manuscripts *Zeredah* [2] Hebrew *their spirit*

7:15–25 Belief that my own hand has saved me (v. 2) is the supreme folly. This mind-set ascribes victory to human strength, great armies, and political kingdoms. By reducing the army to a mere three hundred persons, God's deliverance becomes the only explanation for victory.

Gideon's temptation to fight his own battles, rather than lean on God, reflects a genuine internal struggle for all believers. In the face of injustice, do I commit my way to God and wait for him to act or do I take matters into my own hands (Ps. 37:5–8)? The irony of the battle cry, "A sword for the LORD and for Gideon" (Judg. 7:20), is that the swords mentioned are those which the Midianites turn on one another (Ps. 37:14–15). God is the only hero of this story as he condescends to use human weakness for great victory.

In a similar fashion, God brings ultimate victory over all our sin and circumstances through one man, Jesus Christ. With Gideon's three hundred, as at Christ's cross, we learn that, when circumstances look bleakest and when human weakness is most apparent, God's power and providential care are most evident.

8:1–21 The Lord is prominent in orchestrating the events of the first battle, but his commands are noticeably absent from the second battle. This is not a battle "for

16 [n]ch. 15:4; Gen. 15:17
18 [o][Ex. 14:13, 14; 2 Chr. 20:17]
20 [o][See ver. 18 above]
21 [p][2 Kgs. 7:7]
22 [q][Josh. 6:4, 16, 20] [r][Ps. 83:9; Isa. 9:4] [s]1 Sam. 14:20; [2 Chr. 20:23]
24 [t]ch. 6:35 [u]See Josh. 24:33 [v][ch. 3:28]
25 [w]ch. 8:3; Ps. 83:11 [x]Isa. 10:26 [y]ch. 8:4

Chapter 8
1 [z][ch. 12:1; 2 Sam. 19:41]
2 [a]Isa. 24:13; Jer. 49:9; Obad. 5; Mic. 7:1
3 [b]ch. 7:24, 25 [c][Prov. 15:1]
4 [d]ch. 7:6
5 [e]Gen. 33:17; Ps. 60:6

people who follow me, for they are exhausted,
and I am pursuing after Zebah and Zalmunna,
the kings of Midian." 6 And the officials of
Succoth said, [f]"Are the hands of Zebah and
Zalmunna already in your hand, [g]that we
should give bread to your army?" 7 So Gideon
said, "Well then, when the LORD has given
Zebah and Zalmunna into my hand, [h]I will
flail your flesh with the thorns of the wilderness and with briers." 8 And from there he went
up to [i]Penuel, and spoke to them in the same
way, and the men of Penuel answered him as
the men of Succoth had answered. 9 And he
said to the men of Penuel, [j]"When I come again
in peace, [k]I will break down this tower."

10 Now Zebah and Zalmunna were in Karkor
with their army, about 15,000 men, all who
were left of all the army of [l]the people of the
East, for there had fallen 120,000 men [m]who
drew the sword. 11 And Gideon went up by the
way of the tent dwellers east of [n]Nobah and
Jogbehah and attacked the army, for the army
felt [o]secure. 12 And Zebah and Zalmunna fled,
and he pursued them [p]and captured the two
kings of Midian, Zebah and Zalmunna, and
he threw all the army into a panic.

13 Then Gideon the son of Joash returned
from the battle by the ascent of Heres. 14 And
he captured a young man of Succoth and questioned him. And he wrote down for him the
officials and elders of Succoth, seventy-seven
men. 15 And he came to the men of Succoth
and said, "Behold Zebah and Zalmunna, about
whom you taunted me, saying, [q]'Are the hands
of Zebah and Zalmunna already in your hand,
that we should give bread to your men who
are exhausted?' " 16 And he took the elders of
the city, and he took thorns of the wilderness
and briers and with them taught the men of
Succoth a lesson. 17 [r]And he broke down the
tower of Penuel and killed the men of the city.

18 Then he said to Zebah and Zalmunna,
"Where are the men whom you killed at
[s]Tabor?" They answered, "As you are, so were
they. Every one of them resembled the son of
a king." 19 And he said, "They were my brothers, the sons of my mother. [t]As the LORD lives,
if you had saved them alive, I would not kill
you." 20 So he said to Jether his firstborn, "Rise
and kill them!" But the young man did not
draw his sword, for he was afraid, because
he was still a young man. 21 Then Zebah
and Zalmunna said, "Rise yourself and fall
upon us, for as the man is, so is his strength."
And Gideon arose and [u]killed Zebah and
Zalmunna, and he took [v]the crescent ornaments that were on the necks of their camels.

Gideon's Ephod

22 Then the men of Israel said to Gideon,
"Rule over us, you and your son and your
grandson also, for you have saved us from the
hand of Midian." 23 Gideon said to them, "I will
not rule over you, and my son will not rule
over you; [w]the LORD will rule over you." 24 And
Gideon said to them, "Let me make a request
of you: every one of you give me the earrings
from his spoil." (For they had golden earrings,
[x]because they were Ishmaelites.) 25 And they
answered, "We will willingly give them." And
they spread a cloak, and every man threw in
it the earrings of his spoil. 26 And the weight
of the golden earrings that he requested was
1,700 shekels[1] of gold, besides [y]the crescent
ornaments and [z]the pendants and the purple

[1] A *shekel* was about 2/5 ounce or 11 grams

6 [f][1 Kgs. 20:11] [g][1 Sam. 25:11]
7 [h]ver. 16
8 [i]Gen. 32:30, 31; 1 Kgs. 12:25
9 [j][1 Kgs. 22:27, 28] [k]ver. 17
10 [l]See ch. 6:3 [m]ch. 20:2, 15, 17, 25, 35, 46; 2 Sam. 24:9; 2 Kgs. 3:26; 1 Chr. 21:5
11 [n]Num. 32:35, 42 [o]ch. 18:27
12 [p]Ps. 83:11
15 [q]ver. 6
17 [r][1 Kgs. 12:25]
18 [s][ch. 4:6]
19 [t]See Ruth 3:13
21 [u]Ps. 83:11 [v]ver. 26; Isa. 3:18
23 [w][1 Sam. 8:7; 10:19; 12:12, 17, 19]
24 [x][Gen. 37:25, 28, 36; 39:1]
26 [y]ver. 21 [z]Isa. 3:19

the Lord" but violence of Gideon's own making (v. 4) as he ruthlessly mistreats his own people (vv. 7–8; vv. 13–17) and seeks vengeance for personal injuries (vv. 18–21).

Again we learn that Gideon's victories cannot be attributed to his own heroic nature. In fact, we are meant to understand that his leadership methods, though common in many places in the world, are not honoring to God and must be countered and overcome by God's grace. Leaders in all nations, both inside and outside of the church, must be those who serve (Luke 22:24–27). This is the pattern laid down by our Savior, who himself served us by suffering in our place and restoring us to God (1 Pet. 3:18).

8:22–28 God is the ultimate source of our success. The Israelites want Gideon to begin a kingly dynasty to include "your son and your grandson" (v. 22). With his words, Gideon rightly rejects this desire, indicating that the Lord alone is king (v. 23; cf. Deut. 33:1–5; Ps. 10:16; 29:10; 95:3). But we learn that Gideon's words do not reflect his heart, when he later names his son Abimelech (translated, "My father is the king"; see Judg. 9:1). The failure of Israel (and Gideon) truly to recognize that God alone is their king strikes at the heart of their covenantal relationship with God (1 Sam. 10:19).

garments worn by the kings of Midian, and besides the collars that were around the necks of their camels. 27 And Gideon [a]made an ephod of it and put it in his city, [b]in Ophrah. And all Israel [c]whored after it there, and it became a [d]snare to Gideon and to his family. 28 So Midian was subdued before the people of Israel, and they raised their heads no more. [e]And the land had rest forty years in the days of Gideon.

The Death of Gideon

29 [f]Jerubbaal the son of Joash went and lived in his own house. 30 Now Gideon had [g]seventy sons, his own offspring,[1] for he had many wives. 31 And his concubine [h]who was in Shechem also bore him a son, and he called his name Abimelech. 32 And Gideon the son of Joash died [i]in a good old age and was buried in the tomb of Joash his father, [j]at Ophrah of the Abiezrites.

33 [k]As soon as Gideon died, the people of Israel turned again and [l]whored after the Baals and made [m]Baal-berith their god. 34 And the people of Israel [n]did not remember the LORD their God, who had delivered them from the hand of all their enemies on every side, 35 [o]and they did not show steadfast love to the family of Jerubbaal (that is, Gideon) in return for all the good that he had done to Israel.

Abimelech's Conspiracy

9 Now Abimelech the son of Jerubbaal went to Shechem to [p]his mother's relatives and said to them and to the whole clan of his mother's family, 2 "Say in the ears of all the leaders of Shechem, 'Which is better for you, that all [q]seventy of the sons of Jerubbaal rule over you, or that one rule over you?' Remember also that [p]I am [r]your bone and your flesh."

3 And his mother's relatives spoke all these words on his behalf in the ears of all the leaders of Shechem, and their hearts inclined to follow Abimelech, for they said, [s]"He is our brother." 4 And they gave him seventy pieces of silver out of the house of [t]Baal-berith with which Abimelech hired [u]worthless and reckless fellows, who followed him. 5 And he went to his father's house at [v]Ophrah [w]and killed his brothers the sons of Jerubbaal, seventy men, on one stone. But Jotham the youngest son of Jerubbaal was left, for he hid himself. 6 And all the leaders of Shechem came together, and all [x]Beth-millo, and they went and made Abimelech king, by the oak of the pillar at Shechem.

7 When it was told to Jotham, he went and stood on top of [y]Mount Gerizim and cried aloud and said to them, "Listen to me, you leaders of Shechem, that God may listen to you. 8 [z]The trees once went out to anoint a king over them, and they said to the olive tree, [a]'Reign over us.' 9 But the olive tree said to them, 'Shall I leave my abundance, by which gods and men are honored, and go hold sway over the trees?' 10 And the trees said to the fig tree, 'You come and reign over us.' 11 But the fig tree said to them, 'Shall I leave my sweetness and my good fruit and go hold sway over the trees?' 12 And the trees said to the vine, 'You

[1] Hebrew *who came from his own loins*

We tend to elevate the instrument of God rather than God himself. Personal success may breed a sense of personal privilege and invincibility. In contrast to his initial rejection of kingship, Gideon now requests symbols of monarchy: gold and the purple garments (Judg. 8:24–26). And, in an additional and startling betrayal of his God, Gideon uses spoils from the victory God has just provided to devise a form of idolatry that ensnares this "hero's" family and people (v. 27). Still, the mercy of God prevails for Gideon (v. 32), although his family will suffer sad consequences for the sinful path he blazes for them (vv. 33–35; and see the following chapters). Thus, we learn that God is the giver of all good gifts and we must employ power, wealth, and status to glorify him and serve others rather than to create personal idols that ensnare ourselves, our family, and our community (vv. 27–28; Neh. 9:33–37; James 1:17–18). God is gracious to us in so alerting us to the dangers of sin and idolatry. We are also reminded that only Jesus was the warrior-king who proved faithful to the end.

9:7–21 Judges 9 is the center of the second section of the book (3:7–16:31) and the longest chapter. At this moment in Israel's story, Jotham's fable illustrates several features of Abimelech's reign and instructs God's people moving forward.

The wrong kind of king fails to promote "good faith and integrity" (9:16, 19) and instead motivates God's people to devour one another (vv. 20–21; cf. vv. 46–57; Gal.

27[a] ch. 17:5; 18:14, 17; See Ex. 28:6-35 [b] ch. 6:24 [c] ver. 33; ch. 2:17; Ex. 34:15; Ps. 106:39 [d] Ex. 23:33; Deut. 7:16
28[e] [ch. 3:11; 5:31]
29[f] ch. 6:32; 7:1
30[g] ch. 9:2, 5
31[h] ch. 9:1, 2
32[i] Gen. 15:15; 25:8; Job 5:26 [j] ch. 6:24
33[k] [ch. 2:19] [l] See ver. 27 [m] ch. 9:4, 46
34[n] Ps. 78:11, 42; 106:13, 21
35[o] See ch. 9:16-18
Chapter 9
1[p] ch. 8:31
2[q] ch. 8:30 [p] [See ver. 1 above] [r] Gen. 29:14
3[s] ver. 18
4[t] ch. 8:33; [ver. 46] [u] ch. 11:3; 2 Chr. 13:7; [Prov. 12:11; Acts 17:5]
5[v] ch. 6:24 [w] [2 Kgs. 11:1, 2]
6[x] ver. 20; [2 Sam. 5:9]
7[y] Deut. 11:29; 27:12; Josh. 8:33; [John 4:20]
8[z] [2 Kgs. 14:9] [a] ch. 8:22, 23

come and reign over us.' 13 But the vine said to them, 'Shall I leave my wine that [b]cheers God and men and go hold sway over the trees?' 14 Then all the trees said to the bramble, 'You come and reign over us.' 15 And the bramble said to the trees, 'If in good faith you are anointing me king over you, then come and [c]take refuge in my shade, but if not, [d]let fire come out of the bramble and devour [e]the cedars of Lebanon.'

16 "Now therefore, if you acted in good faith and integrity when you made Abimelech king, and if you have dealt well with [f]Jerubbaal and his house and have done to him [g]as his deeds deserved— 17 for my father fought for you and risked his life and delivered you from the hand of Midian, 18 and you have risen up against my father's house this day [h]and have killed his sons, seventy men on one stone, and have made [i]Abimelech, the son of his female servant, king over the leaders of Shechem, [j]because he is your relative— 19 if you then have acted in good faith and integrity with Jerubbaal and with his house this day, then [k]rejoice in Abimelech, and let him also rejoice in you. 20 But if not, [l]let fire come out from Abimelech and devour the leaders of Shechem and Beth-millo; and let fire come out from the leaders of Shechem and from Beth-millo and devour Abimelech." 21 And Jotham ran away and fled and went to [m]Beer and lived there, because of Abimelech his brother.

The Downfall of Abimelech

22 Abimelech ruled over Israel three years. 23 [n]And God sent an evil spirit between Abimelech and the leaders of Shechem, and the leaders of Shechem [o]dealt treacherously with Abimelech, 24 [p]that the violence done to the seventy sons of Jerubbaal might come, and their blood be laid on Abimelech their brother, who killed them, and on the men of Shechem, who strengthened his hands to kill his brothers. 25 And the leaders of Shechem put men in ambush against him on the mountaintops, and they robbed all who passed by them along that way. And it was told to Abimelech.

26 And Gaal the son of Ebed moved into Shechem with his relatives, and the leaders of Shechem put confidence in him. 27 And they went out into the field and gathered the grapes from their vineyards and trod them and held a festival; and they went into [q]the house of their god and ate and drank and reviled Abimelech. 28 And Gaal the son of Ebed said, [r]"Who is Abimelech, and who are we of Shechem, that we should serve him? Is he not the son of Jerubbaal, and is not Zebul his officer? Serve the men of [s]Hamor the father of Shechem; but why should we serve him? 29 Would that this people were under my hand! Then I would remove Abimelech. I would say[1] to Abimelech, 'Increase your army, and come out.' "

30 When Zebul the ruler of the city heard the words of Gaal the son of Ebed, his anger was kindled. 31 And he sent messengers to Abimelech secretly,[2] saying, "Behold, Gaal the son of Ebed and his relatives have come to Shechem, and they are stirring up[3] the city against you. 32 Now therefore, go by night, you and the people who are with you, and set an ambush in the field. 33 Then in the morning, as soon as the sun is up, rise early and rush upon the city. And when he and the people who are with him come out against you, you may do to them [t]as your hand finds to do."

34 So Abimelech and all the men who were with him rose up by night and set an ambush against Shechem in four companies. 35 And Gaal the son of Ebed went out and stood in the entrance of the gate of the city, and Abimelech and the people who were with him rose from the ambush. 36 And when Gaal saw the people, he said to Zebul, "Look, people are coming down from [u]the mountaintops!" And Zebul said to him, "You mistake[4] the shadow of the mountains for men." 37 Gaal spoke again and

[1] Septuagint; Hebrew *and he said* [2] Or *at Tormah* [3] Hebrew *besieging*, or *closing up* [4] Hebrew *You see*

13 [b] Ps. 104:15
15 [c] Dan. 4:12; Hos. 14:7; [Isa. 30:2] [d] ver. 20; [Num. 21:28; Ezek. 19:14] [e] 1 Kgs. 4:33; 2 Kgs. 14:9; 19:23; Ps. 104:16; Isa. 2:13; 37:24
16 [f] See ch. 6:32 [g] Prov. 12:14; Isa. 3:11; [ch. 8:35]
18 [h] ver. 5, 6 [i] ch. 8:31 [j] ver. 3
19 [k] [Isa. 8:6]

5:15). God loves his people too much to allow this mutual destroying to continue indefinitely. We need the king of God's own choosing (1 Sam. 16:1; Mark 1:9–11; Luke 9:35). In the rule of King Jesus—the ultimate righteous King that Israel desired and truly needed but could not find in her human ranks—we have a shepherd under whom we flourish, who frees us to love one another well rather than feeding upon one another (Jer. 23:1–6; Gal. 5:13–15). Our freedom comes because King Jesus loved and led *us* well, even to the point of dying for us (2 Cor. 5:14–15).

20 [l] ver. 15; [ver. 56, 57] **21** [m] Num. 21:16 **23** [n] [1 Sam. 16:14; 18:10; 19:9] [o] Isa. 33:1 **24** [p] ver. 56; [1 Kgs. 2:32; Esth. 9:25; Ps. 7:16; Matt. 23:35, 36] **27** [q] ver. 4, 46 **28** [r] [1 Sam. 25:10] [s] Gen. 34:2, 6 **33** [t] Eccles. 9:10 **36** [u] ver. 7, 25

said, “Look, people are coming down from
the center of the land, and one company is
coming from the direction of the Diviners’
Oak.” 38 Then Zebul said to him, “Where
is your mouth now, you who said, [v]‘Who is
Abimelech, that we should serve him?’ Are
not these the people whom you despised? Go
out now and fight with them.” 39 And Gaal
went out at the head of the leaders of Shechem
and fought with Abimelech. 40 And Abimelech
chased him, and he fled before him. And many
fell wounded, up to the entrance of the gate.
41 And Abimelech lived at Arumah, and Zebul
drove out Gaal and his relatives, so that they
could not dwell at Shechem.

42 On the following day, the people went out
into the field, and Abimelech was told. 43 He
took his people and divided them into three
companies and set an ambush in the fields.
And he looked and saw the people coming out
of the city. So he rose against them and killed
them. 44 Abimelech and the company that was
with him [w]rushed forward and stood at the
entrance of the gate of the city, while the two
companies rushed upon all who were in the
field and killed them. 45 And Abimelech fought
against the city all that day. He captured the
city and killed the people who were in it, and
[x]he razed the city and [y]sowed it with salt.

46 When all the leaders of the Tower of
Shechem heard of it, they entered [z]the stronghold of the house of [a]El-berith. 47 Abimelech
was told that all the leaders of the Tower
of Shechem were gathered together. 48 And
Abimelech went up to Mount [b]Zalmon, he
and all the people who were with him. And
Abimelech took an axe in his hand and cut
down a bundle of brushwood and took it up
and laid it on his shoulder. And he said to the
men who were with him, “What you have
seen me do, hurry and do as I have done.” 49 So
every one of the people cut down his bundle
and following Abimelech put it against [c]the
stronghold, and they set the stronghold on
fire over them, so that all the people of the
Tower of Shechem also died, about 1,000 men
and women.

50 Then Abimelech went to Thebez and
encamped against Thebez and captured it.
51 But there was a strong tower within the
city, and all the men and women and all the
leaders of the city fled to it and shut themselves in, and they went up to the roof of the
tower. 52 And Abimelech came to the tower
and fought against it and drew near to the
door of the tower to burn it with fire. 53 [d]And
a certain woman threw an upper millstone
on Abimelech’s head and crushed his skull.
54 [e]Then he called quickly to the young man
his armor-bearer and said to him, “Draw
your sword and kill me, lest they say of me,
‘A woman killed him.’ ” And his young man
thrust him through, and he died. 55 And when
the men of Israel saw that Abimelech was
dead, everyone departed to his home. 56 [f]Thus
God returned the evil of Abimelech, which he
committed against his father in killing his seventy brothers. 57 And God also made all the evil
of the men of Shechem return on their heads,
and upon them came [g]the curse of Jotham the
son of Jerubbaal.

Tola and Jair

10 After Abimelech there arose to [h]save
Israel Tola the son of Puah, son of Dodo,
a man of Issachar, and he lived at Shamir in
[i]the hill country of Ephraim. 2 And he judged
Israel twenty-three years. Then he died and
was buried at Shamir.

3 After him arose Jair the Gileadite, who
judged Israel twenty-two years. 4 And he had
thirty sons who [j]rode on thirty donkeys, and
they had thirty cities, called Havvoth-jair to
this day, [k]which are in the land of Gilead. 5 And
Jair died and was buried in Kamon.

Further Disobedience and Oppression

6 [l]The people of Israel again did what was evil
in the sight of the LORD [m]and served the Baals
and the Ashtaroth, the gods of Syria, [n]the gods
of Sidon, the gods of Moab, the gods of the
Ammonites, and the gods of the Philistines.
And they [o]forsook the LORD and did not serve
him. 7 So the anger of the LORD was kindled
against Israel, and [p]he sold them into the

10:6–16 This major summary prepares us for the final two major judges. The Ammonites oppress Israel from the east during Jephthah’s days (chapters 11–12) while the Philistines arise from the west during the time of Samson (chapters 13–16). The relationship of Israel with their Lord continues to deteriorate. Limited idolatry that

38 [v] ver. 28, 29
44 [w] ch. 20:37
45 [x] 2 Kgs. 3:25 [y] Deut. 29:23
46 [z] ver. 49 [a] ver. 4; ch. 8:33
48 [b] Ps. 68:14
49 [c] ver. 46

53 [d] 2 Sam. 11:21 54 [e] [1 Sam. 31:4] 56 [f] [Job 31:8; Ps. 94:23; Prov. 5:22]; See ver. 24 57 [g] ver. 20 Chapter 10 1 [h] ver. 12, 13; See ch. 2:16 [i] See Josh. 24:33 4 [j] ch. 5:10; 12:14 [k] Deut. 3:14 6 [l] See ch. 2:11 [m] See ch. 2:13 [n] 1 Kgs. 11:5, 7, 33; 2 Kgs. 23:13 [o] ver. 10, 13; Deut. 31:16 7 [p] See ch. 2:14

hand of the Philistines and into the hand of the Ammonites, 8 and they crushed and oppressed the people of Israel that year. For eighteen years they oppressed all the people of Israel who were beyond the Jordan in the land of the Amorites, which is in Gilead. 9 And the Ammonites crossed the Jordan to fight also against Judah and against Benjamin and against the house of Ephraim, so that Israel was severely distressed.

10 And the people of Israel [q]cried out to the LORD, saying, "We have sinned against you, because [r]we have forsaken our God and have served the Baals." 11 And the LORD said to the people of Israel, "Did I not save you [s]from the Egyptians and [t]from the Amorites, [u]from the Ammonites and [v]from the Philistines? 12 The Sidonians also, and [w]the Amalekites and the Maonites oppressed you, and you cried out to me, and I [x]saved you out of their hand. 13 Yet you have [y]forsaken me and served other gods; therefore I will save you no more. 14 Go and cry out [z]to the gods whom you have chosen; let them save you in the time of your distress." 15 And the people of Israel said to the LORD, "We have sinned; do to us whatever seems good to you. Only please deliver us this day." 16 So they put away the foreign gods from among them and served the LORD, and [a]he became impatient over the misery of Israel.

17 Then the Ammonites were called to arms, and they encamped in Gilead. And the people of Israel came together, and they encamped at [b]Mizpah. 18 And the people, the leaders of Gilead, said one to another, "Who is the man who will begin to fight against the Ammonites? [c]He shall be head over all the inhabitants of Gilead."

Jephthah Delivers Israel

11 Now [d]Jephthah the Gileadite was [e]a mighty warrior, but he was the son of a prostitute. Gilead was the father of Jephthah. 2 And Gilead's wife also bore him sons. And when his wife's sons grew up, they drove Jephthah out and said to him, "You shall not have an inheritance in our father's house, for you are the son of another woman." 3 Then Jephthah fled from his brothers and lived in the land of [f]Tob, and [g]worthless fellows collected around Jephthah and went out with him.

4 After a time the Ammonites made war against Israel. 5 And when the Ammonites made war against Israel, the elders of Gilead went to bring Jephthah from the land of [f]Tob. 6 And they said to Jephthah, "Come and be our leader, that we may fight against the Ammonites." 7 But Jephthah said to the elders of Gilead, "Did you not hate me and drive me out of my father's house? Why have you come

10[q] See ch. 3:9 [r] ver. 6, 13
11[s] Ex. 14:30 [t] See Num. 21:21-32 [u] [ch. 3:13] [v] ch. 3:31
12[w] [ch. 3:13; 6:3] [x] See ch. 2:16
13[y] ver. 6, 10; [Deut. 32:15; Jer. 2:13]
14[z] Deut. 32:37, 38
16[a] ch. 2:18; Isa. 63:9
17[b] ch. 11:11, 29
18[c] [ch. 11:5, 6, 8, 11]
Chapter 11
1[d] Heb. 11:32 [e] ch. 6:12; 2 Kgs. 5:1
3[f] 2 Sam. 10:6, 8 [g] See ch. 9:4; [1 Sam. 22:2]
5[f] [See ver. 3 above]

goes unchecked eventually results in pervasive idolatry. Israel no longer serves only the Baals and the Ashtaroth; they have added to their pantheon the gods of surrounding peoples while forsaking their covenant-keeping God (10:6–7).

God is patient and longsuffering (Ex. 34:6–7), and yet his patience has reached its end as he uses godless foreign enemies to oppress his people (Judg. 10:7–8). Oppression, suffering, and difficulty are intended to drive God's people (then and now) to him. For the first and only time in Judges we have the clear corporate confession: *we have sinned* (vv. 10, 15). Genuine repentance follows: confession of sin, without condition, *to* God; the cry for deliverance, without manipulation, *from* God; and the abandonment of idols that are attempts to live *without* God (vv. 15–16).

11:1–28 Jephthah is a complicated judge. His name means "he will open," which describes a foolish action later clarified (vv. 35–36). His maternal lineage causes him to be rejected by his people (vv. 1–2). As an outcast, he attracts "worthless fellows" (v. 3; cf. 9:4). However, he is also a "mighty warrior" (11:1) with a God-centered understanding of Israel's history and his role in it (vv. 12–28). Like God himself, Jephthah is rejected by his people who later, when in grave distress, appeal to him only for the benefits he provides (vv. 5–8; cf. 10:11–14). The treatment of God's chosen deliverer by his people often reflects their treatment of God himself (John 8:18–19; 14:7–11).

The full extent of God's faithfulness pulses through all phases of redemptive history. Features of Jephthah point ahead to the Savior Jesus, whose lineage made his wisdom and works suspect (Matt. 13:55–58), who was rejected by his people (Isa. 53:3; Acts 4:11), who was thrust outside the camp (Heb. 13:11–13), and yet who was welcomed by those despised by society (Mark 2:15–17). We come to Jesus not only for the benefits he provides; we trust him because he is the King approved and empowered by God (John 6:25–27).

to me now when you are in distress?" 8 And the elders of Gilead said to Jephthah, "That is why we have turned to you now, that you may go with us and fight against the Ammonites and [h]be our head over all the inhabitants of Gilead." 9 Jephthah said to the elders of Gilead, "If you bring me home again to fight against the Ammonites, and the LORD gives them over to me, I will be your head." 10 And the elders of Gilead said to Jephthah, [i]"The LORD will be witness between us, if we do not do as you say." 11 So Jephthah went with the elders of Gilead, and the people [j]made him head and leader over them. And Jephthah spoke all his words [k]before the LORD at [l]Mizpah.

12 Then Jephthah sent messengers to the king of the Ammonites and said, "What do you have against me, that you have come to me to fight against my land?" 13 And the king of the Ammonites answered the messengers of Jephthah, [m]"Because Israel on coming up from Egypt took away my land, from the [n]Arnon to the [o]Jabbok and to the Jordan; now therefore restore it peaceably." 14 Jephthah again sent messengers to the king of the Ammonites 15 and said to him, "Thus says Jephthah: [p]Israel did not take away the land of Moab or the land of the Ammonites, 16 but when they came up from Egypt, Israel went through the wilderness [q]to the Red Sea and [r]came to Kadesh. 17 [s]Israel then sent messengers to the king of Edom, saying, 'Please let us pass through your land,' [t]but the king of Edom would not listen. And they sent also to the king of Moab, but he would not consent. So Israel [u]remained at Kadesh.

18 "Then they journeyed through the wilderness and [v]went around the land of Edom and the land of Moab and [w]arrived on the east side of the land of Moab and [x]camped on the other side of the Arnon. But they did not enter the territory of Moab, for the Arnon was the boundary of Moab. 19 [y]Israel then sent messengers to Sihon king of the Amorites, king of Heshbon, and Israel said to him, 'Please let us pass through your land to our country,' 20 but Sihon did not trust Israel to pass through his territory, so Sihon gathered all his people together and encamped at Jahaz and fought with Israel. 21 And the LORD, the God of Israel, gave Sihon and all his people into the hand of Israel, and they defeated them. So Israel took possession of all the land of the Amorites, who inhabited that country. 22 And they took possession of all the territory of the Amorites from the Arnon to the Jabbok and from the wilderness to the Jordan. 23 So then the LORD, the God of Israel, dispossessed the Amorites from before his people Israel; and are you to take possession of them? 24 Will you not possess what [z]Chemosh your god gives you to possess? [a]And all that the LORD our God has dispossessed before us, we will possess. 25 Now are you any better than [b]Balak the son of Zippor, king of Moab? Did he ever contend against Israel, or did he ever go to war with them? 26 While Israel lived [c]in Heshbon and its villages, and [d]in Aroer and its villages, and in all the cities that are on the banks of the Arnon, 300 years, why did you not deliver them within that time? 27 I therefore have not sinned against you, and you do me wrong by making war on me. [e]The LORD, the Judge, decide this day between the people of Israel and the people of Ammon." 28 But the king of the Ammonites did not listen to the words of Jephthah that he sent to him.

Jephthah's Tragic Vow

29 [f]Then the Spirit of the LORD was upon Jephthah, and he passed through Gilead and Manasseh and passed on to Mizpah of Gilead, and from Mizpah of Gilead he passed on to the Ammonites. 30 And Jephthah [g]made a vow to the LORD and said, "If you will give the

11:29–40 The intention of Jephthah's vow (vv. 30–31) is debated. Unquestionably, child sacrifice is among the "abominable practices" of the nations (Deut. 18:9–12) and is abhorrent to God (2 Kings 16:2–3; 17:17; 21:6; 23:10; Ps. 106:37–39; Jer. 19:5). Despite Jephthah's claim that he must fulfill the vow to sacrifice his only child (Judg. 11:34–35), impulsive oaths require repentance, not fulfillment (Lev. 5:4–6; cf. Lev. 19:12). Still, in light of God's prohibitions against human sacrifice and in light of the daughter's grieving over her virginity—i.e., a life without children, not the loss of her own life—it is likely that Jephthah dedicated his daughter to the Lord in temple service rather than in blood sacrifice.

8 [h] ch. 10:18
10 [i] Jer. 42:5
11 [j] ver. 6, 8; ch. 10:18 [k] 1 Sam. 10:19, 25; 11:15; 12:7; [ch. 20:1; 1 Sam. 10:17] [l] ch. 10:17
13 [m] See Num. 21:24-26 [n] Num. 21:13 [o] Gen. 32:22
15 [p] Deut. 2:9, 19
16 [q] Num. 14:25; Deut. 1:40 [r] Num. 13:26
17 [s] Num. 20:14 [t] See Num. 20:18-21 [u] Num. 20:1; Deut. 1:46

18 [v] Num. 21:4; See Deut. 2:1-8 [w] Num. 21:11 [x] Num. 21:13; 22:36 **19** [y] For ver. 19-22, see Num. 21:21-26; Deut. 2:26-37 **24** [z] Num. 21:29; 1 Kgs. 11:7 [a] Deut. 9:5; 18:12; Josh. 3:10 **25** [b] Num. 22:2; Josh. 24:9; Mic. 6:5 **26** [c] Num. 21:25 [d] Deut. 2:36 **27** [e] Gen. 16:5; 18:25; 31:53; 1 Sam. 24:12, 15 **29** [f] See ch. 3:10 **30** [g] Gen. 28:20; 1 Sam. 1:11

Ammonites into my hand, 31 then whatever[1] comes out from the doors of my house to meet me when I return in peace from the Ammonites [h]shall be the LORD's, and [i]I will offer it[2] up for a burnt offering." 32 So Jephthah crossed over to the Ammonites to fight against them, and the LORD gave them into his hand. 33 And he struck them from Aroer to the neighborhood of [j]Minnith, twenty cities, and as far as Abel-keramim, with a great blow. So the Ammonites were subdued before the people of Israel.

34 Then Jephthah came to his home at [k]Mizpah. And behold, his daughter came out to meet him [l]with tambourines and with dances. She was his only child; besides her he had neither son nor daughter. 35 And as soon as he saw her, he tore his clothes and said, "Alas, my daughter! You have brought me very low, and you have become the cause of great trouble to me. For I have opened my mouth to the LORD, [m]and I cannot take back my vow." 36 And she said to him, "My father, you have opened your mouth to the LORD; do to me according to what has gone out of your mouth, now that the LORD has avenged you on your enemies, on the Ammonites." 37 So she said to her father, "Let this thing be done for me: leave me alone two months, that I may go up and down on the mountains and weep for my virginity, I and my companions." 38 So he said, "Go." Then he sent her away for two months, and she departed, she and her companions, and wept for her virginity on the mountains. 39 And at the end of two months, she returned to her father, [n]who did with her according to his vow that he had made. She had never known a man, and it became a custom in Israel 40 that the daughters of Israel went year by year to lament the daughter of Jephthah the Gileadite four days in the year.

Jephthah's Conflict with Ephraim

12 [o]The men of Ephraim were called to arms, and they crossed to Zaphon and said to Jephthah, "Why did you cross over to fight against the Ammonites and did not call us to go with you? We will burn your house over you with fire." 2 And Jephthah said to them, "I and my people had a great dispute with the Ammonites, and when I called you, you did not save me from their hand. 3 And when I saw that you would not save me, [p]I took my life in my hand and crossed over against the Ammonites, and the LORD gave them into my hand. Why then have you come up to me this day to fight against me?" 4 Then Jephthah gathered all the men of Gilead and fought with Ephraim. And the men of Gilead struck Ephraim, because they said, [q]"You are fugitives of Ephraim, you Gileadites, in the midst of Ephraim and Manasseh." 5 And the Gileadites captured [r]the fords of the Jordan against the Ephraimites. And when any of the fugitives of Ephraim said, "Let me go over," the men of Gilead said to him, "Are you an Ephraimite?" When he said, "No," 6 they said to him, "Then say Shibboleth," and he said, "Sibboleth," for he could not pronounce it right. Then they seized him and slaughtered him at [r]the fords of the Jordan. At that time 42,000 of the Ephraimites fell.

7 Jephthah judged Israel six years. Then Jephthah the Gileadite died and was buried in his city in Gilead.[3]

Ibzan, Elon, and Abdon

8 After him Ibzan of Bethlehem judged Israel. 9 He had thirty sons, and thirty daughters he gave in marriage outside his clan, and thirty daughters he brought in from outside for his sons. And he judged Israel seven years. 10 Then Ibzan died and was buried at Bethlehem.

[1] Or *whoever* [2] Or *him* [3] Septuagint; Hebrew *in the cities of Gilead*

31 [h] [Lev. 27:2; 1 Sam. 1:28] [i] Ps. 66:13
33 [j] Ezek. 27:17
34 [k] ver. 11; ch. 10:17 [l] Ex. 15:20; 1 Sam. 18:6; Ps. 68:25; Jer. 31:4
35 [m] Num. 30:2; [Eccles. 5:4, 5]
39 [n] ver. 31

Chapter 12
1 [o] ch. 8:1
3 [p] 1 Sam. 19:5; 28:21; Job 13:14; [Ps. 119:109]
4 [q] [1 Sam. 25:10]
5 [r] See ch. 3:28
6 [r] [See ver. 5 above]

Whatever actually occurred, the ironies of the narrative make it clear that Jephthah's vow was foolish and was not something of which God or Israel approved (Judg. 11:40). In this era, prior to kings and with only sporadic prophets, much foolishness prevailed that is not consistent with the gospel priorities ultimately revealed—and, in fact, the foolishness speaks loudly of the need for gospel clarity and revelation.

That clarity and revelation come in an altogether unique offering acceptable to God. Jesus, Lamb and Shepherd, fully God and fully man (John 1:14–18), willingly gave his life, the shepherd for the sheep (John 1:29; 10:14–18). He did so to make the great exchange of our sin for his holiness (2 Cor. 5:21; 1 Pet. 3:18). What scandalous mercy! With hearts filled with loving gratitude, those trusting in Jesus now exist as living sacrifices (Rom. 12:1), offering acts of praise and service that please God (Phil. 4:18; Heb. 13:15–16).

11 After him Elon the Zebulunite judged
Israel, and he judged Israel ten years. 12 Then
Elon the Zebulunite died and was buried at
Aijalon in the land of Zebulun.
13 After him Abdon the son of Hillel the
Pirathonite judged Israel. 14 He had forty [s]sons
and thirty grandsons, who [t]rode on seventy
donkeys, and he judged Israel eight years.
15 Then Abdon the son of Hillel the Pirathonite
died and was buried at Pirathon in the land of
Ephraim, in the hill country of the Amalekites.

The Birth of Samson

13 And the people of Israel again [u]did
what was evil in the sight of the LORD,
so the LORD gave them [v]into the hand of the
Philistines for forty years.
2 There was a certain man of [w]Zorah, of the
tribe of the Danites, whose name was Manoah.
[x]And his wife was barren and had no children.
3 [y]And the angel of the LORD appeared to the
woman and said to her, "Behold, you are barren and have not borne children, but you shall
conceive and bear a son. 4 Therefore be careful [z]and drink no wine or strong drink, and
eat nothing unclean, 5 for behold, you shall
conceive and bear a son. [a]No razor shall come
upon his head, for the child shall be [z]a Nazirite
to God from the womb, and he shall [b]begin to
save Israel from the hand of the Philistines."
6 Then the woman came and told her husband,
[c]"A man of God came to me, and his appearance was like the appearance of the angel of
God, very awesome. [d]I did not ask him where
he was from, and he did not tell me his name,
7 but he said to me, [e]'Behold, you shall conceive and bear a son. So then drink no wine
or strong drink, and eat nothing unclean, for
the child shall be a Nazirite to God from the
womb to the day of his death.'"
8 Then Manoah prayed to the LORD and said,
"O Lord, please let the man of God whom you
sent come again to us and teach us what we
are to do with the child who will be born."
9 And God listened to the voice of Manoah, and
the angel of God came again to the woman as
she sat in the field. But Manoah her husband
was not with her. 10 So the woman ran quickly
and told her husband, "Behold, the man who
came to me the other day has appeared to me."
11 And Manoah arose and went after his wife
and came to the man and said to him, "Are you
the man who spoke to this woman?" And he
said, "I am." 12 And Manoah said, "Now when
your words come true, [f]what is to be the child's
manner of life, and what is his mission?"
13 And the angel of the LORD said to Manoah,
"Of all that I said to the woman let her be careful. 14 She may not eat of anything that comes
from the vine, [g]neither let her drink wine or
strong drink, or eat any unclean thing. All that
I commanded her let her observe."
15 Manoah said to the angel of the LORD,
"Please let us detain you and [h]prepare a young
goat for you." 16 And the angel of the LORD said
to Manoah, "If you detain me, I will not eat of
your food. But if you prepare a burnt offering, then offer it to the LORD." (For Manoah
did not know that he was the angel of the
LORD.) 17 And Manoah said to the angel of the

13:1–25 More than anywhere else in Judges, the stories of Samson demonstrate: (1) the presence of God with his people, (2) the sinfulness of people who need salvation, (3) the Spirit of God who empowers his servants, and (4) the self-sacrificing act of God who provides salvation.

The birth announcement of Samson reveals the presence of God with his people. While "the angel of the LORD" engages Israel elsewhere in Judges (2:1–4; 5:23; 6:11–12, 21–22), Judges 13 evidences the highest concentration of that title in the Old Testament (cf. Numbers 22). He is initially acknowledged as a "man of God" (Judg. 13:6, 8) and is later associated with a "wonderful" name (vv. 18–19; Isa. 9:6; Rev. 19:12–13). Gradually, as with Gideon (Judg. 6:21–22), the visage of the angel of the Lord is recognized as God himself (13:21–22). This experience, expected to bring death (cf. 6:23; Ex. 33:17–20), instead leads to worship (Judg. 13:20).

Central to discipleship is the increasing recognition of the identity of Christ (Matt. 16:13–17; John 12:34–36) leading to worship (Matt. 14:22–33; Rev. 5:6–14). The New Testament understands Jesus Christ as the visible representation of the invisible God (Ex. 3:14; John 8:58; Col. 1:15). In Judges, God's presence is most evident when his people are most helpless. This pattern finds its completion in the coming of Jesus Christ, whose light shines upon his people at their moment of deepest darkness (Matt. 4:13–17; John 3:19–21; Rom. 5:6; Gal. 4:3–5). Our hopeless circumstances are not a hindrance to the God of all grace.

14 [s] Job 18:19; Isa. 14:22; [1 Tim. 5:4] [t] ch. 5:10

Chapter 13

1 [u] See ch. 2:11 [v] [ch. 3:31; 10:7; 1 Sam. 12:9]
2 [w] Josh. 19:41; [Josh. 15:33] [x] [1 Sam. 1:2; Luke 1:7]
3 [y] ch. 6:12; Luke 1:11, 13
4 [z] ver. 7, 14; [Num. 6:2, 3; Luke 1:15]
5 [a] ch. 16:17; 1 Sam. 1:11; [Num. 6:5] [z] [See ver. 4 above] [b] [1 Sam. 7:13; 2 Sam. 8:1; 1 Chr. 18:1]
6 [c] See Deut. 33:1 [d] [ver. 17, 18]
7 [e] ver. 3-5
12 [f] [Luke 1:66]
14 [g] ver. 4, 7
15 [h] ch. 6:19; [Gen. 18:5-8]

LORD, [i]"What is your name, so that, when your
words come true, we may honor you?" 18 And
the angel of the LORD said to him, [j]"Why do
you ask my name, seeing [k]it is wonderful?"
19 So [l]Manoah took the young goat with the
grain offering, and offered it on the rock to
the LORD, to the one who works[1] wonders, and
Manoah and his wife were watching. 20 And
when the flame went up toward heaven from
the altar, the angel of the LORD went up in the
flame of the altar. Now Manoah and his wife
were watching, [m]and they fell on their faces
to the ground.

21 The angel of the LORD appeared no more
to Manoah and to his wife. [n]Then Manoah
knew that he was the angel of the LORD. 22 And
Manoah said to his wife, [n]"We shall surely die,
for we have seen God." 23 But his wife said to
him, "If the LORD had meant to kill us, he
would not have accepted a burnt offering and
a grain offering at our hands, or shown us all
these things, or now announced to us such
things as these." 24 And the woman bore a son
and called his name Samson. [o]And the young
man grew, and the LORD blessed him. 25 [p]And
the Spirit of the LORD began to stir him in
Mahaneh-dan, between [q]Zorah and Eshtaol.

Samson's Marriage

14 [r]Samson went down to [s]Timnah, and at
Timnah he saw one of the daughters of
the Philistines. 2 Then he came up and told his
father and mother, "I saw one of the daughters
of the Philistines at Timnah. [t]Now get her for
me as my wife." 3 But his father and mother
said to him, "Is there not a woman among the
daughters [u]of your relatives, or among all our
people, that you must go to take a wife from
the [v]uncircumcised Philistines?" But Samson
said to his father, "Get her for me, for she is
right in my eyes."

4 His father and mother did not know that
it was [w]from the LORD, for he was seeking an
opportunity against the Philistines. [x]At that
time the Philistines ruled over Israel.

5 Then Samson went down with his father
and mother to Timnah, and they came to the
vineyards of Timnah. And behold, a young
lion came toward him roaring. 6 [y]Then the
Spirit of the LORD rushed upon him, and
although he had nothing in his hand, he tore
the lion in pieces as one tears a young goat.
But he did not tell his father or his mother
what he had done. 7 Then he went down and
talked with the woman, and she was right in
Samson's eyes.

8 After some days he returned to take her.
And he turned aside to see the carcass of the
lion, and behold, there was a swarm of bees in
the body of the lion, and honey. 9 He scraped it
out into his hands and went on, eating as he
went. And he came to his father and mother
and gave some to them, and they ate. But he
did not tell them that he had scraped the
honey from the carcass of the lion.

10 His father went down to the woman, and
Samson prepared a feast there, for so the
young men used to do. 11 As soon as the people

[1] Septuagint, Vulgate; Hebrew *LORD, and working*

17 [i] [ver. 6]
18 [j] Gen. 32:29 [k] [Isa. 9:6]
19 [l] ch. 6:19-21
20 [m] Lev. 9:24; 1 Chr. 21:16; Ezek. 1:28
21 [n] ch. 6:22
22 [n] [See ver. 21 above]
24 [o] 1 Sam. 2:21; 3:19; Luke 1:80; [Luke 2:52]
25 [p] See ch. 3:10 [q] ch. 18:11; Josh. 15:33

Chapter 14
1 [r] Heb. 11:32 [s] Gen. 38:12, 13; Josh. 15:10; 19:43
2 [t] [Gen. 34:4]
3 [u] [Gen. 24:3, 4; 28:1, 2] [v] ch. 15:18; 1 Sam. 14:6; 17:26, 36; 31:4; 2 Sam. 1:20
4 [w] Josh. 11:20 [x] ch. 13:1; 15:11
6 [y] ver. 19; ch. 15:14; 1 Sam. 11:6; [ch. 3:10]

14:1–20 The life of Samson embodies the sinfulness of a people who need salvation. God ordained that Samson's Nazirite vow extend from birth to death (13:4–5, 14; Numbers 6). Samson breaks each Nazirite regulation. He touches a dead body (Judg. 14:8–9), comes into contact with products of the vineyard (v. 5; cf. Num. 6:3–4), and provides an occasion for drinking wine (Judg. 14:10). In Judges 16 his hair is cut (vv. 17, 19). Not every person in Israel took the Nazirite vow, but the vow expressed God's wider desire that his people be holy and separate in response to his grace (Lev. 11:44–45; 1 Pet. 1:16).

However, the idea of seeing Samson as the embodiment of Israel's need for salvation extends beyond his breaking of the Nazirite vow. Like Israel, he is governed by what is right in his own eyes (Judg. 14:1–3, 7; 17:6; 21:25), a mind-set that is deeply evil in God's sight (Num. 15:39; see note on Judg. 2:11–15). His pursuit of foreign women (14:3; 16:4–5) and a prostitute (16:1) mimic the spiritual whoredom of Israel pursuing foreign wives and gods (3:6; Ex. 34:15–16; Deut. 7:3–4; Jer. 3:1–2). Neither Samson nor his parents have the spiritual vision to see God sovereignly working his salvation even through the sinful choices of a man (Judg. 14:4; Acts 2:23). Israel's spiritual blindness (Isa. 42:18–20), mirrored in Samson's physical blindness (Judg. 16:21), requires the healing touch of a Savior (Matt. 9:27–30; 13:15–16). Like Israel, Samson is confident in his own strength, assuming that past blessing and God's presence will continue unabated (Judg. 16:20; Deut. 29:18–19; Jer. 7:1–4; Matt. 3:9).

saw him, they brought thirty companions to be with him. 12 And Samson said to them, [z]"Let me now put a riddle to you. If you can tell me what it is, within [a]the seven days of the feast, and find it out, then I will give you thirty linen garments and thirty [b]changes of clothes, 13 but if you cannot tell me what it is, then you shall give me thirty linen garments and thirty changes of clothes." And they said to him, "Put your riddle, that we may hear it." 14 And he said to them,

"Out of the eater came something to eat.
Out of the strong came something sweet."

And in three days they could not solve the riddle.

15 On the fourth[1] day they said to Samson's wife, [c]"Entice your husband to tell us what the riddle is, [d]lest we burn you and your father's house with fire. Have you invited us here to impoverish us?" 16 And Samson's wife wept over him and said, [e]"You only hate me; you do not love me. You have put a riddle to my people, and you have not told me what it is." And he said to her, "Behold, I have not told my father nor my mother, and shall I tell you?" 17 She wept before him the seven days that their feast lasted, and on the seventh day he told her, because [f]she pressed him hard. Then she told the riddle to her people. 18 And the men of the city said to him on the seventh day before the sun went down,

"What is sweeter than honey?
What is stronger than a lion?"

And he said to them,

"If you had not plowed with my heifer,
you would not have found out my riddle."

19 [g]And the Spirit of the LORD rushed upon him, and he went down to [h]Ashkelon and struck down thirty men of the town and took their spoil and gave the garments to those who had told the riddle. In hot anger he went back to his father's house. 20 And Samson's wife was given to [i]his companion, [j]who had been his best man.

Samson Defeats the Philistines

15 After some days, at the time of wheat harvest, Samson went to visit his wife with [k]a young goat. And he said, "I will go in to my wife in the chamber." But her father would not allow him to go in. 2 And her father said, "I really thought that you utterly hated her, [l]so I gave her to your companion. Is not her younger sister more beautiful than she? Please take her instead." 3 And Samson said to them, "This time I shall be innocent in regard to the Philistines, when I do them harm." 4 So Samson went and caught 300 foxes and took torches. And he turned them tail to tail and put a torch between each pair of tails. 5 And when he had set fire to the torches, he let the foxes go into the standing grain of the Philistines and set fire to the stacked grain and the standing grain, as well as the olive orchards. 6 Then the Philistines said, "Who has done this?" And they said, "Samson, the son-in-law of the Timnite, because he has taken his wife [m]and given her to his companion." And the Philistines came up and [n]burned her and her father with fire. 7 And Samson said to them, "If this is what you do, I swear I will be avenged on you, and after that I will quit." 8 And he struck them hip and thigh with a great blow, and he went down and stayed in the [o]cleft of the rock of Etam.

9 Then the Philistines came up and encamped in Judah and [p]made a raid on [q]Lehi. 10 And the men of Judah said, "Why have you come up against us?" They said, "We have come up to bind Samson, to do to him as he did to us." 11 Then 3,000 men of Judah went down to the cleft of the rock of Etam, and said to Samson,

[1] Septuagint, Syriac; Hebrew *seventh*

15:1–20 God's mission finds no success without the Spirit of the Lord empowering his servants, despite their obvious failings and disservice to him. Deliverance from the attacking lion (14:5–6) and several initial defeats of the Philistines are attributed to the Spirit who "rushes" upon Samson (14:19; 15:14–15). As with other judges, this demonstrates the legitimacy of Samson's saving mission (13:5, 12) and is later echoed when the Spirit "rushes upon" the first two kings of Israel, enabling their feats of deliverance (1 Sam. 11:6; 16:13).

The culmination and continuation of God's saving mission comes by means of the Spirit who confirms King Jesus for his work of salvation (Matt. 3:16–17). The Spirit likewise empowers those in the church (despite their obvious failings and disservice to him) to testify to their Lord's life, death, resurrection, and reign (Acts 1:8).

12 [z]Ezek. 17:2; [1 Kgs. 10:1; Ps. 78:2; Prov. 1:6] [a]Gen. 29:27 [b]Gen. 45:22; 2 Kgs. 5:5, 22, 23
15 [c]ch. 16:5 [d]ch. 15:6
16 [e][ch. 16:15]
17 [f][ch. 16:16]
19 [g]See ver. 6 [h]ch. 1:18
20 [i]ch. 15:2, 6 [j]John 3:29
Chapter 15
1 [k][Gen. 38:17]
2 [l]ver. 6; ch. 14:20
6 [m]ver. 2 [n]ch. 14:15
8 [o]ver. 11; Isa. 2:21; 57:5
9 [p]2 Sam. 5:18, 22 [q]ver. 14, 17, 19

"Do you not know that [r]the Philistines are rulers over us? What then is this that you have done to us?" And he said to them, "As they did to me, so have I done to them." 12 And they said to him, "We have come down to bind you, that we may give you into the hands of the Philistines." And Samson said to them, "Swear to me that you will not attack me yourselves." 13 They said to him, "No; we will only bind you and give you into their hands. We will surely not kill you." So they bound him with two [s]new ropes and brought him up from the rock.

14 When he came to Lehi, the Philistines came shouting to meet him. [t]Then the Spirit of the LORD rushed upon him, and the ropes that were on his arms became as flax that has caught fire, and his bonds melted off his hands. 15 And he found a fresh jawbone of a donkey, and put out his hand and took it, [u]and with it he struck 1,000 men. 16 And Samson said,

"With the jawbone of a donkey,
heaps upon heaps,
with the jawbone of a donkey
have I struck down a thousand men."

17 As soon as he had finished speaking, he threw away the jawbone out of his hand. And that place [v]was called Ramath-lehi.[1]

18 And he was very thirsty, and he called upon the LORD and said, [w]"You have granted this great salvation by the hand of your servant, and shall I now die of thirst and fall into the hands of the uncircumcised?" 19 And God split open the hollow place that is [v]at Lehi, and water came out from it. And when he drank, [x]his spirit returned, and he revived. Therefore the name of it was called En-hakkore;[2] it is at Lehi to this day. 20 And he judged Israel [y]in the days of the Philistines twenty years.

Samson and Delilah

16 Samson went to [z]Gaza, and there he saw a prostitute, and he went in to her. 2 The Gazites were told, "Samson has come here." And they [a]surrounded the place and set an ambush for him all night at the gate of the city. They kept quiet all night, saying, "Let us wait till the light of the morning; then we will kill him." 3 But Samson lay till midnight, and at midnight he arose and took hold of the doors of the gate of the city and the two posts, and pulled them up, bar and all, and put them on his shoulders and carried them to the top of the hill that is in front of Hebron.

4 After this he loved a woman in the Valley of Sorek, whose name was Delilah. 5 And [b]the lords of the Philistines came up to her and said to her, [c]"Seduce him, and see where his great strength lies, and by what means we may overpower him, that we may bind him to [d]humble him. And we will each give you 1,100 pieces of silver." 6 So Delilah said to Samson, "Please tell me where your great strength lies, and how you might be bound, that one could [d]subdue you."

7 Samson said to her, "If they bind me with seven fresh bowstrings that have not been dried, [e]then I shall become weak and be like any other man." 8 Then the lords of the Philistines brought up to her seven fresh bowstrings that had not been dried, and she bound him with them. 9 Now she had men lying in ambush in an inner chamber. And she said to him, "The Philistines are upon you, Samson!" But he snapped the bowstrings, as a thread of flax snaps when it touches the fire. So the secret of his strength was not known.

10 Then Delilah said to Samson, "Behold, you have mocked me and told me lies. Please tell me how you might be bound." 11 And he said to her, "If they bind me with [f]new ropes that have not been used, then I shall become weak and be like any other man." 12 So Delilah took new ropes and bound him with them and said to him, "The Philistines are upon you, Samson!" And the men lying in ambush were in an inner chamber. But he snapped the ropes off his arms like a thread.

[1] *Ramath-lehi* means *the hill of the jawbone* [2] *En-hakkore* means *the spring of him who called*

11 [r]ch. 13:1; 14:4
13 [s]ch. 16:11, 12
14 [t]ch. 14:6, 19; 1 Sam. 11:6; [ch. 3:10]
15 [u]Josh. 23:10; [ch. 3:31; Lev. 26:8]
17 [v]ver. 9, 14
18 [w][Ps. 3:7]
19 [v][See ver. 17 above] [x]Gen. 45:27
20 [y]ch. 13:1

16:1–31 The final days and death of Samson display the kind of character that honors God by providing deliverance for others through self-sacrifice. Samson's *blinding* is here coupled with his *binding* (v. 21), a key word in these narratives (15:10, 12, 13; 16:5–13). For Samson, both blindness and bondage are the result of an arrogance that presumes upon God's grace (v. 20). That this is the spiritual condition of God's people is reflected in the fact that the same treatment of "blinding" and "binding" befalls their representative Zedekiah, the final king of Judah at the time of Israel's great bondage in exile (2 Kings 25:7).

Chapter 16 1 [z]Josh. 15:47 2 [a][1 Sam. 23:26; Ps. 118:10-12; Acts 9:24] 5 [b]Josh. 13:3 [c]ch. 14:15 [d]ver. 19 6 [d][See ver. 5 above] 7 [e]ver. 11, 17 11 [f]ch. 15:13, 14

13 Then Delilah said to Samson, "Until now you have mocked me and told me lies. Tell me how you might be bound." And he said to her, "If you weave the seven locks of my head with the web and fasten it tight with the pin, then I shall become weak and be like any other man." 14 So while he slept, Delilah took the seven locks of his head and wove them into the web.[1] And she made them tight with the pin and said to him, "The Philistines are upon you, Samson!" But he awoke from his sleep and pulled away the pin, the loom, and the web.

15 And she said to him, [g]"How can you say, 'I love you,' when your heart is not with me? You have mocked me these three times, and you have not told me where your great strength lies." 16 And [h]when she pressed him hard with her words day after day, and urged him, his soul was vexed to death. 17 And he told her all his heart, and said to her, [i]"A razor has never come upon my head, for I have been a Nazirite to God from my mother's womb. If my head is shaved, then my strength will leave me, and I shall become weak and be like any other man."

18 When Delilah saw that he had told her all his heart, she sent and called the lords of the Philistines, saying, "Come up again, for he has told me all his heart." Then the lords of the Philistines came up to her and brought [j]the money in their hands. 19 She made him sleep on her knees. And she called a man and had him shave off the seven locks of his head. Then she began [k]to torment him, and his strength left him. 20 And she said, "The Philistines are upon you, Samson!" And he awoke from his sleep and said, "I will go out as at other times and shake myself free." But he did not know that [l]the LORD had left him. 21 And the Philistines seized him and gouged out his eyes and brought him down to Gaza and bound him with bronze shackles. [m]And he ground at the mill in the prison. 22 But the hair of his head began to grow again after it had been shaved.

The Death of Samson

23 Now the lords of the Philistines gathered to offer a great sacrifice to [n]Dagon their god and to rejoice, and they said, "Our god has given Samson our enemy into our hand." 24 And when the people saw him, [o]they praised their god. For they said, "Our god has given our enemy into our hand, the ravager of our country, who has killed many of us."[2] 25 And [p]when their hearts were merry, they said, "Call Samson, that he may entertain us." So they called Samson out of the prison, and he entertained them. They made him stand between the pillars. 26 And Samson said to the young man who held him by the hand, "Let me feel the pillars on which the house rests, that I may lean against them." 27 Now the house was full of men and women. All the lords of the Philistines were there, and [q]on the roof there were about 3,000 men and women, who looked on while Samson entertained.

28 Then Samson called to the LORD and said, "O Lord GOD, [r]please remember me and please strengthen me only this once, O God, that I may be avenged on the Philistines for my two eyes." 29 And Samson grasped the two middle pillars on which the house rested, and he leaned his weight against them, his right hand on the one and his left hand on the other. 30 And Samson said, "Let me die with the Philistines." Then he bowed with all his strength, and the house fell upon the lords and upon all the people who were in it. So the dead whom he killed at his death were more than those whom he had killed during his life. 31 Then his brothers and all his family came down and took him and brought him up and buried him [s]between Zorah and Eshtaol in the tomb of Manoah his father. He had judged Israel twenty years.

[1] Compare Septuagint; Hebrew lacks *and fasten it tight . . . into the web* [2] Or *who has multiplied our slain*

Israel continues in bondage to the Philistines, the chief antagonists in the books of Samuel (1 Samuel 4–6). Eventually, it is David who is raised up by a gracious God to free Israel from Philistine subjugation (1 Samuel 17; 2 Sam. 5:17–25; 19:9).

Jesus Christ, the final Judge and Savior and the final Son of David, is neither blind nor unwillingly bound. He who sees all and enables sight (John 1:48; 9:15) selflessly submitted himself to humiliation by his enemies. As the definitive covenant representative, Jesus saves his people from blindness (John 9:35–41) and identifies with their bondage (Mark 5:1–20; Matt. 27:2). In all this he accomplishes the work of the messianic servant: to open blind eyes and free those in bondage (Luke 4:16–21).

15[g] ch. 14:16
16[h] [ch. 14:17]
17[i] [ch. 13:5]
18[j] ver. 5
19[k] ver. 5, 6
20[l] 1 Sam. 28:15, 16
21[m] [Ex. 11:5; Matt. 24:41]
23[n] 1 Chr. 10:10; See 1 Sam. 5:2-7
24[o] [Dan. 5:4]
25[p] ch. 19:6; [2 Sam. 13:28]
27[q] [Deut. 22:8; 2 Sam. 11:2; Neh. 8:16; Matt. 24:17; Mark 13:15; Luke 17:31] **28**[r] Jer. 15:15 **31**[s] ch. 13:25

Micah and the Levite

17 There was a man of [t]the hill country of Ephraim, whose name was Micah. 2 And he said to his mother, "The 1,100 pieces of silver that were taken from you, about which you uttered a curse, and also spoke it in my ears, behold, the silver is with me; I took it." And his mother said, [u]"Blessed be my son by the LORD." 3 And he restored the 1,100 pieces of silver to his mother. And his mother said, "I dedicate the silver to the LORD from my hand for my son, to make [v]a carved image and [w]a metal image. Now therefore I will restore it to you." 4 So when he restored the money to his mother, his mother [x]took 200 pieces of silver and gave it to the silversmith, who made it into a carved image and a metal image. And it was in the house of Micah. 5 And the man Micah had a shrine, and he made [y]an ephod and [z]household gods, and [a]ordained[1] one of his sons, who became his priest. 6 [b]In those days there was no king in Israel. [c]Everyone did what was right in his own eyes.

7 Now there was a young man of [d]Bethlehem in Judah, of the family of Judah, who was a Levite, and he sojourned there. 8 And the man departed from the town of Bethlehem in Judah to sojourn where he could find a place. And as he journeyed, he came to [e]the hill country of Ephraim to the house of Micah. 9 And Micah said to him, "Where do you come from?" And he said to him, "I am a Levite of Bethlehem in Judah, and I am going to sojourn where I may find a place." 10 And Micah said to him, "Stay with me, and be to me [f]a father and a priest, and I will give you ten pieces of silver a year and a suit of clothes and your living." And the Levite went in. 11 And the Levite [g]was content to dwell with the man, and the young man became to him like one of his sons. 12 And Micah [h]ordained the Levite, and the young man [i]became his priest, and was in the house of Micah. 13 Then Micah said, "Now I know that the LORD will prosper me, because I have a Levite as priest."

[1] Hebrew *filled the hand of*; also verse 12

Chapter 17
1 [t] ver. 8; ch. 18:2; See Josh. 24:33
2 [u] Ruth 3:10; 1 Sam. 15:13
3 [v] [Ex. 20:4] [w] [Lev. 19:4]
4 [x] [Isa. 46:6]
5 [y] ch. 8:27; 18:14, 17; See Ex. 28:6-35 [z] [Gen. 31:19; Hos. 3:4] [a] ver. 12; [1 Kgs. 13:33]
6 [b] ch. 18:1; 19:1; 21:25 [c] [Deut. 12:8]
7 [d] ch. 19:1; Ruth 1:1, 2; Mic. 5:2; Matt. 2:1, 5, 6
8 [e] See Josh. 24:33
10 [f] ch. 18:19
11 [g] [Ex. 2:21]
12 [h] ver. 5 [i] [ch. 18:30]

17:1–21:25 Statements concerning the need for a king and rejection of divine authority conclude each of the final narratives in Judges (17:6; 18:1; 19:1; 21:25). The profound idolatries of the surrounding pagan nations are now *internal* to the people of God, as he graciously warns us in his Word of the thoroughness of corruption when we live outside his will. We learn from these passages that we abandon God when we do only what seems good to us: creating private religion (17:1–6), abandoning our personal calling (17:7–18:1), pursuing individual desire (18:1–19:1), and choosing personal preservation over justice (19:1–21:25).

17:1–6 Micah is a man from the "hill country of Ephraim" (v. 1; 19:1; 1 Sam. 1:1). His orthodox name, meaning "who is like Yahweh," belies his violation of the Lord's commandments. Micah steals from his mother (Judg. 17:2), who creates idols with the money he later returns (v. 3). He then establishes a private house of worship with "household gods" and a priest from his own family (v. 5; cf. Ex. 20:3–4).

The unrelenting testimony of the Scriptures is that idolatry is harmful (Jer. 7:6; 25:6–7), dehumanizing and bringing death rather than life (Ezek. 14:6–8; 33:25–29; Eph. 5:5). Genuine inheritance comes only through wholehearted devotion to the Lord (Deut. 30:5–6; Isa. 57:13; Matt. 5:5). What we worship and how we worship matters, for what we worship reveals what we most deeply trust (Ps. 115:4–8). Either we will become blind, deaf, dumb, and ineffective like the idols of our own making (Isa. 45:16; Jer. 10:5, 14), or we will worship the one true God and be conformed to his image—ultimately revealed in Christ (Rom. 8:29; 2 Cor. 4:4). These are our only two options, and only the God revealed in Christ is worthy of our adoration (Rev. 5:11–14; Matt. 28:8–9; Phil. 2:9–11). Only he is the true "Micah"—the one "who is like Yahweh."

17:7–13 The abhorrent agreement between Micah and the young Levite reveals the failure of an unfaithful priest who places the desire for private gain above his calling from a holy God. In place of priestly ordination (Leviticus 8), the Levite chooses private ordination and compensation (Judg. 17:10–12). He exchanges his holy garments (Exodus 28) for a new "suit of clothes" (Judg. 17:10), and his place and payment in Micah's house (vv. 9–10) supplants the Lord as his true inheritance (Deut. 18:1–5; Num. 18:8–24). Meanwhile Micah incorrectly believes that having his own personal

Danites Take the Levite and the Idol

18 [j]In those days there was no king in
Israel. And in those days [k]the tribe of
the people of Dan was seeking for itself an
inheritance to dwell in, for until then no
inheritance among the tribes of Israel had
fallen to them. 2 So the people of Dan sent
five able men from the whole number of their
tribe, [l]from Zorah and from Eshtaol, [m]to spy
out the land and to explore it. And they said
to them, "Go and explore the land." And they
came [n]to the hill country of Ephraim, to the
house of Micah, and lodged there. 3 When they
were by the house of Micah, they recognized
the voice of the young Levite. And they turned
aside and said to him, "Who brought you here?
What are you doing in this place? What is your
business here?" 4 And he said to them, "This is
how Micah dealt with me: [o]he has hired me,
and I have become his priest." 5 And they said
to him, [p]"Inquire of God, please, that we may
know whether the journey on which we are
setting out will succeed." 6 And the priest said
to them, [q]"Go in peace. The journey on which
you go is under the eye of the LORD."
7 Then the five men departed and came to
[r]Laish and saw the people who were there,
how they lived in security, after the manner
of the Sidonians, [s]quiet and unsuspecting,
lacking[1] nothing that is in the earth and possessing wealth, and how [t]they were far from
the Sidonians and had no dealings with anyone. 8 And when they came to their brothers
at [u]Zorah and Eshtaol, their brothers said
to them, "What do you report?" 9 They said,
[v]"Arise, and let us go up against them, for we
have seen the land, and behold, it is very good.
[w]And will you do nothing? [x]Do not be slow to
go, to enter in and possess the land. 10 As soon
as you go, you will come to an [y]unsuspecting
people. The land is spacious, for God has given
it into your hands, [z]a place where there is no
lack of anything that is in the earth."
11 So 600 men of the tribe of Dan, [a]armed
with weapons of war, set out from Zorah
and Eshtaol, 12 and went up and encamped
at Kiriath-jearim in Judah. On this account
that place is called [b]Mahaneh-dan[2] to this day;
behold, it is west of [c]Kiriath-jearim. 13 And they
passed on from there to [d]the hill country of
Ephraim, and came to the house of Micah.
14 Then the five men who had gone to scout
out the country of Laish said to their brothers,
"Do you know that [e]in these houses there are
an ephod, household gods, a carved image,
and a metal image? Now therefore consider
what you will do." 15 And they turned aside
there and came to the house of the young
Levite, at the home of Micah, and [f]asked him
about his welfare. 16 Now the 600 men of the
Danites, [g]armed with their weapons of war,
stood by the entrance of the gate. 17 And [h]the
five men who had gone to scout out the land
went up and entered and took [i]the carved
image, the ephod, the household gods, and
the metal image, while the priest stood by the
entrance of the gate with the 600 men armed
with weapons of war. 18 And when these went
into Micah's house and took [i]the carved image,
the ephod, the household gods, and the metal
image, the priest said to them, "What are you
doing?" 19 And they said to him, "Keep quiet;

[1] Compare 18:10; the meaning of the Hebrew word is uncertain [2] *Mahaneh-dan* means *camp of Dan*

priest will lead to prosperity (Judg. 17:13; cf. 18:21–26). He makes the mistake made by many today, assuming that piety is all about using spiritual leverage for personal gain.

We praise God for Jesus Christ, our better and faithful priest (Heb. 2:17). At great personal cost—and for no personal gain—Jesus fulfilled his own calling to be the ransom and mediator for all God's flock (John 10:17–18; 1 Tim. 2:5; Heb. 9:15). As a royal priesthood (1 Pet. 2:9), following Christ's example and in gratitude for it, we should also testify selflessly to the nations concerning his Word and deeds (Rom. 16:25–27). And, we are granted a true "suit of clothes" (Judg. 17:10; cf. Zech. 3:3–5), cleansed by the blood of his sacrifice (Rev. 7:13–14). Christ is secured as the priest who intercedes for us not through what we individually pay but through what he offered (Heb. 9:11–15).

18:1–31 The interwoven lives of the young Levite, the Danites, and Micah show that where God is dethroned, individual desire reigns. Within this web of relationships, unhealthy desire leads to sin as idolatry moves from an individual household to an entire tribe (vv. 30–31; cf. James 1:14–15). The fourfold repetition of "an ephod, household gods, a carved image, and a metal image" (Judg. 18:14, 17–18, 20) expresses the folly of idolatry. God's concern for his people then and now inspires the warnings against idolatry implicit in these accounts.

Chapter 18
1 [j]ch. 17:6; 21:25 [k][ch. 1:34; Josh. 19:47, 48]
2 [l]ver. 8, 11; ch. 13:25 [m][Num. 13:17; Josh. 2:1] [n]ch. 17:1, 8; See Josh. 24:33
4 [o]ch. 17:10
5 [p]Num. 27:21
6 [q]1 Sam. 1:17; [1 Kgs. 22:6]
7 [r][Josh. 19:47] [s]ver. 10, 27 [t]ver. 28
8 [u]ver. 2, 11
9 [v][Num. 13:20; Josh. 2:23, 24] [w]1 Kgs. 22:3 [x][Josh. 18:3]
10 [y]ver. 7, 27 [z][ch. 19:19; Deut. 8:9]
11 [a]ver. 16
12 [b]ch. 13:25 [c]Josh. 15:60
13 [d]ver. 2
14 [e]ch. 17:4, 5
15 [f]Gen. 43:27
16 [g]ver. 11
17 [h]ver. 2, 14 [i]ver. 14; ch. 17:4, 5
18 [i][See ver. 17 above]

[j]put your hand on your mouth and come with us and be to us [k]a father and a priest. Is it better for you to be priest to the house of one man, or to be priest to a tribe and clan in Israel?" 20 And the priest's heart was glad. He took the ephod and the household gods and the carved image and went along with the people.

21 So they turned and departed, putting the little ones and the livestock and [l]the goods in front of them. 22 When they had gone a distance from the home of Micah, the men who were in the houses near Micah's house were called out, and they overtook the people of Dan. 23 And they shouted to the people of Dan, who turned around and said to Micah, "What is the matter with you, that you come with such a company?" 24 And he said, [m]"You take my gods that I made and the priest, and go away, and what have I left? How then do you ask me, 'What is the matter with you?' " 25 And the people of Dan said to him, "Do not let your voice be heard among us, lest angry fellows fall upon you, and you lose your life with the lives of your household." 26 Then the people of Dan went their way. And when Micah saw that they were too strong for him, he turned and went back to his home.

27 But the people of Dan took what Micah had made, and the priest who belonged to him, and they came to Laish, to a people [n]quiet and unsuspecting, and [o]struck them with the edge of the sword and burned the city with fire. 28 And there was no deliverer because it was [p]far from Sidon, and they had no dealings with anyone. It was in the valley that belongs to [q]Beth-rehob. Then they rebuilt the city and lived in it. 29 And they named the city [r]Dan, after the name of Dan their ancestor, who was born to Israel; but [s]the name of the city was Laish at the first. 30 And the people of Dan set up the carved image for themselves, and Jonathan the son of Gershom, [t]son of Moses,[1] [u]and his sons were priests to the tribe of the Danites until the day [v]of the captivity of the land. 31 So they set up Micah's carved image that he made, [w]as long as the house of God was at Shiloh.

A Levite and His Concubine

19 In those days, [x]when there was no king in Israel, a certain Levite was sojourning in the remote parts of [y]the hill country of Ephraim, who took to himself a concubine from [z]Bethlehem in Judah. 2 And his concubine was unfaithful to[2] him, and she went away from him to her father's house at Bethlehem in Judah, and was there some four months. 3 Then her husband arose and went after her, to speak kindly to her and bring her back. He had with him his servant and a cou-

[1] Or *Manasseh* [2] Septuagint, Old Latin *became angry with*

19 [j] Job 21:5; 29:9; 40:4; Prov. 30:32; Mic. 7:16 [k] ch. 17:10
21 [l] [1 Sam. 17:22; Isa. 10:28]
24 [m] [Gen. 31:30]
27 [n] ver. 7, 10 [o] Josh. 19:47
28 [p] ver. 7 [q] 2 Sam. 10:6; [Num. 13:21; Josh. 19:28]
29 [r] ch. 20:1; Gen. 14:14; 1 Kgs. 12:29, 30; 15:20 [s] ver. 7
30 [t] Ex. 2:22; 18:3 [u] [ch. 17:12] [v] ch. 13:1; 1 Sam. 4:2, 3, 10, 11; See Ps. 78:60-64
31 [w] Josh. 18:1; 1 Sam. 1:3
Chapter 19
1 [x] ch. 17:6; 18:1; 21:25 [y] See Josh. 24:33 [z] See ch. 17:7

Once we abandon our personal calling from the Lord in favor of private gain (17:10), the pursuit of personal ambition thrives (18:19). No longer satisfied to serve one family, the Levite quickly participates in the Danites' thievery, agreeing to be priest for an entire tribe—an outcome in which he rejoices (v. 20). Meanwhile the Danites take what is not theirs; no longer satisfied with an inheritance previously granted by the Lord (Josh. 19:40–48; Judg. 1:34), they seize land that was never given to them (18:27–29). Micah raises the rhetorical question that drives the application of the passage: what remains when my personal idols are taken away from me (v. 24)?

The people of God exist in an intricate web of relationships in which the spiritual health of the individual matters to the community and vice versa. Because our Lord is our true and righteous King (Rev. 19:16), he calls us to subordinate private gain and personal ambition to kingdom concerns (Matt. 6:25–34; Acts 2:43–45; James 3:14–18). Rather than seeking an idolatrous inheritance of our own creation that cannot sustain or satisfy us, we are called to seek the inheritance Christ gained for us. He himself is the only inheritance that is truly secure and the only one that really satisfies (Col. 1:11–14; 1 Pet. 1:3–5). Where our Lord reigns in the hearts of individuals and communities, we recognize that personal idols upon which we rely (e.g., private addictions, family background, self-righteousness, appearances, etc.) are to be put to death, as was signified and accomplished at the cross (Gal. 6:12–16).

19:1–21:25 Judges concludes with a final long and complicated story of God's people devouring one another (see note on 9:7–21) through widespread lawlessness. The men of Gibeah are driven by illicit sexual desire (19:22); a Levite is more concerned with personal preservation than the welfare of his wife (19:25–26); and Israel extinguishes their own people rather than the Canaanites (21:8–12).

ple of donkeys. And she brought him into her
father's house. And when the girl's father saw
him, he came with joy to meet him. 4 And his
father-in-law, the girl's father, made him stay,
and he remained with him three days. So they
ate and drank and spent the night there. 5 And
on the fourth day they arose early in the morning, and he prepared to go, but the girl's father
said to his son-in-law, [a]"Strengthen your heart
with a morsel of bread, and after that you may
go." 6 So the two of them sat and ate and drank
together. And the girl's father said to the man,
"Be pleased to spend the night, and [b]let your
heart be merry." 7 And when the man rose up
to go, his father-in-law pressed him, till he
spent the night there again. 8 And on the fifth
day he arose early in the morning to depart.
And the girl's father said, [c]"Strengthen your
heart and wait until the day declines." So they
ate, both of them. 9 And when the man and his
concubine and his servant rose up to depart,
his father-in-law, the girl's father, said to him,
"Behold, now the day has waned toward evening. Please, spend the night. Behold, the day
draws to its close. Lodge here and let your
heart be merry, and tomorrow you shall arise
early in the morning for your journey, and
go home."

10 But the man would not spend the night.
He rose up and departed and arrived opposite
[d]Jebus (that is, Jerusalem). He had with him a
couple of saddled donkeys, and his concubine
was with him. 11 When they were near Jebus,
the day was nearly over, and the servant said
to his master, "Come now, let us turn aside to
this city of the Jebusites and spend the night
in it." 12 And his master said to him, "We will
not turn aside into the city of foreigners, who
do not belong to the people of Israel, but we
will pass on to [e]Gibeah." 13 And he said to his
young man, "Come and let us draw near to one
of these places and spend the night at Gibeah
or at [f]Ramah." 14 So they passed on and went
their way. And the sun went down on them
near Gibeah, which belongs to Benjamin,
15 and they turned aside there, to go in and
spend the night at Gibeah. And he went in
and sat down in the open square of the city,
[g]for no one took them into his house to spend
the night.

16 And behold, an old man was coming from
his work in the field at evening. The man was
from [h]the hill country of Ephraim, and he
was sojourning in Gibeah. [i]The men of the
place were Benjaminites. 17 And he lifted up his
eyes and saw the traveler in the open square
of the city. And the old man said, "Where are
you going? And where do you come from?"
18 And he said to him, "We are passing from
Bethlehem in Judah to the remote parts of

What is most striking about this sordid account is the way it recapitulates things that, earlier in Israel's history, were true only of godless Gentiles. The astute Hebrew reader of Judges 19 could not miss the way this story echoes Genesis 19—another account involving a visitor being sought out to be raped by the men of the city. Only that time, the horrid events took place in Sodom, the city that came to represent the epitome of godlessness. Here in Judges 19, the repugnance of Sodom is repeated in Gibeah, a city of Benjamin. Israel has become like her pagan neighbors. Only Israel's united stand against Benjamin's wickedness (20:1, 8, 11) and explicit pursuit of God's will and his response (20:18, 23, 28) provide any glimmer of hope.

We are silenced and then outraged by the unspeakably awful sexual abuse and death experienced by the unnamed innocent woman (19:22–29). Guilt, shame, fear, and many other latent emotions arise in those who have experienced such wickedness at the hands of others. The pain of those wronged by people who claim to be Christians may persuade them to walk away from the Lord. In light of such injustice there are no easy answers. Yet if God does not abandon his people in the face of such horrible sin, then we are helped to understand that he never will abandon us.

We must also consider that if fallen but redeemed men and women sense the depravity of these events, then how much greater is the pain to our Lord and how amazing is the grace he provides to atone for such sin. Jesus, the King, has come and conquered our rejection of his reign (John 1:9–13). His suffering with us enables us to bear up in our own suffering (John 16:33; Rom. 8:21–39). The painful experiences of being both sinner and sinned against propel us to plead with God for the return of our true King. Our prayer must be, "Lord, under your reign, empower me to do my part in promoting the flourishing of your people." And so the prayer of the Davidic king (Ps. 22:19) becomes our prayer: "Our Lord, come!" (1 Cor. 16:22).

5[a] ver. 8; Gen. 18:5
6[b] ver. 9, 22; ch. 16:25; Ruth 3:7; 2 Sam. 13:28
8[c] ver. 5
10[d] See Josh. 15:8, 63
12[e] Josh. 18:28
13[f] Josh. 18:25
15[g] ver. 18
16[h] ver. 1; See Josh. 24:33 [i] ver. 14; ch. 20:4

the hill country of Ephraim, from which I come. I went to Bethlehem in Judah, and I am going[j] to the house of the LORD,[1] [g]but no one has taken me into his house. 19 We have straw and feed for our donkeys, with bread and wine for me and your female servant and the young man with your servants. [k]There is no lack of anything." 20 And the old man said, [l]"Peace be to you; I will care for all your wants. [m]Only, do not spend the night in the square." 21 So he brought him into his house and gave the donkeys feed. [n]And they washed their feet, and ate and drank.

Gibeah's Crime

22 As they were [o]making their hearts merry, behold, the men of the city, worthless fellows, [p]surrounded the house, beating on the door. And they said to the old man, the master of the house, "Bring out the man who came into your house, that we may know him." 23 And the man, the master of the house, went out to them and said to them, "No, my brothers, [q]do not act so wickedly; since this man has come into my house, [r]do not do this vile thing. 24 [s]Behold, here are my virgin daughter and his concubine. Let me bring them out now. [t]Violate them and do with them what seems good to you, but against this man [r]do not do this outrageous thing." 25 But the men would not listen to him. So the man seized his concubine and made her go out to them. And they knew her and abused her all night until the morning. And as the dawn began to break, they let her go. 26 And as morning appeared, the woman came and fell down at the door of the man's house where her master was, until it was light.

27 And her master rose up in the morning, and when he opened the doors of the house and went out to go on his way, behold, there was his concubine lying at the door of the house, with her hands on the threshold. 28 He said to her, "Get up, let us be going." [u]But there was no answer. Then he put her on the donkey, and the man rose up and went away to his home. 29 And when he entered his house, he took a knife, and taking hold of his concubine he [v]divided her, limb by limb, into twelve pieces, and sent her throughout all the territory of Israel. 30 [w]And all who saw it said, "Such a thing has never happened or been seen from the day that the people of Israel came up out of the land of Egypt until this day; [x]consider it, take counsel, and speak."

Israel's War with the Tribe of Benjamin

20 Then [y]all the people of Israel came out, [z]from Dan to Beersheba, including the land of Gilead, and the congregation assembled as one man to the LORD at [a]Mizpah. 2 And the [b]chiefs of all the people, of all the tribes of Israel, presented themselves in the assembly of the people of God, 400,000 men on foot [c]that drew the sword. 3 (Now the people of Benjamin heard that the people of Israel had gone up to Mizpah.) And the people of Israel said, "Tell us, how did this evil happen?" 4 And the Levite, the husband of the woman who was murdered, answered and said, [d]"I came to Gibeah that belongs to Benjamin, I and my concubine, to spend the night. 5 [e]And the leaders of Gibeah rose against me and surrounded the house against me by night. They meant to kill me, and they violated my concubine, and she is dead. 6 [f]So I took hold of my concubine and cut her in pieces and sent her throughout all the country of the inheritance of Israel, for they have committed abomination and [g]outrage in Israel. 7 Behold, you people of Israel, all of you, [h]give your advice and counsel here."

8 And all the people arose as one man, saying, "None of us will go to his tent, and none of us will return to his house. 9 But now this is what we will do to Gibeah: we will go up against it by lot, 10 and we will take ten men of a hundred throughout all the tribes of Israel, and a hundred of a thousand, and a thousand of ten thousand, to bring provisions for the people, that when they come they may repay Gibeah of Benjamin, for all the outrage that they have committed in Israel." 11 So all the men of Israel gathered against the city, united as one man.

12 [i]And the tribes of Israel sent men through all the tribe of Benjamin, saying, "What evil is this that has taken place among you? 13 Now therefore give up the men, [j]the worthless fellows in Gibeah, that we may put them to death [k]and purge evil from Israel." But the Benjaminites would not listen to the voice

[1] Septuagint *my home*; compare verse 29

18 [j]ch. 18:31 [g][See ver. 15 above] **19** [k][ch. 18:10] **20** [l]Gen. 43:23 [m]Gen. 19:2 **21** [n]Gen. 18:4; 24:32; 43:24; [John 13:5] **22** [o]See ver. 6 [p]ch. 20:5; [Gen. 19:4] **23** [q]Gen. 19:7 [r]ch. 20:6; Gen. 34:7; Deut. 22:21; 2 Sam. 13:12; [Josh. 7:15] **24** [s][Gen. 19:8] [t]Gen. 34:2; Deut. 21:14 [r][See ver. 23 above] **28** [u][ch. 20:5] **29** [v]ch. 20:6; [1 Sam. 11:7] **30** [w][Hos. 9:9; 10:9] [x]ch. 20:7 **Chapter 20** **1** [y]ch. 21:5; [Josh. 22:12; 1 Sam. 11:7] [z]1 Sam. 3:20; 2 Sam. 3:10; 24:2 [a][1 Sam. 7:5; 10:17] **2** [b]1 Sam. 14:38 [c]ver. 15, 17, 25, 35, 46; See ch. 8:10 **4** [d]ch. 19:15 **5** [e]ch. 19:22, 25, 26 **6** [f]ch. 19:29 [g]See ch. 19:23 **7** [h]ch. 19:30 **12** [i][Deut. 13:14; Josh. 22:13, 16] **13** [j]ch. 19:22; See Deut. 13:13 [k]Deut. 13:5; 17:2

of their brothers, the people of Israel. 14 Then
the people of Benjamin came together out
of the cities to Gibeah to go out to battle
against the people of Israel. 15 And the people
of Benjamin mustered out of their cities on
that day [l]26,000 men [m]who drew the sword,
besides the inhabitants of Gibeah, who mustered 700 chosen men. 16 Among all these were
700 chosen men who were [n]left-handed; every
one could sling a stone at a hair and not miss.
17 And the men of Israel, apart from Benjamin,
mustered [m]400,000 men who drew the sword;
all these were men of war.

18 The people of Israel arose and went up to
[o]Bethel and inquired of God, [p]"Who shall go
up first for us to fight against the people of
Benjamin?" And the LORD said, [p]"Judah shall
go up first."

19 Then the people of Israel rose in the morning and encamped against Gibeah. 20 And
the men of Israel went out to fight against
Benjamin, and the men of Israel drew up the
battle line against them at Gibeah. 21 [q]The
people of Benjamin came out of Gibeah and
destroyed on that day 22,000 men of the
Israelites. 22 But the people, the men of Israel,
took courage, and again formed the battle line
in the same place where they had formed it on
the first day. 23 [r]And the people of Israel went
up and wept before the LORD until the evening. And they inquired of the LORD, "Shall we
again draw near to fight against our brothers,
the people of Benjamin?" And the LORD said,
"Go up against them."

24 So the people of Israel came near against
the people of Benjamin the second day. 25 And
Benjamin [s]went against them out of Gibeah
the second day, and destroyed 18,000 men of
the people of Israel. All these were men who
[t]drew the sword. 26 Then all the people of
Israel, the whole army, went up and came to
[u]Bethel and wept. They sat there before the
LORD and fasted that day until evening, and
offered burnt offerings and peace offerings
before the LORD. 27 And the people of Israel
inquired of the LORD [v](for the ark of the covenant of God was there in those days, 28 and
[w]Phinehas the son of Eleazar, son of Aaron,
[x]ministered before it in those days), saying,
"Shall we go out once more to battle against
our brothers, the people of Benjamin, or shall
we cease?" And the LORD said, "Go up, for
tomorrow I will give them into your hand."

29 [y]So Israel set men in ambush around
Gibeah. 30 And the people of Israel went
up against the people of Benjamin on the
third day and set themselves in array against
Gibeah, as at other times. 31 And the people of
Benjamin went out against the people and
were drawn away from the city. And as at other
times they began to strike and kill some of the
people in the highways, [z]one of which goes
up to [a]Bethel and the other to Gibeah, and in
the open country, about thirty men of Israel.
32 And the people of Benjamin said, [b]"They are
routed before us, as at the first." But the people
of Israel said, "Let us flee and draw them away
from the city to the highways." 33 And all the
men of Israel rose up out of their place and
set themselves in array at Baal-tamar, and the
men of Israel who were in ambush rushed out
of their place from Maareh-geba.[1] 34 And there
came against Gibeah 10,000 chosen men out
of all Israel, and the battle was hard, [c]but the
Benjaminites did not know that disaster was
close upon them. 35 And the LORD defeated
Benjamin before Israel, and the people of
Israel destroyed 25,100 men of Benjamin that
day. All these were men who [d]drew the sword.
36 So the people of Benjamin saw that they
were defeated.

The men of Israel gave ground to Benjamin,
because they trusted the men in ambush
whom they had set against Gibeah. 37 [e]Then
the men in ambush hurried and rushed
against Gibeah; the men in ambush moved
out and struck all the city with the edge of the
sword. 38 Now the appointed signal between
the men of Israel and the men in the main
ambush was that when they made a great
cloud of smoke rise up out of the city 39 the
men of Israel should turn in battle. Now
Benjamin had begun to strike and kill about
thirty men of Israel. They said, [f]"Surely they
are defeated before us, as in the first battle."
40 But when the signal began to rise out of the
city in a column of smoke, the Benjaminites
looked behind them, and behold, [g]the whole
of the city went up in smoke to heaven. 41 Then
the men of Israel turned, and the men of
Benjamin were dismayed, [h]for they saw that
disaster was close upon them. 42 Therefore

[1] Some Septuagint manuscripts *place west of Geba*

15 [l][Num. 1:37; 26:41] [m]ver. 2 **16** [n]ch. 3:15; [1 Chr. 12:2] **17** [m][See ver. 15 above] **18** [o]ver. 26, 31 [p][ch. 1:1] **21** [q]ver. 25 **23** [r]ver. 26-28 **25** [s]ver. 21 [t]ver. 2 **26** [u]ver. 18, 31 **27** [v][Josh. 18:1; 1 Sam. 4:3, 4] **28** [w]Num. 25:7; 31:6; Josh. 24:33 [x]Deut. 10:8; 18:5, 7 **29** [y][Josh. 8:4] **31** [z]ch. 21:19 [a]ver. 18, 26 **32** [b][Josh. 8:5, 6] **34** [c]ver. 41 **35** [d]ver. 2 **37** [e][Josh. 8:19] **39** [f]ver. 31, 32 **40** [g][Josh. 8:20] **41** [h]ver. 34

they turned their backs before the men of
Israel in [i]the direction of the wilderness, but
the battle overtook them. And those who came
out of the cities were destroying them in their
midst. 43 Surrounding the Benjaminites, they
pursued them and trod them down from
Nohah[1] as far as opposite Gibeah on the east.
44 Eighteen thousand men of Benjamin fell,
all of them men of valor. 45 And they turned
[i]and fled toward the wilderness to the rock of
[j]Rimmon. Five thousand men of them were
cut down in the highways. And they were
pursued hard to Gidom, and 2,000 men of
them were struck down. 46 So all who fell that
day of Benjamin were 25,000 men who drew
the sword, all of them men of valor. 47 But
600 men turned and [i]fled toward the wilderness to the rock of [j]Rimmon and remained at
the rock of Rimmon four months. 48 And the
men of Israel turned back against the people
of Benjamin and struck them with the edge
of the sword, the city, men and beasts and all
that they found. And all the towns that they
found they set on fire.

Wives Provided for the Tribe of Benjamin

21 Now the men of Israel had sworn [k]at
Mizpah, "No one of us shall give his
daughter in marriage to Benjamin." 2 And
the people came to [l]Bethel and sat there till
evening before God, and they lifted up their
voices and wept bitterly. 3 And they said, "O
LORD, the God of Israel, why has this happened in Israel, that today there should be
one tribe lacking in Israel?" 4 And the next day
the people rose early and [m]built there an altar
and offered burnt offerings and peace offerings. 5 And the people of Israel said, "Which of
all the tribes of Israel did not come up in the
assembly to the LORD?" [n]For they had taken a
great oath concerning him who did not come
up to the LORD to Mizpah, saying, "He shall
surely be put to death." 6 And the people of
Israel [o]had compassion for Benjamin their
brother and said, "One tribe is cut off from
Israel this day. 7 [p]What shall we do for wives
for those who are left, since we have sworn by
the LORD that we will not give them any of
our daughters for wives?"
8 And they said, "What one is there of the
tribes of Israel that did not come up to the
LORD to Mizpah?" And behold, no one had
come to the camp from [q]Jabesh-gilead, to the
assembly. 9 For when the people were mustered, behold, not one of the inhabitants of
[q]Jabesh-gilead was there. 10 So the congregation sent 12,000 of their bravest men there
and commanded them, [r]"Go and strike the
inhabitants of Jabesh-gilead with the edge of
the sword; also the women and the little ones.
11 This is what you shall do: [s]every male and
every woman that has lain with a male you
shall devote to destruction." 12 And they found
among the inhabitants of Jabesh-gilead 400
young virgins who had not known a man by
lying with him, and they brought them to the
camp at [t]Shiloh, which is in the land of Canaan.
13 Then the whole congregation sent word to
the people of Benjamin who were at the [u]rock
of Rimmon and [v]proclaimed peace to them.
14 And Benjamin returned at that time. And
they gave them the women whom they had
saved alive of the women of Jabesh-gilead, but
they were not enough for them. 15 And the people [w]had compassion on Benjamin because the
LORD had made a breach in the tribes of Israel.
16 Then the elders of the congregation said,
[x]"What shall we do for wives for those who
are left, since the women are destroyed out of
Benjamin?" 17 And they said, "There must be
an inheritance for the survivors of Benjamin,
that a tribe not be blotted out from Israel. 18 Yet
we cannot give them wives from our daughters." [y]For the people of Israel had sworn,
"Cursed be he who gives a wife to Benjamin."
19 So they said, "Behold, there is the yearly
feast of the LORD at Shiloh, which is north of
Bethel, on the east of [z]the highway that goes
up from Bethel to Shechem, and south of
Lebonah." 20 And they commanded the people
of Benjamin, saying, "Go and lie in ambush in
the vineyards 21 and watch. If the daughters of
Shiloh come out to [a]dance in the dances, then
come out of the vineyards and snatch each
man his wife from the daughters of Shiloh,
and go to the land of Benjamin. 22 And when
their fathers or their brothers come to complain to us, we will say to them, 'Grant them
graciously to us, because we did not take for
each man of them his wife in battle, neither
did you give them to them, else you would
now be guilty.'" 23 And the people of Benjamin

[1] Septuagint; Hebrew [at their] *resting place*

42 [i] [Josh. 8:15, 24] **45** [i] [See ver. 42 above] [j] ch. 21:13; Josh. 15:32 **47** [i] [See ver. 42 above] [j] [See ver. 45 above] **Chapter 21** **1** [k] ver. 18; ch. 20:1
2 [l] ch. 20:18, 26, 31 **4** [m] [2 Sam. 24:25] **5** [n] [ch. 5:23] **6** [o] ver. 15 **7** [p] ver. 16 **8** [q] 1 Sam. 11:1; 31:11-13 **9** [q] [See ver. 8 above] **10** [r] [ver. 5] **11** [s] Num. 31:17
12 [t] Josh. 18:1 **13** [u] ch. 20:47 [v] Deut. 20:10 **15** [w] ver. 6 **16** [x] ver. 7 **18** [y] ver. 1 **19** [z] [ch. 20:31] **21** [a] ch. 11:34; Ex. 15:20

did so and took their wives, according to their
number, from the dancers whom they carried
off. Then they went and returned to their
inheritance [b]and rebuilt the towns and lived
in them. 24 And the people of Israel departed
from there at that time, every man to his tribe
and family, and they went out from there every
man to his inheritance.

25 [c]In those days there was no king in Israel.
Everyone did what was right in his own eyes.

23[b] [ch. 20:48] **25**[c] ch. 17:6; 18:1; 19:1

Introduction to Ruth

Author and Date

The story of Ruth takes place in the time of the judges (after the conquest of Canaan and before c. 1050 B.C.). No author is named, but the mention of David and his genealogy (4:17–22) places the writing sometime after David became king (2 Samuel 2) in c. 1010 B.C.

The Gospel in Ruth

Ruth is the story of a young Moabite widow who comes to know the covenant love of the one true God and the joy of belonging to his people through her Jewish mother-in-law, Naomi. As these two women navigate through difficult as well as ordinary circumstances, there is unmistakable evidence of God's sovereign hand at work to redeem a people for himself. He is the hero of the story as the faithful God who with great loving kindness (*hesed*) cares for his own and provides what they need. In Ruth's story we see a reflection of our own. For we too were "alienated from the commonwealth of Israel and strangers to the covenants of promise, having no hope and without God in the world" (Eph. 2:12). Like Ruth, we too need a Kinsman-Redeemer who will do what is necessary to remedy our helpless condition.

The language of redemption permeates the story of Ruth: words built on the root "redeem" (*ga-al*) appear 23 times. Key to understanding the narrative is the concept of the kinsman-redeemer, the closest living male relative who had the duty to preserve the family name and land. He could do this in a number of ways: buying back either land that a poor relative had to sell or the family member that had sold himself into slavery to pay debts (Lev. 25:25, 47–49), avenging the death of a family member (Num. 35:19–21), or marrying the widow of a deceased relative (Deut. 25:5–10). All of these duties could be refused, including marriage to the late relative's widow (now known as "levirate" marriage, *levir* being the Latin translation of the Hebrew word for brother-in-law). In certain cases, one could be a *goel* (Hebrew for "close relative" or "redeemer") without being a *levir* (one who would provide an heir to the deceased relative through marrying his widow). In Ruth's case, the kinsman-redeemer Boaz elects to carry out the duties of both, buying her estate and taking her as his bride.

Readers of the New Testament will recognize Jesus Christ as the ultimate Kinsman-Redeemer who voluntarily paid the price for the redemption of his people and takes them as his beloved bride (Eph. 5:23–32; Rev. 19:7).

Outline

I. Introduction: Naomi's Family Dies (1:1–5)

II. Scene 1: Naomi Returns to Bethlehem with Ruth (1:6–22)

III. Scene 2: Ruth Gleans in Boaz's Field (2:1–23)
IV. Scene 3: Ruth, at the Threshing Floor, Asks Boaz to Marry Her (3:1–18)
V. Scene 4: Boaz Arranges Redemption at the Gate (4:1–12)
VI. Conclusion: Naomi Blessed with a New Family (4:13–17)
VII. Genealogy: Extended Blessing (4:18–22)

Ruth

Naomi Widowed

1 In the days [a]when the judges ruled there
was [b]a famine in the land, and a man of
[c]Bethlehem in Judah went to sojourn in the
country of Moab, he and his wife and his two
sons. 2 The name of the man was Elimelech and
the name of his wife Naomi, and the names of
his two sons were Mahlon and Chilion. They
were [d]Ephrathites from Bethlehem in Judah.
They went into the country of Moab and
remained there. 3 But Elimelech, the husband
of Naomi, died, and she was left with her two
sons. 4 These took Moabite wives; the name of
the one was Orpah and the name of the other
Ruth. They lived there about ten years, 5 and
both Mahlon and Chilion died, so that the
woman was left without her two sons and her
husband.

Ruth's Loyalty to Naomi

6 Then she arose with her daughters-in-law
to return from the country of Moab, for she
had heard in the fields of Moab that [e]the LORD
had visited his people and [f]given them food.
7 So she set out from the place where she was
with her two daughters-in-law, and they went
on the way to return to the land of Judah. 8 But
Naomi said to her two daughters-in-law, "Go,
return each of you to her mother's house.
May the LORD [g]deal kindly with you, as you
have dealt with [h]the dead and with me. 9 The
LORD grant that you may find [i]rest, each of
you in the house of her husband!" Then she
kissed them, and they lifted up their voices
and wept. 10 And they said to her, "No, we will
return with you to your people." 11 But Naomi
said, "Turn back, my daughters; why will you
go with me? Have I yet sons in my womb [j]that
they may become your husbands? 12 Turn back,
my daughters; go your way, for I am too old to
have a husband. If I should say I have hope,
even if I should have a husband this night and
should bear sons, 13 would you therefore wait
till they were grown? Would you therefore
refrain from marrying? No, my daughters, for
it is exceedingly bitter to me for your sake that
[k]the hand of the LORD has gone out against
me." 14 Then they lifted up their voices and
wept again. And Orpah kissed her mother-in-
law, but Ruth clung to her.
15 And she said, "See, your sister-in-law has

1:1–5 Although the times of the judges were dark, when "everyone did what was right in his own eyes" (Judg. 17:6), God still was calling to himself a believing remnant. Through Elimelech's decision to take his family to Moab (whether right or wrong), God would work to fulfill his promise to Abraham, "In you all the families of the earth shall be blessed" (Gen. 12:3). This story is an important piece of the overarching story of redemptive history. The last word in the book will make this abundantly clear.

1:6–13 Naomi hears that the Lord had shown favor to his people by ending their famine in Judah. She starts on the return journey from Moab with Orpah and Ruth, but then considers their situation and pleads with them to turn back. Using the language of covenant love, "deal kindly" (*hesed*, v. 8), she prays that the Lord will give them the security of home and family in Moab. She has no other sons to fulfill the levirate marriage law, and at her age she cannot provide them now. She grieves that her own circumstances have affected them so disastrously, feeling that the Lord's hand was against her.

But death of loved ones is ultimately the result of living in a fallen world; it comes to all. Far from being against her, the Lord is working through Naomi's grievous circumstances to bring into the world One who ultimately will redeem her and all his people from death forever (Col. 2:13–15; 2 Tim. 1:10; Rev. 21:4).

Chapter 1
1 [a] Judg. 2:16 [b] Gen. 12:10; 26:1; 43:1; 2 Kgs. 8:1 [c] See Judg. 17:7
2 [d] Gen. 35:19
6 [e] Ex. 3:16; 4:31; Luke 1:68 [f] Ps. 132:15
8 [g] Josh. 2:12, 14; Judg. 1:24 [h] ver. 5; ch. 2:20
9 [i] ch. 3:1
11 [j] Gen. 38:11; Deut. 25:5
13 [k] Judg. 2:15; [Job 19:21; Ps. 32:4; 38:2; 39:10]

gone back to her people and to [l]her gods; return after your sister-in-law." 16 But Ruth said, "Do not urge me to leave you or to return from following you. For where you go I will go, and where you lodge I will lodge. [m]Your people shall be my people, and your God my God. 17 Where you die I will die, and there will I be buried. [n]May the LORD do so to me and more also if anything but death parts me from you." 18 [o]And when Naomi saw that she was determined to go with her, she said no more.

Naomi and Ruth Return

19 So the two of them went on until they came to Bethlehem. And when they came to Bethlehem, [p]the whole town was stirred because of them. And the women said, "Is this Naomi?" 20 She said to them, "Do not call me Naomi;[1] call me [q]Mara,[2] for the Almighty has dealt very bitterly with me. 21 [r]I went away full, and the LORD has brought me back empty. Why call me Naomi, when the LORD has testified against me and the Almighty has brought calamity upon me?"

22 So Naomi returned, and Ruth the Moabite her daughter-in-law with her, who returned from the country of Moab. And they came to Bethlehem [s]at the beginning of barley harvest.

Ruth Meets Boaz

2 Now Naomi had [t]a relative of her husband's, a worthy man of the clan of Elimelech, whose name was [u]Boaz. 2 And Ruth the Moabite said to Naomi, "Let me go to the field and [v]glean among the ears of grain after him [w]in whose sight I shall find favor." And she said to her, "Go, my daughter." 3 So she set out and went and gleaned in the field after the reapers, and she happened to come to the part of the field belonging to Boaz, who was of the clan of Elimelech. 4 And behold, Boaz came from Bethlehem. And he said to the reapers, [x]"The LORD be with you!" And they answered, "The LORD bless you." 5 Then Boaz said to his young man who was in charge of the reapers, "Whose young woman is this?" 6 And the servant who was in charge of the reapers answered, "She is the young Moabite woman, [y]who came back with Naomi from the country of Moab. 7 She said, 'Please let me glean and gather among the sheaves after the reapers.' So she came, and she has continued from early morning until now, except for a short rest."[3]

[1] *Naomi* means *pleasant* [2] *Mara* means *bitter* [3] Compare Septuagint, Vulgate; the meaning of the Hebrew phrase is uncertain

15[l] Judg. 11:24; 1 Kgs. 11:7; Jer. 48:7, 13, 46
16[m] [ch. 2:11, 12]
17[n] 1 Sam. 3:17; 25:22; 2 Sam. 19:13; 1 Kgs. 2:23
18[o] [Acts 21:14]
19[p] [Matt. 21:10]
20[q] Ex. 15:23
21[r] Job 1:21
22[s] 2 Sam. 21:9; [ch. 2:23]

Chapter 2
1[t] ch. 3:2, 12 [u] ch. 4:21; Matt. 1:5
2[v] [Deut. 24:19] [w] ver. 10, 13
4[x] Ps. 129:7, 8
6[y] ch. 1:22

1:14–18 Orpah tearfully kisses Naomi good-bye, but Ruth insists on staying with Naomi. She declares her faithful, loving commitment to Naomi, her people, and her God until death. Ruth is willing to leave her native country and its worship of the pagan god Chemosh to become a part of the people of God in the land of Judah—despite poor earthly prospects there. In these ways, Ruth not only demonstrates the reality of her faith in God by her actions, she also becomes a living demonstration of his covenant love to Naomi.

1:19–22 Naomi rightly attributes her circumstances to the sovereign Lord, but she sees only what he has taken away. Her grief blinds her to what he has provided: in his grace God had given her a husband, two sons, and two daughters-in-law. She is returning to Bethlehem with one of them, and with Ruth her life is anything but empty. God's timing is also gracious and full of hope as they return at the beginning of the barley harvest.

2:1 By introducing Boaz here, the author prepares us for what is coming so that as the story unfolds we will recognize the overruling hand of God administering his gracious plan.

2:2–13 Biblical law provides grace for those who struggle by instructing reapers to leave a portion of the field unharvested. The purpose of this was to allow the poor, widows, and sojourners to provide for themselves by gleaning (Lev. 19:9–10; 23:22; Deut. 24:19–22). Ruth does not presume this will apply to her, but in hopes of finding "favor" (Ruth 2:2, 10, 13, often translated "grace"), she asks permission from the young man in charge of Boaz's reapers to glean in his field (v. 7; cf. v. 2). She finds favor not only with him but also with Boaz, who has heard of her faith in the Lord and her faithfulness to her mother-in-law. Boaz gives instruction for her protection and provision, then prays the Lord's rewards on her as one who has found refuge under his wings (cf. Deut. 32:11ff.; Ps. 17:8; 36:7ff.; 57:1; 63:7; 91:1–4).

8 Then Boaz said to Ruth, "Now, listen, my
daughter, do not go to glean in another field
or leave this one, but keep close to my young
women. 9 Let your eyes be on the field that
they are reaping, and go after them. Have
I not charged the young men not to touch
you? And when you are thirsty, go to the vessels
and drink what the young men have drawn."
10 Then [z]she fell on her face, bowing to the
ground, and said to him, "Why have I found
favor in your eyes, that you should [a]take notice
of me, since I am a foreigner?" 11 But Boaz
answered her, [b]"All that you have done for your
mother-in-law since the death of your husband has been fully told to me, and how you
left your father and mother and your native
land and came to a people that you did not
know before. 12 [c]The LORD repay you for what
you have done, and a full reward be given you
by the LORD, the God of Israel, under whose
wings you have come to take refuge!" 13 Then
she said, [d]"I have found favor in your eyes, my
lord, for you have comforted me and spoken
kindly to your servant, though I am not one
of your servants."
14 And at mealtime Boaz said to her, "Come
here and eat some bread and dip your morsel
in the wine." So she sat beside the reapers, and
he passed to her roasted grain. And she ate
until [e]she was satisfied, and she had some left
over. 15 When she rose to glean, Boaz instructed
his young men, saying, "Let her glean even
among the sheaves, and do not reproach her.
16 And also pull out some from the bundles
for her and leave it for her to glean, and do
not rebuke her."
17 So she gleaned in the field until evening.
Then she beat out what she had gleaned, and
it was about an ephah[1] of barley. 18 And she
took it up and went into the city. Her mother-
in-law saw what she had gleaned. She also
brought out and gave her what food she
had left over [f]after being satisfied. 19 And her
mother-in-law said to her, "Where did you
glean today? And where have you worked?
Blessed be the man [g]who took notice of you."
So she told her mother-in-law with whom
she had worked and said, "The man's name
with whom I worked today is Boaz." 20 And
Naomi said to her daughter-in-law, [h]"May he
be blessed by the LORD, whose kindness has
not forsaken [i]the living or the dead!" Naomi
also said to her, "The man is a close relative
of ours, one of [j]our redeemers." 21 And Ruth
the Moabite said, "Besides, he said to me,
'You shall keep close by my young men until
they have finished all my harvest.'" 22 And
Naomi said to Ruth, her daughter-in-law, "It
is good, my daughter, that you go out with
his young women, lest in another field you
be assaulted." 23 So she kept close to the young
women of Boaz, gleaning until the end of the
barley and wheat harvests. And she lived with
her mother-in-law.

[1] An *ephah* was about 3/5 bushel or 22 liters

Ruth is overwhelmed by such grace given to "a foreigner" (v. 10). As a Moabite, she would have been considered an enemy of God's people and forbidden to enter the assembly of the Lord (Deut. 23:3). But as one who put her faith in the Lord and his covenant promises—ultimately fulfilled in the Lord Jesus Christ—she is a child of Abraham by faith (Rom. 4:13–16; Gal. 3:7–9).

10[z] [1 Sam. 25:23, 41] [a] ver. 19
11[b] ch. 1:14, 16, 17
12[c] [1 Sam. 24:19]
13[d] ver. 2, 10; Gen. 33:15; 1 Sam. 1:18
14[e] ver. 18
18[f] ver. 14
19[g] ver. 10
20[h] ch. 3:10; Judg. 17:2; 1 Sam. 15:13; 23:21; 2 Sam. 2:5 [i] ch. 1:8 [j] ch. 3:9; 4:14

2:14–23 Boaz continues to shower his favor on Ruth by having her sit with his reapers at mealtime and by serving her more than she can consume. He instructs his young men to let her glean among the sheaves—not just at the edge of the field—and to leave extra grain for her to gather. When Naomi sees the large amount of barley and the leftover food that Ruth brings home and learns that Boaz is the generous landowner who has taken notice of Ruth in this way, her bitterness and despair dissipate. She prays blessing on Boaz and praises the Lord for his covenant kindness (*hesed*, v. 20) that never forsakes his own. Naomi reveals to Ruth that Boaz is a close relative, one of their redeemers (*goel*). For them such a *goel* holds the promise of help, protection, security, and redemption—a future and a hope (Jer. 29:11).

The same is true of us when we hear for the first time that there exists a Redeemer who may save us from our spiritual poverty and hopelessness, who can take away our guilt of sin and its wages of death and give us right standing before God, bringing us into his very family (Rom. 6:23; 8:16).

Ruth and Boaz at the Threshing Floor

3 Then Naomi her mother-in-law said to
her, "My daughter, should I not seek [k]rest
for you, that it may be well with you? 2 Is not
Boaz [l]our relative, [m]with whose young women
you were? See, he is winnowing barley tonight
at the threshing floor. 3 [n]Wash therefore and
anoint yourself, and put on your cloak and go
down to the threshing floor, but do not make
yourself known to the man until he has finished eating and drinking. 4 But when he lies
down, observe the place where he lies. Then
go and uncover his feet and lie down, and he
will tell you what to do." 5 And she replied, "All
that you say I will do."

6 So she went down to the threshing floor
and did just as her mother-in-law had commanded her. 7 And when Boaz had eaten and
drunk, and [o]his heart was merry, he went to
lie down at the end of the heap of grain. Then
she came softly and uncovered his feet and
lay down. 8 At midnight the man was startled
and turned over, and behold, a woman lay at
his feet! 9 He said, "Who are you?" And she
answered, "I am Ruth, your servant. [p]Spread
your wings[1] over your servant, for you are [q]a
redeemer." 10 And he said, [r]"May you be blessed
by the LORD, my daughter. You have made this
last kindness greater than [s]the first in that you
have not gone after young men, whether poor
or rich. 11 And now, my daughter, do not fear.
I will do for you all that you ask, for all my
fellow townsmen know that you are [t]a worthy woman. 12 And now it is true that I am [u]a
redeemer. Yet there is a redeemer nearer than
I. 13 Remain tonight, and in the morning, if he
will [v]redeem you, good; let him do it. But if
he is not willing to redeem you, then, [w]as the
LORD lives, I will redeem you. Lie down until
the morning."

14 So she lay at his feet until the morning, but
arose before one could recognize another. And
he said, "Let it not be known that the woman
came to the threshing floor." 15 And he said,
"Bring the garment you are wearing and hold
it out." So she held it, and he measured out

[1] Compare 2:12; the word for *wings* can also mean *corners of a garment*

Chapter 3
1 [k] ch. 1:9
2 [l] ch. 2:1 [m] ch. 2:8
3 [n] 2 Sam. 12:20; 14:2
7 [o] See Judg. 19:6
9 [p] Ezek. 16:8; [Deut. 22:30] [q] ch. 2:20
10 [r] See ch. 2:20 [s] ch. 1:8
11 [t] Prov. 12:4; 31:10
12 [u] ch. 4:1
13 [v] ch. 4:5; [Deut. 25:5] [w] Judg. 8:19; 1 Sam. 14:39; 2 Sam. 4:9; 12:5; 2 Kgs. 2:2, 6

3:1–9 Naomi's hope gives birth to a plan by which Ruth may ask Boaz to enter into a levirate marriage with her and take on the duty of being their redeemer. As strange as it may seem to modern readers, there is nothing questionable or unseemly in the plan; we are assured repeatedly of the quality of Boaz's and Ruth's character (2:1, 11–12; 3:11). Few reputable scholars believe the phrase "uncovered his feet and lay down" (v. 7) indicates that a sexual sin was committed or that anything more was intended than a sign of service and devotion. When Boaz awakens and asks her identity, Ruth's delicate request that he marry her reflects the same language that he used of her taking refuge under the God of Israel's wings (v. 9; cf. 2:12). In this way, she is asking Boaz not only to marry her but also to become a demonstration of the Lord's covenant love.

This same language would be used by the prophet Ezekiel in describing the Lord's covenant love for his bride, Jerusalem (Ezek. 16:8), and it recalls the imagery of Christ and his bride, the church, in the new Jerusalem (Rev. 19:7–9; 21:2, 9; cf. Luke 13:34). It is under his wings that we are to find rest and security (cf. Ps. 91:4; Matt. 23:37).

3:10–18 In response to Ruth's proposal, Boaz commends her for her kindness (*hesed*, v. 10) in favoring him over a younger man. He assures her that he will do everything to make sure that she has a redeemer (v. 13). Although he is not the first in line to fulfill this duty, he promises to investigate as soon as possible whether or not the nearer relative is willing to do so; if not, Boaz promises to be that redeemer. Ruth and Naomi are proven right to put their trust in Boaz's own kindness and generosity. He is careful to protect Ruth's reputation (v. 14). He makes sure that Ruth does "not go back *empty*-handed" to her mother-in-law (vv. 15–17), giving an abundant gift for the one who thought the Lord had brought her "back *empty*" from Moab (1:20–21).

This is a beautiful picture of the ultimate Kinsman-Redeemer, Jesus Christ. This true and final Redeemer willingly did everything necessary for the redemption of his bride, the church—"for the joy that was set before him [Christ] endured the cross, despising the shame, and is seated at the right hand of the throne of God" (Heb. 12:2). In him, God, in his covenant love and mercy, provided redemption from our sins, "so that in the coming ages he might show the immeasurable riches of his grace in kindness toward us in Christ Jesus" (Eph. 2:4–7). We are right to put our trust in such covenant kindness and generosity.

six measures of barley and put it on her. Then she went into the city. 16 And when she came to her mother-in-law, she said, "How did you fare, my daughter?" Then she told her all that the man had done for her, 17 saying, "These six measures of barley he gave to me, for he said to me, 'You must not go back empty-handed to your mother-in-law.'" 18 She replied, "Wait, my daughter, until you learn how the matter turns out, for the man will not rest but will settle the matter today."

Boaz Redeems Ruth

4 Now Boaz had gone up to [x]the gate and sat down there. And behold, [y]the redeemer, of whom Boaz had spoken, came by. So Boaz said, "Turn aside, friend; sit down here." And he turned aside and sat down. 2 And he took ten men [z]of the elders of the city and said, "Sit down here." So they sat down. 3 Then he said to the redeemer, "Naomi, who has come back from the country of Moab, is selling the parcel of land that belonged to our relative Elimelech. 4 So I thought I would tell you of it and say, [a]'Buy it in the presence of those sitting here and in the presence of the elders of my people.' If you will redeem it, redeem it. But if you[1] will not, tell me, that I may know, for there is no one besides you to redeem it, and I come after you." And he said, "I will redeem it." 5 Then Boaz said, "The day you buy the field from the hand of Naomi, you also acquire Ruth[2] the Moabite, the widow of the dead, in order [b]to perpetuate the name of the dead in his inheritance." 6 [c]Then the redeemer said, "I cannot redeem it for myself, lest I impair my own inheritance. Take my right of redemption yourself, for I cannot redeem it."

7 [d]Now this was the custom in former times in Israel concerning redeeming and exchanging: to confirm a transaction, the one drew off his sandal and gave it to the other, and this was the manner of attesting in Israel. 8 So when the redeemer said to Boaz, "Buy it for yourself," he drew off his sandal. 9 Then Boaz said to the elders and all the people, "You are witnesses this day that I have bought from the hand of Naomi all that belonged to Elimelech and all that belonged to [e]Chilion and to Mahlon. 10 Also Ruth the Moabite, the widow of Mahlon, I have bought to be my wife, [f]to perpetuate the name of the dead in his inheritance, that the name of the dead may not be cut off from among his brothers and from the gate of his native place. You are witnesses this day." 11 Then all the people who

[1] Hebrew *he* [2] Masoretic Text *you also buy it from Ruth*

4:1–6 Boaz tells the next of kin that Naomi is selling land that belonged to her late husband, Elimelech (v. 3). If Naomi were the only surviving relative, the land would be all there was to redeem because she was beyond childbearing age and therefore the duty of the redeemer would not include a levirate marriage. Boaz makes clear up front that if the relative will not redeem it, he will do so as the next closest kin. After the relative agrees to redeem the land, Boaz lets him know that this also involves marrying Naomi's daughter-in-law, Ruth, *the Moabite*, the widow of Elimelech's son Mahlon, in order to continue the family line (v. 5). This is more than the relative can accept (whether the cost is too high because of an existing family or insufficient funds or some other reason, we do not know), and he yields the "right of redemption" to Boaz (v. 6).

Boaz is the only one who has the willingness and the ability to redeem Ruth. In this respect he represents the nature of grace ultimately found in the Lord Jesus Christ, who was under no obligation to redeem sinners, and could have left them all to their just condemnation, but willingly took on human flesh and paid the required redemption price: death on a cross (Rom. 6:23; Phil. 2:5–11).

4:7–12 The witnesses verify that Boaz has done everything necessary to redeem Naomi's land to continue the legacy of her husband Elimelech and that of his sons, and to perpetuate their line by taking Ruth to be his wife. In evoking the Lord's blessing of offspring, the witnesses first refer to Israel's wives Rachel and Leah, and then to the unsavory story of Perez's parentage. This was another levirate marriage situation, but whereas Judah's son had refused Tamar's legitimate claim (Genesis 38), Boaz has honored the obligation.

The story of God's people has always been one of human frailty and God's overriding grace (2 Cor. 12:9–10). Contrary to our natural instincts and the way the world intuitively operates, God delights to draw near to and magnificently use those whom the world considers weak, needy, helpless, and marginalized.

Chapter 4
1 [x]2 Sam. 15:2; 18:4, 24, 33; 19:8; Ps. 127:5 [y]ch. 2:20
2 [z]1 Kgs. 21:8; Prov. 31:23
4 [a]Lev. 25:25; [Jer. 32:7, 8]
5 [b]ver. 10; ch. 3:13; Deut. 25:5, 6
6 [c]ch. 3:12, 13
7 [d]See Deut. 25:7-10
9 [e]ch. 1:2, 4, 5
10 [f]ver. 5

were [g]at the gate and the elders said, "We are
witnesses. May the LORD make the woman,
who is coming into your house, like Rachel
and Leah, [h]who together [i]built up the house of
Israel. May you act worthily in [j]Ephrathah and
[k]be renowned in Bethlehem, 12 and may your
house be like the house of Perez, [l]whom Tamar
bore to Judah, because [m]of the offspring that
the LORD will give you by this young woman."

Ruth and Boaz Marry

13 So Boaz took Ruth, and she became his
wife. And he went in to her, [n]and the LORD
gave her conception, and she bore a son.
14 [o]Then the women said to Naomi, "Blessed
be the LORD, who has not left you this day
without [p]a redeemer, and may his name [q]be
renowned in Israel! 15 He shall be to you a
restorer of life and a nourisher of your old age,
for your daughter-in-law who loves you, [r]who
is more to you than seven sons, has given birth
to him." 16 Then Naomi took the child and laid
him on her lap and became his nurse. 17 [s]And
the women of the neighborhood gave him a
name, saying, "A son has been born to Naomi."
They named him Obed. He was the father of
Jesse, the father of David.

The Genealogy of David

18 Now these are the generations of Perez:
[t]Perez fathered Hezron, 19 Hezron fathered
Ram, Ram fathered Amminadab, 20 [u]Ammin-
adab fathered Nahshon, Nahshon fathered
Salmon, 21 Salmon fathered Boaz, Boaz
fathered Obed, 22 Obed fathered Jesse, and
Jesse fathered David.

11 [g]See ver. 1 [h]See Gen. 29:31–30:24; 35:16-18 [i]Deut. 25:9 [j]Gen. 35:16, 19 [k]ver. 14
12 [l]Gen. 38:29; 1 Chr. 2:4; Matt. 1:3 [m]1 Sam. 2:20
13 [n]Gen. 29:31; 33:5
14 [o][Luke 1:58] [p]ch. 2:20 [q]ver. 11
15 [r]1 Sam. 1:8
17 [s]Luke 1:59
18 [t]For ver. 18-22, see 1 Chr. 2:4-15; Matt. 1:3-6
20 [u]Num. 1:7; [Ex. 6:23]

4:13–17 After a son is born to Boaz and Ruth, the very women whom Naomi had told to call her Mara ("bitter") after she returned "empty" from Moab (1:20–21) now celebrate with her. They bless the Lord, who has provided a redeemer, and who has restored Naomi's life and nourished her old age through Ruth and her son.

Like Naomi, so often we look at our outward circumstances and feel bitter toward the Lord because we cannot see beyond our situation to what he is doing or why. Yet, as he did for Naomi, God still provides for us a Redeemer, who is the Restorer of Life and nourishes us by his faithful loving kindness as he works out the plan for our lives and for our part in the proclamation of his gospel.

4:18–22 This final genealogy that terminates in David, the royal forefather of Jesus, reveals marvelous aspects of God's gracious nature that may be hidden to modern eyes. First, it reminds us that grace flows where the world may see only shame or cause for rejection. Boaz's father was Salmon, who married Rahab, the harlot who saved the spies at Jericho (see Matt. 1:5). Boaz continues the line of Judah by marrying Ruth, a Gentile woman from one of Israel's ancient enemies, Moab. And Judah, though privileged to be prophesied as the head of the line from which the messianic King would come (Gen. 49:10), initiated the line by impregnating Tamar, his widowed daughter-in-law. He thus fathered twins (Genesis 38) whose illegitimacy would have kept his seed from citizenship in Israel until the tenth generation (see Deut. 23:2)—represented by Boaz. So the line of Christ is replete with scandalous grace.

Note that this genealogy is symbolic as well as chronological. Ten key figures are mentioned from Judah to David (with some names obviously skipped in the time frame from Judah to Boaz). This shows that David's kingly line is an echo of the covenant purposes of God represented in ten generations from Adam to Noah (in Genesis 5 and 1 Chronicles 1) and, again, from Noah to Abraham (in Genesis 11 and 1 Chronicles 1). Here again these are symbolic and not purely chronological lists, as is indicated when Matthew chooses to represent the line another way to demonstrate God's covenant faithfulness to and through David (see Matt. 1:17).

Thus, this genealogy shows us the Lord's sovereignty over our private and seemingly ordinary decisions, such as Ruth's decision to go with Naomi and worship the God of Israel. Little did she know when she set out from Moab that day that she would become great-grandmother to Israel's King David, ancestor to David's Greater Son, the Lord Jesus Christ, the Kinsman-Redeemer of all of God's people.

Introduction to 1–2 Samuel

Author and Date

The author or authors of 1 and 2 Samuel are not known. These books recount the stories of Samuel, Saul, and David. Saul's reign began between 1050–1030 B.C. and ended in 1010. David then reigned until 971. The books were probably written soon after the end of David's reign.

The Gospel in 1–2 Samuel

The books of Samuel are about Israel's first kings, Saul and David: who they were, how they came to the throne, and how they fared. But more than that, the books are about the great King, God himself. In the riveting stories of 1 and 2 Samuel we catch glimpses of who God is, what he does, what life is like with him and without him, and what life can become by his grace and in the power of his Spirit. These stories are part of our family history as children of Abraham by faith (Gal. 3:7–9, 14). They are meant to instruct us, "on whom the end of the ages has come" (1 Cor. 10:11), to teach us endurance and, "through the encouragement of the Scriptures," to give us hope, in order that we may "with one voice glorify the God and Father of our Lord Jesus Christ" (Rom. 15:4, 6).

These are gospel-filled stories, unflinchingly honest about sin and society, but saturated with hope of salvation. The two key characters (apart from Samuel the prophet) are both royal sinners. But Saul and David are as different from one another as darkness is from light. For Saul, God does not appear to be a major concern, perhaps not a reality at all. For David, God is his ultimate concern. For David, God is the ultimate reality. And he carries ultimate weight. This is what it means to "honor" God. By the criteria established early in the books—"those who honor me I will honor, and those who despise me shall be lightly esteemed" (1 Sam. 2:30)—Saul is destined to fall and David to rise.

Because stories tend to convey their messages indirectly—which is to say, we see what characters do and hear what they say but are seldom offered explicit commentary—they are susceptible to misunderstanding. One common misunderstanding sees Saul as all bad and David as all good. Another reverses the approach and sees Saul as not so bad and David as little more than an unscrupulous political animal.

A careful reading disallows both misinterpretations. Saul is not all bad, at least at first. He exhibits some "good faith" at the beginning, but because he is devoid of "true faith" in God this good faith erodes over time into self-centeredness and suicide. David is certainly not all good, and the accounts of 1 and 2 Samuel make no attempt to hide his sins!

But David's relationship with God is fundamentally sound. He knows God, prays to God, confesses to God, and finds strength in God. He knows himself to be a sinner, and he knows what it means to be saved by grace. Does he also sense that God, in putting him on the throne, is about much more than just establishing a limited, local kingdom? Surely he has some sense of this, even if without full discernment. After all, God's promise to Abraham (Gen. 12:1–3), which finds numerous echoes in the promise to David (2 Sam. 7:4–17), culminates with the prophecy that "in you all the families of the earth shall be blessed" (Gen. 12:3). David cannot foresee just how this blessing will work out, but he seems aware that something grand and glorious is underway (2 Sam. 7:18–29).

Only to us, those privileged to live after the coming of the true King, the Lord's Anointed (Messiah) from David's line, is it given to understand that "the kingdom of this world is become the kingdom of our Lord, and of his Christ; and he shall reign for ever and ever . . . Hallelujah!" (from Handel's *Messiah*).

1 Samuel Outline

I. The Story of Samuel (1:1–7:17)

II. Transition to the Monarchy (8:1–22)

III. The Story of Saul (9:1–15:35)

IV. The Story of Saul and David (16:1–31:13)

2 Samuel Outline

I. The Story of King David (1:1–20:26)

II. Epilogue (21:1–24:25)

1 Samuel

The Birth of Samuel

1 There was a certain man of [a]Ramathaim-
zophim of [b]the hill country of Ephraim
whose name was Elkanah the son of Jeroham,
son of Elihu, son of Tohu, son of Zuph, [c]an
Ephrathite. 2 He had two wives. The name
of the one was Hannah, and the name of the
other, Peninnah. And Peninnah had children,
but Hannah had no children.
3 Now this man used to go up [d]year by year
from his city [e]to worship and to sacrifice to the
LORD of hosts [f]at Shiloh, where the two sons
of Eli, Hophni and Phinehas, were priests of
the LORD. 4 On the day when Elkanah sacrificed, [g]he would give portions to Peninnah his
wife and to all her sons and daughters. 5 But
to Hannah he gave a double portion, because
he loved her, though the LORD had closed her
womb.[1] 6 And her rival used to provoke her
grievously to irritate her, because the LORD
had closed her womb. 7 So it went on year by
year. As often as she went up to the house of
the LORD, she used to provoke her. Therefore
Hannah wept and would not eat. 8 And
Elkanah, her husband, said to her, "Hannah,
why do you weep? And why do you not eat?
And why is your heart sad? [h]Am I not more to
you than ten sons?"
9 After they had eaten and drunk in Shiloh,
Hannah rose. Now Eli the priest was sitting
on the seat beside the doorpost of [i]the temple
of the LORD. 10 She was [j]deeply distressed and

[1] Syriac; the meaning of the Hebrew is uncertain. Septuagint *And, although he loved Hannah, he would give Hannah only one portion, because the LORD had closed her womb*

1:1–20 The book of 1 Samuel opens with the story of a woman in pain. Such a beginning may seem curious in a book that will go on to recount perhaps the most significant political shift in Israel's history, from tribal society to monarchy. But in God's economy, seemingly small things are not to be discounted (cf. Zech. 4:10). God delights in reversing expectations. He delights in choosing "what is weak in the world to shame the strong" (1 Cor. 1:27). Indeed, Christ himself is the ultimate instance of God using unimpressive weakness to accomplish a great thing (2 Cor. 13:4).

Hannah is weak in several respects. She is childless in a culture where bearing children was considered one of the chief roles of a wife (1 Sam. 1:2). She finds herself in a polygamous marriage, where her rival takes every opportunity to mock her pain (v. 6). Her husband's attempts to ease her pain are ineffectual (vv. 5, 8). And even her own actions are misunderstood by those who should know better (v. 13). But Hannah is strong in faith. While she might have used her standing as favored wife to take revenge on her rival or simply to repress her pain, she chooses rather to take her sorrow to God. Hannah must have understood that no trial, however heavy, can "outweigh" God and his grace and that God honors those who honor him (cf. 2:29–30). A word of encouragement that God has heard her prayer is all it takes to lift her spirits (1:18).

Of Hannah, the prophet Samuel will be born (v. 20), and this Samuel will be used of God to bring to the throne a king, a man of God's own choosing (13:14). Dramatically demonstrated in the life of Hannah is the fact that everyday faithfulness by ordinary people can, by God's grace, change history forever. Just such faithfulness surrounds the eventual coming of the great King, Jesus. In response to prayer (Luke 1:13), childless Elizabeth is promised and receives a child, John, who like Samuel before him heralds the coming of God's King. The birth of that King, Jesus, involves the humble obedience of yet another faithful woman, Mary (Luke 1:38).

Chapter 1
1 [a][ver. 19] [b]See Josh. 24:33 [c][1 Kgs. 11:26]
3 [d]ver. 21; Ex. 23:14; Deut. 16:16; [Luke 2:41] [e]See Deut. 12:5-7 [f][Josh. 18:1]
4 [g]Deut. 12:17, 18; 16:11; [Neh. 8:10, 12]
8 [h]Ruth 4:15
9 [i]ch. 3:3
10 [j]Job 7:11; 10:1

prayed to the LORD and wept bitterly. 11 And
she [k]vowed a vow and said, "O LORD of hosts,
if you will indeed [l]look on the affliction of
your servant and [m]remember me and not forget your servant, but will give to your servant
a son, then I will give him to the LORD all
the days of his life, [n]and no razor shall touch
his head."
12 As she continued praying before the LORD,
Eli observed her mouth. 13 Hannah was speaking in her heart; only her lips moved, and her
voice was not heard. Therefore Eli took her to
be a drunken woman. 14 And Eli said to her,
"How long will you go on being drunk? Put
your wine away from you." 15 But Hannah
answered, "No, my lord, I am a woman troubled in spirit. I have drunk neither wine nor
strong drink, but [o]I have been pouring out my
soul before the LORD. 16 Do not regard your
servant as [p]a worthless woman, for all along
I have been speaking out of my great anxiety
and vexation." 17 Then Eli answered, [q]"Go in
peace, and the God of Israel [r]grant your petition that you have made to him." 18 And she
said, [s]"Let your servant find favor in your eyes."
Then the woman [t]went her way and ate, and
her face was no longer sad.
19 They rose early in the morning and worshiped before the LORD; then they went back
to their house at [u]Ramah. And Elkanah knew
Hannah his wife, and the LORD [v]remembered
her. 20 And in due time Hannah conceived
and bore a son, and she called his name
Samuel, for she said, "I have asked for him
from the LORD."[1]

Samuel Given to the LORD

21 The man Elkanah and all his house [w]went
up to offer to the LORD the yearly sacrifice
and to pay his vow. 22 But Hannah did not go
up, for she said to her husband, "As soon as
the child is weaned, I will bring him, so that
he may appear in the presence of the LORD
[x]and dwell there forever." 23 [y]Elkanah her
husband said to her, "Do what seems best to
you; wait until you have weaned him; [z]only,
may the LORD establish his word." So the
woman remained and nursed her son until
she weaned him. 24 And when she had weaned
him, [a]she took him up with her, along with a
three-year-old bull,[2] an ephah[3] of flour, and
a skin of wine, and she brought him to [b]the
house of the LORD at Shiloh. And the child
was young. 25 Then they slaughtered the bull,
and they brought the child to Eli. 26 And she
said, "Oh, my lord! [c]As you live, my lord, I am
the woman who was standing here in your
presence, praying to the LORD. 27 For this child
I prayed, [d]and the LORD has granted me my
petition that I made to him. 28 Therefore I have
lent him to the LORD. As long as he lives, he is
lent to the LORD."
[e]And he worshiped the LORD there.

Hannah's Prayer

2 And Hannah prayed and said,

[f]"My heart exults in the LORD;
[g]my horn is exalted in the LORD.
My mouth derides my enemies,
because [h]I rejoice in your salvation.

[1] *Samuel* sounds like the Hebrew for *heard of God* [2] Dead Sea Scroll, Septuagint, Syriac; Masoretic Text *three bulls* [3] An *ephah* was about 3/5 bushel or 22 liters

11 [k]Gen. 28:20; Judg. 11:30 [l]Gen. 29:32 [m]ver. 19; [Gen. 30:22] [n]Judg. 13:5; [Num. 6:5]
15 [o]Job 30:16; Ps. 42:4; Lam. 2:19; [Ps. 62:8]
16 [p]ch. 2:12; Judg. 19:22
17 [q]ch. 20:42; Judg. 18:6; 2 Kgs. 5:19; Mark 5:34 [r]Ps. 20:4, 5
18 [s]Gen. 33:15; Ruth 2:13 [t][Eccles. 9:7]
19 [u]ch. 2:11; [ver. 1] [v]ver. 11
21 [w]ver. 3
22 [x]ver. 11, 28; [ch. 2:11, 18; 3:1]
23 [y][Num. 30:7] [z]2 Sam. 7:25
24 [a]Deut. 12:5, 6, 11 [b]ver. 3, 9; [Josh. 18:1]
26 [c]ch. 17:55; 20:3; 2 Sam. 11:11; 2 Kgs. 2:2, 4, 6; 4:30
27 [d]ver. 17; [Ps. 6:9]
28 [e]Gen. 24:26, 52

Chapter 2

1 [f]For ver. 1-10, see Luke 1:46-53 [g]ver. 10; Ps. 75:10; 89:17, 24; 92:10; 112:9; 148:14 [h]Ps. 9:14; 13:5; 20:5; 35:9

2:1–10 Hannah's prayer sets the theological tone of the books of Samuel and, indeed, anticipates in many respects the later "Magnificat" that Mary, the mother of Jesus, would one day pray (Luke 1:46–55). Both Hannah and Mary rejoice over the Lord's deliverance, proclaim the Lord's uniqueness and holiness, condemn prideful boasting, and celebrate the Lord's right and ability to abase the proud and exalt the humble. In short, both of them extol the Lord's faithful care for those who place their trust in him and his judgment on those who don't (see note on 1 Sam. 2:12–36). At the end of her prayer, Hannah stresses that it is not by human strength that one prevails and that opposing God will inevitably lead to ruin. To his king, by contrast, the Lord himself "will give strength" (v. 10). In the books of Samuel, the Lord's king will be David; in the fullness of time, it will be Jesus, the Messiah (Matt. 1:1; Luke 1:32).

Hannah's story and her prayer reflect key truths of the gospel. First, God must be at the center! When he is, even life's greatest battles can become the ground of blessing (Rom. 8:28), for God delights to embrace and encourage his own even in the midst of severe trial (cf. Isa. 40:11). Second, Hannah's story and her prayer reflect the gospel truth of God's strange reversal of what the world holds dear and counts significant. God delights to show favor to the weak and the socially marginalized. His power interlocks with human weakness and resists flaunted human strength (2 Cor.

2 [i]"There is none holy like the LORD:
for there is none besides you;
there is [j]no rock like our God.
3 Talk no more so very proudly,
let not arrogance come from your mouth;
for the LORD is a God of knowledge,
and by him actions are weighed.
4 [k]The bows of the mighty are broken,
but the feeble bind on strength.
5 Those who were full have hired themselves out for bread,
but those who were hungry have ceased to hunger.
[l]The barren has borne seven,
[m]but she who has many children is forlorn.
6 [n]The LORD kills and brings to life;
he brings down to Sheol and raises up.
7 [o]The LORD makes poor and makes rich;
[p]he brings low and he exalts.
8 [q]He raises up the poor from the dust;
he lifts the needy from the ash heap
[r]to make them sit with princes
and inherit a seat of honor.
[s]For the pillars of the earth are the LORD's,
and on them he has set the world.
9 [t]"He will guard the feet of his faithful ones,
but the wicked shall be cut off in darkness,
for not by might shall a man prevail.
10 [u]The adversaries of the LORD shall be broken to pieces;
[v]against them he will thunder in heaven.
[w]The LORD will judge the ends of the earth;
he will give strength to his king
[x]and exalt the horn of his anointed."

11 Then Elkanah went home [y]to Ramah. [z]And
the boy[1] was ministering to the LORD in the
presence of Eli the priest.

Eli's Worthless Sons

12 Now the sons of Eli were [a]worthless men.
[b]They did not know the LORD. 13 The custom
of the priests with the people was that when
any man offered sacrifice, the priest's servant
would come, while the meat was boiling, with
a three-pronged fork in his hand, 14 and he
would thrust it into the pan or kettle or cauldron or pot. All that the fork brought up the
priest would take for himself. This is what
they did at Shiloh to all the Israelites who
came there. 15 Moreover, [c]before the fat was
burned, the priest's servant would come and
say to the man who was sacrificing, "Give meat
for the priest to roast, for he will not accept
boiled meat from you but only raw." 16 And if
the man said to him, "Let them burn the fat
first, and then take as much as you wish," he
would say, "No, you must give it now, and if
not, I will take it by force." 17 Thus the sin of
the young men was very great [d]in the sight of

[1] Hebrew *na'ar* can be rendered *boy* (2:11, 18, 21, 26; 3:1, 8), *servant* (2:13, 15), or *young man* (2:17), depending on the context

12:9). The supreme example of this principle is the gospel itself—where God delights to accept and approve of those who trust in his Son by faith, rather than those who bring the strength of their own performance to the table.

2:12–36 Standing in marked contrast to righteous Hannah and her son are the wicked sons of Eli, who "did not know" ("did not recognize," "had no regard for") the Lord (v. 12). Their lot is judgment (v. 25). Eli, too, is judged, for though he rebuked his sons (vv. 22–25) he did not restrain them (3:13)—something he, as high priest, could and should have done. Specifically, Eli is charged with honoring his sons above the Lord (2:29). To "honor" someone is to give him "weight," and it is a fine irony that in the present instance the spiritual infraction has a physical manifestation—both father and sons have put on weight!

God's desire to be honored, or glorified, may on a shallow reading seem vainglorious. But that God should require his creatures to honor him, to give him weight, is no more vainglorious than that the law of gravity requires to be acknowledged. Simply put, God has weight! To neglect this fact is to lose one's own center of gravity. Giving God the center is at the heart of accepting the gospel. Every line of the prayer Jesus taught his followers to pray manifestly gives weight and centrality to God (Matt. 6:9–13). As our hearts are gripped with the magnitude of what God has done for his people in the gospel of grace, we are compelled to gladly ascribe all honor and glory to God alone.

2 [i] Ex. 15:11; Ps. 86:8; 89:6, 8 [j] Deut. 32:30, 31
4 [k] Ps. 37:15; 46:9; 76:3
5 [l] Ps. 113:9; Isa. 54:1 [m] Jer. 15:9
6 [n] Deut. 32:39
7 [o] [Job 1:21] [p] Job 5:11; Ps. 75:7
8 [q] Ps. 113:7, 8; [Dan. 4:17; Luke 1:52] [r] Job 36:7 [s] [Job 38:4-6; Ps. 24:2; 102:25; 104:5]
9 [t] Ps. 121:3; Prov. 3:26; [Ps. 91:11]
10 [u] Ps. 2:9 [v] ch. 7:10; Ps. 18:13; [2 Sam. 22:14] [w] Ps. 96:10, 13; 98:9 [x] ver. 1; [Ps. 89:24]
11 [y] ch. 1:19 [z] ver. 18; ch. 3:1
12 [a] See ch. 1:16 [b] Judg. 2:10
15 [c] Lev. 3:5, 16; 7:23, 25, 31
17 [d] [Gen. 6:11]

the LORD, [e]for the men treated the offering of the LORD with contempt.

18 [f]Samuel was ministering before the LORD, a boy [g]clothed with a linen ephod. 19 And his mother used to make for him a little robe and take it to him each year [h]when she went up with her husband to offer the yearly sacrifice. 20 Then Eli would bless Elkanah and his wife, and say, "May the LORD give you children by this woman [i]for the petition she asked of the LORD." So then they would return to their home.

21 [j]Indeed the LORD visited Hannah, and she conceived and bore three sons and two daughters. [k]And the boy Samuel grew in the presence of the LORD.

Eli Rebukes His Sons

22 Now Eli was very old, and he kept hearing all that his sons were doing to all Israel, and how they lay with the women who [l]were serving at the entrance to the tent of meeting. 23 And he said to them, "Why do you do such things? For I hear of your evil dealings from all these people. 24 No, my sons; it is no good report that I hear the people of the LORD spreading abroad. 25 If someone sins against a man, God will mediate for him, but if someone sins against the LORD, who can intercede for him?" But they would not listen to the voice of their father, [m]for it was the will of the LORD to put them to death.

26 Now the boy Samuel [n]continued to grow both in stature and in favor with the LORD and also with man.

The LORD Rejects Eli's Household

27 And there came [o]a man of God to Eli and said to him, "Thus says the LORD, [p]'Did I indeed reveal myself to the house of your father when they were in Egypt subject to the house of Pharaoh? 28 [q]Did I choose him out of all the tribes of Israel to be my priest, to go up to my altar, to burn incense, [r]to wear an ephod before me? [s]I gave to the house of your father all my offerings by fire from the people of Israel. 29 Why then do you [t]scorn[1] my sacrifices and my offerings that I commanded for my dwelling, and honor your sons above me by fattening yourselves on the choicest parts of every offering of my people Israel?' 30 Therefore the LORD, the God of Israel, declares: [v]'I promised that your house and the house of your father should go in and out before me forever,' [w]but now the LORD declares: 'Far be it from me, for those who honor me I will honor, and those who despise me shall be lightly esteemed. 31 Behold, [x]the days are coming when I will cut off your strength and the strength of your father's house, so that there will not be an old man in your house. 32 Then [y]in distress you will look with envious eye on all the prosperity that shall be bestowed on Israel, [z]and there shall not be an old man in your house forever. 33 The only one of you whom I shall not cut off from my altar shall be spared to weep his[2] eyes out to grieve his heart, and all the descendants[3] of your house shall die by the sword of men.[4] 34 [a]And this that shall come upon your two sons, Hophni and Phinehas, shall be the sign to you: both of them shall die [b]on the same day. 35 [c]And I will raise up for myself a faithful priest, who shall do according to what is in my heart and in my mind. [d]And I will build him a sure house, and he shall go in and out before [e]my anointed forever. 36 And everyone who is left in your house shall come to implore him for a piece of silver or a loaf of bread and shall say, "Please put me in one of the priests' places, that I may eat a morsel of bread."'"

The LORD Calls Samuel

3 [f]Now the boy Samuel was ministering to the LORD in the presence of Eli. [g]And the word of the LORD was rare in those days; there was no frequent vision.

2 At that time Eli, [h]whose eyesight had begun

[1] Hebrew *kick at* [2] Septuagint; Hebrew *your*; twice in this verse [3] Hebrew *increase* [4] Septuagint; Hebrew *die as men*

17[e] [Mal. 2:8]
18[f] ver. 11; ch. 3:1 [g] Ex. 28:4; 2 Sam. 6:14; 1 Chr. 15:27
19[h] ch. 1:3
20[i] ch. 1:28
21[j] Gen. 21:1 [k] ver. 26; ch. 3:19; [Judg. 13:24; Luke 1:80; 2:40]
22[l] Ex. 38:8

3:1–21 Though one is not to *presume on* the grace of God (cf. 2:25), God's grace and patience toward his people are remarkable. Even in the dark days of Eli, God does not allow his "lamp" to go out completely (3:3; for the metaphorical uses of "lamp" in the books of Samuel, see 2 Sam. 21:17; 22:29). Eli must be rejected, but the Lord raises up Samuel, so that he might reveal himself "by the word of the LORD" (1 Sam. 3:21). Eli's rejection from office is irrevocable, and he will eventually die under his own

25[m] [Josh. 11:20] **26**[n] Luke 2:52 **27**[o] 1 Kgs. 13:1 [p] [Ex. 3–12] **28**[q] Ex. 28:1; Num. 18:1, 7 [r] [ch. 14:3; 22:18] [s] Lev. 2:3, 10; 6:16; 7:7, 8, 34; 10:14, 15; Num. 5:9, 10; See Num. 18:8-19 **29**[t] Deut. 32:15 **30**[v] Ex. 27:21; 29:9 [w] [Jer. 18:9, 10] **31**[x] 1 Kgs. 2:27; [ch. 4:11, 18, 20; 22:18, 19] **32**[y] ch. 4:11; [Judg. 18:30]; See Ps. 78:59-64 [z] [Zech. 8:4] **34**[a] 1 Kgs. 13:3 [b] ch. 4:11 **35**[c] 1 Kgs. 2:35; 1 Chr. 29:22 [d] ch. 25:28; 1 Kgs. 11:38; [2 Sam. 7:11, 27] [e] 2 Sam. 22:51; Ps. 18:50; [Ps. 89:20]
Chapter 3 **1**[f] ch. 2:11, 18 [g] [ver. 21; Ps. 74:9; Amos 8:11] **2**[h] ch. 4:15; Gen. 27:1; 48:10; [Deut. 34:7]

to grow dim so that he could not see, was lying down in his own place. 3 [j]The lamp of God had not yet gone out, and Samuel was lying down [j]in the temple of the LORD, where the ark of God was.

4 Then the LORD called Samuel, and he said, "Here I am!" 5 and ran to Eli and said, "Here I am, for you called me." But he said, "I did not call; lie down again." So he went and lay down. 6 And the LORD called again, "Samuel!" and Samuel arose and went to Eli and said, "Here I am, for you called me." But he said, "I did not call, my son; lie down again." 7 Now Samuel did not yet know the LORD, and the word of the LORD had not yet been revealed to him. 8 And the LORD called Samuel again the third time. And he arose and went to Eli and said, "Here I am, for you called me." Then Eli perceived that the LORD was calling the boy. 9 Therefore Eli said to Samuel, "Go, lie down, and if he calls you, you shall say, 'Speak, LORD, for your servant hears.'" So Samuel went and lay down in his place.

10 And the LORD came and stood, calling as at other times, "Samuel! Samuel!" And Samuel said, "Speak, for your servant hears." 11 Then the LORD said to Samuel, "Behold, I am about to do a thing in Israel [k]at which the two ears of everyone who hears it will tingle. 12 On that day I will fulfill against Eli [l]all that I have spoken concerning his house, from beginning to end. 13 [l]And I declare to him that I am about to punish his house forever, for the iniquity that he knew, [m]because his sons were blaspheming God,[1] [n]and he did not restrain them. 14 Therefore I swear to the house of Eli [o]that the iniquity of Eli's house shall not be atoned for by sacrifice or offering forever."

15 Samuel lay until morning; then he opened the doors of the house of the LORD. And Samuel was afraid to tell the vision to Eli. 16 But Eli called Samuel and said, "Samuel, my son." And he said, "Here I am." 17 And Eli said, "What was it that he told you? Do not hide it from me. [p]May God do so to you and more also if you hide anything from me of all that he told you." 18 So Samuel told him everything and hid nothing from him. And he said, [q]"It is the LORD. Let him do what seems good to him."

19 [r]And Samuel grew, and the LORD was with him [s]and let none of his words fall to the ground. 20 And all Israel [t]from Dan to Beersheba knew that Samuel was established as a prophet of the LORD. 21 And the LORD appeared again at Shiloh, for the LORD revealed himself to Samuel [u]at Shiloh [v]by the word of the LORD.

The Philistines Capture the Ark

4 And the word of Samuel came to all Israel.

Now Israel went out to battle against the Philistines. They encamped at [w]Ebenezer, and the Philistines encamped at [x]Aphek. 2 The Philistines drew up in line against Israel, and when the battle spread, Israel was defeated before the Philistines, who killed about four thousand men on the field of battle. 3 And when the people came to the camp, the elders of Israel said, "Why has the LORD defeated us today before the Philistines? Let us bring the ark of the covenant of the LORD here [y]from Shiloh, that it[2] may come among us and save

[1] Or *blaspheming for themselves* [2] Or *he*

unrighteously accrued weight (4:18), yet there are nevertheless hints in the narrative that his spiritual life may have experienced some healing from the God who abundantly pardons (Isa. 55:7). For instance, Eli humbly submits to his rejection (1 Sam. 3:18) and, despite his physical—and formerly spiritual—blindness (4:15), he is described in 4:13 as "watching" and "trembling" for the ark of God.

Because God's grace is persistent, even one whose life has been marked by failure can have hope for renewal (cf. Jesus' words to the thief on the cross; Luke 23:39–43). Our sin can never outstrip God's grace if we will simply persist in coming to him (Rom. 5:20).

4:1–11 In the aftermath of Israel's first defeat by the Philistines, the elders ask the right question, recognizing that the outcome of the battle is in the Lord's hands. But they don't wait for an answer. Instead, they try to force the Lord's hand by bringing "the ark of the covenant" into battle with them (v. 3). How easy it is to know that our security is in God's hands and yet to try to secure our own safety by taking matters into our own hands. Israel's manipulative efforts are entirely unsuccessful (v. 10), and the ark of the covenant falls into Philistine hands (v. 11). Soon enough, the Philistines themselves will feel the "weight" of the Lord's hand (5:6, 11).

3 [j]Ex. 27:20, 21; Lev. 24:2, 3; 2 Chr. 13:11 [j]ch. 1:9
11 [k]2 Kgs. 21:12; Jer. 19:3
12 [l]See ch. 2:30-36
13 [l][See ver. 12 above] [m]ch. 2:12, 17, 22 [n]ch. 2:23-25
14 [o][Isa. 22:14]
17 [p][Ruth 1:17]
18 [q][2 Sam. 10:12; Job 1:21; 2:10; Ps. 39:9; Isa. 39:8]
19 [r]See ch. 2:21 [s][ch. 9:6]
20 [t]See 2 Sam. 3:10
21 [u][Josh. 18:1] [v]ver. 1, 4

Chapter 4
1 [w][ch. 5:1; 7:12] [x]ch. 29:1; Josh. 12:18
3 [y]Josh. 18:1

us from the power of our enemies." 4 So the people sent to Shiloh and brought from there the ark of the covenant of the LORD of hosts, [z]who is enthroned on the cherubim. And the two sons of Eli, Hophni and Phinehas, were there with the ark of the covenant of God.

5 As soon as the ark of the covenant of the LORD came into the camp, all Israel [a]gave a mighty shout, so that the earth resounded. 6 And when the Philistines heard the noise of the shouting, they said, "What does this great shouting in the camp of the Hebrews mean?" And when they learned that the ark of the LORD had come to the camp, 7 the Philistines were afraid, for they said, "A god has come into the camp." And they said, "Woe to us! For nothing like this has happened before. 8 Woe to us! Who can deliver us from the power of these mighty gods? These are the gods who struck the Egyptians with every sort of plague in the wilderness. 9 [b]Take courage, and be men, O Philistines, lest you become slaves to the Hebrews [c]as they have been to you; be men and fight."

10 So the Philistines fought, [d]and Israel was defeated, [e]and they fled, every man to his home. And there was a very great slaughter, for thirty thousand foot soldiers of Israel fell. 11 [f]And the ark of God was captured, [g]and the two sons of Eli, Hophni and Phinehas, died.

The Death of Eli

12 A man of Benjamin ran from the battle line and came to Shiloh the same day, [h]with his clothes torn and with dirt on his head. 13 When he arrived, [i]Eli was sitting on his seat by the road watching, for his heart trembled for the ark of God. And when the man came into the city and told the news, all the city cried out. 14 When Eli heard the sound of the outcry, he said, "What is this uproar?" Then the man hurried and came and told Eli. 15 Now Eli was ninety-eight years old [j]and his eyes were set so that he could not see. 16 And the man said to Eli, "I am he who has come from the battle; I fled from the battle today." And he said, [k]"How did it go, my son?" 17 He who brought the news answered and said, "Israel has fled before the Philistines, and there has also been a great defeat among the people. Your two sons also, Hophni and Phinehas, are dead, and the ark of God has been captured." 18 As soon as he mentioned the ark of God, Eli fell over backward [l]from his seat by the side of the gate, and his neck was broken and he died, for the man was old and heavy. He had judged Israel forty years.

19 Now his daughter-in-law, the wife of Phinehas, was pregnant, about to give birth. And when she heard the news that the ark of God was captured, and that her father-in-law and her husband were dead, she bowed and gave birth, for her pains came upon her. 20 And about the time of her death the women attending her said to her, [m]"Do not be afraid, for you have borne a son." But she did not answer or pay attention. 21 And she named the child [n]Ichabod, saying, [o]"The glory has departed[1] from Israel!" because [p]the ark of God had been captured and because of her father-in-law and her husband. 22 And she said, "The glory has departed from Israel, [p]for the ark of God has been captured."

The Philistines and the Ark

5 When the Philistines captured the ark of God, they brought it from [q]Ebenezer to [r]Ashdod. 2 Then the Philistines took the ark of God and brought it into the house of Dagon and set it up beside [s]Dagon. 3 And when the people of Ashdod rose early the next day, behold, [t]Dagon had fallen face downward on the ground before the ark of the LORD. So they took Dagon and put him back in his place.

[1] Or *gone into exile*; also verse 22

4[z] Ex. 25:22; 2 Sam. 6:2; Ps. 80:1; 99:1; [Num. 7:89]
5[a] Josh. 6:5, 20
9[b] [2 Sam. 10:12; 1 Cor. 16:13] [c] Judg. 13:1
10[d] ver. 2; Ps. 78:62; [Lev. 26:17; Deut. 28:25] [e] 2 Sam. 18:17; 19:8; 2 Kgs. 14:12; 2 Chr. 25:22
11[f] [ch. 2:32; Ps. 78:60, 61] [g] ch. 2:34; Ps. 78:64
12[h] See Josh. 7:6
13[i] ver. 18; ch. 1:9
15[j] 1 Kgs. 14:4; [ch. 3:2]

4:12–22 The key word "weight" ("honor," "glory"), introduced in 2:29–30, figures prominently in this section. Eli, after a lifetime of spiritual carelessness, dies under his own weight (4:18). And when hearing of the ark's "capture" by the Philistines causes Eli's daughter-in-law to give premature birth to a son, she names him "Ichabod" ("no honor/glory/weight"), explaining that the "weighty one" had departed (vv. 21–22). The theme of giving God due weight, which is ultimate weight, continues to build.

5:1–12 The Lord wastes no time in putting the chief "god" of the Philistines, Dagon, on his face (vv. 3–4) and bringing the Philistines to their knees by a visitation of plague (v. 6). Unable to bear the weight of God's hand, the Philistines move the ark from

16[k] 2 Sam. 1:4 18[l] ver. 13 20[m] Gen. 35:17 21[n] ch. 14:3 [o] Ps. 78:61; [Ps. 26:8] [p] ver. 11 22[p] [See ver. 21 above] **Chapter 5** 1[q] ch. 4:1; 7:12 [r] Josh. 13:3 2[s] Judg. 16:23 3[t] [Isa. 46:1, 2]

4 But when they rose early on the next morning, behold, Dagon had fallen face downward
on the ground before the ark of the LORD, [u]and
the head of Dagon and both his hands were
lying cut off on the threshold. Only the trunk
of Dagon was left to him. 5 This is why the
priests of Dagon and all who enter the house
of Dagon [v]do not tread on the threshold of
Dagon in Ashdod to this day.
6 [w]The hand of the LORD was heavy against
the people of Ashdod, and he terrified and
afflicted them with [x]tumors, both Ashdod and
its territory. 7 And when the men of Ashdod
saw how things were, they said, "The ark of
the God of Israel must not remain with us,
for his hand is hard against us and against
Dagon our god." 8 So they sent and gathered
together all [y]the lords of the Philistines and
said, "What shall we do with the ark of the
God of Israel?" They answered, "Let the ark of
the God of Israel be brought around to Gath."
So they brought the ark of the God of Israel
there. 9 But after they had brought it around,
[z]the hand of the LORD was against the city,
causing a very great panic, and he afflicted the
men of the city, both young and old, so that
[x]tumors broke out on them. 10 So they sent the
ark of God to Ekron. But as soon as the ark of
God came to Ekron, the people of Ekron cried
out, "They have brought around to us the ark
of the God of Israel to kill us and our people."
11 [y]They sent therefore and gathered together
all the lords of the Philistines and said, "Send
away the ark of the God of Israel, and let it
return to its own place, that it may not kill us
and our people." For there was a deathly panic
throughout the whole city. [w]The hand of God
was very heavy there. 12 The men who did not
die were struck with [x]tumors, and the cry of
the city went up to heaven.

The Ark Returned to Israel

6 The ark of the LORD was in the country
of the Philistines seven months. 2 And the
Philistines called for the priests and [a]the diviners and said, "What shall we do with the ark of
the LORD? Tell us with what we shall send it to
its place." 3 They said, "If you send away the ark
of the God of Israel, do not send it empty, but
by all means return him [b]a guilt offering. Then
you will be healed, and it will be known to you
why [c]his hand does not turn away from you."
4 And they said, "What is the guilt offering
that we shall return to him?" They answered,
"Five golden [d]tumors and five golden mice,
[e]according to the number of the lords of the
Philistines, for the same plague was on all of
you and on your lords. 5 So you must make
images of your [d]tumors and images of your
mice that ravage the land, [f]and give glory to
the God of Israel. Perhaps [g]he will lighten his
hand from off you [h]and your gods and your
land. 6 Why should you harden your hearts as
[i]the Egyptians and [j]Pharaoh hardened their
hearts? After he had dealt severely with them,
[k]did they not send the people away, and they

city to city, always with the same result, "very great panic" (v. 9). In a great reversal, what appeared to be a Philistine victory turns out to be a resounding defeat. The ark's travels from city to city ultimately become a kind of victory march for Israel.

God can neither be manipulated by those who confess him nor managed by those who defy him. Christ's death and resurrection constituted the greatest reversal of all time, as seeming defeat was turned to resounding victory (Col. 2:15; Heb. 2:14). Because God is personal, powerful, and providentially in charge, we must not judge by short-term appearances but trust in his revealed character and word (ultimately revealed in his covenant promises and provision of Christ). False gods—whether of the Egyptians (Ex. 12:12), of the Philistines, or of our own age—will all be judged and brought to nothing.

6:1–20 Through bitter experience, the Philistines learn that God is not to be trifled with, and they determine to "give glory [weight] to the God of Israel" (v. 5). The Israelites, by contrast, apparently still need to learn this lesson, as they greet the Philistines' return of the ark by looking upon it (or perhaps "inside it"; v. 19)! Only a "great blow" brings them to their senses regarding their act of desecration and reminds them that it is no small thing to "stand before the LORD, this holy God" (vv. 19–20). Even sincere actions can be presumptuous, if done in neglect of what God has explicitly said (cf. another story of the ark in 2 Sam. 6:1–11). Depending on our wisdom rather than God's is yet another way in which we make human ability or acumen a substitute for trust in his provision.

4[u] [Jer. 50:2; Ezek. 6:4, 6; Mic. 1:7]
5[v] [Zeph. 1:9]
6[w] [Ex. 9:3; Ps. 32:4; Acts 13:11] [x] ch. 6:5
8[y] Josh. 13:3
9[z] ch. 7:13; 12:15; Deut. 2:15 [x] [See ver. 6 above]
11[y] [See ver. 8 above] [w] [See ver. 6 above]
12[x] [See ver. 6 above]
Chapter 6
2[a] Deut. 18:10; [Gen. 41:8; Ex. 7:11; Dan. 2:2; 5:7]
3[b] [Lev. 5:15, 16] [c] ver. 9
4[d] ch. 5:6, 9, 12 [e] ver. 17, 18; Josh. 13:3; Judg. 3:3
5[d] [See ver. 4 above] [f] [Josh. 7:19] [g] [ch. 5:6, 9, 11] [h] ch. 5:3, 4, 7
6[i] [Ex. 14:17] [j] Ex. 8:15, 32; [Ex. 7:13; 9:7, 35; 10:1] [k] Ex. 12:31

departed? 7 Now then, take and prepare [l]a new cart and two milk cows [m]on which there has never come a yoke, and yoke the cows to the cart, but take their calves home, away from them. 8 And take the ark of the LORD and place it on the cart and put in a box at its side [n]the figures of gold, which you are returning to him as [b]a guilt offering. Then send it off and let it go its way 9 and watch. If it goes up on the way to its own land, to [o]Beth-shemesh, then it is he who has done us this great harm, but if not, then we shall know that it is not [p]his hand that struck us; it happened to us by coincidence."

10 The men did so, and took two milk cows and yoked them to the cart and shut up their calves at home. 11 And they put the ark of the LORD on the cart and the box with the golden mice and the images of their tumors. 12 And the cows went straight in the direction of [q]Beth-shemesh along [r]one highway, lowing as they went. They turned neither to the right nor to the left, and the lords of the Philistines went after them as far as the border of [q]Beth-shemesh. 13 Now the people of [q]Beth-shemesh were reaping their wheat harvest in the valley. And when they lifted up their eyes and saw the ark, they rejoiced to see it. 14 The cart came into the field of Joshua of Beth-shemesh and stopped there. [s]A great stone was there. And they split up the wood of the cart and offered the cows as a burnt offering to the LORD. 15 And the Levites took down the ark of the LORD and the box that was beside it, in which were the golden figures, and set them upon [s]the great stone. And the men of [q]Beth-shemesh offered burnt offerings and sacrificed sacrifices on that day to the LORD. 16 And when [t]the five lords of the Philistines saw it, they returned that day to Ekron.

17 These are the golden tumors that the Philistines returned as a [u]guilt offering to the LORD: one for Ashdod, one for Gaza, one for Ashkelon, one for Gath, one for Ekron, 18 and the golden mice, according to the number of all the cities of the Philistines belonging to the five lords, [v]both fortified cities and unwalled villages. [w]The great stone beside which they set down the ark of the LORD is a witness to this day in the field of Joshua of Beth-shemesh.

19 [x]And he struck some of the men of Beth-shemesh, because they looked upon the ark of the LORD. He struck seventy men of them,[1] and the people mourned because the LORD had struck the people with a great blow. 20 Then the men of Beth-shemesh said, [y]"Who is able to stand before the LORD, this holy God? And to whom shall he go up away from us?" 21 So they sent messengers to the inhabitants of [z]Kiriath-jearim, saying, "The Philistines have returned the ark of the LORD. Come down and take it up to you."

7 And the men of Kiriath-jearim came and took up the ark of the LORD and brought it to the house of [a]Abinadab on the hill. And they consecrated his son Eleazar to have charge of the ark of the LORD. 2 From the day that the ark was lodged at Kiriath-jearim, a long time passed, some twenty years, and all the house of Israel lamented after the LORD.

Samuel Judges Israel

3 And Samuel said to all the house of Israel, [b]"If you are returning to the LORD with all your heart, then [c]put away the foreign gods and the [d]Ashtaroth from among you and [e]direct your heart to the LORD [f]and serve him only, and he will deliver you out of the hand of the Philistines." 4 So the people of Israel put

[1] Most Hebrew manuscripts *struck of the people seventy men, fifty thousand men*

7 [l][2 Sam. 6:3] [m][Num. 19:2]
8 [n]ver. 4, 5 [b][See ver. 3 above]
9 [o]Josh. 15:10 [p]ver. 3
12 [q]Josh. 21:16 [r]Num. 20:19
13 [q][See ver. 12 above]
14 [s]ver. 18
15 [s][See ver. 14 above] [q][See ver. 12 above]
16 [t]See ver. 4
17 [u]ver. 3, 8
18 [v][Deut. 3:5] [w]ver. 14, 15
19 [x][Ex. 19:21; Num. 4:15, 20; 2 Sam. 6:7]
20 [y][2 Sam. 6:9]
21 [z]1 Chr. 13:5, 6; [Josh. 9:17; 18:14]
Chapter 7
1 [a]2 Sam. 6:3

Our calling as followers of Christ is not merely to be sincere (cf. Prov. 21:2) but to be attentive and obedient to God's revealed Word (cf. Deut. 12:8–11), and to live our lives trusting the God of that Word. For this is the same God who sent his own Son as a sacrifice for our sins. If he did that, how could we not trust him in all other matters (Rom. 8:32)?

7:2–17 This chapter bears the imprint of gospel principles. Samuel makes an appeal to the Israelites, who after 20 years of neglecting the Lord now show signs of wanting to return (v. 2). Samuel exhorts the people to return with all their heart, to demonstrate their repentance by putting away false gods, and to serve God alone. Such full-hearted, active conversion is their only hope of salvation from all that threatens them (v. 3). The people respond in all sincerity (vv. 4–6), but instead of their situation immediately improving, circumstances get worse! Perhaps alarmed

3 [b]1 Kgs. 8:48; Isa. 55:7; Hos. 6:1; Joel 2:12; See Deut. 30:2-10 [c]Gen. 35:2; Josh. 24:14, 23; [Judg. 10:16] [d]Judg. 2:13 [e][2 Chr. 19:3; 30:19; Ezra 7:10] [f]Deut. 6:13; 10:20; 13:4; Cited Matt. 4:10; Luke 4:8

away the Baals and the Ashtaroth, and they
served the LORD only.
5 Then Samuel said, "Gather all Israel at
[g]Mizpah, and I will pray to the LORD for
you." 6 So they gathered at [g]Mizpah [h]and
drew water and poured it out before the LORD
[i]and fasted on that day and said there, [j]"We
have sinned against the LORD." And Samuel
judged the people of Israel at Mizpah. 7 Now
when the Philistines heard that the people
of Israel had gathered at Mizpah, the lords
of the Philistines went up against Israel. And
when the people of Israel heard of it, they were
afraid of the Philistines. 8 And the people of
Israel said to Samuel, "Do not cease to cry
out to the LORD our God for us, that he may
save us from the hand of the Philistines." 9 So
Samuel took a nursing lamb and offered it
as a whole burnt offering to the LORD. And
[k]Samuel cried out to the LORD for Israel, and
the LORD answered him. 10 As Samuel was
offering up the burnt offering, the Philistines
drew near to attack Israel. [l]But the LORD thundered with a mighty sound that day against
the Philistines and threw them into confusion,
and they were defeated before Israel. 11 And
the men of Israel went out from Mizpah and
pursued the Philistines and struck them, as
far as below Beth-car.
12 Then Samuel [m]took a stone and set it up
between Mizpah and Shen[1] and called its name
Ebenezer;[2] for he said, "Till now the LORD has
helped us." 13 [n]So the Philistines were subdued
and did not again enter the territory of Israel.
And the hand of the LORD was against the
Philistines all the days of Samuel. 14 The cities that the Philistines had taken from Israel
were restored to Israel, from Ekron to Gath,
and Israel delivered their territory from the
hand of the Philistines. There was peace also
between Israel and the Amorites.
15 [o]Samuel judged Israel all the days of his
life. 16 And he went on a circuit year by year
to Bethel, Gilgal, and Mizpah. And he judged
Israel in all these places. 17 Then he would
return to [p]Ramah, for his home was there, and
there also he judged Israel. [q]And he built there
an altar to the LORD.

Israel Demands a King

8 When Samuel became old, [r]he made
his sons judges over Israel. 2 The name
of his firstborn son was Joel, and the name
of his second, Abijah; they were judges in
Beersheba. 3 Yet his sons did not walk in his
ways [s]but turned aside after gain. [t]They took
bribes and perverted justice.
4 Then all the elders of Israel gathered

[1] Hebrew; Septuagint, Syriac *Jeshanah* [2] *Ebenezer* means *stone of help*

by the Israelite assembly at Mizpah (v. 5), the Philistines come out in force with hostile intent (v. 7).

There is a gospel reality to this part of the story. How many new converts, perhaps expecting immediate resolution to problems in their lives, discover that in the short term things get worse! But also true to the gospel pattern, deliverance is forthcoming in God's perfect timing, which can be delayed beyond human expectations. Consider Paul's words to the Thessalonians about turning and waiting: "you turned to God from idols to serve the living and true God, and to wait for his Son from heaven, . . . Jesus who delivers us from the wrath to come" (1 Thess. 1:9–10).

Helpless to save themselves, and led by Samuel, the people cast themselves on God for rescue, and he saves them. Samuel sets up a stone to mark the deliverance, names it Ebenezer ("stone of help"), and makes a pronouncement: "Till now the LORD has helped us" (1 Sam. 7:12). This phrase not only reminds the people that their past deliverance has been by the Lord's hand, but also that they can go forward in confidence as they continue to walk with him and depend upon him alone.

"Till now the LORD has helped us." Looking at what Christ has done, how much more can believers today say this very thing.

8:1–22 Against the backdrop of chapter 7's description of the Lord's deliverance—recall "Till now the LORD has helped us" (7:12)—chapter 8 comes as a shock. "Appoint for us a king to judge us like all the nations" (8:5) is the elders' demand to Samuel. In actual time, this episode did not immediately follow the events of chapter 7—Samuel by now is "old" (8:1)—but in "narrative time" the immediate juxtaposition of the two chapters raises eyebrows. How can the people of God, who have experienced his deliverance, seek security in lesser powers like human kings?

5 [g][Judg. 20:1]
6 [g][See ver. 5 above] [h][2 Sam. 14:14] [i]ch. 31:13; Neh. 9:1 [j]Judg. 10:10
9 [k]Ps. 99:6; Jer. 15:1
10 [l]ch. 2:10; [2 Sam. 22:14, 15; Ps. 18:13]
12 [m]Gen. 28:18; 31:45; 35:14; Josh. 4:9; 24:26
13 [n][Judg. 13:1]
15 [o]ver. 6; ch. 12:11; [Judg. 2:16]
17 [p]ch. 1:19 [q][ch. 14:35; Judg. 21:4]

Chapter 8
1 [r]Deut. 16:18
3 [s][Ex. 18:21] [t][Ex. 23:8; Deut. 16:19; Ps. 15:5]

together and came to Samuel at [p]Ramah [5]and said to him, "Behold, you are old and your sons do not walk in your ways. [u]Now appoint for us a king to judge us like all the nations." [6]But the thing displeased Samuel when they said, "Give us a king to judge us." And Samuel prayed to the LORD. [7]And the LORD said to Samuel, "Obey the voice of the people in all that they say to you, [v]for they have not rejected you, [w]but they have rejected me from being king over them. [8]According to all the deeds that they have done, from the day I brought them up out of Egypt even to this day, forsaking me and serving other gods, so they are also doing to you. [9]Now then, obey their voice; only you shall solemnly warn them [x]and show them the ways of the king who shall reign over them."

Samuel's Warning Against Kings

[10]So Samuel told all the words of the LORD to the people who were asking for a king from him. [11]He said, [y]"These will be the ways of the king who will reign over you: [z]he will take your sons and appoint them to his chariots and to be his horsemen and to run before his chariots. [12]And he will appoint for himself commanders of thousands and commanders of fifties, and some [a]to plow his ground and to reap his harvest, and to make his implements of war and the equipment of his chariots. [13]He will take your daughters to be perfumers and cooks and bakers. [14][b]He will take the best of your fields and vineyards and olive orchards and give them to his servants. [15]He will take the tenth of your grain and of your vineyards and give it to his officers and to his servants. [16]He will take your male servants and female servants and the best of your young men[1] and your donkeys, and put them to his work. [17]He will take the tenth of your flocks, and you shall be his slaves. [18]And in that day you will cry out because of your king, whom you have chosen for yourselves, [c]but the LORD will not answer you in that day."

The LORD Grants Israel's Request

[19]But the people refused to obey the voice of Samuel. And they said, "No! But there shall be a king over us, [20][d]that we also may be like all the nations, and that our king may judge us and go out before us and fight our battles." [21]And when Samuel had heard all the words of the people, he repeated them in the ears of the LORD. [22]And the LORD said to Samuel, [e]"Obey their voice and make them a king." Samuel then said to the men of Israel, "Go every man to his city."

Saul Chosen to Be King

9 There was a man of Benjamin whose name was [f]Kish, the son of Abiel, son of Zeror, son of Becorath, son of Aphiah, a Benjaminite, a man of wealth. [2]And he had a son whose

[1] Septuagint *cattle*

4[p] [See ch. 7:17 above]
5[u] ver. 19, 20; [Deut. 17:14; Hos. 13:10; Acts 13:21]
7[v] [Ex. 16:8] [w] ch. 10:19
9[x] See ver. 11-18
11[y] ch. 10:25; See Deut. 17:16-20 [z] ch. 14:52
12[a] See Gen. 45:6
14[b] 1 Kgs. 21:7; [Ezek. 46:18]
18[c] Prov. 1:28; Isa. 1:15; Mic. 3:4
20[d] ver. 5
22[e] ver. 7; [Hos. 13:11]
Chapter 9
1[f] ch. 14:51; 1 Chr. 8:33; 9:39

The elders offer reasons: Samuel is old, and his sons and successors are corrupt (vv. 4–5). But these are not the real issues. Samuel hears their request for a "king to judge us" and, as Israel's "judge," feels personally affronted (v. 6). The actual offence, though, is much more serious. God tells Samuel, "they have rejected me from being king over them" (v. 7).

Such is the tendency of the human heart, to seek safety and security in governments, bank accounts, human relationships, insurance policies, health plans—all kinds of things that can never ultimately deliver. True security can be found only in God and in his King, Jesus himself (cf. Mic. 5:4; Rom. 8:31–39). The gospel call is always to resist becoming conformed to worldly thinking and to be transformed in our thinking and living (Rom. 12:2) by the power of the indwelling Holy Spirit (Rom. 8:5–6). "To set the mind on the Spirit is life and peace" (Rom. 8:6).

9:1–25 Having insisted on having a king like those of all the nations, the elders get what they asked for in Saul, son of Kish. The story of Saul is one of the least well understood (and hence one of the more troubling) of any in the Bible. But by attending to clues within the text, we can come to a better understanding of why he was chosen and why he failed. And the lessons to be learned from his rise and fall are immense.

Saul is outwardly impressive when we first meet him (v. 2) but largely ignorant of and insensitive to the things of God; even Saul's servant seems more aware of an important "man of God" than Saul is (v. 6). And when Saul encounters the prophet Samuel face-to-face precisely where Saul had been told he would meet the seer (v. 13), Saul fails to recognize him and asks, rather obtusely, where the seer might be

name was Saul, [g]a handsome young man.
There was not a man among the people of
Israel more handsome than he. [h]From his
shoulders upward he was taller than any of
the people.

3 Now the donkeys of Kish, Saul's father, were
lost. So Kish said to Saul his son, "Take one of
the young men with you, and arise, go and
look for the donkeys." 4 And he passed through
[i]the hill country of Ephraim and passed
through the land of [j]Shalishah, but they did
not find them. And they passed through the
land of Shaalim, but they were not there. Then
they passed through the land of Benjamin, but
did not find them.

5 When they came to the land of Zuph, Saul
said to his servant[1] who was with him, "Come,
let us go back, [k]lest my father cease to care
about the donkeys and become anxious about
us." 6 But he said to him, "Behold, there is [l]a
man of God in this city, and he is a man who
is held in honor; [m]all that he says comes true.
So now let us go there. Perhaps he can tell us
the way we should go." 7 Then Saul said to his
servant, "But if we go, [n]what can we bring the
man? For the bread in our sacks is gone, and
there is no present to bring to the man of God.
What do we have?" 8 The servant answered
Saul again, "Here, I have with me a quarter
of a shekel[2] of silver, and I will give it to the
man of God to tell us our way." 9 (Formerly in
Israel, when a man [o]went to inquire of God, he
said, "Come, let us go to the seer," for today's
"prophet" was formerly called a seer.) 10 And
Saul said to his servant, "Well said; come, let
us go." So they went to the city where the man
of God was.

11 As they went up the hill to the city, [p]they
met young women coming out to draw water
and said to them, "Is the seer here?" 12 They
answered, "He is; behold, he is just ahead of
you. Hurry. He has come just now to the city,
because the people [q]have a sacrifice today on
[r]the high place. 13 As soon as you enter the city
you will find him, before he goes up to the
high place to eat. For the people will not eat
till he comes, since he must bless the sacrifice;
afterward those who are invited will eat. Now
go up, for you will meet him immediately."
14 So they went up to the city. As they were
entering the city, they saw Samuel coming out
toward them on his way up to the high place.

15 Now the day before Saul came, [s]the LORD
had [t]revealed to Samuel: 16 "Tomorrow about
this time I will send to you a man from the
land of Benjamin, [u]and you shall anoint him to
be prince[3] over my people Israel. He shall save
my people from the hand of the Philistines.
[v]For I have seen[4] my people, because their cry
has come to me." 17 When Samuel saw Saul, the
LORD told him, [w]"Here is the man of whom
I spoke to you! He it is who shall restrain my
people." 18 Then Saul approached Samuel in
the gate and said, "Tell me where is the house
of the seer?" 19 Samuel answered Saul, "I am
the seer. Go up before me to the high place, for
today you shall eat with me, and in the morning I will let you go and will tell you all that
is on your mind. 20 [x]As for your donkeys that
were lost three days ago, do not set your mind
on them, for they have been found. And for
whom is all that is desirable in Israel? Is it not
for you and for all your father's house?" 21 Saul
answered, "Am I not a Benjaminite, [y]from the
least of the tribes of Israel? [z]And is not my clan
the humblest of all the clans of the tribe of
Benjamin? Why then have you spoken to me
in this way?"

22 Then Samuel took Saul and his young
man and brought them into the hall and gave
them a place at the head of those who had been
invited, who were about thirty persons. 23 And
Samuel said to the cook, "Bring the portion
I gave you, of which I said to you, 'Put it aside.'"
24 So the cook took up [a]the leg and what was
on it and set them before Saul. And Samuel

[1] Hebrew *young man*; also verses 7, 8, 10, 27 [2] A *shekel* was about 2/5 ounce or 11 grams [3] Or *leader* [4] Septuagint adds *the affliction of*

lodging (v. 18). Given these hints of Saul's inward deficiency, which will become more evident as the story unfolds, why would God choose him in the first place? The short answer is that he conceded to the elders' persistent demand, ultimately to teach them and us of the insufficiency of all purely human deliverance—no matter how noble and capable it may at first appear. Persisting in a demand contrary to the will of God may bring us what we ask for, even though it may be far from what we need. The good news is that God understands our weakness and gives us the Spirit to help us "in our weakness. For we do not know what to pray for as we ought" (Rom. 8:26).

2 [g] [ch. 8:16] [h] ch. 10:23
4 [i] See Josh. 24:33 [j] 2 Kgs. 4:42
5 [k] ch. 10:2
6 [l] Deut. 33:1; Judg. 13:6; 1 Kgs. 13:1 [m] ch. 3:19
7 [n] [1 Kgs. 14:3; 2 Kgs. 4:42; 8:8]
9 [o] Gen. 25:22
11 [p] Gen. 24:11
12 [q] ch. 16:2; 20:29; Gen. 31:54 [r] ch. 10:5; 1 Kgs. 3:2-4

15 [s] ch. 15:1; [Acts 13:21] [t] Ruth 4:4 **16** [u] ch. 10:1 [v] Ex. 2:25; 3:7, 9 **17** [w] [ch. 16:12] **20** [x] ver. 3 **21** [y] [Judg. 20:46; 21:6; Ps. 68:27] [z] ch. 15:17; [Judg. 6:15]
24 [a] Ex. 29:22, 27; Lev. 7:32, 33; [Ezek. 24:4]

said, "See, what was kept is set before you.
Eat, because it was kept for you until the hour
appointed, that you might eat with the guests."[1]
So Saul ate with Samuel that day. 25 And
when they came down from the high place
into the city, a bed was spread for Saul[2] [b]on
the roof, and he lay down to sleep. 26 Then
at the break of dawn[3] Samuel called to Saul
on the roof, "Up, that I may send you on your
way." So Saul arose, and both he and Samuel
went out into the street.

27 As they were going down to the outskirts
of the city, Samuel said to Saul, "Tell the servant to pass on before us, and when he has
passed on, stop here yourself for a while, that
I may make known to you the word of God."

Saul Anointed King

10 [c]Then Samuel took a flask of oil and
poured it on his head [d]and kissed him
and said, "Has not the LORD anointed you to
be prince[4] over [e]his people Israel? And you
shall reign over the people of the LORD and
you will save them from the hand of their surrounding enemies. And this shall be the sign
to you that the LORD has anointed you to be
prince[5] over his heritage. 2 When you depart
from me today, you will meet two men by
[f]Rachel's tomb in the territory of Benjamin at
Zelzah, and they will say to you, [g]'The donkeys that you went to seek are found, and
now [h]your father has ceased to care about
the donkeys and is anxious about you, saying, "What shall I do about my son?"' 3 Then
you shall go on from there farther and come
to the [i]oak of Tabor. Three men [j]going up [k]to
God at Bethel will meet you there, one carrying three young goats, another carrying three
loaves of bread, and another carrying a skin of
wine. 4 And they will greet you and give you
two loaves of bread, which you shall accept
from their hand. 5 After that you shall come
to [l]Gibeath-elohim,[6] [m]where there is a garrison of the Philistines. And there, as soon as
you come to the city, you will meet a group
of prophets coming down [n]from the high
place with harp, tambourine, flute, and lyre
before them, prophesying. 6 [o]Then the Spirit
of the LORD will rush upon you, [p]and you
will prophesy with them and be turned into
another man. 7 Now when [q]these signs meet
you, do what your hand finds to do, [r]for God is
with you. 8 Then go down before me [s]to Gilgal.
And behold, I am coming down to you to offer
burnt offerings and [t]to sacrifice peace offerings. [u]Seven days you shall wait, until I come
to you and show you what you shall do."

9 When he turned his back to leave Samuel,
God gave him another heart. And all these
signs came to pass that day. 10 When they came
to [v]Gibeah,[7] behold, a group of prophets met
him, [o]and the Spirit of God rushed upon him,

[1] Hebrew *appointed, saying, 'I have invited the people'* [2] Septuagint; Hebrew *and he spoke with Saul* [3] Septuagint; Hebrew *And they arose early and at the break of dawn* [4] Or *leader* [5] Septuagint; Hebrew lacks *over his people Israel? And you shall. . . . to be prince* [6] *Gibeath-elohim* means *the hill of God* [7] *Gibeah* means *the hill*

25 [b][Deut. 22:8; 2 Sam. 11:2; 16:22; Neh. 8:16; Matt. 24:17; Acts 10:9]
Chapter 10
1 [c]ch. 9:16; 16:13; 2 Sam. 2:4; 1 Kgs. 1:34, 39; 2 Kgs. 9:1, 3, 6 [d][Ps. 2:12] [e]Deut. 32:9; Ps. 78:71
2 [f]Gen. 35:19, 20 [g]ch. 9:3, 4 [h]ch. 9:5
3 [i]Gen. 13:18 [j][Judg. 20:31] [k]Gen. 28:22; 35:1, 3, 7
5 [l]ver. 10 [m]ch. 13:3, 4 [n][ch. 9:12]
6 [o]ver. 10; ch. 11:6; 16:13; [Num. 11:25; Judg. 3:10; 14:6, 19] [p]ver. 10; ch. 19:23, 24
7 [q]Ex. 4:8; Judg. 6:17; Luke 2:12 [r]Josh. 1:5; Judg. 6:12
8 [s]ch. 11:14, 15; 13:4 [t]ch. 11:15 [u]ch. 13:8
10 [v]ver. 5 [o][See ver. 6 above]

9:26–10:13 Despite Saul's obtuseness, God is gracious to him and provides him everything he needs to succeed: anointing by Samuel (10:1), signs confirming his new status (10:2–6), and instructions regarding how he is to proceed (10:7–8).

The instructions consist of a two-part charge. First, as soon as the confirming signs are fulfilled, Saul is to "do what your hand finds to do," assured that "God is with you" (10:7). In light of the context, it seems clear that Saul should attack the Philistine garrison mentioned in 10:5 (cf. Jonathan's deed in 13:3) and thereby come to public attention as Israel's new leader. Secondly, as the effect of such an action would be to anger Israel's archenemies, the Philistines, and provoke a war, Saul is to rendezvous with Samuel, in order to receive further instructions from the Lord (10:8). How well Saul accommodates himself to this all-important authority structure whereby God continues to rule will be a key test of Saul's fitness to be king in Israel.

In the event, Saul fails to execute the first part of his charge, despite being "turned into another man" (10:6), or given "another heart" (10:9). Such language is not to be understood in New Testament terms as spiritual regeneration, but as a temporary alteration of Saul's normal behavior, in order that all the signs might be fulfilled (10:9). To prophesy was so out of character for Saul that those who knew him were astonished (10:11–13). And they coined an expression for such situations: "Is Saul also [or, Is even Saul] among the prophets?" This saying will recur in 19:24, where the ironic contrast between outward appearance and inward reality will be obvious. The consistent call of the gospel is to focus not on outward appearance but on the true condition of the heart (cf. 16:7; Rom. 2:28; 2 Cor. 5:12).

and he prophesied among them. 11 And when
all who knew him previously saw how he
prophesied with the prophets, the people said
to one another, "What has come over the son
of Kish? [w]Is Saul also among the prophets?"
12 And a man of the place answered, [x]"And who
is their father?" Therefore it became a proverb,
[w]"Is Saul also among the prophets?" 13 When
he had finished prophesying, he came to the
high place.

14 [y]Saul's uncle said to him and to his servant,
"Where did you go?" And he said, [z]"To seek
the donkeys. And when we saw they were not
to be found, we went to Samuel." 15 And Saul's
uncle said, "Please tell me what Samuel said
to you." 16 And Saul said to his uncle, [a]"He
told us plainly that the donkeys had been
found." But about the matter of the kingdom,
of which Samuel had spoken, he did not tell
him anything.

Saul Proclaimed King

17 Now Samuel called the people together
[b]to the LORD [c]at Mizpah. 18 And he said to the
people of Israel, [d]"Thus says the LORD, the God
of Israel, 'I brought up Israel out of Egypt, and
I delivered you from the hand of the Egyptians
and from the hand of all the kingdoms that
were oppressing you.' 19 [e]But today you have
rejected your God, who saves you from all your
calamities and your distresses, and you have
said to him, 'Set a king over us.' Now therefore
[f]present yourselves before the LORD by your
tribes and by your thousands."

20 Then Samuel [g]brought all the tribes
of Israel near, and the tribe of Benjamin
was taken by lot. 21 He brought the tribe of
Benjamin near by its clans, and the clan of
the Matrites was taken by lot;[1] and Saul the
son of Kish was taken by lot. But when they
sought him, he could not be found. 22 [h]So they
inquired again of the LORD, "Is there a man
still to come?" and the LORD said, "Behold,
he has hidden himself among the baggage."
23 Then they ran and took him from there.
And when he stood among the people, [i]he
was taller than any of the people from his
shoulders upward. 24 And Samuel said to all
the people, "Do you see him [j]whom the LORD
has chosen? There is none like him among
all the people." And all the people shouted,
[k]"Long live the king!"

25 Then Samuel told the people [l]the rights
and duties of the kingship, and he wrote them
in a book and laid it up before the LORD. Then
Samuel sent all the people away, each one to
his home. 26 Saul also went to his home [m]at
Gibeah, and with him went men of valor
whose hearts God had touched. 27 But some
[n]worthless fellows said, "How can this man
save us?" And they despised him and brought
him no present. But he held his peace.

Saul Defeats the Ammonites

11 [o]Then Nahash the Ammonite went up
and besieged [p]Jabesh-gilead, and all
the men of Jabesh said to Nahash, [q]"Make a
treaty with us, and we will serve you." 2 But

[1] Septuagint adds *finally he brought the family of the Matrites near, man by man*

10:14–27 Both Saul's conversation with his uncle (vv. 14–16) and Samuel's public lot-casting (vv. 17–27) demonstrate Saul's unwillingness to get on with the task the Lord has given him. The lot-casting was made necessary when Saul's failure to carry out the first part of his charge (see preceding note) meant that he remained unknown to the people. What accounts for Saul's failure to obey? The short answer is his failure to trust. The deficiency of Saul's faith in God will become ever more apparent as the narrative continues.

The story of Saul illustrates a fundamental gospel truth, namely, that "without faith [trust] it is impossible to please [God], for whoever would draw near to God must believe that he exists and that he rewards those who seek him" (Heb. 11:6). How often is our unwillingness to obey rooted in our lack of trust in God, his Word, and his provision? On the tight link between believing/trusting and obeying, see Deuteronomy 9:23; John 3:36; Romans 10:16.

11:1–11 Saul's great victory over the Ammonites and his rescue of the citizens of Jabesh-gilead might seem to contradict the view that Saul was lacking in genuine faith. But the text suggests not only that Saul, in neglect of his calling to lead Israel, has returned to farming (v. 5) but also that the coming of the divine spirit on Saul effects an outward change of behavior but not necessarily inward transformation (cf. similar incidents at 10:10; 18:10; 19:23–24). The heart of the gospel is about the state of the

11 [w] ch. 19:24; [Matt. 13:54, 55; John 7:15]
12 [x] [Isa. 54:13; John 6:45] [w] [See ver. 11 above]
14 [y] ch. 14:50 [z] See ch. 9:4-6
16 [a] ch. 9:20
17 [b] [ch. 11:15] [c] ch. 7:5, 6
18 [d] Judg. 6:8, 9; [ch. 12:8]
19 [e] ch. 8:7, 19; 12:12 [f] Josh. 24:1
20 [g] Josh. 7:14, 16, 17
22 [h] See ch. 22:10
23 [i] ch. 9:2
24 [j] 2 Sam. 21:6 [k] 2 Sam. 16:16; 1 Kgs. 1:25, 39; 2 Kgs. 11:12; 2 Chr. 23:11
25 [l] See ch. 8:11-18; Deut. 17:14-20
26 [m] ch. 11:4
27 [n] ch. 2:12; Deut. 13:13

Chapter 11
1 [o] ch. 12:12 [p] Judg. 21:8 [q] Gen. 26:28; 1 Kgs. 20:34; Ezek. 17:13; [Ex. 23:32; 34:12, 15; Deut. 7:2]

Nahash the Ammonite said to them, "On this
condition I will make a treaty with you, [r]that
I gouge out all your right eyes, and thus [s]bring
disgrace on all Israel." 3 The elders of Jabesh
said to him, "Give us seven days' respite that
we may send messengers through all the territory of Israel. Then, if there is no one to save
us, we will give ourselves up to you." 4 When
the messengers came to [t]Gibeah of Saul, they
reported the matter in the ears of the people,
[u]and all the people wept aloud.
5 Now, behold, Saul was coming from the
field behind the oxen. And Saul said, "What is
wrong with the people, that they are weeping?"
So they told him the news of the men of Jabesh.
6 [v]And the Spirit of God rushed upon Saul when
he heard these words, and his anger was greatly
kindled. 7 He took a yoke of oxen [w]and cut them
in pieces and sent them throughout all the territory of Israel by the hand of the messengers,
saying, [x]"Whoever does not come out after Saul
and Samuel, so shall it be done to his oxen!"
Then the dread of the LORD fell upon the people, and they came out [y]as one man. 8 When he
mustered them at [z]Bezek, [a]the people of Israel
were three hundred thousand, and the men of
Judah thirty thousand. 9 And they said to the
messengers who had come, "Thus shall you
say to the men of Jabesh-gilead: 'Tomorrow,
by the time the sun is hot, you shall have [b]sal-
vation.' " When the messengers came and told
the men of Jabesh, they were glad. 10 Therefore
the men of Jabesh said, [c]"Tomorrow we will
give ourselves up to you, and you may do to
us whatever seems good to you." 11 [d]And the
next day Saul put the people [e]in three companies. And they came into the midst of the
camp in the morning watch and struck down
the Ammonites until the heat of the day. And
those who survived were scattered, so that no
two of them were left together.

The Kingdom Is Renewed

12 Then the people said to Samuel, [f]"Who is it
that said, 'Shall Saul reign over us?' [g]Bring the
men, that we may put them to death." 13 But
Saul said, [h]"Not a man shall be put to death this
day, for today [i]the LORD has worked [j]salvation
in Israel." 14 Then Samuel said to the people,
"Come, let us go to Gilgal and there renew the
kingdom." 15 So all the people went to [k]Gilgal,
and there they made Saul king [l]before the
LORD in Gilgal. There [m]they sacrificed peace
offerings before the LORD, and there Saul and
all the men of Israel rejoiced greatly.

Samuel's Farewell Address

12 And Samuel said to all Israel, "Behold,
I have obeyed [n]your voice in all that you
have said to me [o]and have made a king over
you. 2 And now, behold, the king [p]walks before
you, [q]and I am old and gray; and behold, my
sons are with you. I have walked before you
from my youth until this day. 3 Here I am; testify against me before the LORD and before
[r]his anointed. [s]Whose ox have I taken? Or
whose donkey have I taken? Or whom have
I defrauded? Whom have I oppressed? Or from
whose hand have I taken a bribe to blind my
eyes with it? Testify against me[1] and I will
restore it to you." 4 They said, "You have not
defrauded us or oppressed us or taken any-

[1] Septuagint; Hebrew lacks *Testify against me*

2 [r][Num. 16:14] [s]ch. 17:26; Gen. 34:14
4 [t]ch. 10:26 [u]Judg. 2:4; 21:2
6 [v]See ch. 10:6, 10
7 [w][Judg. 19:29] [x]Judg. 21:5, 8, 10 [y]Judg. 20:1
8 [z]Judg. 1:5 [a][Judg. 20:15-17; 2 Sam. 24:9]
9 [b]ver. 13
10 [c]ver. 3
11 [d][ch. 31:11] [e]Judg. 7:16
12 [f]ch. 10:27 [g][Luke 19:27]
13 [h]2 Sam. 19:22 [i][ch. 19:5; Ex. 14:13] [j]ver. 9
15 [k]ch. 10:8 [l]ch. 15:33; [ch. 10:17; Judg. 11:11] [m]ch. 10:8

Chapter 12
1 [n]ch. 8:5, 19, 20 [o]ch. 10:24; 11:14, 15
2 [p][ch. 8:20; Num. 27:17] [q]ch. 8:1, 5
3 [r]ch. 24:6; 26:9, 11, 16; 2 Sam. 1:14, 16; [ch. 10:1] [s][Ex. 20:17; Num. 16:15]

heart. Paul's prayer for believers is that God "may grant you to be strengthened with power through his Spirit in your inner being, so that Christ may dwell in your hearts through faith," so that you may "know the love of Christ that surpasses knowledge, that you may be filled with all the fullness of God" (Eph. 3:16–17, 19). Overwhelmed by an external working of God's Spirit, Saul on this occasion does the right thing, but his heart is not right with God.

11:12–12:25 A hint that Samuel remains concerned about Saul's suitability to be king under the great King is that, while "Saul and all the men of Israel rejoiced greatly" (11:15), Samuel is not mentioned as joining the celebration. Instead, Samuel issues a stern warning: "if both you and the king who reigns over you will follow the LORD your God, it will be well" (12:14), but "if you still do wickedly, you shall be swept away, both you and your king" (12:25).

Drawing together some threads from the story of Saul, we discover a clear gospel balance: just as works without faith count for little with God, so also claims to faith that do not issue in active obedience are meaningless. As James later writes, "faith apart from works is useless" (James 2:20). It is faith alone that puts us right with God. Yet the kind of faith that puts us right with God is never alone.

thing from any man's hand." 5 And he said to
them, "The LORD is witness against you, and
[r]his anointed is witness this day, that you have
not found anything [t]in my hand." And they
said, "He is witness."

6 And Samuel said to the people, [u]"The LORD
is witness,[1] who appointed Moses and Aaron
and brought your fathers up out of the land
of Egypt. 7 Now therefore stand still that I may
plead with you before the LORD concerning all
the righteous deeds of the LORD that he performed for you and for your fathers. 8 [v]When
Jacob went into Egypt, and the Egyptians
oppressed them,[2] [w]then your fathers cried out
to the LORD and [x]the LORD sent Moses and
Aaron, [y]who brought your fathers out of Egypt
and made them dwell in this place. 9 But [z]they
forgot the LORD their God. [a]And he sold them
into the hand of Sisera, commander of the
army of Hazor,[3] [b]and into the hand of the
Philistines, [c]and into the hand of the king of
Moab. And they fought against them. 10 [d]And
they cried out to the LORD and said, 'We have
sinned, because we have forsaken the LORD
[e]and have served the Baals and the Ashtaroth.
But now [f]deliver us out of the hand of our enemies, that we may serve you.' 11 And the LORD
sent [g]Jerubbaal [h]and Barak[4] [i]and Jephthah and
[j]Samuel and delivered you out of the hand of
your enemies on every side, and you lived in
safety. 12 And when you saw that [k]Nahash the
king of the Ammonites came against you, [l]you
said to me, 'No, but a king shall reign over us,'
[m]when the LORD your God was your king.
13 And now [n]behold the king whom you have
chosen, for whom you have asked; behold, [o]the
LORD has set a king over you. 14 If you will [p]fear
the LORD and serve him and obey his voice and
not rebel against the commandment of the
LORD, and if both you and the king who reigns
over you will follow the LORD your God, it will
be well. 15 But [q]if you will not obey the voice
of the LORD, but rebel against the commandment of the LORD, then [r]the hand of the LORD
will be against you and [s]your king.[5] 16 Now
therefore [t]stand still and see this great thing
that the LORD will do before your eyes. 17 [u]Is it
not wheat harvest today? [v]I will call upon the
LORD, that he may send thunder and rain. And
you shall know and see that [w]your wickedness
is great, which you have done in the sight of
the LORD, in asking for yourselves a king." 18 So
Samuel called upon the LORD, and the LORD
sent thunder and rain that day, [x]and all the
people greatly feared the LORD and Samuel.

19 And all the people said to Samuel, [y]"Pray
for your servants to the LORD your God, that
we may not die, for we have added to all our
sins this evil, to ask for ourselves a king."
20 And Samuel said to the people, "Do not be
afraid; you have done all this evil. Yet [z]do not
turn aside from following the LORD, but serve
the LORD with all your heart. 21 And [z]do not
turn aside after [a]empty things that cannot
profit or deliver, for they are empty. 22 [b]For the
LORD will not forsake his people, [c]for his great
name's sake, because [d]it has pleased the LORD
to make you a people for himself. 23 Moreover,
as for me, far be it from me that I should sin
against the LORD by ceasing [e]to pray for you,
[f]and I will instruct you in the good and the
right way. 24 [g]Only fear the LORD and serve
him faithfully with all your heart. For consider
[h]what great things he has done for you. 25 But
if you still do wickedly, [i]you shall be swept
away, [j]both you and your king."

Saul Fights the Philistines

13 Saul lived for one year and then became
king, and when he had reigned for two
years over Israel,[6] 2 Saul chose three thousand men of Israel. Two thousand were with

[1] Septuagint; Hebrew lacks *is witness* [2] Septuagint; Hebrew lacks *and the Egyptians oppressed them* [3] Septuagint *the army of Jabin king of Hazor* [4] Septuagint, Syriac; Hebrew *Bedan* [5] Septuagint; Hebrew *fathers* [6] Hebrew *Saul was one year old when he became king, and he reigned two years over Israel* (see 1 Samuel 10:6); some Greek manuscripts give Saul's age when he began to reign as thirty years

13:1–15 Saul's official reign begins with a test still to be passed. Does God carry weight with Saul, such that no circumstances can compel him to disobey his charge to wait for divine instruction? Recall that to "honor" God is to give him weight (2:12–36); and recall that Saul's first charge was to attack the Philistine garrison and then to wait for Samuel's further instructions at Gilgal (9:26–10:13). In this episode, Jonathan attacks the garrison, and Saul goes to Gilgal. When Samuel is late in arriving and Saul's

5[r] [See ver. 3 above] [t] Ex. 21:16; 22:4
6[u] [Mic. 6:4]
8[v] Gen. 46:5, 6 [w] Ex. 2:23 [x] Ex. 3:10; 4:14-16 [y] [ch. 10:18]
9[z] Judg. 3:7 [a] Judg. 4:2 [b] Judg. 10:7; 13:1; [Judg. 3:31] [c] Judg. 3:12

10[d] Judg. 10:10; [Judg. 3:9] [e] Judg. 2:13 [f] Judg. 10:15 **11**[g] Judg. 6:14, 32 [h] Judg. 4:6, 8, 10 [i] Judg. 11:1 [j] See ch. 7:10-13 **12**[k] ch. 11:1 [l] ch. 8:5, 19 [m] [ch. 8:7; 10:19; Judg. 8:23] **13**[n] ch. 10:24 [o] ch. 9:16, 17; [Hos. 13:11] **14**[p] ver. 24; Deut. 6:2; Josh. 24:14 **15**[q] Lev. 26:14, 15; Deut. 28:15; Josh. 24:20 [r] ch. 5:9 [s] [ver. 9] **16**[t] Ex. 14:13 **17**[u] [Prov. 26:1] [v] ch. 7:9, 10; [James 5:16-18] [w] ch. 8:7 **18**[x] Ex. 14:31; [Ezra 10:9] **19**[y] ver. 23; [Ex. 9:28; 10:17; Jer. 15:1] **20**[z] Deut. 11:16 **21**[z] [See ver. 20 above] [a] Jer. 16:19; Hab. 2:18; [1 Cor. 8:4] **22**[b] 1 Kgs. 6:13; Ps. 94:14; [1 Kgs. 8:57] [c] Josh. 7:9; Ps. 106:8; Jer. 14:21; Ezek. 20:9, 14, 22 [d] Deut. 7:7, 8; 14:2; [1 Pet. 2:9] **23**[e] See ver. 19 [f] 1 Kgs. 8:36; 2 Chr. 6:27; Ps. 27:11; [Prov. 4:11; Jer. 6:16] **24**[g] ver. 14; [Eccles. 12:13] [h] Deut. 10:21; Ps. 126:2, 3 **25**[i] Josh. 24:20; [Num. 16:26] [j] [Deut. 28:36]

Saul in [k]Michmash and the hill country of Bethel, and a thousand were with Jonathan in [l]Gibeah of Benjamin. The rest of the people he sent home, every man to his tent. 3 Jonathan defeated [m]the garrison of the Philistines that was [n]at Geba, and the Philistines heard of it. And Saul [o]blew the trumpet throughout all the land, saying, "Let the Hebrews hear." 4 And all Israel heard it said that Saul had defeated the garrison of the Philistines, and also that Israel had become a stench to the Philistines. And the people were called out to join Saul at Gilgal.

5 And the Philistines mustered to fight with Israel, thirty thousand chariots and six thousand horsemen and troops [p]like the sand on the seashore in multitude. They came up and encamped in Michmash, to the east of [q]Beth-aven. 6 When the men of Israel saw that they were in trouble (for the people were hard pressed), the people hid themselves [r]in caves and in holes and in rocks and in tombs and in cisterns, 7 and some Hebrews crossed the fords of the Jordan to the land of Gad and Gilead. Saul was still at Gilgal, and all the people followed him trembling.

Saul's Unlawful Sacrifice

8 [s]He waited seven days, the time appointed by Samuel. But Samuel did not come to Gilgal, and the people were scattering from him. 9 So Saul said, "Bring the burnt offering here to me, and the peace offerings." And he offered the burnt offering. 10 As soon as he had finished offering the burnt offering, behold, Samuel came. And Saul went out to meet him and greet him. 11 Samuel said, "What have you done?" And Saul said, "When I saw that the people were scattering from me, and that you did not come within the days appointed, and that the Philistines had mustered at Michmash, 12 I said, 'Now the Philistines will come down against me at Gilgal, and I have not sought the favor of the LORD.' So I forced myself, and offered the burnt offering." 13 And Samuel said to Saul, [t]"You have done foolishly. [u]You have not kept the command of the LORD your God, with which he commanded you. For then the LORD would have established your kingdom over Israel forever. 14 But now [v]your kingdom shall not continue. The LORD has sought out a man [w]after his own heart, and the LORD has commanded him to be prince[1] over his people, because you have not kept what the LORD commanded you." 15 And Samuel arose and went up from Gilgal. The rest of the people went up after Saul to meet the army; they went up from Gilgal[2] to [x]Gibeah of Benjamin.

And Saul numbered the people who were present with him, [y]about six hundred men. 16 And Saul and Jonathan his son and the people who were present with them stayed in [z]Geba of Benjamin, but the Philistines encamped in Michmash. 17 And [a]raiders came out of the

[1] Or *leader* [2] Septuagint; Hebrew lacks *The rest of the people . . . from Gilgal*

Chapter 13
2 [k] ver. 5, 11, 16, 23; ch. 14:31 [l] ver. 15; ch. 10:26
3 [m] ch. 10:5 [n] ver. 16; ch. 14:5 [o] [Judg. 3:27]
5 [p] Josh. 11:4 [q] ch. 14:23
6 [r] Judg. 6:2; Heb. 11:38
8 [s] ch. 10:8
13 [t] 2 Sam. 24:10; 1 Chr. 21:8; 2 Chr. 16:9 [u] ch. 15:11
14 [v] ch. 15:28 [w] Cited Acts 13:22
15 [x] ver. 2 [y] ch. 14:2
16 [z] ver. 3; ch. 14:5
17 [a] ch. 14:15

troops are deserting, Saul acts foolishly by getting on with battle preparations (i.e., sacrifices) in Samuel's absence. This shows that, for Saul, hearing from God is not an ultimate concern. In a tight spot, Saul apparently considers other factors to outweigh his obligation, as king, to hear from the great King.

How tempting it is in pressured situations to seek security by almost any means other than by waiting on God. But the safest place to be is always in a position of trust in the Lord, whatever circumstantial storms may be raging all around us. "The fear of man lays a snare, but whoever trusts in the LORD is safe" (Prov. 29:25). A big view of God brings peace of mind (Ps. 4:8), for "the beloved of the LORD dwells in safety" (Deut. 33:12). The promise of the gospel is not a life free of problems and challenges. God's people are called to suffering, some even to martyrdom. But despite all the hurts, they never suffer ultimate harm. For the Lord stands by his people, strengthens them, and empowers their witness (cf. Paul's experience recounted in 2 Tim. 4:17).

Ultimately, the promise of the gospel is eternal life, as Paul testifies: "The Lord will rescue me from every evil deed and bring me safely into his heavenly kingdom" (2 Tim. 4:18). The suffering that believers undergo is never the punishment of a wrathful judge but always discipline, guidance, or opportunity from the hand of a tender Father, for Christ himself took our punishment in our place.

Saul's folly betrays his small view of God (1 Sam. 13:13). Saul fails to keep the "command [charge] of the LORD your God, with which he commanded you," and the Lord appoints (charges) "a man after his own heart" (v. 14).

camp of the Philistines in three companies. One company turned toward Ophrah, to the land of Shual; 18 another company turned toward [b]Beth-horon; and another company turned toward the border that looks down on the Valley of [c]Zeboim toward the wilderness.

19 [d]Now there was no blacksmith to be found throughout all the land of Israel, for the Philistines said, "Lest the Hebrews make themselves swords or spears." 20 But every one of the Israelites went down to the Philistines to sharpen his plowshare, his mattock, his axe, or his sickle,[1] 21 and the charge was two-thirds of a shekel[2] for the plowshares and for the mattocks, and a third of a shekel[3] for sharpening the axes and for setting the goads.[4] 22 So on the day of the battle [e]there was neither sword nor spear found in the hand of any of the people with Saul and Jonathan, but Saul and Jonathan his son had them. 23 And [f]the garrison of the Philistines went out to the [g]pass of [h]Michmash.

Jonathan Defeats the Philistines

14 One day Jonathan the son of Saul said to the young man who carried his armor, "Come, let us go over to the Philistine garrison on the other side." But he did not tell his father. 2 Saul was staying in the outskirts of Gibeah in the pomegranate cave[5] at [h]Migron. The people who were with him were about [i]six hundred men, 3 including [j]Ahijah the son of Ahitub, [k]Ichabod's brother, son of Phinehas, son of Eli, the priest of the LORD [l]in Shiloh, [m]wearing an ephod. And the people did not know that Jonathan had gone. 4 Within [n]the passes, by which Jonathan sought to go over to the Philistine garrison, there was a rocky crag on the one side and a rocky crag on the other side. The name of the one was Bozez, and the name of the other Seneh. 5 The one crag rose on the north in front of Michmash, and the other on the south in front of [o]Geba.

6 Jonathan said to the young man who carried his armor, "Come, let us go over to the garrison of these [p]uncircumcised. It may be that the LORD will work for us, [q]for nothing can hinder the LORD from saving by many or by few." 7 And his armor-bearer said to him, "Do all that is in your heart. Do as you wish.[6] Behold, I am with you heart and soul." 8 Then Jonathan said, "Behold, we will cross over to the men, and we will show ourselves to them. 9 If they say to us, 'Wait until we come to you,' then we will stand still in our place, and we will not go up to them. 10 But if they say, 'Come up to us,' then we will go up, for the LORD has given them into our hand. And this shall be the sign to us." 11 So both of them showed themselves to the garrison of the Philistines. And the Philistines said, "Look, Hebrews are coming [r]out of the holes where they have hidden themselves." 12 And the men of the garrison hailed Jonathan and his armor-bearer and said, "Come up to us, and we will show you a thing." And Jonathan said to his armor-bearer, "Come up after me, for the LORD has given them into the hand of Israel." 13 Then Jonathan climbed up on his hands and feet, and his armor-bearer after him. And they fell before Jonathan, and his armor-bearer killed them after him. 14 And that first strike, which Jonathan and his armor-bearer made, killed about twenty men within as it were half a furrow's length

[1] Septuagint; Hebrew *plowshare* [2] Hebrew *was a pim* [3] A *shekel* was about 2/5 ounce or 11 grams [4] The meaning of the Hebrew verse is uncertain [5] Or *under the pomegranate* [tree] [6] Septuagint *Do all that your mind inclines to*

14:1–14 Unlike his father in the preceding chapter, for whom loss of troop strength outweighed the necessity of waiting for the prophet Samuel and hearing from God, Jonathan is convinced that "nothing can hinder the LORD from saving by many or by few" (v. 6). This conviction, however, does not by itself propel Jonathan into action; he first waits to discern God's will (vv. 8–12). Having received a clear sign from the Lord, Jonathan and his armor-bearer go out in faith and, though greatly outnumbered, win a great victory (vv. 13–14). A consistent theme, not only in the books of Samuel but throughout Scripture, is that God's strength "is made perfect in weakness" (2 Cor. 12:9; cf. 1 Cor. 1:25, 27; Heb. 11:34). Faith like Jonathan's will be displayed also by David in confronting Goliath (1 Samuel 17). This whole-Bible theme of strength through weakness follows a trajectory that ultimately and supremely is filled out by Christ himself (2 Cor. 13:4).

As we fill our minds with the truths of the gospel that are secured in Christ, we come to see that God is bigger than anything life can throw against us. When God calls us to step out in faith, with the help of God's Spirit we can face any odds.

18[b] See Josh. 10:10 [c] Neh. 11:34
19[d] [2 Kgs. 24:14]
22[e] [Judg. 5:8]
23[f] ch. 14:1, 4, 6, 11; 2 Sam. 23:14 [g] ch. 14:4, 5; Isa. 10:28, 29 [h] Isa. 10:28

Chapter 14
2[h] [See ch. 13:23 above] [i] ch. 13:15
3[j] ch. 22:9, 11, 20 [k] ch. 4:21 [l] See Josh. 18:1 [m] ch. 2:28
4[n] ch. 13:23
5[o] ch. 13:3, 16
6[p] ch. 17:26; Judg. 14:3 [q] [Judg. 7:4, 7; 2 Chr. 14:11]
11[r] ch. 13:6

in an acre[1] of land. 15 And there was a panic
in the camp, in the field, and among all the
people. The garrison and even [s]the raiders
trembled, the earth quaked, and it became a
very great panic.[2]

16 And the watchmen of Saul in Gibeah of
Benjamin looked, and behold, the multitude
[t]was dispersing here and there.[3] 17 Then Saul
said to the people who were with him, "Count
and see who has gone from us." And when they
had counted, behold, Jonathan and his armor-
bearer were not there. 18 So Saul said to Ahijah,
"Bring the ark of God here." For the ark of God
went at that time with the people[4] of Israel.
19 Now [u]while Saul was talking to the priest,
the tumult in the camp of the Philistines
increased more and more. So Saul said to the
priest, "Withdraw your hand." 20 Then Saul
and all the people who were with him rallied
and went into the battle. And behold, [v]every
Philistine's sword was against his fellow, and
there was very great confusion. 21 Now the
Hebrews who had been with the Philistines
before that time and who had gone up with
them into the camp, [w]even they also turned
to be with the Israelites who were with Saul
and Jonathan. 22 Likewise, when all the men
of Israel [x]who had hidden themselves [y]in
the hill country of Ephraim heard that the
Philistines were fleeing, they too followed
hard after them in the battle. 23 [z]So the LORD
saved Israel that day. And the battle passed
beyond [a]Beth-aven.

Saul's Rash Vow

24 And the men of Israel had been hard
pressed that day, [b]so Saul had laid an oath on
the people, saying, "Cursed be the man who
eats food until it is evening and I am avenged
on my enemies." So none of the people had
tasted food. 25 Now when all the people[5] came
to the forest, behold, there was honey on the
ground. 26 And when the people entered the
forest, behold, the honey was dropping, but
no one put his hand to his mouth, for the people feared the oath. 27 But Jonathan had not
heard his father charge the people with the
oath, [c]so he put out the tip of the staff that was
in his hand and dipped it in the honeycomb
and put his hand to his mouth, and his eyes
became bright. 28 Then one of the people said,
"Your father strictly charged the people with
an oath, saying, 'Cursed be the man who eats
food this day.'" And the people were [d]faint.
29 Then Jonathan said, "My father has troubled the land. See how my eyes have become
bright because I tasted a little of this honey.
30 How much better if the people had eaten
freely today of the spoil of their enemies that
they found. For now the defeat among the
Philistines has not been great."

31 They struck down the Philistines that day
from [e]Michmash to [f]Aijalon. And the people
were very [d]faint. 32 The people [g]pounced on the
spoil and took sheep and oxen and calves and
slaughtered them on the ground. And the people ate them [h]with the blood. 33 Then they told
Saul, "Behold, the people are sinning against
the LORD by eating [h]with the blood." And he
said, "You have dealt treacherously; roll a great
stone to me here."[6] 34 And Saul said, "Disperse
yourselves among the people and say to them,
'Let every man bring his ox or his sheep and
slaughter them here and eat, and do not sin
against the LORD by eating with the blood.'"
So every one of the people brought his ox with
him that night and they slaughtered them

[1] Hebrew *a yoke* [2] Or *became a panic from God* [3] Septuagint; Hebrew *they went here and there* [4] Hebrew; Septuagint *"Bring the ephod." For at that time he wore the ephod before the people* [5] Hebrew *land* [6] Septuagint; Hebrew *this day*

15 [s] ch. 13:17
16 [t] Josh. 2:9
19 [u] Num. 27:21
20 [v] [Judg. 7:22; 2 Chr. 20:23]
21 [w] [ch. 29:4]
22 [x] ver. 11; ch. 13:6 [y] See Josh. 24:33
23 [z] Ex. 14:30 [a] ch. 13:5
24 [b] [Josh. 6:26]
27 [c] ver. 43
28 [d] Judg. 8:4, 5
31 [e] ch. 13:2 [f] Josh. 10:12 [d] [See ver. 28 above]
32 [g] ch. 15:19 [h] [Lev. 3:17]
33 [h] [See ver. 32 above]

14:15–46 In this section, Jonathan's successes contrast with Saul's failures. Saul's continuing folly (v. 24) almost costs Jonathan his life (vv. 27–28, 42–44), save for the intervention of the people (v. 45). Moreover, Saul's willingness to wait on the Lord, already in question after chapter 13, shows a pattern of decline. In 14:18–19, Saul calls for an oracular inquiry in order to discover God's will but, when the situation gets too intense, breaks it off before receiving an answer ("withdraw your hand"). Later, in verse 36, Saul apparently forgets to inquire of the Lord altogether and must be reminded by the priest.

How true this pattern can be in the lives of those who don't take God seriously. When God does not occupy first place, he seldom remains long in second, but is quickly relegated to ever lower standing, until he is forgotten altogether. By contrast, those responsive to the gospel are encouraged to "hold fast the confession of our hope without wavering, for he who promised is faithful," and they are enjoined to "consider how to stir up one another to love and good works" (Heb. 10:23–24).

there. 35 And Saul [i]built an altar to the LORD;
it was the first altar that he built to the LORD.
36 Then Saul said, "Let us go down after the
Philistines by night and plunder them until
the morning light; let us not leave a man of
them." And they said, "Do whatever seems
good to you." But [j]the priest said, "Let us draw
near to God here." 37 And Saul inquired of God,
"Shall I go down after the Philistines? Will
you give them into the hand of Israel?" [k]But
he did not answer him that day. 38 And Saul
said, "Come here, all you leaders of the people, and know and see how this sin has arisen
today. 39 For [l]as the LORD lives who saves Israel,
[m]though it be in Jonathan my son, he shall
surely die." But there was not a man among all
the people who answered him. 40 Then he said
to all Israel, "You shall be on one side, and I and
Jonathan my son will be on the other side."
And the people said to Saul, "Do what seems
good to you." 41 Therefore Saul said, "O LORD
God of Israel, why have you not answered
your servant this day? If this guilt is in me or
in Jonathan my son, O LORD, God of Israel, give
Urim. But if this guilt is in your people Israel,
give Thummim."[1] [n]And Jonathan and Saul
were taken, but the people escaped. 42 Then
Saul said, [n]"Cast the lot between me and my son
Jonathan." And Jonathan was taken.
43 Then Saul said to Jonathan, [o]"Tell me what
you have done." And Jonathan told him, [p]"I
tasted a little honey with the tip of the staff
that was in my hand. Here I am; I will die."
44 And Saul said, [q]"God do so to me and more
also; [r]you shall surely die, Jonathan." 45 Then
the people said to Saul, "Shall Jonathan die,
who has worked this great salvation in Israel?
Far from it! [l]As the LORD lives, [s]there shall
not one hair of his head fall to the ground,
for he has worked with God this day." So the
people ransomed Jonathan, so that he did not
die. 46 Then Saul went up from pursuing the
Philistines, and the Philistines went to their
own place.

Saul Fights Israel's Enemies

47 When Saul had taken the kingship over
Israel, he fought against all his enemies on
every side, against Moab, [t]against the Ammonites, against Edom, against the kings of
[u]Zobah, and against the Philistines. Wherever
he turned he routed them. 48 And he did valiantly [v]and struck the Amalekites and delivered Israel out of the hands of those who
plundered them.
49 [w]Now the sons of Saul were Jonathan,
Ishvi, and Malchi-shua. And the names of his
two daughters were these: the name of the
firstborn was [x]Merab, and the name of the
younger Michal. 50 And the name of Saul's wife
was Ahinoam the daughter of Ahimaaz. [y]And
the name of the commander of his army was
Abner the son of Ner, [z]Saul's uncle. 51 [a]Kish was
the father of Saul, and Ner the father of Abner
was the son of [a]Abiel.
52 There was hard fighting against the
Philistines all the days of Saul. And when Saul
saw any strong man, or any valiant man, [b]he
attached him to himself.

The LORD Rejects Saul

15 And Samuel said to Saul, [c]"The LORD
sent me to anoint you king over his
people Israel; now therefore listen to the
words of the LORD. 2 Thus says the LORD of
hosts, 'I have noted what Amalek did to Israel
[d]in opposing them on the way when they came
up out of Egypt. 3 Now go and strike Amalek
and [e]devote to destruction[2] all that they have.

[1] Vulgate and Septuagint; Hebrew *Therefore Saul said to the LORD, the God of Israel, "Give Thummim."* [2] That is, set apart (devote) as an offering to the Lord (for destruction); also verses 8, 9, 15, 18, 20, 21

15:1–30 That Saul receives yet another chance to hear and obey God's instructions (v. 1) is remarkable evidence of God's grace. After Saul's repeated failures in the preceding chapters, beginning with his failure to step out in faith and "do what his hand found to do" at the time of his anointing (cf. 10:7), Samuel stresses the importance of Saul's paying very close attention to the word of God (15:1). Sadly, Saul's conduct in the battle against the Amalekites (quintessential enemies of God; see Ex. 17:8–16) removes any doubt that Saul's main concern is not with God's honor but with his own. His obedience is partial at best, which is tantamount to disobedience (1 Sam. 15:8–9); he builds a "monument to himself" (v. 12); he attempts to shift the blame for any infractions from himself to the people (vv. 13–15; 20–21); his first confession is insincere, as evidenced by Samuel's reaction (vv. 24–26); and ultimately Saul admits that all he actually cares about is his own honor (v. 30).

35 [i] [ch. 7:12, 17]
36 [j] ver. 3, 18, 19
37 [k] ch. 28:6
39 [l] See Ruth 3:13 [m] ver. 44
41 [n] [ch. 10:20, 21; Josh. 7:16-18; Acts 1:24-26]
42 [n] [See ver. 41 above]
43 [o] [Josh. 7:19] [p] ver. 27
44 [q] See Ruth 1:17 [r] ver. 39
45 [l] [See ver. 39 above] [s] 2 Sam. 14:11; 1 Kgs. 1:52; Luke 21:18; Acts 27:34; [Matt. 10:30; Luke 12:7]
47 [t] ch. 11:11 [u] 2 Sam. 8:3; 10:6
48 [v] ch. 15:3, 7
49 [w] [ch. 31:2; 2 Sam. 2:8-10; 1 Chr. 8:33; 9:39] [x] ch. 18:17, 19

50 [y] 2 Sam. 2:8 [z] [ch. 10:14] **51** [a] ch. 9:1 **52** [b] ch. 8:11 **Chapter 15** **1** [c] ch. 9:16 **2** [d] See Ex. 17:8-16; Deut. 25:17-19 **3** [e] Lev. 27:28, 29; Josh. 6:17, 21

Do not spare them, [f]but kill both man and
woman, child and infant, ox and sheep, camel
and donkey.' "
4 So Saul summoned the people and numbered them in Telaim, two hundred thousand
men on foot, and ten thousand men of Judah.
5 And Saul came to the city of Amalek and lay
in wait in the valley. 6 Then Saul said to [g]the
Kenites, "Go, depart; go down from among
the Amalekites, lest I destroy you with them.
[h]For you showed kindness to all the people of
Israel when they came up out of Egypt." So the
Kenites departed from among the Amalekites.
7 [i]And Saul defeated the Amalekites from
[j]Havilah as far as [k]Shur, which is east of Egypt.
8 And he took Agag the king of the Amalekites
alive [l]and devoted to destruction all the people
with the edge of the sword. 9 [m]But Saul and the
people spared Agag and the best of the sheep
and of the oxen and of the fattened calves[1] and
the lambs, and all that was good, and would
not utterly destroy them. All that was despised
and worthless they devoted to destruction.
10 The word of the LORD came to Samuel:
11 [n]"I regret[2] that I have made Saul king, for
he has turned back from following me and
[o]has not performed my commandments."
And Samuel was angry, and he cried to the
LORD all night. 12 And Samuel rose early to
meet Saul in the morning. And it was told
Samuel, "Saul came to [p]Carmel, and behold,
he set up a monument for himself and turned
and passed on and went down to Gilgal."
13 And Samuel came to Saul, and Saul said
to him, [q]"Blessed be you to the LORD. I have
performed the commandment of the LORD."
14 And Samuel said, "What then is this bleat-
ing of the sheep in my ears and the lowing of
the oxen that I hear?" 15 Saul said, "They have
brought them from the Amalekites, [r]for the
people spared the best of the sheep and of
the oxen to sacrifice to the LORD your God,
and the rest we have devoted to destruction."
16 Then Samuel said to Saul, "Stop! I will tell
you what the LORD said to me this night."
And he said to him, "Speak."
17 And Samuel said, [s]"Though you are little
in your own eyes, are you not the head of the
tribes of Israel? The LORD anointed you king
over Israel. 18 And the LORD sent you on a mission and said, 'Go, devote to destruction the
sinners, the Amalekites, and fight against
them until they are consumed.' 19 Why then
did you not obey the voice of the LORD? [t]Why
did you pounce on the spoil and do what was
evil in the sight of the LORD?" 20 And Saul said
to Samuel, [u]"I have obeyed the voice of the
LORD. I have gone on the mission on which the
LORD sent me. I have brought Agag the king
of Amalek, and I have devoted the Amalekites
to destruction. 21 [v]But the people took of the
spoil, sheep and oxen, the best of the things
devoted to destruction, to sacrifice to the LORD
your God in Gilgal." 22 And Samuel said,

[w]"Has the LORD as great delight in burnt
    offerings and sacrifices,
  as in obeying the voice of the LORD?
Behold, [x]to obey is better than sacrifice,
  and to listen than the fat of rams.
23 For rebellion is as the sin of divination,
  and presumption is as iniquity and
    [y]idolatry.

[1] The meaning of the Hebrew term is uncertain [2] See also verses 29, 35

3 [f][ch. 22:19]
6 [g]ch. 27:10; Judg. 1:16 [h][Ex. 18:10, 19; Num. 10:29, 32]
7 [i]ch. 14:48 [j]Gen. 2:11; 25:18 [k]ch. 27:8; [Gen. 16:7; Ex. 15:22]
8 [l][ch. 27:8, 9; 30:1]
9 [m]ver. 15, 21; [ch. 28:18]
11 [n]See Gen. 6:6 [o]ver. 3, 9; [ch. 13:13]
12 [p]Josh. 15:55
13 [q]See Ruth 2:20
15 [r]ver. 9, 21
17 [s][ch. 9:21]
19 [t]ch. 14:32
20 [u]ver. 13
21 [v]ver. 15
22 [w]Ps. 40:6-8; 50:8, 9; Prov. 21:3; Isa. 1:11-13, 16, 17; Jer. 7:22, 23; Mic. 6:6-8; Heb. 10:6-9 [x]Eccles. 5:1; Hos. 6:6; Matt. 9:13; 12:7; Mark 12:33
23 [y]See Gen. 31:19, 34

In view of Saul's consistent rejection of the word of the Lord (v. 23a and prior episodes), it is no surprise that he is rejected from being king (v. 23b). When Saul attempts to gain control of the situation by seizing Samuel's robe, the robe tears, and Samuel uses this as a sign of the fact that "The LORD has torn the kingdom of Israel from you this day and has given it to a neighbor of yours, who is better than you" (v. 28).

This episode, and indeed the entire career of Saul, has much to teach us regarding what it means to be a godly leader. First and foremost, as was explicitly stated in the story of Eli, it means giving God proper honor, that is, giving God ultimate weight in every circumstance and in every decision (cf. 2:29–30). Our obedience to God is not to be trimmed down to our own liking. And we are not to assume that God can be manipulated: "he is not a man, that he should have regret" (15:29).

Despite the finality of Saul's failure, this episode also teaches us something about God's gracious provision of leadership—specifically, the "neighbor" better than Saul, whom we meet in the next chapter. And ultimately our hearts are brought to rest in the Leader who was descended from David and who, unlike even David, unfailingly and sinlessly leads his people as their champion (Acts 5:31; Heb. 2:10; 12:2).

Because [z]you have rejected the word of
the LORD,
[a]he has also rejected you from being
king."

24 Saul said to Samuel, [b]"I have sinned, for
I have transgressed the commandment of the
LORD and your words, because I feared the
people and obeyed their voice. 25 Now therefore, please pardon my sin and [c]return with
me that I may bow before the LORD." 26 And
Samuel said to Saul, "I will not return with
you. [d]For you have rejected the word of the
LORD, [e]and the LORD has rejected you from
being king over Israel." 27 [f]As Samuel turned to
go away, Saul seized the skirt of his robe, and
it tore. 28 And Samuel said to him, [g]"The LORD
has torn the kingdom of Israel from you this
day and has given it to a neighbor of yours,
who is better than you. 29 And also the Glory of
Israel [h]will not lie or have regret, for he is not
a man, that he should have regret." 30 Then he
said, "I have sinned; yet [i]honor me now before
the elders of my people and before Israel, [j]and
return with me, that I may bow before the
LORD your God." 31 So Samuel turned back
after Saul, and Saul bowed before the LORD.

32 Then Samuel said, "Bring here to me Agag
the king of the Amalekites." And Agag came
to him cheerfully.[1] Agag said, "Surely the bitterness of death is past." 33 And Samuel said,
[k]"As your sword has made women childless,
so shall your mother be childless among
women." And Samuel hacked Agag to pieces
before the LORD [l]in Gilgal.

34 Then Samuel went [m]to Ramah, and Saul
went up to his house in [n]Gibeah of Saul.
35 [o]And Samuel did not see Saul again until
the day of his death, [p]but Samuel grieved
over Saul. [q]And the LORD regretted that he
had made Saul king over Israel.

David Anointed King

16 The LORD said to Samuel, [r]"How long
will you grieve over Saul, since [s]I have
rejected him from being king over Israel? [t]Fill
your horn with oil, and go. I will send you to
Jesse the Bethlehemite, [u]for I have provided
for myself a king among his sons." 2 And
Samuel said, "How can I go? If Saul hears it,
he will kill me." And the LORD said, "Take a
heifer with you and say, [v]'I have come to sacrifice to the LORD.' 3 And invite Jesse to the
sacrifice, and I will show you what you shall
do. [w]And you shall anoint for me him whom
I declare to you." 4 Samuel did what the LORD
commanded and came to Bethlehem. The
elders of the city [x]came to meet him trembling

[1] Or *haltingly* (compare Septuagint); the Hebrew is uncertain

16:1–13 Some commentators assume that Samuel wanted Saul to fail, but the texts do not support this assumption. After Saul's definitive rejection as king in chapter 15, Samuel grieves for Saul (15:35), and as chapter 16 opens, the Lord has to exhort him to move on (16:1). God has not abandoned his people. Having provided for the people a king of the sort they demanded in chapter 8, God now provides "for myself a king" (16:1). Samuel is afraid of what Saul might do if he discovers that Samuel is being sent to anoint his replacement, and the Lord instructs him to take a heifer and say, "I have come to sacrifice to the LORD" (v. 2).

This apparent half-truth, suggested by the Lord himself, seems troubling. But perhaps it will help to recall the larger context. In the preceding chapter, Saul repeatedly claimed that the best of the Amalekite livestock was spared only "to sacrifice to the LORD your God" (15:15, 21). Is there a hint of just deserts in the "sacrifice-explanation" being turned back on Saul? Perhaps. After all, "God is not mocked, for whatever one sows, that will he also reap" (Gal. 6:7).

Who is the Lord's king? Not the tall and impressive (1 Sam. 16:7), but the smallest of Jesse's sons (v. 11; "smallest" and "youngest" render the same word in Hebrew). For "the LORD sees not as man sees; man looks on the outward appearance, but the LORD looks on the heart" (v. 7). The opening frame of 1 Samuel included Hannah's declaration that it is not by human might that one prevails (2:9). Rather, where true faith and trust are, God's "power is made perfect in weakness" (2 Cor. 12:9; cf. note on 1 Sam. 14:1–14). David may seem insignificant—the youngest, left to tend the sheep—but God sees in him something special. As his story unfolds, we will encounter sin and failure—David, unlike the Son of David to come, was not sinless. But David had a heart for God. Of equal, or greater, importance, he had the "Spirit of the LORD" powerfully working within him "from that day forward" (16:13).

23 [z]ver. 26 [a]ch. 13:14
24 [b][2 Sam. 12:13]
25 [c]ver. 30
26 [d]ver. 23 [e]ch. 16:1
27 [f][1 Kgs. 11:30, 31]
28 [g]ch. 28:17, 18
29 [h]Num. 23:19; [Ezek. 24:14]
30 [i][John 5:44; 12:43] [j]ver. 25
33 [k][Judg. 1:7] [l]ver. 12, 21
34 [m][ch. 1:19] [n]ch. 11:4
35 [o][ch. 19:24] [p]ch. 16:1 [q]ver. 11
Chapter 16
1 [r]ch. 15:35 [s]ch. 15:23, 26 [t]See ch. 10:1 [u]Ps. 78:70; 89:19, 20; Acts 13:22
2 [v][ch. 9:12; 20:29]
3 [w]ch. 9:16
4 [x]ch. 21:1

and said, [y]"Do you come peaceably?" 5 And he said, "Peaceably; I have come to sacrifice to the LORD. [z]Consecrate yourselves, and come with me to the sacrifice." And he consecrated Jesse and his sons and invited them to the sacrifice.

6 When they came, he looked on [a]Eliab and thought, "Surely the LORD's anointed is before him." 7 But the LORD said to Samuel, [b]"Do not look on his appearance or on the height of his stature, because I have rejected him. For the LORD sees not as man sees: man looks on the outward appearance, [c]but the LORD looks on the heart." 8 Then Jesse called [d]Abinadab and made him pass before Samuel. And he said, "Neither has the LORD chosen this one." 9 Then Jesse made [d]Shammah pass by. And he said, "Neither has the LORD chosen this one." 10 And Jesse made seven of his sons pass before Samuel. And Samuel said to Jesse, "The LORD has not chosen these." 11 Then Samuel said to Jesse, "Are all your sons here?" And he said, [e]"There remains yet the youngest,[1] but behold, he is keeping the sheep." And Samuel said to Jesse, [f]"Send and get him, for we will not sit down till he comes here." 12 And he sent and brought him in. Now he was [g]ruddy and had beautiful eyes and was handsome. And the LORD said, [h]"Arise, anoint him, for this is he." 13 Then Samuel took [i]the horn of oil [j]and anointed him in the midst of his brothers. [k]And the Spirit of the LORD rushed upon David from that day forward. And Samuel rose up and went to Ramah.

David in Saul's Service

14 [l]Now the Spirit of the LORD departed from Saul, [m]and a harmful spirit from the LORD tormented him. 15 And Saul's servants said to him, "Behold now, a harmful spirit from God is tormenting you. 16 Let our lord now command your servants [n]who are before you to seek out a man who is skillful in playing the lyre, and when the harmful spirit from God is upon you, he will [o]play it, and you will be well." 17 So Saul said to his servants, "Provide for me a man who can play well and bring him to me." 18 One of the young men answered, "Behold, I have seen a son of Jesse the Bethlehemite, who is skillful in playing, [p]a man of valor, a man of war, prudent in speech, and a man of good presence, [q]and the LORD is with him." 19 Therefore Saul sent messengers to Jesse and said, "Send me David your son, [r]who is with the sheep." 20 [s]And Jesse took a donkey laden with bread and a skin of wine and a young goat and sent them by David his son to Saul. 21 And David came to Saul [t]and entered his service. And Saul loved him greatly, and he became his armor-bearer. 22 And Saul sent to Jesse, saying, "Let David remain in my service, for he has found favor in my sight." 23 And [u]whenever the harmful spirit from God was upon Saul, David took the lyre [o]and played it with his hand. So Saul was refreshed and was well, and the harmful spirit departed from him.

David and Goliath

17 Now the Philistines [v]gathered their armies for battle. And they were gathered at [w]Socoh, which belongs to Judah, and encamped between Socoh and [x]Azekah, in [y]Ephes-dammim. 2 And Saul and the men of Israel were gathered, and encamped in [z]the Valley of Elah, and drew up in line of battle against the Philistines. 3 And the Philistines

[1] Or *smallest*

4 [y]1 Kgs. 2:13; [2 Kgs. 9:22]
5 [z]Josh. 3:5
6 [a]ch. 17:13
7 [b]Ps. 147:10, 11 [c]1 Kgs. 8:39; 1 Chr. 28:9; Ps. 7:9; Jer. 11:20; 17:10; 20:12; [Acts 1:24]
8 [d]ch. 17:13
9 [d][See ver. 8 above]
11 [e]ch. 17:13; [2 Sam. 13:3; 1 Chr. 2:13] [f][2 Sam. 7:8; Ps. 78:70, 71]
12 [g]ch. 17:42 [h][ch. 9:17]
13 [i]ver. 1 [j][ch. 10:1; Ps. 89:20] [k]ch. 10:6, 10; 11:6; See Judg. 3:10
14 [l]ch. 18:12; 28:15, 16; [Judg. 16:20] [m]ch. 18:10; 19:9; [Judg. 9:23]
16 [n]ver. 21, 22; 1 Kgs. 10:8

16:14–23 The spirit that at the time of Saul's anointing changed him "into another man" (10:6, 9–10) and that had intermittently overwhelmed him to propel him into action, is now removed, and Saul is tormented by "a harmful spirit from the LORD" (16:14). To grieve the Spirit of the Lord is to invite calamity (Isa. 63:10; Eph. 4:30). But even still the Lord extends a measure of kindness to Saul by bringing David into Saul's court to soothe him with music (1 Sam. 16:23).

17:1–51 For those who see only as mortals see (cf. 16:7), every aspect of Goliath's description inspires fear—his giant proportions, his oversized armor and military equipment, his mocking words. "Saul and all Israel" are certainly "dismayed and greatly afraid" (17:11). David, however, arrives on the scene of battle with different eyes and ears. He sees Goliath's size but measures it not against a human standard but against a big God. He hears Goliath's words but finds them ridiculous when one considers that they are aimed at the "armies of the living God" (v. 26). In David's eyes, Goliath

[o]ch. 18:10; 19:9; [2 Kgs. 3:15] **18** [p]See ch. 17:32, 34-36 [q]ch. 3:19; 18:12, 14 **19** [r]ver. 11; ch. 17:15, 34 **20** [s][ch. 17:18] **21** [t]See ver. 16 **23** [u]ver. 14, 16 [o][See ver. 16 above] **Chapter 17** **1** [v]ch. 13:5 [w]Josh. 15:35 [x]Josh. 10:10; Neh. 11:30 [y][1 Chr. 11:13] **2** [z]ver. 19; ch. 21:9

stood on the mountain on the one side, and
Israel stood on the mountain on the other side,
with a valley between them. 4 And there came
out from the camp of the Philistines a champion named [a]Goliath of [b]Gath, whose height
was six[1] cubits[2] and a span. 5 He had a helmet
of bronze on his head, and he was armed with
a coat of mail, and the weight of the coat was
five thousand shekels[3] of bronze. 6 And he
had bronze armor on his legs, and a [c]javelin
of bronze slung between his shoulders. 7 The
shaft of his spear was like a weaver's beam, and
his spear's head weighed six hundred shekels of iron. [d]And his shield-bearer went before
him. 8 He stood and shouted to the ranks of
Israel, "Why have you come out to draw up for
battle? Am I not a Philistine, and [e]are you not
servants of Saul? Choose a man for yourselves,
and let him come down to me. 9 If he is able
to fight with me and kill me, then we will be
your servants. But if I prevail against him and
kill him, then you shall be our servants [f]and
serve us." 10 And the Philistine said, [g]"I defy the
ranks of Israel this day. Give me a man, that we
may fight together." 11 When Saul and all Israel
heard these words of the Philistine, they were
dismayed and greatly afraid.

12 Now David was [h]the son of an [i]Ephrathite
of Bethlehem in Judah, [j]named Jesse, [k]who
had eight sons. In the days of Saul the man
was already old and advanced in years.[4] 13 The
three oldest sons of Jesse had followed Saul
to the battle. And [l]the names of his three sons
who went to the battle were Eliab the firstborn, and next to him Abinadab, and the third
Shammah. 14 [m]David was the youngest. The
three eldest followed Saul, 15 but David went
back and forth from Saul [n]to feed his father's
sheep at Bethlehem. 16 For forty days the
Philistine came forward and took his stand,
morning and evening.

17 And Jesse said to David his son, "Take for
your brothers an ephah[5] of this parched grain,
and these ten loaves, and carry them quickly to
the camp to your brothers. 18 [o]Also take these
ten cheeses to the commander of their thousand. [p]See if your brothers are well, and bring
some token from them."

19 Now Saul and they and all the men of Israel
were in the Valley of Elah, fighting with the
Philistines. 20 And David rose early in the
morning and left the sheep with a keeper
and took the provisions and went, as Jesse
had commanded him. And he came to [q]the
encampment as the host was going out to the
battle line, shouting the war cry. 21 And Israel
and the Philistines drew up for battle, army
against army. 22 And David left the [r]things in
charge of the keeper of the [r]baggage and ran to
the ranks and went and greeted his brothers.
23 As he talked with them, behold, [s]the champion, the Philistine of Gath, Goliath by name,
came up out of the ranks of the Philistines and
spoke [t]the same words as before. And David
heard him.

24 All the men of Israel, when they saw the
man, fled from him and were much afraid.
25 And the men of Israel said, "Have you seen
this man who has come up? Surely he has come
up to [u]defy Israel. And the king will enrich the
man who kills him with great riches [v]and will
give him his daughter and make his father's
house free in Israel." 26 And David said to the
men who stood by him, "What shall be done

[1] Hebrew; Septuagint, Dead Sea Scroll and Josephus *four* [2] A *cubit* was about 18 inches or 45 centimeters [3] A *shekel* was about 2/5 ounce or 11 grams [4] Septuagint, Syriac; Hebrew *advanced among men* [5] An *ephah* was about 3/5 bushel or 22 liters

is no more threatening than one of the brute beasts from which God had rescued him (vv. 34–37; cf. 2 Pet. 2:12).

To see as God sees is the calling of every Christian, but it can sometimes evoke misunderstanding and even rebuke from those who don't so see. David's oldest brother, Eliab, charges David with irresponsibility, presumption (arrogance), and a downright evil heart (1 Sam. 17:28). Christians should expect no less, and Jesus pronounces a blessing on those who suffer such abuse, as he, too, suffered (Matt. 5:11–12).

Saul's attempt to clothe David in his own armor (1 Sam. 17:38) is further evidence of his failure to see what actually matters in God's economy. David, on the other hand, understands that "the LORD saves not with sword and spear" and that "the battle is the LORD's" (v. 47). Armed with the tools of a shepherd, not a soldier, and with faith "in the name of the Lord" (v. 45), David rushes to meet Goliath and fells him with "a sling and with a stone" (v. 50)—as it happens, a rather effective long-range weapon. However modest our native abilities and acquired skills, God can empower them to accomplish his work.

4[a] [2 Sam. 21:19; 1 Chr. 20:4] [b] ch. 21:10; Josh. 11:22; 13:3
6[c] ver. 45
7[d] ver. 41
8[e] ch. 8:17
9[f] [ch. 11:1]
10[g] ver. 25, 26, 36, 45; [2 Sam. 21:21]
12[h] ver. 58; ch. 16:1, 18; Ruth 4:22 [i] Gen. 35:19 [j] ver. 58; ch. 16:1, 18 [k] ch. 16:10, 11; [1 Chr. 2:13-15]
13[l] ch. 16:6, 8, 9; [1 Chr. 2:13]
14[m] ch. 16:11
15[n] ch. 16:19
18[o] [ch. 16:20] [p] [Gen. 37:14]
20[q] ch. 26:5, 7
22[r] [Isa. 10:28; Acts 21:15]
23[s] ver. 4 [t] ver. 8
25[u] ver. 10, 36, 45 [v] [Josh. 15:16]

for the man who kills this Philistine and takes away [w]the reproach from Israel? For who is this [x]uncircumcised Philistine, that he should [u]defy the armies of [y]the living God?" 27 And the people answered him in the same way, [z]"So shall it be done to the man who kills him."

28 Now Eliab his eldest brother heard when he spoke to the men. And Eliab's anger was kindled against David, and he said, "Why have you come down? And with whom have you left those few sheep in the wilderness? I know your presumption and the evil of your heart, for you have come down to see the battle." 29 And David said, "What have I done now? Was it not but a word?" 30 And he turned away from him toward another, and spoke [b]in the same way, and the people answered him again as before.

31 When the words that David spoke were heard, they repeated them before Saul, and he sent for him. 32 And David said to Saul, [c]"Let no man's heart fail because of him. [d]Your servant will go and fight with this Philistine." 33 And Saul said to David, "You are not able to go against this Philistine to fight with him, for you are but a youth, and he has been a man of war from his youth." 34 But David said to Saul, "Your servant used to keep sheep for his father. And when there came a lion, or a bear, and took a lamb from the flock, 35 I went after him and struck him and delivered it out of his mouth. And if he arose against me, I caught him by his beard and struck him and killed him. 36 Your servant has struck down both lions and bears, and this uncircumcised Philistine shall be like one of them, [e]for he has defied the armies of the living God." 37 And David said, [f]"The LORD who delivered me from the paw of the lion and from the paw of the bear will deliver me from the hand of this Philistine." And Saul said to David, "Go, [g]and the LORD be with you!"

38 Then Saul clothed David with his armor. He put a helmet of bronze on his head and clothed him with a coat of mail, 39 and David strapped his sword over his armor. And he tried in vain to go, for he had not tested them. Then David said to Saul, "I cannot go with these, for I have not tested them." So David put them off. 40 Then he took his staff in his hand and chose five smooth stones from the brook and put them in his shepherd's pouch. His sling was in his hand, and he approached the Philistine.

41 And the Philistine moved forward and came near to David, [h]with his shield-bearer in front of him. 42 And when the Philistine looked and saw David, he disdained him, for he was but a youth, [i]ruddy and handsome in appearance. 43 And the Philistine said to David, "Am I [j]a dog, that you come to me with sticks?" And the Philistine cursed David by his gods. 44 The Philistine said to David, "Come to me, and I will give your flesh [k]to the birds of the air and to the beasts of the field." 45 Then David said to the Philistine, "You come to me with a sword and with a spear and with [l]a javelin, but I come to you in the name of the LORD of hosts, the God of the armies of Israel, [e]whom you have defied. 46 This day the LORD will deliver you into my hand, and I will strike you down and cut off your head. [m]And I will give the dead bodies of the host of the Philistines this day [n]to the birds of the air and to the wild beasts of the earth, [o]that all the earth may know that there is a God in Israel, 47 and that all this assembly may know that [p]the LORD saves not with sword and spear. [q]For the battle is the LORD's, and he will give you into our hand."

48 When the Philistine arose and came and drew near to meet David, David ran quickly toward the battle line to meet the Philistine. 49 And David put his hand in his bag and took out a stone and slung it and struck the Philistine on his forehead. The stone sank

26 [w]ch. 11:2 [x]See Judg. 14:3 [u][See ver. 25 above] [y]Deut. 5:26; Josh. 3:10
27 [z]ver. 25
30 [b]ver. 26, 27
32 [c][Deut. 20:3] [d][ch. 16:18]
36 [e]ver. 10, 26
37 [f][2 Tim. 4:17] [g][ch. 20:13; 1 Chr. 22:11, 16]
41 [h]ver. 7
42 [i]ch. 16:12
43 [j]ch. 24:14; 2 Sam. 3:8; 9:8; 16:9; 2 Kgs. 8:13

The main takeaway for believers today involves seeing parallels between what David did and what Jesus does for us today. David, by his confidence in and relationship with God, functions as a representative champion of his cowering people. Christ, similarly, is the representative champion of his cowering people. Both David and Christ win a victory the results of which are imputed to their people. Christians today are not meant to read the story of David and Goliath and mainly identify with David, but with the people who need saving.

Reflecting on the rescue that our true and final champion, Jesus himself, has won on our behalf, our hearts are moved to worship and to greater trust in him.

44 [k]ver. 46 **45** [l]ver. 6 [e][See ver. 36 above] **46** [m]Deut. 28:26 [n]ver. 44 [o]1 Kgs. 18:36; [Josh. 4:24] **47** [p]Hos. 1:7; [Ps. 44:6, 7; Zech. 4:6] [q]2 Chr. 20:15

into his forehead, and he fell on his face to the ground.

50 So David prevailed over the Philistine with a sling and with a stone, and struck the Philistine and killed him. There was no sword in the hand of David. 51 Then David ran and stood over the Philistine [r]and took his sword and drew it out of its sheath and killed him and cut off his head with it. When the Philistines saw that their champion was dead, [s]they fled. 52 And the men of Israel and Judah rose with a shout and pursued the Philistines as far as Gath[1] and the gates of [t]Ekron, so that the wounded Philistines fell on the way from [u]Shaaraim as far as [v]Gath and Ekron. 53 And the people of Israel came back from chasing the Philistines, and they plundered their camp. 54 And David took [w]the head of the Philistine [x]and brought it to Jerusalem, but he put his armor in his tent.

55 As soon as Saul saw David go out against the Philistine, he said to Abner, [y]the commander of the army, "Abner, [z]whose son is this youth?" And Abner said, [a]"As your soul lives, O king, I do not know." 56 And the king said, "Inquire whose son the boy is." 57 And as soon as David returned from the striking down of the Philistine, Abner took him, and brought him before Saul [b]with the head of the Philistine in his hand. 58 And Saul said to him, "Whose son are you, young man?" And David answered, [c]"I am the son of your servant Jesse the Bethlehemite."

David and Jonathan's Friendship

18 As soon as he had finished speaking to Saul, the soul of Jonathan was knit to the soul of David, and Jonathan [d]loved him as his own soul. 2 And Saul took him that day [e]and would not let him return to his father's house. 3 Then Jonathan made a covenant with David, because [d]he loved him as his own soul. 4 And Jonathan stripped himself of the robe that was on him and gave it to David, and his armor, and even his sword and his bow and his belt. 5 And David went out [f]and was successful wherever Saul sent him, so that Saul set him over the men of war. And this was good in the sight of all the people and also in the sight of Saul's servants.

Saul's Jealousy of David

6 As they were coming home, when David returned from striking down the Philistine, [g]the women came out of all the cities of Israel, singing and dancing, to meet King Saul, with tambourines, with songs of joy, and with musical instruments.[2] 7 And the women [h]sang to one another as they celebrated,

[i]"Saul has struck down his thousands,
and David his ten thousands."

8 And Saul was very angry, and this saying

[1] Septuagint; Hebrew *Gai* [2] Or *triangles*, or *three-stringed instruments*

18:1–30 A question seldom asked is, "Where was Jonathan in chapter 17?" Surely, the brave warrior of chapter 14, David-like in his faith, was not shrinking back in fear before Goliath. Nor was he likely absent from the scene of battle, for he is on the scene immediately after David's victory (18:1). Perhaps we are to assume that Jonathan, knowing that the house of Saul had been rejected (cf. 13:14; 15:23), was hanging back, waiting to see if God's new appointee, the "neighbor" better than Saul (15:28), would show himself. If so, he was not disappointed. David came, and won, and "the soul of Jonathan was knit to the soul of David" (18:1; cf. Jacob's attachment to his son Benjamin in Gen. 44:30). Jonathan defers to David, makes a covenant with him, and even gives him the regalia that distinguished him as crown prince (1 Sam. 18:3–4). In short, Jonathan loves David "as his own soul" (vv. 1, 3).

Such selflessness is possible only for those in sync with the purposes of God. Believers today are called to just this kind of selflessness: "Do nothing from selfish ambition or conceit, but in humility count others more significant than yourselves" (Phil. 2:3). In his self-emptying, Jonathan anticipates the far greater act of love rendered by the son of David to come. "Though he was in the form of God," Jesus "did not count equality with God a thing to be grasped, but emptied himself, by taking the form of a servant" (Phil. 2:6–7).

Like Jonathan, Saul senses that David is to replace him as king (1 Sam. 18:8). But Saul's reaction is the precise opposite: anger (v. 8), aggression (v. 11), fear (v. 12), scheming (vv. 17, 25), and enmity (v. 28). Being at odds with God puts one at odds with God's purpose in other people's lives. Recognizing that "the LORD was with David," Saul becomes "David's enemy continually" (vv. 28–29).

51 [r] ch. 21:9; [2 Sam. 23:21] [s] [Heb. 11:34]
52 [t] Josh. 15:11 [u] Josh. 15:36 [v] See ver. 4
54 [w] ver. 57 [x] [2 Sam. 5:6, 7]
55 [y] 2 Sam. 2:8 [z] [ch. 16:21, 22] [a] See ch. 1:26
57 [b] ver. 54
58 [c] ver. 12
Chapter 18
1 [d] ch. 20:17; Deut. 13:6; [ch. 19:2; 2 Sam. 1:26]
2 [e] [ch. 17:15]
3 [d] [See ver. 1 above]
5 [f] ver. 14, 15, 30
6 [g] Ex. 15:20; Judg. 11:34
7 [h] [Ex. 15:21] [i] ch. 21:11; 29:5

displeased him. He said, "They have ascribed
to David ten thousands, and to me they have
ascribed thousands, and what more can he
have but [j]the kingdom?" 9 And Saul eyed David
from that day on.

10 The next day [k]a harmful spirit from God
rushed upon Saul, and [l]he raved within his
house while David was [m]playing the lyre, as he
did day by day. [n]Saul had his spear in his hand.
11 And Saul [o]hurled the spear, for he thought, "I
will pin David to the wall." But David evaded
him twice.

12 [p]Saul was afraid of David because [q]the
LORD was with him [r]but had departed from
Saul. 13 So Saul removed him from his presence and made him a commander of a thousand. [s]And he went out and came in before
the people. 14 And David [t]had success in all his
undertakings, [q]for the LORD was with him.
15 And when Saul saw that [t]he had great success, he stood in fearful awe of him. 16 [u]But all
Israel and Judah loved David, for he went out
and came in before them.

David Marries Michal

17 Then Saul said to David, "Here is [v]my elder
daughter Merab. [w]I will give her to you for
a wife. Only be valiant for me [x]and fight the
LORD's battles." For Saul thought, "Let not my
hand be against him, [y]but let the hand of the
Philistines be against him." 18 And David said
to Saul, [z]"Who am I, and who are my relatives,
my father's clan in Israel, that I should be son-
in-law to the king?" 19 But at the time when
Merab, Saul's daughter, should have been
given to David, she was given to [a]Adriel the
[b]Meholathite for a wife.

20 Now [v]Saul's daughter Michal [c]loved David.
And they told Saul, and the thing pleased him.
21 Saul thought, "Let me give her to him, that
she may [d]be a snare for him [e]and that the
hand of the Philistines may be against him."
Therefore Saul said to David a second time,[1]
[f]"You shall now be my son-in-law." 22 And Saul
commanded his servants, "Speak to David in
private and say, 'Behold, the king has delight
in you, and all his servants love you. Now
then become the king's son-in-law.'" 23 And
Saul's servants spoke those words in the ears
of David. And David said, [g]"Does it seem to
you a little thing to become the king's son-
in-law, since I am a poor man and have no
reputation?" 24 And the servants of Saul told
him, "Thus and so did David speak." 25 Then
Saul said, "Thus shall you say to David, 'The
king desires no [h]bride-price except a hundred
foreskins of the Philistines, [i]that he may be
avenged of the king's enemies.'" [j]Now Saul
thought to make David fall by the hand of
the Philistines. 26 And when his servants told
David these words, it pleased David well to
be the king's son-in-law. [k]Before the time
had expired, 27 David arose and went, [l]along
with his men, and killed two hundred of the
Philistines. [m]And David brought their foreskins, which were given in full number to the
king, that he might become the king's son-in-
law. And Saul gave him his daughter Michal
for a wife. 28 But when Saul saw and knew that
[n]the LORD was with David, [o]and that Michal,
Saul's daughter, loved him, 29 Saul was even
more afraid of David. So Saul was David's
enemy continually.

30 [p]Then the commanders of the Philistines
came out to battle, and as often as they came
out [q]David had more success than all the servants of Saul, so that his name was highly
esteemed.

Saul Tries to Kill David

19 And Saul spoke to Jonathan his son and
to all his servants, that they should kill
David. [r]But Jonathan, Saul's son, delighted
much in David. 2 And Jonathan told David,
"Saul my father seeks to kill you. Therefore
be on your guard in the morning. Stay in a

[1] Hebrew *by two*

8[j] ch. 15:28
10[k] ch. 16:14; [Judg. 9:23] [l] ch. 19:23, 24; [1 Kgs. 18:29; Acts 16:16] [m] See ch. 16:16 [n] ch. 19:9
11[o] ch. 19:10; 20:33
12[p] ver. 15, 29 [q] ver. 28; ch. 16:18 [r] ch. 16:14; 28:15
13[s] ver. 16; [Num. 27:17; 2 Sam. 5:2]
14[t] ver. 5 [q] [See ver. 12 above]
15[t] [See ver. 14 above]

19:1–20:42 Earlier in the book, Eli set the pattern of how one is to respond to divine rejection from office—namely, give in (see comment on 3:18, in the note on 3:1–21). Saul refuses to give in to God, and this costs him dearly. He is progressively alienated from his family (Michal in 19:11–17; Jonathan in 20:13, 16; etc.), from his supporters (22:17), and even from his own mental capacities. With respect to the latter, Saul at first is willing to listen to Jonathan (19:4–6) but ends up cursing him (20:30) and even trying to kill him (20:33), hurling his spear at him, as he had more than once done to David (18:11; 19:10). Consumed with fear, Saul can think of little else than killing

16[u] [ver. 5] **17**[v] ch. 14:49 [w] ch. 17:25 [x] ch. 25:28 [y] ver. 21, 25 **18**[z] ver. 23; 2 Sam. 7:18 **19**[a] [2 Sam. 21:8] [b] Judg. 7:22 **20**[v] [See ver. 17 above] [c] ver. 28 **21**[d] Ex. 10:7 [e] ver. 17 [f] [ver. 26] **23**[g] [Num. 16:9] **25**[h] Gen. 34:12; Ex. 22:17 [i] ch. 14:24 [j] ver. 17, 21 **26**[k] [ver. 21] **27**[l] ver. 13 [m] 2 Sam. 3:14 **28**[n] ver. 12 [o] ver. 20 **30**[p] ch. 19:8; [2 Sam. 11:1] [q] ver. 5 **Chapter 19** **1**[r] ch. 18:1

secret place and hide yourself. 3 And I will go
out and stand beside my father in the field
where you are, and I will speak to my father
about you. And if I learn anything I will tell
you." 4 And Jonathan spoke well of David to
Saul his father and said to him, "Let not the
king [s]sin against his servant David, because
he has not sinned against you, and because his
deeds have brought good to you. 5 For [t]he took
his life in his hand [u]and he struck down the
Philistine, [v]and the LORD worked a great salvation for all Israel. You saw it, and rejoiced. Why
then will you sin against [w]innocent blood by
killing David without cause?" 6 And Saul listened to the voice of Jonathan. Saul swore, [x]"As
the LORD lives, he shall not be put to death."
7 And Jonathan called David, and Jonathan
reported to him all these things. And Jonathan
brought David to Saul, and he was in his presence [y]as before.

8 And there was war again. And David went
out and fought with the Philistines and struck
them with a great blow, so that they fled before
him. 9 [z]Then a harmful spirit from the LORD
came upon Saul, as he sat in his house with
his spear in his hand. [a]And David was playing
the lyre. 10 [b]And Saul sought to pin David to
the wall with the spear, but he eluded Saul,
so that he struck the spear into the wall. And
David fled and escaped that night.

11 [c]Saul sent messengers to David's house
to watch him, that he might kill him in the
morning. But Michal, David's wife, told him,
"If you do not escape with your life tonight,
tomorrow you will be killed." 12 [d]So Michal
let David down through the window, and
he fled away and escaped. 13 Michal took [e]an
image[1] and laid it on the bed and put a pillow
of goats' hair at its head and covered it with
the clothes. 14 And when Saul sent messengers
to take David, she said, "He is sick." 15 Then
Saul sent the messengers to see David, saying,
"Bring him up to me in the bed, that I may kill
him." 16 And when the messengers came in,
behold, [e]the image was in the bed, with the
pillow of goats' hair at its head. 17 Saul said to
Michal, "Why have you deceived me thus and
let my enemy go, so that he has escaped?" And
Michal answered Saul, "He said to me, 'Let me
go. [f]Why should I kill you?' "

18 Now David fled and escaped, and he came
to Samuel at [g]Ramah and told him all that
Saul had done to him. And he and Samuel
went and lived at Naioth. 19 And it was told
Saul, "Behold, David is at Naioth in Ramah."
20 Then Saul sent messengers to take David,
and when they saw the company of the prophets prophesying, and Samuel standing as head
over them, [h]the Spirit of God came upon the
messengers of Saul, [i]and they also prophesied.
21 When it was told Saul, he sent other messengers, [i]and they also prophesied. And Saul sent
messengers again the third time, [i]and they
also prophesied. 22 Then he himself went to
Ramah and came to the great well that is in
Secu. And he asked, "Where are Samuel and
David?" And one said, "Behold, they are at
Naioth in [g]Ramah." 23 And he went there to
Naioth in Ramah. [j]And the Spirit of God came
upon him also, and as he went he prophesied
until he came to Naioth in Ramah. 24 [k]And he
too stripped off his clothes, and he too prophesied before Samuel and lay naked all that day
and all that night. Thus it is said, [l]"Is Saul also
among the prophets?"

Jonathan Warns David

20 Then David fled from Naioth [m]in
Ramah and came and said before
Jonathan, "What have I done? What is my
guilt? And what is my sin before your father,
that he seeks my life?" 2 And he said to him,

[1] Or *a household god*

David. But the Spirit of God prevents him, overwhelms him, divests him of his royal robe, and puts him on his face before Samuel (19:23–24). Saul is, we might say, out of his mind. Prophesying in a posture of worship is so out of character for Saul that the people, with considerable irony, again take up the saying of 10:11: "Is Saul also among the prophets?" (19:24).

How different is the work of the Spirit on those who trust God. To them God gives "a spirit not of fear but of power and love and self-control" (2 Tim. 1:7). Those, like Saul, who refuse to "humble [themselves] . . . under the mighty hand of God" soon find themselves under the sway of a very different spirit, one which "prowls around like a roaring lion, seeking someone to devour" (1 Pet. 5:6, 8).

4 [s] [Gen. 42:22]
5 [t] ch. 28:21; Judg. 12:3; [Judg. 9:17] [u] ch. 17:49, 50 [v] [ch. 11:13; 1 Chr. 11:14] [w] Matt. 27:4
6 [x] See Ruth 3:13
7 [y] ch. 16:21; 18:2, 13
9 [z] See ch. 16:14 [a] See ch. 16:16
10 [b] ch. 18:11; 20:33
11 [c] See Ps. 59
12 [d] [Josh. 2:15; Acts 9:24, 25]; 2 Cor. 11:33
13 [e] See Gen. 31:19
16 [e] [See ver. 13 above]
17 [f] [2 Sam. 2:22]

18 [g] ch. 1:19 **20** [h] [ch. 10:5, 6, 10] [i] [Num. 11:25; Joel 2:28] **21** [i] [See ver. 20 above] **22** [g] [See ver. 18 above] **23** [j] [ch. 18:10] **24** [k] Isa. 20:2; Mic. 1:8; [2 Sam. 6:20] [l] ch. 10:11, 12 **Chapter 20** **1** [m] ch. 1:19

"Far from it! You shall not die. Behold, my father does nothing either great or small without disclosing it to me. And why should my father hide this from me? It is not so." 3 But David vowed again, saying, "Your father knows well that [n]I have found favor in your eyes, and he thinks, 'Do not let Jonathan know this, lest he be grieved.' But truly, [o]as the LORD lives and [p]as your soul lives, there is but a step between me and death." 4 Then Jonathan said to David, "Whatever you say, I will do for you." 5 David said to Jonathan, "Behold, tomorrow is [q]the new moon, and I should not fail to sit at table with the king. But let me go, [r]that I may hide myself in the field till the third day at evening. 6 [s]If your father misses me at all, then say, 'David earnestly asked leave of me to run [t]to Bethlehem his city, for there is a yearly [u]sacrifice there for all the clan.' 7 If he says, 'Good!' it will be well with your servant, but if he is angry, then know that [v]harm is determined by him. 8 Therefore deal kindly with your servant, [w]for you have brought your servant into a covenant of the LORD with you. [x]But if there is guilt in me, kill me yourself, for why should you bring me to your father?" 9 And Jonathan said, "Far be it from you! If I knew that [v]it was determined by my father that harm should come to you, would I not tell you?" 10 Then David said to Jonathan, "Who will tell me if your father answers you roughly?" 11 And Jonathan said to David, "Come, let us go out into the field." So they both went out into the field.

12 And Jonathan said to David, "The LORD, the God of Israel, be witness![1] When I have sounded out my father, about this time tomorrow, or the third day, behold, if he is well disposed toward David, shall I not then send and disclose it to you? 13 But should it please my father to do you harm, [y]the LORD do so to Jonathan and more also if I do not disclose it to you and send you away, that you may go in safety. [z]May the LORD be with you, as he has been with my father. 14 If I am still alive, show me the steadfast love of the LORD, that I may not die; 15 [a]and do not cut off[2] your steadfast love from my house forever, when the LORD cuts off every one of the enemies of David from the face of the earth." 16 And Jonathan made a covenant with the house of David, saying, [b]"May[3] the LORD take vengeance on David's enemies." 17 And Jonathan made David swear again by his love for him, [c]for he loved him as he loved his own soul.

18 Then Jonathan said to him, [d]"Tomorrow is the new moon, and [e]you will be missed, because [f]your seat will be empty. 19 On the third day go down quickly to the place where you hid yourself when the matter was in hand, and remain beside the stone heap.[4] 20 And I will shoot three arrows to the side of it, as though I shot at a mark. 21 And behold, I will send the boy, saying, 'Go, find the arrows.' If I say to the boy, 'Look, the arrows are on this side of you, take them,' then you are to come, for, [g]as the LORD lives, it is safe for you and there is no danger. 22 But if I say to the youth, [h]'Look, the arrows are beyond you,' then go, for the LORD has sent you away. 23 [i]And as for the matter of which you and I have spoken, behold, [j]the LORD is between you and me forever."

24 So David hid himself in the field. And when the new moon came, the king sat down to eat food. 25 The king sat on his seat, as at other times, on the seat by the wall. Jonathan sat opposite,[5] and Abner sat by Saul's side, [k]but David's place was empty.

26 Yet Saul did not say anything that day, for he thought, "Something has happened to him. [l]He is not clean; surely he is not clean." 27 But on [m]the second day, the day after the new moon, [k]David's place was empty. And Saul said to Jonathan his son, "Why has not the son of Jesse come to the meal, either yesterday or today?" 28 Jonathan answered Saul, [n]"David earnestly asked leave of me to go to Bethlehem. 29 He said, 'Let me go, for our clan holds a sacrifice in the city, and my brother has commanded me to be there. So now, if I have found favor in your eyes, let me get away and see my brothers.' For this reason he has not come to the king's table."

30 Then Saul's anger was kindled against Jonathan, and he said to him, "You son of a perverse, rebellious woman, do I not know that you have chosen the son of Jesse to your own shame, and to the shame of your mother's

[1] Hebrew lacks *be witness* [2] Or *but if I die, do not cut off* [3] Septuagint *earth,* **16** *let not the name of Jonathan be cut off from the house of David. And may* [4] Septuagint; Hebrew *the stone Ezel* [5] Compare Septuagint; Hebrew *stood up*

3 [n] See Gen. 33:15 [o] ch. 25:26; 2 Kgs. 2:2, 4, 6; 4:30; See Ruth 3:13 [p] ch. 1:26 **5** [q] ver. 18; Num. 10:10; 28:11 [r] ch. 19:2, 3 **6** [s] ver. 18 [t] ch. 16:4 [u] [ch. 9:12] **7** [v] ch. 25:17; Esth. 7:7; [ver. 33] **8** [w] ver. 16, 42; ch. 18:3; 23:18; [2 Sam. 21:7] [x] 2 Sam. 14:32 **9** [v] [See ver. 7 above] **13** [y] [Ruth 1:17] [z] Josh. 1:5, 17; 1 Kgs. 1:37; 1 Chr. 22:11, 16; [ch. 17:37] **15** [a] 2 Sam. 9:1, 3, 7; 21:7 **16** [b] [ch. 25:22; Josh. 22:23] **17** [c] ch. 18:1, 3 **18** [d] ver. 5 [e] ver. 6 [f] ver. 25, 27 **21** [g] ver. 3; See Ruth 3:13 **22** [h] ver. 37 **23** [i] ver. 14, 15 [j] ver. 42 **25** [k] ver. 18 **26** [l] Lev. 7:21; See Lev. 11:24-28; 15:1-4 **27** [m] [ver. 34] [k] [See ver. 25 above] **28** [n] ver. 6

nakedness? 31 For as long as the son of Jesse
lives on the earth, neither you nor your kingdom shall be established. Therefore send
and bring him to me, for he shall surely die."
32 Then Jonathan answered Saul his father,
[o]"Why should he be put to death? What has
he done?" 33 [p]But Saul hurled his spear at him
to strike him. So Jonathan knew [q]that his
father was determined to put David to death.
34 And Jonathan rose from the table in fierce
anger and ate no food the second day of the
month, for he was grieved for David, because
his father had disgraced him.

35 In the morning Jonathan went out into
the field to the appointment with David, and
with him a little boy. 36 And he said to his boy,
"Run and find the arrows that I shoot." As the
boy ran, he shot an arrow beyond him. 37 And
when the boy came to the place of the arrow
that Jonathan had shot, Jonathan called after
the boy and said, [r]"Is not the arrow beyond
you?" 38 And Jonathan called after the boy,
"Hurry! Be quick! Do not stay!" So Jonathan's
boy gathered up the arrows and came to his
master. 39 But the boy knew nothing. Only
Jonathan and David knew the matter. 40 And
Jonathan gave his weapons to his boy and said
to him, "Go and carry them to the city." 41 And
as soon as the boy had gone, David rose from
beside the stone heap[1] and fell on his face to
the ground and bowed three times. And they
kissed one another and wept with one another,
David weeping the most. 42 Then Jonathan
said to David, [s]"Go in peace, because we have
sworn both of us in the name of the LORD,
saying, [t]'The LORD shall be between me and
you, [u]and between my offspring and your offspring, forever.'" And he rose and departed,
and Jonathan went into the city.[2]

David and the Holy Bread

21 [3] Then David came to [v]Nob to [w]Ahime-
lech the priest. And Ahimelech [x]came
to meet David trembling and said to him,
"Why are you alone, and no one with you?"
2 And David said to Ahimelech the priest, "The
king has charged me with a matter and said to
me, 'Let no one know anything of the matter
about which I send you, and with which I have
charged you.' I have made an appointment
with the young men for such and such a place.
3 Now then, what do you have on hand? Give
me five loaves of bread, or whatever is here."
4 And the priest answered David, "I have no
common bread on hand, but there is [y]holy
bread—[z]if the young men have kept themselves from women." 5 And David answered
the priest, "Truly women have been kept from
us as always when I go on an expedition. The
vessels of the young men are holy even when it
is an ordinary journey. How much more today
will their vessels be holy?" 6 So the priest gave
him [y]the holy bread, for there was no bread
there but the bread of the Presence, [a]which is
removed from before the LORD, to be replaced
by hot bread on the day it is taken away.

7 Now a certain man of the servants of Saul
was there that day, detained before the LORD.
His name was [b]Doeg the Edomite, the chief of
Saul's herdsmen.

8 Then David said to Ahimelech, "Then have
you not here a spear or a sword at hand? For
I have brought neither my sword nor my
weapons with me, because the king's business
required haste." 9 And the priest said, [c]"The
sword of Goliath the Philistine, whom you
struck down in [d]the Valley of Elah, behold, it
is here wrapped in a cloth behind the ephod.
If you will take that, take it, for there is none

[1] Septuagint; Hebrew *from beside the south* [2] This sentence is 21:1 in Hebrew [3] Ch 21:2 in Hebrew

21:1–22:5 Taking one's eyes off God invites fear to rush in. And fear can lead to desperate and dangerous actions. Fleeing from Saul, David not only deceives the Lord's priest at Nob (21:2–3) but, after receiving food and Goliath's sword (21:9), goes to Goliath's hometown (21:10)! It seems an insane step—did David hope to enter the city unnoticed, with Goliath's sword tucked under his belt? As it happens, David is quickly recognized (as Israel's "king"! 21:11) and escapes death only by feigning insanity. He flees into the wilderness (cf. 22:1), and there he begins a training course in trust.

In the life of a believer, the wilderness is often just the place to learn bedrock trust. "When I am afraid," writes David in a psalm linked to his misadventure in Gath, "I put my trust in you" (Ps. 56:3). "What can man do to me?" (Ps. 56:11; cf. v. 4). Or, as the apostle Paul later writes, "If God is for us, who can be against us" (Rom. 8:31). The bedrock certainty of believers in Jesus is that we are "more than conquerors through him who loved us" (Rom. 8:37). Nothing in all creation—no hardship, no earthly or heavenly power, no extremity of life or death, no "Saul," absolutely nothing—"will be able to separate us from the love of God in Christ Jesus our Lord" (Rom. 8:39).

32 [o] ch. 19:5
33 [p] ch. 18:11; 19:10 [q] ver. 7
37 [r] ver. 22
42 [s] ver. 13; ch. 1:17 [t] ver. 23 [u] ver. 15

Chapter 21
1 [v] ch. 22:9, 11, 19; Neh. 11:32; Isa. 10:32 [w] [ch. 14:3; Mark 2:26] [x] [ch. 16:4]
4 [y] Ex. 25:30; Lev. 24:5; Matt. 12:3, 4; Mark 2:25, 26; Luke 6:3, 4 [z] Ex. 19:15
6 [y] [See ver. 4 above] [a] Lev. 24:8, 9
7 [b] ch. 22:9; See Ps. 52
9 [c] ch. 17:51 [d] ch. 17:2

but that here." And David said, "There is none
like that; give it to me."

David Flees to Gath

[10]And David rose and fled that day from Saul
and went to [e]Achish the king of Gath. [11]And
the servants of Achish said to him, "Is not this
David the king of the land? [f]Did they not sing
to one another of him in dances,

'Saul has struck down his thousands,
and David his ten thousands'?"

[12]And David [g]took these words to heart and
was much afraid of Achish the king of Gath.
[13]So he changed his behavior before them
and pretended to be insane in their hands
and made marks on the doors of the gate and
let his spittle run down his beard. [14]Then
Achish said to his servants, "Behold, you see
the man is mad. Why then have you brought
him to me? [15]Do I lack madmen, that you have
brought this fellow to behave as a madman
in my presence? Shall this fellow come into
my house?"

David at the Cave of Adullam

22 David departed from there and escaped
to [h]the cave of [i]Adullam. And when his
brothers and all his father's house heard it,
they went down there to him. [2][j]And everyone
who was in distress, and everyone who was
in debt, and everyone who was bitter in soul,[1]
gathered to him. And he became commander
over them. And there were with him [k]about
four hundred men.
[3]And David went from there to Mizpeh of
Moab. And he said to the king of Moab, "Please
let my father and my mother stay[2] with you,
till I know what God will do for me." [4]And
he left them with the king of Moab, and they
stayed with him all the time that David was
in the stronghold. [5]Then the prophet [l]Gad
said to David, "Do not remain in the stronghold; depart, and go into the land of Judah."
So David departed and went into the forest
of Hereth.

Saul Kills the Priests at Nob

[6]Now Saul heard that David was discovered,
and the men who were with him. Saul was
sitting at Gibeah under [m]the tamarisk tree on
the height with his spear in his hand, and all
his servants were standing about him. [7]And
Saul said to his servants who stood about
him, "Hear now, people of Benjamin; will the
son of Jesse [n]give every one of you fields and
vineyards, will he make you all commanders
of thousands and commanders of hundreds,
[8]that all of you have conspired against me?
No one discloses to me [o]when my son makes
a covenant with the son of Jesse. None of you
[p]is sorry for me or discloses to me that my son
has stirred up my servant against me, [q]to lie
in wait, as at this day." [9]Then answered [r]Doeg
the Edomite, who stood by the servants of
Saul, "I saw the son of Jesse [s]coming to Nob,
to [t]Ahimelech the son of Ahitub, [10][u]and he
inquired of the LORD for him and [v]gave him
provisions and gave him the sword of Goliath
the Philistine."

[1] Or *discontented* [2] Syriac, Vulgate; Hebrew *go out*

10[e] See Ps. 34
11[f] ch. 18:7; 29:5
12[g] [Luke 2:19]
Chapter 22
1[h] See Ps. 57; 142 [i] 2 Sam. 23:13; 1 Chr. 11:15
2[j] [Judg. 9:4; 11:3] [k] [ch. 23:13; 25:13]
5[l] 2 Sam. 24:11, 18, 19; 1 Chr. 21:9, 11, 13, 18, 19; 29:29; 2 Chr. 29:25
6[m] [ch. 31:13; Gen. 21:33]
7[n] [ch. 8:14]
8[o] ch. 18:3 [p] [ch. 23:21] [q] ver. 13
9[r] ch. 21:7; See Ps. 52 [s] ch. 21:1 [t] [ch. 14:3]
10[u] ch. 23:2, 4; 30:8; 2 Sam. 5:19, 23; [Num. 27:21] [v] ch. 21:6, 9

22:6–19 Despite occasional lapses (see, e.g., the note on 27:1–12), David's big view of God builds trust, even when David is on the run (see the preceding episode). Saul's small-to-nonexistent concern for God, by contrast, leads only to paranoia, even on the throne. One never sees life's circumstances rightly when one's view of God is too small. Defective theological vision can lead to alienation and sin. Alienation: refusing to listen to Ahimelech's legitimate defense of having helped David, Saul orders his servants to destroy the priests of Nob (22:17), but they refuse to obey! Sin: frustrated by his servants' refusal to lift a hand against the Lord's priests, Saul turns to the villainous Edomite Doeg, who puts the whole town to the sword, including "man and woman, child and infant, ox, donkey and sheep" (v. 19; ironically echoing 15:3).

The fate of those who, like Saul, refuse "to acknowledge God" is alienation and sin. As Paul warns in Romans 1:28–32, God gives up such persons "to a debased mind to do what ought not to be done," to be filled with "envy, murder, [and] strife," to become "foolish, faithless, heartless, ruthless," and to approve (like Saul) those who (like Doeg) commit crimes worthy of death.

The hope and promise of the gospel, by contrast, is a renewed mind, capable of discerning the will of God and, by grace, obeying it (Rom. 12:2). For we are not who we once were. We have been adopted into God's family, utterly by grace. We have been given a new identity as children of God.

11 Then the king sent to summon Ahimelech
the priest, the son of Ahitub, and all his father's
house, the priests who were at Nob, and all of
them came to the king. 12 And Saul said, "Hear
now, son of Ahitub." And he answered, "Here
I am, my lord." 13 And Saul said to him, "Why
have you conspired against me, you and the
son of Jesse, in that you have given him bread
and a sword and [u]have inquired of God for
him, so that he has risen against me, [w]to lie
in wait, as at this day?" 14 Then Ahimelech
answered the king, "And who among all
your servants is so faithful as David, who is
the king's son-in-law, and captain over[1] your
bodyguard, and honored in your house? 15 Is
today the first time [u]that I have inquired of
God for him? No! Let not the king impute anything to his servant or to all the house of my
father, for your servant has known nothing of
all this, [x]much or little." 16 And the king said,
"You shall surely die, Ahimelech, you and all
your father's house." 17 And the king said to
[y]the guard who stood about him, "Turn and
kill the priests of the LORD, because their
hand also is with David, and they knew that
he fled and did not disclose it to me." But the
servants of the king would not put out their
hand to strike the priests of the LORD. 18 Then
the king said to Doeg, "You turn and strike
the priests." And Doeg the Edomite turned
and struck down the priests, [z]and he killed
on that day eighty-five persons who wore the
linen ephod. 19 And Nob, the city of the priests,
he put to the sword; [a]both man and woman,
child and infant, ox, donkey and sheep, he put
to the sword.

20 But one of the sons of Ahimelech the son
of Ahitub, named [b]Abiathar, escaped and fled
after David. 21 And Abiathar told David that
Saul had killed the priests of the LORD. 22 And
David said to Abiathar, "I knew on that day,
[c]when Doeg the Edomite was there, that he
would surely tell Saul. I have occasioned the
death of all the persons of your father's house.
23 [d]Stay with me; do not be afraid, for he who
seeks my life seeks your life. With me you shall
be in safekeeping."

David Saves the City of Keilah

23 Now they told David, "Behold, the Philistines are fighting against [e]Keilah and
are robbing the threshing floors." 2 Therefore
David [f]inquired of the LORD, "Shall I go and
attack these Philistines?" And the LORD said
to David, "Go and attack the Philistines and
save Keilah." 3 But David's men said to him,
"Behold, we are afraid here in Judah; how
much more then if we go to Keilah against
the armies of the Philistines?" 4 Then David
[f]inquired of the LORD again. And the LORD
answered him, "Arise, go down to Keilah, [g]for
I will give the Philistines into your hand."
5 And David and his men went to Keilah and
fought with the Philistines and brought
away their livestock and struck them with a
great blow. So David saved the inhabitants
of Keilah.

6 [h]When Abiathar the son of Ahimelech had
fled to David to Keilah, he had come down
with an ephod in his hand. 7 Now it was told
Saul that David had come to Keilah. And Saul
said, "God has given him into my hand, for he
has shut himself in by entering a town that
has gates and bars." 8 And Saul summoned all
the people to war, to go down to Keilah, to
besiege David and his men. 9 David knew that

[1] Septuagint, Targum; Hebrew *and has turned aside to*

22:20–23:6 A mark of someone for whom God carries weight and who has experienced God's forgiveness is the ability to honestly admit failings. When Abiathar, the son of the priest Ahimelech and the sole survivor from Nob, arrives in David's camp, David readily admits that his own actions contributed to the massacre, and he offers Abiathar safe haven (22:22–23).

By the end of this section, David has been joined by both the prophet Gad, who guides him (22:5), and the priest Abiathar, who brought with him the priestly "ephod" (23:6), a further instrument of God's guidance. Clearly, the Lord is providentially providing for David in the wilderness (cf. Psalm 63).

Believers can be assured, even "in the wilderness," that as they give God weight and seek his kingdom he will guide them and provide all they need (Matt. 6:31–33; cf. Phil. 4:19). For Jesus himself went through the wilderness, afflicted by the Enemy, so that all our wilderness experiences can be endured not as punishment but as the kind purposes of God to cultivate perseverance in his beloved children (Matt. 4:1–11; Rom. 5:3–5).

13[u] [See ver. 10 above] [w] ver. 8
15[u] [See ver. 10 above] [x] ch. 25:36
17[y] [2 Kgs. 10:25; 11:4, 6; 2 Chr. 12:10]
18[z] [ch. 2:31]
19[a] [ch. 15:3]
20[b] ch. 23:6, 9
22[c] ch. 21:7
23[d] [1 Kgs. 2:26]

Chapter 23
1[e] Josh. 15:44
2[f] See ch. 22:10
4[f] [See ver. 2 above] [g] ver. 14; Josh. 24:11; Judg. 7:7; 20:28
6[h] ch. 22:20

Saul was plotting harm against him. And he
said to Abiathar the priest, [i]"Bring the ephod
here." 10 Then David said, "O LORD, the God of
Israel, your servant has surely heard that Saul
seeks to come to Keilah, to destroy the city on
my account. 11 Will the men of Keilah surrender
me into his hand? Will Saul come down, as
your servant has heard? O LORD, the God of
Israel, please tell your servant." And the LORD
said, "He will come down." 12 Then David said,
"Will the men of Keilah surrender me and my
men into the hand of Saul?" And the LORD
said, [j]"They will surrender you." 13 Then David
and his men, [k]who were about six hundred,
arose and departed from Keilah, and they went
[l]wherever they could go. When Saul was told
that David had escaped from Keilah, he gave
up the expedition. 14 And David remained in
the strongholds in the wilderness, in the hill
country [m]of the wilderness of [n]Ziph. And Saul
sought him every day, but God did not give
him into his hand.

Saul Pursues David

15 David saw that Saul had come out to seek
his life. David was in the wilderness of Ziph at
Horesh. 16 And Jonathan, Saul's son, rose and
went to David at Horesh, and strengthened
his hand in God. 17 And he said to him, "Do
not fear, for the hand of Saul my father shall
not find you. You shall be king over Israel,
and I shall be next to you. [o]Saul my father also
knows this." 18 [p]And the two of them made a
covenant before the LORD. David remained at
Horesh, and Jonathan went home.

19 [q]Then the Ziphites went up to Saul at
Gibeah, saying, "Is not David hiding among
us in the strongholds at Horesh, on the hill
of Hachilah, which is south of [r]Jeshimon?
20 Now come down, O king, according to all
your heart's desire to come down, [s]and our
part shall be to surrender him into the king's
hand." 21 And Saul said, [t]"May you be blessed
by the LORD, [u]for you have had compassion
on me. 22 Go, make yet more sure. Know and
see the place where his foot is, and who has
seen him there, for it is told me that he is very
cunning. 23 See therefore and take note of all
the lurking places where he hides, and come
back to me with sure information. Then I will
go with you. And if he is in the land, I will
search him out among all the thousands of
Judah." 24 And they arose and went to Ziph
ahead of Saul.

Now David and his men were [v]in the wilderness of Maon, [w]in the Arabah to the south
of [r]Jeshimon. 25 And Saul and his men went
to seek him. And David was told, so he went
down to the rock and lived in the wilderness
of Maon. And when Saul heard that, he pursued after David in the wilderness of Maon.
26 Saul went on one side of the mountain,
and David and his men on the other side
of the mountain. And David was hurrying
to get away from Saul. As Saul and his men
were closing in on David and his men to
capture them, 27 a messenger came to Saul,
saying, "Hurry and come, for the Philistines
have made a raid against the land." 28 So Saul
returned from pursuing after David and went
against the Philistines. Therefore that place
was called the Rock of Escape.[1] 29 [2] And David
went up from there and lived in the strongholds of [x]Engedi.

[1] Or *Rock of Divisions* [2] Ch 24:1 in Hebrew

9 [i] ch. 30:7; [Num. 27:21]
12 [j] ver. 20
13 [k] ch. 25:13; 27:2; [ch. 22:2; 30:9, 10] [l] [2 Sam. 15:20]
14 [m] See Ps. 63 [n] Josh. 15:24
17 [o] ch. 24:20; [ch. 20:31]
18 [p] ch. 18:3; 20:8, 16, 42; [2 Sam. 21:7]
19 [q] ch. 26:1; See Ps. 54 [r] Num. 21:20
20 [s] ver. 12
21 [t] See Ruth 2:20 [u] [ch. 22:8]
24 [v] ch. 25:2; Josh. 15:55 [w] See Deut. 1:1 [r] [See ver. 19 above]
29 [x] Josh. 15:62; 2 Chr. 20:2; Song 1:14; Ezek. 47:10

23:16–17 A true friend does not minimize or make light of the sorrow or difficulty another may be experiencing but, rather, helps the other find strength in God. Jonathan's encouragement of David in the present circumstances, "strengthening his hand in God" (v. 16), helps prepare him for a later dire situation, where David will again find strength in God (30:6). "The sweetness of a friend comes from his earnest counsel" (Prov. 27:9).

In the present episode, Jonathan encourages David by reminding him of God's purpose to make David king (1 Sam. 23:17). How much grander is the Christian hope: "We have this as a sure and steadfast anchor of the soul, a hope that enters into the inner place behind the curtain, where Jesus has gone as a forerunner on our behalf" (Heb. 6:19–20; see the broader context). The calling of all Christians is to "encourage one another and build one another up" (1 Thess. 5:11). Yet we do this ultimately because we ourselves have been befriended by God himself in the person of Jesus. In Jesus we have a friend, the great friend, the friend of sinners (Luke 7:34). "No longer do I call you servants . . . but I have called you friends" (John 15:15).

David Spares Saul's Life

24 [1] [y]When Saul returned from following
the Philistines, he was told, "Behold,
David is in the wilderness of Engedi." 2 Then
Saul took [z]three thousand chosen men out of
all Israel and went to seek David and his men
in front of the Wildgoats' Rocks. 3 And he came
to the sheepfolds by the way, where there was
a cave, and Saul went in [a]to relieve himself.[2]
Now David and his men were sitting in the
innermost parts [b]of the cave. 4 And the men of
David said to him, [c]"Here is the day of which
the LORD said to you, 'Behold, I will give your
enemy into your hand, and you shall do to
him as it shall seem good to you.'" Then David
arose and stealthily cut off a corner of Saul's
robe. 5 And afterward [d]David's heart struck
him, because he had cut off a corner of Saul's
robe. 6 He said to his men, [e]"The LORD forbid
that I should do this thing to my lord, the
LORD's anointed, to put out my hand against
him, seeing he is [f]the LORD's anointed." 7 So
David persuaded his men with these words
[g]and did not permit them to attack Saul. And
Saul rose up and left the cave and went on
his way.

8 Afterward David also arose and went out
of the cave, and called after Saul, "My lord the
king!" And when Saul looked behind him,
David bowed with his face to the earth and
paid homage. 9 And David said to Saul, "Why
do you listen to the words of men who say,
'Behold, David seeks your harm'? 10 Behold,
this day your eyes have seen how the LORD
gave you today into my hand in the cave. [h]And
some told me to kill you, but I spared you.[3]
I said, 'I will not put out my hand against
my lord, [f]for he is the LORD's anointed.' 11 See,
my father, see the corner of your robe in my
hand. For by the fact that I cut off the corner of your robe and did not kill you, you
may know and see that [i]there is no wrong
or treason in my hands. I have not sinned
against you, though [j]you hunt my life to take
it. 12 [k]May the LORD judge between me and
you, may the LORD avenge me against you,
but my hand shall not be against you. 13 As
the proverb of the ancients says, 'Out of the
wicked comes wickedness.' But my hand shall
not be against you. 14 After whom has the king
of Israel come out? After whom do you pur-
sue? [l]After a dead dog! [m]After a flea! 15 [k]May the
LORD therefore be judge and give sentence
between me and you, and see to it and [n]plead
my cause and deliver me from your hand."

16 As soon as David had finished speaking
these words to Saul, Saul said, [o]"Is this your
voice, my son David?" And Saul lifted up his
voice and wept. 17 He said to David, "You are
more righteous than I, [p]for you have repaid
me good, whereas I have repaid you evil. 18 And
you have declared this day how you have dealt
well with me, in that you did not kill me when
the LORD put me into your hands. 19 For if a
man finds his enemy, will he let him go away
safe? So may the LORD reward you with good
for what you have done to me this day. 20 And
now, behold, [q]I know that you shall surely
be king, and that the kingdom of Israel shall
be established in your hand. 21 [r]Swear to me
therefore by the LORD that you will not cut off
my offspring after me, and [s]that you will not
destroy my name out of my father's house."
22 And David swore this to Saul. Then Saul
went home, but David and his men went up
[t]to the stronghold.

[1] Ch 24:2 in Hebrew [2] Hebrew *cover his feet* [3] Septuagint, Syriac, Targum; Hebrew *it* [my eye] *spared you*

24:1–26:25 The similar themes of chapters 24 and 26 are obvious—both recount episodes in which David has an opportunity to kill Saul but refuses to do so because Saul is the "LORD's anointed" (24:6, 10; 26:9, 11, 23). But what about chapter 25? Here David has cause and opportunity to avenge himself on the wicked Nabal, a man much like Saul in some respects but not enjoying anointed status. Only by the intervention of a wise woman, Abigail, is David prevented from bloodying his hands (25:23–35). In due course, "the LORD struck Nabal, and he died" (25:38).

The clear teaching of both Old and New Testaments is that believers should never exact a personal vengeance, but should "wait for the LORD, and he will deliver" (Prov. 20:22). "Vengeance is mine, I will repay, says the Lord" (Rom. 12:19; cf. Heb. 10:30; both citing Deut. 32:35). While "vengeance" can sound negative, in the Bible vengeance predominantly has to do with the establishment of lawful justice, and God is its rightful agent. The believer can have confidence that, at the right time and in the right way, the "God of vengeance" will "shine forth" (Ps. 94:1), and full justice will be achieved.

Chapter 24
1 [y] ch. 23:28
2 [z] ch. 26:2
3 [a] Judg. 3:24 [b] See Ps. 57; 142
4 [c] ver. 7; [ch. 26:8]
5 [d] 2 Sam. 24:10
6 [e] ch. 26:11 [f] See ch. 12:3
7 [g] [Ps. 7:4]
10 [h] ver. 4 [f] [See ver. 6 above]
11 [i] Ps. 7:3 [j] ch. 26:20
12 [k] Gen. 16:5; Judg. 11:27
14 [l] See ch. 17:43 [m] ch. 26:20
15 [k] [See ver. 12 above] [n] ch. 25:39; Ps. 35:1; 43:1; 119:154
16 [o] ch. 26:17
17 [p] [ch. 26:21]
20 [q] ch. 23:17
21 [r] [Gen. 21:23] [s] [2 Sam. 21:7]
22 [t] ch. 23:29

The Death of Samuel

25 [u]Now Samuel died. And all Israel
assembled [v]and mourned for him, and
they buried him [w]in his house at [x]Ramah.

David and Abigail

Then David rose and went down to [y]the wilderness of Paran. 2 And there was a man in
[z]Maon whose business was in [a]Carmel. The
man was very rich; he had three thousand
sheep and a thousand goats. [b]He was shearing his sheep in Carmel. 3 Now the name
of the man was Nabal, and the name of his
wife Abigail. The woman was discerning and
beautiful, but the man was harsh and badly
behaved; [c]he was a Calebite. 4 David heard
in the wilderness that Nabal [b]was shearing
his sheep. 5 So David sent ten young men.
And David said to the young men, "Go up
to Carmel, and go to Nabal and greet him
in my name. 6 And thus you shall greet him:
[d]'Peace be to you, and peace be to your house,
and peace be to all that you have. 7 I hear that
you have shearers. Now your shepherds have
been with us, and we did them no harm, [e]and
they missed nothing all the time they were
in Carmel. 8 Ask your young men, and they
will tell you. Therefore let my young men find
favor in your eyes, for we come [f]on a feast day.
Please give whatever you have at hand to your
servants and to your son David.'"

9 When David's young men came, they said
all this to Nabal in the name of David, and
then they waited. 10 And Nabal answered
David's servants, [g]"Who is David? Who is the
son of Jesse? [h]There are many servants these
days who are breaking away from their masters. 11 Shall I take [i]my bread and my water and
my meat that I have killed for my shearers and
give it to [j]men who come from I do not know
where?" 12 So David's young men turned away
and came back and told him all this. 13 And
David said to his men, "Every man strap on his
sword!" And every man of them strapped on
his sword. David also strapped on his sword.
And [k]about four hundred men went up after
David, [k]while two hundred [l]remained with
the baggage.

14 But one of the young men told Abigail,
Nabal's wife, "Behold, David sent messengers
out of the wilderness to greet our master, and
he railed at them. 15 Yet the men were very
good to us, and we suffered no harm, [n]and we
did not miss anything when we were in the
fields, as long as we went with them. 16 They
were [o]a wall to us both by night and by day,
all the while we were with them keeping the
sheep. 17 Now therefore know this and consider
what you should do, [p]for harm is determined
against our master and against all his house,
and he is such [q]a worthless man that one cannot speak to him."

18 Then Abigail made haste and took two
hundred loaves and two skins of wine and
five sheep already prepared and five seahs[1] of
parched grain and a hundred clusters of raisins and two hundred cakes of figs, and laid
them on donkeys. 19 And she said to her young
men, "Go on before me; behold, I come after
you." But she did not tell her husband Nabal.
20 And as she rode on the donkey and came
down under cover of the mountain, behold,
David and his men came down toward her,
and she met them. 21 Now David had said,
"Surely in vain have I guarded all that this
fellow has in the wilderness, [r]so that nothing
was missed of all that belonged to him, and
he has [s]returned me evil for good. 22 [t]God do
so to the enemies of David[2] and more also, if
by morning I leave so much as one male of all
who belong to him."

23 When Abigail saw David, she hurried [u]and
got down from the donkey [v]and fell before
David on her face and bowed to the ground.
24 She fell at his feet and said, [w]"On me alone,
my lord, be the guilt. Please let your servant
speak in your ears, and hear the words of your
servant. 25 Let not my lord regard [q]this worthless fellow, Nabal, for as his name is, so is he.
Nabal[3] is his name, and folly is with him. But
I your servant did not see the young men of
my lord, whom you sent. 26 Now then, my
lord, [x]as the LORD lives, and as your soul lives,
because [y]the LORD has restrained you from
bloodguilt and from [z]saving with your own
hand, now then [a]let your enemies and those
who seek to do evil to my lord be as Nabal.
27 And now let this [b]present that your servant
has brought to my lord be given to the young

[1] A *seah* was about 7 quarts or 7.3 liters [2] Septuagint *to David* [3] *Nabal* means *fool*

Chapter 25 **1** [u]ch. 28:3 [v]Gen. 50:10; [Num. 20:29; Deut. 34:8] [w][1 Kgs. 2:34] [x]ch. 1:19 [y]Num. 10:12 **2** [z]ch. 23:24 [a]Josh. 15:55 [b][Gen. 38:13; 2 Sam. 13:23] **3** [c][ch. 30:14] **4** [b][See ver. 2 above] **6** [d][1 Chr. 12:18; Matt. 10:13; Luke 10:5] **7** [e]ver. 15, 21 **8** [f]Esth. 8:17; 9:19, 22 **10** [g][Judg. 9:28] [h][Judg. 12:4] **11** [i][Judg. 8:6] [j][ch. 22:2] **13** [k]ch. 23:13; 27:2; [ch. 22:2] [l]ch. 30:24 **15** [n]ver. 7, 21 **16** [o][Job 1:10] **17** [p][ch. 20:7] [q]Deut. 13:13 **21** [r]ver. 7, 15 [s]Ps. 109:5; [Prov. 17:13] **22** [t]See Ruth 1:17 **23** [u]Josh. 15:18; Judg. 1:14; [Gen. 24:64] [v]ver. 41; Ruth 2:10 **24** [w][2 Sam. 14:9] **25** [q][See ver. 17 above] **26** [x]See ch. 20:3 [y][Gen. 20:6] [z][Rom. 12:19; Heb. 10:30] [a][2 Sam. 18:32] **27** [b]ch. 30:26; Gen. 33:11; [2 Kgs. 5:15]

men who follow my lord. 28 Please forgive the
trespass of your servant. For the LORD will
certainly make my lord [c]a sure house, because
my lord [d]is fighting the battles of the LORD,
and evil shall not be found in you so long as
you live. 29 If men rise up to pursue you and
to seek your life, the life of my lord shall be
bound in the bundle of the living in the care
of the LORD your God. And the lives of your
enemies [e]he shall sling out as from the hollow
of a sling. 30 And when the LORD has done to
my lord according to all the good that he has
spoken concerning you and has appointed
you prince[1] over Israel, 31 my lord shall have
no cause of grief or pangs of conscience for
having shed blood without cause or for my
lord [z]working salvation himself. And when
the LORD has dealt well with my lord, then
remember your servant."

32 And David said to Abigail, [f]"Blessed be the
LORD, the God of Israel, who sent you this
day to meet me! 33 Blessed be your discretion,
and blessed be you, [y]who have kept me this
day from bloodguilt [z]and from working salvation with my own hand! 34 For as surely [g]as
the LORD, the God of Israel, lives, [y]who has
restrained me from hurting you, unless you
had hurried and come to meet me, truly by
morning there had not been left to Nabal so
much as one male." 35 Then David received
from her hand what she had brought him.
And he said to her, [h]"Go up in peace to your
house. See, I have obeyed your voice, and
I have granted your petition."

36 And Abigail came to Nabal, and behold, [i]he
was holding a feast in his house, like the feast
of a king. And Nabal's heart [j]was merry within
him, for he was very drunk. So she told him
nothing [k]at all until the morning light. 37 In
the morning, when the wine had gone out
of Nabal, his wife told him these things, and
his heart died within him, and he became as
a stone. 38 And about ten days later [l]the LORD
struck Nabal, and he died.

39 When David heard that Nabal was dead, he
said, [f]"Blessed be the LORD who has [m]avenged
the insult I received at the hand of Nabal, [n]and
has kept back his servant from wrongdoing.
[o]The LORD has returned the evil of Nabal on
his own head." Then David sent and [p]spoke
to Abigail, to take her as his wife. 40 When the
servants of David came to Abigail at Carmel,
they said to her, "David has sent us to you to
take you to him as his wife." 41 And she rose
[q]and bowed with her face to the ground and
said, "Behold, your handmaid is a servant
to wash the feet of the servants of my lord."
42 And Abigail hurried and rose and mounted
a donkey, and her five young women attended
her. She followed the messengers of David and
became his wife.

43 David also took Ahinoam of [r]Jezreel, [s]and
both of them became his wives. 44 Saul had
given Michal his daughter, David's wife, to
Palti the son of Laish, who was of Gallim.

David Spares Saul Again

26 [t]Then the Ziphites came to Saul at
Gibeah, saying, "Is not David hiding
himself on the hill of Hachilah, which is on
the east of Jeshimon?" 2 So Saul arose and
went down to [u]the wilderness of Ziph with
[v]three thousand chosen men of Israel to seek
David in the wilderness of Ziph. 3 And Saul
encamped on the hill of Hachilah, which is
beside the road on the east of Jeshimon. But
David remained in the wilderness. When he
saw that Saul came after him into the wilderness, 4 David sent out spies and learned that
Saul had indeed come. 5 Then David rose and
came to the place where Saul had encamped.
And David saw the place where Saul lay, with
[w]Abner the son of Ner, the commander of his
army. Saul was lying within [x]the encampment,
while the army was encamped around him.

6 Then David said to Ahimelech the Hittite,
and to Joab's brother [y]Abishai the son of
Zeruiah, [z]"Who will go down with me into
the camp to Saul?" And Abishai said, "I will
go down with you." 7 So David and Abishai
went to the army by night. And there lay Saul
sleeping within [x]the encampment, with his
spear stuck in the ground [a]at his head, and
Abner and the army lay around him. 8 Then
Abishai said to David, [b]"God has given your
enemy into your hand this day. Now please
let me pin him to the earth with one stroke of
the spear, and I will not strike him twice." 9 But
David said to Abishai, "Do not destroy him, for

[1] Or *leader*

28[c] 1 Kgs. 11:38; [ch. 2:35; 2 Sam. 7:11, 27; 1 Kgs. 9:5; 1 Chr. 17:10, 25] [d] ch. 18:17 **29**[e] Jer. 10:18 **31**[z] [See ver. 26 above] **32**[f] Gen. 24:27; Ps. 41:13; 72:18; Luke 1:68 **33**[y] [See ver. 26 above] [z] [See ver. 26 above] **34**[g] See Ruth 3:13 [y] [See ver. 26 above] **35**[h] See ch. 1:17 **36**[i] [2 Sam. 13:23] [j] [2 Sam. 13:28; 1 Kgs. 21:7] [k] ch. 22:15 **38**[l] ch. 26:10 **39**[f] [See ver. 32 above] [m] See ch. 24:15 [n] ver. 26, 33, 34 [o] 1 Kgs. 2:44; [Ps. 7:16; Ezek. 17:19] [p] [Song 8:8] **41**[q] [Ruth 2:10] **43**[r] Josh. 15:56 [s] ch. 27:3; 30:5; 2 Sam. 2:2; 3:2, 3; 1 Chr. 3:1 **Chapter 26** **1**[t] ch. 23:19; See Ps. 54 **2**[u] ch. 23:14 [v] ch. 24:2 **5**[w] ch. 14:50; 17:55; 2 Sam. 2:8 [x] ch. 17:20 **6**[y] 2 Sam. 2:18; 3:39; 16:10; 19:22; 1 Chr. 2:16 [z] [Judg. 7:9-11] **7**[x] [See ver. 5 above] [a] ver. 11, 16 **8**[b] [ch. 24:4, 18]

who can put out his hand [c]against the LORD's anointed and be guiltless?" 10 And David said, [d]"As the LORD lives, [e]the LORD will strike him, or [f]his day will come to die, [g]or he will go down into battle and perish. 11 [h]The LORD forbid that I should put out my hand against the LORD's anointed. But take now the spear that is [i]at his head and the jar of water, and let us go." 12 So David took the spear and the jar of water from Saul's head, and they went away. No man saw it or knew it, nor did any awake, for they were all asleep, because [j]a deep sleep from the LORD had fallen upon them.

13 Then David went over to the other side and stood far off on the top of the hill, with a great space between them. 14 And David called to the army, and to Abner the son of Ner, saying, "Will you not answer, Abner?" Then Abner answered, "Who are you who calls to the king?" 15 And David said to Abner, "Are you not a man? Who is like you in Israel? Why then have you not kept watch over your lord the king? For one of the people came in to destroy the king your lord. 16 This thing that you have done is not good. [k]As the LORD lives, you deserve to die, because you have not kept watch over your lord, the LORD's anointed. And now see where the king's spear is and the jar of water that was [l]at his head."

17 Saul recognized David's voice and said, [m]"Is this your voice, my son David?" And David said, "It is my voice, my lord, O king." 18 And he said, [n]"Why does my lord pursue after his servant? For what have I done? What evil is on my hands? 19 Now therefore let my lord the king hear the words of his servant. If it is the LORD who has stirred you up against me, may he accept an offering, but if it is men, may they be cursed before the LORD, [o]for they have driven me out this day that I should have no share in [p]the heritage of the LORD, saying, 'Go, serve other gods.' 20 Now therefore, let not my blood fall to the earth away from the presence of the LORD, for the king of Israel has come out to seek [q]a single flea like one who hunts a partridge in the mountains."

21 Then Saul said, [r]"I have sinned. Return, my son David, for I will no more do you harm, because my life was precious in your eyes this day. Behold, I have acted foolishly, and have made a great mistake." 22 And David answered and said, "Here is the spear, O king! Let one of the young men come over and take it. 23 [s]The LORD rewards every man for his righteousness and his faithfulness, for the LORD gave you into my hand today, and I would not put out my hand against the LORD's anointed. 24 Behold, as your life was precious this day in my sight, so may my life be precious in the sight of the LORD, and may he deliver me out of all tribulation." 25 Then Saul said to David, "Blessed be you, my son David! You will do many things and will [t]succeed in them." So David went his way, and Saul returned to his place.

David Flees to the Philistines

27 Then David said in his heart, "Now I shall perish one day by the hand of Saul. There is nothing better for me than that I should escape to the land of the Philistines. Then Saul will despair of seeking me any longer within the borders of Israel, and I shall escape out of his hand." 2 So David arose and went over, he and [u]the six hundred men who

9 [c] ver. 11, 16, 23; ch. 24:6, 10; [2 Sam. 1:16]
10 [d] [Ruth 3:13] [e] [ch. 25:38] [f] [Gen. 47:29; Deut. 31:14] [g] ch. 31:6
11 [h] ch. 24:6 [i] ver. 7, 16
12 [j] Gen. 2:21; 15:12
16 [k] [Ruth 3:13] [l] ver. 7, 11
17 [m] ch. 24:16
18 [n] ch. 24:9, 11
19 [o] [Ps. 120:5] [p] 2 Sam. 14:16; 20:19; 21:3
20 [q] ch. 24:14
21 [r] ch. 15:24; [ch. 24:17, 18]
23 [s] [Ps. 7:8; 18:20]
25 [t] [Gen. 32:28]
Chapter 27
2 [u] ch. 23:13; [2 Sam. 15:18]

27:1–12 Even men and women of great faith can falter. David's regular practice in the books of Samuel is to turn to God for guidance (23:2, 4; 30:8; 2 Sam. 2:1; 5:19, 23), to trust him, and to obey him. But in this episode, we hear nothing of David seeking God's guidance through prayer or any other means. Despite recent assurances by Abigail that he is "bound in the bundle of the living in the care of the LORD" (1 Sam. 25:29) and even by Saul that he "will do many things and will succeed in them" (26:25), David turns inward (27:1), his faith falters, and he heads for Philistine territory! During his 16 months there (v. 7), he engages in dubious activities, lying to his Philistine benefactor, Achish, and massacring whole populations in non-Israelite villages in the Negeb.

The biblical writers are not in the business of sugar-coating even their more laudable human characters. David was a sinner, as will become much more painfully evident in 2 Samuel 11 and following. But David was also a man in honest relationship with God and capable of genuine repentance. Only the Greater Son of David, Jesus, was without sin (Heb. 4:15). God's desire for his people is that we lean not on our own understanding but, rather, get to know and trust him with all our hearts (Prov. 3:5–6). But even when we fail, the good news is that "we have an advocate with the Father, Jesus Christ the righteous" (1 John 2:1).

were with him, [v]to Achish the son of Maoch,
king of Gath. 3 And David lived with Achish
at Gath, he and his men, every man with his
household, and David with [w]his two wives,
Ahinoam of Jezreel, and Abigail of Carmel,
Nabal's widow. 4 And when it was told Saul
that David had fled to Gath, he no longer
sought him.

5 Then David said to Achish, "If [x]I have found
favor in your eyes, let a place be given me in
one of the country towns, that I may dwell
there. For why should your servant dwell in
the royal city with you?" 6 So that day Achish
gave him [y]Ziklag. Therefore Ziklag has
belonged to the kings of Judah to this day.
7 [z]And the number of the days that David lived
in the country of the Philistines was a year and
four months.

8 Now David [a]and his men went up and
made raids against [b]the Geshurites, [c]the
Girzites, and [d]the Amalekites, for these were
the inhabitants of the land from of old, [e]as
far as Shur, to the land of Egypt. 9 And David
would strike the land and would leave neither
man nor woman alive, but would take away
the sheep, the oxen, the donkeys, the camels,
and the garments, and come back to Achish.
10 When Achish asked, "Where have you [f]made
a raid today?" David would say, "Against the
Negeb of Judah," or, "Against the Negeb of
[g]the Jerahmeelites," or, "Against the Negeb of
[h]the Kenites." 11 And David would leave neither
man nor woman alive to bring news to Gath,
thinking, "lest they should tell about us and
say, 'So David has done.'" Such was his custom all the while he lived in the country of the
Philistines. 12 And Achish trusted David, thinking, "He has made himself an utter stench to
his people Israel; therefore he shall always be
my servant."

Saul and the Medium of En-dor

28 In those days [i]the Philistines gathered
their forces for war, to fight against
Israel. And Achish said to David, "Understand
that you and your men are to go out with me
in the army." 2 David said to Achish, "Very well,
you shall know what your servant can do." And
Achish said to David, "Very well, I will make
you my bodyguard for life."

3 Now [j]Samuel had died, and all Israel had
mourned for him and buried him [k]in Ramah,
his own city. And Saul had put [l]the mediums and the necromancers out of the land.
4 The Philistines assembled and came and
encamped [m]at Shunem. And Saul gathered all
Israel, and they encamped [n]at Gilboa. 5 When
Saul saw the army of the Philistines, he was
afraid, and his heart trembled greatly. 6 And
when Saul inquired of the LORD, [o]the LORD
did not answer him, either [p]by dreams, or [q]by
Urim, or by prophets. 7 Then Saul said to his
servants, [r]"Seek out for me a woman who is a
medium, that I may go to her and inquire of
her." And his servants said to him, "Behold,
there is a medium at [s]En-dor."

8 So Saul [t]disguised himself and put on other
garments and went, he and two men with him.
And they came to the woman by night. And he
said, [u]"Divine for me by a spirit and bring up

28:1–29:11 A person's true character is often most evident when the person is under great pressure. The looming Philistine battle with which chapter 28 begins puts both David and Saul under great pressure. Saul is terrified (28:5) and, having ignored or rejected the word of the Lord all his life, he now seeks it in desperation (28:6). When God remains silent, however, instead of asking what in his life may have caused this, Saul turns to a medium, specifically a necromancer (28:7). Saul is not concerned with repentance or a relationship with God, but only with rescue. David, too, is in an untenable position. About to be drawn into battle on the side of the Philistines (28:1; 29:2), he is saved from having to raise his hand against the Lord's anointed only by providential rescue through the agency of suspicious Philistines (29:3–6).

God is not, however, an impersonal power to be accessed at will, as Saul's sad tale illustrates. How far Saul has fallen! His royal career began with a special meal prepared by Samuel, after which Saul went forth to become king (9:19, 24; 10:1). Now he eats his last meal, prepared by a witch, and goes forth to certain death (28:19, 24–25). A lifetime of dishonoring ("underweighting") God can lead only to ruin (cf. 2:29–30). By contrast, David, though flawed and sometimes failing, honors God by living in genuine relationship with him, and in return God gives him weight and rescues him (29:6–11). Without such a relationship, one is, like Saul, without God and without hope in the world (Eph. 2:12), but "for those who love God" and, like David, "are called according to his purpose," "all things work together for good" (Rom. 8:28).

2 [v]ch. 21:10; [1 Kgs. 2:39]
3 [w]See ch. 25:43
5 [x]See Gen. 33:15
6 [y]Josh. 15:31
7 [z][ch. 29:3]
8 [a]See 1 Chr. 12 [b]Josh. 13:2 [c][Josh. 16:10; Judg. 1:29] [d][ch. 15:7, 8] [e]See ch. 15:7
10 [f][ch. 23:27] [g]ch. 30:29 [h]See Judg. 1:16

Chapter 28
1 [i][ch. 29:1]
3 [j]ch. 25:1 [k]ch. 1:19 [l][Ex. 22:18; Lev. 19:31; 20:27; Deut. 18:10, 11]
4 [m]Josh. 19:18 [n]ch. 31:1
6 [o]ver. 15; ch. 14:37 [p]Num. 12:6 [q][Ex. 28:30; Num. 27:21; Deut. 33:8]
7 [r][1 Chr. 10:13] [s]Josh. 17:11; Ps. 83:10
8 [t]1 Kgs. 20:38; 22:30; 2 Chr. 18:29; 35:22 [u][Deut. 18:10]

for me whomever I shall name to you." 9 The
woman said to him, "Surely you know what
Saul has done, [l]how he has cut off the mediums and the necromancers from the land. Why
then are you laying a trap for my life to bring
about my death?" 10 But Saul swore to her by
the LORD, [v]"As the LORD lives, no punishment
shall come upon you for this thing." 11 Then the
woman said, "Whom shall I bring up for you?"
He said, "Bring up Samuel for me." 12 When
the woman saw Samuel, she cried out with a
loud voice. And the woman said to Saul, "Why
have you deceived me? You are Saul." 13 The
king said to her, "Do not be afraid. What do
you see?" And the woman said to Saul, "I see
a god coming up out of the earth." 14 He said
to her, "What is his appearance?" And she said,
"An old man is coming up, and he is wrapped
[w]in a robe." And Saul knew that it was Samuel,
and he bowed with his face to the ground and
paid homage.

15 Then Samuel said to Saul, "Why have
you disturbed me by bringing me up?" Saul
answered, "I am in great distress, for the
Philistines are warring against me, and [x]God
has turned away from me and [y]answers me
no more, either by prophets or by dreams.
Therefore I have summoned you to tell me
what I shall do." 16 And Samuel said, "Why then
do you ask me, since the LORD has turned from
you and become your enemy? 17 The LORD has
done to you as he spoke by me, for [z]the LORD
has torn the kingdom out of your hand and
given it to your neighbor, David. 18 [a]Because
you did not obey the voice of the LORD and did
not carry out his fierce wrath against Amalek,
therefore the LORD has done this thing to you
this day. 19 Moreover, the LORD will give Israel
also with you into the hand of the Philistines,
and tomorrow you [b]and your sons shall be
with me. The LORD will give the army of Israel
also into the hand of the Philistines."

20 Then Saul fell at once full length on the
ground, filled with fear because of the words
of Samuel. And there was no strength in him,
for he had eaten nothing all day and all night.
21 And the woman came to Saul, and when
she saw that he was terrified, she said to him,
"Behold, your servant has obeyed you. [c]I have
taken my life in my hand and have listened
to what you have said to me. 22 Now therefore, you also obey your servant. Let me set
a morsel of bread before you; and eat, that
you may have strength when you go on your
way." 23 He refused and said, "I will not eat."
But his servants, together with the woman,
urged him, and he listened to their words. So
he arose from the earth and sat on the bed.
24 Now the woman had a fattened calf in the
house, and she quickly killed it, and she took
flour and kneaded it and baked unleavened
bread of it, 25 and she put it before Saul and
his servants, and they ate. Then they rose and
went away that night.

The Philistines Reject David

29 [d]Now the Philistines had gathered
all their forces at [e]Aphek. And the
Israelites were encamped by [f]the spring that
is in [g]Jezreel. 2 As [h]the lords of the Philistines
were passing on by hundreds and by thousands, and David and his men were passing
on in the rear [i]with Achish, 3 the commanders of the Philistines said, "What are these
Hebrews doing here?" And Achish said to the
commanders of the Philistines, "Is this not
David, the servant of Saul, king of Israel, who
has been with me [j]now for days and years, and
since he deserted to me [k]I have found no fault
in him to this day." 4 But [h]the commanders of
the Philistines were angry with him. And the
commanders of the Philistines said to him,
"Send the man back, that he may return [l]to
the place to which you have assigned him. He
shall not go down with us to battle, [m]lest in the
battle he become an adversary to us. For how
could this fellow reconcile himself to his lord?
Would it not be with the heads of the men
here? 5 Is not this David, of whom they sing
to one another in dances,

> [n]'Saul has struck down his thousands,
> and David his ten thousands'?"

6 Then Achish called David and said to him,
[o]"As the LORD lives, you have been honest, and
to me it seems right that [p]you should march
out and in with me in the campaign. For I have
found nothing wrong in you from the day of
your coming to me to this day. Nevertheless,
the lords do not approve of you. 7 So go back
now; and go peaceably, that you may not displease the lords of the Philistines." 8 And David
said to Achish, "But what have I done? What

9 [l][See ver. 3 above] **10** [v]See Ruth 3:13 **14** [w]ch. 15:27 **15** [x]ch. 16:14; 18:12 [y]ver. 6 **17** [z]ch. 15:28 **18** [a]ch. 15:9 **19** [b]ch. 31:2 **21** [c]See Judg. 12:3
Chapter 29 **1** [d]ch. 28:1 [e]ch. 4:1; Josh. 12:18 [f]Judg. 7:1 [g]Josh. 17:16 **2** [h]Josh. 13:3 [i]ch. 28:1, 2 **3** [j][ch. 27:7] [k][Dan. 6:5] **4** [h][See ver. 2 above] [l]ch. 27:6; 30:1 [m][ch. 14:21] **5** [n]ch. 18:7; 21:11 **6** [o]See ch. 20:3 [p]2 Sam. 3:25; 2 Kgs. 19:27; Ps. 121:8; Isa. 37:28

have you found in your servant from the day I entered your service until now, that I may not go and fight against the enemies of my lord the king?" 9 And Achish answered David and said, "I know that you are as blameless in my sight [q]as an angel of God. Nevertheless, [r]the commanders of the Philistines have said, 'He shall not go up with us to the battle.' 10 Now then rise early in the morning [s]with the servants of your lord who came with you, and start early in the morning, and depart as soon as you have light." 11 So David set out with his men early in the morning to return to the land of the Philistines. But the Philistines went up to [t]Jezreel.

David's Wives Are Captured

30 Now when David and his men came to [u]Ziklag on the third day, [v]the Amalekites had [w]made a raid against the Negeb and against Ziklag. They had overcome Ziklag and burned it with fire 2 and taken captive the women and all[1] who were in it, both small and great. They killed no one, but carried them off and went their way. 3 And when David and his men came to the city, they found it burned with fire, and their wives and sons and daughters taken captive. 4 Then David and the people who were with him raised their voices and wept until they had no more strength to weep. 5 David's [x]two wives also had been taken captive, Ahinoam of Jezreel and Abigail the widow of Nabal of Carmel. 6 And David was greatly distressed, for the people spoke [y]of stoning him, because all the people were bitter in soul,[2] each for his sons and daughters. But David strengthened himself in the LORD his God.

7 [z]And David said to Abiathar the priest, the son of Ahimelech, "Bring me the ephod." So Abiathar brought the ephod to David. 8 [a]And David inquired of the LORD, "Shall I pursue after this [b]band? Shall I overtake them?" He answered him, "Pursue, for you shall surely overtake [c]and shall surely rescue." 9 So David set out, and [d]the six hundred men who were with him, and they came to the brook Besor, where those who were left behind stayed. 10 But David pursued, he and four hundred men. [e]Two hundred stayed behind, who were too exhausted to cross the brook Besor.

11 They found an Egyptian in the open country and brought him to David. And they gave him bread and he ate. They gave him water to drink, 12 and they gave him a piece of a cake of figs and two clusters of raisins. And when he had eaten, [f]his spirit revived, for he had not eaten bread or drunk water for three days and three nights. 13 And David said to him, "To whom do you belong? And where are you from?" He said, "I am a young man of Egypt, servant to an Amalekite, and my master left me behind because I fell sick three days ago. 14 [g]We had made a raid against the Negeb of [h]the Cherethites and against that which belongs to Judah and against the Negeb of Caleb, and we burned Ziklag with fire." 15 And David said to him, "Will you take me down to this band?" And he said, "Swear to me by God that you will not kill me or deliver me into the

[1] Septuagint; Hebrew lacks *and all* [2] Compare 22:2

30:1–31:13 The contrast between David and Saul continues to the end of Saul's life. In chapter 30, David is in peril of his life at the hands of his own men, but he "strengthens himself in the LORD his God" (30:6). In chapter 31, Saul is also in peril of his life—at the hands of the Philistines—and he finds no strength. Wounded, he is terrified that "these uncircumcised" will come and torture him, and so he asks his armor-bearer to run him through. When the latter refuses, Saul falls on his own sword (31:4). The habits of a lifetime show themselves in extreme circumstances. From an early age, David was convinced that even a giant among the "uncircumcised Philistines" was no match for his big God (17:26). Through the encouragement of a faithful friend like Jonathan, David had developed the habit of finding strength in God (cf. 23:16). Saul, by contrast, had developed the habit of thinking little of God and regularly giving more weight to circumstances. This meant that he vacillated between overwhelming fear and overweening pride, depending on the circumstances. Threats from "uncircumcised Philistines" held little fear for David but literally scared Saul to death.

The magnificent truth of the gospel is that to fear God (to give him ultimate weight) is to dispel all other fears (cf. Ex. 20:20; Rom. 8:35–39), even the fear of death: "If the Spirit of him who raised Jesus from the dead dwells in you, he who raised Christ Jesus from the dead will also give life to your mortal bodies through his Spirit who dwells in you" (Rom. 8:11; cf. Isa. 25:8; 1 Corinthians 15; Heb. 2:14–15; Rev. 21:4).

9 [q]2 Sam. 14:17, 20; 19:27 [r]Josh. 13:3
10 [s][1 Chr. 12:19, 22]
11 [t]Josh. 17:16
Chapter 30
1 [u]ch. 29:4, 11 [v]ch. 27:8; [ch. 15:3, 7] [w]ver. 14
5 [x]See ch. 25:42, 43
6 [y][Ex. 17:4; Num. 14:10]
7 [z]ch. 23:6, 9
8 [a]See ch. 22:10 [b][1 Chr. 12:21] [c]ver. 18
9 [d]See ch. 23:13
10 [e]ver. 21
12 [f]Judg. 15:19; [ch. 14:27]
14 [g]ver. 1 [h]2 Sam. 8:18; 15:18; 20:7, 23; 1 Kgs. 1:38, 44; 1 Chr. 18:17; [Ezek. 25:16; Zeph. 2:5]

hands of my master, and I will take you down to this [i]band."

David Defeats the Amalekites

16 And when he had taken him down, behold, they were spread abroad over all the land, eating and drinking and dancing, because of all the great spoil they had taken from the land of the Philistines and from the land of Judah. 17 And David struck them down from twilight until the evening of the next day, and not a man of them escaped, except four hundred young men, who mounted camels and fled. 18 [j]David recovered all that the Amalekites had taken, and David rescued his two wives. 19 Nothing was missing, whether small or great, sons or daughters, spoil or anything that had been taken. [j]David brought back all. 20 David also captured all the flocks and herds, and the people drove the livestock before him,[1] and said, "This is David's spoil."

21 Then David came to [k]the two hundred men who had been too exhausted to follow David, and who had been left [k]at the brook Besor. And they went out to meet David and to meet the people who were with him. And when David came near to the people he greeted them. 22 Then all the wicked and worthless fellows among the men who had gone with David said, "Because they did not go with us, we will not give them any of the spoil that we have recovered, except that each man may lead away his wife and children, and depart." 23 But David said, "You shall not do so, my brothers, with what the LORD has given us. He has preserved us and given into our hand the band that came against us. 24 Who would listen to you in this matter? [l]For as his share is who goes down into the battle, so shall his share be who stays by the baggage. They shall share alike." 25 And he made it a statute and a rule for Israel from that day forward to this day.

26 When David came to Ziklag, he sent part of the spoil to his friends, the elders of Judah, saying, "Here is a present for you from the spoil of the enemies of the LORD." 27 It was for those in [m]Bethel, in Ramoth of the Negeb, in [n]Jattir, 28 in [o]Aroer, in Siphmoth, in [p]Eshtemoa, 29 in Racal, in the cities of [q]the Jerahmeelites, in the cities of [r]the Kenites, 30 in [s]Hormah, in Bor-ashan, in Athach, 31 in [t]Hebron, for all the places where David and his men had roamed.

The Death of Saul

31 [u]Now the Philistines were fighting against Israel, and the men of Israel fled before the Philistines and fell slain [v]on Mount Gilboa. 2 And the Philistines overtook Saul and his sons, and the Philistines struck down [w]Jonathan and [x]Abinadab and Malchi-shua, the sons of Saul. 3 [y]The battle pressed hard against Saul, and the archers found him, and he was badly wounded by the archers. 4 [z]Then Saul said to his armor-bearer, "Draw your sword, and thrust me through with it, lest these [a]uncircumcised come and thrust me through, and mistreat me." But his armor-bearer would not, [b]for he feared greatly. Therefore Saul took his own sword [c]and fell upon it. 5 And when his armor-bearer saw that Saul was dead, he also fell upon his sword and died with him. 6 Thus Saul died, and his three sons, and his armor-bearer, and all his men, on the same day together. 7 And when the men of Israel who were on the other side of the valley and those beyond the Jordan saw that the men of Israel had fled and that Saul and his sons were dead, they abandoned their cities and fled. And the Philistines came and lived in them.

8 The next day, when the Philistines came to strip the slain, they found Saul and his three sons fallen on Mount Gilboa. 9 So they cut off his head and stripped off his armor and sent messengers throughout the land of the Philistines, [d]to carry the good news [e]to the house of their idols and to the people. 10 [f]They put his armor in the temple of [g]Ashtaroth, and they fastened his body to the wall of [h]Beth-shan. 11 [i]But when the inhabitants of Jabesh-gilead heard what the Philistines had done to Saul, 12 [j]all the valiant men arose and went all night and took the body of Saul and the bodies of his sons from the wall of Beth-shan, and they came to Jabesh [k]and burned them there. 13 And they took their bones [l]and buried them under [m]the tamarisk tree in Jabesh and [n]fasted seven days.

[1] The meaning of the Hebrew clause is uncertain

15 [i][ch. 25:3] **18** [j]ver. 8 **19** [j][See ver. 18 above] **21** [k]ver. 10 **24** [l][Num. 31:27; Josh. 22:8] **27** [m]Gen. 28:19; See Judg. 1:22-26 [n]Josh. 15:48 **28** [o]Deut. 2:36; Josh. 13:16 [p]Josh. 15:50 **29** [q]ch. 27:10 [r]See Judg. 1:16 **30** [s]Judg. 1:17 **31** [t]Josh. 14:13-15; Judg. 1:10; 2 Sam. 2:1-4 **Chapter 31** **1** [u]For ver. 1-13, see 1 Chr. 10:1-12 [v]ch. 28:4; [2 Sam. 1:6, 21; 21:12] **2** [w]1 Chr. 8:33 [x][ch. 14:49] **3** [y][2 Sam. 1:6] **4** [z][Judg. 9:54] [a]See Judg. 14:3 [b][2 Sam. 1:14] [c][2 Sam. 1:10] **9** [d][2 Sam. 1:20] [e][Judg. 16:23, 24] **10** [f][ch. 21:9] [g]See Judg. 2:13 [h]Josh. 17:11 **11** [i]2 Sam. 21:10; See ch. 11:1-11 **12** [j]2 Sam. 2:4-7 [k][2 Chr. 16:14; 21:19; Jer. 34:5] **13** [l]2 Sam. 21:12, 14 [m][ch. 22:6] [n][Gen. 50:10]

2 Samuel

David Hears of Saul's Death

1 After the death of Saul, when David had returned [a]from striking down the Amalekites, David remained two days in Ziklag. 2 And on the third day, behold, [b]a man came from Saul's camp, [c]with his clothes torn and dirt on his head. And when he came to David, [d]he fell to the ground and paid homage. 3 David said to him, "Where do you come from?" And he said to him, "I have escaped from the camp of Israel." 4 And David said to him, [e]"How did it go? Tell me." And he answered, "The people fled from the battle, and also many of the people have fallen and are dead, and Saul and his son Jonathan are also dead." 5 Then David said to the young man who told him, "How do you know that Saul and his son Jonathan are dead?" 6 And the young man who told him said, [f]"By chance I happened to be on Mount Gilboa, and there was Saul leaning on his spear, and behold, the chariots and the horsemen were close upon him. 7 And when he looked behind him, he saw me, and called to me. And I answered, 'Here I am.' 8 And he said to me, 'Who are you?' I answered him, 'I am an Amalekite.' 9 And he said to me, [g]'Stand beside me and kill me, for anguish has seized me, and yet my life still lingers.' 10 So I stood beside him and killed him, because I was sure that he could not live after he had fallen. [h]And I took the crown that was on his head and the armlet that was on his arm, and I have brought them here to my lord."

11 Then David took hold of his clothes and [i]tore them, and so did all the men who were with him. 12 And they mourned and wept [j]and fasted until evening for Saul and for Jonathan his son and for the people of the LORD and for the house of Israel, because they had fallen by the sword. 13 And David said to the young man who told him, "Where do you come from?"

1:1–5:5 It is often remarked that "good things come to those who wait." Anointed to be king already in 1 Samuel 16, David has nevertheless waited—waited on the Lord through years of difficulty and danger in the wilderness. Even when given opportunities in 1 Samuel 24 and 26 to rid the kingdom of the rejected king Saul—who refuses to step down—David resists temptation and waits.

Now, in the section before us, David is finally made king over all Israel, south and north (5:4–5). Blood is spilt on David's way to the throne but, as the biblical writers are at pains to point out, not by David. In fact, even when Saul dies in battle (Saul, who for many years thought about little else than sending David to an early grave), David takes no pleasure in his death and deals harshly with the opportunistic Amalekite who seeks to benefit from it by falsely *claiming* to have killed Saul (1:2–16). Readers already know from 1 Samuel 31 that Saul fell on his own sword.

Then, in one of the most moving eulogy-laments of world literature (2 Sam. 1:17–27), David honors Saul right alongside his beloved and loyal friend Jonathan. David has no desire to gain the throne by just any means or tactic. When the power-hungry former captain of Saul's army, Abner (3:6), is treacherously murdered by Joab (3:27), David does not rejoice but, rather, places a curse on Joab (3:28–29) and forces him and all the people to "put on sackcloth and mourn before Abner" (3:31). When the surviving son of Saul, Ish-bosheth, is assassinated in his sleep by Rechab and Baanah and his head removed as evidence of the deed (4:7), David rewards the assassins with their own deaths and the removal of their hands, which had done the deed, and their feet, which had brought their grisly prize to David (4:12).

Chapter 1
1 [a]See 1 Sam. 30:17-20
2 [b]ch. 4:10 [c]See Josh. 7:6 [d]ch. 14:4
4 [e][1 Sam. 4:16]
6 [f]For ver. 6-10, see 1 Sam. 31:1-4; 1 Chr. 10:1-6
9 [g][Judg. 9:54]
10 [h][2 Kgs. 11:12]
11 [i]ch. 13:31; [ch. 3:31]; See Josh. 7:6
12 [j][ch. 3:35]

And he answered, "I am the son of a sojourner,
an Amalekite." 14 David said to him, "How is it
you were not [k]afraid to put out your hand to
destroy [l]the LORD's anointed?" 15 Then [m]David
called one of the young men and said, "Go,
execute him." And he struck him down so that
he died. 16 And David said to him, [n]"Your blood
be on your head, for your own mouth has testified against you, saying, 'I have killed [o]the
LORD's anointed.'"

David's Lament for Saul and Jonathan

17 And David [p]lamented with this lamentation over Saul and Jonathan his son, 18 and
he said it[1] should be taught to the people of
Judah; behold, it is written in [q]the Book of
Jashar.[2] He said:

19 "Your glory, O Israel, is slain on your high places!
[r]How the mighty have fallen!
20 [s]Tell it not in Gath,
[t]publish it not in the streets of Ashkelon,
[u]lest the daughters of the Philistines rejoice,
lest the daughters of [v]the uncircumcised exult.

21 [w]"You mountains of Gilboa,
let there be no dew or rain upon you,
nor fields of offerings![3]
For there the shield of the mighty was defiled,
the shield of Saul, not [x]anointed with oil.

22 "From the blood of the slain,
from the fat of the mighty,
[y]the bow of Jonathan turned not back,
and the sword of Saul returned not empty.

23 "Saul and Jonathan, beloved and lovely!
In life and in death they were not divided;
they were [z]swifter than eagles;
they were [a]stronger than lions.

24 "You daughters of Israel, weep over Saul,
who clothed you luxuriously in scarlet,
[b]who put ornaments of gold on your apparel.

25 [c]"How the mighty have fallen
in the midst of the battle!

"Jonathan lies slain on your high places.
26 I am distressed for you, my brother Jonathan;
very pleasant have you been to me;
[d]your love to me was extraordinary,
surpassing the love of women.

27 [c]"How the mighty have fallen,
and the weapons of war perished!"

David Anointed King of Judah

2 After this David [e]inquired of the LORD,
"Shall I go up into any of the cities of
Judah?" And the LORD said to him, "Go up."
David said, "To which shall I go up?" And
he said, "To [f]Hebron." 2 So David went up
there, and [g]his two wives also, Ahinoam of
Jezreel and Abigail the widow of Nabal of
Carmel. 3 And David brought up [h]his men
who were with him, everyone with his house-
hold, and they lived in the towns of Hebron.

[1] Septuagint; Hebrew *the Bow*, which may be the name of the lament's tune [2] Or *of the upright* [3] Septuagint *firstfruits*

14[k] [1 Sam. 24:6, 10; 26:9; 31:4] [l]See 1 Sam. 12:3
15[m] ch. 4:10
16[n] [ch. 3:29; Josh. 2:19; 1 Kgs. 2:32, 37; Matt. 27:25] [o]See 1 Sam. 12:3
17[p] [ch. 3:33; 2 Chr. 35:25]
18[q] Josh. 10:13
19[r] ver. 25, 27
20[s] Mic. 1:10 [t][1 Sam. 31:9; Amos 3:9] [u][Ex. 15:20; Judg. 11:34] [v]See Judg. 14:3
21[w] 1 Sam. 31:1 [x][1 Sam. 10:1]
22[y] [1 Sam. 18:4]
23[z] [Jer. 4:13; Hab. 1:8] [a][Judg. 14:18]
24[b] [Ezek. 16:11]
25[c] ver. 19
26[d] See 1 Sam. 18:1, 3
27[c] [See ver. 25 above]
Chapter 2
1[e] See 1 Sam. 22:10 [f]See Josh. 14:13
2[g] See 1 Sam. 25:42, 43
3[h] 1 Sam. 27:2, 3; 30:1; See 1 Chr. 12:1-22

Yes, "good things come to those who wait." But it depends, of course, on what or whom one is waiting for. David waited for the Lord. David's world and his mind were infused with the reality of God. David was patient, because he knew that nothing and no one could thwart the good purposes of God for him or for any who are the Lord's. Because God carried (and carries!) more weight than any threat, challenge, or enemy, David had confidence that "evildoers shall be cut off, but those who wait for the LORD shall inherit the land" (Ps. 37:9).

Throughout the Scriptures, the call to believers is the same: "Wait for the LORD; be strong, and let your heart take courage" (Ps. 27:14); hope in his word (Ps. 130:5); "Do not say, 'I will repay evil'; wait for the LORD, and he will deliver you" (Prov. 20:22). Our calling as Christians is to wait expectantly and in great joy for the "revealing of our Lord Jesus Christ" (1 Cor. 1:7). Indeed, our "blessed hope" is "the appearing of the glory of our great God and Savior Jesus Christ, who gave himself for us to redeem us from all lawlessness and to purify for himself a people for his own possession who are zealous for good works" (Titus 2:13–14; see also Heb. 9:28; Jude 21). We wait for Christ. We trust him. He is our refuge.

4 And the men of Judah came, and there they anointed David [i]king over the house of Judah.

When they told David, [j]"It was the men of Jabesh-gilead who buried Saul," 5 David sent messengers to the men of Jabesh-gilead and said to them, [k]"May you be blessed by the LORD, because you showed this loyalty to Saul your lord and buried him. 6 Now may the LORD show steadfast love and faithfulness to you. And I will do good to you because you have done this thing. 7 Now therefore let your hands be strong, and be valiant, for Saul your lord is dead, and [i]the house of Judah has anointed me king over them."

Ish-bosheth Made King of Israel

8 But [l]Abner the son of Ner, commander of Saul's army, took Ish-bosheth the son of Saul and brought him over to [m]Mahanaim, 9 and he made him king over Gilead and the Ashurites and Jezreel and Ephraim and Benjamin and all Israel. 10 Ish-bosheth, Saul's son, was forty years old when he began to reign over Israel, and he reigned two years. But the house of Judah followed David. 11 [n]And the time that David was king in Hebron over [i]the house of Judah was seven years and six months.

The Battle of Gibeon

12 Abner the son of Ner, and the servants of Ish-bosheth the son of Saul, went out from Mahanaim to Gibeon. 13 And Joab the son of Zeruiah and the servants of David went out and met them at [o]the pool of Gibeon. And they sat down, the one on the one side of the pool, and the other on the other side of the pool. 14 And Abner said to Joab, "Let the young men arise and compete before us." And Joab said, "Let them arise." 15 Then they arose and passed over by number, twelve for Benjamin and Ish-bosheth the son of Saul, and twelve of the servants of David. 16 And each caught his opponent by the head and thrust his sword in his opponent's side, so they fell down together. Therefore that place was called Helkath-hazzurim,[1] which is at Gibeon. 17 And the battle was very fierce that day. And Abner and the men of Israel were beaten before the servants of David.

18 And the [p]three sons of Zeruiah were there, Joab, Abishai, and Asahel. Now Asahel was [q]as swift of foot as a wild gazelle. 19 And Asahel pursued Abner, and as he went, he turned neither to the right hand nor to the left from following Abner. 20 Then Abner looked behind him and said, "Is it you, Asahel?" And he answered, "It is I." 21 Abner said to him, "Turn aside to your right hand or to your left, and seize one of the young men and take his spoil." But Asahel would not turn aside from following him. 22 And Abner said again to Asahel, "Turn aside from following me. Why should I strike you to the ground? How then could I lift up my face to your brother Joab?" 23 But he refused to turn aside. Therefore Abner struck him [r]in the stomach with the butt of his spear, so that the spear came out at his back. And he fell there and died where he was. And all who came to the place where Asahel had fallen and died, stood still.

24 But Joab and Abishai pursued Abner. And as the sun was going down they came to the hill of Ammah, which lies before Giah on the way to the wilderness of Gibeon. 25 And the people of Benjamin gathered themselves together behind Abner and became one group and took their stand on the top of a hill. 26 Then Abner called to Joab, "Shall the sword

[1] *Helkath-hazzurim* means *the field of sword-edges*

We sometimes say, "Patience is a virtue." More biblically, we should say, patience is a mark of the fruit of the Spirit (Gal. 5:22). David suffered much at the hand of Saul—hardship, dishonor, and slander—but he refused to return evil for evil (cf. Rom. 12:17; 1 Thess. 5:15; 1 Pet. 3:9). David chose rather to bless and not curse (Rom. 12:14) and even to eulogize Saul in his death. Such conduct is possible only for those filled with and empowered by the Spirit of God (cf. 1 Sam. 16:13). In the end, ever true to his purposes and promises, the Lord "established [David] king over Israel, and . . . exalted his kingdom for the sake of his people Israel"—and David knew it (2 Sam. 5:12)! In God's economy, suffering ends in exaltation. As Christians, we must expect suffering ("in the world you will have tribulation"; John 16:33), but our hope at the far side of suffering is even grander than David's: "after you have suffered a little while, the God of all grace, who has called you to his eternal glory in Christ, will himself restore, confirm, strengthen, and establish you" (1 Pet. 5:10). Our response? "Humble yourselves, therefore, under the mighty hand of God so that at the proper time he may exalt you, casting all your anxieties on him, because he cares for you" (1 Pet. 5:6–7).

4 [i]ch. 5:5 [j]1 Sam. 31:11-13
5 [k]See Ruth 2:20
7 [i][See ver. 4 above]
8 [l]1 Sam. 14:50 [m]See Josh. 13:26
11 [n]ch. 5:5; 1 Kgs. 2:11 [i][See ver. 4 above]
13 [o][Jer. 41:12]
18 [p]1 Chr. 2:16; [1 Sam. 26:6] [q][ch. 22:34; 1 Chr. 12:8; Ps. 18:33; Song 2:17; 8:14; Hab. 3:19]
23 [r]ch. 3:27; 4:6; 20:10

devour forever? Do you not know that the end will be bitter? How long will it be before you tell your people to turn from the pursuit of their brothers?" 27 And Joab said, "As God lives, if [s]you had not spoken, surely the men would not have given up the pursuit of their brothers until the morning." 28 So Joab blew the trumpet, and all the men stopped and pursued Israel no more, nor did they fight anymore.

29 And Abner and his men went all that night through [t]the Arabah. They crossed the Jordan, and marching the whole morning, they came to [u]Mahanaim. 30 Joab returned from the pursuit of Abner. And when he had gathered all the people together, there were missing from David's servants nineteen men besides Asahel. 31 But the servants of David had struck down of Benjamin 360 of Abner's men. 32 And they took up Asahel and buried him in the tomb of his father, which was at Bethlehem. And Joab and his men marched all night, and the day broke upon them at Hebron.

Abner Joins David

3 There was a long war between the house of Saul and the house of David. And David grew stronger and stronger, while the house of Saul became weaker and weaker.

2 [v]And sons were born to David at Hebron: his firstborn was Amnon, of [w]Ahinoam of Jezreel; 3 and his second, Chileab, of [w]Abigail the widow of Nabal of Carmel; and the third, Absalom the son of Maacah [x]the daughter of Talmai king of [y]Geshur; 4 and the fourth, [z]Adonijah the son of Haggith; and the fifth, Shephatiah the son of Abital; 5 and the sixth, Ithream, of Eglah, David's wife. These were born to David in Hebron.

6 While there was war between the house of Saul and the house of David, Abner was making himself strong in the house of Saul. 7 Now Saul had a concubine whose name was [a]Rizpah, the daughter of Aiah. And Ish-bosheth said to Abner, [b]"Why have you gone in to my father's concubine?" 8 Then Abner was very angry over the words of Ish-bosheth and said, "Am I [c]a dog's head of Judah? To this day I keep showing steadfast love to the house of Saul your father, to his brothers, and to his friends, and have not given you into the hand of David. And yet you charge me today with a fault concerning a woman. 9 [d]God do so to Abner and more also, if I do not accomplish for David [e]what the LORD has sworn to him, 10 to transfer the kingdom from the house of Saul and set up the throne of David over Israel and over Judah, [f]from Dan to Beersheba." 11 And Ish-bosheth could not answer Abner another word, because he feared him.

12 And Abner sent messengers to David on his behalf,[1] saying, "To whom does the land belong? Make your covenant with me, and behold, my hand shall be with you to bring over all Israel to you." 13 And he said, "Good; I will make a covenant with you. But one thing I require of you; that is, [g]you shall not see my face unless you first bring [h]Michal, Saul's daughter, when you come to see my face." 14 Then David sent messengers to Ish-bosheth, Saul's son, saying, "Give me my wife Michal, [i]for whom I paid the bridal price of a hundred foreskins of the Philistines." 15 And Ish-bosheth sent and took her from her husband Paltiel the son of Laish. 16 But her husband went with her, weeping after her all the way to [j]Bahurim. Then Abner said to him, "Go, return." And he returned.

17 And Abner conferred with the elders of Israel, saying, "For some time past you have been seeking David as king over you. 18 Now then bring it about, [k]for the LORD has promised David, saying, 'By the hand of my servant David I will save my people Israel from the hand of the Philistines, and from the hand of all their enemies.'" 19 Abner also spoke to [l]Benjamin. And then Abner went to tell David at Hebron all that Israel and the whole house of Benjamin thought good to do.

20 When Abner came with twenty men to David at Hebron, David made a feast for Abner and the men who were with him. 21 And Abner said to David, "I will arise and go and [m]will gather all Israel to my lord the king, that they may make a covenant with you, and that you may [n]reign over all that your heart desires." So David sent Abner away, and he went in peace.

22 Just then the servants of David arrived with Joab from a raid, bringing much spoil with them. But Abner was not with David at Hebron, for he had sent him away, and he

[1] Or *where he was*; Septuagint *at Hebron*

27 [s]ver. 14; [Prov. 17:14] **29** [t]See Deut. 1:1 [u]ver. 8; See Josh. 13:26 **Chapter 3** **2** [v]For ver. 2-5, see 1 Chr. 3:1-4 [w]1 Sam. 25:42, 43 **3** [w][See ver. 2 above] [x]ch. 13:37, 38 [y]ch. 14:32; 15:8; [1 Sam. 27:8] **4** [z]1 Kgs. 1:5 **7** [a]ch. 21:8-10 [b][ch. 16:21] **8** [c]See 1 Sam. 17:43 **9** [d]ver. 35; See Ruth 1:17 [e]1 Sam. 15:28; 16:1, 12; 28:17; 1 Chr. 12:23 **10** [f]ch. 17:11; 24:2, 15; Judg. 20:1; 1 Sam. 3:20; 1 Kgs. 4:25 **13** [g][Gen. 43:3] [h]1 Sam. 14:49 **14** [i]1 Sam. 18:25, 27 **16** [j]ch. 16:5; 17:18; 19:16; 1 Kgs. 2:8 **18** [k]See ver. 9 **19** [l][1 Chr. 12:29] **21** [m]ver. 12 [n]1 Kgs. 11:37

had gone in peace. [23] When Joab and all the
army that was with him came, it was told Joab,
"Abner the son of Ner came to the king, and
he has let him go, and he has gone in peace."
[24] Then Joab went to the king and said, "What
have you done? Behold, Abner came to you.
Why is it that you have sent him away, so that
he is gone? [25] You know that Abner the son of
Ner came to deceive you and to know [o]your
going out and your coming in, and to know
all that you are doing."

Joab Murders Abner

[26] When Joab came out from David's presence, he sent messengers after Abner, and they
brought him back from the cistern of Sirah.
But David did not know about it. [27] And when
Abner returned to Hebron, Joab took him
aside into the midst of the gate to speak with
him privately, [p]and there he struck him [q]in
the stomach, so that he died, for the blood of
Asahel his brother. [28] Afterward, when David
heard of it, he said, "I and my kingdom are
forever guiltless before the LORD for the blood
of Abner the son of Ner. [29] [r]May it fall upon the
head of Joab and upon all his father's house,
and may the house of Joab never be without
[s]one who has a discharge or who is [t]leprous or
who holds a spindle or who falls by the sword
or who lacks bread!" [30] So Joab and Abishai his
brother killed Abner, because [u]he had put their
brother Asahel to death in the battle at Gibeon.

David Mourns Abner

[31] Then David said to Joab and to all the people who were with him, [v]"Tear your clothes
and [w]put on sackcloth and mourn before
Abner." And King David followed the bier.
[32] They buried Abner at Hebron. And the king
lifted up his voice and wept at the grave of
Abner, and all the people wept. [33] And the king
[x]lamented for Abner, saying,

> [y]"Should Abner die [z]as a fool dies?
> [34] Your hands were not bound;
> your feet were not fettered;
> as one falls before the wicked
> you have fallen."

And all the people wept again over him. [35] Then
all the people came [a]to persuade David to eat
bread while it was yet day. But David swore,
saying, [b]"God do so to me and more also, if
I taste bread or anything else [c]till the sun goes
down!" [36] And all the people took notice of it,
and it pleased them, as everything that the
king did pleased all the people. [37] So all the
people and all Israel understood that day that
it had not been the king's will to put to death
Abner the son of Ner. [38] And the king said to
his servants, "Do you not know that a prince
and a great man has fallen this day in Israel?
[39] And I was gentle today, though anointed
king. [d]These men, the sons of Zeruiah, are
more severe than I. [e]The LORD repay the evildoer according to his wickedness!"

Ish-bosheth Murdered

4 When Ish-bosheth, Saul's son, heard that
Abner had died at Hebron, [f]his courage
failed, and all Israel was dismayed. [2] Now
Saul's son had two men who were captains
of raiding bands; the name of the one was
Baanah, and the name of the other Rechab,
sons of Rimmon a man of Benjamin from
Beeroth ([g]for Beeroth also is counted part of
Benjamin; [3] [h]the Beerothites fled [i]to Gittaim
and have been sojourners there to this day).

[4] [j]Jonathan, the son of Saul, had a son who was
crippled in his feet. He was five years old when
the news about Saul and Jonathan [k]came from
Jezreel, and his nurse took him up and fled,
and as she fled in her haste, he fell and became
lame. And his name was Mephibosheth.

[5] Now the sons of Rimmon the Beerothite,
Rechab and Baanah, set out, and about the
heat of the day they came to the house of Ish-
bosheth as he was taking his noonday rest.
[6] And they came into the midst of the house
as if to get wheat, and they stabbed him [l]in
the stomach. Then Rechab and Baanah his
brother escaped.[1] [7] When they came into the
house, as he lay on his bed in his bedroom,
they struck him and put him to death and
beheaded him. They took his head and went
by the way of [m]the Arabah all night, [8] and
brought the head of Ish-bosheth to David at
Hebron. And they said to the king, "Here is
the head of Ish-bosheth, the son of Saul, your
enemy, [n]who sought your life. The LORD has
avenged my lord the king this day on Saul

[1] Septuagint *And behold, the doorkeeper of the house had been cleaning wheat, but she grew drowsy and slept. So Rechab and Baanah his brother slipped in*

25 [o] See 1 Sam. 29:6 **27** [p] 1 Kgs. 2:5, 32; [ch. 20:9, 10] [q] See ch. 2:23 **29** [r] See ch. 1:16 [s] Lev. 15:2 [t] Lev. 14:2 **30** [u] ch. 2:23 **31** [v] See Josh. 7:6 [w] Gen. 37:34; 1 Kgs. 20:31 **33** [x] [ch. 1:17; 2 Chr. 35:25] [y] [Eccles. 2:16] [z] ch. 13:12, 13 **35** [a] ch. 12:17 [b] See Ruth 1:17 [c] [ch. 1:12] **39** [d] [ch. 16:10; 19:22] [e] [Ps. 28:4; 2 Tim. 4:14]
Chapter 4 **1** [f] Ezra 4:4; Isa. 13:7; Jer. 6:24 **2** [g] Josh. 18:25 **3** [h] [1 Sam. 31:7] [i] Neh. 11:33 **4** [j] ch. 9:3, 6 [k] 1 Sam. 29:1, 11 **6** [l] See ch. 2:23 **7** [m] ch. 2:29; See Deut. 1:1 **8** [n] 1 Sam. 19:10, 11; 23:15

and on his offspring." 9 But David answered Rechab and Baanah his brother, the sons of Rimmon the Beerothite, [o]"As the LORD lives, [p]who has redeemed my life out of every adversity, 10 [q]when one told me, 'Behold, Saul is dead,' and thought he was bringing good news, [r]I seized him and killed him at Ziklag, which was the reward I gave him for his news. 11 How much more, when wicked men have killed a righteous man in his own house on his bed, shall I not now [s]require his blood at your hand and destroy you from the earth?" 12 And David commanded his young men, and they killed them and cut off their hands and feet and hanged them beside the pool at Hebron. But they took the head of Ish-bosheth and buried it [t]in the tomb of Abner at Hebron.

David Anointed King of Israel

5 Then all the tribes of Israel [u]came to David at Hebron and said, "Behold, [v]we are your bone and flesh. 2 In times past, when Saul was king over us, [w]it was you who led out and brought in Israel. And the LORD said to you, [x]'You shall be shepherd of my people Israel, and you shall be prince[1] over Israel.'" 3 So all the elders of Israel came to the king at Hebron, [y]and King David made a covenant with them at Hebron [z]before the LORD, and they anointed David king over Israel. 4 David was thirty years old when he began to reign, and [a]he reigned forty years. 5 [a]At Hebron he reigned over Judah [b]seven years and six months, and at Jerusalem he reigned over all Israel and Judah thirty-three years.[2]

6 [c]And the king and his men went to Jerusalem [d]against the Jebusites, the inhabitants of the land, who said to David, "You will not come in here, but the blind and the lame will ward you off"—thinking, "David cannot come in here." 7 Nevertheless, David took the stronghold of Zion, [e]that is, the city of David. 8 And David said on that day, "Whoever would strike the Jebusites, let him get up the water shaft to attack 'the lame and the blind,' who are hated by David's soul." Therefore it is said, "The blind and the lame shall not come into the house." 9 And David lived in the stronghold and called it [e]the city of David. And David built the city all around from the [f]Millo inward. 10 And David became greater and greater, for the LORD, the God of hosts, was with him.

11 [g]And [h]Hiram king of Tyre sent messengers to David, and cedar trees, also carpenters and masons who built David a house. 12 And David knew that the LORD had established him king over Israel, and that he had exalted his kingdom for the sake of his people Israel.

13 And David took more [i]concubines and wives from Jerusalem, after he came from Hebron, and more sons and daughters were born to David. 14 [j]And these are the names of

[1] Or *leader* [2] Dead Sea Scroll lacks verses 4–5

9[o] See Ruth 3:13 [p]1 Kgs. 1:29
10[q] See ch. 1:4-10 [r]ch. 1:15
11[s] [Gen. 9:5, 6]
12[t] ch. 3:32
Chapter 5
1[u] For ver. 1-3, see 1 Chr. 11:1-3 [v]See Gen. 29:14
2[w] [1 Sam. 18:13] [x]ch. 7:7; 1 Chr. 17:6; Ps. 78:71, 72; [Matt. 2:6]
3[y] ch. 3:12, 13, 21; [2 Kgs. 11:17] [z]Judg. 11:11; 1 Sam. 23:18
4[a] 1 Kgs. 2:11; 1 Chr. 3:4; 29:27
5[a] [See ver. 4 above] [b]ch. 2:11
6[c] For ver. 6-10, see 1 Chr. 11:4-9 [d]Judg. 19:11; [Josh. 15:63; Judg. 1:21]
7[e] ch. 6:12, 16
9[e] [See ver. 7 above] [f]1 Kgs. 9:15, 24; 11:27; 2 Kgs. 12:20; 2 Chr. 32:5
11[g] For ver. 11-25, see 1 Chr. 14:1-16 [h]1 Kgs. 5; 6
13[i] [1 Chr. 3:9]
14[j] [1 Chr. 3:5-8]

5:6–6:23 After years of struggle and waiting, David has "arrived." Indeed, he has become "greater and greater, for the LORD, the God of hosts, was with him" (5:10). Apart from one reference to the young Samuel (1 Sam. 3:19), it is of David alone in the books of Samuel that we hear that "the LORD was with him" (1 Sam. 16:18; 18:14, 28). David is indeed the "man of God's own choosing" or, as the phrase is more traditionally rendered, a "man after God's own heart" (cf. 1 Sam. 13:14). Saul, by contrast, slighted God repeatedly, until the "Spirit of the LORD departed" to be replaced by a "harmful spirit from the LORD" (1 Sam. 16:14). Thereafter, it might well be said of Saul, as it was in fact said of Nabal, that "folly [was] with him" (1 Sam. 25:25). To grieve the Spirit of God is to divorce oneself from the source of wisdom and blessing (Isa. 63:10; Eph. 4:30; James 1:17).

David is going from strength to strength, because the Lord is with him. Among David's successes in this section are the capture of Jerusalem from Jebusite control to become his capital city (2 Sam. 5:6–9); the final defeat of the long-time archenemy of the people of God, the Philistines (5:17–25); and the eventually successful bringing of the ark, the symbol of God's presence, into the city of Jerusalem. Successes all, but there are also failures. David remains fully human, and the biblical writers make no attempt to mask his flaws.

David's expression of animosity toward the "blind and the lame" (5:8) may be such a failure, unless he is simply tossing the mocking words of the Jebusites back in their faces (5:6). In any case, when the true King, the ultimate son of David, Jesus, enters Jerusalem, he comes not to curse but to heal the "blind and the lame" (Matt. 21:14).

those who were born to him in Jerusalem:
Shammua, Shobab, Nathan, Solomon, 15 Ibhar,
Elishua, Nepheg, Japhia, 16 Elishama, Eliada,
and Eliphelet.

David Defeats the Philistines

17 When the Philistines heard that David
had been anointed king over Israel, all the
Philistines went up to search for David. But
David heard of it and went down [k]to the
stronghold. 18 Now the Philistines had come
and spread out in [l]the Valley of Rephaim.
19 And David [m]inquired of the LORD, "Shall I go
up against the Philistines? Will you give them
into my hand?" And the LORD said to David,
"Go up, for I will certainly give the Philistines
into your hand." 20 And David came to Baal-
perazim, and David defeated them there.
And he said, "The LORD has broken through
my enemies before me like a breaking flood."
[n]Therefore the name of that place is called
Baal-perazim.[1] 21 And the Philistines left their
idols there, and David and his men carried
them away.
22 And the Philistines came up yet again
[o]and spread out in the Valley of Rephaim.
23 [p]And when David inquired of the LORD,
he said, "You shall not go up; go around to
their rear, and come against them opposite
the balsam trees. 24 And [q]when you hear the
sound of marching in the tops of the balsam
trees, then rouse yourself, [r]for then the LORD
has gone out before you to strike down the
army of the Philistines." 25 And David did as
the LORD commanded him, and struck down
the Philistines from Geba [s]to Gezer.

The Ark Brought to Jerusalem

6 [t]David again gathered all the chosen men
of Israel, thirty thousand. 2 And David
arose and went with all the people who were
with him from [u]Baale-judah [v]to bring up
from there the ark of God, which is called
by the name of the LORD of hosts [w]who sits
enthroned on the cherubim. 3 And they carried
the ark of God [x]on a new cart and brought
it [y]out of the house of Abinadab, which was
on the hill. And Uzzah and Ahio,[2] the sons of
Abinadab, were driving the new cart,[3] 4 with
the ark of God, and Ahio went before the ark.

Uzzah and the Ark

5 And David and all the house of Israel were
celebrating before the LORD, with [z]songs[4] and
lyres and harps and tambourines and casta-
nets and cymbals. 6 And when they came to
the threshing floor of [a]Nacon, Uzzah [b]put
out his hand to the ark of God and took hold
of it, for the oxen stumbled. 7 And the anger
of the LORD was kindled against Uzzah, and
[c]God struck him down there because of his
error, and he died there beside the ark of God.
8 And David was angry because the LORD had
broken out against Uzzah. And that place is
called Perez-uzzah[5] to this day. 9 And David
was afraid of the LORD that day, and he said,

[1] *Baal-perazim* means *lord of bursting through* [2] Or *and his brother*; also verse 4 [3] Compare Septuagint; Hebrew *the new cart, and brought it out of the house of Abinadab, which was on the hill* [4] Septuagint, 1 Chronicles 13:8; Hebrew *fir trees* [5] *Perez-uzzah* means *the breaking out against Uzzah*

Another failure may be David's acquisition of more "concubines and wives from Jerusalem" (2 Sam. 5:13; contrary to the instruction of Deut. 17:17). A most obvious failure in this section of 2 Samuel is in his transport of the ark to Jerusalem. The move was right in intention but wrong in execution. The ark was to be carried (Ex. 25:12–14; Num. 4:5–6, 15), so to place it on a cart, in neglect of the specific divine instruction, proved a costly mistake (2 Sam. 6:6–8). Even the best of intentions become presumption when the word of God is neglected. And finally, there is the matter of Michal. A true daughter of Saul, she cares little for David's unguarded display of love and loyalty for God—far too undignified! David's abandon in caring more for God's honor than his own is laudable. But what of his sharp response to Michal's criticism? Might this have been the place for a soft answer (Prov. 15:1), rather than a sarcastic recasting of Michal's comment about the servant girls (cf. 2 Sam. 6:20 and 22)? And whose decision was Michal's perpetual childlessness (6:23), the Lord's or David's? And beyond this portion of 2 Samuel, further and more devastating failures await (ch. 11).

David was no cardboard saint, but a flesh-and-blood, flawed man of deep faith. The good news for other flawed people of faith is that it is precisely with such people that God chooses to build his kingdom. Ultimately this is the case only because the true and final son of David took the punishment for all the flaws of his people, so that now all that qualifies us to be used of God is contrite acknowledgment of those flaws and trust in Christ (Isa. 66:1–2; Luke 18:9–14).

17 [k]ch. 23:14; 1 Sam. 22:4, 5
18 [l]ver. 22; ch. 23:13; Josh. 15:8; 18:16; [Josh. 17:15]
19 [m]See ch. 2:1
20 [n]Isa. 28:21
22 [o]ver. 18
23 [p]See 1 Sam. 22:10
24 [q][2 Kgs. 7:6] [r][Judg. 4:14]
25 [s]Josh. 10:33

Chapter 6
1 [t]For ver. 1-11, see 1 Chr. 13:6-14
2 [u]Josh. 15:9, 60 [v]2 Chr. 1:4 [w]Ex. 25:22; 1 Sam. 4:4; Ps. 80:1
3 [x][1 Sam. 6:7] [y][1 Sam. 7:1]
5 [z][1 Chr. 13:8]; See Ps. 150:3-5
6 [a][1 Chr. 13:9] [b][Num. 4:15; 1 Chr. 15:2]
7 [c][1 Sam. 6:19]

"How can the ark of the LORD come to me?" 10 So David was not willing to take the ark of the LORD into the city of David. But David took it aside [d]to the house of Obed-edom the Gittite. 11 And the ark of the LORD remained in the house of Obed-edom the Gittite three months, [e]and the LORD blessed Obed-edom and all his household.

12 And it was told King David, "The LORD has blessed the household of Obed-edom and all that belongs to him, because of the ark of God." [f]So David went and brought up the ark of God from the house of Obed-edom [g]to the city of David with rejoicing. 13 And when [h]those who bore the ark of the LORD had gone six steps, [i]he sacrificed an ox and a fattened animal. 14 And David [j]danced before the LORD with all his might. And David was [k]wearing a linen ephod. 15 So David and all the house of Israel brought up the ark of the LORD with shouting and with the sound of the horn.

David and Michal

16 As the ark of the LORD came into the city of David, Michal the daughter of Saul looked out of the window and saw King David leaping and dancing before the LORD, and she despised him in her heart. 17 And they brought in the ark of the LORD and set it [l]in its place, inside the tent that David had pitched for it. [m]And David offered burnt offerings and peace offerings before the LORD. 18 And when David had finished offering the burnt offerings and the peace offerings, [n]he blessed the people in the name of the LORD of hosts 19 and distributed among all the people, the whole multitude of Israel, both men and women, a cake of bread, a portion of meat,[1] and a cake of raisins to each one. [o]Then all the people departed, each to his house.

20 And David returned to bless his household. But Michal the daughter of Saul came out to meet David and said, "How the king of Israel honored himself today, [p]uncovering himself today before the eyes of his servants' female servants, as one of the [q]vulgar fellows shamelessly uncovers himself!" 21 And David said to Michal, "It was before the LORD, [r]who chose me above your father and above all his house, to appoint me as prince[2] over Israel, the people of the LORD—and I will celebrate before the LORD. 22 I will make myself yet more contemptible than this, and I will be abased in your[3] eyes. But by the female servants of whom you have spoken, by them I shall be held in honor." 23 And Michal the daughter of Saul had no child to the day of her death.

The LORD's Covenant with David

7 [s]Now when the king lived in his house and the LORD [t]had given him rest from all his surrounding enemies, 2 the king said to [u]Nathan the prophet, "See now, I dwell [v]in a house of cedar, but the ark of God dwells [w]in a tent." 3 And Nathan said to the king, [x]"Go, do all that is in your heart, for the LORD is with you."

4 But that same night the word of the LORD came to Nathan, 5 "Go and tell my servant David, 'Thus says the LORD: [y]Would you build me a house to dwell in? 6 I have not lived in a house [z]since the day I brought up the people of Israel from Egypt to this day, but I have been moving about [a]in a tent for my dwelling. 7 In all places where [b]I have moved with all the people of Israel, did I speak a word with [c]any of the judges[4] of Israel, whom I commanded

[1] Vulgate; the meaning of the Hebrew term is uncertain [2] Or *leader* [3] Septuagint; Hebrew *my* [4] Compare 1 Chronicles 17:6; Hebrew *tribes*

10[d] [1 Chr. 15:25]
11[e] 1 Chr. 26:5
12[f] For ver. 12-19, see 1 Chr. 15:25–16:3 [g] [1 Kgs. 8:1]
13[h] [Num. 4:15; 7:9; Josh. 3:3; 1 Chr. 15:2, 15] [i] [1 Kgs. 8:5]
14[j] [Ex. 15:20; Ps. 30:11; 150:4] [k] 1 Sam. 2:18
17[l] [1 Chr. 15:1; 2 Chr. 1:4; Ps. 132:8] [m] [1 Kgs. 8:5, 62, 63]
18[n] [1 Kgs. 8:14, 55]
19[o] 1 Chr. 16:43
20[p] ver. 14, 16; [1 Sam. 19:24] [q] Judg. 9:4
21[r] 1 Sam. 13:14; 15:28

Chapter 7
1[s] For ver. 1-29, see 1 Chr. 17:1-27 [t] See Josh. 11:23
2[u] ver. 17; ch. 12:1 [v] ch. 5:11

7:1–29 Well settled in his own "house" (palace), David decides it is high time that he build a "house" (temple) for the Lord (vv. 1–2). It seems such a good idea that the prophet Nathan readily agrees (v. 3). But the Lord, whose thoughts and ways are different and higher than ours (cf. Isa. 55:8–9), has a very different building plan in mind. David is not to build a house for God (2 Sam. 7:5). Rather, the Lord will build a house (dynasty/kingdom) for David. And what a house it will be, a house and kingdom "made sure forever before me" (v. 16). Even David's sinful descendants will not derail God's grand design (v. 14): "Your throne shall be established forever" (v. 16). Stunned, David lays aside his own blueprint and simply sits in the presence of the Lord (v. 18), marveling at the amazing plan the Lord has just unrolled before him. How easily our imaginations can be captured by and our energies exhausted by what we want to build for God, when what he really wants is for us to sit attentively, witnessing what he is building so that we may marvel and give him thanks!

[w] Ex. 26:1 **3**[x] 1 Kgs. 8:17, 18; 1 Chr. 22:7; 28:2; [Acts 7:46] **5**[y] 1 Kgs. 5:3; 8:19; 1 Chr. 22:8; 28:3 **6**[z] 1 Kgs. 8:16 [a] Ex. 40:18, 19, 34 **7**[b] Lev. 26:11, 12; Deut. 23:14 [c] [1 Chr. 17:6]

[d]to shepherd my people Israel, saying, "Why have you not built me a house of cedar?"' 8 Now, therefore, thus you shall say to my servant David, 'Thus says the LORD of hosts, [e]I took you from the pasture, from following the sheep, that you should be prince[1] over my people Israel. 9 [f]And I have been with you wherever you went and have cut off all your enemies from before you. And I will make for you a great name, like the name of the great ones of the earth. 10 And I will appoint a place for my people Israel [g]and will plant them, so that they may dwell in their own place [h]and be disturbed no more. [i]And violent men shall afflict them no more, as formerly, 11 [j]from the time that I appointed judges over my people Israel. And [k]I will give you rest from all your enemies. Moreover, the LORD declares to you that [l]the LORD will make you a house. 12 [m]When your days are fulfilled and [n]you lie down with your fathers, [o]I will raise up your offspring after you, who shall come from your body, and I will establish his kingdom. 13 [p]He shall build a house for my name, and [q]I will establish the throne of his kingdom forever. 14 [r]I will be to him a father, and he shall be to me a son. When he commits iniquity, [s]I will discipline him with the rod of men, with the stripes of the sons of men, 15 [s]but my steadfast love will not depart from him, [t]as I took it from Saul, whom I put away from before you. 16 [u]And your house and your kingdom shall be made sure forever before me.[2] [u]Your throne shall be established forever.'" 17 In accordance with all these words, and in accordance with all this vision, Nathan spoke to David.

David's Prayer of Gratitude

18 Then King David went in and sat before the LORD and said, [v]"Who am I, O Lord GOD, and what is my house, that you have brought me thus far? 19 And yet this was a small thing in your eyes, O Lord GOD. [w]You have spoken also of your servant's house for a great while to come, and this is instruction for mankind, O Lord GOD! 20 And what more can David say to you? [x]For you know your servant, O Lord GOD! 21 Because of your promise, and according to your own heart, you have brought about all this greatness, to make your servant know it. 22 [y]Therefore you are great, O LORD God. [z]For there is none like you, and there is no God besides you, according to all that we have heard with our ears. 23 [a]And who is like your people Israel, the one nation on earth whom God went to redeem to be his people, making himself a name [b]and doing for them[3] great and awesome things by driving out[4] before your people, whom [c]you redeemed for yourself from Egypt, a nation and its gods? 24 [d]And you established for yourself your people Israel to be your people forever. And you, O LORD, became their God. 25 And now, O LORD God, confirm forever the word that you have spoken concerning your servant and concerning his house, and do as you have spoken. 26 And

[1] Or *leader* [2] Septuagint; Hebrew *you* [3] With a few Targums, Vulgate, Syriac; Hebrew *you* [4] Septuagint (compare 1 Chronicles 17:21); Hebrew *for your land*

Against the backdrop of this marvelous promise of an enduring Davidic kingdom, subsequent historical events caused angst among the people of God. The division of the united kingdom, then the Assyrian conquest of the northern kingdom, then finally the fall of the southern kingdom and the Babylonian exile all seemed to call into question God's grand design for the house of David. Events in our own lives can sometimes cause us to wonder if God is as good as his promises. But, as noted, God's thoughts and ways are different and higher than ours. From our post–New Testament perspective, we can now see that "all the promises of God find their Yes" in Jesus Christ (2 Cor. 1:20)! It is he, "the Son of the Most High," who is on "the throne of his father David"; "of his kingdom there will be no end" (Luke 1:32–33; cf. Isa. 9:1–7; Luke 1:69–70; Acts 2:30–31; 13:22–23; Rom. 1:1–4; 2 Tim. 2:8; Rev. 22:16). When the circumstances of life tempt us to become anxious, that is the time to join David in his simple, profound confession: "O Lord GOD, you are God, and your words are true" (2 Sam. 7:28)!

In the amazing promise to David in 2 Samuel 7, the earlier promise to Abraham (Gen. 12:1–3) is gathered up and refocused. And in a far grander sense all these promises are gathered up and finally fulfilled in Jesus, Son of David and Son of God. The promises of 2 Samuel 7 are finally clinched in the Son of David who will indeed reign forever.

7 [d]See ch. 5:2
8 [e]1 Sam. 16:11; Ps. 78:70
9 [f]ch. 5:10; 8:6, 14; 1 Sam. 18:14
10 [g]Ps. 44:2; 80:8; Jer. 24:6; Amos 9:15 [h]2 Kgs. 21:8 [i][Ps. 89:22]
11 [j]See Judg. 2:14-16; 1 Sam. 12:9-11 [k]ver. 1; See Josh. 11:23 [l]ver. 27; 1 Kgs. 11:38; [Ex. 1:21; 1 Sam. 2:35]
12 [m][1 Kgs. 2:1] [n]1 Kgs. 1:21; 2:10; Acts 13:36; [Deut. 31:16] [o]1 Kgs. 8:20; Ps. 132:11
13 [p]1 Kgs. 5:5; 6:12; 8:19; 1 Chr. 22:10; 28:6 [q]ver. 16; Ps. 89:4, 29, 36, 37
14 [r]Ps. 89:26, 27; Cited Heb. 1:5 [s]Ps. 89:32, 33
15 [s][See ver. 14 above] [t]1 Sam. 15:23, 28; [1 Kgs. 11:13, 34]
16 [u]ver. 13; Ps. 89:36, 37; [Luke 1:33]
18 [v][Gen. 32:10]
19 [w]ver. 12, 13; 1 Chr. 17:17
20 [x]See Ps. 139:1-4
22 [y]1 Chr. 16:25; 2 Chr. 2:5 [z]Ex. 15:11; Deut. 3:24; Ps. 86:8; 89:6, 8; Isa. 45:5; Jer. 10:6 **23** [a]Deut. 4:7, 34; 33:29; Ps. 147:20 [b]Deut. 10:21 [c]Deut. 9:26; Neh. 1:10 **24** [d]ver. 13, 16, 26; Deut. 26:18

your name will be magnified forever, saying,
'The LORD of hosts is God over Israel,' and
the house of your servant David will be established before you. 27 For you, O LORD of hosts,
the God of Israel, have made this revelation to
your servant, saying, 'I will build you a house.'
Therefore your servant has found courage to
pray this prayer to you. 28 And now, O Lord
GOD, you are God, and [e]your words are true,
and you have promised this good thing to
your servant. 29 Now therefore may it please
you to bless the house of your servant, so that
it may continue forever before you. For you,
O Lord GOD, have spoken, [f]and with your
blessing shall the house of your servant be
blessed forever."

David's Victories

8 [g]After this David defeated the Philistines
and subdued them, and David took
[h]Metheg-ammah out of the hand of the
Philistines.

2 [i]And he defeated Moab and he measured
them with a line, making them lie down on
the ground. Two lines he measured to be put
to death, and one full line to be spared. And
the Moabites [j]became servants to David and
[k]brought tribute.

3 David also defeated [l]Hadadezer the son of
Rehob, king of [m]Zobah, as he went to restore
his power at the river Euphrates. 4 [n]And David
took from him 1,700 horsemen, and 20,000
foot soldiers. And David [o]hamstrung all the
chariot horses but left enough for 100 chariots. 5 [p]And when the [q]Syrians of Damascus
came to help [l]Hadadezer king of [m]Zobah,
David struck down 22,000 men of the
Syrians. 6 Then David put garrisons in Aram
of Damascus, and the Syrians [r]became servants to David and brought tribute. [s]And the
LORD gave victory to David wherever he went.
7 And David took [t]the shields of gold that
were carried by the servants of Hadadezer
and brought them to Jerusalem. 8 And from
Betah and from Berothai, cities of Hadadezer,
King David took very much bronze.

9 When Toi king of [u]Hamath heard that
David had defeated the whole army of
Hadadezer, 10 Toi sent his son Joram to King
David, to ask about his health and to bless him
because he had fought against Hadadezer and
defeated him, for Hadadezer had often been
at war with Toi. And Joram brought with
him articles of silver, of gold, and of bronze.
11 [v]These also King David dedicated to the
LORD, together with the silver and gold that
he dedicated from all the nations he subdued,
12 from Edom, [w]Moab, [x]the Ammonites, [y]the
Philistines, [z]Amalek, and from the spoil of
Hadadezer the son of Rehob, king of [m]Zobah.

13 And David made a name for himself when
he returned from striking down 18,000
Edomites in [a]the Valley of Salt. 14 Then he put
garrisons in Edom; throughout all Edom he
put garrisons, [b]and all the Edomites became
David's servants. And the LORD gave victory to
David wherever he went.

David's Officials

15 So David reigned over all Israel. And
David administered justice and equity to all
his people. 16 [c]Joab the son of Zeruiah was
over the army, and [d]Jehoshaphat the son of
Ahilud was recorder, 17 and [e]Zadok the son
of Ahitub and Ahimelech the son of Abiathar
were priests, and [f]Seraiah was secretary, 18 and

8:1–10:19 As a first indication that God's building plan (ch. 7) for the house of David is on track, chapter 8 summarizes his many past victories: "the LORD gave victory to David wherever he went" (8:14). The Lord gives, and David gratefully gives back, dedicating to the Lord silver and gold "from all the nations he subdued" (8:11). A further indication that the building plan is on track is that David uses his royal power not for self-aggrandizement but to provide "justice and equity to all his people" (8:15). Even to the unlikely, David extends grace: to the crippled grandson of Saul (ch. 9) and to the foolish son of the Ammonite king, Nahash (ch. 10). The former, Mephibosheth, gratefully receives David's generosity, while the latter, suspicious and cynical, rebuffs David's attempted kindness, and suffers the consequences.

Two key gospel truths are reflected in these episodes from the reign of David, the king anointed to represent God to his people. First, as recipients of God's free grace, we are called to extend grace freely to others: "you received without paying; give without pay" (Matt. 10:8). Secondly, grace is a gift offered, with no condition imposed, but to reject the King's offer of grace is to incur his wrath (John 3:36).

28 [e] John 17:17
29 [f] ch. 22:51; Ps. 89:28, 29
Chapter 8
1 [g] For ver. 1-18, see 1 Chr. 18:1-17; Ps. 60 [h] [1 Chr. 18:1]
2 [i] Num. 24:17 [j] ver. 6, 14; [Ps. 60:8] [k] [1 Sam. 10:27; 2 Kgs. 17:3; Ps. 72:10]
3 [l] [ch. 10:16, 19; 1 Chr. 18:3] [m] ch. 10:6; 1 Sam. 14:47; 1 Kgs. 11:23
4 [n] [1 Chr. 18:4] [o] See Josh. 11:6
5 [p] [1 Kgs. 11:23-25] [q] See Josh. 11:6 [l] [See ver. 3 above] [m] [See ver. 3 above]
6 [r] ver. 2, 14 [s] ver. 14
7 [t] [2 Kgs. 11:10; 2 Chr. 23:9; Song 4:4]
9 [u] 1 Kgs. 8:65; 2 Kgs. 18:34
11 [v] 1 Kgs. 7:51; 1 Chr. 26:26
12 [w] ver. 2 [x] ch. 10:14; 12:30 [y] See ch. 5:17-25 [z] 1 Sam. 30:20 [m] [See ver. 3 above] **13** [a] 2 Kgs. 14:7; [Josh. 15:62] **14** [b] Gen. 25:23; 27:29, 37, 40; Num. 24:18 **16** [c] For ver. 16-18, see ch. 20:23-26 [d] 1 Kgs. 4:3 **17** [e] 1 Chr. 24:3, 6 [f] [1 Chr. 18:16]

[g]Benaiah the son of Jehoiada was over[1] the
[h]Cherethites and the Pelethites, and David's
sons were priests.

David's Kindness to Mephibosheth

9 And David said, "Is there still anyone left
of the house of Saul, that I may [i]show him
kindness for Jonathan's sake?" 2 Now there was
a servant of the house of Saul whose name
was [j]Ziba, and they called him to David. And
the king said to him, "Are you Ziba?" And he
said, "I am your servant." 3 And the king said,
"Is there not still someone of the house of
Saul, that I may show [k]the kindness of God
to him?" Ziba said to the king, "There is still
a son of [l]Jonathan; he is crippled in his feet."
4 The king said to him, "Where is he?" And
Ziba said to the king, "He is in the house of
[m]Machir the son of Ammiel, at Lo-debar."
5 Then King David sent and brought him
from the house of Machir the son of Ammiel,
at Lo-debar. 6 And [n]Mephibosheth the son of
Jonathan, son of Saul, came to David and fell
on his face and paid homage. And David said,
"Mephibosheth!" And he answered, "Behold,
I am your servant." 7 And David said to him,
"Do not fear, [i]for I will show you kindness for
the sake of your father Jonathan, and I will
restore to you all the land of Saul your father,
and [o]you shall eat at my table always." 8 And he
paid homage and said, "What is your servant,
that you should show regard for [p]a dead dog
such as I?"

9 Then the king called Ziba, Saul's servant,
and said to him, "All that belonged to Saul
and to all his house I have given to your
master's grandson. 10 And you and your sons
and your servants shall till the land for him
and shall bring in the produce, that your
master's grandson may have bread to eat.
But Mephibosheth your master's grandson
[o]shall always eat at my table." Now Ziba had
[q]fifteen sons and twenty servants. 11 Then
Ziba said to the king, "According to all that
my lord the king commands his servant, so
will your servant do." So Mephibosheth [o]ate
at David's[2] table, like one of the king's sons.
12 And Mephibosheth had a young son, [r]whose
name was Mica. And all who lived in Ziba's
house became Mephibosheth's servants. 13 So
Mephibosheth lived in Jerusalem, for [o]he ate
always at the king's table. Now [l]he was lame
in both his feet.

David Defeats Ammon and Syria

10 [s]After this the king of the Ammonites
died, and Hanun his son reigned in
his place. 2 And David said, "I will deal loyally[3] with Hanun the son of [t]Nahash, as his
father dealt loyally with me." So David sent
by his servants to console him concerning his
father. And David's servants came into the
land of the Ammonites. 3 But the princes of
the Ammonites said to Hanun their lord, "Do
you think, because David has sent comforters
to you, that he is honoring your father? Has
not David sent his servants to you to search
the city and to spy it out and to overthrow it?"
4 So Hanun took David's servants and shaved
off half the beard of each and cut off their garments in the middle, [u]at their hips, and sent
them away. 5 When it was told David, he sent to
meet them, for the men were greatly ashamed.
And the king said, "Remain at Jericho until
your beards have grown and then return."

6 When the Ammonites saw that they had
become a stench to David, the Ammonites sent
and hired the Syrians of [v]Beth-rehob, and [w]the
Syrians of Zobah, 20,000 foot soldiers, and
the king of [x]Maacah with 1,000 men, and the
men of [y]Tob, 12,000 men. 7 And when David
heard of it, he sent Joab and all the host of [z]the
mighty men. 8 And the Ammonites came out
and drew up in battle array at the entrance
of the gate, and [w]the Syrians of Zobah and of
Rehob and [y]the men of Tob and Maacah were
by themselves in the open country.

9 When Joab saw that the battle was set
against him both in front and in the rear,
he chose some of the best men of Israel and
arrayed them against the Syrians. 10 The rest
of his men he put in the charge of Abishai
his brother, and he arrayed them against the
Ammonites. 11 And he said, "If the Syrians are
too strong for me, then you shall help me, but
if the Ammonites are too strong for you, then
I will come and help you. 12 [a]Be of good courage, and [b]let us be courageous for our people,
and for the cities of our God, and [c]may the
LORD do what seems good to him." 13 So Joab

[1] Compare 20:23, 1 Chronicles 18:17, Syriac, Targum, Vulgate; Hebrew lacks *was over* [2] Septuagint; Hebrew *my* [3] Or *kindly*; twice in this verse

18 [g]1 Kgs. 4:4; [ch. 23:20-23] [h]ch. 15:18; 20:7; 1 Sam. 30:14; 1 Kgs. 1:38 **Chapter 9** **1** [i]1 Sam. 18:3; 20:14, 15, 42 **2** [j]ch. 16:1-4; 19:17, 29 **3** [k]1 Sam. 20:14 [l]ch. 4:4 **4** [m]ch. 17:27 **6** [n]ch. 16:4; 19:24, 25, 30; 21:7; [1 Chr. 8:34; 9:40] **7** [i][See ver. 1 above] [o]ch. 19:28; 1 Kgs. 2:7; [2 Kgs. 25:29] **8** [p]ch. 16:9; 1 Sam. 24:14 **10** [o][See ver. 7 above] [q]ch. 19:17 **11** [o][See ver. 7 above] **12** [r]1 Chr. 8:34 **13** [o][See ver. 7 above] [l][See ver. 3 above] **Chapter 10** **1** [s]For ver. 1-19, see 1 Chr. 19:1-19 **2** [t]1 Sam. 11:1 **4** [u][Isa. 20:4] **6** [v]Judg. 18:28 [w]ch. 8:3, 5 [x][Josh. 13:11, 13] [y]Judg. 11:3, 5 **7** [z]ch. 23:8 **8** [w][See ver. 6 above] [y][See ver. 6 above] **12** [a]See Deut. 31:6 [b]1 Sam. 4:9; [1 Cor. 16:13] [c]1 Sam. 3:18

and the people who were with him drew
near to battle against the Syrians, and they
fled before him. 14 And when the Ammonites
saw that the Syrians fled, they likewise fled
before Abishai and entered the city. Then
Joab returned from fighting against the
Ammonites and came to Jerusalem.
15 But when the Syrians saw that they had
been defeated by Israel, they gathered themselves together. 16 And Hadadezer sent and
brought out the Syrians who were beyond
[d]the Euphrates.[1] They came to Helam, with
[e]Shobach the commander of the army of
Hadadezer at their head. 17 And when it was
told David, he gathered all Israel together and
crossed the Jordan and came to Helam. The
Syrians arrayed themselves against David and
fought with him. 18 And the Syrians fled before
Israel, and David killed of the Syrians the men
of 700 chariots, and 40,000 horsemen, and
wounded [f]Shobach the commander of their
army, so that he died there. 19 And when all
the kings who were servants of Hadadezer
saw that they had been defeated by Israel, they
made peace with Israel [g]and became subject to
them. So the Syrians were afraid to save the
Ammonites anymore.

David and Bathsheba

11 [h, i]In the spring of the year, the time
when kings go out to battle, David
sent Joab, and his servants with him, and
all Israel. And they ravaged the Ammonites
and besieged [j]Rabbah. But David remained
at Jerusalem.
2 It happened, late one afternoon, when David
arose from his couch and was walking on [k]the
roof of the king's house, that he saw from the
roof a woman bathing; and the woman was
very beautiful. 3 And David sent and inquired
about the woman. And one said, "Is not this
[l]Bathsheba, the daughter of Eliam, the wife of
[m]Uriah the Hittite?" 4 So David sent messengers
and took her, and she came to him, and he lay
with her. ([n]Now she had been purifying herself
from her uncleanness.) Then she returned to
her house. 5 And the woman conceived, and she
sent and told David, "I am pregnant."
6 So David sent word to Joab, "Send me Uriah
the Hittite." And Joab sent Uriah to David.
7 When Uriah came to him, David asked how
Joab was doing and how the people were
doing and how the war was going. 8 Then
David said to Uriah, "Go down to your house
and [o]wash your feet." And Uriah went out of
the king's house, and there followed him a
present from the king. 9 But Uriah slept at the
door of the king's house with all the servants
of his lord, and did not go down to his house.
10 When they told David, "Uriah did not go
down to his house," David said to Uriah, "Have
you not come from a journey? Why did you
not go down to your house?" 11 Uriah said to
David, [p]"The ark and Israel and Judah dwell
in booths, and my lord Joab and [q]the servants
of my lord are camping in the open field. Shall

[1] Hebrew *the River*

16[d] [ch. 8:3] [e] [1 Chr. 19:16]
18[f] [1 Chr. 19:18]
19[g] ch. 8:6
Chapter 11
1[h] 1 Chr. 20:1 [i] 1 Kgs. 20:22, 26; 2 Chr. 36:10 [j] ch. 12:26; Deut. 3:11
2[k] See 1 Sam. 9:25
3[l] [1 Chr. 3:5] [m] ch. 23:39
4[n] Lev. 15:19, 28; 18:19
8[o] See Gen. 18:4
11[p] ch. 7:2, 6 [q] ch. 20:6; 1 Kgs. 1:33

11:1–27 There is no point in life's journey so dangerous as when one has arrived at a comfortable place and lowers one's guard. David has arrived at such a place, and his baser instincts, only hinted at here and there during the challenging wilderness years, are about to burst forth in vivid, lurid color. Strangely for the man so accustomed to praying before acting, David in this episode simply sends others to do his bidding—and his taking (first of another man's wife, then of the man's life).

Surely, David did not arise from his afternoon nap (v. 2) planning to become an adulterer, a conspirator, a murderer, and a hypocrite. Sin seldom shows itself all at once, or even as sin at all. The temptation to sin is usually more subtle than that. But once in its grip, one is taken to places one never intended to go and held longer than one ever intended to stay. In violating his position of power, David harms everyone around him, including the consciences of the messengers who do his bidding and of his coconspirator Joab (if such a conscience actually existed). The Lord, who is often elsewhere reported to be "with David," is not even mentioned until the final line of the chapter: "But the thing that David had done displeased the LORD" (v. 27).

Sin is serious, and no one is entirely out of danger. Where relational ties with God grow lax, success can lead to pride. And "pride goes before . . . a fall" (Prov. 16:18; cf. 1 Tim. 3:6). "Therefore let anyone who thinks that he stands take heed lest he fall" (1 Cor. 10:12).

I then go to my house, to eat and to drink and
to lie with my wife? As you live, and [r]as your
soul lives, I will not do this thing." 12 Then
David said to Uriah, "Remain here today also,
and tomorrow I will send you back." So Uriah
remained in Jerusalem that day and the next.
13 And David invited him, and he ate in his
presence and drank, [s]so that he made him
drunk. And in the evening he went out to lie
on his couch with [q]the servants of his lord, but
he did not go down to his house.

14 In the morning David [t]wrote a letter to
Joab and sent it by the hand of Uriah. 15 In
the letter he wrote, "Set Uriah in the forefront
of the hardest fighting, and then draw back
from him, [u]that he may be struck down, and
die." 16 And as Joab was besieging the city, he
assigned Uriah to the place where he knew
there were valiant men. 17 And the men of the
city came out and fought with Joab, and some
of the servants of David among the people
fell. Uriah the Hittite also died. 18 Then Joab
sent and told David all the news about the
fighting. 19 And he instructed the messenger, "When you have finished telling all the
news about the fighting to the king, 20 then,
if the king's anger rises, and if he says to you,
'Why did you go so near the city to fight? Did
you not know that they would shoot from
the wall? 21 [v]Who killed Abimelech the son of
Jerubbesheth? Did not a woman cast an upper
millstone on him from the wall, so that he
died at Thebez? Why did you go so near the
wall?' then you shall say, 'Your servant Uriah
the Hittite is dead also.'"

22 So the messenger went and came and told
David all that Joab had sent him to tell. 23 The
messenger said to David, "The men gained
an advantage over us and came out against
us in the field, but we drove them back to the
entrance of the gate. 24 Then the archers shot
at your servants from the wall. Some of the
king's servants are dead, and your servant
Uriah the Hittite is dead also." 25 David said
to the messenger, "Thus shall you say to Joab,
'Do not let this matter displease you, for the
sword devours now one and now another.
Strengthen your attack against the city and
overthrow it.' And encourage him."

26 When the wife of Uriah heard that Uriah
her husband was dead, she lamented over
her husband. 27 And when the mourning was
over, David sent and brought her to his house,
and [w]she became his wife and bore him a son.
But the thing that David had done displeased
the LORD.

Nathan Rebukes David

12 And the LORD sent [x]Nathan to David.
He came to him and said to him,
[y]"There were two men in a certain city, the
one rich and the other poor. 2 The rich man had
very many flocks and herds, 3 but the poor man
had nothing but one little ewe lamb, which he
had bought. And he brought it up, and it grew
up with him and with his children. It used to
eat of his morsel and drink from his cup and

The good news of this tragic chapter is that the history of God's people did not finally rest even on David. Despite being a man after God's own heart, and despite the fact that David knows how to repent sincerely in the wake of grievous sin (Psalm 51), David cannot save God's people. He too is weak. He fails. A son of David needs to come who will not fail. In Jesus Christ, this Davidic heir arrives.

12:1–31 God wants to capture hearts as well as minds. In order to elicit not just intellectual but also emotional agreement from David, the Lord sends Nathan to tell him a story. Not noticing subtleties such as the reference to the poor man's one lamb being to him like a "daughter" (Hebrew *bath*, the first element in the name Bathsheba), David is outraged by what he takes to be a criminal case requiring royal judgment. He pronounces a death sentence on the powerful culprit (v. 5).

"You are the man!" are Nathan's famous next words (v. 7). How good God is to devise means to engage the whole person through persuasion rather than simply coercing outward conformity through power. David's response, "I have sinned against the LORD" (v. 13), is profound in its simplicity. In Psalm 51, linked by its superscription to this event, David confesses, "Against you, you only, have I sinned" (51:4). But with collateral damage to so many lives, how can David say this? The simple answer is that, before lifting a hand against a fellow human being, we first shake our fist in God's face. If love of God precedes and enables love of neighbor (Luke 10:27), defiance of God precedes and enables abuse of neighbor.

11 [r]See 1 Sam. 1:26
13 [s][Gen. 19:33, 35] [q][See ver. 11 above]
14 [t]1 Kgs. 21:8, 9
15 [u]ch. 12:9
21 [v]Judg. 9:53
27 [w]ch. 12:9

Chapter 12
1 [x]ver. 7, 13, 15, 25; ch. 7:2, 4, 17; 1 Kgs. 1:10, 22, 34; 4:5; 1 Chr. 29:29; 2 Chr. 9:29 [y][ch. 14:5-7; Judg. 9:8-15]; 1 Kgs. 20:35-41

lie in his arms,[1] and it was like a daughter to him. 4 Now there came a traveler to the rich man, and he was unwilling to take one of his own flock or herd to prepare for the guest who had come to him, but he took the poor man's lamb and prepared it for the man who had come to him." 5 Then David's anger was greatly kindled against the man, and he said to Nathan, [z]"As the LORD lives, the man who has done this deserves to die, 6 and he shall restore the lamb [a]fourfold, because he did this thing, and because he had no pity."

7 Nathan said to David, "You are the man! Thus says the LORD, the God of Israel, [b]'I anointed you king over Israel, and I delivered you out of the hand of Saul. 8 And I gave you your master's house and your master's wives into your arms and gave you the house of Israel and of Judah. And if this were too little, I would add to you as much more. 9 [c]Why have you despised the word of the LORD, [d]to do what is evil in his sight? [e]You have struck down Uriah the Hittite with the sword and [f]have taken his wife to be your wife and have killed him with the sword of the Ammonites. 10 Now therefore the sword shall never depart from your house, because you have despised me and have taken the wife of Uriah the Hittite to be your wife.' 11 Thus says the LORD, 'Behold, I will raise up evil against you out of your own house. And I will take your wives before your eyes and give them to your neighbor, and he shall lie with your wives in the sight of this sun. 12 For you did it secretly, [g]but I will do this thing before all Israel and before the sun.'" 13 [h]David said to Nathan, [i]"I have sinned against the LORD." And Nathan said to David, [j]"The LORD also has put away your sin; you shall not die. 14 Nevertheless, because by this deed you have utterly [k]scorned the LORD,[2] the child who is born to you shall die." 15 Then Nathan went to his house.

David's Child Dies

And the LORD afflicted the child that Uriah's wife bore to David, and he became sick. 16 David therefore sought God on behalf of the child. And David [l]fasted and went in [m]and lay all night on the ground. 17 And the elders of his house stood beside him, to raise him from the ground, but he would not, nor did he eat food with them. 18 On the seventh day the child

[1] Hebrew *bosom*; also verse 8 [2] Masoretic Text *the enemies of the LORD*; Dead Sea Scroll *the word of the LORD*

5[z] See Ruth 3:13
6[a] [Ex. 22:1; Luke 19:8]
7[b] 1 Sam. 16:13
9[c] Num. 15:31 [d] 1 Sam. 15:19 [e] ch. 11:15, 17 [f] ch. 11:27
12[g] ch. 16:22
13[h] [1 Sam. 15:24] [i] ch. 24:10; Ps. 32:5; 51:4 [j] Ps. 32:1; Mic. 7:18; Zech. 3:4
14[k] Isa. 52:5; [Ezek. 36:20, 23; Rom. 2:24]
16[l] [1 Kgs. 21:27] [m] ch. 13:31

Sin is serious and carries consequences in its train (cf. 2 Sam. 12:10–12, 14). Sin earns the death sentence (Rom. 3:23). But the wonderful good news is that "if we confess our sins, [God] is faithful and just to forgive us our sins and to cleanse us from all unrighteousness" (1 John 1:9). "The LORD . . . has put away your sin," Nathan says to David, "you shall not die" (2 Sam. 12:13).

We struggle to see grace where Nathan promises forgiveness from the same God who disciplines the king with the death of David's son. Some explanation lies in Nathan's comment that David's sin "utterly scorned the Lord" (i.e., brought the Lord into contempt before others; see v. 14). As Israel's king, David has a special role of representing God to his people and the watching world. For David to commit such grievous sins without consequence would be to besmirch the character of God in whom all people must trust. The consequence that David experiences is not evidence of the absence of grace but of an eternal perspective whereby God enables his people to maintain their trust in his righteous character.

The difficult lesson for us is that while God's grace erases the guilt of our sin before him, there may be consequences of sin that yet occur in this temporal realm. Divine forgiveness (desiring and acting for another's ultimate good despite their guilt) is not the same as pardon from all earthly consequences; bank robbers may still need to serve prison terms even if they become believers. It also helps to have an eternal perspective in considering that David's child would still be with him and the Lord forever in the heavenly kingdom, freed of all earthly trauma (v. 23).

God's "sendings" in this episode are designed not only to bring David to his knees but to reawaken his concern for others (v. 24), his consciousness of God's love (v. 25), and his commitment to his duties (vv. 27–28). No one is beyond the reach of God's grace, no matter what they have done. The only way they can forfeit God's profound grace is either by denying their need for it or by attempting to earn it. Honest, contrite acknowledgment of failure, and looking to Christ, is all that is needed to be right with God and utterly cleansed.

died. And the servants of David were afraid
to tell him that the child was dead, for they
said, "Behold, while the child was yet alive,
we spoke to him, and he did not listen to us.
How then can we say to him the child is dead?
He may do himself some harm." 19 But when
David saw that his servants were whispering
together, David understood that the child was
dead. And David said to his servants, "Is the
child dead?" They said, "He is dead." 20 Then
David arose from the earth [n]and washed and
anointed himself and changed his clothes.
And he went into the house of the LORD [o]and
worshiped. He then went to his own house.
And when he asked, they set food before him,
and he ate. 21 Then his servants said to him,
"What is this thing that you have done? You
fasted and wept for the child while he was
alive; but when the child died, you arose and
ate food." 22 He said, "While the child was
still alive, I fasted and wept, for I said, [p]'Who
knows whether the LORD will be gracious to
me, that the child may live?' 23 But now he is
dead. Why should I fast? Can I bring him back
again? I shall go to him, [q]but he will not return
to me."

Solomon's Birth

24 Then David comforted his wife, Bathsheba,
and went in to her and lay with her, and [r]she
bore a son, and he called his name [s]Solomon.
And the LORD loved him 25 and sent a message
by Nathan the prophet. So he called his name
Jedidiah,[1] because of the LORD.

Rabbah Is Captured

26 [t]Now Joab [u]fought against [v]Rabbah of the
Ammonites and took the royal city. 27 And
Joab sent messengers to David and said, "I
have fought against Rabbah; moreover, I have
taken the city of waters. 28 Now then gather the
rest of the people together and encamp against
the city and take it, lest I take the city and it be
called by my name." 29 So David gathered all
the people together and went to Rabbah and
fought against it and took it. 30 And he took the
crown of their king from his head. The weight
of it was a talent[2] of gold, and in it was a precious stone, and it was placed on David's head.
And he brought out the spoil of the city, a very
great amount. 31 And he brought out the people
who were in it and set them to labor with saws
and iron picks and iron axes and made them
toil at[3] the brick kilns. And thus he did to all
the cities of the Ammonites. Then David and
all the people returned to Jerusalem.

Amnon and Tamar

13 Now [w]Absalom, David's son, had a beautiful sister, whose name was [x]Tamar.
And after a time Amnon, David's son, loved
her. 2 And Amnon was so tormented that he
made himself ill because of his sister Tamar,
for she was a virgin, and it seemed impossible
to Amnon to do anything to her. 3 But Amnon
had a friend, whose name was Jonadab, the
son of [y]Shimeah, David's brother. And Jonadab
was a very crafty man. 4 And he said to him,
"O son of the king, why are you so haggard
morning after morning? Will you not tell me?"
Amnon said to him, "I love Tamar, my brother
Absalom's sister." 5 Jonadab said to him, "Lie
down on your bed and pretend to be ill. And
when your father comes to see you, say to him,
'Let my sister Tamar come and give me bread
to eat, and prepare the food in my sight, that
I may see it and eat it from her hand.'" 6 So
Amnon lay down and pretended to be ill. And

[1] *Jedidiah* means *beloved of the LORD* [2] A *talent* was about 75 pounds or 34 kilograms [3] Hebrew *pass through*

13:1–14:33 Sin is indeed serious, and even when forgiven can still have crippling effects. Nathan had prophesied that David's sins of sexual abuse and murder would find their evil counterparts within his own family (12:10–12). In Amnon's rape of his half sister Tamar (13:1–19) and in Absalom's patiently plotted murder of Amnon in defense of his full sister Tamar's honor, we witness the sins of the father replicated in the lives of his sons (cf. Ex. 20:5; 34:7; Num. 14:18; Deut. 5:9).

Sin is never a private affair; it always has ripple effects (if not tidal-wave effects!), particularly within a household. When David hears of Amnon's lust-turned-to-hate crime (2 Sam. 13:15), he is "very angry" (13:21) but, apparently, does nothing. As father and as king he had a double duty to impose justice. He is similarly ineffective in dealing with Absalom, when the latter visits a vigilante justice on the scoundrel Amnon (13:28–29). The sense that David has become crippled in his fathering is reinforced by a later notice with respect to yet another son, Adonijah: "His father had never at any time displeased him by asking, 'Why have you done thus and so?'" (1 Kings 1:6).

20 [n]Ruth 3:3 [o]Job 1:20
22 [p][Jonah 3:9]
23 [q]Job 7:8-10
24 [r]Matt. 1:6 [s]1 Chr. 22:9
26 [t]For ver. 26-31, see 1 Chr. 20:1-3 [u]ch. 11:1 [v]Deut. 3:11

Chapter 13
1 [w]ch. 3:2, 3; 1 Chr. 3:2 [x]1 Chr. 3:9
3 [y]1 Chr. 2:13; [1 Sam. 16:9; 17:13]

when the king came to see him, Amnon said
to the king, "Please let my sister Tamar come
and [z]make a couple of cakes in my sight, that
I may eat from her hand."
7 Then David sent home to Tamar, saying,
"Go to your brother Amnon's house and prepare food for him." 8 So Tamar went to her
brother Amnon's house, where he was lying
down. And she took dough and kneaded it and
made cakes in his sight and baked the cakes.
9 And she took the pan and emptied it out
before him, but he refused to eat. And Amnon
said, [a]"Send out everyone from me." So everyone went out from him. 10 Then Amnon said
to Tamar, "Bring the food into the chamber,
that I may eat from your hand." And Tamar
took the cakes she had made and brought
them into the chamber to Amnon her brother.
11 But when she brought them near him to eat,
he took hold of her and said to her, "Come,
lie with me, my sister." 12 She answered him,
"No, my brother, do not violate[1] me, for [b]such
a thing is not done in Israel; do not do this
[c]outrageous thing. 13 As for me, where could
I carry my shame? And as for you, you would
be as one of [d]the outrageous fools in Israel.
Now therefore, please speak to the king, for
he will not withhold me from you." 14 But he
would not listen to her, and being stronger
than she, he violated her and lay with her.
15 Then Amnon hated her with very great
hatred, so that the hatred with which he hated
her was greater than the love with which he
had loved her. And Amnon said to her, "Get up!
Go!" 16 But she said to him, "No, my brother,
for this wrong in sending me away is greater
than the other that you did to me."[2] But he
would not listen to her. 17 He called the young
man who served him and said, "Put this
woman out of my presence and bolt the door
after her." 18 Now she was wearing [e]a long robe[3]
with sleeves, for thus were the virgin daughters of the king dressed. So his servant put her
out and bolted the door after her. 19 And Tamar
[f]put ashes on her head and [g]tore the long robe
that she wore. And [h]she laid her hand on her
head and went away, crying aloud as she went.
20 And her brother Absalom said to her, "Has
Amnon your brother been with you? Now
hold your peace, my sister. He is your brother;
do not take this to heart." So Tamar lived, a
desolate woman, in her brother Absalom's
house. 21 When King David heard of all these
things, he was very angry.[4] 22 But Absalom
spoke to Amnon [i]neither good nor bad, for
Absalom hated Amnon, because he had violated his sister Tamar.

Absalom Murders Amnon

23 After two full years Absalom had [j]sheep-
shearers at Baal-hazor, which is near Ephraim,
and Absalom invited all the king's sons. 24 And
Absalom came to the king and said, "Behold,
your servant has sheepshearers. Please let the
king and his servants go with your servant."

[1] Or *humiliate*; also verses 14, 22, 32 [2] Compare Septuagint, Vulgate; the meaning of the Hebrew is uncertain [3] Or *a robe of many colors* (compare Genesis 37:3); also verse 19 [4] Dead Sea Scroll, Septuagint add *But he would not punish his son Amnon, because he loved him, since he was his firstborn*

6 [z] Gen. 18:6
9 [a] [Gen. 45:1]
12 [b] Lev. 18:9, 11; 20:17 [c] Gen. 34:7; Judg. 19:23; 20:6
13 [d] [ch. 3:33]
18 [e] Gen. 37:3; Judg. 5:30; Ps. 45:14
19 [f] See Josh. 7:6 [g] See ch. 1:11 [h] Jer. 2:37
22 [i] Gen. 24:50; 31:24
23 [j] Gen. 31:19; 38:12, 13; 1 Sam. 25:4

David's emotions appear to be about as ambiguous as the Hebrew text describing them in 2 Sam. 13:39; does his spirit go out against Absalom, because he is angry over Amnon's death, or does it reach out to Absalom, because David is consoled concerning Amnon's death. Neither the text nor David's further actions in this section makes this very clear. After three years in exile, Absalom is finally allowed back into Jerusalem but not into the king's presence (13:38; 14:23–24). After a further two years estranged, Absalom finally manages to force a meeting with David (14:28–33). And what happens? All we read is that "the king kissed Absalom" (14:33)—no discussion of past wrongs on both sides, no forgiveness, and, as subsequent events make painfully obvious, no reconciliation.

If "two wrongs don't make a right," then wrongs upon wrongs certainly do not do so. Whatever may have contributed to David's crippling as a father (his sense of shame; his loss of the moral high ground; his inability to forgive himself, though forgiven by God), only the gospel can break the vicious cycle of alienation. The glorious truth for guilty sinners (that's all of us) is that "if anyone is in Christ, he is a new creation. The old has passed away; behold the new has come. All this is from God, who through Christ reconciled us to himself and gave us the ministry of reconciliation" (2 Cor. 5:17–18). The call, then, for saved sinners is to forget what lies behind (whether personal victories or defeats) and to press forward in the power of the Holy Spirit (cf. Phil. 3:13).

25 But the king said to Absalom, "No, my son,
let us not all go, lest we be burdensome to
you." He pressed him, but he would not go but
gave him his blessing. 26 Then Absalom said,
"If not, please let my brother Amnon go with
us." And the king said to him, "Why should
he go with you?" 27 But Absalom pressed him
until he let Amnon and all the king's sons
go with him. 28 Then Absalom commanded
his servants, "Mark when Amnon's [k]heart is
merry with wine, and when I say to you, 'Strike
Amnon,' then kill him. Do not fear; have I not
commanded you? Be courageous and be valiant." 29 So the servants of Absalom did to
Amnon as Absalom had commanded. Then
all the king's sons arose, and each mounted
his mule and fled.

30 While they were on the way, news came to
David, "Absalom has struck down all the king's
sons, and not one of them is left." 31 Then the
king arose and [l]tore his garments and [m]lay on
the earth. And all his servants who were standing by tore their garments. 32 But [n]Jonadab the
son of Shimeah, David's brother, said, "Let not
my lord suppose that they have killed all the
young men, the king's sons, for Amnon alone
is dead. For by the command of Absalom this
has been determined from the day he violated
his sister Tamar. 33 Now therefore let not my
lord the king so [o]take it to heart as to suppose
that all the king's sons are dead, for Amnon
alone is dead."

Absalom Flees to Geshur

34 [p]But Absalom fled. And the young man
who kept the watch lifted up his eyes and
looked, and behold, many people were coming from the road behind him[1] by the side of
the mountain. 35 And Jonadab said to the king,
"Behold, the king's sons have come; as your
servant said, so it has come about." 36 And as
soon as he had finished speaking, behold, the
king's sons came and lifted up their voice and
wept. And the king also and all his servants
wept very bitterly.

37 [q]But Absalom fled and went to [r]Talmai
the son of Ammihud, king of [s]Geshur. And
David mourned for his son day after day. 38 [q]So
Absalom fled and went to Geshur, and was
there three years. 39 And the spirit of the king[2]
longed to go out[3] to Absalom, because [t]he was
comforted about Amnon, since he was dead.

Absalom Returns to Jerusalem

14 Now Joab the son of Zeruiah knew [u]that
the king's heart went out to Absalom.
2 And Joab sent to [v]Tekoa and brought from
there a wise woman and said to her, "Pretend
to be a mourner and put on mourning garments. [w]Do not anoint yourself with oil, but
behave like a woman who has been mourning
many days for the dead. 3 Go to the king and
speak thus to him." So Joab [x]put the words in
her mouth.

4 When the woman of Tekoa came to the
king, [y]she fell on her face to the ground and
paid homage and said, [z]"Save me, O king."
5 And the king said to her, "What is your trouble?" She answered, [a]"Alas, I am a widow; my
husband is dead. 6 And your servant had two
sons, and they quarreled with one another in
the field. There was no one to separate them,
and one struck the other and killed him.
7 And now the whole clan has risen against
your servant, and they say, 'Give up the man
who struck his brother, that we may put him
to death for the life of his brother whom he
killed.' And so they would [b]destroy the heir
also. Thus they would quench my coal that is
left and leave to my husband neither name nor
[c]remnant on the face of the earth."

8 Then the king said to the woman, "Go to
your house, and I will give orders concerning
you." 9 And the woman of Tekoa said to the
king, [d]"On me be the guilt, my lord the king,
and on my father's house; let the king and his
throne be guiltless." 10 The king said, "If anyone says anything to you, bring him to me,
and he shall never touch you again." 11 Then
she said, "Please let the king invoke the LORD
your God, that [e]the avenger of blood kill no
more, and my son be not destroyed." He said,
[f]"As the LORD lives, [g]not one hair of your son
shall fall to the ground."

12 Then the woman said, "Please let your servant speak a word to my lord the king." He
said, "Speak." 13 And the woman said, "Why
then have you planned such a thing against
[h]the people of God? For in giving this decision the king convicts himself, inasmuch as

[1] Septuagint *the Horonaim Road* [2] Dead Sea Scroll, Septuagint; Hebrew *David* [3] Compare Vulgate *ceased to go out*

28 [k]See Judg. 19:6 **31** [l]See ch. 1:11 [m]ch. 12:16 **32** [n]ver. 3 **33** [o]ch. 19:19 **34** [p]ver. 37, 38 **37** [q]ver. 34 [r]ch. 3:3; 1 Chr. 3:2 [s]ch. 14:23, 32; 15:8 **38** [q][See ver. 37 above] **39** [t]Gen. 24:67; 38:12; [Gen. 37:35] **Chapter 14** **1** [u]ch. 13:39 **2** [v]2 Chr. 11:6; 20:20; Amos 1:1 [w][ch. 12:20; Ruth 3:3] **3** [x]ver. 19; [Ex. 4:15] **4** [y]ch. 1:2 [z]2 Kgs. 6:26 **5** [a]See ch. 12:1 **7** [b][Matt. 21:38; Mark 12:7; Luke 20:14] [c][Gen. 45:7] **9** [d]1 Sam. 25:24 **11** [e]Num. 35:19, 21; Deut. 19:12 [f]See Ruth 3:13 [g]1 Sam. 14:45; Acts 27:34 **13** [h]Judg. 20:2

the king does not bring [i]his banished one home again. 14 We must all die; we are [j]like water spilled on the ground, which cannot be gathered up again. But God will not take away life, and he devises means [k]so that the banished one will not remain an outcast. 15 Now I have come to say this to my lord the king because the people have made me afraid, and your servant thought, 'I will speak to the king; it may be that the king will perform the request of his servant. 16 For the king will hear and deliver his servant from the hand of the man who would destroy me and my son together from [l]the heritage of God.' 17 And your servant thought, 'The word of my lord the king will set me at rest,' for my lord the king is [m]like the angel of God to discern good and evil. The LORD your God be with you!"

18 Then the king answered the woman, "Do not hide from me anything I ask you." And the woman said, "Let my lord the king speak." 19 The king said, "Is the hand of Joab with you in all this?" The woman answered and said, [n]"As surely as you live, my lord the king, one cannot turn to the right hand or to the left from anything that my lord the king has said. It was your servant Joab who commanded me; [o]it was he who put all these words in the mouth of your servant. 20 In order to change the course of things your servant Joab did this. But my lord has wisdom like the wisdom of [m]the angel of God to know all things that are on the earth."

21 Then the king said to Joab, "Behold now, I grant this; go, bring back the young man Absalom." 22 And Joab fell on his face to the ground and paid homage [p]and blessed the king. And Joab said, "Today your servant knows that I have found favor in your sight, my lord the king, in that the king has granted the request of his servant." 23 So Joab arose and went to [q]Geshur and brought Absalom to Jerusalem. 24 And the king said, "Let him dwell apart in his own house; he is not to come into my presence." So Absalom lived apart in his own house and did not come into the king's presence.

25 Now in all Israel there was no one so much to be praised for his handsome appearance as Absalom. [r]From the sole of his foot to the crown of his head there was no blemish in him. 26 And when he cut the hair of his head (for at the end of every year he used to cut it; when it was heavy on him, he [s]cut it), he weighed the hair of his head, two hundred shekels[1] by the king's weight. 27 There were born [t]to Absalom three sons, and one daughter whose name was Tamar. She was a beautiful woman.

28 So Absalom lived two full years in Jerusalem, without coming into the king's presence. 29 Then Absalom sent for Joab, to send him to the king, but Joab would not come to him. And he sent a second time, but Joab would not come. 30 Then he said to his servants, "See, Joab's field is next to mine, and he has barley there; go and set it on fire." So Absalom's servants set the field on fire.[2] 31 Then Joab arose and went to Absalom at his house and said to him, "Why have your servants set my field on fire?" 32 Absalom answered Joab, "Behold, I sent word to you, 'Come here, that I may send you to the king, to ask, "Why have I come from [q]Geshur? It would be better for me to be there still." Now therefore let me go into the presence of the king, [u]and if there is guilt in me, let him put me to death.'" 33 Then Joab went to the king and told him, and he summoned Absalom. So he came to the king and bowed himself on his face to the ground before the king, and the king kissed Absalom.

Absalom's Conspiracy

15 After this Absalom [v]got himself a chariot and horses, and fifty men to run before him. 2 And Absalom used to rise early and stand beside [w]the way of the gate. And when any man had a dispute to come before

[1] A *shekel* was about 2/5 ounce or 11 grams [2] Septuagint, Dead Sea Scroll add *So Joab's servants came to him with their clothes torn, and they said to him, "The servants of Absalom have set your field on fire."*

13[i] [ch. 13:37, 38]
14[j] [1 Sam. 7:6] [k] Num. 35:15, 25, 28
16[l] See 1 Sam. 26:19
17[m] ch. 19:27; 1 Sam. 29:9
19[n] 1 Sam. 1:26 [o] ver. 3
20[m] [See ver. 17 above]
22[p] 1 Kgs. 8:66
23[q] ch. 13:38
25[r] Deut. 28:35; Job 2:7; Isa. 1:6
26[s] Ezek. 44:20
27[t] [ch. 18:18] **32**[q] [See ver. 23 above] [u] 1 Sam. 20:8 **Chapter 15** **1**[v] 1 Kgs. 1:5 **2**[w] See Ruth 4:1

15:1–18:30 Seemingly small sins of omission can spawn rather large sins of commission. The sin of commission in chapter 15 is Absalom's: an insurrection against his own father. The sins of omission, however, are arguably David's in chapters 13–14. The "kiss" of 14:33, unaccompanied by hard-but-healing conversation, clearly achieved no true reconciliation between David and Absalom. The latter, quite evidently still aggrieved that justice was never done by David in the case of Tamar (ch. 13) and unsatisfied by a mere kiss, foments a rebellion over the very issue of "justice" and steals the hearts of the people of Israel with a "kiss" (15:3–6).

the king for judgment, Absalom would call to
him and say, "From what city are you?" And
when he said, "Your servant is of such and
such a tribe in Israel," 3 Absalom would say
to him, "See, your claims are good and right,
but there is no man designated by the king
to hear you." 4 Then Absalom would say, [x]"Oh
that I were judge in the land! Then every man
with a dispute or cause might come to me,
and I would give him justice." 5 And whenever a man came near to pay homage to him,
he would put out his hand and take hold of
him and kiss him. 6 Thus Absalom did to all of
Israel who came to the king for judgment. So
Absalom stole the hearts of the men of Israel.
7 And at the end of four[1] years Absalom said
to the king, "Please let me go and pay my vow,
which I have vowed to the LORD, in Hebron.
8 For your servant [z]vowed a vow [a]while I lived
at Geshur in Aram, saying, 'If the LORD will
indeed bring me back to Jerusalem, then I will
offer worship to[2] the LORD.'" 9 The king said
to him, [b]"Go in peace." So he arose and went
to Hebron. 10 But Absalom sent secret messengers throughout all the tribes of Israel, saying,
"As soon as you hear the sound of the trumpet, then say, 'Absalom is king at Hebron!'"
11 With Absalom went two hundred men from
Jerusalem [c]who were invited guests, and they
went in their innocence and knew nothing.
12 And while Absalom was offering the sacrifices, he sent for[3] [d]Ahithophel the Gilonite,
[e]David's counselor, from his city [f]Giloh. And
the conspiracy grew strong, and the people
with Absalom [g]kept increasing.

David Flees Jerusalem

13 And a messenger came to David, saying,
[h]"The hearts of the men of Israel have gone
after Absalom." 14 Then David said to all his
servants who were with him at Jerusalem,
"Arise, and let us [i]flee, or else there will be no
escape for us from Absalom. Go quickly, lest
he overtake us quickly and bring down ruin
on us and strike the city with the edge of the
sword." 15 And the king's servants said to the
king, "Behold, your servants are ready to do
whatever my lord the king decides." 16 So the
king went out, and all his household after
him. And the king left [j]ten concubines to keep
the house. 17 And the king went out, and all
the people after him. And they halted at the
last house.
18 And [k]all his servants passed by him, and
all the Cherethites, and all the Pelethites, and
all the six hundred Gittites who had followed
him from [l]Gath, passed on before the king.
19 Then the king said to [m]Ittai the Gittite, "Why
do you also go with us? Go back and stay with

[1] Septuagint, Syriac; Hebrew *forty* [2] Or *will serve* [3] Or *sent*

In his flight from Jerusalem, David encounters both friends and foes and hears of a former friend who has become a foe (Ahithophel, 15:12; cf. the laments of Ps. 41:9; 55:12–14). Caught in a series of unfortunate events set in motion by his own sins, David at times seems disoriented—unable or unwilling, for instance, to judge between competing stories by Ziba (2 Sam. 16:1–4) and Mephibosheth (19:24–29). Through it all, however, he begins to reorient to what matters: to God (e.g., 15:25–26, 31; 16:10–12); to family, albeit tragically late (e.g., 18:5, 33); and to responsibility (e.g., 21:15). The swath of misery that sin cuts through David's family and kingdom is heart-wrenching, not least in regard to his concubines, violated (16:21–22), then isolated (20:3).

But God never abandons David. When David prays (15:31; something he is not mentioned as doing in chs. 13–14), God answers (17:14; contrast Saul's experience in 1 Sam. 28:6). David refuses to use God (contrast his return of the ark in 2 Sam. 15:25 with Israel's attempt to manipulate the ark in 1 Samuel 4) but, rather, humbly submits to whatever "seems good to [God]" (2 Sam. 15:25–26; cf. Eli in 1 Sam. 3:18). He patiently endures cursings, reasoning that God may be speaking to him something he needs to hear (2 Sam. 16:10–12).

All in all, it's a messy, costly business—events set in train by sin always are. Carelessness in the palace has landed David in the wilderness again! Only Saul's death brought his wilderness years to a close the first time. This time it is the death of his own son, Absalom. But through it all God preserves David, literally preparing "a table before" him in the wilderness (17:27–29; cf. Ps. 23:5). And God restores David to his throne, even if it includes more political turmoil and gruesome death (2 Samuel 20).

Sin is never trivial, and grace is never cheap. But God never leaves or forsakes those who are truly his. These are key gospel truths vividly illustrated by the life of David.

4 [x] Judg. 9:29
8 [z] Gen. 28:20, 21; 1 Sam. 1:11 [a] ch. 13:38
9 [b] 1 Sam. 1:17
11 [c] [1 Sam. 9:13; 16:3, 5]
12 [d] ver. 31; ch. 16:20; 17:1, 14, 23 [e] 1 Chr. 27:33; [Ps. 41:9; 55:12-14] [f] Josh. 15:51 [g] Ps. 3:1
13 [h] Judg. 9:3
14 [i] ch. 19:9
16 [j] ch. 16:21, 22; 20:3
18 [k] See ch. 8:18 [l] 1 Sam. 27:2
19 [m] ch. 18:2

the king, for you are a foreigner and also an
exile from your home. 20 You came only yesterday, and shall I today make you wander about
with us, since I go [n]I know not where? Go back
and take your brothers with you, and may the
LORD show[1] steadfast love and faithfulness
to you." 21 But Ittai answered the king, [o]"As
the LORD lives, and as my lord the king lives,
[p]wherever my lord the king shall be, whether
for death or for life, there also will your servant be." 22 And David said to Ittai, "Go then,
pass on." So Ittai the Gittite passed on with all
his men and all the little ones who were with
him. 23 And all the land wept aloud as all the
people passed by, and the king crossed [q]the
brook [r]Kidron, and all the people passed on
toward [s]the wilderness.
24 And [t]Abiathar came up, and behold,
[u]Zadok came also with all the Levites, [v]bear-
ing the ark of the covenant of God. And they
set down the ark of God until the people had
all passed out of the city. 25 Then the king said
to Zadok, "Carry the ark of God back into the
city. If I find favor in the eyes of the LORD, he
will [w]bring me back and let me see both it and
his [x]dwelling place. 26 But if he says, 'I have no
[y]pleasure in you,' behold, here I am, [z]let him
do to me what seems good to him." 27 The king
also said to Zadok the priest, "Are you not a
[a]seer? Go back[2] to the city in peace, with [b]your
two sons, Ahimaaz your son, and Jonathan the
son of Abiathar. 28 See, I will wait at [c]the fords
of [s]the wilderness until word comes from you
to inform me." 29 So Zadok and Abiathar carried the ark of God back to Jerusalem, and they
remained there.
30 But David went up the ascent of the Mount
of Olives, weeping as he went, [d]barefoot and
[e]with his head covered. And all the people who
were with him covered their heads, and they
went up, [f]weeping as they went. 31 And it was
told David, "Ahithophel is among the con-
spirators with Absalom." And David said, "O
LORD, please [g]turn the counsel of Ahithophel
into foolishness."
32 While David was coming to the summit,
where God was worshiped, behold, Hushai
[h]the Archite came to meet him [i]with his coat
torn and [i]dirt on his head. 33 David said to him,
"If you go on with me, you will be [j]a burden
to me. 34 But if you return to the city and say
to Absalom, [k]'I will be your servant, O king;
as I have been your father's servant in time
past, so now I will be your servant,' then you
will defeat for me the counsel of Ahithophel.
35 Are not Zadok and Abiathar the priests
with you there? So whatever you hear from
the king's house, [l]tell it to Zadok and Abiathar
the priests. 36 Behold, [m]their two sons are
with them there, Ahimaaz, Zadok's son, and
Jonathan, Abiathar's son, [m]and by them you
shall send to me everything you hear." 37 So
Hushai, [n]David's friend, came into the city,
[o]just as Absalom was entering Jerusalem.

David and Ziba

16 When David had passed a little beyond
[p]the summit, [q]Ziba the servant of
Mephibosheth met him, with a couple of donkeys saddled, bearing two hundred loaves of
bread, [r]a hundred bunches of raisins, a hundred of summer fruits, and a skin of wine.
2 And the king said to Ziba, "Why have you
brought these?" Ziba answered, [s]"The donkeys
are for the king's household to ride on, the
bread and summer fruit for the young men to
eat, and the wine for those who [t]faint in the
wilderness to drink." 3 And the king said, "And
where is your master's son?" [u]Ziba said to the
king, "Behold, he remains in Jerusalem, for he
said, 'Today the house of Israel will give me
back the kingdom of my father.'" 4 Then the
king said to Ziba, "Behold, all that belonged
to Mephibosheth is now yours." And Ziba said,
"I pay homage; let me ever find favor in your
sight, my lord the king."

Shimei Curses David

5 When King David came to [v]Bahurim, there
came out a man of the family of the house
of Saul, whose name was [w]Shimei, the son of
Gera, and as he came [x]he cursed continually.
6 And he threw stones at David and at all the
servants of King David, and all the people
and all the mighty men were on his right
hand and on his left. 7 And Shimei said as he
[x]cursed, "Get out, get out, you man of blood,
you worthless man! 8 The LORD [y]has avenged

[1] Septuagint; Hebrew lacks *may the LORD show* [2] Septuagint *The king also said to Zadok the priest, "Look, go back*

20[n] [1 Sam. 23:13] **21**[o] See Ruth 3:13 [p] [Ruth 1:16, 17] **23**[q] 1 Kgs. 2:37; 15:13; 2 Kgs. 23:4, 6, 12 [r] [John 18:1] [s] ch. 16:2; 17:16, 29 **24**[t] Num. 4:15 [u] 1 Sam. 22:20 [v] ch. 8:17; 20:25 **25**[w] Ps. 43:3 [x] Ex. 15:13; Jer. 25:30 **26**[y] ch. 22:20; Num. 14:8; 1 Kgs. 10:9; 2 Chr. 9:8; Ps. 18:19; 22:8; Isa. 62:4 [z] 1 Sam. 3:18 **27**[a] See 1 Sam. 9:9 [b] ch. 17:17 **28**[c] ch. 17:16 [s] [See ver. 23 above] **30**[d] Isa. 20:2-4 [e] ch. 19:4; Esth. 6:12; Jer. 14:3, 4 [f] Ps. 126:6 **31**[g] ch. 16:23; 17:14, 23 **32**[h] Josh. 16:2 [i] See Josh. 7:6 **33**[j] ch. 19:35 **34**[k] ch. 16:19 **35**[l] ch. 17:15, 16 **36**[m] ch. 17:17 **37**[n] ch. 16:16; 1 Chr. 27:33 [o] ch. 16:15 **Chapter 16** **1**[p] ch. 15:30, 32 [q] See ch. 9:2-13 [r] [1 Sam. 25:18] **2**[s] [Judg. 5:10; 10:4] [t] ver. 14; ch. 17:29 **3**[u] ch. 19:26, 27 **5**[v] See ch. 3:16 [w] ch. 19:16; See 1 Kgs. 2:8, 36-46 [x] ch. 19:21 **7**[x] [See ver. 5 above] **8**[y] Judg. 9:24, 56, 57; 1 Kgs. 2:32, 33

on you all [z]the blood of the house of Saul, in whose place you have reigned, and the LORD has given the kingdom into the hand of your son Absalom. See, your evil is on you, for you are a man of blood."

9 Then Abishai the son of Zeruiah said to the king, "Why should this [a]dead dog [b]curse my lord the king? Let me go over and take off his head." 10 But the king said, [c]"What have I to do with you, [d]you sons of Zeruiah? If he is cursing because the LORD has said to him, 'Curse David,' who then shall say, 'Why have you done so?'" 11 And David said to Abishai and to all his servants, "Behold, [e]my own son seeks my life; how much more now may this Benjaminite! Leave him alone, and let him curse, for the LORD has told him to. 12 It may be that the LORD will look on the wrong done to me,[1] and that the LORD will repay me with good for his cursing today." 13 So David and his men went on the road, while Shimei went along on the hillside opposite him and [f]cursed as he went and threw stones at him and flung dust. 14 And the king, and all the people who were with him, [g]arrived weary at the Jordan.[2] And there he refreshed himself.

Absalom Enters Jerusalem

15 [h]Now Absalom and all the people, the men of Israel, came to Jerusalem, and Ahithophel with him. 16 And when Hushai the Archite, [h]David's friend, came to Absalom, Hushai said to Absalom, [i]"Long live the king! Long live the king!" 17 And Absalom said to Hushai, "Is this your loyalty to your friend? [j]Why did you not go with your friend?" 18 And Hushai said to Absalom, "No, for whom the LORD and this people and all the men of Israel have chosen, his I will be, and with him I will remain. 19 And again, [k]whom should I serve? Should it not be his son? As I have served your father, so I will serve you."

20 Then Absalom said to Ahithophel, "Give your counsel. What shall we do?" 21 Ahithophel said to Absalom, "Go in to [l]your father's concubines, whom he has left to keep the house, and all Israel will hear that you have made yourself a stench to your father, and [m]the hands of all who are with you will be strengthened." 22 So they pitched a tent for Absalom [n]on the roof. And Absalom went in to his father's concubines [o]in the sight of all Israel. 23 Now in those days the counsel that Ahithophel gave was as if one consulted the word of God; so was all the counsel of Ahithophel esteemed, [p]both by David and by Absalom.

Hushai Saves David

17 Moreover, Ahithophel said to Absalom, "Let me choose twelve thousand men, and I will arise and pursue David tonight. 2 I will come upon him while he is [q]weary and discouraged and throw him into a panic, and all the people who are with him will flee. [r]I will strike down only the king, 3 and I will bring all the people back to you as a bride comes home to her husband. You seek the life of only one man,[3] and all the people will be at peace." 4 And the advice seemed right in the eyes of Absalom and all the elders of Israel.

5 Then Absalom said, "Call [s]Hushai the Archite also, and let us hear what he has to say." 6 And when Hushai came to Absalom, Absalom said to him, "Thus has Ahithophel spoken; shall we do as he says? If not, you speak." 7 Then Hushai said to Absalom, "This time the counsel that Ahithophel has given is not good." 8 Hushai said, "You know that your father and his men are mighty men, and that they are enraged,[4] [t]like a bear robbed of her cubs in the field. Besides, your father is expert in war; he will not spend the night with the people. 9 Behold, even now he has hidden himself in one of the pits or in some other place. And as soon as some of the people fall[5] at the first attack, whoever hears it will say, 'There has been a slaughter among the people who follow Absalom.' 10 Then even the valiant man, whose heart is like the heart of a lion, will utterly [u]melt with fear, for all Israel knows that your father is a mighty man, and that those who are with him are valiant men. 11 But my counsel is that all Israel be gathered to you, [v]from Dan to Beersheba, [w]as the sand by the sea for multitude, and that you go to battle in person. 12 So we shall come upon him in some place where he is to be found, and we shall light upon him as the dew falls on the ground,

[1] Septuagint, Vulgate *will look upon my affliction* [2] Septuagint; Hebrew lacks *at the Jordan* [3] Septuagint; Hebrew *back to you. Like the return of the whole is the man whom you seek* [4] Hebrew *bitter of soul* [5] Or *And as he falls on them*

8 [z] See ch. 1:16 **9** [a] ch. 9:8; 1 Sam. 24:14; [ch. 3:8] [b] [Ex. 22:28] **10** [c] ch. 19:22 [d] See 1 Sam. 26:6 **11** [e] ch. 12:11 **13** [f] ch. 19:21 **14** [g] ver. 2 **15** [h] ch. 15:37 **16** [h] [See ver. 15 above] [i] 1 Sam. 10:24; 1 Kgs. 1:25, 39; 2 Kgs. 11:12 **17** [j] [ch. 19:25] **19** [k] ch. 15:34 **21** [l] ch. 15:16; 20:3 [m] ch. 2:7; Zech. 8:9, 13 **22** [n] See 1 Sam. 9:25 [o] ch. 12:11, 12 **23** [p] ch. 15:12 **Chapter 17** **2** [q] ch. 16:14; [Deut. 25:18] [r] [1 Kgs. 22:31] **5** [s] ch. 16:16-18 **8** [t] Prov. 17:12; Hos. 13:8 **10** [u] See Josh. 2:11 **11** [v] See ch. 3:10 [w] See Gen. 22:17

and of him and all the men with him not one
will be left. 13 If he withdraws into a city, then
all Israel will bring ropes to that city, and we
shall drag it into the valley, until not even a
pebble is to be found there." 14 And Absalom
and all the men of Israel said, "The counsel of
Hushai the Archite is better than the counsel
of Ahithophel." [x]For the LORD had ordained[1] to
defeat the good counsel of Ahithophel, so that
the LORD might bring harm upon Absalom.

15 [y]Then Hushai said to Zadok and Abiathar the priests, "Thus and so did Ahithophel
counsel Absalom and the elders of Israel, and
thus and so have I counseled. 16 Now therefore send quickly and tell David, 'Do not stay
tonight at [z]the fords of the wilderness, but by
all means pass over, lest the king and all the
people who are with him be [a]swallowed up.' "
17 Now [b]Jonathan and Ahimaaz were waiting
at [c]En-rogel. A female servant was to go and
tell them, and they were to go and tell King
David, for they were not to be seen entering
the city. 18 But a young man saw them and told
Absalom. So both of them went away quickly
and came to the house of a man at [d]Bahurim,
who had a well in his courtyard. And they
went down into it. 19 [e]And the woman took and
spread a covering over the well's mouth and
scattered grain on it, and nothing was known
of it. 20 When Absalom's servants came to the
woman at the house, they said, "Where are
Ahimaaz and Jonathan?" And the woman said
to them, "They have gone over the brook[2] of
water." And when they had sought and could
not find them, they returned to Jerusalem.

21 After they had gone, the men came up out
of the well, and went and told King David.
They said to David, [f]"Arise, and go quickly
over the water, for thus and so has Ahithophel
counseled against you." 22 Then David arose,
and all the people who were with him, and
they crossed the Jordan. By daybreak not one
was left who had not crossed the Jordan.

23 When Ahithophel saw that his counsel was
not followed, he saddled his donkey and went
off home to [g]his own city. He [h]set his house in
order and [i]hanged himself, and he died and
was buried in the tomb of his father.

24 Then David came to [j]Mahanaim. And
Absalom crossed the Jordan with all the men
of Israel. 25 Now Absalom had set [k]Amasa over
the army instead of Joab. Amasa was the son
of a man named Ithra the Ishmaelite,[3] who
had married Abigal the daughter of [l]Nahash,
sister of Zeruiah, Joab's mother. 26 And Israel
and Absalom encamped in the land of Gilead.

27 When David came to Mahanaim, [m]Shobi
the son of Nahash from [n]Rabbah of the
Ammonites, and [o]Machir the son of Ammiel
from Lo-debar, and [p]Barzillai the Gileadite
from Rogelim, 28 brought beds, basins, and
earthen vessels, wheat, barley, flour, parched
grain, beans and lentils,[4] 29 honey and curds
and sheep and cheese from the herd, for David
and the people with him to eat, for they said,
"The people are hungry and [q]weary and thirsty
[r]in the wilderness."

Absalom Killed

18 Then David mustered the men who
were with him and set over them commanders of thousands and commanders of
hundreds. 2 And David sent out the army, one
third under the command of Joab, one third
under the command of Abishai the son of
Zeruiah, Joab's brother, and one third under
the command of [s]Ittai the Gittite. And the
king said to the men, "I myself will also go
out with you." 3 [t]But the men said, "You shall
not go out. For if we flee, they will not care
about us. If half of us die, they will not care
about us. But you are worth ten thousand
of us. Therefore it is better that you send us
help from the city." 4 The king said to them,
"Whatever seems best to you I will do." So the
king stood at the side of the gate, while all
the army marched out by hundreds and by
thousands. 5 And the king ordered Joab and
Abishai and Ittai, "Deal gently for my sake
with the young man Absalom." [u]And all the
people heard when the king gave orders to all
the commanders about Absalom.

6 So the army went out into the field against
Israel, and the battle was fought in the [v]for-
est of Ephraim. 7 And the men of Israel were
defeated there by the servants of David, and
the loss there was great on that day, twenty
thousand men. 8 The battle spread over the
face of all the country, and the forest devoured
more people that day than the sword.

[1] Hebrew *commanded* [2] The meaning of the Hebrew word is uncertain [3] Compare 1 Chronicles 2:17; Hebrew *Israelite* [4] Hebrew adds *and parched grain*

14 [x] ch. 15:31, 34 **15** [y] ch. 15:35, 36 **16** [z] ch. 15:28 [a] ch. 20:19 **17** [b] ch. 15:27, 36 [c] Josh. 15:7; 18:16 **18** [d] See ch. 3:16 **19** [e] [Josh. 2:6] **21** [f] ver. 15, 16 **23** [g] ch. 15:12 [h] [2 Kgs. 20:1] [i] [Matt. 27:5] **24** [j] See Josh. 13:26 **25** [k] ch. 19:13; 20:9, 12; 1 Kgs. 2:5, 32 [l] [1 Chr. 2:13, 16] **27** [m] [ch. 10:1, 2] [n] ch. 12:26, 29 [o] ch. 9:4 [p] ch. 19:31, 32; 1 Kgs. 2:7; [Ezra 2:61] **29** [q] ch. 16:2 [r] ch. 15:23 **Chapter 18** **2** [s] ch. 15:19 **3** [t] ch. 21:17 **5** [u] ver. 12 **6** [v] ver. 17; [Josh. 17:15, 18]

9 And Absalom happened to meet the servants of David. Absalom was riding on his
mule, and the mule went under the thick
branches of a great oak,[1] [w]and his head caught
fast in the oak, and he was suspended between
heaven and earth, while the mule that was
under him went on. 10 And a certain man saw
it and told Joab, "Behold, I saw Absalom hanging in an oak." 11 Joab said to the man who told
him, "What, you saw him! Why then did you
not strike him there to the ground? I would
have been glad to give you ten pieces of silver
and a belt." 12 But the man said to Joab, "Even
if I felt in my hand the weight of a thousand
pieces of silver, I would not reach out my hand
against the king's son, for [x]in our hearing the
king commanded you and Abishai and Ittai,
'For my sake protect the young man Absalom.'
13 On the other hand, if I had dealt treacherously against his life[2] (and there is nothing
hidden from the king), then you yourself
would have stood aloof." 14 Joab said, "I will
not waste time like this with you." And he took
three javelins in his hand and thrust them into
the heart of Absalom while he was still alive in
the oak. 15 And ten young men, Joab's armor-
bearers, surrounded Absalom and struck him
and killed him.

16 Then Joab blew the trumpet, and the
troops came back from pursuing Israel,
for Joab restrained them. 17 And they took
Absalom and threw him into a great pit in the
forest and raised over him [y]a very great heap
of stones. And all Israel [z]fled every one to his
own home. 18 Now Absalom in his lifetime had
taken and set up for himself [a]the pillar that is
in [b]the King's Valley, for he said, [c]"I have no son
to keep my name in remembrance." He called
the pillar after his own name, and it is called
Absalom's monument[3] to this day.

David Hears of Absalom's Death

19 Then Ahimaaz the son of Zadok said, [d]"Let
me run and carry news to the king that [e]the
LORD has delivered him from the hand of his
enemies." 20 And Joab said to him, "You are
not to carry news today. You may carry news
another day, but today you shall carry no news,
because the king's son is dead." 21 Then Joab said
to the Cushite, "Go, tell the king what you have
seen." The Cushite bowed before Joab, and ran.
22 Then Ahimaaz the son of Zadok said again to
Joab, "Come what may, let me also run after the
Cushite." And Joab said, "Why will you run, my
son, seeing that you will have no reward for the
news?" 23 "Come what may," he said, "I will run."
So he said to him, "Run." Then Ahimaaz ran by
the way of [f]the plain, and outran the Cushite.

24 Now David [g]was sitting between the two
gates, and [h]the watchman went up to the roof
of the gate by the wall, and when he lifted up
his eyes and looked, he saw a man running
alone. 25 The watchman called out and told the
king. And the king said, "If he is alone, there
is news in his mouth." And he drew nearer
and nearer. 26 The watchman saw another man
running. And the watchman called to the gate
and said, "See, another man running alone!"
The king said, "He also brings news." 27 The
watchman said, "I think the running of the
first is [i]like the running of Ahimaaz the son
of Zadok." And the king said, [j]"He is a good
man and comes with good news."

28 Then Ahimaaz cried out to the king, "All is
well." And he bowed before the king with his
face to the earth and said, [k]"Blessed be the LORD
your God, who has delivered up the men who
raised their hand against my lord the king."
29 And the king said, [l]"Is it well with the young
man Absalom?" Ahimaaz answered, "When
Joab sent the king's servant, your servant, I saw
a great commotion, but I do not know what
it was." 30 And the king said, "Turn aside and
stand here." So he turned aside and stood still.

David's Grief

31 And behold, the Cushite came, and the
Cushite said, "Good news for my lord the
king! For [m]the LORD has delivered you this
day from the hand of all who rose up against
you." 32 The king said to the Cushite, [l]"Is it
well with the young man Absalom?" And the

[1] Or *terebinth*; also verses 10, 14 [2] Or *at the risk of my life* [3] Or *Absalom's hand*

18:31–33 It is a moving scene indeed when David finally hears of Absalom's fate: his son has died. Absalom has proven a thorn in his father's side for years, yet deeper than this father/son dysfunction is the love of the father for his son. David even laments, "Would that I had died instead of you, O Absalom, my son, my son!" (v. 33). David expresses a similar desire later in 2 Samuel, as the people suffer pestilence due to David's sinful census (24:17).

9[w] [ch. 14:26]
12[x] ver. 5
17[y] Josh. 7:26; 8:29 [z] ch. 19:8; 20:1, 22; 1 Sam. 4:10; 2 Kgs. 8:21
18[a] Gen. 28:18 [b] [Gen. 14:17] [c] ch. 14:27
19[d] ch. 15:36 [e] ver. 31
23[f] [Deut. 34:3]

24[g] ch. 19:8 [h] [ch. 13:34; 2 Kgs. 9:17] **27**[i] [2 Kgs. 9:20] [j] [1 Kgs. 1:42] **28**[k] See Gen. 14:20 **29**[l] ch. 20:9 **31**[m] ver. 19 **32**[l] [See ver. 29 above]

Cushite answered, [n]"May the enemies of my
lord the king and all who rise up against you
for evil be like that young man." 33 [1] And the
king was deeply moved and went up [g]to the
chamber over the gate and wept. And as he
went, he said, [o]"O my son Absalom, my son,
my son Absalom! Would I had died instead of
you, O Absalom, my son, my son!"

Joab Rebukes David

19 It was told Joab, "Behold, the king is
weeping and mourning for Absalom."
2 So the victory that day was turned into
mourning for all the people, for the people
heard that day, "The king is grieving for his
son." 3 And the people stole into the city that
day as people steal in who are ashamed when
they flee in battle. 4 The king [p]covered his face,
and the king cried with a loud voice, [q]"O my
son Absalom, O Absalom, my son, my son!"
5 Then Joab came into the house to the king
and said, "You have today covered with shame
the faces of all your servants, who have this day
saved your life and the lives of your sons and
your daughters and the lives of your wives and
your concubines, 6 because you love those who
hate you and hate those who love you. For you
have made it clear today that commanders and
servants are nothing to you, for today I know
that if Absalom were alive and all of us were
dead today, then you would be pleased. 7 Now
therefore arise, go out and speak [r]kindly to
your servants, for I swear by the LORD, if you
do not go, not a man will stay with you this
night, and this will be worse for you than all
the evil that has come upon you from your
youth until now." 8 Then the king arose and
took his [s]seat in the gate. And the people were
all told, "Behold, the king is sitting in the
gate." And all the people came before the king.

David Returns to Jerusalem

Now Israel had [t]fled every man to his own
home. 9 And all the people were arguing
throughout all the tribes of Israel, saying,
[u]"The king delivered us from the hand of our
enemies and [v]saved us from the hand of the
Philistines, and now [w]he has fled out of the
land from Absalom. 10 But Absalom, whom we
anointed over us, is dead in battle. Now therefore why do you say nothing about bringing
the king back?"

11 And King David sent this message to
[x]Zadok and Abiathar the priests: "Say to the
elders of Judah, 'Why should you be the last
to bring the king back to his house, when the
word of all Israel has come to the king?[2] 12 You
are my brothers; [y]you are my bone and my
flesh. Why then should you be the last to bring
back the king?' 13 And say to Amasa, [z]'Are you
not my bone and my flesh? [a]God do so to me
and more also, if you are not [b]commander of
my army from now on in place of Joab.'" 14 And
he swayed the heart of all the men of Judah [c]as
one man, so that they sent word to the king,
"Return, both you and all your servants." 15 So
the king came back to the Jordan, and Judah
came to Gilgal to meet the king and to bring
the king over the Jordan.

David Pardons His Enemies

16 And [d]Shimei the son of Gera, the Benjaminite, from Bahurim, hurried to come down
with the men of Judah to meet King David.
17 And with him were a thousand men from
Benjamin. And [e]Ziba the servant of the house
of Saul, with his fifteen sons and his twenty
servants, rushed down to the Jordan before
the king, 18 and they crossed the ford to bring
over the king's household and to do his pleasure. And Shimei the son of Gera fell down
before the king, as he was about to cross the
Jordan, 19 and said to the king, [f]"Let not my
lord hold me guilty or remember how your
servant [g]did wrong on the day my lord the
king left Jerusalem. Do not let the king take it
to heart. 20 For your servant knows that I have
sinned. Therefore, behold, I have come this

[1] Ch 19:1 in Hebrew [2] Septuagint; Hebrew *to the king, to his house*

32 [n] 1 Sam. 25:26
33 [g] [See ver. 24 above] [o] ch. 19:4
Chapter 19
4 [p] ch. 15:30 [q] ch. 18:33
7 [r] Gen. 34:3 (Heb.)
8 [s] ch. 18:4, 24, 33; See Ruth 4:1 [t] See ch. 18:17
9 [u] See ch. 8:1-14 [v] ch. 5:20; 8:1 [w] ch. 15:14

The pain that is inflicted on and by fallen human beings in this diseased world often elicits the cry for such substitution. Seeing a loved one in pain prompts us to wish we could bear the pain in their place. Moses, for example, wishes he could bear the punishment due the Israelites (Ex. 32:30–32). Paul expresses the same wish (Rom. 9:3).

The true climax and fulfillment of this desire to take on oneself the pain of the beloved is when God himself does this for his people in the death of his Son. Jesus bore our punishment in our place, to restore us to God (Gal. 3:13; 1 Pet. 3:18).

11 [x] ch. 15:29 12 [y] ch. 5:1; [Gen. 29:14] 13 [z] ch. 17:25 [a] See Ruth 1:17 [b] ch. 8:16 14 [c] [Judg. 20:1] 16 [d] ch. 16:5; 1 Kgs. 2:8 17 [e] ch. 9:2, 10; See ch. 16:1-4
19 [f] [1 Sam. 22:15] [g] See ch. 16:5-13

day, the first [h] of all the house of Joseph to come
down to meet my lord the king." 21 Abishai the
son of Zeruiah answered, "Shall not Shimei be
put to death for this, because [i] he cursed the
LORD's anointed?" 22 But David said, [j]"What
have I to do with you, you sons of Zeruiah,
that you should this day be as an adversary to
me? [k] Shall anyone be put to death in Israel this
day? For do I not know that I am this day king
over Israel?" 23 [l] And the king said to Shimei,
"You shall not die." And the king gave him
his oath.

24 And [m] Mephibosheth the son of Saul came
down to meet the king. He had neither taken
care of his feet nor trimmed his beard nor
washed his clothes, from the day the king
departed until the day he came back in safety.
25 And when he came to Jerusalem to meet the
king, the king said to him, [n]"Why did you not
go with me, Mephibosheth?" 26 He answered,
"My lord, O king, my servant deceived me,
for your servant said to him, 'I will saddle a
donkey for myself,[1] that I may ride on it and
go with the king.' For [o] your servant is lame.
27 [p] He has slandered your servant to my lord
the king. But my lord the king is [q] like the
angel of God; do therefore what seems good
to you. 28 For all my father's house were but
men doomed to death before my lord the king,
but [r] you set your servant among those who
eat at your table. What further right have I,
then, to cry to the king?" 29 And the king said
to him, "Why speak any more of your affairs?
I have decided: you and Ziba shall divide the
land." 30 And Mephibosheth said to the king,
"Oh, let him take it all, since my lord the king
has come safely home."

31 Now [s] Barzillai the Gileadite had come
down from Rogelim, and he went on with
the king to the Jordan, to escort him over the
Jordan. 32 Barzillai was a very aged man, eighty
years old. [t] He had provided the king with food
while he stayed at Mahanaim, for he was a very
wealthy man. 33 And the king said to Barzillai,
"Come over with me, and I will provide for
you with me in Jerusalem." 34 But Barzillai
said to the king, [u]"How many years have I still
to live, that I should go up with the king to
Jerusalem? 35 I am this day [v] eighty years old.
Can I discern what is pleasant and what is not?
Can your servant taste what he eats or what he
drinks? Can I still listen to the voice of singing
men and singing women? Why then should
your servant be [w] an added burden to my lord
the king? 36 Your servant will go a little way
over the Jordan with the king. Why should the
king repay me with such a reward? 37 Please
let your servant return, that I may die in my
own city near the grave of my father and my
mother. But here is your servant [x] Chimham.
Let him go over with my lord the king, and do
for him whatever seems good to you." 38 And
the king answered, "Chimham shall go over
with me, and I will do for him whatever seems
good to you, and all that you desire of me I will
do for you." 39 Then all the people went over
the Jordan, and the king went over. And [y] the
king kissed Barzillai and blessed him, and he
returned to his own home. 40 The king went
on to Gilgal, and Chimham went on with him.
All the people of Judah, and also half the people of Israel, brought the king on his way.

41 Then all the men of Israel came to the king
and said to the king, "Why have our brothers the men of Judah stolen you away and
[z] brought the king and his household over the
Jordan, and all David's men with him?" 42 All
the men of Judah answered the men of Israel,
"Because the king is [a] our close relative. Why
then are you angry over this matter? Have we
eaten at all at the king's expense? Or has he
given us any gift?" 43 And the men of Israel
answered the men of Judah, "We have [b] ten
shares in the king, and in David also we have
more than you. Why then did you despise us?
Were we not the first to speak of bringing
back our king?" [c] But the words of the men
of Judah were fiercer than the words of the
men of Israel.

The Rebellion of Sheba

20 Now there happened to be there [d] a
worthless man, whose name was
Sheba, the son of Bichri, a Benjaminite. And
he blew the trumpet and said,

> [e]"We have no portion in David,
> and we have no inheritance in the son of Jesse;
> [f] every man to his tents, O Israel!"

2 So all the men of Israel withdrew from David

[1] Septuagint, Syriac, Vulgate *Saddle a donkey for me*

20 [h] [ch. 16:5] **21** [i] [Ex. 22:28] **22** [j] ch. 16:10 [k] [1 Sam. 11:13] **23** [l] [1 Kgs. 2:8, 9, 37, 46] **24** [m] ch. 9:6 **25** [n] [ch. 16:17] **26** [o] ch. 9:3 **27** [p] ch. 16:3 [q] ch. 14:17, 20; 1 Sam. 29:9 **28** [r] ch. 9:7, 10, 13 **31** [s] 1 Kgs. 2:7 **32** [t] ch. 17:27-29 **34** [u] Gen. 47:8 **35** [v] [Ps. 90:10] [w] ch. 15:33 **37** [x] 1 Kgs. 2:7; Jer. 41:17 **39** [y] See ch. 14:33 **41** [z] ver. 15 **42** [a] ver. 12 **43** [b] [1 Kgs. 11:30, 31] [c] Isa. 9:21; 11:13 **Chapter 20** **1** [d] See Deut. 13:13 [e] [ch. 19:43] [f] ver. 22; 1 Kgs. 12:16; 2 Chr. 10:16

and followed Sheba the son of Bichri. But the
men of Judah followed their king steadfastly
from the Jordan to Jerusalem.

3 And David came to his house at Jerusalem.
And the king took [g]the ten concubines whom
he had left to care for the house and put them
in a house under guard and provided for
them, but did not go in to them. So they were
shut up until the day of their death, living as
if in widowhood.

4 Then the king said to [h]Amasa, "Call the
men of Judah together to me within three
days, and be here yourself." 5 So Amasa went
to summon Judah, but he delayed beyond the
set time that had been appointed him. 6 And
David said to Abishai, "Now Sheba the son of
Bichri will do us more harm than Absalom.
Take [i]your lord's servants and pursue him, lest
he get himself to fortified cities and escape
from us."[1] 7 And there went out after him Joab's
men and the [j]Cherethites and the Pelethites,
and all the mighty men. They went out from
Jerusalem to pursue Sheba the son of Bichri.
8 When they were at the great stone that is in
Gibeon, Amasa came to meet them. Now Joab
was wearing a soldier's garment, and over it
was a belt with a sword in its sheath fastened
on his thigh, and as he went forward it fell
out. 9 And Joab said to Amasa, "Is it well with
you, my brother?" And Joab took Amasa by the
beard with his right hand [k]to kiss him. 10 But
Amasa did not observe the sword that was in
Joab's hand. [l]So Joab struck him with it [m]in the
stomach and spilled his entrails to the ground
without striking a second blow, and he died.

Then Joab and Abishai his brother pursued
Sheba the son of Bichri. 11 And one of Joab's
young men took his stand by Amasa and said,
"Whoever favors Joab, and whoever is for
David, let him follow Joab." 12 And Amasa lay
wallowing in his blood in the highway. And
anyone who came by, seeing him, stopped.
And when the man saw that all the people
stopped, he carried Amasa out of the highway
into the field and threw a garment over him.
13 When he was taken out of the highway, all
the people went on after Joab to pursue Sheba
the son of Bichri.

14 And Sheba passed through all the tribes of
Israel to [n]Abel of [n]Beth-maacah,[2] and all [o]the
Bichrites[3] assembled and followed him in.
15 And all the men who were with Joab came
and besieged him in [n]Abel of Beth-maacah.
[p]They cast up a mound against the city, and
it stood against the rampart, and they were
battering the wall to throw it down. 16 Then
a wise woman called from the city, "Listen!
Listen! Tell Joab, 'Come here, that I may speak
to you.'" 17 And he came near her, and the
woman said, "Are you Joab?" He answered,
"I am." Then she said to him, "Listen to the
words of your servant." And he answered, "I
am listening." 18 Then she said, "They used to
say in former times, 'Let them but ask counsel
at [n]Abel,' and so they settled a matter. 19 I am
one of those who are peaceable and faithful
in Israel. You seek to destroy a city that is a
mother in Israel. Why will you [q]swallow up
[r]the heritage of the LORD?" 20 Joab answered,
"Far be it from me, far be it, that I should
[q]swallow up or destroy! 21 That is not true. But
a man of [s]the hill country of Ephraim, called
Sheba the son of Bichri, has lifted up his hand
against King David. Give up him alone, and
I will withdraw from the city." And the woman
said to Joab, "Behold, his head shall be thrown
to you over the wall." 22 Then the woman went
to all the people [t]in her wisdom. And they cut
off the head of Sheba the son of Bichri and
threw it out to Joab. So he blew the trumpet,
and they dispersed from the city, [u]every man
to his home. And Joab returned to Jerusalem
to the king.

23 [v]Now Joab was in command of all the army
of Israel; and Benaiah the son of Jehoiada
was in command of the Cherethites and the
Pelethites; 24 and [w]Adoram was in charge of
the forced labor; and Jehoshaphat the son of
Ahilud was the recorder; 25 and Sheva was secretary; and [x]Zadok and Abiathar were priests;
26 and [y]Ira the Jairite was also David's priest.

David Avenges the Gibeonites

21 Now there was a famine in the days
of David for three years, year after
year. And David [z]sought the face of the LORD.
And the LORD said, "There is bloodguilt on
Saul and on his house, because he put the
Gibeonites to death." 2 So the king called
the Gibeonites and spoke to them. Now the

[1] Hebrew *and snatch away our eyes* [2] Compare 20:15; Hebrew *and Beth-maacah* [3] Hebrew *Berites*

3 [g] ch. 15:16; 16:21, 22 **4** [h] ch. 17:25; 19:13 **6** [i] ch. 11:11; 1 Kgs. 1:33 **7** [j] ver. 23; See ch. 8:18 **9** [k] [Matt. 26:49; Mark 14:45; Luke 22:47] **10** [l] 1 Kgs. 2:5 [m] See ch. 2:23 **14** [n] [2 Kgs. 15:29] [o] Num. 21:16 **15** [n] [See ver. 14 above] [p] 2 Kgs. 19:32; Isa. 37:33; Jer. 6:6; Ezek. 4:2; 26:8 **18** [n] [See ver. 14 above] **19** [q] ch. 17:16 [r] See 1 Sam. 26:19 **20** [q] [See ver. 19 above] **21** [s] See Josh. 24:33 **22** [t] ver. 16; [Eccles. 9:14, 15] [u] See 1 Sam. 4:10 **23** [v] For ver. 23-26, see ch. 8:16-18; 1 Kgs. 4:3-6 **24** [w] [1 Kgs. 12:18] **25** [x] ch. 15:24; 19:11 **26** [y] [ch. 23:38] **Chapter 21** **1** [z] [Num. 27:21]

Gibeonites were not of the people of Israel
but [a]of the remnant of the Amorites. Although
the people of Israel had sworn to spare them,
Saul had sought to strike them down in his
zeal for the people of Israel and Judah. 3And
David said to the Gibeonites, "What shall I do
for you? And how shall I make atonement,
that you may bless [b]the heritage of the LORD?"
4The Gibeonites said to him, "It is not a matter
of silver or gold between us and Saul or his
house; neither is it for us to put any man to
death in Israel." And he said, "What do you say
that I shall do for you?" 5They said to the king,
"The man who consumed us and planned to
destroy us, so that we should have no place
in all the territory of Israel, 6let seven of his
sons be given to us, so that we may hang them
before the LORD at [c]Gibeah of Saul, [d]the chosen of the LORD." And the king said, "I will
give them."

7But the king spared Mephibosheth, the son
of Saul's son Jonathan, because of [e]the oath
of the LORD that was between them, between
David and Jonathan the son of Saul. 8The king
took the two sons of [f]Rizpah the daughter of
Aiah, whom she bore to Saul, Armoni and
Mephibosheth; and the five sons of Merab[1] the
daughter of Saul, whom [g]she bore to [h]Adriel the
son of Barzillai the Meholathite; 9and he gave
them into the hands of the Gibeonites, and
they hanged them on the mountain before the
LORD, and the seven of them perished together.
They were put to death in the first days of harvest, [i]at the beginning of barley harvest.

10[j]Then Rizpah the daughter of Aiah took
sackcloth and spread it for herself on the
rock, from the beginning of harvest until
rain fell upon them from the heavens. And
she did not allow the birds of the air to come
upon them by day, or the beasts of the field by
night. 11When David was told what Rizpah the
daughter of Aiah, the concubine of Saul, had
done, 12David went and took the bones of Saul
and the bones of his son Jonathan from the
men of Jabesh-gilead, [k]who had stolen them
from the public square of [l]Beth-shan, where
the Philistines had hanged them, on the day
the Philistines killed Saul on Gilboa. 13And
he brought up from there the bones of Saul
and the bones of his son Jonathan; and they
gathered the bones of those who were hanged.
14And they buried the bones of Saul and his
son Jonathan in the land of Benjamin in [m]Zela,
in the tomb of Kish his father. And they did all
that the king commanded. And after that [n]God
responded to the plea for the land.

War with the Philistines

15There was war again between the Philistines and Israel, and David went down
together with his servants, and they fought
against the Philistines. And David grew weary.
16And Ishbi-benob, one of the descendants [o]of
the giants, whose spear weighed three hundred shekels[2] of bronze, and who was armed
with a new sword, thought to kill David. 17But
Abishai the son of Zeruiah came to his aid
and attacked the Philistine and killed him.
Then David's men swore to him, [p]"You shall
no longer go out with us to battle, lest you
quench [q]the lamp of Israel."

18[r]After this there was again war with
the Philistines at Gob. Then [s]Sibbecai [t]the
Hushathite struck down Saph, who was

[1] Two Hebrew manuscripts, Septuagint; most Hebrew manuscripts *Michal* [2] A *shekel* was about 2/5 ounce or 11 grams

21:1–24:17 The Christian life is lived out in the real world, where sin remains a problem, where the support of others remains a necessity, and where more than all else we need God. The "epilogue" to the books of Samuel is structured in such a way as to make just these points. Gathering its materials from various times and places in David's life, it is framed by two accounts of royal sinners: Saul and (especially) David. In the first account (21:1–14), David is guilty of being inconstant in prayer (cf. 21:1, 3), and in the second (24:1–25), he is guilty of wanting to number his troops and, it seems, put confidence in his own prowess rather than in God. Inside these framing narratives are two lists of David's supporters and their victories (21:15–22; 23:8–39).

Even here, we are not allowed to lose sight of the fact that David was a sinner—the second, longer list concludes with "Uriah the Hittite" (23:39), recalling the sad and sordid events of chapters 11–12. But David was a sinner saved by God's magnificent grace: this is the theme of the two poems at the center of the epilogue, poems by David, chosen to epitomize the heart of who he was. First, he was a recipient of the Lord's "steadfast love," the Lord promising to be a "tower of salvation" not just to David but to his descendants after him (22:51, ESV footnote). Second, David was the recipient of an "everlasting covenant, ordered in all things and secure" (23:5).

2[a] See Josh. 9:3-17
3[b] See 1 Sam. 26:19
6[c] 1 Sam. 10:26; 11:4 [d] 1 Sam. 10:24
7[e] 1 Sam. 20:8, 42; 23:18
8[f] ch. 3:7 [g] [Gen. 50:23] [h] [1 Sam. 18:19]
9[i] Ruth 1:22
10[j] [Deut. 21:23]
12[k] 1 Sam. 31:10-13; [ch. 2:4] [l] Josh. 17:11
14[m] Josh. 18:28 [n] ch. 24:25
16[o] ver. 18, 20, 22
17[p] [ch. 18:3] [q] ch. 22:29; 1 Kgs. 11:36; 15:4; 2 Kgs. 8:19; 2 Chr. 21:7; Ps. 132:17
18[r] For ver. 18-22, see 1 Chr. 20:4-8 [s] 1 Chr. 11:29; 27:11 [t] ch. 23:27

one of the descendants [u]of the giants. 19 And
there was again war with the Philistines at
Gob, and [v]Elhanan the son of Jaare-oregim,
the Bethlehemite, struck down Goliath the
Gittite, [w]the shaft of whose spear was like a
weaver's beam.[1] 20 And there was again war at
Gath, where there was a man of great stature,
who had six fingers on each hand, and six toes
on each foot, twenty-four in number, and he
also was descended [x]from the giants. 21 And
when [y]he taunted Israel, Jonathan the son of
Shimei, David's brother, struck him down.
22 These four were descended [x]from the giants
in Gath, and they fell by the hand of David and
by the hand of his servants.

David's Song of Deliverance

22 And David spoke [z]to the LORD the words of this song on the day when the LORD delivered him from the hand of all his enemies, and from the hand of Saul. 2 [a]He said,

[b]"The LORD is my rock and my fortress
and my deliverer,
3 [c]my[2] God, my rock, [d]in whom I take
refuge,
[e]my shield, and [f]the horn of my salvation,
[g]my stronghold and [h]my refuge,
my savior; you save me from violence.
4 I call upon the LORD, who is [i]worthy to
be praised,
and I am saved from my enemies.

5 [j]"For the waves of death encompassed me,
the torrents of destruction assailed me;[3]
6 [k]the cords of Sheol entangled me;
the snares of death confronted me.

7 [l]"In my distress I called upon the LORD;
to my God I called.
From his temple he heard my voice,
and my cry [m]came to his ears.

8 "Then [n]the earth reeled and rocked;
[o]the foundations of the heavens trembled
and quaked, because he was angry.
9 Smoke went up from his nostrils,[4]
and devouring fire from his mouth;
[p]glowing coals flamed forth from
him.
10 [q]He bowed the heavens and [r]came down;
[s]thick darkness was under his feet.
11 He rode on a cherub and flew;
he was seen on [t]the wings of the
wind.
12 He made [s]darkness around him [u]his canopy,
thick clouds, a gathering of water.
13 Out of the brightness before him
[v]coals of fire flamed forth.
14 [w]The LORD thundered from heaven,
and the Most High uttered his voice.
15 And he sent out [x]arrows and scattered
them;
lightning, and routed them.
16 Then the channels of the sea were seen;
the foundations of the world were
laid bare,
at the rebuke of the LORD,
at the [y]blast of the breath of his nostrils.

17 [z]"He sent from on high, he took me;
he drew me out of many waters.
18 He rescued me from my strong enemy,
from those who hated me,
for they were too mighty for me.
19 They confronted me in the day of my
calamity,
but the LORD was my support.
20 [a]He brought me out into a broad place;
he rescued me, because [b]he delighted
in me.

[1] Contrast 1 Chronicles 20:5, which may preserve the original reading [2] Septuagint (compare Psalm 18:2); Hebrew lacks *my* [3] Or *terrified me*
[4] Or *in his wrath*

18 [u]ver. 16, 20, 22
19 [v][ch. 23:24] [w]1 Sam. 17:7; 1 Chr. 20:5
20 [x]ver. 16, 18
21 [y]1 Sam. 17:10, 25, 26, 36, 45
22 [x][See ver. 20 above]

Chapter 22

1 [z][Ex. 15:1; Judg. 5:1; 1 Chr. 16:7]
2 [a]For ver. 1-51, see Ps. 18:2-50 [b]Deut. 32:4; Ps. 31:3; 71:3; 91:2; 144:2

The gospel is unblinkingly realistic about our sin, about our need for others, and, most importantly, about our need for God at the center of our lives. Only God can save us and give us security. Only he is a "tower of salvation." Only he is completely "steadfast" in love. Only he offers an "everlasting covenant" in which he orders and secures our lives. To deliver on these promises, more than a king of David's stature was necessary. That king was the Greater Son of David, King Jesus, God the Son. "All the promises of God find their Yes in him" (2 Cor. 1:20). In the light of all that God is, our calling is to give him weight in every quarter of our lives and to "hold fast the confession of our hope without wavering, for he who promised is faithful" (Heb. 10:23).

3 [c]ver. 32, 47 [d][Heb. 2:13] [e]ver. 31; Gen. 15:1 [f]Luke 1:69 [g]Ps. 9:9; 59:9, 16, 17; 62:2, 6; [Prov. 18:10] [h]Ps. 14:6; 46:7, 11; 71:7; Jer. 16:19 **4** [i]1 Chr. 16:25; Ps. 48:1; 96:4 **5** [j][Ps. 42:7; 93:4; Jonah 2:3] **6** [k]Ps. 116:3 **7** [l]Ps. 116:4; 120:1; Jonah 2:2 [m]Ps. 18:6 **8** [n]Judg. 5:4; Ps. 77:18; 97:4 [o][Job 26:11] **9** [p]ver. 13 **10** [q]Ps. 144:5 [r]Isa. 64:1 [s][Ex. 20:21; 1 Kgs. 8:12; Ps. 97:2] **11** [t]Ps. 104:3 **12** [s][See ver. 10 above] [u]Job 36:29 **13** [v]ver. 9 **14** [w]Job 37:4; Ps. 29:3 **15** [x]Deut. 32:23; Ps. 7:13; 77:17; 144:6; Hab. 3:11 **16** [y]Ex. 15:8 **17** [z]Ps. 144:7 **20** [a]Ps. 31:8; 118:5 [b]See ch. 15:26

21 "The LORD [c]dealt with me according to
my righteousness;
according to the [d]cleanness of my
hands he rewarded me.
22 [e]For I have kept the ways of the LORD
and have not wickedly departed from
my God.
23 [f]For all his rules were before me,
and from his statutes I did not turn
aside.
24 I was [g]blameless before him,
and I kept myself from guilt.
25 [d]And the LORD has rewarded me according to my righteousness,
according to my cleanness in his sight.

26 [h]"With the merciful you show yourself
merciful;
with the [g]blameless man you show
yourself blameless;
27 with the purified you deal purely,
and with the crooked you make yourself seem tortuous.
28 [i]You save a humble people,
[j]but your eyes are on the haughty to
bring them down.
29 [k]For you are my lamp, O LORD,
and my God lightens my darkness.
30 For by you I can run against a troop,
and by my God I can leap over a wall.
31 This God—[l]his way is perfect;
the [m]word of the LORD proves true;
he is [n]a shield for all those who take
refuge in him.

32 "For who is God, but the LORD?
[o]And who is a rock, except our God?
33 This God is my [p]strong refuge
and has made my[1] way blameless.[2]
34 [q]He made my feet like the feet of a deer
and set me secure [r]on the heights.
35 [s]He trains my hands for war,
so that my arms can bend a bow of
bronze.
36 You have given me the shield of your
salvation,
and your gentleness made me great.
37 [t]You gave a wide place for my steps
under me,
and my feet[3] did not slip;
38 I pursued my enemies and destroyed
them,
and did not turn back until they were
consumed.
39 I consumed them; I thrust them
through, so that they did not rise;
they fell [u]under my feet.
40 For you equipped me with strength for
the battle;
you made [v]those who rise against me
sink under me.
41 You [w]made my enemies turn their backs
to me,[4]
those who hated me, and I destroyed
them.
42 They looked, but there was none to save;
they cried to the LORD, but [x]he did
not answer them.
43 I beat them fine [y]as the dust of the earth;
I crushed them and stamped them
down [z]like the mire of the streets.

44 "You delivered me from strife with my
people;[5]
you kept me as the head of [a]the
nations;
[b]people whom I had not known served
me.
45 Foreigners came cringing to me;
as soon as they heard of me, they
obeyed me.
46 Foreigners lost heart
and came trembling[6] [c]out of their fortresses.

47 "The LORD lives, and blessed be my rock,
and exalted be [d]my God, [e]the rock of
my salvation,
48 the God who gave me vengeance
and [f]brought down peoples under
me,
49 who brought me out from my enemies;
you exalted me above [v]those who rose
against me;
you delivered me from [g]men of violence.

50 [h]"For this I will praise you, O LORD,
among the nations,
and sing praises to your name.

[1] Or *his*; also verse 34 [2] Compare Psalm 18:32; Hebrew *he has blamelessly set my way free*, or *he has made my way spring up blamelessly* [3] Hebrew *ankles* [4] Or *You gave me my enemies' necks* [5] Septuagint *with the peoples* [6] Compare Psalm 18:45; Hebrew *equipped themselves*

21[c] 1 Sam. 26:23; 1 Kgs. 8:32; Ps. 7:8 [d][Ps. 24:4] **22**[e] Gen. 18:19; Prov. 8:32 **23**[f] Ps. 119:30, 102 **24**[g] [Gen. 6:9; 17:1; Job 1:1] **25**[d] [See ver. 21 above] **26**[h] [Matt. 5:7] [g][See ver. 24 above] **28**[i] [Ps. 72:12, 13] [j][Isa. 2:11, 12, 17; Luke 1:51] **29**[k] Job 29:3; Ps. 27:1; [ch. 21:17] **31**[l] Deut. 32:4; Matt. 5:48 [m]Prov. 30:5 [n]ver. 3; Ps. 5:12; 33:20; 59:11; 84:9 **32**[o] See ver. 2 **33**[p] ver. 2; Ps. 28:8; 31:3, 4 **34**[q] See ch. 2:18 [r]Deut. 32:13; 33:29; Isa. 58:14 **35**[s] Ps. 144:1 **37**[t] Prov. 4:12 **39**[u] [Mal. 4:3] **40**[v] Ps. 44:5; 59:1 **41**[w] Ex. 23:27 **42**[x] 1 Sam. 28:6; Prov. 1:28; [Isa. 1:15; Mic. 3:4] **43**[y] 2 Kgs. 13:7 [z]Isa. 10:6; Mic. 7:10; Zech. 10:5 **44**[a] See ch. 8:1-14 [b]Isa. 55:5 **46**[c] Mic. 7:17 **47**[d] ver. 3, 32 [e]Deut. 32:15; Ps. 89:26; 95:1 **48**[f] Ps. 144:2 **49**[v] [See ver. 40 above] [g]Ps. 140:1 **50**[h] Cited Rom. 15:9

51 [i]Great salvation he brings[1] to his king,
and shows steadfast love to [j]his
anointed,
to David and his offspring [k]forever."

The Last Words of David

23 Now these are the last words of David:

The oracle of David, the son of Jesse,
the oracle of [l]the man who was raised
on high,
[j]the anointed of the God of Jacob,
the sweet psalmist of Israel:[2]

2 [m]"The Spirit of the LORD speaks by me;
his word is on my tongue.
3 The God of Israel has spoken;
[n]the Rock of Israel has said to me:
When one rules justly over men,
ruling [o]in the fear of God,
4 he [p]dawns on them like the morning
light,
like the sun shining forth on a cloudless morning,
like rain[3] that makes grass to sprout
from the earth.

5 "For does not my house stand so with God?
[q]For he has made with me an everlasting covenant,
ordered in all things and secure.
For will he not cause to prosper
all my help and my desire?
6 But worthless men[4] are all like thorns
that are thrown away,
for they cannot be taken with the hand;
7 but the man who touches them
arms himself with iron and the shaft
of a spear,
and they are utterly consumed with
fire."[5]

David's Mighty Men

8 [r]These are the names of the mighty men
whom David had: [s]Josheb-basshebeth a
Tahchemonite; he was chief of the three.[6]
He wielded his spear[7] against eight hundred
whom he killed at one time.
9 And next to him among the three mighty
men was Eleazar the son of [t]Dodo, son of
[u]Ahohi. He was with David when they defied
the Philistines who were gathered there for
battle, and the men of Israel withdrew. 10 He
rose and struck down the Philistines until his
hand was weary, and his hand clung to the
sword. And the LORD brought about a great
victory that day, and the men returned after
him only to strip the slain.
11 And next to him was Shammah, the son of
Agee the [v]Hararite. The Philistines gathered
together at Lehi, where there was a plot of
ground full of lentils, and the men fled from
the Philistines. 12 But he took his stand in the
midst of the plot and defended it and struck
down the Philistines, and the LORD worked a
great victory.
13 And three of the thirty chief men went
down and came about harvest time to David
at the [w]cave of Adullam, when a band of
Philistines was encamped [x]in the Valley of
Rephaim. 14 David was then [y]in the stronghold,
and [z]the garrison of the Philistines was then
at Bethlehem. 15 And David said longingly,
"Oh, that someone would give me water to
drink from the well of Bethlehem that is by
the gate!" 16 Then the three mighty men broke
through the camp of the Philistines and drew
water out of the well of Bethlehem that was by
the gate and carried and brought it to David.
But he would not drink of it. He poured it out
to the LORD 17 and said, "Far be it from me,
O LORD, that I should do this. Shall I drink [a]the
blood of the men who went at the risk of their
lives?" Therefore he would not drink it. These
things the three mighty men did.
18 Now Abishai, the brother of Joab, the son
of Zeruiah, was chief of the thirty.[8] And he
wielded his spear against three hundred men[9]
and killed them and won a name beside the
three. 19 He was the most renowned of the
thirty[10] and became their commander, but he
did not attain to [b]the three.
20 And [c]Benaiah the son of Jehoiada was a valiant man[11] of [d]Kabzeel, a doer of great deeds. He
struck down two ariels[12] of Moab. He also went
down and struck down a lion in a pit on a day
when snow had fallen. 21 And he struck down an
Egyptian, a handsome man. The Egyptian had

[1] Or *He is a tower of salvation* [2] Or *the favorite of the songs of Israel* [3] Hebrew *from rain* [4] Hebrew *worthlessness* [5] Hebrew *consumed with fire in the sitting* [6] Or *of the captains* [7] Compare 1 Chronicles 11:11; the meaning of the Hebrew expression is uncertain [8] Two Hebrew manuscripts, Syriac; most Hebrew manuscripts *three* [9] Or *slain ones* [10] Compare 1 Chronicles 11:25; Hebrew *Was he the most renowned of the three?* [11] Or *the son of Ishhai* [12] The meaning of the word *ariel* is unknown

51 [i][Ps. 144:10] [j][1 Sam. 16:12, 13; Ps. 89:20] [k]ch. 7:12, 13; Ps. 89:29 **Chapter 23** **1** [l][ch. 7:8, 9; Ps. 78:70, 71] [j][See ch. 22:51 above] **2** [m][2 Pet. 1:21] **3** [n]See ch. 22:2, 3, 32, 47 [o]Ex. 18:21; 2 Chr. 19:7, 9 **4** [p][Judg. 5:31; Prov. 4:18; Hos. 6:5] **5** [q]ch. 7:15, 16; Ps. 89:29; Isa. 55:3 **8** [r]For ver. 8-39, see 1 Chr. 11:11-47 [s][1 Chr. 27:2, 3] **9** [t]1 Chr. 27:4 [u]ver. 28 **11** [v]ver. 33 **13** [w]See 1 Sam. 22:1 [x]See ch. 5:18 **14** [y]1 Sam. 22:4, 5 [z][1 Sam. 13:23] **17** [a][Lev. 17:10] **19** [b]1 Chr. 11:21 **20** [c]ch. 8:18; 20:23 [d]Josh. 15:21

a spear in his hand, but Benaiah went down to him with a staff and snatched the spear out of the Egyptian's hand and killed him with his own spear. 22 These things did Benaiah the son of Jehoiada, and won a name beside the three mighty men. 23 He was renowned among the thirty, but he did not attain to the three. And David set him over his bodyguard.

24 [e]Asahel the brother of Joab was one of the thirty; Elhanan the son of Dodo of Bethlehem, 25 [f]Shammah of Harod, Elika of Harod, 26 Helez the Paltite, Ira the son of Ikkesh [g]of Tekoa, 27 Abiezer [h]of Anathoth, Mebunnai [i]the Hushathite, 28 Zalmon [j]the Ahohite, Maharai [k]of Netophah, 29 Heleb the son of Baanah [k]of Netophah, Ittai the son of Ribai of [l]Gibeah of the people of Benjamin, 30 Benaiah [m]of Pirathon, Hiddai of the brooks of [n]Gaash, 31 Abi-albon the Arbathite, Azmaveth of [o]Bahurim, 32 Eliahba the Shaalbonite, the sons of Jashen, Jonathan, 33 [p]Shammah the Hararite, Ahiam the son of Sharar the Hararite, 34 Eliphelet the son of Ahasbai [q]of Maacah, [r]Eliam the son of [s]Ahithophel of Gilo, 35 Hezro[1] [t]of Carmel, Paarai the Arbite, 36 Igal the son of Nathan [u]of Zobah, Bani the Gadite, 37 Zelek the Ammonite, Naharai [v]of Beeroth, the armor-bearer of Joab the son of Zeruiah, 38 [w]Ira the [x]Ithrite, Gareb the Ithrite, 39 [y]Uriah the Hittite: thirty-seven in all.

David's Census

24 [z, a]Again the anger of the LORD was kindled against Israel, and he incited David against them, saying, [b]"Go, number Israel and Judah." 2 So the king said to Joab, the commander of the army,[2] who was with him, "Go through all the tribes of Israel, [c]from Dan to Beersheba, and number the people, that I may know the number of the people." 3 But Joab said to the king, [d]"May the LORD your God add to the people a hundred times as many as they are, while the eyes of my lord the king still see it, but why does my lord the king delight in this thing?" 4 But the king's word prevailed against Joab and the commanders of the army. So Joab and the commanders of the army went out from the presence of the king to number the people of Israel. 5 They crossed the Jordan and began from [e]Aroer,[3] and from the city that is in the middle of the [f]valley, toward Gad and on to [g]Jazer. 6 Then they came to Gilead, and to Kadesh in the land of the Hittites;[4] and they came to Dan, and from Dan[5] they went around to [h]Sidon, 7 and came to the fortress of Tyre and to all the cities of the [i]Hivites and [i]Canaanites; and they went out to the Negeb of Judah at Beersheba. 8 So when they had gone through all the land, they came to Jerusalem at the end of nine months and twenty days. 9 And Joab gave the sum of the numbering of the people to the king: in Israel there were 800,000 valiant men [j]who drew the sword, and the men of Judah were 500,000.

The LORD's Judgment of David's Sin

10 But [k]David's heart struck him after he had numbered the people. And David said to the LORD, [l]"I have sinned greatly in what I have done. But now, O LORD, please take away the iniquity of your servant, for I have done [m]very foolishly." 11 And when David arose in the morning, the word of the LORD came to [n]the prophet Gad, David's [o]seer, saying, 12 "Go and say to David, 'Thus says the LORD, Three things I offer[6] you. Choose one of them, that I may do it to you.'" 13 So Gad came to David and told him, and said to him, "Shall [p]three[7] years of famine come to you in your land? Or will you flee three months before your foes while they pursue you? Or shall there be three days' pestilence in your land? Now consider, and decide what answer I shall return to him who sent me." 14 Then David said to Gad, "I am in great distress. Let us fall into the hand of the LORD, [q]for his mercy is great; but let me not fall into the hand of man."

15 [r]So the LORD sent a pestilence on Israel from the morning until the appointed time. And there died of the people from [s]Dan to Beersheba 70,000 men. 16 And when [t]the angel stretched out his hand toward Jerusalem [u]to destroy it, [v]the LORD relented from the calamity and said to the angel [u]who was working destruction among the people, "It is enough; now stay your hand." And [t]the

[1] Or *Hezrai* [2] Septuagint *to Joab and the commanders of the army* [3] Septuagint; Hebrew *encamped in Aroer* [4] Septuagint; Hebrew *to the land of Tahtim-hodshi* [5] Septuagint; Hebrew *they came to Dan-jaan and* [6] Or *hold over* [7] Compare 1 Chronicles 21:12, Septuagint; Hebrew *seven*

24 [e] ch. 2:18; 1 Chr. 27:7 **25** [f] [1 Chr. 11:27; 27:8] **26** [g] See ch. 14:2 **27** [h] Josh. 21:18 [i] ch. 21:18 **28** [j] ver. 9 [k] 2 Kgs. 25:23 **29** [k] [See ver. 28 above] [l] Josh. 18:28; Judg. 19:14 **30** [m] Judg. 12:13, 15; 1 Chr. 27:14 [n] Josh. 24:30; Judg. 2:9 **31** [o] [ch. 3:16] **33** [p] ver. 11 **34** [q] ch. 10:6, 8 [r] ch. 11:3 [s] ch. 15:12 **35** [t] Josh. 15:55 **36** [u] ch. 8:3 **37** [v] ch. 4:2 **38** [w] [ch. 20:26] [x] 1 Chr. 2:53 **39** [y] ch. 11:3, 6 **Chapter 24** **1** [z] For ver. 1-25, see 1 Chr. 21:1-28 [a] [1 Chr. 21:1] [b] [1 Chr. 27:23, 24] **2** [c] ver. 15; See ch. 3:10 **3** [d] Deut. 1:11 **5** [e] Deut. 2:36; Josh. 13:9, 16 [f] [Num. 13:23] [g] Num. 21:32; 32:1, 3 **6** [h] Josh. 19:28; Judg. 18:28 **7** [i] Josh. 11:3; Judg. 3:3 **9** [j] Judg. 8:10 **10** [k] 1 Sam. 24:5 [l] ch. 12:13 [m] See 1 Sam. 13:13 **11** [n] See 1 Sam. 22:5 [o] See 1 Sam. 9:9 **13** [p] [1 Chr. 21:12] **14** [q] Ps. 119:156 **15** [r] 1 Chr. 27:24 [s] ver. 2 **16** [t] 2 Kgs. 19:35; 2 Chr. 32:21; Isa. 37:36; Acts 12:23 [u] Ex. 12:13, 23 [v] Gen. 6:6; 1 Sam. 15:11; Joel 2:13, 14; Jonah 3:10

angel of the LORD was by the threshing floor
of [w]Araunah the Jebusite. 17 Then David spoke
to the LORD when he saw the angel who was
striking the people, and said, "Behold, I have
sinned, and I have done wickedly. But these
sheep, what have they done? Please let your
hand be against me and against my father's
house."

David Builds an Altar

18 And Gad came that day to David and said
to him, "Go up, raise an altar to the LORD on
the threshing floor of [x]Araunah the Jebusite."
19 So David went up at Gad's word, as the
LORD commanded. 20 And when Araunah
looked down, he saw the king and his servants coming on toward him. And Araunah
went out and paid homage to the king with
his face to the ground. 21 And Araunah said,
"Why has my lord the king come to his servant?" David said, "To buy the threshing floor
from you, in order to build an altar to the
LORD, that the plague [y]may be averted from
the people." 22 Then Araunah said to David,
"Let my lord the king take and offer up what
seems good to him. Here are the oxen for the
burnt offering and the [z]threshing sledges
and the yokes of the oxen for the wood. 23 All
this, O king, Araunah gives to the king." And
Araunah said to the king, "May the LORD
your God [a]accept you." 24 But the king said
to Araunah, "No, but I will buy it from you
for a price. I will not offer burnt offerings to
the LORD my God that cost me nothing." So
David bought the threshing floor and the
oxen for fifty shekels[1] of silver. 25 And David
built there an altar to the LORD and offered
burnt offerings and peace offerings. [b]So the
LORD responded to the plea for the land, and
the plague was averted from Israel.

[1] A *shekel* was about 2/5 ounce or 11 grams

16[w] [2 Chr. 3:1]
18[x] [2 Chr. 3:1]
21[y] Num. 16:48, 50
22[z] 1 Kgs. 19:21
23[a] Deut. 33:11; [Ps. 20:3]
25[b] ch. 21:14

24:18–25 The book of 2 Samuel closes with David building an altar to the Lord and thus averting the plague that has come on the people due to David's sin in taking a census (here again the king is representative of and for the people of God—this time negatively, a concept less familiar to us but important for the covenant people at that time). Thus, in a fitting conclusion, the book ends with that theme that resounds so often through the pages of the Old Testament—the ongoing need for reconciliation between God and his people. Reconciliation is needed because God's own people—even great kings such as David—so often prove fickle and faithless. The entire Old Testament sacrificial system, with its altars and offerings, represents the ever-heightening need for restoration between God and his people.

This snowballing theme is brought to climactic fulfillment and resolution in the coming of Jesus Christ. He is the propitiation that turns away God's wrath (Rom. 3:25). He is the lamb offered as the sacrifice for the sins of the people (1 Cor. 5:7). He is the Great High Priest who not only atones for the sins of his people but who does not need to atone for his own sins—and who intercedes for his people forever (Heb. 7:23–28). Indeed, he is the very tabernacle and temple for the people, the place where God's presence dwells and where the people are restored to God (John 1:14; 2:19–22).

Introduction to 1–2 Kings

Author and Date

The author or authors of these two books are unknown. As the titles of the books indicate, 1–2 Kings describe the period of the monarchy in ancient Israel (970–586 B.C.), concentrating on the kings who ruled after David.

The Gospel in 1–2 Kings

The book of Kings belongs to a larger group of books in the Old Testament, Joshua through Kings (the so-called Former Prophets). Together, these books record the faithfulness of Israel's covenant God to keep all of his covenant promises with regard to the establishment of his people in the Promised Land. There are two important texts that summarize this reality. The first is Joshua 21:44–45: "And the LORD gave them rest on every side just as he had sworn to their fathers. . . . Not one word of all the good promises that the LORD had made to the house of Israel had failed; all came to pass." The second is 1 Kings 8:56: "Blessed be the LORD who has given rest to his people Israel, according to all that he promised. Not one word has failed of all his good promise, which he spoke by Moses his servant." These two texts provide the two theological lenses through which we are invited to read the book of Kings. The Lord was faithful to *give his people rest* and to *keep all of his covenant promises*. In contrast, the history of God's people was characterized as one of covenant breaking and ever increasing infidelity.

The clear contrast between God's covenant keeping and Israel's covenant breaking, particularly among Israel's kings, is perhaps the most important theme in the book of Kings. For this stark contrast highlights the gracious and underserved nature of God's faithfulness to his people. The biblical term for this reality is "steadfast love" (see Ex. 34:6–7; 1 Kings 3:6; 8:23), sometimes translated as mercy, loyalty, faithfulness, or graciousness. Behind the variety of terms used to express this idea in the Bible is one central idea: God does not treat his people as their sins deserve.

But how is this gracious behavior of the Lord possible? We know that God is flawlessly faithful to his covenant promises, yet part of those promises include the promise to curse covenant breakers: "Cursed be anyone who does not confirm the words of this law by doing them" (Deut. 27:26; cf. 27:15–26; 28:15–19). How can God be both merciful to his people but also faithful to curse covenant breakers, especially since all of God's people have broken the covenant? The book of Kings hints at the answer with the small but important expression "for the sake of my servant David" (cf. 1 Kings 11:11–13, 32, 34; 2 Kings 8:19; 19:34; Isa. 37:35).

Because the Lord made a covenant with David to establish an eternal kingdom through his offspring (cf. 2 Sam. 7:9–16; 1 Kings 3:6; 9:4–5; 11:4, 34; 14:8; 15:3), the nation of Israel was repeatedly treated in gracious mercy, in ways it did not deserve. Ultimately, however, the sins of Israel increased to such a point that the covenant curses of destruction and exile were required by the Lord's faithfulness to his own covenant obligations (cf. 2 Kings 17 and 25), but even these disciplinary measures were sovereignly administered in such a way as not to undo the Davidic promise that would remain Israel's hope.

As Christians, we are reminded through 1 and 2 Kings of God's faithfulness to us as his covenant people in spite of our own transgressions and covenant infidelity. We must understand that God's grace and mercy to us is rooted in the same hope expressed by the book of Kings, that God does not treat us as our sins deserve because of the faithfulness of another David, Jesus Christ, the root and offspring (or Seed) of David (Matt. 1:1, 17; 9:27; 12:23; 15:22; 20:30–31; 21:9; John 7:42; Rom. 1:3; 2 Tim. 2:8; Rev. 22:16). But Jesus is not just any son (offspring) of David. He is the true and better David. Not only did his obedience merit our righteousness before God, but he also bore the consequences of our covenant breaking. "For our sake he made him to be sin who knew no sin, so that in him we might become the righteousness of God" (2 Cor. 5:21; cf. Rom. 8:1). In Christ, we are guaranteed that God's steadfast love will never run out, because the necessary curse for covenant disobedience has been endured by another on our behalf. Now, we rest in God's faithfulness, for he has kept all of his covenant promises, and "all the promises of God find their Yes in him" (2 Cor. 1:20).

1 Kings Outline

I. The Reign of King Solomon (1:1–11:43)
II. The Kingdom Is Divided (12:1–14:31)
III. Abijam and Asa (15:1–24)
IV. From Nadab to Ahab (15:25–16:34)
V. Elijah and Ahab (17:1–22:40)
VI. Jehoshaphat and Ahaziah (22:41–53)

2 Kings Outline

I. The Death of Ahaziah (1:1–18)
II. Elisha and Israel (2:1–10:36)
III. Joash (11:1–12:21)
IV. Jehoahaz and Jehoash (13:1–25)
V. Amaziah, Jeroboam II, and Azariah (14:1–15:7)
VI. Israel's Last Days (15:8–31)
VII. Jotham and Ahaz (15:32–16:20)
VIII. The End of Israel (17:1–41)
IX. Hezekiah (18:1–20:21)
X. Manasseh and Amon (21:1–26)
XI. Josiah (22:1–23:30)
XII. The End of Judah (23:31–25:30)

1 Kings

David in His Old Age

1 Now King David was old and advanced in years. And although they covered him with clothes, he could not get warm. 2 Therefore his servants said to him, "Let a young woman be sought for my lord the king, and let her wait on the king and be in his service. Let her lie in your arms,[1] that my lord the king may be warm." 3 So they sought for a beautiful young woman throughout all the territory of Israel, and found Abishag the [a]Shunammite, and brought her to the king. 4 The young woman was very beautiful, and she was of service to the king and attended to him, but the king knew her not.

Adonijah Sets Himself Up as King

5 Now [b]Adonijah the son of Haggith exalted himself, saying, "I will be king." [c]And he prepared for himself chariots and horsemen, and fifty men to run before him. 6 His father had never at any time displeased him by asking, "Why have you done thus and so?" He was also a very handsome man, [d]and he was born next after Absalom. 7 He conferred with [e]Joab the son of Zeruiah and with [f]Abiathar the priest. And they followed Adonijah and helped him. 8 But [f]Zadok the priest and [g]Benaiah the son of Jehoiada and [h]Nathan the prophet and [i]Shimei and Rei and [j]David's mighty men were not with Adonijah.

9 Adonijah sacrificed sheep, oxen, and fattened cattle by the Serpent's Stone, which is beside [k]En-rogel, and he invited all his brothers, the king's sons, and all the royal officials of Judah, 10 but he did not invite Nathan the prophet or Benaiah or the mighty men or [l]Solomon his brother.

Nathan and Bathsheba Before David

11 Then Nathan said to Bathsheba the mother of Solomon, "Have you not heard that [b]Adonijah the son of Haggith has become king and David our lord does not know it? 12 Now therefore come, let me give you advice, that you may save your own life and the life of your

[1] Or *in your bosom*

1:1–53 King David was old, and his earthly days were drawing to a close. It was time to anoint the next king of Israel, David's successor. First Kings 1 presents two possible successors to David's throne: Adonijah and Solomon.

Adonijah represented, at least in human terms, the most likely candidate. He was the oldest living male child, he was physically attractive, and he had the support of the leading political officials in the kingdom (vv. 6–7). Because of his status and position, Adonijah "exalted himself" and presumed to make himself David's successor (v. 5).

Solomon, on the other hand, lacked the credentials of his older brother. In fact, Solomon's status as a royal son was rooted in scandal (2 Samuel 11–12). His mother had become a royal wife through David's acts of adultery and murder. As such, Solomon's claim to kingship was not based on his status or position as the rightful heir but rather on the promise of his father (1 Kings 1:17, 30; cf. 1 Chron. 22:9).

These two men represent a study in contrasts. Adonijah stood to inherit the kingdom according to worldly, external standards. Solomon, in contrast, would become king according to the promise of his father, by grace alone. The choice of Solomon over Adonijah should not surprise us. Rather, it reminds us of the Lord's choice of David over all of his older brothers: "But the LORD said to Samuel, 'Do not look on his appearance or on the height of his stature, because I have rejected him. For the LORD sees not as man sees: man looks on the outward appearance, but the LORD looks on the heart'" (1 Sam. 16:7).

Chapter 1
3[a] Josh. 19:18
5[b] 2 Sam. 3:4 [c] 2 Sam. 15:1
6[d] 2 Sam. 3:3, 4; 1 Chr. 3:2
7[e] 2 Sam. 2:13, 18 [f] 2 Sam. 20:25
8[f] [See ver. 7 above] [g] 2 Sam. 8:18 [h] 2 Sam. 12:1 [i] ch. 4:18 [j] See 2 Sam. 23:8-39
9[k] Josh. 15:7; 2 Sam. 17:17
10[l] 2 Sam. 12:24
11[b] [See ver. 5 above]

son Solomon. 13 Go in at once to King David, and say to him, 'Did you not, my lord the king, swear to your servant, saying, [m]"Solomon your son shall reign after me, and he shall sit on my throne"? Why then is Adonijah king?' 14 Then while you are still speaking with the king, I also will come in after you and confirm[1] your words."

15 So Bathsheba went to the king in his chamber (now the king was very old, and Abishag the Shunammite was attending to the king). 16 Bathsheba bowed and paid homage to the king, and the king said, "What do you desire?" 17 She said to him, "My lord, you swore to your servant by the LORD your God, saying, [m]'Solomon your son shall reign after me, and he shall sit on my throne.' 18 And now, behold, Adonijah is king, although you, my lord the king, do not know it. 19 [n]He has sacrificed oxen, fattened cattle, and sheep in abundance, and has invited all the sons of the king, [f]Abiathar the priest, and Joab the commander of the army, but [l]Solomon your servant he has not invited. 20 And now, my lord the king, the eyes of all Israel are on you, to tell them who shall sit on the throne of my lord the king after him. 21 Otherwise it will come to pass, when my lord the king [o]sleeps with his fathers, that I and my son Solomon will be counted offenders."

22 While she was still speaking with the king, Nathan the prophet came in. 23 And they told the king, "Here is Nathan the prophet." And when he came in before the king, he bowed before the king, with his face to the ground. 24 And Nathan said, "My lord the king, have you said, 'Adonijah shall reign after me, and he shall sit on my throne'? 25 For he has gone down this day and [n]has sacrificed oxen, fattened cattle, and sheep in abundance, and has invited all the king's sons, the commanders[2] of the army, and Abiathar the priest. And behold, they are eating and drinking before him, and saying, [p]'Long live King Adonijah!' 26 [q]But me, your servant, and Zadok the priest, and Benaiah the son of Jehoiada, and your servant Solomon he has not invited. 27 Has this thing been brought about by my lord the king and you have not told your servants who should sit on the throne of my lord the king after him?"

Solomon Anointed King

28 Then King David answered, "Call Bathsheba to me." So she came into the king's presence and stood before the king. 29 And the king swore, saying, [r]"As the LORD lives, who has redeemed my soul out of every adversity, 30 [s]as I swore to you by the LORD, the God of Israel, saying, 'Solomon your son shall reign after me, and he shall sit on my throne in my place,' even so will I do this day." 31 Then Bathsheba bowed with her face to the ground and paid homage to the king and said, [t]"May my lord King David live forever!"

32 King David said, "Call to me Zadok the priest, Nathan the prophet, and Benaiah the son of Jehoiada." So they came before the king. 33 And the king said to them, "Take with you [u]the servants of your lord and have Solomon my son ride on my own mule, and bring him down to [v]Gihon. 34 And let Zadok the priest and Nathan the prophet there [w]anoint him king over Israel. [x]Then blow the trumpet and say, [y]'Long live King Solomon!' 35 You shall then come up after him, and he shall come and sit on my throne, for he shall be king in my place. And I have appointed him to be ruler over Israel and over Judah." 36 And Benaiah the son of Jehoiada answered the king, "Amen! May the LORD, the God of my lord the king, say so. 37 [z]As the LORD has been with my lord the king, even so may he be with Solomon, [a]and make his throne greater than the throne of my lord King David."

38 So Zadok the priest, Nathan the prophet,

[1] Or *expand on* [2] Hebrew; Septuagint *Joab the commander*

13[m] ver. 30; [1 Chr. 22:9]
17[m] [See ver. 13 above]
19[n] ver. 9 [f] [See ver. 7 above] [l] [See ver. 10 above]
21[o] ch. 2:10; 2 Sam. 7:12; [Deut. 31:16]
25[n] [See ver. 19 above] [p] See 1 Sam. 10:24
26[q] ver. 8, 10, 32
29[r] See Ruth 3:13
30[s] ver. 13, 17
31[t] Neh. 2:3; Dan. 2:4; 3:9; 5:10; 6:6, 21
33[u] 2 Sam. 11:11; 20:6 [v] 2 Chr. 32:30; 33:14

However, the Lord's choice of Solomon over Adonijah was not intended simply to subvert human expectations. Rather, the display of grace in Solomon's life through this unmerited promise bore fruit. In the ancient world, a rival to the throne would have certainly been executed. But Solomon, who came to the throne by grace, exhibited grace to his brother, sending him home in peace (1 Kings 1:53; cf. David's dealings with Mephibosheth in 2 Sam. 9:6–13).

As Christians, we too have becomes heirs to the kingdom of God not by our own qualifications but by grace because of God's promise—in much the same way as Solomon inherited the kingship. Only those who know God's grace can bear the fruit of grace in the lives of others. We love as we have been loved.

34[w] See 1 Sam. 10:1 [x] 2 Sam. 15:10; 2 Kgs. 9:13; 11:14 [y] [ver. 25]; See 1 Sam. 10:24 37[z] See 1 Sam. 20:13 [a] ver. 47

and Benaiah the son of Jehoiada, [b]and the Cherethites and the Pelethites went down and had Solomon ride on King David's mule and brought him to Gihon. 39 There Zadok the priest took the horn of [c]oil from the tent and [d]anointed Solomon. [x]Then they blew the trumpet, and all the people said, [y]"Long live King Solomon!" 40 And all the people went up after him, playing on pipes, and rejoicing with great joy, so that the earth was split by their noise.

41 Adonijah and all the guests who were with him heard it as they finished feasting. And when Joab heard the sound of the trumpet, he said, "What does this uproar in the city mean?" 42 While he was still speaking, behold, [e]Jonathan the son of Abiathar the priest came. And Adonijah said, "Come in, [f]for you are a worthy man and bring good news." 43 Jonathan answered Adonijah, "No, for our lord King David has made Solomon king, 44 and the king has sent with him Zadok the priest, Nathan the prophet, and Benaiah the son of Jehoiada, and the [b]Cherethites and the Pelethites. And they had him ride on the king's mule. 45 And Zadok the priest and Nathan the prophet have anointed him king at [v]Gihon, and they have gone up from there rejoicing, so that the city is in an uproar. This is the noise that you have heard. 46 [g]Solomon sits on the royal throne. 47 Moreover, the king's servants came to congratulate our lord King David, saying, [h]'May your God make the name of Solomon more famous than yours, and make his throne greater than your throne.' And the king [i]bowed himself on the bed. 48 And the king also said, 'Blessed be the LORD, the God of Israel, [j]who has granted someone[1] to sit on my throne this day, my own eyes seeing it.'"

49 Then all the guests of Adonijah trembled and rose, and each went his own way. 50 And Adonijah feared Solomon. So he arose and went [k]and took hold of [l]the horns of the altar. 51 Then it was told Solomon, "Behold, Adonijah fears King Solomon, for behold, he has laid hold of the horns of the altar, saying, 'Let King Solomon swear to me first that he will not put his servant to death with the sword.'" 52 And Solomon said, "If he will show himself a worthy man, [m]not one of his hairs shall fall to the earth, but if wickedness is found in him, he shall die." 53 So King Solomon sent, and they brought him down from the altar. And he came and paid homage to King Solomon, and Solomon said to him, "Go to your house."

David's Instructions to Solomon

2 [n]When David's time to die drew near, he commanded Solomon his son, saying, 2 [o]"I am about to go the way of all the earth. [p]Be strong, and show yourself a man, 3 and keep the charge of the LORD your God, walking in his ways and keeping his statutes, his commandments, his rules, and his testimonies, as it is written in the Law of Moses, [q]that you may prosper in all that you do and wherever you turn, 4 that the LORD may [r]establish his word that he spoke concerning me, saying, [s]'If your sons pay close attention to their way, [t]to walk before me in faithfulness with all their heart and with all their soul, [u]you shall not lack[2] a man on the throne of Israel.'

5 "Moreover, you also know what Joab the son of Zeruiah [v]did to me, how he dealt with the two commanders of the armies of Israel, [w]Abner the son of Ner, [x]and Amasa the son of Jether, whom he killed, avenging[3] in time of peace for blood that had been shed in war, and putting the blood of war[4] on the belt around his[5] waist and on the sandals on his feet. 6 Act therefore [y]according to your wisdom, but do not let his gray head go down

[1] Septuagint *one of my offspring* [2] Hebrew *there shall not be cut off for you* [3] Septuagint; Hebrew *placing* [4] Septuagint *innocent blood* [5] Septuagint *my*; twice in this verse

2:1–4 As the representative head of a covenant nation, a king had a particularly important obligation of covenant obedience. Saul's disobedience resulted in the destruction of his royal dynasty (1 Sam. 13:13–14). David's disobedience in the taking of a census resulted in the death of 70,000 men in Israel (2 Samuel 24). Later, Solomon's disobedience would divide the kingdom of Israel (1 Kings 11), and the disobedience of the kings who followed would eventually lead to the nation's destruction and the exile of God's people (2 Kings 17; 25). A king's obedience and the security of his people went hand-in-hand. Given this track record, our frequent despair in human leadership is not unwarranted.

38 [b]See 2 Sam. 8:18
39 [c][Ps. 89:20]; See Ex. 30:23-32 [d]1 Chr. 29:22 [x][See ver. 34 above] [y][See ver. 34 above]
42 [e]2 Sam. 15:27, 36; 17:17 [f]2 Sam. 18:27
44 [b][See ver. 38 above]
45 [v][See ver. 33 above]
46 [g]1 Chr. 29:23
47 [h]ver. 37 [i][Gen. 47:31]
48 [j]ch. 3:6; [Ps. 132:11, 12]
50 [k]ch. 2:28 [l]Ex. 27:2

52 [m]See 1 Sam. 14:45 **Chapter 2** **1** [n][Gen. 47:29] **2** [o]Josh. 23:14 [p]See Josh. 1:6, 7 **3** [q]Deut. 29:9; 1 Chr. 22:12, 13 **4** [r]2 Sam. 7:25 [s]Ps. 132:12 [t][ch. 3:6; 9:4; 2 Kgs. 20:3] [u]ch. 8:25; 9:5; 2 Sam. 7:12, 13 **5** [v]2 Sam. 18:5, 12, 14; [2 Sam. 3:39] [w]ver. 32; 2 Sam. 3:27 [x]2 Sam. 20:10 **6** [y][ver. 9]

to Sheol in peace. 7 But deal loyally with the sons of [z]Barzillai the Gileadite, and let them be [a]among those who eat at your table, [b]for with such loyalty[1] they met me when I fled from Absalom your brother. 8 And there is also with you [c]Shimei the son of Gera, the Benjaminite from Bahurim, who cursed me with a grievous curse on the day [d]when I went to Mahanaim. [e]But when he came down to meet me at the Jordan, I swore to him by the LORD, saying, 'I will not put you to death with the sword.' 9 Now therefore do not hold him guiltless, [f]for you are a wise man. You will know what you ought to do to him, and you shall [g]bring his gray head down with blood to Sheol."

The Death of David

10 [h]Then David slept with his fathers and was buried in [i]the city of David. 11 And the time that David reigned over Israel was [j]forty years. He reigned seven years in Hebron and thirty-three years in Jerusalem. 12 [k]So Solomon sat on the throne of David his father, and his kingdom was firmly established.

Solomon's Reign Established

13 Then Adonijah the son of Haggith came to Bathsheba the mother of Solomon. And she said, [l]"Do you come peacefully?" He said, "Peacefully." 14 Then he said, "I have something to say to you." She said, "Speak." 15 He said, "You know that [m]the kingdom was mine, and that all Israel fully expected me to reign. However, the kingdom has turned about and become my brother's, [n]for it was his from the LORD. 16 And now I have one request to make of you; do not refuse me." She said to him, "Speak." 17 And he said, "Please ask King Solomon—he will not refuse you—to give me [o]Abishag the Shunammite as my wife." 18 Bathsheba said, "Very well; I will speak for you to the king."

19 So Bathsheba went to King Solomon to speak to him on behalf of Adonijah. And the king rose to meet her and bowed down to her. Then he sat on his throne and had a seat brought for the king's mother, [p]and she sat on his right. 20 Then she said, "I have one small request to make of you; do not refuse me." And the king said to her, "Make your request, my mother, for I will not refuse you." 21 She said, "Let [o]Abishag the Shunammite be given to Adonijah your brother as his wife." 22 King Solomon answered his mother, "And why do you ask [o]Abishag the Shunammite for Adonijah? Ask for him the kingdom also, [q]for he is my older brother, and on his side [r]are Abiathar[2] the priest and Joab the son of Zeruiah." 23 Then King Solomon swore by the LORD, saying, [s]"God do so to me and more also if this word does not cost Adonijah his life! 24 Now therefore [t]as the LORD lives, who has established me and placed me on the throne of David my father, and who has made me a house, [u]as he promised, Adonijah shall be put to death today." 25 So King Solomon sent [v]Benaiah the son of Jehoiada, and he struck him down, and he died.

26 And to Abiathar the priest the king said, "Go to [w]Anathoth, to your estate, for you deserve death. But I will not at this time put you to death, [x]because you carried the ark of the Lord GOD before David my father, [y]and because you shared in all my father's affliction." 27 [z]So Solomon expelled Abiathar from being priest to the LORD, thus fulfilling [a]the word of the LORD that he had spoken concerning the house of Eli in Shiloh.

28 When the news came to Joab—for Joab [b]had supported Adonijah although [c]he had not supported Absalom—Joab fled to the tent of the LORD and caught hold of the [d]horns of the altar. 29 And when it was told King Solomon, "Joab has fled to the tent of the LORD, and behold, he is beside the altar," Solomon sent Benaiah the son of Jehoiada,

[1] Or *steadfast love* [2] Septuagint, Syriac, Vulgate; Hebrew *and for him and for Abiathar*

7 [z]See 2 Sam. 19:31-38 [a]2 Sam. 9:7, 10 [b]2 Sam. 17:27-29
8 [c]2 Sam. 16:5 [d]2 Sam. 17:24 [e]2 Sam. 19:18
9 [f][ver. 6] [g][Gen. 42:38; 44:31]
10 [h]ch. 1:21; Acts 2:29; 13:36 [i]ch. 3:1; 9:24
11 [j]2 Sam. 5:4, 5; 1 Chr. 29:26, 27
12 [k]1 Chr. 29:23; 2 Chr. 1:1

When Christians worship Jesus as the "King of kings" (1 Tim. 6:15; Rev. 17:14; 19:16), however, our despair turns to delight. What motivates such worship is the fact that Jesus was perfectly obedient, fulfilling all the kingly virtues detailed in 1 Kings 2:2–4. Additionally, our obedient King reigns eternally at the right hand of God the Father, securing unending blessing and security. Ultimately, the flawed and temporary kingship presented to us through Israel's kings shines the bright spotlight of contrast onto the eternal and flawless kingship of Jesus, reminding each of us why we worship Jesus as our King.

13 [l]1 Sam. 16:4 15 [m][ch. 1:5, 25] [n]1 Chr. 22:9, 10; 28:5-7 17 [o]ch. 1:3, 4 19 [p][Ps. 45:9] 21 [o][See ver. 17 above] 22 [o][See ver. 17 above] [q]ch. 1:6; 1 Chr. 3:2, 5 [r]ch. 1:7 23 [s]See Ruth 1:17 24 [t]See Ruth 3:13 [u]2 Sam. 7:11, 13; 1 Chr. 22:10 25 [v]2 Sam. 8:18 26 [w]Josh. 21:18 [x]1 Sam. 23:6; 2 Sam. 15:24, 29 [y]See 1 Sam. 22:20-23 27 [z][ver. 35] [a]See 1 Sam. 2:27-36 28 [b]ch. 1:7 [c]2 Sam. 17:25; 18:2 [d]ch. 1:50

saying, "Go, strike him down." 30 So Benaiah
came to the tent of the LORD and said to
him, "The king commands, 'Come out.'" But
he said, "No, I will die here." Then Benaiah
brought the king word again, saying, "Thus
said Joab, and thus he answered me." 31 The
king replied to him, [e]"Do as he has said, strike
him down and bury him, [f]and thus take away
from me and from my father's house the guilt
for the blood that Joab shed without cause.
32 The LORD will [g]bring back his bloody deeds
on his own head, because, without the knowledge of my father David, he attacked and
killed with the sword two men [h]more righteous and better than himself, [i]Abner the son
of Ner, commander of the army of Israel, and
[j]Amasa the son of Jether, commander of the
army of Judah. 33 [g]So shall their blood come
back on the head of Joab and on the head of
his descendants forever. But for David and
for his descendants and for his house and
for his throne there shall be peace from the
LORD forevermore." 34 Then Benaiah the son
of Jehoiada went up and struck him down
and put him to death. And he was buried in
his own house in the wilderness. 35 [k]The king
put Benaiah the son of Jehoiada over the army
in place of Joab, and the king put [l]Zadok the
priest [m]in the place of Abiathar.

36 Then the king sent and summoned
[n]Shimei and said to him, "Build yourself a
house in Jerusalem and dwell there, and do
not go out from there to any place whatever.
37 For on the day you go out and cross [o]the
brook Kidron, know for certain that you shall
die. [p]Your blood shall be on your own head."
38 And Shimei said to the king, "What you say
is good; as my lord the king has said, so will
your servant do." So Shimei lived in Jerusalem
many days.

39 But it happened at the end of three years
that two of Shimei's servants ran away to
[q]Achish, son of Maacah, king of Gath. And
when it was told Shimei, "Behold, your servants are in Gath," 40 Shimei arose and saddled
a donkey and went to Gath to Achish to seek
his servants. Shimei went and brought his servants from Gath. 41 And when Solomon was
told that Shimei had gone from Jerusalem to
Gath and returned, 42 the king sent and summoned Shimei and said to him, "Did I not
make you swear by the LORD and solemnly
warn you, saying, 'Know for certain that on
the day you go out and go to any place whatever, you shall die'? And you said to me, 'What
you say is good; I will obey.' 43 Why then have
you not kept your oath to the LORD and the
commandment with which I commanded
you?" 44 The king also said to Shimei, "You
know in your own heart [r]all the harm that
you did to David my father. So the LORD will
[s]bring back your harm on your own head.
45 But King Solomon shall be blessed, [t]and the
throne of David shall be established before the
LORD forever." 46 Then the king commanded
Benaiah the son of Jehoiada, and he went out
and struck him down, and he died.

[u]So the kingdom was established in the hand
of Solomon.

Solomon's Prayer for Wisdom

3 [v]Solomon made a marriage alliance with
Pharaoh king of Egypt. He took Pharaoh's
daughter and brought her into [w]the city of
David until he had finished [x]building his own
house [y]and the house of the LORD [z]and the
wall around Jerusalem. 2 [a]The people were sacrificing at the high places, however, because
no house had yet been built for the name of
the LORD.

3 Solomon [b]loved the LORD, [c]walking in the
statutes of David his father, only he sacrificed
and made offerings at the high places. 4 And
the king went to Gibeon to sacrifice there, [d]for
that was the great high place. Solomon used to
offer a thousand burnt offerings on that altar.

3:3–14 Without a doubt, this is one of the most remarkable passages in all of the Old Testament. The tale of Aladdin's lamp pales in comparison! Here, the true and living God, the Creator of heaven and earth, stoops down and offers Solomon anything that his heart might have desired.

Solomon's request for wisdom was certainly admirable, but it is even more important to note that he understood that the wisdom he needed to navigate life was from God. Apart from God's provision, a blessed life would be unknowable—a point consistently reiterated in the wisdom literature of both the Old and New Testaments (cf. Prov. 2:6; James 1:5). Solomon's request for wisdom embodied the important

31 [e][Ex. 21:14] [f]Num. 35:33; Deut. 19:13; 21:8, 9
32 [g]See Judg. 9:24 [h]2 Chr. 21:13 [i]ver. 5; 2 Sam. 3:27 [j]2 Sam. 20:9, 10
33 [g][See ver. 32 above]
35 [k]ch. 4:4 [l]1 Chr. 29:22 [m]ver. 27
36 [n]ver. 8
37 [o]2 Sam. 15:23 [p]See 2 Sam. 1:16
39 [q][1 Sam. 27:2]
44 [r]See 2 Sam. 16:5-14 [s]See 1 Sam. 25:39

45 [t][Prov. 25:5] **46** [u]ver. 12; [2 Chr. 1:1] **Chapter 3** **1** [v]ch. 7:8; 9:16, 24; 2 Chr. 8:11 [w]See ch. 2:10 [x]ch. 7:1 [y]See ch. 6 [z]ch. 9:15 **2** [a]ch. 22:43; [Deut. 12:2, 3] **3** [b]Deut. 6:5; 30:16, 20; [Ps. 31:23] [c]ver. 6, 14 **4** [d]2 Chr. 1:3, 6, 13; [1 Chr. 16:39; 21:29]

5 [e]At Gibeon [f]the LORD appeared to Solomon [g]in a dream by night, and God said, "Ask what I shall give you." 6 And Solomon said, "You have shown great and steadfast love to your servant David my father, because [h]he walked before you in faithfulness, in righteousness, and in uprightness of heart toward you. And you have kept for him this great and steadfast love and [i]have given him a son to sit on his throne this day. 7 And now, O LORD my God, [j]you have made your servant king in place of David my father, [k]although I am but a little child. I do not know [l]how to go out or come in. 8 [m]And your servant is in the midst of your people whom you have chosen, a great people, [n]too many to be numbered or counted for multitude. 9 [o]Give your servant therefore an understanding mind [p]to govern your people, that I may [q]discern between good and evil, for who is able to govern this your great people?"

10 It pleased the Lord that Solomon had asked this. 11 And God said to him, "Because you have asked this, and have not asked for yourself long life or riches or the life of your enemies, but have asked for yourself understanding to discern what is right, 12 behold, [r]I now do according to your word. Behold, [s]I give you a wise and discerning mind, so that none like you has been before you and none like you shall arise after you. 13 [t]I give you also what you have not asked, [u]both riches and honor, so that no other king shall compare with you, all your days. 14 And if you will walk in my ways, keeping my statutes and my commandments, [v]as your father David walked, then [w]I will lengthen your days."

15 And Solomon [x]awoke, and behold, it was a dream. Then he came to Jerusalem and stood before the ark of the covenant of the Lord, and offered up burnt offerings and peace offerings, and made a feast for all his servants.

Solomon's Wisdom

16 Then two prostitutes came to the king [y]and stood before him. 17 The one woman said, "Oh, my lord, this woman and I live in the same house, and I gave birth to a child while she was in the house. 18 Then on the third day after I gave birth, this woman also gave birth. And we were alone. There was no one else with us in the house; only we two were in the house. 19 And this woman's son died in the night, because she lay on him. 20 And she arose at midnight and took my son from beside me, while your servant slept, and laid him at her breast, and laid her dead son at my breast. 21 When I rose in the morning to nurse my child, behold, he was dead. But when I looked at him closely in the morning, behold, he was not the child that I had borne." 22 But the other woman said, "No, the living child is mine, and the dead child is yours." The first said, "No, the dead child is yours, and the living child is mine." Thus they spoke before the king.

23 Then the king said, "The one says, 'This is my son that is alive, and your son is dead'; and the other says, 'No; but your son is dead, and my son is the living one.'" 24 And the king said, "Bring me a sword." So a sword was brought before the king. 25 And the king said, "Divide the living child in two, and give half to the one and half to the other." 26 Then the woman

5 [e]For ver. 5-14, see 2 Chr. 1:7-12 [f]ch. 9:2; 11:9 [g][Num. 12:6; Matt. 1:20; 2:13, 19]
6 [h]ch. 2:4; 9:4; [Ps. 15:2] [i]ch. 1:48
7 [j][1 Chr. 28:5] [k][1 Chr. 29:1] [l]Num. 27:17
8 [m]Deut. 7:6 [n]Gen. 13:16; 15:5
9 [o][Prov. 2:6, 9; James 1:5] [p]Ps. 72:1, 2 [q][2 Sam. 14:17; Isa. 7:15; Heb. 5:14]
12 [r][1 John 5:14, 15] [s]ch. 4:29-31; 5:12; 10:23, 24; Eccles. 1:16
13 [t][Matt. 6:33] [u]ch. 4:21-24; 10:23, 27; [Prov. 3:16]
14 [v]ver. 6; ch. 15:5 [w][Ps. 91:16; Prov. 3:2]
15 [x]Gen. 41:7
16 [y]Num. 27:2

kingdom ethic that Jesus would later set before his disciples: "Seek first the kingdom of God and his righteousness, and all these things will be added to you" (Matt. 6:33). And so it was. Solomon's request was kingdom-centered, and God added to it (1 Kings 3:13–14).

Perhaps the most amazing aspect of this account is Solomon's description of what motivated his request for wisdom: the "steadfast love" of the Lord (twice in 1 Kings 3:6). Solomon's humble request for wisdom was grounded in the reality that he had already received the greatest treasure in life—the steadfast love of his covenant Lord. Those who seek first the kingdom of God are those who first realize that they have been made members of that kingdom by God's grace. The same steadfast love of the Lord that Solomon experienced some three thousand years ago has been made ours, all through the work of the human embodiment of this steadfast love: Jesus Christ.

3:16–28 The case regarding the ownership of the living baby represents the first recorded display of Solomon's wisdom. Observe that the king of Israel, the highest official in the land, was considering the case of two prostitutes. We do not know what other feats of wisdom may have preceded or followed this one, but we do know that the author of Kings wanted to highlight this particular administration of Solomon's wisdom. When the Lord gives gifts to his people, they are to be administered to all

whose son was alive said to the king, because
[z]her heart yearned for her son, "Oh, my lord,
give her the living child, and by no means put
him to death." But the other said, "He shall be
neither mine nor yours; divide him." 27 Then
the king answered and said, "Give the living
child to the first woman, and by no means
put him to death; she is his mother." 28 And
all Israel heard of the judgment that the king
had rendered, and they stood in awe of the
king, because they perceived that [a]the wisdom
of God was in him to do justice.

Solomon's Officials

4 King Solomon was king over all Israel,
2 and these were his high officials: Azariah
the son of Zadok was [b]the priest; 3 Elihoreph
and Ahijah the sons of Shisha were secretaries;
[c]Jehoshaphat the son of Ahilud was recorder;
4 [d]Benaiah the son of Jehoiada was in command of the army; [e]Zadok and Abiathar were
priests; 5 Azariah the son of Nathan was over
[f]the officers; Zabud the son of Nathan was
priest and [g]king's friend; 6 Ahishar was in
charge of the palace; and [h]Adoniram the son
of Abda was in charge of [i]the forced labor.
7 Solomon had twelve officers over all
Israel, who provided food for the king and
his household. Each man had to make provision for one month in the year. 8 These were
their names: Ben-hur, in [j]the hill country of
Ephraim; 9 Ben-deker, in Makaz, Shaalbim,
Beth-shemesh, and Elonbeth-hanan; 10 Ben-
hesed, in Arubboth (to him belonged Socoh
and all the land of Hepher); 11 Ben-abinadab, in
all [k]Naphath-dor (he had Taphath the daughter of Solomon as his wife); 12 Baana the son of
Ahilud, in [l]Taanach, Megiddo, and all [l]Beth-
shean that is beside Zarethan below Jezreel,
and from Beth-shean to Abel-meholah, as far
as the other side of Jokmeam; 13 Ben-geber,
[m]in Ramoth-gilead (he had [n]the villages of
Jair the son of Manasseh, which are in Gilead,
and he had [o]the region of Argob, which is
in Bashan, sixty great cities with walls and
bronze bars); 14 Ahinadab the son of Iddo, in
Mahanaim; 15 Ahimaaz, in Naphtali (he had
taken Basemath the daughter of Solomon
as his wife); 16 Baana the son of Hushai, in
Asher and Bealoth; 17 Jehoshaphat the son of
Paruah, in Issachar; 18 [p]Shimei the son of Ela,
in Benjamin; 19 Geber the son of Uri, in the
land of Gilead, [q]the country of Sihon king of
the Amorites and of Og king of Bashan. And
there was one governor who was over the land.

Solomon's Wealth and Wisdom

20 Judah and Israel were as many [r]as the sand
by the sea. They ate and drank and were happy.
21 [s]Solomon ruled over all the kingdoms from
the [t]Euphrates[2] to the land of the Philistines
and to the border of Egypt. [u]They brought
tribute and served Solomon all the days of
his life.
22 Solomon's provision for one day was thirty
cors[3] of fine flour and sixty cors of meal, 23 ten
fat oxen, and twenty pasture-fed cattle, a hundred sheep, besides deer, gazelles, roebucks,
and fattened fowl. 24 For he had dominion
over all the region west of the Euphrates[4] from
Tiphsah to [v]Gaza, over all the kings west of
the Euphrates. [w]And he had peace on all sides
around him. 25 And Judah and Israel [x]lived in
safety, [y]from Dan even to Beersheba, [z]every
man under his vine and under his fig tree,
all the days of Solomon. 26 [a]Solomon also had
40,000[5] stalls of horses for his chariots, and
12,000 horsemen. 27 And those officers supplied provisions for King Solomon, and for
all who came to King Solomon's table, each

[1] Ch 5:1 in Hebrew [2] Hebrew *the River* [3] A *cor* was about 6 bushels or 220 liters [4] Hebrew *the River*; twice in this verse [5] Hebrew; one Hebrew manuscript (see 2 Chron. 9:25 and Septuagint of 1 Kings 10:26) *4,000*

of the people in his kingdom without discrimination, even to prostitutes. We must not withhold what God has graciously given us for the service of his people. Nor must we reserve it for only those whom we might deem worthy. Solomon knew this because he was able to distinguish between his own wisdom and the sufficiency of God's equipping gift. He considered himself unqualified to lead God's people, a veritable lost child (1 Kings 3:7), but he also considered the gift of God in him sufficient for service.

It could be a crushing weight to consider ourselves the agents of God's grace. Who could bear such a burden? It is altogether freeing, however, when we recognize that we are simply the instruments through which God's grace flows—and that we have his grace not because of our ability but because of our desperate need.

26[z] Gen. 43:30; Jer. 31:20; [Isa. 49:15]
28[a] ver. 9, 11, 12; [Ezra 7:25]
Chapter 4
2[b] 1 Chr. 6:10
3[c] 2 Sam. 8:16; 20:24
4[d] ch. 2:35 [e] 2 Sam. 20:25; [ch. 2:27, 35]
5[f] ver. 7 [g] [2 Sam. 15:37; 16:16; 1 Chr. 27:33]
6[h] ch. 5:14; [ch. 12:18; 2 Sam. 20:24; 2 Chr. 10:18] [i] [ch. 9:15]
8[j] See Josh. 24:33
11[k] Josh. 11:2

12[l] [Josh. 17:11] **13**[m] [ch. 22:3] [n] Num. 32:41 [o] Deut. 3:4 **18**[p] ch. 1:8 **19**[q] Deut. 3:8-10 **20**[r] Gen. 22:17; [ch. 3:8; 2 Chr. 1:9] **21**[s] 2 Chr. 9:26 [t] Gen. 15:18; Ex. 23:31; Josh. 1:4; Ps. 72:8 [u] Ps. 68:29; 72:10, 11 **24**[v] Gen. 10:19 [w] 1 Chr. 22:9 **25**[x] Jer. 23:6; 32:37; Ezek. 28:26 [y] See 2 Sam. 3:10 [z] Mic. 4:4; Zech. 3:10; [2 Kgs. 18:31; Isa. 36:16] **26**[a] [ch. 10:26; 2 Chr. 1:14; 9:25]

one in his month. They let nothing be lacking. 28 Barley also and straw for the horses and [b]swift steeds they brought to the place where it was required, each according to his duty.

29 [c]And God gave Solomon wisdom and understanding beyond measure, and breadth of mind [d]like the sand on the seashore, 30 so that Solomon's wisdom surpassed the wisdom of all [e]the people of the east [f]and all the wisdom of Egypt. 31 For he was [c]wiser than all other men, wiser than Ethan the Ezrahite, and Heman, Calcol, and Darda, the sons of Mahol, and his fame was in all the surrounding nations. 32 [g]He also spoke 3,000 proverbs, [h]and his songs were 1,005. 33 He spoke of trees, from the cedar that is in Lebanon to the hyssop that grows out of the wall. He spoke also of beasts, and of birds, and of reptiles, and of fish. 34 And people of all nations came to hear the wisdom of Solomon, and from [i]all the kings of the earth, who had heard of his wisdom.

Preparations for Building the Temple

5 [1] Now [j]Hiram king of Tyre sent his servants to Solomon when he heard that they had anointed him king in place of his father, [k]for Hiram always loved David. 2 And Solomon sent word to Hiram, 3 [l]"You know that David my father could not build a house for the name of the LORD his God [m]because of the warfare with which his enemies surrounded him, until the LORD put them under the soles of his feet. 4 [n]But now the LORD my God has given me rest on every side. There is neither adversary nor misfortune. 5 And so I intend to build a house for the name of the LORD my God, [o]as the LORD said to David my father, 'Your son, whom I will set on your throne in your place, shall build the house for my name.' 6 Now therefore command that cedars of Lebanon be cut for me. And my servants will join your servants, and I will pay you for your servants such wages as you set, for you know that there is no one among us who knows how to cut timber like the Sidonians."

7 As soon as Hiram heard the words of Solomon, he rejoiced greatly and said, "Blessed be the LORD this day, who has given to David a wise son to be over this great people." 8 And Hiram sent to Solomon, saying, "I have heard the message that you have sent to me. I am ready to do all you desire in the matter of cedar and cypress timber. 9 My servants shall bring it down to the sea from Lebanon, and I will make it into rafts to go by sea to the place you direct. And I will have them broken up there, and you shall receive it. And you shall meet my wishes [p]by providing food for my household." 10 So Hiram supplied Solomon with all the timber of cedar and cypress that he desired, 11 while Solomon gave Hiram 20,000 cors[2] of wheat

[1] Ch 5:15 in Hebrew [2] A *cor* was about 6 bushels or 220 liters

28 [b]Esth. 8:10, 14; Mic. 1:13
29 [c]ch. 3:12 [d][ver. 20]
30 [e]Judg. 6:3 [f]Acts 7:22; [Isa. 19:11]
31 [c][See ver. 29 above]
32 [g]Prov. 1:1; Eccles. 12:9 [h]Song 1:1
34 [i]2 Chr. 9:23; [ch. 10:1]
Chapter 5
1 [j][2 Chr. 2:3] [k]2 Sam. 5:11; 1 Chr. 14:1
3 [l]For ver. 3-11, see 2 Chr. 2:3-16 [m]1 Chr. 22:8; 28:3
4 [n][ch. 4:24; 1 Chr. 22:9]
5 [o]2 Sam. 7:13; 1 Chr. 17:12; 22:10; 28:6
9 [p][Ezra 3:7; Ezek. 27:17; Acts 12:20]

5:1–12 The gift of Solomon's wisdom continued to grow and flourish. In 1 Kings 3, Solomon's wisdom governed the kingdom, even at the lowest levels. By the end of 1 Kings 4 (vv. 29–34), the fame of Solomon's wisdom had spread throughout the nations. Now, in chapter 5, the wisdom of Solomon was to be employed in the building of God's house, the famed temple of Yahweh, the place where God would cause his name to dwell. It almost seems as if there would be no end to what God was doing through his servant Solomon.

As believers, we might be tempted to read accounts of this type and despair by comparison. How could we ever measure up to the type of service Solomon performed for the kingdom of God? Our own service seems so small and insignificant by comparison. But our Lord never desired us to be like Solomon. In fact, we will soon read that even Solomon, when his dependence on God waned, could not bear the magnitude of kingly service without crumbling under its weight and falling into sin.

Though Solomon was a son of David, more importantly he pointed beyond himself to another son of David, a son even greater than himself (Rom. 1:3). Like Solomon, this King Jesus would surpass all with regard to wisdom (Luke 2:52; 1 Cor. 1:30). Like Solomon, King Jesus would serve God's people (Matt. 20:28). Like Solomon, King Jesus would build God's kingdom and make known his name (John 17:26). But this King would also become the temple of God and provide everlasting rest for all of God's people (Matt. 11:28; Rev. 21:22). King Jesus would not be crushed under the weight of his service, but rather he would be crushed under the weight of *our sin* (Isa. 53:5; 2 Cor. 5:21). We may be impressed for a moment by what Solomon did for the kingdom of God, but it certainly pales in comparison to what David's Greater Son has accomplished.

as food for his household, and 20,000[1] cors of beaten oil. Solomon gave this to Hiram year by year. 12 And the LORD gave Solomon wisdom, [q]as he promised him. And there was peace between Hiram and Solomon, and the two of them made a treaty.

13 King Solomon drafted [r]forced labor out of all Israel, and the draft numbered 30,000 men. 14 And he sent them to Lebanon, 10,000 a month in shifts. They would be a month in Lebanon and two months at home. [s]Adoniram was in charge of the draft. 15 Solomon also [t]had 70,000 burden-bearers and 80,000 stonecutters in the hill country, 16 besides Solomon's 3,300 [u]chief officers who were over the work, [v]who had charge of the people who carried on the work. 17 At the king's command [w]they quarried out great, costly stones in order to lay the foundation of the house with dressed stones. 18 So Solomon's builders and Hiram's builders and [x]the men of Gebal did the cutting and prepared the timber and the stone to build the house.

Solomon Builds the Temple

6 [y]In the four hundred and eightieth year after the people of Israel came out of the land of Egypt, in the fourth year of Solomon's reign over Israel, in the month of Ziv, which is the second month, [z]he began to build the house of the LORD. 2 [a]The house that King Solomon built for the LORD was sixty cubits[2] long, twenty cubits wide, and thirty cubits high. 3 The vestibule in front of the nave of the house was twenty cubits long, equal to the width of the house, and ten cubits deep in front of the house. 4 And [b]he made for the house windows with recessed frames.[3] 5 [c]He also built a structure[4] against the wall of the house, running around the walls of the house, both the nave and [d]the inner sanctuary. And he made [e]side chambers all around. 6 The lowest story[5] was five cubits broad, the middle one was six cubits broad, and the third was seven cubits broad. For around the outside of the house he made offsets on the wall in order that the supporting beams should not be inserted into the walls of the house.

7 When the house was built, [f]it was with stone prepared at the quarry, so that neither hammer nor axe nor any tool of iron was heard in the house while it was being built.

8 The entrance for the lowest[6] story was on the south side of the house, and one went up by stairs to the middle story, and from the middle story to the third. 9 [g]So he built the house and finished it, and he made the ceiling of the house of beams and planks of cedar. 10 He built the structure against the whole house, five cubits high, and it was joined to the house with timbers of cedar.

11 Now the word of the LORD came to Solomon, 12 "Concerning this house that you are building, [h]if you will walk in my statutes and obey my rules and keep all my commandments and walk in them, then I will establish my word with you, [i]which I spoke to David your father. 13 And [j]I will dwell among the children of Israel [k]and will not forsake my people Israel."

14 [l]So Solomon built the house and finished it. 15 He lined the walls of the house on the inside with boards of cedar. From the floor of the house to the walls of the ceiling, he covered them on the inside with wood, [m]and he covered the floor of the house with boards of cypress. 16 [n]He built twenty cubits of the rear

[1] Septuagint; Hebrew *twenty* [2] A *cubit* was about 18 inches or 45 centimeters [3] Or *blocked lattice windows* [4] Or *platform*; also verse 10 [5] Septuagint; Hebrew *structure*, or *platform* [6] Septuagint, Targum; Hebrew *middle*

6:11–13 It took seven years and tremendous amounts of wealth and resources to complete the temple building project. The summary of temple construction presented in chapter 6 staggers the imagination. In the midst of this account, we might wonder if all of that time, effort, and expense was really worth it.

But consider the reason for all of this effort and expense. The Lord had determined to dwell in the midst of his people, and this temple was to be the house of that presence (v. 13), the central place from which God would make his name known to all the nations. But we also read that the continuation of God's presence was contingent upon the obedience of the king (v. 12).

As people living thousands of years after the events recorded in 1 Kings 6, we understand that Solomon, and all of the kings who followed him, did not fully obey the Lord or keep his statutes and ordinances. For this reason, the Lord's presence abandoned the temple, and it was eventually destroyed (2 Kings 25).

12 [q]ch. 3:12
13 [r]ch. 4:6; 9:15
14 [s]See ch. 4:6
15 [t]2 Chr. 2:18; [ch. 9:20-22]
16 [u]ch. 4:5 [v]ch. 9:23
17 [w][ch. 6:7; 1 Chr. 22:2]
18 [x]Josh. 13:5; Ezek. 27:9

Chapter 6
1 [y]2 Chr. 3:1, 2 [z]Acts 7:47
2 [a]2 Chr. 3:3, 4; See Ezek. 40-42
4 [b]Ezek. 40:16; 41:16, 26
5 [c]Ezek. 41:6 [d]ver. 16, 19, 20, 23, 31; ch. 7:49; 8:6, 8; 2 Chr. 4:20; 5:7, 9; Ps. 28:2 [e]Ezek. 41:5, 6
7 [f]ch. 5:18; Deut. 27:5, 6
9 [g]ver. 14, 38
12 [h]ch. 9:4; [ch. 2:4] [i]2 Sam. 7:13; 1 Chr. 22:10 **13** [j]Ex. 25:8 [k]Deut. 31:6, 8; Josh. 1:5 **14** [l]ver. 9, 38 **15** [m][ch. 7:7] **16** [n]2 Chr. 3:8

of the house with boards of cedar from the
floor to the walls, and he built this within as
an inner sanctuary, as [o]the Most Holy Place.
17 The house, that is, the nave in front of the
inner sanctuary, was forty cubits long. 18 The
cedar within the house was carved in the form
of [p]gourds and open flowers. All was cedar; no
stone was seen. 19 The inner sanctuary he prepared in the innermost part of the house, to
set there the ark of the covenant of the LORD.
20 The inner sanctuary[1] was twenty cubits
long, twenty cubits wide, and twenty cubits
high, and he overlaid it with pure gold. He
also overlaid[2] an altar of cedar. 21 And Solomon
overlaid the inside of the house with pure
gold, and he drew chains of gold across, in
front of the inner sanctuary, and overlaid it
with gold. 22 And he overlaid the whole house
with gold, until all the house was finished.
[q]Also the whole altar that belonged to the
inner sanctuary he overlaid with gold.

23 [r]In the inner sanctuary [s]he made two
cherubim of olivewood, each ten cubits high.
24 Five cubits was the length of one wing of
the cherub, and five cubits the length of the
other wing of the cherub; it was ten cubits
from the tip of one wing to the tip of the other.
25 The other cherub also measured ten cubits;
both cherubim had the same measure and the
same form. 26 The height of one cherub was
ten cubits, and so was that of the other cherub.
27 He put the cherubim in the innermost part
of the house. [t]And the wings of the cherubim
were spread out so that a wing of one touched
the one wall, and a wing of the other cherub
touched the other wall; their other wings
touched each other in the middle of the house.
28 And he overlaid the cherubim with gold.

29 Around all the walls of the house he carved
engraved figures of cherubim and palm trees
and open flowers, in the inner and outer
rooms. 30 The floor of the house he overlaid
with gold in the inner and outer rooms.

31 For the entrance to the inner sanctuary
he made doors of olivewood; the lintel and
the doorposts were five-sided.[3] 32 He covered
the two doors of olivewood with carvings of
cherubim, palm trees, and open flowers. He
overlaid them with gold and spread gold on
the cherubim and on the palm trees.

33 So also he made for the entrance to the
nave doorposts of olivewood, in the form of a
square, 34 and two doors of cypress wood. [u]The
two leaves of the one door were folding, and
the two leaves of the other door were folding.
35 On them he carved cherubim and palm trees
and open flowers, and he overlaid them with
gold evenly applied on the carved work. 36 [v]He
built the inner court with three courses of cut
stone and one course of cedar beams.

37 [w]In the fourth year the foundation of the
house of the LORD was laid, in the month of
Ziv. 38 And in the eleventh year, in the month
of Bul, which is the eighth month, the house
was finished in all its parts, and according to
all its specifications. He was seven years in
building it.

Solomon Builds His Palace

7 Solomon was [x]building his own house
thirteen years, and he finished his entire
house.

2 He built [y]the House of the Forest of
Lebanon. Its length was a hundred cubits[4] and
its breadth fifty cubits and its height thirty
cubits, and it was built on four[5] rows of cedar
pillars, with cedar beams on the pillars. 3 And
it was covered with cedar above the chambers
that were on the forty-five pillars, fifteen in
each row. 4 There were window frames in three
rows, and window opposite window in three
tiers. 5 All the doorways and windows[6] had
square frames, and window was opposite window in three tiers.

6 And he made [z]the Hall of Pillars; its length
was fifty cubits, and its breadth thirty cubits.
There was a porch in front with pillars, and [a]a
canopy in front of them.

[1] Vulgate; Hebrew *and before the inner sanctuary* [2] Septuagint *made* [3] The meaning of the Hebrew phrase is uncertain [4] A *cubit* was about 18 inches or 45 centimeters [5] Septuagint *three* [6] Septuagint; Hebrew *posts*

16 [o]ch. 7:50; 8:6; Ex. 26:33, 34; 2 Chr. 3:8; Ezek. 45:3; Heb. 9:3
18 [p]ch. 7:24
22 [q]Ex. 30:1, 3, 6
23 [r]For ver. 23-27, see 2 Chr. 3:10-12 [s]Ex. 37:7-9
27 [t]ch. 8:7; Ex. 25:20; 37:9; 2 Chr. 5:8
34 [u][Ezek. 41:24]

We now live within a new covenant, but the same principles apply. God still desires to dwell among his people, and his presence is still contingent upon the obedience of the king. In the new covenant, however, the obedience of the king is no longer in question. It is a reality (Rom. 5:19; Heb. 5:7–9). The promised presence of God is therefore perfectly secure for each and every believer. Our obedience to Christ flows out of our rest in Christ, the one who obeyed on our behalf. True obedience, then, is the loving response—not the necessary prerequisite—to God's abundant favor.

36 [v]ch. 7:12 **37** [w]ver. 1 **Chapter 7** **1** [x]ch. 3:1; 9:10; 2 Chr. 8:1 **2** [y]ch. 10:17, 21 **6** [z][ver. 12] [a]Ezek. 41:25, 26

7 And he made the Hall of the Throne where
he was to pronounce judgment, even the Hall
of Judgment. [b]It was finished with cedar from
floor to rafters.[1]

8 His own house where he was to dwell, in
the other court back of the hall, was of like
workmanship. Solomon also made a house
like this hall for Pharaoh's daughter [c]whom
he had taken in marriage.

9 All these were made of costly stones, cut
according to measure, sawed with saws, back
and front, even from the foundation to the
coping, and from the outside to the great
court. 10 The foundation was of costly stones,
huge stones, stones of eight and ten cubits.
11 And above were costly stones, cut according
to measurement, and cedar. 12 [d]The great court
had three courses of cut stone all around, and
a course of cedar beams; so had the inner court
of the house of the LORD and [e]the vestibule
of the house.

The Temple Furnishings

13 And King Solomon sent and brought
[f]Hiram from Tyre. 14 He was the son of a widow
of the tribe of Naphtali, and his father was a
man of Tyre, a worker in bronze. And [g]he was
full of wisdom, understanding, and skill for
making any work in bronze. He came to King
Solomon and did all his work.

15 [h]He cast [i]two pillars of bronze. [j]Eighteen
cubits was the height of one pillar, and a line
of twelve cubits measured its circumference.
It was hollow, and its thickness was four fingers. The second pillar was the same.[2] 16 He also
made two capitals of cast bronze to set on the
tops of the pillars. The height of the one capital was five cubits, and [j]the height of the other
capital was five cubits. 17 There were lattices of
checker work with wreaths of chain work for
the capitals on the tops of the pillars, a lattice[3]
for the one capital and a lattice for the other
capital. 18 Likewise he made pomegranates[4] in
two rows around the one latticework to cover
the capital that was on the top of the pillar,
and he did the same with the other capital.
19 Now the capitals that were on the tops of
the pillars in the vestibule were of lily-work,
four cubits. 20 The capitals were on the two
pillars and also above the rounded projection
which was beside the latticework. There were
[k]two hundred pomegranates in two rows all
around, and so with the other capital. 21 [l]He set
up the pillars at the vestibule of the temple.
He set up the pillar on the south and called
its name Jachin, and he set up the pillar on
the north and called its name Boaz. 22 And on
the tops of the pillars was lily-work. Thus the
work of the pillars was finished.

23 [m]Then he made [n]the sea of cast metal. It
was round, ten cubits from brim to brim, and
five cubits high, and a line of thirty cubits
measured its circumference. 24 Under its brim
were [o]gourds, for ten cubits, compassing the
sea all around. The gourds were in two rows,
cast with it when it was cast. 25 It stood on
[p]twelve oxen, three facing north, three facing west, three facing south, and three facing
east. The sea was set on them, and all their
rear parts were inward. 26 Its thickness was a
handbreadth,[5] and its brim was made like the
brim of a cup, like the flower of a lily. It held
two thousand baths.[6]

27 He also made the [q]ten stands of bronze.
Each stand was four cubits long, four cubits
wide, and three cubits high. 28 This was the
construction of the stands: they had panels,
and the panels were set in the frames, 29 and
on the panels that were set in the frames
were lions, oxen, and cherubim. On the
frames, both above and below the lions and
oxen, there were wreaths of beveled work.
30 Moreover, each stand had four bronze
wheels and axles of bronze, and at the four
corners were supports for a basin. The supports were cast with wreaths at the side of
each. 31 Its opening was within a crown that
projected upward one cubit. Its opening was
round, as a pedestal is made, a cubit and a half
deep. At its opening there were carvings, and
its panels were square, not round. 32 And the
four wheels were underneath the panels. The
axles of the wheels were of one piece with
the stands, and the height of a wheel was a
cubit and a half. 33 The wheels were made like
a chariot wheel; their axles, their rims, their
spokes, and their hubs were all cast. 34 There
were four supports at the four corners of each
stand. The supports were of one piece with the

[1] Syriac, Vulgate; Hebrew *floor* [2] Targum, Syriac (compare Septuagint and Jeremiah 52:21); Hebrew *fingers. And a line of twelve cubits measured the circumference of the second pillar* [3] Septuagint; Hebrew *seven*; twice in this verse [4] Two manuscripts (compare Septuagint); Hebrew *pillars* [5] A *handbreadth* was about 3 inches or 7.5 centimeters [6] A *bath* was about 6 gallons or 22 liters

7[b] ch. 6:15, 16 **8**[c] ch. 3:1; 2 Chr. 8:11 **12**[d] ch. 6:36 [e] [ver. 6] **13**[f] [2 Chr. 2:14] **14**[g] [Ex. 31:3-5; 35:31] **15**[h] For ver. 15-21, see 2 Chr. 3:15-17 [i] 2 Kgs. 25:17; 1 Chr. 18:8; 2 Chr. 4:12; Jer. 52:21-23 [j] ver. 41 **16**[j] [See ver. 15 above] **20**[k] [ver. 42; 2 Chr. 3:16; 4:13; Jer. 52:23] **21**[l] 2 Chr. 3:17 **23**[m] For ver. 23-26, see 2 Chr. 4:2-5 [n] 2 Kgs. 16:17; 25:13; 1 Chr. 18:8; Jer. 52:17; [Ex. 30:18] **24**[o] [ch. 6:18] **25**[p] Jer. 52:20 **27**[q] 2 Kgs. 25:13; 2 Chr. 4:14; Jer. 52:17

stands. 35 And on the top of the stand there was a round band half a cubit high; and on the top of the stand its stays and its panels were of one piece with it. 36 And on the surfaces of its stays and on its panels, he carved cherubim, lions, and palm trees, according to the space of each, with wreaths all around. 37 After this manner he made [q]the ten stands. All of them were cast alike, of the same measure and the same form.

38 And he made [r]ten basins of bronze. Each basin held forty baths, each basin measured four cubits, and there was a basin for each of the ten stands. 39 And he set the stands, five on the south side of the house, and five on the north side of the house. And he set the sea at the southeast corner of the house.

40 [s]Hiram also made [t]the pots, the shovels, and the basins. So Hiram finished all the work that he did for King Solomon on the house of the LORD: 41 the two pillars, the two bowls of the capitals that were on the tops of the pillars, and the two [u]latticeworks to cover the two bowls of the capitals that were on the tops of the pillars; 42 and the [v]four hundred pomegranates for the two latticeworks, two rows of pomegranates for each latticework, to cover the two bowls of the capitals that were on the pillars; 43 the ten stands, and the ten basins on the stands; 44 and [w]the one sea, and the twelve oxen underneath the sea.

45 Now [x]the pots, the shovels, and the basins, all these vessels in the house of the LORD, which Hiram made for King Solomon, were of burnished bronze. 46 In the plain of the Jordan the king cast them, in the clay ground between [y]Succoth and [z]Zarethan. 47 And Solomon left all the vessels unweighed, because there were so many of them; [a]the weight of the bronze was not ascertained.

48 So Solomon made all the vessels that were in the house of the LORD: [b]the golden altar, [c]the golden table for [d]the bread of the Presence, 49 [e]the lampstands of pure gold, five on the south side and five on the north, before the inner sanctuary; [f]the flowers, the lamps, and the tongs, of gold; 50 the cups, snuffers, basins, dishes for incense, and [g]fire pans, of pure gold; and the sockets of gold, for the doors of the innermost part of the house, [h]the Most Holy Place, and for the doors of the nave of the temple.

51 Thus all the work that King Solomon did on the house of the LORD was finished. And Solomon brought in [i]the things that David his father had dedicated, the silver, the gold, and the vessels, and stored them in the treasuries of the house of the LORD.

The Ark Brought into the Temple

8 [j]Then Solomon assembled the elders of Israel and all the heads of the tribes, [k]the leaders of the fathers' houses of the people of Israel, before King Solomon in Jerusalem, [l]to bring up the ark of the covenant of the LORD out of [m]the city of David, which is Zion. 2 And all the men of Israel assembled to King Solomon at [n]the feast in the month Ethanim, which is the seventh month. 3 And all the elders of Israel came, and [o]the priests took up the ark. 4 And they brought up the ark of the LORD, [p]the tent of meeting, and all the holy vessels that were in the tent; the priests and the Levites brought them up. 5 And King Solomon and all the congregation of Israel, who had assembled before him, were with him before the ark, [q]sacrificing so many sheep and oxen that they could not be counted or numbered. 6 [r]Then the priests brought the ark of the covenant of the LORD [s]to its place in [t]the inner sanctuary of the house, in the Most Holy Place, underneath the wings of the cherubim. 7 For the cherubim spread out their wings over the place of the ark, so that the cherubim overshadowed the ark and its poles. 8 [u]And the poles were so long that the ends of the poles were seen from the Holy Place before [t]the inner sanctuary; but they could not be seen from outside. And they are there to this day. 9 There was nothing in the ark except [v]the two tablets of stone that Moses put there at Horeb, where [w]the LORD made a covenant with the people of Israel, when they came out of the land of Egypt. 10 And when the priests came out of the Holy Place, [x]a cloud filled the house of the LORD, 11 so that the priests could not stand to minister because of the cloud, for the glory of the LORD filled the house of the LORD.

37 [q][See ver. 27 above] **38** [r]2 Chr. 4:6; [Ex. 30:18] **40** [s]For ver. 40-51, see 2 Chr. 4:11–5:1 [t]Ex. 27:3; 38:3 **41** [u]ver. 17, 18 **42** [v][ver. 20] **44** [w]ver. 23, 25 **45** [x]Ex. 27:3; 38:3 **46** [y]Josh. 13:27 [z]Josh. 3:16 **47** [a][1 Chr. 22:3, 14] **48** [b]See Ex. 37:25-29 [c][2 Chr. 4:8]; See Ex. 37:10-16 [d]Ex. 25:30; See Lev. 24:5-8 **49** [e]2 Chr. 4:7 [f]See Ex. 25:31-38 **50** [g]Ex. 27:3 [h]See ch. 6:16 **51** [i]2 Sam. 8:11 **Chapter 8** **1** [j]For ver. 1-9, see 2 Chr. 5:2-10 [k]Num. 1:16 [l][2 Sam. 6:17] [m]See 2 Sam. 5:7 **2** [n]ver. 65; Lev. 23:34; See 2 Chr. 7:8-10 **3** [o][Num. 4:15; Deut. 31:9; Josh. 3:3, 6; 1 Chr. 15:14, 15] **4** [p][ch. 3:4; 2 Chr. 1:3] **5** [q][2 Sam. 6:13] **6** [r]2 Sam. 6:17 [s]Ex. 26:33, 34 [t]See ch. 6:5 **8** [u]Ex. 25:13-15 [t][See ver. 6 above] **9** [v]Ex. 25:21; 40:20; Deut. 10:2, 5; Heb. 9:4 [w]Ex. 34:27, 28; Deut. 4:13 **10** [x]Ex. 40:34, 35; 2 Chr. 5:13, 14; 7:1, 2; [Ezek. 10:3, 4]

Solomon Blesses the LORD

12 [y]Then Solomon said, "The LORD[1] has
said that he would dwell [z]in thick darkness.
13 [a]I have indeed built you an exalted house,
[b]a place for you to dwell in forever." 14 Then
the king turned around and [c]blessed all the
assembly of Israel, while all the assembly of
Israel stood. 15 And he said, [d]"Blessed be the
LORD, the God of Israel, who with his hand has
fulfilled [e]what he promised with his mouth
to David my father, saying, 16 [f]'Since the day
that I brought my people Israel out of Egypt,
I chose no city out of all the tribes of Israel in
which to build a house, [g]that my name might
be there. [h]But I chose David to be over my people Israel.' 17 [i]Now it was in the heart of David
my father to build a house for the name of the
LORD, the God of Israel. 18 But the LORD said to
David my father, 'Whereas it was in your heart
to build a house for my name, you did well
that it was in your heart. 19 [j]Nevertheless, you
shall not build the house, but your son who
shall be born to you shall build the house for
my name.' 20 Now the LORD has fulfilled his
promise that he made. For I have risen in the
place of David my father, and sit on the throne
of Israel, [k]as the LORD promised, and I have
built the house for the name of the LORD, the
God of Israel. 21 And there I have provided a
place for the ark, [l]in which is the covenant of
the LORD that he made with our fathers, when
he brought them out of the land of Egypt."

Solomon's Prayer of Dedication

22 Then Solomon [m]stood before the altar of
the LORD in the presence of all the assembly
of Israel and [n]spread out his hands toward
heaven, 23 and said, "O LORD, God of Israel,
[o]there is no God like you, in heaven above
or on earth beneath, [p]keeping covenant and
showing steadfast love to your servants who
walk before you with all their heart; 24 you
have kept with your servant David my father
what you declared to him. [e]You spoke with
your mouth, and with your hand have fulfilled
it this day. 25 Now therefore, O LORD, God of
Israel, keep for your servant David my father
what you have promised him, saying, [q]'You
shall not lack a man to sit before me on the
throne of Israel, if only your sons pay close
attention to their way, to walk before me as
you have walked before me.' 26 [r]Now therefore,
O God of Israel, let your word be confirmed,
which you have spoken to your servant David
my father.

27 "But will God indeed dwell on the earth?
Behold, [s]heaven and the highest heaven cannot contain you; how much less this house
that I have built! 28 Yet have regard to the
prayer of your servant and to his plea, O LORD
my God, listening to the cry and to the prayer
that your servant prays before you this day,
29 [t]that your eyes may be open night and day
toward this house, the place of which you have
said, [u]'My name shall be there,' that you may
listen to the prayer that your servant offers
toward this place. 30 And listen to the plea of
your servant and of your people Israel, when
they pray toward this place. And listen in
heaven your dwelling place, and when you
hear, forgive.

31 "If a man sins against his neighbor and is
made to take [v]an oath and comes and swears
his oath before your altar in this house,
32 then hear in heaven and act and judge your

[1] Septuagint *The LORD has set the sun in the heavens, but*

8:22–61 One of the most remarkable realities about the temple Solomon built was that it was designed and constructed to be the place where the Lord (Yahweh) would dwell, not symbolically or metaphorically, but really and truly—"for the glory of the LORD filled the house of the LORD" (v. 11). Solomon recognized the incomprehensible wonder of this reality. "But will God indeed dwell on the earth? Behold, heaven and the highest heaven cannot contain you; how much less this house that I have built!" (v. 27).

Perhaps equally remarkable is the purpose or function for which the temple was designed. This house of the Lord was not simply a place to offer sacrifices or to store the treasures of the kingdom. Rather, the temple of the Lord was designed to be a house of prayer (cf. Isa. 56:7; Matt. 21:13), where the Lord would both hear and forgive his people. These two themes dominate the prayer of Solomon. Fourteen times, Solomon indicates that from this house the Lord would hear the prayers of his people (1 Kings 8:28–30, 32, 34, 36, 39, 42–43, 45, 49, 52). Five more times, Solomon prayed that when the Lord heard these prayers, he would forgive the sins of his people (vv. 30, 34, 36, 39, 50).

12 [y] For ver. 12-50, see 2 Chr. 6:1-39 [z] Ps. 18:11; 97:2; [Lev. 16:2]
13 [a] 2 Sam. 7:13 [b] Ex. 15:17; [Ps. 132:14]
14 [c] ver. 55; 2 Sam. 6:18
15 [d] Luke 1:68 [e] ch. 6:12
16 [f] See 2 Sam. 7:4-16, 25 [g] ver. 29; Deut. 12:11 [h] 1 Sam. 16:1; 2 Sam. 7:8; 1 Chr. 28:4
17 [i] 2 Sam. 7:2, 3; 1 Chr. 17:1, 2
19 [j] ch. 5:3, 5; 2 Sam. 7:5, 12, 13
20 [k] 1 Chr. 28:5, 6
21 [l] ver. 9; Deut. 31:26
22 [m] ver. 54; 2 Chr. 6:12, 13 [n] [Ex. 9:33; Ezra 9:5; Isa. 1:15]
23 [o] Ex. 15:11; 2 Sam. 7:22 [p] See Deut. 7:9
24 [e] [See ver. 15 above]
25 [q] See ch. 2:4
26 [r] 2 Sam. 7:25

27 [s] 2 Chr. 2:6; [Isa. 66:1; Jer. 23:24; Acts 7:49; 17:24] **29** [t] ver. 52; [2 Chr. 7:15; Neh. 1:6] [u] ver. 16; ch. 9:3; Deut. 12:11 **31** [v] [Ex. 22:11]

servants, [w]condemning the guilty by bringing
his conduct on his own head, and vindicating
the righteous by rewarding him according to
his righteousness.
33 [x]"When your people Israel are defeated
before the enemy because they have sinned
against you, and [y]if they turn again to you and
acknowledge your name and pray and plead
with you in this house, 34 then hear in heaven
and forgive the sin of your people Israel and
bring them again to the land that you gave to
their fathers.
35 [z]"When heaven is shut up and there is no
rain because they have sinned against you, if
they pray toward this place and acknowledge
your name and turn from their sin, when you
afflict them, 36 then hear in heaven and forgive
the sin of your servants, your people Israel,
when [a]you teach them [b]the good way in which
they should walk, and grant rain upon your
land, which you have given to your people as
an inheritance.
37 [c]"If there is famine in the land, if there
is pestilence or blight or mildew or locust or
caterpillar, if their enemy besieges them in the
land at their gates,[1] whatever plague, whatever
sickness there is, 38 whatever prayer, whatever
plea is made by any man or by all your people
Israel, each knowing the affliction of his own
heart and stretching out his hands toward this
house, 39 then hear in heaven your dwelling
place and forgive and act and render to each
whose heart you know, according to all his
ways ([d]for you, you only, know the hearts of
all the children of mankind), 40 that they may
fear you [e]all the days that they live in the land
that you gave to our fathers.

41 "Likewise, when a foreigner, who is not of
your people Israel, comes from a far country
for your name's sake 42 (for they shall hear of
your great name [f]and your mighty hand, and
of your outstretched arm), when he comes
and prays toward this house, 43 hear in heaven
your dwelling place and do according to all for
which the foreigner calls to you, in order [g]that
all the peoples of the earth may know your
name and [h]fear you, as do your people Israel,
and that they may know that this house that
I have built is called by your name.
44 "If your people go out to battle against
their enemy, by whatever way you shall send
them, and they pray to the LORD [i]toward the
city that you have chosen and the house that
I have built for your name, 45 then hear in
heaven their prayer and their plea, and maintain their cause.
46 "If they sin against you—[j]for there is no
one who does not sin—and you are angry
with them and give them to an enemy, so
that they are carried away captive [k]to the land
of the enemy, far off or near, 47 yet [l]if they turn
their heart in the land to which they have been
carried captive, and repent and plead with you
in the land of their captors, saying, [m]'We have
sinned and have acted perversely and wickedly,' 48 [n]if they repent with all their mind
and with all their heart in the land of their
enemies, who carried them captive, and pray
to you [o]toward their land, which you gave to
their fathers, the city that you have chosen,
and the house that I have built for your name,
49 then hear in heaven your dwelling place
their prayer and their plea, and maintain their
cause 50 and forgive your people who have

[1] Septuagint, Syriac *in any of their cities*

32 [w] Deut. 25:1
33 [x] Lev. 26:17; Deut. 28:45 [y] Lev. 26:40; [Neh. 1:9]
35 [z] Deut. 11:17; Luke 4:25; [Lev. 26:17; Deut. 28:25]
36 [a] [Ps. 25:4; 27:11; 86:11] [b] 1 Sam. 12:23
37 [c] [Lev. 26:16, 25, 26; Deut. 28:21, 22, 37, 38, 42, 52; 2 Chr. 20:9]
39 [d] 1 Chr. 28:9; Acts 1:24; [1 Sam. 16:7; Jer. 17:10]
40 [e] Deut. 12:1
42 [f] Deut. 3:24; 2 Chr. 6:32
43 [g] ver. 60; [Josh. 4:24] [h] Ps. 102:15
44 [i] [ver. 48]
46 [j] Prov. 20:9; Eccles. 7:20; Rom. 3:23; James 3:2; 1 John 1:8, 10 [k] Lev. 26:34, 44; Deut. 28:36, 64
47 [l] Lev. 26:40 [m] Neh. 1:6; Ps. 106:6; Dan. 9:5
48 [n] 1 Sam. 7:3; Jer. 29:12-14 [o] Dan. 6:10; [ver. 44; Ps. 5:7; Jonah 2:4]

Our covenant Lord, the Creator of heaven and earth, came to dwell among his people in the Promised Land that he had provided in order to hear their prayers and forgive their sins. In light of this reality, Solomon was able to declare that the Lord had fulfilled all that he promised through Moses his servant (v. 56). Only then, after all of God's goodness to his people was thoroughly rehearsed, does Solomon encourage the people to obedience (vv. 58–61), but it is an obedience motivated by God's grace. Our obedience to God, in both the Old and New Testaments, is always motivated by God's grace and his steadfast love. He has kept all of his promises (cf. 2 Cor. 1:20), he comes to hear our prayers and forgive our sins, and so his people long to live in fellowship and communion with him, rejoicing in the "obedience of faith" (Rom. 1:5; 16:26).

Solomon asked of the temple, "But will God indeed dwell on the earth?" (1 Kings 8:27). Beyond what Solomon may ever have imagined, the answer would come resounding back one thousand years later: yes. In Christ's incarnation, God came to dwell on earth. Jesus is the true and final temple (John 1:14), where God and man, heaven and earth, are brought together once more.

sinned against you, and all their transgressions that they have committed against you, and [p]grant them compassion in the sight of those who carried them captive, that they may have compassion on them 51 ([q]for they are your people, and your heritage, which you brought out of Egypt, [r]from the midst of the iron furnace). 52 [s]Let your eyes be open to the plea of your servant and to the plea of your people Israel, giving ear to them whenever they call to you. 53 For you separated them from among all the peoples of the earth to be your heritage, [t]as you declared through Moses your servant, when you brought our fathers out of Egypt, O Lord GOD."

Solomon's Benediction

54 [u]Now as Solomon finished offering all this prayer and plea to the LORD, he arose from before the altar of the LORD, where he had [v]knelt with hands outstretched toward heaven. 55 And he stood and [w]blessed all the assembly of Israel with a loud voice, saying, 56 "Blessed be the LORD who has given rest to his people Israel, according to all that he promised. [x]Not one word has failed of all his good promise, which he spoke by Moses his servant. 57 The LORD our God be with us, as he was with our fathers. [y]May he not leave us or forsake us, 58 that he may [z]incline our hearts to him, to walk in all his ways and to keep his commandments, his statutes, and his rules, which he commanded our fathers. 59 Let these words of mine, with which I have pleaded before the LORD, be near to the LORD our God day and night, and may he maintain the cause of his servant and the cause of his people Israel, as each day requires, 60 that [a]all the peoples of the earth may know that [b]the LORD is God; there is no other. 61 [c]Let your heart therefore be wholly true to the LORD our God, walking in his statutes and keeping his commandments, as at this day."

Solomon's Sacrifices

62 [d]Then [e]the king, and all Israel with him, offered sacrifice before the LORD. 63 Solomon offered as peace offerings to the LORD 22,000 oxen and 120,000 sheep. So the king and all the people of Israel dedicated the house of the LORD. 64 The same day the king consecrated the middle of the court that was before the house of the LORD, for there he offered the burnt offering and the grain offering and the fat pieces of the peace offerings, because [f]the bronze altar that was before the LORD was too small to receive the burnt offering and the grain offering and the fat pieces of the peace offerings.

65 So Solomon held [g]the feast at that time, and all Israel with him, a great assembly, from [h]Lebo-hamath to [i]the Brook of Egypt, before the LORD our God, seven days.[1] 66 On the eighth day he sent the people away, and they blessed the king and went to their homes joyful and glad of heart for all the goodness that the LORD had shown to David his servant and to Israel his people.

The LORD Appears to Solomon

9 [j]As soon as Solomon had finished building the house of the LORD [k]and the king's house and [l]all that Solomon desired to build, 2 [m]the LORD appeared to Solomon a second time, as he had appeared to him at Gibeon. 3 And the LORD said to him, "I have heard your prayer and your plea, which you have made before me. I have consecrated this house that you have built, [n]by putting my name there forever. [o]My eyes and my heart will be there for all time. 4 And as for you, if you will [p]walk before me, [q]as David your father walked, with integrity of heart and uprightness, doing according to all that I have commanded you, and keeping my statutes and my rules, 5 [r]then I will establish your royal throne over Israel forever, as I promised David your father, saying, 'You

[1] Septuagint; Hebrew *seven days and seven days, fourteen days*

9:4–9 The theme of obedience plays a significant role in the account of Solomon's career as recorded in chapters 1–11. The obedience required of Solomon and his heirs was, however, an obedience motivated by God's grace. In chapter 1, Solomon received his kingship by promise, not by right. In chapter 8, Solomon confessed that the Lord had fulfilled all of his promises and had come to dwell among his people in order to hear their prayers and forgive their sins. Solomon's obedience, like ours, is always to be motivated by God's steadfast love, that is, his willingness to keep his promises to us in spite of our inability to respond in obedience with all of our heart, soul, mind, and strength.

50 [p] Ps. 106:46
51 [q] Deut. 9:29; [Neh. 1:10] [r] Deut. 4:20; Jer. 11:4
52 [s] [ver. 29]
53 [t] Ex. 19:5, 6; Deut. 9:26, 29; 14:2
54 [u] 2 Chr. 7:1 [v] [2 Chr. 6:13]
55 [w] ver. 14
56 [x] Josh. 21:45; 23:14
57 [y] [Deut. 31:6; Josh. 1:5; 1 Sam. 12:22]

58 [z] Ps. 119:36 **60** [a] ver. 43 [b] Deut. 4:35, 39; [ch. 18:39] **61** [c] 2 Kgs. 20:3; [ch. 11:4; 15:3, 14] **62** [d] For ver. 62-66, see 2 Chr. 7:4-10 [e] [Ezra 6:16, 17] **64** [f] See 2 Chr. 4:1 **65** [g] ver. 2; Lev. 23:34 [h] Num. 13:21; 34:8 [i] Num. 34:5; 2 Kgs. 24:7 **Chapter 9** **1** [j] For ver. 1-9, see 2 Chr. 7:11-22 [k] ch. 7:1; 2 Chr. 8:1 [l] ver. 19; 2 Chr. 8:6 **2** [m] ch. 3:5; 11:9 **3** [n] ch. 8:16, 29 [o] Deut. 11:12 **4** [p] [Gen. 17:1] [q] ch. 11:4, 6, 38; 14:8; 15:5 **5** [r] ch. 6:12; 1 Chr. 22:10; See ch. 2:4

shall not lack a man on the throne of Israel.'
6 [s]But if you turn aside from following me,
you or your children, and do not keep my
commandments and my statutes that I have
set before you, but go and serve other gods
and worship them, 7 [t]then I will cut off Israel
from the land that I have given them, [u]and the
house that I have consecrated for my name
I will cast out of my sight, [v]and Israel will
become a proverb and a byword among all
peoples. 8 And this house will become a heap
of ruins.[1] Everyone passing by it will be astonished and will hiss, and they will say, [w]'Why
has the LORD done thus to this land and to
this house?' 9 Then they will say, 'Because [x]they
abandoned the LORD their God who brought
their fathers out of the land of Egypt and laid
hold on other gods and worshiped them and
served them. Therefore the LORD has brought
all this disaster on them.'"

Solomon's Other Acts

10 [y]At the end of [z]twenty years, in which
Solomon had built the two houses, the house
of the LORD and the king's house, 11 and Hiram
king of Tyre had supplied Solomon with
cedar and cypress timber and gold, as much
as he desired, King Solomon gave to Hiram
twenty cities in the land of Galilee. 12 But when
Hiram came from Tyre to see the cities that
Solomon had given him, they did not please
him. 13 Therefore he said, "What kind of cities
are these that you have given me, my brother?"
So they are called the land of [a]Cabul to this
day. 14 Hiram had sent to the king 120 talents[2]
of gold.
15 And this is the account of [b]the forced labor
that King Solomon drafted to build the house
of the LORD and his own house and [c]the Millo
and the wall of Jerusalem and [d]Hazor and
[e]Megiddo and Gezer 16 (Pharaoh king of Egypt
had gone up and captured Gezer and burned it
with fire, and had killed [f]the Canaanites who
lived in the city, and had given it as dowry to
[g]his daughter, Solomon's wife; 17 so Solomon
rebuilt Gezer) and [h]Lower Beth-horon 18 and
Baalath and Tamar in the wilderness, in the
land of Judah,[3] 19 and all the store cities that
Solomon had, and [i]the cities for his chariots,
and the cities for [j]his horsemen, and whatever
Solomon [k]desired to build in Jerusalem, in
Lebanon, and in all the land of his dominion.
20 All the people who were left of the Amorites,
the Hittites, the Perizzites, the Hivites, and
the Jebusites, who were not of the people of
Israel— 21 [l]their descendants who were left
after them in the land, [m]whom the people of
Israel were unable to devote to destruction[4]—
[n]these Solomon drafted to be [o]slaves, and so
they are to this day. 22 But [p]of the people of
Israel Solomon made no slaves. They were the
soldiers, they were his officials, his commanders, his captains, his chariot commanders and
his horsemen.
23 These were the chief officers who were over
Solomon's work: [q]550 [r]who had charge of the
people who carried on the work.
24 But [g]Pharaoh's daughter went up from the
city of David to [s]her own house that Solomon
had built for her. [t]Then he built [u]the Millo.
25 Three times a year Solomon used to offer
up burnt offerings and peace offerings on the
altar that he built to the LORD, making offerings with it[5] before the LORD. So he finished
the house.
26 King Solomon built a fleet of ships at
[v]Ezion-geber, which is near Eloth on the shore
of the Red Sea, in the land of Edom. 27 And

[1] Syriac, Old Latin; Hebrew *will become high* [2] A *talent* was about 75 pounds or 34 kilograms [3] Hebrew lacks *of Judah* [4] That is, set apart (devote) as an offering to the Lord (for destruction) [5] Septuagint lacks *with it*

6 [s][2 Sam. 7:14; Ps. 89:30, 32]
7 [t]Deut. 4:26; 2 Kgs. 17:23; 25:21 [u]Jer. 7:14 [v]Deut. 28:37; [Ps. 44:14]
8 [w]Deut. 29:24-26; Jer. 22:8, 9
9 [x]ch. 18:18
10 [y]For ver. 10-28, see 2 Chr. 8:1-18 [z][ch. 6:37, 38; 7:1]
13 [a][Josh. 19:27]
15 [b]ch. 5:13 [c]ver. 24; See 2 Sam. 5:9 [d]Josh. 11:1 [e]Josh. 17:11
16 [f]Josh. 16:10 [g]ch. 3:1; 7:8
17 [h]See Josh. 10:10
19 [i]ch. 10:26; 2 Chr. 1:14; 9:25 [j]ch. 4:26 [k]ver. 1

In addition to highlighting God's grace, the repeated theme of obedience also highlights God's justice. The Lord does in fact require obedience from us, and that is our just response to his grace. However, if the account of Solomon's life teaches us anything, it teaches us that the type of obedience required by God is impossible for us to achieve. But God has provided a way to achieve our obedience outside of our own individual ability. He sent his Son, the King of heaven and the offspring of David (Rom. 1:3), to obey on our behalf. As the apostle Paul said, "For our sake he made him to be sin who knew no sin, so that in him we might become the righteousness of God" (2 Cor. 5:21). In other words, God's remedy to our inability to respond in obedience to his grace is *more grace*. The pathway to heartfelt, authentic obedience is always the path of God's mercy and grace.

21 [l][Judg. 1:21, 27, 29; 3:1] [m][Josh. 15:63; 17:12] [n]Judg. 1:28 [o]Ezra 2:55-58; Neh. 7:57-60; 11:3 22 [p]Lev. 25:39 23 [q][2 Chr. 8:10] [r]ch. 5:16 24 [g][See ver. 16 above] [s]ch. 7:8 [t]ch. 11:27; [2 Sam. 5:9; 2 Chr. 32:5] [u]See ver. 15 26 [v]ch. 22:48; Num. 33:35; Deut. 2:8

Hiram sent [w]with the fleet his servants, sea-
men who were familiar with the sea, together
with the servants of Solomon. 28 And they went
to [x]Ophir and brought from there gold, 420
talents, and they brought it to King Solomon.

The Queen of Sheba

10 [y]Now when [z]the queen of [a]Sheba heard
of the fame of Solomon concerning
the name of the LORD, she came [b]to test him
with hard questions. 2 She came to Jerusalem
with a very great retinue, with camels [c]bear-
ing spices and very much gold and precious
stones. And when she came to Solomon, she
told him all that was on her mind. 3 And
Solomon answered all her questions; there
was nothing hidden from the king that he
could not explain to her. 4 And when the queen
of Sheba had seen all the wisdom of Solomon,
the house that he had built, 5 the food of his
table, the seating of his officials, and the attendance of his servants, their clothing, his cupbearers, and his burnt offerings that he offered
at the house of the LORD, there was no more
breath in her.

6 And she said to the king, "The report was
true that I heard in my own land of your words
and of your wisdom, 7 but I did not believe the
reports until I came and my own eyes had seen
it. And behold, the half was not told me. Your
wisdom and prosperity surpass the report that
I heard. 8 [e]Happy are your men! Happy are
your servants, who continually stand before
you and hear your wisdom! 9 [f]Blessed be the
LORD your God, who has delighted in you
and set you on the throne of Israel! [g]Because
the LORD loved Israel forever, he has made
you king, [h]that you may execute justice and
righteousness." 10 [i]Then she gave the king 120
talents[1] of gold, and a very great quantity of
spices and precious stones. Never again came
such an abundance of spices as these that the
queen of Sheba gave to King Solomon.

11 Moreover, [j]the fleet of Hiram, which
brought [k]gold from Ophir, brought from
Ophir a very great amount of almug wood
and precious stones. 12 And the king made of
the almug wood supports for the house of the
LORD and for the king's house, also lyres and
harps for the singers. No such almug wood has
come or been seen to this day.

13 And King Solomon gave to the queen of
Sheba all that she desired, whatever she asked
besides what was given her by the bounty of
King Solomon. So she turned and went back
to her own land with her servants.

Solomon's Great Wealth

14 [l]Now the weight of gold that came to
Solomon in one year was 666 talents of gold,
15 besides that which came from the explorers and from the business of the merchants,
and from all the kings of the west and from
the governors of the land. 16 King Solomon
made 200 large shields of beaten gold; 600
shekels[2] of gold went into each shield. 17 And
he made 300 [m]shields of beaten gold; three
minas[3] of gold went into each shield. And the
king put them in [n]the House of the Forest of
Lebanon. 18 The king also made a great ivory
throne and overlaid it with the finest gold.
19 The throne had six steps, and the throne
had a round top,[4] and on each side of the seat
were armrests and two lions standing beside
the armrests, 20 while twelve lions stood there,
one on each end of a step on the six steps. The
like of it was never made in any kingdom. 21 All
King Solomon's drinking vessels were of gold,
and all the vessels of [n]the House of the Forest
of Lebanon were of pure gold. None were of
silver; silver was not considered as anything
in the days of Solomon. 22 For the king had [o]a
fleet of ships of Tarshish at sea with the fleet
of Hiram. Once every three years the fleet of
ships of Tarshish used to come bringing gold,
silver, ivory, apes, and peacocks.[5]

23 [p]Thus King Solomon excelled all the
kings of the earth in riches and in wisdom.
24 And the whole earth sought the presence
of Solomon to hear his wisdom, which God
had put into his mind. 25 Every one of them
brought his present, articles of silver and gold,
garments, myrrh, spices, horses, and mules, so
much year by year.

26 [q]And Solomon gathered together [r]chari-
ots and horsemen. He had 1,400 chariots and
12,000 horsemen, whom he stationed in the
[s]chariot cities and with the king in Jerusalem.
27 And the king made silver as common in

[1] A *talent* was about 75 pounds or 34 kilograms [2] A *shekel* was about 2/5 ounce or 11 grams [3] A *mina* was about 1 1/4 pounds or 0.6 kilogram [4] Or *and at the back of the throne was a calf's head* [5] Or *baboons*

27[w] ch. 10:11 **28**[x] ch. 10:11; 22:48; 1 Chr. 29:4; Job 22:24; 28:16; Ps. 45:9; Isa. 13:12 **Chapter 10** **1**[y] For ver. 1-13, see 2 Chr. 9:1-12 [z] [Matt. 12:42; Luke 11:31] [a] Ps. 72:10, 15; Isa. 60:6; Jer. 6:20; Ezek. 27:22, 23; 38:13; Joel 3:8 [b] See Judg. 14:12 **2**[c] ver. 10 **8**[e] [Prov. 8:34] **9**[f] ch. 5:7 [g] 2 Chr. 2:11 [h] 2 Sam. 8:15; [Ps. 72:2] **10**[i] ver. 2 **11**[j] ch. 9:27 [k] See ch. 9:28 **14**[l] For ver. 14-28, see 2 Chr. 9:13-28 **17**[m] ch. 14:26 [n] ch. 7:2 **21**[n] [See ver. 17 above] **22**[o] ch. 22:48; Gen. 10:4; 1 Chr. 1:7; 2 Chr. 20:36, 37; Ps. 48:7; 72:10 **23**[p] [ch. 3:12, 13; 4:30] **26**[q] For ver. 26-29, see 2 Chr. 1:14-17 [r] [ch. 4:26; 2 Chr. 9:25] [s] ch. 9:19

Jerusalem as stone, and he made cedar as
plentiful as [t]the sycamore of the Shephelah.
28 And Solomon's [u]import of horses was from
Egypt and Kue, and the king's traders received
them from Kue at a price. 29 A chariot could be
imported from Egypt for 600 shekels of silver
and a horse for 150, and so through the king's
traders they were exported to all the kings of
[v]the Hittites and the kings of Syria.

Solomon Turns from the LORD

11 Now [w]King Solomon loved many foreign women, along with the daughter
of Pharaoh: Moabite, Ammonite, Edomite,
Sidonian, and Hittite women, 2 from the
nations concerning which the LORD had said
to the people of Israel, [x]"You shall not enter
into marriage with them, neither shall they
with you, for surely they will turn away your
heart after their gods." Solomon clung to
these in love. 3 He had 700 wives, who were
princesses, and 300 concubines. And his wives
turned away his heart. 4 For when Solomon
was old his wives turned away his heart after
other gods, and [y]his heart was not wholly true
to the LORD his God, [z]as was the heart of David
his father. 5 For Solomon went after [a]Ashto-
reth the goddess of the Sidonians, and after
[b]Milcom the abomination of the Ammonites.
6 So Solomon did what was evil in the sight of
the LORD and did not wholly follow the LORD,
as David his father had done. 7 Then Solomon
built a high place for [c]Chemosh the abomination of Moab, and for [d]Molech the abomination of the Ammonites, on the mountain east
of Jerusalem. 8 And so he did for all his foreign
wives, who made offerings and sacrificed to
their gods.

The LORD Raises Adversaries

9 And the LORD was angry with Solomon,
because [e]his heart had turned away from the
LORD, the God of Israel, [f]who had appeared
to him twice 10 and [g]had commanded him
concerning this thing, that he should not go
after other gods. But he did not keep what the
LORD commanded. 11 Therefore the LORD said
to Solomon, "Since this has been your practice
and you have not kept my covenant and my
statutes that I have commanded you, [h]I will
surely tear the kingdom from you and will
give it to your servant. 12 Yet for the sake of
David your father I will not do it in your days,
but I will tear it out of the hand of your son.
13 However, [i]I will not tear away all the kingdom, but [j]I will give one tribe to your son, for
the sake of David my servant and for the sake
of Jerusalem [k]that I have chosen."
14 And the LORD raised up an adversary
against Solomon, Hadad the Edomite. He was
of the royal house in Edom. 15 For [l]when David
was in Edom, and Joab the commander of
the army went up to bury the slain, he struck
down every male in Edom 16 (for Joab and all
Israel remained there six months, until he had
cut off every male in Edom). 17 But Hadad fled
to Egypt, together with certain Edomites of
his father's servants, Hadad still being a little
child. 18 They set out from Midian and came
to [m]Paran and took men with them from
Paran and came to Egypt, to Pharaoh king of
Egypt, who gave him a house and assigned
him an allowance of food and gave him land.
19 And Hadad found great favor in the sight of
Pharaoh, so that he gave him in marriage the
sister of his own wife, the sister of Tahpenes
the queen. 20 And the sister of Tahpenes bore

27 [t]1 Chr. 27:28
28 [u]2 Chr. 9:28; [Deut. 17:16]
29 [v]Judg. 1:26
Chapter 11
1 [w]Neh. 13:26; [Deut. 17:17]
2 [x]See Ex. 34:16
4 [y][ch. 8:61] [z]ch. 9:4
5 [a]ver. 33; Judg. 2:13; 2 Kgs. 23:13 [b][ver. 7]
7 [c]Num. 21:29; 2 Kgs. 23:13 [d]Lev. 18:21; 20:2-4; 2 Kgs. 23:10; Acts 7:43; [ver. 5]
9 [e]ver. 2, 4 [f]ch. 3:5; 9:2
10 [g]ch. 6:12; 9:6
11 [h]ver. 31; [ch. 12:15, 16]
13 [i][2 Sam. 7:15; Ps. 89:33] [j]ver. 32, 36; [ch. 12:20] [k]Deut. 12:5, 11
15 [l]2 Sam. 8:14; 1 Chr. 18:12, 13
18 [m]Num. 10:12; Deut. 33:2

11:1–40 In Deuteronomy 17:14–20, the Lord established the "law of the king," stipulating that Israel's king should not acquire many horses (especially from Egypt), multiple wives, or excessive amounts of silver or gold. In other words, Israel's king was denied political, military, and economic security in order that his trust might be in the Lord and his law. But 1 Kings 10 and 11 make it very clear that Solomon did exactly what the Lord had forbidden in Deuteronomy. He amassed horses and chariots (from Egypt) and incalculable amounts of silver and gold (10:14–29) and, most famously, a thousand wives and concubines (11:1–8). This accumulation of worldly wealth and security certainly yielded its crop of infidelity—"So Solomon did what was evil in the sight of the LORD and did not wholly follow the LORD" (11:6; cf. vv. 4–9). In fact, Solomon's disobedience resulted in the division of the kingdom of Israel and marked the beginning of Israel's ultimate decline toward destruction and exile.

It may be difficult to believe, but the tragedy of Solomon's disobedience should also give us a measure of hope. First, Solomon's life reminds us that neither faith and obedience nor satisfaction and happiness are ever the sure result of material blessing. To Solomon belonged all the resources of life: health, wealth, wisdom, power, fame, sex, and anything else that might satisfy us in this life (cf. Ecclesiastes 2). But all of

him Genubath his son, whom Tahpenes
weaned in Pharaoh's house. And Genubath
was in Pharaoh's house among the sons of
Pharaoh. 21 But when Hadad heard in Egypt
[n]that David slept with his fathers and that Joab
the commander of the army was dead, Hadad
said to Pharaoh, "Let me depart, that I may
go to my own country." 22 But Pharaoh said to
him, "What have you lacked with me that you
are now seeking to go to your own country?"
And he said to him, "Only let me depart."
23 God also raised up as an adversary to him,
Rezon the son of Eliada, who had fled from his
master [o]Hadadezer king of Zobah. 24 And he
gathered men about him and became leader of
a marauding band, [p]after the killing by David.
And they went to Damascus and lived there
and made him king in Damascus. 25 He was
an adversary of Israel all the days of Solomon,
doing harm as Hadad did. And he loathed
Israel and reigned over Syria.
26 [q]Jeroboam the son of Nebat, [r]an Ephraimite of Zeredah, a servant of Solomon, whose
mother's name was Zeruah, a widow, also
[s]lifted up his hand against the king. 27 And
this was the reason why he lifted up his hand
against the king. [t]Solomon built the Millo,
and closed up the breach of the city of David
his father. 28 The man Jeroboam was very able,
and when Solomon saw that the young man
was industrious he gave him charge over all
the forced labor of the house of Joseph. 29 And
at that time, when Jeroboam went out of
Jerusalem, the prophet [u]Ahijah the Shilonite
found him on the road. Now Ahijah had
dressed himself in a new garment, and the
two of them were alone in the open country.
30 Then Ahijah laid hold of the new garment
that was on him, [v]and tore it into twelve
pieces. 31 And he said to Jeroboam, "Take for
yourself ten pieces, for thus says the LORD,
the God of Israel, 'Behold, [w]I am about to tear
the kingdom from the hand of Solomon and
will give you ten tribes 32 (but [x]he shall have
one tribe, for the sake of my servant David and
for the sake of Jerusalem, [y]the city that I have
chosen out of all the tribes of Israel), 33 because
they have[1] forsaken me [z]and worshiped
Ashtoreth the goddess of the Sidonians,
Chemosh the god of Moab, and Milcom the
god of the Ammonites, and they have not
walked in my ways, doing what is right in
my sight and keeping my statutes and my
rules, as David his father did. 34 Nevertheless,
I will not take the whole kingdom out of his
hand, but I will make him ruler all the days
of his life, for the sake of David my servant
whom I chose, who kept my commandments
and my statutes. 35 [a]But I will take the kingdom out of his son's hand and will give it to
you, ten tribes. 36 Yet to his son [x]I will give
one tribe, that David my servant may always
have [b]a lamp before me in Jerusalem, [y]the city
where I have chosen to put my name. 37 And
I will take you, and you shall reign over all
that your soul desires, and you shall be king
over Israel. 38 And if you will listen to all that
I command you, and will walk in my ways,
and do what is right in my eyes by keeping
my statutes and my commandments, as David
my servant did, [c]I will be with you and [d]will
build you a sure house, as I built for David,
and I will give Israel to you. 39 And I will afflict
the offspring of David because of this, but not
forever.'" 40 Solomon sought therefore to kill
Jeroboam. But Jeroboam arose and fled into
Egypt, to [e]Shishak king of Egypt, and was in
Egypt until the death of Solomon.
41 [f]Now the rest of the acts of Solomon, and all
that he did, and his wisdom, are they not written in the Book of the Acts of Solomon? 42 And
the time that Solomon reigned in Jerusalem
over all Israel was forty years. 43 And Solomon
[g]slept with his fathers and was buried in the

[1] Septuagint, Syriac, Vulgate *he has*; twice in this verse

this could not provide fulfillment or prevent infidelity. Rather, it might even be said that all of these "things" got in the way and impeded Solomon's ability to follow or enjoy the Lord fully.

By way of contrast, David's Greater Son, Jesus, came without all of these resources, but he showed us what a life of obedience and contentment should look like. In Christ we learn that neither wealth nor power saves (nor do poverty or weakness, in themselves). Rather, salvation and fulfillment have come to us through the Prince of heaven, who became poor in order that we might become heirs of the kingdom of God together with him (Rom. 8:17).

21 [n] ch. 2:10
23 [o] [2 Sam. 10:16]
24 [p] 2 Sam. 8:3; 10:8, 18
26 [q] ch. 12:2; 2 Chr. 13:6 [r] 1 Sam. 1:1 [s] 2 Sam. 20:21
27 [t] ch. 9:24; [2 Sam. 5:9]
29 [u] ch. 12:15; 14:2; 15:29; 2 Chr. 9:29
30 [v] [1 Sam. 15:27]
31 [w] ver. 11-13
32 [x] ver. 13; ch. 12:21 [y] ch. 14:21; See Deut. 12:5
33 [z] ver. 5, 7

35 [a] ver. 12; ch. 12:16, 17 36 [x] [See ver. 32 above] [b] ch. 15:4; 2 Sam. 21:17; 2 Kgs. 8:19; 2 Chr. 21:7 [y] [See ver. 32 above] 38 [c] Josh. 1:5 [d] 1 Sam. 2:35; 2 Sam. 7:11, 27 40 [e] ch. 14:25; 2 Chr. 12:2, 5, 7, 9 41 [f] For ver. 41-43, see 2 Chr. 9:29-31 43 [g] ch. 2:10; 14:20

city of David his father. And [h]Rehoboam his
son reigned in his place.

Rehoboam's Folly

12 [i]Rehoboam went to [j]Shechem, for all
Israel had come to Shechem to make
him king. [2]And as soon as [k]Jeroboam the son
of Nebat heard of it (for [l]he was still in Egypt,
where he had fled from King Solomon), then
Jeroboam returned from[1] Egypt. [3]And they
sent and called him, and Jeroboam and all the
assembly of Israel came and said to Rehoboam,
[4] [m]"Your father made our yoke heavy. Now
therefore lighten the hard service of your
father and his heavy yoke on us, and we will
serve you." [5]He said to them, [n]"Go away for
three days, then come again to me." So the
people went away.
[6]Then King Rehoboam took counsel with
the old men, who had stood before Solomon
his father while he was yet alive, saying, "How
do you advise me to answer this people?" [7]And
they said to him, "If you will be a servant to
this people today and serve them, and speak
good words to them when you answer them,
then they will be your servants forever." [8]But
he abandoned the counsel that the old men
gave him and took counsel with the young
men who had grown up with him and stood
before him. [9]And he said to them, "What do
you advise that we answer this people who
have said to me, 'Lighten the yoke that your
father put on us'?" [10]And the young men who
had grown up with him said to him, "Thus
shall you speak to this people who said to you,
'Your father made our yoke heavy, but you
lighten it for us,' thus shall you say to them,
'My little finger is thicker than my father's
thighs. [11]And now, whereas [m]my father laid on
you a heavy yoke, I will add to your yoke. My
father disciplined you with whips, but I will
discipline you with scorpions.'"
[12]So Jeroboam and all the people came to
Rehoboam the third day, as the king said,
[o]"Come to me again the third day." [13]And
the king answered the people harshly, and
forsaking the counsel that the old men had
given him, [14]he spoke to them according to
the counsel of the young men, saying, [m]"My
father made your yoke heavy, but I will add
to your yoke. My father disciplined you with
whips, but I will discipline you with scorpions." [15]So the king did not listen to the people,
for [p]it was a turn of affairs brought about by
the LORD that he might fulfill his word, which
[q]the LORD spoke by Ahijah the Shilonite to
Jeroboam the son of Nebat.

The Kingdom Divided

[16]And when all Israel saw that the king did
not listen to them, the people answered the
king, "What portion do we have in David? We
have no inheritance in the son of Jesse. [r]To
your tents, O Israel! Look now to your own
house, David." So Israel went to their tents.
[17]But Rehoboam reigned over [s]the people of
Israel who lived in the cities of Judah. [18]Then
King Rehoboam sent [t]Adoram, who was taskmaster over the forced labor, and all Israel
stoned him to death with stones. And King
Rehoboam hurried to mount his chariot to
flee to Jerusalem. [19] [u]So Israel has been in rebellion against the house of David to this day.
[20]And when all Israel heard that Jeroboam
had returned, they sent and called him to the
assembly and made him king over all Israel.
There was none that followed the house of
David but [v]the tribe of Judah only.
[21] [w]When Rehoboam came to Jerusalem, he
assembled all the house of Judah and the tribe
of Benjamin, 180,000 chosen warriors, to fight

[1] Septuagint, Vulgate (compare 2 Chronicles 10:2); Hebrew *lived in*

12:1–33 The grandeur and scope of the kingdom under David and Solomon was now lost to a divided kingdom, ten tribes for Israel in the north and two tribes for Judah in the south. The heart of Rehoboam no longer desired to serve the people (vv. 7–8), and the heart of Jeroboam led the people back into the idolatry of the wilderness with the worship of golden calves (vv. 28–29).

And yet even these tragic events were from the Lord, part of his plan and design for the earthly kingdom of Israel so that the need and provision of God's greater kingdom would be understood over time (vv. 15, 24). Even the bad things that happen in life, as terrible as they can be, always remain under the supervision and care of our covenant Lord. Trusting in God's good providence sustains the believer in a life full of catastrophe and hardship.

43 [h]Matt. 1:7
Chapter 12
1 [i]For ver. 1-19, see 2 Chr. 10:1-19 [j][Judg. 9:6]
2 [k]ch. 11:26 [l]ch. 11:40
4 [m]ch. 4:7, 22; 9:15; See 1 Sam. 8:11-18
5 [n]ver. 12
11 [m][See ver. 4 above]
12 [o]ver. 5
14 [m][See ver. 4 above]
15 [p]ver. 24 [q]ch. 11:11, 31
16 [r]See 2 Sam. 20:1
17 [s]ch. 11:13, 36
18 [t]ch. 4:6; 5:14
19 [u]2 Kgs. 17:21
20 [v]ch. 11:13, 32, 36 **21** [w]For ver. 21-24, see 2 Chr. 11:1-4

against the house of Israel, to restore the
kingdom to Rehoboam the son of Solomon.
22 But the word of God came to [x]Shemaiah the
man of God: 23 "Say to Rehoboam the son of
Solomon, king of Judah, and to all the house
of Judah and Benjamin, and to the [y]rest of the
people, 24 'Thus says the LORD, You shall not
go up or fight against your relatives the people
of Israel. Every man return to his home, [z]for
this thing is from me.'" So they listened to
the word of the LORD and went home again,
according to the word of the LORD.

Jeroboam's Golden Calves

25 Then Jeroboam [a]built Shechem in the hill
country of Ephraim and lived there. And he
went out from there and [b]built Penuel. 26 And
Jeroboam said in his heart, "Now the kingdom
will turn back to the house of David. 27 If this
people [c]go up to offer sacrifices in the temple
of the LORD at Jerusalem, then the heart of
this people will turn again to their lord, to
Rehoboam king of Judah, and they will kill me
and return to Rehoboam king of Judah." 28 So
the king took counsel and [d]made two calves
of gold. And he said to the people, "You have
gone up to Jerusalem long enough. [e]Behold
your gods, O Israel, who brought you up out
of the land of Egypt." 29 And he set one in
Bethel, and the other he put in Dan. 30 Then
[f]this thing became a sin, for the people went
as far as Dan to be before one.[1] 31 He also made
[g]temples on high places and [h]appointed priests
from among all the people, who were not of
the Levites. 32 And Jeroboam appointed a feast
on the fifteenth day of the eighth month like
[i]the feast that was in Judah, and he offered sacrifices on the altar. So he did in Bethel, sacrificing to the calves that he made. And he placed
in Bethel [j]the priests of the high places that
he had made. 33 He went up to the altar that
he had made in Bethel on the fifteenth day in
the eighth month, in the month that he had
devised from his own heart. And he instituted
a feast for the people of Israel and went up to
the altar [k]to make offerings.

A Man of God Confronts Jeroboam

13 And behold, [l]a man of God came out
of Judah by the word of the LORD to
Bethel. Jeroboam was standing by the altar [m]to
make offerings. 2 [n]And the man cried against
the altar by the word of the LORD and said, "O
altar, altar, thus says the LORD: 'Behold, a son
shall be born to the house of David, [o]Josiah by
name, and he shall sacrifice on you the priests
of the high places who make offerings on you,
and human bones shall be burned on you.'"
3 And he gave [p]a sign the same day, saying,
"This is the sign that the LORD has spoken:
'Behold, the altar shall be torn down, and
the ashes that are on it shall be poured out.'"
4 And when the king heard the saying of the
man of God, which he cried against the altar
at Bethel, Jeroboam stretched out his hand
from the altar, saying, "Seize him." And his
hand, which he stretched out against him,
dried up, so that he could not draw it back to
himself. 5 The altar also was torn down, and
the ashes poured out from the altar, according
to the sign that the man of God had given by
the word of the LORD. 6 And the king said to
the man of God, [q]"Entreat now the favor of the
LORD your God, and pray for me, that my hand
may be restored to me." And the man of God
entreated the LORD, and the king's hand was
restored to him and became as it was before.
7 And the king said to the man of God, "Come
home with me, and refresh yourself, and [r]I will
give you a reward." 8 And the man of God said
to the king, [s]"If you give me half your house,
[t]I will not go in with you. And I will not eat
bread or drink water in this place, 9 for so was
it commanded me by the word of the LORD,
saying, 'You shall neither eat bread nor drink
water nor return by the way that you came.'"

[1] Septuagint *went to the one at Bethel and to the other as far as Dan*

13:1–32 Chapter 13 drives home the sacred importance of the word of the Lord. Through the stories of two very different prophets—one who faithfully serves the Lord (vv. 1–10) and one who does not and is killed as a result (vv. 11–32)—the reader is brought to see the fundamental significance and all-encompassing authority of God's word. The faithful prophet explains his actions by saying, "for it was said to me by the word of the LORD" (v. 17), and this theme of the Lord's word resounds all through the narrative. The crucial mistake of the faithless prophet, however, was deceitfully attributing a statement to the word of the Lord that was no such thing (vv. 18–19).

22 [x] 2 Chr. 12:5, 7, 15
23 [y] [ver. 17]
24 [z] ver. 15
25 [a] [Judg. 9:45] [b] [Judg. 8:17]
27 [c] Deut. 12:5, 6
28 [d] 2 Kgs. 10:29; 17:16; 2 Chr. 11:15; 13:8; Hos. 8:5, 6; 10:5; 13:2; [ch. 14:9] [e] [Ex. 32:4, 8]
30 [f] ch. 13:34; 2 Kgs. 17:21
31 [g] ch. 13:32 [h] ch. 13:33; 2 Kgs. 17:32; 2 Chr. 11:14, 15; 13:9

32 [i] Lev. 23:33, 34; Num. 29:12 [j] ch. 13:2; [Amos 7:13] **33** [k] ch. 13:1 **Chapter 13** **1** [l] 2 Kgs. 23:17 [m] ch. 12:33 **2** [n] ver. 32 [o] 2 Kgs. 23:15, 16 **3** [p] See Judg. 6:17
6 [q] Ex. 8:8; 9:28; 10:17; Num. 21:7; Acts 8:24 **7** [r] [1 Sam. 9:7; 2 Kgs. 5:15] **8** [s] Num. 22:18; 24:13 [t] ver. 16, 17

10 So he went another way and did not return by the way that he came to Bethel.

The Prophet's Disobedience

11 Now [u]an old prophet lived in Bethel. And his sons[1] came and told him all that the man of God had done that day in Bethel. They also told to their father the words that he had spoken to the king. 12 And their father said to them, "Which way did he go?" And his sons showed him the way that the man of God who came from Judah had gone. 13 And he said to his sons, "Saddle the donkey for me." So they saddled the donkey for him and he mounted it. 14 And he went after the man of God and found him sitting under an oak. And he said to him, "Are you the man of God who came from Judah?" And he said, "I am." 15 Then he said to him, "Come home with me and eat bread." 16 And he said, [v]"I may not return with you, or go in with you, neither will I eat bread nor drink water with you in this place, 17 for it was said to me [w]by the word of the LORD, 'You shall neither eat bread nor drink water there, nor return by the way that you came.'" 18 And he said to him, "I also am a prophet as you are, and an angel spoke to me by the word of the LORD, saying, 'Bring him back with you into your house that he may eat bread and drink water.'" But he lied to him. 19 So he went back with him and ate bread in his house and drank water.

20 And as they sat at the table, the word of the LORD came to the prophet who had brought him back. 21 And he cried to the man of God who came from Judah, "Thus says the LORD, 'Because you have disobeyed the word of the LORD and have not kept the command that the LORD your God commanded you, 22 but have come back and have eaten bread and drunk water in the place of which he said to you, "Eat no bread and drink no water," your body shall not come to the tomb of your fathers.'" 23 And after he had eaten bread and drunk, he saddled the donkey for the prophet whom he had brought back. 24 And as he went away [x]a lion met him on the road and killed him. And his body was thrown in the road, and the donkey stood beside it; the lion also stood beside the body. 25 And behold, men passed by and saw the body thrown in the road and the lion standing by the body. And they came and told it in the city where [y]the old prophet lived.

26 And when the prophet who had brought him back from the way heard of it, he said, "It is the man of God who disobeyed the word of the LORD; therefore the LORD has given him to the lion, which has torn him and killed him, according to the word that the LORD spoke to him." 27 And he said to his sons, "Saddle the donkey for me." And they saddled it. 28 And he went and found his body thrown in the road, and the donkey and the lion standing beside the body. The lion had not eaten the body or torn the donkey. 29 And the prophet took up the body of the man of God and laid it on the donkey and brought it back to the city[2] to mourn and to bury him. 30 And he laid the body in his own grave. And they mourned over him, saying, [z]"Alas, my brother!" 31 And after he had buried him, he said to his sons, "When I die, bury me in the grave in which the man of God is buried; [a]lay my bones beside his bones. 32 [b]For the saying that he called out by the word of the LORD against the altar in Bethel and against [c]all the houses of the high places that are in the cities of [d]Samaria shall surely come to pass."

33 After this thing Jeroboam did not turn from his evil way, but made priests for the

[1] Septuagint, Syriac, Vulgate; Hebrew *son* [2] Septuagint; Hebrew *he came to the city of the old prophet*

11[u] ver. 25; [2 Kgs. 23:18]
16[v] ver. 8, 9
17[w] ch. 20:35; 1 Thess. 4:15
24[x] ch. 20:36
25[y] ver. 11
30[z] [Jer. 22:18]
31[a] [2 Kgs. 23:17, 18]
32[b] ver. 2; See 2 Kgs. 23:16-19 [c] ch. 12:31 [d] [ch. 16:24]

Immediate submission to the Lord's word is clearly the high calling of God's people. His word not only carries his authority but also the instruction needed for God's glory and the ultimate safety and care of his people. What is so striking about the Bible's message, however, when taken as a whole, is that at the climax of human history the word of the Lord did not come merely in a message but in a man. John says Jesus *is* the Word (John 1:1, 14). And when the climactic word of God showed up, he did not berate us into submission. He wooed us with grace. He said, "Come to me, all who labor and are heavy laden, and I will give you rest" (Matt. 11:28). The one place in all four Gospels where Jesus tells us about his heart, he says that he is "gentle and lowly in heart" (Matt. 11:29). And indeed, ultimately he suffers and dies in our place (1 Pet. 3:18).

God's word to you, in Jesus, is: bow the knee to him—not because he is a harsh taskmaster, but because he is a gentle and merciful friend. God's word to you is one of hope.

high places again from among all the people.
Any who would, he ordained to be priests of
the high places. 34 [e]And this thing became sin
to the house of Jeroboam, [f]so as to cut it off
and to destroy it from the face of the earth.

Prophecy Against Jeroboam

14 At that time Abijah the son of Jeroboam
fell sick. 2 And Jeroboam said to his
wife, "Arise, and disguise yourself, that it not
be known that you are the wife of Jeroboam,
and go to [g]Shiloh. Behold, Ahijah the prophet
is there, [h]who said of me that I should be king
over this people. 3 [i]Take with you ten loaves,
some cakes, and a jar of honey, and go to him.
He will tell you what shall happen to the
child."

4 Jeroboam's wife did so. She arose and went
to [g]Shiloh and came to the house of [j]Ahijah.
Now [j]Ahijah could not see, for his eyes were
dim because of his age. 5 And the LORD said to
[j]Ahijah, "Behold, the wife of Jeroboam is coming to inquire of you concerning her son, for
he is sick. Thus and thus shall you say to her."

When she came, she pretended to be another
woman. 6 But when [j]Ahijah heard the sound
of her feet, as she came in at the door, he said,
"Come in, wife of Jeroboam. Why do you pretend to be another? For I am charged with
unbearable news for you. 7 Go, tell Jeroboam,
'Thus says the LORD, the God of Israel:
[k]"Because I exalted you from among the people and made you leader over my people Israel
8 and [l]tore the kingdom away from the house
of David and gave it to you, and yet you have
not been [m]like my servant David, who kept my
commandments and followed me with all his
heart, doing only that which was right in my
eyes, 9 but you have done evil above all who
were before you and have gone and [n]made for
yourself other gods and [o]metal images, provoking me to anger, and [p]have cast me behind
your back, 10 therefore behold, I will bring
harm upon the house of Jeroboam and [q]will
cut off from Jeroboam every male, [r]both bond
and free in Israel, and [s]will burn up the house
of Jeroboam, as a man burns up dung until it
is all gone. 11 [t]Anyone belonging to Jeroboam
who dies in the city the dogs shall eat, and
anyone who dies in the open country the birds
of the heavens shall eat, for the LORD has spoken it."' 12 Arise therefore, go to your house.
[u]When your feet enter the city, the child shall
die. 13 And all Israel shall mourn for him and
bury him, for he only of Jeroboam shall come
to the grave, because in him [v]there is found
something pleasing to the LORD, the God of
Israel, in the house of Jeroboam. 14 [w]Moreover,
the LORD will raise up for himself a king over
Israel who shall cut off the house of Jeroboam
today. And henceforth, 15 the LORD will strike
Israel as a reed is shaken in the water, and
[x]root up Israel out of [y]this good land that he
gave to their fathers and scatter them [z]beyond
the Euphrates,[1] because they have made their
[a]Asherim, provoking the LORD to anger. 16 And
he will give Israel up because of the sins of
Jeroboam, which he sinned and made Israel
to sin."

17 Then Jeroboam's wife arose and departed
and came to [b]Tirzah. And [c]as she came to the

[1] Hebrew *the River*

14:1–16 This final account of Jeroboam's life is terribly tragic, a lesson in the destructive power of sin. His apostasy resulted in the death of his son, the annihilation of his dynasty, and the promise of destruction and exile for the ten northern tribes of Israel. Jeroboam's sin spread like a cancer though the northern tribes. We are reminded once again that the faithfulness of the king and the faithfulness of the people are inseparably linked.

The issue of Jeroboam's disobedience and sin is a complicated matter. For example, consider the origin of his kingship. Back in chapter 11, Jeroboam was chosen by the Lord to reign over the 10 northern tribes of Israel because of Solomon's disobedience. The Lord showed great favor to Jeroboam and set before him grand promises: "And I will take you, and you shall reign over all that your soul desires, and you shall be king over Israel. . . . I will be with you and will build you a sure house, as I built for David, and I will give Israel to you" (11:37–38). But Jeroboam forfeited these promises by his disobedience.

As Christians we learn two important lessons from Jeroboam. First, the ability to respond to God's grace and rest in his promises requires the miracle of conversion. We cannot force this reality upon ourselves, our spouses, our children, or our friends. Without a new heart, the sinner remains unaffected by the gracious promises of God in his Word.

34 [e]ch. 12:30; 2 Kgs. 17:21 [f]ch. 14:10; [ch. 15:29, 30]

Chapter 14

2 [g]See Josh. 18:1 [h]See ch. 11:29-31
3 [i][1 Sam. 9:7, 8]
4 [g][See ver. 2 above] [j]ch. 11:29
5 [j][See ver. 4 above]
6 [j][See ver. 4 above]
7 [k]ch. 16:2; [2 Sam. 12:7, 8]
8 [l]ch. 11:31 [m]ch. 11:33, 38; 15:5; [ch. 9:4]
9 [n]ch. 12:28; 2 Chr. 11:15 [o][Ex. 34:17] [p]Ezek. 23:35; [Neh. 9:26; Ps. 50:17]
10 [q]ch. 21:21; 2 Kgs. 9:8 [r]Deut. 32:36; 2 Kgs. 14:26 [s]ch. 16:3
11 [t]ch. 16:4; 21:24
12 [u]ver. 17
13 [v]2 Chr. 12:12; 19:3
14 [w]See ch. 15:27-29
15 [x]Deut. 29:28; Ps. 52:5; Prov. 2:22 [y]Josh. 23:15, 16 [z][2 Kgs. 15:29] [a]Ex. 34:13; Deut. 12:3
17 [b]ch. 15:21, 33; 16:6, 8, 15, 23 [c]ver. 12

threshold of the house, the child died. 18 And
all Israel buried him and mourned for him,
[d]according to the word of the LORD, which
he spoke by his servant Ahijah the prophet.

The Death of Jeroboam

19 Now the rest of the acts of Jeroboam, [e]how
he warred and how he reigned, behold, they
are written in the Book of the Chronicles
of the Kings of Israel. 20 And the time that
Jeroboam reigned was twenty-two years. And
he slept with his fathers, and Nadab his son
reigned in his place.

Rehoboam Reigns in Judah

21 [f]Now Rehoboam the son of Solomon
reigned in Judah. Rehoboam was forty-one
years old when he began to reign, and he
reigned seventeen years in Jerusalem, [g]the
city that the LORD had chosen out of all the
tribes of Israel, to put his name there. [h]His
mother's name was Naamah the Ammonite.
22 [i]And Judah did what was evil in the sight of
the LORD, and they [j]provoked him to jealousy
with their sins that they committed, more
than all that their fathers had done. 23 For
they also built for themselves [k]high places
[l]and pillars and [m]Asherim on every high hill
and [n]under every green tree, 24 and there were
also [o]male cult prostitutes in the land. They
did according to all the abominations of the
nations that the LORD drove out before the
people of Israel.
25 [p]In the fifth year of King Rehoboam,
Shishak king of Egypt came up against
Jerusalem. 26 He took away the treasures of
the house of the LORD and the treasures of
the king's house. [q]He took away everything.
He also took away all the shields of gold [r]that
Solomon had made, 27 and King Rehoboam
made in their place shields of bronze, and
committed them to the hands of the officers
of the guard, who kept the door of the king's
house. 28 And as often as the king went into
the house of the LORD, the guard carried them
and brought them back to the guardroom.
29 [s]Now the rest of the acts of Rehoboam
and all that he did, are they not written in the
Book of the Chronicles of the Kings of Judah?
30 [t]And there was war between Rehoboam
and Jeroboam continually. 31 And Rehoboam
slept with his fathers and was buried with
his fathers in the city of David. [u]His mother's
name was Naamah the Ammonite. And [v]Abi-
jam his son reigned in his place.

Abijam Reigns in Judah

15 [w]Now in the eighteenth year of King
Jeroboam the son of Nebat, Abijam
began to reign over Judah. 2 He reigned for
three years in Jerusalem. His mother's name
was Maacah the daughter of Abishalom. 3 And
he walked in all the sins that his father did
before him, and [x]his heart was not wholly true
to the LORD his God, as the heart of David
his father. 4 Nevertheless, for David's sake the
LORD his God gave him [y]a lamp in Jerusalem,
setting up his son after him, and establishing
Jerusalem, 5 because [z]David did what was right
in the eyes of the LORD and did not turn aside
from anything that he commanded him all the
days of his life, [a]except in the matter of Uriah
the Hittite. 6 [b]Now there was war between
Rehoboam and Jeroboam all the days of his
life. 7 [c]The rest of the acts of Abijam and all
that he did, are they not written in the Book

18 [d]ver. 13
19 [e]See 2 Chr. 13:2-20
21 [f]2 Chr. 12:13 [g]ch. 11:32, 36 [h]2 Chr. 12:13
22 [i][2 Chr. 12:1, 14] [j]See Num. 25:11
23 [k]See Deut. 12:2 [l]See Ex. 23:24 [m]ver. 15 [n]Deut. 12:2; 2 Kgs. 16:4; Isa. 57:5; Jer. 2:20
24 [o]See Deut. 23:17
25 [p]2 Chr. 12:2, 9-11
26 [q][ch. 15:18] [r]ch. 10:17
29 [s]For ver. 29-31, see 2 Chr. 12:15, 16
30 [t]ch. 15:6; [ch. 12:21-24]
31 [u]2 Chr. 12:13 [v][Matt. 1:7]

Chapter 15
1 [w]2 Chr. 13:1, 2
3 [x]ch. 11:4; [ver. 14; ch. 8:61]
4 [y]See ch. 11:36
5 [z]ch. 9:4; 14:8 [a]2 Sam. 11:4, 15; 12:9
6 [b]ch. 14:30
7 [c][2 Chr. 13:22]

Second, we must remember the connection between kings and their people as presented throughout the Bible and pointedly highlighted here. The disobedience of Jeroboam resulted in the disobedience and destruction of his people. As Christians, however, we have been transferred into a kingdom where Jesus is King—the ever living and ever faithful King. Because of the close connection between king and people, we have the treasured assurance that the faithfulness of Jesus will impact our own Christian living, shaping our affections and producing the fruit of obedience. As went Jeroboam, so went the people—to destruction. But as goes Jesus, so go his people—to salvation.

15:4 From the reign of Solomon in 1 Kings 11 to the final reigns of Jehoiachin and Zedekiah in 2 Kings 24–25, the history of Israel's kings represents a tragic downward spiral into disobedience and destruction, with only brief glimpses of faithfulness and zeal for the Lord. Given such a history, we might wonder why the Lord waited more than three hundred years to bring judgment on the land and its people. Or, to put it another way, why does the Lord not always treat us as our sins deserve?

of the Chronicles of the Kings of Judah? [d]And
there was war between Abijam and Jeroboam.
8 [e]And Abijam slept with his fathers, and they
buried him in the city of David. And Asa his
son reigned in his place.

Asa Reigns in Judah

9 In the twentieth year of Jeroboam king of
Israel, Asa began to reign over Judah, 10 and
he reigned forty-one years in Jerusalem. His
mother's name was Maacah the daughter of
Abishalom. 11 [f]And Asa did what was right in
the eyes of the LORD, as David his father had
done. 12 He put away the [g]male cult prostitutes
out of the land and removed [h]all the idols
that his fathers had made. 13 [i]He also removed
Maacah his mother from being queen mother
because she had made an abominable image
for Asherah. And Asa cut down her image and
[j]burned it at the brook Kidron. 14 [k]But the high
places were not taken away. Nevertheless, [l]the
heart of Asa was wholly true to the LORD all
his days. 15 And [m]he brought into the house of
the LORD the sacred gifts of his father and his
own sacred gifts, silver, and gold, and vessels.
16 [n]And there was war between Asa and
Baasha king of Israel all their days. 17 [o]Baasha
king of Israel went up against Judah and
[p]built Ramah, [q]that he might permit no one to
go out or come in to Asa king of Judah. 18 Then
Asa took all the silver and the gold [r]that were
left in the treasures of the house of the LORD
and the treasures of the king's house and gave
them into the hands of his servants. [s]And
King Asa sent them to Ben-hadad the son of
Tabrimmon, the son of Hezion, king of Syria,
[t]who lived in Damascus, saying, 19 "Let there be
[u]a covenant[1] between me and you, as there was
between my father and your father. Behold,
I am sending to you a present of silver and
gold. Go, break your covenant with Baasha
king of Israel, that he may withdraw from me."
20 And Ben-hadad listened to King Asa and
sent the commanders of his armies against
the cities of Israel and conquered [v]Ijon, [w]Dan,
[x]Abel-beth-maacah, and all [y]Chinneroth, with
all the land of Naphtali. 21 And when Baasha
heard of it, [z]he stopped building Ramah, and
he lived in [a]Tirzah. 22 Then King Asa made a
proclamation to all Judah, none was exempt,
and they carried away the stones of Ramah
and its timber, with which Baasha had been
building, and with them King Asa built [b]Geba
of Benjamin and [c]Mizpah. 23 [d]Now the rest of
all the acts of Asa, all his might, and all that
he did, and the cities that he built, are they
not written in the Book of the Chronicles of
the Kings of Judah? But in his old age he was
diseased in his feet. 24 And Asa slept with his
fathers and was buried with his fathers in the
city of David his father, and [e]Jehoshaphat his
son reigned in his place.

[1] Or *treaty*; twice in this verse

The author of the book of Kings is well aware of this tension, and, on several occasions, he tells us why God works in this way. It is an important theme running through the book of Kings, beginning, once again, with Solomon and working its way through Hezekiah in 2 Kings 20. In short, the Lord continually extends mercy to his people "for the sake of David" (cf. 1 Kings 11:12–13, 34; 15:4; 2 Kings 8:19; 19:34; 20:6; Isa. 37:35), that is, "because David did what was right in the eyes of the LORD and did not turn aside from anything that he commanded him all the days of his life, except in the matter of Uriah the Hittite" (1 Kings 15:5). In other words, the Lord is treating subsequent generations of Israelites with mercy because of the obedience of one man, David.

Of course, even David's obedience was only partial. Moreover, the Lord's mercy to Israel as a nation in the Promised Land expired with the destruction of Jerusalem and the exile (2 Kings 25). Nevertheless, it is remarkable to consider the impact that this one man, David, had on the lives of so many people hundreds of years after his death. Because of David's obedience, the Lord actually treated people differently, in a way that they did not deserve. This same principle becomes very important for our understanding of the person and work of Jesus in the New Testament.

While the obedience of David was partial, the obedience of Jesus was full, or complete (cf. Rom. 5:19). The impact of David's obedience was temporary, but the impact of Christ's obedience is permanent, without end. So the Christian is equipped with every confidence. Our standing before God is secure "for the sake of Jesus." Because of this one man's obedience, we stand righteous before God, treated in a way that we certainly do not deserve.

7 [d]See 2 Chr. 13:2-20
8 [e]2 Chr. 14:1
11 [f]2 Chr. 14:2
12 [g]See ch. 14:24 [h][2 Chr. 15:8]
13 [i]For ver. 13-15, see 2 Chr. 15:16-18 [j][Ex. 32:20]
14 [k]ch. 22:43; [2 Kgs. 12:3; 14:4] [l][ver. 3]
15 [m][ch. 7:51]
16 [n]ver. 32
17 [o]For ver. 17-22, see 2 Chr. 16:1-6 [p]ver. 21, 22 [q][ch. 12:27]
18 [r]ch. 14:26 [s][2 Kgs. 12:18] [t]ch. 11:24
19 [u][2 Chr. 16:7]
20 [v]2 Kgs. 15:29 [w]Judg. 18:29 [x]2 Sam. 20:14; 2 Kgs. 15:29 [y]See Josh. 11:2
21 [z]ver. 17 [a]ch. 14:17; 16:6, 9
22 [b]Josh. 21:17 [c]Josh. 18:26
23 [d]For ver. 23, 24, see 2 Chr. 16:11-14
24 [e]2 Chr. 17:1; [Matt. 1:8]

Nadab Reigns in Israel

25 [f]Nadab the son of Jeroboam began to reign
over Israel in the second year of Asa king of
Judah, and he reigned over Israel two years.
26 He did what was evil in the sight of the
LORD [g]and walked in the way of his father,
and in his sin [h]which he made Israel to sin.

27 [i]Baasha the son of Ahijah, of the house of
Issachar, conspired against him. And Baasha
struck him down at [j]Gibbethon, which
belonged to the Philistines, for Nadab and all
Israel were laying siege to Gibbethon. 28 So
Baasha killed him in the third year of Asa king
of Judah and reigned in his place. 29 And as
soon as he was king, he killed all the house of
Jeroboam. He left to the house of Jeroboam
not one that breathed, until he had destroyed
it, [k]according to the word of the LORD that he
spoke by his servant Ahijah the Shilonite. 30 It
was for the sins of Jeroboam that he sinned
and [h]that he made Israel to sin, and because
of the anger to which he provoked the LORD,
the God of Israel.

31 Now the rest of the acts of Nadab and all
that he did, are they not written in the Book
of the Chronicles of the Kings of Israel? 32 [l]And
there was war between Asa and Baasha king of
Israel all their days.

Baasha Reigns in Israel

33 In the third year of Asa king of Judah,
Baasha the son of Ahijah began to reign over
all Israel at Tirzah, and he reigned twenty-four
years. 34 He did what was evil in the sight of
the LORD [m]and walked in the way of Jeroboam
and in his sin which he made Israel to sin.

16 And the word of the LORD came to [n]Jehu
the son of [o]Hanani against Baasha, saying, 2 "Since I [p]exalted you out of the dust and
made you leader over my people Israel, and
[q]you have walked in the way of Jeroboam
and have made my people Israel to sin, provoking me to anger with their sins, 3 behold,
I will utterly [r]sweep away [s]Baasha and his
house, and I will make your house [t]like the
house of Jeroboam the son of Nebat. 4 [u]Anyone
belonging to Baasha who dies in the city the
dogs shall eat, and anyone of his who dies in
the field the birds of the heavens shall eat."

5 Now the rest of the acts of Baasha and what
he did, and his might, are they not written
in the Book of the Chronicles of the Kings
of Israel? 6 And Baasha slept with his fathers
and was buried at [v]Tirzah, and Elah his son
reigned in his place. 7 Moreover, the word of
the LORD came by the prophet [n]Jehu the son
of Hanani against Baasha and his house, both
because of all the evil that he did in the sight
of the LORD, provoking him to anger with the
work of his hands, in being like the house of
Jeroboam, and also because [w]he destroyed it.

Elah Reigns in Israel

8 In the twenty-sixth year of Asa king of
Judah, Elah the son of Baasha began to reign
over Israel in Tirzah, and he reigned two years.
9 But his servant [x]Zimri, commander of half
his chariots, conspired against him. When he
was at Tirzah, drinking himself drunk in the
house of Arza, [y]who was over the household in
Tirzah, 10 Zimri came in and struck him down
and killed him, in the twenty-seventh year of
Asa king of Judah, and reigned in his place.

11 When he began to reign, as soon as he
had seated himself on his throne, he struck
down [z]all the house of Baasha. He [a]did not
leave him a single male of his relatives or his
friends. 12 Thus Zimri destroyed all the house
of Baasha, [b]according to the word of the LORD,
which he spoke against Baasha by [n]Jehu the
prophet, 13 for all the sins of Baasha and the
sins of Elah his son, which they sinned and
which they made Israel to sin, [c]provoking the
LORD God of Israel to anger with their idols.
14 Now the rest of the acts of Elah and all that
he did, are they not written in the Book of the
Chronicles of the Kings of Israel?

Zimri Reigns in Israel

15 In the twenty-seventh year of Asa king of
Judah, Zimri reigned seven days in Tirzah.
Now the troops were encamped against
[d]Gibbethon, which belonged to the Philistines,
16 and the troops who were encamped heard it

25[f] ch. 14:20
26[g] [ver. 34] [h] ver. 30; ch. 12:30; 14:16
27[i] ch. 14:14 [j] ch. 16:15; Josh. 19:44; 21:23
29[k] ch. 14:10, 14
30[h] [See ver. 26 above]

16:1–34 Throughout chapter 16, hope steadily builds for a king who will not fail as one king after another does here. The subtle but ever-heightening question the reader is brought to ask is, when will a real king show up? How will Israel ever get on the right track in light of the miserable moral record of its leaders? That King would one day come (Matt. 1:1; Luke 19:38–40).

32[l] ver. 16 **34**[m] [ver. 26] **Chapter 16** **1**[n] 2 Chr. 19:2; 20:34 [o] 2 Chr. 16:7 **2**[p] [ch. 14:7] [q] ch. 15:34 **3**[r] [ch. 14:10; 21:21] [s] ver. 11 [t] [ch. 15:29] **4**[u] [ch. 14:11; 21:24] **6**[v] ch. 14:17; 15:21 **7**[n] [See ver. 1 above] [w] ch. 15:27, 29; [Hos. 1:4] **9**[x] 2 Kgs. 9:31 [y] [ch. 18:3] **11**[z] [ver. 3] [a] [1 Sam. 25:22] **12**[b] ver. 3 [n] [See ver. 1 above] **13**[c] ver. 26; Deut. 32:21 **15**[d] ch. 15:27

said, "Zimri has conspired, and he has killed the king." Therefore all Israel made Omri, the commander of the army, king over Israel that day in the camp. [17]So Omri went up from Gibbethon, and all Israel with him, and they besieged Tirzah. [18]And when Zimri saw that the city was taken, he went into the citadel of the king's house and burned the king's house over him with fire and died, [19]because of his sins that he committed, doing evil in the sight of the LORD, [e]walking in the way of Jeroboam, and for his sin which he committed, making Israel to sin. [20]Now the rest of the acts of Zimri, and the conspiracy that he made, are they not written in the Book of the Chronicles of the Kings of Israel?

Omri Reigns in Israel

[21]Then the people of Israel were divided into two parts. Half of the people followed Tibni the son of Ginath, to make him king, and half followed Omri. [22]But the people who followed Omri overcame the people who followed Tibni the son of Ginath. So Tibni died, and Omri became king. [23]In the thirty-first year of Asa king of Judah, Omri began to reign over Israel, and he reigned for twelve years; six years he reigned in Tirzah. [24]He bought the hill of [f]Samaria from Shemer for two talents[1] of silver, and he fortified the hill and called the name of the city that he built [g]Samaria, after the name of Shemer, the owner of the hill.

[25][h]Omri did what was evil in the sight of the LORD, and did more evil [i]than all who were before him. [26]For [e]he walked in all the way of Jeroboam the son of Nebat, and in the sins that he made Israel to sin, [j]provoking the LORD, the God of Israel, to anger by their idols. [27]Now the rest of the acts of Omri that he did, and the might that he showed, are they not written in the Book of the Chronicles of the Kings of Israel? [28]And Omri slept with his fathers and was buried in Samaria, and Ahab his son reigned in his place.

Ahab Reigns in Israel

[29]In the thirty-eighth year of Asa king of Judah, Ahab the son of Omri began to reign over Israel, and Ahab the son of Omri reigned over Israel in Samaria twenty-two years. [30]And Ahab the son of Omri did evil in the sight of the LORD, [k]more than all who were before him. [31]And as if it had been a light thing for him to walk in the sins of Jeroboam the son of Nebat, [l]he took for his wife Jezebel the daughter of Ethbaal king of the [m]Sidonians, [n]and went and served Baal and worshiped him. [32]He erected an altar for Baal in [o]the house of Baal, which he built in Samaria. [33]And Ahab made an [p]Asherah. Ahab did more to provoke the LORD, the God of Israel, to anger [k]than all the kings of Israel who were before him. [34][q]In his days Hiel of Bethel built [r]Jericho. He laid its foundation at the cost of Abiram his firstborn, and set up its gates at the cost of his youngest son Segub, according to the word of the LORD, which he spoke by Joshua the son of Nun.

Elijah Predicts a Drought

17 Now Elijah the Tishbite, of [s]Tishbe[2] in Gilead, said to Ahab, [t]"As the LORD, the God of Israel, lives, [u]before whom I stand, [v]there shall be neither dew nor rain these years, except by my word." [2]And the word of the LORD came to him: [3]"Depart from here and turn eastward and hide yourself by the brook Cherith, which is east of the Jordan. [4]You shall drink from the brook, and I have commanded the ravens to feed you there." [5]So he went and did according to the word of the LORD. He went and lived by the brook Cherith that is east of the Jordan. [6]And the ravens brought him bread and meat in the morning, and bread and meat in the evening, and he drank from the brook. [7]And after a while the brook dried up, because there was no rain in the land.

The Widow of Zarephath

[8]Then the word of the LORD came to him, [9]"Arise, go to [w]Zarephath, which belongs to Sidon, and dwell there. Behold, I have commanded a widow there to feed you." [10]So he arose and went to [w]Zarephath. And when he came to the gate of the city, behold, a widow was there [x]gathering sticks. And he called to

[1] A *talent* was about 75 pounds or 34 kilograms [2] Septuagint; Hebrew *of the settlers*

17:1–24 From the end of chapter 11 all the way to the end of chapter 16, the author has been tracking the fall of the northern kingdom of Israel. Destruction and exile were coming, but first God would send the prophets Elijah and Elisha to prepare the

19[e] [ch. 15:26, 34]
24[f] [ch. 13:32] [g] ver. 28, 29, 32
25[h] Mic. 6:16 [i] ver. 30
26[e] [See ver. 19 above] [j] ver. 13

30[k] ch. 21:25; [ver. 25] **31**[l] [Ex. 34:16; Deut. 7:3] [m] Judg. 18:7 [n] ch. 21:25, 26; [2 Kgs. 3:2; 10:18; 17:16] **32**[o] 2 Kgs. 10:21, 26, 27 **33**[p] ch. 18:19; 2 Kgs. 13:6; 17:10; 21:3; 2 Chr. 14:3; [Ex. 34:13; Jer. 17:2] [k] [See ver. 30 above] **34**[q] [Josh. 6:26] [r] See 2 Kgs. 2:4, 18-22 **Chapter 17** **1**[s] [Judg. 12:4] [t] ch. 18:10, 15; 22:14; 2 Kgs. 3:14; 5:16; See Ruth 3:13 [u] ch. 18:15; [Deut. 10:8] [v] Luke 4:25; James 5:17; [ch. 18:1] **9**[w] Obad. 20; Luke 4:26 **10**[w] [See ver. 9 above] [x] Num. 15:32, 33

her and said, "Bring me a little water in a vessel, that I may drink." 11 And as she was going
to bring it, he called to her and said, "Bring
me a morsel of bread in your hand." 12 And
she said, [t]"As the LORD your God lives, I have
nothing baked, only a handful of flour in a jar
and a little oil in a jug. And now I am gathering a couple of sticks that I may go in and
prepare it for myself and my son, that we may
eat it and die." 13 And Elijah said to her, "Do not
fear; go and do as you have said. But first make
me a little cake of it and bring it to me, and
afterward make something for yourself and
your son. 14 For thus says the LORD, the God
of Israel, 'The jar of flour shall not be spent,
and the jug of oil shall not be empty, until the
day that the LORD sends rain upon the earth.'"
15 And she went and did as Elijah said. And
she and he and her household ate for many
days. 16 The jar of flour was not spent, neither
did the jug of oil become empty, according to
the word of the LORD that he spoke by Elijah.

Elijah Raises the Widow's Son

17 After this the son of the woman, the mistress of the house, became ill. And his illness
was so severe that there was no breath left in
him. 18 And she said to Elijah, [y]"What have you
against me, O [z]man of God? You have come
to me to bring my sin to remembrance and to
cause the death of my son!" 19 And he said to
her, "Give me your son." And he took him from
her arms and carried him up into the upper
chamber where he lodged, and laid him on his
own bed. 20 And he cried to the LORD, "O LORD
my God, have you brought calamity even upon
the widow with whom I sojourn, by killing
her son?" 21 [a]Then he stretched himself upon
the child three times and cried to the LORD,
"O LORD my God, let this child's life[1] come
into him again." 22 And the LORD listened to
the voice of Elijah. And the life of the child
came into him again, and [b]he revived. 23 And
Elijah took the child and brought him down
from the upper chamber into the house and
delivered him to his mother. And Elijah said,
"See, your son lives." 24 And the woman said
to Elijah, [c]"Now I know that you are a man of
God, and that the word of the LORD in your
mouth is truth."

Elijah Confronts Ahab

18 [d]After many days the word of the LORD
came to Elijah, in the third year, saying,
"Go, show yourself to Ahab, and I will send
rain upon the earth." 2 So Elijah went to show
himself to Ahab. Now the famine was severe
in Samaria. 3 And Ahab called Obadiah, who
was [e]over the household. (Now Obadiah feared
the LORD greatly, 4 and [f]when Jezebel cut off
the prophets of the LORD, Obadiah took a
hundred prophets and hid them by fifties in
a cave and fed them with bread and water.)
5 And Ahab said to Obadiah, "Go through the
land to all the springs of water and to all the
valleys. Perhaps we may find grass and save
the horses and mules alive, and not lose some
of the animals." 6 So they divided the land
between them to pass through it. Ahab went
in one direction by himself, and Obadiah went
in another direction by himself.
7 And as Obadiah was on the way, behold,

[1] Or *soul*; also verse 22

12[t] [See ver. 1 above] **18**[y] [Luke 4:34; 5:8] [z] See Deut. 33:1 **21**[a] 2 Kgs. 4:34, 35; Acts 20:10 **22**[b] [Heb. 11:35] **24**[c] [John 3:2]
Chapter 18
1[d] See ch. 17:1 **3**[e] ch. 16:9 **4**[f] ver. 13

people for their grim future. Because of Israel's sin and the Lord's just anger, you might expect a prophet like Elijah to cast shadows of dark gloom and despair, but this is not the case.

From this first account of Elijah we learn two things about how God will treat his people in exile. First, God will always provide for his people, even by extraordinary means—with ravens or poor widows from foreign countries. Second, exile is not the final word when it comes to the Lord's dealings with his people. As the resurrection of the widow's son demonstrates, God is able to fully restore his people, even by supernatural feats of resurrection (cf. Ezekiel 37).

The hope represented by Elijah is also applicable to the Christian life. We live in exile on this earth as aliens and sojourners (Heb. 11:13; 1 Pet. 2:11), but the Lord is able to provide for our every need (Matt. 6:25–34; 1 Tim. 6:17), even in miraculous ways. Like Israel, we share in the hope of restoration through resurrection, when our covenant Lord will make all things new (Rom. 6:5; 1 Cor. 15:21, 42; Phil. 3:10–11). Even in the dark hours of Israel's sin, the Lord was compelled to give hope. How much more should we be encouraged by these same realities in our own day of greater light, living on this side of Christ's coming.

Elijah met him. And Obadiah recognized him and fell on his face and said, "Is it you, my lord Elijah?" 8 And he answered him, "It is I. Go, tell your lord, 'Behold, Elijah is here.'" 9 And he said, "How have I sinned, that you would give your servant into the hand of Ahab, to kill me? 10 [g]As the LORD your God lives, there is no nation or kingdom where my lord has not sent to seek you. And when they would say, 'He is not here,' he would take an oath of the kingdom or nation, that they had not found you. 11 And now you say, 'Go, tell your lord, "Behold, Elijah is here."' 12 And as soon as I have gone from you, [h]the Spirit of the LORD will carry you I know not where. And so, when I come and tell Ahab and he cannot find you, he will kill me, although I your servant have feared the LORD from my youth. 13 Has it not been told my lord what I did [i]when Jezebel killed the prophets of the LORD, how I hid a hundred men of the LORD's prophets by fifties in a cave and fed them with bread and water? 14 And now you say, 'Go, tell your lord, "Behold, Elijah is here"'; and he will kill me." 15 And Elijah said, [g]"As the LORD of hosts lives, before whom I stand, I will surely show myself to him today." 16 So Obadiah went to meet Ahab, and told him. And Ahab went to meet Elijah.

17 When Ahab saw Elijah, Ahab said to him, [j]"Is it you, you [k]troubler of Israel?" 18 And he answered, "I have not troubled Israel, but you have, and your father's house, because you have [l]abandoned the commandments of the LORD and [m]followed the Baals. 19 Now therefore send and gather all Israel to me at Mount [n]Carmel, and the [o]450 prophets of Baal and [p]the 400 prophets of Asherah, [q]who eat at Jezebel's table."

The Prophets of Baal Defeated

20 So Ahab sent to all the people of Israel and gathered the prophets together at Mount Carmel. 21 And Elijah came near to all the people and said, "How long [r]will you go limping between two different opinions? [s]If the LORD is God, follow him; but if Baal, then follow him." And the people did not answer him a word. 22 Then Elijah said to the people, [t]"I, even I only, am left a prophet of the LORD, but Baal's prophets are [u]450 men. 23 Let two bulls be given to us, and let them choose one bull for themselves and cut it in pieces and lay it on the wood, but put no fire to it. And I will prepare the other bull and lay it on the wood and put no fire to it. 24 And you call upon the name of your god, and I will call upon the name of the LORD, and the God who [v]answers by fire, he is God." And all the people answered, "It is well spoken." 25 Then Elijah said to the prophets of Baal, "Choose for yourselves one bull and prepare it first, for you are many, and call upon

18:17–40 The competition between Elijah and the prophets of Baal was certainly dramatic: a single prophet of Yahweh versus 450 prophets of Baal. It hardly seemed fair, and the consolation prize for the losing side was death! But all of this drama had a purpose, and that purpose was to produce repentance and to change the hearts of God's people, in order "that this people may know that you, O LORD, are God, and that you have turned their hearts back" (v. 37).

In verse 21, Elijah set the stage with a question: "How long will you go limping between two different opinions? If the LORD is God, follow him; but if Baal, then follow him." The people responded with silence. It appears that their concerns related to the famine, and their persistence in idolatry had hardened their hearts to the reality that Yahweh alone was God (cf. Deut. 6:4). As such, this competition between Elijah and the prophets of Baal was motivated by the Lord's desire to make himself known as the God of Israel, the only true God, and this is exactly what transpired: "When all the people saw it, they fell on their faces and said, 'The LORD, he is God; the LORD, he is God'" (1 Kings 18:39).

One of the remarkable features of this narrative is the fact that the Lord changed the hearts of his people by answering Elijah's prayer and demonstrating his incredible power. We are reminded that God's good news, whether in the Old or New Testament, constitutes a proclamation of his mighty deeds in real time and space. This is one reason why so much of the Bible consists of a narrative history. Over and over again, our covenant God is demonstrating to his people that he alone is the only true God. As such, he is to be trusted, turned to, and obeyed. As these events were intended to bring spiritual change to God's people in the days of Elijah, so the record of these events in Scripture is intended to have the same effect on us—to change our hearts and move us to authentic repentance.

10[g] See ch. 17:1
12[h] 2 Kgs. 2:16; Ezek. 3:12, 14; 8:3; Acts 8:39
13[i] ver. 4
15[g] [See ver. 10 above]
17[j] [ch. 21:20] [k] [Josh. 7:25]
18[l] ch. 9:9; 2 Chr. 15:2; 24:20 [m] ch. 16:31
19[n] See Josh. 19:26 [o] ver. 22 [p] See ch. 16:33 [q] [2 Kgs. 3:13]
21[r] [2 Kgs. 17:41] [s] Josh. 24:15; [Matt. 6:24]
22[t] ch. 19:10, 14 [u] ver. 19
24[v] See ver. 38

the name of your god, but put no fire to it." 26 And they took the bull that was given them, and they prepared it and called upon the name of Baal from morning until noon, saying, "O Baal, answer us!" But there was no voice, and no one answered. And they limped around the altar that they had made. 27 And at noon Elijah mocked them, saying, "Cry aloud, for he is a god. Either he is musing, or he is relieving himself, or he is on a journey, or perhaps he is asleep and must be awakened." 28 And they cried aloud and [w]cut themselves after their custom with swords and lances, until the blood gushed out upon them. 29 And as midday passed, they raved on until the time of [x]the offering of the oblation, but there was no voice. No one answered; no one paid attention.

30 Then Elijah said to all the people, "Come near to me." And all the people came near to him. And he repaired the altar of the LORD that had been [y]thrown down. 31 Elijah took twelve stones, according to the number of the tribes of the sons of Jacob, to whom the word of the LORD came, saying, [z]"Israel shall be your name," 32 and with the stones he built an altar in the name of the LORD. And he made a trench about the altar, as great as would contain two seahs[1] of seed. 33 [a]And he put the wood in order and cut the bull in pieces and laid it on the wood. And he said, "Fill four jars with water and [b]pour it on the burnt offering and on the wood." 34 And he said, "Do it a second time." And they did it a second time. And he said, "Do it a third time." And they did it a third time. 35 And the water ran around the altar and filled the trench also with water.

36 And at the time of [c]the offering of the oblation, Elijah the prophet came near and said, "O LORD, [d]God of Abraham, Isaac, and Israel, let it be known this day that [e]you are God in Israel, and that I am your servant, and that [f]I have done all these things at your word. 37 Answer me, O LORD, answer me, that this people may know that you, O LORD, are God, and that you have turned their hearts back." 38 [g]Then the fire of the LORD fell and consumed the burnt offering and the wood and the stones and the dust, and licked up the water that was in the trench. 39 And when all the people saw it, they fell on their faces and said, [h]"The LORD, he is God; the LORD, he is God." 40 And Elijah said to them, "Seize the prophets of Baal; let not one of them escape." And they seized them. And Elijah brought them down to [i]the brook Kishon and [j]slaughtered them there.

The LORD Sends Rain

41 And Elijah said to Ahab, "Go up, eat and drink, for there is a sound of the rushing of rain." 42 So Ahab went up to eat and to drink. And Elijah went up to the top of Mount Carmel. [k]And he bowed himself down on the earth and put his face between his knees. 43 And he said to his servant, "Go up now, look toward the sea." And he went up and looked and said, "There is nothing." And he said, "Go again," seven times. 44 And at the seventh time he said, "Behold, [l]a little cloud like a man's hand is rising from the sea." And he said, "Go up, say to Ahab, 'Prepare your chariot and go down, lest the rain stop you.'" 45 And in a little while the heavens grew black with clouds and wind, and there was a great rain. And Ahab rode and went to [m]Jezreel. 46 [n]And the hand of the LORD was on Elijah, [o]and he gathered up his garment and ran before Ahab to the entrance of [p]Jezreel.

Elijah Flees Jezebel

19 Ahab told Jezebel all that Elijah had done, and how [q]he had killed all the prophets with the sword. 2 Then Jezebel sent a messenger to Elijah, saying, [r]"So may the gods do to me and more also, if I do not make your life as the life of one of them by this time tomorrow." 3 Then he was afraid, and he arose and ran for his life and came to [s]Beersheba, which belongs to Judah, and left his servant there.

4 But he himself went a day's journey into the wilderness and came and sat down under a broom tree. [t]And he asked that he might die, saying, "It is enough; now, O LORD, take away my life, for I am no better than my fathers." 5 And he lay down and slept under a broom tree. And behold, an angel touched him and said to him, "Arise and eat." 6 And he looked, and behold, there was at his head a cake baked on hot stones and a jar of water. And he ate and drank and lay down again. 7 And the angel of the LORD came again a second time and

[1] A *seah* was about 7 quarts or 7.3 liters

28 [w] [Lev. 19:28; Deut. 14:1] **29** [x] [Ex. 29:39, 41] **30** [y] ch. 19:10, 14 **31** [z] Gen. 32:28; 35:10; 2 Kgs. 17:34 **33** [a] Gen. 22:9; Lev. 1:7 [b] [Judg. 6:20] **36** [c] ver. 29 [d] See Ex. 3:6 [e] Josh. 4:24; 1 Sam. 17:46 [f] [Num. 16:28] **38** [g] ver. 24; See Lev. 9:24 **39** [h] ver. 24 **40** [i] Judg. 4:7 [j] [2 Kgs. 10:25] **42** [k] [James 5:17, 18] **44** [l] [Luke 12:54] **45** [m] Josh. 17:16 **46** [n] 2 Kgs. 3:15; Ezek. 1:3; 3:14 [o] Ex. 12:11; 2 Kgs. 4:29; 9:1; Jer. 1:17 [p] Josh. 17:16 **Chapter 19** **1** [q] ch. 18:40 **2** [r] [ch. 20:10]; See Ruth 1:17 **3** [s] See Gen. 21:31 **4** [t] [Num. 11:15; Jonah 4:3, 8]

touched him and said, "Arise and eat, for the journey is too great for you." 8 And he arose and ate and drank, and went in the strength of that food [u]forty days and forty nights to [v]Horeb, the mount of God.

The LORD Speaks to Elijah

9 There he came to a cave and lodged in it. And behold, [w]the word of the LORD came to him, and he said to him, "What are you doing here, Elijah?" 10 He said, "I have been very [x]jealous for the LORD, the God of hosts. For the people of Israel have forsaken your covenant, [y]thrown down your altars, and [z]killed your prophets with the sword, [a]and I, even I only, am left, and they seek my life, to take it away." 11 And he said, "Go out and [b]stand on the mount before the LORD." And behold, the LORD passed by, and [c]a great and strong wind tore the mountains and broke in pieces the rocks before the LORD, but the LORD was not in the wind. And after the wind [d]an earthquake, but the LORD was not in the earthquake. 12 And after the earthquake a fire, but the LORD was not in the fire. And after the fire the sound of a low whisper.[1] 13 And when Elijah heard it, [e]he wrapped his face in his cloak and went out and stood at the entrance of the cave. And behold, [f]there came a voice to him and said, "What are you doing here, Elijah?" 14 He said, [x]"I have been very jealous for the LORD, the God of hosts. For the people of Israel have forsaken your covenant, [y]thrown down your altars, and killed your prophets with the sword, and I, even I only, am left, and they seek my life, to take it away." 15 And the LORD said to him, "Go, return on your way to the wilderness of Damascus. And when you arrive, you shall anoint Hazael to be king over Syria. 16 [g]And Jehu the son of Nimshi you shall anoint to be king over Israel, and [h]Elisha the son of Shaphat of Abel-meholah you shall anoint to be prophet in your place. 17 And the one who escapes from [i]the sword of Hazael [j]shall Jehu put to death, and the one who escapes from the sword of Jehu [k]shall Elisha put to death. 18 [l]Yet I will leave seven thousand in Israel, all the knees that have not bowed to Baal, and every mouth that has not [m]kissed him."

The Call of Elisha

19 So he departed from there and found Elisha the son of Shaphat, who was plowing with twelve yoke of oxen in front of him, and he was with the twelfth. Elijah passed by him and cast [n]his cloak upon him. 20 And he left the oxen and ran after Elijah and said, [o]"Let me kiss my father and my mother, and then I will follow you." And he said to him, "Go back again, for what have I done to you?"

[1] Or *a sound, a thin silence*

19:4 After the events recorded in chapters 17 and 18, it is hard to believe that Elijah should despair of his life and make a statement like, "I am no better than my fathers." In fact, Elijah twice states his zeal for the Lord and laments that there appears to be none like him who have remained faithful (cf. 19:10, 14). So what was happening here? Was Elijah wrongfully conflicted? Not at all.

We must first recall that Elijah had spent the last three years of his life swimming in the miracles of the Lord: fed by ravens, provided for by a poor widow, seeing the dead raised, and the cessation of rain by his word, and then the dramatic events with the prophets of Baal. These encounters with God's majesty had a profound impact on Elijah. Even as a faithful prophet, he recognized the great divide between himself and his covenant Lord to such a degree that he could only identify with the sinfulness of his fathers. In other words, the power and grace of God displayed in his own life had produced true and genuine humility. We are reminded of the apostle Paul. Paul had experienced the dramatic power of God in his own life (cf. Acts 9), and this encounter left a lasting impression. He called himself the foremost of sinners (1 Tim. 1:15) and the least of all the apostles (1 Cor. 15:9).

As Christians, we certainly recognize the importance of humility in living the Christian life (cf. James 4:6, 10; 1 Pet. 3:8; 5:5–6). But we must also remember that true humility is always the product of our encounter with God's majesty and grace. Real humility is never something we can create on our own. This is good news! For not only do we have the record of God's majesty in the days of Elijah, but we have a Bible filled to the brim with events of this kind. Each one is recorded for us to experience over and over again by the power of the Holy Spirit. Do you need humility? Dare to study God's Word to experience the majesty of his power and grace!

8 [u]Ex. 24:18; 34:28; Deut. 9:9, 18; Matt. 4:2; Mark 1:13; Luke 4:2 [v]Ex. 3:1
9 [w]ver. 13
10 [x]Num. 25:11, 13 [y]ch. 18:30; Cited Rom. 11:3 [z]ch. 18:4 [a]ch. 18:22
11 [b]Ex. 24:12; 34:2 [c]Ezek. 1:4 [d]Ezek. 37:7
13 [e][Ex. 3:6] [f]ver. 9
14 [x][See ver. 10 above] [y][See ver. 10 above]
16 [g]See 2 Kgs. 9:1-6 [h][ver. 19-21; 2 Kgs. 2:9, 15]
17 [i]2 Kgs. 8:12; 13:3, 22 [j]See 2 Kgs. 9–10 [k][Hos. 6:5]
18 [l]Cited Rom. 11:4 [m][Hos. 13:2]
19 [n]2 Kgs. 2:8
20 [o][Matt. 8:21, 22; Luke 9:61, 62]

21 And he returned from following him and
took the yoke of oxen and sacrificed them and
boiled their flesh [p]with the yokes of the oxen
and gave it to the people, and they ate. Then he
arose and went after Elijah and assisted him.

Ahab's Wars with Syria

20 [q]Ben-hadad the king of Syria gathered
all his army together. [r]Thirty-two kings
were with him, and horses and chariots. And
he went up and closed in on [s]Samaria and
fought against it. 2 And he sent messengers
into the city to Ahab king of Israel and said to
him, "Thus says Ben-hadad: 3 'Your silver and
your gold are mine; your best wives and children also are mine.'" 4 And the king of Israel
answered, "As you say, my lord, O king, I am
yours, and all that I have." 5 The messengers
came again and said, "Thus says Ben-hadad:
'I sent to you, saying, "Deliver to me your silver and your gold, your wives and your children." 6 Nevertheless I will send my servants
to you tomorrow about this time, and they
shall search your house and the houses of your
servants and lay hands on whatever pleases
you and take it away.'"

7 Then the king of Israel called all the [t]elders
of the land and said, [u]"Mark, now, and see how
this man is seeking trouble, for he sent to me
for my wives and my children, and for my silver and my gold, and I did not refuse him."
8 And all the elders and all the people said to
him, "Do not listen or consent." 9 So he said to
the messengers of Ben-hadad, "Tell my lord
the king, 'All that you first demanded of your
servant I will do, but this thing I cannot do.'"
And the messengers departed and brought
him word again. 10 Ben-hadad sent to him and
said, [v]"The gods do so to me and more also, if
the dust of Samaria shall suffice for handfuls
for all the people [w]who follow me." 11 And the
king of Israel answered, "Tell him, 'Let not
him who straps on his armor boast himself
as he who takes it off.'" 12 When Ben-hadad
heard this message as [x]he was drinking with
the kings in the booths, he said to his men,
"Take your positions." And they took their
positions against the city.

Ahab Defeats Ben-hadad

13 And behold, a prophet came near to
Ahab king of Israel and said, "Thus says the
LORD, Have you seen all this great multitude? Behold, [y]I will give it into your hand
this day, [z]and you shall know that I am the
LORD." 14 And Ahab said, "By whom?" He said,
"Thus says the LORD, By the servants of the
governors of the districts." Then he said, "Who
shall begin the battle?" He answered, "You."
15 Then he mustered the servants of the governors of the districts, and they were 232. And
after them he mustered all the people of Israel,
seven thousand.

16 And they went out at noon, while Ben-
hadad [x]was drinking himself drunk in the
booths, he and the thirty-two kings who
helped him. 17 The servants of the governors
of the districts went out first. And Ben-hadad
sent out scouts, and they reported to him,
"Men are coming out from Samaria." 18 He
said, "If they have come out for peace, take
them alive. Or if they have come out for war,
take them alive."

19 So these went out of the city, the servants
of the governors of the districts and the army
that followed them. 20 And each struck down
his man. The Syrians fled, and Israel pursued
them, but Ben-hadad king of Syria escaped
on a horse with horsemen. 21 And the king of
Israel went out and struck the horses and chariots, and struck the Syrians with a great blow.

22 Then [a]the prophet came near to the king
of Israel and said to him, "Come, strengthen
yourself, and consider well what you have to
do, for [b]in the spring the king of Syria will
come up against you."

23 And the servants of the king of Syria said
to him, "Their gods are gods of the hills, and
so they were stronger than we. But let us fight
against them in the plain, and surely we shall
be stronger than they. 24 And do this: remove
the kings, each from his post, and put commanders in their places, 25 and muster an
army like the army that you have lost, horse
for horse, and chariot for chariot. Then we will
fight against them in the plain, and surely we
shall be stronger than they." And he listened
to their voice and did so.

Ahab Defeats Ben-hadad Again

26 [b]In the spring, Ben-hadad mustered the
Syrians and went up to [c]Aphek to fight against
Israel. 27 And the people of Israel were mustered and were provisioned and went against
them. The people of Israel encamped before
them like two little flocks of goats, but the

21[p] [2 Sam. 24:22] **Chapter 20** 1[q] 2 Kgs. 6:24; 8:7; [ch. 15:18] [r] ch. 22:31 [s] ch. 16:24 7[t] ch. 21:8, 11 [u] [2 Kgs. 5:7] 10[v] ch. 19:2 [w] [Ex. 11:8] 12[x] [ch. 16:9] 13[y] ver. 28 [z] [ch. 18:36] 16[x] [See ver. 12 above] 22[a] ver. 13 [b] 2 Sam. 11:1 26[b] [See ver. 22 above] [c] 2 Kgs. 13:17

Syrians filled the country. 28 And a [d]man of God came near and said to the king of Israel, "Thus says the LORD, 'Because the Syrians have said, [e]"The LORD is a god of the hills but he is not a god of the valleys," therefore [f]I will give all this great multitude into your hand, and you shall know that I am the LORD.' " 29 And they encamped opposite one another seven days. Then on the seventh day the battle was joined. And the people of Israel struck down of the Syrians 100,000 foot soldiers in one day. 30 And the rest fled into the city of [c]Aphek, and the wall fell upon 27,000 men who were left.

Ben-hadad also fled and entered [g]an inner chamber in the city. 31 And his servants said to him, "Behold now, we have heard that the kings of the house of Israel are merciful kings. Let us [h]put sackcloth around our waists and ropes on our heads and go out to the king of Israel. Perhaps he will spare your life." 32 So they [h]tied sackcloth around their waists and put ropes on their heads and went to the king of Israel and said, "Your servant Ben-hadad says, 'Please, let me live.' " And he said, "Does he still live? He is my brother." 33 Now the men were watching for a sign, and they quickly took it up from him and said, "Yes, your brother Ben-hadad." Then he said, "Go and bring him." Then Ben-hadad came out to him, and he caused him to come up into the chariot. 34 And Ben-hadad said to him, [i]"The cities that my father took from your father I will restore, and you may establish bazaars for yourself in [j]Damascus, as my father did in Samaria." And Ahab said, "I will let you go on these terms." So he made a covenant with him and let him go.

A Prophet Condemns Ben-hadad's Release

35 And a certain man of [k]the sons of the prophets said to his fellow [l]at the command of the LORD, "Strike me, please." But the man refused to strike him. 36 Then he said to him, "Because you have not obeyed the voice of the LORD, behold, as soon as you have gone from me, a lion shall strike you down." And as soon as he had departed from him, [m]a lion met him and struck him down. 37 Then he found another man and said, "Strike me, please." And the man struck him—struck him and wounded him. 38 So the prophet departed and waited for the king by the way, [n]disguising himself with a bandage over his eyes. 39 And as the king passed, he cried to the king and said, "Your servant went out into the midst of the battle, and behold, a soldier turned and brought a man to me and said, 'Guard this man; if by any means he is missing, [o]your life shall be for his life, or else you shall pay a talent[1] of silver.' 40 And as your servant was busy here and there, he was gone." The king of Israel said to him, "So shall your judgment be; you yourself have decided it." 41 Then he hurried to take the bandage away from his eyes, and the king of Israel recognized him as one of the prophets. 42 And he said to him, "Thus says the LORD, 'Because you have let go out of your hand the man whom I had devoted to destruction,[2] therefore [o]your life shall be for his life, and your people for his people.' " 43 And the king of Israel [p]went to his house vexed and sullen and came to Samaria.

Naboth's Vineyard

21 Now Naboth the Jezreelite had a vineyard in [q]Jezreel, beside the palace of Ahab king of Samaria. 2 And after this Ahab said to Naboth, [r]"Give me your vineyard, that I may have it for a vegetable garden, because it is near my house, and I will give you a better vineyard for it; or, if it seems good to you, I will give you its value in money." 3 But Naboth said to Ahab, "The LORD forbid [s]that I should give you the inheritance of my fathers." 4 And Ahab [t]went into his house vexed and sullen because of what Naboth the Jezreelite had said to him, for he had said, "I will not give you the inheritance of my fathers." And he lay down on his bed and turned away his face and would eat no food.

5 But Jezebel his wife came to him and said to him, "Why is your spirit so vexed that you eat no food?" 6 And he said to her, "Because I spoke to Naboth the Jezreelite and said to him, 'Give me your vineyard for money, or else, if it please you, I will give you another vineyard for it.' And he answered, 'I will not give you my vineyard.' " 7 And Jezebel his wife said to him, "Do you now govern Israel? Arise and eat bread and let your heart be cheerful; I will give you the vineyard of Naboth the Jezreelite."

8 [u]So she wrote letters in Ahab's name and

[1] A *talent* was about 75 pounds or 34 kilograms [2] That is, set apart (devoted) as an offering to the Lord (for destruction)

28 [d] ch. 17:18 [e] ver. 23 [f] ver. 13 **30** [c] [See ver. 26 above] [g] ch. 22:25; 2 Kgs. 9:2; 2 Chr. 18:24 **31** [h] See 2 Sam. 3:31 **32** [h] [See ver. 31 above] **34** [i] ch. 15:20 [j] [ch. 11:24] **35** [k] 2 Kgs. 2:3, 5, 7, 15 [l] ch. 13:17, 18 **36** [m] [ch. 13:24] **38** [n] 1 Sam. 28:8 **39** [o] [2 Kgs. 10:24] **42** [o] [See ver. 39 above] **43** [p] ch. 21:4
Chapter 21 **1** [q] ch. 18:45, 46 **2** [r] [1 Sam. 8:14] **3** [s] Lev. 25:23; Num. 36:7; Ezek. 46:18 **4** [t] ch. 20:43 **8** [u] [Esth. 3:12]

sealed them with his seal, and she sent the letters to [v]the elders and the leaders who lived with Naboth in his city. 9 And she wrote in the letters, "Proclaim a fast, and set Naboth at the head of the people. 10 And set two [w]worthless men opposite him, and let them bring a charge against him, saying, [x]'You have cursed[1] God and the king.' Then take him out and stone him to death." 11 And the men of his city, [v]the elders and the leaders who lived in his city, did as Jezebel had sent word to them. As it was written in the letters that she had sent to them, 12 [y]they proclaimed a fast and set Naboth at the head of the people. 13 And the two worthless men came in and sat opposite him. And the worthless men brought a charge against Naboth in the presence of the people, saying, "Naboth cursed God and the king." So they took him outside the city and stoned him to death with stones. 14 Then they sent to Jezebel, saying, "Naboth has been stoned; he is dead."

15 As soon as Jezebel heard that Naboth had been stoned and was dead, Jezebel said to Ahab, "Arise, take possession of the vineyard of Naboth the Jezreelite, which he refused to give you for money, for Naboth is not alive, but dead." 16 And as soon as Ahab heard that Naboth was dead, Ahab arose to go down to the vineyard of Naboth the Jezreelite, to take possession of it.

The Lord Condemns Ahab

17 [z]Then the word of the Lord came to Elijah the Tishbite, saying, 18 "Arise, go down to meet Ahab king of Israel, who is in [a]Samaria; behold, he is in the vineyard of Naboth, where he has gone to take possession. 19 And you shall say to him, 'Thus says the Lord, "Have you killed and also taken possession?"' And you shall say to him, 'Thus says the Lord: [b]"In the place where dogs licked up the blood of Naboth shall dogs lick your own blood."'"

20 Ahab said to Elijah, [c]"Have you found me, O my enemy?" He answered, "I have found you, because [d]you have sold yourself to do what is evil in the sight of the Lord. 21 Behold, I will bring disaster upon you. I will utterly burn you up, and [e]will cut off from Ahab every male, bond or free, in Israel. 22 And I will make your house like [f]the house of Jeroboam the son of Nebat, and like [g]the house of Baasha the son of Ahijah, for the anger to which you have provoked me, and because you [h]have made Israel to sin. 23 And of Jezebel the Lord also said, [i]'The dogs shall eat Jezebel within [j]the walls of Jezreel.' 24 [k]Anyone belonging to Ahab who dies in the city the dogs shall eat, and anyone of his who dies in the open country the birds of the heavens shall eat."

Ahab's Repentance

25 ([l]There was none who sold himself to do what was evil in the sight of the Lord like Ahab, whom Jezebel his wife incited. 26 He acted very abominably in going after [m]idols, as [n]the Amorites had done, whom the Lord cast out before the people of Israel.)

27 And when Ahab heard those words, he [o]tore his clothes and [p]put sackcloth on his flesh and [q]fasted and lay in sackcloth and went about dejectedly. 28 And the word of the Lord came to Elijah the Tishbite, saying, 29 "Have you seen how Ahab has humbled himself before me? Because he has humbled himself before me, I will not bring the disaster in his days; [r]but in his son's days I will bring the disaster upon his house."

Ahab and the False Prophets

22 For three years Syria and Israel continued without war. 2 [s]But in the third year [t]Jehoshaphat the king of Judah came down to the king of Israel. 3 And the king of Israel said to his servants, "Do you know that [u]Ramoth-gilead belongs to us, and we keep quiet and do not take it out of the hand of the king of

[1] Hebrew *blessed*; also verse 13

8 [v]ch. 20:7; Ruth 4:2
10 [w]See Deut. 13:13 [x]Ex. 22:28; Lev. 24:16; [Acts 6:11; 23:5]
11 [v][See ver. 8 above]
12 [y][Isa. 58:4]
17 [z][Ps. 9:12]
18 [a]ch. 16:24
19 [b]ch. 22:38; 2 Kgs. 9:26
20 [c][ch. 18:17] [d]ver. 25; 2 Kgs. 17:17; Rom. 7:14
21 [e]2 Kgs. 9:8; [ch. 14:10]
22 [f]ch. 15:29 [g]ch. 16:3, 11 [h]ch. 14:16

21:25–29 If anyone ever doubted the extent of Ahab's evil character, they need only read the summary provided in verses 25–26: "There was none who sold himself to do what was evil in the sight of the Lord like Ahab. . . . He acted very abominably in going after idols." Because of Ahab's extreme wickedness, the Lord had promised to obliterate his dynasty in the manner first observed with Jeroboam (vv. 20–24; cf. 14:7–16). Finally now, the repeated assaults on the heart of Ahab found a breach, causing what appears to be genuine repentance (21:27–29). But it is even more astounding to observe the Lord's willingness to act in light of Ahab's repentance, withholding the execution of his judgment until the next generation.

23 [i]2 Kgs. 9:36 [j][2 Sam. 20:15] **24** [k][ch. 14:11; 16:4] **25** [l]See ch. 16:30-33 **26** [m][ch. 15:12; 2 Kgs. 17:12; 21:11] [n]Gen. 15:16 **27** [o]2 Kgs. 6:30 [p]See 2 Sam. 3:31 [q]2 Sam. 12:16 **29** [r]2 Kgs. 9:25 **Chapter 22** **2** [s]For ver. 1-35, see 2 Chr. 18:2-34 [t]ch. 15:24 **3** [u]Deut. 4:43; Josh. 21:38; 2 Kgs. 8:28; 9:1, 14; 2 Chr. 22:5

Syria?" 4 And he said to Jehoshaphat, "Will you
go with me to battle at Ramoth-gilead?" And
Jehoshaphat said to the king of Israel, [v]"I am as
you are, my people as your people, my horses
as your horses."
5 And Jehoshaphat said to the king of Israel,
"Inquire first for the word of the LORD." 6 Then
the king of Israel [w]gathered the prophets
together, about four hundred men, and said
to them, "Shall I go to battle against Ramoth-
gilead, or shall I refrain?" And they said, "Go
up, for the Lord will give it into the hand of
the king." 7 But [x]Jehoshaphat said, "Is there
not here another prophet of the LORD of
whom we may inquire?" 8 And the king of
Israel said to Jehoshaphat, "There is yet one
man by whom we may inquire of the LORD,
Micaiah the son of Imlah, but I hate him, for
he never prophesies good concerning me, but
evil." And Jehoshaphat said, "Let not the king
say so." 9 Then the king of Israel summoned
an officer and said, "Bring quickly Micaiah
the son of Imlah." 10 Now the king of Israel
and Jehoshaphat the king of Judah were sitting on their thrones, arrayed in their robes,
at the threshing floor [y]at the entrance of the
gate of Samaria, and all the prophets were
prophesying before them. 11 And Zedekiah the
son of Chenaanah made for himself [z]horns
of iron and said, "Thus says the LORD, 'With
these [a]you shall push the Syrians until they
are destroyed.'" 12 And all the prophets prophesied so and said, "Go up to Ramoth-gilead
and triumph; the LORD will give it into the
hand of the king."

Micaiah Prophesies Against Ahab

13 And the messenger who went to summon
Micaiah said to him, "Behold, the words of the
prophets with one accord are favorable to the
king. Let your word be like the word of one of
them, and speak favorably." 14 But Micaiah said,
[b]"As the LORD lives, [c]what the LORD says to me,
that I will speak." 15 And when he had come
to the king, the king said to him, "Micaiah,
shall we go to Ramoth-gilead to battle, or shall
we refrain?" And he answered him, "Go up
and triumph; the LORD will give it into the
hand of the king." 16 But the king said to him,
"How many times shall I make you swear that
you speak to me nothing but the truth in the
name of the LORD?" 17 And he said, "I saw all
Israel scattered on the mountains, [d]as sheep
that have no shepherd. And the LORD said,
'These have no master; let each return to his
home in peace.'" 18 And the king of Israel said
to Jehoshaphat, [e]"Did I not tell you that he
would not prophesy good concerning me, but
evil?" 19 And Micaiah said, "Therefore hear the
word of the LORD: [f]I saw the LORD sitting on
his throne, [g]and all the host of heaven standing beside him on his right hand and on his
left; 20 and the LORD said, 'Who will entice
Ahab, that he may go up and fall at Ramoth-
gilead?' And one said one thing, and another
said another. 21 Then a spirit came forward and
stood before the LORD, saying, 'I will entice
him.' 22 And the LORD said to him, 'By what
means?' And he said, 'I will go out, and will be
[h]a lying spirit in the mouth of all his prophets.'
And he said, 'You are to entice him, and you
shall succeed; go out and do so.' 23 Now therefore behold, the LORD has put a lying spirit
in the mouth of all these your prophets; the
LORD has declared disaster for you."
24 Then Zedekiah the son of Chenaanah came
near [i]and struck Micaiah on the cheek and said,
"How did the Spirit of the LORD go from me
to speak to you?" 25 And Micaiah said, "Behold,
you shall see on that day when you go [j]into
an inner chamber to hide yourself." 26 And the
king of Israel said, "Seize Micaiah, and take
him back to Amon the governor of the city and
to Joash the king's son, 27 and say, 'Thus says
the king, [k]"Put this fellow in prison and feed
him meager rations of bread and water, [l]until

The final verses in this chapter give readers an important glimpse into God's willingness to respond to repentance, even the repentance of a great sinner. Thus, in those moments when our hearts lie to us, causing us to believe that we have sinned beyond the hope of repentance and mercy, we remember the repentance of Ahab, the murdering idolater of Israel, and we repent yet again.

We cannot out-sin God's grace. God would have to "de-God" himself to turn his back on those who come to him in penitent faith, for his Son has paid for the failures of all who trust him. God turned his back on his own Son so that he would never have to turn his back on his adopted sons and daughters. This is our hope, provided by the marvelous grace that goes deeper than all our sin and weakness.

4 [v] 2 Kgs. 3:7
6 [w] ch. 18:19
7 [x] 2 Kgs. 3:11
10 [y] See Ruth 4:1
11 [z] [Zech. 1:18, 19] [a] [Deut. 33:17]
14 [b] See ch. 17:1 [c] Num. 22:18; 24:13
17 [d] Num. 27:17; Matt. 9:36
18 [e] ver. 8
19 [f] Isa. 6:1; Dan. 7:9; Rev. 4:2 [g] [Deut. 33:2; Job 1:6; 2:1; Ps. 103:21; Dan. 7:10; Heb. 12:22]
22 [h] [Judg. 9:23; Ezek. 14:9; 2 Thess. 2:11]

24 [i] [Lam. 3:30; Mic. 5:1; Matt. 5:39; Acts 23:2] 25 [j] ch. 20:30 27 [k] [2 Chr. 16:10] [l] [Judg. 8:9]

I come in peace.'" 28 And Micaiah said, "If you
return in peace, [m] the LORD has not spoken by
me." And he said, [n] "Hear, all you peoples!"

Ahab Killed in Battle

29 So the king of Israel and Jehoshaphat the
king of Judah went up to Ramoth-gilead.
30 And the king of Israel said to Jehoshaphat,
[o] "I will disguise myself and go into battle, but
you wear your robes." And the king of Israel
disguised himself and went into battle. 31 Now
the king of Syria had commanded [p] the thirty-
two captains of his chariots, "Fight with neither small nor great, but only with the king of
Israel." 32 And when the captains of the chariots saw Jehoshaphat, they said, "It is surely the
king of Israel." So they turned to fight against
him. And Jehoshaphat cried out. 33 And when
the captains of the chariots saw that it was
not the king of Israel, they turned back from
pursuing him. 34 But a certain man drew his
bow at random[1] and struck the king of Israel
between the scale armor and the breastplate.
Therefore he said to the driver of his chariot,
"Turn around and carry me out of the battle,
[q] for I am wounded." 35 And the battle continued that day, and the king was propped up in
his chariot facing the Syrians, until at evening
he died. And the blood of the wound flowed
into the bottom of the chariot. 36 And about
sunset a cry went through the army, "Every
man to his city, and every man to his country!"

37 So the king died, and was brought to
Samaria. And they buried the king in Samaria.
38 And they washed the chariot by the pool of
Samaria, and the dogs licked up his blood,
and the prostitutes washed themselves in it,
[r] according to the word of the LORD that he
had spoken. 39 Now the rest of the acts of Ahab
and all that he did, and [s] the ivory house that
he built and all the cities that he built, are
they not written in the Book of the Chronicles
of the Kings of Israel? 40 So Ahab slept with
his fathers, and Ahaziah his son reigned in
his place.

Jehoshaphat Reigns in Judah

41 [t] Jehoshaphat the son of [u] Asa began to reign
over Judah in the fourth year of Ahab king
of Israel. 42 Jehoshaphat was thirty-five years
old when he began to reign, and he reigned
twenty-five years in Jerusalem. His mother's
name was Azubah the daughter of Shilhi.
43 [v] He walked in all the way of Asa his father.
He did not turn aside from it, doing what was
right in the sight of the LORD. Yet [w] the high
places were not taken away, and the people
still sacrificed and made offerings on the high
places. 44 [x] Jehoshaphat also made peace with
the king of Israel.

45 Now the rest of the acts of Jehoshaphat,
and his might that he showed, and how he
warred, are they not written [y] in the Book of
the Chronicles of the Kings of Judah? 46 And
from the land he exterminated the remnant
[z] of the male cult prostitutes who remained in
the days of his father Asa.

47 [a] There was no king in Edom; a deputy was
king. 48 Jehoshaphat made [b] ships of Tarshish
to go to [c] Ophir for gold, but they did not go,
for the ships were wrecked at [d] Ezion-geber.
49 Then Ahaziah the son of Ahab said to
Jehoshaphat, "Let my servants go with your
servants in the ships," but Jehoshaphat was
not willing. 50 [e] And Jehoshaphat slept with
his fathers and was buried with his fathers in
the city of David his father, and Jehoram his
son reigned in his place.

Ahaziah Reigns in Israel

51 Ahaziah the son of Ahab [f] began to reign
over Israel in Samaria in the seventeenth year
of Jehoshaphat king of Judah, and he reigned
two years over Israel. 52 He did what was evil
in the sight of the LORD [g] and walked in the
way of his father and in the way of his mother
and in the way of Jeroboam the son of Nebat,
who made Israel to sin. 53 [h] He served Baal and
worshiped him and provoked the LORD, the
God of Israel, to anger [i] in every way that his
father had done.

[1] Hebrew *in his innocence*

28 [m] [Num. 16:29; Deut. 18:22] [n] Mic. 1:2 **30** [o] 2 Chr. 35:22 **31** [p] [ch. 20:1, 16, 24] **34** [q] [2 Chr. 35:23] **38** [r] ch. 21:19 **39** [s] [Amos 3:15] **41** [t] For ver. 41-43, see 2 Chr. 20:31-33 [u] ver. 51 **43** [v] [2 Chr. 17:3] [w] [ch. 15:14; 2 Kgs. 12:3] **44** [x] [2 Chr. 18:1; 20:35, 36] **45** [y] [2 Chr. 20:34] **46** [z] ch. 14:24; 15:12 **47** [a] [2 Sam. 8:14; 2 Kgs. 3:9; 8:20] **48** [b] See ch. 10:22 [c] See ch. 9:28 [d] See ch. 9:26 **50** [e] 2 Chr. 21:1 **51** [f] ver. 40 **52** [g] [ch. 15:26] **53** [h] ch. 16:30 [i] [ch. 16:31, 32]

2 Kings

Elijah Denounces Ahaziah

1 [a]After the death of Ahab, Moab [b]rebelled
against Israel.
2 Now Ahaziah fell through the lattice in his
upper chamber in Samaria, and lay sick; so he
sent messengers, telling them, "Go, inquire of
[c]Baal-zebub, the god of Ekron, [d]whether I shall
recover from this sickness." 3 But the angel of
the LORD said to Elijah [e]the Tishbite, "Arise,
go up to meet the messengers of the king of
Samaria, and say to them, 'Is it because there is
no God in Israel that you are going to inquire
of [c]Baal-zebub, the god of Ekron? 4 Now therefore thus says the LORD, [f]You shall not come
down from the bed to which you have gone
up, but you shall surely die.'" So Elijah went.
5 The messengers returned to the king, and
he said to them, "Why have you returned?"
6 And they said to him, "There came a man to
meet us, and said to us, 'Go back to the king
who sent you, and say to him, Thus says the
LORD, Is it because there is no God in Israel
that you are sending to inquire of [c]Baal-zebub,
the god of Ekron? Therefore you shall not
come down from the bed to which you have
gone up, but you shall surely die.'" 7 He said
to them, "What kind of man was he who came
to meet you and told you these things?" 8 They
answered him, [g]"He wore a garment of hair,
with a belt of leather about his waist." And he
said, "It is Elijah the Tishbite."
9 Then the king sent to him a captain of fifty
men with his fifty. He went up to Elijah, who
was sitting on the top of a hill, and said to him,
[h]"O man of God, the king says, 'Come down.'"
10 But Elijah answered the captain of fifty, "If
I am a man of God, [i]let fire come down from
heaven and consume you and your fifty." Then
fire came down from heaven and consumed
him and his fifty.
11 Again the king sent to him another captain
of fifty men with his fifty. And he answered

1:2–16 This is not the first time that Elijah had called down fire from heaven. Back in 1 Kings 18, Israel was worshiping Baal instead of Yahweh, and so Elijah initiated a test to demonstrate that Baal was a false God and Yahweh was the true God—"the God who answers by fire, he is God" (1 Kings 18:24). Now, in 2 Kings 1, Israel's king has rejected Yahweh as God by sending his messengers to Ekron to consult Baal-zebub (lord of the flies). Elijah's interception of the messengers, his rebuke of the king, and the deliverance of the Lord's judgment does not sit well with the king, and so Elijah is summoned. When Elijah responds with fire to the king's summons, the point is clear: Yahweh, not Baal-zebub, is the true God.

As Christians, the events recorded in 1 Kings 18 and 2 Kings 1 may seem overly harsh. We may cringe when we read that the Lord was willing to kill more than five hundred men just to prove that he was the one true God. But these events make an important point: the recognition of the one true God is a matter of life and death. These temporal consequences are severe, but the eternal consequences of false religion and rejecting the true God are more so, making God's display of his true power a merciful warning to all.

The New Testament makes this same point. There came a time during the ministry of Jesus when a certain town rejected him. Two of the disciples wanted, like Elijah, to call down fire from heaven and destroy the town (Luke 9:51–56). After all, Jesus is the one true God, and his disciples were zealous to make that known. But Jesus rebuked his disciples. Why? Because this time, God himself would suffer death in order to make it known that he alone is God. In this instance, the severity of God's wrath toward his own Son becomes the demonstration of his steadfast love toward us. Yes, knowing

Chapter 1
1 [a]ch. 3:5 [b][2 Sam. 8:2]
2 [c][Matt. 10:25; 12:24, 27; Mark 3:22; Luke 11:15, 18, 19] [d][ch. 8:8]
3 [e]1 Kgs. 17:1; 21:17 [c][See ver. 2 above]
4 [f]ver. 6, 16
6 [c][See ver. 2 above]
8 [g][Zech. 13:4; Matt. 3:4; Mark 1:6]
9 [h]Deut. 33:1; Judg. 13:6; 1 Sam. 2:27; 9:6
10 [i]Luke 9:54

and said to him, "O man of God, this is the
king's order, 'Come down quickly!'" 12 But
Elijah answered them, "If I am a man of God,
[j]let fire come down from heaven and consume
you and your fifty." Then the fire of God came
down from heaven and consumed him and
his fifty.
13 Again the king sent the captain of a third
fifty with his fifty. And the third captain of
fifty went up and came and fell on his knees
before Elijah and entreated him, "O man of
God, please let my life, and the life of these
fifty servants of yours, [k]be precious in your
sight. 14 Behold, fire came down from heaven
and consumed the two former captains of fifty
men with their fifties, but now let my life be
precious in your sight." 15 Then the angel of
the LORD said to Elijah, "Go down with him;
do not be afraid of him." So he arose and went
down with him to the king 16 and said to him,
"Thus says the LORD, 'Because you have sent
messengers to inquire of [c]Baal-zebub, the god
of Ekron—is it because there is no God in
Israel to inquire of his word?—therefore you
shall not come down from the bed to which
you have gone up, but you shall surely die.'"
17 So he died according to the word of the
LORD that Elijah had spoken. Jehoram became
king in his place [l]in the second year of Jehoram
the son of Jehoshaphat, king of Judah, because
Ahaziah had no son. 18 Now the rest of the acts
of Ahaziah that he did, are they not written
in the Book of the Chronicles of the Kings of
Israel?

Elijah Taken to Heaven

2 Now when the LORD was about to [m]take
Elijah up to heaven by a whirlwind, Elijah
and [n]Elisha were on their way from [o]Gilgal.
2 And Elijah said to Elisha, [p]"Please stay here,
for the LORD has sent me as far as Bethel." But
Elisha said, [q]"As the LORD lives, and as you
yourself live, I will not leave you." So they went
down to Bethel. 3 And [r]the sons of the prophets
who were in Bethel came out to Elisha and
said to him, "Do you know that today the
LORD will take away your master from over
you?" And he said, "Yes, I know it; keep quiet."
4 Elijah said to him, "Elisha, [p]please stay here,
for the LORD has sent me to [t]Jericho." But he
said, [q]"As the LORD lives, and as you yourself
live, I will not leave you." So they came to
Jericho. 5 [r]The sons of the prophets who were
at Jericho drew near to Elisha and said to him,
"Do you know that today the LORD will take
away your master from over you?" And he
answered, "Yes, I know it; keep quiet."
6 Then Elijah said to him, [p]"Please stay here,
for the LORD has sent me to the Jordan." But
he said, "As the LORD lives, and as you yourself live, I will not leave you." So the two of
them went on. 7 Fifty men of [r]the sons of the
prophets also went and stood at some distance
from them, as they both were standing by the
Jordan. 8 Then Elijah [u]took his cloak and rolled
it up and struck the water, [v]and the water was
parted to the one side and to the other, till
the two of them could go over on dry ground.
9 When they had crossed, Elijah said to

12[j] Job 1:16
13[k] [1 Sam. 26:21; Ps. 72:14]
16[c] [See ver. 2 above]
17[l] [ch. 3:1; 8:16]

Chapter 2
1[m] [Gen. 5:24] [n] See 1 Kgs. 19:19-21 [o] ch. 4:38; [Josh. 5:9]
2[p] [Ruth 1:15, 16] [q] See Ruth 3:13
3[r] ch. 4:1, 38; 5:22; 6:1; 9:1; 1 Kgs. 20:35
4[p] [See ver. 2 above] [t] [Josh. 6:26; 1 Kgs. 16:34] [q] [See ver. 2 above]
5[r] [See ver. 3 above]
6[p] [See ver. 2 above]
7[r] [See ver. 3 above]
8[u] [1 Kgs. 19:19] [v] [Ex. 14:21; Josh. 3:16]

God is a matter of life and death. But the gravity of this knowledge is matched by the depth of God's love: he was willing to die in order to make himself known to us.

If we long to make the one true God known to the world, then we too must answer with "fire": the fire of the Father's love for us, as demonstrated in the death of his Son.

2:1–22 Hope is something God's people need, and hope is something we have in abundance. Sometimes, however, the pictures of hope presented in the Old Testament can be difficult to understand, like the one presented in this text.

First, we must remember that the ministries of Elijah and Elisha were preparing God's people for exile. Because of Israel's rejection of the Lord, judgment was coming, and that judgment was destruction and exile. The ministry of Elijah was presented in such a way as to teach God's people that he was able to protect and provide for them, even while they were in exile—but this did not change the fact that exile was coming. Consider the way in which the ministry of Elijah comes to an end. He departs the Promised Land through Jericho and across the Jordan River, retracing the route through which God's people first entered the land back in the book of Joshua. Exile was coming, and Elijah's actions became a prophetic picture of it.

We must also consider the way in which Elisha's ministry began. He crossed the Jordan River on dry ground, came to the city of Jericho, and reversed the curse of the bitter water in that town (vv. 19–22; cf. Josh. 6:26; 1 Kings 16:34). In this way, Elisha foretold of Israel's return from exile and the reversal of that curse with a retelling of

Elisha, "Ask what I shall do for you, before I am taken from you." And Elisha said, "Please let there be a double portion of your spirit on me." 10 And he said, "You have asked a hard thing; yet, if you see me as I am being taken from you, it shall be so for you, but if you do not see me, it shall not be so." 11 And as they still went on and talked, behold, [w]chariots of fire and horses of fire separated the two of them. And Elijah went up by a whirlwind into heaven. 12 And Elisha saw it and he cried, "My father, my father! [x]The chariots of Israel and its horsemen!" And he saw him no more.

Then he took hold of his own clothes [y]and tore them in two pieces. 13 And he took up the cloak of Elijah that had fallen from him and went back and stood on the bank of the Jordan. 14 Then he took the cloak of Elijah that had fallen from him and struck the water, saying, "Where is the LORD, the God of Elijah?" And when he had struck the water, [v]the water was parted to the one side and to the other, and Elisha went over.

Elisha Succeeds Elijah

15 Now when [r]the sons of the prophets who were at Jericho saw him opposite them, they said, "The spirit of Elijah rests on Elisha." And they came to meet him and bowed to the ground before him. 16 And they said to him, "Behold now, there are with your servants fifty strong men. Please let them go and seek your master. It may be that [z]the Spirit of the LORD has caught him up and cast him upon some mountain or into some valley." And he said, "You shall not send." 17 But when they urged him [a]till he was ashamed, he said, "Send." They sent therefore fifty men. And for three days they sought him but did not find him. 18 And they came back to him while he was staying at Jericho, and he said to them, "Did I not say to you, 'Do not go'?"

19 Now the men of the city said to Elisha, "Behold, the situation of this city is pleasant, as my lord sees, but the water is bad, and the land is unfruitful." 20 He said, "Bring me a new bowl, and put salt in it." So they brought it to him. 21 Then he went to the spring of water and [b]threw salt in it and said, "Thus says the LORD, I have healed this water; from now on neither death nor miscarriage shall come from it." 22 So the water has been healed to this day, according to the word that Elisha spoke.

23 He went up from there to Bethel, and while he was going up on the way, some small boys came out of the city and jeered at him, saying, "Go up, you baldhead! Go up, you baldhead!" 24 And he turned around, and when he saw them, [c]he cursed them in the name of the LORD. And two she-bears came out of the woods and tore forty-two of the boys. 25 From there he went on to [d]Mount Carmel, and from there he returned [e]to Samaria.

Moab Rebels Against Israel

3 [f]In the eighteenth year of Jehoshaphat king of Judah, Jehoram the son of Ahab became king over Israel in Samaria, and he reigned twelve years. 2 He did what was evil in the sight of the LORD, though not like his father and mother, for he put away the [g]pillar of Baal [h]that his father had made. 3 Nevertheless, he clung to [i]the sin of Jeroboam the son of Nebat, [j]which he made Israel to sin; he did not depart from it.

4 Now Mesha king of Moab was a sheep breeder, [k]and he had to deliver to the king of Israel 100,000 lambs and the wool of 100,000 rams. 5 But [l]when Ahab died, the king of Moab rebelled against the king of Israel. 6 So King Jehoram marched out of Samaria at that time and mustered all Israel. 7 And he went and sent word to Jehoshaphat king of Judah, "The king of Moab has rebelled against me. Will you go

Israel's initial entry into the land in the time of Joshua. In other words, the events recorded in 2 Kings 2 were written to provide hope for God's people. Even as the Lord brings judgment, he insists on giving his covenant people hope. Whether before or during exile, then, God's people had before them a clear picture of the hope their faithful God provided.

Our covenant Lord is a God of hope. Christians need not despair despite the difficulties and failings of this life. We are reminded by this text that the Lord protects and provides for his people. He promises to bring us home and reverse the curse of our alienation (cf. Eph. 2:19). Israel had the picture of Elisha's miraculous river crossing to give them hope. To this we today add the much deeper reason for hope: Christ's bodily resurrection, our picture of the final reversal of the curse (Acts 23:6; 24:15; 1 Pet. 1:3).

11 [w] See ch. 6:17
12 [x] ch. 13:14 [y] [1 Kgs. 11:30]
14 [v] [See ver. 8 above]
15 [r] [See ver. 3 above]
16 [z] See 1 Kgs. 18:12
17 [a] ch. 8:11
21 [b] [ch. 4:41; Ex. 15:25]
24 [c] [Neh. 13:25]
25 [d] Josh. 19:26; 1 Kgs. 18:19, 20 [e] [ch. 3:11]

Chapter 3
1 [f] [ch. 1:17]
2 [g] [ch. 10:26, 27; Ex. 23:24] [h] 1 Kgs. 16:31, 32
3 [i] 1 Kgs. 12:28, 31, 32 [j] See 1 Kgs. 14:16
4 [k] [Isa. 16:1, 2]
5 [l] ch. 1:1

with me to battle against Moab?" And he said, "I will go. [m]I am as you are, my people as your people, my horses as your horses." 8 Then he said, "By which way shall we march?" Jehoram answered, "By the way of the wilderness of Edom."

9 So the king of Israel went with the king of Judah and [n]the king of Edom. And when they had made a circuitous march of seven days, there was no water for the army or for the animals that followed them. 10 Then the king of Israel said, "Alas! [o]The LORD has called these three kings to give them into the hand of Moab." 11 [p]And Jehoshaphat said, "Is there no prophet of the LORD here, through whom we may inquire of the LORD?" Then one of the king of Israel's servants answered, [q]"Elisha the son of Shaphat is here, [r]who poured water on the hands of Elijah." 12 And Jehoshaphat said, "The word of the LORD is with him." So the king of Israel and Jehoshaphat and the king of Edom went down to him.

13 And Elisha said to the king of Israel, [s]"What have I to do with you? Go to [t]the prophets of your father and to [u]the prophets of your mother." But the king of Israel said to him, "No; it is [o]the LORD who has called these three kings to give them into the hand of Moab." 14 And Elisha said, [v]"As the LORD of hosts lives, before whom I stand, were it not that I have regard for Jehoshaphat the king of Judah, I would neither look at you nor see you. 15 But now [w]bring me a musician." And when the musician played, [x]the hand of the LORD came upon him. 16 And he said, "Thus says the LORD, 'I will make this dry streambed full of pools.' 17 For thus says the LORD, 'You shall not see wind or rain, but that streambed shall be filled with water, so that you shall drink, you, your livestock, and your animals.' 18 This is a light thing in the sight of the LORD. He will also give the Moabites into your hand, 19 and you shall attack every fortified city and every choice city, and shall fell every good tree and stop up all springs of water [y]and ruin every good piece of land with stones." 20 The next morning, about the time of [z]offering the sacrifice, behold, water came from the direction of Edom, till the country was filled with water.

21 When all the Moabites heard that the kings had come up to fight against them, all who were able to put on armor, from the youngest to the oldest, were called out and were drawn up at the border. 22 And when they rose early in the morning and the sun shone on the water, the Moabites saw the water opposite them as red as blood. 23 And they said, "This is blood; the kings have surely fought together and struck one another down. Now then, Moab, to the spoil!" 24 But when they came to the camp of Israel, the Israelites rose and struck the Moabites, till they fled before them. And

7 [m]1 Kgs. 22:4
9 [n][1 Kgs. 22:47]
10 [o][Josh. 7:7]
11 [p]1 Kgs. 22:7 [q][ch. 2:25] [r][1 Kgs. 19:21; John 13:4, 5]
13 [s][Ezek. 14:3] [t]1 Kgs. 22:6 [u]1 Kgs. 18:19 [o][See ver. 10 above]
14 [v]ch. 5:16; 1 Kgs. 17:1
15 [w][1 Sam. 10:5; 1 Chr. 25:1] [x]1 Kgs. 18:46; Ezek. 1:3; 3:14, 22; 8:1; 37:1; 40:1
19 [y][ver. 25; Isa. 25:2]
20 [z][Ex. 29:39, 40]

3:13–20 A major theme that runs through the book of Kings is God's steadfast love for his covenant people. The Lord remains committed to the covenant even when his people persist in acts of covenant breaking. In other words, the Lord treats his people graciously, in ways that they (and we) certainly do not deserve.

These few verses in 2 Kings 3 remind us of this important aspect of grace. Elisha treats the evil king of Israel graciously, in a way that he does not deserve. The reason for this treatment is the immediate connection between Jehoram, king of Israel, and Jehoshaphat, king of Judah: "were it not that I have regard for Jehoshaphat the king of Judah, I would neither look at you nor see you" (v. 14).

Elisha's regard for Jehoram did not stem from Elisha's relationship with Jehoram, but rather through Jehoshaphat as a mediator. In other words, Jehoram benefited from the good relationship between Jehoshaphat and Elisha. The pattern of mercy and grace exhibited here is a small picture of a larger reality appearing in the New Testament. The Lord continues to treat his covenant people according to his steadfast love, in ways that we do not deserve. The reality that undergirds this type of gracious treatment also remains the same. It is rooted in the consideration of another, a mediator. But in the New Testament, the mediator is not another flawed king. It is the Lord himself, Jesus Christ (cf. 1 Tim. 2:5; Heb. 9:15; 12:24). The hope of each Christian, the grounds for our assurance, achieved by virtue of our union with Christ, is that the heavenly Father treats his people with grace, mercy, and compassion because of our unbreakable connection with his Son. Were it not that the Father has regard for Jesus, the King of kings, he would neither look at us nor see us (see again 2 Kings 3:14). This connection alone produces peace, joy, and assurance in the Christian life.

they went forward, striking the Moabites as they went.[1] 25 And they overthrew the cities, and [a]on every good piece of land every man threw a stone until it was covered. They stopped every spring of water and felled all the good trees, till only its stones were left in [b]Kir-hareseth, and the slingers surrounded and attacked it. 26 When the king of Moab saw that the battle was going against him, he took with him 700 [c]swordsmen to break through, opposite the king of Edom, but they could not. 27 Then he took his oldest son who was to reign in his place [d]and offered him for a burnt offering on the wall. And there came great wrath against Israel. And they withdrew from him and returned to their own land.

Elisha and the Widow's Oil

4 Now the wife of one of the [e]sons of the prophets cried to Elisha, "Your servant my husband is dead, and you know that your servant feared the LORD, [f]but the creditor has come to take my two children to be his slaves." 2 And Elisha said to her, "What shall I do for you? Tell me; what have you in the house?" And she said, "Your servant has nothing in the house except a jar of oil." 3 Then he said, "Go outside, borrow vessels from all your neighbors, empty vessels and not too few. 4 Then go in and shut the door behind yourself and your sons and pour into all these vessels. And when one is full, set it aside." 5 So she went from him and shut the door behind herself and her sons. And as she poured they brought the vessels to her. 6 When the vessels were full, she said to her son, "Bring me another vessel." And he said to her, "There is not another." Then the oil stopped flowing. 7 She came and told the [g]man of God, and he said, "Go, sell the oil and pay your debts, and you and your sons can live on the rest."

Elisha and the Shunammite Woman

8 One day Elisha went on to [h]Shunem, where a [i]wealthy woman lived, who urged him to eat some food. So whenever he passed that way, he would turn in there to eat food. 9 And she said to her husband, "Behold now, I know that this is a holy [g]man of God who is continually passing our way. 10 Let us make a small room on the roof with walls and put there for him a bed, a table, a chair, and a lamp, so that whenever he comes to us, he can go in there."

11 One day he came there, and he turned into the chamber and rested there. 12 And he said to [j]Gehazi his servant, "Call this Shunammite." When he had called her, she stood before him. 13 And he said to him, "Say now to her, 'See, you have taken all this trouble for us; what is to be done for you? Would you have a word spoken on your behalf to the king or to [k]the commander of the army?'" She answered, "I dwell among my own people." 14 And he said, "What then is to be done for her?" Gehazi answered, "Well, she has no son, and her husband is old." 15 He said, "Call her." And when he had called her, she stood in the doorway. 16 And he said, "At this season, [l]about this time next year, you shall embrace a son." And she said, "No, my lord, [g]O man of God; [m]do not lie to your servant." 17 But the woman conceived, and she bore a son about that time [l]the following spring, as Elisha had said to her.

Elisha Raises the Shunammite's Son

18 When the child had grown, he went out one day to his father among the reapers. 19 And he said to his father, "Oh, [n]my head, my head!" The father said to his servant, "Carry him to

[1] Septuagint; the meaning of the Hebrew is uncertain

4:1–44 The author of Kings was writing to an audience perhaps already experiencing the tragedy and difficulty of life in exile. As such, the several miracles recorded in this lengthy chapter would have functioned to remind God's people of his power to restore the blessings forfeited due to repeated infidelity and covenant breaking. Even in the midst of famine or the death of a husband, the Lord can and will provide. He can make the barren fertile and restore life by the power of resurrection.

Until our Lord returns to make all things new, his people will live like aliens in a world to which they do not fully belong. For believers living in this fallen world, we live in exile. As resident aliens, tragedy and suffering will be a normal part of our lives in this fallen world (John 16:33; 1 Pet. 4:12). But even here, the Lord desires to set before the eyes of his people the hope of all things being made new. The miracles recorded in this chapter continue to remind us that we look forward to greater things. One day we will be satisfied at the table of the Lord. Death, hunger, and debt will no longer have any place.

25 [a][ver. 19] [b]Isa. 16:7; [Isa. 15:1; 16:11; Jer. 48:31, 36]
26 [c][Judg. 20:2]
27 [d]Amos 2:1; [Mic. 6:7]
Chapter 4
1 [e]See ch. 2:3 [f][Lev. 25:39-41; 1 Sam. 22:2; Neh. 5:5; Matt. 18:25]
7 [g]See Deut. 33:1
8 [h]Josh. 19:18 [i][1 Sam. 25:2; 2 Sam. 19:32]
9 [g][See ver. 7 above]
12 [j]ch. 5:20, 21, 25; 8:4, 5
13 [k]2 Sam. 19:13; [ch. 5:1]
16 [l]Gen. 18:14; [Gen. 17:21] [g][See ver. 7 above] [m]ver. 28
17 [l][See ver. 16 above]
19 [n][Ps. 121:6]

his mother." 20 And when he had lifted him
and brought him to his mother, the child sat
on her lap till noon, and then he died. 21 And
she went up [o]and laid him on the bed of the
[g]man of God and shut the door behind him
and went out. 22 Then she called to her husband and said, "Send me one of the servants
and one of the donkeys, that I may quickly
go to [g]the man of God and come back again."
23 And he said, "Why will you go to him today?
It is neither [p]new moon nor Sabbath." She said,
"All is well." 24 Then she saddled the donkey,
and she said to her servant, "Urge the animal
on; do not slacken the pace for me unless I tell
you." 25 So she set out and came to the man of
God [q]at Mount Carmel.

When the man of God saw her coming, he
said to Gehazi his servant, "Look, there is the
Shunammite. 26 Run at once to meet her and
say to her, 'Is all well with you? Is all well with
your husband? Is all well with the child?'" And
she answered, "All is well." 27 And when she
came [r]to the mountain to the man of God,
she caught hold of his feet. And Gehazi came
to push her away. But the man of God said,
"Leave her alone, for she is in bitter distress,
and the LORD has hidden it from me and has
not told me." 28 Then she said, "Did I ask my
lord for a son? [s]Did I not say, 'Do not deceive
me?'" 29 He said to Gehazi, [t]"Tie up your garment and [u]take my staff in your hand and go.
If you meet anyone, [v]do not greet him, and
if anyone greets you, do not reply. And [u]lay
my staff on the face of the child." 30 Then the
mother of the child said, [w]"As the LORD lives
and as you yourself live, I will not leave you."
So he arose and followed her. 31 Gehazi went
on ahead and laid the staff on the face of the
child, but there was no sound or sign of life.
Therefore he returned to meet him and told
him, "The child [x]has not awakened."

32 When Elisha came into the house, he saw
the child lying dead on his bed. 33 So he went
in and [y]shut the door behind the two of them
[z]and prayed to the LORD. 34 Then he went
up and lay on the child, putting his mouth
on his mouth, his eyes on his eyes, and his
hands on his hands. And as [a]he stretched himself upon him, the flesh of the child became
warm. 35 Then he got up again and walked
once back and forth in the house, and went up
[a]and stretched himself upon him. The child
sneezed seven times, and the child opened his
eyes. 36 Then he summoned Gehazi and said,
"Call this Shunammite." So he called her. And
when she came to him, he said, "Pick up your
son." 37 She came and fell at his feet, bowing
to the ground. [b]Then she picked up her son
and went out.

Elisha Purifies the Deadly Stew

38 And Elisha came again to [c]Gilgal when
[d]there was a famine in the land. And as [e]the
sons of the prophets [f]were sitting before him,
he said to his servant, [g]"Set on the large pot,
and boil stew for the sons of the prophets."
39 One of them went out into the field to
gather herbs, and found a wild vine and gathered from it his lap full of wild gourds, and
came and cut them up into the pot of stew, not
knowing what they were. 40 And they poured
out some for the men to eat. But while they
were eating of the stew, they cried out, "O man
of God, there is death in the pot!" And they
could not eat it. 41 He said, "Then bring flour."
[h]And he threw it into the pot and said, "Pour
some out for the men, that they may eat." And
there was no harm in the pot.

42 A man came from [i]Baal-shalishah, [j]bring-
ing the man of God bread of the firstfruits,
twenty loaves of barley and fresh ears of grain
in his sack. And Elisha said, [k]"Give to the men,

21 [o] ver. 32 [g] [See ver. 7 above]
22 [g] [See ver. 7 above]
23 [p] [Num. 28:11]
25 [q] ch. 2:25
27 [r] ver. 25
28 [s] ver. 16
29 [t] See 1 Kgs. 18:46 [u] [Ex. 7:19; 14:16; Acts 19:12] [v] Luke 10:4
30 [w] See Ruth 3:13
31 [x] [John 11:11]
33 [y] ver. 4; Matt. 6:6; [Matt. 9:25; Mark 5:37, 40; Luke 8:51] [z] 1 Kgs. 17:20
34 [a] 1 Kgs. 17:21; [Acts 20:10]
35 [a] [See ver. 34 above]
37 [b] 1 Kgs. 17:23; Heb. 11:35; [ch. 8:1, 5]

5:1–27 The account of the healing of Naaman's leprosy is a lesson in the unexpected nature of God's grace and mercy. To begin with, Naaman was a foreigner. But he was not just any foreigner. He was the leader of the Syrian army, the enemy of God's people. For a prophet of the Lord to heal an Israelite leper was one thing, but to restore the very person whose job it was to oppress you—that was altogether outrageous! Yet this is who the Lord *is*. He is lavishly generous with his grace, pouring it out upon those who are especially undeserving.

We are also *warned* by this account. Notice how the king of Israel was terrified by Naaman's request. He did not believe in the promises of God or the power of his grace to be a blessing (cf. Gen. 12:2). And what about Elisha's servant, Gehazi? He had seen God's grace in action but used it to exploit and steal. These two men should

38 [c] ch. 2:1 [d] ch. 8:1 [e] See ch. 2:3 [f] Deut. 33:3; Luke 10:39; Acts 22:3; [ch. 2:3, 5] [g] Ezek. 24:3 **41** [h] [ch. 2:21; Ex. 15:25] **42** [i] [1 Sam. 9:4] [j] [1 Sam. 9:7] [k] See Matt. 14:16-21; 15:32-38; Mark 6:37-44; 8:4-9; Luke 9:13-17; John 6:5-13

that they may eat." [43]But his servant said,
"How can I set this before a hundred men?"
So he repeated, "Give them to the men, that
they may eat, for thus says the LORD, 'They
shall eat and have some left.'" [44]So he set it
before them. And they ate and had some left,
according to the word of the LORD.

Naaman Healed of Leprosy

5 [l]Naaman, [m]commander of the army of
the king of Syria, was a great man with
his master and in high favor, because by him
the LORD had given victory to Syria. He was a
mighty man of valor, but he was a leper.[1] [2]Now
the Syrians on [n]one of their raids had carried
off a little girl from the land of Israel, and she
worked in the service of Naaman's wife. [3]She
said to her mistress, "Would that my lord were
with the prophet who is in Samaria! He would
cure him of his leprosy." [4]So Naaman went
in and told his lord, "Thus and so spoke the
girl from the land of Israel." [5]And the king of
Syria said, "Go now, and I will send a letter to
the king of Israel."

So he went, [o]taking with him ten talents of
silver, six thousand shekels[2] of gold, and ten
[p]changes of clothing. [6]And he brought the
letter to the king of Israel, which read, "When
this letter reaches you, know that I have sent
to you Naaman my servant, that you may cure
him of his leprosy." [7]And when the king of
Israel read the letter, [q]he tore his clothes and
said, [r]"Am I God, to kill and to make alive, that
this man sends word to me to cure a man of
his leprosy? Only [s]consider, and see how he is
seeking a quarrel with me."

[8]But when Elisha the [t]man of God heard
that the king of Israel had torn his clothes, he
sent to the king, saying, "Why have you torn
your clothes? Let him come now to me, that
he may know that there is a prophet in Israel."
[9]So Naaman came with his horses and chariots
and stood at the door of Elisha's house. [10]And
Elisha sent a messenger to him, saying, [u]"Go
and wash in the Jordan seven times, and your
flesh shall be restored, and you shall be clean."
[11]But Naaman was angry and went away, saying, "Behold, I thought that he would surely
come out to me and stand and call upon the
name of the LORD his God, and wave his hand
over the place and cure the leper. [12]Are not
Abana[3] and Pharpar, the rivers of [v]Damascus,
better than all the waters of Israel? Could I not
wash in them and be clean?" So he turned and
went away in a rage. [13]But his servants came
near and said to him, [w]"My father, it is a great
word the prophet has spoken to you; will you
not do it? Has he actually said to you, 'Wash,
and be clean'?" [14]So he went down and dipped
himself seven times in the Jordan, according
to the word of the man of God, [x]and his flesh
was restored like the flesh of a little child, [y]and
he was clean.

Gehazi's Greed and Punishment

[15]Then he returned to the man of God, he
and all his company, and he came and stood
before him. And he said, "Behold, I know that
[z]there is no God in all the earth but in Israel;
so [a]accept now a present from your servant."
[16]But he said, [b]"As the LORD lives, before
whom I stand, [c]I will receive none." And he
urged him to take it, but he refused. [17]Then
Naaman said, "If not, please let there be given
to your servant two mule loads of earth, for
from now on your servant will not offer burnt
offering or sacrifice to any god but the LORD.
[18]In this matter may the LORD pardon your

[1] *Leprosy* was a term for several skin diseases; see Leviticus 13 [2] A *talent* was about 75 pounds or 34 kilograms; a *shekel* was about 2/5 ounce or 11 grams [3] Or *Amana*

have known better than most about the nature of God's grace, but they were blind to it. It is humbling to observe that these men, so closely connected to the work of God in the world, were oblivious to its power in their own lives.

But even if the expected heralds of God's goodness have become blind, we need not despair. The Lord is not limited by such obstacles. Take note of the unexpected conduits of God's power and goodness in this narrative: the little Israelite slave girl, and Naaman's servants. These "second class citizens" are the heroes of the story. They are the ones who encourage Naaman to seek help in Israel and submit to washing in the Jordan River. God has chosen the weak and foolish things of this world to make himself known (cf. 1 Cor. 1:27).

Because the Lord has been generous with his grace to us (Rom. 5:10), we are free to be gracious with others, even desiring to see God's grace poured out in the lives of our enemies. May we never become blind or callous to this grace, but rather see it in all of life, especially in the weak, humble, and foolish things.

Chapter 5
1[l]Luke 4:27 [m][ch. 4:13]
2[n]ch. 6:23
5[o][ch. 4:42; 8:8, 9; 1 Sam. 9:7] [p]ver. 22, 23; [Judg. 14:12]
7[q]See Gen. 44:13 [r][Gen. 30:2; Deut. 32:39; 1 Sam. 2:6] [s][1 Kgs. 20:7]
8[t]See Deut. 33:1
10[u][John 9:7]
12[v][1 Kgs. 11:24]
13[w][ch. 6:21; 8:9; Judg. 17:10]
14[x]ver. 10; [Job 33:25] [y]Luke 4:27
15[z][Dan. 2:47; 3:29; 6:26, 27] [a][Gen. 33:11]
16[b]ch. 3:14; 1 Kgs. 17:1 [c][Gen. 14:23]

servant: when my master goes into the house
of [d]Rimmon to worship there, [e]leaning on
my arm, and I bow myself in the house of
Rimmon, when I bow myself in the house of
Rimmon, the LORD pardon your servant in
this matter." 19 He said to him, [f]"Go in peace."
But when Naaman had gone from him
a short distance, 20 [g]Gehazi, the servant of
Elisha the man of God, said, "See, my master has spared this Naaman the Syrian, in not
accepting from his hand what he brought. [h]As
the LORD lives, I will run after him and get
something from him." 21 So Gehazi followed
Naaman. And when Naaman saw someone
running after him, he got down from the
chariot to meet him and said, [i]"Is all well?"
22 And he said, "All is well. My master has sent
me to say, 'There have just now come to me
from [j]the hill country of Ephraim two young
men of the sons of the prophets. Please give
them a talent of silver and [k]two changes of
clothing.'" 23 And Naaman said, [l]"Be pleased
to accept two talents." And he urged him and
tied up two talents of silver in two bags, with
two changes of clothing, and laid them on two
of his servants. And they carried them before
Gehazi. 24 And when he came to the hill, he
took them from their hand and put them
in the house, and he sent the men away, and
they departed. 25 He went in and stood before
his master, and Elisha said to him, "Where
have you been, Gehazi?" And he said, "Your
servant went nowhere." 26 But he said to him,
"Did not my heart go when the man turned
from his chariot to meet you? Was it a time to
accept money and garments, olive orchards
and vineyards, sheep and oxen, male servants
and female servants? 27 Therefore the leprosy
of Naaman shall cling to you and to your
descendants forever." So he went out from his
presence [m]a leper, like snow.

The Axe Head Recovered

6 Now [n]the sons of the prophets said to
Elisha, "See, the place where we dwell
under your charge is too small for us. 2 Let us
go to the Jordan and each of us get there a log,
and let us make a place for us to dwell there."
And he answered, "Go." 3 Then one of them
said, "Be pleased to go with your servants."
And he answered, "I will go." 4 So he went with
them. And when they came to the Jordan, they
cut down trees. 5 But as one was felling a log,
his axe head fell into the water, and he cried
out, "Alas, my master! It was borrowed." 6 Then
the man of God said, "Where did it fall?" When
he showed him the place, [o]he cut off a stick
and threw it in there and made the iron float.
7 And he said, "Take it up." So he reached out
his hand and took it.

Horses and Chariots of Fire

8 Once when the king of Syria was warring
against Israel, he took counsel with his servants, saying, "At such and such a place shall
be my camp." 9 But the man of God sent word
to the king of Israel, "Beware that you do not
pass this place, for the Syrians are going down
there." 10 And the king of Israel sent to the
place about which the man of God told him.
Thus he used to warn him, so that he saved
himself there more than once or twice.
11 And the mind of the king of Syria was
greatly troubled because of this thing, and
he called his servants and said to them, "Will
you not show me who of us is for the king of

18 [d][1 Kgs. 15:18; Zech. 12:11] [e]ch. 7:2, 17
19 [f]1 Sam. 1:17
20 [g]ch. 4:12 [h]See Ruth 3:13
21 [i]ch. 9:11
22 [j]See Josh. 24:33 [k]ver. 5
23 [l]ch. 6:3
27 [m]Ex. 4:6; Num. 12:10; [ch. 15:5]
Chapter 6
1 [n]See ch. 2:3
6 [o][ch. 2:21]

6:15–17 Oftentimes our fear and anxiety are the result of spiritual blindness. Here, the servant of Elisha is terrified by the presence of the army of the enemy. With his physical eyes, he sees only one army. But Elisha prays that his servant might see all of reality, not just the visible but the invisible too. Once the veil of the invisible world is peeled back, Elisha's servant perceives the fullness of reality, and the reason for his fear no longer exists.

We might be thinking that if God would only do the same thing for us, and show us the power of his invisible kingdom, we too would no longer fear or be anxious. But this is exactly what he has done. Did not the Father send the Son, the fullness of his kingdom and power, into this world? Has not the invisible God become visible in the incarnation? Our Lord did not just peel back the curtain of his invisible kingdom. He came *from* it and lived in our midst, as a flesh-and-blood man. With Jesus Christ, we see clearly the power of God's invisible kingdom in its fullness. In fact, compared with what Elisha's servant saw on that day, we have seen so much more!

When fear and anxiety strike at our hearts, we must pray that God would open our eyes by faith to the fullness of reality that can be found only in his Son, "For from his fullness we have all received, grace upon grace" (John 1:16).

Israel?" 12 And one of his servants said, "None,
my lord, O king; but Elisha, the prophet who
is in Israel, tells the king of Israel the words
that you speak in your bedroom." 13 And he
said, "Go and see where he is, that I may send
and seize him." It was told him, "Behold, he
is in [p]Dothan." 14 So he sent there horses and
chariots and a great army, and they came by
night and surrounded the city.

15 When the servant of the man of God rose
early in the morning and went out, behold, an
army with horses and chariots was all around
the city. And the servant said, "Alas, my master! What shall we do?" 16 He said, "Do not be
afraid, [q]for those who are with us are more
than those who are with them." 17 Then Elisha
prayed and said, "O LORD, please [r]open his eyes
that he may see." So the LORD opened the eyes
of the young man, and he saw, and behold, the
mountain was full of [s]horses and chariots of
fire all around Elisha. 18 And when the Syrians
came down against him, Elisha prayed to the
LORD and said, "Please strike this people with
blindness." [t]So he struck them with blindness
in accordance with the prayer of Elisha. 19 And
Elisha said to them, "This is not the way, and
this is not the city. Follow me, and I will bring
you to the man whom you seek." And he led
them to Samaria.

20 As soon as they entered Samaria, Elisha
said, "O LORD, [r]open the eyes of these men,
that they may see." So the LORD opened their
eyes and they saw, and behold, they were in
the midst of Samaria. 21 As soon as the king
of Israel saw them, he said to Elisha, [u]"My
father, shall I strike them down? Shall I strike
them down?" 22 He answered, "You shall not
strike them down. Would you strike down
those whom you have taken captive [v]with
your sword and with your bow? [w]Set bread
and water before them, that they may eat and
drink and go to their master." 23 So he prepared
for them a great feast, and when they had
eaten and drunk, he sent them away, and they
went to their master. And the Syrians did not
come again [x]on raids into the land of Israel.

Ben-hadad's Siege of Samaria

24 Afterward [y]Ben-hadad king of Syria
mustered his entire army and went up and
besieged Samaria. 25 And there was a great
famine in Samaria, as they besieged it, until a
donkey's head was sold for eighty shekels of
silver, and the fourth part of a kab[1] of dove's
dung for five shekels of silver. 26 Now as the
king of Israel was passing by on the wall, a
woman cried out to him, saying, "Help, my
lord, O king!" 27 And he said, "If the LORD will
not help you, how shall I help you? From the
threshing floor, or from the winepress?" 28 And
the king asked her, "What is your trouble?"
She answered, "This woman said to me, 'Give
your son, that we may eat him today, and we
will eat my son tomorrow.' 29 [z]So we boiled my
son and ate him. And on the next day I said
to her, 'Give your son, that we may eat him.'
But she has hidden her son." 30 When the king
heard the words of the woman, [a]he tore his
clothes—now he was passing by on the wall—
and the people looked, and behold, [a]he had
sackcloth beneath on his body— 31 and he said,
[b]"May God do so to me and more also, if the
head of Elisha the son of Shaphat remains on
his shoulders today."

32 Elisha was sitting in his house, [c]and the
elders were sitting with him. Now the king
had dispatched a man from his presence, but
before the messenger arrived Elisha said to
the elders, "Do you see how this [d]murderer
has sent to take off my head? Look, when the
messenger comes, shut the door and hold the
door fast against him. Is not the sound of his

[1] A *shekel* was about 2/5 ounce or 11 grams; a *kab* was about 1 quart or 1 liter

6:32–7:20 The good news from our covenant Lord is that he has accomplished for us what we could not do for ourselves. When we think about the gospel, or God's good news, our minds probably run straight to the person and work of Jesus. And rightly so! Certainly the person and work of Jesus on our behalf is the best news ever told. But God's good news is not limited to the New Testament. The Old Testament prepares us to expect it. The entire Bible is a unified saving message of God's merciful redemption of sinners through his Son.

The siege of the Syrian army and the famine that accompanied it were so severe that mothers were eating their children. Things didn't just look hopeless. Things *were* hopeless, tragically so. But God intervened and did for Israel what it could not do for itself. He sent the foreign invaders packing and fed all of Samaria with the contents from the enemy's camp. It is even more amazing to discover how God accomplished

13 [p] Gen. 37:17
16 [q] 2 Chr. 32:7; [Ps. 55:18; Rom. 8:31]
17 [r] ver. 20 [s] ch. 2:11; [Ps. 34:7; 68:17]; See Zech. 1:8-10; 6:1-7
18 [t] [Gen. 19:11]
20 [r] [See ver. 17 above]
21 [u] ch. 5:13; 8:9; Judg. 17:10
22 [v] Gen. 48:22 [w] Rom. 12:20
23 [x] ver. 8, 9; ch. 5:2; 24:2
24 [y] 1 Kgs. 20:1
29 [z] [Lev. 26:29; Deut. 28:53, 57; Ezek. 5:10]
30 [a] 1 Kgs. 21:27
31 [b] [1 Kgs. 19:2]; See Ruth 1:17
32 [c] Ezek. 8:1; 14:1; 20:1 [d] [1 Kgs. 18:4; 21:13]

master's feet behind him?" [33] And while he
was still speaking with them, the messenger
came down to him and said, "This trouble is
from the LORD! [e]Why should I wait for the
LORD any longer?"

Elisha Promises Food

7 But Elisha said, "Hear the word of the
LORD: thus says the LORD, [f]Tomorrow
about this time a seah[1] of fine flour shall be
sold for a shekel,[2] and two seahs of barley for
a shekel, at the gate of Samaria." [2] Then [g]the
captain on whose hand the king leaned said to
the man of God, [h]"If the LORD himself should
make windows in heaven, could this thing
be?" But he said, "You shall see it with your
own eyes, but you shall not eat of it."

The Syrians Flee

[3] Now there were four men who were lepers[3]
[i]at the entrance to the gate. And they said to
one another, "Why are we sitting here until
we die? [4] If we say, 'Let us enter the city,' the
famine is in the city, and we shall die there.
And if we sit here, we die also. So now come,
let us go over to the camp of the Syrians. If
they spare our lives we shall live, and if they
kill us we shall but die." [5] So they arose at
twilight to go to the camp of the Syrians. But
when they came to the edge of the camp of the
Syrians, behold, there was no one there. [6] For
the Lord had made the army of the Syrians
[j]hear the sound of chariots and of horses, the
sound of a great army, so that they said to one
another, "Behold, the king of Israel has hired
against us [k]the kings of the Hittites and the
kings of Egypt to come against us." [7] [l]So they
fled away in the twilight and abandoned their
tents, their horses, and their donkeys, leaving the camp as it was, and fled for their lives.
[8] And when these lepers came to the edge of
the camp, they went into a tent and ate and
drank, and they carried off silver and gold and
clothing and went and hid them. Then they
came back and entered another tent and carried off things from it and went and hid them.
[9] Then they said to one another, "We are not
doing right. This day is a day of good news. If
we are silent and wait until the morning light,
punishment will overtake us. Now therefore
come; let us go and tell the king's household."
[10] So they came and called to the gatekeepers
of the city and told them, "We came to the
camp of the Syrians, and behold, there was
no one to be seen or heard there, nothing but
the horses tied and the donkeys tied and the
tents as they were." [11] Then the gatekeepers
called out, and it was told within the king's
household. [12] And the king rose in the night
and said to his servants, "I will tell you what
the Syrians have done to us. They know that
we are hungry. Therefore they have gone out
of the camp to hide themselves in the open
country, thinking, 'When they come out of
the city, we shall take them alive and get into
the city.'" [13] And one of his servants said, "Let
some men take five of the remaining horses,
seeing that those who are left here will fare
like the whole multitude of Israel who have
already perished. Let us send and see." [14] So
they took two horsemen, and the king sent
them after the army of the Syrians, saying,
"Go and see." [15] So they went after them as far

[1] A *seah* was about 7 quarts or 7.3 liters [2] A *shekel* was about 2/5 ounce or 11 grams [3] *Leprosy* was a term for several skin diseases; see Leviticus 13

33[e] [Job 2:9]
Chapter 7
1[f] ver. 18
2[g] ver. 17, 19; [ch. 5:18] [h] Mal. 3:10; [Gen. 7:11]
3[i] [Lev. 13:46]
6[j] [ch. 6:17; 2 Sam. 5:24; Job 15:21] [k] [1 Kgs. 10:29]
7[l] [Ps. 48:4-6; Prov. 28:1]

this great deliverance—not with sword, spear, chariot, or even a single warrior, but with a rumor. God mocked the enemy with the power of his whisper, defeating them with almost no effort at all. The incalculable nature of God's power is demonstrated by his ability to deliver us from the greatest of terrors with almost no effort at all; indeed, with what might appear to be weakness.

The trouble with deliverance of this kind, however, is that it is almost impossible for us to believe. Observe that the account of God's deliverance in 2 Kings 7 is framed by references to the king's captain. In 2 Kings 7:2, the captain did not believe the declaration of the prophet's good news because it seemed ridiculously impossible. Then at the very end, in verse 17, the captain perished because of his unbelief. We are reminded that our salvation depends not only on God's willingness to do for us what we cannot do for ourselves, but also, because his deliverance is so great, it depends on hearts ready to believe that his salvation is true. When God's outrageous free grace seems just too good to be true, believe it! It was designed to be outrageous and remarkable. Grace involves no balancing of the scales, no careful weighing of merits and demerits. Because of Christ's atoning work, God's grace washes over us and into our lives regardless of what we deserve or do not deserve. Humble yourself. Receive it.

as the Jordan, and behold, all the way was lit-
tered with garments and equipment that the
Syrians had thrown away in their haste. And
the messengers returned and told the king.
16 Then the people went out and plundered
the camp of the Syrians. So a seah of fine flour
was sold for a shekel, and two seahs of barley
for a shekel, [m]according to the word of the
LORD. 17 Now the king had appointed [n]the captain on whose hand he leaned to have charge
of the gate. And the people trampled him in
the gate, so that he died, as the man of God had
said [o]when the king came down to him. 18 For
when the man of God had said to the king,
"Two seahs of barley shall be sold for a shekel,
and a seah of fine flour for a shekel, about this
time tomorrow in the gate of Samaria," 19 [n]the
captain had answered the man of God, "If
the LORD himself should make windows in
heaven, could such a thing be?" And he had
said, [p]"You shall see it with your own eyes, but
you shall not eat of it." 20 And so it happened
to him, for the people trampled him in the
gate and he died.

The Shunammite's Land Restored

8 Now Elisha had said to the woman [q]whose
son he had restored to life, "Arise, and
depart with your household, and sojourn
wherever you can, for the LORD [r]has called
for a famine, and it will come upon the land
for [s]seven years." 2 So the woman arose and did
according to the word of the man of God. She
went with her household and sojourned in
the land of the Philistines seven years. 3 And at
the end of the seven years, when the woman
returned from the land of the Philistines, she
went to appeal to the king for her house and
her land. 4 Now the king was talking with
[t]Gehazi the servant of the man of God, saying,
"Tell me all the great things that Elisha has
done." 5 And while he was telling the king how
[q]Elisha had restored the dead to life, behold,
the woman whose son he had restored to life
appealed to the king for her house and her
land. And Gehazi said, "My lord, O king, here
is the woman, and here is her son whom Elisha
restored to life." 6 And when the king asked the
woman, she told him. So the king appointed
an official for her, saying, "Restore all that was
hers, together with all the produce of the fields
from the day that she left the land until now."

Hazael Murders Ben-hadad

7 Now Elisha came to [u]Damascus. [v]Ben-hadad
the king of Syria was sick. And when it was
told him, "The man of God has come here,"
8 the king said to [w]Hazael, [x]"Take a present
with you and go to meet the man of God,
[y]and inquire of the LORD through him, saying, 'Shall I recover from this sickness?'" 9 So
Hazael went to meet him, and took a present
with him, all kinds of goods of Damascus,
forty camels' loads. When he came and stood
before him, he said, [z]"Your son Ben-hadad
king of Syria has sent me to you, saying, 'Shall
I recover from this sickness?'" 10 And Elisha
said to him, [a]"Go, say to him, 'You shall certainly recover,' but[1] the LORD has shown me
that [b]he shall certainly die." 11 And he fixed his
gaze and stared at him, [c]until he was embarrassed. And the man of God wept. 12 And
Hazael said, "Why does my lord weep?" He
answered, "Because I know [d]the evil that you
will do to the people of Israel. You will set on
fire their fortresses, and you will kill their
young men with the sword [e]and dash in pieces
their little ones and rip open their pregnant
women." 13 And Hazael said, "What is your servant, [f]who is but a dog, that he should do this
great thing?" Elisha answered, [g]"The LORD has
shown me that you are to be king over Syria."
14 Then he departed from Elisha and came to
his master, who said to him, "What did Elisha
say to you?" And he answered, "He told me
[h]that you would certainly recover." 15 But the
next day he took the bed cloth[2] and dipped it
in water and spread it over his face, till he died.
And Hazael became king in his place.

Jehoram Reigns in Judah

16 In the fifth year of [i]Joram the son of Ahab,
king of Israel, when Jehoshaphat was king
of Judah,[3] Jehoram the son of Jehoshaphat,
king of Judah, began to reign. 17 He was [j]thirty-
two years old when he became king, and he
reigned eight years in Jerusalem. 18 And he
walked in the way of the kings of Israel, as
the house of Ahab had done, for [k]the daughter
of Ahab was his wife. And he did what was evil

[1] Some manuscripts *say, 'You shall certainly not recover,' for* [2] The meaning of the Hebrew is uncertain [3] Septuagint, Syriac lack *when Jehoshaphat was king of Judah*

16[m] ver. 1 **17**[n] ver. 2 [o] ch. 6:32 **19**[n] [See ver. 17 above] [p] ver. 2 **Chapter 8** **1**[q] ch. 4:35 [r] Ps. 105:16; Hag. 1:11 [s] [Gen. 41:27] **4**[t] See ch. 4:12 **5**[q] [See ver. 1 above] **7**[u] [1 Kgs. 11:24] [v] ch. 6:24; 1 Kgs. 20:1 **8**[w] 1 Kgs. 19:15, 17 [x] See 1 Sam. 9:7 [y] [ch. 1:2] **9**[z] [ch. 5:13] **10**[a] ver. 14 [b] ver. 15 **11**[c] ch. 2:17 **12**[d] ch. 10:32; 12:17; 13:3, 7, 22; Amos 1:3, 4 [e] Isa. 13:16; Hos. 13:16; Nah. 3:10; [Ps. 137:9; Hos. 10:14] **13**[f] See 1 Sam. 17:43 [g] [1 Kgs. 19:15] **14**[h] ver. 10 **16**[i] [ch. 1:17; 3:1] **17**[j] For ver. 17-24, see 2 Chr. 21:5-10 **18**[k] [ver. 26]

in the sight of the LORD. 19 Yet the LORD was
not willing to destroy Judah, for the sake of
David his servant, [l]since he promised to give
[m]a lamp to him and to his sons forever.
20 In his days Edom revolted from the rule of
Judah and set up [n]a king of their own. 21 Then
Joram[1] passed over to Zair with all his chariots
and rose by night, and he and his chariot commanders struck the Edomites who had surrounded him, but his army [o]fled home. 22 [p]So
Edom revolted from the rule of Judah to this
day. Then [q]Libnah revolted at the same time.
23 Now the rest of the acts of Joram, and all that
he did, are they not written in the Book of the
Chronicles of the Kings of Judah? 24 So Joram
slept with his fathers and was buried [r]with his
fathers in the city of David, and [s]Ahaziah his
son reigned in his place.

Ahaziah Reigns in Judah

25 [t]In the [u]twelfth year of Joram the son
of Ahab, king of Israel, Ahaziah the son of
Jehoram, king of Judah, began to reign.
26 Ahaziah was [v]twenty-two years old when
he began to reign, and he reigned one year in
Jerusalem. His mother's name was Athaliah;
she was [w]a granddaughter of Omri king of
Israel. 27 He also walked in the way of the house
of Ahab and did what was evil in the sight of
the LORD, as the house of Ahab had done, for
he was son-in-law to the house of Ahab.
28 He went with Joram the son of Ahab to
make war against [x]Hazael king of Syria at
[y]Ramoth-gilead, and the Syrians wounded
Joram. 29 [z]And King Joram returned to be
healed in Jezreel of the wounds that the
Syrians had given him at [a]Ramah, when he
fought against Hazael king of Syria. And [b]Aha-
ziah the son of Jehoram king of Judah went
down to see Joram the son of Ahab in Jezreel,
because he was sick.

Jehu Anointed King of Israel

9 Then Elisha the prophet called one of [c]the
sons of the prophets and said to him, [d]"Tie
up your garments, and take this [e]flask of oil in
your hand, and go to [f]Ramoth-gilead. 2 And
when you arrive, look there for Jehu [g]the son
of Jehoshaphat, son of Nimshi. And go in and
have him rise from among [h]his fellows, and
lead him to an inner chamber. 3 Then take the
flask of oil and pour it on his head and say,
'Thus says the LORD, [i]I anoint you king over
Israel.' Then open the door and flee; do not
linger."
4 So the young man, the servant of the
prophet, went to Ramoth-gilead. 5 And when
he came, behold, the commanders of the
army were in council. And he said, "I have a
word for you, O commander." And Jehu said,
"To which of us all?" And he said, "To you,
O commander." 6 So he arose and went into the
house. And the young man poured the oil on
his head, saying to him, "Thus says the LORD,
the God of Israel, [i]I anoint you king over the
people of the LORD, over Israel. 7 And you shall
strike down the house of Ahab your master,
so that I may avenge [j]on Jezebel the blood of
my servants the prophets, and the blood of
all the servants of the LORD. 8 For the whole
house of Ahab shall perish, [k]and I will cut off
from Ahab [l]every male, [m]bond or free, in Israel.
9 And I will make the house of Ahab like [n]the
house of Jeroboam the son of Nebat, and like
[o]the house of Baasha the son of Ahijah. 10 [p]And
the dogs shall eat Jezebel in the territory of
Jezreel, and none shall bury her." Then he
opened the door and fled.
11 When Jehu came out to the servants of his
master, they said to him, [q]"Is all well? Why did
[r]this mad fellow come to you?" And he said
to them, "You know the fellow and his talk."
12 And they said, "That is not true; tell us now."
And he said, "Thus and so he spoke to me,
saying, 'Thus says the LORD, I anoint you king
over Israel.'" 13 Then in haste [s]every man of
them took his garment and put it under him
on the bare[2] steps, and they blew the trumpet
and proclaimed, [t]"Jehu is king."

Jehu Assassinates Joram and Ahaziah

14 Thus Jehu the son of Jehoshaphat the son
of Nimshi conspired against Joram. ([u]Now
Joram with all Israel had been on guard at

[1] *Joram* is an alternate spelling of *Jehoram* (the son of Jehoshaphat) as in verse 16; also verses 23, 24 [2] The meaning of the Hebrew word is uncertain

19[l] 2 Sam. 7:12, 13; Ps. 132:11

8:19 See note on 1 Kings 15:4.

[m] 1 Kgs. 11:36; 15:4; [2 Sam. 21:17] **20**[n] ch. 3:9; [1 Kgs. 22:47] **21**[o] See 2 Sam. 18:17 **22**[p] [Gen. 27:40] [q] Josh. 10:29, 30 **24**[r] [2 Chr. 21:20] [s] [2 Chr. 21:17; 22:6; 25:23] **25**[t] For ver. 25-29, see 2 Chr. 22:1-6 [u] [ch. 9:29] **26**[v] [2 Chr. 22:2] [w] [1 Kgs. 15:10] **28**[x] ver. 15 [y] [1 Kgs. 22:3] **29**[z] ch. 9:15 [a] 2 Chr. 22:6; [ver. 28; 2 Chr. 22:5] [b] ch. 9:16 **Chapter 9** **1**[c] See ch. 2:3 [d] See 1 Kgs. 18:46 [e] 1 Sam. 10:1 [f] ch. 8:28; [1 Kgs. 22:3] **2**[g] ver. 14; [ver. 20; 1 Kgs. 19:16] [h] [ver. 5, 11] **3**[i] [1 Kgs. 19:16; 2 Chr. 22:7] **6**[i] [See ver. 3 above] **7**[j] [1 Kgs. 18:4]; See 1 Kgs. 21:5-15 **8**[k] ch. 10:17; 1 Kgs. 21:21; [1 Kgs. 14:10] [l] See 1 Sam. 25:22 [m] Deut. 32:36 **9**[n] 1 Kgs. 14:10; 15:29; 21:22 [o] 1 Kgs. 16:3, 11; 21:22 **10**[p] ver. 35, 36; 1 Kgs. 21:23 **11**[q] ch. 5:21 [r] Jer. 29:26; Hos. 9:7; [John 10:20; Acts 26:24] **13**[s] [Matt. 21:8; Mark 11:8] [t] [1 Kgs. 1:34] **14**[u] [ch. 8:28]

Ramoth-gilead against [v]Hazael king of Syria, 15 [w]but King Joram had returned to be healed in Jezreel of the wounds that the Syrians had given him, when he fought with Hazael king of Syria.) So Jehu said, "If this is your decision, then let no one slip out of the city to go and tell the news in Jezreel." 16 Then Jehu mounted his chariot and went to Jezreel, for Joram lay there. And Ahaziah king of Judah had come down to visit Joram.

17 Now the watchman was standing on the tower in Jezreel, and he saw the company of Jehu as he came and said, "I see a company." And Joram said, "Take a horseman and send to meet them, and let him say, 'Is it peace?'" 18 So a man on horseback went to meet him and said, "Thus says the king, 'Is it peace?'" And Jehu said, "What do you have to do with peace? Turn around and ride behind me." And the watchman reported, saying, "The messenger reached them, but he is not coming back." 19 Then he sent out a second horseman, who came to them and said, "Thus the king has said, 'Is it peace?'" And Jehu answered, "What do you have to do with peace? Turn around and ride behind me." 20 Again the watchman reported, "He reached them, but he is not coming back. And the driving [x]is like the driving of Jehu [y]the son of Nimshi, for he drives furiously."

21 Joram said, [z]"Make ready." And they made ready his chariot. [a]Then Joram king of Israel and Ahaziah king of Judah set out, each in his chariot, and went to meet Jehu, and met him [b]at the property of Naboth the Jezreelite. 22 And when Joram saw Jehu, he said, "Is it peace, Jehu?" He answered, "What peace can there be, so long as [c]the whorings and the sorceries of your mother Jezebel are so many?" 23 Then Joram reined about and fled, saying to Ahaziah, "Treachery, O Ahaziah!" 24 And Jehu drew his bow with his full strength, and shot Joram between the shoulders, so that the arrow pierced his heart, and he sank in his chariot. 25 Jehu said to Bidkar [d]his aide, "Take him up and throw him [b]on the plot of ground belonging to Naboth the Jezreelite. For remember, when you and I rode side by side behind Ahab his father, how [e]the LORD made this [f]pronouncement against him: 26 'As surely as I saw yesterday the blood of Naboth and the blood of his sons—declares the LORD—I will repay you on this plot of ground.' Now therefore take him up and throw him on the plot of ground, in accordance with the word of the LORD."

27 [g]When Ahaziah the king of Judah saw this, he fled in the direction of Beth-haggan. And Jehu pursued him and said, "Shoot him also." And they shot him[1] in the chariot at the ascent of Gur, which is by [h]Ibleam. And he fled to [h]Megiddo and died there. 28 [i]His servants carried him in a chariot to Jerusalem, and buried him in his tomb with his fathers in the city of David.

29 In the [j]eleventh year of Joram the son of Ahab, Ahaziah began to reign over Judah.

Jehu Executes Jezebel

30 When Jehu came to Jezreel, Jezebel heard of it. And [k]she painted her eyes and adorned her head and looked out of the window. 31 And as Jehu entered the gate, she said, [l]"Is it peace, you Zimri, murderer of your master?" 32 And he lifted up his face to the window and said, "Who is on my side? Who?" Two or three eunuchs looked out at him. 33 He said, "Throw her down." So they threw her down. And some of her blood spattered on the wall and on the horses, and they trampled on her. 34 Then he went in and ate and drank. And he said, "See now to this cursed woman and

[1] Syriac, Vulgate (compare Septuagint); Hebrew lacks *and they shot him*

9:14–10:17 A difficult but important aspect of the gospel is that good news for God's people will constitute bad news for those who don't belong to him. In these verses, God brings his promised judgment upon the house of Ahab for its sins, exterminating the royal family that had excelled beyond all others in the promotion of idolatry and the persecution of God's servants.

As Christians, we live as aliens and strangers in a world to which we do not belong, often under rulers and authorities hostile toward God and his people. We are reminded here, however, that our Lord will return at the time he knows is best and will put an end to those who stand in opposition to him, as he did to Joram in this text. Our enduring hope of such judgment upon evil can help us to persevere in difficult times.

But as we witness the judgment of Joram and the extermination of his family, we should also remember that we deserve the very same judgment because of our own

14 [v][1 Kgs. 19:17]
15 [w]ch. 8:29
20 [x][2 Sam. 18:27] [y]1 Kgs. 19:17; [ver. 2, 14]
21 [z]1 Kgs. 18:44 [a]2 Chr. 22:7 [b]1 Kgs. 21:1; [ver. 26]
22 [c][2 Chr. 21:13]
25 [d][ch. 7:2] [b][See ver. 21 above] [e]1 Kgs. 21:19, 29 [f]See Isa. 13:1
27 [g][2 Chr. 22:9] [h]Josh. 17:11
28 [i][ch. 23:30; 2 Chr. 35:24]
29 [j][ch. 8:25]
30 [k][Jer. 4:30; Ezek. 23:40]
31 [l]See 1 Kgs. 16:9-20

bury her, [m]for she is a king's daughter." 35 But when they went to bury her, they found no more of her than the skull and the feet and the palms of her hands. 36 When they came back and told him, he said, "This is the word of the LORD, which he spoke by his servant Elijah the Tishbite: [n]'In the territory of Jezreel the dogs shall eat the flesh of Jezebel, 37 and the corpse of Jezebel shall be [o]as dung on the face of the field in the territory of Jezreel, so that no one can say, This is Jezebel.'"

Jehu Slaughters Ahab's Descendants

10 Now Ahab had seventy sons in [p]Samaria. So Jehu wrote letters and sent them to Samaria, to the rulers of the city,[1] to the elders, and to [q]the guardians of the sons[2] of Ahab, saying, 2 "Now then, as soon as this letter comes to you, seeing your master's sons are with you, and there are with you chariots and horses, fortified cities also, and weapons, 3 select the best and fittest of your master's sons and set him on his father's throne and fight for your master's house." 4 But they were exceedingly afraid and said, "Behold, the two kings could not stand before him. How then can we stand?" 5 So he who was over the palace, and he who was over the city, together with the elders and the guardians, sent to Jehu, saying, [r]"We are your servants, and we will do all that you tell us. We will not make anyone king. Do whatever is good in your eyes." 6 Then he wrote to them a second letter, saying, "If you are on my side, and if you are ready to obey me, take the heads of your master's sons and come to me at Jezreel tomorrow at this time." Now the king's sons, seventy persons, were with the great men of the city, [q]who were bringing them up. 7 And as soon as the letter came to them, they took the king's sons [s]and slaughtered them, seventy persons, and put their heads in baskets and sent them to him at Jezreel. 8 When the messenger came and told him, "They have brought the heads of the king's sons," he said, "Lay them in two heaps at the entrance of the gate until the morning." 9 Then in the morning, when he went out, he stood and said to all the people, "You are innocent. [t]It was I who conspired against my master and killed him, but who struck down all these? 10 Know then that there shall [u]fall to the earth nothing of the word of the LORD, which the LORD spoke concerning the house of Ahab, for the LORD has done [v]what he said by his servant Elijah." 11 So Jehu struck down all who remained of the house of Ahab in Jezreel, all his great men and his close friends and his priests, until he left him none remaining.

12 Then he set out and went to Samaria. On the way, when he was at Beth-eked of the Shepherds, 13 Jehu met [w]the relatives of Ahaziah king of Judah, and he said, "Who are you?" And they answered, "We are the relatives of Ahaziah, and we came down to visit the royal princes and the sons of the queen mother." 14 He said, "Take them alive." And they took them alive and slaughtered them at the pit of Beth-eked, forty-two persons, and he spared none of them.

15 And when he departed from there, he met [x]Jehonadab the son of [y]Rechab coming to meet him. And he greeted him and said to him, "Is your heart true to my heart as mine is to yours?" And Jehonadab answered, "It is." Jehu said,[3] "If it is, [z]give me your hand." So he gave him his hand. And Jehu took him up with him into the chariot. 16 And he said, "Come with me, and see [a]my zeal for the LORD." So he[4] had him ride in his chariot. 17 And when he came to Samaria, [b]he struck down all who remained to Ahab in Samaria, till he had wiped them out, according to the word of the LORD [v]that he spoke to Elijah.

[1] Septuagint, Vulgate; Hebrew *rulers of Jezreel* [2] Hebrew lacks *of the sons* [3] Septuagint; Hebrew lacks *Jehu said* [4] Septuagint, Syriac, Targum; Hebrew *they*

34 [m] 1 Kgs. 16:31
36 [n] 1 Kgs. 21:23
37 [o] [Ps. 83:10; Jer. 8:2; 9:22; 16:4; 25:33]
Chapter 10
1 [p] 1 Kgs. 16:24 [q] [Esth. 2:7]
5 [r] Josh. 9:8, 11
6 [q] [See ver. 1 above]
7 [s] [1 Kgs. 21:21]
9 [t] ch. 9:14, 24
10 [u] [1 Sam. 3:19] [v] 1 Kgs. 21:19, 21, 29
13 [w] [ch. 8:29; 9:16; 2 Chr. 22:8]

sins. Were it not for the fact that another King would come and take upon himself the judgment that we deserve, we would be lying dead next to Joram in the vineyard of Naboth. King Joram died for his sins and for the sins of his father, but King Jesus died for *our* sins in order that we might know *his* Father. It is only by God's grace that we have escaped this judgment. So we must not despise those around us who persist in the sins of Ahab and Joram, but rather declare to them the hope God has granted to us through our *own* forgiveness. Jesus has changed the bad news of our judgment into the good news of our salvation. He can do the same for anyone else who comes to him in contrition and trust.

15 [x] See Jer. 35:6-10, 14, 16, 18 [y] 1 Chr. 2:55 [z] Ezra 10:19; Ezek. 17:18 16 [a] [1 Kgs. 19:10] 17 [b] ch. 9:8; 2 Chr. 22:8 [v] [See ver. 10 above]

Jehu Strikes Down the Prophets of Baal

18 Then Jehu assembled all the people and
said to them, [c]"Ahab served Baal a little, but
Jehu will serve him much. 19 Now therefore call
to me all the [d]prophets of Baal, all his worshipers and all his priests. Let none be missing, for
I have a great sacrifice to offer to Baal. Whoever
is missing shall not live." But Jehu did it with
cunning in order to destroy the worshipers
of Baal. 20 And Jehu ordered, [e]"Sanctify [f]a solemn assembly for Baal." So [g]they proclaimed
it. 21 And Jehu sent throughout all Israel, and
all the worshipers of Baal came, so that there
was not a man left who did not come. And
they entered [h]the house of Baal, and the house
of Baal was filled from one end to the other.
22 He said to him who was in charge of the
wardrobe, "Bring out the vestments for all
the worshipers of Baal." So he brought out
the vestments for them. 23 Then Jehu went
into the house of Baal with Jehonadab the son
of Rechab, and he said to the worshipers of
Baal, "Search, and see that there is no servant
of the LORD here among you, but only the
worshipers of Baal." 24 Then they[1] went in to
offer sacrifices and burnt offerings.

Now Jehu had stationed eighty men outside
and said, "The man who allows any of those
whom I give into your hands to escape [i]shall
forfeit his life." 25 So as soon as he had made an
end of offering the burnt offering, Jehu said
to the guard and to the officers, [j]"Go in and
strike them down; let not a man escape." So
when they put them to the sword, the guard
and the officers cast them out and went into
the inner room of the house of Baal, 26 and they
brought out the [k]pillar that was in [h]the house
of Baal and burned it. 27 And they demolished
the [k]pillar of Baal, and demolished the house
of Baal, and made it [l]a latrine to this day.

Jehu Reigns in Israel

28 Thus Jehu wiped out Baal from Israel.
29 But Jehu did not turn aside from [m]the sins
of Jeroboam the son of Nebat, [n]which he made
Israel to sin—that is, the golden calves that
were in Bethel and in Dan. 30 And the LORD
said to Jehu, "Because you have done well in
carrying out what is right in my eyes, and have
done to the house of Ahab according to all that
was in my heart, [o]your sons of the fourth generation shall sit on the throne of Israel." 31 But
Jehu was not careful to walk in the law of the
LORD, the God of Israel, with all his heart. [p]He
did not turn from the sins of Jeroboam, which
he made Israel to sin.

32 In those days the LORD [q]began to cut off
parts of Israel. [r]Hazael defeated them throughout the territory of Israel: 33 from the Jordan
eastward, all the land of Gilead, the Gadites,
and the Reubenites, and the Manassites, from
[s]Aroer, which is by the Valley of the Arnon,
that is, [t]Gilead and Bashan. 34 Now the rest of
the acts of Jehu and all that he did, and all his
might, are they not written in the Book of the
Chronicles of the Kings of Israel? 35 So Jehu
slept with his fathers, and they buried him in
Samaria. And Jehoahaz his son reigned in his
place. 36 The time that Jehu reigned over Israel
in Samaria was twenty-eight years.

Athaliah Reigns in Judah

11 [u]Now when [v]Athaliah the mother of
Ahaziah saw that her son was dead, she
arose and destroyed all the royal family. 2 But
Jehosheba, the daughter of King Joram, sister
of Ahaziah, took [w]Joash the son of Ahaziah
and stole him away from among the king's
sons who were being put to death, and she
put[2] him and his nurse in a bedroom. Thus
they[3] hid him from Athaliah, so that he was
not put to death. 3 And he remained with her
six years, hidden in the house of the LORD,
while Athaliah reigned over the land.

Joash Anointed King in Judah

4 [x]But in the seventh year [y]Jehoiada sent and
brought the captains of [z]the Carites and of
the guards, and had them come to him in the
house of the LORD. And he made a covenant

[1] Septuagint *he* (compare verse 25) [2] Compare 2 Chronicles 22:11; Hebrew lacks *and she put* [3] Septuagint, Syriac, Vulgate (compare 2 Chronicles 22:11) *she*

11:1–3 A theme that runs across the pages of Scripture is the crisis of the "seed" (or "offspring") of promise (Gen. 3:15). Cain kills Abel, so God provides Seth. Abraham is promised offspring, but Sarah is barren. Miraculously, Sarah gives birth to a son, Isaac, but God commands Abraham to kill him (Genesis 22). Next we find that Rebekah, the wife of Isaac, is also barren. In Egypt, Pharaoh orders all of the male children to

18 [c] 1 Kgs. 16:31, 32
19 [d] 1 Kgs. 18:19; 22:6
20 [e] [Joel 1:14] [f] [Lev. 23:36] [g] [Ex. 32:5]
21 [h] ch. 11:18; 1 Kgs. 16:32
24 [i] [1 Kgs. 20:39, 42]
25 [j] [1 Kgs. 18:40]

26 [k] ch. 3:2; 1 Kgs. 14:23 [h] [See ver. 21 above] **27** [k] [See ver. 26 above] [l] [Ezra 6:11; Dan. 2:5; 3:29] **29** [m] See 1 Kgs. 12:28-31 [n] See 1 Kgs. 14:16 **30** [o] ch. 15:12; [ver. 35; ch. 13:1, 10; 14:23; 15:8] **31** [p] ver. 29 **32** [q] [ch. 13:25; 14:25] [r] [ch. 8:12; 1 Kgs. 19:17] **33** [s] Deut. 2:36 [t] [Amos 1:3, 4] **Chapter 11** **1** [u] For ver. 1-3, see 2 Chr. 22:10-12 [v] ch. 8:26 **2** [w] [ver. 21; ch. 12:1] **4** [x] For ver. 4-20, see 2 Chr. 23:1-21 [y] ver. 9 [z] ver. 19

with them and put them under oath in the
house of the LORD, and he showed them the
king's son. 5 And he commanded them, "This
is the thing that you shall do: one third of you,
[a]those who come off duty on the Sabbath and
guard the king's house 6 ([b]another third being
at the gate Sur and a third at the gate behind
the guards) shall guard the palace.[1] 7 And the
two divisions of you, which come on duty in
force on the Sabbath and guard the house of
the LORD on behalf of the king, 8 shall surround the king, each with his weapons in his
hand. And whoever approaches the ranks is
to be put to death. Be with the king [c]when he
goes out and when he comes in."

9 The captains did according to all that
Jehoiada the priest commanded, and they each
brought his men who were to go off duty on
the Sabbath, with those who were to come on
duty on the Sabbath, and came to Jehoiada
the priest. 10 And the priest gave to the captains the spears and [d]shields that had been
King David's, which were in the house of the
LORD. 11 And the guards stood, every man with
his weapons in his hand, from the south side
of the house to the north side of the house,
around the altar and the house on behalf of
the king. 12 Then he brought out the king's son
and put [e]the crown on him and gave him [f]the
testimony. And they proclaimed him king and
anointed him, and they clapped their hands
and said, [g]"Long live the king!"

13 When Athaliah heard the noise of the
guard and of the people, she went into the
house of the LORD to the people. 14 And when
she looked, there was the king standing [h]by
the pillar, according to the custom, and the
captains and the trumpeters beside the king,
and all the people of the land rejoicing and
[i]blowing trumpets. And Athaliah [j]tore her
clothes and cried, "Treason! Treason!" 15 Then
Jehoiada the priest commanded the captains
who were set over the army, "Bring her out
between the ranks, and put to death with the
sword anyone who follows her." For the priest
said, "Let her not be put to death in the house
of the LORD." 16 So they laid hands on her; and
she went through the horses' entrance to the
king's house, and there she was put to death.

17 And Jehoiada [k]made a covenant between
the LORD and the king and people, that
they should be the LORD's people, and also
[l]between the king and the people. 18 Then all
the people of the land went to [m]the house
of Baal and tore it down; [n]his altars and his
images they broke in pieces, and they killed
Mattan the priest of Baal before the altars. And
the priest posted watchmen over the house
of the LORD. 19 And he took the captains, [o]the
Carites, the guards, and all the people of the
land, and they brought the king down from
the house of the LORD, marching through [p]the
gate of the guards to the king's house. And he
took his seat on the throne of the kings. 20 So
all the people of the land rejoiced, and the city
was quiet after Athaliah had been put to death
with the sword at the king's house.

Jehoash Reigns in Judah

21[2] [q]Jehoash[3] was seven years old when he
began to reign.

12 In the seventh year of Jehu, Jehoash[4]
began to reign, and he reigned forty
years in Jerusalem. His mother's name was
Zibiah of Beersheba. 2 And Jehoash did what
was right in the eyes of the LORD all his days,

[1] The meaning of the Hebrew word is uncertain [2] Ch 12:1 in Hebrew [3] *Jehoash* is an alternate spelling of *Joash* (son of Ahaziah) as in verse 2 [4] *Jehoash* is an alternate spelling of *Joash* (son of Ahaziah) as in 11:2; also verses 2, 4, 6, 7, 18

5[a] [1 Chr. 9:25]
6[b] [2 Chr. 23:5]
8[c] [Num. 27:17]
10[d] 2 Sam. 8:7; 1 Chr. 18:7
12[e] [2 Sam. 1:10] [f] Ex. 25:16; 31:18; See Deut. 17:18-20 [g] 1 Sam. 10:24; 2 Sam. 16:16; 1 Kgs. 1:39
14[h] ch. 23:3; [2 Chr. 34:31] [i] 1 Kgs. 1:34 [j] See Gen. 44:13
17[k] [Josh. 24:25] [l] 2 Sam. 5:3
18[m] ch. 10:21, 23, 26 [n] [Deut. 12:3]
19[o] ver. 4 [p] ver. 6; [2 Chr. 23:20]
21[q] For ch. 11:21-12:15, see 2 Chr. 24:1-14

be killed at birth (Exodus 1). Here, in this text, we discover that almost all of the royal line of Judah was destroyed by Athaliah, the mother of Ahaziah.

The crisis of the seed of promise highlights the ongoing cosmic antagonism (stretching back to Genesis 3) between the seed of the woman and the seed of the serpent. These crises should sharpen our focus on God's preserving, redemptive work to provide for and protect the line of the seed of promise. The Lord may provide a ram as a substitute (Genesis 22), or faithful midwives who refuse to follow the command of the pharaoh (Exodus 1), or, in this case, a faithful sister who hides the one last son.

Events of this kind ultimately point forward to the climactic crisis of the Seed of promise: Jesus, born under a decree of death as in the days of Egypt, but saved from Herod's infanticide by the intervention of his heavenly Father. Finally, on a hill named Golgotha, this royal Seed was sent to be sacrificed just as God sent Abraham to sacrifice his son, Isaac, on Mount Moriah. This time, however, no substitute was provided. Jesus *was* the substitute. Yet God intervened again and resurrected this Son, who now reigns with the Father as our Mediator. The crisis of this Seed of promise

because Jehoiada the priest instructed him. 3 Nevertheless, [r]the high places were not taken away; the people continued to sacrifice and make offerings on the high places.

Jehoash Repairs the Temple

4 Jehoash said to the priests, "All the money of the holy things [s]that is brought into the house of the LORD, the money for which each man is assessed—the money from the assessment of persons—and [t]the money that a man's heart prompts him to bring into the house of the LORD, 5 let the priests take, each from his donor, and let them repair the house wherever any need of repairs is discovered." 6 But by the twenty-third year of King Jehoash, the priests had made no repairs on the house. 7 Therefore King Jehoash summoned Jehoiada the priest and the other priests and said to them, "Why are you not repairing the house? Now therefore take no more money from your donors, but hand it over for the repair of the house." 8 So the priests agreed that they should take no more money from the people, and that they should not repair the house.

9 Then Jehoiada the priest took [u]a chest and bored a hole in the lid of it and set it beside the altar on the right side as one entered the house of the LORD. And the priests who guarded the threshold put in it all the money that was brought into the house of the LORD. 10 And whenever they saw that there was much money in the chest, the king's secretary and the high priest came up and they bagged and counted [v]the money that was found in the house of the LORD. 11 Then they would give the money that was weighed out into the hands of the workmen who had the oversight of the house of the LORD. And they paid it out to the carpenters and the builders who worked on the house of the LORD, 12 and [w]to the masons and the stonecutters, as well as to buy timber and quarried stone for making repairs on the house of the LORD, and for any outlay for the repairs of the house. 13 [x]But there were not made for the house of the LORD [y]basins of silver, snuffers, bowls, trumpets, or any vessels of gold, or of silver, from the money that was brought into the house of the LORD, 14 for that was given to the workmen who were repairing the house of the LORD with it. 15 And [z]they did not ask for an accounting from the men into whose hand they delivered the money to pay out to the workmen, for they dealt honestly. 16 The money from [a]the guilt offerings and the money from the [b]sin offerings was not brought into the house of the LORD; [c]it belonged to the priests.

17 At that time [d]Hazael king of Syria went up and fought against Gath and took it. But when Hazael set his face [e]to go up against Jerusalem, 18 Jehoash king of Judah [f]took all the sacred gifts that Jehoshaphat and Jehoram and Ahaziah his fathers, the kings of Judah, had dedicated, [g]and his own sacred gifts, and all the gold that was found in the treasuries of the house of the LORD and of the king's house, and sent these to Hazael king of Syria. Then Hazael went away from Jerusalem.

The Death of Joash

19 Now the rest of the acts of Joash and all that he did, are they not written in the Book of the Chronicles of the Kings of Judah? 20 [h]His servants arose and made a conspiracy [i]and struck down Joash in the house of [j]Millo, on the way that goes down to Silla. 21 It was [k]Jozacar the son of Shimeath and Jehozabad the son of [k]Shomer, his servants, who struck him down, so that he died. And they buried him with his fathers in the city of David, [l]and Amaziah his son reigned in his place.

Jehoahaz Reigns in Israel

13 In the twenty-third year of Joash the son of Ahaziah, king of Judah, Jehoahaz the son of Jehu began to reign over Israel in

is the means by which God's people have come to experience the forgiveness of sin, the hope of eternal life, and the restoration of fellowship with the God who created us for his glory and good pleasure.

13:1–6 Once again we encounter a king of Israel, Jehoahaz, who persists in evil and infidelity. Yet, with his back against the wall of human oppression, the king seeks the help of the covenant God whom he has forsaken. Remarkably, the Lord responds with mercy and sends a savior to deliver his people (v. 5). It is certainly true, therefore, that the Lord is "merciful and gracious, slow to anger, and abounding in steadfast love and faithfulness" (Ex. 34:6).

Chapter 12
3 [r]ch. 14:4; 15:35; 1 Kgs. 15:14; 22:43
4 [s]ch. 22:4 [t][Ex. 35:5; 1 Chr. 29:9]
9 [u][Mark 12:41; Luke 21:1]
10 [v][ch. 22:4]
12 [w][ch. 22:5, 6]
13 [x][2 Chr. 24:14] [y]1 Kgs. 7:50
15 [z]ch. 22:7
16 [a]Lev. 5:15, 18 [b]Lev. 4:24, 29 [c]Lev. 7:7; Num. 18:19
17 [d]ch. 8:12; [1 Kgs. 19:17] [e][2 Chr. 24:23, 24]

18 [f]ch. 16:8; 18:15, 16; 1 Kgs. 15:18; [ch. 14:14; 1 Kgs. 14:26] [g]ver. 4 **20** [h]For ver. 20, 21, see 2 Chr. 24:25-27 [i]ch. 14:5 [j][2 Sam. 5:9] **21** [k][2 Chr. 24:26] [l]ch. 14:1

Samaria, and he reigned seventeen years. 2 He did what was evil in the sight of the LORD and followed the sins of Jeroboam the son of Nebat, [m]which he made Israel to sin; he did not depart from them. 3 [n]And the anger of the LORD was kindled against Israel, and he gave them continually into the hand of [o]Hazael king of Syria and into the hand of [p]Ben-hadad the son of Hazael. 4 Then Jehoahaz [q]sought the favor of the LORD, and the LORD listened to him, [r]for he saw the oppression of Israel, how the king of Syria oppressed them. 5 (Therefore the LORD gave Israel [s]a savior, so that they escaped from the hand of the Syrians, and the people of Israel lived in [t]their homes as formerly. 6 Nevertheless, they did not depart from the sins of the house of Jeroboam, [m]which he made Israel to sin, but walked[1] in them; and [u]the Asherah also remained in Samaria.) 7 For there was not left to Jehoahaz an army of more than fifty horsemen and ten chariots and ten thousand footmen, for the king of Syria had destroyed them and made them like the dust [v]at threshing. 8 Now the rest of the acts of Jehoahaz and all that he did, and his might, are they not written in the Book of the Chronicles of the Kings of Israel? 9 So Jehoahaz slept with his fathers, and they buried him in Samaria, and Joash his son reigned in his place.

Jehoash Reigns in Israel

10 In the thirty-seventh year of Joash king of Judah, Jehoash[2] the son of Jehoahaz began to reign over Israel in Samaria, and he reigned sixteen years. 11 He also did what was evil in the sight of the LORD. He did not depart from all the sins of Jeroboam the son of Nebat, [m]which he made Israel to sin, but he walked in them. 12 [w]Now the rest of the acts of Joash [x]and all that he did, [y]and the might with which he fought against Amaziah king of Judah, are they not written in the Book of the Chronicles of the Kings of Israel? 13 So Joash slept with his fathers, and Jeroboam sat on his throne. And Joash was buried in Samaria with the kings of Israel.

The Death of Elisha

14 Now when Elisha had fallen sick with the illness of which he was to die, Joash king of Israel went down to him and wept before him, crying, [z]"My father, my father! The chariots of Israel and its horsemen!" 15 And Elisha said to him, "Take a bow and arrows." So he took a bow and arrows. 16 Then he said to the king of Israel, "Draw the bow," and he drew it. And Elisha laid his hands on the king's hands. 17 And he said, "Open the window eastward," and he opened it. Then Elisha said, "Shoot," and he shot. And he said, "The LORD's arrow of victory, the arrow of victory over Syria! For you shall fight the Syrians in [a]Aphek until you have made an end of them." 18 And he said, "Take the arrows," and he took them. And he said to the king of Israel, "Strike the ground with them." And he struck three times and stopped. 19 Then [b]the man of God was angry with him and said, "You should have struck five or six times; then you would have struck down Syria until you had made an end of it, but now you will strike down Syria only [c]three times."

[1] Septuagint, Syriac, Targum, Vulgate; Hebrew *he walked* [2] *Jehoash* is an alternate spelling of *Joash* (son of Jehoahaz) as in verses 9, 12–14; also verse 25

Chapter 13
2 [m]See 1 Kgs. 14:16
3 [n][Judg. 2:14] [o]ch. 8:12; [1 Kgs. 19:17] [p]ver. 24, 25
4 [q]Ex. 32:11; [Ps. 78:34] [r]ch. 14:26; Ex. 3:7, 9
5 [s][Judg. 3:9; Neh. 9:27] [t]See 2 Sam. 18:17
6 [m][See ver. 2 above] [u]1 Kgs. 16:33
7 [v][Amos 1:3]
11 [m][See ver. 2 above]
12 [w]ch. 14:15 [x]See ver. 14-19, 25 [y]See ch. 14:8-14
14 [z]ch. 2:12
17 [a]1 Kgs. 20:26
19 [b]See Deut. 33:1 [c]ver. 25

Having been delivered from the enemy by the Lord's savior, we might have expected both king and people to respond to the Lord's grace with renewed devotion and fidelity, but that did not happen. In the very next verse (2 Kings 13:6), we read that they did not turn from their sins but rather persisted in gross idolatry.

As we read through the accounts in the book of Kings, we might be tempted to become frustrated with the mercy of the Lord toward his people. They sin, become ensnared in their sin, cry out for help, the Lord delivers them, and then they return to their sin. The grace and mercy of the Lord in the midst of so much sin seems almost ridiculous, defiant of all moral equilibrium.

But this is exactly the point. The grace and mercy of the Lord shines brightest when it appears against the backdrop of our darkest sins. Our temptation in life is to minimize our sin so that we might appear more acceptable to those around us, especially those around us in the church. But facades of this kind only shroud the greatness of God's mercy and grace. As God's people learn to boast in God's grace, we will become less preoccupied with fabricating fig leaves to hide our sin. The masks come off. We are free to stop pretending.

20 So Elisha died, and they buried him. Now
bands of [d]Moabites used to invade the land in
the spring of the year. 21 And as a man was being
buried, behold, a marauding band was seen and
the man was thrown into the grave of Elisha,
and as soon as the man touched the bones of
Elisha, he revived and stood on his feet.
22 [e]Now Hazael king of Syria oppressed Israel
all the days of Jehoahaz. 23 [f]But the LORD was
gracious to them and had compassion on
them, [g]and he turned toward them, [h]because
of his covenant with Abraham, Isaac, and
Jacob, and would not destroy them, nor has
he cast them from his presence until now.
24 When Hazael king of Syria died, Ben-
hadad his son became king in his place. 25 Then
Jehoash the son of Jehoahaz took again from
Ben-hadad the son of Hazael the cities [i]that
he had taken from Jehoahaz his father in war.
[j]Three times Joash defeated him and recovered
the cities of Israel.

Amaziah Reigns in Judah

14 [k]In the [l]second year of Joash the son
of Joahaz, king of Israel, [m]Amaziah the
son of Joash, king of Judah, began to reign.
2 He was twenty-five years old when he began
to reign, and he reigned twenty-nine years in
Jerusalem. His mother's name was Jehoaddin
of Jerusalem. 3 And he did what was right
in the eyes of the LORD, yet not like David
his father. He did in all things as Joash his
father had done. 4 [n]But the high places were
not removed; [o]the people still sacrificed and
made offerings on the high places. 5 And as
soon as the royal power was [p]firmly in his
hand, he struck down his servants [q]who had
struck down the king his father. 6 But he did
not put to death the children of the murderers, according to what is written in the Book
of the Law of Moses, where the LORD commanded, [r]"Fathers shall not be put to death
because of their children, nor shall children
be put to death because of their fathers. But
each one shall die for his own sin."
7 [s]He struck down ten thousand Edomites
in [t]the Valley of Salt and took [u]Sela by storm,
and called it [v]Joktheel, which is its name to
this day.
8 [w]Then Amaziah sent messengers to Jehoash[1]
the son of Jehoahaz, son of Jehu, king of Israel,
saying, "Come, [x]let us look one another in the
face." 9 And Jehoash king of Israel sent word to
Amaziah king of Judah, [y]"A thistle on Lebanon
sent to a cedar on Lebanon, saying, 'Give your
daughter to my son for a wife,' and a wild beast
of Lebanon passed by and trampled down the
thistle. 10 You have indeed [z]struck down Edom,
[a]and your heart has lifted you up. Be content
with your glory, and stay at home, for why
should you provoke trouble so that you fall,
you and Judah with you?"
11 But Amaziah would not listen. So Jehoash
king of Israel went up, and he and Amaziah
king of Judah [x]faced one another in battle at
[b]Beth-shemesh, which belongs to Judah. 12 And
Judah was defeated by Israel, [c]and every man
fled to his home. 13 And Jehoash king of Israel
captured Amaziah king of Judah, the son of
Jehoash, son of Ahaziah, at Beth-shemesh, and
came to Jerusalem and broke down the wall of
Jerusalem for four hundred cubits,[2] from [d]the

[1] *Jehoash* is an alternate spelling of *Joash* (son of Jehoahaz) as in 13:9, 12–14; also verses 9, 11–16 [2] A *cubit* was about 18 inches or 45 centimeters

13:20–21 To fully appreciate the significance of the incident recorded in these two verses, it is important to remember that the Elijah and Elisha narratives were written to prepare God's people for judgment and exile from the land. Soon, the Israelites would be living in foreign lands. As the final narrative concerning the prophet Elisha, this passage sets before God's people the means by which ultimate restoration would occur: resurrection from the dead.

Israel's experience of exile in Babylon, Egypt, and various other nations is not unlike the Christian life. We too live as aliens and strangers in a world to which we do not belong (cf. 1 Pet. 2:11; Eph. 2:19). This world is not our home, and living as if it were will only lead to disappointment and despair. We must always remember the hope evidenced through the bones of Elisha: God's ability to fulfill his promises is not limited by death (Acts 23:6; 24:15; Rom. 6:5; 1 Cor. 15:12–42), and so we are free to live fearlessly and hopefully in this world that will soon pass away. And we do so mindful that the Son of God himself became a stranger and a sojourner on this earth, becoming one of us for our salvation. Living as exiles in this world, and as those who are already at home in the next, we follow in the footsteps of the Savior.

20 [d]ch. 1:1; 3:7; 24:2
22 [e]ch. 8:12
23 [f]ch. 14:27 [g][Ex. 2:24, 25] [h]Ex. 32:13
25 [i][ch. 10:32; 14:25] [j]ver. 18, 19; [Amos 1:4]

Chapter 14
1 [k]For ver. 1-6, see 2 Chr. 25:1-4 [l][ch. 13:10] [m]ch. 12:21
4 [n]See ch. 12:3 [o][ch. 16:4]
5 [p][ch. 15:19] [q]ch. 12:20
6 [r]Deut. 24:16; [Jer. 31:30; Ezek. 18:4, 20]
7 [s]2 Chr. 25:11 [t]2 Sam. 8:13; 1 Chr. 18:12; See Ps. 60 [u]Isa. 16:1 [v][Josh. 15:38]
8 [w]For ver. 8-14, see 2 Chr. 25:17-24 [x][ch. 23:29]
9 [y][Judg. 9:8-15]
10 [z]ver. 7 [a]Deut. 8:14; 2 Chr. 26:16; 32:25; Ezek. 28:2, 5, 17
11 [x][See ver. 8 above] [b]Josh. 15:10

12 [c]See 1 Sam. 4:10 **13** [d]Neh. 8:16; 12:39

Ephraim Gate to [e]the Corner Gate. 14 And he seized [f]all the gold and silver, and all the vessels that were found in the house of the LORD and in the treasuries of the king's house, also hostages, and he returned to Samaria.

15 [g]Now the rest of the acts of Jehoash that he did, and his might, and how he fought with Amaziah king of Judah, are they not written in the Book of the Chronicles of the Kings of Israel? 16 And Jehoash slept with his fathers and was buried in Samaria with the kings of Israel, and Jeroboam his son reigned in his place.

17 [h]Amaziah the son of Joash, king of Judah, lived fifteen years after the death of Jehoash son of Jehoahaz, king of Israel. 18 Now the rest of the deeds of Amaziah, are they not written in the Book of the Chronicles of the Kings of Judah? 19 And they made a conspiracy against him in Jerusalem, and he fled to [i]Lachish. But they sent after him to Lachish and put him to death there. 20 And they brought him on horses; and he was buried in Jerusalem with his fathers in the city of David. 21 And all the people of Judah took Azariah, who was sixteen years old, and made him king instead of his father Amaziah. 22 He built [j]Elath and restored it to Judah, after the king slept with his fathers.

Jeroboam II Reigns in Israel

23 In the fifteenth year of Amaziah the son of Joash, king of Judah, Jeroboam the son of Joash, king of Israel, began to reign in Samaria, and he reigned forty-one years. 24 And he did what was evil in the sight of the LORD. He did not depart from all the sins of Jeroboam the son of Nebat, [k]which he made Israel to sin. 25 [l]He restored the border of Israel [m]from Lebo-hamath as far as the Sea of [n]the Arabah, according to the word of the LORD, the God of Israel, which he spoke by his servant [o]Jonah the son of Amittai, the prophet, who was from [p]Gath-hepher. 26 For the LORD [q]saw that the affliction of Israel was very bitter, [r]for there was none left, bond or free, and there was none to help Israel. 27 [s]But the LORD had not said that he would blot out the name of Israel from under heaven, so he saved them by the hand of Jeroboam the son of Joash.

28 Now the rest of the acts of Jeroboam and all that he did, and his might, how he fought, and how he restored [t]Damascus and [u]Hamath to Judah in Israel, are they not written in the Book of the Chronicles of the Kings of Israel? 29 And Jeroboam slept with his fathers, the kings of Israel, and Zechariah his son reigned in his place.

Azariah Reigns in Judah

15 [v]In the twenty-seventh year of Jeroboam king of Israel, [w]Azariah the son of Amaziah, king of Judah, began to reign. 2 He was [x]sixteen years old when he began to reign, and he reigned fifty-two years in Jerusalem. His mother's name was Jecoliah of Jerusalem. 3 And he did what was right in the eyes of the LORD, according to all that his father Amaziah had done. 4 [y]Nevertheless, the high places were not taken away. The people still sacrificed and made offerings on the high places. 5 [z]And the LORD touched the king, so that he was a leper[1] to the day of his death, [a]and he lived in a separate house.[2] And Jotham the king's son was over the household, governing the people of the land. 6 Now the rest of the acts of Azariah, and all that he did, are they not written in the Book of the Chronicles of the Kings of Judah? 7 And Azariah slept with his fathers, and they buried him with his fathers [b]in the city of David, and Jotham his son reigned in his place.

Zechariah Reigns in Israel

8 In the thirty-eighth year of Azariah king of Judah, Zechariah the son of Jeroboam reigned over Israel in Samaria six months. 9 And he did what was evil in the sight of the LORD, as his fathers had done. He did not depart from

[1] *Leprosy* was a term for several skin diseases; see Leviticus 13 [2] The meaning of the Hebrew word is uncertain

14:23–27 Once again, an evil king was raised up to shepherd the ten northern tribes of Israel. Soon, the sin of the king and the people led to their affliction. Then, when Israel was helpless, the Lord used this evil king to save Israel from destruction.

The mercy of the Lord is not limited by human power. In fact, all human authority exists by the command of the Lord, as the instrument of his will (Rom. 13:1). Whether our leaders are virtuous or evil at any given time, God is still in control, and we should not despair.

13 [e] 2 Chr. 25:23; 26:9; Jer. 31:38; Zech. 14:10
14 [f] ch. 12:18; 1 Kgs. 7:51
15 [g] ch. 13:12, 13
17 [h] For ver. 17-22, see 2 Chr. 25:25–26:2
19 [i] See Josh. 10:3
22 [j] ch. 16:6; Deut. 2:8; [2 Chr. 8:17; 26:2]
24 [k] See 1 Kgs. 14:16

25 [l] [ch. 10:32; 13:25] [m] See 1 Kgs. 8:65 [n] See Deut. 3:17 [o] Jonah 1:1; [Matt. 12:39, 40] [p] Josh. 19:13 **26** [q] Ex. 3:7; [ch. 13:4] [r] See Deut. 32:36 **27** [s] [ch. 13:5, 23] **28** [t] [2 Sam. 8:6; 1 Kgs. 11:24; 1 Chr. 18:5, 6] [u] 2 Chr. 8:3 **Chapter 15** **1** [v] [ch. 14:17] [w] [ver. 13, 30, 32, 34; 2 Chr. 26:1] **2** [x] 2 Chr. 26:3, 4 **4** [y] See ch. 12:3 **5** [z] For ver. 5-7, see 2 Chr. 26:21-23 [a] See Lev. 13:46 **7** [b] [2 Chr. 26:23]

the sins of Jeroboam the son of Nebat, [c]which
he made Israel to sin. 10 Shallum the son of
Jabesh conspired against him and [d]struck
him down at Ibleam and put him to death
and reigned in his place. 11 Now the rest of the
deeds of Zechariah, behold, they are written
in the Book of the Chronicles of the Kings of
Israel. 12 (This was [e]the promise of the LORD
that he gave to Jehu, "Your sons shall sit on
the throne of Israel to the fourth generation."
And so it came to pass.)

Shallum Reigns in Israel

13 Shallum the son of Jabesh began to reign in
the thirty-ninth year of [f]Uzziah[1] king of Judah,
and he reigned one month in [g]Samaria. 14 Then
Menahem the son of Gadi came up from
[h]Tirzah and came to Samaria, and he struck
down Shallum the son of Jabesh in Samaria
and put him to death and reigned in his place.
15 Now the rest of the deeds of Shallum, and
the conspiracy that he made, behold, they are
written in the Book of the Chronicles of the
Kings of Israel. 16 At that time Menahem sacked
Tiphsah and all who were in it and its territory
from Tirzah on, because they did not open it
to him. Therefore he sacked it, [i]and he ripped
open all the women in it who were pregnant.

Menahem Reigns in Israel

17 In the thirty-ninth year of Azariah king
of Judah, Menahem the son of Gadi began
to reign over Israel, and he reigned ten years
in Samaria. 18 And he did what was evil in the
sight of the LORD. He did not depart all his
days from all the sins of Jeroboam the son
of Nebat, which he made Israel to sin. 19 [j]Pul[2]
the king of Assyria came against the land, and
Menahem gave [j]Pul a thousand talents[3] of silver, that he might help him [k]to confirm his
hold on the royal power. 20 Menahem exacted
the money from Israel, that is, from all the
wealthy men, fifty shekels[4] of silver from every
man, to give to the king of Assyria. So the
king of Assyria turned back and did not stay
there in the land. 21 Now the rest of the deeds
of Menahem and all that he did, are they not
written in the Book of the Chronicles of the
Kings of Israel? 22 And Menahem slept with
his fathers, and Pekahiah his son reigned in
his place.

Pekahiah Reigns in Israel

23 In the fiftieth year of Azariah king of
Judah, Pekahiah the son of Menahem began
to reign over Israel in Samaria, and he reigned
two years. 24 And he did what was evil in the
sight of the LORD. He did not turn away from
the sins of Jeroboam the son of Nebat, [c]which
he made Israel to sin. 25 And Pekah the son of
Remaliah, his captain, conspired against him
with fifty men of the people of Gilead, and
struck him down in Samaria, in the citadel of
the king's house with Argob and Arieh; he put
him to death and reigned in his place. 26 Now
the rest of the deeds of Pekahiah and all that
he did, behold, they are written in the Book of
the Chronicles of the Kings of Israel.

Pekah Reigns in Israel

27 In the fifty-second year of Azariah king of
Judah, Pekah the son of Remaliah began to
reign over Israel in Samaria, and he reigned
twenty years. 28 And he did what was evil in
the sight of the LORD. He did not depart from
the sins of Jeroboam the son of Nebat, [l]which
he made Israel to sin.
29 In the days of Pekah king of Israel,
[m]Tiglath-pileser king of Assyria came and
captured [n]Ijon, [o]Abel-beth-maacah, Janoah,
[p]Kedesh, [q]Hazor, Gilead, and [r]Galilee, all the
land of Naphtali, and he carried the people
captive to Assyria. 30 Then Hoshea the son of
Elah made a conspiracy against Pekah the son
of Remaliah and struck him down and put
him to death and reigned in his place, [s]in the
twentieth year of Jotham the son of Uzziah.
31 Now the rest of the acts of Pekah and all that

[1] Another name for *Azariah* [2] Another name for *Tiglath-pileser III* (compare verse 29) [3] A *talent* was about 75 pounds or 34 kilograms
[4] A *shekel* was about 2/5 ounce or 11 grams

15:1–16:20 One by one, the kings of Israel and Judah come and go—Azariah, Zechariah, Shallum, Menahem, Pekahiah, Pekah, Jotham, Ahaz. And with each passing king, the same old problems remain among God's people: "The people still sacrificed and made offerings on the high places" (15:35).

A king to supersede and counter all kings is needed—a king who will not only lead the people out of sin but will provide a way for the people who have followed these kings (and others like them) not to have their sins count against them.

9 [c] See 1 Kgs. 14:16
10 [d] [Amos 7:9]
12 [e] ch. 10:30
13 [f] [ver. 1] [g] 1 Kgs. 16:24
14 [h] 1 Kgs. 14:17
16 [i] See ch. 8:12
19 [j] 1 Chr. 5:26 [k] [ch. 14:5]
24 [c] [See ver. 9 above]
28 [l] See 1 Kgs. 14:16
29 [m] ch. 16:7; [1 Chr. 5:6, 26; 2 Chr. 28:20] [n] 1 Kgs. 15:20 [o] 2 Sam. 20:14, 15 [p] Josh. 19:37 [q] Josh. 11:1; Judg. 4:2; 1 Kgs. 9:15 [r] Isa. 9:1
30 [s] [ch. 17:1]

he did, behold, they are written in the Book of
the Chronicles of the Kings of Israel.

Jotham Reigns in Judah

32 In the second year of Pekah the son of
Remaliah, king of Israel, Jotham the son of
Uzziah, king of Judah, began to reign. 33 He
was [t]twenty-five years old when he began
to reign, and he reigned sixteen years in
Jerusalem. His mother's name was Jerusha
the daughter of Zadok. 34 And he did what
was right in the eyes of the LORD, [u]accord-
ing to all that his father Uzziah had done.
35 [v]Nevertheless, the high places were not
removed. The people still sacrificed and
made offerings on the high places. He built
[w]the upper gate of the house of the LORD.
36 Now the rest of the acts of Jotham and all
that he did, are they not written in the Book
of the Chronicles of the Kings of Judah? 37 In
those days the LORD began to send [x]Rezin the
king of Syria and [x]Pekah the son of Remaliah
against Judah. 38 Jotham slept with his fathers
and was buried with his fathers in the city of
David his father, and Ahaz his son reigned in
his place.

Ahaz Reigns in Judah

16 In the seventeenth year of Pekah the
son of Remaliah, Ahaz the son of
Jotham, king of Judah, began to reign. 2 Ahaz
was [y]twenty years old when he began to reign,
and he reigned sixteen years in Jerusalem. And
he did not do what was right in the eyes of
the LORD his God, as his father David had
done, 3 but he walked in the way of the kings
of Israel. [z]He even burned his son as an offering,[1] [a]according to the despicable practices of
the nations whom the LORD drove out before
the people of Israel. 4 [b]And he sacrificed and
made offerings [c]on the high places and on the
hills and under every green tree.

5 [d]Then Rezin king of Syria and [d]Pekah the
son of Remaliah, king of Israel, came up to
wage war on Jerusalem, and they besieged
Ahaz [e]but could not conquer him. 6 At that
time Rezin the king of Syria recovered [f]Elath
for Syria and drove the men of Judah from
[f]Elath, and the Edomites came to Elath, where
they dwell to this day. 7 [g]So Ahaz sent messengers to [h]Tiglath-pileser king of Assyria, saying,
"I am your servant and your son. Come up and
rescue me from the hand of the king of Syria
and from the hand of the king of Israel, who
are attacking me." 8 Ahaz also [i]took the silver
and gold that was found in the house of the
LORD and in the treasures of the king's house
and sent a present to the king of Assyria. 9 [j]And
the king of Assyria listened to him. The king
of Assyria marched up against Damascus [k]and
took it, carrying its people captive to [l]Kir, and
he killed Rezin.

10 When King Ahaz went to Damascus to
meet [m]Tiglath-pileser king of Assyria, he saw
the altar that was at Damascus. And King
Ahaz sent to [n]Uriah the priest a model of the
altar, and its pattern, exact in all its details.
11 And Uriah the priest built the altar; in accordance with all that King Ahaz had sent from
Damascus, so Uriah the priest made it, before
King Ahaz arrived from Damascus. 12 And
when the king came from Damascus, the king
viewed the altar. [o]Then the king drew near
to the altar and went up on it 13 and burned
his burnt offering and his grain offering and
poured his drink offering and threw the blood
of his peace offerings on the altar. 14 And [p]the
bronze altar that was before the LORD he
removed [q]from the front of the house, from
the place between [r]his altar and the house of
the LORD, and put it on the north side of [r]his
altar. 15 And King Ahaz commanded Uriah the
priest, saying, "On the great altar burn [s]the
morning burnt offering and the evening grain
offering and the king's burnt offering and his
grain offering, with the burnt offering of all
the people of the land, and their grain offering and their drink offering. And throw on it
all the blood of the burnt offering and all the
blood of the sacrifice, but [t]the bronze altar
shall be for me to inquire by." 16 Uriah the
priest did all this, as King Ahaz commanded.

17 And King Ahaz cut off the frames of the
stands and removed the basin from them, and
he took down [u]the sea[2] from off the bronze
oxen that were under it and put it on a stone
pedestal. 18 And the covered way for the
Sabbath that had been built inside the house
and the outer entrance for the king he caused
to go around the house of the LORD, because of
the king of Assyria. 19 Now the rest of the acts of

[1] Or *made his son pass through the fire* [2] Compare 1 Kings 7:23

33 [t] For ver. 33, 34, see 2 Chr. 27:1, 2 **34** [u] ver. 3; [2 Chr. 27:6] **35** [v] See ch. 12:3 [w] 2 Chr. 23:20; 27:3 **37** [x] ch. 16:5; Isa. 7:1 **Chapter 16** **2** [y] For ver. 2-4, see 2 Chr. 28:1-4 **3** [z] [Ps. 106:37, 38]; See Lev. 18:21 [a] ch. 21:2; [Deut. 12:31; 18:9] **4** [b] [ch. 14:4] [c] Deut. 12:2; 1 Kgs. 14:23 **5** [d] ch. 15:37 [e] [2 Chr. 28:5, 6] **6** [f] See ch. 14:22 **7** [g] See 2 Chr. 28:16 [h] See ch. 15:29 **8** [i] See ch. 12:18 **9** [j] [2 Chr. 28:21] [k] [Amos 1:5] [l] Isa. 22:6; Amos 1:5; 9:7 **10** [m] See ch. 15:29 [n] Isa. 8:2 **12** [o] See 2 Chr. 26:16-19 **14** [p] 2 Chr. 4:1 [q] [Ex. 40:6, 29] [r] ver. 11 **15** [s] Ex. 29:39-41 [t] ver. 14 **17** [u] 1 Kgs. 7:23, 25

Ahaz that he did, are they not written [v]in the Book of the Chronicles of the Kings of Judah? 20 And Ahaz slept with his fathers and [w]was buried with his fathers in the city of David, and Hezekiah his son reigned in his place.

Hoshea Reigns in Israel

17 In the twelfth year of Ahaz king of Judah, [x]Hoshea the son of Elah began to reign in Samaria over Israel, and he reigned nine years. 2 And he did what was evil in the sight of the LORD, yet not as the kings of Israel who were before him. 3 [y]Against him came up [z]Shalmaneser king of Assyria. And Hoshea became his vassal and paid him tribute. 4 But the king of Assyria found treachery in Hoshea, for he had sent messengers to So, king of Egypt, and offered no tribute to the king of Assyria, as he had done year by year. Therefore the king of Assyria shut him up and bound him in prison. 5 Then the king of Assyria invaded all the land and came to Samaria, and for three years he besieged it.

The Fall of Israel

6 In the ninth year of Hoshea, the king of Assyria [a]captured Samaria, [b]and he carried the Israelites away to Assyria [c]and placed them in Halah, and on the Habor, the river of [d]Gozan, and in the cities of [e]the Medes.

Exile Because of Idolatry

7 And this occurred because the people of Israel had sinned against the LORD their God, [f]who had brought them up out of the land of Egypt from under the hand of Pharaoh king of Egypt, and had feared other gods 8 [g]and walked in the customs of the nations whom the LORD drove out before the people of Israel, [h]and in the customs that the kings of Israel had practiced. 9 And the people of Israel did secretly against the LORD their God things that were not right. They built for themselves high places in all their towns, [i]from watchtower to fortified city. 10 They set up for themselves [j]pillars and Asherim on every high hill and under every green tree, 11 and there they made offerings on all the high places, as the nations did whom the LORD carried away before them. And they did wicked things, provoking the LORD to anger, 12 and they served idols, [k]of which the LORD had said to them, "You shall not do this." 13 Yet the LORD [l]warned Israel and Judah [m]by every prophet [n]and every seer, saying, [o]"Turn from your evil ways and keep my commandments and my statutes, in accordance with all the Law that I commanded your fathers, and that I sent to you by my servants the prophets."

14 But they would not listen, [p]but were stubborn, as their fathers had been, who did not believe in the LORD their God. 15 They despised his statutes [q]and his covenant that he made with their fathers and the warnings that he gave them. They went after [r]false idols [s]and became false, and they followed the nations that were around them, concerning whom the [t]LORD had commanded them that they should not do like them. 16 And they abandoned all the commandments of the LORD their God,

17:6–40 For God's people, judgment is just the beginning of his mercy. The events recorded in 2 Kings 17 describe the fall, destruction, and exile of the northern kingdom of Israel, but note that the actual description of this act of judgment is quite brief: "In the ninth year of Hoshea, the king of Assyria captured Samaria, and he carried the Israelites away to Assyria and placed them in Halah, and on the Habor, the river of Gozan, and in the cities of the Medes" (v. 6). In this particular account, the author has chosen to focus not on the act of God's judgment but rather on the reasons for it.

It may be tempting to regard Israel's destruction as the Lord's inability to protect and provide for his people. In fact, the Lord anticipated such explanation some seven hundred years earlier, when he predicted that his conquered people would say, "Have not these evils come upon us because our God is not among us?" (Deut. 31:17). But the text is clear; Israel's destruction comes because of Israel's sin: "And this occurred because the people of Israel had sinned against the LORD their God" (2 Kings 17:7; see also vv. 7–12)—and because by this sin they broke covenant with the Lord their God (vv. 34–40; cf. 18:11–12).

But why did Israel persist in their idolatry and sin? What prevented their obedience to the covenant? The answer gets to the "heart" of the issue. Israel sinned because they lacked faith. They did not believe or trust in the Lord (17:14). We are reminded that both sin and its accompanying judgment are really the fruit of unbelief. Sin is a lack of genuine faith; faith is the true path to obedience.

19 [v][2 Chr. 28:26]
20 [w][2 Chr. 28:27]

Chapter 17

1 [x][ch. 15:30]
3 [y]For ver. 3-7, see ch. 18:9-12 [z][Hos. 10:14]
6 [a][Hos. 13:16] [b][Lev. 26:32, 33; Deut. 28:36, 64; 29:27, 28] [c]ch. 18:11; [1 Chr. 5:26] [d]Isa. 37:12 [e]Ezra 6:2; Isa. 13:17; 21:2; Jer. 51:11, 28
7 [f]ver. 36; Lev. 25:38; See Ex. 20:2
8 [g]Lev. 18:3; Deut. 18:9 [h]ver. 19; ch. 16:3
9 [i]ch. 18:8
10 [j]See Ex. 23:24
12 [k]See Ex. 20:4
13 [l]Neh. 9:30 [m]ver. 23 [n]See 1 Sam. 9:9 [o]Jer. 18:11; 25:5; 35:15
14 [p]Deut. 9:6; 2 Chr. 30:8; [Deut. 31:27; Acts 7:51]
15 [q]Deut. 29:25 [r]Deut. 32:21; [1 Kgs. 16:13] [s]Jer. 2:5; Rom. 1:21 [t]Deut. 12:30, 31

and made for themselves metal images of
[u]two calves; and they [v]made an Asherah and
[w]worshiped all the host of heaven and served
[x]Baal. 17 [y]And they burned their sons and their
daughters as offerings[1] and used [z]divination
and [a]omens and [b]sold themselves to do evil
in the sight of the LORD, provoking him to
anger. 18 Therefore the LORD was very angry
with Israel and removed them out of his sight.
None was left but [c]the tribe of Judah only.

19 [d]Judah also did not keep the commandments of the LORD their God, but walked in
the customs that Israel had introduced. 20 And
the LORD rejected all the descendants of Israel
and afflicted them [e]and gave them into the
hand of plunderers, until he had cast them
out of his sight.

21 [f]When he had torn Israel from the house of
David, [g]they made Jeroboam the son of Nebat
king. And Jeroboam drove Israel from following the LORD [h]and made them commit great
sin. 22 The people of Israel walked in all the
sins that Jeroboam did. They did not depart
from them, 23 until the LORD removed Israel
out of his sight, [i]as he had spoken by all his
servants the prophets. [j]So Israel was exiled
from their own land to Assyria until this day.

Assyria Resettles Samaria

24 [k]And the king of Assyria brought people
from [l]Babylon, Cuthah, [m]Avva, [n]Hamath, and
[o]Sepharvaim, and placed them in the cities of
Samaria instead of the people of Israel. And
they took possession of Samaria and lived
in its cities. 25 And at the beginning of their
dwelling there, they did not fear the LORD.
Therefore the LORD sent lions among them,
which killed some of them. 26 So the king
of Assyria was told, "The nations that you
have carried away and placed in the cities of
Samaria do not know the law of the god of
the land. Therefore he has sent lions among
them, and behold, they are killing them,
because they do not know the law of the god
of the land." 27 Then the king of Assyria commanded, "Send there one of the priests whom
you carried away from there, and let him[2] go
and dwell there and teach them the law of the
god of the land." 28 So one of the priests whom
they had carried away from Samaria came and
lived in [p]Bethel and taught them how they
should fear the LORD.

29 But every nation still made gods of its own
and put them [q]in the shrines of the high places
that the Samaritans had made, every nation
in the cities in which they lived. 30 The men
of [r]Babylon made Succoth-benoth, the men
of Cuth made Nergal, the men of Hamath
made Ashima, 31 and the Avvites made Nibhaz
and Tartak; and the Sepharvites [s]burned
their children in the fire to [t]Adrammelech
and Anammelech, the gods of [u]Sepharvaim.
32 [v]They also feared the LORD [w]and appointed
from among themselves all sorts of people as
priests of the high places, who sacrificed for
them in the shrines of [x]the high places. 33 So
they feared the LORD but also served their own
gods, after the manner of the nations from
among whom they had been carried away.

34 To this day they do according to the former manner. They do not fear the LORD, and
they do not follow the statutes or the rules or
the law or the commandment that the LORD
commanded the children of Jacob, [y]whom he
named Israel. 35 The LORD made a covenant
with them and commanded them, [z]"You shall
not fear other gods [a]or bow yourselves to them
or serve them or sacrifice to them, 36 but [b]you

[1] Or *made their sons and their daughters pass through the fire* [2] Syriac, Vulgate; Hebrew *them*

16 [u]See 1 Kgs. 12:28 [v]1 Kgs. 14:15, 23; 15:13; 16:33 [w]ch. 21:3; 23:5; [Deut. 4:19] [x]ch. 11:18; 1 Kgs. 16:31; 22:53
17 [y]ch. 16:3; [Lev. 18:21; Ezek. 23:37] [z][Deut. 18:10] [a][Lev. 19:26] [b]See 1 Kgs. 21:20
18 [c][1 Kgs. 11:13, 32; 12:20]
19 [d][Jer. 3:8]
20 [e]Judg. 2:14; [ch. 13:3; 15:29]
21 [f]1 Kgs. 11:11, 31 [g]1 Kgs. 12:20 [h]See 1 Kgs. 14:16
23 [i]ver. 13 [j]ver. 6
24 [k]Ezra 4:2, 10 [l]ver. 30 [m][ch. 18:34] [n]See 1 Kgs. 8:65 [o]ver. 31; ch. 18:34; 19:13
28 [p]1 Kgs. 12:29
29 [q]1 Kgs. 12:31; 13:32
30 [r]ver. 24
31 [s]See ver. 17 [t][ch. 19:37]

The good news about Israel's judgment is that the Lord's judgment of his covenant people at this time is not the final word. After judgment, God also promised restoration, but restoration by means of a changed heart and, therefore, the gift of faith in order to believe: "And the LORD your God will circumcise your heart and the heart of your offspring, so that you will love the LORD your God with all your heart and with all your soul, that you may live" (Deut. 30:6; see also Deut. 30:1–10). Because the Lord is faithful to keep all of his covenant promises, we can look upon the Lord's judgment of Israel as the beginning of a new work, the Lord's work to circumcise (i.e., purify) the heart.

This work was accomplished by yet another act of judgment, the crucifixion of the Son of God. Thus, by faith, with circumcised hearts, we look upon Christ's judgment as the source of our own hope. For God's people, Christ's judgment on the cross two thousand years ago is our day of judgment—and it is already behind us.

[u]ver. 24 **32** [v][Zeph. 1:5] [w]See 1 Kgs. 12:31 [x]ver. 29 **34** [y]Gen. 32:28; 35:10; 1 Kgs. 18:31 **35** [z]Judg. 6:10 [a]See Ex. 20:5 **36** [b]Deut. 6:13

shall fear the LORD, [c]who brought you out of
the land of Egypt with great power and [d]with
an outstretched arm. You shall bow yourselves
to him, and to him you shall sacrifice. 37 And
the statutes and the rules and the law and the
commandment that he wrote for you, [e]you
shall always be careful to do. [z]You shall not
fear other gods, 38 and [f]you shall not forget the
covenant that I have made with you. [z]You shall
not fear other gods, 39 but [b]you shall fear the
LORD your God, and he will deliver you out
of the hand of all your enemies." 40 However,
they would not listen, but they did according
to their former manner.

41 [g]So these nations feared the LORD and also
served their carved images. Their children did
likewise, and their children's children—as
their fathers did, so they do to this day.

Hezekiah Reigns in Judah

18 [h]In the third year of Hoshea son of
Elah, king of Israel, [i]Hezekiah the son
of Ahaz, king of Judah, began to reign. 2 He
was [j]twenty-five years old when he began to
reign, and he reigned twenty-nine years in
Jerusalem. His mother's name was [k]Abi the
daughter of Zechariah. 3 [l]And he did what was
right in the eyes of the LORD, according to all
that David his father had done. 4 [m]He removed
the high places and broke the [n]pillars and cut
down [o]the Asherah. And he broke in pieces
[p]the bronze serpent that Moses had made,
for until those days the people of Israel had
made offerings to it (it was called Nehushtan).[1]
5 [q]He trusted in the LORD, the God of Israel, [r]so
that there was none like him among all the
kings of Judah after him, nor among those
who were before him. 6 [s]For he held fast to the
LORD. He did not depart from following him,
but kept the commandments that the LORD
commanded Moses. 7 [t]And the LORD was with
him; wherever he went out, [u]he prospered.
He rebelled against the king of Assyria and
would not serve him. 8 [v]He struck down the
Philistines as far as Gaza and its territory,
[w]from watchtower to fortified city.

9 In the fourth year of King Hezekiah, which
was the seventh year of Hoshea son of Elah,
king of Israel, [x]Shalmaneser king of Assyria
came up against Samaria and besieged it,
10 and at the end of three years he took it. In
the sixth year of Hezekiah, which was the
ninth year of Hoshea king of Israel, Samaria
was taken. 11 The king of Assyria carried the
Israelites away to Assyria and put them in
[y]Halah, and on the [y]Habor, [y]the river of Gozan,
and in the cities of the Medes, 12 because they
did not obey the voice of the LORD their God
but transgressed his covenant, even all that
Moses the servant of the LORD commanded.
They neither listened nor obeyed.

Sennacherib Attacks Judah

13 [z]In the fourteenth year of King Hezekiah,
Sennacherib king of Assyria came up against
all the fortified cities of Judah and took them.
14 And Hezekiah king of Judah sent to the king
of Assyria at Lachish, saying, "I have done
wrong; withdraw from me. Whatever you
impose on me I will bear." [a]And the king of
Assyria required of Hezekiah king of Judah
three hundred talents[2] of silver and thirty talents of gold. 15 And Hezekiah [b]gave him all the
silver that was found in the house of the LORD
and in the treasuries of the king's house. 16 At
that time Hezekiah stripped the gold from
the doors of the temple of the LORD and from
the doorposts that Hezekiah king of Judah
had overlaid and gave it to the king of Assyria.
17 And the king of Assyria sent the [c]Tartan,
the Rab-saris, and the Rabshakeh with a
great army from Lachish to King Hezekiah
at Jerusalem. And they went up and came to
Jerusalem. When they arrived, they came and

[1] *Nehushtan* sounds like the Hebrew for both *bronze* and *serpent* [2] A *talent* was about 75 pounds or 34 kilograms

18:13–19:37 In whom do we trust, really trust, when we encounter the great trials of life? This is the important question set before God's people in 2 Kings 18 and 19—"In whom do you now trust?" (18:20; cf. 19:10). The northern ten tribes of Israel had been destroyed and sent into exile by Assyria. Now, only Judah remained in the south, and the southern kingdom was also confronted by the threat from Assyria. It appears that in Judah there were fewer than two thousand men able to mount horses and defend the land (18:23). By way of contrast, there were more than 185,000 people in the Assyrian army. By any human estimate, Judah did not stand a chance.

36 [c] ver. 7 [d] Ex. 6:6; Deut. 4:34
37 [e] Deut. 5:32 [z] [See ver. 35 above]
38 [f] Deut. 4:23 [z] [See ver. 35 above]
39 [b] [See ver. 36 above]
41 [g] [Zeph. 1:5]

Chapter 18
1 [h] [ch. 16:2; 17:1] [i] 2 Chr. 28:27; Matt. 1:9
2 [j] For ver. 2, 3, see 2 Chr. 29:1, 2 [k] [2 Chr. 29:1]
3 [l] ch. 20:3; 2 Chr. 31:20 **4** [m] ver. 22; 2 Chr. 31:1 [n] ch. 17:10; See Ex. 23:24 [o] ch. 17:16; See Deut. 16:21 [p] Num. 21:8, 9 **5** [q] ch. 19:10 [r] ch. 23:25 **6** [s] [Deut. 10:20; Josh. 23:8] **7** [t] 2 Chr. 15:2 [u] [ch. 16:7] **8** [v] [Isa. 14:29] [w] ch. 17:9 **9** [x] For ver. 9-12, see ch. 17:3-7 **11** [y] ch. 17:6; 1 Chr. 5:26 **13** [z] For ver. 13-37, see 2 Chr. 32:1-20; Isa. 36:1-22 **14** [a] [ch. 23:33] **15** [b] [ch. 12:18; 16:8] **17** [c] Isa. 20:1

stood by [d]the conduit of the upper pool, which is on the highway to the Washer's Field. 18 And when they called for the king, there came out to them [e]Eliakim the son of Hilkiah, who was over the household, and [f]Shebnah the secretary, and Joah the son of Asaph, the recorder.

19 And the Rabshakeh said to them, "Say to Hezekiah, 'Thus says the great king, the king of Assyria: On what do you rest this trust of yours? 20 Do you think that mere words are strategy and power for war? In whom do you now trust, that you have rebelled against me? 21 Behold, you are trusting now in Egypt, that broken reed of [g]a staff, which will pierce the hand of any man who leans on it. Such is Pharaoh king of Egypt to all who trust in him. 22 But if you say to me, "We trust in the LORD our God," is it not he [h]whose high places and altars Hezekiah has removed, saying to Judah and to Jerusalem, "You shall worship before this altar in Jerusalem"? 23 Come now, make a wager with my master the king of Assyria: I will give you two thousand horses, if you are able on your part to set riders on them. 24 How then can you repulse a single captain among the least of my master's servants, when you trust in Egypt for chariots and for horsemen? 25 Moreover, is it without the LORD that I have come up against this place to destroy it? The LORD said to me, Go up against this land, and destroy it.'"

26 Then [e]Eliakim the son of Hilkiah, and [f]Shebnah, and Joah, said to the Rabshakeh, "Please speak to your servants in [i]Aramaic, for we understand it. Do not speak to us in the language of Judah within the hearing of the people who are on the wall." 27 But the Rabshakeh said to them, "Has my master sent me to speak these words to your master and to you, and not to the men sitting on the wall, who are doomed with you to eat their own dung and to drink their own urine?"

28 Then the Rabshakeh stood and called out in a loud voice in the language of Judah: "Hear the word of the great king, the king of Assyria! 29 Thus says the king: 'Do not let Hezekiah deceive you, for he will not be able to deliver you out of my[1] hand. 30 Do not let Hezekiah make you trust in the LORD by saying, The LORD will surely deliver us, and this city will not be given into the hand of the king of Assyria.' 31 Do not listen to Hezekiah, for thus says the king of Assyria: 'Make your peace with me[2] and come out to me. Then [j]each one of you will eat of his own vine, and each one of his own fig tree, and each one of you will drink the water of his own cistern, 32 until I come and take you away to a land like your own land, [k]a land of grain and wine, a land of bread and vineyards, a land of olive trees and [l]honey, that you may live, and not die. And do not listen to Hezekiah when he misleads you by saying, "The LORD will deliver us." 33 [m]Has any of the gods of the nations ever delivered his land out of the hand of the king of Assyria? 34 [n]Where are the gods of [o]Hamath and [p]Arpad? Where are the gods of Sepharvaim, Hena, and [q]Ivvah? Have they delivered Samaria out of my hand? 35 Who among all the gods of the lands have delivered their lands out of my hand, [r]that the LORD should deliver Jerusalem out of my hand?'"

36 But the people were silent and answered him not a word, for the king's command was, "Do not answer him." 37 Then [s]Eliakim the son of Hilkiah, who was over the household, and Shebna the secretary, and Joah the son of Asaph, the recorder, came to Hezekiah [t]with their clothes torn and told him the words of the Rabshakeh.

Isaiah Reassures Hezekiah

19 [u]As soon as King Hezekiah heard it, [t]he tore his clothes and [v]covered himself with sackcloth and went into the house of the LORD. 2 And he sent Eliakim, who was

[1] Hebrew *his* [2] Hebrew *Make a blessing with me*

17[d] Isa. 7:3; [ch. 20:20]
18[e] Isa. 22:20 [f] Isa. 22:15
21[g] [Ezek. 29:6, 7]; See Isa. 30:2, 3, 7
22[h] [ver. 4; 2 Chr. 31:1]
26[e] [See ver. 18 above] [f] [See ver. 18 above] [i] [Ezra 4:7; Dan. 2:4]
31[j] [1 Kgs. 4:25]
32[k] Deut. 8:7, 8 [l] See Ex. 3:8
33[m] ch. 19:12; [Isa. 10:10, 11]
34[n] [ch. 19:13] [o] See 1 Kgs. 8:65 [p] Isa. 10:9 [q] [ch. 17:24]
35[r] [Dan. 3:15]
37[s] ver. 18, 26; ch. 19:2 [t] See Josh. 7:6
Chapter 19
1[u] For ver. 1-37, see 2 Chr. 32:20-22; Isa. 37:1-38 [t] [See ch. 18:37 above] [v] See 2 Sam. 3:31

The conflict began as a battle of words, almost like something that occurs in our own minds as we face difficulties: "Thus says the great king, the king of Assyria" (18:19) versus "Thus says the LORD" (19:6). The battle rages as we listen to various competing voices. The foreign king promises godlike deliverance for Judah, even a new promised land (18:31–32). The foreign king mocks the gods of his former rivals and characterizes the one true God in the same manner (18:33–35). But in those times when all other hope is exhausted, the Lord is pleased to deliver his people as they seek his face in prayer (19:14–19).

over the household, and Shebna the secretary,
and the senior priests, [v]covered with sackcloth,
to the prophet Isaiah the son of Amoz. 3 They
said to him, "Thus says Hezekiah, This day is
a day of distress, of rebuke, and of disgrace;
children have come to the point of birth, and
there is no strength to bring them forth. 4 [w]It
may be that the LORD your God heard all the
words of the Rabshakeh, whom his master
the king of Assyria has sent [x]to mock the living God, and will rebuke the words that the
LORD your God has heard; therefore lift up
your prayer for [y]the remnant that is left."
5 When the servants of King Hezekiah came
to Isaiah, 6 Isaiah said to them, "Say to your
master, 'Thus says the LORD: Do not be afraid
because of the words that you have heard, with
which [z]the servants of the king of Assyria have
[a]reviled me. 7 Behold, I will put a spirit in him,
so that [b]he shall hear a rumor and return to
his own land, and I will make him [c]fall by the
sword in his own land.' "

Sennacherib Defies the LORD

8 The Rabshakeh returned, and found the
king of Assyria fighting against [d]Libnah,
for he heard that the king had left [e]Lachish.
9 [f]Now the king heard concerning Tirhakah
king of Cush, "Behold, he has set out to fight
against you." So he sent messengers again to
Hezekiah, saying, 10 "Thus shall you speak to
Hezekiah king of Judah: 'Do not let your God
[g]in whom you trust deceive you by promising that [h]Jerusalem will not be given into the
hand of the king of Assyria. 11 Behold, you have
heard what the kings of Assyria have done to
all lands, devoting them to destruction. And
shall you be delivered? 12 [i]Have the gods of the
nations delivered them, the nations that my
fathers destroyed, [j]Gozan, [k]Haran, Rezeph,
and the people of [l]Eden who were in Telassar?
13 [m]Where is the king of Hamath, the king of
Arpad, the king of the city of Sepharvaim, the
king of Hena, or the king of Ivvah?' "

Hezekiah's Prayer

14 Hezekiah received [n]the letter from the
hand of the messengers and read it; and
Hezekiah went up to the house of the LORD
and spread it before the LORD. 15 And Hezekiah
prayed before the LORD and said: "O LORD, the
God of Israel, [o]enthroned above the cherubim,
[p]you are the God, you alone, of all the kingdoms of the earth; you have made heaven and
earth. 16 [q]Incline your ear, O LORD, and hear;
[r]open your eyes, O LORD, and see; and hear
the words of Sennacherib, which he has sent
[s]to mock the living God. 17 Truly, O LORD, the
kings of Assyria have laid waste the nations
and their lands 18 and have cast their gods into
the fire, for they were not gods, [t]but the work
of men's hands, wood and stone. Therefore
they were destroyed. 19 So now, O LORD our
God, save us, please, from his hand, [u]that all
the kingdoms of the earth may know that
[p]you, O LORD, are God alone."

Isaiah Prophesies Sennacherib's Fall

20 Then Isaiah the son of Amoz sent to
Hezekiah, saying, "Thus says the LORD,
the God of Israel: Your prayer to me about
Sennacherib king of Assyria [v]I have heard.
21 This is the word that the LORD has spoken
concerning him:

"She despises you, she scorns you—
[w]the virgin daughter of Zion;
she [x]wags her head behind you—
the daughter of Jerusalem.

22 "Whom have you [y]mocked and [z]reviled?
Against whom have you raised your
voice

When the Lord delivers in this way, he does so to make known his own greatness (19:19), for his own sake, and for the sake of the promises he made to David (19:34). At first glance this might seem selfish, but it is really great news for the family of God as its members encounter trials and difficulties in life. As the adopted children of the living God, we also bear his name and exult in his greatness. Since we are united to Christ, the true and better David (cf. Rom. 1:3; 2 Tim. 2:8; Rev. 22:16), we share in the promises to God's people. By God's grace, because we bear his name and have received his promises, we can be assured of his great salvation. To prove this point, the Lord went out and instantly killed 185,000 Assyrian soldiers, exalting his name and delivering his people. But just in case the execution of the Assyrian army fails to impress, consider the Father's execution of his only Son in order to exalt his name and deliver his people. In whom do you trust?

2 [v][See ver. 1 above]
4 [w][2 Sam. 16:12] [x]ver. 16 [y][Isa. 1:9]
6 [z]ch. 18:17 [a]See ch. 18:22-25, 30-35
7 [b]ver. 9 [c]ver. 37
8 [d]Josh. 10:29 [e]ch. 18:14; Josh. 10:31
9 [f][1 Sam. 23:27]
10 [g]ch. 18:5 [h]ch. 18:30
12 [i]ch. 18:33 [j]ch. 17:6 [k]Gen. 11:31; Ezek. 27:23 [l]Ezek. 27:23; Amos 1:5
13 [m]ch. 18:34
14 [n][2 Chr. 32:17]
15 [o]See Ex. 25:22 [p]1 Kgs. 18:39; Neh. 9:6; Ps. 86:10; Isa. 37:16, 20; 44:6; Jer. 10:10, 12 **16** [q]Ps. 31:2; 71:2; Dan. 9:18 [r]2 Chr. 6:40; Dan. 9:18 [s]ver. 4 **18** [t]2 Chr. 32:19; Ps. 115:4 **19** [u]Josh. 4:24; Ps. 83:18 [p][See ver. 15 above] **20** [v][ch. 20:5] **21** [w]Lam. 2:13 [x]Job 16:4; Ps. 22:7; 109:25; Lam. 2:15 **22** [y]ver. 4 [z]ver. 6

and lifted your eyes to the heights?
Against [a]the Holy One of Israel!
23 [b]By your messengers you have mocked
the Lord,
and you have said, [c]'With my many
chariots
I have gone up the heights of the mountains,
to the far recesses of [d]Lebanon;
I felled its tallest cedars,
its choicest cypresses;
I entered its farthest lodging place,
its most [e]fruitful forest.
24 I dug wells
and drank foreign waters,
and I dried up with the sole of my foot
all the streams [f]of Egypt.'

25 "Have you not heard
that [g]I determined it long ago?
I planned from days of old
what [h]now I bring to pass,
that you should turn fortified cities
into heaps of ruins,
26 while their inhabitants, shorn of strength,
are dismayed and confounded,
and have become [i]like plants of the field
and like tender grass,
like grass on the housetops,
blighted before it is grown.

27 "But I know your sitting down
[j]and your going out and coming in,
and your raging against me.
28 Because you have raged against me
and your complacency has come into
my ears,
I will [k]put my hook in your nose
and my bit in your mouth,
and [l]I will turn you back on the way
by which you came.

29 "And this shall be [m]the sign for you: this
year eat what grows of itself, and in the second
year what springs of the same. Then in the
third year sow and reap and plant vineyards,
and eat their fruit. 30 [n]And the surviving remnant of the house of Judah shall again take
root downward and bear fruit upward. 31 For
out of Jerusalem shall go a remnant, and out
of Mount Zion [o]a band of survivors. [p]The zeal
of the LORD will do this.

32 "Therefore thus says the LORD concerning
the king of Assyria: He shall not come into this
city or shoot an arrow there, or come before it
with a shield or [q]cast up a siege mound against
it. 33 [r]By the way that he came, by the same he
shall return, and he shall not come into this
city, declares the LORD. 34 [s]For I will defend
this city to save it, for my own sake [t]and for
the sake of my servant David."

35 And that night [u]the angel of the LORD
went out and struck down 185,000 in the
camp of the Assyrians. And when people arose
early in the morning, behold, these were all
dead bodies. 36 Then Sennacherib king of
Assyria departed and went home and lived
at [v]Nineveh. 37 And as he was worshiping in
the house of Nisroch his god, [w]Adrammelech
and Sharezer, his sons, struck him down with
the sword and escaped into the land of Ararat.
And Esarhaddon his son reigned in his place.

Hezekiah's Illness and Recovery

20 [x]In those days [y]Hezekiah became sick
and was at the point of death. And
Isaiah the prophet the son of Amoz came to
him and said to him, "Thus says the LORD,
[z]'Set your house in order, for you shall die; you
shall not recover.'" 2 Then Hezekiah turned his
face to the wall and prayed to the LORD, saying, 3 "Now, O LORD, [a]please remember how
I have walked before you in faithfulness and
[b]with a whole heart, [c]and have done what is
good in your sight." [d]And Hezekiah wept bitterly. 4 And before Isaiah had gone out of the
middle court, the word of the LORD came to

20:1–6 The events recorded in these few verses are quite amazing. Hezekiah was sick, and the Lord sent Isaiah the prophet to deliver a message of death: "you shall die; you shall not recover" (v. 1). The king quickly responded with prayer, and then the Lord answered that prayer: "Behold, I will heal you" (v. 5). Yes, the Lord answers prayer. But that is not the whole story.

Even before Isaiah delivered the first prophetic word of death, the Lord certainly knew that he would heal Hezekiah from his sickness. This was his plan all along. But if this was the plan, then why send the first message about death? Why not just send the message of healing? The answer to these questions, at least according to the

22 [a]Ps. 71:22; Isa. 5:24; 60:9; Jer. 51:5
23 [b]ch. 18:17 [c]Ps. 20:7 [d]See Judg. 9:15 [e]2 Chr. 26:10; [Isa. 10:18]
24 [f]Isa. 19:6
25 [g][Isa. 45:7] [h][Isa. 10:5]
26 [i]Ps. 129:6
27 [j][1 Sam. 29:6]
28 [k]Ezek. 29:4; 38:4; [Job 41:2; Isa. 30:28; Amos 4:2] [l]ver. 33, 36
29 [m]ch. 20:8, 9; 1 Sam. 2:34; Isa. 7:11, 14 **30** [n][2 Chr. 32:22, 23] **31** [o][Isa. 10:20] [p]Isa. 9:7 **32** [q]2 Sam. 20:15 **33** [r]ver. 28 **34** [s]ch. 20:6; [Isa. 31:5] [t]1 Kgs. 11:13 **35** [u][Ex. 12:23; 2 Sam. 24:16] **36** [v]Gen. 10:11; Jonah 1:2 **37** [w][ch. 17:31] **Chapter 20** **1** [x]For ver. 1-11, see Isa. 38:1-22 [y]2 Chr. 32:24 [z][2 Sam. 17:23] **3** [a][Neh. 5:19; 13:14, 22, 31] [b]See 1 Kgs. 8:61 [c]ch. 18:3 [d][Ps. 39:12, 13]

him: 5 “Turn back, and say to Hezekiah [e]the
leader of my people, Thus says the LORD, the
God of David your father: [f]I have heard your
prayer; [g]I have seen your tears. Behold, I will
heal you. On the third day you shall go up to
the house of the LORD, 6 and I will add fifteen
years to your life. I will deliver you and this
city out of the hand of the king of Assyria,
[h]and I will defend this city for my own sake
and for my servant David’s sake.” 7 And Isaiah
said, “Bring a cake of figs. And let them take
and lay it on the boil, that he may recover.”
8 And Hezekiah said to Isaiah, “What shall be
the sign that the LORD will heal me, and that
I shall go up to the house of the LORD on the
third day?” 9 And Isaiah said, “This shall be
[i]the sign to you from the LORD, that the LORD
will do the thing that he has promised: shall
the shadow go forward ten steps, or go back
ten steps?” 10 And Hezekiah answered, “It is
an easy thing for the shadow [j]to lengthen ten
steps. Rather let the shadow go back ten steps.”
11 And Isaiah the prophet called to the LORD,
[k]and he brought the shadow back ten steps, by
which it had gone down on the steps of Ahaz.

Hezekiah and the Babylonian Envoys

12 [l]At that time [m]Merodach-baladan the son
of Baladan, king of Babylon, [n]sent envoys with
letters and a present to Hezekiah, for he heard
that Hezekiah had been sick. 13 And Hezekiah
welcomed them, and he showed them [o]all his
treasure house, the silver, the gold, the spices,
the precious oil, his armory, all that was found
in his storehouses. There was nothing in his
house or in all his realm that Hezekiah did not
show them. 14 Then Isaiah the prophet came
to King Hezekiah, and said to him, “What did
these men say? And from where did they come
to you?” And Hezekiah said, “They have come
from a far country, from Babylon.” 15 He said,
“What have they seen in your house?” And
Hezekiah answered, “They have seen all that
is in my house; there is nothing in my storehouses that I did not show them.”
16 Then Isaiah said to Hezekiah, “Hear the
word of the LORD: 17 Behold, the days are coming, when [p]all that is in your house, and that
which your fathers have stored up till this day,
shall be carried to Babylon. Nothing shall be
left, says the LORD. 18 [q]And some of your own
sons, who shall be born to you, shall be taken
away, [r]and they shall be eunuchs in the palace
of the king of Babylon.” 19 Then Hezekiah said
to Isaiah, [s]“The word of the LORD that you have
spoken is good.” For he thought, “Why not, if
there will be peace and security in my days?”
20 [t]The rest of the deeds of Hezekiah and all
his might and how he made [u]the pool and the
conduit [v]and brought water into the city, are
they not written in the Book of the Chronicles
of the Kings of Judah? 21 [w]And Hezekiah slept
with his fathers, and Manasseh his son reigned
in his place.

Manasseh Reigns in Judah

21 [x]Manasseh was twelve years old when
he began to reign, and he reigned fifty-
five years in Jerusalem. His mother’s name was
Hephzibah. 2 And he did what was evil in the
sight of the LORD, [y]according to the despicable
practices of the nations whom the LORD drove
out before the people of Israel. 3 For he rebuilt
the high places [z]that Hezekiah his father had
destroyed, and he erected altars for Baal and
made [a]an Asherah, [b]as Ahab king of Israel had
done, [c]and worshiped all the host of heaven
and served them. 4 [d]And he built altars in the
house of the LORD, of which the LORD had
said, [e]“In Jerusalem will I put my name.” 5 And
he built altars [c]for all the host of heaven in
[f]the two courts of the house of the LORD.
6 [g]And he burned his son as an offering[1] and
[h]used fortune-telling and [i]omens and dealt

[1] Hebrew *made his son pass through the fire*

biblical text, is that the Lord wanted to provoke Hezekiah to prayer, the expression of dependence and the orientation of biblical hope. When we encounter suffering and sickness in life, the Lord is not punishing but rather provoking his people to prayer, to communion with the living God. Therefore, “Count it all joy, my brothers, when you meet trials of various kinds, for you know that the testing of your faith produces steadfastness. And let steadfastness have its full effect, that you may be perfect and complete, lacking in nothing” (James 1:2–4). Do not forget that the grace of the Lord is present is every aspect of life, even in our suffering and sickness.

5 [e]1 Sam. 9:16; 10:1 [f]ch. 19:20; [Ps. 65:2] [g]Ps. 39:12; 56:8
6 [h]ch. 19:34
9 [i]See ch. 19:29
10 [j]Ps. 102:11
11 [k][Josh. 10:12, 13]
12 [l]For ver. 12-19, see Isa. 39:1-8 [m][Isa. 39:1] [n][2 Chr. 32:31]
13 [o][2 Chr. 32:27]
17 [p]ch. 24:13; Jer. 20:5; [ch. 25:13]; See Jer. 27:19-22

18 [q]ch. 24:12; 2 Chr. 33:11 [r][Dan. 1:3] **19** [s]1 Sam. 3:18; [2 Chr. 32:25, 26] **20** [t][2 Chr. 32:32] [u]ch. 18:17; Neh. 2:14; 3:16 [v]2 Chr. 32:30; [Isa. 22:9, 11] **21** [w]2 Chr. 32:33 **Chapter 21** **1** [x]For ver. 1-9, see 2 Chr. 33:1-9 **2** [y][ch. 16:3] **3** [z]ch. 18:4 [a]See Deut. 16:21 [b]1 Kgs. 16:32, 33 [c]ch. 17:16; 23:5; [Deut. 4:19] **4** [d]Jer. 7:30; 32:34 [e]ver. 7; ch. 23:27; 2 Sam. 7:13; 1 Kgs. 8:29; 9:3; [Deut. 12:11] **5** [c][See ver. 3 above] [f]ch. 23:12; 1 Kgs. 6:36; 7:12 **6** [g]See Lev. 18:21 [h]See Lev. 19:26 [i]ch. 17:17

[j]with mediums and with necromancers. He
did much evil in the sight of the LORD, provoking him to anger. 7 And the carved image
of [a]Asherah that he had made he set in the
house of which the LORD said to David and
to Solomon his son, "In this house, [e]and in
Jerusalem, which I have chosen out of all the
tribes of Israel, I will put my name forever.
8 [k]And I will not cause the feet of Israel to
wander anymore out of the land that I gave to
their fathers, if only they will be careful to do
according to all that I have commanded them,
and according to all the Law that my servant
Moses commanded them." 9 But they did not
listen, and Manasseh led them astray to do
more evil than the nations had done whom
the LORD destroyed before the people of Israel.

Manasseh's Idolatry Denounced

10 And the LORD said by his servants the
prophets, 11 [l]"Because Manasseh king of
Judah has committed these abominations
and has done things [m]more evil than all that
the Amorites did, who were before him, [n]and
has made Judah also to sin [o]with his idols,
12 therefore thus says the LORD, the God of
Israel: Behold, I am bringing upon Jerusalem
and Judah such disaster[1] that the ears of everyone who hears of it [p]will tingle. 13 [q]And I will
stretch over Jerusalem the measuring line of
Samaria, and the plumb line of the house of
Ahab, and I will wipe Jerusalem as one wipes
a dish, wiping it and turning it upside down.
14 And I will forsake the remnant of my heritage and give them into the hand of their enemies, and they shall become a prey and a spoil
to all their enemies, 15 because they have done
what is evil in my sight and have provoked me
to anger, since the day their fathers came out
of Egypt, even to this day."
16 [r]Moreover, Manasseh shed very much innocent blood, till he had filled Jerusalem from
one end to another, besides the sin [s]that he
made Judah to sin so that they did what was
evil in the sight of the LORD.
17 [t]Now the rest of the acts of Manasseh and
all that he did, and the sin that he committed, are they not written in the Book of the
Chronicles of the Kings of Judah? 18 [u]And
Manasseh slept with his fathers and was buried in the garden of his house, [v]in the garden of
Uzza, and Amon his son reigned in his place.

Amon Reigns in Judah

19 Amon was twenty-two years old when he
began to reign, and he reigned two years in
Jerusalem. His mother's name was Meshul-
lemeth the daughter of Haruz of Jotbah.
20 And he did what was evil in the sight of
the LORD, [w]as Manasseh his father had done.
21 He walked in all the way in which his father
walked and served [x]the idols that his father
served and worshiped them. 22 [y]He abandoned
the LORD, the God of his fathers, and did not
walk in the way of the LORD. 23 And the servants of Amon conspired against him and
put the king to death in his house. 24 But the
people of the land struck down all those who
had conspired against King Amon, and the
people of the land made Josiah his son king in
his place. 25 Now the rest of the acts of Amon
that he did, are they not written in the Book
of the Chronicles of the Kings of Judah? 26 And
he was buried in his tomb [z]in the garden of
Uzza, and Josiah his son reigned in his place.

Josiah Reigns in Judah

22 [a]Josiah was eight years old when he
began to reign, and he reigned thirty-
one years in Jerusalem. His mother's name was
Jedidah the daughter of Adaiah of [b]Bozkath.
2 And he did what was right in the eyes of the
LORD and walked in all the way of David his
father, [c]and he did not turn aside to the right
or to the left.

Josiah Repairs the Temple

3 In the eighteenth year of King Josiah, the
king sent Shaphan the son of Azaliah, son of
Meshullam, the secretary, to the house of the
LORD, saying, 4 "Go up to [d]Hilkiah the high

[1] Or *evil*

22:3–20 After two generations of gross wickedness (cf. ch. 21), a new king arrived on the scene and began to repair the house of the Lord (22:3–7). In the midst of this repair work, the high priest "found" the Book of the Law of the Lord (v. 8). Can you imagine this—God's people living without God's covenant word? It is no wonder, then, that Judah's condition had become worse than that of the nations previously expelled from the land (cf. 21:9). As such, judgment was coming, and coming quickly.

6 [j]ch. 23:24; See Lev. 19:31 **7** [a][See ver. 3 above] [e][See ver. 4 above] **8** [k][2 Sam. 7:19] **11** [l]ver. 2; ch. 23:26; 24:3, 4; Jer. 15:4 [m]1 Kgs. 21:26 [n]ver. 16 [o]ver. 21 **12** [p]1 Sam. 3:11; Jer. 19:3 **13** [q]Isa. 34:11; [Isa. 28:17; Lam. 2:8; Amos 7:7, 8] **16** [r]ch. 24:4 [s]ver. 11 **17** [t]See 2 Chr. 33:11-19 **18** [u]For ver. 18-24, see 2 Chr. 33:20-25 [v]ver. 26 **20** [w]See ver. 2-6, 11 **21** [x]ver. 11 **22** [y]ch. 22:17; [1 Kgs. 11:33] **26** [z]ver. 18 **Chapter 22** **1** [a]See 2 Chr. 34:1, 2 [b]Josh. 15:39 **2** [c]See Deut. 5:32 **4** [d][ch. 12:10]

priest, that he may count the money [e]that has been brought into the house of the LORD, which [f]the keepers of the threshold have collected from the people. 5 [g]And let it be given into the hand of the workmen who have the oversight of the house of the LORD, and let them give it to the workmen who are at the house of the LORD, repairing the house 6 (that is, to the carpenters, and to the builders, and to the masons), and let them use it for buying timber and quarried stone to repair the house. 7 But [h]no accounting shall be asked from them for the money that is delivered into their hand, for they deal honestly."

Hilkiah Finds the Book of the Law

8 And Hilkiah the high priest said to Shaphan the secretary, "I have found [i]the Book of the Law in the house of the LORD." And Hilkiah gave the book to Shaphan, and he read it. 9 And Shaphan the secretary came to the king, and reported to the king, "Your servants have emptied out the money that was found in the house and have delivered it into the hand of the workmen who have the oversight of the house of the LORD." 10 Then Shaphan the secretary told the king, "Hilkiah the priest has given me a book." And Shaphan read it before the king.

11 When the king heard the words of the Book of the Law, [j]he tore his clothes. 12 And the king commanded Hilkiah the priest, and [k]Ahikam the son of Shaphan, and [l]Achbor the son of [l]Micaiah, and Shaphan the secretary, and Asaiah the king's servant, saying, 13 "Go, inquire of the LORD for me, and for the people, and for all Judah, concerning the words of this book that has been found. For great is [m]the wrath of the LORD that is kindled against us, because our fathers have not obeyed the words of this book, to do according to all that is written concerning us."

14 So Hilkiah the priest, and Ahikam, and Achbor, and Shaphan, and Asaiah went to Huldah the prophetess, the wife of Shallum the son of [n]Tikvah, son of [n]Harhas, keeper of the wardrobe (now she lived in Jerusalem in [o]the Second Quarter), and they talked with her. 15 And she said to them, "Thus says the LORD, the God of Israel: 'Tell the man who sent you to me, 16 Thus says the LORD, Behold, I will bring disaster upon this place and upon its inhabitants, all the words of the book that the king of Judah has read. 17 [p]Because they have forsaken me and have made offerings to other gods, that they might provoke me to anger with all the work of their hands, therefore [m]my wrath will be kindled against this place, and it will not be quenched. 18 But to the king of Judah, who sent you to inquire of the LORD, thus shall you say to him, Thus says the LORD, the God of Israel: Regarding the words that you have heard, 19 [q]because your heart was penitent, and you [r]humbled yourself before the LORD, when you heard how I spoke against this place and against its inhabitants, that they should become [s]a desolation and [t]a curse, and you [u]have torn your clothes and wept before me, I also have heard you, declares the LORD. 20 Therefore, behold, I will gather you to your fathers, and [v]you shall be gathered to your grave in peace, and your eyes shall not see all the disaster that I will bring upon this place.'" And they brought back word to the king.

Josiah's Reforms

23 [w]Then the king sent, and all the elders of Judah and Jerusalem were gathered to him. 2 And the king went up to the house of the LORD, and with him all the men of Judah and all the inhabitants of Jerusalem and the priests and the prophets, all the people, both small and great. And [x]he read in their hearing

But though judgment was coming, it was not too late to repent of wickedness and seek the favor of the Lord. Having encountered the Word of God, King Josiah repented and humbled himself before the Lord, tearing his clothes and weeping.

We are reminded that though judgment is still coming for unrepented evil—and for more than merely the tribe of Judah in the final judgment—yet there is hope. We can be assured that the Lord, who has displayed his forgiving nature in this passage, will continue to look in mercy upon the humble and repentant. He hears prayer and delivers those who turn to him in faith. Consider the marvelous promise of the Lord: "But this is the one to whom I will look: he who is humble and contrite in spirit and trembles at my word" (Isa. 66:2). Such a promise is rooted in the very character of God. For he is "merciful and gracious, slow to anger, and abounding in steadfast love and faithfulness" (Ex. 34:6).

4 [e]ch. 12:4 [f]ch. 12:9
5 [g]ch. 12:11, 12, 14
7 [h]ch. 12:15
8 [i]Deut. 31:24-26; 2 Chr. 34:14
11 [j]See Josh. 7:6
12 [k]ch. 25:22; Jer. 26:24; 39:14; 40:5 [l][2 Chr. 34:20]
13 [m]Deut. 29:27
14 [n][2 Chr. 34:22] [o]Zeph. 1:10
17 [p]ch. 21:22; Deut. 29:25, 26 [m][See ver. 13 above]
19 [q][Ps. 51:17; Isa. 57:15] [r]1 Kgs. 21:29 [s]Lev. 26:31, 32; 2 Chr. 30:7; Jer. 25:18; 44:22; Mic. 6:16 [t]Jer. 24:9; 26:6; 44:22 [u]ver. 11
20 [v]Ps. 37:37; Isa. 57:1, 2

Chapter 23 **1** [w]For ver. 1-3, see 2 Chr. 34:29-32 **2** [x]See Deut. 31:11

all the words of the Book of the Covenant [y]that
had been found in the house of the LORD.
3 And the king stood [z]by the pillar and [a]made
a covenant before the LORD, [b]to walk after the
LORD and to keep his commandments and his
testimonies and his statutes with all his heart
and all his soul, to perform the words of this
covenant that were written in this book. And
all the people joined in the covenant.

4 And the king commanded Hilkiah the high
priest and the priests [c]of the second order and
the keepers of the threshold to bring out of
the temple of the LORD all the vessels made
for [d]Baal, for [e]Asherah, and for all the host of
heaven. [f]He burned them outside Jerusalem
in the fields of the Kidron and carried their
ashes to Bethel. 5 And he deposed the priests
whom the kings of Judah had ordained to
make offerings in the high places at the cities of Judah and around Jerusalem; those also
who burned incense to Baal, to the sun and
the moon and the constellations [g]and all the
host of the heavens. 6 And he brought out [h]the
Asherah from the house of the LORD, outside
Jerusalem, to the brook Kidron, [i]and burned
it at the brook Kidron [j]and beat it to dust and
cast the dust of it upon the graves [k]of the common people. 7 And he broke down the houses
of [l]the male cult prostitutes who were in the
house of the LORD, [m]where the women wove
hangings for [h]the Asherah. 8 And he brought
all the priests out of the cities of Judah, and
defiled the high places where the priests had
made offerings, from [n]Geba to Beersheba.
And he broke down the high places of the
gates that were at the entrance of the gate of
Joshua the governor of the city, which were
on one's left at the gate of the city. 9 [o]However,
the priests of the high places did not come
up to the altar of the LORD in Jerusalem, but
they ate unleavened bread among their brothers. 10 And he defiled [p]Topheth, which is [q]in
the Valley of the Son of Hinnom, [r]that no one
might burn his son or his daughter as an offering to [s]Molech.[1] 11 And he removed the horses
that the kings of Judah had dedicated to the
sun, at the entrance to the house of the LORD,
by the chamber of Nathan-melech the chamberlain, which was in the precincts.[2] And he
burned the chariots of the sun with fire. 12 And
the altars [t]on the roof of the upper chamber
of Ahaz, which the kings of Judah had made,
and the altars [u]that Manasseh had made in the
two courts of the house of the LORD, he pulled
down and broke in pieces[3] and cast the dust
of them [v]into the brook Kidron. 13 And the
king defiled the high places that were east of
Jerusalem, to the south of [w]the mount of corruption, which Solomon the king of Israel had
built for [x]Ashtoreth the abomination of the
Sidonians, and for [y]Chemosh the abomination
of Moab, and for [z]Milcom the abomination of
the Ammonites. 14 And he broke in pieces the
[a]pillars and cut down the Asherim and filled
their places with the bones of men.

15 Moreover, the altar at Bethel, the high place
erected [b]by Jeroboam the son of Nebat, [c]who
made Israel to sin, [d]that altar with the high
place he pulled down and burned,[4] reducing it
to dust. He also burned the Asherah. 16 And as
Josiah turned, he saw the tombs there on the
mount. And he sent and took the bones out of
the tombs and burned them on the altar and
defiled it, [e]according to the word of the LORD
that the man of God proclaimed, who had predicted these things. 17 Then he said, "What is
that monument that I see?" And the men of
the city told him, [f]"It is the tomb of the man
of God who came from Judah and predicted[5]
these things that you have done against the
altar at Bethel." 18 And he said, "Let him be; let
no man move his bones." So they let his bones
alone, with the bones [g]of the prophet who
came out of Samaria. 19 And Josiah removed
all the shrines also of the high places that were
[h]in the cities of Samaria, which kings of Israel

[1] Hebrew *might cause his son or daughter to pass through the fire for Molech* [2] The meaning of the Hebrew word is uncertain
[3] Hebrew *pieces from there* [4] Septuagint *broke in pieces its stones* [5] Hebrew *called*

23:21–23 Among Josiah's many reforms, one key reform was the reinstitution of the Passover. This was a key celebration and memorial for Israel, but one which, strangely, had not "been kept since the days of the judges" (v. 22). The Passover had been instituted when God graciously and powerfully redeemed Israel from Egyptian slavery, "passing over" the home of every Israelite whose doorway was smeared with blood, to spare the firstborn from heaven's righteous wrath.

2 [y] ch. 22:8
3 [z] ch. 11:14 [a] [ch. 11:17] [b] Deut. 13:4
4 [c] [ch. 25:18; Jer. 52:24] [d] ch. 21:3 [e] See Deut. 16:21 [f] ver. 15
5 [g] ch. 21:3
6 [h] See Deut. 16:21 [i] ver. 15 [j] ver. 15; [2 Chr. 15:16]

[k] [2 Chr. 34:4] **7** [l] 1 Kgs. 14:24; 15:12; See Deut. 23:17 [m] [Ezek. 16:16] [h] [See ver. 6 above] **8** [n] 1 Kgs. 15:22 **9** [o] See Ezek. 44:10-14 **10** [p] Isa. 30:33; Jer. 7:31, 32; 19:6, 11-14 [q] See Josh. 15:8 [r] See Lev. 18:21 [s] See 1 Kgs. 11:7 **12** [t] [Jer. 19:13; 32:29; Zeph. 1:5] [u] ch. 21:5 [v] ver. 4, 6 **13** [w] [1 Kgs. 11:7] [x] See 1 Kgs. 11:5 [y] [Num. 21:29] [z] [1 Kgs. 11:5] **14** [a] See Ex. 23:24 **15** [b] 1 Kgs. 12:28, 29, 33 [c] See 1 Kgs. 14:16 [d] ver. 6 **16** [e] 1 Kgs. 13:2 **17** [f] 1 Kgs. 13:1, 30 **18** [g] 1 Kgs. 13:11, 31 **19** [h] [2 Chr. 34:6, 7]

had made, provoking the LORD to anger. He did to them according to all that he had done at Bethel. 20 And [i]he sacrificed all the priests of the high places who were there, on the altars, [j]and burned human bones on them. Then he returned to Jerusalem.

Josiah Restores the Passover

21 And the king commanded all the people, [k]"Keep the Passover to the LORD your God, [l]as it is written in this Book of the Covenant." 22 [m]For no such Passover had been kept since the days of the judges who judged Israel, or during all the days of the kings of Israel or of the kings of Judah. 23 But in the eighteenth year of King Josiah this Passover was kept to the LORD in Jerusalem.

24 Moreover, Josiah put away [n]the mediums and the necromancers and [o]the household gods and [p]the idols and all the abominations that were seen in the land of Judah and in Jerusalem, that he might establish [q]the words of the law that were written in the book [r]that Hilkiah the priest found in the house of the LORD. 25 [s]Before him there was no king like him, who turned to the LORD with all his heart and with all his soul and with all his might, according to all the Law of Moses, nor did any like him arise after him.

26 Still the LORD did not turn from the burning of his great wrath, by which his anger was kindled against Judah, [t]because of all the provocations with which Manasseh had provoked him. 27 And the LORD said, "I will remove Judah also out of my sight, [u]as I have removed Israel, and I will cast off this city that I have chosen, Jerusalem, [v]and the house of which I said, My name shall be there."

Josiah's Death in Battle

28 Now the rest of the acts of Josiah and all that he did, are they not written in the Book of the Chronicles of the Kings of Judah? 29 [w]In his days [x]Pharaoh Neco king of Egypt went up to the king of Assyria to the river Euphrates. King Josiah went to meet him, and Pharaoh Neco killed him at [y]Megiddo, as soon as he saw him. 30 [z]And his servants carried him dead in a chariot from [y]Megiddo and brought him to Jerusalem and buried him in his own tomb. [a]And the people of the land took Jehoahaz the son of Josiah, and anointed him, and made him king in his father's place.

Jehoahaz's Reign and Captivity

31 [b]Jehoahaz was twenty-three years old when he began to reign, and he reigned three months in Jerusalem. His mother's name was [c]Hamutal the daughter of Jeremiah of Libnah. 32 And he did what was evil in the sight of the LORD, [d]according to all that his fathers had done. 33 And [x]Pharaoh Neco put him in bonds at [e]Riblah in the land of [f]Hamath, that he might not reign in Jerusalem, and laid on the land a tribute of a hundred talents[1] of silver and a talent of gold. 34 And [x]Pharaoh Neco made Eliakim the son of Josiah king in the place of Josiah his father, and [g]changed his name to Jehoiakim. But he took Jehoahaz away, [h]and he came to Egypt and died there. 35 And Jehoiakim [i]gave the silver and the gold to Pharaoh, but he taxed the land to give the money according to the command of Pharaoh. He exacted the silver and the gold of the people of the land, from everyone according to his assessment, to give it to Pharaoh Neco.

Jehoiakim Reigns in Judah

36 [j]Jehoiakim was twenty-five years old when he began to reign, and he reigned eleven years in Jerusalem. His mother's name was Zebidah the daughter of Pedaiah of Rumah. 37 And he did what was evil in the sight of the LORD, [d]according to all that his fathers had done.

24 [k]In his days, Nebuchadnezzar king of Babylon came up, and Jehoiakim became his servant for three years. Then he turned and rebelled against him. 2 And the LORD sent against him bands of the [l]Chaldeans and [m]bands of the Syrians and bands of the Moabites and bands of the Ammonites, and sent them against Judah to destroy it,

[1] A *talent* was about 75 pounds or 34 kilograms

The reinstitution of the Passover by Josiah is a major sign and anticipation of the redemption that would one day be accomplished by Christ. He himself is the final Passover lamb (1 Cor. 5:7). By his blood, all who take refuge in him are spared from the righteous wrath of God.

20 [i][ch. 11:18; Ex. 22:20; 1 Kgs. 18:40] [j]2 Chr. 34:5
21 [k]See 2 Chr. 35:1-17 [l]See Ex. 12:3-11; Lev. 23:5, 8; Num. 9:2-4; Deut. 16:2-8

22 [m]2 Chr. 35:18, 19 **24** [n]ch. 21:6; See Lev. 19:31 [o]See Gen. 31:19 [p]ch. 21:11, 21 [q]Lev. 19:31; 20:27; Deut. 18:11 [r]ch. 22:8 **25** [s][ch. 18:5] **26** [t]ch. 21:11; 24:3, 4; Jer. 15:4 **27** [u]ch. 17:18, 20; 18:11; 21:13 [v]See ch. 21:4 **29** [w]For ver. 29, 30, see 2 Chr. 35:20-24 [x]Jer. 46:2 [y][Judg. 5:19; Zech. 12:11] **30** [z][ch. 9:28] [y][See ver. 29 above] [a]For ver. 30-34, see 2 Chr. 36:1-4 **31** [b][1 Chr. 3:15; Jer. 22:11] [c]ch. 24:18 **32** [d][ch. 24:9, 19] **33** [x][See ver. 29 above] [e]ch. 25:6, 20, 21; Jer. 39:5, 6; 52:9, 10, 26, 27 [f]See 1 Kgs. 8:65 **34** [x][See ver. 29 above] [g][ch. 24:17; Dan. 1:7] [h]Jer. 22:11, 12; [Ezek. 19:3, 4] **35** [i]ver. 33 **36** [j]2 Chr. 36:5 **37** [d][See ver. 32 above] **Chapter 24** **1** [k]2 Chr. 36:6; Jer. 25:1, 9; Dan. 1:1 **2** [l]ch. 25:4; Jer. 32:28, 29; 35:11; [Ezek. 19:8] [m]Jer. 35:11

[n]according to the word of the LORD that he
spoke by his servants the prophets. 3 Surely
this came upon Judah at the command of the
LORD, to remove them out of his sight, [o]for
the sins of Manasseh, according to all that he
had done, 4 and also [p]for the innocent blood
that he had shed. For he filled Jerusalem with
innocent blood, and the LORD would not pardon. 5 [q]Now the rest of the deeds of Jehoiakim
and all that he did, are they not written in the
Book of the Chronicles of the Kings of Judah?
6 So Jehoiakim [r]slept with his fathers, and
Jehoiachin his son reigned in his place. 7 [s]And
the king of Egypt did not come again out of
his land, [t]for the king of Babylon had taken all
that belonged to the king of Egypt [u]from the
Brook of Egypt to the river Euphrates.

Jehoiachin Reigns in Judah

8 [v]Jehoiachin was [w]eighteen years old when he
became king, and he reigned three months in
Jerusalem. His mother's name was Nehushta
the daughter of Elnathan of Jerusalem. 9 And
he did what was evil in the sight of the LORD,
[x]according to all that his father had done.

Jerusalem Captured

10 At that time the servants of [y]Nebuchad-
nezzar king of Babylon came up to Jerusalem,
and the city was besieged. 11 And [y]Nebuchad-
nezzar king of Babylon came to the city while
his servants were besieging it, 12 [z]and Jehoiachin the king of Judah gave himself up to the
king of Babylon, himself and his mother and
his servants and his officials and his palace officials. [a]The king of Babylon took him prisoner
[b]in the eighth year of his reign 13 and carried
off all the treasures of the house of the LORD
[c]and the treasures of the king's house, [d]and cut
in pieces all the vessels of gold in the temple
of the LORD, [e]which Solomon king of Israel
had made, [f]as the LORD had foretold. 14 [g]He
carried away all Jerusalem and all the officials
and all the mighty men of valor, [h]10,000 captives, [i]and all the craftsmen and the smiths.
None remained, [j]except the poorest people of
the land. 15 [k]And he carried away Jehoiachin to
Babylon. The king's mother, the king's wives,
his officials, and the chief men of the land he
took into captivity from Jerusalem to Babylon.
16 And the king of Babylon brought captive to
Babylon all the men of valor, [l]7,000, and the
craftsmen and the metal workers, 1,000, all of
them strong and fit for war. 17 [m]And the king of
Babylon [n]made Mattaniah, [o]Jehoiachin's uncle,
king in his place, [p]and changed his name to
Zedekiah.

Zedekiah Reigns in Judah

18 [q]Zedekiah was twenty-one years old when
he became king, and he reigned eleven years in
Jerusalem. His mother's name was [r]Hamutal
the daughter of Jeremiah of Libnah. 19 And he
did what was evil in the sight of the LORD,
[s]according to all that Jehoiakim had done.
20 For because of the anger of the LORD it came
to the point in Jerusalem and Judah that he
cast them out from his presence.

[t]And Zedekiah rebelled against the king of
Babylon.

Fall and Captivity of Judah

25 [u]And in the ninth year of his reign, in
the tenth month, on the tenth day of
the month, [v]Nebuchadnezzar king of Babylon
came with all his army against Jerusalem and
laid siege to it. [w]And they built siegeworks all
around it. 2 So the city was besieged till the
eleventh year of King Zedekiah. 3 On the ninth
day of the fourth month [x]the famine was so
severe in the city that there was no food for
the people of the land. 4 Then a breach was

25:1–26 This final chapter in the book of Kings records the tragic termination of Israel's occupation of the Promised Land. Leaders were executed, kings were exiled, treasures were stolen, and the temple of the Lord that Solomon had built was burned to the ground. But remember, all of this destruction and death came about at the Lord's command (24:3) and was something designed by God long ago (24:2, 13; cf. Deuteronomy 29–31). In other words, though the calamities detailed in these final verses of the book of Kings are shocking, they are not unexpected. From the very beginning (Deuteronomy 29–31), Israel's tenure in the land of Canaan was intended to be temporary, because God had something so much better in mind—not a single nation limited to a single geographical location but people from all nations spread throughout a new earth (cf. Gen. 12:3; Isa. 19:16–25; 49:6; Revelation 21).

2 [n] ch. 20:17; 21:12-14; 23:27
3 [o] ch. 21:11; 23:26
4 [p] ch. 21:16
5 [q] 2 Chr. 36:8
6 [r] [2 Chr. 36:6; Jer. 22:18, 19; 36:30]
7 [s] Jer. 37:5-7 [t] [Jer. 46:2, 20, 24, 26] [u] See Num. 34:5
8 [v] [1 Chr. 3:16; Esth. 2:6; Jer. 22:24, 28; 24:1; 37:1] [w] [2 Chr. 36:9]
9 [x] ch. 23:37
10 [y] Dan. 1:1
11 [y] [See ver. 10 above]
12 [z] [Jer. 24:1; 29:1, 2; Ezek. 17:12] [a] [2 Chr. 36:10] [b] [ch. 25:27] **13** [c] ch. 20:17; Isa. 39:6 [d] 2 Chr. 36:7; Ezra 1:7; Dan. 1:2; 5:2, 3 [e] See 1 Kgs. 7:48-50 [f] Jer. 20:5 **14** [g] Jer. 24:1 [h] [ver. 16; Jer. 52:28] [i] Jer. 24:1; 29:2; [1 Sam. 13:19, 22] [j] ch. 25:12 **15** [k] 2 Chr. 36:10; Esth. 2:6; [Jer. 22:24-26] **16** [l] [ver. 14] **17** [m] For ver. 17-20, see 2 Chr. 36:10-13 [n] [Jer. 37:1] [o] [1 Chr. 3:15] [p] [ch. 23:34; 2 Chr. 36:4] **18** [q] For ch. 24:18–25:21, see Jer. 52:1-27 [r] ch. 23:31 **19** [s] ch. 23:37 **20** [t] [Ezek. 17:18] **Chapter 25** **1** [u] For ver. 1-7, see 2 Chr. 36:17-20; Jer. 39:1-7; 52:4-11 [v] Jer. 34:1, 2; 39:1, 2; Ezek. 24:2 [w] [Ezek. 21:22; 26:8] **3** [x] [Lam. 4:9, 10]

made in the city, and all the men of war fled by night by the way of the gate between the two walls, by [y]the king's garden, and [z]the Chaldeans were around the city. And they went in the direction of the [a]Arabah. 5 But the army of the Chaldeans pursued the king and overtook him in the plains of Jericho, and all his army was scattered from him. 6 Then they captured the king [b]and brought him up to the king of Babylon at [c]Riblah, and they passed sentence on him. 7 They slaughtered the sons of Zedekiah before his eyes, [d]and put out the eyes of Zedekiah and bound him in chains and took him to Babylon.

8 [e]In the fifth month, on [f]the seventh day of the month—that was the nineteenth year of King Nebuchadnezzar, king of Babylon—Nebuzaradan, the captain of the bodyguard, a servant of the king of Babylon, came to Jerusalem. 9 [g]And he burned the house of the LORD [h]and the king's house and all the houses of Jerusalem; every great house he burned down. 10 And all the army of the Chaldeans, who were with the captain of the guard, [i]broke down the walls around Jerusalem. 11 [j]And the rest of the people who were left in the city and the deserters who had deserted to the king of Babylon, together with the rest of the multitude, Nebuzaradan the captain of the guard carried into exile. 12 But the captain of the guard left [k]some of the poorest of the land to be vinedressers and plowmen.

13 [l]And the pillars [m]of bronze that were in the house of the LORD, and [n]the stands and [o]the bronze sea that were in the house of the LORD, the Chaldeans broke in pieces and carried the bronze to Babylon. 14 [p]And they took away the pots and the shovels and the snuffers and the dishes for incense and all the vessels of bronze used in the temple service, 15 the fire pans also and the bowls. What was of gold the captain of the guard took away as gold, and what was of silver, as silver. 16 As for the two pillars, the one sea, and the stands that Solomon had made for the house of the LORD, [q]the bronze of all these vessels was beyond weight. 17 [r]The height of the one pillar was eighteen cubits,[1] and on it was a capital of bronze. The height of the capital was three cubits. A latticework and pomegranates, all of bronze, were all around the capital. And the second pillar had the same, with the latticework.

18 [s]And the captain of the guard took [t]Seraiah the chief priest and [u]Zephaniah the second priest and the three keepers of the threshold; 19 and from the city he took an officer who had been in command of the men of war, and [v]five men of the king's council who were found in the city; and the secretary of the commander of the army, who mustered the people of the land; and sixty men of the people of the land, who were found in the city. 20 And Nebuzaradan the captain of the guard took them and brought them to the king of Babylon at [w]Riblah. 21 And the king of Babylon struck them down and put them to death at [w]Riblah in the land of Hamath. [x]So Judah was taken into exile out of its land.

Gedaliah Made Governor of Judah

22 And over the people who remained in the land of Judah, whom Nebuchadnezzar king of Babylon had left, he appointed [y]Gedaliah the son of [z]Ahikam, son of Shaphan, governor. 23 [a]Now when all the captains and their men heard that the king of Babylon had appointed Gedaliah governor, they came with their men to Gedaliah at [b]Mizpah, namely, Ishmael the son of Nethaniah, and Johanan the son of

[1] A *cubit* was about 18 inches or 45 centimeters

When Christians look upon God's wrath and judgment, we shudder to observe his abhorrence of sin. We are brought to grieve over our own sins. But our grief turns to gladness (Jer. 31:13) as we recognize that the punishment we so rightly deserve has been endured, paid for, and eliminated by the work of Jesus Christ on our behalf (2 Cor. 5:21). Never forget the theme that runs through the book of Kings: "for the sake of my servant David" (cf. 1 Kings 11:32, 34; 15:4; 2 Kings 8:19; 19:34; 20:6; Isa. 37:35). This is our only hope, too—that God will deal with us according to the merits of another David, the true and better David, King Jesus (2 Tim. 2:8; Rev. 22:16). Seek that refuge, to which this book points, from such judgment as this book records. For "There is therefore now no condemnation for those who are in Christ Jesus" (Rom 8:1).

4 [y] Neh. 3:15 [z] See ch. 24:2 [a] See Deut. 1:1
6 [b] Jer. 32:4 [c] [ch. 23:33]
7 [d] [Ezek. 12:13]
8 [e] For ver. 8-12, see Jer. 39:8-12; 52:12-16 [f] [Jer. 52:12]
9 [g] 2 Chr. 36:19; Ps. 79:1 [h] [Hos. 8:14; Amos 2:5]
10 [i] Neh. 1:3
11 [j] 2 Chr. 36:20
12 [k] ch. 24:14; Jer. 40:7
13 [l] [Jer. 27:19, 22]; For ver. 13-17, see 2 Chr. 36:18-20; Jer. 52:17-23 [m] 1 Kgs. 7:15 [n] 1 Kgs. 7:27 [o] 1 Kgs. 7:23

14 [p] Ex. 27:3; 1 Kgs. 7:45, 50 **16** [q] 1 Kgs. 7:47 **17** [r] [1 Kgs. 7:15-18; 2 Chr. 3:15] **18** [s] For ver. 18-21, see Jer. 52:24-27 [t] 1 Chr. 6:14; Ezra 7:1 [u] Jer. 21:1; 29:25; 37:3 **19** [v] Esth. 1:14; [Jer. 52:25] **20** [w] ch. 23:33 **21** [w] [See ver. 20 above] [x] [ch. 23:27; Lev. 26:33; Deut. 28:64] **22** [y] Jer. 39:14; 40:5 [z] ch. 22:12 **23** [a] For ver. 23, 24, see Jer. 40:7-9 [b] Josh. 18:26

Kareah, and Seraiah the son of Tanhumeth the Netophathite, and Jaazaniah the son of the Maacathite. 24 And Gedaliah swore to them and their men, saying, "Do not be afraid because of the Chaldean officials. Live in the land and serve the king of Babylon, and it shall be well with you." 25 [c]But in the seventh month, [d]Ishmael the son of Nethaniah, son of Elishama, of the royal family, came with ten men and struck down Gedaliah and put him to death along with the Jews and the Chaldeans who were with him at Mizpah. 26 [e]Then all the people, both small and great, and the captains of the forces arose and went to Egypt, for they were afraid of the Chaldeans.

Jehoiachin Released from Prison

27 [f]And in the thirty-seventh year of [g]the exile of Jehoiachin king of Judah, in the twelfth month, on the twenty-seventh day of the month, Evil-merodach king of Babylon, in the year that he began to reign, graciously [h]freed[1] Jehoiachin king of Judah from prison. 28 And he spoke kindly to him and gave him a seat above the seats of the kings who were with him in Babylon. 29 So Jehoiachin put off his prison garments. And every day of his life [i]he dined regularly at the king's table, 30 and for his allowance, a regular allowance was given him by the king, according to his daily needs, as long as he lived.

[1] Hebrew *reign, lifted up the head of*

25[c] Jer. 41:1, 2 [d] Jer. 40:14, 15 **26**[e] See Jer. 43:4-7 **27**[f] For ver. 27-30, see Jer. 52:31-34 [g] ch. 24:12, 15 [h] Gen. 40:13, 20 **29**[i] 2 Sam. 9:7, 13

Introduction to 1–2 Chronicles

Author and Date

The text of 1 and 2 Chronicles nowhere directly identifies its author, but traditionally he has been called "the Chronicler." He was either a priest or a Levite who was employed in the service of the temple during the Persian period (539–332 B.C.), after God's people had returned from exile.

The Gospel in 1–2 Chronicles

As the last books in the Hebrew Old Testament, the books of 1–2 Chronicles prepare God's people for the arrival of Jesus. This preparation begins with genealogies. But these genealogies are not random, wandering collections of paternity records. Rather, they represent the carefully crafted lens through which we observe the one plan of God's redemption. They teach us to rest in the unwavering commitment of God to fulfill all of his covenant promises.

The genealogies in 1 Chronicles give attention to each of the tribes of Israel, but clearly focus on two tribes: Judah (2:3–4:23 [110 verses]) and Levi (6:1–81). They focus on the tribes of Judah and Levi to identify the royal and priestly lines of Israel, searching for a rightful king and priest for God's people. The genealogies in Matthew (and Luke) find what Chronicles was searching for: Jesus, the true King (Rom. 1:3; 2 Tim. 2:8; Rev. 19:16) and Priest (Heb. 4:14; 5:5–6; 8:1) for God's people.

The summary of the history of Israel that follows the genealogies is shaped by the emphases of the genealogies—kingship and priesthood—expressed through Israel's inheritance of the land and worship in the temple. The presentations of David and Solomon focus on the building of the temple in Jerusalem. But we quickly encounter royal infidelity and idolatry, eventually resulting in the forfeiture of the land and the destruction of the temple. At the end, we are then left waiting for the true and better Priest-King of Israel to come and restore all things.

1-2 Chronicles Outline

I. A Genealogical Presentation of the Tribes of Israel (1 Chron. 1:1–9:44)

   A. Adam to Esau (1:1–54)

   B. The sons of Israel (2:1–2)

   C. The tribe of Judah (2:3–4:23)

   D. The tribe of Simeon (4:24–43)

   E. The Transjordanian tribes (5:1–26)

   F. The tribe of Levi (6:1–81)

G. Other northern tribes (7:1–40)

H. The tribe of Benjamin (8:1–40)

I. The resettlement of Jerusalem (9:1–34)

J. The genealogy of Saul (9:35–44)

II. The United Kingdom of David and Solomon (1 Chron. 10:1–2 Chron. 9:31)

A. David's rise to power over Israel (1 Chron. 10:1–12:40)

B. David's transfer of the ark of the covenant to Jerusalem (13:1–16:43)

C. The dynastic promise to David (17:1–27)

D. David's wars (18:1–20:8)

E. David's census and preparation for the temple (21:1–29:30)

F. Solomon's temple preparations (2 Chron. 1:1–2:18)

G. Solomon's building of the temple (3:1–5:1)

H. The dedication of the temple (5:2–7:22)

I. Solomon's other accomplishments (8:1–16)

J. Solomon's international relations and renown (8:17–9:31)

III. The Kingdom of Judah down to the Exile (2 Chron. 10:1–36:23)

A. Rehoboam (10:1–12:16)

B. Abijah (13:1–14:1)

C. Asa (14:2–16:14)

D. Jehoshaphat (17:1–21:1)

E. Jehoram and Ahaziah (21:2–22:12)

F. Joash (23:1–24:27)

G. Amaziah (25:1–28)

H. Uzziah (26:1–23)

I. Jotham (27:1–9)

J. Ahaz (28:1–27)

K. Hezekiah (29:1–32:33)

L. Manasseh (33:1–20)

M. Amon (33:21–25)

N. Josiah (34:1–35:27)

O. The last four kings (36:1–21)

P. Restoration (36:22–23)

1 Chronicles

From Adam to Abraham

1 [1] [a]Adam, Seth, Enosh; 2 [b]Kenan, Mahalalel,
Jared; 3 Enoch, Methuselah, Lamech; 4 Noah,
[c]Shem, Ham, and Japheth.
5 [d]The sons of Japheth: Gomer, Magog,
Madai, Javan, Tubal, Meshech, and Tiras.
6 The sons of Gomer: Ashkenaz, Riphath,[2]
and Togarmah. 7 The sons of Javan: Elishah,
Tarshish, Kittim, and Rodanim.
8 [e]The sons of Ham: Cush, Egypt, Put, and
Canaan. 9 The sons of Cush: Seba, Havilah,
Sabta, Raama, and Sabteca. The sons of
Raamah: Sheba and Dedan. 10 Cush fathered
Nimrod. He was the first on earth to be a
mighty man.[3]
11 [f]Egypt fathered Ludim, Anamim, Lehabim,
Naphtuhim, 12 Pathrusim, Casluhim (from
whom the Philistines came), and Caphtorim.
13 Canaan fathered Sidon his firstborn and
Heth, 14 and the Jebusites, the Amorites, the
Girgashites, 15 the Hivites, the Arkites, the
Sinites, 16 the Arvadites, the Zemarites, and
the Hamathites.
17 [g]The sons of Shem: Elam, Asshur, Arpachshad, Lud, and Aram. And the sons of Aram:[4]
Uz, Hul, Gether, and Meshech. 18 Arpachshad
fathered Shelah, and Shelah fathered Eber.
19 To Eber were born two sons: the name of
the one was Peleg[5] (for in his days the earth
was divided), and his brother's name was
Joktan. 20 Joktan fathered Almodad, Sheleph,
Hazarmaveth, Jerah, 21 Hadoram, Uzal, Diklah,
22 Obal,[6] Abimael, Sheba, 23 Ophir, Havilah, and
Jobab; all these were the sons of Joktan.
24 [h]Shem, Arpachshad, Shelah; 25 Eber, Peleg,
Reu; 26 Serug, Nahor, Terah; 27 Abram, that is,
Abraham.

From Abraham to Jacob

28 The sons of Abraham: [i]Isaac and [j]Ishmael.
29 [k]These are their genealogies: the firstborn
of Ishmael, Nebaioth, and Kedar, Adbeel,
Mibsam, 30 Mishma, Dumah, Massa, Hadad,
Tema, 31 Jetur, Naphish, and Kedemah. These
are the sons of Ishmael. 32 [l]The sons of Keturah,
Abraham's concubine: she bore Zimran,
Jokshan, Medan, Midian, Ishbak, and Shuah.
The sons of Jokshan: Sheba and Dedan. 33 The

[1] Many names in these genealogies are spelled differently in other biblical books [2] Septuagint; Hebrew *Diphath* [3] Or *He began to be a mighty man on the earth* [4] Septuagint; Hebrew lacks *And the sons of Aram* [5] *Peleg* means *division* [6] Septuagint, Syriac (compare Genesis 10:28); Hebrew *Ebal*

1:1 By beginning with Adam, Chronicles, the last book in the Hebrew Old Testament, connects itself to Genesis, the first book in the Hebrew Old Testament. This connection between Genesis and Chronicles is intended to demonstrate the fundamental unity of the story line carefully set forth in the pages of the Old Testament. In fact, Israel's experiences echoed those of Adam, through God's creation of a people, provision of special land and law, rest from labor, subsequent sin, and ejection from the land.

The same God who created the universe and granted humanity (Adam) royal dominion over the earth in Genesis was still working to accomplish his redemptive plan in 1–2 Chronicles; even while his people suffered as a community longing to experience the restoration of Davidic kingship, the Aaronic priesthood, and covenant blessings.

The appearance of Adam at the head of the genealogies of Chronicles not only grounded God's work of restoration in the past; it also began to prepare God's people for the arrival of *the* second Adam—Jesus, the son of Adam, the son of God (Luke 3:38; cf. Rom. 5:15–21; 1 Cor. 15:22, 45–49). These genealogies unite the two Testaments by identifying Jesus as the long-anticipated Seed of the woman who would come as our Savior (Acts 13:23) and crush the head of the Serpent (Gen. 3:15).

Chapter 1
1 [a]Gen. 4:25, 26; 5:3, 6
2 [b]For ver. 2-4, see Gen. 5:9-32
4 [c]Gen. 6:10; 9:18
5 [d]For ver. 5-7, see Gen. 10:2-4
8 [e]For ver. 8-10, see Gen. 10:6-8
11 [f]For ver. 11-16, see Gen. 10:10-18
17 [g]For ver. 17-23, see Gen. 10:22-29
24 [h]For ver. 24, 27, see Gen. 11:10-26; Luke 3:34-36
28 [i]Gen. 21:2, 3 [j]Gen. 16:11, 15
29 [k]For ver. 29-31, see Gen. 25:13-16
32 [l]For ver. 32, 33, see Gen. 25:1-4

sons of Midian: Ephah, Epher, Hanoch, Abida,
and Eldaah. All these were the descendants
of Keturah.
34 Abraham fathered [l]Isaac. The sons of
Isaac: [m]Esau and [n]Israel. 35 [o]The sons of Esau:
Eliphaz, Reuel, Jeush, Jalam, and Korah. 36 The
sons of Eliphaz: Teman, Omar, Zepho, Gatam,
Kenaz, and of Timna,[1] Amalek. 37 The sons of
Reuel: Nahath, Zerah, Shammah, and Mizzah.
38 [p]The sons of Seir: Lotan, Shobal, Zibeon,
Anah, Dishon, Ezer, and Dishan. 39 The sons
of Lotan: Hori and Hemam;[2] and Lotan's sister was Timna. 40 The sons of Shobal: Alvan,[3]
Manahath, Ebal, Shepho,[4] and Onam. The
sons of Zibeon: Aiah and Anah. 41 The son[5] of
Anah: Dishon. The sons of Dishon: Hemdan,[6]
Eshban, Ithran, and Cheran. 42 The sons of
Ezer: Bilhan, Zaavan, and Akan.[7] The sons of
Dishan: Uz and Aran.
43 [q]These are the kings who reigned in the
land of Edom before any king reigned over
the people of Israel: Bela the son of Beor, the
name of his city being Dinhabah. 44 Bela died,
and Jobab the son of Zerah of [r]Bozrah reigned
in his place. 45 Jobab died, and Husham of the
land of the [s]Temanites reigned in his place.
46 Husham died, and Hadad the son of Bedad,
who defeated Midian in the country of Moab,
reigned in his place, the name of his city being
Avith. 47 Hadad died, and Samlah of Masrekah
reigned in his place. 48 Samlah died, and Shaul
of Rehoboth on the Euphrates[8] reigned in
his place. 49 Shaul died, and Baal-hanan, the
son of Achbor, reigned in his place. 50 Baal-
hanan died, and Hadad reigned in his place,
the name of his city being Pai; and his wife's
name was Mehetabel, the daughter of Matred,
the daughter of Mezahab. 51 And Hadad died.
The chiefs of Edom were: chiefs Timna,
Alvah, Jetheth, 52 Oholibamah, Elah, Pinon,
53 Kenaz, Teman, Mibzar, 54 Magdiel, and Iram;
these are the chiefs of Edom.

A Genealogy of David

2 These are the sons of [t]Israel: [u]Reuben,
Simeon, Levi, Judah, [v]Issachar, Zebulun,
2 [w]Dan, [x]Joseph, [y]Benjamin, [z]Naphtali, [a]Gad,
and Asher. 3 [b]The sons of Judah: [c]Er, Onan and
Shelah; these three Bath-shua the Canaanite
bore to him. Now Er, Judah's firstborn, was
evil in the sight of the LORD, and he put him to
death. 4 His daughter-in-law [d]Tamar also bore
him Perez and Zerah. Judah had five sons in all.
5 The [e]sons of Perez: Hezron and Hamul.

[1] Septuagint (compare Genesis 36:12); Hebrew lacks *and of* [2] Septuagint (compare Genesis 36:22); Hebrew *Homam* [3] Septuagint (compare Genesis 36:23); Hebrew *Alian* [4] Septuagint (compare Genesis 36:23); Hebrew *Shephi* [5] Hebrew *sons* [6] Septuagint (compare Genesis 36:26); Hebrew *Hamran* [7] Septuagint (compare Genesis 36:27); Hebrew *Jaakan* [8] Hebrew *the River*

34 [l] [See ver. 28 above] [m] Gen. 25:25, 26 [n] Gen. 32:28
35 [o] For ver. 35-37, see Gen. 36:4, 5, 9-13
38 [p] For ver. 38-42, see Gen. 36:20-28
43 [q] For ver. 43-54, see Gen. 36:31-43
44 [r] Isa. 34:6; 63:1
45 [s] Gen. 36:11; Job 2:11; Jer. 49:7, 20; Ezek. 25:13
Chapter 2
1 [t] ch. 1:34 [u] Gen. 29:32-35 [v] Gen. 30:18-20
2 [w] Gen. 30:6 [x] Gen. 30:22-24 [y] Gen. 35:18 [z] Gen. 30:8 [a] Gen. 30:10-13
3 [b] Gen. 38:2-5; 46:12 [c] Gen. 38:7
4 [d] Gen. 38:11, 14, 29, 30; Ruth 4:12; Matt. 1:3
5 [e] Gen. 46:12; Ruth 4:18

2:1–2 The broad, sweeping genealogies of 1 Chronicles 1 come to an end by focusing on Israel (Jacob) and his 12 sons, for whom the 12 tribes of Israel were named. This dual focus, both on the nations in general and then more specifically on Israel, is characteristic of the Old Testament. God's concern for the whole world is not negated by the attention given to Israel in the Old Testament. Rather, it is helpful here to understand that God's care for the world is expressed by and mediated through his attention to Israel. This is one of the major components of the promise God made early on to Abraham, "in you *all the families of the earth* shall be blessed" (Gen. 12:3). And this same promise is upheld by God through his servant Israel, even in the midst of the nation's failure to keep the covenant, "I will make you as a light *for the nations*, that my salvation may reach to *the end of the earth*" (Isa. 49:6b; cf. Isa. 49:5–7). Thus, aspects of God's saving and multiplying grace are evident in the way the history of Israel is chronicled.

2:3–4:23 The genealogies in 1 Chronicles continue to narrow their focus. We have moved from the nations in general (1:1–54) to the specific nation of Israel and her 12 tribes (2:1–2). The rest of chapter 2 focuses on the tribe of Judah, the royal line of Israel from which the Messiah will come (Gen. 49:10). In fact, the genealogical material for Judah extends from 1 Chronicles 2:3 to 4:23, including some 110 verses, more than any other tribe. This type of emphasis clearly highlights the central role that the tribe of Judah will occupy in the upcoming narratives of God's unfolding grace.

During the exilic and postexilic period, a concern for the restoration of the Davidic dynasty occupied center stage in Israel's hope for the future. However, this hope was never fully realized in Israel's postexilic era. It was not until Jesus, the descendant of David according to the flesh (Rom. 1:3), ascended to the throne of the heavenly Father, that this hope began to find a satisfying expression (cf. Luke 22:69; Acts 2:25, 33–34; 5:31; 7:56; Rom. 8:34; Eph. 1:20; Heb. 1:3; 1 Pet. 3:22).

6 The sons of Zerah: Zimri, Ethan, Heman,
Calcol, and Dara, five in all. 7 The son[1] of
Carmi: Achan, the troubler of Israel, who
[f]broke faith in the matter of the devoted thing;
8 and Ethan's son was Azariah.

9 The sons of Hezron that were born to him:
Jerahmeel, [g]Ram, and [h]Chelubai. 10 [g]Ram
fathered Amminadab, and [i]Amminadab
fathered [j]Nahshon, prince of the sons of
Judah. 11 Nahshon fathered [k]Salmon,[2] Salmon
fathered [l]Boaz, 12 Boaz fathered Obed, [l]Obed
fathered Jesse. 13 [m]Jesse fathered Eliab his
firstborn, Abinadab the second, [n]Shimea the
third, 14 Nethanel the fourth, Raddai the fifth,
15 Ozem the sixth, [o]David the seventh. 16 And
their sisters were Zeruiah and Abigail. [p]The
sons of Zeruiah: Abishai, Joab, and Asahel,
three. 17 [q]Abigail bore Amasa, and the father
of Amasa was [q]Jether the Ishmaelite.

18 [r]Caleb the son of Hezron fathered children by his wife Azubah, and by Jerioth;
and these were her sons: Jesher, Shobab, and
Ardon. 19 When Azubah died, [r]Caleb married
[s]Ephrath, who bore him [t]Hur. 20 Hur fathered
Uri, and Uri fathered [u]Bezalel.

21 Afterward Hezron went in to the daughter of [v]Machir the father of Gilead, whom he
married when he was sixty years old, and she
bore him Segub. 22 And Segub fathered Jair,
who had twenty-three cities in the land of
Gilead. 23 [w]But Geshur and Aram took from
them Havvoth-jair, Kenath, and its villages,
sixty towns. All these were descendants of
Machir, the father of Gilead. 24 After the death
of Hezron, [x]Caleb went in to Ephrathah,[3] the
wife of Hezron his father, and she bore him
[y]Ashhur, the father of Tekoa.

25 The sons of [z]Jerahmeel, the firstborn of
Hezron: Ram, his firstborn, Bunah, Oren,
Ozem, and Ahijah. 26 Jerahmeel also had
another wife, whose name was Atarah; she
was the mother of Onam. 27 The sons of Ram,
the firstborn of Jerahmeel: Maaz, Jamin, and
Eker. 28 The sons of Onam: Shammai and Jada.
The sons of Shammai: Nadab and Abishur.
29 The name of Abishur's wife was Abihail, and
she bore him Ahban and Molid. 30 The sons
of Nadab: Seled and Appaim; and Seled died
childless. 31 The son[4] of Appaim: Ishi. [a]The son
of Ishi: Sheshan. The son of Sheshan: Ahlai.
32 The sons of Jada, Shammai's brother: Jether
and Jonathan; and Jether died childless. 33 The
sons of Jonathan: Peleth and Zaza. These were
the descendants of Jerahmeel. 34 Now Sheshan
had no sons, only daughters, but Sheshan had
an Egyptian slave whose name was Jarha.
35 So Sheshan gave his daughter in marriage
to Jarha his slave, and she bore him Attai.
36 Attai fathered Nathan, and Nathan fathered
[b]Zabad. 37 [b]Zabad fathered Ephlal, and Ephlal
fathered [c]Obed. 38 Obed fathered Jehu, and
Jehu fathered Azariah. 39 Azariah fathered
Helez, and Helez fathered Eleasah. 40 Eleasah
fathered Sismai, and Sismai fathered Shallum.
41 Shallum fathered Jekamiah, and Jekamiah
fathered [d]Elishama.

42 The sons of [e]Caleb the brother of Jerahmeel:
Mareshah[5] his firstborn, who fathered Ziph.
The son[6] of Mareshah: [f]Hebron.[7] 43 The sons
of Hebron: Korah, Tappuah, Rekem and
Shema. 44 Shema fathered Raham, the father
of Jorkeam; and Rekem fathered Shammai.
45 The son of Shammai: Maon; and Maon
fathered Beth-zur. 46 Ephah also, Caleb's concubine, bore Haran, Moza, and Gazez; and
Haran fathered Gazez. 47 The sons of Jahdai:

[1] Hebrew *sons* [2] Septuagint (compare Ruth 4:21); Hebrew *Salma* [3] Septuagint, Vulgate; Hebrew *in Caleb Ephrathah* [4] Hebrew *sons*; three times in this verse [5] Septuagint; Hebrew *Mesha* [6] Hebrew *sons* [7] Hebrew *the father of Hebron*

2:15 In 1 Samuel 17:12–14, David is identified as the eighth son of Jesse, the youngest son. Here, however, David is identified as the seventh son of Jesse, omitting Elihu from the list of Jesse's sons (cf. 1 Chron. 27:18). It is unlikely that the author of Chronicles has made a mistake. Rather, he may be making the theological point that David represents the seventh son, the son who would become the vehicle of God's sabbatical rest for God's people (cf. Gen. 2:1–3; 2 Sam. 7:1, 12–13).

The rest that David received from God as he reigned over Israel continues a whole-Bible trajectory beginning with day 7 of creation in Genesis 2 and ultimately culminating in the rest that the greater David, Jesus, would secure for his people. Recall the words of Jesus: "Come to me, all who labor and are heavy laden, and I will give you *rest*. Take my yoke upon you, and learn from me, for I am gentle and lowly in heart, and you will find *rest for your souls*" (Matt. 11:28–29; cf. Heb. 4:1–13).

7 [f] Josh. 6:18; 7:1
9 [g] Ruth 4:19; Matt. 1:3, 4 [h] [ver. 13, 42]
10 [g] [See ver. 9 above] [i] Ruth 4:19; Matt. 1:4 [j] Num. 1:7; 2:3
11 [k] [Ruth 4:20, 21; Matt. 1:4] [l] Ruth 4:21, 22; Matt. 1:5, 6
12 [l] [See ver. 11 above]
13 [m] 1 Sam. 16:6, 8; 17:13 [n] [1 Sam. 16:9; 17:13]
15 [o] [1 Sam. 16:10; 17:12, 14]
16 [p] 2 Sam. 2:18
17 [q] [2 Sam. 17:25]
18 [r] [ver. 9]
19 [r] [See ver. 18 above] [s] [ver. 50] [t] Ex. 17:10, 12; 24:14
20 [u] Ex. 31:2
21 [v] Num. 27:1

23 [w] [Num. 32:41, 42; Deut. 3:14; Josh. 13:30] **24** [x] ver. 19, 50 [y] ch. 4:5 **25** [z] ver. 9 **31** [a] [ver. 34, 35] **36** [b] ch. 11:41 **37** [b] [See ver. 36 above] [c] [2 Chr. 23:1]
41 [d] 2 Kgs. 25:25 **42** [e] ver. 9 [f] See Josh. 14:13

Regem, Jotham, Geshan, Pelet, Ephah, and Shaaph. 48 Maacah, Caleb's concubine, bore Sheber and Tirhanah. 49 She also bore Shaaph the father of Madmannah, Sheva the father of Machbenah and the father of Gibea; and the [g]daughter of Caleb was Achsah. 50 These were the descendants of Caleb.

The sons[1] of Hur the firstborn of [h]Ephrathah: Shobal the father of Kiriath-jearim, 51 [i]Salma, the father of Bethlehem, and Hareph the father of Beth-gader. 52 Shobal the father of Kiriath-jearim had other sons: [j]Haroeh, half of the Menuhoth. 53 And the clans of Kiriath-jearim: the Ithrites, the Puthites, the Shumathites, and the Mishraites; from these came the [k]Zorathites and the Eshtaolites. 54 The sons of Salma: Bethlehem, the Netophathites, Atroth-beth-joab and half of the Manahathites, the Zorites. 55 The clans also of the scribes who lived at Jabez: the Tirathites, the Shimeathites and the Sucathites. These are the [l]Kenites who came from Hammath, the father of [m]the house of Rechab.

Descendants of David

3 [n]These are the sons of David who were born to him in Hebron: the firstborn, Amnon, by Ahinoam the Jezreelite; the second, [o]Daniel, by Abigail the Carmelite, 2 the third, Absalom, whose mother was Maacah, the daughter of Talmai, king of Geshur; the fourth, Adonijah, whose mother was Haggith; 3 the fifth, Shephatiah, by Abital; the sixth, Ithream, by his wife Eglah; 4 six were born to him in Hebron, [p]where he reigned for seven years and six months. [q]And he reigned thirty-three years in Jerusalem. 5 [r]These were born to him in Jerusalem: [s]Shimea, Shobab, Nathan and [t]Solomon, four by [u]Bath-shua, the daughter of [u]Ammiel; 6 then Ibhar, [v]Elishama, Eliphelet, 7 Nogah, Nepheg, Japhia, 8 Elishama, [w]Eliada, and Eliphelet, nine. 9 All these were David's sons, besides the sons of the concubines, [x]and Tamar was their sister.

10 The son of Solomon was [y]Rehoboam, [z]Abijah his son, [a]Asa his son, [b]Jehoshaphat his son, 11 [c]Joram his son, [d]Ahaziah his son, [e]Joash his son, 12 [f]Amaziah his son, [g]Azariah his son, [h]Jotham his son, 13 [i]Ahaz his son, [j]Hezekiah his son, [k]Manasseh his son, 14 [l]Amon his son, [m]Josiah his son. 15 The sons of Josiah: [n]Johanan the firstborn, the second [o]Jehoiakim, the third [p]Zedekiah, the fourth Shallum. 16 The descendants of [q]Jehoiakim: [r]Jeconiah his son, [s]Zedekiah his son; 17 and the sons of Jeconiah, the [t]captive: [u]Shealtiel his son, 18 Malchiram, Pedaiah, Shenazzar, Jekamiah, Hoshama and Nedabiah; 19 and the sons of Pedaiah: [v]Zerubbabel and Shimei; and the sons of [v]Zerubbabel: Meshullam and Hananiah, and Shelomith was their sister; 20 and Hashubah, Ohel, Berechiah, Hasadiah, and Jushab-hesed, five. 21 The sons of Hananiah: Pelatiah and Jeshaiah, his son[2] Rephaiah, his son Arnan, his son Obadiah, his son Shecaniah. 22 The son[3] of Shecaniah: [w]Shemaiah. And the sons of Shemaiah: [x]Hattush, Igal, Bariah, Neariah, and Shaphat, six. 23 The sons of Neariah: Elioenai, Hizkiah, and Azrikam, three. 24 The sons of Elioenai: Hodaviah, Eliashib, Pelaiah, Akkub, Johanan, Delaiah, and Anani, seven.

Descendants of Judah

4 [y]The sons of Judah: [z]Perez, Hezron, [a]Carmi, Hur, and Shobal. 2 [b]Reaiah the son of Shobal fathered Jahath, and Jahath fathered Ahumai and Lahad. These were the clans of the [c]Zorathites. 3 These were the sons[4] of Etam: Jezreel, Ishma, and Idbash; and the name of their sister was Hazzelelponi, 4 and [d]Penuel fathered [e]Gedor, and Ezer fathered Hushah. These were the sons of Hur, the firstborn of [f]Ephrathah, the father of Bethlehem. 5 [g]Ashhur, the father of Tekoa, had two wives, Helah and Naarah; 6 Naarah bore him Ahuzzam, Hepher, Temeni, and Haahashtari. These were the sons of Naarah. 7 The sons of Helah: Zereth, Izhar, and Ethnan. 8 Koz fathered Anub, Zobebah, and the clans of Aharhel, the son of Harum. 9 Jabez was [h]more honorable than his brothers; and his mother called his name Jabez, saying, "Because I bore him in pain."[5] 10 Jabez called upon the God of Israel, saying, "Oh that you would bless me and enlarge my border, and that your hand might be with me, and that you would keep me from

[1] Septuagint, Vulgate; Hebrew *son* [2] Septuagint (compare Syriac, Vulgate); Hebrew *sons of*; four times in this verse [3] Hebrew *sons*
[4] Septuagint (compare Vulgate); Hebrew *father* [5] *Jabez* sounds like the Hebrew for *pain*

49[g] [Josh. 15:17; Judg. 1:13] **50**[h] ch. 4:4; [ver. 19] **51**[i] [ch. 4:4] **52**[j] [ch. 4:2] **53**[k] ch. 4:2 **55**[l] Judg. 1:16 [m] 2 Kgs. 10:15; Jer. 35:2 **Chapter 3** **1**[n] For ver. 1-4, see 2 Sam. 3:2-5 [o] [2 Sam. 3:3] **4**[p] 2 Sam. 2:11 [q] 2 Sam. 5:5 **5**[r] For ver. 5-8, see ch. 14:4-7; 2 Sam. 5:14-16 [s] [ch. 14:4; 2 Sam. 5:14] [t] 2 Sam. 12:24 [u] [2 Sam. 11:3] **6**[v] [ch. 14:5; 2 Sam. 5:15] **8**[w] [ch. 14:7] **9**[x] 2 Sam. 13:1 **10**[y] 1 Kgs. 11:43 [z] [1 Kgs. 14:31; 15:1] [a] 1 Kgs. 15:8 [b] 1 Kgs. 15:24 **11**[c] 2 Kgs. 8:16 [d] 2 Kgs. 8:24; [2 Chr. 21:17; 22:6] [e] 2 Kgs. 11:2 **12**[f] 2 Kgs. 12:21 [g] [2 Kgs. 15:30] [h] 2 Kgs. 15:7 **13**[i] 2 Kgs. 15:38 [j] 2 Kgs. 16:20 [k] 2 Kgs. 20:21 **14**[l] 2 Kgs. 21:18 [m] 2 Kgs. 21:26 **15**[n] [2 Kgs. 23:30] [o] [2 Kgs. 23:34] [p] [2 Kgs. 24:17] **16**[q] [Matt. 1:11] [r] [2 Kgs. 24:6; Jer. 22:24] [s] [2 Kgs. 24:17] **17**[t] 2 Kgs. 24:15 [u] Ezra 3:2; 5:2; Hag. 1:1, 12, 14; 2:2, 23; Matt. 1:12; Luke 3:27 **19**[v] Ezra 2:2; Hag. 1:1, 12, 14; Zech. 4:6 **22**[w] Neh. 3:29 [x] Ezra 8:2 **Chapter 4** **1**[y] [Gen. 46:12] [z] Gen. 38:29 [a] ch. 2:7 **2**[b] [ch. 2:52] [c] ch. 2:53 **4**[d] [ver. 18] [e] ver. 18, 39 [f] [Gen. 35:19; ch. 2:50, 51] **5**[g] ch. 2:24 **9**[h] [Gen. 34:19]

harm[1] so that it might not bring me pain!"
And God granted what he asked. 11 Chelub,
the brother of Shuhah, fathered Mehir, who
fathered Eshton. 12 Eshton fathered Beth-
rapha, Paseah, and Tehinnah, the father of
Ir-nahash. These are the men of Recah. 13 The
sons of [i]Kenaz: [j]Othniel and Seraiah; and the
sons of Othniel: Hathath and Meonothai.[2]
14 Meonothai fathered Ophrah; and Seraiah
fathered Joab, the father of Ge-harashim,[3] so-
called because they were craftsmen. 15 The sons
of [k]Caleb the son of Jephunneh: Iru, Elah, and
Naam; and the son[4] of Elah: Kenaz. 16 The sons
of Jehallelel: Ziph, Ziphah, Tiria, and Asarel.
17 The sons of Ezrah: Jether, Mered, Epher, and
Jalon. These are the sons of Bithiah, the daughter of Pharaoh, whom Mered married;[5] and
she conceived and bore[6] Miriam, Shammai,
and Ishbah, the father of Eshtemoa. 18 And his
Judahite wife bore [l]Jered the father of Gedor,
Heber the father of Soco, and Jekuthiel the
father of Zanoah. 19 The sons of the wife of
Hodiah, the sister of Naham, were the fathers
of Keilah the Garmite and Eshtemoa the
Maacathite. 20 The sons of Shimon: Amnon,
Rinnah, Ben-hanan, and Tilon. The sons of
Ishi: Zoheth and Ben-zoheth. 21 The sons of
[m]Shelah the son of Judah: Er the father of
Lecah, Laadah the father of Mareshah, and
the clans of the house of linen workers at Beth-
ashbea; 22 and Jokim, and the men of Cozeba,
and Joash, and Saraph, who ruled in Moab
and returned to Lehem[7] (now the records[8] are
ancient). 23 These were the potters who were
inhabitants of Netaim and Gederah. They
lived there in the king's service.

Descendants of Simeon

24 [n]The sons of Simeon: Nemuel, Jamin,
Jarib, Zerah, Shaul; 25 Shallum was his son,
Mibsam his son, Mishma his son. 26 The sons
of Mishma: Hammuel his son, Zaccur his son,
Shimei his son. 27 Shimei had sixteen sons and
six daughters; but his brothers did not have
many children, [o]nor did all their clan multi-
ply [p]like the men of Judah. 28 [q]They lived in
Beersheba, Moladah, Hazar-shual, 29 [r]Bilhah,
Ezem, [s]Tolad, 30 [s]Bethuel, Hormah, Ziklag,
31 Beth-marcaboth, [t]Hazar-susim, [t]Beth-biri,
and [t]Shaaraim. These were their cities until
David reigned. 32 And their villages were
Etam, Ain, Rimmon, Tochen, and Ashan, five

[1] Or *evil* [2] Septuagint, Vulgate; Hebrew lacks *Meonothai* [3] *Ge-harashim* means *valley of craftsmen* [4] Hebrew *sons* [5] The clause *These are . . . married* is transposed from verse 18 [6] Hebrew lacks *and bore* [7] Vulgate (compare Septuagint); Hebrew *and Jashubi-lahem* [8] Or *matters*

4:9–10 Among those listed in the genealogies of Judah, the author of Chronicles chose to highlight Jabez as one who "was more honorable than his brothers." In addition to his honor and the account of how the circumstances of his birth resulted in his name, the author of Chronicles took the time to record one of Jabez's prayers. In the context of the exile and the difficulty of returning home, this prayer reminded God's people that his gracious hand remained upon them to deliver from pain and to restore the blessings of the covenant.

4:24–5:26 In this section, the genealogies of Simeon, Reuben, Gad, and the half-tribe of Manasseh are presented. Though these tribes were smaller in number and not as prominent as some of the larger tribes in terms of the history of God's people as recorded in Scripture, Chronicles is concerned to demonstrate that God's salvation is for all of God's people, even for those who appear, at first glance, to play a minor role in the story (cf. 1 Cor. 1:27–29). By including these smaller, lesser-known tribes, the author reminds us about the nature of Israel's election: "It was not because you were more in number than any other people that the LORD set his love on you and chose you, *for you were the fewest of all peoples*" (Deut. 7:7). We are further reminded, then, of what Christ had to become for us, in order that he might help his weak and needy people: "For he was crucified in *weakness*, but lives by the *power of God*. For we also are *weak* in him, but in dealing with you we will live with him by the *power of God*" (2 Cor. 13:4).

This section also describes the devastating impact that sin can have in the lives of God's people. In 1 Chronicles 5:1 it is explained that Reuben's sin caused the forfeiting of his birthright. Then, in 5:25–26, these tribes are removed from the lands of their inheritance and sent into exile because they "whored after the gods of the peoples of the land." Left to our own sinful devices, we would be utterly doomed and completely helpless. But thanks be to God "that Christ Jesus came into the world to save sinners" (1 Tim. 1:15).

13 [i]Josh. 15:17 [j]Judg. 1:13; 3:9, 11
15 [k]Num. 13:6
18 [l][ver. 4]
21 [m]ch. 2:3; Gen. 38:1, 5; 46:12; Num. 26:20
24 [n]Num. 26:12
27 [o][ver. 38] [p][Num. 2:4, 13; 26:14, 22]
28 [q]For ver. 28-33, see Josh. 19:2-8
29 [r][Josh. 19:3] [s][Josh. 19:4]
30 [s][See ver. 29 above]
31 [t][Josh. 19:5, 6]

cities, 33 along with all their villages that were around these cities as far as [u]Baal. These were their settlements, and they kept a genealogical record.

34 Meshobab, Jamlech, Joshah the son of Amaziah, 35 Joel, Jehu the son of Joshibiah, son of Seraiah, son of Asiel, 36 Elioenai, Jaakobah, Jeshohaiah, Asaiah, Adiel, Jesimiel, Benaiah, 37 Ziza the son of Shiphi, son of Allon, son of Jedaiah, son of Shimri, son of Shemaiah— 38 these mentioned by name were princes in their clans, [v]and their fathers' houses increased greatly. 39 They journeyed to the entrance of [w]Gedor, to the east side of the valley, to seek pasture for their flocks, 40 where they found rich, good pasture, and the land was very broad, [x]quiet, and peaceful, for the former inhabitants there belonged to Ham. 41 [y]These, registered by name, came in the days of Hezekiah, king of Judah, and destroyed their tents and the Meunites who were found there, and marked them for destruction to this day, [z]and settled in their place, because there was pasture there for their flocks. 42 And some of them, five hundred men of the Simeonites, went to [a]Mount Seir, having as their leaders Pelatiah, Neariah, Rephaiah, and Uzziel, the sons of Ishi. 43 And they defeated [b]the remnant of the Amalekites who had escaped, and they have lived there to this day.

Descendants of Reuben

5 The sons of Reuben the firstborn of Israel ([c]for he was the firstborn, but because [d]he defiled his father's couch, [e]his birthright was given to the sons of Joseph the son of Israel, so that he could not be enrolled as the oldest son; 2 [f]though Judah became strong among his brothers and a [g]chief came from him, yet the birthright belonged to Joseph), 3 the [h]sons of Reuben, the firstborn of Israel: Hanoch, Pallu, Hezron, and Carmi. 4 The sons of Joel: Shemaiah his son, Gog his son, Shimei his son, 5 Micah his son, Reaiah his son, Baal his son, 6 Beerah his son, whom [i]Tiglath-pileser[1] king of Assyria carried away into exile; he was a chief of the Reubenites. 7 And his kinsmen by their clans, [j]when the genealogy of their generations was recorded: the chief, Jeiel, and Zechariah, 8 and Bela the son of Azaz, son of [k]Shema, son of Joel, who lived in [l]Aroer, as far as [m]Nebo and [n]Baal-meon. 9 He also lived to the east as far as the entrance of the desert this side of the Euphrates, because their livestock had multiplied [o]in the land of Gilead. 10 And in the days of Saul they waged war against the [p]Hagrites, who fell into their hand. And they lived in their tents throughout all the region east of Gilead.

Descendants of Gad

11 The sons of Gad lived over against them in the land of Bashan as far as [q]Salecah: 12 Joel the chief, Shapham the second, Janai, and Shaphat in Bashan. 13 And their kinsmen according to their fathers' houses: Michael, Meshullam, Sheba, Jorai, Jacan, Zia and Eber, seven. 14 These were the sons of Abihail the son of Huri, son of Jaroah, son of Gilead, son of Michael, son of Jeshishai, son of Jahdo, son of Buz. 15 Ahi the son of Abdiel, son of Guni, was chief in their fathers' houses, 16 and they lived in Gilead, in Bashan and in its towns, and in all the pasturelands of [r]Sharon to their limits. 17 All of these were recorded in genealogies in the days of [s]Jotham king of Judah, and in the days of [t]Jeroboam king of Israel.

18 The Reubenites, the Gadites, and the half-tribe of Manasseh had valiant men who carried shield and sword, and drew the bow, [u]expert in war, 44,760, able to go to war. 19 They waged war against the [v]Hagrites, [w]Jetur, Naphish, and Nodab. 20 And when they prevailed[2] over them, the Hagrites and all who were with them were given into their hands, [x]for they cried out to God in the battle, and he granted their urgent plea [y]because they trusted in him. 21 They carried off their livestock: 50,000 of their camels, 250,000 sheep, 2,000 donkeys, and 100,000 men alive. 22 For many fell, because the war was of God. And they lived [z]in their place until [a]the exile.

The Half-Tribe of Manasseh

23 The members of the half-tribe of Manasseh lived in the land. They were very numerous from Bashan to Baal-hermon, [b]Senir, and Mount Hermon. 24 These were the heads of their fathers' houses: Epher,[3] Ishi, Eliel, Azriel, Jeremiah, Hodaviah, and Jahdiel, mighty

[1] Hebrew *Tilgath-pilneser*; also verse 26 [2] Or *they were helped to prevail* [3] Septuagint, Vulgate; Hebrew *and Epher*

33[u] [Josh. 19:8] **38**[v] [ver. 27] **39**[w] ver. 4, 18 **40**[x] [Judg. 18:7, 27] **41**[y] See ver. 34-38 [z] [ch. 5:22] **42**[a] Gen. 36:8 **43**[b] [1 Sam. 15:8; 30:17]
Chapter 5 **1**[c] Gen. 29:32; 49:3 [d] Gen. 35:22; 49:4 [e] See Gen. 48:15-22 **2**[f] See Gen. 49:8-10 [g] Mic. 5:2; Matt. 2:6 **3**[h] Gen. 46:9; Ex. 6:14; Num. 26:5, 6 **6**[i] 2 Chr. 28:20 **7**[j] ver. 17 **8**[k] [ver. 4] [l] Deut. 2:36; Josh. 13:16 [m] Num. 32:3 [n] Num. 32:38 **9**[o] Josh. 22:9 **10**[p] ver. 19, 20; ch. 11:38; 27:30 **11**[q] Josh. 12:5; 13:11 **16**[r] ch. 27:29 **17**[s] 2 Kgs. 15:5, 32 [t] 2 Kgs. 14:16, 28 **18**[u] Num. 1:3 **19**[v] See ver. 10 [w] ch. 1:31; [Gen. 25:15] **20**[x] [2 Chr. 14:11; 18:31] [y] Ps. 22:4, 5 **22**[z] ch. 4:41 [a] ver. 6; 2 Kgs. 15:29; 17:6 **23**[b] Deut. 3:9; Ezek. 27:5

warriors, famous men, heads of their fathers' houses. 25 But they broke faith with the God of their fathers, and [c]whored [d]after the gods of the peoples of the land, whom God had destroyed before them. 26 So the God of Israel stirred up the spirit of [e]Pul king of Assyria, the spirit of [f]Tiglath-pileser king of Assyria, and he took them into exile, namely, the Reubenites, the Gadites, and the half-tribe of Manasseh, and brought them [g]to Halah, [g]Habor, Hara, and [g]the river Gozan, to this day.

Descendants of Levi

6 1[1] [h]The sons of Levi: Gershon, Kohath, and Merari. 2 [i]The sons of Kohath: Amram, Izhar, Hebron, and Uzziel. 3 [j]The children of Amram: Aaron, Moses, and Miriam. [k]The sons of Aaron: Nadab, Abihu, Eleazar, and Ithamar. 4 [l, m]Eleazar fathered [n]Phinehas, Phinehas fathered Abishua, 5 Abishua fathered Bukki, Bukki fathered Uzzi, 6 Uzzi fathered Zerahiah, Zerahiah fathered [o]Meraioth, 7 Meraioth fathered Amariah, Amariah fathered Ahitub, 8 [p]Ahitub fathered [q]Zadok, Zadok fathered Ahimaaz, 9 Ahimaaz fathered Azariah, Azariah fathered Johanan, 10 and Johanan fathered Azariah ([r]it was he who served as priest [s]in the house that Solomon built in Jerusalem). 11 [l]Azariah fathered [t]Amariah, Amariah fathered Ahitub, 12 Ahitub fathered Zadok, Zadok fathered [u]Shallum, 13 Shallum fathered [v]Hilkiah, Hilkiah fathered Azariah, 14 Azariah fathered [w]Seraiah, Seraiah fathered Jehozadak; 15 and [x]Jehozadak went into exile when the LORD sent Judah and Jerusalem into exile [y]by the hand of Nebuchadnezzar.

16[2] The [z]sons of Levi: Gershom, Kohath, and Merari. 17 And these are the names of the sons of Gershom: [a]Libni and Shimei. 18 [b]The sons of Kohath: Amram, Izhar, Hebron and Uzziel. 19 [c]The sons of Merari: Mahli and Mushi. These are the clans of the Levites according to their fathers. 20 [d]Of Gershom: Libni his son, [e]Jahath his son, Zimmah his son, 21 Joah his son, Iddo his son, Zerah his son, Jeatherai his son. 22 [f]The sons of Kohath: Amminadab his son, Korah his son, Assir his son, 23 Elkanah his son, Ebiasaph his son, Assir his son, 24 Tahath his son, Uriel his son, Uzziah his son, and Shaul his son. 25 The sons of Elkanah: Amasai and Ahimoth, 26 Elkanah his son, Zophai his son, Nahath his son, 27 Eliab his son, Jeroham his son, Elkanah his son. 28 The sons of Samuel: Joel[3] his firstborn, the second Abijah.[4] 29 [g]The sons of Merari: Mahli, Libni his son, Shimei his son, Uzzah his son, 30 Shimea his son, Haggiah his son, and Asaiah his son.

31 These are the men [h]whom David put in charge of the service of song in the house of the LORD [i]after the ark rested there. 32 They ministered with song before the tabernacle of the tent of meeting until Solomon built the house of the LORD in Jerusalem, and they performed their service according to their order. 33 These are the men who served and their sons. Of the sons of the Kohathites: Heman the singer the son of Joel, son of [j]Samuel, 34 son of Elkanah, son of Jeroham, son of Eliel, son of Toah, 35 son of Zuph, son of Elkanah, son of Mahath, son of Amasai, 36 son of Elkanah, son of Joel, son of Azariah, son of Zephaniah, 37 son of Tahath, son of Assir, son of Ebiasaph, son of Korah, 38 son of Izhar, son of Kohath, son of Levi, son of Israel; 39 and his brother [k]Asaph, who stood on his right hand, namely, Asaph the son of Berechiah, son of Shimea, 40 son of Michael, son of Baaseiah, son of Malchijah, 41 son of Ethni, son of Zerah, son of Adaiah, 42 son of Ethan, son of Zimmah, son of Shimei, 43 son of Jahath, son of Gershom, son of Levi. 44 On the left hand were their brothers, the sons of Merari: Ethan the son of Kishi, son of Abdi, son of Malluch, 45 son of Hashabiah, son of Amaziah, son of Hilkiah, 46 son of Amzi, son of Bani, son of Shemer, 47 son of Mahli, son of

[1] Ch 5:27 in Hebrew [2] Ch 6:1 in Hebrew [3] Septuagint, Syriac (compare verse 33 and 1 Samuel 8:2); Hebrew lacks *Joel* [4] Hebrew *and Abijah*

6:1–81 At the center of the genealogies in 1 Chronicles, the tribe of Levi appears, occupying 81 verses of text, an amount second only to the royal tribe of Judah at 110 verses. By placing the Levitical genealogies at the center and providing this detailed account, the author highlights the importance of worship for God's people, as they respond to his gracious provision with thanksgiving, sacrifice, and praise. In the New Testament, the importance of worship continues, and it will become the center of activity in the new heavens and new earth (cf. John 4:20–24; Rom. 12:1; Heb. 12:28–29; Rev. 21:22–26; 22:3–5).

25 [c]See Ex. 34:15 [d]2 Kgs. 17:7 **26** [e]2 Kgs. 15:19 [f]See ver. 6 [g]2 Kgs. 17:6; 18:11

Chapter 6

1 [h]ch. 23:6; Gen. 46:11; Ex. 6:16; Num. 26:57 **2** [i]Ex. 6:18; [ver. 22] **3** [j]Ex. 6:20; 15:20 [k]Lev. 10:1, 12 **4** [l]For ver. 4-6, 11-14, see Ezra 7:1-5 [m]For ver. 4-8, see ver. 50-53 [n]See Ex. 6:25 **6** [o][ch. 9:11; Neh. 11:11] **8** [p]2 Sam. 8:17 [q]2 Sam. 15:27 **10** [r]2 Chr. 26:17, 18 [s]See 1 Kgs. 6; 2 Chr. 3 **11** [l][See ver. 4 above] [t]2 Chr. 19:11; Ezra 7:3 **12** [u][Neh. 11:11] **13** [v]2 Kgs. 22:4; Ezra 7:1 **14** [w]2 Kgs. 25:18 **15** [x][Ezra 3:2] [y]See 2 Kgs. 25:8-21 **16** [z]For ver. 16-19, see Ex. 6:16-19 **17** [a][ch. 23:7] **18** [b]ch. 23:12 **19** [c]ch. 23:21; [ver. 44, 47] **20** [d]For ver. 20, 21, see ver. 41-43 [e]ver. 43 **22** [f]For ver. 22-28, see ver. 33-38 **29** [g][ver. 19, 44-47] **31** [h]See ch. 16:4-6 [i]See ch. 15:25–16:1; 2 Sam. 6:12-17 **33** [j][ver. 28] **39** [k]ch. 15:17, 19; 2 Chr. 5:12; Ezra 2:41; Neh. 7:44

Mushi, son of Merari, son of Levi. 48 And their
brothers the Levites were appointed for all the
service of the tabernacle of the house of God.
49 But Aaron and his sons made offerings
[l]on the altar of burnt offering and on [m]the
altar of incense for all the work of the Most
Holy Place, and [n]to make atonement for Israel,
according to all that Moses the servant of
God had commanded. 50 [o]These are the sons
of Aaron: Eleazar his son, Phinehas his son,
Abishua his son, 51 Bukki his son, Uzzi his
son, Zerahiah his son, 52 Meraioth his son,
Amariah his son, Ahitub his son, 53 Zadok his
son, Ahimaaz his son.
54 These are their dwelling places according
to their [p]settlements within their borders: to
the sons of Aaron of the [q]clans of Kohathites,
for theirs was the first lot, 55 to them they gave
Hebron in the land of Judah and its surrounding pasturelands, 56 [r]but the fields of the city
and its villages they gave to Caleb the son of
Jephunneh. 57 [s]To the sons of Aaron they gave
the cities of refuge: Hebron, Libnah with its
pasturelands, Jattir, Eshtemoa with its pasturelands, 58 Hilen with its pasturelands,
Debir with its pasturelands, 59 Ashan with its
pasturelands, and Beth-shemesh with its pasturelands; 60 and from the tribe of Benjamin,
Gibeon,[1] Geba with its pasturelands, Alemeth
with its pasturelands, and Anathoth with its
pasturelands. All their cities throughout their
clans were thirteen.
61 [t]To the rest of the Kohathites were given
by lot out of the clan of the tribe, out of the
half-tribe, the half of Manasseh, ten cities.
62 To the Gershomites according to their clans
were allotted thirteen cities out of the tribes
of Issachar, Asher, Naphtali and Manasseh in
Bashan. 63 [u]To the Merarites according to their
clans were allotted twelve cities out of the tribes
of Reuben, Gad, and Zebulun. 64 [v]So the people
of Israel gave the Levites the cities with their
pasturelands. 65 They gave by lot out of the
tribes of Judah, Simeon, and Benjamin [w]these
cities that are mentioned by name.
66 [x]And some of the clans of the sons of
Kohath had cities of their territory out of the
tribe of Ephraim. 67 They were given the cities of refuge: Shechem with its pasturelands
in the hill country of Ephraim, Gezer with
its pasturelands, 68 [y]Jokmeam with its pasturelands, Beth-horon with its pasturelands,
69 Aijalon with its pasturelands, Gath-rimmon
with its pasturelands, 70 and out of the half-
tribe of Manasseh, Aner with its pasturelands,
and Bileam with its pasturelands, for the rest
of the clans of the Kohathites.
71 [z]To the Gershomites were given out of the
clan of the half-tribe of Manasseh: Golan in
Bashan with its pasturelands and [a]Ashtaroth
with its pasturelands; 72 and out of the tribe
of Issachar: Kedesh with its pasturelands,
Daberath with its pasturelands, 73 Ramoth
with its pasturelands, and Anem with its pasturelands; 74 out of the tribe of Asher: Mashal
with its pasturelands, Abdon with its pasturelands, 75 Hukok with its pasturelands, and
Rehob with its pasturelands; 76 and out of the
tribe of Naphtali: Kedesh in Galilee with its
pasturelands, Hammon with its pasturelands,
and Kiriathaim with its pasturelands. 77 [b]To
the rest of the Merarites were allotted out of
the tribe of Zebulun: [c]Rimmono with its pasturelands, [c]Tabor with its pasturelands, 78 and
[d]beyond the Jordan at Jericho, on the east side
of the Jordan, out of the tribe of Reuben: Bezer
in the wilderness with its pasturelands, Jahzah
with its pasturelands, 79 Kedemoth with its
pasturelands, and Mephaath with its pasturelands; 80 and out of the tribe of Gad: [e]Ramoth
in Gilead with its pasturelands, [f]Mahanaim
with its pasturelands, 81 [g]Heshbon with its
pasturelands, and [h]Jazer with its pasturelands.

Descendants of Issachar

7 The sons[2] of Issachar: Tola, [i]Puah, [j]Jashub,
and Shimron, four. 2 The sons of Tola: Uzzi,
Rephaiah, Jeriel, Jahmai, Ibsam, and Shemuel,
heads of their fathers' houses, namely of Tola,
mighty warriors of their generations, their
number [k]in the days of David being 22,600.
3 The son[3] of Uzzi: Izrahiah. And the sons of
Izrahiah: Michael, Obadiah, Joel, and Isshiah,
all five of them were chief men. 4 And along
with them, by their generations, according to
their fathers' houses, were units of the army
for war, 36,000, for they had many wives and
sons. 5 Their kinsmen belonging to all the

[1] Septuagint, Syriac (compare Joshua 21:17); Hebrew lacks *Gibeon* [2] Syriac (compare Vulgate); Hebrew *And to the sons* [3] Hebrew *sons*; also verses 10, 12, 17

49 [l] Lev. 1:7, 9 [m] Ex. 30:7 [n] Ex. 30:10; Lev. 4:20 **50** [o] For ver. 50-53, see ver. 4-8 **54** [p] Gen. 25:16; Num. 31:10 [q] Josh. 21:4, 10 **56** [r] [Josh. 14:13; 15:13] **57** [s] For ver. 57-60, see Josh. 21:13-19 **61** [t] [ver. 66-70; Josh. 21:5] **63** [u] Josh. 21:7 **64** [v] Josh. 21:3 **65** [w] See ver. 57-60 **66** [x] For ver. 66-70, see Josh. 21:20-26 **68** [y] Josh. 12:22; 1 Kgs. 4:12 **71** [z] For ver. 71-76, see Josh. 21:27-33 [a] Josh. 9:10 **77** [b] For ver. 77-81, see Josh. 21:34-39 [c] [Josh. 19:12, 13] **78** [d] Josh. 13:32 **80** [e] 1 Kgs. 22:3, 4; 2 Kgs. 9:1, 14 [f] See Gen. 32:2 **81** [g] Josh. 13:17; 21:39 [h] Num. 21:32; Josh. 21:39 **Chapter 7** **1** [i] [Num. 26:23] [j] [Gen. 46:13] **2** [k] 2 Sam. 24:1, 2, 9

clans of Issachar were in all 87,000 mighty
warriors, enrolled by genealogy.

Descendants of Benjamin

6 [l]The sons of Benjamin: Bela, Becher, and
Jediael, three. 7 The sons of Bela: Ezbon, Uzzi,
Uzziel, Jerimoth, and Iri, five, heads of fathers'
houses, mighty warriors. And their enrollment by genealogies was 22,034. 8 The sons of
Becher: Zemirah, Joash, Eliezer, Elioenai, Omri,
Jeremoth, Abijah, [m]Anathoth, and Alemeth.
All these were the sons of Becher. 9 And their
enrollment by genealogies, according to
their generations, as heads of their fathers'
houses, mighty warriors, was 20,200. 10 The
son of Jediael: Bilhan. And the sons of Bilhan:
Jeush, Benjamin, Ehud, Chenaanah, Zethan,
Tarshish, and Ahishahar. 11 All these were the
sons of Jediael according to the heads of their
fathers' houses, mighty warriors, 17,200, able
to go to war. 12 And Shuppim and Huppim were
the sons of Ir, Hushim the son of [n]Aher.

Descendants of Naphtali

13 [o]The sons of Naphtali: [p]Jahziel, Guni, Jezer
and [q]Shallum, the descendants of Bilhah.

Descendants of Manasseh

14 [r]The sons of Manasseh: Asriel, whom his
Aramean concubine bore; she bore [s]Machir
the father of Gilead. 15 And Machir took a wife
for Huppim and for Shuppim. The name of
his sister was Maacah. And the name of the
second was Zelophehad, and [t]Zelophehad had
daughters. 16 And Maacah the wife of Machir
bore a son, and she called his name Peresh;
and the name of his brother was Sheresh; and
his sons were Ulam and Rakem. 17 The son of
Ulam: [u]Bedan. These were the sons of Gilead
the son of Machir, son of Manasseh. 18 And his
sister Hammolecheth bore Ishhod, Abiezer
and Mahlah. 19 The sons of Shemida were
Ahian, Shechem, Likhi, and Aniam.

Descendants of Ephraim

20 The [v]sons of Ephraim: Shuthelah, and
Bered his son, Tahath his son, Eleadah his son,
Tahath his son, 21 Zabad his son, Shuthelah
his son, and Ezer and Elead, whom the men
of Gath who were born in the land killed,
because they came down to raid their livestock. 22 And Ephraim their father mourned
many days, and his brothers came to comfort
him. 23 And Ephraim went in to his wife, and
she conceived and bore a son. And he called
his name Beriah, because disaster had befallen
his house.[1] 24 His daughter was Sheerah, who
built both Lower and Upper [w]Beth-horon,
and Uzzen-sheerah. 25 Rephah was his son,
Resheph his son, Telah his son, Tahan his son,
26 Ladan his son, Ammihud his son, [x]Elishama
his son, 27 Nun[2] his son, [y]Joshua his son.
28 [z]Their possessions and settlements were
Bethel and its towns, and to the east Naaran,
and to the west [a]Gezer and its towns, Shechem
and its towns, and Ayyah and its towns; 29 [b]also
in possession of the Manassites, [c]Beth-shean
and its towns, Taanach and its towns, Megiddo
and its towns, Dor and its towns. In these lived
the sons of Joseph the son of Israel.

Descendants of Asher

30 [d]The sons of Asher: Imnah, Ishvah, Ishvi,
Beriah, and their sister Serah. 31 The sons of
Beriah: Heber, and Malchiel, who fathered
Birzaith. 32 Heber fathered Japhlet, Shomer,
Hotham, and their sister Shua. 33 The sons of
Japhlet: Pasach, Bimhal, and Ashvath. These
are the sons of Japhlet. 34 The sons of Shemer
his brother: Rohgah, Jehubbah, and Aram.
35 The sons of Helem his brother: Zophah,
Imna, Shelesh, and Amal. 36 The sons of
Zophah: Suah, Harnepher, Shual, Beri, Imrah.
37 Bezer, Hod, Shamma, Shilshah, Ithran, and
Beera. 38 The sons of Jether: Jephunneh, Pispa,
and Ara. 39 The sons of Ulla: Arah, Hanniel, and
Rizia. 40 All of these were men of Asher, heads
of fathers' houses, approved, mighty warriors,
chiefs of the princes. Their number enrolled by
genealogies, for service in war, was 26,000 men.

A Genealogy of Saul

8 [e]Benjamin fathered Bela his firstborn,
Ashbel the second, [f]Aharah the third,
2 Nohah the fourth, and Rapha the fifth. 3 And

[1] *Beriah* sounds like the Hebrew for *disaster* [2] Hebrew *Non*

7:1–40 On these genealogies, see the note on 4:24–5:26.

8:1–40 It should be shocking to discover the position of prominence allotted to the tribe of Benjamin in the genealogies of Chronicles, ranking third in length after Judah

6[l]Gen. 46:21; Num. 26:38; See ch. 8:1-40
8[m][ch. 6:60]
12[n][ch. 8:1]
13[o]Num. 26:48-50
[p][Num. 26:48] [q][Num. 26:49] **14**[r]For ver. 14-19, see Num. 26:29-33 [s]See Josh. 17:1 **15**[t]Num. 27:1; 36:11; Josh. 17:3 **17**[u]1 Sam. 12:11 **20**[v]Num. 26:35
24[w]See Josh. 10:10, 11 **26**[x]Num. 1:10; 7:48 **27**[y]Num. 13:8, 16 **28**[z]Josh. 16:2, 3 [a]Josh. 16:3 **29**[b]Josh. 17:7 [c]Josh. 17:11 **30**[d]Gen. 46:17; Num. 26:44
Chapter 8 **1**[e][ch. 7:6; Gen. 46:21; Num. 26:38] [f][ch. 7:12]

Bela had sons: Addar, Gera, Abihud, 4 Abishua,
[g]Naaman, Ahoah, 5 Gera, [h]Shephuphan, and
Huram. 6 These are the sons of Ehud (they
were heads of fathers' houses of the inhabitants of Geba, and they were carried into
exile to [i]Manahath): 7 Naaman,[1] Ahijah, and
Gera, that is, Heglam,[2] who fathered Uzza
and Ahihud. 8 And Shaharaim fathered sons
in the country of Moab after he had sent away
Hushim and Baara his wives. 9 He fathered
sons by Hodesh his wife: Jobab, Zibia, Mesha,
Malcam, 10 Jeuz, Sachia, and Mirmah. These
were his sons, heads of fathers' houses. 11 He
also fathered sons by Hushim: Abitub and
Elpaal. 12 The sons of Elpaal: Eber, Misham,
and Shemed, who built [j]Ono and [k]Lod with
its towns, 13 and Beriah and [l]Shema (they were
heads of fathers' houses of the inhabitants of
[m]Aijalon, who caused the inhabitants of Gath
to flee); 14 and Ahio, Shashak, and Jeremoth.
15 Zebadiah, Arad, Eder, 16 Michael, Ishpah,
and Joha were sons of Beriah. 17 Zebadiah,
Meshullam, Hizki, Heber, 18 Ishmerai,
Izliah, and Jobab were the sons of Elpaal.
19 Jakim, Zichri, Zabdi, 20 Elienai, Zillethai,
Eliel, 21 Adaiah, Beraiah, and Shimrath were
the sons of Shimei. 22 Ishpan, Eber, Eliel,
23 Abdon, Zichri, Hanan, 24 Hananiah, Elam,
Anthothijah, 25 Iphdeiah, and Penuel were the
sons of Shashak. 26 Shamsherai, Shehariah,
Athaliah, 27 Jaareshiah, Elijah, and Zichri were
the sons of Jeroham. 28 These were the heads of
fathers' houses, according to their generations,
chief men. These lived in Jerusalem.

29 [n, o]Jeiel[3] the father of Gibeon lived in Gibeon,
and the name of his wife was Maacah. 30 His
firstborn son: Abdon, then Zur, Kish, Baal,
Nadab, 31 Gedor, Ahio, Zecher, 32 and Mikloth
(he fathered Shimeah). Now these also lived
opposite their kinsmen in Jerusalem, with their
kinsmen. 33 [p]Ner was the father of Kish, Kish of
Saul, Saul of [q]Jonathan, Malchi-shua, Abinadab
and Eshbaal; 34 and the son of Jonathan was
Merib-baal; and Merib-baal was the father of
[r]Micah. 35 The sons of Micah: Pithon, Melech,
Tarea, and Ahaz. 36 Ahaz fathered Jehoaddah,
and Jehoaddah fathered Alemeth, Azmaveth,
and Zimri. Zimri fathered Moza. 37 Moza
fathered Binea; Raphah was his son, Eleasah
his son, Azel his son. 38 Azel had six sons, and
these are their names: Azrikam, Bocheru,
Ishmael, Sheariah, Obadiah, and Hanan. All
these were the sons of Azel. 39 The sons of
Eshek his brother: Ulam his firstborn, Jeush
the second, and Eliphelet the third. 40 The sons
of Ulam were men who were mighty warriors,
bowmen, having many sons and grandsons,
150. All these were Benjaminites.

A Genealogy of the Returned Exiles

9 So all Israel was recorded in genealogies,
and these are written in the Book of the
Kings of Israel. And [s]Judah was taken into
exile in Babylon because of their breach of
faith. 2 [t]Now the first to [u]dwell again in their
possessions in their cities were Israel, the
priests, the Levites, and the [v]temple servants.
3 And some of the people of Judah, Benjamin,
Ephraim, and Manasseh lived in Jerusalem:
4 Uthai the son of Ammihud, son of Omri, son
of Imri, son of Bani, from the sons of [w]Perez
the son of Judah. 5 And of the Shilonites:
Asaiah the firstborn, and his sons. 6 Of the sons
of Zerah: Jeuel and their kinsmen, 690. 7 Of the
Benjaminites: Sallu the son of Meshullam, son
of Hodaviah, son of Hassenuah, 8 Ibneiah the
son of Jeroham, Elah the son of Uzzi, son of
Michri, and Meshullam the son of Shephatiah,

[1] Hebrew *and Naaman* [2] Or *he carried them into exile* [3] Compare 9:35; Hebrew lacks *Jeiel*

4 [g] Num. 26:40
5 [h] [ch. 7:12]
6 [i] [ch. 2:52, 54]
12 [j] Ezra 2:33; Neh. 6:2; 7:37; 11:35 [k] [Acts 9:32, 35, 38]
13 [l] [ver. 21] [m] Josh. 10:12
29 [n] [ch. 9:35] [o] For ver. 29-32, see ch. 9:35-38
33 [p] For ver. 33-38, see ch. 9:39-44; [1 Sam. 9:1; 14:51] [q] ch. 10:2; 1 Sam. 31:2
34 [r] 2 Sam. 9:12

Chapter 9
1 [s] ch. 5:25, 26
2 [t] For ver. 2-22, see Neh. 11:3-22 [u] Ezra 2:70; Neh. 7:73 [v] Ezra 2:43, 58; 7:7; 8:17, 20; Neh. 3:26; 7:60, 73; 10:28; 11:3, 21; [Josh. 9:27]
4 [w] [ch. 2:5, 6]

and Levi. In the book of Judges, the sinfulness of the tribe of Benjamin was so great that Israel was compelled to wage war against it, bringing this tribe to the brink of extinction (Judges 19–20). Then, in the books of Samuel, the tribe of Benjamin forfeited its royal status because of the sinful disobedience of King Saul, a Benjaminite. And so when we encounter in 1 Chronicles the prominence of the genealogy of Benjamin, the last in order and rank among Jacob's sons, we are truly reminded of the good news of God's abundant grace: "The steadfast love of the LORD never ceases; his mercies never come to an end" (Lam. 3:22).

9:1 We are reminded in this verse that Israel's exile was precipitated by her unfaithfulness to the Mosaic covenant. The events of the exile, though disciplinary, should also remind us of God's faithfulness to keep his covenant promises, even if that promise means exile for the sake of producing repentance and obedience (Deut. 4:25–31). When God disciplines his people, it is always with the intent of restoration rather than annihilation (cf. Heb. 12:5–6).

son of Reuel, son of Ibnijah; 9 and their kinsmen according to their generations, [x]956. All
these were heads of fathers' houses according
[y]to their fathers' houses.

10 [z]Of the priests: Jedaiah, Jehoiarib, Jachin,
11 and Azariah the son of Hilkiah, son of
Meshullam, son of Zadok, son of Meraioth,
son of Ahitub, the [a]chief officer of the house of
God; 12 and Adaiah the son of Jeroham, son of
Pashhur, son of Malchijah, and Maasai the son
of Adiel, son of Jahzerah, son of Meshullam,
son of Meshillemith, son of Immer; 13 besides
their kinsmen, heads of their fathers' houses,
1,760, mighty men for the work of the service
of the house of God.

14 [b]Of the Levites: Shemaiah the son of
Hasshub, son of Azrikam, son of Hashabiah, of
the sons of Merari; 15 and Bakbakkar, Heresh,
Galal and Mattaniah the son of Mica, son of
Zichri, son of Asaph; 16 and Obadiah the son
of Shemaiah, son of Galal, son of Jeduthun,
and Berechiah the son of Asa, son of Elkanah,
who lived in the villages of the Netophathites.

17 The gatekeepers were Shallum, Akkub,
Talmon, Ahiman, and their kinsmen (Shallum
was the chief); 18 until then they were [c]in the
king's gate on the east side as the gatekeepers of the camps of the Levites. 19 Shallum the
son of Kore, son of [d]Ebiasaph, son of Korah,
and his kinsmen of his fathers' house, the
[e]Korahites, were in charge of the work of the
service, keepers of the thresholds of the tent,
as their fathers had been in charge of the camp
of the LORD, keepers of the entrance. 20 And
[f]Phinehas the son of Eleazar was the chief officer over them in time past; the LORD was with
him. 21 [g]Zechariah the son of Meshelemiah
was gatekeeper at the entrance of the tent
of meeting. 22 All these, who were chosen as
gatekeepers at the thresholds, were 212. They
were enrolled by genealogies in their villages.
[h]David and Samuel [i]the seer established them
in their office of trust. 23 So they and their sons
were in charge of the gates of the house of the
LORD, that is, the house of the tent, as guards.
24 The gatekeepers were on the four sides, east,
west, north, and south. 25 And their kinsmen
who were [j]in their villages were obligated to
come [k]in every seven days, in turn, to be with
these, 26 for the four chief gatekeepers, who
were Levites, were entrusted to be over [l]the
chambers and the treasures of the house of
God. 27 And they lodged around the house of
God, for on them lay the duty of watching, and
[m]they had charge of opening it every morning.

28 Some of them had charge of the utensils
of service, for they were required to count
them when they were brought in and taken
out. 29 Others of them were appointed over
the furniture and over all the holy utensils,
also over the [n]fine flour, the wine, the oil, the
incense, and the spices. 30 Others, of the sons of
the priests, [o]prepared the mixing of the spices,
31 and Mattithiah, one of the Levites, the firstborn of [p]Shallum the [e]Korahite, was entrusted
with [q]making the flat cakes. 32 Also some of
their kinsmen of the Kohathites had [r]charge
of the showbread, to prepare it every Sabbath.

33 Now these, the [s]singers, the heads of
fathers' houses of the Levites, were in the
chambers of the temple free from other service, for they were on duty day and night.
34 These were heads of fathers' houses of the
Levites, according to their generations, leaders. These lived in Jerusalem.

Saul's Genealogy Repeated

35 [t]In Gibeon lived the father of Gibeon,
Jeiel, and the name of his wife was Maacah,
36 and his firstborn son Abdon, then Zur, Kish,
Baal, Ner, Nadab, 37 Gedor, Ahio, Zechariah,
and Mikloth; 38 and Mikloth was the father of
Shimeam; and these also lived opposite their
kinsmen in Jerusalem, with their kinsmen.
39 [u]Ner fathered Kish, Kish fathered Saul, Saul
fathered Jonathan, Malchi-shua, Abinadab,
and Eshbaal. 40 And the son of Jonathan was
[v]Merib-baal, and Merib-baal fathered Micah.
41 The sons of Micah: Pithon, Melech, Tahrea,
and [w]Ahaz.[1] 42 And Ahaz fathered [x]Jarah, and
Jarah fathered Alemeth, Azmaveth, and Zimri.
And Zimri fathered Moza. 43 Moza fathered
Binea, and [y]Rephaiah was his son, Eleasah his
son, Azel his son. 44 Azel had six sons and these
are their names: Azrikam, Bocheru, Ishmael,
Sheariah, Obadiah, and Hanan; these were the
sons of Azel.

[1] Compare 8:35; Hebrew lacks *and Ahaz*

9[x] [Neh. 11:8] [y] [2 Chr. 35:4, 5] **10**[z] For ver. 10-13, see Neh. 11:10-14 **11**[a] [Jer. 20:1; Acts 4:1] **14**[b] For ver. 14-17, see Neh. 11:15-19 **18**[c] Ezek. 46:1, 2 **19**[d] [ch. 26:1] [e] ch. 12:6; Num. 26:58; 2 Chr. 20:19 **20**[f] [Num. 25:11-13] **21**[g] ch. 26:2 **22**[h] [ch. 26:1, 2] [i] See 1 Sam. 9:9 **25**[j] ver. 16 [k] [2 Kgs. 11:5] **26**[l] [1 Kgs. 6:5, 8] **27**[m] See Num. 1:53 **29**[n] ch. 23:29; Lev. 6:20, 21 **30**[o] See Ex. 30:23-25 **31**[p] ver. 19 [e] [See ver. 19 above] [q] ch. 23:29 **32**[r] See Lev. 24:5-8 **33**[s] ch. 6:31; 25:1 **35**[t] For ver. 35-38, see ch. 8:29-32 **39**[u] For ver. 39-44, see ch. 8:33-38 **40**[v] [2 Sam. 4:4; 9:6, 10] **41**[w] ch. 8:35 **42**[x] [ch. 8:36] **43**[y] [ch. 8:37]

The Death of Saul and His Sons

10 [z]Now the Philistines fought against
Israel, and the men of Israel fled
before the Philistines and fell slain on Mount
Gilboa. 2 And the Philistines overtook Saul
and his sons, and the Philistines struck down
Jonathan and Abinadab and Malchi-shua, the
sons of Saul. 3 The battle pressed hard against
Saul, and the archers found him, and he was
wounded by the archers. 4 Then Saul said to his
armor-bearer, "Draw your sword and thrust
me through with it, lest these uncircumcised
come and mistreat me." But his armor-bearer
would not, for he feared greatly. Therefore
Saul took his own sword and fell upon it. 5 And
when his armor-bearer saw that Saul was dead,
he also fell upon his sword and died. 6 Thus
Saul died; he and his three sons and all his
house died together. 7 And when all the men
of Israel who were in the valley saw that the
army[1] had fled and that Saul and his sons were
dead, they abandoned their cities and fled, and
the Philistines came and lived in them.

8 The next day, when the Philistines came to
strip the slain, they found Saul and his sons
fallen on Mount Gilboa. 9 And they stripped
him and took his head and his armor, and
sent messengers throughout the land of the
Philistines to carry the good news to their
idols and to the people. 10 And they put his
armor in the temple of their gods and fastened
his head in the temple of Dagon. 11 But when
all Jabesh-gilead heard all that the Philistines
had done to Saul, 12 all the valiant men arose
and took away the body of Saul and the bodies of his sons, and brought them to Jabesh.
And they buried their bones under the oak in
Jabesh and fasted seven days.

13 So Saul died [a]for his breach of faith. He
broke faith with the LORD in that he did not
keep the command of the LORD, and also [b]con-
sulted a medium, seeking guidance. 14 He [c]did
not seek guidance from the LORD. Therefore
the LORD put him to death and [d]turned the
kingdom over to David the son of Jesse.

David Anointed King

11 [e]Then all Israel gathered together to
David at Hebron and said, "Behold, we
are your bone and flesh. 2 In times past, even
when Saul was king, it was you who led out
and brought in Israel. And the LORD your
God said to you, [f]'You shall be shepherd of my
people Israel, and you shall be prince over my
people Israel.'" 3 So all the elders of Israel came
to the king at Hebron, and David made a covenant with them at Hebron before the LORD.
And they anointed David king over Israel,
[g]according to the word of the LORD by Samuel.

David Takes Jerusalem

4 And David and all Israel went to Jerusalem,
[h]that is, Jebus, where the Jebusites were, [i]the
inhabitants of the land. 5 The inhabitants of
Jebus said to David, "You will not come in
here." Nevertheless, David took the stronghold of Zion, that is, the city of David. 6 David
said, "Whoever strikes the Jebusites first [j]shall
be chief and commander." And Joab the son
of Zeruiah went up first, so he became chief.
7 And David lived in the stronghold; therefore
it was called the city of David. 8 And he built
the city all around from the Millo in complete
circuit, and Joab repaired the rest of the city.
9 And David [k]became greater and greater, for
the LORD of hosts was with him.

[1] Hebrew *they*

Chapter 10
1[z] For ver. 1-12, see 1 Sam. 31:1-13
13[a] 1 Sam. 13:13, 14; 15:23 [b] 1 Sam. 28:7
14[c] [1 Sam. 28:6] [d] ch. 12:23; 1 Sam. 15:28; 2 Sam. 3:9, 10

Chapter 11
1[e] For ver. 1-9, see 2 Sam. 5:1-3, 6-10
2[f] Ezek. 34:23
3[g] ver. 10; ch. 12:23; 1 Sam. 16:1, 3, 12, 13
4[h] See Josh. 15:8 [i] Judg. 1:21
6[j] 2 Sam. 8:16
9[k] Esth. 9:4

10:1–14 This account of Saul's death includes two important facts. First, Saul died because of his sin (vv. 13–14). Second, the text is clear to point out that God himself executed Saul (v. 14). Thus, we are instructed to view the Philistines as the mere instruments of God's just hand.

By contrast, in the New Testament, we encounter another King who was put to death by God, Jesus the Messiah. (Acts 2:23; 4:27–28; Rom 8:32). But this King was not put to death for his own sin. Rather, he died because of the sins of his people, those united to him by faith (Rom. 4:24–25). When King Saul died, he forfeited the kingdom and his heirs perished with him. When King Jesus died, his heirs received the power of eternal life and rights to the eternal kingdom of God.

11:1–9 David's accession to the throne establishes the royal line of Judah, the line through which the eternal King of God's people would one day come. In this account, the prophecy of Jacob's ancient blessing begins to find fulfillment: the acclaim of David by his brothers (the tribes of Israel), the subjugation of his enemies, and his royal dominion (Gen. 49:8–10).

David's Mighty Men

10 [l]Now these are the chiefs of David's mighty
men, who gave him strong support in his
kingdom, together with all Israel, to make him
king, [m]according to the word of the LORD concerning Israel. 11 This is an account of David's
mighty men: [n]Jashobeam, a [n]Hachmonite,
was [o]chief of the three.[1] He wielded his spear
against 300 whom he killed at one time.
12 And next to him among the three mighty
men was Eleazar the son of [p]Dodo, the Ahohite. 13 He was with David at Pas-dammim
[q]when the Philistines were gathered there
for battle. There was a plot of ground full of
barley, and the men fled from the Philistines.
14 But he took his[2] stand in the midst of the
plot and defended it and killed the Philistines.
And the LORD saved them by a great victory.
15 Three of the thirty chief men went down
to the rock to David at the cave of Adullam,
when the army of Philistines was encamped
in the [r]Valley of Rephaim. 16 David was then
in the stronghold, and the [s]garrison of the
Philistines was then at Bethlehem. 17 And
David said longingly, "Oh that someone
would give me water to drink from the well
of Bethlehem that is by the gate!" 18 Then the
three mighty men broke through the camp of
the Philistines and drew water out of the well
of Bethlehem that was by the gate and took it
and brought it to David. But David would not
drink it. He poured it out to the LORD 19 and
said, "Far be it from me before my God that
I should do this. Shall I drink the lifeblood of
these men? For at the risk of their lives they
brought it." Therefore he would not drink it.
These things did the three mighty men.
20 Now Abishai, the brother of Joab, was chief
of the thirty.[3] And he wielded his spear against
300 men and killed them and won a name
beside the three. 21 He was the most renowned[4]
of the thirty[5] and became their commander,
but he did not attain to the three.
22 And Benaiah the son of Jehoiada was
a valiant man[6] of Kabzeel, a doer of great
deeds. He struck down two heroes of Moab.
He also went down and struck down a lion
in a pit on a day when snow had fallen. 23 And
he struck down an Egyptian, a man of great
stature, five cubits[7] tall. The Egyptian had in
his hand a spear [t]like a weaver's beam, but
Benaiah went down to him with a staff and
snatched the spear out of the Egyptian's hand
and killed him with his own spear. 24 These
things did Benaiah the son of Jehoiada and
won a name beside the three mighty men.
25 He was renowned among the thirty, but he
did not attain to the three. And David set him
over his bodyguard.
26 The mighty men were [u]Asahel the brother
of Joab, Elhanan the son of Dodo of Bethlehem,
27 Shammoth of Harod,[8] Helez the Pelonite,
28 Ira the son of Ikkesh of Tekoa, Abiezer of
Anathoth, 29 Sibbecai the Hushathite, Ilai the
Ahohite, 30 Maharai of Netophah, Heled the
son of Baanah of Netophah, 31 Ithai the son
of Ribai of Gibeah of the people of Benjamin,
Benaiah of Pirathon, 32 Hurai of the brooks
of Gaash, Abiel the Arbathite, 33 Azmaveth of
Baharum, Eliahba the Shaalbonite, 34 Hashem[9]
the Gizonite, Jonathan the son of Shagee
the Hararite, 35 Ahiam the son of Sachar the
Hararite, Eliphal the son of Ur, 36 Hepher the
Mecherathite, Ahijah the Pelonite, 37 Hezro
of Carmel, Naarai the son of Ezbai, 38 Joel the
brother of Nathan, Mibhar the son of [v]Hagri,
39 Zelek the Ammonite, Naharai of Beeroth,
the armor-bearer of Joab the son of Zeruiah,
40 Ira the Ithrite, Gareb the Ithrite, 41 Uriah
the Hittite, [w]Zabad the son of Ahlai, 42 Adina
the son of Shiza the Reubenite, a leader of the
Reubenites, and thirty with him, 43 Hanan the
son of Maacah, and Joshaphat the Mithnite,
44 Uzzia the Ashterathite, Shama and Jeiel
the sons of Hotham the Aroerite, 45 Jediael
the son of Shimri, and Joha his brother, the
Tizite, 46 Eliel the Mahavite, and Jeribai, and
Joshaviah, the sons of Elnaam, and Ithmah

[1] Compare 2 Samuel 23:8; Hebrew *thirty*, or *captains* [2] Compare 2 Samuel 23:12; Hebrew *they . . . their* [3] Syriac; Hebrew *three* [4] Compare 2 Samuel 23:19; Hebrew *more renowned among the two* [5] Syriac; Hebrew *three* [6] Syriac; Hebrew *the son of a valiant man* [7] A *cubit* was about 18 inches or 45 centimeters [8] Compare 2 Samuel 23:25; Hebrew *the Harorite* [9] Compare Septuagint and 2 Samuel 23:32; Hebrew *the sons of Hashem*

What is David's honor to inaugurate is Jesus' greater honor to consummate as the true and better Shepherd King (Ezek. 37:24; Matt. 2:2; Mark 15:2; John 10:14; 1 Tim. 1:17; Heb. 13:20; Rev. 7:17; 19:16). May God's people find rest by seeing this aspect of the great plan of redemption faithfully being established by God throughout history, from Genesis to Malachi and then from Matthew to Revelation!

10[l] For ver. 10-41, see 2 Sam. 23:8-39 [m] ver. 3
11[n] [2 Sam. 23:8] [o] [ch. 12:18]
12[p] [ch. 27:4]
13[q] [2 Sam. 23:11, 12]
15[r] ch. 14:8
16[s] [1 Sam. 10:5]

23[t] 1 Sam. 17:7 **26**[u] ch. 27:7 **38**[v] [ch. 5:10] **41**[w] [ch. 2:36]

the Moabite, 47 Eliel, and Obed, and Jaasiel the Mezobaite.

The Mighty Men Join David

12 [x]Now these are the men who came to David at Ziklag, while he could not move about freely because of Saul the son of Kish. And they were among the mighty men who helped him in war. 2 They [y]were bowmen and could shoot arrows and sling stones with either the right or the [z]left hand; they were Benjaminites, [a]Saul's kinsmen. 3 The chief was Ahiezer, then Joash, both sons of Shemaah of [b]Gibeah; also Jeziel and Pelet, the sons of Azmaveth; Beracah, Jehu of [c]Anathoth, 4 Ishmaiah of [d]Gibeon, a mighty man among the thirty and a leader over the thirty; Jeremiah,[1] Jahaziel, Johanan, Jozabad of Gederah, 5 Eluzai,[2] Jerimoth, Bealiah, Shemariah, Shephatiah the Haruphite; 6 Elkanah, Isshiah, Azarel, Joezer, and Jashobeam, the [e]Korahites; 7 And Joelah and Zebadiah, the sons of Jeroham of Gedor.

8 From the Gadites there went over to David at the stronghold in the wilderness mighty and experienced warriors, expert with shield and spear, whose faces were like the faces of lions and who were [f]swift as gazelles upon the mountains: 9 Ezer the chief, Obadiah second, Eliab third, 10 Mishmannah fourth, Jeremiah fifth, 11 Attai sixth, Eliel seventh, 12 Johanan eighth, Elzabad ninth, 13 Jeremiah tenth, Machbannai eleventh. 14 These Gadites were officers of the army; the least was a [g]match for a hundred men and the greatest for a thousand. 15 These are the men who crossed the Jordan in the first month, when it was [h]overflowing all its banks, and put to flight all those in the valleys, to the east and to the west.

16 And some of the men of Benjamin and Judah came to the stronghold to David. 17 David went out to meet them and said to them, "If you have come to me in friendship to help me, my heart will be joined to you; but if to betray me to my adversaries, although there is no wrong in my hands, then may the God of our fathers see and rebuke you." 18 Then [i]the Spirit clothed [j]Amasai, chief of the thirty, and he said,

"We are yours, O David,
and with you, O son of Jesse!
[k]Peace, peace to you,
and peace to your helpers!
For your God helps you."

Then David received them and made them officers of his troops.

19 Some of the men of Manasseh deserted to David [l]when he came with the Philistines for the battle against Saul. (Yet he did not help them, for the rulers of the Philistines took counsel and sent him away, saying, [m]"At peril to our heads he will desert to his master Saul.") 20 As he went to Ziklag, these men of Manasseh deserted to him: Adnah, Jozabad, Jediael, Michael, Jozabad, Elihu, and Zillethai, chiefs of thousands in Manasseh. 21 They helped David against [n]the band of raiders, for they were all mighty men of valor and were commanders in the army. 22 For from day to day men came to David to help him, until there was a great army, like an army of God.

23 These are the numbers of the divisions of the armed troops [o]who came to David in Hebron [p]to turn the kingdom of Saul over to him, [q]according to the word of the LORD. 24 The men of Judah bearing shield and spear were 6,800 armed troops. 25 Of the Simeonites, mighty men of valor for war, 7,100. 26 Of the Levites 4,600. 27 The prince Jehoiada, of the house of Aaron, and with him 3,700. 28 [r]Zadok, a young man mighty in valor, and twenty-two commanders from his own fathers' house. 29 Of the Benjaminites, [s]the kinsmen of Saul, 3,000, of whom the [t]majority had to that point kept their allegiance to the house of Saul. 30 Of the Ephraimites 20,800, mighty men of valor, famous men in their fathers' houses. 31 Of the half-tribe of Manasseh 18,000, who were [u]expressly named to come and make David king. 32 Of Issachar, men who [v]had understanding of the times, to know what Israel ought to do, 200 chiefs, and all their kinsmen under their command. 33 Of Zebulun 50,000 seasoned troops, [w]equipped for battle with all the weapons of war, to help David[3] with [x]singleness of purpose. 34 Of Naphtali 1,000 commanders with whom were 37,000 men armed with shield and spear. 35 Of the Danites 28,600 men equipped for battle. 36 Of [y]Asher 40,000 [z]seasoned troops [z]ready for battle. 37 Of the Reubenites and Gadites and the half-tribe

[1] Hebrew verse 5 [2] Hebrew verse 6 [3] Septuagint; Hebrew lacks *David*

Chapter 12 **1** [x]See 1 Sam. 27:2-6 **2** [y]2 Chr. 17:17; Ps. 78:9 [z][Judg. 3:15; 20:16] [a]ver. 29 **3** [b]Josh. 18:28 [c]ch. 11:28; 27:12 **4** [d]Josh. 9:3 **6** [e]ch. 9:19 **8** [f]2 Sam. 2:18 **14** [g][Lev. 26:8] **15** [h]See Josh. 3:15 **18** [i]See Judg. 3:10 [j][2 Sam. 17:25] [k][1 Sam. 25:6] **19** [l]See 1 Sam. 29:2-9 [m][1 Sam. 29:4] **21** [n]1 Sam. 30:1 **23** [o]ch. 11:1; 2 Sam. 2:3, 4; 5:1 [p]ch. 10:14 [q]ch. 11:3, 10; 1 Sam. 16:1, 3 **28** [r]ch. 6:8; 2 Sam. 8:17 **29** [s]ver. 2 [t][2 Sam. 2:8, 9] **31** [u]See Num. 1:17 **32** [v][Esth. 1:13] **33** [w]ver. 36, 38 [x][Ps. 12:2] **36** [y][2 Sam. 2:9] [z]ver. 33

of Manasseh from beyond the Jordan, 120,000
men armed with all the weapons of war.
38 All these, men of war, arrayed in battle
order, came to Hebron with [a]a whole heart
to make David king over all Israel. Likewise,
all the rest of Israel were of a [b]single mind
to make David king. 39 And they were there
with David for three days, eating and drinking, for their brothers had made preparation
for them. 40 And also their relatives, from as far
as Issachar and Zebulun and Naphtali, came
bringing food on donkeys and on camels and
on mules and on oxen, abundant provisions
of flour, [c]cakes of figs, clusters of raisins, and
wine and oil, oxen and sheep, for there was
joy in Israel.

The Ark Brought from Kiriath-Jearim

13 David consulted with the commanders of thousands and of hundreds, with
every leader. 2 And David said to all the assembly of Israel, "If it seems good to you and from
the LORD our God, let us send abroad to our
brothers [d]who remain in all the lands of Israel,
as well as to the priests and Levites in the cities that have pasturelands, that they may be
gathered to us. 3 Then let us bring again the
ark of our God to us, [e]for we did not seek it[1]
in the days of Saul." 4 All the assembly agreed
to do so, for the thing was right in the eyes of
all the people.

Uzzah and the Ark

5 [f]So David assembled all Israel [g]from the
[h]Nile[2] of Egypt to Lebo-hamath, to bring the
ark of God [i]from Kiriath-jearim. 6 [j]And David
and all Israel went up to [k]Baalah, that is, to
Kiriath-jearim that belongs to Judah, to bring
up from there the ark of God, which is called
by the name of the LORD who [l]sits enthroned
above the cherubim. 7 And they carried the
ark of God on a new cart, from the house of
[m]Abinadab, and Uzzah and Ahio[3] were driving the cart. 8 And David and all Israel were
celebrating before God with all their might,
with song and [n]lyres and harps and tambourines and cymbals and trumpets.
9 And when they came to the threshing floor
of [o]Chidon, Uzzah put out his hand to take
hold of the ark, for the oxen stumbled. 10 And
the anger of the LORD was kindled against
Uzzah, and he struck him down [p]because he
put out his hand to the ark, and [q]he died there
before God. 11 And David was angry because the

[1] Or *him* [2] Hebrew *Shihor* [3] Or *and his brother*

12:39–40 Just as the tribes of Israel brought abundant provisions (supplied by God) for the celebration of David's kingship in Jerusalem, so will all the nations one day bring forth glorious provisions to a new Jerusalem for an eternal celebration of the kingdom of Jesus, the ultimate fulfillment of the Davidic kingdom promises (cf. Rom. 1:3; Rev. 21:22–26).

13:3–6 In the account of Chronicles, David's first concern as king is to bring the ark of the covenant to Jerusalem. This is significant because the ark of God represented the rule of Yahweh in the midst of his people (28:2; Ps. 132:7) as the one "who sits enthroned above the cherubim" (1 Chron. 13:6). By bringing the ark of the covenant to the royal city, David was submitting his own kingship to the Lord. In this way, David demonstrated that he was a *temporary* and *secondary* (vassal) king over Israel. David's great son, the true and final King, was yet to come (cf. 2 Sam. 7:12–13; Matt. 1:1; 9:7; Rom. 1:1–3; Acts 2:29–36).

13:9–12; 15:12–13 The death of Uzzah and the resulting fear of David remind us of God's awesome holiness and the danger of inappropriate worship. Recall the catastrophe of the golden calf in Exodus 32 or the deaths of Nadab and Abihu in Leviticus 10. Remember Saul's unlawful sacrifice in 1 Samuel 13, which resulted in the removal of his royal dynasty. When it came to worship in the Old Testament, God demanded perfection.

In the New Testament this standard remains, but it has been met, perfectly and eternally, once for all in Jesus Christ (Rom. 6:10; Heb. 7:27; 9:12, 26; 10:10). We now rest in the finished work of our faithful High Priest, and so "Let us then *with confidence* draw near to the throne of *grace*, that we may receive *mercy* and find *grace* to help in time of need" (Heb. 4:16). In the new covenant, fear of not fulfilling our obligations perfectly is not the motivating factor in worship. Rather, we now come with confidence that is rooted in the very grace and mercy of God because of Christ's work on our behalf.

38[a] [1 Kgs. 8:61] [b] [ver. 33]
40[c] [1 Sam. 25:18; 30:12]
Chapter 13
2[d] [1 Sam. 31:1]
3[e] [1 Sam. 7:1, 2]
5[f] ch. 15:3; 2 Sam. 6:1 [g] [1 Kgs. 8:65] [h] See Num. 34:5 [i] [1 Sam. 6:21; 7:1]
6[j] For ver. 6-14, see 2 Sam. 6:2-11 [k] Josh. 15:9, 60 [l] See 1 Sam. 4:4
7[m] [1 Sam. 7:1]
8[n] [ch. 15:16]
9[o] [2 Sam. 6:6]
10[p] [ch. 15:13, 15; Num. 4:15] [q] Lev. 10:2

LORD had broken out against Uzzah. And that place is called Perez-uzza[1] to this day. [12] And David was afraid of God that day, and he said, "How can I bring the ark of God home to me?" [13] So David did not take the ark home into the city of David, but took it aside to the house [r] of Obed-edom the Gittite. [14] And the ark of God remained with the household of Obed-edom in his house three months. [s] And the LORD blessed the household of Obed-edom and all that he had.

David's Wives and Children

14 [t] And Hiram king of Tyre sent messengers to David, and cedar trees, also masons and carpenters to build a house for him. [2] And David knew that the LORD had established him as king over Israel, and that his kingdom was highly exalted for the sake of his people Israel.

[3] And David took more wives in Jerusalem, and David fathered more sons and daughters. [4] [u] These are the names of the children born to him in Jerusalem: [v] Shammua, Shobab, Nathan, Solomon, [5] Ibhar, Elishua, Elpelet, [6] Nogah, Nepheg, Japhia, [7] Elishama, [w] Beeliada and [x] Eliphelet.

Philistines Defeated

[8] When the Philistines heard that David had been anointed king over all Israel, all the Philistines went up to search for David. But David heard of it and went out against them. [9] Now the Philistines had come and [y] made a raid in the [z] Valley of Rephaim. [10] And David inquired of God, "Shall I go up against the Philistines? Will you give them into my hand?" And the LORD said to him, "Go up, and I will give them into your hand." [11] And he went up to Baal-perazim, and David struck them down there. And David said, "God has broken through[2] my enemies by my hand, like a bursting flood." Therefore the name of that place is called Baal-perazim. [12] And they left their gods there, and David gave command, and they were burned.

[13] And the Philistines yet again [a] made a raid in the valley. [14] And when David again inquired of God, [b] God said to him, "You shall not go up after them; go around and come against them opposite the balsam trees. [15] And when you hear the sound of marching in the tops of the balsam trees, then go out to battle, for God has gone out before you to strike down the army of the Philistines." [16] And David did as God commanded him, and they struck down the Philistine army from Gibeon to Gezer. [17] And the fame of David went out into all lands, and the LORD brought the [c] fear of him upon all nations.

The Ark Brought to Jerusalem

15 David[3] built houses for himself in the city of David. And he prepared a place for the ark of God and [d] pitched a tent for it. [2] Then David said that no one but the Levites may carry [e] the ark of God, for the LORD had chosen them to carry the ark of the LORD and to minister to him forever. [3] [f] And David assembled all Israel at Jerusalem to bring up the ark of the LORD [g] to its place, which he had prepared for it. [4] And David gathered together the sons of Aaron and [h] the Levites: [5] of the sons of Kohath, Uriel the chief, with 120 of his brothers; [6] of the sons of Merari, Asaiah the chief, with 220 of his brothers; [7] of the sons of Gershom, Joel the chief, with 130 of his brothers; [8] of the sons of Elizaphan, Shemaiah the chief, with 200 of his brothers; [9] of the sons of Hebron, Eliel the chief, with 80 of his brothers; [10] of the sons of Uzziel, Amminadab the chief, with 112 of his brothers. [11] Then David summoned the priests [i] Zadok and [j] Abiathar, and the Levites Uriel, Asaiah, Joel, Shemaiah, Eliel, and Amminadab, [12] and said to them, "You are the heads of the fathers' houses of the Levites. [k] Consecrate yourselves, you and your brothers, so that you may bring up the ark of the LORD, the God of Israel, [l] to the place that I have prepared for it. [13] [m] Because you did not carry it the first time, the LORD our God broke out against us, because we did not seek him according to the rule." [14] So the priests and the Levites consecrated themselves to bring up the ark of the LORD, the God of Israel. [15] And the Levites carried the ark of God on their shoulders [n] with the poles, [o] as Moses had commanded according to the word of the LORD.

[16] David also commanded the chiefs of the Levites to appoint their brothers as the singers who should play loudly on [p] musical

[1] *Perez-uzza* means *the breaking out against Uzzah* [2] *Baal-perazim* means *Lord of breaking through* [3] Hebrew *He*

13 [r] [2 Chr. 25:24] **14** [s] [ch. 26:4, 5] **Chapter 14** **1** [t] For ver. 1-16, see 2 Sam. 5:11-25 **4** [u] For ver. 4-7, see ch. 3:5-8 [v] [ch. 3:5] **7** [w] [ch. 3:8] [x] 2 Sam. 5:16 **9** [y] ver. 13 [z] ch. 11:15 **13** [a] ver. 9 **14** [b] ver. 16 **17** [c] [Deut. 2:25] **Chapter 15** **1** [d] ch. 16:1 **2** [e] ver. 15, 26; Num. 4:2, 15 **3** [f] ch. 13:5; [1 Kgs. 8:1] [g] ver. 1, 12; 2 Sam. 6:17 **4** [h] See ch. 6:16-30 **11** [i] ch. 6:8; 16:39 [j] 1 Sam. 22:20; 1 Kgs. 2:26 **12** [k] 2 Chr. 35:6 [l] ver. 1, 3 **13** [m] ch. 13:7; 2 Sam. 6:3 **15** [n] Ex. 25:14 [o] Num. 4:15; 7:9 **16** [p] [ch. 13:8; 16:5, 42]

instruments, on harps and lyres and cymbals, to raise sounds of joy. 17 So the Levites
appointed [q]Heman the son of Joel; and of his
brothers [r]Asaph the son of Berechiah; and
of the sons of Merari, their brothers, [s]Ethan
the son of Kushaiah; 18 and with them their
brothers of the second order, Zechariah,
Jaaziel, Shemiramoth, Jehiel, Unni, Eliab,
Benaiah, Maaseiah, Mattithiah, Eliphelehu,
and Mikneiah, and the gatekeepers Obed-
edom and Jeiel. 19 The singers, Heman,
Asaph, and Ethan, were to sound bronze
cymbals; 20 Zechariah, [t]Aziel, Shemiramoth,
Jehiel, Unni, Eliab, Maaseiah, and Benaiah
were to play harps according to [u]Alamoth;
21 but Mattithiah, Eliphelehu, Mikneiah,
[v]Obed-edom, Jeiel, and Azaziah were to
lead with lyres according to [w]the Sheminith.
22 Chenaniah, leader of the Levites in music,
should direct the music, for he understood
it. 23 Berechiah and Elkanah were to be gatekeepers for the ark. 24 Shebaniah, Joshaphat,
Nethanel, Amasai, Zechariah, Benaiah, and
Eliezer, the priests, should [x]blow the trumpets
before the ark of God. [v]Obed-edom and Jehiah
were to be gatekeepers for the ark.

25 [y]So David and the elders of Israel and the
commanders of thousands went to bring up
the ark of the covenant of the LORD from the
house of [v]Obed-edom with rejoicing. 26 And
because God helped the Levites who were carrying the ark of the covenant of the LORD, they
sacrificed [z]seven bulls and seven rams. 27 David
was clothed with a robe of fine linen, as also
were all the Levites who were carrying the ark,
and the singers and Chenaniah the leader of
the music of the singers. And David wore a
linen ephod. 28 So all Israel brought up the ark
of the covenant of the LORD with shouting, to
the sound of the horn, [a]trumpets, and cymbals, and made loud music on [b]harps and lyres.

29 And as the ark of the covenant of the LORD
came to the city of David, Michal the daughter of Saul looked out of the window and saw
King David dancing and celebrating, and she
despised him in her heart.

The Ark Placed in a Tent

16 And they brought in the ark of God and
set it inside [c]the tent that David had
pitched for it, and they offered burnt offerings and peace offerings before God. 2 And
when David had finished offering the burnt
offerings and the peace offerings, he blessed
the people in the name of the LORD 3 and distributed to all Israel, both men and women,
to each a loaf of bread, a portion of meat,[1] and
a cake of raisins.

4 Then he appointed some of the Levites as
ministers before the ark of the LORD, to invoke,
to thank, and to praise the LORD, the God of
Israel. 5 [d]Asaph was the chief, and second to

[1] Compare Septuagint, Syriac, Vulgate; the meaning of the Hebrew is uncertain

16:1–43 This chapter describes a series of events surrounding the arrival of the ark of the covenant in the city of David. There was rejoicing that included feasting, singing, and prayers of thanksgiving. God's people were celebrating because they recognized the arrival of the ark in the city of David as a sign of God's covenant faithfulness to the very covenant he made with Abraham, Isaac, and Jacob (vv. 15–17).

The events of this chapter are framed by the statement that David was a blessing, first to God's people (v. 2) and then to his household (v. 43). David was a blessing to God's people for at least two reasons. First, David brought the ark, the footstool of God's throne, to the city of Jerusalem, the city in which God would cause his name to dwell (Deut. 12:11; 14:23; 16:2, 6, 11; 26:2). Second, David was a blessing to God's people because he recognized that his temporary, geographically limited reign was but a mere shadow of God's eternal, universal kingship. In the midst of his song of thanksgiving, David declared that the Lord was King over the nations (1 Chron. 16:31) and the judge of the earth (v. 33). This was David's good news, and he exulted in the fact that he stood at the earthly center of this reality as the Lord's royal ambassador.

As we reflect on the extravagant celebration and worship detailed in this chapter, we understand that this celebration eventually came to an end, and so did David's earthly reign. We also know that the ark of the covenant no longer is displayed in the earthly Jerusalem. But the failure of these shadows to sustain our hope gives way to a greater joy. The temporary joy of God's people over the first David gives way to our eternal joy in the true and better David (Matt. 1:1; Rom. 1:3; 2 Tim. 2:8). Likewise, joy in the first Jerusalem must give way to an ever increasing joy in the new Jerusalem (Rev. 3:12; 21:2), where feasting, thanksgiving, and blessing will never cease.

17 [q]ch. 6:33 [r]ch. 6:39 [s]ch. 6:44
20 [t][ver. 18] [u]See Ps. 46, title
21 [v]ch. 26:4 [w]See Ps. 6, title
24 [x]ver. 28; ch. 16:6; Num. 10:8 [v][See ver. 21 above]
25 [y]For ver. 25-28, see 2 Sam. 6:12-15 [v][See ver. 21 above]
26 [z]Num. 23:1; Job 42:8
28 [a][ver. 24] [b]ver. 16
Chapter 16
1 [c]ch. 15:1
5 [d]ch. 6:39

him were Zechariah, Jeiel, Shemiramoth,
Jehiel, Mattithiah, Eliab, Benaiah, Obed-
edom, and Jeiel, who were to play harps and
lyres; Asaph was to sound the cymbals, 6 and
Benaiah and Jahaziel the priests were to blow
trumpets regularly before the ark of the covenant of God. 7 Then on that day [e]David first
appointed that thanksgiving be sung to the
LORD by Asaph and his brothers.

David's Song of Thanks

8 [f]Oh give thanks to the LORD; [g]call upon
his name;
[h]make known his deeds among the
peoples!
9 Sing to him, sing praises to him;
tell of all his wondrous works!
10 Glory in his holy name;
let the hearts of those who seek the
LORD rejoice!
11 [i]Seek the LORD and his strength;
seek his presence continually!
12 [j]Remember the wondrous works that he
has done,
[k]his miracles and the judgments he
uttered,
13 O offspring of Israel his servant,
children of Jacob, his chosen ones!

14 He is the LORD our God;
[l]his judgments are in all the earth.
15 Remember his covenant forever,
the word that he commanded, for a
thousand generations,
16 the covenant [m]that he made with
Abraham,
his sworn promise to Isaac,
17 which [n]he confirmed to Jacob as a statute,
to Israel as an everlasting covenant,
18 saying, [o]"To you I will give the land of
Canaan,
as your portion for an inheritance."

19 When you were [p]few in number,
of little account, and [q]sojourners in it,
20 wandering from nation to nation,
from one kingdom to another people,
21 he allowed no one to oppress them;
he [r]rebuked kings on their account,
22 saying, "Touch not my anointed ones,
do my [s]prophets no harm!"

23 [t]Sing to the LORD, all the earth!
Tell of his salvation from day to day.
24 Declare his glory among the nations,
his marvelous works among all the
peoples!
25 For [u]great is the LORD, and greatly to be
praised,
and he is to be feared [v]above all gods.
26 For all the gods of the peoples are
worthless idols,
[w]but the LORD made the heavens.
27 Splendor and majesty are before him;
strength and joy are in his place.

28 Ascribe to the LORD, O families of the
peoples,
[x]ascribe to the LORD glory and strength!
29 Ascribe to the LORD the glory due his
name;
bring an offering and come before him!
[y]Worship the LORD in the splendor of
holiness;[1]
30 tremble before him, all the earth;
yes, the world is established; it shall
never be moved.
31 [z]Let the heavens be glad, and let the earth
rejoice,
and let them say among the nations,
[a]"The LORD reigns!"
32 [b]Let the sea roar, and all that fills it;
let the field exult, and everything in it!
33 Then shall the trees of the forest sing for
joy
before the LORD, for he comes to
judge the earth.
34 Oh give thanks to the LORD, for he is
good;
for his steadfast love endures forever!

35 [c]Say also:

"Save us, O God of our salvation,
and gather and deliver us from
among the nations,
that we may give thanks to your holy
name
and glory in your praise.
36 [d]Blessed be the LORD, the God of Israel,
from everlasting to everlasting!"

[e]Then all the people said, "Amen!" and praised
the LORD.

[1] Or *in holy attire*

7[e] [2 Sam. 22:1; 23:1] **8**[f] For ver. 8-22, see Ps. 105:1-15 [g] Isa. 12:4 [h] [Ps. 145:11, 12] **11**[i] Ps. 24:6; 27:8 **12**[j] [Ps. 77:11; 143:5] [k] Ps. 78:43 **14**[l] Isa. 26:9 **16**[m] Gen. 17:2; 22:16; 26:3; 28:13; [Luke 1:73] **17**[n] Gen. 35:11, 12 **18**[o] Gen. 13:15; 15:18-21 **19**[p] Deut. 7:7; 26:5 [q] Heb. 11:9 **21**[r] [Gen. 12:17; 20:3] **22**[s] [Gen. 20:7] **23**[t] For ver. 23-33, see Ps. 96:1-13 **25**[u] Ps. 145:3 [v] [Ps. 95:3] **26**[w] [Ps. 115:15; Isa. 42:5; 44:24; Jer. 10:11, 12] **28**[x] [Ps. 29:1] **29**[y] [Ps. 110:3] **31**[z] [Isa. 49:13] [a] Ps. 93:1; 97:1; 99:1; [Isa. 52:7; Rev. 11:15, 17; 19:6] **32**[b] Ps. 98:7 **35**[c] For ver. 35, 36, see Ps. 106:47, 48 **36**[d] Ps. 41:13; [1 Kgs. 8:15] [e] [Deut. 27:15; Ps. 106:48]

Worship Before the Ark

37 So David left Asaph and his brothers there
[f]before the ark of the covenant of the LORD
to minister regularly before the ark [g]as each
day required, 38 and also [h]Obed-edom and his[1]
sixty-eight brothers, while [h]Obed-edom, the
son of Jeduthun, and [i]Hosah were to be gatekeepers. 39 And he left [j]Zadok the priest and his
brothers the priests before the tabernacle of
the LORD [k]in the high place that was at Gibeon
40 to offer burnt offerings to the LORD [l]on the
altar of burnt offering [m]regularly morning
and evening, to do all that is written in the
Law of the LORD that he commanded Israel.
41 With them were [n]Heman and Jeduthun
[o]and the rest of those chosen and [p]expressly
named to give thanks to the LORD, [q]for his
steadfast love endures forever. 42 Heman and
Jeduthun had trumpets and cymbals for the
music and instruments [r]for sacred song. The
sons of Jeduthun were appointed to the gate.
43 [s]Then all the people departed each to his
house, and David went home to bless his
household.

The LORD's Covenant with David

17 [t]Now when David lived in his house,
David said to Nathan the prophet,
"Behold, I dwell in a house of cedar, but the
ark of the covenant of the LORD is under a
tent." 2 And Nathan said to David, "Do all that
is in your heart, for God is with you."
3 But that same night the word of the LORD
came to Nathan, 4 "Go and tell my servant
David, 'Thus says the LORD: [u]It is not you who
will build me a house to dwell in. 5 For I have
not lived in a house since the day I brought up
Israel to this day, [v]but I have gone from tent
to tent and from dwelling to dwelling. 6 In
all places where I have moved with all Israel,
did I speak a word with any of the judges of
Israel, whom I commanded to shepherd my
people, saying, "Why have you not built me a
house of cedar?"' 7 Now, therefore, thus shall
you say to my servant David, 'Thus says the
LORD of hosts, I took you from the pasture,
from following the sheep, to be prince over
my people Israel, 8 and I have been with you
wherever you have gone and have cut off all
your enemies from before you. And I will
make for you a name, like the name of the
great ones of the earth. 9 And I will appoint a
place for my people Israel and will plant them,
that they may dwell in their own place and
be disturbed no more. And violent men shall
waste them no more, as formerly, 10 from the
time that I appointed judges over my people
Israel. And I [w]will subdue all your enemies.
Moreover, I declare to you that the LORD will
build you a house. 11 When your days are fulfilled to walk with your fathers, I will raise
up your offspring after you, one of your own
sons, and I will establish his kingdom. 12 He
shall build a house for me, and I will establish
his throne forever. 13 [x]I will be to him a father,
and he shall be to me a son. I will not take
my steadfast love from him, [y]as I took it from
him who was before you, 14 but I will confirm
him in my house and in my kingdom forever,
and his throne shall be established forever.'"
15 In accordance with all these words, and in

[1] Hebrew *their*

17:1–27 At first glance, David's desire to express gratitude by building a house for the Lord appears appropriate, even noble. However, the Lord is not someone whom we can pay back for his blessings, and it should not appear that the kingdom promise he is about to give to David for the redemption of humanity has been purchased by any man's gift. The Lord is no man's debtor. Divine grace is not for sale nor offered in return for any human favor. So the Lord rejects David's desire to build a house for him (vv. 4–6), and then he counters with the grand promise to build a house (dynasty) for David (vv. 7–14).

The house that the Lord promised to build for David, the least son of Jesse, outstripped any mansion, estate, or castle that can be imagined. This "house" of the Lord would include eternal dynasty, eternal sonship, and eternal love (vv. 11–14), a reality far exceeding even the glory of the kingdom of Solomon, David's *lesser* son.

The promises of God to David in this chapter are remarkable. Their fulfillment in Jesus Christ is even more remarkable (cf. 2 Tim. 2:8). However, equally important to note is the fact that the Lord taught David about grace and mercy by lavishing upon him even more grace and mercy. Such divine generosity brought Israel's king to his knees, taught him to boast in the greatness of God (1 Chron. 17:17–27), and gave him the courage to pray (v. 25).

37 [f]ver. 4, 5 [g]2 Chr. 31:16
38 [h]ch. 26:4 [i]ch. 26:10, 16
39 [j]ch. 15:11 [k]See 1 Kgs. 3:4
40 [l]Ex. 27:1 [m]See Ex. 29:38-41; Num. 28:3-8
41 [n]See ch. 6:33 [o][ch. 25:1, 3, 6] [p]Num. 1:17 [q]2 Chr. 5:13; 7:3, 6; 20:21; Ezra 3:11; Jer. 33:11; See ver. 34
42 [r][ch. 25:7; 2 Chr. 29:27]
43 [s]2 Sam. 6:19, 20

Chapter 17
1 [t]For ver. 1-27, see 2 Sam. 7:1-29
4 [u]ch. 28:3
5 [v][2 Sam. 7:6]
10 [w][2 Sam. 7:11]
13 [x]Cited Heb. 1:5 [y][1 Sam. 15:23, 28]

accordance with all this vision, Nathan spoke
to David.

David's Prayer

16 Then King David went in and sat before
the LORD and said, "Who am I, O LORD God,
and what is my house, that you have brought
me thus far? 17 And this was a small thing in
your eyes, O God. You have also spoken of your
servant's house for a great while to come, and
have shown me future generations,[1] O LORD
God! 18 And what more can David say to you
for honoring your servant? For you know your
servant. 19 [z]For your servant's sake, O LORD, and
according to your own heart, you have done
all this greatness, in making known all these
great things. 20 There is none like you, O LORD,
and there is no God besides you, according to
all that we have heard with our ears. 21 And who
is like your people Israel, the one[2] nation on
earth whom God went to redeem to be his people, making for yourself a name for great and
awesome things, in driving out nations before
your people whom you redeemed from Egypt?
22 And you made your people Israel to be your
people forever, and you, O LORD, became their
God. 23 And now, O LORD, let the word that you
have spoken concerning your servant and concerning his house be established forever, and
do as you have spoken, 24 and your name will
be established and magnified forever, saying,
'The LORD of hosts, the God of Israel, is Israel's
God,' and the house of your servant David will
be established before you. 25 For you, my God,
have revealed to your servant that you will
build a house for him. Therefore your servant
has found courage to pray before you. 26 And
now, O LORD, you are God, and you have promised this good thing to your servant. 27 Now
you have been pleased to bless the house of
your servant, that it may continue forever
before you, for it is you, O LORD, who have
blessed, and it is blessed forever."

David Defeats His Enemies

18 [a]After this David defeated the Philistines and subdued them, and he took
Gath and its villages out of the hand of the
Philistines.
2 And he defeated Moab, and the Moabites
became servants to David and brought tribute.
3 David also defeated [b]Hadadezer king of
[c]Zobah-Hamath, as he went to set up his
monument[3] at the river Euphrates. 4 And
David took from him 1,000 chariots, [d]7,000
horsemen, and 20,000 foot soldiers. And
David hamstrung all the chariot horses, but
left enough for 100 chariots. 5 And when the
Syrians of Damascus came to help Hadadezer
king [e]of Zobah, David struck down 22,000
men of the Syrians. 6 Then David put garrisons[4] in Syria of Damascus, and the Syrians
became servants to David and brought tribute.
And the LORD gave victory to David[5] wherever
he went. 7 And David took the shields of gold
that were carried by the servants of Hadadezer
and brought them to Jerusalem. 8 And from
[f]Tibhath and from Cun, cities of Hadadezer,
David took a large amount of bronze. [g]With it
Solomon made the bronze sea and the pillars
and the vessels of bronze.
9 When [h]Tou king of Hamath heard that
David had defeated the whole army of
Hadadezer, king [e]of Zobah, 10 he sent his
son [i]Hadoram to King David, to ask about
his health and to bless him because he had
fought against [b]Hadadezer and defeated him;
for [b]Hadadezer had often been at war with
Tou. And he sent all sorts of articles of gold, of
silver, and of bronze. 11 These also King David
dedicated to the LORD, together with the silver
and gold that he had carried off from all the
nations, from [j]Edom, Moab, the Ammonites,
the Philistines, and Amalek.
12 And [k]Abishai, the son of Zeruiah, killed
18,000 Edomites in the Valley of Salt.
13 Then he put garrisons in Edom, and all the
Edomites became David's servants. And the
LORD gave victory to David wherever he went.

David's Administration

14 So David reigned over all Israel, and he
administered justice and equity to all his people. 15 And [l]Joab the son of Zeruiah was over the
army; and Jehoshaphat the son of Ahilud was
recorder; 16 [m]and Zadok the son of Ahitub and
[n]Ahimelech the son of Abiathar were priests;
and [o]Shavsha was secretary; 17 and Benaiah the
son of Jehoiada was over the Cherethites and
the Pelethites; and David's sons were the [p]chief
officials in the service of the king.

[1] The meaning of the Hebrew is uncertain [2] Septuagint, Vulgate *other* [3] Hebrew *hand* [4] Septuagint, Vulgate, 2 Samuel 8:6 (compare Syriac); Hebrew lacks *garrisons* [5] Hebrew *the LORD saved David*; also verse 13

19 [z] [2 Sam. 7:21] **Chapter 18** **1** [a] For ver. 1-17, see 2 Sam. 8:1-18 **3** [b] [2 Sam. 8:3] [c] See 1 Kgs. 8:65 **4** [d] [2 Sam. 8:4] **5** [e] ch. 19:6 **8** [f] [2 Sam. 8:8] [g] 1 Kgs. 7:15, 23; 2 Chr. 4:12, 15, 16 **9** [h] [2 Sam. 8:9] [e] [See ver. 5 above] **10** [i] [2 Sam. 8:10] [b] [See ver. 3 above] **11** [j] [2 Sam. 8:12] **12** [k] 1 Sam. 26:6; [2 Sam. 8:13] **15** [l] [ch. 11:6] **16** [m] [2 Sam. 8:17; 20:25] [n] [ch. 24:3, 6] [o] [2 Sam. 8:17; 1 Kgs. 4:3] **17** [p] [2 Sam. 8:18]

The Ammonites Disgrace David's Men

19 [q]Now after this Nahash the king of the Ammonites died, and his son reigned in his place. 2 And David said, "I will deal kindly with Hanun the son of Nahash, for his father dealt kindly with me." So David sent messengers to console him concerning his father. And David's servants came to the land of the Ammonites to Hanun to console him. 3 But the princes of the Ammonites said to Hanun, "Do you think, because David has sent comforters to you, that he is honoring your father? Have not his servants come to you to search and to overthrow and to spy out the land?" 4 So Hanun took David's servants and shaved them and cut off their garments in the middle, at their hips, and sent them away; 5 and they departed. When David was told concerning the men, he sent messengers to meet them, for the men were greatly ashamed. And the king said, "Remain at Jericho until your beards have grown and then return."

6 When the Ammonites saw that they had become a stench to David, Hanun and the Ammonites sent 1,000 talents[1] of silver to hire chariots and horsemen [r]from Mesopotamia, from Aram-maacah, and from [s]Zobah. 7 They hired 32,000 chariots and the king of Maacah with his army, who came and encamped before [t]Medeba. And the Ammonites were mustered from their cities and came to battle. 8 When David heard of it, he sent Joab and all the army of the mighty men. 9 And the Ammonites came out and drew up in battle array at the entrance of the city, and the kings who had come were by themselves in the open country.

Ammonites and Syrians Defeated

10 When Joab saw that the battle was set against him both in front and in the rear, he chose some of the best men of Israel and arrayed them against the Syrians. 11 The rest of his men he put in the charge of [u]Abishai his brother, and they were arrayed against the Ammonites. 12 And he said, "If the Syrians are too strong for me, then you shall help me, but if the Ammonites are too strong for you, then I will help you. 13 Be strong, and let us use our strength for our people and for the cities of our God, and may the LORD do what seems good to him." 14 So Joab and the people who were with him drew near before the Syrians for battle, and they fled before him. 15 And when the Ammonites saw that the Syrians fled, they likewise fled before [u]Abishai, Joab's brother, and entered the city. Then Joab came to Jerusalem.

16 But when the Syrians saw that they had been defeated by Israel, they sent messengers and brought out the Syrians who were beyond the Euphrates,[2] with [v]Shophach the commander of the army of [w]Hadadezer at their head. 17 And when it was told to David, he gathered all Israel together and crossed the Jordan and came to them and drew up his forces against them. And when David set the battle in array against the Syrians, they fought with him. 18 And the Syrians fled before Israel, and David killed of the Syrians the men of [x]7,000 chariots and 40,000 [x]foot soldiers, and put to death also [v]Shophach the commander of their army. 19 And when the servants of [w]Hadadezer saw that they had been defeated by Israel, they made peace with David and became subject to him. So the Syrians were not willing to save the Ammonites anymore.

The Capture of Rabbah

20 [y]In the spring of the year, the time when kings go out to battle, Joab led out the army and ravaged the country of the Ammonites and came and besieged Rabbah. But David remained at Jerusalem. And [z]Joab

[1] A *talent* was about 75 pounds or 34 kilograms [2] Hebrew *the River*

19:1–5 Over the course of the past several chapters, the Lord has dealt kindly and compassionately with David. Now, in this chapter, we see David dealing out kindness and compassion to others. David's life of mercy and compassion is a response to the Lord's favorable treatment of him, and such should be our response to grace (Matt. 25:40).

It is also important to observe how King Hanun responded to David's overture of mercy and compassion: rejection, humiliation, and hostility. Christians should pray that they would become the *willing recipients* of God's mercy and compassion. Then they should pray that they would be courageous enough to dispense the very same, even if it is rejected or results in injury, for it is the rejection and injury of Christ on our behalf that now makes us willing to do such things.

Chapter 19
1 [q]For ver. 1-19, see 2 Sam. 10:1-19
6 [r][2 Sam. 10:6] [s]ch. 18:5, 9
7 [t]Num. 21:30; Josh. 13:9, 16
11 [u]ch. 18:12
15 [u][See ver. 11 above]
16 [v][2 Sam. 10:16, 18] [w]2 Sam. 10:16
18 [x][2 Sam. 10:18] [v][See ver. 16 above]
19 [w][See ver. 16 above]
Chapter 20
1 [y]2 Sam. 11:1 [z]2 Sam. 12:26

struck down Rabbah and overthrew it. 2 [a]And
David took the crown of their king from his
head. He found that it weighed a talent[1] of
gold, and in it was a precious stone. And it
was placed on David's head. And he brought
out the spoil of the city, a very great amount.
3 And he brought out the people who were in
it and set them to labor[2] [b]with saws and iron
picks and axes.[3] And thus David did to all the
cities of the Ammonites. Then David and all
the people returned to Jerusalem.

Philistine Giants Killed

4 [c]And after this there arose war with the
Philistines at Gezer. Then Sibbecai the
Hushathite struck down Sippai, who was
one of the descendants of the giants, and the
Philistines were subdued. 5 And there was
again war with the Philistines, and Elhanan
the son of [d]Jair struck down Lahmi [d]the
brother of Goliath the Gittite, the shaft of
whose spear was like a weaver's beam. 6 And
there was again war at Gath, where there was
a man of great stature, who had six fingers on
each hand and six toes on each foot, twenty-
four in number, and he also was descended
from the giants. 7 And when he taunted Israel,
Jonathan the son of [e]Shimea, David's brother,
struck him down. 8 These were descended
from the giants in Gath, and they fell by the
hand of David and by the hand of his servants.

David's Census Brings Pestilence

21 [f]Then [g]Satan stood against Israel and
incited David to number Israel. 2 So
David said to Joab and the commanders of the
army, "Go, number Israel, from Beersheba to
Dan, and bring me a report, that I may know
their number." 3 But Joab said, "May the LORD
add to his people a hundred times as many
as they are! Are they not, my lord the king,
all of them my lord's servants? Why then
should my lord require this? Why should it
be a cause of guilt for Israel?" 4 But the king's
word prevailed against Joab. So Joab departed
and went throughout all Israel and came back
to Jerusalem. 5 And Joab gave the sum of the
numbering of the people to David. In all
Israel there were [h]1,100,000 men who drew
the sword, and in Judah [h]470,000 who drew
the sword. 6 [i]But he did not include Levi and
Benjamin in the numbering, for the king's
command was abhorrent to Joab.

7 But God was displeased with this thing,
and he struck Israel. 8 And David said to
God, "I have sinned greatly in that I have
done this thing. But now, please [j]take away
the iniquity of your servant, for I have acted
very foolishly." 9 And the LORD spoke to
Gad, David's [k]seer, saying, 10 "Go and say to
David, 'Thus says the LORD, Three things
I offer you; choose one of them, that I may
do it to you.'" 11 So Gad came to David and
said to him, "Thus says the LORD, 'Choose
what you will: 12 either [l]three years of famine,
or three months of devastation by your foes
while the sword of your enemies overtakes
you, or else three days of the sword of the
LORD, pestilence on the land, with the angel
of the LORD destroying throughout all the
territory of Israel.' Now decide what answer
I shall return to him who sent me." 13 Then
David said to Gad, "I am in great distress. Let
me fall into the hand of the LORD, for his
mercy is very great, but do not let me fall into
the hand of man."

14 So the LORD sent a pestilence on Israel,
and 70,000 men of Israel fell. 15 And God sent
the angel to Jerusalem to destroy it, but as he
was about to destroy it, the LORD saw, and he
[m]relented from the calamity. And he said to
the angel who was working destruction, "It is
enough; now stay your hand." And the angel of
the LORD was standing by the threshing floor
of Ornan the Jebusite. 16 And David lifted his
eyes and saw the angel of the LORD standing
between earth and heaven, and in his hand a
drawn sword stretched out over Jerusalem.

[1] A *talent* was about 75 pounds or 34 kilograms [2] Compare 2 Samuel 12:31; Hebrew *he sawed* [3] Compare 2 Samuel 12:31; Hebrew *saws*

2[a] For ver. 2, 3, see 2 Sam. 12:30, 31
3[b] [2 Sam. 12:31]
4[c] For ver. 4-8, see 2 Sam. 21:18-22
5[d] [2 Sam. 21:19]
7[e] ch. 2:13; 2 Sam. 13:3; [1 Sam. 16:9; 17:13]
Chapter 21
1[f] For ver. 1-28, see 2 Sam. 24:1-25 [g] Zech. 3:1, 2; [2 Sam. 24:1]; See Job 1:6-12; 2:1-7 **5**[h] [2 Sam. 24:9] **6**[i] ch. 27:24 **8**[j] [2 Sam. 12:13] **9**[k] ch. 29:29; See 1 Sam. 9:9 **12**[l] [2 Sam. 24:13] **15**[m] See Gen. 6:6

20:2 The accounts of war and battle recorded in the Old Testament can be difficult to understand and apply. Remember, these things do *not* teach us about how we must live in this world now. Rather, they remind us of the battle that our God wages on our behalf—ultimately through Christ—as he defeats all his and our spiritual foes. Here, in this text, we see the Lord's anointed king, David, taking the crown of another in subjugation. This event, while paling in comparison, points to something we must learn about David's future Son, the true and better David, before whom all crowns will one day be removed (Rev. 4:10; cf. 6:2; 14:14).

Then David and the elders, [n]clothed in sackcloth, fell upon their faces. 17 And David said to God, "Was it not I who gave command to number the people? It is I who have sinned and done great evil. But these sheep, what have they done? Please let your hand, O LORD my God, be against me and against my father's house. But do not let the plague be on your people."

David Builds an Altar

18 Now [o]the angel of the LORD had commanded Gad to say to David that David should go up and raise an altar to the LORD on the threshing floor of Ornan the Jebusite.
19 So David went up at Gad's word, which he had spoken in the name of the LORD. 20 Now Ornan was threshing wheat. He turned and saw the angel, and his four sons who were with him hid themselves. 21 As David came to Ornan, Ornan looked and saw David and went out from the threshing floor and paid homage to David with his face to the ground.
22 And David said to Ornan, "Give me the site of the threshing floor that I may build on it an altar to the LORD—give it to me at its full price—that the plague may be averted from the people." 23 Then Ornan said to David, "Take it, and let my lord the king do what seems good to him. See, I give the oxen for burnt offerings and the threshing sledges for the wood and the wheat for a grain offering; I give it all." 24 But King David said to Ornan, "No, but I will buy them for the full price. I will not take for the LORD what is yours, nor offer burnt offerings that cost me nothing." 25 So David paid Ornan [p]600 shekels[1] of gold by weight for the site. 26 And David built there an altar to the LORD and presented burnt offerings and peace offerings and called on the LORD, and the LORD[2] [q]answered him with fire from heaven upon the altar of burnt offering.
27 Then the LORD commanded the angel, and he put his sword back into its sheath.

28 At that time, when David saw that the LORD had answered him at the threshing floor of Ornan the Jebusite, he sacrificed there. 29 For the tabernacle of the LORD, which Moses had made in the wilderness, and the altar of burnt offering [r]were at that time in the high place at Gibeon, 30 but David could not go before it to inquire of God, for he was afraid of the sword of the angel of the LORD.

22

Then David said, [s]"Here shall be the house of the LORD God and here the altar of burnt offering for Israel."

David Prepares for Temple Building

2 David commanded to gather together the [t]resident aliens who were in the land of Israel, and he [u]set stonecutters to prepare dressed stones for building the house of God. 3 David also provided great quantities of iron for nails for the doors of the gates and for clamps, [v]as well as bronze in quantities beyond weighing, 4 and cedar timbers without number, [w]for the Sidonians and Tyrians brought great quantities of cedar to David. 5 For David said, [x]"Solomon my son is young and inexperienced, and the house that is to be built for the LORD must be exceedingly magnificent, of fame and glory throughout all lands. I will therefore make preparation for it." So David provided materials in great quantity before his death.

Solomon Charged to Build the Temple

6 Then he called for Solomon his son and charged him to build a house for the LORD, the God of Israel. 7 David said to Solomon, "My son, [y]I had it in my heart to build a house

[1] A *shekel* was about 2/5 ounce or 11 grams [2] Hebrew *he*

21:17 After repenting of his sin, David offers his life (and the life of his household) as a substitute for the people of Jerusalem who are now teetering on the very brink of destruction (cf. v. 16). This should remind us of Moses, who after Israel's great sin with the golden calf in Exodus 32:32 offered his own life as a substitute for the lives of God's people, who were facing total extermination.

As noble and exemplary as are these offers of human mediation (for at times we will be called upon to give ourselves for others), it is amazing to observe that these two Old Testament heroes were denied their requests to endure God's wrath in the place of God's people. Why? Because these two men were sinners themselves, in need of their own substitute. It was not until Jesus, the perfect substitute, arrived that God would grant the request for substitution: "For our sake he made him to be sin who knew no sin, so that in him we might become the righteousness of God" (2 Cor. 5:21).

16 [n]1 Kgs. 20:31; See 2 Sam. 3:31
18 [o][2 Chr. 3:1]
25 [p][2 Sam. 24:24]
26 [q]See Lev. 9:24
29 [r]ch. 16:39; 2 Chr. 1:3; [1 Kgs. 3:4]

Chapter 22
1 [s]ch. 21:18, 19, 26, 28; 2 Chr. 3:1; [Deut. 12:5]
2 [t][1 Kgs. 9:20, 21; 2 Chr. 2:17] [u][1 Kgs. 5:17]
3 [v]ver. 14; 1 Kgs. 7:47
4 [w][1 Kgs. 5:6]
5 [x]ch. 29:1; [1 Kgs. 3:7; Prov. 4:3]
7 [y]ch. 17:1, 2; 28:2; 2 Sam. 7:2, 3; 1 Kgs. 8:17; See Ps. 132:1-5

to the name of the LORD my God. 8 But the word of the LORD came to me, saying, [z]'You have shed much blood and have waged great wars. You shall not build a house to my name, because you have shed so much blood before me on the earth. 9 Behold, a son shall be born to you who shall be a man of rest. [a]I will give him rest from all his surrounding enemies. [b]For his name shall be Solomon, and I will give peace and quiet to Israel in his days. 10 [c]He shall build a house for my name. [d]He shall be my son, and I will be his father, and I will establish his royal throne in Israel forever.'

11 "Now, my son, [e]the LORD be with you, so that you may succeed in building the house of the LORD your God, as he has spoken concerning you. 12 [f]Only, may the LORD grant you discretion and understanding, that when he gives you charge over Israel you may keep the law of the LORD your God. 13 [g]Then you will prosper if you are careful to observe the statutes and the rules that the LORD commanded Moses for Israel. [h]Be strong and courageous. Fear not; do not be dismayed. 14 With great pains I have provided for the house of the LORD [i]100,000 talents[1] of gold, a million talents of silver, and [j]bronze and iron beyond weighing, for there is so much of it; timber and stone, too, I have provided. To these you must add. 15 You have an abundance of workmen: stonecutters, masons, carpenters, and all kinds of craftsmen without number, skilled in working 16 gold, silver, bronze, and iron. Arise and work! [k]The LORD be with you!"

17 David also commanded [l]all the leaders of Israel to help Solomon his son, saying, 18 "Is not the LORD your God with you? And [m]has he not given you peace on every side? For he has delivered the inhabitants of the land into my hand, and the land is subdued before the LORD and his people. 19 Now [n]set your mind and heart to seek the LORD your God. Arise and build the sanctuary of the LORD God, [o]so that the ark of the covenant of the LORD and the holy vessels of God may be brought into a house built [p]for the name of the LORD."

David Organizes the Levites

23 [q]When David was old and full of days, [r]he made Solomon his son king over Israel.

2 David[2] assembled all the leaders of Israel and the priests and the Levites. 3 The Levites, [s]thirty years old and upward, were numbered, and [t]the total was [u]38,000 men. 4 "Twenty-four thousand of these," David said,[3] [v]"shall have charge of the work in the house of the LORD, 6,000 shall be [w]officers and judges, 5 4,000 gatekeepers, and 4,000 shall offer praises to the LORD with the instruments [x]that I have made for praise." 6 [y]And David organized them in divisions [z]corresponding to the sons of Levi: Gershon, Kohath, and Merari.

7 [a]The sons of Gershon[4] were Ladan and

[1] A *talent* was about 75 pounds or 34 kilograms [2] Hebrew *He* [3] Hebrew lacks *David said* [4] Vulgate (compare Septuagint, Syriac); Hebrew *to the Gershonite*

8[z] ch. 28:3; [1 Kgs. 5:3]
9[a] 1 Kgs. 5:4; [ver. 18; 1 Kgs. 4:25] [b] 2 Sam. 12:24
10[c] See 2 Sam. 7:13 [d] ch. 28:6; 2 Sam. 7:14; Heb. 1:5
11[e] ver. 16; [1 Sam. 20:13]
12[f] [1 Kgs. 3:9, 12; Ps. 72:1]
13[g] ch. 28:7 [h] ch. 28:20; [Deut. 31:6, 7; Josh. 1:6, 7, 9]
14[i] [ch. 29:4] [j] ver. 3
16[k] ver. 11
17[l] See ch. 28:1-6
18[m] ch. 23:25; [Deut. 12:10; Josh. 21:44; 23:1; 2 Sam. 7:1]; See ver. 9
19[n] [2 Chr. 20:3] [o] 1 Kgs. 8:6, 21; 2 Chr. 5:7; 6:11 [p] ver. 7; 1 Kgs. 5:3

Chapter 23
1[q] ch. 29:28 [r] [ch. 28:5; 29:22, 28]; See 1 Kgs. 1:33-39
3[s] Num. 4:3, 47 [t] ver. 24; Num. 1:2 [u] [Num. 4:47, 48]
4[v] [2 Chr. 2:2, 18; 34:12; Ezra 3:8, 9] [w] ch. 26:29; [Deut. 16:18; 2 Chr. 19:8]
5[x] 2 Chr. 29:25, 26; Neh. 12:36; Amos 6:5
6[y] [2 Chr. 8:14; 23:18; 35:4; Ezra 6:18] [z] ch. 6:1, 16; Ex. 6:16; Num. 26:57
7[a] ch. 26:21

22:8–9 When God established Israel as a nation, he did so in two phases—first with David, the man of war, and then with Solomon, the man of peace. These verses identify and summarize this pattern. By recognizing this important pattern in redemptive history, perhaps we can understand the confusion of the religious leaders and the disciples in Jesus' day. As Jesus repeatedly proclaimed the arrival of the kingdom of God (kingdom of heaven), they would have naturally expected the Messiah to begin with war (stage 1) and then usher in peace (stage 2). Quite unexpectedly, Jesus brought forth his kingdom by first coming as the man of peace (in the Gospels) and he will come as the man of war who secures our peace at the end of history.

In the Old Testament era, Israel lost its kingdom because, though their land had been secured by God, their sinfulness continued. However, when Jesus ushered in his eternal kingdom, he subdued our sin as the man of peace, securing our place in his kingdom by paying the price for our sin and imputing his own righteousness to us. Thus, it is now impossible for the believer to forfeit this kingdom. What good is citizenship in a kingdom that can be lost or surrendered through sin or death?

23:1–27:34 At first glance, the detailed recounting of David's organization of the temple (chs. 23–26) and civil administration (ch. 27) appears odd and perhaps out of place to modern readers. In fact, one might even wonder what relevance this type of information would have had for the postexilic community living hundreds of years after the events recorded. How should we understand this information in light of the work of Christ and the new covenant?

Shimei. 8 The sons of Ladan: [b]Jehiel the chief,
and Zetham, and Joel, three. 9 The sons of
Shimei: Shelomoth, Haziel, and Haran, three.
These were the heads of the fathers' houses
of Ladan. 10 And the sons of Shimei: Jahath,
Zina, and Jeush and Beriah. These four were
the sons of Shimei. 11 Jahath was the chief, and
Zizah the second; but Jeush and Beriah did
not have many sons, therefore they became
counted as a single father's house.

12 [c]The sons of Kohath: Amram, Izhar,
Hebron, and Uzziel, four. 13 [d]The sons of
Amram: Aaron and Moses. [e]Aaron was set
apart to dedicate the most holy things, that
he and his sons forever should [f]make offerings before the LORD and [g]minister to him
and [h]pronounce blessings in his name forever.
14 But the sons of Moses the [i]man of God were
named among the [j]tribe of Levi. 15 The [k]sons
of Moses: Gershom and Eliezer. 16 The sons
of Gershom: [l]Shebuel the chief. 17 The sons of
Eliezer: Rehabiah the chief. Eliezer had no
other sons, but the sons of Rehabiah were
very many. 18 The sons of Izhar: Shelomith the
chief. 19 The [m]sons of Hebron: Jeriah the chief,
Amariah the second, Jahaziel the third, and
Jekameam the fourth. 20 [n]The sons of Uzziel:
Micah the chief and Isshiah the second.

21 [o]The sons of Merari: Mahli and Mushi. The
sons of Mahli: Eleazar and [p]Kish. 22 Eleazar
died [q]having no sons, but only daughters;
their [r]kinsmen, the sons of Kish, married
them. 23 [s]The sons of Mushi: Mahli, Eder, and
Jeremoth, three.

24 [t]These were the sons of Levi by their
fathers' houses, the heads of fathers' houses
[u]as they were listed according to the number of the names of the individuals from
[v]twenty years old and upward who were to
do the work for the service of the house of
the LORD. 25 For David said, "The LORD, the
God of Israel, [w]has given rest to his people,
and he dwells in Jerusalem forever. 26 And so
the Levites no longer need [x]to carry the tabernacle or any of the things for its service."
27 For by the last words of David the sons of
Levi were numbered from [v]twenty years old
and upward. 28 For their duty was to assist the
sons of Aaron for the service of the house of
the LORD, having the care of the courts and
the chambers, the cleansing of all that is holy,
and any work for the service of the house of
God. 29 Their duty was also to assist with the
[y]showbread, the [z]flour for the grain offering,
the wafers of unleavened bread, the [a]baked
offering, the [b]offering mixed with oil, and all
[c]measures of quantity or size. 30 And they were
to stand every morning, thanking and praising the LORD, and likewise at evening, 31 and
whenever burnt offerings were offered to the
LORD [d]on Sabbaths, [e]new moons, and feast
days, [f]according to the number required of
them, regularly before the LORD. 32 Thus [g]they
were to keep charge of the tent of meeting
and the sanctuary, and to attend the sons of
Aaron, their brothers, for the [h]service of the
house of the LORD.

David Organizes the Priests

24 The divisions of the sons of Aaron
were these. The sons of [i]Aaron: Nadab,
Abihu, Eleazar, and Ithamar. 2 [j]But Nadab
and Abihu died before their father and had
no children, so Eleazar and Ithamar became
the priests. 3 With the help of [k]Zadok of the
sons of Eleazar, and Ahimelech of the sons of

We should remember the focus of the genealogies in chapters 1–9. In those genealogies, two tribes garnered special attention, Judah and Levi. These tribes represented the royal and priestly families in Israel. Thus, the emphasis at the beginning of 1 Chronicles is the same as the emphasis at the end of 1 Chronicles—the worship of Yahweh, and his reign through an earthly, Davidic king. The significance of worship and Yahweh's royal dominion over his people are two themes that span both the Old and New Testaments. What the author of Chronicles sets before us in these chapters was succinctly summarized and thereby affirmed by Jesus hundreds of years later, "But seek first the kingdom of God and his righteousness" (Matt. 6:33).

From the garden of Eden in Genesis 2 to the city of God in Revelation 21, we are reminded of the significance and centrality of Yahweh's kingship and our worship of him. It is good for us to remember that from the beginning of time, and then stretching into eternity, the centrality and significance of these two biblical themes will never change or fail to satisfy God's people.

8 [b] ch. 15:18; 29:8; [ch. 26:21]
12 [c] ch. 6:18; 26:23; Ex. 6:18; Num. 3:19
13 [d] Ex. 6:20 [e] Ex. 28:1; [Heb. 5:4] [f] Ex. 30:7; Num. 16:40; 1 Sam. 2:28 [g] Deut. 21:5 [h] Num. 6:23
14 [i] [ch. 26:23-25] [j] Deut. 33:1
15 [k] Ex. 2:22; 18:3, 4
16 [l] ch. 26:24
19 [m] ch. 24:23; [ch. 26:31]
20 [n] ch. 24:24, 25
21 [o] ch. 6:19, 29; 24:26; Ex. 6:19; [Num. 26:58] [p] ch. 24:29
22 [q] ch. 24:28 [r] [Num. 36:6, 8]
23 [s] ch. 24:30
24 [t] [Num. 10:17, 21] [u] ver. 3 [v] 2 Chr. 31:17; Ezra 3:8; [ver. 3; Num. 4:3; 8:24]
25 [w] See ch. 22:18

26 [x] See Num. 4:5-15 **27** [v] [See ver. 24 above] **29** [y] See Lev. 24:5-8 [z] ch. 9:29; Lev. 6:20, 21 [a] ch. 9:31 [b] Lev. 6:21; 7:12 [c] [Lev. 19:35] **31** [d] Isa. 1:13 [e] See Num. 28:11 [f] See Lev. 23:2, 4 **32** [g] Num. 1:53 [h] See Num. 3:6-9 **Chapter 24** **1** [i] Lev. 10:1, 6; Num. 26:60 **2** [j] Lev. 10:2; Num. 26:61 **3** [k] ver. 31; 2 Sam. 8:17

Ithamar, David organized them according to
the appointed duties in their service. 4 Since
more chief men were found among the sons
of Eleazar than among the sons of Ithamar,
they organized them under sixteen heads
of fathers' houses of the sons of Eleazar, and
eight of the sons of Ithamar. 5 They divided
them [l]by lot, all alike, for there were sacred
officers and officers of God among both the
sons of Eleazar and the sons of Ithamar. 6 And
the scribe Shemaiah, the son of Nethanel, a
Levite, recorded them in the presence of the
king and the princes and Zadok the priest and
[m]Ahimelech the son of Abiathar and the heads
of the fathers' houses of the priests and of the
Levites, one father's house being chosen for
Eleazar and one chosen for Ithamar.
7 The first lot fell to Jehoiarib, the second
to Jedaiah, 8 the third to Harim, the fourth to
Seorim, 9 the fifth to Malchijah, the sixth to
Mijamin, 10 the seventh to Hakkoz, the eighth
to [n]Abijah, 11 the ninth to Jeshua, the tenth to
Shecaniah, 12 the eleventh to Eliashib, the
twelfth to Jakim, 13 the thirteenth to Huppah,
the fourteenth to Jeshebeab, 14 the fifteenth to
Bilgah, the sixteenth to Immer, 15 the seventeenth to Hezir, the eighteenth to Happizzez,
16 the nineteenth to Pethahiah, the twentieth
to Jehezkel, 17 the twenty-first to Jachin, the
twenty-second to Gamul, 18 the twenty-third
to Delaiah, the twenty-fourth to Maaziah.
19 These had as their appointed duty in their
service [o]to come into the house of the LORD
according to the procedure established for
them by Aaron their father, as the LORD God
of Israel had commanded him.
20 And of the rest of the sons of Levi: [p]of
the sons of Amram, Shubael; of the sons of
Shubael, Jehdeiah. 21 [q]Of Rehabiah: of the
sons of Rehabiah, Isshiah the chief. 22 Of
the Izharites, Shelomoth; of the sons of
Shelomoth, Jahath. 23 [r]The sons of Hebron:[1]
Jeriah the chief,[2] Amariah the second, Jahaziel
the third, Jekameam the fourth. 24 [s]The sons of
Uzziel, Micah; of the sons of Micah, Shamir.
25 The brother of Micah, Isshiah; of the sons
of Isshiah, Zechariah. 26 [t]The sons of Merari:
Mahli and Mushi. The sons of Jaaziah: Beno.[3]
27 The sons of Merari: of Jaaziah, Beno,
Shoham, Zaccur, and Ibri. 28 Of Mahli: Eleazar,
[u]who had no sons. 29 Of Kish, the sons of Kish:
Jerahmeel. 30 [v]The sons of Mushi: Mahli,
Eder, and Jerimoth. These were the sons of
the Levites according to their fathers' houses.
31 These also, the head of each father's house
and his younger brother alike, [w]cast lots, just
as their brothers the sons of Aaron, in the presence of King David, [x]Zadok, Ahimelech, and
the heads of fathers' houses of the priests and
of the Levites.

David Organizes the Musicians

25 David and the chiefs of the service
also set apart for the service the sons
of [y]Asaph, and of [z]Heman, and of [a]Jeduthun,
who [b]prophesied with lyres, with [c]harps, and
with cymbals. The list of those who did the
work and of their duties was: 2 Of the sons
of Asaph: Zaccur, Joseph, Nethaniah, and
Asharelah, sons of Asaph, under the direction
of Asaph, who [b]prophesied under the direction of the king. 3 Of Jeduthun, the sons of
Jeduthun: Gedaliah, Zeri, Jeshaiah, Shimei,[4]
Hashabiah, and Mattithiah, six, under the
direction of their father Jeduthun, [b]who
prophesied with the lyre in thanksgiving and
praise to the LORD. 4 Of Heman, the sons of
Heman: Bukkiah, Mattaniah, Uzziel, Shebuel
and Jerimoth, Hananiah, Hanani, Eliathah,
Giddalti, and Romamti-ezer, Joshbekashah,
Mallothi, Hothir, Mahazioth. 5 All these were
the sons of Heman [d]the king's seer, according
to the promise of God to exalt him, for God
had given Heman fourteen sons and three
daughters. 6 They were all under the direction
of their father in the music in the house of the
LORD with cymbals, [c]harps, and lyres for the
service of the house of God. Asaph, Jeduthun,
and Heman were under the order of the king.
7 The number of them along with their brothers, who were trained in singing to the LORD,
all who were skillful, was [e]288. 8 And they cast
lots for their duties, [f]small and great, teacher
and pupil alike.
9 The first lot fell for Asaph to Joseph; the
second to Gedaliah, to him and his brothers
and his sons, twelve; 10 the third to Zaccur, his
sons and his brothers, twelve; 11 the fourth to
Izri, his sons and his brothers, twelve; 12 the
fifth to Nethaniah, his sons and his brothers,

[1] Compare 23:19; Hebrew lacks *Hebron* [2] Compare 23:19; Hebrew lacks *the chief* [3] Or *his son*; also verse 27 [4] One Hebrew manuscript, Septuagint; most Hebrew manuscripts lack *Shimei*

5 [l] ver. 31 **6** [m] 2 Sam. 8:17; [ch. 18:16; 1 Sam. 22:20; 23:6] **10** [n] Luke 1:5 **19** [o] ch. 9:25 **20** [p] ch. 23:13 **21** [q] ch. 23:17 **23** [r] ch. 23:19 **24** [s] ch. 23:20 **26** [t] ch. 23:21 **28** [u] ch. 23:22 **30** [v] ch. 23:23 **31** [w] ver. 5; ch. 25:8; 26:13, 14; Neh. 11:1 [x] ver. 6 **Chapter 25** **1** [y] See ch. 6:39 [z] See ch. 6:33 [a] ch. 16:41 [b] [Ex. 15:20; 2 Kgs. 3:15] [c] ch. 15:16; Neh. 12:27 **2** [b] [See ver. 1 above] **3** [b] [See ver. 1 above] **5** [d] [2 Sam. 24:11] **6** [c] [See ver. 1 above] **7** [e] [ch. 23:5] **8** [f] ch. 26:13

twelve; 13 the sixth to Bukkiah, his sons and his
brothers, twelve; 14 the seventh to Jesharelah,
his sons and his brothers, twelve; 15 the eighth
to Jeshaiah, his sons and his brothers, twelve;
16 the ninth to Mattaniah, his sons and his
brothers, twelve; 17 the tenth to Shimei, his
sons and his brothers, twelve; 18 the eleventh
to Azarel, his sons and his brothers, twelve;
19 the twelfth to Hashabiah, his sons and his
brothers, twelve; 20 to the thirteenth, Shubael,
his sons and his brothers, twelve; 21 to the fourteenth, Mattithiah, his sons and his brothers,
twelve; 22 to the fifteenth, to Jeremoth, his sons
and his brothers, twelve; 23 to the sixteenth, to
Hananiah, his sons and his brothers, twelve;
24 to the seventeenth, to Joshbekashah, his
sons and his brothers, twelve; 25 to the eighteenth, to Hanani, his sons and his brothers,
twelve; 26 to the nineteenth, to Mallothi, his
sons and his brothers, twelve; 27 to the twentieth, to Eliathah, his sons and his brothers,
twelve; 28 to the twenty-first, to Hothir, his
sons and his brothers, twelve; 29 to the twenty-
second, to Giddalti, his sons and his brothers,
twelve; 30 to the twenty-third, to Mahazioth,
his sons and his brothers, twelve; 31 to the
twenty-fourth, to Romamti-ezer, his sons and
his brothers, twelve.

Divisions of the Gatekeepers

26 As for the divisions of the gatekeepers: of the Korahites, Meshelemiah
the son of Kore, of the sons of Asaph. 2 And
Meshelemiah had sons: [g]Zechariah the firstborn, Jediael the second, Zebadiah the third,
Jathniel the fourth, 3 Elam the fifth, Jehohanan
the sixth, Eliehoenai the seventh. 4 And [h]Obed-
edom had sons: Shemaiah the firstborn,
Jehozabad the second, Joah the third, Sachar
the fourth, Nethanel the fifth, 5 Ammiel the
sixth, Issachar the seventh, Peullethai the
eighth, [i]for God blessed him. 6 Also to his son
Shemaiah were sons born who were rulers in
their fathers' houses, for they were men of
great ability. 7 The sons of Shemaiah: Othni,
Rephael, Obed and Elzabad, whose brothers
were able men, Elihu and Semachiah. 8 All
these were of the sons of Obed-edom with
their sons and brothers, able men qualified
for the service; sixty-two of Obed-edom. 9 And
Meshelemiah had sons and brothers, able
men, eighteen. 10 And [j]Hosah, of the sons of
Merari, had sons: Shimri the chief (for though
he was not the firstborn, his father made him
chief), 11 Hilkiah the second, Tebaliah the third,
Zechariah the fourth: all the sons and brothers
of Hosah were thirteen.

12 These divisions of the gatekeepers, corresponding to their chief men, had duties, just
as their brothers did, ministering in the house
of the LORD. 13 And they cast lots by fathers'
houses, [k]small and great alike, for their gates.
14 The lot for the east fell to Shelemiah. They
cast lots also for his son Zechariah, a shrewd
counselor, and his lot came out for the north.
15 Obed-edom's came out for the south, and
to his sons was allotted [l]the gatehouse. 16 For
Shuppim and [j]Hosah it came out for the west,
at the gate of Shallecheth on the road that goes
up. Watch corresponded to watch. 17 On the
east there were six each day,[1] on the north four
each day, on the south four each day, as well
as two and two at the gatehouse. 18 And for
the [n]colonnade[2] on the west there were four
at the road and two at the colonnade. 19 These
were the divisions of the gatekeepers among
the Korahites and the sons of Merari.

Treasurers and Other Officials

20 And of the Levites, Ahijah had charge of
[o]the treasuries of the house of God and the
treasuries of the dedicated gifts. 21 The sons
of Ladan, the sons of the Gershonites belonging to Ladan, the heads of the fathers' houses
belonging to Ladan the Gershonite: [p]Jehieli.[3]
22 [q]The sons of Jehieli, Zetham, and Joel his
brother, were in charge of the treasuries of the
house of the LORD. 23 [r]Of the Amramites, the
Izharites, the Hebronites, and the Uzzielites—
24 and [s]Shebuel the son of Gershom, son of
Moses, was chief officer in charge of the treasuries. 25 His brothers: from [t]Eliezer were his
son Rehabiah, and his son [u]Jeshaiah, and his
son Joram, and his son Zichri, and his son
[v]Shelomoth. 26 This Shelomoth and his brothers were in charge of all the treasuries of the
dedicated gifts that David the king and the
heads of the fathers' houses and the officers of
the thousands and the hundreds and the commanders of the army [w]had dedicated. 27 From
spoil won in battles they dedicated gifts for
the maintenance of the house of the LORD.

[1] Septuagint; Hebrew *six Levites* [2] Or *court*; Hebrew *parbar* (meaning unknown); twice in this verse [3] The Hebrew of verse 21 is uncertain

Chapter 26 **2** [g]ch. 9:21 **4** [h]ch. 15:18, 24; 16:38 **5** [i]ch. 13:14; 2 Sam. 6:11 **10** [j]ch. 16:38 **13** [k]ch. 25:8 **15** [l]Neh. 12:25; [2 Chr. 25:24] **16** [j][See ver. 10 above] **18** [n]2 Kgs. 23:11 **20** [o]ver. 22, 24, 26; ch. 28:12; Ezra 2:69; Neh. 10:38 **21** [p][ch. 29:8] **22** [q][ch. 23:8] **23** [r]ch. 23:12 **24** [s]ch. 23:16; [ch. 24:20] **25** [t][ch. 23:17] [u][ch. 24:21] [v][ch. 23:18] **26** [w]2 Sam. 8:11

28 Also all that [x]Samuel the seer and Saul the
son of Kish and Abner the son of Ner and Joab
the son of Zeruiah had dedicated—all dedicated gifts were in the care of [v]Shelomoth[1] and
his brothers.

29 Of the Izharites, Chenaniah and his sons
were appointed to [y]external duties for Israel,
[z]as officers and judges. 30 Of the Hebronites,
[a]Hashabiah and his brothers, 1,700 men of
ability, had the oversight of Israel westward
of the Jordan for all the work of the LORD and
for the service of the king. 31 Of the Hebronites,
[b]Jerijah was chief of the Hebronites of whatever genealogy or fathers' houses. (In the fortieth year of David's reign search was made and
men of great ability among them were found
at [c]Jazer in Gilead.) 32 King David appointed
him and his brothers, 2,700 men of ability,
heads of fathers' houses, to have the oversight
of the Reubenites, the Gadites and the half-
tribe of the Manassites for everything pertaining to God and for [d]the affairs of the king.

Military Divisions

27 This is the number of the people of
Israel, the heads of fathers' houses, the
commanders of thousands and hundreds, and
their officers who served the king in all matters concerning the divisions that came and
went, month after month throughout the
year, each division numbering 24,000:

2 [e]Jashobeam the son of Zabdiel was in charge
of the first division in the first month; in his
division were 24,000. 3 He was a [f]descendant
of Perez and was chief of all the commanders. He served for the first month. 4 [g]Dodai the
Ahohite[2] was in charge of the division of the
second month; in his division were 24,000.
5 The third commander, for the third month,
was [h]Benaiah, the son of Jehoiada the chief
priest; in his division were 24,000. 6 This is the
Benaiah [i]who was a mighty man of the thirty
and in command of the thirty; Ammizabad
his son was in charge of his division.[3] 7 [j]Asahel
the brother of Joab was fourth, for the fourth
month, and his son Zebadiah after him; in
his division were 24,000. 8 The fifth commander, for the fifth month, was [k]Shamhuth
the Izrahite; in his division were 24,000.
9 Sixth, for the sixth month, was [l]Ira, the son
of Ikkesh the Tekoite; in his division were
24,000. 10 Seventh, for the seventh month, was
[m]Helez the Pelonite, of the sons of Ephraim;
in his division were 24,000. 11 Eighth, for the
eighth month, was [n]Sibbecai the Hushathite,
of the Zerahites; in his division were 24,000.
12 Ninth, for the ninth month, was [o]Abiezer
of Anathoth, a Benjaminite; in his division
were 24,000. 13 Tenth, for the tenth month,
was [p]Maharai of Netophah, of the Zerahites;
in his division were 24,000. 14 Eleventh, for the
eleventh month, was [q]Benaiah of Pirathon,
of the sons of Ephraim; in his division were
24,000. 15 Twelfth, for the twelfth month, was
[r]Heldai the Netophathite, of [s]Othniel; in his
division were 24,000.

Leaders of Tribes

16 Over the tribes of Israel, for the Reubenites,
Eliezer the son of Zichri was chief officer; for
the Simeonites, Shephatiah the son of Maacah;
17 for Levi, [t]Hashabiah the son of Kemuel; for
Aaron, [u]Zadok; 18 for Judah, Elihu, one of
David's brothers; for Issachar, Omri the son
of Michael; 19 for Zebulun, Ishmaiah the son of
Obadiah; for Naphtali, Jeremoth the son of
Azriel; 20 for the Ephraimites, Hoshea the son
of Azaziah; for the half-tribe of Manasseh,
Joel the son of Pedaiah; 21 for the half-tribe of
Manasseh in Gilead, Iddo the son of Zechariah;
for Benjamin, Jaasiel the son of Abner; 22 for
Dan, Azarel the son of Jeroham. These were
the [v]leaders of the tribes of Israel. 23 David did
not count those below twenty years of age,
for the [w]LORD had promised to make Israel as
many as the stars of heaven. 24 Joab the son of
Zeruiah began to count, but [x]did not finish.
Yet [y]wrath came upon Israel for this, and the
number was not entered in the chronicles of
King David.

25 Over the king's treasuries was [z]Azmaveth
the son of Adiel; and over the treasuries in the
country, in the cities, in the villages, and in
the towers, was Jonathan the son of Uzziah;
26 and over those who did the work of the
field for tilling the soil was Ezri the son of
Chelub; 27 and over the vineyards was Shimei
the Ramathite; and over the produce of the

[1] Hebrew *Shelomith* [2] Septuagint; Hebrew *Ahohite and his division and Mikloth the chief officer* [3] Septuagint, Vulgate; Hebrew *was his division*

28 [x] ch. 29:29; See 1 Sam. 9:9 [v] [See ver. 25 above] **29** [y] Neh. 11:16 [z] ch. 23:4; See Deut. 16:18 **30** [a] ch. 27:17 **31** [b] ch. 24:23; [ch. 23:19] [c] ch. 6:81; Num. 21:32; Josh. 21:39 **32** [d] 2 Chr. 19:11 **Chapter 27** **2** [e] ch. 11:11; [2 Sam. 23:8] **3** [f] Num. 26:20 **4** [g] 2 Sam. 23:9; [ch. 11:12] **5** [h] 2 Sam. 8:18 **6** [i] ch. 11:24, 25; 2 Sam. 23:20-28 **7** [j] ch. 11:26; 2 Sam. 23:24 **8** [k] [ch. 11:27; 2 Sam. 23:25] **9** [l] ch. 11:28 **10** [m] ch. 11:27 **11** [n] ch. 11:29; 20:4; 2 Sam. 21:18 **12** [o] ch. 11:28 **13** [p] ch. 11:30 **14** [q] ch. 11:31 **15** [r] [2 Sam. 23:29] [s] ch. 4:13; Judg. 1:13; 3:9 **17** [t] ch. 26:30 [u] ch. 24:3 **22** [v] ch. 28:1 **23** [w] See Gen. 15:5 **24** [x] [ch. 21:5, 6] [y] ch. 21:7; 2 Sam. 24:12-15 **25** [z] ch. 11:33; 2 Sam. 23:31

vineyards for the wine cellars was Zabdi the
Shiphmite. 28 Over the olive and [a]sycamore
trees in the Shephelah was Baal-hanan the
Gederite; and over the stores of oil was Joash.
29 Over the herds that pastured in [b]Sharon was
Shitrai the Sharonite; over the herds in the
valleys was Shaphat the son of Adlai. 30 Over
the camels was Obil the Ishmaelite; and over
the donkeys was Jehdeiah the Meronothite.
Over the flocks was Jaziz the [c]Hagrite. 31 All
these were stewards of King David's property.
32 Jonathan, David's uncle, was a counselor,
being a man of understanding and a scribe.
He and Jehiel the son of Hachmoni attended
the king's sons. 33 [d]Ahithophel was the [e]king's
counselor, and Hushai the Archite was the
king's friend. 34 Ahithophel was succeeded by
Jehoiada the son of [f]Benaiah, and [g]Abiathar.
Joab was [h]commander of the king's army.

David's Charge to Israel

28 [i]David assembled at Jerusalem all the
officials of Israel, the [j]officials of the
tribes, the officers of the divisions that served
the king, the [k]commanders of thousands, the
commanders of hundreds, the [l]stewards of
all the property and livestock of the king and
his sons, together with the palace officials, the
[m]mighty men and all the seasoned warriors.
2 Then King David rose to his feet and said:
"Hear me, my brothers and my people. [n]I had
it in my heart to build a house of rest for the
ark of the covenant of the LORD and for the
[o]footstool of our God, and I made preparations for building. 3 But God said to me, [p]'You
may not build a house for my name, for you
are a man of war and have shed blood.' 4 Yet
the LORD God of Israel [q]chose me from all my
father's house to be king over Israel [r]forever.
[s]For he chose Judah as leader, and in the house
of Judah my father's [t]house, and among my
father's sons he took pleasure in me to make
me king over all Israel. 5 And of [u]all my sons
(for the LORD has given me many sons) he [v]has
chosen Solomon my son to sit on the throne of
the kingdom of the LORD over Israel. 6 He said
to me, 'It is [w]Solomon your son who shall build
my house and my courts, for I have chosen him
to be my son, and I will be his father. 7 I will
establish his kingdom [r]forever [x]if he continues
strong in keeping my commandments and my
rules, as he is today.' 8 Now therefore in the
sight of all Israel, the assembly of the LORD,
and in the hearing of our God, observe and
seek out all the commandments of the LORD
your God, that you may possess this good land
and leave it for an inheritance to your children
after you forever.

David's Charge to Solomon

9 "And you, Solomon my son, know the God
of your father and serve him with a [y]whole
heart and with a willing mind, [z]for the LORD
searches all hearts and understands every plan
and thought. [a]If you seek him, he will be found
by you, but if you forsake him, he will cast you
off forever. 10 Be careful now, for the LORD has
chosen you to build a house for the sanctuary;
[b]be strong and do it."
11 Then David gave Solomon his son the
[c]plan of the [d]vestibule of the temple,[1] and
of its houses, its treasuries, its upper rooms,
and its inner chambers, and of the room for
the [e]mercy seat; 12 and the plan of all that he
had in mind for the courts of the house of
the LORD, all the surrounding chambers,
[f]the treasuries of the house of God, and the
treasuries for dedicated gifts; 13 for the [g]divi-
sions of the priests and of the [h]Levites, and
all the work of the service in the house of the
LORD; for all the vessels for the service in the
house of the LORD, 14 the weight of gold for

[1] Hebrew lacks *of the temple*

28:7–9 Note the strong emphasis placed on the obedience of the king, who should have been exemplary and representative for the people. Because of their failure fully to assume these roles, both Saul and David experienced the severe consequences of sin with consequent impact on their families, kingdom, and people. Likewise, the book of 1 Kings records that Solomon's life was overtaken by sin, eventually leading to the tearing apart of the kingdom in 922 B.C.

It was not until almost 1,000 years later that a King would arrive whose obedience would overcome the failure of previous generations, "so that, as *sin reigned in death*, grace also might *reign through righteousness* leading to eternal life through Jesus Christ our Lord" (Rom. 5:21).

28 [a]1 Kgs. 10:27; 2 Chr. 1:15; 9:27
29 [b]ch. 5:16
30 [c]See ch. 5:10
33 [d]See 2 Sam. 15:12 [e]See 2 Sam. 15:37
34 [f][ver. 5] [g]1 Kgs. 1:7; [ch. 24:6] [h][ch. 11:6]

Chapter 28

1 [i]ch. 23:2 [j]See ch. 27:16-22 [k]See ch. 27:1-15 [l]See ch. 27:25-31 [m]See ch. 11:10-47
2 [n]See ch. 22:7 [o]Ps. 99:5; 132:7; Isa. 66:1; Lam. 2:1; [Ps. 110:1] **3** [p]See 2 Sam. 7:5, 13 **4** [q]1 Sam. 16:12, 13 [r]ch. 17:23, 27 [s]ch. 5:2; Gen. 49:8; Ps. 78:68 [t]1 Sam. 16:1 **5** [u]See ch. 3:1-9; 14:3-7 [v]ch. 22:9; 23:1
6 [w]See 2 Sam. 7:13, 14 **7** [r][See ver. 4 above] [x][ch. 22:13] **9** [y][1 Kgs. 8:61] [z]See 1 Sam. 16:7 [a]See 2 Chr. 15:2 **10** [b]ver. 20; Ezra 10:4; Hag. 2:4 **11** [c]ver. 19; See Ex. 25:40 [d]1 Kgs. 6:3; 2 Chr. 3:4 [e]Ex. 25:17 **12** [f]See ch. 26:20 **13** [g]ch. 24:1 [h]ch. 23:6

all golden vessels for each service, the weight of silver vessels for each service, 15 the weight of the golden [l]lampstands and their lamps, the weight of gold for each lampstand and its lamps, the weight of silver for a lampstand and its lamps, according to the use of each lampstand in the service, 16 the weight of gold for each table for the showbread, the silver for the silver tables, 17 and pure gold for the forks, the basins and the cups; for the golden bowls and the weight of each; for the silver bowls and the weight of each; 18 for the [j]altar of incense made of refined gold, and its weight; also his plan for the golden chariot of the [k]cherubim that spread their wings and covered the ark of the covenant of the LORD. 19 "All this he made clear to me in writing from the hand of the LORD, [l]all the work to be done according to the plan."

20 Then David said to Solomon his son, [m]"Be strong and courageous and do it. Do not be afraid and do not be dismayed, for the LORD God, even my God, is with you. He will not leave you or forsake you, until all the work for the service of the house of the LORD is finished. 21 And behold the [n]divisions of the priests and the Levites for all the service of the house of God; and with you in all the work will be [o]every willing man who has skill for any kind of service; also the officers and all the people will be wholly at your command."

Offerings for the Temple

29 And David the king said to all the assembly, "Solomon my son, whom alone God has chosen, is [p]young and inexperienced, and the work is great, for [q]the palace will not be for man but for the LORD God. 2 So I have provided for the house of my God, so far as I was able, the gold for the things of gold, the silver for the things of silver, and the bronze for the things of bronze, the iron for the things of iron, and wood for the things of wood, besides great quantities of [r]onyx and stones for setting, antimony, colored stones, all sorts of precious stones and marble. 3 Moreover, in addition to all that I have provided for the holy house, I have a treasure of my own of gold and silver, and because of my devotion to the house of my God I give it to the house of my God: 4 [s]3,000 talents[1] of gold, of the gold of [t]Ophir, and 7,000 talents of refined silver, for overlaying the walls of the house,[2] 5 and for all the work to be done by craftsmen, gold for the things of gold and silver for the things of silver. Who then will offer willingly, consecrating himself[3] today to the LORD?"

6 Then [u]the leaders of fathers' houses made their freewill offerings, as did also the leaders of the tribes, the commanders of thousands and of hundreds, and [v]the officers over the king's work. 7 They gave for the service of the house of God 5,000 talents and 10,000 [w]darics[4] of gold, 10,000 talents of silver, 18,000 talents of bronze and 100,000 talents of iron. 8 And whoever had precious stones gave them to the treasury of the house of the LORD, in the care of [x]Jehiel the Gershonite. 9 Then the people rejoiced because they had given willingly, for with a [y]whole heart they had offered freely to the LORD. David the king also rejoiced greatly.

David Prays in the Assembly

10 Therefore David blessed the LORD in the presence of all the assembly. And David said: [z]"Blessed are you, O LORD, the God of Israel our father, forever and ever. 11 [a]Yours, O LORD, is the greatness and the power and the glory and the victory and the majesty, for all that is in the heavens and in the earth is yours. Yours is the kingdom, O LORD, and you are exalted as head above all. 12 [b]Both riches and honor come from you, and you rule over all. [c]In your hand are power and might, and in your hand it is to make great and to give strength to all. 13 And now we thank you, our God, and praise your glorious name.

14 "But who am I, and what is my people, that we should be able thus to offer willingly? For all things come from you, and of your own have we given you. 15 [d]For we are strangers before you and sojourners, as all our fathers were. Our days on the earth are [e]like a shadow, and there is no abiding.[5] 16 O LORD our God, all this abundance that we have provided for building you a house for your holy name comes from your hand and is all your own. 17 I know, my God, [f]that you test the heart and [g]have pleasure in uprightness. In the uprightness of my heart I have freely offered all these

[1] A *talent* was about 75 pounds or 34 kilograms [2] Septuagint; Hebrew *houses* [3] Or *ordaining himself*; Hebrew *filling his hand* [4] A *daric* was a coin weighing about 1/4 ounce or 8.5 grams [5] Septuagint, Vulgate; Hebrew *hope*, or *prospect*

15[i] See Ex. 25:31-37 **18**[j] See Ex. 30:1 [k] See Ex. 25:18-22; 1 Kgs. 6:23-28 **19**[l] ver. 11, 12; Ex. 25:40 **20**[m] See ch. 22:13; Josh. 1:5 **21**[n] ver. 13; See ch. 24-26 [o] [Ex. 35:25, 26; 36:1, 2] **Chapter 29** **1**[p] ch. 22:5; [1 Kgs. 3:7] [q] ver. 19 **2**[r] [Isa. 54:11, 12; Rev. 21:19-21] **4**[s] [ch. 22:14] [t] See 1 Kgs. 9:28 **6**[u] ch. 27:1; 28:1 [v] See ch. 27:25-31 **7**[w] Ezra 2:69; 8:27; Neh. 7:70-72 **8**[x] ch. 23:8; [ch. 26:21] **9**[y] [2 Kgs. 12:4; 2 Cor. 9:7] **10**[z] Luke 1:68 **11**[a] [1 Tim. 1:17; Rev. 5:13] **12**[b] [1 Kgs. 3:13; 2 Chr. 1:12; Rom. 11:36] [c] 2 Chr. 20:6 **15**[d] See Lev. 25:23 [e] Job 14:2; Ps. 102:11; 144:4 **17**[f] ch. 28:9; Prov. 17:3; [1 Sam. 16:7] [g] [Prov. 11:20]

things, and now I have seen your people, who are present here, offering freely and joyously to you. [18]O LORD, the God of Abraham, Isaac, and Israel, our fathers, keep forever such purposes and thoughts in the hearts of your people, and direct their hearts toward you. [19][h]Grant to Solomon my son a whole heart that he may keep your commandments, your testimonies, and your statutes, performing all, and that he may [i]build the palace [j]for which I have made provision."

[20]Then David said to all the assembly, [k]"Bless the LORD your God." And all the assembly blessed the LORD, the God of their fathers, [l]and bowed their heads and paid homage to the LORD and to the king. [21]And they offered sacrifices to the LORD, and on the next day offered burnt offerings to the LORD, 1,000 bulls, 1,000 rams, and 1,000 lambs, with their [m]drink offerings, and sacrifices in abundance for all Israel. [22]And they ate and drank before the LORD on that day with great gladness.

Solomon Anointed King

And they made Solomon the son of David king [n]the second time, and they [o]anointed him as prince for the LORD, and [p]Zadok as priest.

[23][q]Then Solomon sat on the [r]throne of the LORD as king in place of David his father. And he prospered, and all Israel obeyed him. [24]All the leaders and the mighty men, and also all the sons of King David, pledged their allegiance to King Solomon. [25]And the LORD made Solomon very [s]great in the sight of all Israel and [t]bestowed on him such royal majesty as had not been on any king before him in Israel.

The Death of David

[26]Thus David the son of Jesse reigned over all Israel. [27]The [u]time that he reigned over Israel was forty years. He reigned seven years in Hebron and thirty-three years in Jerusalem. [28]Then he died [v]at a good age, [w]full of days, riches, and honor. And Solomon his son reigned in his place. [29]Now the acts of King David, from first to last, are written in the Chronicles [x]of Samuel the seer, and in the Chronicles of [y]Nathan the prophet, and in the Chronicles of [z]Gad the seer, [30]with accounts of all his rule and his might and of the circumstances [a]that came upon him and upon Israel and upon all the kingdoms of the countries.

29:15 At the height of his power, and at the peak of national security, David makes the astonishing confession that he remains a stranger and alien in the land (cf. Ps. 119:19) and that his days on this earth are fleeting. In this way, David joins himself to the patriarchs of old, especially Abraham, who "was looking forward to the city that has foundations, whose designer and builder is God" (Heb. 11:10).

We often think that God's people in the Old Testament focused only on earthly and temporal blessings. Yet these earthly blessings always pointed beyond themselves to the promised eternal blessings of the coming kingdom of God. Abraham, David, and ultimately Jesus lived as aliens and strangers on this earth, confident of a better kingdom coming in the future. And so we too now join in this temporary procession of life (cf. 1 Pet. 2:11) as we wait for the consummation of the kingdom and the satisfaction of all things.

19[h] [Ps. 72:1] [i]ver. 1, 2 [j]ch. 22:14
20[k] See Josh. 22:33 [l]See Ex. 4:31
21[m] Gen. 35:14
22[n] [ch. 23:1] [o]See 1 Kgs. 1:38, 39 [p]1 Kgs. 2:35
23[q] 1 Kgs. 2:12 [r]ch. 28:5; [2 Chr. 9:8]
25[s] 2 Chr. 1:1; [Josh. 3:7] [t]1 Kgs. 3:13; 2 Chr. 1:12; [Eccles. 2:9]
27[u] 2 Sam. 5:4, 5; 1 Kgs. 2:11
28[v] [Gen. 15:15; 25:8] [w]ch. 23:1
29[x] ch. 26:28; [1 Sam. 9:9] [y]See 2 Sam. 12:1 [z]See 1 Sam. 22:5
30[a] [Dan. 4:23, 25]

2 Chronicles

Solomon Worships at Gibeon

1 [a]Solomon the son of David established
himself in his kingdom, [b]and the LORD
his God was with him and made him exceedingly great.
2 Solomon spoke to all Israel, to the [c]com-
manders of thousands and of hundreds, to the
judges, and to all the leaders in all Israel, the
heads of fathers' houses. 3 And Solomon, and
all the assembly with him, went to [d]the high
place that was at Gibeon, [e]for [f]the tent of meeting of God, which Moses the servant of the
LORD had made in the wilderness, was there.
4 [g](But David had brought up the ark of God
from Kiriath-jearim to the place that David
had prepared for it, for he had pitched a tent
for it in Jerusalem.) 5 Moreover, [h]the bronze
altar that [i]Bezalel the son of Uri, son of Hur,
had made, was there before the tabernacle of
the LORD. And Solomon and the assembly
[j]sought it[1] out. 6 And Solomon went up there
to the bronze altar before the LORD, which was
at the tent of meeting, [k]and offered a thousand
burnt offerings on it.

Solomon Prays for Wisdom

7 [l]In that night God appeared to Solomon,
and said to him, "Ask what I shall give you."
8 And Solomon said to God, "You have shown
great and steadfast love to David my father,
[m]and have made me king in his place. 9 O LORD
God, [n]let your word to David my father be now
fulfilled, for you have made me king over a
people as numerous [o]as the dust of the earth.
10 Give me now wisdom and knowledge to [p]go
out and come in before this people, for who
can govern this people of yours, which is so
great?" 11 God answered Solomon, "Because
this was in your heart, and you have not asked
for [q]possessions, wealth, honor, or the life of
those who hate you, and have not even asked
for long life, but have asked for wisdom and
knowledge for yourself that you may govern
my people over whom I have made you king,
12 wisdom and knowledge are granted to you.
I will also give you [q]riches, possessions, and
honor, [r]such as none of the kings had who
were before you, and none after you shall have
the like." 13 So Solomon came from[2] the [s]high
place at Gibeon, from before [t]the tent of meeting, to Jerusalem. And he reigned over Israel.

Solomon Given Wealth

14 [u]Solomon gathered together chariots and
horsemen. [v]He had 1,400 chariots and 12,000
horsemen, whom he stationed [w]in the chariot
cities and with the king in Jerusalem. 15 And
the king made silver and gold as common in

[1] Or *him* [2] Septuagint, Vulgate; Hebrew *to*

1:1–13 Solomon's request for wisdom and knowledge is world famous, and we may be tempted to attribute Solomon's early success to the way in which he responded to the Lord's question in verse 7, "Ask what I shall give you." But consider the context. Before Solomon was given the opportunity to make such a request, the Lord was with him and the Lord had made him great (v. 1). Additionally, the Lord appeared to Solomon, and Solomon (v. 7) recognized that his kingship stemmed from the steadfast love of the Lord shown to his father's house (v. 8). Thus, Solomon's request for wisdom and knowledge was not an attempt to curry favor with the Lord. Rather, it was a sanctified response to the abundant grace already poured out into his life. This same reality appears in the New Testament, when believers are united to Christ through faith, "in whom are hidden all the treasures of *wisdom* and *knowledge*" (Col. 2:3).

Chapter 1
1 [a]1 Kgs. 2:46 [b]1 Chr. 29:25
2 [c]1 Chr. 27:1
3 [d]See 1 Kgs. 3:4 [e]1 Chr. 16:39; 21:29 [f]Ex. 29:10; Lev. 10:7; Num. 14:10
4 [g]See 2 Sam. 6:2-17; 1 Chr. 15:25–16:1
5 [h]Ex. 27:1, 2; 38:1, 2 [i]Ex. 31:2 [j][1 Chr. 13:3]
6 [k]1 Kgs. 3:4
7 [l]For ver. 7-12, see 1 Kgs. 3:5-14
8 [m]1 Chr. 28:5
9 [n]ch. 6:17; 1 Kgs. 8:26 [o]Gen. 13:16
10 [p][Num. 27:17; Deut. 31:2] **11** [q]Eccles. 5:19; 6:2 **12** [q][See ver. 11 above] [r]ch. 9:22; [1 Chr. 29:25] **13** [s]See 1 Kgs. 3:4 [t]ver. 3 **14** [u]For ver. 14-17, see ch. 9:25-28; 1 Kgs. 10:26-29 [v][1 Kgs. 4:26] [w][1 Kgs. 9:19]

Jerusalem as stone, and he made cedar as plentiful as the sycamore of the Shephelah. 16 And
Solomon's import of horses was from Egypt
and Kue, and the king's traders would buy
them from Kue for a price. 17 They imported a
chariot from Egypt for 600 shekels[1] of silver,
and a horse for 150. Likewise through them
these were exported to all the kings of the
Hittites and the kings of Syria.

Preparing to Build the Temple

2 [2] [x]Now Solomon purposed to build a temple for the name of the LORD, and a royal
palace for himself. 2 [3] [y]And Solomon assigned
70,000 men to bear burdens and 80,000 to
quarry in the hill country, and [z]3,600 to oversee them. 3 [a]And Solomon sent word to Hiram
the king of Tyre: [b]"As you dealt with David my
father and sent him cedar to build himself a
house to dwell in, so deal with me. 4 Behold,
I am about to build a house for the name of
the LORD my God and dedicate it to him for
the burning of [c]incense of sweet spices before
him, and for [d]the regular arrangement of the
showbread, and for [e]burnt offerings morning
and evening, [f]on the Sabbaths and the new
moons and the appointed feasts of the LORD
our God, as ordained forever for Israel. 5 The
house that I am to build will be great, [g]for
our God is greater than all gods. 6 [h]But who
is able to build him a house, since [h]heaven,
even highest heaven, cannot contain him?
Who am I to build a house for him, except as
a place to make offerings before him? 7 So now
[i]send me a man skilled to work in gold, silver, bronze, and iron, and in purple, crimson,
and blue fabrics, trained also in engraving,
to be with the skilled workers who are with
me in Judah and Jerusalem, [j]whom David my
father provided. 8 Send me also cedar, cypress,
and algum timber from Lebanon, for I know
that [k]your servants know how to cut timber in
Lebanon. And my servants will be with your
servants, 9 to prepare timber for me in abundance, for the house I am to build will be great
and wonderful. 10 [l]I will give for your servants,
the woodsmen who cut timber, 20,000 cors[4] of
crushed wheat, 20,000 cors of barley, 20,000
baths[5] of wine, and 20,000 baths of oil."

11 Then Hiram the king of Tyre answered in a
letter that he sent to Solomon, [m]"Because the
LORD loves his people, he has made you king
over them." 12 Hiram also said, "Blessed be the
LORD God of Israel, [n]who made heaven and
earth, who has given King David a wise son,
who has discretion and understanding, [o]who
will build a temple for the LORD and a royal
palace for himself.

13 "Now I have sent a skilled man, who has
understanding, Huram-abi, 14 [p]the son of a
woman of the daughters of Dan, and his father
was a man of Tyre. He is [q]trained to work in
gold, silver, bronze, iron, stone, and wood,
and in purple, blue, and crimson fabrics and
fine linen, and to do all sorts of engraving and
execute any design that may be assigned him,
with your craftsmen, the craftsmen of my lord,
David your father. 15 Now therefore the wheat
and barley, oil and wine, [r]of which my lord has
spoken, let him send to his servants. 16 [s]And
we will cut whatever timber you need from
Lebanon and bring it to you in rafts by sea to
[t]Joppa, so that you may take it up to Jerusalem."

17 Then Solomon counted all the resident
aliens who were in the land of Israel, [u]after
the census of them that David his father
had taken, and there were found 153,600.

[1] A *shekel* was about 2/5 ounce or 11 grams [2] Ch 1:18 in Hebrew [3] Ch 2:1 in Hebrew [4] A *cor* was about 6 bushels or 220 liters [5] A *bath* was about 6 gallons or 22 liters

Chapter 2
1 [x]1 Kgs. 5:5
2 [y]ver. 18; 1 Kgs. 5:15, 16; [ch. 8:7, 8; 1 Kgs. 9:20, 21] [z][1 Kgs. 5:16]
3 [a]For ver. 3-16, see 1 Kgs. 5:2-11 [b]1 Chr. 14:1
4 [c]See Ex. 30:7 [d]See Lev. 24:5-8 [e]See Num. 28:3-8 [f]ch. 8:13; Num. 28:9, 11, 19, 26
5 [g]Ps. 135:5; [Ex. 15:11; 1 Chr. 16:25; Ps. 86:8]
6 [h]ch. 6:18; 1 Kgs. 8:27; Isa. 66:1; Acts 7:49
7 [i]ver. 13, 14 [j]1 Chr. 22:15
8 [k]ch. 9:10, 11
10 [l][1 Kgs. 5:11]
11 [m]ch. 9:8; 1 Kgs. 10:9
12 [n]See Gen. 1:1 [o][ver. 1] **14** [p]1 Kgs. 7:14 [q][ver. 7] **15** [r]ver. 10 **16** [s][1 Kgs. 5:9] [t]See Josh. 19:46 **17** [u][1 Chr. 22:2]

2:5 Solomon understood that the temple of God must reflect God's greatness, and that no human being had the capacity to build such a structure for the Creator of the universe (cf. Acts 17:25). Thus, like the tabernacle before it (cf. Ex. 25:40; Heb. 8:5–6), the temple built by Solomon was designed to point beyond itself to an even greater reality. Ultimately, nothing in this creation *or the next* could possibly contain and communicate the greatness of our God, except God himself. That is why there is no temple in the new earth: "And I saw *no temple* in the city, for its temple is the Lord God the Almighty and the Lamb" (Rev. 21:22). Remember, what we read in these Old Testament passages, or what we see here now on this earth, all point beyond themselves to the ultimate reality (2 Cor 4:6). Whether it is the tabernacle in the wilderness, the temple in Jerusalem, or the Lamb in the new Jerusalem, all of this points to God's unwavering commitment to restore and sustain fellowship with his people, something secured eternally by the blood of his Son.

18 [v]Seventy thousand of them he assigned to bear burdens, 80,000 to quarry in the hill country, and 3,600 as overseers to make the people work.

Solomon Builds the Temple

3 [w]Then Solomon began to build the house of the LORD in Jerusalem [x]on Mount Moriah, where the LORD[1] had appeared to David his father, at the place that David had appointed, [y]on the threshing floor of Ornan the Jebusite. 2 He began to build in the second month of the fourth year of his reign. 3 These are Solomon's [z]measurements[2] for building the house of God: [a]the length, in cubits[3] of the old standard, was sixty cubits, and the breadth twenty cubits. 4 The vestibule in front of the nave of the house was twenty cubits long, equal to the width of the house,[4] and its height was 120 cubits. He overlaid it on the inside with pure gold. 5 [b]The nave he lined with cypress and covered it with fine gold [c]and made palms and chains on it. 6 He adorned the house with settings of precious stones. The gold was gold of Parvaim. 7 So he lined the house with gold—its beams, its thresholds, its walls, and its doors—[c]and he carved cherubim on the walls.

8 [d]And he made the Most Holy Place. Its length, corresponding to the breadth of the house, was twenty cubits, and its breadth was twenty cubits. He overlaid it with 600 talents[5] of fine gold. 9 The weight of gold for the nails was fifty shekels.[6] And he overlaid [e]the upper chambers with gold.

10 [f]In the Most Holy Place he made two cherubim of wood[7] and overlaid[8] them with gold. 11 The wings of the cherubim together extended twenty cubits: one wing of the one, of five cubits, touched the wall of the house, and its other wing, of five cubits, touched the wing of the other cherub; 12 and of this cherub, one wing, of five cubits, touched the wall of the house, and the other wing, also of five cubits, was joined to the wing of the first cherub. 13 The wings of these cherubim extended twenty cubits. The cherubim[9] stood on their feet, [g]facing the nave. 14 [h]And he made the veil of blue and purple and crimson fabrics and fine linen, and he worked cherubim on it.

15 [i]In front of the house he made two pillars thirty-five cubits high, with a capital of five cubits on the top of each. 16 He made chains like a necklace[10] and put them on the tops of the pillars, and he made a hundred pomegranates and put them on the chains. 17 [j]He set up the pillars in front of the temple, one on the south, the other on the north; that on the south he called Jachin, and that on the north Boaz.

The Temple's Furnishings

4 He made [k]an altar of bronze, twenty cubits[11] long and twenty cubits wide and ten cubits high. 2 [l]Then he made the sea of cast metal. It was round, ten cubits from brim to brim, and five cubits high, and a line of thirty cubits measured its circumference. 3 Under it were figures of gourds,[12] for ten cubits, compassing the sea all around. The gourds were in two rows, cast with it when it was cast. 4 It stood on twelve oxen, three facing north, three facing west, three facing south, and three facing east. The sea was set on them, and all their

[1] Septuagint; Hebrew lacks *the* LORD [2] Syriac; Hebrew *foundations* [3] A *cubit* was about 18 inches or 45 centimeters [4] Compare 1 Kings 6:3; the meaning of the Hebrew is uncertain [5] A *talent* was about 75 pounds or 34 kilograms [6] A *shekel* was about 2/5 ounce or 11 grams [7] Septuagint; the meaning of the Hebrew is uncertain [8] Hebrew *they overlaid* [9] Hebrew *they* [10] Hebrew *chains in the inner sanctuary* [11] A *cubit* was about 18 inches or 45 centimeters [12] Compare 1 Kings 7:24; Hebrew *oxen*; twice in this verse

3:1 The location of the temple, described briefly in this verse, is of singular importance. First, the location in Jerusalem is identified as Mount Moriah. The only other instance in the Bible where this biblical place name appears is Genesis 22:2, where it is named as the mountain on which Abraham was commanded to sacrifice his "only son" but was provided a substitute. Second, this is the plot of ground acquired by David from Ornan the Jebusite—the place where the Lord had stopped pouring out his wrath on Israel (precipitated by David's census in 1 Chronicles 21).

By describing the location of the temple in these ways, the author of Chronicles is weaving together a tapestry of events that ultimately points forward to the person and work of Christ—who, being the "only son" of God, comes as our substitute in order to prevent our complete destruction from the wrath of God through sacrifice. This single verse helps us to comprehend the real significance of the Old Testament sacrificial system, and to understand why that system was temporary (cf. Heb. 9:6; 10:12).

18 [v]See ver. 2
Chapter 3
1 [w]For ver. 1, 2, see 1 Kgs. 6:1 [x]Gen. 22:2, 14 [y][1 Chr. 21:15, 18, 28]
3 [z][Ezra 3:11] [a]For ver. 3, 4, see 1 Kgs. 6:2, 3
5 [b]1 Kgs. 6:17 [c]1 Kgs. 6:29, 32
7 [c][See ver. 5 above]
8 [d][1 Kgs. 6:16]
9 [e]1 Chr. 28:11
10 [f]For ver. 10-13, see 1 Kgs. 6:23-28
13 [g][Ezek. 40:9]
14 [h]See Ex. 26:31
15 [i]For ver. 15, 16, see 1 Kgs. 7:15-20; [1 Kgs. 7:15; 2 Kgs. 25:17; Jer. 52:21]
17 [j]1 Kgs. 7:21

Chapter 4 **1** [k]ch. 7:7; 8:12; [ch. 15:8; 1 Kgs. 8:64; 2 Kgs. 16:14]; See Ezek. 43:13-17 **2** [l]For ver. 2-5, see 1 Kgs. 7:23-26

rear parts were inward. 5 Its thickness was a handbreadth.[1] And its brim was made like the brim of a cup, like the flower of a lily. [m]It held 3,000 baths.[2] 6 [n]He also made ten basins in which to wash, and set five on the south side, and five on the north side. In these they were to rinse off what was used for the burnt offering, and the sea was for the priests to wash in.

7 And he made ten golden lampstands [o]as prescribed, and set them in the temple, five on the south side and five on the north. 8 [p]He also made ten tables and placed them in the temple, five on the south side and five on the north. And he made a hundred basins of gold. 9 He made [q]the court of the priests [r]and the great court and doors for the court and overlaid their doors with bronze. 10 [s]And he set the sea at the southeast corner of the house.

11 [t, u]Hiram also made the pots, the shovels, and the basins. [u]So Hiram finished the work that he did for King Solomon on the house of God: 12 the two pillars, [v]the bowls, and the two capitals on the top of the pillars; and the two latticeworks to cover the two bowls of the capitals that were on the top of the pillars; 13 [w]and the 400 pomegranates for the two latticeworks, two rows of pomegranates for each latticework, to cover the two bowls of the capitals that were on the pillars. 14 [n]He made the stands also, and the basins on the stands, 15 and the one sea, and the twelve oxen underneath it. 16 The pots, the shovels, [x]the forks, and all the equipment for these [t, y]Huram-abi made of burnished bronze for King Solomon for the house of the LORD. 17 In the plain of the Jordan the king cast them, in the clay ground between Succoth and Zeredah.[3] 18 [z]Solomon made all these things in great quantities, for the weight of the bronze was not sought.

19 So Solomon made all the vessels that were in the house of God: the golden altar, [a]the tables for the bread of the Presence, 20 the lampstands and their lamps of pure gold [b]to burn before the inner sanctuary, as prescribed; 21 the flowers, the lamps, and the tongs, of purest gold; 22 the snuffers, basins, dishes for incense, and fire pans, of pure gold, and the sockets[4] of the temple, for the inner doors to the Most Holy Place and for the doors of the nave of the temple were of gold.

5 [c]Thus all the work that Solomon did for the house of the LORD was finished. And Solomon brought in the things that David his father had dedicated, and stored the silver, the gold, and all the vessels in the treasuries of the house of God.

The Ark Brought to the Temple

2 Then Solomon assembled the elders of Israel and all the heads of the tribes, the leaders of the fathers' houses of the people of Israel, in Jerusalem, to bring up the ark of the covenant of the LORD out of [d]the city of David, which is Zion. 3 And all the men of Israel assembled before the king at the feast that is in the seventh month. 4 And all the elders of Israel came, [e]and the Levites took up the ark. 5 And they brought up the ark, the tent of meeting, and all the holy vessels that were in the tent; [f]the Levitical priests brought them up. 6 And King Solomon and all the congregation of Israel, who had assembled before him, were before the ark, sacrificing so many sheep and oxen that they could not be counted or numbered. 7 Then the priests brought the ark of the covenant of the LORD to its place, in the inner sanctuary of the house, in the Most Holy Place, underneath the wings of the cherubim. 8 The cherubim spread out their wings over the place of the ark, so that the cherubim made a covering above the ark and its poles. 9 And the poles were so long that the ends of the poles were seen [g]from the Holy Place before the inner sanctuary, but they could not be seen from outside. And they are[5] there to this day. 10 There was nothing in the ark except the two tablets [h]that Moses put there at Horeb, where the LORD made a covenant with the people of Israel, when they came out of Egypt. 11 And when the priests came out of the Holy Place (for all the priests who were present had consecrated themselves, without regard to [i]their divisions, 12 and all the Levitical [j]singers, [k]Asaph, [l]Heman, and Jeduthun, their sons and kinsmen, arrayed in fine linen, with [m]cymbals, harps, and lyres, stood east of the altar with 120 [n]priests who

[1] A *handbreadth* was about 3 inches or 7.5 centimeters [2] A *bath* was about 6 gallons or 22 liters [3] Spelled *Zarethan* in 1 Kings 7:46
[4] Compare 1 Kings 7:50; Hebrew *the entrance of the house* [5] Hebrew *it is*

5[m] [1 Kgs. 7:26] **6**[n] 1 Kgs. 7:38, 39 **7**[o] ver. 20; 1 Kgs. 7:49; See Ex. 25:31-39; 27:20, 21 **8**[p] ver. 19; [1 Kgs. 7:48] **9**[q] 1 Kgs. 6:36 [r] [ch. 6:13; 2 Kgs. 21:5] **10**[s] 1 Kgs. 7:39 **11**[t] For ch. 4:11–5:1, see 1 Kgs. 7:40-51 [u] [1 Kgs. 7:13, 14] **12**[v] 1 Kgs. 7:41 **13**[w] [1 Kgs. 7:20] **14**[n] [See ver. 6 above] **16**[x] 1 Chr. 28:17 [t] [See ver. 11 above] [y] ch. 2:13; [1 Kgs. 7:14] **18**[z] 1 Kgs. 7:47 **19**[a] ver. 8 **20**[b] ver. 7 **Chapter 5** **1**[c] For ver. 1-10, see 1 Kgs. 7:51–8:9 **2**[d] 2 Sam. 6:12 **4**[e] [ver. 7; 1 Kgs. 8:3] **5**[f] ch. 23:18; 30:27 **9**[g] [1 Kgs. 8:8] **10**[h] Deut. 10:2, 5; [ch. 6:11] **11**[i] 1 Chr. 24:1, 5; [Luke 1:5] **12**[j] See 1 Chr. 25:1-4 [k] See 1 Chr. 6:39 [l] See 1 Chr. 6:33 [m] 1 Chr. 15:16; Ps. 150:3-5 [n] ch. 7:6; 1 Chr. 15:24

were trumpeters; 13 and it was the duty of the
trumpeters and singers to make themselves
heard in unison in praise and thanksgiving
to the LORD), and when the song was raised,
[o]with trumpets and cymbals and other musical instruments, in praise to the LORD,

> [p]"For he is good,
> for his steadfast love endures forever,"

the house, the house of the LORD, was filled
with a cloud, 14 so that the priests could not
stand to minister because of the cloud, [q]for
the glory of the LORD filled the house of God.

Solomon Blesses the People

6 [r]Then Solomon said, "The LORD has said
that he would dwell in thick darkness.
2 But I have built you [s]an exalted house, a place
for you to dwell in forever." 3 Then the king
turned around and blessed all the assembly
of Israel, while all the assembly of Israel stood.
4 And he said, "Blessed be the LORD, the God of
Israel, who with his hand has fulfilled what he
promised with his mouth to David my father,
saying, 5 'Since the day that I brought my people out of the land of Egypt, I chose no city
out of all the tribes of Israel in which to build
a house, that my name might be there, and
I chose no man as prince over my people Israel;
6 [t]but I have chosen Jerusalem that my name
may be there, [u]and I have chosen David to be
over my people Israel.' 7 [v]Now it was in the
heart of David my father to build a house for
the name of the LORD, the God of Israel. 8 But
the LORD said to David my father, 'Whereas
[v]it was in your heart to build a house for my
name, you did well that it was in your heart.
9 Nevertheless, it is not you who shall build
the house, but your son who shall be born to
you shall build the house for my name.' 10 Now
the LORD has fulfilled his promise that he
made. For I have risen in the place of David
my father and sit on the throne of Israel, as
the LORD promised, and I have built the house
for the name of the LORD, the God of Israel.
11 And there I have set the ark, [w]in which is the
covenant of the LORD that he made with the
people of Israel."

Solomon's Prayer of Dedication

12 Then Solomon stood before the altar of the
LORD in the presence of all the assembly of
Israel and spread out his hands. 13 [x]Solomon
had made a bronze platform five cubits[1] long,
five cubits wide, and three cubits high, and
had set it in the court, and he stood on it. [y]Then
he knelt on his knees in the presence of all the
assembly of Israel, and spread out his hands
toward heaven, 14 and said, "O LORD, God of
Israel, [z]there is no God like you, in heaven

[1] A *cubit* was about 18 inches or 45 centimeters

5:13–6:2 Ever since Adam and Eve were expelled from the garden of Eden, God has been working to restore his people to his all-satisfying presence. The Lord's presence guided Israel through the wilderness, residing in the tabernacle and moving out as a column of smoke during the day and a pillar of fire by night (cf. Ex. 40:34–38). This same presence was subsequently manifest in the Jerusalem temple, the place where God caused his name to dwell.

However, the Israelites, like Adam and Eve, were eventually expelled from the Land of Promise, a new Eden, because of their continued disobedience. Thus, for God's people to dwell in God's presence, the problem of sin must first be eradicated. With Christ's first coming, the problem of sin was dealt the fatal blow. Restoration to God's all-satisfying presence was decisively secured. And so, when Christ returns in order to bring us home, back into the presence of God for which we were created, we can be assured that this reality will never change (cf. Rev. 21:3).

6:4–6 This was a great day for Israel. First, the Lord had fulfilled his promise to establish his name and a permanent place of worship in Israel (cf. Deut. 12:3, 5, 11, 21; 16:11). Second, the Lord had established the royal line of Judah through David's line in Solomon, the king who would build the temple (cf. Gen. 49:10; 1 Sam 7:12–17). Solomon stood forth at this high point in redemptive history and proclaimed the good news of God's faithfulness to always keep his promises (cf. 2 Chron. 6:14–17).

6:14–42 The house of Yahweh built by Solomon was to be a house of prayer (cf. Matt. 21:13; Mark 11:17; Luke 19:47 [all quoting Isa. 56:7]). In these few verses, the idea of prayer, petition, thanksgiving, or plea occurs some 25 times to emphasize the dependence of God's people upon his grace.

13 [o]1 Chr. 16:42 [p]See 1 Chr. 16:34
14 [q]ch. 7:2; 1 Kgs. 8:11; [Ex. 40:35; Ezek. 10:3, 4]
Chapter 6
1 [r]For ver. 1-39, see 1 Kgs. 8:12-50; [Ex. 20:21; Heb. 12:18]
2 [s][Ps. 135:21]
6 [t]ch. 12:13; Ps. 78:68 [u]1 Chr. 28:4; See 1 Sam. 16:11-13
7 [v]2 Sam. 7:2; 1 Chr. 17:1; 28:2
8 [v][See ver. 7 above]
11 [w][ch. 5:10]
13 [x][2 Kgs. 11:14; 23:3] [y][1 Kgs. 8:54]
14 [z]See Ex. 15:11

or on earth, [a]keeping covenant and showing
steadfast love to your servants who walk before
you with all their heart, 15 [b]who have kept
with your servant David my father what you
declared to him. You spoke with your mouth,
and with your hand have fulfilled it this day.
16 Now therefore, O LORD, God of Israel, keep
for your servant David my father what you
have promised him, saying, [c]'You shall not lack
a man to sit before me on the throne of Israel,
[d]if only your sons pay close attention to their
way, to walk in my law as you have walked
before me.' 17 Now therefore, O LORD, God of
Israel, let your word be confirmed, which you
have spoken to your servant David.

18 "But will God indeed dwell with man on
the earth? Behold, [e]heaven and the highest
heaven cannot contain you, how much less
this house that I have built! 19 Yet have regard
to the prayer of your servant and to his plea,
O LORD my God, listening to the cry and to
the prayer that your servant prays before you,
20 [f]that your eyes may be open day and night
toward this house, the place where you have
promised to set your name, that you may
listen to the prayer that your servant offers
toward this place. 21 And listen to the pleas of
your servant and of your people Israel, when
they pray toward this place. And listen from
heaven your dwelling place, [g]and when you
hear, forgive.

22 "If a man sins against his neighbor and is
made to take an oath and comes and swears his
oath before your altar in this house, 23 then hear
from heaven and act and judge your servants,
repaying the guilty by bringing his conduct on
his own head, and vindicating the righteous by
rewarding him according to his righteousness.

24 "If your people Israel are defeated before
the enemy because they have sinned against
you, and they turn again and acknowledge
your name and pray and plead with you in this
house, 25 [g]then hear from heaven and forgive
the sin of your people Israel and bring them
again to the land that you gave to them and
to their fathers.

26 [h]"When heaven is shut up and there is no
rain because they have sinned against you, if
they pray toward this place and acknowledge
your name and turn from their sin, when
you afflict[1] them, 27 [g]then hear in heaven and
forgive the sin of your servants, your people
Israel, when you teach them the good way[2] in
which they should walk, and grant rain upon
your land, which you have given to your people as an inheritance.

28 [i]"If there is famine in the land, if there
is pestilence or blight or mildew or locust
or caterpillar, if their enemies besiege them
in the land at their gates, whatever plague,
whatever sickness there is, 29 whatever prayer,
whatever plea is made by any man or by all
your people Israel, each knowing his own
affliction and his own sorrow and stretching
out his hands toward this house, 30 [g]then hear
from heaven your dwelling place and forgive
and render to each whose heart you know,
according to all his ways, [j]for you, you only,
know the hearts of the children of mankind,
31 that they may fear you and walk in your
ways all the days that they live in the land
that you gave to our fathers.

32 "Likewise, when a foreigner, who is not
of your people Israel, comes from a far country for the sake of your great name and your
mighty hand and your outstretched arm,
when he comes and prays toward this house,
33 hear from heaven your dwelling place and
do according to all for which the foreigner
calls to you, in order that all the peoples of
the earth may know your name and fear you,
as do your people Israel, and that they may

[1] Septuagint, Vulgate; Hebrew *answer* [2] Septuagint, Syriac, Vulgate (compare 1 Kings 8:36); Hebrew *toward the good way*

14[a] See Deut. 7:9
15[b] 1 Chr. 22:9, 10
16[c] ch. 7:18; See 1 Kgs. 2:4 [d] Ps. 132:12
18[e] See ch. 2:6
20[f] [ver. 40]
21[g] [Dan. 9:19]
25[g] [See ver. 21 above]
26[h] ch. 7:13; [1 Kgs. 17:1]
27[g] [See ver. 21 above]
28[i] [ch. 20:9]
30[g] [See ver. 21 above] [j] See 1 Sam. 16:7

The use of this house was not restricted to Israel. It was intended for all of the nations (2 Chron. 6:32–33), and from this house God would hear the prayers of all peoples (vv. 19–21, 23, 25, 27, 30, 33, 35, 39) and grant forgiveness (vv. 21, 25, 27, 30, 39) to those who would repent from their sins (vv. 24, 26, 37, 38). This house represented, in a visible fashion, the Lord's desire to dwell among his people and make himself known to them through prayer, repentance, and forgiveness (cf. John 1:14; 2:19; 1 Cor. 6:19).

Solomon's temple is now gone, but our access to the throne of grace has been enabled and strengthened by the work of Christ on our behalf: "I am writing these things to you so that you may not sin. But if anyone does sin, we have an advocate with the Father, Jesus Christ the righteous. He is the propitiation for our sins, and not for ours only but also for the sins of the whole world" (1 John 2:1–2).

know that this house [k]that I have built is called
by your name.
34 "If your people go out to battle against their
enemies, by whatever way you shall send them,
and they pray to you toward this city that you
have chosen and the house that I have built
for your name, 35 then hear from heaven their
prayer and their plea, and maintain their cause.
36 "If they sin against you—[l]for there is no
one who does not sin—and you are angry
with them and give them to an enemy, so
that they are carried away captive to a land
far or near, 37 yet if they turn their heart in the
land to which they have been carried captive,
and repent and plead with you in the land of
their captivity, saying, 'We have sinned and
have acted perversely and wickedly,' 38 if they
repent with all their mind and with all their
heart in the land of their captivity to which
they were carried captive, and pray toward
their land, which you gave to their fathers, the
city that you have chosen and the house that
I have built for your name, 39 then hear from
heaven your dwelling place their prayer and
their pleas, and maintain their cause and forgive your people who have sinned against you.
40 Now, O my God, [m]let your eyes be open [n]and
your ears attentive to the prayer of this place.

41 "And now arise, O LORD God, and go to
your [o]resting place,
you and the ark of your might.
Let your priests, O LORD God, be
[p]clothed with salvation,
and let your saints [q]rejoice in your
goodness.
42 O LORD God, [r]do not turn away the face
of your anointed one!
[s]Remember your steadfast love for
David your servant."

Fire from Heaven

7 [t]As soon as Solomon finished his prayer,
[u]fire came down from heaven and consumed the burnt offering and the sacrifices,
[v]and the glory of the LORD filled the temple.
2 And the priests could not enter the house
of the LORD, because the glory of the LORD
filled the LORD's house. 3 When all the people
of Israel saw the fire come down and the glory
of the LORD on the temple, they bowed down
with their faces to the ground on the pavement and worshiped and gave thanks to the
LORD, saying, "For he is good, [w]for his steadfast love endures forever."

The Dedication of the Temple

4 [x]Then the king and all the people offered
sacrifice before the LORD. 5 King Solomon
offered as a sacrifice 22,000 oxen and 120,000
sheep. So the king and all the people dedicated
the house of God. 6 The priests stood at their
posts; [y]the Levites also, with the instruments
for music to the LORD that King David had
made for giving thanks to the LORD—[w]for
his steadfast love endures forever—whenever
David offered praises by their ministry;[1] [z]oppo-
site them the priests sounded trumpets, and
all Israel stood.
7 [a]And Solomon consecrated the middle of
the court that was before the house of the
LORD, for there he offered the burnt offering
and the fat of the peace offerings, because the
bronze altar Solomon had made could not
hold the burnt offering and the grain offering and the fat.
8 At that time Solomon held the feast for
seven days, and all Israel with him, a very great
assembly, from [b]Lebo-hamath to the [c]Brook
of Egypt. 9 And on the eighth day they held a
solemn assembly, for they had kept the dedication of the altar seven days and the feast seven
days. 10 On the twenty-third day of the seventh
month he sent the people away to their homes,
joyful and glad of heart for the prosperity
that the LORD had granted to David and to
Solomon and to Israel his people.

If My People Pray

11 [d]Thus Solomon finished the house of the
LORD and the king's house. All that Solomon
had planned to do in the house of the
LORD and in his own house he successfully
accomplished. 12 Then the LORD appeared to
Solomon in the night and said to him: "I have
heard your prayer [e]and have chosen this place
for myself as a house of sacrifice. 13 [f]When
I shut up the heavens so that there is no rain,
or command the locust to devour the land,
or send pestilence among my people, 14 if my
people who are called by my name [g]humble

[1] Hebrew *by their hand*

33[k] ch. 7:14; [James 2:7] **36**[l] Eccles. 7:20; James 3:2; 1 John 1:8 **40**[m] Neh. 1:6, 11; [ver. 20; ch. 7:15] [n] Ps. 130:2 **41**[o] Ps. 132:8, 9; [1 Chr. 28:2] [p] [Isa. 61:10] [q] [ch. 7:10; Neh. 9:25] **42**[r] Ps. 132:10 [s] [Ps. 132:1] **Chapter 7** **1**[t] 1 Kgs. 8:54 [u] Lev. 9:24; 1 Kgs. 18:38; 1 Chr. 21:26 [v] See ch. 5:13 **3**[w] See ch. 5:13 **4**[x] 1 Kgs. 8:62; 63 **6**[y] [1 Chr. 15:16] [w] [See ver. 3 above] [z] ch. 5:12 **7**[a] For ver. 7-10, see 1 Kgs. 8:64-66 **8**[b] See Num. 34:8 [c] See Num. 34:5 **11**[d] For ver. 11-22, see 1 Kgs. 9:1-9 **12**[e] See Deut. 12:5 **13**[f] [ch. 6:26, 28] **14**[g] [ch. 12:7]

themselves, and pray and seek my face and
turn from their wicked ways, then I will hear
from heaven and will forgive their sin and heal
their land. 15 [h]Now my eyes will be open and
my ears attentive to the prayer that is made
in this place. 16 [e]For now I have chosen and
consecrated this house that my name may be
there forever. My eyes and my heart will be
there for all time. 17 And as for you, if you will
walk before me as David your father walked,
doing according to all that I have commanded
you and keeping my statutes and my rules,
18 then I will establish your royal throne, as
I covenanted with David your father, saying,
[i]'You shall not lack a man to rule Israel.'

19 [j]"But if you[1] turn aside and forsake my statutes and my commandments that I have set
before you, and go and serve other gods and
worship them, 20 [k]then I will pluck you[2] up
from my land that I have given you, and this
house that I have consecrated for my name,
I will cast out of my sight, and I will make it
[l]a proverb and a byword among all peoples.
21 And at this house, which was exalted, everyone passing by will be astonished and say,
[m]'Why has the LORD done thus to this land and
to this house?' 22 Then they will say, 'Because
they abandoned the LORD, the God of their
fathers who brought them out of the land of
Egypt, and laid hold on other gods and worshiped them and served them. Therefore he
has brought all this disaster on them.'"

Solomon's Accomplishments

8 [n]At the end of twenty years, in which
Solomon had built the house of the LORD
and his own house, 2 Solomon rebuilt the cities
that Hiram had given to him, and settled the
people of Israel in them.

3 And Solomon went to Hamath-zobah and
took it. 4 He built Tadmor in the wilderness
and all the store cities that he built in Hamath.
5 He also built [o]Upper Beth-horon and Lower
Beth-horon, [p]fortified cities [p]with walls, gates,
and bars, 6 and Baalath, and all the store cities that Solomon had and all the cities for
his chariots and the cities for his horsemen,
and whatever Solomon desired to build in
Jerusalem, in Lebanon, and in all the land of
his dominion. 7 [q]All the people who were left
of the Hittites, the Amorites, the Perizzites,
the Hivites, and the Jebusites, who were not
of Israel, 8 from their descendants who were
left after them in the land, whom the people
of Israel had not destroyed—these Solomon
drafted [r]as forced labor, and so they are to this
day. 9 But of the people of Israel Solomon made
no slaves for his work; they were soldiers, and
his officers, the commanders of his chariots,
and his horsemen. 10 And these were the chief
officers of King Solomon, 250, who exercised
authority over the people.

11 [s]Solomon brought Pharaoh's daughter up
from the city of David to the house that he
had built for her, for he said, "My wife shall
not live in the house of David king of Israel,
for the places to which the ark of the LORD has
come are holy."

12 Then Solomon offered up burnt offerings
to the LORD on the altar of the LORD [t]that he
had built before the vestibule, 13 [u]as the duty of
each day required, offering [v]according to the
commandment of Moses for the Sabbaths, the
new moons, and the [w]three annual feasts—
the Feast of Unleavened Bread, the Feast of
Weeks, and the Feast of Booths. 14 According
to the ruling of David his father, he appointed

[1] The Hebrew for *you* is plural here [2] Hebrew *them*; twice in this verse

15[h] See ch. 6:40
16[e] [See ver. 12 above]
18[i] 1 Kgs. 8:25; See ch. 6:16
19[j] [Lev. 26:14; Deut. 28:15]
20[k] [Deut. 29:28] [l] See Deut. 28:37
21[m] Deut. 29:24; Jer. 22:8, 9

Chapter 8
1[n] For ver. 1-18, see 1 Kgs. 9:10-28
5[o] See Josh. 16:3, 5 [p] ch. 14:7; Deut. 3:5
7[q] See Gen. 15:18-21
8[r] ch. 10:18; 1 Kgs. 4:6; 9:21; 12:18; [Josh. 16:10]
11[s] 1 Kgs. 3:1; 7:8; 9:24
12[t] ch. 4:1; 15:8
13[u] [Ex. 29:38] [v] Num. 28:3, 9, 11, 26; 29:2 [w] Ex. 23:14; Deut. 16:16

7:17–20 How can the Lord make an unconditional promise to David, but then make the fulfillment of that promise conditioned upon the obedience of the kings that follow? We know that Solomon forsook the Lord, worshiped other gods, and turned his heart away from the law of God. In fact, Solomon's gross disobedience resulted in the division of the kingdom (922 B.C.). The sins of the kings that followed Solomon eventually precipitated the total destruction of both Israel (722 B.C.) and Judah (586/587 B.C.). These human kings brought the curse of God upon the land of inheritance because of their sin. Thus, God was initially faithful to keep his promise of judgment for disobedience.

But if we can count on God to be faithful to judge disobedience, then we can also count on God to be faithful to render blessing for obedience. In the New Testament, we learn that obedience was, in fact, achieved by a second Adam, the offspring of David, the incarnate Son of God, and that this obedience was applied to God's people (Rom. 1:1–3; 5:19; 2 Cor. 5:21). This is the good news! Everything that God requires from us for blessing, he has provided for us through grace and faith in Christ, the one who came to fulfill God's unconditional promise to David.

[x]the divisions of the priests for their service, [y]and the Levites for their offices of praise and [z]ministry before the priests [u]as the duty of each day required, and [a]the gatekeepers in their divisions at each gate, for so David [b]the man of God had commanded. 15 And they did not turn aside from what the king had commanded the priests and Levites concerning any matter and concerning the treasuries.

16 Thus was accomplished all the work of Solomon from[1] the day the foundation of the house of the LORD was laid until it was finished. So the house of the LORD was completed.

17 Then Solomon went to [c]Ezion-geber and [d]Eloth on the shore of the sea, in the land of Edom. 18 And Hiram sent to him by the hand of his servants ships and servants familiar with the sea, and they went to Ophir together with the servants of Solomon and brought from there [e]450 talents[2] of gold and brought it to King Solomon.

The Queen of Sheba

9 [f]Now when [g]the queen of Sheba heard of the fame of Solomon, she came to Jerusalem to test him with hard questions, having a very great retinue and camels bearing spices and very much gold and precious stones. And when she came to Solomon, she told him all that was on her mind. 2 And Solomon answered all her questions. There was nothing hidden from Solomon that he could not explain to her. 3 And when [g]the queen of Sheba had seen the wisdom of Solomon, the house that he had built, 4 the food of his table, the seating of his officials, and the attendance of his servants, and their clothing, his cupbearers, and their clothing, and his burnt offerings that he offered at the house of the LORD, there was no more breath in her.

5 And she said to the king, "The report was true that I heard in my own land of your words and of your wisdom, 6 but I did not believe the[3] reports until I came and my own eyes had seen it. And behold, half the greatness of your wisdom was not told me; you surpass the report that I heard. 7 Happy are your wives![4] Happy are these your servants, who continually stand before you and hear your wisdom! 8 Blessed be the LORD your God, who has delighted in you [h]and set you on his throne as king for the LORD your God! [i]Because your God loved Israel and would establish them forever, he has made you king over them, that you may execute justice and righteousness." 9 Then she gave the king 120 talents[5] of gold, and a very great quantity of spices, and precious stones. There were no spices such as those that the queen of Sheba gave to King Solomon.

10 Moreover, the servants of Hiram and the servants of Solomon, [j]who brought gold from Ophir, brought algum wood and precious stones. 11 And the king made from the algum wood [k]supports for the house of the LORD and for the king's house, lyres also and harps for the singers. There never was seen the like of them before in the land of Judah.

12 And King Solomon gave to the queen of Sheba all that she desired, whatever she asked [l]besides what she had brought to the king. So she turned and went back to her own land with her servants.

Solomon's Wealth

13 [m]Now the weight of gold that came to Solomon in one year was 666 talents of gold,

[1] Septuagint, Syriac, Vulgate; Hebrew *to* [2] A *talent* was about 75 pounds or 34 kilograms [3] Hebrew *their* [4] Septuagint (compare 1 Kings 10:8); Hebrew *men* [5] A *talent* was about 75 pounds or 34 kilograms

9:1–28 The report of Solomon's wisdom had spread well beyond the borders of Israel, attracting the attention of foreign rulers (vv. 22–23) like the famed queen of Sheba (vv. 1–13). God had been faithful to his promise by making Solomon the wisest of men (1:1–13) and prospering his kingdom in countless ways.

It is almost shocking, therefore, when Jesus declares of himself, "The queen of the South [Sheba] will rise up at the judgment with this generation and condemn it, for she came from the ends of the earth to hear the wisdom of Solomon, and behold, *something greater than Solomon is here*" (Matt. 12:42; cf. Luke 11:31). Jesus, the poor peasant preacher from Nazareth, "in whom are hidden all the treasures of wisdom and knowledge" (Col. 2:3), is indeed greater than Solomon.

As believers who daily live in light of God's rich grace, we are transformed more and more into the image of our Lord (2 Cor. 3:18). As this transformation occurs, we grow in wisdom and discernment (Rom. 12:2), possessing with Christ treasures of wisdom and knowledge.

14[x] See 1 Chr. 24 [y] See 1 Chr. 25 [z] ch. 7:6 [u] [See ver. 13 above] [a] See 1 Chr. 9:17-23, 26 [b] Neh. 12:24, 36
17[c] 1 Kgs. 9:26 [d] [Deut. 2:8; 2 Kgs. 14:22]
18[e] ch. 9:10; [1 Kgs. 9:28]
Chapter 9
1[f] For ver. 1-12, see 1 Kgs. 10:1-13 [g] [Matt. 12:42; Luke 11:31]
3[g] [See ver. 1 above]
8[h] 1 Chr. 29:23 [i] ch. 2:11
10[j] ch. 8:18
11[k] [1 Kgs. 10:12]
12[l] [1 Kgs. 10:13]
13[m] For ver. 13-28, see 1 Kgs. 10:14-28

14 besides that which the explorers and merchants brought. [n]And all the kings of Arabia
and the governors of the land brought gold
and silver to Solomon. 15 King Solomon made
200 large shields of beaten gold; 600 shekels[1]
of beaten gold went into each shield. 16 And he
made 300 shields of beaten gold; [o]300 shekels
of gold went into each shield; and the king put
them in the House of the Forest of Lebanon.
17 The king also made a great ivory throne and
overlaid it with pure gold. 18 The throne had
six steps and a footstool of gold, which were
attached to the throne, and on each side of
the seat were armrests and two lions standing beside the armrests, 19 while twelve lions
stood there, one on each end of a step on the
six steps. Nothing like it was ever made for
any kingdom. 20 All King Solomon's drinking
vessels were of gold, and all the vessels of the
House of the Forest of Lebanon were of pure
gold. Silver was not considered as anything
in the days of Solomon. 21 For the king's ships
went to [p]Tarshish with the servants of Hiram.
Once every three years the ships of Tarshish
used to come bringing gold, silver, ivory, apes,
and peacocks.[2]

22 Thus King Solomon [q]excelled all the kings
of the earth in riches and in wisdom. 23 And
all the kings of the earth sought the presence
of Solomon to hear his wisdom, which God
had put into his mind. 24 Every one of them
brought his present, articles of silver and of
gold, garments, myrrh, spices, horses, and
mules, so much year by year. 25 And Solomon
had [r]4,000 stalls for horses and chariots, and
12,000 horsemen, whom he stationed in the
chariot cities and with the king in Jerusalem.
26 [s]And he ruled over all the kings [t]from the
Euphrates[3] to the land of the Philistines and
to the border of Egypt. 27 [u]And the king made
silver as common in Jerusalem as stone, and
he made cedar as plentiful as the sycamore of
the Shephelah. 28 [v]And horses were imported
for Solomon from Egypt and from all lands.

Solomon's Death

29 [w]Now the rest of the acts of Solomon, from
[x]first to last, are they not written in the history
of [y]Nathan the prophet, and in the prophecy
of [z]Ahijah the Shilonite, and in the visions of
[a]Iddo [b]the seer concerning Jeroboam the son
of Nebat? 30 Solomon reigned in Jerusalem
over all Israel forty years. 31 And Solomon slept
with his fathers and was buried in [c]the city
of David his father, and Rehoboam his son
reigned in his place.

The Revolt Against Rehoboam

10 [d]Rehoboam went to Shechem, for all
Israel had come to Shechem to make
him king. 2 And as soon as Jeroboam the son
of Nebat heard of it (for he was in Egypt,
[e]where he had fled from King Solomon),
then Jeroboam returned from Egypt. 3 And
they sent and called him. And Jeroboam and
all Israel came and said to Rehoboam, 4 [f]"Your
father made our yoke heavy. Now therefore
lighten the hard service of your father and
his heavy yoke on us, and we will serve you."
5 He said to them, "Come to me again in three
days." So the people went away.

6 Then King Rehoboam took counsel with
the old men,[4] who had stood before Solomon
his father while he was yet alive, saying, "How
do you advise me to answer this people?" 7 And
they said to him, [g]"If you will be good to this
people and please them and speak good words
to them, then they will be your servants forever." 8 But he abandoned the counsel that the

[1] A *shekel* was about 2/5 ounce or 11 grams [2] Or *baboons* [3] Hebrew *the River* [4] Or *the elders*; also verses 8, 13

14[n] Ps. 68:29; 72:10
16[o] [1 Kgs. 10:17]
21[p] ch. 20:36, 37
22[q] 1 Kgs. 3:13
25[r] [ch. 1:14; 1 Kgs. 4:26; 10:26]
26[s] 1 Kgs. 4:21 [t] Gen. 15:18; Ex. 23:31; Ps. 72:8
27[u] ch. 1:15
28[v] ch. 1:16
29[w] For ver. 29-31, see 1 Kgs. 11:41-43 [x] 1 Chr. 29:29 [y] 2 Sam. 12:1 [z] 1 Kgs. 11:29 [a] ch. 12:15; 13:22 [b] 2 Sam. 24:11; See 1 Sam. 9:9
31[c] [1 Kgs. 2:10]
Chapter 10
1[d] For ver. 1-19, see 1 Kgs. 12:1-20
2[e] 1 Kgs. 11:40
4[f] [1 Kgs. 5:15]
7[g] [1 Kgs. 12:7]

10:1–14 When Israel first requested a king like all the other nations, the Lord warned them through Samuel that human kings would only bring oppression and slavery (1 Sam. 8:10–18). The Lord's warning had become a reality in Israel, reminding us that choosing any rule but God's over our lives is ultimately some form of bondage.

In contrast to the yoke of oppression and the great burdens described here, the true King of God's people would one day proclaim, "Come to me, all who labor and are heavy laden, and I will give you rest. Take my yoke upon you, and learn from me, for I am gentle and lowly in heart, and you will find rest for your souls. For my yoke is easy, and my burden is light" (Matt. 11:28–30).

This invitation of King Jesus teaches us about the true nature of power, authority, and leadership. By coming under the authority of Jesus' kingship, we are then free to express this same type of loving authority in our own spheres of leadership and responsibility.

old men gave him, and took counsel with the young men who had grown up with him and stood before him. 9 And he said to them, "What do you advise that we answer this people who have said to me, 'Lighten the yoke that your father put on us'?" 10 And the young men who had grown up with him said to him, "Thus shall you speak to the people who said to you, 'Your father made our yoke heavy, but you lighten it for us'; thus shall you say to them, 'My little finger is thicker than my father's thighs. 11 And now, whereas my father laid on you a heavy yoke, I will add to your yoke. My father disciplined you with whips, but I will discipline you with scorpions.'"

12 So Jeroboam and all the people came to Rehoboam the third day, as the king said, "Come to me again the third day." 13 And the king answered them harshly; and forsaking the counsel of the old men, 14 King Rehoboam spoke to them according to the counsel of the young men, saying, "My father made your yoke heavy, but I will add to it. My father disciplined you with whips, but I will discipline you with scorpions." 15 So the king did not listen to the people, for it was a turn of affairs brought about by God that the LORD might fulfill his word, [h]which he spoke by Ahijah the Shilonite to Jeroboam the son of Nebat.

16 And when all Israel saw that the king did not listen to them, the people answered the king, "What portion have we in David? We have no inheritance in the son of Jesse. [i]Each of you to your tents, O Israel! Look now to your own house, David." So all Israel went to their tents. 17 But Rehoboam reigned over the people of Israel who lived in the cities of Judah. 18 Then King Rehoboam sent [j]Hadoram,[1] who was taskmaster over the forced labor, and the people of Israel stoned him to death with stones. And King Rehoboam quickly mounted his chariot to flee to Jerusalem. 19 So Israel has been in rebellion against the house of David to this day.

[1] Spelled *Adoram* in 1 Kings 12:18

Rehoboam Secures His Kingdom

11 [k]When Rehoboam came to Jerusalem, he assembled the house of Judah and Benjamin, 180,000 chosen warriors, to fight against Israel, to restore the kingdom to Rehoboam. 2 But the word of the LORD came to [l]Shemaiah the man of God: 3 "Say to Rehoboam the son of Solomon, king of Judah, and to all Israel in Judah and Benjamin, 4 'Thus says the LORD, You shall not go up or fight against [m]your relatives. Return every man to his home, for this thing is from me.'" So they listened to the word of the LORD and returned and did not go against Jeroboam.

5 Rehoboam lived in Jerusalem, and he built [n]cities for defense in Judah. 6 He built Bethlehem, Etam, Tekoa, 7 Beth-zur, Soco, Adullam, 8 Gath, [o]Mareshah, Ziph, 9 Adoraim, Lachish, Azekah, 10 Zorah, Aijalon, and Hebron, fortified cities that are in Judah and in Benjamin. 11 He made the fortresses strong, and put commanders in them, and stores of food, oil, and wine. 12 And he put shields and spears in all the cities and made them very strong. So he held Judah and Benjamin.

Priests and Levites Come to Jerusalem

13 And the priests and the Levites who were in all Israel presented themselves to him from all places where they lived. 14 For the Levites left [p]their common lands and their holdings and came to Judah and Jerusalem, [q]because Jeroboam and his sons cast them out from serving as priests of the LORD, 15 and he appointed his own [r]priests for the high places and for the goat idols and for [s]the calves that he had made. 16 [t]And those who had set their hearts to seek the LORD God of Israel came after them from all the tribes of Israel to Jerusalem to sacrifice to the LORD, the God of their fathers. 17 [u]They strengthened the kingdom of Judah, and for three years they made Rehoboam the son of Solomon secure, for they walked for three years in the way of David and Solomon.

10:15 Though it might seem like things are quickly deteriorating in the life of God's people after the grandeur of the Solomonic era, it is good to be reminded that this too is a part of God's redemptive plan (cf. 1 Kings 11:29–39). The best days of the united monarchy with human rule could not bring to fulfillment God's ultimate intentions. Thus, the division of the kingdom and its subsequent destruction calls us to look beyond this temporary shadow to the eternal light of the true and better kingdom (Revelation 21–22).

15[h] See 1 Kgs. 11:29-39
16[i] See 2 Sam. 20:1
18[j] [1 Kgs. 4:6; 5:14]

Chapter 11
1[k] For ver. 1-4, see 1 Kgs. 12:21-24
2[l] ch. 12:5, 15
4[m] ch. 28:8, 11
5[n] ver. 23; ch. 8:5; 12:4; 14:6; 17:2, 19; 21:3

8[o] ch. 14:9 **14**[p] Num. 35:2 [q] ch. 13:9 **15**[r] 1 Kgs. 12:31; 13:33 [s] See 1 Kgs. 12:28 **16**[t] ch. 15:9 **17**[u] [ch. 12:1]

Rehoboam's Family

18 Rehoboam took as wife Mahalath the
daughter of Jerimoth the son of David, and of
Abihail the daughter of [v]Eliab the son of Jesse,
19 and she bore him sons, Jeush, Shemariah,
and Zaham. 20 After her he took [w]Maacah the
daughter of Absalom, who bore him [x]Abijah,
Attai, Ziza, and Shelomith. 21 Rehoboam loved
Maacah the daughter of Absalom above all
his wives and concubines (he took eighteen
wives and sixty concubines, and fathered
twenty-eight sons and sixty daughters).
22 [y]And Rehoboam appointed [x]Abijah the son
of Maacah as chief prince among his brothers, for he intended to make him king. 23 And
he dealt wisely and distributed some of his
sons through all the districts of Judah and
Benjamin, in all the fortified cities, and he
gave them abundant provisions and procured
wives for them.[1]

Egypt Plunders Jerusalem

12 [z]When the rule of Rehoboam was
established [a]and he was strong, [b]he
abandoned the law of the LORD, and all
Israel with him. 2 [c]In the fifth year of King
Rehoboam, because they had been unfaithful to the LORD, [d]Shishak king of Egypt came
up against Jerusalem 3 with 1,200 chariots
and 60,000 horsemen. And the people were
without number who came with him from
Egypt—[e]Libyans, Sukkiim, and Ethiopians.
4 And he took [f]the fortified cities of Judah and
came as far as Jerusalem. 5 Then [g]Shemaiah the
prophet came to Rehoboam and to the princes
of Judah, who had gathered at Jerusalem
because of Shishak, and said to them, "Thus
says the LORD, [h]'You abandoned me, so I have
abandoned you to the hand of Shishak.'"
6 Then the princes of [i]Israel and the king
humbled themselves and said, [j]"The LORD
is righteous." 7 When the LORD saw that they
humbled themselves, the word of the LORD
came to Shemaiah: [k]"They have humbled
themselves. I will not destroy them, but I will
grant them some deliverance, [l]and my wrath
shall not be poured out on Jerusalem by the
hand of Shishak. 8 Nevertheless, they shall
be servants to him, [m]that they may know my
service and the service of the kingdoms of the
countries."

9 [n]So Shishak king of Egypt came up against
Jerusalem. He took away the treasures of the
house of the LORD and the treasures of the
king's house. He took away everything. He also
took away [o]the shields of gold that Solomon
had made, 10 and King Rehoboam made in
their place shields of bronze and committed
them to the hands of the officers of the guard,
who kept the door of the king's house. 11 And
as often as the king went into the house of the
LORD, the guard came and carried them and
brought them back to the guardroom. 12 And
when [p]he humbled himself the wrath of the
LORD turned from him, so as not to make a
complete destruction. Moreover, [q]conditions
were good[2] in Judah.

13 [r]So King Rehoboam grew strong in
Jerusalem and reigned. Rehoboam was forty-
one years old when he began to reign, and he
reigned seventeen years in Jerusalem, the city
that the LORD had chosen out of all the tribes
of Israel to put his name there. His mother's
name was Naamah the Ammonite. 14 And he
did evil, [s]for he did not set his heart to seek
the LORD.

[1] Hebrew *and sought a multitude of wives* [2] Hebrew *good things were found*

18[v] 1 Sam. 16:6; 17:13, 28; [1 Chr. 27:18]
20[w] 1 Kgs. 15:2 [x] [1 Kgs. 14:31]
22[y] [Deut. 21:15-17] [x] [See ver. 20 above]
Chapter 12
1[z] ch. 11:17 [a] ch. 26:16 [b] See 1 Kgs. 14:22-24
2[c] 1 Kgs. 14:25 [d] 1 Kgs. 11:40
3[e] ch. 16:8; Nah. 3:9; [Dan. 11:43]
4[f] See ch. 11:5-12
5[g] ch. 11:2; 1 Kgs. 12:22 [h] [ch. 15:2]
6[i] [ch. 21:2] [j] Ex. 9:27
7[k] [ch. 7:14; 1 Kgs. 21:29; James 4:10] [l] [ch. 34:25]
8[m] [Deut. 28:47, 48; Isa. 26:13]
9[n] For ver. 9-11, see 1 Kgs. 14:26-28 [o] ch. 9:15, 16; 1 Kgs. 10:16, 17
12[p] [ch. 7:14; 1 Kgs. 21:29; James 4:10] [q] [ch. 19:3]
13[r] 1 Kgs. 14:21
14[s] [ch. 19:3]

12:1–2 A pattern that emerges among Israel's kings, typified by both Solomon and his son Rehoboam, is that once established and strong they begin to forsake the Lord, abandon his law, and worship other gods. These men had political power, fame, wealth, wives, children, and all of the other trappings associated with success, all stemming from the gracious provision of the Lord. If any group of people ever had the resources and privileges necessary to trust in the Lord, it was these kings of Israel. Their failures show us the inability of external resources as a means for producing true and genuine change in the human heart.

When King Jesus arrived, he did not come with political power, wealth, wives, or heirs. Rather, he came as the impoverished King, but the King who could actually—through his scandalous grace—change our hearts. "For what does it profit a man to gain the whole world and forfeit his soul" (Mark 8:36)? The wealth of human kings impoverish the people, but the poverty of our heavenly King has made us rich beyond calculation (2 Cor. 8:9).

15 [t]Now the acts of Rehoboam, [u]from first to last, are they not written in the chronicles of [v]Shemaiah the prophet and of [w]Iddo [x]the seer?[1] There were continual wars between Rehoboam and Jeroboam. 16 And Rehoboam slept with his fathers and was buried in the city of David, and [y]Abijah[2] his son reigned in his place.

Abijah Reigns in Judah

13 [z]In the eighteenth year of King Jeroboam, [y]Abijah began to reign over Judah. 2 He reigned for three years in Jerusalem. His mother's name was [a]Micaiah[3] the daughter of Uriel of Gibeah.

[b]Now there was war between Abijah and Jeroboam. 3 Abijah went out to battle, having an army of valiant men of war, 400,000 chosen men. And Jeroboam [c]drew up his line of battle against him with 800,000 chosen mighty warriors. 4 Then Abijah stood up on Mount [d]Zemaraim that is in [e]the hill country of Ephraim and said, "Hear me, O Jeroboam and all Israel! 5 Ought you not to know that the LORD God of Israel [f]gave the kingship over Israel forever to David and his sons by [g]a covenant of salt? 6 Yet Jeroboam the son of Nebat, a servant of Solomon the son of David, rose up [h]and rebelled against his lord, 7 and certain [i]worthless scoundrels gathered about him and defied Rehoboam the son of Solomon, when Rehoboam was [j]young and irresolute[4] and could not withstand them.

8 "And now you think to withstand the kingdom of the LORD in the hand of the sons of David, because you are a great multitude and have with you [k]the golden calves that Jeroboam made you for gods. 9 [l]Have you not driven out the priests of the LORD, the sons of Aaron, and the Levites, and made priests for yourselves like the peoples of other lands? Whoever comes [m]for ordination[5] with a young bull or seven rams becomes a priest of what are [n]no gods. 10 But as for us, the LORD is our God, and we have not forsaken him. We have priests ministering to the LORD who are sons of Aaron, and Levites for their service. 11 They offer to the LORD [o]every morning and every evening burnt offerings and incense of sweet spices, set out [p]the showbread on the table of pure gold, [q]and care for the golden lampstand that its lamps may [r]burn every evening. For we [s]keep the charge of the LORD our God, but you have forsaken him. 12 Behold, God is with us at our head, and his priests [t]with their battle trumpets to sound the call to battle against you. O sons of Israel, [u]do not fight against the LORD, the God of your fathers, for you cannot succeed."

13 Jeroboam had sent [v]an ambush around to come upon them from behind. Thus his troops[6] were in front of Judah, and the ambush was behind them. 14 And when Judah looked, behold, the battle was in front of and behind them. [w]And they cried to the LORD, and the priests [t]blew the trumpets. 15 Then the men of Judah raised the battle shout. And when the men of Judah shouted, [x]God defeated Jeroboam and all Israel before Abijah and Judah. 16 The men of Israel fled before Judah,

[1] After *seer*, Hebrew adds *according to genealogy* [2] Spelled *Abijam* in 1 Kings 14:31 [3] Spelled *Maacah* in 1 Kings 15:2 [4] Hebrew *soft of heart* [5] Hebrew *to fill his hand* [6] Hebrew *they*

13:2–18 In the days of Jeroboam, the northern kingdom of Israel had forsaken the Lord, rejected the Levitical priesthood, and erected golden calves as idols for worship (1 Kings 12:25–33; cf. Exodus 32). Additionally, the northern kingdom of Israel had come south to fight against Judah, outnumbering the smaller southern kingdom two to one.

This account reminds us that God himself is the one who fights for his people, especially when the odds are stacked against them (cf. Ex. 14:13–14). The issue was not the size of the force that opposed Judah, but the faith and trust that Judah placed in God. God was head of the army of Judah (2 Chron. 13:12), and God defeated Jeroboam and all Israel (v. 15).

When it comes to earthly demonstrations of strength, God is not impressed by size or numbers. To prove this very point, he arrived as the peasant King in the New Testament, without sword, shield, or army, and he conquered the forces of evil and saved his people from eternal condemnation. Since our great salvation was wrought by God in the form of human weakness, consider what he will do when he returns, mounted for war with the sword of the word in his mouth (cf. Eph. 6:17; Heb. 4:12; Rev. 19:15, 21).

15 [t][1 Kgs. 14:29] [u]ch. 9:29; 1 Chr. 29:29 [v]ver. 5; 1 Kgs. 12:22 [w]ch. 9:29; 13:22 [x]See 1 Sam. 9:9
16 [y][1 Kgs. 14:31]
Chapter 13
1 [z]1 Kgs. 15:1, 2 [y][See ch. 12:16 above]
2 [a][ch. 11:20] [b]1 Kgs. 15:7
3 [c]ch. 14:10; Judg. 20:22; 1 Sam. 17:2
4 [d]Josh. 18:22 [e]See Josh. 24:33
5 [f]2 Sam. 7:12, 13, 16 [g]Num. 18:19
6 [h]1 Kgs. 11:26; 12:19, 20
7 [i]See Judg. 9:4 [j][ch. 12:13; 1 Kgs. 14:21]
8 [k]See 1 Kgs. 12:28
9 [l]ch. 11:14, 15 [m]ch. 29:31 [n]Jer. 5:7
11 [o]ch. 2:4 [p]See Lev. 24:5-9 [q]See Ex. 25:31-39 [r]Ex. 27:20, 21; Lev. 24:2-4 [s]Num. 1:53
12 [t]Num. 10:9 [u][Acts 5:39] **13** [v][Josh. 8:9] **14** [w]ch. 14:11 [t][See ver. 12 above] **15** [x]ch. 14:12

[y]and God gave them into their hand. 17 Abijah
and his people struck them with great force, so
there fell slain of Israel 500,000 chosen men.
18 Thus the men of Israel were subdued at that
time, and the men of Judah prevailed, [z]because
they relied on the LORD, the God of their
fathers. 19 And Abijah pursued Jeroboam [a]and
took cities from him, Bethel with its villages
and Jeshanah with its villages and [b]Ephron[1]
with its villages. 20 Jeroboam did not recover
his power in the days of Abijah. [c]And the LORD
struck him down, [d]and he died. 21 But Abijah
grew mighty. And he took fourteen wives and
had twenty-two sons and sixteen daughters.
22 The rest of the acts of Abijah, his ways and
his sayings, are written in the [e]story of the
prophet [f]Iddo.

Asa Reigns in Judah

14 [2] [g]Abijah slept with his fathers, and they
buried him in the city of David. And
Asa his son reigned in his place. In his days the
land had rest for ten years. 2[3] And Asa did what
was good and right in the eyes of the LORD
his God. 3 He took away the foreign altars
[h]and the high places and broke down [i]the
pillars and cut down the [j]Asherim 4 and commanded Judah to seek the LORD, the God of
their fathers, and to keep the law and the commandment. 5 He also took out of all the cities of Judah [h]the high places and the [k]incense
altars. And the kingdom had rest under him.
6 He built [l]fortified cities in Judah, for the land
had rest. He had no war in those years, [m]for the
LORD gave him peace. 7 And he said to Judah,
"Let us build these cities and surround them
with [n]walls and towers, gates and bars. The
land is still ours, because we have sought the
LORD our God. We have sought him, [m]and
he has given us peace on every side." So they
built and prospered. 8 And Asa had an army
of [o]300,000 from Judah, armed with large
shields and spears, and 280,000 men from
Benjamin that carried shields and drew bows.
All these were mighty men of valor.
9 Zerah [p]the Ethiopian came out against
them with an army of a million men and 300
chariots, and came as far as [q]Mareshah. 10 And
Asa went out to meet him, and [r]they drew up
their lines of battle in the Valley of Zephathah
at [q]Mareshah. 11 And Asa [s]cried to the LORD his
God, "O LORD, there is none like you to help,
between the mighty and the weak. Help us,
O LORD our God, [t]for we rely on you, [u]and in
your name we have come against this multitude. O LORD, you are our God; let not man
prevail against you." 12 [v]So the LORD defeated
the Ethiopians before Asa and before Judah,
and the Ethiopians fled. 13 Asa and the people
who were with him pursued them as far as
[w]Gerar, and the Ethiopians fell until none
remained alive, for they were broken before
the LORD and his army. The men of Judah[4]
carried away very much spoil. 14 And they
attacked all the cities around [w]Gerar, [x]for the
fear of the LORD was upon them. They plundered all the cities, for there was much plunder in them. 15 And they struck down the tents
of those who had livestock and carried away
sheep in abundance and camels. Then they
returned to Jerusalem.

Asa's Religious Reforms

15 [y]The Spirit of God came upon Azariah
the son of Oded, 2 and he went out to
meet Asa and said to him, "Hear me, Asa, and

[1] Or *Ephrain* [2] Ch 13:23 in Hebrew [3] Ch 14:1 in Hebrew [4] Hebrew *They*

14:5–6; 15:1–19 The relationship between faithful leadership and "rest" for the land is an important connection to understand. Consider the book of Judges. As long as a faithful judge lived, the land had rest (cf. Judg. 3:11, 30; 5:31; 8:28). However, once that judge died, the people reverted to idolatry, resulting in foreign oppression. This is one reason why Israel desired a king. The judges were variously raised up by the Lord, but kingship was permanent, enduring through dynastic succession. The problem with kingship, however, was that not all kings were faithful.

In the New Testament, we encounter a King who is both faithful and eternal (John 18:37), securing permanent rest for God's people in a kingdom that will never perish. All of the faithful rulers, judges, and kings in Israel who appear throughout the pages of the Old Testament point beyond themselves to a true and better King. His throne endures on account of his righteousness, and our rest is secure as members of that kingdom.

16[y] ch. 16:8
18[z] [ch. 14:11; 16:7, 8]
19[a] [ch. 15:8; 17:2] [b] [Josh. 15:9]
20[c] 1 Sam. 25:38 [d] 1 Kgs. 14:20
22[e] ch. 24:27 [f] ch. 9:29; 12:15
Chapter 14
1[g] [1 Kgs. 15:8]
3[h] [ch. 15:17; 1 Kgs. 15:14] [i] See Ex. 23:24 [j] Ex. 34:13
5[h] [See ver. 3 above] [k] ch. 34:4, 7; Lev. 26:30; Isa. 17:8; 27:9; Ezek. 6:4, 6
6[l] See ch. 11:5 [m] ch. 15:15; 20:30
7[n] ch. 8:5 [m] [See ver. 6 above]
8[o] [ch. 13:3]
9[p] ch. 12:3; 16:8 [q] ch. 11:8; Josh. 15:44 **10**[r] ch. 13:3 [q] [See ver. 9 above] **11**[s] ch. 13:14; Ex. 14:10 [t] ch. 13:18 [u] [1 Sam. 17:45] **12**[v] ch. 13:15 **13**[w] Gen. 10:19; 20:1; 26:1, 6 **14**[w] [See ver. 13 above] [x] ch. 17:10; 20:29; [Gen. 35:5] **Chapter 15** **1**[y] ch. 20:14; 24:20; Num. 24:2; Judg. 3:10; [ver. 8]

all Judah and Benjamin: [z]The LORD is with you while you are with him. [a]If you seek him, he will be found by you, [b]but if you forsake him, he will forsake you. 3 [c]For a long time Israel was without the true God, and without a teaching priest and without law, 4 [d]but when in their distress they turned to the LORD, the God of Israel, and sought him, he was found by them. 5 In those times there was no peace [e]to him who went out or to him who came in, for great disturbances afflicted all the inhabitants of the lands. 6 They were broken in pieces. Nation was crushed by nation and city by city, for God troubled them with every sort of distress. 7 [f]But you, take courage! Do not let your hands be weak, [g]for your work shall be rewarded."

8 As soon as Asa heard these words, [h]the prophecy of Azariah the son of Oded, he took courage and put away the detestable idols from all the land of Judah and Benjamin and from [i]the cities that he had taken in [j]the hill country of Ephraim, and he repaired the altar of the LORD [k]that was in front of the vestibule of the house of the LORD.[1] 9 And he gathered all Judah and Benjamin, [l]and those from Ephraim, Manasseh, and Simeon who were residing with them, for great numbers had deserted to him from Israel when they saw that the LORD his God was with him. 10 They were gathered at Jerusalem in the third month of the fifteenth year of the reign of Asa. 11 They sacrificed to the LORD on that day [m]from the spoil that they had brought 700 oxen and 7,000 sheep. 12 [n]And they entered into a covenant to seek the LORD, the God of their fathers, with all their heart and with all their soul, 13 but that whoever would not seek the LORD, the God of Israel, [o]should be put to death, whether young or old, man or woman. 14 They swore an oath to the LORD with a loud voice and with shouting and with trumpets and with horns. 15 And all Judah rejoiced over the oath, for they had sworn with all their heart and had sought him with their whole desire, and he was found by them, [p]and the LORD gave them rest all around.

16 [q]Even Maacah, [r]his mother, King Asa removed from being queen mother because she had made a detestable image [s]for Asherah. Asa cut down her image, [t]crushed it, and burned it at the brook Kidron. 17 [u]But the high places were not taken out of Israel. Nevertheless, the heart of Asa was wholly true all his days. 18 And he brought into the house of God the sacred gifts of his father and his own sacred gifts, silver, and gold, and vessels. 19 And there was no more war until the thirty-fifth year of the reign of Asa.

Asa's Last Years

16 [v]In the [w]thirty-sixth year of the reign of Asa, Baasha king of Israel went up against Judah and built Ramah, [x]that he might permit no one to go out or come in to Asa king of Judah. 2 Then Asa took silver and gold from the treasures of the house of the LORD and the king's house and sent them to Ben-hadad king of Syria, who lived in Damascus, saying, 3 "There is a covenant[2] between me and you, as there was between my father and your father. Behold, I am sending to you silver and gold. Go, break your covenant with Baasha king of Israel, that he may withdraw from me." 4 And Ben-hadad listened to King Asa and sent the commanders of his armies against the cities of Israel, and they conquered Ijon, Dan, Abel-maim, and all the

[1] Hebrew *the vestibule of the LORD* [2] Or *treaty*; twice in this verse

16:1–12 All of the faithfulness, zeal, and oath-taking back in 2 Chronicles 15 could not hold back the terrible tide of self-reliance in the heart of Asa, king of Judah. Having experienced the grace, blessing, and protection of the Lord in the past, Asa was quick to forget the true source of his help.

The ebb and flow of the human heart's affections are treacherous and unreliable (cf. Jer. 17:9). This is why it is so important to look outside of ourselves, not only for help in the everyday things of life, but, more importantly, in the steadying of our heart's affections. Consider the example of Jesus who, when assaulted by Satan, did not rely upon himself (though he certainly had the resources), but rather turned in humble dependence to the Scriptures: "Man shall not live by bread alone, but by every word that comes from the mouth of God" (Matt. 4:4; cf. Matt. 4:1–11; Luke 4:1–12). The believer who humbly trusts in the Word of God lives with the resources of grace that are capable of sustaining faith in both good and bad times.

2 [z]ch. 20:17 [a]1 Chr. 28:9; Isa. 55:6; Jer. 29:13 [b]ch. 12:5; 24:20
3 [c][Hos. 3:4]
4 [d]Deut. 4:30, 31
5 [e]Judg. 5:6
7 [f]Josh. 1:6, 7, 9 [g]Gen. 15:1; [Ps. 62:12]
8 [h][ver. 1] [i]ch. 17:2; [ch. 13:19] [j]See Josh. 24:33 [k]ch. 8:12
9 [l]ch. 11:16
11 [m]See ch. 14:13-15
12 [n]ch. 29:10; 34:31; 2 Kgs. 23:3; Neh. 10:29
13 [o]See Deut. 13:6-9
15 [p]ch. 14:7; 20:30
16 [q]For ver. 16-18, see 1 Kgs. 15:13-15 [r][1 Kgs. 15:2, 10] [s]Ex. 34:13 [t][ch. 30:14; 2 Kgs. 23:6, 15]
17 [u][ch. 14:3, 5] **Chapter 16** **1** [v]For ver. 1-6, see 1 Kgs. 15:17-22 [w][1 Kgs. 16:8] [x][ch. 15:9]

[y]store cities of Naphtali. 5 And when Baasha
heard of it, he stopped building Ramah and
let his work cease. 6 Then King Asa took all
Judah, and they carried away the stones of
Ramah and its timber, with which Baasha had
been building, and with them he built Geba
and Mizpah.
7 At that time [z]Hanani [a]the seer came to
Asa king of Judah and said to him, [b]"Because
you relied on the king of Syria, and did not
rely on the LORD your God, the army of the
king of Syria has escaped you. 8 Were not [c]the
Ethiopians and [d]the Libyans a huge army
with very many chariots and horsemen? Yet
[e]because you relied on the LORD, he gave them
into your hand. 9 [f]For the eyes of the LORD
run to and fro throughout the whole earth, to
give strong support to those [g]whose heart is
blameless[1] toward him. [h]You have done foolishly in this, for from now on [i]you will have
wars." 10 Then Asa was angry with the seer and
put him [j]in the stocks in prison, for he was
in a rage with him because of this. And Asa
inflicted cruelties upon some of the people at
the same time.
11 [k]The acts of Asa, from first to last, are
written in the Book of the Kings of Judah
and Israel. 12 In the thirty-ninth year of his
reign Asa was diseased in his feet, and his
disease became severe. Yet even in his disease he did not seek the LORD, but sought
help from physicians. 13 And Asa slept with
his fathers, dying in the forty-first year of his
reign. 14 They buried him in the tomb that
he had cut for himself in the city of David.
They laid him on a bier [l]that had been filled
with various kinds of spices prepared by the
perfumer's art, [m]and they made a very great
fire in his honor.

Jehoshaphat Reigns in Judah

17 Jehoshaphat his son reigned in his
place and strengthened himself against
Israel. 2 He placed forces in all the [n]fortified
cities of Judah and set garrisons in the land
of Judah, and in the cities of Ephraim [o]that
Asa his father had captured. 3 The LORD was
with Jehoshaphat, because he walked in the
earlier ways of his father David. He did not
seek the Baals, 4 but sought the God of his
father and walked in his commandments,
[p]and not according to the practices of Israel.
5 Therefore the LORD established the kingdom
in his hand. And all Judah [q]brought tribute
to Jehoshaphat, [r]and he had great riches and
honor. 6 His heart was courageous in the ways
of the LORD. And furthermore, [s]he took the
high places and the Asherim out of Judah.
7 In the third year of his reign he sent his
officials, Ben-hail, Obadiah, Zechariah,
Nethanel, and Micaiah, [t]to teach in the cities of Judah; 8 [u]and with them the Levites,
Shemaiah, Nethaniah, Zebadiah, Asahel,
Shemiramoth, Jehonathan, Adonijah, Tobijah,
and Tobadonijah; and with these Levites, the
priests Elishama and Jehoram. 9 And [t]they
taught in Judah, having the Book of the Law
of the LORD with them. They went about
through all the cities of Judah and taught
among the people.
10 [v]And the fear of the LORD fell upon
all the kingdoms of the lands that were
around Judah, and they made no war against
Jehoshaphat. 11 Some of the Philistines
[w]brought Jehoshaphat presents and silver
for tribute, and the Arabians also brought
him 7,700 rams and 7,700 goats. 12 And
Jehoshaphat grew steadily greater. He built in
Judah fortresses and store cities, 13 and he had

[1] Or *whole*

4[y] [Ex. 1:11]
7[z] ch. 19:2; 1 Kgs. 16:1 [a] See 1 Sam. 9:9 [b] [Isa. 31:1; Jer. 17:5]
8[c] ch. 14:9 [d] ch. 12:3 [e] [ch. 13:16, 18]
9[f] Zech. 4:10; [Prov. 15:3] [g] [1 Kgs. 8:61] [h] 1 Sam. 13:13 [i] 1 Kgs. 15:16, 32
10[j] [ch. 18:26]
11[k] For ver. 11-14, see 1 Kgs. 15:23, 24
14[l] [Gen. 50:2; Mark 16:1; John 19:39, 40] [m] [ch. 21:19; Jer. 34:5]
Chapter 17
2[n] See ch. 11:5 [o] ch. 15:8
4[p] [1 Kgs. 12:28]
5[q] [ch. 32:23] [r] ch. 18:1

17:7–11 Central to the reign of Jehoshaphat was the commissioning of teachers throughout Judah who would instruct the people in the Book of the Law of the Lord (v. 9). We should carefully note the connection between the teaching of God's Word and Israel's dominance over the surrounding nations, even the Philistines (vv. 10–11).

In modern literary contexts, it is popular to express the power of the pen over the sword. The Bible makes this same connection in powerful ways: "For the word of God is living and active, *sharper than any two-edged sword*, piercing to the division of soul and of spirit, of joints and of marrow, and discerning the thoughts and intentions of the heart" (Heb. 4:12). In the book of Revelation at the end of the Bible, this connection between God's word as a sword and the subjugation of the nations reaches its climax: "*From his mouth comes a sharp sword* with which to strike down the nations" (Rev. 19:15; cf. Isa. 49:2; Rev. 1:16; 2:16). Let each of us take courage, therefore, for the gracious Lord has not left his people unarmed!

6[s] [ch. 15:17; 20:33; 1 Kgs. 22:43] **7**[t] See ch. 35:3 **8**[u] ch. 19:8 **9**[t] [See ver. 7 above] **10**[v] ch. 14:14; 20:29 **11**[w] [ch. 26:8; 2 Sam. 8:2]

large supplies in the cities of Judah. He had
soldiers, mighty men of valor, in Jerusalem.
14 This was the muster of them by fathers'
houses: Of Judah, the commanders of thousands: Adnah the commander, with 300,000
mighty men of valor; 15 and next to him
Jehohanan the commander, with 280,000;
16 and next to him Amasiah the son of Zichri,
[x]a volunteer for the service of the LORD, with
200,000 mighty men of valor. 17 Of Benjamin:
Eliada, a mighty man of valor, with 200,000
men [y]armed with bow and shield; 18 and next
to him Jehozabad with 180,000 armed for war.
19 These were in the service of the king, besides
[z]those whom the king had placed in the fortified cities throughout all Judah.

Jehoshaphat Allies with Ahab

18 Now Jehoshaphat [a]had great riches and
honor, [b]and he made a marriage alliance with Ahab. 2 [c]After some years he went
down to Ahab in Samaria. And Ahab killed
an abundance of sheep and oxen for him
and for the people who were with him, and
induced him to go up against Ramoth-gilead.
3 Ahab king of Israel said to Jehoshaphat king
of Judah, "Will you go with me to Ramoth-
gilead?" He answered him, "I am as you are,
my people as your people. We will be with you
in the war."

4 And Jehoshaphat said to the king of Israel,
"Inquire first for the word of the LORD."
5 Then the king of Israel gathered the prophets together, four hundred men, and said to
them, "Shall we go to battle against Ramoth-
gilead, or shall I refrain?" And they said, "Go
up, for God will give it into the hand of the
king." 6 But Jehoshaphat said, "Is there not
here another prophet of the LORD of whom we
may inquire?" 7 And the king of Israel said to
Jehoshaphat, "There is yet one man by whom
we may inquire of the LORD, Micaiah the son
of Imlah; but I hate him, for he never prophesies good concerning me, but always evil."
And Jehoshaphat said, "Let not the king say
so." 8 Then the king of Israel summoned an
officer and said, "Bring quickly Micaiah the
son of Imlah." 9 Now the king of Israel and
Jehoshaphat the king of Judah were sitting
on their thrones, arrayed in their robes. And
they were sitting at the threshing floor [d]at
the entrance of the gate of Samaria, and all
the prophets were prophesying before them.
10 And Zedekiah the son of Chenaanah made
for himself horns of iron and said, "Thus
says the LORD, 'With these you shall push the
Syrians until they are destroyed.'" 11 And all
the prophets prophesied so and said, "Go up
to Ramoth-gilead and triumph. The LORD will
give it into the hand of the king."

12 And the messenger who went to summon
Micaiah said to him, "Behold, the words of
the prophets with one accord are favorable
to the king. Let your word be like the word
of one of them, and speak favorably." 13 But
Micaiah said, [e]"As the LORD lives, [f]what my
God says, that I will speak." 14 And when he
had come to the king, the king said to him,
"Micaiah, shall we go to Ramoth-gilead to battle, or shall I refrain?" And he answered, "Go
up and triumph; they will be given into your
hand." 15 But the king said to him, "How many
times shall I make you swear that you speak to
me nothing but the truth in the name of the
LORD?" 16 And he said, "I saw all Israel scattered on the mountains, [g]as sheep that have no
shepherd. And the LORD said, 'These have no
master; let each return to his home in peace.'"
17 And the king of Israel said to Jehoshaphat,
"Did I not tell you that he would not prophesy
good concerning me, but evil?" 18 And Micaiah
said, "Therefore hear the word of the LORD:
[h]I saw the LORD sitting on his throne, and all
the host of heaven standing on his right hand
and on his left. 19 And the LORD said, 'Who will
entice Ahab the king of Israel, that he may go
up and fall at Ramoth-gilead?' And one said
one thing, and another said another. 20 Then
a spirit came forward and stood before the
LORD, saying, 'I will entice him.' And the LORD
said to him, 'By what means?' 21 And he said,
'I will go out, and will be [i]a lying spirit in the
mouth of all his prophets.' And he said, 'You
are to entice him, and you shall succeed; go
out and do so.' 22 Now therefore behold, the
LORD has put a lying spirit in the mouth of
these your prophets. The LORD has declared
disaster concerning you."

23 Then Zedekiah the son of Chenaanah came
near [j]and struck Micaiah on the cheek and
said, "Which way did the Spirit of the LORD go
from me to speak to you?" 24 And Micaiah said,
"Behold, you shall see on that day when you go
into an inner chamber to hide yourself." 25 And

16[x] Judg. 5:2, 9; Neh. 11:2 17[y] [1 Chr. 12:2] 19[z] ver. 2 Chapter 18 1[a] ch. 17:5 [b] ch. 21:6; 2 Kgs. 8:18 2[c] For ver. 2-34, see 1 Kgs. 22:2-35 9[d] See Ruth 4:1 13[e] 1 Kgs. 17:1 [f] Num. 22:18; 24:13 16[g] Num. 27:17; Matt. 9:36 18[h] See 1 Kgs. 22:19 21[i] See 1 Kgs. 22:22 23[j] See 1 Kgs. 22:24

the king of Israel said, "Seize Micaiah and take
him back to Amon [k]the governor of the city
and to Joash the king's son, 26 and say, 'Thus
says the king, [l]Put this fellow in prison and
feed him with meager rations of bread and
water until I return in peace.'" 27 And Micaiah
said, "If you return in peace, the LORD has not
spoken by me." And he said, [m]"Hear, all you
peoples!"

The Defeat and Death of Ahab

28 So the king of Israel and Jehoshaphat the
king of Judah went up to Ramoth-gilead.
29 And the king of Israel said to Jehoshaphat,
"I will disguise myself and go into battle, but
you wear your robes." And the king of Israel
disguised himself, and they went into battle.
30 Now the king of Syria had commanded the
captains of his chariots, "Fight with neither
small nor great, but only with the king of
Israel." 31 As soon as the captains of the chariots saw Jehoshaphat, they said, "It is the king
of Israel." So they turned to fight against him.
And Jehoshaphat cried out, and the LORD
helped him; God drew them away from him.
32 For as soon as the captains of the chariots
saw that it was not the king of Israel, they
turned back from pursuing him. 33 But a certain man drew his bow at random[1] and struck
the king of Israel between the scale armor
and the breastplate. Therefore he said to the
driver of his chariot, "Turn around and carry
me out of the battle, for I am wounded." 34 And
the battle continued that day, and the king of
Israel was propped up in his chariot facing the
Syrians until evening. Then at sunset he died.

Jehoshaphat's Reforms

19 Jehoshaphat the king of Judah returned
in safety to his house in Jerusalem. 2 But
[n]Jehu the son of [o]Hanani [p]the seer went out
to meet him and said to King Jehoshaphat,
"Should you [q]help the wicked and love those
who hate the LORD? Because of this, [r]wrath
has gone out against you from the LORD.
3 Nevertheless, [s]some good is found in you, for
[t]you destroyed the Asheroth out of the land,
and have [u]set your heart to seek God."

4 Jehoshaphat lived at Jerusalem. And he
went out again among the people, from
Beersheba to [v]the hill country of Ephraim,
and brought them back to the LORD, the God
of their fathers. 5 He appointed [w]judges in the
land in all [x]the fortified cities of Judah, city by
city, 6 and said to the judges, "Consider what
you do, [y]for you judge not for man but for
the LORD. He is with you in giving judgment.
7 Now then, let the fear of the LORD be upon
you. Be careful what you do, for [z]there is no
injustice with the LORD our God, [a]or partiality
or taking bribes."

8 Moreover, in Jerusalem Jehoshaphat
[b]appointed certain Levites and priests and
heads of families of Israel, [y]to give judgment
for the LORD and to decide disputed cases. They
had their seat at Jerusalem. 9 And he charged
them: [c]"Thus you shall do in the fear of the
LORD, in faithfulness, [d]and with your whole
heart: 10 [e]whenever a case comes to you from
your brothers who live in their cities, concerning bloodshed, law or commandment, statutes
or rules, then you shall warn them, that they
may not incur guilt before the LORD and [f]wrath
may not come upon you and your brothers.
Thus you shall do, and you will not incur guilt.
11 And behold, Amariah the chief priest is over
you [g]in all matters of the LORD; and Zebadiah
the son of Ishmael, the governor of the house of
Judah, in all the king's matters, and the Levites
will serve you as officers. [h]Deal courageously,
and may the LORD be with the upright!"[2]

[1] Hebrew *in his innocence* [2] Hebrew *the good*

19:1–11 There has never been a perfect king in the history of human kings. Even Jehoshaphat lapses in judgment and unites with wicked King Ahab of Israel (vv. 2–3; cf. ch. 18; 20:35–37). However, with Jehoshaphat, the Lord's rebuke by the hand of Jehu the prophet produces repentance and, subsequently, good works. In fact, the work of Jehoshaphat to establish upright judges and bring justice throughout the land in the name of the Lord reminds us of the work of Moses back in Exodus 19.

The Lord will certainly discipline those whom he loves (Heb. 12:4–11), and this discipline is designed to bring repentance and restoration, as it did with Jehoshaphat.

Ultimately, this kindness of the Lord comes to us only because another has endured the wrath that we deserved. Thus, "Consider him who endured from sinners such hostility against himself, so that you may not grow weary or fainthearted" (Heb. 12:3).

25[k] ch. 34:8
26[l] See ch. 16:10
27[m] Mic. 1:2
Chapter 19
2[n] ch. 20:34; 1 Kgs. 16:1 [o] ch. 16:7 [p] See 1 Sam. 9:9 [q] [ch. 18:1; 20:37; Ps. 139:21] [r] ver. 10; ch. 24:18; 32:25
3[s] ch. 12:12; 1 Kgs. 14:13 [t] ch. 17:6 [u] ch. 30:19; Ezra 7:10
4[v] See Josh. 24:33
5[w] [Deut. 16:18] [x] See ch. 11:5
6[y] Deut. 1:17
7[z] Deut. 32:4; Job 8:3; 34:10; [Gen. 18:25; Rom. 9:14] [a] See Deut. 10:17
8[b] ch. 17:8, 9
[y] [See ver. 6 above] **9**[c] 2 Sam. 23:3 [d] 1 Kgs. 8:61 **10**[e] See Deut. 17:8 [f] ver. 2 **11**[g] 1 Chr. 26:30, 32 [h] 1 Chr. 28:10; [Ezra 10:4]

Jehoshaphat's Prayer

20 After this [i]the Moabites and Ammonites, and with them some of the
Meunites,[1] came against Jehoshaphat for battle. 2 Some men came and told Jehoshaphat, "A
great multitude is coming against you from
Edom,[2] from beyond the sea; and, behold,
they are in [j]Hazazon-tamar" (that is, [k]Engedi).
3 Then Jehoshaphat was afraid and set his
face [l]to seek the LORD, and [m]proclaimed a fast
throughout all Judah. 4 And Judah assembled
to seek help from the LORD; from all the cities
of Judah they came to seek the LORD.
5 And Jehoshaphat stood in the assembly
of Judah and Jerusalem, in the house of the
LORD, before the new court, 6 and said, "O
LORD, God of our fathers, are you not [n]God in
heaven? You [o]rule over all the kingdoms of the
nations. [p]In your hand are power and might,
so that none is able to withstand you. 7 Did
you not, our God, [q]drive out the inhabitants
of this land before your people Israel, and give
it forever to the descendants of [r]Abraham your
friend? 8 And they have lived in it and have
built for you in it a sanctuary for your name,
saying, 9 [s]'If disaster comes upon us, the sword,
judgment,[3] or pestilence, or famine, [t]we will
stand before this house and before you—[u]for
your name is in this house—and cry out to
you in our affliction, and you will hear and
save.' 10 And now behold, the men of [v]Ammon
and Moab and [w]Mount Seir, whom [x]you would
not let Israel invade when they came from the
land of Egypt, [y]and whom they avoided and
did not destroy— 11 behold, they reward us
[z]by coming to drive us out of your possession,
which you have given us to inherit. 12 O our
God, will you not [a]execute judgment on them?
For we are powerless against this great horde
that is coming against us. We do not know
what to do, but [b]our eyes are on you."
13 Meanwhile all Judah stood before the
LORD, with their little ones, their wives, and
their children. 14 And [c]the Spirit of the LORD
came upon Jahaziel the son of Zechariah, son
of Benaiah, son of Jeiel, son of Mattaniah, a
Levite of the sons of Asaph, in the midst of
the assembly. 15 And he said, "Listen, all Judah
and inhabitants of Jerusalem and King
Jehoshaphat: Thus says the LORD to you, [d]'Do
not be afraid and do not be dismayed at this
great horde, [e]for the battle is not yours but
God's. 16 Tomorrow go down against them.
Behold, they will come up by the ascent of
Ziz. You will find them at the end of [f]the valley, east of the wilderness of Jeruel. 17 [g]You will
not need to fight in this battle. Stand firm,
hold your position, and see the salvation of the
LORD on your behalf, O Judah and Jerusalem.'
[d]Do not be afraid and do not be dismayed.
Tomorrow go out against them, [h]and the LORD
will be with you."
18 Then Jehoshaphat [i]bowed his head with
his face to the ground, and all Judah and the
inhabitants of Jerusalem fell down before
the LORD, worshiping the LORD. 19 And the
Levites, of the [j]Kohathites and the [k]Korahites,
stood up to praise the LORD, the God of Israel,
with a very loud voice.
20 And they rose early in the morning and
went out into [l]the wilderness of Tekoa. And
when they went out, Jehoshaphat stood
and said, "Hear me, Judah and inhabitants
of Jerusalem! [m]Believe in the LORD your
God, and you will be established; believe
his prophets, and you will succeed." 21 And

[1] Compare 26:7; Hebrew *Ammonites* [2] One Hebrew manuscript; most Hebrew manuscripts *Aram* (Syria) [3] Or *the sword of judgment*

Because of God's free grace to us in Christ, the deserved *destruction* by an enemy has become the *discipline* of a loving father.

20:5–17 When Jehoshaphat encountered the crisis of an enemy threat, he did not fear the future but rather looked to the past. He trusted in the Lord who had driven out the Canaanites to fulfill his covenant with Abraham (vv. 6–7). Jehoshaphat understood that the Lord had done great and amazing feats in order to create and protect his covenant people. Thus, he could continue to trust in the Lord to deliver his people once again.

If Jehoshaphat had reason to trust in the Lord, we have even more. Like Jehoshaphat, we can look to the past and ground our trust in God to protect and provide for his covenant people, the church. Consider him "who did not spare his own Son but gave him up for us all, how will he not also with him graciously give us all things?" (Rom. 8:32). The battle has been won, and now we live as beneficiaries of the spoils of Christ's victory.

Chapter 20
1 [i]2 Kgs. 1:1; 3:4, 7
2 [j]Gen. 14:7 [k]See 1 Sam. 23:29
3 [l]ch. 19:3; [1 Chr. 22:19] [m]Ezra 8:21; Jer. 36:9; Jonah 3:5; [Joel 1:14; 2:15]
6 [n]See Deut. 4:39 [o][Dan. 4:17, 25, 32] [p]1 Chr. 29:12
7 [q]Ps. 44:2 [r]Isa. 41:8; James 2:23
9 [s]ch. 6:28-30; 1 Kgs. 8:33, 37; [Ezek. 14:21] [t][Ezra 10:1] [u]ch. 6:20
10 [v]ver. 1, 22, 23 [w]ch. 25:11, 14; Gen. 32:3; 36:8 [x]Deut. 2:4, 5, 9, 19 [y]Num. 20:21
11 [z]Ps. 83:6, 7, 12
12 [a][1 Sam. 3:13] [b]Ps. 25:15; 123:1, 2; 141:8
14 [c]See ch. 15:1

15 [d]ch. 32:7; [Deut. 1:29, 30; 31:6, 8] [e]1 Sam. 17:47 **16** [f]Num. 13:23 **17** [g][Ex. 14:13, 14] [d][See ver. 15 above] [h]ch. 15:2; 32:8; [Num. 14:9] **18** [i]ch. 29:29, 30; Ex. 4:31; Neh. 8:6 **19** [j]Ex. 6:16, 18 [k]See 1 Chr. 9:19 **20** [l][2 Sam. 14:2] [m]Isa. 7:9

when he had taken counsel with the people,
he appointed those who were to sing to the
LORD and praise him [n]in holy attire, as they
went before the army, and say,

> [o]"Give thanks to the LORD,
> for his steadfast love endures forever."

22 And when they began to sing and praise, the
LORD set [p]an ambush against the men of [q]Ammon, Moab, and Mount Seir, who had come
against Judah, so that they were routed. 23 For
the men of Ammon and Moab rose against the
inhabitants of Mount Seir, devoting them to
destruction, and when they had made an end
of the inhabitants of Seir, [r]they all helped to
destroy one another.

The LORD Delivers Judah

24 When Judah came to the watchtower
of the wilderness, they looked toward the
horde, and behold, there[1] were dead bodies lying on the ground; none had escaped.
25 When Jehoshaphat and his people came
to take their spoil, they found among them,
in great numbers, goods, clothing, and precious things, which they took for themselves
until they could carry no more. They were
three days in taking the spoil, it was so much.
26 On the fourth day they assembled in the
Valley of Beracah,[2] for there they blessed the
LORD. Therefore the name of that place has
been called the Valley of Beracah to this day.
27 Then they returned, every man of Judah
and Jerusalem, and Jehoshaphat at their
head, returning to Jerusalem with joy, [s]for
the LORD had made them rejoice over their
enemies. 28 They came to Jerusalem with harps
and lyres and trumpets, to the house of the
LORD. 29 [t]And the fear of God came on all the
kingdoms of the countries when they heard
that the LORD had fought against the enemies
of Israel. 30 So the realm of Jehoshaphat was
quiet, [u]for his God gave him rest all around.

31 [v]Thus Jehoshaphat reigned over Judah.
He was thirty-five years old when he began
to reign, and he reigned twenty-five years in
Jerusalem. His mother's name was Azubah the
daughter of Shilhi. 32 He walked in the way of
Asa his father and did not turn aside from it,
doing what was right in the sight of the LORD.
33 [w]The high places, however, were not taken
away; [x]the people had not yet set their hearts
upon the God of their fathers.

34 Now the rest of the acts of Jehoshaphat,
from first to last, are written in the chronicles of [y]Jehu the son of Hanani, [z]which are
recorded in the Book of the Kings of Israel.

The End of Jehoshaphat's Reign

35 [a]After this Jehoshaphat king of Judah
joined with Ahaziah king of Israel, who acted
wickedly. 36 He joined him in building ships
to go to [b]Tarshish, and they built the ships
in Ezion-geber. 37 Then Eliezer the son of
Dodavahu of Mareshah prophesied against
Jehoshaphat, saying, [c]"Because you have
joined with Ahaziah, the LORD will destroy
what you have made." And the ships were
wrecked and were not able to go to Tarshish.

Jehoram Reigns in Judah

21 [d]Jehoshaphat slept with his fathers
and was buried with his fathers in the
city of David, and Jehoram his son reigned
in his place. 2 He had brothers, the sons of
Jehoshaphat: Azariah, Jehiel, Zechariah,
Azariah, Michael, and Shephatiah; all these
were the sons of Jehoshaphat king of [e]Israel.[3]
3 Their father gave them great gifts of silver,
gold, and valuable possessions, together with
[f]fortified cities in Judah, but he gave the kingdom to Jehoram, because he was the firstborn.
4 When Jehoram had ascended the throne of
his father and was established, he killed all
his brothers with the sword, and also some of
the princes of [e]Israel. 5 [g]Jehoram was [h]thirty-two years old when he became king, and he
reigned eight years in Jerusalem. 6 [i]And he
walked in the way of the kings of Israel, as the
house of Ahab had done, for [j]the daughter of
Ahab was his wife. And he did what was evil in
the sight of the LORD. 7 Yet the LORD was not

[1] Hebrew *they* [2] *Beracah* means *blessing* [3] That is, Judah

21[n] See 1 Chr. 16:29 [o] See 1 Chr. 16:34
22[p] [ch. 13:13] [q] ver. 10
23[r] [Judg. 7:22; 1 Sam. 14:20]
27[s] Neh. 12:43
29[t] ch. 14:14; 17:10
30[u] [ch. 14:6, 7; 15:15]

21:4–7 Neither dynasty nor paternity could ensure faithful leadership or the protection of the land as Israel's inheritance. Asa and Jehoshaphat were good kings, yet Jehoram followed in the way of Ahab, king of Israel. But even in the midst of egregious fratricide, the Lord holds back from the fullness of his wrath because of his covenant faithfulness (v. 7).

31[v] For ver. 31-33, see 1 Kgs. 22:41-43 **33**[w] [ch. 17:6] [x] ch. 12:14 **34**[y] ch. 19:2 [z] 1 Kgs. 16:1, 7 **35**[a] 1 Kgs. 22:48, 49 **36**[b] ch. 9:21 **37**[c] [ch. 19:2]
Chapter 21 **1**[d] 1 Kgs. 22:50 **2**[e] [ch. 24:5] **3**[f] See ch. 11:5 **4**[e] [See ver. 2 above] **5**[g] For ver. 5-10, see 2 Kgs. 8:17-22 [h] [ver. 20] **6**[i] See 1 Kgs. 12:28-30; 16:31-33 [j] ch. 18:1; 2 Kgs. 8:18

willing to destroy the house of David, because of the covenant that he had made with David, and since he had promised to give [k]a lamp to him and to his sons forever.

8 In his days Edom revolted from the [l]rule of Judah and set up a king of their own. 9 Then Jehoram passed over with his commanders and all his chariots, and he rose by night and struck the Edomites who had surrounded him and his chariot commanders. 10 So Edom revolted from [m]the rule of Judah to this day. At that time Libnah also revolted from his rule, because he had forsaken the LORD, the God of his fathers.

11 Moreover, he made high places in the hill country of Judah and led the inhabitants of Jerusalem [n]into whoredom and made Judah go astray. 12 And a letter came to him from Elijah the prophet, saying, "Thus says the LORD, the God of David your father, [o]'Because you have not walked in the ways of Jehoshaphat your father, or [p]in the ways of Asa king of Judah, 13 [i]but have walked in the way of the kings of Israel and have enticed Judah and the inhabitants of Jerusalem [n]into whoredom, [q]as the house of Ahab led Israel into whoredom, and also you [r]have killed your brothers, of your father's house, who were better than you, 14 behold, the LORD will bring a great plague on your people, your children, your wives, and all your possessions, 15 and you yourself will have a severe sickness [s]with a disease of your bowels, until your bowels come out because of the disease, day by day.'"

16 [t]And the LORD stirred up against Jehoram the anger[1] of the Philistines and of [u]the Arabians who are near the Ethiopians. 17 And they came up against Judah and invaded it and carried away all the possessions they found that belonged to the king's house, and also his sons and his wives, so that no son was left to him except [v]Jehoahaz, his youngest son.

18 And after all this the LORD struck him [w]in his bowels with an incurable disease. 19 In the course of time, at the end of two years, his bowels came out because of the disease, and he died in great agony. His people made no fire in his honor, [x]like the fires made for his fathers. 20 [y]He was thirty-two years old when he began to reign, and he reigned eight years in Jerusalem. And he departed [z]with no one's regret. [a]They buried him in the city of David, but not in the tombs of the kings.

Ahaziah Reigns in Judah

22 [b]And the inhabitants of Jerusalem made Ahaziah, his youngest son, king in his place, for the band of men that came with [c]the Arabians to the camp had killed all the older sons. So Ahaziah the son of Jehoram king of Judah reigned. 2 Ahaziah was twenty-two[2] years old when he began to reign, and he reigned one year in Jerusalem. His mother's name was Athaliah, [d]the granddaughter of Omri. 3 He also walked in the ways of the house of Ahab, for his mother was his counselor in doing wickedly. 4 He did what was evil in the sight of the LORD, as the house of Ahab had done. For after the death of his father they were his counselors, to his undoing. 5 He even followed their counsel and went with Jehoram the son of Ahab king of Israel to make war against Hazael king of Syria at Ramoth-gilead. And the Syrians wounded Joram, 6 and he returned to be healed in Jezreel of the wounds that he had received at Ramah, when he fought against Hazael king of Syria. And Ahaziah the son of Jehoram king of Judah went down to see Joram the son of Ahab in Jezreel, because he was wounded.

7 But it was ordained by God that the downfall of Ahaziah should come about through his going to visit Joram. For when he came there, [e]he went out with Jehoram to meet Jehu the son of Nimshi, [f]whom the LORD had anointed to destroy the house of Ahab.

[1] Hebrew *spirit* [2] See 2 Kings 8:26; Hebrew *forty-two*; Septuagint *twenty*

This picture of God's covenant faithfulness during the darker days of Jehoram should bring us great encouragement. For we have even more cause to rely upon God's mercy than the Old Testament people understood. Under the new covenant, God's wrath has been fully satisfied by the work of Christ on our behalf, securing forever the inheritance for every believer. Additionally, we have a King who is both faithful and eternal, demolishing the instability of any human dynasty. "But as it is, Christ has obtained a ministry that is as much more excellent than the old as the covenant he mediates is better, since it is enacted on better promises" (Heb 8:6; cf. 8:8–13; 9:15).

7 [k]See 1 Kgs. 11:36; [2 Sam. 21:17]
8 [l]ver. 10
10 [m]ver. 8
11 [n]Ex. 34:16; Lev. 17:7; 20:5
12 [o]ch. 17:3 [p]ch. 14:2-5
13 [i][See ver. 6 above] [n][See ver. 11 above] [q]See 1 Kgs. 16:31-33 [r]ver. 4
15 [s]ver. 18, 19
16 [t][1 Kgs. 11:14, 23] [u]ch. 17:11; 22:1; 26:7 **17** [v]ch. 25:23; [ch. 22:6] **18** [w]ver. 15 **19** [x]ch. 16:14 **20** [y][ver. 5] [z][Jer. 22:18] [a][ch. 24:25; 28:27] **Chapter 22** **1** [b]For ver. 1-6, see 2 Kgs. 8:24-29 [c]See ch. 21:16 **2** [d][ch. 21:6] **7** [e]2 Kgs. 9:21 [f]2 Kgs. 9:6, 7

8 [g]And when Jehu was [h]executing judgment
on the house of Ahab, he met the princes of
Judah and the sons of Ahaziah's brothers, who
attended Ahaziah, and he killed them. 9 [i]He
searched for Ahaziah, and he was captured
while hiding in Samaria, and he was brought
to Jehu and put to death. [j]They buried him, for
they said, "He is the grandson of Jehoshaphat,
[k]who sought the LORD with all his heart." And
the house of Ahaziah had no one able to rule
the kingdom.

Athaliah Reigns in Judah

10 [l]Now when Athaliah the mother of Ahaziah saw that her son was dead, she arose and
destroyed all the royal family of the house of
Judah. 11 But Jehoshabeath,[1] the daughter of
the king, took Joash the son of Ahaziah and
stole him away from among the king's sons
who were about to be put to death, and she
put him and his nurse in a bedroom. Thus
Jehoshabeath, the daughter of King Jehoram
and wife of Jehoiada the priest, because
she was a sister of Ahaziah, hid him[2] from
Athaliah, so that she did not put him to
death. 12 And he remained with them six years,
hidden in the house of God, while Athaliah
reigned over the land.

Joash Made King

23 [m]But in the seventh year Jehoiada took
courage and entered into a covenant
with the commanders of hundreds, Azariah
the son of Jeroham, Ishmael the son of
Jehohanan, Azariah the son of Obed, Maaseiah
the son of Adaiah, and Elishaphat the son of
Zichri. 2 And they went about through [n]Judah
and gathered the Levites from all the cities
of Judah, and the heads of fathers' houses of
Israel, and they came to Jerusalem. 3 And all
the assembly made a covenant with the king in
the house of God. And Jehoiada[3] said to them,
"Behold, the king's son! Let him reign, [o]as the
LORD spoke concerning the sons of David.
4 This is the thing that you shall do: [p]of you
priests and Levites who come off duty on the
Sabbath, one third shall be gatekeepers, 5 and
one third shall be at the king's house and one
third at the Gate of the Foundation. And all
the people shall be in the courts of the house
of the LORD. 6 Let no one enter the house of
the LORD except the priests [q]and ministering Levites. They may enter, for they are holy,
but all the people shall keep the charge of the
LORD. 7 The Levites shall surround the king,
each with his weapons in his hand. And whoever enters the house shall be put to death. Be
with the king when he comes in and when he
goes out."

8 The Levites and all Judah did according to
all that Jehoiada the priest commanded, and
they each brought his men, who were to go
off duty on the Sabbath, with those who were
to come on duty on the Sabbath, for Jehoiada
the priest did not dismiss [r]the divisions. 9 And
Jehoiada the priest gave to the captains the
spears and the large and small shields that had
been King David's, which were in the house of
God. 10 And he set all the people as a guard for
the king, every man with his weapon in his
hand, from the south side of the house to the
north side of the house, around the altar and
the house. 11 Then they brought out the king's
son and put the crown on him and gave him
[s]the testimony. And they proclaimed him king,
and Jehoiada and his sons anointed him, and
they said, [t]"Long live the king."

Athaliah Executed

12 When Athaliah heard the noise of the
people running and praising the king, she

[1] Spelled *Jehosheba* in 2 Kings 11:2 [2] That is, Joash [3] Hebrew *he*

8 [g] See 2 Kgs. 10:11-14 [h] [ch. 24:24]
9 [i] [2 Kgs. 9:27] [j] 2 Kgs. 9:28 [k] ch. 17:4
10 [l] For ver. 10-12, see 2 Kgs. 11:1-3

Chapter 23
1 [m] For ver. 1-21, see 2 Kgs. 11:4-20
2 [n] See ch. 21:2
3 [o] See ch. 6:16
4 [p] [1 Chr. 9:25; 24:4]
6 [q] See 1 Chr. 23:27-29
8 [r] See 1 Chr. 24
11 [s] Deut. 17:18, 19 [t] See 1 Sam. 10:24

22:10–12 A theme that runs across the pages of Scripture is the crisis of the seed (offspring) of promise (Gen. 3:15). Cain kills Abel, and so God provides Seth. Abraham is promised offspring, but Sarah is barren. Miraculously, Sarah gives birth to a son, Isaac, but God commands Abraham to kill him (though Isaac is ultimately spared; Genesis 22). Next, we find Rebekah, the wife of Isaac, to be barren. In Egypt, the pharaoh orders all of the male children to be killed at birth. Here, in this text, we discover that almost all of the royal line of Judah was destroyed by Athaliah the mother of Ahaziah.

The crisis of the seed of promise highlights the ongoing cosmic antagonism between the seed of the woman and the seed of the Serpent, stretching back to Genesis 3. These crises should sharpen our focus on God's preserving, redemptive work to provide and protect the line of the seed of promise. The Lord may provide a ram as a substitute (Genesis 22), or faithful midwives who refuse to follow the command of the pharaoh (Exodus 1), or, in this case, a faithful sister who hides one last son.

went into the house of the LORD to the people. 13 And when she looked, there was the king standing by his pillar at the entrance, and the captains and the trumpeters beside the king, and all the people of the land rejoicing and blowing trumpets, and the singers with their musical instruments leading in the celebration. And Athaliah tore her clothes and cried, "Treason! Treason!" 14 Then Jehoiada the priest brought out the captains who were set over the army, saying to them, "Bring her out between the ranks, and anyone who follows her is to be put to death with the sword." For the priest said, "Do not put her to death in the house of the LORD." 15 So they laid hands on her,[1] and she went into the entrance of [u]the horse gate of the king's house, and they put her to death there.

Jehoiada's Reforms

16 And Jehoiada made a covenant between himself and all the people and the king that they should be the LORD's people. 17 Then all the people went to the house of Baal and tore it down; his altars and his images they broke in pieces, [v]and they killed Mattan the priest of Baal before the altars. 18 And Jehoiada posted watchmen for the house of the LORD under the direction of [w]the Levitical priests and the Levites [x]whom David had organized to be in charge of the house of the LORD, to offer burnt offerings to the LORD, [y]as it is written in the Law of Moses, with rejoicing and with singing, [z]according to the order of David. 19 He stationed [a]the gatekeepers at the gates of the house of the LORD so that no one should enter who was in any way unclean. 20 And he took the captains, the nobles, the governors of the people, and all the people of the land, and they brought the king down from the house of the LORD, marching [b]through the upper gate to the king's house. And they set the king on the royal throne. 21 So all the people of the land rejoiced, and the city was quiet after Athaliah had been put to death with the sword.

Joash Repairs the Temple

24 [c]Joash[2] was seven years old when he began to reign, and he reigned forty years in Jerusalem. His mother's name was Zibiah of Beersheba. 2 [d]And Joash did what was right in the eyes of the LORD all the days of Jehoiada the priest. 3 Jehoiada got for him two wives, and he had sons and daughters.

4 After this Joash [e]decided to [f]restore the house of the LORD. 5 And he gathered the priests and the Levites and said to them, "Go out to the cities of [g]Judah and gather from all Israel money to repair the house of your God from year to year, and see that you act quickly." But the Levites did not act quickly. 6 So the king summoned Jehoiada the chief and said to him, "Why have you not required the Levites to bring in from Judah and Jerusalem [h]the tax levied by Moses, the servant of the LORD, and the congregation of Israel for [i]the tent of testimony?" 7 For [j]the sons of Athaliah, that wicked woman, had broken into the house of God, and had also used all [k]the dedicated things of the house of the LORD for the Baals.

8 So the king commanded, and they made a chest and set it outside the gate of the house of the LORD. 9 And [l]proclamation was made throughout Judah and Jerusalem to bring in for the LORD [h]the tax that Moses the servant of God laid on Israel in the wilderness. 10 And all the princes and all the people rejoiced and brought their tax and dropped it into the chest until they had finished.[3] 11 And whenever the chest was brought to the king's officers by the Levites, when they saw that there was much money in it, the king's secretary and the officer of the chief priest

[1] Or *they made a passage for her* [2] Spelled *Jehoash* in 2 Kings 12:1 [3] Or *until it was full*

Events of this type are intended to point us forward to the ultimate crisis of the seed of promise. Jesus, born under a decree of death as in the days of Egypt, was saved from infanticide by the intervention of his heavenly Father. As God called Abraham to sacrifice Isaac, this royal Seed was sent to be sacrificed, but this time no substitute was provided, because he became *our* substitute. Yet God intervened again and resurrected this Son, who now reigns with the Father as our Mediator. The crisis of this Seed of promise is the means by which God's people have come to experience God's unfailing resolve and prevailing providence that provides for the forgiveness of sin, the hope of eternal life, and the restoration of fellowship with the Eternal One who created us for his glory and good pleasure.

15 [u]Neh. 3:28; Jer. 31:40; [2 Kgs. 11:16]
17 [v]Deut. 13:9
18 [w]ch. 5:5; 30:27 [x]1 Chr. 23:6, 30, 31; 24:1 [y]Num. 28:2 [z][1 Chr. 25:2]
19 [a]See 1 Chr. 26:1-19
20 [b][2 Kgs. 11:19; 15:35]

Chapter 24
1 [c]For ver. 1-14, see 2 Kgs. 11:21-12:15
2 [d][ch. 26:5]
4 [e][1 Chr. 22:7] [f]ver. 12
5 [g]See ch. 21:2
6 [h]See Ex. 30:12-16 [i]See Num. 17:7, 8 **7** [j][ch. 21:17] [k][1 Kgs. 15:15] **9** [l][Ezra 1:1] [h][See ver. 6 above]

would come and empty the chest and take
it and return it to its place. Thus they did
day after day, and collected money in abundance. [12] And the king and Jehoiada gave it
to those who had charge of the work of the
house of the LORD, and they hired masons
and carpenters to restore the house of the
LORD, and also workers in iron and bronze to
repair the house of the LORD. [13] So those who
were engaged in the work labored, and the
repairing went forward in their hands, and
they restored the house of God to its proper
condition and strengthened it. [14] And when
they had finished, they brought the rest of
the money before the king and Jehoiada, and
with it [m]were made utensils for the house of
the LORD, both for the service and for the
burnt offerings, and dishes for incense and
vessels of gold and silver. And they offered
burnt offerings in the house of the LORD
regularly all the days of Jehoiada.

[15] But Jehoiada grew old and full of days, and
died. He was 130 years old at his death. [16] And
they buried him in the city of David among
the kings, because he had done good in Israel,
and toward God and his house.

[17] Now after the death of Jehoiada the princes
of Judah came and paid homage to the king.
Then the king listened to them. [18] And they
abandoned the house of the LORD, the God
of their fathers, and served [o]the Asherim and
the idols. And [p]wrath came upon Judah and
Jerusalem for this guilt of theirs. [19] [q]Yet he sent
prophets among them to bring them back to
the LORD. [r]These testified against them, but
they would not pay attention.

Joash's Treachery

[20] [s]Then the Spirit of God clothed Zechariah
[t]the son of Jehoiada the priest, and he stood
above the people, and said to them, "Thus
says God, [u]'Why do you break the commandments of the LORD, so that you cannot prosper? [v]Because you have forsaken the LORD,
he has forsaken you.'" [21] But [w]they conspired
against him, [x]and by command of the king
they stoned him with stones in the court of
the house of the LORD. [22] Thus Joash the king
did not remember the kindness that Jehoiada,
Zechariah's father, had shown him, but killed
his son. And when he was dying, he said, "May
the LORD see [y]and avenge!"[1]

Joash Assassinated

[23] At the end of the year [z]the army of the
Syrians came up against Joash. They came
to Judah and Jerusalem and destroyed all
the princes of the people from among the
people and sent all their spoil to the king of
Damascus. [24] Though the army of the Syrians
had come with few men, [a]the LORD delivered
into their hand a very great army, [v]because
Judah[2] had forsaken the LORD, the God of
their fathers. Thus they [b]executed judgment
on Joash.

[25] When they had departed from him, leaving him [c]severely wounded, [d]his servants
conspired against him because of the blood
of [e]the son[3] of Jehoiada the priest, and killed
him on his bed. So he died, and they buried
him in the city of David, [f]but they did not
bury him in the tombs of the kings. [26] Those
who conspired against him were Zabad
the son of Shimeath the Ammonite, and
Jehozabad the son of Shimrith the Moabite.
[27] Accounts of his sons and of the many oracles against him and of [g]the rebuilding[4] of
the house of God are written in the [h]Story of
the Book of the Kings. And Amaziah his son
reigned in his place.

[1] Hebrew *and seek* [2] Hebrew *they* [3] Septuagint, Vulgate; Hebrew *sons* [4] Hebrew *founding*

24:25–27 The summary of this king's life is tragic! He was rescued from almost certain death as an infant. At seven years of age, the Levites installed him as the king of Judah and executed the murderer of his family. The faithful priest Jehoiada cared for him, provided wives for him, and advised him for years. He even repaired the temple and removed Baal worship from the city. Yet the king's heart remained unchanged by the blessings poured into his life, and so he was executed as a rebel and murderer of God's priest (and prophet).

Thanks be to God, therefore, who changes our hearts and produces real and lasting change in the life of each believer. Though Joash was zealous to follow the law earlier in life, the law could not change his heart (cf. Rom. 7:10–12). Only by grace through faith in Christ can such a change be wrought. "And [so] I am sure of this, that he who began a good work in you will bring it to completion at the day of Jesus Christ" (Phil. 1:6).

14[m] [2 Kgs. 12:13]
18[o] See Deut. 16:21 [p] ch. 19:2, 10; 28:11, 13; 29:8; 32:25
19[q] Jer. 25:4; [Matt. 23:34; Luke 11:49]; See ch. 36:15 [r] Neh. 13:15, 21
20[s] ch. 15:1; 20:14 [t] [Matt. 23:35] [u] [Num. 14:41] [v] ch. 15:2
21[w] [Neh. 9:26] [x] Matt. 23:35; Luke 11:51
22[y] [Gen. 9:5]
23[z] [2 Kgs. 12:17, 18]
24[a] Isa. 30:17; [Lev. 26:8, 36, 37] [v] [See ver. 20 above] [b] [ch. 22:8]
25[c] [Deut. 28:35] [d] For ver. 25-27, see 2 Kgs. 12:20, 21 [e] [ver. 21, 22] [f] [ch. 21:20; 28:27]
27[g] ver. 12 [h] ch. 13:22

Amaziah Reigns in Judah

25 [i]Amaziah was twenty-five years old when he began to reign, and he reigned twenty-nine years in Jerusalem. His mother's name was Jehoaddan of Jerusalem. 2 And he did what was right in the eyes of the LORD, [j]yet not with a whole heart. 3 And as soon as the royal power was firmly his, he killed his servants who had struck down the king his father. 4 But he did not put their children to death, according to what is written in the Law, in the Book of Moses, where the LORD commanded, [k]"Fathers shall not die because of their children, nor children die because of their fathers, but each one shall die for his own sin."

Amaziah's Victories

5 Then Amaziah assembled the men of Judah and set them by fathers' houses under commanders of thousands and of hundreds for all Judah and Benjamin. He mustered those [l]twenty years old and upward, and found that they were [m]300,000 choice men, fit for war, [n]able to handle spear and shield. 6 He hired also 100,000 mighty men of valor from Israel for 100 talents[1] of silver. 7 But [o]a man of God came to him and said, "O king, do not let the army of Israel go with you, for the LORD is not with Israel, with all these Ephraimites. 8 But go, act, be strong for the battle. Why should you suppose that God will cast you down before the enemy? [p]For God has power to help or to cast down." 9 And Amaziah said to the man of God, "But what shall we do about the hundred talents that I have given to the army of Israel?" The man of God answered, "The LORD is able to give you much more than this." 10 Then Amaziah discharged the army that had come to him from Ephraim to go home again. And they became very angry with Judah and returned home in fierce anger. 11 But Amaziah took courage and led out his people and went to the [q]Valley of Salt and struck down [r]10,000 men of Seir. 12 The men of Judah captured another 10,000 alive and took them to the top of a rock and threw them down from the top of the rock, and they were all dashed to pieces. 13 But the men of the army whom Amaziah sent back, not letting them go with him to battle, raided the cities of Judah, [s]from Samaria to Beth-horon, and struck down 3,000 people in them and took much spoil.

Amaziah's Idolatry

14 After Amaziah came from striking down the Edomites, [t]he brought the gods [r]of the men of Seir and set them up as his gods and worshiped them, making offerings to them. 15 Therefore the LORD was angry with Amaziah and sent to him a prophet, who said to him, "Why have you sought the gods of a people [u]who did not deliver their own people from your hand?" 16 But as he was speaking, the king said to him, "Have we made you a royal counselor? Stop! Why should you be struck down?" So the prophet stopped, but said, "I know that [v]God has determined to destroy you, because you have done this and have not listened to my counsel."

Israel Defeats Amaziah

17 [w]Then Amaziah king of Judah took counsel and sent to Joash the son of Jehoahaz, son of Jehu, king of Israel, saying, "Come, let us look one another in the face." 18 And Joash the king of Israel sent word to Amaziah king of Judah, [x]"A thistle on Lebanon sent to a cedar on Lebanon, saying, 'Give your daughter to my son for a wife,' and a wild beast of Lebanon passed by and trampled down the thistle. 19 You say, 'See, I[2] have struck down Edom,' and [y]your heart has lifted you up in boastfulness. But now stay at home. Why should you provoke trouble so that you fall, you and Judah with you?"

20 But Amaziah would not listen, for it was of God, in order that he might give them into the hand of their enemies, [z]because they had sought the gods of Edom. 21 So Joash king of Israel went up, and he and Amaziah king of Judah faced one another in battle at Beth-shemesh, which belongs to Judah. 22 And Judah was defeated by Israel, and every man fled to his home. 23 And Joash king of Israel captured Amaziah king of Judah, the son of Joash, son of [a]Ahaziah, at Beth-shemesh, and brought him to Jerusalem and broke down the wall of Jerusalem for 400 cubits,[3] from [b]the Ephraim Gate to the Corner Gate. 24 And he seized all the gold and silver, and all the

[1] A *talent* was about 75 pounds or 34 kilograms [2] Hebrew *you* [3] A *cubit* was about 18 inches or 45 centimeters

Chapter 25 **1**[i] For ver. 1-4, see 2 Kgs. 14:1-6 **2**[j] [ver. 14] **4**[k] Deut. 24:16; [Jer. 31:30; Ezek. 18:20] **5**[l] Num. 1:3 [m] [ch. 11:1; 13:3; 17:14-18; 26:13] [n] 1 Chr. 12:8 **7**[o] Deut. 33:1 **8**[p] [ch. 20:6] **11**[q] 2 Kgs. 14:7 [r] ch. 20:10 **13**[s] [ch. 15:8; 19:4] **14**[t] [ch. 28:23] [r] [See ver. 11 above] **15**[u] [ver. 11] **16**[v] [Josh. 11:20] **17**[w] For ver. 17-24, see 2 Kgs. 14:8-14 **18**[x] [Judg. 9:8] **19**[y] See ch. 26:16 **20**[z] ver. 14, 15 **23**[a] ch. 21:17 [b] Neh. 8:16

vessels that were found in the house of God,
in the care of [c]Obed-edom. He seized also the
treasuries of the king's house, also hostages,
and he returned to Samaria.
25 [d]Amaziah the son of Joash, king of Judah,
lived fifteen years after the death of Joash the
son of Jehoahaz, king of Israel. 26 Now the rest
of the deeds of Amaziah, from first to last,
are they not written in the Book of the Kings
of Judah and Israel? 27 From the time when
he turned away from the LORD they made
a conspiracy against him in Jerusalem, and
he fled to Lachish. But they sent after him to
Lachish and put him to death there. 28 And
they brought him upon horses, and he was
buried with his fathers in the city of David.[1]

Uzziah Reigns in Judah

26 And all the people of Judah took
Uzziah, who was sixteen years old, and
made him king instead of his father Amaziah.
2 He built Eloth and restored it to Judah, after
the king slept with his fathers. 3 Uzziah was
[e]sixteen years old when he began to reign,
and he reigned fifty-two years in Jerusalem.
His mother's name was Jecoliah of Jerusalem.
4 And he did what was right in the eyes of the
LORD, according to all that his father Amaziah
had done. 5 He set himself to seek God [f]in the
days of Zechariah, [g]who instructed him in the
fear of God, and as long as he sought the LORD,
God made him prosper.
6 He went out and [h]made war against the
Philistines and broke through the wall of
Gath and the wall of Jabneh and the wall
of Ashdod, and he built cities in the territory of
Ashdod and elsewhere among the Philistines.
7 God helped him [i]against the Philistines and
against the Arabians who lived in Gurbaal and
against the [j]Meunites. 8 The Ammonites [k]paid
tribute to Uzziah, and his fame spread even to
the border of Egypt, for he became very strong.
9 Moreover, Uzziah built towers in Jerusalem at
[l]the Corner Gate and at [m]the Valley Gate and at
[n]the Angle, and fortified them. 10 And he built
towers in the wilderness and [o]cut out many
cisterns, for he had large herds, both in the
Shephelah and in the plain, and he had farmers
and vinedressers in the hills and in the fertile
lands, for he loved the soil. 11 Moreover, Uzziah
had an army of soldiers, fit for war, in divisions
according to the numbers in the muster made
by Jeiel the secretary and Maaseiah the officer,
under the direction of Hananiah, one of the
king's commanders. 12 The whole number of
the heads of fathers' houses of mighty men
of valor was 2,600. 13 Under their command
was an army of [p]307,500, who could make war
with mighty power, to help the king against
the enemy. 14 And Uzziah prepared for all the
army shields, spears, helmets, [q]coats of mail,
bows, and stones for slinging. 15 In Jerusalem
he made machines, invented by skillful men,
to be on the towers and the corners, to shoot
arrows and great stones. And his fame spread
far, for he was marvelously helped, till he was
strong.

Uzziah's Pride and Punishment

16 But when [r]he was strong, [s]he grew proud,
to his destruction. For he was unfaithful to the
LORD his God and entered the temple of the
LORD to burn incense on the altar of incense.
17 But [t]Azariah the priest went in after him,

[1] Hebrew *of Judah*

24[c] 1 Chr. 26:15
25[d] For ch. 25:25–26:2, see 2 Kgs. 14:17-22
Chapter 26
3[e] For ver. 3, 4, see 2 Kgs. 15:2, 3
5[f] [ch. 24:2] [g] [Dan. 1:17; 10:1]
6[h] [Isa. 14:29]
7[i] ch. 21:16 [j] [ch. 20:1]
8[k] [ch. 17:11; 2 Sam. 8:2]
9[l] See 2 Kgs. 14:13 [m] Neh. 2:13, 15; 3:13 [n] Neh. 3:19
10[o] Deut. 6:11; Neh. 9:25
13[p] [ch. 25:5]
14[q] Neh. 4:16
16[r] [ch. 12:1; Deut. 32:15] [s] ch. 32:25; Ezek. 28:2, 5, 17; [ch. 25:19; Deut. 8:14; 2 Kgs. 14:10]
17[t] 1 Chr. 6:10

26:4–5, 16; 27:6 The history of many of the kings of Judah is a history of fidelity mixed with infidelity. King Uzziah is one example of this reality. In just a few verses, the author takes us from Uzziah's hopeful beginning to his tragic death as a leper. The text is clear to indicate that the king's prosperity was tied to his obedience, "and as long as he sought the LORD, God made him prosper" (26:5). This does not tie final salvation to our works, but reminds us that the law of God reflects his character and care. As we stay on the path of his instruction, we experience the blessings he intends (which are not necessarily according to the world's values). But there are also consequences to wandering from the path. If God did not love us, he would not so warn us.

In the New Testament, we finally encounter a faithful King in whom there is no infidelity. With regard to this King, the Father says, "Your throne, O God, is forever and ever, the scepter of *uprightness* is the scepter of your kingdom. *You have loved righteousness and hated wickedness*; therefore God, your God, has anointed you with the oil of gladness beyond your companions" (Heb. 1:8–9). Jesus has become our faithful and eternal King. But even better, the righteousness of this King has been reckoned to everyone who has placed their trust in him (Rom. 4:1–8; 1 Cor. 1:30; 2 Cor. 5:21).

with eighty priests of the LORD who were men of valor, 18 and they withstood King Uzziah and said to him, [u]"It is not for you, Uzziah, to burn incense to the LORD, [v]but for the priests, the sons of Aaron, who are consecrated to burn incense. Go out of the sanctuary, for you have done wrong, and it will bring you no honor from the LORD God." 19 Then Uzziah was angry. Now he had a censer in his hand to burn incense, and when he became angry with the priests, [w]leprosy[1] broke out on his forehead in the presence of the priests in the house of the LORD, by the altar of incense. 20 And Azariah the chief priest and all the priests looked at him, and behold, he was leprous in his forehead! And they rushed him out quickly, and he himself hurried to go out, because the LORD had struck him. 21 [x]And King Uzziah was a leper to the day of his death, and being a leper lived [y]in a separate house, for he was excluded from the house of the LORD. And Jotham his son was over the king's household, governing the people of the land.

22 Now the rest of the acts of Uzziah, from first to last, [z]Isaiah the prophet the son of Amoz wrote. 23 And Uzziah slept with his fathers, and they buried him with his fathers in the burial field that belonged to the kings, for they said, "He is a leper." And Jotham his son reigned in his place.

Jotham Reigns in Judah

27 [a]Jotham was twenty-five years old when he began to reign, and he reigned sixteen years in Jerusalem. His mother's name was Jerushah the daughter of Zadok. 2 And he did what was right in the eyes of the LORD according to all that his father Uzziah had done, [b]except he did not enter the temple of the LORD. But the people still followed corrupt practices. 3 He built the upper gate of the house of the LORD and did much building on the wall of [c]Ophel. 4 Moreover, he built cities in the hill country of Judah, and forts and towers on the wooded hills. 5 He fought with the king of the Ammonites and prevailed against them. And the Ammonites gave him that year 100 talents[2] of silver, and 10,000 cors[3] of wheat and 10,000 of barley. The Ammonites paid him the same amount in the second and the third years. 6 So Jotham became mighty, because he ordered his ways before the LORD his God. 7 [d]Now the rest of the acts of Jotham, and all his wars and his ways, behold, they are written in the Book of the Kings of Israel and Judah. 8 He was [e]twenty-five years old when he began to reign, and he reigned sixteen years in Jerusalem. 9 And Jotham slept with his fathers, and they buried him in the city of David, and Ahaz his son reigned in his place.

Ahaz Reigns in Judah

28 [f]Ahaz was twenty years old when he began to reign, and he reigned sixteen years in Jerusalem. And he did not do what was right in the eyes of the LORD, as his father David had done, 2 but he walked in the ways of the kings of Israel. He even made [g]metal images for [h]the Baals, 3 and [i]he made offerings in the [j]Valley of the Son of Hinnom and [k]burned his sons as an offering,[4] according to [l]the abominations of the nations whom the LORD drove out before the people of Israel. 4 And he sacrificed and [i]made offerings on the high places and on the hills and under every green tree.

Judah Defeated

5 [m]Therefore the LORD his God gave him into the hand of the king of Syria, who defeated him and took captive a great number of his people and brought them to Damascus. He was also given into the hand of the king of Israel, who struck him with great force. 6 For [n]Pekah the son of Remaliah killed 120,000 from Judah in one day, all of them men of valor, because they had forsaken the LORD, the God of their fathers. 7 And Zichri, a mighty man of Ephraim, killed Maaseiah the king's son and Azrikam the commander of the palace and Elkanah the next in authority to the king.

8 The men of Israel took captive 200,000 [o]of their relatives, women, sons, and daughters. They also took much spoil from them and brought the spoil to Samaria. 9 But a prophet of the LORD was there, whose name was Oded, and he went out to meet the army that came to Samaria and said to them, "Behold, because the LORD, the God of your fathers, [p]was angry with Judah, he gave them

[1] *Leprosy* was a term for several skin diseases; see Leviticus 13 [2] A *talent* was about 75 pounds or 34 kilograms [3] A *cor* was about 6 bushels or 220 liters [4] Hebrew *made his sons pass through the fire*

18 [u]Num. 16:40; 18:7 [v]Ex. 30:7, 8 **19** [w][Ex. 4:6; Num. 12:10; 2 Kgs. 5:27] **21** [x]For ver. 21-23, see 2 Kgs. 15:5-7 [y][Lev. 13:46; Num. 5:2] **22** [z]Isa. 1:1; 6:1 **Chapter 27** **1** [a]For ver. 1-3, see 2 Kgs. 15:33-35 **2** [b][ch. 26:16] **3** [c]ch. 33:14; Neh. 3:26, 27; 11:21 **7** [d][2 Kgs. 15:36] **8** [e]ver. 1 **Chapter 28** **1** [f]For ver. 1-4, see 2 Kgs. 16:2-4 **2** [g][Ex. 34:17] [h]Judg. 2:11 **3** [i]ver. 25 [j]See Josh. 15:8 [k]ch. 33:6; [Lev. 18:21] [l]ch. 33:2; Deut. 18:9 **4** [i][See ver. 3 above] **5** [m]Isa. 7:1; [2 Kgs. 16:5, 6] **6** [n]2 Kgs. 15:27; 16:5 **8** [o]ch. 11:4 **9** [p]Isa. 47:6; Ezek. 25:12, 15; 26:2

into your hand, but you have killed them in a rage [q]that has reached up to heaven. 10 And now you intend to subjugate the people of Judah and Jerusalem, male and female, as your slaves. Have you not sins of your own against the LORD your God? 11 Now hear me, and send back the captives [o]from your relatives whom you have taken, for the fierce wrath of the LORD is upon you."

12 Certain chiefs also of the men of Ephraim, Azariah the son of Johanan, Berechiah the son of Meshillemoth, Jehizkiah the son of Shallum, and Amasa the son of Hadlai, stood up against those who were coming from the war 13 and said to them, "You shall not bring the captives in here, for you propose to bring upon us guilt against the LORD in addition to our present sins and guilt. For our guilt is already great, and there is fierce wrath against Israel." 14 So the armed men left the captives and the spoil before the princes and all the assembly. 15 And [r]the men who have been mentioned by name rose and took the captives, and with the spoil they clothed all who were naked among them. They clothed them, gave them sandals, [s]provided them with food and drink, and anointed them, and carrying all the feeble among them on donkeys, they brought them to their kinsfolk at Jericho, [t]the city of palm trees. Then they returned to Samaria.

16 [u]At that time King Ahaz sent to the king[1] of Assyria for help. 17 For the Edomites had again invaded and defeated Judah and carried away captives. 18 [v]And the Philistines had made raids on [w]the cities in the Shephelah and the Negeb of Judah, and had taken Beth-shemesh, Aijalon, Gederoth, Soco [x]with its villages, Timnah with its villages, and Gimzo with its villages. And they settled there. 19 For the LORD humbled Judah because of Ahaz king of Israel, for he had made [y]Judah act sinfully[2] and had been very unfaithful to the LORD. 20 So [z]Tiglath-pileser[3] king of Assyria came against him and afflicted him instead of strengthening him. 21 [a]For Ahaz took a portion from the house of the LORD and the house of the king and of the princes, and gave tribute to the king of Assyria, but it did not help him.

Ahaz's Idolatry

22 In the time of his distress he became yet more faithless to the LORD—this same King Ahaz. 23 For [b]he sacrificed to the gods of Damascus that had defeated him and said, [c]"Because the gods of the kings of Syria helped them, I will sacrifice to them that they may help me." But they were the ruin of him and of all Israel. 24 And Ahaz gathered together the vessels of the house of God and [d]cut in pieces the vessels of the house of God, and he shut up the doors of the house of the LORD, and he made himself [e]altars in every corner of Jerusalem. 25 In every city of Judah he made high places to [f]make offerings to other gods, provoking to anger the LORD, the God of his fathers. 26 [g]Now the rest of his acts and all his ways, from first to last, behold, they are written in the Book of the Kings of Judah and Israel. 27 And Ahaz slept with his fathers, and they buried him in the city, in Jerusalem, for [h]they did not bring him into the tombs of the kings of Israel. And Hezekiah his son reigned in his place.

Hezekiah Reigns in Judah

29 [j]Hezekiah began to reign when he was twenty-five years old, and he reigned twenty-nine years in Jerusalem. His mother's name was Abijah[4] the daughter of [k]Zechariah. 2 And he did what was right in the eyes of the LORD, according to all that David his father had done.

Hezekiah Cleanses the Temple

3 In the first year of his reign, in the first month, he [l]opened the doors of the house of the LORD and repaired them. 4 He brought in the priests and the Levites and assembled them in the square on the east 5 and said to them, "Hear me, Levites! Now [m]consecrate yourselves, and consecrate the house of the LORD, the God of your fathers, and carry out the filth from the Holy Place. 6 For our fathers have been unfaithful and have done what was evil in the sight of the LORD our God. They have forsaken him and [n]have turned away their faces from the habitation of the LORD and turned their backs. 7 They also [o]shut the doors of the vestibule and put out the lamps

[1] Septuagint, Syriac, Vulgate (compare 2 Kings 16:7); Hebrew *kings* [2] Or *wildly* [3] Hebrew *Tilgath-pilneser* [4] Spelled *Abi* in 2 Kings 18:2

10 [q]Ezra 9:6; Rev. 18:5 **11** [o][See ver. 8 above] **15** [r]ver. 12; [ch. 31:19; Num. 1:17] [s]2 Kgs. 6:22; Prov. 25:21, 22; Rom. 12:20 [t]Deut. 34:3; Judg. 1:16 **16** [u][2 Kgs. 16:7, 8] **18** [v][Ezek. 16:27, 57] [w]See Josh. 15:33-36 [x][Num. 21:25] **19** [y]See ch. 21:2 **20** [z][2 Kgs. 15:29; 16:7] **21** [a]2 Kgs. 16:8, 9 **23** [b][ch. 25:14] [c][Jer. 44:17, 18] **24** [d][2 Kgs. 16:17] [e][ch. 30:14] **25** [f]ver. 3 **26** [g]For ver. 26, 27, see 2 Kgs. 16:19, 20 **27** [h][ch. 21:20; 24:25] **Chapter 29** **1** [j]For ver. 1, 2, see 2 Kgs. 18:1-3 [k][ch. 26:5] **3** [l][ver. 7; ch. 28:24] **5** [m]ver. 15, 34; ch. 35:6; 1 Chr. 15:12; Ezra 6:20 **6** [n]Jer. 2:27; Ezek. 8:16 **7** [o]ch. 28:24

and have not burned incense or offered burnt
offerings in the Holy Place to the God of Israel.
8 Therefore [p]the wrath of the LORD came on
Judah and Jerusalem, and he has made them
[q]an object of horror, of astonishment, [r]and of
hissing, as you see with your own eyes. 9 For
behold, [s]our fathers have fallen by the sword,
and our sons and our daughters and our wives
are in captivity for this. 10 Now [t]it is in my heart
[u]to make a covenant with the LORD, the God
of Israel, in order that his fierce anger may
turn away from us. 11 My sons, do not now be
negligent, [v]for the LORD has chosen you to
stand in his presence, to minister to him and
to be his ministers and make offerings to him."
12 Then the Levites arose, [w]Mahath the son
of Amasai, and Joel the son of Azariah, of
the sons of [x]the Kohathites; and of the sons
of [x]Merari, Kish the son of Abdi, and Azariah
the son of Jehallelel; and of the [x]Gershonites,
Joah the son of Zimmah, and Eden the son
of Joah; 13 and of the sons of [y]Elizaphan,
Shimri and Jeuel; and of the sons of [z]Asaph,
Zechariah and Mattaniah; 14 and of the sons
of [a]Heman, Jehuel and Shimei; and of the
sons of [b]Jeduthun, Shemaiah and Uzziel.
15 They gathered their brothers and [c]conse-
crated themselves and went in as the king had
commanded, [d]by the words of the LORD, [e]to
cleanse the house of the LORD. 16 The priests
went into the inner part of the house of the
LORD to cleanse it, and they brought out all
the uncleanness that they found in the temple
of the LORD into the court of the house of the
LORD. And the Levites took it and carried it out
to [f]the brook Kidron. 17 They began to consecrate [g]on the first day of the first month, and
on the eighth day of the month they came to
the vestibule of the LORD. Then for eight days
they consecrated the house of the LORD, and
on the sixteenth day of the first month they
finished. 18 Then they went in to Hezekiah the
king and said, "We have cleansed all the house
of the LORD, the altar of burnt offering and all
its utensils, and the table for the showbread
and all its utensils. 19 All the utensils [h]that King
Ahaz discarded in his reign when he was faithless, we have made ready and consecrated, and
behold, they are before the altar of the LORD."

Hezekiah Restores Temple Worship

20 Then Hezekiah the king rose early and
gathered the officials of the city and went up
to the house of the LORD. 21 And they brought
seven bulls, seven rams, seven lambs, and seven
male goats [i]for a sin offering for the kingdom
and for the sanctuary and for Judah. And he
commanded the priests, the sons of Aaron, to
offer them on the altar of the LORD. 22 So they
slaughtered the bulls, and the priests received
the blood [j]and threw it against the altar. And
they slaughtered the rams, and their blood
was thrown against the altar. And they slaughtered the lambs, and their blood was thrown

29:10, 20–24, 31–35 The cycle of infidelity and fidelity continues in 2 Chronicles. One king is unfaithful to the Lord by forsaking the law of the Lord and the regulations for temple worship (cf. Ahaz in 2 Chronicles 28), and then another king comes along who is faithful, keeping the law and reinstituting proper temple worship (cf. Hezekiah in 2 Chronicles 29). In the end, however, every pledge of obedience (2 Chron. 29:10) and all of the temple sacrifices cannot break the cycle that inevitably leads to more sin and God's judgment.

So the question becomes, why can't this cycle be broken under the administration of the Mosaic covenant? The answer: "For since the law has but a shadow of the good things to come instead of the true form of these realities, it can never, by the same sacrifices that are continually offered every year, make perfect those who draw near" (Heb. 10:1). Note the vigor with which sacrifices were made in the Old Testament (e.g., 1 Kings 8:62–64). Even here, it is noted that the sacrifices were so numerous that they were unable to complete the work without additional help.

In the light of this, consider the radical nature of the work of Jesus on our behalf: "But when Christ had offered for all time a single sacrifice for sins, he sat down at the right hand of God. . . . For by a single offering he has perfected for all time those who are being sanctified" (Heb. 10:12, 14). The blood of every Old Testament sacrifice cries out to us, "look to Christ; we were not enough!"

Because of the sacrificial work of Christ on our behalf, believers are no longer condemned because of their own sin. As grace abounds in the life of the believer, sin is put to death. Remember: with the law, sin increased (Rom. 5:20). But now, grace reigns through the righteousness of Christ, leading to eternal life (Rom. 5:21).

8 [p] See ch. 24:18 [q] Deut. 28:25 [r] Jer. 19:8; 25:9, 18; 29:18; Mic. 6:16
9 [s] ch. 28:5, 6, 8, 17
10 [t] See 1 Chr. 22:7 [u] See ch. 15:12
11 [v] Num. 3:6; 8:14; 18:2, 6
12 [w] ch. 31:13 [x] Num. 3:17
13 [y] 1 Chr. 15:8 [z] 1 Chr. 6:39
14 [a] 1 Chr. 6:33 [b] 1 Chr. 9:16
15 [c] See ver. 5 [d] ch. 30:12 [e] [Neh. 13:9]
16 [f] See 2 Sam. 15:23
17 [g] ver. 3
19 [h] [ch. 28:24]
21 [i] [Lev. 4:14]
22 [j] Lev. 8:15, 19, 24; Heb. 9:21; [ch. 35:11]

against the altar. 23 Then the goats for the sin
offering were brought to the king and the
assembly, [k]and they laid their hands on them,
24 and the priests slaughtered them and made
a sin offering with their blood on the altar, [l]to
make atonement for all Israel. For the king
commanded that the burnt offering and the
sin offering should be made for all Israel.

25 [m]And he stationed the Levites in the house
of the LORD with cymbals, harps, and lyres,
[n]according to the commandment of David
and of Gad [o]the king's seer and of [p]Nathan
the prophet, for the commandment was from
the LORD through his prophets. 26 The Levites
stood with [q]the instruments of David, [r]and the
priests with the trumpets. 27 Then Hezekiah
commanded that the burnt offering be offered
on the altar. And when the burnt offering
began, [s]the song to the LORD began also, and
the trumpets, accompanied by the instruments
of David king of Israel. 28 The whole assembly
worshiped, and the singers sang, and the trumpeters sounded. All this continued until the
burnt offering was finished. 29 When the offering was finished, [t]the king and all who were
present with him bowed themselves and worshiped. 30 And Hezekiah the king and the officials commanded the Levites to sing praises to
the LORD with the words of David and of Asaph
the seer. And they sang praises with gladness,
and they bowed down and worshiped.

31 Then Hezekiah said, [u]"You have now consecrated yourselves to[1] the LORD. Come near;
bring sacrifices and thank offerings to the
house of the LORD." And the assembly brought
sacrifices and thank offerings, and all who
were [v]of a willing heart brought burnt offerings. 32 The number of the burnt offerings that
the assembly brought was 70 bulls, 100 rams,
and 200 lambs; all these were for a burnt offering to the LORD. 33 And the consecrated offerings were 600 bulls and 3,000 sheep. 34 But
the priests were too few and could not flay
all the burnt offerings, so until other priests
had consecrated themselves, [w]their brothers
the Levites helped them, until the work was
finished—[x]for the Levites were more upright
in heart than the priests in consecrating themselves. 35 Besides the great number of burnt
offerings, there was [y]the fat of the peace
offerings, and there were [z]the drink offerings
for the burnt offerings. Thus the service of
the house of the LORD was restored. 36 And
Hezekiah and all the people rejoiced because
God had provided for the people, for the thing
came about suddenly.

Passover Celebrated

30 Hezekiah sent to all Israel and Judah,
and wrote letters also to Ephraim
and Manasseh, that they should come to the
house of the LORD at Jerusalem to keep the
Passover to the LORD, the God of Israel. 2 For
the king and his princes and all the assembly
in Jerusalem had taken counsel to keep the
Passover [a]in the second month— 3 for they
could not keep it [b]at that time [c]because the
priests had not consecrated themselves in sufficient number, nor had the people assembled
in Jerusalem— 4 and the plan seemed right
to the king and all the assembly. 5 So they
decreed to make a proclamation throughout
all Israel, [d]from Beersheba to Dan, that the
people should come and keep the Passover to
the LORD, the God of Israel, at Jerusalem, for
they had not kept it as often as prescribed. 6 [e]So
couriers went throughout all Israel and Judah
with letters from the king and his princes, as
the king had commanded, saying, "O people
of Israel, [f]return to the LORD, the God of
Abraham, Isaac, and Israel, that he may turn
again to the remnant of you who have escaped
from the hand of [g]the kings of Assyria. 7 [h]Do
not be like your fathers and your brothers,
who were faithless to the LORD God of their
fathers, so that he made them a desolation, as
you see. 8 [i]Do not now be stiff-necked as your
fathers were, but yield yourselves to the LORD
and come to his sanctuary, which he has consecrated forever, and serve the LORD your God,
[j]that his fierce anger may turn away from you.
9 For [f]if you return to the LORD, your brothers
and your children [k]will find compassion with
their captors and return to this land. For [l]the

[1] Hebrew *filled your hand for*

30:1–22 See the note on 35:1–19 for the significance of the Passover (the Feast of Unleavened Bread) in Chronicles.

23 [k] Lev. 4:15 **24** [l] Lev. 4:26 **25** [m] 1 Chr. 16:4; 25:6; [1 Chr. 15:16] [n] ch. 8:14; 1 Chr. 23:5; 25:1 [o] See 1 Sam. 9:9 [p] 2 Sam. 12:1 **26** [q] 1 Chr. 23:5; [Amos 6:5] [r] See 1 Chr. 15:24 **27** [s] [ch. 23:18] **29** [t] [ch. 20:18] **31** [u] ch. 13:9; [Ex. 28:41] [v] Ex. 35:5, 22 **34** [w] [ch. 35:11] [x] [ch. 30:3] **35** [y] Lev. 3:1, 16 [z] Num. 15:5, 7, 10 **Chapter 30** **2** [a] ver. 13, 15; Num. 9:10, 11 **3** [b] [ch. 29:17; Ex. 12:6, 18] [c] ch. 29:34; [ver. 24] **5** [d] See 2 Sam. 3:10 **6** [e] [Esth. 3:13, 15; 8:10, 14; Jer. 51:31] [f] Jer. 4:1; Joel 2:12, 13 [g] 2 Kgs. 15:19, 29 **7** [h] [Ezek. 20:18] **8** [i] Ex. 32:9; Deut. 9:6; 10:16; 2 Kgs. 17:14; Neh. 9:16, 29; Jer. 7:26; 17:23; [Acts 7:51] [j] ch. 29:10 **9** [f] [See ver. 6 above] [k] [Ps. 106:46] [l] Ex. 34:6; Dan. 9:9

LORD your God is gracious and merciful and
will not turn away his face from you, [m]if you
return to him."
10 [e]So the couriers went from city to city
through the country of [n]Ephraim and
Manasseh, and as far as Zebulun, but [o]they
laughed them to scorn and mocked them.
11 However, [p]some men of Asher, of Manasseh,
and of Zebulun humbled themselves and
came to Jerusalem. 12 The hand of God was
also on Judah to give them one heart to do
what the king and the princes commanded
[q]by the word of the LORD.
13 And many people came together in
Jerusalem to keep the Feast of Unleavened
Bread [r]in the second month, a very great
assembly. 14 They set to work and removed [s]the
altars that were in Jerusalem, and all the altars
for burning incense they took away [t]and threw
into the brook Kidron. 15 [u]And they slaughtered the Passover lamb on the fourteenth
day of the second month. [v]And the priests
and the Levites were ashamed, [w]so that they
consecrated themselves and brought burnt
offerings into the house of the LORD. 16 [x]They
took their accustomed posts according to the
Law of Moses [y]the man of God. The priests
threw the blood that they received from the
hand of the Levites. 17 For there were many in
the assembly who had not consecrated themselves. Therefore the Levites had to slaughter the Passover lamb for everyone who was
not clean, to consecrate it to the LORD. 18 For
a majority of the people, [z]many of them from
Ephraim, Manasseh, Issachar, and Zebulun,
had not cleansed themselves, yet they ate the
Passover otherwise [a]than as prescribed. For
Hezekiah had prayed for them, saying, "May
the good LORD pardon everyone 19 [b]who sets
his heart to seek God, the LORD, the God of
his fathers, even though not according to the
sanctuary's rules of cleanness."[1] 20 And the
LORD heard Hezekiah and healed the people.
21 And the people of Israel who were present
at Jerusalem kept [c]the Feast of Unleavened
Bread seven days with great gladness, and the
Levites and the priests praised the LORD day
by day, singing with all their might[2] to the
LORD. 22 And Hezekiah spoke [d]encouragingly
to all the Levites who showed good skill in the
service of the LORD. So they ate the food of
the festival for seven days, sacrificing [e]peace
offerings and giving thanks to the LORD, the
God of their fathers.
23 Then the whole assembly agreed together
to keep the feast [f]for another seven days. So
they kept it for another seven days with gladness. 24 For Hezekiah king of Judah [g]gave the
assembly 1,000 bulls and 7,000 sheep for
offerings, and the princes gave the assembly
1,000 bulls and 10,000 sheep. And the priests
[h]consecrated themselves in great numbers.
25 The whole assembly of Judah, and the
priests and the Levites, [i]and the whole assembly that came out of Israel, and the sojourners who came out of the land of Israel, and
the sojourners who lived in Judah, rejoiced.
26 So there was great joy in Jerusalem, for [j]since
the time of Solomon the son of David king
of Israel there had been nothing like this in
Jerusalem. 27 Then [k]the priests and the Levites
arose and [l]blessed the people, and their voice
was heard, and their prayer came to [m]his holy
habitation in heaven.

Hezekiah Organizes the Priests

31 Now when all this was finished, all
Israel who were present went out to
the cities of Judah and [n]broke in pieces the
[o]pillars and cut down [p]the Asherim and broke
down the high places and the altars throughout all Judah and Benjamin, and in Ephraim
and Manasseh, until they had destroyed them
all. Then all the people of Israel returned to
their cities, every man to his possession.
2 And Hezekiah appointed [q]the divisions
of the priests and of the Levites, division by
division, each according to his service, the
priests and the Levites, [r]for burnt offerings
and peace offerings, to minister in the gates
of the camp of the LORD and to give thanks
and praise. 3 [s]The contribution of the king
from his own possessions was for the burnt
offerings: the burnt offerings of morning
and evening, and the burnt offerings for the
Sabbaths, the new moons, and the appointed
feasts, [t]as it is written in the Law of the LORD.
4 And he commanded the people who lived
in Jerusalem to give [u]the portion due to the

[1] Hebrew *not according to the cleanness of holiness* [2] Compare 1 Chronicles 13:8; Hebrew *with instruments of might*

9[m] See 1 Sam. 7:3 **10**[e] [See ver. 6 above] [n] ver. 1 [o] [ch. 36:16] **11**[p] ver. 18, 21, 25 **12**[q] [ch. 29:15] **13**[r] ver. 2 **14**[s] ch. 28:24 [t] [ch. 15:16; 2 Kgs. 23:6] **15**[u] ch. 35:11 [v] [ch. 29:34] [w] [Ezra 6:20] **16**[x] ch. 35:10 [y] Deut. 33:1 **18**[z] ver. 11, 25 [a] See Ex. 12:43-49 **19**[b] ch. 19:3 **21**[c] Ex. 12:15; 13:6; Ezra 6:22 **22**[d] ch. 32:6; Isa. 40:2 [e] [Lev. 5] **23**[f] [1 Kgs. 8:65] **24**[g] [ch. 35:7-9] [h] ver. 3; ch. 29:34 **25**[i] ver. 11, 18 **26**[j] See ch. 7:8-10 **27**[k] ch. 5:5; 23:18 [l] See Num. 6:23-27 [m] Deut. 26:15; Ps. 68:5 **Chapter 31** **1**[n] 2 Kgs. 18:4 [o] See Deut. 16:22 [p] See Deut. 16:21 **2**[q] 1 Chr. 23:6; 24:1 [r] 1 Chr. 23:30, 31 **3**[s] [ch. 35:7] [t] See Num. 28:3–29:40 **4**[u] [Neh. 13:10]; See Num. 18:8-24

priests and the Levites, that they might give themselves to the Law of the LORD. 5 As soon as the command was spread abroad, the people of Israel gave in abundance the firstfruits of grain, wine, oil, honey, and of all the produce of the field. And they brought in abundantly [v]the tithe of everything. 6 And the people of Israel and Judah who lived in the cities of Judah also brought in the tithe of cattle and sheep, and [w]the tithe of the dedicated things that had been dedicated to the LORD their God, and laid them in heaps. 7 In the third month they began to pile up the heaps, and finished them in the seventh month. 8 When Hezekiah and the princes came and saw the heaps, they blessed the LORD and his people Israel. 9 And Hezekiah questioned the priests and the Levites about the heaps. 10 Azariah the chief priest, who was [x]of the house of Zadok, answered him, "Since they began to bring the contributions into the house of the LORD, we have eaten and had enough and have plenty left, [y]for the LORD has blessed his people, so that we have this large amount left."

11 Then Hezekiah commanded them to prepare [z]chambers in the house of the LORD, and they prepared them. 12 And they faithfully brought in the contributions, the tithes, and the dedicated things. The chief officer [a]in charge of them was Conaniah the Levite, with [b]Shimei his brother as second, 13 [b]while Jehiel, Azaziah, Nahath, Asahel, Jerimoth, Jozabad, Eliel, Ismachiah, [b]Mahath, and Benaiah were overseers assisting Conaniah and Shimei his brother, by the appointment of Hezekiah the king and [x]Azariah the chief officer of the house of God. 14 And Kore the son of Imnah the Levite, keeper of the east gate, was over the freewill offerings to God, to apportion the contribution reserved for the LORD and the most holy offerings. 15 [b]Eden, Miniamin, Jeshua, Shemaiah, Amariah, and Shecaniah were faithfully assisting him in [d]the cities of the priests, to distribute the portions to their brothers, old and young alike, by divisions, 16 except those enrolled by genealogy, males from three years old and upward—all who entered the house of the LORD [e]as the duty of each day required—for their service according to their offices, by their divisions. 17 The enrollment of the priests was according to their fathers' houses; that of the Levites [f]from twenty years old and upward was according to their offices, by their divisions. 18 They were enrolled with all their little children, their wives, their sons, and their daughters, the whole assembly, for they were faithful in keeping themselves holy. 19 And for the sons of Aaron, the priests, who were in the fields of common land belonging to their cities, there were men in the several cities who were [g]designated by name to distribute portions to every male among the priests and to everyone among the Levites who was enrolled.

20 Thus Hezekiah did throughout all Judah, [h]and he did what was good and right and faithful before the LORD his God. 21 And every work that he undertook in the service of the house of God and in accordance with the law and the commandments, seeking his God, he did with all his heart, and prospered.

Sennacherib Invades Judah

32 [i]After these things and these acts of faithfulness, Sennacherib king of Assyria came and invaded Judah and encamped against the fortified cities, thinking to win them for himself. 2 And when Hezekiah saw that Sennacherib had come and intended to fight against Jerusalem, 3 he planned with his officers and his mighty men to stop the water of the springs that were outside the city; and they helped him. 4 A great many people were gathered, and they stopped all the springs and [j]the brook that flowed through the land, saying, "Why should the kings of Assyria come and find much water?" 5 He set to work resolutely and built up [k]all the wall that was broken down and raised towers upon it,[1] and outside it he built another wall, and he strengthened the [l]Millo in the city of David. He also made weapons and shields in abundance. 6 And he set combat commanders over the people and gathered them together to him in the square at the gate of the city and spoke [m]encouragingly to them, saying, 7 [n]"Be strong

[1] Vulgate; Hebrew *and raised upon the towers*

5[v] Neh. 13:12
6[w] Lev. 27:30; Deut. 14:28

31:20–21 On Hezekiah's kingship, see the notes on 26:4–5, 16; 27:6; and 29:10, 20–24, 31–35.

10[x] 1 Chr. 6:8 [y] [Mal. 3:10] **11**[z] 1 Chr. 9:26, 33; [2 Kgs. 23:11; Neh. 10:39] **12**[a] [ch. 35:9; Neh. 13:13] [b] [ch. 29:12, 14] **13**[b] [See ver. 12 above] [x] [See ver. 10 above] **15**[b] [See ver. 12 above] [d] See Josh. 21:9-19 **16**[e] 1 Kgs. 8:59; Ezra 3:4; Neh. 11:23; 12:47 **17**[f] 1 Chr. 23:24, 27 **19**[g] [ch. 28:15; Num. 1:17]; See ver. 12-15 **20**[h] 2 Kgs. 18:3; 20:3 **Chapter 32** **1**[i] For ver. 1-22, see 2 Kgs. 18:13–19:37; Isa. 36:1–37:38 **4**[j] ver. 30 **5**[k] ch. 25:23; [Isa. 22:9, 10] [l] See 2 Sam. 5:9 **6**[m] ch. 30:22; Isa. 40:2 **7**[n] See Deut. 31:6

and courageous. [o]Do not be afraid or dismayed before the king of Assyria and all the horde that is with him, [p]for there are more with us than with him. 8 With him is [q]an arm of flesh, [r]but with us is the LORD our God, to help us and to fight our battles." And the people took confidence from the words of Hezekiah king of Judah.

Sennacherib Blasphemes

9 After this, Sennacherib king of Assyria, who was besieging Lachish with all his forces, sent his servants to Jerusalem to Hezekiah king of Judah and to all the people of Judah who were in Jerusalem, saying, 10 "Thus says Sennacherib king of Assyria, 'On what are you trusting, that you endure the siege in Jerusalem? 11 Is not Hezekiah misleading you, that he may give you over to die by famine and by thirst, when he tells you, "The LORD our God will deliver us from the hand of the king of Assyria"? 12 [s]Has not this same Hezekiah taken away his high places and his altars and commanded Judah and Jerusalem, "Before one altar you shall worship, and on it you shall burn your sacrifices"? 13 Do you not know what I and my fathers have done to all the peoples of other lands? Were the gods of the nations of those lands at all able to deliver their lands out of my hand? 14 Who among all the gods of those nations that my fathers devoted to destruction was able to deliver his people from my hand, that your God should be able to deliver you from my hand? 15 Now, therefore, do not let Hezekiah deceive you or mislead you in this fashion, and do not believe him, for no god of any nation or kingdom has been able to deliver his people from my hand or from the hand of my fathers. How much less will your God deliver you out of my hand!'"

16 And his servants said still more against the LORD God and against his servant Hezekiah. 17 And he wrote letters to cast contempt on the LORD, the God of Israel, and to speak against him, saying, "Like the gods of the nations of the lands who have not delivered their people from my hands, so the God of Hezekiah will not deliver his people from my hand." 18 And they shouted it with a loud voice in the language of Judah to the people of Jerusalem who were on the wall, to frighten and terrify them, in order that they might take the city. 19 And they spoke of the God of Jerusalem as they spoke of the gods of the peoples of the earth, which are the work of men's hands.

The LORD Delivers Jerusalem

20 Then Hezekiah the king and Isaiah the prophet, the son of Amoz, prayed because of this and cried to heaven. 21 And the LORD sent an angel, who cut off all the mighty warriors and commanders and officers in the camp of the king of Assyria. So he returned with [t]shame of face to his own land. And when he came into the house of his god, some of his own sons struck him down there with the sword. 22 So the LORD saved Hezekiah and the inhabitants of Jerusalem from the hand of Sennacherib king of Assyria and from the hand of all his enemies, and he provided for them on every side. 23 And many [u]brought gifts to the LORD to Jerusalem and precious

32:7–8, 15, 20–21 King Hezekiah calculated his odds in battle using the Bible's testimony of the Lord's faithfulness to fight for his people. This particular aspect of God's faithfulness to his people began at the exodus, when the Lord delivered Israel from Egypt: "And Moses said to the people, 'Fear not, stand firm, and see the salvation of the LORD, which he will work for you today. For the Egyptians whom you see today, you shall never see again. The LORD will fight for you, and you have only to be silent'" (Ex. 14:13–14; cf. Deut. 1:30; 20:4; Josh. 10:25; 2 Chron. 20:17; Isa. 31:4; Zech. 14:3). The prophet Elisha made the same calculation when he said to his servant, "Do not be afraid, for those who are with us are more than those who are with them" (2 Kings 6:16; cf. 6:15–19).

Tremendous acts of deliverance such as these were designed to publicly display the awesome strength of the Lord of hosts (Lord of armies) in battle. But it is not really the nations of this world from which God's people require ultimate deliverance. The greater enemy is the sin and death that separates us from life in God. Like these battles in the Old Testament, the conquering Christ came to slay the cosmic enemies of sin and death for his people—and he won! "If God is for us, who can be against us? . . . Who shall separate us from the love of Christ? Shall tribulation, or distress, or persecution, or famine, or nakedness, or danger, or sword? . . . No, in all these things we are more than conquerors through him who loved us" (Rom. 8:31b, 35, 37).

7 [o]ch. 20:15 [p]2 Kgs. 6:16
8 [q]Jer. 17:5 [r]ch. 15:2; 20:17
12 [s][ch. 31:1]
21 [t][Ps. 44:15; Jer. 7:19]
23 [u][ch. 17:5]

things to Hezekiah king of Judah, so that he
was exalted in the sight of all nations from
that time onward.

Hezekiah's Pride and Achievements

24 [v]In those days Hezekiah became sick and
was at the point of death, and he prayed to the
LORD, and he answered him and gave him a
sign. 25 But Hezekiah [w]did not make return
according to the benefit done to him, for [x]his
heart was proud. Therefore [y]wrath came upon
him and Judah and Jerusalem. 26 But Hezekiah
[z]humbled himself for the pride of his heart,
both he and the inhabitants of Jerusalem, so
that the wrath of the LORD did not come upon
them in the days of Hezekiah.

27 And Hezekiah had very great riches and
honor, and he made for himself treasuries for
silver, for gold, for precious stones, for spices,
for shields, and for all kinds of [a]costly vessels;
28 storehouses also for the yield of grain, wine,
and oil; and stalls for all kinds of cattle, and
sheepfolds. 29 He likewise provided cities for
himself, and flocks and herds in abundance,
for God had given him very great possessions.
30 This same Hezekiah [b]closed the upper out-
let of the waters of [c]Gihon and directed them
down to the west side of the city of David. And
Hezekiah prospered in all his works. 31 And so
in the matter of the envoys of the princes of
Babylon, [d]who had been sent to him to inquire
about [e]the sign that had been done in the land,
God left him to himself, [f]in order to test him
and to know all that was in his heart.

32 Now the rest of the acts of Hezekiah and
his good deeds, behold, they are written [g]in
the vision of Isaiah the prophet the son of
Amoz, [h]in the Book of the Kings of Judah and
Israel. 33 And Hezekiah slept with his fathers,
and they buried him in the [i]upper part of the
tombs of the sons of David, and all Judah and
the inhabitants of Jerusalem did him honor
at his death. And Manasseh his son reigned
in his place.

Manasseh Reigns in Judah

33 [j]Manasseh was twelve years old when
he began to reign, and he reigned fifty-
five years in Jerusalem. 2 And he did what was
evil in the sight of the LORD, according to
[k]the abominations of the nations whom the
LORD drove out before the people of Israel.
3 For he rebuilt the high places [l]that his father
Hezekiah had broken down, and he erected
altars to the Baals, and made [m]Asheroth, and
worshiped all the host of heaven and served
them. 4 And he built altars in the house of
the LORD, of which the LORD had said, [n]"In
Jerusalem shall my name be forever." 5 And he
built altars for all the host of heaven in [o]the
two courts of the house of the LORD. 6 [p]And he
burned his sons as an offering [q]in the Valley of
the Son of Hinnom, and [r]used fortune-telling
and omens and sorcery, and dealt with [s]medi-
ums and with necromancers. He did much evil
in the sight of the LORD, provoking him to
anger. 7 And [t]the carved image of the idol that
he had made he set in the house of God, of
which God said to David and to Solomon his
son, "In this house, and in Jerusalem, which
I have chosen out of all the tribes of Israel, [n]I
will put my name forever, 8 and I will no more
remove the foot of Israel from the land [u]that
I appointed for your fathers, if only they will
be careful to do all that I have commanded
them, all the law, the statutes, and the rules
given through Moses." 9 Manasseh led Judah
and the inhabitants of Jerusalem astray, to do
more evil than the nations whom the LORD
destroyed before the people of Israel.

Manasseh's Repentance

10 The LORD spoke to Manasseh and to
his people, but they paid no attention.
11 [v]Therefore the LORD brought upon them
the commanders of the army of the king of
Assyria, who captured Manasseh with hooks
and [w]bound him with chains of bronze and
brought him to Babylon. 12 And when he was
in distress, he entreated the favor of the LORD
his God [x]and humbled himself greatly before
the God of his fathers. 13 He prayed to him, and
[y]God was moved by his entreaty and heard his
plea and brought him again to Jerusalem into
his kingdom. [z]Then Manasseh knew that the
LORD was God.

14 Afterward he built an outer wall for the city
of David west of [a]Gihon, in the valley, and for
the entrance into [b]the Fish Gate, and carried
it around [c]Ophel, and raised it to a very great
height. He also put commanders of the army

24 [v]See 2 Kgs. 20:1-11; Isa. 38:1-8 **25** [w][Ps. 116:12] [x]See ch. 26:16 [y]ch. 19:2; 24:18 **26** [z]Jer. 26:18, 19; [ch. 33:12] **27** [a]ch. 36:10 **30** [b]2 Kgs. 20:20; [Isa. 22:9, 11] [c]1 Kgs. 1:33 **31** [d]2 Kgs. 20:12; Isa. 39:1 [e]ver. 24 [f]Deut. 8:2 **32** [g]See Isa. 36–39 [h]See 2 Kgs. 18–20 **33** [i][2 Sam. 15:30] **Chapter 33** **1** [j]For ver. 1-9, see 2 Kgs. 21:1-9 **2** [k]ch. 28:3 **3** [l]ch. 30:14; 31:1; 2 Kgs. 18:4 [m]See Deut. 16:21; [Deut. 17:3] **4** [n]ch. 6:6 **5** [o]ch. 4:9 **6** [p]ch. 28:3 [q]See Josh. 15:8 [r]Deut. 18:10 [s]See 1 Sam. 28:3 **7** [t]ver. 15 [n][See ver. 4 above] **8** [u]2 Sam. 7:10 **11** [v][Deut. 28:36] [w][ch. 36:6; Judg. 16:21] **12** [x][ch. 32:26] **13** [y]1 Chr. 5:20; Ezra 8:23 [z][Dan. 4:25] **14** [a]1 Kgs. 1:33 [b]Neh. 3:3; 12:39; Zeph. 1:10 [c]ch. 27:3

in all the fortified cities in Judah. 15 And [d]he
took away the foreign gods and the idol from
the house of the LORD, and all the altars that
he had built on the mountain of the house
of the LORD and in Jerusalem, and he threw
them outside of the city. 16 He also restored the
altar of the LORD and offered on it sacrifices
of peace offerings and of thanksgiving, and
he commanded Judah to serve the LORD, the
God of Israel. 17 [e]Nevertheless, the people still
sacrificed at the high places, but only to the
LORD their God.

18 Now the rest of the acts of Manasseh, and
[f]his prayer to his God, and the words of [g]the
seers who spoke to him in the name of the
LORD, the God of Israel, behold, they are in
the [h]Chronicles of the Kings of Israel. 19 And
his prayer, and how [y]God was moved by his
entreaty, and all his sin and his faithlessness,
and the sites [i]on which he built high places
and set up the [i]Asherim and the images,
before [x]he humbled himself, behold, they are
written in the Chronicles of the Seers.[1] 20 So
Manasseh slept with his fathers, and they
buried him in his house, and Amon his son
reigned in his place.

Amon's Reign and Death

21 [j]Amon was twenty-two years old when he
began to reign, and he reigned two years in
Jerusalem. 22 And he did what was evil in the
sight of the LORD, as Manasseh his father had
done. Amon sacrificed to all the images [k]that
Manasseh his father had made, and served
them. 23 And he did not humble himself before
the LORD, [l]as Manasseh his father had humbled himself, but this Amon incurred guilt
more and more. 24 And his servants conspired
against him and put him to death in his house.
25 But the people of the land struck down all
those who had conspired against King Amon.
And the people of the land made Josiah his son
king in his place.

Josiah Reigns in Judah

34 [m]Josiah was eight years old when he
began to reign, and he reigned thirty-
one years in Jerusalem. 2 And he did what was
right in the eyes of the LORD, and walked in
the ways of David his father; and he did not
turn aside to the right hand or to the left. 3 For
in the eighth year of his reign, while he was
yet a boy, he began to seek the God of David
his father, and in the twelfth year he began to
purge Judah and Jerusalem of the high places,
the [n]Asherim, and the carved and the metal
images. 4 And they chopped down the altars
of the Baals in his presence, and he cut down
the [o]incense altars that stood above them. And
he broke in pieces the [n]Asherim and the carved
and the metal images, and he made dust of
them and [o]scattered it over the graves of those
who had sacrificed to them. 5 [p]He also burned
the bones of the priests on their altars and
cleansed Judah and Jerusalem. 6 And in the
[q]cities of Manasseh, Ephraim, and Simeon, and
as far as Naphtali, in their ruins[2] all around,
7 he broke down the altars and beat the [n]Ashe-
rim and the images [r]into powder and cut down
all the incense altars throughout all the land of
Israel. Then he returned to Jerusalem.

The Book of the Law Found

8 [s]Now in the eighteenth year of his reign,
when he had cleansed the land and the
house, he sent Shaphan the son of Azaliah,
and Maaseiah the [t]governor of the city, and
Joah the son of Joahaz, [u]the recorder, to repair

[1] One Hebrew manuscript, Septuagint; most Hebrew manuscripts *of Hozai* [2] The meaning of the Hebrew is uncertain

34:8–21 A major part of the continuing reforms under Josiah's reign was the discovery of the Book of the Law. Here were the very words of God, perhaps a scroll of Deuteronomy. As God's people are reconsecrating themselves to the Lord and returning to the Lord with earnest seriousness, God's Word comes flooding back into the regular life of the people.

Then or now, a fresh discovery of and commitment to the Word of God is a great gift of grace. Left to ourselves, we have no firm, fixed rock on which to stand. Human cleverness and ingenuity are powerless to surely guide or to give life. God's Word alone guides and enlivens. As Moses told God's people at the end of Deuteronomy, "it is no empty word for you, but your very life" (Deut. 32:47). We need a word from above, a revelation from heaven, something that cannot be humanly mustered up.

The supreme Word of God from heaven is Christ himself (John 1:14). He is the final revelation from God. In him, we see our Savior. He is "our very life."

15 [d]ver. 3, 5, 7
17 [e][ch. 32:12]
18 [f]ver. 13, 19 [g]See 1 Sam. 9:9 [h][2 Kgs. 21:17]
19 [y][See ver. 13 above] [i]ver. 3 [x][See ver. 12 above]
21 [j]For ver. 21-25, see 2 Kgs. 21:19-24
22 [k]ver. 7; [ch. 34:3, 4]
23 [l]ver. 12

Chapter 34
1 [m]For ver. 1, 2, see 2 Kgs. 22:1, 2
3 [n]See ch. 14:3
4 [o][2 Kgs. 23:6] [n][See ver. 3 above]
5 [p]2 Kgs. 23:20; [1 Kgs. 13:2]
6 [q]2 Kgs. 23:15, 19
7 [n][See ver. 3 above] [r][Deut. 9:21]
8 [s]For ver. 8-28, see 2 Kgs. 22:3-20 [t]ch. 18:25 [u]2 Sam. 8:16

the house of the LORD his God. 9 They came
to [v]Hilkiah the high priest and gave him the
money that had been brought into the house
of God, which the Levites, the keepers of the
threshold, had collected from [q]Manasseh and
Ephraim and from all the remnant of Israel
and from all Judah and Benjamin and from
the inhabitants of Jerusalem. 10 And they gave
it to the workmen who were working in the
house of the LORD. And the workmen who
were working in the house of the LORD gave
it for repairing and restoring the house. 11 They
gave it to the carpenters and the builders to
buy quarried stone, and timber for binders
and [w]beams for the buildings that the kings
of Judah had let go to ruin. 12 And the men
did the work faithfully. Over them were set
Jahath and Obadiah the Levites, of the sons of
Merari, and Zechariah and Meshullam, of the
sons of the Kohathites, to have oversight. [x]The
Levites, all who were skillful with instruments
of music, 13 were over [y]the burden-bearers and
directed all who did work in every kind of service, and some of the Levites were scribes and
officials and gatekeepers.

14 While they were bringing out the money
that had been brought into the house of
the LORD, [v]Hilkiah the priest found the
Book of the Law of the LORD given through
Moses. 15 Then Hilkiah answered and said to
Shaphan the secretary, "I have found the Book
of the Law in the house of the LORD." And
Hilkiah gave the book to Shaphan. 16 Shaphan
brought the book to the king, and further
reported to the king, "All that was committed
to your servants they are doing. 17 They have
emptied out the money that was found in the
house of the LORD and have given it into the
hand of the overseers and the workmen."
18 Then Shaphan the secretary told the king,
"Hilkiah the priest has given me a book." And
Shaphan read from it before the king.

19 And when the king heard the words of the
Law, [z]he tore his clothes. 20 And the king commanded Hilkiah, Ahikam the son of Shaphan,
Abdon the son of Micah, Shaphan the secretary, and Asaiah the king's servant, saying,
21 "Go, inquire of the LORD for me and for
those who are left in Israel and in Judah, concerning the words of the book that has been
found. For great is [a]the wrath of the LORD that
is poured out on us, because our fathers have
not kept the word of the LORD, to do according to all that is written in this book."

Huldah Prophesies Disaster

22 So Hilkiah and those whom the king had
sent[1] went to Huldah the prophetess, the
wife of Shallum the son of Tokhath, son of
Hasrah, keeper of the wardrobe (now she lived
in Jerusalem in the Second Quarter) and spoke
to her to that effect. 23 And she said to them,
"Thus says the LORD, the God of Israel: 'Tell
the man who sent you to me, 24 Thus says the
LORD, Behold, I will bring disaster upon this
place and upon its inhabitants, all the curses
that are written in the book that was read
before the king of Judah. 25 Because they have
forsaken me and [b]have made offerings to other
gods, that they might provoke me to anger
with all the works of their hands, therefore
[a]my wrath will be poured out on this place
and will not be quenched. 26 But to the king of
Judah, who sent you to inquire of the LORD,
thus shall you say to him, Thus says the LORD,
the God of Israel: Regarding the words that
you have heard, 27 because your heart was
tender and you humbled yourself before God
when you heard his words against this place
and its inhabitants, and you have humbled
yourself before me and have torn your clothes
and wept before me, I also have heard you,
declares the LORD. 28 Behold, I will gather you
to your fathers, and you shall be gathered to
your grave in peace, and your eyes shall not
see all the disaster that I will bring upon this
place and its inhabitants.'" And they brought
back word to the king.

29 [c]Then the king sent and gathered together
all the elders of Judah and Jerusalem. 30 And
the king went up to the house of the LORD,
with all the men of Judah and the inhabitants
of Jerusalem and the priests and the Levites,
all the people both great and small. And he
read in their hearing all the words of the Book
of the Covenant that had been found in the
house of the LORD. 31 And the king [d]stood in
his place [e]and made a covenant before the
LORD, to walk after the LORD and to keep his
commandments and his testimonies and his
statutes, with all his heart and all his soul, to
perform the words of the covenant that were

[1] Syriac, Vulgate; Hebrew lacks *had sent*

9 [v] ch. 35:8 [q] [See ver. 6 above] **11** [w] Neh. 2:8 **12** [x] 1 Chr. 23:5 **13** [y] ch. 2:2, 18; Neh. 4:10 **14** [v] [See ver. 9 above] **19** [z] See Josh. 7:6 **21** [a] ch. 12:7 **25** [b] ch. 28:3, 4, 25 [a] [See ver. 21 above] **29** [c] For ver. 29-32, see 2 Kgs. 23:1-3 **31** [d] ch. 6:13; 2 Kgs. 11:14; [ch. 30:16] [e] See ch. 15:12

written in this book. 32 Then he made all who were present in Jerusalem and in Benjamin join in it. And the inhabitants of Jerusalem did according to the covenant of God, the God of their fathers. 33 And Josiah took away [f]all the abominations from all the territory that belonged to the people of Israel and made all who were present in Israel serve the LORD their God. All his days they did not turn away from following the LORD, the God of their fathers.

Josiah Keeps the Passover

35 [g]Josiah kept a Passover to the LORD in Jerusalem. And they slaughtered the Passover lamb [h]on the fourteenth day of the first month. 2 He appointed the priests to their offices [i]and encouraged them in the service of the house of the LORD. 3 And he said to the Levites [j]who taught all Israel and who were holy to the LORD, "Put the holy ark in the house that Solomon the son of David, king of Israel, built. You need not carry it on your shoulders. Now serve the LORD your God and his people Israel. 4 Prepare yourselves [k]according to your fathers' houses by your divisions, [l]as prescribed in the writing of David king of Israel [m]and the document of Solomon his son. 5 And [n]stand in the Holy Place [o]according to the groupings of the fathers' houses of your brothers the lay people, and according to the division of the Levites by fathers' household. 6 And slaughter the Passover lamb, and [p]consecrate yourselves, and prepare for your brothers, to do according to the word of the LORD by Moses."

7 Then Josiah contributed to the lay people, as Passover offerings for all who were present, lambs and young goats from the flock to the number of 30,000, and 3,000 bulls; [q]these were from the king's possessions. 8 And his officials contributed willingly to the people, to the priests, and to the Levites. [r]Hilkiah, Zechariah, and Jehiel, the chief officers of the house of God, gave to the priests for the Passover offerings 2,600 Passover lambs and 300 bulls. 9 Conaniah also, and Shemaiah and Nethanel his brothers, and Hashabiah and Jeiel and Jozabad, the chiefs of the Levites, gave to the Levites for the Passover offerings 5,000 lambs and young goats and 500 bulls.

10 When the service had been prepared for, the priests [s]stood in their place, [t]and the Levites in their divisions according to the king's command. 11 [u]And they slaughtered the Passover lamb, and the priests [v]threw the blood that they received from them [w]while the Levites flayed the sacrifices. 12 And they set aside the burnt offerings that they might distribute them according to the groupings of the fathers' houses of the lay people, to offer to the LORD, as it is written in the Book of Moses. And so they did with the bulls. 13 [x]And they roasted the Passover lamb with fire according to the rule; and they [y]boiled the holy offerings

35:1–19 The celebration of the Passover is of special importance in 2 Chronicles—celebrated by Hezekiah in chapter 30 and then by Josiah in chapter 35. In fact, no other book in the Old Testament mentions this feast more. Recall that the Passover was first celebrated by Israel on the evening before their famed exodus from Egypt (Exodus 12; cf. Numbers 9; Deuteronomy 16). The Passover sacrifice gives us a stark reminder that the wages of sin is death, and that the shedding of blood is required to appease God's wrath. But this event also memorializes the Lord's great mercy and power by delivering his people from the bondage of slavery.

As the last book in the Hebrew Old Testament, Chronicles prepares us for the arrival of Christ in a unique and important manner with its emphasis on the Passover. First, the Passover lamb of the Old Testament was merely a shadow or type of the great cost of forgiveness and escape from death. God the Father paid this price for his people when he sent the true and better Passover Lamb, Jesus, as the full and final payment. John the Baptist was given the honor of publicly identifying this Passover Lamb sent by God, when he said of Jesus, "Behold, the Lamb of God, who takes away the sin of the world!" (John 1:29; cf. v. 36; 1 Cor. 5:7).

Secondly, not only is Jesus the Passover Lamb of God, but he is also a new Moses, leading God's people in a new exodus (Luke 9:31), a deliverance not simply from slavery or subjugation in this world, but from the slavery of sin and death to eternal life in a new heavens and earth. The Passover is good news because it sets before us our arrival in the true Land of Promise and the extravagant price our heavenly Father was willing to pay for us to be with him for all eternity.

33 [f]ch. 28:3; 33:2

Chapter 35

1 [g]2 Kgs. 23:21-23 [h]Ex. 12:6; Ezra 6:19
2 [i]ch. 29:11
3 [j]ch. 17:9; Neh. 8:7, 9; [ch. 15:3; 30:22; Lev. 10:11; Deut. 33:10; Ezra 7:10; Mal. 2:7]
4 [k]1 Chr. 9:9 [l]See 1 Chr. 23–26 [m]ch. 8:14
5 [n]Ps. 134:1 [o][Ezra 6:18]
6 [p]See ch. 29:5
7 [q][ch. 31:3]
8 [r]ch. 34:9, 14
10 [s]ch. 30:16 [t]Ezra 6:18
11 [u]ch. 30:15; Ezra 6:20 [v]See ch. 29:22 [w][ch. 29:34]
13 [x]Ex. 12:8, 9; Deut. 16:7 [y][1 Sam. 2:13-15]

in pots, in cauldrons, and in pans, and carried them quickly to all the lay people. 14 And
afterward they prepared for themselves and
for the priests, because the priests, the sons
of Aaron, were offering the burnt offerings
and the fat parts until night; so the Levites
prepared for themselves and for the priests,
the sons of Aaron. 15 The singers, the sons of
Asaph, were in their place [z]according to the
command of David, and Asaph, and Heman,
and Jeduthun the king's [a]seer; [b]and the gatekeepers were at each gate. They did not need
to depart from their service, for their brothers
the Levites prepared for them.

16 So all the service of the LORD was prepared that day, to keep the Passover and to
offer burnt offerings on the altar of the LORD,
according to the command of King Josiah.
17 And the people of Israel who were present kept the Passover at that time, [c]and the
Feast of Unleavened Bread seven days. 18 [d]No
Passover like it had been kept in Israel since
the days of Samuel the prophet. None of the
kings of Israel had kept such a Passover as was
kept by Josiah, and the priests and the Levites,
and all Judah and Israel who were present, and
the inhabitants of Jerusalem. 19 In the eighteenth year of the reign of Josiah this Passover
was kept.

Josiah Killed in Battle

20 [e]After all this, when Josiah had prepared
the temple, Neco king of Egypt went up to
fight at [f]Carchemish on the Euphrates, and
Josiah went out to meet him. 21 But he sent
envoys to him, saying, "What have we to
do with each other, king of Judah? I am not
coming against you this day, but against the
house with which I am at war. And God has
commanded me to hurry. Cease opposing
God, who is with me, lest he destroy you."
22 Nevertheless, Josiah did not turn away from
him, but [g]disguised himself in order to fight
with him. He did not listen to the words of
Neco from the mouth of God, but came to
fight in the plain of [h]Megiddo. 23 And the
archers shot King Josiah. And the king said
to his servants, [i]"Take me away, for I am badly
wounded." 24 So his servants took him out of
the chariot and carried him in his second chariot and brought him to Jerusalem. And he died
and was buried in the tombs of his fathers.
[j]All Judah and Jerusalem mourned for Josiah.
25 [k]Jeremiah also uttered a lament for Josiah;
and all [l]the singing men and singing women
have spoken of Josiah in their laments to this
day. They made these a rule in Israel; behold,
they are written in the Laments. 26 Now the
rest of the acts of Josiah, and his good deeds
according to what is written in the Law of the
LORD, 27 and his acts, first and last, behold,
they are written in the Book of the Kings of
Israel and Judah.

Judah's Decline

36 [m]The people of the land took Jehoahaz
the son of Josiah and made him king
in his father's place in Jerusalem. 2 Jehoahaz
was twenty-three years old when he began
to reign, and he reigned three months in
Jerusalem. 3 Then the king of Egypt deposed
him in Jerusalem and [n]laid on the land a tribute of a hundred talents of silver and a talent[1]
of gold. 4 And the king of Egypt made Eliakim
his brother king over Judah and Jerusalem,
and changed his name to Jehoiakim. But Neco
took Jehoahaz his brother and carried him
to Egypt.

5 [o]Jehoiakim was twenty-five years old when
he began to reign, and he reigned eleven years
in Jerusalem. He did what was evil in the sight
of the LORD his God. 6 [p]Against him came
up Nebuchadnezzar king of Babylon [q]and
bound him in chains [r]to take him to Babylon.
7 [s]Nebuchadnezzar also carried part of the vessels of the house of the LORD to Babylon and
put them in his palace in Babylon. 8 [t]Now the
rest of the acts of Jehoiakim, and the abominations that he did, and what was found against
him, behold, they are written in the Book of
the Kings of Israel and Judah. And Jehoiachin
his son reigned in his place.

9 [u]Jehoiachin was eighteen[2] years old when he
became king, and he reigned three months and
ten days in Jerusalem. He did what was evil in
the sight of the LORD. 10 In [v]the spring of the
year King Nebuchadnezzar sent and brought
him to Babylon, [w]with the precious vessels of
the house of the LORD, and made his brother
[x]Zedekiah king over Judah and Jerusalem.

[1] A *talent* was about 75 pounds or 34 kilograms [2] Septuagint (compare 2 Kings 24:8); most Hebrew manuscripts *eight*

15[z] See 1 Chr. 25 [a] See 1 Sam. 9:9 [b] See 1 Chr. 9:17-29; 26:1-19 **17**[c] See ch. 30:21 **18**[d] 2 Kgs. 23:22, 23 **20**[e] 2 Kgs. 23:29, 30 [f] [Jer. 46:2] **22**[g] [1 Kgs. 22:30] [h] Judg. 5:19 **23**[i] [1 Kgs. 22:34] **24**[j] [Zech. 12:11] **25**[k] Lam. 4:20; [2 Sam. 1:17] [l] 2 Sam. 19:35; Ezra 2:65; Neh. 7:67; [Matt. 9:23] **Chapter 36** **1**[m] For ver. 1-4, see 2 Kgs. 23:30-34 **3**[n] Deut. 22:19 **5**[o] 2 Kgs. 23:36, 37 **6**[p] 2 Kgs. 24:1 [q] [ch. 33:11] [r] [2 Kgs. 24:6; Jer. 22:18, 19; 36:30] **7**[s] 2 Kgs. 24:13; Ezra 1:7; Dan. 1:1, 2; 5:2; [ver. 10, 18] **8**[t] 2 Kgs. 24:5, 6 **9**[u] For ver. 9, 10, see 2 Kgs. 24:8-17 **10**[v] 2 Sam. 11:1 [w] [ver. 7, 18] [x] Jer. 37:1; [2 Kgs. 24:17]

[11] [y]Zedekiah was twenty-one years old when
he began to reign, and he reigned eleven years
in Jerusalem. [12] He did what was evil in the
sight of the LORD his God. He did not humble
himself before [z]Jeremiah the prophet, who
spoke from the mouth of the LORD. [13] [a]He also
rebelled against King Nebuchadnezzar, who
had made him swear by God. [b]He stiffened
his neck and hardened his heart against turning to the LORD, the God of Israel. [14] All the
officers of the priests and the people likewise
were exceedingly unfaithful, following all
the abominations of the nations. And they
polluted the house of the LORD that he had
made holy in Jerusalem.

[15] The LORD, the God of their fathers, [c]sent
persistently to them by his messengers,
because he had compassion on his people
and on his dwelling place. [16] [d]But they kept
mocking the messengers of God, [e]despising
his words and scoffing at his prophets, [f]until
the wrath of the LORD rose against his people,
until there was no remedy.

Jerusalem Captured and Burned

[17] [g]Therefore he brought up against them
the king of the Chaldeans, who killed their
young men with the sword in the house
of their sanctuary and had no compassion
on young man or virgin, old man or aged.
He gave them all into his hand. [18] [h]And all
the vessels of the house of God, great and
small, and the treasures of the house of the
LORD, and the treasures of the king and of
his princes, all these he brought to Babylon.
[19] [i]And they burned the house of God and
broke down the wall of Jerusalem and
burned all its palaces with fire and destroyed
all its precious vessels. [20] He [j]took into exile
in Babylon those who had escaped from the
sword, [k]and they became servants to him and
to his sons until the establishment of the
kingdom of Persia, [21] to fulfill the word of
the LORD by the mouth of Jeremiah, until
the land had [l]enjoyed its Sabbaths. All the
days that it lay desolate [m]it kept Sabbath, to
fulfill seventy years.

The Proclamation of Cyrus

[22] [n]Now in the first year of Cyrus king of
Persia, [o]that the word of the LORD by the
mouth of Jeremiah might be fulfilled, [p]the
LORD stirred up the spirit of Cyrus king
of Persia, so that he made a proclamation
throughout all his kingdom and also put
it in writing: [23] "Thus says Cyrus king of
Persia, 'The LORD, the God of heaven, has
given me all the kingdoms of the earth, and
he has charged me to build him a house at
Jerusalem, which is in Judah. Whoever is
among you of all his people, may the LORD
his God be with him. Let him go up.' "

36:15–16 The New Testament is clear in its assessment of the Old Testament (Mosaic) covenant—namely, that it was a shadow of a better reality, something designed to pass away (Col. 2:17; Heb. 8:5; 10:1).

Nevertheless, God's character does not change, and we observe here the long-suffering compassion of a father working to provide every opportunity for repentance through the prophetic word. Having sent his servants the prophets to no avail, it would soon be time to send his one and only Son (Matt. 21:33–41). And though they would kill the Son as they did the prophets (Acts 7:52), this death would turn out to be the means by which God would bring true and lasting forgiveness to his people, forever breaking the cycles of temporary fidelity with his provision of everlasting righteousness.

11[y] For ver. 11-13, see 2 Kgs. 24:18-20; Jer. 52:1, 2
12[z] See Jer. 21:3-7; 27:12-22; 32:1-5; 37:6-10; 38:17-26
13[a] Jer. 52:3; Ezek. 17:15, 18 [b] See ch. 30:8
15[c] Jer. 7:13, 25; 25:3, 4; 26:5; 29:19; 35:15; 44:4; [Jer. 11:7; 32:33]
16[d] [Jer. 5:12, 13] [e] [Prov. 1:25, 30] [f] [Ezra 5:12]
17[g] For ver. 17-20, see 2 Kgs. 25:1-7; [Deut. 28:49; Ezra 9:7]
18[h] 2 Kgs. 25:13-15; [ver. 7, 10]
19[i] 2 Kgs. 25:9

20[j] 2 Kgs. 25:11 [k] Jer. 27:7 **21**[l] Lev. 26:34, 35, 43; [Dan. 9:2] [m] [Lev. 25:4, 5] **22**[n] For ver. 22, 23, see Ezra 1:1-3 [o] Jer. 25:12, 13; 29:10; 33:10, 11, 14 [p] Isa. 44:28

Introduction to Ezra

Author and Date

The book of Ezra never declares who its author is, and the book's contents make it difficult to determine when it was written. Ezra 1–6 recounts events that occurred long before Ezra's time. Ezra 7:27–9:15 clearly comes from Ezra's own hand, since it is written in the first person. Ezra 7:1–26 and 10:1–44 describe events in Ezra's time, but are written in the third person. It is possible Ezra may have combined the other materials with his autobiographical writings to form the book. Or, a later historian may have collected all the portions to describe Israelite history from c. 538–433 B.C. The events narrated in Ezra-Nehemiah occur over a century: Ezra 1–6 covers 538–515 B.C., while Ezra 7–Nehemiah 13 covers 458–433 B.C.

The Gospel in Ezra

Ezra and Nehemiah offer the final piece of Old Testament history, one last glimpse of God's people living out his redemptive plan before the coming of the Messiah. God's covenant promises are gloriously on display as this weak, struggling remnant returns to Jerusalem after the exile to live together again as his people, according to his Word.

Ezra in particular highlights God's redemptive plan. The opening verse declares that God initiates these events that he himself decreed through his prophets. God's hand is then evident throughout: sovereignly directing the kings and peoples who aim to have a hand in Zerubbabel's return and rebuilding of the temple (chs. 1–6), and personally clearing the path for Ezra's later return to teach the law (chs. 7–10). All the action unfolds God's plan, according to his Word.

God's redemptive plan focuses on a *people*. Ezra makes clear who these people are: Abraham's seed, those whom God promised to make a great nation in whom all the nations would be blessed (Gen. 12:1–3; 15:1–5). In Ezra, this blessed "remnant" (see Isa. 10:20–22) is reassembled and numbered carefully by tribe and genealogy. Ezra's passion to keep them holy and separate reflects not ethnic elitism but rather a concern to honor the Lord who had redeemed them, reflecting his holiness through their own. Ezra thus sought to bring Israel to demonstrate trust in the Lord by obeying his law. This is the blessed way of life given to this chosen people from whom the promised offspring would come, according to God's Word. These exiles did not know Jesus' name, but they carefully traced the seed promises leading to his birth.

God's redemptive plan focuses on a people created to *worship* him—and the plan provides the means. Hope continues to rise in this book as we see struggling, sinful exiles released in waves from Babylon and rebuilding the temple that identified their land as the place of God's people and promise. Their ancient hope for a messianic King was no longer visible in an earthly kingdom (Zerubbabel remained in the line of David, but as the servant of a foreign king). So, by the efforts of the returning remnant of Israel, amid Jerusalem's ruins, hope emerges more clearly for God's promised King, who would rule on an eternal throne, and who would release his people finally and fully from their oppressors. In the meantime, God had provided the temple as a witness to his continuing presence and promises—a temple whose sacrifices also pictured and pointed ahead to the perfect sacrifice that would be needed for the eternal deliverance of God's people.

This perfect sacrifice and final King would come four centuries after Ezra lived. Jesus gathers up all these ancient longings in his coming to earth. The importance of the temple in Ezra makes us look ahead to the one who is himself the temple, providing access into God's presence through his blood (John 2:18–22; Rev. 21:22). The plain appearance of Ezra's rebuilt temple (in contrast to Solomon's magnificent one) helps us anticipate the spiritual temple that will rise as Christ's body, the church (Eph. 2:19–22).

Ultimately, God provided his *Word*, which Ezra the priest set his heart to study and do and teach (Ezra 7:10). Old Testament history comes to a close with a picture of God's people gathered around God's Word, yearning for the ultimate fulfillment of God's promises—the fulfillment that would come with the Word made flesh.

Outline

I. Cyrus's Decree and the Return of Exiles from Babylon (1:1–2:70)
   - A. The decree (1:1–4)
   - B. The exiles respond to the decree (1:5–11)
   - C. The exiles live again in their ancestral homes (2:1–70)

II. The Returned Exiles Rebuild the Temple on Its Original Site (3:1–6:22)
   - A. The foundations of the temple are laid (3:1–13)
   - B. Enemies stall the project by conspiring against it (4:1–24)
   - C. The work is resumed, and local officials seek confirmation of Cyrus's decree (5:1–17)
   - D. King Darius discovers and reaffirms Cyrus's decree, and the work is completed (6:1–22)

III. Ezra the Priest Comes to Jerusalem to Establish the Law of Moses (7:1–8:36)
   - A. King Artaxerxes gives Ezra authority to establish the Mosaic law (7:1–28)
   - B. Ezra journeys to Jerusalem with a new wave of returnees, bearing royal gifts for the temple (8:1–36)

IV. Ezra Discovers and Confronts the Problem of Intermarriage (9:1–10:44)
   - A. Ezra discovers the problem of marriage to idolaters, and prays (9:1–15)
   - B. The people agree to dissolve the marriages (10:1–17)
   - C. List of those who were implicated (10:18–44)

Ezra

The Proclamation of Cyrus

1 [a]In the first year of Cyrus king of Persia,
[b]that the word of the LORD by the mouth
of Jeremiah might be fulfilled, the LORD
stirred up the spirit of Cyrus king of Persia,
so [c]that he made a proclamation throughout
all his kingdom and also put it in writing:
2 "Thus says Cyrus king of Persia: The LORD,
the God of heaven, has given me all the kingdoms of the earth, and [d]he has charged me
to build him a house at Jerusalem, which is
in Judah. 3 Whoever is among you of all his
people, may his God be with him, and let him
go up to Jerusalem, which is in Judah, and
rebuild the house of the LORD, the God of
Israel—[e]he is the God who is in Jerusalem.
4 And let each survivor, in whatever place he
sojourns, be assisted by the men of his place
with silver and gold, with goods and with
beasts, besides freewill offerings for the house
of God that is in Jerusalem."
5 Then rose up the heads of the fathers'
houses of Judah and Benjamin, and the priests
and the Levites, [f]everyone whose spirit [g]God
had stirred to go up to rebuild the house of
the LORD that is in Jerusalem. 6 And all who
were about them [h]aided them with vessels
of silver, with gold, with goods, with beasts,
and with costly wares, besides all that was
freely offered. 7 [i]Cyrus the king also brought
out the vessels of the house of the LORD that
[j]Nebuchadnezzar had carried away from
Jerusalem and placed in the house of his gods.
8 Cyrus king of Persia brought these out in
the charge of [k]Mithredath the treasurer, who
counted them out to [l]Sheshbazzar the prince
of Judah. 9 And this was the number of them:
[m]30 basins of gold, 1,000 basins of silver, 29
censers, 10 30 bowls of gold, 410 bowls of silver, and 1,000 other vessels; 11 all the vessels
of gold and of silver were 5,400. All these did
Sheshbazzar bring up, when the exiles were
brought up from Babylonia to Jerusalem.

The Exiles Return

2 [n]Now these were the people of the province who came up out of the captivity of
those exiles [o]whom Nebuchadnezzar the king

1:1–11 Ezra continues the story of God's people directly from Chronicles (2 Chron. 36:22–23). But it reaches farther back: "The word of the LORD" in Ezra 1:1 might recall Genesis 1, where God's word initiated all these events from the very beginning. A sense of awe for such a God pervades this chapter's details, which show the certainty of God's promises—most immediately, that King Cyrus would after 70 years release the exiles to return to their land (Jer. 25:11–14; 32:36–38). Cyrus is mentioned specifically by the prophet Isaiah, who calls him God's "anointed" (Isa. 45:1–13). This earthly king who fulfilled God's plan offers just a shadowy picture of God's anointed Son, who would finally release God's people from slavery to sin and the exile of separation from God.

God's redemptive plan looms large here, as we see him preserving the people to whom he has given his covenant promises—through Abraham (Gen. 12:1–3) and David (2 Sam. 7:12–17). Those promises were carried through generations of Abraham's seed and channeled through the tribe of Judah (see Ezra 1:5) until they ultimately culminated in Christ. Ezra shows the merciful continuity of God's covenant, even for a sinful people punished by exile for their ugly rebellion against God. God's promises will not fail; they are even more solid and beautiful than all the gold and silver vessels produced here as glorious evidence.

2:1 In offering a simple summary, this verse rings with grace. God punished and purified his rebellious people through the captivity, and God also restored his people

Chapter 1
1 [a]For ver. 1-3, see 2 Chr. 36:22, 23 [b]Jer. 25:12, 13; 29:10 [c]ch. 5:13
2 [d]Isa. 44:28; [Isa. 45:1, 13]
3 [e]Dan. 6:26
5 [f][Phil. 2:13] [g]ver. 1
6 [h][ch. 4:4]; Jer. 38:4
7 [i]ch. 5:14; 6:5 [j]2 Kgs. 24:13; 2 Chr. 36:7
8 [k]ch. 4:7 [l]ch. 5:14
9 [m][ch. 8:27; 1 Chr. 28:17]
Chapter 2
1 [n]For ver. 1-70, see Neh. 7:6-73 [o]2 Kgs. 24:14-16; 25:11; 2 Chr. 36:20

of Babylon had carried captive to Babylonia.
They returned to Jerusalem and Judah, each to
his own town. 2 They came with Zerubbabel,
Jeshua, Nehemiah, Seraiah, Reelaiah, [p]Mor-
decai, Bilshan, Mispar, Bigvai, Rehum, and
Baanah.

The number of the men of the people of
Israel: 3 [q]the sons of Parosh, 2,172. 4 The sons
of Shephatiah, 372. 5 The sons of Arah, 775.
6 The sons of Pahath-moab, namely the sons
of Jeshua and Joab, 2,812. 7 The sons of Elam,
1,254. 8 The sons of Zattu, 945. 9 The sons of
Zaccai, 760. 10 The sons of Bani, 642. 11 The sons
of Bebai, 623. 12 The sons of Azgad, 1,222. 13 The
sons of Adonikam, 666. 14 The sons of Bigvai,
2,056. 15 The sons of Adin, 454. 16 The sons of
Ater, namely of Hezekiah, 98. 17 The sons of
Bezai, 323. 18 The sons of Jorah, 112. 19 The
sons of Hashum, 223. 20 The sons of Gibbar,
95. 21 The sons of Bethlehem, 123. 22 The men
of Netophah, 56. 23 The men of Anathoth, 128.
24 The sons of Azmaveth, 42. 25 The sons of
Kiriath-arim, Chephirah, and Beeroth, 743.
26 The sons of Ramah and Geba, 621. 27 The
men of Michmas, 122. 28 The men of Bethel
and Ai, 223. 29 The sons of Nebo, 52. 30 The
sons of Magbish, 156. 31 The sons of [r]the other
Elam, 1,254. 32 The sons of Harim, 320. 33 The
sons of Lod, Hadid, and Ono, 725. 34 The sons
of Jericho, 345. 35 The sons of Senaah, 3,630.

36 The priests: the [s]sons of Jedaiah, of the
house of Jeshua, 973. 37 The sons of Immer,
1,052. 38 The [t]sons of Pashhur, 1,247. 39 The
sons of Harim, 1,017.

40 The Levites: the sons of [u]Jeshua and
Kadmiel, of the sons of Hodaviah, 74. 41 The
singers: the sons of [v]Asaph, 128. 42 The sons
of the [w]gatekeepers: the sons of Shallum, the
sons of Ater, the sons of Talmon, the sons of
Akkub, the sons of Hatita, and the sons of
Shobai, in all 139.

43 [x]The temple servants: the sons of Ziha,
the sons of Hasupha, the sons of Tabbaoth,
44 the sons of Keros, the sons of Siaha, the sons
of Padon, 45 the sons of Lebanah, the sons of
Hagabah, the sons of Akkub, 46 the sons of
Hagab, the sons of Shamlai, the sons of Hanan,
47 the sons of Giddel, the sons of Gahar, the
sons of Reaiah, 48 the sons of Rezin, the sons
of Nekoda, the sons of Gazzam, 49 the sons
of Uzza, the sons of Paseah, the sons of Besai,
50 the sons of Asnah, the sons of Meunim, the
sons of Nephisim, 51 the sons of Bakbuk,
the sons of Hakupha, the sons of Harhur,
52 the sons of Bazluth, the sons of Mehida, the
sons of Harsha, 53 the sons of Barkos, the sons
of Sisera, the sons of Temah, 54 the sons of
Neziah, and the sons of Hatipha.

55 [y]The sons of Solomon's servants: the
sons of Sotai, the sons of Hassophereth, the
sons of Peruda, 56 the sons of Jaalah, the sons
of Darkon, the sons of Giddel, 57 the sons of
Shephatiah, the sons of Hattil, the sons of
Pochereth-hazzebaim, and the sons of Ami.

58 All the temple servants and the sons of
Solomon's servants were 392.

59 The following were those who came up
from Tel-melah, Tel-harsha, Cherub, Addan,
and Immer, [z]though they could not prove their
fathers' houses or their descent, whether they
belonged to Israel: 60 the sons of Delaiah, the
sons of Tobiah, and the sons of Nekoda, 652.
61 Also, of the sons of the priests: the sons of
Habaiah, the sons of Hakkoz, and the sons
of [a]Barzillai (who had taken a wife from the
daughters of Barzillai the Gileadite, and was
called by their name). 62 These sought their
registration among those enrolled in the genealogies, but they were not found there, and
[b]so they were excluded from the priesthood
as unclean. 63 The [c]governor told them that
they were not [d]to partake of the most holy
food, until there should be a priest to consult
[e]Urim and Thummim.

64 [f]The whole assembly together was 42,360,
65 besides their male and female servants, of

2 [p] Esth. 2:5, 6
3 [q] ch. 8:3; 10:25
31 [r] [ver. 7]
36 [s] For ver. 36-39, see 1 Chr. 24:7-18
38 [t] 1 Chr. 9:12
40 [u] [Neh. 10:9]
41 [v] See 1 Chr. 6:39
42 [w] 1 Chr. 9:17, 18
43 [x] 1 Chr. 9:2; Neh. 11:3
55 [y] Neh. 11:3; [1 Kgs. 9:21]
59 [z] [1 Chr. 9:1]
61 [a] 2 Sam. 17:27
62 [b] [Num. 3:10]
63 [c] Neh. 8:9 [d] Lev. 22:2, 10, 15, 16 [e] See Ex. 28:30
64 [f] Neh. 7:66, 67

from a captivity they could not have escaped on their own, bringing them home to the land of blessing. This gracious pattern of God never abandoning his people but always leading them toward the blessing of dwelling with him comes to ultimate fulfillment and demonstration in Christ.

2:2–70 All these names and numbers are a counting of blessings, a review of God's abundant faithfulness in preserving a previously faithless people—who now respond in renewed faithfulness by ordering themselves according to God's Word and giving themselves to God's work (vv. 68–69). The carefully recorded priests and Levites, who alone are designated by God to serve in the temple, play a crucial role as these exiles rebuild the temple and reestablish proper worship to honor the God who has redeemed them.

whom there were 7,337, and they had 200
male and female [g]singers. 66 Their horses were
736, their mules were 245, 67 their camels were
435, and their donkeys were 6,720.
68 [h]Some of the heads of families, when
they came to the house of the LORD that is
in Jerusalem, made freewill offerings for the
house of God, to erect it on its site. 69 According
to their ability they gave to [i]the treasury of the
work 61,000 darics[1] of gold, 5,000 minas[2] of
silver, and 100 priests' garments.
70 [j]Now the priests, the Levites, some of the
people, the singers, the gatekeepers, and the
temple servants lived in their towns, and all
the rest of Israel[3] in their towns.

Rebuilding the Altar

3 [k]When the seventh month came, and the
children of Israel were in the towns, the
people gathered as one man to Jerusalem.
2 Then arose Jeshua the son of Jozadak, with
his fellow priests, and [l]Zerubbabel the son of
[m]Shealtiel with his kinsmen, and they built
the altar of the God of Israel, to offer burnt
offerings on it, [n]as it is written in the Law of
Moses the [o]man of God. 3 They set the altar in
its place, [p]for fear was on them because of the
peoples of the lands, and [q]they offered burnt
offerings on it to the LORD, burnt offerings
morning and evening. 4 [r]And they kept the
Feast of Booths, [s]as it is written, [t]and offered
the daily burnt offerings by number according
to the rule, as each day required, 5 and after
that the regular burnt [u]offerings, the offerings at the new moon [v]and at all the appointed
feasts of the LORD, and the offerings of everyone who made a freewill offering to the LORD.
6 From the first day of the seventh month they
began to offer burnt offerings to the LORD.
But the foundation of the temple of the LORD
was not yet laid. 7 So they gave money to the
masons and the carpenters, [w]and food, drink,
and oil to the Sidonians and the Tyrians [x]to
bring cedar trees from Lebanon to the sea, to
Joppa, [y]according to the grant that they had
from Cyrus king of Persia.

Rebuilding the Temple

8 Now in the second year after their coming
to the house of God at Jerusalem, in the second month, [z]Zerubbabel the son of Shealtiel
and [z]Jeshua the son of Jozadak made a beginning, together with the rest of their kinsmen,
the priests and the Levites and all who had
come to Jerusalem from the captivity. They
[a]appointed the Levites, from twenty years
old and upward, to [b]supervise the work of
the house of the LORD. 9 And [z]Jeshua with his
sons and his brothers, and Kadmiel and his
sons, the sons of Judah, together [b]supervised
the workmen in the house of God, along with
the [c]sons of Henadad and the Levites, their
sons and brothers.
10 And when the builders laid the foundation
of the temple of the LORD, the priests in their
vestments came forward with trumpets, and

[1] A *daric* was a coin weighing about 1/4 ounce or 8.5 grams [2] A *mina* was about 1 1/4 pounds or 0.6 kilogram [3] Hebrew *all Israel*

As those with unproven genealogies are noted (vv. 59–63), particularly those claiming priesthood, a strong theme emerges: God's people must keep themselves pure and holy according to God's commands—not out of racial superiority or legalistic pride but because God purposed to bring great blessing to them, and through them to the whole earth. Our Lord's gracious commands are always for the purpose of blessing. And through it all we remember that our pursuit of purity and holiness is a response to, not the prerequisite for, God's favor—ultimately shown to us through Christ.

3:1–7 The priority of rebuilding the altar according to God's Word shows what is to be the shape of the Israelites' (and our) lives: centered around the Lord God, listening to his Word, and offering up to him morning and night the sacrifices he desires. In the Old Testament it was lambs and grain and drink, to be offered with hearts of faith. In this new covenant age we now see clearly that even these offerings were ultimately an anticipation of Jesus, who "loved us and gave himself up for us, a fragrant offering and sacrifice to God" (Eph. 5:2). We who are united to Christ, who gave himself for us as the perfect sacrifice, are called now "to be a holy priesthood, to offer spiritual sacrifices acceptable to God through Jesus Christ" (1 Pet. 2:5).

3:10–13 The song celebrating the laying of the temple foundation not only echoes the words sung in anticipation of Solomon's temple (1 Chron. 16:34) but also features the "steadfast love" that God declared to Moses (Ex. 34:6; Deut. 7:9) and that rings out repeatedly in the Psalms. The weeping of those who remember the magnificent

65 [g] See 2 Chr. 35:25
68 [h] Neh. 7:70-72
69 [i] [1 Chr. 26:20]
70 [j] Neh. 7:73
Chapter 3
1 [k] Neh. 7:73; 8:1
2 [l] Matt. 1:12; Luke 3:27 [m] 1 Chr. 3:17; Matt. 1:12; Luke 3:27 [n] Deut. 12:5, 6 [o] See Deut. 33:1
3 [p] [ch. 4:4] [q] Ex. 29:38; Num. 28:3, 4
4 [r] Zech. 14:16; See Neh. 8:14-17 [s] Ex. 23:16; Lev. 23:34 [t] See Num. 29:12-38
5 [u] See Num. 28:11-15 [v] Num. 29:39
7 [w] 1 Kgs. 5:6, 9; 2 Chr. 2:10 [x] 2 Chr. 2:16 [y] ch. 1:3, 4; 6:3
8 [z] ch. 2:2; 4:3 [a] 1 Chr. 23:24 [b] 1 Chr. 23:4
9 [z] [See ver. 8 above] [b] [See ver. 8 above] [c] Neh. 10:9, 10

the Levites, the sons of Asaph, with cymbals,
to praise the LORD, [d]according to the directions of David king of Israel. 11 And they sang
responsively, praising and giving thanks to
the LORD,

> [e]"For he is good,
> for his steadfast love endures forever
> toward Israel."

And all the people shouted with a great shout
when they praised the LORD, because the foundation of the house of the LORD was laid. 12 But
many of the priests and Levites and heads of
fathers' houses, [f]old men who had seen the
first house, wept with a loud voice when they
saw the foundation of this house being laid,
though many shouted aloud for joy, 13 so that
the people could not distinguish the sound of
the joyful shout from the sound of the people's
weeping, for the people shouted with a great
shout, and the sound was heard far away.

Adversaries Oppose the Rebuilding

4 Now when [g]the adversaries of Judah and
Benjamin heard that the returned exiles
were building a temple to the LORD, the God
of Israel, 2 they approached Zerubbabel and
the heads of fathers' houses and said to them,
"Let us build with you, for we worship your
God as you do, and we have been sacrificing
to him ever [h]since the days of [i]Esarhaddon
king of Assyria [j]who brought us here." 3 But
Zerubbabel, Jeshua, and the rest of the heads
of fathers' houses in Israel said to them, [k]"You
have nothing to do with us in building a house
to our God; but we alone will build to the
LORD, the God of Israel, [l]as King Cyrus the
king of Persia has commanded us."

4 Then [m]the people of the land discouraged
the people of Judah and made them afraid to
build 5 and bribed counselors against them to
frustrate their purpose, all the days of Cyrus
king of Persia, even until the reign of Darius
king of Persia.

6 And in the reign of [n]Ahasuerus, in the beginning of his reign, they wrote an accusation
against the inhabitants of Judah and Jerusalem.

The Letter to King Artaxerxes

7 In the days of Artaxerxes, Bishlam and
[o]Mithredath and Tabeel and the rest of their
associates wrote to Artaxerxes king of Persia.
The letter was written [p]in Aramaic and translated.[1] 8 Rehum the commander and Shimshai
the scribe wrote a letter against Jerusalem to
Artaxerxes the king as follows: 9 Rehum the
commander, Shimshai the scribe, and the rest
of their associates, the [q]judges, the [r]governors,
the officials, the Persians, the men of Erech,
the Babylonians, the men of Susa, that is, the
[s]Elamites, 10 and the rest of the nations whom
the great and noble [t]Osnappar deported and
settled in the cities of Samaria and in the
rest of the province Beyond the River. 11 (This
is a copy of the letter that they sent.) "To
Artaxerxes the king: Your servants, the men
of the province Beyond the River, send greeting. And now 12 be it known to the king that

[1] Hebrew *written in Aramaic and translated in Aramaic*, indicating that 4:8–6:18 is in Aramaic; another interpretation is *The letter was written in the Aramaic script and set forth in the Aramaic language*

10[d] 1 Chr. 6:31; 16:4-6; 25:1, 2
11[e] See 1 Chr. 16:34, 41
12[f] Hag. 2:3
Chapter 4
1[g] See ver. 7-10
2[h] 2 Kgs. 17:24, 32, 33 [i] 2 Kgs. 19:37 [j] [ver. 10]
3[k] Neh. 2:20 [l] ch. 1:1-3
4[m] ch. 3:3
6[n] Esth. 1:1; Dan. 9:1
7[o] ch. 1:8 [p] [2 Kgs. 18:26]
9[q] [2 Kgs. 17:24, 30, 31] [r] [ch. 5:6; 6:6] [s] Isa. 11:11
10[t] [ver. 2]

former temple reminds us that this once great nation has lost its visible power and glory. God's people must now trust solely in the power of God's covenant promises—in his steadfast love, and in the glory that would come to this temple only with the arrival of Jesus (see 1 Kings 8:10–11; Hag. 2:7; John 1:14).

At this stage in redemptive history, then, the longing for a true and final temple is heightened. Jesus came as this true and final temple: he is the final place where people may freely enjoy fellowship with God, where earth and heaven meet. And in the vision of the new earth that we are given at the very end of the Bible, we see that there is no longer any need for a physical temple such as the people in Ezra's day longed for, because Christ is there. In him, God forever dwells with his redeemed people (Rev. 21:3, 22–23).

4:1–24 This chapter and the whole rest of the story show how believers in all times live out the tensions Jesus talked about in John 15:18–19—being chosen out of the world and hated by the world. Those offering to help the returned exiles (Ezra 4:1–2) are in fact adversaries, not worshipers of the same God, as they claim. The whole Persian Empire for decades (as shown in the jump forward in time in vv. 6–23) seems aligned against God's people. Zerubbabel's focus on serving the Lord God (v. 3) offers a godly example, though the people's discouragement and fear are responses known and battled by all.

the Jews who came up from you to us have
gone to Jerusalem. They are rebuilding that
rebellious and wicked city. They are [v]finish-
ing the walls and repairing the foundations.
13 Now be it known to the king that if this city
is rebuilt and the walls finished, they will not
pay [w]tribute, custom, or toll, and the royal revenue will be impaired. 14 Now because we eat
the salt of the palace and it is not fitting for
us to witness the king's dishonor, therefore
we send and inform the king, 15 in order that
search may be made in the book of the records
of your fathers. You will find in the book of the
records and learn that this city is a rebellious
city, hurtful to kings and provinces, and that
sedition was stirred up in it from of old. That
was why this city was laid waste. 16 We make
known to the king that if this city is rebuilt
and its walls finished, you will then have no
possession in the province Beyond the River."

The King Orders the Work to Cease

17 The king sent an answer: "To Rehum the
commander and Shimshai the scribe and the
rest of their associates who live in Samaria and
in the rest of the province Beyond the River,
greeting. And now 18 the letter that you sent
to us has been [x]plainly read before me. 19 And
I made a decree, and search has been made,
and it has been found that this city from of old
has risen against kings, and that rebellion and
sedition have been made in it. 20 And mighty
kings have been over Jerusalem, [y]who ruled
over the whole province Beyond the River, to
whom [z]tribute, custom, and toll were paid.
21 Therefore make a decree that these men be
made to cease, and that this city be not rebuilt,
until a decree is made by me. 22 And take care
not to be slack in this matter. Why should
damage grow to the hurt of the king?"

23 Then, when the copy of King Artaxerxes'
letter was read before Rehum and Shimshai
the scribe and their associates, they went in
haste to the Jews at Jerusalem and by force and
power made them cease. 24 Then the work on
the house of God that is in Jerusalem stopped,
and it ceased until the second year of the reign
of Darius king of Persia.

Rebuilding Begins Anew

5 Now the prophets, [a]Haggai and [b]Zechariah
the son of Iddo, prophesied to the Jews
who were in Judah and Jerusalem, in the
name of the God of Israel who was over them.
2 [c]Then Zerubbabel the son of Shealtiel and
[d]Jeshua the son of Jozadak arose and began to

The chapter's last sentence shows God's people temporarily defeated but gives a hint of the victory to come. From our present place in history, we know that the defeat experienced here was not ultimate but was only a chapter in God's book of instruction, leading us to trust in the God who would soon bring a greater victory (the building would resume) and ultimately a greater Victor, from this remnant's efforts. This battle for a physical temple in a physical land against earthly rulers is a picture of the spiritual battle Paul describes, not "against flesh and blood, but against the rulers, against the authorities, against the cosmic powers over this present darkness, against the spiritual forces of evil in the heavenly places" (Eph. 6:12). Thus, from an ultimate perspective, this is the battle Christ himself came to fight *for* us. It is a battle he won on our behalf. Christ "disarmed the rulers and authorities . . . triumphing over them" (Col. 2:15).

We fight, knowing that Christ has won, so that we can by his Spirit put on the "armor of God" and "stand firm" (Eph. 6:12–13). We do not wage our spiritual battle to gain God's love; we do battle because he has promised to love us no matter what.

5:1–5 The role of the prophets is crucial, as they bring God's word to God's people (5:1–2; see also 6:14). In battles then and now, the difference is made by "the sword of the Spirit, which is the word of God" (Eph. 6:17). In this story and in all of history, the ultimate power and help come from the God who breathes out that word, the God who "was over them" (Ezra 5:1) and whose eye was on his people (v. 5).

The prophets Haggai and Zechariah here join a prominent leadership duo: Jeshua the high priest and Zerubbabel the descendant of David (3:2, 8; 4:3). God's people need prophet, priest, and king—a prophet to speak God's word, a priest to represent the people to God, and a king to represent God to them.

This triad of needs is fully met in Jesus. He himself is not only the final prophet (Acts 3:18–24) but the very Word from God spoken to the people (John 1:1, 14). He himself is the final priest (Heb. 7:15–28) as well as the temple within which the priests

12 [v]ch. 5:3, 9
13 [w]ver. 20; ch. 7:24
18 [x][Neh. 8:8]
20 [y]1 Kgs. 4:21; Ps. 72:8; [Gen. 15:18; Josh. 1:4] [z]ver. 13; [ch. 7:24]

Chapter 5

1 [a]Hag. 1:1 [b]Zech. 1:1
2 [c]ch. 3:2 [d]See ch. 3:2

rebuild the house of God that is in Jerusalem, and the prophets of God were [e]with them, supporting them.

[3]At the same time [f]Tattenai the governor of the province Beyond the River and Shethar-bozenai and their associates came to them and spoke to them thus: [g]"Who gave you a decree to build this house and to finish this structure?" [4]They[1] also asked them this: "What are the names of the men who are building this building?" [5]But [h]the eye of their God was on the elders of the Jews, and they did not stop them until the report should reach Darius and then an answer be returned by letter concerning it.

Tattenai's Letter to King Darius

[6]This is a copy of the letter that [f]Tattenai the governor of the province Beyond the River and Shethar-bozenai and his associates, the [i]governors who were in the province Beyond the River, sent to Darius the king. [7]They sent him a report, in which was written as follows: "To Darius the king, all peace. [8]Be it known to the king that we went to the province of Judah, to the house of the great God. It is being built with huge stones, and timber is laid in the walls. This work goes on diligently and prospers in their hands. [9]Then we asked those elders and spoke to them thus: [g]'Who gave you a decree to build this house and to finish this structure?' [10]We also asked them their names, for your information, that we might write down the names of their leaders.[2] [11]And this was their reply to us: 'We are the servants of the God of heaven and earth, and we are rebuilding the house that was built many years ago, [j]which a great king of Israel built and [k]finished. [12][l]But because our fathers had angered the God of heaven, he [m]gave them into the hand of Nebuchadnezzar king of Babylon, the Chaldean, who destroyed this house and carried away the people to Babylonia. [13][n]However, in the first year of Cyrus king of Babylon, Cyrus the king made a decree that this house of God should be rebuilt. [14][o]And the gold and silver vessels of the house of God, which Nebuchadnezzar had taken out of the temple that was in Jerusalem and brought into the temple of Babylon, these Cyrus the king took out of the temple of Babylon, and they were delivered to one whose name was [p]Sheshbazzar, whom he had made governor; [15]and he said to him, "Take these vessels, go and put them in the temple that is in Jerusalem, and let the house of God be rebuilt on its site." [16]Then this [p]Sheshbazzar came and [q]laid the foundations of the house of God that is in Jerusalem, and from that time until now it has been in building, and it is [r]not yet finished.' [17]Therefore, if it seems good to the king, [s]let search be made in the royal archives there in Babylon, to see whether a decree was issued by Cyrus the king for the rebuilding of this house of God in Jerusalem. And let the king send us his pleasure in this matter."

The Decree of Darius

6 Then Darius the king made a decree, and [t]search was made in Babylonia, in the house of the archives where the documents were stored. [2]And in Ecbatana, the citadel that is [u]in the province of Media, a scroll was found on which this was written: "A record. [3]In the first year of Cyrus the king, Cyrus the king issued a decree: Concerning the house of God at Jerusalem, let the house be rebuilt, the place where sacrifices were offered, and let its foundations be retained. Its height shall be sixty cubits[3] and its breadth sixty cubits, [4][v]with three layers of great stones and one layer of timber. Let the cost be paid from the royal treasury. [5]And also [w]let the gold and

[1] Septuagint, Syriac; Aramaic *We* [2] Aramaic *of the men at their heads* [3] A *cubit* was about 18 inches or 45 centimeters

2[e] [ch. 6:14]
3[f] ch. 6:6, 13 [g] ch. 4:12
5[h] Ps. 33:18; [ch. 7:6, 28]
6[f] [See ver. 3 above] [i] [ch. 4:9]
9[g] [See ver. 3 above]
11[j] 1 Kgs. 6:1 [k] ch. 4:12
12[l] 2 Chr. 36:16, 17 [m] 2 Kgs. 24:2; See 2 Kgs. 25:8-11
13[n] ch. 1:1
14[o] ch. 1:7, 8; 6:5 [p] ch. 1:8
16[p] [See ver. 14 above] [q] ch. 3:8, 10 [r] [ch. 6:15]
17[s] ch. 6:1, 2
Chapter 6
1[t] ch. 5:17
2[u] [2 Kgs. 17:6] **4**[v] 1 Kgs. 6:36 **5**[w] ch. 1:7, 8; 5:14

worked (John 2:19–22; Eph. 2:19–22) and the sacrifice offered by the priests in the temple (1 Cor. 5:7; Eph. 5:2). And he is the eternal King, the Messiah, the Anointed One, the Son of David, Lord of all (Matt. 27:11).

5:11–16 Included in this letter to King Darius is a long quotation of the Jewish leaders' words. These words truly affirm their God not just as a local deity, as others around would have believed, but as "God of heaven and earth," a holy God who is angered by and who punishes sin (vv. 11–12). These leaders give bold, faithful witness to the Lord God, not only by their words but by the very fact that they stand again in their land, with people restored and rebuilding, sanctioned by royal decree—all due to the mercy and care of God.

silver vessels of the house of God, which
Nebuchadnezzar took out of the temple that
is in Jerusalem and brought to Babylon, be
restored and brought back to the temple that
is in Jerusalem, each to its place. You shall put
them in the house of God."
6 "Now therefore, [x]Tattenai, governor of the
province Beyond the River, Shethar-bozenai,
[y]and your[1] associates the governors who are
in the province Beyond the River, keep away.
7 Let the work on this house of God alone. Let
the governor of the Jews and the elders of
the Jews rebuild this house of God on its site.
8 Moreover, [z]I make a decree regarding what
you shall do for these elders of the Jews for
the rebuilding of this house of God. The cost
is to be paid to these men in full and without
delay from the royal revenue, the tribute of
the province from Beyond the River. 9 And
whatever is needed—bulls, rams, or sheep for
burnt offerings to the God of heaven, wheat,
salt, wine, or oil, as the priests at Jerusalem
require—let that be given to them day by day
without fail, 10 that they may offer pleasing
sacrifices to the God of heaven [a]and pray for
the life of the king and his sons. 11 Also I make
a decree that if anyone alters this edict, a beam
shall be pulled out of his house, and he shall
be impaled on it, and [b]his house shall be made
a dunghill. 12 May the God [c]who has caused
his name to dwell there overthrow any king
or people who shall put out a hand to alter
this, or to destroy this house of God that is
in Jerusalem. I Darius make a decree; let it be
done with all diligence."

The Temple Finished and Dedicated

13 Then, according to the word sent by Darius
the king, [x]Tattenai, the governor of the province Beyond the River, Shethar-bozenai, and
their associates did with all diligence what
Darius the king had ordered. 14 [d]And the elders
of the Jews built and prospered through the
prophesying of Haggai the prophet and
Zechariah the son of Iddo. They finished their
building by decree of the God of Israel and [e]by
decree of Cyrus and [f]Darius and [g]Artaxerxes
king of Persia; 15 and this house was finished
on the third day of the [h]month of Adar, in the
sixth year of the reign of Darius the king.
16 And the people of Israel, the priests and
the Levites, and the rest of the returned exiles,
celebrated the [i]dedication of this house of God
with joy. 17 They offered at the dedication of
this house of God 100 bulls, 200 rams, 400
lambs, and as a sin offering for all Israel [j]12
male goats, according to the number of the
tribes of Israel. 18 And they set the priests [k]in
their divisions and the Levites [l]in their divisions, for the service of God at Jerusalem, [m]as
it is written in the Book of Moses.

Passover Celebrated

19 [n]On the fourteenth day of the first month,
the returned exiles kept the Passover. 20 [o]For
the priests and the Levites had purified themselves together; all of them were clean. [p]So
they slaughtered the Passover lamb for all the
returned exiles, for their fellow priests, and
for themselves. 21 It was eaten by the people
of Israel who had returned from exile, and
[q]also by every one who had joined them and

[1] Aramaic *their*

6:6–12 Knowingly or unknowingly, King Darius speaks truly of God, who has caused his name to dwell in the temple (v. 12; see Deut. 12:5). These words reverberate with Scripture's continual exaltation of God's name, and especially with Scripture's unfolding of that name as revealed finally in Jesus, who is given "the name that is above every name," to which every knee of every earthly king will one day bow (Phil. 2:9–10).

6:16–22 The dedication of the rebuilt temple has all the marks of the community of God's covenant people. The Word is central (v. 18), and worship happens according to that Word. The sacrifices (v. 17) anticipate the final, perfect sacrifice of Christ on our behalf. The Passover Feast (vv. 19–20) celebrates redemption from Egypt, anticipating God's redemption of his people through the blood of his Son. Included are not only the Jews but all "who had joined them" to serve and worship the one true God (v. 21): here is a picture of God's redeemed people drawn from the nations. God sovereignly cares for them (v. 22) and makes them joyful (vv. 16, 22).

What an encouragement to see the continuity of God's covenant people, as today the worldwide church worships according to the Scriptures, joyfully exalting Jesus Christ in the sacraments given in remembrance of him, who instituted a new covenant in his blood (1 Cor. 11:25).

6 [x] ch. 5:3, 6 [y] ch. 5:6
8 [z] ch. 7:13, 21
10 [a] Jer. 29:7; [1 Tim. 2:2]
11 [b] Dan. 2:5; 3:29
12 [c] 1 Kgs. 9:3
13 [x] [See ver. 6 above]
14 [d] ch. 5:1, 2 [e] ver. 3; ch. 1:1; 5:13 [f] ver. 12; [ch. 4:24] [g] ch. 7:1
15 [h] Esth. 3:7
16 [i] 1 Kgs. 8:63; 2 Chr. 7:5
17 [j] [ch. 8:35]
18 [k] 1 Chr. 24:1; 2 Chr. 35:5 [l] 1 Chr. 23:6 [m] Num. 3:6; 8:9
19 [n] Ex. 12:6
20 [o] 2 Chr. 30:15 [p] 2 Chr. 35:11
21 [q] Neh. 9:2; 10:28; [ch. 9:1]

separated himself [r]from the uncleanness of
the peoples of the land to worship the LORD,
the God of Israel. 22 And they kept the Feast of
Unleavened Bread [s]seven days with joy, for the
LORD had made them joyful [t]and had turned
the heart of [u]the king of Assyria to them, so
that he aided them in the work of the house
of God, the God of Israel.

Ezra Sent to Teach the People

7 Now after this, [v]in the reign of [v]Artaxerxes
king of Persia, [w]Ezra the son of Seraiah, son
of Azariah, son of Hilkiah, 2 son of Shallum,
son of Zadok, son of Ahitub, 3 son of Amariah,
son of Azariah, son of Meraioth, 4 son of
Zerahiah, son of Uzzi, son of Bukki, 5 son of
Abishua, son of Phinehas, son of Eleazar, son
of Aaron the chief priest— 6 this Ezra went up
from Babylonia. He was a scribe [x]skilled in the
Law of Moses that the LORD, the God of Israel,
had given, and the king granted him all that
he asked, [y]for the hand of the LORD his God
was on him.

7 And there went up also to Jerusalem, in the
seventh year of Artaxerxes the king, some of
the people of Israel, and [z]some of the priests
and [a]Levites, the singers and gatekeepers,
and the temple [b]servants. 8 And Ezra[1] came
to Jerusalem in the fifth month, which was
in the seventh year of the king. 9 For on the
first day of the first month he began to go up
from Babylonia, and on the first day of the
fifth month he came to Jerusalem, [c]for the
good hand of his God was on him. 10 For Ezra
had set his heart to study the Law of the LORD,
and to do it [d]and to [e]teach his statutes and
rules in Israel.

11 This is a copy of the letter that King
Artaxerxes gave to Ezra the priest, the scribe,
a man learned in matters of the commandments of the LORD and his statutes for Israel:
12 "Artaxerxes, [f]king of kings, to Ezra the
priest, the [g]scribe of the Law of the God of
heaven. Peace.[2] [h]And now 13 [i]I make a decree
that anyone of the people of Israel or their
priests or Levites in my kingdom, who freely
offers to go to Jerusalem, may go with you.
14 For you are sent by the king [j]and his seven
counselors to make inquiries about Judah and
Jerusalem according to the Law of your God,
which is in your hand, 15 and also to carry the
silver and gold that the king [j]and his counselors have freely offered to the God of Israel,
[k]whose dwelling is in Jerusalem, 16 [l]with all
the silver and gold that you shall find in the
whole province of Babylonia, and [m]with the
freewill offerings of the people and the priests,
vowed willingly for the house of their God
that is in Jerusalem. 17 With this money, then,
you shall with all diligence buy bulls, rams,
and lambs, with their grain offerings and their
drink offerings, and [n]you shall offer them on
the altar of the house of your God that is in
Jerusalem. 18 Whatever seems good to you and
your brothers to do with the rest of the silver
and gold, you may do, according to the will
of your God. 19 The vessels that have been given
you for the service of the house of your God,
you shall deliver before the God of Jerusalem.
20 And whatever else is required for the house
of your God, which it falls to you to provide,
you may provide it out of the king's treasury.

21 "And I, Artaxerxes the king, make a decree
to all the treasurers in the province Beyond
the River: Whatever Ezra the priest, the scribe
of the Law of the God of heaven, requires of
you, let it be done with all diligence, 22 up
to 100 talents[3] of silver, 100 cors[4] of wheat,
100 baths[5] of wine, 100 baths of oil, and salt
without prescribing how much. 23 Whatever is
decreed by the God of heaven, let it be done in
full for the house of the God of heaven, lest his

[1] Aramaic *he* [2] Aramaic *Perfect* (probably a greeting) [3] A *talent* was about 75 pounds or 34 kilograms [4] A *cor* was about 6 bushels or 220 liters [5] A *bath* was about 6 gallons or 22 liters

21[r] ch. 9:11
22[s] Ex. 12:15; 13:6; 2 Chr. 30:21; 35:17 [t] ch. 7:27; [Prov. 21:1] [u] [Neh. 13:6]
Chapter 7
1[v] Neh. 2:1 [w] For ver. 1-5, see 1 Chr. 6:4-14
6[x] ver. 11, 12, 21; Neh. 8:1-3, 13; 12:26, 36 [y] ver. 9, 28; ch. 8:18, 22, 31; Neh. 2:8, 18; [ch. 5:5]
7[z] See ch. 8:1-14 [a] ch. 8:15-19 [b] ch. 8:17, 20; [ch. 2:43]
9[c] See ver. 6

7:1–28 The focus on God's Word continues even as the narrative skips 57 years to Ezra, who leads a second group of exiles back to Jerusalem. Pointedly introduced as a descendant of Aaron the first high priest, this scribe skilled in the law (v. 6) offers to believers in every age the example of studying, doing, and teaching God's Word (v. 10). His effectiveness depends clearly on God's grace, as this chapter is enfolded in affirmations of the hand of God on Ezra (vv. 6, 28). God's grace shines through personally in the chapter's conclusion (vv. 27–28), as Ezra the narrator praises God for his moving the heart of the king (see Prov. 21:1), his "steadfast love," and his hand "on me." Ezra is faithful to God's Word, Ezra takes courage—and, ultimately, God opens his path.

10[d] ver. 25; [Deut. 33:10] [e] [2 Chr. 17:7; Mal. 2:7; Matt. 23:2, 3]; See Neh. 8:1-8 **12**[f] Ezek. 26:7; Dan. 2:37 [g] See ver. 6 [h] ch. 4:11, 17 **13**[i] ch. 6:8 **14**[j] ver. 15, 28; ch. 8:25; [Esth. 1:14] **15**[j] [See ver. 14 above] [k] 2 Chr. 6:2; [Ps. 135:21] **16**[l] ch. 8:25 [m] 1 Chr. 29:6, 9 **17**[n] Deut. 12:5, 11

wrath be against the realm of the king and his
sons. 24 We also notify you that it shall not be
lawful to impose [o]tribute, custom, or toll on
anyone of the priests, the Levites, the singers,
the doorkeepers, the temple servants, or other
servants of this house of God.
25 "And you, Ezra, according to the wisdom
of your God that is in your hand, [p]appoint
magistrates and judges who may judge all
the people in the province Beyond the River,
all such as know the laws of your God. [q]And
those who do not know them, you shall teach.
26 Whoever will not obey the law of your God
and the law of the king, let judgment be
strictly executed on him, whether for death
or for banishment or for confiscation of his
goods or for imprisonment."
27 [r]Blessed be the LORD, the God of our
fathers, [s]who put such a thing as this into
the heart of the king, to beautify the house
of the LORD that is in Jerusalem, 28 [t]and who
extended to me his steadfast love before the
king and his counselors, and before all the
king's mighty officers. I took courage, for
the hand of the LORD my God was on me,
and I gathered leading men from Israel to go
up with me.

Genealogy of Those Who Returned with Ezra

8 These are the heads of their fathers'
houses, and this is the genealogy of those
who went up with me from Babylonia, in the
reign of Artaxerxes the king: 2 Of the sons of
Phinehas, Gershom. Of the sons of [u]Ithamar,
Daniel. Of the sons of David, [v]Hattush. 3 Of
the sons of Shecaniah, who was of the sons of
[w]Parosh, Zechariah, with whom were registered 150 men. 4 [x]Of the sons of Pahath-moab,
Eliehoenai the son of Zerahiah, and with him
200 men. 5 Of the sons of Zattu,[1] Shecaniah the
son of Jahaziel, and with him 300 men. 6 Of
the sons of Adin, Ebed the son of Jonathan,
and with him 50 men. 7 Of the sons of Elam,
Jeshaiah the son of Athaliah, and with him 70
men. 8 Of the sons of Shephatiah, Zebadiah
the son of Michael, and with him 80 men.
9 Of the sons of Joab, Obadiah the son of
Jehiel, and with him 218 men. 10 Of the sons
of Bani,[2] Shelomith the son of Josiphiah, and
with him 160 men. 11 [y]Of the sons of Bebai,
Zechariah, the son of Bebai, and with him 28
men. 12 Of the sons of Azgad, Johanan the son
of Hakkatan, and with him 110 men. 13 Of the
sons of Adonikam, those who came later, their
names being Eliphelet, Jeuel, and Shemaiah,
and with them 60 men. 14 Of the sons of Bigvai,
Uthai and Zaccur, and with them 70 men.

Ezra Sends for Levites

15 I gathered them to the river that runs to
[z]Ahava, and there we camped three days. As
I reviewed the people and the priests, I found
there [a]none of the sons of Levi. 16 Then I sent
for Eliezer, Ariel, Shemaiah, Elnathan,
Jarib, Elnathan, Nathan, Zechariah, and
[b]Meshullam, leading men, and for Joiarib and
Elnathan, who were men of insight, 17 and sent
them to Iddo, the leading man at the place
Casiphia, telling them what to say to Iddo and
his brothers and[3] the temple servants at the
place Casiphia, namely, to send us ministers
for the house of our God. 18 And [c]by the good
hand of our God on us, they brought us a man
of discretion, of the sons of [d]Mahli the son of
Levi, son of Israel, namely Sherebiah with his
sons and kinsmen, 18; 19 also [e]Hashabiah, and

[1] Septuagint; Hebrew lacks *of Zattu* [2] Septuagint; Hebrew lacks *Bani* [3] Hebrew lacks *and*

8:1–36 In these journey details, Ezra's wise decisions are consistently linked to and dependent on God's gracious care. First, Ezra deals with a lack of leaders, specifically leaders for temple worship (v. 17): his well-placed request for help brings a whole group of priests and Levites—"by the good hand of our God on us" (v. 18). Next Ezra addresses the safety of his people and the treasure they transport, deciding not to ask for the king's help but to trust the words of witness he had given the king concerning God's good hand *and* God's wrath (v. 22).

Ezra is clearly unafraid to bear bold witness to the whole truth about God—to approach the God whom he believes is for him (v. 22), and to appeal to God as One who listens to Ezra's prayer for safety (v. 23). Ezra's smart decision to apportion the treasures among the leading priests is rewarded by God's hand, delivering them from enemies along the way and bringing them safely to Jerusalem (v. 31). By the chapter's close, we see the final celebration of burnt offerings and sin offerings not just as an obedient response to God but as God's great provision for the people over whom he watches so faithfully for his redemptive purposes, purposes ultimately fulfilled in Christ.

24 [o] ch. 4:13, 20
25 [p] Ex. 18:21, 22; Deut. 16:18 [q] See ver. 10
27 [r] 1 Chr. 29:10 [s] ch. 6:22
28 [t] ch. 9:9
Chapter 8
2 [u] 1 Chr. 24:3, 4 [v] [1 Chr. 3:22]
3 [w] For ver. 3, see ch. 2:3-15
4 [x] ch. 10:30
11 [y] ch. 10:28
15 [z] ver. 21, 31 [a] [ch. 7:7]
16 [b] ch. 10:15
18 [c] See ch. 7:6 [d] 1 Chr. 6:19
19 [e] Neh. 12:24

with him Jeshaiah of [f]the sons of Merari, with
his kinsmen and their sons, 20; 20 [g]besides 220
of the temple servants, whom David and his
officials had set apart to attend the Levites.
These were all [h]mentioned by name.

Fasting and Prayer for Protection

21 [i]Then I proclaimed a fast there, at the
river [j]Ahava, that we might humble ourselves
before our God, [k]to seek from him a safe journey for ourselves, our children, and all our
goods. 22 For I was ashamed to ask the king for
a band of soldiers and horsemen to protect us
against the enemy on our way, since we had
told the king, [l]"The hand of our God is for
good on [m]all who seek him, and the power of
his wrath is against all who forsake him." 23 So
we fasted and implored our God for this, and
he listened to our entreaty.

Priests to Guard Offerings

24 Then I set apart twelve of the leading
priests: [e]Sherebiah, [e]Hashabiah, and ten of
their kinsmen with them. 25 And I weighed
out to them the [n]silver and the gold and the
vessels, the offering for the house of our God
that the king and his [o]counselors and his lords
and all Israel there present had offered. 26 [p]I
weighed out into their hand 650 talents[1] of silver, and silver vessels worth 200 talents,[2] and
100 talents of gold, 27 20 bowls of gold worth
1,000 darics,[3] and two vessels of fine bright
bronze as precious as gold. 28 And I said to
them, [q]"You are holy to the LORD, and [r]the vessels are holy, and the silver and the gold are a
freewill offering to the LORD, the God of your
fathers. 29 Guard them and keep them until
you weigh them before the chief priests and
the Levites and the heads of fathers' houses in
Israel at Jerusalem, [s]within the chambers of
the house of the LORD." 30 So the priests and
the Levites [p]took over the weight of the silver
and the gold and the vessels, to bring them to
Jerusalem, to the house of our God.

31 Then we departed from the river Ahava
[t]on the twelfth day of the first month, to go
to Jerusalem. [u]The hand of our God was on
us, and he delivered us from the hand of the
enemy and from ambushes by the way. 32 [v]We
came to Jerusalem, and there we remained
three days. 33 On the fourth day, within the
house of our God, the silver and the gold and
the vessels were [w]weighed into the hands
of [x]Meremoth the priest, son of Uriah, and
with him was Eleazar the son of Phinehas,
and with them were the Levites, [y]Jozabad the
son of Jeshua and Noadiah the son of [z]Binnui.
34 The whole was counted and weighed, and
the weight of everything was recorded.

35 At that time [a]those who had come from
captivity, the returned exiles, offered burnt
offerings to the God of Israel, [b]twelve bulls
for all Israel, ninety-six rams, seventy-seven
lambs, and as a sin offering twelve male goats.
All this was a burnt offering to the LORD.
36 [c]They also delivered the king's commissions
to the king's [d]satraps[4] and to the governors of
the province Beyond the River, and they aided
the people and the house of God.

Ezra Prays About Intermarriage

9 After these things had been done, the officials approached me and said, "The people of Israel and the priests and the [e]Levites
have not separated themselves from the
peoples of the lands [f]with their abominations, from the [g]Canaanites, the Hittites, the
Perizzites, the Jebusites, the Ammonites, the
Moabites, the Egyptians, and the Amorites.
2 [h]For they have taken some of their daughters
to be wives for themselves and for their sons,
so that the [i]holy race[5] has [j]mixed itself with
the peoples of the lands. And in this faithlessness the hand of the officials and chief men

[1] A *talent* was about 75 pounds or 34 kilograms [2] Revocalization; the number is missing in the Masoretic Text [3] A *daric* was a coin weighing about 1/4 ounce or 8.5 grams [4] A *satrap* was a Persian official [5] Hebrew *offspring*

19 [f]1 Chr. 6:1, 16
20 [g]ch. 2:43; 7:7 [h]Num. 1:17
21 [i]See 2 Chr. 20:3 [j]ver. 15, 31 [k][Ps. 5:8]
22 [l]See ch. 7:6 [m][2 Chr. 15:2]
24 [e][See ver. 19 above]
25 [n]ch. 7:15, 16 [o]See ch. 7:14
26 [p][ch. 1:9-11]
28 [q]Lev. 21:6 [r]Lev. 22:2, 3
29 [s][ch. 10:6]
30 [p][See ver. 26 above]
31 [t][ch. 7:9] [u]See ch. 7:6
32 [v]Neh. 2:11

9:1–15 Ezra's reaction and prayer of confession expose the seriousness of the people's "faithlessness" (vv. 2, 3) in disobeying God's command not to intermarry with the people of the surrounding nations. (See Deut. 7:1–5 for God's law against marriage with foreigners; see Ezra 6:21 to clarify God's welcome to any foreign convert, like Rahab or Ruth, who believed and worshiped the Lord God.) The term "holy race" (Ezra 9:2) is more literally translated "holy seed" or "holy offspring"—a clear echo of God's covenant with Abraham in Genesis 12 and 15, where blessing and land are promised to and through his offspring, and where most of the nations of Ezra 9:1 are even named (Gen. 15:18–21).

33 [w][ch. 1:9-11] [x]Neh. 3:4, 21 [y]Neh. 11:16 [z]Neh. 3:24 35 [a]ch. 2:1 [b][ch. 6:17] 36 [c]ch. 7:21 [d]Esth. 3:12; 8:9; 9:3; Dan. 3:2, 3, 27; 6:2, 3 **Chapter 9** 1 [e][ch. 6:21; Neh. 9:2] [f]Deut. 12:30, 31 [g]See Ex. 13:5 2 [h]ch. 10:2; Neh. 13:23, 27; [Ex. 34:16; Deut. 7:3; Neh. 10:30] [i]See Deut. 7:6 [j]Ps. 106:35; [2 Cor. 6:14]

has been foremost." 3 As soon as I heard this,
I [k]tore my garment and my cloak and pulled
hair from my head and beard and [l]sat appalled.
4 Then all who [m]trembled at the words of the
God of Israel, because of the faithlessness of
the returned exiles, gathered around me while
I sat [n]appalled until the evening sacrifice. 5 And
at the [n]evening sacrifice I rose from my fasting,
with my garment [k]and my cloak torn, and fell
upon my knees [o]and spread out my hands to
the LORD my God, 6 saying:

"O my God, I am ashamed and blush to lift
my face to you, my God, for our iniquities [p]have
risen higher than our heads, and our [q]guilt has
[r]mounted up to the heavens. 7 [s]From the days
of our fathers to this day we have been in great
[q]guilt. And for our iniquities we, our kings, and
our priests have been given into the hand of
the kings of the lands, to the sword, to captivity, to plundering, [t]and to utter shame, as it is
today. 8 But now for a brief moment favor has
been shown by the LORD our God, to leave us a
[u]remnant and to give us a [v]secure hold[1] within
his holy place, that our God may [w]brighten
our eyes and grant us a little reviving in our
slavery. 9 [x]For we are slaves. Yet our God has not
forsaken us in our slavery, [y]but has extended to
us his steadfast love before the kings of Persia,
to grant us some reviving to set up the house
of our God, to repair its ruins, and to give us
protection[2] in Judea and Jerusalem.

10 "And now, O our God, what shall we say
after this? For we have forsaken your commandments, 11 which you commanded by
your servants the prophets, saying, 'The land
that you are entering, to take possession of
it, is a land impure with the impurity of the
peoples of the lands, with their abominations
that have filled it from end to end with [z]their
uncleanness. 12 [a]Therefore do not give your
daughters to their sons, neither take their
daughters for your sons, and never seek their
peace or prosperity, that you may be strong
and eat the good of the land [b]and leave it for
an inheritance to your children forever.' 13 And
after all that has come upon us for our evil
deeds and for [c]our great guilt, seeing that
you, our [d]God, have punished us less than our
iniquities deserved and have given us such a
[e]remnant as this, 14 shall we break your commandments again and [f]intermarry with the
peoples who practice these abominations?
Would you not be angry with us [g]until you
consumed us, so that there should be no [e]rem-
nant, nor any to escape? 15 O LORD, the God of
Israel, you are just, for we are left a [e]remnant
that has escaped, as it is today. Behold, we are
before you in our [h]guilt, [i]for none can stand
before you because of this."

The People Confess Their Sin

10 [j]While Ezra prayed and [k]made confession, weeping and [l]casting himself
down [m]before the house of God, a very great
assembly of men, women, and children, gathered to him out of Israel, for the people wept

[1] Hebrew *nail*, or *tent-pin* [2] Hebrew *a wall*

Ezra approaches God on the basis of a whole history of God's covenant promises, but also as one who trembles at God's words (Ezra 9:3; 10:3; see also Isa. 66:2, 5). He shows the need for an intercessor on behalf of a sinful people. Ezra himself only foreshadows that role, trusting in God's "favor," or "grace" (Ezra 9:8), which brightens the very heart of this prayer just as it brightened the eyes of these slaves allowed by God to return home (v. 8).

The repetition of "remnant" throughout this chapter (see Isa. 10:20–22), and the reaffirmation of God's "steadfast love" (Ezra 9:9) to his people show Ezra's unshakeable trust in God's great purpose of blessing through the offspring of this remnant people. In effect, Ezra was putting his faith in God's provision being maintained through the remnant that would ultimately produce the Seed of promise, who would come and make his people holy despite their sin (cf. vv. 13–15; 1 Pet. 2:9).

We believers are often more like the people of God in Ezra's day than we care to acknowledge. Yet our faithlessness, like theirs, need not be the last word. For God sent his own Son to live the one truly faithful life, so that faltering sinners who nevertheless put their trust in the Lord can be restored to God and joy.

10:1–44 The unsatisfying way in which the book of Ezra ends is significant. The beauty of the resolution in this moment of Israelite history is marred by the depth of the people's continued sin, sin not against ethnic purity but against God's covenant commands for separation from pagan influences (see note on 9:1–15).

3 [k]See Josh. 7:6 [l][Neh. 1:4]
4 [m]ch. 10:3; Isa. 66:2, 5 [n]Ex. 29:39, 41
5 [n][See ver. 4 above] [k][See ver. 3 above] [o]1 Kgs. 8:22
6 [p][Ps. 38:4] [q]ver. 7, 13, 15; ch. 10:10, 19; 2 Chr. 24:18 [r][2 Chr. 28:9; Rev. 18:5]
7 [s]Ps. 106:6; Dan. 9:5, 6 [q][See ver. 6 above] [t]Dan. 9:7, 8
8 [u]ver. 13, 14, 15 [v]Isa. 22:23 [w]Ps. 13:3
9 [x][Neh. 9:36] [y]ch. 7:28
11 [z]ch. 6:21
12 [a]See ver. 2 [b][Prov. 13:22]
13 [c]ver. 6, 7 [d]Job 11:6; Ps. 103:10 [e]ver. 8
14 [f]See ver. 2 [g][Deut. 9:8] [e][See ver. 13 above]
15 [e][See ver. 13 above] [h]Neh. 9:33; Ps. 119:137; Jer. 12:1; Dan. 9:14 [i]Ps. 130:3

Chapter 10
1 [j]Neh. 1:4, 5 [k]Neh. 1:6; Dan. 9:20 [l]Deut. 9:18 [m][2 Chr. 20:9]

bitterly. 2 And Shecaniah the son of Jehiel, of
the sons of Elam, addressed Ezra: [n]"We have
broken faith with our God and have married
foreign women from the peoples of the land,
but even now there is hope for Israel in spite
of this. 3 Therefore [o]let us make a covenant
with our God to put away all these wives and
[p]their children, according to the counsel of
my lord[1] and of [q]those who tremble at the
commandment of our God, and let it be done
[r]according to the Law. 4 Arise, for it is your
task, and we are with you; [s]be strong and do
it." 5 Then Ezra arose and made the leading
priests and Levites and all Israel [t]take an oath
that they would do as had been said. So they
took the oath.

6 Then Ezra withdrew [u]from before the
house of God and went to the [v]chamber of
[w]Jehohanan the son of [x]Eliashib, where he
spent the night,[2] neither [y]eating bread nor
drinking water, for he was mourning over
the faithlessness of the exiles. 7 And a proclamation was made throughout Judah and
Jerusalem to all the returned exiles that they
should assemble at Jerusalem, 8 and that if
anyone did not come within three days, by
order of the officials and the elders all his
property should be forfeited, and he himself
banned from the congregation of the exiles.

9 Then all the men of Judah and Benjamin
assembled at Jerusalem within the three days.
It was the ninth month, on the twentieth day
of the month. And all the people sat in the
open square before the house of God, trembling because of this matter and because of
the [z]heavy rain. 10 And Ezra the priest stood up
and said to them, "You have broken faith and
married foreign women, and so increased the
guilt of Israel. 11 Now then [a]make confession to
the LORD, the God of your fathers and do his
will. [b]Separate yourselves from the peoples of
the land and from the foreign wives." 12 Then
all the assembly answered with a loud voice,
"It is so; we must do as you have said. 13 But
the people are many, and it is a time of heavy
rain; we cannot stand in the open. Nor is this a
task for one day or for two, for we have greatly
transgressed in this matter. 14 Let our officials
stand for the whole assembly. Let all in our
cities who have taken foreign wives come [c]at
appointed times, and with them the elders
and judges of every city, [d]until the fierce wrath
of our God over this matter is turned away
from us." 15 Only Jonathan the son of Asahel
and Jahzeiah the son of Tikvah opposed this,
and [e]Meshullam and [f]Shabbethai the Levite
supported them.

16 Then the returned exiles did so. Ezra the
priest selected men,[3] heads of fathers' houses,
according to their fathers' houses, each of
them designated by name. On the first day of
the tenth month they sat down to examine the
matter; 17 and by the first day of the first month
they had come to the end of all the men who
had married foreign women.

Those Guilty of Intermarriage

18 Now there were found some of the sons of
the priests who had married foreign women:
Maaseiah, Eliezer, Jarib, and Gedaliah, some
of the sons of [g]Jeshua the son of Jozadak and
his brothers. 19 They [h]pledged themselves to
put away their wives, and their guilt offering
was [i]a ram of the flock for their guilt.[4] 20 [j]Of
the sons of Immer: Hanani and Zebadiah.
21 [k]Of the sons of Harim: Maaseiah, Elijah,

[1] Or *of the Lord* [2] Probable reading; Hebrew *where he went* [3] Syriac; Hebrew *And there were selected Ezra . . .* [4] Or *as their reparation*

2 [n] See ch. 9:2
3 [o] 2 Chr. 34:31 [p] [ver. 44] [q] ch. 9:4 [r] Deut. 7:2, 3
4 [s] 1 Chr. 28:10; [2 Chr. 19:11]
5 [t] Neh. 5:12; 13:25
6 [u] ver. 1 [v] ch. 8:29 [w] Neh. 12:22, 23 [x] Neh. 3:1 [y] Deut. 9:18
9 [z] [1 Sam. 12:18]
11 [a] [Josh. 7:19] [b] ver. 3
14 [c] Neh. 13:31 [d] 2 Chr. 29:10; 30:8; [Num. 25:4]
15 [e] ch. 8:16 [f] Neh. 11:16
18 [g] ch. 3:2
19 [h] See 2 Kgs. 10:15 [i] Lev. 6:6
20 [j] For ver. 20-43, see ch. 2:3-42
21 [k] [ver. 31]

In all this, Ezra tells the true story of all people—for, indeed, our guilt keeps increasing (10:10), and our sin deserves the "fierce wrath" of a holy God (v. 14; see Rom. 1:18; 3:23). The chapter ends with a sad rehearsal of the offenders and an organized but not happy (or even fully explained) separation from the foreign women who did not worship their God. Even the repentant obedience shown by the people seems inadequate; their covenant with a holy God at this point (Ezra 10:3) has a shallow ring, in contrast to God's unfailing covenant with such a sinful people.

But hope is not fully extinguished. For the welfare of the people lies not ultimately in them but in their God. Ezra 10:2 rings out deeply with the words, "even now there is hope for Israel in spite of this." Believers of all times can hold this hope, "even now," even when we continually fail, for God's promises will not fail. Abraham's seed of blessing for the world has appeared in Christ. Unlike the ill-advised intermarriage of Ezra 10, the perfect marriage will come finally, eternally, in Christ and his bride the church, cleansed by him and presented "to himself in splendor, without spot or wrinkle or any such thing . . . holy and without blemish" (Eph. 5:26–27).

Shemaiah, Jehiel, and Uzziah. 22 Of the sons
of Pashhur: Elioenai, Maaseiah, Ishmael,
Nethanel, Jozabad, and Elasah.
23 Of the Levites: Jozabad, Shimei, Kelaiah
(that is, Kelita), Pethahiah, Judah, and Eliezer.
24 Of the singers: Eliashib. Of the gatekeepers:
Shallum, Telem, and Uri.
25 And of Israel: of the sons of Parosh:
Ramiah, Izziah, Malchijah, Mijamin, Eleazar,
Hashabiah,[1] and Benaiah. 26 Of the sons of
Elam: Mattaniah, Zechariah, Jehiel, Abdi,
Jeremoth, and Elijah. 27 Of the sons of Zattu:
Elioenai, Eliashib, Mattaniah, Jeremoth,
Zabad, and Aziza. 28 Of the sons of Bebai were
Jehohanan, Hananiah, Zabbai, and Athlai. 29 Of
the sons of Bani were Meshullam, Malluch,
Adaiah, Jashub, Sheal, and Jeremoth. 30 Of the
sons of Pahath-moab: Adna, Chelal, Benaiah,
Maaseiah, Mattaniah, Bezalel, Binnui, and
Manasseh. 31 Of the [l]sons of Harim: Eliezer,
Isshijah, Malchijah, Shemaiah, Shimeon,
32 Benjamin, Malluch, and Shemariah. 33 Of
the sons of Hashum: Mattenai, Mattattah,
Zabad, Eliphelet, Jeremai, Manasseh, and
Shimei. 34 Of the sons of [m]Bani: Maadai,
Amram, Uel, 35 Benaiah, Bedeiah, Cheluhi,
36 Vaniah, Meremoth, Eliashib, 37 Mattaniah,
Mattenai, Jaasu. 38 Of the sons of Binnui:[2]
Shimei, 39 Shelemiah, Nathan, Adaiah,
40 Machnadebai, Shashai, Sharai, 41 Azarel,
Shelemiah, Shemariah, 42 Shallum, Amariah,
and Joseph. 43 Of the sons of Nebo: Jeiel,
Mattithiah, Zabad, Zebina, Jaddai, Joel, and
Benaiah. 44 All these had married foreign
women, and some of the women [n]had even
borne children.[3]

[1] Septuagint; Hebrew *Malchijah* [2] Septuagint; Hebrew *Bani, Binnui* [3] Or *and they put them away with their children*

31[l] ver. 21 **34**[m] [ver. 29] **44**[n] [ver. 3]

Introduction to Nehemiah

Author and Date

Nehemiah is the central figure in the book that bears his name. It contains some of his own records, but he is not the author of the entire book. The same author probably wrote Nehemiah and portions of Ezra. Nehemiah arrived in Jerusalem in 445 B.C., 13 years after Ezra arrived. He returned for a further visit sometime between 433 and 423 B.C. He may have made several journeys between Persian capitals and Jerusalem in this period of 20 years.

The Gospel in Nehemiah

Nehemiah continues Ezra's final glimpse of God's people mercifully reestablished in their land after the Babylonian exile and before the long, dark intertestamental period of waiting for a greater restoration and revelation of God's deliverance. Many have noted this book's lessons in leadership. Wise, prayerful Nehemiah leads a third group of exiles back to Jerusalem and there unites the people, amid surrounding opposition, to rebuild the city walls and to live as God's people according to his Word. But Nehemiah is about much more than leadership, however inspiring that leadership might be.

In the end, this book leaves us with a leader's failures more than his successes. Rather than focusing mainly on human faithfulness to God, the book of Nehemiah shows God's faithfulness to his unfaithful people. This divine faithfulness is rooted in God's covenant promises. As in Ezra, the remnant of God's people is here recorded carefully by genealogy: this is Abraham's seed, the people God promised to bless and through whom he would bless all the nations of the world. Perhaps at no point in their history had the prospects for this people looked bleaker, with a ruined city to rebuild, hateful enemies all around, and sin always threatening from within.

At this point of weakness, Nehemiah leads the people toward trust in a strong, trustworthy God. The wall rebuilt under Nehemiah's direction pictures not fearful retreat or isolation but rather God's protection of this people whom he has chosen, and through whom he will accomplish his redemptive plan for the human race. The book's climax comes not simply with the finished wall but with worship of the Lord God who has spoken and whose word will not fail. As we see this people rebuilding, so imperfectly and sustained only by God's faithful promises, we cannot help but look ahead to God's people today. For we too, though not working with physical stones, are "like living stones . . . being built up as a spiritual house." And Christ himself is the chief cornerstone (1 Pet. 2:5–6).

Nehemiah's people were waiting for the promised Savior, who now has come according to God's word of promise: "The Word became flesh and dwelt among us, and we have seen his glory, glory as of the only Son from the Father, full of grace and truth" (John 1:14). Even as we see and worship Jesus, God's people today also wait for him—for his second coming. As living stones in God's spiritual house, with Jesus as the cornerstone (Eph. 2:19–22), we also build imperfectly, battling enemies without and sin within. But we also look ahead to God's promise of that "holy city, new Jerusalem," the eternal dwelling of God with his people (Rev. 21:2–3). Safe in that city, around the throne of God and of the Lamb, "his servants will worship him" perfectly and forever (Rev. 22:1–3).

Outline

I. Nehemiah Returns to Jerusalem to Rebuild Its Walls (1:1–2:20)
  - A. Nehemiah learns of Jerusalem's dilapidation (1:1–11)
  - B. Nehemiah gains permission to return and inspects Jerusalem's walls (2:1–16)
  - C. First signs of opposition (2:17–20)

II. The Wall Is Built, Despite Difficulties (3:1–7:4)
  - A. The people work systematically on the walls (3:1–32)
  - B. Opposition intensifies, but the people continue watchfully (4:1–23)
  - C. Nehemiah deals with injustices in the community; Nehemiah's personal contribution to the project (5:1–19)
  - D. A conspiracy against Nehemiah, but the wall is finished (6:1–7:4)

III. A Record of Those Who Returned from Exile (7:5–73)

IV. The Reading of the Law, and Covenant Renewal (8:1–10:39)
  - A. The law is read (8:1–8)
  - B. The people are to be joyful (8:9–12)
  - C. The people keep the Feast of Booths (8:13–18)
  - D. A prayer of confession, penitence, and covenant commitment (9:1–38)
  - E. Signatories and specific commitments (10:1–39)

V. The Population of Jerusalem and the Villages; Priests and Levites (11:1–12:43)
  - A. Those who lived in Jerusalem and the villages of Judah (11:1–36)
  - B. High priests and leading Levites since the time of Zerubbabel (12:1–26)
  - C. Dedication of the walls (12:27–43)

VI. Nehemiah Deals with Problems in the Community (12:44–13:31)
  - A. The administration of offerings for the temple (12:44–47)
  - B. Ejection of Tobiah the Ammonite from the temple (13:1–9)
  - C. Dealing with neglect of the offerings (13:10–14)
  - D. Dealing with Sabbath breaking (13:15–22)
  - E. The problem of intermarriage again (13:23–29)
  - F. Summary of Nehemiah's temple reforms (13:30–31)

Nehemiah

Report from Jerusalem

1 The words of [a]Nehemiah the son of
Hacaliah.
Now it happened in the month of [b]Chislev,
[c]in the twentieth year, as I was in [d]Susa the citadel, 2 that [e]Hanani, one of my brothers, came
with certain men from Judah. And I asked
them concerning the Jews who escaped,
who had survived the exile, and concerning
Jerusalem. 3 And they said to me, "The remnant there in the province who had survived
the exile is in great trouble and [f]shame. [g]The
wall of Jerusalem is broken down, [h]and its
gates are destroyed by fire."

Nehemiah's Prayer

4 As soon as I heard these words I [i]sat down
and wept and mourned for days, and I continued fasting and praying before the [j]God of
heaven. 5 And I said, "O LORD God of heaven,
[k]the great and awesome God who keeps covenant and steadfast love with those who love
him and keep his commandments, 6 [l]let your
ear be attentive and your eyes open, to hear the
prayer of your servant that I now pray before
you day and night for the people of Israel your
servants, [m]confessing the sins of the people of
Israel, which we have sinned against you. Even
[n]I and my father's house have sinned. 7 [o]We
have acted very corruptly against you and have
not kept the commandments, the statutes, and
the rules [p]that you commanded your servant
Moses. 8 Remember the word that you commanded your servant Moses, saying, 'If you
are unfaithful, [q]I will scatter you among the
peoples, 9 [r]but if you return to me and keep my
commandments and do them, [s]though your
outcasts are in the uttermost parts of heaven,
from there I will gather them and bring them
[t]to the place that I have chosen, to make my
name dwell there.' 10 [u]They are your servants
and your people, whom you have redeemed

1:1–11 As the book of Ezra closed, so Nehemiah opens: with the prayer of a godly intercessor. Nehemiah is the last in a progression of Old Testament leaders who in their faithfulness *and* their imperfection teach us to depend on God's faithfulness, and who train us to look ahead to the true Intercessor who will represent God's people perfectly before his Father.

Nehemiah knows God's faithfulness in preserving a remnant and restoring them to Jerusalem, according to his promises (see note on Ezra 1:1–11). Yearning for his people, hearing of their city's broken down wall, Nehemiah leads the third group of returning exiles 13 years after Ezra's return. Before his action comes his prayer, which acknowledges a need for more than the physical protection of walls. His people need the faithful protection of their God.

Here and throughout the book, Nehemiah shows us how to pray: with reverence for such a great and awesome God (Neh. 1:5), knowledge of God's Word, along with confession of disobedience to that Word (vv. 6–10) and requests for mercy (v. 11). His prayer addresses a covenant-keeping God of steadfast love (v. 5; see Ex. 34:6; Deut. 7:9), a God who has "redeemed" his people (Neh. 1:10). Nehemiah is referring to God's redemption of the Israelites from Egypt, but that rescue pictures the greater One to come, not through the blood of a sacrificed lamb but through the death and resurrection of Christ, "our Passover lamb" (1 Cor. 5:7). The word "servant" (Neh. 1:6, 8, 10, 11) emphasizes this people's identity as belonging to this God, not to the earthly king Nehemiah serves. Addressing the Lord, Nehemiah calls the exiles "your people" (v. 10; see Ex. 6:7); they were chosen by God to receive his promises of blessing and to bear the seed of that blessing for all the peoples of the earth (Gen. 12:1–3).

Chapter 1

1 [a]ch. 10:1 [b]Zech. 7:1 [c]ch. 2:1 [d]Esth. 1:2, 5; 2:3, 5
2 [e]ch. 7:2
3 [f]ch. 2:17 [g]ch. 2:13; 2 Kgs. 25:10 [h]ch. 2:3, 13, 17
4 [i][Ezra 9:3] [j]ch. 2:4
5 [k]ch. 9:32; Dan. 9:4; [Deut. 7:21]
6 [l]Dan. 9:18; [1 Kgs. 8:29; 2 Chr. 6:40] [m]Ezra 10:1; Dan. 9:20 [n][Ps. 106:6]
7 [o]Dan. 9:5 [p]Deut. 28:15
8 [q]Lev. 26:33; Deut. 28:64; See Deut. 4:25-27
9 [r]Lev. 26:39-42; Deut. 4:29-31; 30:2, 3 [s]Deut. 30:4 [t]Deut. 12:5
10 [u]Deut. 9:29

by your great power and by your strong hand. 11 O Lord, [l]let your ear be attentive to the prayer of your servant, and to the prayer of your servants who delight to fear your name, and give success to your servant today, and grant him mercy in the sight of this man."

Now I was [v]cupbearer to the king.

Nehemiah Sent to Judah

2 In the month of Nisan, [w]in the twentieth year of King [x]Artaxerxes, when wine was before him, [y]I took up the wine and gave it to the king. Now I had not been sad in his presence. 2 And the king said to me, "Why is your face sad, seeing you are not sick? This is nothing but [z]sadness of the heart." Then I was very much afraid. 3 I said to the king, [a]"Let the king live forever! Why should not my face be sad, [b]when the city, the place of my fathers' graves, lies in ruins, and its gates have been destroyed by fire?" 4 Then the king said to me, "What are you requesting?" So I prayed [c]to the God of heaven. 5 And I said to the king, "If it pleases the king, and if your servant has found favor in your sight, that you send me to Judah, to the city of my fathers' graves, that I may rebuild it." 6 And the king said to me ([d]the queen sitting beside him), "How long will you be gone, and when will you return?" So it pleased the king to send me [e]when I had given him a time. 7 And I said to the king, "If it pleases the king, let letters be given me [f]to the governors of the province Beyond the River, that they may let me pass through until I come to Judah, 8 and a letter to Asaph, the keeper of the king's forest, that he may give me timber to make beams for the gates of [g]the fortress of the temple, and for the wall of the city, and for the house that I shall occupy." And the king granted me what I asked, [h]for the good hand of my God was upon me.

Nehemiah Inspects Jerusalem's Walls

9 Then I came to [i]the governors of the province Beyond the River and gave them the king's letters. Now the king had sent with me officers of the army and horsemen. 10 But when [j]Sanballat the Horonite and [k]Tobiah the Ammonite servant heard this, it displeased them greatly that someone had come to seek the welfare of the people of Israel.

11 [l]So I went to Jerusalem and was there three days. 12 Then I arose in the night, I and a few men with me. And I told no one what my God had put into my heart to do for Jerusalem. There was no animal with me but the one on which I rode. 13 I went out by night by [m]the Valley Gate to the Dragon Spring and to [n]the Dung Gate, and I inspected the walls of Jerusalem [o]that were broken down [p]and its gates that had been destroyed by fire. 14 Then I went on to [q]the Fountain Gate and to [r]the King's Pool, but there was no room for the animal that was under me to pass. 15 Then I went up in the night [s]by the valley and inspected the wall, and I turned back and entered by the Valley Gate, and so returned. 16 And the officials did not know where I had gone or what I was doing, and I had not yet told the Jews, the priests, the nobles, the officials, and the rest who were to do the work.

17 Then I said to them, "You see the trouble we are in, [t]how Jerusalem lies in ruins with its gates burned. Come, let us build the wall of Jerusalem, that we may no longer [u]suffer derision." 18 And I told them [v]of the hand of my

11 [l][See ver. 6 above] [v][ch. 2:1]
Chapter 2
1 [w]ch. 1:1; 5:14 [x]Ezra 7:1 [y][ch. 1:11]
2 [z]Prov. 15:13
3 [a]1 Kgs. 1:31; Dan. 2:4; 5:10; 6:21 [b]ver. 13, 17; ch. 1:3
4 [c]ver. 20; ch. 1:4, 5; Ezra 5:12; Dan. 2:18
6 [d][Ps. 45:9] [e][ch. 5:14; 13:6]
7 [f]Ezra 8:36
8 [g]ch. 7:2 [h]ver. 18; See Ezra 7:6
9 [i]Ezra 8:36
10 [j]ver. 19; ch. 4:1, 7; 6:1, 2, 5, 12, 14; 13:28 [k]ch. 13:4
11 [l]Ezra 8:32
13 [m]ch. 3:13; 2 Chr. 26:9 [n]ch. 3:13, 14; 12:31 [o]ch. 1:3 [p]ver. 3, 17
14 [q]ch. 3:15; 12:37 [r]2 Kgs. 20:20; [ch. 3:16; 2 Chr. 32:3, 30]

2:1–20 Nehemiah shows us how grace and works go together. The sovereign "God of heaven" (1:4; 2:4, 20) graciously directs events for his redemptive purposes. As he did for Joseph, Daniel, and Esther, he brings favor with kings: Artaxerxes grants Nehemiah's requests because of God's hand at work (vv. 8, 18; see Prov. 21:1). Knowing God's grace personally (as the first-person narrative demonstrates), Nehemiah responds with wholehearted service: praying continually, preparing carefully, rousing himself for his nighttime inspection, and wisely articulating his plan of action—even when surrounded by the threats and jeers of hostile enemies (Neh. 2:10, 19). Nehemiah's summary: God makes us prosper, and we his servants arise and build (v. 20). This is the pattern of the gospel: God delivers; we gratefully respond. God acts in marvelous mercy, and we respond accordingly out of hearts transformed by grace.

Constant focus on the city of Jerusalem highlights this place where God displayed his grace, dwelling with his people and making a way, through the temple sacrifices, for them to worship and live as his people. All this grace and favor prepared the way for God's greatest gift, his Son, "from [whose] fullness we have all received, grace upon grace" (John 1:16)—and to whom we respond by rising up and serving.

15 [s]2 Sam. 15:23 **17** [t]ver. 3, 13; ch. 1:3 [u]ch. 1:3; Ps. 44:13; 79:4; Jer. 24:9; Ezek. 5:14, 15; 22:4 **18** [v]ver. 8

God that had been upon me for good, and also
of the words that the king had spoken to me.
And they said, "Let us rise up and build." [w]So
they strengthened their hands for the good
work. 19 But when Sanballat the Horonite and
Tobiah the Ammonite servant and [x]Geshem
the Arab heard of it, [y]they jeered at us and
despised us and said, "What is this thing that
you are doing? [z]Are you rebelling against the
king?" 20 Then I replied to them, [a]"The God
of heaven will make us prosper, and we his
servants will arise and build, but you have no
portion or right or claim[1] in Jerusalem."

Rebuilding the Wall

3 Then [b]Eliashib the high priest rose up
with his brothers the priests, and they
built [c]the Sheep Gate. They consecrated it and
[d]set its doors. They consecrated it as far as the
Tower of the Hundred, as far as the [e]Tower
of Hananel. 2 And next to him [f]the men of
Jericho built. And next to them[2] Zaccur the
son of Imri built.

3 The sons of Hassenaah built [g]the Fish Gate.
[h]They laid its beams and [d]set its doors, its bolts,
and its bars. 4 And next to them [i]Meremoth
the son of Uriah, son of Hakkoz repaired. And
next to them [j]Meshullam the son of Berechiah,
son of Meshezabel repaired. And next to them
Zadok the son of Baana repaired. 5 And next to
them [k]the Tekoites repaired, but their nobles
would not stoop to serve their Lord.[3]

6 Joiada the son of Paseah and Meshullam
the son of Besodeiah [l]repaired the Gate of
Yeshanah.[4] [h]They laid its beams and [d]set its
doors, its bolts, and its bars. 7 And next to them
repaired Melatiah the Gibeonite and Jadon
the Meronothite, the men of Gibeon and of
Mizpah, the seat of [m]the governor of the province Beyond the River. 8 Next to them Uzziel
the son of Harhaiah, goldsmiths, repaired.
Next to him Hananiah, one of the perfumers,
repaired, and they restored Jerusalem as far
as [n]the Broad Wall. 9 Next to them Rephaiah
the son of Hur, [o]ruler of half the district of[5]
Jerusalem, repaired. 10 Next to them Jedaiah
the son of Harumaph repaired opposite his
house. And next to him Hattush the son of
Hashabneiah repaired. 11 Malchijah the son of
Harim and Hasshub the son of Pahath-moab
repaired another section and [p]the Tower of
the Ovens. 12 Next to him Shallum the son
of Hallohesh, [q]ruler of half the district of
Jerusalem, repaired, he and his daughters.

13 Hanun and the inhabitants of Zanoah
repaired [r]the Valley Gate. They rebuilt it
and [s]set its doors, its bolts, and its bars, and
repaired a thousand cubits[6] of the wall, as far
as [t]the Dung Gate.

14 Malchijah the son of Rechab, ruler of the
district of [u]Beth-haccherem, repaired [t]the
Dung Gate. He rebuilt it and [s]set its doors, its
bolts, and its bars.

15 And Shallum the son of Col-hozeh, ruler of
the district of Mizpah, repaired [v]the Fountain
Gate. He rebuilt it and covered it and [s]set its
doors, its bolts, and its bars. And he built the
wall of [w]the Pool of Shelah of [x]the king's garden, as far as [y]the stairs that go down from
the city of David. 16 After him Nehemiah the
son of Azbuk, ruler of half the district of
Beth-zur, repaired to a point opposite [z]the
tombs of David, as far as [a]the artificial pool,
and as far as the house of the mighty men.
17 After him the Levites repaired: Rehum the
son of Bani. Next to him Hashabiah, ruler

[1] Or *memorial* [2] Hebrew *him* [3] Or *lords* [4] Or *of the old city* [5] Or *foreman of half the portion assigned to*; also verses 12, 14, 15, 16, 17, 18
[6] A *cubit* was about 18 inches or 45 centimeters

3:1–32 What a picture of God's people building together! The many details create a vivid illustration that serves as a precursor of the apostle Paul's teaching that all the members of the body are necessary and must work as one (1 Cor. 12:12–26). Here too is enacted Paul's admonition to "count others more significant than yourselves" (Phil 2:3)—a concept not embraced by the Tekoite nobles (Neh. 3:5).

All such principles find their meaning in the promised Seed who came from these workers, the One who unifies a people from many nations, who humbled himself as a servant of all, even unto death: Jesus Christ. In short, in God's wise providence Jerusalem and its people quietly prepared the way for a new building project, a spiritual one that brought all God's saving purposes down through history into culmination at a single point: "the household of God, built on the foundation of the apostles and prophets, Christ Jesus himself being the cornerstone, in whom the whole structure, being joined together, grows into a holy temple in the Lord" (Eph. 2:19–21).

18 [w] [2 Sam. 2:7]
19 [x] [ch. 6:6] [y] ch. 4:1; Ps. 44:13 [z] ch. 6:6
20 [a] ver. 4

Chapter 3
1 [b] ver. 20, 21; ch. 13:4, 7, 28 [c] ver. 32; ch. 12:39; John 5:2 [d] ch. 6:1; 7:1 [e] Jer. 31:38; Zech. 14:10
2 [f] Ezra 2:34
3 [g] ch. 12:39; 2 Chr. 33:14; Zeph. 1:10 [h] [ch. 2:8] [d] [See ver. 1 above]
4 [i] ver. 21; Ezra 8:33 [j] ver. 30; Ezra 8:16
5 [k] ver. 27; [2 Sam. 14:2]
6 [l] ch. 12:39 [h] [See ver. 3 above] [d] [See ver. 1 above]
7 [m] ch. 2:7, 9
8 [n] ch. 12:38 **9** [o] ver. 12 **11** [p] ch. 12:38 **12** [q] ver. 9 **13** [r] ch. 2:13, 15; 2 Chr. 26:9 [s] See ver. 1 [t] ch. 2:13; 12:31 **14** [u] Jer. 6:1 [t] [See ver. 13 above] [s] [See ver. 13 above] **15** [v] ch. 2:14 [s] [See ver. 13 above] [w] [Luke 13:4; John 9:7, 11] [x] 2 Kgs. 25:4 [y] ch. 12:37 **16** [z] 1 Kgs. 2:10; Acts 2:29 [a] 2 Kgs. 20:20; Isa. 22:11

of half the district of Keilah, repaired for his
district. 18 After him their brothers repaired:
Bavvai the son of Henadad, ruler of half the
district of Keilah. 19 Next to him Ezer the son
of Jeshua, ruler of Mizpah, repaired another
section opposite the ascent to the armory at
[b]the buttress.[1] 20 After him Baruch the son of
Zabbai repaired another section from the buttress to the door of the house of [c]Eliashib the
high priest. 21 After him [d]Meremoth the son
of Uriah, son of Hakkoz repaired another section from the door of the house of Eliashib to
the end of the house of Eliashib. 22 After him
the priests, the men of [e]the surrounding area,
repaired. 23 After them Benjamin and Hasshub
repaired opposite their house. After them
Azariah the son of Maaseiah, son of Ananiah
repaired beside his own house. 24 After him
Binnui the son of Henadad repaired another
section, from the house of Azariah to the buttress 25 and to [f]the corner. Palal the son of Uzai
repaired opposite the buttress and the tower
projecting from the upper house of the king
at [g]the court of the guard. After him Pedaiah
the son of Parosh 26 [h]and the temple servants
living on [i]Ophel repaired to a point opposite
[j]the Water Gate on the east and the projecting tower. 27 After him [k]the Tekoites repaired
another section opposite the great projecting
tower as far as the wall of Ophel.
28 Above [l]the Horse Gate the priests repaired,
each one opposite his own house. 29 After them
Zadok the son of Immer repaired opposite his
own house. After him Shemaiah the son of
Shecaniah, the keeper of the East Gate, repaired.
30 After him Hananiah the son of Shelemiah
and Hanun the sixth son of Zalaph repaired
another section. After him [m]Meshullam the son
of Berechiah repaired opposite [n]his chamber.
31 After him Malchijah, one of the goldsmiths,
repaired as far as the house of the temple
servants and of the merchants, opposite the
Muster Gate,[2] and to the upper chamber of the
corner. 32 And between the upper chamber of
the corner and [o]the Sheep Gate the goldsmiths
and the merchants repaired.

Opposition to the Work

4 [3] Now when [q]Sanballat heard that we
were building the wall, he was angry
and greatly enraged, and he jeered at the
Jews. 2 And he said in the presence of his brothers and of the army of [r]Samaria, "What are
these feeble Jews doing? Will they restore it
for themselves?[4] Will they sacrifice? Will they
finish up in a day? Will they revive the stones
out of the heaps of rubbish, and burned ones
at that?" 3 [q]Tobiah the Ammonite was beside
him, and he said, "Yes, what they are building—[s]if a fox goes up on it he will break down
their stone wall!" 4 [t]Hear, O our God, for we are
despised. [u]Turn back their taunt on their own
heads and give them up to be plundered in a
land where they are captives. 5 [v]Do not cover
their guilt, and let not their sin be blotted out
from your sight, for they have provoked you to
anger in the presence of the builders.
6 So we built the wall. And all the wall was
joined together to half its height, for the people had a mind to work.
7 [5] But when [q]Sanballat and Tobiah and
the Arabs and the Ammonites and the
Ashdodites heard that the repairing of the
walls of Jerusalem was going forward and
that the breaches were beginning to be closed,
they were very angry. 8 [w]And they all plotted
together to come and fight against Jerusalem
and to cause confusion in it. 9 And we prayed

[1] Or *corner*; also verses 20, 24, 25 [2] Or *Hammiphkad Gate* [3] Ch 3:33 in Hebrew [4] Or *Will they commit themselves to God?* [5] Ch 4:1 in Hebrew

19[b] 2 Chr. 26:9
20[c] ver. 1
21[d] ver. 4
22[e] ch. 12:28
25[f] [2 Kgs. 14:13] [g] Jer. 32:2; 33:1; 37:21; 38:6, 13, 28; 39:14; [ch. 12:39]
26[h] ch. 11:21 [i] 2 Chr. 27:3 [j] ch. 8:1, 3, 16; 12:37
27[k] ver. 5
28[l] See 2 Chr. 23:15
30[m] ver. 4 [n] [ch. 12:44; 13:7]
32[o] See ver. 1
Chapter 4
1[q] ver. 7; ch. 2:10, 19
2[r] 1 Kgs. 16:24
3[q] [See ver. 1 above]

4:1–23 God's people were "despised" (v. 4), even as God's Son would be despised and rejected (Isa. 53:3; 1 Pet. 2:23). Surrounding peoples "all plotted together" (Neh. 4:8), even as earthly kings have always (vainly) plotted against the Lord's anointed (Ps. 2:1–2). The contours of the story remain, and the weapons of God's people remain: prayer (Neh. 4:4–5, 9) and obedient action (vv. 6, 9, 15–23). But it is all founded on the bedrock of trust in the Lord: "Our God will fight for us" (v. 20; see Ex. 14:14; Deut. 1:30).

The exhortation not to fear (Neh. 4:14) applies to us today, as does the dynamic example of trust and obedience: they prayed and set a guard (v. 9). Nehemiah sums it up: "remember the Lord" *and* "fight" (v. 14). Our God *has* fought for us, in Christ, and has won the victory. As we battle on as his people to the end, often despised and rejected, we must always remember our great and awesome Lord and make every effort to guard and strengthen the household of God.

[s] [Lam. 5:18] 4[t] Ps. 123:3, 4 [u] Ps. 79:12 5[v] Ps. 69:27, 28; 109:14, 15; Jer. 18:23 7[q] [See ver. 1 above] 8[w] See Ps. 83:3-5

to our God and set a guard as a protection
against them day and night.

10 In Judah it was said,[1] "The strength of those
who bear the burdens is failing. There is too
much rubble. By ourselves we will not be able
to rebuild the wall." 11 And our enemies said,
"They will not know or see till we come among
them and kill them and stop the work." 12 At
that time the Jews who lived near them came
from all directions and said to us ten times,
"You must return to us."[2] 13 So in the lowest
parts of the space behind the wall, in open
places, I stationed the people by their clans,
with their swords, their spears, and their bows.
14 And I looked and arose and said to the nobles
and to the officials and to the rest of the people, [x]"Do not be afraid of them. Remember the
Lord, [y]who is great and awesome, [z]and fight
for your brothers, your sons, your daughters,
your wives, and your homes."

The Work Resumes

15 When our enemies heard that it was
known to us [a]and that God had frustrated
their plan, we all returned to the wall, each
to his work. 16 From that day on, half of my
servants worked on construction, and half
held the spears, shields, bows, and [b]coats of
mail. And the leaders stood behind the whole
house of Judah, 17 who were building on the
wall. Those who carried burdens were loaded
in such a way that each labored on the work
with one hand and held his weapon with
the other. 18 And each of the builders had his
sword strapped at his side while he built. The
man who sounded the trumpet was beside
me. 19 And I said to [c]the nobles and to the
officials and to the rest of the people, "The
work is great and widely spread, and we are
separated on the wall, far from one another.
20 In the place where you hear the sound of
the trumpet, rally to us there. [d]Our God will
fight for us."

21 So we labored at the work, and half of them
held the spears from the break of dawn until
the stars came out. 22 I also said to the people at
that time, "Let every man and his servant pass
the night within Jerusalem, that they may be
a guard for us by night and may labor by day."
23 So neither I nor my brothers nor my servants
nor the men of the guard who followed me,
none of us took off our clothes; [e]each kept his
weapon at his right hand.[3]

Nehemiah Stops Oppression of the Poor

5 Now there arose [f]a great outcry of the
people and of their wives [g]against their
Jewish brothers. 2 For there were those who
said, "With our sons and our daughters, we are
many. So let us get grain, that we may eat and
keep alive." 3 There were also those who said,
"We are mortgaging our fields, our vineyards,
and our houses to get grain because of the
famine." 4 And there were those who said, "We
have borrowed money for [h]the king's tax on
our fields and our vineyards. 5 Now [i]our flesh
is as the flesh of our brothers, our children are
as their children. Yet [j]we are forcing our sons
and our daughters to be slaves, and some of
our daughters have already been enslaved, but
it is not in our power to help it, for other men
have our fields and our vineyards."

6 I was very angry when I heard [f]their outcry
and these words. 7 I took counsel with myself,
and I brought charges against the nobles and
the officials. I said to them, [k]"You are exacting
interest, each from his brother." And I held
a great assembly against them 8 and said to

[1] Hebrew *Judah said* [2] The meaning of the Hebrew is uncertain [3] Probable reading; Hebrew *each his weapon the water*

5:1–19 These people obviously hadn't read 1 John 3–4, about showing God's love by loving one another! They had not seen Jesus lay down his life for us, showing us how to lay down our lives for our brothers (1 John 3:16). Yet when Nehemiah confronts their mistreatment of the poor, they respond willingly, reflecting the character of the God on whose grace they (and we) depend (Neh. 5:13).

Throughout history, God has given his Word and called his people to follow him by faith, according to that Word. The call is not just to good behavior, but to walk in "the fear of God" (vv. 9, 15), to live in relationship with our "great and awesome" God (1:5; 4:14). Nehemiah shows the fruit of this relationship not only in his refusal to lord it over those he governs (5:14–18) but also in his personal communion with God (v. 19). Nehemiah understood the great commands: "love the Lord your God with all your heart and with all your soul and with all your mind," and "love your neighbor as yourself" (Matt. 22:35–40). Nehemiah's leadership would one day be filled out and perfected in Jesus, who supremely refused to lord it over others, despite his right to do so as Lord of the cosmos (Mark 10:42–45).

14[x] [Num. 14:9]; Deut. 1:29 [y] Deut. 7:21; 10:17 [z] 2 Sam. 10:12
15[a] [Job 5:12]
16[b] 2 Chr. 26:14
19[c] ver. 14
20[d] Ex. 14:14, 25; Deut. 1:30; 3:22; 20:4; Josh. 23:10
23[e] ver. 17

Chapter 5
1[f] [Ex. 3:9; Isa. 5:7] [g] Lev. 25:35, 37; Deut. 15:7
4[h] Ezra 4:13, 20; 7:24
5[i] Isa. 58:7; [Gen. 29:14] [j] [Ex. 21:7; Lev. 25:39; 2 Kgs. 4:1]
6[f] [See ver. 1 above]
7[k] [Ex. 22:25; Lev. 25:36; Ps. 15:5; Ezek. 22:12]

them, "We, as far as we are able, [l]have bought
back our Jewish brothers who have been sold
to the nations, but you even sell your brothers that they may be sold to us!" They were
silent and could not find a word to say. 9 So
I said, "The thing that you are doing is not
good. Ought you not to walk [m]in the fear of
our God [n]to prevent the taunts of the nations
our enemies? 10 Moreover, I and my brothers
and my servants are lending them money and
grain. Let us abandon this exacting of interest. 11 Return to them this very day their fields,
their vineyards, their olive orchards, and their
houses, and the percentage of money, grain,
wine, and oil that you have been exacting from
them." 12 Then they said, "We will restore these
and [o]require nothing from them. We will do
as you say." And I called the priests and [p]made
them swear [q]to do as they had promised.
13 [r]I also shook out the fold[1] of my garment
and said, "So may God shake out every man
from his house and from his labor who does
not keep this promise. So may he be shaken
out and emptied." [s]And all the assembly said
"Amen" and praised the LORD. And the people
did as they had promised.

Nehemiah's Generosity

14 Moreover, from the time that I was
appointed to be their governor in the land of
Judah, from [t]the twentieth year to [u]the thirty-
second year of Artaxerxes the king, twelve
years, [v]neither I nor my brothers ate the food
allowance of the governor. 15 The former governors who were before me laid heavy burdens
on the people and took from them for their
daily ration[2] forty shekels[3] of silver. Even their
servants lorded it over the people. But I did
not do so, [w]because of the fear of God. 16 I also
persevered in the work on this wall, and we
acquired no land, and all my servants were
gathered there for the work. 17 Moreover, there
were [x]at my table 150 men, Jews and officials,
besides those who came to us from the nations
that were around us. 18 [y]Now what was prepared at my expense[4] for each day was one ox
and six choice sheep and birds, and every ten
days all kinds of wine in abundance. Yet for all
this [v]I did not demand the food allowance of
the governor, because the service was too heavy
on this people. 19 [z]Remember for my good,
O my God, all that I have done for this people.

Conspiracy Against Nehemiah

6 Now when [a]Sanballat and Tobiah and
[b]Geshem the Arab and the rest of our
enemies heard that I had built the wall and
that there was no breach left in it ([c]although
up to that time I had not set up the doors in
the gates), 2 Sanballat and Geshem sent to
me, saying, "Come and let us meet together
at Hakkephirim in the plain of [d]Ono." But they
intended to do me harm. 3 And I sent messengers to them, saying, "I am doing a great work
and I cannot come down. Why should the
work stop while I leave it and come down to
you?" 4 And they sent to me four times in this
way, and I answered them in the same manner.
5 In the same way Sanballat for the fifth time
sent his servant to me with an open letter in
his hand. 6 In it was written, "It is reported
among the nations, and Geshem[5] also says it,
that you and [e]the Jews intend to rebel; that is
why you are building the wall. And according to these reports you wish to become their
king. 7 And you have also set up prophets to
proclaim concerning you in Jerusalem, 'There
is a king in Judah.' And now the king will hear

[1] Hebrew *bosom* [2] Compare Vulgate; Hebrew *took from them with food and wine afterward* [3] A *shekel* was about 2/5 ounce or 11 grams
[4] Or *prepared for me* [5] Hebrew *Gashmu*

8 [l]Lev. 25:48, 49
9 [m]Lev. 25:36 [n]ch. 4:4; [2 Sam. 12:14]
12 [o][ch. 10:31] [p]Ezra 10:5 [q][Jer. 34:8, 9]
13 [r][Acts 18:6] [s]ch. 8:6; [Deut. 27:15]; 1 Chr. 16:36; Ps. 106:48
14 [t]ch. 2:1 [u]ch. 13:6 [v][2 Thess. 3:8]
15 [w]ver. 9
17 [x][2 Sam. 9:7, 10]; 1 Kgs. 18:19
18 [y][1 Kgs. 4:22, 23] [v][See ver. 14 above]
19 [z]ch. 13:14, 22, 31
Chapter 6
1 [a]ch. 2:10, 19; 4:1, 7 [b][ver. 6] [c][ch. 3:1, 3]
2 [d]1 Chr. 8:12
6 [e]ch. 2:19

6:5–7 Sanballat's charge about Nehemiah planning to rebel is false. But the charge that Israelite prophets had proclaimed a king in Judah was essentially true, according to God's covenant with David, wherein God promised that from David would come a king whose throne God would establish forever (2 Sam. 7:12–17). God's redemptive purposes are always greater than the world can grasp. Sanballat spoke more truth than he intended. It would not be the last time unbelieving leaders would do so (cf. John 11:49–52).

6:9–19 Fear is our enemies' great weapon. Nehemiah recognizes their aim to frighten him (vv. 9, 13, 14, 19). His words from 4:14 echo here in chapter 6, calling God's people not to fear but to remember their God.

One of the key strategies of faith is to tackle fear not by belittling the fear or wishing it away but by taking our eyes off of that which makes us afraid and looking to God. For us today, Jesus' words echo: "Do not fear, only believe" (Mark 5:36).

of these reports. So now come and let us take
counsel together." 8 Then I sent to him, saying, "No such things as you say have been
done, for you are inventing them out of your
own mind." 9 For they all wanted to frighten
us, thinking, "Their hands will drop from
the work, and it will not be done." But now,
O God,[1] strengthen my hands.

10 Now when I went into the house of Shemaiah the son of Delaiah, son of Mehetabel,
who was [f]confined to his home, he said, "Let us
meet together in the house of God, within the
temple. Let us close the doors of the temple, for
they are coming to kill you. They are coming
to kill you by night." 11 But I said, "Should such
a man as I run away? And what man such as
I could go into the temple and live?[2] I will not
go in." 12 And I understood and saw that God
had not sent him, [g]but he had pronounced
the prophecy against me because Tobiah and
Sanballat had hired him. 13 For this purpose
he was hired, that I should be afraid and act in
this way and sin, and so they could give me a
bad name in order to taunt me. 14 [h]Remember
Tobiah and Sanballat, O my God, according to
these things that they did, and also [i]the prophetess Noadiah and the rest of the prophets who
wanted to make me afraid.

The Wall Is Finished

15 So the wall was finished on the twenty-
fifth day of the month Elul, in fifty-two days.
16 And [j]when all our enemies heard of it, all the
nations around us were afraid and fell greatly
in their own esteem, [k]for they perceived that
this work had been accomplished with the
help of our God. 17 Moreover, in those days the
nobles of Judah sent many letters to Tobiah,
and Tobiah's letters came to them. 18 For many
in Judah were bound by oath to him, because
he was the son-in-law of Shecaniah the son of
[l]Arah: and his son Jehohanan had taken the
daughter of [m]Meshullam the son of Berechiah
as his wife. 19 Also they spoke of his good deeds
in my presence and reported my words to him.
And Tobiah sent letters to make me afraid.

7 Now when the wall had been built [n]and
I had set up the doors, and the gatekeepers, the singers, and the Levites had been
appointed, 2 I gave [o]my brother Hanani and
Hananiah the governor of [p]the castle charge
over Jerusalem, for he was [q]a more faithful
and God-fearing man than many. 3 And I said
to them, "Let not the gates of Jerusalem be
opened until the sun is hot. And while they are
still standing guard, let them shut and bar the
doors. Appoint guards from among the inhabitants of Jerusalem, some at their guard posts
and some in front of their own homes." 4 The
city was wide and large, but the people within
it were few, and no houses had been rebuilt.

Lists of Returned Exiles

5 Then my God put it into my heart to assemble the nobles and the officials and the people
to be enrolled by genealogy. And I found the
book of the genealogy of [r]those who came up
at the first, and I found written in it:
6 [s]These were the people of the province who
came up out of the captivity of those exiles

[1] Hebrew lacks *O God* [2] Or *would go into the temple to save his life*

The Father's wise ordering of all things in the world and in our own lives is of great comfort. We can bank on God's goodness, for we have seen him send his only Son to die on our behalf. He has done the hard thing; he will surely care for us in the little things (Rom. 5:9–10).

Ironically, when the wall is finished despite the opponents' plots, the surrounding nations are afraid, seeing God's help for his people (Neh. 6:16). Encouragement not to fear comes all the more powerfully through Nehemiah's own narrative, continually interspersed with his "live" prayers to the Lord, whom he always remembers (vv. 9, 14). Living without fear means living in personal relationship with a God who loves his people so much that he has made a way for us to come confidently to him—now not dependent on priests or temple rituals but through Jesus Christ our Savior (Heb. 10:19–22).

7:1–73 Genealogy is crucial for these descendants of Abraham: God plants in Nehemiah's heart the task of tracing the promised seed (v. 5). (See note on Ezra 2:2–70.) This is a reminder that God's grace to his people travels down through history in our space and time. God's work of redemption is not abstract or esoteric or difficult to perceive. His mighty acts of deliverance have always taken place in our space-and-time history. This is supremely the case with the coming of Jesus Christ—a certain man born in a certain place at a certain time.

10 [f][Jer. 36:5]
12 [g][Ezek. 13:17, 22]
14 [h]ch. 13:29 [i][Ezek. 13:17]
16 [j]ch. 2:10; 4:1, 7 [k][Ps. 126:2]
18 [l]Ezra 2:5 [m]Ezra 8:16

Chapter 7

1 [n][ch. 6:1]
2 [o]ch. 1:2 [p]ch. 2:8 [q][ch. 13:13]
5 [r]Ezra 1:11
6 [s]For ver. 6-73, see Ezra 2:1-70

whom Nebuchadnezzar the king of Babylon
had carried into exile. They returned to
Jerusalem and Judah, each to his town. 7 They
came with Zerubbabel, Jeshua, Nehemiah,
[t]Azariah, Raamiah, Nahamani, Mordecai,
Bilshan, Mispereth, Bigvai, Nehum, Baanah.

The number of the men of the people of
Israel: 8 the sons of Parosh, 2,172. 9 The sons
of Shephatiah, 372. 10 The sons of Arah, [u]652.
11 The sons of Pahath-moab, namely the sons
of Jeshua and Joab, 2,818. 12 The sons of [v]Elam,
1,254. 13 The sons of Zattu, 845. 14 The sons of
Zaccai, 760. 15 The sons of [w]Binnui, 648. 16 The
sons of Bebai, 628. 17 The sons of Azgad, 2,322.
18 The sons of Adonikam, 667. 19 The sons of
Bigvai, 2,067. 20 The sons of Adin, 655. 21 The
sons of Ater, namely of Hezekiah, 98. 22 The
sons of Hashum, 328. 23 The sons of [x]Bezai,
324. 24 The sons of Hariph, 112. 25 The sons
of [y]Gibeon, 95. 26 The men of Bethlehem and
Netophah, 188. 27 The men of Anathoth, 128.
28 The men [z]of Beth-azmaveth, 42. 29 The men
of [a]Kiriath-jearim, Chephirah, and Beeroth,
743. 30 The men of Ramah and Geba, 621.
31 The men of Michmas, 122. 32 The men of
Bethel and Ai, 123. 33 The men of the other
Nebo, 52. 34 The sons of [b]the other Elam,
1,254. 35 The sons of Harim, 320. 36 The sons
of Jericho, 345. 37 The sons of Lod, Hadid, and
Ono, 721. 38 The sons of Senaah, 3,930.

39 The priests: the sons of [c]Jedaiah, namely
the house of Jeshua, 973. 40 The sons of
[d]Immer, 1,052. 41 The sons of [e]Pashhur, 1,247.
42 The sons of [f]Harim, 1,017.

43 The Levites: the sons of Jeshua, namely of
Kadmiel of the sons of [g]Hodevah, 74. 44 The
singers: the sons of Asaph, 148. 45 The gatekeepers: the sons of Shallum, the sons of Ater,
the sons of Talmon, the sons of Akkub, the
sons of Hatita, the sons of Shobai, 138.

46 The temple servants: the sons of Ziha,
the sons of Hasupha, the sons of Tabbaoth,
47 the sons of Keros, the sons of [h]Sia, the sons
of Padon, 48 the sons of Lebana, the sons of
[i]Hagaba, the sons of [j]Shalmai, 49 the sons of
Hanan, the sons of Giddel, the sons of Gahar,
50 the sons of Reaiah, the sons of Rezin, the
sons of Nekoda, 51 the sons of Gazzam, the
sons of Uzza, the sons of Paseah, 52 the sons
of Besai, the sons of Meunim, the sons of
[j]Nephushesim, 53 the sons of Bakbuk, the
sons of Hakupha, the sons of Harhur, 54 the
sons of [k]Bazlith, the sons of Mehida, the sons
of Harsha, 55 the sons of Barkos, the sons
of Sisera, the sons of Temah, 56 the sons of
Neziah, the sons of Hatipha.

57 The sons of Solomon's servants: the sons
of Sotai, the sons of Sophereth, the sons of
[l]Perida, 58 the sons of Jaala, the sons of Darkon,
the sons of Giddel, 59 the sons of Shephatiah,
the sons of Hattil, the sons of Pochereth-
hazzebaim, the sons of [m]Amon.

60 All the temple servants and the sons of
Solomon's servants were 392.

61 [n]The following were those who came up
from Tel-melah, Tel-harsha, Cherub, [o]Addon,
and Immer, but they could not prove their
fathers' houses nor their descent, whether
they belonged to Israel: 62 the sons of Delaiah,
the sons of Tobiah, the sons of Nekoda, 642.
63 Also, of the priests: the sons of Hobaiah, the
sons of Hakkoz, the sons of Barzillai (who
had taken a wife of the daughters of Barzillai
the Gileadite and was called by their name).
64 These sought their registration among
those enrolled in the genealogies, but it was
not found there, so they were excluded from
the priesthood as unclean. 65 [p]The [q]governor
told them that they were not to partake of the
most holy food until a priest with Urim and
Thummim should arise.

Totals of People and Gifts

66 The whole assembly together was 42,360,
67 besides their male and female servants, of
whom there were 7,337. And they had 245
singers, male and female. 68 Their horses were
736, their mules 245,[1] 69 their camels 435, and
their donkeys 6,720.

70 Now some of the heads of fathers' houses
gave to the work. The [q]governor gave to the
treasury 1,000 darics[2] of gold, 50 basins, 30
priests' garments and 500 minas[3] of silver.[4]
71 And some of the heads of fathers' houses
gave into the treasury of the work 20,000 darics of gold and 2,200 minas of silver. 72 [r]And
what the rest of the people gave was 20,000
darics of gold, 2,000 minas of silver, and 67
priests' garments.

73 So the priests, the Levites, the gatekeepers,

[1] Compare Ezra 2:66 and the margins of some Hebrew manuscripts; Hebrew lacks *Their horses . . . 245* [2] A *daric* was a coin weighing about 1/4 ounce or 8.5 grams [3] A *mina* was about 1 1/4 pounds or 0.6 kilogram [4] Probable reading; Hebrew lacks *minas of silver*

7[t] [Ezra 2:2] **10**[u] [Ezra 2:5] **12**[v] [ver. 34] **15**[w] [Ezra 2:10] **23**[x] [Ezra 2:17] **25**[y] [Ezra 2:20] **28**[z] [Ezra 2:24] **29**[a] [Ezra 2:25] **34**[b] [ver. 12] **39**[c] 1 Chr. 9:10; 24:7 **40**[d] 1 Chr. 9:12; 24:14 **41**[e] 1 Chr. 9:12 **42**[f] 1 Chr. 24:8 **43**[g] [Ezra 2:40; 3:9] **47**[h] [Ezra 2:44] **48**[i] [Ezra 2:46] **52**[j] [Ezra 2:50] **54**[k] [Ezra 2:52] **57**[l] [Ezra 2:55] **59**[m] [Ezra 2:57] **61**[n] Ezra 2:59 [o] [Ezra 2:59] **65**[p] Ezra 2:63 [q] ch. 8:9; 10:1 **70**[q] [See ver. 65 above] **72**[r] [Ezra 2:69]

the singers, some of the people, the temple
servants, and all Israel, lived in their towns.
[s]And when the seventh month had come, the
people of Israel were in their towns.

Ezra Reads the Law

8 And all the people gathered as one man
into the square before [t]the Water Gate. And
they told [u]Ezra the scribe to bring the Book
of the Law of Moses that the LORD had commanded Israel. 2 So Ezra the priest [v]brought
the Law before the assembly, both men and
women and all who could understand what
they heard, [w]on the first day of the seventh
month. 3 [x]And he read from it facing the square
before the Water Gate from early morning
until midday, in the presence of the men and
the women and those who could understand.
And the ears of all the people were attentive
to the Book of the Law. 4 And Ezra the scribe
stood on a wooden platform that they had
made for the purpose. And beside him stood
Mattithiah, Shema, Anaiah, Uriah, Hilkiah,
and Maaseiah on his right hand, and Pedaiah,
Mishael, Malchijah, Hashum, Hashbaddanah,
Zechariah, and Meshullam on his left hand.
5 And Ezra opened the book in the sight of all
the people, for he was above all the people,
and as he opened it all the people stood. 6 And
Ezra blessed the LORD, the great God, and all
the people answered, [y]"Amen, Amen," [z]lifting
up their hands. [a]And they bowed their heads
and worshiped the LORD with their faces to
the ground. 7 [b]Also Jeshua, Bani, Sherebiah,
Jamin, Akkub, Shabbethai, Hodiah, Maaseiah,
Kelita, Azariah, Jozabad, Hanan, Pelaiah, the
Levites,[1] [c]helped the people to understand
the Law, [d]while the people remained in their
places. 8 They read from the book, from the
Law of God, clearly,[2] and they gave the sense,
so that the people understood the reading.

This Day Is Holy

9 And Nehemiah, who was [e]the governor,
and Ezra [f]the priest and scribe, and the Levites
who taught the people said to all the people,
[g]"This day is holy to the LORD your God; [h]do
not mourn or weep." For all the people wept
as they heard the words of the Law. 10 Then
he said to them, "Go your way. Eat the fat and
drink sweet wine and [i]send portions to anyone
who has nothing ready, for this day is holy to
our Lord. And do not be grieved, for the joy
of the LORD is your strength." 11 So the Levites
calmed all the people, saying, "Be quiet, for
this day is holy; do not be grieved." 12 And all
the people went their way to eat and drink and
to send portions and to make great rejoicing,
because [j]they had understood the words that
were declared to them.

Feast of Booths Celebrated

13 On the second day the heads of fathers'
houses of all the people, with the priests and
the Levites, came together to Ezra the scribe
in order to study the words of the Law. 14 And
they found it written in the Law that the LORD
had commanded by Moses [k]that the people of
Israel should dwell in booths[3] during the feast
of the seventh month, 15 and that they should

[1] Vulgate; Hebrew *and the Levites* [2] Or *with interpretation*, or *paragraph by paragraph* [3] Or *temporary shelters*

8:1–18 The focus of this gathering is the Book of the Law, God's Word delivered by Moses. Especially through Ezra's leadership (see note on Ezra 7:1–28), God's people were reestablished as a people of the book. This meant more to them now than ever, for the visible greatness of impressive institutions such as the former temple had disappeared. Only the promises of God remained. The returned exiles played a great part in compiling the remaining Old Testament books. From this vivid scene we learn much about honoring God's Word (Neh. 8:1–5) and about how that Word speaks to all ("men and women and all who could understand"; vv. 2, 3). *Understanding* God's Word is emphasized (vv. 2, 3, 7, 8, 12), as the people are instructed by priests and Levites. They not only understand; they obey (vv. 13–17). And they rejoice (vv. 10, 12, 17).

Believers today are the recipients of this same, now-complete book passed on and preserved by God's people, a book whose power comes from the God who graciously breathed out its words to give us guidance, safety, and hope on our journey through a fallen world (Ps. 19:7–14; 2 Tim. 3:16). In this Word we are enabled to understand the character of and to actually meet the Word made flesh, the One who was there from the beginning, who was promised, and who came, according to God's Word (John 1:1–2, 14).

Receiving this Word, both inscripturated and incarnated, brings us, far more than Israel in Nehemiah 8, to rejoice.

73 [s]Ezra 3:1
Chapter 8
1 [t]ch. 3:26 [u]See Ezra 7:6
2 [v]See Deut. 31:11 [w]Lev. 23:24
3 [x]See ch. 13:1
6 [y]See ch. 5:13 [z]Ps. 134:2; Lam. 3:41; [1 Tim. 2:8] [a]See 2 Chr. 20:18
7 [b][ch. 9:4] [c]See 2 Chr. 35:3 [d]ch. 9:3
9 [e]ch. 7:65, 70; 10:1; Ezra 2:63 [f]ch. 12:26 [g]ver. 2; Lev. 23:24; Num. 29:1 [h][Eccles. 3:4]
10 [i]Esth. 9:19, 22
12 [j]ver. 7, 8
14 [k]Lev. 23:34, 40, 42

proclaim it and [l]publish it in all their towns
and [m]in Jerusalem, "Go out to the hills and
bring [n]branches of olive, wild olive, myrtle,
palm, and other leafy trees to make booths,
as it is written." 16 So the people went out and
brought them and made booths for themselves, each [o]on his roof, and in their courts
and in the courts of the house of God, and in
the square at [p]the Water Gate and in the square
at [q]the Gate of Ephraim. 17 And all the assembly of those who had returned from the captivity made booths and lived in the booths,
for from the days of Jeshua the son of Nun to
that day [r]the people of Israel had not done so.
And there was [s]very great rejoicing. 18 And day
by day, from the first day to the last day, [t]he
read from the Book of the Law of God. They
kept the feast seven days, and [u]on the eighth
day there was a solemn assembly, according
to the rule.

The People of Israel Confess Their Sin

9 Now on the twenty-fourth day of [v]this
month the people of Israel were assembled [w]with fasting [x]and in sackcloth, [y]and
with earth on their heads. 2 [z]And the Israelites[1]
separated themselves from all foreigners and
stood and confessed their sins and the iniquities of their fathers. 3 [a]And they stood up
in their place and read from the Book of the
Law of the LORD their God for a quarter of
the day; for another quarter of it they made
confession and worshiped the LORD their God.
4 On the stairs of the Levites stood [b]Jeshua,
Bani, Kadmiel, Shebaniah, Bunni, Sherebiah,
Bani, and Chenani; and they cried with a
loud voice to the LORD their God. 5 Then the
Levites, Jeshua, Kadmiel, Bani, Hashabneiah,
Sherebiah, Hodiah, Shebaniah, and Pethahiah,
said, "Stand up and bless the LORD your God
from everlasting to everlasting. [c]Blessed be
your glorious name, which is exalted above
all blessing and praise.

6[2] [d]"You are the LORD, you alone. [e]You have
made heaven, [f]the heaven of heavens, [g]with all
their host, [e]the earth and all that is on it, the
seas and all that is in them; [h]and you preserve
all of them; and the host of heaven worships
you. 7 You are the LORD, the God [i]who chose
Abram and brought him out of [j]Ur of the
Chaldeans [k]and gave him the name Abraham.
8 [l]You found his heart faithful before you, [m]and
made with him the covenant to give to his offspring [n]the land of the Canaanite, the Hittite,
the Amorite, the Perizzite, the Jebusite, and
the Girgashite. [o]And you have kept your promise, for you are righteous.

9 [p]"And you saw the affliction of our fathers
in Egypt and heard [q]their cry at the Red Sea,
10 [r]and performed signs and wonders against
Pharaoh and all his servants and all the people
of his land, for you knew that [s]they acted arrogantly against our fathers. And [t]you made a
name for yourself, as it is to this day. 11 [u]And
you divided the sea before them, so that they
went through the midst of the sea on dry land,
and you cast their pursuers into the depths,
[v]as a stone into mighty waters. 12 By [w]a pillar of cloud you led them in the day, and by
a pillar of fire in the night to light for them
the way in which they should go. 13 [x]You came

[1] Hebrew *the offspring of Israel* [2] Septuagint adds *And Ezra said*

15 [l]Lev. 23:4 [m]Deut. 16:16 [n][Lev. 23:40]
16 [o]See 1 Sam. 9:25 [p]ver. 1, 3; ch. 3:26 [q]ch. 12:39; 2 Kgs. 14:13; 2 Chr. 25:23
17 [r][1 Kgs. 8:2; 2 Chr. 7:9; 8:13; Ezra 3:4] [s][2 Chr. 30:21]
18 [t]Deut. 31:10, 11 [u]Lev. 23:36; Num. 29:35

Chapter 9

1 [v][ch. 8:2] [w][1 Sam. 7:6] [x]See 2 Sam. 3:31 [y]See Josh. 7:6
2 [z]ch. 10:28; 13:3, 30; [Ezra 6:21; 10:11]
3 [a]ch. 8:7, 8
4 [b][ch. 8:7]
5 [c][1 Chr. 29:13]
6 [d]See 2 Kgs. 19:15 [e]See Gen. 1:1 [f]See Deut. 10:14 [g]See Gen. 2:1 [h][Ps. 36:6]
7 [i]See Gen. 11:31 [j]Gen. 11:31 [k]Gen. 17:5
8 [l]Gen. 15:6 [m]Gen. 12:7; 15:18; 17:7-9 [n]See Ex. 13:5 [o][Josh. 23:14] **9** [p]Ex. 3:7 [q]Ex. 14:10 **10** [r]See Ex. 7–14 [s]Ex. 18:11 [t]Isa. 63:12, 14; Jer. 32:20; Dan. 9:15; [Ex. 9:16] **11** [u]Ex. 14:21, 22, 27, 28; Ps. 78:13 [v]Ex. 15:5, 10 **12** [w]ver. 19; Ex. 13:21, 22; Num. 14:14; 1 Cor. 10:1 **13** [x]Ex. 19:20

9:1–38 This is the longest recorded prayer in the Bible. It confesses before a faithful God the history of a faithless people.

As Christ's followers we are grafted into this family (Gal. 3:7–9), and we can share in this prayer for mercy from our covenant-keeping God. The prayer unfolds history as God's acts of grace and mercy—from creation (Neh. 9:6), to the Abrahamic covenant (vv. 7–8), to the deliverance from Egypt (vv. 9–11), to God's wilderness provisions (including the law [vv. 12–15]), to a kingdom in a rich land (vv. 22–25). This outpouring of God's faithfulness is interrupted by two sections which confess the people's rebellion against him (vv. 16–21, 26–31). But there are repeated appeals to a merciful God, "abounding in steadfast love" (v. 17; see also Ex. 34:6; Deut. 7:9). The focus is on God's "covenant and steadfast love" (Neh. 9:32), ever the basis on which his people approach him.

Praise God. We can know and name the Christ in whom all the promises of God are "yes" and "Amen" (2 Cor. 1:20). The Old Testament people of God knew that God was full of grace and truth. We today see grace and truth itself embodied in Jesus Christ (John 1:14–18).

down on Mount Sinai [y]and spoke with them
from heaven and gave them [z]right rules and
true laws, good statutes and commandments,
14 [a]and you made known to them your holy
Sabbath and commanded them commandments and statutes and a law by Moses your
servant. 15 [b]You gave them bread from heaven
for their hunger and [c]brought water for them
out of the rock for their thirst, and you [d]told
them to go in to possess the land that you had
sworn to give them.

16 "But they and our fathers [e]acted presumptuously and stiffened their neck and did not
obey your commandments. 17 They refused to
obey [f]and were not mindful of the wonders
that you performed among them, but they
stiffened their neck and appointed a leader
to return to their slavery in Egypt. But you are
a God ready to forgive, [g]gracious and merciful, slow to anger and abounding in steadfast
love, and did not forsake them. 18 Even [h]when
they had made for themselves a golden[1] calf
and said, 'This is your God who brought you
up out of Egypt,' [i]and had committed great
blasphemies, 19 you [j]in your great mercies did
not forsake them in the wilderness. [k]The pillar of cloud to lead them in the way did not
depart from them by day, [k]nor the pillar of fire
by night to light for them the way by which
they should go. 20 [l]You gave your good Spirit
to instruct them [m]and did not withhold your
manna from their mouth and gave them water
for their thirst. 21 [n]Forty years you sustained
them in the wilderness, and they lacked nothing. Their clothes did not wear out and their
feet did not swell.

22 "And you gave them kingdoms and peoples and allotted to them every corner. [o]So they
took possession of the land of Sihon king of
Heshbon [p]and the land of Og king of Bashan.
23 You multiplied their children [q]as the stars
of heaven, and you brought them into the
land that you had told their fathers to enter
and possess. 24 [r]So the descendants went in
and possessed the land, [s]and you subdued
before them the inhabitants of the land, the
Canaanites, and gave them into their hand,
with their kings and the peoples of the land,
that they might do with them as they would.
25 And they captured [t]fortified cities and [u]a rich
land, and took possession of [v]houses full of all
good things, cisterns already hewn, vineyards,
olive orchards and fruit trees in abundance. So
they ate and were filled [w]and became fat and
delighted themselves in [x]your great goodness.

26 [y]"Nevertheless, they were disobedient
and rebelled against you [z]and cast your law
behind their back [a]and killed your prophets,
who [b]had warned them in order to turn them
back to you, [c]and they committed great blasphemies. 27 [d]Therefore you gave them into the
hand of their enemies, who made them suffer.
[e]And in the time of their suffering they cried
out to you and you heard them from heaven,
and according to your great mercies you gave
them [f]saviors who saved them from the hand
of their enemies. 28 [g]But after they had rest
they did evil again before you, and you abandoned them to the hand of their enemies, so
that they had dominion over them. Yet when
they turned and cried to you, you heard from
heaven, [h]and many times you delivered them
according to your mercies. 29 [b]And you warned
them in order to turn them back to your law.
Yet [i]they acted presumptuously and did not
obey your commandments, but sinned against
your rules, [j]which if a person does them, he
shall live by them, [k]and they turned a stubborn
shoulder [l]and stiffened their neck and would
not obey. 30 Many years [m]you bore with them
[n]and warned them [o]by your Spirit through
your prophets. [p]Yet they would not give ear.
[q]Therefore you gave them into the hand of
the peoples of the lands. 31 Nevertheless, [r]in
your great mercies [s]you did not make an end
of them or forsake them, [t]for you are a gracious and merciful God.

32 "Now, therefore, our God, [u]the great, the
mighty, and the awesome God, who keeps covenant and steadfast love, let not all the hardship seem little to you that has come upon
us, upon our kings, our princes, our priests,
our prophets, our fathers, and all your people,
[v]since the time of the kings of Assyria until

[1] Hebrew *metal*

13 [y]See Ex. 20:1-17 [z]Ps. 19:8, 9; [Rom. 7:12]; See Ps. 119 **14** [a]Ex. 16:23; 20:8-11; [Gen. 2:2, 3; Ezek. 20:12, 20] **15** [b][Ex. 16:14, 15; Ps. 78:25; 105:40; 1 Cor. 10:3]; Cited John 6:31 [c]Ex. 17:6; Num. 20:10; Ps. 78:15-17; 105:41; 1 Cor. 10:4 [d]Deut. 1:8 **16** [e]Ex. 18:11 **17** [f]Ps. 78:11, 42, 43 [g]ver. 31; Ex. 34:6; Num. 14:18; Ps. 86:5, 15; Joel 2:13 **18** [h]Ex. 32:4; Ps. 106:19, 20; Acts 7:41 [i]ver. 26; Ps. 78:41, 58; [Heb. 3:15] **19** [j]ver. 27, 31; Ps. 106:45 [k]See ver. 12 **20** [l]Isa. 63:11; [Num. 11:17] [m][Ex. 16:35]; See ver. 15 **21** [n]Deut. 2:7 **22** [o]See Num. 21:21-31 [p]See Num. 21:33-35 **23** [q]Gen. 15:5; 22:17 **24** [r]See Josh. 1–12 [s]Ps. 44:2, 3 **25** [t]Deut. 3:5; 9:1; Josh. 10:20; 14:12 [u]ver. 35; [Num. 13:20, 27; Deut. 8:7, 8; Ezek. 20:6] [v]Deut. 6:11 [w]Deut. 32:15 [x]ver. 35; Hos. 3:5 **26** [y]Judg. 2:11, 12; Ezek. 20:21 [z]Ps. 50:17; [1 Kgs. 14:9] [a]1 Kgs. 18:4; 19:10; 2 Chr. 24:20, 21; Matt. 23:37; Acts 7:52 [b]See ver. 30 [c]See ver. 18 **27** [d]Judg. 2:14; Ps. 106:41, 42 [e]Ps. 106:44, 45 [f]Judg. 2:16; 3:9 **28** [g]Judg. 3:11, 12, 30; 4:1; 5:31; 6:1 [h]Ps. 106:43 **29** [b][See ver. 26 above] [i]ver. 10, 16 [j]See Lev. 18:5 [k]Zech. 7:11 [l]See ver. 16 **30** [m][Acts 13:18] [n]ver. 26, 29, 34; 2 Kgs. 17:13 [o]1 Pet. 1:10, 11; 2 Pet. 1:21 [p]Acts 7:51 [q]Ezra 9:7; [Isa. 42:24] **31** [r]ver. 19, 27 [s]Jer. 4:27; 5:10, 18 [t]ver. 17 **32** [u]ch. 1:5; Deut. 7:21 [v]2 Kgs. 17:3

this day. 33 [w]Yet you have been righteous in
all that has come upon us, for you have dealt
faithfully [x]and we have acted wickedly. 34 Our
kings, our princes, our priests, and our fathers
have not kept your law or paid attention to
your commandments and your warnings that
you gave them. 35 Even in their own kingdom,
[y]and amid your great goodness that you gave
them, and in the large and [y]rich land that you
set before them, [z]they did not serve you or
turn from their wicked works. 36 Behold, [a]we
are slaves this day; in the land that you gave
to our fathers to enjoy its fruit and its good
gifts, behold, we are slaves. 37 [b]And its rich yield
goes to the kings whom you have set over us
because of our sins. They rule over our bodies
and over our livestock as they please, and we
are in great distress.

38[1] "Because of all this [c]we make a firm covenant in writing; on [d]the sealed document are
the names of[2] our princes, our Levites, and
our priests.

The People Who Sealed the Covenant

10 [3] [e]"On the seals are the names of[4] Nehemiah [f]the governor, [g]the son of Hacaliah, Zedekiah, 2 [h]Seraiah, Azariah, Jeremiah,
3 Pashhur, Amariah, Malchijah, 4 [i]Hattush,
Shebaniah, Malluch, 5 Harim, Meremoth,
Obadiah, 6 Daniel, Ginnethon, Baruch, 7 Meshullam, Abijah, Mijamin, 8 Maaziah, Bilgai,
Shemaiah; these are the priests. 9 And the
Levites: [j]Jeshua the son of Azaniah, Binnui of
the sons of [k]Henadad, Kadmiel; 10 and their
brothers, Shebaniah, Hodiah, Kelita, Pelaiah,
Hanan, 11 Mica, Rehob, Hashabiah, 12 Zaccur,
Sherebiah, Shebaniah, 13 Hodiah, Bani, Beninu.
14 The chiefs of the people: [l]Parosh, Pahath-
moab, Elam, Zattu, Bani, 15 Bunni, Azgad,
Bebai, 16 Adonijah, Bigvai, Adin, 17 Ater, Hezekiah, Azzur, 18 Hodiah, Hashum, Bezai,
19 Hariph, Anathoth, Nebai, 20 Magpiash, Meshullam, Hezir, 21 Meshezabel, Zadok, Jaddua,
22 Pelatiah, Hanan, Anaiah, 23 Hoshea, Hananiah, Hasshub, 24 Hallohesh, Pilha, Shobek,
25 Rehum, Hashabnah, Maaseiah, 26 Ahiah,
Hanan, Anan, 27 Malluch, Harim, Baanah.

The Obligations of the Covenant

28 [m]"The rest of the people, the priests, the
Levites, the gatekeepers, the singers, the
temple servants, [n]and all who have separated
themselves from the peoples of the lands
to the Law of God, their wives, their sons,
their daughters, all who have knowledge and
understanding, 29 join with their brothers,
their nobles, [o]and enter into a curse and an
oath [p]to walk in God's Law that was given
by Moses the servant of God, and to observe
and do all the commandments of the LORD
our Lord and his rules and his statutes. 30 [q]We
will not give our daughters to the peoples
of the land or take their daughters for our
sons. 31 [r]And if the peoples of the land bring
in goods or any grain on the Sabbath day
to sell, we will not buy from them on the
Sabbath or on a holy day. And we will forego
the crops of the [s]seventh year and the [t]exac-
tion of every debt.

32 "We also take on ourselves the obligation to
give yearly [u]a third part of a shekel[5] for the service of the house of our God: 33 [v]for the showbread, [w]the regular grain offering, [w]the regular
burnt offering, the Sabbaths, the new moons,
the appointed feasts, the holy things, and the
sin offerings to make atonement for Israel,
and for all the work of the house of our God.
34 [x]We, the priests, the Levites, and the people,

[1] Ch 10:1 in Hebrew [2] Hebrew lacks *the names of* [3] Ch 10:2 in Hebrew [4] Hebrew lacks *the names of* [5] A *shekel* was about 2/5 ounce or 11 grams

33 [w] See Ezra 9:15 [x] Ps. 106:6; Dan. 9:5
35 [y] ver. 25 [z] Deut. 28:47
36 [a] Ezra 9:9
37 [b] Deut. 28:33, 51
38 [c] 2 Kgs. 23:3; 2 Chr. 29:10; 34:31; Ezra 10:3; [ch. 10:29]; ch. 10:1 [d] [ch. 10:1]
Chapter 10
1 [e] ch. 9:38 [f] See ch. 8:9 [g] ch. 1:1
2 [h] For ver. 2-27, see ch. 12:2-21
4 [i] Ezra 8:2
9 [j] Ezra 2:40 [k] Ezra 3:9
14 [l] See ch. 7:8-42; Ezra 2:3-35
28 [m] See Ezra 2:36-54 [n] See ch. 9:2

10:1–39 After the history just rehearsed, the people's covenant with God seems encouraging but doubtful. Ezra has already uncovered disobedience to laws about marriage (Ezra 9–10; see Deut. 7:1–5). The people's oaths echo those of an earlier generation on the brink of the Promised Land: to their confident promises to serve the Lord, Joshua retorted that they were not able (Josh. 24:16–19).

The scene in Nehemiah 10 is beautiful, with God's people restored, united, and acknowledging his law in the most crucial areas of life and worship. But of course we must read on, looking and longing for the joy of final restoration, the full obedience to God's law that comes only with the Son of God—the One made sin even though he "knew no sin, so that in him we might become the righteousness of God" (2 Cor. 5:21). Through him, believers are assured that one day they will be swept up into the perfect and final restoration of all things (Rev. 21:1–22:5).

29 [o] ch. 5:12, 13; Deut. 29:12, 14; [Ps. 119:106] [p] [2 Kgs. 23:3; 2 Chr. 34:31] **30** [q] Ex. 34:16; Deut. 7:3; Ezra 9:12, 14 **31** [r] Ex. 20:10; Lev. 23:3; Deut. 5:12; See ch. 13:15-22 [s] Ex. 23:10, 11; Lev. 25:4 [t] Deut. 15:1, 2; [ch. 5:12] **32** [u] [Matt. 17:24] **33** [v] 2 Chr. 2:4; [1 Chr. 9:32]; See Lev. 24:5-9 [w] See Num. 28; 29 **34** [x] [ch. 11:1]

have likewise cast lots [y]for the wood offering,
to bring it into the house of our God, according to our fathers' houses, at times appointed,
year by year, to burn on the altar of the LORD
our God, [z]as it is written in the Law. 35 We obli-
gate ourselves [a]to bring the firstfruits of our
ground and the firstfruits of all fruit of every
tree, year by year, to the house of the LORD;
36 also to bring to the house of our God, to the
priests who minister in the house of our God,
the firstborn of our sons and of our cattle, [b]as
it is written in the Law, and the firstborn of
our herds and of our flocks; 37 [c]and to bring
the first of our dough, and our contributions,
the fruit of every tree, the wine and the oil,
to the priests, [d]to the chambers of the house
of our God; and to bring to the Levites the
tithes from our ground, for it is the Levites
who collect the tithes in all our towns where
we labor. 38 And the priest, the son of Aaron,
shall be with the Levites when the Levites
receive the tithes. And the Levites shall bring
up the tithe of the tithes to the house of our
God, to the chambers of [e]the storehouse. 39 For
the people of Israel and the sons of Levi [f]shall
bring the contribution of grain, wine, and oil
to the chambers, where the vessels of the sanctuary are, as well as the priests who minister,
and the gatekeepers and the singers. [g]We will
not neglect the house of our God."

The Leaders in Jerusalem

11 Now the leaders of the people [h]lived in
Jerusalem. And the rest of the people
[i]cast lots to bring one out of ten to live in
Jerusalem [j]the holy city, while nine out of ten[1]
remained in the other towns. 2 And the people
blessed all the men [k]who willingly offered to
live in Jerusalem.
3 [l]These are the chiefs of the province who
lived in Jerusalem; but in the towns of Judah
[m]everyone lived on his property in their towns:
Israel, the priests, the Levites, [n]the temple servants, [o]and the descendants of Solomon's servants. 4 And in Jerusalem lived certain of the
sons of Judah and of the sons of Benjamin. Of
the sons of Judah: Athaiah the son of Uzziah,
son of Zechariah, son of Amariah, son of
Shephatiah, son of Mahalalel, of the sons of
[p]Perez; 5 and Maaseiah the son of Baruch, son
of Col-hozeh, son of Hazaiah, son of Adaiah,
son of Joiarib, son of Zechariah, son of the
Shilonite. 6 All the sons of Perez who lived in
Jerusalem were 468 valiant men.
7 And these are the sons of Benjamin: Sallu
the son of Meshullam, son of Joed, son of
Pedaiah, son of Kolaiah, son of Maaseiah, son
of Ithiel, son of Jeshaiah, 8 and his brothers,
men of valor, 928.[2] 9 Joel the son of Zichri
was their overseer; and Judah the son of
Hassenuah was second over the city.
10 Of the priests: Jedaiah the son of Joiarib,
Jachin, 11 Seraiah the son of Hilkiah, son of
Meshullam, son of Zadok, son of Meraioth,
son of Ahitub, ruler of the house of God,
12 and their brothers who did the work of the
house, 822; and Adaiah the son of Jeroham,
son of Pelaliah, son of Amzi, son of Zechariah,
son of Pashhur, son of Malchijah, 13 and his
brothers, heads of fathers' houses, 242; and
Amashsai, the son of Azarel, son of Ahzai, son
of Meshillemoth, son of Immer, 14 and their
brothers, mighty men of valor, 128; their overseer was Zabdiel the son of Haggedolim.
15 And of the Levites: Shemaiah the son of
Hasshub, son of Azrikam, son of Hashabiah,
son of Bunni; 16 and Shabbethai and [q]Jozabad,
of the chiefs of the Levites, who were over
[r]the outside work of the house of God; 17 and
[s]Mattaniah the son of Mica, son of Zabdi, son

[1] Hebrew *nine hands* [2] Compare Septuagint; Hebrew *Jeshaiah, and after him Gabbai, Sallai, 928*

11:1–36 The returning exiles resettled the land as an ordered and unified people, according to the tribes God had established through Abraham's descendants. The lines of Judah, Benjamin, and Levi continued, lines that contain priests and kings—including David's line leading to the promised King. The "holy city" of Jerusalem with its temple is a central focus (v. 1)—holy only because of the presence and promises of their merciful God.

This city was built and rebuilt on God's promises, which pointed toward Jesus and toward the city Abraham looked for: "the city that has foundations, whose designer and builder is God" (Heb. 11:10). The apostle John saw this city: "the holy city, new Jerusalem, coming down out of heaven from God" (Rev. 21:2), where God will dwell with his people forever. There the final temple is found, though not built with wood and stone but rather existing as Christ himself (Rev. 21:22).

34 [y]ch. 13:31; [Isa. 40:16] [z]Lev. 6:12
35 [a]Ex. 23:19; 34:26; Lev. 19:23, 24; Num. 18:12; Deut. 26:2
36 [b]Ex. 13:2, 12, 13; Lev. 27:26, 27; Num. 18:15, 16
37 [c]Lev. 23:17; Num. 15:20, 21; 18:12; Deut. 18:4 [d]1 Chr. 9:26; 2 Chr. 31:11
38 [e]1 Chr. 26:20
39 [f][ch. 13:12; Deut. 12:6, 11; 2 Chr. 31:12] [g][ch. 13:11]

Chapter 11
1 [h][1 Chr. 9:3] [i]ch. 10:34 [j]ver. 18; Isa. 48:2; 52:1; Matt. 4:5; 27:53
2 [k][Judg. 5:9; 2 Chr. 17:16]
3 [l]For ver. 3-19, see 1 Chr. 9:2-34 [m]ver. 20 [n]Ezra 2:43 [o]Ezra 2:55 **4** [p][Gen. 38:29] **16** [q]Ezra 8:33 [r]1 Chr. 26:29 **17** [s]ch. 12:8, 24

of Asaph, who was the leader of the praise,[1]
who gave thanks, and Bakbukiah, the second among his brothers; and Abda the son of
Shammua, son of Galal, son of Jeduthun. 18 All
the Levites in [t]the holy city were 284.
19 The gatekeepers, Akkub, Talmon and their
brothers, who kept watch at the gates, were
172. 20 And the rest of Israel, and of the priests
and the Levites, were in all the towns of Judah,
[u]every one in his inheritance. 21 [v]But the temple
servants lived on Ophel; and Ziha and Gishpa
were over the temple servants.
22 The overseer of the Levites in Jerusalem
was Uzzi the son of Bani, son of Hashabiah,
son of Mattaniah, son of Mica, of the sons of
Asaph, the singers, over the work of the house
of God. 23 [w]For there was a command from the
king concerning them, and a fixed provision
for the singers, [x]as every day required. 24 And
Pethahiah the son of Meshezabel, of the sons
of Zerah the son of Judah, was at the king's
side[2] in all matters concerning the people.

Villages Outside Jerusalem

25 And as for the villages, with their fields,
some of the people of Judah lived in [y]Kiriath-
arba and its villages, and in Dibon and its villages, and in Jekabzeel and its villages, 26 and
in Jeshua and in Moladah and Beth-pelet, 27 in
Hazar-shual, in Beersheba and its villages,
28 in Ziklag, in Meconah and its villages, 29 in
En-rimmon, in Zorah, in Jarmuth, 30 Zanoah,
Adullam, and their villages, Lachish and its
fields, and Azekah and its villages. So they
encamped from Beersheba to [z]the Valley of
Hinnom. 31 The people of Benjamin also lived
from Geba onward, at Michmash, Aija, Bethel
and its villages, 32 Anathoth, Nob, Ananiah,
33 Hazor, Ramah, Gittaim, 34 Hadid, Zeboim,
Neballat, 35 Lod, and [a]Ono, the valley of craftsmen. 36 And certain divisions of the Levites in
Judah were assigned to Benjamin.

Priests and Levites

12 These are [b]the priests and the Levites
who came up with [c]Zerubbabel the
son of Shealtiel, and [d]Jeshua: [e]Seraiah, Jeremiah, Ezra, 2 Amariah, Malluch, Hattush,
3 Shecaniah, Rehum, Meremoth, 4 Iddo, Ginne-
thoi, Abijah, 5 Mijamin, Maadiah, Bilgah,
6 Shemaiah, Joiarib, Jedaiah, 7 Sallu, Amok,
Hilkiah, Jedaiah. These were the chiefs of the
priests and of their brothers in the days of
Jeshua.
8 And the Levites: Jeshua, Binnui, Kadmiel,
Sherebiah, Judah, and Mattaniah, who with
his brothers was [f]in charge of the songs of
thanksgiving. 9 And Bakbukiah and Unni and
their brothers stood opposite them [g]in the service. 10 And Jeshua was the father of Joiakim,
Joiakim the father of Eliashib, Eliashib
the father of Joiada, 11 Joiada the father of
Jonathan, and Jonathan the father of Jaddua.
12 [h]And in the days of Joiakim were priests,
heads of fathers' houses: of Seraiah, Meraiah;
of Jeremiah, Hananiah; 13 of Ezra, Meshullam; of Amariah, Jehohanan; 14 of Malluchi,
Jonathan; of Shebaniah, Joseph; 15 of Harim,
Adna; of Meraioth, Helkai; 16 of Iddo, Zechariah; of Ginnethon, Meshullam; 17 of Abijah,
Zichri; of Miniamin, of Moadiah, Piltai; 18 of
Bilgah, Shammua; of Shemaiah, Jehonathan;
19 of Joiarib, Mattenai; of Jedaiah, Uzzi; 20 of
Sallai, Kallai; of Amok, Eber; 21 of Hilkiah,
Hashabiah; of Jedaiah, Nethanel.
22 In the days of Eliashib, Joiada, Johanan,
and Jaddua, the Levites were recorded as heads
of fathers' houses; so too were the priests in
the reign of Darius the Persian. 23 As for the
sons of Levi, their heads of fathers' houses
[i]were written in the Book of the Chronicles
until the days of Johanan the son of Eliashib.
24 And the chiefs of the Levites: Hashabiah,
Sherebiah, and [j]Jeshua the son of Kadmiel,

[1] Compare Septuagint, Vulgate; Hebrew *beginning* [2] Hebrew *hand*

18[t] See ver. 1
20[u] ver. 3
21[v] ch. 3:26
23[w] Ezra 6:8, 9; 7:20 [x] ch. 12:47; 2 Chr. 31:16
25[y] Josh. 14:15; 21:11
30[z] See Josh. 15:8
35[a] ch. 6:2; 1 Chr. 8:12
Chapter 12
1[b] Ezra 2:1, 2 [c] ver. 47; See 1 Chr. 3:19 [d] See Ezra 3:2 [e] For ver. 1-7, see ver. 12-21; ch. 10:2-8
8[f] ver. 24; ch. 11:17; [2 Chr. 5:13]
9[g] [ver. 24]

12:1–26 Before the climactic dedication of the wall, the book looks back to trace one strong thread through the story of the returning exiles. The unbroken Levitical line shows God's preservation of the people's ability to worship and be purified as he intended. God's faithfulness makes the way for his people to worship him, as they do in the subsequent scene.

12:27–43 Here is a glimpse of God's people doing what we were created to do: worship him! Purification and sacrifices enfold this celebration (vv. 30, 43), showing the need for cleansing and mercy from a holy God. The celebration overflows with a joy that God intends and enables (see esp. v. 43). Music erupts, both vocal and instrumental.

12[h] ver. 26 **23**[i] See 1 Chr. 9:14-16 **24**[j] ch. 10:9; Ezra 2:40

with their brothers who stood opposite them,
[k]to praise and to give thanks, [l]according to the
commandment of David [m]the man of God,
[n]watch by watch. 25 Mattaniah, Bakbukiah,
Obadiah, Meshullam, Talmon, and Akkub
were gatekeepers standing guard at [o]the storehouses of the gates. 26 These were in the days of
Joiakim the son of Jeshua son of Jozadak, and
in the days of [p]Nehemiah the governor and of
[p]Ezra, the priest and scribe.

Dedication of the Wall

27 And at [q]the dedication of the wall of
Jerusalem they sought the Levites in all their
places, to bring them to Jerusalem to celebrate
the dedication with gladness, with thanksgivings and with singing, [r]with cymbals, harps,
and lyres. 28 And the sons of the singers gathered together from the district surrounding Jerusalem and from the villages of the
Netophathites; 29 also from Beth-gilgal and
from the region of Geba and Azmaveth, for
the singers had built for themselves villages
around Jerusalem. 30 And the priests and the
Levites [s]purified themselves, and they purified
the people and the gates and the wall.
31 Then I brought the leaders of Judah up
onto the wall and appointed two great choirs
that gave thanks. [t]One went to the south
on the wall to [u]the Dung Gate. 32 And after
them went Hoshaiah and half of the leaders
of Judah, 33 and Azariah, Ezra, Meshullam,
34 Judah, Benjamin, Shemaiah, and Jeremiah,
35 and certain of the priests' sons [v]with trumpets: Zechariah the son of Jonathan, son of
Shemaiah, son of Mattaniah, son of Micaiah,
son of Zaccur, son of Asaph; 36 and his relatives, Shemaiah, Azarel, Milalai, Gilalai, Maai,
Nethanel, Judah, and Hanani, [w]with the musical instruments of David [x]the man of God. And
Ezra the scribe went before them. 37 At [y]the
Fountain Gate they went up straight before
them by [z]the stairs of the city of David, at the
ascent of the wall, above the house of David,
to [a]the Water Gate on the east.
38 [b]The other choir of those who gave thanks
went to the north, and I followed them with
half of the people, on the wall, above [c]the
Tower of the Ovens, to [d]the Broad Wall,
39 and above [e]the Gate of Ephraim, and by
[f]the Gate of Yeshanah,[1] and by [g]the Fish Gate
and [h]the Tower of Hananel and [h]the Tower
of the Hundred, to [i]the Sheep Gate; and they
came to a halt at [j]the Gate of the Guard. 40 So
both choirs of those who gave thanks stood
in the house of God, and I and half of the
officials with me; 41 and the priests Eliakim,
Maaseiah, Miniamin, Micaiah, Elioenai,
Zechariah, and Hananiah, [k]with trumpets;
42 and Maaseiah, Shemaiah, Eleazar, Uzzi,
Jehohanan, Malchijah, Elam, and Ezer. And
the singers sang with Jezrahiah as their leader.
43 And they offered great sacrifices that day
and rejoiced, for God had made them rejoice
with great joy; the women and children also
rejoiced. And the joy of Jerusalem was heard
far away.

Service at the Temple

44 [l]On that day men were appointed over
the storerooms, the contributions, the firstfruits, and the tithes, to gather into them the
portions required by the Law for the priests
and for the Levites according to the fields of
the towns, for Judah rejoiced over the priests
and the Levites who ministered. 45 And they
performed the service of their God and the
service of purification, as did the singers and
the gatekeepers, [m]according to the command
of David and his son Solomon. 46 For long ago

[1] Or *of the old city*

What a heritage for believers who aim to let the word of Christ dwell in us richly, "singing psalms and hymns and spiritual songs, with thankfulness in your hearts to God" (Col. 3:16). "Psalms" recalls King David; indeed David is much mentioned (Neh. 12:36–37, 45–46), in glimpses back to God's faithfulness and ahead to God's promises of an eternal King (2 Sam. 7:12–17). The "joy of Jerusalem" (Neh. 12:43) echoes far and wide, both geographically and throughout time. This is the spreading joy of a people redeemed through Christ our King—echoing and climaxing with the worship in heaven (see Rev. 5:8–14).

12:44–13:31 After a transition (12:44–13:3) showing the people's trusting obedience to God's law, the remaining verses (13:4–31) make a dramatic contrast, as the people disobey the law in Nehemiah's absence. Each promise from chapter 10 is broken: regarding the temple (vv. 7–13; see 10:32–39), the Sabbath (13:15–22; see 10:31), and marriage (13:23–27; see 10:30; see also Ezra 9–10 and notes).

24 [k]ch. 11:17; [2 Chr. 5:13] [l]See 1 Chr. 25 [m]ver. 36 [n][ver. 9; Ezra 3:11]
25 [o][1 Chr. 26:15]
26 [p]ch. 8:9
27 [q]See Num. 7:10 [r]See 1 Chr. 15:16
30 [s]ch. 13:22, 30
31 [t][ver. 38] [u]ch. 2:13; 3:13
35 [v]See 1 Chr. 15:24
36 [w]1 Chr. 23:5 [x]ver. 24
37 [y]ch. 2:14; 3:15 [z]ch. 3:15 [a]ch. 3:26; 8:1, 3, 16
38 [b][ver. 31] [c]ch. 3:11 [d]ch. 3:8
39 [e]See ch. 8:16 [f]ch. 3:6 [g]See ch. 3:3 [h]ch. 3:1 [i]See ch. 3:1 [j]See ch. 3:25
41 [k]See 1 Chr. 15:24
44 [l]ch. 13:5, 12, 13; [2 Chr. 31:11, 12]
45 [m]See 1 Chr. 25; 26

in the days of David and [n]Asaph there were
directors of the singers, and there were songs[1]
of praise and thanksgiving to God. 47 And all
Israel in the days of Zerubbabel and in the
days of Nehemiah gave the [o]daily portions for
the singers and the gatekeepers; [p]and they set
apart that which was for the Levites; [q]and the
Levites set apart that which was for the sons
of Aaron.

Nehemiah's Final Reforms

13 On that day [r]they read from the Book of
Moses in the hearing of the people. And
in it was found written [s]that no Ammonite
or Moabite should ever enter the assembly
of God, 2 for they did not meet the people of
Israel with bread and water, but hired Balaam
against them to curse them—yet our God
turned the curse into a blessing. 3 As soon as
the people heard the law, [t]they separated from
Israel all [u]those of foreign descent.

4 Now before this, [v]Eliashib the priest, who
[w]was appointed over the chambers of the
house of our God, and who was related to
[x]Tobiah, 5 prepared for Tobiah a large chamber where they had previously put the grain
offering, the frankincense, the vessels, and
the tithes of grain, wine, and oil, [y]which were
given by commandment to the Levites, singers, and gatekeepers, and the contributions for
the priests. 6 While this was taking place, I was
not in Jerusalem, for [z]in the thirty-second year
of Artaxerxes [a]king of Babylon I went to the
king. And after some time I asked leave of
the king 7 and came to Jerusalem, and I then
discovered the evil that Eliashib had done
for Tobiah, [b]preparing for him a chamber in
the courts of the house of God. 8 And I was
very angry, and I threw all the household furniture of Tobiah out of the chamber. 9 Then
I gave orders, and they [c]cleansed the chambers,
and I brought back there the vessels of the
house of God, with the grain offering and the
frankincense.

10 I also found out that [d]the portions of the
Levites had not been given to them, so that
the Levites and the singers, who did the work,
had fled each [e]to his field. 11 [f]So I confronted the
officials and said, [g]"Why is the house of God
forsaken?" And I gathered them together and
set them in their stations. 12 Then all Judah
brought [h]the tithe of the grain, wine, and oil
into the storehouses. 13 And [i]I appointed as
treasurers over the storehouses Shelemiah
the priest, Zadok the scribe, and Pedaiah of
the Levites, and as their assistant Hanan the
son of Zaccur, son of Mattaniah, [j]for they were
considered reliable, and their duty was to distribute to their brothers. 14 [k]Remember me,
O my God, concerning this, and do not wipe
out my good deeds that I have done for the
house of my God and for his service.

15 In those days I saw in Judah people treading winepresses [l]on the Sabbath, and bringing
in heaps of grain and loading them on donkeys, and also wine, grapes, figs, and all kinds
of loads, [m]which they brought into Jerusalem
on the Sabbath day. And [n]I warned them on
the day when they sold food. 16 Tyrians also,
who lived in the city, brought in fish and all
kinds of goods and sold them on the Sabbath
to the people of Judah, in Jerusalem itself!
17 [o]Then I confronted the nobles of Judah and
said to them, "What is this evil thing that you
are doing, [p]profaning the Sabbath day? 18 [q]Did
not your fathers act in this way, and did not
our God bring all this disaster[2] on us and on
this city? Now you are bringing more wrath
on Israel by profaning the Sabbath."

[1] Or *leaders* [2] The Hebrew word can mean *evil*, *harm*, or *disaster*, depending on the context

This book thus lowers a dark final curtain at the onset of that intertestamental waiting period, before the promised "light of life" comes to shine in the darkness (John 1:4–5). In Scripture's full light, it is clear that only the one who is himself the temple can make these wrongs right (John 2:18–22). Nehemiah's interspersed prayers offer a thread of hope, asking God to "remember" (Neh. 13:14, 22, 29, 31)—both the good and the evil, all of which God will bring to light. The greatest hope comes in Nehemiah's final claiming of "the greatness of your steadfast love" (v. 22), God's covenant love for his people that culminates in the death and resurrection of Jesus Christ. In reading the book of Nehemiah, we too are brought to reflect on the greatness of God's steadfast love, which for us has been decisively secured in Jesus on our behalf. We have been adopted into God's family. We are no longer orphans. Let us lift our heads and rejoice.

46 [n]1 Chr. 25:1; 2 Chr. 29:30
47 [o]ch. 11:23; 2 Chr. 31:16 [p]Num. 18:21, 24 [q]See Num. 18:26-28

Chapter 13

1 [r]ch. 8:3, 8, 9, 18; 9:3; [Deut. 31:11, 12; 2 Kgs. 23:2] [s]See Deut. 23:3-5
3 [t]See ch. 9:2 [u][Ex. 12:38; Num. 11:4]
4 [v]ver. 28; ch. 3:1 [w][ch. 12:44] [x]ch. 2:10
5 [y]Num. 18:21, 24
6 [z]ch. 5:14 [a]Ezra 6:22
7 [b]ver. 5
9 [c]2 Chr. 29:15, 16, 18
10 [d]2 Chr. 31:4; [Mal. 3:8] [e]ch. 12:28, 29
11 [f]ver. 17, 25 [g][ch. 10:39]
12 [h][ch. 10:38, 39; 12:44]
13 [i][2 Chr. 31:12, 13] [j]ch. 7:2; [1 Cor. 4:2]
14 [k]ver. 22, 31; ch. 5:19
15 [l][Ex. 20:10] [m]See ch. 10:31 [n]ver. 21
17 [o]ver. 11 [p][Matt. 12:5]
18 [q]See Jer. 17:19-23

19 As soon as it [r]began to grow dark at the
gates of Jerusalem before the Sabbath, I commanded that the doors should be shut and
gave orders that they should not be opened
until after the Sabbath. And I stationed some
of my servants at the gates, that no load might
be brought in on the Sabbath day. 20 Then the
merchants and sellers of all kinds of wares
lodged outside Jerusalem once or twice.
21 [s]But I warned them and said to them, "Why
do you lodge outside the wall? If you do so
again, I will lay hands on you." From that
time on they did not come on the Sabbath.
22 Then I commanded the Levites [t]that they
should purify themselves and come and
guard the gates, to keep the Sabbath day holy.
[u]Remember this also in my favor, O my God,
and spare me according to the greatness of
your steadfast love.

23 In those days also I saw the Jews [v]who had
married women [w]of Ashdod, [x]Ammon, and
[x]Moab. 24 And half of their children spoke
the language of Ashdod, and they could not
speak the language of Judah, but only the
language of each people. 25 [o]And I confronted
them and cursed them and beat some of them
and pulled out their hair. [y]And I made them
take an oath in the name of God, saying, "You
shall not give your daughters to their sons,
or take their daughters for your sons or for
yourselves. 26 [z]Did not Solomon king of Israel
sin on account of such women? [a]Among the
many nations there was no king like him, and
he was [b]beloved by his God, and God made
him king over all Israel. Nevertheless, foreign
women made even him to sin. 27 Shall we then
listen to you and do all this great evil and [c]act
treacherously against our God by marrying
foreign women?"

28 And one of the sons of [d]Jehoiada, the son
of [e]Eliashib the high priest, was the son-in-law
of [f]Sanballat the Horonite. Therefore I chased
him from me. 29 [g]Remember them, O my God,
because they have desecrated the priesthood
[h]and the covenant of the priesthood and the
Levites.

30 [i]Thus I cleansed them from everything foreign, and I established the duties of the priests
and Levites, each in his work; 31 and I provided
[j]for the wood offering [k]at appointed times, and
for the firstfruits.

[l]Remember me, O my God, for good.

19 [r] Lev. 23:32 **21** [s] ver. 15 **22** [t] ch. 12:30 [u] [ver. 14, 31] **23** [v] Ezra 9:2; 10:10 [w] [ch. 4:7] [x] [ver. 1; Ezra 9:1] **25** [o] [See ver. 17 above] [y] Ezra 10:5; [ch. 10:29, 30] **26** [z] See 1 Kgs. 11:1-8 [a] 1 Kgs. 3:13; 2 Chr. 1:12 [b] [2 Sam. 12:24] **27** [c] Ezra 10:2 **28** [d] ch. 12:10, 11, 22 [e] ver. 4, 7; ch. 3:1 [f] ch. 2:10, 19 **29** [g] [ch. 6:14] [h] Mal. 2:4 **30** [i] ch. 10:30 **31** [j] ch. 10:34 [k] Ezra 10:14 [l] ver. 14, 22

Introduction to Esther

Author and Date

Like many Old Testament books, Esther is an anonymous work. It is possible that the author was someone like Mordecai, who had access to historical documents (2:23; 6:1). The events of Esther took place after the Babylonian exile, when Persia had replaced Babylon as the ruling power in the Near East, including Judea. The story is set in Susa, one of the Persian capitals, during the reign of King Ahasuerus, better known by his Greek name, Xerxes I (486–464 B.C.). While many Jews had returned home to Judea after the exile, many others chose to remain in Persia. As a minority group, they were viewed with suspicion and sometimes faced threats to their existence.

The Gospel in Esther

It is natural to read Esther as a morality tale about cousins who stand in the gap to save a nation. As a consequence, women may be told, "Be compliant and brave like Esther!" Men are encouraged, "Be faithful and wise like Mordecai!" We're all admonished, "Don't be proud like Haman—you might end up on the gallows!" But is Esther fundamentally a morality tale about how we should stand tall in the midst of our earthly captivity? Or is it a gospel message ultimately about our need for dependence upon Jesus Christ, our Mediator who himself stood in the gap and accomplished our deliverance?

For believers today, the significance of the book of Esther is that it coordinates with the rest of the Old Testament to foreshadow Jesus as deliverer and mediator for God's people (Luke 24:27, 44; John 5:39, 46). Yet, strikingly, neither the Messiah nor even God is mentioned at all in Esther. It is the only book in Scripture in which God seems to be missing. The point being made may well be captured in this key observation: when everything seems to be under the control of a godless despot; when God's people, because of their own sin, have lost all memory of him, of their true identity, and of their land; God is nevertheless at work to fulfill his promise of ultimate triumph over his enemies (Gen. 3:15). The triumph of God's kingdom is not dependent upon the faithfulness of God's people. Even when they think that the only way to survive is to blend in or keep quiet, God is yet able and willing to deliver.

Esther is laced with irony. In fact, it could be read as a satire on the futility of attempting to thwart God's plan. The Lord scoffs at the seemingly invincible power of political parties, great armies, or immense wealth. With ease he displays his manifold wisdom to the "rulers and authorities in the heavenly places" (Eph. 3:10). He is ruling sovereignly, accomplishing his purposes whether we see him or not. And that's good news for all believers who wonder where he is in their suffering. We might not see him. He may be absent from mind, mention, or memory. And it might appear that he's forgotten us or that our sins have finally turned him away. But that is not the truth. The truth is that God is defending his people and building his church, and nothing—not even the "gates of hell" (Matt. 16:18)—will prevail against him.

There is something even deeper happening in the book of Esther, beneath the drama of court intrigues and character models. God is ruling in heaven, undisturbed by the defiance of those on earth who persist in trusting in their power, beauty, rituals, and ambitions. We remember that God himself chose to accomplish the greatest triumph of human history through the lowliest of means: a pregnant virgin, a rejected and crucified man, bread and wine, and the foolishness of a message that abases mankind and exalts a crucified Savior. God delights in crushing his Enemy through the weakness of the cross, using sinners to accomplish his will and make his glory great. When we read of Ahasuerus's great wealth and seemingly invincible power, we're meant to laugh sardonically: Sure Ahasuerus is powerful, but what can he do to separate God's people from his love? What can God's enemies do to separate us from the love of Christ that will result from God's preservation of this covenant people? Who can stop God's plan to bless?

The book of Esther is not simply a morality tale about a few faithful Jewish people who stand up for God in the midst of a pagan land. More fundamentally and splendidly, it is the story of God's desire to glorify himself and make his Son beautiful in the lives of alienated, weak exiles from covenant faithfulness—like us.

Outline

I. Introduction (1:1–2:23)

II. Main Action (3:1–9:19)

III. Conclusion (9:20–10:3)

Esther

The King's Banquets

1 Now in the days of Ahasuerus, the Ahasuerus who reigned [a]from India to Ethiopia over [b]127 provinces, 2 in those days when King Ahasuerus [c]sat on his royal throne in [d]Susa, the citadel, 3 in the third year of his reign [e]he gave a feast for all his officials and servants. The army of Persia and Media and the nobles and governors of the provinces were before him, 4 while he showed the riches of his royal glory and the splendor and pomp of his greatness for many days, 180 days. 5 And when these days were completed, the king gave for all the people present in Susa the citadel, both great and small, a feast lasting for seven days in the court of [f]the garden of the king's palace. 6 There were white cotton curtains and violet hangings fastened with cords of fine linen and purple to silver rods[1] and marble pillars, and also [g]couches of gold and silver on a mosaic pavement of porphyry, marble, mother-of-pearl and precious stones. 7 Drinks were served in golden vessels, vessels of different kinds, and the royal wine was lavished according to the bounty of the king. 8 And drinking was according to this edict: "There is no compulsion." For the king had given orders to all the staff of his palace to do as each man desired. 9 Queen Vashti also gave a feast for the women in the palace that belonged to King Ahasuerus.

Queen Vashti's Refusal

10 On the seventh day, [h]when the heart of the king was merry with wine, he commanded Mehuman, Biztha, [i]Harbona, [j]Bigtha and Abagtha, Zethar and Carkas, the seven eunuchs who served in the presence of King Ahasuerus, 11 to bring Queen Vashti before the king with [k]her royal crown,[2] in order to show the peoples and the princes her beauty, for she was lovely to look at. 12 But Queen Vashti refused to come at the king's command delivered by the eunuchs. At this the king became enraged, and his anger burned within him.

13 Then the king said to [l]the wise men [m]who knew the times (for this was the king's procedure toward all who were versed in law and judgment, 14 the men next to him being Carshena, Shethar, Admatha, Tarshish, Meres, Marsena, and [n]Memucan, [o]the seven princes of Persia and Media, [p]who saw the king's face, and sat first in the kingdom): 15 "According to the law, what is to be done to Queen Vashti, because she has not performed the command of King Ahasuerus delivered by the eunuchs?" 16 Then Memucan said in the presence of the king and the officials, "Not only against the king has Queen Vashti done wrong, but also against all the officials and all the peoples who are in all the provinces of King Ahasuerus. 17 For the queen's behavior will be made known to all women, causing them to look at their

[1] Or *rings* [2] Or *headdress*

1:1–12 In gaudy display, Ahasuerus, king of Persia, hosts a 180-day-long party, culminating in the call to his wife, Vashti, to flaunt her beauty before him and his cohorts. Vashti refuses to oblige, and the king is enraged. This is more than the story of a dysfunctional royal marriage. It is the hand of the sovereign God who is orchestrating events to bring Esther, a Jewish woman, into a position of authority so that God's people will be preserved. Right from the start of the book of Esther, God's sovereign grace is guiding all events, down to every last detail. Sovereign irony is also meant to be on display here: the king who had so much earthly authority was powerless over his own wife!

Chapter 1
1 [a]ch. 8:9 [b]ch. 8:9; 9:30; [Dan. 6:1]
2 [c]1 Kgs. 1:46 [d]See Neh. 1:1
3 [e]ch. 2:18; [Gen. 40:20; 1 Kgs. 3:15; Mark 6:21]
5 [f]ch. 7:7, 8
6 [g][Ezek. 23:41; Amos 6:4]
10 [h][2 Sam. 13:28] [i]ch. 7:9 [j][ch. 2:21; 6:2]
11 [k]ch. 2:17; 6:8
13 [l]Jer. 10:7; Dan. 2:12, 13; Matt. 2:1 [m]1 Chr. 12:32
14 [n]ver. 16, 21 [o]Ezra 7:14 [p]2 Kgs. 25:19

husbands with contempt, since they will say,
'King Ahasuerus commanded Queen Vashti to
be brought before him, and she did not come.'
18 This very day the noble women of Persia and
Media who have heard of the queen's behavior
will say the same to all the king's officials, and
there will be contempt and wrath in plenty.
19 If it please the king, let a royal order go out
from him, and let it be written among the
laws of the Persians and the Medes so [q]that it
may not be repealed, that Vashti is never again
to come before King Ahasuerus. And let the
king give her royal position to another who
is better than she. 20 So when the decree made
by the king is proclaimed throughout all his
kingdom, for it is vast, [r]all women will give
honor to their husbands, high and low alike."
21 This advice pleased the king and the princes,
and the king did as Memucan proposed. 22 He
sent letters to all the royal provinces, [s]to every
province in its own script and to every people
in its own language, that every man be master
in his own household and speak according to
the language of his people.

Esther Chosen Queen

2 After these things, [t]when the anger of
King Ahasuerus had abated, he remembered Vashti [u]and what she had done and
what had been decreed against her. 2 Then the
king's young men who attended him said, "Let
beautiful young virgins be sought out for the
king. 3 And let the king appoint officers in all
the provinces of his kingdom to gather all the
beautiful young virgins to the harem in Susa
the citadel, under custody of [v]Hegai, the king's
eunuch, who is in charge of the women. [w]Let
their cosmetics be given them. 4 And let the
young woman who pleases the king be queen
instead of Vashti." This pleased the king, and
he did so.

5 Now there was a Jew in Susa the citadel
whose name was [x]Mordecai, the son of Jair, son
of Shimei, son of Kish, a Benjaminite, 6 [y]who
had been carried away from Jerusalem among
the captives carried away with Jeconiah king
of Judah, whom Nebuchadnezzar king of
Babylon had carried away. 7 He was bringing
up Hadassah, that is Esther, [z]the daughter
of his uncle, for she had neither father nor
mother. The young woman had a beautiful
figure and was lovely to look at, and when
her father and her mother died, Mordecai
took her as his own daughter. 8 So when the
king's order and his edict were proclaimed,
and [a]when many young women were gathered
in Susa the citadel in custody of [b]Hegai, Esther
also was taken into the king's palace and put
in custody of Hegai, who had charge of the
women. 9 And the young woman pleased him
and won his favor. And he quickly provided
her [c]with her cosmetics and her portion of
food, and with seven chosen young women
from the king's palace, and advanced her and
her young women to the best place in the
harem. 10 [d]Esther had not made known her
people or kindred, for Mordecai had commanded her not to make it known. 11 And every
day Mordecai walked in front of the court of
the harem to learn how Esther was and what
was happening to her.

12 Now when the turn came for each young

19 [q] ch. 8:8; Dan. 6:8, 12, 15
20 [r] [Eph. 5:22, 24, 33; Col. 3:18; 1 Tim. 2:12; 1 Pet. 3:1]
22 [s] ch. 3:12; 8:9
Chapter 2
1 [t] [ch. 7:10] [u] ch. 1:19, 20
3 [v] ver. 8, 15 [w] ver. 9, 12
5 [x] [Ezra 2:2]
6 [y] 2 Kgs. 24:14, 15; 2 Chr. 36:10, 20; Jer. 24:1; 29:1, 2
7 [z] ver. 15
8 [a] ver. 3 [b] ver. 3
9 [c] ver. 3, 12
10 [d] ver. 20

1:19–22 The king decreed that, "every man be master in his own household" (v. 22). Once again, we're meant to smile at the tin-pot dictator who commands that every husband do what he himself is unable to do: be a master in his own household. Jewish readers in later generation were to understand the contrast: Only God is all-powerful, doing whatever he wants—and not in a rash or fickle way, as Ahasuerus does.

2:1–14 Following the counsel of his young men (and God's sovereign plan), Ahasuerus gathered beautiful young virgins from his vast kingdom to be placed in his harem, so that they might have a one-night audition with the king. It is here that we meet Mordecai, a self-identified Jew, and his orphaned cousin, Esther, who was chosen because she "had a beautiful figure and was lovely to look at" (v. 7). We learn that Mordecai worried about his cousin, for "every day Mordecai walked in front of the court of the harem to learn how Esther was and what was happening to her" (v. 11).

To bolster his reputation and salve his wounded pride, wicked Ahasuerus gathers the captive girls he considers beautiful to select his queen. In contrast, from a Jewish perspective, Esther spoils and demeans herself by acceding to the pagan king's desires. Yet as queen, Esther will be used of God, despite her impurity and shame, to protect the lineage of the "seed of the woman," Jesus Christ, who will ultimately crush the head of the Serpent (Gen. 3:15; Rom. 16:20).

woman to go in to King Ahasuerus, after being twelve months under the regulations for the women, since this was the regular period of their beautifying, six months with oil of myrrh and six months with spices and ointments for women— 13 when the young woman went in to the king in this way, she was given whatever she desired to take with her from the harem to the king's palace. 14 In the evening she would go in, and in the morning she would return to the second harem in custody of Shaashgaz, the king's eunuch, who was in charge of the concubines. She would not go in to the king again, unless the king delighted in her and she was summoned by name.

15 When the turn came for Esther [e]the daughter of Abihail the uncle of Mordecai, who had taken her as his own daughter, to go in to the king, she asked for nothing except what [f]Hegai the king's eunuch, who had charge of the women, advised. Now Esther was winning favor in the eyes of all who saw her. 16 And when Esther was taken to King Ahasuerus, into his royal palace, in the tenth month, which is the month of Tebeth, in the seventh year of his reign, 17 the king loved Esther more than all the women, and she won grace and favor in his sight more than all the virgins, so that he set [g]the royal crown[1] on her head and made her queen instead of Vashti. 18 Then the king [h]gave a great feast for all his officials and servants; it was Esther's feast. He also granted a remission of taxes to the provinces and gave gifts with royal generosity.

Mordecai Discovers a Plot

19 Now when the virgins were gathered together [i]the second time, Mordecai was sitting [j]at the king's gate. 20 [k]Esther had not made known her kindred or her people, as Mordecai had commanded her, for Esther obeyed Mordecai just [l]as when she was brought up by him. 21 In those days, as Mordecai was sitting at the king's gate, [m]Bigthan and [n]Teresh, two of the king's eunuchs, who guarded the threshold, became angry and sought to lay hands on King Ahasuerus. 22 And this came to the knowledge of Mordecai, [o]and he told it to Queen Esther, and Esther told the king in the name of Mordecai. 23 When the affair was investigated and found to be so, the men were both hanged on the gallows.[2] And it was recorded in [p]the book of the chronicles in the presence of the king.

Haman Plots Against the Jews

3 After these things King Ahasuerus [q]promoted Haman [r]the Agagite, the son of Hammedatha, [s]and advanced him and set his throne above all the officials who were with him. 2 And all the king's servants who were at the king's gate bowed down and paid homage to Haman, for the king had so commanded concerning him. [t]But Mordecai did not bow down or pay homage. 3 Then the king's servants who were [u]at the king's gate said to Mordecai, "Why do you transgress [v]the king's command?" 4 And when they spoke to him day after day and he would not listen to them, they told Haman, in order to see whether Mordecai's words would stand, for he had told them that he was a Jew. 5 And when Haman saw that [t]Mordecai did not bow down or pay homage to him, Haman was [w]filled with fury. 6 But he disdained to lay hands on Mordecai alone. So, as they had made known to him the

[1] Or *headdress* [2] Or *suspended on a stake*

2:19–23 God continues behind the scenes, as Mordecai becomes aware of a plot against Ahasuerus and communicates it to the king. Although Mordecai should have been rewarded for his allegiance, he was forgotten for the time being—like Joseph before him (Gen. 40:23). But God is ruling sovereignly and will use these events in his own time. The invisible hand of God continues to work toward his people's preservation.

God's timing may not be what we prefer, given the limited knowledge we have, but he is always "on time" according to his own sovereign plan. Observing this, believers today take heart in the confidence that, whatever our circumstances, God has promised to preserve those who are in Christ (1 Cor. 1:8; Phil. 1:6).

3:1–6 Many times throughout God's story of redemption down through history, the wicked have sought to lay hands on the godly, as Haman sought to do to Mordecai and to the Jews. We see this, for example, in the lives of Joseph (Gen. 37:23–24), Moses (Ex. 2:15), David (1 Sam. 18:10–11; 24:1–2), Daniel (Dan. 2:13), and Jeremiah (Jer. 38:6). Evil may have its day, but God will have the final say. The ultimate example of this is Christ himself, whom wicked men seized and wrongfully crucified.

15 [e] ver. 7; ch. 9:29 [f] ver. 3, 8
17 [g] ch. 1:11; 6:8
18 [h] See ch. 1:3
19 [i] ver. 3, 4 [j] ver. 21; ch. 3:2, 3; 5:9, 13; 6:10, 12
20 [k] ver. 10 [l] ver. 7
21 [m] [ch. 1:10; 6:2] [n] ch. 6:2
22 [o] ch. 6:2; [ch. 7:9]
23 [p] ch. 6:1; 10:2
Chapter 3
1 [q] ch. 5:11 [r] ver. 10; ch. 8:3, 5; 9:24 [s] ch. 5:11
2 [t] ch. 5:9
3 [u] See ch. 2:19 [v] ver. 2
5 [t] [See ver. 2 above] [w] Dan. 3:19

people of Mordecai, Haman sought to destroy
all the Jews, the people of Mordecai, throughout the whole kingdom of Ahasuerus.
7 In the first month, which is the month of
Nisan, in the twelfth year of King Ahasuerus,
[x]they cast Pur (that is, they cast lots) before
Haman day after day; and they cast it month
after month till the twelfth month, which is
[y]the month of Adar. 8 Then Haman said to
King Ahasuerus, "There is a certain people
scattered abroad and dispersed among the
peoples in all the provinces of your kingdom.
[z]Their laws are different from those of every
other people, and they do not keep the king's
laws, so that it is not to the king's profit to
tolerate them. 9 If it please the king, let it be
decreed that they be destroyed, and I will pay
10,000 talents[1] of silver into the hands of those
who have charge of the king's business, that
they may put it into the king's treasuries."
10 [a]So the king took his signet ring from his
hand and gave it to Haman [b]the Agagite, the
son of Hammedatha, [c]the enemy of the Jews.
11 And the king said to Haman, "The money is
given to you, the people also, to do with them
as it seems good to you."
12 [d]Then the king's scribes were summoned
on the thirteenth day of the first month, and
an edict, according to all that Haman commanded, was written to the king's [e]satraps
and to the governors over all the provinces
and to the officials of all the peoples, [f]to every
province in its own script and every people in
its own language. It was written [g]in the name
of King Ahasuerus [h]and sealed with the king's
signet ring. 13 Letters were sent [i]by couriers
to all the king's provinces with instruction
[j]to destroy, to kill, and to annihilate all Jews,
young and old, women and children, [k]in one
day, the thirteenth day of the twelfth month,
which is the month of Adar, [l]and to plunder
their goods. 14 [m]A copy of the document was
to be issued as a decree in every province by
proclamation to all the peoples to be ready for
that day. 15 [i]The couriers went out hurriedly by
order of the king, and the decree was issued
in Susa the citadel. And the king and Haman
sat down to drink, [n]but the city of Susa was
thrown into confusion.

Esther Agrees to Help the Jews

4 When Mordecai learned all that had been
done, Mordecai tore his clothes [o]and put
on sackcloth and ashes, and went out into the
midst of the city, and he cried out with a loud
and bitter cry. 2 He went up to the entrance
of the king's gate, for no one was allowed to
enter the king's gate clothed in sackcloth.
3 And in every province, wherever the king's
command and his decree reached, there was
great mourning among the Jews, [p]with fasting and weeping and lamenting, and many
of them [q]lay in sackcloth and ashes.
4 When Esther's young women and her
eunuchs came and told her, the queen was
deeply distressed. She sent garments to clothe
Mordecai, so that he might take off his sackcloth, but he would not accept them. 5 Then
Esther called for Hathach, one of the king's
eunuchs, who had been appointed to attend
her, and ordered him to go to Mordecai to
learn what this was and why it was. 6 Hathach
went out to Mordecai in the open square
of the city in front of the king's gate, 7 and
Mordecai told him all that had happened
to him, [r]and the exact sum of money that

[1] A *talent* was about 75 pounds or 34 kilograms

7 [x]ch. 9:24, 26 [y]Ezra 6:15
8 [z][Ezra 4:12, 13; Acts 16:20, 21]
10 [a]ch. 8:2; Gen. 41:42 [b]ver. 1 [c]ch. 7:6; 8:1; 9:10, 24
12 [d]ch. 8:9 [e]See Ezra 8:36 [f]ch. 1:22; 8:9 [g]ch. 8:8, 10; [1 Kgs. 21:8] [h]ch. 8:8, 10
13 [i]ch. 8:10; [2 Chr. 30:6] [j]ch. 7:4; 8:11 [k]ch. 8:12; [ch. 9:1] [l]ch. 8:11
14 [m]ch. 8:13, 14
15 [i][See ver. 13 above] [n][ch. 8:15]

Chapter 4
1 [o]See 2 Sam. 3:31
3 [p]ver. 16; ch. 9:31 [q]Dan. 9:3; [Isa. 58:5]
7 [r]ch. 3:9

3:7–15 Like the religious leaders in Christ's day (John 12:19), Haman couldn't stand the thought of losing the approval of the masses, so he promised Ahasuerus 10,000 talents of silver for an unchangeable edict that would ensure the annihilation of the Jews. Ironically, Haman unintentionally declared war on the queen, who herself was Jewish; his yearlong superstitious casting of lots (the Pur) did not ensure his success or protect him from God's judgment (see Prov. 16:33). We are to be reminded that humans plan and God laughs (Ps. 2:2–4), for his ways are far beyond ours (Isa. 55:8–9).

Again, although annihilation of the covenant people seemed inevitable, God was at work. Haman is rejoicing as all his plans come together, but he's in for an unexpected reversal. Such surprising reversals have often been the way the Lord has worked down through history. Indeed, grace itself, the core message of the Bible, is a matter of surprising reversal. The supreme reversal is when Satan rejoiced at the supposed demise of the Christ and the end of God's plans on Calvary; it was Christ's very death that accomplished the greatest victory for his people.

Haman had promised to pay into the king's
treasuries for the destruction of the Jews.
8 Mordecai also gave him [s]a copy of the written decree issued in Susa for their destruction,
that he might show it to Esther and explain
it to her and command her to go to the king
to beg his favor and plead with him on behalf
of her people. 9 And Hathach went and told
Esther what Mordecai had said. 10 Then Esther
spoke to Hathach and commanded him to go
to Mordecai and say, 11 "All the king's servants
and the people of the king's provinces know
that if any man or woman goes to the king
inside [t]the inner court without being called,
[u]there is but one law—to be put to death,
except the one [v]to whom the king holds out
the golden scepter so that he may live. But as
for me, I have not been called to come in to
the king these thirty days."

12 And they told Mordecai what Esther had
said. 13 Then Mordecai told them to reply to
Esther, "Do not think to yourself that in the
king's palace you will escape any more than
all the other Jews. 14 For if you keep silent at
this time, relief and deliverance will rise for
the Jews from another place, but you and your
father's house will perish. And who knows
whether you have not come to the kingdom
for such a time as this?" 15 Then Esther told
them to reply to Mordecai, 16 "Go, gather
all the Jews to be found in Susa, and hold a
fast on my behalf, and do not eat or drink
for [w]three days, night or day. I and my young
women will also fast as you do. Then I will
go to the king, though it is against the law,
[x]and if I perish, I perish." 17 Mordecai then
went away and did everything as Esther had
ordered him.

Esther Prepares a Banquet

5 [y]On the third day Esther put on her royal
robes and stood in [z]the inner court of the
king's palace, in front of the king's quarters,
while the king was sitting on his royal throne
inside the throne room opposite the entrance
to the palace. 2 And when the king saw Queen
Esther standing in the court, [a]she won favor
in his sight, [b]and he held out to Esther the
golden scepter that was in his hand. Then
Esther approached and touched the tip of the
scepter. 3 And the king said to her, "What is it,
Queen Esther? What is your request? It shall be
given you, even [c]to the half of my kingdom."
4 And Esther said, "If it please the king, let the
king and Haman come today to a feast that
I have prepared for the king." 5 Then the king
said, "Bring Haman quickly, so that we may do
as Esther has asked." So the king and Haman
came to the feast that Esther had prepared.
6 [d]And as they were drinking wine after the
feast, the king said to Esther, [e]"What is your
wish? It shall be granted you. And what is your
request? [c]Even to the half of my kingdom, it
shall be fulfilled." 7 Then Esther answered, "My
wish and my request is: 8 [f]If I have found favor
in the sight of the king, and if it please the
king to grant my wish and fulfill my request,
let the king and Haman come to [g]the feast that
I will prepare for them, and tomorrow I will
do as the king has said."

Haman Plans to Hang Mordecai

9 And Haman went out that day [h]joyful and
glad of heart. But when Haman saw Mordecai
[i]in the king's gate, [j]that he neither rose nor
trembled before him, he was filled with wrath
against Mordecai. 10 Nevertheless, Haman

4:14 Mordecai encourages Esther that now, in the time of the Jews' need, "who knows whether you have not come to the kingdom for such a time as this?" By his own merciful initiative, God delights to raise up deliverers for his people when they need him most (1 Cor. 1:27–28). We think especially here of the judges and then the kings down through Israel's history, who frequently deliver God's people, yet just as frequently are themselves corrupt. And all of them, eventually, die.

The King who never dies is Jesus himself, who, like Esther, was raised up at just the right moment in history (Rom. 5:6; Gal. 4:4), "for such a time as this"—or as Paul elsewhere says, "when the fullness of time had come" (Gal. 4:4).

4:16–5:1 "If I perish, I perish" are the words of Esther's Gethsemane (4:16). Unlike our Savior, however, Esther had to be threatened with destruction before she would act. Again, we see here how the Bible is honest about the flaws of its heroes. No one is without the need of God's grace in their lives.

Once Esther does act, she has the support of all the Jews in Susa standing with her. She dresses herself in her royal robes and goes in before the king. The disgraced Jewish girl is about to be used of God to deliver his people.

8 [s] ch. 3:14; 8:13
11 [t] ch. 5:1; [ch. 6:4] [u] Dan. 2:9 [v] ch. 5:2; 8:4
16 [w] [ch. 5:1] [x] [Gen. 43:14]

Chapter 5
1 [y] [ch. 4:16] [z] ch. 4:11; [ch. 6:4]
2 [a] [ch. 2:9] [b] ch. 4:11; 8:4
3 [c] ch. 7:2; [Mark 6:23]
6 [d] ch. 7:2 [e] ver. 3; ch. 7:2; 9:12 [c] [See ver. 3 above]
8 [f] ch. 7:3; 8:5 [g] ch. 6:14
9 [h] 1 Kgs. 8:66 [i] See ch. 2:19 [j] ch. 3:5

restrained himself and went home, and he sent and brought his friends and [k]his wife Zeresh. 11 And Haman recounted to them the splendor of his riches, [l]the number of his sons, all the promotions with which [m]the king had honored him, and how he had advanced him above the officials and the servants of the king. 12 Then Haman said, "Even Queen Esther let no one but me come with the king to the feast she prepared. And tomorrow also I am invited by her together with the king. 13 Yet all this is worth nothing to me, so long as I see Mordecai the Jew sitting [i]at the king's gate." 14 Then [k]his wife Zeresh and all his friends said to him, [n]"Let a gallows[1] fifty cubits[2] high be made, and in the morning tell the king to have Mordecai hanged upon it. Then go joyfully with the king to the feast." This idea pleased Haman, and he had the gallows made.

The King Honors Mordecai

6 On that night the king could not sleep. And he gave orders to bring [o]the book of memorable deeds, the chronicles, and they were read before the king. 2 And it was found written how [p]Mordecai had told about [q]Bigthana[3] and [r]Teresh, two of the king's eunuchs, who guarded the threshold, and who had sought to lay hands on King Ahasuerus. 3 And the king said, "What honor or distinction has been bestowed on Mordecai for this?" The king's young men who attended him said, "Nothing has been done for him." 4 And the king said, "Who is in the court?" Now Haman had just entered [s]the outer court of the king's palace to speak to the king about having Mordecai hanged on [t]the gallows[4] that he had prepared for him. 5 And the king's young men told him, "Haman is there, standing in the court." And the king said, "Let him come in." 6 So Haman came in, and the king said to him, "What should be done to the man [u]whom the king delights to honor?" And Haman said to himself, "Whom would the king delight to honor more than me?" 7 And Haman said to the king, "For the man whom the king delights to honor, 8 let royal robes be brought, which the king has worn, [v]and the horse that the king has ridden, and on whose head [w]a royal crown[5] is set. 9 And let the robes and the horse be handed over to one of the king's most noble officials. Let them dress the man whom the king delights to honor, and let them lead him on the horse through the square of the city, [x]proclaiming before him: 'Thus shall it be done to the man whom the king delights to honor.'" 10 Then the king said to Haman, "Hurry; take the robes and the horse, as you have said, and do so to Mordecai the Jew, who sits [y]at the king's gate. Leave out nothing that you have mentioned." 11 So Haman took the robes and the horse, and he dressed Mordecai and led him through the square of the city, proclaiming before him, "Thus shall it be done to the man whom the king delights to honor."

12 Then Mordecai returned to the king's gate. But Haman hurried to his house, mourning [z]and with his head covered. 13 And Haman told [a]his wife Zeresh and all his friends everything that had happened to him. Then his wise men and his wife Zeresh said to him, "If Mordecai, before whom you have begun to fall, is of the Jewish people, you will not overcome him but will surely fall before him."

Esther Reveals Haman's Plot

14 While they were yet talking with him, the king's eunuchs arrived and hurried to bring Haman [b]to the feast that Esther had prepared.

7 So the king and Haman went in to feast with Queen Esther. 2 And on the second day, as they were drinking wine after the feast, the king again said to Esther, [c]"What is your wish, Queen Esther? It shall be granted you.

[1] Or *stake*; twice in this verse [2] A *cubit* was about 18 inches or 45 centimeters [3] *Bigthana* is an alternate spelling of *Bigthan* (see 2:21) [4] Or *suspended on a stake* [5] Or *headdress*

10[k] ch. 6:13
11[l] See ch. 9:7-10 [m] ch. 3:1
13[i] [See ver. 9 above]
14[k] [See ver. 10 above]
[n] ch. 6:4; 7:9, 10; [ch. 8:7; 9:13, 25]
Chapter 6
1[o] ch. 2:23; 10:2
2[p] ch. 2:22 [q] [ch. 1:10; 2:21]
[r] ch. 2:21
4[s] [ch. 4:11; 5:1] [t] ch. 5:14
6[u] ver. 7, 9, 11
8[v] [1 Kgs. 1:33] [w] ch. 1:11; 2:17

6:1–4 A seemingly inconsequential night of restlessness results in deliverance for God's people as Ahasuerus is reminded of Mordecai's faithfulness and Haman, who has just constructed gallows on which to hang Mordecai, is forced to exalt him instead.

Two gospel reminders are embedded in this event. First, we see once more that God is working behind the scenes for the good of his people. The king just "happened" to have a sleepless night, and just "happened" to hear of Mordecai's saving of the king! Second, we remember that God humbles those who exalt themselves, yet he delights to exalt those who humble themselves (Luke 18:14; James 4:10). The supreme example of this upside-down principle is Christ himself (Phil. 2:6–11).

9[x] [Gen. 41:43] **10**[y] See ch. 2:19 **12**[z] See 2 Sam. 15:30 **13**[a] ch. 5:10, 14 **14**[b] ch. 5:8 **Chapter 7** **2**[c] ch. 5:6; 9:12

And what is your request? [d]Even to the half of my kingdom, it shall be fulfilled." 3 Then Queen Esther answered, [e]"If I have found favor in your sight, O king, and if it please the king, let my life be granted me for my wish, and my people for my request. 4 [f]For we have been sold, I and my people, [g]to be destroyed, to be killed, and to be annihilated. If we had been sold merely as slaves, men and women, I would have been silent, for our affliction is not to be compared with the loss to the king." 5 Then King Ahasuerus said to Queen Esther, "Who is he, and where is he, who has dared[1] to do this?" 6 And Esther said, [h]"A foe and enemy! This wicked Haman!" Then Haman was terrified before the king and the queen.

Haman Is Hanged

7 And the king arose in his wrath from the wine-drinking and went into [i]the palace garden, but Haman stayed to beg for his life from Queen Esther, for he saw that harm was determined against him by the king. 8 And the king returned from [i]the palace garden to the place where they were drinking wine, as Haman was falling on [j]the couch where Esther was. And the king said, "Will he even assault the queen in my presence, in my own house?" As the word left the mouth of the king, they covered Haman's face. 9 Then [k]Harbona, one of the eunuchs in attendance on the king, said, "Moreover, [l]the gallows[2] that Haman has prepared for Mordecai, [m]whose word saved the king, is standing at Haman's house, fifty cubits[3] high." 10 And the king said, "Hang him on that." [n]So they hanged Haman on the gallows that he had prepared for Mordecai. [o]Then the wrath of the king abated.

Esther Saves the Jews

8 On that day King Ahasuerus gave to Queen Esther the house of Haman, [h]the enemy of the Jews. And Mordecai came before the king, for Esther had told [p]what he was to her. 2 [q]And the king took off his signet ring, which he had taken from Haman, and gave it to Mordecai. And Esther set Mordecai over the house of Haman.

3 Then Esther spoke again to the king. She fell at his feet and wept and pleaded with him to avert the evil plan of Haman [r]the Agagite and the plot that he had devised against the Jews. 4 [s]When the king held out the golden scepter to Esther, 5 Esther rose and stood before the king. And she said, "If it please the king, [t]and if I have found favor in his sight, and if the thing seems right before the king, and I am pleasing in his eyes, let an order be written to revoke [u]the letters devised by Haman [r]the Agagite, the son of Hammedatha, which he wrote to destroy the Jews who are in all the provinces of the king. 6 For how can I bear [v]to see the calamity that is coming to my people? Or how can I bear to see the destruction of my kindred?" 7 Then King Ahasuerus said to Queen Esther and to Mordecai the Jew,

[1] Hebrew *whose heart has filled him* [2] Or *stake*; also verse 10 [3] A *cubit* was about 18 inches or 45 centimeters

7:3–4 Esther cunningly appeals to Ahasuerus, revealing Haman's plan to annihilate her and her people. Haman's treachery is nothing new: From the beginning, the Serpent has sought again and again to destroy God's people, but God honors his covenant and preserves the lineage of the Seed of the woman so that we would have life through his death (John 10:10–14). Though we might not see his hand, God is at work even in circumstances that seem doomed.

7:5–10 The terror that Haman experienced (v. 6) is analogous to the terror that will be known by all who have futilely plotted against God (2 Cor. 2:15–16; Col. 2:15). This reality makes us grateful for the gospel through which even Haman-like wickedness can be fully and freely forgiven. For in God's plan, Christ hung not on a gallows, as did Haman, but on a cross, where the penalty for the sin of all who trust in him was fully paid.

8:1–14 Although Haman has been hanged, the edict to destroy God's people was still in effect. How will God change what seems unchangeable? Yet Mordecai is elevated to a position of authority and writes a new law so that God's people are freed to defend themselves. Again, we see how the sovereign plan of God overcomes the seemingly insurmountable opposition to his people. The point of all of this is to demonstrate the nature of God so that we will trust him when he promises that his mercy and provision for his people continues, as he knows is best. Back then, and today, the Lord refuses to abandon those who are his.

2 [d]ch. 5:3
3 [e]ch. 5:8
4 [f]ch. 3:9; 4:7 [g]ch. 3:13; 8:11
6 [h]See ch. 3:10
7 [i]ch. 1:5
8 [i][See ver. 7 above] [j][ch. 1:6]
9 [k]ch. 1:10 [l]See ch. 5:14 [m][ch. 2:22]
10 [n][Ps. 7:16; Prov. 11:5, 6; Dan. 6:24] [o][ch. 2:1]
Chapter 8
1 [h][See ch. 7:6 above] [p][ch. 2:7, 15]
2 [q]ch. 3:10
3 [r]ch. 3:1; 9:24
4 [s]ch. 4:11; 5:2
5 [t]ch. 5:8; 7:3 [u][ch. 3:13] [r][See ver. 3 above]
6 [v][ch. 7:4]

"Behold, [w]I have given Esther the house of Haman, and they have hanged him on the gallows,[1] because he intended to lay hands on the Jews. 8 But you may write as you please with regard to the Jews, in the name of the king, [x]and seal it with the king's ring, for an edict written in the name of the king and sealed with the king's ring [y]cannot be revoked."

9 [z]The king's scribes were summoned at that time, in the third month, which is the month of Sivan, on the twenty-third day. And an edict was written, according to all that Mordecai commanded concerning the Jews, to [a]the satraps and the governors and the officials of the provinces [b]from India to Ethiopia, [b]127 provinces, [c]to each province in its own script and to each people in its own language, and also to the Jews in their script and their language. 10 [d]And he wrote in the name of King Ahasuerus [e]and sealed it with the king's signet ring. Then he sent the letters by mounted couriers riding on [f]swift horses that were used in the king's service, bred from the royal stud, 11 saying that the king allowed the Jews who were in every city [g]to gather and defend their lives, [h]to destroy, to kill, and to annihilate any armed force of any people or province that might attack them, children and women included, [i]and to plunder their goods, 12 [j]on one day throughout all the provinces of King Ahasuerus, on the thirteenth day of the twelfth month, which is the month of Adar. 13 [k]A copy of what was written was to be issued as a decree in every province, being publicly displayed to all peoples, and the Jews were to be ready on that day to take vengeance on their enemies. 14 So the couriers, mounted on their [f]swift horses that were used in the king's service, rode out hurriedly, urged by the king's command. And the decree was issued in Susa the citadel.

15 Then Mordecai went out from the presence of the king [l]in royal robes of blue and white, with a great golden crown[2] and [m]a robe of fine linen and purple, [n]and the city of Susa shouted and rejoiced. 16 The Jews had [o]light and gladness and joy and honor. 17 And in every province and in every city, wherever the king's command and his edict reached, there was gladness and joy among the Jews, a feast and [p]a holiday. [q]And many from the peoples of the country declared themselves Jews, [r]for fear of the Jews had fallen on them.

The Jews Destroy Their Enemies

9 [s]Now in the twelfth month, which is the month of Adar, [t]on the thirteenth day of the same, [u]when the king's command and edict were about to be carried out, [j]on the very day when the enemies of the Jews hoped to gain the mastery over them, the reverse occurred: the Jews gained mastery over those who hated them. 2 [v]The Jews gathered in their cities throughout all the provinces of King Ahasuerus to lay hands on those who sought their harm. And no one could stand against them, [w]for the fear of them had fallen on all peoples. 3 All the officials of the provinces and [x]the satraps and the governors and the royal agents also helped the Jews, for the fear of Mordecai had fallen on them. 4 For Mordecai was great in the king's house, and his fame spread throughout all the provinces, for the man Mordecai grew [y]more and more powerful. 5 The Jews struck all their enemies with the sword, killing and destroying them, and did as they pleased to those who hated them. 6 In Susa the citadel

[1] Or *stake* [2] Or *headdress*

7 [w] ver. 1
8 [x] ver. 10; ch. 3:12 [y] [ch. 1:19; Dan. 6:8, 12, 15]
9 [z] ch. 3:12 [a] See Ezra 8:36 [b] ch. 1:1 [c] ch. 1:22; 3:12
10 [d] ch. 3:12, 13 [e] ch. 3:12 [f] 1 Kgs. 4:28
11 [g] ch. 9:2, 15, 16, 18 [h] ch. 3:13; 7:4 [i] [ch. 9:10, 15, 16]
12 [j] ch. 3:13; 9:1
13 [k] ch. 3:14; 4:8
14 [f] [See ver. 10 above]
15 [l] [Gen. 41:42; Dan. 5:29] [m] [1 Chr. 15:27] [n] [ch. 3:15]
16 [o] [Ps. 97:11]
17 [p] ch. 9:19, 22; 1 Sam. 25:8 [q] ch. 9:27 [r] ch. 9:2
Chapter 9
1 [s] ch. 8:12 [t] ver. 17 [u] ch. 3:13 [j] [See ch. 8:12 above] **2** [v] ver. 15, 16, 18; ch. 8:11 [w] ch. 8:17 **3** [x] See Ezra 8:36 **4** [y] [2 Sam. 3:1]; 1 Chr. 11:9

8:16 The Jews had light, gladness, joy, honor, and victory because Esther had stepped into the gap to risk all for them. But her saving actions were made possible only by the supernatural intervention of God controlling the events of her life and the lives of her people. The message of the gospel is that this same God (who demonstrates his nature in the life of Esther) still intervenes to deliver his people from the sin and miseries of this present world.

9:1 ". . . the reverse occurred." Just when God's enemies think that they have finally gained mastery over his people, the reverse occurs and God's people are victorious (2 Cor. 6:9–10). Again, we see that God's ways are not our ways. Human weakness is the channel through which divine power is manifested. The gospel truth is given its richest meaning in Jesus, who won the greatest victory of all just when his enemies thought they had vanquished him (Col. 2:14–15). And God yet uses jars of clay such as us to display the glories of his grace (2 Cor. 4:7).

itself the Jews killed and destroyed 500 men,
[7]and also killed Parshandatha and Dalphon
and Aspatha [8]and Poratha and Adalia and
Aridatha [9]and Parmashta and Arisai and
Aridai and Vaizatha, [10][z]the ten sons of Haman
the son of Hammedatha, [a]the enemy of the
Jews, [b]but they laid no hand on the plunder.
[11]That very day the number of those killed
in Susa the citadel was reported to the king.
[12]And the king said to Queen Esther, "In Susa
the citadel the Jews have killed and destroyed
500 men and also the ten sons of Haman.
What then have they done in the rest of the
king's provinces! [c]Now what is your wish?
It shall be granted you. And what further
is your request? It shall be fulfilled." [13]And
Esther said, "If it please the king, let the Jews
who are in Susa be allowed [d]tomorrow also
to do according to this day's edict. And let
the ten sons of Haman be hanged on the gallows."[1]
[14]So the king commanded this to be
done. A decree was issued in Susa, and the ten
sons of Haman were hanged. [15]The Jews who
were in Susa gathered also on the fourteenth
day of the month of Adar and they killed
300 men in Susa, but they laid no hands on
the plunder.
[16][e]Now the rest of the Jews who were in
the king's provinces also [f]gathered to defend
their lives, and got relief from their enemies
and killed 75,000 of those who hated them,
but they laid no hands on the plunder. [17]This
was [g]on the thirteenth day of the month of
Adar, and on the fourteenth day they rested
and made that a day of feasting and gladness.
[18]But the Jews who were in Susa gathered [g]on
the thirteenth day and on the fourteenth, and
rested [h]on the fifteenth day, making that a day
of feasting and gladness. [19]Therefore the Jews
of the villages, who live in [i]the rural towns,
hold the fourteenth day of the month of Adar
as a day for gladness and feasting, as [j]a holiday,
and [k]as a day on which they send gifts of food
to one another.

The Feast of Purim Inaugurated

[20]And Mordecai recorded these things and
sent letters to all the Jews who were in all the
provinces of King Ahasuerus, both near and
far, [21]obliging them to keep the fourteenth
day of the month Adar and also the fifteenth
day of the same, year by year, [22]as the days on
which the Jews got relief from their enemies,
and as the month that had been turned for
them from sorrow into gladness and from
mourning into [j]a holiday; that they should
make them days of feasting and gladness, days
for sending gifts of food to one another and
gifts to the poor.
[23]So the Jews accepted what they had
started to do, and what Mordecai had written
to them. [24]For Haman the Agagite, the
son of Hammedatha, [l]the enemy of all the
Jews, [m]had plotted against the Jews to destroy
them, and [n]had cast Pur (that is, cast lots),
to crush and to destroy them. [25]But when it
came before the king, he gave orders in writing
[o]that his evil plan that he had devised
against the Jews [p]should return on his own
head, and that he and his sons should be
hanged on the gallows.[2] [26]Therefore they
called these days Purim, after the term [n]Pur.
Therefore, because of all that was written in
[q]this letter, and of what they had faced in
this matter, and of what had happened to
them, [27]the Jews firmly obligated themselves
and their offspring and [r]all who joined them,
that without fail they would keep [s]these two
days according to what was written and at the
time appointed every year, [28]that these days
should be remembered and kept throughout
every generation, in every clan, province,
and city, and that these days of Purim should
never fall into disuse among the Jews, nor
should the commemoration of these days
cease among their descendants.
[29]Then Queen Esther, [t]the daughter of
Abihail, and Mordecai the Jew gave full written
authority, confirming [u]this second letter
about Purim. [30]Letters were sent to all the
Jews, [v]to the 127 provinces of the kingdom
of Ahasuerus, in words of peace and truth,
[31]that these days of Purim should be observed
at their appointed seasons, as Mordecai the
Jew and Queen Esther obligated them, and
as they had obligated themselves and their
offspring, with regard to [w]their fasts and their
lamenting. [32]The command of Queen Esther
confirmed these practices of [x]Purim, and it was
recorded in writing.

[1] Or *stake* [2] Or *suspended on a stake*

10[z] ver. 13, 14; [ch. 5:11] [a] See ch. 3:10 [b] [ch. 8:11] **12**[c] ch. 5:6; 7:2 **13**[d] ver. 15; ch. 8:11 **16**[e] ver. 2 [f] ver. 2; [ch. 8:11] **17**[g] ver. 1 **18**[g] [See ver. 17 above] [h] ver. 21 **19**[i] Deut. 3:5; Ezek. 38:11; Zech. 2:4 [j] ch. 8:17 [k] Neh. 8:10, 12 **22**[j] [See ver. 19 above] **24**[l] See ch. 3:10 [m] ch. 3:6 [n] ch. 3:7 **25**[o] ch. 7:9, 10; 8:3, 7 [p] [Ps. 7:16] **26**[n] [See ver. 24 above] [q] ver. 20 **27**[r] [Isa. 56:3, 6; Zech. 2:11] [s] ver. 21 **29**[t] ch. 2:15 [u] ver. 20; ch. 8:10 **30**[v] ch. 1:1; 8:9 **31**[w] ch. 4:3 **32**[x] ver. 26

The Greatness of Mordecai

10 King Ahasuerus imposed tax on
the land and on [y]the coastlands of
the sea. 2 And all the acts of his power and
might, and the full account of the high
honor of Mordecai, [z]to which the king
advanced him, are they not written in [a]the
Book of the Chronicles of the kings of Media
and Persia? 3 For Mordecai the Jew was [b]sec-
ond in rank to King Ahasuerus, and he was
great among the Jews and popular with the
multitude of his brothers, for he [c]sought
the welfare of his people and spoke peace
to all his people.

Chapter 10
1[y]Isa. 11:11; 24:15
2[z]ch. 8:15; 9:4 [a]ch. 2:23; 6:1
3[b]2 Chr. 28:7; [Gen. 41:40]
[c][Neh. 2:10; Ps. 122:8, 9]

10:1–3 Mordecai sought the welfare of others rather than himself. The commendation of the narrator reflects the ethic and nature of the Lord who inspired the text by the Holy Spirit. The supreme and ultimate expression of this nature is Jesus Christ, who supremely loved others ahead of himself and whom God therefore showered with honor (John 13:1; 17:4–5). Jesus is the true and final Mordecai, who, as the last verse of Esther says, "sought the welfare of his people and spoke peace to all his people" (Est. 10:3).

Introduction to Job

Author and Date

The unknown author presents Job as a person living in Uz (1:1), location unknown. Job was a godly man who clearly knew the God of Israel (1:21). The events of the book seem to be set in the time of Abraham, Isaac, and Jacob.

The Gospel in Job

The core complaint of "Everyman" Job is, "Why do the wicked prosper, and the righteous—like me!—suffer?" The book of Job attempts to help us understand the deficiencies of a worldview simply based upon the "merit," or value, of good conduct, and the "*de*-merit," or negative value, of bad conduct. Job engages in a passionate and persistent complaint, expressed both to God directly and also to his three friends, Eliphaz, Bildad, and Zophar. His complaint is that a world in which suffering could be visited on *him*, an innocent Everyman, rather than on heedless, ambitious people who seem to succeed at success, is either a meaningless world or a *malignant* world governed by a *malignant* God.

Job's "world"—that is, his conception of the world—is a world based on a simplistic view of law: God rewards the innocent and punishes the guilty. Job is so attached to his "consequentialist" theory of reality, and especially of God's reality, that it is impossible for him to see an eternal Reality *behind* his experienced reality of works and consequences.

Job's three friends speak "'peace, peace,' when there is no peace" (Jer. 6:14). They try to refute Job's complaint against the fairness of God either by *defending* God's fairness in the face of an "unfair" reality, or by attempting to discover what bad thing Job has (unconsciously) done that would make Job's suffering "fair," or by lecturing Job for even wondering about his circumstances. Job's indignant replies to his friends are justified. He accuses them of not taking his questions seriously enough, and rebukes them for not taking his suffering, and therefore human suffering in general, seriously enough. Job speaks rightly, we might say, *as far as he goes*. He lobs verbal grenades back at his three accusing friends and appears to beat them at their own game, which is accusation, defense, and counter-accusation.

From a gospel point of view, both Job and his friends argue on the wrong basis. Job accuses God; his friends defend God. But all four of them are viewing God in action-consequence terms. The gospel teaches a different version of God: God loves his own with a love that operates apart from and beyond questions of merit. "God shows his love for us in that while we were still sinners, Christ died for us" (Rom. 5:8). The gospel insight, which emerges like a supernova in the appearance of Jesus Christ, puts a person's moral standing before God on the basis of God's grace alone. Job becomes able, before the book ends, to hear something of this. He hears it first from Elihu, who intervenes in the argumentative deadlock with which the first 31 chapters of Job conclude. According to Elihu, the whole world, the "guilty" as well as the "innocent," are convicted before the Reality of God. "None is righteous, no, not one" (Rom. 3:10; Ps. 14:3).

After Elihu speaks, for six full chapters without interruption, the Lord comes down! Answering Job "out of the whirlwind" (Job 38:1) and with the evidences of his greatness displayed in creation, the Lord embodies and declares the nature of his Reality, which is beyond what Job has conceived. The Lord concludes by describing at length a most unusual creature he has created—Leviathan. The incomparable majesty and marvel of God's work stops Job in his tracks. He responds with newfound humility: "Therefore I despise myself, and repent in dust and ashes" (42:6).

Readers of Job can apply this book as a stunning corrective to ideas about God that conceive of him as operating according to human ideas of fairness and reward—that is, meritorious law. Moreover, God's nature is revealed to be benign and compassionate rather than malignant and contemptuous. We read at the end of the book that "Job died, an old man, and full of days" (42:17), having seen his sons' sons, down to four generations. The book of Job helps free us from believing in a "score-keeping" God. We are brought to see the God who is, who is all, and who is love.

Outline

I. Narrative Introduction (1:1–2:13)
II. Job's Complaint (3:1–26)
III. The Intervention of Eliphaz (4:1–5:27)
IV. Job's First Response to Eliphaz (6:1–7:21)
V. The Intervention of Bildad (8:1–22)
VI. Job's First Response to Bildad (9:1–10:22)
VII. The Intervention of Zophar (11:1–20)
VIII. Job's First Response to Zophar (12:1–14:22)
IX. The Second Intervention of Eliphaz (15:1–35)
X. Job's Second Response to Eliphaz (16:1–17:16)
XI. The Second Intervention of Bildad (18:1–21)
XII. Job's Second Response to Bildad (19:1–29)
XIII. The Second Intervention of Zophar (20:1–29)
XIV. Job's Second Response to Zophar (21:1–34)
XV. The Third Intervention of Eliphaz (22:1–30)
XVI. Job's Third Response to Eliphaz (23:1–24:25)
XVII. The Third Intervention of Bildad (25:1–6)
XVIII. Job's Third Response to Bildad (26:1–14)
XIX. Job's Parting Shot (27:1–31:40)
XX. The Intervention of Elihu (32:1–37:24)
XXI. The Lord's Intervention (38:1–41:34)
XXII. Job's Response to the Lord (42:1–6)
XXIII. The Lord Addresses Eliphaz, Bildad, and Zophar (42:7–9)
XXIV. How Job's Life Turned Out (42:10–17)

Job

Job's Character and Wealth

1 There was a man in the land of [a]Uz whose
name was [b]Job, and that man was [c]blame-
less and upright, one who [d]feared God and
[e]turned away from evil. 2 There were born to
him [f]seven sons and three daughters. 3 He possessed 7,000 sheep, 3,000 camels, 500 yoke of
oxen, and 500 female donkeys, and very many
servants, so that this man was the greatest of
all [g]the people of the east. 4 His sons used to
go and hold a feast in the house of each one
on his day, and they would send and invite
their three sisters to eat and drink with them.
5 And when the days of the feast had run their
course, Job would send and [h]consecrate them,
and he would rise early in the morning and
[i]offer burnt offerings according to the number
of them all. For Job said, "It may be that my
children have sinned, and [j]cursed[1] God in their
hearts." Thus Job did continually.

Satan Allowed to Test Job

6 Now there was a day when [k]the sons of
God came to present themselves before the
LORD, and [l]Satan[2] also came among them.
7 The LORD said to Satan, "From where have
you come?" Satan answered the LORD and
said, "From [m]going to and fro on the earth,
and from walking up and down on it." 8 And
the LORD said to Satan, "Have you [n]considered

[1] The Hebrew word *bless* is used euphemistically for *curse* in 1:5, 11; 2:5, 9 [2] Hebrew *the Accuser* or *the Adversary*; so throughout chapters 1–2

1:1–2:13 The first two chapters of Job set the stage for a great and climactic meeting: the encounter with God of a passionate man, filled with passionate rage concerning his life.

The background to this meeting is God's allowing Satan to test Job's faith—Job's entire attitude to life—by tearing him down. Explaining to Satan that Job is "a blameless and upright man, who fears God and turns away from evil" (1:8; 2:3), God puts "all that [Job] has" in Satan's power, *except* Job's self (1:12). Satan duly takes away every *possession* Job has, both things and family. Despite this, Job stays faithful to God: "Blessed be the name of the LORD" (1:21).

Then, however, God gives Job's *body* to be put under Satan's power, again with one exception: "only spare his life" (2:6). God exempts Job's breathing existence from Satan's strategy of demolition. God is more interested in Job as a person—in Job's soul, we might say, the enduring essence of him—than he is in Job's things, or even Job's body. What goes on inside Job is more important to God than what goes on outside him. Job's consequent skin disease (2:7) makes him repulsive to himself, and also to his wife. She shows him utter contempt: "Curse God and die" (2:9).

Job has three friends—Eliphaz, Bildad, and Zophar—all of whom care enough about him to sit with him—for seven days!—and commiserate. They see that Job's suffering is very great (2:13).

The question for Christians here is this: Where is God in our suffering? Not in conceptual suffering, nor in the suffering of people over *there*; but in actual, personal, experienced suffering. Where is God when our lives are dismantled by inconsolable grief or crushing disappointment? The book of Job does not deny the reality of our sufferings. Indeed, at one level this book complicates our perception of God by making us aware that God may permit suffering. But the reality that Job will ultimately perceive through his suffering also makes us aware that our lives are not beyond God's attention and our difficulties are not beyond his purposes.

Chapter 1
1 [a]Jer. 25:20; Lam. 4:21 [b]Ezek. 14:14, 20; James 5:11 [c]ver. 8; ch. 2:3; [ch. 9:20; Gen. 6:9; 17:1] [d]ch. 4:6; Prov. 16:6 [e][ch. 28:28; Ps. 34:14]
2 [f]ch. 42:13
3 [g]See Judg. 6:3
5 [h]1 Sam. 16:5 [i]ch. 42:8; Gen. 8:20 [j]ch. 2:5; [Ps. 10:3]
6 [k]ch. 2:1; 38:7; Gen. 6:2, 4 [l][1 Chr. 21:1; Zech. 3:1; Rev. 12:9, 10]
7 [m]ch. 2:2; [1 Pet. 5:8]
8 [n]ch. 2:3

my [o]servant Job, that there is none like him on the earth, [p]a blameless and upright man, who fears God and turns away from evil?" 9 Then Satan answered the LORD and said, "Does Job fear God for no reason? 10 Have you not put [q]a hedge around him and his house and all that he has, on every side? You have [r]blessed the work of his hands, and his possessions have increased in the land. 11 But [s]stretch out your hand and [t]touch all that he has, and he will [u]curse you [v]to your face." 12 And the LORD said to Satan, "Behold, all that he has is in your hand. Only against him do not stretch out your hand." So Satan went out from the presence of the LORD.

Satan Takes Job's Property and Children

13 Now there was a day when his sons and daughters were eating and drinking wine in their oldest brother's house, 14 and there came a messenger to Job and said, "The oxen were plowing and the donkeys feeding beside them, 15 and [w]the Sabeans fell upon them and took them and struck down the servants[1] with the edge of the sword, and I alone have escaped to tell you." 16 While he was yet speaking, there came another and said, [x]"The fire of God fell from heaven and burned up the sheep and the servants and consumed them, and I alone have escaped to tell you." 17 While he was yet speaking, there came another and said, [y]"The Chaldeans formed [z]three groups and made a raid on the camels and took them and struck down the servants with the edge of the sword, and I alone have escaped to tell you." 18 While he was yet speaking, there came another and said, [a]"Your sons and daughters were eating and drinking wine in their oldest brother's house, 19 and behold, a great wind came across [b]the wilderness and struck the four corners of the house, and it fell upon the young people, and they are dead, and I alone have escaped to tell you."

20 Then Job arose and [c]tore his [d]robe and [e]shaved his head [f]and fell on the ground and worshiped. 21 And he said, [g]"Naked I came from my mother's womb, and naked shall I [h]return. The LORD [i]gave, and the LORD has taken away; [j]blessed be the name of the LORD."

22 [k]In all this Job did not sin or charge God with [l]wrong.

Satan Attacks Job's Health

2 Again [m]there was a day when the sons of God came to present themselves before the LORD, and Satan also came among them to present himself before the LORD. 2 And the LORD said to Satan, "From where have you come?" Satan answered the LORD and said, "From going to and fro on the earth, and from walking up and down on it." 3 And the LORD said to Satan, "Have you considered my servant Job, that there is none like him on the earth, a blameless and upright man, who fears God and turns away from evil? He still [n]holds fast his integrity, although you incited me against him to destroy him [o]without reason." 4 Then Satan answered the LORD and said, "Skin for skin! All that a man has he will give for his life. 5 But [p]stretch out your hand and touch his bone and his flesh, and he will [q]curse you to your face." 6 And the LORD said to Satan, "Behold, he is in your hand; only spare his life."

7 So Satan went out from the presence of the LORD and struck Job with loathsome [r]sores

[1] Hebrew *the young men*; also verses 16, 17

8 [o] Num. 12:7; 2 Sam. 7:5; Isa. 20:3 [p] ver. 1
10 [q] [Ps. 3:3; 34:7] [r] [Ps. 128:1, 2]
11 [s] ch. 2:5 [t] ch. 19:21; Isa. 53:4 (Heb.) [u] ver. 5 [v] Isa. 65:3
15 [w] ch. 6:19; See 1 Kgs. 10:1
16 [x] 2 Kgs. 1:12
17 [y] Gen. 11:28; 2 Kgs. 24:2 [z] [Judg. 7:16; 1 Sam. 11:11]
18 [a] ver. 4, 13
19 [b] Isa. 21:1; Jer. 4:11; Hos. 13:15
20 [c] See Gen. 37:29 [d] Ezra 9:3 [e] Jer. 7:29 [f] [1 Pet. 5:6]
21 [g] Eccles. 5:15; [Ps. 49:17; 1 Tim. 6:7] [h] [Gen. 3:19; Ps. 90:3; Eccles. 12:7] [i] [Eccles. 5:19; James 1:17] [j] Ps. 113:2; Dan. 2:20; [Eph. 5:20; 1 Thess. 5:18]
22 [k] ch. 2:10 [l] ch. 24:12

The ultimate answer to questions about God's nature and love in the midst of suffering will not come until the New Testament points us to the cross of Christ. Where is God when suffering is great and all seems lost? The gospel says God is *there*, in *that man*. Since God is there in that man's unfair suffering, when we suffer the "slings and arrows of outrageous fortune," we are close to God, drawing comfort from his presence (cf. 2 Cor. 1:5). And because there was purpose beyond the fathoming of those who witnessed Christ's suffering—despite its horrific unfairness—we can believe there is purpose in our difficulties, and eternal care beyond them, even if there is no fairness evident in them.

Job and also Job's friends start out—and actually continue, until very late in the game—believing that God is normally present only in blessing and prosperity. Job and his friends (but only at the last) are eventually given a vision of God's presence that is beyond a vision of worldly success. It is a vision outside and beyond human judging. It is also a vision that includes all things. "He's got the whole world in his hands."

Chapter 2 **1** [m] ch. 1:6 **3** [n] ver. 9; [ch. 27:5, 6] [o] ch. 9:17 **5** [p] ch. 1:11 [q] ch. 1:5 **7** [r] Ex. 9:9; Lev. 13:18; [Deut. 28:27]

from [s]the sole of his foot to the crown of his
head. 8 And he took [t]a piece of broken pottery
with which to scrape himself while he sat in
[u]the ashes.

9 Then his wife said to him, "Do you still
[v]hold fast your integrity? [q]Curse God and die."
10 But he said to her, "You speak as one of the
[w]foolish women would speak. [x]Shall we receive
good from God, and shall we not receive evil?"[1]
[y]In all this Job did not [z]sin with his lips.

Job's Three Friends

11 Now when Job's three [a]friends heard of
all this evil that had come upon him, they
came each from his own place, Eliphaz [b]the
Temanite, Bildad [c]the Shuhite, and Zophar
the Naamathite. They made an appointment
together to come to [d]show him sympathy and
comfort him. 12 And when they saw him from
a distance, they did not recognize him. And
they raised their voices and wept, and they
[e]tore their robes and sprinkled [f]dust on their
heads toward heaven. 13 And they sat with him
on the ground [g]seven days and seven nights,
and no one spoke a word to him, for they saw
that his suffering was very great.

Job Laments His Birth

3 After this Job [h]opened his mouth and
cursed the day of his birth. 2 And Job said:

3 [i]"Let the day perish on which I was born,
and the night that said,
'A man is conceived.'
4 Let that day be darkness!
May God above not seek it,
nor light shine upon it.
5 Let gloom and [j]deep darkness claim it.
Let clouds dwell upon it;
let the blackness of the day terrify it.
6 That night—let thick darkness seize it!
Let it not rejoice among the days of
the year;
let it not come into the number of the
months.
7 Behold, let that night be barren;
let no joyful cry enter it.
8 Let those curse it who curse the day,
who are ready to rouse up [k]Leviathan.
9 Let the stars of its dawn be dark;
let it hope for light, but have none,
nor see [l]the eyelids of the morning,
10 because it did not shut the doors of my
mother's womb,
nor hide trouble from my eyes.

11 "Why [m]did I not die at birth,
come out from the womb and expire?
12 Why did [n]the knees receive me?
Or why the breasts, that I should
nurse?
13 For then I would have lain down and
been quiet;
I would have slept; then I would have
been at rest,
14 with kings and counselors of the earth
who [o]rebuilt ruins for themselves,
15 or with princes who had gold,
who filled their houses with silver.
16 Or why was I not as a hidden [p]stillborn
child,
as infants who never see the light?
17 There the wicked cease from troubling,
and there the weary are at [q]rest.

[1] Or *disaster*; also verse 11

3:1–26 In light of the devastation visited upon Job's possessions and also his body, Job complains bitterly to his three friends. He wishes he had never been born (vv. 3, 11–12). He regards the dead as having ceased from all trouble and oppression (vv. 17–19). He also regards the present moment in his life—and who could not identify at some point with Job's words?—as being "not at ease, nor am I quiet; I have no rest, but trouble comes" (v. 26). Job believes that having *no* life would be preferable to his life of suffering. His existence in the world having come undone, he wants out!

For Christians, the fact that the Bible includes such unvarnished words of despair as Job's is a good thing. We sometimes hear the counsel, "first thought, best thought." This is another way of saying, stick to your initial reaction to a situation, emotionally speaking, since it tells the truth of what is going on inside you. Job is able to tell the truth here, about his inner life; and *we* can tell the truth about ours. As Paul said later, "I am speaking the truth in Christ—I am not lying; . . . that I have great sorrow and unceasing anguish in my heart" (Rom. 9:1–2).

We have a Savior who welcomes our unfiltered questions and laments. He is the Friend to the perplexed.

7[s] Deut. 28:35; Isa. 1:6
8[t] ch. 41:30 [u] ch. 42:6; Ezek. 27:30; Jonah 3:6; Matt. 11:21
9[v] ver. 3 [q] [See ver. 5 above]
10[w] [Ps. 74:18, 22] [x] [James 5:10, 11] [y] ch. 1:22 [z] [Ps. 39:1]
11[a] [Prov. 17:17] [b] See 1 Chr. 1:45 [c] Gen. 25:2; 1 Chr. 1:32 [d] ch. 42:11; [Rom. 12:15]
12[e] See Gen. 37:29 [f] See Josh. 7:6; Neh. 9:1; Lam. 2:10; Ezek. 27:30
13[g] Ezek. 3:15; [Gen. 50:10]

Chapter 3
1[h] ch. 33:2; Ps. 78:2
3[i] [ch. 10:18, 19]; See Jer. 20:14-18
5[j] ch. 10:21, 22; 12:22; 24:17; 28:3; 34:22; 38:17; Ps. 23:4; Isa. 9:2; Matt. 4:16
8[k] ch. 41:1
9[l] ch. 41:18
11[m] ch. 10:18, 19
12[n] Gen. 30:3; 50:23; Isa. 66:12

14[o] [Isa. 58:12] **16**[p] Ps. 58:8; Eccles. 6:3; [1 Cor. 15:8] **17**[q] ch. 17:16

18 There the prisoners are at ease together;
they hear not the voice of [r]the taskmaster.
19 The small and the great are there,
and the slave is free from his master.

20 "Why is light given to him who is in misery,
and life to [s]the bitter in soul,
21 who [t]long for death, but it comes not,
and dig for it more than for [u]hidden
treasures,
22 who rejoice exceedingly
and are glad when they find the grave?
23 Why is light given to a man whose [v]way
is hidden,
whom God has [w]hedged in?
24 For my sighing comes [x]instead of[1] my
bread,
and my [y]groanings are poured out
like water.
25 [z]For the thing that I fear comes upon me,
and what I dread befalls me.
26 I am not at ease, nor am I quiet;
I have no rest, but trouble comes."

Eliphaz Speaks: The Innocent Prosper

4 Then Eliphaz the Temanite answered and
said:

2 "If one ventures a word with you, will
you be impatient?
Yet who can keep from speaking?
3 Behold, you have instructed many,
and you have [a]strengthened the weak
hands.
4 Your words have upheld him who was
stumbling,
and you have [a]made firm the feeble
knees.
5 But now it has come to you, and you are
impatient;
it touches you, and you are dismayed.
6 [b]Is not your fear of God[2] your [c]confi-
dence,
and the integrity of your ways your
hope?

7 "Remember: [d]who that was innocent ever
perished?
Or where were the upright cut off?
8 As I have seen, those who [e]plow iniquity
and sow trouble reap the same.
9 By [f]the breath of God they perish,
and by [g]the blast of his anger they are
consumed.
10 The roar of the lion, the voice of the
fierce lion,
[h]the teeth of the young lions are broken.
11 The strong lion perishes for lack of prey,
and the cubs of the lioness are scattered.

12 "Now a word was brought to me stealthily;
my ear received [i]the whisper of it.
13 Amid [j]thoughts from [k]visions of the
night,
when [k]deep sleep falls on men,
14 dread came upon me, and trembling,
which made all my bones shake.
15 A spirit glided past my face;
the hair of my flesh stood up.
16 It stood still,
but I could not discern its appearance.
[l]A form was before my eyes;
there was silence, then I heard [m]a voice:
17 [n]'Can mortal man be in the right before[3]
God?
Can a man be pure before his Maker?
18 Even in his servants [o]he puts no trust,
and his angels he charges with error;
19 how much more those who dwell in
houses of [p]clay,
whose foundation is in [q]the dust,
who are crushed like [r]the moth.
20 Between [s]morning and evening they are
beaten to pieces;
they perish forever [t]without anyone
regarding it.
21 Is not their tent-cord plucked up within
them,
[u]do they not die, and that without wisdom?'

5 "Call now; is there anyone who will
answer you?
To which of [v]the holy ones will you
turn?
2 Surely vexation kills the fool,
and jealousy slays the simple.

[1] Or *like*; Hebrew *before* [2] Hebrew lacks *of God* [3] Or *more than*; twice in this verse

18[r] Ex. 3:7 **20**[s] Prov. 31:6 **21**[t] Rev. 9:6 [u] Prov. 2:4 **23**[v] Isa. 40:27 [w] [ch. 1:10]; See ch. 19:8 **24**[x] [Ps. 42:3; 80:5; 102:9] [y] Ps. 22:1; 38:8 **25**[z] [Prov. 10:24] **Chapter 4** **3**[a] Isa. 35:3; [Heb. 12:12] **4**[a] [See ver. 3 above] **6**[b] ch. 1:1 [c] ch. 31:24; Prov. 3:26 **7**[d] [Ps. 37:25] **8**[e] Hos. 10:13; [Ps. 7:14; Prov. 22:8; Gal. 6:7, 8] **9**[f] Isa. 30:33 [g] ch. 15:30; Ex. 15:8; Ps. 18:15; [Isa. 11:4; 2 Thess. 2:8] **10**[h] Ps. 58:6; [ch. 29:17; Ps. 3:7] **12**[i] ch. 26:14 **13**[j] ch. 20:2 [k] ch. 33:15; Gen. 2:21; 15:12; 1 Sam. 26:12; Isa. 29:10 **16**[l] Num. 12:8 [m] [1 Kgs. 19:12] **17**[n] ch. 9:2; 10:4; 25:4; 32:2 **18**[o] ch. 15:15 **19**[p] ch. 10:9; 13:12; 33:6; Isa. 64:8; 2 Cor. 4:7; 5:1 [q] Gen. 2:7; 3:19; 18:27 [r] [ch. 13:28] **20**[s] [Ps. 90:5, 6; Isa. 38:12] [t] [Isa. 42:25; 57:1] **21**[u] ch. 36:12; Prov. 5:23; 10:21; [Hos. 4:6] **Chapter 5** **1**[v] ch. 15:15; Ps. 89:5, 7; Zech. 14:5

3 [w]I have seen the fool taking root,
but suddenly I cursed his dwelling.
4 His children are [x]far from safety;
they are crushed in [y]the gate,
and there is no one to deliver them.
5 The hungry eat his harvest,
and he takes it even out of thorns,[1]
and the thirsty pant[2] after his[3] wealth.
6 For affliction does not come from the
dust,
nor does trouble sprout from the
ground,
7 but man is [z]born to trouble
as the sparks fly upward.

8 "As for me, I would seek God,
and to God would I commit my cause,
9 who [a]does great things and [b]unsearch-
able,
[c]marvelous things without number:
10 he gives [d]rain on the earth
and sends waters on the fields;
11 he [e]sets on high those who are lowly,
and those who mourn are lifted to
safety.
12 He [f]frustrates the devices of the crafty,
so that their hands achieve no success.
13 He [g]catches the wise in their own craftiness,
and the schemes of the wily are
brought to a quick end.
14 They meet with darkness in the daytime
and [h]grope at noonday as in the night.
15 But he [i]saves the needy from the sword
of their mouth
and from the hand of the mighty.
16 So the poor have hope,
and [j]injustice shuts her mouth.

17 "Behold, [k]blessed is the one whom God
reproves;
therefore [l]despise not the discipline of
the [m]Almighty.
18 For he wounds, but he [n]binds up;
he [o]shatters, but his hands heal.
19 He will [p]deliver you from six troubles;
in seven no [q]evil[4] shall touch you.
20 [r]In famine he will redeem you from death,
and in war from the power of the
sword.
21 You shall be [s]hidden from the lash of the
tongue,
and shall not fear destruction when it
comes.
22 At destruction and famine you shall
laugh,
and shall not fear [t]the beasts of the
earth.
23 For you shall be in league with the
stones of the field,
and the beasts of the field shall be at
peace with you.

[1] The meaning of the Hebrew is uncertain [2] Aquila, Symmachus, Syriac, Vulgate; Hebrew could be read as *and the snare pants* [3] Hebrew *their* [4] Or *disaster*

5:8–27 The first intervention of Job's friend Eliphaz is a mistaken speech, and on two counts. First, it is spoken under the heading of "If *I* were *you*, I'd . . ." (v. 8). In other words, Eliphaz presents himself as superior to the sufferer in front of him. Sufferers are seldom able to hear such an attitude from another person no matter how well-meaning the person is. Eliphaz is telling Job what to do on the basis, supposedly, of Eliphaz's deeper understanding. He therefore presents himself as superior from the start, disqualifying himself from any true empathy that would really *help* his friend.

Second, Eliphaz's words reek of piety, in the negative sense of that word. Much of what Eliphaz says sounds good—and, to a Christian ear, true. But it is so full of platitudes that it falls flat. It sounds like one boasting of his own righteousness while giving a theology lecture about God's nature (cf. v. 8; Luke 18:11), and by doing so demonstrating that he cannot really sense the seriousness of Job's pain. Rather, Eliphaz is like one who says, "'Peace, peace,' when there is no peace" (Jer. 6:14; 8:11).

It is for us a good and graceful thing that the Word of God gives this example of Eliphaz, this portrait of a mistaken man. We can see in Eliphaz how *not* to go about comforting our fellow sufferers. We don't detach ourselves from and thereby look down on the sufferings of another human being.

We can't tell someone who is unwell that all will *be* well, even if, like Julian of Norwich, we know that it is true. This is because unwell people will probably receive such encouragement as a judgment on *their* experience, and therefore close their ears. Sufferers do not require the theological statements of those whose lives are currently easy. They require the graceful presence of friends who are wise enough to "weep with those who weep" (Rom. 12:15).

3[w] Jer. 12:2, 3; [Ps. 37:35, 36; 73:18-20]
4[x] [Ps. 119:155] [y] ch. 29:7; Ps. 127:5; Prov. 22:22; [Josh. 20:4; Amos 5:12]; See Ruth 4:1
7[z] ch. 14:1; Gen. 3:17-19; Eccles. 2:23
9[a] ch. 9:10; [ch. 37:5; Ps. 40:5; 72:18; Rom. 11:33; Rev. 15:3] [b] ch. 9:10; 11:7; 34:24 [c] [ch. 10:16]
10[d] Ps. 65:9, 10; 147:8; Jer. 5:24; 14:22; Acts 14:17; [Ps. 104:10, 13; Matt. 5:45]
11[e] 1 Sam. 2:7; [Ps. 113:7]
12[f] [Neh. 4:15; Ps. 33:10; Isa. 8:10]
13[g] Cited 1 Cor. 3:19; [Ps. 9:15, 16]
14[h] ch. 12:25; Deut. 28:29; [Isa. 59:10]
15[i] Ps. 35:10
16[j] Ps. 107:42; [Ps. 63:11]
17[k] Ps. 94:12; [James 1:12] [l] Prov. 3:11; Heb. 12:5; Rev. 3:19 [m] Gen. 17:1
18[n] Isa. 30:26; 61:1; Hos. 6:1 [o] [Deut. 32:39]
19[p] Ps. 34:19; 91:3; 1 Cor. 10:13 [q] Ps. 91:10
20[r] Ps. 33:19; 37:19
21[s] [Ps. 31:20]
22[t] [Isa. 11:8, 9; 35:9; 65:25; Ezek. 34:25; Hos. 2:18]

24 You shall know that your [u]tent is at
peace,
and you shall inspect your fold and
miss nothing.
25 You shall know also that your [v]offspring
shall be many,
and your descendants as [w]the grass of
the earth.
26 You shall come to your grave in [x]ripe old
age,
like a sheaf gathered up in its season.
27 Behold, this we have [y]searched out; it is
true.
Hear, and know it for your good."[1]

Job Replies: My Complaint Is Just

6 Then Job answered and said:

2 "Oh that my vexation were weighed,
and all my calamity laid in the balances!
3 For then it would be heavier than [z]the
sand of the sea;
therefore my words have been rash.
4 For [a]the arrows of the Almighty are in
me;
my spirit drinks their poison;
the terrors of God are arrayed against
me.
5 Does the wild donkey bray when he has
grass,
or the ox low over his fodder?
6 Can that which is tasteless be eaten
without salt,
or is there any taste in the juice of the
mallow?[2]
7 My appetite refuses to touch them;
they are as food that is loathsome to
me.[3]

8 "Oh that I might have my request,
and that God would fulfill my hope,
9 that it would [b]please God to crush me,
that he would let loose his hand and
cut me off!
10 This would be my comfort;
I would even exult[4] in pain [c]unspar-
ing,
for I have not denied the words of
[d]the Holy One.
11 What is my strength, that I should wait?
And what is my end, that I should be
patient?
12 Is my strength the strength of stones, or
is my flesh bronze?
13 Have I any help in me,
when resource is driven from me?

14 "He who [e]withholds[5] kindness from a
[f]friend
forsakes the fear of the Almighty.
15 My [g]brothers are [h]treacherous as a torrent-bed,
as torrential [i]streams that pass away,
16 which are dark with ice,
and where the snow hides itself.
17 When they melt, they disappear;
when it is hot, they vanish from their
place.
18 The caravans turn aside from their
course;
they go up into [j]the waste and perish.
19 The caravans of [k]Tema look,
the travelers of [l]Sheba hope.
20 They are [m]ashamed because they were
confident;
they come there and are [m]disappointed.
21 For you have now become nothing;
you see my calamity and are afraid.
22 Have I said, 'Make me a gift'?
Or, 'From your wealth offer a bribe for
me'?
23 Or, 'Deliver me from the adversary's
hand'?
Or, 'Redeem me from the hand of [n]the
ruthless'?

24 "Teach me, and I will be silent;
make me understand how I have gone
astray.
25 How forceful are upright words!
But what does reproof from you
reprove?
26 Do you think that you can reprove words,
when the speech of a despairing man
is [o]wind?
27 You would even [p]cast lots over the
fatherless,
and bargain over your friend.

[1] Hebrew *for yourself* [2] The meaning of the Hebrew word is uncertain [3] The meaning of the Hebrew is uncertain [4] The meaning of the Hebrew word is uncertain [5] Syriac, Vulgate (compare Targum); the meaning of the Hebrew word is uncertain

24[u] [ch. 21:9] **25**[v] ch. 21:8; Ps. 112:2 [w] Ps. 72:16 **26**[x] [Gen. 15:15; 25:8; 35:29; Prov. 9:11; 10:27] **27**[y] [Ps. 111:2] **Chapter 6** **3**[z] [Prov. 27:3] **4**[a] Ps. 38:2 **9**[b] 1 Kgs. 19:4; [Num. 11:15] **10**[c] [Isa. 30:14] [d] Lev. 19:2; Isa. 57:15; Hos. 11:9 **14**[e] [Prov. 11:24] [f] [Prov. 17:17] **15**[g] [Ps. 38:11; 41:9] [h] [1 Sam. 14:33] [i] [Jer. 15:18] **18**[j] [Gen. 1:2; Jer. 4:23] **19**[k] Gen. 25:15; 1 Chr. 1:30; Isa. 21:14; Jer. 25:23 [l] See 1 Kgs. 10:1 **20**[m] Isa. 1:29; Jer. 14:3 **23**[n] ch. 15:20; 27:13 **26**[o] ch. 7:7; Isa. 41:29 **27**[p] Joel 3:3; Nah. 3:10

28 “But now, be pleased to look at me,
for I will not lie to your face.
29 [q]Please turn; let no injustice be done.
Turn now; my vindication is at stake.
30 Is there any injustice on my tongue?
Cannot my palate discern the cause of
calamity?

Job Continues: My Life Has No Hope

7 “Has not man [r]a hard service on earth,
and are not his [s]days like the days of a
hired hand?
2 Like a slave who longs for [t]the shadow,
and like [u]a hired hand who looks for
his [v]wages,
3 so I am allotted months of [w]emptiness,
[x]and nights of misery are apportioned
to me.
4 [y]When I lie down I say, ‘When shall I arise?’
But the night is long,
and I am full of tossing till the dawn.
5 My flesh is clothed with [z]worms and [a]dirt;
my skin hardens, then [b]breaks out
afresh.
6 My days are [c]swifter than [d]a weaver’s
shuttle
and come to their end without hope.

7 “Remember that my life is a [e]breath;
my eye will never again see good.
8 [f]The eye of him who sees me will behold
me no more;
while your eyes are on me, [g]I shall be
gone.
9 As [h]the cloud fades and vanishes,
so he who [i]goes down to Sheol does
not come up;
10 he [j]returns no more to his house,
nor does his [k]place know him anymore.

11 “Therefore I will not [l]restrain my mouth;
I will speak in the anguish of my spirit;
I will [m]complain in [n]the bitterness of
my soul.
12 Am I the sea, or [o]a sea monster,
that you set a guard over me?
13 [p]When I say, ‘My bed will comfort me,
my couch will ease my complaint,’
14 then you scare me with dreams
and terrify me with visions,
15 so that I would choose strangling
and death rather than my [q]bones.
16 I [r]loathe my life; I would not live forever.
[s]Leave me alone, for my days are [t]a
breath.
17 [u]What is man, that you make so much of
him,
and that you set your heart on him,
18 [v]visit him every morning
and [w]test him every moment?
19 How long will you not [x]look away from
me,
nor leave me alone till I swallow my
spit?
20 If I sin, what do I do to you, you watcher
of mankind?
Why have you made me [y]your mark?
Why have I become a burden to you?
21 Why do you not pardon my transgression
and take away my iniquity?
For now I shall lie in [z]the earth;
you will [a]seek me, [b]but I shall not be.”

Bildad Speaks: Job Should Repent

8 Then [c]Bildad the Shuhite answered and
said:

2 “How long will you say these things,
and the words of your mouth be a
[d]great wind?
3 [e]Does God pervert justice?
Or does the Almighty pervert the
right?
4 If your [f]children have sinned against
him,
he has delivered them into the hand
of their transgression.

8:1, 11–18 Like Eliphaz’s speech before him, the first intervention by Job’s second friend, Bildad, is an attempted “refutation” of Job’s state of mind. But it is a mistaken refutation, because it is coming from a place of anger. Bildad speaks harshly to his friend’s complaint: “How long will you say these things, and the words of your mouth be a great wind?” (v. 2).

The Bible tells us that, “a bruised reed [my servant] will not break” (Isa. 42:3; Matt. 12:20). “Softly and tenderly, Jesus is calling.” Whenever we find ourselves getting

29[q] ch. 17:10

Chapter 7

1[r] ch. 14:14; Isa. 40:2 [s] ch. 14:5; Ps. 39:4
2[t] Song 2:17; 4:6; Jer. 6:4 [u] ch. 14:6 [v] Lev. 19:13
3[w] ver. 16 [x] [ch. 30:17]
4[y] Deut. 28:67
5[z] Isa. 14:11 [a] [ch. 2:8] [b] [ch. 2:7]

6[c] ch. 9:25 [d] [Isa. 38:12] **7**[e] ch. 6:26; Ps. 78:39 **8**[f] ch. 20:9; [ch. 8:18; Ps. 37:36] [g] [ver. 2] **9**[h] ch. 30:15 [i] See ch. 21:13 **10**[j] ch. 10:21; 2 Sam. 12:23 [k] ch. 20:9; Ps. 103:16; [ch. 8:18] **11**[l] Ps. 40:9 [m] ch. 21:4; Ps. 77:3 [n] ch. 10:1; 21:25; 1 Sam. 1:10; Isa. 38:15; [ch. 3:20] **12**[o] Gen. 1:21 **13**[p] [ch. 9:27] **15**[q] [ch. 19:20; 30:17] **16**[r] [ch. 9:21; 10:1] [s] ch. 10:20; 14:6; Ex. 14:12; [Ps. 39:13] [t] ver. 3 **17**[u] Ps. 8:4; 144:3; Heb. 2:6 **18**[v] Ps. 17:3 [w] Ps. 11:4, 5 **19**[x] ch. 14:6 **20**[y] ch. 16:12; Lam. 3:12 **21**[z] Dan. 12:2 [a] [ch. 8:5; 24:5; Prov. 1:28] [b] [ver. 8] **Chapter 8** **1**[c] ch. 2:11 **2**[d] 1 Kgs. 19:11; [ch. 15:2] **3**[e] ch. 34:12; [Gen. 18:25; Deut. 32:4; 2 Chr. 19:7; Ezra 9:15; Dan. 9:14; Rom. 3:5] **4**[f] ch. 1:5, 18, 19

5 If you will seek God
and [g]plead with the Almighty for mercy,
6 if you are pure and upright,
surely then he will [h]rouse himself for you
and [i]restore your rightful habitation.
7 And though your beginning was small,
[j]your latter days will be very great.

8 "For [k]inquire, please, of bygone ages,
and consider what [l]the fathers have searched out.
9 For we are but of yesterday and know nothing,
for our days on earth are [m]a shadow.
10 Will they not teach you and tell you
and utter words out of their understanding?

11 "Can papyrus grow where there is no marsh?
Can reeds flourish where there is no water?
12 While yet in flower and not cut down,
they [n]wither before any other plant.
13 Such are the paths of all who [o]forget God;
[p]the hope of [q]the godless shall perish.
14 His confidence is severed,
and his trust is [r]a spider's web.[1]
15 He leans against his [s]house, but it does not stand;
he lays hold of it, but it does not endure.
16 He is a lush plant before the sun,
and his [t]shoots spread over his garden.
17 His roots entwine the stone heap;
he looks upon a house of stones.
18 If he is destroyed from his [u]place,
then it will deny him, saying, 'I have never [v]seen you.'
19 Behold, this is the joy of his way,
and out of [w]the soil others will spring.

20 "Behold, God will not reject a blameless man,
nor take the hand of evildoers.
21 He will yet [x]fill your mouth with laughter,
and your lips with shouting.
22 Those who hate you will be [y]clothed with shame,
and the tent of the wicked will be no more."

Job Replies: There Is No Arbiter

9 Then Job answered and said:

2 "Truly I know that it is so:
But how can a man be [z]in the right before God?
3 If one wished to [a]contend with him,
one could not answer him once in a thousand times.
4 He is [b]wise in heart and mighty in strength
—who has [c]hardened himself against him, and succeeded?—
5 he who removes mountains, and they know it not,
when he overturns them in his anger,
6 who [d]shakes the earth out of its place,
and [e]its pillars tremble;
7 who commands the sun, and it does not rise;
who seals up the stars;
8 who alone [f]stretched out the heavens
and trampled the waves of the sea;
9 who [g]made [h]the Bear and [i]Orion,
the Pleiades [j]and the chambers of the south;

[1] Hebrew *house*

5 [g]ch. 9:15
6 [h]See Ps. 7:6 [i][Prov. 3:33]
7 [j][ch. 42:12; James 5:11]
8 [k]Deut. 4:32; 32:7; [ch. 15:18] [l]ch. 15:18
9 [m]ch. 14:2; 17:7; 1 Chr. 29:15; Ps. 102:11; 109:23; 144:4; Eccles. 6:12
12 [n][Ps. 37:2; 129:6]
13 [o]See Ps. 9:17 [p]Prov. 10:28; 11:7 [q]ch. 13:16; 15:34; 27:8
14 [r][Isa. 59:5, 6]
15 [s]ch. 27:18
16 [t]Ps. 80:11
18 [u]See ch. 7:10 [v]ch. 7:8
19 [w][1 Sam. 2:7, 8; Ps. 103:16; 113:7] **21** [x]Ps. 126:2 **22** [y]Ps. 35:26; 132:18; [Ps. 109:29] **Chapter 9** **2** [z]ch. 4:17 **3** [a][ch. 10:2; Ps. 143:2; Rom. 3:20] **4** [b][ch. 12:13; 36:5] [c][Ex. 7:13; 32:9] **6** [d]Isa. 2:19, 21; 13:13; Hag. 2:6, 21; Heb. 12:26 [e]ch. 26:11; Ps. 75:3 **8** [f]ch. 26:7; Ps. 104:2; Jer. 10:12; 51:15; Zech. 12:1 **9** [g]Gen. 1:16 [h]ch. 38:32 [i]ch. 38:31; Amos 5:8 [j]ch. 37:9

exasperated, or plain mad, at someone we think needs to be "straightened out," we should consider whether we need to wait awhile before responding to them. Not only will we probably make things worse if we speak from impatience, but God has been patient with *us* in the gospel, giving us all the more reason to be patient with others (Matt. 18:23–35).

The second reason Bildad's words are unhelpful is that they assume Job has in fact done something *wrong*, and that Job's fate is therefore deserved (Job 8:11–13). The implication—and Bildad repeats it again and again—is that Job has forgotten God. The reader already knows this is untrue, for "in all this Job did not sin" (1:22; 2:10). Bildad's speech is a good example, like Eliphaz's, of how not to treat a sufferer. Bildad is angry, and is insinuating something for which he has no evidence.

10 who does [k]great things beyond searching out,
and marvelous things beyond number.
11 Behold, he passes by me, and I [l]see him not;
he moves on, but I do not perceive him.
12 Behold, he snatches away; [m]who can turn him back?
[n]Who will say to him, 'What are you doing?'

13 "God will not turn back his anger;
beneath him bowed the helpers of [o]Rahab.
14 [p]How then can I [q]answer him,
choosing my words with him?
15 [r]Though I am in the right, I cannot answer him;
I must [s]appeal for mercy to my accuser.[1]
16 If I summoned him and he answered me,
I would not believe that he was listening to my voice.
17 For he crushes me with a tempest
and multiplies my wounds [t]without cause;
18 he will not let me get my breath,
but fills me with bitterness.
19 If it is a contest of [u]strength, behold, he is mighty!
If it is a matter of justice, who can [v]summon him?[2]
20 Though I am in the right, [w]my own mouth would condemn me;
though I am blameless, he would prove me perverse.
21 I am [x]blameless; I regard not myself;
I [y]loathe my life.
22 It is all one; therefore I say,
'He [z]destroys both the blameless and the wicked.'
23 When [a]disaster brings sudden death,
he mocks at the calamity[3] of the innocent.
24 [b]The earth is given into the hand of the wicked;
he [c]covers the faces of its judges—
[d]if it is not he, who then is it?

25 "My [e]days are swifter than [f]a runner;
they flee away; they see no good.
26 They go by like [g]skiffs of reed,
like [h]an eagle swooping on the prey.
27 If I say, [i]'I will forget my complaint,
I will put off my sad face, and [j]be of good cheer,'
28 I become [k]afraid of all my suffering,
for I know you will not [l]hold me innocent.
29 I shall be [m]condemned;
why then do I labor in vain?
30 If I wash myself with snow
and [n]cleanse my hands with lye,
31 yet you will plunge me into a pit,
and my own clothes will [o]abhor me.
32 For he is not a man, as I am, that I might answer him,
that we should [p]come to trial together.
33 [q]There is no[4] arbiter between us,
who might lay his hand on us both.
34 [r]Let him take his [s]rod away from me,
and let [t]not dread of him terrify me.
35 Then I would speak without fear of him,
for I am not so in myself.

Job Continues: A Plea to God

10

"I [u]loathe my life;
I will give free utterance to my [v]complaint;
I will speak in [w]the bitterness of my soul.
2 I will say to God, Do not [x]condemn me;
let me know why you [y]contend against me.
3 [z]Does it seem good to you to oppress,
to despise [a]the work of your hands
[b]and favor the designs of the wicked?
4 Have you [c]eyes of flesh?
[d]Do you see as man sees?
5 Are your days as the days of man,
or your [e]years as a man's years,
6 that you [f]seek out my iniquity
and search for my sin,
7 although you [g]know that I am not guilty,
and there is [h]none to deliver out of your hand?

[1] Or *to my judge* [2] Compare Septuagint; Hebrew *me* [3] The meaning of the Hebrew word is uncertain [4] Or *Would that there were an*

10[k] See ch. 5:9 **11**[l] ch. 23:8, 9 **12**[m] ch. 11:10; 23:13 [n] Isa. 45:9; [Jer. 18:6; Rom. 9:20] **13**[o] ch. 26:12; Ps. 87:4; 89:10; Isa. 30:7; 51:9 **14**[p] ch. 15:16 [q] ver. 3 **15**[r] ch. 10:15 [s] ch. 8:5 **17**[t] ch. 2:3; [ch. 34:6] **19**[u] [ver. 4] [v] Jer. 49:19; 50:44 **20**[w] ch. 15:6 **21**[x] ch. 1:1 [y] ch. 7:16 (Heb.); [ch. 10:1] **22**[z] Eccles. 9:2, 3; Ezek. 21:3 **23**[a] Isa. 10:26 **24**[b] [ch. 10:3] [c] See ch. 12:17 [d] [ch. 24:25] **25**[e] ch. 7:6 [f] [2 Chr. 30:6; Jer. 51:31] **26**[g] [Isa. 18:2] [h] Hab. 1:8 **27**[i] [ch. 7:13] [j] Ps. 39:13 **28**[k] [Ps. 119:120] [l] ch. 10:14 **29**[m] [ch. 10:2] **30**[n] Isa. 1:25; Jer. 2:22; See ch. 22:30 **31**[o] ch. 19:19; 30:10 **32**[p] Eccles. 6:10; Rom. 9:20 **33**[q] ver. 19; 1 Sam. 2:25; [ch. 16:21] **34**[r] [Ps. 39:10] [s] ch. 21:9; Ps. 89:32; Isa. 10:24 [t] [ch. 13:21; 33:7] **Chapter 10** **1**[u] [ch. 7:16; 9:21; Num. 11:15; 1 Kgs. 19:4] [v] ch. 21:4; 23:2 [w] See ch. 7:11 **2**[x] ch. 9:29 [y] ch. 9:3 **3**[z] ch. 13:9; Ps. 89:38 [a] ch. 14:15; Ps. 138:8; Isa. 64:8 [b] [ch. 9:24] **4**[c] [John 8:15] [d] 1 Sam. 16:7 **5**[e] ch. 36:26; Ps. 77:10; [Ps. 90:4; 2 Pet. 3:8] **6**[f] [ch. 14:16] **7**[g] [ch. 2:3, 9] [h] Deut. 32:39; Isa. 43:13

8 [i]Your hands fashioned and made me,
and now you have destroyed me altogether.
9 Remember that you have made me like [j]clay;
and will you return me to the [k]dust?
10 Did you not pour me out like milk
and curdle me like cheese?
11 You clothed me with skin and flesh,
and knit me together with bones and sinews.
12 You have granted me life and steadfast love,
and your care has preserved my spirit.
13 Yet these things you hid in your heart;
I know that [l]this was your purpose.
14 If I sin, you [m]watch me
and do not [n]acquit me of my iniquity.
15 [o]If I am guilty, woe to me!
If I am [p]in the right, I cannot lift up my head,
for I am filled with disgrace
and [q]look on my affliction.
16 And were my head lifted up,[1] you would hunt me like [r]a lion
and again work [s]wonders against me.
17 You renew your [t]witnesses against me
and increase your vexation toward me;
you [u]bring fresh troops against me.

18 [v]"Why did you bring me out from the womb?
Would that I had died before any eye had seen me
19 [w]and were as though I had not been,
carried from the womb to the grave.
20 [x]Are not my days few?
[y]Then cease, and leave me alone, [z]that I may find a little cheer
21 before I go—and [a]I shall not return—
to the land of [b]darkness and [c]deep shadow,
22 the land of gloom like thick darkness,
like deep shadow without any order,
where light is as thick darkness."

Zophar Speaks: You Deserve Worse

11 Then [d]Zophar the Naamathite answered and said:

2 "Should [e]a multitude of words go unanswered,
and a man full of talk be judged right?
3 Should your babble silence men,
and when you mock, shall no one shame you?
4 For [f]you say, 'My [g]doctrine is pure,
and I am clean in God's[2] eyes.'
5 But oh, that God would speak
and open his lips to you,
6 and that he would tell you the secrets of wisdom!
For he is manifold in [h]understanding.[3]
Know then that God [i]exacts of you less than your guilt deserves.

7 [j]"Can you find out the deep things of God?
Can you find out the limit of the Almighty?
8 It is [k]higher than heaven[4]—what can you do?
Deeper than Sheol—what can you know?
9 Its measure is longer than the earth
and broader than the sea.
10 If he [l]passes through and [m]imprisons
and summons the court, who can [n]turn him back?

[1] Hebrew lacks *my head* [2] Hebrew *your* [3] The meaning of the Hebrew is uncertain [4] Hebrew *The heights of heaven*

11:6–12:20 If words could kill a man, the words of Job's third friend, Zophar, would do it! Zophar says that "God exacts of you less than your guilt deserves" (11:6). He suggests that Job is "a stupid man" (11:12). Zophar goes so far as to imply that Job is in reality a "wicked" man, that "all way of escape [is] lost to [him]," and, recalling the contemptuous words of Job's wife, the best thing Job could do is just die (11:20). With friends like this, who needs enemies!

The "double jeopardy" of Zophar's thinking is the idea that not only is Job suffering acutely, but that Job's suffering is Job's own fault. Zophar doesn't even believe his friend *meant well in life*: Job must be hiding some whopper of iniquity and worthlessness (11:11), which God's court of law will consider soon enough.

8[i] Ps. 119:73
9[j] See ch. 4:17 [k] ch. 34:15; Gen. 2:7; 3:19; Ps. 146:4; Eccles. 12:7
13[l] ch. 23:14; 27:11
14[m] ch. 13:27; 33:11; Ps. 130:3 [n] ch. 9:28
15[o] Isa. 3:11 [p] ch. 9:15 [q] [Ps. 25:18]
16[r] ch. 28:8; Hos. 5:14; 13:7; [Isa. 38:13] [s] [ch. 5:9]
17[t] [ch. 16:8; Ruth 1:21] [u] [ch. 19:12]
18[v] ch. 3:11; [ch. 3:3]
19[w] Obad. 16
20[x] See ch. 14:1 [y] See ch. 7:16 [z] ch. 9:27; Ps. 39:13 **21**[a] [ch. 16:22; 2 Sam. 12:23] [b] ch. 30:26; Ps. 88:12 [c] See ch. 3:5 **Chapter 11** **1**[d] ch. 2:11 **2**[e] Prov. 10:19; Eccles. 5:3 **4**[f] ch. 10:7 [g] Deut. 32:2; Prov. 4:2; Isa. 29:24 **6**[h] ch. 5:12 (Heb.) [i] [Ezra 9:13] **7**[j] ch. 5:9; Eccles. 3:11; 8:17; [Ps. 145:3; Rom. 11:33] **8**[k] [ch. 22:12; Ps. 139:8] **10**[l] See ch. 9:11-16 [m] See ch. 12:14 [n] ch. 9:12; 23:13

11 For he knows [o]worthless men;
when he sees iniquity, will he not consider it?
12 But a stupid man will get understanding
when [p]a wild donkey's colt is [q]born a man!

13 "If you [r]prepare your heart,
you will [s]stretch out your hands toward him.
14 If iniquity is in your hand, put it far away,
and let not injustice dwell in your tents.
15 Surely then you will [t]lift up your face without [u]blemish;
you will be secure and will not fear.
16 You will [v]forget your misery;
you will remember it as waters that have passed away.
17 And your life will be [w]brighter than the noonday;
its darkness will be like the morning.
18 And you will feel secure, because there is hope;
you will look around and [x]take your rest in security.
19 You will [x]lie down, and none will make you afraid;
many will [y]court your favor.
20 But [z]the eyes of the wicked will fail;
all way of escape will be lost to them,
and their hope is [a]to breathe their last."

Job Replies: The LORD Has Done This

12 Then Job answered and said:
2 "No doubt you are the people,
and wisdom will die with you.
3 But I have [b]understanding as well as you;
I am not inferior to you.
Who does not know [c]such things as these?
4 I am [d]a laughingstock to my friends;
I, who [e]called to God and he answered me,
a just and blameless man, am a laughingstock.
5 In the thought of one who is [f]at ease
there is contempt for misfortune;
it is ready for those whose feet slip.
6 [g]The tents of robbers are at peace,
and those who provoke God are secure,
who bring their god in their hand.[1]

7 "But ask the beasts, and they will teach you;
the birds of the heavens, and they will tell you;
8 or the bushes of the earth,[2] and they will teach you;
and the fish of the sea will declare to you.
9 Who among all these does not know
that [h]the hand of the LORD has done this?
10 In [i]his hand is the life of every living thing
and the breath of all mankind.
11 Does not [j]the ear test words
as the palate tastes food?
12 Wisdom is with [k]the aged,
and understanding in length of days.

13 [l]"With God[3] are wisdom and might;
he has counsel and understanding.
14 If he tears down, none can rebuild;
if he [m]shuts a man in, none can open.
15 If he [n]withholds the waters, they dry up;
if he [o]sends them out, they overwhelm the land.
16 With him are strength and [p]sound wisdom;
the deceived and the deceiver are his.
17 He leads [q]counselors away stripped,
and [r]judges he makes fools.
18 He [s]looses the bonds of kings
and binds a waistcloth on their hips.

[1] The meaning of the Hebrew is uncertain [2] Or *speak to the earth* [3] Hebrew *him*

When we treat sufferers this way—and we have all probably done so at one time or another, if only in our thoughts—we are acting as divine Sherlock Holmeses and divine "hanging judges." When people set themselves up to make judgments for God, they can become malicious, like Zophar; and un-*healing*, like all three of Job's friends. In response to such pride, Jesus says, "Judge not, that you be not judged" (Matt. 7:1).

11[o] Ps. 26:4 **12**[p] See ch. 39:5-8 [q] [Ps. 73:22; Eccles. 3:18] **13**[r] Ps. 78:8; See 1 Sam. 7:3 [s] Ps. 44:20; 88:9; 143:6 **15**[t] ch. 22:26; [Gen. 4:5; Ps. 119:6; 1 John 3:21] [u] ch. 31:7; 2 Pet. 3:14 **16**[v] [Isa. 65:16] **17**[w] [Ps. 37:6; Isa. 58:8, 10] **18**[x] Lev. 26:5, 6; Ps. 4:8; Prov. 3:24; Isa. 17:2; Zeph. 3:13 **19**[x] [See ver. 18 above] [y] Ps. 45:12 **20**[z] ch. 17:5; 31:16 [a] Jer. 15:9 **Chapter 12** **3**[b] [ch. 13:2; 15:9] [c] ch. 16:2 **4**[d] ch. 16:10; 17:2, 6; 21:3; 30:1 [e] Ps. 91:15 **5**[f] ch. 3:18 **6**[g] See ch. 21:7 **9**[h] Isa. 41:20; [ch. 1:21] **10**[i] Num. 16:22; Dan. 5:23; Acts 17:28 **11**[j] ch. 34:3 **12**[k] ch. 32:7; [Ps. 119:100] **13**[l] [ch. 9:4; 36:5] **14**[m] ch. 11:10; [Isa. 22:22; Rev. 3:7] **15**[n] [Deut. 11:17; 1 Kgs. 8:35; 17:1] [o] [Gen. 7:11-24; Ps. 147:18; Amos 9:6] **16**[p] [ch. 5:12] **17**[q] [2 Sam. 17:23] [r] ch. 9:24; Isa. 40:23; [Isa. 29:14; 44:25; 1 Cor. 1:19] **18**[s] Ps. 116:16

19 He leads priests away stripped
and overthrows the mighty.
20 He deprives of speech those who are trusted
[t]and takes away the discernment of the elders.
21 He [u]pours contempt on princes
and loosens the belt of the strong.
22 He [v]uncovers the deeps out of darkness
and brings [w]deep darkness to light.
23 He [x]makes nations great, and he destroys them;
he enlarges nations, and [y]leads them away.
24 He takes away understanding from the chiefs of the people of the earth
and [z]makes them wander in a trackless waste.
25 They [a]grope in the dark without light,
and he makes them [b]stagger like a drunken man.

Job Continues: Still I Will Hope in God

13 "Behold, my eye has seen all this,
my ear has heard and understood it.
2 [c]What you know, I also know;
I am not inferior to you.
3 [d]But I would speak to the Almighty,
and I desire to [e]argue my case with God.
4 As for you, [f]you whitewash with lies;
[g]worthless physicians are you all.
5 Oh that you would [h]keep silent,
and it would be your wisdom!
6 Hear now my argument
and listen to the pleadings of my lips.
7 Will you [i]speak falsely for God
and speak [i]deceitfully for him?
8 Will you show partiality toward him?
Will you [j]plead the case for God?
9 Will it be well with you when he [k]searches you out?
Or [l]can you deceive him, as one deceives a man?
10 He will surely rebuke you
if in secret you show partiality.
11 Will not his [m]majesty terrify you,
and the dread of him fall upon you?
12 Your maxims are proverbs of [n]ashes;
your defenses are defenses of clay.

13 "Let me have silence, and I will speak,
and let come on me what may.
14 Why should I take my flesh in my teeth
and [o]put my life in my hand?
15 [p]Though he slay me, I will [q]hope in him;[1]
yet I will [r]argue my ways to his face.
16 This will be my salvation,
that the godless shall not come before him.
17 [s]Keep listening to my words,
and let my declaration be in your ears.
18 Behold, I have [t]prepared my case;
I know that I shall be in the right.
19 [u]Who is there who will contend with me?
For then I would be silent and die.
20 Only grant me two things,
then I will not [v]hide myself from your face:
21 [w]withdraw your hand far from me,
and let not [x]dread of you terrify me.
22 [y]Then call, and I will answer;
or let me speak, and you reply to me.
23 How many are my iniquities and my sins?
[z]Make me know my transgression and my sin.
24 Why [a]do you hide your face
and [b]count me as your enemy?
25 Will you frighten [c]a driven leaf
and pursue dry [d]chaff?
26 For you [e]write bitter things against me
and make me inherit [f]the iniquities of my youth.
27 You put my feet in [g]the stocks
and [h]watch all my paths;
you set a limit for[2] the soles of my feet.
28 Man[3] wastes away like [i]a rotten thing,
like a garment that is [j]moth-eaten.

[1] Or *Behold, he will slay me; I have no hope* [2] Or *you marked* [3] Hebrew *He*

13:1–12 Job responds to his friends, initially at least, with dazzling truth. First, he tells them he has heard nothing new from them: "What you know, I also know" (v. 2). Then Job resolves to take his case directly to God (v. 3). Next Job declares his friends' words to be "worthless," a "whitewash" (v. 4), explaining that if they'd only sat by him *in silence*, it would have been the way of wisdom (v. 5). Their platitudes amount to ashes; their defenses of God are mere putty (v. 12).

20[t] [ch. 32:9]
21[u] Ps. 107:40
22[v] Dan. 2:22; 1 Cor. 4:5 [w] See ch. 3:5
23[x] Isa. 9:3; 26:15 [y] [2 Kgs. 18:11]
24[z] Ps. 107:40; [ch. 6:18]
25[a] See ch. 5:14 [b] Ps. 107:27; Isa. 19:14 **Chapter 13** **2**[c] [ch. 12:3; 15:9] **3**[d] ch. 23:4; 31:35 [e] [ver. 15, 18] **4**[f] Ps. 119:69 [g] [ch. 16:2] **5**[h] Prov. 17:28 **7**[i] ch. 27:4 **8**[j] [Judg. 6:31] **9**[k] Prov. 28:11 [l] Gal. 6:7 **11**[m] ch. 31:23 **12**[n] Isa. 44:20 **14**[o] See Judg. 12:3 **15**[p] [Prov. 14:32] [q] ch. 14:14 [r] [ver. 3; ch. 27:5] **17**[s] ch. 21:2 **18**[t] See ch. 33:5 **19**[u] Isa. 50:8, 9 **20**[v] [Gen. 3:8] **21**[w] ch. 9:34; Ps. 39:10 [x] ch. 9:34; 33:7 **22**[y] ch. 14:15 **23**[z] [Ps. 19:12] **24**[a] Deut. 32:20 [b] ch. 19:11; 33:10; [Lam. 2:5] **25**[c] Lev. 26:36 [d] ch. 21:18; Ps. 83:13 **26**[e] [Ps. 149:9] [f] Ps. 25:7 **27**[g] [ch. 33:11] [h] See ch. 10:14 **28**[i] Prov. 12:4; 14:30; Hab. 3:16 [j] ch. 4:19

Job Continues: Death Comes Soon to All

14 "Man who is [k]born of a woman
is [l]few of days and [m]full of trouble.
2 He comes out like [n]a flower and [o]withers;
he flees like [p]a shadow and continues not.
3 And do you [q]open your eyes on such a one
and [r]bring me into judgment with you?
4 Who can bring [s]a clean thing out of an unclean?
There is not one.
5 Since his [t]days are determined,
and [u]the number of his months is with you,
and you have appointed his limits that he cannot pass,
6 [v]look away from him and leave him alone,[1]
that he may enjoy, like [w]a hired hand, his day.

7 "For there is hope for a tree,
if it be cut down, that it will sprout again,
and that its shoots will not cease.
8 Though its root grow old in the earth,
and [x]its stump die in the soil,
9 yet at the scent of water it will bud
and put out [y]branches like a young plant.
10 But a man dies and is laid low;
man breathes his last, and [z]where is he?
11 [a]As waters fail from a lake
and a river wastes away and dries up,
12 so a man lies down and rises not again;
till [b]the heavens are no more he will not awake
or be [c]roused out of his sleep.
13 Oh that you would [d]hide me in [e]Sheol,
that you would [d]conceal me [f]until your wrath be past,
that you would appoint me a set time, and remember me!
14 If a man dies, shall he live again?
All the days of my [g]service I would [h]wait,
till my renewal[2] should come.
15 You would [i]call, and I would answer you;
you would long for the [j]work of your hands.
16 For then you would [k]number my steps;
you would not keep [l]watch over my sin;
17 my transgression would be [m]sealed up in a bag,
and you would cover over my iniquity.

18 "But the mountain falls and [n]crumbles away,
and [o]the rock is removed from its place;
19 the waters wear away the stones;
the torrents wash away the soil of the earth;
so you destroy the hope of man.
20 You prevail forever against him, and he passes;
you change his countenance, and send him away.
21 His sons come to honor, and he [p]does not know it;
they are brought low, and he perceives it not.
22 He feels only the pain of his own body,
and he mourns only for himself."

Eliphaz Accuses: Job Does Not Fear God

15 Then [q]Eliphaz the Temanite answered and said:

2 "Should [r]a wise man answer with [s]windy knowledge,
and fill his [t]belly with [u]the east wind?
3 Should he argue in unprofitable talk,
or in words with which he can do no good?

[1] Probable reading; Hebrew *look away from him, that he may cease* [2] Or *relief*

Silence is golden. A caring presence can be far more helpful than thoughtless words or arrogant assumptions that our wise words can fix others' brokenness. When we have nothing to say, we should say nothing. God can defend himself from others' expressions of anger or frustration. Or rather, God will declare himself—which he does, in the book of Job, soon enough. Moreover, we don't help a sufferer by assuming a superior position. The gospel says that our ultimate healing occurred when God "emptied himself, by taking the form of a servant, being born in the likeness of men" (Phil. 2:7).

Chapter 14
1[k] ch. 15:14; 25:4; Matt. 11:11 [l] ch. 10:20; 16:22; Gen. 47:9; Ps. 39:5; 89:47 [m] See ch. 5:7 **2**[n] Ps. 103:15; Isa. 40:6, 7; James 1:10; 1 Pet. 1:24 [o] Ps. 37:2; 90:6 [p] See ch. 8:9; 17:7; Ps. 109:23 **3**[q] [Ps. 8:4; 144:3] [r] ch. 22:4; Ps. 143:2 **4**[s] ch. 15:14; [Ps. 51:5; John 3:6] **5**[t] [ch. 7:1; Ps. 39:4] [u] ch. 21:21 **6**[v] ch. 7:19 [w] ch. 7:1 **8**[x] Isa. 11:1 **9**[y] [ch. 29:19] **10**[z] ch. 29:7 **11**[a] Isa. 19:5 **12**[b] Deut. 11:21; Ps. 89:29; [Ps. 72:5; Matt. 5:18] [c] [John 11:11] **13**[d] [Ps. 27:5; 31:20] [e] See ch. 21:13 [f] [Isa. 26:20] **14**[g] ch. 7:1 [h] ch. 13:15 **15**[i] ch. 13:22 [j] See ch. 10:3 **16**[k] ch. 31:4; 34:21 [l] [ch. 10:6] **17**[m] Deut. 32:34; [Hos. 13:12] **18**[n] Isa. 34:4 [o] ch. 18:4 **21**[p] [Eccles. 9:5] **Chapter 15** **1**[q] ch. 2:11 **2**[r] [ch. 12:3] [s] ch. 16:3 [t] ver. 35 [u] ch. 6:26; 8:2; Hos. 12:1

4 But you are doing away with the fear of
God[1]
and hindering meditation before God.
5 For your iniquity teaches your mouth,
and you choose the tongue of the
crafty.
6 Your [v]own mouth condemns you, and
not I;
[w]your own lips testify against you.

7 [x]"Are you the first man who was born?
Or [y]were you brought forth [z]before
the hills?
8 Have you listened in [a]the council of God?
And do you limit wisdom to yourself?
9 [b]What do you know that we do not know?
What do you understand that is not
clear to us?
10 [c]Both the gray-haired and the aged are
among us,
older than your father.
11 Are the comforts of God too small for
you,
or the word that deals gently with you?
12 Why does your heart carry you away,
and why do your eyes flash,
13 that you turn your [d]spirit against God
and bring such words out of your
mouth?
14 [e]What is man, [f]that he can be pure?
Or he who is [g]born of a woman, that
he can be righteous?
15 Behold, God[2] [h]puts no trust in his [i]holy
ones,
and the heavens are not pure in his
sight;
16 [j]how much less one who is abominable
and [k]corrupt,
a man who [l]drinks injustice like water!

17 "I will show you; hear me,
and what I have seen I will declare
18 (what wise men have told,
without hiding it [m]from their fathers,
19 to whom alone the land was given,
and no [n]stranger passed among them).
20 The wicked man writhes in pain all his
days,
through all the [o]years that are laid up
for [p]the ruthless.
21 [q]Dreadful sounds are in his ears;
in [r]prosperity the destroyer will come
upon him.
22 He does not believe that he will return
out of darkness,
and he is marked for the sword.
23 He [s]wanders abroad for bread, saying,
'Where is it?'
He knows that a day of darkness is
ready at his hand;
24 distress and anguish terrify him;
they [t]prevail against him, like a king
ready for battle.
25 Because he has stretched out his hand
against God
and defies the Almighty,
26 [u]running [v]stubbornly against him
with a thickly bossed shield;
27 because he has [w]covered his face with his
fat
and gathered fat upon his waist
28 and has lived in desolate cities,
in houses that none should inhabit,
which were ready to become heaps of
ruins;
29 he will not be rich, and his wealth will
not endure,
nor will his possessions spread over
the earth;[3]
30 he will not depart from darkness;
the flame will dry up his shoots,
and by [x]the breath of his mouth he
will depart.
31 Let him not [y]trust in emptiness, deceiving himself,
for emptiness will be his payment.
32 It will be paid in full [z]before his time,
and his branch will not be green.
33 He will shake off his unripe grape like
the vine,
and cast off his blossom like the olive
tree.
34 For [a]the company of the godless is barren,
and [b]fire consumes the tents of brib-
ery.
35 They [c]conceive trouble and give birth to
evil,
and their [d]womb prepares deceit."

[1] Hebrew lacks *of God* [2] Hebrew *he* [3] Or *nor will his produce bend down to the earth*

6[v] ch. 9:20; Luke 19:22 [w] 2 Sam. 1:16 **7**[x] [ch. 38:21] [y] Prov. 8:25 [z] Ps. 90:2 **8**[a] ch. 29:4; Jer. 23:18; [Gen. 1:26; 3:22] **9**[b] ch. 12:3; 13:2 **10**[c] [ch. 12:12; 32:6, 7] **13**[d] [ch. 21:4] **14**[e] For ver. 14-16, see ch. 25:4-6 [f] [ch. 14:4; Ps. 14:3; Prov. 20:9; Eccles. 7:20; 1 John 1:8, 10] [g] See ch. 14:1 **15**[h] ch. 4:18 [i] See ch. 5:1 **16**[j] ch. 9:14 [k] [Ps. 14:3; 53:1] [l] ch. 34:7; [Prov. 19:28; 26:6] **18**[m] [ch. 8:8]; See Ps. 44:1 **19**[n] Joel 3:17 **20**[o] [ch. 21:19; 24:1] [p] ch. 6:23; 27:13 **21**[q] See ch. 18:11 [r] [1 Thess. 5:3] **23**[s] Ps. 59:15; 109:10 **24**[t] ch. 14:20 **26**[u] [ch. 16:14; Dan. 8:6] [v] Ps. 75:5 **27**[w] See Ps. 17:10 **30**[x] ch. 4:9 **31**[y] [Isa. 59:4] **32**[z] ch. 22:16; Eccles. 7:17; [Ps. 55:23; 102:24] **34**[a] ch. 16:7 [b] [ch. 20:26] **35**[c] Ps. 7:14; Isa. 59:4; [Hos. 10:13] [d] See ver. 2

Job Replies: Miserable Comforters Are You

16 Then Job answered and said:
2 "I have heard [e]many such things;
[f]miserable comforters are you all.
3 Shall [g]windy words have an end?
Or what provokes you that you
answer?
4 I also could speak as you do,
if you were in my place;
I could join words together against you
and [h]shake my head at you.
5 I could strengthen you with my mouth,
and the solace of my lips would
assuage your pain.

6 "If I speak, my pain is not assuaged,
and if I forbear, how much of it leaves
me?
7 Surely now God has worn me out;
[i]he has[1] made desolate all my company.
8 And he has shriveled me up,
which is [j]a witness against me,
and my [k]leanness has risen up against
me;
it testifies to my face.
9 He has [l]torn me in his wrath [m]and hated
me;
he has [n]gnashed his teeth at me;
my adversary sharpens his eyes
against me.
10 Men have [o]gaped at me with their mouth;
they have [p]struck me insolently on the
cheek;
they [q]mass themselves together
against me.
11 God gives me up to the ungodly
and casts me into the hands of the
wicked.
12 I was at ease, and he broke me apart;
he seized me by the neck and dashed
me to pieces;
he set me up as his [r]target;
13 his [s]archers surround me.
He slashes open my kidneys [t]and does
not spare;
he [u]pours out my gall on the ground.
14 He breaks me with [v]breach upon breach;
he [w]runs upon me like a warrior.
15 I have sewed [x]sackcloth upon my skin
and have laid [y]my strength [z]in the dust.
16 My face is red with weeping,
and on my eyelids is [a]deep darkness,
17 although there is no [b]violence in my
hands,
and my prayer is pure.

18 "O earth, [c]cover not my blood,
and let my [d]cry find no resting place.
19 Even now, behold, my [e]witness is in
heaven,
and he who testifies for me is [f]on high.
20 My friends [g]scorn me;
my eye pours out tears to God,
21 that he would [h]argue the case of a man
with God,
as[2] a son of man does with his neighbor.
22 For when a few years have come
I shall go the way [i]from which I shall
not return.

Job Continues: Where Then Is My Hope?

17 "My spirit is broken; my days are
[j]extinct;
[k]the graveyard is ready for me.
2 Surely there are mockers about me,
and my eye dwells on their [l]provoca-
tion.

[1] Hebrew *you have*; also verse 8 [2] Hebrew *and*

16:1–5 In his response to Eliphaz, Job looks underneath the words of his friend: "Shall windy words have an end? Or what provokes you that you answer?" (v. 3). What is causing his friends to answer with heat but little light? Job adds that if the roles were reversed, he would try to "strengthen" and "assuage" (v. 5).

It is easy for believers to get angry "for" God. There's a lot in the world to get angry about! And when the merciful cause of Christ is misunderstood and abused, either by its adherents or by its elite despisers, it is easy to become adversarial. But rarely are God's purposes advanced or his people helped by means of an "answer" which is provoked by indignation. The gospel comes as help to the helpless, love to the loveless, strength to the weak, a raft to the drowning, and water to the thirsty. Rage and blame spoil it.

Chapter 16
2[e] [ch. 12:3] [f] [ch. 13:4]
3[g] [ch. 15:2]
4[h] 2 Kgs. 19:21; Ps. 22:7; 109:25; Isa. 37:22; Jer. 18:16; Lam. 2:15; Matt. 27:39; Mark 15:29
7[i] [ch. 15:34]; See ch. 1:15-19
8[j] ch. 10:17; [Ruth 1:21] [k] [Ps. 109:24]
9[l] ch. 18:4; Hos. 6:1; Amos 1:11 [m] ch. 30:21 [n] Ps. 35:16; 37:12; 112:10; Lam. 2:16; Acts 7:54
10[o] Ps. 22:13 [p] Ps. 3:7; Isa. 50:6; Lam. 3:30; Mic. 5:1; [1 Kgs. 22:24; Acts 23:2]
[q] Ps. 35:15 **12**[r] Lam. 3:12; [ch. 7:20] **13**[s] Jer. 50:29 [t] ch. 27:22 [u] ch. 20:25; [Lam. 2:11] **14**[v] ch. 30:14 [w] ch. 15:26 **15**[x] See 2 Sam. 3:31 [y] [Ps. 75:10] [z] [Ps. 7:5] **16**[a] See ch. 3:5 **17**[b] Isa. 53:9 **18**[c] Isa. 26:21; Ezek. 24:7 [d] [Gen. 4:10] **19**[e] Ps. 89:37; Rom. 1:9 [f] [Ps. 148:1] **20**[g] [ch. 12:5] **21**[h] [ch. 31:35] **22**[i] See ch. 10:21 **Chapter 17** **1**[j] [ch. 18:5, 6] [k] [Ps. 88:3, 4] **2**[l] 1 Sam. 1:6, 7; [ch. 12:6]

3 "Lay down a pledge for me with you;
who is there who will put up [m]security for me?
4 Since you have closed their hearts to understanding,
therefore you will not let them triumph.
5 He who informs against his friends to get a share of their property—
the [n]eyes of his children will fail.

6 "He has made me [o]a byword of the peoples,
and I am one before whom men spit.
7 My [p]eye has grown dim from vexation,
and all my members are like [q]a shadow.
8 The upright are [r]appalled at this,
and the innocent stirs himself up against the godless.
9 Yet the righteous holds to his way,
and he who has [s]clean hands grows stronger and stronger.
10 But you, [t]come on again, all of you,
and I shall not find a wise man among you.
11 My [u]days are past; my plans are broken off,
the desires of my heart.
12 They [v]make night into day:
'The light,' they say, 'is near to the darkness.'[1]
13 If I hope for [w]Sheol as [x]my house,
if I make my bed in darkness,
14 if I say to the pit, 'You are my father,'
and to the worm, 'My mother,' or 'My sister,'
15 where then is my hope?
Who will see my hope?
16 Will it go down to the bars of [w]Sheol?
Shall we [y]descend together [z]into the dust?"

Bildad Speaks: God Punishes the Wicked

18 Then [a]Bildad the Shuhite answered and said:

2 "How long will you [b]hunt for words?
Consider, and then we will speak.
3 Why are we counted as [c]cattle?
Why are we stupid in your sight?
4 You who [d]tear yourself in your anger,
shall the earth be forsaken for you,
or [e]the rock be removed out of its place?

5 "Indeed, [f]the light of the wicked is put out,
and the flame of his fire does not shine.
6 The light is [g]dark in his tent,
and his lamp above him is put out.
7 His strong steps are shortened,
and his [h]own schemes throw him down.
8 For he is cast into a net by his own feet,
and he walks on its mesh.
9 [i]A trap seizes him by the heel;
a snare lays hold of him.
10 A rope is hidden for him in the ground,
a trap for him in the path.
11 [j]Terrors frighten him on every side,
and chase him at his heels.
12 His strength is famished,
and calamity is [k]ready for his stumbling.
13 It consumes the parts of his skin;
[l]the firstborn of death consumes his limbs.
14 He is torn from the tent in which he trusted
and is brought to [m]the king of terrors.
15 In his tent dwells that which is none of his;
[n]sulfur is scattered over his habitation.
16 His [o]roots dry up beneath,
and his branches [p]wither above.
17 His [q]memory perishes from the earth,
and he has no name in the street.
18 [r]He is thrust from light into darkness,
and driven out of the world.
19 He has no [s]posterity or progeny among his people,
and no survivor where he used to live.
20 They of the west are appalled at his [t]day,
and [u]horror seizes them of the east.
21 Surely such are the dwellings of the unrighteous,
such is the place of him who [v]knows not God."

[1] The meaning of the Hebrew is uncertain

3[m] Ps. 119:122; Isa. 38:14; Heb. 7:22 **5**[n] [ch. 11:20; 31:16] **6**[o] ch. 30:9; Deut. 28:37; [Ps. 44:14; 69:11] **7**[p] [Ps. 6:7; 31:9] [q] See ch. 14:2 **8**[r] Isa. 52:14 **9**[s] See ch. 22:30 **10**[t] ch. 6:29 **11**[u] ch. 7:6; 9:25 **12**[v] [ch. 11:17] **13**[w] See ch. 21:13 [x] [Eccles. 12:5] **16**[w] [See ver. 13 above] [y] [ch. 3:17-19] [z] ch. 21:26; 40:13
Chapter 18 **1**[a] ch. 2:11; 8:1 **2**[b] [Matt. 22:15; Mark 12:13; Luke 20:20] **3**[c] Ps. 73:22 **4**[d] ch. 16:9 [e] ch. 14:18 **5**[f] ch. 21:17; Prov. 13:9; 20:20; 24:20; See Ps. 18:28 **6**[g] ch. 10:22 **7**[h] [ch. 5:13] **9**[i] Ps. 140:5 **11**[j] ch. 15:21; 20:25; 27:20; 30:15; Jer. 6:25; 46:5; 49:29 **12**[k] Ps. 38:17 **13**[l] Isa. 14:30 **14**[m] [Rev. 9:11] **15**[n] See Ps. 11:6; Ezek. 38:22 **16**[o] ch. 29:19; Hos. 9:16 [p] ch. 14:2 **17**[q] Ps. 34:16; Prov. 10:7; [Ps. 109:13, 15] **18**[r] ch. 10:21, 22 **19**[s] Isa. 14:22 **20**[t] Ps. 37:13; Jer. 50:27; Ezek. 21:25, 29; Obad. 12; [1 Sam. 26:10] [u] [ch. 21:6] **21**[v] Judg. 2:10; Jer. 9:3; 10:25; 1 Thess. 4:8; 2 Thess. 1:8

Job Replies: My Redeemer Lives

19 Then Job answered and said:
2 "How long will you torment me
and break me in pieces with words?
3 These [w]ten times you have cast reproach
upon me;
are you not ashamed to wrong me?
4 And even if it be true that I have erred,
my error remains with myself.
5 If indeed you [x]magnify yourselves
against me
and make my disgrace an argument
against me,
6 know then that God has [y]put me in the
wrong
and closed his net about me.
7 Behold, I [z]cry out, 'Violence!' but I am
not answered;
I call for help, but there is no justice.
8 He has [a]walled up my way, so that I cannot pass,
and he has set darkness upon my paths.
9 He has [b]stripped from me my glory
and taken the [c]crown from my head.
10 He breaks me down on every side, and
I [d]am gone,
and my hope has he pulled up like a
tree.
11 He has kindled his wrath against me
and [e]counts me as his adversary.
12 His [f]troops come on together;
they have [g]cast up their siege ramp[1]
against me
and encamp around my tent.
13 "He has put my [h]brothers far from me,
and [i]those who knew me are wholly
estranged from me.
14 My relatives [j]have failed me,
my close [k]friends have forgotten me.
15 The guests [l]in my house and my maidservants count me as a stranger;
I have become a foreigner in their eyes.
16 I call to my servant, but he gives me no
answer;
I must plead with him with my
mouth for mercy.
17 My breath is strange to my [m]wife,
and I am a stench to the children of
[n]my own mother.
18 Even young [o]children despise me;
when I rise they talk against me.
19 All my [p]intimate friends abhor me,
and those whom I loved have turned
against me.
20 My [q]bones stick to my skin and to my
flesh,
and I have escaped by the skin of my
teeth.
21 Have mercy on me, have mercy on me,
O you my friends,
for the hand of God has [r]touched me!
22 Why do you, like God, [s]pursue me?
Why are you not satisfied with my
flesh?
23 "Oh that my words were written!
Oh that they were [t]inscribed in a book!
24 Oh that with an iron [u]pen and lead
they were engraved in the rock forever!
25 For I [v]know that my [w]Redeemer lives,
and at the last he will stand upon the
[x]earth.[2]
26 And after my skin has been thus
destroyed,
yet in[3] my flesh I shall [y]see God,

[1] Hebrew *their way* [2] Hebrew *dust* [3] Or *without*

19:25–27 In Job's replies to his friends' statements to him, he sometimes tries to beat them at their own game. He tries to refute their refutations, or defend himself against their defenses (of God). Seldom does he get outside the boxing ring of verbal punches and counterpunches.

Here, toward the end of Job's second response to Bildad, Job is given something wonderful to say. Recognizing the place of despair out of which Job has been speaking up to now, right up to the very hem of these verses, it is a lovely wonder that he is inspired to declare what he says next.

Job says that he believes he shall one day see God as his Redeemer and not his enemy. He shall see God with his own eyes (v. 27), "in my flesh" (v. 26). In faith Job predicts this, even "after my skin has been thus destroyed" (v. 26). Job's pre-vision of the direct presence of God, ultimately fulfilled in Christ, has been quoted often, most famously in Handel's "Messiah" and in the Book of Common Prayer.

Chapter 19
3[w] Gen. 31:7
5[x] Ps. 35:26; 38:16; 55:12
6[y] [ch. 8:3; 34:12; Lam. 3:36]
7[z] ch. 24:12; Hab. 1:2; [Lam. 3:8]
8[a] Lam. 3:7, 9; Hos. 2:6; [ch. 3:23; 13:27]
9[b] Ps. 89:44 [c] Ps. 89:39; Lam. 5:16; [ch. 29:14]
10[d] ch. 27:21; [ch. 10:21; 14:20]
11[e] See ch. 13:24
12[f] [ch. 10:17; 25:2] [g] ch. 30:12
13[h] Ps. 69:8; [ch. 6:15] [i] [Ps. 31:11; 88:8, 18]
14[j] Ps. 38:11 [k] Ps. 55:13
15[l] [Gen. 17:27; Matt. 10:36]
17[m] ch. 2:9 [n] ch. 3:10
18[o] [2 Kgs. 2:23]
19[p] [Ps. 41:9; 55:13, 14]
20[q] Ps. 102:5; [Lam. 4:8] **21**[r] ch. 1:11; Isa. 53:4 **22**[s] [Ps. 69:26] **23**[t] Isa. 30:8 **24**[u] Jer. 17:1 **25**[v] ch. 30:23 [w] Isa. 43:14; 44:6, 24; 49:7; [Gen. 48:16; Ps. 19:14; 103:4; 1 Thess. 1:10] [x] ch. 41:33 **26**[y] Ps. 17:15; 1 Cor. 13:12; 1 John 3:2

27 whom I shall see for myself,
and my eyes shall behold, and not [z]another.
My heart [a]faints within me!
28 If you say, 'How we will [s]pursue him!'
and, 'The root of the matter is found in him,'
29 be afraid of the sword,
for wrath brings the punishment of the sword,
that you may know there is [b]a judgment."

Zophar Speaks: The Wicked Will Suffer

20 Then [c]Zophar the Naamathite answered and said:

2 "Therefore my [d]thoughts answer me,
because of my haste within me.
3 I hear censure that insults me,
and out of my understanding a spirit answers me.
4 Do you not know this from of old,
[e]since man was placed on earth,
5 [f]that the exulting of the wicked is short,
and the joy of the godless but for a moment?
6 [g]Though his height mount up to the heavens,
and his head reach to the clouds,
7 he will perish forever like his own [h]dung;
those who have seen him will say, [i]'Where is he?'
8 He will fly away like [j]a dream and not be found;
he will be chased away like a vision of the night.
9 [k]The eye that saw him will see him no more,
nor will his place any more behold him.
10 His children will seek the favor of the poor,
and his hands will [l]give back his wealth.
11 His bones are full of his [m]youthful vigor,
but it will lie [n]down with him in the dust.

12 "Though evil is sweet in his mouth,
though he hides it [o]under his tongue,
13 though he is loath to let it go
and holds it in his mouth,
14 yet his food is turned in his stomach;
it is the venom of [p]cobras within him.
15 He swallows down riches and vomits them up again;
God casts them out of his belly.
16 He will suck the poison of cobras;
[q]the tongue of a viper will kill him.
17 He will not look upon [r]the rivers,
the streams flowing with [s]honey and [t]curds.
18 He will [u]give back the fruit of his toil
and will not [v]swallow it down;
from the profit of his trading
he will get no enjoyment.
19 For he has crushed and abandoned the poor;
he has seized a house that he did not build.

20 "Because he [w]knew no [x]contentment in his belly,
[y]he will not let anything in which he delights escape him.
21 There was nothing left after he had eaten;
therefore his prosperity will not endure.
22 In the fullness of his sufficiency he will be in distress;
the hand of everyone in misery will come against him.
23 To fill his belly to the full,
God[1] will send his burning anger against him
and rain it upon him [z]into his body.
24 [a]He will flee from an iron weapon;
[b]a bronze arrow will strike [c]him through.

[1] Hebrew *he*

For Christians, the mighty hope of a physical resurrection culminates with a glorious exultation from the apostle Paul that echoes Job's words: "O death, where is your victory? O death, where is your sting?" (1 Cor. 15:55). We therefore give great thanks to God, "who gives us the victory through our Lord Jesus Christ" (1 Cor. 15:57; Isa. 25:8; Hos. 13:14).

27[z] [Prov. 27:2] [a] [Ps. 73:26]
28[s] [See ver. 22 above]
29[b] Eccles. 12:14; See Ps. 58:11

Chapter 20
1[c] ch. 2:11
2[d] ch. 4:13

4[e] [Deut. 4:32] **5**[f] Ps. 37:35, 36 **6**[g] [Isa. 14:13, 14; Obad. 3, 4] **7**[h] Ps. 83:10; Zeph. 1:17; [1 Kgs. 14:10; 2 Kgs. 9:37] [i] ch. 14:10 **8**[j] Ps. 73:20; 90:5; Isa. 29:7, 8 **9**[k] See ch. 7:8, 10 **10**[l] ver. 18 **11**[m] [ch. 13:26; Ps. 25:7] [n] ch. 21:26 **12**[o] Ps. 10:7 **14**[p] Deut. 32:33; Ps. 140:3 **16**[q] Isa. 59:5; [Prov. 23:32] **17**[r] [Ps. 36:8; Jer. 17:6] [s] [Deut. 32:13, 14] [t] [ch. 29:6] **18**[u] ver. 10 [v] ver. 15 **20**[w] Isa. 59:8 [x] Prov. 17:1 [y] [Eccles. 5:13, 14] **23**[z] [Num. 11:33; Ps. 78:30, 31] **24**[a] [Isa. 24:18; Jer. 48:44; Amos 5:19] [b] 2 Sam. 22:35 [c] Judg. 5:26

25 It[d] is drawn forth and comes out of his body;
[e] the glittering point comes out of his [f] gallbladder;
[g] terrors come upon him.
26 Utter darkness is laid up for his treasures;
[h] a fire not fanned will devour him;
what is left in his tent will be consumed.
27 [i] The heavens will reveal his iniquity,
and the earth will rise up against him.
28 The possessions of his house will be carried away,
dragged off in the day of God's[1] wrath.
29 [j] This is the wicked man's portion from God,
[j] the heritage decreed for him by God."

Job Replies: The Wicked Do Prosper

21 Then Job answered and said:
2 [k]"Keep listening to my words,
and let this be your comfort.
3 Bear with me, and I will speak,
and after I have spoken, [l] mock on.
4 As for me, is my [m] complaint against man?
Why should I not be impatient?
5 Look at me and be appalled,
and [n] lay your hand over your mouth.
6 When I remember, I am dismayed,
and shuddering seizes my flesh.
7 [o] Why do the wicked live,
reach old age, and grow mighty in power?
8 Their [p] offspring are established in their presence,
and their descendants before their eyes.
9 Their houses are [q] safe from fear,
and [r] no rod of God is upon them.
10 Their bull breeds without fail;
their cow calves and [s] does not miscarry.
11 They send out their [t] little boys like a flock,
and their children dance.
12 They sing to [u] the tambourine and [v] the lyre
and rejoice to the sound of [v] the pipe.
13 They [w] spend their days in prosperity,
and in [x] peace they go down to [y] Sheol.
14 They say to God, [z]'Depart from us!
We do not desire the knowledge of your ways.
15 [a] What is the Almighty, that we should serve him?
And what [b] profit do we get if we pray to him?'
16 Behold, is not their prosperity in their hand?
[c] The counsel of the wicked is far from me.
17 "How often is it that [d] the lamp of the wicked is put out?
That their calamity comes upon them?
That God[2] distributes pains in his anger?
18 That they are like [e] straw before the wind,
and like [f] chaff that the storm carries away?

[1] Hebrew *his* [2] Hebrew *he*

21:7–26 This chapter distills the essence of Job's argument against believing in the goodness of God. Not only does Job think that he, an innocent man, has suffered unjustly. But he also believes that the guilty—in other words, the *wicked*—do not suffer. Job even believes the wicked *prosper* and that they end their lives in prosperity. He speaks at length about this, looking at his conceptualized group "the wicked" from the cradle to the grave. Bitterly, Job concludes that the wicked person "dies in his full vigor, being wholly at ease and secure" (v. 23).

As another character, Elihu, points out later (36:17), Job is reeking with judgments, especially on the supposedly thriving class of people whom he categorizes as "the wicked."

Job is mistaken in two ways. Both of his mistakes apply to the application of the gospel of God's grace in real life. First, Job's perception that "the wicked" are unscathed and protected is not true to life. Maybe he hasn't spent enough time with them! Everyone, "wicked" and "innocent," bleeds the same, mourns the loss of their children the same, and dies the same. Shakespeare described many characters who, though having a crown, were as troubled, lonely, and vulnerable as persons who have no crown (cf. Eccles. 9:2). Later in the Bible Paul wrote, "there is no distinction; for all have sinned and fall short of the glory of God" (Rom. 3:22–23).

25[d] Judg. 3:22 [e] Deut. 32:41 [f] ch. 16:13 [g] See ch. 18:11
26[h] [ch. 15:34; Ps. 21:9]
27[i] [ch. 16:18, 19]
29[j] ch. 27:13; [ch. 18:21; 31:2, 3]
Chapter 21
2[k] ch. 13:17
3[l] [ch. 16:10, 20; 17:2]
4[m] ch. 10:1; 23:2
5[n] ch. 29:9; 40:4; Judg. 18:19
7[o] ch. 12:6; Ps. 17:14; 37:1, 35; 73:3, 5; 92:7; Eccles. 8:14; Jer. 12:1, 2; Hab. 1:13, 16; Mal. 3:14, 15
8[p] [ch. 5:25]
9[q] [ch. 5:24] [r] See ch. 9:34
10[s] Ex. 23:26
11[t] [Ps. 17:14]
12[u] Ex. 15:20 [v] ch. 30:31; Gen. 4:21
13[w] ch. 36:11 [x] ch. 34:20; [ch. 24:19] [y] ch. 7:9; 14:13; 17:13; See Ps. 16:10
14[z] ch. 22:17
15[a] [Ex. 5:2] [b] See ch. 34:9
16[c] ch. 22:18; [Ps. 1:1]
17[d] See ch. 18:5, 6
18[e] ch. 13:25; Ps. 83:13 [f] Ps. 1:4; 35:5; Isa. 17:13; 29:5

19 You say, 'God [g]stores up their iniquity
for their [h]children.'
Let him pay it out to them, that they
may [i]know it.
20 Let their own eyes see their destruction,
and let them [j]drink of the wrath of
the Almighty.
21 For what do they care for their houses
after them,
when [k]the number of their months is
cut off?
22 [l]Will any teach God knowledge,
seeing that he [m]judges those who are
on high?
23 One dies in his full vigor,
being wholly at ease and secure,
24 his pails[1] full of milk
and [n]the marrow of his bones moist.
25 Another dies in [o]bitterness of soul,
never having tasted of prosperity.
26 They [p]lie down alike in the dust,
and [q]the worms cover them.

27 "Behold, I know your thoughts
and your schemes to wrong me.
28 For you say, [r]'Where is the house of the
prince?
Where is [s]the tent in which the
wicked lived?'
29 Have you not asked those who travel the
roads,
and do you not accept their testimony
30 that [t]the evil man is spared in the day of
calamity,
that he is rescued in the day of wrath?
31 Who declares his way [u]to his face,
and who [v]repays him for what he has
done?
32 When he is [w]carried to the grave,
watch is kept over his tomb.
33 [x]The clods of the valley are sweet to him;
[y]all mankind follows after him,
and those who go before him are
innumerable.
34 How then will you comfort me with
empty nothings?
There is nothing left of your answers
but falsehood."

Eliphaz Speaks: Job's Wickedness Is Great

22 Then [z]Eliphaz the Temanite answered
and said:

2 [a]"Can a man be profitable to God?
Surely he who is wise is profitable to
himself.
3 Is it any pleasure to the Almighty if you
are in the right,
or is it gain to him if you [b]make your
ways blameless?
4 Is it for your fear of him that he reproves
you
and [c]enters into judgment with you?
5 Is not your evil abundant?
There is no end to your iniquities.
6 For you have [d]exacted pledges of your
brothers for nothing
[e]and stripped the naked of their clothing.
7 You have given no water to the weary to
drink,
and you have [f]withheld bread from
the hungry.
8 [g]The man with power possessed the land,
and [h]the favored man lived in it.

[1] The meaning of the Hebrew word is uncertain

19[g] ch. 15:20 [h] Ex. 20:5 [i] Isa. 9:9; Ezek. 25:14; Hos. 9:7
20[j] Ps. 60:3; 75:8; Isa. 51:17, 22; Jer. 25:15; Obad. 16; Rev. 14:10
21[k] ch. 14:5
22[l] Isa. 40:14; Rom. 11:34; 1 Cor. 2:16 [m] [ch. 4:18; 15:15]
24[n] Prov. 3:8; [Isa. 58:11; 66:14]
25[o] See ch. 7:11
26[p] ch. 20:11; [Eccles. 9:2] [q] Isa. 14:11
28[r] [ch. 20:6, 7] [s] [ch. 8:22; 15:34]
30[t] [Prov. 16:4; 2 Pet. 2:9]
31[u] Deut. 7:10; Hos. 5:5; Gal. 2:11 [v] Deut. 7:10
32[w] ch. 10:19
33[x] ch. 38:38 [y] [ch. 30:23; Heb. 9:27]

Second, Job is extremely judgmental in passages like this. It's "they," "they," "they" who are terrible; "they" who are the unending source of comparison with himself and his situation. This feature of Job's repeating words of vindication is usually called self-righteousness. The gospel (and the ultimate revelation of God's glory in the book of Job) dismantles self-righteousness, because it places *everyone* at a parallel point of spiritual need. No one can stand proud and unflinching before the awesome holiness and power of God. People's life situations differ for as many cases as there are people in the world. Yet God uses these varieties of circumstances to bring us to, and meet us at, our point of need. Everyone has a point of need. This practical insight is an essential step in discerning why we suffer and in acquiring compassion for our fellow-sufferers.

From the standpoint of Christian faith, one perfect Man has already suffered, "the righteous for the unrighteous" (1 Pet. 3:18), and he did so because of his infinitely far-reaching compassion for *everyone's* suffering.

Chapter 22 **1**[z] ch. 2:11 **2**[a] See ch. 35:7 **3**[b] See Ps. 18:32 **4**[c] ch. 14:3; [Ps. 143:2] **6**[d] ch. 24:3, 9; Ex. 22:26; Deut. 24:6, 17; Ezek. 18:12, 16 [e] [ch. 31:16] **7**[f] [ch. 31:17; Isa. 58:7; Ezek. 18:7, 16; Matt. 25:42] **8**[g] [ch. 35:9] [h] 2 Kgs. 5:1; Isa. 9:15

9 You have [i]sent widows away empty,
and [j]the arms of [k]the fatherless were crushed.
10 Therefore [l]snares are all around you,
and sudden terror overwhelms you,
11 or [m]darkness, so that you cannot see,
and a [n]flood of [o]water covers you.

12 "Is not God high in the heavens?
See [p]the highest stars, how lofty they are!
13 But you say, [q]'What does God know?
Can he judge through [r]the deep darkness?
14 [s]Thick clouds veil him, so that he does not see,
and he walks on the vault of heaven.'
15 Will you keep to the old way
that wicked men have trod?
16 They were snatched away [t]before their time;
their foundation was washed away.
17 They said to God, [u]'Depart from us,'
and [v]'What can the Almighty do to us?'[1]
18 Yet he filled their houses with good things—
but [w]the counsel of the wicked is far from me.
19 [x]The righteous see it and are glad;
the innocent one [y]mocks at them,
20 saying, 'Surely our adversaries are cut off,
and what they left [z]the fire has consumed.'

21 [a]"Agree with God, and [b]be at peace;
thereby good will come to you.
22 Receive instruction from [c]his mouth,
and [d]lay up his words in your heart.
23 If you [e]return to the Almighty you will be [f]built up;
if you [g]remove injustice far from your tents,
24 if you lay gold in [h]the dust,
and gold of [i]Ophir among the stones of the torrent-bed,
25 then the Almighty will be your gold
and your precious silver.
26 For then you [j]will delight yourself in the Almighty
and [k]lift up your face to God.
27 You will [l]make your prayer to him, and he will hear you,
and you will [m]pay your vows.
28 You will decide on a matter, and it will be established for you,
and [n]light will shine on your ways.
29 For when they are humbled you say, 'It is because of pride';[2]
but he saves [o]the lowly.
30 He [p]delivers even the one who is not innocent,
who will be delivered through [q]the cleanness of your hands."

Job Replies: Where Is God?

23 Then Job answered and said:

2 "Today also my [r]complaint is bitter;[3]
my [s]hand is heavy on account of my groaning.
3 Oh, [t]that I knew where I might find him,
that I might come even to his [u]seat!
4 I would [v]lay my case before him
and fill my mouth with arguments.
5 I would know what he would answer me
and understand what he would say to me.
6 Would he [w]contend with me in the greatness of his power?
No; he would pay attention to me.
7 There an upright man could argue with him,
and I would be acquitted forever by my judge.

8 "Behold, [x]I go forward, but he is not there,
and backward, but I do not perceive him;
9 on the left hand when he is working,
I do not behold him;
he turns to the right hand, but I do not see him.
10 But he [y]knows [z]the way that I [a]take;
when he has [b]tried me, I shall come out as gold.

[1] Hebrew *them* [2] Or *you say, 'It is exaltation'* [3] Or *defiant*

9[i] [Luke 1:53] [j] [ch. 38:15] [k] ch. 31:21; Isa. 10:2; Ezek. 22:7 **10**[l] ch. 18:8-10 **11**[m] [Ex. 10:22, 23] [n] ch. 38:34 [o] [ch. 27:20; Ps. 69:1, 2, 14, 15; 124:5; Lam. 3:54; Jonah 2:3, 5] **12**[p] [ch. 11:8] **13**[q] Ps. 73:11; [Ps. 10:11; 59:7; 64:5; 94:7; Isa. 29:15; Ezek. 8:12; 9:9] [r] ch. 38:9 **14**[s] [Ps. 139:11, 12]; [Prov. 8:27; Isa. 40:22] **16**[t] See ch. 15:32 **17**[u] ch. 21:14 [v] [Ps. 4:6] **18**[w] ch. 21:16 **19**[x] Ps. 52:6; 58:10; 107:42; [Ps. 64:10] [y] Ps. 2:4 **20**[z] ch. 1:16 **21**[a] See Ps. 119:45 [b] [Prov. 3:2] **22**[c] Prov. 2:6; [Mal. 2:7] [d] Ps. 119:11 **23**[e] [ch. 8:5, 6; 11:13, 14; Mal. 3:7] [f] Jer. 24:6; 33:7 [g] ch. 11:14 **24**[h] ch. 20:11; 21:26 [i] See 1 Kgs. 9:28 **26**[j] ch. 27:10; Ps. 37:4; Isa. 58:14 [k] See ch. 11:15 **27**[l] ch. 33:26; Ps. 50:14, 15; Isa. 58:9 [m] Ps. 50:14 **28**[n] Prov. 4:18 **29**[o] Ps. 138:6; Prov. 3:34; 29:23; Matt. 23:12; Luke 1:52; James 4:6; 1 Pet. 5:5 **30**[p] [Gen. 18:26] [q] ch. 17:9; Ps. 18:20, 24; 24:4; 26:6; [ch. 9:30] **Chapter 23** **2**[r] ch. 10:1; 21:4 [s] [Ps. 32:4] **3**[t] [ch. 13:3; 16:21] [u] [Ps. 9:7, 8; Isa. 57:15, 16] **4**[v] See ch. 33:5 **6**[w] [ch. 9:34; 13:21] **8**[x] ch. 9:11; 35:14 **10**[y] Ps. 139:1-3 [z] Ps. 139:24 [a] [ch. 9:35] [b] Ps. 17:3; 26:2; 66:10; 139:23; Zech. 13:9; Mal. 3:3; 1 Pet. 1:7; Rev. 3:18; [James 1:12]

11 My foot [c]has held fast to his steps;
I have kept his way and have [d]not turned aside.
12 I have not departed from the commandment of his lips;
I have [e]treasured the words of his mouth more than my [f]portion of food.
13 But he is unchangeable,[1] and [g]who can turn him back?
What he [h]desires, that he does.
14 For he will complete what he [i]appoints for me,
and many such things are [j]in his mind.
15 Therefore I am terrified at his presence;
when I consider, I am in dread of him.
16 God has made my [k]heart faint;
the Almighty has terrified me;
17 yet I am not silenced because of the darkness,
nor because thick darkness covers my face.

24 "Why are [l]not times of judgment [m]kept by the Almighty,
and why do those who know him never see his [n]days?
2 Some move [o]landmarks;
they seize flocks and pasture them.
3 They drive away the donkey of the fatherless;
they [p]take the widow's ox for a pledge.
4 They [q]thrust the poor off the road;
the poor of the earth [r]all hide themselves.
5 Behold, like wild donkeys in the desert
the poor[2] [s]go out to their toil, [t]seeking game;
the wasteland yields food for their children.
6 They gather their[3] fodder in the field,
and they glean the vineyard of the wicked man.
7 They [u]lie all night naked, without clothing,
and have no covering in the cold.
8 They are wet with the rain of the mountains
and [v]cling to the rock for lack of shelter.
9 (There are those who snatch the fatherless child from the breast,
and they take a pledge against the poor.)
10 They go about naked, without clothing;
hungry, they [w]carry the sheaves;
11 among the olive rows of the wicked[4] they make oil;
they tread the winepresses, but suffer thirst.
12 From out of the city the dying groan,
and the soul of [x]the wounded cries for help;
yet God charges no one with [y]wrong.

13 "There are those who rebel [z]against the light,
who are not acquainted with its ways,
and do not stay in its paths.
14 The murderer rises before it is light,
that he [a]may kill the poor and needy,
and in the night he is like a thief.
15 The eye of the adulterer also waits for [b]the twilight,
saying, 'No [c]eye will see me';
and he veils his face.
16 In the dark they [d]dig through houses;
by day they shut themselves up;
they do not know the light.
17 For [e]deep darkness is morning to all of them;
for they are friends with the terrors of deep darkness.

18 "You say, [f]'Swift are they on the face of the waters;
their portion is cursed in the land;
no treader turns toward their vineyards.
19 Drought and heat snatch away the snow waters;
so does [g]Sheol those who have sinned.
20 The womb forgets them;
the worm finds them sweet;
they are [h]no longer remembered,
so wickedness is broken like [i]a tree.'
21 "They wrong the barren, childless woman,
and do no good to the widow.

[1] Or *one* [2] Hebrew *they* [3] Hebrew *his* [4] Hebrew *their olive rows*

11[c] Ps. 17:5; 44:18 [d] Ps. 125:5 **12**[e] [Ps. 119:11] [f] [Ps. 119:103; John 4:32, 34] **13**[g] [ch. 9:12; 12:14] [h] Ps. 115:3 **14**[i] [1 Thess. 3:3] [j] [ch. 10:13; 27:11] **16**[k] Deut. 20:3; [Ps. 22:14] **Chapter 24** **1**[l] Eccles. 9:12; Isa. 13:22; Jer. 27:7; Ezek. 22:3; 30:3 [m] ch. 15:20 [n] Isa. 2:12; 13:6, 9; Joel 1:15; 2:1; Amos 5:18; See ch. 18:20 **2**[o] See Deut. 19:14 **3**[p] See ch. 22:6 **4**[q] Amos 2:7; 5:12; Mal. 3:5 [r] Prov. 28:28; [ch. 30:5, 6] **5**[s] Ps. 104:23 [t] Ps. 104:21 **7**[u] [Ex. 22:26, 27; Deut. 24:12, 13] **8**[v] Lam. 4:5 **10**[w] [2 Tim. 2:6; James 5:4] **12**[x] Jer. 51:52; Ezek. 30:24 [y] ch. 1:22 **13**[z] John 3:19, 20 **14**[a] [Ps. 10:8] **15**[b] Prov. 7:9 [c] Ps. 10:11 **16**[d] Ex. 22:2; Matt. 6:20; [ch. 31:9] **17**[e] See ch. 3:5 **18**[f] [ch. 9:26; Hos. 10:7] **19**[g] See ch. 21:13 **20**[h] [Prov. 10:7] [i] [ch. 18:16]

22 Yet God[1] [i]prolongs the life of the mighty
by his power;
they rise up when they despair of life.
23 He gives them security, and they are
supported,
and his [j]eyes are upon their ways.
24 They are exalted [k]a little while, and then
[l]are gone;
they are brought low and gathered up
like all others;
they are [m]cut off like the heads of grain.
25 If it is [n]not so, who will prove me a liar
and show that there is nothing in
what I say?"

Bildad Speaks: Man Cannot Be Righteous

25 Then [o]Bildad the Shuhite answered
and said:

2 "Dominion and fear are with God;[2]
he makes peace in his high heaven.
3 Is there any number to his [p]armies?
Upon whom does his [q]light not arise?
4 How then can man be [r]in the right
before God?
How can he who is [s]born of woman
be [t]pure?
5 Behold, even the moon is not bright,
and the stars are not pure in his eyes;
6 [u]how much less man, who is [v]a maggot,
and [w]the son of man, who is a worm!"

Job Replies: God's Majesty Is Unsearchable

26 Then Job answered and said:

2 "How you have [x]helped him who has no
power!
How you have saved [y]the arm that has
no strength!
3 How you have [z]counseled him who has
no wisdom,
and plentifully declared sound
knowledge!
4 With whose help have you uttered
words,
and whose breath [a]has come out from
you?
5 The [b]dead tremble
under the waters and their inhabitants.
6 Sheol is [c]naked before God,[3]
and [d]Abaddon has no covering.
7 He [e]stretches out the north over [f]the void
and hangs the earth on nothing.
8 He [g]binds up the waters in his thick
clouds,
and the cloud is not split open under
them.
9 He covers the face of the full moon[4]
and [h]spreads over it his cloud.
10 He has inscribed [i]a circle on the face of
the waters
at the boundary between light and
darkness.
11 [j]The pillars of heaven tremble
and are astounded at his [k]rebuke.
12 By his power he [l]stilled the sea;
by his understanding he shattered
[m]Rahab.
13 [n]By his wind the heavens were made fair;
his hand pierced [o]the fleeing serpent.
14 Behold, these are but the outskirts of his
[p]ways,
and how small [q]a whisper do we hear
of him!
But the thunder of his power who can
understand?"

[1] Hebrew *he* [2] Hebrew *him* [3] Hebrew *him* [4] Or *his throne*

26:1–3 Job's sarcasm directed at the three who have now been seen to be false comforters affirms *by implication* what a true comforter should be like. A true comforter would have "helped him who has no power" (v. 2). A true comforter would have "saved the arm that has no strength" (v. 2). A true comforter would have "counseled him who has no wisdom" (v. 3). A true comforter would have "plentifully declared sound knowledge" (v. 3). A helper, a saver, a counselor, a proclaimer: all those things a true comforter would be—as our Savior ultimately demonstrated.

Note the *no* in "no power . . . no strength . . . no wisdom" (vv. 2–3). True comfort comes to us when we are at the end of the road, with no gas in the engine and no human *possibility* of gas for thousands of miles around. Grace doesn't add to what's already there. Grace comes to our aid when there is *nothing* there. This is the comforting grace that Jesus Christ embodied in his life and ministry. He is the Comforter for all who have broken down and have nothing left to run on.

23 [j]See Ps. 11:4; Prov. 15:3
24 [k]Ps. 37:10 [l][ch. 27:19] [m]ch. 14:2
25 [n][ch. 9:24]
Chapter 25
1 [o]ch. 2:11
3 [p]ch. 19:12; Ps. 103:21 [q]Matt. 5:45; James 1:17
4 [r]ch. 4:17-19; 9:2; 15:14-16; Ps. 130:3; 143:2 [s]See ch. 14:1 [t]ch. 14:4
6 [u]ch. 9:14; 15:16 [v]Ps. 22:6; Isa. 41:14 [w]ch. 35:8
Chapter 26
2 [x]Isa. 40:29 [y]Gen. 49:24; Hos. 7:15
3 [z]Ps. 73:24; James 1:5
4 [a]Gen. 2:7
5 [b]Ps. 88:10

6 [c]Ps. 139:8; Prov. 15:11 [d]Rev. 9:11 **7** [e]See ch. 9:8 [f][Gen. 1:2] **8** [g]Prov. 30:4 **9** [h][ch. 36:29] **10** [i]Prov. 8:29; [ch. 38:8-11; Ps. 33:7; Jer. 5:22] **11** [j]ch. 9:6; Ps. 75:3 [k]Ps. 104:7 **12** [l]Isa. 51:15; Jer. 31:35 [m]See ch. 9:13 **13** [n][Ps. 33:6] [o]Isa. 27:1 **14** [p]ch. 40:19 [q]ch. 4:12

Job Continues: I Will Maintain My Integrity

27 And Job again [r]took up his discourse, and said:

2 "As God lives, who has [s]taken away my right,
and the Almighty, who has [t]made my soul bitter,
3 as long as my breath is in me,
and [u]the spirit of God is in my nostrils,
4 my lips will not speak [v]falsehood,
and my tongue will not utter [v]deceit.
5 Far be it from me to say that you are right;
till I die I will not put away my [w]integrity from me.
6 I [x]hold fast my righteousness and will not let it go;
my heart does not [y]reproach me for any of my days.

7 "Let my enemy be as the wicked,
and let him who rises up against me be as the unrighteous.
8 [z]For what is the hope of the godless
[a]when God cuts him off,
when God takes away his life?
9 [b]Will God hear his cry
when distress comes upon him?
10 Will he [c]take delight in the Almighty?
Will he call upon God at all times?
11 I will teach you concerning the hand of God;
[d]what is with the Almighty I will not conceal.
12 Behold, all of you have seen it yourselves;
why then have you become altogether vain?

13 [e]"This is the portion of a wicked man with God,
and the heritage that [f]oppressors receive from the Almighty:
14 If his [g]children are multiplied, it is for [h]the sword,
and his descendants have not enough bread.
15 Those who survive him the pestilence buries,
and his [i]widows do not weep.
16 Though he [j]heap up silver like dust,
and pile up clothing like clay,
17 he may pile it up, but the righteous will wear it,
and [k]the innocent will divide the silver.
18 He builds his [l]house like a moth's,
like [m]a booth that [n]a watchman makes.
19 He goes to bed rich, but will [o]do so no more;
he opens his eyes, and [p]his wealth is gone.
20 [q]Terrors overtake him like [r]a flood;
in the night a whirlwind [s]carries him off.
21 [t]The east wind lifts him up and he is gone;
it [u]sweeps him out of his place.
22 It[1] hurls at him [v]without pity;
he flees from its[2] power in headlong flight.
23 It [w]claps its hands at him
and [x]hisses at him from its place.

Job Continues: Where Is Wisdom?

28 "Surely there is a mine for silver,
and a place for gold that they [y]refine.
2 Iron is taken out of the earth,
and copper is smelted from the ore.
3 Man puts an end to darkness
and searches out to the farthest limit
the ore in [z]gloom and [a]deep darkness.
4 He opens shafts in a valley away from where anyone lives;
they are forgotten by travelers;
they hang in the air, far away from mankind; they swing to and fro.
5 As for the earth, [b]out of it comes bread,
but underneath it is turned up as by fire.
6 Its stones are the place of [c]sapphires,[3]
and it has dust of gold.

7 "That path no bird of prey knows,
and the falcon's eye has not seen it.
8 [d]The proud beasts have not trodden it;
[e]the lion has not passed over it.

9 "Man puts his hand to [f]the flinty rock
and overturns mountains by the roots.
10 He cuts out channels in the rocks,
and his eye sees every precious thing.

[1] Or *He* (that is, God); also verse 23 [2] Or *his*; also verse 23 [3] Or *lapis lazuli*; also verse 16

Chapter 27 **1** [r]ch. 29:1; See Num. 23:7 **2** [s]ch. 34:5 [t][Ruth 1:20; 2 Kgs. 4:27] **3** [u]ch. 33:4; [Gen. 2:7] **4** [v]ch. 13:7 **5** [w]ch. 2:3, 9; [ch. 13:15] **6** [x]ch. 2:3 [y][Acts 23:1; 24:16; 1 Cor. 4:4] **8** [z]See ch. 8:13 [a]Matt. 16:26; [Luke 12:20] **9** [b]Ps. 18:41; Prov. 1:28; 15:29; Isa. 1:15; Jer. 11:11; 14:12; Ezek. 8:18; Mic. 3:4; Zech. 7:13; [ch. 35:12, 13]; See Ps. 66:18 **10** [c]See ch. 22:26 **11** [d]ch. 10:13; 23:14 **13** [e]ch. 20:29; [ch. 18:21; 31:2] [f]ch. 6:23; 15:20 **14** [g]Deut. 28:41; Hos. 9:13, 16 [h]Jer. 15:2 **15** [i]Ps. 78:64 **16** [j]Zech. 9:3 **17** [k][Prov. 13:22; Eccles. 2:26] **18** [l]ch. 8:14, 15 [m]Isa. 1:8 [n]Song 1:6; 8:11, 12 **19** [o]Jer. 8:2; Ezek. 29:5 [p]ch. 24:24 **20** [q]See ch. 18:11 [r]See ch. 22:11 [s]ch. 34:20, 25; 36:20 **21** [t][ch. 30:22] [u]ch. 8:18 **22** [v]ch. 16:13 **23** [w]Lam. 2:15; Ezek. 25:6; Nah. 3:19 [x][2 Chr. 29:8; Jer. 49:17; Lam. 2:15; Ezek. 27:36; Zeph. 2:15] **Chapter 28** **1** [y][Mal. 3:3] **3** [z]ch. 10:22 [a]See ch. 3:5 **5** [b]Ps. 104:14 **6** [c]Ex. 24:10 **8** [d]ch. 41:34 [e]ch. 10:16 **9** [f]Deut. 8:15; 32:13; Ps. 114:8

11 He dams up the streams so that they do not trickle,
and the thing that is hidden he brings out to light.

12 [g]"But where shall wisdom be found?
And where is the place of understanding?
13 Man does not know its worth,
and it is not found in [h]the land of the living.
14 [i]The deep says, 'It is not in me,'
and the sea says, 'It is not with me.'
15 It [j]cannot be bought for gold,
and silver cannot be weighed as its price.
16 It cannot be valued in [k]the gold of [l]Ophir,
in precious [m]onyx or [n]sapphire.
17 Gold and glass cannot equal it,
nor can it be exchanged for jewels of fine gold.
18 No mention shall be made of [o]coral or of crystal;
the price of wisdom is above [o, p]pearls.
19 [q]The topaz of Ethiopia cannot equal it,
nor can it be valued in pure gold.

20 "From where, then, does wisdom come?
And where is the place of understanding?
21 It is hidden from the eyes of [r]all living
and concealed from the birds of the air.
22 [s]Abaddon and Death say,
'We have heard a rumor of it with our ears.'

23 [t]"God understands the way to it,
and he knows its place.
24 For he [u]looks to the ends of the earth
and sees everything under the heavens.
25 When he [v]gave to the wind its weight
and apportioned the waters by measure,
26 when he made a decree for the rain
and [w]a way for the lightning of the thunder,
27 then he saw it and declared it;
he established it, and searched it out.
28 And he said to man,
'Behold, [x]the fear of the Lord, that is wisdom,
and to [y]turn away from evil is understanding.'"

Job's Summary Defense

29 And Job again [z]took up his discourse, and said:

2 "Oh, that I were as in the months of old,
as in the days when God watched over me,
3 when his [a]lamp shone upon my head,
and by his light I walked through darkness,
4 as I was in my prime,[1]
when the [b]friendship of God was upon my tent,
5 when the Almighty was yet with me,
when my [c]children were all around me,
6 when my steps were [d]washed with [e]butter,
and [f]the rock poured out for me streams of [g]oil!
7 When I went out to [h]the gate of the city,
when I prepared my seat in the square,

[1] Hebrew *my autumn days*

29:1–25 A poignant note of loss is sounded toward the end of Job's concluding speech in reply to his friends. Job looks back at the "seven fat years" of his life (cf. Gen. 41:29) and rhapsodizes about them: "Oh, that I were as in the months of old, as in the days when God watched over me" (Job 29:2). "Men listened to me and waited and kept silence for my counsel" (v. 21). "I lived like a king among his troops" (v. 25).

When someone says they're at the "top of their game," watch out. For them! The kind of self-congratulation that Job apparently *thought*, even if he didn't say it, "back in the day," was the prelude to his fall. Successful people start giving themselves credit and pat themselves on the back. Then one day, sometimes sooner rather than later, "all fall down."

No wonder Job's success was snatched out of his hand. He'd evidently begun to think the self-importance "myth" was true: The Myth of Job the Magnificent. Now he is nostalgic for the Myth, "(for) now they laugh at me, men who are younger than I, whose fathers I would have disdained to set with the dogs of my flock" (30:1).

12[g] [Prov. 16:16; Eccles. 7:24]
13[h] See Ps. 27:13
14[i] Gen. 49:25
15[j] Prov. 3:14; 8:10, 11, 19; 16:16
16[k] Ps. 45:9; Isa. 13:12 [l] See 1 Kgs. 9:28 [m] Gen. 2:12 [n] Ex. 24:10
18[o] Ezek. 27:16 [p] Prov. 3:15; 8:11; 20:15; 31:10; Lam. 4:7
19[q] Ex. 28:17; 39:10; Ezek. 28:13
21[r] ch. 12:10; 30:23
22[s] See ch. 26:6
23[t] For ver. 23-28, see Prov. 8:22-31
24[u] [Prov. 15:3; Zech. 4:10]
25[v] [Ps. 135:7]
26[w] ch. 38:25
28[x] Deut. 4:6; Ps. 111:10; Prov. 1:7; [Eccles. 12:13] [y] Prov. 3:7; 14:16; 16:6

Chapter 29 **1**[z] ch. 27:1; See Num. 23:7 **3**[a] ch. 18:6; 2 Sam. 21:17; Ps. 18:28 **4**[b] Ps. 25:14; Prov. 3:32; See ch. 15:8 **5**[c] ch. 1:2; [Ps. 128:3] **6**[d] [Gen. 49:11] [e] ch. 20:17 [f] Deut. 32:13, 14; Ps. 81:16 [g] [Deut. 33:24] **7**[h] See ch. 5:4

8 the young men saw me and withdrew,
and the aged rose and stood;
9 the princes refrained from talking
and [i]laid their hand on their mouth;
10 the voice of the nobles was hushed,
and their [j]tongue stuck to the roof of their mouth.
11 When the ear heard, it called me blessed,
and when the eye saw, it approved,
12 because I [k]delivered the poor who cried for help,
and the fatherless who had none to help him.
13 [l]The blessing of him who was [m]about to perish came upon me,
and I caused [n]the widow's heart to sing for joy.
14 I [o]put on righteousness, and it clothed me;
my justice was like a robe and [p]a turban.
15 I was [q]eyes to the blind
and feet to the lame.
16 I was a father to the needy,
and I searched out [r]the cause of him whom I did not know.
17 I [s]broke [t]the fangs of the unrighteous
and made him drop his prey from his teeth.
18 [u]Then I thought, 'I shall die in my [v]nest,
and I shall multiply my days as [w]the sand,
19 my [x]roots spread out to [y]the waters,
with the dew all night on my [z]branches,
20 my glory fresh with me,
and my [a]bow ever [b]new in my hand.'

21 "Men listened to me and waited
and kept silence for my counsel.
22 After I spoke they did not speak again,
and my word [c]dropped upon them.
23 They waited for me as for the rain,
and they [d]opened their mouths as for the [e]spring rain.
24 I smiled on them when they had no confidence,
and [f]the light of my [g]face they did not cast down.
25 I chose their way and sat as chief,
and I lived like [h]a king among his troops,
like one who comforts mourners.

30 "But now they [i]laugh at me,
men who are [j]younger than I,
whose fathers I would have disdained
to set with the dogs of my flock.
2 What could I gain from the strength of their hands,
[k]men whose [l]vigor is gone?
3 Through want and hard hunger
they [m]gnaw [n]the dry ground by night
in [o]waste and desolation;
4 they pick saltwort and the leaves of bushes,
and the roots of the broom tree for their food.[1]
5 [p]They are driven out from human company;
they shout after them as after a thief.
6 In the gullies of the torrents they must dwell,
in holes of the earth and of [q]the rocks.
7 Among the bushes they [r]bray;
under [s]the nettles they huddle together.
8 A senseless, a nameless brood,
they have been whipped out of the land.

9 "And now I have become their [t]song;
I am [u]a byword to them.
10 They [v]abhor me; they keep aloof from me;
they do not hesitate to [w]spit at the sight of me.

[1] Or *warmth*

9[i] See ch. 21:5
10[j] Ps. 22:15; 137:6; Lam. 4:4; Ezek. 3:26
12[k] Ps. 72:12
13[l] ch. 31:20 [m] Prov. 31:6; Isa. 27:13 [n] [Ruth 2:20]
14[o] Ps. 132:9; Isa. 59:17; 61:10; [Isa. 11:5; Eph. 6:14; 1 Thess. 5:8] [p] Isa. 62:3; Zech. 3:5; [ch. 19:9]

The gospel does not assess success as does the world but rather, in a direction Job is just barely beginning to learn, "God chose what is foolish in the world to shame the wise; God chose what is weak in the world to shame the strong; God chose what is low and despised in the world, even things that are not, to bring to nothing things that are, so that no human being might boast in the presence of God. And because of him you are in Christ Jesus . . . so that, as it is written, 'Let the one who boasts, boast in the Lord'" (1 Cor. 1:27–31).

15[q] Num. 10:31 **16**[r] [Prov. 29:7] **17**[s] Ps. 3:7 [t] Ps. 58:6; Prov. 30:14 **18**[u] [Ps. 30:6] [v] Num. 24:21; See ch. 39:27 [w] Gen. 22:17 **19**[x] ch. 18:16 [y] See Ps. 1:3 [z] [ch. 14:9] **20**[a] Gen. 49:24 [b] [Isa. 40:31; 41:1] **22**[c] [Deut. 32:2; 33:28] **23**[d] Ps. 119:131; [Isa. 5:14] [e] Prov. 16:15; Jer. 3:3; Zech. 10:1; [Deut. 11:14] **24**[f] Prov. 16:15 [g] Gen. 4:5 **25**[h] ch. 15:24 **Chapter 30** **1**[i] See ch. 12:4 [j] ch. 32:6; [ch. 32:4] **2**[k] For ver. 2-8, see ch. 24:4-8 [l] [ch. 5:26] **3**[m] [ver. 17] [n] Jer. 2:6 [o] ch. 38:27; Zeph. 1:15 **5**[p] [1 Sam. 26:19] **6**[q] 1 Sam. 13:6; Jer. 4:29 **7**[r] ch. 6:5 [s] Prov. 24:31; Zeph. 2:9 **9**[t] Ps. 69:12; Lam. 3:14, 63 [u] See ch. 17:6 **10**[v] Ps. 88:8; [ch. 17:6] [w] Num. 12:14; Isa. 50:6; Matt. 26:67; 27:30

11 Because God has loosed my cord and
humbled me,
they have cast off restraint[1] in my
presence.
12 On my [x]right hand the rabble rise;
they push away my feet;
they [y]cast up against me their ways of
destruction.
13 They break up my path;
they promote my [z]calamity;
they need no one to help them.
14 As through a wide [a]breach they come;
amid the crash they roll on.
15 [b]Terrors are turned upon me;
my honor is pursued as by the wind,
and my prosperity has passed away
like [c]a cloud.

16 "And now my soul is [d]poured out within
me;
days of affliction have taken hold of
me.
17 [e]The night [f]racks my bones,
and the pain that [g]gnaws me takes no
rest.
18 With great force my garment is [h]disfig-
ured;
it binds me about like the collar of my
tunic.
19 God[2] has cast me into the mire,
and I have become like [i]dust and
ashes.
20 I cry to you for help and you do not
answer me;
I stand, and you only look at me.
21 You have [j]turned cruel to me;
with the might of your hand you [k]per-
secute me.
22 [l]You lift me up on the wind; you make
me ride on it,
and you toss me about in the roar of
the storm.
23 [m]For I know that you will bring me to
death
and to the house appointed for [n]all
living.

24 "Yet does not one in a [o]heap of ruins
stretch out his hand,
and in his disaster cry for help?[3]
25 Did not I [p]weep for him whose day was
hard?
Was not my soul grieved for the needy?
26 But [q]when I hoped for good, evil came,
and when I waited for light, [r]darkness
came.
27 My inward parts are in turmoil and
never still;
days of affliction [s]come to meet me.
28 I [t]go about darkened, but not by the sun;
I stand up in [u]the assembly and cry for
help.
29 I am a brother of [v]jackals
and a companion of [w]ostriches.
30 My [x]skin turns black and falls from me,
and my [y]bones burn with heat.
31 My [z]lyre is [a]turned to mourning,
and my [z]pipe to the voice of those
who weep.

Job's Final Appeal

31 "I have made a covenant with my
[b]eyes;
how then could I gaze at a virgin?
2 What would be [c]my portion from God
above
and [c]my heritage from the Almighty
on high?
3 Is not calamity for the unrighteous,
and disaster for the workers of iniquity?
4 [d]Does not he see my ways
and [e]number all my steps?

5 "If I have walked with falsehood
and my foot has hastened to deceit;
6 (Let me be [f]weighed in a just balance,
and let God know my integrity!)
7 if my step has turned aside from the way
and [g]my heart has gone after my eyes,
and if any [h]spot has stuck to my
hands,
8 then let me [i]sow, and another eat,
and let what grows for me[4] be rooted
out.

9 "If my heart has been enticed toward a
woman,
and I have [j]lain in wait at my neighbor's door,

[1] Hebrew *the bridle* [2] Hebrew *He* [3] The meaning of the Hebrew is uncertain [4] Or *let my descendants*

12[x] Ps. 109:6 [y] ch. 19:12 **13**[z] ch. 6:2 **14**[a] ch. 16:14 **15**[b] See ch. 18:11 [c] ch. 7:9; Isa. 44:22 **16**[d] 1 Sam. 1:15; [ch. 10:1] **17**[e] [ch. 7:3] [f] ch. 33:19 [g] ver. 3 **18**[h] [1 Sam. 28:8; 1 Kgs. 20:38] **19**[i] ch. 42:6; [Gen. 18:27] **21**[j] Lam. 4:3; [Isa. 63:10] [k] ch. 16:9 **22**[l] [ch. 27:21] **23**[m] ch. 19:25 [n] ch. 28:21 **24**[o] Ps. 79:1; Jer. 26:18; Mic. 1:6; 3:12 **25**[p] Ps. 35:13, 14; Rom. 12:15 **26**[q] Jer. 8:15; 14:19 [r] ch. 10:21, 22 **27**[s] 2 Sam. 22:6; Ps. 18:5 **28**[t] Ps. 38:6; 42:9; 43:2 [u] Prov. 26:26 **29**[v] Mic. 1:8 [w] Isa. 13:21; 34:13; Jer. 50:39; Mic. 1:8 **30**[x] [Ps. 119:83; Lam. 4:8; 5:10] [y] Ps. 102:3 **31**[z] ch. 21:12 [a] Lam. 5:15 **Chapter 31** **1**[b] [Isa. 33:15; Matt. 5:28] **2**[c] See ch. 20:29 **4**[d] ch. 14:16; 34:21; 2 Chr. 16:9; Prov. 5:21; 15:3; Jer. 16:17; 32:19; Zech. 4:10 [e] ch. 14:16 **6**[f] Dan. 5:27 **7**[g] Num. 15:39; Eccles. 11:9 [h] [ch. 11:15] **8**[i] Lev. 26:16; Deut. 28:30, 38; [John 4:37] **9**[j] [ch. 24:15]

10 then let my wife [k]grind for another,
and let others [l]bow down on her.
11 For that would be a heinous crime;
that would be an iniquity [m]to be punished by the judges;
12 for that would be a fire [n]that consumes as far as Abaddon,
and it would burn to the root all my increase.

13 "If I have rejected the cause of my manservant or my maidservant,
when they brought a complaint against me,
14 what then shall I do when God rises up?
When he [o]makes inquiry, what shall I answer him?
15 Did [p]not he who made me in the womb make him?
And did not one fashion us in the womb?

16 "If I have [q]withheld anything that the poor desired,
or have [r]caused the eyes of the widow to fail,
17 or have eaten my morsel alone,
and the fatherless has not eaten of it
18 (for from my youth the fatherless[1] grew up with me as with a father,
and from my mother's womb I guided the widow[2]),
19 if I have seen anyone [s]perish for [t]lack of clothing,
or the needy without [t]covering,
20 if his body has not [u]blessed me,[3]
and if he was not warmed with the fleece of my sheep,
21 if I have raised my hand against [v]the fatherless,
because I saw my help in [w]the gate,
22 then let my shoulder blade fall from my shoulder,
and let my arm be broken from its socket.
23 For I was [x]in terror of calamity from God,
and I could not have faced his [x]majesty.

24 [y]"If I have made gold my [z]trust
or called [a]fine gold my confidence,
25 if I have [b]rejoiced because my wealth was abundant
or because [c]my hand had found much,
26 [d]if I have looked at the sun[4] when it shone,
or [e]the moon moving in splendor,
27 and my heart has been secretly enticed,
and my mouth has kissed my hand,
28 this also would be [f]an iniquity to be punished by the judges,
for I would have been false to God above.

29 "If I have [g]rejoiced at the ruin of him who hated me,
or exulted when evil overtook him
30 ([h]I have not let my mouth sin
by asking for his life with a curse),
31 if the men of my tent have not said,
'Who is there that has not been filled with his [i]meat?'
32 ([j]the sojourner has not lodged in the street;
I have opened my doors to the traveler),
33 if I [k]have concealed my transgressions [l]as others do[5]
by hiding my iniquity in my heart,
34 because I stood in great fear of [m]the multitude,
and the contempt of families terrified me,
so that I kept silence, and did not go out of doors—
35 Oh, that I had one to hear me!
(Here is my signature! Let the Almighty [n]answer me!)
Oh, that I had [o]the indictment written by my adversary!
36 Surely I would carry it on my [p]shoulder;
I would [q]bind it on me as [r]a crown;
37 I would give him an account of all my steps;
like a prince I would approach him.

38 "If my land has cried out against me
and its furrows have wept together,
39 [s]if I have eaten its yield without payment
and made its owners [t]breathe their last,

[1] Hebrew *he* [2] Hebrew *her* [3] Hebrew *if his loins have not blessed me* [4] Hebrew *the light* [5] Or *as Adam did*

10[k] [Ex. 11:5; Isa. 47:2] [l] [2 Sam. 12:11; Jer. 8:10] **11**[m] ver. 28; [Lev. 20:10; Deut. 22:22] **12**[n] See Prov. 6:27-29 **14**[o] Ps. 17:3 **15**[p] ch. 34:19; Prov. 14:31; 22:2; [Eph. 6:9] **16**[q] [ch. 22:7] [r] ch. 11:20; 17:5 **19**[s] ch. 29:13 [t] ch. 24:7, 10 **20**[u] ch. 29:13; Deut. 24:13 **21**[v] ch. 22:9 [w] See ch. 5:4 **23**[x] ch. 13:11 **24**[y] Mark 10:24, 25 [z] ch. 4:6 [a] ch. 28:16 **25**[b] Ps. 62:10 [c] Deut. 8:17 **26**[d] Deut. 4:19; [Deut. 17:3; 2 Kgs. 23:5, 11; Ezek. 8:16] [e] See Jer. 44:17-19 **28**[f] ver. 11 **29**[g] Prov. 17:5 **30**[h] [Matt. 5:44; Rom. 12:14] **31**[i] Ex. 16:12; 1 Sam. 25:11 **32**[j] [Gen. 19:2, 3; Judg. 19:20, 21; Matt. 25:35; Heb. 13:2] **33**[k] Prov. 28:13 [l] Gen. 3:8, 12 **34**[m] [Ex. 23:2] **35**[n] ch. 13:22 [o] [ch. 19:23] **36**[p] Isa. 9:6; 22:22 [q] Prov. 6:21 [r] Zech. 6:11 **39**[s] [ch. 22:6-9; Luke 10:7; 2 Tim. 2:6; James 5:4] [t] [1 Kgs. 21:16, 19]

40 let [u]thorns grow instead of wheat,
and foul weeds instead of barley."

The words of Job are ended.

Elihu Rebukes Job's Three Friends

32 So these three men ceased to answer
Job, because he was [v]righteous in his
own eyes. 2 Then Elihu the son of Barachel
[w]the Buzite, of the family of Ram, burned with
anger. He burned with anger at Job because he
justified himself [x]rather than God. 3 He burned
with anger also at Job's three friends because
they had found no answer, although they had
[y]declared Job to be in the wrong. 4 Now Elihu
had waited to speak to Job because they were
older than he. 5 And when Elihu saw that there
was no answer in the mouth of these three
men, he burned with anger.
6 And Elihu the son of Barachel the Buzite
answered and said:

"I am young in years,
and you are [z]aged;
therefore I was timid and afraid
to declare my opinion to you.
7 I said, 'Let days speak,
and many years teach wisdom.'
8 But it is [a]the spirit in man,
[b]the breath of the Almighty, that makes him [c]understand.
9 [d]It is not the old[1] who are wise,
nor the aged who understand what is right.
10 Therefore I say, 'Listen to me;
let me also declare my opinion.'

11 "Behold, I waited for your words,
I listened for your wise sayings,
while you searched out what to say.
12 I gave you my attention,
and, behold, there was none among you who refuted Job
or who answered his words.
13 Beware [e]lest you say, 'We have found wisdom;
God may vanquish him, not a man.'
14 He has not directed his words against me,
and I will not answer him with your speeches.

15 "They are dismayed; they answer no more;
they have not a word to say.
16 And shall I wait, because they do not speak,
because they stand there, and answer no more?
17 I also will answer with my share;
I also will declare my opinion.
18 For I am full of words;
the spirit within me constrains me.
19 Behold, my belly is like wine that has no vent;
like new [f]wineskins ready to burst.
20 [g]I must speak, that I may find [h]relief;
I must open my lips and answer.
21 I will not [i]show partiality to any man
or use flattery toward any person.
22 For I do not know how to flatter,
else my Maker would soon take me away.

Elihu Rebukes Job

33 "But now, hear my speech, O Job,
and listen to all my words.
2 Behold, I [j]open my mouth;
the tongue in my mouth speaks.
3 My words declare the uprightness of my heart,
and what my lips know they speak sincerely.
4 [k]The Spirit of God has made me,
and [l]the breath of the Almighty gives me life.
5 [m]Answer me, if you can;
[n]set your words in order before me;
take your stand.
6 Behold, I am toward God as you are;
I too was pinched off from a piece of [o]clay.
7 Behold, no [p]fear of me need terrify you;
my [q]pressure will not be heavy upon you.

8 "Surely you have spoken in my ears,
and I have heard the sound of your words.
9 You say, 'I am [r]pure, without [s]transgression;
I am clean, and there is no iniquity in me.

[1] Hebrew *many* [in years]

40 [u]Gen. 3:18 **Chapter 32** **1** [v]See ch. 33:9 **2** [w]Gen. 22:21; Jer. 25:23 [x]ch. 4:17; [ch. 34:5; 35:2; 40:8] **3** [y]ch. 8:6; 22:5 **6** [z]ch. 15:10 **8** [a]ch. 33:4; 34:14 [b]ch. 33:4; Gen. 2:7 [c]ch. 35:11; 38:36; 39:17; 1 Kgs. 3:12; 4:29; Prov. 2:6; Eccles. 2:26; Dan. 1:17; 2:21; James 1:5 **9** [d]1 Cor. 1:26; [ch. 12:20; Matt. 11:25] **13** [e]Jer. 9:23 **19** [f]Matt. 9:17; [Josh. 9:4] **20** [g][Ps. 39:3] [h]1 Sam. 16:23 **21** [i]Lev. 19:15 **Chapter 33** **2** [j]ch. 3:1 **4** [k]ch. 27:3 [l]ch. 32:8; Gen. 2:7; [Ezek. 37:9; Acts 17:25] **5** [m]ver. 32 [n]ch. 13:18; 23:4; [Ps. 5:3] **6** [o]See ch. 4:19 **7** [p]ch. 9:34, 35; 13:21 [q][ch. 23:2] **9** [r]ch. 9:21; 10:7; 11:4; 12:4; 13:18; 16:17; 23:10, 11; 27:5; 29:14; 32:1; 34:5 [s]ch. 34:6

10 Behold, he finds occasions against me,
he [t]counts me as his enemy,
11 he [u]puts my feet in the stocks
and [v]watches all my paths.'

12 "Behold, in this you are not right. I will
answer you,
for God is greater than man.
13 Why do you [w]contend against him,
saying, 'He [x]will answer none of
man's[1] words'?[2]
14 For God [y]speaks in one way,
[z]and in two, though man [a]does not
perceive it.
15 In [b]a dream, in [c]a vision of [d]the night,
when [c]deep sleep falls on men,
while they slumber on their beds,
16 then he [e]opens the ears of men
and terrifies them with warnings,
17 that he may turn man aside from his
[f]deed
and conceal pride from a man;
18 he keeps back his soul from the pit,
his life from [g]perishing by the sword.

19 "Man is also rebuked with pain on his bed
and with continual strife in his [h]bones,
20 so that his [i]life loathes bread,
and his appetite [j]the choicest food.
21 His flesh is so wasted away that it cannot
be seen,
and his bones that were not seen
[k]stick out.
22 His soul draws near [l]the pit,
and his life to [m]those who bring death.
23 If there be for him [n]an angel,
[o]a mediator, [p]one of the thousand,
to declare to man what is [q]right for
him,
24 and he is merciful to him, and says,
'Deliver him from going down into
the pit;
I have found [r]a ransom;
25 let his flesh [s]become fresh with youth;
let him return to the days of his
youthful vigor';
26 then man[3] [t]prays to God, and he accepts
him;
he [u]sees his face with a shout of joy,
and he [v]restores to man his righteousness.
27 He sings before men and says:
'I [w]sinned and perverted what was right,
and it was not repaid to me.
28 He has redeemed my [x]soul from going
down [y]into the pit,
and my life shall [z]look upon the light.'

29 "Behold, God does all these things,
twice, [a]three times, with a man,
30 to bring back his soul from the pit,
that he may be lighted with [b]the light
of life.
31 Pay attention, O Job, listen to me;
be silent, and I will speak.
32 If you have any words, [c]answer me;
[d]speak, for I desire to justify you.
33 If not, [e]listen to me;
be silent, and I will teach you wisdom."

[1] Hebrew *his* [2] Or *He will not answer for any of his own words* [3] Hebrew *he*

33:29–33 The Christian contemplative Meister Eckhart said that people's defenses against truth, particularly truth about themselves, are equivalent to "thirty or forty skins or hides, like an ox's or a bear's, so thick and hard." The young man Elihu, who emerged "out of the blue" in chapter 32, says something like that here: "God does all these things" (i.e., events and frustrations to get a person's attention) "twice, three times, with a man, to bring back his soul from the pit, that he may be lighted with the light of life" (33:29–30).

Next, Elihu calls on Job to *stop talking*! He claims to be able to teach Job a little wisdom, but only if Job can "be silent" (v. 33).

Two points of gospel application here: The first work of God in a person's life is *archaeological*. God must get beneath the surface to our foundations. For, if they are founded on self then they require undermining. "For it is written, 'I will destroy the wisdom of the wise, and the discernment of the discerning I will thwart'" (1 Cor. 1:19; Isa. 29:14). The operation of repentance and self-knowledge is the beginning of wisdom.

Second, we have to stop listening to ourselves in order to listen to the truth that sets us free (John 8:32). We need a holiday from self-expression. "Be silent, and I will teach you wisdom" (Job 33:33).

10[t] See ch. 13:24
11[u] ch. 13:27 [v] ch. 10:14; 14:16; 31:4
13[w] ch. 13:3; 16:21; 31:35; 40:2 [x] See ch. 9:12
14[y] [ch. 40:5; Ps. 62:11] [z] ver. 29 [a] [1 Sam. 3:4, 6]
15[b] See Num. 12:6 [c] ch. 4:13 [d] Ps. 17:3
16[e] ch. 36:10, 15; Ps. 40:6; Isa. 50:5
17[f] ch. 36:9
18[g] ch. 36:12
19[h] ch. 30:17
20[i] Ps. 107:18 [j] Prov. 23:3
21[k] [Ps. 22:17]
22[l] ver. 24, 28 [m] 2 Sam. 24:16, 17; Ps. 78:49
23[n] Gen. 16:7; 22:11; 48:16; Ps. 34:7; Isa. 63:9; [Mal. 3:1] [o] Gen. 42:23; Isa. 43:27 [p] Eccles. 7:28; [Song 5:10] [q] [Prov. 14:2; Ezek. 18:21, 22]
24[r] ch. 36:18; Ps. 49:7
25[s] 2 Kgs. 5:14; [Heb. 9:12]
26[t] See ch. 22:27 [u] Ps. 17:15 [v] [2 Sam. 12:13; Prov. 28:13; Luke 15:21-24; 1 John 1:9] **27**[w] Ps. 106:6; [Rom. 6:21] **28**[x] Isa. 38:17 [y] ver. 22, 24 [z] [ch. 3:9] **29**[a] ver. 14 **30**[b] Ps. 56:13 **32**[c] ver. 5 [d] ch. 34:33
33[e] Ps. 34:11

Elihu Asserts God's Justice

34 Then Elihu answered and said:

2 "Hear my words, you wise men,
and give ear to me, you who know;
3 for [g]the ear tests words
as the palate tastes food.
4 Let us choose [h]what is right;
let us know among ourselves what is good.
5 For Job has said, 'I am [i]in the right,
and [j]God has taken away my right;
6 in spite of my right I am counted a liar;
my wound is incurable, though I am [k]without transgression.'
7 What man is like Job,
who [l]drinks up scoffing like water,
8 who travels in company with evildoers
and walks [m]with wicked men?
9 For [n]he has said, 'It profits a man nothing
that he should take delight in God.'

10 "Therefore, hear me, you men of understanding:
far be it from God that he should [o]do wickedness,
and from the Almighty that he should do wrong.
11 For according to [p]the work of a man he will repay him,
and [q]according to his ways he will make it befall him.
12 Of a truth, God will not do wickedly,
and [r]the Almighty will not pervert justice.
13 Who gave him charge over the earth,
and who [s]laid on him[1] the whole world?
14 If he should [t]set his heart to it
and [u]gather to himself his [v]spirit and his breath,
15 all flesh would perish together,
and man would [w]return to dust.

16 "If you have understanding, hear this;
listen to what I say.
17 [x]Shall one who hates justice govern?
Will you condemn him who is righteous and mighty,
18 who [y]says to a king, 'Worthless one,'
and to nobles, 'Wicked man,'
19 who [z]shows no partiality to princes,
nor regards the rich [a]more than the poor,
for [b]they are all the work of his hands?
20 In a moment [c]they die;
at [d]midnight the people are shaken and pass away,
and the mighty are taken away by [e]no human hand.

21 "For his eyes are on [f]the ways of a man,
and he sees all his [f]steps.
22 There is no [g]gloom or [h]deep darkness
where evildoers may hide themselves.
23 For God[2] has no need to consider a man further,
that he should go before God in [i]judgment.
24 He [j]shatters the mighty without investigation
and sets [l]others in their place.
25 Thus, knowing their works,
he [m]overturns them in the night, and they are crushed.
26 He strikes them for their wickedness
in a place for all to see,
27 because they turned aside from [n]following him
and had no regard for any of his ways,
28 so that they [o]caused the cry of the poor to come to him,
and he [p]heard the cry of the afflicted—
29 When he is quiet, who can condemn?
When he hides his face, who can behold him,
whether it be a nation or a man?—
30 that a godless man should not reign,
that he should not ensnare the people.

31 "For has anyone said to God,
'I have borne punishment; I will not offend any more;
32 [r]teach me what I do not see;
if I have done iniquity, I will do it no more'?
33 Will he then make repayment to suit you,
because you reject it?

[1] Hebrew lacks *on him* [2] Hebrew *he*

Chapter 34 **3**[g] ch. 12:11 **4**[h] 1 Thess. 5:21, 22 **5**[i] See ch. 33:9 [j] ch. 27:2 **6**[k] ch. 33:9 **7**[l] See ch. 15:16 **8**[m] [Ps. 1:1] **9**[n] ch. 9:22, 23, 30, 31; 21:7, 15; 24:1; [ch. 35:3; Mal. 3:14] **10**[o] ch. 36:23; Gen. 18:25; Deut. 32:4; 2 Chr. 19:7; Ps. 92:15; Rom. 9:14 **11**[p] Ps. 62:12; Prov. 24:12; Matt. 16:27; Rom. 2:6; 2 Cor. 5:10; 1 Pet. 1:17; Rev. 22:12 [q] Jer. 17:10; 32:19; Ezek. 33:20 **12**[r] See ch. 8:3 **13**[s] See ch. 38:4-7 **14**[t] [ch. 2:3] [u] Ps. 104:29; [Ps. 146:4] [v] ch. 32:8 **15**[w] See ch. 10:9 **17**[x] [Gen. 18:25] **18**[y] Ex. 22:28 **19**[z] Deut. 10:17; 2 Chr. 19:7; Acts 10:34; Rom. 2:11; Gal. 2:6; Eph. 6:9; Col. 3:25; 1 Pet. 1:17 [a] [James 2:5] [b] See ch. 31:15 **20**[c] ch. 21:13 [d] Ex. 11:4; [ch. 27:20; 36:20] [e] Dan. 8:25; [Lam. 4:6] **21**[f] ch. 14:16; See ch. 31:4 **22**[g] [Ps. 139:12; Amos 9:2, 3; Heb. 4:13] [h] See ch. 3:5 **23**[i] ch. 14:3 **24**[j] Ps. 2:9 [l] See ch. 8:19 **25**[m] Prov. 12:7 **27**[n] 1 Sam. 15:11; Ps. 28:5; Isa. 5:12 **28**[o] ch. 35:9; James 5:4; [Gen. 18:20, 21] [p] Ex. 3:7; 22:23; Isa. 32:17 **32**[r] ch. 35:11; 36:22; Ps. 19:12; 86:11

For you must choose, and not I;
therefore [s]declare what you know.[1]
34 Men of understanding will say to me,
and the wise man who hears me will say:
35 'Job [t]speaks without knowledge;
his words are without insight.'
36 Would that Job were tried to the end,
because he answers like wicked men.
37 For he adds rebellion to his sin;
he [u]claps his hands among us
and multiplies his words against God."

Elihu Condemns Job

35 And Elihu answered and said:

2 "Do you think this to be just?
Do you say, [v]'It is my right before God,'
3 that you ask, [w]'What advantage have I?
How am I better off than if I had sinned?'
4 I will answer you
and [x]your friends with you.
5 [y]Look at the heavens, and see;
and behold the clouds, which are higher than you.
6 If you have sinned, [z]what do you accomplish against him?
And if your transgressions are multiplied, what do you do to him?
7 [a]If you are righteous, what do you give to him?
Or what does he receive from your hand?
8 Your wickedness concerns a man like yourself,
and your righteousness [b]a son of man.

9 "Because of the multitude of [c]oppressions people [d]cry out;
they call for help because of the arm of [e]the mighty.[2]
10 But none says, 'Where is God my [f]Maker,
who gives [g]songs in the night,
11 who teaches us [h]more than the beasts of the earth
and makes us wiser than the birds of the heavens?'
12 There they [i]cry out, but he does not answer,
because of the pride of evil men.
13 Surely God does not hear an empty cry,
nor does the Almighty regard it.
14 How much less when you say that you [j]do not see him,
that the case is before him, and you are [k]waiting for him!
15 And now, because [l]his anger does not punish,
and he does not take much note of transgression,[3]

[1] The meaning of the Hebrew in verses 29–33 is uncertain [2] Or *the many* [3] Theodotion, Symmachus (compare Vulgate); the meaning of the Hebrew word is uncertain

33[s] ch. 33:32
35[t] See ch. 35:16
37[u] See ch. 27:23
Chapter 35
2[v] See ch. 32:2
3[w] See ch. 34:9
4[x] ch. 34:8, 36
5[y] [ch. 22:12]
6[z] Prov. 8:36; Jer. 7:19
7[a] ch. 22:2, 3; Prov. 9:12; Luke 17:10; [ch. 41:11; Rom. 11:35]
8[b] ch. 25:6
9[c] Amos 3:9 [d] Ex. 2:23; [ch. 34:28] [e] [ch. 22:8]
10[f] ch. 4:17; Deut. 32:6 [g] Ps. 42:8; 77:6; 149:5; [Acts 16:25]
11[h] ch. 36:22; Ps. 94:12; Isa. 28:26
12[i] See ch. 27:9
14[j] ch. 9:11; 23:8, 9 [k] [ch. 13:15]
15[l] Num. 16:29; Ps. 89:32

35:15 Elihu "blows the whistle" on Job's main character flaw. Job is *angry*! We can understand Job's anger at his life, at his life's "result"; and even share it. But anger accomplishes nothing that lastingly satisfies.

Moreover, Job misunderstands the nature of God's anger. Elihu says, "[God's] anger does not punish, and he does not take much note of transgression." Here is a theme that was stated at the start. In 1:12 and 2:6, the Lord gave Satan permission to dismantle Job's things, his works, and his body; but *not* his life, *not* his person or self. The Lord permitted all the foregoing "theater" of deconstruction in the life of his servant in order to save Job's true self and true interest. According to Elihu, God "does not take much note of transgression" nor is it the intention of God's anger to "punish." The intention of God's anger is to save lost people.

Behind the whole drama of Job's humiliation is God's motive: to save a man. This is the gospel: "While we were still sinners," (but we have to know we are sinners, and Job is not yet there) "Christ died for us" (Rom. 5:8).

36:1–17 Elihu's qualifications as an interventionist are never questioned in the book of Job. Elihu's assertion, speaking of himself, that "one who is perfect in knowledge is with you" (v. 4) is never refuted. It is refuted neither by Job's three friends nor by Job himself. We are meant to believe what Elihu says.

Elihu makes a timeless point when he observes that God "delivers the afflicted by their affliction and opens their ear by adversity" (v. 15). It is *through* Job's suffering that Job will be delivered, and through no other vehicle. Through the suffering of persons, "[God] opens their ears to instruction" (v. 10).

16 Job opens his mouth in empty talk;
he [m]multiplies words [n]without knowledge."

Elihu Extols God's Greatness

36 And Elihu continued, and said:

2 "Bear with me a little, and I will show you,
for I have yet something to say on God's behalf.
3 I will get my knowledge from [o]afar
and ascribe [p]righteousness to my [q]Maker.
4 For truly my words are not false;
one who is [r]perfect in knowledge is with you.

5 "Behold, God is mighty, and [s]does not despise any;
he is [t]mighty in strength of understanding.
6 He does not keep the wicked alive,
but gives [u]the afflicted their right.
7 He does not withdraw his [v]eyes from the righteous,
but with [w]kings on the throne
he sets them forever, and they are [x]exalted.
8 And if they are [y]bound in chains
and caught in the cords of affliction,
9 then he declares to them their work
and their transgressions, that they are [z]behaving arrogantly.
10 He [a]opens their ears to instruction
and commands that they [b]return from iniquity.
11 [c]If they listen and serve him,
they [d]complete their days in prosperity,
and their years in pleasantness.
12 But if they do not listen, they [e]perish by the sword
and die [f]without knowledge.

13 "The [g]godless in heart cherish anger;
they do not cry for help when he [h]binds them.
14 They [i]die in youth,
and their life ends among the cult prostitutes.
15 He delivers [j]the afflicted by their affliction
and [k]opens their ear by adversity.
16 He also allured you out of distress
into [l]a broad place where there was no cramping,
and what was set on your [m]table was full of [n]fatness.

17 "But you are full of the judgment on the wicked;
judgment and justice seize you.
18 Beware lest wrath entice you into scoffing,
and let not the greatness of [o]the ransom turn you aside.
19 Will your [p]cry for help avail to keep you from distress,
or all the force of your strength?
20 Do not long for [q]the night,
when peoples vanish [r]in their place.
21 Take care; [s]do not turn to iniquity,
for this you have chosen rather than affliction.

In 1518 Martin Luther wrote in the Heidelberg Disputation, "He deserves to be called a theologian, who comprehends the visible and manifest things of God seen through suffering and the cross." According to Elihu, God is working in Job's life by *waking Job up*, through his defeats, to the twin facts of his arrogance (v. 9) and his lack of knowledge (v. 12).

Elihu also makes mention of Job's judgmental spirit (v. 17). Of what effect is all your anger at other people? Elihu asks Job. You seem to be judging everyone but yourself.

We tend to understand things by means of appearances. And then we make massive judgments concerning what we think we see. "The natural person does not accept the things of the Spirit of God, for they are folly to him, and he is not able to understand them because they are spiritually discerned" (1 Cor. 2:14). It seems we need to be "broken"—often by means of a two-by-four—of the "natural" pattern that avoids the defeats and runs toward the apparent victories of our lives.

In the kingdom of God, what seems a bad circumstance is ultimately good. The supreme instance of this is the death of Christ on *Good* Friday, through which an apparent catastrophe became the means by which the sin of the world was taken away (John 1:29).

16[m] ch. 34:37 [n] ch. 34:35; 36:12; 38:2; 42:3

Chapter 36

3[o] [Ps. 78:2] [p] [Rev. 15:3, 4; 16:5, 7; 19:1, 2] [q] ch. 35:10
4[r] ch. 37:16
5[s] ch. 8:20 (Heb.); [Ps. 138:6] [t] ch. 9:4; 12:13, 16
6[u] ver. 15; ch. 34:28
7[v] [Ps. 33:18; 34:15] [w] Ps. 132:12; [Ps. 113:8] [x] Ps. 75:10
8[y] ver. 13; Ps. 107:10
9[z] ch. 15:25
10[a] ch. 33:16 [b] Jer. 18:11
11[c] For ver. 11, 12, see Isa. 1:19, 20 [d] ch. 21:13
12[e] ch. 33:18 [f] [ch. 4:21]; See ch. 35:16
13[g] ch. 15:34 [h] ver. 8
14[i] ch. 15:32; 22:16; Ps. 55:23
15[j] ver. 6; See ch. 33:15-28 [k] ver. 10; [Ps. 119:67, 71]
16[l] [ch. 37:10; Ps. 4:1; 18:19; 31:8; 118:5] [m] Ps. 23:5 [n] Ps. 36:8
18[o] ch. 33:24

19[p] Prov. 11:4 **20**[q] ch. 27:20; 34:20, 25 [r] ch. 40:12 **21**[s] Ps. 66:18

22 Behold, God is exalted in his power;
who is [t]a teacher like him?
23 Who has [u]prescribed for him his way,
or who can say, [v]'You have done wrong'?

24 "Remember to [w]extol his work,
of which men have [x]sung.
25 All mankind has looked on it;
man beholds it from afar.
26 Behold, God is great, and we [y]know him not;
the number of his [z]years is unsearchable.
27 For he draws up the drops of water;
they distill his [a]mist in [b]rain,
28 which [c]the skies pour down
and drop on mankind abundantly.
29 Can anyone understand [d]the spreading of the clouds,
the thunderings of his [e]pavilion?
30 Behold, he scatters his lightning about him
and covers the roots of the sea.
31 For by these he [f]judges peoples;
he gives [g]food in abundance.
32 He covers his [h]hands with the lightning
and commands it to strike the mark.
33 Its crashing declares his presence;[1]
the cattle also declare that he rises.

Elihu Proclaims God's Majesty

37 "At this also my heart trembles
and leaps out of its place.
2 Keep listening to the thunder of his voice
and the rumbling that comes from his mouth.
3 Under the whole heaven he lets it go,
and his [i]lightning to the [j]corners of the earth.
4 After it [k]his voice roars;
[l]he thunders with his majestic voice,
and he does not restrain the lightnings[2] when his voice is heard.
5 God thunders wondrously with his voice;
he does [m]great things that we cannot [n]comprehend.
6 For to [o]the snow he says, 'Fall on the earth,'
likewise to the downpour, his mighty downpour.
7 He [p]seals up the hand of every man,
that all men whom he made may [q]know it.
8 Then the beasts go into their [r]lairs,
and remain in their [s]dens.
9 From [t]its chamber [u]comes the whirlwind,
and [v]cold from the scattering winds.
10 By the breath of God [w]ice is given,
and [x]the broad waters are frozen fast.
11 He loads the thick cloud with moisture;
the clouds scatter his lightning.
12 They [y]turn around and around by his [z]guidance,
[z]to accomplish all that he commands them
on the face of [a]the habitable world.
13 Whether for [b]correction or for his [c]land
or for [d]love, he causes it to happen.

14 "Hear this, O Job;
stop and [e]consider the wondrous works of God.
15 Do you know how God lays his command upon them
and causes the lightning of his cloud to shine?
16 Do you know the balancings[3] of the clouds,
the wondrous works of him who is [f]perfect in knowledge,
17 you whose garments are hot
when the earth is still because of the south wind?
18 Can you, like him, [g]spread out the skies,
hard as a cast metal [h]mirror?
19 Teach us what we shall say to him;
we cannot draw up our case because of [i]darkness.
20 Shall it be told him that I would speak?
Did a man ever wish that he would be swallowed up?

21 "And now no one looks on the light
when it is bright in the skies,
when the wind has passed and cleared them.
22 Out of the north comes golden splendor;
God is clothed with [j]awesome majesty.

[1] Hebrew *declares concerning him* [2] Hebrew *them* [3] Or *hoverings*

22[t] ch. 34:32; 35:11 **23**[u] ch. 34:13; [Isa. 40:13, 14; Rom. 11:34; 1 Cor. 2:16] [v] [ch. 34:10] **24**[w] Luke 1:46; [Ps. 92:5; Rev. 15:3] [x] [ch. 33:27; Ps. 104:33] **26**[y] [ch. 37:5; 1 Cor. 13:12] [z] Ps. 90:2; 102:27 **27**[a] Gen. 2:6 (Heb.) [b] Ps. 147:8 **28**[c] Prov. 3:20; [Deut. 33:28] **29**[d] [ch. 26:9] [e] Ps. 18:11; 105:39 **31**[f] ch. 37:13 [g] Ps. 104:27, 28; 136:25; 145:15; 147:9; Acts 14:17 **32**[h] Hab. 3:4 **Chapter 37** **3**[i] ch. 36:30, 32 [j] ch. 38:13; [Isa. 11:12; Ezek. 7:2] **4**[k] ch. 40:9; Ps. 68:33; See Ps. 29:3-9 [l] Ps. 18:13 **5**[m] See ch. 5:9 [n] ch. 36:26 **6**[o] Ps. 147:16, 17 **7**[p] Dan. 12:9; [ch. 14:17] [q] Ps. 109:27 **8**[r] ch. 38:40 [s] Ps. 104:22 **9**[t] ch. 9:9 [u] Isa. 21:1; [ch. 1:19] [v] Ps. 147:17 **10**[w] ch. 38:29, 30; Ps. 147:17 [x] [ch. 36:16] **12**[y] Gen. 3:24 [z] Ps. 148:8 [a] [Prov. 8:31] **13**[b] Ex. 9:18, 23; 1 Sam. 12:18, 19; Ezra 10:9; [ch. 36:31; 38:22, 23] [c] ch. 38:26, 27 [d] 1 Kgs. 18:45 **14**[e] [Ps. 111:2] **16**[f] ch. 36:4; [1 Sam. 2:3] **18**[g] Isa. 42:5; 44:24; [Gen. 1:6] [h] [Ex. 38:8] **19**[i] Isa. 60:2; [Eph. 4:18] **22**[j] [Ps. 104:1]

23 The Almighty—we [k]cannot find him;
he is [l]great in power;
[m]justice and abundant righteousness
he will not [n]violate.
24 Therefore men [o]fear him;
he does not regard any who are [p]wise
in their own conceit."[1]

The Lord Answers Job

38 Then the Lord [q]answered Job out of
the whirlwind and said:

2 "Who is this that [r]darkens counsel by
words [s]without knowledge?
3 [t]Dress for action[2] like a man;
I will question you, and you make it
known to me.

4 "Where were you when I [u]laid the foundation of the earth?
Tell me, if you have understanding.
5 Who determined its measurements—
surely you know!
Or who stretched the line upon it?
6 On what were its bases sunk,
or who laid its cornerstone,
7 when the morning stars [v]sang together
and all [w]the sons of God [x]shouted for
joy?

8 "Or who [y]shut in the sea with doors
when it burst out from the womb,
9 when I made clouds its garment
and [z]thick darkness its swaddling
band,
10 and prescribed [a]limits for it
and set bars and doors,
11 and said, 'Thus far shall you come, and
no farther,
and here shall your [b]proud waves be
stayed'?

12 "Have you [c]commanded the morning
since your days began,
and caused the dawn to know its
place,
13 that it might take hold of [d]the skirts of
the earth,
and the wicked be [e]shaken out of it?
14 It is changed like clay under the seal,
and its features stand out like a garment.
15 From the wicked their [f]light is withheld,
and [g]their uplifted arm is broken.

16 "Have you [h]entered into the springs of
the sea,
or walked in the recesses of the deep?
17 Have [i]the gates of death been revealed to
you,
or have you seen the gates of [j]deep
darkness?
18 Have you comprehended the expanse of
the earth?
Declare, if you know all this.

19 "Where is the way to the dwelling of
light,
and where is the place of darkness,
20 that you may take it to its territory
and that you may discern [k]the paths
to its home?
21 You know, for [l]you were born then,
and the number of your days is great!

22 "Have you entered [m]the storehouses of
the snow,
or have you seen [m]the storehouses of
the hail,
23 which I have reserved [n]for the time of
trouble,
[n]for the day of battle and war?
24 What is the way to the place where the
light is distributed,
or where the east wind is scattered
upon the earth?

25 "Who has cleft a channel for the torrents
of rain
and [o]a way for the thunderbolt,
26 to bring rain on [p]a land where no man is,
on [q]the desert in which there is no man,
27 to satisfy the waste and desolate land,
and to make the ground sprout with
[r]grass?

28 "Has [s]the rain a father,
or who has begotten the drops of dew?
29 From whose womb did [t]the ice come
forth,
and who has given birth to [t]the frost
of heaven?
30 The waters become hard like stone,
and the face of the deep is [u]frozen.

[1] Hebrew *in heart* [2] Hebrew *Gird up your loins*

23[k] 1 Tim. 6:16 [l] ch. 36:5 [m] Ps. 99:4 [n] Lam. 3:33 **24**[o] Ps. 130:4; [Matt. 10:28] [p] [Isa. 5:21; Matt. 11:25; 1 Cor. 1:26] **Chapter 38** **1**[q] ch. 40:6; [ch. 13:22] **2**[r] ch. 42:3 [s] See ch. 35:16 **3**[t] 1 Kgs. 18:46 **4**[u] Ps. 104:5; [Prov. 30:4; Isa. 40:12-14]; See Prov. 8:24-29 **7**[v] [Ps. 19:1-4] [w] See ch. 1:6 [x] [Luke 2:13, 14] **8**[y] Gen. 1:9; Ps. 33:7; 104:8, 9; Jer. 5:22 **9**[z] ch. 22:13 **10**[a] [ver. 33 (Heb.)] **11**[b] [Ps. 65:7; 89:9; 93:4] **12**[c] Ps. 65:8; 74:16 **13**[d] ch. 37:3 [e] [Neh. 5:13] **15**[f] ch. 18:5; [Matt. 6:23]; See ch. 24:13-17 [g] Ps. 10:15; 37:17; Ezek. 30:21, 22 **16**[h] Ps. 77:19 **17**[i] Ps. 9:13; 107:18; [Isa. 38:10; Matt. 16:18] [j] See ch. 3:5 **20**[k] ch. 24:13 **21**[l] [ch. 15:7] **22**[m] [Ps. 135:7] **23**[n] Josh. 10:11; Isa. 28:17; 30:30; Ezek. 13:11, 13; 38:22; Rev. 16:21; [ch. 37:13] **25**[o] ch. 28:26 **26**[p] [ch. 37:13] [q] Ps. 107:35 **27**[r] Gen. 1:11; 2 Sam. 23:4 **28**[s] Ps. 147:8; Jer. 14:22 **29**[t] Ps. 147:16, 17 **30**[u] [ch. 37:10]

31 “Can you bind the chains of [v]the Pleiades
or loose the cords of [v]Orion?
32 Can you lead forth the Mazzaroth[1] in their season,
or can you guide [v]the Bear with its children?
33 Do you know [w]the ordinances of the heavens?
Can you establish their rule on the earth?

34 “Can you lift up your voice to the clouds,
that [x]a flood of waters may cover you?
35 Can you send forth lightnings, that they may go
and say to you, ‘Here we are’?
36 Who has [y]put wisdom in [z]the inward parts[2]
or given understanding to the mind?[3]
37 Who can number the clouds by wisdom?
Or who can tilt the waterskins of the heavens,
38 when the dust runs into a mass
and [a]the clods stick fast together?

39 “Can you hunt the prey for the lion,
or [b]satisfy the appetite of the young lions,
40 when they crouch in their [c]dens
or lie in wait [d]in their thicket?
41 Who provides for [e]the raven its prey,
when its young ones cry to God for help,
and wander about for lack of food?

39

“Do you know when [f]the mountain goats give birth?
Do you observe [g]the calving of the does?
2 Can you number the months that they fulfill,
and do you know the time when they give birth,
3 when they [h]crouch, bring forth their offspring,
and are delivered of their young?
4 Their young ones become strong; they grow up in the open;
they go out and [i]do not return to them.

5 “Who has let the wild donkey go free?
Who has [j]loosed the bonds of the swift donkey,
6 to whom I have given [k]the arid plain for his home
and [l]the salt land for his dwelling place?
7 He scorns the tumult of the city;
he hears not the shouts of the driver.
8 He ranges the mountains as his pasture,
and he searches after every green thing.

9 “Is [m]the wild ox willing to serve you?
Will he spend the night at your [n]manger?
10 Can you bind [m]him in the furrow with ropes,
or will he harrow the valleys after you?
11 Will you depend on him because his strength is great,
and will you leave to him your labor?
12 Do you have faith in him that he will return your grain
and gather it to your threshing floor?

13 “The wings of the ostrich wave proudly,
but are they the pinions and plumage of love?[4]
14 For she leaves her eggs to the earth
and lets them be warmed on the ground,
15 forgetting that a foot may crush them
and that the wild beast may trample them.
16 She [o]deals cruelly with her young, as if they were not hers;
though her [p]labor be in vain, yet she has no fear,
17 because God has made her forget wisdom
and [q]given her no share in understanding.
18 When she rouses herself to flee,[5]
she laughs at the horse and his rider.

19 “Do you give the horse his might?
Do you clothe his neck with a mane?
20 Do you make him leap like the locust?
His majestic [r]snorting is terrifying.
21 He paws[6] in the valley and exults in his strength;
he [s]goes out to meet the weapons.
22 He laughs at fear and is not dismayed;
he does not turn back from the sword.
23 Upon him rattle the quiver,
the flashing spear, and the javelin.

[1] Probably the name of a constellation [2] Or *in the ibis* [3] Or *rooster* [4] The meaning of the Hebrew is uncertain [5] The meaning of the Hebrew is uncertain [6] Hebrew *They paw*

31[v] ch. 9:9; Amos 5:8 **32**[v] [See ver. 31 above] **33**[w] Jer. 31:35 **34**[x] ch. 22:11 **36**[y] See ch. 32:8 [z] Ps. 51:6 **38**[a] ch. 21:33 **39**[b] [Ps. 104:21] **40**[c] ch. 37:8 [d] Ps. 17:12 **41**[e] Ps. 147:9; Luke 12:24; [Matt. 6:26] **Chapter 39** **1**[f] 1 Sam. 24:2; Ps. 104:18 [g] Ps. 29:9 **3**[h] 1 Sam. 4:19 **4**[i] [Gen. 8:12] **5**[j] [ch. 12:18; Ps. 116:16] **6**[k] ch. 24:5; Jer. 2:24 [l] Ps. 107:34; Jer. 17:6; [Deut. 29:23] **9**[m] Num. 23:22 [n] Prov. 14:4; Isa. 1:3 **10**[m] [See ver. 9 above] **16**[o] [Lam. 4:3] [p] Isa. 49:4; 65:23 **17**[q] [ch. 35:11] **20**[r] Jer. 8:16 **21**[s] [Jer. 8:6]

24 With fierceness and rage he swallows the ground;
he cannot stand still at [t]the sound of the trumpet.
25 When the trumpet sounds, he says 'Aha!'
He smells the battle from afar,
the thunder of the captains, and the shouting.

26 "Is it by your understanding that the hawk soars
and spreads his wings toward the south?
27 Is it at your command that the eagle mounts up
and makes his [u]nest on high?
28 On the rock he dwells and makes his home,
on [v]the rocky crag and stronghold.
29 From there he spies out the prey;
his eyes behold it from far away.
30 His young ones suck up blood,
and [w]where the slain are, there is he."

40 And the LORD [x]said to Job:

2 "Shall a faultfinder [y]contend with the Almighty?
He who argues with God, let him answer it."

Job Promises Silence

3 Then Job answered the LORD and said:

4 "Behold, I am [z]of small account; what shall I answer you?
[a]I lay my hand on my mouth.
5 I have spoken [b]once, and I will not answer;
[b]twice, but I will proceed no further."

The LORD Challenges Job

6 Then the LORD [c]answered Job out of the whirlwind and said:

7 [d]"Dress for action[1] like a man;
[e]I will question you, and you make it known to me.
8 Will you even put me in the wrong?
Will you condemn me that [f]you may be in the right?
9 Have you [g]an arm like God,
and can you thunder with [h]a voice like his?

10 "Adorn yourself with majesty and dignity;
[i]clothe yourself with glory and splendor.
11 Pour out the overflowings of your anger,
and look on everyone who is [j]proud and abase him.
12 Look on everyone who is proud and bring him low
and [k]tread down the wicked [l]where they stand.
13 [m]Hide them all in [n]the dust together;
bind their faces in the world below.[2]
14 Then will I also acknowledge to you
that your own [o]right hand can save you.

15 "Behold, Behemoth,[3]
which I made as I made you;
he eats [p]grass like an ox.
16 Behold, his strength in his loins,
and his power in the muscles of his belly.
17 He makes his tail stiff like a cedar;
the sinews of his thighs are knit together.
18 His bones are tubes of bronze,
his limbs like bars of iron.

[1] Hebrew *Gird up your loins* [2] Hebrew *in the hidden place* [3] A large animal, exact identity unknown

40:1–24 After Elihu's words have "softened up" Job, the Lord addresses Job for the first time, directly and in person (chs. 38–41). Right away Job responds and whispers, "I will not answer . . . I will proceed no further" (40:5). The Lord then spotlights Job's wrong, with light of the highest possible power. God asks Job simply whether he would compare himself with the Author of Life (vv. 8–14). As an example of his incomparable and measureless power, the Lord reminds Job of Behemoth: "Behold, Behemoth" (v. 15), a primeval monster, "the first of the works of God" (v. 19).

The way that God engages with and humbles Job reminds us that we really have nothing to say before such a great Creator: nothing of an availing defense, nothing of an extenuating self-justification, nothing of self-preservation, just nothing. When we have nothing to say, we should say nothing, recognizing that in human silence the divine voice will speak to and for us. God so speaks to and for Job by these descriptions of divine greatness, in order that finally, like Ebenezer Scrooge wakened from his self-preoccupation and self-dependence at the end of *A Christmas Carol*, Job would begin to bow down and wise up (42:1–6; Ps. 111:10; Prov. 9:10).

24[t] Jer. 4:19; Amos 3:6
27[u] [Num. 24:21; Jer. 49:16; Obad. 4; Hab. 2:9]
28[v] 1 Sam. 14:5
30[w] Matt. 24:28; Luke 17:37
Chapter 40
1[x] ch. 38:1
2[y] See ch. 33:13
4[z] [ch. 42:6; Ezra 9:6] [a] ch. 21:5; 29:9; Judg. 18:19
5[b] ch. 33:14; Ps. 62:11
6[c] ch. 38:1
7[d] ch. 38:3 [e] ch. 38:3; 42:4
8[f] See ch. 32:2
9[g] Ps. 89:13; Isa. 63:12 [h] See ch. 37:4
10[i] [Ps. 93:1; 104:1]
11[j] [Dan. 4:37]; See Isa. 2:11-17
12[k] Isa. 63:3 [l] [ch. 36:20]
13[m] Isa. 2:10 [n] ch. 21:26
14[o] Ps. 98:1; Isa. 59:16; 63:5
15[p] Num. 22:4

19 "He is [q]the first of [r]the works[1] of God;
let him who made him bring near his sword!
20 For the mountains yield food for him
where all the wild beasts play.
21 Under the lotus plants he lies,
in the shelter of [s]the reeds and in the marsh.
22 For his shade the lotus trees cover him;
the willows of the brook surround him.
23 Behold, if the river is turbulent he is not frightened;
he is confident though Jordan rushes against his mouth.
24 Can one take him by his eyes,[2]
or pierce his nose with a snare?

41 [3] "Can you draw out [u]Leviathan[4] with a fishhook
or press down his tongue with a cord?
2 Can you put [v]a rope in his nose
or pierce his jaw with [v]a hook?
3 Will he make many pleas to you?
Will he speak to you soft words?
4 Will he make a covenant with you
to take him for [w]your servant forever?
5 Will you play with him as with a bird,
or will you put him on a leash for your girls?
6 Will traders bargain over him?
Will they divide him up among the merchants?
7 Can you fill his skin with harpoons
or his head with fishing spears?
8 Lay your hands on him;
remember the battle—you will not do it again!
9[5] Behold, the hope of a man is false;
he is laid low even at the sight of him.
10 No one is so fierce that he dares to stir him up.
Who then is he who can stand before me?
11 [x]Who has first given to me, that I should repay him?
[y]Whatever is under the whole heaven is mine.

12 "I will not keep silence concerning his limbs,
or his mighty strength, or his goodly frame.
13 Who can strip off his outer garment?
Who would come near him with a bridle?
14 Who can open the doors of his face?
Around his teeth is terror.
15 His back is made of[6] rows of shields,
shut up closely as with a seal.
16 One is so near to another
that no air can come between them.
17 They are [z]joined one to another;
they clasp each other and cannot be separated.
18 His sneezings flash forth light,
and his eyes are like [a]the eyelids of the dawn.
19 Out of his mouth go flaming torches;
sparks of fire leap forth.
20 Out of his nostrils comes forth smoke,
as from a boiling pot and burning rushes.
21 His breath [b]kindles coals,
and a flame comes forth from his mouth.

[1] Hebrew *ways* [2] Or *in his sight* [3] Ch 40:25 in Hebrew [4] A large sea animal, exact identity unknown [5] Ch 41:1 in Hebrew [6] Or *His pride is in his*

19[q] [Prov. 8:22] [r] ch. 26:14
21[s] Ps. 68:30
Chapter 41
1[u] ch. 3:8; Ps. 74:14; 104:26; Isa. 27:1
2[v] [2 Kgs. 19:28; Isa. 37:29]
4[w] Ex. 21:6; Deut. 15:17
11[x] Rom. 11:35; [ch. 35:7] [y] See Ps. 24:1
17[z] ver. 23
18[a] ch. 3:9
21[b] 2 Sam. 22:13; [Ps. 18:8]

41:1–34 The Lord's speech to Job concludes on an unusual note. The Lord devotes the entire last chapter of his speech, 34 verses in all, to a description of Leviathan. To modern ears this Leviathan sounds like some kind of "Loch Ness Monster" which God has made. Various commentators seek to identify the animal as a crocodile, a whale, an extinct creature only known to the ancients, or an "allegorical" beast representative of the forces of both nature and evil that God subdues and surpasses. Whatever its identity, this creature's great power is yet governed by God's greater power. Is this odd, that the words of God to his servant Job, whose life and soul he has worked so hard to save, should dwell at the end upon a sea monster?

No, for the Word of God takes us sometimes straight into the mysterious in order to upset our preconceptions and disorder our "order." We might have expected a cascade of life-correctives directed at Job. Nothing like it! Rather, Job receives a strange and awesome message: "Out of his mouth go flaming torches; sparks of fire leap forth. Out of his nostrils comes forth smoke. . . . and a flame comes forth from his mouth" (vv. 19–21). "Behold, the hope of a man is false; he is laid low even at the sight of him" (v. 9).

22 In his neck abides strength,
and terror dances before him.
23 The folds of his flesh [c]stick together,
firmly cast on him and immovable.
24 His heart is hard as a stone,
hard as the lower millstone.
25 When he raises himself up the mighty[1]
are afraid;
at the crashing they are beside themselves.
26 Though the sword reaches him, it does
not avail,
nor the spear, the dart, or the javelin.
27 He counts iron as straw,
and bronze as rotten wood.
28 The arrow cannot make him flee;
for him sling stones are turned to
stubble.
29 Clubs are counted as stubble;
he laughs at the rattle of javelins.
30 His underparts are like sharp [d]potsherds;
he spreads himself like [e]a threshing
sledge on the mire.
31 He makes the deep boil like a pot;
he makes the sea like a pot of ointment.
32 Behind him he leaves a shining wake;
one would think the deep to be white-
haired.
33 [f]On earth there is not his like,
a creature without fear.
34 He sees everything that is high;
he is king over all the [g]sons of pride."

Job's Confession and Repentance

42 Then Job answered the LORD and said:
2 "I know that you can [h]do all things,
and that no purpose of yours can be
thwarted.
3 [i]'Who is this that hides counsel without
knowledge?'
Therefore I have uttered what I did not
understand,
things [j]too wonderful for me, which
I did not know.
4 'Hear, and I will speak;
[k]I will question you, and you make it
known to me.'
5 I had heard of you by the hearing of the
ear,
but now my eye sees you;
6 therefore I despise myself,
and repent[2] in [l]dust and ashes."

The LORD Rebukes Job's Friends

7 After the LORD had spoken these words to
Job, the LORD said to Eliphaz [m]the Temanite:

[1] Or *gods* [2] Or *and am comforted*

The creature whose description is meant to humble Job reminds us that God speaks to us *against* our fixed ideas of almost anything. "None of the rulers of this age understood this, for if they had, they would not have crucified the Lord of glory" (1 Cor. 2:8). The gospel of grace confounds our intuitive expectations of how this world, and especially God himself, functions. He is Lord of all and he rules, beyond our control or expectations, as he alone knows is best.

42:1–6 Job has nothing more to say in response to God's word, though he does make an overwhelming admission: *"I didn't know what I was talking about."* Job "hid" wisdom by his questions and complaints that were "without knowledge" (cf. 38:2; 42:3a). Job "uttered what [he] did not understand" and said things "which [he] did not know" (42:3b). There is only one thing for Job to "do": "[I] repent in dust and ashes" (v. 6).

Job's repentance reflects what happens when the realities of God's power, holiness, and provision pull the rug out from under a person. The way that these aspects of the gospel were revealed to Job also reminds us that they cannot be earned. There is nothing we can do to make ourselves worthy of God's grace. It is a gift, and generally comes to someone when they stop trying to "make it" by themselves. We have to give up, often after having hit bottom through pride, selfishness, or self-dependence. Some people seem to have a "high bottom"—blessed are they!—while other people have a "low bottom." Suffering has to go deep in order to reach people with a low bottom. Job had a low bottom. It took a lot to break through. But that is God's grace. As in the incarnation of God in Jesus, so in Job's life, God went all the way to the bottom needed to bring the repentance required.

42:7–9 The grace of God also extends to Job's three foolish friends. They hear the truth from God about their faulty "comfort": "You have not spoken of me what is right"

23[c] ver. 17
30[d] ch. 2:8 [e] Isa. 28:27; 41:15
33[f] ch. 19:25
34[g] ch. 28:8
Chapter 42
2[h] Gen. 18:14; Matt. 19:26
3[i] ch. 38:2 [j] Ps. 40:5; 131:1; 139:6
4[k] ch. 38:3; 40:7
6[l] [ch. 30:19; Gen. 18:27]; See ch. 2:8
7[m] ch. 2:11; 1 Chr. 1:45

"My anger burns against you and against
your two friends, for you have not spoken
of me what is right, as my servant Job has.
8 Now therefore take [n]seven bulls and seven
rams and go to my servant Job and [o]offer up
a burnt offering for yourselves. And my servant Job shall [p]pray for you, for I will accept
his prayer not to deal with you according to
your folly. For you have not spoken of me
what is right, as my servant Job has." 9 [q]So
Eliphaz the Temanite and Bildad the Shuhite
and Zophar the Naamathite went and did
what the LORD had told them, and the LORD
accepted Job's prayer.

The LORD Restores Job's Fortunes

10 And the LORD [r]restored the fortunes of Job,
when he had prayed for his friends. And the
LORD gave Job [s]twice as much as he had before.
11 Then came to him all his [t]brothers and sisters and all who had [t]known him before, and
ate bread with him in his house. And they
[u]showed him sympathy and comforted him
for all the evil[1] that the LORD had brought
upon him. And each of them gave him [v]a piece
of money[2] and [w]a ring of gold.

12 And the LORD blessed [x]the latter days of
Job more than his beginning. And he had
[y]14,000 sheep, 6,000 camels, 1,000 yoke of
oxen, and 1,000 female donkeys. 13 He had
also [z]seven sons and three daughters. 14 And he
called the name of the first daughter Jemimah,
and the name of the second Keziah, and the
name of the third Keren-happuch. 15 And in
all the land there were no women so beautiful as Job's daughters. And their father gave
them an inheritance [a]among their brothers.
16 And after this Job lived 140 years, and [b]saw
his sons, and his sons' sons, four generations.
17 And Job died, an old man, and [c]full of days.

[1] Or *disaster* [2] Hebrew *a qesitah*; a unit of money of unknown value

8 [n] Num. 23:1; 1 Chr. 15:26 [o] ch. 1:5 [p] Gen. 20:7; 1 Sam. 12:23; James 5:16; 1 John 5:16
9 [q] ch. 2:11
10 [r] See Ps. 14:7 [s] Isa. 40:2; 61:7
11 [t] ch. 19:13 [u] ch. 2:11 [v] Gen. 33:19; Josh. 24:32 [w] Gen. 24:22
12 [x] ch. 8:7 [y] [ver. 10; ch. 1:3]
13 [z] ch. 1:2
15 [a] See Num. 27:1-8
16 [b] Gen. 50:23; [Ps. 128:6; Isa. 53:10]
17 [c] See ch. 5:26

(v. 7). You have spoken "folly" (v. 8). But they are also given a gift: Job's prayer for them, which God accepts (v. 9).

Even if we have spoken from "self," acted from "self," and defended our "self," it doesn't mean God is done with us yet. His grace covers even the pain-exacerbating drivel of Eliphaz, Bildad, and Zophar.

42:10–17 Is the book of Job's "happy ending" tacked on? Is it a sort of reassurance, to make the reader breathe easy again after emerging from the wringer? No. Job's happy ending is a resolution that deserves the word "profound." As ever with God's work in a person's life, Job's character or *inner* self is more important to God than Job's "doings." Thus, the provided-for life that Job ended up with was not provided until he prayed in selfless fashion for his three unworthy friends (v. 10).

We are also told that Job's sufferings were "all the evil that the LORD had brought upon him" (v. 11). *Everything* that happens to us comes from God. "He's got the whole world in his hands." Such truths challenge us no less than they challenged Job, but they are also responsible for leading Job (and us) to a right understanding of the God who provides eternity—even if it is through earthly difficulties. God's purposes are eternal as he weans us from earth and woos us to heaven.

Finally, Elihu's prediction of how Job's life was *supposed* to end, actually came true: "If [people] listen and serve [God], they complete their days in prosperity, and their years in pleasantness" (36:11). "Job died, an old man, and full of days" (42:17), with his losses restored and possessions increased (vv. 12–16). Even his children were doubled, if one considers the existence of those already in eternity with those new on earth. As the expression goes, "It's never too late." We could also say, on the basis of Job, that things are never so bad that God is not present and "able to do far more abundantly than all that we ask or think" (Eph. 3:20). Of course, for many of those who suffer in this world, prosperity and pleasantness await fulfillment in the new heavens and new earth, but this reality is no less real for those of faith. Through Job we learn that God will do whatever is necessary to claim the hearts of those he loves. His eternal love is solace, sufficiency, and satisfaction for all whose ultimate hope is in him.

It's the old, old story, of Mary Magdalene, Zacchaeus the tax collector, Peter the denier, James and John the Sons of (raging) Thunder, Paul the Christian-tracker, and Cornelius the sideliner. And us. "We love because he first loved us" (1 John 4:19).

Introduction to
The Psalms

Author and Date

Individual psalms come from different periods of Israel's history, but at every stage they served as the songbook of God's people. David wrote about half of the Psalms. His role as king was more than that of a ruler. He was to represent and even embody the people, and their well-being was tied to his faithfulness.

The Gospel in the Psalms

The risen Jesus said to his disciples that "everything written about me in the Law of Moses and the Prophets *and the Psalms* [i.e., the Old Testament Poetical Books] must be fulfilled" (Luke 24:44). Jesus considered the book of Psalms to be ultimately about him. To read the Psalms in a non-gospel way, therefore, is to fail to read them the way Jesus himself told us to.

How then do we read the Psalms in a way that honors Jesus' own words? We do so by understanding that this book of the Bible, like all books of the Bible, plays a contributing role in the history of redemption that culminates in Jesus. The Bible is in essence a message of what God has done to redeem and restore sinners, and this is done preeminently in the person and work of Christ. Each book of the Bible carries forward that supreme redemptive purpose, a purpose that comes to a decisive climax in Jesus.

Psalms, however, is unique in some ways. Perhaps more than any other book in the Old Testament, this book clearly anticipates the coming of the Messiah. This is done in various ways. The Psalms predict the coming Savior in a fairly straightforward way, such as in Psalm 2, where the Messiah's rule over the nations is prophesied. Other times Jesus himself takes on his own lips the words of a psalm. In this way he "fulfills" the psalm even though the psalm does not self-consciously look toward the future. Psalm 22:1 ("My God, my God, why have you forsaken me?") is an example of this. Still other times, psalms pick up earlier promises to God's covenant people, especially the Davidic promise of an eternal reign from 2 Samuel 7. Jesus fulfills these psalms (such as in Ps. 45:6) because he is the Davidic Son, the heir of the promises to David that he would never lack a son to sit on the throne.

Stepping back and viewing the Psalms more broadly, we should see that they are not "about" Jesus (to use his own word from Luke 24) merely by a verse here and a verse there anticipating him. Though the Christ-centeredness of the Psalms are surely not *less* than this, a full understanding of the Christ-focus of the Psalms must understand what these 150 poems *are*—namely, the heart-cries of God's covenant people. They cry to him for forgiveness (Psalms 32; 51; 130), out of lament (Psalms 12; 13), with praise (Psalms 8; 93; 145), with thanksgiving (Psalm 9; 106; 138), to exult in God's law (Psalms 19; 119), to express confidence (Psalm 23), and to recount the merciful dealings of God with his people throughout Israel's history (Psalms 78; 107).

In all these ways we see the hearts of God's people laid bare before him in song. Yet as believers on this side of the first coming of Christ, we must understand that Christ fulfilled all such cries to God. *Jesus is God's definitive answer to the cries of his people.* Jesus provides the forgiveness cried out for. Jesus underwent the ultimate lament, crying out as he was forsaken by the Father on the cross, so that we need not lament separation from God. Jesus' substitutionary work gives us supreme reason to praise God and to thank him. Jesus perfectly lived out God's law so that we law-breakers can be exonerated freely and then changed from the inside out so that we can delight in God's law truly. Looking to Jesus, we have full cause for confidence in God; if God did not spare his own Son, what can we ever possibly lack (Rom. 8:32)? And Jesus is himself the fulfillment of all God's ways with his people in our space-and-time history.

Reading the Psalms mindful of Jesus is not a clever way to read this book of the Bible, nor is it one way to do so among others. It is *the* way. A gospel-lens to reading the Psalms is how Jesus himself teaches us to read them. As you read this portion of God's Word, make these prayers to God your own, and consider the ways these Psalms are good news to us—expressing the full range of our emotions, and ultimately bringing our minds to rest on the finished work of Christ on behalf of sinners.

The Psalms

Book One

The Way of the Righteous and the Wicked

1 Blessed is the man[1]
who [a]walks not in [b]the counsel of the wicked,
nor stands in [c]the way of sinners,
nor [d]sits in [e]the seat of [f]scoffers;
2 but his [g]delight is in the law[2] of the Lord,
and on his [h]law he meditates day and night.

3 He is like [i]a tree
planted by [j]streams of water
that yields its fruit in its season,
and its [k]leaf does not wither.
[l]In all that he does, he prospers.
4 The wicked are not so,
but are like [m]chaff that the wind drives away.

5 Therefore the wicked [n]will not stand in the judgment,
nor sinners in [o]the congregation of the righteous;
6 for the Lord [p]knows [q]the way of the righteous,
but the way of the wicked will perish.

The Reign of the Lord's Anointed

2 [r]Why do [s]the nations rage[3]
and the peoples plot in vain?
2 The kings of the earth set themselves,
and the rulers take counsel together,
against the Lord and against his [t]Anointed, saying,
3 "Let us [u]burst their bonds apart
and cast away their cords from us."

4 He who [v]sits in the heavens [w]laughs;
the Lord holds them in derision.

[1] The singular Hebrew word for *man* (*ish*) is used here to portray a representative example of a godly person; see Preface [2] Or *instruction*
[3] Or *nations noisily assemble*

Psalm 1 This psalm could be seen as introducing key concerns of the whole Bible, since it describes the two fundamental classes of mankind—sinners and righteous. It also addresses concepts ultimately revealed in the perfectly blessed man, Jesus Christ, who stands at the crossroads of two ways (v. 1; Matt. 7:13). He is anticipated in the first word of this psalm because "blessing" in Scripture references the redemptive presence of God. That presence was perfectly realized when Mary was called "blessed . . . among women," because Jesus, "God with us," had finally been conceived in her (Luke 1:42).

The "righteous" man is blessed when he consciously lives in the presence of the Word, which we, on this side of the cross, know would become flesh and would cause his "law" to be written on our hearts for our instruction (Ps. 1:2; John 20:31; 1 Cor. 10:11). Thus the believer's life is blessed by the presence and care of Christ, bearing eternally significant fruit by being grafted into the "tree of life" (Ps. 1:3; Rev. 2:7; 22:2).

On the other hand, those who follow the broad way that "leads to destruction" become hollow persons whose lives count for nothing beyond the grave, and who perish at the judgment day (Ps. 1:5; Matt. 25:41–46). But even in the Old Testament context of this psalm, what separates the righteous from the wicked is not ultimately good works but the grace of the Lord, who "knows" the righteous (Ps. 1:6; Matt. 7:23).

Psalm 2 Psalm 2 ushers the worshiper into God's throne room. It reminds us that David's emergence as a king from Judah was a midcourse confirmation between God's promise to Abraham and his descendant bringing the final kingdom to earth (Gen. 49:10; cf. Gen. 12:1–3; Matt. 3:2). The first hint that the psalm refers to David's

Psalm 1
1 [a]Prov. 4:14, 15 [b]Job 21:16 [c]Prov. 1:10 [d]Ps. 26:4; Jer. 15:17 [e][Ps. 107:32] [f]Prov. 1:22; 3:34; 19:29; 21:24; 29:8; [Isa. 28:14]
2 [g]Ps. 112:1; 119:35, 47, 92 [h]Ps. 119:1, 97; Josh. 1:8
3 [i]Jer. 17:8; Ezek. 19:10; [Num. 24:6; Job 29:19] [j]Ps. 46:4 [k]Ezek. 47:12; [Isa. 34:4] [l]Gen. 39:3, 23; [Ps. 128:2; Isa. 3:10]
4 [m]See Job 21:18
5 [n]Ps. 5:5; 76:7; Nah. 1:6; Luke 21:36; Eph. 6:13 [o][Ezek. 13:9]
6 [p]Ps. 31:7; 37:18; 144:3; Nah. 1:7; [John 10:14; 2 Tim. 2:19] [q]Ps. 37:5

Psalm 2
1 [r]Cited Acts 4:25, 26 [s][Ps. 46:6]
2 [t]Ps. 18:50; 20:6; 45:7; 89:20
3 [u]Jer. 5:5
4 [v]Ps. 11:4; 29:10; [Isa. 40:22] [w]Ps. 37:13; 59:8; Job 22:19; Prov. 1:26

5 Then he will speak to them in his [x]wrath,
and terrify them in his fury, saying,
6 "As for me, I have [y]set my King
on [z]Zion, my [a]holy hill."

7 I will tell of the decree:
The LORD said to me, [b]"You are my Son;
today I have begotten you.
8 Ask of me, and I will make the nations
your heritage,
and [c]the ends of the earth your possession.
9 You shall [d]break[1] them with [e]a rod of iron
and dash them in pieces like [f]a potter's vessel."

10 Now therefore, O kings, be wise;
be warned, O rulers of the earth.
11 [g]Serve the LORD with [h]fear,
and [i]rejoice with [h]trembling.
12 [j]Kiss [k]the Son,
lest he be angry, and you perish in the way,
for his [l]wrath is quickly kindled.
[m]Blessed are all who take refuge in him.

Save Me, O My God

3

A PSALM OF DAVID, [n]WHEN HE FLED FROM ABSALOM HIS SON.

1 O LORD, [o]how many are my foes!
Many are [p]rising against me;
2 many are saying of my soul,
[q]there is no salvation for him in God. *Selah*[2]

3 But you, O LORD, are [r]a shield [s]about me,
my glory, and [t]the lifter of my head.
4 I [u]cried aloud to the LORD,
and he [v]answered me from his [w]holy hill. *Selah*

5 I [x]lay down and slept;
I woke again, for the LORD sustained me.
6 I [y]will not be afraid of many thousands of people
who have [z]set themselves against me all around.

7 [a]Arise, O LORD!
Save me, O my God!

[1] Revocalization yields (compare Septuagint) *You shall rule* [2] The meaning of the Hebrew word *Selah*, used frequently in the Psalms, is uncertain. It may be a musical or liturgical direction

5 [x]Rev. 6:16, 17
6 [y]Prov. 8:23 [z]2 Sam. 5:7; Ps. 110:2 [a]Ps. 3:4; 15:1; 43:3; 99:9
7 [b]Rom. 1:4; Cited Acts 13:33; Heb. 1:5; 5:5
8 [c][Ps. 72:8; 89:27; Dan. 7:14]
9 [d]Ps. 89:23; Job 34:24 [e]Rev. 2:27; 12:5; 19:15 [f]Isa. 30:14; Jer. 19:11
11 [g]Heb. 12:28 [h]Phil. 2:12 [i]Phil. 4:4
12 [j]1 Sam. 10:1; 1 Kgs. 19:18; [John 5:23] [k]Prov. 31:2 [l]ver. 5 [m]Ps. 34:8; 84:12; Prov. 16:20; Jer. 17:7; [Ps. 146:5; Isa. 30:18]

Psalm 3
[n]See 2 Sam. 15:14-17
1 [o]2 Sam. 15:12 [p]2 Sam. 18:31, 32
2 [q]Ps. 71:11; [2 Sam. 16:8]
3 [r]Ps. 28:7; 84:9; 119:114; Gen. 15:1 [s]Job 1:10 [t]Ps. 27:5, 6; [Job 10:15]
4 [u]Ps. 77:1; 142:1 [v]Ps. 34:4; 60:5; 108:6; [Ps. 6:8; 34:6] [w]See Ps. 2:6
5 [x]Ps. 4:8; [Lev. 26:6; Job 11:18, 19; Prov. 3:24]
6 [y][Ps. 23:4; 27:3] [z]Isa. 22:7; [1 Kgs. 20:12]
7 [a]Ps. 7:6; 9:19; 10:12; Num. 10:35

Greater Son is in the title "Anointed," which is *Messiah* in Hebrew and *Christ* in Greek (Ps. 2:2; Acts 10:38).

Another clue is the prophecy of worldwide rule that demands a King with infinitely greater powers than David, but which also accords with God's promise to David of an eternal and worldwide kingdom established by his descendant (cf. Ps. 2:8–9; 2 Sam. 7:12–14; Rev. 2:27; 12:5; 19:15). The apostles preached the gospel from this psalm. The author of Hebrews explained that Christ was this "Son" whom God sent into the world—the only Son who could truly fulfill the promises to David (Ps. 2:7; Heb. 1:5).

Peter preached that Christ's cross was the epitome of the nations' rage (Ps. 2:1; Acts 4:25–27). Paul revealed that Christ's coronation occurred after his resurrection (Ps. 2:6; Acts 13:33; Rom. 1:4) and that he blesses the nations as they obey him by faith (Ps. 2:10; Rom. 1:5). John showed that salvation or damnation depends on one's relationship to the Son (Ps. 2:12a; John 3:36). And Ephesians calls Christians to live courageously in the face of worldwide spiritual rebellion because Christ is actively ruling over all of reality (Ps. 2:12b; Eph. 1:20–22). In these various ways the New Testament reveals that ultimately Christ himself is the King who fulfills Psalm 2.

Psalm 3 Whereas in Psalm 2 David offers terms and images whose full meaning becomes represented in the life and ministry of King Jesus, Psalm 3 exemplifies saving faith. David's faith focuses ultimately on his Lord, whose name and actions in this Psalm will be personified in Christ (v. 8; Luke 1:31). David's deliverance comes from that same "holy hill" of sacrifice—that hill on which Christ would ultimately die for his people (Ps. 3:4; John 19:17).

All of the requirements for saving faith are in this prayer: knowledge, agreement, and authentic commitment. First, the believer must acknowledge that salvation belongs exclusively to the Lord (Ps. 3:2, 8; John 14:6). Then he must agree that he needs the "shield" provided by God alone—ultimately, the shield of Christ's faithfulness (Ps. 3:3a; Eph. 6:11–13)—and must welcome the glory promised in him (Ps. 3:3b; 2 Cor. 4:4). And thirdly, if the believer's faith is real, it will be followed by actions consistent with such commitment.

For you [b]strike all my enemies on the
cheek;
you [c]break the teeth of the wicked.

8 [d]Salvation belongs to the LORD;
your blessing be on your people! *Selah*

Answer Me When I Call

4 TO THE [e]CHOIRMASTER: WITH [e]STRINGED INSTRUMENTS. A PSALM OF DAVID.

1 Answer me when I call, O God of my
[f]righteousness!
You have [g]given me relief when I was
in distress.
Be gracious to me and hear my prayer!

2 O men,[1] how long shall my honor be
turned into shame?
How long will you love vain words
and seek after [h]lies? *Selah*
3 But know that the LORD has [i]set apart
[j]the godly for himself;
the LORD hears when I call to him.

4 [k]Be angry,[2] and do not sin;
[l]ponder in your own hearts [m]on your
beds, and be silent. *Selah*
5 Offer [n]right sacrifices,
and put your [o]trust in the LORD.

6 There are many who say, "Who will
show us some good?
[p]Lift up [q]the light of your face upon us,
O LORD!"
7 You have put [r]more joy in my heart
than they have when their grain and
wine abound.

8 In peace I will both [s]lie down and sleep;
for you alone, O LORD, make me
[t]dwell in safety.

Lead Me in Your Righteousness

5 TO THE CHOIRMASTER: FOR THE FLUTES. A PSALM OF DAVID.

1 Give ear to my words, O LORD;
consider my [u]groaning.

[1] Or *O men of rank* [2] Or *Be agitated*

On the one hand, David entrusts his safekeeping to one who neither slumbers nor sleeps (Ps. 3:5; 121:4). On the other hand, he pushes through his fear into the face of danger, refusing to be intimidated by enemies God promises to defeat (Ps. 3:6–7; Rev. 12:8). This promise for the ultimate defeat of King David's foes was achieved by the cross and will be finally complete in the day of judgment. Thus, we have even more cause than David to face our spiritual enemies—with faith in the God who has so provided for us (1 Cor. 15:57–58; Col. 2:14–15).

Psalm 4 This is an "evening psalm," reflecting on the events of the day. God's redemption in the past (v. 1; cf. 3:5) provides hope for the future (4:8). David confesses his sole dependence on God's "righteousness"—his commitment to do what is right and to rescue his covenant people. Because his confidence is in the Redeemer's righteousness rather than his own, David boldly asks God to be "gracious" (v. 1; cf. Heb. 4:14–16).

Confidence in God further explains how David can ask for vindication before his enemies (Ps. 4:2). Rather than fret about his reputation, David asks God to defend his own name because he has "set apart" the "godly" for himself (v. 3). This principle of God establishing his name through his people assures Christians that God will answer their "call" (v. 3). Though we will not always understand the ways or timing of the Lord, he is zealous to advance his own name through us. This knowledge of the Redeemer's priorities for his people frees believers to call upon God with trust, and provides them security to live without anger (vv. 4–5, 8; Eph. 4:26).

The light of God's face brings joy to his children but fear to their enemies (Ps. 4:6–7; Ex. 14:24; Deut. 30:6–7). The shepherd boy turned king finally rests in the promise that the Good Shepherd makes us "dwell in safety" (Ps. 4:8; John 10:11). Faith in a Savior who loves us with such tender care nurtures communion with One who is gracious toward sinners, leading us into quiet peace of mind (Ps. 4:8).

Psalm 5 During morning worship (v. 3), God grants David a right perspective on his enemies. Despite the grave wickedness of those who are hostile toward David (vv. 8–9), David seeks refuge in God. For David knows of God's utter moral integrity: "evil may not dwell with you" (v. 4). This would be not only a comfort to David regarding his enemies, but also an indictment of David himself—but for one thing: David does not enter into fellowship with God through his own uprightness. Rather, "But I, through

7[b] See Job 16:10 [c] Ps. 58:6; Job 29:17
8[d] Ps. 37:39; 62:7; Isa. 43:11; 45:21; Jer. 3:23; Hos. 13:4; Jonah 2:9; Rev. 7:10; 19:1
Psalm 4
[e] Ps. 61, title; Hab. 3:19
1[f] Isa. 54:17; Jer. 23:6 [g] See Job 36:16
2[h] [Ps. 5:6]
3[i] [Ex. 11:7] [j] [Ps. 50:5]
4[k] Cited Eph. 4:26 [l] Ps. 77:6 [m] See Ps. 42:8
5[n] Ps. 51:19; Deut. 33:19 [o] Ps. 37:3; 62:8
6[p] Num. 6:26 [q] Ps. 89:15; [Ps. 31:16; 67:1; 80:3, 7, 19; 119:135]
7[r] [Isa. 9:3; 16:10; Jer. 48:38]
8[s] See Ps. 3:5 [t] Ps. 16:9; Lev. 25:18, 19; 26:5; Deut. 33:28
Psalm 5
1[u] [Ps. 39:3]

2 Give attention to the sound of my cry,
my [v]King and my God,
for [w]to you do I pray.
3 O LORD, in [x]the morning you hear my voice;
in the morning I prepare a sacrifice for you[1] and [y]watch.

4 For you are not a God who delights in wickedness;
evil may not dwell with you.
5 The [z]boastful shall not [a]stand before your eyes;
you [b]hate all evildoers.
6 You destroy those who speak [c]lies;
the LORD abhors [d]the bloodthirsty and deceitful man.

7 But I, through the abundance of your steadfast love,
will enter your house.
I will [e]bow down [f]toward your [g]holy temple
in the fear of you.
8 [h]Lead me, O LORD, in your righteousness
because of my enemies;
[i]make your way straight before me.

9 For there is no truth in their mouth;
their inmost self is [j]destruction;
[k]their throat is [l]an open grave;
they [m]flatter with their tongue.
10 [n]Make them bear their guilt, O God;
let them [o]fall by their own counsels;
because of the abundance of their transgressions cast them out,
for they have rebelled against you.

11 But let all who [p]take refuge in you [q]rejoice;
let them ever sing for joy,
and spread your protection over them,
that those who love your name may [r]exult in you.
12 For you [s]bless the righteous, O LORD;
you [t]cover him with favor as with [u]a shield.

O LORD, Deliver My Life

6 TO THE CHOIRMASTER: WITH STRINGED INSTRUMENTS; ACCORDING TO [v]THE SHEMINITH.[2] A PSALM OF DAVID.

1 O LORD, [w]rebuke me not in your anger,
nor [x]discipline me in your wrath.
2 Be gracious to me, O LORD, for I am languishing;
[y]heal me, O LORD, [z]for my bones are troubled.
3 My [a]soul also is greatly troubled.
But you, O LORD—[b]how long?

4 Turn, O LORD, deliver my life;
save me for the sake of your steadfast love.

[1] Or *I direct my prayer to you* [2] Probably a musical or liturgical term

2[v] Ps. 84:3 [w] Ps. 65:2
3[x] Ps. 88:13; 119:147; 130:6 [y] [Hab. 2:1]
5[z] Ps. 73:3; 75:4; [Hab. 1:13] [a] See Ps. 1:5 [b] Ps. 11:5
6[c] [Ps. 4:2]; Rev. 21:8; 22:15 [d] Ps. 55:23
7[e] Ps. 132:7 [f] 1 Kgs. 8:29, 30 [g] Ps. 11:4; 79:1
8[h] [Ps. 23:3; 25:4, 5] [i] [Ezra 8:21]
9[j] Ps. 52:2 [k] Cited Rom. 3:13 [l] Jer. 5:16 [m] Ps. 12:2; Prov. 2:16; 7:5
10[n] [Isa. 24:6] [o] [2 Sam. 15:31; 17:14, 23]
11[p] Ps. 2:12 [q] Ps. 33:21 [r] [Ps. 9:2; 1 Sam. 2:1]
12[s] Ps. 115:13 [t] [Ps. 103:4] [u] [Ps. 35:2]
Psalm 6
[v] 1 Chr. 15:21
1[w] Ps. 38:1 [x] [Ps. 94:12; 118:18; Prov. 3:11, 12; Jer. 30:11; 46:28]; See Heb. 12:3-11
2[y] Ps. 30:2; 41:4; 103:3 [z] See Ps. 31:10
3[a] [John 12:27] [b] Ps. 90:13

the abundance of your steadfast love, will enter your house" (v. 7). It is through God's grace, not David's merit, that the king communes with God. On the other hand, the wicked who do not penitently seek refuge in the Lord will find justice, not mercy: "Make them bear their guilt, O God" (v. 10).

David sought refuge in God (v. 11) because he was confident that the Lord would "cover him with favor as with a shield" (v. 12). This truth of God's covering those who take refuge in him is ultimately fulfilled in Jesus Christ. Through his death and resurrection, those who trust in Christ are covered with the favor and the very righteousness of God. No one can bring any charge against such a one (Rom. 8:33).

Psalm 6 No other faith has a holy book whose writers talk to God as the psalmists do. Particularly when it comes to suffering, the psalmists make bold complaints. In the case of this psalm, David's affliction is so intense that he does not immediately know whether it comes from God or from his enemies, but he asks God to forestall his anger nonetheless (vv. 1, 3). He does not plead his innocence, but only God's grace (v. 2). He is emboldened to do so because he knows God's essential nature is to be merciful (v. 4; Ex. 34:6–7; Rom. 9:15).

When it resembles the Messiah's suffering and enhances faith, suffering can actually prove that a person belongs to God (cf. 1 Pet. 1:6–12). Despite his deep grief, David's torment drives him closer to the Lord, not farther away (Ps. 6:9). Paul will call such grief "godly" because it produces repentance (i.e., a turning to God) rather than mere regret (2 Cor. 7:10). Since they are united to Christ by faith, the suffering of believers throughout redemptive history is intimately connected with their Savior's suffering (Ps. 22:14; Phil. 3:10). David thus provides the follower of Christ an inspired

5 For in [c]death there is no remembrance
of you;
in Sheol who will give you praise?

6 I am [d]weary with my [e]moaning;
every night I flood my bed with tears;
I drench my couch with my weeping.
7 My [f]eye wastes away because of grief;
it grows weak because of all my foes.

8 [g]Depart from me, all you [h]workers of evil,
for the LORD [i]has heard the sound of
my weeping.
9 The LORD has heard my [j]plea;
the LORD accepts my prayer.
10 All my enemies shall be ashamed and
greatly troubled;
they shall [k]turn back and be put to
shame in a moment.

In You Do I Take Refuge

7 A [l]SHIGGAION[1] OF DAVID, WHICH HE SANG TO THE LORD CONCERNING THE WORDS OF CUSH, A BENJAMINITE.

1 O LORD my God, in you do I [m]take refuge;
[n]save me from all my pursuers and
deliver me,
2 lest like [o]a lion they tear my soul apart,
rending it in pieces, with [p]none to
deliver.

3 O LORD my God, [q]if I have done this,
if there is [r]wrong in my hands,
4 if I have repaid [s]my friend[2] with evil
or [t]plundered my enemy without
cause,
5 let the enemy pursue my soul and overtake it,
and let him [u]trample my life to the
ground
and lay my glory in the dust. *Selah*

6 [v]Arise, O LORD, in your anger;
[w]lift yourself up against the fury of my
enemies;
[x]awake for me; you have appointed a
judgment.
7 Let the assembly of the peoples be gathered about you;
over it return on high.
8 The LORD [y]judges the peoples;
[z]judge me, O LORD, according to my
righteousness
and according to the integrity that is
in me.
9 Oh, let the evil of the wicked come to an
end,
and may you establish the righteous—
you who [a]test [b]the minds and hearts,[3]
O righteous God!
10 My shield is [c]with God,
who saves [d]the upright in heart.
11 God is [e]a righteous judge,
and a God who feels [f]indignation
every day.

[1] Probably a musical or liturgical term [2] Hebrew *the one at peace with me* [3] Hebrew *the hearts and kidneys*

vocabulary to express his or her frustration with God's painful providence. David also leaves a legacy of faith by demonstrating that, when we flee to God alone for mercy, our conscience finds lasting relief from the trouble of our sins (cf. Heb. 10:12–14). We lean ultimately on God's "steadfast love" (Ps. 6:4)—love that is fulfilled in Jesus Christ.

Psalm 7 David's sufferings are not only anticipatory of Christ's sufferings. They are also an example of how all of God's children suffer in union with their Savior (Matt. 10:16–25; 1 Pet. 1:3–12). Like his descendant Lord, David is the victim of betrayal by a fellow Israelite from a friendly tribe (cf. Matt. 26:23; Ps. 41:9). Honest about his own heart, however, David invites God to scrutinize his conscience (7:3–5).

David can make that bold request because he ultimately trusts in the righteousness of his Redeemer, not in his own spotless character. David's is the same confidence as Paul's; they both trusted in their God's righteousness to be their shield (vv. 8–10; Eph. 6:16). By virtue of being in God's forgiven army, David cries out to his warring Lord Deliverer to "arise" and do battle with the enemy of the good news of grace (Ps. 7:6; Num. 10:35; Gal. 1:8–9).

While he anticipates his Lord's mercy, David also knows that God will execute judgment against all who do not repent (Ps. 7:12–16; Rev. 6:16). At the Great Day, only God will be Most High above his enemies. His people will give "thanks due to his righteousness" and sing praise to the name of the Lord (Ps. 7:17)—a promise fulfilled in the ultimate victory of Christ.

5 [c]Ps. 30:9; 88:10-12; 115:17; Isa. 38:18
6 [d]Ps. 69:3 [e]Ps. 38:9
7 [f]Ps. 31:9; 88:9; [Ps. 38:10; Job 17:7; Lam. 2:11; 5:17]
8 [g]Ps. 119:115; 139:19; Matt. 7:23; 25:41; Luke 13:27 [h]Ps. 94:4 [i][Ps. 3:4]
9 [j]Ps. 55:1; 1 Kgs. 8:38
10 [k]Ps. 40:14; 56:9
Psalm 7
[l]Hab. 3:1
1 [m]See Ps. 11:1 [n]Ps. 31:15
2 [o]See Job 10:16 [p]Ps. 50:22
3 [q][2 Sam. 16:7, 8] [r]1 Sam. 24:11; 26:18; [Ps. 59:3]
4 [s]Ps. 55:20 [t]1 Sam. 24:7; 26:9
5 [u]Dan. 8:7; [Ps. 89:39]
6 [v]See Ps. 3:7 [w]Ps. 94:2; Isa. 33:10 [x]Ps. 35:23; 44:23; 59:4; Job 8:6
8 [y]See Ps. 58:11 [z]Ps. 26:1; 35:24; 43:1; [Ps. 18:20]
9 [a]Ps. 11:5; Job 23:10; [Ps. 139:1; 1 Sam. 16:7; 1 Chr. 28:9] [b]Ps. 26:2; Jer. 11:20; 17:10; 20:12; Rev. 2:23
10 [c][Ps. 62:8] [d]2 Chr. 29:34
11 [e][Job 8:3] [f]Nah. 1:2, 6

12 If a man[1] does not repent, God[2] will
[g]whet his sword;
he has [h]bent and [i]readied his bow;
13 he has prepared for him his deadly
weapons,
making his [j]arrows [k]fiery shafts.
14 Behold, the wicked man [l]conceives evil
and is [l]pregnant with mischief
and gives birth to lies.
15 He makes [m]a pit, digging it out,
and falls into the hole that he has
made.
16 His [n]mischief returns upon his own
head,
and on his own skull his violence
descends.

17 I will give to the LORD the thanks due to
his righteousness,
and I will [o]sing praise to the name of
the LORD, the Most High.

How Majestic Is Your Name

8 TO THE CHOIRMASTER: ACCORDING TO THE [p]GITTITH.[3] A PSALM OF DAVID.

1 O LORD, our Lord,
how majestic is your [q]name in all the
earth!
You have set your [r]glory above the heavens.
2 [s]Out of the mouth of babies and
infants,
you have established [t]strength because
of your foes,
to still [u]the enemy and the avenger.
3 When I [v]look at your heavens, the work
of your [w]fingers,
the moon and the stars, [x]which you
have set in place,
4 [y]what is man that you are [z]mindful of
him,
and [a]the son of man that you [b]care for
him?

5 Yet you have made him a little lower
than [c]the heavenly beings[4]
and crowned him with [d]glory and
honor.
6 You have given him [e]dominion over the
works of your hands;
[f]you have put all things under his
feet,
7 all sheep and oxen,
and also the beasts of the field,
8 the birds of the heavens, and the fish of
the sea,
whatever passes along the paths of
the seas.

9 O LORD, our Lord,
how majestic is your name in all the
earth!

I Will Recount Your Wonderful Deeds

9[5] TO THE CHOIRMASTER: ACCORDING TO MUTH-LABBEN.[6] A PSALM OF DAVID.

1 I will give thanks to the LORD with my
whole heart;
I will recount all of your [g]wonderful
deeds.

[1] Hebrew *he* [2] Hebrew *he* [3] Probably a musical or liturgical term [4] Or *than God*; Septuagint *than the angels* [5] Psalms 9 and 10 together follow an acrostic pattern, each stanza beginning with the successive letters of the Hebrew alphabet. In the Septuagint they form one psalm [6] Probably a musical or liturgical term

12[g] Deut. 32:41 [h] Ps. 11:2; 37:14 [i] Ps. 21:12
13[j] See Ps. 18:14 [k] [Eph. 6:16]
14[l] Job 15:35; Isa. 59:4; [Isa. 33:11; James 1:15]
15[m] Ps. 9:15; 57:6; 119:85; Prov. 26:27; 28:10; Eccles. 10:8
16[n] [Ps. 94:23; 141:10; Judg. 9:24; 1 Kgs. 2:32; Esth. 7:10; 9:25; Prov. 5:22]
17[o] Ps. 9:2
Psalm 8
[p] Ps. 81, title; 84, title
1[q] Ps. 148:13; Isa. 12:4; [Ex. 34:5] [r] Ps. 113:4
2[s] Cited Matt. 21:16; [Matt. 11:25; 1 Cor. 1:27] [t] Jer. 16:19 [u] Ps. 44:16
3[v] [Ps. 111:2] [w] Ex. 8:19; 31:18 [x] Gen. 1:16
4[y] Cited Heb. 2:6-8; [Ps. 144:3; Job 7:17; 25:6] [z] [Gen. 8:1] [a] Ps. 80:17 [b] Ps. 65:9; Gen. 21:1; 50:24

Psalm 8 The Bible's worldview restores human dignity. Here David outlines that worldview by alluding to creation, fall, redemption, and consummation. Singing God's covenant name *Yahweh* while reflecting on his "glory above the heavens" (v. 1) reminds the worshiper that God created the world as an act of covenant love (Gen. 1:26–27). An infinite God's particular care for humans should overwhelm anyone contemplating the heavenly expanse (Ps. 8:3–4).

The references to "foes," "enemy," and "avenger" in the course of praising God for his creation remind us that there was also a fall (v. 2; Gen. 3:1–24). Thoughts of God's creation kindness in contrast to the wrath he could have justly poured out against such fallen humanity should move the sinner to repentance (Rom. 1:18–20; 2:4). Despite their fall into sin, God still dignifies his people as the stewards of his creation (Ps. 8:5–8; Gen. 1:28–31). But as Moses prophesied, man would need a Savior to overcome not only personal sin but also the fallen condition of the creation (Gen. 3:15, 18–19). By quoting this psalm, the writer of the book of Hebrews later clarifies that Christ, our Savior, is the perfect representation of the humanity described in this psalm (Heb. 2:6–8).

5[c] [Gen. 1:26] [d] Ps. 21:5 **6**[e] Gen. 1:26, 28 [f] Cited 1 Cor. 15:27; [Matt. 28:18] **Psalm 9** **1**[g] Ps. 26:7; 40:5; 96:3; 105:5

2 I will be glad and [h]exult in you;
I will [i]sing praise to your name, [j]O Most High.

3 When my enemies turn back,
they stumble and perish before[1] your presence.
4 For you have [k]maintained my just cause;
you have [l]sat on the throne, giving righteous judgment.

5 You have [m]rebuked the nations; you have made the wicked perish;
you have [n]blotted out their name forever and ever.
6 The enemy came to an end in everlasting ruins;
their cities you rooted out;
the very memory of them has perished.

7 But the LORD sits enthroned forever;
he has established his throne for justice,
8 and he [o]judges the world with righteousness;
he [p]judges the peoples with uprightness.

9 The LORD is [q]a stronghold for [r]the oppressed,
a stronghold in [s]times of trouble.
10 And those who [t]know your name put their trust in you,
for you, O LORD, have not forsaken those who seek you.

11 Sing praises to the LORD, who [u]sits enthroned in Zion!
Tell among the peoples his [v]deeds!
12 For he who [w]avenges blood is mindful of them;
he [x]does not forget the cry of the afflicted.

13 [y]Be gracious to me, O LORD!
See my affliction from those who hate me,
O you who lift me up from [z]the gates of death,
14 that I may recount all your praises,
that in the gates of [a]the daughter of Zion
I may [b]rejoice in your salvation.

15 The nations have sunk in [c]the pit that they made;
in [d]the net that they hid, their own foot has been caught.
16 The LORD has made himself [e]known; he has executed judgment;
the wicked are snared in the work of their own hands. *Higgaion.*[2] *Selah*

17 The wicked shall [f]return to Sheol,
all the nations that [g]forget God.

18 For the needy shall not always be forgotten,
and [h]the hope of the poor shall not perish forever.

19 [i]Arise, O LORD! Let not [j]man prevail;
let the nations be judged before you!
20 Put them in fear, O LORD!
Let the nations know that they are but [j]men! *Selah*

[1] Or *because of* [2] Probably a musical or liturgical term

The One through whom the world was created (John 1:3; Heb. 1:2) came to restore the image marred at the fall (Col. 1:15). He empowers even the weakest to participate in his redemptive plan (1 Cor. 1:26–31). Verses 1 and 9 of Psalm 8 serve not only as bookends for the psalm; they also anticipate the end of all things, when Christ's enemies will be made a footstool for his feet, and his name will be majestic through all the earth (Eph. 1:22).

Psalm 9 David's "whole heart" is moved to praise his King (v. 1), for the Lord has upheld David's cause and has given "righteous judgment" (v. 4). Here we see blended the infinite greatness and wonderful gentleness of God. He "sits enthroned forever" (v. 7) and "judges the world with righteousness" (v. 8). He is supreme in glory and might. And yet he is not aloof or uncaring. Instead, he is "a stronghold for the oppressed, a stronghold in times of trouble" (v. 9). For this reason, "the needy shall not always be forgotten" (v. 18).

In Jesus Christ we see these marks of God in beautiful flesh-and-blood reality. For Christ is both a lion and a lamb (Rev. 5:5–6). He is both supremely powerful (2 Thess. 1:7–10) and supremely gentle (Matt. 11:29). He is a strong refuge and a tender friend. In

2[h] Ps. 5:11 [i] Ps. 7:17 [j] See Ps. 83:18
4[k] Ps. 140:12 [l] Ps. 29:10
5[m] Ps. 68:30 [n] Deut. 9:14; 29:20; [Prov. 10:7]
8[o] Ps. 58:11; 96:13; 98:9 [p] Ps. 96:10
9[q] 2 Sam. 22:3; [Prov. 18:10] [r] Ps. 10:18; 74:21 [s] Ps. 10:1
10[t] Ps. 91:14
11[u] Ps. 76:2 [v] Ps. 77:12; [Ps. 107:22]
12[w] Gen. 9:5; [Ps. 10:13]; See 1 Kgs. 21:17-19 [x] ver. 18; Ps. 10:12; [Ps. 12:5]
13[y] Ps. 4:1 [z] See Job 38:17
14[a] 2 Kgs. 19:21; Isa. 37:22 [b] Ps. 13:5; 20:5; 21:1; 35:9; 1 Sam. 2:1
15[c] See Ps. 7:15 [d] See Job 18:8
16[e] Ex. 7:5; 14:4
17[f] [Gen. 3:19] [g] Ps. 50:22; Job 8:13; Isa. 51:13
18[h] [Prov. 23:18; 24:14]
19[i] See Ps. 3:7 [j] [Ps. 10:18]
20[j] [See ver. 19 above]

Why Do You Hide Yourself?

10 Why, O LORD, do you stand [k]far away?
Why [l]do you hide yourself in [m]times of trouble?

2 In arrogance the wicked hotly pursue the poor;
let them [n]be caught in the schemes that they have devised.
3 For the wicked [o]boasts of the desires of his soul,
and the one greedy for gain [p]curses[1] and [q]renounces the LORD.
4 In the pride of his face[2] the wicked does not [q]seek him;[3]
all his thoughts are, [r]"There is no God."
5 His ways prosper at all times;
your judgments are on high, [s]out of his sight;
as for all his foes, he [t]puffs at them.
6 He [u]says in his heart, "I shall not be moved;
throughout all generations I [v]shall not meet adversity."
7 [w]His mouth is filled with cursing and [x]deceit and [y]oppression;
[z]under his tongue are [a]mischief and [b]iniquity.
8 He sits in ambush in the villages;
in [c]hiding places he murders the innocent.
His eyes stealthily watch for the helpless;
9 he lurks in ambush like [d]a lion in his [e]thicket;
he [f]lurks that he may seize the poor;
he seizes the poor when he draws him into his [g]net.
10 The helpless are crushed, sink down, and fall by his might.
11 He says in his heart, "God has forgotten,
he has [h]hidden his face, he [i]will never see it."

12 [j]Arise, O LORD; O God, [k]lift up your hand;
[l]forget not the afflicted.
13 Why does the wicked [m]renounce God
and say in his heart, "You will not [n]call to account"?
14 But you do see, for you [o]note mischief and vexation,
that you may take it into your hands;
to you the helpless [p]commits himself;
you have been [q]the helper of the fatherless.
15 [r]Break the arm of the wicked and evildoer;
[s]call his wickedness to account till you find none.

16 [t]The LORD is king forever and ever;
the [u]nations perish from his land.
17 O LORD, you hear the desire of the afflicted;
you will [v]strengthen their heart; you will incline your ear
18 to [w]do justice to the fatherless and [x]the oppressed,
so that [y]man who is of the earth may strike terror no more.

[1] Or *and he blesses the one greedy for gain* [2] Or *of his anger* [3] Or *the wicked says, "He will not call to account"*

Jesus, we see concretely the God of Psalm 9. Jesus is "a stronghold for the oppressed" (Ps. 9:9). He came to preach good news to the poor (v. 18; Luke 4:18).

Psalm 10 Psalms 9 and 10 are regarded as companions in biblical tradition. They refer to the same messianic King who will reign "forever and ever," bringing justice to the oppressed (vv. 16–18). Unlike David in Psalm 9, this anonymous author laments God's apparent absence (10:1). Nevertheless, this psalmist calls on the Lord as his only hope for salvation. Recognizing the same godless mistreatment of the poor noted by David in Psalm 9, this forlorn soul cries out to Immanuel, as warrior, to "arise" and do battle on behalf of the afflicted (10:12). By the end of the psalm, the writer has recovered his vision of the coming Messiah who "inclines" his ear to the cry of the oppressed, does justice for the "fatherless," and will reign as King over all the earth (vv. 16–18).

Not only does this Psalm provide encouragement for Christians who grow overwhelmed with evil in their world; it calls them to pursue what the Lord calls true religion—to care for the "orphans and widows in their affliction" (James 1:27). This is the happy privilege of those who have been rescued from their own distressing sin and darkness by our Messiah.

Psalm 10
1[k] Ps. 22:1, 11, 19; 35:22; 38:21 [l] Ps. 13:1 [m] Ps. 9:9
2[n] [Ps. 7:15, 16]
3[o] Ps. 94:4; [Isa. 3:9] [p] ver. 13 [q] Job 1:5, 11
4[q] [See ver. 3 above] [r] Ps. 14:1; 53:1
5[s] [Isa. 26:11] [t] Ps. 12:5
6[u] ver. 11, 13 [v] [Rev. 18:7]
7[w] Cited Rom. 3:14 [x] Ps. 36:3 [y] Ps. 55:11; 72:14 [z] Job 20:12; [Ps. 140:3; Song 4:11] [a] Ps. 7:14 [b] Ps. 5:5; 6:8
8[c] Ps. 17:12; 64:4; [Hab. 3:14]
9[d] Ps. 17:12 [e] Job 38:40 [f] Ps. 59:3; Mic. 7:2 [g] Ps. 9:15
11[h] [Ps. 73:11]; Job 22:13 [i] Ps. 94:7; Ezek. 8:12; 9:9; [Zeph. 1:12]
12[j] See Ps. 3:7 [k] Mic. 5:9 [l] Ps. 9:12, 18
13[m] ver. 3 [n] Ps. 9:12
14[o] Ps. 33:13 [p] 2 Tim. 1:12; 1 Pet. 4:19 [q] Ps. 68:5; 146:9; Hos. 14:3
15[r] See Ps. 37:17 [s] [Ps. 37:36; Isa. 41:12] **16**[t] Ps. 29:10; Ex. 15:18; Jer. 10:10; Lam. 5:19; Dan. 4:34; 6:26; 1 Tim. 1:17; Rev. 11:15 [u] Deut. 8:20 **17**[v] 1 Chr. 29:18
18[w] Ps. 82:3; [Isa. 1:17; 11:4] [x] Ps. 9:9; 74:21 [y] Ps. 9:19, 20; 17:14

The Lord Is in His Holy Temple

11 To the choirmaster. Of David.
In the Lord I take refuge;
how can you say to my soul,
[z]"Flee like a bird to your mountain,
2 for behold, the wicked [a]bend the bow;
[b]they have fitted their arrow to the string
to shoot in the dark at the upright in heart;
3 if [c]the foundations are destroyed,
what can the righteous do?"[1]

4 [d]The Lord is in his holy temple;
the Lord's [e]throne is in heaven;
his eyes see, his eyelids [f]test the children of man.
5 The Lord [g]tests the righteous,
but [h]his soul hates the wicked and the one who loves violence.
6 Let him rain coals on the wicked;
[i]fire and sulfur and a scorching wind shall be [j]the portion of their cup.
7 For the Lord is righteous;
he [k]loves righteous deeds;
[l]the upright shall behold his face.

The Faithful Have Vanished

12 To the choirmaster: according to The Sheminith.[2] A Psalm of David.

1 Save, O Lord, for [m]the godly one is gone;
for the faithful have vanished from among the children of man.
2 Everyone [n]utters lies to his neighbor;
with [o]flattering lips and [p]a double heart they speak.

3 May the Lord cut off all [o]flattering lips,
the tongue that makes [q]great boasts,
4 those who say, "With our tongue we will prevail,
our lips are with us; who is master over us?"

5 "Because [r]the poor are plundered,
because the needy groan,
[s]I will now arise," says the Lord;
"I will place him in the [t]safety for which he longs."
6 [u]The words of the Lord are pure words,
like silver refined in a furnace on the ground,
purified seven times.

[1] Or *for the foundations will be destroyed; what has the righteous done?* [2] Probably a musical or liturgical term

Psalm 11 The idea that God is the believer's "refuge" was a precious truth to the hunted David (v. 1). Most of the psalm depicts the otherness of God, who sits on a heavenly throne in a holy temple (vv. 4–6); however, God's transcendence strengthens faith against enemies who are bent on David's destruction (v. 2).

Jesus came to reveal this kind of God, so he calls his people to pray to the "Father" who is "in heaven," but whose will is done "on earth" (Matt. 6:9–10). Wielding his power to care for his children, the Father brings all enemies under Christ's and his followers' feet (Rom. 16:20; 1 Thess. 5:2–5). Though the billows of suffering come against his life, the believer will not be shaken if he is built on Christ as his foundation (Ps. 11:3; Matt. 7:25–27). But Christ is also a just King (Ps. 11:5–7; Matt. 12:18). God's omniscience reassures the lonely disciple that his righteous deeds are not only noticed but are loved by the Lord (Ps. 11:4, 7; Rev. 19:8). And to keep the persecuted follower from growing disheartened, the Lord threatens Sodom-like judgment against the violent (Ps. 11:5–6; cf. 2 Thess. 1:5–9). Vindication at the end of the world is promised for the "upright," who will "behold [God's] face" (Ps. 11:7). Implicitly, that right standing is offered to any who receive by faith the righteousness earned by the one who drank the "cup" of God's wrath (v. 6; John 18:11)—namely, Jesus, in whose face we see the very glory of God (John 14:9; 2 Cor. 4:6).

Psalm 12 This Psalm begins with "save," the Hebrew word that would one day provide the name "Jesus" (Matt. 1:21). Then follows David's desperate lament over the absence of a godly man and lack of faithful leaders. From neighborhood conversations to the halls of government, lying is systemic in the realm of Israel (Ps. 12:2–4; cf. Rom. 3:12–13). It is hopeless even to confront the lying leaders, because they have created a parallel universe in which hypocrisy is the norm (Ps. 12:2, 8; cf. James 1:8). And because there is no apparent judgment, the impudent deceivers believe that they are the masters of their fate (Ps. 12:4; 2 Pet. 3:4). So David petitions the Lord to make things right (Ps. 12:3–4). The Savior must be a righteous man (cf. v. 5 and 1 Pet. 3:18), whose words are truth (cf. Ps. 12:6 and John 5:24), a sovereign judge (cf. Ps. 12:3 and 5 with John 8:26), and an eternal protector (cf. Ps. 12:7 and John 10:28). Ultimately, this can only

Psalm 11
1[z] [1 Sam. 23:14, 19; 24:2; 26:19, 20]
2[a] Ps. 7:12; 64:4; [Jer. 9:3] [b] Ps. 21:12; 58:7; See Ps. 7:10
3[c] Ps. 82:5; Ezek. 30:4
4[d] Ps. 18:6; Mic. 1:2; Hab. 2:20 [e] Ps. 2:4; Isa. 66:1; Matt. 5:34; 23:22; Acts 7:49 [f] See Job 23:10
5[g] Gen. 22:1; James 1:12 [h] Ps. 5:5
6[i] Gen. 19:24; Job 18:15; Ezek. 38:22 [j] Ps. 75:8; [Job 21:20]
7[k] See Ps. 33:5 [l] [Ps. 17:15; 140:13; 1 John 3:2; Rev. 22:4]

Psalm 12
1[m] Isa. 57:1; Mic. 7:2
2[n] Ps. 41:6; 144:8 [o] Ps. 5:9; Jer. 9:8; Rom. 16:18 [p] 1 Chr. 12:33; James 1:8
3[o] [See ver. 2 above] [q] Dan. 7:8; Rev. 13:5; [Ps. 17:10]
5[r] Ps. 9:12 [s] Isa. 33:10; [Ps. 82:8] [t] See Ps. 55:18
6[u] Ps. 18:30; 119:140; Prov. 30:5; [Ps. 19:8]

7 You, O LORD, will keep them;
you will guard us[1] from this generation forever.
8 On every side the wicked prowl,
as vileness is exalted among the children of man.

How Long, O LORD?

13 TO THE CHOIRMASTER. A PSALM OF DAVID.
[v]How long, O LORD? Will you [w]forget me forever?
How long will you [x]hide your face from me?
2 How long must I take [y]counsel in my soul
and have sorrow in my heart all the day?
How long shall my enemy be exalted over me?

3 [z]Consider and answer me, O LORD my God;
[a]light up my eyes, lest [b]I sleep the sleep of death,
4 [c]lest my enemy say, "I have prevailed over him,"
lest my foes rejoice because I am [d]shaken.

5 But I have [e]trusted in your steadfast love;
my heart shall [f]rejoice in your salvation.
6 I will sing to the LORD,
because he has dealt bountifully with me.

The Fool Says, There Is No God

14 TO THE CHOIRMASTER. OF DAVID.
[g]The [h]fool says in his heart, [i]"There is no God."
They are [j]corrupt, they do abominable deeds,
[k]there is none who does good.

2 The LORD [l]looks down from heaven on the children of man,
to see if there are any who understand,[2]
who [m]seek after God.

3 They have all turned aside; together they have become [n]corrupt;
there is none who does good,
not even one.

4 Have they no [o]knowledge, all the evildoers
who [p]eat up my people as they eat bread
and [q]do not call upon the LORD?

[1] Or *guard him* [2] Or *that act wisely*

Psalm 13
1[v] Ps. 79:5; 89:46; [Rev. 6:10] [w] Ps. 10:12; 44:24; 74:19, 23; Lam. 5:20 [x] See Job 13:24
2[y] [Ps. 77:6]
3[z] Ps. 5:1; 119:153 [a] Ps. 19:8; Ezra 9:8; Prov. 29:13; Eph. 1:18; [1 Sam. 14:27] [b] [Jer. 51:39]
4[c] Deut. 32:27 [d] See Ps. 10:6
5[e] See Ps. 11:1 [f] See Ps. 9:14

Psalm 14
1[g] For ver. 1-7, see Ps. 53:1-6 [h] Ps. 74:18, 22; Job 2:10 [i] Ps. 10:4 [j] Gen. 6:5, 11, 12 [k] Cited Rom. 3:10-12
2[l] Ps. 102:19; [Ps. 11:4] [m] 2 Chr. 15:2; 19:3
3[n] Job 15:16
4[o] Ps. 82:5; [Isa. 1:3; Jer. 4:22] [p] Prov. 30:14; Jer. 10:25; Hos. 7:7; [Ps. 27:2; Amos 8:4; Mic. 3:3] [q] Ps. 79:6; Jer. 10:25; Hos. 7:7; [Isa. 64:7]

be Jesus. Proof that the Savior is this promised Messiah is how he responds when he sees ruthless leaders plundering the poor (Luke 16:14–17, 19–31).

Though for a time the wicked are exalted in this fallen world, God's covenantal protection of his people will last from generation to generation. When the believer feels overwhelmed by systemic evil and is disheartened as an apparent minority standing for truth, this psalm will lead him to the only one who can save. In the meantime, Christ's promise of justice provides hope: "Behold, I am coming soon, bringing recompense with me, to repay each one for what he has done" (Rev. 22:12).

Psalm 13 Only a sovereign Father would allow his suffering children to complain in order to draw them to greater faith (vv. 1–2). Even more magnanimous is the Lord's endurance of David's demand to "consider" (v. 3). Like a lawyer interrogating a witness, David demands an "answer" (v. 3), for he is afraid of dying at the hands of God's mockers (v. 4). By the end of the prayer, the Father's strategy works. Being drawn to the Father's knee, David remembers that God's love is "steadfast" (cf. v. 5a and Ex. 34:6–7), as our God acts according to covenant commitment that we now know would ultimately be sealed in Christ's blood (cf. Ps. 13:5b and Luke 22:20). David also knows that "salvation" will come from God alone, which will cause David to "rejoice" (Ps. 13:5). We remember that a salvation was indeed announced, to a group of shepherds, as "news of great joy" (Luke 2:10).

David is so confident that God will deliver him that he begins to "sing" even before resolution has occurred (Ps. 13:6). We have an even greater basis for such confidence because we know this salvation hope finds its final fulfillment in Christ, who provides "hope" that "does not put us to shame" (Rom. 5:3–5). Such an honest prayer by David invites Christians to express all of their pain to the heavenly Father. After all, Christ's substitution means that the believer can never be rejected (2 Cor. 5:21). Our experience of God's goodness will be the same as the psalmist's—never mere sustenance, but bountiful blessing from an extravagant God who "graciously" gives us "all things," because he gave his Son for us all (Rom. 8:32).

5 There they are in great terror,
for God is with [r]the generation of the righteous.
6 You would shame the plans of the poor,
but[1] the LORD is his [s]refuge.

7 Oh, that salvation for Israel would come out of Zion!
When the LORD [t]restores the fortunes of his people,
let Jacob rejoice, let Israel be glad.

Who Shall Dwell on Your Holy Hill?

15 A PSALM OF DAVID.
O LORD, [u]who shall sojourn in your [v]tent?
Who shall dwell on your [w]holy hill?

2 He who [x]walks blamelessly and [y]does what is right
and [z]speaks truth in his heart;
3 who [a]does not slander with his tongue
and does no evil to his neighbor,
nor [b]takes up a reproach against his friend;
4 [c]in whose eyes a vile person is despised,
but who honors those who fear the LORD;
who [d]swears to his own hurt and does not change;
5 who [e]does not put out his money at interest
and [f]does not take a bribe against the innocent.
He who does these things shall never be [g]moved.

[1] Or *for*

5 [r] Ps. 24:6; 73:15
6 [s] Ps. 46:1; 61:3; 62:7, 8; 91:2; 142:5
7 [t] Ps. 85:1; 126:1; Job 42:10; Jer. 30:18; Ezek. 16:53; 39:25; Hos. 6:11; Joel 3:1

Psalm 15
1 [u] For ver. 1-5, see Ps. 24:3-5; Isa. 33:14-16 [v] Ps. 61:4 [w] See Ps. 2:6
2 [x] Prov. 28:18 [y] Ps. 106:3; [Matt. 6:1] [z] Zech. 8:16; Eph. 4:25; [John 1:47; Col. 3:9]
3 [a] Lev. 19:16; [Ps. 34:13] [b] Ex. 23:1
4 [c] [Esth. 3:2] [d] [Judg. 11:35]
5 [e] Ex. 22:25; Lev. 25:36; Deut. 23:19; Ezek. 18:8; 22:12 [f] Ex. 23:8; Deut. 16:19 [g] See Ps. 10:6

Psalm 14 An atheist is a "fool" because he acts contrary to true understanding (vv. 1–2). Elsewhere David says that God's self-revelation through creation is a universal language producing "knowledge" (19:1–4). Paul adds that even God's "invisible attributes" can be "perceived" in what God has made (Rom. 1:18–20). Even the "law is written on their hearts" (Rom. 2:15–16). So to deny that God exists requires "suppressing the truth," which produces foolish and conflicting thoughts (Rom. 1:18, 2:15; Titus 1:16).

While not everyone professes atheism, all practice it at some level by refusing to do good or seek after God—as though he did not exist (Ps. 14:1–3; Rom. 3:10–12). Consequently, the "wrath of God" revealed from heaven against such willingly blind arrogance is a theme throughout Scripture (Ps. 31:13; Jer. 6:16–26; Josh. 10:10; Phil. 1:28). God must punish the sin of those who deny what creation and their own hearts attest. And yet he who is "the God of all grace" (1 Pet. 5:10) will rise up for his people and be a refuge for the poor (Ps. 14:6; 35:10). The "righteous" therefore do not fear, because their God is Immanuel (14:5). For them he provides "refuge," "salvation," "fortunes," and gladness (vv. 6–7).

David's confidence was more than emotional; he looked ahead to a man who would come from of a place called "Zion" (v. 7). Zion with its temple represented the intersection of heaven and earth—God's down payment on the incarnation. On the cross, Immanuel, Jesus Christ, tore down the dividing curtain of the temple, making that intersection an unhindered highway (Matt. 27:51–54; Heb. 10:20) and also removing the wall of ethnic separation. As a consequence, sinners from every race may stand righteously and safely in God's presence and have their joy restored according to the promises made to the patriarchs of Israel (Ps. 14:7; Eph. 2:11–22).

Psalm 15 This is a portrait of an upright man. He keeps all the "weightier matters of the law"—justice, mercy, and faithfulness (cf. Matt. 23:23). He judges rightly between the "vile" and those who "fear the Lord" (Ps. 15:4; Deut. 10:17). He avoids usury (Ps. 15:5; Deut. 23:19–20) and deals faithfully with his "neighbor" (Ps. 15:3).

These are the requirements of righteousness, and God threatens judgment against any who fail to meet them (Isa. 33:14–16). Everyone will receive what is justly "due for what he has done in the body, whether good or evil" (2 Cor. 5:10). No mercy will come to him who has "shown no mercy" (James 2:13). And the unfaithful will be "paid back for the wrong he has done" (Col. 3:25).

Confrontation with these high standards drives every reader back to David's question: "Who shall dwell on your holy hill?" (Ps. 15:1). The answer drives us to look for someone unlike us, knowing we cannot perfectly keep such standards. That one is finally revealed only in God's own Son, who lived the life we should have lived and

You Will Not Abandon My Soul

16 A [h]MIKTAM[1] OF DAVID.
Preserve me, O God, for in you
I [i]take refuge.
2 I say to the LORD, "You are my Lord;
[j]I have no good apart from you."
3 As for [k]the saints in the land, they are
the excellent ones,
in whom is all my delight.[2]
4 The sorrows of those who run after[3]
another god shall multiply;
their drink offerings of blood I will
not pour out
or [l]take their names on my lips.
5 The LORD is [m]my chosen portion and my
[n]cup;
you hold my [o]lot.
6 [p]The lines have fallen for me in pleasant
places;
indeed, I have a beautiful inheritance.
7 I bless the LORD who [q]gives me counsel;
in [r]the night also my [s]heart instructs
me.[4]
8 [t]I have [u]set the LORD always before me;
because he is at my [v]right hand, I shall
not be [w]shaken.
9 Therefore my heart is glad, and my
[x]whole being[5] rejoices;
my flesh also dwells secure.
10 For you will not abandon my soul to
[y]Sheol,
[z]or let your [a]holy one see [b]corruption.[6]
11 You make known to me [c]the path of life;
in your presence there is [d]fullness of
joy;
at your right hand are [e]pleasures forevermore.

In the Shadow of Your Wings

17 A [f]PRAYER OF DAVID.
Hear a just cause, O LORD; [g]attend
to my cry!
Give ear to my prayer from lips free of
deceit!
2 From your presence [h]let my vindication
come!
Let your eyes behold the right!

[1] Probably a musical or liturgical term [2] Or *To the saints in the land, the excellent in whom is all my delight, I say:* [3] Or *who acquire*
[4] Hebrew *my kidneys instruct me* [5] Hebrew *my glory* [6] Or *see the pit*

Psalm 16
[h][Ps. 56, title; 57, title; 60, title]
1 [i]See Ps. 11:1
2 [j][Ps. 73:25]
3 [k][Ex. 19:6; Deut. 7:6; 1 Pet. 2:9]
4 [l]Ex. 23:13; Josh. 23:7
5 [m]Ps. 73:26; 119:57; 142:5; Num. 18:20; Lam. 3:24; [Deut. 32:9; Jer. 10:16; 51:19] [n]Ps. 23:5; 116:13 [o]Ps. 125:3
6 [p]Mic. 2:5
7 [q]See 1 Sam. 23:9-12; 2 Sam. 5:18, 19 [r]Ps. 17:3; See Ps. 42:8 [s]Ps. 7:9
8 [t]Cited Acts 2:25-28 [u]Ps. 119:30 [v]Ps. 109:31; 110:5; 121:5 [w]Ps. 10:6; 15:5
9 [x]Ps. 30:12; 57:8; 108:1; Gen. 49:6
10 [y]See Job 21:13 [z]Cited Acts 13:35 [a]Ps. 89:18; [Mark 1:24] [b]Ps. 49:9; 103:4
11 [c]Matt. 7:14 [d][Ps. 21:6] [e]Ps. 36:8

Psalm 17
[f][Ps. 86, title; 142, title]
1 [g]Ps. 142:6; [Ps. 61:1; Jer. 7:16]
2 [h][Ps. 26:1]

died a death that paid the penalty for our failures. It is good that David begins such a challenging psalm with reference to the "holy hill," representing Zion, where the temple for atoning sacrifices stood. Jesus dwelled on God's holy hill by *becoming* the temple. By his atoning sacrifice, Jesus himself is the place where God and man are reconciled (John 2:19–22). Built on the unshakeable rock of Christ's life, and united to Christ as part of that holy temple (Eph. 2:19–22), the believer "shall never be moved" (Ps. 15:5).

Psalm 16 The Lord provides infallible protection. David the refugee knew what made for a sure sanctuary. First, one must enter it. At some point David said "yes" to the Lord and "no" to all contrary allegiances (vv. 1–4). Second, one must trust that momentary discomforts of the sanctuary are far better than the danger outside. The believer must accept his current condition as God's gracious design for his "good" (v. 2).

Elsewhere that good is described as *shalom* or "peace" (Isa. 52:7; Jer. 8:15). In this haven, with nothing but the sound of his beating heart, David tunes the ear of his conscience to the "counsel" (Ps. 16:7) of God's Word. Thus focused, the eyes of faith see that God is present at David's "right hand" (vv. 7–8). The blessed alternative to self-trust is to be set on a solid foundation that not even death can unsettle (vv. 9–10). Death becomes a door instead of a wall; an entrance ramp, not an exit, into the "presence" of God (v. 11).

The God who came to David's side is the God who came to be "with us" through Christ and who will exalt the Christian to his right hand (v. 11). Here is the doctrine of the two ways. The way of self-trust results in sorrows, blood, abandonment, and corruption. But the way of the gospel provides refuge, good, excellence, delight, pleasantness, beauty, counsel, instruction, stability, gladness, security, fullness of joy, and pleasures forevermore. Peter revealed that in Psalm 16 David was speaking ultimately about Jesus Christ (Acts 2:25–33). The believer's union with Jesus' resurrection and exaltation to the right of God is the ultimate source of our infallible protection.

Psalm 17 Combining the themes of Psalms 15 and 16, in this psalm David praises his Savior as vindicator and refuge. David's petition to be vindicated in the Lord's

3 You have [i]tried my heart, you have [j]visited me by [k]night,
you have [l]tested me, and you will find nothing;
I have purposed that my mouth will not transgress.
4 With regard to the works of man, by the word of your lips
I have avoided the ways of the violent.
5 My steps have [m]held fast to your paths;
my feet have not slipped.

6 I [n]call upon you, for you will answer me, O God;
[o]incline your ear to me; hear my words.
7 [p]Wondrously show[1] your steadfast love,
O Savior of those who seek refuge
from [q]their adversaries at your right hand.

8 Keep me as [r]the apple of your eye;
hide me in [s]the shadow of your wings,
9 from the wicked who do me violence,
my deadly enemies who [t]surround me.

10 [u]They close their hearts to pity;
with their mouths they [v]speak arrogantly.
11 They have now surrounded our [w]steps;
they set their eyes to [x]cast us to the ground.
12 He is like a lion eager to tear,
as a young lion [y]lurking in ambush.

13 Arise, O LORD! Confront him, subdue him!
Deliver my soul from the wicked by your sword,
14 from men by your hand, O LORD,
from [z]men of the world whose [a]portion is in this life.[2]
You fill their womb with treasure;[3]
they are satisfied with [b]children,
and they leave their abundance to their infants.

15 As for me, I shall [c]behold your face in righteousness;
when I [d]awake, I shall be [e]satisfied with your likeness.

The LORD Is My Rock and My Fortress

18

TO THE CHOIRMASTER. A PSALM OF DAVID, [f]THE SERVANT OF THE LORD, [g]WHO ADDRESSED THE WORDS OF THIS [h]SONG TO THE LORD ON THE DAY WHEN THE LORD RESCUED HIM FROM THE HAND OF ALL HIS ENEMIES, AND FROM THE HAND OF SAUL. HE SAID:

1 I love you, O LORD, my strength.
2 The LORD is my [i]rock and my [j]fortress and my deliverer,
my God, my [i]rock, in [k]whom I take refuge,
my [l]shield, and [m]the horn of my salvation, my [n]stronghold.

[1] Or *Distinguish me by* [2] Or *from men whose portion in life is of the world* [3] Or *As for your treasured ones, you fill their womb*

"presence" and before his "eyes" (Ps. 17:2) reveals the uniqueness of his Savior. This uniqueness that David knew spiritually became a physical reality in God's only Son. Jesus brought the presence of God to man, as his followers saw him with their "eyes" and "touched" him with their "hands" (1 John 1:1–4). By his incarnation and death, Jesus "made manifest" God's vindication for sinners and refuge for the spiritually oppressed (1 John 1:2, 5–9; 4:4).

As one of those who saw and touched Christ, Peter disclosed that the ultimate purpose for David's plea in this psalm was for the sake of his Greater Son. David beseeched the Lord to preserve him as the forefather of the Messiah (cf. the "inheritance" of Ps. 16:3–6; Acts 2:34–35). By delivering David, God preserved the line of the Messiah and "wondrously" assured his people forever that he is their refuge (Ps. 17:7).

While their bitter enemies mercilessly seek to harm them (vv. 9–12, 14), God's people can rest quietly and confidently in the knowledge that they are peculiarly treasured. God himself rises and fights for them (v. 13; Num. 10:35), jealously guarding them as one protects the apple of his eye (Ps. 17:8). No matter what he suffers in this life, the believer must know that his "witness is in heaven" (Job 16:19). No matter how miserable the fight here and now, one look at Christ's face will one day make it all worthwhile (Ps. 17:15; Rev. 22:4).

Psalm 18 The Lord's strong deliverance of David from Saul elicits from David a song of love (v. 1). Two metaphors convey God's strength: warrior and rock. Expanding on the war cry in 17:13, David first imagines his Savior to be a fortress, deliverer, shield,

3[i] See Job 23:10 [j] Job 31:14 [k] Ps. 16:7; [Job 33:15] [l] Judg. 7:4; Zech. 13:9; 1 Pet. 1:7; [Ps. 139:1; Mal. 3:2, 3]
5[m] Job 23:11; [Ps. 44:18]
6[n] Ps. 86:6, 7; 116:1, 2 [o] See Ps. 31:2
7[p] Ps. 31:21 [q] Ps. 44:5; 59:1; 139:21
8[r] Deut. 32:10; Zech. 2:8 [s] Ps. 36:7; 57:1; 63:7; 91:4; [Matt. 23:37; Luke 13:34]; See Ruth 2:12
9[t] [1 Sam. 23:26]
10[u] [Ps. 119:70] [v] Ps. 31:18; 1 Sam. 2:3
11[w] [Ps. 89:51] [x] Ps. 62:4
12[y] [Ps. 10:8, 9]
14[z] [Ps. 10:18; Luke 16:8; 20:34] [a] Matt. 6:2, 5, 16; Luke 16:25 [b] [Job 21:11]
15[c] Job 33:26; 1 John 3:2; [Ps. 11:7] [d] Isa. 26:19; Dan. 12:2 [e] [Ps. 16:11]

Psalm 18
[f] Ps. 36, title; 89:3, 20; [2 Sam. 3:18; 7:5] [g] See 2 Sam. 22 [h] Ex. 15:1; Deut. 31:30
2[i] ver. 31, 46; Ps. 19:14; 31:3 [j] Ps. 91:2; 144:2 [k] [Heb. 2:13] [l] ver. 30; Gen. 15:1 [m] Ps. 112:9; Luke 1:69 [n] See Ps. 9:9

3 I call upon the LORD, who is [o]worthy to
be praised,
and I am saved from my enemies.

4 [p]The cords of death encompassed me;
[q]the torrents of destruction assailed me;[1]
5 [p]the cords of Sheol entangled me;
the snares of death confronted me.

6 [r]In my distress I called upon the LORD;
to my God I cried for help.
From his [s]temple he heard my voice,
and my cry to him reached his ears.

7 Then the earth [t]reeled and rocked;
the foundations also of the mountains trembled
and quaked, because he was angry.
8 Smoke went up from his nostrils,[2]
and devouring [u]fire from his mouth;
glowing coals flamed forth from him.
9 He [v]bowed the heavens and [w]came down;
[x]thick darkness was under his feet.
10 He rode on a cherub and flew;
he came swiftly on [z]the wings of the
wind.
11 He made darkness his covering, his [a]can-
opy around him,
thick clouds [b]dark with water.
12 Out of the brightness before him
[c]hailstones and coals of fire broke
through his clouds.

13 The LORD also [d]thundered in the heavens,
and the Most High uttered his [e]voice,
hailstones and coals of fire.

14 And he sent out his [f]arrows and scattered them;
he flashed forth lightnings and
[g]routed them.
15 Then [h]the channels of the sea were seen,
and the foundations of the world
were laid bare
at your [i]rebuke, O LORD,
at the blast of [j]the breath of your nostrils.

16 He [k]sent from on high, he took me;
he [l]drew me out of [m]many waters.
17 He rescued me from my strong enemy
and from those who hated me,
for they were [n]too mighty for me.
18 They confronted me in the day of my
calamity,
but the LORD was my support.
19 He brought me out into [o]a broad place;
he rescued me, because he [p]delighted
in me.

20 The LORD dealt with me [q]according to
my righteousness;
according to [r]the cleanness of my
hands he rewarded me.
21 For I have [s]kept the ways of the LORD,
and have not wickedly departed from
my God.
22 For [t]all his rules[3] were before me,
and his statutes I did not put away
from me.
23 I was [u]blameless before him,
and I kept myself from my guilt.

[1] Or *terrified me* [2] Or *in his wrath* [3] Or *just decrees*

3[o] Ps. 48:1; 96:4; 113:3; 145:3
4[p] Ps. 116:3; [Ps. 119:61] [q] See Ps. 32:6
5[p] [See ver. 4 above]
6[r] Ps. 66:14; 102:2; 120:1; [Jonah 2:2] [s] See Ps. 11:4
7[t] [Judg. 5:4; Acts 4:31; 16:26]
8[u] See Ps. 21:9
9[v] Ps. 144:5 [w] Isa. 64:1 [x] See Ex. 20:21
10[z] Ps. 104:3
11[a] Job 36:29; [Ps. 97:2] [b] [Ps. 29:3]
12[c] [Ps. 148:8; Josh. 10:11]
13[d] 1 Sam. 2:10; 7:10; See Job 37:4 [e] Isa. 30:30; See Ps. 29:3-9
14[f] Ps. 7:13; 64:7; 77:17; 144:6; Deut. 32:23, 42; Hab. 3:11 [g] Ex. 14:24; Josh. 10:10
15[h] Ps. 42:1; Joel 1:20 (Heb.); [Job 36:30] [i] Ps. 106:9; Nah. 1:4 [j] [Ex. 15:8]
16[k] [Ps. 144:7] [l] [Ex. 2:10] [m] See Ps. 32:6; Job 22:11
17[n] Ps. 142:6

horn, and stronghold who avenges, subdues, saves, rescues and gives victories (18:1–3, 46–50; cf. Rev. 19:11–21).

As a rock, God provides shade from natural disasters, refuge from human enemies, and a foundation for a stable life (Ps. 18:2, 31, 46). But the psalm is not merely biographical of David, nor is it simply pietistic words for the worshiper. When David spoke similar words elsewhere, it was apparent that the purpose of the preservation of his line was to provide a Redeemer for the world (2 Sam. 7:4–17; 22:1–51).

These features of God's gracious character and care find their ultimate revelation in Christ Jesus. Eventually Paul explained that Psalm 18 is prophetic of Jesus and shows that God's plan was always to redeem the Gentiles through the Seed of Abraham (Rom. 15:9; Gal. 3:17, 18). The Christian should see that such infallible promises of protection and strength are not to be hoarded, but leveraged for God's service. Christ the rock is a citadel from which to launch missions across the world. And Christ the warrior leads the church into battles for souls throughout the nations. Because Christ is the commander of this kingdom operation, victory is assured: "the kingdom of the world has become the kingdom of our Lord and of his Christ, and he shall reign forever and ever" (Rev. 11:15).

19[o] Ps. 31:8; 118:5; [ver. 36] [p] Ps. 22:8; 2 Sam. 15:26 **20**[q] Ps. 7:8; 1 Sam. 24:19; 26:23; 1 Kgs. 8:32 [r] See Job 22:30 **21**[s] [Gen. 18:19; Prov. 8:32] **22**[t] Ps. 119:30, 102 **23**[u] Gen. 17:1; [1 Kgs. 14:8]

24 So the LORD has rewarded me according
to my righteousness,
according to the cleanness of my
hands in his sight.

25 With [v]the merciful you show yourself
merciful;
with the blameless man you show
yourself blameless;
26 with the purified you show yourself
pure;
and with [w]the crooked you make
yourself seem tortuous.
27 For you save [x]a humble people,
but [y]the haughty eyes you bring
down.
28 For it is you who light my [z]lamp;
the LORD my God lightens my darkness.
29 For by you I can run against a troop,
and by my God I can [a]leap over [b]a
wall.
30 This God—his way is [c]perfect;[1]
the word of the LORD [d]proves true;
he is [e]a shield for all those who [f]take
refuge in him.

31 For [g]who is God, but the LORD?
And who is [h]a rock, except our
God?—
32 the God who [i]equipped me with
strength
and made my way [j]blameless.
33 He made my feet like the feet of a [k]deer
and set me secure on [l]the heights.
34 He [m]trains my hands for war,
so that my arms can bend a bow of
bronze.
35 You have given me the shield of your
salvation,
and your right hand [n]supported me,
and your [o]gentleness made me great.
36 You [p]gave a wide place for my steps
under me,
and my feet did not slip.
37 I pursued my enemies and overtook
them,
and did not turn back till they were
consumed.
38 I thrust them through, so that they were
not able to rise;
they fell under my feet.
39 For you equipped me with strength for
the battle;
you made those who rise against me
sink under me.
40 You made my enemies [q]turn their backs
to me,[2]
and those who hated me I destroyed.
41 [r]They cried for help, but there was none
to save;
they cried to the LORD, but he did not
answer them.
42 I beat them fine as [s]dust before the
wind;
I cast them out like [t]the mire of the
streets.

43 You delivered me from [u]strife with the
people;
you made me [v]the head of the
nations;
[w]people whom I had not known served
me.
44 As soon as they heard of me they obeyed
me;
[x]foreigners [y]came cringing to me.
45 [x]Foreigners lost heart
and [z]came trembling out of their fortresses.

46 The LORD lives, and blessed be my rock,
and exalted be the God of my salvation—
47 the God who gave me vengeance
and [a]subdued peoples under me,
48 who delivered me from my enemies;
yes, you [b]exalted me above those who
rose against me;
you rescued me from [c]the man of violence.

49 [d]For this I will praise you, O LORD,
among the nations,
and [e]sing to your name.
50 Great [f]salvation he brings to his king,
and shows steadfast love to his
[g]anointed,
to [h]David and his offspring forever.

[1] Or *blameless* [2] Or *You gave me my enemies' necks*

25[v] Matt. 5:7 **26**[w] Ps. 81:12; Lev. 26:23, 24; Prov. 3:34; Acts 7:42; Rom. 1:28 **27**[x] [Ex. 3:7] [y] See Ps. 101:5 **28**[z] Ps. 132:17; 1 Kgs. 11:36; 15:4; 2 Kgs. 8:19; [2 Sam. 21:17]; See Job 18:5, 6 **29**[a] [Isa. 35:6] [b] See 2 Sam. 5:6-9 **30**[c] Deut. 32:4; Dan. 4:37; Matt. 5:48; [Rev. 15:3] [d] See Ps. 12:6 [e] ver. 2 [f] Ps. 17:7 **31**[g] [Ps. 86:8] [h] See ver. 2 **32**[i] 1 Sam. 2:4; Isa. 45:5 [j] Ps. 101:2, 6; 119:1; Job 22:3 **33**[k] Hab. 3:19 [l] Deut. 32:13; Isa. 58:14 **34**[m] Ps. 144:1 **35**[n] Ps. 20:2 [o] [Isa. 63:9] **36**[p] Ps. 31:8; Prov. 4:12; [ver. 19] **40**[q] Ex. 23:27; [Ps. 21:12] **41**[r] See Job 27:9 **42**[s] 2 Kgs. 13:7 [t] Isa. 10:6; Mic. 7:10; Zech. 10:5 **43**[u] [2 Sam. 3:1; 19:9, 43; 20:1] [v] [Ps. 2:8]; See 2 Sam. 8:1-14 [w] Isa. 55:5; [Ps. 22:27] **44**[x] Ps. 144:7 [y] Ps. 66:3; 81:15; Deut. 33:29 **45**[x] [See ver. 44 above] [z] Mic. 7:17 **47**[a] Ps. 47:3; 144:2; [Isa. 45:1] **48**[b] Ps. 59:1 [c] Ps. 140:1 **49**[d] Cited Rom. 15:9 [e] Ps. 66:4 **50**[f] Ps. 144:10 [g] See Ps. 2:2 [h] [Ps. 89:29; 2 Sam. 7:12, 13, 29]

The Law of the LORD Is Perfect

19

TO THE CHOIRMASTER. A PSALM OF DAVID.
1 [i]The heavens declare the glory of
God,
and the sky above[1] proclaims his handiwork.
2 Day to day pours out speech,
and night to night reveals knowledge.
3 There is no speech, nor are there words,
whose voice is not heard.
4 [j]Their [k]voice[2] goes out through all the
earth,
and their words to the end of the
world.
In them he has set a tent for [l]the sun,
5 [m]which comes out like [n]a bridegroom
leaving his chamber,
and, like a strong man, runs its course
with joy.
6 Its rising is from the end of the heavens,
and its circuit to the end of them,
and there is nothing hidden from its
heat.

7 [o]The law of the LORD is perfect,[3]
[p]reviving the soul;
[q]the testimony of the LORD is [r]sure,
[s]making wise [t]the simple;
8 [u]the precepts of the LORD are right,
rejoicing the heart;
the commandment of the LORD is [v]pure,
[w]enlightening the eyes;
9 the fear of the LORD is clean,
enduring forever;
the rules[4] of the LORD are [x]true,
and righteous altogether.
10 More to be desired are they than [y]gold,
even much [z]fine gold;
[a]sweeter also than honey
and drippings of [b]the honeycomb.
11 Moreover, by them is your servant
warned;
[c]in keeping them there is great reward.

12 [d]Who can discern his errors?
[e]Declare me innocent from [f]hidden
faults.
13 [g]Keep back your servant also from [h]pre-
sumptuous sins;
let them not have [i]dominion over me!
Then I shall be blameless,
and innocent of great transgression.

14 Let the words of my mouth and the meditation of my heart
be acceptable in your sight,
O LORD, my [j]rock and my [k]redeemer.

[1] Hebrew *the expanse*; compare Genesis 1:6–8 [2] Or *Their measuring line* [3] Or *blameless* [4] Or *just decrees*

Psalm 19
1 [i] Ps. 50:6; [Rom. 1:19, 20]
4 [j] Cited Rom. 10:18 [k] [Isa. 28:10] [l] [Eccles. 1:5]
5 [m] [Judg. 5:31] [n] Joel 2:16
7 [o] Rom. 7:12 [p] Ps. 23:3; [2 Tim. 3:16] [q] Ex. 25:16; See Ps. 78:5 [r] Ps. 111:7 [s] [Matt. 11:25; 1 Cor. 1:27; 2 Tim. 3:15] [t] Ps. 119:130; Prov. 1:4
8 [u] Ps. 103:18; 111:7; 119:4, 27 [v] [Ps. 12:6] [w] See Ps. 13:3
9 [x] Ps. 119:142, 151, 160
10 [y] Ps. 119:72, 127; Prov. 8:10 [z] Job 28:17; Prov. 8:19 [a] Ps. 119:103 [b] Prov. 16:24
11 [c] [Prov. 29:18]
12 [d] Ps. 40:12; [1 Cor. 4:4] [e] [Lev. 4:2; Num. 15:27] [f] Ps. 90:8; See Job 34:32
13 [g] Gen. 20:6; 1 Sam. 25:33, 34, 39 [h] [Num. 15:30] [i] Ps. 119:133; Rom. 6:12, 14
14 [j] See Ps. 18:2 [k] See Job 19:25

Psalm 19 As in Psalm 18, David calls the Lord his "rock" (19:14). Only here the "rock" is God's revelation of himself. Through his handiwork, everyone gains knowledge of God's glory (vv. 1–2; cf. Rom. 1:18–23). Through the creation and within the creature, God has generally disclosed enough about himself that everyone has an obligation to turn toward him for salvation (Rom. 2:15; 10:18). God has revealed himself by natural revelation (Ps. 19:1–6), and since the fall of humanity he has revealed himself more perfectly in the special revelation of his inspired Word (vv. 7–13). When embraced by faith, the Scriptures are gracious, "reviving the soul" (v. 7). Because their "testimony" is sure, they make us wise by warning us away from danger (vv. 7, 11; James 1:25). Because they are refreshing, their "precepts" rejoice the heart (Ps. 19:8; Prov. 25:13). Because they are "clean," "enduring," "true," and "righteous," they are more desirable than gold or honey (Ps. 19:9, 10; Rev. 16:7). In essence, God's Word is representative of his own character—a fitting reason why Jesus will be identified as God's Word in the New Testament (John 1:1).

By faithful adherence to God's Word, the believer may expect "great reward" (Ps. 19:11). The problem is that no one naturally repents or obeys. Rather than turn to God who graciously reveals himself in creation, everyone suppresses the truth (Rom. 1:18). Rather than heed warnings written on his heart, everyone rebels against the law through "hidden faults" if not by "presumptuous sins" and "great transgression" (Ps. 19:12–13). Like the scorching sun, the written Word exposes every meditation of the heart (v. 14; Heb. 4:12). How is it possible then to be "blameless," "innocent," and "acceptable" (Ps. 19:13–14)? Only through Christ. He himself is the Word through whom the world was created (John 1:1–3). He has ultimately become the "redeemer" (Ps. 19:14) whose righteous record is the "rock" of a believer's life (Matt. 7:25).

Trust in the Name of the LORD Our God

20 TO THE CHOIRMASTER. A PSALM OF DAVID.
May the LORD [l]answer you in the
day of trouble!
May [m]the name of the God of Jacob
[n]protect you!
2 May he send you help from [o]the sanctuary
and give you support from [p]Zion!
3 May he [q]remember all your offerings
and regard with favor your burnt sacrifices! *Selah*

4 May he [r]grant you your heart's desire
and fulfill all your plans!
5 May we shout for joy over [s]your salvation,
and in the name of our God set up our
[t]banners!
May the LORD fulfill all your petitions!

6 Now I know that the LORD saves his
anointed;
he will answer him from his holy
heaven
with [u]the saving might of his right
hand.
7 Some trust in [v]chariots and some in
[w]horses,
[x]but we trust in the name of the LORD
our God.
8 They collapse and fall,
but we rise and stand upright.

9 O LORD, save [y]the king!
May he answer us when we call.

The King Rejoices in the LORD's Strength

21 TO THE CHOIRMASTER. A PSALM OF DAVID.
O LORD, in your [z]strength the king
rejoices,
and in your [a]salvation how greatly he
exults!
2 You have [b]given him his heart's desire
and have not withheld the request of
his lips. *Selah*
3 For you [c]meet him with rich blessings;
you set [d]a crown of [e]fine gold upon
his head.
4 He asked life of you; you [f]gave it to him,
[g]length of days forever and ever.
5 His [h]glory is great through your salvation;
[i]splendor and majesty you bestow on
him.
6 For you make him most blessed forever;[1]
you make him glad with the [j]joy of
your presence.
7 For the king trusts in the LORD,
and through the steadfast love of the
Most High he shall not be [k]moved.

[1] Or *make him a source of blessing forever*

Psalm 20 Psalms 20 and 21 form a pair: one a prayer and the other praise for the answer to the prayer. First, in Psalm 20, the congregation appeals to the Lord to bless the "king" (v. 9). Immediately in focus is the Davidic king (in this case, David himself), but these petitions are so theologically supercharged that they can only be answered fully in the last "anointed" one, the Messiah (v. 6; John 1:41).

Confident in God's principle of representation, the worshipers pray for the anointed one to be saved from danger, which will vicariously benefit them (cf. Rom. 5:18). "Help from the sanctuary" (like angelic support) enabled Christ to accomplish his work on the cross (Ps. 20:2; Matt. 4:11; Luke 22:43; Heb. 5:7). And God's remembrance of Christ's sacrifice earned "favor" for sinners (Ps. 20:3; Isa. 61:2).

As God answered the "heart's desire" of godly kings, the people experienced the joy of salvation, recognizing by faith that each deliverance moved them closer to God's eternal purpose (Ps. 20:4–5; Eph. 3:11). Every victory won for his people in redemptive history proved the superiority of God's "right hand" and that his Messiah's "name" was above every name (Ps. 20:6–8; Phil. 2:9). The Lord's undefeated record of saving his anointed (Ps. 20:6) assures the believer that God will answer when he calls—because he is united to Christ the King (v. 9; Acts 4:26–29).

Psalm 21 One mark of God's people is that he delivers them when they call for help (20:9). Here is the record of God's answer to the prayer of Psalm 20. However, it is not merely an answer regarding individual protection from the occasional struggles of life. God's answer to the "request of [David's] lips" ultimately provided eternal salvation for the nation according to the larger "plans" of the Davidic covenant (20:4; 2:8; 2 Sam. 7:14; Acts 2:33).

As the full significance of this psalm is seen in light of Christ's ministry fulfilling David's plans, we understand that, having saved his people from their sins by Christ's

Psalm 20
1 [l][Gen. 35:3] [m]Prov. 18:10 [n]Ps. 59:1; 69:29
2 [o]Ps. 73:17; 2 Chr. 20:8 [p]Ps. 128:5
3 [q][Acts 10:4]
4 [r]Ps. 21:2
5 [s]Ps. 9:14 [t]Ps. 60:4; Song 6:4, 10
6 [u][Ps. 28:8]
7 [v]Isa. 31:1; 36:9 [w]Prov. 21:31 [x][1 Sam. 17:45; 2 Chr. 32:8]
9 [y]Ps. 48:2

Psalm 21
1 [z]Ps. 8:2; 28:7, 8 [a]Ps. 9:14
2 [b]Ps. 20:4, 5
3 [c]Ps. 59:10 [d][2 Sam. 12:30; 1 Chr. 20:2] [e]Ps. 19:10
4 [f]Ps. 61:6; [2 Sam. 7:19] [g]Ps. 91:16; [1 Kgs. 1:31; Neh. 2:3]
5 [h]Ps. 8:5 [i]Ps. 45:3; 96:6
6 [j]Ps. 45:7; See Ps. 16:11
7 [k]Ps. 10:6; 16:8

8 Your hand will [l]find out all your enemies;
your right hand will find out those who hate you.
9 You will make them as [m]a blazing oven when you appear.
The LORD will swallow them up in his [n]wrath,
and [o]fire will consume them.
10 You [p]will destroy their [q]descendants from the earth,
and their offspring from among the children of man.
11 Though they plan evil against you,
though they [r]devise mischief, they will not succeed.
12 For you will put them [s]to flight;
you will [t]aim at their faces with your bows.

13 Be exalted, O LORD, in your strength!
We will sing and praise your power.

Why Have You Forsaken Me?

22

TO THE CHOIRMASTER: ACCORDING TO THE DOE OF THE DAWN. A PSALM OF DAVID.

1 [u]My God, my God, why have you forsaken me?
Why are you so [v]far from saving me,
from the words of my [w]groaning?
2 O my God, I cry by [x]day, but you do not answer,
and by night, but I find no rest.

3 Yet you are [y]holy,
[z]enthroned on [a]the praises[1] of Israel.
4 In you our fathers trusted;
they trusted, and you delivered them.
5 To you they [b]cried and were rescued;
in you they [c]trusted and were not put to shame.

6 But I am [d]a worm and not a man,
[e]scorned by mankind and [f]despised by the people.
7 All who see me [g]mock me;
they make mouths at me; they [h]wag their heads;
8 [i]"He trusts in the LORD; let him [j]deliver him;
let him rescue him, for he [k]delights in him!"

9 Yet you are he who [l]took me from the womb;
you made me trust you at my mother's breasts.
10 On you was I cast from my birth,
and from [m]my mother's womb you have been my God.
11 Be not [n]far from me,
for trouble is near,
and there is [o]none to help.

12 Many bulls encompass me;
[p]strong bulls of [q]Bashan surround me;
13 they [r]open wide their mouths at me,
like a ravening and roaring lion.

14 I am [s]poured out like water,
and all my bones are [t]out of joint;

[1] Or *dwelling in the praises*

8[l] [Isa. 10:10]
9[m] Mal. 4:1; [Ps. 83:14] [n] Ps. 2:5 [o] Ps. 18:8; 50:3; 97:3; Isa. 26:11; [Job 20:26; Dan. 7:10; Hab. 3:5]
10[p] Ps. 34:16; 1 Kgs. 13:34 [q] Ps. 37:28; 109:13; Job 18:16, 17, 19; Isa. 14:20
11[r] Ps. 2:1; 10:2
12[s] Ps. 18:40 [t] Ps. 7:12; 11:2
Psalm 22
1[u] Cited Matt. 27:46; Mark 15:34 [v] ver. 11 [w] Ps. 32:3; 38:8; Job 3:24; Isa. 59:11; [Heb. 5:7]
2[x] Ps. 88:1
3[y] Lev. 19:2 [z] [Ps. 80:1; 99:1] [a] [Ps. 9:11, 14; 65:1; 102:21; 147:12]
5[b] See Judg. 3:9 [c] Ps. 25:2; 31:1; 71:1; Isa. 49:23; Rom. 9:33
6[d] Job 25:6; Isa. 41:14

sacrifice, God raised him and granted him eternal life (Ps. 21:4; Rom. 4:23–25). As the risen victor over death, Christ earned authority to convey all the blessings he earned to his people whom he saves (Ps. 21:5–8; Acts 13:34). His "crown of fine gold" signifies his power to defeat all the enemies of his church (Ps. 21:3, 9–12; Rev. 14:14). Because Christ submitted himself to God's will through his sufficient sacrifice, God enforces his authority to bring all of his enemies into submission (Ps. 21:7; Heb. 10:12–13).

Christ was then exalted to the right hand of his Father, and the "joy of [his] presence" was restored (Ps. 21:6; Heb. 1:3). The joy of that reconciliation and the "power" of that co-regency explain the believer's eternal song of "praise" (Ps. 21:13; Rev. 5:9–14). David trains believers to pray for more than just everyday nuisances. We must also pray "your kingdom come, your will be done" (Matt. 6:10), and this psalm assures us that these things will happen.

Psalm 22 While Jesus quoted only the first verse of this psalm (Matt. 27:46), he adopted all of David's words as his own. This is seen by the Gospels' identification

[e] Ps. 69:19; 109:25 [f] Isa. 49:7; 53:3 **7**[g] See Matt. 27:39-43; Mark 15:29-32; Luke 23:35, 36 [h] Ps. 109:25; [Ps. 44:14; 2 Kgs. 19:21; Isa. 37:22; Lam. 2:15] **8**[i] [Ps. 37:5; Prov. 16:3] [j] Ps. 91:14 [k] Ps. 18:19; Matt. 3:17; Mark 1:11; Luke 3:22 **9**[l] Ps. 71:6 **10**[m] Isa. 46:3; 49:1; Gal. 1:15 **11**[n] See ver. 1; Ps. 10:1 [o] Ps. 107:12; 2 Kgs. 14:26; Isa. 63:5 **12**[p] [Ps. 68:30 (Heb.)] [q] Amos 4:1 **13**[r] Ps. 35:21; Job 16:10; Lam. 2:16; 3:46 **14**[s] [Lam. 2:11] [t] [Dan. 5:6]

my [u]heart is like [v]wax;
it is melted within my breast;
15 my strength is [w]dried up like a potsherd,
and my [x]tongue sticks to my jaws;
you lay me in the dust of death.

16 For [y]dogs encompass me;
a company of evildoers [z]encircles me;
they have [a]pierced my hands and feet[1]—
17 I can count all my bones—
they [b]stare and gloat over me;
18 [c]they divide my garments among them,
and for my clothing they cast lots.

19 But you, O LORD, [n]do not be far off!
O you my help, [d]come quickly to my aid!
20 Deliver my soul from the sword,
my precious life from the power of [e]the dog!
21 Save me from [f]the mouth of the lion!
You have rescued[2] me from the horns of [g]the wild oxen!

22 [h]I will tell of your name to my [i]brothers;
in the midst of the congregation I will praise you:
23 You who [j]fear the LORD, praise him!
All you offspring of Jacob, [k]glorify him,
and stand in awe of him, all you offspring of Israel!
24 For he has not despised or abhorred
the affliction of [l]the afflicted,
and he has not [m]hidden his face from him,
but has heard, when he [n]cried to him.

25 From you comes my praise in the great [o]congregation;
my [p]vows I will [q]perform before those who fear him.
26 [r]The afflicted[3] shall [s]eat and be satisfied;
those who seek him shall praise the LORD!
May your hearts [t]live forever!

27 All [u]the ends of the earth shall remember
and turn to the LORD,
and all [v]the families of the nations
shall worship before you.
28 For [w]kingship belongs to the LORD,
and he rules over the nations.

29 All [x]the prosperous of the earth eat and worship;
before him shall [y]bow all who go down to the dust,
even the one who could not [z]keep himself alive.
30 Posterity shall serve him;
it shall be told of the Lord to the coming [a]generation;
31 they shall [b]come and proclaim his righteousness to a people yet [c]unborn,
that he has done it.

[1] Some Hebrew manuscripts, Septuagint, Vulgate, Syriac; most Hebrew manuscripts *like a lion* [they are at] *my hands and feet* [2] Hebrew *answered* [3] Or *The meek*

as prophetic the incidental detail that Jesus' garments were divided (Ps. 22:18; cf. Matt. 27:35).

The psalmist also describes the faithful attributes of God that have been universal principles for believers throughout history. For instance, he gives "justice to his elect, who cry to him day and night" (Luke 18:7; cf. Ps. 22:2, 24, 31). His holiness provokes his people to praise because he is trustworthy and preserves them from "shame" (vv. 3–5, 23–26; Rom. 5:5). He remains faithful to covenant children all the days of their lives (Ps. 22:10–12, 30; 1 Tim. 3:14–16). And he saves his elect from "every nation, from all tribes and peoples and languages" (Rev. 7:9; cf. Ps. 22:27–29; Mark 13:27).

It is the suffering of Christ that has secured these patterns of faithfulness for the unfaithful. Jesus did this by carrying out God's eternal plan to provide "righteousness" through his own sacrificial death (Ps. 22:31; Rev. 13:8). His cry of forsakenness from the cross was the announcement that he had become a "curse" for his people, which "redeemed us from the curse of the law" and fulfilled the Abrahamic promise to bring salvation to the nations (Gal. 3:13–14; cf. Ps. 22:1). Those who put their faith in Christ can therefore be assured that they will never be cursed.

14[u] [Job 23:16; Nah. 2:10]; See Josh. 2:11 [v] See Ps. 68:2
15[w] Prov. 17:22 [x] [John 19:28; See Job 29:10]
16[y] [Phil. 3:2; Rev. 22:15] [z] Ps. 88:17 [a] Matt. 27:35; Mark 15:24; Luke 23:33; 24:40; John 19:23, 37; 20:25; [Zech. 12:10]
17[b] Luke 23:35
18[c] Cited John 19:24; [Matt. 27:35; Luke 23:34]
19[n] [See ver. 11 above] [d] Ps. 38:22
20[e] [Phil. 3:2; Rev. 22:15]
21[f] 2 Tim. 4:17 [g] See Num. 23:22
22[h] Cited Heb. 2:12; [Ps. 102:21; John 17:6] [i] Matt. 28:10; John 20:17; Rom. 8:29
23[j] Ps. 135:20 [k] Ps. 50:15, 23
24[l] [Isa. 53:4, 7] [m] Ps. 10:1; 13:1; See Job 13:24 [n] Heb. 5:7
25[o] Ps. 35:18; 40:9, 10; 111:1 [p] Lev. 7:16 [q] Ps. 66:13; Jonah 2:9; See Ps. 50:14
26[r] Ps. 69:32 [s] Isa. 25:6; 65:13 [t] John 6:51 **27**[u] Ps. 2:8; 67:7 [v] Ps. 96:7 **28**[w] Obad. 21; [Ps. 47:8; Zech. 14:9] **29**[x] [Ps. 45:12] [y] Ps. 72:9; [Phil. 2:10] [z] Ezek. 18:27 **30**[a] Ps. 48:13; 71:18 **31**[b] Ps. 86:9; [Isa. 60:3] [c] Ps. 78:6; 102:18

The Lord Is My Shepherd

23 A Psalm of David.
The Lord is my [d]shepherd; I shall
not [e]want.
2 He makes me lie down in green [f]pastures.
He leads me beside still waters.[1]
3 He [g]restores my soul.
He [h]leads me in [i]paths of righteousness[2]
for his [j]name's sake.

4 Even though I [k]walk through the valley
of [l]the shadow of death,[3]
I will [m]fear no evil,
for [n]you are with me;
your [o]rod and your staff,
they comfort me.

5 You [p]prepare a table before me
in [q]the presence of my enemies;
you [r]anoint my head with oil;
my [s]cup overflows.
6 Surely[4] goodness and mercy[5] shall follow me
all the days of my life,
and I shall [t]dwell[6] in the house of the
Lord
[u]forever.[7]

The King of Glory

24 A Psalm of David.
[v]The earth is the Lord's and the
fullness thereof,[8]
the world and those who dwell
therein,
2 for he has [w]founded it upon [x]the seas
and established it upon the rivers.

3 [y]Who shall ascend the hill of the Lord?
And who shall stand in his [z]holy
place?
4 [a]He who has [b]clean hands and [c]a pure
heart,
who does not [d]lift up his soul to [e]what
is false
and does not swear deceitfully.
5 He will receive [f]blessing from the Lord
and [g]righteousness from [h]the God of
his salvation.
6 Such is [i]the generation of those who
seek him,
who [j]seek the face of the God of
Jacob.[9] *Selah*

7 [k]Lift up your heads, O gates!
And be lifted up, O ancient doors,
that [l]the King of glory may come in.

[1] Hebrew *beside waters of rest* [2] Or *in right paths* [3] Or *the valley of deep darkness* [4] Or *Only* [5] Or *steadfast love* [6] Or *shall return to dwell* [7] Hebrew *for length of days* [8] Or *and all that fills it* [9] Septuagint, Syriac, and two Hebrew manuscripts; Masoretic Text *Jacob, who seek your face*

Psalm 23
1 [d]Ps. 78:52; 80:1; Isa. 40:11; Jer. 31:10; Ezek. 34:11, 12, 23; John 10:11; Heb. 13:20; 1 Pet. 2:25; 5:4 [e]Ps. 34:9, 10; [Matt. 6:33]
2 [f]Ezek. 34:14; John 10:9
3 [g]Ps. 19:7 [h]Ps. 5:8; 31:3; 139:10, 24; 143:10; Isa. 40:11; 49:10 [i]Prov. 4:11; 8:20 [j]Ps. 25:11; 31:3; 79:9; 109:21; Ezek. 20:9, 14
4 [k]Ps. 138:7 [l]See Job 3:5 [m]Ps. 3:6; 27:1, 3; 118:6 [n]Ex. 3:12; Isa. 43:2 [o]Mic. 7:14
5 [p]Ps. 78:19; [Prov. 9:2; John 6:51]; See 2 Sam. 17:27-29 [q][Ps. 31:19] [r]Ps. 45:7; 133:2; Luke 7:46; [Ps. 92:10] [s]Ps. 16:5
6 [t]Ps. 27:4 [u]Ps. 21:4

Psalm 24
1 [v]Ps. 50:12; 89:11; Ex. 9:29; 19:5; Deut. 10:14; Job 41:11; Cited 1 Cor. 10:26
2 [w]Ps. 104:5; Job 38:6; Prov. 8:29 [x]Ps. 136:6; Gen. 1:9
3 [y]For ver. 3-5, see Ps. 15:1-5 [z]Ps. 2:6
4 [a][Deut. 10:12; Isa. 33:15, 16; Mic. 6:8] [b]See Job 22:30 [c]Ps. 73:1; Matt. 5:8 [d][Ezek. 18:6] [e]Ps. 31:6; 119:37
5 [f][Gen. 22:17, 18] [g]Isa. 46:13; 56:1 [h]Ps. 27:9; 38:22; 51:14; 88:1
6 [i]Ps. 14:5 [j]Ps. 27:8; 105:4
7 [k][Ps. 118:19, 20; Isa. 26:2] [l][1 Cor. 2:8]

Psalm 23 Just as a shepherd provides food, water, and respite to his flocks, God fills the creaturely needs of his children (vv. 1–3; Matt. 6:25–34). As a shepherd leads his sheep down carefully chosen paths, God providentially guides his children (Ps. 23:3; John 16:13). As a shepherd guards his sheep from danger, God protects his children from "evil" and eternal "death" (Ps. 23:4; Luke 1:79).

However, God also does something that no ordinary shepherd can do: he shares a fellowship meal with his sheep (Ps. 23:5; Lev. 7:15–18; 1 Cor. 5:7–8). In the presence of enemies, these table guests are honored by anointing and overwhelmed by extravagance (Ps. 23:5; Eph. 2:7). They receive the "goodness and mercy" which form the core of God's character (Ps. 23:6; Ex. 34:6–7). As the compassionate character of God is revealed in this precious psalm, we are prepared to see how the steadfast love of the final sacrificial Lamb enables wayward sheep to dwell with a holy God (Isa. 53:6). He was the scapegoat who carried away the sins of God's people to provide goodness and mercy (Ps. 23:6; Ex. 34:6; Lev. 16:22).

But this Lamb who laid down his life is also the Good Shepherd (John 10:1–18). Recognizing his sheep's voice, Christ meets our needs, leads us in the way, and protects us from disaster (John 10:5, 10). Listening to the Chief Shepherd's voice, the believer's soul is restored. And we will "dwell in the house of the Lord forever" (Ps. 23:6; cf. 1 Pet. 5:4; Rev. 22:4).

Psalm 24 The greatness of God humbles the human being who lives in his presence, but the Creator's ownership of the earth assures the believer that all its resources are gifts from a gracious sovereign (v. 1; cf. 1 Cor. 10:26). Kind welcome into the presence of God is not universal, however. The Lord demands a sincere heart and is not pleased with perfunctory, arid worship (Ps. 15:1–5; Isa. 1:11–17).

Who then can enter God's sanctuary with "clean hands," innocent of misdeeds, or with a "pure heart," guiltless of impure motives (Ps. 24:3–4; Matt. 5:8)? Only the one

8 Who is this King of glory?
The LORD, strong and mighty,
the LORD, [m]mighty in battle!
9 Lift up your heads, O gates!
And lift them up, O ancient doors,
that the King of glory may come in.
10 Who is this King of glory?
[n]The LORD of hosts,
he is the King of glory! *Selah*

Teach Me Your Paths

25[1] OF DAVID.
To you, O LORD, I [o]lift up my soul.
2 O my God, in you I [p]trust;
[q]let me not be put to shame;
[r]let not my enemies exult over me.
3 Indeed, [s]none who wait for you shall be put to shame;
they shall be ashamed who are [t]wantonly [u]treacherous.

4 [v]Make me to know your ways, O LORD;
teach me your paths.
5 Lead me in your [w]truth and teach me,
for you are the God of my salvation;
for you I wait all the day long.

6 Remember your [x]mercy, O LORD, and your steadfast love,
[y]for they have been from of old.
7 Remember not [z]the sins of my youth or my transgressions;
according to your [a]steadfast love remember me,
for the sake of your goodness, O LORD!

8 [b]Good and upright is the LORD;
therefore he [c]instructs sinners in the way.
9 He leads the humble in what is right,
and teaches the humble his way.
10 All the paths of the LORD are [d]steadfast love and faithfulness,
for those who keep his covenant and his testimonies.

11 For your [e]name's sake, O LORD,
pardon my guilt, for it is [f]great.
12 Who is the man who fears the LORD?
Him [c]will he instruct in the way that he should choose.
13 His soul shall [g]abide in well-being,
and his [h]offspring [i]shall inherit the land.

[1] This psalm is an acrostic poem, each verse beginning with the successive letters of the Hebrew alphabet

who receives such "righteousness" as a gift from the God of "salvation" (Ps. 24:5, 6; Rom. 1:17; 1 Tim. 1:1). Only those who know such grace actually "seek the things that are above" (Col. 3:1). They seek the God who made even "Jacob," the cheat, a true worshiper when he called upon the Lord for mercy (Gen. 35:15).

David may have reflected on this grace as he led the ark into the sanctuary (2 Samuel 6). Through this visual event, his faith would have been launched to heaven, where he could see the day when his Greater Son, who brought the face of God to earth, would be welcomed back to heaven upon his ascension, after securing his people's salvation (Luke 24:51; Heb. 9:24). The one united to Christ by faith has then been brought into the throne room of God's grace and may therefore enter boldly by prayer (Heb. 4:16).

Psalm 25 Salvation has many facets not only because grace is so beautiful but also because there are so many dangers in the world. In the biblical world, to be put to shame often meant being humiliatingly exposed for trusting in the wrong deity. On occasion an idol could appear to bring rain or provide a crop. But David boasts that "none who wait" for the Lord will ever be put to shame (vv. 1–3, 19–22).

Obviously, the child of God needs protection from enemies, because their mockery is cruel and their treachery is unpredictable (vv. 1–3, 19). Emotional dangers also warrant God's help (vv. 16–17). But God's people also need refuge from the less obvious enemies of their own sinful and dishonest hearts (v. 21). That relief can be supplied only by a gracious God who forgives sins (vv. 16, 18). Forgiveness is not conditioned on dutiful service or sacrifices (Heb. 7:27); it is based entirely on God's own "steadfast love" (Ps. 25:6–7).

This love ultimately came to expression in Christ, who was broken because sinners broke the covenant (Matt. 26:26). The main distinction David sees between the believer and the unbeliever is instruction, another facet of salvation (Ps. 25:5; John 14:26). God's children prosper as they pursue a long obedience to God's truth (Ps. 25:4–5, 8–10; John 3:36).

8 [m] [Ex. 15:3]
10 [n] Mal. 1:14
Psalm 25
1 [o] Ps. 86:4; 143:8; Lam. 3:41; [Ps. 24:4]
2 [p] See Ps. 11:1 [q] ver. 20; Ps. 31:1, 17; 71:1 [r] [Ps. 13:4]
3 [s] Isa. 49:23; [Rom. 5:5; Phil. 1:20] [t] [Ps. 59:3, 4] [u] [Jer. 3:20]
4 [v] Ps. 27:11; 86:11; 143:8, 10; Ex. 33:13; [Ps. 5:8; 119:35]
5 [w] Ps. 26:3; 86:11
6 [x] Ps. 51:1; [Ps. 103:17; Isa. 63:15] [y] [Gen. 8:1; 9:15; 19:29]
7 [z] Job 13:26; 20:11; Jer. 3:25 [a] Ps. 51:1
8 [b] Ps. 100:5 [c] Ps. 32:8
10 [d] [John 1:17]
11 [e] See Ps. 23:3 [f] [Rom. 5:20]
12 [c] [See ver. 8 above]
13 [g] [Prov. 1:33; 19:23] [h] Ps. 112:2 [i] See Ps. 37:9

14 [j]The friendship[1] of the LORD is for those who fear him,
and he makes known to them his covenant.
15 My [k]eyes are ever toward the LORD,
for he will [l]pluck my feet out of the net.

16 [m]Turn to me and be gracious to me,
for I am lonely and afflicted.
17 The troubles of my heart are enlarged;
bring me out of my distresses.
18 [n]Consider my affliction and my trouble,
and forgive all my sins.

19 Consider how many are my foes,
and with what violent hatred they hate me.
20 Oh, guard my soul, and deliver me!
[o]Let me not be put to shame, for I take refuge in you.
21 May integrity and uprightness preserve me,
for I wait for you.

22 [p]Redeem Israel, O God,
out of all his troubles.

I Will Bless the LORD

26

OF DAVID.

1 [q]Vindicate me, O LORD,
for I have [r]walked in my integrity,
and I have [s]trusted in the LORD without wavering.
2 [t]Prove me, O LORD, and try me;
test my heart and [u]my mind.[2]
3 For your [v]steadfast love is before my eyes,
and I [w]walk in your [v]faithfulness.

4 I do not [x]sit with men of [y]falsehood,
nor do I consort with hypocrites.
5 I [z]hate the assembly of evildoers,
and I will not sit with the wicked.

6 I [a]wash my hands in innocence
and go around your altar, O LORD,
7 proclaiming thanksgiving aloud,
and telling all your [b]wondrous deeds.

8 O LORD, I [c]love the habitation of your house
and the place where your glory dwells.
9 [d]Do not sweep my soul away with sinners,
nor my life with bloodthirsty men,
10 in whose hands are evil devices,
and whose right hands are full of [e]bribes.

11 But as for me, I shall walk in my integrity;
redeem me, and be gracious to me.
12 My foot stands on [f]level ground;
in [g]the great assembly I will bless the LORD.

The LORD Is My Light and My Salvation

27

OF DAVID.

1 The LORD is my [h]light and my [i]salvation;
[j]whom shall I fear?
The LORD is the stronghold[3] of my life;
of whom shall I be afraid?

[1] Or *The secret counsel* [2] Hebrew *test my kidneys and my heart* [3] Or *refuge*

14[j] [Amos 3:7; See Job 29:4]
15[k] Ps. 123:1, 2; 141:8; [2 Chr. 20:12] [l] Ps. 31:4
16[m] Ps. 69:16; 86:16; 119:132
18[n] [Job 10:15]
20[o] See ver. 2
22[p] Ps. 34:22; 71:23; 130:8; Lam. 3:58; [2 Sam. 4:9]

Psalm 26
1[q] See Ps. 7:8 [r] ver. 11 [s] See Ps. 11:1
2[t] See Ps. 7:9; 17:3; 139:23 [u] Ps. 7:9
3[v] [Ps. 25:10] [w] 2 Kgs. 20:3; [Ps. 86:11]
4[x] See Ps. 1:1 [y] Job 11:11
5[z] Ps. 31:6; 139:21, 22
6[a] Ps. 73:13; [Ex. 30:19, 20; Deut. 21:6]
7[b] See Ps. 9:1
8[c] [Ps. 27:4]
9[d] [Ps. 28:3]
10[e] Ex. 23:8; Deut. 16:19
12[f] See Ps. 27:11 [g] Ps. 22:25

Psalm 27
1[h] Isa. 60:20; Mic. 7:8; [Ps. 84:11] [i] Ps. 118:14; Ex. 15:2; Isa. 12:2; 62:11 [j] See Ps. 23:4

Psalm 26 To be in God's presence as a worshiper is to see the glory of his love, and to see his love is to be motivated to faithfulness (v. 3; Ex. 33:18–19; 34:6–7). Motivation is one thing, however, but ability is another. So David pleads to be vindicated or distinguished from "hypocrites" and "evildoers" (Ps. 26:1, 4–5). Far from boasting, David's pronouncements are implicit prayers for help in his pursuit of holiness. Recognition of God's threat of judgment against the unholy should be enough to keep anyone from boasting (vv. 9–10).

With the Lord's "steadfast love" before his eyes of faith, David sees God to be a gracious redeemer (vv. 3, 11), which emboldens him to ask for vindication (v. 1). With God's grace as his focal point, he has pursued a publicly worshipful life of gratitude (v. 7). The result has been "integrity" in his dealings (v. 1), moral separation in his social life (vv. 4–5), and humble passion in his worship (vv. 6–8, 12). Yet this determination to walk uprightly is not a moralistic, self-generated effort (v. 11a); David knows he needs redemption and grace (v. 11b). Because of this grace, whatever happens, David stands on level ground (v. 12). The ultimate way in which God secured this redemption and grace was in the sending of his own Son, to whom God was *not* gracious, so that grace could be extended to sinners such as David—and us.

Psalm 27 Already we have learned in the Psalms that friendship with the Lord is everything anyone needs (cf. 25:14). While God is everywhere present, only believers experience the *blessings* of his presence. Topping those benefits are "light" and

2 When evildoers assail me
to [k]eat up my flesh,
my adversaries and foes,
it is they who stumble and fall.

3 [l]Though an army encamp against me,
my heart shall not fear;
though war arise against me,
yet[1] I will be confident.

4 [m]One thing have I asked of the LORD,
that will I seek after:
that I may [n]dwell in the house of the LORD
all the days of my life,
to gaze upon [o]the beauty of the LORD
and to inquire[2] in his temple.

5 For he will [p]hide me in his shelter
in the day of trouble;
he will conceal me under the cover of his tent;
he will [q]lift me high upon a rock.

6 And now my [r]head shall be lifted up
above my enemies all around me,
and I will offer in his tent
sacrifices with shouts of [s]joy;
[t]I will sing and make melody to the LORD.

7 [u]Hear, O LORD, when I cry aloud;
be gracious to me and answer me!
8 You have said, [v]"Seek[3] my face."
My heart says to you,
"Your face, LORD, do I seek."[4]
9 [w]Hide not your face from me.
Turn not your servant away in anger,
O you who have been my help.
Cast me not off; forsake me not,
[x]O God of my salvation!
10 For [y]my father and my mother have forsaken me,
but the LORD will [z]take me in.

11 [a]Teach me your way, O LORD,
and lead me on [b]a level path
because of my enemies.
12 [c]Give me not up to the will of my adversaries;
for [d]false witnesses have risen against me,
and they [e]breathe out violence.

13 I believe[5] that I shall look upon [f]the goodness of the LORD
in [g]the land of the living!
14 [h]Wait for the LORD;
[i]be strong, and let your heart take courage;
wait for the LORD!

The LORD Is My Strength and My Shield

28

OF DAVID.

To you, O LORD, I call;
[j]my rock, be not deaf to me,
lest, if you [k]be silent to me,
I become like those who [l]go down to the pit.
2 [m]Hear the voice of my pleas for mercy,
when I cry to you for help,

[1] Or *in this* [2] Or *meditate* [3] The command (*seek*) is addressed to more than one person [4] The meaning of the Hebrew verse is uncertain [5] Other Hebrew manuscripts *Oh! Had I not believed*

"salvation" (27:1). To have light in the impenetrable darkness of the ancient Near East was salvation, because it exposed one's enemies and one's resources. God also saves his people from spiritual dangers lurking in the dark by exposing them in the light and provision of his Word (vv. 1–2, 11; 2 Cor. 10:4–6).

To be in the friendly presence of God is a privilege afforded only to the holy (Ps. 27:4–9). Bad things—even death—can happen when people defile God's consecrated space (Lev. 10:1–3; Joshua 7–8; Acts 5:1–11; 1 Cor. 11:17–34). God is good, and the goodness of his grace overwhelms fear to the point of making us joyful worshipers in this evil world (Ps. 27:6, 13). God's beautiful presence comforts the abandoned (v. 10), vindicates the falsely accused (v. 12), and makes brave the cowardly (v. 14). In fact, waiting on the realization of God's presence is always the formula for courage in Scripture (e.g., Josh. 1:5–9). God's people waited until his presence became flesh in Jesus Christ. No one could find fault in Christ's perfection (Matt. 26:59). So, joined to him, believers now serve through their words and work as holy priests before the presence of God (1 Pet. 2:9; Heb. 10:19–25).

Psalm 28 When one is convinced that he is God's heir, he can speak to God as boldly as David did: Answer, or I will "go down to the pit" is one sure way to win an answer from a Father who cannot fail his "heritage" and a Shepherd who cannot abandon his sheep (vv. 1, 9; Deut. 32:9). David prays toward the "most holy sanctuary" (Ps. 28:2). An outpost of heaven, the sanctuary was the temple, the successor to the first holy

2[k] Ps. 14:4
3[l] Ps. 3:6
4[m] [Ps. 26:8; 84:1, 2] [n] Ps. 23:6; 65:4; [Luke 2:37] [o] Ps. 90:17
5[p] Ps. 31:20; [Ps. 91:1; Job 5:21; Isa. 4:6] [q] Ps. 40:2
6[r] Ps. 3:3 [s] [Num. 10:10] [t] Eph. 5:19; Col. 3:16
7[u] Ps. 30:10
8[v] Ps. 24:6; 105:4
9[w] Ps. 69:17; 102:2; 143:7 [x] See Ps. 24:5
10[y] [Isa. 49:15; 63:16] [z] [Isa. 40:11]
11[a] See Ps. 25:4 [b] [Ps. 5:8]
12[c] Ps. 41:2 [d] Ps. 35:11; [1 Kgs. 21:13; Matt. 26:59, 60; Mark 14:55, 56] [e] Acts 9:1
13[f] Ex. 33:19 [g] Ps. 52:5; 116:9; 142:5; Job 28:13
14[h] Ps. 37:34; 62:5; Prov. 20:22 [i] Ps. 31:24; Deut. 31:7; Josh. 1:6, 9, 18

Psalm 28
1[j] See Ps. 18:2 [k] Ps. 35:22; 39:12; 83:1; 109:1 [l] Ps. 88:4; 143:7
2[m] Ps. 140:6

when I [n]lift up my hands
[o]toward your most holy sanctuary.[1]
3 Do not [p]drag me off with the wicked,
with the workers of evil,
[q]who speak peace with their neighbors
while evil is in their hearts.
4 [r]Give to them according to their work
and according to the evil of their deeds;
give to them according to the work of their hands;
[s]render them their due reward.
5 Because they [t]do not regard the works of the LORD
or the work of his hands,
he will tear them down and build them up no more.

6 Blessed be the LORD!
For he has [u]heard the voice of my pleas for mercy.
7 The LORD is my strength and [v]my shield;
in him my heart [w]trusts, and I am helped;
my heart exults,
and with my [x]song I give thanks to him.
8 The LORD is the strength of his people;[2]
he is [y]the saving refuge of his anointed.
9 Oh, save your people and bless [z]your heritage!
[a]Be their shepherd and [b]carry them forever.

Ascribe to the LORD Glory

29 A PSALM OF DAVID.
Ascribe to the LORD, O heavenly beings,[3]
[c]ascribe to the LORD glory and strength.
2 Ascribe to the LORD the glory due his name;
worship the LORD in [d]the splendor of holiness.[4]

3 The voice of the LORD is over [e]the waters;
the God of glory [f]thunders,
the LORD, over many waters.
4 The voice of the LORD is [g]powerful;
the voice of the LORD is full of majesty.

5 The voice of the LORD breaks the cedars;
the LORD breaks [h]the cedars of Lebanon.
6 He makes Lebanon to [i]skip like a calf,
and [j]Sirion like a young [k]wild ox.

[1] Hebrew *your innermost sanctuary* [2] Some Hebrew manuscripts, Septuagint, Syriac; most Hebrew manuscripts *is their strength* [3] Hebrew *sons of God*, or *sons of might* [4] Or *in holy attire*

2 [n] Ps. 134:2; 141:2; Lam. 2:19; 1 Tim. 2:8; [Ps. 119:48] [o] Ps. 5:7; 138:2; [1 Kgs. 8:29]
3 [p] [Ps. 26:9; Ezek. 32:20] [q] Jer. 9:8; [Ps. 5:9; 12:2; 55:21; 62:4]
4 [r] Jer. 50:15, 29; Rev. 18:6; [2 Tim. 4:14] [s] [Ps. 137:8]
5 [t] Isa. 5:12; [Job 34:27]
6 [u] ver. 2
7 [v] See Ps. 3:3 [w] See Ps. 11:1 [x] Ps. 69:30
8 [y] Ps. 140:7; [Ps. 20:6]
9 [z] Deut. 9:29; 32:9 [a] Ps. 78:71, 72 [b] Isa. 40:11; 46:3; 63:9

Psalm 29
1 [c] Ps. 96:7, 8; 1 Chr. 16:28, 29; [Ps. 68:34]
2 [d] Ps. 110:3; 1 Chr. 16:29; [Ex. 28:2]
3 [e] [Ps. 18:11] [f] Job 37:4, 5
4 [g] Ps. 68:33
5 [h] Ps. 104:16; Judg. 9:15
6 [i] Ps. 114:4, 6 [j] Deut. 3:9 [k] Num. 23:22

place, Eden, from which Adam and Eve had been driven. David now prays that the wicked will likewise be driven from the Holy Land (vv. 3–5; 2 Tim. 4:15; Acts 12:20–23). The sanctuary held out the promise of a renewed relationship with the Creator. Today the Holy Spirit makes the believer a new holy place (1 Cor. 6:19).

In the Old Testament, God was accessible only vicariously, through a priest—the office David represented when he lifted his hands on behalf of the people (Ps. 28:2); but the New Testament believer may gain audience with God at any time through prayer (Heb. 4:16). We have full access. For, as David foresaw, there would be ultimate refuge and salvation for his "anointed" line (Ps. 28:8; Luke 4:18). The nation he represented and the lineage he represented had assurance of God's covenant provision. As it did for David, our assurance of God's promises to save his people settles our hearts into quiet joy, even before the difficulties of our immediate situation are resolved (Ps. 28:6–7; 1 Pet. 1:8–9).

Psalm 29 The biblical formula for peace is glory plus strength. As David observes a storm moving inland from the Mediterranean, he imagines a Redeemer riding the winds like a warrior on a horse. Rather than cower from this awesome vision, David concludes that this warrior comes to bring peace. No true worshiper could read "glory" (vv. 1, 2, 3, 9) and not recall the Lord's revelation to Moses on Mount Sinai. Hiding his servant in the rock, God passed by, revealing his "glory" (Ex. 33:18–23). Surprisingly, his glory was expressed in that moment not merely as judgment on idolaters but as mercy toward sinners (Ex. 34:6–7). Thereafter, prophets and psalmists recognize that God's sovereignty over seen and unseen worlds (Ps. 29:1–10) is mainly to prove that he is sufficiently powerful to have compassion on whomever he will (cf. Ex. 33:19). "Glory" then becomes the watermark of God's redeeming love (Acts 7:2–4), describing loving kindness that can break stiff-necked rebels and forgiveness that can melt hearts of stone.

7 The voice of the LORD flashes forth
flames of fire.
8 The voice of the LORD shakes the wilderness;
the LORD shakes the wilderness of
[l]Kadesh.
9 The voice of the LORD makes [m]the deer
give birth[1]
and strips the forests bare,
and in his temple all cry, "Glory!"
10 The LORD sits enthroned over [n]the flood;
the LORD sits enthroned [o]as king forever.
11 May the LORD give [p]strength to his people!
May the LORD bless[2] his people with
[q]peace!

Joy Comes with the Morning

30

A PSALM OF DAVID. A SONG AT THE DEDICATION OF [r]THE TEMPLE.

1 I will [s]extol you, O LORD, for you have
drawn me up
and have not let my foes [t]rejoice over
me.
2 O LORD my God, I [u]cried to you for help,
and you have [v]healed me.
3 O LORD, you have brought up my soul
from [w]Sheol;
you restored me to life from among
those who [x]go down to the pit.[3]
4 Sing praises to the LORD, O you [y]his
saints,
and [z]give thanks to his holy name.[4]
5 [a]For his anger is but for a moment,
and [b]his favor is for a lifetime.[5]
[c]Weeping may tarry for the night,
but [d]joy comes with the morning.
6 As for me, I said in my [e]prosperity,
"I shall never be [f]moved."
7 By your favor, O LORD,
you made my [g]mountain stand
strong;
you [h]hid your face;
I was [i]dismayed.
8 To you, O LORD, I cry,
and [j]to the Lord I plead for mercy:
9 "What profit is there in my death,[6]
if I go down to the pit?[7]
Will [k]the dust praise you?
Will it tell of your faithfulness?
10 [l]Hear, O LORD, and be merciful to me!
O LORD, be my helper!"

[1] Revocalization yields *makes the oaks to shake* [2] Or *The LORD will give . . . The LORD will bless* [3] Or *to life, that I should not go down to the pit* [4] Hebrew *to the memorial of his holiness* (see Exodus 3:15) [5] Or *and in his favor is life* [6] Hebrew *in my blood* [7] Or *to corruption*

Finally, in Christ we have "seen his glory, glory as of the only Son from the Father, full of grace and truth" (John 1:14). His sovereign ability to bring "peace" within the seen world was proven when he calmed the storm on the Sea of Galilee (Mark 4:39). And the one risen from the dead has unique authority to command "peace" to his disciples surrounded by spiritual enemies (Ps. 29:11; John 20:26).

Psalm 30 Meditating on the future temple provokes David to recall its representation of God's presence. Immanuel protects (v. 1), heals (v. 2), restores (v. 3), shows mercy to (vv. 8–10), and produces joy for (vv. 11–12) his people. David pompously forgot these blessings, so God withdrew the awareness of his presence (v. 6). From the Lord, such dismay is a gift, confronting us with our own insufficiency (v. 7). Ironically, the weaker we feel, the stronger the Lord can make us (2 Cor. 12:10), like a house built on a rock (Matt. 7:26), or like a mountain (Ps. 30:7). Grace of such quality does not come cheaply; one must plead for it like a dying man pleads for life.

But this is not just any dying man; he is God's child, whose cry our Lord cannot ignore. In effect David says, "You'll miss me when I'm gone" (vv. 8–10). His repentance is furious, and his praise vigorous. God responds, and turns "mourning" over spiritual death into "dancing" because of eternal life (vv. 5, 11, 12)—a kind of resurrection (v. 3)! What kind of God transforms such an impudent sinner? One whose glory it is to overwhelm judgment with steadfast love, which lasts for thousands of generations (v. 5; Ex. 34:6–7). God's glory evoked from David's "glory" (Ps. 30:12) an exuberant song.

But there was to come still a greater glory, "glory as of the only Son from the Father" (John 1:14). God raised Christ from the dead, triumphantly conquering death. When God hid his face from him, Jesus cried, "Why have you forsaken me?" (Matt. 27:46). Heeding the Son's cry, God saved him from the pit and brought up his soul from Sheol (Ps. 30:3). Those who are united with Christ share in the same victory (Col 3:1).

8[l] Num. 13:26
9[m] [Job 39:1-3]
10[n] [Gen. 6:17] [o] Ps. 10:16
11[p] Ps. 68:35; [Isa. 40:29] [q] Phil. 4:7
Psalm 30
[r] 2 Sam. 5:11; 1 Chr. 22:1
1[s] Ps. 107:32 [t] Ps. 25:2; 35:19, 24; [Ps. 13:4]
2[u] Ps. 88:13 [v] See Ps. 6:2
3[w] See Ps. 16:10 [x] Ps. 28:1
4[y] Ps. 50:5 [z] Ps. 97:12; [1 Chr. 16:4]
5[a] [Ps. 103:9; Job 33:26; Isa. 26:20; 54:7, 8] [b] Ps. 63:3 [c] [2 Cor. 4:17, 18] [d] Ps. 126:5 (Heb.)
6[e] [Job 29:18; Prov. 1:32] [f] Ps. 10:6
7[g] [2 Sam. 5:9] [h] Ps. 104:29; [Deut. 31:17] [i] [2 Sam. 24:10]
8[j] Ps. 142:1
9[k] See Ps. 6:5
10[l] Ps. 27:7

11 You have turned for me my mourning
into [m]dancing;
you have loosed my sackcloth
and clothed me with gladness,
12 that my [n]glory may sing your praise and
not be silent.
O LORD my God, I will give thanks to
you forever!

Into Your Hand I Commit My Spirit

31

TO THE CHOIRMASTER. A PSALM OF DAVID.

[o]In you, O LORD, do I [p]take refuge;
[q]let me never be put to shame;
in your [r]righteousness deliver me!
2 Incline your ear to me;
rescue me speedily!
Be [s]a rock of [t]refuge for me,
a strong fortress to save me!

3 For you are my rock and my fortress;
and for your [u]name's sake you lead me
and guide me;
4 you [v]take me out of [w]the net they have
hidden for me,
for you are my [x]refuge.
5 [y]Into your hand I commit my spirit;
you have redeemed me, O LORD,
[z]faithful God.

6 I [a]hate[1] those who pay [b]regard to worthless [c]idols,
but I trust in the LORD.
7 I will rejoice and be glad in your steadfast love,
because you have seen my affliction;
you have [d]known the distress of my
soul,
8 and you have not [e]delivered me into the
hand of the enemy;
you have set my feet in [f]a broad place.

9 Be gracious to me, O LORD, for I am [g]in
distress;
[h]my eye is wasted from grief;
my soul and my body also.
10 For my life is spent with sorrow,
and my years with sighing;
my strength fails because of my iniquity,
and [i]my bones waste away.

11 Because of all my adversaries I have
become [j]a reproach,
especially to my [k]neighbors,
and an object of dread to my acquaintances;
those who see me in the street [l]flee
from me.
12 I have been [m]forgotten like one who is
dead;
I have become like [n]a broken vessel.
13 For I [o]hear the whispering of many—
terror on every side!—
[p]as they scheme together against me,
as they plot to take my life.

14 But I [q]trust in you, O LORD;
I say, "You are my God."
15 My [r]times are in your hand;
[s]rescue me from the hand of my enemies and from my persecutors!
16 [t]Make your face shine on your servant;
save me in your steadfast love!
17 O LORD, [u]let me not be put to shame,
for I call upon you;

[1] Masoretic Text; one Hebrew manuscript, Septuagint, Syriac, Jerome *You hate*

11[m] Ex. 15:20; 2 Sam. 6:14; Jer. 31:4, 13; [Ps. 149:3; 150:4; Lam. 5:15]
12[n] See Ps. 16:9
Psalm 31
1[o] For ver. 1-3, see Ps. 71:1-3 [p] See Ps. 11:1 [q] ver. 17 [r] Ps. 143:1
2[s] See Ps. 18:2 [t] [Ps. 91:2]
3[u] See Ps. 23:3
4[v] Ps. 25:15 [w] See Job 18:8 [x] Ps. 43:2
5[y] Cited Luke 23:46; [Acts 7:59] [z] Deut. 32:4
6[a] Ps. 26:5 [b] Jonah 2:8 [c] Deut. 32:21; Jer. 8:19; 14:22
7[d] See Ps. 1:6
8[e] [Deut. 32:30] [f] See Job 36:16
9[g] Ps. 66:14 [h] See Ps. 6:7
10[i] Ps. 6:2; 32:3; 38:3; 102:3
11[j] [Ps. 41:7, 8; Isa. 53:3] [k] See Job 19:13, 14 [l] [Matt. 26:56; Mark 14:50]
12[m] Ps. 88:5; Eccles. 9:5
[n] Isa. 30:14 **13**[o] Jer. 20:10 [p] [Matt. 27:1]; See 2 Sam. 17:1-4 **14**[q] ver. 1, 6 **15**[r] 1 Chr. 29:30; Job 24:1 [s] Ps. 7:1 **16**[t] See Ps. 4:6 **17**[u] ver. 1

Psalm 31 Faith in the goodness of God may sometimes seem counterintuitive, but God's "stored up" provision—ultimately seen in Christ's life, death, and resurrection—is all the proof we need of it (v. 19; Titus 3:4). The Lord's faithfulness and steadfast love convinced David of God's goodness even when his closest friends were plotting to kill him and the stress of it broke his health (Ps. 31:5, 7, 9–14, 16). His prayer also reflects meditation on God's grand scheme of redemption, a perspective that focuses more on God's reputation than one's own (vv. 1, 14–18). David had learned these lessons through past rescues, and he now understood more deeply that God refines faith through suffering (vv. 7–8, 21–22; 1 Pet. 1:6–7).

David also learned that no one is ever completely innocent; each one needs the same grace for his "iniquity" (Ps. 31:10). Without suffering personal anguish over betrayal or moral failure, it is impossible to grow in the Lord. Christ came to teach us this (John 12:27; Heb. 2:10–11). The more one acknowledges that his rescue has come only due to God's abundant grace, the more the believer will love the Lord and hate all that detracts from him (Ps. 31:6; 1 Pet. 1:8). He will remain confident that God will bring justice on the wicked (Ps. 31:6, 23; 1 Kings 16:13; 2 Thess. 1:6). And he will "be strong" in his conviction that God is present regardless of who abandons him (Ps. 31:20, 24; Josh. 10:25).

let the wicked be put to shame;
let them go [v]silently to Sheol.
18 Let the lying lips be mute,
which [w]speak [x]insolently against the righteous
in pride and contempt.

19 Oh, how abundant is your goodness,
which you have stored up for those who fear you
and worked for those who take refuge in you,
[y]in the sight of the children of mankind!
20 In [z]the cover of your presence you hide them
from the plots of men;
you [a]store them in your shelter
from the strife of tongues.

21 Blessed be the LORD,
for he has wondrously [b]shown his steadfast love to me
when I was in [c]a besieged city.
22 I had said in my [d]alarm,[1]
"I am [e]cut off from [f]your sight."
But you heard the voice of my pleas for mercy
when I cried to you for help.

23 Love the LORD, all you his [g]saints!
The LORD preserves the faithful
but abundantly [h]repays the one who acts in pride.
24 [i]Be strong, and let your heart take courage,
all you who wait for the LORD!

Blessed Are the Forgiven

32 A MASKIL[2] OF DAVID.
[j]Blessed is the one whose
[k]transgression is forgiven,
whose sin is covered.
2 Blessed is the man against whom the LORD [l]counts no iniquity,
and in whose spirit [m]there is no deceit.

3 For when I kept silent, my [n]bones wasted away
through my [o]groaning all day long.
4 For day and night your [p]hand was heavy upon me;
my strength was dried up[3] as by the heat of summer. *Selah*

5 I [q]acknowledged my sin to you,
and I did not cover my iniquity;
I said, "I [r]will confess my transgressions to the LORD,"
and you forgave the iniquity of my sin. *Selah*

6 Therefore let everyone who is [s]godly
offer prayer to you at a time when you [t]may be found;
surely in the rush of [u]great waters,
they shall not reach him.

[1] Or *in my haste* [2] Probably a musical or liturgical term [3] Hebrew *my vitality was changed*

Psalm 32 David explains two important concepts in this psalm: joy and righteousness (v. 11). Both are created by one divine action—forgiveness (v. 5). "Righteous" or "upright" (v. 11) cannot possibly describe those who have merited the title by their sinless perfection. Rather, the upright are made so by God's forgiveness of their sins. It has always been this way (Rom. 4:1–8). This is the gospel preached even to Abraham (Gal. 3:8). Understandably, the justified are happy or "blessed" (Ps. 32:1). Before forgiveness, they are rebels against God's will ("transgression"; v. 1), wrongdoers ("sin"; v. 1), evil men ("iniquity"; v. 2), and liars ("deceit"; v. 2). As long as we deny the truth of who we are in our heart of hearts ("spirit"; v. 2), a guilty conscience will eventually take its toll on our body (vv. 3–4). But if we confess our sin to the Lord, we will find God's grace to be perfectly matched to our need. After all, it is the Lord's glory and delight to forgive "iniquity and transgression and sin" (see Ex. 34:6–7).

Reflecting on the power of God's grace to cover every blemish and failure due to the depth of sin, David is confident that God can also provide refuge from any earthly "trouble" (Ps. 32:6–7). Furthermore, his memory of God's deliverances provides a platform for encouraging his fellow worshipers to find joy and righteousness in God's forgiveness (vv. 8–9). Contrary to the wicked, who have many sorrows, the Lord "surrounds" those who trust in him with "steadfast love" (v. 10). This refuge is ultimately provided only in Jesus Christ—the man who bore our transgression, sin, iniquity, and deceit—so that we can be freely forgiven.

17[v] 1 Sam. 2:9; [Ps. 94:17; 115:17]
18[w] [Jude 15] [x] Ps. 17:10
19[y] Ps. 23:5
20[z] See Ps. 32:7 [a] See Ps. 27:5
21[b] Ps. 17:7 [c] [1 Sam. 23:7]
22[d] Ps. 116:11; [2 Sam. 15:14] [e] Isa. 38:11, 12; Lam. 3:54 [f] Jonah 2:4
23[g] Ps. 30:4 [h] Deut. 32:41
24[i] See Ps. 27:14
Psalm 32
1[j] Cited Rom. 4:7, 8; [Ps. 85:2] [k] [Ex. 34:7; John 1:29]
2[l] [2 Cor. 5:19] [m] John 1:47
3[n] See Ps. 31:10 [o] See Ps. 22:1
4[p] 1 Sam. 5:6, 11; [Ps. 38:2]
5[q] Ps. 51:3 [r] Ps. 38:18; Job 33:27; Prov. 28:13; [Luke 15:18, 21; 1 John 1:9]
6[s] Ps. 30:4 [t] See Ps. 69:13 [u] [Ps. 18:4, 16; 42:7; 69:1; 144:7]; See Job 22:11

7 You are a [v]hiding place for me;
you preserve me from [w]trouble;
you surround me with [x]shouts of
deliverance. *Selah*

8 I will [y]instruct you and teach you in the
way you should go;
I will [z]counsel you with my eye upon
you.
9 [a]Be not like a horse or a mule, without
understanding,
which must be curbed with [b]bit and
bridle,
or it will not stay near you.

10 [c]Many are the sorrows of the wicked,
but steadfast love surrounds the one
who [d]trusts in the LORD.
11 [e]Be glad in the LORD, and rejoice, O righteous,
and [f]shout for joy, all you [g]upright in
heart!

The Steadfast Love of the LORD

33 [h]Shout for joy in the LORD, O you
righteous!
[i]Praise befits the upright.
2 Give thanks to the LORD with the [j]lyre;
make melody to him with [j]the harp of
[k]ten strings!
3 Sing to him [l]a new song;
play skillfully on the strings, with
loud shouts.

4 For the word of the LORD is upright,
and all his work is done in [m]faithful-
ness.
5 He [n]loves righteousness and justice;
[o]the earth is full of the steadfast love of
the LORD.

6 By [p]the word of the LORD the heavens
were made,
and by [q]the breath of his mouth all
[r]their host.
7 He gathers the waters of the sea as [s]a
heap;
he [t]puts the deeps in storehouses.

8 Let all the earth fear the LORD;
let all the inhabitants of the world
stand in awe of him!
9 For [u]he spoke, and it came to be;
he commanded, and it stood firm.

10 The LORD [v]brings the counsel of the
nations to nothing;
he frustrates the plans of the peoples.
11 [w]The counsel of the LORD stands forever,
the plans of his heart to all generations.
12 [x]Blessed is the nation whose God is the
LORD,
the people whom he has [y]chosen as
his heritage!

13 The LORD [z]looks down from heaven;
he sees all the children of man;
14 from [a]where he sits enthroned he [b]looks
out
on all the inhabitants of the earth,
15 he who fashions the hearts of them all
and observes all their deeds.

7[v] Ps. 91:1; 119:114; [Ps. 27:5; 31:20] [w] Ps. 9:9 [x] [Ps. 18, title]; See Ex. 15:1-18; Judg. 5:1-31
8[y] Ps. 25:8, 12 [z] Ps. 73:24
9[a] Prov. 26:3; [Job 35:11] [b] James 3:3
10[c] [Prov. 13:21; Rom. 2:9] [d] Ps. 34:8; 84:12; Prov. 16:20; Jer. 17:7
11[e] Ps. 64:10; 68:3; 97:12; [Ps. 33:1] [f] Deut. 32:43 [g] See Ps. 7:10

Psalm 33
1[h] [Ps. 32:11] [i] Ps. 147:1
2[j] Ps. 71:22 [k] Ps. 144:9
3[l] Ps. 40:3; 96:1; Isa. 42:10
4[m] Ps. 119:75
5[n] Ps. 11:7; 36:5, 6; 45:7; 89:14 [o] Ps. 119:64
6[p] Gen. 1:6, 7; Heb. 11:3; 2 Pet. 3:5; [John 1:3] [q] [Job 26:13; Isa. 11:4] [r] Gen. 2:1
7[s] Ps. 78:13; Ex. 15:8; Josh. 3:13, 16 [t] See Job 38:8
9[u] Ps. 148:5, 6; Gen. 1:3; [Ps. 147:15, 18]

Psalm 33 There are six commands to worship in this psalm (vv. 1–3). By piling up imperatives, the psalmist tells the believers they must always praise God for salvation, because God is always redeeming (v. 5). It is a law woven into the fabric of history that God alone saves; all other trusts he "frustrates" and brings to naught (vv. 10–19).

Specific commands in verses 1–3 also teach that God's grace is worthy of our skill, freshness, and fervor. Playing "skillfully" implies mastery and excellence (v. 3). A "new song" calls experienced worshipers to renew their praise for the Savior (v. 3; cf. Eph. 5:19; Rev. 14:3). And shouting connotes fervent preparation of mind and body to engage in worship energetically. Inspiration for such vigor in worship is not peripheral to the biblical vision of Christian worship. Because of who God is, supremely in the incarnate Christ who was given for us and for our salvation, he deserves our all (cf. Rom. 12:1–2).

Furthermore, God's work on behalf of his children is "upright" (Ps. 33:4). God's eyes are always on those who trust him, to ensure that they are nurtured spiritually and physically and know the joy of being faithfully loved (vv. 13–14, 18–22). Jesus came teaching and healing in order to convince us that it is our "Father's good pleasure to give you the kingdom" (Luke 12:32). Through the gospel, we have all we could ever want or need, and all for free.

10[v] Isa. 19:3; Luke 1:51; [2 Sam. 15:34; 17:14; Neh. 4:15; Job 5:12; Isa. 8:10] **11**[w] Prov. 19:21; Isa. 46:10 **12**[x] Ps. 144:15; Deut. 33:29 [y] Ps. 65:4; Deut. 7:6; [Ex. 19:5] **13**[z] Job 28:24; See Ps. 11:4 **14**[a] 1 Kgs. 8:39, 43, 49 [b] [Prov. 15:3; Jer. 32:19]

16 [c]The king is not saved by his great army;
a warrior is not delivered by his great strength.
17 [d]The war horse is a false hope for salvation,
and by its great might it cannot rescue.

18 Behold, [e]the eye of the LORD is on those who fear him,
[f]on those who hope in his steadfast love,
19 that he may [g]deliver their soul from death
and keep them alive in [h]famine.

20 Our soul [i]waits for the LORD;
he is our [j]help and [k]our shield.
21 For our heart is [l]glad in him,
because we [m]trust in his holy name.
22 Let your steadfast love, O LORD, be upon us,
even as we hope in you.

Taste and See That the LORD Is Good

34

[1] OF DAVID, WHEN HE [n]CHANGED HIS BEHAVIOR BEFORE [o]ABIMELECH, SO THAT HE DROVE HIM OUT, AND HE WENT AWAY.

1 I will bless the LORD [p]at all times;
his praise shall continually be in my mouth.
2 My soul [q]makes its boast in the LORD;
let the humble hear and [r]be glad.
3 Oh, [s]magnify the LORD with me,
and let us exalt his name together!

4 I [t]sought the LORD, and he answered me
and delivered me from all my fears.
5 Those who look to him are [u]radiant,
and their faces shall never be ashamed.
6 [v]This poor man cried, and the LORD heard him
and [w]saved him out of all his troubles.
7 [x]The angel of the LORD [y]encamps
around those who fear him, and delivers them.

8 Oh, [z]taste and see that [a]the LORD is good!
[b]Blessed is the man who takes refuge in him!
9 Oh, fear the LORD, you his saints,
for those who fear him have no lack!
10 [c]The young lions suffer want and hunger;
but those who [d]seek the LORD lack no good thing.

11 [e]Come, O children, listen to me;
[f]I will teach you the fear of the LORD.
12 [g]What man is there who desires life
and loves many days, that he may [h]see good?
13 [i]Keep your tongue from evil
and your lips from [j]speaking deceit.
14 [k]Turn away from evil and do good;
seek peace and [l]pursue it.

15 [m]The eyes of the LORD are toward the righteous
[n]and his ears toward their cry.
16 [o]The face of the LORD is against those who do evil,
to [p]cut off the memory of them from the earth.
17 [n]When the righteous cry for help, the LORD hears
and delivers them out of all their troubles.
18 The LORD is near to [q]the brokenhearted
and saves [r]the crushed in spirit.

[1] This psalm is an acrostic poem, each verse beginning with the successive letters of the Hebrew alphabet

Psalm 34 Reflecting on his miraculous escape from a near death experience at the hand of Abimelech, David invites every worshiper to bless the Lord who "redeems the life of his servants" (vv. 1–3, 22; cf. 1 Sam. 21:10–15). The Lord undergirds his "brokenhearted" saints by readily drawing near to their cries (Ps. 34:17–19). Our Lord's proximity to and identification with the broken is realized most fully in Christ's earthly ministry. He entered into our suffering and pain to rescue us from their ultimate claim on our eternities.

Suffering brings believers into communion with the suffering Savior and a paradoxical kind of comfort that is found only in the difficult times of life (2 Cor. 1:5; 2 Tim. 3:11). God's future vengeance satisfies the persecuted person's desire for justice (Ps. 34:15–16, 21; John 9:31). With the Lord's presence surrounding him, even the believer's body is nourished and his countenance is put at ease (Ps. 34:4–10; Heb. 1:14; 1 Pet. 2:3).

16[c] [Ps. 44:6]
17[d] Ps. 20:7; 147:10; Prov. 21:31; Hos. 1:7
18[e] Ps. 34:15; Job 36:7; 1 Pet. 3:12 [f] Ps. 147:11
19[g] [Acts 12:11] [h] Ps. 37:19; Job 5:20
20[i] Ps. 62:1, 5; 130:6; Isa. 8:17 [j] Ps. 115:9-11 [k] See Ps. 3:3
21[l] Zech. 10:7; See Ps. 9:14 [m] See Ps. 11:1

Psalm 34
[n] 1 Sam. 21:13 [o] [1 Sam. 21:10, 11, 12, 14]
1[p] [Eph. 5:20; 1 Thess. 5:18]
2[q] Ps. 44:8; 1 Sam. 2:1; Jer. 9:24 [r] Ps. 119:74

3[s] Ps. 35:27; 40:16; 69:30; 70:4; Luke 1:46 **4**[t] 2 Chr. 15:2; [Matt. 7:7] **5**[u] Isa. 60:5; [Ps. 4:6] **6**[v] ver. 15, 17 [w] ver. 17, 19; 2 Sam. 22:1 **7**[x] Dan. 6:22; Heb. 1:14 [y] [Gen. 32:1, 2; 2 Kgs. 6:17] **8**[z] Heb. 6:5; 1 Pet. 2:3 [a] Ps. 100:5 [b] See Ps. 2:12 **10**[c] Job 4:10, 11 [d] [Ps. 84:11] **11**[e] Ps. 66:16 [f] [Ps. 32:8] **12**[g] Cited 1 Pet. 3:10-12 [h] Eccles. 3:13; 6:6 **13**[i] Ps. 15:3; 39:1; 141:3; Prov. 13:3; 21:23; James 1:26; 3:2; 1 Pet. 2:1, 22 [j] John 1:47; Rev. 14:5 **14**[k] Ps. 37:27; Isa. 1:16, 17; [Job 28:28] [l] Rom. 14:19; Heb. 12:14; [Rom. 12:18] **15**[m] See Ps. 33:18 [n] ver. 6, 8; Ps. 145:18; [John 9:31] **16**[o] Jer. 44:11; Amos 9:4 [p] See Ps. 21:10 **17**[n] [See ver. 15 above] **18**[q] Ps. 51:17; 147:3; Isa. 61:1 [r] Isa. 57:15; 66:2; See Luke 15:17-24

19 [s]Many are the afflictions of the righteous,
[t]but the LORD delivers him out of them all.
20 He keeps all his bones;
[u]not one of them is broken.
21 [v]Affliction will slay the wicked,
and those who hate the righteous will be condemned.
22 The LORD [w]redeems the life of his servants;
none of those who take refuge in him will be [x]condemned.

Great Is the LORD

35 OF DAVID.
Contend, O LORD, with those who [y]contend with me;
[z]fight against those who fight against me!
2 Take hold of [a]shield and buckler
and rise for my help!
3 Draw the spear and javelin[1]
against my pursuers!
Say to my soul,
"I am your salvation!"

4 [b]Let them be [c]put to shame and dishonor
who seek after my life!
Let them be [d]turned back and disappointed
who devise evil against me!
5 Let them be like [e]chaff before the wind,
with the angel of the LORD driving them away!
6 Let their way be dark and [f]slippery,
with the angel of the LORD pursuing them!

7 For [g]without cause [h]they hid their net for me;
without cause they dug [i]a pit for my life.[2]
8 Let [j]destruction come upon him [k]when he does not know it!
And let the net that he hid ensnare him;
let him fall into it—to his destruction!

9 Then my soul will rejoice in the LORD,
[l]exulting in his salvation.
10 All my [m]bones shall say,
"O LORD, [n]who is like you,
delivering the poor
from him who is too strong for him,
the poor and needy from him who robs him?"

11 [o]Malicious[3] witnesses rise up;
they ask me of things that I do not know.

[1] Or *and close the way* [2] The word *pit* is transposed from the preceding line; Hebrew *For without cause they hid the pit of their net for me; without cause they dug for my life* [3] Or *Violent*

19[s] 2 Tim. 3:11, 12 [t] ver. 6, 17, 22; [Acts 12:11]
20[u] John 19:36
21[v] Ps. 94:23; Prov. 24:16; [Ps. 7:15, 16]
22[w] See Ps. 25:22 [x] [Rom. 8:33, 34]
Psalm 35
1[y] Isa. 49:25 [z] [Ex. 14:25; Isa. 42:13]
2[a] Ps. 91:4; [Ps. 5:12]
4[b] For ver. 4-8, see Ps. 69:22-28; 109:6-15 [c] ver. 26; Ps. 40:14; 70:2; 71:13; 83:17 [d] Ps. 129:5
5[e] See Job 21:18
6[f] Ps. 73:18; Jer. 23:12
7[g] See Ps. 69:4 [h] See Job 18:8 [i] See Ps. 7:15
8[j] [1 Thess. 5:3] [k] Isa. 47:11
9[l] Luke 1:47; See Ps. 9:14
10[m] Ps. 51:8 [n] Ps. 71:19; 86:8; 89:6, 8; 113:5; Ex. 15:11
11[o] See Ps. 27:12

Ultimate physical healing is guaranteed by the believer's union with the crucified and resurrected Christ, whose body was preserved by the Father (Ps. 34:20; John 19:36; 1 Cor. 15:20–23). Knowing these undeserved kindnesses of the Father moves us to dread displeasing him. In love we surrender thought, word, and deed to holiness (Ps. 34:11–14; James 1:26). Grace has always been the motivation of such holiness (Lev. 20:7–8), and Christ has always been the enablement (1 Pet. 3:10–12, 16).

Psalm 35 While some dismiss "imprecatory" psalms (prayers for cursing) like this one as inappropriate, the Bible's own testimony is that David wrote by the inspiration of the Holy Spirit (2 Sam. 23:1–2; Mark 12:36; Acts 1:16). David's inspired words reveal his Greater Son's passion for his rule to come to earthly expression. That passion calls believers to submit their wills to the same ultimate goal. Christ prays for his enemies to be defeated so that his kingdom and our salvation would not be interrupted (Ps. 35:1–18; Rom. 11:9–10). As they echo David's prayer, Christians will be diverted from personal vengeance (Rom. 12:17–21). Surrendering all vengeance to Christ means that Christians are prepared even to suffer, if that is how Christ chooses to defeat their enemies (Ps. 35:19–25; John 15:25; Rom. 12:15). Their constant prayer must be that all of Christ's enemies would be conquered first by conversion. The goal of God's threats is always conversion—that, rather than being "clothed with shame," his enemies would come to be among those who proclaim, "Great is the LORD, who delights in the welfare of his servant" (Ps. 35:26–28; Jer. 18:7–10).

Whatever difficulties imprecatory psalms such as this one raise, the ultimate truth they teach is that the curses David pronounces really should fall on us. Our sin deserves cursing. But such curses have fallen instead on the Savior. He substituted himself in our place, so that the Father can truly say to our souls, "I am your salvation!" (Ps. 35:3).

12 [p]They repay me evil for good;
my soul is bereft.[1]
13 But I, [q]when they were sick—
I [r]wore sackcloth;
I [s]afflicted myself with fasting;
I prayed [t]with head bowed[2] on my chest.
14 I went about as though I grieved for my friend or my brother;
as one who laments his mother,
I [u]bowed down in mourning.

15 But at my stumbling they rejoiced and gathered;
they gathered together against me;
[v]wretches whom I did not know
tore at me without ceasing;
16 like profane mockers at a feast,[3]
they [w]gnash at me with their teeth.

17 How long, O Lord, will you [x]look on?
Rescue me from their destruction,
[y]my precious life from the lions!
18 I will thank you in [z]the great congregation;
in the mighty throng I will praise you.

19 [a]Let not those rejoice over me
who are [b]wrongfully my foes,
and let not those [c]wink the eye
who [d]hate me [e]without cause.
20 For they do not speak peace,
but against those who are quiet in the land
they devise words of deceit.
21 They [f]open wide their mouths against me;
they say, [g]"Aha, Aha!
Our eyes have seen it!"

22 [h]You have seen, O LORD; [i]be not silent!
O Lord, [j]be not far from me!
23 Awake and [k]rouse yourself for [l]my vindication,
for my cause, my God and my Lord!
24 [m]Vindicate me, O LORD, my God,
according to your righteousness,
and [n]let them not rejoice over me!
25 Let them not say in their hearts,
[o]"Aha, our heart's desire!"
Let them not say, [p]"We have swallowed him up."

26 Let them be [q]put to shame and disappointed altogether
who rejoice at my calamity!
Let them be [r]clothed with shame and dishonor
who [s]magnify themselves against me!

27 Let those who delight in my righteousness
shout for joy and be glad
[t]and say evermore,
[u]"Great is the LORD,
who [v]delights in the welfare of his servant!"
28 Then my [w]tongue shall tell of your righteousness
and of your praise all the day long.

How Precious Is Your Steadfast Love

36

TO THE CHOIRMASTER. OF DAVID, THE [x]SERVANT OF THE LORD.

1 Transgression speaks to the wicked
deep in his heart;[4]
[y]there is no fear of God
before his eyes.
2 [z]For he flatters himself in his own eyes
that his iniquity cannot be found out and hated.
3 The words of his mouth are [a]trouble and deceit;
[b]he has ceased to act wisely and do good.
4 He [c]plots [d]trouble while on his bed;
he sets himself in [e]a way that is not good;
[f]he does not reject evil.

[1] Hebrew *it is bereavement to my soul* [2] Or *my prayer shall turn back* [3] The meaning of the Hebrew phrase is uncertain [4] Some Hebrew manuscripts, Syriac, Jerome (compare Septuagint); most Hebrew manuscripts *in my heart*

Psalm 36 In this oracle on transgression, David paints a frightening portrait of the reprobate (v. 1; cf. Rom. 3:18). The picture unfolds through a slow progression. First comes the sinner trying sin and experiencing no pain. Gradually losing fear, he infers that the absence of any immediate judgment means it will never come (Ps. 36:2; 2 Pet. 3:4–7). Then he pursues sin more devotedly (Ps. 36:3). Finally, when most consciences are tender at night, his is so seared that he plans his next transgression (v. 4). He is utterly lost.

12[p] Ps. 38:20; 109:4; Jer. 18:20; [John 10:32] **13**[q] [Job 30:25] [r] Ps. 69:11; [1 Kgs. 20:31] [s] Ps. 69:10; Num. 29:7 [t] [Matt. 10:13]; Luke 10:6 **14**[u] See Ps. 38:6 **15**[v] Job 30:1, 8, 12 **16**[w] Ps. 37:12; Job 16:9; Lam. 2:16

17[x] Hab. 1:13 [y] Ps. 22:20 **18**[z] Ps. 22:25 **19**[a] ver. 24; See Ps. 13:4 [b] Ps. 38:19; 69:4; 119:78, 86 [c] Prov. 6:13; 10:10 [d] Ps. 69:4; Cited John 15:25 [e] ver. 7 **21**[f] See Ps. 22:13 [g] ver. 25; Ps. 40:15; 70:3 **22**[h] [Ex. 3:7] [i] Ps. 28:1 [j] See Ps. 10:1 **23**[k] Ps. 44:23; 59:4; 80:2 [l] Ps. 7:6 **24**[m] Ps. 7:8 [n] ver. 19 **25**[o] ver. 21 [p] 2 Sam. 17:16; Lam. 2:16 **26**[q] See ver. 4 [r] See Job 8:22 [s] See Job 19:5 **27**[t] Ps. 40:16; 70:4 [u] Ps. 34:3 [v] Ps. 149:4 **28**[w] Ps. 51:14; 71:8, 15, 24 **Psalm 36** [x] See Ps. 18, title **1**[y] Cited Rom. 3:18 **2**[z] Deut. 29:19; [Ps. 10:3; 49:18] **3**[a] [Ps. 12:2] [b] [Jer. 4:22] **4**[c] Mic. 2:1; [Prov. 4:16] [d] Ps. 10:7 [e] Isa. 65:2 [f] [Ps. 97:10]

5 Your steadfast love, O LORD, extends to
the heavens,
your faithfulness to the clouds.
6 [g]Your righteousness is like the mountains of God;
[h]your judgments are like the great deep;
man and beast you [i]save, O LORD.

7 [j]How precious is your steadfast love,
O God!
The children of mankind take refuge
[k]in the shadow of your wings.
8 They feast on [l]the abundance of your
house,
and you give them drink from [m]the
river of [n]your delights.
9 For with you is [o]the fountain of life;
[p]in your light do we see light.

10 Oh, continue your steadfast love to those
who [q]know you,
and your righteousness to [r]the
upright of heart!
11 Let not the foot of arrogance come upon
me,
nor the hand of the wicked drive me
away.
12 There [s]the evildoers lie fallen;
they are thrust down, [t]unable to rise.

He Will Not Forsake His Saints

37[1] OF DAVID.
[u]Fret not yourself because of
evildoers;
be not [v]envious of wrongdoers!
2 For they will soon [w]fade like [x]the grass
and wither [y]like the green herb.

3 [z]Trust in the LORD, and do good;
[a]dwell in the land and befriend faithfulness.[2]
4 [b]Delight yourself in the LORD,
and he will [c]give you the desires of
your heart.

5 [d]Commit your way to the LORD;
[z]trust in him, and he will act.
6 [e]He will bring forth your righteousness
as the light,
and your justice as [f]the noonday.

7 [g]Be still before the LORD and wait
patiently for him;
[h]fret not yourself over the one who
[i]prospers in his way,
over the man who carries out evil
devices!

8 [j]Refrain from anger, and forsake wrath!
[h]Fret not yourself; it tends only to evil.

[1] This psalm is an acrostic poem, each stanza beginning with the successive letters of the Hebrew alphabet [2] Or *and feed on faithfulness*, or *and find safe pasture*

6[g] [Ps. 71:19] [h] Ps. 92:5; Rom. 11:33 [i] Ps. 104:14, 15; 145:9, 15, 16; Neh. 9:6
7[j] [Ps. 31:19] [k] See Ruth 2:12
8[l] Ps. 23:5; 27:4; 65:4; Isa. 25:6; See Jer. 31:12-14 [m] Ps. 46:4; Rev. 22:1 [n] Ps. 16:11
9[o] Jer. 2:13; John 4:10, 14; 5:26 [p] John 1:9; Acts 26:18; 1 Pet. 2:9
10[q] Jer. 22:16; Gal. 4:9; [Ps. 79:6] [r] See Ps. 7:10
12[s] Ps. 94:4 [t] See Ps. 1:5
Psalm 37
1[u] ver. 7, 8; Prov. 24:19 [v] Ps. 73:3; Prov. 3:31; 23:17; 24:1, 19
2[w] Job 14:2; See Job 27:13-23 [x] Ps. 90:5, 6 [y] Ps. 129:6
3[z] Ps. 62:8; 115:9-11; Prov. 3:5; Isa. 26:4 [a] Lev. 26:5; Prov. 2:21
4[b] Job 22:26; Isa. 58:14; [Phil. 3:1; 4:4] [c] Matt. 6:33
5[d] Ps. 22:8; 55:22; Prov. 16:3; 1 Pet. 5:7 [z] [See ver. 3 above]
6[e] Isa. 58:8, 10; Mic. 7:9 [f] Job 11:17
7[g] [Ps. 62:1; Isa. 30:15; Lam. 3:26] [h] ver. 1 [i] Jer. 12:1
8[j] [Eph. 4:26] [h] [See ver. 7 above]

Only God's grace can rescue such a lost soul. That explains why David turns dramatically to God's attributes (vv. 5–9). God's faithful love is like a guiding star in the heavens, beckoning to wayfaring sinners (v. 5; 103:11). No matter how deep one's sin, God's grace is deeper still; no matter how high his moral debt, God's righteous mountains are taller still (36:6; Rom. 5:20).

This effulgence of blessings is personified in Christ (Ps. 36:8, 9; Eph. 1:3). As in the past, God will save "man and beast" in his new world (Ps. 36:6; Isa. 11:6–9; Jonah 4:11; 2 Pet. 2:5). In fact, the Father's love is so tender it is like a mother bird's, whose wings offer refuge (Ps. 36:7; 10–12). Through tears, Christ similarly invited an apostate Jerusalem to return to him (Matt. 23:37). The heart of Jesus is gentleness and lowliness (Matt. 11:29).

Psalm 37 Despite the temporary success of "evildoers," dependence on God will bring eternal reward (vv. 1–2, 7–11). Rather than "fretting," David prescribes meekness just as Jesus did in the third beatitude (v. 22; Matt. 5:5; James 1:20; Rom. 12:21). While the New Testament speaks only occasionally of meekness (e.g., Gal. 5:22–23; Col. 3:12; 1 Pet. 3:15; James 1:21), this psalm is nearly encyclopedic. Meekness is strength from trust in a sovereign God, and David imagines the first step to be rolling his burdens onto the Lord (Ps. 37:5).

God's intimate knowledge of his children explains why disaster and famine cannot eternally destroy them (vv. 18–19; Gen. 18:19; Jer. 1:5). On the other hand, eternal anonymity will be the lot of the wicked, beginning with the words, "I never knew you" (Matt. 7:23). Judgment has already begun on the wicked as God "laughs" at their smugness, readies his vengeance, and neutralizes their significance (Ps. 37:12–20, 35–36; Matt. 3:10; Acts 7:54; Heb. 11:40). Their existence is vacuous in contrast to the righteous, who are "generous" (Ps. 37:21; 2 Cor. 9:12, 13) because of their abundance in the Lord (Ps. 37:23–26, 37–40).

9 [k]For the evildoers shall be cut off,
but those who wait for the LORD shall
[l]inherit the land.
10 In [m]just a little while, the wicked will be
no more;
though you look carefully at [n]his
place, he will not be there.
11 But [o]the meek shall inherit the land
and delight themselves in [p]abundant
peace.

12 The wicked [q]plots against the righteous
and [r]gnashes his teeth at him,
13 but the Lord [s]laughs at the wicked,
for he sees that his [t]day is coming.

14 The wicked draw the sword and [u]bend
their bows
to bring down the poor and needy,
to slay those whose [v]way is upright;
15 their sword shall enter their own heart,
and their [w]bows shall be broken.

16 [x]Better is the little that the righteous has
than the abundance of many wicked.
17 For [y]the arms of the wicked shall be broken,
but the LORD [z]upholds the righteous.

18 The LORD [a]knows the days of the blameless,
and their [b]heritage will remain forever;
19 they are not put to shame in evil times;
in [c]the days of famine they have abundance.

20 But the wicked will perish;
the enemies of the LORD are like [d]the
glory of the pastures;
they vanish—like [e]smoke they vanish
away.
21 The wicked borrows but does not pay
back,
but the righteous [f]is generous and
gives;
22 for those blessed by the LORD[1] shall
[g]inherit the land,
but those cursed by him [h]shall be cut
off.

23 The [i]steps of a man are [j]established by
the LORD,
when he delights in his way;
24 [k]though he fall, he shall not be cast headlong,
for the LORD [l]upholds his hand.

25 I have been young, and now am old,
yet I have not seen the righteous forsaken
or his children [m]begging for bread.
26 He is ever [n]lending generously,
and his children become a blessing.

27 [o]Turn away from evil and do good;
so shall you [p]dwell forever.
28 For the LORD [q]loves justice;
he will not forsake his [r]saints.
They are preserved forever,
but the children of the wicked shall
be [s]cut off.
29 The righteous shall inherit the land
and [p]dwell upon it forever.

30 The mouth of the righteous utters wisdom,
and his tongue speaks justice.
31 [t]The law of his God is in his heart;
his [u]steps do not slip.

32 The wicked [v]watches for the righteous
and seeks to put him to death.
33 The LORD will not [w]abandon him to his
power
or let him [x]be condemned when he is
brought to trial.

34 [y]Wait for the LORD and keep his way,
and he will exalt you to inherit the
land;
you will look on [z]when the wicked are
cut off.

[1] Hebrew *by him*

In the New Testament, our motivation for generosity comes into full bloom as we see the generosity of God himself. For the eternal second person of the triune God came to earth, becoming poor in the incarnation so that we might become rich (2 Cor. 8:9). This lavish generosity of God in the gospel is the supreme motivation for believers today to likewise be radically generous.

9[k] ver. 2, 22 [l] Ps. 25:13; Prov. 2:21; Isa. 57:13; 60:21 **10**[m] Job 24:24 [n] Job 7:10 **11**[o] Cited Matt. 5:5 [p] Ps. 119:165; [Isa. 32:17] **12**[q] Ps. 31:13 [r] See Ps. 35:16 **13**[s] See Ps. 2:4 [t] See Job 18:20

14[u] Ps. 7:12 [v] See Ps. 7:10 **15**[w] See 1 Sam. 2:4 **16**[x] Prov. 15:16; 16:8; [1 Tim. 6:6] **17**[y] Ps. 10:15; Job 38:15; Ezek. 30:21, 22 [z] ver. 24 **18**[a] See Ps. 1:6 [b] ver. 9 **19**[c] Ps. 33:19; Job 5:20 **20**[d] [Matt. 6:30; James 1:11] [e] Ps. 68:2; 102:3; Hos. 13:3 **21**[f] ver. 26 **22**[g] See ver. 9 [h] ver. 2 **23**[i] Ps. 25:12; 1 Sam. 2:9 [j] Ps. 40:2; 119:5 **24**[k] Prov. 24:16; Mic. 7:8; 2 Cor. 4:9 [l] ver. 17 **25**[m] [Ps. 109:10; Job 15:23] **26**[n] Ps. 112:5, 9; Deut. 15:8, 10; Matt. 5:42; Luke 6:35 **27**[o] See Ps. 34:14 [p] [Ps. 102:28] **28**[q] See Ps. 11:7 [r] See Ps. 16:10 [s] ver. 2, 9; Ps. 21:10; Prov. 2:22; Isa. 14:20 **29**[p] [See ver. 27 above] **31**[t] Ps. 40:8; 119:11; Deut. 6:6; Isa. 51:7; Jer. 31:33; [Rom. 7:22] [u] [Ps. 73:2] **32**[v] Ps. 10:8 **33**[w] [2 Pet. 2:9] [x] Ps. 109:31 **34**[y] ver. 9; See Ps. 27:14 [z] Ps. 52:5, 6; 91:8

35 [a]I have seen a wicked, ruthless man,
spreading himself like [b]a green laurel tree.[1]
36 But he passed away,[2] and behold, [c]he was no more;
though I sought him, he could not be found.
37 Mark the blameless and behold the upright,
for there is a future for the man of [d]peace.
38 But [e]transgressors shall be altogether destroyed;
the future of the wicked [f]shall be cut off.
39 [g]The salvation of the righteous is from the LORD;
he is their stronghold in [h]the time of trouble.
40 The LORD helps them and [i]delivers them;
[j]he delivers them from the wicked and saves them,
because they [k]take refuge in him.

Do Not Forsake Me, O LORD

38

A PSALM OF DAVID, [l]FOR THE MEMORIAL OFFERING.

1 O LORD, [m]rebuke me not in your anger,
nor discipline me in your wrath!
2 For your [n]arrows have sunk into me,
and your hand [o]has come down on me.
3 There is [p]no soundness in my flesh
because of your indignation;
there is no health in my [q]bones
because of my sin.
4 For my [r]iniquities have gone over my head;
like a heavy burden, they are too heavy for me.
5 My wounds stink and fester
because of my foolishness,
6 I am [s]utterly bowed down and [t]prostrate;
all the day I [u]go about mourning.
7 For my sides are filled with burning,
and there is [p]no soundness in my flesh.
8 I am feeble and crushed;
I [v]groan because of the tumult of my heart.
9 O Lord, all my longing is before you;
my [w]sighing is not hidden from you.
10 My heart throbs; my strength fails me,
and [x]the light of my eyes—it also has gone from me.
11 My [y]friends and companions [z]stand aloof from my [a]plague,
and my nearest kin [b]stand far off.
12 Those who seek my life [c]lay their snares;
those who seek my hurt [d]speak of ruin
and meditate [e]treachery all day long.
13 But I am like a deaf man; I do not hear,
like [f]a mute man who does not open his mouth.
14 I have become like a man who does not hear,
and in whose mouth are no [g]rebukes.

[1] The identity of this tree is uncertain [2] Or *But one passed by*

35[a] See Job 5:3 [b] [Ps. 52:8]
36[c] ver. 10; Job 20:5
37[d] ver. 11; Ps. 119:165; Isa. 57:2
38[e] [Ps. 52:5; 104:35; Prov. 2:22] [f] Ps. 73:17; Job 18:17
39[g] See Ps. 3:8 [h] Ps. 9:9
40[i] [Isa. 31:5; Acts 12:11] [j] [1 Chr. 5:20; Dan. 3:17, 28; 6:23] [k] See Ps. 11:1

Psalm 38
[l] Ps. 70, title; [1 Chr. 16:4]
1[m] Ps. 6:1
2[n] Job 6:4 [o] See Ps. 32:4
3[p] Isa. 1:6 [q] See Ps. 31:10
4[r] Ps. 40:12; Ezra 9:6
6[s] Ps. 35:14; 42:5, 6, 11; 43:5 [t] Isa. 21:3 [u] [Job 30:28]
7[p] [See ver. 3 above]
8[v] See Ps. 22:1
9[w] Ps. 6:6
10[x] See Ps. 6:7
11[y] Ps. 88:18; See Job 19:13-20 [z] [Luke 10:31, 32] [a] Ps. 39:10; Isa. 53:4, 8 [b] [Matt. 27:55; Mark 15:40; Luke 23:49]

Psalm 38 This is an explicit confession of personal sin against God (vv. 1, 3, 18). The Lord had to discipline David before he could smell the stench of his sin, feel the agony of his iniquity, suffer the shame of his guilt, and realize the numbness of his spiritual senses (vv. 5–12; Luke 23:49; Rom. 6:21). God's discipline of a believer is meant to soften the heart and ultimately restore fellowship. When we are in the midst of divine discipline, we are called to wait on the Lord (Ps. 38:15).

David's own sin, however, is not his only trouble. David is also suffering the hostility of his enemies (vv. 16–20). His pain is increased because he knows that his foes hate him wrongfully; what David has done does not deserve their hatred. We are reminded of David's Greater Son, the Lord Jesus himself, who similarly suffered wrongful hostility. Perhaps you have, also.

David's refuge is ours as well—the Lord who saves us and who loves as he knows is best. Based on the help and deliverance of God, David ends this psalm on a hopeful though desperate note (vv. 21–22). We today can similarly call on God to help and deliver us, though we need not be anxious as to whether God will answer us. For we see Jesus Christ himself, God incarnate, come to earth. God has drawn near, in the person of his own Son.

12[c] [Matt. 22:15]; Mark 12:13; Luke 20:20; See 2 Sam. 17:1-3 [d] [2 Sam. 16:7, 8] [e] Ps. 35:20 **13**[f] Ps. 39:2, 9; Isa. 53:7; 1 Pet. 2:23 **14**[g] [Job 23:4]

15 But for [h]you, O LORD, do I wait;
it is you, O Lord my God, who will
answer.
16 For I said, "Only [i]let them not rejoice
over me,
who [j]boast against me when my [k]foot
slips!"

17 For I am [l]ready to fall,
and my pain is ever before me.
18 I [m]confess my iniquity;
I am [n]sorry for my sin.
19 But my foes are vigorous, they are mighty,
and many are those who hate me
[o]wrongfully.
20 Those who [p]render me evil for good
[q]accuse me because I [r]follow after good.

21 Do not forsake me, O LORD!
O my God, be not [s]far from me!
22 [t]Make haste to help me,
O Lord, my [u]salvation!

What Is the Measure of My Days?

39

TO THE CHOIRMASTER: TO [v]JEDUTHUN. A PSALM OF DAVID.

1 I said, "I will [w]guard my ways,
that I [x]may not sin with my tongue;
I will [y]guard my mouth with a muzzle,
so long as the wicked are in my presence."
2 I was [z]mute and silent;
I held my peace to no avail,
and my distress grew worse.
3 My [a]heart became hot within me.
As I mused, the fire burned;
then I spoke with my tongue:

4 "O LORD, [b]make me know my end
and what is the measure of my days;
let me know how fleeting I am!
5 Behold, you have made my days a few
handbreadths,
and [c]my lifetime is as nothing before
you.
Surely [d]all mankind stands as a mere
breath! *Selah*
6 Surely a man [e]goes about as a
shadow!
Surely for nothing[1] they are in turmoil;
man [f]heaps up wealth and does not
know who will gather!

7 "And now, O Lord, for what do I wait?
[g]My hope is in you.
8 Deliver me from all my transgressions.
[h]Do not make me the scorn of the
fool!
9 [i]I am mute; I do not open my mouth,
[j]for it is you who have done it.
10 [k]Remove your stroke from me;
I am spent by the hostility of your
hand.
11 When you discipline a man
with [l]rebukes for sin,
you [m]consume like a [n]moth what is dear
to him;
[o]surely all mankind is a mere breath!
Selah

12 [p]"Hear my prayer, O LORD,
and give ear to my cry;
hold not your peace at my tears!
For I am [q]a sojourner with you,
[q]a guest, like all my fathers.

[1] Hebrew *Surely as a breath*

Psalm 39 Perhaps this psalm has in view the occasion that gave rise to David's confession in the previous psalm. And perhaps the sin of his "tongue" was his attributing injustice to God for allowing transgressors to prosper (vv. 1–3; cf. Psalm 37). Regardless of the specific cause, God's merciful discipline comes here by reminding David that his life is a vapor compared to God's eternality (39:4–6, 12; cf. Luke 12:21; Heb. 11:13). God shuts the mouth of the insolent by making him feel his finitude before the fire of God's just wrath (Ps. 39:7–11, 13; cf. James 4:14). When self-righteous anger is extinguished, the believer is able to confess his sin of scorn, wait in hope for God's justice, cry for peace, and pray for God's smile (Ps. 39:7–8, 12–13).

Psalm 39 is the cry of one who suddenly feels the futility and shortness of his own time on earth. Indeed, the fall in Genesis 3 did introduce a futility and frustration into our earthly lives. In the gospel, however, we are promised that this earthly life is not all we have. Rather, those united to Christ stand to inherit the entire world (Matt. 5:5; 25:34; 1 Cor. 3:21). Here and now, we are "sojourners," strangers (Ps. 39:12). But it will not always be so.

15[h] Ps. 39:7; [2 Sam. 16:12]
16[i] [Ps. 13:4] [j] See Job 19:5 [k] Ps. 94:18
17[l] Ps. 35:15; Jer. 20:10
18[m] See Ps. 32:5 [n] [2 Cor. 7:9, 10]
19[o] Ps. 35:19
20[p] See Ps. 35:12 [q] Ps. 109:4 [r] [3 John 11]
21[s] See Ps. 10:1
22[t] See Ps. 40:13 [u] See Ps. 27:1
Psalm 39
[v] Ps. 62, title; 77, title; 1 Chr. 16:41; 25:1
1[w] 1 Kgs. 2:4; 2 Kgs. 10:31 [x] Job 2:10 [y] See Ps. 34:13
2[z] ver. 9; Job 40:4, 5; See Ps. 38:13
3[a] Jer. 20:9; Luke 24:32; [Job 32:18, 19]
4[b] Ps. 90:12
5[c] Ps. 89:47; 90:4 [d] ver. 11; [Job 14:2] **6**[e] [1 Cor. 7:31; James 4:14] [f] Ps. 49:10; Job 27:16, 17; Luke 12:20; [Eccles. 2:18, 21, 26; Jer. 17:11] **7**[g] Ps. 38:15 **8**[h] See Ps. 44:13 **9**[i] ver. 2 [j] 2 Sam. 16:10; Job 2:10 **10**[k] Job 9:34; 13:21 **11**[l] Ps. 80:16 [m] Ps. 49:14 [n] Job 13:28; Isa. 50:9 [o] See ver. 5 **12**[p] Ps. 102:1 [q] Ps. 119:19; Lev. 25:23; 1 Chr. 29:15; Heb. 11:13; 1 Pet. 2:11; [Gen. 47:9]

13 [r]Look away from me, that I may smile
again,
[s]before I depart and [t]am no more!"

My Help and My Deliverer

40 To the choirmaster. A Psalm of David.
I [u]waited patiently for the LORD;
he inclined to me and [v]heard my cry.
2 He drew me up from [w]the pit of destruction,
out of [x]the miry bog,
and [y]set my feet upon a rock,
[z]making my steps secure.
3 He put [a]a new song in my mouth,
a song of praise to our God.
Many will [b]see and fear,
and put their trust in the LORD.

4 Blessed is the man who [c]makes
the LORD his trust,
who does not turn to the proud,
to those who [d]go astray after a lie!
5 You have multiplied, O LORD my God,
your [e]wondrous deeds and your
[f]thoughts toward us;
none can compare with you!
I will proclaim and tell of them,
yet they are [g]more than can be told.

6 [h]In sacrifice and offering you have not
delighted,
but you have given me an open [i]ear.[1]
Burnt offering and sin offering
you have not required.
7 Then I said, "Behold, I have come;
in the scroll of the book it is written
[j]of me:
8 [k]I delight to do your will, O my God;
your law is [l]within my heart."

9 I have told the glad news of deliverance[2]
in [m]the great congregation;
behold, I have not [n]restrained my lips,
[o]as you know, O LORD.
10 I have not hidden your deliverance
within my heart;
I have spoken of your faithfulness and
your salvation;
I have not concealed your steadfast love
and your faithfulness
from the great congregation.

11 As for you, O LORD, you will not
restrain
your mercy from me;
your [p]steadfast love and your faithfulness will
ever preserve me!
12 For evils have [q]encompassed me
beyond number;
my [r]iniquities have overtaken me,
and I cannot [s]see;
they are [t]more than the hairs of my
head;
my heart [u]fails me.

[1] Hebrew *ears you have dug for me* [2] Hebrew *righteousness*; also verse 10

13[r]Job 7:19 [s]Job 10:21 [t]Job 7:8; 14:10-12; 20:9
Psalm 40
1[u]Ps. 27:14; 37:7 [v]Ps. 39:12
2[w][Jer. 38:6] [x]Ps. 69:2, 14 [y]Ps. 27:5 [z]Ps. 37:23
3[a]See Ps. 33:3 [b]Ps. 52:6; 64:8, 9; Deut. 13:11
4[c]See Ps. 2:12 [d]Ps. 101:3; 125:5; Lev. 19:4; Deut. 29:18; Job 23:11; Hos. 3:1
5[e]Ps. 9:1; Ex. 15:11 [f]Ps. 92:5; 139:17; Isa. 55:8 [g]Ps. 71:15; 139:18
6[h]Ps. 51:16; 1 Sam. 15:22; Cited Heb. 10:5-7; See Prov. 21:3 [i]See Job 33:16
7[j]Luke 24:44
8[k]Ps. 119:16, 24, 35, 92; [John 4:34] [l]See Ps. 37:31
9[m]See Ps. 22:25 [n]Ps. 119:13; [Acts 20:20, 27] [o]Josh. 22:22
11[p]Ps. 57:3; 61:7; Prov. 20:28; See Ps. 36:5
12[q]Ps. 116:3 [r]Ps. 38:4 [s][Ps. 38:10] [t]Ps. 69:4 [u]Ps. 73:26

Psalm 40 In its immediate context, this psalm of David teaches that the Lord hears the cries of his children and responds, but they must wait "patiently" for him since their perception of timeliness is not always the same as his perfect providence. More distantly, this is a psalm that will be lived out by David's Greater Son. Throughout history, Christians have viewed the Psalter ultimately as a collection of Christ's prayers. The way this psalm occurs in the New Testament reinforces that conviction. In fact, Hebrews 10:5–7 quotes Psalm 40:6–7 and attributes the words to Christ.

With this perspective, the psalm also provides insight into our Redeemer's earthly experience, which melts our hearts and shapes our service for him. The opening stanza can also be used to describe Christ being delivered from the "miry bog" of death and raised to "set [his] feet" upon a "rock" of God's provision (vv. 1–2). From that place, our risen King empowers our worship (v. 3; cf. Heb. 2:12) and enables us to work "wondrous deeds" (Ps. 40:5; cf. John 14:12). As an obedient Son, Jesus humbled himself to save the world his Father loved (Ps. 40:6–8). Jesus the Prophet taught God's "love" and "faithfulness" (Ps. 40:9–10; cf. John 17:8, 14).

Verses 12–17 of Psalm 40 poignantly anticipate Christ's own Gethsemane experience and death on the cross. The Priest himself became sin on our behalf. That substitution must move our hearts to "love [his] salvation" and to "say continually, 'Great is the LORD!'" (vv. 12–17). Believers should read through this psalm first with the effort to make it their own prayer. Then we should read it again with the comfort that, because Christ prayed it perfectly, he can enable his disciples where our faith is weak.

13 [v]Be pleased, O LORD, to [w]deliver me!
O LORD, [x]make haste to help me!
14 [y]Let those be put to shame and disappointed altogether
who seek to snatch away my life;
let those be [z]turned back and brought to dishonor
who delight in my hurt!
15 Let those be appalled because of their shame
who [a]say to me, "Aha, Aha!"

16 But may all who seek you
rejoice and be glad in you;
may those who love your salvation
[b]say continually, "Great is the LORD!"
17 As for me, I am [c]poor and needy,
but [d]the Lord takes thought for me.
You are my help and my deliverer;
do not delay, O my God!

O LORD, Be Gracious to Me

41

TO THE CHOIRMASTER. A PSALM OF DAVID.

[e]Blessed is the one who considers the poor![1]
[f]In the day of trouble the LORD delivers him;
2 the LORD protects him and keeps him alive;
he is called blessed in the land;
you [g]do not give him up to the will of his enemies.
3 The LORD sustains him on his sickbed;
in his illness you restore him to full health.[2]

4 As for me, I said, "O LORD, [h]be gracious to me;
[i]heal me,[3] for I have sinned against you!"
5 My enemies say of me in malice,
"When will he die, and his name perish?"
6 And when one comes to see me, [j]he utters empty words,
while his heart gathers iniquity;
when he goes out, he tells it abroad.
7 All who hate me whisper together about me;
they imagine the worst for me.[4]

8 They say, "A deadly thing is poured out[5] on him;
he will not rise again from where he lies."
9 Even my [k]close friend in whom I trusted,
who [l]ate my bread, has lifted his heel against me.
10 But you, O LORD, be gracious to me,
and raise me up, that I may repay them!
11 By this I know that [m]you delight in me:
my enemy will not shout in triumph over me.
12 But [n]you have upheld me because of [o]my integrity,
and [p]set me in your presence [q]forever.

13 [r]Blessed be the LORD, the God of Israel,
from everlasting to everlasting!
Amen and Amen.

[1] Or *weak* [2] Hebrew *you turn all his bed* [3] Hebrew *my soul* [4] Or *they devise evil against me* [5] Or *has fastened*

Psalm 41 Here David voices every person's need for redeeming grace. All are physically "poor" (v. 1). If that realization does not dawn on us through the "sickbed" (v. 3), it will certainly come whenever we face death (v. 2). Such experiences should drive us to David's Greater Son, who came to provide holistic salvation. Jesus went about healing in his day to provide a foretaste for what life in his future kingdom would look like (Luke 4:17–19; James 5:15).

But a person is more than a body; we have a spirit too. While unreconciled with God, that spirit is at enmity with God. Physical death threatens the lost soul with eternal damnation (Rom. 6:23; 1 Cor. 15:50). However, Christ's mercy, received through repentance, will "heal" us at least by the day of resurrection (Ps. 41:4; 1 Cor. 15:52). As image-bearers of a Trinitarian God, we were made to live in community. But sin has fragmented relationships. Christ, who suffered betrayal by a "close friend," comes to the aid of the brokenhearted (Ps. 41:7–9; Heb. 2:17; John 13:18).

Jesus also redeems our emotions. Because God was pleased with his Son, he is pleased with those who are united to him (Matt. 3:17; 17:5). Living in that pleasure enabled Christ to persevere through his mission to save, and it motivates us to obey the Lord with confidence that he will vindicate us (Luke 1:71; 10:19; Heb. 10:13).

13[v] For ver. 13-17, see Ps. 70:1-5 [w]Ps. 22:20 [x]Ps. 22:19; 38:22; 71:12; 141:1
14[y] Ps. 35:4, 26; 71:13 [z]Ps. 6:10
15[a] Ps. 35:21, 25; 70:3
16[b] Ps. 35:27
17[c] Ps. 86:1; 109:22 [d][1 Pet. 5:7]

Psalm 41
1[e] Prov. 14:21 [f]Ps. 37:19
2[g] Ps. 27:12
4[h] Ps. 4:1 [i]Ps. 6:2; 147:3; 2 Chr. 30:20
6[j] Ps. 12:2; 144:8
9[k] Ps. 55:12, 13, 20; Job 19:13, 14, 19; Jer. 9:4; 20:10; Mic. 7:5; [2 Sam. 15:12] [l]Cited John 13:18
11[m] [2 Sam. 15:25, 26]
12[n] Ps. 63:8 [o]Ps. 26:1 [p]Job 36:7 [q]Ps. 23:6
13[r] Luke 1:68; [Ps. 72:18, 19; 89:52; 106:48; 150:6]

Book Two

Why Are You Cast Down, O My Soul?

42 TO THE CHOIRMASTER. A MASKIL[1] OF [s]THE SONS OF KORAH.

1 [t]As a deer pants for flowing streams,
so pants my soul for you, O God.
2 [u]My soul thirsts for God,
for [v]the living God.
When shall I come and [w]appear before God?[2]
3 [x]My tears have been my food
day and night,
[y]while they say to me all the day long,
"Where is your God?"
4 These things I remember,
as I [z]pour out my soul:
[a]how I would go [b]with the throng
and lead them in procession to the house of God
with glad shouts and songs of praise,
[c]a multitude keeping festival.

5 [d]Why are you cast down, O my soul,
and why are you [e]in turmoil within me?
[f]Hope in God; for I shall again praise him,
my salvation[3] 6 and my God.

My soul is cast down within me;
therefore I [g]remember you
[h]from the land of Jordan and of [i]Hermon,
from Mount Mizar.
7 Deep calls to deep
at the roar of your waterfalls;
[j]all your breakers and your [k]waves
have gone over me.
8 By day the LORD [l]commands his steadfast love,
and at [m]night his song is with me,
a prayer to the God of my life.
9 I say to God, [n]my rock:
"Why have you forgotten me?
[o]Why do I go mourning
because of the oppression of the enemy?"
10 As with a deadly wound in my bones,
my adversaries taunt me,
[p]while they say to me all the day long,
"Where is your God?"

11 [q]Why are you cast down, O my soul,
and why are you in turmoil within me?
Hope in God; for I shall again praise him,
my salvation and my God.

Send Out Your Light and Your Truth

43 [r]Vindicate me, O God, and [s]defend my cause
against an ungodly people,
from [t]the deceitful and unjust man
deliver me!
2 For you are [u]the God in whom I take refuge;
why have you [v]rejected me?

[1] Probably a musical or liturgical term [2] Revocalization yields *and see the face of God* [3] Hebrew *the salvation of my face*; also verse 11 and 43:5

Psalm 42
[s]1 Chr. 6:33, 37
1[t][Joel 1:20]
2[u]Ps. 63:1; John 7:37; [Isa. 41:17; 55:1]; See Ps. 84:2 [v]Ps. 84:2; Josh. 3:10; Dan. 6:26 [w]Ps. 84:7; [Ex. 23:17]
3[x]Ps. 80:5; 102:9 [y]ver. 10; Ps. 79:10; 115:2; Joel 2:17; Mic. 7:10
4[z]Ps. 62:8; 1 Sam. 1:15; Job 30:16; Lam. 2:19 [a][Isa. 30:29] [b]Ps. 55:14 [c][2 Sam. 6:15]
5[d]ver. 11; Ps. 43:5; [Matt. 26:38; John 12:27] [e]Ps. 77:3 [f]Lam. 3:24
6[g]Jonah 2:7 [h]2 Sam. 17:22, 24 [i]Deut. 3:9
7[j]Jonah 2:3 [k]Ps. 88:7; See Ps. 32:6
8[l]Ps. 44:4; 68:28; 71:3; 133:3 [m]Job 35:10; [Ps. 4:4; 16:7; 63:6; 77:6; 119:55, 62, 148; 149:5]
9[n]See Ps. 18:2; 2 Sam. 22:2 [o]Ps. 38:6; 43:2
10[p]See ver. 3
11[q]See ver. 5

Psalm 43
1[r]Ps. 7:8; 26:1 [s]See 1 Sam. 24:15 [t]Ps. 5:6
2[u]Ps. 31:4 [v]See Ps. 44:9

Psalm 42 Only a soul indwelt by the Spirit "pants" for God (v. 1; cf. John 3:3; 1 Cor. 2:14). And only one loved by God will exhort his soul to "hope in God" (Ps. 42:5; cf. Rom. 5:5). This is the kind of intimate relationship with God that Christ came to bring (John 14:21). More fully and deeply than any other, he can empathize with the devastating feeling of being forsaken by God (Ps. 42:1–4; Mark 15:34).

The sons of Korah refer to God with three names rich in redemptive significance: *God*, *salvation*, and *rock*. Because this God is living, the psalmist hopes that his thirst for satisfaction in worship will be quenched (Ps. 42:4, 5). Christ personally came to bring this ever-living God—and the fullness of his joy—to spiritually dead people (Matt. 22:32; John 15:11; 17:13). The particular aspect of "salvation" that the psalmist pines for—the very presence of God (Ps. 42:2–3)—is precisely what the Savior provided. The psalmist needs around-the-clock protection (v. 8); Jesus promises it (Matt. 28:20). The psalmist mourns for a "rock" to give stability to his life (Ps. 42:9); Christ became the cornerstone (Matt. 21:42; cf. Psalm 118:22–23; Matt. 7:24; Eph. 2:13–22). If we suffer from spiritual depression, we can find relief in the Savior anticipated in this psalm. We must call our souls to build their confidence on the living Rock who stabilizes, protects, and provides the only basis for joy.

Psalm 43 The Psalter provides all the vocabulary necessary to articulate our deepest emotions. This psalm encourages us to express without fear even our disappointments with God. Though God has not rejected him, the psalmist feels as though he has. But God uses even our mistaken beliefs about him to draw us to himself.

Why do I [w]go about mourning
because of the oppression of the
enemy?
3 [x]Send out your light and your truth;
let them lead me;
let them bring me to your [y]holy hill
and to your [z]dwelling!
4 Then I will go to the altar of God,
to God my exceeding joy,
and I will praise you with the lyre,
O God, my God.

5 [a]Why are you cast down, O my soul,
and why are you in turmoil within
me?
[b]Hope in God; for I shall again praise
him,
my salvation and my God.

Come to Our Help

44

To the choirmaster. [c]A Maskil[1] of the Sons of Korah.

1 O God, we have heard with our ears,
[d]our fathers have told us,
what deeds you performed in their days,
[e]in the days of old:
2 you with your own hand [f]drove out the
nations,
but [g]them you planted;
you afflicted the peoples,
but [h]them you set free;
3 for not [i]by their own sword did they win
the land,
nor did their own arm save them,
but your right hand and your arm,
and [j]the light of your face,
[k]for you delighted in them.

4 [l]You are my King, O God;
[m]ordain salvation for Jacob!
5 Through you we [n]push down our foes;
through your name we [o]tread down
those who rise up against us.
6 For not in [p]my bow do I trust,
nor can my sword save me.
7 But you have saved us from our foes
and have [q]put to shame those who
hate us.
8 [r]In God we have boasted continually,
and we will give thanks to your name
forever. *Selah*

9 But you have [s]rejected us and disgraced us
and [t]have not gone out with our
armies.
10 You have made us [u]turn back from the
foe,
and those who hate us have gotten
spoil.
11 You have made us like [v]sheep for slaughter
and have [w]scattered us among the
nations.

[1] Probably a musical or liturgical term

In Christ, God will ultimately show us the relief from despair for which the psalmist longs ("salvation"; v. 5). By committing his spirit into God's hands, the suffering servant experienced vindication (v. 1; Isa. 50:7–9; Luke 23:46). Because the Lord upheld him in his righteousness, his "light" could not be overwhelmed, and the "truth" he personified could not be discredited (Ps. 43:3; John 1:5; John 18:37). After Christ's life provided justification, he was raised in holiness and later ascended to God's "altar" (Ps. 43:3, 4). And there he has received with "joy" the inheritance of the nations (v. 4; Acts 4:25, 26).

Those who are united to Christ by faith may anticipate the same trajectory of "hope in God" (Ps. 43:5). While many languages do not have an equivalent expression to "my God," this Hebrew poet assures us that God offers himself to be possessed by faith (John 20:17). Complete consignment to Jesus as our Redeemer will result in vindicating righteousness, guiding light, liberating truth, and emboldening access to God's throne room in prayer (Rom. 3:21–26; Eph. 4:20–24; John 8:32; Heb. 4:16).

Psalm 44 Verses 1–8 of the psalm are a recollection of God's deliverance of his covenant people by mighty acts. However, the mood changes in verse 9 to a complaint that, without apparent reason, God rejected his people and broke his promises of care. This psalm's movements actually reflect the unfolding drama of redemptive history, with the people of God experiencing what Christ will actually experience in their behalf to save his covenant people—with whom the Lord will never truly break faith, despite their sin. Israel thus undergoes what Jesus himself does, reinforcing a pattern of mighty deeds followed by abandonment that Christ eventually fulfills.

2 [w]Ps. 42:9
3 [x]Ps. 40:11; 57:3 [y]See Ps. 2:6; 46:4 [z]Ps. 84:1
5 [a]See Ps. 42:5 [b]Ps. 42:5, 11

Psalm 44
[c]Ps. 42, title
1 [d]Ps. 78:3; Ex. 10:2; 12:26, 27; 13:8, 14, 15; Judg. 6:13; See Deut. 6:20-23 [e]See Ps. 77:5
2 [f]Ps. 78:55; 80:8; Josh. 3:10 [g]Ex. 15:17; 2 Sam. 7:10 [h]Ps. 80:9-11; [Jer. 17:8]
3 [i]Josh. 24:12; Hos. 1:7 [j]See Ps. 4:6 [k]Deut. 4:37; 7:7, 8; 10:15
4 [l]Ps. 74:12 [m]See Ps. 42:8
5 [n][Deut. 33:17; Dan. 8:4] [o]Ps. 60:12
6 [p][Ps. 33:16; 1 Sam. 17:47]
7 [q]See Ps. 35:4
8 [r]See Ps. 34:2
9 [s]ver. 23; Ps. 43:2; 60:1, 10; 74:1; 108:11; See Ps. 89:38-45 [t][Judg. 4:14; 2 Sam. 5:24]
10 [u]Lev. 26:17; Deut. 28:25; Josh. 7:8, 12
11 [v][ver. 22] [w]Ps. 106:27; Lev. 26:33; Deut. 4:27; 28:64; Isa. 52:3; Ezek. 20:23; [John 7:35; 1 Pet. 1:1]

12 [x]You have sold your people for a trifle,
demanding no high price for them.
13 You have made us [y]the taunt of our neighbors,
the derision and [z]scorn of those around us.
14 You have made us [a]a byword among the nations,
[b]a laughingstock[1] among the peoples.
15 All day long my disgrace is before me,
and [c]shame has covered my face
16 at the sound of the taunter and reviler,
at the sight of [d]the enemy and the avenger.

17 [e]All this has come upon us,
though we have not forgotten you,
and we have not been false to your covenant.
18 Our heart has not turned back,
nor have our [f]steps [g]departed from your way;
19 yet you have [h]broken us in the place of [i]jackals
and covered us with [j]the shadow of death.
20 If we had forgotten the name of our God
or [k]spread out our hands to [l]a foreign god,
21 [m]would not God discover this?
[n]For he knows the secrets of the heart.
22 Yet [o]for your sake we are killed all the day long;
we are regarded as sheep to be slaughtered.

23 [p]Awake! Why are you sleeping, O Lord?
Rouse yourself! [q]Do not reject us forever!
24 Why [r]do you hide your face?
Why do you forget our affliction and oppression?
25 For our [s]soul is bowed down to the dust;
our belly clings to the ground.
26 Rise up; [t]come to our help!
[u]Redeem us for the sake of your steadfast love!

Your Throne, O God, Is Forever

45

To the choirmaster: according to Lilies. A Maskil[2] of [v]the Sons of Korah; a love song.

1 My heart overflows with a pleasing theme;
I address my verses to the king;
my tongue is like the pen of [w]a ready scribe.

2 You are [x]the most handsome of the sons of men;
[y]grace is poured upon your lips;
therefore God has blessed you forever.

[1] Hebrew *a shaking of the head* [2] Probably a musical or liturgical term

12[x] [Deut. 32:30; Judg. 2:14; 3:8; Jer. 15:13]
13[y] Ps. 39:8; 79:4; 89:41; 119:22; [Neh. 2:17] [z] [Ps. 80:6]
14[a] Jer. 24:9; See Job 17:6 [b] See Job 16:4
15[c] 2 Chr. 32:21
16[d] Ps. 8:2
17[e] Dan. 9:13
18[f] Ps. 37:31 [g] Ps. 119:51, 157; Job 23:11
19[h] Ps. 51:8 [i] See Job 30:29 [j] See Job 3:5
20[k] Ps. 68:31; Job 11:13 [l] See Ps. 81:9
21[m] Ps. 139:1; Jer. 17:10 [n] [John 2:25; Heb. 4:13]
22[o] ver. 11; Cited Rom. 8:36
23[p] See Ps. 35:23 [q] ver. 9
24[r] See Job 13:24
25[s] Ps. 119:25
26[t] Ps. 63:7 [u] See Ps. 25:22

Psalm 45
[v] Ps. 42, title
1[w] [Ezra 7:6]
2[x] [Isa. 33:17] [y] [Luke 4:22]; See Isa. 61:1-3

Verses 1–8 call believers to confidence because they summarize God's eternal plan to rescue a people and empower them to "push down" all enemies who serve the Serpent (v. 5; Gen. 3:15). But it must be a humble confidence: the whole plan will be accomplished in such a way as to redound to the praise of the Lord's "great might" through the "light" which came into darkness, and was the "delight" of his Father (Ps. 44:3; Eph. 1:19; John 1:9; Matt. 12:18).

Obeying despite his suffering, Christ received the "name" which is above every name and which alone saves (Ps. 44:5, 8; Phil. 2:9; Acts 4:12). Like our Savior, Christians must endure suffering on the path to eternal victory (Heb. 2:17–18). Nevertheless, the Shepherd welcomes the cry of his beloved sheep being led to slaughter (Ps. 44:9–22) and provides the words of this psalm, so that they can voice their pain while they bear the dignity of suffering with Christ. Comfort comes to the church when God draws near to his people as he did in the pillar, the cloud, and ultimately in Jesus Christ (Ps. 44:23–26; Num. 10:35).

Psalm 45 Initially descriptive of David's throne, this psalm was perfectly fulfilled at Christ's ascension according to Hebrews 1:5–9, which connects the "Son" (Ps. 2:7) to the Davidic King (2 Sam. 7:14) to "God" (Psalm 45). This King is "handsome" because he reigns righteously and "grace is poured upon [his] lips" (v. 2). Christ executes his reign by graciously speaking the Word, a Word that is "sharper than any two-edged sword" (Heb. 4:12; cf. Ps. 45:2–3, 5). But he is a meek King, "gentle and lowly in heart" (Matt. 11:29; cf. Ps. 45:4, 6). As such, he woos us to submit rather than wielding a sword of servile fear. All who "labor and are heavy laden" from slavery to the law must come to him (Matt. 11:28).

3 [z]Gird your [a]sword on your thigh,
O [b]mighty one,
in [c]your splendor and majesty!

4 In your majesty [d]ride out victoriously
for the cause of truth and meekness
and righteousness;
let your right hand teach you [e]awe-
some deeds!
5 Your arrows are sharp
in the heart of the king's enemies;
the peoples fall under you.

6 [f]Your throne, O God, is forever and ever.
The [g]scepter of your kingdom is a
scepter of uprightness;
7 [h]you have loved righteousness and
hated wickedness.
Therefore [i]God, your God, has [j]anointed
you
with the oil of [k]gladness [l]beyond your
companions;
8 your robes are all fragrant with
[m]myrrh and aloes and cassia.
From ivory palaces [n]stringed instruments make you glad;
9 daughters of kings are among your
ladies of honor;
[o]at your right hand stands the queen
in [p]gold of Ophir.

10 Hear, O daughter, and consider, and
incline your ear:
forget your people and your father's
house,
11 and the king will desire your beauty.
Since he is your [q]lord, [r]bow to him.
12 The people[1] of Tyre will [s]seek your
favor with [t]gifts,
[u]the richest of the people.[2]

13 All glorious is [v]the princess in her chamber, with robes interwoven with
gold.
14 [w]In many-colored robes [x]she is led to
the king,
with her virgin companions following behind her.
15 With joy and gladness they are led along
as they enter the palace of the king.

16 In place of your fathers shall be your sons;
you will make them [y]princes in all the
earth.
17 [z]I will cause your name to be remembered in all generations;
therefore nations will praise you forever and ever.

God Is Our Fortress

46

To the choirmaster. Of [a]the Sons of Korah. According to [b]Alamoth.[3] A Song.

1 God is our [c]refuge and strength,
a very [d]present[4] help in [e]trouble.
2 Therefore we will not fear [f]though the
earth gives way,
though the mountains be moved into
[g]the heart of the sea,
3 though [h]its waters roar and foam,
though the mountains tremble at its
swelling. *Selah*

[1] Hebrew *daughter* [2] Or *The daughter of Tyre is here with gifts, the richest of people seek your favor* [3] Probably a musical or liturgical term [4] Or *well proved*

The king of this psalm is also one who makes his bride beautiful (Ps. 45:10–14). Her clothing is stunning because his tastes are extravagant—but also because he wants his bride to reflect his attributes: "righteousness" and hatred of wickedness (vv. 7, 13–15; cf. Rev. 19:8). Because the Old Testament kings typologically represented Christ, we may see in this bride a reflection of the church as the bride of Christ (Eph. 5:25–27; Rev. 21:9). And *her* countenance is joyful because *his* shines with the "oil of gladness" (Ps. 45:7, 15; cf. 104:15). This marriage will result in a line of succession culminating in an innumerable host from every nation gathered in heaven to "praise [him] forever and ever" (45:16–17; Rev. 7:9–12). As this bride submits to her husband/king, so also any Christian who recognizes the true nature of Christ's sovereignty will desire to submit with humility, live in moral beauty, and pass on his or her faith with joy (Ps. 45:11–15).

Psalm 46 As Immanuel ("God with us"), Jesus is the personification of this psalm. For Jesus himself is our present refuge and future victory. God's past record of strong protection for his people is a present comfort to the psalmist; it is "well proved" (v. 1). Even if the unthinkable should occur—even the implosion of the earth—God's faithfulness to his promises drives away fear (vv. 2–3).

3 [z]Ex. 32:27 [a][Isa. 49:2; Heb. 4:12; Rev. 1:16; 19:15] [b][Ps. 24:8; Isa. 9:6] [c]Ps. 21:5; 96:6, 7
4 [d][Rev. 16:2] [e]See Ps. 65:5
6 [f]Ps. 93:2; 110:2; Cited Heb. 1:8, 9 [g][Ps. 67:4; 96:10]
7 [h]See Ps. 11:7 [i]Isa. 61:1 [j]Ps. 2:2; 1 Kgs. 1:39; [Acts 10:38] [k][Ps. 21:6] [l][1 Kgs. 3:13]
8 [m]John 19:39; [Matt. 2:11] [n]Ps. 150:4
9 [o][1 Kgs. 2:19; Neh. 2:6] [p]See Job 28:16
11 [q]Isa. 54:5 [r]Ps. 95:6
12 [s][Job 11:19] [t]Ps. 96:8 [u]Ps. 22:29; 68:29; 72:10; Isa. 49:7
13 [v][Rev. 19:7, 8]
14 [w][Judg. 5:30; Ezek. 16:18; 26:16] [x][Song 1:4]
16 [y]1 Pet. 2:9; Rev. 1:6; 5:10; 20:6
17 [z][Mal. 1:11]

Psalm 46 [a]Ps. 42, title [b]1 Chr. 15:20 **1** [c]See Ps. 14:6 [d]Ps. 145:18; Deut. 4:7 [e]Ps. 9:9 **2** [f][Ps. 18:7] [g]Ezek. 27:26 **3** [h][Ps. 93:3, 4; Jer. 5:22]

4 There is [i]a river whose streams make
glad [j]the city of God,
the holy [k]habitation of the Most
High.
5 [l]God is in the midst of her; she shall not
be moved;
God will help her when morning
dawns.
6 [m]The nations rage, the kingdoms totter;
he [n]utters his voice, the earth [o]melts.
7 [p]The LORD of hosts is with us;
the God of Jacob is our fortress. *Selah*

8 [q]Come, behold the works of the LORD,
how he has brought desolations on
the earth.
9 [r]He makes wars cease to the end of the
earth;
he [s]breaks the bow and shatters the
spear;
[t]he burns the chariots with fire.
10 [u]"Be still, and know that I am God.
[v]I will be exalted among the nations,
I will be exalted in the earth!"
11 [p]The LORD of hosts is with us;
the God of Jacob is our fortress. *Selah*

God Is King over All the Earth

47

TO THE CHOIRMASTER. A PSALM OF [w]THE SONS OF KORAH.

1 [x]Clap your hands, all peoples!
[y]Shout to God with loud songs of joy!
2 For the LORD, the Most High, [z]is to be
feared,
[a]a great king over all the earth.
3 He [b]subdued peoples under us,
and nations under our feet.
4 He chose our [c]heritage for us,
[d]the pride of Jacob whom he loves.
Selah

5 God [e]has gone up with a shout,
the LORD with the sound of a trumpet.
6 Sing praises to God, sing praises!
Sing praises to our King, sing praises!
7 For God is [f]the King of all the earth;
sing praises [g]with a psalm![1]

8 God [h]reigns over the nations;
God sits on his holy throne.
9 [i]The princes of the peoples gather
as the people of the God of Abraham.

[1] Hebrew *maskil*

4 [i]Ps. 36:8; 65:9; [Isa. 8:6; 33:21; Rev. 22:1, 2] [j]Ps. 48:1; 87:3; [Isa. 60:14] [k]Ps. 43:3; 84:1
5 [l]Lev. 26:12; Deut. 23:14; Isa. 12:6; Ezek. 43:7, 9; Hos. 11:9; Joel 2:27; Zeph. 3:15; Zech. 2:5, 10, 11; 8:3
6 [m]Ps. 2:1 [n]Ps. 18:13; 68:33; 76:8; Jer. 25:30; Joel 2:11; 3:16; Amos 1:2 [o]Ex. 15:15; Josh. 2:9, 24; Amos 9:5
7 [p]ver. 11; 2 Chr. 13:12; 20:17; [Num. 14:9]
8 [q]Ps. 66:5
9 [r]Isa. 2:4; Mic. 4:3 [s]Ps. 76:3; 1 Sam. 2:4 [t]Ezek. 39:9
10 [u][Ex. 14:13] [v]Isa. 2:11, 17; 33:10
11 [p][See ver. 7 above]

Psalm 47
[w]Ps. 42, title
1 [x]2 Kgs. 11:12; Isa. 55:12; Nah. 3:19 [y]Ps. 95:1; [1 Sam. 10:24]
2 [z]Ps. 66:3, 5; 68:35; Deut. 7:21 [a]Mal. 1:14
3 [b]See Ps. 18:47
4 [c]Ps. 2:8; [1 Pet. 1:4] [d]Amos 6:8; 8:7; Nah. 2:2
5 [e]2 Sam. 6:15; [Ps. 68:18]
7 [f]Zech. 14:9 [g]1 Cor. 14:15
8 [h]Ps. 22:28; 1 Chr. 16:31
9 [i][Ps. 72:11; Isa. 49:7, 23]

The Christian's confidence is even more certain because Christ personally promised to be with us to the "end of the age" (Matt. 28:20). Like a secret aqueduct to a besieged city, God's grace convinces the psalmist that the church will not only survive any onslaught but also will thrive in joy (Ps. 46:4–7). Jesus specifically revealed that the Holy Spirit is that means of grace who causes "rivers of living water" to flow from the heart of the believer (John 7:37–39).

Amid "wars and rumors of wars" (Matt. 24:6), both Old and New Testament believers are buttressed with the confidence that all the kingdoms of this world will one day become the "kingdom of our Lord and of his Christ, and he shall reign forever and ever" (Rev. 11:15), thus fulfilling God's covenant promise to Abraham (Gen. 12:1–3). Keeping our eyes on King Jesus, we must courageously witness for Christ to the ends of the earth (cf. Ps. 46:9) until the nations are given to Christ as his inheritance (2:7; Acts 1:8; 2:34–35).

Psalm 47 Because the "king over all the earth" is the one true God, the psalmist calls on all humanity to worship him expressively (vv. 1, 6). Christ not only incarnated the psalmist's vision of this loving conqueror (v. 4), he sovereignly provoked such energetic worship even among children (Matt. 21:15). Not only does Christ harness people's emotions for worship, he "subdues" their wills to be blessed in reflection of the truths of this psalm (Ps. 47:3–4).

The blessing is not merely provincial; it is for the nations, the "other sheep" of Jesus' fold (John 10:16; cf. Ps. 47:8; Gen. 12:3). Alluding to the procession of the ark of the covenant up to Jerusalem, the psalmist understood that it represented the blessed presence of God (cf. Ps. 47:5–6; 2 Sam. 6:15). Its lid and the blood that covered it once a year represented God's mercy (Lev. 16:13–16). As God looked down from heaven on his people in relationship to the law, he could see them only through the blood of a goat on the altar (cf. Ps. 47:8; Heb. 9:5).

For [j]the shields of the earth belong to
God;
he is highly exalted!

Zion, the City of Our God

48

A SONG. A PSALM OF [k]THE SONS OF KORAH.

[l]Great is the LORD and greatly to be
praised
in [m]the city of our God!
His [n]holy mountain, 2 [o]beautiful in ele-
vation,
is [p]the joy of all the earth,
Mount Zion, in the far north,
[q]the city of the great King.
3 Within her citadels God
has made himself known as a fortress.

4 For behold, [r]the kings assembled;
they came on together.
5 As soon as they saw it, they were
astounded;
they were in panic; they took to
flight.
6 [s]Trembling took hold of them there,
anguish [t]as of a woman in labor.
7 By [u]the east wind you [v]shattered
the ships of [w]Tarshish.
8 As we have heard, so have we seen
in the city of the LORD of hosts,
in [m]the city of our God,
which God will [x]establish forever.
Selah

9 We have thought on your [y]steadfast love,
O God,
in the midst of your temple.
10 As your [z]name, O God,
so your praise reaches to [a]the ends of
the earth.
Your right hand is filled with righteousness.
11 Let Mount [b]Zion be glad!
Let [b]the daughters of Judah rejoice
because of your judgments!

12 Walk about Zion, go around her,
number her towers,
13 consider well her [c]ramparts,
go through her citadels,
[d]that you may tell the next generation
14 that this is God,
our God forever and ever.
He will [e]guide us forever.[1]

[1] Septuagint; another reading is (compare Jerome, Syriac) *He will guide us beyond death*

Christ, the last Lamb, went up to Jerusalem to become that altar-sacrifice for his people by dying on the cross. He tore down the dividing curtain in the Most Holy Place (Mark 15:38). Reflecting images of this psalm, Christ's love at Calvary explains our present "loud songs of joy" and moves us to "fear"—that is, reverent trust—out of love because our sins are forgiven (Ps. 47:1–2, 5–7; 130:4).

Psalm 48 Cities are important to God (Jonah 4:11). Throughout redemptive history God has reached out to them. Patriarchs interceded for them (Gen. 18:16–33). Prophets called them to repentance (Jonah 1:1–2). And righteous kings ensured justice for their citizens (Isa. 45:13)—especially King David, who established Jerusalem as a staging ground for God's worldwide kingdom (Psalm 122).

The priestly writer of this psalm described God's special plans for Jerusalem and thus prepared God's people for the day when it would be the "city of the great King" (cf. Ps. 48:2; Matt. 5:35)—the one Christ wept for, was condemned in, and died outside of (Luke 19:41; Heb. 13:12). Jesus came there to establish a newer city of God, which would spread to the "ends of the earth" (Ps. 48:10). As a "city set on a hill" (Matt. 5:14), the church now shines the light of the gospel wherever her members live and work. This light comes from Christ in glory (Rev. 21:23).

God has historically preserved Jerusalem as an earthly illustration of his eternal protection of the "heavenly Jerusalem" (Heb. 12:22). Likewise Christ protects the church against cosmic enemies (Ps. 48:5; 1 John 4:4) and provides laws that "guide" rather than burden his subjects (Ps. 48:14). Such "steadfast love" moves kingdom citizens, generation after generation, to "be glad" and "rejoice" (vv. 9–11). Christians must look beyond the comforts or terrors of earthly cities to the "city that has foundations, whose designer and builder is God" (Heb. 11:10). Living self-consciously as citizens of that city will make Christians courageous and generous citizens within their earthly cities (Prov. 11:10–11; Heb. 13:13–14).

9 [j]Ps. 89:18
Psalm 48
[k]Ps. 42, title; 46, title
1 [l]Ps. 96:4; 145:3 [m]See Ps. 46:4 [n]Ps. 2:6; 87:1; Zech. 8:3; [Isa. 2:3; Mic. 4:1]
2 [o]See Ps. 50:2 [p]Lam. 2:15; [Ezek. 20:6] [q]Matt. 5:35
4 [r]See 2 Sam. 10:6-19
6 [s][Ex. 15:15] [t]Isa. 13:8; Hos. 13:13
7 [u]Jer. 18:17 [v]1 Kgs. 22:48; Ezek. 27:26 [w]1 Kgs. 10:22
8 [m][See ver. 1 above] [x]Ps. 87:5; Isa. 2:2; Mic. 4:1
9 [y]Ps. 26:3; 40:10
10 [z]Ps. 113:3; [Ex. 34:5, 6; Deut. 28:58; Mal. 1:11, 14] [a]See Ps. 22:27
11 [b]Ps. 97:8
13 [c]Ps. 122:7 [d][Ps. 78:4-6]
14 [e]Ps. 23:3, 4

Why Should I Fear in Times of Trouble?

49 To the choirmaster. A Psalm of [f]the Sons of Korah.

1 [g]Hear this, all peoples!
Give ear, all inhabitants of the world,
2 [h]both low and high,
rich and poor together!
3 My mouth shall speak [i]wisdom;
the meditation of my heart shall be understanding.
4 I will incline my ear to [j]a proverb;
I will solve my [k]riddle to the music of the lyre.

5 [l]Why should I fear in [m]times of trouble,
when the iniquity of those who cheat me surrounds me,
6 those who [n]trust in their wealth
and boast of the abundance of their riches?
7 Truly no man [o]can ransom another,
or [p]give to God [q]the price of his life,
8 for [r]the ransom of their life is costly
and can never suffice,
9 that he should live on forever
and [s]never see the pit.

10 For he sees [t]that even the wise die;
[u]the fool and the stupid alike must perish
and [v]leave their wealth to others.
11 Their [w]graves are their homes forever,[1]
their dwelling places [x]to all generations,
though they [y]called lands by their own names.
12 Man in his pomp [z]will not remain;
[a]he is like the beasts that perish.

13 This is the path of those who have [b]foolish confidence;
yet after them people approve of their boasts.[2] *Selah*
14 Like sheep they are appointed for Sheol;
death shall be their shepherd,
and the upright [c]shall rule over them in the morning.
[d]Their form shall be consumed [e]in Sheol, with no place to dwell.
15 But God will [f]ransom my soul from the power of Sheol,
for he will [g]receive me. *Selah*

16 Be not afraid when a man becomes rich,
when the glory of his house increases.
17 [h]For when he dies he will [i]carry nothing away;
his glory will not go down after him.
18 For though, while he lives, he counts himself [j]blessed
—and though you get praise when you do well for yourself—
19 his soul will [k]go to the generation of his fathers,
who will never again [l]see light.
20 [m]Man in his pomp yet without understanding is like the beasts that perish.

God Himself Is Judge

50 A Psalm of [n]Asaph.

1 [o]The Mighty One, God the Lord,
speaks and summons the earth
[p]from the rising of the sun to its setting.

[1] Septuagint, Syriac, Targum; Hebrew *Their inward thought was that their homes were forever* [2] Or *and of those after them who approve of their boasts*

Psalm 49
[f]Ps. 42, title
1[g]Ps. 78:1; Isa. 1:2; Mic. 1:2
2[h]Ps. 62:9
3[i]Prov. 1:20; 9:1
4[j][Ps. 78:2; Matt. 13:35]
[k]Num. 12:8; Prov. 1:6
5[l][Ps. 37:1] [m]Ps. 94:13
6[n]Ps. 52:7; Prov. 11:28; Mark 10:24, 25; [Job 31:24]
7[o][Matt. 25:9] [p][Matt. 16:26]
[q]See Job 33:24
8[r]Job 36:18, 19
9[s]Ps. 16:10; [Ps. 89:48]
10[t]Eccles. 2:16 [u]Ps. 73:22; 92:6; 94:8; Prov. 30:2 [v]See Ps. 39:6
11[w]Ps. 5:9; 64:6 [x]Ps. 10:6
[y][Gen. 4:17]
12[z]ver. 20; [Ps. 39:5; 82:7]
[a]ver. 20; Eccles. 3:19

Psalm 49 The psalmists provide three strategies for combatting bitterness toward pompous unbelievers. The first is to follow God's Word. When disciples meditate on the promises of God's Word, they will focus less on material inequity and more on the certainty of God's promises (vv. 1–3; Matt. 6:33–34).

Furthermore, they will sing God's Word. Worship through song fertilizes the Word in the deepest parts of the heart (Ps. 49:4). The psalmist refuses to be intimidated by those who claim superiority and put their trust in their moral portfolio. Viewing God with the eyes of faith minimizes even the most foreboding threat (vv. 5–7).

When one feels like the way of righteousness is a waste of time, eternity is the third place to which one must focus one's eyes of faith. No matter how valuable the unbeliever believes his worldly possessions to be, they do not equal the cost to ransom a soul (vv. 17–20). The soul itself is of inestimable worth; therefore, to ransom it from eternal death required an infinite price (vv. 7–9). The costliness of the sacrifice denotes

13[b][Luke 12:20] **14**[c][Dan. 7:22; Mal. 4:3; Luke 22:30; 1 Cor. 6:2; Rev. 2:26; 20:4] [d]Ps. 39:11 [e]Job 24:19, 20 **15**[f]Hos. 13:14; [Dan. 12:2] [g]Ps. 16:11; 17:15; 73:24; [Gen. 5:24] **17**[h][Job 27:19] [i]1 Tim. 6:7 **18**[j]Ps. 10:3; 36:2; Deut. 29:19; Luke 12:19 **19**[k]Gen. 15:15 [l]Ps. 56:13; Job 33:30 **20**[m]ver. 12 **Psalm 50**
[n]1 Chr. 6:39; 15:17; 16:5, 7; 25:2; 2 Chr. 29:30 **1**[o]Josh. 22:22 [p]Ps. 113:3

2 Out of Zion, [q]the perfection of beauty,
[r]God shines forth.

3 Our God comes; he [s]does not keep silence;[1]
before him is a devouring [t]fire,
around him a mighty tempest.
4 [u]He calls to the heavens above
and to the earth, that he may judge his people:
5 "Gather to me my faithful ones,
who made [v]a covenant with me by sacrifice!"
6 [w]The heavens declare his righteousness,
for [x]God himself is judge! *Selah*

7 [y]"Hear, O my people, and I will speak;
O Israel, I will testify against you.
[z]I am God, your God.
8 Not for your sacrifices [a]do I rebuke you;
your burnt offerings are continually before me.
9 I will not accept a bull from your house
or goats from your folds.
10 For every beast of the forest is mine,
the cattle on a thousand hills.
11 [b]I know all the birds of the hills,
and all that moves in the field is mine.

12 "If I were hungry, I would not tell you,
[c]for the world and its fullness are mine.
13 Do I eat the flesh of bulls
or drink the blood of goats?
14 [d]Offer to God a sacrifice of thanksgiving,[2]
and [e]perform your vows to the Most High,
15 and [f]call upon me in the day of trouble;
I will [g]deliver you, and you shall [h]glorify me."

16 But to the wicked God says:
"What right have you to recite my statutes
or take my covenant on your lips?
17 [i]For you hate discipline,
[j]and you cast my words behind you.
18 If you see a thief, [k]you are pleased with him,
[l]and you keep company with adulterers.

19 "You give your mouth free rein for evil,
[m]and your tongue frames deceit.
20 You sit and speak against your brother;
you slander your own mother's son.
21 These things you have done, and I [n]have been silent;
you thought that I[3] was one like yourself.
But now I [o]rebuke you and [p]lay the charge before you.

[1] Or *May our God come, and not keep silence* [2] Or *Make thanksgiving your sacrifice to God* [3] Or *that the* I AM

the efficacy of salvation in contrast to the "foolish confidence" of the unbeliever, and it explains the believer's fearlessness (vv. 10–16). The price Jesus paid to ransom lost souls was given with love, to create friends who would serve God in warmhearted gratitude for grace (Mark 10:45; John 15:13; 1 Tim. 2:6; 1 Pet. 1:18–19).

Psalm 50 Speaking on behalf of God, Asaph warns the church to repent of her perfunctory worship or else face judgment (vv. 5, 16, 22). The unrepentant will be proven in a covenant lawsuit to be the "wicked" rather than true disciples (vv. 6–7, 16–21). Without negating the sacrificial system, God expresses his greater desire for worshipers who are grateful for salvation (vv. 8, 23). He has no need for food or drink; he wants a heartfelt relationship with his children (vv. 9–15).

At this point in redemptive history, God's ways had been most significantly revealed at Sinai. Through "devouring fire" and "tempest," God proved that he was near as the mighty Savior (vv. 1, 3). There he also provided commandments to guide his children into a righteous life. Three of those commands—against stealing, adultery, and lying—are presented here as shorthand for all ten (vv. 18–20). God rebukes his people for breaking, and even hating, his decrees (vv. 17, 21).

On Mount Sinai God also prescribed the sacrificial system, because he knew the law was impossible to keep. The law has always driven sinners to the end of themselves and thus to the sacrifices as means of grace. Offerings which could never save did, however, prepare the way for the slaughter of the last Lamb on "Zion" (v. 2; cf. 1 Cor. 5:7). This once-and-for-all sacrifice by Christ demands a life of public and private gratitude in response (Ps. 50:20–21). The One perfect in beauty and righteousness will generate such beauty and righteousness in us as we seek him (vv. 2, 6).

2[q] [Lam. 2:15]; See Ps. 48:2 [r] Ps. 80:1; 94:1; Deut. 33:2
3[s] [Ex. 19:16] [t] Ps. 21:9; 97:3; Lev. 10:2; Num. 16:35; Dan. 7:10
4[u] Deut. 4:26; 31:28; 32:1; Isa. 1:2; Mic. 6:1, 2
5[v] Ex. 24:7, 8; See Gen. 15:9-18
6[w] Ps. 89:5; 97:6; [Rev. 16:5, 7; 19:2] [x] Ps. 58:11; 75:7
7[y] Ps. 81:8; [Ps. 49:1] [z] Ex. 20:2
8[a] See Ps. 40:6
11[b] [Matt. 10:29]
12[c] See Ps. 24:1
14[d] ver. 23; Ps. 27:6; 69:30; 107:22; Heb. 13:15; [Hos. 14:2; Rom. 12:1] [e] Ps. 22:25; 61:8; 65:1; 76:11; 116:14, 18; Num. 30:2; Deut. 23:21; Job 22:27; Eccles. 5:4, 5
15[f] Ps. 81:7; Zech. 13:9; [Ps. 107:6] [g] Ps. 91:15 [h] ver. 23; Ps. 22:23
17[i] [Rom. 2:21, 22] [j] 1 Kgs. 14:9; Neh. 9:26
18[k] Rom. 1:32 [l] [1 Tim. 5:22]
19[m] [Ps. 52:2]
21[n] Eccles. 8:11; Isa. 57:11 [o] Ps. 90:8; 2 Kgs. 19:4 [p] Job 13:18; 23:4

22 "Mark this, then, you who [q]forget God,
lest I tear you apart, and there be
[r]none to deliver!
23 The one who [s]offers thanksgiving as his
sacrifice glorifies me;
to one who [t]orders his way rightly
I will show the [u]salvation of God!"

Create in Me a Clean Heart, O God

51 To the choirmaster. A Psalm of David, when [v]Nathan the prophet went to him, after he had gone in to Bathsheba.

1 [w]Have mercy on me,[1] O God,
according to your steadfast love;
according to your [x]abundant mercy
[y]blot out my transgressions.
2 [z]Wash me thoroughly from my iniquity,
and [a]cleanse me from my sin!

3 [b]For I know my transgressions,
and my sin is ever before me.
4 [c]Against you, you only, have I sinned
and done what is evil [d]in your sight,
[e]so that you may be justified in your words
and blameless in your judgment.
5 Behold, [f]I was brought forth in iniquity,
and in sin did my mother conceive me.
6 Behold, you delight in truth in [g]the
inward being,
and you teach me wisdom in the
secret heart.
7 Purge me [h]with hyssop, and I shall be
clean;
[z]wash me, and I shall be [i]whiter than
snow.
8 Let me hear joy and gladness;
[j]let the bones [k]that you have broken
rejoice.
9 [l]Hide your face from my sins,
and [y]blot out all my iniquities.
10 [m]Create in me a [n]clean heart, O God,
and [o]renew a right[2] spirit within me.
11 [p]Cast me not away from your presence,
and take not [q]your Holy Spirit from
me.
12 Restore to me the joy of your salvation,
and uphold me with a willing spirit.

13 Then I will teach transgressors your ways,
and sinners will [r]return to you.
14 Deliver me from [s]bloodguiltiness, O God,
O [t]God of my salvation,
and [u]my tongue will sing aloud of
your [v]righteousness.
15 O Lord, open my lips,
and my mouth will declare your praise.
16 [w]For you will not delight in sacrifice, or
I would give it;
you will not be pleased with a burnt
offering.
17 The sacrifices of God are [x]a broken spirit;
a broken and contrite heart, O God,
you will not despise.

[1] Or *Be gracious to me* [2] Or *steadfast*

22[q]See Ps. 9:17 [r]Ps. 7:2
23[s]ver. 14, 15 [t][Gal. 6:16] [u]Ps. 91:16
Psalm 51 [v]2 Sam. 12:1
1[w]See Ps. 4:1 [x]See Ps. 106:45 [y]ver. 9; Isa. 43:25; 44:22; Acts 3:19; Col. 2:14
2[z]ver. 7; Isa. 1:16; Jer. 4:14; Mal. 3:3; Acts 22:16 [a]Heb. 9:14; 1 John 1:7, 9; [Lev. 13:6]
3[b]Ps. 32:5; [Prov. 28:13]
4[c]Gen. 20:6; 39:9; 2 Sam. 12:13; [1 Cor. 8:12] [d]Luke 15:18, 21 [e]Cited Rom. 3:4
5[f]Rom. 5:12, 19; Eph. 2:3; See Job 14:4; 15:14
6[g]Job 38:36
7[h]Ex. 12:22; Lev. 14:4; Num. 19:18; Heb. 9:19 [z][See ver. 2 above] [i]Isa. 1:18
8[j]Ps. 35:10 [k]Ps. 44:19; Isa. 38:13
9[l]Jer. 16:17 [y][See ver. 1 above]
10[m]1 Sam. 10:9; Jer. 24:7; Ezek. 11:19; 36:26; Eph. 4:23, 24 [n]Ps. 24:4; Matt. 5:8; Acts 15:9 [o]Lam. 5:21
11[p]Ps. 102:10; 2 Kgs. 13:23; 17:20; 24:20; Jer. 7:15 [q]Rom. 8:9; Eph. 4:30 **13**[r][Luke 22:32] **14**[s]2 Sam. 11:17; 12:9 [t]Ps. 24:5 [u]Ps. 35:28; 71:8, 15, 24 [v][1 John 1:9] **16**[w]See Ps. 40:6
17[x]See Ps. 34:18

Psalm 51 That David's personal confession of adultery and murder could be turned into a divinely inspired congregational hymn proves that "whoever comes" to Christ will never be "cast out" (John 6:37). After Nathan's rebuke, David went straight to the Lord, who had revealed himself as "merciful" and "abounding in steadfast love" (Ex. 34:6; cf. Ps. 51:1). David's psalm is no proposal for rehabilitation, only a plea for cleansing (Ps. 51:2, 7; Titus 3:5).

There is no self-justification, only affirmation of God's justice (Ps. 51:3–6; cf. 1 John 1:9). David does not blame his upbringing; he was a sinner before he was born (Ps. 51:5; Rom. 3:4). He does not claim mitigating circumstances; these were "sins" and "iniquities" (Ps. 51:9; 1 Cor. 6:9, 10). Only God can qualify a sinner to stand in his presence (Ps. 51:11). As a priest, God cleanses the confessing sinner (vv. 2, 7, 17; Num. 19:6). As a judge, he blots out his guilty record (Ps. 51:9, 14). As the Creator, he remakes his heart (v. 10).

But the gore of the sacrificial system hinted to David that supplying these needed graces would cost God personally (vv. 1, 4, 9, 12, 14). Only Christ's innocent blood could ultimately erase human guilt (Heb. 9:14, 22). Only Christ's perfect record of "righteousness" can substitute for iniquities (cf. Ps. 51:14). And only Christ's Spirit can regenerate wills (vv. 12, 19; Titus 3:8). Christ's is the only sacrifice God has permanently delighted in (Ps. 51:16; Heb. 10:5–10). Salvation is a gift granted by God's "good pleasure," never in response to merit or desert (Ps. 51:18; Phil. 2:13). Joyful obedience—never pride—is the response to grace (Ps. 51:12, 15).

18 [y]Do good to Zion in your good pleasure;
[z]build up the walls of Jerusalem;
19 then will you delight in [a]right sacrifices,
in burnt offerings and [b]whole burnt offerings;
then bulls will be offered on your altar.

The Steadfast Love of God Endures

52 To the choirmaster. A Maskil[1] of David, when [c]Doeg, the Edomite, came and told Saul, "David has come to the house of Ahimelech."

1 Why do you boast of evil, O mighty man?
The steadfast love of God endures all the day.
2 Your [d]tongue plots destruction,
like [e]a sharp razor, you [f]worker of deceit.
3 You love evil more than good,
and [g]lying more than speaking what is right. *Selah*
4 You love all words that devour,
O deceitful tongue.

5 But God will break you down forever;
he will snatch and [h]tear you from your tent;
he will uproot you from [i]the land of the living. *Selah*
6 The righteous shall [j]see and fear,
and shall [k]laugh at him, saying,
7 "See the man who would not make God his refuge,
but [l]trusted in the abundance of his riches
and sought refuge in his own destruction!"[2]

8 But I am like [m]a green olive tree
in the house of God.
I trust in the steadfast love of God
forever and ever.
9 I will thank you forever,
because you have done it.
I will wait for your name, [n]for it is good,
in the presence of the [o]godly.

There Is None Who Does Good

53 To the choirmaster: according to [p]Mahalath. A Maskil[3] of David.

1 [q]The fool says in his heart, "There is no God."
They are corrupt, doing abominable iniquity;
there is none who does good.

2 God looks down from heaven
on the children of man
to see if there are any who understand,[4]
who seek after God.

3 They have all fallen away;
together they have become corrupt;
there is none who does good,
not even one.

[1] Probably a musical or liturgical term [2] Or *in his work of destruction* [3] Probably musical or liturgical terms [4] Or *who act wisely*

Psalm 52 God's steadfast love endures longer than the worst evil, even the insidious betrayal of Doeg (superscription and v. 1), and David's blessed life proves that God's love is more trustworthy than wealth (vv. 7–9). God's love is enduring and trustworthy because its promises are founded on his character, which is absolute truth as personified in Jesus Christ (John 17:17). As such, God's steadfast love stands in contrast to human devotion, which is fallible even when presented with the best appearances (Ps. 52:2–4; Rom. 3:4). The believer should be comforted to know that God will prove the truthfulness of his love, not least by destroying the deceitfulness of the wicked (Ps. 52:5; 2 Thess. 1:10).

God displays the superior nature of his love by the fruit it produces in a believer's life. Love then produces courage instead of panic, contentment rather than avarice, vitality in place of death, and joy as opposed to bitterness (Ps. 52:6–9). Christ was eventually revealed to be the true "olive tree," which gives life to everyone grafted into him by faith (cf. Ps. 52:8; John 15:1; Rom. 11:17). The psalmist's establishment "in the house of God" (Ps. 52:8) reminds us that ultimately Christ's love will make each believer a pillar there (Rev. 3:12).

Psalm 53 There are only two major differences between this psalm and Psalm 14. Rather than referring to God by his covenant name "the LORD" (e.g., Ps. 14:2), Psalm 53 refers to Israel's Savior as "God" throughout. The second difference is that 53:5 focuses on God's judgment on his enemies versus his care for the poor in 14:5–6. God comforts his people by describing his eventual terrifying subjugation of all those who attack them.

18[y] [Ps. 69:35; 122:6] [z] Ps. 147:2
19[a] Ps. 4:5; [Mal. 3:3] [b] Deut. 33:10
Psalm 52
[c] 1 Sam. 22:9
2[d] Ps. 50:19 [e] [Ps. 57:4] [f] Ps. 101:7
3[g] [Jer. 9:4, 5]
5[h] Prov. 2:22 [i] See Ps. 27:13
6[j] See Ps. 40:3 [k] See Ps. 2:4
7[l] See Ps. 49:6
8[m] Jer. 11:16; [Ps. 1:3; 37:35; 92:12, 13; 128:3; 144:12; Hos. 14:6]
9[n] Ps. 54:6 [o] See Ps. 50:5
Psalm 53
[p] Ps. 88, title
1[q] For ver. 1-6, see Ps. 14:1-7

4 Have those who work evil no knowledge,
who eat up my people as they eat bread,
and do not call upon God?

5 There they are, in great terror,
[r]where there is no terror!
For God [s]scatters the bones of him who encamps against you;
you put them to shame, for God has rejected them.

6 Oh, that salvation for Israel would come out of Zion!
When God restores the fortunes of his people,
let Jacob rejoice, let Israel be glad.

The Lord Upholds My Life

54 To the choirmaster: with [t]stringed instruments. A Maskil[1] of David, [u]when the Ziphites went and told Saul, "Is not David hiding among us?"

1 O God, save me by your [v]name,
and vindicate me by your might.
2 O God, [w]hear my prayer;
give ear to the words of my mouth.

3 [x]For [y]strangers[2] have risen against me;
ruthless men [z]seek my life;
they do not set God before themselves. *Selah*

4 Behold, [a]God is my helper;
the Lord is the upholder of my life.
5 He will return the evil to my enemies;
in your [b]faithfulness [c]put an end to them.

6 With a freewill offering I will sacrifice to you;
I will give thanks to your name,
O Lord, [d]for it is good.
7 For he has delivered me from every trouble,
and my eye has [e]looked in triumph on my enemies.

Cast Your Burden on the Lord

55 To the choirmaster: with [f]stringed instruments. A Maskil[3] of David.

1 [g]Give ear to my prayer, O God,
and hide not yourself from my plea for mercy!

[1] Probably a musical or liturgical term [2] Some Hebrew manuscripts and Targum *insolent men* (compare Psalm 86:14) [3] Probably a musical or liturgical term

5[r] [Lev. 26:17, 36; Prov. 28:1] [s] Ps. 89:10; 141:7; Jer. 8:1, 2; Ezek. 6:5
Psalm 54
[t] Ps. 4, title [u] 1 Sam. 23:19; 26:1
1[v] Ps. 5:11; 52:9
2[w] See Ps. 55:1
3[x] Ps. 86:14 [y] Ps. 18:44; 144:7; Isa. 25:5 [z] [1 Sam. 23:15]
4[a] Ps. 118:7
5[b] [Ps. 89:49] [c] Ps. 143:12
6[d] Ps. 52:9
7[e] Ps. 59:10; 92:11; 112:8; 118:7
Psalm 55
[f] Ps. 4, title
1[g] Ps. 54:2; 61:1; 86:6

Throughout redemptive history, God has shown his ability to instill direct fear in the enemies of his people through acts of judgment. For no obvious reason, God's enemies have been sent into a panic (53:5; cf. Josh. 10:10; Judg. 7:22; 1 Sam. 14:15; 18:12). Though rare, God occasionally "scatters the bones" (Ps. 53:5), serving as a preview of the coming Great Day (2 Kings 19:35–37; Acts 5:5, 11; Rev. 19:21). However, until Christ returns such fear is intended to drive all to the "salvation" that comes out of "Zion"—where Christ died and rose to life (Ps. 53:6; Mark 5:36; 1 John 4:18; Rev. 14:7).

Psalm 54 When David is betrayed, he seeks the Lord rather than seeking revenge (vv. 1–2; 1 Sam. 23:19). It is a poignant pain when, like a "stranger," a countryman/neighbor sells you out (note the superscription to Psalm 54, as well as v. 3). So here is a hymn for a believer to sing when such an unthinkable thing occurs. No matter how close the treachery, God is closer still as a "helper," like Eve to Adam (v. 4; Gen. 2:18).

Since God's "might" (Ps. 54:1) is greater than the strength of the worst enemies, he is not only near but powerful enough to help. And since he is faithful, the believer can wait for God to bring justice on traitors at the end of time (v. 5; 2 Thess. 1:5, 6; Rev. 6:10). In contrast to the short-sightedness of his enemies, David "set God before" himself, which produced a defiant hope (Ps. 54:5). Hope enables a believer to rejoice in an invincible future even in the midst of trouble.

God's almighty and present grace even provokes David to generosity. Since he is responding to grace, his offering is a "freewill" offering, celebrating the peace he has with a reconciling God (v. 6; Lev. 7:16). So sure is David of final deliverance from all evil, he can speak of it as if it has already come. What makes him confident in future grace is his prophetic vision that his Lord (ultimately revealed in Christ) will triumph over all enemies on the cross and will make his children their judges (cf. Matt. 22:43; 1 Cor. 2:15; 6:2).

2 Attend to me, and answer me;
I am restless [h]in my complaint and
I [i]moan,
3 because of the noise of the enemy,
because of the oppression of the
wicked.
For they [j]drop trouble upon me,
and in anger they bear a grudge
against me.

4 My heart is in anguish within me;
[k]the terrors of death have fallen upon
me.
5 Fear and trembling come upon me,
and [l]horror [m]overwhelms me.
6 And I say, "Oh, that I had wings like a
dove!
I would fly away and be at rest;
7 [n]yes, I would wander far away;
I would lodge in the wilderness; *Selah*
8 I would hurry to find a shelter
from [o]the raging wind and tempest."

9 Destroy, O Lord, [p]divide their tongues;
for I see [q]violence and strife in the city.
10 Day and night they go around it
on its walls,
and [r]iniquity and trouble are within it;
11 ruin is in its midst;
[s]oppression and fraud
do not depart from its marketplace.

12 For it is not an enemy who taunts me—
then I could bear it;
it is not an adversary who [t]deals insolently with me—
then I could hide from him.
13 [u]But it is you, a man, my equal,
my companion, my familiar friend.
14 We used to take sweet counsel together;
within God's house we walked in [v]the
throng.
15 Let death steal over them;
let them go down to Sheol [w]alive;
for evil is in their dwelling place and
in their heart.

16 But I call to God,
and the LORD will save me.
17 [x]Evening and [y]morning and at [z]noon
I [a]utter my complaint and moan,
and he hears my voice.
18 He redeems my soul in safety
from the battle that I wage,
for [b]many are arrayed against me.
19 God will give ear and humble them,
he who is [c]enthroned from of old,
Selah
because they do not [d]change
and do not fear God.

20 My companion[1] [e]stretched out his hand
against his friends;
he violated his covenant.
21 His [f]speech was [g]smooth as butter,
yet war was in his heart;
his words were softer than oil,
yet they were [h]drawn swords.

22 [i]Cast your burden on the LORD,
and he will sustain you;
[j]he will never permit
the righteous to be moved.

23 But you, O God, [k]will cast them down
into [l]the pit of destruction;
men of [m]blood and treachery
shall not [n]live out half their days.
But I will [o]trust in you.

[1] Hebrew *He*

Psalm 55 Previously David alluded to the angst caused when countrymen become traitors (Psalm 54). In this psalm he describes the pain of being betrayed by a close friend (55:12–14, 20, 21; cf. 2 Sam. 15:1–12; 16:15–23). His hymn gives voice to the panic-stricken (Ps. 55:2–6). He articulates the escapist thoughts of the anxious (vv. 7, 8). He fashions imprecations to express anger to the Lord rather than storing it up in bitterness or acting on it in rage (vv. 9, 10, 15).

Recalling that God is King allows the believer to calm his emotions (v. 19). He is calmed by the realization that his Shepherd-King "gives ear" to his "voice" and protects his soul in the battle (vv. 16–19; 78:72). The believer's faith is reawakened when he remembers that God will bring justice upon the treacherous (55:23). A fresh vision of a benevolent and all-powerful King creates a stable and steadfast faith, inviting other anxious souls to "cast [their] burden" upon the Lord rather than be cast about on the waves of doubt or even be cast down into the "pit of destruction" (vv. 22–23; 1 Pet. 5:6–7). Even now, Christ rules over all (Phil. 2:9).

2[h] ver. 17; Ps. 64:1 [i][Isa. 38:14; 59:11]
3[j] [2 Sam. 16:7, 8]
4[k] Ps. 116:3
5[l] Job 21:6; Isa. 21:4; Ezek. 7:18 [m] Ps. 78:53
7[n] [Jer. 9:2]
8[o] Ps. 83:15
9[p] [Gen. 11:9] [q] Jer. 6:7
10[r] Ps. 5:9
11[s] [Ps. 10:7]
12[t] Job 19:5
13[u] [2 Sam. 15:12; 16:23]; See Ps. 41:9
14[v] Ps. 42:4
15[w] Num. 16:30, 33; Prov. 1:12; [Ps. 124:3]
17[x] Ps. 141:2; Acts 3:1; 10:3, 30 [y] Ps. 5:3; 88:13; 92:2 [z] Acts 10:9; [Dan. 6:10] [a] ver. 2
18[b] [Ps. 56:2]

19[c] Deut. 33:27 [d] Job 10:17; See Job 21:7-15 **20**[e] Acts 12:1 **21**[f] See Ps. 28:3 [g] Prov. 5:3, 4 [h] See Ps. 57:4 **22**[i] See Ps. 37:5 [j] Ps. 10:6 **23**[k] ver. 15; Ps. 56:7; 59:11 [l] Ps. 69:15; 94:13 [m] Ps. 5:6 [n] Prov. 10:27; See Job 15:32 [o] See Ps. 11:1

In God I Trust

56 To the choirmaster: according to The Dove on Far-off Terebinths. A [p]Miktam[1] of David, when the [q]Philistines seized him in Gath.

1 [r]Be gracious to me, O God, for man
[s]tramples on me;
all day long an attacker oppresses me;
2 my enemies trample on me all day long,
for many attack me proudly.
3 When I am afraid,
I [t]put my trust in you.
4 In God, whose word I praise,
in God I trust; [u]I shall not be afraid.
What can flesh do to me?

5 All day long they injure my cause;[2]
all their thoughts are against me for evil.
6 They [v]stir up strife, they [w]lurk;
they [x]watch my steps,
as they have waited for my life.
7 For their crime will they escape?
[y]In wrath [z]cast down the peoples,
O God!

8 You have kept count of my tossings;[3]
[a]put my tears in your bottle.
[b]Are they not in your book?
9 Then my enemies will turn back
[c]in the day when I call.
This I know, that[4] [d]God is for me.
10 In God, whose word I praise,
in the LORD, whose word I praise,
11 in God I trust; [u]I shall not be afraid.
What can man do to me?

12 I must perform my [e]vows to you, O God;
I will [e]render thank offerings to you.
13 [f]For you have delivered my soul from death,
yes, my feet from falling,
[g]that I may walk before God
[h]in the light of life.

Let Your Glory Be over All the Earth

57 To the choirmaster: according to [i]Do Not Destroy. A [j]Miktam[5] of David, when he fled from Saul, in [k]the cave.

1 [l]Be merciful to me, O God, be merciful to me,
for in you my soul [m]takes refuge;
in [n]the shadow of your wings I will take refuge,
[o]till the storms of destruction pass by.
2 I cry out to God Most High,
to God who [p]fulfills his purpose for me.

[1] Probably a musical or liturgical term [2] Or *they twist my words* [3] Or *wanderings* [4] Or *because* [5] Probably a musical or liturgical term

Psalm 56
[p]Ps. 16, title; 57, title
[q][1 Sam. 21:10, 11; 22:1]
1 [r]Ps. 57:1; See Ps. 4:1 [s]Ps. 57:3
3 [t]See Ps. 11:1
4 [u]Ps. 27:1; 118:6; Isa. 51:12; Heb. 13:6
6 [v]Ps. 59:3; 140:2; Isa. 54:15 [w]Ps. 10:8 [x]Ps. 71:10
7 [y]Ps. 7:6; 59:5 [z]See Ps. 55:23
8 [a][Ps. 39:12; 2 Kgs. 20:5] [b][Mal. 3:16]
9 [c]Ps. 102:2 [d]Ps. 118:6; [Rom. 8:31]
11 [u][See ver. 4 above]
12 [e]See Ps. 50:14
13 [f]Ps. 49:15; 116:8 [g]Ps. 116:9 [h][Ps. 49:19]

Psalm 57
[i][Ps. 58, title; 59, title; 75, title] [j]Ps. 16, title; 56, title [k]1 Sam. 22:1; 24:1-3; [Ps. 142, title]
1 [l]Ps. 56:1; See Ps. 4:1 [m]Ps. 91:4 [n]See Ps. 17:8 [o]Isa. 26:20
2 [p]Ps. 138:8

Psalm 56 Realizing that God is for you is the antidote to fear (vv. 9, 13). Throughout his life, David was so convinced of the Lord's gracious character that he would choose even God's judgment over man's oppression (v. 1; 2 Sam. 24:13–14). David's imprecations are bold because his enemy's hostility threatens his "cause," which is to continue the line through which the Messiah will come (Ps. 56:5; Acts 2:29–32). Prayers for the success of Christ's kingdom will always be answered (Ps. 56:6, 7, 9; Luke 11:2). But prayerfully trusting and not fearing is a perennial battle. While David asserts, "I shall not be afraid," he admits that there will be times when he fails to trust (Ps. 56:4, 11). In those times he must return to God's Word and trust his promises (vv. 4, 10).

There are two other "pills to take" for fear in this psalm. One is logic. Often the Bible commands us to "consider" or "reason." In this instance, David considers, "What can man do to me?" (see vv. 4, 11). Of course men can kill, but David says we must trust the One who has "delivered my soul from death" (v. 13). The second is worship. Even before experiencing God's answer, David worships the Lord with thanksgiving and obedience (vv. 4, 11, 12). How much greater reason is there for the Christian to be courageous! God's Word became flesh. Through his apostles he caused even more to be written down, and he has given us the Holy Spirit to lead us in the "light" of life (v. 13; John 1:1–4).

Psalm 57 God's glory is his mercy, and his mercy evokes a believer's "glory" (vv. 1, 8; Ex. 34:6). Anyone else looking at David's situation would have concluded that he was utterly vulnerable, cowering as he was in a cave, hiding from Saul (1 Sam. 22:1). But with his eyes of faith set on the Lord, David felt himself to be hidden in the "shadow" of God's wings (Ps. 57:1).

3 [q]He will send from heaven and save me;
he will put to shame [r]him who tramples on me. *Selah*
[s]God will send out [t]his steadfast love and his faithfulness!

4 My soul is in the midst of [u]lions;
I lie down amid fiery beasts—
the children of man, whose [v]teeth are spears and arrows,
whose [w]tongues are sharp swords.

5 [x]Be exalted, O God, above the heavens!
Let your glory be over all the earth!

6 They set [y]a net for my steps;
my soul was [z]bowed down.
They [a]dug a pit in my way,
but they have fallen into it themselves. *Selah*

7 [b]My heart is [c]steadfast, O God,
my heart is steadfast!
I will sing and make melody!
8 [d]Awake, [e]my glory![1]
Awake, [f]O harp and lyre!
I will awake the dawn!
9 I will give thanks to you, O Lord, among the peoples;
I will sing praises to you among the nations.
10 For your [g]steadfast love is great to the heavens,
your faithfulness to the clouds.

11 [x]Be exalted, O God, above the heavens!
Let your glory be over all the earth!

God Who Judges the Earth

58

To the choirmaster: according to [h]Do Not Destroy. A [i]Miktam[2] of David.

1 Do you indeed decree what is right, you gods?[3]
Do you judge the children of man uprightly?
2 No, in your hearts you devise wrongs;
your hands [j]deal out violence on earth.

3 The wicked are [k]estranged from the womb;
they go astray from birth, speaking lies.
4 [l]They have venom like the venom of a serpent,
like the deaf adder that stops its ear,
5 so that it [m]does not hear the voice of charmers
or of the cunning enchanter.

6 O God, [n]break the teeth in their mouths;
tear out the fangs of the young lions, O Lord!
7 Let them [o]vanish like water that runs away;
when he [p]aims his arrows, let them be blunted.

[1] Or *my whole being* [2] Probably a musical or liturgical term [3] Or *you mighty lords* (by revocalization; Hebrew *in silence*)

The secret to David's confidence is getting God's attributes in clear view. Recalling God's sovereignty assures David that God will "fulfill his purpose" to bring the Savior from David's line (v. 2). A clear view of God's grace in Christ inspires Christians to pursue with faithfulness God's purpose for their lives (Acts 11:23). His omnipotence means God will humiliate all the enemies of his church (Ps. 57:3, 4, 6). And his omnipresence implies that his "steadfast love and his faithfulness" are sent forth to every corner of the earth and heavens, to accomplish his purposes on behalf of his people (vv. 3, 10, 11).

The glorious steadfastness of God's character makes for a steadfast heart (v. 7). God's purpose for David's life was fulfilled in Jesus Christ, who triumphed over all the enemies of God's church through his resurrection—which makes us "steadfast, immovable, always abounding in the work of the Lord" (1 Cor. 15:58).

Psalm 58 The problem with these civil authorities is what they are *not* doing (Prov. 31:1–9; cf. Isa. 61:1–4; Luke 4:16–21). They are not pursuing justice. Knowledge of wrong obligates one to action (Lev. 5:1; Deut. 22:1, 4). By refusing to promote justice, one becomes complicit with violence (Ps. 58:1–2). Even if nothing else can be done, the righteous must pray for their leaders to do right (1 Tim. 2:1–3). To pray against injustice is to express solidarity with what burdens the heart of God, because God loves justice (Isa. 61:8). Conversely, these judges tolerate evil because their hearts—like the hearts of all the unregenerate—are estranged from God from birth (Ps. 58:2–3; 51:5). Unbelievers are dangerous, like deaf cobras that ignore correction (58:4, 5). In fact, instruction only exacerbates their rebellion and makes them "stupid" (Prov. 12:1; Rom. 7:7–12).

3 [q]Ps. 144:5, 7; [Ps. 18:16] [r]See Ps. 56:1 [s]Ps. 43:3 [t]See Ps. 36:5; 40:11
4 [u]Ps. 58:6 [v]Prov. 30:14 [w]Ps. 55:21; 59:7; 64:3; Prov. 12:18; [Ps. 52:2; Jer. 9:8]
5 [x]Ps. 108:5; [Ps. 113:4]
6 [y]See Job 18:8 [z]Ps. 145:14; 146:8 [a]See Ps. 7:15
7 [b]For ver. 7-11, see Ps. 108:1-5 [c]Ps. 112:7
8 [d]Judg. 5:12 [e]See Ps. 16:9 [f]1 Chr. 15:16
10 [g]See Ps. 36:5
11 [x][See ver. 5 above]
Psalm 58
[h]See Ps. 57, title [i]See Ps. 16, title
2 [j][Ps. 94:20]
3 [k]Ps. 51:5; Isa. 48:8
4 [l]Ps. 140:3; [Deut. 32:33]
5 [m]Jer. 8:17
6 [n]Ps. 3:7; Job 4:10; 29:17
7 [o]Ps. 112:10; Josh. 7:5 [p]Ps. 64:3

8 Let them be like the snail [o]that dissolves into slime,
like [q]the stillborn child who never sees the sun.
9 Sooner than your pots can feel the heat of [r]thorns,
whether green or ablaze, may he [s]sweep them away![1]

10 [t]The righteous will rejoice when he sees the vengeance;
he will [u]bathe his feet in the blood of the wicked.
11 Mankind will say, "Surely there is [v]a reward for the righteous;
surely there is a God who [w]judges on earth."

Deliver Me from My Enemies

59 To the choirmaster: according to [x]Do Not Destroy. A [y]Miktam[2] of David, [z]when Saul sent men to watch his house in order to kill him.

1 [a]Deliver me from my enemies, O my God;
[b]protect me from those who [c]rise up against me;
2 deliver me from [d]those who work evil,
and save me from [e]bloodthirsty men.

3 For behold, they [f]lie in wait for my life;
fierce men [g]stir up strife against me.
[h]For no transgression or sin of mine, O Lord,
4 for no fault of mine, they run and make ready.
[i]Awake, come to meet me, and see!
5 You, [j]Lord God of hosts, are God of Israel.
Rouse yourself to punish all the nations;
spare none of those who treacherously plot evil. *Selah*

6 Each evening they [k]come back,
howling like dogs
and prowling about the city.
7 There they are, [l]bellowing with their mouths
with [m]swords in their lips—
for [n]"Who," they think,[3] "will hear us?"

8 But you, O Lord, [o]laugh at them;
you hold all the nations in derision.

[1] The meaning of the Hebrew verse is uncertain [2] Probably a musical or liturgical term [3] Hebrew lacks *they think*

8[o] [See ver. 7 above] [q] See Job 3:16
9[r] Ps. 118:12; Eccles. 7:6 [s] [Job 27:21; See Prov. 10:25]
10[t] Deut. 32:43; See Job 22:19 [u] Ps. 68:23
11[v] Isa. 3:10 [w] Ps. 67:4; 94:2; Gen. 18:25; Job 19:29; Eccles. 12:14
Psalm 59
[x] Ps. 57, title [y] Ps. 16, title [z] [1 Sam. 19:11]
1[a] Ps. 143:9; [Ps. 18:48] [b] See Ps. 20:1 [c] See Ps. 17:7
2[d] Ps. 94:4 [e] Ps. 5:6
3[f] Ps. 10:9 [g] See Ps. 56:6 [h] 1 Sam. 24:11; [Ps. 7:3; 69:4]
4[i] See Ps. 35:23
5[j] Ps. 80:4; 84:8
6[k] [Ps. 22:16]
7[l] Prov. 15:2, 28; [Ps. 94:4] [m] See Ps. 57:4 [n] See Job 22:13
8[o] See Ps. 2:4

David's imprecations in verses 6–9 of Psalm 58 are not bloodthirsty; they are pleas for the failure of wickedness. Broken teeth, vanishing water, and a stillborn child are cries for evil to be undone. David's personal example proves that the goal of his prayer was for unjust rulers to repent (1 Sam. 18:1; 19:10; 24:16–22; 26:21–25). To "bathe" in "blood" (Ps. 58:10) was a common manner of speech describing a warrior's share in an enemy's defeat. Indeed, the righteous will share the Lamb's victory in the end (68:21–23; Isa. 63:3; Rev. 14:19, 20; 19:14, 15).

Psalm 59 David's grasp of God's redemptive plan provides a counterintuitive perspective on a terrifying siege by Saul's men (1 Sam. 19:11). By faith David understands that his situation must be desperate in order to prove that God is the only fortress (Ps. 59:16–17). The utter evil of his enemies' hearts had to be turned inside out to serve as a foil against which God's steadfast love could be clearly displayed (vv. 1–3, 9–11).

David compares Saul's henchmen to a pack of ravenous dogs terrorizing a closely compacted city (vv. 6, 7, 14, 15). While dogs were useful in the ancient Near East, these had turned fierce because of hunger (Job 30:1; Isa. 56:10). Likewise, these fellow Israelites had abandoned their covenant fidelity and had become as bloodthirsty as Gentile aggressors (Ps. 59:5, 8). As such, they had joined the "nations" outside of Israel—those later to be identified as armies of the "kings of the earth" (148:11), whose ranks Christ is raiding today through the preaching of the gospel (Acts 4:25–29).

David calls for God to display his grace by consuming his enemies with exhibitions of superior power, until all "know that God rules over Jacob to the ends of the earth" (Ps. 59:13). The ultimate exhibition of such gospel power in Scripture are the "signs and wonders" of the New Testament, whose apex is the resurrection (Acts 4:30; 1 Corinthians 15). In union with Christ, believers may still suffer unjustly as they participate in the expansion of the kingdom (cf. Ps. 59:4, 12; Rom. 8:17). But their apparent weakness in suffering only provides further evidence of God's infinite power to use the weakest instruments to "shield" them from harm and make a mockery of the Enemy (cf. Ps. 59:11; 1 Sam. 19:12–13; 1 Cor. 1:27; Col. 2:15).

9 O my Strength, I will watch for you,
for you, O God, are [p]my fortress.
10 [q]My God in his steadfast love[1] [r]will meet
me;
God will let me [s]look in triumph on
my enemies.

11 Kill them not, lest my people forget;
make them totter[2] by your power and
[t]bring them down,
O Lord, our [u]shield!
12 For [v]the sin of their mouths, the words
of their lips,
let them be trapped in their pride.
For the cursing and lies that they utter,
13 [w]consume them in wrath;
consume them till they are no more,
that they may [x]know that God rules over
Jacob
to [y]the ends of the earth. *Selah*

14 [z]Each evening they come back,
howling like dogs
and prowling about the city.
15 They [a]wander about for food
and growl if they do not get their fill.

16 But I will sing of your strength;
I will sing aloud of your steadfast love
in the morning.
For you have been to me [b]a fortress
and [c]a refuge in [d]the day of my distress.
17 O my Strength, I will sing praises to you,
for you, O God, [b]are my fortress,
[e]the God who shows me steadfast love.

He Will Tread Down Our Foes

60 To the choirmaster: according to [f]Shushan Eduth. A [g]Miktam[3] of David; [h]for instruction; when he [i]strove with Aram-naharaim and with Aram-zobah, and when Joab on his return struck down twelve thousand of Edom in the Valley of Salt.

1 O God, [j]you have rejected us, [k]broken
our defenses;
you have been angry; [l]oh, restore us.
2 You have made the land to quake; you
have torn it open;
[m]repair its breaches, for it totters.
3 [n]You have made your people see hard
things;
[o]you have given us [p]wine to drink that
made us stagger.

4 You have set up [q]a banner for those who
fear you,
that they may flee to it [r]from the bow.[4]
Selah
5 [s]That your [t]beloved ones may be delivered,
give salvation by your right hand and
answer us!

6 God has spoken [u]in his holiness:[5]
"With exultation [v]I will divide up
[w]Shechem
and portion out the Vale of [x]Succoth.
7 [y]Gilead is mine; Manasseh is mine;
[z]Ephraim is [a]my helmet;
Judah is my [b]scepter.

[1] Or *The God who shows me steadfast love* [2] Or *wander* [3] Probably musical or liturgical terms [4] Or *that it may be displayed because of truth* [5] Or *sanctuary*

Psalm 60 Like a disillusioned child, David erupts with complaints against his Father, accusing him of rejection, defeat, anger, natural disaster, intoxication, and abandonment (vv. 1–3, 9, 10). Apparently this is the petition David taught his people to pray in a conflict (2 Sam. 8:1–14). The rush of rash and confused words demonstrates that a believer does not have to have his thoughts straight before he prays. When he turns to the Lord, the Lord will order his thoughts and comfort his heart.

As David's spiritual eyes gain their focus, God's attributes come more clearly into view and his accusations against God are substituted with words of trust (Ps. 60:11–12). Seeing God as a refuge, David understands that God protects his people because he loves them, not because they are worthy of his love (vv. 4, 5; Rom. 5:8; Rev. 1:5, 6).

Finally, David recalls that God is sovereign over the nations (Ps. 60:6–8). This absolute sovereignty oversees all of salvation history, finally culminating in Christ. God does not capriciously use natural forces to punish humans (Luke 21:25–28). Confessing God's sovereign grace turns the believer away from the vain threats and toward a valiant courage that only our Lord, the ultimate conqueror, can give (Rom. 8:37; Phil. 4:13).

9[p] ver. 16, 17; See Ps. 9:9
10[q] ver. 17 [r]Ps. 21:3 [s]See Ps. 54:7
11[t] See Ps. 55:23 [u]See Ps. 3:3
12[v] See Prov. 12:13
13[w] [Ps. 7:9] [x]Ps. 83:18 [y]Ps. 22:27
14[z] [Ps. 22:16]
15[a] Ps. 109:10; Job 15:23
16[b] ver. 9 [c]2 Sam. 22:3 [d]Ps. 18:6
17[b] [See ver. 16 above] [e]ver. 10
Psalm 60
[f]Ps. 80, title [g]See Ps. 16, title [h]Deut. 31:19 [i][2 Sam. 8:3, 13, 14; 10:16; 1 Chr. 18:3, 12]
1[j] ver. 10; See Ps. 44:9 [k][2 Sam. 5:20] [l]See Ps. 80:3
2[m] [2 Chr. 7:14]
3[n] Ps. 71:20 [o]Job 21:20 [p]Isa. 51:17, 22
4[q] Isa. 5:26; 11:12; 13:2; [Ps. 20:5] [r]Prov. 22:21 **5**[s] For ver. 5-12, see Ps. 108:6-13 [t]Deut. 33:12; Jer. 11:15 **6**[u] Ps. 89:35; Amos 4:2 [v][Josh. 1:6] [w]Gen. 12:6; 33:18; Josh. 17:7 [x]Gen. 33:17; Josh. 13:27 **7**[y] Josh. 13:31 [z]Deut. 33:17 [a]Ps. 140:7 [b]Gen. 49:10

8 [c]Moab is my washbasin;
upon Edom I [d]cast my shoe;
over [e]Philistia I shout in triumph."[1]

9 Who will bring me to the fortified city?
[f]Who will lead me to Edom?
10 Have you not [g]rejected us, O God?
You [h]do not go forth, O God, with our armies.
11 Oh, grant us help against the foe,
for [i]vain is the salvation of man!
12 With God we shall [j]do valiantly;
it is he who will [k]tread down our foes.

Lead Me to the Rock

61

TO THE CHOIRMASTER: WITH [l]STRINGED INSTRUMENTS. OF DAVID.

1 Hear my cry, O God,
[m]listen to my prayer;
2 from the end of the earth I call to you
when my heart is [n]faint.
Lead me to [o]the rock
that is higher than I,
3 for you have been [p]my refuge,
a strong [q]tower against the enemy.

4 Let me [r]dwell in your tent forever!
Let me take refuge under [s]the shelter of your wings! *Selah*

5 For you, O God, have heard my vows;
you have given me the heritage of those who fear your name.

6 [t]Prolong [u]the life of the king;
may his years endure to all generations!
7 May he be enthroned forever before God;
appoint [v]steadfast love and faithfulness to watch over him!

8 So will I ever sing praises to your name,
as I [w]perform my vows day after day.

My Soul Waits for God Alone

62

TO THE CHOIRMASTER: ACCORDING TO [x]JEDUTHUN. A PSALM OF DAVID.

1 For God alone [y]my soul [z]waits in silence;
from him comes my salvation.
2 [a]He alone is my rock and my salvation,
my [b]fortress; [c]I shall not be greatly shaken.

3 How long will all of you attack a man
to batter him,
like [d]a leaning wall, a tottering fence?
4 They only plan to thrust him down from his [e]high position.
They take pleasure in falsehood.

[1] Revocalization (compare Psalm 108:10); Masoretic Text *over me, O Philistia, shout in triumph*

8[c][2 Sam. 8:2] [d][Matt. 3:11] [e][2 Sam. 8:1]
9[f][2 Sam. 8:14]
10[g]ver. 1 [h]See Ps. 44:9
11[i][Ps. 146:3]
12[j]Ps. 108:13; 118:15, 16; Num. 24:18 [k]Ps. 44:5; Isa. 63:3
Psalm 61
[l]Ps. 4, title
1[m]Ps. 55:1, 2
2[n]Ps. 77:3 [o][Ps. 18:2]
3[p]See Ps. 14:6 [q]Prov. 18:10
4[r]See Ps. 15:1; 27:4 [s]See Ps. 17:8
6[t]See Ps. 21:4 [u]Ps. 63:11
7[v]See Ps. 40:11
8[w]See Ps. 50:14
Psalm 62
[x]See Ps. 39, title
1[y]See Ps. 33:20 [z][Ps. 37:7]
2[a]Ps. 18:2 [b]See Ps. 9:9 [c]See Ps. 10:6
3[d][Isa. 30:13]
4[e]Job 13:11

Psalm 61 That one can bless many is a critically important principle in Scripture (Rom. 5:15). David leads his people to pray for the king to be faithful to God (Ps. 61:4, 5). If their king's heart finds its courage in God's protection, their nation will be secure (vv. 1–3). They appeal not merely for longevity but for covenant succession. If this is true in their rulers, then generations of citizens will experience the steadfastness of God's love and observe the faithfulness of their Great Shepherd (vv. 6–7).

David's very act of teaching his people to pray for him reminds every believer that no one is capable of performing his vows "day after day" unless the Lord "appoints" soul-guarding grace (vv. 7–8; Eph. 2:10). Believers have a priestly responsibility to pray for their leaders to be just (Isa. 1:23–26). But it must not be self-serving. Such prayers are meant to be an act of mercy toward the leader and ultimately for the whole nation (Prov. 14:34; 1 Tim. 2:1–4). The effects that our lives have on others should remind us that believers must also "sanctify" themselves not merely to avoid judgment but as a loving act toward others who would be blessed by their holiness (cf. John 17:19; 1 Pet. 2:9–12). Ultimately, as David prepared his people to anticipate a saving King, this psalm exhorts us to pray for Christ's worldwide mission to succeed so that citizens will be summoned by grace into his kingdom from every tribe, tongue, people, and nation (Rev. 7:9–11).

Psalm 62 Salvation comes by trusting God alone. But trusting God alone brings disciples into conflict with a world that trusts itself (vv. 3–4; 1 John 3:1, 13). Ultimately, David's trust is in a God who alone "is my rock and my salvation" (Ps. 62:6). These words describe the character and heart of God, whose full provision will ultimately be revealed in the coming Savior, who will overcome the world for his people (John 16:33). He will enable believers to overcome the world by providing a more sure foundation and a more enduring hope (Ps. 62:2–6; 1 John 5:5). The world's focus is to gain power and possessions, which will vanish (Ps. 62:4, 10; James 5:3), but the

[f]They bless with their mouths,
but inwardly they curse. *Selah*

5 For God alone, O [y]my soul, wait in silence,
for my hope is from him.
6 [a]He only is my rock and my salvation,
my fortress; I shall not be shaken.
7 On God rests my [g]salvation and my glory;
my mighty rock, [h]my refuge is God.

8 [i]Trust in him at all times, O people;
[j]pour out your heart before him;
God is [h]a refuge for us. *Selah*

9 [k]Those of low estate are but a breath;
those of high estate [l]are a delusion;
in the balances they go up;
[k]they are together lighter than a breath.
10 Put no trust in extortion;
[m]set no vain hopes on robbery;
[n]if riches increase, set not your heart
on them.

11 [o]Once God has spoken;
[o]twice have I heard this:
that [p]power belongs to God,
12 and that to you, O Lord, [q]belongs
steadfast love.
For you will [r]render to a man
according to his work.

My Soul Thirsts for You

63

A Psalm of David, [s]when he was in the wilderness of Judah.

1 O God, you are my God; [t]earnestly I seek
you;
[u]my soul thirsts for you;
my flesh faints for you,
as in [v]a dry and weary land where
there is no water.
2 So I have looked upon you in the sanctuary,
beholding [w]your power and glory.
3 Because your [x]steadfast love is better
than life,
my lips will praise you.
4 So I will bless you [y]as long as I live;
in your [z]name I will [a]lift up my hands.

5 My soul will be [b]satisfied as with fat and
rich food,
and my mouth will praise you with
joyful lips,
6 when I remember you [c]upon my bed,
and meditate on you in [c]the watches
of the night;
7 for you have been my help,
and in [d]the shadow of your wings
I will sing for joy.

hope of believers is eternally secure, because their honor and riches are safely stored in heaven (Ps. 62:7; Matt. 6:19–20).

David reasons that if God can be trusted for salvation, then he can be entrusted with everything else, even one's reputation (Ps. 62:7–9). True faith is not only bolstered by a strong God; it is emboldened by his love. We need not only strength for our wills but fuel for our emotions. God provides both (vv. 11–12; 2 Cor. 1:3–4).

When believers remember God's steadfast love, they will actually look forward to judgment, because that love has taken their sins away, as the scapegoat symbolized on the Day of Atonement (Ex. 34:6–7; Lev. 16:1–34). On that same day the blood of the other goat symbolized the atoning righteousness to be provided through the final Lamb (1 Pet. 1:19). The believer can look forward to the judgment because it will be the day on which all wrong is put right (Matt. 16:27; Rom. 2:6). In Christ, we have nothing to fear.

Psalm 63 For the believer, awareness of the presence of God is better than life itself (v. 3). In contrast to the rebel, who squirms at the nearness of God, the reconciled worship Immanuel (v. 2; cf. Rom. 2:15). At times, the Father proves the necessity of that dependence by hiding his face. In this way, the believer's dependence on union with the life of God (ultimately made possible through Christ) is as real as the human need for water and confirms the reality of God's love, which is more real than our present circumstances (Ps. 63:1; cf. 1 Pet. 1:8).

David's experience of blessing *while* he thirsts illustrates Jesus' beatitude, "Blessed are those who hunger and thirst for righteousness" (Matt. 5:6). Any suffering Christian can testify to the quiet assurance that comes from realizing that there would be no such longings for righteousness if the faith were not real. Even while he lay awake in his anguish, David knew the peace that surpasses understanding under God's wings and in the clutches of his embrace (Ps. 63:6–8; Phil. 4:7).

4[f] See Ps. 28:3
5[y] [See ver. 1 above]
6[a] [See ver. 2 above]
7[g] See Ps. 3:8 [h] See Ps. 14:6
8[i] See Ps. 37:3 [j] See Ps. 42:4 [h] [See ver. 7 above]
9[k] Ps. 39:5; [Isa. 40:17] [l] [Ps. 116:11]
10[m] See Prov. 1:10-19 [n] Luke 12:15; See Ps. 49:6
11[o] Job 33:14; 40:5 [p] Rev. 19:1; [Ps. 59:9, 17]
12[q] Ps. 86:5, 15; 103:8; Dan. 9:9 [r] See Job 34:11

Psalm 63
[s] [2 Sam. 16:14; 17:2, 29]
1[t] Ps. 78:34; Isa. 26:9 [u] See Ps. 84:2 [v] Ps. 143:6; Isa. 32:2
2[w] Ps. 78:61; [Ps. 27:4]
3[x] [Ps. 69:16]
4[y] Ps. 104:33; 146:2 [z] Ps. 20:1, 5 [a] See Ps. 28:2
5[b] See Ps. 36:8
6[c] See Ps. 42:8
7[d] See Ps. 17:8

8 My soul [e]clings to you;
your right hand [f]upholds me.

9 But those who seek to destroy my life
[g]shall go down into [h]the depths of the earth;
10 they shall be given over to the power of the sword;
they shall be a portion for jackals.
11 But [i]the king shall rejoice in God;
all who [j]swear by him shall exult,
[k]for the mouths of [l]liars will be stopped.

Hide Me from the Wicked

64 To the choirmaster. A Psalm of David.
Hear my voice, O God, in my [m]complaint;
preserve my life from dread of the enemy.
2 Hide me from [n]the secret plots of the wicked,
from the throng of evildoers,
3 who [o]whet their tongues like swords,
who [p]aim bitter words like arrows,
4 shooting from [q]ambush at the blameless,
shooting at him suddenly and [r]without fear.
5 They [s]hold fast to their evil purpose;
they talk of [t]laying snares secretly,
thinking, [u]"Who can see them?"
6 They search out injustice,
saying, "We have accomplished a diligent search."
For [v]the inward mind and heart of a man are deep.

7 [w]But God shoots his arrow at them;
they are wounded suddenly.
8 They are brought to ruin, with their own [x]tongues turned against them;
all who [y]see them will [z]wag their heads.
9 Then all mankind [y]fears;
they [a]tell what God has brought about
and ponder what he has done.

10 Let [b]the righteous one rejoice in the LORD
and [c]take refuge in him!
Let all [d]the upright in heart exult!

O God of Our Salvation

65 To the choirmaster. A Psalm of David. A Song.

1 Praise [e]is due to you,[1] O God, in Zion,
and to you shall [f]vows be performed.
2 O you who [g]hear prayer,
to you [h]shall all flesh come.
3 When [i]iniquities prevail against me,
you [j]atone for our transgressions.

[1] Or *Praise waits for you in silence*

8[e] [Num. 14:24] [f] See Ps. 41:12
9[g] Ps. 9:17; 55:15 [h] Ezek. 26:20; 31:14; Eph. 4:9
11[i] Ps. 61:6 [j] Deut. 6:13; Isa. 45:23; 65:16 [k] Ps. 107:42; Job 5:16; [Rom. 3:19] [l] [Ps. 38:12; 41:5-8]

Psalm 64
1[m] Ps. 55:2
2[n] [Ps. 55:14]
3[o] See Ps. 57:4 [p] See Ps. 11:2
4[q] [Ps. 10:8] [r] Ps. 55:19
5[s] Jer. 23:14; Ezek. 13:22 [t] See Ps. 140:5 [u] See Job 22:13
6[v] Ps. 49:11
7[w] Ps. 7:12, 13; [Ps. 58:7]
8[x] See Prov. 12:13; 18:7 [y] See Ps. 40:3 [z] Jer. 18:16; 48:27; See Ps. 22:7
9[y] [See ver. 8 above] [a] Jer. 50:28; 51:10
10[b] See Ps. 32:11; Job 22:19 [c] See Ps. 11:1 [d] See Ps. 7:10

Psalm 65
1[e] Ps. 62:1 [f] See Ps. 50:14
2[g] 2 Kgs. 19:20 [h] See Ps. 86:9
3[i] See Ps. 38:4 [j] Ps. 79:9; Isa. 6:7; See Ps. 51:2

Living in the same blessed faith that Jesus articulated on the mount, David confirmed that those who hunger and thirst for righteousness "will be satisfied," while the enemies of God's people will be destroyed (Ps. 63:5, 9, 10). God's people will "rejoice" not merely because their persecutors are conquered; they will rejoice *in the Lord* because his truth is vindicated as he fulfills his redemptive promises (v. 11; John 15:11; Rom. 4:11–12).

Psalm 64 There are few places in Scripture where the destructive power of the tongue is more vividly described than here. Accusations conjured up in a sinister plot to ruin a righteous man's reputation are deadly to the soul and directly attack the image of God (vv. 1–6; Rom. 3:13; James 3:9). But the one who finds his refuge in God's justice rather than in taking revenge will be comforted to know that God will someday judge in such a way as to vindicate his children before the whole world (Ps. 64:7–9; Matt. 24:30). Reviled Christians are invited to rejoice that they have the privilege of carrying on the line of the prophets, and of being so identified with Christ that they suffer for his name (Ps. 64:10; Matt. 5:11–12). In the meantime, believers must keep their eyes on the future and patiently wait for Christ to come and judge all evildoing. Such faith will ensure that our speech does not fall to the level of our tormentors (James 5:7–12)—an exercise in patience that follows in the footsteps of Christ himself (1 Pet. 2:23).

Psalm 65 Like any good father, God provides reasons for doing what we ought to do (Rom. 12:1–2). In this case he explains why we should praise and obey him. God "hears" the prayers of those who come to him (Ps. 65:2; Rom. 10:13). But how can he listen to the prayers of sinful people? He can do so because he "atones" for transgressions and iniquities (Ps. 65:3; Rom. 3:23–26). And who will come to him for atonement? Only those whom God chooses to "bring near" and give new hearts to desire "holiness" (Ps. 65:4; John 6:44–45; Eph. 6:6).

4 [k]Blessed is the one you choose and bring
near,
to [l]dwell in your courts!
We shall be [m]satisfied with the goodness
of your house,
the holiness of your temple!

5 By [n]awesome deeds you answer us with
righteousness,
O God of our salvation,
the hope of all [o]the ends of the earth
and of the farthest seas;
6 the one who by his strength established
the mountains,
being [p]girded with might;
7 who [q]stills the roaring of the seas,
the roaring of their waves,
[r]the tumult of the peoples,
8 so that those who dwell at the ends of
the earth are in awe at your signs.
You make the going out of the morning
and the evening to shout for joy.

9 You visit the earth and [s]water it;[1]
you greatly enrich it;
[t]the river of God is full of water;
[u]you provide their grain,
for so you have prepared it.
10 You water its furrows abundantly,
settling its ridges,
softening it with [v]showers,
and blessing its growth.
11 You crown the year with your bounty;
your wagon tracks [w]overflow with
abundance.
12 [x]The pastures of the wilderness overflow,
the hills [y]gird themselves with joy,
13 [z]the meadows clothe themselves with
flocks,
the valleys deck themselves with
grain,
they [a]shout and sing together for joy.

How Awesome Are Your Deeds

66 To the choirmaster. A Song. A Psalm.
[b]Shout for joy to God, all the earth;
2 sing the glory of his name;
[c]give to him glorious praise!
3 Say to God, [d]"How awesome are your
deeds!
So great is your power that your enemies [e]come cringing to you.
4 [f]All the earth worships you
and sings praises to you;
they sing praises to your name." *Selah*

5 [g]Come and see what God has done:
[d]he is awesome in his deeds toward the
children of man.
6 He [h]turned the sea into dry land;
they [i]passed through the river on
foot.
There did we rejoice in him,
7 who rules by his might forever,

[1] *Or and make it overflow*

Unlike false gods, whose promises are mystical and unseen, God has performed his "awesome deeds" of redemption within creation (Ps. 65:5; 1 Cor. 10:1–5). Unlike those philosophies that teach that divine power can be accessed only by transcending physical reality, the believer worships the true God whose decrees are carried out within creation.

Rather than despising the creation and seeking "true spirituality," the Christian looks at the wonders of nature and exclaims, "This is my Father's world!" Christians do so because the same God who provides atonement for sins is the One through whom the world was created. From the testimony of the New Testament, we know even more precisely what this means. John says not only that Christ was "in the beginning with God" but that "without him was not any thing made that was made" (John 1:1–3). Behind the physical science of rainfall and germination, the believer sees Christ's provision of daily bread (Ps. 65:9–11). And beyond the beautiful vistas of mountains and valleys, meadows and pastures, the Christian sees God rejoicing over his good creation (vv. 12–13), a creation that will one day be perfectly restored and cleansed of all that is fallen.

Psalm 66 This is an example of what some have called "doxological evangelism." As persons created by God, all are born into a relationship of creational (human) lordship under their Creator, but all have rebelled against this divine lordship by sinning (Rom. 3:23). Whom he worships reveals whether a person is living in faithfulness or in rebellion (Rom. 1:25). Therefore, the psalmists issue God's call to all of his creatures to worship the one true God (Ps. 66:1–4).

4[k][Ps. 33:12] [l]Ps. 84:4; See Ps. 27:4 [m]See Ps. 16:11
5[n]Ps. 45:4; 106:22; Deut. 10:21; 2 Sam. 7:23; [Rev. 15:3] [o]See Ps. 22:27
6[p]Ps. 93:1
7[q]Ps. 89:9; 93:3, 4; 107:29; Matt. 8:26; [Jer. 5:22] [r]Ps. 74:23; Isa. 17:12, 13
9[s]Ps. 68:9; 72:6; Lev. 26:4; See Job 5:10 [t][Ps. 46:4] [u][Ps. 147:14]
10[v]Deut. 32:2
11[w]Job 36:28
12[x]Joel 2:22; [Job 38:26, 27] [y]Isa. 55:12
13[z]Isa. 30:23 [a]Ps. 98:8; [Isa. 44:23]
Psalm 66
1[b]Ps. 81:1; 95:1; 98:4; 100:1
2[c][Josh. 7:19; Isa. 42:12]
3[d]See Ps. 65:5 [e]See Ps. 18:44
4[f]See Ps. 22:27
5[g]ver. 16; Ps. 46:8 [d][See ver. 3 above]
6[h][Ex. 14:21] [i]Ps. 74:15; See Josh. 3:14-17

whose [j]eyes keep watch on the nations—
let not the rebellious exalt themselves. *Selah*

8 Bless our God, O peoples;
let the sound of his praise be heard,
9 who has kept our soul among the living
and [k]has not let our feet slip.
10 For you, O God, have [l]tested us;
you have tried us as silver is tried.
11 You brought us into [m]the net;
you laid a crushing burden on our backs;
12 you let men [n]ride over our heads;
we went through fire and through [o]water;
yet you have brought us out to a place of abundance.

13 I will come into your house with burnt offerings;
I will [p]perform my vows to you,
14 that which my lips uttered
and my mouth promised [q]when I was in trouble.
15 I will offer to you burnt offerings of fattened animals,
with the smoke of the sacrifice of rams;
I will make an offering of bulls and goats. *Selah*

16 [r]Come and hear, all you who fear God,
and I will tell what he has done for my soul.
17 I cried to him with my mouth,
and high praise was on[1] my tongue.[2]
18 If I had [s]cherished iniquity in my heart,
[t]the Lord would not have listened.
19 But truly [u]God has listened;
he has attended to the voice of my prayer.

20 Blessed be God,
because he has not rejected my prayer
or removed his steadfast love from me!

Make Your Face Shine upon Us

67

To the choirmaster: with [v]stringed instruments. A Psalm. A Song.

1 May God [w]be gracious to us and bless us
and make his face to [x]shine upon us, *Selah*
2 that [y]your way may be known on earth,
your [z]saving power among all nations.
3 [a]Let the peoples praise you, O God;
let all the peoples praise you!

[1] Hebrew *under* [2] Or *and he was exalted with my tongue*

7[j] See Ps. 11:4
9[k] See Ps. 121:3
10[l] See Job 23:10
11[m] Lam. 1:13; Ezek. 12:13
12[n] Isa. 51:23 [o] Isa. 43:2
13[p] See Ps. 50:14
14[q] See Ps. 18:6
16[r] ver. 5; Ps. 34:11
18[s] Job 36:21 [t] [Prov. 28:9; Isa. 59:2; John 9:31; James 4:3; See Job 27:9]
19[u] Ps. 116:1, 2
Psalm 67
[v] Ps. 4, title
1[w] Num. 6:25 [x] See Ps. 4:6
2[y] [Acts 18:25] [z] Ps. 98:3; Luke 2:30; Titus 2:11
3[a] See Ps. 22:27

God's purpose with Israel was to work not only in them but through them. Their very purpose as a nation was to be a light to the world (Ps. 66:5–8; Ex. 19:5–6). They were a prototype of the kingdom God would build with citizens from every nation (Heb. 8:10; Rev. 7:4). So what God did for Israel was not exclusive to her but rather was a foretaste of what he planned to do for the Gentiles too (Rom. 15:11). Even Israel's suffering demonstrated that God never lets go of his people (Ps. 66:8–12), a truth that believing Gentiles would one day embrace.

The modern worshiper praying this psalm ultimately realizes that God's preservation of Israel brought Christ into the world (vv. 13–16). He is faithful to save at all times and in every place (Eph. 2:11–13; 1 Tim. 2:1–4). His kindness should draw to repentance and his mercy should inspire holiness. The psalmist is not declaring that perfection is necessary for answered prayer, but rather that all who have tasted of God's grace cannot cherish that which is abhorrent to the God they love (Ps. 66:17–20; 1 John 3:4–10).

Psalm 67 God's blessings are intended to create people with an outward-oriented, missional impulse (Gen. 12:1–3). Attaching a purpose clause (Ps. 67:2) to the traditional Aaronic blessing (Num. 6:22–27) forms a prayer for evangelistic success to the ends of the earth. There are three parts to this news that make it good for all the peoples of the earth. The first is that God makes himself known (Ps. 67:2; Acts 17:27). In contrast to false gods, whose ways are fickle and whose wills are difficult to discern, God shines his grace into the world (Isa. 44:9–20). Ultimately, that light shone perfectly in Jesus Christ (John 8:12).

Another reason the news of the gospel is good is that the Lord is an utterly fair judge (Ps. 67:4–5). The nations will be glad to live under his authority, because it saves (John 12:47). Unlike pagan rulers, God's judges protected the weak and brought liberation to the downtrodden (Judg. 2:16–19). They prepared the way for Christ the

4 Let the nations be glad and sing for joy,
for you [b]judge the peoples with equity
and guide the nations upon earth. *Selah*
5 [a]Let the peoples praise you, O God;
let all the peoples praise you!

6 The earth has [c]yielded its increase;
God, our God, shall bless us.
7 God shall bless us;
let [d]all the ends of the earth fear him!

God Shall Scatter His Enemies

68

To the choirmaster. A Psalm of David. A Song.

1 [e]God shall arise, his enemies shall be [f]scattered;
and those who hate him shall flee before him!
2 As [g]smoke is driven away, so you shall drive them away;
[h]as wax melts before fire,
so the wicked shall perish before God!
3 But [i]the righteous shall be glad;
they shall exult before God;
they shall be jubilant with joy!

4 Sing to God, [j]sing praises to his name;
[k]lift up a song to him who [l]rides through [m]the deserts;
his name is [n]the LORD;
exult before him!

5 [o]Father of the fatherless and [p]protector of widows
is God in his holy habitation.
6 God [q]settles the solitary in a home;
he [r]leads out the prisoners to prosperity,
but [s]the rebellious dwell in [t]a parched land.

7 O God, when you [u]went out before your people,
[v]when you marched through [w]the wilderness, *Selah*
8 [x]the earth quaked, the heavens poured down rain,
before God, the One of Sinai,
before God, the God of Israel.
9 [y]Rain in abundance, O God, you shed abroad;
you restored your inheritance as it languished;
10 your flock[1] found a dwelling in it;
in your goodness, O God, you [z]provided for the needy.

11 The Lord gives [a]the word;
[b]the women who announce the news are a great host:
12 [c]"The kings of the armies—they flee, they flee!"
The women at home [d]divide the spoil—
13 though you men lie among [e]the sheepfolds—

[1] Or *your congregation*

Judge, whose arrival brought "good news of great joy that will be for all the people" (Luke 2:10; cf. Ps. 67:4–5).

Finally, God supplies the creaturely needs of all human beings (Ps. 67:6; Acts 14:17). He provides "life and breath and everything"(Acts 17:25). But this common grace has a redemptive purpose. Sinners must not presume on God's patience, who "commands all people everywhere to repent" (Acts 17:30). If they repent now, they will be "glad and sing for joy" (Ps. 67:4); if they wait, they will be judged in "righteousness" and found wanting (Acts 17:31).

Psalm 68 God is uniquely praiseworthy because he protects weaklings and pursues nobodies (vv. 3–4). With language reminiscent of Moses' war cry, David reminds the covenant people that God's power over their enemies is like wind to smoke, and fire to wax (vv. 1–2). God rode "through the deserts" (v. 4) on the cloud, which was a foretaste of his tabernacling presence in Christ (John 1:14). Through the cloud, God showed that he defends against human and natural enemies (Ps. 105:39; Dan. 7:13–14). Such total care is endearing and strengthening (Ps. 68:5–6).

With a highly compressed montage of scenes from Israel's history, David reminds believers that God preserves his people—even as a remnant (vv. 7–10). The desert, Sinai, the defeat of Sisera (Judg. 4:7; 5:4), the arrival in Canaan, and the displacement of bloodthirsty enemies are all events in which God moved heaven and earth to prove that salvation comes from the Lord (Ps. 68:11–14; Jonah 2:9; Matt. 12:39–41).

4[b] See Ps. 58:11
5[a] [See ver. 3 above]
6[c] Ps. 85:12; Lev. 26:4; Ezek. 34:27; [Hos. 2:22]
7[d] See Ps. 22:27
Psalm 68
1[e] Num. 10:35; Isa. 33:3 [f] [Ps. 89:10; 92:9]
2[g] See Ps. 37:20 [h] Ps. 22:14; 97:5; Mic. 1:4
3[i] See Ps. 32:11
4[j] Ps. 66:4 [k] [Isa. 62:10] [l] ver. 33; [Ps. 18:10] [m] Isa. 40:3 [n] Ps. 89:8
5[o] See Ps. 10:14 [p] Deut. 10:18
6[q] Ps. 113:9; 1 Sam. 2:5 [r] Ps. 69:33; 107:10, 14; 146:7; Acts 12:7; 16:26 [s] ver. 18 [t] [Ps. 107:33, 40]
7[u] Ex. 13:21; Judg. 4:14; Hab. 3:13; Zech. 14:3 [v] Judg. 5:4 [w] Ps. 78:40
8[x] Ex. 19:18; Judg. 5:4
9[y] See Ps. 65:9, 10
10[z] Ps. 65:9; 78:20
11[a] [Ps. 33:9] [b] [Ex. 15:20; 1 Sam. 18:6]
12[c] Ps. 110:5; [Num. 31:8; Josh. 10:16; Judg. 5:19]; See Josh. 12:7-24 [d] Judg. 5:30
13[e] [Gen. 49:14; Judg. 5:16]

the wings of a dove covered with silver,
its pinions with shimmering gold.
14 When the Almighty scatters kings there,
let snow fall on [f]Zalmon.

15 O mountain of God, mountain of Bashan;
O many-peaked[1] mountain, mountain of Bashan!
16 Why do you look with hatred, O many-peaked mountain,
at the mount that God [g]desired for his abode,
yes, where the LORD will dwell forever?
17 [h]The chariots of God are twice ten thousand,
thousands upon thousands;
the Lord is among them; Sinai is now in the sanctuary.
18 [i]You ascended on high,
[j]leading a host of captives in your train
and [k]receiving gifts among men,
even among [l]the rebellious, [m]that the LORD God may dwell there.

19 Blessed be the Lord,
who daily [n]bears us up;
God is our salvation. *Selah*
20 Our God is a God of salvation,
[o]and to GOD, the Lord, belong deliverances from death.
21 [p]But God will strike the heads of his enemies,
the hairy crown of him who walks in his guilty ways.
22 The Lord said,
"I will bring them back [q]from Bashan,
[r]I will bring them back from the depths of the sea,
23 that you may [s]strike your feet in their blood,
that [t]the tongues of your dogs may have their portion from the foe."
24 Your procession is[2] seen, O God,
the procession of my God, my King,
into the sanctuary—
25 [u]the singers in front, [v]the musicians last,
between them [w]virgins playing tambourines:
26 [x]"Bless God in the great congregation,
the LORD, O you[3] who are of [y]Israel's fountain!"
27 There is [z]Benjamin, the least of them, in the lead,
the princes of Judah in their throng,
the princes of [a]Zebulun, the princes of Naphtali.

28 [b]Summon your power, O God,[4]
the power, O God, by which you have worked for us.
29 Because of your temple at Jerusalem
kings shall [c]bear gifts to you.
30 Rebuke [d]the beasts that dwell among the reeds,
the herd of [e]bulls with the calves of the peoples.
[f]Trample underfoot those who lust after tribute;
scatter the peoples who delight in war.[5]
31 Nobles shall come from [g]Egypt;
[h]Cush shall hasten to [i]stretch out her hands to God.

32 [j]O kingdoms of the earth, sing to God;
sing praises to the Lord, *Selah*
33 to him [k]who rides in [l]the heavens, the ancient heavens;
behold, he [m]sends out his voice, his mighty voice.
34 [n]Ascribe power to God,
whose majesty is over Israel,
and whose [o]power is in [p]the skies.

[1] Or *hunch-backed*; also verse 16 [2] Or *has been* [3] The Hebrew for *you* is plural here [4] By revocalization (compare Septuagint); Hebrew *Your God has summoned your power* [5] The meaning of the Hebrew verse is uncertain

God's preferred way of overtaking unbelievers is by summoning them into his kingdom through saving faith, as he did with Rahab, Naaman, and other formerly unrighteous people (Ps. 68:11–14; 1 Cor. 6:9–11). What is most startling about God's battle plan—illustrated in these historical skirmishes—is that he assembles a ragtag band of warriors from a weak and persecuted people to execute it (Ps. 68:18). Similarly surrounding himself with orphans, widows, aliens, prisoners, poor, unwise, and weak sinners, Christ will bring humiliating defeat to hell itself (vv. 15–18; 2 Cor. 12:9; Eph. 4:8–9).

14[f] Judg. 9:48 **16**[g] Ps. 132:13, 14; [Ps. 78:54; 87:1, 2; Deut. 12:5] **17**[h] 2 Kgs. 6:17; Hab. 3:8 **18**[i] Ps. 7:7; 47:5; Cited Eph. 4:8; [Acts 1:9] [j] Judg. 5:12 [k] [Acts 2:4, 33] [l] [Rom. 5:8; 1 Tim. 1:13] [m] Ps. 78:60; Ex. 29:45; Rev. 21:3; [John 14:23] **19**[n] [Isa. 46:4] **20**[o] Deut. 32:39; Eccles. 7:18; Rev. 1:18 **21**[p] Ps. 110:6; Hab. 3:13 **22**[q] Num. 21:33 [r] See Amos 9:2-4 **23**[s] Ps. 58:10 [t] [1 Kgs. 21:19; 22:38] **25**[u] Ps. 47:5; 1 Chr. 13:8; 15:16 [v] See Ps. 33:3 [w] Ex. 15:20; Judg. 11:34 **26**[x] Ps. 22:25; 26:12 [y] Deut. 33:28; Isa. 48:1; [Isa. 51:1] **27**[z] [1 Sam. 9:21] [a] [Judg. 5:18] **28**[b] See Ps. 42:8 **29**[c] Ps. 45:12; 76:11; 1 Kgs. 10:10, 25; 2 Chr. 32:23; Isa. 18:7 **30**[d] Job 40:21; Isa. 19:6; Ezek. 29:3, 4; [Ezek. 32:2] [e] Ps. 22:12 [f] [2 Sam. 8:2, 6] **31**[g] Isa. 19:19, 21 [h] Ps. 87:4; Isa. 45:14; Zeph. 3:10 [i] Ps. 44:20 **32**[j] Ps. 102:22 **33**[k] Ps. 18:10; 104:3; Deut. 33:26 [l] Deut. 10:14; 1 Kgs. 8:27 [m] Ps. 29:4; See Ps. 46:6 **34**[n] Ps. 29:1 [o] Ps. 150:1 [p] Ps. 36:5; 57:10; 108:4

35 [q]Awesome is God from his[1] [r]sanctuary;
the God of Israel—he is the one who gives [s]power and strength to his people.
Blessed be God!

Save Me, O God

69 To the choirmaster: according to [t]Lilies. Of David.

1 Save me, O God!
For [u]the waters have come up to my neck.[2]
2 I sink in deep [v]mire,
where there is no foothold;
I have come into deep waters,
and the flood [w]sweeps over me.
3 [x]I am weary with my crying out;
[y]my throat is parched.
[z]My eyes grow dim
with [a]waiting for my God.

4 [b]More in number than the hairs of my head
are [c]those who hate me [d]without cause;
mighty are those who would destroy me,
[e]those who attack me with lies.
What I did not steal
must I now restore?
5 O God, you know my folly;
the wrongs I have done are not hidden from you.

6 Let not those who hope in you [f]be put to shame through me,
O Lord GOD of hosts;
let not those who seek you be brought to dishonor through me,
O God of Israel.
7 For it is [g]for your sake that I have borne reproach,
that dishonor has covered my face.
8 I have become [h]a stranger to my brothers,
an alien to my mother's sons.

9 For [i]zeal for your house has consumed me,
and [j]the reproaches of those who reproach you have fallen on me.
10 When I wept and humbled[3] my soul with fasting,
it became my reproach.
11 When I made [k]sackcloth my clothing,
I became [l]a byword to them.
12 I am the talk of those who [m]sit in the gate,
and the drunkards make [n]songs about me.

13 But as for me, my [o]prayer is to you, O LORD.
At [p]an acceptable time, O God,
in the abundance of your steadfast love answer me in your saving faithfulness.
14 Deliver me
from sinking in [q]the mire;
[r]let me be delivered from my enemies
and from [s]the deep waters.
15 Let not the flood sweep over me,
or the deep swallow me up,
or [t]the pit close [u]its mouth over me.

[1] Septuagint; Hebrew *your* [2] Or *waters threaten my life* [3] Hebrew lacks *and humbled*

Psalm 69 David provides the believer with words to express a lament when falsely persecuted. However, the New Testament's application of these verses to the Messiah also teaches the worshiper that his ultimate vindication can come only through his union with Christ.

The psalm opens loudly with the cries of a drowning man (vv. 1–5). Though he reaches for a handhold, he only sinks deeper and deeper. The Savior felt like this as a victim of man's mockery and estrangement from his Father (vv. 4, 9, 19–21; John 15:25). The only time Jesus did not address God as his Father was when he felt his abandonment (Mark 15:34). However, all of his suffering was out of zeal for the glory of his Father and love for those he came to save (Ps. 69:9, 13–18; Ex. 34:6; John 2:17; Rom. 15:3).

David poignantly describes how suffering cruelty can affect a person (Ps. 69:11, 12, 20, 29). In his pain he can lash out in uncharacteristic anger (vv. 9, 24–28). Applied to Christ, this explains the mystery of the "wrath of the Lamb" (Rev. 6:16; cf. John 2:17). An otherwise peaceful man became violent as he battled hell (Ps. 69:22–28; Acts 1:20; Rom. 11:9–10). The consequences of sin also alienate and dehumanize (Ps. 69:7–8). Since there is no way to avoid the messianic nature of this psalm, we conclude that Christ bore our reproach and became sin for us (cf. v. 9; 2 Cor. 5:21). David and his Greater Son lead the spiritually depressed out of their grief into praise for the God who saves the humble (Ps. 69:30–36; Matt. 11:28–30).

35[q] [Ps. 65:5]; See Ps. 47:2 [r] [Ps. 110:2] [s] Isa. 40:29; See Ps. 29:11
Psalm 69
[t] Ps. 45, title
1[u] ver. 14, 15; See Ps. 32:6; 130:1; Job 22:11
2[v] ver. 14; Ps. 40:2 [w] Ps. 124:4
3[x] Ps. 6:6 [y] [Ps. 22:15] [z] Ps. 119:82, 123; Deut. 28:32; Isa. 38:14 [a] See Ps. 31:24
4[b] Ps. 40:12 [c] Cited John 15:25 [d] [Ps. 35:7; 59:3, 4; 109:3; 119:161] [e] Ps. 35:19; 38:19
6[f] See Ps. 25:2
7[g] Jer. 15:15; [Ps. 44:22]
8[h] [Ps. 31:11; 38:11; Job 19:13; John 1:11]
9[i] Cited John 2:17; [Ps. 119:139]; See Ps. 132:1-5 [j] Cited Rom. 15:3; [Ps. 89:41, 50]
11[k] See Ps. 35:13 [l] See Job 17:6
12[m] [Gen. 19:1; Esth. 2:19] [n] See Job 30:9
13[o] Ps. 109:4 [p] Isa. 49:8; 2 Cor. 6:2; [Ps. 32:6]
14[q] ver. 2 [r] Ps. 144:7 [s] ver. 1, 2
15[t] Ps. 55:23 [u] Num. 16:33

16 Answer me, O LORD, for your [v]steadfast love is good;
according to your abundant [w]mercy, [x]turn to me.
17 [y]Hide not your face from your servant;
[z]for I am in distress; [a]make haste to answer me.
18 Draw near to my soul, redeem me;
ransom me because of my enemies!

19 You know my [b]reproach,
and my shame and my dishonor;
my foes are all known to you.
20 [b]Reproaches have broken my heart,
so that I am in [c]despair.
I [d]looked for [e]pity, but there was none,
and for [f]comforters, but I found none.
21 They gave me [g]poison for food,
and for my thirst they gave me [h]sour wine to drink.

22 [i]Let their own [j]table before them become a snare;
[k]and when they are at peace, let it become a trap.[1]
23 [l]Let their eyes be darkened, so that they cannot see,
[m]and make their loins tremble continually.
24 Pour out your indignation upon them,
and let your burning anger overtake them.
25 [n]May their camp be a desolation;
let no one dwell in their tents.
26 For they [o]persecute him whom [p]you have struck down,
and they recount the pain of [q]those you have wounded.
27 [r]Add to them punishment upon punishment;
may they have no acquittal from you.[2]
28 Let them be [s]blotted out of the book of the living;
let them not be [t]enrolled among the righteous.

29 But I am afflicted and in pain;
let your salvation, O God, [u]set me on high!

30 I will [v]praise the name of God with a song;
I will [w]magnify him with [x]thanksgiving.
31 This will [y]please the LORD more than an ox
or a bull [z]with horns and hoofs.
32 When [a]the humble see it they will be glad;
you who seek God, [a]let your hearts revive.
33 For the LORD hears the needy
and [b]does not despise his own people who are prisoners.

34 Let [c]heaven and earth praise him,
the seas and everything that moves in them.
35 For [d]God will save Zion
and build up the cities of Judah,
and people shall dwell there and possess it;
36 [e]the offspring of his servants shall inherit it,
and those who love his name shall dwell in it.

O LORD, Do Not Delay

70

TO THE CHOIRMASTER. OF DAVID, [f]FOR THE MEMORIAL OFFERING.

1 [g]Make haste, O God, to deliver me!
O LORD, make haste to help me!
2 Let them be put to shame and confusion
who seek my life!

[1] Hebrew; a slight revocalization yields (compare Septuagint, Syriac, Jerome) *a snare, and retribution and a trap* [2] Hebrew *may they not come into your righteousness*

16[v] Ps. 63:3; 109:21 [w] Ps. 106:45 [x] See Ps. 25:16
17[y] See Ps. 27:9 [z] See Ps. 18:6 [a] Ps. 102:2; 143:7
19[b] ver. 10, 11; [Heb. 12:2]; See Ps. 22:6
20[b] [See ver. 19 above] [c] [Matt. 26:37] [d] Ps. 142:4; [Isa. 63:5] [e] Jer. 15:5 [f] Job 16:2
21[g] Deut. 29:18; Matt. 27:34 [h] Matt. 27:48; Luke 23:36; John 19:29; [Mark 15:23]
22[i] Cited Rom. 11:9, 10; See Ps. 35:4-8; 109:6-15 [j] Ps. 23:5 [k] [1 Thess. 5:3] **23**[l] Isa. 6:10; [Matt. 13:14] [m] Dan. 5:6; Nah. 2:10 **25**[n] Cited Acts 1:20; [Matt. 23:38; Luke 13:35] **26**[o] [Zech. 1:15] [p] Isa. 53:4 [q] [Job 19:21] **27**[r] Neh. 4:5 **28**[s] Ex. 32:32; Rev. 3:5; [Phil. 4:3] [t] [Ezek. 13:9; Luke 10:20; Heb. 12:23] **29**[u] Ps. 20:1 **30**[v] Ps. 28:7 [w] See Ps. 34:3 [x] See Ps. 50:14, 23 **31**[y] Ps. 50:13 [z] Lev. 11:3 **32**[a] Ps. 22:26; 34:2 **33**[b] [Ps. 68:6] **34**[c] Ps. 96:11; 98:7; Isa. 44:23; 49:13; See Ps. 148:1-12 **35**[d] See Ps. 51:18; [Isa. 44:26] **36**[e] Ps. 102:28; Isa. 65:9; [Ps. 37:29] **Psalm 70** [f] Ps. 38, title; [1 Chr. 16:4] **1**[g] For ver. 1-5, see Ps. 40:13-17

Psalm 70 David's cry for help in this psalm is virtually the same as Psalm 40:14–17, only with a greater sense of urgency. A portion of the earlier verses from Psalm 40 are attributed to Christ in Hebrews 10:5–7. Thus the psalm ultimately draws the worshiper nearer to the God of grace not only because of insights into the suffering his Son would experience, but also because it shows how willing and able God is to help the desperate.

Though similarly translated, David's first line here is more compact than in Psalm 40:14. Literally it reads, "God, to deliver me; Lord, to my help, hurry"—as if David is on the run. One gripped by panic like a cornered animal can find a voice in these verses (70:2–3; Matt. 27:39–43).

Let them be turned back and brought to dishonor
who delight in my hurt!
3 Let them turn back because of their shame
who say, "Aha, Aha!"

4 May all who seek you
rejoice and be glad in you!
May those who love your salvation
say evermore, "God is great!"
5 But I am poor and needy;
[h]hasten to me, O God!
You are my help and my deliverer;
O LORD, do not delay!

Forsake Me Not When My Strength Is Spent

71 [i]In you, O LORD, do I take refuge;
let me never be put to shame!
2 In your righteousness deliver me and rescue me;
incline your ear to me, and save me!
3 Be to me a rock of [j]refuge,
to which I may continually come;
you have [k]given the command to save me,
for you are my [l]rock and my fortress.

4 [m]Rescue me, O my God, from the hand of the wicked,
from the grasp of the unjust and cruel man.
5 For you, O Lord, are my [n]hope,
my trust, O LORD, from my youth.
6 Upon you I have leaned [o]from before my birth;
you are he who [p]took me from my mother's womb.
My praise is continually of you.

7 I have been as [q]a portent to many,
but you are my strong refuge.
8 My [r]mouth is filled with your praise,
and with your glory all the day.
9 [s]Do not cast me off in the time of old age;
forsake me not when my strength is spent.
10 For my enemies speak concerning me;
those who [t]watch for my life [u]consult together
11 and say, "God has forsaken him;
pursue and seize him,
for there is none to deliver him."

12 O God, be not [v]far from me;
O my God, [w]make haste to help me!
13 May my accusers be [x]put to shame and consumed;
[y]with scorn and disgrace may they be covered
who [z]seek my hurt.
14 But I will [a]hope continually
and will [b]praise you yet more and more.

The tension between "God is great!" (Ps. 70:4) and "I am poor and needy" (v. 5) is a realistic demonstration of contradicting desires even within believing souls. While the flesh wishes to flee hardship, the Spirit enables the believer to remain faithful. Consistent with the character of this God of grace in the Old Testament, Jesus promised help to the weak, not those who fake strength: "Blessed are the poor in spirit, for theirs is the kingdom of heaven" (Matt. 5:3). Looking to future redemption produces perseverance, not escapism. This is the Old Testament version of the New Testament cry, "Maranatha! Come, Lord Jesus" (Rev. 22:20; cf. 1 Cor. 16:22; Ps. 70:1, 5). And the promise is that, in answer to that plea, the "grace of the Lord Jesus" will "be with all" (Rev. 22:21).

Psalm 71 God's mercy is more than sufficient for every stage of life. Straining his memory to childhood, the psalmist cannot remember a day without mercy (vv. 5–6; cf. 22:9–10). Early in life, he learned from the Scriptures to trust God prayerfully for his future: he was never disappointed (71:1–3; 31:1–3). These were among the same "sacred writings" Timothy would have learned from his childhood, which made him "wise for salvation through faith in Christ Jesus" (2 Tim. 3:15). A long history of proving God's faithfulness buttresses one against hostile peers (Ps. 71:4–9). At the end of the ages, the believer will "shout for joy" and his enemies will be "put to shame" (vv. 23–24).

Since verses 12 and 13 are quoted in numerous other psalms attributed to David, this middle portion could be his testimony to God's mercy in his mid-life battles (v. 17; 22:11; 35:4, 22, 26; 38:21, 22; 40:13, 14; 109:29). The believer's eternal hope is stronger than conspiracy and fear because it is based on God's unassailable character, finally personified in Jesus (71:10–16; Heb. 6:13–20).

5[h] Ps. 141:1
Psalm 71
1[i] For ver. 1-3, see Ps. 31:1-3
3[j] [Ps. 90:1; 91:9; Deut. 33:27] [k] See Ps. 42:8 [l] See Ps. 18:2
4[m] Ps. 140:1, 4
5[n] Jer. 14:8; 17:13; 50:7; 1 Tim. 1:1
6[o] See Ps. 22:10 [p] Ps. 22:9
7[q] Isa. 8:18; [1 Cor. 4:9]
8[r] ver. 24
9[s] ver. 18
10[t] Ps. 56:6 [u] Ps. 83:5; [Ps. 41:7, 8]
12[v] See Ps. 10:1 [w] Ps. 70:5; See Ps. 40:13
13[x] ver. 24; See Ps. 35:4, 26 [y] Ps. 109:29 [z] ver. 24; Esth. 9:2; [Ps. 70:2]
14[a] ver. 5 [b] ver. 22

15 My [c]mouth will tell of your righteous
acts,
of your deeds of salvation all the day,
for [d]their number is past my knowledge.
16 With the mighty deeds of the Lord GOD
I will come;
I will remind them of your righteousness, yours alone.

17 O God, from my youth you have taught
me,
and I still proclaim your wondrous
deeds.
18 So even to [e]old age and gray hairs,
O God, [f]do not forsake me,
until I proclaim your might to another
generation,
your power to all those to come.
19 Your [g]righteousness, O God,
reaches the high heavens.
You who have done [h]great things,
O God, [i]who is like you?
20 You who have [j]made me see many troubles and calamities
will [k]revive me again;
from the depths of the earth
you will bring me up again.
21 You will increase my greatness
and comfort me again.

22 I will also praise you with [l]the harp
for your faithfulness, O my God;
I will sing praises to you with the lyre,
O [m]Holy One of Israel.
23 My lips will shout for joy,
when I sing praises to you;
my soul also, which you have
[n]redeemed.
24 And my [o]tongue will talk of your righteous help all the day long,
for they have been [p]put to shame and
disappointed
who sought to do me hurt.

Give the King Your Justice

72

OF [q]SOLOMON.

Give the king your [r]justice, O God,
and your righteousness to the royal
son!
2 May he [s]judge your people with righteousness,
and your poor with justice!
3 Let the mountains bear [t]prosperity for
the people,
and the hills, in righteousness!
4 May he defend the cause of the poor of
the people,
give deliverance to the children of the
needy,
and crush the oppressor!

5 May they fear you[1] while [u]the sun
endures,
and as long as the moon, [v]throughout
all generations!

[1] Septuagint *He shall endure*

15[c] ver. 8, 24 [d] See Ps. 40:5
18[e] Isa. 46:4 [f] ver. 9
19[g] Ps. 36:5 [h] Ps. 126:2; 1 Sam. 12:24; Luke 1:49 [i] Ps. 35:10
20[j] Ps. 60:3 [k] Ps. 80:18; 85:6; 119:25; 138:7; 143:11; Hos. 6:2
22[l] Ps. 33:2 [m] Ps. 78:41; 89:18; 2 Kgs. 19:22; Isa. 60:9
23[n] Ps. 34:22
24[o] [ver. 8, 15]; See Ps. 35:28 [p] [ver. 13]
Psalm 72
[q] Ps. 127, title
1[r] [1 Chr. 22:12]
2[s] Isa. 9:7; 11:2-4; 32:1; See Ps. 122:5
3[t] [Ps. 85:10; Isa. 32:17; 52:7]
5[u] ver. 7, 17; Ps. 89:36, 37; Jer. 31:35, 36; [Jer. 33:20, 25] [v] Ps. 89:4; [Luke 1:33]

Finally, the old saint recognizes that he must tell his story to the next generation. An elderly saint's greatest responsibility to the young is teaching them how to die well (Ps. 71:18–19; 2 Tim. 4:9). Courage to meet the last enemy comes only from the promise of the resurrection, which the Spirit enabled the Old Testament saint anticipate with hope (Ps. 71:20–21; Job 19:26; Acts 2:27). Not only does the psalmist foresee the resurrection, he understands that the judgment will bring commendation for those united to Christ (Ps. 71:21; Rom. 2:29; 9:21–23).

Psalm 72 The first verse of this psalm prays for justice for the king of Israel, the son of David (in this case, Solomon; see superscription). While we must pray for all rulers to be righteous, this prayer will be completely answered only in Christ, the ultimate Son of David (vv. 1–2; cf. Matt. 20:31; Mark 12:35).

By praying that the people would be "blessed *in him*," the psalmist is asking to be hidden in the righteousness God provides through Israel's king (Ps. 72:1, 17). Ultimately this prayer is answered in Christ, who was typified in the Old Testament kings before actually becoming the "righteousness of God" for everyone who receives him "through faith" (Rom. 3:21–22). Solomon also prays for earthly justice (Ps. 72:3–7, 12–14). The Old Testament believer pleaded for God to vindicate his name by effecting justice on the earth (Psalm 7; Isa. 56:1; Amos 5:24). Likewise, Solomon imagines a land in which people flourish economically and the needy are protected (Ps. 72:3, 4). By his word and example, Jesus announced a kingdom that brings relief, healing, and life to people physically as well as spiritually (Luke 4:18–19).

6 May he be like [w]rain that falls on [x]the
mown grass,
like [y]showers that water the earth!
7 In his days may [z]the righteous flourish,
and [a]peace abound, till the moon be
no more!

8 May he have dominion from [b]sea to sea,
and from [b]the River[1] to the [c]ends of
the earth!
9 May desert tribes [d]bow down before
him,
and his enemies [e]lick the dust!
10 May the kings of [f]Tarshish and of [g]the
coastlands
render him [h]tribute;
may the kings of [i]Sheba and [j]Seba
bring gifts!
11 May all kings [k]fall down before him,
all nations serve him!

12 For he delivers [l]the needy when he calls,
the poor and him who has no helper.
13 He has pity on the weak and the needy,
and saves the lives of the needy.
14 From oppression and violence he
redeems their life,
and [m]precious is their blood in his
sight.

15 Long may he live;
may [n]gold of Sheba be given to him!
May prayer be made [o]for him continually,
and blessings invoked for him all the
day!

16 May there be abundance of grain in the
land;
on the tops of the mountains may it
wave;
may its fruit be like Lebanon;
and may people [p]blossom in the cities
like the [q]grass of the field!
17 [r]May his name endure forever,
his fame continue as long as the sun!
[s]May people be blessed in him,
[t]all nations call him blessed!

18 [u]Blessed be the LORD, the God of Israel,
who alone does [v]wondrous things.
19 Blessed be his [w]glorious name forever;
may [x]the whole earth be filled with
his glory!
[y]Amen and Amen!

20 [z]The prayers of [a]David, the son of Jesse,
are ended.

Book Three

God Is My Strength and Portion Forever

73 A PSALM OF [b]ASAPH.
Truly God is good to [c]Israel,
to those who are [d]pure in heart.
2 But as for me, my feet had almost stumbled,
my steps had nearly slipped.
3 [e]For I was [f]envious of the arrogant
when I saw the [g]prosperity of the
wicked.

4 For they have no pangs until death;
their bodies are fat and sleek.

[1] That is, the Euphrates

Prophetically, Solomon understood that his Greater Son's kingdom will extend far beyond *his* kingdom geographically, ethnically, and chronologically (Ps. 72:8–11, 15–20; Acts 10:47). To the believer this is a comforting thought (Ps. 139:1–16). With this cosmic vision, we are strengthened to live in a kingdom that is "now but not yet" (see Heb. 12:28).

Psalm 73 The psalmists arrive at accurate perspectives on the world by voicing their complaints to God. Asaph shows believers how to express doubts, questions, or anger to God, and the goodness of God makes it safe to do so. The core complaint is that the wicked seem never to suffer disappointment (vv. 4–5) or consequences for their ungodly actions (vv. 4–12). Asaph is even so bold as to accuse the Lord of turning a blind eye to the actions of the ungodly, thus removing all incentive for pursuing godliness (vv. 13–14).

Asaph expressed his doubts to God (vv. 15–16) in the context of worship (vv. 17–20). That is, he went to the tabernacle with the full expectation that he would receive an answer, rather than pulling back in self-pity and bitterness (v. 21).Throughout redemptive history, worshipers have been encouraged to remember that, while God's time line for justice is not short, it progresses with steady assurances. In these last days, Christ is the absolute guarantee that the triune God will fulfill all of his promises of justice for the godly and judgment on the wicked (2 Pet. 3:8–10).

6 [w]2 Sam. 23:4; Hos. 6:3 [x]Amos 7:1 [y]Deut. 32:2; [Ps. 65:10; Job 5:10]
7 [z]See Ps. 92:12 [a]Isa. 2:4; [Eph. 2:14]
8 [b]Ex. 23:31; 1 Kgs. 4:21, 24; Zech. 9:10; [Ps. 80:11; 89:25] [c]See Ps. 2:8
9 [d]Ps. 22:29 [e]Isa. 49:23; Mic. 7:17
10 [f]1 Kgs. 10:22 [g]Isa. 42:10, 12; 51:5; 60:9 [h]See Ps. 68:29; 1 Sam. 10:27 [i]See 1 Kgs. 10:1 [j]Gen. 10:7; Isa. 43:3; 45:14
11 [k]Isa. 49:7, 23
12 [l]See Job 29:12-17
14 [m]Ps. 116:15; 2 Kgs. 1:13
15 [n]1 Kgs. 10:10 [o]Deut. 9:20
16 [p]Ps. 92:7 [q]Job 5:25
17 [r]Ps. 104:31; [Ps. 89:36] [s]Gen. 12:3; 18:18; 22:18; 26:4 [t]Luke 1:48
18 [u]See Ps. 41:13 [v]Ps. 77:14; 86:10; 136:4; Ex. 15:11; See Job 5:9
19 [w]Neh. 9:5 [x]Num. 14:21 [y]Ps. 41:13
20 [z]Ps. 17, title; 55:1; 86, title [a]2 Sam. 23:1

Psalm 73 [b]See Ps. 50, title **1** [c]John 1:47 [d]See Ps. 24:4 **3** [e]See Job 21:7 [f]Ps. 37:1; Prov. 23:17 [g][Ps. 37:7; 92:7; Jer. 12:1]

5 They are not in trouble as others are;
they are not [h]stricken like the rest of mankind.
6 Therefore pride is [i]their necklace;
violence covers them as [j]a garment.
7 Their [k]eyes swell out through fatness;
their hearts overflow with follies.
8 They scoff and [l]speak with malice;
loftily they threaten oppression.
9 They set their mouths against the heavens,
and their tongue struts through the earth.
10 Therefore his people turn back to them,
and find [m]no fault in them.[1]
11 And they say, [n]"How can God know?
Is there knowledge in the Most High?"
12 Behold, these are the wicked;
always at ease, they [o]increase in riches.
13 All in vain have I [p]kept my heart clean
and [q]washed my hands in innocence.
14 For all the day long I have been [h]stricken
and [r]rebuked [s]every morning.
15 If I had said, "I will speak thus,"
I would have betrayed [t]the generation of your children.

16 But when I thought how to understand this,
it seemed to me [u]a wearisome task,
17 until I went into [v]the sanctuary of God;
then I discerned their [w]end.

18 Truly you set them in [x]slippery places;
you make them fall to ruin.
19 How they are destroyed [y]in a moment,
swept away utterly by [z]terrors!
20 Like [a]a dream when one awakes,
O Lord, when [b]you rouse yourself, you despise them as phantoms.
21 When my soul was embittered,
when I was pricked in heart,
22 I was [c]brutish and ignorant;
I was like [d]a beast toward you.

23 Nevertheless, I am continually with you;
you [e]hold my right hand.
24 You [f]guide me with your counsel,
and afterward you will [g]receive me to glory.
25 [h]Whom have I in heaven but you?
And there is nothing on earth that I desire besides you.
26 [i]My flesh and my heart may fail,
but God is [j]the strength[2] of my heart and my [k]portion [l]forever.

27 For behold, those who are [m]far from you shall perish;
you put an end to everyone who is [n]unfaithful to you.
28 But for me it is good to [o]be near God;
I have made the Lord GOD my [p]refuge,
that I may [q]tell of all your works.

Arise, O God, Defend Your Cause

74 A MASKIL[3] OF [r]ASAPH.

1 O God, why do you [s]cast us off forever?
Why does your anger [t]smoke against [u]the sheep of your pasture?

[1] Probable reading; Hebrew *the waters of a full cup are drained by them* [2] Hebrew *rock* [3] Probably a musical or liturgical term

5[h] [Isa. 53:4]
6[i] [Judg. 8:26] [j] [Ps. 109:18]
7[k] See Job 15:27
8[l] [2 Pet. 2:18; Jude 16]
10[m] [Job 15:16]
11[n] See Job 22:13
12[o] [ver. 3]
13[p] [ver. 1]; See Job 34:9 [q] See Ps. 26:6
14[h] [See ver. 5 above] [r] Rev. 3:19 [s] [Ps. 101:8]
15[t] [Ps. 14:5]
16[u] Eccles. 8:17
17[v] Ps. 20:2 [w] Ps. 37:38
18[x] Ps. 35:6
19[y] [Num. 16:21] [z] See Job 18:11
20[a] See Job 20:8 [b] Ps. 78:65
22[c] See Ps. 49:10 [d] Job 18:3; [Job 11:12]
23[e] Ps. 63:8; [Ps. 41:12]

Bitterness obscures rationality, and ingratitude blinds us to God's grace that is ultimately seen again (Ps. 73:23–28) after Asaph confesses his narrowed vision (vv. 16–20) and sin (vv. 21–22). Bitterness and ingratitude cause us to forget the unique comfort of God's nearness (vv. 23, 27), neglect the transformative power of his Word (v. 24), fail to look to our advocate in heaven (v. 25), and lose the assurance of eternal life (v. 26).

Psalm 74 The tabernacle represents God's presence among his people, so when Asaph sees prophetically the day when the temple will be destroyed, he is emotionally undone, wondering if God has abandoned his people (vv. 1–11). Asaph thus provides a pattern for how to trust God when your world is falling apart. One must first recall God's faithfulness in the past by reading biblical stories of God's mighty acts, remembering testimonies from contemporaries, and recalling God's personal help in one's own life—supremely through the gospel of grace.

24[f] Ps. 32:8 [g] See Ps. 49:15 **25**[h] Ps. 16:2; [Phil. 3:8] **26**[i] Ps. 40:12; See Ps. 84:2 [j] Ps. 18:2 [k] See Ps. 16:5 [l] [Dan. 12:3] **27**[m] Ps. 119:155 [n] Ps. 106:39; Ex. 34:15; Num. 15:39; James 4:4 **28**[o] James 4:8; [Heb. 10:22] [p] See Ps. 14:6 [q] See Ps. 118:17 **Psalm 74** [r] See Ps. 50, title **1**[s] See Ps. 44:9 [t] Deut. 29:20; [Ps. 18:8] [u] Ps. 79:13; 100:3; Jer. 23:1; Ezek. 34:31; [Ps. 95:7]

2 [v]Remember your congregation, which
you have [w]purchased of old,
which you have [x]redeemed to be [y]the
tribe of your heritage!
Remember Mount Zion, [z]where you
have dwelt.
3 Direct your steps to [a]the perpetual
ruins;
the enemy has destroyed everything
in the sanctuary!

4 Your foes have [b]roared in the midst of
your meeting place;
[c]they set up their [d]own signs for
[e]signs.
5 They were like those who swing [f]axes
in a forest of trees.[1]
6 And all its [g]carved wood
they broke down with hatchets and
hammers.
7 They [h]set your sanctuary on fire;
they [i]profaned [j]the dwelling place of
your name,
bringing it down to the ground.
8 They [k]said to themselves, "We will
utterly subdue them";
they burned all the meeting places of
God in the land.

9 We do not see our [l]signs;
[m]there is no longer any prophet,
and there is none among us who
knows how long.
10 How long, O God, [n]is the foe to scoff?
Is the enemy to revile your name forever?
11 Why [o]do you hold back your hand, your
right hand?
Take it from the fold of your garment[2] and destroy them!

12 Yet [p]God my King is from of old,
working salvation in the midst of the
earth.
13 You [q]divided the sea by your might;
you [r]broke the heads of [s]the sea mon-
sters[3] on the waters.
14 You crushed the heads of [t]Leviathan;
you gave him as food for the creatures
of the wilderness.
15 You [u]split open springs and brooks;
you [v]dried up ever-flowing streams.
16 Yours is the day, yours also the night;
you have established [w]the heavenly
lights and the sun.
17 You have [x]fixed all the boundaries of the
earth;
you have made [y]summer and winter.

18 [z]Remember this, O LORD, how the enemy
scoffs,
and [a]a foolish people reviles your
name.
19 Do not deliver the soul of your [b]dove to
the wild beasts;
[c]do not forget the life of your poor forever.

20 Have regard for [d]the covenant,
for [e]the dark places of the land are full
of the habitations of violence.
21 Let not [f]the downtrodden [g]turn back in
shame;
let [h]the poor and needy praise your
name.

22 Arise, O God, [i]defend your cause;
[j]remember how the foolish scoff at
you all the day!
23 Do not forget the clamor of your foes,
[k]the uproar of those who rise against
you, which goes up continually!

[1] The meaning of the Hebrew is uncertain [2] Hebrew *from your bosom* [3] Or *the great sea creatures*

Like a lawyer, Asaph argues for why God must act. On the one hand, Asaph asks God to defend his own reputation (vv. 3–8, 10–11, 22–23). Then he appeals to God's covenant promises to his children (vv. 1–2, 12–17, 20). Such appeals represent a believer's love for his Father's name, arising from his past experience of God's love.

Christ surpassed the temple by bringing God's presence to earth tangibly (John 2:18–22). Recalling God's demonstration of love and faithfulness in Christ quiets all fears that God could disappoint us (Rom. 8:31–38). In Christ, we are utterly secure. In Christ, God has supremely had "regard for the covenant" (Ps. 74:20). Christ has paid for the curses of covenant disobedience, and we covenant breakers are put right with God for free, because of Jesus (Gal. 3:10–14).

2[v] ver. 18, 22 [w] Ex. 15:16; Deut. 32:6; [Ps. 78:54] [x] Ps. 77:15; Isa. 63:9 [y] Isa. 63:17; Jer. 10:16; 51:19 [z] Ps. 9:11
3[a] [Isa. 61:4]
4[b] Lam. 2:6, 7 [c] [Matt. 24:15] [d] Num. 2:2 [e] [ver. 9]
5[f] [Jer. 46:22]
6[g] [1 Kgs. 6:18, 29, 32, 35]
7[h] 2 Kgs. 25:9; [Ps. 79:1] [i] Ps. 89:39; [Lam. 2:2] [j] [Ps. 26:8]
8[k] Ps. 83:4
9[l] [ver. 4] [m] [1 Sam. 3:1; Lam. 2:9; Ezek. 7:26; Amos 8:11]

10[n] ver. 18, 22; Ps. 79:12; 89:51 **11**[o] Lam. 2:3 **12**[p] Ps. 44:4 **13**[q] Ex. 14:21 [r] Isa. 51:9 [s] Isa. 27:1 **14**[t] See Job 41:1 **15**[u] Ps. 78:15; 105:41; Ex. 17:5, 6; Num. 20:11; Isa. 48:21 [v] Josh. 2:10; 4:23; Isa. 51:10; [Ps. 66:6]; See Ex. 14:21-25; Josh. 3:13-17 **16**[w] Ps. 104:19; See Gen. 1:14-16 **17**[x] Deut. 32:8; [Acts 17:26] [y] Gen. 8:22 **18**[z] ver. 2, 22; Ps. 89:50; Rev. 16:19; 18:5 [a] Ps. 39:8; Deut. 32:6 **19**[b] Song 2:14 [c] [Ps. 68:10] **20**[d] Ps. 106:45; Gen. 17:7, 8; Lev. 26:44, 45; Jer. 33:21 [e] [Ps. 10:8] **21**[f] Ps. 9:9; 10:18 [g] [Ps. 6:10] [h] Ps. 86:1 **22**[i] [1 Sam. 24:15] [j] ver. 2, 18 **23**[k] See Ps. 65:7

God Will Judge with Equity

75

To the choirmaster: according to [l]Do Not Destroy. [m]A Psalm of Asaph. A Song.

1 We give thanks to you, O God;
we give thanks, for your name is [n]near.
We[1] recount your wondrous deeds.

2 "At [o]the set time that I appoint
I will judge [p]with equity.
3 When the earth [q]totters, and all its inhabitants,
it is I who keep steady its [r]pillars. *Selah*
4 I say to the boastful, 'Do not boast,'
and to the wicked, [s]'Do not lift up your horn;
5 do not lift up your horn on high,
or speak with haughty neck.'"

6 For not from the east or from the west
and not from the wilderness comes [t]lifting up,
7 but it is [u]God who executes judgment,
[v]putting down one and lifting up another.
8 [w]For in the hand of the LORD there is [x]a cup
with foaming wine, [y]well mixed,
and he pours out from it,
and all the wicked of the earth
shall [z]drain it down to the dregs.

9 But I will declare it forever;
I will sing praises to the God of Jacob.
10 [a]All the horns of the wicked I will cut off,
[b]but the horns of the righteous shall be lifted up.

Who Can Stand Before You?

76

To the choirmaster: with [c]stringed instruments. A Psalm of [d]Asaph. A Song.

1 In Judah God is [e]known;
his name is great in Israel.
2 His [f]abode has been established in [g]Salem,
his [h]dwelling place in Zion.
3 There he [i]broke the flashing arrows,
the shield, the sword, and the weapons of war. *Selah*

4 Glorious are you, more majestic
[j]than the mountains full of [k]prey.
5 [l]The stouthearted were stripped of their spoil;
[m]they sank into sleep;

[1] Hebrew *They*

Psalm 75
[l]See Ps. 57, title [m]See Ps. 50, title
1[n]Ps. 145:18
2[o]Dan. 8:19; Hab. 2:3; See Ps. 102:13 [p]Ps. 17:2
3[q]Isa. 24:19 [r]1 Sam. 2:8
4[s]ver. 10; Zech. 1:21
6[t]See Ps. 3:3
7[u]See Ps. 50:6 [v]1 Sam. 2:7; Dan. 2:21
8[w]See Job 21:20 [x]Ps. 11:6 [y]Prov. 23:30 [z]Ps. 73:10
10[a]Jer. 48:25 [b]ver. 4; Ps. 89:17; 112:9; 1 Sam. 2:1
Psalm 76
[c]Ps. 4, title [d]See Ps. 50, title
1[e]Ps. 48:3
2[f]Ps. 27:5; Lam. 2:6 [g]Gen. 14:18 [h]Ps. 9:11; 74:2
3[i]Ps. 46:9; [Ezek. 39:9]
4[j][Isa. 14:25; Ezek. 39:4] [k]Nah. 2:13
5[l]Isa. 46:12 [m]Ps. 13:3; 2 Kgs. 19:35; Jer. 51:39; Nah. 3:18

Psalm 75 In this psalm, four parties testify that God is trustworthy. First, God's people testify that his "name," which encapsulates all of his attributes, is always near (v. 1). God's name was ultimately personified in Jesus Christ (Matt. 1:23). From other Scripture we understand that the church may cite not only its own experience of God but also the testimonies of skeptics who are forced to profess the greatness of God's deeds (Josh. 2:8–13; Luke 23:47).

Second, God himself is summoned for testimony (Ps. 75:2–5). First, he assures that he sustains the basic structures of the cosmos and society (Gen. 8:22; Dan. 2:21; Mal. 2:13–16; Rom. 13:1). The second assurance God gives is a warning to the wicked (Ps. 75:4–5). He judges them by allowing them to condemn themselves (Gen. 15:16; Ex. 9:16; Rom. 9:17). In the meantime, his kindness allows time to repent (Rom. 2:3–4).

Third (Ps. 75:6–7), a preacher is summoned who challenges the believer to look away from those who seem to be powerful now. Majorities, victories, and consensuses do not determine what is right. Right is right regardless of who subscribes or does not subscribe to it. The preacher, reflecting the earlier testimony of God, turns to the dreadful end of the unbelievers and warns that unless they repent, God's vengeful judgment will "foam" against them (see v. 8; cf. Isa. 51:17; Jer. 25:15–38; 49:12; 51:7; Rev. 18:6).

Finally (Ps. 75:9–10), an individual declares his trust in the Lord. He expresses confidence in the same Redeemer who, according to Job's testimony, "lives, and at the last . . . will stand upon the earth" (Job 19:25). Ultimately, this one is Christ, the righteous One who conquered death and now rules at God's right hand (Heb. 1:3; 8:1).

Psalm 76 Second only to the exodus as the most significant redemptive event in the Old Testament is God's defeat of the Assyrians under Sennacherib, when God's angel slew 185,000 Assyrian soldiers (vv. 5–6; 2 Kings 19:14–37). Ancient tradition relates this psalm to that event—interwoven with references to other redeeming events in Israel's history. By either prophecy or reflection, the psalmist recounts the mighty

all the men of war
were unable to use their hands.
6 At your rebuke, O God of Jacob,
both [n]rider and horse lay stunned.

7 [o]But you, you are to be feared!
Who can [p]stand before you
when once your anger is roused?
8 From the heavens you uttered judgment;
[q]the earth feared and was still,
9 when God [r]arose to establish judgment,
to save all the humble of the earth.
Selah

10 Surely [s]the wrath of man shall praise you;
the remnant[1] of wrath you will put on
like a belt.
11 [t]Make your vows to the LORD your God
and perform them;
let all around him [u]bring gifts
to him who [v]is to be feared,
12 who [w]cuts off the spirit of princes,
who [x]is to be feared by the kings of
the earth.

In the Day of Trouble I Seek the Lord

77

TO THE CHOIRMASTER: ACCORDING TO [y]JEDUTHUN. A PSALM OF [z]ASAPH.

1 I [a]cry aloud to God,
aloud to God, and he will hear me.
2 [b]In the day of my trouble I seek the Lord;
in [c]the night my [d]hand is stretched
out without wearying;
my soul [e]refuses to be comforted.
3 When I remember God, I [f]moan;
when I meditate, my spirit faints. *Selah*

4 You hold my eyelids open;
I am so [g]troubled that I cannot speak.
5 I consider [h]the days of old,
the years long ago.
6 I said,[2] "Let me remember my [i]song in
the night;
let me [j]meditate in my heart."
Then my spirit made a diligent search:
7 "Will the Lord [k]spurn forever,
and never again [l]be favorable?
8 Has his steadfast love forever ceased?
Are his [m]promises at an end for all
time?
9 [n]Has God forgotten to be gracious?
[o]Has he in anger shut up his compassion?" *Selah*

10 Then I said, "I will appeal to this,
to the years of the [p]right hand of the
Most High."[3]

11 I will remember the deeds of the LORD;
yes, I will [q]remember your wonders of
old.

[1] Or *extremity* [2] Hebrew lacks *I said* [3] Or *This is my grief: that the right hand of the Most High has changed*

deeds of God (Ps. 76:7–9; cf. Luke 1:49). However, it should be even more amazing to all believers that this mighty God graciously makes himself knowable (Ps. 76:1–2). He tabernacles among his people to live with them and be their God.

Asaph sees that, at the end of time, the Lord will so dominate his enemies that he will wear the "wrath of man" like a "belt" (vv. 10–12). Asaph's vision was a glimpse of the man Daniel saw, who also wore a belt of glorious triumph (Dan. 10:5). John would later see the same man but recognize him as Jesus in his glory as Judge on the Great Day (Rev. 1:12–16). The Lord's all-powerful preservation of his people in the past, and his indestructible promise of their glorification in the future, provides indescribable "Salem"—that is, "peace" (Ps. 76:2; Heb. 7:2). This peace can be enjoyed even now, because of Christ (Rom. 5:1).

Psalm 77 In times of soul disturbance, we must seek God (v. 1). Though Asaph refers to himself nine times in the first four verses and to God only twice, God seems pleased that at least Asaph is still praying. When he does focus on God, he makes six complaints, all basically asking if God has rejected his people (vv. 7–9). The rest of the Bible answers unequivocally that, "the LORD will not forsake his people, for his great name's sake, because it has pleased the LORD to make you a people for himself" (1 Sam. 12:22; cf. Ps. 94:14; Rom. 11:2).

After he unloads his heart, Asaph begins to calm down and submit his will to the Lord. By doing so, a believer will gain a more patient perspective on God's future redemptive plans (2 Pet. 3:9; James 5:11). Remembering God's past deeds will also build confidence in God's justice by revealing three of God's attributes: his holiness (Ps. 77:13), greatness (vv. 13–14), and care (v. 15). These attributes of the Lord are finally given flesh-and-blood reality in Jesus of Nazareth.

6[n] Ex. 15:1, 21
7[o] Ps. 47:2 [p] Ps. 130:3
8[q] 2 Chr. 20:29, 30; [Hab. 2:20]
9[r] [Ps. 9:7, 8]
10[s] [Ex. 9:16]
11[t] See Ps. 50:14 [u] See Ps. 68:29 [v] Ps. 89:7; Gen. 31:42, 53; Isa. 8:13
12[w] [Isa. 18:5] [x] See Ps. 47:2
Psalm 77
[y] Ps. 39, title [z] Ps. 50, title
1[a] See Ps. 3:4
2[b] Ps. 86:7; [Ps. 20:1; 50:15; Isa. 26:16] [c] Ps. 63:6; Isa. 26:9 [d] [Ps. 143:6] [e] Gen. 37:35
3[f] Ps. 42:5, 11; 43:5
4[g] [Gen. 41:8]
5[h] ver. 10, 11; Ps. 44:1; 143:5; Deut. 32:7; Isa. 51:9
6[i] See Ps. 42:8 [j] Ps. 4:4
7[k] See Ps. 44:9 [l] Ps. 85:1
8[m] [Rom. 9:6]
9[n] [Isa. 49:15] [o] [Hab. 3:2]
10[p] [Ps. 118:15]
11[q] ver. 5; Ps. 105:5

12 I will ponder all your [r]work,
and meditate on your [s]mighty deeds.
13 Your way, O God, is [t]holy.
[u]What god is great like our God?
14 You are the God who [v]works wonders;
you have [w]made known your might
among the peoples.
15 You [x]with your arm redeemed your people,
the children of Jacob and Joseph. *Selah*

16 When [y]the waters saw you, O God,
when the waters saw you, they were afraid;
indeed, the deep trembled.
17 The clouds poured out water;
the skies [z]gave forth thunder;
your [a]arrows flashed on every side.
18 [b]The crash of your thunder was in the whirlwind;
[c]your lightnings lighted up the world;
the earth [d]trembled and shook.
19 Your [e]way was through the sea,
your path through the great waters;
yet your footprints [f]were unseen.[1]
20 You [g]led your people like a flock
by the hand of Moses and Aaron.

Tell the Coming Generation

78 A MASKIL[2] OF [h]ASAPH.
[i]Give ear, O my people, to my teaching;
incline your ears to the words of my mouth!
2 [j]I will open my mouth [k]in a parable;
I will utter dark sayings from of old,
3 things that we have heard and known,
that our [l]fathers have told us.
4 We will not [m]hide them from their children,
but [n]tell to the coming generation
the glorious deeds of the LORD, and his might,
and [o]the wonders that he has done.

5 He established [p]a testimony in [q]Jacob
and appointed a law in [q]Israel,
which he commanded our fathers
to teach to their children,
6 that [r]the next generation might know them,
the children yet unborn,
and arise and tell them to their children,
7 so that they should set their hope in God
and not forget [s]the works of God,
but [t]keep his commandments;
8 and that they should not be [u]like their fathers,
[v]a stubborn and rebellious generation,
a generation [w]whose heart was not steadfast,
whose spirit was not faithful to God.

9 The Ephraimites, armed with[3] the bow,
[x]turned back on the day of battle.
10 They [y]did not keep God's covenant,
but refused to walk according to his law.
11 They [z]forgot his works
and [a]the wonders that he had shown them.
12 In the sight of their fathers [b]he performed wonders
in the land of Egypt, in [c]the fields of Zoan.
13 He [d]divided the sea and let them pass through it,
and made the waters [e]stand like a heap.

[1] Hebrew *unknown* [2] Probably a musical or liturgical term [3] Hebrew *armed and shooting*

12[r] Ps. 90:16 [s] Ps. 9:11
13[t] Ps. 73:17 [u] See Ps. 35:10
14[v] See Ps. 72:18 [w] Ps. 106:8
15[x] [Ps. 74:2; Ex. 6:6; Deut. 9:29]
16[y] Ps. 114:3; Ex. 14:21; Josh. 3:15, 16; Hab. 3:10
17[z] [Ps. 68:33] [a] See Ps. 18:14
18[b] Ps. 104:7 [c] Ps. 97:4 [d] See Ps. 18:7
19[e] Hab. 3:15 [f] See Ps. 36:6
20[g] Ps. 78:52, 53; 80:1; Ex. 13:21; 14:19; Isa. 63:11, 12
Psalm 78
1[h] Ps. 50, title [i] [Isa. 51:4]; See Ps. 49:1; 50:7 **2**[j] Cited Matt. 13:35; See Ps. 49:4 [k] [Num. 21:27] **3**[l] See Ps. 44:1 **4**[m] Job 15:18 [n] [Ex. 12:26, 27; 13:8, 14; Deut. 11:19; Josh. 4:6, 7; Joel 1:3] [o] ver. 11, 32 **5**[p] Ps. 19:7; [Ps. 81:5] [q] Ps. 147:19 **6**[r] ver. 4; Ps. 102:18 **7**[s] Ps. 77:12 [t] Ps. 105:45 **8**[u] 2 Kgs. 17:14; 2 Chr. 30:7; Ezek. 20:18 [v] Ex. 32:9; 33:3; Deut. 9:7, 24; 31:27; Jer. 5:23 [w] ver. 37; Job 11:13 **9**[x] ver. 57 **10**[y] [2 Kgs. 17:15] **11**[z] See Ps. 106:13 [a] ver. 4 **12**[b] ver. 43; See Ex. 7-12; Ps. 72:18 [c] ver. 43; Num. 13:22; Isa. 19:11, 13; Ezek. 30:14 **13**[d] Ps. 136:13; Ex. 14:21 [e] Ex. 15:8

Asaph's final comfort is that God "led [his] people like a flock by the hand of Moses and Aaron" (v. 20). How did the Lord do this? "Your way was through the sea" (v. 19). This is an allusion to the exodus, when God opened the Red Sea to deliver his people. Then as now, God performs miracles to deliver his beloved people—the greatest miracle of all being the incarnation, life, death, and resurrection of the Son of God, for sinners such as us.

Psalm 78 The recurring theme of Scripture is God's persistent redemption of an ungratefully forgetful people. When God's people forget to be thankful for his sovereign grace, they become cowardly (vv. 9–11; Gal. 2:12), discontented (Ps. 78:17–22, 40–44; Heb. 13:5), embarrassed (Ps. 78:32–37; Rom. 1:16), and idolatrous (Ps. 78:56–58; Rom. 1:21).

14 [f]In the daytime he led them with a cloud,
and all the night with a fiery light.
15 He [g]split rocks in the wilderness
and gave them drink abundantly as from the deep.
16 He made streams come out of [h]the rock
and caused waters to flow down like rivers.

17 Yet they sinned still more against him,
[i]rebelling against the Most High in the desert.
18 They [j]tested God in their heart
by demanding the food they craved.
19 They spoke against God, saying,
[k]"Can God [l]spread a table in the wilderness?
20 [m]He struck the rock so that water gushed out
and streams overflowed.
Can he also give bread
or provide meat for his people?"

21 Therefore, when the LORD heard, he was full of wrath;
[n]a fire was kindled against Jacob;
his anger rose against Israel,
22 because they [o]did not believe in God
and did not trust his saving power.
23 Yet he commanded the skies above
and [p]opened the doors of heaven,
24 and he [q]rained down on them manna to eat
and gave them [r]the grain of heaven.
25 Man ate of the bread of [s]the angels;
he sent them food [t]in abundance.
26 He [u]caused the east wind to blow in the heavens,
and by his power he led out the south wind;
27 he rained meat on them like [v]dust,
winged birds like [w]the sand of the seas;
28 he [x]let them fall in the midst of their camp,
all around their dwellings.
29 And they [y]ate and were well filled,
for he gave them what they [z]craved.
30 But before they had satisfied their craving,
[a]while the food was still in their mouths,
31 the anger of God rose against them,
and he killed [b]the strongest of them
and laid low [c]the young men of Israel.

32 In spite of all this, they [d]still sinned;
[e]despite his wonders, they did not believe.
33 So he made [f]their days [g]vanish like[1] a breath,[2]
and their years in terror.
34 When he killed them, they [h]sought him;
they repented and sought God earnestly.
35 They remembered that God was their [i]rock,
the Most High God their [j]redeemer.
36 But they [k]flattered him with their mouths;
they [l]lied to him with their tongues.
37 Their [m]heart was not [n]steadfast toward him;
they were not faithful to his covenant.
38 Yet he, being [o]compassionate,
[p]atoned for their iniquity
and did not destroy them;
he restrained his anger often
and did not stir up all his wrath.
39 He [q]remembered that they were but [r]flesh,
[s]a wind that passes and comes not again.
40 How often they [t]rebelled against him in the wilderness
and [u]grieved him in [v]the desert!

[1] Hebrew *in* [2] Or *vapor*

If they persist in that ungrateful amnesia, it will spread to their children (Judg. 2:10). Therefore, all members of the covenant community must listen to the Word so that they can teach it (Ps. 78:1–6; Matt. 13:35). God so dignifies parents and pastors with the responsibility of the next generation's faith that he holds them accountable when their actions or neglect lead to covenant children growing up not knowing the Lord (Jer. 2:8, 9; Hos. 4:6).

14[f] See Ps. 105:39
15[g] ver. 20; Ps. 105:41; 114:8; Ex. 17:6; Isa. 48:21
16[h] Num. 20:8, 10, 11
17[i] ver. 40, 56; Deut. 9:22; Isa. 63:10
18[j] ver. 41, 56; Ps. 95:9; 106:14; Deut. 6:16; 1 Cor. 10:9

19[k] [Ex. 16:3; Num. 11:4; 20:3; 21:5] [l] See Ps. 23:5 **20**[m] ver. 15, 16 **21**[n] Num. 11:1 **22**[o] ver. 8, 32, 37 **23**[p] Gen. 7:11; [Mal. 3:10] **24**[q] Ex. 16:4 [r] Ps. 105:40; [John 6:31] **25**[s] Ps. 103:20 [t] [ver. 29] **26**[u] Num. 11:31 **27**[v] [Gen. 13:16] [w] [Gen. 22:17] **28**[x] Ex. 16:13; Num. 11:31 **29**[y] Num. 11:19, 20 [z] Num. 11:4, 34 **30**[a] Num. 11:33; [Job 20:23] **31**[b] Isa. 10:16 [c] ver. 63 **32**[d] See Num. 14; 16; 17 [e] ver. 22; Num. 14:11 **33**[f] Num. 14:29, 35; 26:64, 65 [g] Ps. 39:5 **34**[h] Hos. 5:15 **35**[i] Deut. 32:4, 15, 31 [j] Ex. 15:13; See Ps. 74:2 **36**[k] Isa. 29:13; Ezek. 33:31 [l] Isa. 57:11 **37**[m] ver. 8 [n] Ps. 51:10 **38**[o] Ex. 34:6 [p] Num. 14:20 **39**[q] [Ps. 103:14; Job 10:9] [r] Gen. 6:3 [s] Job 7:7 **40**[t] ver. 17, 56; Ps. 107:11 [u] [Eph. 4:30] [v] Ps. 106:14

41 They [w]tested God again and again
and provoked [x]the Holy One of Israel.
42 They [y]did not remember his power[1]
or the day when he redeemed them from the foe,
43 [z]when he performed his [a]signs in Egypt
and his [b]marvels in [c]the fields of Zoan.
44 He [d]turned their rivers to blood,
so that they could not drink of their streams.
45 He sent among them swarms of [e]flies,
which devoured them,
and [f]frogs, which destroyed them.
46 He gave their crops to [g]the destroying locust
and the fruit of their labor to the locust.
47 He destroyed their vines with [h]hail
and their sycamores with frost.
48 He gave over their [i]cattle to the hail
and their flocks to thunderbolts.
49 He let loose on them his burning anger,
wrath, indignation, and distress,
a company of [j]destroying angels.
50 He made a path for his anger;
he did not spare them from death,
but gave their lives over to the plague.
51 He struck down every [k]firstborn in Egypt,
the firstfruits of their strength in the tents of [l]Ham.
52 Then he led out his people [m]like sheep
and guided them in the wilderness like a flock.
53 [n]He led them in safety, so that they [o]were not afraid,
but [p]the sea overwhelmed their enemies.
54 And he brought them to his [q]holy land,
[r]to the mountain which his right hand had [s]won.
55 He [t]drove out nations before them;
he [u]apportioned them for a possession
and settled the tribes of Israel in their tents.

56 Yet they [v]tested and [w]rebelled against the Most High God
and did not keep his testimonies,
57 but turned away and acted treacherously like their fathers;
they twisted like [x]a deceitful bow.
58 For they [y]provoked him to anger with their [z]high places;
they [a]moved him to jealousy with their [b]idols.
59 When God heard, he was full of [c]wrath,
and he utterly rejected Israel.
60 He [d]forsook his dwelling at [e]Shiloh,
the tent where he dwelt among mankind,
61 and delivered his [f]power to captivity,
his [g]glory to the hand of the foe.
62 He [h]gave his people over to the sword
and [i]vented his wrath on his heritage.
63 [j]Fire devoured their young men,
and their young women had no [k]marriage song.
64 Their [l]priests fell by the sword,
and their [m]widows made no lamentation.
65 Then the Lord [n]awoke as from sleep,
like a strong man shouting because of wine.

[1] Hebrew *hand*

41[w] See ver. 18 [x] See Ps. 71:22
42[y] Judg. 8:34
43[z] For ver. 43-51, see Ps. 105:27-36 [a] Ex. 7:3; [Ps. 106:22]; Acts 7:36 [b] Ex. 4:21; 11:9, 10 [c] See ver. 12
44[d] See Ex. 7:17-24
45[e] See Ex. 8:21-24 [f] See Ex. 8:2-14
46[g] See Ex. 10:12-15
47[h] See Ex. 9:23-25
48[i] See Ex. 9:19-21
49[j] Ex. 12:13, 23; [2 Sam. 24:16]
51[k] Ex. 12:29; [Ps. 105:36; 135:8; 136:10] [l] Ps. 105:23, 27; 106:22
52[m] See Ps. 77:20
53[n] [Ex. 14:19, 20] [o] [Ex. 14:13] [p] Ex. 14:27, 28; 15:10

Motivation for this eternally significant task must come from grace, not guilt. Biblical reflection on God's powerful deliverance in the past (Ps. 78:12–16, 45–55), generous sustenance in the present (vv. 23–31; John 6:31), and gracious vindication in the future (Ps. 78:59–72) generates heartfelt, grateful obedience. But at the center of the passage is the central message of the Bible for those who will fail: "he, being compassionate, atoned for their iniquity" (v. 38, Rom. 3:25; 1 John 2:2). This is who God is. He delights to shower sinners with favor, if they will simply humble themselves enough to receive it.

When God took the tabernacle out of Shiloh and away from the tribe of Ephraim, he gave it to the tribe of Judah (Ps. 78:67–72; Rev. 2:5; 3:16). From that tribe came David, who in spite of his failures shepherded the children of Israel with integrity and skill. And from David came Jesus the "faithful high priest," who atoned for our sins in the temple of his body (Heb. 2:17).

54[q] Ex. 15:17 [r] Isa. 11:9; 57:13; [Ps. 68:16] [s] Ps. 74:2 **55**[t] See Ps. 44:2 [u] Josh. 23:4; [Ps. 135:12; 136:21, 22; Acts 13:19] **56**[v] ver. 18; Judg. 2:11, 12 [w] ver. 40 **57**[x] Hos. 7:16; [ver. 9] **58**[y] Deut. 31:29 [z] Lev. 26:30; Deut. 12:2; 1 Kgs. 11:7; 12:31; Ezek. 20:28 [a] Num. 25:11; Deut. 32:16, 21; Judg. 2:12 [b] Deut. 7:5, 25; 12:3 **59**[c] ver. 62; Ps. 106:40; Deut. 3:26 **60**[d] 1 Sam. 4:11; Jer. 7:12, 14; 26:6 [e] Josh. 18:1 **61**[f] Ps. 132:8; [Ps. 63:2; 96:6] [g] [1 Sam. 4:21] **62**[h] [1 Sam. 4:10] [i] ver. 59 **63**[j] [Ps. 79:5; 89:46] [k] [Jer. 7:34] **64**[l] 1 Sam. 4:11 [m] Job 27:15 **65**[n] Ps. 73:20; See Ps. 35:23

66 And he [o]put his adversaries to rout;
he put them to everlasting shame.

67 He rejected the tent of [p]Joseph;
he did not choose the tribe of
Ephraim,
68 but he chose the tribe of Judah,
Mount Zion, which he [q]loves.
69 He [r]built his sanctuary like the high
heavens,
like the earth, which he has founded
forever.
70 He [s]chose David his servant
and took him from the sheepfolds;
71 from [t]following the nursing ewes he
brought him
to [u]shepherd Jacob his people,
Israel his [v]inheritance.
72 With [w]upright heart he shepherded
them
and [x]guided them with his skillful
hand.

How Long, O LORD?

79 A PSALM OF [y]ASAPH.
O God, [z]the nations have come into
your [a]inheritance;
they have defiled your [b]holy temple;
they have [c]laid Jerusalem in ruins.
2 They have given [d]the bodies of your servants
to the birds of the heavens for food,
the flesh of your [e]faithful to [f]the
beasts of the earth.
3 They have poured out their blood like
water
all around Jerusalem,
and there was [g]no one to bury them.
4 We have become [h]a taunt to our neighbors,
[h]mocked and derided by those around
us.

5 [i]How long, O LORD? Will you be angry
[j]forever?
Will your [k]jealousy [l]burn like fire?
6 [m]Pour out your anger on the nations
that [n]do not know you,
and on the kingdoms
that [o]do not call upon your name!
7 For they have devoured Jacob
and laid waste his habitation.

8 [p]Do not remember against us [q]our former
iniquities;[1]
let your compassion come speedily to
meet us,
for we are [r]brought very low.
9 [s]Help us, O God of our salvation,
for the glory of your name;
deliver us, and [t]atone for our sins,
for your [u]name's sake!
10 [v]Why should the nations say,
"Where is their God?"
Let [w]the avenging of the outpoured
blood of your servants
be known among the nations before
our eyes!

[1] Or *the iniquities of former generations*

Psalm 79 Confronted with a world broken because of relational distress with God and one another, every believer will eventually exclaim, "How long, O LORD?" (vv. 5–9). Eventually God did restore Israel's temple that had been defiled by the nation's enemies, but not before he showed his prophets that his redemptive plan transcended that earthly structure (Zech. 8:3; Eph. 2:18–22). One day God himself would come to earth to dwell among his people not in a building but in a body (John 1:14).

In the meantime, Israel was not prepared for God to answer her prayer for righteous vindication by sending judgment on unbelieving Israel itself (Ps. 79:1–7; cf. Amos 3:2; Luke 12:47–48). That drives Asaph to a prayer for atonement (cf. Leviticus 16). Though he cannot envision how God is going to answer, he prays to the only One who can offer hope. God finally answered by sending Jesus Christ, who became the perfect atoning sacrifice (1 John 4:10).

In desperate times, godly people must plead for God to glorify himself. Asaph is so abandoned to the glory of God that he prays that even forgiveness of sins would be a reflection of God's greatness (Ps. 79:9–10). Reflecting on God's glory puts all injustices in perspective (vv. 11–13). Asaph's ultimate "leverage" in his prayer is to remind God of his love for his people. But of course God does not need reminding; *we* need reminding of God's regard for us. We are his inheritance (v. 1; Ex. 34.9; Col. 1:12), his holy temple (Ps. 79:7; 1 Pet. 2:4), his dignified servants (Ps. 79:10; 1 Pet. 2:16), his chosen people (Ps. 79:13; 1 Thess. 1:4), and his sheep (Ps. 79:13; John 10:1–17)—all supremely so for those in Christ.

66 [o] [Ps. 40:14]
67 [p] Ps. 80:1; 81:5
68 [q] Ps. 87:2
69 [r] See 1 Kgs. 6
70 [s] 1 Sam. 16:12, 13
71 [t] 2 Sam. 7:8 [u] 2 Sam. 5:2; [Ps. 28:9] [v] 1 Sam. 10:1
72 [w] Ps. 101:2; 1 Kgs. 9:4 [x] [Ps. 77:20]

Psalm 79
[y] Ps. 50, title
1 [z] Lam. 1:10 [a] Ex. 15:17; See Ps. 74:2 [b] [Ps. 74:7] [c] Jer. 26:18; Mic. 3:12; [2 Kgs. 25:9, 10]; 2 Chr. 36:19
2 [d] Deut. 28:26; Jer. 7:33; 16:4; 19:7; 34:20 [e] See Ps. 50:5 [f] Ps. 74:19
3 [g] Jer. 14:16; [2 Kgs. 9:10]
4 [h] Dan. 9:16; See Ps. 44:13
5 [i] [Ps. 74:10; 80:4] [j] [Ps. 74:1; 85:5]; See Ps. 13:1 [k] Ps. 78:58 [l] Ps. 78:21; 89:46
6 [m] Cited Jer. 10:25; [Zeph. 3:8] [n] 2 Thess. 1:8 [o] See Ps. 14:4
8 [p] Isa. 64:9 [q] Jer. 11:10 [r] Ps. 116:6; 142:6
9 [s] 2 Chr. 14:11 [t] See Ps. 65:3 [u] Jer. 14:7, 21; See Ps. 23:3
10 [v] See Ps. 42:3 [w] See Ps. 94:1

11 Let [x]the groans of the prisoners come before you;
according to your great power, preserve those [y]doomed to die!
12 Return [z]sevenfold into the [a]lap of our neighbors
the [b]taunts with which they have taunted you, O Lord!
13 But we your people, the [c]sheep of your pasture,
will [d]give thanks to you forever;
from generation to generation we will recount your praise.

Restore Us, O God

80

To the choirmaster: according to [e]Lilies. A Testimony. Of [f]Asaph, a Psalm.

1 Give ear, O Shepherd of Israel,
you who lead [g]Joseph like [h]a flock.
You who are [i]enthroned upon the cherubim, [j]shine forth.
2 Before [k]Ephraim and Benjamin and Manasseh,
[l]stir up your might
and [m]come to save us!

3 [n]Restore us,[1] O God;
[o]let your face shine, that we may be saved!

4 O [p]Lord God of hosts,
[q]how long will you be angry with your people's prayers?
5 You have fed them with [r]the bread of tears
and given them tears to drink in full measure.
6 [s]You make us an object of contention for our [s]neighbors,
and our enemies laugh among themselves.

7 [n]Restore us, O God of hosts;
let your face shine, that we may be saved!

8 You brought [t]a vine out of Egypt;
you [u]drove out the nations and planted it.
9 You [v]cleared the ground for it;
it took deep root and filled the land.
10 The mountains were covered with its shade,
the mighty cedars with its branches.
11 It sent out its branches to [w]the sea
and its shoots to [w]the River.[2]
12 Why then have you [x]broken down its walls,
so that all who pass along the way pluck its fruit?
13 [y]The boar from the forest ravages it,
and all that move in the field feed on it.

14 Turn again, O God of hosts!
[z]Look down from heaven, and see;

[1] Or *Turn us again*; also verses 7, 19 [2] That is, the Euphrates

11[x]Ps. 102:20 [y][1 Sam. 20:31]
12[z]Gen. 4:15, 24; Lev. 26:21, 28; Prov. 6:31 [a]Isa. 65:6, 7; Jer. 32:18 [b]See Ps. 74:10
13[c]See Ps. 74:1 [d]Isa. 43:21
Psalm 80
[e]Ps. 60, title [f]Ps. 50, title
1[g]Ps. 78:67; 81:5 [h][Ps. 95:7]; See Ps. 77:20 [i]Ps. 99:1; Ex. 25:22; 1 Sam. 4:4; 2 Sam. 6:2 [j]See Ps. 50:2
2[k]See Num. 2:18-24 [l]See Ps. 35:23 [m][Ps. 118:14, 21]
3[n]ver. 19; Ps. 60:1; 85:4; Lam. 5:21 [o]Num. 6:25; See Ps. 4:6
4[p]See Ps. 59:5 [q][Ps. 74:10; 79:5]
5[r]Ps. 42:3; 102:9; [1 Kgs. 22:27; Isa. 30:20]
6[s]See Ps. 44:13
7[n][See ver. 3 above]
8[t]Isa. 5:1; 27:2; Jer. 2:21; 12:10; Ezek. 17:6; Matt. 21:33; Mark 12:1; Luke 20:9 [u]See Ps. 44:2
9[v][Josh. 24:12]
11[w]See Ps. 72:8
12[x]Ps. 89:40; Isa. 5:5
13[y][Jer. 5:6]
14[z][Isa. 63:15]

Psalm 80 Through familiar prayer, believers have access to a sovereign Shepherd when they are distressed (vv. 1–2; Isa. 40:11). As he did with Joseph, the Good Shepherd sometimes leads his people into deep valleys. But when he does so, this "great shepherd of the sheep" will "equip you with everything good that you may do his will, working in us that which is pleasing in his sight," for the eternal glory of his grace (Heb. 13:20–21).

Though rare in the Psalter, the main purpose of "vine" imagery (Ps. 80:8, 14) is to comfort believers with the promise that God will save them from fruitlessness and will restore their health (cf. Gen. 49:22). Such tender care by God for his prized plants makes their sin against grace all the more heinous (Isa. 5:1–7; 27:2–6; Jer. 2:21; Hos. 10:1; 14:7).

God was faithful to redeem his people in the past by transplanting them as a tender shoot from Egypt to the Promised Land (Ps. 80:8–11). Changing metaphors, Asaph assures that the Father will restore vitality to his favored "son" in the future (vv. 14–18). While Israel is the immediate referent, the Son of Man eventually fulfilled all righteousness for God's people (Matt. 2:15).

While the past and future are clear, present suffering can be perplexing (Ps. 80:4–6, 12–13). If God is a faithful Shepherd, loving Father, and tender Vinedresser, why is his current discipline so painful? The answer is because he rescues straying sheep who would not otherwise be turned from the sin that threatens them (1 Pet. 2:25). He disciplines his children in love (Heb. 12:3–11). And he prunes his vines to bear more fruit (John 15:1–7).

have regard for this vine,
15 the stock that your right hand planted,
and for the son whom you made strong for yourself.
16 They have [a]burned it with fire; they have [a]cut it down;
may they perish at [b]the rebuke of your face!
17 But [c]let your hand be on the man of your right hand,
the son of man whom you have made strong for yourself!
18 Then we shall not turn back from you;
[d]give us life, and we will call upon your name!

19 [e]Restore us, O LORD God of hosts!
Let your face shine, that we may be saved!

Oh, That My People Would Listen to Me

81

TO THE CHOIRMASTER: ACCORDING TO [f]THE GITTITH.[1] OF [g]ASAPH.

1 [h]Sing aloud to God our strength;
[i]shout for joy to the God of Jacob!
2 Raise a song; sound [j]the tambourine,
[k]the sweet lyre with [k]the harp.
3 Blow the trumpet at [l]the new moon,
at the full moon, on our feast day.

4 For it is a statute for Israel,
a rule[2] of the God of Jacob.
5 He made it [m]a decree in [n]Joseph
when he [o]went out over[3] the land of Egypt.
[p]I hear a language [q]I had not known:
6 "I [r]relieved your[4] shoulder of [s]the burden;
your hands were freed from the basket.
7 In distress you [t]called, and I delivered you;
I [u]answered you in the secret place of thunder;
I [v]tested you at the waters of Meribah. *Selah*
8 [w]Hear, O my people, while I admonish you!
O Israel, if you would but listen to me!
9 There shall be no [x]strange god among you;
you shall not bow down to a [y]foreign god.
10 [z]I am the LORD your God,
who brought you up out of the land of Egypt.
[a]Open your mouth wide, and I will fill it.

11 "But my people did not listen to my voice;
Israel [b]would not submit to me.
12 So I [c]gave them over to their [d]stubborn hearts,
to follow their own [e]counsels.
13 [f]Oh, that my people would listen to me,
that Israel would [g]walk in my ways!
14 I would soon subdue their enemies
and [h]turn my hand against their foes.

[1] Probably a musical or liturgical term [2] Or *just decree* [3] Or *against* [4] Hebrew *his*; also next line

Psalm 81 The only lasting motivation for obedience is grace. So Asaph focuses the worshiper's attention on redemption (vv. 1–8). Between the Feast of Trumpets and the Feast of Tabernacles, the Israelites observed the Day of Atonement, which portrayed through two goats—one slain and the other released—both the price and the success of their forgiveness (v. 3; Lev. 23:23–44). Atonement should prick the hearts of those whose worship is perfunctory and whose lives are hypocritical (Ps. 81:11; Isa. 29:13; Matt. 15:8). True obedience begins with a covenant relationship with God, who rescues us from spiritual slavery. Asaph needs only to rehearse the preface and first command of the Decalogue (Ps. 81:9–10), because they summarize both the spirit that contextualizes God's grace and the content of the law that reflects his character and care. When the believer's heart is warmed to love the God who delivered him, he will reject all idols.

The law is God's gift to his people. It is fatherly instruction intended for our well-being (Deut. 16:18–20; Isa. 54:5, 6; Dan. 9:10; Hos. 2:16, 19, 20; Prov. 1:8). Jesus explained that even the Psalms were "Law" (or "teaching"), which cannot be understood merely as stale legislation (John 10:34). Christ confirmed that the "Law of Moses and the Prophets and the Psalms" were written about him and therefore include blessing and direct us toward our need of faith in him (Luke 24:44). Like Elijah, Asaph is begging God's people to return to him with all their hearts so that he might bless them (Ps. 81:12–16; 1 Kings 18:37). In Christ, God did bless his people—beyond anything Elijah or Asaph could have imagined.

16[a] Isa. 33:12 [b] Ps. 76:6; [Ps. 39:11]
17[c] Ps. 89:21
18[d] See Ps. 71:20
19[e] ver. 3, 7
Psalm 81
[f] Ps. 8, title; 84, title [g] Ps. 50, title
1[h] [Deut. 32:43] [i] See Ps. 66:1
2[j] Ex. 15:20 [k] Ps. 71:22
3[l] Lev. 23:24; Num. 10:10; 29:1
5[m] Ps. 122:4; [Ps. 78:5] [n] Ps. 77:15; 78:67; 80:1 [o] Ex. 11:4 [p] Ps. 114:1 [q] [Deut. 28:49; Jer. 5:15]
6[r] Isa. 9:4; 10:27 [s] Ex. 1:11
7[t] Ps. 50:15; [Ex. 2:23; 14:10] [u] Ex. 19:19; See Ps. 18:11-14 [v] Ex. 17:7; Num. 20:13
8[w] See Ps. 50:7
9[x] Ps. 44:20; Isa. 43:12; [Ex. 20:3] [y] Deut. 32:12
10[z] Ex. 20:2 [a] [Ps. 37:3, 4]
11[b] Ex. 32:1; Deut. 32:15, 18; Prov. 1:25, 30
12[c] Job 8:4; [Acts 7:42; 14:16; Rom. 1:24, 26] [d] [Deut. 29:19] [e] Ps. 106:43; Jer. 7:24; Mic. 6:16
13[f] Deut. 5:29; 32:29; Isa. 48:18 [g] Deut. 5:33
14[h] Amos 1:8

15 Those who hate the LORD would [i]cringe
toward him,
and their fate would last forever.
16 But he would feed you[1] with [j]the finest
of the wheat,
and with [k]honey from the rock
I would satisfy you."

Rescue the Weak and Needy

82

A PSALM OF [l]ASAPH.
[m]God [n]has taken his place in the
divine council;
in the midst of [p]the gods he [q]holds
judgment:
2 "How long will you judge unjustly
and [r]show partiality to [s]the wicked?
Selah
3 [t]Give justice to [u]the weak and the fatherless;
[v]maintain the right of the afflicted and
the destitute.
4 [w]Rescue the weak and the needy;
[x]deliver them from the hand of the
wicked."

5 [y]They have neither knowledge nor
understanding,
[z]they walk about in darkness;
[a]all the foundations of the earth are
[b]shaken.

6 [c]I said, "You are gods,
sons of the Most High, all of you;
7 nevertheless, like men [d]you shall die,
and fall like any prince."[2]

8 [e]Arise, O God, judge the earth;
for you shall [f]inherit all the nations!

O God, Do Not Keep Silence

83

A SONG. A PSALM OF [g]ASAPH.
O God, do not keep silence;
[h]do not hold your peace or be still,
O God!
2 For behold, your enemies [i]make an
uproar;
those who hate you have [j]raised their
heads.
3 They lay [k]crafty plans against your people;
they consult together against your
[l]treasured ones.
4 They say, "Come, [m]let us wipe them out
as a nation;
let the name of Israel be remembered
no more!"
5 For they conspire with one accord;
against you they make a covenant—
6 the tents of [n]Edom and [o]the Ishmaelites,
[p]Moab and [q]the Hagrites,
7 [r]Gebal and [p]Ammon and [s]Amalek,
[t]Philistia with the inhabitants of [u]Tyre;
8 [v]Asshur also has joined them;
they are the strong arm of [w]the children of Lot. *Selah*

9 Do to them as you did to [x]Midian,
as to [y]Sisera and Jabin at [z]the river
Kishon,
10 who were destroyed at [a]En-dor,
who became [b]dung for the ground.
11 Make their nobles like [c]Oreb and Zeeb,
all their princes like [d]Zebah and
Zalmunna,
12 who said, [e]"Let us take possession for
ourselves
of the pastures of God."

[1] That is, Israel; Hebrew *him* [2] Or *fall as one man, O princes*

15[i] Ps. 18:44
16[j] Ps. 147:14; Deut. 32:14 [k] Deut. 32:13; [Job 29:6; Ezek. 16:19]
Psalm 82 [l] See Ps. 50, title
1[m] [2 Chr. 19:5, 6; Eccles. 5:8] [n] Isa. 3:13 [p] [1 Sam. 28:13] [q] See Ps. 58:11
2[r] Deut. 1:17 [s] Prov. 18:5
3[t] Ps. 10:18 [u] Ps. 41:1 [v] Jer. 22:3
4[w] Job 29:12 [x] Prov. 24:11
5[y] [Mic. 3:1]; See Ps. 14:4 [z] Prov. 2:13 [a] See Ps. 11:3 [b] Ps. 10:6
6[c] ver. 1; Cited John 10:34
7[d] Ps. 49:12; Job 21:32; Ezek. 31:14; See Ezek. 28:2-10

Psalm 82 Leaders who are responsible for others who bear the image of God are called to imitate God's justice and compassion (vv. 2–5; 1 Chron. 29:23; 2 Chron. 19:6, 7). Elsewhere, he even refers to civic rulers as his "ministers" (Rom. 13:6). God's personification of justice in human rulers points to his ultimate incarnation of peace and justice in Jesus (John 10:34–35).

However, a civil authority is not God's minister by divine right; he is appointed by, and rules under, God himself. So when he fails to carry out biblical justice, he abrogates his authority (Ps. 82:5). His justice must be impartial (v. 2; Lev. 19:35–36; Deut. 1:17; Prov. 11:1). And it must be proactive toward the defenseless (Ps. 82:3–5; Amos. 4:1–6). In fact, advocacy for the weak is a convincing sign of righteousness (Job 29:16; 1 John 3:17–18). Ignoring the poor is as repugnant to God as idolatry and adultery, and is a sin that will be punished (Ps. 82:1, 6–7; Amos 2:6, 7; Prov. 14:31).

8[e] See Ps. 12:5 [f] Ps. 2:8; [Rev. 11:15] **Psalm 83** [g] See Ps. 50, title **1**[h] See Ps. 28:1 **2**[i] [Ps. 2:1] [j] Judg. 8:28 **3**[k] [Neh. 4:8] [l] See Ps. 27:5; 31:20 **4**[m] Jer. 48:2; [Ps. 74:8; Esth. 3:6] **6**[n] Ps. 137:7; See 2 Chr. 20:10 [o] See Gen. 25:12-16 [p] 2 Chr. 20:10 [q] 1 Chr. 5:10 **7**[r] Josh. 13:5 [p] [See ver. 6 above] [s] 1 Sam. 15:2 [t] 1 Sam. 4:1; [Amos 1:6] [u] Ezek. 27:3; [Amos 1:9] **8**[v] 2 Kgs. 15:19 [w] Deut. 2:9, 19 **9**[x] Num. 31:7; See Isa. 9:4 [y] Judg. 4:15, 24 [z] Judg. 4:7; 5:21 **10**[a] Josh. 17:11; 1 Sam. 28:7 [b] See Job 20:7 **11**[c] Judg. 7:25; 8:3 [d] See Judg. 8:5-21 **12**[e] [2 Chr. 20:11]

13 O my God, make them like [f]whirling
dust,[1]
like [g]chaff before the wind.
14 As [h]fire consumes the forest,
as the flame [i]sets the mountains
ablaze,
15 so may you pursue them [j]with your tempest
and terrify them with your hurri-
cane!
16 [k]Fill their faces with shame,
that they may seek your name,
O LORD.
17 Let them be [l]put to shame and dismayed
forever;
let them perish in disgrace,
18 that they may [m]know that you alone,
[n]whose name is the LORD,
are [o]the Most High over all the earth.

My Soul Longs for the Courts of the LORD

84

TO THE CHOIRMASTER: ACCORDING TO [p]THE GITTITH.[2] A PSALM OF [q]THE SONS OF KORAH.

1 How [r]lovely is your [s]dwelling place,
O LORD of hosts!
2 My soul [t]longs, yes, [u]faints
for the courts of the LORD;
my heart and flesh sing for joy
to [v]the living God.

3 Even the sparrow finds a home,
and the swallow a nest for herself,
where she may lay her young,
at your altars, O LORD of hosts,
[w]my King and my God.
4 [x]Blessed are those who dwell in your
house,
ever [y]singing your praise! *Selah*

[1] Or *like a tumbleweed* [2] Probably a musical or liturgical term

13[f] Isa. 17:13 [g] Job 13:25; 21:18; [Ps. 1:4]
14[h] [Isa. 9:18]; See Isa. 10:16-19 [i] Deut. 32:22
15[j] Job 9:17
16[k] [Ps. 35:4, 26; Job 10:15]
17[l] Ps. 35:4
18[m] Ps. 59:13 [n] Ex. 6:3 [o] Ps. 9:2; 18:13; 97:9

Psalm 84
[p] Ps. 8, title; 81, title [q] Ps. 42, title
1[r] [Ps. 27:4] [s] Ps. 43:3; 132:5
2[t] [Ps. 42:1, 2; 63:1] [u] [Ps. 73:26; 119:81; 143:6; Job 19:27] [v] See Ps. 42:2
3[w] Ps. 5:2
4[x] See Ps. 65:4 [y] Ps. 42:5, 11; 43:5

Whereas the psalm begins in heaven, it ends on earth, where God is called upon to judge the earth and inherit the nations, a promise the New Testament locates in Christ's person and ministry (cf. Ps. 82:8; Matt. 25:31–46; Acts 17:31; Rev. 21:3). Believers must not only pray for their leaders to represent God's kingdom justice; they must live out that justice themselves, lest they become like Sodom (James 5:1–6). Among Sodom's sins was injustice toward the most disenfranchised members of society: "She and her daughters had pride, excess of food, and prosperous ease, but did not aid the poor and needy" (Ezek. 16:49–50). In Christ, we who are so spiritually "poor and needy" have been lavishly cared for; how can we fail to care for those who are poor and needy in our own communities?

Psalm 83 God sometimes hides his face to draw his children closer to himself. Asaph's prayer is evidence that this divine strategy is effective (vv. 1–2). Jesus similarly tested his disciples' faith when he slept during a storm (Luke 8:22–23).

In the case of this psalm, God had another purpose for apparently withdrawing. God's silence lured in ten nations, symbolizing all the opponents of God's people, so that he might destroy them with one blow (Ps. 83:3–8; cf. 2 Chron. 20:13–23; Rev. 11:18). Despite all efforts to wipe them out, God has always preserved his people (Ps. 83:4–5; Rom. 11:1–6). Grafted into their olive tree, Gentiles are now heirs to the same promises of protection (Rom. 11:24). They are his "treasured" property (Ps. 83:3, 12; Rom. 9:23).

Not only does God promise to preserve his disadvantaged people, he delights in prevailing over their opponents for the sake of his people's deliverance. Asaph's first example of an unlikely victory is Midian's defeat by Gideon, the youngest leader of the weakest tribe of Israel (Judg. 6:1–40). Second is the defeat of Sisera. The mighty commander of Jabin, who had tormented Israel for twenty years, was destroyed by a homemaker (Judg. 4:17–22).

The ultimate reason to live confidently in a hostile world is that Jesus Christ has prevailed over our greatest enemies: sin, guilt, Satan, and death. In Christ, we are invincible. For Jesus was raised bodily, and we are now united to him, by faith. Our future could not be brighter, whatever adversity washes over us in this fallen world.

Psalm 84 When we trust the Lord of hosts, we are perfectly blessed with everything needed for human flourishing. The first two beatitudes of this psalm outline blessings of being. The first is what pragmatists think they can live without, what C. S. Lewis called the "fair beauty of the Lord" (vv. 1–2). The second is the treasure of knowing that one belongs to God and is as safe as the sparrow in the shelter of the temple

5 Blessed are those whose strength is in
you,
[z] in whose heart are the highways to
Zion.[1]
6 As they go through the Valley of Baca
they make it a place of springs;
[a] the early rain also covers it with [b] pools.
7 They go [c] from strength to strength;
each one [d] appears before God in Zion.

8 O [e] LORD God of hosts, hear my prayer;
give ear, O God of Jacob! *Selah*
9 [f] Behold our [g] shield, O God;
look on the face of your anointed!

10 For a day [h] in your courts is better
than a thousand elsewhere.
I would rather be [i] a doorkeeper in the
house of my God
than dwell in the tents of wickedness.
11 For the LORD God is [j] a sun and [g] shield;
the LORD bestows favor and honor.
[k] No good thing does he withhold
from those who [l] walk uprightly.
12 O LORD of hosts,
[m] blessed is the one who trusts in you!

Revive Us Again

85

TO THE CHOIRMASTER. A PSALM OF [n] THE SONS OF KORAH.

1 LORD, you were [o] favorable to your land;
you [p] restored the fortunes of Jacob.
2 You [q] forgave the iniquity of your people;
you [q] covered all their sin. *Selah*
3 You withdrew all your wrath;
you [r] turned from your hot anger.

4 [s] Restore us again, O God of our salvation,
and put away your indignation
toward us!
5 [t] Will you be angry with us forever?
Will you prolong your anger to all
generations?
6 Will you not [u] revive us again,
that your people may [v] rejoice in you?
7 Show us your steadfast love, O LORD,
and grant us your salvation.

8 [w] Let me hear what God the LORD will
speak,
for he will [x] speak peace to his people,
to his [y] saints;
but let them not [z] turn back to [a] folly.
9 Surely his [b] salvation is near to those who
fear him,
that [c] glory may dwell in our land.

10 [d] Steadfast love and faithfulness meet;
[e] righteousness and peace kiss each
other.
11 Faithfulness springs up from the
ground,
and righteousness looks down from
the sky.

[1] Hebrew lacks *to Zion*

5[z] [Ps. 122:1]
6[a] Joel 2:23 [b] Ezek. 34:26
7[c] Prov. 4:18; Isa. 40:31; [John 1:16; 2 Cor. 3:18] [d] See Ps. 42:2
8[e] See Ps. 59:5
9[f] Ps. 80:14 [g] See Ps. 3:3
10[h] ver. 2 [i] 1 Chr. 26:19
11[j] Isa. 60:19, 20; See Ps. 27:1; Mal. 4:2; Rev. 21:23 [g] [See ver. 9 above] [k] Ps. 85:12; [Ps. 34:9, 10; Matt. 6:33; 7:11] [l] Ps. 15:2; Prov. 2:7
12[m] See Ps. 2:12

Psalm 85
[n] Ps. 42, title
1[o] Ps. 77:7 [p] Ps. 14:7
2[q] Ps. 32:1
3[r] Ps. 78:38; 106:23; Ex. 32:12; Deut. 13:17; Jonah 3:9
4[s] See Ps. 80:3
5[t] [Ps. 79:5]
6[u] Ps. 71:20 [v] Ps. 90:14; 149:2
8[w] [Hab. 2:1] [x] Zech. 9:10; [Hag. 2:9] [y] See Ps. 50:5 [z] [2 Pet. 2:21] [a] [Ps. 49:13]
9[b] Isa. 46:13 [c] Zech. 2:5; [John 1:14]
10[d] Ps. 89:14; See Ps. 40:11 [e] [Isa. 45:8]; See Ps. 72:3

(vv. 3–4). The psalmists conclude, as later Jesus would teach his disciples, that if God can take notice of a sparrow, he can take care of his church (Matt. 10:29).

The last two beatitudes outline blessings of vocation. First the psalmists recount the joy of knowing there is a redemptive purpose in suffering. Imagining the children of Israel coming from their scattered places to the temple to worship as commanded, they remember that the approach is unpleasant from every direction (Ps. 84:5–9; Deut. 16:16). Every pilgrim must endure a troubled and dangerous earthly trek to heaven. Jesus promised troubles but explained that suffering confirms the reality of our faith (John 16:33; cf. 1 Pet. 1:7). Finally, the Korahites rejoice in the dignity of their vocation as doorkeepers, regardless of its menial nature. God blesses his children with the dignity of causing his kingdom to advance through their individual callings. There are no little people in God's family, and no small things in his redemptive plan (Zech. 4:10). Indeed, it is those who serve who are the greatest (Matt. 18:1–4; John 13:12–16)—as was the case for Jesus' own life (Phil. 2:6–11).

Psalm 85 God reveals his glory through mercy (Ex. 34:6–7; Eph. 1:6). While God expresses "anger" toward his people when they turn aside to idols (Ps. 85:3; Deut. 29:25–29), he promises to "restore" their "fortunes" if they repent (see Ps. 85:1; Deut. 30:1–5). And he did so, time and again (Ps. 85:2). Remembering God's mercy in the past inspires these worshipers to plead for the completion of his redemptive work in the future, in this case the blessings of temple worship (vv. 4–7; Heb. 11:10). For God to "restore us again" would represent the "turning" of God to his people who had "turned" to him (see Ps. 85:3–4, 6, 8; Matt. 13:15).

12 Yes, [f]the LORD will give what is good,
and our land [g]will yield its increase.
13 [h]Righteousness will go before him
and make his footsteps a way.

Great Is Your Steadfast Love

86 [i]A PRAYER OF DAVID.
[j]Incline your ear, O LORD, and
answer me,
for I am [k]poor and needy.
2 Preserve my life, for I am [l]godly;
save your servant, who [m]trusts in
you—you are my God.
3 [n]Be gracious to me, O Lord,
for to you do I cry all the day.
4 Gladden the soul of your servant,
for [o]to you, O Lord, do I lift up my
soul.
5 For you, O Lord, are good and [p]forgiv-
ing,
[q]abounding in steadfast love to all who
call upon you.
6 [r]Give ear, O LORD, to my prayer;
listen to my plea for grace.
7 In [s]the day of my trouble I call upon
you,
[t]for you answer me.
8 There is [u]none like you among the gods,
O Lord,
[v]nor are there any works like yours.
9 [w]All the nations you have made shall come
and worship before you, O Lord,
and shall glorify your name.
10 For [x]you are great and [y]do wondrous
things;
[z]you alone are God.
11 [a]Teach me your way, O LORD,
that I may [b]walk in your truth;
[c]unite my heart to fear your name.
12 I give thanks to you, O Lord my God,
with my whole heart,
and I will glorify your name forever.
13 [d]For great is your steadfast love toward
me;
you have [e]delivered my soul from the
depths of Sheol.

14 O God, insolent men have [f]risen up
against me;
a band of ruthless men seeks my life,
and they do not set you before them.
15 But you, O Lord, are a God [g]merciful and
gracious,
slow to anger and abounding in
steadfast love and faithfulness.

Love and peace form the bookends of God's qualities that express his compassion on sinners (Ps. 85:10). However, the middle characteristics—faithfulness and righteousness—demand punishment of sin. God's harmonizing grace is represented as a "kiss" (v. 10). He is at harmony with himself because he righteously deals with our sin by carrying it away and covering it.

Ultimately, this "kiss" took place on the cross of Calvary, through the blood of the last Lamb (vv. 4, 6, 8; Rom. 3:25–26). God is at harmony with his people by finally bringing a grace-based salvation "near" in Immanuel (Ps. 85:9; Matt. 1:23). And redeemed humanity is at harmony with itself as God's righteousness is conveyed to it by faith (Ps. 85:11–13; Rom. 4:22–25).

Psalm 86 God's self-revelation to Moses in Exodus 34:6–7 is the north star of the Bible (Neh. 9:17; Joel 2:13; Jonah 4:2) and the refrain of the Psalter (Ps. 103:8; 145:8). Setting his gaze on this divine mercy that defines who the Lord is, the believer will find hope when he prays from the depths (86:15).

David catalogs promises to be claimed. First, he begs God to answer, because the Lord is prejudiced toward the "poor and needy" (v. 1; cf. 113:7; Luke 4:18). Then he asks for preservation, because God guards the loyal (Ps. 86:2; 1 Sam. 7:3; Luke 12:8). Finally, he pleads for mercy, joy, and a hearing, because God answers importunate prayer (Ps. 86:3–4, 6–7; 4:3; Luke 18:1–8). These prayers find their "Yes" and "Amen" in Jesus (2 Cor. 1:20), who is "full of grace and truth" (John 1:14). The grace exemplified in the promises of God is revealed most fully in Christ.

David's boldness in prayer is further explained by the fact that his God not only makes promises but is sovereignly powerful to fulfill them (Ps. 86:8–10). In the face of arrogant, ruthless, and God-denying enemies who oppose his people, it is especially comforting to remember that God will conquer all of these enemies on the Great Day (cf. v. 9; Isa. 19:21; Zech. 8:20–22; Rev. 15:4). The clock is ticking on evil. Those who do not turn to Christ in trusting faith will nevertheless be forced to confess him

12[f]Ps. 84:11; [James 1:17] [g]See Ps. 67:6
13[h]Ps. 89:14; Isa. 58:8
Psalm 86
[i][Ps. 72:20]
1[j]See Ps. 31:2 [k]Ps. 40:17
2[l]See Ps. 50:5 [m]See Ps. 11:1
3[n]ver. 16; Ps. 56:1; 57:1; See Ps. 4:1
4[o]See Ps. 25:1
5[p]Ps. 130:4 [q]ver. 15; Ps. 103:8; 145:8, 9; Ex. 34:6; Joel 2:13
6[r]Ps. 55:1, 2
7[s]See Ps. 77:2 [t]Ps. 17:6
8[u][Ps. 89:6; Ex. 15:11] [v]Deut. 3:24
9[w]Ps. 66:4; [Ps. 22:31; 65:2; Isa. 66:23; Zech. 14:18; Rev. 15:4]
10[x]Ps. 77:13 [y]See Ps. 72:18 [z]Deut. 6:4; Isa. 37:16; 44:6, 8; 1 Cor. 8:4, 6
11[a]See Ps. 25:4 [b]Ps. 26:3 [c][Jer. 32:39]
13[d][ver. 5] [e]Ps. 30:3; [Ps. 88:6; Ezek. 26:20]
14[f]Ps. 54:3
15[g]ver. 5; Ps. 111:4; 112:4; Num. 14:18; Neh. 9:17; Jonah 4:2; See Ps. 62:12

16 [h]Turn to me and be gracious to me;
give your strength to [i]your servant,
and save [i]the son of your maidservant.
17 [j]Show me a sign of your [k]favor,
that those who hate me may see and
be put to shame
because you, LORD, have helped me
and comforted me.

Glorious Things of You Are Spoken

87

A PSALM OF [l]THE SONS OF KORAH. A SONG.

On [m]the holy mount [n]stands the city
he founded;
2 the LORD [o]loves the gates of Zion
more than all the dwelling places of
Jacob.
3 [p]Glorious things of you are spoken,
O [q]city of God. *Selah*

4 Among those who [r]know me I mention
[s]Rahab and Babylon;
behold, Philistia and Tyre, with
[t]Cush[1]—
"This one was born there," they say.
5 And of Zion it shall be said,
"This one and that one were born in
her";
for the Most High himself will [u]establish her.
6 The LORD records as he [v]registers the
peoples,
"This one was born there." *Selah*

7 [w]Singers and [x]dancers alike say,
"All my [y]springs are in you."

I Cry Out Day and Night Before You

88

A SONG. A PSALM OF [z]THE SONS OF KORAH. TO THE CHOIRMASTER: ACCORDING TO [a]MAHALATH LEANNOTH. A MASKIL[2] OF [b]HEMAN THE EZRAHITE.

1 O LORD, [c]God of my salvation;
I [d]cry out day and night before you.
2 Let my prayer come before you;
[e]incline your ear to my cry!

3 For my soul is full of troubles,
and [f]my life draws near to [g]Sheol.

[1] Probably *Nubia* [2] Probably musical or liturgical terms

16[h] See Ps. 25:16 [i]See Ps. 116:16
17[j] [Judg. 6:17] [k]Neh. 5:19; 13:31
Psalm 87
[l]Ps. 42, title
1[m] See Ps. 48:1 [n]Isa. 28:16
2[o] Ps. 78:67, 68
3[p] [Isa. 60:1]; See Isa. 54:1-3 [q]Ps. 46:4
4[r] Ps. 36:10; [John 10:14] [s]See Job 9:13; See Isa. 19:22-25 [t]See Ps. 68:31
5[u] Ps. 48:8
6[v] See Ps. 69:28
7[w] Ps. 68:25 [x]2 Sam. 6:14 [y]Ps. 36:9; Isa. 12:3; Rev. 21:6
Psalm 88
[z]Ps. 42, title [a]Ps. 53, title [b]1 Kgs. 4:31; 1 Chr. 2:6
1[c] See Ps. 24:5 [d]Ps. 22:2; Luke 18:7
2[e] See Ps. 31:2
3[f] [Ps. 107:18] [g]See Ps. 16:10

at that time (Phil. 2:9–11). That clear view of a victorious future redemption made possible by a God who is "merciful and gracious, slow to anger and abounding in steadfast love and faithfulness" gives a believer resolve to live and worship joyfully in the present (Ps. 86:11–16).

Psalm 87 The covenant nation is "glorious" because she is loved by the God whose glory is his mercy (vv. 1–3). Given the degraded nature of those who will finally make up the church, it is essential that a sovereignly gracious God be the foundation of God's people (v. 4; Heb. 11:10). "Rahab" (which here means "arrogant one" in Hebrew) refers to Egypt (cf. Ps. 89:10), but someday her citizens would bow the knee to God. Babylon represents confusion, yet God promises that her citizens will see the light. Though a wrathful opponent, Philistia would come to peace with God. A commercial city, Tyre represented covetousness, but she would someday make God her soul's chief treasure. Though Ethiopia (Cush) represented the most remote and spiritually illiterate nation of the known world, God's good news would someday come even to them, enabling them to identify with God's people and setting them free.

God will see to it by his Spirit that his chosen ones will be reborn as citizens in his city (cf. Gal. 4:26–27). In the fullness of time, God will ultimately unveil that he was drawing his people to a person, not a place—"to Jesus, the mediator of a new covenant" (Heb. 12:24). The Father will ensure that they are transferred from the kingdom of darkness to the kingdom of his beloved Son (Col. 1:13). He will himself write in his book, "This one was born [in Zion]" (Ps. 87:5–6). Experiencing God's grace ignites exuberant living (v. 7; John 7:38). If this deliverance really is true, how could our response be anything less?

Psalm 88 Proof of life even in a despondent child of God is prayer. While this desperate psalmist frankly describes his sense of abandonment, he utters only one petition, "Let my prayer come before you" (v. 2). Sometimes it is enough to be heard. What follows is a list of emotions which indirectly form Heman's reasons for why God should answer him.

First, Heman suggests that God is responsible for his anguish (vv. 3–9). Heman knows that such a claim will make an impact on his merciful God, because Scripture

4 I am counted among those who [h]go
down to the pit;
I am a man who has no strength,
5 like one set loose among the dead,
like the slain that lie in the grave,
like those whom [i]you remember no
more,
for they are [j]cut off from your hand.
6 You have put me in [k]the depths of the
pit,
in the [l]regions dark and [m]deep.
7 Your wrath [n]lies heavy upon me,
and you overwhelm me with [o]all your
waves. *Selah*

8 You have caused [p]my companions to
shun me;
you have made me [q]a horror[1] to them.
I am [r]shut in so that I cannot escape;
9 [s]my eye grows dim through sorrow.
Every day I call upon you, O LORD;
I [t]spread out my hands to you.
10 Do you work wonders for the dead?
[u]Do the departed rise up to praise you?
Selah
11 Is your steadfast love declared in the
grave,
or your faithfulness in Abaddon?
12 Are your [v]wonders known in [w]the darkness,
or your righteousness in the land of
[x]forgetfulness?
13 But I, O LORD, cry [y]to you;
[z]in the morning my prayer comes
before you.
14 O LORD, why [a]do you cast my soul
away?
Why [b]do you hide your face from
me?
15 Afflicted and close to death from my
youth up,
I suffer your terrors; I am helpless.[2]
16 Your wrath has swept over me;
your [c]dreadful assaults destroy me.
17 They [d]surround me like a flood [e]all day
long;
they [f]close in on me together.
18 You have caused [g]my beloved and my
friend to shun me;
my companions have become darkness.[3]

I Will Sing of the Steadfast Love of the LORD

89 A MASKIL[4] OF [h]ETHAN THE EZRAHITE.
[i]I will sing of [j]the steadfast love of
the LORD, forever;
with my mouth I will make known
your [k]faithfulness to all generations.
2 For I said, [j]"Steadfast love will be built
up forever;
in the heavens [l]you will establish your
[k]faithfulness."

[1] Or *an abomination* [2] The meaning of the Hebrew word is uncertain [3] Or *darkness has become my only companion* [4] Probably a musical or liturgical term

assures that the pain of God's children moves him (Gen. 6:6, 7; Isa. 49:15; Jer. 31:3, 20; Hos. 11:8). The second reason God should save Heman from despair is that if he dies because of despair, he will not fulfill his primary purpose on earth—to glorify God (Ps. 88:10–12). Those who are loved by God long for his presence when he hides his face (Matt. 27:46; 2 Cor. 12:8–9).

By the end of the prayer, Heman reveals that abandonment by a "beloved friend" was the catalyst for his spiritual depression (Ps. 88:18). Though shunned by the friend, Heman cries out to God day and night (vv. 9, 13), because in his heart, despite the pain that finds no resolution in the course of the Psalm, he knows the Lord is unchanging in his steadfast love and faithfulness, and will never really forsake him (vv. 11–12; Ex. 34:6–7; Heb. 13:5–6). The Lord is the "God of my salvation" (Ps. 88:1). The light of redemption is quite faint in this psalm, but the Redeemer is still the One sought because there is no other to seek in such pain (Heb. 4:15; Luke 22:42–44; Matt. 28:19–20). Such authentic expression of deep depression in Scripture assures us that we can approach God with our hurts and doubts, never wondering if he will reject us. He is not threatened by our raw honesty with him. He welcomes it. In Jesus, he has himself entered into our pain and darkness.

Psalm 89 God's sovereignty confirms his gracious promises, promises that prompt prayer in dark times. The means by which Ethan seeks to lift his heart to the Lord is a mosaic of God's redemptive attributes: strong love (vv. 1–4; Rom. 8:37), creational might (Ps. 89:5–13; Jer. 31:35–37; Rom. 8:21), righteous mediation (Ps. 89:14, 18–29; Heb.

4[h] See Ps. 28:1
5[i] [Ps. 31:12] [j] Isa. 53:8
6[k] [Ps. 63:9] [l] ver. 12, 18; Ps. 143:3; Lam. 3:6 [m] Ps. 69:15
7[n] [Ps. 32:4] [o] Ps. 42:7
8[p] ver. 18; Ps. 142:4; See Job 19:13 [q] Job 30:10 [r] Jer. 32:2
9[s] [Ps. 6:7] [t] See Job 11:13
10[u] [Ps. 6:5]
12[v] Ps. 89:5 [w] ver. 6; Job 10:21 [x] [Eccles. 9:5]
13[y] Ps. 30:2 [z] See Ps. 5:3
14[a] See Ps. 44:9 [b] See Job 13:24
16[c] Job 6:4; 9:34
17[d] See Ps. 118:10-12 [e] Ps. 86:3 [f] Ps. 18:4; 22:16; [Ps. 118:10]
18[g] See Job 19:13, 14
Psalm 89
[h] 1 Kgs. 4:31; 1 Chr. 2:6
1[i] Ps. 101:1 [j] ver. 14, 24, 28, 33, 49; [Isa. 55:3] [k] ver. 5, 8, 24, 33, 49; Ps. 88:11; 119:90
2[j] [See ver. 1 above] [l] See Ps. 36:5 [k] [See ver. 1 above]

3 You have said, "I have made [m]a covenant
with my [n]chosen one;
I have [o]sworn to David my servant:
4 'I will establish your [p]offspring forever,
and build your [q]throne for all generations.'" *Selah*

5 Let [r]the heavens praise your [s]wonders, O LORD,
your faithfulness in the assembly of
[t]the holy ones!
6 For [u]who in the skies can be compared to
the LORD?
[u]Who among the heavenly beings[1] is
like the LORD,
7 a God greatly [v]to be feared in the council
of [t]the holy ones,
and awesome above all [w]who are
around him?
8 O LORD God of hosts,
[x]who is mighty as you are, O [y]LORD,
with your faithfulness all around
you?
9 You rule the raging of the sea;
when its waves rise, you [z]still them.
10 You [a]crushed [b]Rahab like a carcass;
you [c]scattered your enemies with your
mighty arm.
11 [d]The heavens are yours; the earth also is
yours;
[e]the world and all that is in it, you
have [f]founded them.
12 [g]The north and the south, you have created them;
[h]Tabor and [i]Hermon [j]joyously praise
your name.
13 You have a mighty arm;
strong is your hand, high your right
hand.
14 [k]Righteousness and justice are the foundation of your throne;
[l]steadfast love and faithfulness go
before you.
15 Blessed are the people who know [m]the
festal shout,
who walk, O LORD, in [n]the light of
your face,
16 who exult in your [o]name all the day
and in your righteousness are
[p]exalted.
17 For you are [q]the glory of their strength;
by your favor our [r]horn is exalted.
18 For our [s]shield belongs to the LORD,
our king to [t]the Holy One of Israel.

19 [u]Of old you spoke in a vision to your
godly one,[2] and said:
"I have [v]granted help to one who is
[w]mighty;
I have exalted one [x]chosen from the
people.
20 [y]I have found David, my servant;
with my holy oil I have [z]anointed
him,

[1] Hebrew *the sons of God*, or *the sons of might* [2] Some Hebrew manuscripts *godly ones*

3 [m]ver. 28, 34, 39 [n]ver. 19; 1 Kgs. 8:16; Isa. 42:1 [o]ver. 35, 49; Ps. 132:11; See 2 Sam. 7:8-16; 1 Chr. 17:7-14; Jer. 33:17-21
4 [p]ver. 29, 36; John 12:34 [q]ver. 29, 36; [Isa. 9:7; Luke 1:32, 33]
5 [r]Ps. 19:1; 50:6; 97:6; See Rev. 7:10-12 [s]Ps. 88:12 [t]ver. 7; Job 5:1; 15:15; [Job 1:6]
6 [u]ver. 8; [Ps. 86:8]
7 [v]See Ps. 47:2 [t][See ver. 5 above] [w][Ps. 103:20, 21]
8 [x][1 Sam. 2:2]; See Ps. 35:10 [y]See Ps. 68:4
9 [z]Ps. 65:7; Job 38:11
10 [a][Ex. 14:30] [b]See Job 9:13 [c]See Ps. 53:5
11 [d]Gen. 1:1; 1 Chr. 29:11 [e]See Ps. 24:1 [f]See Ps. 104:5
12 [g]Job 26:7 [h]Jer. 46:18 [i]Deut. 3:9 [j]Ps. 98:8
14 [k]Ps. 97:2 [l]ver. 2; [Ps. 85:13]
15 [m]See Ps. 66:1 [n]See Ps. 4:6
16 [o][Ps. 20:5, 7] [p][Job 36:7]
17 [q][Ps. 78:61] [r]ver. 24; See Ps. 75:10
18 [s]Ps. 47:9 [t]See Ps. 71:22
19 [u][ver. 3, 4] [v][Ps. 21:5] [w]2 Sam. 17:10 [x]See ver. 3
20 [y]Cited Acts 13:22 [z]1 Sam. 16:13

12:22–24), joy-giving presence (Ps. 89:15–17; John 3:29–30), and fatherly discipline (Ps. 89:30–37; Heb. 12:7). All these traits have been fulfilled and climactically embodied in Christ, who embodies all of God's promises (Rom. 1:1–6).

With God's character stated clearly for disillusioned believers, Ethan teaches us to pray for God to exercise his sovereignty and "establish the work of [his] hands" (Ps. 90:17; cf. 89:2, 4, 29). Accusing God of renouncing his covenant promises (vv. 38–45) might seem to border on irreverence. But this is the undeniable felt experience of the psalmist, and it is the felt experience of the saints down through the ages. In giving voice to the pain and despair we often pass through, however, the psalmist also guides us into hope. For we are reminded that even when all looks dark, God has made a promise to David of an eternal throne (vv. 35–37). The bottom line, therefore, is, "Blessed be the LORD forever!" (v. 52). Reading this psalm today, moreover, we are reminded that God kept this promise in Jesus, the long-anticipated Davidic heir. Jesus underwent the ultimate pain—condemnation and separation from God—so that we never need to.

Believers can pray so brazenly because they know a gracious Father (vv. 38–46). This Father's "compassion grows warm and tender" when his children are in pain (Hos. 11:8), and there comes a time when he can no longer bear the anguish of his children (Ps. 89:50–51; Judg. 10:16). So God welcomes honest and heartfelt prayer; he does not punish it, for he is "steadfast" in his love and faithful in his care (Ps. 89:49; Luke 18:1–5).

21 so that my [a]hand shall be established
with him;
my arm also shall strengthen him.
22 The enemy shall not outwit him;
[b]the wicked shall not humble him.
23 I will [c]crush his foes before him
and strike down those who hate him.
24 My [d]faithfulness and my [d]steadfast love
shall be with him,
and in my name shall his [e]horn be
exalted.
25 I will set his hand on [f]the sea
and his right hand on [f]the rivers.
26 He shall cry to me, 'You are my [g]Father,
my God, and [h]the Rock of my salvation.'
27 And I will make him the [i]firstborn,
[j]the highest of the kings of the earth.
28 My steadfast love I will keep for him forever,
and my [k]covenant will stand firm[1] for
him.
29 I will establish his [l]offspring forever
and his [l]throne as [m]the days of the
heavens.
30 [n]If his children forsake my law
and do not walk according to my
rules,[2]
31 if they violate my statutes
and do not keep my commandments,
32 then I will punish their transgression
with [o]the rod
and their iniquity with stripes,
33 but I will not remove from him my
steadfast love
or be false to my faithfulness.
34 I will not violate my [k]covenant
or alter the word that went forth from
my lips.
35 Once for all I have sworn [p]by my holiness;
I will not [q]lie to David.
36 His [l]offspring shall endure forever,
[r]his [l]throne as long as [s]the sun before
me.
37 Like [s]the moon it shall be established
forever,
[t]a faithful witness in the skies." *Selah*

38 But now you have [u]cast off and rejected;
you are full of wrath against your
[v]anointed.
39 You have [w]renounced [x]the covenant with
your servant;
you have [y]defiled his [z]crown in the
dust.
40 You have [a]breached all his walls;
you have laid his strongholds in ruins.
41 [a]All who pass by plunder him;
he has become [b]the scorn of his neighbors.
42 You have exalted the right hand of his
foes;
you have made all his enemies rejoice.
43 You have also turned back the edge of
his sword,
and you have not made him stand in
battle.
44 You have made his splendor to cease
and cast his throne to the ground.
45 You have cut short [c]the days of his youth;
you have [d]covered him with shame.
Selah

46 [e]How long, O LORD? Will you hide yourself forever?
How long will your wrath [f]burn like
fire?
47 [g]Remember [h]how short my [i]time is!
For what vanity you have created all
the children of man!
48 [j]What man can live and never [k]see death?
Who can deliver his soul from the
power of [l]Sheol? *Selah*

49 Lord, where is your [m]steadfast love of old,
which by your [m]faithfulness you
swore to David?
50 [n]Remember, O Lord, how your servants
are mocked,
and how I bear in my [o]heart the
insults[3] of all the many nations,
51 with which your enemies mock, O LORD,
with which they mock [p]the footsteps
of your [q]anointed.

52 [r]Blessed be the LORD forever!
Amen and Amen.

[1] Or *will remain faithful* [2] Or *my just decrees* [3] Hebrew lacks *the insults*

21[a] Ps. 80:17 **22**[b] [2 Sam. 7:10] **23**[c] [2 Sam. 7:9]; See Ps. 2:9 **24**[d] ver. 1 [e] ver. 17 **25**[f] See Ps. 72:8 **26**[g] [2 Sam. 7:14] [h] [Ps. 18:2] **27**[i] Ex. 4:22; [Rom. 8:29; Col. 1:15, 18; Heb. 1:5] [j] Num. 24:7; [Rev. 19:16] **28**[k] See ver. 3 **29**[l] See ver. 4 [m] See Job 14:12 **30**[n] 2 Sam. 7:14; 1 Kgs. 2:4 **32**[o] See Job 9:34 **34**[k] [See ver. 28 above] **35**[p] See Ps. 60:6 [q] [Heb. 6:18] **36**[l] [See ver. 29 above] [r] See ver. 4 [s] See Ps. 72:5 **37**[s] [See ver. 36 above] [t] See Job 16:19 **38**[u] See Ps. 44:9 [v] ver. 20, 51 **39**[w] Lam. 2:7 [x] See ver. 3 [y] See Ps. 74:7 [z] Job 19:9 **40**[a] See Ps. 80:12 **41**[a] [See ver. 40 above] [b] [ver. 50]; See Ps. 44:13; 69:9, 19 **45**[c] Ps. 102:23 [d] Ps. 71:13; 109:29 **46**[e] See Ps. 13:1 [f] Ps. 78:63; 79:5 **47**[g] Job 7:7; 10:9 [h] [Job 14:1] [i] Ps. 39:5 **48**[j] [Ps. 49:9] [k] [Luke 2:26; Heb. 11:5] [l] See Ps. 16:10 **49**[m] [ver. 1, 2] **50**[n] [ver. 41]; See Ps. 74:18, 22 [o] Ps. 79:12 **51**[p] [Ps. 17:11; 56:6] [q] ver. 20, 38 **52**[r] See Ps. 41:13

Book Four

From Everlasting to Everlasting

90 A [s]Prayer of Moses, the [t]man of God.
Lord, you have been our [u]dwelling place[1]
in all generations.
2 [v]Before the [w]mountains were brought forth,
or ever you had formed the earth and the world,
[x]from everlasting to everlasting you are God.

3 You return man to dust
and say, [y]"Return, [z]O children of man!"[2]
4 For [a]a thousand years in your sight
are but as [b]yesterday when it is past,
or as [c]a watch in the night.

5 You [d]sweep them away as with a flood;
they are like [e]a dream,
like [f]grass that is renewed in the morning:
6 in [i]the morning it flourishes and is renewed;
in the evening it [j]fades and [k]withers.

7 For we are brought to an end by your anger;
by your wrath we are dismayed.
8 You have [l]set our iniquities before you,
our [m]secret sins in the light of your presence.

9 For all our days pass away under your wrath;
we bring our years to an end like a sigh.
10 The years of our life are seventy,
or even by reason of strength eighty;
yet their span[3] is but toil and trouble;
they are soon gone, and we fly away.
11 Who considers the power of your anger,
and your wrath according to the fear of you?

12 [n]So teach us to number our days
that we may get a heart of wisdom.
13 [o]Return, O LORD! [p]How long?
Have [q]pity on your servants!
14 Satisfy us in the [s]morning with your steadfast love,
that we may [t]rejoice and be glad all our days.
15 Make us glad for as many days as you have [u]afflicted us,
and for as many years as we have seen evil.
16 Let your [v]work be shown to your servants,
and your glorious power to their children.
17 Let the [x]favor[4] of the Lord our God be upon us,
and establish [y]the work of our hands upon us;
yes, establish the work of our hands!

My Refuge and My Fortress

91 He who dwells in [a]the shelter of the Most High
will abide in [b]the shadow of the Almighty.

[1] Some Hebrew manuscripts (compare Septuagint) *our refuge* [2] Or *of Adam* [3] Or *pride* [4] Or *beauty*

Psalm 90
[s]Ps. 17, title; 55:1 [t]Deut. 33:1; Josh. 14:6; Ezra 3:2
1[u]See Ps. 71:3
2[v]Prov. 8:25 [w][Deut. 33:15; Job 15:7] [x]See Job 36:26
3[y]Gen. 3:19 [z]Eccles. 12:7
4[a]2 Pet. 3:8 [b][Ps. 39:5] [c]Ex. 14:24; Judg. 7:19
5[d]Ps. 58:9 [e]See Job 20:8 [f]Ps. 37:2; 103:15; 2 Kgs. 19:26; Isa. 40:6-8; 1 Pet. 1:24
6[i]See Job 4:20 [j]Job 14:2; [Ps. 92:7] [k]James 1:11
8[l]Jer. 16:17; Heb. 4:13 [m]Ps. 19:12
12[n]Ps. 39:4
13[o]Ps. 6:4 [p]See Ps. 74:9, 10 [q]Ps. 106:45; 135:14; Ex. 32:12; Deut. 32:36; Judg. 2:18; Jonah 3:10; See Gen. 6:6
14[s]See Ps. 46:5 [t]See Ps. 85:6
15[u][Deut. 8:2]
16[v]Ps. 77:12; 92:4; 95:9; Deut. 32:4; Hab. 3:2
17[x]Ps. 27:4 [y][Ps. 128:2]; [Isa. 26:12]

Psalm 91
1[a]See Ps. 32:7 [b]Ps. 121:5; [Isa. 25:4; 32:2]

Psalm 90 Looking at earthly suffering against the backdrop of God's eternal plan of redemption provides hope. Over the course of Moses' leadership, he was regularly faced with man's temporal and sinful nature (vv. 4–6, 10; Num. 20:2–9; James 4:14). Though painful, this knowledge of man produces wisdom when it leads to knowledge of God as a "dwelling place" (Ps. 90:1; Rev. 21:3). Different from a refuge, which is temporary, a dwelling is where one lives in good times and bad.

Dwelling in the presence of God results in an eternally significant life (Rom. 8:18). God graciously adopts the believer's work and makes it "glorious" and "favored" (Ps. 90:16–17; 1 Cor. 3:9). Those works done for the glory of Christ will be proven by fire to be as enduring and beautiful as gold (1 Cor. 3:12–14).

God's "pity" reveals humanity's brokenness but also God's compassion, leading to merciful deliverance (Ps. 90:7–9, 11, 13; Rom. 5:12). His parental emotions are stirred when he looks at our brokenness (Ps. 90:12–13; Matt. 14:14). Turning his wrath away, he grants the repentant "steadfast love" (Ps. 90:14). Then love produces "gladness" that more than makes up for the years spent in agony living outside of God's grace (v. 15). The previous psalm explains that those who experience this gladness exult in God's righteousness (Ps. 89:15–16; Heb. 1:9). That is, God substitutes righteousness for sin. Ultimately he made that possible at great cost to himself at the high point of history through the gift of his only Son (Rom. 8:3–4).

2 I will say[1] to the LORD, "My [c]refuge and
my [d]fortress,
my God, in whom I [e]trust."
3 For he will deliver you from [f]the snare of
the fowler
and from the deadly pestilence.
4 He will [g]cover you with his pinions,
and under his [h]wings you will [i]find
refuge;
his [j]faithfulness is [k]a shield and buckler.
5 [l]You will not fear [m]the terror of the night,
nor the arrow that flies by day,
6 nor the pestilence that stalks in darkness,
nor the destruction that wastes at
noonday.
7 A thousand may fall at your side,
ten thousand at your right hand,
but it will not come near you.
8 You will only look with your eyes
and [n]see the recompense of the wicked.
9 Because you have made the LORD your
[o]dwelling place—
the Most High, who is my [c]refuge[2]—
10 [p]no evil shall be allowed to befall you,
[q]no plague come near your tent.
11 [r]For he will command his [s]angels concerning you
to [t]guard you in all your ways.
12 On their hands they will bear you up,
lest you [u]strike your foot against a
stone.
13 You will tread on [v]the lion and the
[w]adder;
the young lion and [x]the serpent you
will [y]trample underfoot.
14 "Because he [z]holds fast to me in love,
I will deliver him;
I will protect him, because he [a]knows
my name.
15 When he [b]calls to me, I will answer
him;
I will be with him in trouble;
I will rescue him and [c]honor him.
16 With [d]long life I will satisfy him
and [e]show him my salvation."

How Great Are Your Works

92 A PSALM. A SONG FOR THE SABBATH.
[f]It is good to give thanks to the
LORD,
to sing praises to your name, [g]O Most
High;

[1] Septuagint *He will say* [2] Or *For you, O LORD, are my refuge! You have made the Most High your dwelling place*

2[c] ver. 9; See Ps. 14:6 [d] See Ps. 18:2 [e] See Ps. 11:1
3[f] Ps. 124:7; 140:5; 141:9; Prov. 6:5
4[g] [1 Kgs. 8:7] [h] See Ps. 17:8 [i] Ps. 57:1 [j] See Ps. 36:5 [k] See Ps. 35:2
5[l] Prov. 3:23; Isa. 43:1; See Job 5:19-23 [m] Song 3:8
8[n] See Ps. 37:34
9[o] See Ps. 71:3 [c] [See ver. 2 above]
10[p] [ver. 5]; See Prov. 12:21 [q] Ps. 38:11
11[r] Cited Matt. 4:6; Luke 4:10, 11 [s] See Ps. 34:7 [t] Ex. 23:20
12[u] Prov. 3:23; [Ps. 37:24]
13[v] [Dan. 6:23] [w] [Acts 28:5] [x] See Ps. 74:13 [y] Luke 10:19; [Mark 16:18]
14[z] Deut. 7:7; 10:15 [a] Ps. 9:10
15[b] Job 12:4; See Ps. 50:15 [c] 1 Sam. 2:30; John 12:26
16[d] Ps. 21:4; Deut. 6:2; 1 Kgs. 3:14; Prov. 3:2, 16 [e] Ps. 50:23; [Ps. 118:14, 21]

Psalm 92
1[f] Ps. 147:1; [Ps. 71:22] [g] [Gen. 14:19, 20]

Psalm 91 When someone experiences God's grace, he cannot keep it to himself. Consequently, the psalmist's pronouns quickly shift from "I" to "you" (vv. 1–3; cf. Rom. 1:5–7). God's titles explain why his grace is commendable. The one who regularly lives in the shelter of the "Most High" will find rest in the shadow of the "Almighty" (Ps. 91:1). This was especially meaningful to Israel, who was homeless for much of the Old Testament. Her refuge was the "LORD," the "I AM" who met Moses in the burning bush and who is all-sufficient in resources (Ex. 3:14). Even so, he is the believer's intimate companion ("my God," v. 2).

The psalmist assures us of God's aggressive defense against every kind of threat: terror at night, arrows by day, pestilence in darkness, destruction at noon (Ps. 91:5–6), along with the lion, the adder, the young lion, and the serpent (v. 13; Luke 10:19; Acts 28:1–6). Yet God's protection is as tender as a mother bird's (Ps. 91:4; Deut. 32:11; Matt. 23:37). The "snare of the fowler" represents hidden plots, and "pestilence" represents everything else that threatens in this life (Ps. 91:3; 2 Cor. 4:7–11). Finally, the psalmist prophesies regarding what only a Messiah can deliver: shelter from the future judgment (Ps. 91:7–8; John 12:47).

Misapplying this text, the devil urged Jesus to provoke God to an additional proof of his love (Matt. 4:6; cf. Ps. 91:11–12). But God's pronouncement at Jesus' baptism was sufficient (Luke 3:22). Likewise, the believer united to Christ is also perpetually assured of loving protection by God's angels, who represent his presence (Ps. 91:11–13; 34:7; John 14:21). So what began with a human testimony to God's deliverance from trouble ends with a divine pledge of a "long life" (for those in Christ, eternal life) and of "rescue" and "honor" for the one who "holds fast to [him] in love" (Ps. 91:14–16; John 15:26).

Psalm 92 It should be every believer's delight to worship morning and evening, indicating the commitment of the whole day to God's honor. Throughout redemptive history, believers have practiced morning and evening prayer, especially on the

2 to declare your [h]steadfast love in [i]the
morning,
and your [h]faithfulness by [i]night,
3 to the music of [j]the lute and [j]the harp,
to the melody of [j]the lyre.
4 For you, O LORD, have made me glad by
your [k]work;
at [l]the works of your hands I sing for
joy.

5 How [m]great are your works, O LORD!
Your [n]thoughts are very [o]deep!
6 The stupid man cannot know;
the fool cannot understand this:
7 that though [p]the wicked sprout like grass
and all [q]evildoers flourish,
they are doomed to destruction forever;
8 but you, O LORD, are [r]on high forever.
9 For behold, your enemies, O LORD,
for behold, your enemies shall perish;
all evildoers shall be [s]scattered.

10 But you have exalted my [t]horn like that
of [u]the wild ox;
you have [v]poured over me[1] fresh oil.
11 My [w]eyes have seen the downfall of my
enemies;
my ears have heard the doom of my
evil assailants.

12 [x]The righteous flourish like the palm tree
and grow like a cedar in Lebanon.
13 They are planted in the house of the
LORD;
they flourish in [y]the courts of our God.
14 They still bear fruit in old age;
they are ever full of sap and green,
15 [z]to declare that the LORD is upright;
he is my [a]rock, and there is [b]no
unrighteousness in him.

The LORD Reigns

93 [c]The LORD reigns; he is [d]robed in
majesty;
the LORD is [e]robed; he has [f]put on
strength as his belt.
[g]Yes, the world is established; [h]it shall
never be moved.
2 [i]Your throne is established from of old;
[j]you are from everlasting.

3 [k]The floods have lifted up, O LORD,
the floods have lifted up their voice;
the floods lift up their roaring.
4 Mightier than the thunders of many
waters,
mightier than the waves of the sea,
[l]the LORD [m]on high is mighty!

[1] Compare Syriac; the meaning of the Hebrew is uncertain

2 [h]See Ps. 36:5 [i][Ps. 119:147, 148]
3 [j]See Ps. 33:2
4 [k]See Ps. 90:16 [l]Ps. 8:6
5 [m]Ps. 111:2; Rev. 15:3 [n]Ps. 40:5; 139:17 [o][Rom. 11:33]; See Ps. 36:6
7 [p]See Job 21:7 [q]Ps. 94:4; 125:5
8 [r]Ps. 93:4
9 [s]See Ps. 68:1
10 [t]See Ps. 75:10; 1 Sam. 2:1 [u]Num. 23:22 [v]See Ps. 23:5
11 [w]See Ps. 37:34; 54:7
12 [x]Ps. 1:3; 52:8; 72:7; Prov. 11:28; [Num. 24:6; Isa. 61:3]; See Hos. 14:5-8
13 [y]Ps. 100:4; 116:19; 135:2
15 [z][Ps. 58:11] [a]See Ps. 18:2 [b]See Job 34:10

Psalm 93
1 [c]Ps. 96:10; See 1 Chr. 16:31 [d]Ps. 104:1 [e]Isa. 51:9 [f]Ps. 65:6 [g]Ps. 96:10; [Ps. 46:5] [h]See Ps. 125:1
2 [i][Ps. 45:6] [j]Ps. 90:2
3 [k][Ps. 98:7, 8; Hab. 3:10]
4 [l]See Ps. 65:6, 7 [m]Ps. 92:8

Sabbath (e.g., superscription; 2 Chron. 13:11; Ex. 29:39–41). In the New Testament, "Lord's Day" captures the idea that one particular day is to be set aside for rest and worship (Acts 20:7; 1 Cor. 16:2; Rev. 1:10). Praising God for his "good" gift of a day of rest (Ps. 92:1), the psalmist illustrates that God graciously made the Sabbath for man, not man for the Sabbath (cf. Mark 2:27). Beyond "good," the original language says the Sabbath is "delectable" (vv. 1–2). In celebrating a Sabbath, we acknowledge that God can provide by his grace more than we can accomplish with non-stop striving.

Every morning, a believer can "declare [the] steadfast love" of the Lord for safekeeping through the night (v. 2). Such gratitude should remind him of his dependence on the Lord for the whole day ahead (James 4:13–17). The very existence of the morning convinces him that God's "work" of redemption is ongoing (Ps. 92:4; Jer. 31:35; Rev. 6:12–13). On the Lord's Day in particular, Christians should give praise for the work of Christ's resurrection, which guarantees their own resurrection in the future (John 20:1; 1 Cor. 15:12), since they are united to Christ (Eph. 2:6; Col. 3:1). The spirit of all these morning reflections must be one of joy in God's grace, especially on the Lord's Day (Ps. 92:3–4; Luke 24:1, 13, 41, 52).

As the day dies, the believer should remember his protection from enemies but should also confess his need to die to his own sin (Ps. 92:9–12; Luke 1:74; 1 Pet. 2:24). By living according to this rhythm of morning and evening worship, God's children will be fruitful and will fulfill his purposes for their lives (Ps. 92:13–14; Eph. 5:7–14).

Psalm 93 The believer's great comfort is that God is a benevolent king. As sustainer of the universe, God is all-powerful, unchangeable, and eternal. His perfect sovereignty joined with absolute goodness answers every need for his people's sustenance (vv. 1–2; Phil. 4:19–20). Not only so, but perfect sovereignty joined to passionate love makes him triumphant over his children's enemies (Ps. 93:3–4; Rev. 11:16–18). No force of nature, nations, or culture can threaten the eternal security of believers (Rom. 8:38–39).

5 Your [n]decrees are very trustworthy;
[o]holiness befits your house,
O LORD, forevermore.

The LORD Will Not Forsake His People

94 O LORD, God of [p]vengeance,
O God of vengeance, [q]shine forth!
2 [r]Rise up, O [s]judge of the earth;
repay to the [t]proud what they deserve!
3 O LORD, [u]how long shall the wicked,
how long shall [v]the wicked exult?
4 They pour out their [w]arrogant words;
all [x]the evildoers boast.
5 They [y]crush your people, O LORD,
and afflict your heritage.
6 They kill [z]the widow and the sojourner,
and murder [z]the fatherless;
7 [a]and they say, "The LORD does not see;
the God of Jacob does not perceive."

8 [b]Understand, O dullest of the people!
Fools, when will you be wise?
9 [c]He who planted the ear, does he not
hear?
He who formed the eye, does he not see?
10 He who [d]disciplines the nations, does he
not rebuke?
He who [e]teaches man knowledge—
11 [f]the LORD—knows the thoughts of
man,
that they are [g]but a breath.[1]

12 [h]Blessed is the man whom you [i]discipline, O LORD,
and whom you teach out of your law,
13 to give him [j]rest from [k]days of trouble,
until [l]a pit is dug for the wicked.
14 [m]For the LORD will not forsake his [n]people;
he will not abandon his [n]heritage;
15 for [o]justice will return to the righteous,
and all the upright in heart will [p]follow it.

16 [q]Who rises up for me against the wicked?
Who stands up for me against evildoers?
17 [r]If the LORD had not been my help,
my soul would soon have lived in the
land of [s]silence.
18 When I thought, [t]"My foot slips,"
your steadfast love, O LORD, [u]held me
up.
19 When the cares of my heart are many,
your consolations cheer my soul.

[1] Septuagint *they are futile*

The eternality of God's rule pointed the Old Testament saint forward to Christ (Ps. 93:2; Heb. 1:10–12). Calling his subjects "friends" not "servants," Christ in his eternal kingdom provides security, which fosters loving familiarity and freedom (John 15:15; 8:36).

"Decrees" (Ps. 93:5) could be translated "testimonies," because God's laws, instructions, promises, rebukes, and encouragements are all testimonies of his gracious rule. At the same time, his kingdom is not a democracy. God's holiness demands that all his creatures submit to his law. But his loving promise is that life for those who submit to him will be under the control of One who is mightier than the waters he subdued in creation (v. 5; Gen. 1:2; Deut. 4:40; Rom. 6:16). Ultimately, God's righteousness and might were revealed in Jesus, whom God sent with the power to resist sin and defeat Satan. The result is that, as we place our trust in him day by day, walking with by the Spirit (Gal. 5:25), we begin to live the life of love to which the law always pointed, and we experience the blessings always promised (Rom. 8:3; 13:8–10).

Psalm 94 In the hands of God, vengeance is just punishment for sins (vv. 1–2; Jer. 51:56; Rom. 12:19). But when believers petition God for justice, their anger is replaced with comfort (Eph. 4:26). Comfort comes from the fact that God does not change, so we can wait for his justice (Heb. 13:8–9). But waiting patiently means prayerfulness, not passivity (Lam. 3:25–26; James 5:7–11).

One must learn to wait prayerfully for God's purification of the church as well. Israel's leaders were proudly abusing the disenfranchised, which is contrary to "religion that is pure" (James 1:26–27; cf. Ps. 94:4–7). While his children wait, God disciplines them (v. 12; Rom. 8:25). His fatherly teaching includes allowing them to see the contrast between the misery of sin and the blessing of living by his "law" (Ps. 94:12; Rom. 7:12). Examples of this contrast include sinful entanglement versus "rest" (Ps. 94:13; Heb. 12:1–2), betrayal versus loyalty (Ps. 94:14; Rom. 11:2), and judgment versus vindication (Ps. 94:15; Phil. 2:10–11).

5[n] [Ps. 89:28, 37] [o] See Ps. 29:2
Psalm 94
1[p] Deut. 32:35, 41, 43; Isa. 35:4; Jer. 51:56; Nah. 1:2; Rom. 12:19 [q] See Ps. 50:2
2[r] See Ps. 7:6 [s] See Ps. 58:11 [t] Luke 1:51
3[u] Rev. 6:10; See Ps. 74:10 [v] [Job 20:5]
4[w] Ps. 31:18; 1 Sam. 2:3; [Jude 15] [x] Ps. 92:7, 9; 125:5
5[y] [Prov. 22:22; Isa. 3:15]
6[z] [Isa. 10:2]
7[a] See Job 22:13
8[b] See Ps. 49:10
9[c] [Ex. 4:11; Prov. 20:12]
10[d] [Job 12:23] [e] See Job 35:11
11[f] Cited 1 Cor. 3:20 [g] [Ps. 30:5, 11]
12[h] Prov. 3:11, 12; Heb. 12:5, 6; See Job 5:17 [i] Deut. 8:5; 1 Cor. 11:32
13[j] Job 34:29 [k] Ps. 49:5 [l] Ps. 55:23
14[m] 1 Sam. 12:22; Rom. 11:2 [n] Deut. 32:9
15[o] [Isa. 42:3] [p] 1 Sam. 12:14; 1 Kgs. 14:8
16[q] See Ps. 12:5
17[r] Ps. 124:1, 2 [s] See Ps. 31:17
18[t] Ps. 38:16; [Ps. 73:2] [u] [Ps. 20:2]

20 Can [w]wicked rulers be allied with you,
those who frame injustice by [x]statute?
21 They [y]band together against the life of
the righteous
and condemn [z]the innocent to death.[1]
22 But the LORD has become my [a]stronghold,
and my God [b]the rock of my [c]refuge.
23 He will bring back on them [d]their iniquity
and [e]wipe them out for their wickedness;
the LORD our God will wipe them out.

Let Us Sing Songs of Praise

95 Oh come, let us sing to the LORD;
let us [f]make a joyful noise to [g]the
rock of our salvation!
2 Let us [h]come into his presence with
thanksgiving;
let us [f]make a joyful noise to him with
songs of praise!
3 For the LORD is [i]a great God,
and a great King [j]above all gods.
4 In his hand are the depths of the earth;
the heights of the mountains are his
also.
5 The sea is his, for [k]he made it,
and his hands formed [k]the dry land.
6 Oh come, let us worship and bow down;
let us [l]kneel before the LORD, our
[m]Maker!
7 For he is our [n]God,
and we are the people of his [o]pasture,
and the sheep of his hand.
[p]Today, if you [q]hear his voice,
8 [r]do not harden your hearts, as at
[s]Meribah,
as on the day at [t]Massah in the wilderness,
9 when your fathers put me to the [u]test
and put me to the proof, though they
had seen my [v]work.
10 [w]For forty years I loathed that generation
and said, "They are a people who go
astray in their heart,
and they have not known [x]my ways."
11 Therefore I [y]swore in my wrath,
"They shall not enter [z]my rest."

Worship in the Splendor of Holiness

96 [a]Oh sing to the LORD [b]a new song;
sing to the LORD, all the earth!
2 Sing to the LORD, bless his name;
[c]tell of his salvation from day to day.
3 Declare his glory among the nations,
his marvelous works among all the
peoples!

[1] Hebrew *condemn innocent blood*

20[w] [Amos 6:3] [x] Ps. 50:16; 58:2; Isa. 10:1
21[y] Matt. 27:1 [z] Matt. 27:4
22[a] See Ps. 9:9 [b] See Ps. 18:2 [c] See Ps. 14:6
23[d] See Ps. 7:16; 34:21; [Prov. 2:22] [e] [Ps. 92:9]

Psalm 95
1[f] See Ps. 66:1 [g] Ps. 89:26; [Ps. 94:22]
2[h] Mic. 6:6 [f] [See ver. 1 above]
3[i] Ps. 93:4; 135:5 [j] Ps. 86:8; 96:4; 97:9; 2 Chr. 2:5
5[k] Gen. 1:9, 10; Jonah 1:9
6[l] 2 Chr. 6:13; Dan. 6:10 [m] Ps. 100:3; 149:2; Deut. 32:6, 15, 18
7[n] Ps. 48:14 [o] See Ps. 74:1 [p] Cited Heb. 3:7-11, 15; 4:7 [q] Num. 14:22
8[r] Ex. 9:34; 1 Sam. 6:6; 2 Chr. 36:13; Prov. 28:14 [s] Ex. 17:7; Num. 20:13 [t] Ex. 17:7; Deut. 6:16
9[u] 1 Cor. 10:9; [Ps. 78:18, 41, 56] [v] See Ps. 90:16; [Num. 14:22]
10[w] Acts 7:36; 13:18; Heb. 3:17; [Deut. 9:7] [x] [Ps. 81:13]
11[y] Num. 14:23, 28, 30; Deut. 1:35; Cited Heb. 3:11; 4:3, 5 [z] Deut. 12:9

Psalm 96
1[a] For ver. 1-13, see 1 Chr. 16:23-33 [b] Ps. 98:1; See Ps. 33:3
2[c] [Isa. 52:7; 60:6]

No matter who deserts the believer, God will always be with him, and his presence supplies every need. When he is defenseless, God is the helper (Ps. 94:16–17; 2 Tim. 4:16–17). When he slips, God is his loving support (Ps. 94:18; 1 Sam. 20:3). When he is anxious, God is his consolation (Ps. 94:19; 2 Cor. 1:3–5). And when he despairs of justice, God promises total war on wickedness at the Great Day (Ps. 94:20–23; Rev. 11:18). God's attributes perfectly match our need. And these attributes all find perfect fulfillment in his Son, Jesus Christ our Lord (Heb. 1:3).

Psalm 95 God's grace as "the rock of our salvation" (v. 1) provokes the believer to joyful and humble worship. The first sign of joyful worship is singing, which expresses the full range of human emotion, especially love (vv. 1–2; Eph. 5:19–21; Col. 3:16). Humble prayer also characterizes godly worship. Kneeling (Ps. 95:6) is a common posture for prayer in the Bible because it is a physical expression of humility before someone great, especially one greater than demons (v. 3), creation (vv. 4–5), and all people (v. 6). The believer bows to God out of a heart overflowing with gratefulness for who God is and what he has done (vv. 3–7; Eph. 3:14).

At the same time, God will not be presumed upon by our adopting any practice that becomes superficial or superstitious. The psalmist reminds the worshipers of the "test" at Massah, when the Israelites grumbled that they had no water (Ps. 95:7b–11). Commenting on this passage, the writer of Hebrews interprets "today" to mean whenever someone hears the call to repentance and "rest" as referring to eternal salvation through Jesus Christ (Heb. 3:7–15; 4:3–7).

The opposite of repentance (i.e., turning from sin to God) is going "astray" (Ps. 95:10). Straying begins with discontentment and ends in direct disobedience. Straying sinners do the opposite of what they know God commands. In contrast, joyful obedience results from worshiping God as the great King, Maker, and Shepherd. And it will

4 For [d]great is the LORD, and [e]greatly to be praised;
he is to be feared above [f]all gods.
5 For all the gods of the peoples are worthless idols,
but the LORD [g]made the heavens.
6 Splendor and majesty are before him;
[h]strength and beauty are in his sanctuary.

7 Ascribe to the LORD, O [i]families of the peoples,
[j]ascribe to the LORD glory and strength!
8 Ascribe to the LORD [k]the glory due his name;
bring [l]an offering, and [m]come into his courts!
9 Worship the LORD in [n]the splendor of holiness;[1]
[o]tremble before him, all the earth!

10 Say among the nations, [p]"The LORD reigns!
Yes, the world is established; it shall never be moved;
he will [q]judge the peoples with equity."

11 Let [r]the heavens be glad, and let [s]the earth rejoice;
let [t]the sea roar, and all that fills it;
12 let [u]the field exult, and everything in it!
Then shall all [v]the trees of the forest sing for joy
13 before the LORD, for he comes,
for he comes [w]to judge the earth.
He will judge the world in righteousness,
and the peoples in his faithfulness.

The LORD Reigns

97 [x]The LORD reigns, [y]let the earth rejoice;
let the many [z]coastlands be glad!
2 [a]Clouds and thick darkness are all around him;
[b]righteousness and justice are the foundation of his throne.
3 [c]Fire goes before him
and burns up his adversaries all around.
4 His [d]lightnings light up the world;
the earth sees and [e]trembles.

[1] Or *in holy attire*

be the remembrance of his abundant kindness that will melt ungrateful hearts (cf. v. 7; Rom. 2:4)—kindness that finds supreme expression in the sending of his own Son in the fullness of time.

Psalm 96 That the good news crosses all geographical borders and will infiltrate every people group is reason enough to rejoice all over the world (vv. 1–3; Rom. 16:26–27). David sang this hymn as he brought the ark back to Jerusalem from Obed-edom (1 Chron. 16:23–34). His "new song" (Ps. 96:1) announces to his Jewish congregation that God is revealing his glory to the nations in a new way. The difference from this and the "new song" in the New Testament is the latter's clarity that the message of the cross will "turn" the world "upside down" (Rev. 5:9–10; Acts 17:3, 6), but both songs make clear God's intention to claim the nations beyond Israel.

God commands all people to believe; he does not beg, because he has no competitors (Rom. 1:5). Idols are literally "no-things" (Ps. 96:5–6). Not only is God the only deity, he is the most impressive of all conceivable alternatives (Isa. 8:7; 40:5). God's "glory" comprises his proactive and powerful presence in the world (Ps. 19:1; Ezek. 28:22). These qualities demand exclusive worship and produce heroic disciples (Ps. 96:7, 9; Acts 7:2, 55).

The Lord's sovereignty over creation demands material surrender, too. By bringing offerings, the worshiper acknowledges that all possessions come as gifts from the Lord and therefore portions should be returned in gratitude (Ps. 96:8–9, 11–12; 2 Cor. 9:6–15). The glory of God's sovereign grace also compels the worshiper to offer himself as a testimony to the world (Ps. 96:3–6; 1 Thess. 1:4–5). After all, Jesus Christ offered himself up for *us*. In calm assurance that our victorious Lord will have dominion, we will be emboldened to witness (Ps. 96:10–13; Acts 1:7–8).

Psalm 97 Because God is the good King, believers must rejoice in his reign by loving righteousness and hating sin (vv. 1–2). God's standards flow from his character and are revealed through his Word. The fire, lightning, and earthquake at Sinai not only accompanied the Ten Commandments to reveal God's holy glory; they also confirmed Moses as a prophet (vv. 3–6; Ex. 19:9–20; Acts 7:37–38).

4[d] See Ps. 48:1 [e] Ps. 18:3 [f] See Ps. 95:3
5[g] Ps. 115:15; Isa. 42:5; 44:24; Jer. 10:12
6[h] [Ps. 78:61]
7[i] Ps. 22:27 [j] See Ps. 29:1
8[k] Ps. 29:2 [l] [Ps. 45:12]; See Ps. 68:29; 72:10 [m] Ps. 100:4
9[n] See Ps. 29:2 [o] Ps. 114:7
10[p] See Ps. 93:1 [q] ver. 13; See Ps. 9:8; 58:11
11[r] See Ps. 69:34 [s] Ps. 97:1 [t] Ps. 98:7
12[u] [Isa. 35:1] [v] [Isa. 55:12]
13[w] See Isa. 11:1-9
Psalm 97
1[x] See Ps. 93:1 [y] Ps. 96:11 [z] See Ps. 72:10
2[a] Ex. 19:9; Deut. 4:11; 5:22; 1 Kgs. 8:12; See Ps. 18:11 [b] Ps. 89:14
3[c] See Ps. 21:9; 50:3
4[d] Ps. 77:18 [e] [Ps. 96:9]

5 The mountains [f]melt like [g]wax before
the LORD,
before [h]the Lord of all the earth.

6 [i]The heavens proclaim his righteousness,
and all [j]the peoples see his glory.
7 All worshipers of images are [k]put to shame,
who make their boast in [l]worthless idols;
[m]worship him, all you gods!

8 Zion hears and [n]is glad,
and the daughters of Judah rejoice,
because of your judgments, O LORD.
9 For you, O LORD, are [o]most high over all the earth;
you are exalted far above [p]all gods.

10 O you who love the LORD, [q]hate evil!
He [r]preserves the lives of his [s]saints;
he [t]delivers them from the hand of the wicked.
11 [u]Light [v]is sown[1] for the righteous,
and joy for the upright in heart.
12 [w]Rejoice in the LORD, O you righteous,
and [x]give thanks to his holy name!

Make a Joyful Noise to the LORD

98

A PSALM.

Oh sing to the LORD [y]a new song,
for he has done [z]marvelous things!
His [a]right hand and his holy arm
have worked salvation for him.
2 The LORD has [b]made known his salvation;
he has [c]revealed his righteousness in
[d]the sight of the nations.
3 He has [e]remembered his [f]steadfast love
and faithfulness
to the house of Israel.
All [g]the ends of the earth have seen
[h]the salvation of our God.

4 [i]Make a joyful noise to the LORD, all the earth;
[j]break forth into joyous song and sing praises!
5 Sing praises to the LORD with the lyre,
with the lyre and the [k]sound of melody!

[1] Most Hebrew manuscripts; one Hebrew manuscript, Septuagint, Syriac, Jerome *Light dawns*

5[f] Nah. 1:5; [Judg. 5:5] [g] See Ps. 68:2 [h] Josh. 3:11
6[i] See Ps. 50:6 [j] Isa. 40:5; 66:18; [Ps. 96:3]
7[k] Isa. 42:17; 44:9 [l] Ps. 96:5 [m] Heb. 1:6
8[n] Ps. 48:11
9[o] See Ps. 83:18 [p] See Ps. 95:3
10[q] Prov. 8:13; Amos 5:15; Rom. 12:9; See Ps. 34:14 [r] Ps. 31:23; 37:28; 121:4; 145:20; Prov. 2:8 [s] See Ps. 30:4 [t] Dan. 3:28; 6:27; Acts 12:11
11[u] Ps. 112:4; 118:27; Prov. 4:18 [v] [Prov. 11:18; Hos. 10:12; James 3:18]
12[w] See Ps. 32:11 [x] See Ps. 30:4

Psalm 98
1[y] See Ps. 33:3 [z] [Ps. 96:3]; Ps. 72:18 [a] [Ex. 15:6; Luke 1:51]; See Job 40:14
2[b] Isa. 49:6; 52:10; Luke 2:30, 31; [Isa. 59:16; 63:5] [c] Isa. 62:2; Rom. 3:25, 26 [d] Ps. 96:2, 3
3[e] Luke 1:54, 72 [f] See Ps. 36:5 [g] Ps. 22:27 [h] ver. 2
4[i] See Ps. 66:1 [j] Isa. 44:23
5[k] Isa. 51:3

That experience defined Moses' authority for the rest of his ministry. When his teaching was questioned, he appealed to Sinai (Deut. 4:9, 12, 33–36). When disputes had to be settled, Moses entered the tabernacle where the ark of the covenant was, and the cloud hovered overhead (Num. 12:5, 8; 16:19). When he left, his face shone as well. All of those signs were reminiscent of Sinai, which verified Moses' prophecies for all time, including that of the Prophet who would complete God's revelation to his people (Deut. 18:15–22; Acts 3:22–26). In grace, God made plain to his people his authority so that they did not doubt him and would not doubt the Word that would guide them in life and for eternity (Ps. 97:10).

Since God's reign is spiritual, it is not yet completely revealed to our eyes (Heb. 2:9; 1 Cor. 15:24). God is not slow in keeping his promises, but we are often impatient (2 Pet. 3:8–9). Therefore, believers must not lose heart (Titus 2:13; 2 Cor. 4:16). While the believer waits for the consummation, his love for God is manifested by hating evil and rejoicing in the Lord by praise of his holiness (Ps. 97:10–12; Rom. 12:9). As we walk with God, "light is sown" (Ps. 97:11)—that is, the radiant resplendence of what we will one day be is ignited in an unstoppable process.

Psalm 98 God will utterly save his people (vv. 1–3; Rom. 11:11–12). The new song announced in Psalm 96 is "remixed" here with a reminder that Israel is an essential partner in God's missional expansion to the Gentiles (Ps. 67:1–2). God reiterates that he is conducting a great international campaign of redemption. He will make his salvation known even to the Gentiles, while remembering his loving kindness to the Jews. As Paul the apostle would later say, "Oh, the depth of the riches and wisdom and knowledge of God!" (Rom. 11:33).

Their mission strategy will be unconventional. God will conquer the nations through the worship of his people (Ps. 98:4–6). As others see the enthusiasm, energy, and sense of expectation, they will be attracted to God's reality (1 Cor. 14:24–25). But if they are going to be convinced of God's greatness, the redeemed must worship with glad enthusiasm. The shouts of Old Testament worshipers could sometimes be heard far away (2 Chron. 29:25–30; Ezek. 3:10–13).

6 With [l]trumpets and the sound of [m]the
horn
[l]make a joyful noise before the King,
the LORD!

7 [n]Let the sea roar, and [o]all that fills it;
[o]the world and those who dwell in it!
8 Let the rivers [p]clap their hands;
let [q]the hills sing for joy together
9 before the LORD, for he comes
to [r]judge the earth.
He will judge the world with righteousness,
and the peoples with equity.

The LORD Our God Is Holy

99 [s]The LORD reigns; [t]let the peoples
tremble!
He [u]sits enthroned upon the cherubim; [v]let the earth quake!
2 The LORD is [w]great in Zion;
he is [x]exalted over all the peoples.
3 Let them praise your [y]great and awesome name!
[z]Holy is he!

4 [a]The King in his might [b]loves justice.[1]
You have established equity;
you have executed justice
and righteousness in Jacob.
5 [c]Exalt the LORD our God;
[d]worship at his [e]footstool!
[z]Holy is he!

6 [f]Moses and Aaron were among his
[g]priests,
Samuel also was among those who
[h]called upon his name.
They [i]called to the LORD, and he
answered them.
7 In [j]the pillar of the cloud he spoke to
them;
they [k]kept his testimonies
and the statute that he gave them.

8 O LORD our God, you answered them;
you were [l]a forgiving God to them,
but [m]an avenger of their wrongdoings.
9 Exalt the LORD our God,
and worship at his [n]holy mountain;
for the LORD our God is holy!

[1] Or *The might of the King loves justice*

Not only do God's people testify to the reality of the fall and redemption, the creation does as well (Ps. 98:7–9). The world was crafted by God to be the arena of redemption (Eph. 3:9–10). Nature then helps tell the story and will someday announce when it is complete (Rom. 8:19–23). God will fully restore this fallen world, all through the work of his Son.

Psalm 99 God's holiness means he is superior to all other creatures in his being and sovereignty (vv. 5, 9; Isa. 6:3; Rev. 4:8). But that holiness brings redemptive benefits to true worshipers. His enthronement "upon the cherubim" (Ps. 99:1) means mercy for those who trust him for salvation. With a reference to the mercy seat, which rested just under the wings of angels atop the ark of the covenant, the psalmist reminds the singer of that place where blood made yearly atonement for lawbreakers (v. 1; Lev. 16:15–16; Luke 18:13; 1 Cor. 11:25). Furthermore, God's holy reign extends to his "footstool," the earth (Ps. 99:5; Isa. 66:1). Thus God is not only transcendent but also present and active in his world, as symbolized by the pillar of cloud that guided Israel in the wilderness and descended in glory upon the temple at its dedication (Ps. 99:7; 1 Kings 8:10–13; 1 Cor. 10:1–4). And believers can be glad that God is actively present, because with might he executes loving justice (Ps. 99:4; 1 Kings 10:9; cf. Luke 11:42).

Prayer is the major means through which God executes his decrees on earth. So the psalmist provides examples of men who received exceptional answers to their petitions (Ps. 99:6–7). Each example prepares us to understand the mediating work of Christ. God granted the revelation of his glory to Moses, who would intercede for the people (Ex. 33:12–23; 34:6–7; Heb. 9:24). Aaron saved the Israelites by mediation (Num. 16:41–50; 1 Tim. 2:5). And Samuel prayed down terror on the Philistines (1 Sam. 7; Rev. 6:10). So how does a holy God answer the prayers of sinful men? He reigns from a holy mountain, the place of atonement (Ps. 99:8–9; Heb. 12:22–24). And this atonement finds ultimate expression in the final Mediator, Jesus himself, who reconciles God to humanity with his own blood.

6[l] Num. 10:10; 1 Chr. 15:24 [m] 2 Chr. 15:14 [l] [See ver. 4 above]
7[n] Ps. 96:11 [o] Ps. 24:1
8[p] Isa. 55:12; [Ps. 93:3] [q] Ps. 89:12
9[r] Ps. 96:13; See Ps. 58:11

Psalm 99
1[s] Ps. 93:1; See 1 Chr. 16:31 [t] [Ps. 96:9] [u] See Ps. 80:1 [v] [Isa. 24:19, 20]
2[w] [Isa. 24:23] [x] Ps. 113:4; [Ps. 92:8; 93:4]
3[y] [Ps. 111:9; Deut. 28:58] [z] Josh. 24:19; Isa. 6:3; Rev. 15:4
4[a] [ver. 1] [b] Ps. 11:7; Isa. 61:8; [Job 36:5-7]
5[c] Ps. 107:32; 118:28; Ex. 15:2; Isa. 25:1 [d] Ps. 132:7; 1 Chr. 28:2 [e] Isa. 60:13; Lam. 2:1; Ezek. 43:7 [z] [See ver. 3 above]
6[f] [Jer. 15:1] [g] See Ex. 24:6-8; 40:22-27; Lev. 8:1-30 [h] 1 Sam. 7:9; 12:18; See Ps. 105:1 [i] Ps. 106:23; Ex. 14:15; 17:11, 12; 32:30; Num. 12:13; 16:48; Deut. 9:18
7[j] Ex. 33:9; Num. 12:5 [k] [Ps. 105:28]
8[l] Num. 14:20 [m] Ex. 32:35; Num. 20:12; Deut. 9:20; [Jer. 46:28]
9[n] See Ps. 2:6

His Steadfast Love Endures Forever

100 A Psalm for [o]giving thanks.
[p]Make a joyful noise to the Lord,
all the earth!
2 [q]Serve the Lord with gladness!
[r]Come into his presence with singing!

3 Know that [s]the Lord, he is God!
It is he who [t]made us, and [u]we are his;[1]
we are his [v]people, and [w]the sheep of
his pasture.

4 [x]Enter his gates with thanksgiving,
and his [y]courts with praise!
Give thanks to him; [z]bless his name!

5 [a]For the Lord is good;
his steadfast love endures forever,
and his [b]faithfulness to all generations.

I Will Walk with Integrity

101 A Psalm of David.
I will sing of [c]steadfast love and
justice;
to you, O Lord, I will make music.
2 I will [d]ponder the way [e]that is blameless.
Oh when will you [f]come to me?
I will [g]walk with [h]integrity of heart
within my house;
3 I will not set before my eyes
anything [i]that is worthless.
I hate the work of those who [j]fall away;
it shall not cling to me.
4 [k]A perverse heart shall be far from me;
I will [l]know nothing of evil.

5 Whoever slanders his neighbor [m]secretly
I will [n]destroy.
Whoever has a [o]haughty look and an
[p]arrogant heart
I will not endure.

6 I will look with favor on the faithful in
the land,
that they may dwell with me;
he who walks in [q]the way that is blameless
shall minister to me.

7 No one who [r]practices deceit
shall dwell in my house;
no one who utters lies
shall [s]continue before my eyes.

[1] Or *and not we ourselves*

Psalm 100
[o][Ps. 50:14]
1 [p]See Ps. 66:1
2 [q][Ps. 2:11] [r][Ps. 95:2]
3 [s]1 Kgs. 18:39 [t]See Ps. 95:6; Job 10:3, 8 [u]Isa. 43:1 [v]Ezek. 34:30 [w]See Ps. 74:1
4 [x][Ps. 66:13] [y]Ps. 96:8 [z]Ps. 96:2
5 [a]Ps. 25:8; 106:1; 119:68; 2 Chr. 5:13; Ezra 3:11; Jer. 33:11; Nah. 1:7 [b]See Ps. 36:5

Psalm 101
1 [c][Ex. 34:7]
2 [d][Ps. 4:4] [e]Ps. 119:1; Prov. 11:20; [Matt. 5:48] [f][Ex. 20:24; John 14:23] [g]1 Kgs. 9:4 [h]Ps. 78:72
3 [i]Deut. 15:9 [j]See Ps. 40:4
4 [k]Prov. 11:20; 17:20 [l][1 Cor. 5:11]
5 [m]Ps. 15:3 [n]ver. 8 [o]Ps. 18:27; 131:1; Prov. 6:17; 21:4; 30:13 [p]Prov. 16:5
6 [q]Ps. 119:1; Prov. 11:20; [Matt. 5:48]
7 [r]Ps. 52:2 [s]Ps. 102:28

Psalm 100 Providing seven ways to give thanks, the psalmist exhorts worshipers to be grateful at all times. The most obvious expression of gratitude is singing, which is the joyful expression of love and overflows from a liberated heart (vv. 1–2; Isa. 51:11; Col. 3:13–16). The redeemed also act gratefully when they pursue knowledge of God through his Word and works (Ps. 100:3; Rom. 16:25–27). Knowing God not only humbles dependent creatures, it heartens them to realize that he is willing to make himself known, and ultimately he does so through Jesus Christ, revealing our God as a Father and Good Shepherd (cf. Ps. 100:3, 5; Matt. 6:9; John 10:14).

The psalmist then commands God's people to express their gratitude (Ps. 100:2, 4). In Hebrew there is no distinction between serving in church or at work. The same word describes worship in every place (Col. 3:17). All of life in every realm is an opportunity to "give thanks to him" and "bless his name" (Ps. 100:4).

The Father also provides reasons for his commands. The most obvious is that he is good in all his roles. He is the good Creator who endowed us with his image, which requires treating every person with dignity (v. 3; James 3:9). His universal rule reminds us of his protection (Ex. 6:7; Isa. 3:15), calls us to bold prayer (Isa. 64:9; John 17:6–9), and motivates us to discipleship as those purchased at a great price (Titus 2:14). That purchase was made out of the "steadfast love" that epitomizes God's character and which finds full expression in the death and resurrection of Jesus. He is the Good Shepherd who cares for his sheep all the days of their lives (Ps. 100:5; 23:6; John 10:11; Rev. 7:17).

Psalm 101 Book 4 of the Psalter (Psalms 90–106) contains two psalms of David: Psalms 101 and 103. Psalm 101 is a royal psalm that tells of the Greater Son of David who will reign with righteousness and justice. Because of the perfect righteousness of this King (vv. 2–4), his commitment to live in peace with his own people (v. 6), and the complete vanquishing of God's enemies he will bring about (vv. 5, 7–8), this psalm must refer ultimately and only fully to Jesus. He is the King from the line of David to fulfill all that the Messiah was to do.

8 [t]Morning by morning I will destroy
all the wicked in the land,
[u]cutting off all [v]the evildoers
from [w]the city of the LORD.

Do Not Hide Your Face from Me

102

A PRAYER OF ONE AFFLICTED, WHEN HE IS [x]FAINT AND [y]POURS OUT HIS COMPLAINT BEFORE THE LORD.

1 [z]Hear my prayer, O LORD;
let my cry [a]come to you!
2 [b]Do not hide your face from me
in [c]the day of my distress!
[d]Incline your ear to me;
[e]answer me speedily [f]in the day when
I call!

3 For my days [g]pass away like smoke,
and my [h]bones burn like a furnace.
4 My heart is [i]struck down like grass and
[j]has withered;
I [k]forget to eat my bread.
5 Because of my loud groaning
my [l]bones cling to my flesh.
6 I am like [m]a desert owl of the wilderness,
like an owl[1] of the waste places;
7 I [n]lie awake;
I am like a lonely sparrow on the
housetop.
8 All the day my enemies taunt me;
those who [o]deride me [p]use my name
for a curse.
9 For I eat ashes like bread
and [q]mingle tears with my drink,
10 because of your indignation and anger;
for you have [r]taken me up and
[s]thrown me down.
11 My days are like [t]an evening shadow;
I [j]wither away like grass.

12 But you, O LORD, are [u]enthroned forever;
you [v]are remembered throughout all
generations.
13 You will [w]arise and have [x]pity on Zion;
it is the time to favor her;
[y]the appointed time has come.
14 For your servants hold her [z]stones dear
and have pity on her dust.
15 Nations will [a]fear the name of the LORD,
and all [b]the kings of the earth will
fear your glory.
16 For the LORD [c]builds up Zion;
he [d]appears in his glory;
17 he [e]regards the prayer of the destitute
and does not despise their prayer.

18 Let this be [f]recorded for [g]a generation to
come,
so that [h]a people yet to be created may
praise the LORD:

[1] The precise identity of these birds is uncertain

The king opens the psalm pledging to sing and make music to God (v. 1). He will extol the "steadfast love and justice" of the Lord (v. 1), which anticipates the incarnation of the final King who comes displaying the "grace and truth" of his Father (John 1:14, 17). Christ, the true King, will embody the very character here extolled, all for the purpose of saving his people and conquering his enemies. The perfection of his own life surpasses any other person, including David himself. This King will display "integrity of heart" (Ps. 101:2) while declaring that he will not set before his eyes "anything that is worthless" (v. 3) and will "know nothing of evil" (v. 4).

Here is one, then, who lives a perfect life, sinless and obedient, which qualifies him to save his people from their sins. But he not only will save and purify his people (v. 7; cf. Eph. 5:25–27), he also will judge the wicked (Ps. 101:5, 7–8; cf. Psalm 2). Only Christ, the perfect Savior and Judge, can fulfill the vision of this glorious psalm.

Psalm 102 This psalm is an individual lament that captures the weakness, plight, and distress God's people often feel. Such weakness is in contrast to the eternal greatness of God, who delights to pledge himself to weak and needy believers. The confidence in God expressed by Paul amid his weakness—"when I am weak, then I am strong" (2 Cor. 12:10)—echoes the struggle and hope of this psalm.

The psalmist begins with a plea for the Lord to hear his cry and come to his aid (Ps. 102:1–2). Great internal distresses, even despair, mark his experiences. Pain, groaning, and sleeplessness (vv. 3–7) are coupled with the taunting and derision of his enemies (vv. 8–11), leaving him almost utterly without hope. But then the psalmist contemplates the greatness of God who has promised to be with his people in every

8[t] [Ps. 73:14] [u] Ps. 75:10 [v] Ps. 94:4 [w] Ps. 48:1, 8; [Isa. 52:1]
Psalm 102 [x] Ps. 61:2 [y] Ps. 142:2
1[z] Ps. 39:12 [a] Ps. 18:6; Ex. 2:23; 1 Sam. 9:16
2[b] See Ps. 27:9 [c] See Ps. 18:6 [d] See Ps. 31:2 [e] See Ps. 69:17 [f] Ps. 56:9
3[g] [James 4:14]; See Ps. 37:20 [h] Job 30:30; Lam. 1:13; See Ps. 31:10
4[i] Ps. 121:6 [j] Ps. 37:2; Isa. 40:7; [James 1:10, 11] [k] [1 Sam. 1:7; 2 Sam. 12:17; 1 Kgs. 21:4; Job 33:20]
5[l] See Job 19:20
6[m] Isa. 34:11; Zeph. 2:14; [Job 30:29]
7[n] Ps. 77:4
8[o] [Acts 26:11] [p] Isa. 65:15; Jer. 29:22
9[q] See Ps. 42:3
10[r] Ezek. 3:12, 14 [s] Ps. 51:11
11[t] Ps. 109:23; 144:4; Job 8:9 [j] [See ver. 4 above]
12[u] ver. 26; See Ps. 9:7 [v] Ps. 135:13; Ex. 3:15
13[w] Ps. 68:1 [x] Isa. 60:10; Zech. 1:12 [y] Ps. 75:2; Jer. 29:10; Dan. 9:2; [Isa. 40:2]
14[z] Neh. 4:2; [Lam. 4:1]
15[a] 1 Kgs. 8:43; Isa. 59:19 [b] Ps. 138:4; Isa. 60:3
16[c] Ps. 147:2 [d] Isa. 60:1, 2
17[e] Neh. 1:6, 11 **18**[f] [Deut. 31:19; Rom. 15:4; 1 Cor. 10:1] [g] Ps. 48:13; See Ps. 78:4, 6 [h] See Ps. 22:31; [Isa. 43:21]

19 that he [i]looked down from his holy
height;
from heaven the LORD looked at the
earth,
20 to hear [j]the groans of the prisoners,
to set free [k]those who were doomed to
die,
21 that they may [l]declare in Zion the name
of the LORD,
and in Jerusalem his praise,
22 when [m]peoples gather together,
and kingdoms, to worship the LORD.

23 He has broken my strength in midcourse;
he [n]has shortened my days.
24 "O my God," [o]I say, "take me not away
in the midst of my days—
[p]you whose years endure
throughout all generations!"

25 [q]Of old you laid the foundation of the
earth,
and [r]the heavens are the work of your
hands.
26 [s]They will perish, but [t]you will remain;
they will all wear out like a garment.
You will change them like a robe, and
they will pass away,
27 but [u]you are the same, and your years
have no end.
28 [v]The children of your servants [w]shall
dwell secure;
[x]their offspring shall be established
before you.

Bless the LORD, O My Soul

103 OF DAVID.
[y]Bless the LORD, O my soul,
and all that is within me,
bless his holy name!
2 [y]Bless the LORD, O my soul,
and [z]forget not all his benefits,
3 who [a]forgives all your iniquity,
who [b]heals all your diseases,
4 who [c]redeems your life from the pit,
who [d]crowns you with steadfast love
and mercy,
5 who [e]satisfies you with good
so that your youth is renewed like [f]the
eagle's.

6 The LORD works [g]righteousness
and justice for all who are oppressed.
7 He made known his [h]ways to Moses,
his [i]acts to the people of Israel.
8 The LORD is [j]merciful and gracious,
slow to anger and abounding in
steadfast love.
9 [k]He will not always chide,
nor will he [l]keep his anger forever.

19[i] See Ps. 11:4
20[j] Ps. 79:11 [k] Ps. 79:11
21[l] See Ps. 22:22
22[m] [Isa. 45:14]; See Ps. 22:27
23[n] Ps. 89:45
24[o] [Isa. 38:10] [p] Ps. 90:2; Job 36:26; Hab. 1:12
25[q] Gen. 1:1; 2:1; Cited Heb. 1:10 [r] See Ps. 96:5
26[s] Isa. 34:4; 51:6; Matt. 24:35; 2 Pet. 3:7, 10, 12; Rev. 20:11; 21:1; Cited Heb. 1:11, 12 [t] ver. 12
27[u] Isa. 41:4; 48:12; Mal. 3:6; [Heb. 13:8; James 1:17]
28[v] See Ps. 69:36 [w] Ps. 37:29 [x] Ps. 112:2

Psalm 103
1[y] ver. 22; Ps. 104:1
2[y] [See ver. 1 above] [z] Deut. 6:12; 8:11
3[a] Ex. 34:7; Isa. 33:24; Matt. 9:2; Mark 2:5; [Luke 7:47] [b] Ps. 107:20; 147:3; Ex. 15:26; [Matt. 8:17]
4[c] See Ps. 56:13 [d] [Ps. 5:12]
5[e] Ps. 107:9 [f] Isa. 40:31
6[g] Ps. 146:7
7[h] Ex. 33:13; [Ps. 25:4] [i] [Ps. 78:11; Ex. 34:10]
8[j] See Ps. 86:15
9[k] Isa. 57:16 [l] Ps. 30:5; Jer. 3:5, 12; Mic. 7:18

generation (v. 12). God has covenanted with Zion, the people of Israel (vv. 13–16), so that his people can know that God will not fail to come to their aid. With renewed hope, the weary psalmist declares, "he regards the prayer of the destitute" (v. 17), so even generations yet future may also find their hope in this merciful and saving God (vv. 18–24). The constancy and faithfulness of God is an assured reality. Whereas even the apparently stable earth and heavens can perish (vv. 25–26), more permanent and fixed even than these is God himself. He is the same, and his years have no end (v. 27). Hebrews 1:10–12 quotes these verses (Ps. 102:25–27) and applies them to Christ, through whom God created (cf. Heb. 1:2) and redeemed (cf. Heb. 2:17–18) the world.

Believers of all generations may put their hope in Christ, who is the same yesterday, today, and forever (cf. Heb. 13:8). He is their salvation. He is their hope. In him the people of God "shall dwell secure" (Ps. 102:28).

Psalm 103 This hymn of praise reflects on the faithfulness and goodness of God, who delivered Israel from Egypt under Moses (vv. 6–7). It calls people to praise God for his continued acts of merciful forgiveness and sustaining grace. The psalm's theme is announced at the outset: "Bless the LORD, O my soul, and forget not all his benefits" (v. 2). Indeed, these benefits are astonishing! Everything from physical healing, prosperity, and well-being, to spiritual forgiveness, peace, and hope, are grounded in the constancy of God's covenant faithfulness to his people (vv. 3–5). Even when God disciplines his children, they can know that such punishment will give way to forgiveness and restoration. "He does not deal with us according to our sins" (v. 10) but instead casts our sins as far away as the east is from the west (vv. 11–12). After all, our heavenly Father knows our frame (v. 14) and is eager to show compassion to all who rely wholly upon his grace (v. 13).

10 He does not deal with us [m]according to
our sins,
nor repay us according to our iniquities.
11 For [n]as high as the heavens are above the
earth,
so great is his [o]steadfast love toward
[p]those who fear him;
12 as far as the east is from the west,
so far does he [q]remove our transgressions from us.
13 As [r]a father shows compassion to his
children,
so the LORD shows compassion [p]to
those who fear him.
14 For he knows our frame;[1]
he [s]remembers that we are dust.

15 As for man, his days are like [t]grass;
he flourishes like [u]a flower of the field;
16 for [v]the wind passes over it, and [w]it is
gone,
and [x]its place knows it no more.
17 But [y]the steadfast love of the LORD is
from everlasting to everlasting
on [p]those who fear him,
and his righteousness to [z]children's
children,
18 to those who [a]keep his covenant
and [b]remember to do his commandments.
19 The LORD has [c]established his throne in
the heavens,
and his [d]kingdom rules over all.

20 Bless the LORD, O you [e]his angels,
you [f]mighty ones who [g]do his word,
obeying the voice of his word!
21 Bless the LORD, all his [h]hosts,
his [i]ministers, who do his will!
22 [j]Bless the LORD, all his works,
in all places of his dominion.
[k]Bless the LORD, O my soul!

O LORD My God, You Are Very Great

104 [l]Bless the LORD, O my soul!
O LORD my God, you are [m]very
great!
[n]You are clothed with splendor and majesty,
2 covering yourself with light as with a
garment,
[o]stretching out the heavens [p]like a tent.
3 He [q]lays the beams of his [r]chambers on
the waters;
he makes [s]the clouds his chariot;
he rides on [t]the wings of the wind;
4 he [u]makes his messengers winds,
his [v]ministers [w]a flaming fire.

5 He [x]set the earth on its foundations,
so that it should never be moved.
6 You [y]covered it with the deep as with a
garment;
the waters stood above the mountains.
7 At [z]your rebuke they fled;
at [a]the sound of your thunder they
[b]took to flight.
8 The mountains rose, the valleys sank
down
to the place that you [c]appointed for
them.
9 You set [d]a boundary that they may not
pass,
so that they [e]might not again cover
the earth.

10 You make springs gush forth in the valleys;
they flow between the hills;

[1] Or *knows how we are formed*

Although our lives are frail and fleeting (vv. 15–16), God and his love are from everlasting (v. 17). God has promised to bless those who fear his name, and nothing can hinder the accomplishment of his will (vv. 18–19). In light of such magnificent mercy and such covenant faithfulness, all of creation should stand in awe and give praise to his name (vv. 20–22).

Psalm 104 God is worthy of praise and glory in part because of the splendor and variety of the creation he has made and which he sustains. The created order serves, as it were, to clothe God and provide for him a theatre suitable for the display of his majesty, beauty, and glory (vv. 1–4). Creation is also the object of God's meticulous (v. 14) and ominous (v. 32) provision, protection, and governance.

10[m] Ezra 9:13
11[n] See Ps. 36:5 [o] Ps. 117:2 [p] ver. 13, 17; Luke 1:50
12[q] [Isa. 38:17; 43:25; Mic. 7:19]
13[r] Mal. 3:17 [p] [See ver. 11 above]
14[s] Ps. 78:39
15[t] Ps. 90:5 [u] See Job 14:2
16[v] Isa. 40:7 [w] Ps. 37:36 [x] See Job 7:10
17[y] Ps. 25:6 [p] [See ver. 11 above] [z] Ex. 20:5, 6
18[a] Deut. 7:9 [b] Ps. 19:8
19[c] Ps. 11:4; 93:2 [d] Ps. 47:2; Dan. 4:17
20[e] Ps. 148:2; [Luke 2:13]

[f] Ps. 78:25 [g] Matt. 6:10 **21**[h] Gen. 32:2; Josh. 5:14; 1 Kgs. 22:19 [i] Ps. 104:4; Dan. 7:10; Heb. 1:14 **22**[j] Ps. 145:10 [k] ver. 1, 2 **Psalm 104** **1**[l] Ps. 103:1, 2, 22 [m] See 2 Sam. 7:22 [n] Ps. 93:1; Job 40:10; [Job 37:22] **2**[o] See Job 9:8 [p] Isa. 40:22 **3**[q] Amos 9:6 [r] ver. 13 [s] Isa. 19:1 [t] Ps. 18:10; 2 Sam. 22:11 **4**[u] Cited Heb. 1:7; [Ps. 148:8] [v] Ps. 103:21 [w] [2 Kgs. 1:10; 2:11] **5**[x] Ps. 24:2; 89:11; 136:6; See Job 38:4 **6**[y] Gen. 7:19 **7**[z] Ps. 18:15; [Ps. 106:9; Gen. 1:9; 8:1, 5; Matt. 8:26] [a] Ps. 77:18 [b] Ps. 48:5 **8**[c] [Job 38:8, 10, 11] **9**[d] See Job 26:10 [e] See Gen. 9:11-16

11 they [f]give drink to every beast of the field;
the wild donkeys quench their thirst.
12 Beside them the birds of the heavens dwell;
they sing among the branches.
13 [g]From your lofty abode you [h]water the mountains;
the earth is satisfied with the fruit of your work.

14 You cause [i]the grass to grow for the livestock
and [j]plants for man to cultivate,
that he may bring forth [k]food from the earth
15 and [l]wine to gladden the heart of man,
[m]oil to make his face shine
and bread to [n]strengthen man's heart.

16 The trees of the LORD are watered abundantly,
[o]the cedars of Lebanon [p]that he planted.
17 In them the birds build their nests;
the stork has her home in the fir trees.
18 The high mountains are for [q]the wild goats;
the rocks are a refuge for [r]the rock badgers.

19 He made the moon to mark the [s]seasons;[1]
the sun knows its time for setting.
20 [t]You make darkness, and it is night,
when all the beasts of the forest creep about.
21 [u]The young lions roar for their prey,
seeking their food from God.
22 When the sun rises, they steal away
and lie down in their [v]dens.
23 [w]Man goes out to his work
and to his labor until the evening.

24 O LORD, how manifold are your works!
In [x]wisdom have you made them all;
the earth is full of your creatures.
25 Here is the sea, great and wide,
[y]which teems with creatures innumerable,
living things both small and great.
26 There go the ships,
and [z]Leviathan, which you formed to [a]play in it.[2]

27 These [b]all look to you,
to [c]give them their food in due season.
28 When you give it to them, they gather it up;
when you [d]open your hand, they are filled with good things.
29 When you [e]hide your face, they are [f]dismayed;
when you [g]take away their breath, they die
and [h]return to their dust.
30 When you [i]send forth your Spirit,[3] they are created,
and you [j]renew the face of the ground.

31 May the glory of the LORD [k]endure forever;
may the LORD [l]rejoice in his works,
32 who looks on the earth and it [m]trembles,
who [n]touches the mountains and they smoke!
33 I will sing to the LORD [o]as long as I live;
I will sing praise to my God while I have being.

[1] Or *the appointed times* (compare Genesis 1:14) [2] Or *you formed to play with* [3] Or *breath*

11[f] [ver. 13]
13[g] ver. 3 [h] [Ps. 65:9; 147:8; Deut. 11:11; Job 5:10; Jer. 10:13; 14:22]
14[i] Ps. 147:8, 9 [j] Gen. 1:11, 29, 30; 3:18; 9:3 [k] Job 28:5; [Ps. 136:25; 147:9]
15[l] Judg. 9:13; Eccles. 10:19; [Prov. 31:6, 7] [m] [Ps. 23:5; Judg. 9:9] [n] [Gen. 18:5]
16[o] See Judg. 9:15 [p] [Num. 24:6]
18[q] See Job 39:1 [r] Lev. 11:5; Prov. 30:26
19[s] Gen. 1:14; Lev. 23:4
20[t] Isa. 45:7
21[u] Job 38:39
22[v] Job 37:8
23[w] [Gen. 3:19]
24[x] Prov. 3:19
25[y] Ps. 69:34

When one recalls the earlier claim in the Psalms that "by the word of the LORD the heavens were made, and by the breath of his mouth all their host" (Ps. 33:6), one comes to see a passage like Psalm 104 as depicting the role of the "Word" of God who creates and sustains all that is created. The New Testament clearly understands the roles of creator and sustainer as applying to Christ, the eternal Son of the Father, "through whom also he created the world" (Heb. 1:2), and the One who "upholds the universe by the word of his power" (Heb. 1:3). This eternal Son was designated by his Father to create all that the Father designed (cf. Col. 1:16) and then to hold together and sustain all that he has made (cf. Col. 1:17). Psalm 104 celebrates the wisdom and love this Creator has over all that he has made and which he sustains. Every aspect of creation exists in complete dependence upon him. Creation, then, provides a basis for the eternal Creator Son to rejoice in the works that he has brought forth (v. 31), while it provides us reason to offer praise and honor to this Christ for his care for us and all of creation (v. 33).

26[z] See Job 41:1 [a] [Job 40:20] **27**[b] Ps. 145:15 [c] [ver. 14]; See Job 36:31 **28**[d] Ps. 145:16 **29**[e] Ps. 30:7; [Deut. 31:17] [f] Job 23:15 [g] See Job 34:14 [h] See Job 10:9 **30**[i] See Job 33:4 [j] [Rev. 21:5] **31**[k] Ps. 72:17 [l] [Gen. 1:31; Prov. 8:31] **32**[m] [Hab. 3:10] [n] Ps. 144:5; Ex. 19:18; [Amos 9:5] **33**[o] See Ps. 63:4

34 May my [p]meditation be pleasing to him,
for I rejoice in the LORD.
35 Let [q]sinners be consumed from the earth,
and let the wicked be no more!
[r]Bless the LORD, O my soul!
[s]Praise the LORD!

Tell of All His Wonderful Works

105 [t]Oh give thanks to the LORD; [u]call upon his name;
[v]make known his deeds among the peoples!
2 Sing to him, sing praises to him;
[w]tell of all his wondrous works!
3 Glory in his holy name;
let the hearts of those who seek the LORD rejoice!
4 Seek the LORD and his [x]strength;
[y]seek his presence continually!
5 Remember the [z]wondrous works that he has done,
his miracles, and [a]the judgments he uttered,
6 O offspring of [b]Abraham, his servant,
children of Jacob, his [c]chosen ones!

7 He is the LORD our God;
his [d]judgments are in all the earth.
8 He [e]remembers his covenant forever,
the word that he commanded, for [f]a thousand generations,
9 [g]the covenant that he made with Abraham,
his [h]sworn promise to Isaac,
10 which he confirmed to [i]Jacob as a statute,
to Israel as an everlasting covenant,
11 saying, [j]"To you I will give the land of Canaan
as [k]your portion for an inheritance."

12 When they were [l]few in number,
of little account, and [m]sojourners in it,
13 wandering from nation to nation,
from one kingdom to another people,
14 he [n]allowed no one to oppress them;
he [o]rebuked kings on their account,
15 saying, [p]"Touch not my anointed ones,
do my prophets no harm!"

16 When he [q]summoned a famine on the land
and [r]broke all supply[1] of bread,
17 he had [s]sent a man ahead of them,
Joseph, who was [t]sold as a slave.
18 His [u]feet were hurt with fetters;
his neck was put in a collar of iron;
19 until [v]what he had said came to pass,
the word of the LORD [w]tested him.
20 [x]The king sent and [y]released him;
the ruler of the peoples set him free;
21 he [z]made him lord of his house
and ruler of all his possessions,
22 to bind[2] his princes at his pleasure
and to teach his elders wisdom.

[1] Hebrew *staff* [2] Septuagint, Syriac, Jerome *instruct*

Psalm 105 We see here the gracious, covenant-keeping God of Israel, who elects, calls, delivers, protects, and cares for his people. Whereas the people are once admonished to "remember the wondrous works that he has done" (v. 5), twice it is said of God that *he* remembers: "he remembers his covenant forever" (v. 8) and "he remembered his holy promise, and Abraham, his servant" (v. 42).

The God who remembered his covenant with his chosen people Israel is the same God who pledges himself always to care for those whom he calls now into the new covenant (see Heb. 10:15–25). His word is sure, his promise is secure, and his commitment to his own people—to love, forgive, protect, and provide for them—endures now through the finished work of Christ, whose death and resurrection secured every good thing for his people forever.

Part of what gives the people of God this confidence is the history of God's constant care for his own people, as Psalm 105 records. When wandering without a permanent home in the Promised Land (vv. 12–15), seeking food to survive during famine (vv. 16–22), living as slaves in Egypt (vv. 23–38), wandering in the wilderness following the exodus (vv. 39–42), and finally fulfilling the promised conquest of the land given them by God (vv. 43–44)—in all these episodes of the life of Israel, the constant commitment and care of God is evident. How right it is, then, to "remember the wondrous works that he has done" (v. 5), and to trust that this same God who has shown his faithfulness will continue to care for his people—who continue to be his own chosen covenant people, through entrance by faith into the new covenant Christ has purchased for us.

34[p] Job 15:4
35[q] See Ps. 37:38 [r] See ver. 1 [s] Ps. 105:45; 106:48; 113:9; 150:6
Psalm 105
1[t] Ps. 106:1; 1 Chr. 16:34; Isa. 12:4; For ver. 1-15, see 1 Chr. 16:8-22 [u] Ps. 99:6; 116:13, 17; [Gen. 4:26] [v] Ps. 145:4, 5, 11, 12
2[w] Ps. 77:12
4[x] See Ps. 78:61 [y] [Ps. 27:8]
5[z] Ps. 77:11; See Ps. 72:18 [a] Ex. 6:6; 7:4
6[b] ver. 42 [c] ver. 43; Ps. 106:5; [Ps. 135:4]
7[d] Isa. 26:9
8[e] ver. 42; Ps. 106:45; 111:5; Luke 1:72 [f] Deut. 7:9
9[g] Gen. 17:2; See Gen. 22:15-18 [h] Gen. 26:3
10[i] Gen. 28:13, 14; 35:11, 12
11[j] Gen. 13:15; 15:18 [k] Ps. 78:55
12[l] Gen. 34:30; Deut. 7:7; 26:5 [m] Heb. 11:9
14[n] [Gen. 35:5] [o] Gen. 12:17; 20:3
15[p] Gen. 20:6, 7; [Gen. 26:11]
16[q] Gen. 41:54; [2 Kgs. 8:1; Hag. 1:11] [r] Lev. 26:26; Isa. 3:1; Ezek. 4:16; [Ps. 104:15]
17[s] Gen. 45:5; 50:20 [t] Gen. 37:28, 36; Acts 7:9
18[u] [Gen. 39:20] **19**[v] Gen. 40:20, 21; 41:53, 54 [w] [Judg. 7:4] **20**[x] Gen. 41:14 [y] Ps. 146:7 **21**[z] Gen. 41:40

23 Then [a]Israel came to Egypt;
Jacob [b]sojourned in [c]the land of Ham.
24 And the LORD [d]made his people very fruitful
and made them stronger than their foes.
25 He [e]turned their hearts to hate his people,
to [f]deal craftily with his servants.

26 He [g]sent Moses, his servant,
and Aaron, [h]whom he had chosen.
27 [i]They performed his signs among them
and miracles in [c]the land of Ham.
28 He [j]sent darkness, and made the land dark;
they [k]did not rebel[1] against his words.
29 He turned their waters into blood
and [l]caused their fish to die.
30 Their land swarmed with frogs,
even in [m]the chambers of their kings.
31 He spoke, and there came [n]swarms of flies,
[o]and gnats throughout their country.
32 He gave them hail for rain,
and fiery [p]lightning bolts through their land.
33 He struck down their vines and fig trees,
and [q]shattered the trees of their country.
34 He spoke, and the [r]locusts came,
young locusts without number,
35 which devoured all the vegetation in their land
and ate up the fruit of their ground.
36 He [s]struck down all the firstborn in their land,
[s]the firstfruits of all their strength.

37 Then he brought out Israel with [t]silver and gold,
and there was none among his tribes who stumbled.
38 [u]Egypt was glad when they departed,
for [v]dread of them had fallen upon it.

39 He [w]spread a cloud for a covering,
and fire to give light by night.
40 [x]They asked, and he [y]brought quail,
and gave them [z]bread from heaven in abundance.
41 He opened the rock, and [a]water gushed out;
it flowed through [b]the desert like a river.
42 For he [c]remembered his holy promise,
and [d]Abraham, his servant.

43 So he brought his people out with joy,
his [d]chosen ones with [e]singing.
44 And he [f]gave them the lands of the nations,
and they took possession of the fruit of the peoples' toil,
45 that they might [g]keep his statutes
and [h]observe his laws.
[i]Praise the LORD!

Give Thanks to the LORD, for He Is Good

106 [i]Praise the LORD!
[j]Oh give thanks to the LORD, [k]for he is good,
[l]for his steadfast love endures forever!
2 Who can utter the mighty deeds of the LORD,
or declare all his praise?
3 Blessed are they who observe justice,
who [m]do righteousness at all times!

[1] Septuagint, Syriac omit *not*

23[a] Gen. 46:6; Acts 7:15 [b] Acts 13:17 [c] Ps. 106:22; [Ps. 78:51]
24[d] Ex. 1:7; Deut. 26:5
25[e] [Ex. 9:12; Rom. 11:8]; See Ex. 1:8-14 [f] Ex. 1:10; Acts 7:19
26[g] Ex. 3:10; 4:12 [h] Num. 16:5; 17:5
27[i] For ver. 27-36, see Ps. 78:43-51 [c] [See ver. 23 above]
28[j] Ex. 10:21-23 [k] Ps. 99:7
29[l] Ex. 7:21
30[m] Ex. 8:3
31[n] Ex. 8:21 [o] Ex. 8:16
32[p] Ex. 9:23
33[q] Ex. 9:25
34[r] See Ex. 10:12-15
36[s] See Ps. 78:51

Psalm 106 This psalm carries forward the historical narrative summarized also in Psalms 78 and 105. This psalm highlights the contrast between the faithfulness of God and the faithlessness of his people. Over and again, although his people turn from him, disobey, rebel, and go after other gods, the covenant God of Israel demonstrates his commitment and steadfast love, even though discipline and judgment sometimes must precede reconciliation and restoration.

God's final word to his people—that is, to his disobedient, wayward people—is not the word of judgment they deserve. Rather, it is a word of their gracious renewal and glorious restoration. No wonder, then, his people are beckoned to "praise the LORD" and "give thanks to the LORD" (Ps. 106:1). His steadfast love indeed endures forever, and his mighty deeds indeed display the wonder of his righteous character (vv. 1–3).

37[t] Ex. 12:35, 36 **38**[u] Ex. 12:23 [v] Ex. 15:16 **39**[w] [Job 36:20; Isa. 4:5]; See Ex. 13:21 **40**[x] Ps. 78:18, 27 [y] Ex. 16:13 [z] Ps. 78:24, 25; [John 6:31] **41**[a] See Ps. 78:15 [b] See Ps. 63:1 **42**[c] ver. 8, 9; Ex. 2:24 [d] [Gen. 15:14]; See ver. 6 **43**[d] [See ver. 42 above] [e] [Isa. 35:10]; See Ex. 15:1-21 **44**[f] Josh. 24:13; [Ps. 78:55] **45**[g] Deut. 4:1, 40 [h] Ps. 78:7 [i] See Ps. 104:35 **Psalm 106** **1**[i] [See Ps. 105:45 above] [j] See Ps. 105:1 [k] See Ps. 100:5 [l] See 1 Chr. 16:34, 41 **3**[m] [Ps. 15:2]

4 [n]Remember me, O LORD, when you show
favor to your people;
help me when you save them,[1]
5 that I may look upon the prosperity of
your [o]chosen ones,
that I may rejoice in the gladness of
your nation,
that I may glory with your inheritance.

6 [p]Both we and [q]our fathers have sinned;
we have committed iniquity; we have
done wickedness.
7 Our fathers, when they were in Egypt,
did not consider your wondrous
works;
they [r]did not remember the abundance
of your steadfast love,
but [s]rebelled by the sea, at the Red Sea.
8 Yet he saved them [t]for his name's sake,
[u]that he might make known his
mighty power.
9 He [v]rebuked the Red Sea, and it [w]became
dry,
and he [x]led them through the deep as
through a desert.
10 So he [y]saved them from the hand of the
foe
and [z]redeemed them from the power
of the enemy.
11 And [a]the waters covered their adversaries;
not one of them was left.
12 Then [b]they believed his words;
they [c]sang his praise.

13 But they soon [d]forgot his works;
they did not wait for [e]his counsel.
14 But they had [f]a wanton craving in the
wilderness,
and [g]put God to the test in the desert;
15 he [h]gave them what they asked,
but sent [i]a wasting disease among
them.

16 When men in the camp [j]were jealous of
Moses
and Aaron, [k]the holy one of the LORD,
17 [l]the earth opened and swallowed up
Dathan,
and covered the company of Abiram.
18 [m]Fire also broke out in their company;
the flame burned up the wicked.

19 They [n]made a calf in Horeb
and worshiped a metal image.
20 They [o]exchanged the glory of God[2]
for the image of an ox that eats grass.
21 They [p]forgot God, their Savior,
who had done great things in Egypt,
22 wondrous works in [q]the land of Ham,
and awesome deeds by the Red Sea.
23 Therefore [r]he said he would destroy
them—
had not Moses, his [s]chosen one,
[t]stood in the breach before him,
to turn away his wrath from destroying them.

24 Then they [u]despised [v]the pleasant land,
having [w]no faith in his promise.
25 They [x]murmured in their tents,
and did not obey the voice of the
LORD.
26 Therefore he [y]raised his hand and swore
to them
that he would make them fall in the
wilderness,
27 and would make their offspring fall
among the nations,
[z]scattering them among the lands.

[1] Or *Remember me, O LORD, with the favor you show to your people; help me with your salvation* [2] Hebrew *exchanged their glory*

Although the justice and judgment of God are on display in this psalm in response to the nearly continual rebellion of his people, in the end God does not forsake those who are his own. Rather, even in the distress brought upon them by God's own judgment of them, we read, "Nevertheless, he looked upon their distress, when he heard their cry. For their sake he remembered his covenant, and relented according to the abundance of his steadfast love" (vv. 44–45). What horrid sin his people have committed! But what amazing grace was granted them for their forgiveness and renewal—and we know this grace in its apex appearance in Christ. The words of Paul, "where sin increased, grace abounded all the more" (Rom. 5:20), surely do capture the final message of this psalm. Indeed, "let all the people say, 'Amen!' Praise the LORD!" (Ps. 106:48).

4[n] [Ps. 119:132]
5[o] Ps. 105:6, 43
6[p] 1 Kgs. 8:47; Ezra 9:6; Neh. 1:6, 7; 9:16; Jer. 3:25; 14:20; Dan. 9:5 [q] Ps. 79:8; Lev. 26:40
7[r] [ver. 13, 21] [s] Ex. 14:11, 12
8[t] Ezek. 20:9, 14 [u] Ex. 9:16
9[v] [Ps. 18:15; 104:7] [w] Ex. 14:21; [Isa. 50:2; 51:10] [x] Isa. 63:13
10[y] Ex. 14:30 [z] Ps. 107:2
11[a] Ex. 14:28; 15:5
12[b] Ex. 14:31 [c] See Ex. 15:1-21
13[d] Ps. 78:11; [Ex. 15:24; 16:2; 17:2] [e] [Ps. 107:11]

14[f] Num. 11:4; 1 Cor. 10:6; [Ps. 78:18] [g] Ex. 17:2; 1 Cor. 10:9 **15**[h] Ps. 78:29 [i] Isa. 10:16 **16**[j] See Num. 16:1-3 [k] Deut. 33:2; Zech. 14:5; Jude 14 **17**[l] Num. 16:31, 32; Deut. 11:6 **18**[m] Num. 16:35 **19**[n] Ex. 32:4; Deut. 9:8; Acts 7:41 **20**[o] Jer. 2:11; [Rom. 1:23] **21**[p] ver. 7, 13; Ps. 78:11; Deut. 32:18 **22**[q] Ps. 105:23, 27; [Ps. 78:51] **23**[r] Ex. 32:10; Deut. 9:14; Ezek. 20:8 [s] Ps. 105:6 [t] Ezek. 22:30 **24**[u] Num. 14:31 [v] Zech. 7:14 [w] Deut. 1:32; 9:23 **25**[x] Num. 14:2; Deut. 1:27 **26**[y] Ex. 6:8; Num. 14:30; Deut. 32:40; Ezek. 20:6, 15, 23; [Ps. 95:11] **27**[z] See Ps. 44:11

28 Then they [a]yoked themselves to the
[a]Baal of Peor,
and ate sacrifices offered to [b]the dead;
29 they provoked the LORD to anger with
their deeds,
and a plague broke out among them.
30 Then [c]Phinehas stood up and intervened,
and the plague was stayed.
31 And that was [d]counted to him as righteousness
from generation to generation forever.

32 They [e]angered him at the waters of
Meribah,
and it went ill with Moses on their
account,
33 for they [f]made his spirit bitter,[1]
and he [g]spoke rashly with his lips.

34 They did not [h]destroy the peoples,
[i]as the LORD commanded them,
35 but they [j]mixed with the nations
and learned to do as they did.
36 They served their idols,
which became [k]a snare to them.
37 They [l]sacrificed their sons
and their daughters to [m]the demons;
38 they poured out innocent blood,
the blood of their sons and daughters,
whom they sacrificed to the idols of
Canaan,
and the land was [n]polluted with
blood.
39 Thus they [o]became unclean by their
acts,
and [p]played the whore in their deeds.

40 Then [q]the anger of the LORD was kindled against [r]his people,
and he abhorred his [r]heritage;
41 he [s]gave them into the hand of the
nations,
so that those who hated them ruled
over them.
42 Their enemies [t]oppressed them,
and they were brought into subjection under their power.
43 [u]Many times he delivered them,
but they were rebellious in their [v]pur-
poses
and were [w]brought low through their
iniquity.

44 Nevertheless, he looked upon their distress,
when he [x]heard their cry.
45 For their sake he [y]remembered his covenant,
and [z]relented according to [a]the abundance of his steadfast love.
46 He caused them to be [b]pitied
by all those who held them captive.

47 [c]Save us, O LORD our God,
and [d]gather us from among the
nations,
that we may give thanks to your holy
name
and glory in your praise.

48 [e]Blessed be the LORD, the God of Israel,
from everlasting to everlasting!
[e]And let all the people say, "Amen!"
[f]Praise the LORD!

Book Five

Let the Redeemed of the LORD Say So

107 [g]Oh give thanks to the LORD, [h]for
he is good,
for his steadfast love endures forever!
2 Let [i]the redeemed of the LORD say so,
whom he has [j]redeemed from trouble[2]
3 and [k]gathered in from the lands,
from the east and from the west,
from the north and from the south.

4 Some [l]wandered in desert wastes,
finding no way [m]to a city to dwell in;
5 hungry and thirsty,
their soul [n]fainted within them.

[1] Or *they rebelled against God's Spirit* [2] Or *from the hand of the foe*

28[a] Num. 25:3; Hos. 9:10 [b] Isa. 8:19
30[c] Num. 25:7, 8
31[d] [Gen. 15:6]; See Num. 25:10-13

Psalm 107 Although Psalm 107 begins the fifth and final book of the Psalter, it continues the themes of the despicable sinfulness of God's people along with the gracious and restorative mercy of God that are also described in the narrative depictions of Psalms 105 and 106.

32[e] See Num. 20:2-13; Deut. 1:37 **33**[f] Ps. 107:11; [Ps. 78:40; Isa. 63:10] [g] Num. 20:10 **34**[h] See Judg. 1:21, 27-36 [i] Deut. 7:2, 16; Judg. 2:2 **35**[j] Judg. 3:5, 6; [Ezra 9:2] **36**[k] Ex. 23:33; Deut. 7:16; Judg. 2:3 **37**[l] 2 Kgs. 16:3; Isa. 57:5; Ezek. 16:20; 20:26 [m] Deut. 32:17; [1 Cor. 10:20] **38**[n] Isa. 24:5 **39**[o] Ezek. 20:18, 30, 31 [p] See Ps. 73:27 **40**[q] Ps. 78:59, 62; Judg. 2:14 [r] See Ps. 28:9 **41**[s] Neh. 9:27 **42**[t] Judg. 4:3; 10:12 **43**[u] Judg. 2:16 [v] See Ps. 81:12 [w] Lev. 26:39 **44**[x] Judg. 3:9; 4:3; 6:7; 10:10 **45**[y] Ps. 105:8; Lev. 26:42 [z] See Ps. 90:13 [a] ver. 7; Ps. 51:1; 69:16; Isa. 63:7; Lam. 3:32 **46**[b] 1 Kgs. 8:50; 2 Chr. 30:9; Ezra 9:9; Neh. 1:11; Jer. 42:12 **47**[c] For ver. 47, 48, see 1 Chr. 16:35, 36 [d] See Ps. 107:3 **48**[e] See Ps. 41:13 [f] See Ps. 104:35 **Psalm 107** **1**[g] See Ps. 105:1 [h] See Ps. 100:5 **2**[i] Ps. 106:10 [j] Isa. 62:12; 63:4 **3**[k] Ps. 106:47; Deut. 30:3; Isa. 11:12; 43:5; 56:8; Jer. 29:14; 31:8, 10; Ezek. 20:34, 41; 39:27 **4**[l] ver. 40; [Deut. 32:10] [m] ver. 36 **5**[n] Ps. 77:3

6 Then they [o]cried to the LORD in their trouble,
and he delivered them from their distress.
7 He led them by [p]a straight way
till they reached [m]a city to dwell in.
8 [q]Let them thank the LORD for his steadfast love,
for his wondrous works to the children of man!
9 For he [r]satisfies the longing soul,
[s]and the hungry soul he fills with good things.

10 [t]Some sat in darkness and in [u]the shadow of death,
prisoners in [v]affliction and in irons,
11 for they [w]had rebelled against the words of God,
and [x]spurned the counsel of the Most High.
12 So he bowed their hearts down with hard labor;
they fell down, [y]with none to help.
13 [z]Then they cried to the LORD in their trouble,
and he delivered them from their distress.
14 He brought them out of [a]darkness and the shadow of death,
and [b]burst their bonds apart.
15 [c]Let them thank the LORD for his steadfast love,
for his wondrous works to the children of man!
16 For he [d]shatters the doors of bronze
and cuts in two the bars of iron.

17 Some were [e]fools through their sinful ways,
and because of their iniquities suffered affliction;
18 [f]they loathed any kind of food,
and they [g]drew near to [h]the gates of death.
19 [i]Then they cried to the LORD in their trouble,
and he delivered them from their distress.
20 He [j]sent out his word and [k]healed them,
and [l]delivered them from their destruction.
21 [m]Let them thank the LORD for his steadfast love,
for his wondrous works to the children of man!
22 And let them [n]offer sacrifices of thanksgiving,
and [o]tell of his deeds in [p]songs of joy!

23 Some [q]went down to the sea in ships,
doing business on the great waters;
24 they saw the deeds of the LORD,
his wondrous works in the deep.
25 For he [r]commanded and [s]raised the stormy wind,
which lifted up the waves of the sea.
26 They mounted up to heaven; they went down to the depths;
their courage [t]melted away in their evil plight;

The opening verses announce the overarching message of the psalm: because God's goodness and steadfast love endures forever, those redeemed by the Lord, wherever they may be (i.e., in their homeland or in exile), give thanks to him and look to him for future deliverance and restoration (Ps. 107:1–3). The psalm then focuses on four groupings (the "some" of vv. 4, 10, 17, 23) of God's people who, in their respective situations of distress and need, look to God for help. Each group's affliction differs, but each calls upon God for deliverance (vv. 6, 13, 19, 28), and God hears and answers their humble cries for help. Each, then, is encouraged to offer a response of thanksgiving to God (vv. 8, 15, 21, 31), expressing the praise and worth of God in light of his gracious and powerful deliverance.

God's faithfulness to his own people, to hear and help in times of distress, is the repeated theme of this psalm. As God's people learn that he "raises up the needy out of affliction" (v. 41), they will begin to "consider the steadfast love of the LORD" (v. 43). There is such good news here; although God's people are feeble, needy, afflicted, and often sinful, yet his steadfast love never ceases. The grace we see here prepares us to understand its expression and fulfillment in Christ, by whom God has once and for all answered the cry of the needy. The steadfast love of the Lord becomes flesh-and-blood reality, before our very eyes, in Christ.

6[o] ver. 13, 19, 28; Ps. 106:44
7[p] Ezra 8:21 [m] [See ver. 4 above]
8[q] ver. 15, 21, 31
9[r] [Ps. 34:10; 146:7] [s] Luke 1:53
10[t] Luke 1:79; [Isa. 42:7; 49:9; Mic. 7:8] [u] ver. 14; Job 10:21 [v] [Job 36:8]
11[w] Ps. 106:7, 33, 43; See Ps. 78:40 [x] Prov. 1:30; 5:12; 15:5; [Deut. 31:20; Luke 7:30]
12[y] See Ps. 22:11
13[z] ver. 6, 19, 28
14[a] See ver. 10 [b] [Ps. 2:3]
15[c] ver. 8, 21, 31
16[d] Isa. 45:2
17[e] Prov. 1:7; 14:9
18[f] Job 33:20 [g] Ps. 88:3; Job 33:22 [h] See Job 38:17
19[i] ver. 6, 13, 28
20[j] Ps. 147:15, 18; [Matt. 8:8] [k] Ps. 30:2, 3; 2 Kgs. 20:5; Job 33:29, 30 [l] Ps. 103:4
21[m] ver. 8, 15, 31
22[n] See Ps. 50:14 [o] Ps. 9:11; See Ps. 118:17 [p] Ps. 105:43

23[q] Isa. 42:10 **25**[r] Ps. 105:31, 34 [s] Ps. 148:8; Jonah 1:4 **26**[t] Ps. 119:28; See Ps. 22:14

27 they reeled and [u]staggered like drunken men
and [v]were at their wits' end.[1]
28 [w]Then they cried to the LORD in their trouble,
and he delivered them from their distress.
29 He [x]made the storm be still,
and the waves of the sea were hushed.
30 Then they were glad that the waters[2] were quiet,
and he brought them to their desired haven.
31 [y]Let them thank the LORD for his steadfast love,
for his wondrous works to the children of man!
32 Let them [z]extol him in [a]the congregation of the people,
and praise him in the assembly of the elders.

33 He [b]turns rivers into a desert,
springs of water into thirsty ground,
34 [c]a fruitful land into a salty waste,
because of the evil of its inhabitants.
35 He [d]turns a desert into pools of water,
[e]a parched land into springs of water.
36 And there he lets the hungry dwell,
and they establish [f]a city to live in;
37 they sow fields and plant vineyards
and get a fruitful yield.
38 [g]By his blessing they multiply greatly,
and he does not let their livestock diminish.

39 When they are diminished and brought low
through oppression, evil, and sorrow,
40 [h]he pours contempt on princes
and [i]makes them wander [j]in trackless wastes;
41 but [k]he raises up the needy out of affliction
and [l]makes their families like flocks.
42 [m]The upright see it and are glad,
and [n]all wickedness shuts its mouth.

43 [o]Whoever is wise, let him attend to these things;
let them consider the steadfast love of the LORD.

With God We Shall Do Valiantly

108 A SONG. A PSALM OF DAVID.
[p]My heart is steadfast, O God!
I will sing and make melody with all my being![3]
2 Awake, O harp and lyre!
I will awake the dawn!
3 I will give thanks to you, O LORD,
among the peoples;
I will sing praises to you among the nations.
4 For your steadfast love is great [q]above the heavens;
your faithfulness reaches to the clouds.

5 Be exalted, O God, above the heavens!
Let your glory be over all the earth!
6 [r]That your beloved ones may be delivered,
give salvation by your right hand and answer me!

[1] Hebrew *and all their wisdom was swallowed up* [2] Hebrew *they* [3] Hebrew *with my glory*

27[u] Isa. 24:20; 29:9; See Job 12:25 [v] Isa. 19:3
28[w] ver. 6, 13, 19
29[x] See Ps. 65:7
31[y] ver. 8, 15, 21
32[z] See Ps. 99:5 [a] Ps. 22:22, 25
33[b] Isa. 50:2; [Isa. 42:15]
34[c] [Gen. 13:10; 14:3; Deut. 29:23]; See Gen. 19:24-28
35[d] Ps. 114:8; Isa. 41:18; [Isa. 35:6, 7; 43:19, 20] [e] Job 38:26, 27
36[f] ver. 4, 7
38[g] Gen. 12:2; 17:20; Ex. 1:7
40[h] Job 12:21 [i] Job 12:24 [j] [Deut. 32:10]
41[k] Ps. 113:7, 8; 1 Sam. 2:8 [l] Job 21:11
42[m] See Job 22:19 [n] See Ps. 63:11
43[o] [Ps. 64:9; Jer. 9:12; Hos. 14:9]
Psalm 108
1[p] For ver. 1-5, see Ps. 57:7-11
4[q] [Ps. 113:4]
6[r] For ver. 6-13, see Ps. 60:5-12

Psalm 108 Psalms 108, 109, and 110 are all psalms of David, the first two being psalms of lament, and the third a coronation or royal psalm. The lament of Psalm 108 combines elements of both individual (vv. 1–5) and community lament (vv. 6–13). While David clearly does lament the apparent absence of the Lord in the face of his enemies (vv. 10–12), the overarching tone and message of the psalm is hope in God. The opening line expresses this hope: "My heart is steadfast, O God!" (v. 1). And the psalm ends with this confident declaration: "With God we shall do valiantly; it is he who will tread down our foes" (v. 13).

Even though King David is facing formidable opposition from surrounding enemy nations, he also knows that God has promised victory for Israel (e.g., vv. 7–8) over neighboring foes (v. 9), so long as David looks to God who alone can "give salvation" by his strong and merciful right hand (v. 6). The effect of God's final triumph over Israel's enemies is underscored in the early verses of the psalm. David longs for the "peoples" and "nations" to see the glory of God (vv. 3–4) expressed in God's steadfast love for his own people.

Because of God's faithfulness, and because of the certainty of his triumph, David is filled with song and praise and hope. David's hope finds fulfillment in Jesus, through whom God has, at the culmination of human history, triumphed decisively over all

7 God has promised in his holiness:[1]
"With exultation I will divide up
Shechem
and portion out the Valley of Succoth.
8 Gilead is mine; Manasseh is mine;
Ephraim is my helmet,
Judah my scepter.
9 Moab is my washbasin;
upon Edom I cast my shoe;
[s] over Philistia I shout in triumph."

10 Who will bring me to the fortified city?
Who will lead me to Edom?
11 Have you not rejected us, O God?
You do not go out, O God, with our
armies.
12 Oh grant us help against the foe,
for vain is the salvation of man!
13 With God we shall do valiantly;
it is he who will tread down our foes.

Help Me, O Lord My God

109

To the choirmaster.
A Psalm of David.

1 [t] Be not silent, O [u] God of my praise!
2 For wicked and [v] deceitful mouths are
opened against me,
speaking against me with lying
tongues.
3 They encircle me with words of hate,
and attack me [w] without cause.
4 In return for my love they [x] accuse me,
but I [y] give myself to prayer.[2]
5 So they [z] reward me evil for good,
and hatred for my love.

6 [a] Appoint a wicked man [b] against him;
let an accuser stand [c] at his right hand.
7 When he is tried, let him come forth
guilty;
let his [d] prayer be counted as sin!
8 May his [e] days be few;
may [f] another take his [g] office!
9 May his [h] children be fatherless
and his wife a widow!
10 May his children [i] wander about and beg,
[j] seeking food far from the ruins they
inhabit!
11 May [k] the creditor seize all that he has;
may [k] strangers plunder the fruits of
his toil!
12 Let there be none to [l] extend kindness to
him,
nor any to [m] pity his fatherless children!
13 May his [n] posterity be cut off;
may his [o] name be blotted out in the
second generation!
14 May [p] the iniquity of his fathers be
remembered before the Lord,
and let not the sin of his mother be
[q] blotted out!
15 [r] Let them be before the Lord continually,
that he may [s] cut off the memory of
them from the earth!

16 For he did not remember to show kindness,
but pursued [t] the poor and needy
and [u] the brokenhearted, to put them
to death.

[1] Or *sanctuary* [2] Hebrew *but I am prayer*

his foes (Col. 2:14–15). Psalm 108 expresses lament with trust, instructing the people of God to keep their eyes fixed on the immeasurable love and power of God—the love and power supremely seen on Calvary.

Psalm 109 In this personal psalm of lament, David reflects upon his great need for and dependence on the Lord in the face of the relentless cursings and threats the wicked pour out on him. Though David has shown love and kindness (vv. 2–5), these wicked men return evil for good.

In this respect, this psalm from Israel's king anticipates something of the opposition King Jesus himself experienced from many of those to whom he showed kindness. The most notable example is Judas, whom Jesus chose as one of his disciples, yet who betrayed Jesus and plotted to gain monetarily as he handed him over to be killed. There is reason to think of Judas from this psalm in light of the quotation of verse 8 in Acts 1:20, where Judas's suicide presents the need for another to take his place. So, while much of this psalm reflects the specific reality of bitterness and opposition David faced, it likewise foreshadows the opposition Jesus, the Greater Son of David, would face in even greater ways.

The most difficult part of the psalm is the extended curse upon and woe to the wicked themselves (Ps. 109:6–20). Some would like to dismiss these as rash, ungodly cursings. We must recall, however, the similar woes Jesus pronounced upon

9[s] [Ps. 60:8]
Psalm 109
1[t] See Ps. 28:1 [u] Deut. 10:21; [Ps. 71:6; Jer. 17:14]
2[v] Ps. 52:4
3[w] See Ps. 69:4
4[x] Ps. 38:20 [y] [Ps. 69:13]
5[z] See Ps. 35:12
6[a] For ver. 6-15, see Ps. 35:4-8; 69:22-28 [b] [1 Chr. 21:1; Zech. 3:1] [c] Job 30:12
7[d] Prov. 28:9; [Prov. 15:8; 21:27]
8[e] [Ps. 55:23] [f] Cited Acts 1:20 [g] Num. 4:16; [1 Chr. 24:3]
9[h] Ex. 22:24
10[i] [Gen. 4:12]; See Ps. 59:15 [j] [Ps. 37:25]
11[k] [Deut. 28:43, 44]
12[l] [Ps. 36:10] [m] [Job 5:4]
13[n] See Ps. 21:10 [o] Prov. 10:7
14[p] Ex. 20:5 [q] Neh. 4:5; Jer. 18:23
15[r] [Ps. 90:8] [s] Ps. 34:16
16[t] ver. 22; Ps. 40:17 [u] See Ps. 34:18

17 [v]He loved to curse; let curses come[1] upon him!
He did not delight in blessing; may it be far[2] from him!
18 He [w]clothed himself with cursing as his coat;
may it [x]soak[3] into his body like water,
like oil into his bones!
19 May it be like a garment that he wraps around him,
like a belt that he puts on every day!
20 May this be the reward of my [y]accusers from the LORD,
of those who speak evil against my life!

21 But you, O GOD my Lord,
deal on my behalf [z]for your name's sake;
because your [a]steadfast love is good, deliver me!
22 For I am [b]poor and needy,
and my heart is stricken within me.
23 I am gone like [c]a shadow at evening;
I am [d]shaken off like a locust.
24 My knees are weak [e]through fasting;
my [f]body has become gaunt, with no fat.
25 I am [g]an object of scorn to my accusers;
when they see me, they [h]wag their heads.
26 [i]Help me, O LORD my God!
Save me according to your steadfast love!
27 Let them [j]know that this is your hand;
you, O LORD, have done it!
28 [k]Let them curse, but you will bless!
They arise and are put to shame, but [l]your servant will be glad!
29 May my accusers be [m]clothed with dishonor;
may they [n]be wrapped in their own shame as in a cloak!

30 With my mouth I will give great thanks to the LORD;
I will [o]praise him in the midst of the throng.
31 For he stands [p]at the right hand of the needy one,
to save him from those who condemn his soul to death.

Sit at My Right Hand

110

A PSALM OF DAVID.

[q]The LORD says to my Lord:
[r]"Sit at my right hand,
[s]until I make your enemies your [t]footstool."

2 The LORD sends forth [u]from Zion
[v]your mighty scepter.
[w]Rule in the midst of your enemies!

[1] Revocalization; Masoretic Text *curses have come* [2] Revocalization; Masoretic Text *it is far* [3] Revocalization; Masoretic Text *it has soaked*

17[v] [Prov. 14:14; Ezek. 35:6]
18[w] [ver. 29; Ps. 73:6] [x] [Num. 5:22]
20[y] ver. 6, 29
21[z] [Jer. 14:7]; See Ps. 23:3 [a] Ps. 69:16; [Ps. 63:3]
22[b] ver. 16
23[c] See Ps. 102:11 [d] Ex. 10:19; [Neh. 5:13; Job 38:13]
24[e] Ps. 35:13 [f] [Job 16:8]
25[g] Ps. 22:6; 69:19 [h] See Ps. 22:7
26[i] Ps. 119:86
27[j] [Job 37:7]
28[k] [2 Sam. 16:12] [l] [Isa. 65:14]
29[m] ver. 18; See Job 8:22 [n] Ps. 71:13; [Ps. 35:26]
30[o] [Ps. 22:25]
31[p] ver. 6; See Ps. 16:8

Psalm 110
1[q] Cited Matt. 22:44; Mark 12:36; Luke 20:42, 43; Acts 2:34, 35 [r] Cited Heb. 1:13; [Matt. 26:64; Eph. 1:20; Col. 3:1; Heb. 1:3; 8:1; 10:12; 12:2] [s] Heb. 10:13; [1 Cor. 15:25; Eph. 1:22; Heb. 2:8; 1 Pet. 3:22] [t] [Ps. 8:6; 18:38; Josh. 10:24]
2[u] [Ps. 68:35] [v] Jer. 48:17; Ezek. 19:14; [Ps. 45:6] [w] Ps. 72:8; [Dan. 7:13, 14]

the scribes and Pharisees (Matt. 23:1–36). It is not rash to denounce evil, for evil deserves denouncing. In the end, David trusts in God to deliver him (Ps. 109:21–29) while he pledges to praise and thank God for his goodness (vv. 30–31). In these ways David anticipates the trust that the Savior puts in God, who will vindicate him in the face of his accusers.

Psalm 110 This psalm of David, has two parts: (1) verses 1–3 announce Yahweh's declaration of the Lord whom he will set at his right hand as king over all, to rule even over his enemies; and (2) verses 4–7 announce Yahweh's unchangeable oath that this Lord, this anointed King, will likewise be an eternal Priest of the people. This psalm, then, is fundamentally about David's Greater Son who will be both King (v. 1) and Priest (v. 4), a dual role that none of the previous kings of Israel or Judah could play.

God had established the kingly line from Judah (Gen. 49:10), and more specifically through David (2 Sam. 7:12–13), whereas the priestly line ran through Levi (Num. 3:5–13; 8:5–22; 18:1–7), and particularly through the line of Aaron (Ex. 28:1–2; 29:1–9). But finally in Jesus we see One whose kingly line runs from David (Matt. 1:6; Luke 1:32–33; 3:31) but who is established as priest forever after the greater priestly order of Melchizedek (Heb. 5:5–6; 7:1–28). Another reason for seeing this psalm as fundamentally about David's Son, fulfilled in Jesus, comes from the opening verse. Since David (the highest human authority) is writing this psalm, the second "Lord" (of "the LORD says to my Lord"; Ps. 110:1) must refer to a divine figure rather than to David himself. Thus, this second "Lord" must be the One whom we know as the Son of the Father, Jesus himself (cf. Matt. 22:41–45; Acts 2:34–36).

3 [x]Your people will [y]offer themselves freely
on the day of your [z]power,[1]
in [a]holy garments;[2]
from the womb of the morning,
the dew of your youth will be yours.[3]
4 [b]The LORD has [c]sworn
and will [d]not change his mind,
[e]"You are [f]a priest [g]forever
after the order of [h]Melchizedek."

5 The Lord is at your [i]right hand;
he will [j]shatter kings on [k]the day of
his wrath.
6 He will [l]execute judgment among the
nations,
[m]filling them with corpses;
he will [n]shatter chiefs[4]
over the wide earth.
7 He will [o]drink from the brook by the
way;
therefore he will lift up his head.

Great Are the LORD's Works

111 [5] [p]Praise the LORD!
I [q]will give thanks to the LORD
with my whole heart,
in the company of [r]the upright, in the
congregation.
2 Great are the [s]works of the LORD,
[t]studied by all who delight in them.
3 [u]Full of splendor and majesty is his
work,
and his [v]righteousness endures forever.
4 He has [w]caused his wondrous works to
be remembered;
the LORD is gracious and merciful.
5 He provides food for those who fear
him;
he [x]remembers his covenant forever.
6 He has shown his people the power of
his works,
in giving them the inheritance of the
nations.
7 The works of his hands are faithful and
just;
all his precepts are [y]trustworthy;
8 they are [z]established forever and ever,
to be performed with [a]faithfulness
and uprightness.
9 He sent [b]redemption to his people;
he has [c]commanded his covenant forever.
[d]Holy and awesome is his name!
10 [e]The fear of the LORD is the beginning of
wisdom;
all those who practice it have [f]a good
understanding.
His [g]praise endures forever!

[1] Or *on the day you lead your forces* [2] Masoretic Text; some Hebrew manuscripts and Jerome *on the holy mountains* [3] The meaning of the Hebrew is uncertain [4] Or *the head* [5] This psalm is an acrostic poem, each line beginning with the successive letters of the Hebrew alphabet

But his role as this King-Priest will be as the incarnate God-man. Notice that in executing his judgment, he will "drink from the brook by the way" (Ps. 110:7), indicating he comes as a man, the Son of David, who nonetheless is David's "Lord" and hence, also, fully God (v. 1). Jesus, the God-man, then, is the subject of Psalm 110, the glorious and final King and Priest over his own people and over the whole world.

Psalm 111 This is a corporate psalm of praise to God for his faithfulness to his people and for the wondrous works he has done. God's glorious works are expressions of his character. God's righteousness (v. 3), grace and mercy (v. 4), power (v. 6), and faithfulness and justice (vv. 7–8) are emphasized as those qualities exhibited in the work that he does.

Among the works of God that display the glory of his character are his giving the nations to his people as their inheritance (v. 6) and the covenant redemption he has provided for them. These character qualities and attending works anticipate the even greater works—and hence greater display of his character—that he shows forth in the redeeming work of his Son. All the qualities mentioned in this psalm—God's righteousness, grace, mercy, power, faithfulness, justice—are seen in even greater measure in the cross and resurrection of Christ. Just as God should be praised by the corporate assembly for the redemption he carried out in the exodus, now there is even greater reason to praise this glorious God for the redemption he has won for his people in Christ. The bondage from which we have been freed through Christ is not physical slavery in Egypt but ultimate slavery to sin.

3[x] Judg. 5:2; Neh. 11:2 [y][Ex. 35:29] [z][Isa. 13:3, 4] [a][Rev. 19:14]; See 1 Chr. 16:29
4[b] Cited Heb. 7:21 [c]Ps. 132:11; Heb. 6:17, 18 [d]Num. 23:19 [e]Cited Heb. 5:6; 7:17, 21; [Heb. 6:20] [f]Zech. 6:13 [g]Heb. 7:24, 28; [John 12:34] [h]Gen. 14:18
5[i] See Ps. 16:8 [j][Ps. 68:14] [k]Rom. 2:5; Rev. 6:17; [Ps. 2:5, 12]
6[l] Isa. 2:4; Joel 3:12; Mic. 4:3 [m]See Ezek. 39:17-19; Rev. 19:17, 18 [n][Ps. 68:21]
7[o] [Judg. 7:5, 6]
Psalm 111
1[p] See Ps. 104:35 [q]Ps. 138:1 [r][Ps. 149:1]
2[s] Ps. 92:5; Rev. 3:2; [Ps. 139:14] [t]Ps. 119:45, 94, 155; [Ps. 112:1; 143:5]
3[u] Ps. 145:5 [v]Ps. 112:3, 9
4[w] [Ps. 78:4]
5[x] See Ps. 105:8
7[y] Ps. 93:5; [Ps. 19:7]
8[z] Isa. 40:8; Matt. 5:18 [a]Ps. 19:9; Rev. 15:3
9[b] [Matt. 1:21]; Luke 1:68 [c][Ps. 133:3] [d]Ps. 99:3; Luke 1:49; [Ps. 8:1]
10[e] Prov. 9:10; See Prov. 1:7 [f][Prov. 3:4; 13:15; John 7:17] [g][Ps. 44:8]

The Righteous Will Never Be Moved

112 [1] [h]Praise the LORD!
[i]Blessed is the man who fears the LORD,
who [j]greatly delights in his commandments!
2 His [k]offspring will be mighty in the land;
[l]the generation of the upright will be blessed.
3 [m]Wealth and riches are in his house,
and his [n]righteousness endures forever.
4 Light dawns in the darkness [o]for the upright;
he is gracious, merciful, and [p]righteous.
5 It is well with the man who [q]deals generously and lends;
who conducts his affairs with justice.
6 For the righteous will [r]never be moved;
[s]he will be remembered forever.
7 He is not [t]afraid of bad news;
his [u]heart is firm, [v]trusting in the LORD.
8 His heart is steady; he will not be afraid,
until he looks in triumph on his adversaries.
9 He has [w]distributed freely; he has given to the poor;
his righteousness endures forever;
his [x]horn is exalted in honor.
10 The wicked man sees it and is angry;
he [y]gnashes his teeth and [z]melts away;
[a]the desire of the wicked will perish!

Who Is like the LORD Our God?

113 [b]Praise the LORD!
[c]Praise, O [d]servants of the LORD,
praise the name of the LORD!
2 [e]Blessed be the name of the LORD
from this time forth and forevermore!
3 [f]From the rising of the sun to its setting,
[g]the name of the LORD is [h]to be praised!
4 The LORD is [i]high above all nations,
and his [j]glory above the heavens!
5 [k]Who is like the LORD our God,
who is seated on high,

[1] This psalm is an acrostic poem, each line beginning with the successive letters of the Hebrew alphabet

Psalm 112
1 [h]See Ps. 104:35 [i]Ps. 128:1, 4; [Ps. 111:10; 115:13] [j]See Ps. 1:2
2 [k][Ps. 25:13; 102:28; Prov. 11:21; 20:7] [l]Ps. 37:26
3 [m]See Prov. 3:16 [n][Ps. 111:3]
4 [o][Job 11:17]; See Ps. 97:11 [p][Matt. 1:19]
5 [q]See Ps. 37:26
6 [r]Ps. 55:22 [s][Prov. 10:7]
7 [t]Prov. 1:33 [u]Ps. 57:7 [v]Ps. 11:1; 64:10
9 [w]Cited 2 Cor. 9:9 [x]See Ps. 75:10
10 [y][Matt. 8:12; Luke 13:28]; See Job 16:9 [z][Ps. 58:8] [a]See Job 8:13

Psalm 113
1 [b]See Ps. 104:35 [c]Ps. 135:1 [d]Ps. 34:22; 69:36; 102:28
2 [e]Ps. 115:18; See Job 1:21
3 [f]Ps. 50:1; Isa. 59:19; Mal. 1:11 [g]See Ps. 48:10 [h]See Ps. 18:3
4 [i]Ps. 99:2 [j]Ps. 8:1; 57:5, 11; 148:13
5 [k]See Ps. 35:10

Psalm 112 This psalm is reminiscent of Psalm 1 with its extolling of the benefits God has in store for those who fear the Lord and greatly delight in his commandments (112:1). The wicked are contrasted (as in Psalm 1), but only in the final verse (112:10), as they revolt against the righteous—to their peril and demise. What characterizes the righteous? They are gracious and merciful while maintaining their righteousness before God and others. In essence, they reflect the grace and goodness of their God (v. 4). They do not fear distressing news or shrewd adversaries but remain steadfast in their trust in God (vv. 7–8). They are lavish in their generosity toward those in need (vv. 5, 9). God's favor rests on them, causing their offspring to multiply (v. 2), their wealth to increase (v. 3), their pathway to be lighted (v. 4), and their name to be remembered (v. 6). All of these blessings follow proper regard for the Lord (v. 1) in an imperfect world where "darkness" (v. 4), "bad news" (v. 7), and "adversaries" (v. 8) still exist. The reason for such blessing in this fallen world is not merely human achievement or resolve. The language used to describe the righteous man in Psalm 112 is very similar to the description of God in Psalm 111. If the two psalms are read in tandem, they can be seen to prefigure the nature of grace that allows the righteousness of God to become our own, and through which we ultimately know the blessing of God.

No doubt righteous kings like David, Uzziah, Hezekiah, and Josiah could testify that God's favor indeed rested on them as they walked in his ways. But the fullness of the truth of this passage is seen only with one who is perfectly righteous, one who thus is perfectly blessed by God. Jesus alone fills that description, and this psalm must lift our gaze ultimately to the only perfectly righteous man, who shares his righteousness with us (2 Cor. 5:21). As Philippians 2:6–11 indicates, because of his perfect obedience he was highly exalted by God. Jesus, then, epitomizes the righteous man of which Psalm 112 speaks.

Psalm 113 This is a hymn of praise to God for his greatness and supremacy over all nations and above all creation (vv. 4–6), and also for his kindness and compassion to the needy and destitute (vv. 7–9). That God is both great *and* gracious, majestic *and* merciful, is strong reason to offer to him ceaseless praise, as the psalmist declares,

6 who [l]looks far down
on the heavens and the earth?
7 He [m]raises the poor from the dust
and lifts the needy from the ash
heap,
8 to make them [n]sit with princes,
with the princes of his people.
9 He [o]gives the barren woman a home,
making her the joyous mother of children.
[b]Praise the LORD!

Tremble at the Presence of the Lord

114 When [p]Israel went out from
Egypt,
the house of Jacob from [q]a people of
strange language,
2 Judah became his [r]sanctuary,
Israel his dominion.

3 [s]The sea looked and fled;
[t]Jordan turned back.
4 [u]The mountains skipped like rams,
the hills like lambs.

5 What [v]ails you, O sea, that you flee?
O Jordan, that you turn back?
6 O mountains, that you skip like rams?
O hills, like lambs?

7 [w]Tremble, O earth, at the presence of the
Lord,
at the presence of the God of Jacob,
8 who turns [x]the rock into [y]a pool of
water,
[z]the flint into a spring of water.

"from the rising of the sun to its setting" (vv. 1–3). That such a great and awesome God should care so deeply for hopeless and helpless people should fill our minds and hearts with a deep sense of awe, wonder, and thanksgiving.

This is especially true when we consider how highly exalted God is ("high above all nations, and his glory above the heavens"; v. 4), and in contrast how impoverished are the objects of his favor. That they live in the "dust" and the "ash heap" (v. 7) indicates the most severe of conditions. The "barren woman" (v. 9) is totally incapable of bringing about the offspring she so desperately wants. But the mercy of God is shown to his needy creatures as he raises the poor from the ash heap and seats them with princes (v. 8), and as he grants the barren woman the joy of motherhood (v. 9). As Hannah of old praised God for his answer to her prayers in the birth of Samuel (1 Sam. 2:1–10), so all who know their destitute condition should praise God for daily and everlasting grace. Ceaseless praise, indeed, should mark our lives.

The God who showed his grace to those so in need in this Psalm magnifies that grace in the provision of Christ. Because God has proved himself in Jesus to be not only great but also exceedingly and eternally good, we look to him with a sure and fixed confidence.

Psalm 114 This hymn of praise reveals God as the Ruler of the forces of nature, who chose the people of Israel as the focal point of his dominion over all. It shows God's greatness and power alongside his intimate love and care for his people. We read of the miraculous ways in which God delivered his people out of bondage in Egypt by parting the sea (vv. 1, 3), preserving them with water and drink in the rugged land of their wanderings (vv. 4, 6, 8), and opening a pathway through the Jordan River to enter their Promised Land (v. 5).

God's control over sea, river, rock, and hill demonstrates his sovereign power over all his created order, yet this very power is exercised not for mere show but for the express purpose of delivering, protecting, and providing for the people of his covenant love. That the preincarnate Christ may indeed be understood as the God who controlled nature to provide for them is suggested especially by the last verse, where we see God turn "the rock into a pool of water, the flint into a spring of water" (v. 8). Paul instructs us that the rock of their provision of water in the wilderness (Ex. 17:6–7; Num. 20:8–13) was none other than Christ, their God and Provider (1 Cor. 10:4). Indeed, Christ the Creator, Sustainer, and Ruler of creation (Col. 1:16–17; Heb. 1:1–3) gives himself also to provide food (John 6:35) and water (John 4:13–14) for his own. What Israel experienced in the miraculous deliverance and provision on their behalf shows forth the glory of Christ. He rules over creation in part to provide—in love and grace—for his people.

6 [l] See Ps. 11:4; [Ps. 138:6]
7 [m] [Ps. 136:23]; See Ps. 107:41
8 [n] [Job 36:7]
9 [o] Ps. 68:6; 1 Sam. 2:5; [Ex. 1:21; Isa. 54:1] [b] [See ver. 1 above]

Psalm 114
1 [p] Ex. 12:37 [q] Ps. 81:5; [Gen. 42:23]
2 [r] Ps. 78:68, 69; [Ex. 15:17; 25:8]
3 [s] See Ps. 77:16 [t] See Josh. 3:13-16
4 [u] [Ps. 18:7; 29:6; Ex. 19:18]
5 [v] [Hab. 3:8]
7 [w] Ps. 96:9
8 [x] Num. 20:11; See Ps. 78:15 [y] See Ps. 107:35 [z] Deut. 8:15

To Your Name Give Glory

115 [a]Not to us, O LORD, not to us, but
to your name give glory,
[b]for the sake of your steadfast love and
your faithfulness!

2 Why should the nations say,
[c]"Where is their God?"
3 [d]Our God is in the heavens;
[e]he does all that he pleases.

4 [f]Their idols are silver and gold,
[g]the work of human hands.
5 They have mouths, [h]but do not speak;
eyes, but do not see.
6 They have ears, but do not hear;
noses, but do not smell.
7 They have hands, but do not feel;
feet, but do not walk;
and they do not make a sound in their
throat.
8 [i]Those who make them become like them;
so do all who trust in them.

9 O [j]Israel,[1] [k]trust in the LORD!
He is their [l]help and their shield.
10 O [j]house of Aaron, trust in the LORD!
He is their help and [m]their shield.
11 You [n]who fear the LORD, trust in the
LORD!
He is their help and their shield.

12 The LORD has remembered us; he will
bless us;
he will bless [o]the house of Israel;
he will bless [o]the house of Aaron;
13 he will [p]bless those who fear the LORD,
[q]both the small and the great.

14 May the LORD [r]give you increase,
you and your children!
15 May [s]you be blessed by the LORD,
[t]who made heaven and earth!

16 The heavens are the LORD's heavens,
but the earth he has given to the children of man.
17 [u]The dead do not praise the LORD,
nor do any who go down into [v]silence.
18 But [w]we will bless the LORD
from this time forth and forevermore.
[x]Praise the LORD!

I Love the LORD

116 I [y]love the LORD, because he has
[z]heard
my voice and my pleas for mercy.

[1] Masoretic Text; many Hebrew manuscripts, Septuagint, Syriac *O house of Israel*

Psalm 115
1[a] [Isa. 48:11; Ezek. 36:22; Dan. 9:18, 19] [b] See Ps. 36:5
2[c] [Ex. 32:12; Num. 14:13, 14]; See Ps. 42:3
3[d] See Ps. 11:4 [e] Ps. 135:6; Dan. 4:35
4[f] For ver. 4-8, see Ps. 135:15-18 [g] Deut. 4:28; 2 Kgs. 19:18; Isa. 37:19; Acts 19:26; See Isa. 44:10-20; Jer. 10:3-5
5[h] [Isa. 46:7; Hab. 2:18]
8[i] [Isa. 44:9]
9[j] [Ps. 118:2-4; 135:19, 20] [k] Ps. 37:3; 62:8 [l] Ps. 33:20
10[j] [See ver. 9 above] [m] See Ps. 3:3
11[n] Ps. 22:23; 103:11, 13, 17
12[o] [Ps. 118:2-4; 135:19, 20]
13[p] See Ps. 112:1 [q] Jer. 16:6; 31:34
14[r] Deut. 1:11
15[s] See Ruth 2:20 [t] Ps. 121:2; 124:8; 134:3; 146:6; Acts 14:15; Rev. 14:7; [Gen. 1:1; 14:19; Jer. 10:11]
17[u] See Ps. 6:5 [v] See Ps. 31:17
18[w] Ps. 113:2 [x] See Ps. 104:35
Psalm 116
1[y] Ps. 18:1 [z] Ps. 66:19; 118:21

Psalm 115 God's people are called to celebrate the truth that their God, the God of Israel, is the one and only true and living God. Although the peoples of the nations may ask cynically of Israel, "Where is their God?" (v. 2), the truth is this: their God, the only true God, "is in the heavens; he does all that he pleases" (v. 3). The contrast with the idols of the nations could not be more painfully clear. These pretender deities, though fashioned often to appear as personal beings, have only man-made mouths that cannot speak, eyes that cannot see, ears that cannot hear, noses that cannot smell, hands that cannot feel, and feet that cannot walk (vv. 4–7). These are the creations of man, fully incapable of doing anything whatsoever, and those who make them will be as impotent and inglorious as the idols themselves (v. 8).

The God of Israel, on the other hand, is full of steadfast love and faithfulness. Hence this God alone, the true and living God, the God of Israel, should receive all glory (v. 1). He can be trusted (vv. 10–11), for he will not fail to remember his people in their need, to bless and favor them as they look to him (vv. 12–15).

This psalm reflects the core of the good news that the people of God have always been told: our hope is in God, and not in ourselves. His abundant mercy, his faithful commitment, his inexorable power, and his steadfast love provide his people with the basis for full assurance of his care for them. For this reason we place our hope and trust in God alone. Because of who God is—not because of who we are or anything of our making—"we will bless the LORD from this time forth and forevermore" (v. 18). The supreme reason we will bless the Lord is that his powerful care for us has been decisively proven in his sending his only Son to redeem sinners and restore them back to himself.

Psalm 116 This psalm is a personal hymn of thanksgiving to God for the gracious compassion and powerful deliverance he has extended toward his servant who hopes and trusts in the Lord. Only two passages in the Psalter directly express love for God (the other being Psalm 18:1), so the intimacy of the opening expression—"I love the

2 Because he [a]inclined his ear to me,
therefore I will call on him as long as I live.
3 [b]The snares of death encompassed me;
the pangs of Sheol laid hold on me;
I suffered distress and anguish.
4 Then [c]I called on the name of the LORD:
"O LORD, I pray, deliver my soul!"

5 [d]Gracious is the LORD, and [e]righteous;
our God is [f]merciful.
6 The LORD preserves [g]the simple;
when [h]I was brought low, he saved me.
7 Return, O my soul, to your [i]rest;
for the LORD has [j]dealt bountifully with you.

8 For [k]you have delivered my soul from death,
my eyes from tears,
my feet from stumbling;
9 I will walk before the LORD
[l]in the land of the living.

10 [m]I believed, [n]even when[1] I spoke:
"I am greatly afflicted";
11 [o]I said in my alarm,
[p]"All mankind are liars."

12 What shall I [q]render to the LORD
for all his benefits to me?
13 I will lift up [r]the cup of salvation
and [s]call on the name of the LORD,
14 I will [t]pay my vows to the LORD
in the presence of all his people.

15 [u]Precious in the sight of the LORD
is the death of his [v]saints.
16 O LORD, I am your [w]servant;
I am your servant, [x]the son of your maidservant.
You have [y]loosed my bonds.
17 I will [z]offer to you the sacrifice of thanksgiving
and [s]call on the name of the LORD.
18 I will [t]pay my vows to the LORD
in the presence of all his people,
19 in [a]the courts of the house of the LORD,
in your midst, O Jerusalem.
[b]Praise the LORD!

The LORD's Faithfulness Endures Forever

117 [c]Praise the LORD, all nations!
Extol him, all peoples!
2 For [d]great is his steadfast love toward us,
and [e]the faithfulness of the LORD endures forever.
[b]Praise the LORD!

[1] Or *believed, indeed*; Septuagint *believed, therefore*

LORD" (Ps. 116:1)—indicates the depth of the psalmist's warmth and gratitude toward God. Indeed, God has shown this psalmist such kindness, care, and protection amid agonizing affliction (vv. 3, 8); he therefore wants to express his deep and abiding thanksgiving.

Two observations are noteworthy: (1) The psalmist's expression of thanksgiving is not just personal; he feels the need to express his gratitude "in the presence of all his people" (v. 14). Public worship rightly includes expressions of public praise and thanksgiving to God for personal deliverance. (2) As the psalmist reflects on what he may best "render to the LORD for all his benefits" (v. 12) to him, the answer is surprising. He responds, "I will lift up the cup of salvation and call on the name of the LORD" (v. 13). Lifting up the cup of salvation is a means of putting on public display that it is *God* who has heard, and come, and delivered, and saved. And calling on the name of the Lord indicates the psalmist's determination to trust God in the days ahead.

The ultimate "benefit" (v. 12) for believers today is the redemptive work of Jesus Christ. When we call on the name of the Lord, it is on Christ that we call (Rom. 10:13–17). The "cup of salvation" (Ps. 116:13) that is ours has been granted to us by virtue of God's free grace in Christ.

Psalm 117 While the gracious promises of God are, in a particular way, for his chosen people Israel, they are promises that God intends to extend to the whole world (see, e.g., Gen. 12:1–3; Isa. 2:1–4). The psalm begins from this assumption: "Praise the LORD all *nations*! Extol him, all *peoples*! (Ps. 117:1).

Why should the nations of the world join in the praise of Yahweh, the God of Israel? Because the very steadfast love and faithfulness he has shown over and again to Israel (v. 2) are the very qualities he longs to express also to the nations. Here, then, is the

2[a] [Ps. 31:2]
3[b] See Ps. 18:4
4[c] Ps. 118:5; See Ps. 18:6
5[d] See Ps. 86:15 [e] Ps. 7:9; 119:137; 145:17; Ezra 9:15; Neh. 9:8; Jer. 12:1; Dan. 9:7 [f] See Ps. 62:12
6[g] See Ps. 19:7 [h] Ps. 79:8; 142:6
7[i] Jer. 6:16; [Matt. 11:28] [j] See Ps. 13:6
8[k] Ps. 49:15; 56:13; [Ps. 86:13]
9[l] See Ps. 27:13
10[m] Cited 2 Cor. 4:13 [n] [Ps. 39:3]
11[o] Ps. 31:22 [p] [Ps. 62:9]
12[q] 2 Chr. 32:25
13[r] [Ps. 16:5] [s] See Ps. 99:6; 105:1
14[t] See Ps. 50:14
15[u] See Ps. 72:14 [v] See Ps. 50:5
16[w] Ps. 119:125; 143:12; [Ps. 113:1] [x] Ps. 86:16 [y] [Job 12:18]
17[z] See Ps. 50:14 [s] [See ver. 13 above]
18[t] [See ver. 14 above]
19[a] See Ps. 92:13 [b] See Ps. 104:35

Psalm 117
1[c] Cited Rom. 15:11
2[d] Ps. 103:11; [Ps. 116:5] [e] [Ps. 100:5] [b] [See Ps. 116:19 above]

His Steadfast Love Endures Forever

118 [f]Oh give thanks to the LORD, for
he is good;
for his steadfast love endures forever!

2 [g]Let Israel say,
"His steadfast love endures forever."
3 [g]Let the house of Aaron say,
"His steadfast love endures forever."
4 [g]Let those who fear the LORD say,
"His steadfast love endures forever."

5 [h]Out of my distress I [i]called on the LORD;
the LORD answered me and set me
[j]free.
6 [k]The LORD is on my side; [l]I will not fear.
What can man do to me?
7 [m]The LORD is on my side as my helper;
I shall [n]look in triumph on those who
hate me.

8 [o]It is better to take refuge in the LORD
[p]than to trust in man.
9 It is better to take refuge in the LORD
[p]than to trust in princes.

10 [q]All nations surrounded me;
in the name of the LORD I cut them off!
11 They surrounded me, surrounded me on
every side;
in the name of the LORD I cut them off!
12 [r]They surrounded me like bees;
they went out like [s]a fire among
thorns;
in the name of the LORD I cut them off!
13 I was [t]pushed hard,[1] so that I was falling,
but the LORD helped me.

14 The LORD is my strength and my song;
[u]he has become my salvation.
15 Glad songs of salvation
are in the tents of the righteous:
[v]"The right hand of the LORD [w]does valiantly,
16 the right hand of the LORD exalts,
the right hand of the LORD [w]does valiantly!"

17 [x]I shall not die, but I shall live,
and [y]recount the deeds of the LORD.
18 The LORD has [z]disciplined me severely,
but he has not given me over to death.

19 [a]Open to me the gates of righteousness,
that I may enter through them
and give thanks to the LORD.
20 This is the gate of the LORD;
[b]the righteous shall enter through it.
21 I thank you that [c]you have
answered me
[u]and have become my salvation.
22 [d]The stone that the builders rejected
has become the cornerstone.[2]
23 This is the LORD's doing;
it is marvelous in our eyes.
24 This is the day that the LORD has made;
let us rejoice and be glad in it.

25 Save us, we pray, O LORD!
O LORD, we pray, give us success!

[1] Hebrew *You* (that is, the enemy) *pushed me hard* [2] Hebrew *the head of the corner*

Psalm 118
1[f] ver. 29; See Ps. 100:5
2[g] [Ps. 115:9, 10, 11]
3[g] [See ver. 2 above]
4[g] [See ver. 2 above]
5[h] [Jonah 2:1] [i] [Ps. 116:4] [j] See Ps. 18:19
6[k] Ps. 56:9; Cited Heb. 13:6 [l] See Ps. 23:4; 56:4, 11
7[m] Ps. 54:4 [n] See Ps. 54:7
8[o] [Ps. 40:4; 62:8] [p] Ps. 146:3
9[p] [See ver. 8 above]
10[q] [Ps. 88:17]
12[r] Deut. 1:44 [s] [Ps. 58:9]
13[t] [Ps. 140:4]
14[u] See Ps. 27:1
15[v] Ex. 15:6; Luke 1:51 [w] Ps. 60:12
16[w] [See ver. 15 above]
17[x] [Hab. 1:12] [y] Ps. 73:28; 107:22; [Ps. 6:5]
18[z] [Jer. 30:11; 2 Cor. 6:9]
19[a] Isa. 26:2; [Ps. 24:7, 9]
20[b] Rev. 21:27; 22:14; [Isa. 35:8]
21[c] Ps. 116:1 [u] [See ver. 14 above]
22[d] Cited Matt. 21:42; Mark 12:10, 11; Luke 20:17; [Isa. 28:16]; Acts 4:11; Eph. 2:20; 1 Pet. 2:4-7

saving God of all the earth, the covenant-making/keeping God who through Israel will reach the nations (see Paul's quotation of Ps. 117:1 in Rom. 15:11).

Consider two implications of this truth: (1) Even though other nations and peoples do not recognize the God of Israel and, by extension, the God of the Christian faith, as their God, he nonetheless *is* their God since he is the only true and living God. He has rights over them, both in judgment and in salvation, whether they ever acknowledge this or not. (2) Because God has promised to bless the nations of the world through the seed of Israel, we can be confident that as the gospel goes forth, God will not fail to bring in people from "every tribe and language and people and nation" (Rev. 5:9). What gospel confidence and hope these twin implications offer. God is the only true and living God, and his intent is to save men and women from all the nations. May the gospel of grace go forth in power under the banner of this saving God, who has come to earth in Christ to redeem a people for himself from all the nations of the world.

Psalm 118 Clearly, this psalm centers on praise of the God of Israel. It begins (v. 1) and ends (vv. 28–29) with praise and thanksgiving. What stands behind these expressions of praise are both the character and the works of God. By character, God is faithful, gracious, loving, powerful, and steadfast in his love for his people (vv. 1–4, 14–16, 29). By works, God has saved and delivered his people by his covenant faithfulness and inexorable power (vv. 5–18). He is, then, the faithful God and the saving God.

26 [e]Blessed is he who comes in the name of
the LORD!
We [f]bless you from the house of the
LORD.
27 The LORD is God,
and he has made [g]his light to shine
upon us.
Bind the festal sacrifice with cords,
up to [h]the horns of the altar!

28 You are my God, and I will give thanks
to you;
you are my God; I will [i]extol you.
29 [j]Oh give thanks to the LORD, for he is
good;
for his steadfast love endures forever!

Your Word Is a Lamp to My Feet

ALEPH

119[1] Blessed are those whose [k]way is
blameless,
who [l]walk in the law of the LORD!
2 Blessed are those who [m]keep his [n]testi-
monies,
who [o]seek him with their whole heart,
3 who also [p]do no wrong,
but walk in his ways!
4 You have commanded your [q]precepts
to be kept diligently.
5 Oh that my ways may [r]be steadfast
in keeping your statutes!
6 [s]Then I shall not be put to shame,
having my eyes fixed on all your commandments.
7 I will praise you with an upright heart,
when I learn [t]your righteous rules.[2]
8 I will keep your statutes;
[u]do not utterly forsake me!

BETH

9 How can [v]a young man keep his way
pure?
By guarding it according to your word.
10 [w]With my whole heart I seek you;
let me not [x]wander from your commandments!
11 I have [y]stored up your word in my heart,
that I might not sin against you.
12 Blessed are you, O LORD;
[z]teach me your statutes!
13 With my lips I [a]declare
all the rules[3] of your mouth.
14 In the way of your testimonies I [b]delight
as much as in all [c]riches.
15 I will [d]meditate on your precepts
and fix my eyes on your [e]ways.
16 I will [f]delight in your statutes;
I will not forget your word.

GIMEL

17 [g]Deal bountifully with your servant,
[h]that I may live and keep your word.
18 Open my eyes, that I may behold
wondrous things out of your law.
19 I am [i]a sojourner on the earth;
[j]hide not your commandments from
me!
20 My soul is consumed with [k]longing
for your rules[4] at all times.

[1] This psalm is an acrostic poem of twenty-two stanzas, following the letters of the Hebrew alphabet; within a stanza, each verse begins with the same Hebrew letter [2] Or *your just and righteous decrees*; also verses 62, 106, 160, 164 [3] Or *all the just decrees* [4] Or *your just decrees*; also verses 30, 39, 43, 52, 75, 102, 108, 137, 156, 175

God can be trusted implicitly because of the constancy of his character and the sovereign grace shown in his works. Key statements in Psalm 118:22–23 deserve special comment due to their Christological application. The "stone that the builders rejected" (v. 22) in context here likely refers to Israel, who was afflicted and rejected by the nations. But we understand from the New Testament use of these verses (see Matt. 21:42; Acts 4:11; Eph. 2:20; 1 Pet. 2:4–7) that this rejected stone, though typified by Israel, is fulfilled directly in Christ who, ironically, was rejected by the very people of Israel who themselves had been rejected by the other nations. But unlike the rejected stone Israel (also identified as God's "firstborn son," prefiguring Christ; see Ex. 4:22), the rejected stone Christ became the cornerstone and fulfilled all the wondrous things God had envisioned to be brought about through him. Where Israel failed, Christ succeeded. Where Israel sinned, Christ obeyed. Christ's accomplishment of bringing an end to sin and oppression and guilt and misery truly was, then, "the LORD's doing" and is "marvelous in our eyes" (Ps. 118:23).

Psalm 119 The written Word of God stands as one of the greatest and most precious of all of God's gifts to his people! Psalm 119 celebrates the wisdom, truthfulness, clarity, grace, direction, and power of this written revelation of God.

26[e] Matt. 21:9; 23:39; Mark 11:9; Luke 13:35; 19:38 [f] Ps. 129:8
27[g] Ps. 18:28; 97:11; [Esth. 8:16; 1 Pet. 2:9] [h] See Ex. 27:2
28[i] See Ps. 99:5
29[j] ver. 1
Psalm 119
1[k] Prov. 11:20; 13:6; [Ps. 101:2, 6] [l] Ps. 128:1; [Gen. 17:1]
2[m] [ver. 22] [n] [Ps. 78:5] [o] [ver. 10; 2 Chr. 15:2]
3[p] 1 John 3:9; 5:18
4[q] Ps. 19:8
5[r] Ps. 37:23; [Prov. 16:9; Jer. 10:23]
6[s] ver. 80; [1 John 2:28]
7[t] ver. 62, 106; Ex. 24:3
8[u] Ps. 38:21; 71:9, 18
9[v] [Ps. 25:7]
10[w] [2 Chr. 15:2] [x] [ver. 21, 118]
11[y] Luke 2:19, 51; See Ps. 37:31
12[z] ver. 26, 64, 68, 108, 124, 135, 171; See Ps. 25:4
13[a] Ps. 40:9; [Deut. 6:7]
14[b] ver. 111, 162 [c] See Prov. 3:13-15; 8:10, 11, 18, 19

15[d] ver. 23, 78, 97 [e] Ps. 25:4 **16**[f] ver. 24, 47, 70, 77, 92, 143, 174 **17**[g] See Ps. 13:6 [h] ver. 144 **19**[i] See Ps. 39:12 [j] [Isa. 6:9, 10] **20**[k] ver. 40, 131, 174; [Ps. 42:1, 2]

21 You rebuke [l]the insolent, [m]accursed ones,
who [n]wander from your commandments.
22 Take away from me [o]scorn and contempt,
[p]for I have kept your testimonies.
23 Even though [q]princes sit plotting against me,
your servant will [r]meditate on your statutes.
24 Your testimonies are my [s]delight;
they are my [t]counselors.

DALETH

25 [u]My soul clings to the dust;
[v]give me life [w]according to your word!
26 When [x]I told of my ways, you answered me;
[y]teach me your statutes!
27 [z]Make me understand the way of your precepts,
and I will [a]meditate on your wondrous works.
28 [b]My soul melts away for sorrow;
strengthen me according to your word!
29 Put false ways far from me
and graciously [c]teach me your law!
30 I have chosen the way of faithfulness;
I [d]set your rules before me.
31 I cling to your testimonies, O LORD;
[e]let me not be put to shame!
32 I will run in the way of your commandments
when you [f]enlarge my heart![1]

HE

33 [g]Teach me, O LORD, the way of your statutes;
and I will keep it [h]to the end.[2]
34 [i]Give me understanding, that I may keep your law
and observe it with my whole heart.
35 [j]Lead me in the path of your commandments,
for I [k]delight in it.
36 [l]Incline my heart to your testimonies,
and not to [m]selfish gain!
37 [n]Turn my eyes from looking at worthless things;
and [o]give me life in your ways.
38 [p]Confirm to your servant your promise,
[q]that you may be feared.
39 Turn away the [r]reproach that I dread,
for your rules are good.
40 Behold, I [s]long for your precepts;
[t]in your righteousness give me life!

WAW

41 Let your [u]steadfast love come to me, O LORD,
your salvation [v]according to your promise;
42 then [w]shall I have an answer for him [r]who taunts me,
for I trust in your word.
43 And take not the word of truth utterly out of my mouth,
for my [x]hope is in your rules.
44 I will keep your law continually,
forever and ever,

[1] Or *for you set my heart free* [2] Or *keep it as my reward*

21[l] See ver. 51 [m] Deut. 27:26 [n] [ver. 10]
22[o] See Ps. 44:13 [p] [ver. 2]
23[q] ver. 161; [Dan. 6:4] [r] ver. 15, 27, 28
24[s] [Rom. 7:22]; See ver. 16 [t] [ver. 104]
25[u] Ps. 44:25 [v] ver. 37, 40, 88, 107, 149, 154, 156, 159; See Ps. 71:20 [w] ver. 65
26[x] [Ps. 37:5] [y] ver. 12
27[z] ver. 18, 34, 73, 125, 144, 169; [Job 32:8] [a] ver. 15, 23, 78
28[b] See Ps. 22:14
29[c] [ver. 27]
30[d] [Ps. 16:8]
31[e] ver. 116
32[f] 1 Kgs. 4:29; Isa. 60:5; 2 Cor. 6:11, 13
33[g] ver. 12, 26 [h] ver. 112; [Matt. 10:22; Heb. 3:6; Rev. 2:26]
34[i] ver. 27; Prov. 2:6; James 1:5
35[j] See Ps. 25:4, 5 [k] ver. 16; See Ps. 1:2

The main focus of the psalm is the "Torah," the graciously given "instruction" or "law" of the Lord given particularly in the first five books of the Bible (the "Books of Moses"). By extension, however, what is said here of God's law and precepts and testimonies and statutes should be seen as referring to all that God has revealed to his people in the Law, the Prophets, and the Writings (see Luke 24:44 for this threefold designation of the whole of the Old Testament Scriptures). But of course we realize also that this written Word of God both speaks of (Luke 24:25–26, 44–45) and anticipates (Heb. 1:1–2) the greatest of all of the revelations of God to his people—namely, the revelation of the "Word made flesh" (see John 1:14, 18). Christ himself is the living Word of God who embodies in life and speech and mission the very content and truth of that written Word.

So, reading Psalm 119 should bring Christ to mind in at least two ways. First, he lived out the principles and commandments of this psalm perfectly as he loved the law of the Lord and meditated on it day and night (Ps. 119:97; cf. 1:2). Second, his very life gave the fuller and indeed fullest expression possible of this Word, as he came as the very living Word of God himself. Jesus is himself God's message to the world.

36[l] ver. 112; 1 Kgs. 8:58; [Ps. 141:4] [m] [Luke 12:15; 1 Tim. 6:10; Heb. 13:5] **37**[n] [Prov. 23:5; Isa. 33:15] [o] ver. 25 **38**[p] 2 Sam. 7:25 [q] [Ps. 25:10; 112:1; 128:1; 130:4] **39**[r] ver. 22 **40**[s] ver. 20 [t] [ver. 149, 156] **41**[u] ver. 77; [Ps. 106:4] [v] ver. 58, 65, 76, 116, 170 **42**[w] Prov. 27:11 [r] [See ver. 39 above] **43**[x] ver. 49, 74, 81, 114, 147; [Ps. 31:24]

45 and I shall walk [y]in a wide place,
for I have [z]sought your precepts.
46 I will also speak of your testimonies
[a]before kings
and shall not be put to shame,
47 for I [b]find my delight in your commandments,
which I love.
48 I will [c]lift up my hands toward your
commandments, which I love,
and I will [d]meditate on your statutes.

ZAYIN

49 Remember [e]your word to your servant,
in which you have made me [f]hope.
50 This is [g]my comfort in my affliction,
that your promise [h]gives me life.
51 [i]The insolent utterly deride me,
but I do not [j]turn away from your
law.
52 When I think of your rules from of old,
I take comfort, O LORD.
53 [k]Hot indignation seizes me because of
the wicked,
who forsake your law.
54 Your statutes have been my songs
in the house of my [l]sojourning.
55 I [m]remember your name in the night,
O LORD,
and keep your law.
56 This blessing has fallen to me,
that [n]I have kept your precepts.

HETH

57 [o]The LORD is my portion;
I promise to keep your words.
58 I [p]entreat your favor with all my heart;
be gracious to me [q]according to your
promise.
59 When I [r]think on my ways,
I turn my feet to your testimonies;
60 I hasten and do not delay
to keep your commandments.
61 Though [s]the cords of the wicked ensnare
me,
I do not [t]forget your law.
62 At [u]midnight I rise to praise you,
because of your [v]righteous rules.
63 [w]I am a companion of all who fear you,
of those who keep your precepts.
64 [x]The earth, O LORD, is full of your steadfast love;
[y]teach me your statutes!

TETH

65 You have dealt well with your servant,
O LORD, [z]according to your word.
66 Teach me [a]good judgment and knowledge,
for I believe in your commandments.
67 [b]Before I was afflicted I went astray,
but now I keep your word.
68 [c]You are good and do good;
[d]teach me your statutes.
69 [e]The insolent [f]smear me with lies,
but with my whole heart I [g]keep your
precepts;
70 their heart is unfeeling [h]like fat,
but I [i]delight in your law.
71 It is [j]good for me that I was afflicted,
that I might learn your statutes.
72 [k]The law of your mouth is better to me
than thousands of gold and silver
pieces.

YODH

73 [l]Your hands have made and fashioned
me;
[m]give me understanding that I may
learn your commandments.
74 Those who fear you shall see me and
[n]rejoice,
because I have [o]hoped in your word.
75 I know, O LORD, that your rules are
[p]righteous,
and that in [q]faithfulness you have
afflicted me.
76 Let your steadfast love comfort me
according to your promise to your servant.
77 Let your [r]mercy come to me, that I may
live;
for your law is my [s]delight.
78 Let [t]the insolent be put to [u]shame,
because they have [v]wronged me with
falsehood;
as for me, I will [w]meditate on your
precepts.
79 Let those who fear you [x]turn to me,
that they may know your testimonies.

45[y] Prov. 4:12 [z] ver. 94, 155 **46**[a] [Matt. 10:18; Acts 26:1, 2] **47**[b] ver. 16 **48**[c] See Ps. 28:2 [d] ver. 13 **49**[e] ver. 41, 42, 43 [f] ver. 43 **50**[g] [Rom. 15:4] [h] ver. 25; See Ps. 71:20 **51**[i] ver. 69, 78, 85, 122; Jer. 20:7; [Ps. 42:3; 123:4] [j] ver. 157; Ps. 44:18; Job 23:11 **53**[k] [Neh. 13:25] **54**[l] See Ps. 39:12 **55**[m] See Ps. 42:8 **56**[n] ver. 22, 69, 100 **57**[o] See Ps. 16:5 **58**[p] Ps. 45:12 [q] ver. 41 **59**[r] [Luke 15:17] **61**[s] ver. 110 [t] ver. 83 **62**[u] [Acts 16:25] [v] ver. 7 **63**[w] [Ps. 101:6] **64**[x] Ps. 33:5 [y] ver. 12 **65**[z] [ver. 41] **66**[a] Phil. 1:9; [James 1:5] **67**[b] ver. 71, 75; Jer. 31:18, 19; See Heb. 12:5-11 **68**[c] Ps. 106:1 [d] ver. 12 **69**[e] ver. 51 [f] Job 13:4; [Ps. 109:2] [g] ver. 56 **70**[h] Isa. 6:10; See Ps. 17:10 [i] ver. 16 **71**[j] [ver. 67] **72**[k] ver. 127; Ps. 19:10; Prov. 8:10 **73**[l] Job 10:8; See Ps. 95:6; Job 31:15 [m] ver. 27 **74**[n] Ps. 34:2; 35:27; 107:42 [o] ver. 43; Ps. 130:5 **75**[p] ver. 138 [q] Ps. 33:4; See ver. 67 **77**[r] ver. 41 [s] ver. 24, 47, 174 **78**[t] See ver. 51 [u] Ps. 25:3 [v] ver. 86 [w] ver. 15, 23 **79**[x] [Jer. 15:19]

80 May my heart be [y]blameless in your statutes,
[z]that I may not be put to shame!

KAPH

81 My soul [a]longs for your salvation;
I [b]hope in your word.
82 My [c]eyes long for your promise;
I ask, [d]"When will you comfort me?"
83 For I have [e]become like a [f]wineskin in the smoke,
yet I have not forgotten your statutes.
84 [g]How long must your servant endure?[1]
[h]When will you judge those who persecute me?
85 [i]The insolent have [j]dug pitfalls for me;
they do not live according to your law.
86 All your commandments are [k]sure;
they persecute me [l]with falsehood;
[m]help me!
87 They have almost made an end of me on earth,
but I have not forsaken your precepts.
88 In your steadfast love [n]give me life,
that I may keep the testimonies of your mouth.

LAMEDH

89 Forever, O LORD, your [o]word
is firmly fixed in the heavens.
90 Your [p]faithfulness endures to all generations;
you have [q]established the earth, and it [r]stands fast.
91 By your [s]appointment they stand this day,
for all things are your servants.
92 If your law had not been my [t]delight,
I would have perished in my affliction.
93 I will never forget your precepts,
for by them you have [u]given me life.
94 I am yours; save me,
[v]for I have sought your precepts.
95 The wicked lie in wait to destroy me,
but I consider your testimonies.
96 I have seen a limit to all perfection,
but your commandment is exceedingly [w]broad.

MEM

97 Oh how [x]I love your law!
It is my [y]meditation all the day.
98 Your commandment makes me [z]wiser than my enemies,
for it is ever with me.
99 I have more understanding than all my teachers,
for [a]your testimonies are my meditation.
100 I understand more than [b]the aged,[2]
for I [c]keep your precepts.
101 I [d]hold back my feet from every evil way,
in order to keep your word.
102 I do not turn aside from your rules,
for you have taught me.
103 How [e]sweet are your words to my taste,
sweeter than honey to my mouth!
104 Through your precepts I get understanding;
therefore [f]I hate every false way.

NUN

105 [g]Your word is a lamp to my feet
and a light to my path.
106 I have [h]sworn an oath and confirmed it,
to keep your [i]righteous rules.
107 I am severely [j]afflicted;
[k]give me life, O LORD, according to your word!
108 Accept [l]my freewill offerings of praise, O LORD,
and [m]teach me your rules.
109 I hold my life [n]in my hand continually,
but I do not [o]forget your law.
110 The wicked have laid [p]a snare for me,
but [q]I do not stray from your precepts.
111 Your testimonies are [r]my heritage forever,
for they are [s]the joy of my heart.
112 I [t]incline my heart to perform your statutes
forever, [u]to the end.[3]

SAMEKH

113 I hate [v]the double-minded,
but I love [w]your law.
114 You are my [x]hiding place and my [y]shield;
I [z]hope in your word.
115 [a]Depart from me, you evildoers,
that I may [b]keep the commandments of my God.

[1] Hebrew *How many are the days of your servant?* [2] Or *the elders* [3] Or *statutes; the reward is eternal*

80[y] ver. 1 [z] ver. 6 **81**[a] See Ps. 84:2 [b] ver. 74, 114 **82**[c] See Ps. 69:3 [d] [Ps. 101:2] **83**[e] [Job 30:30] [f] [Matt. 9:17; Mark 2:22] **84**[g] [Ps. 39:4] [h] Rev. 6:10; [Zech. 1:12] **85**[i] ver. 51 [j] See Ps. 7:15 **86**[k] ver. 138 [l] ver. 78; Ps. 35:19 [m] Ps. 109:26 **88**[n] ver. 25; See Ps. 71:20 **89**[o] ver. 152; [Matt. 24:35; 1 Pet. 1:25]; [Jer. 31:35-37] **90**[p] See Ps. 36:5 [q] [Ps. 148:6] [r] Eccles. 1:4 **91**[s] Jer. 33:25 **92**[t] ver. 77 **93**[u] ver. 25; See Ps. 71:20 **94**[v] ver. 45 **96**[w] [Ps. 18:19] **97**[x] ver. 113, 163, 165; [Ps. 1:2] [y] ver. 15 **98**[z] [Deut. 4:6] **99**[a] [2 Tim. 3:15] **100**[b] See Job 32:7-9 [c] ver. 56, 69 **101**[d] Prov. 1:15 **103**[e] Ps. 19:10 **104**[f] ver. 128 **105**[g] Prov. 6:23 **106**[h] Neh. 10:29 [i] ver. 7 **107**[j] [ver. 25, 50] [k] ver. 88; See Ps. 71:20 **108**[l] [Hos. 14:2] [m] ver. 12 **109**[n] See Judg. 12:3 [o] ver. 83 **110**[p] See Ps. 91:3 [q] ver. 10 **111**[r] Deut. 33:4 [s] ver. 14, 162 **112**[t] ver. 36 [u] See ver. 33 **113**[v] [1 Kgs. 18:21; James 1:8; 4:8] [w] ver. 97 **114**[x] See Ps. 32:7 [y] See Ps. 3:3 [z] ver. 74 **115**[a] See Ps. 6:8 [b] [ver. 22]

116 Uphold me [c]according to your promise,
that I may live,
and let me not be [d]put to shame in my
[e]hope!
117 [f]Hold me up, that I may be safe
and have regard for your statutes continually!
118 You [g]spurn all who [h]go astray from your
statutes,
for their cunning is in vain.
119 All the wicked of the earth you discard
like [i]dross,
therefore [j]I love your testimonies.
120 My flesh [k]trembles for fear of you,
and I am afraid of your judgments.

AYIN

121 I have done what is just and right;
do not leave me to my oppressors.
122 Give your servant [l]a pledge of good;
let not [m]the insolent oppress me.
123 My [n]eyes long for your salvation
and for the fulfillment of your righteous promise.
124 Deal with your servant according to
your steadfast love,
and [o]teach me your statutes.
125 I am your [p]servant; [q]give me understanding,
that I may know your testimonies!
126 It is time for the LORD to act,
for your law has been broken.
127 Therefore I [r]love your commandments
above gold, above fine gold.
128 Therefore I consider all your precepts to
be right;
I hate every [s]false way.

PE

129 Your testimonies are [t]wonderful;
therefore my soul [u]keeps them.
130 The unfolding of your words gives
light;
it imparts [v]understanding to the simple.
131 I [w]open my mouth and [x]pant,
because I [y]long for your commandments.
132 [z]Turn to me and be gracious to me,
as is your way with those who love
your name.
133 [a]Keep steady my steps according to your
promise,
and let no iniquity [b]get dominion
over me.
134 [c]Redeem me from man's oppression,
that I may keep your precepts.
135 [d]Make your face shine upon your servant,
and [e]teach me your statutes.
136 My eyes [f]shed streams of tears,
because people [g]do not keep your law.

TSADHE

137 [h]Righteous are you, O LORD,
and right are your rules.
138 You have appointed your testimonies in
[i]righteousness
and in all [j]faithfulness.
139 My [k]zeal consumes me,
because my foes forget your words.
140 Your promise is well [l]tried,
and your servant [m]loves it.
141 I am small and despised,
yet I do not [n]forget your precepts.
142 Your righteousness is righteous forever,
and your law is [o]true.
143 Trouble and anguish have found me out,
but your commandments are my
[p]delight.
144 Your testimonies are righteous forever;
[q]give me understanding that I may [r]live.

QOPH

145 With my [s]whole heart I cry; answer me,
O LORD!
I will [t]keep your statutes.
146 I call to you; save me,
that I may observe your testimonies.
147 I rise before [u]dawn and cry for help;
I [v]hope in your words.
148 My eyes are awake before [w]the watches
of the night,
that I may meditate on your promise.
149 Hear my voice according to your steadfast love;
O LORD, [x]according to your justice
[y]give me life.
150 They draw near who persecute me with
evil purpose;
they are far from your law.
151 But [z]you are near, O LORD,
and all your commandments are [a]true.

116[c] ver. 41 [d] ver. 31; See Ps. 25:2 [e] Ps. 146:5 **117**[f] [Ps. 20:2] **118**[g] Lam. 1:15 [h] ver. 10, 21, 110 **119**[i] Isa. 1:25; [Ezek. 22:18; Mal. 3:2, 3] [j] ver. 97 **120**[k] [Job 4:14; Hab. 3:16] **122**[l] See Job 17:3 [m] ver. 51 **123**[n] ver. 82 **124**[o] ver. 12 **125**[p] See Ps. 116:16 [q] ver. 27 **127**[r] ver. 72; Ps. 19:10 **128**[s] ver. 104 **129**[t] ver. 18, 27 [u] ver. 22 **130**[v] See Ps. 19:7 **131**[w] Ps. 81:10; Job 29:23 [x] Ps. 42:1 [y] ver. 20 **132**[z] See Ps. 25:16 **133**[a] [Ps. 17:5] [b] Ps. 19:13 **134**[c] [Luke 1:74] **135**[d] See Ps. 4:6 [e] ver. 12 **136**[f] Jer. 9:1, 18; 14:17; Lam. 3:48; [Ezek. 9:4; Phil. 3:18] [g] ver. 158 **137**[h] See Ps. 116:5 **138**[i] ver. 75, 172; See Ps. 19:7-9 [j] ver. 86 **139**[k] See Ps. 69:9 **140**[l] See Ps. 12:6 [m] ver. 97 **141**[n] ver. 83 **142**[o] ver. 151, 160; John 17:17; [Ps. 19:2] **143**[p] ver. 24 **144**[q] ver. 27 [r] ver. 17 **145**[s] ver. 2, 10 [t] ver. 22, 33 **147**[u] See Ps. 5:3 [v] ver. 74 **148**[w] See Ps. 42:8 **149**[x] ver. 156; [ver. 40] [y] ver. 25; See Ps. 71:20 **151**[z] See Ps. 145:18 [a] See ver. 142

152 Long have I known from your testimonies
that you have [b]founded them forever.

RESH

153 Look on my [c]affliction and deliver me,
for [d]I do not forget your law.
154 [e]Plead my cause and redeem me;
[f]give me life according to your promise!
155 [g]Salvation is far from the wicked,
[h]for they do not seek your statutes.
156 [i]Great is your mercy, O LORD;
[f]give me life according to your rules.
157 [j]Many are my persecutors and my adversaries,
but I do not [k]swerve from your testimonies.
158 I look at [l]the faithless with [m]disgust,
because they do not keep your commands.
159 Consider how I [n]love your precepts!
[f]Give me life according to your steadfast love.
160 [o]The sum of your word is [p]truth,
and every one of your [q]righteous rules
endures forever.

SIN AND SHIN

161 [r]Princes persecute me [s]without cause,
but my heart [t]stands in awe of your words.
162 I [t]rejoice at your word
like one who [u]finds great spoil.
163 I hate and abhor falsehood,
but I love [v]your law.
164 Seven times a day I praise you
for your [q]righteous rules.
165 Great [w]peace have those who love your law;
[x]nothing can make them stumble.
166 I [y]hope for your salvation, O LORD,
and I do your commandments.
167 My soul keeps your testimonies;
I [v]love them exceedingly.
168 I keep your precepts and testimonies,
[z]for all my ways are before you.

TAW

169 Let my [a]cry come before you, O LORD;
[b]give me understanding [c]according to your word!
170 Let my plea come before you;
[d]deliver me according to your word.
171 My lips will [e]pour forth praise,
for you [f]teach me your statutes.
172 My tongue will sing of your word,
for [g]all your commandments are right.
173 Let your hand be ready to help me,
for I have [h]chosen your precepts.
174 I [i]long for your salvation, O LORD,
and your law is my [j]delight.
175 Let my soul live and praise you,
and let your rules help me.
176 I have [k]gone astray like a lost sheep; seek your servant,
for I do not [l]forget your commandments.

Deliver Me, O LORD

120

A SONG OF [m]ASCENTS.

In my distress I called to the LORD,
and he answered me.
2 Deliver me, O LORD,
from lying lips,
from a deceitful tongue.

3 What shall be given to you,
[n]and what more shall be done to you,
you deceitful tongue?

Psalm 120 Psalms 120–134 comprise the "psalms [or "songs"] of ascent," thought to be recited by pilgrims ascending to Jerusalem for sacred festivals and other times of worship. Many of these psalms express the affliction of life that the people of God undergo, while also extolling God as their only hope and joy and source of life.

Psalm 120 begins by recalling prior distresses and God's faithfulness and deliverance. Evidently, the psalmist has been exiled and is living with pagan peoples who do not worship the God of Israel (see vv. 5–7). Furthermore, these foreigners promote war instead of peace, and the psalmist has cried out to the God of peace to frustrate their plans for war and oppression. Due to God's past faithfulness in answering when called upon (v. 1), the psalmist now is emboldened to cry out for deliverance once again. That God alone is Savior, and faithful, and powerful gives the psalmist confidence over the deception of his opponents. God's power and grace, in the end, are what will bring victory to God's people; God can be relied upon to bring the lasting and permanent peace the psalmist longs to experience.

152[b] ver. 89, 160; [Matt. 5:18]
153[c] Job 36:15 [d] ver. 83
154[e] Ps. 35:1 [f] ver. 25
155[g] Job 5:4 [h] [ver. 150]
156[i] 2 Sam. 24:14 [f] [See ver. 154 above]
157[j] Ps. 3:1, 2 [k] See ver. 51
158[l] [Jer. 3:20] [m] Ps. 139:21; [ver. 136]
159[n] ver. 97 [f] [See ver. 154 above]
160[o] Ps. 139:17 [p] [ver. 142, 172] [q] ver. 7
161[r] ver. 23; [1 Sam. 24:11; 26:18] [s] See Ps. 69:4 [t] [Ps. 2:11]
162[t] [See ver. 161 above] [u] 1 Sam. 30:16; Isa. 9:3; [Matt. 13:44]
163[v] ver. 97
164[q] [See ver. 160 above]

165[w] Ps. 37:11, 37; [Prov. 3:2] [x] Prov. 3:23; 1 John 2:10; [Matt. 13:41] **166**[y] ver. 174; Gen. 49:18 **167**[v] [See ver. 163 above] **168**[z] Ps. 139:3; Prov. 5:21
169[a] [ver. 145] [b] See ver. 34 [c] ver. 65 **170**[d] ver. 41 **171**[e] Ps. 145:7 [f] ver. 12 **172**[g] [ver. 160] **173**[h] Josh. 24:22; [Prov. 1:29] **174**[i] ver. 20 [j] ver. 24
176[k] Isa. 53:6; 1 Pet. 2:25; [Matt. 18:12; Luke 15:4] [l] ver. 83 **Psalm 120** [m] Ex. 34:24; 1 Kgs. 12:27; Isa. 30:29 **3**[n] [1 Sam. 3:17]

4 [o]A warrior's [p]sharp arrows,
with glowing [q]coals of the broom tree!
5 Woe to me, that I sojourn in [r]Meshech,
that I dwell among [s]the tents of [t]Kedar!
6 Too long have I had my dwelling
among those who hate peace.
7 [u]I am for peace,
but when I speak, they are for war!

My Help Comes from the LORD

121 A SONG OF [m]ASCENTS.
I [v]lift up my eyes to [w]the hills.
From where does my help come?
2 [x]My help comes from the LORD,
who [y]made heaven and earth.
3 He will not [z]let your foot be moved;
he who [a]keeps you will not slumber.
4 Behold, he who keeps Israel
will neither slumber nor sleep.
5 The LORD is your keeper;
the LORD is your [b]shade on your
[c]right hand.
6 [d]The sun shall not [e]strike you by day,
nor the moon by night.
7 The LORD will [a]keep you from all evil;
he will [a]keep your life.
8 The LORD will keep
your [f]going out and your coming in
from this time forth and forevermore.

Let Us Go to the House of the LORD

122 A SONG OF [m]ASCENTS. OF DAVID.
I was glad when they said to me,
[g]"Let us go to the house of the LORD!"
2 Our feet have been standing
within your gates, O Jerusalem!
3 Jerusalem—[h]built as a city
that is [i]bound firmly together,
4 to which the tribes [j]go up,
the tribes of the LORD,
as was [k]decreed for[1] Israel,
to give thanks to the name of the LORD.
5 There [l]thrones for judgment were set,
the thrones of the house of David.
6 [m]Pray for the peace of Jerusalem!
"May they be secure who love you!
7 Peace be within your [n]walls
and security within your [n]towers!"

[1] Or *as a testimony for*

Jesus himself is the supreme instance of a man who came in peace but who experienced undeserved hostility. And yet in a marvel of God's providence and grace, the act of hostility that put Christ to death is the very means by which sinners, naturally hostile to God, can be reconciled to God and receive undeserved peace.

Psalm 121 In their ascent to Jerusalem, pilgrims traveled dangerous roads and pathways. Their confidence along the way was focused on the destination point—not merely the "hills" (v. 1) where Jerusalem lay but more importantly the God of those hills and of that city. For this was the covenant God who had promised his people his care, provision, and protection as they walked faithfully with him. Indeed, their help came from the Lord, Yahweh, the God who made the heavens and the earth (v. 2). As they traveled uncertain paths, they knew his presence would never fail (vv. 3–4). Day and night, he would watch over them (vv. 5–6).

As people traveled down the Jordan Valley southwards and then turned west to ascend the steep roadway to Jerusalem, the sun would be to their left side. The Lord, then, was likened to the shade on their right hand (v. 5), where comfort and protection was felt. God would keep them from danger as they traveled to and then from the city of God, and throughout all the days of their lives (vv. 7–8). We see, then, the covenant care and grace of God toward his people. As they follow faithfully in his ways, and do what he has called them to do, they can be assured of his watchful presence. The good news of God's grace toward his people, then, involves not only their past—i.e., forgiveness of sin—but also their futures—i.e., trusting his watchful care of their lives daily as they walk by faith in his power, his promise, and his presence. For we have been united to Christ, whose invincible care for us will never fail—"from this time forth and forevermore" (v. 8; cf. Heb. 13:5–8).

Psalm 122 With the pilgrims' journey of Psalm 121 complete, these followers of Yahweh now stand within the gates of Jerusalem (Ps. 122:1–2). How glad they are to be in this place, this city and temple that mark the covenant promises of God to his own people!

4 [o]Ps. 127:4; Jer. 50:9 [p]Ps. 45:5 [q]Ps. 140:10; Prov. 25:22
5 [r]Gen. 10:2; Ezek. 27:13; 38:2, 3; 39:1 [s]Song 1:5 [t]Gen. 25:13; Isa. 60:7; Jer. 49:28; Ezek. 27:21
7 [u][Ps. 109:4]

Psalm 121
[m][See Ps. 120, title]
1 [v]See Ps. 123:1 [w]Ps. 87:1; 133:3; Jer. 3:23; [Ps. 48:1]
2 [x]Ps. 124:8; [Ps. 20:2] [y]See Ps. 115:15
3 [z]Ps. 66:9; Prov. 3:23, 26; [1 Sam. 2:9] [a]Ps. 41:2; 127:1; [Isa. 27:3]; See Ps. 97:10
5 [b]Ps. 91:1 [c]See Ps. 16:8
6 [d]Isa. 49:10; Rev. 7:16 [e]2 Kgs. 4:19; Jonah 4:8
7 [a][See ver. 3 above]
8 [f]Deut. 28:6; 31:2; [Num. 27:17; 1 Sam. 29:6; 1 Kgs. 3:7; Acts 1:21]

Psalm 122
[m][See Ps. 120, title]
1 [g]Isa. 2:3; Mic. 4:2; Zech. 8:21
3 [h]Ps. 147:2 [i]Neh. 4:6
4 [j]Deut. 16:16 [k]Ps. 78:5
5 [l]Deut. 17:8; 2 Sam. 15:2; 1 Kgs. 3:16; 7:7; 2 Chr. 19:8
6 [m][Ps. 51:18; Jer. 29:7]
7 [n]Ps. 48:13

8 For my brothers and companions' sake
I will say, [o]"Peace be within you!"
9 For the sake of the house of the LORD our God,
I will [p]seek your good.

Our Eyes Look to the LORD Our God

123

A SONG OF [m]ASCENTS.
To you I [q]lift up my eyes,
O you who are [r]enthroned in the heavens!
2 Behold, as the eyes of servants
look to the hand of their master,
as the eyes of a maidservant
to the hand of her mistress,
so our eyes look to the LORD our God,
till he has mercy upon us.

3 [s]Have mercy upon us, O LORD, have mercy upon us,
for we have had more than enough of [t]contempt.
4 Our soul has had more than enough
of [u]the scorn of [v]those who are at ease,
of the contempt of [w]the proud.

Our Help Is in the Name of the LORD

124

A SONG OF [m]ASCENTS. OF DAVID.
[x]If it had not been the LORD who was on our side—
[y]let Israel now say—
2 if it had not been the LORD who was on our side
when people rose up against us,
3 then they would have [z]swallowed us up alive,
when their anger was kindled against us;
4 then [a]the flood would have [b]swept us away,
the torrent would have gone [c]over us;
5 then over us would have gone
the raging waters.

6 Blessed be the LORD,
who has not given us
as prey to their teeth!
7 We have escaped like a bird
from [d]the snare of the fowlers;
the snare is broken,
and we have escaped!

8[o] [1 Sam. 25:6; Ps. 85:8]
9[p] Neh. 2:10; Esth. 10:3
Psalm 123
[m] [See Ps. 120, title]
1[q] Ps. 121:1; [Ps. 141:8]; See Ps. 25:15 [r] See Ps. 2:4
3[s] Ps. 4:1 [t] [Neh. 4:4]
4[u] [Neh. 2:19] [v] Isa. 32:9, 11; Amos 6:1 [w] See Ps. 119:51
Psalm 124
[m] [See Ps. 120, title]
1[x] Ps. 94:17 [y] Ps. 129:1
3[z] See Ps. 56:1
4[a] See Ps. 32:6; Job 22:11 [b] Ps. 69:2; Isa. 8:8 [c] Ps. 69:1
7[d] See Ps. 91:3

Among the most precious of those promises is God's declaration to David that he would forever have a son (i.e., descendant) sitting on the throne of Israel (see 2 Sam. 7:12–13). As the tribes of Israel ascend to Jerusalem, they acknowledge the special place the tribe of Judah plays in the outworking of God's covenant promises. They praise God for the throne of David that will not fail (Ps. 122:3–5). Yet these pilgrims realize the opposition Jerusalem and its king have faced. They pray for peace for this covenantal city, for the temple and for the throne that reside within (vv. 6–9). All of this reminds us that the line of the kings of David came to an abrupt end with the destruction of Jerusalem in 586 B.C. at the hands of Nebuchadnezzar, king of Babylon.

Yet this was not the final end! No, indeed, for God has brought forth the Greater Son of David, born of Mary, to take that throne and once again to reign over Jerusalem and all of the earth (see Luke 1:31–33). So what the pilgrims of old longed to see we now understand is fulfilled in the coming of Christ. Though the fullness of his reign is yet to be displayed, the certainty of it has been established—the King of Israel and of all the earth has come!

Psalm 123 Those faithful to God often feel the contempt of those who stand against God, and hence against them. So it is in this corporate psalm of lament. Those obeying God in their endeavor to come and worship at the temple in Jerusalem find themselves the objects of scorn and ridicule. The proud are mocking the humble, and those humble faithful feel the weight of the derision being heaped upon them (vv. 3–4).

But their hope is in the Lord! He is enthroned in the heavens as God over all (v. 1)! The images used in verse 2 are telling—they express the hope of those who are dependent entirely on the good will of the one in authority over them. The master must provide, or the servants surely lack; the mistress must show kindness, lest the maidservants despair. So here, those faithful to the Lord await the good that he, and only he, can give. To God and God alone they lift up their eyes (v. 1). There is good news proclaimed from God to his people, but this good news of grace and strength and salvation is found in only one place and through only one Lord. Only he who is enthroned in the heavens is worthy of our trust, and only he can deliver. Indeed, at the climax of all of history, God did indeed deliver—by sending his own Son so that sinners can be made right with God based on what Christ has done.

8 [e]Our help is in the name of the LORD,
who made heaven and earth.

The LORD Surrounds His People

125

A SONG OF [m]ASCENTS.
Those who [f]trust in the LORD are
like Mount Zion,
which [g]cannot be moved, but abides
forever.
2 As the mountains surround Jerusalem,
so [h]the LORD surrounds his people,
from this time forth and forevermore.
3 For [i]the scepter of wickedness shall not
[j]rest
on [k]the land allotted to the righteous,
lest the righteous [l]stretch out
their hands to do wrong.
4 [m]Do good, O LORD, to those who are good,
and to those who are [n]upright in their
hearts!
5 But those who [o]turn aside to their
[p]crooked ways
the LORD will lead away with [q]evildo-
ers!
[r]Peace be upon Israel!

Restore Our Fortunes, O LORD

126

A SONG OF [m]ASCENTS.
When the LORD [s]restored the
fortunes of Zion,
we were like those who [t]dream.
2 Then our [u]mouth was filled with laughter,
and our tongue with shouts of joy;

Psalm 124 This psalm continues the theme of the previous psalm. In even more explicit terms, the psalmist declares the exclusivity of the God of Israel, the covenant God of his people. He alone can deliver them from those who oppress them.

If the Lord had not been on the side of his people—i.e., if the covenant God of Israel, the Lord who revealed himself in Exodus 3:14 as the eternal "I AM" who is forever committed to his people for their good and their salvation—if this eternal and exclusively true God had not been on his people's side, they would have been destroyed (Ps. 124:1–5). But he *is* the true God, he *is* their God, and he *did* watch over them for their good (vv. 6–8). The psalmist likely reflects back on the exodus from Egypt, where God saved his people from the waters of the Red Sea (vv. 3–5), and he sees in this a basis for continued trust in this same saving and merciful God. As their past help has been from the Lord, so their present and future hope is in this true God—their God, who is the covenant God of Israel, who made heaven and earth (v. 8).

What amazing strength and hope there is in these words: the true and living God, the God who made heaven and earth, is none other than our God, the God of covenant faithfulness and mercy to his own people. This covenant faithfulness and mercy was clinched in the coming of Jesus Christ. There, in Christ, the demands of the covenant were kept on our behalf so that we can receive God's promised blessings even though we have failed and do not deserve them.

Psalm 125 The faithful of the Lord have strong reason for confidence. For those who trust in Yahweh—the Lord, the covenant God of Israel—are like Mount Zion (Jerusalem), which cannot be moved (v. 1). As Jerusalem is surrounded by protecting mountains, so God's people are surrounded by the presence of the Lord himself. God will not—indeed, he cannot—renounce his commitment to his own people. And so as Jerusalem is founded upon God's promise, his people likewise bask in the strength and confidence of his promise and covenant commitment to preserve them (vv. 2–4).

But we must recall that God's covenant promise is for those who truly are his people. And what marks those who are his? They are, by God's rich grace, good and upright in heart (v. 4), whereas those who have falsely professed their faith in God turn aside to crooked ways (v. 5). Peace, then, is promised and pledged to those who comprise the true Israel, the true people of God, those who follow him faithfully and seek to do his will. These we understand by God's further revelation are those who have been united to Christ by faith (Rom. 9:5; Gal. 3:7, 14).

Psalm 126 The covenant faithfulness and sovereign grace of God that preserved Jerusalem in the past (vv. 1–3) are the basis for confident expectation that the same powerful and gracious covenant God will restore Jerusalem in the future, come what may (vv. 4–6).

8 [e]Ps. 121:2
Psalm 125
[m][See Ps. 120, title]
1 [f]Ps. 25:2, 3 [g]Ps. 93:1; 104:5; [Prov. 10:30]
2 [h][2 Kgs. 6:17; Zech. 2:5]
3 [i]Isa. 14:5 [j]Isa. 30:30 [k]See Ps. 16:5 [l]Gen. 3:22; Ex. 22:8
4 [m]Ps. 119:68 [n]See Ps. 7:10
5 [o]See Ps. 40:4 [p]Prov. 2:15 [q]Ps. 92:7, 9; 94:4 [r]Ps. 128:6; Gal. 6:16
Psalm 126
[m][See Ps. 120, title]
1 [s]See Ps. 14:7 [t][Acts 12:9]
2 [u]Job 8:21

then they said among the nations,
[v]"The LORD has done great things for them."
3 The LORD has done great things for us;
we are glad.

4 Restore our fortunes, O LORD,
like streams in the Negeb!
5 [w]Those who sow in tears
shall reap with shouts of joy!
6 He who goes out weeping,
bearing the seed for sowing,
shall come home with shouts of joy,
bringing his sheaves with him.

Unless the LORD Builds the House

127 A SONG OF [m]ASCENTS. OF SOLOMON.
Unless the LORD builds the house,
those who build it labor in vain.
Unless the LORD [x]watches over the city,
the watchman stays awake in vain.
2 It is in vain that you rise up early
and go late to rest,
eating the bread of anxious [y]toil;
for he gives to his [z]beloved [a]sleep.

3 Behold, [b]children are a heritage from the LORD,
[c]the fruit of the womb a reward.
4 Like arrows in the hand of [d]a warrior
are the children[1] of one's youth.
5 Blessed is the man
who fills his quiver with them!
He shall not be put to shame
when he speaks with his enemies [e]in the gate.[2]

Blessed Is Everyone Who Fears the LORD

128 A SONG OF [m]ASCENTS.
[f]Blessed is everyone who fears the LORD,
who [g]walks in his ways!

[1] Or *sons* [2] Or *They shall not be put to shame when they speak with their enemies in the gate*

2[v] See Ps. 71:19
5[w] [Ezra 6:22; Neh. 12:43; Jer. 31:9; Gal. 6:9]; See Hag. 2:3-9
Psalm 127
[m] [See Ps. 120, title]
1[x] See Ps. 121:4
2[y] Gen. 3:17, 19 [z] Ps. 60:5
[a] [Mark 4:26, 27]
3[b] [Gen. 33:5] [c] Deut. 28:4; [Ps. 132:11]
4[d] Ps. 120:4
5[e] See Job 5:4
Psalm 128
[m] [See Ps. 120, title]
1[f] See Ps. 112:1 [g] Ps. 119:1; [Prov. 8:32]

Perhaps the psalmist was reflecting on some specific time of divine deliverance of Jerusalem—perhaps when David first brought the ark of the covenant into Jerusalem (2 Sam. 6:12–19), or when Jerusalem was spared from destruction by Sennacherib during the reign of Hezekiah (2 Kings 18–19). In a sense, the City of God had been under assault perpetually, and God had spared her over and again. The only reason for this was God's own commitment to this city, its temple, and most importantly, its chosen people. Even though Jerusalem would later be destroyed, first under Nebuchadnezzar in 586 B.C. and again by a Roman army in A.D. 70, yet God will do precisely what the psalmist declares in Psalm 126:4. God will restore the fortunes of Jerusalem and of his people. The Bible ends with the account of the new Jerusalem coming down from the sky, new and better than Jerusalem ever had been before (Revelation 21–22). No temple will be found there, "for its temple is the Lord God the Almighty and the Lamb" (Rev. 21:22). God will indeed restore the Holy City. In the light of Christ's coming and the great promises for the future, God's people have strong reason to trust him with resilient hope.

Psalm 127 Although the people of God are commanded to "build" (v. 1a) and "watch" (v. 1b) and "toil" (v. 2) and bring forth children (vv. 3–5), they must always remember that their labors are in vain apart from the enabling and sustaining grace and power of God. As our Lord Jesus reminds us, "apart from me you can do nothing" (John 15:5).

We exercise our human responsibility along with complete and utter dependence on God. Neither one cancels out the other. Our labor does not preclude either the need for or the legitimacy of God's sovereign oversight, just as the display of God's sovereign and gracious power does not render our labor superfluous. Psalm 127 reminds us that as we labor to build, and watch to protect, and toil to eat, and bring forth children for blessing, our ultimate and perpetual dependence must be on the God who alone can make these efforts succeed and bear fruit for eternity.

How good God is to give us meaningful work! But how good God is also to strengthen our hand, and instruct our minds, and direct our steps so that what we do will accomplish what he alone knows is best. This psalm places a special emphasis on the blessing of children (vv. 3–5). Those who are led to marry and then granted the privilege to raise children should see these little ones as evidence of God's blessing—they are, in the end, his children, not ours. Yes, we bear and raise them, but then we shoot them out as arrows (v. 4) to land in the places God designs. Indeed, even

2 You [h]shall eat the fruit of the labor of
your hands;
you shall be blessed, and it shall be
well with you.
3 Your wife will be like [i]a fruitful vine
within your house;
your children will be like [j]olive shoots
around your table.
4 Behold, thus shall the man be blessed
who fears the LORD.
5 [k]The LORD bless you [l]from Zion!
May you see [m]the prosperity of
Jerusalem
all the days of your life!
6 May you see your [n]children's children!
[o]Peace be upon Israel!

They Have Afflicted Me from My Youth

129 A SONG OF [m]ASCENTS.
"Greatly[1] have they [p]afflicted me
[q]from my youth"—
[r]let Israel now say—
2 "Greatly have they [p]afflicted me [q]from my
youth,
[s]yet they have not prevailed against
me.
3 [t]The plowers plowed [u]upon my back;
they made long their furrows."
4 The LORD is righteous;
he has cut [v]the cords of the wicked.
5 May all who hate Zion
be [w]put to shame and turned backward!
6 Let them be like [x]the grass on the housetops,
which [y]withers before it grows up,
7 with which the reaper does not fill his
hand
nor the binder of sheaves his arms,
8 nor do those who pass by say,
[a]"The blessing of the LORD be upon
you!
We [b]bless you in the name of the
LORD!"

[1] Or *Often*; also verse 2

our children, the fruit of our most consistent and diligent labor, come from God, are matured by God, and are to be used by God. All of life is God's abundant grace to us.

Psalm 128 We see here a blessing upon Zion, the City of God, and also upon the man who fears the Lord. The psalm opens generically: "Blessed is *everyone* who fears the LORD" (v. 1). This promise, then, is for every believer: to live in the fear of God is to invite his blessing upon one's life.

But as the psalm continues, its application is directed particularly at a believing husband and father who fears the Lord (i.e., gives God proper regard). A man's work (v. 2), his wife (v. 3a), and his children (v. 3b) all will prosper due to the fact that *he*—not they—fear the Lord (v. 4). What grace there is here! How kind God is! While he does visit the sins of the father on the third and fourth generations (Ex. 20:5), he shows kindness to "thousands" (Ex. 20:6) because of faithfulness to him in this generation; the consequences of sin are ultimately exceeded by and eclipsed by grace toward those who follow God. Psalm 128 expresses this important truth with further implications for all those responsible for the nurture of others. As this man, this husband and father, lives by God's grace a life in the fear of God, he can expect God's blessing to rest on his labor, on his wife, and on his children. Call this the "umbrella principle," perhaps. One man holds the umbrella faithfully, and, by God's grace, countless others are protected under the cover it provides. The switch, then, in verses 5–6, seems to be this: as a man fears God, his children are blessed, and so his city and nation likewise are blessed. As goes the husband and father, so go the children and nation. May we see our children's children (v. 6), because of God's blessing and the faithfulness of God's people!

Psalm 129 Pilgrims who ascend the pathway to Jerusalem understand that this city and nation have been afflicted from the very beginning by those opposed to the God of Israel. So the psalmist begins, "Greatly have they afflicted me from my youth" (v. 1), personifying the affliction of Israel herself.

Yet, despite their regular and severe affliction (v. 3), the enemies of Israel have not prevailed (v. 2), because the Lord has cut the cords the wicked used to hold Israel in bondage (v. 4). This may be a reference to the exodus, where God delivered his people from the bondage of slavery, but it probably refers to this and more. God

2[h] Isa. 3:10; [Ps. 109:11]
3[i] Ezek. 19:10; [Gen. 49:22] [j] See Ps. 52:8
5[k] Ps. 134:3 [l] Ps. 20:2; 135:21 [m] [Ps. 122:9]
6[n] Prov. 17:6; See Job 42:16 [o] Ps. 125:5

Psalm 129
[m] [See Ps. 120, title]
1[p] [Ex. 1:14; Judg. 3:8, 14; 4:3; 6:2; 10:8] [q] Isa. 47:12; Jer. 2:2; 22:21; Hos. 2:15 [r] Ps. 124:1
2[p] [See ver. 1 above] [q] [See ver. 1 above] [s] [2 Cor. 4:8-10]
3[t] Mic. 3:12 [u] [Isa. 50:6; 51:23]
4[v] Ps. 2:3
5[w] See Ps. 35:4
6[x] 2 Kgs. 19:26; Isa. 37:27 [y] Ps. 37:2; Job 8:12
8[a] Ruth 2:4 [b] Ps. 118:26

My Soul Waits for the Lord

130 A Song of [m]Ascents.
Out of [c]the depths I cry to you,
O Lord!
2 O Lord, hear my voice!
[d]Let your ears be attentive
to [e]the voice of my pleas for mercy!

3 If you, O Lord, should [f]mark iniquities,
O Lord, who could [g]stand?
4 But with you there is [h]forgiveness,
[i]that you may be feared.

5 I [j]wait for the Lord, [k]my soul waits,
and [l]in his word I hope;
6 my soul [m]waits for the Lord
more than [n]watchmen for [o]the morning,
more than watchmen for the morning.

7 O Israel, [p]hope in the Lord!
For [q]with the Lord there is steadfast love,
and with him is plentiful redemption.
8 And he will [r]redeem Israel
from all his iniquities.

I Have Calmed and Quieted My Soul

131 A Song of [m]Ascents. Of David.
O Lord, my heart is not [s]lifted up;
my eyes are not [t]raised too high;
I do not [u]occupy myself with things
too great and [v]too marvelous for me.
2 But I have calmed and quieted my soul,
like a weaned [w]child with its mother;
like a weaned child is my soul within me.

Psalm 130
[m] [See Ps. 120, title]
1 [c] Ps. 69:2, 14; Lam. 3:55; Jonah 2:2
2 [d] Ps. 86:6; 2 Chr. 6:40 [e] Ps. 140:6
3 [f] [Ps. 90:8]; See Job 10:14 [g] Ps. 76:7; Amos 2:15; Nah. 1:6; Mal. 3:2; Eph. 6:13; Rev. 6:17; [Ps. 143:2]
4 [h] ver. 7; Isa. 55:7; Dan. 9:9; See Ps. 86:5, 15 [i] 1 Kgs. 8:39, 40; Jer. 33:8, 9; [Rom. 2:4]
5 [j] Ps. 40:1; Isa. 8:17; 26:8 [k] See Ps. 33:20 [l] Ps. 119:74, 81
6 [m] [Ps. 123:2] [n] [Ps. 63:6; 119:147] [o] See Ps. 5:3
7 [p] Ps. 131:3 [q] ver. 4
8 [r] Ps. 111:9; Luke 1:68; Titus 2:14; [Matt. 1:21]; See Ps. 25:22

Psalm 131
[m] [See Ps. 120, title]
1 [s] [Ps. 138:6; Isa. 57:15] [t] See Ps. 101:5 [u] [Jer. 45:5; Rom. 12:16] [v] See Job 42:3
2 [w] [Matt. 18:3; 1 Cor. 14:20]

always protects and preserves his people, and he will save them even from their deepest and most severe bondage. We read these words not only in the context of Israel's immediate condition but also in the context of God's wider redemptive plan. As Israel's Messiah comes, who himself was afflicted beyond description (Isa. 52:14; 53:5, 7), he will deliver them from everlasting affliction (Isa. 53:10–11). With confidence, then, the psalmist declares that all who hate Zion will be put to shame (Ps. 129:5). They will fail in their attempts to destroy the people of God because they will not be able to preserve themselves (vv. 6–8), and God himself will show his continued favor and blessing to his covenant people (vv. 5–8). What grace and power the true God has; his people can always hope and trust in him.

Psalm 130 This individual psalm of lament focuses on the psalmist's own sin (vv. 1–3) but then generalizes at the psalm's conclusion to celebrate the forgiveness God brings to redeem Israel of all its iniquities (v. 8). Today this psalm of both narrow and wide deliverance brings great hope and healing to sinners individually and to the people of God corporately.

Given the covenant commitment of God to his people, one might wonder if there was something about the people, Israel, which elicited God's favor. Perhaps they were more righteous than other nations, and that's why he took them as his own people. Nothing could be further from the truth! The fact is, every individual Israelite, and all of them taken together, must acknowledge this truth: "If you, O Lord, should mark iniquities, O Lord, who could stand?" (v. 3). The implied answer, obviously, is "no one—not even one!" How remarkable, then, is the verse that follows: "But with you there is forgiveness, that you may be feared" (i.e., be given proper regard; v. 4). Both personal (v. 4) and corporate (v. 8) forgiveness is celebrated as the wondrous and gracious gift of God to an undeserving people.

But notice what this forgiveness is to produce. Those who bask in God's merciful forgiveness are to fear God. That is, those redeemed by grace walk in his ways with joyous reverence and a determination to turn from evil (v. 4). They are marked by waiting tirelessly and expectantly on the Lord (v. 6), and they place their hope in God and in him alone (v. 7). What sinners we are, and what grace God has shown—ultimately and lavishly expressed in Christ. How his followers should be marked, then, by faithful lives of trust and obedience.

Psalm 131 Some might wonder how the opening of this psalm of ascent can fit with expressions in other psalms of ascent. Here we read, "O Lord, my heart is not lifted up; my eyes are not raised too high" (v. 1), whereas elsewhere we read, "I lift up my eyes to the hills" (121:1), and, "To you I lift up my eyes, O you who are enthroned in the heavens!" (123:1). But as we consider these statements, we realize there is no conflict.

3 [x]O Israel, hope in the LORD
from this time forth and forevermore.

The LORD Has Chosen Zion

132 A SONG OF [m]ASCENTS.
Remember, O LORD, in David's favor,
all [y]the hardships he endured,
2 how he swore to the LORD
and [z]vowed to [a]the Mighty One of Jacob,
3 "I will not enter my house
or get into my bed,
4 I will not [b]give sleep to my eyes
or slumber to my eyelids,
5 until I [c]find a place for the LORD,
a dwelling place for [a]the Mighty One of Jacob."

6 Behold, we heard of it in [d]Ephrathah;
we found it in [e]the fields of Jaar.
7 "Let us go to his dwelling place;
let us [f]worship at his [g]footstool!"

8 [h]Arise, O LORD, and go to your [i]resting place,
you and the ark of your [j]might.
9 Let your [k]priests be [l]clothed with righteousness,
and let your [m]saints shout for joy.
10 For the sake of your servant David,
[n]do not turn away the face of [o]your anointed one.

11 [p]The LORD swore to David a sure oath
[q]from which he will not turn back:
[r]"One of the sons of your body[1]
I will set on your throne.
12 If your sons keep my covenant
and my testimonies that I shall teach them,
their sons also forever
shall [s]sit on your throne."

13 For the LORD has [t]chosen Zion;
he has [u]desired it for his dwelling place:
14 "This is my [v]resting place forever;
here I will [w]dwell, for I have desired it.
15 I will abundantly [x]bless her provisions;
I will [y]satisfy her poor with bread.
16 Her [z]priests I will clothe with salvation,
and her [z]saints will shout for joy.
17 There I will make [a]a horn to sprout for David;
I have prepared [b]a lamp for [c]my anointed.
18 His enemies I will [d]clothe with shame,
but on him his crown will shine."

[1] Hebrew *of your fruit of the womb*

In fact, precisely because the psalmist has his eyes lifted high to the hills, gazing on the One enthroned in the heavens, he is able to understand himself in proper perspective. His gaze toward God is high, but his consideration of himself is measured and modest. He recognizes that there is much he simply cannot understand rightly (131:1b), so he can be at peace entrusting those things to God. The calm and quiet of his soul (v. 2) is not an expression of resignation and defeat. Rather, he experiences this calm precisely as he expresses all of his hope in the superior greatness and majesty of the Lord (v. 3).

He longs, then, for the whole of the nation of Israel to experience the joy of this peace and calm, and so he calls them, "from this time forth and forevermore," to "hope in the LORD" (v. 3).

Psalm 132 God is a promise *making* and promise *keeping* God. There are few things taught in the Scriptures about God that are more central to his self-revelation to his people of who he is than this: God is faithful to his word, his oath, his promise, indeed, his covenant.

The background to Psalm 132 is 2 Samuel 7, where David expressed to Nathan his longing to build a house (i.e., temple) where the ark of the covenant would dwell (2 Sam. 7:2; Ps. 132:1–5). God revealed to Nathan that, while the temple would later be built, God had made a covenant with David that he would have a son (i.e., a descendant) who would sit on his throne forever (2 Sam. 7:12–13; Ps. 132:8–12). The pilgrims ascending to the temple in Jerusalem remind themselves, through this psalm, that God had chosen to show his favor to David, and to the city of Jerusalem where the kingship of David's Son would be manifest (Ps. 132:13–18).

But what those pilgrims of old longed for, we now have seen! Their longings were fulfilled in Jesus! When the angel Gabriel came to Mary to reveal to her that she was

3[x] Ps. 130:7
Psalm 132
[m] [See Ps. 120, title]
1[y] 1 Chr. 22:14
2[z] Ps. 50:14 [a] ver. 5; Gen. 49:24; Isa. 49:26; 60:16
4[b] Prov. 6:4
5[c] 1 Chr. 22:7; Acts 7:46 [a] [See ver. 2 above]
6[d] 1 Sam. 17:12; [Gen. 35:19] [e] [1 Sam. 7:1]
7[f] Ps. 5:7 [g] See Ps. 99:5
8[h] Ps. 68:1; 2 Chr. 6:41, 42 [i] ver. 14 [j] Ps. 78:61
9[k] ver. 16 [l] See Job 29:14 [m] [Ps. 149:5]
10[n] [2 Kgs. 18:24] [o] ver. 17; [1 Kgs. 1:39]
11[p] Ps. 89:3, 34 [q] Ps. 110:4 [r] 2 Sam. 7:12; 2 Chr. 6:16; Luke 1:32; Acts 2:30
12[s] 1 Kgs. 8:25; [Job 36:7]
13[t] Ps. 78:68; [Ps. 135:21] [u] See Ps. 68:16
14[v] ver. 8 [w] Matt. 23:21
15[x] Ps. 147:14 [y] Ruth 1:6
16[z] ver. 9
17[a] Ezek. 29:21; [Luke 1:69] [b] 1 Kgs. 11:36; 15:4; 2 Kgs. 8:19; 2 Chr. 21:7 [c] ver. 10
18[d] See Job 8:22

When Brothers Dwell in Unity

133 A Song of [m]Ascents. Of David.
Behold, how good and pleasant it is
when [e]brothers dwell in unity![1]
2 It is like the precious [f]oil on [g]the head,
running down on the beard,
on the beard of Aaron,
running down on [h]the collar of his robes!
3 It is like [i]the dew of [j]Hermon,
which falls on [k]the mountains of Zion!
For there the Lord [l]has commanded the blessing,
life forevermore.

Come, Bless the Lord

134 A Song of [m]Ascents.
Come, bless the Lord, all you [m]servants of the Lord,
who [n]stand [o]by night in the house of the Lord!
2 [p]Lift up your hands to [q]the holy place
and bless the Lord!

[1] Or *dwell together*

Psalm 133
[m] [See Ps. 120, title]
1 [e] [Gen. 13:8; Heb. 13:1]
2 [f] Ex. 30:25, 30 [g] Ex. 29:7; Lev. 8:12 [h] Ex. 28:33; 39:24; [Ex. 28:32; 39:23; Job 30:18]
3 [i] Prov. 19:12; Mic. 5:7 [j] Deut. 3:9; 4:48 [k] See Ps. 48:1 [l] Lev. 25:21; Deut. 28:8; See Ps. 42:8

Psalm 134
[m] [See Ps. 120, title]
1 [m] Ps. 135:1 [n] Deut. 10:8; 18:7; 1 Chr. 23:30; 2 Chr. 29:11; 35:5 [o] 1 Chr. 9:33; [Lev. 8:35]
2 [p] See Ps. 28:2 [q] Ps. 63:2

chosen to give birth to the long-awaited Messiah, Gabriel reminded Mary that, "the Lord God will give to him the throne of his father David, and he will reign over the house of Jacob forever, and of his kingdom there will be no end" (Luke 1:32–33). Surely God is faithful to his promise; he keeps his word. Both in the coming of Christ and in the gospel that announces what Christ has accomplished, God demonstrates that he is absolutely and unequivocally faithful.

Psalm 133 The unity of God's people has been, and continues to be, a sign of God's rich blessing. Here the psalmist reflects on those who are bound together in the worship of Yahweh at the temple, and he revels in their union in faith and practice as the true people of God.

He likens this unity to two different but equally important parts of their lives: unity in their holiness, as they submit to the practices of the priesthood by which their sins are forgiven and they are represented to God (v. 2); and unity in their dependence on God for his physical blessing, bringing moisture from the higher mountains in the north to water the needy land of Palestine (v. 3). Both the priestly and the natural images also depict things distant from one another being joined by another element flowing down (the oil uniting Aaron's head and collar; and dew uniting a northern, high mountain with southern, lower hills). Spiritual and physical blessings are both good gifts from God above, and those who see God's hand at work in both ways unite in their common praise of their gracious God.

As believers on this side of the cross, our minds are naturally brought to the unity we have in Christ (e.g., John 17:21–23). The basis for our unity is even greater now that the fulfillment of those priestly laws has come, and the true Mediator of God's people with their heavenly Father intercedes for us. If there was beauty in the unity of God's people at the temple, how much more is the glory of our union shown as we, in Christ, display our devotion and love for him.

Psalm 134 This final psalm of the psalms of ascent calls the people of God generally, and those ministering at the temple on behalf of the people specifically, to join together in offering praise to their God. The lifting up of holy hands (v. 2) is an outward expression of adoration and worship. It acknowledges the true greatness, not of the people themselves, but of the God whom they love, serve, and worship.

Yet in their very worship of God they recognize how very much they need his continued blessing on their lives. Their worship therefore leads naturally to expectation of God's continued blessing on them (v. 3). Rightly seen, both the offering to God of worship, and the receiving from God of what we need, are the twin sides of all true worship. God is honored both as we give expression to his greatness and glory, and as we open our hearts and hands to receive from him what only he can give. After all, he alone "made heaven and earth" (v. 3), and hence he alone stands above all need. What a marvelous conclusion to the songs of ascent—a reminder of the obligation and joy of God's people both to offer praise worthy of God's greatness and to receive his blessing which we need day by day. We, the needy ones, give glory to God as we receive what he graciously shares out of the bounty of his infinite fullness—a grace ultimately made manifest in his own Son.

3 May the LORD [r]bless you [s]from Zion,
he who [t]made heaven and earth!

Your Name, O LORD, Endures Forever

135 [u]Praise the LORD!
Praise the name of the LORD,
give praise, O [v]servants of the LORD,
2 who [n]stand in the house of the LORD,
in [w]the courts of the house of our God!
3 Praise the LORD, for [x]the LORD is good;
sing to his name, [y]for it is pleasant![1]
4 For the LORD has [z]chosen Jacob for himself,
Israel as his [a]own possession.

5 For I know that [b]the LORD is great,
and that our Lord is above all gods.
6 [c]Whatever the LORD pleases, he does,
in heaven and on earth,
in the seas and all deeps.
7 [d]He it is who makes the clouds rise at the end of the earth,
who [e]makes lightnings for the rain
and brings forth the wind from his [f]storehouses.

8 He it was who [g]struck down the firstborn of Egypt,
both of man and of beast;
9 who in your midst, O Egypt,
sent [h]signs and wonders
against Pharaoh and all his servants;
10 [i]who struck down many nations
and killed mighty kings,
11 [j]Sihon, king of the Amorites,
and [k]Og, king of Bashan,
and [l]all the kingdoms of Canaan,
12 and [m]gave their land as a heritage,
a heritage to his people Israel.

13 [n]Your name, O LORD, endures forever,
[o]your renown,[2] O LORD, throughout all ages.
14 [p]For the LORD will vindicate his people
and [q]have compassion on his servants.

15 [r]The idols of the nations are silver and gold,
the work of human hands.
16 They have mouths, but do not speak;
they have eyes, but do not see;
17 they have ears, but do not hear,
nor is there any breath in their mouths.
18 Those who make them become like them,
so do all who trust in them.

19 [s]O house of Israel, bless the LORD!
O house of Aaron, bless the LORD!
20 O house of Levi, bless the LORD!
You who fear the LORD, bless the LORD!
21 Blessed be the LORD [t]from Zion,
he who [u]dwells in Jerusalem!
[v]Praise the LORD!

[1] Or *for he is beautiful* [2] Or *remembrance*

Psalm 135 The God of Israel, the only true and living God, is worthy of all praise (vv. 1–3), for he has chosen Israel as his own possession (v. 4), he is the sovereign ruler of all of the world that he has made (vv. 5–7), and he is the gracious and powerful redeemer of these people of his choosing (vv. 8–12). What fools other peoples and nations are, who worship their idols. Those false, pretender deities cannot see or hear or speak or act (vv. 13–17), and those who worship them become as empty as their gods themselves are (v. 18).

In contrast, how blessed the people of Israel are! Their God truly is God, and they truly are his chosen people. The privilege of their position as the people of God has nothing to do with them and rather has everything to do with the sovereign grace and power of God. Oh what mercy is shown in the gracious love of God. What hope should fill the hearts of the people of God to know that they are saved and secured by the same God who controls the natural forces of the world (vv. 7–12). And, because they are the people he has rescued, he is committed to them, with sovereign power that rules heaven and earth, to bring about all the good he intends for them.

We can know for certain that everything that washes into our lives is for our good because this same God who controls creation and nations sent Jesus Christ for us. Even when we cannot make sense of our circumstances, we know the character and power of our God revealed in his redemption and creation. Therefore we trust him, believing all that we experience is from the hand of a sovereign God, who is also a heavenly Father. In the plan and provision of Christ, our God has infallibly demonstrated that he loves us eternally and, by his sovereign rule over creation, he assures us that he can direct all things necessary for our ultimate good. We could not be more secure.

3 [r]Num. 6:24 [s]Ps. 128:5 [t]See Ps. 115:15
Psalm 135
1 [u]See Ps. 104:35 [v]See Ps. 113:1
2 [n][See Ps. 134:1 above] [w]Ps. 92:13
3 [x]See Ps. 100:5 [y]Ps. 147:1; [Ps. 52:9]
4 [z]Deut. 7:6, 7; 10:15; See Ps. 105:6 [a]Ex. 19:5
5 [b]Ps. 95:3
6 [c]Ps. 115:3
7 [d]Jer. 10:13; 51:16 [e][Job 28:25, 26; 38:25; Zech. 10:1] [f]Job 38:22
8 [g]See Ps. 78:51
9 [h]Deut. 6:22
10 [i]For ver. 10-12, see Ps. 136:17-22
11 [j]Deut. 29:7; See Num. 21:21-26 [k]See Num. 21:33-35 [l]See Josh. 12:7-24
12 [m]Deut. 29:8; See Ps. 78:55
13 [n]Ex. 3:15 [o]Ps. 102:12
14 [p]Deut. 32:36 [q]See Ps. 90:13
15 [r]For ver. 15-18, see Ps. 115:4-8
19 [s]See Ps. 115:9
21 [t]Ps. 128:5 [u]Ps. 132:13, 14 [v]ver. 1

His Steadfast Love Endures Forever

136 [w]Give thanks to the LORD, for he
is good,
[x]for his steadfast love endures forever.
2 Give thanks to [y]the God of gods,
for his steadfast love endures forever.
3 Give thanks to [y]the Lord of lords,
for his steadfast love endures forever;

4 to him who alone [z]does great wonders,
for his steadfast love endures forever;
5 to him who [a]by understanding [b]made
the heavens,
for his steadfast love endures forever;
6 to him who [c]spread out the earth [d]above
the waters,
for his steadfast love endures forever;
7 to him who [e]made the great lights,
for his steadfast love endures forever;
8 the sun to rule over the day,
for his steadfast love endures forever;
9 the moon and stars to rule over the night,
for his steadfast love endures forever;

10 to him who [f]struck down the firstborn
of Egypt,
for his steadfast love endures forever;
11 and [g]brought Israel out from among
them,
for his steadfast love endures forever;
12 with [h]a strong hand and an outstretched
arm,
for his steadfast love endures forever;
13 to him who [i]divided the Red Sea in two,
for his steadfast love endures forever;
14 [j]and made Israel pass through the midst
of it,
for his steadfast love endures forever;
15 but [k]overthrew[1] Pharaoh and his host in
the Red Sea,
for his steadfast love endures forever;
16 to him who [l]led his people through the
wilderness,
for his steadfast love endures forever;

17 to him [m]who struck down great kings,
for his steadfast love endures forever;
18 and killed mighty kings,
for his steadfast love endures forever;
19 Sihon, king of the Amorites,
for his steadfast love endures forever;
20 and Og, king of Bashan,
for his steadfast love endures forever;
21 and gave their land as a heritage,
for his steadfast love endures forever;
22 a heritage to Israel his [n]servant,
for his steadfast love endures forever.

23 It is he who [o]remembered us in our low
estate,
for his steadfast love endures forever;
24 and [p]rescued us from our foes,
for his steadfast love endures forever;
25 he who [q]gives food to all flesh,
for his steadfast love endures forever.

26 Give thanks to [r]the God of heaven,
for his steadfast love endures forever.

[1] Hebrew *shook off*

Psalm 136
1[w] Ps. 106:1; 107:1; 118:1 [x] See 1 Chr. 16:41
2[y] Deut. 10:17
3[y] [See ver. 2 above]
4[z] See Ps. 72:18
5[a] Prov. 3:19; Jer. 10:12; 51:15 [b] See Gen. 1:1
6[c] Isa. 42:5; 44:24 [d] Ps. 24:2
7[e] Gen. 1:16
10[f] See Ps. 78:51
11[g] Ex. 12:51; 13:3
12[h] Deut. 4:34
13[i] See Ps. 78:13
14[j] Ex. 14:21, 22
15[k] Ex. 14:27; [Ps. 78:53]
16[l] Ex. 15:22; Deut. 8:15; See Ps. 77:20
17[m] For ver. 17-22, see Ps. 135:10-12
22[n] Ps. 105:6, 26
23[o] Gen. 8:1; [Deut. 32:36]
24[p] Ps. 107:2
25[q] Ps. 104:27; See Job 36:31
26[r] Ezra 5:12; Neh. 1:4; Dan. 2:18

Psalm 136 This psalm is unique in the Psalter in having the same refrain ("for his steadfast love endures forever") for every verse of the psalm. The Hebrew word translated "steadfast love" is *hesed* and refers to the covenant commitment and loyal, faithful love that originates in God and is resolutely expressed toward his people.

The psalmist reflects mostly on three areas of God's work and ties each area to God's steadfast love. After beginning with a note of thanksgiving to this God of steadfast love (vv. 1–3), he then declares that God created and rules over the heavens and earth, the sun, moon, and stars (vv. 4–9); that God saw the affliction of his people in Egypt and moved in to save them from their oppressors (vv. 10–16); and that God preserved his people in their wilderness wanderings, fulfilling his promise to them by bringing them into the Promised Land (vv. 17–25).

A final note of thanksgiving takes us back to where we began: "Give thanks to the God of heaven, for his steadfast love endures forever" (v. 26). Each of these three main areas—God as creator, redeemer, and protector/provider—elicit from the psalmist the same response: "for his steadfast love endures forever." Were it not for the faithfulness of God to his people, they would have no hope. God does not show his care to them, provide for them, protect them from harm, fulfill good for them, because they deserve these kindnesses from the Lord! Indeed, though they (and we!) are totally undeserving of any good thing from God's hand, he nonetheless showers his people with his loyal and steadfast love. The steadfast love of the Lord is supremely revealed in the sending of his own Son to suffer and die for the sins of his people.

How Shall We Sing the LORD's Song?

137 By the waters of Babylon,
there we sat down and wept,
when we remembered Zion.
2 On the willows[1] there
we hung up our lyres.
3 For there our captors
required of us songs,
and our tormentors, mirth, saying,
"Sing us one of the songs of Zion!"

4 [s]How shall we sing the LORD's song
in a foreign land?
5 If I forget you, O Jerusalem,
[t]let my right hand forget its skill!
6 Let my [u]tongue stick to the roof of my mouth,
if I do not remember you,
if I do not set Jerusalem
above my highest joy!

7 Remember, O LORD, against the [v]Edomites
[w]the day of Jerusalem,
how they said, [x]"Lay it bare, lay it bare,
down to its foundations!"
8 O daughter of Babylon, [y]doomed to be destroyed,
blessed shall he be who [z]repays you
with what you have done to us!
9 Blessed shall he be who takes your little ones
and [a]dashes them against the rock!

Give Thanks to the LORD

138 OF DAVID.
[b]I give you thanks, O LORD, with my whole heart;
before [c]the gods I sing your praise;
2 I bow down [d]toward your [e]holy temple
and give thanks to your name for
your steadfast love and your faithfulness,
for you have exalted above all things
your name and your word.[2]
3 On the day I called, you answered me;
my strength of soul you increased.[3]

[1] Or *poplars* [2] Or *you have exalted your word above all your name* [3] Hebrew *you made me bold in my soul with strength*

Psalm 137 This psalm gives expression to the longing of God's people, now in exile in Babylon, for the restoration of their beloved Jerusalem and the vindication of God's justice against their oppressors. In 586 B.C., Nebuchadnezzar and the Babylonian army destroyed Jerusalem, its temple and wall, and took most of its residents captive in Babylon. The psalm portrays the ways their captors mock them by demanding that they sing songs of Zion by the waters of Babylon (vv. 1–6). These godly Israelites long for justice; they long for God to vindicate his holy name and bring vengeance upon those who have destroyed the city of God, its temple, and families—killing wives, husbands, and children. The Edomites (descendants of Esau), on the east side of the Dead Sea, joined the Babylonians in the destruction of Jerusalem, so the psalm calls for vengeance also on Edom (v. 7).

But the stronger denunciation is against Babylon herself (vv. 8–9). Is it right for godly people to request what we read in Psalm 137:9? If we believe that salvation is by sovereign grace, this means that God chooses to save some who deserve condemnation. But the other side of God's gracious choice to save some—on the other side of the gospel itself—is God's righteous choice to judge others who likewise deserve condemnation.

The cry of Psalm 137:9 is the cry for justice to be served upon those who have abused and killed the children of Israel. Still, the words calling for retributive execution of children shock us. The words may simply reflect the idioms of warfare language from ancient times, or may be the expression of unrepressed anger and agony from the heart of one who has been victimized by such cruelty. Yet before we would ever utter such words, we should take careful notice that this verse comes in the context of an appeal for *God* to bring about a just sentence upon Israel's oppressors (see v. 8). As Jesus, who "when he was reviled, . . . did not revile in return; when he suffered, . . . did not threaten, but continued entrusting himself to him who judges justly" (1 Pet. 2:23), so God's people may call upon God to enact the justice he knows is right. But we leave this in his hands to enact, in his way, in his time, and by authorities of his appointment.

Psalm 138 Psalms 138–145 comprise the final set of psalms in the Psalter attributed to David. Here, David focuses on God's faithfulness to him personally (138:1–3, 7–8), which extends, then, to God's faithfulness to Israel as a whole through whom the nations of the world will one day bow in thanksgiving to Yahweh, the God of Israel (vv. 4–6).

Psalm 137
4[s] [Neh. 2:3]
5[t] [Ps. 76:5]
6[u] Job 29:10; Ezek. 3:26
7[v] Isa. 34:5, 6; Lam. 4:21, 22; Ezek. 35:2; [Amos 1:11, 12]; See Jer. 49:7-22; Ezek. 25:12-14; Obad. 8-14 [w] See Job 18:20 [x] Hab. 3:13; Zeph. 2:14
8[y] Isa. 21:9; 47:1-15; Jer. 25:12; 50:1-46; 51:1-64; See Isa. 13:1-22 [z] Jer. 51:24, 56; [Ps. 28:4]
9[a] 2 Kgs. 8:12; Isa. 13:16; Hos. 10:14; Nah. 3:10

Psalm 138
1[b] Ps. 111:1 [c] Ps. 95:3; 96:5
2[d] Ps. 28:2; 1 Kgs. 8:29 [e] Ps. 5:7

4 [f]All the kings of the earth shall give you thanks, O LORD,
for they have heard the words of your mouth,
5 and they shall sing of [g]the ways of the LORD,
for great is the glory of the LORD.
6 [h]For though the LORD is high, he regards the lowly,
but the haughty he knows from afar.

7 [i]Though I walk in the midst of trouble,
you [j]preserve my life;
you [k]stretch out your hand against the wrath of my enemies,
and your [l]right hand delivers me.
8 The LORD will [m]fulfill his purpose for me;
[n]your steadfast love, O LORD, endures forever.
Do not forsake [o]the work of your hands.

Search Me, O God, and Know My Heart

139

TO THE CHOIRMASTER. A PSALM OF DAVID.

1 O LORD, you have [p]searched me and known me!
2 You [q]know when I sit down and when I rise up;
you [r]discern my thoughts from afar.
3 You search out my path and my lying down
and are acquainted with all my ways.
4 Even before a word is on my tongue,
behold, O LORD, [s]you know it altogether.
5 You [t]hem me in, behind and before,
and [u]lay your hand upon me.
6 [v]Such knowledge is [w]too wonderful for me;
it is high; I cannot attain it.

7 [x]Where shall I go from your Spirit?
Or where [y]shall I flee from your presence?
8 [z]If I ascend to heaven, you are there!
[a]If I make my bed in Sheol, you are there!
9 If I take the wings of the morning
and dwell in the uttermost parts of the sea,
10 even there your hand shall [b]lead me,
and your right hand shall hold me.
11 If I say, [c]"Surely the darkness shall cover me,
and the light about me be night,"
12 [d]even the darkness is not dark to you;
the night is bright as the day,
for darkness is as light with you.

13 For you [e]formed my inward parts;
you [f]knitted me together in my mother's womb.
14 I praise you, for I am fearfully and wonderfully made.[1]
[g]Wonderful are your works;
my soul knows it very well.

[1] Or *for I am fearfully set apart*

4[f] See Ps. 102:15
5[g] Ps. 103:7
6[h] [Ps. 131:1; Prov. 3:34; Luke 1:48; James 4:6]; See Ps. 113:5, 6
7[i] [Ps. 23:4] [j] See Ps. 71:20 [k] [1 Sam. 24:6; Job 1:12] [l] Ps. 60:5
8[m] Ps. 57:2; [Phil. 1:6] [n] Ps. 136:1; See 1 Chr. 16:41 [o] See Ps. 100:3

Psalm 139
1[p] Jer. 12:3; See Ps. 7:9; 17:3; 44:21
2[q] 2 Kgs. 19:27; Lam. 3:63 [r] [Job 14:16; 31:4; Matt. 9:4; John 2:24, 25]
4[s] Heb. 4:13
5[t] Job 19:8 [u] Job 9:33
6[v] Rom. 11:33 [w] Job 42:3
7[x] [Jer. 23:24] [y] Jonah 1:3
8[z] [Amos 9:2] [a] [Job 26:6]
10[b] ver. 24; Ps. 23:3
11[c] [Job 22:14]
12[d] Job 34:22; [Dan. 2:22]
13[e] Deut. 32:6 [f] [Job 10:11]
14[g] See Ps. 72:18

The "steadfast love" highlighted in Psalm 136 is back in view here. Of the many reasons David has for offering thanks to the Lord, God's faithfulness, his loyal and committed love to David and to the nation of Israel, ranks high on the list. David's personal testimony of God's unwavering faithfulness and steadfast love is given here: "On the day I called, you answered me; my strength of soul you increased" (Ps. 138:3), and, "Though I walk in the midst of trouble, you preserve my life; you stretch out your hand against the wrath of my enemies, and your right hand delivers me" (v. 7). In light of God's faithfulness in the past, David concludes with hope in God for the future: "The LORD will fulfill his purpose for me; your steadfast love, O LORD, endures forever. Do not forsake the work of your hands" (v. 8). The gospel is founded on the faithfulness of God to his promise. Were it not for God's sovereign commitment to bring about the salvation of his chosen ones through the coming of Christ, we would have no hope. And were God to promise but fail to fulfill what he said, we likewise would be without hope. But God is faithful; he keeps his word; his steadfast love indeed never fails. The work of Jesus Christ is the ultimate proof of this.

Psalm 139 The intimacy of David's relationship with God is put on beautiful display through this psalm. David knows that God's care for him is so deep and thorough that every step he takes (vv. 1–3), every word he speaks (v. 4), is known fully by the Lord who has numbered all of his days before they began (v. 16). Indeed, his days began as God formed him while yet in his mother's womb (v. 13). His very inward parts and every aspect of his life have been designed by God himself (vv. 14–16). No matter

15 [h]My frame was not hidden from you,
when I was being made in secret,
intricately woven in [i]the depths of the earth.
16 Your eyes saw my unformed substance;
in your [j]book were written, every one of them,
the days that were formed for me,
when as yet there was none of them.
17 How precious to me are your [k]thoughts, O God!
How vast is the sum of them!
18 [l]If I would count them, they are more than [m]the sand.
I awake, and I am still with you.
19 Oh that you would [n]slay the wicked, O God!
O [o]men of blood, [p]depart from me!
20 They [q]speak against you with malicious intent;
your enemies [r]take your name in vain.[1]
21 [s]Do I not hate those who hate you, O LORD?
And do I not [t]loathe those who [u]rise up against you?
22 I hate them with complete hatred;
I count them my enemies.
23 Search me, O God, and know my heart!
[v]Try me and know my thoughts![2]
24 And see if there be any grievous way in me,
and [w]lead me in [x]the way everlasting![3]

Deliver Me, O LORD, from Evil Men

140

TO THE CHOIRMASTER. A PSALM OF DAVID.

1 [y]Deliver me, O LORD, from evil men;
preserve me from [z]violent men,
2 who plan evil things in their heart
and [a]stir up wars continually.
3 They make [b]their tongue sharp as [c]a serpent's,
and [d]under their lips is the [e]venom of asps. *Selah*
4 Guard me, O LORD, from the hands of the wicked;
preserve me from [z]violent men,
who have planned to trip up my feet.
5 The arrogant have [f]hidden a trap for me,
and with cords they have spread [g]a net;[4]
beside the way they have set [h]snares for me. *Selah*
6 [i]I say to the LORD, You are my God;
give ear to [j]the voice of my pleas for mercy, O LORD!
7 O LORD, my Lord, [k]the strength of my salvation,
you have covered my head in the day of battle.

[1] Hebrew lacks *your name* [2] Or *cares* [3] Or *in the ancient way* (compare Jeremiah 6:16) [4] Or *they have spread cords as a net*

where David may travel, far or wide, he knows that God's Spirit is always with him, that God always knows the situations he is in (vv. 7–12). To imagine the detailed and exhaustive nature of God's thoughts toward his own children, as David here exemplifies, truly is precious (vv. 17–18).

How could such a great and glorious God care so deeply, so intimately, for little creatures such as we are? This is exactly what astonishes David. God is so great, and yet he shows extraordinary care for his own. The greatness of God, then, is the backdrop for understanding verses 19–22. Given how glorious God is, and how good he is to his undeserving children, who have been adopted as his own through the work of Christ, how deeply wrong it is for others to mock and belittle them.

David rightly longs for God's name to be exalted, which means that those who mock his name will themselves be put to shame. The longing to see God glorified has, then, another expression. Those who love God and his glory likewise hate all that stands against God and his ways (vv. 21–22). To love God and to hate evil are two sides of the same coin. David knows this, and prays in the end for God to search his heart—to see if both his "love" and his "hatred" is as it ought to be. Only then can he have assurance that he is walking in the way everlasting—a principle that also applies to us and calls upon us to test our hearts, to see whether their loves and hates reflect Christ in us.

Psalm 140 The theme of this psalm of David is seen most clearly in its final verses: "I know that the LORD will maintain the cause of the afflicted, and will execute justice for the needy. Surely the righteous shall give thanks to your name; the upright shall dwell in your presence" (vv. 12–13).

15[h] [Job 10:8-10; Eccles. 11:5] [i] Ps. 63:9
16[j] Ps. 56:8
17[k] Ps. 92:5
18[l] Ps. 40:5 [m] Gen. 22:17
19[n] Isa. 11:4; [Ps. 9:17] [o] Ps. 5:6 [p] See Ps. 6:8
20[q] [Jude 15] [r] Ex. 20:7
21[s] See Ps. 26:5 [t] Ps. 119:158 [u] Ps. 59:1
23[v] Ps. 26:2
24[w] ver. 10 [x] [Jer. 6:16; 18:15]
Psalm 140
1[y] Ps. 71:4; 119:153, 170 [z] Ps. 18:48; Prov. 3:31
2[a] See Ps. 56:6
3[b] [Ps. 52:2] [c] Ps. 58:4 [d] Ps. 10:7 [e] Cited Rom. 3:13
4[z] [See ver. 1 above]
5[f] Ps. 35:7; 141:9; 142:3; Jer. 18:22 [g] Job 18:8-10 [h] Ps. 64:5
6[i] Ps. 142:5 [j] Ps. 28:2; 31:22; 130:2
7[k] Ps. 28:8

8 [l]Grant not, O LORD, the desires of the wicked;
do not further their[1] evil plot, or [m]they will be exalted! *Selah*

9 As for the head of those who surround me,
let [n]the mischief of their lips overwhelm them!
10 Let [o]burning coals fall upon them!
Let them be cast into fire,
into miry pits, no more to rise!
11 Let not the slanderer be established in the land;
let evil hunt down the violent man speedily!

12 I know that the LORD will [p]maintain the cause of the afflicted,
and [q]will execute justice for the needy.
13 Surely [r]the righteous shall give thanks to your name;
[s]the upright shall dwell in your presence.

Give Ear to My Voice

141

A PSALM OF DAVID.
O LORD, I call upon you; [t]hasten to me!
Give ear to my voice when I call to you!
2 Let [u]my prayer be counted as incense before you,
and [v]the lifting up of my hands as [w]the evening sacrifice!

3 [x]Set a guard, O LORD, over my mouth;
[y]keep watch over the door of my lips!
4 [z]Do not let my heart incline to any evil,
to busy myself with wicked deeds
in company with men who [a]work iniquity,
and [b]let me not eat of their delicacies!

5 [c]Let a righteous man strike me—it is a kindness;
let him rebuke me—it is oil for my head;
let my head not refuse it.
Yet [d]my prayer is continually against their evil deeds.

[1] Hebrew *his*

8[l][Ps. 35:25] [m]Isa. 14:21
9[n][Prov. 12:13; 18:7]; See Ps. 7:16
10[o][Ps. 11:6; 18:13]
12[p]Ps. 9:4 [q]1 Kgs. 8:45, 49, 59
13[r][Ps. 64:10] [s][Ps. 11:7]
Psalm 141
1[t]Ps. 40:13; 70:5
2[u]Luke 1:10; Rev. 5:8; 8:3, 4 [v]See Ps. 28:2 [w]See Ex. 29:41
3[x]Ps. 34:13 [y]Mic. 7:5
4[z]Ps. 119:36 [a]ver. 9; Ps. 94:4 [b]Prov. 23:6
5[c][Prov. 9:8; 19:25; 25:12; 27:6; Eccles. 7:5] [d][Ps. 109:4]

David wrote this psalm during a time when he was under attack and fearing for his life. His enemies are powerful and deceitful. They plan evil and speak venomous words of hatred and spite (vv. 1–5). Despite the force and wickedness of those who oppose him, David's trust is in the Lord. "You are my God," he declares, "give ear to the voice of my pleas for mercy, O LORD!" (v. 6). He pleads with God to turn the evil of the wicked back on themselves and to vindicate him, the righteous king of Israel.

In very similar ways, the greater King of David, our Lord Jesus, trusted in his Father to vindicate him amid vicious accusations and assaults. The trust and hope in God that David shows here is typical of the truly godly, but is perfectly carried out only in Jesus. Even David must trust in his Lord, as "the strength of my salvation" (v. 7), because only David's Greater Son unfailingly entrusted his soul to God, even to the point of his death on the cross. As with David, and as shown with greatest clarity in Christ, so all who follow the path of righteousness by faith in God may have this same confidence: "Surely the righteous shall give thanks to your name; the upright shall dwell in your presence" (v. 13).

Psalm 141 The psalmist here expresses his heart's desire to live with integrity and righteousness before God. His call to the Lord (vv. 1–2) is not here primarily because he is being oppressed and afflicted, as is the case in many of the other psalms of David. Rather, the earnestness with which he approaches God is to convey his deep longing for God's enablement to withstand the temptations of the "delicacies" of the wicked (vv. 3–4).

He is more than happy to receive the rebuke of a righteous man (v. 5), for he knows such a rebuke or correction only serves to keep him on the path of righteousness himself. But he longs also for the wicked themselves to be shown for what they are, to receive the judgment that they well deserve (vv. 6–7). His prayer, then, is for God to keep him faithful and not to be caught in the snares of the ungodly, so that as the wicked fall due to their own devising, he rather may walk "safely" in the ways of God (vv. 8–10). All of this speaks highly of God's character and his ways that truly are best. Yes, the delicacies of the wicked are ever present. But one can resist these enticements knowing that there is a better, indeed, an infinitely superior way of life.

6 When their judges are [e]thrown over the cliff,[1]
then they shall hear my words, for they are pleasant.
7 As when one plows and breaks up the earth,
so shall our bones [f]be scattered at the mouth of Sheol.[2]

8 But [g]my eyes are toward you, O GOD, my Lord;
[h]in you I seek refuge; leave me not defenseless![3]
9 Keep me from [i]the trap that they have laid for me
and from the snares of evildoers!
10 Let the wicked [j]fall into their own nets,
while I pass by safely.

You Are My Refuge

142

A MASKIL[4] OF DAVID, WHEN HE WAS IN [k]THE CAVE. A PRAYER.

1 With my voice I [l]cry out to the LORD;
with my voice I [m]plead for mercy to the LORD.
2 I [n]pour out my complaint before him;
I tell my trouble before him.

3 When my spirit [o]faints within me,
you know my way!
In the path where I walk
they have [p]hidden a trap for me.
4 [q]Look to the [r]right and see:
[s]there is none who takes notice of me;
[t]no refuge remains to me;
no one cares for my soul.

5 I cry to you, O LORD;
I say, "You are my [u]refuge,
my [v]portion in [w]the land of the living."
6 [x]Attend to my cry,
for [y]I am brought very low!
Deliver me from my persecutors,
[z]for they are too strong for me!
7 [a]Bring me out of prison,
that I may give thanks to your name!
The righteous will surround me,
for you will [b]deal bountifully with me.

My Soul Thirsts for You

143

A PSALM OF DAVID.

Hear my prayer, O LORD;
[c]give ear to my pleas for mercy!
In your [d]faithfulness answer me, in your [d]righteousness!

[1] Or *When their judges fall into the hands of the Rock* [2] The meaning of the Hebrew in verses 6, 7 is uncertain [3] Hebrew *refuge; do not pour out my life!* [4] Probably a musical or liturgical term

God's own goodness and God's righteous path provide the real beauty and glory that alone will satisfy the godly person's desire. God's grace is here seen in granting this man vision to see the true good that is God, ultimately manifested in Christ, and to desire him above all else.

Psalm 142 This psalm of lament expresses David's cry for God's deliverance when he feared for his life while hiding in a cave. This may refer to a time when he was fleeing from Saul, who was seeking to kill him (cf. 1 Samuel 24), or perhaps a similar occasion. David's trust in God during this situation is remarkable. Although he was an able warrior, and while he had keen wit and ability, he also realized that his only hope of living and fulfilling what God had called him to do was as God intervened and brought about his deliverance—a realization of saving grace that ultimately must be embraced by believers in every age.

David is desperate. He feels there is no escape (Ps. 142:1–4), so he cries to the Lord, who alone is his refuge (v. 5). He recognizes the superior strength of those who oppose him (v. 6), but with confidence he lays his life before the Lord, expressing his complete trust and hope. The future tense verbs that end the psalm are telling: "The righteous *will* surround me, for you *will* deal bountifully with me" (v. 7). Here is staggering confidence in God! No matter what the wicked plot and how powerful they are, God is greater and he *will* deliver.

Is this not the heart of the message of the gospel itself? No matter how great is our opponent—which, among other things, includes the sin and guilt of our own lives—God is greater, and his provision more fully revealed in Jesus Christ for our deliverance cannot fail. In Christ we know that the righteous will surround us, that God will deal bountifully with us. In Christ, we are invincible.

Psalm 143 This psalm, much like Psalm 142, envisions David desperately asking God to spare his life in the face of strong and wicked enemies. As David calls out to God,

6 [e] 2 Chr. 25:12; [Luke 4:29]
7 [f] Ps. 53:5; [Ezek. 37:1]
8 [g] Ps. 25:15 [h] See Ps. 11:1
9 [i] See Ps. 140:5
10 [j] [Ps. 7:15]

Psalm 142
[k] Ps. 57, title
1 [l] Ps. 3:4 [m] Ps. 30:8
2 [n] [Isa. 26:16]; See Ps. 102, title
3 [o] See Ps. 77:3 [p] Ps. 140:5
4 [q] Ps. 69:20 [r] Ps. 16:8 [s] [Ps. 31:11] [t] Job 11:20; Jer. 25:35
5 [u] See Ps. 14:6 [v] Ps. 16:5 [w] Ps. 27:13
6 [x] Ps. 17:1 [y] Ps. 79:8 [z] Ps. 18:17
7 [a] Isa. 42:7; [Ps. 143:11] [b] Ps. 13:6

Psalm 143
1 [c] Ps. 140:6 [d] 1 John 1:9; [Ps. 31:1]

2 [e]Enter not into judgment with your servant,
for no one living is righteous [f]before you.

3 For the enemy has pursued my soul;
[g]he has crushed my life to the ground;
[h]he has made me sit in darkness like those long dead.
4 Therefore my spirit [i]faints within me;
my heart within me is appalled.

5 [j]I remember the days of old;
[k]I meditate on all that you have done;
I ponder the work of your hands.
6 [l]I stretch out my hands to you;
[m]my soul thirsts for you like [n]a parched land. *Selah*

7 [o]Answer me quickly, O LORD!
[p]My spirit fails!
[q]Hide not your face from me,
[r]lest I be like those who go down to the pit.
8 [s]Let me hear in the morning of your steadfast love,
for in you I [t]trust.
[u]Make me know the way I should go,
[v]for to you I lift up my soul.

9 [w]Deliver me from my enemies, O LORD!
I have fled to you for refuge.[1]
10 [x]Teach me to do your will,
for you are my God!
[y]Let your good Spirit [z]lead me
on [a]level ground!

11 [b]For your name's sake, O LORD, [c]preserve my life!
In your righteousness [d]bring my soul out of trouble!
12 And in your steadfast love you will [e]cut off my enemies,
and you will destroy all the adversaries of my soul,
for I am your [f]servant.

My Rock and My Fortress

144 OF DAVID.
Blessed be the LORD, my [g]rock,
[h]who trains my hands for war,
and my fingers for battle;
2 he is my [i]steadfast love and my [j]fortress,
my [k]stronghold and my deliverer,
my [l]shield and he in whom I take refuge,
who [m]subdues peoples[2] under me.

3 O LORD, [n]what is man that you [o]regard him,
or the son of man that you think of him?
4 [p]Man is like a breath;
his days are like [q]a passing [r]shadow.

[1] One Hebrew manuscript, Septuagint; most Hebrew manuscripts *To you I have covered* [2] Many Hebrew manuscripts, Dead Sea Scroll, Jerome, Syriac, Aquila; most Hebrew manuscripts *subdues my people*

2[e] [Job 14:3] [f] Ps. 130:3; 1 Kgs. 8:46; Job 9:2; 15:14; 25:4; Eccles. 7:20; Rom. 3:23; 1 Cor. 4:4
3[g] See Ps. 88:3-6 [h] Lam. 3:6
4[i] See Ps. 77:3
5[j] Ps. 77:5, 11 [k] Ps. 77:12; 111:2
6[l] See Job 11:13 [m] Ps. 42:2 [n] [Ps. 63:1]
7[o] Ps. 69:17; 102:2 [p] [Ps. 84:2] [q] Ps. 27:9 [r] Ps. 28:1; 88:4
8[s] [Ps. 90:14] [t] Ps. 11:1; 25:2 [u] Ps. 25:4 [v] Ps. 25:1
9[w] Ps. 59:1; 142:6
10[x] [Ps. 119:12] [y] Neh. 9:20 [z] See Ps. 23:3 [a] Isa. 26:10; [Ps. 27:11]
11[b] Ps. 23:3; 25:11 [c] See Ps. 71:20 [d] Ps. 142:7
12[e] Ps. 54:5 [f] See Ps. 116:16
Psalm 144
1[g] See Ps. 18:2, 31, 46 [h] Ps. 18:34
2[i] [Ps. 59:10, 17; Jonah 2:8] [j] Ps. 18:2; 91:2 [k] Ps. 18:2; 59:9 [l] Ps. 7:10; 18:2 [m] Ps. 18:47
3[n] See Ps. 8:4 [o] See Ps. 31:7
4[p] Ps. 39:5 [q] Ps. 102:11; 109:23 [r] Job 8:9

he realizes he cannot do so from the basis of his own perfect obedience before God; rather, he acknowledges that no one, including himself, is truly righteous before God (Ps. 143:1–2). So the basis of his plea is the character of God as shown in his past actions. David recalls the past goodness of God, his past deliverances, and he meditates on God's gracious character and powerful intervention (vv. 5–6).

From the standpoint, then, of God's character, his faithfulness, his track record of acting on behalf of his own people, David puts his trust in God yet again. And as with Psalm 142, this psalm ends with future tense verbs expressing David's confidence that God will not fail: "And in your steadfast love you will cut off my enemies, and you will destroy all the adversaries of my soul, for I am your servant" (Ps. 143:12). Here is grace! Here is the gospel! For here is the faithful God who would ultimately provide triumph over all of David's (and our) enemies in the life, death, and resurrection of his Son (Col. 2:14–15).

Psalm 144 With echoes of Psalm 8 ("what is man that you are mindful of him . . . ?"; Ps. 8:4; cf. Ps. 144:3), this psalm of David reflects on the absolute dependence the king must place on the all-sufficient and gracious enablement of God. The Lord is his rock who trains him for battle, who is his own fortress, shield, refuge, and deliverer (Ps. 144:1–2). Man, in contrast, is as breath; his days are like a passing shadow (v. 4). God alone, then, can bring the victory desired. He alone can bow the heavens, touch the mountains, send forth lightning, and rout the enemy (vv. 5–8). David pledges, then, following the victory God will bring, to sing to him a "new song" (v. 9), signaling the new work of deliverance and might that God will bring for this new challenge.

5 [s]Bow your heavens, O LORD, and come down!
[t]Touch the mountains so that they smoke!
6 [u]Flash forth the lightning and scatter them;
[u] send out your arrows and rout them!
7 [v]Stretch out your hand from on high;
[w]rescue me and deliver me from the many waters,
from the hand [x]of foreigners,
8 whose mouths speak [y]lies
and whose right hand is [z]a right hand of falsehood.

9 I will sing [a]a new song to you, O God;
upon [a]a ten-stringed harp I will play to you,
10 who gives victory to kings,
who [b]rescues David his servant from the cruel sword.
11 Rescue me and deliver me
from the hand [x]of foreigners,
whose mouths speak [y]lies
and whose right hand is a right hand of falsehood.

12 May our sons in their youth
be like [c]plants full grown,
our daughters like [d]corner pillars
cut for the structure of a palace;
13 [e]may our granaries be full,
[f]providing all kinds of produce;
may our sheep bring forth thousands
and ten thousands in our fields;
14 may our cattle be heavy with young,
suffering no mishap or failure in bearing;[1]
may there be no [g]cry of distress in our streets!
15 [h]Blessed are the people to whom such blessings fall!
[i]Blessed are the people whose God is the LORD!

Great Is the LORD

145 [2] A SONG OF PRAISE. OF DAVID.
[j]I will extol you, my God and [k]King,
and bless your name forever and ever.
2 Every day I will bless you
[l]and praise your name forever and ever.
3 [m]Great is the LORD, and greatly to be praised,
and his [n]greatness is unsearchable.

4 [o]One generation shall commend your works to another,
and shall declare your mighty acts.
5 On [p]the glorious splendor of your majesty,
and on your wondrous works, I will meditate.
6 They shall speak of [q]the might of your awesome deeds,
and I will declare your greatness.
7 They shall pour forth the fame of your [r]abundant goodness
and shall sing aloud of your righteousness.

[1] Hebrew *with no breaking in or going out* [2] This psalm is an acrostic poem, each verse beginning with the successive letters of the Hebrew alphabet

New opposition (from the enemy), new trust (in the ever-faithful God), new victory (brought by God's grace and power), new song (written new for this most recent victory for which God is rightly glorified)—this is the order David follows. And this order of act and attitude provides God's people in every generation a God-glorifying pattern for their lives as well. The psalm therefore concludes looking forward to generations to come (vv. 12–15). May they also not only benefit from this present victory of God; may they trust God in their afflictions and distresses as David has. In this way God's people see afresh the victory of God in their lives—a victory accomplished decisively and finally in Christ's death and resurrection, through which God triumphed over the powers of hell.

Psalm 145 This last of the psalms of David hits the high-water mark of praise to God for his exalted greatness and steadfast love. Because of the "unsearchable" greatness of God, David pledges to bless him every day, to praise his name forever and ever (vv. 1–3). And because God's greatness endures, every generation will see and praise God for his character and works (vv. 4, 10–13).

While the greatness of God's sovereignty is included in David's litany of praise (v. 13), clearly what gets repeated mention is the compassion, kindness, forgiveness, provision, protection, grace, and mercy of God toward those who look to him. God

5[s] Ps. 18:9; [Isa. 64:1] [t] See Ps. 104:32
6[u] See Ps. 18:14
7[v] Ps. 18:16 [w] Ps. 69:14 [x] Ps. 18:44, 45
8[y] Ps. 12:2; 41:6 [z] [Ps. 106:26; Gen. 14:22; Deut. 32:40; Isa. 62:8]
9[a] Ps. 33:2, 3
10[b] Ps. 18:50
11[x] [See ver. 7 above] [y] [See ver. 8 above]
12[c] [Ps. 128:3] [d] [Zech. 9:15]
13[e] [Joel 2:24] [f] [Isa. 30:23]
14[g] [Isa. 24:11; Jer. 14:2; 46:12]
15[h] Deut. 33:29 [i] Ps. 33:12; 146:5

Psalm 145
1[j] Ps. 99:5, 9 [k] Ps. 98:6
2[l] [Ps. 146:2]
3[m] Ps. 48:1 [n] Job 5:9; [Isa. 40:28]
4[o] Isa. 38:19
5[p] ver. 12
6[q] [Ps. 78:4]
7[r] Isa. 63:7

8 The LORD is [s]gracious and merciful,
slow to anger and abounding in
steadfast love.
9 The LORD is [t]good to all,
and his mercy is over all that he has
made.

10 [u]All your works shall give thanks to you,
O LORD,
and all your [v]saints shall bless you!
11 They shall speak of the glory of your
kingdom
and tell of your power,
12 to [w]make known to the children of man
your[1] [x]mighty deeds,
and [y]the glorious splendor of your
kingdom.
13 [z]Your kingdom is an everlasting kingdom,
and your dominion endures throughout all generations.

[The LORD is faithful in all his words
and kind in all his works.][2]
14 The LORD [a]upholds all who are falling
and [b]raises up all who are bowed down.
15 The eyes of all [c]look to you,
and you give them their food in due
season.
16 You [d]open your hand;
you [e]satisfy the desire of every living
thing.
17 The LORD is [f]righteous in all his ways
and [g]kind in all his works.
18 The LORD is [h]near to all who call on him,
to all who call on him [i]in truth.
19 He [j]fulfills the desire of those who fear
him;
he also [k]hears their cry and saves them.
20 The LORD [l]preserves all who love him,
but all the wicked he will destroy.

21 My mouth will speak the praise of the
LORD,
and [m]let all flesh bless his holy name
forever and ever.

Put Not Your Trust in Princes

146 [n]Praise the LORD!
Praise the LORD, O my soul!
2 I will praise the LORD [o]as long as I live;
[p]I will sing praises to my God while
I have my being.

3 [q]Put not your trust in princes,
[r]in a son of man, in whom there is [s]no
salvation.

[1] Hebrew *his*; also next line [2] These two lines are supplied by one Hebrew manuscript, Septuagint, Syriac (compare Dead Sea Scroll)

8[s] See Ps. 86:5, 15
9[t] See Ps. 100:5
10[u] [Ps. 19:1; 103:22] [v] [Ps. 132:9, 16]
12[w] Ps. 105:1 [x] ver. 4; Ps. 150:2; Deut. 3:24 [y] ver. 5
13[z] See Ps. 10:16
14[a] [Ps. 37:17, 24] [b] Ps. 146:8
15[c] Ps. 104:27
16[d] Ps. 104:28 [e] [Ps. 104:21; 147:8]
17[f] See Ps. 116:5 [g] Ps. 18:25; Jer. 3:12
18[h] [Ps. 34:18; 119:151; Deut. 4:7] [i] John 4:23, 24
19[j] Prov. 10:24; [John 9:31] [k] Ps. 31:22
20[l] See Ps. 97:10
21[m] [Ps. 150:6]

Psalm 146
1[n] See Ps. 135:1
2[o] Ps. 63:4; [Ps. 145:2] [p] Ps. 104:33
3[q] Ps. 118:9 [r] Ps. 118:8; [Isa. 2:22; Jer. 17:5] [s] Ps. 60:11; 108:12

raises those who fall, he feeds the hungry, he satisfies the desires of all living things (vv. 14–16). Perhaps verse 17 comes the closest to summarizing the heart of this psalm: "The LORD is righteous in all his ways and kind in all his works." Notice the joining together of qualities in this declaration. God is both righteous (v. 17a) *and* kind (v. 17b). God is great *and* gracious, majestic *and* merciful, glorious *and* good. But these qualities, as amazing as they are, are reserved for those who truly seek and trust him and love him. God is near to those "who call on him" (v. 18), he fulfills the desire of those "who fear him" (i.e., give him proper regard; v. 19), he preserves all those "who love him" (v. 20).

We see here, then, the heart expression of this godly king who knows his God! This vision of God—of his greatness and goodness—is what compels David to praise him every day. And this greatness and goodness is what ultimately culminates in the sending of Jesus Christ to redeem sinners.

Psalm 146 The final five psalms of the Psalter all begin and end with the same imperative: the Hebrew words, Hallelu-jah! That is, "Praise the LORD!" But the emphasis of Psalm 145 on the greatness of God's goodness toward those who trust in him is continued here. After the opening declaration, announcing an imperative for all of the people of God to "Praise the LORD!" (Ps. 146:1), the psalmist enumerates a multitude of ways in which God shows his kindness and compassion to his people. He alone is their salvation. Trust in mere humans—even in mighty yet mortal princes—is vain, but trust in the true and living God is the pathway of blessing (vv. 3–4).

How do we know it makes sense to trust in God? Answer: God has made the heavens and earth, the sea and all in them! He truly is God, and hence, all hope and trust in him is validated fully. As the true God that he is, he alone is able to execute justice for the oppressed, to give food to the hungry, to set prisoners free, to open the eyes of the blind, to lift up those bowed down and to watch over the sojourner, the widow, the fatherless (vv. 7–9). In each of these mercies, our God reflects his gra-

4 When [t]his breath departs, he returns to
the earth;
on that very day his plans perish.
5 [u]Blessed is he whose help is the God of
Jacob,
whose [v]hope is in the LORD his God,
6 [w]who made heaven and earth,
the sea, and all that is in them,
[x]who keeps faith forever;
7 [y]who executes justice for the oppressed,
[z]who gives food to the hungry.

[a]The LORD sets the prisoners free;
8 [b]the LORD opens the eyes of the blind.
[c]The LORD lifts up those who are bowed
down;
[d]the LORD loves the righteous.
9 [e]The LORD watches over the sojourners;
[f]he upholds the widow and the fatherless,
but [g]the way of the wicked he brings
to ruin.
10 [h]The LORD will reign forever,
your God, O Zion, to all generations.
[n]Praise the LORD!

He Heals the Brokenhearted

147 [i]Praise the LORD!
For [j]it is good to sing praises to
our God;
for [k]it is pleasant,[1] and [l]a song of
praise is fitting.
2 The LORD [m]builds up Jerusalem;
he [n]gathers the outcasts of Israel.
3 He heals [o]the brokenhearted
and [p]binds up their wounds.
4 He [q]determines the number of the stars;
he [r]gives to all of them their names.
5 [s]Great is our Lord, and [t]abundant in
power;
[u]his understanding is beyond measure.
6 The LORD [v]lifts up the humble;[2]
he casts the wicked to the ground.

7 [w]Sing to the LORD with thanksgiving;
make melody to our God on [x]the lyre!
8 He covers the heavens with clouds;
he prepares [y]rain for the earth;
he makes [z]grass grow on the hills.
9 He [a]gives to the beasts their food,
and to [b]the young ravens that cry.
10 His delight is not in [c]the strength of the
horse,
nor his pleasure in the legs of a man,
11 but the LORD [d]takes pleasure in those
who fear him,
in those who [e]hope in his steadfast
love.

12 Praise the LORD, O Jerusalem!
Praise your God, O Zion!
13 For he strengthens [f]the bars of your gates;
he blesses your children within you.
14 He [g]makes peace in your borders;
he [h]fills you with the [i]finest of the
wheat.
15 He [j]sends out his command to the earth;
his word runs swiftly.

[1] Or *for he is beautiful* [2] Or *afflicted*

cious character. And as God, he alone reigns over every and all generations. So, let all peoples, at all times, praise the Lord! (v. 10). In the provision of his Son Jesus Christ, our God makes the fullest and greatest declaration of the grace he has demonstrated through the ages, as reflected in this psalm.

Psalm 147 There are innumerable reasons why it is both right and good to praise the Lord. Psalm 147 alternates between two broad categories of the praise of God. On the one hand, the God of Israel is the one true God who has made and who rules the heavens and the earth. To pick out one sample statement, "He [Yahweh] determines the number of the stars; he gives to all of them their names" (v. 4). The vastness and scope of the galaxies and starry hosts of the universe are the result of God's planning, design, and determined will, and his naming all the stars (there are 100 billion stars in the Milky Way galaxy alone!) indicates his rightful jurisdiction over them all. On the other hand, this same God, the Creator and providential Ruler of all, is also the God of his own people, Israel. Again, to pick out one poignant statement: "He has not dealt thus [good and gracious, providing and protecting] with any other nation; they do not know his rules" (v. 20). Indeed, how kind God was to give this people, the people of his choosing, his word, his law, his rules that are a reflection of his character and care, in that God's commands outline a safe and good path for God's people (cf. Ps. 19:7–11; Psalm 119).

4[t] Ps. 104:29; [Eccles. 12:7]; See Job 10:9; 34:14, 15
5[u] [Ps. 144:15] [v] Ps. 119:116; See Ps. 2:12
6[w] See Ps. 115:15 [x] [Ps. 100:5; 117:2]
7[y] Ps. 103:6 [z] Ps. 107:9; 145:15 [a] Ps. 105:20; Isa. 61:1; [Ps. 68:6]
8[b] Matt. 9:30; John 9:7 [c] Ps. 145:14; [Ps. 147:6] [d] Ps. 11:7
9[e] [Ex. 22:21] [f] Deut. 10:18; [Ex. 22:22]; See Ps. 10:14 [g] [Ps. 147:6]
10[h] See Ps. 10:16 [n] [See ver. 1 above]

Psalm 147
1[i] See Ps. 135:1 [j] Ps. 92:1 [k] Ps. 135:3 [l] Ps. 33:1
2[m] Ps. 51:18; 102:16 [n] Deut. 30:3; Isa. 11:12; 27:13; 56:8; Ezek. 39:28
3[o] Ps. 34:18 [p] Ezek. 34:16
4[q] [Gen. 15:5] [r] Isa. 40:26
5[s] Ps. 48:1 [t] Nah. 1:3 [u] Isa. 40:28; [Job 5:9]
6[v] [Ps. 146:8, 9]

7[w] Ex. 15:21; [Ps. 95:1, 2] [x] See 1 Chr. 15:16 **8**[y] See Job 5:10 [z] Ps. 104:14; Job 38:27 **9**[a] Ps. 104:27, 28 [b] See Job 38:41 **10**[c] Ps. 33:17 **11**[d] Ps. 149:4 [e] Ps. 33:18 **13**[f] Neh. 7:3 **14**[g] Ex. 34:24; Prov. 16:7; Isa. 60:17, 18 [h] Ps. 132:15 [i] Ps. 81:16; Deut. 32:14 **15**[j] [Ps. 148:8]

16 He gives [k]snow like wool;
he scatters [l]frost like ashes.
17 He hurls down his crystals of [m]ice like crumbs;
who can stand before his [n]cold?
18 He [o]sends out his word, and melts them;
he makes his wind blow and the waters flow.
19 He declares his word to Jacob,
his [p]statutes and rules[1] to Israel.
20 He [q]has not dealt thus with any other nation;
they do not know his rules.[2]
[r]Praise the LORD!

Praise the Name of the LORD

148 [r]Praise the LORD!
Praise the LORD [s]from the heavens;
praise him [t]in the heights!
2 Praise him, all his angels;
praise him, all his [u]hosts!

3 Praise him, sun and moon,
praise him, all you shining stars!
4 Praise him, you [v]highest heavens,
and you [w]waters above the heavens!

5 [x]Let them praise the name of the LORD!
For [y]he commanded and they were created.
6 And he [z]established them forever and ever;
he gave [a]a decree, and it shall not [b]pass away.[3]

7 Praise the LORD [c]from the earth,
you [d]great sea creatures and all deeps,
8 [e]fire and hail, [f]snow and mist,
[g]stormy wind [h]fulfilling his word!

9 [i]Mountains and all hills,
[j]fruit trees and all [k]cedars!
10 [l]Beasts and all livestock,
creeping things and [m]flying birds!

11 Kings of the earth and [n]all peoples,
princes and all rulers of the earth!

[1] Or *and just decrees* [2] Or *his just decrees* [3] Or *it shall not be transgressed*

16[k] Job 37:6 [l][Job 38:29]
17[m] Job 37:10 [n] Job 37:9
18[o] ver. 15; [Job 37:12]; See Ps. 33:9; 107:20
19[p] Mal. 4:4; [Ps. 78:5]; See Deut. 33:2-4
20[q] Deut. 4:7; See Deut. 4:32-34 [r] See Ps. 135:1

Psalm 148
1[r] [See Ps. 147:20 above] [s] [ver. 7]; See Ps. 69:34 [t] Matt. 21:9
2[u] See Ps. 103:20, 21
4[v] Ps. 68:33; Deut. 10:14; Neh. 9:6; See 1 Kgs. 8:27 [w] Gen. 1:7
5[x] ver. 13 [y] See Ps. 33:6, 9
6[z] Ps. 119:90, 91 [a] [Job 28:26; Jer. 31:35, 36; 33:25] [b] [Ps. 104:9; Esth. 1:19; Job 14:5]
7[c] [ver. 1] [d] [Gen. 1:21]; See Ps. 74:13
8[e] Ps. 18:12; 105:32 [f] Ps. 147:16 [g] Ps. 107:25 [h] Ps. 103:20; See Ps. 147:15-18
9[i] Isa. 44:23; 49:13; 55:12 [j] Gen. 1:11 [k] Ps. 104:16
10[l] Gen. 1:24 [m] Gen. 1:20, 21
11[n] [Rev. 7:9]

These, then, are some of the reasons why God should be praised and why his people should be thrilled, awe-struck, and amazed, that they are his people and he is their God. What a God this is! What a privilege to be the people of God, ultimately the very body of Christ! The one true and living God, the Creator and Ruler of all, is *our* God. Praise be to the Lord!

Psalm 148 The psalmist decrees that praise for Yahweh, the God of his people Israel, should be expressed by three groupings of God's creation: the heavens, the earth, and all people on the earth. First, all inhabitants of the heavens are called to praise the Lord. The angels, the hosts of the heavens, sun and moon, starry hosts, highest heaven, and the waters above the heavens (vv. 1–4)—all are to praise the Lord, because "he commanded and they were created" (v. 5), he established them and decreed that they not pass away (vv. 5–6). Second, all on earth are to praise the Lord. The creatures of the sea, fire, hail, snow, mist, storms, mountains, trees, beasts, livestock, birds (vv. 7–10)—all are to praise the Lord. Aspects of the earth's weather, in particular, give praise to God because they fulfill his will (v. 8). Third, kings, princes, rulers, old men, children, indeed all peoples (plural) are to praise the Lord (vv. 11–12).

The psalm ends with the ultimate basis for why the Lord should be praised: "for his name alone is exalted; his majesty is above earth and heaven. He has raised up a horn for his people, praise for all his saints, for the people of Israel who are near to him" (vv. 13–14). The "horn" language is unfamiliar to us but it refers to the dignity of a person or nation established by some innate strength. In this case, it is important to note that God raises up the dignity of his people. Their glory is not from themselves but from the Creator God whose redeeming love provides for their honor.

God as Creator, and God as Redeemer, then, are both bases for praise to God. The people of God in particular should see how right and good it is to praise him, for he not only made them but he has, in his mercy and kindness, raised up a horn (of salvation) for them. Psalm 18:2 identifies the horn of salvation as God himself (cf. 112:9). As the provider of their honor, God declares himself to be his people's Redeemer. He not only made all things, but he has condescended to rescue his needy people and give them the honor that he alone deserves. This is accomplished finally and most truly in the sending of his own Son. In Jesus Christ the people of God are redeemed

12 Young men and maidens together,
old men and children!

13 [o]Let them praise the name of the LORD,
for [p]his name alone is exalted;
[q]his majesty is above earth and heaven.
14 He has [r]raised up a horn for his people,
[s]praise for all his saints,
for the people of Israel who are [t]near to him.
[u]Praise the LORD!

Sing to the LORD a New Song

149 [u]Praise the LORD!
Sing to the LORD [v]a new song,
his praise in [w]the assembly of the godly!
2 Let Israel [x]be glad in [y]his Maker;
let the children of Zion rejoice in their [z]King!
3 Let them praise his name with [a]dancing,
making melody to him with [b]tambourine and [c]lyre!
4 For the LORD [d]takes pleasure in his people;
he [e]adorns the humble with salvation.
5 Let the godly exult in glory;
let them [f]sing for joy on their [g]beds.
6 Let [h]the high praises of God be in their throats
and [i]two-edged swords in their hands,
7 to execute vengeance on the nations
and punishments on the peoples,
8 to bind their kings with [j]chains
and their nobles with fetters of iron,
9 to execute on them the judgment [k]written!
[l]This is honor for all his godly ones.
[u]Praise the LORD!

Let Everything Praise the LORD

150 [u]Praise the LORD!
Praise God in his [m]sanctuary;
praise him in [n]his mighty heavens![1]

[1] Hebrew *expanse* (compare Genesis 1:6–8)

from sin and death, and given the glorious and eternal righteousness of God—truly, God has "raised up a horn for his people" (148:14)!

Psalm 149 Two aspects of the praise of God are highlighted here. First, the people of God who express praise to their God should do so with great passion, intensity, zeal, and emotion. That they sing a "new song" (v. 1) indicates awareness of fresh bestowments of God's blessing, for which they now offer enthusiastic praise. They are to be glad and rejoice, to dance and exult (vv. 2–5), showing the depth of their heart's delight in bringing praise to their great, gracious, and saving God. For indeed, "the LORD takes pleasure in his people; he adorns the humble with salvation" (v. 4). There is no place, then, for apathy or merely formalistic worship. No, this God is worthy of heart-felt praise and joyous singing!

Second, cause for the praise of God is shown in the coming judgment that God's people will execute on the nations. Verse 6 is the hinge of these two themes: "Let the high praises of God be in their throats [strong, emotional praise of God] and two-edged swords in their hands [preparedness for retributive judgment]" (v. 6). Amazingly, then, the praise of God here is associated with the day, not only when God will judge the wicked of the nations, but when he will execute this judgment through his own people. That God has designed this judgment to be carried out in this fashion is an "honor" for his people and a basis for praising him (v. 9).

The good news of salvation that God's people receive, then, implies also the corresponding harsh news of judgment for all who reject God and his ways. God is exalted in saving those who deserve judgment (his people) and in bringing that very judgment on others who oppose his purposes, oppress his people, and reject his offer of mercy. Let us look to Christ, at whose cross God's judgment was poured out for all who trust in Jesus as their Savior and Lord.

Psalm 150 The Psalter ends with a portrayal of the people of God involved in joyous worship of the One who alone deserves the fullest and most glorious expression of praise that can possibly be offered. This praise is corporate, for it finds expression in his sanctuary, but immediately we see that it cannot be contained there for it expands into the highest heavens as well (v. 1). And the praise of God is not only for his "mighty deeds" but also for his "excellent greatness" (v. 2)—that is, for both the works and the

13 [o]ver. 5 [p]Ps. 8:1 [q]See Ps. 113:4
14 [r]See 1 Sam. 2:1 [s][Deut. 10:21; Jer. 17:14] [t]Deut. 4:7; Eph. 2:17 [u]See Ps. 135:1
Psalm 149
1 [u][See Ps. 148:14 above] [v]See Ps. 33:3 [w]Ps. 89:5, 7
2 [x]Ps. 85:6 [y]See Ps. 95:6; Job 35:10 [z]1 Sam. 12:12; Zech. 9:9
3 [a]Ps. 150:4; [Ps. 30:11] [b]Ps. 150:4; Ex. 15:20 [c]Ps. 150:3
4 [d]Ps. 35:27; 147:11 [e][Isa. 61:3]
5 [f]See Job 35:10 [g]Ps. 4:4; 63:6; [Hos. 7:14]
6 [h][Ps. 66:17] [i]Heb. 4:12; Rev. 1:16; 2:12; [Prov. 5:4]
8 [j][Job 36:8]
9 [k]Isa. 65:6; [Job 13:26] [l][Ps. 148:14] [u][See Ps. 148:14 above]
Psalm 150
1 [u][See Ps. 148:14 above] [m][Ps. 11:4; 134:2] [n][Ps. 68:34]

2 Praise him for his [o]mighty deeds;
praise him according to his excellent
[p]greatness!
3 Praise him with [q]trumpet sound;
praise him with [r]lute and [r]harp!
4 Praise him with [s]tambourine and [s]dance;
praise him with [t]strings and [u]pipe!
5 Praise him with sounding [v]cymbals;
praise him with loud clashing cymbals!
6 Let [w]everything that has breath praise
the LORD!
[x]Praise the LORD!

2 [o]Ps. 145:12 [p]Deut. 3:24
3 [q]Ps. 98:6 [r]Ps. 33:2; 71:22
4 [s]Ps. 149:3 [t]Ps. 45:8; [Isa. 38:20] [u]Job 21:12
5 [v]2 Sam. 6:5; 1 Chr. 15:16, 19, 28; 25:1, 6
6 [w][Ps. 145:21] [x]ver. 1

worth, the outward actions and inward character, of God. Because of the greatness of God, every rightful manner of expression of his praise should be employed. Bring forth the trumpets, the lute, and the harp; the tambourine, the strings, and the pipes; the loud and sounding cymbals; and all with the joyous dancing of God's people (vv. 3–5). Indeed, "let everything that has breath praise the LORD! Praise the LORD!" (v. 6).

What a fitting conclusion to the Psalter. God, who is great and glorious, who has acted over and again for the welfare and salvation of his people, is indeed infinitely worthy. He must be the object of his people's deepest affections and their highest adoration. We praise the Lord today supremely for what he has done to deliver his people through Jesus Christ. Rescued from ourselves through the grace won for us by Christ, our hearts are moved to do what the psalmist says: praise the Lord!

Proverbs

The Beginning of Knowledge

1 [a]The proverbs of Solomon, son of David,
king of Israel:

2 To know wisdom and instruction,
to understand words of insight,
3 to receive instruction in wise dealing,
in [b]righteousness, justice, and equity;
4 to give prudence to [c]the simple,
knowledge and [d]discretion to the youth—
5 Let the wise hear and [e]increase in learning,
and the one who understands obtain guidance,
6 to understand a proverb and a saying,
[f]the words of the wise and their [g]riddles.
7 [h]The fear of the LORD is the beginning of knowledge;
fools despise wisdom and instruction.

The Enticement of Sinners

8 [i]Hear, my son, your father's instruction,
and forsake not your mother's teaching,
9 for they are [j]a graceful garland for your head
and [k]pendants for your neck.
10 My son, if sinners [l]entice you,
do not consent.
11 If they say, "Come with us, [m]let us lie in wait for blood;
[n]let us ambush the innocent without reason;
12 like Sheol let us [o]swallow them alive,
and whole, like [p]those who go down to the pit;
13 we shall find all precious goods,
we shall fill our houses with plunder;
14 throw in your lot among us;
we will all have one purse"—

1:1–7 The word "proverbs" alerts us to the style of this book. A biblical proverb is a briefly stated, time-tested insight into real life. The mention of Solomon, David's son, locates this book within the biblical story leading to Jesus, the ultimate Son of David, and history's greatest expert on foolish sinners who need help from beyond themselves.

Verses 2–6 explain how this book helps us. Wisdom, the primary goal, is skill for living daily life well. Starting with beginners—the simple, the youth—and including the mature—the wise, the one who understands—everyone is invited to grow in wisdom together. All anyone needs is an open mind.

Verse 7 defines that openness: the fear of the Lord. We begin our journey into wisdom by revering the Lord with holy awe, and we never grow beyond it, because all true wisdom is his alone. We do not master it by our giftedness; he gives it by his grace. The fear of the Lord makes us repentant (3:7), decisive against sin (8:13), stable (14:26), refreshed (14:27), humble (15:33), and satisfied (19:23). We struggle with the Hebrew word "fear," because there is not a close English equivalent. So it is important to recall that Jesus also came in, and delighted in, "the fear of the LORD" (Isa. 11:2–3). This description of the loving and respectful relationship that the eternal Son had for his Father reminds us that holy "fear" is not terror or dread of harm, but proper and worshipful regard for all that God is in his wisdom, power, holiness, mercy, and love.

1:8–19 We grow not in isolation but in community. But wisdom refuses sinful community (1 Cor. 15:33). "Greedy for unjust gain" (Prov. 1:19) marks those who are out for themselves, willing to step on people to get their way. They recruit others: "Come with us" (v. 11). By contrast, God calls us to purity and safety, ultimately expressed in Jesus' call for us to come to himself (Matt. 11:28). He did not lie in wait for our blood (Prov. 1:11); he gave his own, leaving us a beautiful example (1 Pet. 2:21).

Chapter 1
1 [a]ch. 10:1; 25:1; 1 Kgs. 4:32; Eccles. 12:9
3 [b]ch. 2:9
4 [c]ch. 8:5; 14:15, 18 [d]ch. 2:11; 3:21
5 [e]ch. 9:9
6 [f]ch. 22:17 [g]Judg. 14:12; Ps. 78:2
7 [h]ch. 9:10; [ch. 15:33]; See Job 28:28
8 [i]ch. 6:20; [Ps. 34:11; Eph. 6:1, 2]
9 [j]ch. 4:9; [ch. 3:22] [k][Gen. 41:42; Dan. 5:29]
10 [l]ch. 16:29
11 [m]ver. 18; ch. 12:6; Jer. 5:26 [n]ver. 18; Ps. 10:8; 64:5
12 [o]Ps. 124:3; [Num. 16:32, 33] [p]Ps. 28:1

15 my son, [q]do not walk in the way with
them;
[r]hold back your foot from their paths,
16 for [s]their feet run to evil,
and they make haste to shed blood.
17 [t]For in vain is a net spread
in the sight of any bird,
18 but these men [u]lie in wait for their own
blood;
they [u]set an ambush for their own
lives.
19 [v]Such are the ways of everyone who is
[w]greedy for unjust gain;
[x]it takes away the life of its possessors.

The Call of Wisdom

20 [y]Wisdom cries aloud in the street,
in the markets she raises her voice;
21 at the head of the noisy streets she cries
out;
at [z]the entrance of the city gates she
speaks:
22 "How long, O [a]simple ones, will you love
being simple?
How long will [b]scoffers delight in their
scoffing
and fools [c]hate knowledge?
23 If you turn at my reproof,[1]
behold, I will [d]pour out my spirit to you;
I will make my words known to you.
24 [e]Because I have called and [f]you refused to
listen,
have [g]stretched out my hand and no
one has heeded,
25 because you have [h]ignored all my counsel
and [i]would have none of my reproof,
26 I also [j]will laugh at your calamity;
I will mock when [k]terror strikes you,
27 when terror strikes you like [l]a storm
and your calamity comes like a whirlwind,
when distress and anguish come
upon you.
28 [m]Then they will call upon me, but I will
not answer;
they will seek me diligently but will
not find me.
29 Because they [c]hated knowledge
and [n]did not choose the fear of the
LORD,
30 [h]would have none of my counsel
and [i]despised all my reproof,
31 therefore they shall eat [o]the fruit of their
way,
and have [p]their fill of their own devices.
32 For the simple are killed by [q]their turning away,
and [r]the complacency of fools
destroys them;
33 but [s]whoever listens to me will dwell
secure
and will be [t]at ease, without dread of
disaster."

The Value of Wisdom

2 [u]My son, [v]if you receive my words
and treasure up my commandments
with you,
2 making your ear attentive to wisdom
and inclining your heart to understanding;
3 yes, if you call out for insight
and raise your voice [w]for understanding,
4 if you seek it like [x]silver
and search for it as for [y]hidden treasures,

[1] Or *Will you turn away at my reproof?*

1:20–33 This is the first of two appeals from Wisdom personified as an elegant lady, obviously worthy of our admiration (cf. 8:4–36). Right where we live our daily lives (1:20–21), Wisdom shouts above the noise and offers us her spirit and words (v. 23). But if we trifle with the message, judgment will come like a storm, like a whirlwind (v. 27). God hides his wisdom from the proud (vv. 24–32; cf. Matt. 11:25; 13:12). But listening to him we will dwell secure—as Jesus, God's ultimate wisdom, promises (Matt. 7:24–27).

2:1–4 These verses describe a growing believer. In contrast to "the complacency of fools" (1:32), the fear of the Lord creates an openness (2:1–2) and even an eagerness (vv. 3–4) to change. The word "if" (vv. 1, 3, and 4) does not mean we have to deserve God's blessing, but it does mean we have to pursue his blessing (Phil. 3:12–14). No one drifts into wisdom.

15[q]ch. 4:14; 24:1; Ps. 1:1 [r][Ps. 119:101]
16[s]ch. 6:18; Isa. 59:7; [Rom. 3:15]
17[t][Job 40:24]
18[u]ver. 11
19[v][Job 8:13] [w]ch. 15:27 [x][1 Tim. 6:10]
20[y]ch. 8:1; 9:3; [John 7:37]
21[z]ch. 8:3
22[a]See ver. 4 [b]See Ps. 1:1 [c]ver. 29; ch. 5:12; [Job 21:14]
23[d]Joel 2:28; Acts 2:17
24[e]Isa. 65:12; 66:4; Jer. 7:13 [f]Zech. 7:11 [g]Rom. 10:21
25[h]See Ps. 107:11 [i][Ps. 81:11; Luke 7:30]

26[j]See Ps. 2:4 [k]ch. 10:24; Jer. 48:43; 49:5 **27**[l][Zeph. 1:15] **28**[m]See 1 Sam. 8:18; Job 27:9 **29**[c][See ver. 22 above] [n][Job 21:14] **30**[h][See ver. 25 above] [i][See ver. 25 above] **31**[o]Jer. 6:19 [p]ch. 14:14; Isa. 3:11; [Job 4:8] **32**[q]Jer. 2:19 [r][Ps. 73:18, 19] **33**[s][Ps. 25:12, 13] [t]Ps. 112:7, 8 **Chapter 2** **1**[u]See ch. 1:8 [v][ch. 4:1, 10, 20; 7:1] **3**[w]ch. 4:1, 5, 7 **4**[x]ch. 3:14 [y]Job 3:21; [Matt. 13:44]

5 then [z]you will understand the fear of the
LORD
and find the knowledge of God.
6 For [a]the LORD gives wisdom;
from his mouth come knowledge and
understanding;
7 he stores up sound wisdom for the
upright;
he is [b]a shield to those who [c]walk in
integrity,
8 guarding the paths of justice
and [d]watching over the way of his
[e]saints.
9 [f]Then you will understand [g]righteous-
ness and justice
and equity, every good path;
10 for wisdom will come into your heart,
and knowledge will be pleasant to
your soul;
11 [h]discretion will [i]watch over you,
understanding will guard you,
12 delivering you from the way of evil,
from men of perverted speech,
13 who forsake the paths of uprightness
to [j]walk in the ways of darkness,
14 who [k]rejoice in doing evil
and [l]delight in the perverseness of
evil,
15 men whose [m]paths are crooked,
[n]and who are [o]devious in their ways.
16 So [p]you will be delivered from the forbidden[1] woman,
from [q]the adulteress[2] with [r]her
smooth words,
17 who forsakes [s]the companion of her
youth
and forgets [t]the covenant of her God;
18 [u]for her house sinks down to death,
and her paths to the departed;[3]
19 none who go to her come back,
nor do they regain the paths of life.
20 So you will walk in the way of the good
and keep to the paths of the righteous.
21 For the upright [v]will inhabit the land,
and those with integrity will remain
in it,
22 but the wicked will be [w]cut off from the
land,
and the treacherous will be [x]rooted
out of it.

Trust in the LORD with All Your Heart

3 [y]My son, do not forget my teaching,
[z]but let your heart keep my
commandments,
2 for [a]length of days and years of life
and [b]peace they will add to you.
3 Let not [c]steadfast love and [d]faithfulness
forsake you;
[e]bind them around your neck;
[f]write them on the tablet of your heart.

[1]Hebrew *strange* [2]Hebrew *foreign woman* [3]Hebrew *to the Rephaim*

2:5–11 After the "if" statements in verses 1–4, verses 5–11 are marked by the word "then" (vv. 5, 9). Growing believers can expect two things. First, according to verses 5–8, we "will understand the fear of the LORD and find the knowledge of God" (v. 5). True wisdom is not an abstract principle. It is our walk with the living God. Second, according to verses 9–11, wisdom will come into our hearts (v. 10). We will not need external pressure to turn toward what is right, for we ourselves will change from within (1:23; Ezek. 36:26–27). Our hearts will have a taste for the wise choice.

2:12–19 With a heart newly awakened to God's wisdom, a growing believer is fortified against two dangers. First, in verses 12–15, "men of perverted speech" (v. 12). Such people twist words around, to sneak things in that honesty would be ashamed of—in politics or in advertising, for example. But a heart made wise will not be fooled. Second, in verses 16–19, "the adulteress with her smooth words" (v. 16). However she might flatter, there is no "safe sex," except in marriage. "Her house sinks down to death" (v. 18). By contrast, our risen Lord is "a life-giving spirit" (1 Cor. 15:45), and our spirits have been eternally joined to him as our loving husband (1 Cor. 6:17).

2:20–22 But wisdom is more than avoiding trouble. It is also a path into life, and the only path into life. Rather than going to the place of death (vv. 18–19), the upright "will inhabit the land" (v. 21), the place of blessing—in New Testament terms, Jesus himself, who said, "Abide in me" (John 15:4).

3:1–12 God our Father urges us toward a rewarding life. He gives us counsel in the odd-numbered verses of this section and offers us incentives in the even-numbered

5[z] [Ps. 25:14; John 7:17; 14:21]
6[a] Job 32:8
7[b] ch. 30:5; See Ps. 3:3 [c] Ps. 84:11
8[d] 1 Sam. 2:9; Ps. 66:9; 97:10 [e] See Ps. 30:4
9[f] [ver. 5] [g] ch. 1:3
11[h] ch. 1:4 [i] ch. 6:22
13[j] Ps. 82:5; [John 3:19, 20]
14[k] Jer. 11:15; [ch. 10:23] [l] [Ps. 50:18; Rom. 1:32]
15[m] Ps. 125:5; [ch. 21:8] [n] ch. 14:2 [o] ch. 3:32
16[p] ch. 7:5 [q] ch. 6:24; 23:27 [r] ch. 6:24; Ps. 5:9
17[s] Jer. 3:4; [Ps. 55:13] [t] [Mal. 2:14, 15]
18[u] ch. 7:27
21[v] ch. 10:30
22[w] See Ps. 37:38 [x] ch. 15:25; Deut. 28:63; Ps. 52:5

Chapter 3
1[y] See ch. 1:8 [z] Deut. 8:1; 30:16, 20
2[a] ver. 16; ch. 4:10; 9:11; 10:27; See Ps. 91:16 [b] ch. 1:33; Ps. 119:165
3[c] [Ps. 85:10] [d] [ch. 20:28; Isa. 59:14] [e] [ch. 1:9; 6:21; 7:3] [f] ch. 7:3; [Jer. 17:1; 2 Cor. 3:3]

4 So you will [g]find favor and [h]good success[1]
in the sight of God and man.

5 [i]Trust in the LORD with all your heart,
and [j]do not lean on your own understanding.
6 In all your ways [k]acknowledge him,
and he [l]will make straight your paths.
7 [m]Be not wise in your own eyes;
[n]fear the LORD, and turn away from evil.
8 It will be [o]healing to your flesh[2]
and [p]refreshment[3] to your bones.

9 Honor the LORD with your wealth
and with [q]the firstfruits of all your produce;
10 then your [r]barns will be filled with plenty,
and your vats will be bursting with wine.

11 [s]My son, do not despise the LORD's discipline
or be weary of his reproof,
12 for the LORD reproves him whom he loves,
as [t]a father the son in whom he delights.

Blessed Is the One Who Finds Wisdom

13 [u]Blessed is the one who finds wisdom,
and the one who gets understanding,
14 [v]for the gain from her is better than gain from silver
and her profit better than [w]gold.
15 She is more precious than [x]jewels,
and [y]nothing you desire can compare with her.
16 [z]Long life is in her right hand;
in her left hand are [a]riches and honor.
17 Her [b]ways are ways of pleasantness,
and all her paths are peace.
18 She is [c]a tree of life to those who [d]lay hold of her;
those who hold her fast are called blessed.

19 [e]The LORD by wisdom founded the earth;
by understanding [e]he established the heavens;
20 by his knowledge [f]the deeps broke open,
and [g]the clouds drop down the dew.

21 My son, [h]do not lose sight of these—
keep sound wisdom and discretion,
22 and they will be [i]life for your soul
and [j]adornment for your neck.
23 [k]Then you will walk on your way securely,
[l]and your foot will not stumble.
24 [m]If you lie down, you will not be afraid;
when you lie down, [n]your sleep will be sweet.
25 [o]Do not be afraid of sudden terror
or of [p]the ruin[4] of the wicked, when it comes,

[1] Or *repute* [2] Hebrew *navel* [3] Or *medicine* [4] Hebrew *storm*

4[g] [1 Sam. 2:26; Luke 2:52; Rom. 14:18] [h] See Ps. 111:10
5[i] Ps. 37:3, 5 [j] [Jer. 9:23]
6[k] 1 Chr. 28:9 [l] [Ps. 73:24]
7[m] [Rom. 12:16]; See ch. 12:15 [n] Job 1:1; 28:28
8[o] [ch. 4:22] [p] See Job 21:24
9[q] Ex. 23:19; 34:26; Deut. 26:2
10[r] Deut. 28:8
11[s] Cited Heb. 12:5, 6; See Job 5:17
12[t] Deut. 8:5; [1 Cor. 11:32]
13[u] ch. 8:34, 35
14[v] See Job 28:15-19 [w] ch. 8:10, 19; 16:16; Ps. 19:10
15[x] Job 28:18 [y] ch. 8:11
16[z] ver. 2 [a] ch. 8:18; 22:4
17[b] [Matt. 11:29, 30]
18[c] ch. 11:30; 13:12; 15:4; Gen. 2:9; 3:22; Rev. 2:7; 22:2 [d] ch. 4:13
19[e] ch. 8:27; Ps. 104:5, 24; 136:5
20[f] Gen. 7:11; [Job 38:8] [g] Job 36:28
21[h] ch. 4:21
22[i] See ch. 4:22 [j] [ch. 1:9]
23[k] ch. 10:9; [ch. 28:18; Ps. 91:11] [l] ch. 4:12; Ps. 91:12
24[m] [ch. 6:22; Ps. 3:5; 4:8]; See Job 11:19 [n] Jer. 31:26 **25**[o] [1 Pet. 3:14]; See Ps. 91:5 [p] [Job 5:21]

verses. His counsel is not bare ethical principles but a call to himself: "Trust in the LORD" (v. 5), "fear the LORD" (v. 7), "honor the LORD" (v. 9). His incentives are not worldly but the life and peace that result from obeying his commands (v. 2; cf. John 10:10; 14:27). Even the pain of his discipline and reproof (Prov. 3:11) opens our hearts more deeply to his love (Heb. 12:5–11; Rev. 3:19). The commands and the discipline are ultimately seen as coming from the same father-like love that provides the Christ we need for our disobedience and lack of discipline (Prov. 3:12).

3:13–26 This passage strengthens the Father's appeals in vv. 1–12. His wisdom matters for three reasons. First, according to verses 13–18, "blessed is the one who finds wisdom" (v. 13). The word "blessed" describes a person to be admired. As "a tree of life" (v. 18), God's wisdom, ultimately revealed in Christ, restores the ideal we lost in Eden (Gen. 3:22–24; Rev. 2:7; 22:2). Second, according to Proverbs 3:19, "the LORD by wisdom founded the earth." His wisdom is embedded in how the creation works. Ignoring him cannot succeed. Trusting him cannot fail. Third, according to verses 21–26, "you will walk on your way securely" (v. 23), because the Lord will "keep your foot from being caught" (v. 26; cf. 2 Tim. 4:18). "Do not lose sight of . . . sound wisdom and discretion" (Prov. 3:21) calls for diligent attention to our lives, moment by moment, confident in the Lord's protection.

26 for the LORD will be your confidence
and will [q]keep your foot from being
caught.
27 [r]Do not withhold good from those to
whom it is due,[1]
when it is in your power to do it.
28 [s]Do not say to your neighbor, "Go, and
come again,
tomorrow I will give it"—when you
have it with you.
29 [t]Do not plan evil against your neighbor,
who [u]dwells trustingly beside you.
30 [v]Do not contend with a man for no reason,
when he has done you no harm.
31 [w]Do not envy [x]a man of violence
and do not choose any of his ways,
32 for [y]the devious person is an abomination to the LORD,
but the upright are [z]in his confidence.
33 [a]The LORD's curse is on the house of the
wicked,
but he [b]blesses the dwelling of the
righteous.
34 Toward the [c]scorners he [d]is scornful,
[e]but to the humble he gives favor.[2]
35 The wise will inherit honor,
but fools get[3] disgrace.

A Father's Wise Instruction

4 [f]Hear, O sons, a father's instruction,
and be attentive, that you may [g]gain[4]
insight,
2 for I give you good [h]precepts;
do not forsake my teaching.
3 When I was a son with my father,
[i]tender, [j]the only one in the sight of
my mother,
4 he [k]taught me and said to me,
[l]"Let your heart hold fast my words;
[m]keep my commandments, and live.
5 [n]Get wisdom; get [g]insight;
do not forget, and do not turn away
from the words of my mouth.
6 Do not forsake her, and she will keep you;
[o]love her, and she will guard you.
7 [p]The beginning of wisdom is this: Get
wisdom,
and whatever you get, get [g]insight.
8 Prize her highly, and she will exalt you;
she will [q]honor you [r]if you embrace
her.
9 She will place on your head [s]a graceful
garland;
she will bestow on you a beautiful
crown."

10 [f]Hear, [t]my son, and accept my words,
that [u]the years of your life may be
many.

[1] Hebrew *Do not withhold good from its owners* [2] Or *grace* [3] The meaning of the Hebrew word is uncertain [4] Hebrew *know*

3:27–35 Now the Father explains the point of Proverbs chapter 3—how we treat one another. God's wisdom creates relationships of responsible generosity (vv. 27–28), trusting safety (vv. 29–30), and careful discernment (vv. 31–32). The Lord is active among his people, with both blessing and discipline (vv. 33–35). James 4:6 and 1 Peter 5:5 draw upon verse 34 as a practical application of the gospel. Humility started in heaven and came down to us in Jesus (Phil. 2:5–8). The humble find favor with the Lord, not because they demand it by their merits but because he gives it to those who are open.

4:1–27 Surprisingly, God is nowhere mentioned in chapter 4. But he is everywhere present, speaking through the wise father as he introduces his son to their family tradition of sacred wisdom (vv. 1, 10, 20).

4:1–9 In the Old Testament, the priests taught the *law* of God, and the prophets declared the *word* of God (Jer. 18:18). But the fathers and mothers gave their children the *wisdom* of God (Prov. 1:8; 6:20). Their tone is urgent: "The beginning of wisdom is this: Get wisdom" (4:7). The strong expressions "hold fast," "keep," "get," "love," "prize," and "embrace" set the tone of the section. We grow wise not by brains but by bold decisiveness. Do we want the mind of God, ultimately revealed in Christ? We may, we must, receive his wisdom through the gospel. Getting it will cost us, but not getting it would cost us infinitely more (Matt. 13:44–46).

4:10–19 This passage locates us at a fork in the road, with two paths before us. "The path of the wicked" (v. 14) leads away from the Father and into compulsive cravings (v. 16; cf. John 8:34), which the wicked cannot explain even to themselves (Prov. 4:19;

26[q] See 1 Sam. 2:9
27[r] Gal. 6:10
28[s] [Lev. 19:13; Deut. 24:15]
29[t] ch. 6:14; 12:20; 14:22 [u][Judg. 18:7, 27]
30[v] [Rom. 12:18]
31[w] See Ps. 37:1 [x] Ps. 18:48; 140:1
32[y] ch. 2:15 [z] See Job 29:4
33[a] Ps. 37:22; Zech. 5:4; Mal. 2:2; See Lev. 26:14-39 [b][Job 8:6]
34[c] See Ps. 1:1 [d][James 4:6; 1 Pet. 5:5; See Ps. 138:6] [e][James 4:6; 1 Pet. 5:5]; See Ps. 138:6
Chapter 4
1[f] ch. 1:8; [ch. 5:7; 7:24; 8:33; Ps. 34:11] [g] ch. 2:2
2[h] Job 11:4
3[i] See 1 Chr. 22:5 [j] Zech. 12:10
4[k] 1 Chr. 28:9; [Eph. 6:4] [l][ch. 3:1] [m] ch. 7:2; Lev. 18:5; Isa. 55:3
5[n] ch. 2:2 [g][See ver. 1 above]
6[o][2 Thess. 2:10]
7[p][ch. 1:7] [g][See ver. 1 above]
8[q] 1 Sam. 2:30 [r][Song 2:6]
9[s] ch. 1:9
10[f][See ver. 1 above] [t] ch. 2:1 [u] See ch. 3:2

11 I have [v]taught you the way of wisdom;
I have led you in the paths of uprightness.
12 When you walk, [w]your step will not be hampered,
and [x]if you run, you will not stumble.
13 [y]Keep hold of instruction; do not let go;
guard her, for she is your [z]life.
14 [a]Do not enter the path of the wicked,
and do not walk in the way of the evil.
15 Avoid it; do not go on it;
turn away from it and pass on.
16 For they [b]cannot sleep unless they have done wrong;
they are robbed of sleep unless they have made someone stumble.
17 For they eat the bread of wickedness
[c]and drink the wine of violence.
18 But [d]the path of the righteous is like [e]the light of dawn,
which shines [f]brighter and brighter until [g]full day.
19 [h]The way of the wicked is like deep [i]darkness;
they do not know over what they [j]stumble.

20 [k]My son, be attentive to my words;
incline your ear to my sayings.
21 [l]Let them not escape from your sight;
[m]keep them within your heart.
22 For they are [n]life to those who find them,
and healing to all their[1] flesh.
23 Keep your heart with all vigilance,
for [o]from it flow [p]the springs of life.
24 Put away from you [q]crooked speech,
and put [r]devious talk far from you.
25 [s]Let your eyes look directly forward,
and your gaze be straight before you.
26 [t]Ponder[2] the path of your feet;
[u]then all your ways will be sure.
27 [v]Do not swerve to the right or to the left;
turn your foot away from evil.

Warning Against Adultery

5 [w]My son, be attentive to my wisdom;
[x]incline your ear to my understanding,
2 that you may keep [y]discretion,
and your lips may [z]guard knowledge.
3 For the lips of [a]a forbidden[3] woman drip honey,
and her speech[4] is [b]smoother than oil,
4 but in the end she is [c]bitter as [d]wormwood,
[e]sharp as [f]a two-edged sword.
5 Her feet [g]go down to death;
her steps follow the path to[5] Sheol;
6 she [h]does not ponder the path of life;
her ways wander, and she does not know it.

7 And [i]now, O sons, listen to me,
and do not depart from the words of my mouth.

[1] Hebrew *his* [2] Or *Make level* [3] Hebrew *strange*; also verse 20 [4] Hebrew *palate* [5] Hebrew *lay hold of*

11[v] See 1 Sam. 12:23
12[w] [Job 18:7; Ps. 18:36; 119:45] [x] ch. 3:23
13[y] ch. 3:18 [z] ver. 22; [John 1:4; 1 John 5:12]
14[a] ch. 1:15; Ps. 1:1
16[b] [Ps. 36:4]
17[c] [Amos 2:8]
18[d] Job 11:17; 22:28; Isa. 60:3; 62:1, 2; Dan. 12:3 [e] 2 Sam. 23:4; See Ps. 97:11 [f] [Ps. 84:7] [g] [1 John 3:2]
19[h] 1 Sam. 2:9; Isa. 59:9, 10; Jer. 23:12; John 12:35; [Job 18:5] [i] [Matt. 6:23] [j] [John 11:10; 1 John 2:10]
20[k] ver. 10
21[l] ch. 3:21 [m] [ch. 2:1]
22[n] ver. 13; ch. 8:35; 21:21; Deut. 32:47; [1 Tim. 4:8]
23[o] [Matt. 12:35] [p] [Ps. 16:11]
24[q] ch. 6:12 [r] ch. 2:15
25[s] [Heb. 12:2]
26[t] ch. 5:6, 21; [Heb. 12:13] [u] [Ps. 119:5]
27[v] Deut. 5:32; 28:14; Josh. 1:7; 1 Kgs. 15:5
Chapter 5
1[w] ch. 4:20; [ch. 2:1, 2] [x] ch. 22:17

cf. 1 John 2:11). "The path of the righteous" (Prov. 4:18) may be, for now, only a glimmer of dawn; but the glory of full day is coming (2 Cor. 3:18; Phil. 1:6; Rev. 22:5). All who by God's grace follow the path of wisdom are in the early morning of their lives. All who take the other path are already in the lengthening shadows of their afternoon.

4:20–27 We make progress toward wisdom by staying intensely focused: "Let your eyes look directly forward" (v. 25). Many distractions in this world would draw us away. How can we remain loyal to God through it all? "Keep your heart with all vigilance, for from it flow the springs of life" (v. 23). Jesus may have been thinking of verse 23b in John 7:38: "Whoever believes in me, as the Scripture has said, 'Out of his heart will flow rivers of living water.'" True life does not flow *into* us from external circumstances; true life flows *out of* us from the internal fullness of the Holy Spirit.

5:1–6 The Father warns us against sexual sin, pointing out its surface appeal but its hidden destruction.

5:7–14 "Keep your way far from her" (v. 8) is decisive and safe. Sexual sin carries unforeseeable but inevitable impact, painfully felt (vv. 9–14). God, in grace, redeems the consequences of our sins; but, by the same grace, he also warns us against sinning in the first place (1 Cor. 4:14; Gal. 5:19–21; Heb. 13:4). Warning is part of the ministry of the gospel.

2[y] ch. 1:4 [z] Mal. 2:7 **3**[a] See ch. 2:16 [b] Ps. 55:21 **4**[c] [Eccles. 7:26] [d] Deut. 29:18; Jer. 9:15; Lam. 3:15, 19; Rev. 8:11 [e] Ps. 57:4; [Ps. 55:21] [f] See Ps. 149:6
5[g] See ch. 7:27 **6**[h] ver. 21; ch. 4:26 **7**[i] See ch. 4:1

8 Keep your way far from her,
and do not go near the door of her house,
9 lest you give your honor to others
and your years to the merciless,
10 lest strangers take their fill of your strength,
and your [j]labors go to the house of a foreigner,
11 and at the end of your life you [k]groan,
when your flesh and body are consumed,
12 and you say, [l]"How I hated discipline,
and my heart [m]despised reproof!
13 I did not listen to the voice of my teachers
or incline my ear to my instructors.
14 [n]I am at the brink of utter ruin
in the assembled congregation."

15 Drink [o]water from your own cistern,
flowing water from your own well.
16 Should your [p]springs be scattered abroad,
streams of water [q]in the streets?
17 [r]Let them be for yourself alone,
and not for strangers with you.
18 Let your [o]fountain be blessed,
and [s]rejoice in [t]the wife of your youth,
19 a lovely [u]deer, a graceful doe.
Let her breasts [v]fill you at all times with delight;
be intoxicated[1] always in her love.
20 Why should you be intoxicated, my son, with [w]a forbidden woman
and embrace the bosom of [w]an adulteress?[2]
21 For [x]a man's ways are [y]before the eyes of the LORD,
and he [z]ponders[3] all his paths.
22 The [a]iniquities of the wicked [b]ensnare him,
and he is held fast in the cords of his sin.
23 [c]He dies for lack of discipline,
and because of his great folly he is [d]led astray.

Practical Warnings

6 My son, if you have put up [e]security for your neighbor,
have [e]given your pledge for a stranger,
2 if you are [f]snared in the words of your mouth,
caught in the words of your mouth,
3 then do this, my son, and save yourself,
for you have come into the hand of your neighbor:
go, hasten,[4] and [g]plead urgently with your neighbor.

[1] Hebrew *be led astray*; also verse 20 [2] Hebrew *a foreign woman* [3] Or *makes level* [4] Or *humble yourself*

5:15–19 The wise alternative to sexual chaos outside marriage is sexual satisfaction within marriage (1 Cor. 7:2). "Drink water from your own cistern" (Prov. 5:15) means to satisfy your sexual thirst within the privacy of marriage. Our sexuality is not public property (vv. 16–17), but within marriage the Father blesses uninhibited sexual joys (vv. 18–19). The words "at all times" and "always" (v. 19) remove limits from a married couple's sexual enjoyment of each other (1 Cor. 7:3–5). The gospel highly honors marriage as a picture of Christ and his church in love together (cf. notes on The Song of Solomon; Eph. 5:31–32).

5:20–23 After the positive affirmation of married sex in 5:15–19, to violate it would be shocking (v. 20). Human sexuality is very personal, but not off-limits to the Lord (v. 21; cf. Luke 12:2). He who created us male and female (Gen. 1:27) has every right to guide us by his Word. His judgments of sin, moreover, are not arbitrary additions. Sinful folly works with its own dark powers: The iniquities of the wicked ensnare him (Prov. 5:22). May God enable us to say, "I will arise and go to my father" (Luke 15:18). However foolish we have been, we still have a Father who will receive us and rejoice over us in our repentance (Luke 15:20).

6:1–19 With down-to-earth practicality, the gracious wisdom of the Father guides us away from three forms of folly.

One, "if you have put up security for your neighbor" (v. 1), that is, if we have guaranteed someone else's debt, we should swallow our pride, take immediate action, and get free (vv. 1–5). Why would we put our financial future in the control of another? The grace of financial integrity keeps us available to serve God. We want to be in his hand only, not at all in the hand of our neighbor (v. 3).

10[j] Ps. 127:2
11[k] Ezek. 24:23
12[l] ch. 1:22, 29; See ch. 12:1 [m] ch. 1:25; See Ps. 107:11
14[n] [Ps. 94:17]
15[o] ver. 18; [ch. 9:17; Song 4:12, 15; Jer. 2:13]
16[p] See Ps. 68:26 [q] [Jer. 9:21; Zech. 8:5]
17[r] [ch. 14:10]
18[o] [See ver. 15 above] [s] Deut. 24:5 [t] Mal. 2:14
19[u] Song 2:9, 17; 8:14 [v] [Jer. 31:14]
20[w] See ch. 2:16
21[x] Ps. 119:168 [y] Hos. 7:2; Heb. 4:13; See Job 14:16; Ps. 11:4 [z] ver. 6
22[a] See Ps. 7:15, 16 [b] ch. 6:2
23[c] See Job 4:21 [d] [Job 12:24]
Chapter 6
1[e] See Job 17:3
2[f] [ch. 5:22]
3[g] [Luke 11:8; 18:5]

4 [h]Give your eyes no sleep
and your eyelids no slumber;
5 save yourself like a gazelle from the
hand of the hunter,[1]
[i]like a bird from the hand of the
fowler.

6 [j]Go to [k]the ant, O [l]sluggard;
consider her ways, and [m]be wise.
7 [n]Without having any chief,
[o]officer, or ruler,
8 she prepares her bread [p]in summer
and [q]gathers her food in harvest.
9 [r]How long will you lie there, [l]O sluggard?
When will you arise from your sleep?
10 [s]A little sleep, a little slumber,
[t]a little [s]folding of the hands to rest,
11 [u]and poverty will come upon you like a
robber,
and want like an armed man.

12 [v]A worthless person, a wicked man,
goes about with [w]crooked speech,
13 [x]winks with his eyes, signals[2] with his
feet,
points with his finger,
14 with [y]perverted heart [z]devises evil,
continually [a]sowing discord;
15 therefore calamity will come upon him
suddenly;
[b]in a moment he will be broken
[c]beyond healing.

16 There are [d]six things that the LORD hates,
[d]seven that are an abomination to him:
17 [e]haughty eyes, [f]a lying tongue,
and [g]hands that shed innocent blood,
18 [h]a heart that devises wicked plans,
[i]feet that make haste to run to evil,
19 [j]a false witness who [k]breathes out lies,
and one who [a]sows discord among
brothers.

Warnings Against Adultery

20 [l]My son, keep your father's commandment,
[l]and forsake not your mother's teaching.
21 [m]Bind them on your heart always;
[n]tie them around your neck.
22 [o]When you walk, they[3] will lead you;
[o]when you lie down, they will [p]watch
over you;
and when you awake, they will talk
with you.
23 For the commandment is [q]a lamp and
the teaching a light,
and the [r]reproofs of discipline are the
way of life,
24 to preserve you from the evil woman,[4]
from the smooth tongue of [s]the adulteress.[5]
25 [t]Do not desire her beauty in your heart,
and do not let her capture you with
her [u]eyelashes;

[1] Hebrew lacks *of the hunter* [2] Hebrew *scrapes* [3] Hebrew *it*; three times in this verse [4] Revocalization (compare Septuagint) yields *from the wife of a neighbor* [5] Hebrew *the foreign woman*

4[h] ch. 20:13; Ps. 132:4
5[i] See Ps. 91:3
6[j] [Job 12:7] [k] ch. 30:25 [l] ch. 10:26 [m] ch. 23:19; 27:11
7[n] [ch. 30:27] [o] Ex. 5:6, 15
8[p] [ch. 10:5] [q] [ch. 10:5]
9[r] [Jonah 1:6] [l] [See ver. 6 above]
10[s] ch. 24:33 [t] Eccles. 4:5
11[u] ch. 24:34
12[v] ch. 16:27 [w] ch. 4:24
13[x] ch. 10:10; Ps. 35:19
14[y] See ch. 2:12 [z] [Mic. 2:1]; See ch. 3:29 [a] [ch. 16:28]
15[b] Isa. 30:13, 14; Jer. 19:11 [c] ch. 29:1; 2 Chr. 36:16
16[d] See Job 5:19
17[e] [ch. 8:13; 16:5; 21:4]; See Ps. 101:5 [f] ch. 12:22; 17:7; Ps. 31:18; 120:2 [g] Deut. 19:10; Isa. 1:15; 59:3, 7
18[h] Gen. 6:5 [i] See ch. 1:16
19[j] See Ps. 27:12 [k] ch. 12:17; 14:5, 25; 19:5, 9 [a] [See ver. 14 above]
20[l] See ch. 1:8
21[m] See ch. 3:3 [n] [Job 31:36]
22[o] See ch. 3:23, 24 [p] ch. 2:11
23[q] Ps. 119:105; [Ps. 13:3] [r] [ch. 10:17]
24[s] See ch. 2:16
25[t] [Matt. 5:28] [u] [2 Kgs. 9:30]

Two, "Go to the ant, O sluggard" (v. 6) warns us against laziness (vv. 6–11). The opportunity of life can slip through our fingers a little at a time (v. 10), but the accumulated losses are not little (v. 11). Jesus worked hard (John 9:4), his grace makes us hard workers (1 Cor. 15:10; Eph. 4:28), and our labors in him will matter forever (1 Cor. 15:58).

Three, "sowing discord" and "one who sows discord" (Prov. 6:14, 19) warn us not to violate the grace of divinely provided fellowship (vv. 12–19). The folly of sowing discord among brothers is so serious, the warning is repeated (vv. 12–15, 16–19). The strong word "abomination" (v. 16) sets a troublemaker apart with the same moral stigma as a prostitute (Deut. 23:17–18). But "Blessed are the peacemakers, for they shall be called sons of God" (Matt. 5:9).

6:20–35 The Father returns to the subject of our sexuality. Here the Father bases his appeal on the practical impact of sexual sin: the pain is personally inescapable (v. 27), and the anger and jealousy it can cause may find no remedy (v. 34). The world glorifies sexual adventurism. Only God our Father loves us enough to tell us the hard truth about the actual cost of sexual sin. Even while we stand, let us take heed lest we fall, trusting in our faithful Lord to keep us in his grace (1 Cor. 10:12–13; Jude 24–25).

The Father addresses our sexuality repeatedly because sexual sin betrays his grace and sexual faithfulness displays the greatness of his love, finally revealed in Christ and the church (1 Cor. 6:12–20; Eph. 5:22–33). The gospel is the ultimate reason why our sexual integrity matters.

26 for [v]the price of a prostitute is only [w]a
loaf of bread,[1]
but a married woman[2] [x]hunts down a
precious life.
27 Can a man carry [y]fire next to his [z]chest
and his clothes not be burned?
28 Or can one [a]walk on hot coals
and his feet not be scorched?
29 So is he who goes in to his neighbor's wife;
none who touches her [b]will go
unpunished.
30 People do not despise a thief if he steals
to [c]satisfy his appetite when he is
hungry,
31 but [d]if he is caught, he will pay [e]sevenfold;
he will give all the goods of his house.
32 He who commits adultery lacks sense;
he who does it destroys himself.
33 He will get wounds and dishonor,
and his disgrace will not be wiped away.
34 For [f]jealousy makes a man furious,
and he will not spare when [g]he takes
revenge.
35 He will accept no compensation;
he will refuse though you multiply
gifts.

Warning Against the Adulteress

7 [h]My son, keep my words
and [h]treasure up my commandments
with you;
2 [i]keep my commandments and live;
keep my teaching as [j]the apple of your
eye;
3 [k]bind them on your fingers;
[k]write them on the tablet of your
heart.
4 Say to wisdom, "You are my sister,"
and call insight your intimate friend,
5 to keep you from [l]the forbidden[3]
woman,
from [l]the adulteress[4] with her smooth
words.

6 For at [m]the window of my house
I have looked out through my lattice,
7 and I have seen among [n]the simple,
I have perceived among the youths,
a young man [o]lacking sense,
8 passing along the street [p]near her corner,
taking the road to her house
9 in [q]the twilight, in the evening,
at [r]the time of night and darkness.

10 And behold, the woman meets him,
[s]dressed as a prostitute, wily of heart.[5]
11 She is [t]loud and [u]wayward;
[v]her feet do not stay at home;
12 now in the street, now in the market,
and [w]at every corner she [x]lies in wait.
13 She seizes him and kisses him,
and with [y]bold face she says to him,
14 "I had to [z]offer sacrifices,[6]
and today I have [a]paid my vows;
15 so now I have come out to meet you,
to seek you eagerly, and I have found
you.
16 I have spread my couch with [b]coverings,
colored linens from [c]Egyptian linen;

[1] Or (compare Septuagint, Syriac, Vulgate) *for a prostitute leaves a man with nothing but a loaf of bread* [2] Hebrew *a man's wife* [3] Hebrew *strange* [4] Hebrew *the foreign woman* [5] Hebrew *guarded in heart* [6] Hebrew *peace offerings*

7:1–27 For the final time in the introductory chapters 1–9, the Father aims to safeguard our sexual purity. As in chapter 4, God is not mentioned; but still he is present in the voice of the wise father. Speaking to his beloved son, he is saying, "Here is how you will be tempted. Get ready." We need realism about this world (1 John 2:15–17). The chapter begins and ends with a call to pay close attention (Prov. 7:1–5, 24–27), as a matter of life and death (vv. 2, 27). In the body of the chapter, we are warned about the approach of sexual temptation (vv. 6–13), the words of sexual temptation (vv. 14–20), and the impact of giving in to sexual temptation (vv. 21–23).

7:6–13 The simple (v. 7) are uncommitted people who see themselves as smart and in control. The Father sees them as gullible, and so they prove to be. This young man's self-assurance is no match for the prostitute, "wily of heart" (v. 10), who approaches him. If these two are caught in their sin, she already has a plan for getting out of it. She can easily accuse him of rape (cf. Gen. 39:11–18). But he is not thinking beyond the impulses of the moment. In this way, a loving father warns his children of the consequences of waywardness while also acknowledging their susceptibility to it. Such is the nature of a wise and gracious heart.

7:14–20 She offers the young man an exotic sexual experience (vv. 14–17), with no fear of discovery (vv. 18–20). "I had to offer sacrifices" (v. 14) implies she has a good meal

26 [v] [ch. 29:3] [w] ch. 28:21; 1 Sam. 2:36 [x] Ezek. 13:18
27 [y] Job 31:12 [z] Ps. 79:12
28 [a] Isa. 43:2
29 [b] ch. 16:5
30 [c] Job 38:39
31 [d] [Ex. 22:4] [e] See Ps. 79:12
34 [f] ch. 27:4; Song 8:6 [g] [Lev. 20:10]

Chapter 7
1 [h] See ch. 2:1
2 [i] See ch. 4:4 [j] Deut. 32:10
3 [k] See ch. 3:3
5 [l] See ch. 2:16
6 [m] Judg. 5:28
7 [n] See ch. 1:4 [o] See ch. 6:32
8 [p] ver. 12
9 [q] Job 24:15 [r] ch. 20:20
10 [s] [Gen. 38:14]
11 [t] ch. 9:13 [u] [Hos. 4:16] [v] 1 Tim. 5:13; [Titus 2:5]
12 [w] ver. 8 [x] ch. 23:28
13 [y] ch. 21:29
14 [z] Lev. 7:11 [a] See Ps. 50:14
16 [b] ch. 31:22 [c] [Isa. 19:9]

17 I have perfumed my bed with [d]myrrh,
aloes, and [e]cinnamon.
18 Come, let us take our fill of love till
morning;
let us delight ourselves with love.
19 For [f]my husband is not at home;
he has gone on a long journey;
20 he took a bag of money with him;
at full moon he will come home."

21 With much seductive speech she persuades him;
with [g]her smooth talk she compels
him.
22 All at once he follows her,
as an ox goes to the slaughter,
or as a stag is caught fast[1]
23 till an arrow pierces its liver;
as [h]a bird rushes into a snare;
he does not know that it will cost him
his life.

24 And [i]now, O sons, listen to me,
and be attentive to the words of my
mouth.
25 Let not your heart turn aside to her
ways;
do not stray into her paths,
26 for many a victim has she laid low,
and all her slain are [j]a mighty throng.
27 Her house is [k]the way to Sheol,
going down to the chambers of
death.

The Blessings of Wisdom

8 Does not [l]wisdom call?
Does not [m]understanding raise her voice?
2 On [n]the heights beside the way,
at the crossroads she takes her stand;
3 beside [o]the gates in front of [p]the town,
at the entrance of the portals she cries
aloud:
4 "To you, O [q]men, I call,
and my cry is to [q]the children of man.
5 O [r]simple ones, learn [s]prudence;
O [t]fools, learn sense.
6 Hear, for I will speak [u]noble things,
and from my lips will come [v]what is
right,
7 for my [w]mouth will utter truth;
wickedness is an abomination to my
lips.
8 All the words of my mouth are righteous;
there is nothing [x]twisted or crooked
in them.
9 They are all [y]straight to him who understands,
and right to those who find knowledge.
10 [z]Take my instruction instead of silver,
and knowledge rather than choice
gold,
11 [a]for wisdom is better than jewels,
and [b]all that you may desire cannot
compare with her.

[1] Probable reading (compare Septuagint, Vulgate, Syriac); Hebrew *as an anklet for the discipline of a fool*

17[d] Ps. 45:8 [e] Ex. 30:23
19[f] Matt. 20:11
21[g] ch. 5:3; 6:24; See Ps. 12:2
23[h] Eccles. 9:12
24[i] See ch. 4:1
26[j] [Neh. 13:26]; See Judg. 16:1-5
27[k] [ch. 2:18; 5:5; 9:18]
Chapter 8
1[l] See ch. 1:20 [m] Job 28:12
2[n] ch. 9:3, 14
3[o] ch. 1:21 [p] Job 29:7
4[q] [Ps. 49:1, 2]
5[r] See ch. 1:4 [s] ver. 12 [t] [ch. 1:22]
6[u] [ch. 22:20] [v] ch. 23:16
7[w] Ps. 37:30
8[x] Deut. 32:5
9[y] [ch. 14:6; 1 Cor. 2:10]
10[z] ver. 19; ch. 3:14; Ps. 119:72, 127
11[a] [ch. 16:16]; See Job 28:12-19 [b] ch. 3:15

to share—with a veneer of religion, too (Lev. 7:16). Religious observance sometimes accompanies blatant evil (e.g., John 18:28). "I have found you" (Prov. 7:15) flatters this youth as her ideal man. Her proposition in verse 18 parodies the satisfactions of true love in 5:18–19. Her empty assurances in 7:19–20 are as believable as saying, "God is not at home in his universe right now, and he won't be back until next month."

7:21–23 "It will cost him his life" (v. 23) is the gospel frankly warning us, "The wages of sin is death" (Rom. 6:23). But the free gift of God, even to those who have been sexual fools, is eternal life in Christ Jesus our Lord, if we will listen to him (Prov. 7:1–5, 24–27).

8:1–36 The Father speaks directly to us in verses 1–3, appealing to us to pay attention to Wisdom's call. In verses 4–36, as in 1:22–33, we hear the voice of Wisdom herself—wisdom personified as a lovely lady, the opposite of the brash adulteress in chapter 7. The four paragraphs in chapter 8 commend the wisdom God provides for us as attractive, rewarding, ancient, and a matter of life and death.

8:1–11 Wisdom is attractive. Like the temptress in chapter 7, Lady Wisdom also approaches us, but offering noble things (8:6). Unlike the "seductive speech" of the prostitute (7:21), there is nothing twisted or crooked in Wisdom's words. For similar reasons, we can open our hearts to "the word of the truth, the gospel" (Col. 1:5) with no fear of betrayal. Wisdom graciously appeals not to geniuses but to simple ones and fools (Prov. 8:5). All she asks is that we would listen—"Hear, for I will speak" (v. 6)—and choose—"Take my instruction" (v. 10).

12 “I, wisdom, dwell with prudence,
and I find knowledge and [c]discretion.
13 [d]The fear of the LORD is [e]hatred of evil.
[f]Pride and arrogance and the way of evil
and [g]perverted speech I hate.
14 I have [h]counsel and [i]sound wisdom;
I have insight; [j]I have strength.
15 By me [k]kings reign,
and rulers decree what is just;
16 by me princes rule,
and nobles, all who govern justly.[1]
17 [l]I love those who love me,
and [m]those who seek me diligently find me.
18 [n]Riches and honor are with me,
[o]enduring wealth and [o]righteousness.
19 My fruit is [p]better than [q]gold, even fine gold,
and my yield than [r]choice silver.
20 I walk in the way of righteousness,
in the paths of justice,
21 granting an inheritance to those who love me,
and filling their treasuries.

22 [s]“The LORD [t]possessed[2] me at the beginning of his work,[3]
the first of his acts [u]of old.
23 Ages ago I was [v]set up,
at the first, [w]before the beginning of the earth.
24 When there were no [x]depths I was [y]brought forth,
when there were no springs abounding with water.
25 Before the mountains [z]had been shaped,
[a]before the hills, I was brought forth,
26 before he had made the earth with its fields,
or the first of the dust of the world.
27 When he [b]established the heavens, I was there;
when he drew [c]a circle on the face of the deep,
28 when he [d]made firm the skies above,
when he established[4] the fountains of the deep,
29 when he [e]assigned to the sea its [f]limit,
so that the waters might not transgress his command,
when he marked out [g]the foundations of the earth,
30 then [h]I was beside him, like a master workman,
and I was daily his[5] [i]delight,
rejoicing before him always,
31 [j]rejoicing in his [k]inhabited world
and delighting in the children of man.

32 “And now, [l]O sons, listen to me:
[m]blessed are those who keep my ways.
33 [n]Hear instruction and be wise,
and do not neglect it.

[1] Most Hebrew manuscripts; many Hebrew manuscripts, Septuagint *govern the earth* [2] Or *fathered*; Septuagint *created* [3] Hebrew *way* [4] The meaning of the Hebrew is uncertain [5] Or *daily filled with*

8:12–21 Wisdom is rewarding. She prepares us for leadership: “By me kings reign; . . . by me princes rule” (vv. 15, 16). She is generous to the unworthy: “Riches and honor are with me” (v. 18). But we must value her above all else. That bold decisiveness is obvious in the words “hatred” and “hate” (v. 13) and “love” (vv. 17, 21; cf. Phil. 3:7–14).

8:22–31 Wisdom is ancient. We cannot make reality up, according to our own likes and dislikes. Wisdom was here first and is deeply embedded in the way reality is designed: “The Lord possessed me at the beginning of his work” (v. 22). But Wisdom is not haughty or stuffy; she is fun. She welcomed us into God’s creation with a glad heart, “delighting in the children of man” (v. 31; cf. Gen. 1:31).

The world foolishly suppresses the truth about who God really is and who we really are, replacing it with human versions of reality; but these human theories only make life worse (Rom. 1:18–32). Humility means accepting our place in God’s creation as a joyous privilege. The gospel opposes pious negativity (1 Tim. 4:1–5) and promises us a glorious new creation, where we will forever be happily at home (Rev. 21:1–4; 22:1–5).

8:32–36 Wisdom is far more than an optional extra, to enhance our lifestyles somewhat; wisdom is a matter of life and death. “Whoever finds me finds life; . . . all who hate me love death” (vv. 35, 36; cf. 1 John 5:12).

12[c] ch. 1:4
13[d] [ch. 16:6] [e] See Ps. 97:10 [f] [ch. 6:17; 16:5] [g] ch. 2:12; 4:24
14[h] Isa. 11:2; [Isa. 9:6] [i] [ch. 2:7] [j] Eccles. 7:19; [Ps. 89:19]
15[k] [Dan. 2:21; Rom. 13:1; Rev. 19:16]
17[l] Ps. 91:14; John 14:21; [1 Sam. 2:30] [m] James 1:5; [ch. 1:28]
18[n] ch. 3:16 [o] Ps. 112:3; [Matt. 6:33; Luke 16:11; Eph. 3:8]
19[p] ch. 3:14 [q] ver. 10 [r] ch. 10:20
22[s] See Job 28:25-28 [t] Gen. 14:19, 22; [Ps. 104:24; 136:5] [u] Ps. 93:2
23[v] Ps. 2:6 [w] [John 17:5]
24[x] ver. 27, 28; ch. 3:20; Gen. 1:2 [y] Job 15:7; Ps. 51:5
25[z] Job 38:6 (Heb.) [a] Ps. 90:2
27[b] ch. 3:19 [c] Job 26:10
28[d] Gen. 1:6
29[e] Gen. 1:9, 10 [f] See Job 26:10 [g] See Ps. 104:5
30[h] Zech. 13:7; [John 1:1, 2] [i] Ps. 16:3; [Matt. 3:17]
31[j] [Gen. 1:31; Ps. 104:31] [k] Isa. 45:18

32[l] ch. 5:7; 7:24; [1 John 3:1] [m] Ps. 119:1, 2; 128:1, 2; [Luke 11:28] **33**[n] See ch. 4:1

34 [o]Blessed is the one who listens to me,
watching daily at my gates,
waiting beside my doors.
35 For [p]whoever finds me [q]finds life
and [r]obtains favor from the LORD,
36 but he who fails to find me [s]injures himself;
all who [t]hate me [u]love death."

The Way of Wisdom

9 [v]Wisdom has built her house;
she has hewn her [w]seven [x]pillars.
2 She has [y]slaughtered her beasts; she has [z]mixed her wine;
she has also [a]set her table.
3 She has [b]sent out her young women to [c]call
from [d]the highest places in the town,
4 [e]"Whoever is simple, let him turn in here!"
[f]To him who lacks sense she says,
5 "Come, [g]eat of my bread
and [h]drink of [z]the wine I have mixed.
6 Leave [i]your simple ways,[1] and [j]live,
[k]and walk in the way of insight."

7 Whoever corrects a scoffer gets himself abuse,
and he who reproves a wicked man incurs injury.
8 [l]Do not reprove a scoffer, or he will hate you;
[m]reprove a wise man, and he will love you.
9 Give instruction[2] to a wise man, and he will be [n]still wiser;
teach a righteous man, and he will [o]increase in learning.
10 [p]The fear of the LORD is the beginning of wisdom,
and [q]the knowledge of the Holy One is insight.
11 For by me [r]your days will be multiplied,
and years will be added to your life.
12 [s]If you are wise, you are wise for yourself;
if you scoff, you alone will bear it.

The Way of Folly

13 [t]The woman Folly is [u]loud;
she is seductive[3] and [v]knows nothing.
14 She sits at the door of her house;
she takes a seat on [w]the highest places of the town,
15 calling to those who pass by,
who are [x]going straight on their way,
16 [y]"Whoever is simple, let him turn in here!"
And to him who lacks sense she says,
17 [z]"Stolen water is sweet,
and [a]bread eaten in secret is pleasant."

[1] Or *Leave the company of the simple* [2] Hebrew lacks *instruction* [3] Or *full of simpleness*

34[o] [ch. 3:13]
35[p] ch. 3:18; See ch. 4:22 [q] John 1:4; 17:3 [r] ch. 12:2; 18:22
36[s] [ch. 15:32; 20:2; 29:24] [t] ch. 12:1 [u] ch. 21:6
Chapter 9
1[v] [Matt. 16:18; 1 Pet. 2:5]; See Eph. 2:20-22 [w] [Rev. 1:4] [x] [1 Tim. 3:15]
2[y] [Matt. 22:4] [z] ch. 23:30; Song 8:2 [a] Ps. 23:5; [Luke 14:17]
3[b] [Ps. 68:11; Matt. 22:3; 23:34] [c] ch. 8:1, 2 [d] ver. 14; ch. 8:2; [Matt. 10:27]
4[e] ver. 16; [Matt. 11:25; 1 Cor. 1:26] [f] ch. 6:32
5[g] [Song 5:1; Isa. 55:1; John 6:27] [h] [John 7:37] [z] [See ver. 2 above]
6[i] See ch. 1:4 [j] [ver. 11] [k] [ch. 23:19]
8[l] [Matt. 7:6] [m] See Ps. 141:5
9[n] [Matt. 13:12] [o] ch. 1:5
10[p] See ch. 1:7 [q] ch. 30:3
11[r] [ch. 10:27]; See ch. 3:2
12[s] [Job 22:2, 3; 1 Cor. 3:8; Gal. 6:5]
13[t] For ver. 13-18, see ch. 7:7-27 [u] ch. 7:11 [v] ch. 5:6
14[w] ver. 3
15[x] [ver. 6]
16[y] ver. 4
17[z] [ch. 5:15] [a] [ch. 20:17; 30:20]

9:1–18 As the introductory chapters 1–9 conclude, the Father calls us to a decision. The alternatives are clear. On one side of our path is Wisdom, inviting us into the lavish banquet of blessings made available by God's grace (9:1–6). On the other side is Folly, waving us over into the guilty pleasures of sin (vv. 13–18). If we choose Wisdom, we will be ready to study chapters 10–31 with eternal benefit.

9:1–6 With costly personal investment, Wisdom prepares her best and sends out an open invitation: "Whoever is simple, let him turn in here!" (v. 4). God is so good, he makes even repentance into a feast: "My bread" and "the wine I have mixed" find their ultimate fulfillment in Jesus himself (John 6:51, 53–55).

9:7–12 These verses contrast what a person will become, depending on his choice of Wisdom or Folly. A scoffer is so proud he considers Wisdom's appeal an insult and attacks the messenger, but a wise man humbly welcomes the opportunity to learn even more and keep growing (vv. 7–9; cf. Matt. 13:12; Acts 28:23–29; 2 Cor. 2:15–16). What makes the difference is the fear of the Lord (Prov. 9:10; cf. the section on 1:7 in the note on 1:1–7).

The wise do not debate the Lord over this or that question but bow down to him in reverence. Then they get traction for deeper obedience (Phil. 2:12–13). But what we choose does forecast our future, and no one else can choose for us (Prov. 9:12).

9:13–18 Unlike gracious Wisdom, who sends out her servants with invitations (v. 3), pompous Folly sits there like the queen of the town and expects us to be impressed (v. 14). She does have an undeniable appeal: "Stolen water is sweet" (v. 17). Our foolish hearts relish sin as exciting and glamorous. But the truth is this: folly's menu is water and bread (v. 17), sweetened only by "the fleeting pleasures of sin" (Heb. 11:25), while Wisdom's feast is wine and meat (Prov. 9:2), leading to eternal life (v. 6).

18 But he does not know [b]that the dead[1] are
there,
that her guests are in the depths of
Sheol.

The Proverbs of Solomon

10 [c]The proverbs of Solomon.

[d]A wise son makes a glad father,
[e]but a foolish son is a sorrow to his
mother.
2 [f]Treasures gained by wickedness do not
profit,
[g]but righteousness delivers from
death.
3 [h]The LORD does not let the righteous go
hungry,
[i]but he thwarts the craving of the
wicked.
4 A slack hand [j]causes poverty,
[k]but the hand of the diligent makes
rich.
5 He who [l]gathers in summer is a prudent
son,
but he who sleeps in harvest is [m]a son
who brings shame.
6 Blessings are on the head of the righteous,
but [n]the mouth of the wicked conceals
violence.
7 [o]The memory of the righteous is a blessing,
but [p]the name of the wicked will rot.
8 [q]The wise of heart will receive commandments,
but a babbling fool will come to ruin.
9 [r]Whoever walks in integrity walks
securely,
but he who makes his ways crooked
[s]will be found out.
10 Whoever [t]winks the eye causes trouble,
and a babbling fool will come to
ruin.
11 [u]The mouth of the righteous is [v]a fountain of life,
but the mouth of the wicked [n]conceals
violence.
12 Hatred stirs up strife,
but [w]love covers all offenses.
13 On the lips of him who has understanding, wisdom is found,
but [x]a rod is for the back of him who
[y]lacks sense.
14 The wise [z]lay up knowledge,
but [a]the mouth of a fool brings ruin
near.
15 [b]A rich man's wealth is his strong city;
the poverty of the poor is their ruin.
16 The wage of the righteous leads [c]to life,
the gain of the wicked to sin.
17 Whoever heeds instruction is on [d]the
path to life,
but he who rejects reproof leads others astray.
18 The one who conceals hatred has lying
lips,
and whoever utters slander is a fool.
19 [e]When words are many, transgression is
not lacking,
[f]but whoever restrains his lips is prudent.

[1] Hebrew *Rephaim*

There is nothing disappointing in God's wisdom, ultimately revealed in Jesus; but outside him, everything is death (v. 18). Will we become decisive about following Jesus? Will we meditate on Proverbs 10–31 with the fear of the Lord opening our hearts? (The proverbs and sayings of chapters 10–31 are here divided into the following topics: the tongue, humility, emotions, family, work and money, and friendship and conflict.)

10:11 *The tongue.* How we use words is a major theme in Proverbs 10–31. Every day we speak words, each one marked by either wisdom or folly. Jesus said we will give account even "for every careless word" (Matt. 12:36). The book of Proverbs guides us toward wise words that can be a fountain of life to others.

Our words, not just our deeds, matter to God. For example, "Lying lips are an abomination to the LORD" (Prov. 12:22). Telling a lie might not bother us that much, but true words count heavily with God. He created the universe by his word (Ps. 33:6). He saves us by his word (1 Pet. 1:23–25). He will judge the world by the sword of his mouth (Rev. 1:16; 19:15). He *is* the Word (John 1:1, 14), and he never lies (Titus 1:2). But the Devil is "a liar and the father of lies" (John 8:44; cf. Acts 5:3).

18[b] See ch. 7:27
Chapter 10
1[c] See ch. 1:1 [d] See ch. 29:3 [e] ch. 17:25; 29:15
2[f] [ch. 21:6; Ezek. 7:19; Luke 12:19, 20] [g] ch. 11:4, 6
3[h] Ps. 34:9, 10; 37:25; [Matt. 6:33] [i] [Ps. 112:10; James 4:3]
4[j] [ch. 6:11; 12:24; 13:4] [k] ch. 21:5
5[l] [ch. 6:8] [m] ch. 17:2; 19:26
6[n] ver. 32
7[o] Ps. 112:6 [p] [Ps. 9:5]
8[q] [Matt. 7:24, 25]
9[r] ch. 3:23; 28:18; Ps. 23:4; Isa. 33:15, 16 [s] [Matt. 10:26; 1 Tim. 5:25]
10[t] ch. 6:13
11[u] Ps. 37:30 [v] ch. 13:14; Ps. 36:9 [n] [See ver. 6 above]
12[w] 1 Pet. 4:8; [James 5:20]
13[x] ch. 19:29; 26:3 [y] See ch. 6:32
14[z] [ver. 8; ch. 12:23] [a] ch. 18:7

15[b] ch. 18:11; [Ps. 52:7; Mark 10:24, 25] **16**[c] ch. 11:19; 19:23 **17**[d] [ch. 6:23] **19**[e] [Matt. 12:36, 37] [f] ch. 17:27; [James 3:2]

20 The tongue of the righteous is [g]choice
silver;
the heart of the wicked is of little
worth.
21 The lips of the righteous feed many,
but fools die for [h]lack of sense.
22 [i]The blessing of the LORD makes rich,
and he adds no sorrow with it.[1]
23 Doing wrong is [j]like a joke to a fool,
but [k]wisdom is pleasure to a man of
understanding.
24 [l]What the wicked dreads [m]will come
upon him,
but [n]the desire of the righteous will
be granted.
25 When [o]the tempest passes, the wicked is
no more,
but [p]the righteous is established forever.
26 Like vinegar to the teeth and smoke to
the eyes,
so is the sluggard to those who send
him.
27 [q]The fear of the LORD prolongs life,
[r]but the years of the wicked will be
short.
28 [s]The hope of the righteous brings joy,
[t]but the expectation of the wicked will
perish.
29 [u]The way of the LORD is a stronghold to
the blameless,
but destruction to evildoers.
30 [v]The righteous will never be removed,
but [w]the wicked will not dwell in the
land.
31 [x]The mouth of the righteous brings forth
wisdom,
but the perverse tongue will be cut off.
32 The lips of the righteous [y]know what is
acceptable,
but the mouth of the wicked, [z]what is
perverse.

11 [a]A false balance is an abomination to
the LORD,
[b]but a just weight is his delight.
2 [c]When pride comes, then comes disgrace,
but with [d]the humble is wisdom.
3 [e]The integrity of the upright guides them,
[f]but the crookedness of the treacherous destroys them.
4 [g]Riches do not profit in the day of wrath,
[h]but righteousness delivers from death.
5 The righteousness of the blameless
[i]keeps his way straight,
but the wicked falls by his own wickedness.
6 [h]The righteousness of the upright delivers them,
but the treacherous [j]are taken captive
by their lust.
7 When the wicked dies, his [k]hope will
perish,
and [l]the expectation of wealth[2] perishes too.
8 [m]The righteous is delivered from trouble,
and the wicked walks into it instead.
9 With his mouth the godless man would
destroy his neighbor,
but by knowledge the righteous are
delivered.

[1] Or *and toil adds nothing to it* [2] Or *of his strength*, or *of iniquity*

20[g] ch. 8:19; 16:16
21[h] [Hos. 4:6]
22[i] [Gen. 24:35; 26:12; Deut. 8:18]
23[j] ch. 2:14; 15:21 [k] [ch. 8:30]
24[l] Isa. 66:4; Heb. 10:27; [Job 15:21] [m] Job 3:25 [n] Ps. 145:19; Matt. 5:6; 1 John 5:14, 15
25[o] [Job 21:18; Ps. 58:9]; See Matt. 7:26, 27 [p] ch. 12:3; Ps. 15:5; [Matt. 7:24, 25]
27[q] See ch. 3:2 [r] See Job 15:32, 33
28[s] [Luke 21:28] [t] See Job 8:13
29[u] [Ps. 25:12; Matt. 22:16; Acts 9:2]
30[v] ver. 25; Ps. 37:22, 29; 125:1 [w] ch. 2:21, 22
31[x] Ps. 37:30
32[y] [Eccles. 10:12] [z] ch. 2:12

The wise understand that we are caught up in a great spiritual battle of truth versus lies. If we tell a lie, we are taking sides against "the Amen, the faithful and true witness" (Rev. 3:14), betraying him and one another (Col. 3:9). It is because of who Jesus is that "Truthful lips endure forever, but a lying tongue is but for a moment" (Prov. 12:19). Lying can have a certain appeal, as it offers a shortcut to getting one's way. But the Bible reveals how important words really are. True and loving words from God bind us to him in covenant (Ex. 24:8), and true and loving words among ourselves bind us together in community (Eph. 4:15–16).

Wisdom transforms how we use words. "The lips of knowledge are a precious jewel" (Prov. 20:15). Thoughtful words are a rare treasure in this world of trivial chatter. When "a precious jewel" comes from the lips of a wise person, others pay attention. Literal jewels might catch people's eyes, but jewel-like words catch people's ears. It was said of Jesus, "No one ever spoke like this man!" (John 7:46).

Chapter 11 **1**[a] ch. 16:11; 20:10, 23; See Lev. 19:35, 36 [b] [ch. 12:22] **2**[c] ch. 16:18; 18:12; 29:23; [Dan. 4:30, 31] [d] Mic. 6:8 **3**[e] ch. 13:6 [f] ch. 19:3 **4**[g] Zeph. 1:18; See ch. 10:2 [h] [Gen. 7:1] **5**[i] ch. 3:6 **6**[h] [See ver. 4 above] [j] See Ps. 7:15, 16 **7**[k] ch. 10:28 [l] See Job 8:13, 14 **8**[m] ver. 6; [ch. 21:18]

10 [n]When it goes well with the righteous,
the city rejoices,
and when the wicked perish there are
shouts of gladness.
11 By the blessing of the upright a city is
exalted,
but [o]by the mouth of the wicked [p]it is
overthrown.
12 Whoever [q]belittles his neighbor lacks
sense,
but a man of understanding remains
silent.
13 Whoever [r]goes about slandering reveals
secrets,
but he who is trustworthy in spirit
keeps a thing covered.
14 Where there is [s]no guidance, a people
falls,
[s]but in an abundance of counselors
there is safety.
15 [t]Whoever puts up security for a stranger
will surely suffer harm,
but he who hates striking hands in
pledge is secure.
16 [u]A gracious woman gets honor,
and [v]violent men get riches.
17 [w]A man who is kind benefits himself,
but a cruel man hurts himself.
18 The wicked earns deceptive wages,
but one who [x]sows righteousness gets
a sure reward.
19 Whoever is steadfast in righteousness
[y]will live,
but [z]he who pursues evil will die.
20 Those of [a]crooked heart are [b]an abomination to the LORD,
but those of [c]blameless ways are [d]his
delight.
21 [e]Be assured, [f]an evil person will not go
unpunished,
but [g]the offspring of the righteous
will be delivered.
22 Like [h]a gold ring in a pig's snout
is a beautiful woman without discretion.
23 The desire of the righteous ends only in
good;
[i]the expectation of the wicked in wrath.
24 [j]One gives [k]freely, yet grows all the richer;
another withholds what he should
give, and only suffers want.
25 [l]Whoever brings blessing [m]will be
enriched,
and [n]one who waters will himself be
watered.
26 [o]The people curse him who holds back
grain,
but [p]a blessing is on the head of him
who [q]sells it.
27 Whoever diligently seeks good seeks
favor,[1]
but evil comes to [r]him who searches
for it.
28 Whoever [s]trusts in his riches will fall,
but the righteous will [t]flourish like a
green leaf.
29 Whoever [u]troubles his own household
will [v]inherit the wind,
and the fool will be servant to the
wise of heart.
30 The fruit of the righteous is [w]a tree of life,
and whoever [x]captures souls is wise.
31 If [y]the righteous is repaid on earth,
how much more the wicked and the
sinner!

12

Whoever loves discipline loves
knowledge,
but he who [z]hates reproof is [a]stupid.
2 A good man [b]obtains favor from the
LORD,
but a man of evil devices he condemns.
3 No one is established by wickedness,
but the root of [c]the righteous will
never be moved.
4 [d]An excellent wife is [e]the crown of her
husband,
but she who [f]brings shame is like [g]rot-
tenness in his bones.
5 [h]The thoughts of the righteous are just;
the counsels of the wicked are deceitful.
6 The words of the wicked [i]lie in wait for
blood,
but [j]the mouth of the upright delivers
them.

[1] Or *acceptance*

10[n] [ch. 28:12; Esth. 8:15] **11**[o] Ps. 10:7 [p] [ch. 14:1; 29:8] **12**[q] ch. 14:21; [Matt. 7:1] **13**[r] ch. 20:19; Lev. 19:16 **14**[s] ch. 15:22; 20:18; 24:6 **15**[t] [ch. 6:1; Job 17:3] **16**[u] [ch. 31:30] [v] [Luke 11:21] **17**[w] [Matt. 5:7]; See Matt. 25:34-40 **18**[x] Hos. 10:12; Gal. 6:8, 9; [James 3:18] **19**[y] ch. 10:16; 19:23 [z] [Rom. 6:23; Gal. 6:8] **20**[a] [ch. 17:20] [b] ch. 12:22; 16:5 [c] ch. 13:6; Ps. 119:1 [d] 1 Chr. 29:17 **21**[e] ch. 16:5 [f] ch. 12:7; [Ps. 37:2, 9]; See Isa. 28:15-18 [g] See Ps. 112:2 **22**[h] [Gen. 24:47; Isa. 3:21; Ezek. 16:12] **23**[i] Rom. 2:8, 9 **24**[j] ch. 13:7 [k] Ps. 37:21; 112:9; [ch. 19:17] **25**[l] See 2 Cor. 9:6-11 [m] ch. 13:4; 28:25 [n] [Matt. 7:2] **26**[o] ch. 24:24 [p] [Job 29:13] [q] [Gen. 42:6] **27**[r] See Ps. 7:16 **28**[s] See Ps. 49:6 [t] Jer. 17:8; See Ps. 92:12 **29**[u] ch. 15:27 [v] [Eccles. 5:16] **30**[w] See ch. 3:18 [x] Dan. 12:3; James 5:20; See 1 Cor. 9:19-22 **31**[y] [Jer. 25:29; 1 Pet. 4:18] **Chapter 12** **1**[z] ch. 5:12; 15:10 [a] Ps. 49:10 **2**[b] ch. 8:35 **3**[c] See ch. 10:25 **4**[d] See ch. 31:10 [e] Song 3:11 [f] ch. 10:5 [g] ch. 14:30 **5**[h] [Matt. 12:35] **6**[i] See ch. 1:11 [j] ch. 14:3

7 [k]The wicked are [l]overthrown and are no more,
[m]but the house of the righteous will stand.
8 A man is commended according to his good sense,
but one of twisted mind is [n]despised.
9 Better to be lowly and have a servant
than to play the great man and lack bread.
10 [o]Whoever is righteous has regard for the life of his beast,
but the mercy of the wicked is cruel.
11 [p]Whoever works his land [q]will have plenty of bread,
[r]but he who follows [s]worthless pursuits lacks sense.
12 Whoever is wicked covets [t]the spoil of evildoers,
but the root of the righteous bears fruit.
13 An evil man is ensnared [u]by the transgression of his lips,
[v]but the righteous escapes from trouble.
14 From the fruit of his mouth [w]a man is satisfied with good,
[x]and the work of a man's hand comes back to him.
15 [y]The way of a fool is right in his own eyes,
but a wise man listens to advice.
16 [z]The vexation of a fool is known at once,
but the prudent ignores an insult.
17 [a]Whoever speaks[1] the truth gives honest evidence,
but [b]a false witness utters deceit.
18 [c]There is one whose rash words are like sword thrusts,
but the tongue of the wise brings [d]healing.
19 Truthful lips endure forever,
but [e]a lying tongue is but for a moment.
20 Deceit is in the heart of [f]those who devise evil,
but those who plan peace have joy.
21 [g]No ill befalls the righteous,
but the wicked are filled with trouble.
22 [h]Lying lips are [i]an abomination to the LORD,
[j]but those who act faithfully are his delight.
23 [k]A prudent man conceals knowledge,
[k]but the heart of fools proclaims folly.
24 [l]The hand of the diligent will rule,
while the slothful will be [m]put to forced labor.
25 [n]Anxiety in a man's heart weighs him down,
but a good word makes him glad.
26 One who is righteous is a guide to his neighbor,[2]
but the way of the wicked leads them astray.
27 [o]Whoever is slothful will not roast his game,
but the diligent man will get precious wealth.[3]

[1] Hebrew *breathes out* [2] Or *The righteous chooses his friends carefully* [3] Or *but diligence is precious wealth*

7[k] See ch. 11:21 [l] Job 34:25 [m] [ch. 10:25, 30]
8[n] [1 Sam. 20:30]
10[o] [Deut. 25:4]
11[p] ch. 28:19 [q] ch. 20:13 [r] ch. 28:19 [s] Judg. 9:4
12[t] [Ps. 10:9]
13[u] ch. 18:7; [Ps. 64:8; Matt. 12:37] [v] ch. 21:23
14[w] ch. 13:2; 14:14; 18:20 [x] ch. 19:17; Isa. 3:10, 11; [Judg. 9:16, 56]
15[y] ch. 3:7; 16:2; 21:2; 26:12; [ch. 14:12; 16:25]
16[z] [ch. 14:33; 29:11]
17[a] ch. 14:5 [b] See ch. 6:19
18[c] See Ps. 57:4 [d] See ch. 4:22
19[e] ch. 19:9; [Ps. 52:4, 5]
20[f] ch. 3:29
21[g] Ps. 91:10; [1 Pet. 3:13; 2 Pet. 2:9]
22[h] [Rev. 22:15]; See ch. 6:17 [i] ch. 11:20 [j] [ch. 11:1]
23[k] [ch. 13:16; 15:2]
24[l] [ch. 10:4; 13:4] [m] [Gen. 49:15; 1 Kgs. 9:21]
25[n] ch. 15:13; [ch. 17:22] 27[o] [ver. 24]

12:11 *Work and money.* The book of Proverbs takes a positive view of work and money. God created this world, with its many opportunities and rich treasures, and called it "very good" (Gen. 1:31). But by what practical means does his bounty enter into our possession? Through our own hard work: "Whoever works his land will have plenty of bread." There are rare exceptions, but the pattern God has wisely established is that he provides for us through our own efforts. "A slack hand causes poverty, but the hand of the diligent makes rich" (Prov. 10:4; cf. 1 Thess. 4:11–12; 2 Thess. 3:6–12). Wisdom, therefore, rejoices in the dignity and benefit of hard work—mindful that the land and the strength to work it are from God (Prov. 2:21–22; 8:14; 10:30).

Wisdom cautions us against "worthless pursuits" (12:11). Not every career dream or business venture is realistic, no matter how hard we work. The word "follows" in this proverb is a strong word, suggesting intense effort. But by their nature, the only bounty some pursuits will produce is "plenty of poverty" (Prov. 28:19).

Nor can get-rich-quick schemes or gambling help us make money God's way. "Wealth gained hastily will dwindle, but whoever gathers little by little will increase it" (Prov. 13:11; cf. 28:20). Windfalls rarely make a lasting difference for good. But faithful, steady effort deepens our character even as it builds our wealth.

28 [p]In the path of righteousness is life,
and in its pathway there is no death.

13 A wise son hears his father's instruction,
but [q]a scoffer does not listen to rebuke.
2 From the fruit of his mouth a man [r]eats what is good,
but the desire of the treacherous [s]is for violence.
3 [t]Whoever guards his mouth preserves his life;
[u]he who opens wide his lips [v]comes to ruin.
4 [w]The soul of the sluggard craves and gets nothing,
while the soul of the diligent [x]is richly supplied.
5 The righteous hates falsehood,
but the wicked brings shame[1] and disgrace.
6 [y]Righteousness guards him whose [z]way is blameless,
but sin overthrows the wicked.
7 [a]One pretends to be rich, yet has nothing;
[b]another pretends to be poor, yet has great wealth.
8 The ransom of a man's life is his wealth,
but a poor man [c]hears no threat.
9 [d]The light of the righteous rejoices,
but [e]the lamp of the wicked will be put out.
10 [f]By insolence comes nothing but strife,
but with those who take advice is wisdom.
11 [g]Wealth gained hastily[2] will dwindle,
but whoever gathers little by little will increase it.
12 Hope deferred makes the heart sick,
[h]but a desire fulfilled is [i]a tree of life.
13 Whoever [j]despises [k]the word brings destruction on himself,
but he who reveres the commandment will be [l]rewarded.
14 The teaching of the wise is [m]a fountain of life,
that one may [n]turn away from the snares of death.
15 [o]Good sense wins [p]favor,
but the way of the treacherous is their ruin.[3]
16 [q]In everything the prudent acts with knowledge,
[r]but a fool flaunts his folly.
17 A wicked messenger falls into trouble,
but [s]a faithful envoy brings healing.
18 Poverty and disgrace come to him who [t]ignores instruction,
[u]but whoever [v]heeds reproof is honored.
19 [w]A desire fulfilled is sweet to the soul,
but to turn away from evil is an abomination to fools.
20 Whoever walks with the wise becomes wise,
but the companion of fools will suffer harm.
21 [x]Disaster[4] pursues sinners,
[y]but the righteous are rewarded with good.
22 [z]A good man leaves an inheritance to his children's children,
but [a]the sinner's wealth is laid up for the righteous.

[1] Or *stench* [2] Or *by fraud* [3] Probable reading (compare Septuagint, Syriac, Vulgate); Hebrew *is rugged*, or *is an enduring rut* [4] Or *Evil*

When we have financial problems, our primary business is not with man but with God, for "the blessing of the LORD makes rich" (10:22). Our employers do not provide for us; God does. Let us fulfill our financial obligations, but let us trust in the Lord alone. And let us always remember this: "Better is a little with the fear of the LORD than great treasure and trouble with it" (15:16; cf. 15:17; 1 Tim. 6:6–10).

Through all the ups and downs, in good times and bad, here is our unfailing assurance: "Keep your life free from love of money, and be content with what you have, for he has said, 'I will never leave you nor forsake you'" (Heb. 13:5). Moreover, there is one pursuit that cannot possibly prove worthless. Jesus said, "If anyone would come after me, let him deny himself and take up his cross and follow me. For whoever would save his life will lose it, but whoever loses his life for my sake will find it. For what will it profit a man if he gains the whole world and forfeits his soul?" (Matt. 16:24–26). Jesus himself is the only treasure that cannot fail.

28[p] See ch. 10:2
Chapter 13
1[q] ch. 1:22; See Ps. 1:1
2[r] ch. 12:14 [s] [ch. 1:31; 26:6]
3[t] ch. 21:23; [ch. 12:13; 18:21; James 3:2] [u] ch. 20:19 [v] ch. 18:7
4[w] See ch. 6:9-11 [x] ch. 11:25
6[y] ch. 11:3, 5, 6 [z] ch. 11:20
7[a] ch. 11:24; [Luke 12:21; Rev. 3:17] [b] [Luke 12:33; 2 Cor. 6:10; James 2:5]
8[c] [ver. 1]
9[d] [Job 29:3] [e] See Job 18:5
10[f] [ch. 28:25]
11[g] [ch. 10:2; 20:21; 21:6; 28:20, 22]
12[h] [ver. 19] [i] See ch. 3:18
13[j] [ch. 19:16; Num. 15:31; 2 Chr. 36:16] [k] ch. 16:20; Deut. 30:14 [l] [ver. 21] **14**[m] See ch. 10:11 [n] ch. 14:27; [Ps. 18:5; 2 Tim. 2:26] **15**[o] [Luke 2:52]; See Ps. 111:10 [p] ch. 3:4; 22:1 **16**[q] [ch. 12:23; 15:2] [r] [ch. 18:2; Eccles. 10:3] **17**[s] ch. 25:13; [ch. 14:5] **18**[t] [ch. 15:5, 31, 32] [u] [ch. 15:5] [v] [ch. 15:31] **19**[w] [ver. 12] **21**[x] [Ps. 11:6; 32:10] [y] [ver. 13; Luke 6:38] **22**[z] [Ezra 9:12; Ps. 37:25] [a] ch. 28:8; See Job 27:16, 17

23 The fallow ground of the poor would yield much food,
but it is swept away through [b]injustice.
24 [c]Whoever spares the rod hates his son,
but he who loves him is diligent to discipline him.[1]
25 [d]The righteous has enough to satisfy his appetite,
but the belly of the wicked suffers want.

14 [e]The wisest of women [f]builds her house,
but folly with her own hands [g]tears it down.
2 Whoever [h]walks in uprightness fears the LORD,
but he who is [i]devious in his ways despises him.
3 By the mouth of a fool comes [j]a rod for his back,[2]
[k]but the lips of the wise will preserve them.
4 Where there are no oxen, the manger is clean,
but abundant crops come by the strength of the ox.
5 [l]A faithful witness does not lie,
but [m]a false witness breathes out lies.
6 [n]A scoffer seeks wisdom [o]in vain,
but [p]knowledge is easy for a man of understanding.
7 Leave the presence of a fool,
for there you do not meet words of knowledge.
8 The wisdom of the prudent is to discern his way,
but the folly of fools is deceiving.
9 [q]Fools mock at the guilt offering,
but the upright enjoy acceptance.[3]
10 The heart knows its own [r]bitterness,
and no stranger shares its joy.
11 [s]The house of the wicked will be destroyed,
but the tent of the upright will flourish.
12 [t]There is a way that seems right to a man,
but [u]its end is the way to death.[4]
13 Even in laughter the heart may ache,
and [v]the end of joy may be [w]grief.
14 The backslider in heart will be [x]filled with the fruit of his ways,
and [y]a good man will be filled with the fruit of his ways.
15 [z]The simple believes everything,
but the prudent gives thought to his steps.
16 [a]One who is wise is cautious[5] and [b]turns away from evil,
but a fool is reckless and careless.
17 A man of [c]quick temper acts foolishly,
and a man of evil devices is hated.
18 The simple inherit folly,
but the prudent are crowned with knowledge.
19 [d]The evil bow down before the good,
the wicked at the gates of the righteous.
20 [e]The poor is disliked even by his neighbor,
[f]but the rich has many friends.

[1] Or *who loves him disciplines him early* [2] Or *In the mouth of a fool is a rod of pride* [3] Hebrew *but among the upright is acceptance* [4] Hebrew *ways of death* [5] Or *fears* [the LORD]

14:29 *Emotions.* "Slow to anger" is the God-like quality of calm patience (Ex. 34:6). A person of great understanding can avoid being goaded into an angry outburst by an annoying person. But a hasty temper puts folly on public display.

Not all anger is foolish. The Lord of Israel got angry (Deut. 32:15–22). Jesus got angry (Mark 3:5). He will someday return to judge the world in his fury (Rev. 19:11–16). All the sins of mankind must be judged under the wrath of God—either at the cross or in hell. But the Bible never says, "God is wrath." The Bible does say, "God is love" (1 John 4:8, 16). We, by our sins, have to provoke him to wrath, but we do not have to provoke him to love us. Love is his spontaneous response to us, and his loving heart is slow to anger.

The book of Proverbs counsels us against unruly anger (Prov. 16:32). In fact, "Good sense makes one slow to anger, and it is his glory to overlook an offense" (Prov. 19:11). That word *glory* means beauty. Wisdom has a higher goal than getting even. Wisdom displays the beauty of God by overlooking an insult. After all, God overlooks many offenses in us, for Jesus' sake.

23[b] [ch. 16:8]
24[c] [ch. 19:18; 22:15; 23:13, 14; 29:15, 17]
25[d] See ch. 10:3
Chapter 14
1[e] [ch. 9:1; 24:3] [f] Deut. 25:9; Ruth 4:11 [g] [ch. 11:11]
2[h] ch. 19:1; 28:6 [i] ch. 2:15
3[j] [Jer. 18:18] [k] ch. 12:6
5[l] [Ex. 23:1] [m] See ch. 6:19
6[n] [ch. 24:7] [o] [Ps. 25:9; 1 Pet. 5:5] [p] [ch. 8:9; 15:14; 17:24]
9[q] [ch. 10:23]
10[r] [1 Sam. 1:10]; See Job 3:20
11[s] [ch. 3:33; 15:25; Job 8:15; 21:28]
12[t] ch. 16:25; See ch. 12:15 [u] [ch. 5:5; Rom. 6:21]; See ch. 7:27
13[v] [Eccles. 2:2; Luke 6:25] [w] ch. 10:1
14[x] [ch. 1:31; Matt. 6:2, 5] [y] ch. 12:14; Isa. 3:10
15[z] See ch. 1:4 **16**[a] [ch. 22:3; 27:12] [b] [ch. 3:7]; See Job 28:28; Ps. 34:14 **17**[c] [ver. 29] **19**[d] [Gen. 42:6; 1 Sam. 2:36] **20**[e] ch. 19:7 [f] ch. 19:4

21 Whoever [g]despises his neighbor is a sinner,
but [h]blessed is he who is generous to the poor.
22 Do they not go astray who [i]devise evil?
Those who devise good meet[1] [j]steadfast love and faithfulness.
23 In all toil there is profit,
but mere talk [k]tends only to poverty.
24 The crown of the wise is their wealth,
but the folly of fools brings folly.
25 A truthful witness saves lives,
but one who [l]breathes out lies is deceitful.
26 In the fear of the LORD one has [m]strong confidence,
and [n]his children will have [o]a refuge.
27 The fear of the LORD is [p]a fountain of life,
that one may [q]turn away from the snares of death.
28 In [r]a multitude of people is the glory of a king,
but without people a prince is ruined.
29 Whoever is [s]slow to anger has great understanding,
but he who has a hasty temper exalts folly.
30 A tranquil[2] heart gives [t]life to the flesh,
but [u]envy[3] makes [v]the bones rot.
31 Whoever oppresses a poor man [w]insults his [x]Maker,
[y]but he who is generous to the needy honors him.
32 [z]The wicked is overthrown through his evildoing,
but [a]the righteous finds refuge in his death.
33 Wisdom [b]rests in the heart of a man of understanding,
but it makes itself known even in the midst of fools.[4]
34 Righteousness exalts a nation,
but sin is a reproach to any people.
35 A servant who deals wisely has [c]the king's favor,
but his wrath falls on one who acts shamefully.

15 [d]A soft answer turns away wrath,
but [e]a harsh word stirs up anger.
2 The tongue of the wise commends knowledge,
but [f]the mouths of fools pour out folly.
3 [g]The eyes of the LORD are in every place,
keeping watch on the evil and the good.
4 [h]A gentle[5] tongue is [i]a tree of life,
but [j]perverseness in it breaks the spirit.
5 [k]A fool [l]despises his father's instruction,
but [m]whoever heeds reproof is prudent.
6 In the house of the righteous there is much treasure,
but trouble befalls the income of the wicked.
7 [n]The lips of the wise spread knowledge;
[n]not so the hearts of fools.[6]
8 [o]The sacrifice of the wicked is an abomination to the LORD,
but [p]the prayer of the upright is acceptable to him.
9 The way of the wicked is an abomination to the LORD,
but he loves him [q]who pursues righteousness.
10 There is [r]severe discipline for him who forsakes the way;
[s]whoever hates reproof will die.
11 Sheol and Abaddon lie open before the LORD;
how much more [t]the hearts of the children of man!

[1] Or *show* [2] Or *healing* [3] Or *jealousy* [4] Or *Wisdom rests quietly in the heart of a man of understanding, but makes itself known in the midst of fools* [5] Or *healing* [6] Or *the hearts of fools are not steadfast*

Anger is a judging emotion. Many wrongs do deserve judgment, but wisdom brings our judgments themselves under a higher judgment. The gospel moderates our own angry judgments by prophesying to us God's final judgment (Rev. 20:11–15). God will judge, and no one will get away with anything. And in the meantime, God is watching over us (Prov. 2:8). Let us trust his wise wrath, rather than unleash our own foolish wrath. And may the peace of Christ rule in our hearts (Col. 3:15).

21[g] ch. 11:12 [h] Ps. 41:1 **22**[i] See ch. 3:29 [j] ch. 3:3 **23**[k] [ch. 11:24; 21:5; 22:16] **25**[l] ver. 5 **26**[m] [ch. 1:33] [n] [Ps. 73:15] [o] See Ps. 14:6 **27**[p] See ch. 10:11 [q] See ch. 13:14 **28**[r] [1 Kgs. 4:20] **29**[s] ch. 16:32; 19:11; [ver. 17; Eccles. 7:9; James 1:19] **30**[t] See ch. 4:22 [u] [Ps. 112:10] [v] ch. 12:4 **31**[w] ch. 17:5; [Matt. 25:40, 45] [x] ch. 22:2; See Job 35:10 [y] ch. 28:8 **32**[z] ch. 24:16 [a] Gen. 49:18; Ps. 16:11; 17:15; 23:4; 2 Cor. 1:9; 5:8; 2 Tim. 4:18; [Num. 23:10]; See Job 19:25-27 **33**[b] Eccles. 7:9; ch. 12:16; 29:11 **35**[c] [ch. 16:13; 22:11]; See Matt. 24:45-47 **Chapter 15** **1**[d] [ch. 25:15]; See Judg. 8:1-3 [e] See 1 Sam. 25:10-13; 1 Kgs. 12:13-16 **2**[f] [ver. 28; ch. 12:23; 13:16; 18:2] **3**[g] See Job 31:4 **4**[h] [ch. 12:18] [i] See ch. 3:18 [j] ch. 11:3 **5**[k] [ch. 10:1] [l] [Ps. 107:11] [m] [ch. 13:18] **7**[n] [Matt. 12:34, 35] **8**[o] ch. 21:27; Eccles. 5:1; Isa. 1:11, 15 [p] [ver. 29] **9**[q] ch. 21:21; 1 Tim. 6:11; [ch. 11:19] **10**[r] [Isa. 1:5] [s] See ch. 12:1 **11**[t] 2 Chr. 6:30; Ps. 44:21; John 2:24; See 1 Sam. 16:7

12 [u]A scoffer [v]does not like to be reproved;
he will not go to the wise.
13 [w]A glad heart makes a cheerful face,
but by [x]sorrow of heart the spirit is [y]crushed.
14 [z]The heart of him who has understanding seeks knowledge,
but the mouths of fools feed on folly.
15 All the days of the afflicted are evil,
but [a]the cheerful of heart has a continual feast.
16 [b]Better is a little with the fear of the LORD
than great treasure and trouble with it.
17 [c]Better is a dinner of herbs where love is
than [d]a fattened ox and hatred with it.
18 [e]A hot-tempered man [f]stirs up strife,
but he who is [g]slow to anger quiets contention.
19 The way of [h]a sluggard is like a hedge of [i]thorns,
but the path of the upright is [j]a level highway.
20 [k]A wise son makes a glad father,
but a foolish man despises his mother.
21 [l]Folly is a joy to him who lacks sense,
but a man of understanding [m]walks straight ahead.
22 [n]Without counsel plans fail,
but with many advisers they succeed.
23 To make an apt answer is a joy to a man,
and [o]a word in season, how good it is!
24 The path of life leads upward [p]for the prudent,
that he may turn away from Sheol beneath.
25 The LORD tears down the house of [q]the proud
but [r]maintains [s]the widow's boundaries.
26 [t]The thoughts of the wicked are an abomination to the LORD,
but [u]gracious words are pure.
27 Whoever is [v]greedy for unjust gain
[w]troubles his own household,
but he who hates [x]bribes will live.
28 The heart of the righteous [y]ponders how to answer,
but [z]the mouth of the wicked pours out evil things.
29 The LORD is [a]far from the wicked,
but he [b]hears the prayer of the righteous.
30 [c]The light of the eyes rejoices the heart,
and [d]good news refreshes[1] the bones.
31 [e]The ear that listens to [f]life-giving reproof
will dwell among the wise.
32 Whoever [g]ignores instruction [h]despises himself,
but he who listens to reproof [i]gains intelligence.
33 [j]The fear of the LORD is instruction in wisdom,
and [k]humility comes before honor.

[1] Hebrew *makes fat*

12[u] See Ps. 1:1 [v] Amos 5:10 **13**[w] [ver. 15; ch. 17:22] [x] See ch. 12:25 [y] ch. 18:14 **14**[z] ch. 14:6; 19:24 **15**[a] ver. 13 **16**[b] ch. 16:8; Ps. 37:16; [1 Tim. 6:6] **17**[c] ch. 17:1 [d] [Matt. 22:4; Luke 15:23] **18**[e] ch. 29:22; [ch. 16:28; 26:21] [f] ch. 28:25 [g] See ch. 14:29 **19**[h] ch. 19:24; 22:13 [i] ch. 22:5 [j] Jer. 18:15 **20**[k] See ch. 29:3 **21**[l] ch. 10:23 [m] [Eph. 5:15] **22**[n] ch. 11:14; [ch. 20:18] **23**[o] ch. 25:11; [Isa. 50:4] **24**[p] Col. 3:1, 2; [ch. 2:18, 19; Phil. 3:20] **25**[q] [ch. 29:23] [r] [ch. 23:10] [s] [Ps. 68:5; 146:9] **26**[t] ch. 6:16, 18 [u] ch. 16:24 **27**[v] ch. 1:19; [Isa. 5:8; Jer. 17:11] [w] ch. 11:29; [Josh. 7:25] [x] ch. 17:23 **28**[y] Ps. 37:30 [z] [1 Pet. 3:15]; See ver. 2 **29**[a] [Ps. 18:41; 34:16]

15:15 *Emotions.* Cheerfulness is wise—and surprising. This proverb does not contrast the afflicted with the cheerful of heart. Rather, this cheerful person *is* an afflicted believer, going through evil days, who nevertheless enjoys a spiritual feast within (cf. Acts 5:40–41; 16:25; 2 Cor. 4:8; 6:10; Heb. 10:34).

Joy comes naturally to the wise (Prov. 8:30–31), and joyous vitality grows within us through the fear of the Lord (3:7–8), humble contentment (15:16–17), and frequent exposure to the good news of the gospel (v. 30). The joy of believers' fellowship is also contagious: "The light of the eyes [of a radiant, glowing believer] rejoices the heart [of someone else]" (v. 30). Ultimately, "Blessed are the people who . . . walk, O LORD, in the light of your face" (Ps. 89:15; cf. John 15:11).

With so much pain in this world, we need to know that misery is not ultimate, but that the joy of Christ *is* ultimate and final and victorious. We can look at the saddest thing that has ever happened—the cross—and see the greater joy beyond it: "[Christ] for the joy that was set before him endured the cross, despising the shame, and is seated at the right hand of the throne of God" (Heb. 12:2). His victory is ours too. As we suffer, we have an assurance from him to cheer our way: "Let not your hearts be troubled, neither let them be afraid. . . . In the world you will have tribulation. But take heart; I have overcome the world" (John 14:27; 16:33).

[b] Ps. 145:18, 19; [ver. 8] **30**[c] Ps. 38:10 [d] [ch. 25:25] **31**[e] ver. 5; ch. 20:12; 25:12 [f] [ch. 6:23] **32**[g] [ch. 8:33] [h] See ch. 8:36 [i] [ch. 19:8] **33**[j] See ch. 1:7 [k] ch. 18:12

16 The plans of the heart belong to man,
but [l]the answer of the tongue is
from the LORD.
2 [m]All the ways of a man are pure in his
own eyes,
but the LORD [n]weighs the spirit.
3 [o]Commit your work to the LORD,
and your plans will be established.
4 [p]The LORD has made everything for its
purpose,
even [q]the wicked for the day of trouble.
5 Everyone who is arrogant in heart is [r]an
abomination to the LORD;
[s]be assured, he will not go unpunished.
6 By [t]steadfast love and faithfulness iniquity is atoned for,
and by [u]the fear of the LORD one
[v]turns away from evil.
7 When a man's ways please the LORD,
[w]he makes even his enemies to be at
peace with him.
8 [x]Better is a little with righteousness
than great revenues with injustice.
9 [y]The heart of man plans his way,
but [z]the LORD establishes his steps.
10 [a]An oracle is on the lips of a king;
his mouth does not sin in judgment.
11 [b]A just balance and scales are the LORD's;
all the weights in the bag are his
work.
12 It is an abomination to kings to do evil,
for [c]the throne is established by righteousness.
13 [d]Righteous lips are the delight of a king,
and he loves him who speaks what is
right.
14 [e]A king's wrath is a messenger of death,
and a wise man will [f]appease it.
15 [g]In the light of a king's face there is life,
and his [d]favor is like [h]the clouds that
bring the spring rain.
16 [i]How much better to get wisdom than
[j]gold!
To get understanding is to be chosen
rather than [k]silver.
17 The highway of the upright [l]turns aside
from evil;
whoever guards his way preserves his
life.
18 [m]Pride goes before destruction,
and a haughty spirit before a fall.
19 [n]It is better to be of a lowly spirit with the
poor
than to [o]divide the spoil with the
proud.
20 Whoever gives thought to the word[1]
[p]will discover good,
and blessed is he [q]who trusts in the
LORD.
21 The wise of heart is called discerning,
and sweetness of speech [r]increases
persuasiveness.
22 Good sense is [s]a fountain of life to him
who has it,
but the instruction of fools is folly.

[1] *Or to a matter*

15:20 *Family.* God so values the family that he includes in the Ten Commandments "Honor your father and your mother" (Ex. 20:12). He reaffirms this in the New Testament (Eph. 6:2–3). The opposite of that honor is the word "despises" in this proverb, that is, to treat a parent as irrelevant. It is a grief to a godly parent to be dismissed by a haughty child. Whether he or she knows it or not, that foolish child is dismissing the Lord himself. Family life is typically where our true feelings for the Lord become most clear. For that very reason, it is a joy for a parent to see a child grow up to be wise (Prov. 23:15–16, 24–25; 27:11). This proverb does not say, "A *rich* son makes a glad father," but a *wise* son, that is, a son who fears the Lord (1:7; 9:10). A child's career choice is important, but it is nothing compared with his having a heart for the Lord.

The Lord asked his foolish people, "If then I am a father, where is my honor?" (Mal. 1:6). If your child dishonors you, there is pain. But there is also a blessing hidden in that sorrow: you can enter more deeply into the heart of the Father. Through our tears, we parents learn how God really feels about us all. And as we think about his patient forgiveness of the ways we dishonor him as our ultimate Father, we are helped to forgive our own children.

Some of us *are* the son or daughter who has dishonored our earthly parents. We may bring our failure to the Son who unfailingly honored his Father. Our folly within the family need not be the last word, for our identity is renewed by Another.

Chapter 16
1[l][Matt. 10:19, 20]
2[m]ch. 21:2; [ch. 12:15]; See ch. 30:12 [n]ch. 24:12; See 1 Sam. 16:7
3[o]See Ps. 37:5
4[p]Rom. 11:36 [q]Job 21:30; [Ex. 9:16]
5[r]ch. 6:16, 17; 8:13; Luke 16:15 [s]ch. 11:21; [ch. 28:20]
6[t]Dan. 4:27 [u]ch. 14:16 [v]ver. 17; Job 28:28
7[w][Gen. 26:28; 2 Chr. 17:10]
8[x]See ch. 15:16
9[y][ver. 1; ch. 19:21] [z]ch. 20:24; [Ps. 37:23; Jer. 10:23]
10[a][1 Kgs. 3:28]
11[b]See ch. 11:1
12[c]ch. 25:5; [ch. 20:28; 29:14; Isa. 16:5]
13[d][ch. 14:35; 22:11]
14[e]ch. 19:12; 20:2 [f][ch. 25:15]
15[g][Job 29:24] [d][See ver. 13 above] [h][Ps. 72:6]; See Job 29:23
16[i]ch. 8:10, 11, 19 [j]See ch. 3:14 [k]ch. 10:20
17[l]ver. 6
18[m]See ch. 11:2
19[n]ch. 29:23; Isa. 57:15 [o]See Ex. 15:9 **20**[p]ch. 19:8 [q]See Ps. 2:12 **21**[r]ver. 23 **22**[s]See ch. 10:11

23 [t]The heart of the wise makes his speech
judicious
and adds persuasiveness to his lips.
24 [u]Gracious words are like [v]a honeycomb,
sweetness to the soul and [w]health to
the body.
25 There is a way that seems right to a man,
but its end is the way to death.[1]
26 A worker's appetite works for him;
his [x]mouth urges him on.
27 [y]A worthless man plots evil,
and his speech[2] is like [z]a scorching fire.
28 [a]A dishonest man spreads strife,
and [b]a whisperer [c]separates close
friends.
29 A man of violence [d]entices his neighbor
and leads him in a way that is not good.
30 Whoever winks his eyes plans[3] [e]dishonest
things;
he who [f]purses his lips brings evil to
pass.
31 [g]Gray hair is [h]a crown of glory;
it [i]is gained in a righteous life.
32 [j]Whoever is slow to anger is better than
the mighty,
and he who rules his spirit than he
who takes a city.
33 [k]The lot is cast into the lap,
but its every decision is [l]from the LORD.

17 [m]Better is a dry morsel with quiet
than a house full of feasting[4] with
strife.
2 A servant who deals wisely will rule over
[n]a son who acts shamefully
and [o]will share the inheritance as one
of the brothers.
3 [p]The crucible is for silver, and the furnace
is for gold,
[q]and the LORD tests hearts.
4 An evildoer listens to wicked lips,
and a liar gives ear to a mischievous
tongue.
5 Whoever mocks the poor [r]insults his
Maker;
he who is [s]glad at calamity will not go
[t]unpunished.
6 [u]Grandchildren are [v]the crown of the
aged,
and the glory of children is their
fathers.
7 Fine speech is not [w]becoming to a fool;
still less is [x]false speech to a prince.
8 [y]A bribe is like a magic stone in the eyes
of the one who gives it;
wherever he turns he prospers.
9 Whoever [z]covers an offense seeks love,
but he who repeats a matter [a]sepa-
rates close friends.
10 A rebuke goes deeper into a man of
understanding
than a hundred blows into a fool.
11 An evil man seeks only rebellion,
and [b]a cruel messenger will be sent
against him.
12 Let a man meet [c]a she-bear robbed of her
cubs
[d]rather than a fool in his folly.
13 If anyone [e]returns evil for good,
[f]evil will not depart from his house.
14 The beginning of strife is like letting out
water,
so [g]quit before the quarrel breaks out.

[1] Hebrew *ways of death* [2] Hebrew *what is on his lips* [3] Hebrew *to plan* [4] Hebrew *sacrifices*

23[t] [Ps. 37:30; Matt. 12:34]
24[u] ch. 15:26 [v] Ps. 19:10 [w] See ch. 4:22
26[x] [Eccles. 6:7]
27[y] [ch. 6:12, 14, 19] [z] James 3:6
28[a] See ch. 15:18 [b] [ch. 18:8; 26:20, 22] [c] ch. 17:9
29[d] ch. 1:10
30[e] See ch. 2:12 [f] [ch. 6:13]
31[g] ch. 20:29 [h] ch. 17:6 [i] See ch. 3:1, 2
32[j] ch. 14:29; [ch. 19:11; 25:28]
33[k] [Acts 1:26] [l] ch. 29:26
Chapter 17
1[m] ch. 15:17
2[n] ver. 21, 25; ch. 10:5; 19:26 [o] [2 Sam. 16:4]
3[p] ch. 27:21 [q] 1 Chr. 29:17; Ps. 26:2; Jer. 17:10; Mal. 3:3
5[r] ch. 14:31; [Matt. 25:40, 45] [s] Job 31:29; Obad. 12; [ch. 24:17] [t] ch. 16:5

17:4 *The tongue.* Speaking wicked words is folly, but so is listening to them. Without a willing audience, foolish talk dies. But with listening ears, it spreads. Listening to wicked lips is the behavior of an evildoer. In fact, the listener is himself a liar: ". . . a liar gives ear." We might tell ourselves that we disapprove of a mischievous tongue, but by listening we get involved. The New Testament echoes these truths, reminding us that the gospel deeply saves us, so that we no longer rejoice at wrongdoing but rejoice with the truth (1 Cor. 13:6).

The words we speak, and the words we accept, reveal the true condition of our hearts (Matt. 12:34). For example, "The words of a whisperer are like delicious morsels" (Prov. 18:8). Gossip and controversy can be tasty. When this appetite for negative information spreads, it can separate even close friends (16:28). To safeguard a church, the elders may have to expel a person whose tongue is out of control (22:10; Titus 3:10). But the gospel's positive remedy for gossip is hearts filled, and continually refilled, with the word of Christ (Col. 3:16). Then we will turn the tables on gossip, set a new tone, and speak up for people being falsely accused (Prov. 31:8–9).

6[u] Ps. 128:6; [Ps. 127:3, 4] [v] ch. 16:31 **7**[w] [ch. 19:10; 26:1] [x] ch. 6:17 **8**[y] ver. 23; ch. 18:16; 19:6; 21:14; [Ex. 23:8; Isa. 1:23; Amos 5:12] **9**[z] ch. 10:12 [a] ch. 16:28
11[b] [1 Kgs. 2:29] **12**[c] 2 Sam. 17:8; Hos. 13:8 [d] [ch. 27:3] **13**[e] Ps. 35:12; 109:4, 5; [ch. 20:22; Matt. 5:39] [f] [2 Sam. 12:10] **14**[g] ch. 20:3; 25:8

15 He who [h]justifies the wicked and he who
[i]condemns the righteous
are both alike an abomination to the
LORD.
16 Why should a fool have money in his
hand [j]to buy wisdom
when he has no sense?
17 [k]A friend loves at all times,
and a brother is born for adversity.
18 One who lacks sense gives a pledge
and puts up security in the presence
of his neighbor.
19 Whoever loves transgression loves
strife;
he who [l]makes his door high seeks
destruction.
20 [m]A man of crooked heart does not discover good,
and one with a dishonest tongue falls
into calamity.
21 He who [n]sires a fool gets himself sorrow,
and the father of a fool has no joy.
22 [o]A joyful heart is good medicine,
but a crushed spirit [p]dries up the
bones.
23 The wicked accepts [q]a bribe in secret[1]
to [r]pervert the ways of justice.
24 [s]The discerning sets his face toward wisdom,
but the eyes of a fool are on the ends
of the earth.
25 [n]A foolish son is a grief to his father
[t]and bitterness to [u]her who bore him.
26 [v]To impose a fine on a righteous man is
not good,
nor to strike the noble for their
uprightness.
27 Whoever [w]restrains his words has
knowledge,
and he who has a cool spirit is a man
of understanding.
28 Even a fool [x]who keeps silent is considered wise;
when he closes his lips, he is deemed
intelligent.

18

1 Whoever [y]isolates himself seeks his
own desire;
he breaks out against all sound judgment.
2 A fool takes no pleasure in understanding,
but only [z]in expressing his opinion.
3 When wickedness comes, contempt
comes also,
and with dishonor comes disgrace.
4 The words of a man's mouth are [a]deep
waters;
the fountain of wisdom is a bubbling
brook.
5 It is not good to [b]be partial to[2] the
wicked
or to [c]deprive the righteous of justice.
6 A fool's lips walk into a fight,
and his mouth invites [d]a beating.
7 [e]A fool's mouth is his ruin,
and his lips are a snare to his soul.
8 [f]The words of a whisperer are like delicious morsels;
they go down into [g]the inner parts of
the body.
9 Whoever is slack in his work
is a [h]brother to him who destroys.
10 [i]The name of the LORD is [j]a strong tower;
the righteous man runs into it and [k]is
safe.
11 [l]A rich man's wealth is his strong city,
and like a high wall in his imagination.
12 [m]Before destruction a man's heart is
haughty,
but [n]humility comes before honor.
13 If one gives an answer [o]before he hears,
it is his folly and shame.
14 A man's spirit will endure sickness,
but [p]a crushed spirit who can bear?
15 An intelligent heart acquires knowledge,
and the ear of the wise seeks knowledge.
16 A man's [q]gift makes room for him
and brings him before the great.
17 The one who states his case first seems
right,
until the other comes and examines
him.
18 [r]The lot puts an end to quarrels
and decides between powerful contenders.

[1] Hebrew *a bribe from the bosom* [2] Hebrew *to lift the face of*

15[h] ch. 24:24; Ex. 23:7; Isa. 5:23 [i] Job 34:17; Ps. 94:21; [ver. 26; ch. 18:5] **16**[j] [ch. 23:23] **17**[k] ch. 18:24; 27:10; [Ruth 1:16; Job 6:14] **19**[l] [ch. 11:2; 29:23] **20**[m] [ch. 11:20] **21**[n] ch. 10:1; 19:13 **22**[o] See ch. 15:13 [p] Ps. 22:15; [ch. 12:25] **23**[q] See ver. 8 [r] [Mic. 3:11; 7:3] **24**[s] [ch. 14:6; 15:14; Eccles. 2:14]; See Deut. 30:11-14 **25**[n] [See ver. 21 above] [t] ch. 10:1 [u] ch. 23:25 **26**[v] [ver. 15] **27**[w] ch. 10:19; [James 1:19] **28**[x] Job 13:5 **Chapter 18** **1**[y] [Jude 19] **2**[z] ch. 13:16; [Eccles. 10:3] **4**[a] ch. 20:5 **5**[b] ch. 24:23; 28:21; Lev. 19:15; Deut. 1:17; Ps. 82:2 [c] See ch. 17:15 **6**[d] See ch. 19:29 **7**[e] ch. 10:14; 12:13; 13:3; Ps. 64:8; 140:9; Eccles. 10:12 **8**[f] ch. 26:22; [ch. 16:28] [g] ch. 20:27 **9**[h] [ch. 28:24] **10**[i] See Ex. 34:5-7 [j] Ps. 61:3; [Ps. 18:2]; See 2 Sam. 22:3 [k] [Ps. 20:1] **11**[l] See ch. 10:15 **12**[m] See ch. 11:2 [n] ch. 15:33 **13**[o] [John 7:51] **14**[p] ch. 15:13 **16**[q] [Gen. 32:20; 1 Sam. 25:27]; See ch. 17:8 **18**[r] [ch. 16:33]

19 A brother offended is more unyielding
than a strong city,
and quarreling is like the bars of a
castle.
20 [s]From the fruit of a man's mouth his
stomach is satisfied;
he is satisfied by the yield of his lips.
21 [t]Death and life are in the power of the
tongue,
and those who love it will eat its
fruits.
22 He who finds [u]a wife finds [v]a good
thing
and [w]obtains favor [x]from the LORD.
23 The poor use entreaties,
but [y]the rich answer roughly.
24 A man of many companions may come
to ruin,
but [z]there is a friend who sticks closer
than a brother.

19 [a]Better is a poor person who [b]walks
in his integrity
than one who is crooked in speech
and is a fool.
2 Desire[1] without knowledge is not good,
and whoever [c]makes haste with his
feet misses his way.
3 When a man's folly [d]brings his way to
ruin,
his heart [e]rages against the LORD.
4 [f]Wealth brings many new friends,
[f]but a poor man is deserted by his
friend.
5 [g]A false witness will not go unpunished,
and he who [h]breathes out lies will not
escape.
6 Many seek the favor of a generous man,[2]
and everyone is a friend to a man who
gives [i]gifts.
7 [j]All a poor man's brothers hate him;
[k]how much more do his friends go far
from him!
He pursues them with words, but does
not have them.[3]
8 [l]Whoever gets sense loves his own soul;
he who keeps understanding will
[m]discover good.
9 [g]A false witness will not go unpunished,
and he who [h]breathes out lies will perish.
10 [n]It is not fitting for a fool to live in luxury,
much less for [o]a slave to rule over
princes.
11 [p]Good sense makes one slow to anger,
and it is his glory to overlook an
offense.
12 A king's wrath is like [q]the growling of a
lion,
but his [r]favor is like [s]dew on the grass.
13 [t]A foolish son is ruin to his father,
and [u]a wife's quarreling is [v]a continual
dripping of rain.
14 [w]House and wealth are inherited from
fathers,
but a prudent wife is [x]from the LORD.

[1] Or *A soul* [2] Or *of a noble* [3] The meaning of the Hebrew sentence is uncertain

20[s] See ch. 12:14
21[t] Matt. 12:36, 37; [ch. 4:23; 12:13]
22[u] ch. 12:4; 19:14; See ch. 31:10-31 [v] [Gen. 2:18] [w] ch. 8:35 [x] ch. 19:14
23[y] [James 2:3, 6]
24[z] See ch. 17:17
Chapter 19
1[a] ch. 28:6 [b] ch. 14:2; 20:7; Ps. 26:1, 11
2[c] [ch. 21:5; 28:20; 29:20]
3[d] [ch. 11:3] [e] [Ps. 37:7; Isa. 8:21; Rev. 16:11]
4[f] ch. 14:20
5[g] [ch. 12:19; 21:28]; See Deut. 19:16-19 [h] See ch. 6:19
6[i] See ch. 17:8
7[j] [ver. 4] [k] [Ps. 38:11]
8[l] [ch. 15:32] [m] ch. 16:20
9[g] [See ver. 5 above] [h] [See ver. 5 above]
10[n] [ch. 17:7; 26:1] [o] ch. 30:22; Eccles. 10:6, 7
11[p] See ch. 14:29
12[q] ch. 20:2; [ch. 16:14, 15; 28:15] [r] ch. 14:35 [s] Ps. 133:3; Hos. 14:5; Mic. 5:7
13[t] ch. 10:1; 17:21 [u] See ch. 21:9 [v] ch. 27:15
14[w] [2 Cor. 12:14] [x] ch. 18:22

18:21 *The tongue.* Since "death and life are in the power of the tongue," we must use words carefully. They are easy to say, but hard to take back. Rash words, blurted out on impulse, are "like sword thrusts" (12:18). The outburst itself lasts only a moment, but the pain inflicted remains long after. Therefore, "a fool gives full vent to his spirit, but a wise man quietly holds it back" (29:11). Some things we think and feel are better left unsaid.

But life also is in the power of the tongue. "The tongue of the wise brings healing" (Prov. 12:18). Our words can "give grace to those who hear" (Eph. 4:29). The preaching of the gospel is a wonderful power for good (Luke 4:16–22). The Holy Spirit himself speaks to our hearts with healing assurances of God's love (Rom. 8:16). If deeds are called for, then, of course, mere words will not suffice (Prov. 14:23). And words can be an excuse for a failure to take action (24:12). But still, the wise carefully guide their words with clear awareness of their potential for giving life.

"If anyone does not stumble in what he says, he is a perfect man" (James 3:2). But who of us is perfect? We regret things we have said and things we have left unsaid. But God never stumbles in his words. By his word he "calls into existence the things that do not exist" (Rom. 4:17). The greatest proof that life is in the power of the tongue is God's promise of grace in the gospel, calling into existence a better future for us, despite what we deserve.

15 [y]Slothfulness casts into [z]a deep sleep,
and [a]an idle person will suffer hunger.
16 Whoever [b]keeps the commandment
keeps his life;
he who despises his ways will die.
17 [c]Whoever is generous to the poor lends
to the LORD,
and he [d]will repay him for his [e]deed.
18 [f]Discipline your son, for there is hope;
do not set your heart on [g]putting him
to death.
19 A man of great wrath will pay the penalty,
for if you deliver him, you will only
have to do it again.
20 Listen to advice and accept instruction,
that you may gain wisdom in [h]the
future.
21 [i]Many are the plans in the mind of a man,
but [j]it is the purpose of the LORD
[k]that will stand.
22 What is desired in a man is steadfast
love,
and a poor man is better than a liar.
23 The fear of the LORD [l]leads to life,
and whoever has it rests [m]satisfied;
he will [n]not be visited by harm.
24 [o]The sluggard buries his hand in [p]the dish
and will not even bring it back to his
mouth.
25 [q]Strike [r]a scoffer, and the simple will
[s]learn prudence;
[t]reprove a man of understanding, and
he will gain knowledge.
26 He who does violence to his father and
chases away his mother
is [u]a son who brings shame and
reproach.
27 Cease to hear instruction, my son,
[v]and you will stray from the words of
knowledge.
28 A worthless witness mocks at justice,
and the mouth of the wicked
[w]devours iniquity.
29 Condemnation is ready for [r]scoffers,
and [x]beating for the backs of fools.

20

[y]Wine is a mocker, [z]strong drink a
brawler,
and whoever [a]is led astray by it is not
wise.[1]
2 The terror of a king is like [b]the growling
of a lion;
whoever provokes him to anger [c]forfeits his life.
3 It is an honor for a man to [d]keep aloof
from strife,
but every fool will be quarreling.
4 [e]The sluggard does not plow in the
autumn;
[f]he will seek at harvest and have nothing.
5 The purpose in a man's heart is like
[g]deep water,
but a man of understanding will draw
it out.
6 Many a man [h]proclaims his own steadfast love,
but [i]a faithful man who can find?
7 The righteous who [j]walks in his integrity—
[k]blessed are his children after him!
8 [l]A king who sits on the throne of judgment
[m]winnows all evil with his eyes.

[1] Or *will not become wise*

20:6 *Friendship and conflict.* People can let you down, even when you are suffering. If such companions are all you have, you may well "come to ruin" (18:24). Promises of friendship are common, but steadfast loyalty is rare and precious (20:6). It is wise to choose as a friend one who "sticks closer than a brother" (18:24).

How does the book of Proverbs define a true friend? "A friend loves at all times" (17:17). The gospel creates faithful friends, who "rejoice with those who rejoice" and "weep with those who weep" (Rom. 12:15). This constancy comes from the grace of God reflected in Jesus himself, our ultimate Friend (John 13:1; 2 Tim. 4:16–18). After the disciples promised Jesus their loyalty, they all forsook him (Matt. 26:35, 56). But the risen Lord, when he appeared to them, greeted them not with accusations but with peace (John 20:19, 21, 26). Jesus knows all our weaknesses and still stands by us. One proof that his steadfast love is getting through to us is that we love one another as he has loved us (John 13:34; 15:12–13).

15 [y] See ch. 6:9-11 [z] Job 4:13 [a] [ch. 10:4; 20:4, 13; 23:21] **16** [b] [ch. 13:13; Luke 10:28] **17** [c] [ch. 22:9; 28:27; Eccles. 11:1; Matt. 10:42; Heb. 6:10]; See Deut. 15:7-10; Matt. 25:40; 2 Cor. 9:6-8 [d] [Luke 6:38] [e] See ch. 12:14 **18** [f] See ch. 13:24 [g] [ch. 23:13]; See Deut. 21:18-21 **20** [h] Ps. 37:37 **21** [i] Ps. 33:10, 11 [j] Job 23:13; Isa. 14:26, 27 [k] Isa. 46:10 **23** [l] ch. 10:16; 11:19; [Isa. 38:5; Mark 10:30] [m] [Ps. 25:13] [n] [Lev. 26:6] **24** [o] ch. 26:15; [ch. 15:19; 20:4] [p] [Matt. 26:23; Mark 14:20] **25** [q] ch. 21:11 [r] See Ps. 1:1 [s] See Deut. 13:6-11 [t] [ch. 9:8] **26** [u] ch. 10:5; 17:2

27 [v] [2 Pet. 2:21] **28** [w] Job 15:16; [ch. 18:8; Job 34:7] **29** [r] [See ver. 25 above] [x] ch. 10:13; 18:6; 26:3 **Chapter 20** **1** [y] [Gen. 9:21]; See ch. 23:29-32 [z] ch. 31:4 [a] Isa. 28:7; [Hos. 4:11] **2** [b] See ch. 19:12 [c] Num. 16:38; Hab. 2:10; See ch. 8:36 **3** [d] [ch. 17:14] **4** [e] [ch. 19:24] [f] ch. 19:15; [ch. 6:11] **5** [g] ch. 18:4 **6** [h] [ch. 25:14; Matt. 6:2; Luke 18:11] [i] [Ps. 12:1] **7** [j] See ch. 19:1 [k] [1 Kgs. 15:4; Ps. 37:26; 112:2; Jer. 33:20, 21] **8** [l] [ch. 16:10] [m] [ver. 26; ch. 25:5; Ps. 101:5]

9 [n]Who can say, "I have made my heart
pure;
I am clean from my sin"?
10 [o]Unequal[1] weights and unequal measures
are both alike an abomination to the
LORD.
11 Even a child [p]makes himself known by
his acts,
by whether his conduct is pure and
upright.[2]
12 [q]The hearing ear and the seeing eye,
[r]the LORD has made them both.
13 [s]Love not sleep, lest you [t]come to poverty;
open your eyes, and you will have
[u]plenty of bread.
14 "Bad, bad," says the buyer,
but when he goes away, then he
boasts.
15 There is gold and abundance of [v]costly
stones,
[w]but the lips of knowledge are a precious jewel.
16 [x]Take a man's garment when he has put
up security for a stranger,
and [y]hold it in pledge when he puts
up security for foreigners.[3]
17 [z]Bread gained by deceit is sweet to a man,
but afterward his mouth will be full
of [a]gravel.
18 [b]Plans are established by counsel;
by [c]wise guidance [d]wage war.
19 Whoever [e]goes about slandering reveals
secrets;
therefore do not associate with [f]a simple babbler.[4]
20 [g]If one curses his father or his mother,
[h]his lamp will be put out in utter darkness.
21 [i]An inheritance gained hastily in the
beginning
will not be blessed in the end.
22 Do not say, [j]"I will repay evil";
[k]wait for the LORD, and he will deliver
you.
23 [l]Unequal weights are an abomination to
the LORD,
and [m]false scales are not good.
24 A man's [n]steps are from the LORD;
how then can man understand his
way?
25 It is a snare to say rashly, "It is holy,"
and to reflect only [o]after making
vows.
26 A wise king [p]winnows the wicked
and drives [q]the wheel over them.
27 [r]The spirit[5] of man is the lamp of the
LORD,
[s]searching all [t]his innermost parts.
28 [u]Steadfast love and faithfulness preserve
the king,
and by steadfast love his [v]throne is
upheld.
29 The glory of young men is their
strength,
but [w]the splendor of old men is their
gray hair.
30 [x]Blows that wound cleanse away evil;
strokes make clean [t]the innermost
parts.

21

The king's heart is a stream of water
in the hand of the LORD;
he [y]turns it wherever he will.
2 [z]Every way of a man is right in his own
eyes,
but the LORD [a]weighs the heart.
3 [b]To do righteousness and justice
is more acceptable to the LORD than
sacrifice.
4 [c]Haughty eyes and a proud heart,
[d]the lamp[6] of the wicked, are sin.
5 The plans of [e]the diligent lead surely to
abundance,
but everyone who is [f]hasty comes
[g]only to poverty.
6 [h]The getting of treasures by a lying
tongue
is a [i]fleeting [j]vapor and a [k]snare of
death.[7]
7 The violence of the wicked will [l]sweep
them away,
because they refuse to do what is just.
8 The way of the guilty [m]is crooked,
but the conduct of the pure is
upright.

[1] Or *Two kinds of*; also verse 23 [2] Or *Even a child can dissemble in his actions, though his conduct seems pure and upright* [3] Or *for an adulteress* (compare 27:13) [4] Hebrew *with one who is simple in his lips* [5] Hebrew *breath* [6] Or *the plowing* [7] Some Hebrew manuscripts, Septuagint, Latin; most Hebrew manuscripts *vapor for those who seek death*

9[n] See 1 Kgs. 8:46 **10**[o] ver. 23; See ch. 11:1 **11**[p] [Matt. 7:16] **12**[q] ch. 15:31; 25:12 [r] Ex. 4:11; Ps. 94:9 **13**[s] [ch. 6:4; 19:15; 31:15; Rom. 12:11] [t] [ver. 4] [u] ch. 12:11 **15**[v] Job 28:18 [w] [ch. 3:14, 15] **16**[x] ch. 27:13; [ch. 6:1; 22:26] [y] See Job 22:6 **17**[z] [ch. 9:17] [a] [Lam. 3:16] **18**[b] [ch. 11:14; 15:22] [c] ch. 24:6 [d] Luke 14:31 **19**[e] ch. 11:13 [f] ch. 13:3; [Rom. 16:18] **20**[g] ch. 30:11, 17; See Ex. 21:17 [h] See 2 Sam. 21:17; Job 18:5 **21**[i] See ch. 13:11 **22**[j] ch. 24:29; [ch. 17:13; Matt. 5:39; Rom. 12:17, 19; 1 Thess. 5:15; 1 Pet. 3:9] [k] Ps. 27:14 **23**[l] ver. 10 [m] See ch. 11:1 **24**[n] See ch. 16:9 **25**[o] [Eccles. 5:4, 5] **26**[p] [Matt. 3:12] [q] Isa. 28:27 **27**[r] [1 Cor. 2:11] [s] [Zeph. 1:12] [t] ch. 18:8 **28**[u] ch. 3:3 [v] See ch. 16:12 **29**[w] ch. 16:31 **30**[x] [Isa. 53:5] [t] [See ver. 27 above] **Chapter 21** **1**[y] [Ezra 6:22] **2**[z] ch. 16:2; [ch. 12:15] [a] ch. 24:12; [Luke 16:15; 1 Cor. 4:4]; See 1 Sam. 16:7 **3**[b] See ch. 15:8; 1 Sam. 15:22 **4**[c] See ch. 6:17; Ps. 101:5 [d] 1 Kgs. 11:36 **5**[e] ch. 10:4 [f] [ch. 19:2] [g] [ch. 11:24; 14:23; 22:16] **6**[h] ch. 20:21; See ch. 10:2 [i] [ch. 13:11] [j] Job 13:25 [k] [ch. 8:36] **7**[l] [Jer. 30:23] **8**[m] [ch. 2:15]

9 It is [n]better to live in a corner of the
housetop
than in a house shared with a quarrelsome wife.
10 The soul of the wicked desires evil;
his neighbor finds no mercy in his eyes.
11 When [o]a scoffer is punished, the simple
becomes wise;
when a wise man is instructed, he
gains knowledge.
12 The Righteous One [p]observes the house
of the wicked;
he throws the wicked down to ruin.
13 [q]Whoever closes his ear to the cry of the
poor
will himself call out and not be
answered.
14 [r]A gift in secret averts anger,
and a concealed bribe,[1] strong wrath.
15 When justice is done, it is a joy to the
righteous
[s]but terror to evildoers.
16 One who wanders from the way of good
sense
[t]will rest in the assembly of the dead.
17 Whoever loves pleasure will be a poor
man;
he who loves wine and oil will not be
rich.
18 [u]The wicked is a [v]ransom for the righteous,
and the traitor for the upright.
19 It is [w]better to live in a desert land
than with a quarrelsome and fretful
woman.
20 [x]Precious treasure and oil are in a wise
man's dwelling,
but a foolish man [y]devours it.
21 Whoever [z]pursues righteousness and
kindness
will find [a]life, righteousness, and honor.
22 [b]A wise man scales the city of the mighty
and brings down the stronghold in
which they trust.
23 [c]Whoever keeps his mouth and his tongue
[d]keeps himself out of [e]trouble.
24 [f]"Scoffer" is the name of the arrogant,
haughty man
who acts with arrogant pride.
25 The desire of [g]the sluggard kills him,
for his hands refuse to labor.
26 All day long he craves and craves,
but the righteous [h]gives and does not
hold back.
27 [i]The sacrifice of the wicked is an abomination;
how much more [j]when he brings it
with evil intent.
28 [k]A false witness will perish,
but the word of a man who hears will
endure.
29 A wicked man puts on a bold face,
but the upright [l]gives thought to[2] his
ways.
30 [m]No wisdom, no understanding, no counsel
can avail against the LORD.
31 [n]The horse is made ready for the day of
battle,
but [o]the victory belongs to the LORD.

22 [p]A good name is to be chosen rather
than great riches,
and favor is better than silver or gold.
2 [q]The rich and the poor meet together;
the LORD is [r]the maker of them all.
3 [s]The prudent sees danger and hides himself,
but the simple go on and suffer for it.
4 The reward for humility and fear of the
LORD
is [t]riches and honor and life.[3]

[1] Hebrew *a bribe in the bosom* [2] Or *establishes* [3] Or *The reward for humility is the fear of the LORD, riches and honor and life*

22:4 *Humility.* The foundation of biblical wisdom is humility before God and one another. There is also a false kind of "wisdom," a worldly way to get ahead, driven by pride and selfish ambition (James 3:13–18). This selfish wisdom comes to us naturally, but it offends the Lord (Luke 16:15) and it lets us down. God's wisdom always involves humility, depending upon God for everything we need and crediting him with everything we have (1 Cor. 4:7). This is a difficult adjustment but it is rewarding—with riches and honor and life in the Lord (cf. Col. 2:3; 1 Pet. 1:7). Solomon humbled himself as a child, and God gave him both wisdom and its rewards (1 Kings 3:5–15). Jesus humbled himself all the way to the cross, and God gave him a name above every other name (Phil. 2:5–11). Humility is *the* key to everything we desire in our own deepest intentions.

9[n] ch. 25:24; [ver. 19; ch. 19:13; 27:15]
11[o] ch. 19:25; See Ps. 1:1
12[p] Ps. 37:35, 36
13[q] [James 2:13]; See Matt. 18:30-34
14[r] [ch. 17:8; 18:16]
15[s] [ch. 10:29]
16[t] [Ps. 49:14]
18[u] [ch. 11:8] [v] Isa. 43:3
19[w] [ver. 9]
20[x] [Ps. 112:3] [y] [Job 20:15, 18]
21[z] ch. 15:9; Matt. 5:6; [ch. 3:3] [a] ch. 3:16; 1 Kgs. 3:11; Matt. 6:33; See ch. 4:22

22[b] [ch. 24:5; Eccles. 7:19]; See 2 Sam. 5:6-9; Eccles. 9:14-18 **23**[c] See ch. 13:3 [d] ch. 22:5 [e] ch. 12:13 **24**[f] ch. 1:22; See Ps. 1:1 **25**[g] [ch. 13:4] **26**[h] See Ps. 37:26 **27**[i] Isa. 66:3; See ch. 15:8 [j] [ch. 24:9] **28**[k] ch. 19:5, 9 **29**[l] Ps. 119:5 **30**[m] Isa. 8:9, 10; 1 Cor. 3:19, 20; [ch. 19:21] **31**[n] [Ps. 20:7; 33:17; Isa. 31:1] [o] Jer. 3:23 **Chapter 22** **1**[p] [Eccles. 7:1] **2**[q] [ch. 29:13] [r] ch. 14:31; Job 31:15 **3**[s] ch. 27:12; [ch. 14:16] **4**[t] [ch. 21:20, 21]

5 [u]Thorns and snares are in the way of the crooked;
whoever [v]guards his soul will keep far from them.
6 [w]Train up a child in the way he should go;
even when he is old he will not depart from it.
7 [x]The rich rules over the poor,
and the borrower is the slave of the lender.
8 Whoever [y]sows injustice will reap calamity,
and [z]the rod of his fury will fail.
9 [a]Whoever has a bountiful[1] eye will be blessed,
for he [b]shares his bread with the poor.
10 [c]Drive out a scoffer, [d]and strife will go out,
and [e]quarreling and abuse will cease.
11 He who [f]loves purity of heart,
and whose [g]speech is gracious, [h]will have the king as his friend.
12 The eyes of the LORD keep watch over knowledge,
but he [i]overthrows the words of the traitor.
13 [j]The sluggard says, "There is a lion outside!
I shall be killed in the streets!"
14 The mouth of [k]forbidden[2] women is [l]a deep pit;
[m]he with whom the LORD is angry will fall into it.
15 Folly is bound up in the heart of a child,
but [n]the rod of discipline drives it far from him.
16 Whoever oppresses the poor to increase his own wealth,
or gives to the rich, [o]will only come to poverty.

Words of the Wise

17 [p]Incline your ear, and hear [q]the words of the wise,
[r]and apply your heart to my knowledge,
18 for it will be pleasant if you keep them within you,
if all of them are ready on your lips.
19 That your trust may be in the LORD,
I have made them known to you today, even to you.
20 Have I not written for you [s]thirty sayings of counsel and knowledge,
21 to [t]make you know what is right and true,
that you may give a true answer to those who sent you?

22 [u]Do not rob the poor, because he is poor,
or [v]crush the afflicted at [w]the gate,

[1] Hebrew *good* [2] Hebrew *strange*

5[u]ch. 15:19 [v]ch. 21:23; [1 John 5:18]
6[w]Eph. 6:4; 2 Tim. 3:15
7[x]James 2:6
8[y]Job 4:8; [Hos. 10:13] [z][Isa. 14:6; 30:31]
9[a][ch. 19:17; 2 Cor. 9:6] [b][ch. 19:17; Luke 14:13, 14]
10[c][Gen. 21:9, 10] [d][ch. 26:20] [e]ch. 26:20
11[f][ch. 16:13; Ps. 101:6] [g][Eccles. 10:12] [h][ch. 14:35]
12[i]ch. 21:12; [ch. 11:3]
13[j]ch. 26:13
14[k]See ch. 2:16 [l][ch. 23:27] [m]Eccles. 7:26
15[n]See ch. 13:24
16[o]ch. 28:22
17[p]ch. 5:1 [q]ch. 1:6; 24:23 [r][ch. 23:12]
20[s]ch. 8:6
21[t][Luke 1:3, 4]
22[u][Ex. 23:6; Zech. 7:10; Mal. 3:5] [v]See Job 5:4 [w]Job 31:21

What is humility? It is the fear of the Lord: "The reward for humility and fear of the LORD" (Prov. 22:4) means "The reward for humility, that is, fear of the Lord." Reverence for the Lord changes our focus from self-esteem to joyful Christ-esteem (Phil. 3:4–11). Our own accomplishments and privileges come to mean less to us, replaced with a sense of need that draws us closer to the Lord and his strength (2 Cor. 12:1–10). We submit our problem-solving to the Lord, because he loves us more than we love ourselves (1 Pet. 5:6–7). Rather than brag about our own plans, we humbly entrust our future to the Lord (Prov. 27:1; James 4:13–17). This is the wisdom of humbly fearing the Lord, as Jesus did (cf. the section on Prov. 1:7 in the note on 1:1–7).

When the eternal Word became earthly flesh (John 1:14), humility came down into this proud world as a conquering power, overthrowing human strategies for success (Matt. 23:12; Luke 14:11; 18:14). The humility of Jesus becomes visible today through the humility of his followers (1 Pet. 5:5; cf. Matt. 18:1–4). But at his second coming, the Lord will return not in lowliness but as King of kings and Lord of lords (Rev. 19:11–16). Then the meek will truly inherit the earth (Matt. 5:5).

22:6 *Family.* This proverb is not a sure formula for success in child rearing; it is an assurance of how profound a parent's influence can be—though that influence might be rejected. The Proverbs provide reliable guidance but they do not address every contingency encountered in a sinful world. Wise parents invest in a child during the crucial, early years, because such care typically has godly results. But even the best parenting can result in a prodigal and a prideful son (Luke 15:11–32). Ultimately, the way a child "should go" (Prov. 22:6) is not a college or career choice but an eternal choice to live for God. Such a "way" is profoundly influenced by parents' actions, but is ultimately determined by the child's heart.

23 for [x]the LORD will plead their cause
and rob of life those who rob them.
24 Make no friendship with a man given to
anger,
nor go with a wrathful man,
25 lest you learn his ways
and entangle yourself in a snare.
26 Be not one of those who [y]give pledges,
who put up security for debts.
27 If you have nothing with which to pay,
why should [z]your bed be taken from
under you?
28 Do not move the ancient [a]landmark
that your fathers have set.
29 Do you see a man skillful in his work?
He will [b]stand before kings;
he will not stand before obscure men.

23 When you sit down to eat with a
ruler,
observe carefully what[1] is before you,
2 and put a knife to your throat
if you are given to appetite.
3 [c]Do not desire his delicacies,
for they are deceptive food.
4 [d]Do not toil to acquire wealth;
[e]be discerning enough to desist.
5 When your eyes light on it, it is gone,
[f]for suddenly it sprouts wings,
flying like an eagle toward heaven.
6 [g]Do not eat the bread of a man who is
[h]stingy;[2]
[i]do not desire his delicacies,
7 for he is like one who is inwardly calculating.[3]
"Eat and drink!" he says to you,
but his [j]heart is not with you.
8 You will vomit up the morsels that you
have eaten,
and waste your pleasant words.
9 Do not speak in the hearing of a fool,
for he will despise the good sense of
your words.
10 [k]Do not move an ancient landmark
or enter the fields of the fatherless,
11 for their [l]Redeemer is strong;
he will [m]plead their cause against you.
12 Apply your heart to instruction
and your ear to words of knowledge.
13 Do not withhold [n]discipline from a
child;
[o]if you strike him with a rod, he will
not die.
14 If you strike him with the rod,
you will [p]save his soul from Sheol.
15 [q]My son, if your heart is wise,
my heart too will be glad.
16 My [r]inmost being[4] will exult
when your lips speak [s]what is right.
17 Let not your heart [t]envy sinners,
but continue in [u]the fear of the LORD
all the day.
18 Surely [v]there is a future,
and your [w]hope will not be cut off.
19 Hear, my son, and [x]be wise,
and [y]direct your heart in the way.
20 Be not among [z]drunkards[5]
or among [a]gluttonous eaters of meat,
21 for the drunkard and the glutton will
come to poverty,
and [b]slumber will clothe them with
rags.
22 [c]Listen to your father who gave you life,
[d]and do not despise your mother when
she is old.
23 [e]Buy truth, and do not sell it;
buy wisdom, instruction, and understanding.

[1] Or *who* [2] Hebrew *whose eye is evil* [3] Or *for as he calculates in his soul, so is he* [4] Hebrew *My kidneys* [5] Hebrew *those who drink too much wine*

"Train up" means to dedicate the child to God (cf. 1 Sam. 1:27–28; Eph. 6:4), so this proverb raises the question of the parent's own commitment. The parent's dedication is sustained by remembering that the Lord himself is committed to that family. "He who did not spare his own Son but gave him up for us all, how will he not also with him graciously give us all things?" (Rom. 8:32). Once a Christian family is truly dedicated to the Lord, the practical questions of child rearing find their place. A wise parent is realistic about a child's innate folly (Prov. 22:15). Something deep inside a child wants to demand its own way. But "the rod of discipline" will drive that folly out. Even so, our Father in heaven disciplines us all (Heb. 12:5–11), proving thereby that he cares about us. Wise parents discipline their children with the same love they themselves have received from their gracious heavenly Father.

23[x] ch. 23:11; 1 Sam. 25:39; Ps. 12:5; 35:10; 68:5; 140:12; Jer. 51:36
26[y] See Job 17:3
27[z] [ch. 20:16; Ex. 22:26]
28[a] ch. 23:10; Deut. 19:14; 27:17; Job 24:2; Hos. 5:10
29[b] 1 Kgs. 10:8; See Gen. 41:46
Chapter 23
3[c] ver. 6
4[d] ch. 15:27; 28:20; Matt. 6:19; 1 Tim. 6:9, 10; Heb. 13:5 [e] [ch. 3:5, 7; 26:12; Isa. 5:21; Rom. 12:16]
5[f] ch. 27:24
6[g] [Ps. 141:4] [h] ch. 28:22; Deut. 15:9 [i] ver. 3 **7**[j] [Ps. 12:2] **10**[k] See ch. 22:28 **11**[l] [Ex. 6:6]; See Job 19:25 [m] See ch. 22:23 **13**[n] See ch. 13:24 [o] [ch. 19:18] **14**[p] [1 Cor. 5:5] **15**[q] ver. 24, 25; See ch. 29:3 **16**[r] Ps. 7:9; 73:21 [s] [ch. 8:6] **17**[t] See Ps. 37:1 [u] [ch. 28:14] **18**[v] ch. 24:14, 20 [w] Ps. 9:18 **19**[x] ch. 6:6 [y] [ch. 9:6] **20**[z] [ver. 29, 30; Isa. 5:11, 22; Matt. 24:49; Luke 21:34; Rom. 13:13; Eph. 5:18] [a] ch. 28:7 **21**[b] [ch. 6:10, 11] **22**[c] See ch. 1:8 [d] [ch. 30:17] **23**[e] [ch. 4:5, 7; 18:15; Matt. 13:44]

24 [f]The father of the righteous will greatly
rejoice;
he who fathers a wise son will be glad
in him.
25 [f]Let your father and mother be glad;
let [g]her who bore you rejoice.

26 My son, give me your heart,
and let your eyes observe[1] my ways.
27 For a prostitute is [h]a deep pit;
[i]an adulteress[2] is a narrow [j]well.
28 [k]She lies in wait like a robber
and increases the traitors among
mankind.

29 [l]Who has woe? Who has sorrow?
Who has strife? Who has complaining?
Who has [m]wounds without cause?
Who has [n]redness of eyes?
30 Those who [o]tarry long over wine;
those who go to try [p]mixed wine.
31 Do not look at wine when it is red,
when it sparkles in the cup
and goes down smoothly.
32 In the end it [q]bites like a serpent
and stings like an adder.
33 Your eyes will see strange things,
and your heart utter [r]perverse things.
34 You will be like one who lies down in
the midst of the sea,
like one who lies on the top of a
mast.[3]
35 "They [s]struck me," you will say,[4] "but
I was not hurt;
they beat me, but I did not feel it.
When shall I awake?
I [t]must have another drink."

24

1 Be not [u]envious of evil men,
nor desire to be [v]with them,
2 for their hearts [w]devise violence,
and their lips [x]talk of trouble.

3 By [y]wisdom a house is built,
and by understanding it is established;
4 by knowledge the rooms are filled
with all [z]precious and pleasant riches.
5 [a]A wise man is full of strength,
and a man of knowledge enhances his
might,
6 for by [b]wise guidance you can wage your
war,
and in [c]abundance of counselors there
is victory.
7 Wisdom is [d]too high for a fool;
in [e]the gate he does not open his
mouth.

8 Whoever [f]plans to do evil
will be called a schemer.
9 [g]The devising[5] of folly is sin,
and [h]the scoffer is an abomination to
mankind.

10 If you [i]faint in the day of adversity,
your strength is small.
11 [j]Rescue those who are being taken away
to death;
hold back those who are stumbling to
the slaughter.
12 If you say, "Behold, we did not know
this,"
[k]does not he who [l]weighs the heart
perceive it?
Does not he who [m]keeps watch over your
soul know it,
and will he not repay man [n]according
to his work?

13 My son, [o]eat honey, for it is good,
and [p]the drippings of the honeycomb
are sweet to your taste.
14 Know that wisdom is such to your soul;
if you find it, there will be [q]a future,
and your hope will not be cut off.

15 [r]Lie not in wait as a wicked man against
the dwelling of the righteous;
do no violence to his home;
16 [s]for the righteous falls [t]seven times and
rises again,
but [u]the wicked stumble in times of
calamity.

17 [v]Do not rejoice when your enemy falls,
and let not your heart be glad when
he stumbles,
18 lest the LORD see it and be displeased,
and turn away his anger from him.

19 [w]Fret not yourself because of evildoers,
and be not [x]envious of the wicked,

[1] Or *delight in* [2] Hebrew *a foreign woman* [3] Or *of the rigging* [4] Hebrew lacks *you will say* [5] Or *scheming*

24[f] ver. 15; See ch. 29:3 **25**[f] [See ver. 24 above] [g] ch. 17:25 **27**[h] [ch. 22:14] [i] See ch. 2:16 [j] Ps. 55:23 **28**[k] ch. 7:12; [Eccles. 7:26] **29**[l] [ver. 20, 21] [m] [ver. 35] [n] Gen. 49:12 **30**[o] Isa. 5:11 [p] ch. 9:2, 5; Ps. 75:8; Isa. 5:22; 65:11 **32**[q] Job 20:16 **33**[r] See ch. 2:12 **35**[s] Jer. 5:3; [ver. 29] [t] Isa. 56:12
Chapter 24 **1**[u] ver. 19; See Ps. 37:1 [v] See ch. 1:15 **2**[w] [Isa. 59:13] [x] Ps. 10:7 **3**[y] [ch. 14:1] **4**[z] [ch. 23:23; Luke 16:11] **5**[a] [ch. 21:22] **6**[b] ch. 20:18 [c] See ch. 11:14 **7**[d] [ch. 14:6] [e] See Job 5:4 **8**[f] Rom. 1:30 **9**[g] [ch. 21:27] [h] See Ps. 1:1 **10**[i] [Heb. 12:3] **11**[j] Ps. 82:4; [Isa. 58:6, 7] **12**[k] [Eccles. 5:8] [l] ch. 16:2; See 1 Sam. 16:7 [m] [Ps. 91:11] [n] See Job 34:11 **13**[o] [Ps. 19:10; 119:103; Song 5:1; Isa. 7:15] [p] Song 4:11 **14**[q] See ch. 23:18 **15**[r] Ps. 10:9, 10 **16**[s] See Ps. 37:24 [t] See Job 5:19 [u] ch. 14:32 **17**[v] Ps. 35:15, 19; [Mic. 7:8]; See ch. 17:5 **19**[w] [Jer. 12:1]; See Ps. 37:1 [x] ver. 1

20 for the evil man has no [q]future;
[y]the lamp of the wicked will be put out.

21 My son, [z]fear the LORD and the king,
and do not join with those who do otherwise,
22 for disaster will arise suddenly from them,
and who knows the ruin that will come from them both?

More Sayings of the Wise

23 These also are sayings of [a]the wise.
[b]Partiality in judging is not good.
24 Whoever [c]says to the wicked, "You are in the right,"
[d]will be cursed by peoples, abhorred by nations,
25 but those who rebuke the wicked will have delight,
and a good blessing will come upon them.
26 Whoever gives an honest answer
kisses the lips.
27 [e]Prepare your work outside;
get everything ready for yourself in the field,
and after that build your house.
28 [f]Be not a witness against your neighbor without cause,
and do not deceive with your lips.
29 Do not say, [g]"I will do to him as he has done to me;
I will pay the man back for what he has done."
30 [h]I passed by the field of a sluggard,
by the vineyard of a man [i]lacking sense,
31 and behold, it was all overgrown with thorns;
the ground was covered with nettles,
and its stone [j]wall was broken down.
32 Then I saw and [k]considered it;
I looked and received instruction.
33 [l]A little sleep, a little slumber,
a little folding of the hands to rest,
34 and poverty will come upon you like a robber,
and want like an armed man.

More Proverbs of Solomon

25 These also are [m]proverbs of Solomon which the men of Hezekiah king of Judah copied.

2 It is the glory of God to [n]conceal things,
but the glory of kings is to [o]search things out.
3 As the heavens for height, and the earth for depth,
so the heart of kings is [p]unsearchable.
4 Take away [q]the dross from the silver,
and [r]the smith has material for a vessel;
5 take away [s]the wicked from the presence of the king,
and his [t]throne will be established in righteousness.
6 Do not put yourself forward in the king's presence
or stand in the place of the great,
7 for [u]it is better to be told, "Come up here,"
than to be put lower in the presence of a noble.

24:26 *Friendship and conflict.* A true friend does more than accept us: "whoever gives an honest answer kisses the lips." As a later proverb puts it, "Faithful are the wounds of a friend" (Prov. 27:6). True friends stir us to strive and grow (Heb. 10:24). Wisely, the wounds of a true friend are not rash or reckless but gentle and respectful, for "a brother offended is more unyielding than a strong city" (Prov. 18:19). It is easy to offend, but hard to reconcile.

If someone you love has betrayed your trust and harmed you, the path of God's wisdom for you is this: "Do not say, 'I will repay evil'; wait for the LORD, and he will deliver you" (20:22; 24:29). Waiting for the Lord is not easy, but taking your own revenge can only make matters worse. Far from repaying one evil with more evil, God's counsel is that you unsettle your ex-friend with surprising kindnesses: "If your enemy is hungry, give him bread to eat, and if he is thirsty, give him water to drink, for you will heap burning coals on his head, and the LORD will reward you" (25:21–22; Rom. 12:19–21; 1 Pet. 3:8–17). The Lord does not ask us to trust our enemies, but he does ask us to love them, for he loved us when we were his enemies (Rom. 5:8; 2 Cor. 5:17–20). By this heavenly wisdom, and by this means alone, the love of Christ will be wonderfully seen and felt in our angry world today.

20[q] [See ver. 14 above] [y]ch. 13:9; See Job 18:5
21[z] 1 Pet. 2:17; [Rom. 13:7]
23[a] ch. 1:6; 22:17 [b]See ch. 18:5
24[c] See ch. 17:15 [d]ch. 11:26
27[e] [Luke 14:28]
28[f] [ch. 25:18]
29[g] See ch. 20:22
30[h] [Job 5:3] [i]See ch. 6:32
31[j] Isa. 5:5
32[k] [ch. 22:17]
33[l] For ver. 33, 34, see ch. 6:10, 11

Chapter 25
1[m] See ch. 1:1
2[n] [Deut. 29:29; Rom. 11:33] [o]Job 29:16
3[p] [Ps. 145:3]
4[q] [Ezek. 22:18; 2 Tim. 2:20, 21] [r][Mal. 3:2, 3]
5[s] [ch. 20:8] [t]See ch. 16:12
7[u] See Luke 14:8-11

What your eyes have seen
8 [w]do not hastily bring into court,
for[1] what will you do in the end,
when your neighbor puts you to shame?
9 [x]Argue your case with your neighbor himself,
and do not reveal another's secret,
10 lest he who hears you bring shame upon you,
and your ill repute have no end.

11 [y]A word fitly spoken
is like apples of gold in a setting of silver.
12 Like [z]a gold ring or an ornament of gold
is a wise reprover to [a]a listening ear.
13 Like the cold of snow in the time of harvest
is [b]a faithful messenger to those who send him;
he refreshes the soul of his masters.
14 Like [c]clouds and wind without rain
is a man who [d]boasts of a gift he does not give.

15 With [e]patience a ruler may be persuaded,
and a soft tongue will break a bone.
16 If you have [f]found honey, eat [g]only enough for you,
lest you have your fill of it and vomit it.
17 Let your foot be seldom in your neighbor's house,
lest he have his fill of you and hate you.
18 A man who [h]bears false witness against his neighbor
is like a war club, or [i]a sword, or a sharp arrow.
19 Trusting in a treacherous man in time of trouble
is like a bad tooth or a foot that slips.
20 Whoever [j]sings songs to a heavy heart
is like one who takes off a garment on a cold day,
and like vinegar on soda.
21 [k]If your enemy is hungry, give him bread to eat,
and if he is thirsty, give him water to drink,
22 for you will heap [l]burning coals on his head,
and the LORD will reward you.
23 The north wind brings forth rain,
and a backbiting tongue, angry looks.
24 [m]It is better to live in a corner of the housetop
than in a house shared with a quarrelsome wife.
25 Like cold water to [n]a thirsty soul,
so is [o]good news from a far country.
26 Like [p]a muddied spring or a polluted fountain
is a righteous man who gives way before the wicked.
27 It is [q]not good to eat much honey,
nor is it glorious to [r]seek one's own glory.[2]
28 A man [s]without self-control
is like [t]a city broken into and left without walls.

26 Like snow in summer or [u]rain in harvest,
so [v]honor is [w]not fitting for a fool.
2 Like [x]a sparrow in its flitting, like a swallow in its flying,
[y]a curse that is causeless does not alight.
3 [z]A whip for the horse, a bridle for the donkey,
and [a]a rod for the back of fools.
4 [b]Answer not a fool according to his folly,
lest you be like him yourself.
5 [c]Answer a fool according to his folly,
lest he be [d]wise in his own eyes.
6 Whoever sends a message by the hand of a fool
cuts off his own feet and [e]drinks violence.
7 Like a lame man's legs, which hang useless,
is a proverb in the mouth of fools.
8 Like one who binds the stone in the sling
is [f]one who gives honor to a fool.
9 Like [g]a thorn that goes up into the hand of a drunkard
is a proverb in the mouth of fools.

[1] Hebrew *or else* [2] The meaning of the Hebrew line is uncertain

8[w] Matt. 5:25; Luke 12:58; [ch. 17:14] **9**[x] Matt. 18:15 **11**[y] ch. 15:23; [Isa. 50:4] **12**[z] [Gen. 24:22] [a] ch. 15:31; 20:12 **13**[b] ch. 13:17 **14**[c] Jude 12 [d] ch. 20:6 **15**[e] ch. 15:1; 16:14; [Eccles. 10:4] **16**[f] [Judg. 14:8; 1 Sam. 14:25] [g] [ver. 27] **18**[h] [ch. 24:28] [i] ch. 12:18; See Ps. 57:4 **20**[j] [Rom. 12:15] **21**[k] Cited Rom. 12:20; [2 Kgs. 6:22; 2 Chr. 28:15]; See Ex. 23:4, 5 **22**[l] Ps. 140:10 **24**[m] ch. 21:9 **25**[n] [Ps. 42:2] [o] ch. 15:30 **26**[p] [Ezek. 32:2; 34:18, 19] **27**[q] [ver. 16] [r] [ch. 27:2] **28**[s] [ch. 16:32] [t] [2 Chr. 32:5; 36:19; Neh. 1:3] **Chapter 26** **1**[u] [1 Sam. 12:17] [v] [ver. 8] [w] ch. 17:7; 19:10 **2**[x] ch. 27:8; Ps. 84:3 [y] [Num. 23:8; Deut. 23:5; 2 Sam. 16:12] **3**[z] [Ps. 32:9] [a] See ch. 19:29 **4**[b] [2 Sam. 16:11; 2 Kgs. 18:36; Luke 23:9] **5**[c] See Matt. 16:1-4; 21:24-27 [d] ch. 28:11; [Rom. 12:16] **6**[e] [ch. 13:2; Job 15:16] **8**[f] [ver. 1] **9**[g] [ch. 23:35]

10 Like an archer who wounds everyone
is one who hires a passing fool or
drunkard.[1]
11 Like [h]a dog that returns to his vomit
is [i]a fool who repeats his folly.
12 Do you see a man who is [j]wise in his own
eyes?
[k]There is more hope for a fool than for
him.
13 [l]The sluggard says, "There is a lion in the
road!
There is a lion in the streets!"
14 As a door turns on its hinges,
so does a sluggard on his bed.
15 [m]The sluggard buries his hand in the
dish;
it wears him out to bring it back to his
mouth.
16 The sluggard is [j]wiser in his own eyes
[n]than seven men who can answer sen-
sibly.
17 Whoever meddles in a quarrel not his
own
is like one who takes a passing dog by
the ears.
18 Like a madman who throws [o]firebrands,
arrows, and death
19 is the man who deceives his neighbor
and says, "I am only joking!"
20 For lack of wood the fire goes out,
and where there is no [p]whisperer,
[q]quarreling ceases.
21 As charcoal to hot embers and wood to
fire,
so is [r]a quarrelsome man for kindling
strife.
22 [s]The words of [p]a whisperer are like delicious morsels;
they go down into the inner parts of
the body.
23 [t]Like the [u]glaze[2] covering an earthen vessel
are fervent lips with an evil heart.
24 Whoever hates disguises himself with
his lips
and harbors deceit in his heart;
25 [v]when he speaks graciously, believe him
not,
for there are [w]seven abominations in
his heart;
26 though his hatred be covered with
deception,
his wickedness will be exposed in the
assembly.
27 [x]Whoever digs a pit will fall into it,
and a stone will come back on him
who starts it rolling.
28 A lying tongue hates its victims,
and a flattering mouth works ruin.

27

Do not boast about tomorrow,
[y]for you do not know what a day
may bring.
2 Let [z]another praise you, and not your
own mouth;
a stranger, and not your own lips.
3 A stone is heavy, and sand is weighty,
but [a]a fool's provocation is heavier
than both.
4 Wrath is cruel, anger is overwhelming,
but who can stand before [b]jealousy?
5 [c]Better is open rebuke
than hidden love.
6 Faithful are [d]the wounds of a friend;
profuse are the kisses of an enemy.

[1] Or *hires a fool or passersby* [2] By revocalization; Hebrew *silver of dross*

27:4 *Emotions.* There is a good kind of jealousy, the opposite of indifference (Ex. 34:14). But this proverb is pondering a selfish and vindictive kind of jealousy. The proverb points out that the impact of wrath and anger can be hard to bear, but jealousy goes beyond both. Wrath and anger react to something that is wrong, but jealousy reacts to something that is right and good. Cain did not murder Abel because Abel had wronged him but because Abel had outshone him (1 John 3:12). It was jealousy that aroused the enemies of Jesus against him (Matt. 27:18). It was jealousy that moved the enemies of Jesus against Lazarus (John 12:9–11). The early church was persecuted out of jealousy (Acts 5:17–18; 13:44–45). Wrath and anger are irrational, but jealousy is calculating and therefore more sinister.

The gospel comforts us when we are mistreated in this way. It reminds us of the greater judgment of God (Prov. 24:19–20). Moreover, the gospel teaches us to look for, and humbly rejoice in, the overruling glory of God that culminates in Christ's victory, even when others are acting out of jealous motives (Phil. 1:12–18). Wisdom says, "He must increase, but I must decrease" (John 3:30).

11[h] Cited 2 Pet. 2:22 [i][Ex. 8:15]
12[j] ch. 28:11; [Rom. 12:16] [k] ch. 29:20
13[l] ch. 22:13
15[m] ch. 19:24
16[j] [See ver. 12 above] [n] [ver. 25; ch. 6:16]; See Job 5:19
18[o] [Isa. 50:11]
20[p] ch. 16:28 [q] ch. 22:10
21[r] See ch. 15:18
22[s] ch. 18:8 [p] [See ver. 20 above]
23[t] [Matt. 23:27; Luke 11:39] [u] See ch. 25:4
25[v] See Ps. 28:3 [w] [ver. 16]
27[x] [ch. 28:10]; See Ps. 7:15
Chapter 27
1[y] Luke 12:19, 20; James 4:13, 14
2[z] 2 Cor. 10:12, 18; [ch. 25:27; 2 Cor. 12:11]
3[a] [ch. 12:16; 17:12]
4[b] ch. 6:34
5[c] [ch. 28:23] **6**[d] Ps. 141:5

7 One who is full loathes [e]honey,
but to one who is hungry everything
bitter is sweet.
8 Like [f]a bird that strays from its nest
is a man who strays from his home.
9 [g]Oil and perfume make the heart glad,
and the sweetness of a friend comes
from his earnest counsel.[1]
10 Do not forsake your friend and [h]your
father's friend,
and do not go to your brother's house
in the day of your calamity.
[i]Better is a neighbor who is near
than a brother who is far away.
11 [j]Be wise, [k]my son, and [l]make my heart
glad,
that I may [m]answer him who
reproaches me.
12 [n]The prudent sees danger and hides himself,
but [o]the simple go on and suffer for it.
13 [p]Take a man's garment when he has put
up security for a stranger,
and hold it in pledge when he puts up
security for an adulteress.[2]
14 Whoever blesses his neighbor with a
loud voice,
rising early in the morning,
will be counted as cursing.
15 [q]A continual dripping on a rainy day
and a quarrelsome wife are alike;
16 to restrain her is to restrain the wind
or to grasp[3] oil in one's right hand.
17 Iron sharpens iron,
and one man sharpens another.[4]
18 [r]Whoever tends a fig tree will eat its
fruit,
and he who [s]guards his master will be
honored.
19 As in water face reflects face,
so the heart of man reflects the man.
20 [t]Sheol and Abaddon are [u]never satisfied,
and [v]never satisfied are the eyes of
man.
21 [w]The crucible is for silver, and the furnace
is for gold,
and a man is tested by his praise.
22 [x]Crush a fool in a mortar with a pestle
along with crushed grain,
yet his folly will not depart from him.
23 [y]Know well the condition of your flocks,
and [y]give attention to your herds,
24 for [z]riches do not last forever;
and does a crown endure to all generations?
25 [a]When the grass is gone and the new
growth appears
and the vegetation of the mountains
is gathered,
26 [b]the lambs will provide your clothing,
and the goats the price of a field.
27 [b]There will be enough goats' milk for
your food,
for the food of your household
and maintenance for your girls.

28

[c]The wicked flee when no one
pursues,
but [d]the righteous are bold as a lion.
2 When a land transgresses, [e]it has many
rulers,
but with a man of understanding and
knowledge,
its stability will long continue.
3 [f]A poor man who oppresses the poor
is a beating rain that leaves no food.
4 Those who forsake the law [g]praise the
wicked,
but those who keep the law [h]strive
against them.
5 Evil men [i]do not understand justice,
but those who seek the LORD [j]under-
stand it completely.
6 [k]Better is a poor man who [l]walks in his
integrity
than a rich man who is [l]crooked in his
ways.
7 The one who keeps the law is a son with
understanding,
but [m]a companion of gluttons shames
his father.
8 Whoever multiplies his wealth [n]by interest and profit[5]
[o]gathers it for him who is [p]generous to
the poor.

[1] Or *and so does the sweetness of a friend that comes from his earnest counsel* [2] Hebrew *a foreign woman*; a slight emendation yields (compare Vulgate; see also 20:16) *foreigners* [3] Hebrew *to meet with* [4] Hebrew *sharpens the face of another* [5] That is, profit that comes from charging interest to the poor

7[e] [ch. 25:16] **8**[f] ch. 26:2 **9**[g] [Ps. 23:5] **10**[h] See 1 Kgs. 12:6-8; 2 Chr. 10:6-8 [i] See ch. 17:17 **11**[j] ch. 6:6 [k] ch. 10:1; 23:15, 24 [l] See ch. 29:3 [m] Ps. 119:42; [Ps. 127:5] **12**[n] ch. 22:3 [o] See ch. 1:4 **13**[p] See ch. 20:16 **15**[q] ch. 19:13 **18**[r] Song 8:12; 1 Cor. 3:8; 9:7; 2 Tim. 2:6 [s] [Matt. 25:21] **20**[t] ch. 15:11; See Job 26:6 [u] ch. 30:15, 16; Hab. 2:5; [ch. 1:12] [v] Eccles. 1:8; 4:8 **21**[w] ch. 17:3 **22**[x] [ch. 23:35; Isa. 1:5; Jer. 5:3] **23**[y] [John 10:3, 14; Acts 20:28; 1 Pet. 5:2, 4] **24**[z] ch. 23:5 **25**[a] Ps. 37:2; 90:5, 6 **26**[b] [1 Tim. 6:8] **27**[b] [See ver. 26 above] **Chapter 28** **1**[c] Lev. 26:17; Ps. 53:5 [d] Lev. 26:8; 1 Sam. 17:32 **2**[e] [1 Kgs. 15:27]; See 1 Kgs. 16:8-28; 2 Kgs. 15:8-15 **3**[f] [Matt. 18:28] **4**[g] Ps. 10:3; Rom. 1:32 [h] [1 Kgs. 18:18, 21; Neh. 13:11, 15; Matt. 3:7; 14:4; Eph. 5:11] **5**[i] Ps. 92:6; [John 12:39, 40] [j] Ps. 119:100; [John 7:17; 1 Cor. 2:15; James 1:5; 1 John 2:20, 27] **6**[k] ch. 19:1 [l] ver. 18 **7**[m] [ch. 23:20; 29:3] **8**[n] Ex. 22:25; Lev. 25:36 [o] See Job 27:17 [p] ch. 14:31

9 If one turns away his ear from hearing
the law,
even his [q]prayer is an abomination.
10 Whoever misleads the upright into an
evil way
[r]will fall into his own pit,
but the blameless [s]will have a goodly
inheritance.
11 A rich man is wise in his [t]own eyes,
but a poor man who has understanding
[u]will find him out.
12 When [v]the righteous triumph, there is
great glory,
but when [w]the wicked rise, people
hide themselves.
13 Whoever [x]conceals his transgressions
will not prosper,
but he who [y]confesses and forsakes
them will obtain mercy.
14 Blessed is the one who [z]fears the LORD
always,
but whoever [a]hardens his heart will
fall into calamity.
15 Like [b]a roaring lion or [c]a charging bear
is [d]a wicked ruler over a poor people.
16 A ruler who [e]lacks understanding is a
cruel oppressor,
but he who hates unjust gain will
prolong his days.
17 If one is burdened with [f]the blood of
another,
he will be a fugitive until death;[1]
let no one help him.
18 [g]Whoever [h]walks in integrity will be
delivered,
but he who is crooked in his ways will
suddenly fall.
19 [i]Whoever works his land will have plenty
of bread,
but he who follows worthless pursuits
will have plenty of poverty.
20 A faithful man will abound with blessings,
but whoever hastens to be rich [j]will
not go unpunished.
21 To show [k]partiality is not good,
but for [l]a piece of bread a man will do
wrong.
22 A [m]stingy man[2] [n]hastens after wealth
and does not know that [o]poverty will
come upon him.
23 Whoever [p]rebukes a man will afterward
find more favor
than [q]he who flatters with his tongue.
24 Whoever robs his father or his mother
and says, "That is no transgression,"
is [r]a companion to a man who
destroys.
25 A greedy man [s]stirs up strife,
but the one who trusts in the LORD
will [t]be enriched.
26 Whoever [u]trusts in his own mind is a fool,
but he who walks in wisdom will be
delivered.
27 Whoever [v]gives to the poor will not want,
but he who [w]hides his eyes will get
many a curse.

[1] Hebrew *until the pit* [2] Hebrew *A man whose eye is evil*

28:25 *Work and money.* Our feelings about money make an impact on our relationships. A greedy man stirs up strife because of his unrestrained appetites, expectations, and demands. His heart is not contented with God's provision, so he oversteps his bounds with others, who are understandably offended (James 4:1–3). But the one who trusts in the Lord is not out for himself. His heart is given over to the Lord first and foremost. And he will be enriched, in the way Jesus promised (Matt. 6:33).

Greed spreads conflict, while generosity spreads friendship: "Whoever brings blessing will be enriched, and one who waters will himself be watered" (Prov. 11:25). Many investments are uncertain, and some will come to nothing. But godly generosity cannot fail to bless and be blessed—ultimately, and most wonderfully, with God himself (11:24; 19:17; 22:9; Matt. 25:40; Luke 16:9; 2 Cor. 9:6–11; 1 Tim. 6:17–19; Heb. 13:16). Every aspect of our new life in Christ, including generosity, grows by use and withers by neglect (Matt. 25:29).

How can we become less greedy and more generous? By the power of the gospel: "For you know the grace of our Lord Jesus Christ, that though he was rich, yet for your sake he became poor, so that you by his poverty might become rich" (2 Cor. 8:9). The most powerful motivation for generosity is not a threat or a demand but the grace of God made plain in Jesus. How can we be selfish, when he is so generous?

9[q] [Ps. 109:7]; See ch. 15:8
10[r] See Ps. 7:15 [s] [Matt. 6:33]
11[t] ch. 26:5, 16 [u] Job 13:9
12[v] ch. 11:10 [w] ver. 28; [ch. 29:2; Eccles. 10:5, 6]
13[x] [Job 31:33; Ps. 32:3]; See 1 John 1:8-10 [y] Ps. 32:5; 1 John 1:9
14[z] ch. 23:17; Isa. 66:2; Phil. 2:12 [a] See Ps. 95:8
15[b] ch. 19:12; 1 Pet. 5:8 [c] [2 Kgs. 2:24] [d] [Ex. 1:14, 16, 22; Matt. 2:16]
16[e] See ch. 6:32
17[f] [Gen. 9:6]
18[g] [ch. 3:23; 10:9] [h] ver. 6
19[i] ch. 12:11
20[j] ch. 16:5
21[k] See ch. 18:5 [l] Ezek. 13:19
22[m] See ch. 23:6 [n] [ver. 20] [o] ch. 22:16
23[p] ch. 27:5, 6 [q] ch. 29:5
24[r] [ch. 18:9]
25[s] See ch. 15:18 [t] ch. 11:25; 13:4
26[u] [1 Cor. 3:18]
27[v] [ch. 11:24]; See ch. 19:17 [w] [ch. 29:7]

28 When [x]the wicked rise, [y]people hide
themselves,
but when they perish, the righteous
increase.

29 [z]He who is often reproved, yet
stiffens his neck,
will suddenly be [a]broken [b]beyond
healing.
2 When [c]the righteous increase, the people
rejoice,
but when [d]the wicked rule, the people
groan.
3 He who [e]loves wisdom makes his father
glad,
but [f]a companion of prostitutes
[g]squanders his wealth.
4 By justice a king [h]builds up the land,
but he who exacts gifts[1] tears it down.
5 [i]A man who flatters his neighbor
spreads [j]a net for his feet.
6 An evil man is [k]ensnared in his transgression,
but a righteous man [l]sings and rejoices.
7 A righteous man [m]knows the rights of
the poor;
a wicked man does not [n]understand
such knowledge.
8 [o]Scoffers set a city aflame,
but the wise turn away wrath.
9 If a wise man has an argument with a
fool,
the fool only rages and laughs, and
there is [p]no quiet.
10 Bloodthirsty men [q]hate one who is
blameless
and seek the life of the upright.[2]
11 A fool gives full vent to his spirit,
but a wise man quietly holds it back.
12 If a ruler listens to falsehood,
all his officials will be wicked.
13 The poor man and the oppressor [r]meet
together;
the LORD [s]gives light to the eyes of
both.
14 If a king [t]faithfully judges the poor,
his throne will [u]be established forever.
15 [v]The rod and reproof give wisdom,
but a child left to himself [w]brings
shame to his mother.
16 When the wicked increase, transgression
increases,
but [x]the righteous will look upon
their downfall.
17 [y]Discipline your son, and he will give you
rest;
he will give delight to your heart.
18 Where [z]there is no prophetic vision the
people [a]cast off restraint,[3]
but blessed is he who [b]keeps the law.
19 By mere words a servant is not disciplined,
for though he understands, he will
not respond.
20 Do you see a man who is hasty in his
words?
[c]There is more hope for a fool than for
him.
21 Whoever pampers his servant from
childhood
will in the end find him his heir.[4]
22 [d]A man of wrath stirs up strife,
and one given to anger causes much
transgression.
23 [e]One's pride will bring him low,
[f]but he who is lowly in spirit will
obtain honor.

[1] Or *who taxes heavily* [2] Or *but the upright seek his soul* [3] Or *the people are discouraged* [4] The meaning of the Hebrew word rendered *his heir* is uncertain

29:23 *Humility.* The surprise of God's wisdom is that it outfoxes our own intuitive formulas for success. Pride feels smart, but is foolish (26:12). Inevitably, pride goes before a fall (16:18). "There is a way that seems right to a man, but its end is the way to death" (14:12; 16:25). This is so because in selfishness and impatience our pride overreaches. Pride even hastens judgment, because it scorns the saving Word of God (13:13). By contrast, "he who is lowly in spirit will obtain honor" (29:23). The lowly might be highly talented people, but they are teachable before the Lord (15:31–33).

This theme of humility-before-honor opens up the heart of the gospel. Jesus himself walked this path—first the cross, then the crown—and now he is giving us the privilege of following him there (1 Pet. 1:10–11; 4:12–13). Sometimes, when we are bearing the cross of humility, it can be heavy. That is when we can remember that the glorious crown of honor is coming to us just as surely as it came to Jesus himself.

28 [x]See ver. 12 [y]Job 24:4
Chapter 29
1 [z][1 Sam. 2:25]; See ch. 1:24-27 [a][Isa. 30:14; Jer. 19:11] [b]ch. 6:15
2 [c]ch. 11:10; 28:12, 28; [Esth. 8:15] [d][Esth. 3:15]
3 [e][ch. 10:1; 15:20; 27:11; 28:7] [f][ch. 5:9, 10; 6:26] [g]Luke 15:13, 30
4 [h][ver. 14; 2 Chr. 9:8]
5 [i]ch. 28:23 [j][Ps. 9:15]
6 [k][Eccles. 9:12] [l][Ex. 15:1, 21; Ps. 35:27]
7 [m]Job 29:16; Ps. 41:1 [n][ch. 28:27]
8 [o][ch. 11:11]
9 [p][Eccles. 4:6] **10** [q][Gen. 4:5, 8; 1 John 3:12] **13** [r][ch. 22:2] [s]Ps. 13:3; See Job 25:3 **14** [t][Ps. 72:4] [u][ver. 4]; See ch. 16:12 **15** [v]See ver. 17 [w]ch. 10:1; 17:25 **16** [x]Ps. 37:34, 36; 58:10; 91:8; 92:11 **17** [y]See ch. 13:24 **18** [z]1 Sam. 3:1; [2 Chr. 15:3; Ps. 74:9; Amos 8:11, 12] [a]Ex. 32:25 [b]Luke 11:28; John 13:17; James 1:25 **20** [c]ch. 26:12 **22** [d]See ch. 15:18 **23** [e]ch. 17:19; 2 Sam. 22:28; Matt. 23:12; James 4:6; See ch. 11:2 [f]ch. 15:33; 18:12

24 The partner of a thief [g]hates his own
life;
[h]he hears the curse, but discloses nothing.
25 [i]The fear of man lays a snare,
but whoever trusts in the LORD is safe.
26 Many [j]seek the face of a ruler,
but it is from the LORD that a man
[k]gets justice.
27 [l]An unjust man is an abomination to the
righteous,
but one whose way is straight is an
abomination to the wicked.

The Words of Agur

30 The words of Agur son of Jakeh. The oracle.[1]

The man declares, I am weary, O God;
I am weary, O God, and worn out.[2]
2 Surely I am too [m]stupid to be a man.
I have not the understanding of a man.
3 I have not learned wisdom,
nor have I knowledge of [n]the Holy One.
4 Who has [o]ascended to heaven and come
down?
Who has [p]gathered the wind in his
fists?
Who has [q]wrapped up the waters in a
garment?
Who has established all [r]the ends of
the earth?
[s]What is his name, and what is his son's
name?
Surely you know!

5 [t]Every word of God proves true;
he is [u]a shield to those who take refuge in him.
6 [v]Do not add to his words,
lest he rebuke you and you be found a
liar.
7 Two things I ask of you;
deny them not to me [w]before I die:
8 Remove far from me falsehood and
lying;
give me neither poverty nor riches;
feed me with the food that is [x]needful
for me,
9 lest I be [y]full and [z]deny you
and say, [a]"Who is the LORD?"
or lest I be poor and steal
[b]and profane the name of my God.

10 [c]Do not slander a servant to his master,
[d]lest he curse you, and you be held
guilty.

11 There are those[3] who [e]curse their fathers
and do not bless their mothers.
12 There are those who are [f]clean in their
own eyes
but are not washed of their filth.
13 There are those—how [g]lofty are their
eyes,
how high their eyelids lift!
14 There are those whose teeth are [h]swords,
whose [i]fangs are knives,
to [j]devour the poor from off the earth,
the needy from among mankind.

15 The leech has two daughters:
Give and Give.[4]
[k]Three things are never satisfied;
[k]four never say, "Enough":
16 [l]Sheol, [m]the barren womb,
the land never satisfied with water,
and the fire that never says, "Enough."

17 The eye that [n]mocks a father
and [o]scorns to obey a mother
will [p]be picked out by [q]the ravens of the
valley
and eaten by the vultures.

[1] Or *Jakeh, the man of Massa* [2] Revocalization; Hebrew *The man declares to Ithiel, to Ithiel and Ucal* [3] Hebrew *There is a generation*; also verses 12, 13, 14 [4] Or *"Give, give," they cry*

One of the practical ways we can walk in humility together is to confess our sins to one another: "Whoever conceals his transgressions will not prosper, but he who confesses and forsakes them will obtain mercy" (Prov. 28:13; cf. James 5:16). Rather than save face, we can humbly own up to our sins, because God has justified us by his grace as a gift (Rom. 3:24). The curse of the law's condemnation fell not on us but on Christ at the cross (Gal. 3:13). We are now free to be honest with God, and with one another, about our real problems. When we walk humbly together in this gospel light, we experience renewed fellowship and fresh cleansing (1 John 1:7). Truly, we will "obtain mercy."

24[g] See ch. 8:36 [h] See Lev. 5:1
25[i] Luke 12:4; [Gen. 12:12, 13; 20:2, 11; 26:7; John 12:42, 43]
26[j] ch. 19:6 [k] Isa. 49:4; 1 Cor. 4:4, 5
27[l] [2 Cor. 6:14]
Chapter 30
2[m] See Ps. 49:10
3[n] ch. 9:10
4[o] John 3:13 [p] [Isa. 40:12]; See Job 38:4-11; Ps. 104:3-6 [q] Job 26:8 [r] Ps. 22:27

[s] [Rev. 19:12] **5**[t] Ps. 12:6; 18:30 [u] See Ps. 3:3 **6**[v] Deut. 4:2; 12:32; [Rev. 22:18] **7**[w] Gen. 45:28 **8**[x] Job 23:12; Matt. 6:11; Luke 11:3 **9**[y] Deut. 8:12; 31:20; 32:15; Neh. 9:25; [ver. 22] [z] Josh. 24:27 [a] Ex. 5:2 [b] [Job 21:14, 15]; See Ex. 20:7 **10**[c] [Ps. 15:3; 101:5] [d] Eccles. 7:21 **11**[e] ch. 20:20; [ver. 17]; See Ex. 21:17 **12**[f] ch. 16:2; [Luke 18:11; Rev. 3:17] **13**[g] See Ps. 101:5 **14**[h] See Ps. 57:4 [i] Job 29:17 [j] See Ps. 14:4 **15**[k] ver. 18, 21, 29; [ch. 6:16] **16**[l] See ch. 27:20 [m] [Gen. 30:1] **17**[n] [ver. 11; Gen. 9:22] [o] [ch. 23:22] [p] [Num. 16:14] [q] [Jer. 16:4]

18 [k]Three things are [r]too wonderful for me;
[k]four I do not understand:
19 the way of an eagle in the sky,
the way of a serpent on a rock,
the way of a ship on the high seas,
and the way of a man with a virgin.

20 This is the way of an adulteress:
she eats and wipes her mouth
and says, "I have done no wrong."

21 Under [k]three things [s]the earth trembles;
under [k]four it cannot bear up:
22 [t]a slave when he becomes king,
and a fool when he is [u]filled with food;
23 [v]an unloved woman when she [w]gets a husband,
and a maidservant when she displaces her mistress.

24 [k]Four things on earth are small,
but they are exceedingly wise:
25 [x]the ants are a people not strong,
yet they provide their food in the summer;
26 [y]the rock badgers are a people not mighty,
yet they make their homes in the cliffs;
27 the locusts have no [z]king,
yet all of them march in [a]rank;
28 the lizard you can take in your hands,
yet it is in kings' palaces.

29 [b]Three things are stately in their tread;
[b]four are stately in their stride:
30 the lion, which is mightiest among beasts
and [c]does not turn back before any;
31 the [d]strutting rooster,[1] the he-goat,
and a king whose army is with him.[2]

32 If you have been foolish, exalting yourself,
or if you have been devising evil,
[e]put your hand on your mouth.
33 For pressing milk produces curds,
pressing the nose produces blood,
and pressing anger produces strife.

The Words of King Lemuel

31 The words of King Lemuel. An oracle that his mother taught him:

2 What are you doing, my son?[3] What are you doing, [f]son of my womb?
What are you doing, [g]son of my vows?
3 Do [h]not give your strength to women,
your ways to those [i]who destroy kings.
4 [j]It is not for kings, O Lemuel,
it is not for kings [k]to drink wine,
or for rulers to take [l]strong drink,
5 lest they drink and forget what has been decreed
and [m]pervert the rights of all the afflicted.
6 Give strong drink to the one who [n]is perishing,
and wine to [o]those in bitter distress;[4]
7 [p]let them drink and forget their poverty
and remember their misery no more.
8 [q]Open your mouth for the mute,
for the rights of all who are destitute.[5]
9 Open your mouth, [r]judge righteously,
[s]defend the rights of [t]the poor and needy.

The Woman Who Fears the LORD

10[6] [u]An excellent wife who can find?
She is far more precious than [v]jewels.
11 The heart of her husband trusts in her,
and he will have no lack of gain.

[1] Or *the magpie*, or *the greyhound*; Hebrew *girt-of-loins* [2] Or *against whom there is no rising up* [3] Hebrew *What, my son?* [4] Hebrew *those bitter in soul* [5] Hebrew *are sons of passing away* [6] Verses 10–31 are an acrostic poem, each verse beginning with the successive letters of the Hebrew alphabet

18[k] [See ver. 15 above] [r]See Job 42:3
21[k] [See ver. 15 above] [s]Joel 2:10; Amos 8:8
22[t] ch. 19:10 [u][ver. 9]
23[v] Deut. 21:15 [w][Isa. 54:1; 62:4]
24[k] [See ver. 15 above]
25[x] ch. 6:6-8
26[y] Lev. 11:5; Ps. 104:18
27[z] [ch. 6:7] [a][Joel 2:7, 8, 25]
29[b] ver. 15, 18, 21; [ch. 6:16]
30[c] [Job 39:22]
31[d] [Job 40:16]

31:10–31 *Family.* The book of Proverbs concludes with a family scene both impressive and heartwarming. At the center of this ideal family is a strong woman of wide-ranging capabilities, fully involved in the challenges of life. The glowingly positive message here is that "a woman who fears the LORD is to be praised" (v. 30). The word "praise" occurs three times in verses 28–31, setting an overall tone of encouragement in this home. The children rise up in respect and speak well of their mother (v. 28). The husband, never a faultfinder, gently praises her for her outstanding qualities (v. 28). This remarkable woman gives herself diligently to her family and her community (vv. 10–27), and her family communicates how they admire her (vv. 28–31). This wise family sees through the false glories that inevitably disappoint: "Charm is deceitful,

32[e] Mic. 7:16; See Job 21:5 **Chapter 31** **2**[f] Isa. 49:15 [g][1 Sam. 1:27] **3**[h] [ch. 5:9] [i][ch. 7:26; Deut. 17:17; 1 Kgs. 11:1; Neh. 13:26] **4**[j] Eccles. 10:17; [1 Kgs. 16:9; 20:16] [k][Hos. 4:11] [l]ch. 20:1 **5**[m] [Isa. 5:22, 23] **6**[n] Job 29:13 [o]Job 3:20 **7**[p] [Ps. 104:15] **8**[q] Job 29:12, 15, 16; [Isa. 1:17] **9**[r] Lev. 19:15; Deut. 1:16 [s]Jer. 22:16; [Isa. 1:17] [t]ver. 20; Ps. 40:17; 86:1 **10**[u] ch. 12:4; Ruth 3:11; [ch. 18:22; 19:14] [v]Job 28:18

12 She does him good, and not harm,
all the days of her life.
13 She [w]seeks wool and flax,
and works with willing hands.
14 She is like the ships of the merchant;
she brings her food from afar.
15 She [x]rises while it is yet night
and [y]provides food for her household
and portions for her maidens.
16 She considers a field and buys it;
with the fruit of her hands she plants
a vineyard.
17 She [z]dresses herself[1] with strength
and makes her arms strong.
18 She perceives that her merchandise is
profitable.
Her lamp does not go out at night.
19 She puts her hands to the distaff,
and her hands hold the spindle.
20 She [a]opens her hand to [b]the poor
and reaches out her hands to [b]the
needy.
21 She is not afraid of snow for her household,
for all her household are clothed in
[c]scarlet.[2]
22 She makes [d]bed coverings for herself;
her clothing is [e]fine linen and [f]purple.
23 Her husband is known in [g]the gates
when he sits among the elders of the
land.
24 She makes [h]linen garments and sells
them;
she delivers sashes to the merchant.
25 [i]Strength and dignity are her clothing,
and she laughs at the time to come.
26 She opens her mouth with wisdom,
and the teaching of kindness is on her
tongue.
27 She looks well to the ways of her household
and does not eat the bread of idleness.
28 Her children rise up and call her blessed;
her husband also, and he praises her:
29 "Many [j]women have done [k]excellently,
but you surpass them all."
30 [l]Charm is deceitful, and beauty is vain,
but a woman who fears the LORD is to
be praised.
31 Give her of the fruit of her hands,
and let her works praise her in the
gates.

[1] Hebrew *She girds her loins* [2] Or *in double thickness*

and beauty is vain" (v. 30). Their mother, who "has devoted herself to every good work" (1 Tim. 5:10), embodies the godly wisdom of her entire family.

Clearly, the life of wisdom is not just for men, but for all. It is not just for Sunday, but for every aspect of life. It is not austere and grim, but attractive with a sincere enjoyment that flows from one human heart to another. Best of all, the life of wisdom will matter forever. When we are with the Lord in heaven above, we will find that our deeds will have followed us, transformed by his grace into eternal blessing (Rev. 14:13).

But "who is sufficient for these things?" (2 Cor. 2:16). We are not. Even the "excellent wife" of Proverbs 31 is not sufficient in herself, but she "fears the LORD" (v. 30). Her ultimate regard is not for her beauty, goodness, or accomplishment, but for the One who provides for her every need and loved one (cf. the section on 1:7 in the note on 1:1–7). We are prepared by such an example to remember that God must make us sufficient for what we face and for what he requires. Ultimately, in Christ, he does so. What he commands, he also gives. Therefore, we may receive his counsels in the book of Proverbs with this wonderful assurance: "Not that we are sufficient in ourselves to claim anything as coming from us, but our sufficiency is from God" (2 Cor. 3:5).

13[w] [ver. 21, 22, 24]
15[x] [ch. 20:13] [y] Luke 12:42; [Ps. 111:5]
17[z] [ver. 25]
20[a] [Rom. 12:13; Eph. 4:28] [b] [ver. 9]
21[c] 2 Sam. 1:24
22[d] ch. 7:16 [e] Gen. 41:42; Rev. 19:8, 14 [f] Judg. 8:26
23[g] See Ruth 4:1, 2
24[h] Judg. 14:12; Isa. 3:23
25[i] [ver. 17]
29[j] Song 6:9 [k] [ver. 10]
30[l] [ch. 11:16]

Introduction to Ecclesiastes

Author

The author of Ecclesiastes calls himself "the Preacher" (1:1). Some interpreters have concluded that this was Solomon, while others think he was a writer later than Solomon. Either way, the book claims that its wisdom comes from the "one Shepherd" (12:11), the Lord himself.

The Gospel in Ecclesiastes

Jesus taught us to read our Bibles with him in mind—"everything written about *me* in the Law of Moses and the Prophets and the Psalms" (Luke 24:44). Even "the Psalms" or "the Writings," which include Ecclesiastes, bear witness to him (John 5:39) and can "make [us] *wise* for salvation" (2 Tim. 3:15). For the Christian, what Jesus taught in John 15:10–11 is an excellent summary of the wisdom of Ecclesiastes: "If you keep my commandments, you will abide in my love, just as I have kept my Father's commandments and abide in his love. These things I have spoken to you, that my joy may be in you, and that your joy may be full."

Our search for eternal life, rest, joy, and justice moves us beyond the creation's subjection to futility (the frequent subject of Ecclesiastes) *to Christ* (Rom. 8:20). The movement to Christ is not by direct statement but by the words of this "son of David" (Eccles. 1:1), revealing the futility of everything that is not of God. Throughout Ecclesiastes we are led forward to other answers, other solutions, and other wisdom than the world's vain promises of satisfaction, happiness, and fulfillment. Our eyes are constantly taken heavenward for God's ultimate and eternal provision of which Christ becomes the ultimate revelation (2 Cor. 4:6; Eph. 1:17). He is the world's supreme sage (e.g., Matt. 7:24–27; 28:20a) as well as the ultimate embodiment and demonstration of the "wisdom of God" (1 Cor. 1:24, 30; Col. 2:3).

Outline

I. Introduction and Theme (1:1–3)
II. First Catalog of "Vanities" (1:4–2:26)
III. Poem: A Time for Everything (3:1–8)
IV. Fear God, the Sovereign One (3:9–15)
V. Second Catalog of "Vanities" (3:16–4:16)
VI. Fear God, the Holy and Righteous One (5:1–7)
VII. Life "Under the Sun" (5:8–7:24)
VIII. The Heart of the Problem: Sin (7:25–29)
IX. More on Life "Under the Sun" (8:1–12:7)
X. Final Conclusion and Epilogue (12:8–14)

Ecclesiastes

All Is Vanity

1 The words of [a]the Preacher,[1] the son of David, [b]king in Jerusalem.

2 [c]Vanity[2] of vanities, says [a]the Preacher,
[c]vanity of vanities! [d]All is vanity.
3 [e]What [f]does man gain by all the toil
at which he toils under the sun?
4 A generation goes, and a generation comes,
but [g]the earth remains forever.
5 [h]The sun rises, and the sun goes down,
and hastens[3] to the place where it rises.
6 [i]The wind blows to the south
and goes around to the north;
around and around goes the wind,
and on its circuits the wind returns.
7 All [j]streams run to the sea,
but the sea is not full;
to the place where the streams flow,
there they flow again.
8 All things are full of weariness;
a man cannot utter it;
[k]the eye is not satisfied with seeing,
nor the ear filled with hearing.
9 [l]What has been is what will be,
and what has been done is what will be done,
and there is nothing new under the sun.
10 Is there a thing of which it is said,
"See, this is new"?
It has been [m]already
in the ages before us.
11 There is no [n]remembrance of former things,[4]
nor will there be any remembrance
of later things[5] yet to be
among those who come after.

The Vanity of Wisdom

12 I [o]the Preacher have been king over Israel
in Jerusalem. 13 And I [p]applied my heart[6] to
seek and to search out by wisdom all that is
done under heaven. It is an unhappy [q]business
that God has given to the children of man to
be busy with. 14 I have seen everything that is

[1] Or *Convener*, or *Collector*; Hebrew *Qoheleth* (so throughout Ecclesiastes) [2] The Hebrew term *hebel*, translated *vanity* or *vain*, refers concretely to a "mist," "vapor," or "mere breath," and metaphorically to something that is fleeting or elusive (with different nuances depending on the context). It appears five times in this verse and in 29 other verses in Ecclesiastes [3] Or *and returns panting* [4] Or *former people* [5] Or *later people* [6] The Hebrew term denotes the center of one's inner life, including mind, will, and emotions

1:2–11 Due to the tyranny of time that erodes and replaces all that distinguishes human accomplishment, our work can be summarized as "nothing new" (v. 9) and nothing remembered. This blanket observation of the futility of human accomplishment makes the heart long for the stark contrast of Jesus' work for, in, and through us that is new and will forever be remembered. When we come to believe in Jesus—partaking of the new covenant that gives new birth, new life, and a new commandment—we enter into a new workforce. Now, what we do matters, as it is done for the sake of the gospel and the glory of God (e.g., Matt. 25:40; 26:10–13). Our labor is not in vain (Psalm 112; 1 Cor. 15:58).

"Vanity of vanities. . . . All is vanity" (Eccles. 1:2; 12:8). True—unless we work "as to the Lord" (Eph. 5:22; 6:7), united to his Son (1 Cor. 15:58; Gal. 2:20).

1:14 Ecclesiastes was written to depress us into dependence on our joyous God and his blessed will for our lives. If we are attempting to live the "meaningful" secular life—a life "under the sun" without reference to God—we are attempting to grasp the unattainable. We are "striving after wind." The only remedy to meaninglessness and

Chapter 1
1[a] ver. 12; ch. 7:27; 12:8-10 [b] ver. 12
2[c] ch. 12:8 [a] [See ver. 1 above] [d] [Rom. 8:20]
3[e] ver. 14; Ps. 144:4; See Job 7:16; Ps. 39:5 [f] ch. 2:11, 22; 3:9; 5:16
4[g] Ps. 104:5; 119:90
5[h] [Ps. 19:4-6]
6[i] [ch. 11:5; John 3:8]
7[j] Ps. 104:8, 9
8[k] ch. 4:8; Prov. 27:20
9[l] ch. 3:15; 6:10; [ch. 2:12]
10[m] ch. 3:15
11[n] ch. 2:16; See ch. 9:5
12[o] ver. 1
13[p] ver. 17; [1 Kgs. 4:33] [q] ch. 2:23, 26; 3:10; [Gen. 3:19]

done under the sun, and behold, all is [r]vanity[1]
and a striving after wind.[2]

15 [s]What is crooked cannot be made straight,
and what is lacking cannot be counted.

16 I said in my heart, "I have acquired great
[t]wisdom, surpassing all who were over
Jerusalem before me, and my heart has had
great experience of wisdom and knowledge."
17 And I [u]applied my heart to know wisdom
and to know [v]madness and folly. I perceived
that this also is but [r]a striving after wind.

18 For [w]in much wisdom is much vexation,
and he who increases knowledge
increases sorrow.

The Vanity of Self-Indulgence

2 I [x]said in my heart, "Come now, I will
test you with pleasure; enjoy yourself."
But behold, this also was vanity.[3] 2 I [y]said of
laughter, "It is mad," and of pleasure, "What
use is it?" 3 I [z]searched with my heart how to
cheer my body with wine—my heart still
guiding me with wisdom—and how to lay
hold on [a]folly, till I might see what was good
for the children of man to do under heaven
during the few days of their life. 4 I made great
works. I [b]built houses and planted [c]vineyards
for myself. 5 I made myself [d]gardens and parks,
and planted in them all kinds of fruit trees.
6 I made myself pools from which to water
the forest of growing trees. 7 I bought male
and female slaves, and had [e]slaves who were
born in my house. I had also great possessions
of [f]herds and flocks, more than any who had
been before me in Jerusalem. 8 I also gathered
for myself silver and [g]gold and the treasure
of [h]kings and [i]provinces. I got [j]singers, both
men and women, and many [k]concubines,[4] the
delight of the sons of man.
9 So I became great and [l]surpassed all who
were before me in Jerusalem. Also my [l]wis-
dom remained with me. 10 And whatever my
eyes desired I did not keep from them. I kept
my heart from no pleasure, for my heart
[m]found pleasure in all my toil, and this was
my [n]reward for all my toil. 11 Then I considered
all that my hands had done and the toil I had
expended in doing it, and behold, all was [o]van-
ity and a striving after wind, and there was
nothing [p]to be gained under the sun.

The Vanity of Living Wisely

12 [q]So I turned to consider [r]wisdom and madness and folly. For what can the man do who
comes after the king? Only [s]what has already
been done. 13 Then I saw that there is more
gain in wisdom than in folly, as there is more
gain in light than in darkness. 14 [t]The wise
person has his eyes in his head, but the fool
walks in darkness. And yet I perceived that
the [u]same event happens to all of them. 15 Then
I said in my heart, [v]"What happens to the fool
will happen to me also. Why then have I been
so very wise?" And I said in my heart that this
also is vanity. 16 For of the wise as of the fool
there is [w]no enduring remembrance, seeing
that in the days to come all will have been long

[1] The Hebrew term *hebel* can refer to a "vapor" or "mere breath" (see note on 1:2) [2] Or *a feeding on wind*; compare Hosea 12:1 (also in Ecclesiastes 1:17; 2:11, 17, 26; 4:4, 6, 16; 6:9) [3] The Hebrew term *hebel* can refer to a "vapor" or "mere breath"; also verses 11, 15, 17, 19, 21, 23, 26 (see note on 1:2) [4] The meaning of the Hebrew word is uncertain

14 [r]ver. 2; ch. 2:11, 17, 26; 4:4; 6:9
15 [s]See ch. 7:13
16 [t]ch. 2:9; [1 Kgs. 3:12, 13; 4:30; 10:7, 23]
17 [u]ver. 13; [ch. 2:3, 12; 7:23, 25] [v]ch. 9:3 [r][See ver. 14 above]
18 [w][ch. 12:12]
Chapter 2
1 [x]Luke 12:19
2 [y][Prov. 14:13]
3 [z][ch. 1:17] [a]ch. 7:25
4 [b]See 1 Kgs. 7:1-12 [c]Song 8:11
5 [d]Song 4:16; 5:1
7 [e]Gen. 14:14; 15:3 [f][1 Kgs. 4:23]
8 [g]1 Kgs. 9:28; 10:10, 14, 21 [h][1 Kgs. 4:21; 10:15] [i]1 Kgs. 20:14; Ezek. 19:8 [j]2 Sam. 19:35; 2 Chr. 35:25 [k]1 Kgs. 11:3
9 [l]1 Chr. 29:25; See ch. 1:16
10 [m][Prov. 8:31] [n]ch. 3:22; 5:18; 9:9
11 [o]See ch. 1:14 [p]See ch. 1:3

the depression caused by a godless life *is God*. In reference to himself, Jesus taught, "whoever would save his life will lose it, but whoever loses his life for my sake and the gospel's will save it. For what does it profit a man to gain the whole world and forfeit his soul?" (Mark 8:35–36).

2:1–11 In contrast to this king's self-indulgence that reflects the natural inclination of the human heart when unchecked (1:1; 2:1–11), Jesus taught and embodied self-denial and loving service to others (John 13:3–14). Through the greatest act of humility, Jesus took the punishment for all our vainglorious desires and ungodly pleasures, so that through faith in this gospel (Phil. 1:27), we might clothe ourselves with all humility (Col. 3:12), die to sin, and live to righteousness (1 Pet. 2:24).

2:16 The despair in Ecclesiastes is due to God's curse on creation, which most notably includes the reality of death. We are to be reminded that "The wages of sin is death" (cf. Gen. 2:17; Rom. 6:23a). Through Christ's death and resurrection, we also know that death has lost its "sting," that we have "victory through our Lord Jesus Christ," that our "labor is not in vain" (1 Cor. 15:55–58), and that someday Jesus, as Creator of all, will reconcile us to God (Col. 1:15–20), reversing completely the curses of the

12 [q]ch. 7:25 [r]See ch. 1:17 [s]ch. 1:9, 10 **14** [t][Prov. 17:24] [u]ch. 3:19; 9:2, 3; Ps. 49:10 **15** [v][ver. 16; ch. 6:8] **16** [w]ch. 1:11; See ch. 9:5

forgotten. [x]How the wise dies just like the fool!
17 So I hated life, because what is done under
the sun was grievous to me, for [o]all is vanity
and a striving after wind.

The Vanity of Toil

18 I hated [y]all my toil in which I toil under
the sun, seeing that I must [z]leave it to the man
who will come after me, 19 and who knows
whether he will be wise or a fool? Yet he will
be master of all for which I toiled and used
my wisdom under the sun. This also is vanity.
20 So I [a]turned about and gave my heart up to
despair [b]over all the toil of my labors under
the sun, 21 because sometimes a person who has
toiled with wisdom and knowledge and skill
must leave everything to be enjoyed by someone who did not toil for it. This also is vanity
and a great evil. 22 What has a man from [c]all the
toil and striving of heart with which he toils
beneath the sun? 23 For [d]all his days are full of
sorrow, and his [e]work is a vexation. Even in the
night his heart does not rest. This also is vanity.
24 [f]There is nothing better for a person than
that he should [g]eat and drink and find enjoyment[1] in his toil. This also, I saw, is [h]from the
hand of God, 25 for apart from him[2] who can
eat or who can have enjoyment? 26 For to the
one who pleases him [i]God has given wisdom
and knowledge and joy, but to the sinner he
has given [e]the business of gathering and collecting, [j]only to give to one who pleases God.
[k]This also is vanity and a striving after wind.

A Time for Everything

3 For everything there is a season, and [l]a
time for every matter under heaven:

2 a time to be born, and a time to [m]die;
a time to plant, and a time to pluck up
what is planted;
3 a time to kill, and a time to heal;
a time to break down, and a time to
build up;
4 a time to [n]weep, and a time to laugh;
a time to mourn, and a time to [o]dance;
5 a time to [p]cast away stones, and a time to
[q]gather stones together;
a time to embrace, and a time to [r]refrain
from embracing;
6 a time to seek, and a time to [s]lose;
a time to keep, and a time to [t]cast away;
7 a time to [u]tear, and a time to sew;
a time to [v]keep silence, and a time to
speak;
8 a time to love, and a time to [w]hate;
a time for war, and a time for peace.

The God-Given Task

9 What [x]gain has the worker from his toil? 10 I
have seen [y]the business that [z]God has given to
the children of man to be busy with. 11 He has
[a]made everything beautiful in its time. Also,
he has put eternity into man's heart, yet so
that he cannot [b]find out what God has done
from the beginning to the end. 12 I perceived
that there is [c]nothing better for them than to
be joyful and to [d]do good as long as they live;
13 also [e]that everyone should eat and drink and
take pleasure in all his toil—this is [f]God's gift
to man.

14 I perceived that whatever God does endures
forever; [g]nothing can be added to it, nor anything taken from it. God has done it, so that
people fear before him. 15 That which is, [h]already

[1] Or *and make his soul see good* [2] Some Hebrew manuscripts, Septuagint, Syriac; most Hebrew manuscripts *apart from me*

fall (Rom. 8:19–22). Thus we affirm with Paul, "to die is gain" (Phil. 1:21; cf. 2 Cor. 5:2), because, as Jesus said, "whoever believes in [him], though he die, yet shall he live" (John 11:25; cf. Rom. 6:23b).

2:24–26a If we neglect God in our pursuit of joy, everything good in life—e.g., health, possessions, sensual pleasures—slips through our grasp or fails to satisfy. But if we see that what we have is God's provision and give "thanks to God the Father"—ultimately through Christ (Col. 3:17)—for all his gifts, then whatever we receive from him is seen as a gift that brings true joy—joy in God. In Jesus' words, "Blessed are those who hunger and thirst for righteousness, for they shall be satisfied" (Matt. 5:6).

3:1–15 These verses remind us that while God's timing is not always ours, it is always best and sufficient for all that must occur in this fallen world. We are not necessarily faithless or cursed because at times we face the vagaries of this life. Rather we face all that we must with the understanding that the God of grace will time all things as

16[x] See ver. 14
17[o] [See ver. 11 above]
18[y] ch. 1:3 [z] Ps. 39:6; 49:10
20[a] ch. 7:25 [b] ch. 1:3
22[c] See ch. 1:3
23[d] Job 5:7; 14:1 [e] See ch. 1:13
24[f] ch. 3:12, 13, 22; 5:18; 8:15; [1 Tim. 6:17] [g] [ch. 9:7; Luke 12:19; 1 Cor. 15:32] [h] [ch. 3:13; 5:19]
26[i] Job 32:8 [e] [See ver. 7 above] [j] [Job 27:16, 17; Prov. 13:22] [k] See ch. 1:14

Chapter 3
1[l] ver. 17; ch. 8:6
2[m] Heb. 9:27
4[n] [Rom. 12:15] [o] [2 Sam. 6:14]; See Ex. 15:20
5[p] [2 Kgs. 3:25] [q] [Isa. 5:2] [r] [Joel 2:16]
6[s] [Matt. 10:39] [t] [Prov. 11:24]
7[u] See Gen. 37:29 [v] Amos 5:13

8[w] [Luke 14:26] **9**[x] See ch. 1:3 **10**[y] See ch. 1:13 [z] See Gen. 3:17-19 **11**[a] [Gen. 1:31] [b] ch. 8:17; [Job 5:9; Rom. 11:33] **12**[c] [ver. 22] [d] Ps. 34:14; 37:3 **13**[e] See ch. 2:24 [f] [ch. 2:24; 5:19] **14**[g] [James 1:17] **15**[h] [ch. 1:9]

has been; that which is to be, already has been;
and God [i]seeks what has been driven away.[1]

From Dust to Dust

16 Moreover, [j]I saw under the sun that in the
place of justice, even [k]there was wickedness,
and in the place of righteousness, even there
was wickedness. 17 I said in my heart, [l]God will
judge the righteous and the wicked, for there
is [m]a time for every matter and for every work.
18 I said in my heart with regard to the children
of man that God is testing them that they may
see that they themselves are but [n]beasts. 19 [o]For
what happens to the children of man and
what happens to the beasts is the same; as one
dies, so dies the other. They all have the same
breath, and man has no advantage over the
beasts, for all is vanity.[2] 20 All go to one place.
All are from [p]the dust, and to dust all return.
21 Who knows whether [q]the spirit of man goes
upward and the spirit of the beast goes down
into the earth? 22 So I saw that there is [r]nothing
better than that a man should rejoice in his
work, for [s]that is his lot. Who can bring him
to see [t]what will be after him?

Evil Under the Sun

4 [u]Again I [v]saw all [w]the oppressions that
are done under the sun. And behold, the
tears of the oppressed, and they had [x]no one
to comfort them! On the side of their oppressors there was power, and there was no one to
comfort them. 2 And I [y]thought the dead who
are already dead more fortunate than the living who are still alive. 3 But [z]better than both
is he who has not yet been and has not seen the
evil deeds that are done under the sun.

4 Then I saw that all toil and all skill in work
come from a man's envy of his neighbor. This
also is [a]vanity[3] and a striving after wind.

5 The fool [b]folds his hands and [c]eats his own
flesh.

6 [d]Better is a handful of [e]quietness than two
hands full of toil and a striving after wind.

7 [u]Again, I saw vanity under the sun: 8 one
person who has no other, either son or brother,
yet there is no end to all his toil, and his [f]eyes
are never satisfied with riches, so that he never
asks, [g]"For whom am I toiling and depriving
myself of pleasure?" This also is vanity and an
unhappy [h]business.

9 Two are better than one, because they have
a good reward for their toil. 10 For if they fall,
one will lift up his fellow. But woe to him who
is alone when he falls and has not another to
lift him up! 11 Again, if two lie together, they
keep warm, [i]but how can one keep warm
alone? 12 And though a man might prevail
against one who is alone, two will withstand
him—a threefold cord is not quickly broken.

13 Better was [j]a poor and wise youth than an
old and foolish king who no longer knew how
[k]to take advice. 14 For he went [l]from prison to

[1] Hebrew *what has been pursued* [2] The Hebrew term *hebel* can refer to a "vapor" or "mere breath" (see note on 1:2) [3] The Hebrew term *hebel* can refer to a "vapor" or "mere breath"; also verses 7, 8, 16 (see note on 1:2)

15 [i] [ch. 12:14]
16 [j] ch. 4:1 [k] ch. 5:8; [ch. 4:1]
17 [l] Matt. 16:27; 2 Cor. 5:10; See Rom. 2:6-11; 2 Thess. 1:6-10 [m] ver. 1; ch. 8:6
18 [n] Ps. 49:12, 20; 73:22
19 [o] See ch. 2:14
20 [p] ch. 12:7; Gen. 3:19
21 [q] [ch. 12:7]
22 [r] See ch. 2:24 [s] See ch. 2:10 [t] ch. 2:19; 6:12; 8:7; 10:14
Chapter 4
1 [u] ch. 9:11 [v] ch. 3:16 [w] ch. 5:8; Job 35:9 [x] Lam. 1:2
2 [y] See Job 3:11-26
3 [z] ch. 6:3
4 [a] See ch. 1:14
5 [b] Prov. 6:10; 24:33 [c] [Isa. 9:20]
6 [d] See Prov. 15:16 [e] ch. 6:5
7 [u] [See ver. 1 above]
8 [f] ch. 1:8; [Prov. 27:20; 1 John 2:16] [g] ch. 2:18; Ps. 39:6 [h] See ch. 1:13
11 [i] See 1 Kgs. 1:1-4
13 [j] [ch. 9:15, 16] [k] [Prov. 12:15]
14 [l] See Gen. 41:14, 41-43

he knows is best. Jesus would also come in "the fullness of time" (Gal. 4:4–5) to fulfill God's perfectly timed plan of salvation (Mark 1:15; John 7:30; 13:1; cf. Rom. 5:6). For Christians, the purpose of time is "to be conformed to the image of his Son" (Rom. 8:29). Such conformity even rejoices in sufferings, knowing that all the moments of our lives "work together" for our good (Rom. 8:28).

3:16–17 Ecclesiastes contains passages that despair over injustice (1:15; 3:16; 4:1–3; 5:8; 7:15–18; 8:14; 9:11), reminding us that this world, as it is, will not provide all that is needed to satisfy, correct, or justify. God must ultimately be the one to vindicate the righteous as well as punish the guilty, because we cannot finally depend on the justice of earthly judgments. As Jesus entrusted himself "to him who judges justly," so we must "follow in his steps" (1 Pet. 2:19–23), longing for "when his glory is revealed" (4:13), and when, as the final judge, he will right every wrong (e.g., John 5:22; 1 Cor. 4:4–5; 1 Pet. 4:5).

4:12 This verse and those surrounding remind us of our need for relationships in a world where no earthly relationships are sure. Such verses reminds us that our Savior willingly identified with us in the loneliness of his passion: He was forsaken by Israel, by the Twelve, and even, in some inexplicable way, by the Father—"My God, my God, why have you forsaken me?" (Matt. 27:46). These same verses remind us of the preciousness of the Savior's promise never to leave or forsake us (Heb. 13:5). They also remind us of the Christian's necessity of fellowship—for church discipline (Matt. 18:15–20), mission (Mark 6:7), and perseverance (Heb. 10:25).

the throne, though in his own kingdom he
had been born poor. 15 I saw all the living who
move about under the sun, along with that[1]
youth who was to stand in the king's[2] place.
16 There was no end of all the people, all of
whom he led. Yet those who come later will
not rejoice in him. Surely this also is [m]vanity
and a striving after wind.

Fear God

5 [3] [n]Guard your steps when you go to [o]the
house of God. To draw near to listen is
better than to [p]offer the sacrifice of fools, for
they do not know that they are doing evil. 2 [4] Be
not rash with your mouth, nor let your heart
be hasty to utter a word before God, for God
is in heaven and you are on earth. Therefore
[q]let your words be few. 3 For a dream comes
with much business, and a fool's voice with
[r]many words.
4 When [s]you vow a vow to God, [t]do not delay
paying it, for he has no pleasure in fools. [u]Pay
what you vow. 5 [v]It is better that you should
not vow than that you should vow and not
pay. 6 Let not your mouth lead you[5] into sin,
and do not say before [w]the messenger[6] that
it was [x]a mistake. Why should God be angry
at your voice and destroy the work of your
hands? 7 For when dreams increase and words
grow many, there is vanity;[7] but[8] [y]God is the
one you must fear.

The Vanity of Wealth and Honor

8 [z]If you see in a province the oppression of
the poor and the violation of justice and righteousness, [a]do not be amazed at the matter,
[b]for the high official is watched by a higher,
and there are yet higher ones over them. 9 But
this is gain for a land in every way: a king committed to cultivated fields.[9]
10 He who loves money will not be satisfied
with money, nor he who loves wealth with
his income; this also is vanity. 11 When goods
increase, they increase who eat them, and what
advantage has their owner but to see them
with his eyes? 12 Sweet is the sleep of a laborer,
whether he eats little or much, but the full
stomach of the rich will not let him sleep.
13 [c]There is a grievous evil that I have seen
under the sun: riches were kept by their owner
to his hurt, 14 and those riches were lost in a
bad venture. And he is father of a son, but he

[1] Hebrew *the second* [2] Hebrew *his* [3] Ch 4:17 in Hebrew [4] Ch 5:1 in Hebrew [5] Hebrew *your flesh* [6] Or *angel* [7] The Hebrew term *hebel* can refer to a "vapor" or "mere breath"; also verse 10 (see note on 1:2) [8] Or *For when dreams and vanities increase, words also grow many; but* [9] The meaning of the Hebrew verse is uncertain

16 [m] See ch. 1:14

Chapter 5

1 [n] [Ex. 3:5; Isa. 1:12] [o] [Gen. 28:17] [p] Prov. 15:8; See 1 Sam. 15:22
2 [q] [Matt. 6:7]
3 [r] Prov. 10:19; [Job 11:2]
4 [s] Num. 30:2 [t] Deut. 23:21; Ps. 50:14; 76:11 [u] [Ps. 66:13, 14]
5 [v] [Prov. 20:25; Acts 5:4]
6 [w] [1 Cor. 11:10] [x] ch. 10:5; Num. 15:25, 26
7 [y] ch. 12:13
8 [z] ch. 3:16; 4:1 [a] [1 Pet. 4:12] [b] [Ps. 12:5; 58:11; 82:1]
13 [c] ch. 6:1

5:1–7 Because life and all that is needed for it are from the Lord, we should be in a constant attitude of humility before him: in worship, listening to his Word; in obligations, quick to obey him; in planning, speaking, and dreaming of what we will do with our lives, ready to honor him. While our public worship should be celebratory—especially on the Lord's Day as we celebrate Christ's resurrection!—nevertheless, "acceptable worship" is filled with "reverence and awe" (Heb. 12:28) as well as humility before the holiness of the exalted Lord and Lamb (Revelation 4–5).

5:1a Mention of "the house of God" (i.e., the temple) reminds us of Jesus' judgment (Matt. 21:13; 23:38; 24:2) and replacement (Matt. 12:6; 26:61; 27:40, 51) of the temple. Christ is the final temple. He is that toward which the temple buildings always pointed. In him we meet with God, a communion that the temple was created to facilitate. Through Jesus' death, we have a perfect and permanent sacrifice and intercessor for our sins (Heb. 7:23–28), as well as the gift of the Spirit who dwells within all (Eph. 2:13–22) who worship God in Spirit and in truth (John 4:23–24).

5:1b For an illustration of "the sacrifice of fools," see Jesus' parable in Luke 18:9–14.

5:2 The admonition to "let your words be few" in prayer because "God is in heaven and you are on earth" fits well with Jesus' teaching on prayer (Matt. 6:5, 7) and his example prayer—the Lord's Prayer (Matt. 6:9–13), an extremely short prayer addressed to "our Father *in heaven*." Such prayer depends upon the grace of God, and does not seek to *gain* grace or to leverage God by the merit of the eloquence or length of our prayers.

5:10–17 This is a return to a recurring theme of Ecclesiastes: the riches of this world will not satisfy. Heap up your marbles and you will not only want more, you will also fear that the heap makes them all the more likely to roll away.

Jesus warned about the deceitfulness of riches (Matt. 6:24; 13:22; Luke 12:15) and futility of greed (Matt. 19:22–24; Luke 12:16–20). Moreover, he admonished us to be

has nothing in his hand. 15 [d]As he came from his mother's womb he shall go again, naked as he came, and shall take nothing for his toil that he may carry away in his hand. 16 This also is a grievous evil: just as he came, so shall he go, and what [e]gain is there to him who [f]toils for the wind? 17 Moreover, all his days he [g]eats in darkness in much vexation and sickness and anger.

18 Behold, what I have seen to be [h]good and fitting is to eat and drink and find enjoyment[1] in all the toil with which one toils under the sun the few days of his life that God has given him, for this is his [i]lot. 19 Everyone also to whom [j]God has given [k]wealth and possessions [l]and power to enjoy them, and to accept his lot and rejoice in his toil—this is [m]the gift of God. 20 For he will not much remember the days of his life because God keeps him occupied with joy in his heart.

6 [n]There is an evil that I have seen under the sun, and it lies heavy on mankind: 2 a man [o]to whom [p]God gives wealth, possessions, and honor, so that he [q]lacks nothing of all that he desires, yet God [r]does not give him power to enjoy them, but a stranger enjoys them. This is vanity;[2] it is a grievous evil. 3 If a man fathers a hundred children and lives many years, so that [s]the days of his years are many, but his soul is not satisfied with life's [t]good things, and he also has no [u]burial, I say that [v]a stillborn child is better off than he. 4 For it comes in vanity and goes in darkness, and in darkness its name is covered. 5 Moreover, it has not [w]seen the sun or known anything, yet it finds [x]rest rather than he. 6 Even though he should live a thousand years twice over, yet enjoy[3] no good—do not all go to the one place? 7 [y]All the toil of man is for his mouth, yet his appetite is not satisfied.[4] 8 For what advantage has the wise man [z]over the fool? And what does the poor man have who knows how to conduct himself before the living? 9 Better [a]is the sight of the eyes than the wandering of the appetite: this also is [b]vanity and a striving after wind.

10 Whatever has come to be has [c]already been named, and it is known what man is, and that he is not able to [d]dispute with one stronger than he. 11 The more words, the more vanity, and what is the advantage to man? 12 For who knows what is good for man while he lives the few days of his [e]vain[5] life, which he passes like [f]a shadow? For who can tell man what will be [g]after him under the sun?

The Contrast of Wisdom and Folly

7 [h]A good name is better than precious ointment,
  and [i]the day of death than the day of birth.
2 It is better to go to the house of mourning
  than to go to the house of feasting,
for this is the end of all mankind,
  and the living will [j]lay it to heart.
3 Sorrow is better than laughter,
  [k]for by sadness of face the heart is made glad.
4 The heart of the wise is in the house of mourning,
  but the heart of fools is in the house of mirth.
5 It is [l]better for a man to hear the rebuke of the wise
  than to hear the song of fools.

[1] Or *and see good* [2] The Hebrew term *hebel* can refer to a "vapor" or "mere breath"; also verses 4, 9, 11 (see note on 1:2) [3] Or *see* [4] Hebrew *filled* [5] The Hebrew term *hebel* can refer to a "vapor" or "mere breath" (see note on 1:2)

15 [d]See Job 1:21
16 [e]See ch. 1:3 [f][Prov. 11:29]
17 [g][Ps. 127:2]
18 [h]See ch. 2:24 [i]See ch. 2:10
19 [j]ch. 6:2; [ch. 2:24] [k]2 Chr. 1:11 [l][ch. 6:2] [m]See ch. 3:13
Chapter 6
1 [n]ch. 5:13
2 [o]ch. 5:19 [p][1 Kgs. 3:13] [q]Ps. 17:14; 73:7; See Job 21:7-13 [r][ch. 5:19; Luke 12:20]
3 [s]Gen. 47:8, 9 [t][ver. 6] [u]Isa. 14:20; Jer. 8:2; 22:19; [2 Kgs. 9:35] [v]ch. 4:3; Job 3:16
5 [w]ch. 7:11; 11:7 [x]ch. 4:6
7 [y][Prov. 16:26]
8 [z][ch. 2:15]
9 [a]ch. 11:9 [b]See ch. 1:14
10 [c]ch. 1:10; 3:15 [d]Job 9:32; Isa. 45:9; [1 Cor. 10:22] **12** [e][ch. 7:15; 9:9] [f]ch. 8:13; See Job 14:2 [g][ch. 2:18; 3:22] **Chapter 7** **1** [h]Prov. 22:1; [Song 1:3] [i]ch. 4:2 **2** [j][Ps. 90:12] **3** [k][2 Cor. 7:10] **5** [l]Prov. 13:18; 15:31, 32; [Ps. 141:5]

"rich toward God" (Luke 12:21), to seek first his kingdom (Luke 12:31), and to trust and thank God for provision (Matt. 6:19–33). Following Jesus (1 Tim. 6:3), Paul speaks of the damnable dangers of the love of money (1 Tim. 6:10) and the uncertainty of riches, and he charges wealthy Christians to "set their hopes . . . on God, who richly provides us with everything to enjoy" (1 Tim. 6:17).

7:1–13 Because of the futility of the world, the counterintuitive is the wisest approach—trusting God over circumstances and appearances. Such wisdom provides more protection than money, and it preserves life (and sanity) when this broken world makes no sense. Such brokenness can make our final days of pain seem more desirable than the day of our birth into this troubled existence. But this wisdom ultimately concludes that it is not within our knowledge or experience to make sense of what God does on an earthly plane.

6 [m]For as the crackling of [n]thorns under a
pot,
so is the laughter of the fools;
this also is vanity.[1]
7 Surely [o]oppression drives the wise into
madness,
and [p]a bribe corrupts the heart.
8 Better is the end of a thing than its
beginning,
and [q]the patient in spirit is better
than the proud in spirit.
9 [r]Be not quick in your spirit to become
angry,
[s]for anger lodges in the heart[2] of fools.
10 Say not, "Why were the former days better than these?"
For it is not from wisdom that you ask
this.
11 Wisdom is good with an inheritance,
an advantage to those who [t]see the sun.
12 For the protection of wisdom is like [u]the
protection of money,
and the advantage of knowledge is
that [v]wisdom preserves the life of
him who has it.
13 Consider [w]the work of God:
[x]who can make straight what he has
made crooked?

14 [y]In the day of prosperity be joyful, and in
the day of adversity consider: God has made
the one as well as the other, [z]so that man may
not find out anything that will be after him.
15 In my [a]vain[3] life I have seen everything.
There is [b]a righteous man who perishes in his
righteousness, and there is a wicked man who
[c]prolongs his life in his evildoing. 16 Be not
overly righteous, and do not [d]make yourself
too wise. Why should you destroy yourself?
17 Be not overly wicked, neither be a fool.
[e]Why should you die before your time? 18 It
is good that you should take hold of [f]this,
and from [g]that [h]withhold not your hand, for
the one who fears God shall come out from
both of them.
19 [i]Wisdom gives strength to the wise man
more than ten rulers who are in a city.
20 Surely [j]there is not a righteous man on
earth who does good and never sins.
21 Do not take to heart all the things that
people say, lest you hear [k]your servant cursing you. 22 Your heart knows that [l]many times
you yourself have cursed others.
23 All this I have tested by wisdom. [m]I said, "I
will be wise," but it was far from me. 24 That
which has been is far off, and [n]deep, very deep;
[o]who can find it out?
25 [p]I turned my heart to know and to search
out and to seek wisdom and the scheme of
things, and to know the wickedness of folly
and the foolishness that is madness. 26 And
I find something more [q]bitter than death:
[r]the woman whose heart is [s]snares and nets,
and whose hands are fetters. He who pleases
God escapes her, but [t]the sinner is taken by
her. 27 Behold, this is what I found, says [u]the
Preacher, while adding one thing to another to
find the scheme of things— 28 which my soul
has sought repeatedly, but I have not found.
[v]One man among a thousand I found, but
[w]a woman among all these I have not found.
29 See, this alone I found, that [x]God made man
upright, but [y]they have sought out many
schemes.

Keep the King's Command

8 Who is like the wise?
And who knows the interpretation of a
thing?
[z]A man's wisdom makes his face shine,
and [a]the hardness of his face is
changed.

[1] The Hebrew term *hebel* can refer to a "vapor" or "mere breath" (see note on 1:2) [2] Hebrew *in the bosom* [3] The Hebrew term *hebel* can refer to a "vapor" or "mere breath" (see note on 1:2)

7:9 Jesus too gave severe warnings about words (Matt. 5:22; 12:37). We must ask God for the wisdom (James 1:5) to be "slow to speak" (James 1:19) and quick to tame our tongues before we destroy others (James 3:3–10; cf. 1:26).

7:20, 22 Ecclesiastes affirms the Bible's view of sin (e.g., Rom. 3:9–10; Mark 7:20–23). We celebrate Jesus as the exception—"who in every respect has been tempted as we are, yet without sin" (Heb. 4:15)—and we rejoice in that "for our sake [God] made him to be sin who knew no sin, so that in him we might become the righteousness of God" (2 Cor. 5:21).

6[m] [Joel 2:5] [n] [Ps. 58:9; 118:12]
7[o] [ch. 4:1] [p] Deut. 16:19; See Prov. 17:8
8[q] See Prov. 14:29
9[r] [Prov. 14:17; 16:32; James 1:19] [s] [Eph. 4:26]
11[t] ch. 6:5; 11:7
12[u] [ch. 10:19] [v] Prov. 3:18
13[w] [ch. 3:11] [x] [ch. 1:15; Job 12:14; Isa. 14:27]
14[y] [ch. 3:4, 22; Deut. 28:47]

[z] [ch. 3:22; 6:12] **15**[a] ch. 6:12; 9:9 [b] See ch. 8:14 [c] ch. 8:12, 13 **16**[d] [Rom. 12:3] **17**[e] [Prov. 10:27]; See Job 22:16 **18**[f] [ver. 17] [g] [ver. 16] [h] ch. 11:6 **19**[i] ch. 9:16, 18; Prov. 21:22; 24:5 **20**[j] See 1 Kgs. 8:46 **21**[k] Prov. 30:10 **22**[l] [Gal. 6:1] **23**[m] [Rom. 1:22] **24**[n] [Rom. 11:33] [o] Job 28:12, 20; [1 Tim. 6:16] **25**[p] See ch. 1:17 **26**[q] Prov. 5:4 [r] See Prov. 2:16 [s] Prov. 12:12; [Prov. 23:28] [t] Prov. 22:14 **27**[u] See ch. 1:1 **28**[v] Job 33:23; [ver. 20] [w] [1 Kgs. 11:3] **29**[x] [Gen. 1:27] [y] [Gen. 3:6, 7] **Chapter 8** **1**[z] Prov. 4:8, 9; [Acts 6:15] [a] Prov. 21:29; [Deut. 28:50]

2 I say:[1] Keep the king's command, because
of [b]God's oath to him.[2] 3 Be not hasty to [c]go
from his presence. Do not take your stand in
an evil cause, for he does whatever he pleases.
4 For the word of the king is supreme, and
[d]who may say to him, "What are you doing?"
5 Whoever keeps a command will know no
evil thing, and the wise heart will know the
proper time and the just way. 6 For there is
a time and a way [e]for everything, although
man's trouble[3] lies heavy on him. 7 For he
[f]does not know what is to be, for [g]who can
tell him how it will be? 8 No man has power
to [h]retain the spirit, [i]or power over the day of
death. There is no [j]discharge from war, nor
will wickedness deliver those who are given
to it. 9 [k]All this I observed while applying my
heart to all that is done under the sun, when
man had power over man to his hurt.

Those Who Fear God Will Do Well

10 Then I saw the wicked buried. They used
to go in and out of [l]the holy place and were
[m]praised[4] in the city where they had done
such things. This also is vanity.[5] 11 Because [n]the
sentence against an evil deed is not executed
speedily, [o]the heart of the children of man is
fully set to do evil. 12 Though a sinner does evil
a hundred times and [p]prolongs his life, yet
I know that [q]it will be well with [r]those who
fear God, because they fear before him. 13 But it
will [s]not be well with the wicked, neither will
he prolong his days like [t]a shadow, because he
does not fear before God.

Man Cannot Know God's Ways

14 There is a vanity that takes place on
earth, that there are righteous people [u]to
whom it happens according to the deeds of
the wicked, and there are wicked people [v]to
whom it happens according to the deeds of
the righteous. I said that this also is vanity.
15 And I commend joy, for man [w]has nothing
better under the sun but to [x]eat and drink
and be joyful, for this will go with him in his
toil through the days of his life that God has
given him under the sun.

16 When I applied my heart to know wisdom,
and to see [y]the business that is done on earth,
how neither [z]day nor night do one's eyes see
sleep, 17 then I saw all the work of God, that
[a]man cannot find out the work that is done
under the sun. However much man may toil
in seeking, he will not find it out. Even though
a wise man claims to know, [b]he cannot find
it out.

Death Comes to All

9 But all this I laid to heart, examining it
all, [c]how the righteous and the wise and
their deeds are [d]in the hand of God. Whether
it is love or hate, man does not know; both are
before him. 2 [e]It is the same for all, since [f]the
same event happens to the righteous and the
wicked, to the good and the evil,[6] to the clean
and the unclean, to him who sacrifices and
him who does not sacrifice. As the good one
is, so is the sinner, and he who [g]swears is as he
who shuns an oath. 3 This is an evil in all that
is done under the sun, that [e]the same event
happens to all. Also, the hearts of the children
of man are full of evil, and [h]madness is in their
hearts while they live, and after that they go
to the dead. 4 But he who is joined with all the
living has hope, for a living dog is better than
a dead lion. 5 For the living know that they
will die, but [i]the dead know nothing, and they
have no more reward, for [j]the memory of them
is forgotten. 6 Their love and their hate and
their envy have already perished, and forever
they have no more share in all that is done
under the sun.

[1] Hebrew lacks *say* [2] Or *because of your oath to God* [3] Or *evil* [4] Some Hebrew manuscripts, Septuagint, Vulgate; most Hebrew manuscripts *forgotten* [5] The Hebrew term *hebel* can refer to a "vapor" or "mere breath"; also twice in verse 14 (see note on 1:2) [6] Septuagint, Syriac, Vulgate; Hebrew lacks *and the evil*

2 [b] Ex. 22:11; 2 Sam. 21:7; 1 Kgs. 2:43; [2 Chr. 36:13; Ezek. 17:18]
3 [c] [ch. 10:4]
4 [d] Dan. 4:35; See Job 9:12
6 [e] ch. 3:1, 17
7 [f] [Prov. 24:22] [g] ch. 3:22; 6:12; 9:12; 10:14
8 [h] [Job 14:5] [i] [ch. 3:19; 9:11] [j] See Deut. 20:5-8

8:12–13 This is the third mention in Ecclesiastes (cf. 3:14; 5:7; 7:18; 12:13) of the central concept of Wisdom Literature: the fear of God. This phrase refers to an attitude of submission to, respect for, dependence on, and worship of the Lord. Therefore, the fear of God and obedience to his word are the two inseparable components of genuine faith—"the obedience of faith" (Rom. 1:5; 16:26). Put differently, Ecclesiastes anticipates the right reaction to the gospel of righteousness: that the just shall live by faith (Hab. 2:4; Rom. 1:16–17; Gal. 3:11; Heb. 10:38).

9 [k] [ch. 1:13] **10** [l] [Neh. 11:1; Matt. 24:15] [m] [ch. 9:5; Prov. 10:7] **11** [n] [Ps. 10:6; 50:21; Isa. 26:10; Rom. 2:4, 5; 2 Pet. 3:9] [o] [Esth. 7:5; Acts 5:3] **12** [p] ch. 7:15; Isa. 65:20 [q] [Deut. 12:25; Isa. 3:10] [r] [Ps. 37:11, 18, 19; Prov. 1:33; Matt. 25:34] **13** [s] Isa. 3:11 [t] ch. 6:12; See Job 14:2 **14** [u] ch. 7:15; [Ps. 73:3]; See ch. 2:14 [v] [Job 21:7; Ps. 17:9, 10; 73:12; Jer. 12:1] **15** [w] See ch. 2:24 [x] 1 Kgs. 4:20 **16** [y] ch. 1:13; 3:10 [z] [Ps. 127:2] **17** [a] [Prov. 25:2]; See ch. 3:11 [b] [Ps. 73:16]
Chapter 9 **1** [c] [ch. 8:14] [d] Deut. 33:3 **2** [e] Job 9:22 [f] See ch. 2:14 [g] Zech. 5:3; [Mal. 3:5] **3** [e] [See ver. 2 above] [h] ch. 1:17 **5** [i] Job 14:21 [j] ch. 1:11; 8:10; Ps. 31:12; 88:5, 12; Isa. 26:14

Enjoy Life with the One You Love

7 Go, [k]eat your bread with joy, and drink your
wine with a merry heart, for God has already
approved what you do.
8 [l]Let your garments be always white. Let not
[m]oil be lacking on your head.
9 Enjoy life with the wife whom you love, all
the days of your [n]vain[1] life that he has given
you under the sun, because that is your [o]por-
tion in life and in your toil at which you toil
under the sun. 10 Whatever your hand finds
to do, [p]do it with your might,[2] [q]for there is no
work or thought or knowledge or wisdom in
Sheol, to which you are going.

Wisdom Better than Folly

11 [r]Again I saw that under the sun [s]the race is
not to the swift, nor [t]the battle to the strong,
nor bread to the wise, nor riches to the intelligent, nor favor to those with knowledge, but
time and [u]chance [v]happen to them all. 12 For
man [w]does not know his time. Like fish that
are taken in an evil net, and [x]like birds that are
caught in a snare, so the children of man are
[y]snared at an evil time, when it suddenly falls
upon them.
13 I have also seen this example of wisdom
under the sun, and it seemed great to me.
14 There was a little city with few men in it,
and a great king came against it and besieged
it, building great siegeworks against it. 15 But
there was found in it [z]a poor, wise man, and
he by his [a]wisdom delivered the city. Yet no
one remembered that poor man. 16 But I say
that [b]wisdom is better than might, though
[c]the poor man's wisdom is despised and his
words are not heard.
17 The words of the wise heard in [d]quiet are
better than the shouting of a ruler among
fools. 18 [e]Wisdom is better than weapons of
war, but [f]one sinner destroys much good.

10 Dead flies make [g]the perfumer's
ointment give off a stench;
so a little folly outweighs wisdom and
honor.
2 [h]A wise man's heart inclines him to the
right,
but a fool's heart to the left.
3 Even when the fool walks on the road,
he lacks sense,
and he [i]says to everyone that he is a
fool.
4 If the anger of the ruler rises against
you, [j]do not leave your place,
[k]for calmness[3] will lay great offenses to
rest.

5 There is an evil that I have seen under the
sun, as it were [l]an error proceeding from the
ruler: 6 [m]folly is set in many high places, and
the rich sit in a low place. 7 [n]I have seen slaves
[o]on horses, and princes walking on the ground
like slaves.

8 He who [p]digs a pit will fall into it,
and [q]a serpent will bite him who
breaks through a wall.
9 [r]He who quarries stones is hurt by them,
and he who [s]splits logs is endangered
by them.
10 If the iron is blunt, and one does not
sharpen the edge,
he must use more strength,
but wisdom helps one to succeed.[4]
11 If the serpent bites before it is [t]charmed,
there is no advantage to the charmer.
12 The words of a wise man's mouth [u]win
him favor,[5]
but [v]the lips of a fool consume him.

[1] The Hebrew term *hebel* can refer to a "vapor" or "mere breath" (see note on 1:2) [2] Or *finds to do with your might, do it* [3] Hebrew *healing* [4] Or *wisdom is an advantage for success* [5] Or *are gracious*

9:7 This verse typifies the positive refrain of Ecclesiastes (cf. 2:10, 24–26; 3:12–13; 5:17–19; 8:15; 9:7–9; 11:7–10), which involves the enjoyment of food and drink as the provision of God in an otherwise undependable world that is beyond human control, understanding, or anticipation. Such gracious provision comes to its richest fulfillment first in the earthly ministry of Jesus (who alone has mastery over the earthly elements). One thinks of his miracle at Cana (John 2:1–11), his dining at Matthew's house (Matt. 9:10–15), the feeding of the multitudes (Matt. 14:14–21; 15:32–38), the Last Supper (Mark 14:17–25), or the post-resurrection breakfast on the beach (John 21:12). Finally, we reflect on the future wedding supper of the Lamb (Rev. 19:9), which we anticipate each time we celebrate the Lord's Supper, "proclaiming the Lord's death *until he comes*" (1 Cor. 11:26).

7 [k] See ch. 2:24
8 [l] [Rev. 3:4] [m] Ps. 23:5
9 [n] ch. 6:12; 7:15 [o] See ch. 2:10
10 [p] Rom. 12:11; Col. 3:23 [q] [ver. 5]
11 [r] ch. 4:1, 7 [s] Amos 2:14, 15; [Rom. 9:16] [t] [2 Chr. 20:15; Jer. 9:23] [u] [1 Kgs. 22:34] [v] See ch. 2:14
12 [w] [ch. 8:7] [x] Prov. 7:23 [y] [Prov. 29:6; Ezek. 12:13; Hos. 7:12; Luke 21:34, 35; 1 Thess. 5:3]
15 [z] [ch. 4:13] [a] ver. 18; [2 Sam. 20:22]
16 [b] See ch. 7:19 [c] [Mark 6:2, 3]

17 [d] ch. 4:6 **18** [e] ver. 16 [f] [Josh. 7:1] **Chapter 10** **1** [g] Ex. 30:25 **2** [h] [ch. 2:14] **3** [i] [Prov. 13:16; 18:2] **4** [j] [ch. 8:3] [k] [1 Sam. 25:24, 32, 33]; See Prov. 25:15 **5** [l] ch. 5:6 **6** [m] [Esth. 3:1; Prov. 28:12; 29:2] **7** [n] Prov. 19:10; [Prov. 30:22] [o] [Esth. 6:8] **8** [p] See Ps. 7:15 [q] Amos 5:19 **9** [r] [1 Chr. 22:2] [s] [Deut. 19:5] **11** [t] [Jer. 8:17] **12** [u] Prov. 10:32; 22:11; [Luke 4:22] [v] See Prov. 18:7

13 The beginning of the words of his
mouth is foolishness,
and the end of his talk is evil madness.
14 [w]A fool multiplies words,
though no man knows what is to be,
and who can tell him [x]what will be
after him?
15 The toil of a fool wearies him,
for he does not know [y]the way to the
city.

16 [z]Woe to you, O land, when your king is a
child,
and your princes feast in the morning!
17 Happy are you, O land, when your king
is the son of the nobility,
and your princes feast at the proper
time,
for strength, and not for [a]drunken-
ness!
18 Through sloth the roof sinks in,
and through indolence the house leaks.
19 Bread is made for laughter,
and [b]wine gladdens life,
and [c]money answers everything.
20 Even in your thoughts, [d]do not curse the
king,
nor in your [e]bedroom curse the rich,
for a bird of the air will carry your voice,
or some winged creature tell the matter.

Cast Your Bread upon the Waters

11 [f]Cast your bread upon the waters,
[g]for you will find it after many days.
2 [h]Give a portion to [i]seven, or even to eight,
[j]for you know not what disaster may
happen on earth.
3 If the clouds are full of rain,
they empty themselves on the earth,
and if a tree falls to the south or to the
north,
in the place where the tree falls, there
it will lie.
4 He who observes the wind will not sow,
and he who regards the clouds will
not reap.

5 As you do not know the way [k]the spirit
comes to [l]the bones in the womb[1] of a woman
with child, so you do not know the work of
God who makes everything.
6 In the morning sow your seed, and at evening [m]withhold not your hand, for you do
not know which will prosper, this or that, or
whether both alike will be good.
7 Light is sweet, and it is pleasant for the eyes
to [n]see the sun.
8 So if a person lives many years, let him
rejoice in them all; but let him remember
[o]that the days of darkness will be many. All
that comes is [p]vanity.[2]
9 [q]Rejoice, O young man, in your youth, and
let your heart cheer you in the days of your
youth. [r]Walk in the ways of your heart and [s]the
sight of your eyes. But know that for all these
things [t]God will bring you into judgment.
10 Remove vexation from your heart, and
[u]put away pain[3] from your body, for youth
and the dawn of life are vanity.

Remember Your Creator in Your Youth

12 Remember also your Creator in [v]the days
of your youth, before [w]the evil days come
and the years draw near of which [x]you will say,
"I have no pleasure in them"; 2 before [y]the sun
and the light and the moon and the stars are
darkened and the clouds return after the rain,
3 in the day when the keepers of the house
tremble, and the strong men are bent, and the
grinders cease because they are few, and [z]those
who look through the windows are dimmed,
4 and [a]the doors on the street are shut—when
[b]the sound of the grinding is low, and one rises
up at the sound of a bird, and all [c]the daughters
of song are brought low— 5 they are afraid also
of what is high, and [d]terrors are in the way; the
almond tree blossoms, the grasshopper drags

[1] Some Hebrew manuscripts, Targum; most Hebrew manuscripts *As you do not know the way of the wind, or how the bones grow in the womb* [2] The Hebrew term *hebel* can refer to a "vapor" or "mere breath"; also verse 10 (see note on 1:2) [3] Or *evil*

14[w] See Prov. 15:2 [x] See ch. 3:22
15[y] [Isa. 35:8]
16[z] Isa. 3:4, 12; [2 Chr. 13:7]
17[a] [Prov. 31:4; Isa. 5:11]
19[b] See Ps. 104:15 [c] [ch. 7:12]
20[d] Ex. 22:28 [e] See 2 Kgs. 6:12; Luke 12:3

12:1 There are many connections between Ecclesiastes and Genesis (e.g., creation and curse—see Eccles. 7:29). Yet this reminder to depend on our Creator for solace in a broken world will ultimately move us forward in our search for wholeness to the culminating truths of salvation history revealed in Jesus (John 1:1–3; 20:17, 30–31). For it is in Christ that we see God's promise of abundant life (John 10:10) and the renewal of all things (Rev. 21:5).

Chapter 11 **1**[f] [Isa. 32:20] [g] [Deut. 15:10; Prov. 19:17; Matt. 10:42; Luke 14:14; 2 Cor. 9:8; Gal. 6:9, 10; Heb. 6:10] **2**[h] [Ps. 112:9; Matt. 5:42; Luke 6:30; 1 Tim. 6:18, 19] [i] Mic. 5:5; See Job 5:19; Prov. 6:16 [j] [Luke 16:9; Eph. 5:16] **5**[k] [ch. 1:6; John 3:8] [l] See Ps. 139:13-16 **6**[m] ch. 7:18 **7**[n] ch. 6:5; 7:11 **8**[o] [ch. 12:1, 2] [p] ch. 2:23; See ch. 1:2 **9**[q] [ch. 2:10; 9:7] [r] [Num. 15:39; Job 31:7] [s] ch. 6:9 [t] See ch. 12:14 **10**[u] 2 Cor. 7:1; 2 Tim. 2:22 **Chapter 12** **1**[v] [Lam. 3:27] [w] [ch. 11:8] [x] [2 Sam. 19:35] **2**[y] [Job 3:9; Isa. 5:30; Ezek. 32:7, 8] **3**[z] [Gen. 27:1; 48:10; 1 Sam. 3:2] **4**[a] [Ps. 141:3] [b] [Jer. 25:10; Rev. 18:22] [c] [ch. 2:8] **5**[d] [Prov. 26:13]

itself along,[1] and desire fails, because man is
going to his [e]eternal [f]home, and the [g]mourn-
ers go about the streets— 6 before the silver
cord is snapped, or [h]the golden bowl is broken,
or the pitcher is [i]shattered at the fountain, or
the wheel broken at the cistern, 7 and [j]the dust
returns to the earth as it was, and [k]the spirit
returns to God [l]who gave it. 8 [m]Vanity[2] of vanities, says [n]the Preacher; all is vanity.

Fear God and Keep His Commandments

9 Besides being wise, [n]the Preacher also
taught the people knowledge, weighing and
studying and arranging [o]many proverbs with
great care. 10 [n]The Preacher sought to find
words of delight, and uprightly he wrote
words of truth.

11 [p]The words of the wise are like goads, and
like [q]nails firmly fixed are the collected sayings; they are [r]given by [s]one Shepherd. 12 My
son, beware of anything beyond these. Of
making [u]many books there is no end, and
[v]much study is a weariness of the flesh.

13 The end of the matter; all has been heard.
[w]Fear God and keep his commandments, for
this is the whole duty of man.[3] 14 For [x]God will
bring every deed into judgment, with[4] every
secret thing, whether good or evil.

[1] Or *is a burden* [2] The Hebrew term *hebel* can refer to a "vapor" or "mere breath" (three times in this verse); see note on 1:2 [3] Or *the duty of all mankind* [4] Or *into the judgment on*

12:10 Like "the Preacher" of Ecclesiastes, Jesus was a wisdom teacher, surpassing even Solomon in his wisdom (Matt. 12:42). He also lived a life of wisdom. From the cradle to the cross, he walked the way of wisdom. Denying himself the usual rewards of godliness—long life, good reputation, strong marriage, healthy children, material prosperity—he submitted to the wise but inexplicable will of his Father, enduring a humiliating death, so that in his sufferings he might become for us the very wisdom and power of God (1 Cor. 1:24).

12:11 If the writer is borrowing from the language of Ezekiel (Ezek. 34:23–24; 37:24–25), the reference to "one shepherd" serves as an anticipation of the coming Davidic shepherd king. The New Testament identifies this as Jesus (Matt. 25:31–46). Jesus called himself, "one shepherd" (John 10:16), as well as "the good shepherd" who laid "down [his] life for the sheep" (John 10:14–15).

12:13–14 In Matthew 10:28, Jesus likewise combines the themes of fearing God and judgment—"And do not fear those who kill the body but cannot kill the soul. Rather fear him who can destroy both soul and body in hell."

12:14 If you have yet to realize that God is the Ruler of this exceedingly complex universe and that therefore you are not, then the door to the kingdom of heaven and a meaningful life remains closed. To you, this verse serves as a final warning with the weight of the warning falling on the words "every" and "secret." Each and every word, action, and thought will be judged by God (cf. 11:9c–12:7; Rom. 2:16).

However, if you have come to Christ in faith and are thus willing to live in dependence upon his wisdom, provision, and grace, then this verse serves as a reminder of the comfort that will come when Jesus balances the scales of justice on the last day. On that day he will vindicate those already declared righteous by him. He will also condemn the wicked who by rejecting him will have every deed, including every secret thing, taken into account (Matt. 25:31–46; 2 Cor. 5:10).

Above all, Ecclesiastes is a call to entrust yourself to God, the only solid truth and reality in this universe. Everything "under the sun" will finally disappoint. But trust in God gives us an "above the sun" perspective that acknowledges the harsh realities of this fallen existence while retaining hope. God will one day cleanse this world and reinstate Eden. In Christ, this new world has already dawned.

5 [e] [Ps. 143:3] [f] [Job 17:13; 30:23; Isa. 14:18] [g] [2 Chr. 35:25; Jer. 9:17; Matt. 9:23]
6 [h] [Zech. 4:2, 3] [i] [Isa. 30:14]
7 [j] Ps. 90:3; 103:14; See ch. 3:20; Job 34:15 [k] [ch. 3:21] [l] [Job 34:14; Isa. 57:16; Zech. 12:1]; See Gen. 2:7
8 [m] ch. 1:2 [n] See ch. 1:1
9 [n] [See ver. 8 above] [o] See Prov. 1:1
10 [n] [See ver. 8 above]
11 [p] Prov. 22:17 [q] Ezra 9:8; Isa. 22:23 [r] Prov. 1:6; 2:6 [s] Ps. 80:1; Ezek. 34:23; John 10:11, 16
12 [u] [1 Kgs. 4:32, 33] [v] [ch. 1:18]
13 [w] ch. 5:7; Deut. 6:2; 10:12
14 [x] ch. 11:9; Job 19:29; Matt. 12:36; Acts 17:31; Rom. 2:16; 14:10, 12; 1 Cor. 4:5; [ch. 3:15, 17; Gen. 18:25; Ps. 58:11]

Introduction to
The Song of Solomon

Author and Date

The wording of the first verse in the Song of Solomon (or Song of Songs) does not necessarily mean that Solomon wrote the book. It may have been written by Solomon himself, or it could have been written in his honor. Whatever the case, the book was probably composed during Solomon's lifetime between c. 960 and 931 B.C.

The Gospel in Song of Solomon

The Song of Solomon is a lyrical poem that celebrates marital love. Through beautiful sensory scenes and sensual imagery, it provides us with God's wisdom on sexual intimacy. For those unmarried, the exhortation is to wait until marriage to express and enjoy such intimacy—"I adjure you . . . that you not stir up or awaken love until it pleases" (2:7; cf. 3:5; 8:4). For those married, it is an admonishment to grow in intimacy—"I am my beloved's and my beloved is mine" (6:3; cf. 2:16; 7:10).

Through the centuries various allegorical interpretations of the Song of Solomon have sought to identify the groom as Christ and the bride as the church (or, the groom as God and the bride as Israel). But we are on safest interpretive ground to recognize that this "poem" of idealized love (probably used in ceremonies related to marriage in Solomon's time), while representing a marriage that God approves, is more a representation of the love he values than an extended metaphor of Christ and his church (or the soul of a believer). As such, this Song tells us what God values: a loving marriage (including its expressions of physical and emotional affection), fidelity to another, protection of another, and the valuing of another—who may even consider herself undeserving of such love. Thus, we gain insight into the loving nature of the God who inspired this Song, and are made able to love him in return although we constantly require his fidelity, protection, and undeserved love.

And yet, because the Song is found in the Bible, we must read it alongside the other Wisdom Literature (Job, Proverbs, and Ecclesiastes) and in light of the ultimate revelation of wisdom and love—our Lord Jesus Christ. Jesus is called both "the bridegroom" (John 3:29) and our "one husband" (2 Cor. 11:2). His kingdom and consummation is like "a wedding feast" (Matt. 22:2; cf. Rev. 19:9). Read in light of Jesus, the Song, like all Scripture, makes us "wise for salvation through faith in Christ Jesus" (2 Tim. 3:15). That is, it reveals to us something of how the "mystery" of marriage (Eph. 5:32) relates to "the mystery of the gospel" itself (Eph. 6:19). For marriage is itself an institution that displays the gospel of grace (Eph. 5:22–33).

Outline

I. Title: The Best of Songs (1:1)

II. The Lovers Yearn for Each Other (1:2–2:17)

III. The Shepherdess Dreams (3:1–6:3)

IV. The Lovers Yearn for Each Other Again (6:4–8:4)

V. The Lovers Join in Marriage (8:5–14)

The Song of Solomon

1 The Song of [a]Songs, which is Solomon's.

The Bride Confesses Her Love

SHE[1]

2 Let him kiss me with the kisses of his
mouth!
For your [b]love is better than wine;
3 your [c]anointing oils are fragrant;
your [d]name is oil poured out;
therefore virgins love you.
4 [e]Draw me after you; [f]let us run.
[g]The king has brought me into his
chambers.

OTHERS

We will [h]exult and rejoice in you;
we will extol [b]your love more than
wine;
rightly do they love you.

SHE

5 I am very dark, but [i]lovely,
O [j]daughters of Jerusalem,
like [k]the tents of [l]Kedar,
like the curtains of Solomon.
6 Do not gaze at me because I am dark,
because the sun has looked upon me.
My [m]mother's sons were angry with me;
they made me [n]keeper of [o]the vineyards,
but [p]my own vineyard I have not kept!
7 Tell me, you [q]whom my soul loves,
where you [r]pasture your flock,
where you make it [s]lie down at noon;
for why should I be like one who veils
herself
beside the flocks of your [t]compan-
ions?

Solomon and His Bride Delight in Each Other

HE

8 If you do not know,
O [u]most beautiful among women,
follow in the tracks of the flock,
and pasture your young goats
beside the shepherds' tents.

[1] The translators have added speaker identifications based on the gender and number of the Hebrew words

1:2–4 Although we are fallen, and thus our sexual desires can easily be distorted and debased, there is still something "very good" (Gen. 1:31) about the desire for physical intimacy.

Within the marriage "chambers" (Song 1:4b), such passion is to be expressed (v. 2), and such love exalted and rejoiced in (v. 4). Within the canon of Scripture, one should not think of marriage without thinking of Christ, and this is because marriage was always intended to point to him (Eph. 5:32). Even our sexual desires are a reflection of what should be our ultimate "desire," that is to be made complete in devotion to another—the reality we taste now by the Holy Spirit but will ultimately experience when we depart to be with Christ (Phil. 1:23).

1:5–2:7 These responsive words of kind affection exchanged between bride and groom reflect not only the regard each has for the other but also the importance of communicating that regard. Here we simply learn that the God who inspired these words approves the approval that we express in order to bless each one that we love. We will all give an account for every careless word we speak (Matt. 12:36–37). The power of words is the prevalent theme in Song of Solomon 1:5–2:7. This poem paints a picture of the transformative power of affirming words. Husbands and wives are to *complement* each other by *complimenting* each other.

Chapter 1
1[a]1 Kgs. 4:32
2[b]ch. 4:10
3[c][Luke 7:46; John 12:3] [d]Eccles. 7:1
4[e][Hos. 11:4; John 6:44; 12:32] [f]Ps. 119:32; See Phil. 3:12-14 [g]Ps. 45:14, 15; [ch. 2:4; John 14:2; Eph. 2:6] [h]Ps. 9:2; 45:15 [b][See ver. 2 above]
5[i]ch. 2:14; 4:3; 6:4 [j]ch. 2:7; 3:5, 10, 11; 5:8, 16; 8:4; Luke 23:28 [k]Ps. 120:5 [l]Isa. 60:7
6[m][Ps. 69:8] [n]Job 27:18; Prov. 27:18 [o]ch. 8:11, 12 [p][1 Cor. 9:27]
7[q]See ch. 3:1-4 [r]ch. 2:16; 6:3; [Ps. 23:1-3; Ezek. 34:14, 15] [s][Isa. 13:20; Jer. 33:12] [t]ch. 8:13
8[u]ch. 5:9; 6:1

9 I compare you, [v]my love,
to [w]a mare among Pharaoh's chariots.
10 [x]Your cheeks are lovely with ornaments,
your neck with strings of jewels.

Others

11 We will make for you[1] ornaments of gold,
studded with silver.

She

12 While [y]the king was on his couch,
my [z]nard gave forth its fragrance.
13 My beloved is to me a sachet of [a]myrrh
that lies between my breasts.
14 My beloved is to me a cluster of [b]henna
blossoms
in the vineyards of [c]Engedi.

He

15 [d]Behold, [e]you are beautiful, [f]my love;
behold, you are beautiful;
your [g]eyes are doves.

She

16 Behold, you are beautiful, [h]my beloved,
truly [i]delightful.
Our couch is green;
17 the beams of our house are [j]cedar;
our rafters are [j]pine.

2 I am a rose[2] of Sharon,
[k]a lily of the valleys.

He

2 As a lily among brambles,
so is [l]my love among the young women.

She

3 As an apple tree among the trees of the
forest,
so is my [m]beloved among the young
men.
With great delight I sat [n]in his shadow,
and his [o]fruit was sweet to my taste.
4 He [p]brought me to the banqueting
house,[3]
and his [q]banner over me was love.
5 Sustain me with [r]raisins;
refresh me with apples,
[s]for I am sick with love.
6 His [t]left hand is under my head,
and his right hand [u]embraces me!
7 I [v]adjure you,[4] O [w]daughters of
Jerusalem,
by [x]the gazelles or the does of the
field,
that you not stir up or awaken love
until it pleases.

The Bride Adores Her Beloved

8 The voice of my beloved!
Behold, he comes,
leaping [y]over the mountains,
bounding over the hills.
9 My beloved is like [z]a gazelle
or a young stag.
Behold, there he stands
behind our wall,
gazing through the windows,
looking through the lattice.
10 My beloved speaks and says to me:
[a]"Arise, my love, my beautiful one,
and come away,
11 for behold, the winter is past;
[b]the rain is over and gone.
12 [c]The flowers appear on the earth,
the time of singing[5] has come,
and the voice of [d]the turtledove
is heard in our land.
13 [e]The fig tree ripens its figs,
and [f]the vines are in blossom;
they give forth fragrance.
[g]Arise, my love, my beautiful one,
and come away.

[1] The Hebrew for *you* is feminine singular [2] Probably a bulb, such as a crocus, asphodel, or narcissus [3] Hebrew *the house of wine* [4] That is, I put you on oath; so throughout the Song [5] Or *pruning*

9[v] See ver. 15 [w] [2 Chr. 1:16, 17]
10[x] [ch. 5:13]; See Ezek. 16:11-14
12[y] [ver. 4] [z] ch. 4:13, 14; [Mark 14:3; John 12:3]
13[a] Ps. 45:8; [John 19:39]
14[b] ch. 4:13 [c] 1 Sam. 23:29
15[d] ch. 4:1 [e] [Ezek. 16:13] [f] ver. 9; ch. 2:2, 10, 13; 4:1, 7; 5:2; 6:4 [g] ch. 4:1; 5:12
16[h] ch. 2:3 [i] [2 Sam. 1:23, 26]
17[j] Isa. 37:24; 60:13; Ezek. 31:8

In doing so, we reflect the character of our Savior, who commends his love to us in kind and affectionate words (e.g., John 15:15; Heb. 2:11). We are to speak the truth in love (Eph. 4:15). We are not to let any unwholesome talk come out of our mouths, but only what is helpful for building each other up (Eph. 4:29). We are to get rid of all bitterness, rage, anger, brawling, and slander (Eph. 4:31). We are to be kind and tenderhearted to one another, forgiving one another, just as God in Christ forgave us (Eph. 4:32).

2:7 The Song's refrain (see also 3:5; 8:4; cf. 5:8) in the midst of allusions to the couple's emotional and sexual joy teaches that pure passion is good and is approved by God, but also that it waits for the proper time (marriage) and the proper person (one's

Chapter 2 **1**[k] Hos. 14:5; [ch. 5:13] **2**[l] See ch. 1:15 **3**[m] ch. 1:16 [n] Isa. 25:4; 32:2 [o] [Rev. 22:2] **4**[p] ch. 1:4 [q] [Ps. 20:5] **5**[r] 2 Sam. 6:19; 1 Chr. 16:3; Hos. 3:1 [s] ch. 5:8 **6**[t] ch. 8:3; [Deut. 33:27] [u] [Prov. 4:8] **7**[v] ch. 3:5; 5:8, 9; 8:4 [w] See ch. 1:5 [x] See ver. 9 **8**[y] [Isa. 52:7] **9**[z] ch. 4:5; 7:3; 8:14; 2 Sam. 2:18; 1 Chr. 12:8; [Ps. 18:33; Hab. 3:19] **10**[a] ver. 13 **11**[b] [Joel 2:23] **12**[c] [2 Sam. 23:4] [d] [Jer. 8:7] **13**[e] [Matt. 24:32] [f] ch. 7:12 [g] ver. 10

14 O my [h]dove, in the [i]clefts of the rock,
in the crannies of the cliff,
let me see your face,
let me [j]hear your voice,
for your voice is sweet,
and your face is [k]lovely.
15 Catch [l]the foxes[1] for us,
the little foxes
that spoil the vineyards,
[f]for our vineyards are in blossom."

16 [m]My beloved is mine, and I am his;
he [n]grazes[2] among the lilies.
17 Until [o]the day breathes
and [p]the shadows flee,
turn, my beloved, be like [q]a gazelle
or a young stag on cleft mountains.[3]

The Bride's Dream

3 On my bed [r]by night
I sought [s]him whom my soul loves;
[t]I sought him, but found him not.
2 I will rise now and go about the city,
in [u]the streets and in the squares;
I will seek [s]him whom my soul loves.
I sought him, but found him not.
3 [v]The watchmen found me
as they went about in the city.
"Have you seen him whom my soul loves?"
4 Scarcely had I passed them
when I found [s]him whom my soul
loves.
I [w]held him, and would not let him go
until I had [x]brought him into my
mother's house,
and into the chamber of [y]her who
conceived me.
5 [z]I adjure you, [a]O daughters of Jerusalem,
[b]by the gazelles or the does of the field,
that you not stir up or awaken love
until it pleases.

Solomon Arrives for the Wedding

6 [c]What is that coming up from the wilderness
like [d]columns of smoke,
perfumed with [e]myrrh and frankincense,
with all the fragrant powders of a
merchant?
7 Behold, it is the litter[4] of Solomon!
Around it are [f]sixty [g]mighty men,
some of the mighty men of Israel,
8 all of them wearing swords
and expert in war,
each with his [h]sword at his thigh,
against [i]terror by night.
9 King Solomon made himself a carriage[5]
from the wood of Lebanon.
10 He made its posts of silver,
its back of gold, its seat of purple;
its interior was inlaid with love
by [j]the daughters of Jerusalem.
11 Go out, O [k]daughters of Zion,
and look upon King Solomon,
with the crown with which his mother
crowned him
on [l]the day of his wedding,
on the day of the gladness of his heart.

Solomon Admires His Bride's Beauty

HE

4 Behold, [m]you are beautiful, my love,
behold, you are beautiful!
[n]Your eyes are doves
[o]behind your veil.
[p]Your hair is like a flock of goats
leaping down [q]the slopes of Gilead.
2 Your [r]teeth are like a flock of shorn ewes
that have come up from the washing,
all of which bear twins,
and not one among them has lost its
young.

[1] Or *jackals* [2] Or *he pastures his flock* [3] Or *mountains of Bether* [4] That is, the couch on which servants carry a king [5] Or *sedan chair*

spouse). In his grace, God provides marriage for deep emotional and physical fulfillment. Indeed, God identifies each as good. And yet our sinfulness and selfishness easily prompt us to pursue others outside of marriage.

What if you haven't waited for marriage? Know that God offers full forgiveness for sins, and cleansing through Jesus. What if your marriage has been damaged by sins and selfishness? Do not think that help and healing are impossible. Jesus did not come "to call the righteous, but sinners" (Matt. 9:13). Consider the salvation story in Luke 7:36–50. If you want to hear the voice of the bridegroom (John 3:29) say, "Your sins are forgiven" (Luke 7:48) and "Go in peace" (Luke 7:50), then come to him in repentance and faith. He who shows love for one who thinks of herself as unlovely in these verses will also love you despite your sin and failure.

14[h] ch. 5:2; 6:9; [ch. 1:15] [i] Jer. 48:28; 49:16; Obad. 3 [j] ch. 8:13 [k] ch. 1:5; 4:3
15[l] [Ezek. 13:4] [f] [See ver. 13 above]
16[m] ch. 6:3; 7:10 [n] ch. 4:5; 6:3
17[o] ch. 4:6; [Gen. 3:8] [p] Jer. 6:4 [q] See ver. 9
Chapter 3
1[r] Isa. 26:9 [s] ch. 1:7 [t] ch. 5:6; [John 7:34]
2[u] Jer. 5:1 [s] [See ver. 1 above]
3[v] ch. 5:7
4[s] [See ver. 1 above] [w] [Job 27:6] [x] ch. 8:2 [y] [Hos. 2:5]
5[z] See ch. 2:7 [a] See ch. 1:5 [b] See ch. 2:9

6[c] ch. 8:5; [ch. 6:10; Isa. 60:8] [d] Ex. 13:21; Joel 2:30 [e] ch. 4:6, 14; Matt. 2:11; John 19:39 **7**[f] ch. 6:8 [g] 2 Sam. 23:8; 1 Chr. 11:10 **8**[h] Ps. 45:3 [i] Ps. 91:5 **10**[j] See ch. 1:5 **11**[k] Isa. 3:16, 17; 4:4 [l] [Isa. 62:5] **Chapter 4** **1**[m] See ch. 1:15 [n] ch. 1:15; 5:12 [o] ch. 6:7 [p] ch. 6:5; [ch. 7:5] [q] Mic. 7:14 **2**[r] ch. 6:6

3 Your lips are like [s]a scarlet thread,
and your mouth is [t]lovely.
Your [u]cheeks are like halves of a pomegranate
[o]behind your veil.
4 Your [v]neck is like the tower of David,
built in [w]rows of stone;[1]
on it [x]hang a thousand shields,
all of [y]them shields of warriors.
5 Your [z]two breasts are like two [a]fawns,
twins of a gazelle,
that [b]graze among the lilies.
6 [c]Until the day breathes
and the shadows flee,
I will go away to the mountain of [d]myrrh
and the hill of [d]frankincense.
7 [e]You are altogether beautiful, my love;
there is no [f]flaw in you.
8 [g]Come with me from [h]Lebanon, my [i]bride;
come with me from [h]Lebanon.
Depart[2] from the peak of Amana,
from the peak of [j]Senir and [k]Hermon,
from the dens of lions,
from the mountains of leopards.

9 You have captivated my heart, my [l]sister,
my bride;
you have captivated my heart with
one glance of your eyes,
with one [m]jewel of your necklace.
10 How beautiful is your love, my [l]sister,
my bride!
How much [n]better is your love than wine,
and [o]the fragrance of your oils than any spice!
11 Your [p]lips drip nectar, my bride;
[q]honey and milk are under your tongue;
the fragrance of your garments is [r]like
the fragrance of [h]Lebanon.
12 A garden locked is my [l]sister, my bride,
a spring locked, [s]a fountain [t]sealed.
13 Your shoots are [u]an orchard of pomegranates
with all [v]choicest fruits,
[w]henna with [x]nard,
14 nard and saffron, [y]calamus and [y]cinnamon,
with all trees of [z]frankincense,
[a]myrrh and [b]aloes,
with all [y]choice spices—
15 a garden fountain, a well of [c]living water,
and flowing streams from [h]Lebanon.

16 Awake, O north wind,
and come, O south wind!
Blow upon my [d]garden,
let its spices flow.

Together in the Garden of Love

SHE

[e]Let my beloved come to his [f]garden,
and eat its [v]choicest fruits.

[1] The meaning of the Hebrew word is uncertain [2] Or *Look*

3[s][Josh. 2:18] [t]ch. 1:5; 2:14 [u]ch. 6:7 [o][See ver. 1 above] **4**[v][ch. 7:4] [w]Neh. 3:19 [x][Ezek. 27:10, 11] [y][2 Sam. 1:21] **5**[z]ch. 7:3; [ch. 8:10; Prov. 5:19] [a]See ch. 2:9 [b]ch. 2:16; 6:3 **6**[c]ch. 2:17 [d]ver. 14; [ch. 3:6] **7**[e]See ch. 1:15 [f]ch. 5:2; [Eph. 5:27] **8**[g][Ps. 45:10, 11] [h]ch. 7:4; See 1 Kgs. 4:33 [i][Isa. 62:5] [j]Deut. 3:9; 1 Chr. 5:23 [k]Ps. 89:12 **9**[l]ch. 5:1, 2 [m][Judg. 8:26] **10**[l][See ver. 9 above] [n]ch. 1:2, 4 [o][ch. 1:3] **11**[p][Prov. 5:3] [q]Prov. 24:13 [r]Hos. 14:6; [Gen. 27:27] [h][See ver. 8 above] **12**[l][See ver. 9 above] [s][Gen. 29:3; Dan. 6:17] [t][Prov. 5:15] **13**[u]Eccles. 2:5 [v]ch. 7:13 [w]ch. 1:14 [x]See ch. 1:12 **14**[y]Ex. 30:23 [z]ver. 6 [a]See ch. 3:6 [b]John 19:39 **15**[c]Jer. 2:13; [John 4:10; 7:38] [h][See ver. 8 above] **16**[d][ch. 5:1; 6:2] [e][ch. 6:2] [f]ch. 6:2 [v][See ver. 13 above]

4:7 For the husband, his wife is "altogether beautiful." As much as his eyes are open to her, we might rightly label his love "blind love." She is not actually flawlessly beautiful; indeed, she sometimes speaks disparagingly of herself (e.g., 1:6). Similarly, God's love for us *in Christ* can be categorized as "blind love." We know ourselves to be blemished by sin and unworthy of his affection. Yet Christians are made beautiful, ironically, through Christ's bloody atoning death. This truth is illustrated in Ephesians 5:25–30, which speaks of the mystery of marriage between Christ and the church and how through Christ's sacrificial love he will present the church to himself "holy and without blemish."

4:12–16 Sexual intimacy is for unity, comfort, offspring, help against sexual temptation, and pleasure. It is also designed to point us to the Lord of love in whom all longings are ultimately satisfied.

This is taught in the Song through all the garden imagery. To the groom, his bride is like the garden of Eden *and* the temple, which was decorated like Eden. To them, lovemaking is the closest thing to the Promised Land. Their love is like being in the presence of God. That is what Eden, the Promised Land, and the temple all have in common. These metaphors are mixed to say that sex is a signpost that points to *God's intimate presence* with his people. In this way, the intimate is the path to the transcendent: through the intimacy of marriage, we learn what it means to be exposed and yet loved; to be separate but one; to be different without distance; to be made most fulfilled by giving ourselves to another; to be made most whole by

HE

5 I [g]came to my garden, my [h]sister, my
bride,
I gathered my [i]myrrh with my spice,
I ate my [j]honeycomb with my honey,
I [k]drank my wine with my milk.

OTHERS

Eat, [l]friends, drink,
and be drunk with love!

The Bride Searches for Her Beloved

SHE

2 I slept, but my heart was awake.
A sound! My beloved is [m]knocking.
"Open to me, my [n]sister, my [o]love,
my [p]dove, my [q]perfect one,
for my head is wet with dew,
my [r]locks with the drops of the
night."
3 [s]I had put off my garment;
how could I put it on?
I had [t]bathed my feet;
how could I soil them?
4 My beloved put his hand to the latch,
and my heart was thrilled within me.
5 I arose to open to my beloved,
and my hands dripped with myrrh,
my fingers with [u]liquid myrrh,
on the handles of the bolt.
6 I opened to my beloved,
but my beloved had turned and gone.
My soul failed me when he [v]spoke.
[w]I sought him, but found him not;
[x]I called him, but he gave no answer.
7 [y]The watchmen found me
as they went about in the city;
they beat me, they bruised me,
they took away my veil,
those watchmen of the walls.
8 I [z]adjure you, O [a]daughters of Jerusalem,
if you find my beloved,
that you tell him
[b]I am sick with love.

OTHERS

9 What is your beloved more than another
beloved,
O [c]most beautiful among women?
What is your beloved more than another
beloved,
that you thus [z]adjure us?

The Bride Praises Her Beloved

SHE

10 My beloved is radiant and [d]ruddy,
[e]distinguished among ten thousand.
11 His head is the finest gold;
[f]his locks are wavy,
black as a raven.

completely sharing ourselves with another; and, to be made most at peace by the caring presence of another who knows we can express none of these things perfectly.

Throughout the Old Testament there is an ongoing theme of Eden restored and transcended, as God comes ever closer to us. The prophets speak of this coming salvation in garden/temple terminology (e.g., Isa. 58:11; Jer. 31:12). In the person of Jesus the very presence of God comes to us in bodily form, and by his Spirit he indwells us. Those who come into his presence now by faith are promised final salvation that is portrayed as a wedding feast (Rev. 19:7, 9; 21:6) in the city of God (which is like a garden, with its river, trees, and fruits). In that place at that time those in Christ "will see his face" (Rev. 22:4a). This will be the ultimate ecstatic encounter with God!

5:1 After Jesus quoted Genesis 2:24 in his argument against easy divorce, he added his simple summary, "So they are no longer two but one flesh," and the God-centered application, "What therefore God has joined together, let not man separate" (Matt. 19:6). In Song of Solomon 4:6–5:1, we have the Song's most vivid description of this pure "flesh of my flesh" (Gen. 2:23) joining—the "undefiled" (Heb. 13:4) yet aflame wedding night, whose expressions of intimacy are reflective of the grace we require (see note on Song 4:12–16).

5:2–6:3 Song of Solomon 5:2–3 is worlds apart from 6:3. While 5:2–3 is dominated by selfish thoughts, 6:3 concludes with mutual selflessness: "I am my beloved's and my beloved is mine." Initially the physical aspects of each of the two lovers result in personal ecstasy that makes the pain of separation unbearable (4:1–5:16). But then, the chasm of the lovers' separation (perhaps caused by selfishness and symbolized in the strange aspect of the bride's dream [5:6–8]) is bridged by self-denial (5:16; 6:2–3, 10–12).

Chapter 5

1 [g][ch. 4:16; 6:2] [h]ch. 4:9, 10, 12 [i]ver. 5, 13; ch. 4:14 [j]ch. 4:11 [k][Prov. 9:5] [l][John 15:14, 15]
2 [m][Rev. 3:20] [n]ch. 4:9, 10, 12 [o]See ch. 1:15 [p]See ch. 2:14 [q]ch. 6:9; [ch. 4:7] [r]ver. 11
3 [s][Luke 11:7] [t]See Gen. 18:4
5 [u]ver. 13
6 [v][ver. 2] [w]ch. 3:1 [x][Prov. 1:28]
7 [y]ch. 3:3
8 [z]See ch. 2:7 [a]See ch. 1:5 [b]ch. 2:5
9 [c]ch. 1:8; 6:1 [z][See ver. 8 above]
10 [d][1 Sam. 16:12] [e][Ps. 45:2]
11 [f]ver. 2

12 His [g]eyes are like doves
beside streams of water,
bathed in milk,
sitting beside a full pool.[1]
13 His [i]cheeks are like [j]beds of spices,
mounds of sweet-smelling herbs.
His lips are [k]lilies,
dripping [u]liquid myrrh.
14 His arms are rods of gold,
set with [l]jewels.
His body is polished ivory,[2]
bedecked with [m]sapphires.[3]
15 His legs are alabaster columns,
set on bases of gold.
His appearance is like [o]Lebanon,
choice as the cedars.
16 His [p]mouth[4] is most sweet,
and he is altogether desirable.
This is my beloved and this is my friend,
O [a]daughters of Jerusalem.

OTHERS

6 Where has your beloved gone,
O [c]most beautiful among women?
Where has your beloved turned,
that we may seek him with you?

Together in the Garden of Love

SHE

2 My beloved has gone down to his [q]garden
to [r]the beds of spices,
to [s]graze[5] in the gardens
and to gather [t]lilies.
3 [u]I am my beloved's and my beloved is mine;
he grazes among the lilies.

Solomon and His Bride Delight in Each Other

HE

4 You are beautiful as [v]Tirzah, [w]my love,
[x]lovely as [y]Jerusalem,
[z]awesome as an army with banners.
5 Turn away your eyes from me,
for they overwhelm me—
[a]Your hair is like a flock of goats
leaping down the slopes of Gilead.
6 [b]Your teeth are like a flock of ewes
that have come up from the washing;
all of them bear twins;
not one among them has lost its young.
7 [c]Your cheeks are like halves of a pomegranate
behind your veil.
8 There are [d]sixty [e]queens and eighty [e]concubines,
and [f]virgins without number.
9 My [g]dove, my [h]perfect one, is the only one,
the only one of her mother,
pure to [i]her who bore her.
[j]The young women saw her and called her blessed;
[e]the queens and [e]concubines also, and they praised her.

10 [k]"Who is this who looks down like the dawn,
beautiful as the moon, bright as the sun,
[l]awesome as an army with banners?"

SHE

11 I went down to the nut orchard
to look at [m]the blossoms of the valley,

[1] The meaning of the Hebrew is uncertain [2] The meaning of the Hebrew word is uncertain [3] Hebrew *lapis lazuli* [4] Hebrew *palate* [5] Or *to pasture his flock*; also verse 3

12[g] ch. 1:15; 4:1
13[i] [ch. 1:10] [j] ch. 6:2 [k] [ch. 2:1] [u] [See ver. 5 above]
14[l] Ex. 28:20; 39:13; Ezek. 1:16 [m] Ex. 24:10; Ezek. 1:26; 10:1
15[o] See 1 Kgs. 4:33
16[p] [ch. 7:9] [a] [See ver. 8 above]
Chapter 6
1[c] [See ch. 5:9 above]
2[q] ch. 4:16; 5:1 [r] ch. 5:13 [s] ch. 1:7 [t] [ch. 2:1]
3[u] ch. 2:16; 7:10
4[v] See 1 Kgs. 14:17 [w] See ch. 1:15 [x] ch. 1:5 [y] Ps. 48:2; 50:2; Lam. 2:15; [Rev. 21:2] [z] ver. 10
5[a] ch. 4:1
6[b] ch. 4:2
7[c] ch. 4:3
8[d] [ch. 3:7] [e] [1 Kgs. 11:3] [f] Ps. 45:9, 14

Jesus will ultimately epitomize the self-denial that results in a more perfect union. In humility he "emptied himself" and "humbled himself by becoming obedient to the point of death . . . on a cross" (see Phil. 2:3–8). Your marriage is designed to look like Christ's crucifixion, where selfless love and selfless submission collide for the sake of another (see Eph. 5:22–33). The result is that both husband and wife can say, "God has given me a lover whose care sings to me the story of our salvation—of God having reconciled selfish sinners through his selfless Son."

6:4–8:4 The word "beautiful" occurs sixteen times in the Song, four of those times in this passage (6:4, 10; 7:1, 6). All four occur in the man's descriptions of his bride's body. In this way the groom gives his bride her beauty by his assessment of her. Beauty is not known if it is not appreciated. Our Lord's delight in the beauty of the human body in marriage is only a dim reflection of the measure of grace he extends to us by calling sinners holy—all through his grace. He gives the beauty he relishes and then credits us with its possession.

9[g] See ch. 2:14 [h] ch. 5:2 [i] Prov. 17:25 [j] [Gen. 30:13] [e] [See ver. 8 above] **10**[k] See ch. 3:6 [l] ver. 4 **11**[m] [Job 8:11, 12]

[n]to see whether the vines had budded,
whether the pomegranates were in bloom.
12 [o]Before I was aware, my desire set me
among [p]the chariots of my kinsman, a prince.[1]

OTHERS

13[2] Return, return, O [q]Shulammite,
return, return, that we may look upon you.

HE

Why should you look upon [q]the Shulammite,
as upon [r]a dance before [s]two armies?[3]

7 How beautiful are your feet in sandals,
O [t]noble daughter!
Your rounded thighs are like [u]jewels,
the work of [v]a master hand.
2 Your navel is a rounded bowl
that never lacks mixed wine.
Your belly is a heap of wheat,
encircled with [w]lilies.
3 [x]Your two breasts are like two fawns,
twins of a gazelle.
4 Your [y]neck is like an ivory tower.
Your [z]eyes are pools in [a]Heshbon,
by the gate of Bath-rabbim.
Your nose is like a tower of [b]Lebanon,
which looks toward [c]Damascus.
5 Your head crowns you like [e]Carmel,
and your [f]flowing locks are like purple;
a king is held captive in the tresses.
6 [g]How beautiful and [h]pleasant you are,
O loved one, with all your delights![4]
7 Your stature is like a palm tree,
and your breasts are like its clusters.
8 I say I will climb the palm tree
and lay hold of its fruit.
Oh may your breasts be like [i]clusters of the vine,
and the scent of your breath like apples,
9 and your [j]mouth[5] like the best wine.

SHE

It goes down smoothly for my beloved,
gliding over lips and teeth.[6]
10 [k]I am my beloved's,
[l]and his desire is for me.

The Bride Gives Her Love

11 [m]Come, my beloved,
let us go out into the fields
and lodge in the villages;[7]
12 let us go out early to the vineyards
[n]and see whether the vines have budded,
whether [o]the grape blossoms have opened
and the pomegranates are in bloom.
There I will give you my love.
13 [p]The mandrakes give forth fragrance,
and beside our doors are all choice fruits,
[q]new as well as old,
which I have laid up for you, O my beloved.

Longing for Her Beloved

8 Oh that you were like a brother to me
who nursed at my mother's breasts!
If I found you outside, I would kiss you,
and none would despise me.
2 I would lead you and [r]bring you
into the house of my mother—
she who used to teach me.
I would give you [s]spiced wine to drink,
the juice of my pomegranate.
3 [t]His left hand is under my head,
and his right hand embraces me!

[1] Or *chariots of Ammi-Nadib* [2] Ch 7:1 in Hebrew [3] Or *dance of Mahanaim* [4] Or *among delights* [5] Hebrew *palate* [6] Septuagint, Syriac, Vulgate; Hebrew *causing the lips of sleepers to speak* [7] Or *among the henna plants*

Yet the beauty of the Lord—"the beauty of all things beautiful," as Augustine put it—transcends the beauty of the body. Ironically, what is most captivating about the incarnation ("in him the whole fullness of deity dwells bodily"; Col. 2:9) is that Jesus "had no form or majesty that we should look at him, and no beauty that we should desire him" (Isa. 53:2) and yet he was "beautiful and glorious" (Isa. 4:2) when crucified upon the tree. Yes, let us "behold the king in his beauty" (Isa. 33:17), a marred beauty that has made many marred sinners beautiful through faith in him (cf. Isa. 60:9).

11[n] ch. 7:12
12[o] [Ps. 35:8; Prov. 5:6] [p] [2 Kgs. 2:12; 13:14]
13[q] [1 Kgs. 1:3; 2 Kgs. 4:12] [r] [Judg. 21:21] [s] Gen. 32:2; 2 Sam. 17:24
Chapter 7
1[t] Ps. 45:13 [u] Prov. 25:12 [v] [Prov. 8:30]
2[w] ch. 2:1
3[x] ch. 4:5

4[y] [ch. 4:4] [z] [ch. 5:12] [a] Num. 21:26 [b] ch. 4:8; See 1 Kgs. 4:33 [c] 1 Kgs. 11:24; 2 Kgs. 5:12 **5**[e] See Josh. 19:26 [f] [ch. 4:1] **6**[g] [ch. 1:15, 16] [h] 2 Sam. 1:23, 26 **8**[i] [ch. 1:14; Mic. 7:1] **9**[j] [ch. 5:16] **10**[k] ch. 2:16; 6:3 [l] [Ps. 45:11] **11**[m] [ch. 2:10; 4:8] **12**[n] ch. 6:11 [o] ch. 2:13, 15 **13**[p] Gen. 30:14; ch. 4:13 [q] [Matt. 13:52]
Chapter 8 **2**[r] ch. 3:4 [s] [Prov. 9:2, 5] **3**[t] ch. 2:6, 7

4 I [u]adjure you, O [v]daughters of Jerusalem,
[w]that you not stir up or awaken love
until it pleases.

5 [x]Who is that coming up from the wilderness,
leaning on her beloved?

Under the apple tree I awakened you.
There your mother was in labor with you;
there she who bore you was in labor.

6 Set me as a seal upon your heart,
as [y]a seal upon your arm,
for [z]love is strong as death,
[a]jealousy[1] is fierce as the grave.[2]
Its flashes are flashes of fire,
the very [b]flame of the LORD.
7 Many waters cannot quench love,
neither can floods drown it.
If a man offered for love
all the wealth of his [c]house,
he[3] would be utterly despised.

Final Advice

OTHERS

8 We have a little sister,
and she [d]has no breasts.
What shall we do for our sister
on the day when she is spoken for?
9 If she is a wall,
we will build on her a battlement of silver,
but if she is a door,
we will enclose her with [e]boards of cedar.

SHE

10 [f]I was a wall,
and my [g]breasts were like towers;
then I was in his eyes
as one who finds[4] peace.

11 Solomon had [h]a vineyard at Baal-hamon;
he [i]let out the vineyard to [j]keepers;
each one was to bring for its fruit [k]a thousand pieces of silver.
12 My vineyard, my very own, is before me;
you, O Solomon, may have the thousand,
and [l]the keepers of the fruit two hundred.

[1] Or *ardor* [2] Hebrew *as Sheol* [3] Or *it* [4] Or *brings out*

4[u] See ch. 2:7 [v] See ch. 1:5 [w] [ch. 2:7]
5[x] See ch. 3:6
6[y] Isa. 49:16; Jer. 22:24; Hag. 2:23 [z] [Rom. 8:35] [a] [Ex. 34:14]; Deut. 4:24 [b] [Job 1:16]
7[c] Prov. 6:35
8[d] [Ezek. 16:7]
9[e] [1 Kgs. 6:15]
10[f] [ch. 4:12, 13] [g] [ch. 4:5; 7:3]
11[h] Eccles. 2:4 [i] [Matt. 21:33] [j] ch. 1:6 [k] [Isa. 7:23]
12[l] See Prov. 27:18

8:6–7 Marriage is an exclusive, lifelong commitment (cf. Matt. 19:6; Rom. 7:2–3). The reasons for this commitment are found in Song of Solomon 8:6. The two images—"death" and "the very flame of the LORD"—are both images of permanence. (We think also of the burning bush that was not consumed and the flaming sword of the angel perpetually guarding the garden of Eden.) This is the only mention of "the LORD" in the Song (the Hebrew for "flame" is likely related to the Hebrew for "the LORD" [*Yahweh*]). Since the marriage relationship of the Song reflects the values of our God, we are here made to understand that he intends for covenant relationships (including his with us) to be permanent—not revoked by the imperfections of any party to the covenant.

Similarly, there is a permanence to our covenant relationship with the Lord Christ, which is not only until death ("till death do us part") but which overcomes death ("O death, where is your victory?"; 1 Cor. 15:55). Because Jesus is "the resurrection and the life" (John 11:25), we who believe in him are "sealed" by the Spirit "for the day of redemption" (Eph. 4:30).

8:8–14 The Song ends with a vignette on virginity, love still unknown (vv. 8–12), followed by a picture of the two lovers wanting to touch but not yet touching (vv. 13–14). Thus, we are left with the same kind of longing that opened the Song (1:2).

This longing leaves us longing for more. The Song intentionally ends abruptly and inconclusively because the love story is not done—the life of love for these two is only at its beginning. The many chapters of the full story of the married couple have yet to be written—where love will deepen and strengthen in the marriage that God intends.

Feeling the longing we all have for a deep and strong love that makes us one with another is a path for the gospel. This Song prepares our hearts by making them long for the deepest and dearest love that God can provide. In this way, this Song of Solomon makes us long for God's greater love song in our lives and the story that is not yet done at this point in the canon of Scripture. Viewed from the perspective of the whole Bible, this longing leads its readers forward to Isaiah, where God's gracious redemption of his people is as clear as anywhere in the Old Testament. From Isaiah

He

13 [m]O you who dwell in the gardens,
with [n]companions listening for your voice;
[o]let me hear it.

She

14 [p]Make haste, my beloved,
and be [q]like a gazelle
or a young stag
on [r]the mountains of spices.

we journey finally to Revelation, which ends as the final Song ends: "Let us rejoice and exult and give him the glory, for the marriage of the Lamb has come, and his Bride has made herself ready" by keeping herself "pure" (Rev. 19:7–8). Then, Jesus/the bridegroom says, "Surely I am coming soon," and the church/the bride says, "Come" (Rev. 22:17), "Amen. Come, Lord Jesus!" (Rev. 22:20).

13[m] [ch. 5:1] [n] ch. 1:7 [o] ch. 2:14
14[p] [Rev. 22:17, 20] [q] See ch. 2:9 [r] [ch. 4:6]

Introduction to Isaiah

Author and Date

Isaiah was called to his prophetic ministry "in the year that King Uzziah died" (6:1), around 740 B.C. He lived long enough to record the death of Sennacherib (37:38), in 681. However, most of the book can be dated only in very general terms because few specific dates are given.

The Gospel in Isaiah

Reading the book of Isaiah takes us into the precarious space between warning and wonder, faithlessness and fidelity, compromise and conviction: this is the world where a fallen people hear the holy God. Divine words come full of truth and grace; they expose sin while offering, beneath all failure, hope and redemption. In Isaiah, God's word calls for a humble response of awe, humble trust, and reverent submission to the Lord and his kingdom.

While the immediate context of Isaiah relates to the dangers posed by Assyria and Babylon as well as the dramatic shifts between exile and return, this prophetic book was always understood to have ongoing relevance. One of the most referenced Old Testament books in the New Testament, later writers look back to Isaiah and unflinchingly identify Jesus as the foretold Messiah who fulfills all the promises in this prophetic book. Isaiah's messianic profile informs Christian worship of Jesus as the suffering servant who brings a new creation through his life-giving resurrection.

God had entered into a covenant with Israel, and with that covenant came the promise of divine blessings for faithfulness and a warning about curses for lack of faithfulness (e.g., Leviticus 26). Sadly, Israel flirted with idols, and when difficulties arose they tended to trust in unrighteous foreign powers rather than their sovereign Lord. Through their hardness of heart they forsook wholehearted trust in the Lord, while showing apathy toward injustice and a lack of concern for the needy. Throughout Isaiah we read sober warnings not only against the idolatrous nations but also against God's own covenant-breaking people. Israel has proven not to be the "light to the nations" they were called to be.

Where then can a foundation for hope and redemption be found? It is grounded on the promises brought home time and again throughout Isaiah—promises ultimately secured only in Jesus Christ (2 Cor. 1:19–20). A sampling of key ideas emerging from Isaiah demonstrates how much our understanding of Christ and his kingdom is informed by this glorious book.

First, a preserved "remnant" becomes the focal point of God's promises in Isaiah, and eventually the remnant is identified through and in its one messianic representative, the Anointed One: Jesus himself.

Second, this Anointed One will suffer on behalf of others: in the New Testament we discover that Jesus the Messiah is the one who absorbs the covenant curses—so that those who are united to him by faith might live in his covenant blessings. But we must turn to Christ, trusting in him as Savior and Lord.

Third, Isaiah reminds us that God's people are meant to reflect God's heart. We repeatedly read about Israel's struggle with disobedience and with not consistently showing a concern for the things that reflect God's heart (e.g., the poor and vulnerable, and matters of justice). In their rebellion they undermine the ancient ceremonies and practices that God instituted to prompt his forgiven people to practice righteousness and mercy. When they do not practice these things, the concern is that they may not have truly feasted on God's grace in the first place.

Fourth, God's call extends beyond Israel to the world. Isaiah keeps a global perspective even as it often focuses on Judah. God is described not merely as the Creator of Israel in particular, but also as the Creator of the world in general (e.g., 17:7; 29:16; 40:28; 43:15; 51:13; 54:5). God wants his people to be a blessing to the world (e.g., Gen. 12:1–3; 18:17–18; 28:14; Jer. 4:2; cf. Acts 3:25; Gal. 3:14). Part of the reason God's judgments so often appear in Isaiah is that his people have been rebellious, creating darkness rather than bringing light. Nevertheless, the Creator, who singularly serves as the Redeemer of Israel, also extends hope to the nations who must repent and look in faith to the only true God (e.g., Isa. 19:16–25; 44:6, 24).

Engrafted into the Messiah and the deliverance he brings, God's people are liberated to love God and neighbor. As this occurs, God's people become a light to the nations, holding out the hope not merely of forgiveness but also of new creation. The message of Isaiah is that God is very great—and yet, astonishingly, his mercy is just as great.

Outline

I. Introduction: "Ah, Sinful Nation!" (1:1–5:30)

II. God Redefines the Future of His People: "Your Guilt Is Taken Away" (6:1–12:6)

III. God's Judgment and Grace for the World: "We Have a Strong City" (13:1–27:13)

IV. God's Sovereign Word Spoken into the World: "Ah!" (28:1–35:10)

V. Historical Transition: "In Whom Do You Now Trust?" (36:1–39:8)

VI. Encouragement for God's Exiles: "The Glory of the Lord Shall Be Revealed" (40:1–55:13)

VII. How to Prepare for the Coming Glory: "Hold Fast My Covenant" (56:1–66:24)

Isaiah

1 The [a]vision of Isaiah the son of Amoz,
which he saw concerning Judah and
Jerusalem [b]in the days of [c]Uzziah, [d]Jotham,
[e]Ahaz, and [f]Hezekiah, kings of Judah.

The Wickedness of Judah

2 [g]Hear, O heavens, and give ear, O [h]earth;
for the LORD has spoken:
"Children[1] [i]have I reared and brought up,
but they have rebelled against me.
3 The ox [j]knows its owner,
and the donkey its master's crib,
but Israel does [j]not know,
my people do not understand."

4 Ah, sinful nation,
a people laden with iniquity,
[k]offspring of evildoers,
children who deal corruptly!
They have forsaken the LORD,
they have [l]despised [m]the Holy One of Israel,
they are utterly [n]estranged.

5 Why will you still be [o]struck down?
Why will you [p]continue to rebel?
The whole head is sick,
and the whole heart faint.
6 [q]From the sole of the foot even to the head,
there is no soundness in it,
but bruises and sores
and raw wounds;
they are [r]not pressed out or bound up
or softened with oil.
7 [s]Your country lies desolate;
your cities are burned with fire;
in your very presence
foreigners devour your land;
it is desolate, as overthrown by foreigners.
8 And [t]the daughter of Zion is left
like a [u]booth in a vineyard,
like a lodge in a cucumber field,
like a besieged city.
9 [v]If the LORD of hosts
had not left us [w]a few survivors,
we should have been like [x]Sodom,
and become like [x]Gomorrah.

10 Hear the word of the LORD,
you rulers of [y, z]Sodom!
Give ear to the teaching[2] of our God,
you people of [z]Gomorrah!

[1] Or *Sons*; also verse 4 [2] Or *law*

1:1–6:13 The first six chapters of Isaiah provide the tone and setting for the entire book. They anticipate some of the main themes, introduce us to prominent imagery, and show how we might see a gospel pattern emerge within the book as a whole.

1:1–31 Isaiah ministered during turbulent times, specifically addressing God's people in Judah and Jerusalem (v. 1). Under the covenant, they were called to be faithful to Yahweh, but we quickly discover in this opening oracle that all is not well. God has treated them as "children" that he lovingly "reared and brought up, but they have rebelled against me" (v. 2). Their actions show that they do not truly know the Lord, and they find themselves "laden with iniquity" (vv. 3–4).

Their leadership, described as "rulers of Sodom" (v. 10), have not led God's people in righteousness and mercy, and thus they have invalidated the worship they continued offering to God. God is the God of the fatherless, he is just and opposes oppression, and he upholds the "widow's cause" (vv. 16–17; cf. vv. 23, 27). While these values reflect God's heart, Judah seems to have rejected them, instead displaying hard-heartedness.

Chapter 1
1[a] ch. 6:1 [b] Hos. 1:1; Mic. 1:1 [c] [2 Kgs. 15:1, 7]; See 2 Chr. 26 [d] See 2 Kgs. 15:32-38; 2 Chr. 27 [e] ch. 7:1, 3, 10, 12; 14:28; See 2 Kgs. 16; 2 Chr. 28 [f] See ch. 37:2–39:8; 2 Kgs. 18-20; 2 Chr. 29–32
2[g] Deut. 32:1; [Deut. 4:26] [h] Mic. 1:2; 6:2 [i] [Deut. 32:6, 10, 15]
3[j] [Jer. 8:7]
4[k] [Matt. 3:7] [l] ch. 5:24 [m] See ch. 31:1 [n] Ezek. 14:5
5[o] Jer. 5:3; [ch. 9:13] [p] ch. 31:6
6[q] Ps. 38:3 [r] [Jer. 8:22]
7[s] ch. 5:5; 6:11, 12; Deut. 28:51, 52
8[t] ch. 10:32; 37:22; Zech. 2:10; 9:9 [u] Job 27:18
9[v] Lam. 3:22 [w] ch. 10:21, 22; Cited Rom. 9:29 [x] ch. 13:19; Gen. 19:24, 25 **10**[y] Ezek. 16:46, 48, 49, 55; [ch. 3:9; Rev. 11:8] [z] [Deut. 32:32]

11 [a]"What to me is the multitude of your sacrifices?
says the LORD;
I have had enough of burnt offerings of rams
and the fat of well-fed beasts;
I do not delight in the blood of bulls,
or of lambs, or of goats.

12 "When you come to [b]appear before me,
who has required of you
this trampling of my courts?
13 Bring no more vain offerings;
incense is an abomination to me.
[c]New moon and Sabbath and the [d]calling of convocations—
I cannot endure [e]iniquity and [f]solemn assembly.
14 Your [c]new moons and your appointed feasts
my soul hates;
they have become a burden to me;
I am weary of bearing them.
15 When you [g]spread out your hands,
I will hide my eyes from you;
[h]even though you make many prayers,
I will not listen;
[i]your hands are full of blood.
16 [j]Wash yourselves; make yourselves clean;
remove the evil of your deeds from before my eyes;
[k]cease to do evil,
17 learn to do good;
[l]seek justice,
correct oppression;
[m]bring justice to the fatherless,
plead the widow's cause.

18 "Come now, [n]let us reason[1] together, says the LORD:
though your sins are like scarlet,
they shall be as [o]white as snow;
though they are red like crimson,
they shall become like wool.
19 [p]If you are willing and obedient,
you shall eat the good of the land;
20 but if you refuse and rebel,
you shall be eaten by the sword;
[q]for the mouth of the LORD has spoken."

The Unfaithful City

21 How the faithful city
[r]has become a whore,[2]
[s]she who was full of justice!
Righteousness lodged in her,
but now murderers.
22 [t]Your silver has become dross,
your best wine mixed with water.
23 Your princes are rebels
and companions of thieves.
Everyone [u]loves a bribe
and runs after gifts.

[1] Or *dispute* [2] Or *become unchaste*

11[a] Prov. 15:8; Jer. 6:20; Mal. 1:10; [ch. 66:3]; See 1 Sam. 15:22
12[b] Ex. 23:17; 34:23
13[c] Num. 28:11; 1 Chr. 23:31 [d] Ex. 12:16; Lev. 23:36 [e] [Jer. 7:9, 10] [f] See Joel 2:15-17
14[c] [See ver. 13 above]
15[g] 1 Kgs. 8:22 [h] Prov. 1:28; Mic. 3:4 [i] ch. 59:3
16[j] [Jer. 2:22] [k] [1 Pet. 3:11]
17[l] Jer. 22:3 [m] [ver. 23; James 1:27]
18[n] Mic. 6:2; [ch. 43:26] [o] Ps. 51:7; [Rev. 7:14]
19[p] Deut. 30:15, 16
20[q] ver. 2; ch. 24:3; 40:5; 58:14; Mic. 4:4; [Num. 23:19]
21[r] Jer. 2:20; [Ex. 34:15] [s] [Jer. 31:23]
22[t] [Jer. 6:30; Ezek. 22:18]
23[u] Mic. 7:3; [Ex. 23:8]

God makes it clear he is not interested merely in religious rituals (vv. 11–14): God desires a true love of him that inevitably overflows to a love of neighbor, especially directed toward the needy (Deut. 6:5; Hos. 6:6; cf. Matt. 9:13; 12:7; Luke 10:27). When divinely sanctioned ceremonies are divorced from an active love and concern for the most vulnerable, they fail to reflect the very truths they were meant to reveal: God's compassion for us in our utmost need. Rituals meant to promote communion with God are now frustrating him, as the divine voice hauntingly declares, "they have become a burden to me; I am weary of bearing them" (Isa. 1:14).

So is there any hope? We will find throughout Isaiah, especially in the first 39 chapters, consistent divine confrontations and warnings, but sprinkled throughout these sober judgments are words of promise and future redemption. Surely their sins are like "scarlet" and "red like crimson," but God can make them "white as snow" and "wool" (v. 18). Nevertheless they must be "willing and obedient" (v. 19), otherwise judgment will fall on Judah.

Despite their unfaithfulness, God will not abandon his people. Hints of the promised future surface even in the first chapter, where God declares, "If the LORD of hosts had not left us a few survivors [i.e., a remnant], we should have been like Sodom, and become like Gomorrah" (v. 9; cf. Genesis 19). But God does preserve a remnant, and out of this remnant will ultimately come the Messiah, who will alone prove to be the embodiment of God's heart, full of love, mercy, justice, and righteousness, with powerful concern directed to the most needy and vulnerable. When Isaiah declares, "Zion shall be redeemed by justice" (Isa. 1:27), the truth is that Christ alone comes to be both the "just and the justifier" (Rom. 3:26).

[v]They do not bring justice to the fatherless,
and the widow's cause does not come to them.

24 Therefore the [w]Lord declares,
the LORD of hosts,
the [x]Mighty One of Israel:
"Ah, I will get relief from my enemies
[y]and avenge myself on my foes.
25 [z]I will turn my hand against you
and will smelt away your [a]dross as with lye
and remove all your alloy.
26 And I will restore your judges [b]as at the first,
and your counselors as at the beginning.
Afterward [c]you shall be called the city of righteousness,
the faithful city."
27 [d]Zion shall be redeemed by justice,
and those in her who repent, by righteousness.
28 [e]But rebels and sinners shall be broken together,
and those who forsake the LORD shall be consumed.
29 [f]For they[1] shall be ashamed of [g]the oaks
that you desired;
and you shall blush for [h]the gardens
that you have chosen.
30 For you shall be [i]like an oak
whose leaf withers,
and like a garden without water.
31 And the strong shall become [j]tinder,
and his work a spark,
and both of them shall burn together,
with [k]none to quench them.

The Mountain of the LORD

2 The word that Isaiah the son of Amoz saw concerning Judah and Jerusalem.

2 [l]It shall come to pass in the latter days
that [m]the mountain of the house of the LORD
shall be established as the highest of the mountains,
and shall be lifted up above the hills;
and [n]all the nations shall flow to it,
3 and [o]many peoples shall come, and say:
"Come, let us go up to the mountain of the LORD,
to the house of the God of Jacob,
that he may teach us his ways
and that we may walk in his paths."
For [p]out of Zion shall go the law,[2]
and the word of the LORD from Jerusalem.

[1] Some Hebrew manuscripts *you* [2] Or *teaching*

2:1–22 Isaiah 2 opens with much-needed promise. Judah was meant to bring hope to the nations by being a light to them, providing a powerful vision of the God of Abraham, Isaac, and Jacob. However, Judah was not displaying the beauty of God's law and love, and thus they were often indistinguishable from the other nations. But in "the latter days," God's home would be established and exalted so that all would see God's house, as if it were on the "highest of the mountains" (v. 2). When this happens, "all the nations shall flow to it," for here they will find God's law, his word going out from Zion (v. 3). Here God will serve as the "judge between the nations," but the outcome of his dealings will be peace rather than war (v. 4). God will humble the people so that they might be freed from "their idols of silver and their idols of gold" which they worship (v. 20). Look not to men who breathe, Isaiah proclaims, but turn to him who is the giver of breath (v. 22).

With the coming of the Messiah, the Word of God becomes flesh (John 1:14), becoming one of the people. In this way, the Son of God becomes the very embodiment of Israel, faithfully loving his Father and his neighbors in a way disobedient Israel has failed to do (cf. Ex. 4:22–23). Not only through his obedient life but also by his substitutionary death, Christ offers himself in Israel's place. Consequently, when he rises from the dead and ascends into heaven he demonstrates that in Christ all things are being made new. The result? As Jesus ascends into the heavens, he pours out his Spirit in Jerusalem, and his disciples are enabled to speak in the tongues of the nations, representatively drawing all the peoples of the earth back to the one true God (Acts 1–2).

We no longer wait for the nations to come to Jerusalem, but in these "last days" (e.g., Acts 2:17; Heb. 1:2) we go out to evangelize, proclaiming the good news from "Jerusalem and in all Judea and Samaria, and to the end of the earth" (Acts 1:8).

23[v] Jer. 5:28; Zech. 7:10; [ver. 17]
24[w] ch. 3:1; 10:33 [x] Ps. 132:2 [y] [Deut. 32:41]
25[z] Ps. 81:14; Amos 1:8; [ch. 5:25] [a] [Ezek. 22:20; Mal. 3:3]
26[b] Jer. 33:7, 11 [c] [Zech. 8:3]
27[d] Jer. 22:3, 4
28[e] Job 31:3; Ps. 1:6
29[f] Hos. 4:19 [g] ch. 57:5; Hos. 4:13 [h] ch. 65:3; 66:17
30[i] [Jer. 17:8]
31[j] Judg. 16:9 [k] ch. 66:24
Chapter 2
2[l] For ver. 2-4, see Mic. 4:1-3 [m] ch. 14:13; 25:6 [n] [ch. 56:7]
3[o] See Zech. 8:20-23 [p] [Luke 24:47; John 4:22]

4 He shall judge between the nations,
and shall decide disputes for many peoples;
[q]and they shall beat their swords into plowshares,
and their spears into pruning hooks;
[r]nation shall not lift up sword against nation,
neither shall they learn war anymore.

5 O house of Jacob,
come, let us walk
in [s]the light of the LORD.

The Day of the LORD

6 For you have rejected your people,
the house of Jacob,
because they are full of things [t]from the east
and [u]of fortune-tellers [v]like the Philistines,
and they [w]strike hands with the children of foreigners.
7 Their land is [x]filled with silver and gold,
and there is no end to their treasures;
their land is [y]filled with horses,
and there is no end to their chariots.
8 Their land is [z]filled with idols;
they bow down to [a]the work of their hands,
to what their own fingers have made.
9 So man [b]is humbled,
and each one [b]is brought low—
do not forgive them!
10 [c]Enter into the rock
and hide in the dust
[d]from before the terror of the LORD,
and from the splendor of his majesty.
11 [e]The haughty looks of man shall be brought low,
and the lofty pride of men shall be humbled,
and the LORD alone will be exalted in that day.

12 [f]For the LORD of hosts has a day
against all that is proud and lofty,
against all that is lifted up—and it shall be brought low;
13 against all the [g]cedars of Lebanon,
lofty and lifted up;
and against all the [h]oaks of Bashan;
14 against all [i]the lofty mountains,
and against all the uplifted hills;
15 against every high tower,
and against every fortified wall;
16 against all [j]the ships of Tarshish,
and against all the beautiful craft.
17 [k]And the haughtiness of man shall be humbled,
and the lofty pride of men shall be brought low,
and the LORD alone will be exalted in that day.
18 [l]And the idols shall utterly pass away.
19 [m]And people shall enter the caves of the rocks
and the holes of the ground,[1]
from before the terror of the LORD,
and from the splendor of his majesty,
[n]when he rises to terrify the earth.

20 In that day [o]mankind will cast away
their idols of silver and their idols of gold,
which they made for themselves to worship,
to the moles and to the [p]bats,
21 [m]to enter the caverns of the rocks
and the clefts of the cliffs,
from before the terror of the LORD,
and from the splendor of his majesty,
[n]when he rises to terrify the earth.
22 [q]Stop regarding man
[r]in whose nostrils is breath,
for of what account is he?

Judgment on Judah and Jerusalem

3 For behold, the [s]Lord GOD of hosts
is taking away from Jerusalem and from Judah
support and supply,[2]
all [t]support of bread,
and all support of water;
2 [u]the mighty man and the soldier,
the judge and the prophet,
the diviner and the elder,
3 the captain of fifty
and the man of rank,

[1] Hebrew *dust* [2] Hebrew *staff*

4[q] [Joel 3:10] [r] ch. 9:7; Ps. 72:3, 7; Hos. 2:18; Zech. 9:10 **5**[s] ch. 60:1, 2; [Eph. 5:8] **6**[t] [2 Kgs. 16:10, 11] [u] Mic. 5:12 [v] 2 Kgs. 1:2 [w] [2 Kgs. 16:7, 8] **7**[x] ch. 39:2; [ch. 22:8, 11; Deut. 17:17] [y] ch. 30:16; [Deut. 17:16; Mic. 5:10] **8**[z] ver. 18, 20; ch. 10:10, 11; Jer. 2:28 [a] See ch. 44:9-17 **9**[b] ch. 5:15 **10**[c] ver. 19, 21; [Rev. 6:15, 16] [d] Cited 2 Thess. 1:9 **11**[e] ver. 17; Ps. 18:27; [Mic. 2:3; 2 Cor. 10:5] **12**[f] [Job 40:11, 12; Mal. 4:1] **13**[g] ch. 14:8; See Judg. 9:15 [h] Ezek. 27:6; Zech. 11:2 **14**[i] [ch. 30:25] **16**[j] ch. 60:9; 1 Kgs. 10:22 **17**[k] Ps. 18:27; [Mic. 2:3; 2 Cor. 10:5] **18**[l] ver. 8 **19**[m] ver. 10; Hos. 10:8; Luke 23:30; Rev. 6:16 [n] [Ps. 76:8, 9; Hab. 3:6] **20**[o] ch. 30:22; 31:7 [p] Lev. 11:19; Deut. 14:18 **21**[m] [See ver. 19 above] [n] [See ver. 19 above] **22**[q] Ps. 146:3 [r] Job 27:3; [James 4:14] **Chapter 3** **1**[s] ch. 1:24 [t] Lev. 26:26; Ezek. 4:16 **2**[u] 2 Kgs. 24:14; Ezek. 17:13, 14

the counselor and the skillful magician
and the expert in charms.
4 [v]And I will make boys their princes,
and infants[1] shall rule over them.
5 [w]And the people will oppress one another,
every one his fellow
and every one his neighbor;
the youth will be insolent to the elder,
and the despised to the honorable.

6 For [x]a man will take hold of his brother
in the house of his father, saying:
"You have a cloak;
you shall be our leader,
and this heap of ruins
shall be under your rule";
7 in that day he will speak out, saying:
"I will not be a [y]healer;[2]
in my house there is neither bread nor cloak;
you shall not make me
leader of the people."
8 For Jerusalem has stumbled,
and Judah has fallen,
because their [z]speech and their deeds are against the LORD,
[a]defying his glorious presence.[3]

9 For the look on their faces bears witness against them;
they proclaim their sin [b]like Sodom;
they do not hide it.
Woe to them!
[c]For they have brought evil on themselves.
10 [d]Tell the righteous that it shall be well with them,
[e]for they shall eat the fruit of their deeds.
11 [f]Woe to the wicked! It shall be ill with him,
for what his hands have dealt out
shall be done to him.
12 My people—[g]infants are their oppressors,
and women rule over them.
O my people, [h]your guides mislead you
and they have swallowed up[4] the course of your paths.

13 The LORD [i]has taken his place to contend;
he stands to judge peoples.
14 The LORD will enter into judgment
with the [j]elders and princes of his people:
"It is you who [k]have devoured[5] the vineyard,
[l]the spoil of the poor is in your houses.
15 What do you mean by [m]crushing my people,
by grinding the face of the poor?"
declares the Lord GOD of hosts.

16 The LORD said:
[n]Because [o]the daughters of Zion are haughty
and walk with outstretched necks,
glancing wantonly with their eyes,
mincing along as they go,
[p]tinkling with their feet,

[1] Or *caprice* [2] Hebrew *binder of wounds* [3] Hebrew *the eyes of his glory* [4] Or *they have confused* [5] Or *grazed over*; compare Exodus 22:5

3:1–26 Sober words of warning continue, with God's particular concern addressing "their speech and their deeds" (v. 8). The rich have feasts in their homes while the deprived workers who labored for this food are crushed and left empty-handed (v. 14). It is as if the rich were "grinding the face of the poor" through these injustices (v. 15). So also, the "daughters of Zion" are living in luxury (v. 16), enjoying as many extravagances as they can while showing hard-heartedness toward those in need. Such sin demonstrates that the wealthy are ultimately "against the LORD, defying his glorious presence" (v. 8), for genuine love of God and love of neighbor are necessarily connected.

In his just love, God will not turn a blind eye to this situation, and he warns of a reversal to come. God will expose the uncaring (v. 17b), taking away all of the false security and comfort they find in their luxury (vv. 18–23); they will come to recognize that they are also the needy, unprotected, and weak (vv. 24–26).

While we may not all suffer material poverty, we are called to recognize that we are "poor in spirit" (Matt. 5:3; cf. Luke 6:20). Thus the church, living in response to God's radical grace, is invited to participate in his generosity. "For you know the grace of our Lord Jesus Christ, that though he was rich, yet for your sake he became poor, so that you by his poverty might become rich" (2 Cor. 8:9). We sacrificially and joyfully give of our time, talents, and treasure to those in need, and in this way we demonstrate the grace and love that mark God's kingdom, as opposed to the kingdoms of this world.

4[v] ver. 12; Eccles. 10:16
5[w] See Mic. 7:3-6
6[x] ch. 4:1
7[y] [ch. 1:6]
8[z] See Ps. 73:9-11 [a] ch. 65:3
9[b] Gen. 13:13; 18:20; Ezek. 16:46, 48, 49 [c] [Rom. 6:23]
10[d] Eccles. 8:12; See Deut. 28:1-14 [e] Ps. 128:2
11[f] Eccles. 8:13; See Deut. 28:15-68
12[g] ver. 4 [h] See ch. 28:14-22
13[i] Ps. 7:6; Hos. 4:1
14[j] Mic. 3:1 [k] Ps. 14:4 [l] Amos 3:10
15[m] [Ps. 94:5]
16[n] See ch. 32:9-11 [o] ch. 4:4; Song 3:11 [p] ver. 18

17 therefore the Lord [q]will strike with a scab
the heads of [o]the daughters of Zion,
and the LORD will lay bare their secret
parts.

18 In that day the Lord will take away [r]the
finery of the anklets, the [s]headbands, and the
[t]crescents; 19 the pendants, the bracelets, and
the scarves; 20 the [u]headdresses, the armlets,
the sashes, the perfume boxes, and the amu-
lets; 21 the signet rings and [v]nose rings; 22 the
[w]festal robes, the mantles, the cloaks, and the
handbags; 23 the mirrors, the linen garments,
the turbans, and the veils.

24 Instead of [x]perfume there will be rottenness;
and instead of a [y]belt, a rope;
and instead of [z]well-set hair, [a]baldness;
and instead of a rich robe, a [b]skirt of
sackcloth;
and [c]branding instead of beauty.
25 Your men shall fall by the sword
and your mighty men in battle.
26 And [d]her gates shall lament and mourn;
empty, she shall [e]sit on the ground.

4 [f]And seven women [g]shall take hold of [f]one
man in that day, saying, "We will eat our
own bread and wear our own clothes, only
let us be called by your name; [h]take away our
reproach."

The Branch of the LORD Glorified

2 In that day [i]the branch of the LORD shall
be beautiful and glorious, and [j]the fruit of the
land shall be the pride and honor of the survivors of Israel. 3 [k]And he who is left in Zion
and remains in Jerusalem will be called [l]holy,
everyone who has [m]been recorded for life in
Jerusalem, 4 when [n]the Lord shall have washed
away the filth of [o]the daughters of Zion and
cleansed the bloodstains of Jerusalem from its
midst by a spirit of judgment and by [p]a spirit
of burning.[1] 5 Then the LORD will create over
the whole site of Mount Zion and over her
assemblies [q]a cloud by day, and smoke and the
shining of a flaming fire by night; for over all
the glory there will be [r]a canopy. 6 [s]There will
be a [t]booth for shade by day from the heat,
and [u]for a refuge and a shelter from the storm
and rain.

The Vineyard of the LORD Destroyed

5 Let me sing for my beloved
my love song concerning his vineyard:
My beloved had [v]a vineyard
on a very fertile hill.
2 He dug it and cleared it of stones,
and planted it with [w]choice vines;
he built a watchtower in the midst of it,
and hewed out a wine vat in it;

[1] Or *purging*

17 [q][Deut. 28:60] [o][See ver. 16 above]
18 [r]ver. 16 [s][1 Pet. 3:3] [t]Judg. 8:21, 26
20 [u]Ex. 39:28; Ezek. 24:17
21 [v]Gen. 24:47; Ezek. 16:12
22 [w][Luke 15:22]
24 [x][Esth. 2:12] [y]Prov. 31:24 [z]1 Pet. 3:3 [a]ch. 15:2; 22:12; Ezek. 27:31; Amos 8:10; Mic. 1:16 [b]ch. 15:3; Gen. 37:34; Lam. 2:10 [c]Lev. 19:28
26 [d]Jer. 14:2; Lam. 1:4 [e]Job 2:13; Lam. 2:10

Chapter 4

1 [f][ch. 13:12] [g]ch. 3:6 [h]See Gen. 30:23
2 [i]Jer. 23:5; 33:15; Zech. 3:8; 6:12 [j][ch. 27:6]
3 [k]ch. 6:13; 10:20 [l]Obad. 17 [m]Ex. 32:32; Luke 10:20; Heb. 12:23; [Ps. 69:28]
4 [n]Ezek. 36:25 [o]ch. 3:16 [p]ch. 33:14; Mal. 3:2; Matt. 3:11; Luke 3:17
5 [q]Ex. 13:21 [r][Rev. 7:15]
6 [s]ch. 25:4 [t]See Ps. 27:5 [u]ch. 25:4

Chapter 5

1 [v]Ps. 80:8; Matt. 21:33; Mark 12:1; Luke 20:9; [Hos. 9:10]
2 [w]Jer. 2:21

4:1–6 In the midst of God's warnings the people are called to turn to him, looking for the "branch of the LORD," who "shall be beautiful and glorious" (v. 2). While some debate the connection, this phrase appears to include a messianic reference, for God has promised to raise up from David "a righteous Branch" who will "reign as king . . . and shall execute justice and righteousness in the land" (Jer. 23:5; cf. 33:15). This one "whose name is the Branch" will "build the temple of the LORD" (Zech. 6:12; cf. 3:8), and as such he will bring renewal and shalom to the land.

The result will be a changed people. They will be "holy," for God shall "have washed away" their filth that came with their arrogant words and deeds; they are "cleansed," interestingly enough, "by a spirit of judgment and by a spirit of burning" (Isa. 4:4). Is this not what John the baptizer spoke of by the river Jordan? He prepared the way for the coming Messiah, who will bring a baptism "with the Holy Spirit and fire" (Matt. 3:11; Luke 3:16).

When God comes and rescues, he does not leave us as we are, but purifies us and changes our lives. This grace of God finds full expression in the work of Christ, as his Spirit makes us new creatures, accomplishing our sanctification through our union to the crucified and risen Lord (Gal. 2:20).

5:1–7 While Isaiah sprinkled in words of promise amid the strong warnings of the first four chapters, here in chapter 5 such hope is hard to find. The first seven verses include what is commonly called the Song of the Vineyard. Isaiah sings on behalf of his "Beloved"—the Lord—who had a vineyard that he loved. He prepared the vineyard, protected it, and tended to its needs with the expectation of fruit. But the vineyard yielded "wild grapes" (v. 4). The divine voice asks, "What more was there to do for my vineyard, that I have not done in it?" (v. 4). A good tree should bear good fruit

and [x]he looked for it to yield grapes,
but it yielded wild grapes.

3 And now, O inhabitants of Jerusalem
and men of Judah,
judge between me and my vineyard.
4 [y]What more was there to do for my vineyard,
that I have not done in it?
[x]When I looked for it to yield grapes,
why did it yield wild grapes?

5 And now I will tell you
what I will do to my vineyard.
I will remove [z]its hedge,
and it shall be devoured;[1]
[a]I will break down its wall,
and it shall be trampled down.
6 I will make it a waste;
it shall not be pruned or hoed,
and [b]briers and thorns shall grow up;
[c]I will also command the clouds
that they rain no rain upon it.

7 [d]For the vineyard of the LORD of hosts
is the house of Israel,
and the men of Judah
are his pleasant planting;
and he looked for justice,
but behold, bloodshed;[2]
for righteousness,
but behold, an outcry![3]

Woe to the Wicked

8 Woe to those who [e]join house to house,
who add field to field,
until there is no more room,
and you are made to dwell alone
in the midst of the land.
9 The LORD of hosts has sworn in my hearing:
[f]"Surely many houses shall be desolate,
large and beautiful houses, without inhabitant.
10 [g]For ten acres[4] of vineyard shall yield but one bath,
and a [h]homer of seed shall yield but an ephah."[5]

11 Woe to those who [i]rise early in the morning,
that they may run after strong drink,
who tarry late into the evening
as wine inflames them!
12 [j]They have lyre and harp,
tambourine and flute and wine at their feasts,
[k]but they do not regard the deeds of the LORD,
or see the work of his hands.

13 Therefore my people go into exile
[l]for lack of knowledge;[6]
their [m]honored men go hungry,[7]
and their multitude is parched with thirst.
14 Therefore Sheol has [n]enlarged its appetite
and opened [o]its mouth beyond measure,
and the nobility of Jerusalem[8] and her multitude will go down,
her revelers and he who [p]exults in her.
15 [q]Man is humbled, and each one is brought low,
and the eyes of the haughty[9] are brought low.
16 [r]But the LORD of hosts is exalted[10] in justice,
and the Holy God shows himself holy in righteousness.

[1] Or *grazed over*; compare Exodus 22:5 [2] The Hebrew words for *justice* and *bloodshed* sound alike [3] The Hebrew words for *righteous* and *outcry* sound alike [4] Hebrew *ten yoke*, the area ten yoke of oxen can plow in a day [5] A *bath* was about 6 gallons or 22 liters; a *homer* was about 6 bushels or 220 liters; an *ephah* was about 3/5 bushel or 22 liters [6] Or *without their knowledge* [7] Or *die of hunger* [8] Hebrew *her nobility* [9] Hebrew *high* [10] Hebrew *high*

(cf. Matt. 7:17–19). "He looked for justice, but behold, bloodshed; for righteousness, but behold, an outcry" (Isa. 5:7).

When Jesus came, he identified himself as the final and true vine (John 15:1). United to him and cleansed in him (John 15:3), we bear fruit (John 15:5).

5:8–30 In light of the failures of the vineyard presented in the previous chapter, we read six "woes" from the Lord, speaking judgment against Judah's greed (vv. 8–10), self-indulgence (vv. 11–13), cynicism (vv. 18–19), moral distortion (v. 20), blinding arrogance (v. 21), and corruption and drunkenness (vv. 22–23). Each of these, in their own way, distorts God's good creation, making a mockery of his wisdom and justice.

2[x] [Matt. 21:19; Mark 11:13; Luke 13:6]
4[y] [Mic. 6:3, 4] [x] [See ver. 2 above]
5[z] [Jer. 5:10] [a] Ps. 80:12; [Prov. 24:31]
6[b] See ch. 7:23-25 [c] [1 Kgs. 17:1; Jer. 14:1, 22]
7[d] [ch. 3:14]; See Ps. 80:8-11
8[e] Mic. 2:2
9[f] ch. 6:12
10[g] [Lev. 26:26; Hag. 1:6; 2:16] [h] Ezek. 45:11
11[i] ver. 22; [Prov. 23:29, 30; Eccles. 10:16, 17] **12**[j] Amos 6:5, 6 [k] ch. 26:11 **13**[l] ch. 1:3; Hos. 4:6 [m] [Lam. 4:2, 7, 8] **14**[n] Hab. 2:5 [o] Ps. 141:7 [p] [ver. 12; Job 1:18, 19] **15**[q] ch. 2:9 **16**[r] ch. 2:11, 17

17 Then shall the lambs graze [s]as in their pasture,
and [t]nomads shall eat among the ruins of the rich.

18 Woe to those who draw iniquity with [u]cords of falsehood,
who draw sin as with cart ropes,
19 who say: [v]"Let him be quick,
let him speed his work
that we may see it;
let the counsel of the Holy One of Israel draw near,
and let it come, that we may know it!"
20 Woe to [w]those who call evil good
and good evil,
[x]who put darkness for light
and light for darkness,
who put bitter for sweet
and sweet for bitter!
21 Woe to those who are [y]wise in their own eyes,
and shrewd in their own sight!
22 Woe to those who are [z]heroes at drinking wine,
and valiant men in mixing strong drink,
23 who [a]acquit the guilty for a bribe,
and deprive the innocent of his right!

24 Therefore, [b]as the tongue of fire devours the stubble,
and as dry grass sinks down in the flame,
so [c]their root will be [d]as rottenness,
and their blossom go up like dust;
for they have [e]rejected the law of the LORD of hosts,
and have [f]despised the word of the Holy One of Israel.

25 Therefore [g]the anger of the LORD was kindled against his people,
and he stretched out his hand against them and struck them,
and [h]the mountains quaked;
and their corpses were [i]as refuse
in the midst of the streets.
[j]For all this his anger has not turned away,
and his hand is stretched out still.

26 He will [k]raise a signal for nations far away,
and [l]whistle for them [m]from the ends of the earth;
and behold, quickly, speedily they come!
27 [n]None is weary, none stumbles,
none slumbers or sleeps,
not a waistband is loose,
not a sandal strap broken;
28 [o]their arrows are sharp,
all their bows bent,
their horses' hoofs seem like flint,
and their wheels [p]like the whirlwind.
29 Their roaring is like a lion,
like young lions they roar;
they growl and [q]seize their prey;
they carry it off, and none can rescue.
30 They will growl over it on that day,
like the growling of the sea.
And if one looks to the land,
behold, [r]darkness and distress;
and the light is darkened by its clouds.

Isaiah's Vision of the Lord

6 In the year that [s]King Uzziah died I [t]saw
the Lord sitting upon a throne, high and
lifted up; and the train[1] of his robe filled the
temple. 2 Above him stood the seraphim. Each
had [u]six wings: with two he covered his face,
and with two he covered his feet, and with two
he flew. 3 And one called to another and said:

[1] Or *hem*

17[s] Mic. 2:12 [t] [Judg. 6:3]
18[u] Prov. 5:22
19[v] [Ezek. 12:22; 2 Pet. 3:4]
20[w] [Amos 5:7] [x] [Job 17:12; Matt. 6:22, 23; Luke 11:34, 35]
21[y] Prov. 3:7; Rom. 12:16
22[z] ver. 11
23[a] Ex. 23:8; Prov. 17:15
24[b] ch. 47:14; Joel 2:5; [Ex. 15:7] [c] Job 18:16 [d] Hos. 5:12 [e] ch. 30:9 [f] ch. 1:4
25[g] 2 Kgs. 22:13, 17 [h] Jer. 4:24; [Ps. 97:5; Hab. 3:6] [i] [2 Kgs. 9:37; Jer. 36:30] [j] ch. 9:12, 17, 21; 10:4
26[k] ch. 11:12; 13:2; 18:3 [l] ch. 7:18; Zech. 10:8 [m] ch. 10:3; Deut. 28:49 **27**[n] See ch. 10:28-31 **28**[o] Ps. 7:12, 13 [p] ch. 21:1 **29**[q] See 2 Kgs. 18:13-16 **30**[r] ch. 8:22 **Chapter 6** **1**[s] ch. 1:1; 2 Chr. 26:16-21 [t] [John 12:41] **2**[u] Rev. 4:8

Similar to the underlying concerns expressed here by Isaiah, Jesus offers strong words against the Pharisees when he gives a list of "woe" declarations to them. While externally carrying out what they believe to be the letter of the law, the religious leaders "neglect justice and the love of God," dishonoring God by making the burdens of others heavier, rather than working to bring them assistance and grace (Luke 11:42–52). But Jesus comes "full of grace and truth" (John 1:14). He promises to set us free from our self-absorbed sin so that we might joyfully put our neighbor above ourselves.

6:1–5 Having expressed the ominous prospects for Judah, the book now turns to Isaiah's call from God. Isaiah has a profound encounter with "the Lord sitting upon a throne," where his splendor is revealed (vv. 1–2). This Lord's glory fills the heavens and the earth, being perfectly complete and unmistakably holy (v. 3).

[u]"Holy, holy, holy is the LORD of hosts;
[v]the whole earth is full of his glory!"[1]

4 And [w]the foundations of the thresholds
shook at the voice of him who called, and [x]the
house was filled with smoke. 5 And I said: "Woe
is me! [y]For I am lost; [z]for I am a man of unclean
lips, and I dwell in the midst of a people of
unclean lips; for my eyes have seen the [a]King,
the LORD of hosts!"

6 Then one of the seraphim flew to me, having in his hand a burning coal that he had
taken with tongs from the altar. 7 And he
[b]touched my mouth and said: "Behold, this
has touched your lips; your guilt is taken away,
and your sin atoned for."

Isaiah's Commission from the Lord

8 And I heard the voice of the Lord saying,
"Whom shall I send, and who will go for [c]us?"
Then I said, "Here I am! Send me." 9 And he
said, "Go, and say to this people:

[d]"'Keep on hearing,[2] but do not understand;
keep on seeing,[3] but do not perceive.'
10 [e]Make the heart of this people [f]dull,[4]
and their ears heavy,
and blind their eyes;
[g]lest they see with their eyes,
and hear with their ears,
and understand with their hearts,
and turn and be healed."
11 Then I said, [h]"How long, O Lord?"
And he said:
"Until [i]cities lie waste
without inhabitant,
and houses without people,
and the land is a desolate waste,
12 and the LORD removes people far away,
and the forsaken places are many in the midst of the land.
13 [j]And though a tenth remain in it,
it will be burned[5] again,

[1] Or *may his glory fill the whole earth* [2] Or *Hear indeed* [3] Or *see indeed* [4] Hebrew *fat* [5] Or *purged*

3[u] [See ver. 2 above] [v]Ps. 72:19
4[w] Amos 9:1 [x]1 Kgs. 8:10, 11; Rev. 15:8; [Ex. 19:18]
5[y] [Judg. 13:22] [z][Luke 5:8] [a]ch. 33:17; Jer. 10:10; [1 Sam. 12:12]
7[b] Jer. 1:9; Dan. 10:16
8[c] See Gen. 1:26
9[d] Cited Matt. 13:14, 15; Acts 28:26, 27; [Mark 4:12; Luke 8:10; Rom. 11:8]
10[e] Cited John 12:40 [f]Ps. 119:70 [g][Jer. 5:21]
11[h] Ps. 79:5; 89:46 [i][ch. 1:7; 27:10]
13[j] [ch. 10:22]

The revelation of the glory of God results in statements of humility and confession from the prophet—regarding both himself and his people (v. 5). Here we discover important truths: real perception of the holiness of God necessarily results in acknowledgment of our sin and our need of his mercy; and, for all who are called to proclaim God's majesty and mercy, we must confess, "Woe is me!" (v. 5). When in the divine presence, Isaiah doesn't stand over against the people to whom he preaches; he identifies with them: "for I am a man of unclean lips, and I dwell in the midst of a people of unclean lips." Isaiah does not promote a deceptive modesty based on comparison to others; instead he experiences genuine humility that comes when his "eyes have seen the King, the LORD of hosts" (v. 5), the thrice holy God (v. 3).

6:6–13 We become emotionally and spiritually able to address the needs of others only after we come to recognize and confess our own great need and dependence upon God. Until that happens we inevitably slip into mere self-help advice, rather than the repentance unto life into which the gospel invites us. Isaiah confesses that he is a man of unclean lips (v. 5) as he realizes that he cannot join in the holy song of the seraphim (v. 3). Thus, the touch of the burning ember (from the altar of atonement) to his lips indicates that he has been made pure by a work beyond himself, so that now he can sing of, and give witness to, his God (vv. 6–7). We too have been touched by the "burning coal" of the altar where the sacrifices were made, having been purified by Christ's atoning sacrifice that put an end to the need of the altar's fire. Restored by his forgiveness and liberated from sin to be sent out, our lips may joyfully testify to the holiness and mercy of our God (v. 8).

Despite Isaiah's vision and message, God tells him that the covenant people will not listen to the message that he has given them yet another opportunity to hear (vv. 9–10); their deliberate deafness further justifies his judgment (vv. 11–13). Jesus draws on Isaiah's words (vv. 9–10; cf. e.g., Matt. 13:13–15) to explain his preference to speak about the kingdom in parables: no one will remain unaffected by their hearing of God's word; their hearts will be either softened and drawn into God's saving grace, or hardened by their refusal to acknowledge their need. Only God can give eyes to see and ears to hear (Matt. 13:16–17).

While Judah may appear hopeless, yet "the holy seed is its stump" (Isa. 6:13), for out of this stump of Jesse will come the heir of David (11:1, 10; Rom. 15:12), our Savior Jesus the Christ (Acts 13:23).

like a terebinth or an oak,
whose stump [k]remains
when it is felled."
[l]The holy seed[1] is its stump.

Isaiah Sent to King Ahaz

7 In the days of [m]Ahaz the son of Jotham, son
of Uzziah, king of Judah, [n]Rezin the king of
Syria and [n]Pekah the son of Remaliah the king
of Israel came up to Jerusalem to wage war
against it, but could not yet mount an attack
against it. 2 When the house of David was told,
[o]"Syria is in league with[2] [p]Ephraim," the heart
of Ahaz[3] and the heart of his people shook as
the trees of the forest shake before the wind.
3 And the LORD said to Isaiah, "Go out to
meet Ahaz, you and [q]Shear-jashub[4] your son,
at the end of [r]the conduit of the upper pool on
the highway to the Washer's Field. 4 And say
to him, [s]'Be careful, [t]be quiet, do not fear, and
do not let your heart be faint because of these
two [u]smoldering stumps of firebrands, at the
fierce anger of Rezin and Syria and [v]the son of
Remaliah. 5 Because Syria, with Ephraim and
[v]the son of Remaliah, has devised evil against
you, saying, 6 "Let us go up against Judah and
terrify it, and let us conquer it[5] for ourselves,
and set up the son of Tabeel as king in the
midst of it," 7 thus says the Lord GOD:

[w]"'It shall not stand,
and it shall not come to pass.
8 For the head of Syria is [x]Damascus,
and the head of Damascus is Rezin.
And within sixty-five years
Ephraim will be shattered from being
a people.
9 And the head of Ephraim is Samaria,
and the head of Samaria is [y]the son of
Remaliah.
[z]If you[6] are not firm in faith,
you will not be firm at all.'"

The Sign of Immanuel

10 Again the LORD spoke to Ahaz, 11 "Ask [a]a
sign of the LORD your[7] God; let it be deep as
Sheol or high as heaven." 12 But Ahaz said, "I
will not ask, and I will not put the LORD to
the test." 13 And he[8] said, "Hear then, O house
of David! Is it too little for you to weary men,
that you [b]weary my God also? 14 Therefore the
[c]Lord himself will give you a sign. [d]Behold,
the [e]virgin shall conceive and bear a son, and
shall call his name [f]Immanuel.[9] 15 He shall
eat [g]curds and honey when he knows how
to refuse the evil and choose the good. 16 [h]For
before the boy knows how to refuse the evil
and choose the good, the land whose two
kings you dread will be [i]deserted. 17 [j]The LORD

[1] Or *offspring* [2] Hebrew *Syria has rested upon* [3] Hebrew *his heart* [4] *Shear-jashub* means *A remnant shall return* [5] Hebrew *let us split it open* [6] The Hebrew for *you* is plural in verses 9, 13, 14 [7] The Hebrew for *you* and *your* is singular in verses 11, 16, 17 [8] That is, Isaiah [9] *Immanuel* means *God is with us*

13 [k][Job 14:7] [l]Ezra 9:2
Chapter 7
1 [m]ch. 1:1 [n]2 Kgs. 15:37; 16:5
2 [o][ch. 8:12] [p]ch. 9:9
3 [q][ch. 8:3, 18] [r]ch. 36:2; 2 Kgs. 18:17
4 [s][ch. 8:12] [t][Ex. 14:13] [u][Amos 4:11; Zech. 3:2] [v]ver. 1
5 [v][See ver. 4 above]
7 [w]ch. 8:10
8 [x]Gen. 14:15
9 [y]ver. 1 [z][2 Chr. 20:20]
11 [a]See 2 Kgs. 19:29
13 [b]ch. 43:24
14 [c]ch. 37:30; 38:7, 8 [d]ch. 9:6; Cited Matt. 1:23; [Luke 1:31, 34] [e]Gen. 24:43 (Heb.); Ex. 2:8 (Heb.); Ps. 68:25 (Heb.); Prov. 30:19 (Heb.) [f]ch. 8:8, 10
15 [g]ver. 22
16 [h][ch. 8:4] [i]ch. 6:12
17 [j]ch. 8:7; [2 Chr. 28:20]

7:1–9 Chapters 7–39 can be understood as dealing with the call (and failure) to trust in God. Will Judah trust foreign powers, their own ingenuity, and handcrafted idols, or will they trust Yahweh, the only true God? Isaiah provides a summary statement for this whole section: "If you are not firm in faith, you will not be firm at all" (7:9).

Ahaz and the people show how fragile their trust in God is, for when the threat of Syria and Ephraim appears, their hearts all "shook as the trees of the forest shake before the wind" (v. 2). What is more foundational to true love than trust? When circumstances grow difficult in our lives, the temptation increases to cease trusting God. James cautions us about difficult seasons when we appear wavering in our clear commitment to God: we become "like a wave of the sea that is driven and tossed by the wind" (James 1:6). Rather than this, we should stand secure in God's promises realized for us in Christ. Thus James continues, "Blessed is the man who remains steadfast under trial, for when he has stood the test he will receive the crown of life, which God has promised to those who love him" (James 1:12).

We are faithful by being full-of-faith, trusting God amid great uncertainties and challenges. In light of the sending of Jesus for our salvation, we have sufficient reason for such trust (Rom. 8:32).

7:10–25 Isaiah tells his audience that "in that day" devastation will come from the hand of Assyria, the very power they decided to lean on instead of trusting God (vv. 18–25). Their short-term solution leads to long-term misery. Although the circumstances seem frightening, with Jerusalem under immediate threat, God again promises deliverance that can come by "the Lord himself" (v. 14). The sign of this promise was "the virgin" who "shall conceive and bear a son," and this son will be called "Immanuel," which means "God is with us" (v. 14; cf. 8:8, 10).

will bring upon you and upon your people
and upon your father's house such days as
have not come since the day that [k]Ephraim
departed from Judah—the king of Assyria."
18 In that day the LORD will [l]whistle for the
fly that is at the end of the streams of Egypt,
and for the bee that is in the land of Assyria.
19 And they will all come and settle in the steep
ravines, and [m]in the clefts of the rocks, and on
all the thornbushes, and on all the pastures.[1]
20 In that day [n]the Lord will [o]shave with a
razor that is [p]hired beyond [q]the River—with
the king of Assyria—the head and the hair of
the feet, and it will sweep away the beard also.
21 [r]In that day a man will keep alive a young
cow and two sheep, 22 and because of the abundance of milk that they give, he will eat curds,
for everyone who is left in the land will eat
[s]curds and honey.
23 In that day every place where there used
to be a thousand vines, worth a thousand
shekels[2] of silver, will become [t]briers and
thorns. 24 [u]With bow and arrows a man will
come there, for all the land will be briers and
thorns. 25 [v]And as for all the hills that used to
be hoed with a hoe, you will not come there
for fear [t]of briers and thorns, but they will
become a place where cattle are let loose and
where sheep tread.

The Coming Assyrian Invasion

8 Then the LORD said to me, "Take a large
tablet [w]and write on it in common characters,[3] 'Belonging to Maher-shalal-hash-baz.'[4]
2 And [x]I will get reliable witnesses, [y]Uriah the
priest and Zechariah the son of Jeberechiah,
to attest for me."
3 And I went to the prophetess, and she conceived and bore a son. Then the LORD said
to me, [z]"Call his name Maher-shalal-hash-
baz; 4 [a]for before the boy knows how to cry
'My father' or 'My mother,' the [a]wealth of
[b]Damascus and the spoil of [b]Samaria will be
carried away before the king of Assyria."
5 The LORD spoke to me again: 6 "Because
this people has refused the waters of [c]Shiloah
that flow gently, and rejoice over [d]Rezin and
the son of Remaliah, 7 therefore, behold, the
Lord is bringing up against them [e]the waters
of [f]the River, mighty and many, the king of
Assyria and all his glory. And it [g]will rise over
all its channels and go over all its banks, 8 and
it will sweep on into Judah, it will overflow
and pass on, [h]reaching even to the neck, and its
[i]outspread wings will fill the breadth of your
land, [j]O Immanuel."

9 Be broken,[5] you peoples, and [k]be shattered;[6]
give ear, all you far countries;

[1] Or *watering holes*, or *brambles* [2] A *shekel* was about 2/5 ounce or 11 grams [3] Hebrew *with a man's stylus* [4] *Maher-shalal-hash-baz* means *The spoil speeds, the prey hastens* [5] Or *Be evil* [6] Or *dismayed*

While there may have been some immediate fulfillment of this promise in the time of Ahaz (perhaps Maher-shalal-hash-baz [8:1, 3], or Hezekiah), Christians rightly recognize, in light of the rest of Scripture, that this promise is ultimately fulfilled in the incarnation of the Son of God. He alone uniquely fulfills God's promise to be "with us" (Matt. 1:23; cf. e.g., Rom. 8:3; Gal. 4:4; Phil. 2:7; 1 John 4:2; 2 John 7). He alone will ground the promises of God, not merely in words but in his life, death, and resurrection. He alone will be faithful even amid the greatest temptations and trials, even unto death. Therefore, he is now the anchor and center of our faith and trust.

8:1–22 Christians are called to live their lives *coram deo* (before God), rather than *coram hominibus* (before man). In other words, we must always recognize that our ultimate audience is God. The Bible thus calls us to fear God and not man. But this can be such a challenge for us when our circumstances and all we see make us fear what others will think and do. In such situations, we must regain Isaiah's perspective: "do not fear" what the world fears (v. 12), "but the LORD of hosts, him you shall honor as holy. Let him be your fear, and let him be your dread" (v. 13). For Isaiah's audience, this meant a call to "wait for the LORD" and a cultivated commitment to "hope in him" (v. 17).

Peter applies these words to his readers, who are facing the challenge of suffering for the gospel. However, whereas Isaiah spoke of honoring *God* as "holy," Peter specifically applies that description and reasoning to Jesus: "Have no fear of them, nor be troubled, but in your hearts honor Christ the Lord as holy" (1 Pet. 3:14–15). Peter puts an eternal perspective on suffering, for "even if you should suffer for righteousness' sake, you will be blessed" (1 Pet. 3:14).

17 [k]1 Kgs. 12:16
18 [l]ch. 5:26
19 [m]ch. 2:19; Jer. 13:4; 16:16
20 [n]ch. 24:1; See 2 Kgs. 18:13-16 [o]Ezek. 5:1 [p][ch. 10:5, 15] [q]ch. 8:7; 11:15
21 [r][ch. 5:17]
22 [s]ver. 15
23 [t]ch. 5:6
24 [u][Judg. 5:11]
25 [v]ch. 32:13, 14 [t][See ver. 23 above]

Chapter 8
1 [w]ch. 30:8
2 [x][ch. 43:10] [y]2 Kgs. 16:10, 11, 15, 16
3 [z][Hos. 1:4]
4 [a][ch. 7:16] [b]See ch. 7:8, 9
6 [c][Neh. 3:15; John 9:7, 11] [d]See ch. 7:1, 4
7 [e][ch. 17:12, 13] [f]See ch. 7:20 [g][Jer. 46:8]
8 [h]ch. 30:28 [i][ch. 36:1] [j]ch. 7:14
9 [k][Dan. 2:34, 35]

strap on your armor and be shattered;
strap on your armor and be shattered.
10 Take counsel together, but it will come to nothing;
speak a word, [l]but it will not stand,
for God [m]is with us.[1]

Fear God, Wait for the LORD

11 For the LORD spoke thus to me with his
strong hand upon me, and [n]warned me not
to walk in the way of this people, saying:
12 "Do not call [o]conspiracy all that this people
calls conspiracy, and [p]do not fear what they
fear, nor be in dread. 13 But the LORD of hosts,
[q]him you shall honor as holy. Let him be your
fear, and let him be your dread. 14 And he will
become a [r]sanctuary and [s]a stone of offense
and a rock of stumbling to both houses of
Israel, a trap and a snare to the inhabitants
of Jerusalem. 15 And many [t]shall stumble on
it. They shall fall and be broken; they shall be
snared and taken."

16 Bind up [u]the testimony; [v]seal the teaching[2] among my disciples. 17 I will [w]wait for the
LORD, who is [x]hiding his face from the house
of Jacob, and I will hope in him. 18 [y]Behold,
I and [z]the children whom the LORD has given
me are signs and portents in Israel from the
LORD of hosts, who dwells on Mount Zion.
19 And when they say to you, "Inquire of the
[a]mediums and the necromancers who chirp
and mutter," should not a people inquire of
their God? Should they inquire of [b]the dead
on behalf of the living? 20 [c]To the teaching
and to the testimony! If they will not speak
according to this word, it is because they have
no [d]dawn. 21 They will pass through the land,[3]
greatly distressed and hungry. And when they
are hungry, they will be enraged and will
speak contemptuously against[4] their king
and their God, and turn their faces upward.
22 [e]And they will look to the earth, but behold,
distress and darkness, the gloom of anguish.
And they will be thrust into [f]thick darkness.

For to Us a Child Is Born

9 [5] But there will be no [g]gloom for her who
was in anguish. In the former time he
[h]brought into contempt the land of [i]Zebulun
and the land of Naphtali, but in the latter time
he [j]has made glorious the way of the sea, the
land beyond the Jordan, Galilee of the nations.[6]

2 [7] [i]The people [k]who walked in darkness
have seen a great light;
those who dwelt in a land of [l]deep darkness,
on them has light shone.
3 [m]You have multiplied the nation;
you have increased its joy;
they rejoice before you
as with [n]joy at the harvest,
as they [o]are glad [p]when they divide the spoil.
4 [q]For the yoke of his burden,
[r]and the staff for his shoulder,
the rod of his oppressor,
you have broken as [s]on the day of Midian.
5 [t]For every boot of the tramping warrior in battle tumult
and every garment rolled in blood
will be burned as fuel for the fire.
6 [u]For to us a child is born,
to us [v]a son is given;
[w]and the government shall be [x]upon[8] his shoulder,
and his name shall be called[9]
Wonderful [y]Counselor, [z]Mighty God,
[a]Everlasting [b]Father, Prince of [c]Peace.
7 Of the increase of his government and of peace
[d]there will be no end,

[1] The Hebrew for *God is with us* is *Immanuel* [2] Or *law*; also verse 20 [3] Hebrew *it* [4] Or *speak contemptuously by* [5] Ch 8:23 in Hebrew [6] Or *of the Gentiles* [7] Ch 9:1 in Hebrew [8] Or *is upon* [9] Or *is called*

9:1–21 Here we read one of the most memorable messianic expectations from the book of Isaiah. For the promise is that a child is coming (v. 6; cf. Matt. 4:15–16), breaking into the darkness and bringing his life-giving light (Isa. 9:2; cf. John 1:9–13; 1 Pet. 2:9). This coming "child," a "son," is the embodiment of Immanuel (Isa. 7:14; 8:8). His character displays his divine identity: he is a Wonderful Counselor (cf. Judg. 13:18; Isa. 28:29), the very Might of God (Deut. 10:17), an Everlasting Father (a royal one who is like a loving father to his people), and the Prince of Peace (Ps. 72:7; cf. Eph. 2:14).

10[l] ch. 7:7 [m] [ver. 8; Rom. 8:31]
11[n] [Ezek. 2:8]
12[o] [ch. 7:2] [p] Cited 1 Pet. 3:14, 15
13[q] See Num. 20:12
14[r] Ezek. 11:16 [s] Cited Rom. 9:33; 1 Pet. 2:8; [ch. 28:16]
15[t] [ch. 28:13; Matt. 21:44; Luke 20:18]
16[u] ver. 1, 2 [v] Dan. 12:4

17[w] Ps. 27:14; 33:20; Hab. 2:3 [x] ch. 1:15; 54:8; Deut. 31:17 **18**[y] Cited Heb. 2:13 [z] [ch. 7:3] **19**[a] ch. 19:3; 2 Kgs. 21:6; 23:24; 2 Chr. 33:6; See Lev. 19:31 [b] [Ps. 106:28]; See 1 Sam. 28:11-14 **20**[c] [Luke 16:29] [d] [ch. 60:1] **22**[e] ch. 5:30 [f] Nah. 1:8 **Chapter 9** **1**[g] [ch. 8:22] [h] [2 Kgs. 15:29; 2 Chr. 16:4] [i] Cited Matt. 4:15, 16 [j] ch. 26:15 **2**[i] [See ver. 1 above] [k] [Luke 1:79; Eph. 5:8, 14] [l] See Job 3:5 **3**[m] ch. 26:15 [n] Ps. 4:7; [John 4:36] [o] Ps. 119:162; [1 Sam. 30:16] [p] [Judg. 5:30] **4**[q] ch. 10:27; 14:25; Nah. 1:13; [Matt. 11:29] [r] ch. 10:5, 24; 14:5 [s] ch. 10:26; Ps. 83:9; See Judg. 7:19-25; 8:10-21 **5**[t] Ezek. 39:9 **6**[u] Luke 2:11; [John 3:16] [v] ch. 7:14 [w] [Matt. 28:18; 1 Cor. 15:25] [x] ch. 22:22 [y] [ch. 28:29] [z] ch. 10:21; Deut. 10:17; Neh. 9:32; Jer. 32:18; [Ps. 45:3] [a] Ps. 72:17 [b] ch. 63:16; [John 14:18] [c] Ps. 72:7; [Eph. 2:14]; See ch. 11:6-9 **7**[d] Ps. 89:4; Luke 1:32, 33

on the throne of David and over his
kingdom,
to establish it and to uphold it
[e]with justice and with righteousness
from this time forth and forevermore.
[f]The zeal of the LORD of hosts will do
this.

Judgment on Arrogance and Oppression

8 The Lord has sent a word against Jacob,
and it will fall on Israel;
9 and all the people will know,
[g]Ephraim and the inhabitants of
Samaria,
who say in pride and in arrogance of
heart:
10 "The bricks have fallen,
but we will build with dressed stones;
the sycamores have been cut down,
but we will put cedars in their place."
11 But the LORD raises the adversaries of
Rezin against him,
and stirs up his enemies.
12 [h]The Syrians on the east and [i]the
Philistines on the west
devour Israel with open mouth.
[j]For all this his anger has not turned
away,
and his hand is stretched out still.

13 The people [k]did not turn to him who
struck them,
nor inquire of the LORD of hosts.
14 So the LORD cut off from Israel [l]head
and tail,
palm branch and reed in one day—
15 [m]the elder and honored man is the head,
and [n]the prophet who teaches lies is
the tail;
16 for those who guide this people have
been leading them astray,
and those who are guided by them are
swallowed up.
17 Therefore the Lord does not [o]rejoice over
their young men,
and has no compassion on their
fatherless and widows;
for everyone is [p]godless and an evildoer,
and every mouth speaks [q]folly.[1]
[j]For all this his anger has not turned away,
and his hand is stretched out still.

18 For wickedness burns like [r]a fire;
it consumes briers and thorns;
it kindles the thickets of the forest,
and they roll upward in a column of
smoke.
19 Through the wrath of the LORD of hosts
the land is scorched,
and [s]the people are like fuel for the fire;
[t]no one spares another.
20 [u]They slice meat on the right, but are still
hungry,
and they devour on the left, but are
not satisfied;
[v]each devours the flesh of his own arm,
21 Manasseh devours Ephraim, and
Ephraim devours Manasseh;
together they are [w]against Judah.
[x]For all this his anger has not turned away,
and his hand is stretched out still.

10 Woe to those who [y]decree
iniquitous decrees,
and the writers who [z]keep writing
oppression,
2 to turn aside the needy from justice
and [a]to rob the poor of my people of
their right,

[1] Or *speaks disgraceful things*

The Gospels are built on this confession that, with the birth of Jesus, the Messiah has come (Luke 2:11). Jesus the King establishes his kingdom, not for a time but for eternity. "Justice" and "righteousness" mark his kingdom, for which there will "be no end" (Isa. 9:7; Rev. 11:15; 21:6). What the gospel makes clear, however, is that in our sin we are dependent on the gift of God's righteousness to us, since as sinners we are not righteous in and of ourselves (Rom. 3:23–24). We need Christ to bear our sin and God to credit his righteousness to our account (2 Cor. 5:21). As God's people who are united to Christ by his Spirit, the church should now be marked by the characteristics of Christ, such as justice, mercy, righteousness, wisdom, and peace (cf. Gal. 5:22–25). In a word, we become known by love. What we have received from God, we gladly extend to others (1 John 4:11).

10:1–4 God's love bends toward those in need, and when the most vulnerable are mistreated, his righteous anger grows fierce. Here we read of warnings against leaders who promote "oppression" and people who carry it out, who "turn aside the needy from justice" and by their action—or inaction—steal from the poor and mistreat the

7[e] Jer. 23:5 [f] ch. 37:32; 2 Kgs. 19:31; [Zech. 1:14]
9[g] ch. 7:2, 5, 8, 9, 17
12[h] [2 Kgs. 16:6] [i] [2 Chr. 28:18] [j] ver. 17, 21; ch. 5:25; 10:4
13[k] [ch. 1:5; Hos. 7:10]
14[l] ch. 19:15; Deut. 28:13
15[m] ch. 3:2, 3 [n] [ch. 28:7; Mic. 3:5]
17[o] Ps. 147:10, 11 [p] ch. 10:6 [q] Gen. 34:7 [j] [See ver. 12 above]
18[r] Ps. 83:14; [James 3:5]
19[s] ch. 24:6 [t] [Mic. 7:2]
20[u] ch. 8:21 [v] ch. 49:26; See Deut. 28:53-57
21[w] [ch. 11:13]; See 2 Chr. 28:6-9 [x] See ver. 12

Chapter 10
1[y] [Ps. 94:20] [z] Jer. 8:8
2[a] ch. 5:23

that widows may be their spoil,
and that they may make the fatherless their prey!
3 What will you do on [b]the day of punishment,
in the ruin that will come [c]from afar?
To whom will you flee for help,
and where will you leave your wealth?
4 Nothing remains but to crouch among the prisoners
or fall among the slain.
[d]For all this his anger has not turned away,
and his hand is stretched out still.

Judgment on Arrogant Assyria

5 Ah, Assyria, [e]the rod of my anger;
the staff in their hands is my fury!
6 Against a [f]godless nation I send him,
and against the people of my wrath I command him,
to take [g]spoil and seize plunder,
and to [h]tread them down like the mire of the streets.
7 But he [i]does not so intend,
and his heart does not so think;
but it is in his heart to destroy,
and to cut off nations not a few;
8 for he says:
[j]"Are not my commanders all kings?
9 [k]Is not [l]Calno like [m]Carchemish?
Is not [n]Hamath like [o]Arpad?
[p]Is not [q]Samaria like Damascus?
10 As my hand has reached to [r]the kingdoms of the idols,
whose carved images were greater than those of Jerusalem and Samaria,
11 shall I not do to Jerusalem and [s]her idols
[t]as I have done to Samaria and her images?"

12 [u]When the Lord has finished all his work
on Mount Zion and on Jerusalem, [v]he[1] will
punish the speech of the arrogant heart of the
king of Assyria and the boastful look in his
eyes. 13 [w]For he says:

"By the strength of my hand I have done it,
and by my wisdom, for I have understanding;
I remove the boundaries of peoples,
and plunder their treasures;
like a bull I bring down those who sit on thrones.
14 My hand has found like a nest
the wealth of the peoples;
and as one gathers eggs that have been forsaken,
so I have gathered all the earth;
and there was none that moved a wing
or opened the mouth or chirped."

15 Shall [x]the axe boast over him who hews with it,
or the saw magnify itself against him who wields it?
As if a rod should wield him who lifts it,
or as if a staff should lift him who is not wood!
16 Therefore the Lord GOD of hosts
will send wasting sickness among his [y]stout warriors,
and under his glory [z]a burning will be kindled,
like the burning of fire.
17 [a]The light of Israel will become a fire,
and [b]his Holy One a flame,

[1] Hebrew *I*

3[b] Jer. 5:29; Hos. 9:7; [Luke 19:44] [c] ch. 5:26
4[d] See ch. 9:12
5[e] ver. 24; ch. 9:4; [Mic. 5:1; 6:9]
6[f] ch. 9:17 [g] See 2 Kgs. 18:14-16 [h] ch. 5:5
7[i] [Mic. 4:12]
8[j] [2 Kgs. 18:24]
9[k] 2 Kgs. 19:12, 13 [l] [Gen. 10:10; Amos 6:2] [m] 2 Chr. 35:20; Jer. 46:2 [n] ch. 11:11; Amos 6:2; Zech. 9:2 [o] 2 Kgs. 18:34 [p] [2 Kgs. 16:9; 17:6] [q] ch. 7:9
10[r] [2 Kgs. 19:17, 18]
11[s] ch. 2:8 [t] 2 Kgs. 18:34
12[u] [ch. 29:4, 5; 30:18; 2 Kgs. 19:31] [v] See 2 Kgs. 19:35-37
13[w] ch. 37:23-25; 2 Kgs. 19:22-24
15[x] [ver. 5; ch. 29:16; 45:9; Rom. 9:17] **16**[y] Ps. 78:31 [z] [ch. 30:33] **17**[a] [Obad. 18] [b] ch. 37:23

widows and fatherless (vv. 1–3). While God promises to be their help, he asks those who mistreat them, "to whom will you flee for help?" (v. 3).

The sovereign God identifies with the weak (e.g., Ps. 12:5; 40:17; Jer. 22:15–16) and has always told his people to be quick to care for the poor and needy (Deut. 15:11), to protect workers against oppression (Deut. 24:14–15), and to uphold justice for the fatherless and widows (Deut. 24:17). Even today, God's people find ministries of mercy an essential outworking of our "religion" (James 1:27). For to neglect these needs is to misunderstand our own utter dependence on God—and his extravagant mercy toward us.

10:5–34 Despite its apparent power, Assyria also is not self-sufficient (v. 15) but is reliant upon God's providential sustenance and patience. Such divine long-suffering, however, is not endless. Consequently, the end of Assyria's reign (vv. 24–34) is contrasted with the promise that "the remnant of Israel" will return to the Lord, their Mighty God (vv. 20–21). "The Lord is not slow to fulfill his promise" (2 Pet. 3:9).

and [c]it will burn and devour
his thorns and briers [d]in one day.
18 The glory of [e]his forest and of his [f]fruitful land
the LORD will destroy, both soul and body,
and it will be as when a sick man wastes away.
19 The remnant of the trees of his forest will be so few
that a child can write them down.

The Remnant of Israel Will Return

20 [g]In that day [h]the remnant of Israel and the
survivors of the house of Jacob will no more
[i]lean on him who struck them, but [j]will lean
on the LORD, the Holy One of Israel, in truth.
21 A remnant will return, the remnant of
Jacob, [k]to the mighty God. 22 [l]For though your
people Israel be as the sand of the sea, [m]only
a remnant of them will return. [n]Destruction
is decreed, overflowing with righteousness.
23 For the Lord GOD of hosts will make a full
end, as decreed, in the midst of all the earth.
24 Therefore thus says the Lord GOD of hosts:
"O my people, [o]who dwell in Zion, [p]be not
afraid of the Assyrians when they strike with
the rod and lift up their staff against you as
[q]the Egyptians did. 25 For [r]in a very little while
my fury will come to an end, and my anger
will be directed to their destruction. 26 And
[s]the LORD of hosts will wield against them a
whip, as when he struck [t]Midian [u]at the rock
of Oreb. And his staff will be over the sea, and
he will lift it [v]as he did in Egypt. 27 And in
that day [w]his burden will depart from your
shoulder, and [x]his yoke from your neck; and
the yoke will be broken because of the fat."[1]

28 He has come to Aiath;
he has passed through [y]Migron;
at Michmash he stores [z]his baggage;
29 they have crossed over [a]the pass;
at [b]Geba they lodge for the night;
[c]Ramah trembles;
[d]Gibeah of Saul has fled.
30 Cry aloud, O daughter of [e]Gallim!
Give attention, O Laishah!
O poor [f]Anathoth!
31 Madmenah is in flight;
the inhabitants of Gebim flee for safety.
32 This very day he will halt at [g]Nob;
he will shake his fist
at the mount of [h]the daughter of Zion,
the hill of Jerusalem.
33 Behold, the Lord GOD of hosts
[i]will lop [j]the boughs with terrifying power;
the great in height will be hewn down,
and the lofty will be brought low.
34 He will cut down [j]the thickets of the forest with an axe,
and [k]Lebanon will fall by the Majestic One.

The Righteous Reign of the Branch

11 There shall come forth a shoot from the stump of [l]Jesse,
and a branch from his roots shall bear fruit.

[1] The meaning of the Hebrew is uncertain

11:1–16 God never abandoned Israel, promising that amid the apparently destitute land there remained "the holy seed" found in a stump (6:13). Coming forth from the line of David (11:1), this "root of Jesse" would signal to the nations a new reality (v. 10).

At Jesus' baptism, as he rose out of the water, the Spirit descended upon him like a dove, and the Gospel writers appear to connect this event with the messianic expectations of Isaiah (see Matt. 3:16; Mark 1:10; Luke 3:22; cf. Isa. 11:2, 61:1). Here is the true fulfillment of this expectation, as the one conceived by the Holy Spirit (Luke 1:35) grows in wisdom, understanding, and counsel, so that "his delight shall be in the fear of the LORD" (Isa. 11:3; cf. Heb. 5:7–9). These words provide one of the most profound definitions of "the fear of the LORD" in the Old Testament. We hardly have a modern word equivalent to this Hebrew word for "fear." The word cannot simply mean "terror," because God's people are called to love their Lord—impossible if they only live in terror of him. Many theologians, therefore, substitute words such as "awe" or "reverence" for this Old Testament use of "fear." Such words help our understanding, but this passage (Isa. 11:2–3) reminds us that Christ will "delight" in the fear of the Lord. So, we are made to understand that the loving regard that the eternal Son has for his Father is the fear of the Lord. This is not merely reverence for divine power but is proper regard for all that God is: just, holy, powerful, wise, loving, compassionate, and merciful.

17 [c]ch. 27:4; [ch. 9:18; Nah. 1:10] [d][ch. 9:14; 2 Kgs. 19:35]
18 [e]ver. 33; [ch. 2:13] [f][Ps. 107:33-34]
20 [g]ver. 27; ch. 2:11 [h]ch. 4:2 [i][2 Kgs. 16:7; 2 Chr. 28:20, 21] [j]2 Kgs. 19:14
21 [k]ch. 9:6
22 [l]Cited Rom. 9:27, 28 [m][ch. 6:13] [n]ch. 28:22
24 [o][ch. 31:5] [p]2 Kgs. 19:6 [q]Ex. 2:23
25 [r][ch. 17:14]
26 [s]2 Kgs. 19:35 [t]ch. 9:4 [u]Judg. 7:25; [ch. 9:4] [v][Ex. 14:30]
27 [w]2 Kgs. 18:14 [x][ch. 9:4; Nah. 1:13]
28 [y]1 Sam. 14:2 [z]Judg. 18:21; 1 Sam. 17:22; Acts 21:15; [ch. 46:1]
29 [a]1 Sam. 13:23 [b]1 Sam. 13:16 [c]1 Sam. 7:17 [d]1 Sam. 11:4
30 [e]1 Sam. 25:44 [f]Jer. 1:1
32 [g]1 Sam. 21:1; 22:19 [h]ch. 1:8; 37:22

33 [i][Nah. 1:12] [j]ver. 18 **34** [j][See ver. 33 above] [k][Ezek. 31:3; Amos 2:9] **Chapter 11** **1** [l]ver. 10; Acts 13:23

2 And [m]the Spirit of the LORD shall rest
upon him,
the Spirit of wisdom and understanding,
the Spirit of counsel and might,
the Spirit of knowledge and the fear
of the LORD.
3 And his delight shall be in the fear of the
LORD.
[n]He shall not judge by [o]what his eyes
see,
or decide disputes by [o]what his ears
hear,
4 but [p]with righteousness he shall judge
the poor,
and decide with equity for the meek
of the earth;
and he shall [q]strike the earth with the
rod of his mouth,
and [r]with the breath of his lips [s]he
shall kill the wicked.
5 Righteousness shall be the belt of his
waist,
and [t]faithfulness the belt of his loins.

6 [u]The wolf shall dwell with the lamb,
and the leopard shall lie down with
the young goat,
and the calf and the lion and the fattened calf together;
and a little child shall lead them.
7 The cow and the bear shall graze;
their young shall lie down together;
and the lion shall eat straw like the ox.
8 The nursing child shall play over the
hole of the cobra,
and the weaned child shall put his
hand on the adder's den.
9 [u]They shall not hurt or destroy
in all [v]my holy mountain;
[w]for the earth shall be full of the knowledge of the LORD
as the waters cover the sea.

10 In that day [x]the root of [y]Jesse, who shall
stand as [z]a signal for the peoples—of him
shall the nations inquire, and his resting place
shall be glorious.
11 [a]In that day the Lord will extend his hand
yet a second time to recover the remnant that
remains of his people, [b]from Assyria, [b]from
Egypt, from [c]Pathros, from [d]Cush,[1] from [e]Elam,
from [f]Shinar, from [g]Hamath, and from [h]the
coastlands of the sea.

12 He will raise [z]a signal for the nations
and will assemble [i]the banished of
Israel,
and gather the dispersed of Judah
from the four corners of the earth.
13 [j]The jealousy of Ephraim shall depart,
and those who harass Judah shall be
cut off;
Ephraim shall not be jealous of Judah,
and Judah shall not harass Ephraim.
14 [k]But they shall swoop down on the shoulder of the Philistines in the west,
and together they shall plunder [l]the
people of the east.
They shall put out their hand [m]against
[n]Edom and [o]Moab,
and [p]the Ammonites shall obey them.
15 And the LORD will utterly destroy[2]
[q]the tongue of the Sea of Egypt,
and will wave his hand over [r]the River
with his scorching breath,[3]

[1] Probably *Nubia* [2] Hebrew *devote to destruction* [3] Or *wind*

2[m] ch. 61:1; Matt. 3:16; Mark 1:10; Luke 3:22
3[n] [John 7:24] [o] [Eccles. 1:8]
4[p] Ps. 72:2, 4 [q] Ps. 2:9; [Mal. 4:6] [r] Job 4:9; 2 Thess. 2:8 [s] Ps. 139:19
5[t] [Eph. 6:14]
6[u] ch. 65:25; [Hos. 2:18]
9[u] [See ver. 6 above] [v] Ps. 78:54 [w] Hab. 2:14
10[x] Cited Rom. 15:12 [y] ver. 1 [z] ch. 49:22; [Ex. 17:15]
11[a] ch. 10:20 [b] ch. 27:13; Mic. 7:12; Zech. 10:10 [c] Jer. 44:1, 15; Ezek. 29:14; 30:14 [d] See Gen. 10:6-12 [e] Gen. 10:22; 14:1, 9; Jer. 25:25; See Jer. 49:34-39 [f] Gen. 11:2 [g] See ch. 10:9 [h] Esth. 10:1
12[z] [See ver. 10 above] [i] ch. 56:8; [Zech. 10:6]

Contributing to this "proper regard" are Isaiah's prophecies of the new world order. After Jesus' death and resurrection, all who believe in him become a part of this promised new creation. With the coming of this "stump of Jesse" a radical shift in the way of the world is expected: chaos will turn to harmony, fear to laughter, death to life (vv. 6–9). We who are new creatures in Christ joyfully participate in the work of the kingdom that we anticipate (vv. 4–10), seeking reconciliation in Jesus' name by pursuing peace, justice, creation care, and life-promoting goodness (cf. Deut. 26:13). In part we do this by putting on the full armor of God, first truly worn by Christ (cf. Isa. 11:5) but now given to us by his Spirit. In so doing we wage the battle not against foreign political powers but against "the schemes of the devil" (Eph. 6:11). Echoing the words of Isaiah, we are encouraged to stand, to put on the "belt of truth, and . . . the breastplate of righteousness," being ready "by the gospel of peace" to hold up "the shield of faith" and the "helmet of salvation," fighting back with the "sword of the Spirit, which is the word of God" (Eph. 6:13–17).

13[j] Ezek. 37:16, 17; [ch. 9:21; Zech. 11:14] **14**[k] [2 Sam. 8:1; 2 Kgs. 18:8] [l] Judg. 6:3; See Jer. 49:28 [m] Ps. 60:8 [n] [2 Sam. 8:14] [o] [2 Sam. 8:2] [p] See 2 Sam. 12:26-31 **15**[q] [Zech. 10:11] [r] See ch. 7:20

and strike it into seven channels,
and he will lead people across in sandals.
16 And there will be [s]a highway from Assyria
for the remnant that remains of his people,
[t]as there was for Israel
when they came up from the land of Egypt.

The LORD Is My Strength and My Song

12 You[1] will say [u]in that day:
"I will give thanks to you, O LORD,
for though you were angry with me,
[v]your anger turned away,
that you might comfort me.

2 "Behold, God is my salvation;
I will trust, and will not be afraid;
for [w]the LORD GOD[2] is my strength and my song,
and he has become my salvation."

3 [x]With joy you[3] will draw water from the
wells of salvation. 4 [y]And you will say in that
day:

[z]"Give thanks to the LORD,
call upon his name,
[a]make known his deeds among the peoples,
proclaim [b]that his name is exalted.

5 [c]"Sing praises to the LORD, for he has done gloriously;
let this be made known[4] in all the earth.
6 Shout, and sing for joy, O inhabitant of Zion,
for great [d]in your[5] midst is [e]the Holy One of Israel."

The Judgment of Babylon

13 The oracle concerning [f]Babylon which [g]Isaiah the son of Amoz saw.

2 On a bare hill [h]raise a signal;
cry aloud to them;
wave the hand for [i]them to enter
the gates of the nobles.
3 I myself have commanded my consecrated ones,
and have summoned my mighty men
to execute my anger,
my proudly exulting ones.[6]

4 The sound [j]of a tumult is on the mountains
as of a great multitude!
The sound of an uproar of kingdoms,
of nations gathering together!
[k]The LORD of hosts is mustering
a host for battle.
5 [l]They come from a distant land,
from the end of the heavens,

[1] The Hebrew for *you* is singular in verse 1 [2] Hebrew *for Yah, the LORD* [3] The Hebrew for *you* is plural in verses 3, 4 [4] Or *this is made known*
[5] The Hebrew for *your* in verse 6 is singular, referring to the *inhabitant of Zion* [6] Or *those who exult in my majesty*

12:1–6 Those who have been rescued from a frightening reality want to tell others about it. Such experiences naturally bring forth song, story, and renewed hope. Isaiah promises that such a time is coming, when God's saving work will be celebrated (v. 3), when trust in Yahweh will replace their fears, and when God's strength—rather than fragile national power—will become the center of their song (v. 2). Courage to face future challenges can be found from the experiences of past deliverances (cf. Ex. 15:1–18).

13:1–23:18 In the next 11 chapters Isaiah turns his warnings about God's judgment to more direct statements about what will happen to nations beyond Israel. This is the judgment that befalls all those, then and now, who refuse to humble themselves and yield to God's gracious rule, ultimately secured in his Son.

13:1–22 Babylon is the first to receive word that God's patience should not be tested, for he will "punish the world for its evil" (v. 11). Plunging from its greatness and glory, Babylon will end up becoming like a wild and abandoned territory, ruled by animals rather than by prideful humans (vv. 19–22; cf. Nebuchadnezzar in Dan. 4:31–33; 5:24–31).

Isaiah's warning, while here applied to Babylon, speaks to all who imagine that the prosperity and ease of their life will continue forever, even as injustices and sin accumulate. There is a coming judgment directed not just against a particular region or country but against the world that has rebelled against God and his good creation. Only by trusting in Christ alone can we rest in the safety of his sanctuary during a coming day of judgment: God will "make the heavens tremble, and the earth will be shaken out of its place" (Isa. 13:13; Hag. 2:6; Matt. 24:29–31; Mark 13:24–27).

16 [s]ch. 19:23; [ch. 35:8] [t]Ex. 14:29

Chapter 12
1 [u]ch. 11:11 [v][ch. 10:4]
2 [w]Ex. 15:2; Ps. 118:14
3 [x][John 4:13, 14; 7:37, 38]
4 [y]ch. 11:11 [z]Ps. 105:1 [a][Ps. 145:4-6] [b]Ps. 148:13
5 [c]Ex. 15:1; Ps. 98:1
6 [d]Ps. 46:5; Hos. 11:9 [e]ch. 5:24; 41:14, 16

Chapter 13
1 [f]ver. 19; ch. 14:4; 21:9; 47:1; See Jer. 51, 52 [g]ch. 1:1
2 [h]ch. 5:26 [i][ch. 41:25]
4 [j][ch. 22:5] [k][Josh. 5:13, 14]
5 [l][ch. 46:11]

the LORD and the weapons of his indignation,
to destroy the whole land.[1]

6 [m]Wail, for [n]the day of the LORD is near;
as destruction from the Almighty[2] it will come!
7 Therefore all hands will be feeble,
and every human heart [o]will melt.
8 They will be dismayed:
[p]pangs and agony will seize them;
[q]they will be in anguish like a woman in labor.
They will look aghast at one another;
their faces will be aflame.

9 Behold, [n]the day of the LORD comes,
cruel, with wrath and fierce anger,
to make the land a desolation
and [r]to destroy its sinners from it.
10 [s]For the stars of the heavens and their constellations
will not give their light;
[t]the sun will be dark at its rising,
and the moon will not shed its light.
11 I will punish [u]the world for its evil,
and the wicked for their iniquity;
I will [v]put an end to the pomp of the arrogant,
[w]and lay low the pompous pride of the ruthless.
12 I will make [x]people more rare than fine gold,
and mankind than the [y]gold of Ophir.
13 Therefore [z]I will make the heavens tremble,
and the earth will be shaken out of its place,
at the wrath of the LORD of hosts
in the day of his fierce anger.
14 And like a hunted gazelle,
or like sheep with none to gather them,
[a]each will turn to his own people,
and each will flee to his own land.
15 Whoever is found will be thrust through,
and whoever is caught will fall by the sword.
16 [b]Their infants will be dashed in pieces before their eyes;
their houses will be plundered
and their wives ravished.

17 Behold, [c]I am stirring up the Medes against them,
who have no regard for silver
and do not delight in gold.
18 [d]Their bows will slaughter[3] the young men;
they will have no mercy on the fruit of the womb;
their eyes will not pity children.
19 And Babylon, [e]the glory of kingdoms,
the splendor and pomp of the Chaldeans,
will be [f]like Sodom and Gomorrah
when God overthrew them.
20 [g]It will never be inhabited
or lived in for all generations;
no [h]Arab will pitch his tent there;
no [i]shepherds will make their flocks lie down there.
21 But [j]wild animals will lie down there,
and their houses will be full of howling creatures;
there [k]ostriches[4] will dwell,
and there wild goats will dance.
22 Hyenas[5] will cry in its towers,
and [l]jackals in [m]the pleasant palaces;
its time is close at hand
and its days will not be prolonged.

The Restoration of Jacob

14 [n]For the LORD will have compassion on
Jacob and will again choose Israel, and
[o]will set them in their own land, and [p]sojourn-
ers will join them and will attach themselves
to the house of Jacob. 2 And [q]the peoples will
take them and bring them to their place, and
the house of Israel will possess them in the

[1] Or *earth*; also verse 9 [2] The Hebrew words for *destruction* and *almighty* sound alike [3] Hebrew *dash in pieces* [4] Or *owls* [5] Or *foxes*

Such a judgment can be marvelously avoided by trusting in the King who died on our behalf. He made the earth tremble and rocks shake as he faced exile for us (cf. Matt. 27:45–54), but then by his resurrection he brought new life to those who are united to him by faith (2 Cor. 5:17).

6[m] ch. 14:31; 15:2, 3, 8; 16:7; Jer. 51:8; Ezek. 30:2 [n] ch. 2:12; Joel 1:15; Zeph. 1:7 **7**[o] See Josh. 2:11 **8**[p] [Nah. 2:10] [q] ch. 26:17; Jer. 4:31; 6:24; Mic. 4:9, 10; John 16:21 **9**[n] [See ver. 6 above] [r] [Ps. 104:35] **10**[s] [ch. 34:4] [t] Ezek. 32:7; Joel 2:31; 3:15; Matt. 24:29; Mark 13:24; Luke 21:25 **11**[u] ch. 24:21 [v] [ch. 24:4] [w] [ch. 2:11, 17] **12**[x] ch. 24:6 [y] 1 Kgs. 10:11; Job 28:16 **13**[z] Hag. 2:6 **14**[a] Jer. 50:16; 51:9; [1 Kgs. 22:36] **16**[b] Ps. 137:9; Nah. 3:10 **17**[c] ch. 21:2; Jer. 51:11, 28; Dan. 5:28, 31 **18**[d] Jer. 50:14, 29; 51:3 **19**[e] [ch. 47:5] [f] ch. 1:9; Gen. 19:24; Jer. 50:40; Amos 4:11 **20**[g] Jer. 51:37, 43 [h] Jer. 3:2 [i] Jer. 33:12 **21**[j] [ch. 34:13, 14] [k] ch. 34:13; Jer. 50:39 **22**[l] ch. 35:7; Jer. 51:37 [m] [ch. 25:2; Amos 3:15] **Chapter 14** **1**[n] Ps. 102:13; Zech. 1:17 [o] 2 Chr. 36:22, 23 [p] Zech. 8:22, 23; See Eph. 2:12-14 **2**[q] ch. 49:22; 60:9; 66:20

LORD's land [r]as male and female slaves.[1] [s]They
will take captive those who were their captors,
[t]and rule over those who oppressed them.

Israel's Remnant Taunts Babylon

3 When the LORD has given you rest from
your pain and turmoil and the hard service
with which you were made to serve, 4 you will
take up this [u]taunt against the king of Babylon:

"How the oppressor has ceased,
 [v]the insolent fury[2] ceased!
5 The LORD has broken the [w]staff of the wicked,
 the [w]scepter of rulers,
6 [x]that struck the peoples in wrath
 with unceasing blows,
that ruled the nations in anger
 with unrelenting persecution.
7 The whole earth is at rest and quiet;
 [y]they break forth into singing.
8 [z, a]The cypresses rejoice at you,
 [b]the cedars of Lebanon, saying,
'Since you were laid low,
 no woodcutter comes up against us.'
9 Sheol beneath is stirred up
 to meet you when you come;
it rouses the shades to greet you,
 all who were leaders of the earth;
it raises from their thrones
 all who were kings of the nations.
10 [c]All of them will answer
 and say to you:
'You too have become as weak as we!
 You have become like us!'
11 Your pomp is brought down to Sheol,
 the sound of your harps;
maggots are laid as a bed beneath you,
 and worms are your covers.

12 "How [d]you are fallen from heaven,
 O Day Star, [e]son of Dawn!
How you are cut down to the ground,
 you who laid the nations low!
13 You said in your heart,
 [f]'I will ascend to heaven;
above the stars of God
 [g]I will set my throne on high;
I will sit on the mount of assembly
 in the far reaches of the north;[3]
14 I will ascend above the heights of the clouds;
 I will make myself like the Most High.'
15 [h]But you are brought down to Sheol,
 to the far reaches of the pit.
16 Those who see you will stare at you
 and ponder over you:
'Is this [i]the man who made the earth tremble,
 who shook kingdoms,

[1] Or *servants* [2] Dead Sea Scroll (compare Septuagint, Syriac, Vulgate); the meaning of the word in the Masoretic Text is uncertain [3] Or *in the remote parts of Zaphon*

14:1–2 As God's judgments are turned against Babylon and the other nations, God's historic promises resurface: he will have "compassion on Jacob and will again choose Israel" (v. 1). We find sober warnings in the Old Testament about covenant unfaithfulness: those who consistently rebel against God can face his discipline to "the third and the fourth generation" (e.g., Ex. 34:7; Num. 14:18).

As harsh as that may sound, we sometimes miss the contrast that is actually given in those contexts. God's very heart is to be "merciful and gracious, slow to anger, and abounding in steadfast love and faithfulness, keeping steadfast love for thousands [of generations], forgiving iniquity and transgression and sin" (Ex. 34:6–7; Num. 14:18). While God never becomes blind to sin, his people must not forget that he is long-suffering and full of grace, and his promises are always there even as he chastens them.

14:3–32 A reversal takes place. Where previously Babylon had taunted Israel, now Israel's remnant stands over their former oppressors (vv. 3–4). God's judgment strikes down this tormentor; a clear outworking of the scriptural principle that God "opposes the proud, but gives grace to the humble" (James 4:6; 1 Pet. 5:5; cf. Prov. 3:34).

How easy it is when in power and during times of prosperity to become like the self-deluded Babylonians who came to imagine that they stood "above the stars of God" when in fact we always remain under Yahweh's sovereign reign and rule (Isa. 14:13–21). When God's judgment comes, what once seemed invincible can easily be swept away (vv. 22–23). Turning to the One who "founded Zion" is the only hope; in the city of God's tender presence and provision, refuge and grace can be enjoyed (v. 32). Such refuge is found only in Christ.

2 [r] ch. 61:5 [s] [Joel 3:8] [t] ch. 60:14
4 [u] Mic. 2:4; Hab. 2:6 [v] [Jer. 51:13; Rev. 18:16]
5 [w] [ch. 9:4]
6 [x] [Jer. 50:23]
7 [y] ch. 44:23; 49:13; 54:1; 55:12
8 [z] [Ezek. 31:16] [a] [ch. 37:24] [b] See ch. 2:13
10 [c] [Jer. 51:48]
12 [d] [ch. 24:21; 34:3] [e] [Job 38:7]
13 [f] Jer. 51:53; Amos 9:2; [Matt. 11:23; Luke 10:15] [g] Dan. 5:22, 23; [2 Thess. 2:4]
15 [h] Ezek. 32:23; Matt. 11:23; Luke 10:15
16 [i] [Jer. 50:23]

17 who made the world like a desert
and overthrew its cities,
[j]who did not let his prisoners go
home?'
18 All the kings of the nations lie in glory,
each in his own tomb;[1]
19 but you are cast out, away from your
grave,
like a loathed branch,
[k]clothed with the slain, those pierced by
the sword,
who go down to the stones of the pit,
like a dead body trampled underfoot.
20 You will not be joined with them in
burial,
because you have destroyed your land,
you have slain your people.

"May [l]the offspring of evildoers
nevermore be named!
21 Prepare slaughter for his sons
[m]because of the guilt of their fathers,
lest they rise and possess the earth,
and fill the face of the world with cities."

22 "I will rise up against them," declares the
LORD of hosts, "and will cut off from Babylon
name and [n]remnant, [o]descendants and posterity," declares the LORD. 23 "And I will make it
a possession of the [p]hedgehog,[2] and pools of
water, and I will sweep it with the broom of
destruction," declares the LORD of hosts.

An Oracle Concerning Assyria

24 The LORD of hosts has sworn:
[q]"As I have planned,
so shall it be,
and as I have purposed,
so shall it stand,
25 that [r]I will break the Assyrian in my land,
and on my mountains trample him
underfoot;
and [s]his yoke shall depart from them,
and [s]his burden from their shoulder."
26 This is the purpose that is purposed
concerning the whole earth,
and this is [t]the hand that is stretched
out
over all the nations.
27 [u]For the LORD of hosts has purposed,
and who will annul it?
[t]His hand is stretched out,
and who will turn it back?

An Oracle Concerning Philistia

28 In the year that [v]King Ahaz died came this
[w]oracle:

29 Rejoice not, [x]O Philistia, all of you,
that [y]the rod that struck you is broken,
for from the serpent's root will come
forth an adder,
and its fruit will be a [z]flying fiery serpent.
30 And the firstborn of [a]the poor will graze,
and [a]the needy lie down in safety;
but I will kill your root with famine,
and your remnant it will slay.
31 [b]Wail, O [c]gate; cry out, O city;
melt in fear, [x]O Philistia, all of you!
[d]For smoke comes out of the north,
and there is no straggler in his ranks.

32 What will one answer the messengers of
the nation?
[e]"The LORD has founded Zion,
and in her the afflicted of his people
find refuge."

An Oracle Concerning Moab

15

An [w]oracle concerning [f]Moab.

Because [g]Ar of Moab is laid waste in a
night,
Moab is undone;
because [h]Kir of Moab is laid waste in a
night,
Moab is undone.

[1] Hebrew *house* [2] Possibly *porcupine*, or *owl*

17[j] [Jer. 50:33]
19[k] [Ezek. 32:20]
20[l] Job 18:19; Ps. 21:10; 109:13
21[m] [Ex. 20:5; Matt. 23:35]
22[n] [Jer. 51:50, 62] [o] Job 18:19; [Gen. 21:23]
23[p] ch. 34:11; Zeph. 2:14
24[q] [Prov. 19:21]
25[r] ch. 37:36 [s] ch. 9:4; 10:27
26[t] [Deut. 4:34]

15:1–9 Moab also is "undone" and filled with humiliation (vv. 1–3). Pride and insolence lead to this verdict of judgment for Moab (see 16:6). Such devastating decrees against the nations are not something God delights in: "My heart cries out for Moab; [for] her fugitives" (15:5). He does not delight even in the death of the wicked (cf. Ezek. 18:23; 33:11). God senses their suffering and pain, and hints of promise can be found even amid this dire situation, but hope will come only from looking to Yahweh for deliverance.

27[u] 2 Chr. 20:6; Job 9:12; Ps. 33:11; Prov. 21:30; Dan. 4:31, 33, 35 [t] [See ver. 26 above] **28**[v] 2 Kgs. 16:20 [w] See ch. 13:1 **29**[x] Ex. 15:14; [Ps. 60:8; 87:4; 108:9] [y] [ch. 10:24] [z] ch. 30:6; Num. 21:6; [Jer. 46:22] **30**[a] [ch. 29:19; Zeph. 3:12] **31**[b] ch. 13:6 [c] ch. 24:12 [x] [See ver. 29 above] [d] [ch. 20:1] **32**[e] Ps. 87:1, 5; 102:16; 132:13; [ch. 28:16] **Chapter 15** **1**[w] [See ch. 14:28 above] [f] See Jer. 48; Ezek. 25:8-11; Amos 2:1-3; Zeph. 2:8, 9 [g] Num. 21:15, 28 [h] [ch. 16:7, 11]

2 He has gone up to the temple,[1] and to
[i]Dibon,
to the high places[2] to weep;
over [j]Nebo and over [i]Medeba
Moab [k]wails.
On every head is [l]baldness;
every beard is shorn;
3 in the streets they wear sackcloth;
on the housetops and in the squares
everyone wails and melts in tears.
4 [m]Heshbon and [m]Elealeh cry out;
their voice is heard as far as [n]Jahaz;
therefore the armed men of Moab cry
aloud;
his soul trembles.
5 My heart cries out for Moab;
her fugitives flee to Zoar,
to [n]Eglath-shelishiyah.
For at the [o]ascent of Luhith
they go up weeping;
on the road to [o]Horonaim
they raise a cry of destruction;
6 the waters of [p]Nimrim
are a desolation;
the grass is withered, the vegetation fails,
the greenery is no more.
7 [q]Therefore the abundance they have
gained
and what they have laid up
they carry away
over the Brook of the Willows.
8 For a cry has gone
around the land of Moab;
her wailing reaches to Eglaim;
her wailing reaches to Beer-elim.
9 For the waters of [r]Dibon[3] are full of blood;
for I will bring upon Dibon even more,
[s]a lion for those of Moab who escape,
for the remnant of the land.

16

1 [t]Send the lamb to the ruler of the
land,
from [u]Sela, by way of the desert,
to the mount of the daughter of Zion.
2 Like fleeing birds,
like a scattered nest,
so are the daughters of Moab
at [v]the fords of the Arnon.

3 "Give counsel;
grant justice;
[w]make your shade like night
at the height of noon;
shelter the outcasts;
do not reveal the fugitive;
4 let [x]the outcasts of Moab
sojourn among you;
be a shelter to them[4]
from the destroyer.
When the oppressor is no more,
and destruction has ceased,
and he who tramples underfoot has vanished from the land,
5 [y]then a throne will be established in
steadfast love,
and on it will sit in faithfulness
in the tent of David
one who judges and seeks justice
and is swift to do righteousness."
6 [z]We have heard of the pride of Moab—
how proud he is!—
[a]of his arrogance, his pride, and his insolence;
in his idle boasting he is not right.
7 Therefore let Moab wail for Moab,
[b]let everyone wail.

[1] Hebrew *the house* [2] Or *temple, even Dibon to the high places* [3] Dead Sea Scroll, Vulgate (compare Syriac); Masoretic Text *Dimon*; twice in this verse [4] Some Hebrew manuscripts, Septuagint, Syriac; Masoretic Text *let my outcasts sojourn among you; as for Moab, be a shelter to them*

16:1–14 Devastation is coming to Moab (vv. 13–14), as she will eat the fruit of her accumulated sins. Moab will look to Zion for "counsel" and "shelter" (vv. 3–4), with the hope of escape. Isaiah points them to Israel's messianic expectation. In contrast to Moab's injustice and arrogance, there will be "a throne" from the line of David that is established "in steadfast love," and he who sits upon that throne will "sit in faithfulness," reigning in justice and righteousness (v. 5). In other words, the messianic hope of Zion actually offered refuge to Gentiles as well if, in trusting faith, they would turn to this "one" who will establish a kingdom governed by love rather than by abusive power.

With the coming of Christ, the King of Zion arrives in Jerusalem (Matt. 21:5; John 12:15). His kingdom will be marked by righteousness and love, and the whole world is called to believe in him so that they may become part of true "Israel" (Hos. 2:23; Rom. 9:25; Gal. 3:7–9). This good news must be universally proclaimed, irrespective of nationality and geography, since all can find refuge in the God of Zion.

2[i] Num. 21:30 [j] Deut. 34:1 [k] ch. 13:6 [l] See ch. 3:24
4[m] Num. 32:37 [n] Jer. 48:34
5[n] [See ver. 4 above] [o] Jer. 48:5
6[p] [Num. 32:36]
7[q] Jer. 48:36
9[r] [ver. 2] [s] [2 Kgs. 17:25; Jer. 50:17]
Chapter 16
1[t] 2 Kgs. 3:4 [u] ch. 42:11; 2 Kgs. 14:7
2[v] Judg. 11:18
3[w] [1 Kgs. 18:4]
4[x] 1 Sam. 22:3
5[y] ch. 32:1, 2; Dan. 7:14, 27; Mic. 4:7; Luke 1:33
6[z] Jer. 48:29; Zeph. 2:10 [a] Judg. 3:14; 2 Kgs. 13:20; [2 Chr. 20:1]
7[b] ch. 15:3

Mourn, utterly stricken,
for the [c]raisin cakes of [d]Kir-hareseth.
8 For the fields of Heshbon languish,
and [e]the vine of Sibmah;
the lords of the nations
have struck down its branches,
which reached to Jazer
and strayed to the desert;
its shoots spread abroad
and passed over the sea.
9 Therefore [f]I weep with [e]the weeping of Jazer
for the vine of Sibmah;
I drench you with my tears,
O Heshbon and Elealeh;
for over [g]your summer fruit and your harvest
the shout has ceased.
10 [h]And joy and gladness are taken away
from [i]the fruitful field,
and in the vineyards no [j]songs are sung,
no cheers are raised;
no [k]treader treads out wine [l]in the presses;
I have put an end to the shouting.
11 Therefore [m]my inner parts moan like a lyre for Moab,
and my inmost self for Kir-hareseth.

12 And when Moab presents himself, when
[n]he wearies himself on [o]the high place, when
he comes to his sanctuary to pray, he will not
prevail.
13 This is the word that the LORD spoke concerning Moab [p]in the past. 14 But now the LORD
has spoken, saying, "In three years, [q]like the
years of a hired worker, the glory of Moab will
be brought into contempt, in spite of all his
great multitude, and those who remain will
be [r]very few and feeble."

An Oracle Concerning Damascus

17 An [s]oracle concerning [t]Damascus.

Behold, Damascus will cease to be a city
and will become a heap of ruins.
2 The cities of [u]Aroer are deserted;
they will be for flocks,
which will lie down, and [v]none will make them afraid.
3 The fortress will disappear from [w]Ephraim,
and the kingdom from [w]Damascus;
and the remnant of Syria will be
like [x]the glory of the children of Israel,
declares the LORD of hosts.

4 And in that day [x]the glory of Jacob will be brought low,
and [y]the fat of his flesh will grow lean.
5 And it shall be [z]as when the reaper gathers standing grain
and his arm harvests the ears,
and as when one gleans the ears of grain
in [a]the Valley of Rephaim.
6 [b]Gleanings will be left in it,
as when an olive tree is beaten—
two or three berries
in the top of the highest bough,
four or five
on the branches of a fruit tree,
declares the LORD God of Israel.

7 [c]In that day man will look to his Maker, and
his eyes will look on the Holy One of Israel.
8 [d]He will not look to the altars, the work of his
hands, and he will not look on what his own
fingers have made, either the [e]Asherim or the
altars of incense.

17:1–7 Northern Israel and Damascus are thrown together here as the stern oracles continue to come down. What they could expect was "a heap of ruins" (v. 1), with the "fortress" and "kingdom" disappearing from their lands (v. 3). What appears so resilient can easily be vanquished when a divine sentencing is uttered and carried out. Again, humiliation becomes reality as they are "brought low" (v. 4).

The shock of the gospel is that God carried out the supreme divine sentencing against his own Son. Those who see this and who humble themselves by trusting him find that their justly deserved sentence of condemnation has already been satisfied—at the cross of Calvary.

17:8–14 We receive hints here of the remnant who will cease to look to their self-crafted idols (v. 8) and will instead return to their Creator, who is none other than "the Holy One of Israel" (v. 7). To forget this God is to forget the hope of salvation and the "Rock of your refuge" (v. 10).

7 [c] 2 Sam. 6:19; [ver. 9] [d] 2 Kgs. 3:25; [ch. 15:1]
8 [e] Jer. 48:32
9 [f] [ch. 15:5] [e] [See ver. 8 above] [g] [ver. 7]
10 [h] Jer. 48:33 [i] [ch. 9:3] [j] [Judg. 9:27] [k] ch. 63:3; Jer. 25:30 [l] ch. 5:2
11 [m] ch. 15:5; Jer. 48:36
12 [n] [1 Kgs. 18:29] [o] ch. 15:2; [Num. 22:41; 23:14, 28]
13 [p] See Amos 2:1-3
14 [q] ch. 21:16 [r] [ch. 10:22]

Chapter 17

1 [s] See ch. 13:1 [t] ch. 7:8; Zech. 9:1; See Jer. 49:23-27; Amos 1:3-5
2 [u] Deut. 2:36; Josh. 13:25 [v] Mic. 4:4
3 [w] ch. 7:16; 8:4 [x] [1 Sam. 4:21]
4 [x] [See ver. 3 above] [y] ch. 10:16
5 [z] [ch. 24:1] [a] See 2 Sam. 5:18
6 [b] ch. 24:13
7 [c] [Hos. 8:14]
8 [d] ch. 27:9; Mic. 5:13, 14 [e] Ex. 34:13; See Deut. 16:21

9 [f]In that day their strong cities will be like the deserted places of the wooded heights and the hilltops, which they deserted because of the children of Israel, and there will be desolation.

10 For [g]you have forgotten the God of your salvation
and have not remembered the [h]Rock of your refuge;
therefore, though you plant pleasant plants
and sow the vine-branch of a stranger,
11 though you make them grow[1] on the day that you plant them,
and make them blossom in the morning that you sow,
yet the harvest will flee away[2]
in a day of grief and incurable pain.

12 Ah, [i]the thunder of many peoples;
they thunder like the thundering of the sea!
Ah, the roar of nations;
they roar like the roaring of mighty waters!
13 [j]The nations roar like the roaring of many waters,
[k]but he will rebuke them, and they will flee far away,
chased [l]like chaff on the mountains before the wind
and [m]whirling dust before the storm.
14 [n]At evening time, behold, terror!
Before morning, they are no more!
This is the portion of those who loot us,
and the lot of those who plunder us.

An Oracle Concerning Cush

18 Ah, land of [o]whirring wings
that is beyond the rivers of [p]Cush,[3]
2 which [q]sends ambassadors by the sea,
in vessels of papyrus on the waters!
Go, you swift messengers,
to a nation [r]tall and smooth,
to a people feared near and far,
a nation [s]mighty and conquering,
whose land the rivers divide.

3 All you inhabitants of the world,
you who dwell on the earth,
when [t]a signal is raised on the mountains, look!
When a trumpet is blown, hear!
4 For thus the LORD said to me:
"I will quietly look [u]from my dwelling
like clear heat in sunshine,
like a cloud of dew in the heat of harvest."
5 [v]For before the harvest, when the blossom is over,
and the flower becomes a ripening grape,
he cuts off the shoots with pruning hooks,
and the spreading branches he lops off and clears away.
6 [v]They shall all of them be left
to the birds of prey of the mountains
and to the beasts of the earth.
And the birds of prey will summer on them,
and all the beasts of the earth will winter on them.

7 [w]At that time tribute will be brought to the LORD of hosts

[1] Or *though you carefully fence them* [2] Or *will be a heap* [3] Probably *Nubia*

18:1–7 How easy it is for us to look at our circumstances and imagine that God is not paying attention. Here God tells Isaiah from his throne room that he is fully aware of everything, and though for a time he will "quietly look from my dwelling" (v. 4), he does not simply observe—he will act. In this case, God's movements against his people's foes come just when it appears that their crop will burst into full harvest (vv. 5–6). During times when it looks as if God has forgotten his people, we resiliently remember that in truth he is always as near as "clear heat in sunshine" (v. 4). He knows. In his good time he will unmistakably act on behalf of his people.

It may appear that Zion is at risk of losing everything, but actually Isaiah prophesies that the time is coming when tribute will not be taken *from* Jerusalem but instead will be brought *to* "Mount Zion, the place of the name of the LORD of hosts" (v. 7). This, as the psalmist exults, is the expectation when "nobles shall come from Egypt, [and] Cush" with their hands stretched out to God, and all the "kingdoms of the earth" will sing to God (Ps. 68:31–32). Yahweh is not merely the God of the Promised Land; the entire world must come to recognize his lordship. At the end of all things, therefore, in the new earth, "the kings of the earth will bring their glory into it" (Rev. 21:24).

9 [f][ch. 27:10]
10 [g]Ps. 106:21 [h]ch. 26:4; [Deut. 32:4, 18, 31]
12 [i]See ch. 22:5-7
13 [j][ch. 33:3] [k]Ps. 9:5; [Joel 3:2] [l]See Ps. 1:4 [m]Ps. 83:13
14 [n][Ps. 30:5]
Chapter 18
1 [o][ch. 8:8; 17:12] [p]2 Kgs. 19:9
2 [q]ch. 30:4 [r]ver. 7 [s][2 Sam. 8:2]
3 [t]See ch. 5:26
4 [u]Ps. 11:4
5 [v][Ezek. 31:3, 12, 13]
6 [v][See ver. 5 above]
7 [w]Ps. 68:31

from a people [x]tall and smooth,
from a people feared near and far,
a nation mighty and conquering,
whose land the rivers divide,

to [y]Mount Zion, the place of the [z]name of the LORD of hosts.

An Oracle Concerning Egypt

19 An [a]oracle concerning [b]Egypt.

Behold, the LORD [c]is riding on a swift cloud
and comes to Egypt;
and [d]the idols of Egypt will tremble at his presence,
and the heart of the Egyptians will [e]melt within them.
2 And I will stir up Egyptians against Egyptians,
[f]and they will fight, each against another
and each against his neighbor,
city against city, kingdom against kingdom;
3 and the spirit of the Egyptians within them will be emptied out,
and I will confound[1] their [g]counsel;
and they will inquire of the idols and the sorcerers,
and [h]the mediums and the necromancers;
4 and I will give over the Egyptians
into the hand of [i]a hard master,
and a fierce king will rule over them,
declares the Lord GOD of hosts.

5 And the waters of the sea will be dried up,
and the river will be dry and parched,
6 and its canals will become foul,
and the branches of Egypt's Nile will diminish and dry up,
reeds and rushes will rot away.
7 There will be bare places by the Nile,
on the brink of the Nile,
and all that is sown by the Nile will be parched,
will be driven away, and will be no more.
8 The [j]fishermen will mourn and lament,
all who cast a hook in the Nile;
and they will languish
who spread nets on the water.
9 The workers in [k]combed flax will be in despair,
and the weavers of white cotton.
10 Those who are the [l]pillars of the land will be crushed,
and all who [m]work for pay will be grieved.

11 The princes of [n]Zoan are utterly foolish;
the wisest counselors of Pharaoh give stupid counsel.
How can you say to Pharaoh,
"I am a son of the wise,
a son of ancient kings"?
12 Where then are your [o]wise men?
Let them tell you
that they might know what the LORD of hosts has purposed against Egypt.
13 The princes of [n]Zoan have become fools,
and the princes of [p]Memphis are deluded;
those who are the [q]cornerstones of her tribes
have made Egypt stagger.
14 The LORD has mingled within her [r]a spirit of confusion,
and they will make Egypt stagger in all its deeds,
[s]as a drunken man staggers in his vomit.

[1] Or *I will swallow up*

7 [x]ver. 2 [y][ch. 25:10] [z]2 Sam. 7:13
Chapter 19
1 [a]See ch. 13:1 [b][Joel 3:19]; See Jer. 46:13-26; Ezek. 29:1-31:2; 31:18-32:32 [c]Ps. 18:10, 11; 104:3; [Matt. 26:64; Rev. 1:7] [d]Ex. 12:12; [1 Sam. 5:3; Jer. 43:12; 50:2] [e]ch. 13:7; See Josh. 2:11
2 [f][Judg. 7:22]
3 [g]ver. 11 [h]ch. 8:19
4 [i]ch. 20:4; Jer. 46:26; Ezek. 29:19

19:1–15 As is often the case in Isaiah, there is a movement between God's strong chastisement for sin and his equally strong promise of deliverance. The first half of chapter 19 makes it clear that Egypt, Israel's long-standing enemy, will face the great divine warrior who comes "riding on a swift cloud" (v. 1). When he comes to fight on behalf of his people, Egypt is reduced from her previous wisdom and strength to utter confusion and weakness (vv. 2–15). Consequently, Egypt's idols will "tremble at his presence, and the heart of the Egyptians will melt within them" (v. 1). No gods or governments can stand against Yahweh's holy supremacy.

This prophecy reminds us that one day every knee will bow to Jesus Christ (45:23; Phil 2:10–11).

8 [j][Num. 11:5] **9** [k][Ezek. 27:7] **10** [l][Gal. 2:9] [m]Jer. 46:21 **11** [n]ch. 30:4; Num. 13:22; Ps. 78:43 **12** [o]1 Kgs. 4:30; Acts 7:22 **13** [n][See ver. 11 above] [p]Jer. 2:16; 44:1; 46:14, 19; Ezek. 30:13, 16 [q][Zech. 10:4] **14** [r][1 Kgs. 22:22] [s][ch. 24:20; 29:9]

15 And there will be nothing for Egypt
that [t]head or tail, palm branch or
reed, may do.

Egypt, Assyria, Israel Blessed

16 In that day the Egyptians will be [u]like women, and [v]tremble with fear before the hand that the LORD of hosts shakes over them. 17 And the land of Judah will become a terror to the Egyptians. Everyone to whom it is mentioned will fear because of the purpose that the LORD of hosts has purposed against them.

18 [w]In that day there will be [x]five cities in the land of Egypt that [y]speak the language of Canaan and swear allegiance to the LORD of hosts. One of these will be called the City of Destruction.[1]

19 In that day there will be an [z]altar to the LORD in the midst of the land of Egypt, and a [a]pillar to the LORD at its border. 20 [a]It will be a sign and a witness to the LORD of hosts in the land of Egypt. When they cry to the LORD because of oppressors, [b]he will send them a savior and defender, and deliver them. 21 [c]And the LORD will make himself known to the Egyptians, and the Egyptians will know the LORD in that day [d]and worship with sacrifice and offering, and they will make vows to the LORD and perform them. 22 [e]And the LORD will strike Egypt, striking and healing, and they will return to the LORD, and he will listen to their pleas for mercy and heal them.

23 [f]In that day there will be a highway from Egypt to Assyria, and Assyria will come into Egypt, and Egypt into Assyria, [g]and the Egyptians will worship with the Assyrians.

24 In that day Israel will be the third with Egypt and Assyria, [h]a blessing in the midst of the earth, 25 whom the LORD of hosts has blessed, saying, "Blessed be Egypt [i]my people, and Assyria [j]the work of my hands, and [k]Israel my inheritance."

A Sign Against Egypt and Cush

20 In the year that [l]the commander in chief, who was sent by Sargon the king of Assyria, came to [m]Ashdod and fought against it and captured it— 2 at that time the LORD spoke by Isaiah the son of Amoz, saying, "Go, and loose the sackcloth from your waist and take off your sandals from your feet," and he did so, walking [n]naked and barefoot.

3 Then the LORD said, "As my servant Isaiah has walked naked and barefoot for three years [o]as a sign and a portent against Egypt and Cush,[2] 4 so shall the [p]king of Assyria lead away the Egyptian captives and the Cushite exiles, both the young and the old, naked and barefoot, with buttocks uncovered, the nakedness

[1] Dead Sea Scroll and some other manuscripts *City of the Sun* [2] Probably *Nubia*

19:16–25 God always has a purpose when he confronts. In an unexpected way, Isaiah quickly turns from judgment to blessing. Look to the future, he promises, because "in that day" (vv. 16, 18, 19, 23, 24; cf. 2:11–12) Yahweh will link together Egypt, Assyria, and Israel in joyful harmony: their antagonism will cease. Moving from a "terror" (19:17) to a "blessing" (v. 24), the divine warrior becomes "a savior and defender" who, by his actions, will achieve peace (v. 20). Harkening back to the exodus, now there will be "a highway from Egypt to Assyria," with Israel happily in the middle (v. 23).

The universal focus of God's grace is realized in bringing Egypt to be "my people" and Assyrians to be "the work of my hands" (vv. 24–25; cf. Gen. 12:1–3; Isa. 11:10). Paul emphasizes this theme of Gentile inclusion as he describes the new age that has dawned in Christ—indeed, Paul calls himself the "apostle to the Gentiles" (Rom. 11:13; 15:4–12; cf. Gal. 2:7–9; 1 Tim. 2:7).

20:1–6 How easy it is for us to put our trust in the powers of this world, be they governments, institutions, people, or wealth. All too often we find that these supposed strengths fail to deliver. While we thought we were protected and secure, we come to realize we are vulnerable and exposed. Isaiah highlights this very dynamic. Egypt had been busy provoking rebellion against Assyria in the Palestinian area. Ashdod decided to trust in Egypt and Cush (713 B.C.) only to find that they were no protection, with Egypt reneging on their promises to Ashdod, once confronted by Assyrian dominance (711 B.C.).

Isaiah personifies this vulnerability by stripping down to his loincloth and going about barefoot (vv. 2–3). Judah should not follow the example of Ashdod, trusting in Egypt rather than trusting in Yahweh. Those who trusted in Egypt for protection

15 [t]ch. 9:14
16 [u]Jer. 50:37; 51:30; Nah. 3:13 [v]ch. 10:32
18 [w]ver. 21 [x][ch. 30:17; 2 Kgs. 7:13] [y][Zeph. 3:9]
19 [z][2 Kgs. 5:17] [a][Gen. 28:18]
20 [a][See ver. 19 above] [b][Obad. 21]
21 [c][ver. 25] [d]Zech. 14:16-18; [ch. 2:2]
22 [e]Jer. 46:25, 26
23 [f]ch. 11:16 [g][ver. 18, 21; Zeph. 3:9]
24 [h][Gen. 12:2, 3]
25 [i][Hos. 2:23] [j]ch. 29:23 [k]Deut. 32:9

Chapter 20
1 [l]2 Kgs. 18:17 [m]1 Sam. 5:1
2 [n]Mic. 1:8, 11; [1 Sam. 19:24]
3 [o][ch. 8:18]
4 [p]ch. 19:4

of Egypt. 5 [q]Then they shall be dismayed and
ashamed because of Cush their hope and of
Egypt their boast. 6 And the inhabitants of
[r]this coastland will say in that day, 'Behold,
this is what has happened to those in whom
we hoped and [s]to whom we fled for help to be
delivered from the king of Assyria! And we,
how shall we escape?'"

Fallen, Fallen Is Babylon

21 The [t]oracle concerning the wilderness of [u]the sea.

[v]As whirlwinds in the Negeb sweep on,
it comes from the wilderness,
from a terrible land.
2 A stern vision is told to me;
[w]the traitor betrays,
and the destroyer destroys.
Go up, O [x]Elam;
lay siege, O [y]Media;
all the [z]sighing she has caused
I bring to an end.
3 Therefore my loins are filled with anguish;
[a]pangs have seized me,
like the pangs of a woman in labor;
I am bowed down so that I cannot hear;
I am dismayed so that I cannot see.
4 My heart staggers; horror has appalled me;
[b]the twilight I longed for
has been turned for me into trembling.
5 [c]They prepare the table,
they spread the rugs,[1]
they eat, they drink.
Arise, O princes;
[d]oil the shield!
6 For thus the Lord said to me:
"Go, set a watchman;
let him announce what he sees.
7 When he sees riders, horsemen in pairs,
riders on donkeys, riders on camels,
let him listen diligently,
very diligently."
8 Then he who saw cried out:[2]
[e]"Upon a watchtower I stand, O Lord,
continually by day,
and at my post I am stationed
whole nights.
9 And behold, here come riders,
horsemen in pairs!"
[f]And he answered,
[g]"Fallen, fallen is Babylon;
[h]and all the carved images of her gods
he has shattered to the ground."
10 O [i]my threshed and winnowed one,
what I have heard from the LORD of hosts,
the God of Israel, I announce to you.

11 The [j]oracle concerning [k]Dumah.

One is calling to me from [l]Seir,
"Watchman, what time of the night?
Watchman, what time of the night?"
12 The watchman says:
"Morning comes, and also [m]the night.
If you will inquire, [n]inquire;
come back again."

13 The [o]oracle concerning [p]Arabia.

In the thickets in [p]Arabia you will lodge,
O [q]caravans of [p]Dedanites.

[1] Or *they set the watchman* [2] Dead Sea Scroll, Syriac; Masoretic Text *Then a lion cried out*, or *Then he cried out like a lion*

5[q] ch. 30:3, 5; [ch. 37:9]
6[r] Jer. 47:7; [ch. 14:29, 31] [s] [ch. 37:6]
Chapter 21
1[t] See ch. 13:1 [u] Jer. 51:36, 42 [v] Jer. 51:1
2[w] ch. 24:16; 33:1 [x] See ch. 11:11 [y] See ch. 13:17 [z] Ezek. 9:4
3[a] See ch. 13:8
4[b] [Deut. 28:67]
5[c] Jer. 51:39, 57 [d] 2 Sam. 1:21
8[e] Hab. 2:1
9[f] [Hab. 2:2] [g] Jer. 51:8; Cited Rev. 14:8; 18:2 [h] ch. 46:1
10[i] Jer. 51:33; Amos 1:3; [Mic. 4:13]
11[j] See ch. 13:1 [k] Gen. 25:14; 1 Chr. 1:30 [l] Deut. 2:8; Ezek. 35:2
12[m] [Job 36:20; Amos 5:8] [n] [Ps. 37:36]
13[o] See ch. 13:1 [p] Gen. 25:3; Jer. 25:23, 24 [q] [Gen. 37:25]

were now being taken into captivity by Assyria, going not with their heads held high but in public humiliation (v. 4). God's people should not trust in such earthly powers (v. 6). They are to lean not on the faithfulness of Egypt nor on the power of Assyria but on the sovereign God who "in that day" can bring Egypt, Assyria, and Israel together under his lordship (19:24).

We must avoid finding our ultimate security in the power of our state, race, or wealth. We must never forget who alone is our strength, for he is the universal King, the One who reigns with grace and goodness, leading to life-giving peace (John 14:27).

21:1–17 With horsemen riding in pairs, the cry echoes, "Fallen, fallen is Babylon" (v. 9; cf. Jer. 25:12). This very call reverberates all the way to Revelation—there, however, "Babylon" applies more broadly than to a mere geographical location (Rev. 14:8; 18:2–3). Babylon becomes a symbol of evil and rebellion against God and his people; it can even symbolize the sinful rebellion of God's own people. Yet Christ the King and his kingdom will not be overcome. Babylon's oppressive and unjust living will not stand (Rev. 18:4–18), for the "great city" will fall (Rev. 18:19–24). As evil collapses, the heavenly city will rise, filling the air with the praises of God's salvation, for his "judgments are true and just" (Rev. 19:1–5).

14 To the thirsty bring water;
meet the fugitive with bread,
O inhabitants of the land of [r]Tema.
15 For they have fled from the swords,
from the drawn sword,
from the bent bow,
and from the press of battle.

16 For thus the Lord said to me, "Within a year,
[s]according to the years of a hired worker, all
the glory of [t]Kedar will come to an end. 17 And
the remainder of the archers of the mighty
men of the sons of [t]Kedar will be few, [u]for the
LORD, the God of Israel, has spoken."

An Oracle Concerning Jerusalem

22 The [v]oracle concerning [w]the valley of
vision.

What do you mean that you have gone
up,
all of you, to the housetops,
2 you who are full of shoutings,
tumultuous city, [x]exultant town?
Your slain are [y]not slain with the sword
or dead in battle.
3 [z]All your leaders have fled together;
without the bow they were captured.
All of you who were found were captured,
though they had fled far away.
4 Therefore I said:
"Look away from me;
[a]let me weep bitter tears;
do not labor to comfort me
concerning the destruction of the
daughter of my people."

5 [b]For the Lord GOD of hosts has [c]a day
of tumult and [d]trampling and [e]confusion
in [w]the valley of vision,
a battering down of walls
and a shouting to the mountains.
6 And [f]Elam bore the quiver
with chariots and horsemen,
and [g]Kir uncovered the shield.
7 Your choicest valleys were full of chariots,
and the horsemen took their stand at
the gates.
8 He has taken away [h]the covering of Judah.

In that day you looked to [i]the weapons of
the House of the Forest, 9 and you saw that
[j]the breaches of the city of David were many.
[k]You collected the waters of the lower pool,
10 and you counted the houses of Jerusalem,
and you broke down the houses to fortify the
wall. 11 [k]You made a reservoir between [l]the two
walls for the water of [m]the old pool. But [n]you
did not look to him who did it, or see him who
planned it long ago.

12 In that day [o]the Lord GOD of hosts
called for weeping and mourning,
for [p]baldness and [q]wearing sackcloth;
13 and behold, joy and gladness,
killing oxen and slaughtering sheep,
eating flesh and drinking wine.

In the meantime, God's people sometimes feel "threshed and winnowed" (Isa. 21:10), yet such suffering will not last forever, for the oppression and pain will be put to an end and the eternal joy of the heavenly hallelujah will become the final reality. Jesus Christ, who was "threshed and winnowed" in an ultimate sense on our behalf on the cross, has secured it.

22:1–25 Attention now turns back to Jerusalem. A strong disconnect is exposed between the superficial merriment and momentary glee of the people (vv. 1–2a, 13) and the timely repentance called for by God (v. 12). Catastrophe was coming to them (vv. 2b–8) in "the valley of vision" (vv. 1, 5), for they resisted turning to Yahweh. Thus, "in that day" their military and domestic preparations for security would not hold, exposing their vulnerability when attacked (vv. 8–14).

What is truly uncovered, however, is the sins of the people which are not atoned for (v. 14). Shebna, a self-possessed and arrogant leader in Jerusalem, is set out as an example of this false trust in the strength of foreign powers with their "glorious chariots" (v. 18). Trusting in Egypt rather than Yahweh is a losing proposition. Shebna will be brought down and replaced by Eliakim, who is called God's "servant" (vv. 20–21). But even Eliakim, who is much more loyal than Shebna, will fall short. The "key of the house of David" will be given to him, and God will "fasten him like a peg in a secure place. . . . And they will hang on him the whole honor of his father's house" (vv. 22–24). Unfortunately, this responsibility and honor will prove too heavy for Eliakim to bear, and the "peg" will "give way" (v. 25).

14 [r] Job 6:19
16 [s] See ch. 16:14 [t] ch. 60:7; Gen. 25:13; Ps. 120:5, 6; Song 1:5; Jer. 2:10; 49:28; Ezek. 27:21
17 [t] [See ver. 16 above] [u] ch. 1:20

Chapter 22
1 [v] See ch. 13:1 [w] ver. 5; Jer. 21:13; [Joel 3:12, 14]
2 [x] ch. 32:13 [y] Lam. 4:9
3 [z] [ch. 1:10]
4 [a] Jer. 9:1; Mic. 1:8
5 [b] ch. 2:12-17 [c] [ch. 37:3] [d] ch. 10:6; 18:2 [e] Mic. 7:4 [w] [See ver. 1 above]
6 [f] See ch. 11:11 [g] 2 Kgs. 16:9
8 [h] ch. 30:1 [i] 1 Kgs. 10:17
9 [j] ver. 5, 10; [2 Chr. 32:5] [k] [Neh. 3:16]
11 [k] [See ver. 9 above] [l] [2 Kgs. 25:4] [m] [ch. 7:3; 2 Kgs. 20:20; 2 Chr. 32:3, 4] [n] [ch. 5:12]
12 [o] [Joel 2:17] [p] See ch. 3:24 [q] See 2 Sam. 3:31

[r]"Let us eat and drink,
for tomorrow we die."
14 The LORD of hosts [s]has revealed himself
in my ears:
"Surely [t]this iniquity will not be atoned
for you [u]until you die,"
says the Lord GOD of hosts.

15 Thus says the Lord GOD of hosts, "Come, go to this steward, to [v]Shebna, who is over the household, and say to him: 16 What have you to do here, and whom have you here, [w]that you have cut out here a tomb for yourself, you [x]who cut out a tomb on the height and carve a dwelling for yourself in the rock? 17 Behold, the LORD will hurl you away violently, O you strong man. [y]He will seize firm hold on you 18 and whirl you around and around, and throw you like a ball into a wide land. There you shall die, and there shall be [z]your glorious chariots, you shame of your master's house. 19 [a]I will thrust you from your office, and you will be pulled down from your station. 20 In that day I will call my servant [b]Eliakim the son of Hilkiah, 21 and [b]I will clothe him with your robe, and will bind your sash on him, and will commit your authority to his hand. And he shall be [c]a father to the inhabitants of Jerusalem and to the house of Judah. 22 And I will place [d]on his shoulder [e]the key of the house of David. [f]He shall open, and none shall shut; and he shall shut, and none shall open. 23 And I will fasten him [g]like a peg in a secure place, and he will become [h]a throne of honor to his father's house. 24 And they will hang on him the whole honor of his father's house, the offspring and issue, every small vessel, from the cups to all the flagons. 25 In that day, declares the LORD of hosts, [g]the peg that was fastened in a secure place will give way, and it will be cut down and fall, and the load that was on it will be cut off, for the LORD has spoken."

An Oracle Concerning Tyre and Sidon

23 The [i]oracle concerning [j]Tyre.

Wail, O [k]ships of Tarshish,
for Tyre is laid waste, [l]without house
or harbor!
From [m]the land of Cyprus[1]
it is revealed to them.
2 Be still, O inhabitants of the coast;
the merchants of [n]Sidon, who cross
the sea, have filled you.
3 And on many waters
your revenue was the grain of Shihor,
the harvest of the Nile;
you were [o]the merchant of the
nations.
4 Be ashamed, O [n]Sidon, for the sea has
spoken,
the stronghold of the sea, saying:
"I have neither labored nor given birth,
I have neither reared young men
nor brought up young women."
5 When the report comes to Egypt,
they will be in anguish[2] over the
report about Tyre.
6 [p]Cross over to Tarshish;
wail, O inhabitants of the coast!

[1] Hebrew *Kittim*; also verse 12 [2] Hebrew *they will have labor pains*

13[r] ch. 56:12; Cited 1 Cor. 15:32
14[s] ch. 5:9 [t][ch. 27:9; 1 Sam. 3:14] [u][ver. 13]
15[v] ch. 36:3, 11, 22; 37:2; 2 Kgs. 18:18, 26, 37; 19:2
16[w] 2 Chr. 16:14 [x] Matt. 27:60
17[y] [Dan. 3:21]
18[z] [ch. 36:9]
19[a] [ver. 25]
20[b] ch. 36:3; 37:2; 2 Kgs. 18:18, 26, 37; 19:2
21[b] [See ver. 20 above] [c] Gen. 45:8
22[d] ch. 9:6 [e] Rev. 3:7 [f][Job 12:14]
23[g] [ch. 33:20; 54:2; Eccles. 12:11] [h][Rev. 3:21]
25[g] [See ver. 23 above]
Chapter 23
1[i] See ch. 13:1 [j][Jer. 25:22; 27:2, 3]; See Ezek. 26:2–28:24; Joel 3:4-8; Amos 1:9, 10; Zech. 9:2-4 [k] ver. 14; 1 Kgs. 10:22; 22:48 [l] ch. 24:10 [m] Jer. 2:10; See Gen. 10:4

Christ is the true holder of the "keys" (Rev. 1:18; cf. Rev. 3:7; 9:1; 20:1). He alone can lead people out of judgment and death and into his resurrection life. Jesus gives Peter the "keys of the kingdom" (Matt. 16:18–19), a gift that is not for Peter alone but for the church, which echoes Peter's confession that Jesus is the Messiah. Jesus is the one around whom all true repentance and forgiveness must be centered (Matt. 18:18–19). The church employs these keys only as an extension of Christ's finished work, for only the King can carry the full weight of his Father's house. He alone is able to bear the weight and not "give way."

23:1–18 Faced with their own destruction, those living in Tyre struggled with a question: "Who has purposed this . . . ?" (v. 8). There must be a reason behind it. There must be a larger narrative explaining this disaster. Isaiah wastes no time in answering their question: "The LORD of hosts has purposed it" (v. 9). Why? Because of the "pompous pride" which aggressively put itself in a position above all others (e.g., "the bestower of crowns"; v. 8) as the "honored of the earth" (v. 9). Such arrogance can become a civic idol; Tyre had sold its soul. Consequently, the final image here is not one of wholesome health and harmonious delight but of a "forgotten prostitute" that would never be mistaken for an innocent or a life-giving beauty (vv. 16–18).

2[n] ver. 4, 12; Gen. 10:15; Josh. 19:28; Jer. 25:22; 27:3; Ezek. 27:8; 32:30; Joel 3:4; Zech. 9:2 **3**[o] See Ezek. 27:3-23 **4**[n] [See ver. 2 above] **6**[p] ver. 12

7 Is this your exultant city
[q]whose origin is from days of old,
whose feet carried her
to settle far away?
8 Who has purposed this
against Tyre, the bestower of crowns,
whose merchants were princes,
whose traders were the honored of
the earth?
9 The LORD of hosts has purposed it,
[r]to defile the pompous pride of all
glory,[1]
to dishonor all the honored of the
earth.
10 Cross over your land like the Nile,
O daughter of Tarshish;
there is no restraint anymore.
11 [s]He has stretched out his hand over the
sea;
he has shaken the kingdoms;
the LORD has given command concerning Canaan
to destroy its strongholds.
12 And he said:
"You will no more exult,
O oppressed virgin daughter of [t]Sidon;
arise, [u]cross over to [v]Cyprus,
even there you will have no rest."

13 Behold the land of [w]the Chaldeans! This is
the people that was not;[2] Assyria destined it
for wild beasts. They erected [x]their siege towers, they stripped her palaces bare, they made
her a ruin.

14 [y]Wail, O ships of Tarshish,
for your stronghold is laid waste.

15 In that day Tyre will be forgotten for [z]sev-
enty years, like the days[3] of one king. At the
end of [z]seventy years, it will happen to Tyre
as in the song of the prostitute:

16 "Take a harp;
go about the city,
O forgotten prostitute!
Make sweet melody;
sing many songs,
that you may be remembered."

17 At the end of [a]seventy years, the LORD will
visit Tyre, and she will return to her wages and
[b]will prostitute herself with all the kingdoms
of the world on the face of the earth. 18 Her
merchandise and her wages will be holy to
the LORD. It will not be stored or hoarded,
but her merchandise will supply abundant
food and fine clothing for those who dwell
before the LORD.

Judgment on the Whole Earth

24 Behold, [c]the LORD will empty the
earth[4] and make it desolate,
and he will twist its surface and scatter its inhabitants.
2 [d]And it shall be, as with the people, so
with the priest;
as with the slave, so with his master;
as with the maid, so with her mistress;
[e]as with the buyer, so with the seller;
as with the lender, so with the borrower;
[f]as with the creditor, so with the
debtor.
3 [g]The earth shall be utterly empty and
utterly plundered;
[h]for the LORD has spoken this word.
4 [i]The earth mourns and withers;
the world languishes and withers;
the highest people of the earth languish.
5 The earth lies [j]defiled
under its inhabitants;
for [k]they have transgressed the laws,
violated the statutes,
broken the everlasting covenant.
6 Therefore [l]a curse devours the earth,
and its inhabitants [m]suffer for their
guilt;

[1] The Hebrew words for *glory* and *hosts* sound alike [2] Or *that has become nothing* [3] Or *lifetime* [4] Or *land*; also throughout this chapter

24:1–27:13 Often referred to as "the Little Apocalypse," chapters 24–27 turn our attention from divine judgment on individual nations to a global apocalyptic vision of the end of the whole earth.

24:1–13 The judgment coming is utterly fair and impartial, treating equally slave and master, maid and mistress, creditor and debtor (v. 2), as the whole earth is emptied (vv. 1, 3). Using strong and often frightening apocalyptic images, Isaiah portrays a scorched earth scenario, where things are utterly destroyed and flattened out (vv. 4–13). Chaos reigns.

7[q] [Gen. 10:15]
9[r] [Ezek. 28:7]
11[s] [Ex. 14:21]
12[t] See ver. 2 [u] ver. 6 [v] ver. 1
13[w] ch. 47:1; 48:14 [x] [2 Kgs. 25:1]
14[y] See ver. 1
15[z] Jer. 25:11, 22
17[a] Jer. 25:11, 22 [b] Rev. 17:1, 2
Chapter 24
1[c] ch. 13:9
2[d] Hos. 4:9; [Lam. 4:16]; See ch. 3:1-3 [e] [Ezek. 7:12, 13] [f] [Jer. 15:10] **3**[g] ver. 1, 6 [h] See ch. 1:20 **4**[i] [ch. 16:8; Hos. 4:3] **5**[j] Num. 35:33 [k] [ch. 2:6, 8] **6**[l] Zech. 5:3, 4 [m] [Ps. 5:10]

therefore the inhabitants of the earth are scorched,
and few men are left.
7 [n]The wine mourns,
the vine languishes,
all the merry-hearted sigh.
8 [o]The mirth of the tambourines is stilled,
the noise of the jubilant has ceased,
the mirth of the lyre is stilled.
9 No more do they drink wine [p]with singing;
strong drink is bitter to those who drink it.
10 [q]The wasted city is broken down;
[r]every house is shut up so that none can enter.
11 [s]There is an outcry in the streets for lack of wine;
[t]all joy has grown dark;
the gladness of the earth is banished.
12 Desolation is left in the city;
the gates are battered into ruins.
13 For thus it shall be in the midst of the earth
among the nations,
[u]as when an olive tree is beaten,
as at the gleaning when the grape harvest is done.

14 They lift up their voices, they sing for joy;
over the majesty of the LORD they shout from the west.[1]
15 [v]Therefore in the east[2] give glory to the LORD;
in the coastlands of the sea, give glory to the name of the LORD, the God of Israel.
16 [w]From the ends of the earth we hear songs of praise,
of glory to [x]the Righteous One.
But I say, "I waste away,
I waste away. Woe is me!
For [y]the traitors have betrayed,
with betrayal the traitors have betrayed."

17 [z]Terror and the pit and the snare[3]
are upon you, O inhabitant of the earth!
18 [z]He who flees at the sound of the terror
shall fall into the pit,
and he who climbs out of the pit
shall be caught in the snare.
For [a]the windows of heaven are opened,
and [b]the foundations of the earth tremble.
19 The earth is utterly broken,
the earth is split apart,
the earth is violently shaken.
20 The earth [c]staggers like a drunken man;
it sways like a hut;
[d]its transgression lies heavy upon it,
and it falls, and will not rise again.

21 On that day the LORD will punish
the host of heaven, in heaven,
and [e]the kings of the earth, on the earth.
22 [f]They will be gathered together
as prisoners in a pit;
they will be shut up in a prison,
and after many days [g]they will be punished.

[1] Hebrew *from the sea* [2] Hebrew *in the realm of light* [3] The Hebrew words for *terror*, *pit*, and *snare* sound alike

7[n] [Joel 1:10, 12]
8[o] Jer. 7:34; Hos. 2:11; [Amos 8:10]
9[p] [Amos 6:5, 6]
10[q] [ch. 34:11] [r] ch. 23:1
11[s] [ver. 7; Ps. 144:14; Joel 1:5] [t] [Joel 1:12]
13[u] ch. 17:6; [Mic. 7:1]
15[v] [ch. 45:6]
16[w] [ver. 14] [x] [ch. 26:2; 60:21] [y] ch. 21:2; 33:1
17[z] Jer. 48:43, 44; [Job 20:24; Amos 5:19]
18[z] [See ver. 17 above] [a] See Gen. 7:11 [b] Ps. 18:7
20[c] [ch. 19:14; 29:9] [d] [ver. 5, 6]
21[e] Ps. 76:12; [ch. 10:12; 31:8]
22[f] Mic. 4:11, 12 [g] ch. 29:6

24:14–16 Only a "few men are left" (v. 6), but this remnant gleaned from the harvest (v. 13) appear to raise their voice in praise to God, joyfully giving him glory (vv. 14–15). A new day is coming, and the result is that "the Righteous One" will be praised from "the ends of the earth" (v. 16). In the end, a song will rise up from those whom God has "ransomed" from "every tribe and language and people and nation" (Rev. 5:9; cf. 7:9).

24:17–23 Isaiah's brief focus on these voices of joyful praise is quickly replaced by his return to an apocalyptic message. "The earth staggers like a drunken man; . . . its transgression lies heavy upon it, and it falls, and will not rise again" (v. 20). Sin has affected not just one person, not just one people, but all of humanity, of every nation. Under the weight of sin we stagger and, like a drunkard, we fail to distinguish the good from the evil. We have plunged into our own ruin (e.g., Hos. 4:10–12; Eph. 5:18).

But the day is coming when all in heaven and on earth will gather together (Isa. 24:21–22), and all shall see and behold God's glory (cf. Rev. 21:22–27). So clear a contrast will it be from this fallen cosmos that even the "moon will be confounded and the sun ashamed" (Isa. 24:23). Paul declares a day coming when this recognition of God's reign will be centered on Christ, before whom every knee will bow and every tongue confess that he is Lord (Phil. 2:9–11).

23 [h]Then the moon will be confounded
and the sun ashamed,
for [i]the LORD of hosts reigns
on Mount Zion and in Jerusalem,
and his glory will be before his elders.

God Will Swallow Up Death Forever

25 O LORD, [j]you are my God;
[k]I will exalt you; I will praise your name,
for you have done wonderful things,
[l]plans formed of old, faithful and sure.
2 For you have made the city [m]a heap,
the fortified city a ruin;
the foreigners' palace is a city no more;
it will never be rebuilt.
3 [n]Therefore strong peoples will glorify you;
cities of ruthless nations will fear you.
4 [o]For you have been a stronghold to the poor,
a stronghold to the needy in his distress,
[p]a shelter from the storm and a shade from the heat;
[q]for the breath of the ruthless is like a storm against a wall,
5 [r]like heat in a dry place.
You subdue the noise of the foreigners;
as heat by the shade of a cloud,
so the song of the ruthless is put down.

6 [s]On this mountain the LORD of hosts will make for all peoples
a feast of rich food, a feast of well-aged wine,
[t]of rich food full of marrow, of aged wine well refined.
7 And he will swallow up [s]on this mountain
the covering that is cast over all peoples,
[u]the veil that is spread over all nations.
8 [v]He will swallow up death forever;
and [w]the Lord GOD will wipe away tears from all faces,
and [x]the reproach of his people he will take away from all the earth,
[y]for the LORD has spoken.

25:1–12 Whereas "ruthless nations" used their strength to bring oppression and foster injustice (vv. 3, 4, 5), God is a "stronghold to the poor, a stronghold to the needy in his distress, a shelter from the storm and a shade from the heat" (v. 4). While they may be forgotten and mistreated by society, God remains a refuge for them.

Biblically, a paradox arises: it is precisely God's *impartiality* that makes him *partial* to the poor (Deut. 10:17–18; cf. James 3:17). We think of fairness as treating everyone the same, yet God sees perfectly the many ways in which things are not the same for all people. The world gives inherent priority to the powerful, wealthy, and beautiful. Impartiality for God does not mean treating everyone the exact same way at all times, since he alone perfectly takes into consideration all things (Rom. 11:33–35). It is in fairness that God favors the forgotten and receives the rejected (Psalm 113; cf. Ps. 107:41; 136:23). God's royal majesty is seen in his tender mercy (Ps. 138:6; cf. Luke 1:52–53). How easy it is for us to forget that God gives priority to the weak, the vulnerable, and the needy (James 2:5). Accordingly, one of the marks of a healthy church, and a healthy Christian, is an impulse to extend God's compassionate care to those most in need—supremely those in spiritual need, but also those in physical need. The church thus becomes a "stronghold" for those must vulnerable, bringing the peace of Christ to trial-ridden lives.

God's mercy to the needy has a flip side here, according to Isaiah: he will not turn a blind eye toward the injustices carried out by the nations. The sovereign Lord, who has "done wonderful things," will act "faithful and sure" (Isa. 25:1), and this includes his plans to carry out a just judgment against the idolatrous and tyrannical nations (vv. 2–5). He will "lay low" the "pompous pride" of such harmful powers (v. 11).

Furthermore, the Lord promises to "swallow up death," not for a time but eternally. He will "wipe away tears from all faces," taking away his people's "reproach" (vv. 8–10; cf. Rev. 7:17; 21:4). Only in his substitutionary death and life-giving resurrection do we see Christ as decisively victorious over the power of sin and death (1 Cor. 15:54; cf. Heb. 9:8–24). United to him by God-given faith, we share in his triumph.

23[h]See ch. 13:10 [i]Ps. 99:1, 2; Mic. 4:7
Chapter 25
1[j]Ex. 15:2 [k][Ps. 107:32] [l][2 Kgs. 19:25]
2[m][ch. 17:1; Jer. 51:37]
3[n][ch. 18:7]
4[o]Nah. 1:7 [p]ch. 4:6 [q][2 Chr. 32:18]
5[r][ch. 32:2]
6[s]ch. 2:2, 3; 11:9; 24:23 [t][Ps. 63:5]
7[s][See ver. 6 above] [u][2 Cor. 3:15]
8[v]Cited 1 Cor. 15:54; [Hos. 13:14] [w]Rev. 7:17; [ch. 30:19] [x][ch. 37:4] [y]See ch. 1:20

9 It will be said on that day,
"Behold, this is our God; [z]we have waited for him, that he might save us.
This is the LORD; we have waited for him;
[a]let us be glad and rejoice in his salvation."
10 For the hand of the LORD will rest [s]on this mountain,
and [b]Moab shall be trampled down in his place,
as straw is trampled down in a dunghill.[1]
11 [c]And he will spread out his hands in the midst of it
as a swimmer spreads his hands out to swim,
but the LORD [d]will lay low his pompous pride together with the skill[2] of his hands.
12 And the high fortifications of his walls he will bring down,
lay low, and cast to the ground, to the dust.

You Keep Him in Perfect Peace

26 In that day [e]this song will be sung in the land of Judah:

"We have a strong city;
he sets up [f]salvation
as walls and bulwarks.
2 [g]Open the gates,
that the righteous nation that keeps faith may enter in.
3 [h]You keep him in perfect peace
whose mind is stayed on you,
because he trusts in you.
4 Trust in the LORD forever,
for the LORD GOD is an everlasting rock.
5 [i]For he has humbled
the inhabitants of the height,
the lofty city.
He lays it low, lays it low to the ground,
casts it to the dust.
6 The foot tramples it,
the feet of [j]the poor,
the steps of [j]the needy."

7 The path of the righteous is level;
[k]you make level the way of the righteous.
8 In the path of your judgments,
O LORD, we wait for you;
[l]your name and [l]remembrance
are the desire of our soul.
9 My soul yearns for you in the night;
my spirit within me earnestly seeks you.
[m]For when your judgments are in the earth,
the inhabitants of the world learn righteousness.
10 [n]If favor is shown to the wicked,
he does not learn righteousness;
in the land of uprightness he deals corruptly
and does not see the majesty of the LORD.
11 O LORD, [o]your hand is lifted up,
but [p]they do not see it.
Let them see your zeal for your people,
and be ashamed.
Let [q]the fire for your adversaries consume them.

[1] The Hebrew words for *dunghill* and for the Moabite town *Madmen* (Jeremiah 48:2) sound alike [2] Or *in spite of the skill*

9[z] ch. 26:8; [Gen. 49:18; Ps. 27:14] [a] Ps. 9:14
10[s] [See ver. 6 above] [b] See ch. 15:1
11[c] [ch. 16:12] [d] [ch. 16:14]
Chapter 26
1[e] [ch. 27:2] [f] [ch. 60:18]
2[g] Ps. 118:19, 20
3[h] [ch. 30:15]
5[i] ch. 25:12
6[j] [ch. 25:4]
7[k] 1 Sam. 2:9; Ps. 37:23
8[l] Ex. 3:15
9[m] ver. 16; [2 Chr. 33:12]
10[n] See Ps. 73:3-11
11[o] [Mic. 5:9] [p] [ch. 5:12] [q] Ps. 21:9; [ch. 33:14]

26:1–21 Judah's song praises God and calls the people to be centered on their Lord. Amid the storms of life, we can be reminded that "the LORD GOD is an everlasting rock," and thus, standing on him, we are kept "in perfect peace" (vv. 3–4). While "other lords besides you have ruled over us," the song proclaims, "your name alone we bring to remembrance" (v. 13; cf. v. 8). Like the psalmist writing during times of difficulty, we see the wisdom of bringing to mind God's faithful actions in the past, since such "remembering" also serves to bring us courage and peace in the present (e.g., Ps. 42:3–11; ch. 77).

God has been faithful, he has not forgotten us, and he will remain faithful through eternity. Hebrews 11 is guided by this very belief, for the examples of "faith" in that chapter ultimately point to God's faithfulness, rather than to mere human loyalty (Heb. 11:1–39; cf. Ps. 91:4). As Hebrews reminds us, we are surrounded by a great "cloud of witnesses" (Heb. 12:1) who trusted God's fidelity amid adversity as they longed for deliverance. The long-anticipated promise has come in "Jesus, the founder and perfecter of our faith, who for the joy that was set before him endured the cross, despising the shame, and is seated at the right hand of the throne of God" (Heb. 12:1–3).

12 O LORD, you will ordain [r]peace for us,
for you have indeed done for us all
our works.
13 O LORD our God,
[s]other lords besides you have ruled
over us,
[t]but your name alone we bring to
remembrance.
14 They are dead, they will not live;
they are shades, they will not arise;
to that end you have visited them with
destruction
and wiped out all remembrance of
them.
15 [u]But you have increased the nation,
O LORD,
you have increased the nation; you are
glorified;
[v]you have enlarged all the borders of
the land.

16 O LORD, [w]in distress they sought you;
they poured out a whispered prayer
when your discipline was upon them.
17 [x]Like a pregnant woman
who writhes and cries out in her pangs
when she is near to giving birth,
so were we because of you, O LORD;
18 [x]we were pregnant, we writhed,
but we have given birth to wind.
We have accomplished no deliverance in
the earth,
and the inhabitants of the world have
not fallen.
19 [y]Your dead shall live; their bodies shall
rise.
You who dwell in the dust, awake and
sing for joy!
For [z]your dew is a dew of light,
and the earth will give birth to the
dead.

20 Come, my people, enter your chambers,
and shut your doors behind you;
hide yourselves [a]for a little while
until the fury has passed by.
21 [b]For behold, the LORD is coming out
from his place
to punish the inhabitants of [c]the
earth for their iniquity,
and the earth will disclose the blood
shed on it,
and will no more cover its slain.

The Redemption of Israel

27 In that day the LORD with his hard and
great and strong [d]sword will punish
[e]Leviathan the fleeing serpent, [e]Leviathan the
twisting serpent, and he will slay [f]the dragon
that is in the sea.

2 In that day,
[g]"A pleasant vineyard,[1] [h]sing of it!
3 I, the LORD, am its keeper;
every moment I water it.
Lest anyone punish it,
I keep it night and day;
4 I have no wrath.
[i]Would that I had thorns and briers to
battle!
I would march against them,
I would burn them up together.
5 Or let them lay hold of my protection,
let them make peace with me,
let them make peace with me."

6 [j]In days to come[2] Jacob shall take root,
Israel shall blossom and put forth
shoots
and fill the whole world with fruit.
7 [k]Has he struck them [l]as he struck those
who struck them?
Or have they been slain [m]as their slay-
ers were slain?

[1] Many Hebrew manuscripts *A vineyard of wine* [2] Hebrew *In those to come*

As in the Passover (Ex. 12:22–23), God's people are invited to "come" into their chambers, so that they may be hidden "until the fury has passed by" against the iniquity of the earth (Isa. 26:20–21; cf. Ps. 57:1). Only now we see that Christ is "our Passover lamb [who] has been sacrificed" for us so that we might be safe and find refuge in him (1 Cor. 5:7).

27:1–13 "Leviathan" represents powers—natural or supernatural—raging against God (cf. Job 41:1; Ps. 74:14; 104:26). God will cast down such powers "in that day," showing that there is only one true sovereign Lord (Isa. 27:1). With the coming of King Jesus and the dawning of his kingdom we find Jesus similarly testifying that he "saw Satan fall like lightning from heaven," cast down by God's authority (Luke 10:18–20).

12[r] ch. 9:7; Mic. 5:5
13[s] [ch. 2:8; 2 Kgs. 16:3, 4] [t] [ch. 2:20; Ps. 20:7]; See 2 Kgs. 18:4-6
15[u] ch. 9:3 [v] [ch. 54:2, 3]
16[w] Hos. 5:15; See ch. 37:1-4
17[x] See ch. 13:8
18[x] [See ver. 17 above]
19[y] [Ezek. 37:12; Dan. 12:2; Hos. 13:14] [z] [Hos. 14:5]
20[a] ch. 10:25
21[b] Mic. 1:3 [c] [ch. 24:5]
Chapter 27
1[d] [Jer. 47:6] [e] Ps. 74:14 [f] ch. 51:9; Ezek. 29:3
2[g] ch. 5:7 [h] [ch. 26:1]

4[i] [ch. 10:17] **6**[j] ch. 37:31; Hos. 14:5, 6 **7**[k] Hos. 6:1, 2 [l] See ch. 37:36-38 [m] ch. 37:18, 19

8 [n]Measure by measure,[1] by exile you contended with them;
[o]he removed them with his fierce breath[2] in the day of the east wind.
9 Therefore by this [p]the guilt of Jacob will be atoned for,
and this will be the full fruit of the removal of his sin:[3]
[q]when he makes all the stones of the altars like chalkstones crushed to pieces,
no [r]Asherim or incense altars will remain standing.
10 [s]For the fortified city is solitary,
a habitation deserted and forsaken, like the wilderness;
there the calf grazes;
there it lies down and strips its branches.
11 When its boughs are dry, they are broken;
women come and make a fire of them.
[t]For this is a people without discernment;
therefore he who made them will not have compassion on them;
he who formed them will show them no favor.

12 In that day [u]from the river Euphrates[4] to
the Brook of Egypt the LORD will thresh out
the grain, and you will be gleaned one by one,
O people of Israel. 13 And in that day [v]a great
trumpet will be blown, [w]and those who were
lost in the land of Assyria and those who were
driven out to the land of Egypt [x]will come and
worship the LORD on the holy mountain at
Jerusalem.

Judgment on Ephraim and Jerusalem

28 Ah, the proud crown of [y]the drunkards of Ephraim,
and the fading flower of its glorious beauty,
which is on the head of the rich valley of those overcome with wine!
2 Behold, the Lord has [z]one who is mighty and strong;
like a storm of hail, a destroying tempest,
like [a]a storm of mighty, overflowing waters,
he casts down to the earth with his hand.
3 [b]The proud crown of the drunkards of Ephraim
will be trodden underfoot;
4 [c]and the fading flower of its glorious beauty,
which is on the head of the rich valley,
will be like [d]a first-ripe fig before the summer:
when someone sees it, he swallows it
as soon as it is in his hand.

[1] Or *By driving her away*; the meaning of the Hebrew word is uncertain [2] Or *wind* [3] Septuagint *and this is the blessing when I take away his sin* [4] Hebrew *from the River*

8[n] [Jer. 10:24] [o] [Jer. 18:17]
9[p] [ch. 22:14] [q] [2 Kgs. 18:4] [r] See Deut. 16:21
10[s] ch. 17:9; 32:14, 19; [Hos. 8:14; Mic. 5:11]
11[t] Deut. 32:28; See ch. 30:16-18
12[u] See Gen. 15:18
13[v] Lev. 25:9; [Matt. 24:31; Rev. 11:15] [w] ch. 11:11, 16; Mic. 7:12 [x] [ch. 2:2]
Chapter 28
1[y] [Hos. 7:5]
2[z] [ch. 8:7] [a] ver. 15, 18
3[b] ver. 1
4[c] [Amos 8:1, 2] [d] Hos. 9:10; Mic. 7:1

Again Isaiah presents the Lord as the owner of the vineyard who "every moment" takes care of it, "lest anyone punish it" (Isa. 27:2–3; cf. 5:7). God's anger here is not against his vineyard but against the "thorns and briers" that compromise his harvest's health (27:4–5).

Our omnipotent and omniscient Lord never forgets us. He is present and concerned for us "night and day" (v. 3). Forgetfulness may mark our lives, but not so with God. He is the one who nourishes his vineyard as well as the one who actively seeks to protect it from dangers that steal into his fields. The Master himself will, in the end, separate the weeds from the wheat (v. 12; cf. Matt. 13:24–30). Until the final harvest, the "weeds" sown by the "evil one" may penetrate the fields (Matt. 13:36–43), but those who look to the Son of Man in faith will bear good fruit (e.g., repentance, humility, grace), showing their connection to the life-giving vine of Christ (John 15:1–17).

28:1–29 The Lord of the harvest is "wonderful in counsel and excellent in wisdom" (v. 29). All he does has purpose, even when that purpose is not immediately clear during times of plowing, planting, pruning, and production (vv. 22–28). God will not abide the pride of nations, and here "the drunkards of Ephraim" will find their once powerful stature diminished and fading (vv. 1–4).

The rest and repose offered by God to his weary people is too often ignored (v. 12); rather than listening to him they seek deliverance from other tongues (vv. 9, 11, 13). Nonetheless, a "remnant" will be preserved; those included will find their strength in "the LORD of hosts," who will be their "crown of glory, and a diadem of beauty" (vv. 5–6).

5 [e]In that day the LORD of hosts will be a
crown of glory,[1]
and a diadem of beauty, to the remnant of his people,
6 and [f]a spirit of justice to him who sits in
judgment,
and [g]strength to those who turn back
the battle at the gate.

7 [h]These also reel with wine
and [i]stagger with strong drink;
the priest and [j]the prophet reel with
strong drink,
they are swallowed by[2] wine,
they stagger with strong drink,
they reel in vision,
they stumble in giving judgment.
8 For all tables are full of filthy vomit,
with no space left.

9 [k]"To whom will he teach knowledge,
and to whom will he explain the message?
Those who are weaned from the milk,
those taken from the breast?
10 For it is precept upon precept, precept
upon precept,
line upon line, line upon line,
here a little, there a little."
11 [l]For by people of strange lips
and with a foreign tongue
the LORD will speak to this people,
12 to whom he has said,
[m]"This is rest;
give rest to the weary;
and this is repose";
yet they would not hear.
13 And the word of the LORD will be to them
precept upon precept, precept upon precept,
line upon line, line upon line,
here a little, there a little,
[n]that they may go, and fall backward,
and be broken, and snared, and taken.

A Cornerstone in Zion

14 Therefore hear the word of the LORD,
you [o]scoffers,
who rule this people in Jerusalem!
15 Because you have said, "We have made a
covenant with death,
and with Sheol we have an agreement,
when the [p]overwhelming whip passes
through
it will not come to us,
for we have made [q]lies our refuge,
and in falsehood we have taken shelter";
16 therefore thus says the Lord GOD,
[r]"Behold, I am the one who has laid[3] as a
foundation [s]in Zion,
a stone, a tested stone,
a precious cornerstone, of a sure foundation:
'Whoever believes will not be in haste.'
17 And I will make justice [t]the line,
and righteousness [t]the plumb line;
and hail will sweep away the refuge of
lies,
and waters will overwhelm the shelter."
18 Then [u]your covenant with death will be
annulled,
and your agreement with Sheol will
not stand;
when the overwhelming scourge passes
through,
you will be beaten down by it.
19 As often as it passes through it will take
you;
[v]for morning by morning it will pass
through,
by day and by night;
and it will be [w]sheer terror to understand the message.

[1] The Hebrew words for *glory* and *hosts* sound alike [2] Or *confused by* [3] Dead Sea Scroll *I am laying*

The church may similarly be tempted to follow every trend of wisdom and "spiritual insight" coming from outside of God's Word. We should never forget that God's final word and self-disclosure is found in Jesus Christ alone (e.g., John 1:16–18). Any voices that lead us away from the incarnate Son of God are voices we should not heed (e.g., 1 John 4:1–2). Christ alone is the true "precious cornerstone, of a sure foundation," and so in him we believe and put our trust (Isa. 28:16; cf. Acts 4:11; Matt. 21:42; Rom. 9:33; Eph. 2:20; 1 Pet. 2:6–7). On Christ alone can we build our houses, and on him alone will the foundation hold (cf. Matt. 7:24–27). For in him we sinners are graced with an undeserved "crown of glory, and a diadem of beauty" (Isa. 28:5).

Forgiven through grace, our frenetic hearts are calmed. As we are restored and put at rest (v. 12), the inner haste of frantic anxiety is soothed (v. 16). We become human again.

5[e] ch. 2:11
6[f] [1 Kgs. 3:28] [g] [ch. 38:6]
7[h] [ch. 3:12] [i] Hos. 4:11 [j] ch. 9:15; 56:10, 12
9[k] Jer. 6:10
11[l] Cited 1 Cor. 14:21; See ch. 5:26-29
12[m] ch. 30:15; [Matt. 11:28, 29]
13[n] ch. 8:15
14[o] ver. 22; ch. 29:20
15[p] ver. 2, 18; [ch. 8:7, 8] [q] [Rom. 1:25]
16[r] Cited Rom. 9:33; 1 Pet. 2:6; [Ps. 118:22; Matt. 21:42; Acts 4:11] [s] ch. 14:32
17[t] [2 Kgs. 21:13]
18[u] ver. 15
19[v] [ch. 50:4] [w] [2 Chr. 32:18]

20 For the bed is too short to stretch oneself
on,
and the covering too narrow to wrap
oneself in.
21 For the LORD will rise up [x]as on Mount
Perazim;
[y]as in the Valley of [z]Gibeon he will be
roused;
to do his deed—strange is his deed!
and to work his work—alien is his
work!
22 Now therefore do not [a]scoff,
lest your bonds be made strong;
for I have heard [b]a decree of destruction
from the Lord GOD of hosts against
the whole land.

23 Give ear, and hear my voice;
give attention, and hear my speech.
24 Does he who plows for sowing plow
continually?
Does he continually open and harrow
his ground?
25 [c]When he has leveled its surface,
does he not scatter dill, sow cumin,
and put in wheat in rows
and barley in its proper place,
and emmer[1] as the border?
26 [d]For he is rightly instructed;
his God teaches him.

27 Dill is not threshed with a threshing
sledge,
nor is a cart wheel rolled over cumin,
but dill is beaten out with a stick,
and cumin with a rod.
28 Does one crush grain for bread?
No, he does not thresh it forever;[2]
when he drives his cart wheel over it
with his horses, he does not crush it.
29 This also comes from the LORD of hosts;
he is [e]wonderful in counsel
and excellent in wisdom.

The Siege of Jerusalem

29 Ah, Ariel, Ariel,
the city [f]where David encamped!
Add year to year;
let the feasts run their round.
2 Yet I will distress Ariel,
and there shall be moaning and lamentation,
and she shall be to me like an Ariel.[3]
3 [g]And I will encamp against you all around,
and will besiege you [h]with towers
and I will raise siegeworks against you.
4 [i]And you will be brought low; from the
earth you shall speak,
and from the dust your speech will be
bowed down;
your voice shall come from the ground
like [j]the voice of a ghost,
and from the dust your speech shall
whisper.

5 But the multitude of your foreign foes
shall be like [k]small dust,
and the multitude of the ruthless like
passing chaff.
[l]And in an instant, suddenly,
6 [m]you will be visited by the LORD of
hosts
with thunder and with earthquake and
great noise,
with whirlwind and tempest, and the
flame of a devouring fire.
7 And [n]the multitude of all the nations
that fight against Ariel,
all that fight against her and her
stronghold and distress her,
shall be [o]like a dream, a vision of the
night.
8 [p]As when a hungry man dreams, and
behold, he is eating
and awakes with his hunger not satisfied,

[1] A type of wheat [2] Or *Grain is crushed for bread; he will surely thresh it, but not forever* [3] *Ariel* could mean *lion of God*, or *hero* (2 Samuel 23:20), or *altar hearth* (Ezekiel 43:15–16)

21[x] [2 Sam. 5:20; 1 Chr. 14:11] [y] See Josh. 10:10-14 [z] 1 Chr. 14:16; See Josh. 9:3
22[a] ver. 14 [b] ch. 10:23
25[c] [ch. 55:10, 11]
26[d] [ch. 21:10]
29[e] Jer. 32:19; [ch. 9:6]
Chapter 29
1[f] [2 Sam. 5:9]
3[g] [2 Kgs. 25:1; Ezek. 4:2] [h] [Ezek. 21:22; 26:8]
4[i] [ch. 2:11, 12] [j] See ch. 8:19
5[k] ch. 17:13; Ps. 18:42 [l] [ch. 17:14; 37:36; 2 Kgs. 19:35]
6[m] [1 Kgs. 19:11, 12] **7**[n] [Zech. 12:9]; See Mic. 4:11-13 [o] ch. 17:14; [Job 20:8] **8**[p] [Ps. 73:20; 90:5]

29:1–9 The people of God must always remember that their Lord has not abandoned them, even when hope is dim. Here the attacking nations appear ready to devour Zion (Ariel), but at the last moment God provides deliverance (vv. 7–8). Probably the initial promise is experienced in 701 B.C., as the divine warrior fights for his people against Sennacherib's attacks (see 37:33–37).

29:10–14 Yet the danger of spiritual blindness remains. It can be self-imposed (v. 9) or it can be a verdict of God (v. 10; cf. 6:9–10), but it always puts one in danger. God warns against fostering hypocrisy, by which the people's mouths claim to "honor" God while in reality their "hearts are far from me" (29:13). God will keep

or as when a thirsty man dreams, and
behold, he is drinking
and awakes faint, with his thirst not
quenched,
so shall the multitude of all the
nations be
that fight against Mount Zion.

9 Astonish yourselves[1] and be astonished;
blind yourselves and be blind!
Be drunk, but not with wine;
[r]stagger, but not with strong drink!
10 [s]For the LORD has poured out upon you
a spirit of deep sleep,
and has closed your eyes (the prophets),
and covered your heads (the seers).

11 And the vision of all this has become to
you like the words of a book that is [t]sealed.
When men give it to one who can read, saying,
"Read this," he says, "I cannot, for it is sealed."
12 And when they give the book to one who
cannot read, saying, "Read this," he says, "I
cannot read."

13 And the Lord said:
"Because [u]this people [v]draw near with
their mouth
and honor me with their lips,
while their hearts are far from me,
and their fear of me is a commandment
taught by men,
14 therefore, behold, [w]I will again
do wonderful things with this people,
with wonder upon wonder;
and [x]the wisdom of their wise men shall
perish,
and the discernment of their discerning men shall be hidden."

15 Ah, [y]you who hide deep from the LORD
your counsel,
whose deeds are [z]in the dark,
and who say, "Who sees us? Who
knows us?"
16 [a]You turn things upside down!
Shall the potter be regarded as the clay,
that the thing made should say of its
maker,
"He did not make me";
or the thing formed say of him who
formed it,
"He has no understanding"?

17 Is it not yet a very little while
[b]until Lebanon shall be turned into a
fruitful field,
and the fruitful field shall be regarded
as a forest?
18 In that day [c]the deaf shall hear
[d]the words of a book,
and out of their gloom and darkness
[e]the eyes of the blind shall see.
19 [f]The meek shall obtain fresh joy in the
LORD,
and the poor among mankind shall
exult in the Holy One of Israel.
20 For the ruthless shall come to nothing
and [g]the scoffer cease,
and all who watch to do evil shall be
cut off,
21 who by a word make a man out to be an
offender,
and [h]lay a snare for him who reproves
in the gate,
and with an empty plea [i]turn aside
him who is in the right.

[1] Or *Linger awhile*

working, doing "wonders," but rather than wholeheartedly embracing Yahweh the people end up appearing foolish though imagining themselves to be wise (v. 14, quoted in 1 Cor. 1:19).

Jesus picks up on Isaiah's concerns and applies them to the Pharisees (Mark 7:6–7). The rituals and words are meant to flow from a broken and contrite spirit, not an arrogant and hard-hearted one (Ps. 51:17).

29:15–24 God remains the Creator, and we the creation (v. 16). And this Creator has no difficulty reversing the brokenness of this world, making the deaf to hear and the blind to see (v. 18). But who is it that hears from God? Who sees? The meek and the poor (v. 19).

That is what we see with Jesus, the Light of the World (John 8:12–30). Religious leaders who were meant to see Jesus were blinded by their sin (John 8:39–59), while the physically blind could, by humble faith, receive the grace of Christ which gave them eyes to see and ears to hear (John 9:1–41). Mindful of God's mercy, let us recognize that we too are by nature blind. It is grace alone that has restored our sight. We too once were blind, but now we see (John 9:25).

9[r] [ch. 19:14; 24:20]
10[s] [ch. 6:10; Rom. 11:8]
11[t] ch. 8:16; Dan. 12:4
13[u] Cited Matt. 15:8, 9; Mark 7:6, 7; [Ezek. 33:31] [v] [ch. 1:12; 58:2]
14[w] Hab. 1:5; See ch. 3:1-4 [x] Jer. 49:7; Cited 1 Cor. 1:19
15[y] [ch. 30:1] [z] Ezek. 8:12
16[a] See ch. 10:15
17[b] [Ps. 107:33, 35]
18[c] [ch. 32:3; 35:5; Matt. 11:5] [d] ver. 12 [e] [ch. 35:5; Matt. 11:5]
19[f] ch. 61:1; [ch. 14:32; Zeph. 3:12; Matt. 5:3]
20[g] ch. 28:14, 22
21[h] Amos 5:10; [Ps. 127:5] [i] Amos 5:12

22 Therefore thus says the LORD, [j]who redeemed Abraham, concerning the house of Jacob:

"Jacob shall no more be ashamed,
no more shall his face grow pale.
23 For when he sees his children,
[k]the work of my hands, in his midst,
they will sanctify my name;
[l]they will sanctify the Holy One of Jacob
and will stand in awe of the God of Israel.
24 And those [m]who go astray in spirit will come to understanding,
and those who murmur will accept instruction."

Do Not Go Down to Egypt

30 "Ah, [n]stubborn children," declares the LORD,
[o]"who carry out a plan, but not mine,
and who make [p]an alliance,[1] but not of my Spirit,
that they may add sin to sin;
2 [q]who set out to go down to Egypt,
without asking for my direction,
to take refuge in the protection of Pharaoh
and to seek shelter in the shadow of Egypt!
3 [r]Therefore shall the protection of Pharaoh turn to your shame,
and the shelter in the shadow of Egypt to your humiliation.
4 For though his officials are at [s]Zoan
and [t]his envoys reach [u]Hanes,
5 everyone comes to shame
through [v]a people that cannot profit them,
that brings neither help nor profit,
but shame and disgrace."

6 An [w]oracle on [x]the beasts of [y]the Negeb.

Through a land of trouble and anguish,
from where come the lioness and the lion,
the adder and the [z]flying fiery serpent,
they carry their riches on the backs of donkeys,
and their treasures on the humps of camels,
to a people that cannot profit them.
7 Egypt's [a]help is worthless and empty;
therefore I have called her
[b]"Rahab who sits still."

A Rebellious People

8 And now, go, [c]write it before them on a tablet
and inscribe it in a book,
that it may be for the time to come
as a witness forever.[2]
9 [d]For they are a rebellious people,
lying children,
children unwilling to hear
the instruction of the LORD;
10 [e]who say to [f]the seers, "Do not see,"
and to the prophets, "Do not prophesy to us what is right;
speak to us [g]smooth things,
prophesy illusions,
11 leave the way, turn aside from the path,
let us hear no more about the Holy One of Israel."
12 Therefore thus says the Holy One of Israel,

[1] Hebrew *who weave a web* [2] Some Hebrew manuscripts, Syriac, Targum, Vulgate, and Greek versions; Masoretic Text *forever and ever*

22[j] [ch. 51:2]
23[k] ch. 19:25; 60:21; [Ps. 100:3] [l] ch. 8:13
24[m] [ch. 28:7]
Chapter 30
1[n] [ch. 1:2, 4] [o] [ch. 29:15] [p] ch. 25:7
2[q] ch. 31:1; 36:6
3[r] [ver. 7; ch. 20:5]
4[s] See ch. 19:11 [t] [Ezek. 17:15] [u] [Jer. 43:7]
5[v] [ver. 7; Jer. 2:36]
6[w] See ch. 13:1 [x] [ch. 51:9; Ps. 68:30] [y] [Acts 8:26] [z] [Deut. 8:15]
7[a] ch. 36:6 [b] ch. 51:9
8[c] Hab. 2:2
9[d] ver. 1
10[e] Amos 2:12; [Amos 7:12, 13] [f] See 1 Sam. 9:9 [g] [1 Kgs. 22:13]; See Jer. 28:1-11; Ezek. 13:8-16

30:1–33 Rather than turning to God, the people "add sin to sin" (v. 1) and apathetically fail to ask for divine direction, instead seeking "shelter in the shadow of Egypt" (vv. 2–3). But what at first appears a safe haven ends up being a position of shame and disgrace (vv. 4–5). What is Egypt in comparison to the Creator? In the long run, her "help is worthless and empty" (v. 7), whereas God is our ever present help in time of need (Ps. 46:1; cf. Heb. 4:16).

We are always tempted to create idols, even provoking our spiritual leaders to ignore God's warnings and instructions. We crave "smooth things," even "illusions" (Isa. 30:8–10). May it not be so! We must be willing to hear the full counsel of the Lord, trusting his word over the perverted powers of the age (vv. 11–12). Sometimes we imagine God prefers punishment to pardon, but Isaiah reminds his listeners, "the LORD waits to be gracious to you, and therefore he exalts himself to show mercy to you" (v. 18). He is exalted as he comes low, forgiving, restoring, and enlivening. Those who "wait for him" experience his merciful justice. Isaiah promises, "in the day when the LORD binds up the brokenness of his people," he will go on to heal the "wounds inflicted by his blow" (v. 26).

"Because you despise this word
and trust in [h]oppression and perverseness
and rely on them,
13 therefore this iniquity shall be to you
[i]like a breach in a high wall, bulging out, and about to collapse,
whose breaking comes suddenly, in an instant;
14 and its breaking is [j]like that of a potter's vessel
that is smashed so ruthlessly
that among its fragments not a shard is found
with which to take fire from the hearth,
or to dip up water out of the cistern."

15 For thus said the Lord GOD, the Holy One of Israel,
"In [k]returning[1] and [l]rest you shall be saved;
in quietness and in trust shall be your strength."
But you were unwilling, 16 and you said,
"No! We will flee upon [m]horses";
therefore you shall flee away;
and, "We will ride upon swift steeds";
therefore your pursuers shall be swift.
17 [n]A thousand shall flee at the threat of one;
at the threat of five you shall flee,
till you are left
like a flagstaff on the top of a mountain,
like a signal on a hill.

The LORD Will Be Gracious

18 Therefore the LORD [o]waits to be gracious to you,
and therefore he [p]exalts himself to show mercy to you.
For the LORD is a God of justice;
[q]blessed are all those who wait for him.

19 For a people shall dwell [r]in Zion, in
Jerusalem; you shall weep no more. He will
surely be gracious to you at the sound of your
cry. As soon as he hears it, he answers you.
20 And though the Lord give you the [s]bread
of adversity and the [s]water of affliction, [t]yet
your Teacher will not hide himself anymore,
but your eyes shall see your Teacher. 21 [u]And
your ears shall hear a word behind you, saying,
"This is [v]the way, walk in it," when you turn to
the right or when you turn to the left. 22 Then
you will defile your carved idols overlaid with
silver and your gold-plated metal images.
[w]You will scatter them as unclean things. You
will say to them, "Be gone!"

23 [x]And he will give [y]rain for the seed with
which you sow the ground, and bread, the
produce of the ground, which will be rich
and plenteous. [z]In that day your livestock will
graze in large pastures, 24 and [a]the oxen and
the donkeys that work the ground will eat seasoned fodder, which has been winnowed with
shovel and fork. 25 And [b]on every lofty moun-
tain and every high hill there will be brooks
running with water, in the day of the great
slaughter, [c]when the towers fall. 26 [d]Moreover,
the light of the moon will be as the light of the
sun, and the light of the sun will be sevenfold,
as the light of seven days, in the day when [e]the
LORD binds up [f]the brokenness of his people,
and heals the wounds inflicted by his blow.

27 Behold, the name of the LORD comes from afar,
burning with his anger, and in thick rising smoke;[2]
his lips are full of fury,
and his tongue is like a devouring fire;
28 [g]his breath is [h]like an overflowing stream
that reaches up to the neck;
to sift the nations with the sieve of destruction,
and to place on the jaws of the peoples [i]a bridle that leads astray.

29 You shall have a song as in the night when
a holy feast is kept, and gladness of heart, [j]as
when one sets out to the sound of the flute to
go to [k]the mountain of the LORD, to [l]the Rock
of Israel. 30 And the LORD [m]will cause his majestic voice to be heard and the descending blow
of his arm to be seen, in furious anger [n]and a

[1] Or *repentance* [2] Hebrew *in weight of uplifted clouds*

These words find their ultimate fulfillment in Christ, as we see that the blow against our sin fell on him, and so the "holy feast is kept" (v. 29); we now eat of his body and drink of his blood in remembrance of what he has done on our behalf (Luke 22:14–23; 1 Cor. 11:23–26). By his wounds we are healed (Isa. 53:5; 1 Pet. 2:24).

12[h] [ch. 5:8, 20]
13[i] Ps. 62:3
14[j] Ps. 2:9
15[k] Hos. 14:1 [l] [Ex. 14:14]
16[m] ch. 31:1, 3; [Hos. 14:3]

17[n] [Lev. 26:8; Deut. 32:30] **18**[o] [Hab. 2:3] [p] ch. 5:16 [q] Ps. 2:12; 34:8; Prov. 16:20; Jer. 17:7 **19**[r] [ch. 14:32] **20**[s] 1 Kgs. 22:27; Ps. 127:2; [Ezek. 4:10, 11] [t] [ch. 3:1, 2] **21**[u] [Jer. 31:33, 34] [v] ch. 35:8; [Acts 9:2] **22**[w] ch. 2:20; 31:7; [Hos. 14:8] **23**[x] [ch. 32:20; Ps. 144:13, 14] [y] [Jer. 5:24] [z] [Ps. 65:13] **24**[a] See Gen. 45:6 **25**[b] [ch. 33:21; Ps. 107:35; Joel 3:18] [c] ch. 32:19; [ch. 2:15] **26**[d] ch. 60:19, 20 [e] [Hos. 6:1] [f] [ch. 1:5, 6] **28**[g] ch. 11:4; 2 Thess. 2:8 [h] [ch. 8:8; Nah. 1:8] [i] ch. 37:29 **29**[j] 1 Sam. 10:5; 1 Kgs. 1:40 [k] ch. 2:3 [l] ch. 26:4; 44:8; Deut. 32:18 **30**[m] Ps. 18:13 [n] ch. 29:6

flame of devouring fire, with a cloudburst[o] and
storm and hailstones. 31 The Assyrians will be
terror-stricken at the voice of the LORD, [p] when
he strikes with his rod. 32 And every stroke of
the appointed staff that the LORD lays on them
[q] will be to the sound of tambourines and lyres.
[r] Battling with brandished arm, he will fight
with them. 33 For [s] a burning place[1] has long
been prepared; indeed, for the king it is made
ready, [t] its pyre made deep and wide, with fire
and wood in abundance; [u] the breath of the
LORD, like a stream of sulfur, kindles it.

Woe to Those Who Go Down to Egypt

31 Woe to [v] those who go down to Egypt for help
and rely on horses,
who [w] trust in chariots because they are many
and in horsemen because they are very strong,
but [x] do not look to the Holy One of Israel
or consult the LORD!
2 And [y] yet he is wise and brings disaster;
[z] he does not call back his words,
but [a] will arise against the house of the evildoers
and against the helpers of [b] those who work iniquity.
3 The Egyptians are man, and not God,
and their horses [c] are flesh, and not spirit.
When the LORD stretches out his hand,
the helper will stumble, and he who is helped will fall,
and they will all perish together.

4 For thus the LORD said to me,
[d] "As a lion or a young lion growls over his prey,
and when a band of shepherds is called out against him
he is not terrified by their shouting
or daunted at their noise,
[e] so the LORD of hosts will come down
to fight[2] on Mount Zion and on its hill.
5 [f] Like birds hovering, so the LORD of hosts
will protect Jerusalem;
he will protect and deliver it;
he will spare and rescue it."

6 [g] Turn to him from whom people[3] have
[h] deeply revolted, O children of Israel. 7 For in
that day [i] everyone shall cast away his idols of
silver and his idols of gold, which your hands
have sinfully made for you.

8 [j] "And the Assyrian shall fall by a sword, not of man;
and a sword, not of man, shall devour him;
and he shall flee from the sword,
and his young men shall be [k] put to forced labor.
9 [l] His rock shall pass away in terror,
and his officers desert the standard in panic,"
declares the LORD, whose [m] fire is in Zion,
and whose [n] furnace is in Jerusalem.

A King Will Reign in Righteousness

32 Behold, [o] a king will reign in righteousness,
and princes will rule in justice.
2 [p] Each will be like a hiding place from the wind,
a shelter from the storm,
[q] like streams of water in a dry place,
like the shade of a great rock in a weary land.
3 [r] Then the eyes of those who see will not be closed,
and the ears of those who hear will give attention.

[1] Or *For Topheth* [2] The Hebrew words for *hosts* and *to fight* sound alike [3] Hebrew *they*

30[o] ch. 28:2; [Josh. 10:11]
31[p] ch. 9:4; [Mic. 6:9]
32[q] Ex. 15:1 [r] ch. 11:15; 19:16; [ch. 2:19]
33[s] 2 Kgs. 23:10; Jer. 7:31 [t] Ezek. 24:9, 10 [u] Ps. 18:8; Ezek. 20:48

Chapter 31
1[v] ch. 30:2; 36:6 [w] Ps. 20:7; [ch. 30:16; 36:9] [x] [ch. 22:11]
2[y] [Ps. 94:8-10] [z] [Num. 23:19] [a] [ch. 22:14] [b] Ps. 94:4
3[c] Jer. 17:5

31:1–9 A common refrain throughout Isaiah is the warning not to trust in political muscle more than in God's provision (v. 1). Egypt again represents military and economic strength (vv. 1–3), yet God will win the battle as he fights on behalf of Zion (vv. 4–5). Trusting in Egypt represents trusting in the "idols" of silver and gold (v. 7), but God's people must instead "turn to him" (v. 6) who created such materials and stands over even the strongest powers (e.g., Assyria; vv. 8–9).

Likewise, in our own day, let us always be mindful to not place our security in any political or military might but rather in the Lord of heaven and earth. Lurking behind well-intentioned patriotism can be ugly idolatry. Christ and his kingdom must always ground our true citizenship and security (Phil. 3:20).

4[d] Hos. 11:10; Amos 1:2; 3:8 [e] [ch. 42:13] **5**[f] Deut. 32:11; [Ps. 91:4] **6**[g] [ch. 30:15] [h] ch. 1:5 **7**[i] ch. 2:20; 30:22 **8**[j] ch. 37:36 [k] [Gen. 49:15; Prov. 12:24] **9**[l] Deut. 32:31; See ch. 30:29 [m] ch. 30:33 [n] Ps. 21:9; Mal. 4:1 **Chapter 32** **1**[o] Ps. 72:1, 2, 4; Jer. 23:5; See ch. 11:1-4 **2**[p] ch. 4:6; 25:4 [q] ch. 33:21 **3**[r] See ch. 29:18

4 The heart of the hasty will understand
and know,
[s]and the tongue of the stammerers
will hasten to speak distinctly.
5 [t]The fool will no more be called noble,
nor the scoundrel said to be honorable.
6 For [u]the fool speaks folly,
and his heart is busy with iniquity,
to practice ungodliness,
to utter error concerning the LORD,
[v]to leave the craving of the hungry unsatisfied,
and to deprive the thirsty of drink.
7 As for the scoundrel—[w]his devices are
evil;
he plans wicked schemes
to ruin the poor with lying words,
even when the plea of the needy is
right.
8 But he who is noble plans noble things,
and on noble things he stands.

Complacent Women Warned of Disaster

9 [x]Rise up, you women [y]who are at ease,
hear my voice;
you complacent daughters, give ear to
my speech.
10 In little more than a year
you will shudder, you complacent
women;
for the grape harvest fails,
the fruit harvest will not come.
11 Tremble, you women [y]who are at ease,
shudder, you complacent ones;
[z]strip, and make yourselves bare,
[a]and tie sackcloth around your waist.
12 [b]Beat your breasts for the pleasant fields,
for the fruitful vine,
13 [c]for the soil of my people
growing up in thorns and briers,
[d]yes, for all the joyous houses
in the exultant city.
14 For the palace is forsaken,
the populous city deserted;
the hill and the watchtower
will become dens forever,
[e]a joy of wild donkeys,
a pasture of flocks;
15 until [f]the Spirit is poured upon us from
on high,
and [g]the wilderness becomes a fruitful field,
and the fruitful field is deemed a forest.
16 Then justice will dwell in the wilderness,
and righteousness abide in the fruitful field.
17 [h]And the effect of righteousness will be
peace,
and the result of righteousness, quietness and trust[1] forever.

[1] Or *security*

32:1–8 A vivid contrast is presented to the reader. The reign of a just and righteous king (vv. 1–2) is juxtaposed with the self-serving rule of the "scoundrel" who hurts the poor and needy (v. 7). "He who is noble plans noble things, and on noble things he stands" (v. 8). Whereas the fool seeks to satisfy his own cravings (vv. 5–7), this glorious king provides shelter and protection for the vulnerable (v. 2).

In Jesus we see with unprecedented clarity and vividness the Lord as a refuge. He helps the poor and needy. He is the friend of failures. The only prerequisite for his glad and delighted favor is the open hands of need and faith.

32:9–20 It can be too easy for us to stand at a distance and blame our leaders for the injustices that occur in this world, even as we are benefitting from those inequities. But Isaiah's warnings are next turned toward those who benefit from the injustices even if they are not legislating them (v. 9). Those "women" who are living in ease should be quick to mourn over their sin (vv. 10–13; cf. 3:16–26). Rather than indulging in ill-gotten or ill-preserved prosperity, they desperately need God's Spirit to be "poured upon us from on high" (32:15).

Here we see an example of how our Messiah King's reign (vv. 1–2) must be framed in terms of a fresh outpouring of the Spirit. In this new age comes the fruit of justice and righteousness (vv. 16–17), and so under his reign and by his Spirit the people can "abide in a peaceful habitation" (v. 18). When Jesus the risen King pours out his Spirit at Pentecost (Acts 2:1–41), God's people immediately begin caring for the needy, bringing together people from every tongue and land in anticipatory expression of Christ's kingdom (Acts 2:42–47; 4:23–37). These are the marks of the King and his Spirit's already reigning presence.

4[s] ch. 35:6
5[t] [ch. 5:20]
6[u] 1 Sam. 24:13 [v] [ch. 3:14, 15]
7[w] Mic. 2:1, 2
9[x] See ch. 3:16–4:1 [y] Amos 6:1
11[y] [See ver. 9 above] [z] [ch. 47:2, 3] [a] See Gen. 37:34
12[b] [ch. 24:7]
13[c] ch. 7:23; 34:13; Hos. 9:6 [d] [ch. 24:11, 12]
14[e] Jer. 2:24
15[f] [ch. 11:2; Joel 2:28] [g] ch. 35:1, 2; [ch. 29:17]
17[h] James 3:18; [ch. 1:27; Ps. 72:3; 119:165]

18 My people will abide in a peaceful habitation,
in secure dwellings, and in quiet resting places.
19 [i]And it will hail when the forest falls down,
[j]and the city will be utterly laid low.
20 [k]Happy are you who sow beside all waters,
who let the feet of the ox and the donkey range free.

O Lord, Be Gracious to Us

33 [l]Ah, you destroyer,
who yourself have not been destroyed,
you traitor,
whom none has betrayed!
When you have ceased to destroy,
you will be destroyed;
and when you have finished betraying,
they will betray you.

2 O Lord, be gracious to us; [m]we wait for you.
Be our arm every morning,
our salvation in the time of trouble.
3 [n]At the tumultuous noise peoples flee;
when you lift yourself up, nations are scattered,
4 and your spoil is gathered as the caterpillar gathers;
[o]as locusts leap, it is leapt upon.
5 [p]The Lord is exalted, for he dwells on high;
he will fill Zion with justice and righteousness,
6 [q]and he will be the stability of your times,
abundance of salvation, wisdom, and knowledge;
the fear of the Lord is Zion's[1] treasure.
7 Behold, their heroes cry in the streets;
[r]the envoys of peace weep bitterly.
8 [s]The highways lie waste;
the traveler ceases.
[t]Covenants are broken;
cities[2] are despised;
there is no regard for man.
9 [u]The land mourns and languishes;
Lebanon is confounded and withers away;
Sharon is like a desert,
and Bashan and Carmel shake off their leaves.

10 [v]"Now I will arise," says the Lord,
"now I will lift myself up;
now I will be exalted.
11 [w]You conceive chaff; you give birth to stubble;
your breath is [x]a fire that will consume you.
12 And the peoples will be as if burned to lime,
[x]like thorns cut down, that are burned in the fire."

13 Hear, you who are far off, what I have done;
and you who are near, acknowledge my might.
14 The sinners in Zion are afraid;
trembling has seized the godless:

[1] Hebrew *his* [2] Masoretic Text; Dead Sea Scroll *witnesses*

19[i] ch. 28:2, 17 [j] ch. 26:5
20[k] Eccles. 11:1; [ch. 30:23]
Chapter 33
1[l] ch. 21:2; [ch. 17:14]
2[m] ch. 25:9; 26:8
3[n] ch. 17:13; [2 Kgs. 19:7]
4[o] [Joel 2:4, 5]
5[p] ch. 2:17; 5:15, 16
6[q] [ch. 39:8]
7[r] [ch. 36:22; 2 Kgs. 18:37]
8[s] [Judg. 5:6] [t] [ver. 1]; See 2 Kgs. 18:14-17
9[u] ch. 24:4; [Nah. 1:4]
10[v] Ps. 12:5; 68:1; [ch. 10:26]
11[w] [ch. 59:4; Ps. 7:14] [x] ch. 10:16, 17; [Ps. 80:16]
12[x] [See ver. 11 above]

33:1–13 While times of disorder come, those who promote such an environment end up destroying and devouring themselves (v. 1). We must echo the people's cry of dependence on the gracious God who provides salvation in such times (v. 2). His exaltation is one governed by the twin characteristics of justice and righteousness, attributes exercised by God to bring "stability" and, in the end, the "abundance of salvation, wisdom, and knowledge" (vv. 5–6).

The "covenants are broken," and humanity's dignity is disregarded (v. 8). Yet Christ comes as the climax of the covenants, faithful to maintain God's covenant promises to his people even when it means he must die on their behalf. In an astonishing exchange, God the Son absorbs the punishment for his faithless covenant partner—us.

33:14–24 God's visitation to Zion will bring purification (v. 14). As with the psalmist who asks, "who shall dwell on your holy hill?" (Ps. 15:1), the answer is only the blameless one whose character reflects the righteousness and values of God (Ps. 15:2–5). So Isaiah asks, who can withstand "the consuming fire" (Isa. 33:14; cf. Heb. 12:29)? His answer likewise points to a unique King (Isa. 33:17) who could represent the people: he must be the blameless One who resists corruption, brutality, and oppression (vv. 15–16).

[y]"Who among us can dwell [z]with the consuming fire?
Who among us can dwell with everlasting burnings?"
15 [a]He who walks righteously and speaks uprightly,
who despises the gain of oppressions,
who shakes his hands, lest they hold a bribe,
who stops his ears from hearing of bloodshed
[b]and shuts his eyes from looking on evil,
16 he will dwell on the heights;
his place of defense will be the fortresses of rocks;
[c]his bread will be given him; his water will be sure.

17 [d]Your eyes will behold the king in his beauty;
[e]they will see a land that stretches afar.
18 [f]Your heart will muse on the terror:
"Where is he who counted, where is [g]he who weighed the tribute?
Where is [h]he who counted the towers?"
19 [i]You will see no more the insolent people,
the people [j]of an obscure speech that you cannot comprehend,
stammering in a tongue that you cannot understand.
20 Behold Zion, the city of our appointed feasts!
[k]Your eyes will see Jerusalem,
an untroubled habitation, an [l]immovable tent,
whose stakes will never be plucked up,
nor will any of its cords be broken.
21 But there the LORD in majesty will be for us
a place of [m]broad rivers and streams,
[n]where no galley with oars can go,
nor majestic ship can pass.
22 For the LORD is our [o]judge; the LORD is our [p]lawgiver;
the LORD is our [q]king; he will save us.

23 Your cords hang loose;
they cannot hold the mast firm in its place
or keep the sail spread out.
[r]Then prey and spoil in abundance will be divided;
even [s]the lame will take the prey.
24 And no inhabitant will say, [t]"I am sick";
[u]the people who dwell there will be forgiven their iniquity.

Judgment on the Nations

34 Draw near, [v]O nations, to hear,
and give attention, O peoples!
Let the earth hear, and all that fills it;
the world, and all that comes from it.
2 For the LORD is enraged against all the nations,
and furious against all their host;
he has [w]devoted them to destruction,[1]
has given them over for slaughter.
3 Their slain shall be cast out,
and [x]the stench of their corpses shall rise;
[y]the mountains shall flow with their blood.

[1] That is, set apart (devoted) as an offering to the Lord (for destruction); also verse 5

Jesus the Messiah is the long-expected One who is God's "judge" (Matt. 25:34; 2 Cor. 5:10), "lawgiver" (cf. James. 4:12), and "king" (cf. Matt. 21:5; Rev. 19:16): "he will save us" (Isa. 33:22). "God exalted him at his right hand as Leader and Savior, to give repentance to Israel and forgiveness of sins" (Acts 5:31; cf. Titus. 3:4–6).

34:1–17 Where is your citizenship? Are you united to the King of Zion, or do you follow the idolatry of others (v. 8)? Isaiah speaks sternly of a coming universal judgment against the nations of the earth (vv. 1–2). Frighteningly, the warning is that the Lord's "sword" will have its way (vv. 5–6). Devastation is coming, threatening a return to the chaos of the unformed "void" of creation that existed before God's Spirit brought about order (Gen. 1:2). Important in these descriptions of judgment is the note that it comes, at least in part, on behalf of God's people (Isa. 34:8, 16–17). We need not exact our own vengeance, or fear that we shall not be vindicated, for wrongs committed against us. God will set right the scales of justice with his ultimate and righteous judgment.

How surprising and glorious to read then that "God so loved the world, that he gave his only Son, that whoever believes in him should not perish but have eternal life"

14[y] [Ps. 15:1; 24:3] [z] ch. 66:15; Heb. 12:29
15[a] [Ps. 15:2; 24:4] [b] Ps. 119:37
16[c] ch. 30:23, 25
17[d] ch. 6:5; [Zech. 9:9] [e] [ch. 54:2, 3]
18[f] [Ps. 37:10] [g] [2 Kgs. 18:14] [h] [Ps. 48:12]
19[i] [2 Kgs. 19:32, 33] [j] ch. 28:11; Deut. 28:49, 50
20[k] ch. 32:18 [l] ver. 6
21[m] Ps. 46:4, 5 [n] [ch. 2:16; Ps. 48:7]
22[o] [Judg. 2:16] [p] James 4:12 [q] [1 Sam. 12:13]
23[r] [Gen. 49:27] [s] [Ps. 68:12]
24[t] [ch. 1:5, 6] [u] ch. 1:25, 26; Jer. 50:20

Chapter 34
1[v] Ps. 49:1; [Joel 3:1, 2]
2[w] [Josh. 6:21]
3[x] Joel 2:20 [y] [Ezek. 39:4]

4 [z]All the host of heaven shall rot away,
and the skies roll up like a scroll.
All their host shall fall,
as leaves fall from the vine,
like leaves falling from the fig tree.

5 For my sword has drunk its fill in the heavens;
behold, it descends for judgment upon [a]Edom,
upon the people [b]I have devoted to destruction.
6 The LORD has a sword; it is sated with blood;
it is gorged with fat,
with the blood of lambs and goats,
with the fat of the kidneys of rams.
[c]For the LORD has a sacrifice in Bozrah,
a great slaughter in the land of Edom.
7 [d]Wild oxen shall [e]fall with them,
and [f]young steers with [f]the mighty bulls.
Their land shall drink its fill of blood,
and their soil shall be gorged with fat.

8 [g]For the LORD has a day of vengeance,
a year of recompense for the cause of Zion.
9 [h]And the streams of Edom[1] shall be turned into pitch,
and her soil into sulfur;
her land shall become burning pitch.
10 Night and day [i]it shall not be quenched;
[j]its smoke shall go up forever.
[k]From generation to generation it shall lie waste;
none shall pass through it forever and ever.
11 [l]But the hawk and the porcupine[2] shall possess it,
the owl and the raven shall dwell in it.
[m]He shall stretch the line of [n]confusion[3] over it,
and the plumb line of emptiness.
12 Its nobles—there is no one there to call it a kingdom,
and all its princes shall be nothing.

13 [o]Thorns shall grow over its strongholds,
nettles and thistles in its fortresses.
It shall be the haunt of [p]jackals,
an abode for ostriches.[4]
14 [q]And wild animals shall meet with hyenas;
the wild goat shall cry to his fellow;
indeed, there the night bird[5] settles
and finds for herself a resting place.

15 There the owl nests and lays
and hatches and gathers her young in her shadow;
indeed, there [r]the hawks are gathered,
each one with her mate.
16 Seek and read from the book of the LORD:
Not one of these shall be missing;
none shall be without her mate.
For the mouth of the LORD has commanded,
and his Spirit has gathered them.
17 [s]He has cast the lot for them;
his hand has portioned it out to them with the line;
they shall possess it forever;
from generation to generation they shall dwell in it.

The Ransomed Shall Return

35 [t]The wilderness and the dry land shall be glad;
[u]the desert shall rejoice and blossom like the crocus;
2 it shall blossom abundantly
and rejoice with joy and singing.

[1] Hebrew *her streams* [2] The identity of the animals rendered *hawk* and *porcupine* is uncertain [3] Hebrew *formlessness* [4] Or *owls* [5] Identity uncertain

4[z] Joel 2:31; 3:15; Matt. 24:29; Acts 2:20; Rev. 6:13, 14; [Ps. 102:26; Heb. 1:11]
5[a] See ch. 63:1-6; Jer. 49:7-22; Obad. 1-21; Mal. 1:2-4 [b][ver. 2]
6[c] ch. 63:1
7[d] Num. 23:22 [e] ch. 47:1 [f] Ps. 22:12
8[g] ch. 61:2; 63:4; Ps. 137:7
9[h] Deut. 29:23
10[i] ch. 66:24 [j] [Rev. 14:11; 18:18; 19:3] [k] Mal. 1:4
11[l] ch. 14:23; Zeph. 2:14; [Rev. 18:2] [m] 2 Kgs. 21:13; Lam. 2:8; See Amos 7:7-9 [n] [ch. 24:10] **13**[o] See ch. 32:13 [p] ch. 13:22; Ps. 44:19; Mal. 1:3 **14**[q] See ch. 13:21 **15**[r] Deut. 14:13 **17**[s] [Ps. 78:55] **Chapter 35**
1[t] ch. 55:12, 13 [u] [ch. 32:15]

(John 3:16). In John's Gospel, the "world" often signifies rebellion against God (e.g., John 7:7; 12:31; 14:17; 15:18–19). The Son came for those who were hostile toward him (Rom. 5:10); he was willing to take the sword for us so that "the world might be saved through him" (John 3:17; cf. 1:29). God's Son has brought light to this dark world, so that salvation could reach throughout the whole world (e.g., John 1:9; 4:42; 6:33, 51; 8:12–30; 9:5). We now go out to the world, not ignorant of their sin but nevertheless confident of Christ's ability to rescue and release those who are in its blinding darkness.

35:1–10 After so many warnings and confrontations, Isaiah offers a glorious word of hope: there is a coming exodus that will exceed the first one. The imagery is of a flower-lined highway of "holiness" (vv. 1–2, 8) reconnecting the people with their

[v]The glory of Lebanon shall be given to it,
the majesty of [w]Carmel and [x]Sharon.
[y]They shall see the glory of the LORD,
the majesty of our God.

3 [z]Strengthen the weak hands,
and make firm the feeble knees.
4 Say to those who have an anxious heart,
"Be strong; fear not!
[a]Behold, your God
will come with vengeance,
with the recompense of God.
He will come and save you."

5 [b]Then the eyes of the blind shall be
opened,
and the ears of the deaf unstopped;
6 [b]then shall the lame man leap like a deer,
and the tongue of the mute sing for joy.
[c]For waters break forth in the wilderness,
and streams in the desert;
7 [d]the burning sand shall become a pool,
and the thirsty ground springs of
water;
in the haunt of [e]jackals, where they lie
down,
the grass shall become reeds and
rushes.
8 [f]And a highway shall be there,
and it shall be called the Way of
Holiness;
[g]the unclean shall not pass over it.
It shall belong to those who walk on
the way;
even if they are fools, they shall not go
astray.[1]
9 No lion shall be there,
nor shall any ravenous beast come up
on it;
they shall not be found there,
but the redeemed shall walk there.
10 [h]And the ransomed of the LORD shall
return
and come to Zion with singing;
[i]everlasting joy shall be upon their heads;
they shall obtain gladness and joy,
and sorrow and sighing shall flee away.

Sennacherib Invades Judah

36 [j]In the fourteenth year of King
Hezekiah, [k]Sennacherib king of Assyria
came up against all the fortified cities of Judah
and took them.
2 [l]And the king of Assyria
sent the Rabshakeh[2] from [m]Lachish to King
Hezekiah at Jerusalem, with a great army. And

[1] Or *if they are fools, they shall not wander in it* [2] *Rabshakeh* is the title of a high-ranking Assyrian military officer

glorious God. They have been "ransomed" by their Lord, securing their return. Such divine deliverance points well beyond the immediate historical restoration from exile, for the anticipation is ultimately of "everlasting joy," singing, and gladness that will become the new reality of the redeemed (vv. 9–10).

What are the signs that the time of God's visitation and liberation has come? The blind will see, the deaf will hear, the lame will walk, and the mute will speak (vv. 5–6). And this is exactly what we find when Jesus answers John the Baptist's question about Jesus' identity and relation to messianic kingdom expectations (Matt. 11:4–5; Luke 7:22).

Hebrews picks up on Isaiah's encouragement to "lift your drooping hands and strengthen your weak knees" (Heb. 12:12; cf. Isa. 35:3), applying it to Christians. As sons and daughters of God we do not stand under divine wrath. But we do experience his loving fatherly discipline, which is "for our good, that we may share his holiness" (Heb. 12:10; cf. Isa. 35:8). God's forgiveness and grace is meant to be life-giving, bringing about the way of holiness and peace rather than immorality and chaos (Heb. 12:14–17).

36:1–39:8 Isaiah 36–39 largely corresponds with 2 Kings 18–20. Isaiah's ministry has warned of compromises and temptations, and now we reach a climax in the narrative: will King Hezekiah trust in Yahweh or will his fear of a threatening political force cause him to lose faith in the God of Israel? Though the circumstances differ, the battle of the heart remains the same for us today.

36:1–22 "On what do you rest this trust of yours?" (v. 4). Like the Assyrian commander taunting Hezekiah and the inhabitants of Jerusalem, we often face voices—internal and external—that tempt us to second-guess God's commitment to us. If we say we trust in God, these voices counter that others have claimed divine protection only to end up helpless and exposed (vv. 7–10). Anticipating Hezekiah's plea to the people, the Assyrian commander intimidates the besieged people in their native tongue,

2 [v]Song 5:15 [w]Song 7:5 [x]ch. 33:9; Song 2:1 [y]ch. 40:5
3 [z]Cited Heb. 12:12; [ch. 40:1]
4 [a][ch. 40:10, 11]
5 [b]ch. 32:3, 4
6 [b][See ver. 5 above] [c][ver. 1; ch. 41:18; 43:19; 44:3, 4; John 7:38, 39]
7 [d]ch. 48:20, 21; 49:10 [e]See ch. 13:22
8 [f]ch. 40:3 [g]ch. 52:1
10 [h]ch. 51:11 [i]ch. 65:19; [ch. 25:8; Rev. 7:17; 21:4]

Chapter 36
1 [j]For ver. 1-22, see 2 Kgs. 18:13, 17-37 [k][2 Chr. 32:1]
2 [l]2 Chr. 32:9 [m]Josh. 15:20, 39

he stood [n]by the conduit of the upper pool on
the highway to the Washer's Field. 3 And there
came out to him [o]Eliakim the son of Hilkiah,
who was over the household, and [o]Shebna
the secretary, and Joah the son of Asaph, the
recorder.

4 And the Rabshakeh said to them, "Say to
Hezekiah, 'Thus says the [p]great king, the king
of Assyria: On what do you rest this trust of
yours? 5 Do you think that mere words are
strategy and power for war? In whom do you
now trust, that you have rebelled against me?
6 [q]Behold, you are trusting in Egypt, that broken reed of a staff, which will pierce the hand
of any man who leans on it. Such is Pharaoh
king of Egypt to all who trust in him. 7 But
if you say to me, "We trust in the LORD our
God," is it not he [r]whose high places and altars
Hezekiah has removed, saying to Judah and
to Jerusalem, "You shall worship before this
altar"? 8 Come now, make a wager with my
master the king of Assyria: I will give you
two thousand horses, if you are able on your
part to set riders on them. 9 How then can you
repulse [s]a single captain among the least of my
master's servants, when [t]you trust in Egypt for
chariots and for horsemen? 10 Moreover, is it
without the LORD that I have come up against
this land to destroy it? [u]The LORD said to me,
Go up against this land and destroy it.'"

11 Then Eliakim, Shebna, and Joah said to
the Rabshakeh, "Please speak to your servants [v]in Aramaic, for we understand it. Do
not speak to us in the language of Judah
within the hearing of the people who are on
the wall." 12 But the Rabshakeh said, "Has my
master sent me to speak these words to your
master and to you, and not to the men sitting
on the wall, who are doomed with you to eat
their own dung and drink their own urine?"
13 Then the Rabshakeh stood and called
out in a loud voice in the language of Judah:
"Hear the words of the great king, the king
of Assyria! 14 Thus says the king: [w]'Do not let
Hezekiah deceive you, for he will not be able
to deliver you. 15 Do not let Hezekiah make you
trust in the LORD by saying, "The LORD will
surely deliver us. This city will not be given
into the hand of the king of Assyria." 16 Do not
listen to Hezekiah. For thus says the king of
Assyria: Make your peace with me[1] and come
out to me. Then each one of you will eat of
his own vine, and each one of his own fig tree,
and each one of you will drink the water of
his own cistern, 17 until [x]I come and take you
away to a land like your own land, a land of
grain and wine, a land of bread and vineyards.
18 Beware lest Hezekiah mislead you by saying, "The LORD will deliver us." Has any of
the gods of the nations delivered his land out
of the hand of the king of Assyria? 19 [y]Where
are the gods of [z]Hamath and [z]Arpad? Where
are the gods of Sepharvaim? [a]Have they delivered Samaria out of my hand? 20 [b]Who among
all the gods of these lands have delivered their
lands out of my hand, that the LORD should
deliver Jerusalem out of my hand?'"

21 But they were silent and answered him
not a word, for the king's command was,
"Do not answer him." 22 [c]Then Eliakim the
son of Hilkiah, who was over the household,
and Shebna the secretary, and Joah the son of
Asaph, the recorder, came to Hezekiah with
their clothes torn, and told him the words of
the Rabshakeh.

Hezekiah Seeks Isaiah's Help

37 [d]As soon as King Hezekiah heard it, he
tore his clothes and covered himself
with sackcloth and went into the house of the
LORD. 2 And he sent Eliakim, who was over
the household, and Shebna the secretary, and

[1] Hebrew *Make a blessing with me*

2 [n]ch. 7:3
3 [o]ch. 22:15, 20, 21
4 [p][ch. 10:8]
6 [q]Ezek. 29:6, 7
7 [r]2 Kgs. 18:4; See Deut. 12:2-5
9 [s][ch. 10:8] [t][ch. 20:5; 30:3, 7; 31:1]
10 [u]ch. 10:5, 6
11 [v]Ezra 4:7; Dan. 2:4
14 [w][ch. 37:10; 2 Chr. 32:6-8]
17 [x]2 Kgs. 18:11
19 [y]ch. 37:13 [z]Jer. 49:23 [a][2 Kgs. 17:6]
20 [b][2 Chr. 32:19]
22 [c]ver. 3; [ch. 33:7]
Chapter 37
1 [d]For ver. 1-38, see 2 Kgs. 19

warning them not to listen to Hezekiah's cries to trust in Yahweh for deliverance. No other god has been able to stand up to the Assyrian forces thus far. What makes them think Yahweh will be any different? (vv. 13–20).

The chapter ends with silence and no response. As readers, we are to identify with Hezekiah, feeling the tension and temptation. How will we respond? Gaining courage from him (ch. 37), we are to break the silence of doubt and disbelief. In repentance we are invited to turn our gaze to the God of the exodus who is not like the other gods, for he alone is the Lord of creation. Sennacherib doesn't frighten the Lord; he shouldn't frighten the Lord's people.

Fear is what happens when we take our eyes off of the Lord (cf. Matt. 14:30). In Jesus we have a tangible picture of what the love and care of God looks like (2 Cor. 4:6). Let us therefore look to Jesus (Heb. 12:2).

the senior priests, covered with sackcloth, to
the prophet [e]Isaiah the son of Amoz. 3 They
said to him, "Thus says Hezekiah, 'This day is
a [f]day of distress, of rebuke, and of disgrace;
[g]children have come to the point of birth, and
there is no strength to bring them forth. 4 [h]It
may be that the LORD your God will hear the
words of the Rabshakeh, whom his master
the king of Assyria has sent to mock the living God, and will rebuke the words that the
LORD your God has heard; therefore lift up
your prayer for [i]the remnant that is left.'"

5 When the servants of King Hezekiah came
to Isaiah, 6 Isaiah said to them, "Say to your
master, 'Thus says the LORD: Do not be afraid
because of the words that you have heard, with
which the young men of the king of Assyria
have reviled me. 7 Behold, [j]I will put a spirit in
him, so that [k]he shall hear a rumor and return
to his own land, and [l]I will make him fall by
the sword in his own land.'"

8 The Rabshakeh returned, and found the
king of Assyria fighting against [m]Libnah, for
he had heard that the king had left [m]Lachish.
9 Now the king heard concerning Tirhakah
king of [n]Cush,[1] "He has set out to fight against
you." And when he heard it, he sent messengers
to Hezekiah, saying, 10 "Thus shall you speak
to Hezekiah king of Judah: [o]'Do not let your
God in whom you trust deceive you by promising that Jerusalem will not be given into the
hand of the king of Assyria. 11 Behold, you have
heard what the kings of Assyria have done to
all lands, devoting them to destruction. And
shall you be delivered? 12 [p]Have the gods of the
nations delivered them, the nations that my
fathers destroyed, [q]Gozan, [r]Haran, Rezeph,
and the people of Eden who were in Telassar?
13 [p]Where is the king of Hamath, the king of
Arpad, the king of the city of Sepharvaim, the
king of Hena, or the king of Ivvah?'"

Hezekiah's Prayer for Deliverance

14 Hezekiah received the letter from the
hand of the messengers, and read it; and
Hezekiah went up to the house of the
LORD, and spread it before the LORD. 15 And
Hezekiah prayed to the LORD: 16 "O LORD of
hosts, God of Israel, [s]enthroned above the
cherubim, you are the God, you alone, of all
the kingdoms of the earth; [t]you have made
heaven and earth. 17 [u]Incline your ear, O LORD,
and hear; open your eyes, O LORD, and see;
and hear [v]all the words of Sennacherib, which
he has sent to mock the living God. 18 Truly,
O LORD, [w]the kings of Assyria have laid waste
all the nations and their lands, 19 and have
cast their gods into the fire. For they were no
gods, but the work of men's hands, wood and
stone. Therefore they were destroyed. 20 So
now, O LORD our God, save us from his hand,
that all the kingdoms of the earth may know
that you alone are the LORD."

Sennacherib's Fall

21 Then Isaiah the son of Amoz sent to
Hezekiah, saying, "Thus says the LORD, the
God of Israel: Because you have prayed to me
concerning Sennacherib king of Assyria, 22 this
is the word that the LORD has spoken concerning him:

[1] Probably *Nubia*

37:1–20 King Hezekiah is here a model of personal and corporate repentance amid weakness and threat (vv. 1–2; cf. 2 Chron. 7:14). While it was a day of "distress," "rebuke," and "disgrace" (Isa. 37:3), it was also a day in which the living God was being publically mocked by the Assyrian leadership (vv. 4, 8–13). Isaiah's prophetic perspective and counsel centers around a consistent message we hear throughout this biblical book: "Do not be afraid" (v. 6, cf. 7:4; 10:24–25; 35:4; 41:10–14; 43:1–2; 51:12–13). Yahweh—not Sennacherib—is alone truly sovereign, and he can be trusted (37:15–16). Confident of God's sovereignty, Hezekiah prays honestly and desperately, asking that God would see, hear, and respond to their dire situation in a way that no idol could (vv. 17–20).

Very often our faith is strongest when we come to see the depth of our need and dependence, for in our weakness the wonder of God's mercy and tender concern gives us hope and strength (cf. Mark 4:35–41; 5:35–42). Above all, we now have Christ as the greatest expression of God's power and mercy. Fear not!

37:21–38 Isaiah tells Hezekiah that "because you have prayed," God responded (v. 21). According to Isaiah, human agency and divine sovereignty are not at odds but rather work in beautiful harmony. God's people are to cry out to him, to honestly make their concerns known. The Lord of Israel delights to act in response to those prayers as he carries out his good and wise purposes (v. 35).

2 [e] See ch. 1:1
3 [f] [ch. 22:5] [g] [ch. 13:8; Hos. 13:13]
4 [h] [ver. 28, 29] [i] ch. 1:9
7 [j] [ch. 19:14] [k] ver. 9 [l] ver. 38
8 [m] Josh. 10:31
9 [n] ch. 18:1, 2; 20:5
10 [o] [ch. 36:14]
12 [p] ch. 36:18, 19 [q] 2 Kgs. 17:6 [r] Gen. 11:31, 32
13 [p] [See ver. 12 above]
16 [s] Ex. 25:22; Ezek. 10:1 [t] Acts 4:24; [Jer. 10:11]
17 [u] [2 Chr. 6:40] [v] 2 Chr. 32:19
18 [w] [ch. 10:13, 14]

"'She despises you, she scorns you—
[x]the virgin daughter of Zion;
she wags her head behind you—
the daughter of Jerusalem.

23 "'Whom have you mocked and reviled?
Against whom have you raised your voice
and lifted your eyes to the heights?
Against [y]the Holy One of Israel!
24 By your servants you have mocked the Lord,
and you have said, [z]With my many chariots
I have gone up the heights of the mountains,
to the far recesses of Lebanon,
[a]to cut down its tallest cedars,
its choicest cypresses,
to come to its remotest height,
its most fruitful forest.
25 I dug wells
and drank waters,
to dry up with the sole of my foot
all [b]the streams [c]of Egypt.

26 [d]"'Have you not heard
that I determined it long ago?
I planned from days of old
what now I bring to pass,
that you should make fortified cities
crash into heaps of ruins,
27 while their inhabitants, shorn of strength,
are dismayed and confounded,
and have become like plants of the field
and like tender grass,
like grass on the housetops,
blighted[1] before it is grown.

28 "'I know your sitting down
and your going out and coming in,
and your raging against me.
29 [e]Because you have raged against me
and your complacency has come to my ears,
I will put my hook in your nose
and my bit in your mouth,
and [f]I will turn you back on the way
by which you came.'

30 "And this shall be the sign for you: this
year you shall eat what grows of itself, and in
the second year what springs from that. Then
in the third year sow and reap, and plant vineyards, and eat their fruit. 31 And the surviving
remnant of the house of Judah [g]shall again
take root downward and bear fruit upward.
32 [h]For out of Jerusalem shall go a remnant,
and out of Mount Zion a band of survivors.
[i]The zeal of the LORD of hosts will do this.
33 "Therefore thus says the LORD concerning
the king of Assyria: He shall not come into this
city or shoot an arrow there or come before it
with a shield or [j]cast up a siege mound against
it. 34 By the way that he came, by the same he
shall return, and he shall not come into this
city, declares the LORD. 35 [k]For I will defend this
city to save it, for my own sake and for [l]the sake
of my servant David."
36 [m]And the angel of the LORD went out
and struck down 185,000 in the camp of the
Assyrians. And when people arose early in the
morning, behold, these were all dead bodies.
37 Then Sennacherib king of Assyria departed
and returned home and lived at [n]Nineveh.
38 And as he was worshiping in the house of
Nisroch his god, Adrammelech and Sharezer,
his sons, struck him down with the sword.
And after they escaped into the land of [o]Ararat,
[p]Esarhaddon his son reigned in his place.

Hezekiah's Sickness and Recovery

38 [q]In those days Hezekiah became [r]sick
and was at the point of death. And
[s]Isaiah the prophet the son of Amoz came to
him, and said to him, "Thus says the LORD:
Set your house in order, for you shall die, you
shall not recover."[2] 2 Then Hezekiah turned his
face to the wall and prayed to the LORD, 3 and

[1] Some Hebrew manuscripts and 2 Kings 19:26; most Hebrew manuscripts *like a field* [2] Or *live*; also verses 9, 21

22[x] [Mic. 4:13]; See ch. 1:8
23[y] ch. 10:17
24[z] [ch. 8:7, 8] [a] [ch. 14:8]
25[b] [ch. 19:6] [c] [ch. 20:4]
26[d] [ch. 10:5, 15; 25:1, 2]
29[e] [ch. 10:12] [f] ver. 34
31[g] ch. 27:6
32[h] [ch. 14:32] [i] See ch. 9:7
33[j] [Hab. 1:10; Luke 19:43]
35[k] ch. 31:5; 38:6 [l] [ch. 29:1]
36[m] ch. 17:14; 30:31; 31:8; [ch. 10:33; 14:25; 29:5]
37[n] Gen. 10:11; Jonah 1:2; 3:3; 4:11 **38**[o] Gen. 8:4 [p] Ezra 4:2 **Chapter 38** **1**[q] For ver. 1-8, see 2 Kgs. 20:1-6, 9-11 [r] 2 Chr. 32:24 [s] See ch. 1:1

The supreme instance of divine sovereignty and human responsibility working together is at the crucifixion of Christ, which the Bible clearly teaches was the sovereign will of God and yet also the culpable wickedness of men (Acts 2:23–24; 4:27–28).

38:1–22 After hearing a sobering divine announcement that his death is imminent (v. 1), Hezekiah doesn't become a passive stoic. Rather, he becomes an active worshiper, knowing that prophesies based on the direction of present circumstances can provide opportunity for prayer for a change of circumstances (e.g., Jer. 18:1–11; Jonah 3:4). He is convinced that God hears and responds to prayer, so from his depths he makes his

said, "Please, O LORD, remember how [t]I have
walked before you in faithfulness and with a
whole heart, and have done what is good in
your sight." And Hezekiah wept bitterly.
4 Then the word of the LORD came to Isaiah:
5 "Go and say to Hezekiah, Thus says the LORD,
the God of David your father: I have heard
your prayer; I have seen your tears. Behold,
I will add [u]fifteen years to your life.[1] 6 [v]I will
deliver you and this city out of the hand of
the king of Assyria, and will defend this city.
7 "This shall be the sign to you from the LORD,
that the LORD will do this thing that he has
promised: 8 [w]Behold, I will make the shadow
cast by the declining sun on the dial of Ahaz
turn back ten steps." So the sun turned back on
the dial the ten steps by which it had declined.[2]

9 A writing of Hezekiah king of Judah, after
he had been sick and had recovered from his
sickness:

10 I said, [x]In the middle[3] of my days
I must depart;
I am consigned to the gates of Sheol
for the rest of my years.
11 I said, I shall not see the LORD,
the LORD [y]in the land of the living;
I shall look on man no more
among the inhabitants of the world.
12 My dwelling is plucked up and removed
from me
[z]like a shepherd's tent;
[a]like a weaver [b]I have rolled up my life;
[c]he cuts me off from the loom;
[d]from day to night you bring me to an end;
13 [e]I calmed myself[4] until morning;
like a lion [f]he breaks all my bones;
from day to night you bring me to an
end.
14 Like [g]a swallow or a crane I chirp;
[h]I moan like a dove.
[i]My eyes are weary with looking upward.
O Lord, I am oppressed; [j]be my pledge
of safety!
15 What shall I say? For he has spoken to me,
and he himself has done it.
[k]I walk slowly all my years
because of the bitterness of my soul.

16 [l]O Lord, by these things men live,
and in all these is the life of my spirit.
Oh restore me to health and make me
live!
17 [m]Behold, it was for my welfare
that I had great bitterness;
[n]but in love you have delivered my life
from the pit of destruction,
[n] for you have cast all my sins
behind your back.
18 [o]For Sheol does not thank you;
death does not praise you;
those who go down to the pit do not hope
for your faithfulness.
19 The living, the living, he thanks you,
as I do this day;
[p]the father makes known to the children
your faithfulness.

20 The LORD will save me,
and we will play my music on
stringed instruments
all the days of our lives,
[q]at the house of the LORD.

21 [r]Now Isaiah had said, "Let them take a cake
of figs and apply it to the boil, that he may
recover." 22 Hezekiah also had said, "What is
the sign that I shall go up to the house of the
LORD?"

[1] Hebrew *to your days* [2] The meaning of the Hebrew verse is uncertain [3] Or *In the quiet* [4] Or (with Targum) *I cried for help*

groans and fears known to God, weeping bitterly in the process (Isa. 38:2–3). God doesn't rebuke Hezekiah for lack of faith here, but instead graciously responds not simply to the sounds of his words but to the reality of his tears (v. 5). Thus, God grants him not only an additional fifteen years of life but also the promise of deliverance for the city from the Assyrians—a deliverance for *his* lifetime (v. 6), accompanied by a miraculous sign as confirmation (vv. 7–8).

In Hezekiah's beautifully written response, he reminds us that ultimately such gracious actions of God point beyond mere physical healing to divine forgiveness: "in love you have delivered my life from the pit of destruction, for you have cast all my sins behind your back" (v. 17; cf. Mic. 7:19).

Like Hezekiah, let us not forget to celebrate God's gracious provision and answers to prayer with music and delight (Isa. 38:20). For we see with supreme clarity something that Hezekiah could never see; we see with utter confidence that God has cast all our sins behind his back—through the substitutionary work of Jesus Christ (2 Cor. 5:21; Gal. 3:13).

3[t] 2 Kgs. 18:5, 6
5[u] 2 Kgs. 18:2, 13
6[v] ch. 37:35
8[w] [2 Kgs. 20:9, 10]
10[x] [Ps. 102:24]
11[y] Ps. 27:13; [Ps. 88:5]
12[z] [2 Cor. 5:1] [a] Job 7:6 [b] [Heb. 1:12] [c] Job 6:9 [d] [Job 4:20; Ps. 73:14]
13[e] [Ps. 30:5] [f] [Ps. 38:3]
14[g] [Jer. 8:7] [h] ch. 59:11 [i] Ps. 69:3 [j] Ps. 119:122; [Ps. 86:17; Heb. 7:22]
15[k] 1 Kgs. 21:27
16[l] Deut. 8:3
17[m] Ps. 119:67, 75 [n] [Ps. 103:12; Mic. 7:19]
18[o] Ps. 88:10-12; 115:17; [Eccles. 9:10]
19[p] Deut. 4:9; 6:7; Ps. 78:3, 4
20[q] 2 Kgs. 20:5
21[r] 2 Kgs. 20:7, 8

Envoys from Babylon

39 [s]At that time Merodach-baladan the son of Baladan, king of Babylon, [t]sent envoys with letters and a present to Hezekiah, for he heard that he had been sick and had recovered. 2 And Hezekiah welcomed them gladly. And he showed them his treasure house, [u]the silver, the gold, the spices, the precious oil, his whole armory, all that was found in his storehouses. [v]There was nothing in his house or in all his realm that Hezekiah did not show them. 3 Then Isaiah the prophet came to King Hezekiah, and said to him, "What did these men say? And from where did they come to you?" Hezekiah said, "They have come to me from a far country, from Babylon." 4 He said, "What have they seen in your house?" Hezekiah answered, "They have seen all that is in my house. There is nothing in my storehouses that I did not show them."

5 Then Isaiah said to Hezekiah, "Hear the word of the LORD of hosts: 6 [w]Behold, the days are coming, when all that is in your house, and that which your fathers have stored up till this day, shall be carried to Babylon. Nothing shall be left, says the LORD. 7 [x]And some of your own sons, who will come from you, whom you will father, shall be taken away, and they shall be eunuchs in the palace of the king of Babylon." 8 Then Hezekiah said to Isaiah, "The word of the LORD that you have spoken is good." For he thought, [y]"There will be peace and security in my days."

Comfort for God's People

40 [z]Comfort, comfort my people, says your God.

2 [a]Speak tenderly to Jerusalem,
and cry to her
that [b]her warfare[1] is ended,
that her iniquity is pardoned,
that she has received from the LORD's hand
double for all her sins.

3 [c]A voice cries:[2]
[d]"In the wilderness prepare the way of the LORD;
[e]make straight in the desert a highway for our God.
4 [f]Every valley shall be lifted up,
and every mountain and hill be made low;
the uneven ground shall become level,
and the rough places a plain.

[1] Or *hardship* [2] Or *A voice of one crying*

Chapter 39
1 [s]For ver. 1-8, see 2 Kgs. 20:12-19 [t][2 Chr. 32:31]
2 [u][2 Kgs. 18:15, 16] [v][2 Chr. 32:25]
6 [w]2 Kgs. 24:13; See 2 Kgs. 25:13-17
7 [x]Dan. 1:2, 3, 7
8 [y][2 Chr. 32:26]

Chapter 40
1 [z]ch. 51:12; [Luke 2:25]
2 [a]Hos. 2:14 [b][2 Chr. 36:22; Jer. 25:12]
3 [c]Cited Matt. 3:3; Mark 1:3; Luke 3:4; John 1:23 [d]Mal. 3:1; [ch. 57:14] [e]Ps. 68:4
4 [f]Cited Luke 3:5; [ch. 49:11]

39:1–8 Even when God has been gracious to us we must be vigilant against reverting back to self-absorption and arrogance.

Having experienced a wonder of God's grace, Hezekiah appears to let down his guard and opens himself up to flattery, boasting as he shows off the glories of the house of Israel (vv. 1–2; cf. 1 Chron. 21:1–4; 1 Kings 10:1–9). Rather than being wise, he acts foolishly. As the apostle Paul would later warn, "let anyone who thinks that he stands take heed lest he fall" (1 Cor. 10:12). We will all be tempted, even after we have received God's grace, but God is faithful and will provide a "way of escape" so that we can endure the trial (1 Cor. 10:13). When we, like Hezekiah, fail to resist, temptation lingers; such sins often lead to pain not only for ourselves but for others as well. By loving himself more than the good of his people, Hezekiah set Judah up to face captivity to Babylon in the future. Exile was still coming, only not from the Assyrians but from Babylon (Isa. 39:5–8).

40:1–55:13 Moving from the first part of Isaiah to the next major section (chs. 40–55), readers will notice a shift in historical concerns and application. Much of the earlier section of Isaiah (e.g., chs. 7–39) presents consistent themes of divine judgment and confrontation, with vital but less extensive pronouncements of divine promises of hope. In the earlier section, the eighth-century Assyrian threat formed the context in which God's people were called to trust in him rather than in political and military power. Unfortunately, they consistently fail to believe, and thus they imitate the nations rather than imitating God.

This failure to trust in Yahweh as King—the only one who can truly defend them—resulted in Israel's tragic exile to Assyria in 722 B.C., yet much of Judah had thus far been spared. As we move from chapter 39 to 40 it is as if, in the blink of an eye, Isaiah moves from addressing the problems in his own day, to anticipating Judah's exile to Babylon (39:5–7). Then, when he opens his eyes again (chs. 40–55), he sees God's people anew, only now he addresses them after the deportation has

5 [g]And the glory of the LORD shall be
revealed,
and all flesh shall see it together,
[h]for the mouth of the LORD has spoken."

The Word of God Stands Forever

6 A voice says, "Cry!"
And I said,[1] "What shall I cry?"
[i]All flesh is grass,
and all its beauty[2] is like the flower of
the field.
7 The grass withers, the flower fades
when the breath of the LORD blows
on it;
surely the people are grass.
8 [j]The grass withers, the flower fades,
but the word of our God will stand
forever.

The Greatness of God

9 Go on up to a high mountain,
O Zion, [k]herald of good news;[3]
lift up your voice with strength,
O Jerusalem, herald of good news;[4]
lift it up, fear not;
say to the cities of Judah,
"Behold your God!"
10 [l]Behold, the Lord GOD comes with might,
and his arm rules for him;
[m]behold, his reward is with him,
and his recompense before him.
11 [n]He will tend his flock like a shepherd;
[o]he will gather the lambs in his arms;
[p]he will carry them in his bosom,
and gently lead those that are with
young.

[1] Revocalization based on Dead Sea Scroll, Septuagint, Vulgate; Masoretic Text *And someone says* [2] Or *all its constancy* [3] Or *O herald of good news to Zion* [4] Or *O herald of good news to Jerusalem*

5[g] [Luke 3:6] [h] ch. 1:20
6[i] Cited 1 Pet. 1:24, 25; [Job 14:2; Ps. 102:11; 103:15; James 1:10]
8[j] Cited James 1:11
9[k] ch. 52:7
10[l] ch. 59:16, 17; [Luke 11:22] [m] ch. 62:11; [Rev. 22:12]
11[n] Ezek. 34:23; Zech. 11:7; [John 10:11; 21:15; Acts 20:28] [o] [Matt. 18:12; Luke 15:5] [p] [Num. 11:12]

already occurred (in 586 B.C.). In short, this section seems to address the people living in exile (after 586), whereas earlier in the book they were living in Judah but fearing exile (after 722 B.C.).

As we move into Isaiah 40, the themes of comfort, deliverance, and the revelation of God's glory explode onto the scene. The exiles would be returning, for Yahweh never forgets his people. Yet the temptation to harden their hearts toward God and neighbor remains.

40:1–11 "Comfort, comfort my people, says your God" (v. 1). When the Babylonians brought their threats of exile to Jerusalem, there was great grief. Out of this context the book of Lamentations emerged, reverberating with sorrows and mourning the pain and loss. Again and again in that context we see a great longing to be consoled, but Jerusalem "has none to comfort her" (Lam. 1:2, 9, 17, 21). As Isaiah records Yahweh's gracious declaration, the promise of comfort has come. It needs to be announced, believed, and rested in. Yet this proclamation was to be given "tenderly," for here was God's promise that "her warfare is ended" and "her iniquity is pardoned" (Isa. 40:2).

"A voice says, 'Cry!'" (v. 6). The command to be a herald reminds us of Isaiah's commissioning, in which he responds to God's question, "Whom shall I send, and who will go for us?" (6:8). For comfort to be received, it needs a voice to serve as the "herald of good news" (40:9). It is interesting, however, that in Isaiah 40:1, the call to "comfort" is in the plural, not singular, making it clear that this comfort was to be offered through a prophetic word echoed by many (see v. 9).

The people who are to receive this news are like "grass" and "the flower" (vv. 7, 8). One withers, and the other fades. But in "the word of our God" confidence can be maintained, for his word "will stand forever" (v. 8). Our comfort rests not in the consistency of human leaders, even ecclesial ones, but in the certainty of the divine word.

Here the "word of God" is spoken, but with the coming of the Messiah, the Word is made flesh. He will come as a shepherd who "will gather the lambs in his arms," carrying them "in his bosom" as a loving Lord (v. 11) despite his great power (see vv. 12–17). Jesus self-identifies with this portrait, describing himself as the "good shepherd" who "lays down his life for the sheep" (John 10:1–18). The Messiah will face a withering, even unto death, but this incarnate Word, with power beyond this world, overcomes death and sin, rising from the grave and making it certain that God's Word will never die and can be trusted unto death. The apostle Peter even describes the unfading word of God of Isaiah 40:8 as the gospel message itself (1 Pet. 1:25).

12 [q]Who has measured the waters in the hollow of his hand
and marked off the heavens with a span,
enclosed the dust of the earth in a measure
and weighed the mountains in scales
and the hills in a balance?
13 [r]Who has measured[1] the Spirit of the LORD,
or what man shows him his counsel?
14 Whom did he consult,
and who made him understand?
[s]Who taught him the path of justice,
and taught him knowledge,
and showed him the way of understanding?
15 Behold, the nations are like a drop from a bucket,
and are accounted [t]as the dust on the scales;
behold, he takes up [u]the coastlands like fine dust.
16 Lebanon would not suffice for fuel,
nor are [v]its beasts enough for a burnt offering.
17 [w]All the nations are as nothing before him,
they are accounted by him as less than nothing and emptiness.

18 [x]To whom then will you liken God,
[y]or what likeness compare with him?
19 [y]An idol! A craftsman casts it,
and a goldsmith overlays it with gold
and casts for it silver chains.
20 [z]He who is too impoverished for an offering
chooses wood[2] that will not rot;
he seeks out a skillful craftsman
to set up an idol that will not move.
21 [a]Do you not know? Do you not hear?
Has it not been told you from the beginning?
Have you not understood from the foundations of the earth?
22 It is he who sits above the circle of the earth,
and its inhabitants are [b]like grasshoppers;
[c]who stretches out the heavens like a curtain,
and spreads them like a tent to dwell in;
23 [d]who brings princes to nothing,
and makes the rulers of the earth as emptiness.

24 Scarcely are they planted, scarcely sown,
scarcely has their stem taken root in the earth,
when he blows on them, and they wither,
[e]and the tempest carries them off like stubble.

25 [f]To whom then will you compare me,
that I should be like him? says the Holy One.
26 Lift up your eyes on high and see:
who created these?
[g]He who brings out their host by number,
calling them all by name,
by the greatness of his might,
and because he is strong in power
not one is missing.

27 Why do you say, O Jacob,
and speak, O Israel,
[h]"My way is hidden from the LORD,
[i]and my right is disregarded by my God"?

[1] Or *has directed* [2] Or *He chooses valuable wood*

12[q] [Prov. 30:4]
13[r] Cited Rom. 11:34; [1 Cor. 2:16]
14[s] Job 21:22
15[t] ch. 29:5 [u] ch. 41:1
16[v] [Ps. 50:10]
17[w] Ps. 62:9; Dan. 4:35; [ch. 41:12]
18[x] ver. 25; ch. 46:5; Acts 17:29 [y] [Hos. 13:2]
19[y] [See ver. 18 above]
20[z] ch. 46:6; Jer. 10:3-5; See ch. 44:9-15
21[a] ver. 28; [Acts 14:17; Rom. 1:19, 20]
22[b] [Num. 13:33] [c] Job 9:8; Ps. 104:2
23[d] Job 12:21; Ps. 107:40
24[e] ch. 41:2; [Ps. 83:13]
25[f] ver. 18
26[g] Ps. 147:4
27[h] [ch. 49:14] [i] [ch. 49:4]

40:12–31 The difference between the Creator and the creature is immeasurable (v. 25). So why look to idols (v. 19) or to other nations (v. 17)? Instead, look to the Creator of the earth who is also the Lord of Israel—their Redeemer (vv. 26–27).

When we are exhausted, when we wonder how we can continue, Isaiah reminds us not to look at ourselves and our own resources. Instead we turn our eyes to the all-knowing (v. 27), sustaining (vv. 22–26), and creating God (v. 28) who "does not faint or grow weary," but rather "gives power to the faint" (vv. 28–29). Strength from God in this context comes not from self-improvement but from waiting on the Lord, who promises to sustain us as we make this pilgrim journey (vv. 30–31).

As new covenant believers, we see with unprecedented clarity exactly why we are free to wait on the Lord. For God used his resources of wisdom, power, and creation to send his own Son to do all that we cannot do, and to suffer the penalty of all that we have done wrongly. Nothing is left but to wait on the Lord, trusting him and walking with him in quiet confidence and courage.

28 Have you not known? Have you not
heard?
The LORD is [j]the everlasting God,
the Creator of the ends of the earth.
He does not faint or grow weary;
[k]his understanding is unsearchable.
29 He gives power to the faint,
and to him who has no might he
increases strength.
30 Even youths shall faint and be weary,
and young men shall fall exhausted;
31 but [l]they who wait for the LORD shall
renew their strength;
they shall mount up with wings [m]like
eagles;
they shall run and not be weary;
they shall walk and not faint.

Fear Not, for I Am with You

41 [n]Listen to me in silence, [o]O coastlands;
let the peoples renew their strength;
let them approach, then let them speak;
let us together draw near for judgment.

2 [p]Who stirred up one from the east
whom victory meets at every [q]step?[1]
[r]He gives up nations before him,
so that he tramples kings underfoot;
he makes them like dust with his sword,
[s]like driven stubble with his bow.
3 He pursues them and passes on safely,
by paths his feet have not trod.
4 [t]Who has performed and done this,
calling the generations from the
beginning?
[u]I, the LORD, the first,
and with the last; I am he.

5 [v]The coastlands have seen and are afraid;
the ends of the earth tremble;
they have drawn near and come.
6 Everyone helps his neighbor
and says to his brother, "Be strong!"
7 [w]The craftsman strengthens the goldsmith,
and he who smooths with the hammer him who strikes the anvil,
saying of the soldering, "It is good";
and they strengthen it with nails [x]so
that it cannot be moved.

8 But you, Israel, [y]my servant,
Jacob, [z]whom I have chosen,
the offspring of Abraham, [a]my friend;
9 you whom I took from the ends of the
earth,
and called [b]from its farthest corners,
saying to you, "You are [y]my servant,
[z]I have chosen you and not cast you off";
10 fear not, for I am with you;
be not dismayed, for I am your God;
I will strengthen you, I will help you,
I will uphold you with [c]my righteous
right hand.

11 [d]Behold, all who are incensed against you
shall be put to shame and confounded;
those who strive against you
shall be as nothing and shall perish.
12 [e]You shall seek those who contend with
you,
but you shall not find them;

[1] Or *whom righteousness calls to follow?*

41:1–29 After quieting the coastlands and reminding the unbelieving nations that Yahweh alone is "the first and the last" (v. 4), words of warmth and comfort are directed to Israel. A beautiful reminder arises in which God's willingness to link himself with the people of Jacob (v. 8) is his people's foundation for comfort. Israel did not choose God; God chose them (v. 9). They must therefore "fear not," since he is their God and is with them: "I will strengthen you, I will help you, I will uphold you with my righteous right hand" (v. 10). When Israel looks around at the dangers, she is prone to anxiety, but when she looks to the sovereign Lord, fear loses its paralyzing power (vv. 13–14).

God acts on behalf of his people, not because they are mighty or wise but out of his good pleasure and love (cf. Deut. 7:6–8). "Your Redeemer is the Holy One of Israel" (Isa. 41:14, 16, 20) who condescends to help the "poor and needy" (v. 17), answering them in the depth of their need and providing the waters of life in the midst of deserts and bare lands (vv. 18–20).

Jesus the Messiah comes as God's Son, bringing true and lasting redemption for the people of God (e.g., Luke 21:28; Rom. 3:24; 1 Cor. 1:30; Heb. 9:12). This redemptive love came not in response to our love for God but as the overflow of God's love for us. Our security is "not that we have loved God but that he loved us and sent his Son to be the propitiation for our sins" (1 John 4:10). We extend his movement of divine love by sacrificially loving others: "We love because he first loved us" (1 John 4:19).

28 [j][Ps. 121:4] [k]Ps. 147:5
31 [l]Ps. 103:5 [m][Ex. 19:4]
Chapter 41
1 [n][Hab. 2:20; Zech. 2:13] [o]See ch. 11:11
2 [p]ch. 46:11; [ch. 45:1] [q][Judg. 4:10] [r]2 Chr. 36:23 [s]ch. 40:24
4 [t][ver. 26] [u]ch. 43:10, 11; 44:6; 48:12; Rev. 1:8, 17; 22:13
5 [v]See ch. 11:11
7 [w]ch. 40:19 [x][ch. 40:20]
8 [y]ch. 44:1, 2 [z]Deut. 7:6; 10:15; 14:2; Ps. 135:4; [1 Pet. 2:9] [a]2 Chr. 20:7; James 2:23
9 [b]ch. 43:5, 6 [y][See ver. 8 above] [z][See ver. 8 above]
10 [c]Ps. 48:10
11 [d][ch. 45:24]
12 [e]Ps. 37:10

[f]those who war against you
shall be as nothing at all.
13 For I, the LORD your God,
hold your right hand;
it is I who say to you, "Fear not,
I am the one who helps you."

14 Fear not, you [g]worm Jacob,
you men of Israel!
I am the one who helps you, declares the LORD;
your [h]Redeemer is the Holy One of Israel.
15 [i]Behold, I make of you a threshing sledge,
new, sharp, and having teeth;
you shall thresh [j]the mountains and crush them,
and you shall make the hills like chaff;
16 [k]you shall winnow them, and [l]the wind shall carry them away,
and the tempest shall scatter them.
[m]And you shall rejoice in the LORD;
in the Holy One of Israel you shall glory.

17 [n]When the poor and needy seek water,
and there is none,
and their tongue is parched with thirst,
I the LORD will answer them;
I the God of Israel will not forsake them.
18 [o]I will open rivers on the bare heights,
and fountains in the midst of the valleys.
[p]I will make the wilderness a pool of water,
and the dry land springs of water.
19 [q]I will put in the wilderness the cedar,
the acacia, the myrtle, and the olive.
I will set in the desert [r]the cypress,
the plane and the pine together,
20 that they may see and know,
may consider and understand together,
that [s]the hand of the LORD has done this,
the Holy One of Israel has created it.

The Futility of Idols

21 Set forth your case, says the LORD;
bring your proofs, says the King of Jacob.
22 Let them bring them, and [t]tell us
what is to happen.
Tell us the former things, what they are,
that we may consider them,
that we may know their outcome;
or declare to us the things to come.
23 [t]Tell us what is to come hereafter,
that we may know that you are gods;
[u]do good, or do harm,
that we may be dismayed and terrified.[1]
24 Behold, [v]you are nothing,
and your work is less than nothing;
an abomination is he who chooses you.

25 [w]I stirred up one from the north, and he has come,
[x]from the rising of the sun, [y]and he shall call upon my name;
he shall trample on rulers as on mortar,
as the potter treads clay.
26 [z]Who declared it from the beginning, that we might know,
and beforehand, that we might say, "He is right"?
There was none who declared it, none who proclaimed,
none who heard your words.
27 [a]I was the first to say[2] to Zion, "Behold, here they are!"
and [b]I give to Jerusalem a herald of good news.
28 [c]But when I look, there is no one;
among these there is no counselor
who, when I ask, gives an answer.
29 [d]Behold, they are all a delusion;
their works are nothing;
their metal images are empty wind.

The LORD's Chosen Servant

42 [e]Behold [f]my servant, whom I uphold,
my chosen, [g]in whom my soul delights;
[h]I have put my Spirit upon him;
[i]he will bring forth justice to the nations.
2 He will not cry aloud or lift up his voice,
or make it heard in the street;
3 [j]a bruised reed he will not break,
and a faintly burning wick he will not quench;
[k]he will faithfully bring forth justice.

[1] Or *that we may both be dismayed and see* [2] Or *Formerly I said*

12[f] ch. 40:17 **14**[g] [Ps. 22:6] [h] ch. 54:5; [Ps. 78:35]; See ch. 43:14 **15**[i] Mic. 4:13 [j] [ch. 2:14] **16**[k] [Jer. 51:2] [l] [ver. 2] [m] ch. 45:25 **17**[n] [ch. 44:3] **18**[o] ch. 35:6, 7 [p] Ps. 107:35 **19**[q] ch. 35:1, 2; 55:12, 13 [r] ch. 60:13 **20**[s] Job 12:9 **22**[t] [ver. 26; ch. 44:7; 45:21; 46:10] **23**[t] [See ver. 22 above] [u] [ch. 45:7] **24**[v] ver. 29; [Ps. 115:8; 1 Cor. 8:4] **25**[w] Jer. 50:3 [x] ver. 2 [y] [Ps. 44:5] **26**[z] [ver. 22] **27**[a] ch. 51:12 [b] ch. 40:9; 52:7 **28**[c] See ver. 21-24 **29**[d] [ver. 12] **Chapter 42** **1**[e] Cited Matt. 12:18-20 [f] ch. 41:8; 43:10; 52:13; 53:11; [ver. 19; Ezek. 34:24; Zech. 3:8; Acts 3:26; 4:27; Phil. 2:7] [g] Matt. 3:17 [h] ch. 11:2; 61:1 [i] [ch. 2:4] **3**[j] [ch. 57:15] [k] Ps. 9:8

4 He will not grow faint or be discouraged[1]
till he has established justice in the earth;
and [l]the coastlands wait for his law.

5 Thus says God, the LORD,
who created the heavens [m]and stretched them out,
who spread out the earth and what comes from it,
[n]who gives breath to the people on it
and spirit to those who walk in it:
6 "I am the LORD; [o]I have called you[2] in righteousness;
I will take you by the hand and keep you;
I will give you [p]as a covenant for the people,
[q]a light for the nations,
7 [r]to open the eyes that are blind,
to bring out the prisoners from the dungeon,
[s]from the prison those who sit in darkness.
8 I am the LORD; that is my name;
[t]my glory I give to no other,
nor my praise to carved idols.
9 Behold, the former things have come to pass,
[u]and new things I now declare;
before they spring forth
I tell you of them."

Sing to the LORD a New Song

10 [v]Sing to the LORD a new song,
his praise from the end of the earth,
[w]you who go down to the sea, and all that fills it,
[l]the coastlands and their inhabitants.
11 Let the desert and its cities lift up their voice,
the villages that [x]Kedar inhabits;
let the habitants of [y]Sela sing for joy,
let them shout from the top of the mountains.
12 Let them give glory to the LORD,
and declare his praise in [l]the coastlands.
13 [z]The LORD goes out like a mighty man,
like a man of war [a]he stirs up his zeal;
he cries out, [b]he shouts aloud,
he shows himself mighty against his foes.

14 For a long time I have held my peace;
I have kept still and restrained myself;
now I will cry out [c]like a woman in labor;
I will gasp and pant.
15 [d]I will lay waste mountains and hills,
and dry up all their vegetation;
I will turn the rivers into islands,[3]
and dry up the pools.
16 [e]And I will lead the blind
in a way that they do not know,
in paths that they have not known
I will guide them.

[1] Or *bruised* [2] The Hebrew for *you* is singular; four times in this verse [3] Or *into coastlands*

42:1–17 This passage is commonly referred to as the first "Servant Song" in Isaiah (42:1–9), and other such "songs" follow in 49:1–13; 50:4–11; and 52:13–53:12 (cf. 51:12–13; 61:1–11). In these texts, one who represents and sacrificially serves others emerges. Here, the suffering servant is most directly associated with Israel (cf. 41:8–10), but in a representative way (the entire nation represented in her king), the image can also point to an individual who is meant to represent the whole (cf. 11:1–5, with Jer. 33:16). The king was expected to represent Israel, and Israel was intended to be a blessing to the nations. Though far too often this had not been the case, the expectation is of a time of renewal brought about by God's "servant" (i.e., the nation), whose hope and identity would ultimately be personified in the Messiah (Isa. 42:1; cf. 49:5–6).

Filled with the Spirit, able to heal, and deeply concerned about justice, Jesus is recognized as the fulfillment of Isaiah's expectation for God's "servant." Matthew picks up on Isaiah 42:1–4, making a direct link with Jesus (Matt. 12:17–21). Gentle yet powerful, this servant is unflinching in his mission, and Matthew reminds us that he "brings justice to victory," not by destroying the nations but by becoming the very hope of the nations (Matt. 12:20–21). The divine warrior has come, and he will bring light where there is darkness (Isa. 42:13, 16). Jesus' mission is the mission of the Creator God who cares for the whole earth (v. 4). Reconstituting Israel in himself, the Messiah comes in righteousness as a blessing to the nations (Gen. 12:3; 17:4) and a light to the world (cf. Luke 2:32). As that blessed light, his servant calling is opening the eyes of the blind and setting the prisoners free (Isa. 42:6–9). We now go out in his name and, in that way, bring his salvation and light to the world (Acts 13:47).

4[l] ch. 60:9; Gen. 10:5; [ch. 2:3; Matt. 12:21]
5[m] ch. 44:24; 45:12 [n] Acts 17:25
6[o] ch. 41:9 [p] ch. 49:6, 8 [q] Luke 2:32
7[r] ch. 35:5; 49:9; 61:1; Heb. 2:14, 15 [s] Luke 1:79
8[t] ch. 48:11
9[u] [ch. 43:19]
10[v] See Ps. 33:3 [w] Ps. 107:23 [l] [See ver. 4 above]
11[x] See ch. 21:16 [y] ch. 16:1
12[l] [See ver. 4 above]
13[z] ch. 40:10 [a] [ch. 9:7; 59:17] [b] Ps. 78:65
14[c] See ch. 13:8
15[d] ch. 50:2
16[e] ch. 35:5, 8

I will turn the darkness before them into light,
[f]the rough places into level ground.
These are the things I do,
and I do not forsake them.
17 [g]They are turned back and utterly put to shame,
who trust in carved idols,
who say to metal images,
"You are our gods."

Israel's Failure to Hear and See

18 Hear, you deaf,
and look, you blind, that you may see!
19 Who is blind but my servant,
or deaf as my messenger whom I send?
Who is blind as my dedicated one,[1]
or blind as the servant of the LORD?
20 [h]He sees many things, but does not observe them;
[i]his ears are open, but he does not hear.
21 The LORD was pleased, for his righteousness' sake,
to magnify his law and make it glorious.
22 But this is a people plundered and looted;
they are all of them trapped in holes
[j]and hidden in prisons;
they have become plunder with none to rescue,
spoil with none to say, "Restore!"
23 Who among you will give ear to this,
will attend and listen for the time to come?
24 Who gave up Jacob to the looter,
and Israel to the plunderers?
Was it not the LORD, against whom we have sinned,
in whose ways they would not walk,
and whose law they would not obey?
25 So he poured on him the heat of his anger
and the might of battle;
it set him on fire all around, [k]but he did not understand;
it burned him up, [l]but he did not take it to heart.

Israel's Only Savior

43 But now thus says the LORD,
[m]he who created you, O Jacob,
he who formed you, O Israel:
[n]"Fear not, for I have redeemed you;
[o]I have called you by name, you are mine.
2 [p]When you pass through the waters,
I will be with you;
and through the rivers, they shall not overwhelm you;
[p]when you walk through fire [q]you shall not be burned,
and the flame shall not consume you.
3 For [r]I am the LORD your God,
the Holy One of Israel, your Savior.

[1] Or *as the one at peace with me*

16[f]ch. 40:4
17[g]ch. 1:29; 44:11; 45:16; Ps. 97:7
20[h]See Rom. 2:21-23 [i][Jer. 6:10]
22[j]ch. 14:17
25[k][ch. 47:11; Hos. 7:9] [l]ch. 57:1, 11
Chapter 43
1[m]ch. 44:2, 21, 24 [n]ch. 41:14 [o]ch. 45:3, 4; [Gen. 32:28]
2[p]Ps. 66:12 [q]ch. 42:25; [Dan. 3:25, 27]
3[r]See Ex. 20:2

42:18–25 Unfortunately, Israel too (and not just the nations) is "deaf" and "blind," so how can this people be God's representative servant, drawing others to Yahweh (vv. 18–20; cf. Rom. 10:14–21)? They are themselves "hidden in prisons" (Isa. 42:22), so how can they set the captives free? How can Israel reveal God's glory and deliverance when God's people themselves have ignored what has been given them (v. 20)?

Only the promised Messiah, ultimately revealed in Jesus, the true servant of God and King of Israel, is able to overcome the predicament (cf. 49:5–7). For God's people need a representative who will draw the nations in, yet who has not himself become, as Israel has, "plunder with none to rescue" (42:22). Jesus stands in for God's people, fully identified with them yet with one crucial difference: he is without any sin of his own (Heb. 4:16).

43:1–21 "Fear not, for I am with you" (v. 5; cf. v. 1). The Redeemer extends his grace by self-identifying with his people even as they walk through their frightening trials: he is their Savior and their God (vv. 1–5). Israel was to serve as his "witnesses" that all gods and foreign powers stand under, not over, the Lord and their Savior (vv. 10–12). Israel's Holy One is not simply the Maker of the world but "the Creator of Israel," and thus he alone is their King (vv. 14–15).

Like God's people in exile who heard this message, we need to be reminded that God can make a way when there is no way, "doing a new thing" so that all will sing his praise (vv. 19, 21; cf. Ps. 96:10–13). In Christ God is indeed, beyond anything Isaiah would have imagined, *with* us. His very name is Immanuel—"God with us" (Isa 7:14; Matt. 1:21–23).

[s]I give Egypt as your ransom,
Cush and [t]Seba in exchange for you.
4 Because you are precious in my eyes,
and honored, and I love you,
I give men in return for you,
peoples in exchange for your life.
5 [u]Fear not, for I am with you;
[v]I will bring your offspring from the east,
and from the west I will gather you.
6 I will say to the north, Give up,
and to the south, Do not withhold;
bring [w]my sons from afar
and [w]my daughters from the end of the earth,
7 everyone who is called by my name,
whom I created for my glory,
whom I formed and made."
8 Bring out [x]the people who are blind, yet have eyes,
who are deaf, yet have ears!
9 [y]All the nations gather together,
and the peoples assemble.
Who among them can declare this,
and show us the former things?
Let them bring their witnesses to prove them right,
and let them hear and say, It is true.
10 [z]"You are my witnesses," declares the LORD,
"and [a]my servant whom I have chosen,
that you may know and believe me
and understand that I am he.
[b]Before me no god was formed,
nor shall there be any after me.
11 [c]I, I am the LORD,
and besides me there is no savior.
12 I declared and saved and proclaimed,
when there was no strange god among you;
and [z]you are my witnesses," declares the LORD, "and I am God.
13 Also [d]henceforth I am he;
there is none who can deliver from my hand;
I work, and who can turn it back?"

14 Thus says the LORD,
your Redeemer, the Holy One of Israel:
[e]"For your sake I send to Babylon
and [f]bring them all down as fugitives,
[g]even the Chaldeans, in the ships in which they rejoice.
15 I am the LORD, your Holy One,
the Creator of Israel, your King."
16 Thus says the LORD,
[h]who makes a way in the sea,
a path in the mighty waters,
17 who [i]brings forth chariot and horse,
army and warrior;
they lie down, they cannot rise,
[j]they are extinguished, [k]quenched like a wick:
18 [l]"Remember not the former things,
nor consider the things of old.
19 [m]Behold, I am doing a new thing;
now it springs forth, do you not perceive it?
[n]I will make a way in the wilderness
[o]and rivers in the desert.
20 The wild beasts will honor me,
[p]the jackals and the ostriches,
[q]for I give water in the wilderness,
rivers in the desert,
to give drink to my chosen people,
21 the people whom I formed for myself
[r]that they might declare my praise.
22 "Yet you did not call upon me, O Jacob;
but [s]you have been weary of me, O Israel!
23 [t]You have not brought me your sheep for burnt offerings,
or honored me with your sacrifices.

43:22–28 Sadly, God's patience and grace can be ignored or taken for granted (vv. 22–23). While God did not weigh the people down with religious requirements (v. 23), they themselves "burdened" him with their sins (v. 24). We must strive to prevent our hearts from growing hard lest the Spirit be quenched in us (Heb. 3:7–4:13; 1 Thess. 5:19). God is the one who can wipe out our sins, not allowing them to clog up his memory; instead of repentance and faith, however, the people risked hardening their hearts and facing God's chastisement (Isa. 43:26–28). We must guard against the same mistake. Reflecting on his unspeakable grace in the gospel, our hearts are repeatedly refreshed, calmed, and softened.

3[s] [ch. 45:14; 52:3, 4] [t]Ps. 72:10
5[u] ch. 41:10, 13, 14; 44:2; Jer. 30:10, 11 [v]ch. 49:12; [ch. 60:8, 9; Ps. 107:3]
6[w] [2 Cor. 6:18]
8[x] ch. 42:19
9[y] ch. 41:1, 21, 22
10[z] ver. 12; ch. 44:8 [a]ch. 42:1 [b]See ch. 41:4
11[c] ch. 45:21; Hos. 13:4
12[z] [See ver. 10 above]
13[d] ch. 41:4; Ps. 90:2; [John 8:58] **14**[e] [ver. 4] [f][ch. 47:1] [g]ch. 23:13 **16**[h] ch. 51:10; Ex. 14:21, 22; Ps. 77:19 **17**[i] See Ex. 14:4-9 [j][Ps. 76:5, 6] [k]ch. 1:31; [Ps. 118:12] **18**[l] [Jer. 16:14; 23:7] **19**[m] [ch. 42:9; 2 Cor. 5:17; Rev. 21:5] [n]ch. 35:8 [o]ch. 41:18; 48:21 **20**[p] See ch. 13:22 [q][ch. 49:10] **21**[r] Ps. 79:13; [Ps. 22:3; 105:1; Luke 1:74, 75; 1 Pet. 2:9] **22**[s] Mic. 6:3 **23**[t] [Amos 5:25]

I have not burdened you with offerings,
[s]or wearied you with frankincense.
24 You have not bought me sweet cane
with money,
or satisfied me with the fat of your
sacrifices.
But you have burdened me with your
sins;
you have wearied me with your iniquities.
25 "I, I am he
[u]who blots out [v]your transgressions for
my own sake,
and I will not remember your sins.
26 Put me in remembrance; [w]let us argue
together;
set forth your case, that you may be
proved right.
27 [x]Your first father sinned,
and [y]your mediators transgressed
against me.
28 Therefore [z]I will profane the princes of
the sanctuary,
and [a]deliver Jacob to utter destruction
and Israel to reviling.

Israel the LORD's Chosen

44 "But now hear, [b]O Jacob my servant,
Israel whom I have chosen!
2 Thus says the LORD who made you,
[c]who formed you from the womb and
will help you:
[d]Fear not, O Jacob my servant,
[e]Jeshurun whom I have chosen.
3 [f]For I will pour water on the thirsty land,
and streams on the dry ground;
I will pour my Spirit upon your offspring,
and my blessing on your descendants.
4 They shall spring up among the grass
[g]like willows by flowing streams.
5 [h]This one will say, 'I am the LORD's,'
another will call on the name of Jacob,
and another will write on his hand, 'The
LORD's,'
and name himself by the name of
Israel."

Besides Me There Is No God

6 Thus says the LORD, the King of Israel
and [i]his Redeemer, the LORD of hosts:
[j]"I am the first and I am the last;
besides me there is no god.
7 [k]Who is like me? Let him proclaim it.[1]
Let him declare and set it before me,
since I appointed an ancient people.
Let them declare what is to come, and
what will happen.
8 Fear not, nor be afraid;
have I not told you from of old and
declared it?
[l]And you are my witnesses!
[m]Is there a God besides me?
There is no [n]Rock; I know not any."

The Folly of Idolatry

9 [o]All who fashion idols are nothing, and the
things they delight in do not profit. Their witnesses neither see nor know, that they may
be put to shame. 10 [p]Who fashions a god or

[1] Or *Who like me can proclaim it?*

23[s] [See ver. 22 above]
25[u] ch. 44:22; [Ezek. 36:25, 26] [v] [ch. 46:8]
26[w] ch. 1:18
27[x] [Ezek. 16:3] [y] [Jer. 5:31]
28[z] Lam. 2:2 [a] [Jer. 24:9; 29:22]
Chapter 44
1[b] See ch. 41:8
2[c] ver. 24; ch. 49:15; [Ps. 71:6; Jer. 1:5; Gal. 1:15] [d] See ch. 43:5 [e] Deut. 32:15
3[f] Joel 2:28; John 7:38; Acts 2:18; See ch. 35:6
4[g] [Ps. 1:3]
5[h] [ch. 14:1]
6[i] See ch. 43:14 [j] ch. 48:12; Rev. 1:8; See ch. 41:4
7[k] ch. 41:26, 27
8[l] ch. 43:10 [m] ch. 45:5; Deut. 4:35, 39; 32:39; 1 Sam. 2:2; Joel 2:27 [n] See ch. 30:29
9[o] ch. 41:24, 29
10[p] [ch. 40:19, 20; 41:6, 7; 46:6, 7; Hab. 2:18]; See Jer. 10:3-5

44:1–25 Why turn to idols, which are mere human creations unable to defend themselves (v. 16)? Their designers are finite, themselves dependent on the true Creator (vv. 9–17). There is no god but Yahweh, who alone is "the first and the last" beyond all created things from which idols come (v. 6). He knows and controls what they cannot (vv. 7–8). And so, he alone is the Rock upon which his people must rest, the refuge enabling them not to be afraid (v. 8). Amazingly, this God has "chosen" and "formed" Israel, promising to sustain and bless her through the generations (vv. 1–3, 21). God's promise thus rings through the silence of exile: "O Israel, you will not be forgotten by me" (v. 21). The coming of Jesus Christ 700 years after Isaiah is proof of this.

There is a significant pattern here of redemption and return: "return to me, for I have redeemed you" (v. 22). God promises remembrance, renewed righteousness, and redemption prior to Israel's return from wayward paths (vv. 22–23). Undeserved deliverance, not mere command or conditional love, fuels repentance. As with the exodus preceding Sinai, here again God's grace is extended to his people in their state of need, reminding us of the grace that is ours even before we return to him—a grace that enables us to repent and rest in his deliverance (cf. 30:15). As the redeemed, we are liberated to obey our Lord's commands. Our response does not secure God's favor but flows from heartfelt gratitude for the provision of his grace.

casts an idol that is profitable for nothing?
11 [q]Behold, all his companions shall be put to
shame, and the craftsmen are only human.
Let them all assemble, let them stand forth.
They shall be terrified; they shall be put to
shame together.
12 [p]The ironsmith takes a cutting tool and
works it over the coals. He fashions it with
hammers and works it with his strong arm.
He becomes hungry, and his strength fails; he
drinks no water and is faint. 13 The carpenter
stretches a line; he marks it out with a pencil.
He shapes it with planes and marks it with a
compass. [r]He shapes it into the figure of a man,
with the beauty of a man, to dwell in a house.
14 [s]He cuts down cedars, or he chooses a cypress
tree or an oak and lets it grow strong among
the trees of the forest. He plants a cedar and the
rain nourishes it. 15 Then it becomes fuel for a
man. He takes a part of it and warms himself;
he kindles a fire and bakes bread. Also he makes
a god and worships it; he makes it an idol and
falls down before it. 16 Half of it he burns in the
fire. Over the half he eats meat; he roasts it and
is satisfied. Also he warms himself and says,
"Aha, I am warm, I have seen the fire!" 17 And
the rest of it he makes into a god, his idol, and
falls down to it and worships it. [t]He prays to
it and says, "Deliver me, for you are my god!"
18 They know not, nor do they discern, for he
has shut their eyes, so that they cannot see, and
their hearts, so that they cannot understand.
19 No one considers, nor is there knowledge or
discernment to say, "Half of it I burned in the
fire; I also baked bread on its coals; I roasted
meat and have eaten. And shall I make the
rest of it an [u]abomination? Shall I fall down
before a block of wood?" 20 [v]He feeds on [w]ashes;
a deluded heart has led him astray, and he cannot deliver himself or say, "Is there not [x]a lie
in my right hand?"

The LORD Redeems Israel

21 Remember these things, O Jacob,
and Israel, for you are [y]my servant;
I formed you; you are my servant;
[z]O Israel, you will not be forgotten by me.
22 [a]I have blotted out your transgressions like a cloud
and your sins like mist;
return to me, for I have redeemed you.
23 [b]Sing, O heavens, for the LORD has done it;
shout, O [c]depths of the earth;
break forth into singing, O mountains,
O forest, and every tree in it!
For the LORD has redeemed Jacob,
[d]and will be glorified[1] in Israel.
24 Thus says the LORD, [e]your Redeemer,
[f]who formed you from the womb:
[g]"I am the LORD, who made all things,
[h]who alone stretched out the heavens,
who spread out the earth by myself,
25 who frustrates the signs of liars
and makes fools of diviners,
[i]who turns wise men back
and makes their knowledge foolish,
26 [j]who confirms the word of his servant
and fulfills the counsel of his messengers,
who says of Jerusalem, 'She shall be inhabited,'
[k]and of the cities of Judah, 'They shall be built,
and I will raise up their ruins';
27 [l]who says to the deep, 'Be dry;
I will dry up your rivers';
28 who says of [m]Cyrus, 'He is [n]my shepherd,
and he shall fulfill all my purpose';
saying of Jerusalem, 'She shall be built,'
[o]and of the temple, 'Your foundation shall be laid.'"

Cyrus, God's Instrument

45 Thus says the LORD to [p]his anointed, to Cyrus,
[q]whose right hand I have grasped,
to subdue nations before him
and [r]to loose the belts of kings,

[1] Or *will display his beauty*

45:1–21 Cyrus is here described as the Lord's "anointed" (v. 1). Later, this title will have particular significance when applied to Jesus as the Anointed One (i.e., the Messiah), but even in this Old Testament text the title is striking. A high priest would be anointed (e.g., Lev. 4:3) or a ruler of Israel (e.g., 1 Sam. 12:3; 24:6), but to apply "anointed" to a foreign leader who did not know Yahweh (Isa. 45:4–5) was somewhat shocking. Such

11 [q] ch. 45:16; Ps. 115:8; See ch. 42:17
12 [p] [See ver. 10 above]
13 [r] See Ps. 115:5-7
14 [s] [ch. 40:20]
17 [t] [ch. 45:20]
19 [u] Deut. 27:15
20 [v] Hos. 12:1 [w] [Job 13:12] [x] Ps. 144:8; [Rom. 1:25] **21** [y] ch. 42:19; See ch. 42:1 [z] [ch. 49:15] **22** [a] ch. 43:25 **23** [b] ch. 49:13; [ch. 55:12; Ps. 69:34; Jer. 51:48] [c] Ps. 63:9; [Hos. 2:21, 22] [d] ch. 49:3; [ch. 55:5; 60:9] **24** [e] See ch. 43:14 [f] See ver. 2 [g] [ch. 42:5] [h] ch. 42:5; 45:12 **25** [i] [ch. 19:3, 14] **26** [j] [2 Chr. 36:22] [k] [Jer. 32:15, 44] **27** [l] ch. 11:15; [ch. 51:10] **28** [m] ch. 45:1 [n] [2 Sam. 5:2; Ps. 78:72] [o] ch. 45:13; See 2 Chr. 36:22, 23; Ezra 1:1-3 **Chapter 45** **1** [p] [ch. 44:28] [q] [ch. 41:13] [r] Job 12:21; [ver. 5; ch. 22:21]

to open doors before him
that gates may not be closed:
2 "I will go before you
and [s]level the exalted places,[1]
[t]I will break in pieces the doors of bronze
and cut through the bars of iron,
3 [u]I will give you the treasures of darkness
and the hoards in secret places,
that you may know that it is I, the LORD,
the God of Israel, [v]who call you by
your name.
4 For the sake of my servant Jacob,
and Israel my chosen,
[v]I call you by your name,
[w]I name you, though you do not know
me.
5 [x]I am the LORD, and there is no other,
besides me there is no God;
[y]I equip you, though you do not know
me,
6 [z]that people may know, from the rising
of the sun
and from the west, that there is none
besides me;
I am the LORD, and there is no other.
7 I form light and create darkness,
I make well-being and [a]create calamity,
I am the LORD, who does all these
things.

8 [b]"Shower, O heavens, from above,
and [c]let the clouds rain down righteousness;
let the earth open, that salvation and
righteousness may bear fruit;
let the earth cause them both to
sprout;
I the LORD have created it.

9 [d]"Woe to him who strives with him who
formed him,
a pot among earthen pots!
[e]Does the clay say to him who forms it,
'What are you making?'
or 'Your work has no handles'?
10 Woe to him who says to a father, 'What
are you begetting?'
or to a woman, 'With what are you in
labor?'"

11 Thus says [f]the LORD,
the Holy One of Israel, and the one
who formed him:
[g]"Ask me of things to come;
will you command me [h]concerning
my children and [i]the work of my
hands?[2]
12 [j]I made the earth
and created man on it;
it was my hands [k]that stretched out the
heavens,
and [l]I commanded all their host.
13 [m]I have stirred him up in righteousness,
[n]and I will make all his ways level;
[o]he shall build my city
[p]and set my exiles free,
not for price or reward,"
says the LORD of hosts.

The LORD, the Only Savior

14 Thus says the LORD:
[q]"The wealth of Egypt and the merchandise of Cush,
and the Sabeans, men of stature,
shall come over to you [r]and be yours;
they shall follow you;
they shall come over in chains and
bow down to you.
They will plead with you, saying:
'Surely God is in you, and there is no
other,
no god besides him.'"
15 [s]Truly, you are a God who hides himself,
O God of Israel, the Savior.

[1] Masoretic Text; Dead Sea Scroll, Septuagint *level the mountains* [2] A slight emendation yields *will you question me about my children, or command me concerning the work of my hands?*

2[s] ch. 40:4 [t] Ps. 107:16
3[u] [Jer. 50:37; 51:13] [v] ch. 43:1
4[v] [See ver. 3 above] [w] [ch. 62:2]
5[x] See ch. 44:8 [y] [Job 12:21; ch. 22:21]
6[z] [ch. 37:20; Mal. 1:11]
7[a] [ch. 41:23; Amos 3:6]
8[b] [Deut. 32:2] [c] Ps. 85:11; [Hos. 10:12]
9[d] [Eccles. 6:10]; See ch. 10:15 [e] ch. 64:8; Cited Rom. 9:20
11[f] Ezek. 39:7 [g] [ch. 41:23]

anointing signified a commissioning from God, and here we see the Lord "grasping" Cyrus's "right hand" with the purpose of subduing the nations (v. 1).

While this can raise various questions, it also reminds us of a key biblical truth. In the ancient world, gods were often tied to territories or specific regions. This is why people wanted to fight in an area where their god would be present, because then he could fight for them. But Yahweh is not confined to a particular geographical location, nor restricted to a particular population. He "made the earth and created man on it; it was my hands that stretched out the heavens, and I commanded all their host" (v. 12; cf. v. 18). A pagan king is as much under God's sovereign hand as is any Israelite.

[h] [Jer. 31:9] [i] ch. 29:23; 64:8 **12**[j] Jer. 27:5 [k] ch. 42:5; 44:24 [l] Gen. 2:1 **13**[m] ch. 41:2 [n] [ver. 2] [o] See ch. 44:28 [p] ch. 49:25; 51:14; 52:3 **14**[q] [ch. 43:3] [r] ch. 14:2
15[s] ch. 57:17

16 [t]All of them are put to shame and confounded;
the makers of idols go in confusion together.
17 But Israel is saved by the LORD
with everlasting salvation;
[u]you shall not be put to shame or confounded
to all eternity.

18 [v]For thus says the LORD,
who created the heavens
(he is God!),
who formed the earth and made it
(he established it;
he [w]did not create it empty,
[x]he formed it to be inhabited!):
"I am the LORD, and there is no other.
19 [y]I did not speak in secret,
in a land of darkness;
I did not say to the offspring of Jacob,
[z]'Seek me in vain.'[1]
I the LORD speak [a]the truth;
I declare what is right.

20 [b]"Assemble yourselves and come;
draw near together,
you survivors of the nations!
[c]They have no knowledge
who [d]carry about their wooden idols,
[e]and keep on praying to a god
that cannot save.
21 [f]Declare and present your case;
let them take counsel together!
Who told this long ago?
Who declared it of old?
Was it not I, the LORD?
And there is no other god besides me,
a righteous God [g]and a Savior;
there is none besides me.

22 "Turn to me and be saved,
[h]all the ends of the earth!
For I am God, and there is no other.
23 [i]By myself I have sworn;
from my mouth has gone out in [j]righteousness
a word that shall not return:
[k]'To me every knee shall bow,
every tongue shall swear allegiance.'[2]

24 [l]"Only in the LORD, it shall be said of me,
are righteousness and [m]strength;
to him shall come and be ashamed
[n]all who were incensed against him.
25 In the LORD all the offspring of Israel
shall be justified and shall glory."

The Idols of Babylon and the One True God

46 [o]Bel bows down; Nebo stoops;
their idols are on beasts and livestock;
these things you carry are borne
as burdens on weary beasts.

[1] Hebrew *in emptiness* [2] Septuagint *every tongue shall confess to God*

45:22–25 "Turn to me and be saved": God does not delight in human rebellion and death, and this text reminds us of his heartfelt invitation to "all the ends of the earth," that they might receive his salvation (v. 22; cf. Gen. 12:1–3; 22:18; Isa. 19:23–25). Since there are no other gods, God simply speaks the truth by calling for the world to return to their Creator and now Redeemer. Those who return become part of the "offspring of Israel," even if they come from the distant four corners of the world (45:25). Isaiah 45:22 may be the best single-verse summary of the entire book of Isaiah, emphasizing God's gracious salvation, its global scope, and the grounding of this comprehensive salvation in the utter supremacy of God.

Significantly, the New Testament applies verse 23b to Jesus: "to me every knee shall bow, every tongue shall swear allegiance." Paul makes it clear that bowing down before God is now understood as bending the knee to Jesus the Messiah. Such will one day be the posture of all creation: all confession, praise, and promise is centered on Jesus, who is the "glory of God the Father" (Phil. 2:9–11; cf. Rom. 14:11).

Looking to the incarnate Son, we see divine faithfulness and grace embodied, and so now by the Spirit we worship the Father through the Son in the freedom of the gospel.

46:1–13 Idols cannot comfort or respond, for they are merely the result of human creativity: "if one cries to it, it does not answer or save him from his trouble" (vv. 6–7; cf. 1 Kings 18:27). Like no other (Isa. 46:5, 9), the Creator's wisdom, eternal plans, and ability to forgive should prompt "the remnant" to "remember this and stand firm (vv. 3, 8–11). They stand secure, however, not on their own righteousness but by God's salvation and righteousness that he will bring "near" (vv. 12–13; cf. Jer. 23:6; 33:16).

16[t] See ch. 42:17
17[u] ch. 54:4
18[v] ch. 42:5 [w] [Gen. 1:2] [x] [Ps. 115:16]
19[y] ch. 48:16; [Deut. 30:11] [z] Jer. 29:13, 14 [a] ver. 23
20[b] [ch. 41:1] [c] [ch. 44:18, 19; 48:5-7] [d] ch. 46:1, 7; Jer. 10:5 [e] [ch. 44:17]
21[f] [ch. 41:22, 26; 43:9] [g] [ch. 43:11]
22[h] ch. 11:12; 43:5, 6
23[i] See Gen. 22:16 [j] ver. 19 [k] Cited Rom. 14:11; [Phil. 2:10]
24[l] [ch. 26:4; 44:8] [m] [ch. 26:4; 44:8] [n] [ch. 41:11]
Chapter 46
1[o] Jer. 50:2; 51:44; [ch. 21:9]

2 They stoop; they bow down together;
they cannot save the burden,
but [p]themselves go into captivity.

3 "Listen to me, O house of Jacob,
all the remnant of the house of Israel,
[q]who have been borne by me from before
your birth,
carried from the womb;
4 [r]even to your old age I am he,
and to gray hairs I will carry you.
I have made, and I will bear;
I will carry and will save.

5 [s]"To whom will you liken me and make
me equal,
and compare me, that we may be alike?
6 [t]Those who lavish gold from the purse,
and weigh out silver in the scales,
hire a goldsmith, and he makes it into a
god;
[u]then they fall down and worship!
7 [v]They lift it to their shoulders, they carry
it,
they set it in its place, and it stands
there;
[w]it cannot move from its place.
If one cries to it, it does not answer
or save him from his trouble.

8 "Remember this and stand firm,
recall it to mind, [x]you transgressors,
9 remember the former things of old;
for I am God, and there is no other;
I am God, and there is none like me,
10 [y]declaring the end from the beginning
and from ancient times things not yet
done,
saying, [z]'My counsel shall stand,
and I will accomplish all my purpose,'
11 [a]calling a bird of prey from the east,
the man of my counsel from a far
country.
[b]I have spoken, and I will bring it to pass;
I have purposed, and I will do it.

12 "Listen to me, you stubborn of heart,
you who are far from righteousness:
13 [c]I bring near my righteousness; it is not
far off,
and my salvation will not delay;
[d]I will put salvation in Zion,
for Israel my glory."

The Humiliation of Babylon

47 [e]Come down and sit in the dust,
O virgin [f]daughter of Babylon;
[g]sit on the ground without a throne,
O daughter of [h]the Chaldeans!
[i]For you shall no more be called
tender and delicate.
2 Take the millstones and [j]grind flour,
[k]put off your veil,
strip off your robe, uncover your legs,
pass through the rivers.
3 Your nakedness shall be uncovered,
and your disgrace shall be seen.
I will take vengeance,
and I will spare no one.
4 [l]Our Redeemer—the LORD of hosts is
his name—
is the Holy One of Israel.
5 [m]Sit in silence, and go into darkness,
O daughter of [h]the Chaldeans;

2[p] [Jer. 48:7; Hos. 10:5, 6]
3[q] [Deut. 1:31; 32:11]
4[r] [Ps. 71:18]
5[s] See ch. 40:18
6[t] See ch. 44:10 [u] ch. 44:15
7[v] See ch. 45:20 [w] Ps. 115:7
8[x] [ch. 43:25]
10[y] ch. 41:26 [z] ch. 44:26, 28; Ps. 33:11; Prov. 19:21; [Heb. 6:17]
11[a] See ch. 41:2 [b] Num. 23:19
13[c] ch. 51:5; [ch. 56:1; Ps. 85:9] [d] ch. 62:11; [Joel 2:32]
Chapter 47
1[e] [ch. 43:14] [f] Ps. 137:8 [g] ch. 3:26 [h] ch. 23:13; 48:14 [i] [ver. 5; ch. 13:19]
2[j] Judg. 16:21; [Matt. 24:41] [k] [ch. 20:4]
4[l] See ch. 43:14
5[m] [Jer. 8:14] [h] [See ver. 1 above]

Our comfort comes from receiving God's righteousness, ultimately revealed as coming through faith in Christ (Rom. 3:21–22; cf. Rom. 8:10–11). We are those who rest in—and are animated by—the "abundance of grace and the free gift of righteousness" which are ours in Christ (Rom. 5:17).

47:1–15 While God did allow his wayward people to be handed over to the Babylonians, who "showed them no mercy" and made their lives a great burden (v. 6), the Lord will not allow this situation to continue forever. He expects the discipline to lead to a renewed dependence on the grace that is his people's eternal hope. By contrast, the Babylonians grow in their foolish arrogance. They begin to believe that they stand above everything, "secure in [their] wickedness," imagining their sins will go unaccounted for (vv. 8–10).

Resembling Elijah mocking the false prophets and their lifeless gods (1 Kings 18:27), God offers a response full of sarcasm. He tells the Babylonians to try and "stand fast" in the powerlessness of their enchantments, sorceries, and false religion: "let them stand forth and save you" (vv. 12–13). Idols often have a trendy nature to them, and individuals and nations can be seduced by the proposed promises associated with them. But as time passes these idols are silenced and exposed as fraudulent (vv. 1–4), whereas the Lord God remains forever faithful and true.

for you shall no more be called
[n]the mistress of kingdoms.
6 [o]I was angry with my people;
I profaned my heritage;
I gave them into your hand;
[p]you showed them no mercy;
on the aged you made your yoke exceedingly heavy.
7 You said, "I shall be [q]mistress forever,"
so that you did not lay these things to heart
or remember their end.

8 Now therefore hear this, [q]you lover of pleasures,
[r]who sit securely,
who say in your heart,
[s]"I am, and there is no one besides me;
[t]I shall not sit as a widow
or know the loss of children":
9 [u]These two things shall come to you
in a moment, [v]in one day;
the loss of children and widowhood
shall come upon you in full measure,
[w]in spite of your many sorceries
and the great power of your enchantments.

10 You felt secure in your wickedness,
you said, "No one sees me";
your wisdom and your knowledge led you astray,
and you said in your heart,
[x]"I am, and there is no one besides me."
11 But evil shall come upon you,
which you will not know how to charm away;
disaster shall fall upon you,
for which you will not be able to atone;
[y]and ruin shall come upon you suddenly,
of which you know nothing.

12 [z]Stand fast in your enchantments
and your many sorceries,
with which you have labored from your youth;
perhaps you may be able to succeed;
perhaps you may inspire terror.
13 You are wearied with your many counsels;
let them stand forth and save you,
[a]those who divide the heavens,
who gaze at the stars,
who at the new moons make known
what shall come upon you.

14 Behold, [b]they are like stubble;
[c]the fire consumes them;
they cannot deliver themselves
from the power of the flame.
No coal for warming oneself is this,
no fire to sit before!
15 Such to you are those with whom you have labored,
who have done business with you from your youth;
they wander about, each in his own direction;
there is no one to save you.

Israel Refined for God's Glory

48 Hear this, O house of Jacob,
[d]who are called by the name of Israel,
and [e]who came from the waters of Judah,
[f]who swear by the name of the LORD
and confess the God of Israel,
but not in truth or right.
2 For they call themselves after the holy city,
[g]and stay themselves on the God of Israel;
the LORD of hosts is his name.

3 "The former things [h]I declared of old;
they went out from my mouth, and I announced them;
then suddenly I did them, and they came to pass.
4 Because I know that [i]you are obstinate,
and your neck is an iron sinew
and your forehead brass,

48:1–22 Darkness had crept into the house of Jacob, for while claiming God, the people were "not in truth or right" (v. 1). Rather than having contrite and thankful hearts, they had become like hardened iron or brass, obstinate rather than repentant (vv. 3–4). Yet again, God's patience shines out of the darkness, for he reaffirms his self-identification with Israel. Like Moses' plea that God relent lest his character be misunderstood (Ex. 32:11–13), so here God declares, "for my name's sake I defer my anger, for the sake of my praise I restrain it for you, that I may not cut you off" (Isa. 48:9).

5[n] [ver. 1]
6[o] [Zech. 1:15] [p] [ch. 14:17; 51:23]
7[q] [ver. 1]
8[q] [See ver. 7 above] [r] Zeph. 2:15 [s] [ch. 45:6, 18; Jer. 50:29] [t] Lam. 1:1; [Rev. 18:7]
9[u] [ch. 51:19] [v] [Jer. 50:31] [w] [ver. 12, 13; Nah. 3:4]
10[x] [ch. 45:6, 18; Jer. 50:29]
11[y] [Ps. 35:8; Jer. 51:41]

12[z] [ver. 9] **13**[a] [ch. 44:25; Dan. 2:2, 10] **14**[b] ch. 41:2; Nah. 1:10; Mal. 4:1 [c] See ch. 10:17 **Chapter 48** **1**[d] ch. 43:1 [e] Ps. 68:26 [f] Jer. 7:9 **2**[g] [Mic. 3:11] **3**[h] ch. 41:26 **4**[i] [Ex. 32:9]

5 [h]I declared them to you from of old,
before they came to pass I announced them to you,
lest you should say, [i]'My idol did them,
my carved image and my metal image commanded them.'

6 "You have heard; now see all this;
and will you not declare it?
From this time forth [k]I announce to you new things,
hidden things that you have not known.
7 They are created now, not long ago;
before today you have never heard of them,
lest you should say, 'Behold, I knew them.'
8 You have never heard, you have never known,
from of old your ear has not been opened.
For I knew that you would surely deal treacherously,
and that [l]from before birth you were called a rebel.

9 [m]"For my name's sake I defer my anger,
for the sake of my praise I restrain it for you,
that I may not cut you off.
10 Behold, I have refined you, [n]but not as silver;
[o]I have tried[1] you in the furnace of affliction.
11 [p]For my own sake, for my own sake, I do it,
for how should my name[2] be profaned?
[q]My glory I will not give to another.

The LORD's Call to Israel

12 "Listen to me, O Jacob,
and Israel, whom I called!
I am he; [r]I am the first,
and I am the last.
13 My hand [s]laid the foundation of the earth,
and my right hand [s]spread out the heavens;
[t]when I call to them,
they stand forth together.

14 "Assemble, all of you, and listen!
[u]Who among them has declared these things?
The LORD loves him;
[v]he shall perform his purpose on Babylon,
and his arm shall be against [w]the Chaldeans.
15 [x]I, even I, have spoken and called him;
I have brought him, and he will prosper in his way.
16 [y]Draw near to me, hear this:
from the beginning I have not spoken in secret,
from the time it came to be I have been there."
And now [z]the Lord GOD has sent me, and his Spirit.

17 Thus says the LORD,
your Redeemer, the Holy One of Israel:
"I am the LORD your God,
who teaches you to profit,
who leads you in the way you should go.
18 [a]Oh that you had paid attention to my commandments!
[b]Then your peace would have been like a river,
and your righteousness like the waves of the sea;
19 [c]your offspring would have been like the sand,
and your descendants like its grains;
their name would never be cut off
or destroyed from before me."

[1] Or *I have chosen* [2] Hebrew lacks *my name*

5[h] [See ver. 3 above] [i] See Jer. 44:15-17
6[k] See ch. 43:19
8[l] ch. 46:8
9[m] [Mal. 3:6]
10[n] [1 Pet. 1:7] [o] [Deut. 4:20; Ezek. 22:18, 20, 22]
11[p] ch. 43:25; Ezek. 20:9 [q] ch. 42:8
12[r] See ch. 41:4
13[s] ch. 51:13; [Ps. 102:25; Heb. 1:10] [t] [ch. 40:26]

Yet the hardness and disobedience of God's people keep them from peace (vv. 18, 22). Similarly, looking over Jerusalem, Jesus' hilltop lament reflects his concern over this long-standing resistance to God's gracious offers (Luke 13:34–35).

Yahweh's holy love assuredly will not leave his people as they are, and thus refinement will be necessary (Isa. 48:10–11). We are to reflect the holy God (cf. Lev. 11:44–45; 1 Pet. 1:15–16). Redemptive purification is carried out by the crucified Messiah, whose blood sanctifies the church. He alone is able to offer us up to the Father "without spot . . . that [the church] might be holy and without blemish" (Eph. 5:25–27, 29).

14[u] [ch. 41:26] [v] ch. 46:10, 11 [w] ch. 23:13; 47:1 15[x] See ch. 45:1-3 16[y] ch. 45:19 [z] ch. 61:1 18[a] Ps. 81:13; Luke 19:42; [Deut. 32:29] [b] ch. 66:12 19[c] ch. 10:22; Gen. 22:17; Hos. 1:10

20 [d]Go out from Babylon, flee from [e]Chaldea,
declare this [f]with a shout of joy, proclaim it,
send it out to the end of the earth;
say, [g]"The LORD has redeemed his servant Jacob!"
21 [h]They did not thirst when he led them through the deserts;
[i]he made water flow for them from the rock;
he split the rock and the water gushed out.
22 [j]"There is no peace," says the LORD, "for the wicked."

The Servant of the LORD

49 Listen to me, [k]O coastlands,
and give attention, you peoples [l]from afar.
[m]The LORD called me from the womb,
from the body of my mother he named my name.
2 [n]He made my mouth like a sharp sword;
[o]in the shadow of his hand he hid me;
he made me a polished arrow;
in his quiver he hid me away.
3 And he said to me, "You are my servant,
Israel, [p]in whom I will be glorified."[1]
4 [q]But I said, "I have labored in vain;
I have spent my strength for nothing and vanity;
yet surely my right is with the LORD,
and my recompense with my God."
5 [r]And now the LORD says,
he [m]who formed me from the womb to be his servant,
to bring Jacob back to him;
and that Israel might be gathered to him—
for [s]I am honored in the eyes of the LORD,
and my God has become my strength—
6 he says:
"It is too light a thing that you should be my servant
to raise up the tribes of Jacob
and to bring back the preserved of Israel;
[t]I will make you [u]as a light for the nations,
that [v]my salvation may reach to the end of the earth."
7 Thus says the LORD,
[w]the Redeemer of Israel and his Holy One,
[x]to one deeply despised, abhorred by the nation,
the servant of rulers:
[y]"Kings shall see and arise;
princes, and they shall prostrate themselves;
because of the LORD, who is faithful,
the Holy One of Israel, who has chosen you."

The Restoration of Israel

8 Thus says the LORD:
[z]"In a [a]time of favor I have answered you;
in a day of salvation I have helped you;
I will keep you [b]and give you
as a covenant to the people,
to establish the land,
[c]to apportion the desolate heritages,

[1] Or *I will display my beauty*

49:1–13 Emerging out of the second "Servant Song" is One who is identified with Israel (v. 3). Yet he is also distinguished from them, for he is uniquely able to restore and gather Israel (v. 5). Filled with God's strength, the servant is empowered to renew Israel and then extend divine salvation "to the end of the earth" (v. 6). Reflecting a biblical pattern, God works through the particular (e.g., Abraham/Israel/church) to reach the universal (the nations/world). Here, this unique chosen one embodies the remnant, faithfully representing the Holy One of Israel, but all the while his ministry is meant to extend well beyond the nation's borders (v. 7).

In the New Testament, Paul draws on Isaiah's reference to "a light for the Gentiles" to make sense of the gospel extending beyond merely the Jews (Acts 13:47). Right after quoting Isaiah 49:8, Paul boldly proclaims, "now is the favorable time; behold, now is the day of salvation" (2 Cor. 6:2). God's ancient promises have been realized in Christ. The new age has dawned (1 Cor. 10:11). Consequently, all believers are involved in the ministry of reconciliation: we serve as ambassadors of Christ, extending God's reconciling love to all the world (2 Cor. 5:18–21). We are reminded that God's redemptive concerns were always global, and his pattern of renewal was always from the particular to the universal (Gen. 12:1–3).

20 [d]ch. 52:11; Jer. 50:8; 51:6, 45; Zech. 2:6, 7 [e]ch. 23:13; 47:1 [f][ch. 35:10; 52:9] [g]ch. 44:23; [Ex. 19:4-6]
21 [h][ch. 35:6; 44:3; Deut. 8:15] [i]ch. 43:19; Ex. 17:6; Num. 20:11
22 [j]ch. 57:21
Chapter 49
1 [k]See ch. 11:11 [l]ch. 33:13 [m]See ch. 44:2
2 [n]ch. 11:4; Hos. 6:5; [Heb. 4:12; Rev. 1:16] [o]ch. 51:16
3 [p]ch. 44:23
4 [q][ch. 65:23]; See ch. 50:6-8; 53:10-12
5 [r][ch. 50:4] [m][See ver. 1 above] [s][ch. 52:13]
6 [t]Cited Acts 13:47 [u]ch. 42:6 [v][Ps. 98:3]
7 [w]ch. 48:17 [x]ver. 1; ch. 53:3; [ch. 50:6, 7] [y]ver. 23
8 [z]Cited 2 Cor. 6:2 [a]Ps. 69:13 [b]ch. 42:6 [c]ch. 61:4

9 [d]saying to the prisoners, 'Come out,'
to those who are in darkness, 'Appear.'
[e]They shall feed along the ways;
on all bare heights shall be their pasture;
10 [f]they shall not hunger or thirst,
neither scorching wind nor sun shall strike them,
for he who has pity on them [g]will lead them,
and by springs of water will guide them.
11 [h]And I will make all my mountains a road,
and my highways shall be raised up.
12 [i]Behold, these shall come from afar,
and behold, [j]these from the north and from the west,[1]
and these from the land of Syene."[2]

13 [k]Sing for joy, O heavens, and exult, O earth;
break forth, O mountains, into singing!
For the LORD [l]has comforted his people
and will have compassion on his afflicted.

14 But Zion said, [m]"The LORD has forsaken me;
my Lord has forgotten me."

15 [n]"Can a woman forget her nursing child,
that she should have no compassion on the son of her womb?
Even these may forget,
yet I will not forget you.
16 Behold, [o]I have engraved you on the palms of my hands;
your walls are continually before me.
17 Your builders make haste;[3]
[p]your destroyers and those who laid you waste go out from you.
18 [q]Lift up your eyes around and see;
they all gather, they come to you.
[r]As I live, declares the LORD,
[s]you shall put them all on as an ornament;
you shall bind them on as a bride does.

19 "Surely your waste and your desolate places
and your devastated land—
[t]surely now you will be too narrow for your inhabitants,
and those who swallowed you up will be far away.
20 [u]The children of your bereavement
will yet say in your ears:
[t]'The place is too narrow for me;
make room for me to dwell in.'
21 Then you will say in your heart:
'Who has borne me these?
[u]I was bereaved and barren,
exiled and put away,
but who has brought up these?
Behold, I was left alone;
from where have these come?'"

22 Thus says the Lord GOD:
"Behold, I will lift up my hand to the nations,
[v]and raise my signal to the peoples;
[w]and they shall bring your sons in their arms,[4]
and your daughters shall be carried on their shoulders.
23 [x]Kings shall be your foster fathers,
and their queens your nursing mothers.
[y]With their faces to the ground they shall bow down to you,
and [z]lick the dust of your feet.
Then you will know that I am the LORD;
[a]those who wait for me [b]shall not be put to shame."

24 Can the prey be taken from the mighty,
or the captives of a tyrant[5] be rescued?

[1] Hebrew *from the sea* [2] Dead Sea Scroll; Masoretic Text *Sinim* [3] Dead Sea Scroll; Masoretic Text *Your children make haste* [4] Hebrew *in their bosom* [5] Dead Sea Scroll, Syriac, Vulgate (see also verse 25); Masoretic Text *of a righteous man*

49:14–50:3 Zion may feel forgotten (49:14), but God is compassionate and sees the depth of his people's struggles and pain, promising that he will deliver those who wait for him (49:15–23). Not only does God see his people's pain; he also sees the wickedness of their oppressors and promises to "contend with those who contend with you" (49:25). While Israel was suffering as a result of her own sin (50:1; 59:1–2), this was not a position to which God would abandon them. God is not short of resources or commitment to redeem his enslaved people (50:1–2).

9[d] ch. 42:7 [e] [ch. 41:18]
10[f] Cited Rev. 7:16 [g] Rev. 7:17; See ch. 40:11
11[h] [ch. 40:4]
12[i] ch. 43:5, 6 [j] [Ps. 107:3]
13[k] See ch. 44:23 [l] ch. 40:1
14[m] [ch. 40:27; 54:6; 62:4]
15[n] [ch. 43:1; Ps. 27:10]
16[o] Song 8:6; Rev. 13:16
17[p] See Zech. 1:18-21

18[q] ch. 60:4 [r] Num. 14:21; See Ezek. 5:11 [s] [Jer. 43:12] **19**[t] [Zech. 10:10] **20**[u] ch. 54:1 [t] [See ver. 19 above] **21**[u] [See ver. 20 above] **22**[v] ch. 11:12 [w] ch. 14:2 **23**[x] ch. 60:3, 16 [y] ch. 60:14 [z] Ps. 72:9; [Mic. 7:17] [a] [ch. 40:31] [b] Ps. 25:3; Joel 2:27

25 For thus says the LORD:
[c]"Even the captives of the mighty shall be taken,
and the prey of the tyrant be rescued,
for I will contend with those who contend with you,
and I will save your children.
26 [d]I will make your oppressors eat their own flesh,
and they shall be drunk [e]with their own blood as with wine.
Then all flesh shall know
that [f]I am the LORD your Savior,
and your Redeemer, the Mighty One of Jacob."

Israel's Sin and the Servant's Obedience

50 Thus says the LORD:
"Where is [g]your mother's certificate of divorce,
with which [h]I sent her away?
Or [i]which of my creditors is it
to whom I have sold you?
[j]Behold, for your iniquities you were sold,
and for your transgressions your mother was sent away.
2 [k]Why, when I came, was there no man;
why, when I called, was there no one to answer?
[l]Is my hand shortened, that it cannot redeem?
Or have I no power to deliver?
[m]Behold, by my rebuke [n]I dry up the sea,
[o]I make the rivers a desert;
[p]their fish stink for lack of water
and die of thirst.
3 [q]I clothe the heavens with blackness
and make sackcloth their covering."

4 The Lord GOD has given [r]me
the tongue of those who are taught,
that [s]I may know how to sustain with a word
[t]him who is weary.
Morning by morning he awakens;
he awakens my ear
to hear as those who are taught.
5 [u]The Lord GOD has opened my ear,
[v]and I was not rebellious;
I turned not backward.
6 [w]I gave my back to those who strike,
and my cheeks to those who pull out the beard;
I hid not my face
from disgrace and spitting.

7 But the Lord GOD helps me;
therefore I have not been disgraced;
[x]therefore I have set my face like a flint,
and I know that I shall not be put to shame.
8 [y]He who vindicates me is near.
Who will contend with me?
Let us stand up together.
Who is my adversary?
Let him come near to me.
9 [z]Behold, the Lord GOD helps me;
who will declare me guilty?
Behold, all of them will wear out like a garment;
the moth will eat them up.

10 Who among you fears the LORD
and obeys [a]the voice of his servant?
[b]Let him who walks in darkness
and has no light
trust in the name of the LORD
and rely on his God.
11 Behold, all you who kindle a fire,
who equip yourselves with burning torches!

50:4–11 The third "Song" (vv. 4–9) portrays the servant not only as personally innocent (v. 5) but also as one who is nevertheless willing to be struck and to take the disgrace and shame for Israel (vv. 6–7). He is able to take on this substitutionary role with God's help, for his vindication and strength come from above (vv. 7–9).

As we recognize these messianic truths as applying to the work of Christ, Scripture is showing us how to respond when our sins testify against us. Our only comfort in such moments comes from looking to the suffering servant: he was innocent yet stricken on our behalf, so that we might be free from condemnation. Paul proclaims, "Who shall bring any charge against God's elect? It is God who justifies. Who is to condemn? Christ Jesus is the one who died—more than that, who was raised—who is at the right hand of God, who indeed is interceding for us" (Rom. 8:33–34).

25[c] [Matt. 12:29; Luke 11:21, 22]
26[d] [ch. 9:20; Zech. 11:9] [e] [Rev. 14:20; 16:6] [f] ch. 43:3; See Ex. 20:2

Chapter 50

1[g] Deut. 24:1 [h] Jer. 3:8; [Hos. 2:2] [i] [2 Kgs. 4:1; Matt. 18:25] [j] ch. 59:2
2[k] [ch. 42:18-23] [l] ch. 59:1; Num. 11:23 [m] Ps. 104:7; 106:9; Nah. 1:4; [ch. 19:5, 6] [n] [Ex. 14:21] [o] Josh. 3:16 [p] [Ex. 7:18, 21]
3[q] Jer. 14:22; Rev. 6:12
4[r] [Ex. 4:11] [s] [ch. 40:1, 2] [t] [Matt. 11:28]
5[u] Ps. 40:6 [v] [John 14:31; Phil. 2:8; Heb. 5:8; 10:7] **6**[w] [ch. 53:5; Matt. 26:67; 27:26; Mark 15:19; Luke 22:63] **7**[x] Ezek. 3:8, 9 **8**[y] Rom. 8:33, 34 **9**[z] ch. 41:10 **10**[a] ver. 4; ch. 49:2, 3 [b] ch. 42:16; [Mic. 7:8]

Walk by the light of your fire,
and by the torches that you have kindled!
[c]This you have from my hand:
you shall lie down in torment.

The LORD's Comfort for Zion

51 [d]"Listen to me, you who pursue righteousness,
you who seek the LORD:
look to the rock from which you were hewn,
and to the quarry from which you were dug.
2 Look to Abraham your father
and to Sarah who bore you;
for [e]he was but one when I called him,
that I might bless him and multiply him.
3 For the LORD [f]comforts Zion;
he comforts all her waste places
and makes her wilderness like [g]Eden,
her desert like [h]the garden of the LORD;
[i]joy and gladness will be found in her,
thanksgiving and the voice of song.

4 [j]"Give attention to me, my people,
and give ear to me, my nation;
[k]for a law[1] will go out from me,
and I will set my justice for a light to the peoples.
5 [l]My righteousness draws near,
my salvation has gone out,
and my arms will judge the peoples;
[m]the coastlands hope for me,
and for my arm they wait.
6 [n]Lift up your eyes to the heavens,
and look at the earth beneath;
[o]for the heavens vanish like smoke,
the earth will wear out like a garment,
and they who dwell in it will die in like manner;[2]
[p]but my salvation will be forever,
and my righteousness will never be dismayed.

7 [q]"Listen to me, you who know righteousness,
the people [r]in whose heart is my law;
[s]fear not the reproach of man,
nor be dismayed at their revilings.
8 [t]For the moth will eat them up like a garment,
and the worm will eat them like wool;
[p]but my righteousness will be forever,
and my salvation to all generations."

9 [u]Awake, awake, [v]put on strength,
O [w]arm of the LORD;
awake, [x]as in days of old,
the generations of long ago.
Was it not you who cut [y]Rahab in pieces,
who pierced [z]the dragon?
10 [a]Was it not you who dried up the sea,
the waters of the great deep,
who made the depths of the sea a way
for the redeemed to pass over?

[1] Or *for teaching*; also verse 7 [2] Or *will die like gnats*

11[c] [John 9:39]
Chapter 51
1[d] ver. 7
2[e] Ezek. 33:24
3[f] ch. 40:1; 52:9 [g] Gen. 2:8; Ezek. 28:13; 31:9; Joel 2:3 [h] Gen. 13:10 [i] ch. 35:10
4[j] Ps. 78:1 [k] ch. 2:3
5[l] ch. 46:13 [m] See ch. 11:11
6[n] ch. 40:26 [o] Ps. 102:26; [Matt. 24:25; 2 Pet. 3:10; Rev. 21:1] [p] [Ps. 102:27, 28]
7[q] ver. 1 [r] Ps. 37:31 [s] ch. 41:14; Matt. 10:28
8[t] ch. 50:9 [p] [See ver. 6 above]
9[u] ver. 17; ch. 52:1 [v] [Ps. 93:1] [w] ch. 40:10; 52:10; 53:1; Luke 1:51 [x] Ps. 44:1 [y] ch. 30:7 [z] ch. 27:1; Ps. 74:13, 14; Ezek. 29:3
10[a] ch. 43:16; Ex. 14:21; Ps. 106:9

51:1–52:12 A pattern emerges with three calls to "Listen" (i.e., "give attention"; 51:1, 4, 7) to the Lord. The sovereign Lord chose his people to be a blessing to many (51:2); as the comforter of Zion, he can reverse the pattern of the fall, returning the deadening "wilderness" to a life-giving "Eden" (51:3). The time is coming when God's "righteousness draws near" even as his "salvation has gone out" to the "coastlands," who will hope in him (51:4–5). Rather than fear the shame that comes from "the reproach of man," the people are reminded that God brings a deliverance that lasts "forever," and this can sustain them amid their current humiliations (51:6–8). With a similar eternal perspective, because of the resurrection of Christ, we can remain spiritually healthy and joyful as we face life's challenges and insecurities. For one day, Eden will be perfectly and invincibly restored, allowing us to live without insecurity, guilt, or shame.

Yet hearing is not enough. One must also "Awake, awake" (51:9). God's comfort is not meant to cultivate passivity but rather to liberate activity. As the Lord's ransomed and rescued (51:11; 52:3), the people are to sing songs of joy rather than allow fear to silence their praise. "Your Maker" is no distant deity but one who self-identifies with Israel (51:13–16). Strength is "put on" when God's message is heard, believed, and acted upon (51:9; 52:1). God's grace changes those it touches, so that with a renewed sense of God's saving presence his people are sent out, not "in haste" or "flight" but secure in his saving power—a power that can bring a new exodus from sin and hopelessness (52:11–12; cf. Ex. 13:21; 14:19).

and as one from whom men hide their
faces[1]
he was despised, and [l]we esteemed
him not.

4 [m]Surely he has borne our griefs
and carried our sorrows;
yet we esteemed him stricken,
[n]smitten by God, and afflicted.
5 [o]But he was pierced for our transgressions;
he was crushed for our iniquities;
upon him was the chastisement that
brought us peace,
[p]and with his wounds we are healed.
6 [q]All we like sheep have gone astray;
we have turned—every one—to his
own way;
[r]and the LORD has laid on him
the iniquity of us all.

7 He was oppressed, and he was afflicted,
[s]yet he opened not his mouth;
[t]like a [u]lamb that is led to the slaughter,
and like a sheep that before its shearers is silent,
so he opened not his mouth.
8 By oppression and judgment he was
taken away;
and as for his generation, [v]who considered
that he was cut off out of the land of the
living,
stricken for the transgression of my
people?
9 And they made his grave with the wicked
[w]and with a rich man in his death,
although [x]he had done no violence,
and there was no deceit in his mouth.

10 Yet [y]it was the will of the LORD to crush
him;
he has put him to grief;[2]
[z]when his soul makes[3] an offering for
guilt,
he shall see his offspring; he shall prolong his days;
[a]the will of the LORD shall prosper in his
hand.
11 Out of the anguish of his soul he shall
see[4] and be satisfied;
by his knowledge shall [b]the righteous
one, my servant,
[c]make many to be accounted righteous,
[d]and he shall bear their iniquities.
12 [e]Therefore I will divide him a portion
with the many,[5]
[f]and he shall divide the spoil with the
strong,[6]
because he poured out his soul to death
and was numbered with the transgressors;
[g]yet he bore the sin of many,
and makes intercession for the transgressors.

The Eternal Covenant of Peace

54 [h]"Sing, O barren one, who did not bear;
break forth into singing and cry
aloud,
you who have not been in labor!
For the children of [i]the desolate one [j]will
be more
than the children of her who is married," says the LORD.
2 [k]"Enlarge the place of your tent,
and let the curtains of your habitations be stretched out;

[1] Or *as one who hides his face from us* [2] Or *he has made him sick* [3] Or *when you make his soul* [4] Masoretic Text; Dead Sea Scroll *he shall see light* [5] Or *with the great* [6] Or *with the numerous*

Few passages in the Old Testament so clearly anticipate and give texture to the person and work of Jesus. These verses helped the apostles make sense of the significance of Jesus' death: he was condemned with sinners so that we might be pardoned (cf. Isa. 53:12; Luke 22:37). God providentially used this passage (Isa. 53:7–8) to allow Philip to explain the gospel to the Ethiopian eunuch (Acts 8:26–40) and encourage his baptism (cf. Isa. 52:15). Peter appears to apply the passage (53:5, 9) to Christ hanging on a tree: "by his wounds you have been healed" (1 Pet. 2:22–24).

For both Isaiah and Peter, such grace transforms the receiver, so that having been healed, believers are called to "die to sin and live to righteousness" (1 Pet. 2:24).

54:1–17 Three times the readers are reminded of God's compassion, which is taken as his great "yes" to his people (cf. 2 Cor. 1:19–20). While Israel had been disobedient, only for a brief time did they experience God's chastisement. Such times always ended with his "great compassion" to gather his people, to draw them up again into

3[l] [John 1:10, 11]
4[m] [Matt. 8:17] [n] Ps. 69:26
5[o] [Rom. 4:25] [p] Cited 1 Pet. 2:24
6[q] Cited 1 Pet. 2:25; [Jer. 50:6, 17] [r] 2 Cor. 5:21; [ver. 10; Col. 2:14]
7[s] Matt. 26:63; Mark 14:61; John 19:9; 1 Pet. 2:23 [t] Cited Acts 8:32 [u] [Jer. 11:19]
8[v] ch. 57:1
9[w] Matt. 27:57, 60 [x] Cited 1 Pet. 2:22; [Heb. 4:15; 1 John 3:5]
10[y] [ver. 4] [z] [ver. 6] [a] [ch. 44:28]
11[b] [1 John 2:1] [c] Acts 13:39; Rom. 5:18, 19 [d] [ver. 5]
12[e] ch. 52:13; [Phil. 2:9] [f] [Col. 2:15] [g] ver. 6, 8, 10

Chapter 54 **1**[h] Cited Gal. 4:27 [i] ch. 62:4 [j] [1 Sam. 2:5] **2**[k] [ch. 49:19, 20]

do not hold back; lengthen your cords
and strengthen your stakes.
3 [l]For you will spread abroad to the right
and to the left,
and your offspring will possess the
nations
and will people the desolate cities.

4 "Fear not, [m]for you will not be ashamed;
be not confounded, for you will not
be disgraced;
for you will forget the shame of your
youth,
and the reproach of your widowhood
you will remember no more.
5 [n]For your Maker is your husband,
the LORD of hosts is his name;
[o]and the Holy One of Israel is your
Redeemer,
[p]the God of the whole earth he is
called.
6 [q]For the LORD has called you
like a wife deserted and grieved in
spirit,
like a wife of youth when she is cast off,
says your God.
7 [r]For a brief moment I deserted you,
but with great compassion I will
gather you.
8 [r]In overflowing anger for a moment
I hid my face from you,
[s]but with everlasting love I will have
compassion on you,"
says the LORD, your Redeemer.

9 "This is like [t]the days of Noah[1] to me:
as I swore that the waters of Noah
should no more go over the earth,
so I have sworn that I will not be angry
with you,
and will not rebuke you.
10 For the mountains may depart
and the hills be removed,
but my steadfast love shall not depart
from you,
and [u]my covenant of peace shall not
be removed,"
says the LORD, who has compassion
on you.

11 [v]"O afflicted one, storm-tossed and not
comforted,
behold, [w]I will set your stones in antimony,
[x]and lay your foundations with sap-
phires.[2]
12 I will make your pinnacles of agate,[3]
your gates of carbuncles,[4]
and all your wall of precious stones.
13 [y]All your children [z]shall be taught by the
LORD,
[a]and great shall be the peace of your
children.
14 In righteousness you shall be established;
you shall be far from oppression, for
you shall not fear;
and from terror, for it shall not come
near you.
15 [b]If anyone stirs up strife,
it is not from me;

[1] Some manuscripts *For this is as the waters of Noah* [2] Or *lapis lazuli* [3] Or *jasper*, or *ruby* [4] Or *crystal*

3[l] [ch. 11:14; Gen. 28:14]
4[m] ch. 45:17
5[n] ch. 62:4, 5; [Hos. 2:7] [o] See ch. 43:14 [p] Zech. 14:9
6[q] ver. 1; [ch. 49:14; 60:15; 62:4]
7[r] [ch. 26:20]
8[r] [See ver. 7 above] [s] ch. 55:3
9[t] Gen. 8:21; 9:11
10[u] Num. 25:12; Ezek. 34:25; 37:26; [Mal. 2:5]
11[v] ch. 51:21 [w] [ch. 60:10] [x] [Rev. 21:19]
13[y] Cited John 6:45 [z] Jer. 31:33, 34 [a] [ch. 9:7; Ps. 119:165]
15[b] [ch. 8:9, 10]

his "everlasting love" out of which his "covenant of peace shall not be removed" (Isa. 54:7, 8, 10; cf. 55:7). This preservation and "vindication" of God's people grows out of the substitutionary sacrifice made by the suffering servant, the One through whom God achieves their redemption (54:5, 8, 17; cf. 52:13–53:12). As seen before, while God is confessed as Creator of the universe, he pledges himself in particular to Israel: "your Maker is your husband," and "the Holy One of Israel is your Redeemer" (54:5). God's people should not be afraid, since God has made his covenant promise: "I have sworn that I will not be angry with you, and will not rebuke you" (v. 9).

In the New Testament, these promises are applied to the church, the "children of promise" who are liberated by the gospel (54:1; Gal. 4:27–31). Set free in Christ from sin's condemnation, we are also freed to live in loving service to others. In this way our lives are conformed to the cross-shaped life of the suffering servant (Gal. 5:1–15).

In the Gospels, Jesus too draws on this text (Isa. 54:13) to make it clear that he has been uniquely sent from the Father. Receiving Jesus' words is recognized as being "taught by God" himself (John 6:42–46). The ancient promises and provision of God (e.g., manna) are now realized in Jesus' very flesh and blood. As the compassionate servant, Jesus anticipates his sacrificial death and promises eternal life to those who trust in him (John 6:47–59).

whoever stirs up strife with you
shall fall because of you.
16 Behold, I have created the smith
who blows the fire of coals
and produces a weapon for its purpose.
I have also created the ravager to destroy;
17 no weapon that is fashioned against
you shall succeed,
and you shall refute every tongue that
rises against you in judgment.
This is the heritage of the servants of the
LORD
[c]and their vindication[1] from me,
declares the LORD."

The Compassion of the LORD

55 [d]"Come, everyone who thirsts,
come to the waters;
and he who has no money,
[e]come, buy and eat!
Come, buy wine and milk
without money and without price.
2 [f]Why do you spend your money for that
which is not bread,
and your labor for that which does
not satisfy?
Listen diligently to me, and eat what is
good,
and delight yourselves in rich food.
3 Incline your ear, and come to me;
[g]hear, that your soul may live;
[h]and I will make with you an everlasting
covenant,
[i]my steadfast, sure love for [j]David.
4 [k]Behold, I made him a witness to the peoples,
[l]a leader and commander for the peoples.
5 [k]Behold, you shall call a nation that you
do not know,
and [m]a nation that did not know you
shall run to you,
because of the LORD your God, and of
the Holy One of Israel,
[n]for he has glorified you.
6 [o]"Seek the LORD while he may be found;
call upon him while he is near;
7 let the wicked forsake his way,
and the unrighteous man his thoughts;
let him return to the LORD, that he may
have compassion on him,
and to our God, for he will abundantly pardon.
8 For my thoughts are not your thoughts,
neither are your ways my ways,
declares the LORD.
9 [p]For as the heavens are higher than the
earth,
so are my ways higher than your ways
and my thoughts than your thoughts.
10 [q]"For as the rain and the snow come down
from heaven
and do not return there but water the
earth,
making it bring forth and sprout,
[r]giving seed to the sower and bread to
the eater,

[1] Or *righteousness*

55:1–13 We are often tempted to think we must clean ourselves up to be worthy of God's concern. But that is to misunderstand God and his saving grace. In our desperate thirst and poverty God says, "Come, buy and eat!" (v. 1). *And all is free*—obtained "without money and without price" (v. 1). His bounteous goodness is only for those who resist the impulse to pay for it. His love and grace come to us not because we have been so good but because he has been so gracious. In light of the mercy secured for God's people by "the arm of the LORD" (53:1), the call for repentance goes out. God's invitation echoes through creation, calling us to seek, hear, and come to the Lord (55:2–11). As we behold God's righteousness and are honest about our sin, we become able to experience his saving forgiveness. We *turn* to the Lord and forsake our unrighteous ways. Then we enter into the movement of divine generosity, proclaiming his grace and caring for others in need (v. 10; 2 Cor. 9:8–15).

Here we find hope and a promise that this good news is meant for the whole world: "a nation that did not know you shall run to you" (Isa. 55:5). And now, as Christians who proclaim Christ crucified and risen (v. 3; cf. Acts 13:34), we go out to the ends of the world, proclaiming his name to all peoples and nations (cf. Ps. 48:10; 65:5–8; Isa. 24:16; Matt. 28:19–20). We go confident in God's promise that when his word goes out, it never fails. It extends his praise across his creation (Isa. 55:11–13).

17[c] ch. 45:24, 25

Chapter 55

1[d] ch. 44:3; John 7:37; [Matt. 5:6] [e] Prov. 9:5
2[f] [John 6:27]
3[g] Prov. 4:4 [h] ch. 61:8; Jer. 32:40; Ezek. 37:26; [ch. 54:8; 59:21] [i] Ps. 89:33-35; [Acts 13:34] [j] Jer. 30:9
4[k] Ps. 18:43 [l] Dan. 9:25; Mic. 5:2; Acts 5:31; Rev. 17:14; 19:16; [ch. 9:6, 7]
5[k] [See ver. 4 above] [m] Zech. 8:22, 23 [n] [ch. 44:23; Acts 3:13]
6[o] Ps. 32:6; Amos 5:4
9[p] Ps. 103:11
10[q] [Ps. 148:8] [r] [2 Cor. 9:10]

11 so shall my word be that goes out from
my mouth;
it shall not return to me empty,
but [s]it shall accomplish that which
I purpose,
and shall succeed in the thing for
which I sent it.

12 [t]"For you shall go out in joy
and be led forth in peace;
[u]the mountains and the hills before you
shall break forth into singing,
and all the trees of the field shall clap
their hands.
13 [v]Instead of the thorn shall come up the
cypress;
instead of the brier shall come up the
myrtle;
and it shall make a name for the LORD,
an everlasting sign that shall not be
cut off."

Salvation for Foreigners

56 Thus says the LORD:
"Keep justice, and do righteousness,
[w]for soon my salvation will come,
and my righteousness be revealed.
2 Blessed is the man who does this,
and the son of man who holds it fast,
[x]who keeps the Sabbath, not profaning it,
and keeps his hand from doing any
evil."

3 Let not [y]the foreigner who has joined
himself to the LORD say,
"The LORD will surely separate me
from his people";
and let not the eunuch say,
"Behold, I am [z]a dry tree."
4 For thus says the LORD:
"To the eunuchs [x]who keep my Sabbaths,
who choose the things that please me
and hold fast my covenant,
5 [a]I will give in my house and within my
walls
a [b]monument and a name
better than sons and daughters;
[c]I will give them an everlasting name
that shall not be cut off.

6 "And [y]the foreigners who join themselves
to the LORD,
to minister to him, to love the name
of the LORD,
and to be his servants,
everyone [x]who keeps the Sabbath and
does not profane it,
and holds fast my covenant—
7 [d]these I will bring to [e]my holy mountain,
and make them joyful in my house of
prayer;
[f]their burnt offerings and their sacrifices
will be accepted on my altar;
for [g]my house shall be called a house of
prayer
for all peoples."
8 The Lord GOD,
[h]who gathers the outcasts of Israel,
declares,
[i]"I will gather yet others to him
besides those already gathered."

11 [s]ch. 40:8
12 [t]ch. 35:10; [ch. 48:20, 21; 52:12] [u]ch. 44:23; Ps. 98:8
13 [v]ch. 35:1, 2; 41:19

Chapter 56
1 [w]ch. 46:12, 13; 51:5, 6
2 [x]ch. 58:13
3 [y]ch. 14:1; [Deut. 23:7, 8] [z][Ezek. 17:24; 20:47]
4 [x][See ver. 2 above]
5 [a][1 Tim. 3:15; Rev. 3:12] [b][2 Sam. 18:18; John 1:12] [c][2 Tim. 2:19]
6 [y][See ver. 3 above] [x][See ver. 2 above]
7 [d]ch. 65:1; [ch. 19:24, 25] [e]ch. 2:2 [f][Rom. 15:16] [g]Cited Matt. 21:13; Mark 11:17; Luke 19:46
8 [h]ch. 11:12 [i]John 10:16; Eph. 1:10; See Eph. 2:11-16

56:1–66:24 Turning from a section of Isaiah where the looming concern is the Babylonian exile (chs. 40–55), we now enter the final section of the book, where attention turns toward Israel's return home (chs. 56–66).

56:1–8 God's saving purposes are ultimately expansive, reaching out beyond the territory of ancient Israel. Symbolized through the "foreigner" and the "eunuch," God shows his redemptive acceptance to those who are "joined" to the Lord, for the Lord's house is not confined within the physical walls of the temple (vv. 3–6).

God's house was always meant to be "a house of prayer for *all* peoples" (v. 7). Given God's particular concern for the neglected and vulnerable, which appears throughout Isaiah, it should be no surprise that the Lord here promises to gather "the outcasts of Israel" as well as those not already within the fold (v. 8).

Jesus takes this text and proclaims it as he cleanses the temple. Embodying God's promises and purposes, the blind and lame come to him to be healed in the now cleansed temple (Matt. 21:12–14). We discover that Jesus himself is God's holy temple, and to come to Christ is to be in God's presence (e.g., John 1:14; 2:19). As the resurrected temple, Jesus becomes the focus of salvation that is now proclaimed by his disciples, not only in Jerusalem and Judah, but from Samaria "to the end of the earth" (Acts 1:8).

Israel's Irresponsible Leaders

9 [j]All you beasts of the field, come to
devour—
all you beasts in the forest.
10 [k]His watchmen are blind;
they are all without knowledge;
they are all silent [l]dogs;
they cannot bark,
dreaming, lying down,
loving to slumber.
11 [m]The dogs have a mighty appetite;
they never have enough.
But [n]they are shepherds who have no
understanding;
they have all turned to their own way,
[o]each to his own gain, one and all.
12 [p]"Come," they say, "let me get wine;
let us fill ourselves with strong drink;
[q]and tomorrow will be like this day,
great beyond measure."

Israel's Futile Idolatry

57 The righteous man perishes,
and no one lays it to heart;
[r]devout men are taken away,
while no one understands.
For the righteous man is taken away
from calamity;
2 [s]he enters into peace;
they rest [t]in their beds
who walk in their uprightness.
3 But you, draw near,
sons of the sorceress,
[u]offspring of the adulterer and the
loose woman.
4 Whom are you mocking?
Against whom [v]do you open your
mouth wide
and stick out your tongue?
Are you not children of [w]transgression,
[x]the offspring of deceit,
5 you who burn with lust among [y]the oaks,[1]
under every green tree,
[z]who slaughter your children in the valleys,
under the clefts of the rocks?
6 Among the smooth stones of [a]the valley
is your portion;
they, they, are your lot;
to them you have poured out a drink
offering,
you have brought a grain offering.
Shall I relent for these things?
7 [b]On a high and lofty mountain
you have set your bed,
and there you went up to offer sacrifice.
8 Behind the door and the doorpost
you have set up your memorial;
for, deserting me, [c]you have uncovered
your bed,
you have gone up to it,
[d]you have made it wide;
and you have made a covenant for yourself with them,
you have loved their bed,
you have looked on nakedness.[2]
9 You journeyed to the king with oil
and multiplied your perfumes;
[e]you sent your envoys far off,
and sent down even to Sheol.
10 You were wearied with the length of
your way,
[f]but you did not say, "It is hopeless";
you found new life for your strength,
and so you were not faint.[3]
11 [g]Whom did you dread and fear,
[h]so that you lied,

[1] Or *among the terebinths* [2] Or *on a monument* (see 56:5); Hebrew *on a hand* [3] Hebrew *and so you were not sick*

56:9–57:13 Even as God extends his promises, there is also the danger that the "watchmen are blind," indulgent and neglectful rather than offering the protection and vigilance of wise shepherds (56:10–12). Consequently, the people are enticed by sorcery, sexual perversion, and false spirituality (57:1–10; cf. 2 Kings 21:1–16), a path that leads to ruin (e.g., the slaughtering of their children; Isa. 57:5; cf. 2 Kings 21:6) rather than life. Idols cannot hear the cries of the people, and they do not bring deliverance (Isa. 57:13).

We must always be mindful of the temptation to turn to trendy forms of spirituality rather than trusting in the God of Abraham, Isaac, and Jacob, who is the God of the living, not the dead (Matt. 22:32). Jesus, the long-promised Seed of Abraham and David, is not trendy. He is "the same yesterday and today and forever" (Heb. 13:8). But unlike idols created by current trends and tastes, he will never let us down. Unlike idols, he always remains a tender and compassionate master (Matt. 11:28–30). Whatever happens in your life, bank on him.

9[j] Jer. 12:9; Ezek. 34:8
10[k] ch. 62:6; Jer. 6:17 [l] [Phil. 3:2]
11[m] Ezek. 34:2, 3 [n] [Jer. 23:1] [o] Jer. 6:13
12[p] [ch. 28:7] [q] [ch. 22:13; Prov. 23:35; Luke 12:19; 1 Cor. 15:32]
Chapter 57
1[r] Ps. 12:1
2[s] [Luke 2:29] [t] 2 Chr. 16:14; Ezek. 32:25
3[u] [John 8:41, 42]
4[v] [Ps. 35:21] [w] ch. 46:8, 9 [x] [ch. 1:4]
5[y] ch. 1:29; 2 Kgs. 16:4 [z] Ezek. 16:20, 21
6[a] [2 Kgs. 23:10]
7[b] 1 Kgs. 14:23; Ezek. 16:16, 24
8[c] Ezek. 16:25; [Hos. 1:2] [d] [Ezek. 23:17] **9**[e] Ezek. 16:26, 28, 29 **10**[f] Jer. 2:25; 18:12 **11**[g] [ch. 51:12, 13] [h] Ps. 78:10, 36

and did not remember me,
did not lay it to heart?
[i]Have I not held my peace, even for a long time,
and you do not fear me?
12 I will declare your righteousness and your deeds,
but they will not profit you.
13 [j]When you cry out, let your collection of idols deliver you!
The wind will carry them all off,
a breath will take them away.
[k]But he who takes refuge in me shall possess the land
and shall inherit [l]my holy mountain.

Comfort for the Contrite

14 And it shall be said,
[m]"Build up, build up, prepare the way,
remove every obstruction from my people's way."
15 For thus says [n]the One who is high and lifted up,
who inhabits eternity, whose name is [o]Holy:
[p]"I dwell in the high and holy place,
and also [q]with him who is of a contrite and lowly spirit,
[r]to revive the spirit of the lowly,
and to revive the heart of the contrite.
16 [s]For I will not contend forever,
nor will I always be angry;
for the spirit would grow faint before me,
and the breath of life that I made.
17 Because of the iniquity of his [t]unjust gain I was angry,
I struck him; I hid my face and was angry,
but he went on backsliding in the way of his own heart.
18 I have seen his ways, [u]but I will heal him;
I will lead him [v]and restore comfort to him and his mourners,
19 [w]creating [x]the fruit of the lips.
[y]Peace, peace, [z]to the far and to the near,"
says the LORD,
[u]"and I will heal him.
20 [a]But the wicked are like the tossing sea;
for it cannot be quiet,
and its waters toss up mire and dirt.
21 [b]There is no peace," says my God, "for the wicked."

True and False Fasting

58 "Cry aloud; do not hold back;
[c]lift up your voice like a trumpet;
[d]declare to my people their transgression,
to the house of Jacob their sins.
2 [e]Yet they seek me daily
and delight to know my ways,
as if they were a nation that did righteousness
and did not forsake the judgment of their God;
they ask of me righteous judgments;
they delight to draw near to God.
3 [f]'Why have we fasted, and you see it not?
Why have we humbled ourselves, and you take no knowledge of it?'

11[i]Ps. 50:21
13[j]Jer. 11:12 [k]Ps. 37:9 [l]ch. 11:9; 56:7; 65:11, 25
14[m]ch. 62:10; [ch. 40:3]
15[n][Mic. 6:6] [o]Luke 1:49 [p]Ps. 113:6 [q]Ps. 34:18; 138:6 [r][ch. 42:3]
16[s]Gen. 6:3; Ps. 103:9
17[t]ch. 56:11; Jer. 6:13
18[u]Jer. 3:22 [v]ch. 61:3
19[w]ch. 50:4 [x]Heb. 13:15 [y][Eph. 2:17] [z]Acts 2:39 [u][See ver. 18 above]
20[a]Jude 13
21[b]ch. 48:22
Chapter 58
1[c]Lev. 25:9; [Joel 2:1] [d]Mic. 3:8
2[e][ch. 1:11; 29:13; Zech. 7:5, 6]
3[f][Mal. 3:14]

57:14–21 God's holiness is seen in his condescension: while dwelling "in the high and holy place" he is also "with him who is of a contrite and lowly spirit" (v. 15). Rather than trust in idols, God's people are called to return to him, not by cleaning themselves up but by confessing their sin. What an amazing and counterintuitive pathway of healing. God offers healing, restoration, and comfort to those who mourn over their fallenness rather than those who seek in a self-generated way to overcome it (v. 18). Those who humbly bow down before the Lord hear his pardon of "Peace, peace" which goes out "to the far and to the near" (v. 19). But the wicked drown out the calls for repentance with their arrogant actions and zealous running after false spiritualities: for them, therefore, "there is no peace" (vv. 20–21).

The gracious character of God revealed by Isaiah reminds us that only in Christ is true peace available (John 14:27). And it is available to any who ask for it.

58:1–14 Echoing the divine concerns highlighted earlier in Isaiah (e.g., 1:2–31), God makes it clear that he is not interested in empty rituals but desires heartfelt humility and life-giving action. Here the perversion of the Sabbath serves as the example. While the people "Sabbath" and fast, they do so in a way that ironically promotes self-righteousness and self-absorption rather than authentic humility and concern for neighbor. Emptied of love, such ritual observance "will not make your voice to be heard on high" (58:4).

Behold, in the day of your fast you seek
your own pleasure,[1]
[g]and oppress all your workers.
4 Behold, you fast only to quarrel and to
fight
and to hit with a wicked fist.
Fasting like yours this day
will not make your voice to be heard
on high.
5 [h]Is such the fast that I choose,
[i]a day for a person to humble himself?
Is it to bow down his head like a reed,
and to spread sackcloth and ashes
under him?
Will you call this a fast,
and a day acceptable to the LORD?

6 "Is not this the fast that I choose:
[j]to loose the bonds of wickedness,
to undo the straps [k]of the yoke,
to let the oppressed[2] go free,
and to break every yoke?
7 Is it not [l]to share your bread with the
hungry
and bring the homeless poor into
your house;
when you see the naked, to cover him,
[m]and not to hide yourself from your
own flesh?
8 [n]Then shall your light break forth like
the dawn,
[o]and your healing shall spring up
speedily;
[p]your righteousness shall go before you;
[q]the glory of the LORD shall be your
rear guard.
9 Then you shall call, and the LORD will
answer;
you shall cry, and he will say, 'Here
I am.'
If you take away [r]the yoke from your
midst,
[s]the pointing of the finger, and speaking wickedness,
10 [t]if you pour yourself out for the hungry
and satisfy the desire of the afflicted,
[n]then shall your light rise in the darkness
and your gloom be as the noonday.
11 And the LORD will guide you continually
and satisfy your desire in scorched
places
and make your bones strong;
and you shall be [u]like a watered garden,
like a spring of water,
whose waters do not fail.
12 [v]And your ancient ruins shall be rebuilt;
you shall raise up the foundations of
many generations;
you shall be called the repairer of the
breach,
the restorer of streets to dwell in.

13 [w]"If you turn back your foot from the
Sabbath,
from doing your pleasure[3] on my holy
day,

[1] Or *pursue your own business* [2] Or *bruised* [3] Or *business*

No, God brings rest for his people, and this is meant to provide "rest" from the chaos and tyranny of a fallen world. Therefore, a genuine Sabbath promotes justice rather than neglect. Such rest seeks to reverse the destabilizing effects of sin by providing food to the hungry and shelter to the homeless (vv. 6–7). Sabbath rest is meant to simultaneously point back to the goodness of creation and forward to the promise of God's new creation.

A wonderful irony emerges. By forgetting yourself and your own pleasures on the Sabbath (v. 13), your pleasure and satisfaction in God increases (v. 14). And this is what Jesus taught all along: "the Sabbath was made for man, not man for the Sabbath" (Mark 2:27). God was not trying to make life miserable or rigid by calling for Sabbath observance, but it was always his desire to foster healing, rest, renewal, and grace. Rightly understood, Sabbath rest promotes communion between God and man, between man and man, and even between humanity and the rest of creation. Only Jesus, the Son of Man, is Lord of the Sabbath (Matt. 12:8; Luke 6:5; cf. Heb. 4:1–16). It was Jesus who "scandalously" worked on this day to forgive the sinner, heal the sick, and enjoy creation (e.g., Matt. 12:1–21; Luke 13:10–16; John 9:13–17). As we find our rest in him, our communion with God and others is properly renewed.

The gospel is God's final, eschatological word of rest. While we will not be finally at rest until the new earth, true soul-rest has broken into this diseased world. The Sabbath points to and anticipates the rest wrought in the gospel of grace, in which Jesus worked for us so that we can rest in him (Matt. 11:28–30; Heb. 3:1–4:13).

3[g] [ch. 60:17]; See Neh. 5:1-8
5[h] Zech. 7:5 [i] Lev. 16:29
6[j] See Neh. 5:10-12 [k] ver. 9
7[l] ver. 10; Ezek. 18:7; [Matt. 25:35] [m] Neh. 5:5
8[n] [Job 11:17] [o] Jer. 30:17 [p] Ps. 85:13 [q] [ch. 52:12]
9[r] ver. 6 [s] Prov. 6:13
10[t] ver. 7, 8 [n] [See ver. 8 above]
11[u] Jer. 31:12
12[v] ch. 61:4; 65:21; [Ezra 6:14; Neh. 4:6]
13[w] ch. 56:2; See Neh. 13:15-21

and call the Sabbath a delight
and the holy day of the LORD honorable;
if you honor it, not going your own ways,
or seeking [x]your own pleasure,[1] or talking idly;[2]
14 then you shall take delight in the LORD,
[y]and I will make you ride on the heights of the earth;[3]
[z]I will feed you with the heritage of Jacob your father,
[a]for the mouth of the LORD has spoken."

Evil and Oppression

59 Behold, [b]the LORD's hand is not shortened, that it cannot save,
or his ear dull, that it cannot hear;
2 [c]but your iniquities have made a separation
between you and your God,
and your sins have hidden his face from you
so that he does not hear.
3 [d]For your hands are defiled with blood
and your fingers with iniquity;
your lips have spoken lies;
your tongue mutters wickedness.
4 [e]No one enters suit justly;
no one goes to law honestly;
they rely on empty pleas, they speak lies,
[f]they conceive mischief and give birth to iniquity.
5 They hatch adders' eggs;
they weave the spider's web;
he who eats their eggs dies,
and from one that is crushed a viper is hatched.
6 [g]Their webs will not serve as clothing;
men will not cover themselves with what they make.
Their works are works of iniquity,
and deeds of violence are in their hands.
7 [h]Their feet run to evil,
and they are swift to shed innocent blood;
their thoughts are thoughts of iniquity;
desolation and destruction are in their highways.
8 The way of peace they do not know,
and there is no justice in their paths;
they have made their roads crooked;
[i]no one who treads on them knows peace.

9 Therefore justice is far from us,
and righteousness does not overtake us;
[j]we hope for light, and behold, darkness,
and for brightness, but we walk in gloom.
10 [k]We grope for the wall like the blind;
we grope like those who have no eyes;
we stumble at noon as in the twilight,
[l]among those in full vigor we are like dead men.

[1] Or *pursuing your own business* [2] Hebrew *or speaking a word* [3] Or *of the land*

13[x] ver. 3
14[y] Deut. 32:13 [z] Jer. 50:19 [a] ch. 1:20
Chapter 59
1[b] ch. 50:2; Num. 11:23
2[c] Jer. 5:25
3[d] ch. 1:15
4[e] [ver. 14] [f] Job 15:35; Ps. 7:14
6[g] Job 8:14
7[h] Prov. 1:16; Cited Rom. 3:15-17
8[i] ch. 48:22; 57:21
9[j] [ver. 11; ch. 60:2]
10[k] Deut. 28:29; Job 5:14; 12:25; See ch. 42:18-20 [l] [1 Cor. 4:9, 10]

59:1–21 Sin gives birth to sin (v. 12; cf. James 1:15). We cannot merely look within ourselves in morbid introspection to properly assess our spiritual state, since often private and public transgressions go together (e.g., Isa. 59:14–15). Here Isaiah places the people's sin and guilt in the public arena. He is again concerned that their apathy about justice is a sign of deeper problems, both for individuals and for the community (e.g., vv. 8, 9, 11, 14, 15; cf. Rom. 3:15–17). Such indifference places them at odds with God, who declares, "I the LORD love justice; I hate robbery and wrong" (Isa. 61:8). When he sees injustice unaddressed, he is "displeased" (59:15). Consequently, when calls for repentance are ignored, such iniquities make "a separation between you and your God" (v. 2).

Out of his commitment to his holy justice, the Creator will act, for his "hand is not shortened, that it cannot save, or his ear dull, that it cannot hear" (v. 1). God will hear and he will act. Seeing none able to make intercession in this situation, God promises that "his own arm" will bring salvation (v. 16). His salvation comes clothed in righteousness, bringing redemption and restoration (vv. 16–17, 20; cf. Rom. 11:26–27). Those filled with God's Spirit go forth as God's offspring, now seeking to reflect his values and grace (Isa. 59:21)

In Isaiah, God arms himself for war (v. 17). In the New Testament, however, it is *believers* who are armed for *spiritual* war (Eph. 6:10–18; 1 Tim. 1:18; 6:12). How can this be? The answer lies in the glorious truth that we are united to Christ, who vanquished the enemy (Col. 2:15) and whose Spirit enables us to do likewise (John 14:12; 16:7).

11 We all growl like bears;
[m]we moan and moan like doves;
[n]we hope for justice, but there is none;
for salvation, but it is far from us.
12 For our transgressions are multiplied before you,
and our sins testify against us;
for our transgressions are with us,
and we know our iniquities:
13 transgressing, and denying the LORD,
and turning back from following our God,
[o]speaking oppression and revolt,
conceiving and uttering from the heart lying words.

Judgment and Redemption

14 [p]Justice is turned back,
and righteousness stands far away;
for truth has stumbled in the public squares,
and uprightness cannot enter.
15 Truth is lacking,
and he who departs from evil makes himself a prey.
The LORD saw it, and it displeased him[1]
that there was no justice.
16 [q]He saw that there was no man,
and wondered that there was no one to intercede;
then his own arm brought him salvation,
and his righteousness upheld him.
17 [r]He put on righteousness as a breastplate,
and a helmet of salvation on his head;
he put on garments of vengeance for clothing,
and wrapped himself in [s]zeal as a cloak.
18 [t]According to their deeds, so will he repay,
wrath to his adversaries, repayment to his enemies;
[u]to the coastlands he will render repayment.
19 [v]So they shall fear the name of the LORD from the west,
and his glory from the rising of the sun;
[w]for he will come like a rushing stream,[2]
which the wind of the LORD drives.

20 [x]"And [y]a Redeemer will come to Zion,
to those in Jacob who turn from transgression," declares the LORD.

21 "And as for me, [z]this is my covenant with
them," says the LORD: "My Spirit that is upon
you, [a]and my words that I have put in your
mouth, shall not depart out of your mouth,
or out of the mouth of your offspring, or out
of the mouth of your children's offspring,"
says the LORD, "from this time forth and
forevermore."

The Future Glory of Israel

60 [b]Arise, shine, for your light has come,
and [c]the glory of the LORD has risen upon you.
2 For behold, darkness shall cover the earth,
and thick darkness the peoples;
but the LORD will arise upon you,
and his glory will be seen upon you.
3 [d]And nations shall come to your light,
and kings to the brightness of your rising.
4 [e]Lift up your eyes all around, and see;
they all gather together, they come to you;
[f]your sons shall come from afar,
and your daughters shall be carried on the hip.

[1] Hebrew *and it was evil in his eyes* [2] Hebrew *a narrow river*

60:1–9 Darkness is contrasted with Zion's light, which arises as the Lord and his glory shine forth (vv. 1–2). Escape from darkness is possible as "nations" and "kings" come to the Lord's light, gathering together from near and far as the call goes forth (vv. 3–4; cf. 55:1; Ps. 67:1–2; Rev. 21:24–26). Seeing the Lord's grace, people are changed, becoming "radiant" with hearts overflowing with worship and confidence in God's promises (Isa. 60:5; cf. Ps. 34:5). God declares that he himself "has made . . . beautiful" his children (Isa. 60:9)—they did not beautify themselves. As always, the message of grace is that God meets us in the moral mud and then cleanses and beautifies us by his own initiative of love.

True radiance comes only from beholding the Christ who makes us shine (2 Cor. 3:18; Phil. 2:15). Look at him. Seek him. Be transformed by his beauty.

11[m] ch. 38:14 [n] [ver. 9; ch. 46:13; 56:1]
13[o] [ver. 3, 4]
14[p] [ch. 51:4, 5]
16[q] [ch. 51:18; 63:5]
17[r] 1 Thess. 5:8; See Eph. 6:13-17 [s] [ch. 9:7]
18[t] ch. 63:4, 6 [u] [ch. 41:1, 5]
19[v] [Ps. 113:3] [w] [ch. 30:27, 28]
20[x] Cited Rom. 11:26, 27; [ch. 40:9; Joel 2:32] [y] ch. 43:14
21[z] Jer. 31:31; Heb. 8:10; 10:16 [a] ch. 51:16; [Deut. 4:10]
Chapter 60
1[b] [Eph. 5:14] [c] ch. 40:5; 58:8; Mal. 4:2

3[d] ch. 42:6; 49:6; Rev. 21:24 **4**[e] ch. 49:18 [f] ver. 9; ch. 66:20

5 Then you shall see and [g]be radiant;
your heart shall thrill and exult,[1]
because the abundance of the sea shall
be turned to you,
[h]the wealth of the nations shall come
to you.
6 A multitude of camels shall cover you,
the young camels of [i]Midian and
[j]Ephah;
all those from [k]Sheba shall come.
[l]They shall bring gold and frankincense,
and shall bring good news, the praises
of the LORD.
7 All the flocks of [m]Kedar shall be gathered
to you;
the rams of [n]Nebaioth shall minister
to you;
[o]they shall come up with acceptance on
my altar,
[p]and I will beautify my beautiful house.

8 Who are these that fly like a cloud,
and [q]like doves to their windows?
9 For [r]the coastlands shall hope for me,
[s]the ships of Tarshish first,
[t]to bring your children from afar,
their silver and gold with them,
for the name of the LORD your God,
and for the Holy One of Israel,
because [u]he has made you beautiful.

10 [v]Foreigners shall build up your walls,
and [v]their kings shall minister to you;
for in my wrath I struck you,
but in my favor I have had mercy on
you.
11 [w]Your gates shall be open continually;
day and night they shall not be shut,
[w]that people may bring to you the wealth
of the nations,
with their kings led in procession.
12 [x]For the nation and kingdom
that will not serve you shall perish;
those nations shall be utterly laid
waste.
13 [y]The glory of Lebanon shall come to you,
the cypress, the plane, and [z]the pine,
to beautify the place of my sanctuary,
and I will make the place of my feet
glorious.
14 [a]The sons of those who afflicted you
shall come bending low to you,
[b]and all who despised you
shall bow down at your feet;
[c]they shall call you the City of the LORD,
the Zion of the Holy One of Israel.

15 [d]Whereas you have been forsaken and
hated,
with no one passing through,
[e]I will make you majestic forever,
a joy from age to age.
16 [f]You shall suck the milk of nations;
you shall nurse at the breast of kings;
and you shall know that [g]I, the LORD,
am your Savior
and your Redeemer, [h]the Mighty One
of Jacob.

17 Instead of bronze I will bring gold,
and instead of iron I will bring silver;
instead of wood, bronze,
instead of stones, iron.
I will make your overseers peace
[i]and your taskmasters righteousness.
18 [j]Violence shall no more be heard in your
land,
devastation or destruction within
your borders;
[k]you shall call your walls Salvation,
and your gates Praise.

[1] Hebrew *your heart shall tremble and grow wide*

5[g] Ps. 34:5 [h] ch. 61:6
6[i] Judg. 6:5 [j] Gen. 25:4 [k] 1 Kgs. 10:1; Ps. 72:10 [l] [Matt. 2:11]
7[m] See ch. 21:16 [n] Gen. 25:13; 28:9; 36:3 [o] ch. 56:7 [p] Hag. 2:7
8[q] Hos. 11:11; [Gen. 8:9]
9[r] ch. 51:5; See ch. 11:11 [s] See ch. 2:16 [t] Gal. 4:26 [u] ch. 44:23; 55:5
10[v] ch. 45:1, 13; Zech. 6:15
11[w] [Rev. 21:25, 26]
12[x] [Zech. 14:17-19]
13[y] ch. 35:2 [z] ch. 41:19
14[a] [ch. 14:1, 2; Zech. 8:23] [b] ch. 49:23; [Rev. 3:9] [c] [ch. 1:26; 62:2]
15[d] ch. 54:6; 62:4 [e] Ps. 47:4; [ch. 65:18]

60:10–16 In the end, the vivid portrait reveals only two options: be part of the city of God that glories in the Lord, or perish (v. 12). Sober as the words are, they also offered Israel comfort and strength in the midst of facing divine chastisement (vv. 10, 15). For a time was coming when those who seemed mighty and able to abuse the people would come to bow down before their victims (v. 14). Ultimate justice for God's people is sure. We can wait on the Lord with patient, calm hope.

60:17–22 Beautiful images portray the Creator as Redeemer, so that earthly elements (e.g., sun, moon) are not necessary, for "the LORD will be your everlasting light" and "glory" (v. 19; cf. 1 Pet. 2:9). Such imagery is richly repeated in the book of Revelation, where the scenes that speak of no sun and moon are not meant as scientific description but rather as the fulfillment of the promise of God's perfect presence: no darkness exists in his all-encompassing grace. His grace is the overarching reality of the new

16[f] [ch. 49:23; 66:11, 12] [g] ch. 43:3; 49:26; [ch. 47:4] [h] Gen. 49:24; Ps. 132:2 **17**[i] [ch. 58:3] **18**[j] ch. 11:9 [k] ch. 26:1

19 [l]The sun shall be no more
your light by day,
nor for brightness shall the moon
give you light;[1]
but the LORD will be your everlasting
light,
and your God will be your glory.[2]
20 Your sun shall no more go down,
nor your moon withdraw itself;
for the LORD will be your everlasting
light,
and [m]your days of mourning shall be
ended.
21 [n]Your people shall all be righteous;
[o]they shall possess the land forever,
[p]the branch of my planting, the work of
my hands,
that I might be glorified.[3]
22 [q]The least one shall become a clan,
and the smallest one a mighty nation;
[r]I am the LORD;
in its time I will hasten it.

The Year of the LORD's Favor

61 [s]The Spirit of the Lord GOD is upon
me,
because the LORD has [t]anointed me
to bring good news to the poor;[4]
he has sent me to bind up the brokenhearted,
to proclaim liberty to the captives,
and [u]the opening of the prison to
those who are bound;[5]
2 [v]to proclaim the year of the LORD's favor,
[w]and the day of vengeance of our God;
to comfort all who mourn;
3 to grant to those who mourn in Zion—
[x]to give them a beautiful headdress
instead of ashes,
[y]the oil of gladness instead of mourning,
the garment of praise instead of a
faint spirit;
[z]that they may be called oaks of righteousness,
the planting of the LORD, [a]that he
may be glorified.[6]
4 [b]They shall build up the ancient ruins;
they shall raise up the former devastations;
they shall repair the ruined cities,
the devastations of many generations.
5 [c]Strangers shall stand and tend your
flocks;
foreigners shall be your plowmen and
vinedressers;
6 [d]but you shall be called the priests of the
LORD;
they shall speak of you as the ministers of our God;
[e]you shall eat the wealth of the nations,
and in their glory you shall boast.
7 [f]Instead of your shame there shall be a
double portion;
instead of dishonor they shall rejoice
in their lot;

[1] Masoretic Text; Dead Sea Scroll, Septuagint, Targum add *by night* [2] Or *your beauty* [3] Or *that I might display my beauty* [4] Or *afflicted*
[5] Or *the opening* [of the eyes] *to those who are blind*; Septuagint *and recovery of sight to the blind* [6] Or *that he may display his beauty*

creation (e.g., Rev. 21:23; 22:5; cf. Isa. 65:17–25). Looking to these promises as they are fulfilled in Christ reminds us why he himself is "the light of the world" (John 8:12), and we patiently await and long for his day of light and rest.

61:1–11 "For I the LORD love justice; I hate robbery and wrong" (v. 8). These words capture key aspects of the mission of the Anointed One described here, and Jesus employs this passage as part of his self-revelation. Before a packed synagogue in Nazareth, Jesus reads from Isaiah 61's description of the Spirit-filled one who uniquely comes to bring good news to the poor, liberty to the captives, and healing to the sick (vv. 1–2; cf. Luke 4:18–19). "Today this Scripture has been fulfilled," Jesus proclaims, making it clear that he is the anticipated Messiah who has come to bring the promised renewal (Luke 4:21; cf. Luke 7:22).

Jesus intentionally combined his ministries of caring for people physically and spiritually, for God is concerned for us as complete creatures of his design. Our bodies, minds, wills, and affections were created for free communion with God, but sin has affected them all. The Messiah's coming marks the time when a new creation is to be ushered in, which is what happens when the "firstborn from the dead" rises on the third day (Col. 1:18; Rev. 1:5). We who are clothed in the "garments of salvation" and are covered "with the robe of righteousness" are his bride, and we wait for the great consummation (Isa. 61:10; cf. Isa. 59:17; Zech. 3:4; Rev. 21:2–7).

19[l] Zech. 14:6, 7; Rev. 21:23; 22:5; [ch. 24:23; 30:26]
20[m] ch. 35:10; 65:19; Rev. 21:4
21[n] ch. 52:1; Jer. 31:34 [o] Ps. 37:9; See Ezek. 37:25 [p] ch. 61:3
22[q] [Matt. 13:31] [r] Hab. 2:3
Chapter 61
1[s] ch. 11:2; 42:1; 48:16; Cited Luke 4:18, 19 [t] Ps. 45:7 [u] ch. 45:13; Ps. 146:7
2[v] [Lev. 25:10] [w] ch. 34:8
3[x] ver. 10; [ch. 28:5] [y] Ps. 45:7; Heb. 1:9 [z] [ch. 60:21] [a] John 15:8
4[b] Amos 9:14; See ch. 58:12
5[c] ch. 14:2; [ch. 60:10]
6[d] Ex. 19:6; 1 Pet. 2:9; [Joel 1:9] [e] ch. 60:5, 11, 16
7[f] ch. 40:2; [ch. 54:7, 8; Zech. 9:12]

therefore in their land they shall possess
a double portion;
they shall have everlasting joy.

8 [g]For I the LORD love justice;
I hate robbery and wrong;[1]
[h]I will faithfully give them their recompense,
[i]and I will make an everlasting covenant with them.
9 Their offspring shall be known among the nations,
and their descendants in the midst of the peoples;
all who see them shall acknowledge them,
that they are an offspring the LORD has blessed.

10 [j]I will greatly rejoice in the LORD;
my soul shall exult in my God,
[k]for he has clothed me with the garments of salvation;
he has covered me with the robe of righteousness,
as a bridegroom decks himself [l]like a priest with a beautiful headdress,
[m]and as a bride adorns herself with her jewels.
11 For as the earth brings forth its sprouts,
and as a garden causes what is sown in it to sprout up,
so the Lord GOD will cause [n]righteousness and praise
to sprout up before all the nations.

Zion's Coming Salvation

62 [o]For Zion's sake I will not keep silent,
and for Jerusalem's sake I will not be quiet,
[p]until her righteousness goes forth as brightness,
and her salvation as a burning torch.
2 [q]The nations shall see your righteousness,
and all the kings your glory,
[r]and you shall be called by a new name
that the mouth of the LORD will give.
3 You shall be [s]a crown of beauty in the hand of the LORD,
and a royal diadem in the hand of your God.
4 [t]You shall no more be termed [u]Forsaken,[2]
and your land shall no more be termed Desolate,[3]
[r]but you shall be called [v]My Delight Is in Her,[4]
and your land Married;[5]
for the LORD delights in you,
and your land shall be married.
5 For as a young man marries a young woman,
so [w]shall your sons marry you,
and as the bridegroom rejoices over the bride,
so [x]shall your God rejoice over you.

[1] Or *robbery with a burnt offering* [2] Hebrew *Azubah* [3] Hebrew *Shemamah* [4] Hebrew *Hephzibah* [5] Hebrew *Beulah*

8[g] Ps. 11:7; [ch. 59:15] [h] ch. 40:10; 49:4 [i] See ch. 55:3
10[j] Hab. 3:18 [k] [ch. 59:17; Zech. 3:4] [l] ver. 3 [m] ch. 49:18; Rev. 21:2
11[n] [ch. 60:18; 62:7]
Chapter 62
1[o] ver. 6, 7 [p] [Prov. 4:18]
2[q] ch. 60:3; Ps. 98:2 [r] ch. 60:14; [Rev. 2:17; 3:12]
3[s] Zech. 9:16; [ch. 54:11, 12]
4[t] Hos. 1:10; 1 Pet. 2:10; See ch. 54:6 [u] ch. 49:14; 54:1, 7; 60:15 [r] [See ver. 2 above] [v] Mal. 3:12
5[w] [ch. 51:18] [x] ch. 65:19

In the meantime, having received the Spirit of Christ, the Anointed One, we experience communion with God (e.g., Rom 8:10). And out of this communion we are set free for the holy work of loving those in need even as Christ has cared for us (Eph. 4:32–5:2). The book of Acts tells the story of the post-Pentecost church: filled with the Spirit of the Resurrected Christ, they carry out the ministry of preaching, showing concern for the needy, and taking God's healing work to all the nations (cf. Isa. 61:11).

62:1–12 The Anointed One will not stay silent; he must speak and act on behalf of his people so that they can experience salvation (v. 1). Though in the past mocked, forsaken, and exposed in her desolation, Zion is his beloved bride: "My Delight Is in Her" (v. 4). God promises a celebration uniting the Lamb and the bride—whom he himself readies for the wedding banquet (Rev. 19:7).

It can be hard for us to believe, but the imagery here is of God rejoicing over his people just like a newly married man's heart leaps as he looks at his resting wife (Isa. 62:5; cf. Zeph. 3:17). We are prone to have hard thoughts of God, but here we are reminded of his tender love and joyful commitment to us. One of the main images in the New Testament for the church is that of the bride of Christ (e.g., John 3:29; Matt. 9:15; 25:1–13; Mark 2:19): the groom has come; he has washed his bride and redeemed her. God is not motivated merely by dispassionate contractual concerns; his heart is moved by a deep love for and delight in his people (e.g., Eph. 5:25; Rev. 19:7). He fully recognizes her sins. But he desires and is able to bring her salvation. And through her, salvation goes out "to the end of the earth" (Isa. 62:11).

6 On your walls, O Jerusalem,
I have set [y]watchmen;
all the day and all the night
they shall never be silent.
You who put the LORD in remembrance,
take no rest,
7 and give him no rest
until he establishes Jerusalem
and makes it [z]a praise in the earth.
8 The LORD has sworn [a]by his right hand
and by his mighty arm:
"I will not again give [b]your grain
to be food for your enemies,
[c]and foreigners shall not drink your wine
for which you have labored;
9 but [d]those who garner it shall eat it
and praise the LORD,
and [d]those who gather it shall drink it
in the courts of my sanctuary."[1]

10 Go through, go through the gates;
[e]prepare the way for the people;
[f]build up, build up the highway;
clear it of stones;
[g]lift up a signal over the peoples.
11 Behold, the LORD has proclaimed
to the end of the earth:
[h]Say to the daughter of Zion,
[i]"Behold, your salvation comes;
behold, his reward is with him,
and his recompense before him."
12 [j]And they shall be called The Holy People,
The Redeemed of the LORD;
[k]and you shall be called Sought Out,
A City Not Forsaken.

The LORD's Day of Vengeance

63 Who is this who comes from [l]Edom,
in crimsoned garments from
[l]Bozrah,
he who is splendid in his apparel,
[m]marching in the greatness of his
strength?
"It is I, speaking in righteousness,
mighty to save."

2 Why is your [n]apparel red,
and your garments like his [o]who
treads in the winepress?

3 [p]"I have trodden the winepress alone,
[q]and from the peoples no one was with
me;
I trod them in my anger
and trampled them in my wrath;
their lifeblood[2] spattered on my garments,
and stained all my apparel.
4 [r]For the day of vengeance was in my
heart,
and my year of redemption[3] had
come.
5 I looked, but [s]there was no one to help;
I was appalled, but there was no one
to uphold;
so my own arm brought me salvation,
and my wrath upheld me.
6 I trampled down the peoples in my
anger;
[t]I made them drunk in my wrath,
and I poured out their lifeblood on
the earth."

[1] Or *in my holy courts* [2] Or *their juice*; also verse 6 [3] Or *the year of my redeemed*

Because of what God accomplishes, the people are given a new name: Holy, Redeemed, Sought Out, and Not Forsaken (vv. 2, 12; cf. Jer. 33:16; 1 Pet. 1:18–19; 2:9; Rev. 2:17). "Christians" are those whose name has been changed because of their union to the risen Lord (Acts 11:26). Such a name change also changes us. Bearing the name of Christ, we are invited to live a cross-shaped life, willing to give ourselves for the glory of his righteousness and to suffer for the joyful spread of the gospel (e.g., 1 Pet. 4:16).

63:1–6 God's vengeance and redemption are here placed together (v. 4; cf. Rev. 19:1–8). Our refuge can be only in the long-promised Messiah, for apart from him we are exposed and open to the just judgment of God against unrighteousness.

In the Bible, salvation is often portrayed in terms of warfare: God must secure the victory in order for the benefits of liberty to be experienced. At the height of human history, Christ himself overcame our three main enemies: sin, death, and the Devil (e.g., 1 Cor. 15:25; Col. 2:15 Heb. 2:14–15; 1 John 3:8). Our battle is not ultimately against flesh and blood, but against the "the cosmic powers over this present darkness" (Eph. 6:12). Christ, the conquering Messiah, alone secured the final victory over these foes. We battle on, then, as those who know that the final outcome is secure.

6[y] ch. 52:8; 56:10
7[z] ch. 60:18; [ch. 61:11; Zeph. 3:20]
8[a] [Heb. 6:13] [b] Deut. 28:33; Jer. 5:17 [c] [ch. 65:21, 22]
9[d] [Deut. 12:12; 14:23, 26]
10[e] ch. 40:3 [f] ch. 57:14 [g] ch. 11:10; 49:22
11[h] Zech. 9:9; [Matt. 21:5; John 12:15] [i] ch. 40:10
12[j] ch. 61:6 [k] ver. 4; [ch. 61:4]
Chapter 63
1[l] ch. 34:6 [m] [Ps. 68:7]
2[n] Rev. 19:13 [o] [Lam. 1:15; Rev. 14:20; 19:15]
3[p] [Joel 3:13] [q] [ch. 59:16]
4[r] ch. 34:8
5[s] [ch. 59:16]
6[t] ch. 49:26

The LORD's Mercy Remembered

7 I will recount the steadfast love of the LORD,
the praises of the LORD,
according to all that the LORD has granted us,
[u]and the great goodness to the house of Israel
that he has granted them according to his compassion,
according to the abundance of his steadfast love.
8 For he said, "Surely they are my people,
children who will not deal falsely."
And he became their Savior.
9 [v]In all their affliction he was afflicted,[1]
and the angel of his presence saved them;
[w]in his love and in his pity he redeemed them;
[x]he lifted them up and carried them all the days of old.

10 [y]But they rebelled
[z]and grieved his Holy Spirit;
therefore he turned to be their enemy,
and himself fought against them.
11 Then he remembered [a]the days of old,
of Moses and his people.[2]
[b]Where is he who brought them up out of the sea
with the shepherds of his flock?
Where is he who put in the midst of them
his Holy Spirit,
12 who caused his glorious arm
to go at the right hand of Moses,
[c]who divided the waters before them
[d]to make for himself an everlasting name,
13 who led them through the depths?
Like a horse in the desert,
they did not stumble.
14 Like livestock that go down into the valley,
[e]the Spirit of the LORD gave them rest.
So you led your people,
[d]to make for yourself a glorious name.

Prayer for Mercy

15 [f]Look down from heaven and see,
[g]from your holy and beautiful[3] habitation.
Where are [h]your zeal and your might?
The stirring of your inner parts and your compassion
are held back from me.
16 For [i]you are our Father,
though Abraham does not know us,
and Israel does not acknowledge us;
you, O LORD, are our Father,
[j]our Redeemer from of old is your name.
17 O LORD, why do you make us wander from your ways
and [k]harden our heart, so that we fear you not?
[l]Return for the sake of your servants,
the tribes of your heritage.
18 [m]Your holy people held possession for a little while;[4]
[n]our adversaries have trampled down your sanctuary.

[1] Or *he did not afflict* [2] Or *Then his people remembered the days of old, of Moses* [3] Or *holy and glorious* [4] Or *They have dispossessed your holy people for a little while*

7[u] Ps. 145:7
9[v] Judg. 10:16 [w] Deut. 7:7, 8; [Ezek. 16:5, 6] [x] See Deut. 32:10-12
10[y] Ex. 15:24; Num. 14:11; Ps. 78:17, 56; 95:9; Ezek. 20:8 [z] Ps. 78:40; Acts 7:51; [Eph. 4:30]
11[a] See Ps. 77:11-20 [b] See Ex. 14:19-22
12[c] Ex. 14:21; Josh. 3:16 [d] 2 Sam. 7:23; Neh. 9:10
14[e] [Num. 10:33] [d] [See ver. 12 above]
15[f] Deut. 26:15 [g] Ps. 33:14 [h] ch. 59:17; [Zech. 1:14]
16[i] ch. 64:8; Deut. 32:6 [j] ch. 43:14
17[k] ch. 6:10; [John 12:40] [l] Ps. 90:13
18[m] [Deut. 4:25, 26] [n] ch. 64:11

63:7–64:12 The sober warnings of 63:1–6 do not cause stoic passivity but rather active intercession. Isaiah calls for "recounting" God's "steadfast love" and compassion (63:7–8), for the God who rescued in the past is still the "Savior," and he remains ready to redeem just as he did in "the days of old" (63:9, 11). Divine chastening may have come against Israel in their fits of rebellion (63:10), but God's commitment remains as that of a Father to his children (63:8, 16).

Informed by God's faithfulness in the past, honest prayers cry out for God's return to his people. He has pledged himself to them, and what happens to them reflects his character to the world (63:17–19; cf. Ex. 32:11–14). As in this prayer, we often fervently pray that just as God has done "awesome things" in the past, so might he work in our day, even in our struggles (Isa. 64:1–3). Confidence comes from the fact that there is no god like the holy God, who amazingly "acts for those who wait [not "work"] for him" (Isa. 64:4; 1 Cor. 2:9). Such prayers are offered from a posture of confession of sin (Isa. 64:6–7), repenting of our uncleanness and resting only in the finished work of Christ, by whose blood we are made clean once and for all (cf. Heb. 7:27; 9:12–28; 10:10).

19 [o]We have become like those over whom
you have never ruled,
like those who are not called by your
name.

64 [p]Oh that you would rend the
heavens and come down,
[q]that the mountains might quake at
your presence—
2[1] as when fire kindles brushwood
and the fire causes water to boil—
[r]to make your name known to your
adversaries,
and that the nations might tremble at
your presence!
3 [s]When you did awesome things that we
did not look for,
you came down, the mountains
quaked at your presence.
4 [t]From of old no one has heard
or perceived by the ear,
[u]no eye has seen a God besides you,
who acts for those who wait for him.
5 You meet him who joyfully works righteousness,
those who remember you in your
ways.
Behold, you were angry, and we sinned;
in our sins we have been a long time,
and shall we be saved?[2]
6 [v]We have all become like one who is
unclean,
and all our righteous deeds are like a
polluted garment.
[w]We all fade like a leaf,
and our iniquities, like the wind, take
us away.
7 [x]There is no one who calls upon your
name,
who rouses himself to take hold of you;
for you have hidden your face from us,
and have made us melt in[3] the hand
of our iniquities.
8 [y]But now, O LORD, you are our Father;
[z]we are the clay, and you are our potter;
[a]we are all the work of your hand.
9 [b]Be not so terribly angry, O LORD,
[c]and remember not iniquity forever.
Behold, please look, we are all your
people.
10 [d]Your holy cities have become a wilderness;
Zion has become a wilderness,
Jerusalem a desolation.
11 [e]Our holy and beautiful[4] house,
where our fathers praised you,
has been burned by fire,
and all our pleasant places have
become ruins.
12 [f]Will you restrain yourself at these
things, O LORD?
Will you keep silent, and afflict us so
terribly?

Judgment and Salvation

65 [g]I was ready to be sought by [h]those
who did not ask for me;
I was ready to be found by those who
did not seek me.
I said, "Here I am, here I am,"
to a nation that was not called by[5] my
name.
2 [i]I spread out my hands all the day
to a rebellious people,
who walk in a way that is not good,
following their own devices;
3 a people who provoke me
to my face continually,

[1] Ch 64:1 in Hebrew [2] Or *in your ways is continuance, that we might be saved* [3] Masoretic Text; Septuagint, Syriac, Targum *have delivered us into* [4] Or *holy and glorious* [5] Or *that did not call upon*

65:1–16 Two options surface in this and the final chapter. One group seeks the Lord and experiences his festive blessing while the other's arrogance leads to dissatisfaction and shame (e.g., vv. 13–16). Quoting Isaiah 65:1–2, Paul applies it to the call to believe that goes out beyond Israel to all the nations (Rom. 10:20–21). He warns Israel of her lingering self-righteous hardness toward God even as he holds out the promise of salvation to any who confess Jesus as risen from the dead (Rom. 10:8–13; cf. Isa. 65:5). God calls out and identifies himself even to those who were rebellious and distant from him (those who "did not ask"; vv. 1–2).

The New Testament manifestation of this promise occurs as, through faith in Christ, Jew and Gentile are brought onto the same path, the new exodus accomplished by King Jesus (e.g., Rom. 3:21–31; Gal. 2:15–21). What a salvation! What a Savior!

19[o] [Jer. 14:8]
Chapter 64
1[p] [2 Sam. 22:10; Ps. 18:9; 144:5] [q] Judg. 5:5; Mic. 1:4
2[r] [Josh. 2:9, 10]
3[s] [Ex. 14:13; 15:11]
4[t] [Ps. 31:19] [u] [1 Cor. 2:9]
6[v] See ch. 59:12-15 [w] Ps. 90:5, 6
7[x] ch. 43:22; Hos. 7:7
8[y] ch. 63:16 [z] ch. 45:9; Rom. 9:20, 21 [a] ch. 29:23; 45:11
9[b] [ch. 57:16; Ps. 74:1, 2] [c] Ps. 79:8
10[d] Neh. 1:3; 2:3
11[e] Hag. 1:9; 2:3; [2 Kgs. 25:9; 2 Chr. 36:19; Ps. 74:7]
12[f] ch. 42:14; [Zech. 1:12] **Chapter 65** **1**[g] Cited Rom. 10:20; [Eph. 2:12, 13] [h] [ch. 2:2, 3; 18:7; 19:19, 25; Zech. 14:16] **2**[i] Rom. 10:21

[j]sacrificing in gardens
and making offerings on bricks;
4 who sit in tombs,
and spend the night in secret places;
[k]who eat pig's flesh,
and broth of tainted meat is in their
vessels;
5 who say, "Keep to yourself,
do not come near me, for I am too
holy for you."
[l]These are a smoke in my nostrils,
a fire that burns all the day.
6 Behold, [m]it is written before me:
[n]"I will not keep silent, but I will repay;
[o]I will indeed repay into their lap
7 both your iniquities [p]and your
fathers' iniquities together,
says the LORD;
[q]because they made offerings on the
mountains
[q]and insulted me on the hills,
I will measure into their lap
payment for their former deeds."[1]

8 Thus says the LORD:
[r]"As the new wine is found in the cluster,
and they say, 'Do not destroy it,
for there is a blessing in it,'
so I will do for my servants' sake,
[s]and not destroy them all.
9 [t]I will bring forth offspring from Jacob,
and from Judah possessors of my
mountains;
my chosen shall possess it,
and my servants shall dwell there.
10 [u]Sharon shall become a pasture for flocks,
and [v]the Valley of Achor a place for
herds to lie down,
for my people [w]who have sought me.
11 But [x]you who forsake the LORD,
who forget [y]my holy mountain,
who [z]set a table for Fortune
and [z]fill cups of mixed wine for
Destiny,
12 I will destine you to the sword,
and all of you shall bow down to the
slaughter,
[a]because, when I called, you did not
answer;
when I spoke, you did not listen,
[b]but you did what was evil in my eyes
and chose what I did not delight in."

13 Therefore thus says the Lord GOD:
"Behold, [c]my servants shall eat,
but you shall be hungry;
behold, my servants shall drink,
but you shall be thirsty;
behold, my servants shall rejoice,
but you shall be put to shame;
14 behold, [d]my servants shall sing for gladness of heart,
but you shall cry out for pain of heart
and shall wail for breaking of spirit.
15 You shall leave your name to [e]my chosen
[f]for a curse,
and the Lord GOD will put you to
death,
but his servants [g]he will call by
another name.
16 So that he who [h]blesses himself in the
land
shall bless himself by [h]the God of
truth,
and he who takes an oath in the land
shall swear by [i]the God of truth;
[j]because the former troubles are forgotten
and are hidden from my eyes.

New Heavens and a New Earth

17 "For behold, [k]I create new heavens
and a new earth,

[1] Or *I will first measure their payment into their lap*

65:17–25 The promise of a new creation is not "new" because it lacks continuity with the past; it is new because it brings about a radical *re*newal of God's fallen creation. The holy God created the "former things" to be good, and he delighted and rejoiced in that original work; he invites people to enter into his joy with his promise of the renewal of shalom on earth (vv. 17–19).

Sin ruptured and compromised God's harmonious creation (Genesis 3), but God promises that the weeping, distress, death, and disorder will be overcome with a life-giving congruence between God, humanity, and the earth (Isa. 65:19–25). The Serpent will face his doom so that this peace may go forth (v. 25; cf. Rev. 12:7–9; 20:7–10; Rom. 16:20).

3[j] ch. 1:29; 66:17; [ch. 57:3-6] **4**[k] ch. 66:17 **5**[l] ch. 1:31; 9:18 **6**[m] [Jer. 2:22; 17:1] [n] Ps. 50:3 [o] Ps. 79:12; [Jer. 16:18] **7**[p] Ex. 20:5; [Matt. 23:35] [q] [Ezek. 20:27, 28] **8**[r] [ch. 17:6] [s] [ch. 2:21] **9**[t] [ch. 27:6; 37:31] **10**[u] ch. 33:9; 35:2 [v] Hos. 2:15; [Josh. 7:26] [w] [ch. 51:1] **11**[x] [Josh. 24:20] [y] ver. 25; Joel 3:17 [z] Ezek. 23:41; [1 Cor. 10:21] **12**[a] ch. 66:4; Prov. 1:24; Jer. 7:13 [b] ch. 66:4 **13**[c] ch. 55:1; Ps. 22:26 **14**[d] [Ps. 5:11] **15**[e] ver. 9 [f] [Deut. 28:37; Jer. 29:22; Zech. 8:13] [g] ch. 62:2 **16**[h] Jer. 4:2 [i] [Deut. 32:4] [j] [ch. 43:18, 19] **17**[k] ch. 66:22; 2 Pet. 3:13; Rev. 21:1

and the former things shall not be
remembered
or come into mind.
18 But be glad and rejoice forever
in that which I create;
for behold, [l]I create Jerusalem to be a joy,
and her people to be a gladness.
19 [m]I will rejoice in Jerusalem
and be glad in my people;
[n]no more shall be heard in it the sound of
weeping
and the cry of distress.
20 No more shall there be in it
an infant who lives but a few days,
or an old man who does not fill out
his days,
for [o]the young man shall die a hundred
years old,
and [p]the sinner a hundred years old
shall be accursed.
21 [q]They shall build houses and inhabit
them;
they shall plant vineyards and eat
their fruit.
22 [q]They shall not build and another
inhabit;
they shall not plant and another eat;
[r]for like the days of a tree shall the days
of my people be,
and my chosen shall long enjoy[1] the
work of their hands.
23 [s]They shall not labor in vain
[t]or bear children for calamity,[2]
for [u]they shall be the offspring of the
blessed of the LORD,
and their descendants with them.
24 [v]Before they call I will answer;
[w]while they are yet speaking I will hear.
25 [x]The wolf and the lamb shall graze
together;
the lion shall eat straw like the ox,
and [y]dust shall be the serpent's food.
[z]They shall not hurt or destroy
in all my holy mountain,"
says the LORD.

The Humble and Contrite in Spirit

66 [a]Thus says the LORD:
[b]"Heaven is my throne,
and the earth is my footstool;
what is the house that you would build
for me,
and what is the place of my rest?
2 [c]All these things my hand has made,
and so all these things came to be,
declares the LORD.
[d]But this is the one to whom I will look:
he who is humble and contrite in spirit
and trembles at my word.
3 [e]"He who slaughters an ox is like one who
kills a man;
he who sacrifices a lamb, like one who
breaks a dog's neck;
he who presents a grain offering, like
one who offers [f]pig's blood;
he who makes a memorial offering of
frankincense, like one who
blesses an idol.
[g]These have chosen their own ways,
and their soul delights in their abominations;
4 [h]I also will choose harsh treatment for
them
and bring [i]their fears upon them,
[j]because when I called, no one answered,
when I spoke, they did not listen;

[1] Hebrew *shall wear out* [2] Or *for sudden terror*

Isaiah's glorious portrait must always remind us that God's restorative salvation will ultimately touch everything, from the physical to the emotional, from the social to the psychological, from the wolf to the lamb (cf. Isa. 11:6–9).

66:1–24 With an ending that reflects the rhythm of the book as a whole as well as the previous chapter, Isaiah closes with two paths, one filled with promise and the other with warning.

Simply engaging in religious activities—even those commanded by God (e.g., offering sacrifices)—is not the mark of faithfulness and love (v. 3; cf. 1:11–20). When divorced from a "humble and contrite" spirit, these rituals become offensive to the Lord (66:2–4; cf. 57:15; Ps. 138:6; Luke 14:11). Such perversion fosters judgmental intolerance rather than gracious neighbor love (Isa. 66:5). The warning is clear: "the LORD will come in fire," and here the particular focus of his judgment is those who are apostate, having claimed the name of God but with hearts and lives far from him (vv. 15–17, 24). Jesus' strong words against certain Pharisees seem to grow out of this divine concern.

18[l] [Jer. 31:7]
19[m] ch. 62:5; 66:10 [n] ch. 35:10; Rev. 21:4
20[o] [Prov. 3:2] [p] Eccles. 8:12
21[q] Ezek. 28:26; [Deut. 28:30]
22[q] [See ver. 21 above] [r] See Ps. 92:12-14
23[s] ch. 49:4 [t] [Deut. 28:41] [u] ch. 61:9; See Ps. 115:12-15
24[v] [Ps. 32:5] [w] [Dan. 9:21]
25[x] ch. 11:6, 7 [y] Gen. 3:14; Mic. 7:17 [z] ch. 11:9

Chapter 66
1[a] Cited Acts 7:49, 50; [1 Kgs. 8:27; Acts 17:24] [b] [Matt. 5:34, 35]
2[c] [1 Chr. 29:14] [d] ch. 57:15; Ps. 34:18
3[e] ch. 1:11 [f] See ch. 65:4 [g] Jer. 7:24
4[h] [ch. 30:16] [i] [ch. 51:12] [j] See ch. 65:12

[k]but they did what was evil in my eyes
and chose that in which I did not
delight."

5 Hear the word of the LORD,
you who tremble at his word:
"Your brothers who hate you
and cast you out for my name's sake
have said, [l]'Let the LORD be glorified,
that we may see your joy';
but it is they who shall be put to shame.

6 "The sound of an uproar from the city!
A sound from the temple!
The sound of the LORD,
[m]rendering recompense to his enemies!

Rejoice with Jerusalem

7 [n]"Before she was in labor
she gave birth;
before her pain came upon her
she delivered a son.
8 Who has heard such a thing?
Who has seen such things?
Shall a land be born in one day?
Shall a nation be brought forth in one
moment?
For [n]as soon as Zion was in labor
she brought forth her children.
9 Shall I bring to the point of birth and
not cause to bring forth?"
says the LORD;
"shall I, who cause to bring forth, shut
the womb?"
says your God.
10 [o]"Rejoice with Jerusalem, and be glad for
her,
all you who love her;
rejoice with her in joy,
all you who mourn over her;
11 that you may nurse and be satisfied
from her consoling breast;
that you may drink deeply with delight
from her glorious abundance."[1]

12 For thus says the LORD:
[p]"Behold, I will extend peace to her like a
river,
and the glory of the nations like an
overflowing stream;
and [q]you shall nurse, you shall be carried
upon her hip,
and bounced upon her knees.
13 As one whom his mother comforts,
so [r]I will comfort you;
you shall be comforted in Jerusalem.
14 You shall see, and your heart shall rejoice;
[s]your bones shall flourish like the grass;
and [t]the hand of the LORD shall be
known to his servants,
and he shall show his indignation
against his enemies.

Final Judgment and Glory of the LORD

15 "For behold, [u]the LORD will come in fire,
and [v]his chariots like the whirlwind,
to render his anger in fury,
and his rebuke with flames of fire.
16 For [w]by fire [x]will the LORD enter into
judgment,
and by his sword, with all flesh;
and those slain by the LORD shall be
many.

17 [y]"Those who sanctify and purify themselves to go into the gardens, following one in

[1] Or *breast*

4[k] [Jer. 7:31]
5[l] ch. 5:19
6[m] ch. 63:4; 65:6
7[n] See ch. 13:8
8[n] [See ver. 7 above]
10[o] ch. 65:19
12[p] [ch. 48:18] [q] ch. 60:16
13[r] ch. 51:12; [ch. 35:10]
14[s] ch. 58:11 [t] [Ezra 8:22, 31]
15[u] ch. 33:14; Mal. 3:1, 2; [2 Thess. 1:7, 8] [v] Ps. 68:17
16[w] Ps. 97:3 [x] Joel 3:2
17[y] ch. 65:3, 5

Judgment is not God's preference, for he delights in life, not death (e.g., Ezek. 18:23, 32; 33:11; 2 Pet. 3:9). He calls us to recognize his holiness and our dependence (Isa. 66:1); when we have fully believed this, we then humbly "tremble" at the sound of his word (vv. 2, 5; cf. Deut. 4:39; Ps. 119:120–161; Phil. 2:12; 1 Pet. 5:5.), thankful to hear the divine voice offering life-giving grace.

The call is to trust in God's coming deliverance that will bring great rejoicing, peace, and comfort (Isa. 66:7–14). A time is anticipated when God's salvation goes to nations far beyond the geography of Israel, bringing "all your brothers from all the nations as an offering to the LORD" (e.g., vv. 19–21). But the offering is the people themselves, not animals (cf. Rom. 12:1–2). There will be a "new heavens and the new earth," for the Creator Lord is reclaiming his creation, bringing Sabbath communion to people across the earth who see his glory and trust in him (Isa. 66:18, 22–23).

God does not "look" (v. 2) to the super-spiritual, the hard workers, the insiders, those esteemed in the world's eyes. He looks to those who humble themselves. Qualification for God's attention comes in this strange way: by admitting our disqualification. This is the nature of the God whose grace is displayed throughout the Bible. This is the God of Isaiah. Trust him.

the midst, [z]eating pig's flesh and the abomination and mice, shall come to an end together,
declares the LORD.

18 "For I know[1] their works and their
thoughts, and the time is coming[2] [a]to gather
all nations and tongues. And they shall come
and shall see my glory, 19 and I will set a sign
among them. And from them [b]I will send
survivors to the nations, to [c]Tarshish, [d]Pul,
and [d]Lud, who draw the bow, to [e]Tubal and
[e]Javan, [f]to the coastlands far away, [g]that have
not heard my fame or seen my glory. And they
shall declare my glory among the nations.
20 [h]And they shall bring all your brothers from
all the nations [i]as an offering to the LORD,
on horses and in chariots and in litters and
on mules and on dromedaries, to my holy
mountain Jerusalem, says the LORD, just as
the Israelites bring their grain offering in a
clean vessel to the house of the LORD. 21 [j]And
some of them also I will take for priests and
for Levites, says the LORD.

22 "For as [k]the new heavens and the new
earth
that I make
shall remain before me, says the LORD,
so [l]shall your offspring and your
name remain.
23 [m]From new moon to new moon,
and from Sabbath to Sabbath,
all flesh shall come to worship before me,
declares the LORD.

24 "And they shall go out and look on the
dead bodies of the men who have rebelled
against me. For [n]their worm shall not die,
[o]their fire shall not be quenched, and they
shall be an abhorrence to all flesh."

[1] Septuagint, Syriac; Hebrew lacks *know* [2] Hebrew *and it is coming*

17 [z]See ch. 65:4 **18** [a]ch. 2:2; Zech. 14:16 **19** [b]ch. 45:20 [c]1 Kgs. 10:22 [d]Jer. 46:9; Ezek. 27:10 [e]Gen. 10:2; Ezek. 27:13 [f]Gen. 10:5 [g][Rom. 15:20, 21] **20** [h]See ch. 14:2; 49:22 [i][Rom. 15:16] **21** [j]ch. 61:6; Ex. 19:6; [1 Pet. 2:9; Rev. 1:6] **22** [k]See ch. 65:17 [l]ch. 53:10; [Ps. 89:29] **23** [m][Ps. 86:9; Zech. 14:16] **24** [n]Mark 9:48 [o][Rev. 21:8]

Introduction to
Jeremiah

Author and Date

Jeremiah was called to be a prophet c. 627 B.C., when he was young (1:6). He served for more than 40 years (1:2–3). Jeremiah had a difficult life. His messages of repentance, delivered at the temple, were not well received (7:1–8:3; 26:1–11). His hometown plotted against him (11:18–23), and he endured much persecution (20:1–6; 37:11–38:13; 43:1–7). Though the book does not reveal the time or place of Jeremiah's death, he probably died in Egypt, where he was taken by his countrymen against his will after the fall of Jerusalem (43:1–7).

The Gospel in Jeremiah

"Long ago, at many times and in many ways, God spoke to our fathers by the prophets, but in these last days he has spoken to us by his Son, whom he appointed the heir of all things, through whom also he created the world" (Heb. 1:1–2). To understand the gospel in Jeremiah we need to see his book in the context of redemptive history. Jeremiah plays a strategic role in God's revelation of his purposes that will be fulfilled in Jesus Christ.

From the beginning and up to the first part of Solomon's rule, we can summarize the main elements of redemptive history thus: creation and fall; the covenant with Abraham; redemption from captivity; the Sinai covenant; entry into and possession of the Promised Land; the Davidic kingship; the temple in Jerusalem. As history unfolds, these elements build a comprehensive picture that foreshadows the kingdom of God and the way into it through redemption in Christ. But following Solomon's defection (1 Kings 11), idolatry and covenant breaking lead to a period of decline for Israel. Despite some valiant attempts to reform by kings such as Hezekiah and Josiah, this process of decline is irreversible and ends with the ultimate destruction of all the visible elements of Israel's covenant relationship with God, such as Jerusalem and the temple.

Jeremiah prophesies in the final stages of this terrible period of decline. He declares the coming destruction of all the visible, tangible evidences of God's presence with the people: the land, the city, the temple, the throne of David. In common with nearly all the Old Testament prophets, Jeremiah had three main points to his message:

1. God's people (in this case, those in Judah) have sinned grievously against the Lord.
2. The Lord will judge his people for their sin, in this case through the onslaught of the Babylonians.
3. Yet God is both unfailingly faithful and bountifully merciful and will bring restoration and salvation.

In various ways the writing prophets, as they prophesy concerning the restoration of Israel and Judah, gather up and repeat all the elements of God's kingdom and redemption that have been revealed in the history of God's people from the beginning up to the glories of Solomon's kingdom. They see this renewal as a future event that some prophets refer to as occurring on the "day of the Lord." Thus, the prophetic view of the future salvation is that it repeats (recapitulates) the pattern of events that has already been revealed. The difference of this future salvation from past patterns of restoration is that the prophets see this coming renewal as being perfect, glorious, and forever.

Of course, no such renewal took place in Old Testament times. Such restoration would dawn only when Jesus of Nazareth came into Galilee proclaiming the gospel of God, and saying, "The time is fulfilled, and the kingdom of God is at hand; repent and believe in the gospel" (Mark 1:14–15). The New Testament picks up the great themes of Old Testament redemptive history and sees them fulfilled in and through the person and work of Jesus.

We should not be put off by Jeremiah's reputation as the gloomy or "weeping" prophet. He has much encouragement to offer the faithful. To be sure, he is remarkable for the way he reveals his feelings and the torment of his soul. This is not surprising given the nature of his message and the constant opposition by most of his fellow Israelites. Yet, even his experience of this sadness and his suffering are a foreshadowing of the anguish of Jesus as he faces even more harrowing torments, again from fellow Israelites, that lead to his death on the cross. Redemption comes through pain, not through avoiding it. The gospel is foreshadowed by Jeremiah's message and his personal involvement in it. By his words and suffering he points to the sovereign grace of God in his control over world history and his faithfulness to his covenant that will be fulfilled in the life, death, and resurrection of Jesus.

Outline

I. Introduction (1:1–19)

II. Israel's Covenantal Adultery (2:1–6:30)

III. False Religion and an Idolatrous People (7:1–10:25)

IV. Jeremiah's Struggles with God and Judah (11:1–20:18)

V. Jeremiah's Confrontations (21:1–29:32)

VI. Restoration for Judah and Israel (30:1–33:26)

VII. God Judges Judah (34:1–45:5)

VIII. God's Judgment on the Nations (46:1–51:64)

IX. Conclusion: The Fall of Jerusalem (52:1–34)

Jeremiah

1 The words of Jeremiah, the son of Hilkiah, one [a]of the priests who were in [b]Ana-
thoth in the land of Benjamin, 2 to whom the
word of the LORD came in the days of [c]Josiah
the son of Amon, king of Judah, in [d]the thirteenth year of his reign. 3 It came also in the
days of [e]Jehoiakim the son of Josiah, king
of Judah, and [f]until the end of the eleventh
year of [g]Zedekiah, the son of Josiah, king of
Judah, [h]until the captivity of Jerusalem in
the fifth month.

The Call of Jeremiah

4 Now the word of the LORD came to me,
saying,

5 [i]"Before I formed you in the womb I knew
you,
and before you were born [j]I consecrated
you;
I appointed you a prophet [k]to the
nations."

6 Then I said, "Ah, Lord GOD! Behold, [l]I do not
know how to speak, [m]for I am only a youth."
7 But the LORD said to me,

"Do not say, 'I am only a youth';
for to all to whom I send you, you shall
go,
and [n]whatever I command you, you shall
speak.

1:1–3 The historical timing of Jeremiah's prophecies is significant. Ever since Solomon's apostasy (1 Kings 11), the fortunes of Judah have been in decline because of the rebellious faithlessness of the people. King Josiah's reforms (2 Kings 22–23) could not stem the tide of evil under his successors. Jeremiah presides over the demise of Judah and the destruction of Jerusalem, the temple, and the Davidic kingship at the hands of the Babylonians in 586 B.C. He thus witnesses to and speaks of the destruction of all the institutions that testified to God's election of the nation.

These introductory verses remind us that Jeremiah's prophecy as a whole is a warning that a nation, a church, or an individual that relies on the externals of religion rather than faith in the redemptive grace of God remains under God's wrath. But he also points to the sovereign purpose of God to save a people for himself.

1:4–10 The call of Jeremiah to be God's prophet demonstrates the sovereignty of God. Before Jeremiah was conceived in the womb, God knew him, consecrated him, and appointed him as his prophet. This foreknowledge of the man is more than foreseeing his future. It establishes a relationship between God and his chosen one that is sure and that will fulfill God's purpose. In this it foreshadows God's foreknowledge of his people as expressed throughout the New Testament (e.g., Rom. 8:29; 11:2; 1 Pet. 1:2).

Jeremiah's timid response, echoed so often in our own hearts, is countered by the divine assurance that God's purpose will be fulfilled. Many times in Scripture we see God choosing the weak, the aged (Abraham), the inarticulate (Moses), the morally blemished (Jacob), the obscure (Gideon), and the persecuted (the suffering servant in Isaiah)—all culminating ultimately in the true suffering servant, Jesus. The apostle Paul also had to learn that God's power is made perfect in our weakness (2 Cor. 12:5–10). Jeremiah needs to be assured that his words will be God's words because his message will have universal significance and will bring both destruction and renewal. The assurance God gives him strikes a theme consistent with the gospel—that God has chosen what is weak to confound the strong (1 Cor. 1:27), for the gospel is the power of God for salvation (Rom. 1:16). This gospel, like Jeremiah's message, speaks of both judgment and redemption.

Chapter 1

1 [a]Ezek. 1:3 [b]ch. 29:27; 32:7; Josh. 21:18
2 [c]See 2 Kgs. 22; 23:1-30 [d]ch. 25:3; 36:2
3 [e]ch. 25:1; 36:1; See 2 Kgs. 23:34–24:6 [f]ch. 39:2 [g]See 2 Kgs. 24:17–25:7 [h]See 2 Kgs. 25:8-11
5 [i]See Isa. 44:2 [j][John 10:36] [k][Isa. 49:6]; See ch. 25:15-29; ch. 46–51
6 [l][Ex. 4:10] [m][1 Kgs. 3:7]
7 [n]ver. 17; Ezek. 2:7

8 [o]Do not be afraid of them,
[p]for I am with you to deliver you,
declares the LORD."

9 [q]Then the LORD put out his hand and
[r]touched my mouth. And the LORD said to me,

"Behold, I have put [s]my words in your
mouth.
10 See, I have set you this day [k]over nations
and over kingdoms,
[t]to pluck up and to break down,
to destroy and to overthrow,
to build and to plant."

11 And the word of the LORD came to me,
saying, [u]"Jeremiah, what do you see?" And
I said, "I see an almond[1] branch." 12 Then the
LORD said to me, "You have seen well, for I am
watching over my word to perform it."
13 The word of the LORD came to me a second
time, saying, "What do you see?" And I said,
"I see [v]a boiling pot, facing away [w]from the
north." 14 Then the LORD said to me, [w]"Out of
the north disaster[2] shall be let loose upon all
the inhabitants of the land. 15 For behold, [x]I
am calling all the tribes of the kingdoms of
the north, declares the LORD, [y]and they shall
come, and every one shall set his throne at the
entrance of the gates of Jerusalem, against all
its walls all around and against all the cities
of Judah. 16 And [z]I will declare my judgments
against them, for all their evil [a]in forsaking
me. [b]They have made offerings to other gods
and [c]worshiped the works of their own hands.
17 But you, [d]dress yourself for work;[3] arise, and
[e]say to them everything that I command you.
[f]Do not be dismayed by them, lest I dismay
you before them. 18 And I, behold, I make you
this day [g]a fortified city, [h]an iron pillar, and
[i]bronze walls, against the whole land, against
the kings of Judah, its officials, its priests,
and the people of the land. 19 [i]They will fight
against you, but they shall not prevail against
you, for [j]I am with you, declares the LORD, to
deliver you."

Israel Forsakes the LORD

2 The word of the LORD came to me, saying, 2 "Go and proclaim in the hearing of
Jerusalem, Thus says the LORD,

"I remember the devotion of [k]your
youth,
your love [l]as a bride,
[m]how you followed me in the wilderness,
[n]in a land not sown.
3 [o]Israel was holy to the LORD,
[p]the firstfruits of his harvest.

[1] *Almond* sounds like the Hebrew for *watching* (compare verse 12) [2] The Hebrew word can mean *evil, harm,* or *disaster*, depending on the context; so throughout Jeremiah [3] Hebrew *gird up your loins*

8 [o]Ezek. 2:6; 3:9 [p]ch. 15:20; See Ex. 3:12
9 [q][Ezek. 2:9] [r][Isa. 6:7] [s]ch. 5:14
10 [k][See ver. 5 above] [t]ch. 18:7; 31:28; 45:4; [2 Cor. 10:4, 5]
11 [u][Amos 7:8]
13 [v]Ezek. 24:3; [Ezek. 22:21] [w]ch. 4:6; 6:1; 10:22
14 [w][See ver. 13 above]
15 [x][ch. 25:9] [y][ch. 39:3; 43:10]
16 [z]ch. 4:12 [a]ch. 19:4; 22:9 [b]ch. 7:9; 44:3 [c]ch. 25:6, 7; Isa. 2:8; Acts 7:41
17 [d][1 Kgs. 18:46; 1 Pet. 1:13] [e]ver. 7 [f]ver. 8; Ezek. 3:9
18 [g][Isa. 50:7] [h]Rev. 3:12 [i]ch. 15:20; [ch. 6:27]
19 [i][See ver. 18 above] [j]ver. 8; [Acts 18:9, 10]

Chapter 2
2 [k]ch. 3:4 [l]Ezek. 16:8, 43, 60; [Rev. 2:4] [m]Deut. 2:7 [n]Deut. 8:2, 3
3 [o]Ex. 28:36; [Ex. 19:5, 6] [p]James 1:18; [Ex. 4:22]

In Jeremiah's weakness—not despite his weakness—God will be with him and will deliver him (Jer. 1:8, 19). This is good news for weak people today who know they need God more than anything else and who cry out for his all-sufficient grace. Such are the ones whom God uses in supernatural ways.

1:11–19 The word of the sovereign God will achieve his purpose, and enable Jeremiah to do the same. As Jeremiah responds to God's command to "say to them [his people] everything that I command you," God promises, "I make you this day a fortified city, an iron pillar, and bronze walls" against his opposition (vv. 17–18). In like manner, Isaiah assured his hearers that God's word is invincible (Isa. 55:11). This word announces both judgment and salvation. The prophetic word foreshadows the Word made flesh, Jesus Christ (John 1:14). He must come because of the difficult thing the word of God must also do: pronounce forgiveness over the lives of those who do not deserve it. Yet this is precisely the message of the gospel, accomplished by Christ's atoning work as that Word invincibly achieves God's redeeming purpose.

Christians should be confident that Jesus cannot fail in his purpose to redeem his people and to judge evil, as the word of God does here in Jeremiah 1. Confidence in the sovereignty of God motivates Christian living and evangelism.

2:1–8 The covenant relationship between God and his people is often described with the metaphor of marriage, the pinnacle of human relationship (Hos. 2:16–20; 2 Cor. 11:2; Rev. 21:2, 9). Mutual love and devotion should exist in such a relationship. Yet Israel has forsaken the Lord. The adulterous faithlessness of Judah ultimately will be removed in the perfecting of the church, the bride of Christ. But until Christ returns, the prophetic word is a warning against turning from God's love. This warning is reinforced for Christians many times in the New Testament (e.g., Heb. 2:1–4).

[q]All who ate of it incurred guilt;
disaster came upon them,
declares the LORD."

4 Hear the word of the LORD, O house of
Jacob, and all the clans of the house of Israel.
5 Thus says the LORD:

[r]"What wrong did your fathers find in me
that they went far from me,
[s]and went after [t]worthlessness, and
became worthless?
6 They did not say, [u]'Where is the LORD
who brought us up from the land of
Egypt,
who led us [v]in the wilderness,
in a land of deserts and pits,
in a land of drought and deep darkness,
in a land that none passes through,
where no man dwells?'
7 [w]And I brought you into a plentiful land
to enjoy its fruits and its good things.
But when you came in, [x]you defiled my
land
and made my heritage an abomination.
8 The priests did not say, 'Where is the
LORD?'
[y]Those who handle the law did not
know me;
[z]the shepherds[1] transgressed against me;
[a]the prophets prophesied by Baal
and went after [b]things that do not
profit.

9 "Therefore [c]I still contend with you,
declares the LORD,
and [d]with your children's children
I will contend.
10 For cross to the coasts of [e]Cyprus and see,
or send to [f]Kedar and examine with
care;
see if there has been such a thing.
11 [g]Has a nation changed its gods,
[h]even though they are no gods?
But my people [i]have changed their glory
for [b]that which does not profit.
12 Be appalled, [j]O heavens, at this;
be shocked, be utterly desolate,
declares the LORD,
13 for my people have committed two evils:
[k]they have forsaken [l]me,
the fountain of [m]living waters,
and hewed out cisterns for themselves,
broken cisterns that can hold no water.

14 [n]"Is Israel a slave? Is he a homeborn servant?
Why then has he become a prey?
15 [o]The lions have roared against him;
they have roared loudly.
They have made his land a waste;
his cities are in ruins, [p]without inhabitant.
16 Moreover, the men of [q]Memphis and
[r]Tahpanhes
[s]have shaved[2] the crown of your head.
17 [t]Have you not brought this upon yourself
by forsaking the LORD your God,
when [u]he led you in the way?

[1] Or *rulers* [2] Hebrew *grazed*

This covenant "marriage" was cemented for Israel in the exodus (Jer. 2:2). How perverse that those who have received such grace—redemption from Egypt's oppression—should forget it and turn to others for sustenance (vv. 2–8 with vv. 11–13). The Christian life can also become arid and fruitless when we forget its basis in the true exodus wrought for us by Christ's resurrection. It is appalling when preachers and teachers forsake the truth for another "gospel" (vv. 12, 17, 19; cf. Gal. 1:6–9).

2:9–13 Even pagans show greater consistency than the people of God, who find only emptiness when they turn their backs on the truth to try things other than the word of God. Cisterns that leak are no substitute for the living water (see 17:13; Isa. 58:11).

When Christ came, he announced that he himself is the one who gives the "living water" that God has repeatedly provided and promised to his people (cf. Jer. 17:13; Exodus 17; Numbers 20; John 4:11–12; 1 Cor. 10:4). Thus for the one who believes in him, "out of his heart will flow rivers of living water" (John 7:38; see also Ezek. 47:1–12). In Eden, rivers flowed from the garden (Gen. 2:10), and in the new earth, rivers will once more flow plentifully (Rev. 22:1). And it is climactically through Christ, the one who provides forgiveness and restoration for his people, that this motif of running, living water passes. Abiding in him, believers today discover the true "fountain of living waters" (Jer. 2:13), the only solid and lasting joy. Only in him is spiritual thirst satisfied and the arid wilderness of sin and death replaced by eternal life with God.

3[q]ch. 12:14; Ezek. 25:12, 13; [Gen. 12:3]
5[r]ver. 31; Isa. 5:4; Mic. 6:3 [s]2 Kgs. 17:15 [t]ch. 10:15; 14:22; 16:19
6[u][Isa. 63:11-13; Hos. 13:4, 5] [v]Deut. 8:15; 32:10
7[w]See Deut. 8:7-10 [x]Ps. 106:38; [Lev. 18:24, 25]
8[y]ch. 18:18; [Mal. 2:7; Rom. 2:20] [z][ch. 5:5] [a]ch. 23:13; [ch. 5:31] [b][Hab. 2:18]
9[c]ver. 35; Ezek. 17:20; 20:35, 36 [d]Ex. 20:5, 6
10[e]See Gen. 10:4 [f]See Isa. 21:16
11[g][Mic. 4:5]; See ch. 18:13-15 [h]ch. 16:20; Isa. 37:19; Gal. 4:8 [i]Ps. 106:20 [b][See ver. 8 above]
12[j]Isa. 1:2
13[k]ch. 17:13 [l]Ps. 36:9 [m]John 4:10
14[n][Ex. 4:22]
15[o]ch. 4:7; Isa. 5:29 [p]ch. 9:11; 46:19
16[q]ch. 44:1; 46:14; Ezek. 30:16 [r]ch. 43:7-9 [s][Deut. 33:20]
17[t]ch. 4:18 [u]ver. 6

18 [v]And now what do you gain by going to
Egypt
to drink the waters of [w]the Nile?
[x]Or what do you gain by going to Assyria
to drink the waters of [y]the Euphrates?[1]
19 [z]Your evil will chastise you,
and [a]your apostasy will reprove you.
Know and see that it is evil and [b]bitter
for [c]you to forsake the LORD your God;
the fear of me is not in you,
declares the Lord GOD of hosts.

20 "For long ago I [d]broke your yoke
and burst your bonds;
but you said, [e]'I will not serve.'
Yes, [f]on every high hill
and under every green tree
you bowed down [g]like a whore.
21 [h]Yet I planted you a choice vine,
wholly of pure seed.
[i]How then have you turned degenerate
and become a wild vine?
22 Though you wash yourself with lye
and use much soap,
[j]the stain of your guilt is still before me,
declares the Lord GOD.
23 [k]How can you say, 'I am not unclean,
I have not gone after the Baals'?
Look at your way [l]in the valley;
know what you have done—
a restless young camel running here and
there,
24 [m]a wild donkey used to the wilderness,
in her heat sniffing the wind!
Who can restrain her lust?
None who seek her need weary themselves;
in her month they will find her.
25 Keep [n]your feet from going unshod
and [o]your throat from thirst.
But you said, 'It is hopeless,
[p]for I have loved foreigners,
and after them I will go.'

26 "As a thief is shamed when caught,
so the house of Israel shall be shamed:
[q]they, their kings, their officials,
their priests, and their prophets,
27 who say to a tree, 'You are my father,'
and to a stone, 'You gave me birth.'
For they have turned their back to me,
and not their face.
But [r]in the time of their trouble they say,
'Arise and save us!'
28 But [s]where are your gods
that you made for yourself?
Let them arise, [t]if they can save you,
in your time of trouble;
for [u]as many as your cities
are your gods, O Judah.

[1] Hebrew *the River*

18[v] ver. 36; Isa. 30:1, 2; 31:1 [w] Isa. 23:3 [x] [Hos. 7:11] [y] Gen. 31:21; Isa. 7:20; 8:7
19[z] Isa. 3:9; Hos. 5:5 [a] ch. 3:22; 5:6; 14:7 [b] ch. 4:18 [c] ver. 13, 17
20[d] ch. 5:5; 30:8 [e] ver. 31 [f] ch. 3:2; 17:2 [g] ch. 3:1; Isa. 1:21
21[h] Ex. 15:17; Ps. 44:2; 80:8; Isa. 5:2 [i] Isa. 5:4; [Deut. 32:32]
22[j] [ch. 17:1]
23[k] ver. 35 [l] ch. 7:31, 32; 19:2, 6
24[m] ch. 14:6
25[n] Deut. 29:5 [o] Ex. 17:6 [p] ch. 3:13; Deut. 32:16
26[q] ch. 13:13; 32:32; [ch. 8:1]
27[r] Judg. 10:9, 10; Isa. 26:16
28[s] Deut. 32:37, 38 [t] Isa. 45:20 [u] ch. 11:13

2:20–21 The imagery of the marriage bond broken by whoredom is linked to that of the wild vine. The vine imagery is used to describe God's people (see 8:13; Isaiah 5; Ezek. 15:1–8; Hos. 10:1). In Jeremiah 2:21 God says that he planted Israel as "a choice vine," yet his people have become "a wild vine." Israel was called to bless the nations with the blessing they themselves had received (Gen. 12:1–3), yet they proved consistently fruitless in this calling. Unfaithfulness and idolatry mean that Israel is worthy only to be destroyed. Thus, Judah is a wild, degenerate vine. God's indictment of Israel as fruitless, however, is a valid allegation not only against faithless Israelites but against all God's people of all times, for none have been the fruitful men and women he created us to be.

In Jesus, however, this tragic history of fruitlessness is wonderfully reversed. Jesus declared himself to be the true Vine, in union with whom fruitless and faltering men and women can once more be fruitful (John 15:1–8). Israel failed to be the "firstfruits" (Jer. 2:3) they were called to be, but Jesus himself has become the firstfruits of all those united to him by faith (1 Cor. 15:20–23). Acknowledging the way we too have "turned degenerate," and looking to Christ and being united to him by faith, we receive the benefits of Christ's work.

2:22–37 The people say they have not sinned. Even the people of God need reminding of the sin "which clings so closely" to us (Heb. 12:1–2). Israel's lack of any sense of guilt (Jer. 2:22, 35) is itself, ironically, proof of their guilt. The seriousness of sin is ever before us in the New Testament (e.g., Rom. 1:18–32; 3:9–20; 1 John 1:8–10). The only sin that cannot be forgiven by the grace of God in Christ is the sin that is denied. Open, contrite acknowledgment of sin, no matter how grievous the transgression, can be fully and permanently covered by the blood of Christ.

29 "Why do you contend with me?
You have all transgressed against me,
declares the LORD.
30 In vain have I [v]struck your children;
they took no correction;
[w]your own sword devoured your prophets
like a ravening lion.
31 And you, O generation, behold the word of the LORD.
Have I been a wilderness to Israel,
or a land of thick darkness?
Why then do my people say, 'We are free,
we will come no more to you'?
32 [x]Can a virgin forget her ornaments,
or a bride her attire?
Yet [y]my people have forgotten me
days without number.
33 "How well you direct your course
to seek love!
So that even to wicked women
you have taught your ways.
34 Also on your skirts is found
[z]the lifeblood of the guiltless poor;
you did not find them [a]breaking in.
Yet in spite of all these things
35 you say, 'I am innocent;
surely his anger has turned from me.'
[b]Behold, I will bring you to judgment
for [c]saying, 'I have not sinned.'
36 [d]How much you go about,
changing your way!
You shall be [e]put to shame by Egypt
as you were put to shame by Assyria.
37 From it too you will come away
with [f]your hands on your head,
for the LORD has rejected those in whom
you trust,
and you will not prosper by them.

3 [g]"If[1] a man divorces his wife
and she goes from him
and becomes another man's wife,
will he return to her?
[h]Would not that land be greatly polluted?
[i]You have played the whore with many
lovers;
and would you return to me?
declares the LORD.
2 Lift up your eyes to [j]the bare heights,
and see!
Where have you not been ravished?
[k]By the waysides you have sat awaiting
lovers
like an Arab in the wilderness.
[h]You have polluted the land
with your vile whoredom.
3 [l]Therefore the showers have been withheld,
and the spring rain has not come;
yet you have [m]the forehead of a whore;
you refuse to be ashamed.
4 Have you not just now [n]called to me,
'My father, you are the friend of my
youth—
5 [o]will he be angry forever,
will he be indignant to the end?'
Behold, you have spoken,
but you have done all the evil that you
could."

[1] Septuagint, Syriac; Hebrew *Saying, "If*

3:1–5 The marriage metaphor returns in reverse (see note on 2:1–8). Faithlessness and a lack of true repentance are characterized as whoredom that pollutes the land. God has called his people into covenant relationship with himself, yet they have forsaken him and senselessly run after other gods.

Yet all is not lost. "Turning" and "returning" to the Lord is the typical way the prophets speak of repentance. True repentance is both turning *from* sin and turning *to* God with a whole heart of dependence upon the fullness of his mercy (not upon the goodness of our repentance). John the Baptist came to call the Jews to repentance, but he saw the shallowness of the response of many: "You brood of vipers! Who warned you to flee from the wrath to come?" (Luke 3:7). Because of our sinful nature, our repentance will never be perfect. But there is One who has shown himself to be the truly repentant person—even though he had no sin to repent of—by being perfectly *turned* to God his Father. Jesus' baptism of repentance justifies our repentance by fulfilling all righteousness for *us*, his own people (Matt. 3:13–15).

Though we have whored after other lovers, God says, "I have loved you with an everlasting love" (Jer. 31:3). Such love, refusing to be put off by our adulterous failures, confounds our hearts. Such love changes us.

30[v] ch. 5:3; Isa. 1:5; 9:13 [w] Neh. 9:26; 1 Thess. 2:15
32[x] Isa. 3:20; 61:10 [y] ch. 3:21; 18:15; Deut. 32:18; Ps. 106:21; Isa. 17:10; Hos. 8:14
34[z] ch. 19:4; 2 Kgs. 21:16; 24:4; Ps. 106:38 [a] Ex. 22:2
35[b] Ps. 143:2 [c] Prov. 28:13; 1 John 1:8, 10
36[d] [ch. 31:22] [e] Isa. 30:3
37[f] 2 Sam. 13:19
Chapter 3
1[g] See Deut. 24:1-4 [h] ver. 9; Ps. 106:38 [i] ch. 2:20
2[j] ver. 21, 23; ch. 4:11; 7:29; Num. 23:3 [k] Ezek. 16:25 [h] [See ver. 1 above]
3[l] ch. 9:12; 14:22; Deut. 28:24 [m] [ch. 6:15]; See Ezek. 3:7, 8
4[n] [Luke 15:18]
5[o] Ps. 103:9

Faithless Israel Called to Repentance

6 The LORD said to me in the days of [p]King
Josiah: "Have you seen what she did, that
faithless one, Israel, [q]how she went up on
every high hill and under every green tree,
and there [i]played the whore? 7 And I thought,
'After she has done all this she will return to
me,' but she did not return, and her treacherous [r]sister Judah saw it. 8 She saw that for all
the adulteries of that faithless one, Israel, [s]I
had sent her away with [t]a decree of divorce.
[u]Yet her treacherous sister Judah did not
fear, but she too went [i]and played the whore.
9 Because she took her whoredom lightly, she
polluted the land, committing adultery with
[v]stone and tree. 10 Yet for all this her treacherous sister Judah did not return to me [w]with
her whole heart, but in pretense, declares
the LORD."

11 And the LORD said to me, [x]"Faithless Israel
has shown herself more righteous than treacherous Judah. 12 Go, and proclaim these words
toward [y]the north, and say,

[z]"'Return, faithless Israel,
declares the LORD.
I will not look on you in anger,
for [a]I am merciful,
declares the LORD;
[b]I will not be angry forever.
13 [c]Only acknowledge your guilt,
that you rebelled against the LORD
your God
and scattered your favors among foreigners under [d]every green tree,
and that you have not obeyed my voice,
declares the LORD.
14 [e]Return, O faithless children,
declares the LORD;
[f]for I am your master;
I will take you, one from a city and two
from a family,
and I will bring you to Zion.

15 "'And [g]I will give you shepherds after my
own heart, [h]who will feed you with knowledge
and understanding. 16 And when you have multiplied and been fruitful in the land, in those
days, declares the LORD, they shall no more
say, "The ark of the covenant of the LORD." It
shall not come to mind or be remembered or
missed; it shall not be made again. 17 At that
time Jerusalem shall be called the throne of the
LORD, [i]and all nations shall gather to it, [j]to the
presence of the LORD in Jerusalem, and they
shall no more stubbornly follow their own evil
heart. 18 [k]In those days the house of Judah shall
join the house of Israel, and together they shall
come from the land [l]of the north to [m]the land
that I gave your fathers for a heritage.

6 [p]ch. 1:2 [q]See ch. 2:20 [i][See ver. 1 above]
7 [r][Ezek. 16:46; 23:4]
8 [s]2 Kgs. 17:18; [Hos. 1:6, 9] [t][Matt. 19:7; Mark 10:4]; See Deut. 24:1-4 [u]Ezek. 23:11 [i][See ver. 1 above]
9 [v]ch. 2:27
10 [w]Hos. 7:14
11 [x]Ezek. 16:51, 52
12 [y]See ver. 18 [z]Prov. 28:13; See Deut. 30:1-10 [a]Ps. 86:5, 15 [b]Ps. 103:9
13 [c]Lev. 26:40 [d]ver. 6
14 [e]ver. 22; Hos. 14:1 [f]Isa. 54:5; 62:5; Hos. 2:19, 20; Mal. 2:11
15 [g]ch. 23:4; Ezek. 34:23; [John 10:11] [h]Acts 20:28
17 [i]Isa. 2:2, 3 [j]Isa. 60:9
18 [k]ch. 50:4; Isa. 11:13; Ezek. 37:21, 22; Hos. 1:11 [l]ver. 12; ch. 16:15; 23:8; 31:8 [m]Amos 9:15

3:6–14 Judah has failed to learn the lesson of Israel's destruction in 722 B.C. The "wrath to come" (Luke 3:7) is a notion the world repudiates and the church often neglects in its preaching and teaching. Yet the theme appears often in the New Testament. God's love, great as it is, does not mean he will take sin lightly in those who remain impenitent.

Jeremiah's condemnations, however, are not the only word he has from the Lord. Jeremiah also declares that God is rich in mercy (Jer. 3:12; cf. Eph. 2:4–6). When faithless Israel returns in repentance, God will delight to show his unfailing mercy. This is who he *is*.

3:15–18 The shepherd in the ancient world ruled his flock and cared for them. The rulers of Israel and Judah were often referred to as shepherds (v. 15; cf. 23:1–4). The evil kings that have led the nation astray are evil shepherds, failing to care for the sheep, God's people. Psalm 23 reminds us that the Lord is the true shepherd. Here God promises to provide rulers "after my own heart" (Jer. 3:15). None truly satisfies and fulfills this promise until Jesus comes and declares, "I am the good shepherd" (John 10:11–14). This is a shepherd who not only rules his flock but also lays down his life for them (John 10:15–18).

Jeremiah was appointed as a prophet over nations and kingdoms (Jer. 1:10). This did not mean that he was to be an itinerant evangelist going from country to country. Rather we see the appointment working out in his message of the nations being under the rule of God. God's works of judgment and salvation will be shown among the nations. The restoration of Jerusalem (3:17) means it will again become the place of God's rule. Jeremiah here reflects the covenant promise to Abraham concerning the nations being blessed through him (Gen. 12:3). The promise will be fulfilled, as Isaiah declared, with the renewal of Jerusalem (Isa. 2:1–4). This foreshadows the gospel going to the nations when Christ brings in the day of the Lord and gives his Spirit.

19 "'I said,
How I would set you among my sons,
and give you a pleasant land,
a heritage most beautiful of all
nations.
And I thought you would [n]call me, My
Father,
and would not turn from following
me.
20 [o]Surely, as a treacherous wife leaves her
husband,
so have you been treacherous to me,
O house of Israel,
declares the LORD.'"
21 A voice on the [p]bare heights is heard,
[q]the weeping and pleading of Israel's
sons
because they have perverted their way;
they have forgotten the LORD their
God.
22 [r]"Return, O faithless sons;
[s]I will heal your faithlessness."
"Behold, we come to you,
for you are the LORD our God.
23 Truly [t]the hills are a delusion,
the orgies[1] on the mountains.
[u]Truly in the LORD our God
is the salvation of Israel.

24 "But from our youth the shameful thing
has devoured all for which our fathers labored,
their flocks and their herds, their sons and
their daughters. 25 [v]Let us lie down in our
shame, and let our dishonor cover us. For [w]we
have sinned against the LORD our God, we
and our fathers, from our youth even to this
day, and we have not obeyed the voice of the
LORD our God."

4 "If you return, O Israel,
declares the LORD,
[x]to me you should return.
If you remove your detestable things
from my presence,
[y]and do not waver,
2 [z]and if you swear, 'As the LORD lives,'
in truth, in justice, and in righteousness,
then [a]nations shall bless themselves in
him,
[b]and in him shall they glory."

3 For thus says the LORD to the men of Judah
and Jerusalem:

[1] Hebrew *commotion*

3:19–23 The covenant love of God is expressed in the tender words of a loving Father's desire for Israel's good. God's judgment is not at odds with his faithfulness to his covenant promises. While the impenitent will indeed be finally judged and punished, God's fatherly hand of discipline operates on his people as "strong love," sent for their ultimate good (see Heb. 12:5–11).

God's people cannot be punished for their sins, for Jesus himself has exhausted all of God's righteous wrath, accepting in full the penalty they deserved. The consequences of sin that we now experience are only a loving Father's discipline. The edifying (not punitive) purpose of his discipline is restoration, righteousness, and peace (Heb. 12:10–11). This fatherly concern of God is echoed in the lament of Jesus over Jerusalem (Matt. 23:37–39). This is the compassion we are called on to have for others in their sin and need, in light of the compassion we ourselves have been shown (2 Cor. 5:14; Eph. 5:2; 1 Pet. 3:8; 1 John 3:17).

4:1–2 The true repentance of Israel would have global results. God promised Abraham, "In you all the families of the earth shall be blessed" (Gen. 12:3; 18:18). Israel's election is God's way of bringing salvation to all nations. Jeremiah 4:2 echoes this but shows that the blessing is in the Lord; that is, the goodness and glory are ultimately his, not Israel's. The New Testament shows us that the truly repentant Israel, the one who is perfectly turned to God and through whom the nations are blessed, is actually Jesus (Matt. 2:15; 3:15; cf. Ex. 4:22; see also note on Isa. 42:1–17). Through him and his astonishing work of redemption, the gospel can be proclaimed to all the nations of the world (Matt. 28:18–20; Luke 24:45–47; Rev. 7:9–12).

4:3–4 The people of Judah are called upon to circumcise their *hearts*. Later on Jeremiah will complain that their ears are uncircumcised (6:10). Circumcision, as the sign of God's covenant promises, was an outward sign in the flesh that achieved no blessings unless it signified the circumcision of the heart (see note on Gen. 17:9–14).

19[n] [Isa. 63:16]
20[o] ver. 7, 8; ch. 5:11
21[p] See ver. 2 [q] ch. 31:9
22[r] ver. 14 [s] ch. 30:17; Isa. 57:18; Hos. 6:1
23[t] ver. 21; [Ps. 121:1, 2] [u] Ps. 3:8
25[v] Ezra 9:6; Job 8:22 [w] Ezra 9:7; Ezek. 2:3
Chapter 4
1[x] Joel 2:12 [y] [1 Kgs. 14:15]
2[z] Deut. 6:13 [a] Isa. 65:16 [b] 1 Cor. 1:31; 2 Cor. 10:17

[c]"Break up your fallow ground,
and [d]sow not among thorns.
4 [e]Circumcise yourselves to the LORD;
remove the foreskin of your hearts,
O men of Judah and inhabitants of
Jerusalem;
[f]lest my wrath go forth like fire,
and burn with none to quench it,
[g]because of the evil of your deeds."

Disaster from the North

5 Declare in Judah, and proclaim in Jerusalem, and say,

[h]"Blow the trumpet through the land;
cry aloud and say,
[i]'Assemble, and let us go
into the fortified cities!'
6 [j]Raise a standard toward Zion,
flee for safety, stay not,
for I bring disaster from [k]the north,
[l]and great destruction.
7 [m]A lion has gone up from his thicket,
a destroyer of nations has set out;
he has gone out from his place
to make your land a waste;
your cities will be ruins
[n]without inhabitant.
8 For this [o]put on sackcloth,
lament and wail,
for [p]the fierce anger of the LORD
has not turned back from us."

9 "In that day, declares the LORD, [q]courage shall
fail both king and officials. The priests shall be
appalled and the prophets astounded." 10 Then
I said, "Ah, Lord GOD, [r]surely you have utterly
deceived this people and Jerusalem, saying, 'It
shall be well with you,' whereas the sword has
reached their very life."

11 At that time it will be said to this people
and to Jerusalem, "A hot wind from [s]the bare
heights in the desert toward the daughter of
my people, not to winnow or cleanse, 12 a wind
too full for this comes for me. Now it is I who
[t]speak in judgment upon them."

13 Behold, he comes up like clouds;
[u]his chariots like the whirlwind;
his horses are [v]swifter than eagles—
woe to us, [w]for we are ruined!
14 O Jerusalem, [x]wash your heart from evil,
that you may be saved.
How long shall your wicked thoughts
lodge within you?
15 For a voice [y]declares from Dan
and proclaims trouble from [z]Mount
Ephraim.
16 Warn the nations that he is coming;
announce to Jerusalem,
"Besiegers come [a]from a distant land;
they shout against the cities of Judah.
17 Like keepers of a field [b]are they against
her all around,
because she has rebelled against me,
declares the LORD.
18 Your ways and your deeds
have brought this upon you.
This is your doom, and [c]it is bitter;
it has reached your very heart."

Anguish over Judah's Desolation

19 [d]My anguish, my anguish! I writhe in
pain!
Oh the walls of my heart!

3[c] Hos. 10:12 [d] Matt. 13:7, 22; Mark 4:7, 18; Luke 8:7, 14
4[e] Deut. 10:16; [ch. 9:26; Rom. 2:28, 29] [f] ch. 21:12 [g] Deut. 28:20
5[h] [ch. 6:1; Hos. 5:8; Joel 2:1] [i] ch. 8:14
6[j] [ch. 50:2; 51:12, 27] [k] See ch. 1:13 [l] [Isa. 1:28]
7[m] ch. 2:15; 5:6; 49:19 [n] ch. 33:10; 34:22; 46:19; Isa. 5:9; 6:11
8[o] ch. 6:26; Isa. 22:12; 32:11 [p] Num. 25:4; Ps. 78:49; See Isa. 13:9-13
9[q] [Ps. 48:4, 5]
10[r] Ezek. 14:9; [1 Kgs. 22:22]
11[s] See ch. 3:2
12[t] ch. 1:16
13[u] Isa. 5:28 [v] 2 Sam. 1:23; Lam. 4:19 [w] ch. 9:19
14[x] Ps. 51:2, 7; Isa. 1:16; James 4:8
15[y] ch. 8:16 [z] See Josh. 24:33
16[a] ch. 5:15

This inner spiritual circumcision meant fearing the Lord and walking in his ways, loving him and serving him with heart and soul.

Even in Moses' day, however, it was recognized that compliance with this ideal was impossible unless God himself performed the miracle of renewal (Deut. 30:6). Ultimately, therefore, the Old Testament foreshadows our union with Christ as our spiritual circumcision—that is, our internal transformation (Col. 2:9–15).

4:19–26 Jeremiah's anguish over his people reflects his perception that destruction is coming to them because of their foolishness. They are clever only in evildoing (v. 22). His constant theme is that Judah's idolatry and attempts to find ways of staving off the threat of Babylon show a godless mind-set. False gods and unwise political alliances demonstrate that the leadership is prey to a worldly way of thinking that is at odds with faith in the Lord.

Such folly persists today. What the world calls wisdom is actually folly, while the gospel as the wisdom of God is written off by the world as foolishness (1 Cor. 1:18–30). As Christians, we are transformed by the renewing of our minds through the true wisdom of the gospel (Rom. 12:1–2).

17[b] ch. 6:3; See 2 Kgs. 25:1-4 18[c] ch. 2:19 19[d] Isa. 16:11; Hab. 3:16; [ch. 9:1; Isa. 22:4]

My heart is beating wildly;
I cannot keep silent,
for I hear the sound of the trumpet,
the alarm of war.
20 [e]Crash follows hard on crash;
the whole land is laid waste.
[f]Suddenly my tents are laid waste,
my curtains in a moment.
21 How long must I see the standard
and hear the sound of the trumpet?

22 "For [g]my people are foolish;
they know me not;
they are stupid children;
they have no understanding.
[h]They are 'wise'—in doing evil!
But how to do good they know not."

23 I looked on the earth, and behold, it was
[i]without form and void;
[j]and to the heavens, and they had no
light.
24 I looked on [k]the mountains, and behold,
they were quaking,
and all the hills moved to and fro.
25 [l]I looked, and behold, there was no man,
and all the birds of the air had fled.
26 I looked, and behold, the [m]fruitful land
was a desert,
and all its cities were laid in ruins
before the LORD, before [n]his fierce
anger.

27 For thus says the LORD, "The whole land
shall be a desolation; [o]yet I will not make a
full end.

28 [p]"For this the earth shall mourn,
[q]and the heavens above be dark;
for I have spoken; I have purposed;
[r]I have not relented, nor will I turn
back."

29 At the noise of horseman and archer
every city takes to flight;
they enter thickets; they climb among
rocks;
all the cities are forsaken,
and [s]no man dwells in them.
30 And you, O desolate one,
what do you mean that you dress in scarlet,
[t]that you adorn yourself with ornaments of gold,
[u]that you enlarge your eyes with
paint?
In vain you beautify yourself.
[v]Your lovers despise you;
they seek your life.
31 For I heard [w]a cry as of a woman in labor,
anguish as of one giving birth to her
first child,
the cry of the daughter of Zion gasping
for breath,
[x]stretching out her hands,
"Woe is me! I am fainting before murderers."

Jerusalem Refused to Repent

5 [y]Run to and fro through the streets of
Jerusalem,
look and take note!

4:23–27 When Adam and Eve sinned, they were exiled from Eden into the wilderness of a world fallen on their account. Exile and wilderness go together in the imagery of the Old Testament.

Here Jeremiah goes further in describing the judgment of the Lord as returning the world to the primeval void at the beginning of creation (Gen. 1:2). He uses the same Hebrew phrase—translated "without form and void"—to underline the horror to come. It is a description of "un-creation" and is echoed in other references to desert and wilderness in relation to the world that awaits its redemption in the new creation (see Isa. 65:17; 2 Pet. 3:10–13). Israel and Judah are perpetually in the wilderness of exile until the day of the Lord brings both final judgment and ultimate renewal.

This judgment and renewal could never, in fact, be accomplished by God's people. This is why Jesus came. Jesus underwent an exile for his people by coming into our fallen world and dying in order to bring in the new creation for us. Until the consummation of the gospel, Christians continue as exiles in the world (Phil. 3:20; 1 Pet. 1:1; 2:11; 2 Pet. 3:11–13; 1 John 2:15). Remembering this frees us from needing to be comfortable in the world and accepted by our neighbors. Our true home is coming. We are not there yet.

5:1–3 Truth and justice are constant themes in Scripture. Yet the prophet declares that in Judah there is only lip service to truth. Truth is usually the casualty in this world. Even among some who claim to be Christian, truth is sacrificed in the name of

20[e] Ezek. 7:26 [f] ch. 10:20; 49:29
22[g] Ps. 82:5; Isa. 1:3 [h] Ps. 36:3; Isa. 1:16, 17; Rom. 16:19
23[i] Gen. 1:2 [j] Isa. 5:30
24[k] Nah. 1:5
25[l] [Zeph. 1:3]
26[m] Ps. 107:34 [n] See ver. 8
27[o] ch. 5:10, 18; 30:11; 46:28; Neh. 9:31; Ezek. 11:13
28[p] ch. 12:4; Hos. 4:3 [q] Isa. 50:3 [r] [Num. 23:19]
29[s] See ver. 7
30[t] [Isa. 61:10] [u] [2 Kgs. 9:30] [v] Lam. 1:2, 19; Ezek. 23:22
31[w] ch. 6:24; See Isa. 13:8 [x] Isa. 1:15; Lam. 1:17
Chapter 5
1[y] [2 Chr. 16:9]

Search her squares to see
[z]if you can find a man,
one who does justice
and seeks truth,
[a]that I may pardon her.
2 [b]Though they say, "As the LORD lives,"
[c]yet they swear falsely.
3 O LORD, do not your eyes look for truth?
[d]You have struck them down,
but they felt no anguish;
you have consumed them,
but they refused to take correction.
[e]They have made their faces harder than rock;
they have refused to repent.

4 Then I said, "These are only the poor;
they have no sense;
[f]for they do not know the way of the LORD,
the justice of their God.
5 I will go to the great
and will speak to them,
for they know the way of the LORD,
the justice of their God."
[g]But they all alike had broken the yoke;
they had burst the bonds.

6 Therefore [h]a lion from the forest shall strike them down;
a [i]wolf from the desert shall devastate them.
[j]A leopard is watching their cities;
everyone who goes out of them shall be torn in pieces,
because their transgressions are many,
their [k]apostasies are great.

7 [l]"How can I pardon you?
Your children have forsaken me
[m]and have sworn by those who are no gods.
[n]When I fed them to the full,
[o]they committed adultery
[p]and trooped to the houses of whores.
8 They were well-fed, lusty stallions,
[q]each neighing [r]for his neighbor's wife.
9 [s]Shall I not punish them for these things?
declares the LORD;
and shall I not avenge myself
on a nation such as this?

10 [t]"Go up through her vine rows and destroy,
[u]but make not a full end;
strip away her branches,
for they are not the LORD's.
11 [v]For the house of Israel and the house of Judah
have been utterly treacherous to me,
declares the LORD.
12 They have spoken falsely of the LORD
and have said, 'He will do nothing;
[w]no disaster will come upon us,
[x]nor shall we see sword or famine.
13 The prophets will become wind;
the word is not in them.
Thus shall it be done to them!'"

The LORD Proclaims Judgment

14 Therefore thus says the LORD, the God of hosts:
"Because you have spoken this word,
behold, [y]I am making my words in your mouth [z]a fire,
and this people wood, and the fire shall consume them.

1[z]See Gen. 18:23-32 [a][ver. 7]
2[b][Titus 1:16] [c]ch. 7:9
3[d]See ch. 2:30 [e]Ezek. 3:8
4[f]ch. 8:7; Mic. 3:1
5[g]ch. 2:20; Ps. 2:3; 107:14
6[h]See ch. 4:7 [i]Hab. 1:8; Zeph. 3:3 [j]Hos. 13:7 [k]ch. 2:19
7[l][ver. 1] [m]Deut. 32:21; Josh. 23:7; 2 Chr. 13:9; Gal. 4:8 [n]Deut. 32:15 [o]ch. 9:2; 23:10 [p]Mic. 5:1
8[q]ch. 13:27; 50:11 [r]Ezek. 22:11
9[s]ver. 29; ch. 9:9; [Rom. 2:2]
10[t][ch. 39:8] [u]See ch. 4:27
11[v]ch. 3:20
12[w][Gen. 3:4] [x][ch. 14:13; Isa. 28:15]
14[y][ch. 1:9, 10] [z][Obad. 18; Zech. 12:6; Rev. 11:5]

tolerance or unity. Jesus warned against those who claim his name but to whom he must say, "I never knew you; depart from me, you workers of lawlessness" (Matt. 7:23).

5:10–13 Jeremiah returns to the metaphor of the vine (see note on 2:20–21). Israel and Judah are together a wild vine, and the branches that do not "abide" in the Lord will be cut off from bearing fruit (John 15:6; cf. Matt. 21:43). The great delusion of the world is that there is no real wrath from God or judgment to come. There are many false prophets in the church who repudiate any suggestion of sin's consequences, hell and damnation. Yet no one spoke of the consequences of sin or the horrors of hell as seriously as Jesus himself (e.g., Matt. 5:22–30; 10:28; 23:33; John 5:14; 8:34).

5:14–31 Given the apostasy of the people, the prophet's words must be consuming words of judgment (v. 14). This judgment will come in the form of invasion by a powerful and ruthless enemy (vv. 15–17), yet it will not mean the end of all things (v. 18).

Throughout Jeremiah there are clear indications of the faithfulness of God to his covenant: there will be a people of God forever (v. 18; see also 3:12–18). But the idolatrous and unrepentant ones will not be part of this people who remain in God's covenant of blessing. Isaiah too spoke of a remnant of the faithful that would return

15 [a]Behold, I am bringing against you
a nation from afar, O house of Israel,
declares the LORD.
It is an enduring nation;
it is an ancient nation,
a nation whose language you do not
know,
[b]nor can you understand what they say.
16 [c]Their quiver is like [d]an open tomb;
they are all mighty warriors.
17 [e]They shall eat up your harvest and your
food;
they shall eat up your sons and your
daughters;
they shall eat up your flocks and your
herds;
they shall eat up your vines and your
fig trees;
your [f]fortified cities in which you trust
they shall beat down with the sword."

18 "But even in those days, declares the LORD,
[u]I will not make a full end of you. 19 And when
your people say, [g]'Why has the LORD our God
done all these things to us?' you shall say to
them, 'As you have forsaken me and served
foreign gods in your land, [h]so you shall serve
foreigners in a land that is not yours.'"

20 Declare this in the house of Jacob;
proclaim it in Judah:
21 "Hear this, [i]O foolish and senseless people,
[j]who have eyes, but see not,
who have ears, but hear not.
22 [k]Do you not fear me? declares the LORD.
Do you not tremble before me?
I placed the sand [l]as the boundary for
the sea,
a perpetual barrier that it cannot pass;
though the waves toss, they cannot prevail;
though [m]they roar, they cannot pass
over it.
23 [n]But this people has a stubborn and
rebellious heart;
they have turned aside and gone away.
24 They do not say in their hearts,
'Let us fear the LORD our God,
[o]who gives the rain in its season,
the autumn rain and the spring rain,
and keeps for us
[p]the weeks appointed for the harvest.'
25 [q]Your iniquities have turned these away,
and your sins have kept good from
you.
26 For wicked men are found among my
people;
[r]they lurk like fowlers lying in wait.[1]
[s]They set a trap;
they catch men.
27 Like a cage full of birds,
their houses are full of deceit;
therefore they have become great and
rich;
28 [t]they have grown fat and sleek.
They know no bounds in deeds of evil;
[u]they judge not with justice
the cause of the fatherless, to make it
prosper,
and they do not defend the rights of
the needy.

[1] The meaning of the Hebrew is uncertain

from exile (e.g., Isa. 10:20–23; 11:11, 16; 46:3). Jeremiah will go on to construct a major part of his teaching on the fact of the faithful remnant. Paul recalls this concept from Isaiah as he deals with the problem of Jewish unbelief in the gospel (Rom. 9:27; see also Rom. 11:5–7, 25–32). The remnant is the faithful Israel/Judah. Since genuine faithfulness was exhibited finally only by Jesus as the true Israel and Son of God (see also note on Jer. 4:1–2), only those united to him can know God's covenant blessings. The dynamic of salvation in the New Testament can be stated thus: Jesus is the true spiritual Israel, the remnant of God's people; the elect Jews believe in Jesus and are thus also joined to the remnant; the Gentiles who are elect come to the restored Israel, that is, they believe in Israel's Savior and are also joined to him.

This section of Jeremiah is like a drama in which the principal player is God, who speaks to his chosen people through the prophet Jeremiah. There are false prophets who speak lies (5:31) and the people's hearts are hardened in sin. The agent of God's judgment, a foreign power, is at hand to wreak destruction. Still God will graciously preserve a remnant from which will come a Savior for many more. This drama will be played out definitively when not a rebellions son but a true and faithful Son will give himself into the hands of wicked men and will suffer the full weight of God's wrath against sin—to deliver many more sons into glory (Rom. 5:6–11; 2 Cor. 5:21; Heb. 2:10).

15[a] ch. 34:21, 22; Deut. 28:49; [ch. 1:15; Amos 6:14] [b] Isa. 33:19
16[c] See Isa. 5:28 [d] Ps. 5:9
17[e] Lev. 26:16; Deut. 28:31, 33, 51 [f] [Hos. 8:14]
18[u] [See ver. 10 above]
19[g] ch. 13:22; 16:10, 11; 22:8, 9; Deut. 29:24, 25; 1 Kgs. 9:8, 9 [h] Deut. 4:27, 28; 28:47, 48, 68
21[i] Deut. 32:6; Isa. 6:9 [j] [Matt. 13:14]
22[k] ch. 10:7 [l] Job 26:10; 38:10, 11; Ps. 104:9 [m] ch. 51:55; [Ps. 46:3]
23[n] ch. 6:28
24[o] ch. 14:22; Deut. 11:14; Job 5:10; Ps. 147:8; Matt. 5:45 [p] Gen. 8:22
25[q] ch. 3:3
26[r] [Prov. 1:11] [s] Ps. 10:9; [Ps. 124:7]
28[t] Deut. 32:15 [u] [ch. 7:6; Isa. 1:23; Zech. 7:10]

29 [v]Shall I not punish them for these things?
declares the LORD,
and shall I not avenge myself
on a nation such as this?"

30 An appalling and [w]horrible thing
has happened in the land:
31 [x]the prophets prophesy falsely,
and the priests rule at their direction;
[y]my people love to have it so,
but what will you do when the end
comes?

Impending Disaster for Jerusalem

6 Flee for safety, [z]O people of Benjamin,
from the midst of Jerusalem!
Blow the trumpet in [a]Tekoa,
and raise a signal on [b]Beth-haccherem,
for disaster looms [c]out of the north,
and great destruction.
2 The lovely and delicately bred I will
destroy,
[d]the daughter of Zion.[1]
3 [e]Shepherds with their flocks shall come
against her;
[f]they shall pitch their tents around her;
they shall pasture, each in his place.
4 [g]"Prepare war against her;
arise, and let us attack [h]at noon!
Woe to us, for the day declines,
for the shadows of evening lengthen!
5 Arise, and let us attack by night
and destroy her palaces!"

6 For thus says the LORD of hosts:
[i]"Cut down her trees;
[j]cast up a siege mound against
Jerusalem.
This is the city that must be [k]punished;
there is nothing but oppression
within her.
7 [l]As a well keeps its water fresh,
so she keeps fresh her evil;
[m]violence and destruction are heard
within her;
sickness and wounds are ever before
me.
8 Be warned, O Jerusalem,
[n]lest I turn from you in disgust,
lest I make you [o]a desolation,
an uninhabited land."

9 Thus says the LORD of hosts:
[p]"They shall glean thoroughly as a vine
the remnant of Israel;
like a grape gatherer pass your hand
again
over its branches."
10 [q]To whom shall I speak and give warning,
that they may hear?
[r]Behold, their ears are uncircumcised,
[s]they cannot listen;
behold, [t]the word of the LORD is to them
an object of scorn;
they take no pleasure in it.
11 Therefore I am full of the wrath of the
LORD;
[u]I am weary of holding it in.
[v]"Pour it out upon the children in the
street,
and upon the gatherings of young
men, also;
[w]both husband and wife [x]shall be taken,
the elderly and the very aged.

[1] Or *I have likened the daughter of Zion to the loveliest pasture*

29[v] See ver. 9
30[w] ch. 23:14; Hos. 6:10
31[x] ch. 6:13; 14:14, 18; 20:6; 23:21, 25; 27:10, 15; 29:9; Ezek. 13:6 [y][Mic. 2:11]
Chapter 6
1[z] [Judg. 1:21] [a] See 2 Sam. 14:2 [b] Neh. 3:14 [c] See ch. 1:14
2[d] See 2 Kgs. 19:21
3[e] [ch. 23:1] [f] ch. 4:17
4[g] ch. 22:7; Joel 3:9; [ch. 51:27] [h] ch. 15:8
6[i] [Deut. 20:20] [j] 2 Kgs. 19:32; Isa. 37:33; Ezek. 26:8; Luke 19:43 [k] Luke 19:44
7[l] Isa. 57:20 [m] Ps. 55:9; Ezek. 7:11, 23
8[n] Ezek. 23:18; [Hos. 9:12] [o] See ch. 4:7
9[p] [Deut. 24:21]
10[q] Isa. 28:9; 53:1 [r] [Ex. 6:12; Acts 7:51] [s] ch. 7:26 [t] ch. 20:8
11[u] ch. 20:9 [v] ch. 9:21 [w] [Lam. 2:21] [x] ch. 8:9

6:1–15 This extended word of disaster contains several important themes. The impending destruction of Jerusalem and the temple, a threat barely averted when the Assyrians failed to take the city a century before, was to most people unthinkable. The city and its temple were symbols of the presence of the God and Lord of all the earth. All the promises of God to his people were represented in them and in David's dynasty.

Tragically, the people are complacent and have refused to hear the Lord's words of warning (v. 10). Worse, the corruption has spread to the religious leaders, who blatantly lie, telling the people that all is well (vv. 13–15). "Peace" (*shalom*; v. 14) is much more than tranquility or lack of conflict. It is the well-being of the whole person in relation to God. It is what Adam and Eve enjoyed in Eden and what will be enjoyed in the new earth. In the end, only the Prince of Peace can heal the wounds of sin and assure his people of peace, since he has made the only peace that matters (John 14:27; Rom. 5:1; 8:6). So Paul begins all his epistles with the greeting "Grace to you and peace" (Rom. 1:7; etc.). But when church leaders follow Jerusalem's leaders and deceive their flocks with words of easy acceptance by a "loving" God, while condoning heresy, immorality, and gospel-neglecting religiosity, things are bad indeed.

12 [y]Their houses shall be turned over to others,
their fields and wives together,
for I will stretch out my hand
against the inhabitants of the land,"
declares the LORD.
13 [z]"For from the least to the greatest of them,
everyone [a]is greedy for unjust gain;
and from [b]prophet to priest,
everyone deals falsely.
14 They have healed the wound of my people lightly,
saying, [c]'Peace, peace,'
[d]when there is no peace.
15 [e]Were they ashamed when they committed abomination?
No, they were not at all ashamed;
they did not know how to blush.
Therefore they shall fall among those who fall;
[f]at the time that I punish them, they shall be overthrown,"
says the LORD.

16 Thus says the LORD:
"Stand by the roads, and look,
and ask for [g]the ancient paths,
where the good way is; and walk in it,
[h]and find rest for your souls.
But they said, 'We will not walk in it.'
17 [i]I set watchmen over you, saying,
'Pay attention to [j]the sound of the trumpet!'
But they said, [k]'We will not pay attention.'
18 Therefore hear, O nations,
and know, O congregation, what will happen to them.
19 Hear, O earth; behold, I am bringing
disaster upon this people,
[l]the fruit of their devices,
because they have not paid attention to my words;
and as for my law, they have rejected it.
20 [m]What use to me is [n]frankincense that comes from [o]Sheba,
or sweet cane from a distant land?
[p]Your burnt offerings are not acceptable,
nor your sacrifices pleasing to me.
21 Therefore thus says the LORD:
[q]'Behold, I will lay before this people
stumbling blocks against which they shall stumble;
fathers and sons together,
neighbor and friend shall perish.'"

22 Thus says the LORD:
[r]"Behold, a people is coming [s]from the north country,
a great nation is stirring from [t]the farthest parts of the earth.
23 They lay hold on bow and javelin;
they are [u]cruel and have no mercy;
[v]the sound of them is like the roaring sea;
they ride on horses,
set in array as a man for battle,
against you, O daughter of Zion!"
24 We have heard the report of it;
[w]our hands fall helpless;
anguish has taken hold of us,
[x]pain as of a woman in labor.
25 Go not out into the field,
nor walk on the road,
for the enemy has a sword;
[y]terror is on every side.
26 O daughter of my people, [z]put on sackcloth,
and [a]roll in ashes;
[b]make mourning as for an only son,
most bitter lamentation,
for suddenly the destroyer
will come upon us.

27 "I have made you [c]a tester of metals among my people,
that you may know and [d]test their ways.

6:16 "Rest for your souls" here is the very phrase repeated by Jesus: "Come to me, all who labor and are heavy laden, and I will give you rest. . . . I am gentle and lowly in heart, and you will find *rest for your souls*" (Matt. 11:28–29). God invited the people of Jeremiah's day to walk with him and enjoy rest for their souls. God is always the source of his people's rest. And in Jesus, this rest is decisively secured. Those who do not pay attention to God's warnings and ways will find not rest but destruction (Jer. 6:16ff.). Such warning is also gracious, because if God did not love his people, he would not so warn them of the consequences of their waywardness.

12[y] For ver. 12-15, see ch. 8:10-12 **13**[z] [ch. 31:34; 44:12; Jonah 3:5] [a] Isa. 56:11 [b] ch. 14:18; 23:11; Mic. 3:11; See ch. 5:31 **14**[c] ch. 4:10; 14:13; 23:17; Ezek. 13:10; Mic. 3:5; [John 14:27] [d] Isa. 48:22; 57:21; Ezek. 7:25 **15**[e] [ch. 3:3; 8:12] [f] [ver. 6] **16**[g] ch. 18:15; [Isa. 8:20; Mal. 4:4; Luke 16:29] [h] Matt. 11:29; [Ps. 116:7] **17**[i] Isa. 56:10; [Isa. 21:11] [j] Isa. 58:1; [ch. 4:19] [k] ch. 44:16 **19**[l] Prov. 1:31 **20**[m] Isa. 1:11 [n] Isa. 43:23; 60:6 [o] See 1 Kgs. 10:1 [p] ch. 7:21, 22; 14:12; Ps. 40:6; Isa. 1:11; Amos 5:21 **21**[q] Ezek. 3:20 **22**[r] For ver. 22-24, see ch. 50:41-43 [s] See ch. 1:13 [t] ch. 25:32; 31:8 **23**[u] Isa. 13:9, 18 [v] Isa. 17:12 **24**[w] ch. 38:4; 49:24; Ezek. 21:7; See 2 Sam. 4:1; Ezek. 7:17 [x] See Isa. 13:8 **25**[y] Ps. 31:13; Lam. 2:22; [Job 18:11] **26**[z] See ch. 4:8; Esth. 4:1 [a] ch. 25:34; Ezek. 27:30; [Lam. 3:16; Mic. 1:10] [b] Amos 8:10; Zech. 12:10 **27**[c] [ch. 1:18] [d] ch. 9:7

28 [e]They are all stubbornly rebellious,
[f]going about with slanders;
they are [g]bronze and iron;
all of them act corruptly.
29 The [g]bellows blow fiercely;
the lead is consumed by the fire;
[h]in vain the refining goes on,
for the wicked are not removed.
30 [i]Rejected silver they are called,
for the LORD has rejected them."

Evil in the Land

7 The word that came to Jeremiah from the
LORD: 2 [j]"Stand in the gate of the LORD's
house, and proclaim there this word, and say,
Hear the word of the LORD, all you men of
Judah who enter these gates to worship the
LORD. 3 Thus says the LORD of hosts, the God
of Israel: [k]Amend your ways and your deeds,
and I will let you dwell in this place. 4 [l]Do not
trust in these deceptive words: 'This is the
temple of the LORD, the temple of the LORD,
the temple of the LORD.'
5 "For if you truly [m]amend your ways and
your deeds, if you truly [n]execute justice one
with another, 6 if you [n]do not oppress the
sojourner, the fatherless, or the widow, [m]or
shed innocent blood in this place, [o]and if you
do not go after other gods to your own harm,
7 [p]then I will let you dwell in this place, [q]in the
land that I gave of old to your fathers forever.
8 "Behold, you trust in deceptive words to no
avail. 9 [r]Will you steal, murder, commit adultery, [s]swear falsely, [t]make offerings to Baal,
[o]and go after other gods that you have not
known, 10 and then come and stand before me
in this house, [u]which is called by my name, and
say, 'We are delivered!'—only to go on doing
all these abominations? 11 [v]Has this house,
[u]which is called by my name, [w]become a den
of robbers in your eyes? Behold, I myself have
seen it, declares the LORD. 12 Go now to [x]my
place that was in Shiloh, [y]where I made my
name dwell at first, and [z]see what I did to it
because of the evil of my people Israel. 13 And
now, because you have done all these things,
declares the LORD, and [a]when I spoke to you
persistently you did not listen, and [b]when
I called you, you did not answer, 14 therefore
I will do to [c]the house [u]that is called by my
name, and in which you trust, and to the
place that I gave to you and to your fathers,
[z]as I did to Shiloh. 15 [c]And I will cast you out
of my sight, [d]as I cast out all your kinsmen,
all the offspring of [e]Ephraim.
16 "As for you, [f]do not pray for this people,
or lift up a cry or prayer for them, and do not
intercede with me, for I will not hear you. 17 Do
you not see what they are doing in the cities
of Judah and in the streets of Jerusalem? 18 The
children gather wood, the fathers kindle fire,
[g]and the women knead dough, to [h]make cakes
for [i]the queen of heaven. And [j]they pour out
drink offerings to other gods, [k]to provoke me
to anger. 19 [l]Is it I whom they provoke? declares
the LORD. Is it not themselves, [m]to their own
shame? 20 Therefore thus says the Lord GOD:
Behold, [n]my anger and my wrath will be
poured out on this place, upon man and beast,
upon the trees of the field and the fruit of the
ground; [o]it will burn and not be quenched."
21 Thus says the LORD of hosts, the God of
Israel: [p]"Add your burnt offerings to your
sacrifices, and eat the flesh. 22 For in the day
that I brought them out of the land of Egypt,
I did not speak to your fathers or command
them [q]concerning burnt offerings and sacri-

28 [e] ch. 5:23 [f] ch. 9:4; [Lev. 19:16] [g] Ezek. 22:18, 20
29 [g] [See ver. 28 above] [h] [Isa. 1:25]
30 [i] Isa. 1:22; Ezek. 22:19, 20
Chapter 7
2 [j] ch. 26:2
3 [k] ch. 18:11; 26:13
4 [l] [ver. 8]
5 [m] ch. 22:3 [n] Deut. 24:14
6 [n] [See ver. 5 above] [m] [See ver. 5 above] [o] ch. 13:10; 25:6; Deut. 6:14
7 [p] Deut. 4:40 [q] ch. 3:18
9 [r] Hos. 4:1, 2 [s] ch. 5:2 [t] ch. 1:16 [o] [See ver. 6 above]
10 [u] ch. 32:34; 34:15

7:1–15 Jeremiah's famous temple sermon most likely was given sometime after Josiah's temple reforms in 621 B.C. (2 Kings 23). As far-reaching as these reforms were, after a book of the law was discovered in the temple, the results were apparently superficial and not long-lasting. Josiah's successors were all evil and would not have helped maintain the reformation. The situation addressed here is rife with formalism, spiritual corruption, and injustice (Jer. 7:3–4). The people's life in the Promised Land is thus put at risk (vv. 5–7). These people were using the Lord's name in vain (vv. 8–11; cf. Ex. 20:7, where the verb usually translated *take* is the verb to *bear, carry, take upon oneself*). They claimed to be called by God's name—claimed to "bear" it—while living godless lives.

This principle remains true for Christians who claim the name of Christ. We are to "walk in a manner worthy of the calling to which you have been called" (Eph. 4:1). Called by his grace, we walk accordingly (Eph. 5:1–2).

11 [v] Isa. 56:7 [u] [See ver. 10 above] [w] Cited Matt. 21:13; Mark 11:17; Luke 19:46; [Ezek. 7:22] **12** [x] Judg. 18:31; 1 Sam. 1:3 [y] Deut. 12:11 [z] ch. 26:6; Ps. 78:60; See 1 Sam. 4:3-12 **13** [a] ver. 25; 2 Chr. 36:15 [b] Prov. 1:24; [ver. 27; Isa. 50:2; 65:12] **14** [c] Deut. 12:5; 1 Kgs. 9:7 [u] [See ver. 10 above] [z] [See ver. 12 above] **15** [c] [See ver. 14 above] [d] 2 Kgs. 17:6, 23 [e] Ps. 78:67; Hos. 4:17; 5:3, 9; 6:4; 12:1 **16** [f] ch. 11:14; 14:11; [Ex. 32:10; Deut. 9:14; 1 John 5:16] **18** [g] Hos. 7:4 [h] ch. 44:17, 19 [i] [2 Kgs. 23:13] [j] ch. 19:13 [k] ch. 11:17; Deut. 32:16, 21; 1 Kgs. 14:9; 16:2; 2 Chr. 34:25 **19** [l] [Job 35:6] [m] ch. 51:51 **20** [n] ch. 42:18; 44:6; 2 Chr. 34:25; Lam. 4:11 [o] ch. 17:27 **21** [p] See ch. 6:20 **22** [q] Hos. 6:6

fices. 23 But this command I gave them: [r]"Obey
my voice, and [s]I will be your God, and you
shall be my people. [t]And walk in all the way
that I command you, [u]that it may be well with
you.' 24 [v]But they did not obey or incline their
ear, [w]but walked in their own counsels and
[x]the stubbornness of their evil hearts, and
[y]went backward and not forward. 25 From the
day that your fathers came out of the land of
Egypt to this day, [z]I have persistently sent all
my servants the prophets to them, day after
day. 26 [v]Yet they did not listen to me or incline
their ear, [a]but stiffened their neck. [b]They did
worse than their fathers.

27 [c]"So you shall speak all these words to
them, but they will not listen to you. [d]You
shall call to them, but they will not answer
you. 28 And you shall say to them, 'This is the
nation that did not obey the voice of the LORD
their God, and did not accept discipline; [e]truth
has perished; it is cut off from their lips.

29 [f]" 'Cut off your hair and cast it away;
raise a lamentation on [g]the bare
heights,
for the LORD has rejected and forsaken
the generation of his wrath.'

The Valley of Slaughter

30 "For the sons of Judah have done evil in my
sight, declares the LORD. They have set [h]their
detestable things in the house [i]that is called by
my name, to [h]defile it. 31 And they have built
the high places of [j]Topheth, which is in [k]the
Valley of the Son of Hinnom, [l]to burn their
sons and their daughters in the fire, [m]which
I did not command, nor did it come into my
mind. 32 [n]Therefore, behold, the days are coming, declares the LORD, when it will no more
be called [j]Topheth, or [k]the Valley of the Son of
Hinnom, but the Valley of Slaughter; [o]for they
will bury in Topheth, because there is no room
elsewhere. 33 [p]And the dead bodies of this people will be food for the birds of the air, and for
the beasts of the earth, [q]and none will frighten
them away. 34 [r]And I will silence in the cities of
Judah and in the streets of Jerusalem the voice
of mirth and the voice of gladness, the voice of
the bridegroom and the voice of the bride, [s]for
the land shall become a waste.

8 "At that time, declares the LORD, the bones
of the kings of Judah, the bones of its officials, the bones of the priests, the bones of the
prophets, and the bones of the inhabitants of
Jerusalem shall be brought out of their tombs.
2 And they shall be spread [t]before the sun and
the moon and all the host of heaven, which
they have loved and served, which they have
gone after, and which they have sought and
worshiped. [u]And they shall not be gathered or
buried. [v]They shall be as dung on the surface
of the ground. 3 [w]Death shall be preferred to
life by all the remnant that remains of this evil
family [x]in all the places where I have driven
them, declares the LORD of hosts.

7:21–29 Spiritual deafness is a fearful thing. To hear God's Word and obey is to be reassured of the gift of grace: "I will be your God, and you shall be my people" (v. 23; see note on 11:1–5). Constant refusal to listen to God's Word (7:25–26) results in total deafness to the truth, as our hearts gradually harden. Indeed, this hardening of ears and hearts is, from the divine perspective, God's very act of judgment (Isa. 6:9–10; Amos 8:11–12). Jesus speaks only to those who are attuned to him as the Word of God, while others cannot hear with the faith required truly to understand (Mark 4:11–12; John 10:24–26; 1 Cor. 2:14).

7:30–8:3 Because of detestable idolatry, the land of fruitfulness and plenty, with the glory of Jerusalem showing the blessing of God, will be desecrated. The defilement of the dead bodies of kings, priests, prophets, and people is a reversal of all the covenant blessings anticipated through God's promise (Gen. 12:1–3). Only the covenant curses remain in evidence (see Deuteronomy 28).

But desolation is not the end of the story. From the wider context of Jeremiah, we know that God yet has a plan for his people despite the desolation they will face—a plan that will result in their ultimate salvation. So it would be again as Jesus warned of the horrors to come on the temple and the land (Matt. 24:1–2; Mark 13:1–2). But, after suffering the curse of the covenant (Gal. 3:13), the true temple will be raised up (John 2:18–22). All the covenant promises came undone in the horrific cross of Christ, so that these promises can now become reality for God's people, despite our failures.

23 [r]ch. 11:4, 7; Ex. 15:26; Deut. 6:3 [s]Lev. 26:12 [t]Deut. 5:33 [u]ch. 42:6; Deut. 4:40
24 [v]Ps. 81:11 [w]Ps. 81:12 [x][ch. 3:17; Hos. 4:16] [y]ch. 2:19, 27; 8:5; 15:6; 32:33
25 [z]2 Chr. 36:15, 16
26 [v][See ver. 24 above] [a]2 Chr. 30:8 [b]ch. 16:12
27 [c]ch. 1:17 [d][ver. 13]
28 [e]ch. 9:3
29 [f][Job 1:20] [g]See ch. 3:2
30 [h]ch. 32:34; Ezek. 5:11; 7:20; [ch. 19:5; 2 Kgs. 21:4, 7] [i]See ver. 10
31 [j]2 Kgs. 23:10 [k][ch. 31:40; Josh. 18:16] [l]Ps. 106:38 [m]Deut. 17:3; [ver. 21, 22]
32 [n]ch. 19:6 [j][See ver. 31 above] [k][See ver. 31 above] [o]ch. 19:11; [Ezek. 6:5]
33 [p]ch. 12:9; 16:4; 19:7; 34:20; Deut. 28:26; Ps. 79:2 [q][Isa. 17:2]
34 [r]ch. 16:9; 25:10; Ps. 78:63; Isa. 24:7, 8; Rev. 18:22, 23; [Ezek. 26:13; Hos. 2:11] [s]ch. 27:17; 44:2, 6; Lev. 26:31, 33

Chapter 8
2 [t]Deut. 4:19; 2 Kgs. 21:3; 23:5; [Job 31:26-28; Ezek. 8:16] [u][Job 27:19] [v]ch. 9:22; 16:4; 25:33 **3** [w][Job 3:21, 22; 7:15, 16; Rev. 9:6] [x]ch. 23:3, 8; 29:14, 18; 32:37; Dan. 9:7

Sin and Treachery

4 "You shall say to them, Thus says the
LORD:
[y]When men fall, do they not rise again?
If one turns away, does he not return?
5 Why then has this people [z]turned away
in perpetual [a]backsliding?
[b]They hold fast to deceit;
they refuse to return.
6 [c]I have paid attention and listened,
but they have not spoken rightly;
no man relents of his evil,
saying, 'What have I done?'
Everyone turns to his own course,
[d]like a horse plunging headlong into
battle.
7 Even the stork in the heavens
knows her times,
and [e]the turtledove, [f]swallow, and crane[1]
keep the time of their coming,
[g]but my people know not
the rules[2] of the LORD.

8 [h]"How can you say, 'We are wise,
and the law of the LORD is with us'?
But behold, the lying pen of the scribes
has made it into a lie.
9 [i]The wise men shall be put to shame;
they shall be dismayed [j]and taken;
behold, they have rejected the word of
the LORD,
so what wisdom is in them?
10 [k]Therefore I will give their wives to others
and their fields to conquerors,
because from the least to the greatest
everyone [l]is greedy for unjust gain;
from prophet to priest,
everyone deals falsely.
11 They have healed [m]the wound of my
people lightly,
saying, 'Peace, peace,'
when there is no peace.
12 Were they ashamed when they committed abomination?
No, [n]they were not at all ashamed;
they did not know how to blush.
[o]Therefore they shall fall among the
fallen;
when I punish them, they shall be
overthrown,
says the LORD.
13 When I would gather them, declares the
LORD,
there are [q]no grapes on the vine,
[r]nor figs on the fig tree;
[s]even the leaves are withered,
and what I gave them has passed away
from them."[3]

14 Why do we sit still?
[t]Gather together; let us go into the fortified cities
and perish there,
for the LORD our God has doomed us to
perish
and has [u]given us [v]poisoned water to
drink,
because we have sinned against the
LORD.
15 [w]We looked for peace, but no good came;
for a time of healing, but behold, terror.

16 [x]"The snorting of their horses is heard
[y]from Dan;
at the sound of the neighing [z]of their
stallions
[a]the whole land quakes.
They come [b]and devour the land and all
that fills it,
the city and those who dwell in it.
17 For behold, I am sending among you
[c]serpents,
adders [d]that cannot be charmed,
[e]and they shall bite you,"
declares the LORD.

[1] The meaning of the Hebrew word is uncertain [2] Or *just decrees* [3] The meaning of the Hebrew is uncertain

8:4–17 Once again Jeremiah delivers a stinging indictment of the people for their hardness of heart. This time he focuses on the claims of wisdom. Under David and Solomon, the wisdom traditions and literature had flourished. But these "wise men" (vv. 8–9) have misled the people with false words of comfort (vv. 10–11). True wisdom is based on the fear of the Lord (Prov. 1:7), and without that vital foundation it becomes worldly cleverness that in God's sight is foolishness. Solomon appears to have forgotten the fear of the Lord (1 Kings 11:1–8) as he plunged Judah into idolatry and faithlessness.

4[y] [Rom. 11:11]
5[z] See ch. 7:24 [a] See ch. 2:19 [b] ch. 9:6
6[c] [2 Pet. 3:9] [d] See Job 39:19-25
7[e] Song 2:12 [f] Isa. 38:14 [g] [ch. 5:4, 5; Isa. 1:3]
8[h] [Rom. 2:17, 18]
9[i] [1 Cor. 1:19, 20] [j] Job 5:13
10[k] For ver. 10-12, see ch. 6:12-15 [l] [Isa. 56:11]

11[m] ver. 21 **12**[n] See ch. 3:3 [o] [Hos. 4:5] **13**[q] Isa. 5:1, 2; Joel 1:7 [r] [Matt. 21:19; Luke 13:6] [s] Isa. 1:30 **14**[t] ch. 4:5 [u] ch. 9:15; 23:15; Lam. 3:15, 19; Amos 6:12; [Rev. 8:11] [v] ch. 23:15; Deut. 29:18 **15**[w] ch. 14:19; Job 30:26 **16**[x] Job 39:20 [y] ch. 4:15 [z] Judg. 5:22 [a] ch. 49:21; 51:29; Ps. 60:2 [b] ch. 10:25; 47:2 **17**[c] [Lev. 26:22] [d] Ps. 58:4, 5; [Eccles. 10:11] [e] Num. 21:6

Jeremiah Grieves for His People

18 My joy is gone; grief is upon me;[1]
[f]my heart is sick within me.
19 Behold, the cry of the daughter of my
people
from [g]the length and breadth of the
land:
"Is the LORD not in Zion?
[h]Is her King not in her?"
[i]"Why have they provoked me to anger
with their carved images
and with their foreign idols?"
20 "The harvest is past, the summer is ended,
and we are not saved."
21 For the wound of [j]the daughter of my
people is my heart wounded;
[k]I mourn, and dismay has taken hold
on me.

22 Is there no [l]balm in Gilead?
Is there no physician there?
Why then has the health of the daughter
of my people
not been restored?

9 [2] [m]Oh that my head were waters,
and my eyes a fountain of tears,
that I might weep day and night
for the slain of [j]the daughter of my
people!
2[3] Oh that I had in the desert
a travelers' lodging place,
that I might leave my people
and go away from them!
For they are all [n]adulterers,
a company of [o]treacherous men.
3 [p]They bend their tongue like a bow;
falsehood and not truth has grown
strong[4] in the land;
for they proceed from evil to evil,
[q]and they do not know me, declares
the LORD.

4 [r]Let everyone beware of his neighbor,
and put no trust in any brother,
for every [s]brother is a deceiver,
and every neighbor [t]goes about as a
slanderer.
5 Everyone deceives his neighbor,
and no one speaks the truth;
they have taught their tongue to speak
lies;
they weary themselves committing
iniquity.
6 Heaping oppression upon oppression,
and deceit upon deceit,
[u]they refuse to know me, declares the
LORD.

7 Therefore thus says the LORD of hosts:
"Behold, [v]I will refine them and [w]test them,
for what else can I do, [j]because of my
people?
8 [x]Their tongue is a deadly arrow;
[y]it speaks deceitfully;
with his mouth [z]each speaks peace to his
neighbor,
but in his heart [a]he plans an ambush
for him.
9 [b]Shall I not punish them for these things?
declares the LORD,
and shall I not avenge myself
on a nation such as this?

10 "I will take up weeping and wailing for
the mountains,
and a lamentation for [c]the pastures of
the wilderness,

[1] Compare Septuagint; the meaning of the Hebrew is uncertain [2] Ch 8:23 in Hebrew [3] Ch 9:1 in Hebrew [4] Septuagint; Hebrew *and not for truth they have grown strong*

The fear of the Lord is supremely revealed in the New Testament as humble trust in Jesus, the true wise man of Israel (Matt. 7:24–29). For in the grace of the gospel, Jesus not only embodies wisdom but has become for us "wisdom from God, righteousness and sanctification and redemption" (1 Cor. 1:30).

8:18–9:3 Jeremiah's anguish and sorrow is not simply empathy with the suffering of his people that will come with the devastation of invasion. He is attuned to the covenant with both its promises of blessing and its curses of judgment on disobedience (Deuteronomy 28). All that the land, the city, the temple, and the kingship stood for is under threat. There is no healing ointment to apply to the wounds of the people. Their waywardness is beyond any self-generated recovery. God must provide what his people cannot provide for themselves, if they are to know his covenant blessings. This is clear from Jesus' own day, as he would grieve over an unrepentant Jerusalem and the coming destruction of the temple because his people would not depend on God's provision (himself) for them (Matt. 23:37–24:2).

18[f] Isa. 1:5; Lam. 1:13, 22; 5:17
19[g] Isa. 39:3 [h] Isa. 33:17 [i] Deut. 32:21
21[j] ver. 11; ch. 14:17 [k] Job 30:30; Lam. 4:8; Joel 2:6; Nah. 2:10
22[l] ch. 46:11; [Gen. 37:25]
Chapter 9
1[m] See ch. 13:17 [j] [See ch. 8:21 above]
2[n] ch. 5:7, 8; 23:10; Hos. 7:4 [o] Isa. 21:2
3[p] [Ps. 64:3] [q] [Judg. 2:10; Hos. 4:1]
4[r] ch. 12:6; Ps. 41:9; Mic. 7:5 [s] [Gen. 27:36] [t] ch. 6:28; [Lev. 19:16]
6[u] ch. 8:5
7[v] Isa. 1:25 [w] ch. 6:27 [j] [See ch. 8:21 above]
8[x] [Ps. 57:4] [y] [Ps. 12:2; 120:3] [z] Ps. 28:3 [a] Hos. 7:6
9[b] ch. 5:9, 29
10[c] ch. 12:4; Ps. 65:12

[d]because they are laid waste so that no
one passes through,
and the lowing of cattle is not heard;
[e]both the birds of the air and the beasts
have fled and are gone.
11 [f]I will make Jerusalem a heap of ruins,
[g]a lair of jackals,
[h]and I will make the cities of Judah a desolation,
without inhabitant."

12 [i]Who is the man so wise that he can understand this? To whom has the mouth of the
LORD spoken, that he may declare it? Why is
the land ruined [j]and laid waste like a wilderness, so that no one passes through? 13 And
the LORD says: [k]"Because they have forsaken
my law that I set before them, and have not
obeyed my voice or walked in accord with it,
14 but [l]have stubbornly followed their own
hearts and have gone after the Baals, as their
fathers taught them. 15 Therefore thus says
the LORD of hosts, the God of Israel: [m]Behold,
I will feed this people with bitter food, and
give them [n]poisonous water to drink. 16 [o]I will
scatter them among the nations [p]whom neither they nor their fathers have known, and
I will [q]send the sword after them, until I have
consumed them."

17 Thus says the LORD of hosts:
[r]"Consider, and call for the mourning
women to come;
send for the skillful women to come;
18 let them make haste [s]and raise a wailing
over us,
[t]that our eyes may run down with tears
and our eyelids flow with water.
19 For a sound of wailing is heard from
Zion:
[u]'How we are ruined!
We are utterly shamed,
because we have left the land,
because they have cast down our
dwellings.'"

20 Hear, O women, the word of the LORD,
and let your ear receive the word of
his mouth;
teach to your daughters a lament,
and each to her neighbor a dirge.
21 For death has come up into our windows;
it has entered our palaces,
[v]cutting off the children from the streets
and the young men from the squares.
22 Speak: "Thus declares the LORD,
[w]'The dead bodies of men shall fall
like dung upon the open field,
[x]like sheaves after the reaper,
and none shall gather them.'"

23 Thus says the LORD: [y]"Let not the wise
man boast in his wisdom, let not the mighty
man boast in his might, let not the rich man
boast in his riches, 24 but [z]let him who boasts
boast in this, that he understands and knows
me, that I am the LORD who practices steadfast love, justice, and righteousness in the
earth. [a]For in these things I delight, declares
the LORD."

25 "Behold, the days are coming, declares the
LORD, when [b]I will punish all those who are
circumcised merely in the flesh— 26 [c]Egypt,
Judah, Edom, the sons of Ammon, Moab,
and [d]all who dwell in the desert who cut the
corners of their hair, for all these nations are

10[d] ver. 12 [e] ch. 4:25
11[f] Isa. 25:2 [g] ch. 10:22; 49:33; 51:37 [h] ch. 34:22; 44:6
12[i] ch. 23:18; Ps. 107:43; Hos. 14:9 [j] ver. 10
13[k] [Ps. 89:30-32]
14[l] See ch. 3:17
15[m] Deut. 29:18; [Ps. 80:5] [n] See ch. 8:14
16[o] Lev. 26:33; Deut. 28:64 [p] ch. 15:14 [q] ch. 14:12; [ch. 49:37; Ezek. 5:2, 12]
17[r] [2 Chr. 35:25]
18[s] Amos 5:16; [Matt. 9:23; Mark 5:38] [t] ver. 1; ch. 14:17
19[u] ch. 4:13
21[v] ch. 6:11
22[w] See ch. 8:2 [x] [Lev. 23:22; Job 5:26]
23[y] Prov. 3:5; 21:30; Eccles. 9:11
24[z] [Ps. 34:2; 1 Cor. 1:31; 2 Cor. 10:17] [a] [Mic. 6:8; 7:18]
25[b] [Isa. 24:21]
26[c] [ch. 25:19-21] [d] ch. 25:23; 49:32; [Lev. 19:27]

9:12–22 Jeremiah asks who has the wisdom to understand this terrible reversal of fortune (v. 12). The Lord's answer is clear: if there is no covenant faithfulness, there will be no covenant blessings (v. 13). The horror and shame of this situation is graphically portrayed (vv. 17–22). The tribulation described foreshadows a greater tribulation to come. The land, city, and temple will be destroyed by the Romans in future generations. But the greatest tribulation of God's people will be experienced by a faithful Israelite who will suffer on behalf of his people and be put to death on a cross.

If you are in Christ, your greatest tribulation—condemnation and hell—has been resolved. Indeed, you can see it, right there at the cross of Christ. That cross was the final judgment and condemnation for everyone who looks in trusting faith to Christ, abandoning their own moral resume and banking their pardoned future on him.

9:23–24 Can a Christian boast? Clearly Jeremiah rejected the worldly boasting of the "wise" men, the rich, and the powerful. There is only one basis for boasting, and that is to boast in knowing the Lord. Even this might sound like pretentious pride. But in the context of God's grace it is not a boasting in oneself but in the Lord. So Paul, without in any way condoning pride (Rom. 3:27–28), quotes Jeremiah and encourages the Christian to boast in the Lord (1 Cor. 1:30–31).

uncircumcised, and all the house of Israel are [e]uncircumcised in heart."

Idols and the Living God

10 Hear the word that the LORD speaks to you, O house of Israel. [2] Thus says the LORD:

"Learn not the way of the nations,
nor be dismayed at the signs of the heavens
because the nations are dismayed at them,
3 [f]for the customs of the peoples are vanity.[1]
[g]A tree from the forest is cut down
and worked with an axe by the hands of a craftsman.
4 [h]They decorate it with silver and gold;
[i]they fasten it with hammer and nails
so that it cannot move.
5 Their idols[2] are like scarecrows in a cucumber field,
and [j]they cannot speak;
[k]they have to be carried,
for they cannot walk.
Do not be afraid of them,
[l]for they cannot do evil,
neither is it in them to do good."
6 [m]There is none like you, O LORD;
you are great, and your name is great in might.
7 [n]Who would not fear you, O King of the nations?
For this is your due;
for among all the wise ones of the nations
and in all their kingdoms
there is none like you.
8 [o]They are both [p]stupid and foolish;
the instruction of idols is but wood!
9 [q]Beaten silver is brought from [r]Tarshish,
and gold from [s]Uphaz.
[q]They are the work of the craftsman and of the hands of the goldsmith;
their clothing is violet and purple;
[t]they are all the work of skilled men.
10 [u]But the LORD is the true God;
[v]he is the living God and the everlasting King.
At his wrath the earth quakes,
and the nations cannot endure his indignation.

[11] Thus shall you say to them: [w]"The gods who did not make the heavens and the earth [x]shall perish from the earth and from under the heavens."[3]

[1] Or *vapor*, or *mist* [2] Hebrew *They* [3] This verse is in Aramaic

How can this be? It is because God provides our wisdom, righteousness, sanctification, and redemption—ultimately in Christ. The boasting that Jeremiah urges as a consequence of one's knowledge of the Lord (and not one's own qualities) anticipates the gospel. Our union with Christ by faith is the basis for any merit that we have before God, as what characterizes Christ's perfect humanity becomes ours—imputed to us by his grace. We have the confidence and comfort of knowing that our acceptance by God is perfect, since it is based on Christ's perfect acceptance by the Father (Rom. 3:21–26; Eph. 2:5–6). God would have to turn his back on his own Son, to turn his back on those who are united to his Son.

10:1–10 Jeremiah reminds the people of Judah that there are two ways to live. One is to trust in idols, a foolish path that leads to futility and destruction. The other is to trust in the Lord. He is sovereign over the affairs of the nations. He is the one true God and everlasting King. His wrath will be shown in the earth among these godless nations.

Babylon, the present threat to Judah, comes to be symbolic of everything in the world that is evil and hostile to God. There are those from among the nations of the world who will find redemption in Israel's God (Acts 10; Rev. 7:9–17). But there are also those who will fall under God's judgment (Rev. 18:1–3). Christians are called upon to keep themselves unstained from the world (James 1:27) and from idols (1 John 5:20–21). We can be either friends with the world and enemies of God, or hated by the world and friends with God. But this need not discourage us. The beauty of the gospel is that we who are natural enemies of God can freely become his friends—indeed, his sons and daughters—because the Son of God allowed himself to be treated as God's enemy (Gal. 3:13).

10:11–13 That God is the Creator of all things is basic to understanding his sovereignty. By contrast, idols have made nothing and will themselves be nothing (v. 11). Creation

26[e] Lev. 26:41; Deut. 10:16; Ezek. 44:7; Rom. 2:28, 29; [ch. 4:4]
Chapter 10
3[f] Isa. 44:9 [g] Isa. 40:20; 45:20
4[h] Isa. 40:19 [i] Isa. 41:7
5[j] Ps. 115:5; 135:16; Hab. 2:18, 19; 1 Cor. 12:2 [k] Ps. 115:7; Isa. 46:7 [l] Isa. 41:23
6[m] ch. 49:19; Ex. 15:11; Ps. 86:8, 10
7[n] ch. 5:22; Rev. 15:4
8[o] [Isa. 41:29; Hab. 2:18; Zech. 10:2] [p] ver. 21
9[q] Isa. 40:19 [r] Gen. 10:4; See 1 Kgs. 10:22 [s] Dan. 10:5 [t] Ps. 115:4
10[u] Deut. 32:4; Ps. 31:5 [v] Ps. 42:2
11[w] [Ps. 96:5] [x] ver. 15; Isa. 2:18; Zech. 13:2

12 [y]It is he who [z]made the earth by his power,
[z]who established the world by his wisdom,
and [a]by his understanding stretched out the heavens.
13 [b]When he utters his voice, there is a tumult of waters in the heavens,
[c]and he makes the mist rise from the ends of the earth.
[c]He makes lightning [d]for the rain,
[c]and he brings forth the wind [e]from his storehouses.
14 [f]Every man is stupid and without knowledge;
[g]every goldsmith is put to shame by his idols,
for his images are false,
[h]and there is no breath in them.
15 They are worthless, a work of delusion;
at the time of their punishment they shall perish.
16 Not like these is he who is [i]the portion of Jacob,
for he is the one who formed all things,
[j]and Israel is the tribe of his inheritance;
[k]the LORD of hosts is his name.

17 [l]Gather up your bundle from the ground,
O you who dwell under siege!
18 For thus says the LORD:
[m]"Behold, I am slinging out the inhabitants of the land
at this time,
[n]and I will bring distress on them,
that they may feel it."

19 Woe is me because of my hurt!
[o]My wound is grievous.
But I said, "Truly this is an affliction,
and I must bear it."
20 [p]My tent is destroyed,
and all my cords are broken;
my children have gone from me,
[q]and they are not;
there is no one to spread my tent again
and [p]to set up my curtains.
21 [r]For the shepherds [s]are stupid
and do not inquire of the LORD;
therefore they have not prospered,
[t]and all their flock is scattered.

22 A voice, a rumor! Behold, it comes!—
[u]a great commotion out of the north country
to make [v]the cities of Judah a desolation,
[v]a lair of jackals.

23 [w]I know, O LORD, that the way of man is not in himself,
that it is not in man who walks to direct his steps.
24 [x]Correct me, O LORD, but in justice;
not in your anger, lest you bring me to nothing.

25 [y]Pour out your wrath on the nations that know you not,
and on the peoples that call not on your name,
[z]for they have devoured Jacob;
they have devoured him and consumed him,
and have laid waste his habitation.

The Broken Covenant

11 The word that came to Jeremiah from
the LORD: 2 [a]"Hear the words of this
covenant, and speak to the men of Judah and
the inhabitants of Jerusalem. 3 You shall say to
them, Thus says the LORD, the God of Israel:
[b]Cursed be the man who does not hear the

demonstrates God's power, his wisdom (see Prov. 8:22–31), and the efficacy of his word (Gen. 1:3, 6, 9; John 1:1–3).

In the New Testament these themes have new force. Christ is the creating Word in the beginning (John 1:1–3; Col. 1:15–17). The creative power, wisdom, and word are exhibited in the gospel and bring about the new creation in Christ (2 Cor. 5:17). Paul thus likens the creation of a Christian to the creation of the world (2 Cor. 4:6). Both bring something out of nothing. Both are a miracle of divine initiative. For both, we praise God.

11:1–5 The covenant involved God's election of Israel, a people upon whom he set his love even though there was no virtue in them that he should desire them (Deut. 7:6–11). It is sheer grace—undeserved gift—that grounds this relationship. The release from captivity in Egypt was also an undeserved gift. The redeemed people were instructed in the covenant at Sinai concerning how they should live. Obedience to this law could

12 [y]For ver. 12-16, see ch. 51:15-19 [z]Gen. 1:1, 6, 9; Ps. 104:5; Prov. 3:19 [a]Job 9:8
13 [b][Job 38:34; Ps. 104:6, 7] [c]Ps. 135:7 [d]ch. 14:22; Job 5:10 [e]Job 38:22
14 [f]ver. 8; Prov. 30:2; [Rom. 1:22] [g]See Isa. 42:17 [h]Ps. 135:17; Hab. 2:19
16 [i]Ps. 16:5 [j]Deut. 32:9 [k]ch. 31:35; 32:18; 50:34
17 [l][ch. 6:1; Ezek. 12:3]
18 [m]1 Sam. 25:29 [n]Deut. 28:20
19 [o]ch. 14:17; 30:12
20 [p]ch. 4:20; [Isa. 54:2] [q]ch. 31:15
21 [r]ch. 23:1; Ezek. 34:2 [s]ver. 8 [t]Ezek. 34:5, 6
22 [u]See ch. 1:13 [v]See ch. 9:11
23 [w]Prov. 16:1; 20:24; Dan. 5:23
24 [x]ch. 30:11; 46:28; Ps. 6:1; 38:1 **25** [y]Ps. 79:6, 7 [z]ch. 8:16; 30:16; Ps. 14:4 **Chapter 11** **2** [a]ver. 6, 8; [2 Kgs. 23:3] **3** [b]Deut. 27:26; Gal. 3:10

words of this covenant 4 that I commanded
your fathers when I brought them out of the
land of Egypt, [c]from the iron furnace, saying,
[d]Listen to my voice, and do all that I command
you. [d]So shall you be my people, and I will be
your God, 5 [e]that I may confirm the oath that
I swore to your fathers, [f]to give them a land
flowing with milk and honey, as at this day."
Then I answered, "So be it, LORD."
6 And the LORD said to me, [g]"Proclaim all
these words in the cities of Judah and in the
streets of Jerusalem: [h]Hear the words of this
covenant and do them. 7 For I solemnly warned
your fathers when I brought them up out of
the land of Egypt, [i]warning them persistently,
even to this day, saying, [d]Obey my voice. 8 [j]Yet
they did not obey or incline their ear, [k]but
everyone walked in the stubbornness of his
evil heart. Therefore I brought upon them
all [h]the words of this covenant, which I commanded them to do, but they did not."
9 Again the LORD said to me, [l]"A conspiracy exists among the men of Judah and the
inhabitants of Jerusalem. 10 They have turned
back to [m]the iniquities of their forefathers,
who refused to hear my words. [m]They have
gone after other gods to serve them. [n]The
house of Israel and the house of Judah have
broken my covenant that I made with their
fathers. 11 Therefore, thus says the LORD,
Behold, I am bringing disaster upon them
that they cannot escape. [o]Though they cry to
me, I will not listen to them. 12 Then the cities
of Judah and the inhabitants of Jerusalem
[p]will go and cry to the gods to whom they
make offerings, [p]but they cannot save them
in the time of their trouble. 13 [p]For your gods
have become as many as your cities, O Judah,
and as many as the streets of Jerusalem are
the altars you have set up to shame, [q]altars
to make offerings to Baal.
14 "Therefore [r]do not pray for this people, or
lift up a cry or prayer on their behalf, [o]for I will
not listen when they call to me in the time of
their trouble. 15 [s]What right has my beloved
in my house, [t]when she has done many vile
deeds? Can even sacrificial flesh avert your
doom? [u]Can you then exult? 16 The LORD
once called you [v]'a green olive tree, beautiful
with good fruit.' But [w]with the roar of a great
tempest he will set fire to it, and [x]its branches
will be consumed. 17 The LORD of hosts, [y]who
planted you, has decreed disaster against you,
because of the evil that the house of Israel and
the house of Judah have done, [z]provoking me
to anger by making offerings to Baal."

not save them (Gal. 2:16; 3:11). But continual and hard-hearted disregard of it brought the consequent curses of the covenant upon them.

Judah is now faced with the disgrace of having scorned its election to be the people of God. Yet to be reminded of this privilege is to be reminded of God's covenant faithfulness. The grace and love of the covenant came to be summarized as, "I will be your God, and you shall be my people" (Jer. 7:23; cf. 24:7; 30:22; Gen. 17:7–8; Lev. 26:12; Ezek. 11:20; 14:11; 36:28; 37:27). Throughout the book of Jeremiah and the books of the other canonical prophets we are startled by repeated reminders that the faithlessness of Israel and Judah cannot frustrate God's sovereign grace. He has determined to have a remnant of faithful people among whom he will dwell in glory. Paul applies this principle, for example, in quoting Leviticus 26:12 in 2 Corinthians 6:14–18. There he uses temple theology and categories to describe the body of Christ, urging Christians to live as God's people and to avoid godless pursuits.

11:14 Three times Jeremiah is told not to pray for this people (see also 7:16; 14:11). This is a terrible indictment of their sin. There comes a time when even prophetic intercession is impotent to reclaim those who persistently rebel against God's word. Then, God may harden hearts and deafen ears to his mercy as part of his judgment against such resistance. As God hardened Pharaoh's heart (Ex. 7:3; 9:12; 10:1, 20, 27; 11:10), so he hardens whom he wills (Rom. 9:14–18). But while God is absolutely sovereign, human responsibility is in no way undermined. We are all fully culpable for our own hardness of heart (Ex. 8:15, 32; 9:34–35). So, while Jesus told his disciples to pray for their enemies (Matt. 5:44), Scripture also declares there will come a time when the opportunity for repentance is past (Heb. 6:4–8) and the vine is cleansed by judgment (John 15:6). Even Jesus, the true Prophet, did not pray for the world that would not repent, but for those God had given him (John 17:6–9).

The gospel is good news only to those who trust in Christ, while in it God's righteousness is revealed and his wrath declared against all unrighteousness (Rom. 1:16–18).

4 [c]Deut. 4:20 [d]ch. 7:22, 23; Lev. 26:3, 12
5 [e]Deut. 7:12, 13; Ps. 105:9, 10 [f]See Ex. 3:8
6 [g][ch. 19:2] [h]ver. 2, 8; [2 Kgs. 23:3]
7 [i]ch. 7:25; See 2 Chr. 36:15 [d][See ver. 4 above]
8 [j]ch. 7:26; 32:23 [k]See ch. 3:17 [h][See ver. 6 above]
9 [l]Ezek. 22:25; [Isa. 8:12; Hos. 6:9]
10 [m][ch. 17:23; Ps. 78:8; 79:8; Ezek. 20:18] [n]Deut. 31:16, 20
11 [o]Prov. 1:28; Isa. 1:15; Ezek. 8:18; Mic. 3:4
12 [p]ch. 2:28; [Acts 17:16]
13 [p][See ver. 12 above] [q][Hos. 9:10]; See Judg. 6:25-32
14 [r]ch. 7:16; [Heb. 10:26; 1 John 5:16] [o][See ver. 11 above]
15 [s]Isa. 1:11, 12 [t][Ezek. 16:25] [u]Prov. 2:14
16 [v]Ps. 52:8; [Hos. 14:6] [w][Ps. 83:2] [x]Rom. 11:17, 20
17 [y]ch. 2:21; Isa. 5:2 [z]See ch. 7:18

18 The LORD made it known to me and
I knew;
then you showed me their deeds.
19 But I was [a]like a gentle lamb
led to the slaughter.
I did not know [b]it was against me
they devised schemes, saying,
"Let us destroy the tree with its fruit,
[c]let us cut him off from [d]the land of
the living,
that his name be remembered no
more."
20 But, O LORD of hosts, who judges righteously,
who [e]tests [f]the heart and the mind,
[g]let me see your vengeance upon them,
for to you have I committed my
cause.

21 Therefore thus says the LORD concerning
the men of [h]Anathoth, [i]who seek your life,
and say, [j]"Do not prophesy in the name of the
LORD, or you will die by our hand"— 22 therefore thus says the LORD of hosts: "Behold,
I will punish them. The young men shall die
by the sword, their sons and their daughters
shall die by famine, 23 and none of them shall
be left. For I will bring disaster upon the men
of [k]Anathoth, [l]the year of their punishment."

Jeremiah's Complaint

12 [m]Righteous are you, O LORD,
when I complain to you;
yet I would plead my case before you.
[n]Why does the way of the wicked prosper?
Why do all [o]who are treacherous
thrive?
2 You plant them, and they take root;
they grow and produce fruit;
[p]you are near in their mouth
and far from their heart.
3 [q]But you, O LORD, know me;
[r]you see me, and test my heart toward
you.
[s]Pull them out like sheep for the slaughter,
and set them apart for [t]the day of
slaughter.
4 [u]How long will the land mourn
and the grass of every field wither?
[v]For the evil of those who dwell in it
[w]the beasts and the birds are swept
away,
because they said, "He will not see our
latter end."

The LORD Answers Jeremiah

5 "If you have raced with men on foot, and
they have wearied you,
how will you compete with horses?
And if in a safe land you are so trusting,
what will you do in [x]the thicket of the
Jordan?
6 For [y]even your brothers and the house of
your father,
[o]even they have dealt treacherously
with you;
they are in full cry after you;

19[a] Isa. 53:7; [Rev. 5:6] [b] ch. 18:18; Lam. 3:60, 61 [c] Ps. 83:4; Isa. 53:8 [d] Ps. 27:13
20[e] ch. 17:10; 20:12; Ps. 7:9; Rev. 2:23 [f] See 1 Sam. 16:7 [g] ch. 15:15; 17:18; 20:12; Lam. 3:64
21[h] Josh. 21:18 [i] [ch. 12:6; Matt. 13:57] [j] Isa. 30:10
23[k] Josh. 21:18 [l] ch. 23:12
Chapter 12
1[m] Ezra 9:15; Ps. 51:4; Lam. 1:18; Dan. 9:7 [n] Job 12:6; Ps. 37:1, 7; 92:7; Hab. 1:13; Mal. 3:15; See Job 21:7-15; Ps. 73:3-12 [o] [Isa. 21:2]
2[p] Isa. 29:13
3[q] ch. 15:15; Ps. 139:1 [r] Ps. 17:3 [s] [2 Pet. 2:12] [t] James 5:5
4[u] ver. 11; ch. 9:10; 23:10 [v] Ps. 107:34 [w] ch. 4:25; 7:20; 9:10; Hos. 4:3; [Rom. 8:22]
5[x] ch. 49:19; 50:44; Zech. 11:3; [Josh. 3:15]
6[y] ch. 9:4; [ch. 11:19, 21] [o] [See ver. 1 above]

12:1–4 Jeremiah's complaint is similar to that of certain Psalms in which the psalmist cries out for vindication, often in the face of persecution (e.g., Psalms 52–57). The problem is the apparent prosperity of the wicked. A similar concern to justify the ways of God is expressed by the prophet Habakkuk (see also Psalm 73). A significant part of the answer given to Habakkuk is that "the righteous shall live by his faith" (Hab. 2:4; cf. Ps. 73:23–28). This great truth is used by Paul to encapsulate the heart of the gospel, which is justification by faith (Rom. 1:17; Gal. 3:1). In a world in which evil prospers, we need the assurance of God's judgment. This includes not only confidence in God's punitive justice that rights all wrongs, but also our being justified by faith in Jesus Christ. In both cases, God is vindicated as supremely just.

12:5–17 The Lord's response to Jeremiah's complaint is that things will get even worse (vv. 5–6). This is because God has forsaken his house and his heritage (vv. 7–9), just as later he would forsake his Son (cf. Ex. 4:22–23) at the moment when Jesus assumed the sins of his people (Matt. 27:46). Desolation comes at the hand of false shepherds and evil neighbors (Jer. 12:10–13), but ultimately it is "the sword of the LORD" that devours them (v. 12). Clearly, the evil destroyers are God's agents even though they have no idea that they are. Furthermore, they are guilty of their evil deeds. God will punish them for what they do to his people (vv. 14–17). At the same time, he will have compassion on the sinful people of Judah and restore them to their heritage. They will once again call on the name of the Lord.

[z]do not believe them,
though they speak friendly words to
you."

7 "I have forsaken my house;
I have abandoned [a]my heritage;
I have given [b]the beloved of my soul
into the hands of her enemies.
8 [a]My heritage has become to me
like a lion in the forest;
she has lifted up her voice against me;
therefore I hate her.
9 Is [a]my heritage to me like [c]a hyena's lair?
Are the [c]birds of prey against her all
around?
Go, [d]assemble all the wild beasts;
bring them to devour.
10 Many shepherds have destroyed my
vineyard;
[e]they have trampled down my portion;
they have made my pleasant portion
a desolate wilderness.
11 They have made it a desolation;
desolate, [u]it mourns to me.
The whole land is made desolate,
[f]but no man lays it to heart.
12 Upon all the bare heights in the desert
destroyers have come,
for the sword of the LORD devours
from one end of the land to the other;
no flesh has peace.
13 [g]They have sown wheat and have reaped
thorns;
[h]they have tired themselves out but
profit nothing.
They shall be ashamed of their[1] harvests
[i]because of the fierce anger of the
LORD."

14 Thus says the LORD concerning all [j]my evil
neighbors [k]who touch the heritage that [l]I have
given my people Israel to inherit: "Behold,
I will pluck them up from their land, and I will
pluck up the house of Judah from among
them. 15 And after I have plucked them up,
I will again have compassion on them, [m]and
I will bring them again each to his heritage
and each to his land. 16 And it shall come to
pass, if they will diligently learn the ways of
my people, [n]to swear by my name, 'As the LORD
lives,' even as they taught my people to swear
by Baal, [o]then they shall be built up in the
midst of my people. 17 [p]But if any nation will
not listen, then I will utterly pluck it up and
destroy it, declares the LORD."

The Ruined Loincloth

13 Thus says the LORD to me, "Go and buy
a linen loincloth and [q]put it around
your waist, and do not dip it in water." 2 So
I bought a loincloth according to the word of
the LORD, and put it around my waist. 3 And
the word of the LORD came to me a second
time, 4 "Take the loincloth that you have
bought, which is around your waist, and arise,
[r]go to the Euphrates and hide it there in [s]a
cleft of the rock." 5 So I went and hid it by the
Euphrates, as the LORD commanded me. 6 And
after many days the LORD said to me, "Arise,
go to the Euphrates, and take from there

[1] Hebrew *your*

Thus, in God's providential use and divine judgment of the evil that humans choose to do, and in his salvation of those who at times choose to walk away from him, we find two seemingly irreconcilable facts: God's sovereignty and human responsibility. In Jeremiah these are brought together without explanation. We are therefore content to receive God's word on this, even if it is beyond our finite capacities to fully understand how they fit together.

Jeremiah also points to the salvation of Israel as a light to the nations. The promise of Genesis 12:3 continues to travel down through redemptive history. In Christ, this promise will explode out to the nations, as the gospel welcomes both insiders and outsiders to leave their moral records behind and come to Christ.

13:1–11 Jeremiah is commanded to act out a parable with a loincloth that is spoiled. The message is that Israel and Judah were intended to cling to the Lord as a loincloth but have refused, and the cloth is rotten (v. 11). Now their pride will be spoiled (v. 9). God's purpose for his people is that they should be a name, a praise, and a glory for him (v. 11). They represent God, reflecting him to a watching world.

In the final analysis, only Jesus was perfectly true to this purpose. Consequently, Christians are chosen "in Christ" from before the foundation of the world to be holy and blameless, to the praise of God's glorious grace (Eph. 1:3–6, 11–12).

6[z] Prov. 26:25
7[a] Isa. 19:25 [b] ch. 11:15
8[a] [See ver. 7 above]
9[a] [See ver. 7 above] [c] Isa. 46:11 [d] ch. 7:33; Isa. 56:9; [Ezek. 39:17; Rev. 19:17]
10[e] Isa. 63:18
11[u] [See ver. 4 above] [f] Isa. 42:25
13[g] [Lev. 26:16; Deut. 28:38; Mic. 6:15; Hag. 1:6] [h] Isa. 55:2; Hab. 2:13 [i] ch. 4:8, 26; 25:37, 38; 30:24; 49:37; 51:45; Lam. 1:12; 4:11
14[j] [Ps. 137:7]; See Ezek. 25 [k] Zech. 2:8 [l] ch. 3:18
15[m] ch. 48:47; 49:6
16[n] ch. 4:2 [o] ch. 24:6; [1 Pet. 2:5]
17[p] [Isa. 60:12]
Chapter 13
1[q] Ex. 28:39; Lev. 16:4; [Acts 21:11]
4[r] [ch. 51:59, 63] [s] Isa. 7:19

[q]the loincloth that I commanded you to hide
there." 7 Then I went to the Euphrates, and
dug, and I took [q]the loincloth from the place
where I had hidden it. And behold, the loincloth was [t]spoiled; it was [u]good for nothing.
8 Then the word of the LORD came to me:
9 "Thus says the LORD: [v]Even so will I spoil
the pride of Judah and the great [w]pride of
Jerusalem. 10 This evil people, who refuse to
hear my words, [x]who stubbornly follow their
own heart and have gone after other gods to
serve them and worship them, shall be like
this loincloth, which is [u]good for nothing.
11 For as the loincloth clings to the waist of a
man, so I made the whole house of Israel and
the whole house of Judah cling to me, declares
the LORD, [y]that they might be for me a people,
[z]a name, a praise, and a glory, but they would
not listen.

The Jars Filled with Wine

12 "You shall speak to them this word: 'Thus
says the LORD, the God of Israel, "Every jar
shall be filled with wine."' And they will say
to you, 'Do we not indeed know that [a]every jar
will be filled with wine?' 13 Then you shall say
to them, 'Thus says the LORD: [b]Behold, I will
fill with drunkenness all the inhabitants of
this land: [c]the kings who sit on David's throne,
[d]the priests, the prophets, and all the inhabitants of Jerusalem. 14 And I will [e]dash them
one against another, fathers and sons together,
declares the LORD. I will not pity or spare or
have compassion, that I should not destroy
them.'"

Exile Threatened

15 Hear and give ear; be not proud,
for the LORD has spoken.
16 [f]Give glory to the LORD your God
[g]before he brings darkness,
before your feet stumble
on the twilight mountains,
and [g]while you look for light
he turns it into gloom
and makes it [h]deep darkness.
17 But if you will not listen,
[i]my soul will weep in secret for your
pride;
my eyes will weep bitterly and run down
with tears,
because the LORD's flock has been
taken captive.

18 Say to [j]the king and [j]the queen mother:
"Take a lowly seat,
for [k]your beautiful crown
has come down from your head."
19 [l]The cities of the Negeb are shut up,
with none to open them;
all Judah is taken into exile,
wholly taken into exile.

20 "Lift up your eyes [m]and see
those who come from the north.
Where is the flock that was given you,
your beautiful flock?
21 What will you say when they set as head
over you
those whom you yourself have taught
to be friends to you?
[n]Will not pangs take hold of you
like those of a woman in labor?
22 And if you say in your heart,
[o]'Why have these things come upon me?'
it is for the greatness of your iniquity
that [p]your skirts are lifted up
and you suffer violence.
23 [q]Can the Ethiopian change his skin
or [q]the leopard his spots?
Then also you can do good
who are accustomed to do evil.
24 I will scatter you[1] [r]like chaff
driven by the wind from the desert.
25 [s]This is your lot,
the portion I have measured out to
you, declares the LORD,

[1] Hebrew *them*

13:15–17 One of a number of threats in this chapter is that exile and captivity loom. Again there is the appeal to turn to the Lord, this time to give him glory before darkness overtakes his people. To give God the glory is to acknowledge and to bow before his greatness as the one who has made all things and who now rules over all. It is to submit to his Word and to praise him for the grace of redemption. It is to give due weight to his majesty and being. Glory belongs to God as the Creator and bringer of light (v. 16), and ultimately to his Son who is his light to the world (John 1:14; 8:12; 9:5; Rev. 4:11; 5:12; 19:1–2; 6–8).

6[q] [See ver. 1 above] **7**[q] [See ver. 1 above] [t] ch. 18:4 [u] [Ezek. 15:4, 5] **9**[v] [Ps. 137:1] [w] Lev. 26:19 **10**[x] [ch. 3:17; 16:11, 12] [u] [See ver. 7 above] **11**[y] [Ex. 19:5] [z] ch. 33:9; Isa. 55:13; Zeph. 3:20 **12**[a] ch. 48:12 **13**[b] Ezek. 23:33 [c] ch. 17:20; 19:3; 22:2 [d] [ch. 18:18] **14**[e] Ps. 2:9; [ch. 19:10, 11] **16**[f] [Josh. 7:19] [g] Isa. 5:30; 8:22; Amos 5:8; 8:9; [John 11:10] [h] Isa. 60:2 **17**[i] ch. 9:1, 18; 14:17; Lam. 1:2, 16; 2:18; 3:49 **18**[j] ch. 22:26; 2 Kgs. 24:12 [k] Prov. 4:9; Isa. 28:5; 62:3; Lam. 5:16 **19**[l] [Josh. 6:1] **20**[m] ch. 1:13, 14; 6:22 **21**[n] See Isa. 13:8 **22**[o] See ch. 5:19 [p] ver. 26; Isa. 3:17; Lam. 1:8; Nah. 3:5; [Hos. 2:10] **23**[q] [Matt. 19:26] **24**[r] Ps. 1:4; 83:13 **25**[s] Job 20:29; Ps. 11:6

because [t]you have forgotten me
and trusted in lies.
26 [p]I myself will lift up your skirts over your face,
and your shame will be seen.
27 I have seen [u]your abominations,
your adulteries and [v]neighings, your lewd whorings,
[w]on the hills in the field.
Woe to you, O Jerusalem!
How long will it be [x]before you are made clean?"

Famine, Sword, and Pestilence

14 The word of the LORD that came to Jeremiah concerning [y]the drought:

2 [z]"Judah mourns,
and [a]her gates languish;
her people lament on the ground,
and [b]the cry of Jerusalem goes up.
3 Her nobles send their servants for water;
they come to the cisterns;
they find no water;
they return with their vessels empty;
they are [c]ashamed and confounded
and [d]cover their heads.
4 Because of the ground that is dismayed,
since there is [e]no rain on the land,
the farmers are ashamed;
they cover their heads.
5 Even [f]the doe in the field forsakes her newborn fawn
because there is no grass.
6 [g]The wild donkeys stand on the bare heights;
they pant for air like jackals;
their eyes fail
because there is no vegetation.

7 "Though our iniquities testify against us,
act, O LORD, [h]for your name's sake;
[i]for our backslidings are many;
[j]we have sinned against you.
8 [k]O you hope of Israel,
its savior in time of trouble,
why should you be like a stranger in the land,
like a traveler who turns aside to tarry for a night?
9 Why should you be like a man confused,
[l]like a mighty warrior who cannot save?
Yet [m]you, O LORD, are in the midst of us,
and [n]we are called by your name;
[o]do not leave us."

10 Thus says the LORD concerning this people:
"They have loved to wander thus;
they have not restrained their feet;
[p]therefore the LORD does not accept them;
[q]now he will remember their iniquity
and punish their sins."

11 The LORD said to me: [r]"Do not pray for the
welfare of this people. 12 Though they fast,
I will not hear their cry, [s]and though they offer
burnt offering and grain offering, I will not
accept them. But I will consume them [t]by the
sword, by famine, and by pestilence."

14:1–12 The drought highlights the theme of exile in the wilderness. The people had inherited a land flowing with milk and honey. This was a fruitful land that, however imperfectly, echoed the fertility of the garden of Eden (Ex. 3:7–8; Deut. 28:1–14). The Promised Land thus foreshadowed the new creation of the messianic age (Isa. 11:1–9; 35:1–7; 65:17–25; Ezek. 36:33–38; 47:1–12). This significant theme of Eden is countered by the present experience of drought.

This fall of creation reflects the sinful fall of humanity. Here it shows up in the dreadful condition of those who should be enjoying the land's plenty but who come under this fearful judgment. When the plea is made that "we are called by your name; do not leave us" (Jer. 14:9), the Lord's response is not only to cite their sin but to withdraw the prophetic intercession (vv. 10–12; see note on 11:14).

Wilderness themes in Scripture often reflect struggle with sin and temptation. Israel wandered in the wilderness after turning back from the Promised Land. John the Baptist went into the wilderness to call Israel to repentance. Jesus went into the wilderness to overcome the Devil's temptations and to provide for his people deliverance from the exile of sin and death. But in Christ you can know that whatever wilderness experience you undergo, it cannot now be to punish you but only to prune you (John 15:2). For Jesus went through the ultimate wilderness in being rejected by men and then forsaken by the Father on the cross, on our behalf.

25 [t]ch. 2:32
26 [p][See ver. 22 above]
27 [u]ch. 6:15 [v]ch. 5:8 [w]See ch. 2:20 [x]Isa. 1:16; [Ezek. 24:13]

Chapter 14
1 [y]ch. 17:8
2 [z]Lam. 1:4 [a]Isa. 3:26; [Lam. 2:8] [b][1 Sam. 5:12]
3 [c]Ps. 40:14 [d][2 Sam. 15:30]
4 [e]ch. 3:3
5 [f]Job 39:1; Ps. 29:9
6 [g]ch. 2:24
7 [h]ver. 21; Ps. 25:11 [i]ch. 2:19 [j]ver. 20
8 [k]ch. 17:13; 50:7; Ps. 71:5
9 [l][Isa. 59:1] [m][Ex. 29:45] [n]Dan. 9:18; [Eph. 3:15] [o]Ps. 119:121
10 [p]Hos. 8:13 [q]Hos. 9:9
11 [r]See ch. 7:16
12 [s]Prov. 1:28; Isa. 1:15; Ezek. 8:18; Mic. 3:4; See ch. 6:20 [t]ch. 16:4; 24:10; 32:24; Ezek. 14:21

Lying Prophets

13 Then I said: "Ah, Lord GOD, behold, the prophets [u]say to them, 'You shall not see the sword, nor shall you have famine, but I will give you assured peace in this place.'" 14 And the LORD said to me: "The [v]prophets are prophesying lies in my name. [w]I did not send them, nor did I command them or speak to them. They are prophesying to you a lying vision, [x]worthless divination, and [y]the deceit of their own minds. 15 Therefore thus says the LORD concerning the prophets who prophesy in my name although [w]I did not send them, and who say, [t]'Sword and famine shall not come upon this land': [z]By sword and famine those prophets shall be consumed. 16 And the people to whom they prophesy shall be cast out in the streets of Jerusalem, victims of famine and sword, [a]with none to bury them—them, their wives, their sons, and their daughters. For I will pour out their evil upon them.

17 "You shall say to them this word:
[b]'Let my eyes run down with tears night
and day,
and let them not cease,
for the virgin [c]daughter of my people is
shattered with a great wound,
[d]with a very grievous blow.
18 [e]If I go out into the field,
behold, those pierced by the sword!
[e]And if I enter the city,
behold, the diseases of famine!
[f]For both prophet and priest ply their
trade through the land
and have no knowledge.'"
19 [g]Have you utterly rejected Judah?
Does your soul loathe Zion?
Why have you struck us down
[h]so that there is no healing for us?
[i]We looked for peace, but no good came;
[i]for a time of healing, but behold, terror.
20 [j]We acknowledge our wickedness,
O LORD,
and the iniquity of our fathers,
[j]for we have sinned against you.
21 Do not spurn us, [k]for your name's sake;
do not dishonor your glorious throne;
[l]remember and do not break your covenant with us.
22 Are there any among [m]the false gods of
the nations [n]that can bring rain?
Or can the heavens give showers?
Are you not he, O LORD our God?
We set our hope on you,
[o]for you do all these things.

The LORD Will Not Relent

15 Then the LORD said to me, [p]"Though [q]Moses [r]and Samuel [s]stood before me, yet my heart would not turn toward this people. Send them out of my sight, and let them go! 2 And when they ask you, 'Where shall we go?' you shall say to them, 'Thus says the LORD:

13[u] [ch. 4:10; 6:14]
14[v] See ch. 5:31 [w] ch. 23:21; 27:15; Deut. 18:20; [Matt. 7:15; Mark 13:22] [x] Ezek. 13:6; [ch. 27:9; 29:8] [y] ch. 23:26
15[w] [See ver. 14 above] [t] [See ver. 12 above] [z] [ch. 23:34]
16[a] Ps. 79:3
17[b] See ch. 13:17 [c] See ch. 8:21 [d] ch. 10:19; 30:12
18[e] Ezek. 7:15 [f] [ch. 5:31]
19[g] Lam. 5:22 [h] [ch. 15:18] [i] ch. 8:15
20[j] [Ps. 106:6; Dan. 9:5, 8]
21[k] ver. 7 [l] Lev. 26:42; Ps. 106:45
22[m] ch. 10:15; [Deut. 32:21] [n] Job 28:26; 38:26, 28; Zech. 10:1, 2 [o] Job 12:9; Isa. 66:2

Chapter 15
1[p] Ps. 99:6; [Ezek. 14:14] [q] [Ps. 106:23]; See Ex. 32:11-13 [r] [1 Sam. 7:9; 8:6; 12:23; 15:11] [s] ch. 35:19; [ver. 19]

14:13–16 Lying or deluded prophets are a continual problem for God's people. When Judah was under the Babylonian threat, such prophets claimed that peace would reign. A prophet not sent by God is both deceived and a liar. This problem has always existed (Deut. 18:20–22). Jesus warned that even the church is not immune in these last days (Matt. 24:11). Christian history bears witness to many who claim to know the day of the Lord's return or to be prophets of a modern religion more suited to our day and age. All claims to prophecy should be tested against God's Word.

15:1–4 Prophetic intercession, beginning with Moses, became an institution in Israel. Moses interceded for the people after the provocation of Aaron's golden calf, as well as on other occasions when the people had sinned (Ex. 33:12–17; Num. 11:2; 21:7; Deut. 9:25–29). Samuel interceded for the people in times of peril (1 Sam. 7:5, 8; 12:19, 23). Now the provocation has become so great that God declares that even the intercession of Moses and Samuel would not have been able to avert disaster.

Today, we live in the glad knowledge that the ultimate prophet and priest of God, Jesus Christ, has come. He now intercedes at God's right hand with total efficacy for his people (John 17:1–26; Rom. 8:31–34; 1 Tim. 2:5; Heb. 7:25). It is this divine intercession that assures those who are in Christ that their prayers are heard.

Jeremiah identifies a particular false shepherd, a descendant of David and thus one from the messianic dynasty: Manasseh, who installed pagan altars in the temple of God (2 Kings 21:1–18). He was so evil that even the reforms of Josiah could not avert the wrath of the Lord because of him (2 Kings 23:26–27; 24:1–3). Only the Good Shepherd is able truly to feed the flock and to keep them in eternal life (John 10:7–18, 26–30).

[t]“ ‘Those who are for pestilence, to pestilence,
and those who are for the sword, to the sword;
those who are for famine, to famine,
and those who are for captivity, to captivity.’

3 [u]I will appoint over them four kinds of
destroyers, declares the LORD: the sword to
kill, the dogs to tear, and [v]the birds of the air
[w]and the beasts of the earth to devour and
destroy. 4 [x]And I will make them a horror to
all the kingdoms of the earth because of what
[y]Manasseh the son of Hezekiah, king of Judah,
did in Jerusalem.

5 [z]“Who will have pity on you, O Jerusalem,
[z]or who will grieve for you?
Who will turn aside
to ask about your welfare?
6 [a]You have rejected me, declares the LORD;
[b]you keep going backward,
so I have stretched out my hand against you and destroyed you—
[c]I am weary of relenting.
7 [d]I have winnowed them with [e]a winnowing fork
in the gates of the land;
I have bereaved them; I have destroyed my people;
[f]they did not turn from their ways.
8 I have made their widows more in number
than [g]the sand of the seas;
I have brought against the mothers of young men
a destroyer at noonday;
I have made anguish and terror
fall upon them suddenly.
9 [h]She who bore seven has grown feeble;
[i]she has fainted away;
[j]her sun went down while it was yet day;
she has been shamed and disgraced.
And the rest of them I will give to the sword
before their enemies,
declares the LORD.”

Jeremiah's Complaint

10 [k]Woe is me, my mother, that you bore me, a
man of strife and contention to the whole land!
[l]I have not lent, nor have I borrowed, yet all of
them curse me. 11 The LORD said, “Have I not[1]
set you free for their good? Have I not pleaded
for you before the enemy in the time of trouble
and in the time of distress? 12 Can one break
iron, iron [m]from the north, and bronze?
13 [n]“Your wealth and your treasures I will
give as [o]spoil, without price, for all your sins,
throughout all your territory. 14 I will make
you serve your enemies [p]in a land that you do
not know, [q]for in my anger a fire is kindled
that shall burn forever.”

15 [r]O LORD, you know;
[s]remember me and visit me,
[s, t]and take vengeance for me on my persecutors.
In your forbearance take me not away;
[u]know that [v]for your sake I bear reproach.
16 Your words were found, [w]and I ate them,
and [x]your words became to me a joy
and the delight of my heart,
[y]for I am called by your name,
O LORD, God of hosts.
17 [z]I did not sit in the company of revelers,
nor did I rejoice;

[1] The meaning of the Hebrew is uncertain

15:10–21 Jeremiah bares the agony of his soul as he must stand against the whole nation in his prophetic condemnation of sin. His lament (v. 10) is like Job's in his suffering (Job 3:1–16). The ambivalence Jeremiah feels comes from the persecution his message invites. Yet at the same time he knows that he is being reproached for God's sake (Jer. 15:15). Like Ezekiel, he found that God's word is for the faithful servant a joy (v. 16; cf. Ezek. 3:1–3). Those who have tasted to see that the Lord is good (Ps. 34:8; 1 Pet. 2:1–3) may still have to face the loneliness and bitterness of persecution for Christ's sake (Rom. 8:35–39). Jeremiah appears to be flagging in his zeal for God because of his bitter message, and he too needs to turn again in repentance to the Lord (Jer. 15:19). Thus he will find strength and deliverance (vv. 20–21).

There is no perfection for the Christian this side of our resurrection. But walking with Jesus Christ, the friend of sinners, is a salve that gets down underneath even the painful sting of rejection by other people. He is enough.

2 [t]ch. 14:12; 16:4; 21:9; 43:11; Ezek. 5:12; 6:11, 12; Zech. 11:9
3 [u]See Lev. 26:16-22 [v]Deut. 28:26 [w]Rev. 6:8
4 [x]ch. 24:9; 29:18; 34:17; Deut. 28:25 [y][2 Kgs. 21:2, 11, 16, 17; 23:26; 24:3, 4]
5 [z]Isa. 51:19; [Nah. 3:7]
6 [a]Deut. 32:15 [b]See ch. 7:24 [c][Hos. 13:14]
7 [d][ch. 51:2; Isa. 41:16; Matt. 3:12; Luke 3:17] [e]Isa. 30:24 [f]ch. 5:3; Isa. 9:13; Amos 4:6, 8-11
8 [g]Gen. 22:17; Ps. 139:18
9 [h]1 Sam. 2:5; [Lam. 1:1] [i]Job 11:20 [j]Amos 8:9
10 [k]ch. 20:14 [l]Ex. 22:25; Ps. 15:5; Isa. 24:2

12 [m]See ch. 1:13 **13** [n]ch. 17:3 [o]Ps. 44:12 **14** [p]ch. 9:16; 16:13; 17:4; 22:28 [q]Deut. 32:22 **15** [r]ch. 12:3 [s][Judg. 16:28] [t]ch. 11:20; 20:12 [u]ch. 17:16 [v]Ps. 69:7 **16** [w]Ezek. 3:1, 3; Rev. 10:9, 10 [x]Ps. 119:111, 162 [y]ch. 14:9 **17** [z]Ps. 26:4

[a]I sat alone, because your hand was upon me,
for you had filled me with indignation.
18 Why is my pain unceasing,
[b]my wound incurable,
refusing to be healed?
Will you be to me [c]like a deceitful brook,
like waters that fail?

19 Therefore thus says the LORD:
[d]"If you return, I will restore you,
and you shall [e]stand before me.
If you utter what is precious, and not what is worthless,
you shall be as my mouth.
They shall turn to you,
but you shall not turn to them.
20 [f]And I will make you to this people
a fortified wall of bronze;
they will fight against you,
[g]but they shall not prevail over you,
[h]for I am with you
to save you and deliver you,
declares the LORD.
21 [g]I will deliver you out of the hand of the wicked,
and redeem you from the grasp of [i]the ruthless."

Famine, Sword, and Death

16 The word of the LORD came to me:
2 "You shall not take a wife, nor shall
you have sons or daughters in this place.
3 For
thus says the LORD concerning the sons and
daughters who are born in this place, and concerning the mothers who bore them and the
fathers who fathered them in this land:
4 [j]They
shall die of deadly diseases. [k]They shall not be
lamented, nor shall they be buried. [l]They shall
be as dung on the surface of the ground. [m]They
shall perish by the sword and by famine, [n]and
their dead bodies shall be food for the birds of
the air and for the beasts of the earth.
5 "For thus says the LORD: [o]Do not enter the
house of mourning, or go to lament or grieve
for them, for I have taken away my peace from
this people, my steadfast love and mercy,
declares the LORD.
6 Both great and small shall
die in this land. [k]They shall not be buried, and
no one shall lament for them or [p]cut himself
[q]or make himself bald for them.
7 No one shall
[r]break bread for the mourner, to comfort him
for the dead, nor shall anyone give him the
cup of consolation to drink for his father or
his mother.
8 You shall not go into the house
of feasting to sit with them, to eat and drink.
9 For thus says the LORD of hosts, the God of
Israel: [s]Behold, I will silence in this place,
before your eyes and in your days, the voice
of mirth and the voice of gladness, the voice
of the bridegroom and the voice of the bride.
10 "And when you tell this people all these
words, and they say to you, [t]'Why has the LORD
pronounced all this great evil against us? What
is our iniquity? What is the sin that we have
committed against the LORD our God?'
11 then
you shall say to them: [u]'Because your fathers
have forsaken me, declares the LORD, and
[v]have gone after other gods and have served
and worshiped them, and have forsaken me
and have not kept my law,
12 and because [w]you
have done worse than your fathers, for behold,
[x]every one of you follows his stubborn, evil

17[a] Ps. 102:7; Lam. 3:28
18[b] ch. 30:15; Job 34:6 [c] Job 6:15; Isa. 58:11
19[d] ch. 3:14 [e] [ver. 1]
20[f] [ch. 1:18; 6:27] [g] ch. 1:19; 20:11 [h] See ch. 1:8
21[g] [See ver. 20 above] [i] Isa. 13:11; 25:4, 5; 29:5
Chapter 16
4[j] See ch. 15:2 [k] ch. 22:18, 19; 25:33 [l] See ch. 8:2 [m] See ch. 14:12 [n] See ch. 7:33
5[o] See Ezek. 24:16-23
6[k] [See ver. 4 above] [p] Lev. 19:28; Deut. 14:1 [q] Job 1:20; [Isa. 3:24]
7[r] Isa. 58:7; Ezek. 24:17; [Deut. 26:14; Hos. 9:4]
9[s] See ch. 7:34
10[t] See ch. 5:19
11[u] ch. 5:19; 22:9; [Deut. 29:25, 26; 2 Kgs. 22:17; 2 Chr. 34:25] [v] ch. 13:10
12[w] ch. 7:26 [x] See ch. 3:17

16:9 Describing the judgment coming on Judah, God says that he will silence the joyful noises that erupt from the bridegroom and the bride and their wedding celebration (cf. 7:34). This is the most joyful event in human culture and was given to us by God as a glimpse of the ultimate relationship, not with another human but with God himself (Eph. 5:31–32). Throughout the Bible, God is the great lover and wooer of his people, his bride (e.g., Jer. 2:2, 32; Isa. 61:10; 62:5). The stilling of the mirth of weddings signifies the great sadness to befall the nation for their sin.

Because of the depth and intimacy of the marriage relationship, and the sense of loss and betrayal when such a covenant is abused or abandoned, spiritual truths are often tied to marriage themes. But as important as is that theme, even more so is the message of God's faithfulness communicated by the analogy. Despite our consistent faithlessness to our covenant Lord, God does not divorce us. He does not abandon us. He proves this in our own space-and-time history in the coming of Christ, the great bridegroom of his people (John 3:29; cf. Eph. 5:23–32; Rev. 19:7–9). For Christ, beyond anyone else, experienced the misery of Jeremiah 16:9. On the cross he was abandoned by his Father (Matt. 27:46), so that in the new earth God's people, his beautified "bride adorned for her husband" (Rev. 21:2; cf. Rev. 21:9), will truly forever rejoice in "the voice of mirth and the voice of gladness" (Jer. 16:9).

will, refusing to listen to me. 13 Therefore [y]I
will hurl you out of this land into [z]a land that
neither you nor your fathers have known, [a]and
there you shall serve other gods day and night,
for I will show you no favor.'

The Lord Will Restore Israel

14 [b]"Therefore, behold, the days are coming,
declares the Lord, when it shall no longer be
said, [c]'As the Lord lives who brought up the
people of Israel out of the land of Egypt,' 15 but
[c]'As the Lord lives who brought up the people
of Israel [d]out of the north country and out of
all the countries where he had driven them.'
For [e]I will bring them back to their own land
that I gave to their fathers.

16 "Behold, [f]I am sending for many fishers,
declares the Lord, and they shall catch them.
And afterward I will send for many hunters,
and they shall hunt them from every mountain and every hill, and out [g]of the clefts of the
rocks. 17 For [h]my eyes are on all their ways. [i]They
are not hidden from me, [i]nor is their iniquity
concealed from my eyes. 18 But first [j]I will doubly repay their iniquity and their sin, because
they have polluted my land with the carcasses
of their detestable idols, and [k]have filled my
inheritance with their abominations."

19 [l]O Lord, my strength and my stronghold,
[m]my refuge in the day of trouble,
[n]to you shall the nations come
from the ends of the earth and say:
"Our fathers have inherited nothing but
lies,
[o]worthless things in which there is no
profit.
20 Can man make for himself [p]gods?
Such are not gods!"

21 "Therefore, behold, I will make them
know, this once I will make them know my
power and my might, and they shall know
that [q]my name is the Lord."

The Sin of Judah

17 "The sin of Judah is written with [r]a pen
of iron; with a point of diamond it is
engraved on [s]the tablet of their heart, and on
[t]the horns of their altars, 2 while [u]their children remember their altars and their [v]Ashe-
rim, [w]beside every green tree and on the high
hills, 3 [x]on the mountains in the open country.
[y]Your wealth and all your treasures I will give
for spoil as the price of your high places for
sin throughout all your territory. 4 You shall
loosen your hand from your heritage that
I gave to you, [z]and I will make you serve your
enemies in a land that you do not know, [a]for
in my anger a fire is kindled that shall burn
forever."

5 Thus says the Lord:
"Cursed is the man [b]who trusts in man
and makes flesh his strength,[1]
whose heart turns away from the
Lord.

[1] Hebrew *arm*

16:14–21 Jeremiah sees the definitive redemptive experience in Israel's past, the exodus from Egypt, as foreshadowing a second exodus. This second exodus would be from the north country, Babylon (vv. 14–15). Described prominently in Isaiah and Ezekiel and in some of the Minor Prophets, this second exodus will also prove to be merely another shadow of the ultimate redemptive act of God in the death and resurrection of Jesus (see 23:5–8; 1 Cor. 5:7; 10:1–4).

Israel's life of faith was focused on what God had done in redeeming his people. For the Christian, the main focus must always be on the work of God for us in Christ. For us, the gospel is an event in the past, accomplished by the person and work of Jesus. Before restoration can be experienced, sin must be judged (Jer. 16:16–21). The resurrection life of the Christian comes only because the wrath of God is poured out upon our sins at the cross of Jesus.

When sin is judged and God's people restored, then the nations shall come and find their blessing in God (v. 19). The ingathering of the nations according to the promises to Abraham is an event of the end times, which began with the coming of Jesus of Nazareth (Mark 1:14–15; 1 Cor. 10:11; 1 John 2:18).

17:5–8 Again the prophet contrasts the life of sin and the life of faith. The desert imagery (vv. 5–6) picks up on the wider theme of the first Adam's exile from the garden of Eden. The return from exile will be truly achieved only when the last Adam

13 [y]ch. 10:18; 22:26; Isa. 22:17, 18; See Deut. 4:26-28; 28:64, 65 [z]See ch. 15:14 [a]Deut. 28:36, 64
14 [b]For ver. 14, 15, see ch. 23:7, 8 [c]ch. 4:2
15 [c][See ver. 14 above] [d][Isa. 43:5, 6]; See ch. 3:18 [e]ch. 24:6; 30:3; 32:37
16 [f][Ezek. 12:13; Amos 4:2; Hab. 1:15] [g]ch. 13:4
17 [h]ch. 32:19; 2 Chr. 16:9; Job 34:21; Prov. 5:21 [i][Ps. 51:9; 90:8]
18 [j]ch. 17:18; Isa. 40:2 [k][Isa. 65:4]; See Ezek. 43:7-9
19 [l]2 Sam. 22:33; Ps. 28:7; 31:3, 4; Isa. 25:4 [m]ch. 17:17 [n][Isa. 9:2; 49:6, 22, 23] [o]See ch. 18:15
20 [p][1 Cor. 8:4]; See ch. 2:11
21 [q]See ch. 33:2
Chapter 17
1 [r]Job 19:24 [s]Prov. 3:3; 7:3; [2 Cor. 3:3] [t]Ex. 27:2; Ps. 118:27
2 [u][ch. 19:5] [v]Judg. 3:7; See Deut. 16:21 [w][Isa. 1:29]; See ch. 2:20
3 [x]Ps. 48:1, 2; 87:1; Isa. 2:3
[y]ch. 15:13 **4** [z]See ch. 15:14 [a]See Deut. 32:22 **5** [b]2 Chr. 32:8; Ps. 146:3

6 [c]He is like a shrub in the desert,
[d]and shall not see any good come.
He shall dwell in the parched places of the wilderness,
in [e]an uninhabited salt land.

7 [f]"Blessed is the man who trusts in the LORD,
[g]whose trust is the LORD.
8 [h]He is like a tree planted by water,
that sends out its roots by the stream,
and does not fear when heat comes,
for its leaves remain green,
and is not anxious in the year of drought,
for it does not cease to bear fruit."

9 The heart is deceitful above all things,
and desperately sick;
who can understand it?
10 [i]"I the LORD search the heart
[j]and test the mind,[1]
[k]to give every man according to his ways,
according to the fruit of his deeds."

11 Like the [l]partridge that gathers a brood that she did not hatch,
so is [m]he who gets riches but not by justice;
[n]in the midst of his days they will leave him,
[o]and at his end he will be a fool.

12 A glorious throne set on high from the beginning
is the place of our sanctuary.
13 O LORD, [p]the hope of Israel,
[q]all who forsake you shall be put to shame;
those who turn away from you[2] [r]shall be written in the earth,
for [s]they have forsaken [t]the LORD, the fountain of living water.

Jeremiah Prays for Deliverance

14 [u]Heal me, O LORD, and I shall be healed;
save me, and I shall be saved,
for [v]you are my praise.
15 [w]Behold, they say to me,
"Where is the word of the LORD?
Let it come!"
16 I have not run away from being your shepherd,
nor have I desired the day of sickness.
[x]You know [x]what came out of my lips;
it was before your face.

[1] Hebrew *kidneys* [2] Hebrew *me*

6[c] ch. 48:6 [d] ch. 29:32; Job 20:17; Ps. 34:12 [e] Deut. 29:23; Job 39:6
7[f] Ps. 25:2; 34:8; 125:1; See Ps. 2:12 [g] Ps. 71:5
8[h] Ps. 1:3; [Ezek. 47:12]
10[i] 1 Sam. 16:7; 1 Chr. 28:9; Ps. 139:23; Rom. 8:27 [j] See ch. 11:20 [k] ch. 32:19; Job 34:11; Ps. 62:12
11[l] [1 Sam. 26:20] [m] Ps. 39:6 [n] [Ps. 55:23] [o] [Luke 12:20]
13[p] See ch. 14:8 [q] Josh. 24:20; Ps. 73:27; Isa. 1:28 [r] [Luke 10:20] [s] ch. 1:16 [t] ch. 2:13; [John 4:10, 14]
14[u] Ps. 6:2 [v] Deut. 10:21
15[w] Isa. 5:19; 2 Pet. 3:4
16[x] ch. 15:15; Ps. 40:9; 139:4

has gone into the wilderness and returns triumphant over death and the Devil. In this way he redeems his sheep that are lost in the wilderness (Rom. 5:12–17; 1 Cor. 15:21–22, 45). Such are those who trust the Lord (Jer. 17:7–8). They experience the sustenance of a watered place (cf. Ps. 1:1–3; Ezek. 47:12). In the fullness of time, Jesus himself would use the imagery of water to indicate the life given by the Spirit of God to all who believe in him (John 4:10–14; 7:37–39).

17:9–10 The heart—that is, the center of willing and desiring that drives all that we do—is so deceitful that none can really understand it. But the Lord can and does search our inmost thoughts, and nothing is hidden from him (cf. 1 Cor. 4:5). Ezekiel saw the need for God to give us cleansed and renewed hearts (Ezek. 36:25–28). Jesus recalls Ezekiel's words when he declares to Nicodemus the need to be born of water and the Spirit (John 3:5).

Sin will continue to cling to us our whole lives long, but the gospel of grace does not simply forgive us and then leave us as we were. God changes us. He gives us a thirst for holiness and re-sensitizes us to true beauty. We become human again.

17:12–13 Jeremiah turns to one of the great themes of the kingdom of God: the throne and the sanctuary. The visible institutions in Jerusalem of the temple and the Davidic throne are symbols of God's presence and rule over all things. These symbols might be removed by the invading Babylonian, but the reality to which they point can never be touched. Even Solomon recognized that his glorious temple was only symbolic, because God dwells in the heavens (1 Kings 8:27–30; see Isa. 66:1–2; Acts 7:47–50). Jesus declares that he fulfills the role of the Jerusalem temple in his coming and particularly in his resurrection (John 2:19–22; cf. Acts 2:30–32). Christ's kingly lordship over all is a consistent theme of the apostles (e.g., Luke 2:11; John 20:28; Acts 10:36; 2 Cor. 4:5).

17 Be not a terror to me;
[y]you are my refuge in the day of disaster.
18 [z]Let those be put to shame who persecute me,
but let me not be put to shame;
[z]let them be dismayed,
but let me not be dismayed;
[a]bring upon them the day of disaster;
destroy them with double destruction!

Keep the Sabbath Holy

19 Thus said the LORD to me: "Go and stand
in the People's Gate, by which [b]the kings of
Judah enter and by which they go out, and in
all the gates of Jerusalem, 20 and say: 'Hear the
word of the LORD, [b]you kings of Judah, and all
Judah, and all the inhabitants of Jerusalem,
who enter by these gates. 21 Thus says the
LORD: Take care for the sake of your lives, and
[c]do not bear a burden on the Sabbath day or
bring it in by the gates of Jerusalem. 22 And
do not carry a burden out of your houses
on the Sabbath [d]or do any work, but [e]keep
the Sabbath day holy, as I commanded your
fathers. 23 Yet [f]they did not listen or incline
their ear, [g]but stiffened their neck, that they
[h]might not hear and receive instruction.
24 "'But if you listen to me, declares the
LORD, and [c]bring in no burden by the gates
of this city on the Sabbath day, but [e]keep the
Sabbath day holy and do no work on it, 25 then
[i]there shall enter by the gates of this city kings
and princes who sit on the throne of David,
riding in chariots and on horses, they and their
officials, the men of Judah and the inhabitants
of Jerusalem. And this city shall be inhabited
forever. 26 And people shall come from [j]the cities of Judah [k]and the places around Jerusalem,
[j]from the land of Benjamin, [k]from the
Shephelah, from the hill country, [k]and from
[l]the Negeb, bringing [m]burnt offerings and
sacrifices, grain offerings and frankincense,
and [m]bringing thank offerings to the house
of the LORD. 27 But if you do not listen to me,
to [e]keep the Sabbath day holy, [c]and not to bear
a burden and enter by the gates of Jerusalem
on the Sabbath day, then I will [n]kindle a fire
in its gates, and it shall [o]devour the palaces of
Jerusalem and [p]shall not be quenched.'"

The Potter and the Clay

18 The word that came to Jeremiah from
the LORD: 2 "Arise, and go down to [q]the
potter's house, and there I will let you hear my
words." 3 So I went down to [r]the potter's house,
and there he was working at his wheel. 4 And
the vessel he was making of clay was [s]spoiled
in the potter's hand, and [t]he reworked it into
another vessel, as it seemed good to the potter to do.
5 Then the word of the LORD came to me: 6 "O
house of Israel, [u]can I not do with you as this
potter has done? declares the LORD. [v]Behold,
like the clay in the potter's hand, so are you in
my hand, O house of Israel. 7 If at any time I

17:24–27 We cannot suppose that the keeping of the Sabbath was all that was required by the law. It clearly represents the covenant stipulations as a whole. Breaking the Sabbath was a very visible form of covenant violation. If the people refuse to live as the redeemed of the Lord, they cannot expect the covenant blessings to flow. Here Jeremiah links faithfulness to the Sinai covenant with the blessings of the Davidic covenant (v. 25; see 2 Sam. 7:12–16).

Ultimately, the rule of the Davidic messiah-king will come only when there is perfect obedience to God's law. Jesus, the faithful Son of David, kept the law perfectly and also ascended to the throne of God at his resurrection (Acts 2:30–32; Rom. 1:3–4). Having the law fulfilled for us by Christ does not mean that the Christian life is lawless. On the contrary, we seek to fulfill the law of Christ, not in order to be saved, but because we *are* saved by grace as a gift (Gal. 6:2; James 1:22–27). Having been loved much, we fulfill the law by loving others (Rom. 13:8–10; Eph. 5:2).

18:1–12 Jeremiah receives an object lesson at the potter's house. If the vessel is spoiled in the making, the potter has the power to reshape it. Israel is like clay in the hands of the divine potter. God's plans cannot be frustrated despite the fact that his people are like a spoiled vessel. The reality behind this imagery is the infallible purpose of God to bring in his kingdom despite the unbelief in the chosen nation and in the world. He will save those whom he has destined to be vessels of honor (Rom. 9:19–23). No human failure can get in his way, for in his own Son he has satisfied the penalty of his people's failure.

17[y] ch. 16:19
18[z] Ps. 35:4; 40:14 [a] ch. 11:20; Ps. 35:8
19[b] See ch. 13:13
20[b] [See ver. 19 above]
21[c] [John 5:10]; See Neh. 13:15-19
22[d] See Num. 15:32-36 [e] Ex. 23:12; 31:13; Isa. 56:2; 58:13; Ezek. 20:12, 20; See Ex. 20:8-11; Deut. 5:12-15
23[f] ch. 7:24, 26; [ch. 11:10] [g] [2 Chr. 30:8; Acts 7:51] [h] See ch. 5:3
24[c] [See ver. 21 above] [e] [See ver. 22 above]
25[i] ch. 22:4
26[j] ch. 32:44; 33:13 [k] Zech. 7:7 [l] Gen. 13:1 [m] Lev. 7:12; 22:29; 2 Chr. 33:16; Ps. 107:22; 116:17
27[e] [See ver. 22 above] [c] [See ver. 21 above] [n] ch. 21:14; 43:12; 49:27; 50:32; Lam. 4:11; Amos 1:14 [o] ch. 52:13; 2 Kgs. 25:9 [p] ch. 7:20

Chapter 18
2[q] ch. 19:1; 1 Chr. 4:23; [Zech. 11:13]
3[r] ch. 19:1; 1 Chr. 4:23; [Zech. 11:13]
4[s] ch. 13:7 [t] [Rom. 9:21]
6[u] Isa. 45:9; See Rom. 9:20-24 [v] Job 10:9; Isa. 64:8

declare concerning a nation or a kingdom, that
I will [w]pluck up and break down and destroy it,
8 and if that nation, concerning which I have
spoken, [x]turns from its evil, [y]I will relent of
the disaster that I intended to do to it. 9 And if
at any time I declare concerning a nation or a
kingdom that I will [w]build and plant it, 10 and
if it does evil in my sight, not listening to my
voice, then I will relent of the good that I had
intended to do to it. 11 Now, therefore, say to the
men of Judah and the inhabitants of Jerusalem: 'Thus says the LORD, Behold, I am shaping
disaster against you and devising a plan against
you. [z]Return, every one from his evil way, and
[a]amend your ways and your deeds.'
12 "But they say, [b]'That is in vain! We will
follow our own plans, and will every one act
according to [c]the stubbornness of his evil heart.'

13 "Therefore thus says the LORD:
[d]Ask among the nations,
Who has heard the like of this?
The virgin Israel
has done [e]a very horrible thing.
14 Does the snow of Lebanon leave
the crags of Sirion?[1]
Do the mountain waters run dry,[2]
the cold flowing streams?
15 [f]But my people have forgotten me;
they make offerings to [g]false gods;
they made them stumble in their ways,
[h]in the ancient roads,
and to walk into side roads,
[i]not the highway,
16 making their land [j]a horror,
a thing [j]to be hissed at forever.
[k]Everyone who passes by it is horrified
[l]and shakes his head.
17 [m]Like the east wind [n]I will scatter them
before the enemy.
[o]I will show them my back, not my face,
in the day of their calamity."

18 Then they said, [p]"Come, let us make plots
against Jeremiah, [q]for the law shall not perish
from the priest, nor counsel from the wise,
nor the word from the prophet. [r]Come, let us
strike him with the tongue, and let us not pay
attention to any of his words."

19 Hear me, O LORD,
and [s]listen to the voice of my adversaries.
20 [t]Should good be repaid with evil?
Yet [u]they have dug a pit for my life.
[v]Remember how I stood before you
to speak good for them,
to turn away your wrath from them.
21 Therefore [w]deliver up their children to
famine;
give them over to the power of the
sword;
let their wives become childless [x]and
widowed.
May their men meet death by pestilence,
their youths be struck down by the
sword in battle.
22 [y]May a cry be heard from their houses,
when you bring the plunderer suddenly upon them!
For [u]they have dug a pit to take me
[z]and laid snares for my feet.
23 Yet [a]you, O LORD, know
all their plotting to kill me.
[b]Forgive not their iniquity,
nor blot out their sin from your sight.
Let them be overthrown before you;
deal with them in the time of your
anger.

The Broken Flask

19 Thus says the LORD, "Go, buy [c]a potter's earthenware [d]flask, and take some
of [e]the elders of the people and some of [e]the

[1] Hebrew *of the field* [2] Hebrew *Are foreign waters plucked up*

19:1–15 Another object lesson is acted out by the prophet himself. After delivering God's message of condemnation, he is to break an earthenware flask before the people. Once again it is made clear that the visible symbols of the covenant blessings—Jerusalem and the Davidic kingship (vv. 10–13)—will be destroyed. These holy places and institutions have no permanence until renewed on the day of the Lord. This permanence will eventually come, though Jeremiah's words in this passage do not say how. But it will come in a surprising way: not in a renewed building and institution but rather in a human, Jesus of Nazareth. He is the dwelling of God, the new temple, the promised Son of David (Matt. 1:21–23; Luke 1:30–33; John 1:14; 2:19–22; Rom. 1:3–4).

7[w] ch. 1:10; 42:10
8[x] Ezek. 18:21 [y] ch. 26:3, 13, 19; Judg. 2:18; Jonah 3:10
9[w] [See ver. 7 above]
11[z] ch. 35:15; 2 Kgs. 17:13; Jonah 3:8 [a] ch. 7:3; 25:5; 35:15
12[b] ch. 2:25 [c] See ch. 3:17
13[d] ch. 2:10, 11 [e] ch. 5:30
15[f] ch. 2:13, 32; 17:13 [g] ch. 2:5; 10:15; 16:19 [h] ch. 6:16 [i] [Isa. 57:14]
16[j] ch. 19:8; 25:9, 11, 18; 49:13, 17; 50:13; 51:37; 2 Chr. 29:8 [k] ch. 50:13; Lam. 2:15 [l] Job 16:4; Ps. 22:7; Matt. 27:39 **17**[m] Gen. 41:6, 23, 27; Ex. 10:13; Job 27:21; Ps. 48:7; Ezek. 27:26; Hos. 13:15; Jonah 4:8 [n] ch. 13:24 [o] [ch. 2:27] **18**[p] ch. 11:19 [q] [ch. 2:8; 5:13, 31; 6:13] [r] ch. 9:3, 8; Job 5:21; [Ps. 31:20] **19**[s] Ps. 35:1; Isa. 49:25 **20**[t] Ps. 35:12 [u] Ps. 35:7; 57:6; 119:85 [v] [Neh. 13:14] **21**[w] Ps. 109:10 [x] Ps. 109:9 **22**[y] [ch. 20:16] [u] [See ver. 20 above] [z] Ps. 140:5 **23**[a] [Ps. 35:22] [b] Neh. 4:5 **Chapter 19**
1[c] See ch. 18:2 [d] ver. 10 [e] 2 Kgs. 19:2; 23:1; Ezek. 8:1

elders of the priests, 2 and go out [f]to the Valley
of the Son of Hinnom at the entry of the
Potsherd Gate, and proclaim there the words
that I tell you. 3 You shall say, [g]'Hear the word
of the LORD, [h]O kings of Judah and inhabitants
of Jerusalem. Thus says the LORD of hosts, the
God of Israel: Behold, I am bringing such disaster upon this place that [i]the ears of everyone
who hears of it will tingle. 4 [j]Because the people
have forsaken me and have profaned this place
by making offerings in it to other gods whom
neither they nor their fathers nor the kings
of Judah have known; [k]and because they have
filled this place with the blood of innocents,
5 [l]and have built the high places of Baal [l]to burn
their sons in the fire as burnt offerings to Baal,
[m]which I did not command or decree, nor did
it come into my mind— 6 therefore, [n]behold,
days are coming, declares the LORD, when this
place shall no more be called Topheth, or [o]the
Valley of the Son of Hinnom, but the Valley of
Slaughter. 7 And in this place [p]I will make void
the plans of Judah and Jerusalem, [q]and will
cause their people to fall by the sword before
their enemies, and by the hand of those who
seek their life. [r]I will give their dead bodies for
food to the birds of the air and to the beasts of
the earth. 8 And I will make this city [s]a horror, [s]a
thing to be hissed at. Everyone who passes by it
will be horrified and will hiss because of all its
wounds. 9 [t]And I will make them eat the flesh
of their sons and their daughters, and everyone
shall eat the flesh of his neighbor [u]in the siege
and in the distress, with which their enemies
and those who seek their life afflict them.'

10 "Then [v]you shall break [w]the flask in the
sight of the men who go with you, 11 and shall
say to them, 'Thus says the LORD of hosts: So
will I break this people and this city, [x]as one
breaks a potter's vessel, [y]so that it can never be
mended. [z]Men shall bury in Topheth because
there will be no place else to bury. 12 Thus will
I do to this place, declares the LORD, and to its
inhabitants, making this city [a]like Topheth.
13 The houses of Jerusalem and the houses of
the kings of Judah—[b]all the houses on whose
[c]roofs offerings have been offered [d]to all the
host of heaven, and [e]drink offerings have been
poured out to other gods—shall be defiled
[a]like the place of Topheth.' "

14 Then Jeremiah came from [f]Topheth, where
the LORD had sent him to prophesy, [g]and he
stood in the court of the LORD's house and
said to all the people: 15 "Thus says the LORD
of hosts, the God of Israel, behold, I am bringing upon this city and upon all its towns all
the disaster that I have pronounced against it,
[h]because they have stiffened their neck, [i]refus-
ing to hear my words."

Jeremiah Persecuted by Pashhur

20 Now [j]Pashhur the priest, the son of
[k]Immer, who was [l]chief officer in the
house of the LORD, heard Jeremiah prophesying these things. 2 Then [j]Pashhur beat
Jeremiah the prophet, and put him [m]in the
stocks that were in the upper [n]Benjamin Gate
of the house of the LORD. 3 The next day, when
[j]Pashhur released Jeremiah from the stocks,
Jeremiah said to him, "The LORD does not call
your name [j]Pashhur, but Terror on Every Side.
4 For thus says the LORD: Behold, I will make
you [o]a terror to yourself and to all your friends.
They shall fall by the sword of their enemies
while you look on. And I will give all Judah
into the hand of the king of Babylon. He shall
carry them captive to Babylon, and shall strike
them down with the sword. 5 Moreover, [p]I will
give all the wealth of the city, all its gains, all
its [q]prized belongings, and all the treasures
of the kings of Judah into the hand of their
enemies, who shall plunder them and seize
them and carry them to Babylon. 6 And you,
[r]Pashhur, and all who dwell in your house,
shall go into captivity. To Babylon you shall
go, and there you shall die, and there you shall
be buried, you and all your friends, [s]to whom
you have prophesied falsely."

7 O LORD, [t]you have deceived me,
and I was deceived;
[u]you are stronger than I,
and you have prevailed.

20:7–18 It is very difficult, perhaps impossible, for us to appreciate Jeremiah's inner turmoil and psychological distress arising from his calling to announce the coming demise of Judah, Jerusalem, the temple, and the Davidic throne. Jeremiah's struggle

2 [f]See Josh. 15:8 **3** [g]ch. 17:20 [h]See ch. 13:13 [i]1 Sam. 3:11; 2 Kgs. 21:12 **4** [j]See ch. 1:16 [k]2 Kgs. 21:16; See ch. 2:34 **5** [l]ch. 7:31; 32:35; Lev. 18:21 [m]ch. 7:31; 32:35; Deut. 17:3 **6** [n]ch. 7:32 [o]ver. 2 **7** [p][Isa. 19:3] [q][Lev. 26:17] [r]See ch. 7:33 **8** [s]See ch. 18:16 **9** [t]Lev. 26:29; Deut. 28:53; Isa. 9:20; Lam. 2:20; 4:10; Ezek. 5:10 [u]Deut. 28:53, 55, 57 **10** [v][ch. 51:63, 64] [w]ver. 1 **11** [x]Ps. 2:9; Isa. 30:14; Lam. 4:2 [y][Prov. 6:15] [z]ch. 7:32 **12** [a][2 Kgs. 23:10] **13** [b]ch. 32:29; 44:18; 2 Kgs. 23:12; Zeph. 1:5 [c]2 Sam. 11:2 [d]Deut. 4:19; Acts 7:42 [e]ch. 7:18; 44:18 [a][See ver. 12 above] **14** [f]ver. 2, 3 [g]ch. 26:2; [2 Chr. 20:5] **15** [h]ch. 7:26; 2 Chr. 30:8 [i]ch. 25:3 **Chapter 20** **1** [j]ch. 21:1; 38:1; 1 Chr. 9:12; [Ezra 2:38] [k]1 Chr. 24:14; Ezra 2:37 [l][ch. 29:26] **2** [j][See ver. 1 above] [m]ch. 29:26; Acts 16:24 [n]ch. 37:13 **3** [j][See ver. 1 above] **4** [o]See ch. 6:25 **5** [p][2 Kgs. 20:17]; See 2 Kgs. 24:12-16; 25:13-17 [q]Job 28:10; Ezek. 22:25 **6** [r]ch. 21:1; 38:1; 1 Chr. 9:12; [Ezra 2:38] [s]See ch. 14:14 **7** [t][Ezek. 14:9] [u][2 Pet. 1:21]

[v]I have become a laughingstock all the day;
everyone mocks me.
8 For whenever I speak, I cry out,
I shout, [w]"Violence and destruction!"
For [x]the word of the LORD has become for me
[y]a reproach and [y]derision all day long.
9 If I say, "I will not mention him,
or speak any more in his name,"
[z]there is in my heart as it were a burning fire
shut up in my bones,
and [a]I am weary with holding it in,
and I cannot.
10 [b]For I hear many whispering.
[c]Terror is on every side!
"Denounce him! [d]Let us denounce him!"
say all my [e]close friends,
[f]watching for [g]my fall.
"Perhaps he will be deceived;
then [h]we can overcome him
and take our revenge on him."
11 But [i]the LORD is with me as a dread warrior;
therefore my persecutors will stumble;
[i]they will not overcome me.
[j]They will be greatly shamed,
for they will not succeed.
Their [k]eternal dishonor
will never be forgotten.
12 O LORD of hosts, who tests the righteous,
[l]who sees the heart and the mind,[1]
let me see your vengeance upon them,
for to you have I committed my cause.

13 [m]Sing to the LORD;
praise the LORD!
For he has delivered the life of the needy
from the hand of evildoers.

14 [n]Cursed be the day
on which I was born!
The day when my mother bore me,
let it not be blessed!
15 Cursed be the man who brought the news to my father,
"A son is born to you,"
[o]making him very glad.
16 Let that man be like [p]the cities
that the LORD overthrew without pity;
[q]let him hear a cry in the morning
and an alarm at noon,
17 [r]because he did not kill me in the womb;
so my mother would have been my grave,
and her womb forever great.
18 [s]Why did I come out from the womb
[t]to see toil and sorrow,
and spend my days in shame?

Jerusalem Will Fall to Nebuchadnezzar

21 This is the word that came to Jeremiah
from the LORD, when King Zedekiah
sent to him [u]Pashhur the son of Malchiah and
[v]Zephaniah the priest, the son of [w]Maaseiah,
saying, 2 [x]"Inquire of the LORD for us, [y]for
Nebuchadnezzar[2] king of Babylon is making
war against us. Perhaps the LORD will deal
with us according to [z]all his wonderful deeds
and will make him withdraw from us."

[1] Hebrew *kidneys* [2] Hebrew *Nebuchadrezzar*, an alternate spelling of *Nebuchadnezzar* (king of Babylon) occurring frequently from Jeremiah 21–52; this latter spelling is used throughout Jeremiah for consistency

7[v] Ps. 119:51; Lam. 3:14
8[w] ch. 6:7 [x] ch. 6:10 [y] Ps. 44:13; 79:4
9[z] Job 32:18, 19; Ps. 39:3 [a] ch. 6:11
10[b] Ps. 31:13 [c] See ch. 6:25 [d] [ch. 36:16, 20] [e] Ps. 41:9; 55:13; [ch. 9:4; 38:22] [f] [Ps. 56:6] [g] Ps. 35:15 [h] ch. 1:19; 5:22
11[i] See ch. 1:8 [j] ch. 17:18; 23:40 [k] ch. 23:40
12[l] See ch. 11:20
13[m] [Ps. 35:9, 10; 109:30, 31]
14[n] ch. 15:10; Job 3:3
15[o] [John 16:21]
16[p] Gen. 19:25; Isa. 13:19 [q] ch. 18:22
17[r] [Job 3:10, 11]
18[s] [Job 3:20] [t] [Lam. 3:1, 2]
Chapter 21
1[u] See ch. 20:1 [v] ch. 29:25; 37:3; 2 Kgs. 25:18 [w] ch. 35:4; 2 Chr. 34:8
2[x] [ch. 37:7] [y] [2 Kgs. 25:1] [z] Ps. 105:2, 5

can be seen as a rebuke to the superficial triumphalism and joyful bravado that some Christians imagine they should exhibit all the time. The peace of God that passes all understanding (Phil. 4:7) does not mean an easy ride. Suffering is a normal part of being a Christian because allegiance to Christ puts us at odds with the world and its thinking (John 16:33; 17:14–17; Rom. 8:17–18; Phil. 1:29).

But it is never unrelieved gloom. Jeremiah points to two aspects that make for genuine joy: evil will be dealt with by our warrior God (Jer. 20:11–12), and we can praise him for our salvation even though it is yet to be consummated (v. 13; see Rom. 13:11–14). The Christian life is the paradox of sober joy—"sorrowful, yet always rejoicing" (2 Cor. 6:10).

21:1–7 The Lord had made himself known to Israel as the divine warrior who fights for his people (Ex. 15:1–3; Ps. 8:1–2; Psalm 124; Isa. 59:15–20). The Israelites possessed the Promised Land because God fought for them against their enemies. Now a horrifying prospect is announced by the prophet: because of their rebellion against him, God the warrior will actually fight *against* the Israelites (Jer. 21:4–7). In light of Judah's hard-heartedness, the tables have been turned. Other prophets were similarly to warn of the "day of the Lord," when he would come in judgment. Thus Malachi 3:1–3 speaks of a time of a purifying advent of the Lord.

3 Then Jeremiah said to them: "Thus you
shall say to Zedekiah, 4 'Thus says the LORD,
the God of Israel: [a]Behold, I will turn back
the weapons of war that are in your hands
and with which you are fighting against the
king of Babylon and against the Chaldeans
who are besieging you outside the walls. [b]And
I will bring them together into the midst of
this city. 5 I myself will fight against you [c]with
outstretched hand and strong arm, [d]in anger
and in fury and in great wrath. 6 And I will
strike down the inhabitants of this city, both
man and beast. They shall die of a great pestilence. 7 Afterward, declares the LORD, [e]I will
give Zedekiah king of Judah and his servants
and the people in this city who survive the
pestilence, sword, and famine into the hand
of Nebuchadnezzar king of Babylon and into
the hand of their enemies, into the hand of
those who seek their lives. He shall strike them
down with the edge of the sword. [f]He shall not
pity them or spare them or have compassion.'
8 "And to this people you shall say: [g]'Thus says
the LORD: Behold, [h]I set before you the way of
life and the way of death. 9 He who stays in this
city shall die [i]by the sword, by famine, and by
pestilence, but he who goes out and [j]surren-
ders to the Chaldeans who are besieging you
shall live [k]and shall have his life as a prize of
war. 10 For [l]I have set my face against this city
for harm and [m]not for good, declares the LORD:
[n]it shall be given into the hand of the king of
Babylon, and he shall burn it with fire.'

Message to the House of David

11 "And to the house of the king of Judah
say, 'Hear the word of the LORD, 12 O house of
David! Thus says the LORD:

[o]"'Execute justice [p]in the morning,
and deliver from the hand of the
oppressor
him who has been robbed,
[q]lest my wrath go forth like fire,
and burn with none to quench it,
because of your evil deeds.'"

13 [r]"Behold, I am against you, O inhabitant
of the valley,
O rock of the plain,
declares the LORD;
you who say, [s]'Who shall come down
against us,
or who shall enter our habitations?'
14 [t]I will punish you according to [u]the fruit
of your deeds,
declares the LORD;
[v]I will kindle a fire in her forest,
[v]and it shall devour all that is around
her."

22 Thus says the LORD: "Go down to the
house of the king of Judah and speak
there this word, 2 and say, [w]'Hear the word of

For those who repent and turn to God, however, this purifying comes ultimately through the cross of Christ. God still wages war against sin, but he also conquers it through the sacrifice of his Son. Now he is for us, not against us (Rom. 8:31). And we will be vindicated in the final judgment, when Christ returns to judge the living and the dead.

21:8–10 For those who choose the way of life, the coming judgment is not the end. Those who hear God's promises and trust in him will live. This means, however, that they are to go into exile in Babylon and not depend on the outward symbols of the land, city, and temple. Jeremiah thus foreshadows the way of life which is union with Jesus, the Way (John 14:6). The Christian life is a continual following of Jesus in his exile (Matt. 10:24–39), depending only on the word of his promise (John 5:24).

21:11–22:30 Prominent in Jeremiah's preaching is the significance of God's covenant with David in 2 Samuel 7:9–14. The earlier covenant promises had been encapsulated in the promises of the Lord "to be God to you" (Gen. 17:7–8); and "I will be your God, and you shall be my people" (Jer. 7:23; 11:4; 24:7; Lev. 26:12; Ezek. 11:20). These were then individualized by focusing the promise on David's son: "I will be to him a father, and he shall be to me a son" (2 Sam. 7:14).

In this long oracle, however, Jeremiah condemns the dynasty of David for faithlessness. It thus invites the discipline of the Lord foreshadowed in the promise to David (2 Sam. 7:14). Yet God is faithful and his purposes sure (2 Sam. 7:15–16). The covenant promises must depend upon God because David's son, Solomon, and his royal successors failed to live as the sons of God, just as Israel, the son of God (Ex. 4:22–23; Hos. 11:1), had constantly failed.

4 [a][ch. 32:5; 37:10] [b][Isa. 13:4]
5 [c]ch. 27:5; 32:17, 21; Ex. 6:6; Deut. 4:34; Ezek. 20:33 [d]ch. 32:37; Deut. 29:28
7 [e]ch. 37:17; 39:5; 52:9 [f]Deut. 28:50; 2 Chr. 36:17; Ezek. 5:11
8 [g]Deut. 30:15, 19 [h]ch. 38:2
9 [i]See ch. 15:2 [j]ch. 37:13, 14 [k]ch. 39:18; 45:5
10 [l]ch. 44:11; Lev. 20:3, 5; Ps. 34:16; Ezek. 14:8; [Amos 9:4] [m][ch. 14:11] [n]ver. 7; ch. 34:2; 37:8, 10; 38:17, 18, 23; 39:8; 52:13; 2 Chr. 36:19
12 [o]ch. 22:3; Zech. 7:9; [ch. 22:16] [p]Ps. 101:8 [q]ch. 4:4
13 [r][ver. 10]; See Ezek. 13:8 [s][ch. 49:4]
14 [t]ch. 9:25 [u]Prov. 1:31; Isa. 3:10 [v]Ezek. 20:47

Chapter 22
2 [w]ch. 21:12

the LORD, O king of Judah, who sits on the
throne of David, you, and your servants, and
your people who enter these gates. 3 Thus says
the LORD: [x]Do justice and righteousness, and
deliver from the hand of the oppressor him
who has been robbed. And [y]do no wrong or
violence [z]to the resident alien, [x]the fatherless,
and the widow, nor [a]shed innocent blood in
this place. 4 For if you will indeed obey this
word, [b]then there shall enter the gates of this
house kings who sit on the throne of David,
riding in chariots and on horses, they and their
servants and their people. 5 But if you will not
obey these words, I [c]swear by myself, declares
the LORD, that [d]this house shall become a desolation. 6 For thus says the LORD concerning
the house of the king of Judah:

"'You are like Gilead to me,
like the summit of [e]Lebanon,
yet surely I will make you a desert,
[f]an uninhabited city.[1]
7 [g]I will prepare destroyers against you,
each with his weapons,
[h]and they shall cut down your choicest cedars
and cast them into the fire.

8 "'And many nations will pass by this city,
and every man will say to his neighbor, [i]"Why
has the LORD dealt thus with this great city?"
9 [j]And they will answer, "Because they have
forsaken the covenant of the LORD their God
and worshiped other gods and served them."'"

10 [k]Weep not for him who is dead,
nor grieve for him,
[l]but weep bitterly for him who goes away,
for he shall return no more
to see his native land.

Message to the Sons of Josiah

11 For thus says the LORD concerning Shallum
the son of Josiah, king of Judah, who reigned
instead of Josiah his father, and [m]who went
away from this place: "He shall return here
no more, 12 but [m]in the place where they have
carried him captive, there shall he die, and he
shall never see this land again."

13 [n]"Woe to him who builds his house by [o]unrighteousness,
and his upper rooms by injustice,
[p]who makes his neighbor serve him for nothing
and does not give him his wages,
14 who says, 'I will build myself a great house
with spacious upper rooms,'
who cuts out windows for it,
paneling it with cedar
and [q]painting it with vermilion.
15 Do you think you are a king
because you compete in cedar?
Did not your father eat and drink
and [r]do justice and righteousness?
[s]Then it was well with him.
16 [t]He judged the cause of the poor and needy;
[s]then it was well.
Is not this [u]to know me?
declares the LORD.
17 But you have eyes and heart
only for your dishonest gain,
[v]for shedding innocent blood,
and for practicing oppression and violence."

18 Therefore thus says the LORD concerning
Jehoiakim the son of Josiah, king of Judah:

[w]"They shall not lament for him, saying,
[x]'Ah, my brother!' or 'Ah, sister!'
They shall not lament for him, saying,
[y]'Ah, lord!' or 'Ah, his majesty!'
19 With the burial of a donkey [z]he shall be buried,
dragged and dumped beyond the gates of Jerusalem."
20 "Go up to Lebanon, and cry out,
and lift up your voice in Bashan;

[1] Hebrew *cities*

3[x] ch. 7:5, 6; 21:12 [y] Lev. 19:33 [z] [Ps. 82:3; Isa. 1:17] [a] ver. 17; [ch. 26:15]
4[b] ch. 17:25
5[c] ch. 49:13; 51:14; Gen. 22:16; Amos 6:8; [Heb. 6:13] [d] ch. 7:34; 25:11, 18; 44:6, 22; Isa. 64:10; Ezek. 5:14
6[e] ver. 20, 23 [f] [ch. 6:8]

The promises of an eternal kingdom to David's heir find their fulfillment, not in his immediate progeny, but in the lineage culminating in Christ. Eventually Jesus came, and God's approving declaration was, "You are my beloved Son; with you I am well pleased" (Mark 1:11). Because we are united by faith to the beloved Son, we receive adoption as sons: "And because you are sons, God has sent the Spirit of his Son into our hearts, crying, 'Abba! Father!'" (Gal. 4:6; see also Rom. 8:14–17).

7[g] ch. 6:4 [h] 2 Kgs. 19:23; Isa. 37:24 **8**[i] See ch. 5:19 **9**[j] Deut. 29:25, 26 **10**[k] [2 Chr. 35:24, 25] [l] ver. 11 **11**[m] [2 Kgs. 23:34; 2 Chr. 36:4; Ezek. 19:4] **12**[m] [See ver. 11 above] **13**[n] Hab. 2:12; See Isa. 5:18-23 [o] [Mic. 3:10] [p] Lev. 19:13; 25:39, 40; Deut. 24:14, 15; James 5:4 **14**[q] Ezek. 23:14 **15**[r] [2 Kgs. 23:25] [s] Ps. 128:2; Eccles. 8:12; Isa. 3:10 **16**[t] Prov. 31:9; [Isa. 1:17] [s] [See ver. 15 above] [u] [Judg. 2:10] **17**[v] ver. 3; [ch. 26:15] **18**[w] Ps. 78:64; See ch. 16:4-6 [x] [1 Kgs. 13:30] [y] [ch. 34:5] **19**[z] ch. 8:2; 36:30; [Isa. 14:19]

cry out from [a]Abarim,
for all [b]your lovers are destroyed.
21 I spoke to you in your prosperity,
but you said, 'I will not listen.'
[c]This has been your way from [d]your youth,
that you have not obeyed my voice.
22 [e]The wind shall shepherd all your shepherds,
and [b]your lovers shall go into captivity;
[f]then you will be ashamed and confounded
because of all your evil.
23 O inhabitant of [g]Lebanon,
nested among the cedars,
how you will be pitied when pangs come upon you,
[h]pain as of a woman in labor!"

24 [i]"As I live, declares the LORD, though
Coniah the son of Jehoiakim, king of Judah,
were [j]the signet ring on my right hand, yet
I would tear you off 25 and [k]give you [l]into the
hand of those who seek your life, into the
hand of those of whom you are afraid, even
into the hand of Nebuchadnezzar king of
Babylon and into the hand of the Chaldeans.
26 [m]I will hurl you and [n]the mother who bore
you into another country, where you were not
born, and there you shall die. 27 But to the land
to which they will long to return, there they
shall not return."

28 Is this man [o]Coniah a despised, broken pot,
a [p]vessel no one cares for?
Why are he and his children hurled and cast
into a [q]land that they do not know?
29 [r]O land, land, land,
hear the word of the LORD!
30 Thus says the LORD:
"Write this man down as [s]childless,
a man who shall not succeed in his days,
[t]for none of his offspring shall succeed
[t]in sitting on the throne of David
and ruling again in Judah."

The Righteous Branch

23 [u]"Woe to the shepherds who destroy
and scatter the sheep of my pasture!"
declares the LORD. 2 Therefore thus says the
LORD, the God of Israel, concerning [u]the shepherds who care for my people: "You have scattered my flock and have driven them away, and
you have not attended to them. [v]Behold, I will
attend to you for your evil deeds, declares the
LORD. 3 [w]Then I will gather the remnant of
my flock [x]out of all the countries where I have
driven them, and I will bring them back to
their fold, [y]and they shall be fruitful and multiply. 4 [z]I will set shepherds over them who will
care for them, and they shall fear no more,

23:1–6 Jeremiah 22 highlights the fact that those who should have been the good shepherds of the people were in fact false. This passage continues that theme but speaks of hope as well as of judgment. The sheep are not safe, but scattered (23:1–2). The remnant (v. 3) is made up of the faithful few who will be the nucleus of a true people of God. The purpose of God is infallibly to save his own out of the faithless and godless multitude, and to give them good shepherds. Furthermore, none shall be missing (v. 4). So, God will one day raise up a descendant of David—"a righteous Branch" (v. 5). He is the Good Shepherd, who infallibly saves his own: none will be missing, because they are God's gift to Jesus (John 6:37–40).

The kingdoms of Israel and Judah will be reunited under one godly King (Jer. 23:6). This will be salvation for the true people of God. The name of the "Branch" is significant: "The LORD is our righteousness" (v. 6). There was no righteousness among the people or their rulers. This brings us to the heart of the gospel: there is no one who is righteous before God (Rom. 3:9–18). "All have sinned and fall short of the glory of God" (Rom. 3:23). To imagine we can have enough righteousness within us is to be deluded (1 John 1:8). We must look outside of ourselves, to the "alien" righteousness of another. The Lord whom Jeremiah prophesies is our righteousness, and the just live by faith in him—ultimately, that is, in Christ (Rom. 1:16–17; 3:21–24; 1 Cor. 1:30). By the grace of God, the righteousness he maintained becomes ours as we are united to Christ by faith (2 Cor. 5:21). Believers have the righteousness of Christ imputed to them as a gift (Rom. 4:5–8). Our record is therefore spotless, clean, perfect.

This is the basis of our assurance: God accepts us on the grounds of the perfect righteousness of Christ. Justification by faith alone is the central truth of the gospel, pointing us to the merits of Christ *for us*.

20 [a]Num. 27:12; Deut. 32:49 [b][ch. 3:1]
21 [c]ch. 3:25 [d]Ps. 129:1, 2
22 [e]ch. 23:1; [Ezek. 34:10] [b][See ver. 20 above] [f]ch. 3:25
23 [g]ver. 6 [h]ch. 6:24; See Isa. 13:8
24 [i]Isa. 49:18; See Ezek. 5:11 [j]1 Kgs. 21:8; Song 8:6; Hag. 2:23
25 [k]ch. 34:20 [l]ch. 39:17; [Deut. 1:17]
26 [m]2 Kgs. 24:15; 2 Chr. 36:10 [n][2 Kgs. 24:8]
28 [o]ver. 24 [p][ch. 48:38; Ps. 31:12; Hos. 8:8] [q]See ch. 15:14
29 [r]Isa. 1:2
30 [s][1 Chr. 3:17; Matt. 1:12] [t]ch. 36:30

Chapter 23
1 [u]ch. 6:3; 10:21; 22:22; 25:34, 36; Isa. 56:11; Ezek. 34:2; Zech. 11:17; [John 10:12, 13]
2 [u][See ver. 1 above] [v]ver. 22; ch. 4:4
3 [w]ch. 29:14; 32:37; Deut. 30:3; Ezek. 20:34, 41; 37:21; [Ps. 107:3]; See Ezek. 34:11-16 [x][ch. 8:3] [y][Gen. 1:28]
4 [z]ch. 3:15

nor be dismayed, neither shall any be missing,
declares the LORD.
5 [a]"Behold, the days are coming, declares the
LORD, when I will raise up for David a righteous [b]Branch, and [c]he shall reign as king and
deal wisely, and shall execute justice and righteousness in the land. 6 In his days Judah will
be saved, and [d]Israel will [e]dwell securely. And
this is the name by which he will be called:
[f]'The LORD is our righteousness.'
7 [g]"Therefore, behold, the days are coming,
declares the LORD, when they shall no longer
say, 'As the LORD lives who brought up the
people of Israel out of the land of Egypt,' 8 but
'As the LORD lives who brought up and led
the offspring of the house of Israel out of the
north country and out of all the countries
where he[1] had driven them.' Then they shall
dwell in their own land."

Lying Prophets

9 Concerning the prophets:

[h]My heart is broken within me;
  [i]all my bones shake;
I am like a drunken man,
  like a man overcome by wine,
because of the LORD
  and because of his holy words.
10 [j]For the land is full of adulterers;
  [k]because of the curse [l]the land mourns,
  and [m]the pastures of the wilderness
    are dried up.
[n]Their course is evil,
  and their might is not right.
11 [o]"Both prophet and priest are ungodly;
  even [p]in my house I have found their
    evil,
        declares the LORD.
12 [q]Therefore their way shall be to them
  like slippery paths [r]in the darkness,
  into which they shall be driven and
    fall,
for I will bring disaster upon them
  [s]in the year of their punishment,
        declares the LORD.
13 In the prophets of [t]Samaria
  [u]I saw an unsavory thing:
[v]they prophesied by Baal
  [w]and led my people Israel astray.
14 But in the prophets of Jerusalem
  I have seen a horrible thing:
[x]they commit adultery and walk in lies;
  [y]they strengthen the hands of evildoers,
  so that no one turns from his evil;
[z]all of them have become like Sodom to
    me,
  [z]and its inhabitants like Gomorrah."

[1] Septuagint; Hebrew *I*

5 [a]For ver. 5, 6, see ch. 33:14-16 [b]Isa. 4:2; 11:1 [c]ch. 30:9; Isa. 32:1; Ezek. 37:24; Hos. 3:5; Zech. 9:9; Matt. 2:2; Luke 1:32; 19:38; John 1:49
6 [d]Deut. 33:28; [Zech. 14:11] [e]ch. 32:37 [f]Rom. 10:4; 1 Cor. 1:30
7 [g]For ver. 7, 8, see ch. 16:14, 15
9 [h]Ezek. 6:9 [i]Hab. 3:16
10 [j]ch. 5:7, 8; 9:2 [k]Ps. 10:7; 59:12; Hos. 4:2, 3 [l]ch. 4:28 [m]ch. 9:10; 12:4; Ps. 107:34 [n][ch. 22:17]
11 [o][ver. 33, 34; Zeph. 3:4]; See ch. 6:13 [p]ch. 7:30; 32:34; Ezek. 8:16; 23:39
12 [q]Ps. 35:6; 73:18 [r]Prov. 4:19; [ch. 13:16] [s]ch. 11:23
13 [t]Isa. 7:9; Ezek. 16:46, 51, 53, 55; 23:4, 33 [u]Lam. 2:14 [v]ch. 2:8 [w]Isa. 9:16; Mic. 3:5
14 [x]ch. 29:23 [y]Ps. 64:5; Ezek. 13:22 [z]Isa. 1:9, 10; 13:19

23:7–8 Jeremiah shifts the focus from the definitive redemptive event in the exodus from Egypt to another redemption to come. The people will one day look back on this second exodus, the return from Babylon, as the basis of their blessing in the land. However this second exodus, like the first, will be but a foreshadowing of the one true exodus from the power of Satan, sin, and death that Jesus accomplishes (Matt. 2:14–15; 1 Cor. 5:7–8; Eph. 4:8; Rev. 16:3).

23:9–22 The Scriptures have many warnings against false prophets. The definitive prophet was Moses, who met with God on Mount Sinai. God promised Israel that he would raise up another prophet like Moses, whose words would come from the Lord (Deut. 18:15–19). Israel was also warned of lying prophets who would seek to deceive them (Deut. 18:20–22). Many true prophets arose in Israel and Judah, Jeremiah being one of them. Yet the promise of a prophet like Moses was never entirely fulfilled by these (Deut. 34:10–12).

The indictment of the false prophets includes the contrast with the true prophet who is one who has "stood in [God's] council" (Jer. 23:22). However the people of Jeremiah's day understood that proviso, we know that Jesus came as that definitive and ultimate prophet from the very presence of his Father. The apostles identified Jesus as the prophet spoken of by Moses (Acts 3:20–24). From our perspective, then, we know the truth of the biblical prophets in that they testify to Christ and his gospel. Jesus came as the very Word of God in the flesh (John 1:14). He has truly "stood in God's council," and his words are true (John 3:31–36) and have the authority of his Father (John 12:44–50; 17:6–8, 14). Jesus' prophetic ministry fulfills and takes over from the Old Testament prophets (Heb. 1:1–2). Because the whole Bible is the Spirit-inspired testimony to Christ and the salvation he brings (2 Tim. 3:15), we can have confidence in it as the very Word of God.

15 Therefore thus says the LORD of hosts
concerning the prophets:
[a]"Behold, I will feed them with bitter food
[a] and give them [b]poisoned water to
drink,
for from the prophets of Jerusalem
ungodliness has gone out into all the
land."

16 Thus says the LORD of hosts: "Do not listen
to the words of the prophets who prophesy
to you, [c]filling you with vain hopes. [d]They
speak visions of their own minds, not from
the mouth of the LORD. 17 They say continually
to those who despise the word of the LORD, [e]'It
shall be well with you'; and to everyone who
[f]stubbornly follows his own heart, they say,
[g]'No disaster shall come upon you.'"

18 For [h]who among them has stood in the
council of the LORD
to see and to hear his word,
or who has paid attention to his word
and listened?
19 [i]Behold, the storm of the LORD!
Wrath has gone forth,
[j]a whirling tempest;
it will burst upon the head of the
wicked.
20 [k]The anger of the LORD will not turn back
until he has executed and [k]accom-
plished
the intents of his heart.
[l]In the latter days you will understand it
clearly.
21 [m]"I did not send the prophets,
yet they ran;
I did not speak to them,
yet they prophesied.
22 [n]But if they had stood in my council,
then they would have proclaimed my
words to my people,
[o]and they would have turned them from
their evil way,
and [p]from the evil of their deeds.

23 [q]"Am I a God at hand, declares the LORD,
and not a God far away? 24 [q]Can a man hide
himself in secret places so that I cannot see
him? declares the LORD. [r]Do I not fill heaven
and earth? declares the LORD. 25 I have heard
what the prophets have said [s]who prophesy
lies in my name, saying, [t]'I have dreamed,
I have dreamed!' 26 How long shall there be
lies in the heart of [u]the prophets who prophesy
lies, and who prophesy the deceit of their own
heart, 27 who think to make my people forget
my name [t]by their dreams that they tell one
another, even as their [v]fathers forgot my name
for Baal? 28 [w]Let the prophet who has a dream
[x]tell the dream, but let him who has my word
speak my word faithfully. [y]What has straw in
common with wheat? declares the LORD. 29 [y]Is
not my word like fire, declares the LORD, and
[z]like a hammer that breaks the rock in pieces?
30 [a]Therefore, behold, I am against the prophets, declares the LORD, who steal my words
from one another. 31 Behold, I am against the
prophets, declares the LORD, who use their
tongues and declare, 'declares the LORD.'
32 Behold, I am against those who prophesy
lying dreams, declares the LORD, and who tell
them and [b]lead my people astray by their lies
and their recklessness, when [c]I did not send
them or charge them. So they do not profit
this people at all, declares the LORD.

33 [d]"When one of this people, or a prophet
or a priest asks you, 'What is the burden of
the LORD?' you shall say to them, 'You are the
burden,[1] and [f]I will cast you off, declares the
LORD.' 34 And as for the prophet, priest, or
one of the people who says, 'The burden of
the LORD,' [d]I will punish that man and his
household. 35 Thus shall you say, every one
to his neighbor and every one to his brother,
'What has the LORD answered?' or 'What has
the LORD spoken?' 36 But 'the burden of the
LORD' you shall mention no more, for the burden is every man's own word, and [g]you pervert the words of [h]the living God, the LORD
of hosts, our God. 37 Thus you shall say to the
prophet, 'What has the LORD answered you?'
or 'What has the LORD spoken?' 38 But if you
say, 'The burden of the LORD,' thus says the
LORD, 'Because you have said these words,
"The burden of the LORD," when I sent to you,
saying, "You shall not say, 'The burden of the
LORD,'" 39 therefore, behold, I will surely lift
you up and [f]cast you away from my presence,
you and the city that I gave to you and your

[1] Septuagint, Vulgate; Hebrew *What burden?*

15[a] ch. 9:15; Prov. 5:4 [b] ch. 8:14 **16**[c] [Ps. 12:2] [d] [ver. 21, 26; Num. 16:28] **17**[e] [Zech. 10:2]; See ch. 6:14 [f] See ch. 3:17 [g] ch. 5:12; Mic. 3:11 **18**[h] ver. 22; Isa. 40:14 **19**[i] ch. 30:23 [j] ch. 25:32 **20**[k] ch. 30:24; [Isa. 55:11] [l] ch. 30:24 **21**[m] See ch. 14:14 **22**[n] ver. 18 [o] ch. 25:5; [Luke 1:17] [p] ver. 2 **23**[q] [Ps. 94:7, 9; Amos 9:2, 3]; See Ps. 139:7-12 **24**[q] [See ver. 23 above] [r] Isa. 66:1; Acts 7:49 **25**[s] See ch. 5:31 [t] [Zech. 10:2] **26**[u] [ver. 16, 21; Num. 16:28] **27**[t] [See ver. 25 above] [v] Judg. 3:7; 8:33, 34 **28**[w] [Num. 12:6] [x] ver. 25 [y] [Luke 3:17] **29**[y] [See ver. 28 above] [z] [Dan. 2:34, 45] **30**[a] Ezek. 13:8; [ch. 14:15; Deut. 18:20] **32**[b] ver. 13 [c] ver. 21; See ch. 14:14 **33**[d] See Ezek. 14:1-11 [f] [Hos. 4:6] **34**[d] [See ver. 33 above] **36**[g] [Matt. 15:6] [h] Ps. 42:2 **39**[f] [See ver. 33 above]

fathers. 40 [i]And I will bring upon you everlasting reproach and [i]perpetual shame, which shall not be forgotten.'"

The Good Figs and the Bad Figs

24 [j]After Nebuchadnezzar king of Babylon had taken into exile from Jerusalem [k]Jeconiah the son of Jehoiakim, king of Judah, together with [l]the officials of Judah, the craftsmen, and the metal workers, and had brought them to Babylon, the LORD showed me this vision: behold, [m]two baskets of figs placed before the temple of the LORD. 2 One basket had very good figs, [n]like first-ripe figs, but the other basket had [o]very bad figs, so bad that they could not be eaten. 3 And the LORD said to me, "What do you see, Jeremiah?" I said, "Figs, the good figs very good, and the bad figs very bad, so bad that they cannot be eaten."

4 Then the word of the LORD came to me: 5 "Thus says the LORD, the God of Israel: Like these good figs, so I will regard as good the exiles from Judah, [p]whom I have sent away from this place to the land of the Chaldeans. 6 [q]I will set my eyes on them for good, and I will bring them back to this land. [r]I will build them up, and not tear them down; [s]I will plant them, and not pluck them up. 7 [t]I will give them a heart to know that I am the LORD, [u]and they shall be my people [u]and I will be their God, [v]for they shall return to me with their whole heart.

8 "But thus says the LORD: Like [w]the bad figs that are so bad they cannot be eaten, so will I treat [x]Zedekiah the king of Judah, his officials, the remnant of Jerusalem who remain in this land, and those who [y]dwell in the land of Egypt. 9 I will make them [z]a horror[1] to all the kingdoms of the earth, to be [a]a reproach, [b]a byword, [a]a taunt, and [c]a curse in all the places where I shall drive them. 10 And I will send [d]sword, famine, and pestilence upon them, until they shall be utterly destroyed from the land that I gave to them and their fathers."

Seventy Years of Captivity

25 [e]The word that came to Jeremiah concerning all the people of Judah, in the fourth year of Jehoiakim the son of Josiah, king of Judah (that was the first year of Nebuchadnezzar king of Babylon), 2 which Jeremiah the prophet spoke to all the people of Judah and all the inhabitants of Jerusalem: 3 "For twenty-three years, [f]from the thirteenth year of Josiah the son of Amon, king of Judah, to this day, the word of the LORD has come to me, and I have spoken [g]persistently to you, [h]but you have not listened. 4 [h]You have neither listened nor inclined your ears to hear, although the LORD [g]persistently sent to you all his servants the prophets, 5 saying, [i]'Turn now, every one of you, [j]from his evil way and evil deeds, and [k]dwell upon the land that the LORD has given to you and your fathers from of old and forever. 6 [l]Do not go after other gods to serve and worship them, [m]or provoke me to anger [m]with the work of your hands. Then I will do you no harm.' 7 [m]Yet you have not listened to me, declares the LORD, [m]that you might provoke me to anger [m]with the work of your hands to your own harm.

8 "Therefore thus says the LORD of hosts: Because you have not obeyed my words, 9 [n]behold, I will send for all the tribes of the north, declares the LORD, and for Nebuchadnezzar the king of Babylon, [o]my servant, and I will bring them against this land and its inhabitants, and against all these surround-

[1] Compare Septuagint; Hebrew *horror for evil*

24:1–10 The exile is now a reality. Jeconiah (Jehoiachin) the king has been taken along with many others to Babylon. Zedekiah, the king's uncle, is placed on the throne as a puppet king. God gives Jeremiah a vision of two baskets of figs, to warn against any further insurrections against the conqueror, Nebuchadnezzar. The good figs are the exiles and the bad figs are those who have stayed in Jerusalem. The encouragement is for the exiles. God will restore them (v. 6) and will give them a new heart (v. 7). Ezekiel has a similar promise of regeneration (Ezek. 36:26–28). It is significant that we are not dealing here with people "turning over a new leaf," but with a supernatural gift of God to change the inner nature of a sinner. It is God's gift to give people a heart to know that he is God. That is how Jesus instructed Nicodemus: a new birth was necessary, but it would be the sovereign work of the Spirit of God (John 3:5–8). Only thus can we become truly repentant people of the covenant.

40 [i]ch. 20:11
Chapter 24
1 [j]2 Kgs. 24:12; 2 Chr. 36:10 [k]Matt. 1:11; [ch. 22:18, 24, 28] [l]ch. 29:2; 2 Kgs. 24:12, 14 [m]Amos 8:1, 2
2 [n][Isa. 28:4] [o]ch. 29:17
5 [p]ch. 29:20
6 [q][Amos 9:4] [r]ch. 12:15; 29:10 [s]ch. 31:28; 42:10; [ch. 1:10; Amos 9:15]
7 [t]ch. 32:39; Deut. 30:6; Ezek. 11:19; 36:26, 27 [u]See ch. 30:22; 31:33 [v]ch. 29:13; Joel 2:12, 13
8 [w]ver. 2; ch. 29:17 [x]ch. 21:1 [y]See ch. 43–44
9 [z]See ch. 15:4 [a]ch. 29:18; 49:13; Neh. 2:17; Isa. 43:28 [b]Deut. 28:37; 2 Chr. 7:20 [c]ch. 25:18; 26:6; 29:22; 2 Kgs. 22:19 **10** [d]See ch. 14:12 **Chapter 25** **1** [e]ch. 1:3; 36:1; [2 Kgs. 24:1] **3** [f]ch. 1:2 [g]ch. 7:13; 11:7, 8; 26:5; 29:19; 32:33; 35:14; 2 Chr. 36:15 [h]See ch. 7:13 **4** [h][See ver. 3 above] [g][See ver. 3 above] **5** [i]See ch. 18:11 [j]ch. 23:22 [k]ch. 7:7 **6** [l]See ch. 7:6 [m][ch. 32:30] **7** [m][See ver. 6 above] **9** [n]ch. 1:15 [o]ch. 27:6; 43:10; [Isa. 44:28; 45:1]; See Ezek. 29:18-20

ing nations. I will devote them to destruction,
[p]and make them a horror, a hissing, and an
everlasting desolation. 10 Moreover, [q]I will
banish from them the voice of mirth and the
voice of gladness, the voice of the bridegroom
and the voice of the bride, [r]the grinding of
the millstones and [s]the light of the lamp.
11 [p]This whole land shall become a ruin and a
waste, and [t]these nations shall serve the king
of Babylon [u]seventy years. 12 Then after [u]sev-
enty years are completed, [v]I will punish the
king of Babylon and that nation, [v]the land of
the Chaldeans, for their iniquity, declares the
LORD, [v]making the land an everlasting waste.
13 I will bring upon that land all the words that
I have uttered against it, everything written
[w]in this book, which Jeremiah prophesied
against all the nations. 14 [x]For many nations
[x]and great kings shall make slaves even of
them, [y]and I will recompense them according
to their deeds and the work of their hands."

The Cup of the LORD's Wrath

15 Thus the LORD, the God of Israel, said to
me: [z]"Take from my hand this cup of the wine
of wrath, and make all the nations to whom
I send you drink it. 16 They shall drink and
stagger and be crazed because of [a]the sword
that I am sending among them."

17 So I took the cup from the LORD's hand,
[b]and made all the nations to whom the LORD
sent me drink it: 18 [c]Jerusalem and the cities of
Judah, its kings and officials, [d]to make them a
desolation and a waste, a hissing and a curse,
as at this day; 19 [e]Pharaoh king of Egypt, his
servants, his officials, all his people, 20 and [f]all
the mixed tribes among them; all the kings of
[g]the land of Uz and all the kings of [h]the land
of the Philistines ([h]Ashkelon, [h]Gaza, Ekron,
and the remnant of [i]Ashdod); 21 [j]Edom, [k]Moab,
and the sons of [l]Ammon; 22 all the kings of
[m]Tyre, all the kings of [m]Sidon, and the kings of
the coastland across [n]the sea; 23 [o]Dedan, [p]Tema,
[q]Buz, and all who cut [r]the corners of their hair;
24 all the [s]kings of Arabia and all the kings of
[f]the mixed tribes who dwell in the desert; 25 all
the kings of Zimri, all the kings of [t]Elam, and
all the kings of [u]Media; 26 all the kings of [v]the
north, far and near, one after another, and all
the kingdoms of the world that are on the
face of the earth. And after them the king of
[w]Babylon[1] shall drink.

27 "Then you shall say to them, 'Thus says
the LORD of hosts, the God of Israel: [x]Drink,
be drunk and vomit, fall and rise no more,
because of [y]the sword that I am sending
among you.'

28 "And if they refuse to accept the cup from
your hand to drink, then you shall say to them,
'Thus says the LORD of hosts: [z]You must drink!
29 For behold, [a]I begin to work disaster at the
city that is called by my name, and shall you
go unpunished? You shall not go unpunished,
[y]for I am summoning a sword against all the
inhabitants of the earth, declares the LORD
of hosts.'

30 "You, therefore, shall prophesy against
them all these words, and say to them:

[b]"'The LORD will roar from on high,
and from his holy habitation utter his
voice;
he will roar mightily against his fold,
[c]and shout, like those who tread
grapes,
against all the inhabitants of the
earth.
31 The clamor will resound to the ends of
the earth,
for [d]the LORD has an indictment
against the nations;
[e]he is entering into judgment with all
flesh,
and the wicked he will put to the
sword,
declares the LORD.'

[1] Hebrew *Sheshach*, a code name for Babylon

25:15–29 The cup of the Lord's wrath is imagery used to describe God's judgment against all who have opposed his kingdom and have done evil (Isa. 51:17, 22; Hab. 2:16; Rev. 14:9–11; 16:17–21). Jesus' cup of suffering was substitutionary and the means of our redemption (Matt. 26:37–39). In drinking that cup he bore our sins and endured the full weight of God's wrath on sin for us (2 Cor. 5:21). It is also a suffering in which we share, until Jesus is revealed in glory (Matt. 20:22–23; Rom. 8:17).

9 [p]See ch. 18:16
10 [q]See ch. 7:34 [r]Eccles. 12:4; Rev. 18:22 [s]Rev. 18:23
11 [p][See ver. 9 above] [t][ch. 28:14]; See ch. 27:3-6 [u]2 Chr. 36:21, 22; Ezra 1:1; Dan. 9:2; [Isa. 23:15]
12 [u][See ver. 11 above] [v]ch. 51:24, 26, 62; Isa. 13:19

13 [w]See ch. 46–51 **14** [x]ch. 27:7; 50:9, 41; 51:27, 28 [y]ch. 50:29; 51:6, 24 **15** [z]ch. 49:12; 51:7; Job 21:20; Ps. 60:3; 75:8; Isa. 51:17; Lam. 4:21; Rev. 14:10 **16** [a][ch. 47:6] **17** [b][Isa. 51:22, 23] **18** [c][Zech. 12:2] [d]See ch. 18:16 **19** [e]ch. 46:25 **20** [f]ch. 50:37; [Ex. 12:38; Ezek. 30:5] [g]Job 1:1; Lam. 4:21 [h]ch. 47:1, 4, 5 [i][Isa. 20:1] **21** [j]ch. 9:26; See ch. 49:7-22 [k]See ch. 48 [l]See ch. 49:1-6 **22** [m]ch. 47:4; Isa. 23:1, 2 [n][ch. 49:23] **23** [o]ch. 49:8; Isa. 21:13 [p]Job 6:19 [q][Job 32:2, 6] [r]See ch. 9:26 **24** [s]2 Chr. 9:14 [f][See ver. 20 above] **25** [t]Isa. 11:11; See ch. 49:34-39 [u][2 Kgs. 17:6] **26** [v]ch. 50:9 [w]ch. 51:41 **27** [x]Hab. 2:16 [y]Ezek. 38:21; [ver. 16] **28** [z]ch. 49:12 **29** [a]Prov. 11:31; Isa. 10:12; Amos 3:2; Obad. 16; [1 Pet. 4:17] [y][See ver. 27 above] **30** [b]Joel 3:16; Amos 1:2 [c][Judg. 9:27; Isa. 16:9] **31** [d]Hos. 4:1 [e]Isa. 66:16; [Joel 3:2]

32 "Thus says the LORD of hosts:
Behold, disaster is going forth
from nation to nation,
[f]and a great tempest is stirring
[g]from the farthest parts of the earth!

33 [h]"And those pierced by the LORD on that
day shall extend from one end of the earth
to the other. [i]They shall not be lamented, [i]or
gathered, or buried; [j]they shall be dung on the
surface of the ground.

34 [k]"Wail, [l]you shepherds, and cry out,
[m]and roll in ashes, you lords of the flock,
for the days of your slaughter and dispersion have come,
and you shall fall like a choice vessel.
35 No refuge will remain [n]for the shepherds,
nor escape for the lords of the flock.
36 A voice—the cry [n]of the shepherds,
[o]and the wail of the lords of the flock!
For the LORD is laying waste their pasture,
37 [p]and the peaceful folds are devastated
[q]because of the fierce anger of the LORD.
38 Like a lion [r]he has left his lair,
for their land has become a waste
because of [s]the sword of the oppressor,
[q]and because of his fierce anger."

Jeremiah Threatened with Death

26 [t]In the beginning of the reign of
[u]Jehoiakim the son of Josiah, king
of Judah, this word came from the LORD:
2 "Thus says the LORD: [v]Stand in the court of
the LORD's house, and speak to all the cities
of Judah that come to worship in the house
of the LORD [w]all the words that I command
you to speak to them; [x]do not hold back a
word. 3 [y]It may be they will listen, and every
one turn from his evil way, [z]that I may relent
of the disaster that I intend to do to them
[a]because of their evil deeds. 4 You shall say to
them, 'Thus says the LORD: [b]If you will not
listen to me, to walk in my law that I have
set before you, 5 [c]and to listen to the words
of my servants the prophets whom I send to
you [c]urgently, [c]though you have not listened,
6 then I will make this house [d]like Shiloh, and
I will make this city [e]a curse for all the nations
of the earth.'"

7 [f]The priests and the prophets and all the
people heard Jeremiah speaking these words
in the house of the LORD. 8 And when Jeremiah
had finished speaking all that the LORD had
commanded him to speak to all the people,
then [f]the priests and the prophets and all the
people laid hold of him, saying, "You shall
die! 9 Why have you prophesied in the name
of the LORD, saying, 'This house shall be [d]like
Shiloh, and this city shall be desolate, [g]without inhabitant'?" And all the people gathered
around Jeremiah in the house of the LORD.

10 When [h]the officials of Judah heard these
things, they came up from the king's house
to the house of the LORD and took their seat
in the [i]entry of the New Gate of the house of
the LORD. 11 Then [f]the priests and the prophets
said to the officials and to all the people, [j]"This
man deserves the sentence of death, because
he has prophesied against this city, as you have
heard with your own ears."

12 Then Jeremiah spoke to all the officials and
all the people, saying, "The LORD sent me to
prophesy against this house and this city all
the words you have heard. 13 Now therefore

32[f] ch. 23:19; 30:23 [g] ch. 6:22
33[h] Isa. 66:16 [i] See ch. 16:4 [j] See ch. 8:2
34[k] ch. 4:8 [l] See ch. 23:1 [m] ch. 6:26
35[n] See ch. 23:1
36[n] [See ver. 35 above] [o] ch. 4:8
37[p] [Isa. 32:18] [q] See ch. 12:13
38[r] [Job 38:40] [s] ch. 46:16; 50:16 [q] [See ver. 37 above]

Chapter 26
1[t] ch. 27:1 [u] 2 Kgs. 23:36; 2 Chr. 36:5
2[v] ch. 19:14 [w] [Ezek. 3:10] [x] Deut. 4:2; 12:32; [Acts 20:27]
3[y] ch. 36:3 [z] ver. 13, 19; See ch. 18:8 [a] ch. 4:4
4[b] Lev. 26:14; Deut. 28:15
5[c] See ch. 25:3, 4
6[d] See ch. 7:12 [e] See ch. 24:9
7[f] ch. 23:33
8[f] [See ver. 7 above]

26:1–11 Once again Jeremiah had to pronounce God's judgment on the people, the temple, and the city. The reaction of the religious leaders and officials to this message was anger. Jeremiah had dared to threaten these outward symbols that had become idols instead of the means of knowing the true and living God.

In speaking against the hypocritical, established leaders, Jeremiah is assuming a responsibility that we will later see Jesus fulfill as he cleanses the temple, displaying righteous anger at the way it had been turned into a trading post (John 2:13–17). Jesus then claimed that the true temple would be his risen body (John 2:18–22). Stephen, likewise, when accused of speaking against the temple, pointed to the need to leave earthly symbols and embrace the reality to which they point, namely Christ (Acts 7:47–56). As the people stoned him, Stephen beheld "the Son of Man standing at the right hand of God" (Acts 7:56). His vision, too, was of the spiritual reality, not the shadows of religious practice and prestige.

It is easy to want to base our hope on our performance of, or regard among, the shadows, the symbols, and/or the activities of worship. But Jesus himself said that "God is spirit, and those who worship him must worship in spirit and truth" (John 4:24).

9[d] [See ver. 6 above] [g] See ch. 4:7 **10**[h] ch. 36:12 [i] ch. 36:10 **11**[f] [See ver. 7 above] [j] ch. 38:4; [ver. 16]

[k]mend your ways and your deeds, [l]and obey the voice of the LORD your God, [z]and the LORD will relent of the disaster that he has pronounced against you. 14 [m]But as for me, behold, I am in your hands. Do with me as seems good and right to you. 15 Only know for certain that if you put me to death, [n]you will bring innocent blood upon yourselves and upon this city and its inhabitants, for in truth the LORD sent me to you to speak all these words in your ears."

Jeremiah Spared from Death

16 [o]Then the officials and all the people said to the priests and the prophets, [p]"This man does not deserve the sentence of death, for he has spoken to us in the name of the LORD our God." 17 [q]And certain of [r]the elders of the land arose and spoke to all the assembled people, saying, 18 "Micah of Moresheth prophesied in the days of Hezekiah king of Judah, and said to all the people of Judah: 'Thus says the LORD of hosts,

[s]"'Zion shall be plowed as a field;
Jerusalem shall become a heap of ruins,
and the mountain of the house a
wooded height.'

19 Did Hezekiah king of Judah and all Judah put him to death? [t]Did he not fear the LORD and entreat the favor of the LORD, [u]and did not the LORD relent of the disaster that he had pronounced against them? [v]But we are about to bring great disaster upon ourselves."

20 There was another man who prophesied in the name of the LORD, Uriah the son of Shemaiah from [w]Kiriath-jearim. He prophesied against this city and against this land in words like those of Jeremiah. 21 And when [x]King Jehoiakim, with all his warriors and all the officials, heard his words, the king sought to put him to death. But when Uriah heard of it, he was afraid and fled and escaped to Egypt. 22 Then [x]King Jehoiakim sent to Egypt certain men, [y]Elnathan the son of [z]Achbor and others with him, 23 and they took Uriah from Egypt and brought him to King Jehoiakim, [a]who struck him down with the sword and dumped his dead body into the burial place of the common people.

24 But the hand of [b]Ahikam the son of Shaphan was with Jeremiah so that he was not given over to the people to be put to death.

The Yoke of Nebuchadnezzar

27 In the beginning of the reign of Zedekiah[1] the son of Josiah, king of Judah, this word came to Jeremiah from the LORD. 2 Thus the LORD said to me: [c]"Make yourself straps and [d]yoke-bars, and put them on your neck. 3 Send word[2] to the king of [e]Edom, the king of [e]Moab, the king of the sons of [e]Ammon, the king of [e]Tyre, and the king of Sidon by the hand of the envoys who have come to Jerusalem to Zedekiah king of Judah. 4 Give them this charge for their masters: 'Thus says the LORD of hosts, the God of Israel: This is what you shall say to your

[1] Or *Jehoiakim* [2] Hebrew *Send them*

27:1–11 In delivering once again the same basic message that Judah must submit to the yoke of Babylon, Jeremiah is told to do some play-acting, with an actual yoke placed on his neck. The emphasis in this oracle is the sovereignty of God. On this subject most Christians agree, until it comes to the question of the extent of God's sovereignty in our own lives. The prophet is uncompromising here. God's rule is absolute, yet human responsibility is real and evildoers must answer to God. To many people this is a problem, yet it is clear in Scripture that both aspects of this apparent paradox are true.

Jeremiah declares the rule of God over the whole creation. This is God's world, and he gives power and possessions to whomever he wills (vv. 4–7). This brings up two considerations for believers today, one concerning Jesus and one concerning us. First, Jesus Christ is true and sovereign God and, at the same time, true and responsible man. Yet these two realities (sovereignty and responsibility) are in perfect harmony. Second, Peter declares that "this Jesus, delivered up according to the definite plan and foreknowledge of God [sovereignty], you crucified and killed by the hands of lawless men [responsibility]" (Acts 2:23). For Christians, Paul urges us to "work out your own salvation with fear and trembling [responsibility], for it is God who works in you, both to will and to work for his good pleasure [sovereignty]" (Phil. 2:12–13). We trust God in the necessity of these conclusions, despite our finite inability to understand how they fully coordinate.

13 [k]See ch. 7:3 [l]Deut. 30:2 [z][See ver. 3 above]
14 [m]Josh. 9:25
15 [n][Matt. 27:24]
16 [o]ver. 8 [p][ver. 11]
17 [q][Acts 5:34] [r]See ch. 19:1
18 [s]Mic. 3:12
19 [t][2 Chr. 32:26] [u]Ex. 32:14; 2 Sam. 24:16; [1 Kgs. 13:6] [v][Acts 5:39]
20 [w]Josh. 9:17; 1 Sam. 6:21; 7:1, 2; 1 Chr. 13:5, 6
21 [x]ver. 1; ch. 27:1
22 [x][See ver. 21 above] [y]ch. 36:12, 25 [z]2 Kgs. 22:12, 14
23 [a][ch. 22:17; Neh. 9:26; Matt. 21:35; 23:37]
24 [b]2 Kgs. 22:12
Chapter 27
2 [c][1 Kgs. 22:11; Ezek. 7:23] [d]ch. 28:10, 12, 13; See Lev. 26:13
3 [e]ch. 25:21, 22

masters: 5 “It is I who [f]by my great power and
my outstretched arm [g]have made the earth,
with the men and animals that are on the
earth, [h]and I give it to whomever it seems
right to me. 6 [i]Now I have given all these lands
into the hand of Nebuchadnezzar, the king of
Babylon, [j]my servant, [k]and I have given him
also the beasts of the field to serve him. 7 [l]All
the nations shall serve him and [m]his son and
[n]his grandson, [o]until the time of his own land
comes. [p]Then many nations and great kings
shall make him their slave.

8 “‘“But if any nation or kingdom will not
serve this Nebuchadnezzar king of Babylon,
[q]and put its neck under the yoke of the king
of Babylon, I will punish that nation [r]with
the sword, with famine, and with pestilence,
declares the LORD, until I have consumed it by
his hand. 9 So [s]do not listen to your [t]prophets,
your diviners, your dreamers, your [u]fortune-
tellers, or your sorcerers, who are saying to
you, ‘You shall not serve the king of Babylon.’
10 [v]For it is a lie that they are prophesying to
you, with the result that you will be removed
far from your land, and I will drive you out,
and you will perish. 11 [w]But any nation that
will bring its neck under the yoke of the king
of Babylon and serve him, I will leave on its
own land, to work it and dwell there, declares
the LORD.”’”

12 To [x]Zedekiah king of Judah I spoke in like
manner: [w]“Bring your necks under the yoke
of the king of Babylon, and [y]serve him and his
people and live. 13 [z]Why will you and your people die [a]by the sword, by famine, and by pestilence, [b]as the LORD has spoken concerning any
nation that will not serve the king of Babylon?
14 [c]Do not listen to the words of the prophets
who are saying to you, ‘You shall not serve the
king of Babylon,’ [v]for it is a lie that they are
prophesying to you. 15 I have not sent them,
declares the LORD, but [v]they are prophesying
falsely in my name, with the result that I will
drive you out and you will perish, you and the
prophets who are prophesying to you.”

16 Then I spoke to the priests and to all this
people, saying, “Thus says the LORD: [c]Do not
listen to the words of your prophets who are
prophesying to you, saying, [d]‘Behold, the vessels of the LORD’s house will now shortly be
brought back from Babylon,’ [v]for it is a lie that
they are prophesying to you. 17 [c]Do not listen
to them; [w]serve the king of Babylon and live.
Why should this city [e]become a desolation?
18 If they are prophets, and if the word of the
LORD is with them, then [f]let them intercede
with the LORD of hosts, [g]that the vessels that
are left in the house of the LORD, in the house
of the king of Judah, and in Jerusalem may
not go to Babylon. 19 [h]For thus says the LORD
of hosts concerning the pillars, the sea, the
stands, and the rest of the vessels that are left
in this city, 20 which Nebuchadnezzar king of
Babylon did not take away, [i]when he took into
exile from Jerusalem to Babylon Jeconiah the
son of Jehoiakim, king of Judah, and all the
nobles of Judah and Jerusalem— 21 thus says
the LORD of hosts, the God of Israel, [h]concern-
ing the vessels that are left in the house of the
LORD, in the house of the king of Judah, and in
Jerusalem: 22 [j]They shall be carried to Babylon
[k]and remain there [l]until the day when I visit
them, declares the LORD. [m]Then I will bring
them back [l]and restore them to this place.”

Hananiah the False Prophet

28 In that same year, at the beginning of
the reign of [n]Zedekiah king of Judah, in
the fifth month of the fourth year, Hananiah
the son of [o]Azzur, the prophet from [p]Gibeon,

27:12–22 The false prophets are predominantly those who proclaim that the Babylonian captivity will be partial and short-lived (e.g., Hananiah; 28:1–3). The fondly held opinion that there is nothing to worry about is ever present. In many churches today, themes of judgment and hell are either glossed over or flatly denied. Jesus confirmed the message of the prophets by himself speaking of judgment and death as the outcome of rebellion against God (Matt. 5:20; 12:36–37; 13:41–43; 25:31–46; Luke 16:19–31).

The world considers the Christian idea of God as a judge (Rom. 1:18) to be either horrendous or ridiculous. Yet if the same people look forward to a life after death, they want it to be just, harmonious, and free of evil. All people ultimately want evil to be judged—we just don’t want our *own* evil to be judged!

5 [f]See ch. 21:5 [g]Ps. 115:15; Isa. 45:12 [h]Ps. 115:16; Dan. 4:17, 25, 32
6 [i][Ezek. 30:21, 25] [j]See ch. 25:9 [k]ch. 28:14; Dan. 2:38
7 [l][Dan. 2:37, 38] [m]ch. 52:31 [n]Dan. 5:1, 30 [o]See ch. 25:12 [p]See ch. 25:14
8 [q]ver. 11, 12; [ch. 30:8] [r]See ch. 14:12
9 [s][ch. 14:14] [t][ch. 29:8] [u][Deut. 18:10; Isa. 2:6]
10 [v]See ch. 5:31
11 [w][ver. 2, 8]
12 [x]ch. 28:1; [ver. 1] [w][See ver. 11 above] [y]ver. 17; [ch. 38:17] **13** [z]Ezek. 18:31 [a]See ch. 14:12 [b]ver. 8 **14** [c][ch. 14:14] [v][See ver. 10 above] **15** [v][See ver. 10 above] **16** [c][See ver. 14 above] [d]ch. 28:3; 2 Kgs. 24:13; 2 Chr. 36:7, 10, 18 [v][See ver. 10 above] **17** [c][See ver. 14 above] [w][See ver. 11 above] [e]See ch. 7:34 **18** [f][Isa. 59:16] [g]Dan. 1:2 **19** [h][2 Kgs. 25:13] **20** [i]2 Kgs. 24:14, 15; Matt. 1:11, 12; See ch. 24:1 **21** [h][See ver. 19 above] **22** [j]ch. 52:17, 20, 21; 2 Kgs. 25:13; 2 Chr. 36:18 [k]ch. 32:5 [l]ch. 29:10; 2 Chr. 36:22; Ezra 1:1 [m]Ezra 1:7, 8; 5:14; 7:19 **Chapter 28** **1** [n]ch. 27:12 [o]Ezek. 11:1 [p]Josh. 9:3; 21:17

spoke to me in the house of the LORD, in the
presence of the priests and all the people, saying, 2 "Thus says the LORD of hosts, the God of
Israel: [q]I have broken the yoke of the king of
Babylon. 3 [r]Within [s]two years I will bring back
to this place all the vessels of the LORD's house,
which Nebuchadnezzar king of Babylon took
away from this place and carried to Babylon.
4 I will also bring back to this place [t]Jeconiah
the son of Jehoiakim, king of Judah, and all
the exiles from Judah who went to Babylon,
declares the LORD, [q]for I will break the yoke
of the king of Babylon."

5 Then the prophet Jeremiah spoke to
Hananiah the prophet in the presence of the
priests and all the people who were standing
in the house of the LORD, 6 and the prophet
Jeremiah said, [u]"Amen! May the LORD do so;
may the LORD make the words that you have
prophesied come true, and bring back to this
place from Babylon the vessels of the house
of the LORD, and all the exiles. 7 Yet hear now
this word that I speak in your hearing and in
the hearing of all the people. 8 [v]The prophets who preceded you and me from ancient
times prophesied war, famine, and pestilence
against many countries and great kingdoms.
9 [w]As for the prophet who prophesies peace,
when the word of that prophet comes to pass,
then it will be known that the LORD has truly
sent the prophet."

10 Then the prophet Hananiah took the
[x]yoke-bars from the neck of Jeremiah the
prophet and broke them. 11 And Hananiah
spoke in the presence of all the people, saying,
[y]"Thus says the LORD: [z]Even so will I break
the yoke of Nebuchadnezzar king of Babylon
from the neck of [a]all the nations within two
years." But Jeremiah the prophet went his way.
12 Sometime after the prophet [b]Hananiah
had broken the yoke-bars from off the neck
of Jeremiah the prophet, the word of the
LORD came to Jeremiah: 13 "Go, tell Hananiah,
'Thus says the LORD: You have broken wooden
bars, but you have made in their place bars
of iron. 14 For thus says the LORD of hosts,
the God of Israel: I have put upon the neck
of all these nations [c]an iron yoke to serve
Nebuchadnezzar king of Babylon, [d]and they
shall serve him, [e]for I have given to him even
the beasts of the field.'" 15 And Jeremiah
the prophet said to the prophet Hananiah,
"Listen, Hananiah, [f]the LORD has not sent you,
[g]and you have made this people trust in a lie.
16 Therefore thus says the LORD: 'Behold, I will
remove you from the face of the earth. This
year you shall die, [h]because you have uttered
rebellion against the LORD.'"

17 In that same year, in the seventh month,
the prophet Hananiah died.

Jeremiah's Letter to the Exiles

29 These are the words of the letter
that Jeremiah the prophet sent from
Jerusalem to [i]the surviving elders of the
exiles, and to [j]the priests, [j]the prophets, and
[j]all the people, whom Nebuchadnezzar had
taken into exile from Jerusalem to Babylon.
2 This was after [k]King Jeconiah and the queen
mother, the eunuchs, the officials of Judah
and Jerusalem, the craftsmen, and the metal
workers had departed from Jerusalem. 3 The
letter was sent by the hand of Elasah the son of
[l]Shaphan and Gemariah the son of [m]Hilkiah,
whom Zedekiah king of Judah sent to Babylon
to Nebuchadnezzar king of Babylon. It said:
4 "Thus says the LORD of hosts, the God of
Israel, to all the exiles whom I have sent into
exile from Jerusalem to Babylon: 5 [n]Build
houses and live in them; plant gardens and

29:1–14 Jeremiah now writes a letter to the exiles in Babylon, continuing the theme of condemnation of the false prophets. One would think that, given the initial Babylonian victory and the first exile in 597, these so-called prophets would have learned from their experience. But they continue to proclaim lies. Jeremiah's message to the exiles is to get on with a normal life where they are, and even to pray for the welfare of Babylon (vv. 4–7). This is important instruction for God's people in all ages as we become the agents of God's righteousness in all the places to which his providence calls us—agents of gospel transformation in the world in which we live.

Jeremiah's letter to the exiles also exhorts them to ignore the lies of the false prophets (vv. 8–9). God controls the length of their exile, after which he will fulfill his promises (v. 10). His plan is to give them wholeness, a future, and a hope (v. 11). As in the New Testament, hope is not merely a fond wish but a certain future based on God's faithfulness to his word (Rom. 5:1–5; Eph. 1:18; Col. 1:5, 27; 1 Thess. 4:13; 5:8; 1 Pet. 1:3, 21).

2 [q] [ch. 27:2, 11, 12]
3 [r] ch. 27:16 [s] ver. 11
4 [t] [ch. 22:10, 12, 26] [q] [See ver. 2 above]
6 [u] 1 Kgs. 1:36
8 [v] [ch. 26:18]
9 [w] Deut. 18:22; See ch. 6:14
10 [x] ch. 27:2
11 [y] [1 Kgs. 22:11] [z] ver. 2, 3 [a] ch. 27:7
12 [b] ver. 1, 10
14 [c] Deut. 28:48 [d] [ch. 25:11] [e] See ch. 27:6
15 [f] ch. 29:31; Deut. 18:20; [Ezek. 13:22, 23] [g] See ch. 5:31
16 [h] ch. 29:32; Deut. 13:5
Chapter 29
1 [i] Ezek. 8:1 [j] [ch. 23:33]
2 [k] ch. 24:1; 2 Kgs. 24:12, 14
3 [l] 2 Chr. 34:8 [m] 1 Chr. 6:13
5 [n] ver. 28

eat their produce. 6 Take wives and have sons and daughters; take wives for your sons, and give your daughters in marriage, that they may bear sons and daughters; multiply there, and do not decrease. 7 But seek the welfare of the city where I have sent you into exile, and [o]pray to the LORD on its behalf, for in its welfare you will find your welfare. 8 For thus says the LORD of hosts, the God of Israel: [p]Do not let your prophets and [q]your diviners who are among you deceive you, and do not listen to the dreams that they dream,[1] 9 for [r]it is a lie that they are prophesying to you in my name; [s]I did not send them, declares the LORD.

10 "For thus says the LORD: [t]When seventy years are completed for Babylon, [u]I will visit you, [v]and I will fulfill to you my promise [v]and bring you back to this place. 11 [w]For I know the plans I have for you, declares the LORD, plans for welfare[2] and not for evil, [x]to give you a future and a hope. 12 [y]Then you will call upon me and come and pray to me, [y]and I will hear you. 13 [z]You will seek me and find me, when you seek me [a]with all your heart. 14 I will be found by you, declares the LORD, [b]and I will restore your fortunes and [c]gather you from all the nations and all the places [d]where I have driven you, declares the LORD, and I will bring you back to the place from which I sent you into exile.

15 "Because you have said, 'The LORD has raised up prophets for us in Babylon,' 16 thus says the LORD concerning [e]the king who sits on the throne of David, and concerning all the people who dwell in this city, your kinsmen who did not go out with you into exile: 17 'Thus says the LORD of hosts, behold, I am sending on them [f]sword, famine, and pestilence, and I will make them like [g]vile figs that are so rotten they cannot be eaten. 18 I will pursue them with [f]sword, famine, and pestilence, [h]and will make them a horror to all the kingdoms of the earth, [i]to be a curse, a terror, a hissing, and a reproach among all the nations [d]where I have driven them, 19 because they did not pay attention to my words, declares the LORD, [j]that I persistently sent to you by my servants the prophets, but you would not listen, declares the LORD.' 20 Hear the word of the LORD, all you exiles [k]whom I sent away from Jerusalem to Babylon: 21 'Thus says the LORD of hosts, the God of Israel, concerning Ahab the son of Kolaiah and Zedekiah the son of Maaseiah, [l]who are prophesying a lie to you in my name: Behold, I will deliver them into the hand of Nebuchadnezzar king of Babylon, and he shall strike them down before your eyes. 22 [m]Because of them [n]this curse shall be used by all the exiles from Judah in Babylon: "The LORD make you like Zedekiah and Ahab, [o]whom the king of Babylon roasted in the fire," 23 because they have done an outrageous thing in Israel, [p]they have committed adultery with their neighbors' wives, and [p]they have spoken in my name lying words that I did not command them. [q]I am the one who knows, [q]and I am witness, declares the LORD.'"

Shemaiah's False Prophecy

24 To [r]Shemaiah of Nehelam you shall say: 25 "Thus says the LORD of hosts, the God of Israel: You have sent letters in your name to all the people who are in Jerusalem, and to [s]Zephaniah the son of [t]Maaseiah the priest, and to all the priests, saying, 26 'The LORD has made you priest instead of Jehoiada the priest, to have [u]charge in the house of the LORD [v]over every madman who prophesies, to put him in [w]the stocks and neck irons. 27 Now why have you not rebuked Jeremiah [x]of Anathoth who

[1] Hebrew *your dreams, which you cause to dream* [2] Or *peace*

7[o] [Ezra 6:10; 1 Tim. 2:1, 2]
8[p] [ch. 5:31; 6:14] [q] ch. 27:9, 15
9[r] See ch. 5:31 [s] ver. 31
10[t] See ch. 25:12 [u] ch. 27:22 [v] ch. 33:14; [ch. 24:6]
11[w] [Isa. 55:8, 9] [x] ch. 31:17
12[y] ch. 33:3; Dan. 9:3
13[z] 2 Chr. 15:2; Ps. 32:6; 78:34; Prov. 8:17; Isa. 55:6; Hos. 3:5; See Lev. 26:39-42; Deut. 30:1-3 [a] ch. 24:7; Deut. 4:29
14[b] ch. 30:3 [c] See ch. 23:3 [d] See ch. 8:3
16[e] See ch. 22:2

Note the way prayer works: God first tells the exiles what he will do and why (Jer. 29:10–11); then they will pray accordingly, and God will hear them (v. 12). Those who seek God with a whole heart will find him, and they will be restored from their exile (vv. 13–14). Prayer is not trying to get God to do something he might not otherwise do; rather it is aligning our thoughts, desires, and will with God's, as we humbly consider our circumstances in the light of the priorities that he reveals in his Word. We ask him to do his will (Matt. 6:10). God speaks first, and we respond to his Word. He initiates prayer by revealing his will. True prayer is always that God will fulfill his revealed will. When we don't know the details of his will, we can follow Jesus' example: "Yet not what I will, but what you will" (Mark 14:36). As his adopted children, we can rest confident that whatever he ordains will ultimately be for our joy and glory.

17[f] See ch. 24:10 [g] ch. 24:8 **18**[f] [See ver. 17 above] [h] See ch. 15:4 [i] ch. 18:16; 42:18; See ch. 24:9 [d] [See ver. 14 above] **19**[j] See ch. 25:4 **20**[k] ch. 24:5 **21**[l] ver. 9; See ch. 14:14 **22**[m] See Isa. 65:15 [n] See ch. 24:9 [o] [Dan. 3:6] **23**[p] ch. 23:14 [q] Mal. 3:5 **24**[r] ver. 31, 32 **25**[s] ch. 21:1; 2 Kgs. 25:18 [t] ch. 35:4 **26**[u] [ch. 20:1] [v] [2 Kgs. 9:11; Acts 26:24] [w] ch. 20:2 **27**[x] ch. 1:1; 32:7

is prophesying to you? [28] For he has sent to us
in Babylon, saying, "Your exile will be long;
[y]build houses and live in them, and plant gardens and eat their produce.'"
[29] [s]Zephaniah the priest read this letter in
the hearing of Jeremiah the prophet. [30] [z]Then
the word of the LORD came to Jeremiah:
[31] "Send to all the exiles, saying, 'Thus says
the LORD concerning [a]Shemaiah of Nehelam:
Because [a]Shemaiah had prophesied to you
[b]when I did not send him, and has made you
trust in a lie, [32] therefore thus says the LORD:
Behold, I will punish [a]Shemaiah of Nehelam
and his descendants. He shall not have anyone living among this people, [c]and he shall
not see the good that I will do to my people,
declares the LORD, [d]for he has spoken rebellion against the LORD.'"

Restoration for Israel and Judah

30 The word that came to Jeremiah from
the LORD: [2] "Thus says the LORD, the
God of Israel: [e]Write in a book all the words
that I have spoken to you. [3] [f]For behold, days
are coming, declares the LORD, [g]when I will
restore [h]the fortunes of my people, [i]Israel and
Judah, says the LORD, [j]and I will bring them
back to the land that I gave to their fathers,
and they shall take possession of it."
[4] These are the words that the LORD spoke
concerning [i]Israel and Judah:

5 "Thus says the LORD:
We have heard a cry of panic,
of terror, and no peace.
6 Ask now, and see,
can a man bear a child?
[k]Why then do I see every man
with his hands on his stomach [k]like a woman in labor?
[l]Why has every face turned pale?
7 Alas! [m]That day is so great
[n]there is none like it;
it is a time of distress for Jacob;
yet he shall be saved out of it.

[8] "And it shall come to pass in that day,
declares the LORD of hosts, that I will [o]break
his [p]yoke from off your neck, and I will [o]burst
your bonds, [q]and foreigners shall no more
make a servant of him.[1] [9] But they shall serve
the LORD their God and [r]David their king,
whom I will raise up for them.

[1] Or *serve him*

30:1–33:26 These four chapters form the literary climax of the book of Jeremiah. they are often called the "Book of Comfort" or "Book of Consolation" because they comprise an extended declaration from God that, despite the people's rebellion, he will *not* forsake them. Only in Jesus are we today able to make sense of how a just and holy God can lavish such mercy and grace upon his people without compromising his righteous standards.

30:1–3 Jeremiah's inner turmoil and his anguish over the message of doom that he has had to announce over Judah and Jerusalem are not by any means the whole story. There are two great truths attached to the covenant promises of God. First, those who reject the grace of God will not know the blessings of the covenant but only the curses. Second, despite the intractable faithlessness and treasonous rebellion of the people, God will infallibly bring in his kingdom, peopled by those whose hearts are made new to love and serve God.

We must understand that the holy city, the temple, and the Davidic throne, in their time of glory under David's son Solomon, were the center of the universe to God's people. The meaning of all creation was summed up in these things. But now they are about to be demolished by the Babylonians. From the ashes God will raise up a new kingdom. From the broken world God will raise up a new creation. Possession of the Promised Land is central to the covenant.

Here the renewal of the old covenant promises points forward to a time when out of the suffering would emerge glory—through the cross and resurrection. For Christians these truths converge to point us to the fact that suffering is but for a time, until renewal in glory (Rom. 8:18–24). All is under the sovereign rule and plan of God as he acts in all the events of human history—past, present, and future.

30:8–11 Whereas in 23:5 Jeremiah speaks of a *descendant* of David as the focus of God's rule among his redeemed, here it is David himself who is named. This is a way of speaking about the One who will fulfill the role of the ideal David (see also Ezek.

28[y] ver. 5
29[s] [See ver. 25 above]
30[z] ver. 1, 20
31[a] ver. 24 [b] ver. 9; See ch. 5:31
32[a] [See ver. 31 above] [c] See ch. 17:6 [d] ch. 28:16

Chapter 30
2[e] ch. 36:2; Hab. 2:2
3[f] Hab. 2:3 [g] ver. 18; ch. 29:14; 31:23; 32:44; 33:7, 11, 26; Job 42:10; Lam. 2:14 [h] Ezra 2:1 [i] Isa. 11:12, 13; Hos. 1:11 [j] ch. 12:15; Ezek. 20:42; See ch. 16:15; 23:3
4[i] [See ver. 3 above]
6[k] See Isa. 13:8 [l] Nah. 2:10; [Joel 2:6]
7[m] Joel 2:11; Zeph. 1:14 [n] Dan. 12:1
8[o] ch. 2:20; Nah. 1:13 [p] See ch. 27:2 [q] Ezek. 34:27
9[r] Isa. 55:3, 4; Ezek. 34:23; 37:24; Hos. 3:5; [Luke 1:69, 70; Acts 13:22, 23]; See ch. 23:5

10 [s]"Then fear not, [t]O Jacob my servant,
declares the LORD,
nor be dismayed, O Israel;
for behold, [s]I will save you from far
away,
[u]and your offspring from the land of
their captivity.
[s]Jacob shall return and have quiet and
ease,
and none shall make him afraid.
11 [v]For I am with you to save you,
declares the LORD;
[v]I will make a full end of all the nations
among whom I scattered you,
but of you I will not make a full end.
[v]I will [w]discipline you in just measure,
and I will by no means leave you
unpunished.

12 "For thus says the LORD:
[x]Your hurt is incurable,
[y]and your wound is grievous.
13 There is none to uphold your cause,
no medicine for your wound,
[z]no healing for you.
14 [a]All your lovers have forgotten you;
they care nothing for you;
for I have dealt you the blow of [b]an
enemy,
the punishment [c]of a merciless foe,
because your guilt is great,
[d]because your sins are flagrant.
15 [x]Why do you cry out over your hurt?
[x]Your pain is incurable.
Because your guilt is great,
[d]because your sins are flagrant,
I have done these things to you.
16 [e]Therefore all who devour you shall be
devoured,
and [f]all your foes, every one of them,
shall go into captivity;
[g]those who plunder you shall be plundered,
[h]and all who prey on you I will make a
prey.
17 [i]For I will restore [j]health to you,
and [k]your wounds I will heal,
declares the LORD,
because [l]they have called you an outcast:
[l]'It is Zion, for whom no one cares!'

18 "Thus says the LORD:
Behold, [m]I will restore the fortunes of
the tents of Jacob
and have compassion on his dwellings;
the city shall be rebuilt on [n]its mound,
and the palace shall stand where it
used to be.
19 [o]Out of them shall come songs of thanksgiving,
and the voices of those who celebrate.
[p]I will multiply them, and they shall not
be few;
I will make them honored, and they
shall not be small.
20 [q]Their children shall be as they were of
old,
and their congregation shall be established before me,
and I will punish all who oppress
them.
21 [r]Their prince shall be one of themselves;
[r]their ruler shall come out from their
midst;

10[s] ch. 42:11; 46:27, 28; See Isa. 43:5 [t] Isa. 41:8 [u] See ch. 3:18
11[v] ch. 46:28 [w] See ch. 10:24
12[x] See ch. 15:18 [y] ch. 10:19; 14:17
13[z] ch. 46:11
14[a] Lam. 1:2; [ch. 4:30] [b] Job 13:24; 19:11; Isa. 63:10; Lam. 2:4 [c] Job 30:21; [ch. 6:23] [d] ch. 5:6
15[x] [See ver. 12 above] [d] [See ver. 14 above]
16[e] [ver. 11; ch. 10:25; Isa. 41:11] [f] [Ex. 23:22] [g] [Isa. 33:1] [h] ch. 2:14
17[i] ch. 33:6 [j] ch. 8:22 [k] Ps. 6:2; Hos. 6:1 [l] [Mic. 4:6, 7; Zeph. 3:19]
18[m] [Amos 9:11]; See ver. 3 [n] Deut. 13:16
19[o] ch. 31:12, 13; 33:11; Isa. 35:10; 51:11 [p] Ezek. 36:10, 37; Zech. 10:8
20[q] Isa. 1:26
21[r] [Gen. 49:10; Deut. 18:18]

34:22–24). He will be a Son of David, and it is this role that is assigned to Jesus in the New Testament (Matt. 1:1, 17; Acts 2:29–36; 13:22–23, 32–39; Rom. 1:3–4).

30:17 An important theme in the Old Testament is the reversal of the physical ills that are the lot of fallen mankind. This is part of the cosmic reversal of the fall, when the creation is renewed (Isa. 35:1–10; 53:5; 65:17–25).

Understanding the comprehensive scope of the cosmic reversal prophesied by Jeremiah helps to underscore the importance of Scripture's testimony that Jesus died bodily, rose bodily, and ascended to heaven bodily. The physical aspects of his victory join with the spiritual realities to guarantee that our salvation includes our total being, both body and soul. The redemption of the creation and the redemption of our bodies go hand in hand (Rom. 8:22–23). The false teaching that Jesus rose only in spirit leads to the idea of the immortality of the soul rather than the resurrection of the body. The Bible teaches that the final, permanent state of God's people is not some kind of disembodied, ethereal existence but rather involves fully physical human beings. It is also clear from the New Testament that total and consummate healing from our fallen state occurs only in the final day of resurrection (Rev. 21:1–5).

[s]I will make him draw near, and he shall
approach me,
[t]for who would dare of himself to
approach me?
declares the LORD.
22 [u]And you shall be my people,
and I will be your God."
23 [v]Behold [w]the storm of the LORD!
Wrath has gone forth,
a whirling tempest;
it will burst upon the head of the
wicked.
24 [x]The fierce anger of the LORD will not
turn back
until he has executed and accomplished
the intentions of his mind.
[y]In the latter days you will understand
this.

The LORD Will Turn Mourning to Joy

31 [z]"At that time, declares the LORD, [a]I will
be the God of all the clans of Israel, and
they shall be my people."
2 Thus says the LORD:
"The people who survived the sword
found grace in the wilderness;
[b]when Israel sought for rest,
3 the LORD appeared to him[1] from far
away.
[c]I have loved you with an everlasting
love;
therefore [d]I have continued [e]my faithfulness to you.
4 [f]Again I will build you, and you shall be
built,
O virgin Israel!
[g]Again you shall adorn yourself with
tambourines
and shall go forth in [h]the dance of the
merrymakers.
5 [i]Again you shall plant vineyards
on the mountains of Samaria;
the planters shall plant
and shall enjoy the fruit.
6 For there shall be a day when watchmen
will call
in [j]the hill country of Ephraim:
[k]'Arise, and let us go up to Zion,
to the LORD our God.'"
7 For thus says the LORD:
[l]"Sing aloud with gladness for Jacob,
and raise shouts for [m]the chief of the
nations;

[1] Septuagint; Hebrew *me*

31:1–3 Israel will be reunited and the covenant promises of God will be realized. In New Testament times the people of Israel lived in the Roman province of Judea. As today, they were then all known as Jews—originally the name of the people of the tribe of Judah. One of the great mysteries of this nation is the extent of their rejection of Jesus their Messiah. How then are such prophecies as this one fulfilled?

The general pattern of the Old Testament promises is that God chooses Israel as his people, but because of their sinful rebellion only a remnant will finally receive the promised blessings. This remnant shall be a light for the Gentiles, of whom many will be saved and share the blessings of Israel. This pattern is maintained in the New Testament. Jesus declares that salvation is from the Jews (John 4:22), and that his mission is to the lost sheep of the house of Israel (Matt. 10:6–7; 15:24). Paul describes the gospel as being "to the Jew first" (Rom. 1:16; 2:10). The advantage to the Jews because of the covenant is great (Rom. 3:1–2; 9:4–5), but they have squandered it through unbelief (Rom. 3:9–18).

Paul wrestles with the problem of Jewish unbelief in Romans 9–11 and shows himself to be a latter-day Jeremiah, grieving over the unbelief of his people (Rom. 9:1–3; 10:1). Paul sees the ultimate fulfillment of the Old Testament promises in believing Jews and believing Gentiles becoming one new man in Christ (Eph. 2:11–21; cf. Jer. 31:15). Because the dividing wall of hostility between Jew and Gentile is broken down in Christ (Eph. 2:13–14), Gentiles become fellow citizens with the Jewish saints (Eph. 2:19–20). God declares through Jeremiah that his love is everlasting (Jer. 31:3), and that God *will* be the God of Israel and they shall be his people (v. 1). His covenant promises will not fail.

31:7–8 The doctrine of the "remnant" is the way the prophets refer to the faithfulness of God in tension with the overwhelming faithlessness of the chosen nation. God will save a people out of the mass of humanity. Paul takes up the remnant doctrine in his

21[s]Num. 16:5 [t]ch. 49:19; [Heb. 5:4]
22[u]ch. 24:7; 31:1; 32:38; See ch. 31:33; Lev. 26:12
23[v]ch. 23:19, 20 [w]ch. 25:32
24[x]See ch. 12:13 [y]Hos. 3:5
Chapter 31
1[z]ch. 30:24 [a][2 Cor. 6:18]; See ch. 30:22
2[b][ch. 30:10; Ps. 95:11; Isa. 63:14]
3[c]Deut. 7:8; 10:15; Mal. 1:2; Rom. 11:28 [d]Ps. 36:10 [e]Hos. 11:4
4[f]ver. 28; ch. 33:7 [g]Isa. 61:10 [h]ver. 13; Ex. 15:20; Judg. 11:34; 21:21; See 2 Sam. 6:14
5[i]Isa. 65:21; Amos 9:14
6[j]See Josh. 24:33 [k]Isa. 2:3; 27:13
7[l]Isa. 12:6; 65:18 [m]Amos 6:1

proclaim, give praise, and say,
[n]'O LORD, save your people,
the remnant of Israel.'
8 Behold, I will bring them [o]from the north country
and [p]gather them from [q]the farthest parts of the earth,
among them [r]the blind and the lame,
the pregnant woman and she who is in labor, together;
a great company, they shall return here.
9 [s]With weeping they shall come,
[t]and with pleas for mercy I will lead them back,
I will make them [u]walk by brooks of water,
[v]in a straight path in which they shall not stumble,
for [w]I am a father to Israel,
and Ephraim is [x]my firstborn.

10 "Hear the word of the LORD, O nations,
and declare it in the coastlands far away;
say, 'He who scattered Israel will [p]gather him,
and will keep him [y]as a shepherd keeps his flock.'
11 [z]For the LORD has ransomed Jacob
and has redeemed him from [a]hands too strong for him.
12 They shall come and sing aloud on the height of Zion,
[b]and they shall be radiant [c]over the goodness of the LORD,
[d]over the grain, the wine, and the oil,
and over the young of the flock and the herd;
[e]their life shall be like a watered garden,
[f]and they shall languish no more.
13 [g]Then shall the young women rejoice in the dance,
and the young men and the old shall be merry.
[h]I will turn their mourning into joy;
I will comfort them, and give them gladness for sorrow.
14 [i]I will feast the soul of the priests with abundance,
and my people shall be satisfied with my goodness,
declares the LORD."

15 Thus says the LORD:
[j]"A voice is heard in [k]Ramah,
lamentation and bitter weeping.

7[n] Ps. 118:25
8[o] See ch. 3:18 [p] See ch. 23:3 [q] See ch. 6:22 [r] Isa. 35:5, 6
9[s] ch. 50:4; [Ezra 3:13; 10:1] [t] ch. 3:21; Zech. 12:10 [u] Isa. 35:6, 7; 49:10; [Ps. 23:2] [v] Isa. 35:8; 43:19; 49:11 [w] Rom. 8:15 [x] [Ex. 4:22; Ps. 89:27]
10[p] [See ver. 8 above] [y] Isa. 40:11
11[z] Isa. 43:1; 44:23; 48:20 [a] [Isa. 49:24, 25]
12[b] Isa. 2:2; Mic. 4:1 [c] Hos. 3:5 [d] [Deut. 12:17] [e] Isa. 58:11 [f] Isa. 35:10
13[g] See ver. 4 [h] [John 16:20]
14[i] [ver. 25]
15[j] Cited Matt. 2:18 [k] Josh. 18:25

concerns over unbelief among his fellow Jews. A remnant is being saved as the true Israel (Rom. 9:6–8, 27; 11:1–7).

Eventually, however, this remnant shrank and shrank. Finally, Jesus came as the embodiment of faithful Israel (cf. Ex. 4:22–23; Matt. 2:15), the truly righteous and suffering servant (see note on Isa. 42:1–17).

31:10–12 The theme of the scattered remnant coming to Zion and being kept safe by the Good Shepherd is repeated. Being redeemed from "hands too strong for him" (v. 11) is a reminder that God's people are helpless to save themselves. God graciously brings his people back from a captivity that they are powerless to oppose.

Being ransomed and redeemed by the power of God alone is the reality that is ultimately fulfilled for God's people in Jesus. Jesus declares his power to save to be the power of the Father (John 5:19–24). True believers are God's gift to Jesus; they are saved and secured, for none shall be able to pluck them from his hand (John 6:37–40). Salvation is God's work from beginning to end, which is why we have assurance of our salvation (John 6:44). Those who are in Christ cannot sin their way beyond his gathering grace (Jer. 31:10).

Jeremiah's use of the theme of the saved of Israel coming to Zion is taken up in Hebrews 12:22–24. The Jewish-raised Christians to whom Hebrews is addressed should understand that by believing in Jesus as their Messiah, they have thereby come to the true Zion (Heb. 12:22). The fulfillment of the promises of the prophets is reached by faith in Jesus. All that Jeremiah and other prophets say about the return from exile to the Promised Land is ultimately fulfilled in the person and work of Jesus. In Isaiah 2:2–4 we are told that the day when Zion is restored is the time when the nations also will come to find salvation with the Jews (also Mic. 4:1–2). Thus, Jeremiah helps us to understand that Hebrews 12:22–24 applies to both Jewish and Gentile Christians.

[l]Rachel is weeping for her children;
she refuses to be comforted for her children,
[m]because they are no more."

16 Thus says the LORD:
"Keep your voice from weeping,
and your eyes from tears,
for there is a reward for your work,
declares the LORD,
and [n]they shall come back from the land of the enemy.
17 [o]There is hope for your future,
declares the LORD,
and your children shall come back to their own country.
18 I have heard [p]Ephraim grieving,
'You have disciplined me, and I was disciplined,
like an untrained calf;
[q]bring me back that I may be restored,
for you are the LORD my God.
19 For after [r]I had turned away, I relented,
and after I was instructed, [s]I struck my thigh;
[t]I was ashamed, and I was confounded,
because I bore the disgrace of my youth.'
20 [p]Is Ephraim my dear son?
[u]Is he my darling child?
For as often as I speak against him,
I do remember him still.
[v]Therefore my heart[1] yearns for him;
I will surely have mercy on him,
declares the LORD.

21 [w]"Set up road markers for yourself;
make yourself guideposts;
[x]consider well the highway,
[w]the road by which you went.
Return, O virgin Israel,
return to these your cities.
22 [y]How long will you waver,
[z]O faithless daughter?
For the LORD has created a new thing on the earth:
a woman encircles a man."

23 Thus says the LORD of hosts, the God of
Israel: "Once more they shall use these words
in the land of Judah and in its cities, [a]when
I restore their fortunes:

[b]" 'The LORD bless you, [c]O habitation of righteousness,
[d]O holy hill!'

24 [e]And Judah and all its cities shall dwell there
together, and [e]the farmers and those who wander with their flocks. 25 For I will [f]satisfy the
weary soul, and every languishing soul I will
replenish."
26 At this I awoke and looked, and my sleep
was pleasant to me.
27 [g]"Behold, the days are coming, declares the
LORD, when [h]I will sow the house of Israel and
the house of Judah with [i]the seed of man and
the seed of beast. 28 And it shall come to pass
that [j]as I have watched over them [k]to pluck up
and break down, to overthrow, destroy, and
bring harm, [j]so I will watch over them [l]to build
and to plant, declares the LORD. 29 In those
days they shall no longer say:

[m]" 'The fathers have eaten sour grapes,
and the children's teeth are set on edge.'

30 [n]But everyone shall die for his own iniquity.

[1] Hebrew *bowels*

31:28–30 The initial call of Jeremiah is recalled here (v. 28; cf. 1:10). The judgment on Adam and Eve was not the last word and, by the grace of God, life continued outside of Eden with the promise of future redemption (Gen. 3:15). So also the judgment on the elect nation is not the last word, and God promises that he will "build" and "plant." While God deals with his people as a corporate entity, there is nevertheless individual responsibility (Jer. 31:29–30).

The New Testament also reflects this relationship of individuality to "body life" in the church. Some Christians stress only the truth of the need for an individual to repent and believe, while neglecting the doctrine of the church as the body of believers within and through which God acts.

The relationship of the individual to the corporate stems from the nature of the covenant itself. Adam failed, and all those who are in Adam were represented by Adam's failure. Yet we have no reason to object to this seeming injustice—for Christ, the second Adam, succeeded, and all those who are in Christ are represented by Christ's success (Rom. 5:12–20).

15 [l][Gen. 35:19, 20; 48:7; 1 Sam. 10:2] [m]ch. 10:20
16 [n]Ezra 1:5; Hos. 1:11
17 [o]ch. 29:11
18 [p][ver. 9] [q]Ps. 80:3; Lam. 5:21
19 [r]Deut. 30:2 [s]Ezek. 21:12 [t][ch. 3:25]
20 [p][See ver. 18 above] [u][Prov. 8:30] [v]Song 5:4; Isa. 16:11
21 [w][Isa. 57:14; 62:10] [x]ch. 50:4, 5
22 [y]ch. 2:18, 23, 36 [z]ch. 49:4
23 [a]See ch. 30:3 [b]Ps. 122:6, 7 [c]ch. 50:7; Isa. 1:26 [d]Zech. 8:3
24 [e]ch. 33:13
25 [f]Ps. 36:8; [ver. 14]
27 [g]ch. 9:25 [h]Ezek. 36:11; Hos. 2:23; Zech. 10:9 [i][Ps. 22:30; Isa. 53:10]
28 [j]ch. 44:27; [ch. 32:42] [k][ver. 40]; See ch. 1:10
[l]See ch. 24:6 **29** [m]Ezek. 18:2, 3; [Lam. 5:7] **30** [n]Ezek. 18:4

Each man who eats sour grapes, his teeth shall
be set on edge.

The New Covenant

31 [o]"Behold, the days are coming, declares the
LORD, when I will make [p]a new covenant with
the house of Israel and the house of Judah,
32 not like the covenant that I made with their
fathers on the day when [q]I took them by the
hand to bring them out of the land of Egypt,
my covenant that they broke, [r]though I was
their husband, declares the LORD. 33 [s]For this
is the covenant that I will make with the house
of Israel after those days, declares the LORD: [s]I
will put my law within them, and I will write
it [t]on their hearts. [u]And I will be their God,
and they shall be my people. 34 And no longer
shall each one teach his neighbor and each his
brother, saying, 'Know the LORD,' [v]for they
shall all know me, [w]from the least of them
to the greatest, declares the LORD. For [x]I will
forgive their iniquity, and [y]I will remember
their sin no more."

35 Thus says the LORD,
who [z]gives the sun for light by day
and [a]the fixed order of the moon and
the stars for light by night,
who stirs up the sea so that its waves
roar—
[b]the LORD of hosts is his name:
36 [c]"If this fixed order departs
from before me, declares the LORD,
then shall the offspring of Israel cease
from being a nation before me forever."

37 Thus says the LORD:
"If the heavens above can be measured,
and the foundations of the earth
below can be explored,
[d]then I will cast off all the offspring of
Israel
for all that they have done,
declares the LORD."

38 [e]"Behold, the days are coming, declares
the LORD, when the city shall be rebuilt for
the LORD [f]from the Tower of Hananel to [g]the
Corner Gate. 39 [h]And the measuring line shall
go out farther, straight to the hill Gareb, and
shall then turn to Goah. 40 [i]The whole valley
of the dead bodies and the ashes, and all the
fields as far as the [j]brook Kidron, to the corner
of [k]the Horse Gate toward the east, [l]shall be
sacred to the LORD. [m]It shall not be plucked
up or overthrown anymore forever."

Jeremiah Buys a Field During the Siege

32 The word that came to Jeremiah from
the LORD [n]in the tenth year of Zedekiah
king of Judah, [o]which was the eighteenth year
of Nebuchadnezzar. 2 At that time the army of
the king of Babylon was besieging Jerusalem,
and Jeremiah the prophet [p]was shut up in
[q]the court of the guard that was in the palace
of the king of Judah. 3 For Zedekiah king of
Judah had imprisoned him, saying, "Why do
you prophesy and say, 'Thus says the LORD:
[r]Behold, I am giving this city into the hand of
the king of Babylon, and he shall capture it;
4 [s]Zedekiah king of Judah shall not escape out

31:31–34 This is one of the most significant passages in Jeremiah. It is quoted (Heb. 8:8–13; 10:15–17) and alluded to a number of times in the New Testament (see Matt. 26:28; Mark 14:24; Luke 22:20; 1 Cor. 11:23–26; 2 Cor. 3:3, 6; Heb. 7:22).

When Jesus, at the Last Supper, refers to the "new covenant in my blood" (Luke 22:20), he picks up the theme of Exodus 24:8, where Moses seals the covenant of Sinai in sacrificial blood. It is this Sinai covenant, written on stone, that Jeremiah indicates needs to be renewed by being written on people's hearts—not merely presumed to be in effect on the basis of the external practices of the Mosaic economy. This corresponds to the regeneration by the Spirit that is spoken of in Ezekiel 36:25–28.

Jesus' own sacrificial blood seals the new covenant of our salvation (Heb. 8:6; 9:11–12). The internalizing of the law on the hearts of the people is the transformation by which the covenant promise will be fulfilled (Jer. 31:33; see 2 Cor. 6:16). God himself asserts that the people "shall all know me" (Jer. 31:34). This is not only an intellectual knowing about God but a relational knowing made possible by regeneration. It means believing in him, trusting him, and obeying him in gratitude for salvation. Those to whom the new covenant applies will have their sins forgiven ("remembered no more"; see v. 34). This perfectly describes the glorious situation of Christians, who know God internally through regeneration and who have had their sins wiped away by his gracious provision.

31 [o]ver. 31-34, cited Heb. 8:8-12 [p]Luke 22:20; 2 Cor. 3:6
32 [q][Deut. 1:31] [r]See ch. 3:14
33 [s]ch. 32:40; Ezek. 37:26; Cited Heb. 10:16 [t]Ps. 37:31; 2 Cor. 3:3 [u]Hos. 2:23; Zech. 8:8; 13:9; Rev. 21:7; See ch. 30:22
34 [v]Isa. 54:13 [w]See ch. 6:13 [x]ch. 33:8; 36:3; 50:20; Mic. 7:18; Acts 10:43; Rom. 11:27; Cited Heb. 10:17 [y]Isa. 43:25
35 [z]Gen. 1:16 [a]See ver. 36 [b]See ch. 10:16
36 [c][Ps. 148:6; Isa. 54:9, 10]; For ver. 36, 37, see ch. 33:20-26
37 [d]Rom. 11:1
38 [e]ver. 27, 31 [f]Neh. 3:1; 12:39; Zech. 14:10 [g]2 Kgs. 14:13
39 [h]Ezek. 40:3; Zech. 1:16; 2:1, 2; [Rev. 11:1]
40 [i][ch. 7:31, 32] [j]See 2 Sam. 15:23 [k]2 Chr. 23:15 [l]Isa. 52:1; Joel 3:17 [m][ver. 28]

Chapter 32
1 [n][ch. 37:5, 11; 39:1, 2; 52:4; 2 Kgs. 25:2] [o][ch. 52:12; 2 Kgs. 25:8]
2 [p]Ps. 88:8 [q]ver. 8, 12; ch. 33:1; 37:21; 38:6, 13; 39:14; [Neh. 3:25] **3** [r]ver. 25, 36, 43; ch. 21:10; 34:2; 37:17; 38:3 **4** [s]ch. 34:3

of the hand of the Chaldeans, [r]but shall surely
be given into the hand of the king of Babylon,
and shall speak with him face to face and see
him eye to eye. 5 And [t]he shall take Zedekiah to
Babylon, and there he shall remain until I visit
him, declares the LORD. [u]Though you fight
against the Chaldeans, you shall not succeed'?"
6 Jeremiah said, "The word of the LORD came
to me: 7 Behold, Hanamel the son of Shallum
your uncle will come to you and say, [v]'Buy
my field that is at [w]Anathoth, [x]for the right
of redemption by purchase is yours.' 8 Then
Hanamel my cousin came to me in [q]the court
of the guard, in accordance with the word of
the LORD, and said to me, 'Buy my field that is
at [w]Anathoth in the land of Benjamin, for the
right of possession and redemption is yours;
buy it for yourself.' Then I knew that this was
the word of the LORD.
9 "And I bought the field at [w]Anathoth from
Hanamel my cousin, and [y]weighed out the
money to him, seventeen shekels of silver. 10 [z]I
signed the deed, [a]sealed it, [b]got witnesses, and
[y]weighed the money on scales. 11 Then I took
the sealed deed of purchase, containing the
terms and conditions and the open copy. 12 And
I gave the deed of purchase to [c]Baruch the son
of Neriah son of Mahseiah, in the presence
of Hanamel my cousin, in the presence of
[d]the witnesses who signed the deed of purchase, and in the presence of all the Judeans
who were sitting in [q]the court of the guard.
13 I charged [c]Baruch in their presence, saying,
14 'Thus says the LORD of hosts, the God of
Israel: Take these deeds, both this sealed deed
of purchase and this open deed, and put them
in an earthenware vessel, that they may last
for a long time. 15 For thus says the LORD of
hosts, the God of Israel: Houses and [e]fields and
vineyards shall again be bought in this land.'

Jeremiah Prays for Understanding

16 "After I had given the deed of purchase
to [f]Baruch the son of Neriah, I prayed to the
LORD, saying: 17 'Ah, Lord GOD! It is [g]you who
have made the heavens and the earth by your
great power and by [h]your outstretched arm!
[i]Nothing is too hard for you. 18 [j]You show
steadfast love to thousands, [j]but you repay
the guilt of fathers [k]to their children after
them, O great and [l]mighty God, whose name
is the [m]LORD of hosts, 19 [n]great in counsel and
[o]mighty in deed, [p]whose eyes are open to all
the ways of the children of man, [q]rewarding
each one according to his ways and according
to the fruit of his deeds. 20 You have shown
[r]signs and wonders in the land of Egypt, and
to this day in Israel and among all mankind,
[s]and have made a name for yourself, as at this
day. 21 [t]You brought your people Israel out of
the land of Egypt with signs and wonders,
with a strong hand and [u]outstretched arm,
[t]and with great terror. 22 And you gave them
this land, [v]which you swore to their fathers

32:6–15 The purchase of a field seems inconsistent with the message of destruction at which King Zedekiah was so offended (see vv. 1–5). It is Jeremiah's expression of his confidence in the reliability of the Lord's promises of an eventual end to the exile and the restoration of the people to their own land. Destruction and renewal are the effects of judgment and redemption.

What Jeremiah describes here foreshadows first the death and resurrection of Jesus and, second, our being crucified with him and raised to newness of life (Rom. 6:1–8; 1 Cor. 15:21–22; Gal. 2:19–20; Col. 3:1–4). As the believing exiles were taught to wait in hope of restoration, so we wait for the return of Jesus to judge the living and the dead and to bring in the fullness of his kingdom.

32:16–25 Jeremiah's humanity is revealed in this prayer, which seems to express some of his concerns about God's instruction to purchase a field even as destruction looms. He first rehearses the greatness of God's actions from creation, through redemption from Egypt, the giving of the Promised Land to Israel, right up to the present situation of disaster. But then he questions, "Yet you, O Lord GOD, have said to me, 'Buy the field . . . though the city is given into the hands of the Chaldeans'" (v. 25). We can readily identify with Jeremiah's desire for reassurance regarding God's will. It is easy to be rattled by events that we do not fully understand even when we have a firm grasp of the gospel. When our faith is thus challenged, we should focus, not on how well we believe, but on how well God has acted for us in Christ (Rom. 8:26–39). Note that Jeremiah's prayer, prior to his questioning statement, rehearses God's saving acts (Jer. 32:16–24).

4 [r][See ver. 3 above]
5 [t]ch. 39:7; 52:11 [u][ch. 21:4; 33:5]
7 [v]ver. 25 [w]ch. 1:1; 29:27; Josh. 21:18 [x]Lev. 25:25; [Ruth 4:4]
8 [q][See ver. 2 above] [w][See ver. 7 above]
9 [w][See ver. 7 above] [y]Gen. 23:16; Zech. 11:12; [Matt. 26:15]
10 [z]ver. 44 [a]Esth. 3:12 [b]ver. 25 [y][See ver. 9 above]
12 [c]ch. 36:4, 8, 10, 14, 26, 32; 43:3, 6; 45:1-3 [d][Isa. 8:2] [q][See ver. 2 above]
13 [c][See ver. 12 above]
15 [e]ver. 43
16 [f]See ver. 12
17 [g]Isa. 37:16 [h]See ch. 21:5 [i]ver. 27; See Gen. 18:14
18 [j]Ex. 20:6; 34:7; Deut. 5:9, 10 [k][Ps. 79:12; Isa. 65:6-7] [l]Isa. 9:6 [m]See ch. 10:16
19 [n]Isa. 28:29 [o][Ps. 66:3, 5] [p]See ch. 16:17 [q]See ch. 17:10
20 [r]Ps. 135:9 [s]2 Sam. 7:23; See Neh. 9:10
21 [t]Ex. 6:6; Deut. 4:34; 1 Chr. 17:21 [u]See ch. 21:5
22 [v]Deut. 26:15; See Ex. 3:8

to give them, [v]a land flowing with milk and honey. 23 And they entered and took possession of it. [w]But they did not obey your voice or walk in your law. They did nothing of all you commanded them to do. Therefore you have made all this disaster come upon them. 24 Behold, [x]the siege mounds have come up to the city to take it, and [y]because of sword and famine and pestilence [z]the city is given into the hands of the Chaldeans who are fighting against it. What you spoke has come to pass, and behold, you see it. 25 Yet you, O Lord GOD, have said to me, [a]"Buy the field for money [b]and get witnesses"—though [z]the city is given into the hands of the Chaldeans.'"

26 The word of the LORD came to Jeremiah: 27 "Behold, I am the LORD, [c]the God of all flesh. [d]Is anything too hard for me? 28 Therefore, thus says the LORD: [e]Behold, I am giving this city into the hands of the Chaldeans and into the hand of Nebuchadnezzar king of Babylon, and he shall capture it. 29 The Chaldeans who are fighting against this city [f]shall come and set this city on fire and burn it, [g]with the houses on whose roofs offerings have been made to Baal [g]and drink offerings have been poured out to other gods, [h]to provoke me to anger. 30 For the children of Israel and the children of Judah have done nothing but evil in my sight [i]from their youth. The children of Israel have done nothing but [h]provoke me to anger [j]by the work of their hands, declares the LORD. 31 This city has aroused my anger and wrath, from the day it was built to this day, [k]so that I will remove it from my sight 32 because of all the evil of the children of Israel and the children of Judah that they did to provoke me to anger—[l]their kings and their officials, their priests and their prophets, the men of Judah and the inhabitants of Jerusalem. 33 [m]They have turned to me their back and not their face. And though I have taught them [n]persistently, they have not listened [o]to receive instruction. 34 They set up [p]their abominations in the house that is called by my name, to defile it. 35 They built the high places of Baal [q]in the Valley of the Son of Hinnom, [r]to offer up their sons and daughters to Molech, [s]though I did not command them, nor did it enter into my mind, that they should do [p]this abomination, [t]to cause Judah to sin.

They Shall Be My People; I Will Be Their God

36 "Now therefore thus says the LORD, the God of Israel, concerning this city of which you say, [u]'It is given into the hand of the king of Babylon by sword, by famine, and by pestilence': 37 [v]Behold, I will gather them from all the countries [w]to which I drove them in [x]my anger and my wrath and in great indignation. I will bring them back to this place, [y]and I will make them dwell in safety. 38 [z]And they shall be my people, and I will be their God. 39 [a]I will give them one heart and one way, that they may fear me forever, [b]for their own good and the good of their children after them. 40 [c]I will make with them an everlasting covenant, that I will not turn away from doing good to them. [d]And I will put the fear of me in their hearts, that they may not turn from me. 41 [e]I will rejoice in doing them good, [f]and I will plant them in this land in faithfulness, with all my heart and all my soul.

42 "For thus says the LORD: [g]Just as I have brought all this great disaster upon this people, so I will bring upon them all the good that

22 [v]Deut. 26:15; See Ex. 3:8
23 [W]Neh. 9:26, 27; See ch. 11:8; Dan. 9:10-14
24 [x]ch. 33:4; See ch. 6:6 [y]ver. 36; See ch. 14:12 [z]See ver. 3
25 [a]ver. 7 [b]ver. 10 [z][See ver. 24 above]
27 [c]Num. 16:22 [d]See Gen. 18:14
28 [e]ver. 3
29 [f]See ch. 21:10 [g]See ch. 19:13 [h]See ch. 7:18
30 [i]ch. 3:25 [h][See ver. 29 above] [j]ch. 25:6, 7
31 [k]2 Kgs. 23:27; 24:3
32 [l]ch. 2:26
33 [m]ch. 2:27; [Ezek. 8:16]; See ch. 7:24 [n]See ch. 25:3 [o]See ch. 5:3
34 [p]See ch. 7:30; 23:11
35 [q]ch. 7:31; See Josh. 18:16 [r]Lev. 18:21 [s]ch. 7:31 [p][See ver. 34 above]

32:26–35 The Lord's reply to Jeremiah is instructive. If there is any rebuke at all, it is muted or implied. He patiently repeats the rationale for the destruction of Judah and the exile of the people. Sometimes we don't need answers to our questions or doubts; we need rather to be reminded of God's grace. As with Paul, who prayed for relief from his illness three times, God's answer to us is often, "My grace is sufficient for you, for my power is made perfect in weakness" (2 Cor. 12:9). This grace is the action of our God in Christ, and the word of the gospel as the Spirit focuses our faith on the sovereign power of a loving, saving God. For Jeremiah it is the reminder of God's revealed plan for the redemption of his people (see Jer. 32:36–44).

32:40–41 The pleasure of God in salvation is noted here. God saw that his creation was good (Gen. 1:31), and he took pleasure in it. It is also his pleasure to bring in the new creation and to give the kingdom to his redeemed people (Ps. 51:18–19; 149:4). What the Lord delights in becomes the delight of those that are with him (Luke 15:7, 10; John 15:11).

[t][1 Kgs. 16:19] **36** [u]See ver. 3 **37** [v]See ch. 23:3 [w]See ch. 8:3 [x]ch. 21:5; Deut. 29:28 [y]ch. 23:6; 33:16; Ezek. 34:25 **38** [z]See ch. 30:22; 31:33 **39** [a]Ezek. 11:19, 20 [b]Deut. 6:24 **40** [c]ch. 50:5; Ps. 89:34; Isa. 55:3; Ezek. 16:60 [d]See ch. 31:33 **41** [e][Deut. 28:63] [f]See ch. 24:6 **42** [g][ch. 31:28]

I promise them. 43 [h]Fields shall be bought in this land [i]of which you are saying, 'It is a desolation, without man or beast; [j]it is given into the hand of the Chaldeans.' 44 Fields shall be bought for money, and [k]deeds shall be signed and [k]sealed and [k]witnessed, [l]in the land of Benjamin, [l]in the places about Jerusalem, [l]and in the cities of Judah, [l]in the cities of the hill country, [l]in the cities of the Shephelah, and in the cities of the Negeb; for [m]I will restore their fortunes, declares the LORD."

The LORD Promises Peace

33 The word of the LORD came to Jeremiah a second time, while he was still [n]shut up in the court of the guard: 2 "Thus says [o]the LORD who made the earth,[1] the LORD who formed it to establish it—[p]the LORD is his name: 3 [q]Call to me and I will answer you, [r]and will tell you great and hidden things that you have not known. 4 For thus says the LORD, the God of Israel, concerning the houses of this city and the houses of the kings of Judah that were torn down to make a defense against [s]the siege mounds and against the sword: 5 They are coming in [t]to fight against the Chaldeans and to fill them[2] with the dead bodies of men whom I shall strike down [u]in my anger and my wrath, [v]for I have hidden my face from this city because of all their evil. 6 [w]Behold, I will bring to it health and healing, and I will heal them and reveal to them abundance of prosperity and security. 7 [x]I will restore the fortunes of Judah and the fortunes of Israel, [y]and rebuild them as they were [z]at first. 8 [a]I will cleanse them from all the guilt of their sin against me, [b]and I will forgive all the guilt of their sin and rebellion against me. 9 [c]And this city[3] shall be to me a name of joy, a praise and a glory before all the nations of the earth who shall hear of all the good that I do for them. They shall [d]fear and tremble because of all the good and all the prosperity I provide for it.

10 "Thus says the LORD: In this place [e]of which you say, 'It is a waste without man or beast,' in the cities of Judah and the streets of Jerusalem that are desolate, without man or inhabitant or beast, there shall be heard again 11 [f]the voice of mirth and the voice of gladness, the voice of the bridegroom and the voice of the bride, the voices of those who sing, as they bring [g]thank offerings to the house of the LORD:

[h]"'Give thanks to the LORD of hosts,
for the LORD is good,
for his steadfast love endures forever!'

[x]For I will restore the fortunes of the land as at first, says the LORD.

12 "Thus says the LORD of hosts: [i]In this place that is waste, without man or beast, and in all of its cities, there shall again be [j]habitations of shepherds [k]resting their flocks. 13 [l]In the cities of the hill country, [l]in the cities of

[1] Septuagint; Hebrew *it* [2] That is, the torn-down houses [3] Hebrew *And it*

Redemption of his people is something God will delight to do, "with all my heart and all my soul" (Jer. 32:41). We penetrate here into the very core of who God is. Such mercy is not merely peripheral to the nature of God. Six centuries later, Jesus reiterated this aspect of the divine nature when he said, "I am gentle and lowly in heart, and you will find rest for your souls" (Matt. 11:29). This is the only place in all the four Gospels where Jesus tells us about his heart. And at the one place where he opens up his heart, he says it is "gentle and lowly."

Are you cowering before the sovereign God of creation? Then remember that he presents himself to us in the person of the risen Lord Christ. Your felt inadequacy, your sins, your anxieties—none of these are hindrances. They are the very things to which the Lord Jesus is drawn, as you look to him. Trust him. Walk with him. He is a gentle Savior—showing mercy with all his heart and with all his soul.

33:6–9 The restoration of Judah is described as healing, prosperity, and security. This is what belongs to a people dwelling safely in the Promised Land. Jesus presents himself as the fulfiller of these promises through his healing miracles (e.g., Matt. 9:2–6). Such miracles were themselves pointers to the consummation of God's promises in his kingdom in the new heaven and the new earth, where there will be neither death nor pain (Rev. 21:3–5). God clearly can and does perform healing miracles in the present. But this power of God must be understood in the light of the teaching of the New Testament that we will suffer and be vulnerable to sickness until Christ's return (e.g., John 16:33; 2 Cor. 4:17; Gal. 4:13–14; 2 Tim. 4:20; 1 Pet. 4:12).

43 [h]ver. 15 [i]ch. 33:10 [j]See ver. 3
44 [k]ver. 10 [l]See ch. 17:26 [m]See ch. 30:3
Chapter 33
1 [n]See ch. 32:2
2 [o][Isa. 37:26] [p][ch. 16:21; Ex. 6:3; Ps. 83:18; Amos 4:13]
3 [q]ch. 29:12; Ps. 91:15 [r]Isa. 48:6
4 [s]ch. 32:24
5 [t][ch. 32:5] [u]Ezek. 22:20 [v]Deut. 31:17, 18
6 [w]ch. 30:17
7 [x]See ch. 30:3 [y]See ch. 24:6 [z]Isa. 1:26
8 [a]Ezek. 36:25; [Ps. 51:2, 7; Heb. 9:13, 14] [b]See ch. 31:34
9 [c]See ch. 13:11 [d][Ps. 130:4; Isa. 60:5]
10 [e]ch. 32:43
11 [f]See ch. 7:34 [g]1 Chr. 16:34; Ps. 106:1; 107:1; Isa. 12:4 [h]ch. 30:19; Lev. 7:12; Ps. 107:22 [x][See ver. 7 above]
12 [i][Ezek. 36:11] [j][ch. 31:24; 50:19; Isa. 65:10; Ezek. 34:14, 15] [k]Song 1:7
13 [l]See ch. 17:26

the Shephelah, [l]and in the cities of the Negeb,
in the land of Benjamin, [l]the places about
Jerusalem, [l]and in the cities of Judah, [m]flocks
shall again pass under the hands [n]of the one
who counts them, says the LORD.

The LORD's Eternal Covenant with David

14 [o]"Behold, the days are coming, declares the
LORD, when [p]I will fulfill the promise I made
to the house of Israel and the house of Judah.
15 In those days and at that time I will cause a
righteous [q]Branch to spring up for David, and
he shall execute justice and righteousness in
the land. 16 In those days Judah will be saved,
[r]and Jerusalem will dwell securely. And this
is the name by which it will be called: [s]'The
LORD is our righteousness.'

17 "For thus says the LORD: [t]David shall never
lack a man to sit on the throne of the house of
Israel, 18 [u]and the Levitical priests shall never
lack a man in my presence to offer burnt offerings, to burn grain offerings, and to make sacrifices forever."

19 The word of the LORD came to Jeremiah:
20 [v]"Thus says the LORD: [w]If you can break my
covenant with the day and my covenant with
the night, [x]so that day and night will not come
at their appointed time, 21 [y]then also my covenant with David my servant may be broken,
so that he shall not have a son to reign on his
throne, and my covenant with the Levitical
priests my ministers. 22 As [z]the host of heaven
cannot be numbered and [z]the sands of the sea
cannot be measured, so I will multiply the offspring of David my servant, and the Levitical
priests who minister to me."

23 The word of the LORD came to Jeremiah:
24 "Have you not observed that these people
are saying, 'The LORD has rejected the two
clans that he chose'? Thus they have despised
my people so that they are no longer a nation
in their sight. 25 Thus says the LORD: [a]If I have
not established my covenant with day and
night and the fixed order of heaven and earth,
26 then I will reject the offspring of Jacob and
David my servant and will not choose one
of his offspring to rule over the offspring of
Abraham, Isaac, and Jacob. [b]For I will restore
their fortunes and will have mercy on them."

Zedekiah to Die in Babylon

34 The word that came to Jeremiah from
the LORD, when [c]Nebuchadnezzar
king of Babylon and all his army [d]and all the

13 [l]See ch. 17:26 [m][Lev. 27:32] [n][John 10:3]
14 [o]For ver. 14-16, see ch. 23:5, 6 [p]ch. 29:10
15 [q]ch. 23:5; [Isa. 4:2; 11:1]
16 [r]ch. 23:6; 32:37 [s]ch. 23:6
17 [t]2 Sam. 7:16; 1 Kgs. 2:4; Ps. 89:3, 4
18 [u][Isa. 66:21]
20 [v]For ver. 20-26, see ch. 31:36, 37 [w]ver. 25; [Isa. 54:9] [x]Gen. 8:22; Ps. 72:5
21 [y]Ps. 89:34
22 [z]Gen. 22:17
25 [a]Ps. 74:16, 17; 104:19
26 [b]ver. 7, 11; See ch. 30:3

Chapter 34
1 [c]ch. 39:1; 52:4; 2 Kgs. 25:1 [d]ch. 1:15; [ch. 51:28]

33:14–22 (See also notes on 23:1–6 and 23:7–8.) A significant restoration theme in Jeremiah concerns God's covenant with David. The Branch theme (33:15) is found in Isaiah 11:1, where the imagery is of a stump, the remnant of the family tree of David's father Jesse, from which sprouts a new branch, who brings in the messianic age (Isa. 11:1–9).

Here in Jeremiah 33 the metaphor signifies that a descendant of David is to be the mediator of justice, righteousness, and salvation (vv. 15–16). Once again we are reminded that "The LORD is our righteousness"—but this time the *nation* receives that name, as it assumes the identity of its Mediator (v. 16; cf. 23:6). The principle of righteous substitution (God's righteousness for his people's sin) has always been true, for there is no righteousness in us as grounds for our acceptance by a holy God. If we are to be saved, it must be purely by God's grace as a gift of his own righteousness in Christ (Rom. 3:21–26).

The new emphasis in this passage, not contained in Jeremiah 23:5–8, is the utter *permanence* of the covenant with David (33:19–21; but see 31:36–37). This assurance, based on the permanence of night followed by day, is repeated in 33:25–26. The "covenant" referenced here is the one expressed in 2 Samuel 7:12–16. It is also referred to in Isaiah 55:3 and is the subject of Psalm 89. Matthew introduces his Gospel with Jesus' genealogy as the Son of David (Matt. 1:1–17). According to the apostle Peter, this covenant with David is ultimately fulfilled in the resurrection of Jesus (Acts 2:29–32). Paul outlines his gospel in Romans 1:1–4, which includes the important fact that it is the gospel "concerning his Son, who was descended from David according to the flesh" (Rom. 1:3). As in 2 Samuel 7:14, the son of God is also the son of David. Paul reiterates this as central to the gospel: the Son of God is the Son of David. Thus the covenant focus moves from Abraham and his descendants as sons of God, through David's descendant as a son of God, to Jesus the Son of God.

Reflecting on God's grace in providing an alien righteousness, our hearts are transformed and we are compelled to love others in light of the way we have been loved.

kingdoms of the earth under his dominion and all the peoples were fighting against Jerusalem and all of its cities: 2 "Thus says the LORD, the God of Israel: Go and speak to [e]Zedekiah king of Judah and say to him, 'Thus says the LORD: [f]Behold, I am giving this city into the hand of the king of Babylon, and he shall burn it with fire. 3 [g]You shall not escape from his hand but shall surely be captured and delivered into his hand. [g]You shall see the king of Babylon eye to eye and speak with him face to face. And you shall go to Babylon.' 4 Yet hear the word of the LORD, O Zedekiah king of Judah! [h]Thus says the LORD concerning you: [h]'You shall not die by the sword. 5 You shall die in peace. [i]And as spices were burned for your fathers, the former kings who were before you, so people shall [j]burn spices for you [k]and lament for you, saying, "Alas, lord!"' For I have spoken the word, declares the LORD."

6 Then Jeremiah the prophet spoke all these words to Zedekiah king of Judah, in Jerusalem, 7 when the army of the king of Babylon was fighting against Jerusalem and against all the cities of Judah that were left, [l]Lachish and [m]Azekah, [n]for these were the only [o]fortified cities of Judah that remained.

8 The word that came to Jeremiah from the LORD, after King Zedekiah [p]had made a covenant with all the people in Jerusalem [q]to make a proclamation of liberty to them, 9 [r]that everyone should set free his Hebrew slaves, male and female, [s]so that no one should enslave a Jew, his brother. 10 And they obeyed, all the officials and all the people who had entered into the covenant that everyone would set free his slave, male or female, so that they would not be enslaved again. They obeyed and set them free. 11 But afterward they turned around and took back the male and female slaves [r]they had set free, and brought them into subjection as slaves. 12 The word of the LORD came to Jeremiah from the LORD: 13 "Thus says the LORD, the God of Israel: I myself made a covenant with your fathers when [t]I brought them out of the land of Egypt, out of the house of slavery, saying, 14 [u]'At the end of seven years each of you must set free the fellow Hebrew who has been sold to you and has served you six years; [r]you must set him free from your service.' But [v]your fathers did not listen to me or incline their ears to me. 15 You recently repented and did what was right in my eyes [q]by proclaiming liberty, each to his neighbor, and [w]you made a covenant before me in the [x]house that is called by my name, 16 but then you turned around [y]and profaned my name when each of you took back his male and female slaves, [z]whom you had set free according to their desire, and

34:1–7 The chain of events in Jeremiah has reached the rule of Zedekiah, last of the Davidic kings of Judah. Ironically, his name means "The Lord is [my] righteousness" (cf. 23:6; 33:16) but he showed that he had learned little from Jeremiah's words. International ferment led him to believe he could successfully rebel against the Babylonians, for whom he was a puppet king.

Once again we see the futility of trying to steer history away from God's intended purposes. God will accomplish what he has designed from the beginning. Not only has Jesus written the definitive human history by which we are accounted righteous according to God's original plan (Gen. 3:15), but the book of Revelation as a whole tells of the end of history and the final victory of God's Christ, who shall rule forever (e.g., Rev. 11:15–18; 18:1–10; 21:1–8).

34:8–16 At a time when many people of Judah had been taken as captives to Babylon, Zedekiah makes a covenant with the people which frees any Hebrews in servitude to them, a principle that had existed since Moses (Deut. 15:12–15). The people agree to the covenant, then renege, thus breaking their covenant made before God. In doing so they profane God's name (Jer. 34:16) and make light of God's being witness to their covenant. They ignore their own history of being freed from captivity in Egypt (vv. 12–14).

This principle that Israel ignores—as God has done to you, so do to others—is amplified in the New Testament. At its base is the fact that we must not treat others in a way that contradicts God's grace towards us (Matt. 6:15; 18:21–35; Rom. 15:7; Eph. 4:32; Col. 3:13). God has shown such marvelous mercy to us sinners. How could we not treat others accordingly? When we love Christ because we have apprehended his grace toward us, then we will love what and whom he loves (the downtrodden, disadvantaged, and discriminated against).

2 [e] 2 Kgs. 25:2 [f] See ch. 21:10
3 [g] See ch. 32:4
4 [h] [ch. 38:17, 20; 39:4, 7]
5 [i] 1 Sam. 31:12; 2 Chr. 21:19 [j] 2 Chr. 16:14 [k] [ch. 22:18]
7 [l] Josh. 10:3 [m] Josh. 10:10; 15:35 [n] 2 Kgs. 18:13 [o] ch. 4:5
8 [p] ver. 15 [q] ver. 15, 17; Ex. 21:2; Lev. 25:10; [Isa. 61:1]
9 [r] See Lev. 25:39-46 [s] [Neh. 5:8]
11 [r] [See ver. 9 above]
13 [t] Ex. 20:2
14 [u] Ex. 21:2; Deut. 15:12 [r] [See ver. 9 above] [v] ch. 7:24, 26; 11:8; 17:23; 25:4; 35:15; 44:5
15 [q] [See ver. 8 above] [w] ver. 8; [2 Kgs. 23:3] [x] See ch. 7:10
16 [y] Lev. 18:21; 19:12 [z] ver. 11

you brought them into subjection to be your slaves.

17 "Therefore, thus says the LORD: You have not obeyed me [q]by proclaiming liberty, every one to his brother and to his neighbor; [a]behold, I proclaim to you liberty [b]to the sword, to pestilence, and to famine, declares the LORD. [c]I will make you a horror to all the kingdoms of the earth. 18 And the men who transgressed my covenant and did not keep the terms of [w]the covenant that they made before me, I will make them like[1] [d]the calf that they cut in two and passed between its parts— 19 the officials of Judah, the officials of Jerusalem, [e]the eunuchs, the priests, and all the people of the land who passed between the parts of the calf. 20 And I will give them into the hand of their enemies [f]and into the hand of those who seek their lives. [g]Their dead bodies shall be food for the birds of the air and the beasts of the earth. 21 And [h]Zedekiah king of Judah and his officials I will give into the hand of their enemies and into the hand of those who seek their lives, into the hand of the army of the king of Babylon [i]which has withdrawn from you. 22 Behold, [j]I will command, declares the LORD, and will [k]bring them back to this city. [k]And they will fight against it and take it and burn it with fire. [l]I will make the cities of Judah a desolation [m]without inhabitant."

The Obedience of the Rechabites

35 The word that came to Jeremiah from the LORD in the days of [n]Jehoiakim the son of Josiah, king of Judah: 2 "Go to the house of the [o]Rechabites and speak with them and bring them to the house of the LORD, into one of [p]the chambers; then offer them wine to drink." 3 So I took Jaazaniah the son of Jeremiah, son of Habazziniah and his brothers and all his sons and the whole house of the Rechabites. 4 I brought them to the house of the LORD into [p]the chamber of the sons of Hanan the son of Igdaliah, [q]the man of God, which was near [p]the chamber of the officials, above [p]the chamber of [r]Maaseiah the son of Shallum, [s]keeper of the threshold. 5 Then I set before the Rechabites pitchers full of wine, and cups, and I said to them, "Drink wine." 6 But they answered, "We will drink no wine, for [t]Jonadab the son of Rechab, our father, commanded us, 'You shall not drink wine, neither you nor your sons forever. 7 You shall not build a house; you shall not sow seed; you shall not plant or have a vineyard; but you shall live in tents all your days, [u]that you may live many days in the land where you sojourn.' 8 We have obeyed the voice of Jonadab the son of Rechab, our father, in all that he commanded us, to drink no wine all our days, ourselves, our wives, our sons, or our daughters, 9 and not to build houses to dwell in. We have no vineyard or field or seed, 10 but we have lived in tents and have obeyed and done all that Jonadab our father commanded us. 11 But [v]when Nebuchadnezzar king of Babylon came up against the land, we said, 'Come, and let us go to Jerusalem for fear of [w]the army of the Chaldeans and [w]the army of the Syrians.' [x]So we are living in Jerusalem."

12 Then the word of the LORD came to Jeremiah: 13 "Thus says the LORD of hosts, the God of Israel: Go and say to the people of Judah and the inhabitants of Jerusalem, [y]Will you not receive instruction and listen to my words? declares the LORD. 14 The command that Jonadab the son of Rechab gave to his sons, to drink no wine, has been kept, and they drink none to this day, for they have obeyed their father's command. I have spoken to you [z]persistently, but you have not listened to me. 15 I have sent to you all my servants the

[1] Hebrew lacks *them like*

17[q] [See ver. 8 above] [a] [Matt. 7:2; Gal. 6:7; James 2:13] [b] See ch. 14:12 [c] See ch. 15:4
18[w] [See ver. 15 above] [d] [Gen. 15:10]
19[e] ch. 29:2
20[f] See ch. 22:25 [g] See ch. 7:33
21[h] [ver. 2, 4, 8] [i] ch. 37:5, 11
22[j] Isa. 10:6 [k] ch. 37:8; 38:3 [l] ch. 9:11 [m] See ch. 4:7
Chapter 35
1[n] ch. 25:1
2[o] 1 Chr. 2:55 [p] 1 Kgs. 6:5, 6; 1 Chr. 9:26, 33
4[p] [See ver. 2 above]

35:1–19 Judah's covenant breaking is now contrasted with the faithfulness of the Rechabites. When a previous king tried to get them to break their covenant of abstinence, they remained faithful to their vow to their leader (v. 14). But the people of Judah have broken their covenant with God (v. 15). The outcome is to be the punishments prescribed in the covenant (v. 17; see also 34:18).

The New Testament has many warnings against scorning the grace of God and being disobedient to our covenant status. Hebrews 3:1–4:13 applies Psalm 95 as a warning to Christians against unbelief and falling away (see also Heb. 2:1–4; 5:11–6:12). Even warnings, stern as they may be, are expressions of God's tender mercy toward wayward sinners. He loves us too much to let us walk in folly.

[q] [Deut. 33:1] [r] ch. 21:1; 29:25; 37:3 [s] 2 Kgs. 12:9; 25:18 **6**[t] 2 Kgs. 10:15, 23 **7**[u] [Ex. 20:12; Eph. 6:2, 3] **11**[v] ch. 46:2; 2 Kgs. 24:1; [ver. 1] [w] 2 Kgs. 24:2 [x] [ver. 7]
13[y] See ch. 5:3 **14**[z] See ch. 25:3

prophets, sending them [z]persistently, saying,
[a]'Turn now every one of you from his evil
way, and amend your deeds, and [b]do not go
after other gods to serve them, and then you
shall dwell in the land that I gave to you and
your fathers.' [c]But you did not incline your
ear or listen to me. 16 The sons of Jonadab the
son of Rechab have kept the command that
their father gave them, but this people has not
obeyed me. 17 Therefore, thus says the LORD,
the God of hosts, the God of Israel: Behold,
I am bringing upon Judah and all the inhabitants of Jerusalem all the disaster that I have
pronounced against them, [d]because I have spoken to them and they have not listened, [d]I have
called to them and they have not answered."

18 But to the house of the Rechabites Jeremiah
said, "Thus says the LORD of hosts, the God of
Israel: Because you have obeyed the command
of Jonadab your father and kept all his precepts and done all that he commanded you,
19 therefore thus says the LORD of hosts, the
God of Israel: Jonadab the son of Rechab shall
never lack a man [e]to stand before me."

Jehoiakim Burns Jeremiah's Scroll

36 In the [f]fourth year of Jehoiakim the
son of Josiah, king of Judah, this word
came to Jeremiah from the LORD: 2 "Take [g]a
scroll and [h]write on it all the words that I have
spoken to you against Israel and [i]Judah [j]and
all the nations, [k]from the day I spoke to you,
from the days of Josiah until today. 3 [l]It may be
that the house of Judah will hear all the disaster that I intend to do to them, [m]so that every
one may turn from his evil way, and [n]that
I may forgive their iniquity and their sin."
4 Then Jeremiah called [o]Baruch the son of
Neriah, and [o]Baruch wrote on [g]a scroll at the
dictation of Jeremiah all the words of the LORD
that he had spoken to him. 5 And Jeremiah
ordered [o]Baruch, saying, [p]"I am banned from
going to the house of the LORD, 6 so you are to
go, and [q]on a day of fasting in the hearing of all
the people in the LORD's house you shall read
the words of the LORD from the scroll that
you have written at my dictation. You shall
read them also in the hearing of all the men
of Judah who come out of their cities. 7 [l]It may
be that their plea for mercy will come before
the LORD, [m]and that every one will turn from
his evil way, for great is the anger and wrath
that the LORD has pronounced against this
people." 8 And Baruch the son of Neriah did all
that Jeremiah the prophet ordered him about
reading from the scroll the words of the LORD
in the LORD's house.

9 [r]In the fifth year of Jehoiakim the son of
Josiah, king of Judah, [s]in the ninth month, all
the people in Jerusalem and all the people who
came from the cities of Judah to Jerusalem
[t]proclaimed a fast before the LORD. 10 Then, in
the hearing of all the people, Baruch read the
words of Jeremiah from the scroll, in the house
of the LORD, in [u]the chamber of Gemariah the
son of Shaphan the secretary, which was in the
upper court, at the entry of the New Gate of
the LORD's house.

11 When Micaiah the son of Gemariah, son
of [v]Shaphan, heard all the words of the LORD
from the scroll, 12 he went down to the king's
house, into the secretary's chamber, and [w]all
the officials were sitting there: [x]Elishama
the secretary, [y]Delaiah the son of Shemaiah,
[y]Elnathan [z]the son of Achbor, [y]Gemariah
the son of [z]Shaphan, Zedekiah the son of

36:1–32 God tells Jeremiah to write down all that he has spoken against Israel and Judah. This is to be a gracious warning and an opportunity for repentance (vv. 1–3). Because Jeremiah's movements have been restricted, he sends Baruch, his scribe, to read the scroll on a day of fasting in the temple (vv. 4–7). When Baruch reads the scroll, it causes much concern (vv. 8–14). Eventually one of the officials reads the scroll to Jehoiakim the king, who contemptuously, and without repentance, cuts off sections of the scroll as they are read and burns them (vv. 23–26). God tells Jeremiah to rewrite the scroll (v. 28), and to pronounce the removal of the blessings of the Davidic covenant from the king (v. 30). Jehoiakim's pride led him to have contempt for God's word and to ignore the warnings of the wrath to come.

Contempt for God's word is ever present in the world. Its most extreme form is contempt for Jesus—the Word of God incarnate—and rejection of his gospel. Nevertheless, God's word cannot be thwarted. "It shall accomplish that which I purpose," says the Lord (Isa. 55:11). The word of our God will stand forever (Isa. 40:8; Matt. 24:35).

15 [z][See ver. 14 above] [a]2 Kgs. 17:13; See ch. 18:11 [b]See ch. 7:6 [c]See ch. 34:14
17 [d][Isa. 50:2]
19 [e]See ch. 15:1
Chapter 36
1 [f]ch. 25:1; 45:1; [ver. 9]
2 [g]Ezra 6:2; Ps. 40:7; Ezek. 2:9; Zech. 5:1, 2 [h]ch. 30:2; [ch. 51:60] [i]ch. 25:2 [j]See ch. 25:15-26; 46–51 [k]ch. 1:2; 25:3
3 [l]ch. 26:3; Ezek. 12:3; Zeph. 2:3; [Amos 5:15] [m][ch. 18:8] [n]See ch. 31:34
4 [o]See ch. 32:12 [g][See ver. 2 above]
5 [o][See ver. 4 above] [p]ch. 32:2; 33:1; 39:15
6 [q][ver. 9]
7 [l][See ver. 3 above] [m][See ver. 3 above] **9** [r][ver. 1] [s]ver. 22 [t][2 Chr. 20:3] **10** [u][ch. 35:2] **11** [v]ch. 26:24; 40:5; 2 Chr. 34:8, 15, 18 **12** [w]ch. 26:10 [x]ver. 20; ch. 41:1; 2 Kgs. 25:25 [y]ver. 25 [z]ch. 26:22

Hananiah, and all the officials. 13 And Micaiah
told them all the words that he had heard,
when Baruch read the scroll in the hearing of
the people. 14 Then all the officials sent Jehudi
the son of Nethaniah, son of [a]Shelemiah, son
of Cushi, to say to Baruch, "Take in your
hand the scroll that you read in the hearing
of the people, and come." So Baruch the son of
Neriah took the scroll in his hand and came to
them. 15 And they said to him, "Sit down and
read it." So Baruch read it to them. 16 When
they heard all the words, they turned one
to another in fear. And they said to Baruch,
[b]"We must report all these words to the king."
17 Then they asked Baruch, "Tell us, please,
how did you write all these words? Was it at
his dictation?" 18 Baruch answered them, "He
dictated all these words to me, [c]while I wrote
them with ink on the scroll." 19 Then the officials said to Baruch, "Go and hide, you and
Jeremiah, and let no one know where you are."

20 So they went into the court to the king,
having put the scroll in [d]the chamber of
Elishama the secretary, and they reported all
the words to the king. 21 Then the king sent
Jehudi to get the scroll, and he took it from
the chamber of Elishama the secretary. And
Jehudi read it to the king and all the officials
who stood beside the king. 22 It was [e]the ninth
month, and the king was sitting in [f]the winter
house, and there was a fire burning in the fire
pot before him. 23 As Jehudi read three or four
columns, the king would cut them off with a
knife and throw them into the fire in the fire
pot, until the entire scroll was consumed in
the fire that was in the fire pot. 24 Yet [g]neither
the king nor any of his servants who heard
all these words was afraid, [h]nor did they tear
their garments. 25 Even when [i]Elnathan and
Delaiah and Gemariah [j]urged the king not to
burn the scroll, he would not listen to them.
26 And the king commanded Jerahmeel the
[k]king's son and Seraiah the son of Azriel and
[l]Shelemiah the son of Abdeel to seize [m]Baruch
the secretary and Jeremiah the prophet, but
the LORD hid them.

27 Now after the king had burned the scroll
with the words that Baruch wrote at Jeremiah's
dictation, the word of the LORD came to
Jeremiah: 28 "Take another scroll and write on
it all the former words that were in the first
scroll, which Jehoiakim the king of Judah has
burned. 29 And concerning Jehoiakim king of
Judah you shall say, 'Thus says the LORD, You
have burned this scroll, saying, [n]"Why have
you written in it that the king of Babylon will
certainly come and destroy this land, and will
cut off from it man and beast?" 30 Therefore
thus says the LORD concerning Jehoiakim king
of Judah: [o]He shall have none [p]to sit on the
throne of David, [q]and his dead body shall be
cast out to the heat by day and the frost by
night. 31 [r]And I will punish him and his offspring and his servants for their iniquity. I will
bring upon them and upon the inhabitants of
Jerusalem and upon the people of Judah all the
disaster that I have pronounced against them,
but they would not hear.'"

32 Then Jeremiah took another scroll and
gave it to [s]Baruch the scribe, the son of Neriah,
who [t]wrote on it at the dictation of Jeremiah
all the words of the scroll that Jehoiakim king
of Judah had burned in the fire. And many
similar words were added to them.

Jeremiah Warns Zedekiah

37 [u]Zedekiah the son of Josiah, [v]whom
Nebuchadnezzar king of Babylon
made king in the land of Judah, reigned
instead of [w]Coniah the son of Jehoiakim. 2 [x]But
neither he nor his servants nor the people of
the land listened to the words of the LORD
that he spoke through Jeremiah the prophet.

3 King Zedekiah sent [y]Jehucal the son of
[z]Shelemiah, and [a]Zephaniah the priest, the son
of [b]Maaseiah, to Jeremiah the prophet, saying, "Please [c]pray for us to the LORD our God."
4 [d]Now Jeremiah was still going in and out
among the people, [e]for he had not yet been put
in prison. 5 [f]The army of Pharaoh had come out
of Egypt. And when [g]the Chaldeans who were
besieging Jerusalem heard news about them,
[h]they withdrew from Jerusalem.

6 Then the word of the LORD came to
Jeremiah the prophet: 7 "Thus says the LORD,
God of Israel: Thus shall you say to the king
of Judah who [i]sent you to me to inquire of me,
'Behold, [j]Pharaoh's army that came to help
you is about to [k]return to Egypt, to its own
land. 8 And [l]the Chaldeans shall come back and
fight against this city. [l]They shall capture it

14 [a] ver. 26; ch. 37:3, 13; 38:1 **16** [b] ver. 20 **18** [c] ver. 32; [Rom. 16:22] **20** [d] ver. 12 **22** [e] ver. 9; [John 10:22] [f] Amos 3:15 **24** [g] [ver. 16] [h] See Josh. 7:6
25 [i] ver. 12 [j] [Isa. 59:16] **26** [k] [1 Kgs. 22:26; Zeph. 1:8] [l] ver. 14 [m] See ch. 45:1-3 **29** [n] See ch. 26:9 **30** [o] [ch. 22:30] [p] [ch. 22:2, 4] [q] [ch. 22:19] **31** [r] [ch. 1:16]
32 [s] See ver. 4 [t] ver. 18 **Chapter 37** **1** [u] 2 Kgs. 24:17; 2 Chr. 36:10 [v] [Ezek. 17:13] [w] ch. 22:24 **2** [x] See 2 Chr. 36:12-14 **3** [y] [ch. 38:1] [z] ver. 13; ch. 38:1 [a] See ch.
21:1 [b] See ch. 35:4 [c] [ch. 21:2] **4** [d] [Num. 27:17] [e] [ch. 32:2; 33:1] **5** [f] [Ezek. 17:15] [g] ch. 32:2 [h] ver. 11; ch. 34:21 **7** [i] [ch. 21:2] [j] [Ezek. 29:2, 6] [k] [ch. 46:17; 2 Kgs.
24:7; Lam. 4:17] **8** [l] ch. 34:22

and burn it with fire. 9 Thus says the LORD, Do
not deceive yourselves, saying, "The Chaldeans
will surely go away from us," for they will not
go away. 10 [m]For even if you should defeat the
whole army of Chaldeans who are fighting
against you, and there remained of them only
wounded men, every man in his tent, they
would rise up and [l]burn this city with fire.'"

Jeremiah Imprisoned

11 Now when [n]the Chaldean army had withdrawn from Jerusalem at the approach of
Pharaoh's army, 12 Jeremiah set out from
Jerusalem to go to [o]the land of Benjamin [p]to
receive his portion there [q]among the people.
13 When he was at [r]the Benjamin Gate, a sen-
try there named Irijah the son of [s]Shelemiah,
son of Hananiah, seized Jeremiah the prophet,
saying, [t]"You are deserting to the Chaldeans."
14 And Jeremiah said, "It is a lie; I am not deserting to the Chaldeans." But Irijah would not listen to him, and seized Jeremiah and brought
him to [u]the officials. 15 And the officials were
enraged at Jeremiah, and they beat him [v]and
imprisoned him in the house of Jonathan the
secretary, for it had been made a prison.

16 [w]When Jeremiah had come to the dungeon
cells and remained there many days, 17 King
Zedekiah sent for him and received him. The
king questioned him [x]secretly in his house
and said, "Is there any word from the LORD?"
Jeremiah said, "There is." Then he said, [y]"You
shall be delivered into the hand of the king
of Babylon." 18 Jeremiah also said to King
Zedekiah, "What wrong have I done to you
or your servants or this people, [v]that you have
put me in prison? 19 [z]Where are your prophets
who prophesied to you, saying, 'The king of
Babylon will not come against you and against
this land'? 20 Now hear, please, O my lord the
king: [a]let my humble plea come before you
and [b]do not send me back to the house of
Jonathan the secretary, lest I die there." 21 So
King Zedekiah gave orders, and they committed Jeremiah to [c]the court of the guard. And
a loaf of bread was given him daily from the
bakers' street, [d]until all the bread of the city
was gone. So Jeremiah remained in [c]the court
of the guard.

Jeremiah Cast into the Cistern

38 Now Shephatiah the son of Mattan,
Gedaliah the son of Pashhur, [e]Jucal
the son of Shelemiah, and [f]Pashhur the son
of Malchiah heard the words that Jeremiah
was saying to all the people, 2 "Thus says the
LORD: [g]He who stays in this city shall die by
the sword, by famine, and by pestilence, [g]but
he who goes out to the Chaldeans shall live.
He shall have his life as a prize of war, and live.
3 Thus says the LORD: [h]This city shall surely be
given into the hand of the army of the king
of Babylon and be taken." 4 Then the officials
said to the king, [i]"Let this man be put to death,
[j]for he is weakening the hands of the soldiers
who are left in this city, and the hands of all
the people, by speaking such words to them.
For this man is not seeking [k]the welfare of
this people, but their harm." 5 King Zedekiah
said, "Behold, he is in your hands, [l]for the king
can do nothing against you." 6 So they took
Jeremiah [m]and cast him into the cistern of
Malchiah, the king's son, which was in [n]the
court of the guard, letting Jeremiah down [o]by
ropes. [p]And there was no water in the cistern,
but only mud, and [q]Jeremiah sank in the mud.

37:15–21 Jeremiah continues to be persecuted for speaking God's words of judgment. The disobedient of the world lose patience with the constant reminders of the coming judgment. As it was then, so it is now. Proclaiming the kingdom of God means speaking judgment for the unrepentant as well as salvation for those who repent and believe. Praying "Your kingdom come" (Matt. 6:10) has serious implications for judgment as well as for joyful hope. The message of the kingdom will inevitably invite rejection and, often, outright persecution of the messengers.

Jesus said, "In the world you will have tribulation. But take heart; I have overcome the world" (John 16:33, see also John 15:18–25; 17:14; Rom. 8:18; Phil. 1:29; 1 Pet. 2:21; 4:12–19; Rev. 1:9). Jeremiah was beaten (Jer. 37:15), and we today will face hazardous hostility from unbelievers, whether physical or verbal or in some other way. But we can take heart in the astonishing fact that Christ himself was beaten with the ultimate beating that we deserved, absorbing God's righteous wrath. The result is that any pain unbelievers inflict on us can only work out for our glory. It is pruning (John 15:2), not punishing (John 15:6).

10 [m][ch. 21:4] [l][See ver. 8 above]
11 [n]ver. 5
12 [o]ch. 1:1; 32:8 [p][ch. 32:9] [q]ver. 4; ch. 39:14
13 [r]ch. 38:7; Zech. 14:10 [s]ver. 3; ch. 38:1 [t][ch. 21:9; 38:19; 39:9; 52:15]
14 [u]ch. 36:12
15 [v][Heb. 11:36]
16 [w]See ch. 38:6-14
17 [x]ch. 38:16 [y]See ch. 21:7
18 [v][See ver. 15 above]
19 [z][ch. 28:2, 11, 17]
20 [a][ch. 38:26] [b][ch. 38:28]
21 [c]See ch. 32:2 [d]ch. 38:9; 52:6; Ezek. 4:10, 16

Chapter 38
1 [e][ch. 37:3] [f]See ch. 20:1
2 [g]ch. 21:9; [ver. 17, 18]
3 [h]See ch. 32:3
4 [i]ch. 26:11 [j]See ch. 6:24

[k][ch. 33:9] **5** [l]See ver. 24-28 **6** [m]ch. 37:16 [n]See ch. 32:2 [o]ver. 11, 13 [p][Gen. 37:24; Zech. 9:11] [q][Ps. 69:14]

Jeremiah Rescued from the Cistern

7 When [r]Ebed-melech [s]the Ethiopian, [t]a eunuch who was in the king's house, heard that they had put Jeremiah into the cistern—the king was sitting [u]in the Benjamin Gate—8 [r]Ebed-melech went from the king's house and said to the king, 9 "My lord the king, these men have done evil in all that they did to Jeremiah the prophet by casting him into the cistern, and he will die there of [v]hunger, [w]for there is no bread left in the city." 10 Then the king commanded [r]Ebed-melech the Ethiopian, "Take thirty men with you from here, and lift Jeremiah the prophet out of the cistern before he dies." 11 So [r]Ebed-melech took the men with him and went to the house of the king, to a wardrobe in the storehouse, and took from there old rags and worn-out clothes, which he let down to Jeremiah in the cistern [x]by ropes. 12 Then [r]Ebed-melech the Ethiopian said to Jeremiah, "Put the rags and clothes between your armpits and [x]the ropes." Jeremiah did so. 13 Then they drew Jeremiah up with [x]ropes and lifted him out of the cistern. And Jeremiah remained in the [n]court of the guard.

Jeremiah Warns Zedekiah Again

14 King Zedekiah sent for Jeremiah the prophet and received him at the third entrance of the temple of the LORD. The king said to Jeremiah, "I will ask you a question; hide nothing from me." 15 Jeremiah said to Zedekiah, "If I tell you, will you not surely put me to death? And if I give you counsel, you will not listen to me." 16 Then King Zedekiah swore [y]secretly to Jeremiah, [z]"As the LORD lives, [a]who made our souls, I will not put you to death or deliver you into the hand of [b]these men who seek your life."

17 Then Jeremiah said to Zedekiah, "Thus says the LORD, the God of hosts, the God of Israel: [c]If you will surrender to [d]the officials of the king of Babylon, [e]then your life shall be spared, and this city shall not be burned with fire, and you and your house shall live. 18 But if you do not surrender to [d]the officials of the king of Babylon, [f]then this city shall be given into the hand of the Chaldeans, [f]and they shall burn it with fire, and you shall not escape from their hand." 19 King Zedekiah said to Jeremiah, "I am afraid of the Judeans [g]who have deserted to the Chaldeans, lest I be handed over to them and they deal cruelly with me." 20 Jeremiah said, "You shall not be given to them. Obey now the voice of the LORD in what I say to you, [h]and it shall be well with you, and your life shall be spared. 21 But if you refuse to [c]surrender, this is the vision which the LORD has shown to me: 22 Behold, all the women left in the house of the king of Judah were being led out to the officials of the king of Babylon and were saying,

[i]"'Your trusted friends have deceived you
and prevailed against you;
now that your feet are sunk in the mud,
they turn away from you.'

23 All your wives and [j]your sons shall be led out to the Chaldeans, and you yourself shall not escape from their hand, but shall be seized by the king of Babylon, and this city shall be burned with fire."

24 Then Zedekiah said to Jeremiah, "Let no one know of these words, and you shall not die. 25 If [k]the officials hear that I have spoken with you and come to you and say to you, 'Tell us what you said to the king and what the king said to you; hide nothing from us and we will not put you to death,' 26 then you shall say to them, [l]'I made a humble plea to the king that he would not send me back to the house of Jonathan to die there.'" 27 Then all the officials came to Jeremiah and asked him, and he answered them as the king had instructed him. So they stopped speaking with him, for the conversation had not been overheard. 28 And Jeremiah remained [m]in the court of the guard until the day that Jerusalem was taken.

7 [r] ch. 39:16 [s] [Acts 8:27] [t] ch. 29:2; Isa. 56:3, 4 [u] See ch. 37:13
8 [r] [See ver. 7 above]
9 [v] ch. 11:22; [ch. 14:16, 18; 19:9] [w] [ch. 37:21]
10 [r] [See ver. 7 above]
11 [r] [See ver. 7 above] [x] ver. 6
12 [r] [See ver. 7 above] [x] [See ver. 11 above]

38:16 King Zedekiah swore not to put Jeremiah to death or deliver him over into the hand of the men seeking his life. This is the very language that would be used to describe the handing over of Jesus to the men who would seek *his* life. Jeremiah was spared; Jesus was not. The same loving Lord ruled over both Jeremiah's life and the life of his own Son (Matt. 11:27). Jeremiah was delivered in this instance, and will be restored perfectly to God in the new earth, because Jesus was not delivered, but was "delivered up for our trespasses" (Rom. 4:25).

13 [x] [See ver. 11 above] [n] [See ver. 6 above] 16 [y] ch. 37:17 [z] See Ruth 3:13 [a] [Isa. 57:16] [b] See ver. 1-9 17 [c] ver. 2, 21; [ch. 27:12, 13; 2 Kgs. 24:12] [d] ch. 39:3 [e] [ch. 34:4, 5] 18 [d] [See ver. 17 above] [f] See ch. 21:10 19 [g] See ch. 37:13 20 [h] ch. 40:9 21 [c] [See ver. 17 above] 22 [i] See ch. 20:10 23 [j] ch. 39:6; 41:10; 43:6 25 [k] [ver. 5] 26 [l] [ch. 37:20] 28 [m] See ch. 32:2

The Fall of Jerusalem

39 [n]In the ninth year of Zedekiah king of
Judah, in the tenth month, Nebuchadnezzar king of Babylon and all his army came
against Jerusalem and besieged it. 2 In the eleventh year of Zedekiah, in the fourth month, on
the ninth day of the month, a breach was made
in the city. 3 Then all [o]the officials of the king
of Babylon came [p]and sat in the middle gate:
Nergal-sar-ezer of Samgar, Nebu-sar-sekim
[q]the Rab-saris, Nergal-sar-ezer the Rab-mag,
with all the rest of the officers of the king of
Babylon. 4 When Zedekiah king of Judah and
all the soldiers saw them, they fled, going out
of the city at night by way of the king's garden
through the gate between the two walls; and
they went toward [r]the Arabah. 5 But the army
of the Chaldeans pursued them and overtook
Zedekiah in [s]the plains of Jericho. And when
they had taken him, they brought him up to
Nebuchadnezzar king of Babylon, at [t]Riblah,
in the land of Hamath; [u]and he passed sentence on him. 6 The king of Babylon [v]slaugh-
tered the sons of Zedekiah at [t]Riblah before
his eyes, and the king of Babylon [v]slaughtered
all the nobles of Judah. 7 [w]He put out the eyes
of Zedekiah and bound him in chains to take
him to Babylon. 8 [x]The Chaldeans burned the
king's house and the house of the people, [y]and
broke down the walls of Jerusalem. 9 Then
[z]Nebuzaradan, the [a]captain of the guard,
carried into exile to Babylon the rest of the
people who were left in the city, [b]those who
had deserted to him, and the people who
remained. 10 Nebuzaradan, the captain of the
guard, [c]left in the land of Judah some of the
poor people who owned nothing, and gave
them vineyards and fields at the same time.

The LORD Delivers Jeremiah

11 Nebuchadnezzar king of Babylon gave
command concerning Jeremiah through
Nebuzaradan, the captain of the guard, saying,
12 [d]"Take him, look after him well, and do him
no harm, but deal with him as he tells you."
13 So [e]Nebuzaradan the captain of the guard,
Nebushazban the Rab-saris, Nergal-sar-ezer
the Rab-mag, [e]and all the chief officers of the
king of Babylon 14 sent and took Jeremiah
from [f]the court of the guard. They entrusted
him to [g]Gedaliah the son of [h]Ahikam, son of
[i]Shaphan, that he should take him home. So
[j]he lived among the people.

15 The word of the LORD came to Jeremiah
[k]while he was shut up in the court of the guard:
16 "Go, and say to [l]Ebed-melech the Ethiopian,
'Thus says the LORD of hosts, the God of Israel:
[m]Behold, I will fulfill my words against this
city for harm and [n]not for good, and they
shall be accomplished before you on that day.
17 But I will deliver you on that day, declares
the LORD, and you shall not be given into the
hand of the men [o]of whom you are afraid. 18 For
I will surely save you, and you shall not fall by
the sword, but you shall have your [p]life as a
prize of war, [q]because you have put your trust
in me, declares the LORD.'"

Jeremiah Remains in Judah

40 The word that came to Jeremiah
from the LORD [r]after Nebuzaradan
the captain of the guard had let him go from
[s]Ramah, when he took him [t]bound in chains

39:1–10 After Jeremiah suffers further imprisonment (38:1–13) and again warns Zedekiah (38:14–28), the inevitable happens and Jerusalem falls to the Babylonian invaders. The word of the Lord can be ridiculed and repudiated only for as long as the Lord himself permits. Then comes the judgment. All the temporal judgments of the Bible foreshadow the final judgment that will take place at the end of time before the judgment seat of Christ (2 Cor. 5:10). For "it is appointed for man to die once, and after that comes judgment" (Heb. 9:27).

39:11–18 Amid the chaos and devastation, Jeremiah's life is spared. He is given a message of deliverance for the Ethiopian who had secured his release from the pit (38:7–13). God's word to the Gentile Ebed-melech is, "I will deliver you on that day . . . because you have put your trust in me, declares the LORD" (39:17–18).

This saving trust is the same as putting one's hope in Christ, God's provision for our deliverance (Eph. 1:12–13). Jeremiah's word of salvation to a Gentile echoes the program of world evangelization originally promised to Abraham and fulfilled in Christian mission (Gen. 17:5; Acts 1:8). God's mercy washes into the life of anyone who will bank on Christ for forgiveness and joy.

Chapter 39
1 [n]For ver. 1-10, see ch. 52:4-16; 2 Kgs. 25:1-12
3 [o]ch. 38:17, 18, 22 [p][ch. 1:15] [q]ver. 13; 2 Kgs. 18:17
4 [r]See Deut. 1:1
5 [s]Josh. 5:10 [t]See 2 Kgs. 23:33 [u][Ezek. 17:15]
6 [v]ch. 52:10 [t][See ver. 5 above]
7 [w][ch. 32:4; Ezek. 12:13]
8 [x]See ch. 21:10 [y]Neh. 1:3; [Ps. 80:12; Isa. 5:5]
9 [z]ch. 40:1; 52:12; 2 Kgs. 25:8 [a]Gen. 37:36 [b]See ch. 37:13
10 [c]ch. 40:7; 2 Kgs. 25:12
12 [d]ch. 40:4
13 [e][ver. 3]
14 [f]ch. 38:28; See ch. 32:2 [g]ch. 43:6; See ch. 40:5-9, 11-16; 41:1-4, 6; 2 Kgs. 25:22-25 [h]2 Kgs. 22:12 [i]2 Kgs. 22:3 [j]ch. 37:12
15 [k]ch. 36:5; 38:13
16 [l]See ch. 38:7 [m]Dan. 9:12 [n]ch. 21:10; [ch. 14:11]
17 [o]ch. 22:25
18 [p]ch. 21:9; 45:5 [q]Ps. 25:2; 37:40
Chapter 40
1 [r][ch. 39:14] [s]Josh. 18:25 [t][Ps. 149:8]

along with all the captives of Jerusalem and Judah who were being exiled to Babylon. 2 The captain of the guard took Jeremiah and said to him, [u]"The LORD your God pronounced this disaster against this place. 3 The LORD has brought it about, and has done as he said. [v]Because you sinned against the LORD and did not obey his voice, this thing has come upon you. 4 Now, behold, I release you today from [t]the chains on your hands. [w]If it seems good to you to come with me to Babylon, come, and I will look after you well, [w]but if it seems wrong to you to come with me to Babylon, do not come. [x]See, the whole land is before you; go wherever you think it good and right to go. 5 If you remain,[1] then return to [y]Gedaliah the son of Ahikam, son of Shaphan, [z]whom the king of Babylon appointed governor of the cities of Judah, and dwell with him among the people. Or go wherever you think it right to go." So the captain of the guard gave him an allowance of food and a present, and let him go. 6 Then Jeremiah went to [y]Gedaliah the son of Ahikam, at [a]Mizpah, and lived with him [b]among the people [c]who were left in the land.

7 [d]When all the captains of the forces in the open country and their men heard that [e]the king of Babylon had appointed Gedaliah the son of Ahikam governor in the land and had committed to him men, women, and children, those of [f]the poorest of the land who had not been taken into exile to Babylon, 8 they went to Gedaliah at [a]Mizpah—[g]Ishmael the son of Nethaniah, [h]Johanan the son of Kareah, Seraiah the son of Tanhumeth, the sons of Ephai the Netophathite, [i]Jezaniah the son of the Maacathite, they and their men. 9 Gedaliah the son of Ahikam, son of Shaphan, swore to them and their men, saying, "Do not be afraid to serve the Chaldeans. Dwell in the land and serve the king of Babylon, [j]and it shall be well with you. 10 As for me, I will dwell at [a]Mizpah, to represent you before the Chaldeans who will come to us. But as for you, [l]gather wine and summer fruits and oil, and store them in your vessels, and dwell in your cities that you have taken." 11 Likewise, when all the Judeans who were in [m]Moab and among [n]the Ammonites and in [o]Edom and in other lands heard that the king of Babylon had left a remnant in Judah and had appointed Gedaliah the son of Ahikam, son of Shaphan, as governor over them, 12 [p]then all the Judeans returned from all the places to which they had been driven and came to the land of Judah, to Gedaliah at Mizpah. And they [q]gathered wine and summer fruits in great abundance.

13 Now [r]Johanan the son of Kareah and [s]all the leaders of the forces in the open country came to Gedaliah at Mizpah 14 and said to him, "Do you know that Baalis the king of [t]the Ammonites has sent Ishmael the son of Nethaniah to take your life?" But Gedaliah the son of Ahikam would not believe them. 15 Then Johanan the son of Kareah spoke secretly to Gedaliah at Mizpah, "Please let me go and strike down Ishmael the son of Nethaniah, and no one will know it. Why should he take your life, so that all the Judeans who are gathered about you would be scattered, [u]and the remnant of Judah would perish?" 16 But Gedaliah the son of Ahikam said to Johanan the son of Kareah, "You shall not do this thing, for you are speaking falsely of Ishmael."

Gedaliah Murdered

41 [v]In the seventh month, Ishmael the son of Nethaniah, son of Elishama, of the royal family, one of the chief officers of the king, came with ten men to Gedaliah the son of Ahikam, at [w]Mizpah. As they [x]ate bread together there at Mizpah, 2 [y]Ishmael the son of Nethaniah and the ten men with him rose up and struck down Gedaliah the son of Ahikam, son of Shaphan, with the sword, and killed him, [z]whom the king of Babylon had appointed governor in the land. 3 Ishmael also struck down all the Judeans who were with

[1] Syriac; the meaning of the Hebrew phrase is uncertain

41:1–18 Confusion and power struggles follow the destruction of Jerusalem. The governor appointed by the Babylonians is murdered (vv. 1–3). Such events show the chaos that ensues when the clear word of God through his prophet is ignored. It is folly to try to control history without consideration for God's sovereign control over all. Proclamation in the New Testament of events yet to come makes it clear that no purpose of God in world history can be eluded.

2[u] [Deut. 29:24, 28] **3**[v] ch. 44:3, 23; Deut. 29:25; See Dan. 9:10-12 **4**[t] [See ver. 1 above] [w] [ch. 39:12] [x] [Gen. 20:15] **5**[y] See ch. 39:14 [z] ch. 41:2 **6**[y] [See ver. 5 above] [a] ch. 41:6; Josh. 18:26 [b] ch. 37:12; 39:14 [c] ch. 39:10

7[d] For ver. 7-9, see 2 Kgs. 25:23, 24 [e] ver. 5 [f] ch. 39:10; 2 Kgs. 25:12 **8**[a] [See ver. 6 above] [g] ver. 14, 15, 16; See ch. 41:1-3 [h] ver. 13, 15, 16; ch. 42:1, 8 [i] ch. 42:1 **9**[j] ch. 38:20 **10**[a] [See ver. 6 above] [l] [ver. 12] **11**[m] [Num. 22:1; 2 Sam. 8:2] [n] 1 Sam. 11:1; 12:12 [o] Gen. 36:8 **12**[p] [ch. 43:5] [q] [ver. 10] **13**[r] ver. 8, 15, 16; ch. 42:1, 8 [s] ch. 41:11; 42:1 **14**[t] [ch. 41:10] **15**[u] [ch. 42:2] **Chapter 41** **1**[v] 2 Kgs. 25:25 [w] See ch. 40:6, 8, 10 [x] [Ps. 41:9] **2**[y] [2 Sam. 13:28, 29] [z] ch. 40:5

Gedaliah at [w]Mizpah, and the Chaldean soldiers who happened to be there.
4 On the day after the murder of Gedaliah,
before anyone knew of it, 5 eighty men arrived
from [a]Shechem and [b]Shiloh and [c]Samaria,
with [d]their beards shaved and [e]their clothes
torn, and [d]their bodies gashed, [f]bringing
grain offerings and incense to present at the
temple of the LORD. 6 And Ishmael the son of
Nethaniah came out from [g]Mizpah to meet
them, weeping as he came. As he met them,
he said to them, "Come in to Gedaliah the son
of Ahikam." 7 When they came into the city,
Ishmael the son of Nethaniah and the men
with him slaughtered them and cast them
into a cistern. 8 But there were ten men among
them who said to Ishmael, "Do not put us to
death, for we have [h]stores of wheat, barley,
oil, and honey hidden in the fields." So he
refrained and did not put them to death with
their companions.
9 Now the cistern into which Ishmael had
thrown all the bodies of the men whom he
had struck down along with[1] Gedaliah was
the large cistern that [i]King Asa had made for
defense against [i]Baasha king of Israel; Ishmael
the son of Nethaniah filled it with the slain.
10 Then Ishmael took captive all the rest
of the people who were in Mizpah, [j]the king's
daughters and all the people who were left
at Mizpah, whom [k]Nebuzaradan, the captain
of the guard, had committed to Gedaliah the
son of Ahikam. Ishmael the son of Nethaniah
took them captive and set out to cross over to
[l]the Ammonites.
11 But when [m]Johanan the son of Kareah and
[n]all the leaders of the forces with him heard of
all the evil that Ishmael the son of Nethaniah
had done, 12 they took all their men and went
to fight against Ishmael the son of Nethaniah.
They came upon him at [o]the great pool that
is in [p]Gibeon. 13 And when all the people who
were with Ishmael saw Johanan the son of
Kareah and [q]all the leaders of the forces with
him, they rejoiced. 14 [r]So all the people whom
Ishmael had carried away captive from Mizpah
turned around and came back, and went to
Johanan the son of Kareah. 15 But Ishmael
the son of Nethaniah escaped from Johanan
with eight men, and went to [s]the Ammonites.
16 Then Johanan the son of Kareah and [q]all
the leaders of the forces with him took from
Mizpah all the rest of the people whom he had
recovered from Ishmael the son of Nethaniah,
after he had struck down Gedaliah the son
of Ahikam—soldiers, [t]women, children, and
eunuchs, whom Johanan brought back from
[u]Gibeon. 17 And they went and stayed at Geruth
[v]Chimham near [w]Bethlehem, intending to go
to Egypt 18 because of the Chaldeans. For they
were afraid of them, because Ishmael the son
of Nethaniah had struck down Gedaliah the
son of Ahikam, [x]whom the king of Babylon
had made governor over the land.

Warning Against Going to Egypt

42 Then [y]all the commanders of the forces,
and [z]Johanan the son of Kareah and
Jezaniah the son of [a]Hoshaiah, and all the
people [b]from the least to the greatest, came
near 2 and said to Jeremiah the prophet, "Let
[c]our plea for mercy come before you, and
[d]pray to the LORD your God for us, for all

[1] Hebrew *by the hand of*

Many today make the mistake of trying to interpret the New Testament message of the gospel and the end of this present age in terms of current historical events. History cannot interpret the Bible; the Bible must interpret history. The history of our broken world is the history of a human race in rebellion against God—a race that tries to order events without heeding God's prophetic word. Because God's plan is to unite (or "sum up") all things in Christ (Eph. 1:10), because all things hold together in him (Col. 1:17), and because Christ is appointed heir of all things and upholds the universe by the word of his power (Heb. 1:2–3), we must conclude that the totality of human history has meaning only in relation to Christ. He is the interpretative key to the history of the world.

42:1–22 When Johanan and the people with him ask Jeremiah to pray that God will have mercy, the prophet agrees to do so (vv. 1–4). He reminds them that God is rich in mercy to those who hear his word and obey (vv. 7–12). Then Jeremiah issues another stern warning from God: the remnant of the people in Judah should not look to Egypt for salvation (vv. 13–22). There is the danger here that the remnant left in Jerusalem will presume on their status as a remnant saved from exile (vv. 17–22). But they are reminded that they must be a *faithful* remnant.

3 [w][See ver. 1 above]
5 [a]Josh. 17:7 [b]Josh. 18:1 [c]1 Kgs. 16:24; See ch. 23:13 [d][ch. 48:37; Deut. 14:1; Isa. 15:2] [e]ch. 36:24 [f][2 Kgs. 25:9]
6 [g]ch. 40:6, 8, 10
8 [h][Judg. 6:11]
9 [i][1 Kgs. 15:22; 2 Chr. 16:6]
10 [j]See ch. 38:23 [k][ch. 40:7] [l][ch. 40:14]
11 [m]See ch. 40:8 [n]ch. 40:13
12 [o][2 Sam. 2:13] [p]Josh. 9:3, 17
13 [q]ch. 40:13
14 [r]ver. 10, 16
15 [s][ch. 40:14]
16 [q][See ver. 13 above] [t]ch. 40:7 [u]Josh. 9:3, 17
17 [v][2 Sam. 19:37, 38] [w][Matt. 2:1, 14]; See Gen. 35:19
18 [x]ver. 2; ch. 40:5

Chapter 42

1 [y]ch. 40:13; 41:11 [z]See ch. 40:8 [a]ch. 43:2 [b][ch. 6:13]
2 [c]See ch. 36:7 [d]ver. 20; [1 Sam. 7:8; 12:19]

[e]this remnant—[f]because we are left with but
a few, as your eyes see us— 3 that [g]the LORD
your God may show us the way we should go,
and the thing that we should do." 4 Jeremiah
the prophet said to them, "I have heard you.
Behold, I will pray to the LORD your God
according to your request, and [h]whatever the
LORD answers you I will tell you. [h]I will keep
nothing back from you." 5 Then they said to
Jeremiah, [i]"May the LORD be a true and [j]faith-
ful witness against us [k]if we do not act according to all the word [l]with which the LORD your
God sends you to us. 6 Whether it is good or
bad, we will obey the voice of the LORD our
God to whom we are sending you, [m]that it may
be well with us when we obey the voice of the
LORD our God."

7 [n]At the end of ten days the word of the
LORD came to Jeremiah. 8 Then he summoned
[z]Johanan the son of Kareah and [y]all the commanders of the forces who were with him, and
all the people [b]from the least to the greatest,
9 and said to them, "Thus says the LORD, the
God of Israel, [o]to whom you sent me to present
your plea for mercy before him: 10 If you will
remain in this land, [p]then I will build you up
and not pull you down; I will plant you, and
not pluck you up; [q]for I relent of the disaster
that I did to you. 11 [r]Do not fear the king of
Babylon, [r]of whom you are afraid. [s]Do not fear
him, declares the LORD, [s]for I am with you, to
save you and to deliver you from his hand. 12 [t]I
will grant you mercy, that he may have mercy
on you and let you remain in your own land.
13 [u]But if you say, 'We will not remain in this
land,' disobeying the voice of the LORD your
God 14 and saying, 'No, [v]we will go to the land
of Egypt, where we shall not see war or [w]hear
the sound of the trumpet or [x]be hungry for
bread, and we will dwell there,' 15 then hear
the word of the LORD, O remnant of Judah.
Thus says the LORD of hosts, the God of Israel:
[y]If you set your faces to enter Egypt [z]and go
to live there, 16 then the sword [a]that you fear
shall overtake you there in the land of Egypt,
and the famine of which you are afraid shall
follow close after you to Egypt, [b]and there you
shall die. 17 All the men who set their faces to
go to Egypt to live there shall die by the sword,
by famine, and by pestilence. They shall have
[c]no remnant or survivor from the disaster that
I will bring upon them.

18 "For thus says the LORD of hosts, the God
of Israel: [d]As my anger and my wrath were
poured out on the inhabitants of Jerusalem,
so my wrath will be poured out on you when
you go to Egypt. [e]You shall become an execra-
tion, a horror, a curse, and a taunt. You shall
see this place no more. 19 The LORD has said to
you, O remnant of Judah, [f]'Do not go to Egypt.'
[g]Know for a certainty that I have warned you
this day 20 that you have gone astray at the cost
of your lives. [h]For you sent me to the LORD
your God, saying, [h]'Pray for us to the LORD
our God, and [i]whatever the LORD our God says
declare to us and we will do it.' 21 And I have
this day declared it to you, but you have not
obeyed the voice of the LORD your God in
anything [j]that he sent me to tell you. 22 [k]Now
therefore know for a certainty that you shall
die by the sword, by famine, and by pestilence
in the place where you desire to go to live."

Jeremiah Taken to Egypt

43 When Jeremiah finished speaking to
all the people all these words of the
LORD their God, with which the LORD their
God had sent him to them, 2 Azariah the son
of [l]Hoshaiah and [m]Johanan the son of Kareah
and [n]all the insolent men said to Jeremiah,
"You are telling a lie. The LORD our God did
not send you to say, [o]'Do not go to Egypt to live

There is a similar danger that we will presume on being the people of God in the world while failing to trust in Christ. At stake here is the integrity of the word of God mediated by the prophet. Unbelief is a culpable refusal to acknowledge God (Rom. 1:18–32). Salvation can be found only in the Lord as he works out his sovereign will according to his word. We have that word now in inspired Scripture. All attempts to find salvation in empires, religions, denominational identities, philosophies, politics, or self-help schemes will inevitably fail.

43:1–13 Johanan and his followers refuse Jeremiah's words of assurance and warning. To the prophet it must seem that he is helpless in the power of these rebellious people. Johanan leads the remnant (that is no true remnant) to Egypt, taking Jeremiah

2[e] [ch. 40:15; Isa. 37:4] [f] [Lev. 26:22]
3[g] [ch. 37:17; Ezra 8:21]
4[h] 1 Sam. 3:18; [Num. 22:18]
5[i] [Gen. 31:50] [j] [Rev. 1:5; 3:14] [k] Judg. 11:10 [l] ver. 21
6[m] ch. 7:23
7[n] [Ezek. 3:16]
8[z] [See ver. 1 above] [y] [See ver. 1 above] [b] [See ver. 1 above]
9[o] ver. 2, 3
10[p] See ch. 24:6 [q] ch. 18:8; Gen. 6:6; [Deut. 32:36]
11[r] [ch. 22:25; 41:18] [s] ch. 30:10, 11; [Rom. 8:31]

12[t] [Neh. 1:11] **13**[u] ch. 43:4; [ch. 44:16, 17] **14**[v] [ch. 41:17] [w] ch. 4:19 [x] [ch. 37:21] **15**[y] ch. 44:12; [ver. 19; Deut. 17:16] [z] ch. 44:27; See ch. 44:1, 12-14
16[a] Ezek. 11:8 [b] ver. 22; ch. 44:12 **17**[c] Lam. 2:22 **18**[d] See ch. 7:20 [e] See ch. 18:16 **19**[f] ch. 43:2; [ver. 14-16] [g] [Ezek. 2:5] **20**[h] ver. 2 [i] ver. 3 **21**[j] ver. 5
22[k] ver. 16, 17 **Chapter 43** **2**[l] ch. 42:1 [m] See ch. 40:8 [n] Ps. 86:14; Isa. 13:11; Mal. 4:1 [o] ch. 42:19

there,' 3 but [p]Baruch the son of Neriah [q]has set
you against us, [r]to deliver us into the hand of
the Chaldeans, that they may kill us or take us
into exile in Babylon." 4 So [m]Johanan the son of
Kareah and all [s]the commanders of the forces
and all the people did not obey the voice of
the LORD, to remain in the land of Judah. 5 But
Johanan the son of Kareah and all the commanders of the forces took [t]all the remnant
of Judah who had returned to live in the land
of Judah from all the nations to which they
had been driven— 6 [u]the men, the women,
the children, [v]the princesses, and every person
whom [w]Nebuzaradan the captain of the guard
had left with [x]Gedaliah the son of Ahikam,
son of Shaphan; also Jeremiah the prophet
and Baruch the son of Neriah. 7 And they came
into the land of Egypt, for they did not obey
the voice of the LORD. And they arrived at
[y]Tahpanhes.

8 Then the word of the LORD came to Jeremiah in [y]Tahpanhes: 9 "Take in your hands
large stones and hide them in the mortar in the
pavement that is at the entrance to Pharaoh's
palace in [y]Tahpanhes, in the sight of the men
of Judah, 10 and say to them, 'Thus says the
LORD of hosts, the God of Israel: Behold, I will
send and take Nebuchadnezzar the king of
Babylon, [z]my servant, [a]and I will set his throne
above these stones that I have hidden, and he
will spread his royal canopy over them. 11 He
shall come [b]and strike the land of Egypt,
[c]giving over to the pestilence those who are
doomed to the pestilence, to captivity those
who are doomed to captivity, and to the sword
those who are doomed to the sword. 12 [d]I shall
kindle a fire [e]in the temples of the gods of
Egypt, and he shall burn them [f]and carry them
away captive. [g]And he shall clean the land of
Egypt [g]as a shepherd cleans his cloak of ver-
min, and he shall go away from there in peace.
13 He shall break the [h]obelisks of Heliopolis,
which is in the land of Egypt, [e]and the temples
of the gods of Egypt he shall burn with fire.'"

Judgment for Idolatry

44 The word that came to Jeremiah concerning all the Judeans who lived in
the land of Egypt, at [i]Migdol, at [j]Tahpanhes, at
Memphis, and in the land of [k]Pathros, 2 "Thus
says the LORD of hosts, the God of Israel: You
have seen all the disaster that I brought upon
Jerusalem and upon all the cities of Judah.
Behold, this day [l]they are a desolation, and no
one dwells in them, 3 because of the evil that
they committed, [m]provoking me to anger, [n]in
that they went to make offerings [o]and serve
other gods that they knew not, neither they,
nor you, nor your fathers. 4 [p]Yet I persistently
sent to you all my servants the prophets, saying, 'Oh, do not do this abomination that
I hate!' 5 [q]But they did not listen [q]or incline
their ear, to turn from their evil and make no
offerings to other gods. 6 [r]Therefore my wrath
and my anger were poured out and kindled
in the cities of Judah and in the streets of
Jerusalem, [s]and they became a waste and a
desolation, as at this day. 7 And now thus says
the LORD God of hosts, the God of Israel:
Why do you commit this great evil [t]against
yourselves, to cut off from you [u]man and
woman, [u]infant and child, from the midst of
Judah, leaving you no remnant? 8 [m]Why do
you provoke me to anger with the works of
your hands, [n]making offerings to other gods
in the land of Egypt where you have come to
live, so that you may be cut off and become [v]a
curse and a taunt among all the nations of the
earth? 9 Have you forgotten the evil of your
fathers, [w]the evil of the kings of Judah, [x]the

with them (vv. 1–7). The prophet continues to proclaim the word of the Lord in the Egyptian city of Tahpanhes (v. 8). The Egyptians who have received the Jerusalem rebels now come under judgment (vv. 9–13). The Babylonian king is referred to by the Lord as "my servant" (v. 10) just as Cyrus is the Lord's "anointed" (Isa. 45:1). He will serve the Lord in bringing judgment to these godless people.

We may not be able to discern the details of God's plan in the world today, but we do know that our God "works all things according to the counsel of his will" (Eph. 1:11). He rules nations and the affairs of men. The bottom line is, we know that God is bringing in his kingdom. Indeed, the kingdom has already quietly dawned in the coming of Christ (Mark 1:15). Man-made plans for salvation will always be overtaken by the infallible purposes of God.

3 [p]See ch. 32:12 [q][ch. 38:22] [r][ch. 37:13]
4 [m][See ver. 2 above] [s]ch. 40:13
5 [t][ch. 40:11, 12]
6 [u]ch. 44:20 [v]See ch. 38:23 [w]ch. 39:10; 40:7 [x]See ch. 39:14
7 [y]ch. 2:16; 44:1; 46:14; [Isa. 30:4]
8 [y][See ver. 7 above]
9 [y][See ver. 7 above]
10 [z]See ch. 25:9 [a]ch. 1:15
11 [b]ch. 44:13; 46:13 [c]See ch. 15:2
12 [d]See ch. 17:27 [e]ch. 46:25; Ezek. 30:13; [Ex. 12:12; Isa. 19:1] [f][ch. 48:7] [g][Ps. 104:2; Isa. 49:18] **13** [h][Ex. 23:24] [e][See ver. 12 above] **Chapter 44** **1** [i]ch. 46:14; Ex. 14:2 [j]See ch. 43:7-9 [k]ver. 15; See Isa. 11:11 **2** [l]ver. 6 **3** [m]ver. 8; See ch. 7:18, 19 [n]See ch. 1:16 [o]ch. 19:4; Deut. 6:14 **4** [p]See 2 Chr. 36:15 **5** [q]See ch. 34:14 **6** [r]See ch. 7:20 [s]See ch. 7:34; 9:11 **7** [t]Hab. 2:10; [Num. 16:38; Prov. 20:2] [u][ch. 38:23; Lam. 2:11] **8** [m][See ver. 3 above] [n][See ver. 3 above] [v]ch. 42:18; See ch. 18:16 **9** [w][ch. 15:4] [x]1 Kgs. 11:1, 8; 15:13; 2 Kgs. 11:1

evil of their[1] wives, your own evil, [y]and the evil
of your wives, which they committed in the
land of Judah and in the streets of Jerusalem?
10 They have not humbled themselves even to
this day, [z]nor have they feared, nor walked in
my law and my statutes that I set before you
and before your fathers.

11 "Therefore thus says the LORD of hosts,
the God of Israel: [a]Behold, I will set my face
against you for harm, to cut off all Judah. 12 I
will take the remnant of Judah who have [b]set
their faces to come to the land of Egypt to
live, and they shall all be consumed. [c]In the
land of Egypt they shall fall; by the sword and
by famine [c]they shall be consumed. [d]From
the least to the greatest, they shall die by the
sword and by famine, [e]and they shall become
an oath, a horror, [v]a curse, and a taunt. 13 [f]I
will punish those who dwell in the land of
Egypt, as I have punished Jerusalem, with
the sword, with famine, and with pestilence,
14 [g]so that none of the remnant of Judah who
have come to live in the land of Egypt shall
escape or survive [h]or return to the land of
Judah, to which they desire to return to dwell
there. For they shall not return, [i]except some
fugitives."

15 Then all the men who knew that [j]their
wives had made offerings to other gods, and
all the women who stood by, a great assembly, all the people who lived in [k]Pathros in
the land of Egypt, answered Jeremiah: 16 "As
for the word that you have spoken to us in
the name of the LORD, [l]we will not listen to
you. 17 [m]But we will do everything that we
have vowed, make offerings to [n]the queen
of heaven [o]and pour out drink offerings to
her, [p]as we did, both we and our fathers, our
kings and our officials, in the cities of Judah
and in the streets of Jerusalem. For then we
had plenty of food, and prospered, and saw
no disaster. 18 But since we left off making
offerings to [n]the queen of heaven and pouring out drink offerings to her, we have lacked
everything [q]and have been consumed by the
sword and by famine." 19 And the women
said,[2] "When we made offerings to the queen
of heaven [r]and poured out drink offerings to
her, was it [s]without our husbands' approval
that we made cakes for her bearing her image
and poured out drink offerings to her?"

20 Then Jeremiah said to all the people, [t]men
and women, all the people who had given
him this answer: 21 [u]"As for the offerings that
you offered in the cities of Judah and in the
streets of Jerusalem, you and your fathers,
your kings and your officials, and the people
of the land, [v]did not the LORD remember
them? Did it not come into his mind? 22 [w]The
LORD could no longer bear your evil deeds
and [x]the abominations that you committed.
[y]Therefore your land has become [z]a desolation and a waste and a curse, [a]without inhabitant, as it is this day. 23 It is because you made
offerings [b]and because you sinned against
the LORD and did not obey the voice of the
LORD or walk in his law and in his statutes
and in his testimonies [c]that this disaster has
happened to you, as at this day."

24 Jeremiah said to all the people and all the
women, "Hear the word of the LORD, [d]all you
of Judah who are in the land of Egypt. 25 Thus
says the LORD of hosts, the God of Israel:
[e]You and your wives have declared with your
mouths, and have fulfilled it with your hands,
saying, 'We will surely perform our vows
that we have made, [f]to make offerings to the
queen of heaven and to pour out drink offerings to her.' Then confirm your vows and perform your vows! 26 Therefore hear the word
of the LORD, [d]all you of Judah who dwell in
the land of Egypt: [g]Behold, I have sworn by
my great name, says the LORD, [h]that my name
shall no more be invoked by the mouth of
any man of Judah in all the land of Egypt,
[i]saying, 'As the Lord GOD lives.' 27 [j]Behold,
I am watching over them for disaster and
not for good. [k]All the men of Judah who are
in the land of Egypt shall be consumed by
the sword and by famine, until there is an
end of them. 28 [l]And those who escape the
sword shall return from the land of Egypt
to the land of Judah, [m]few in number; and
all the remnant of Judah, who came to the
land of Egypt to live, [n]shall know whose word
will stand, mine or theirs. 29 This shall be the
sign to you, declares the LORD, that I will
punish you in this place, in order that you

[1] Hebrew *his* [2] Compare Syriac; Hebrew lacks *And the women said*

9[y] ver. 15, 25 **10**[z] [Prov. 28:14] **11**[a] See ch. 21:10 **12**[b] ch. 42:15 [c] ch. 42:16 [d] See ch. 6:13 [e] See ch. 18:16 [v] [See ver. 8 above] **13**[f] ch. 43:11 **14**[g] ch. 42:17 [h] [ch. 22:27] [i] [ver. 28] **15**[j] ver. 9, 25 [k] See ver. 1 **16**[l] ch. 6:16; 42:13 **17**[m] [Judg. 11:36] [n] ch. 7:18 [o] ch. 19:13 [p] [1 Kgs. 11:33; 2 Kgs. 21:3] **18**[n] [See ver. 17 above] [q] [Lam. 3:22] **19**[r] ch. 7:18 [s] [Num. 30:6, 7] **20**[t] ch. 43:6 **21**[u] ver. 17; [Ezek. 8:10, 11] [v] [Ezek. 21:24] **22**[w] ch. 5:9, 29 [x] Ezek. 8:6 [y] See ch. 7:34 [z] See ch. 18:16 [a] See ch. 4:7 **23**[b] See ch. 40:3 [c] [Deut. 31:29] **24**[d] ver. 15; See ch. 43:5-7 **25**[e] ver. 16 [f] ver. 17 **26**[d] [See ver. 24 above] [g] See ch. 22:5 [h] [Ezek. 20:39] [i] [ch. 4:2] **27**[j] ch. 31:28 [k] ch. 42:16 **28**[l] [ver. 14; Isa. 27:13] [m] Ezek. 6:8 [n] ver. 17, 25, 26

may know that [o]my words will surely stand
against you for harm: 30 Thus says the LORD,
Behold, I will give [p]Pharaoh Hophra king
of Egypt into the hand of his enemies [q]and
into the hand of those who seek his life, as
I gave [r]Zedekiah king of Judah into the hand
of Nebuchadnezzar king of Babylon, who
was his enemy and sought his life."

Message to Baruch

45 The word that Jeremiah the prophet
spoke to [s]Baruch the son of Neriah,
[t]when he wrote these words in a book at the
dictation of Jeremiah, [u]in the fourth year of
Jehoiakim the son of Josiah, king of Judah:
2 "Thus says the LORD, the God of Israel, to
you, O Baruch: 3 You said, [v]'Woe is me! For
the LORD has added sorrow to my pain. [w]I
am weary with my groaning, [x]and I find no
rest.' 4 Thus shall you say to him, Thus says
the LORD: [y]Behold, what I have built I am
breaking down, and what I have planted I am
plucking up—that is, the whole land. 5 And
[z]do you seek great things for yourself? Seek
them not, for behold, [a]I am bringing disaster
upon all flesh, declares the LORD. But I will
give you [b]your life as a prize of war in all places
to which you may go."

Judgment on Egypt

46 The word of the LORD that came to
Jeremiah the prophet [c]concerning the
nations.

2 About Egypt. [d]Concerning the army of
Pharaoh Neco, king of Egypt, which was by
the river Euphrates at Carchemish and which
Nebuchadnezzar king of Babylon defeated in
[e]the fourth year of Jehoiakim the son of Josiah,
king of Judah:

3 [f]"Prepare buckler and shield,
and advance for battle!
4 [g]Harness the horses;
mount, O horsemen!
Take your stations with your helmets,
[f]polish your spears,
put on your armor!
5 Why have I seen it?
They are dismayed
and have turned backward.
Their [h]warriors are beaten down
and have fled in haste;
[i]they look not back—
[j]terror on every side!
declares the LORD.

6 "The swift cannot flee away,
nor the warrior escape;

45:1–5 As Jeremiah had been, so Baruch his scribe was affected deeply by the message he had to write down. He too needed the assurance that his suffering was not forever. The gospel of the kingdom can never be reduced to a message of peace when there is no peace (6:13–14). Peace in a fallen world comes only through judgment. Peace with God comes through the judgment on our sins at the cross of Christ. Having been justified by faith alone, then and only then do we find peace with God (Rom. 5:1; Eph. 2:13–19).

The words of assurance to Baruch are still applicable to the Lord's servants who struggle. It is assurance that does not gloss over the solemnity of judgment. What can Baruch take away after his suffering? His life; that is, he will survive this judgment (Jer. 45:5). The fiery trials will not consume God's faithful servants (Isa. 43:1–2; Rom. 8:31–39; 2 Cor. 11:21–30). Even if our lives are taken, our souls are secure. We will be restored in the new earth one day.

45:5 Jeremiah's scribe, Baruch, had important work to do. But he was apparently wearied from the trials bound up with being the secretary to a controversial prophet, and he also apparently wished to be more than a mere scribe (vv. 1–4). Jeremiah's message to Baruch is direct: "And do you seek great things for yourself? Seek them not" (v. 5). The heart of human sin is *self*—the quest for self-glory instead of God's glory (Rom. 3:23). In the upside-down framework of the gospel, our Lord consistently teaches that the way to glory is through servanthood (Mark 10:43). "The last will be first, and the first last" (Matt. 20:16).

Jesus not only taught this. He also embodied it (Mark 10:45). The path to which he calls us is one he himself blazed. Leaving behind his heavenly glory, he became a servant to all (John 13:14–15; Phil. 2:6–8). Following our Master, we likewise gladly lay down our lives (John 15:12–13).

29 [o]Prov. 19:21
30 [p]ch. 46:17; See Ezek. 29:2-5; 30:21-24 [q]ch. 46:26 [r][ch. 39:5]

Chapter 45
1 [s]See ch. 32:12 [t]See ch. 36:4, 18 [u]ch. 36:1
3 [v][ch. 36:26] [w]Ps. 6:6 [x]Lam. 1:3; 5:5
4 [y]ch. 31:28; [Isa. 5:5]
5 [z][Ps. 131:1, 2; Rom. 12:16] [a][ch. 25:26, 29] [b]ch. 21:9; 39:18

Chapter 46
1 [c][ch. 1:5; 25:13]; See ch. 25:15-26
2 [d]2 Kgs. 23:29; 2 Chr. 35:20 [e]ch. 25:1; 36:1; 45:1
3 [f][ch. 51:11]
4 [g][Nah. 3:2] [f][See ver. 3 above]
5 [h][2 Sam. 1:19, 25] [i]ver. 21; ch. 47:3 [j]See ch. 6:25

[d]in the north by the river Euphrates
[k]they have stumbled and fallen.

7 “Who is this, [l]rising like the Nile,
like rivers [m]whose waters surge?
8 Egypt rises like the Nile,
like rivers [m]whose waters surge.
He said, ‘I will rise, I will cover the earth,
I will destroy cities and their inhabitants.’
9 [n]Advance, O horses,
and rage, O chariots!
Let the warriors go out:
men of Cush and [o]Put who handle the shield,
[p]men of Lud, skilled in handling the bow.
10 [q]That day is the day of the Lord GOD of hosts,
[r]a day of vengeance,
[s]to avenge himself on his foes.
[t]The sword shall devour and be sated
and drink its fill of their blood.
For the Lord GOD of hosts holds [u]a sacrifice
[v]in the north country [w]by the river Euphrates.
11 [x]Go up to Gilead, and take [x]balm,
O virgin daughter of Egypt!
In vain you have used many medicines;
[y]there is no healing for you.
12 The nations have heard of your shame,
and the earth is full of your cry;
[z]for warrior has stumbled against warrior;
they have both fallen together.”

13 The word that the LORD spoke to Jeremiah the prophet about the coming of [a]Nebuchadnezzar king of Babylon to strike the land of Egypt:

14 “Declare in Egypt, and proclaim in [b]Migdol;
proclaim in [b]Memphis and [b]Tahpanhes;
say, [c]‘Stand ready and be prepared,
for [d]the sword shall devour around you.’
15 Why are your mighty ones face down?
They do not stand[1]
because the LORD thrust them down.
16 He made many stumble, [f]and they fell,
and they said one to another,
‘Arise, and let us go back to our own people
and to the land of our birth,
[g]because of the sword of the oppressor.’
17 Call the name of [h]Pharaoh, king of Egypt,
‘Noisy one who lets the hour go by.’

18 [i]“As I live, declares the King,
[j]whose name is the LORD of hosts,
like [k]Tabor among the mountains
and like [l]Carmel by the sea, shall one come.
19 [m]Prepare yourselves baggage for exile,
O [n]inhabitants of Egypt!
For [o]Memphis shall become a waste,
a ruin, [p]without inhabitant.

20 “A beautiful [q]heifer is Egypt,
but a biting fly [r]from the north has come upon her.
21 Even her hired soldiers in her midst
are like [s]fattened calves;
yes, they have turned and fled together;
they did not stand,
for the day of their calamity has come upon them,
[t]the time of their punishment.

[1] Hebrew *He does not stand*

6[d] [See ver. 2 above] [k] [Dan. 11:19]
7[l] [ch. 47:2; Isa. 8:7, 8; Dan. 11:22] [m] [Ezek. 32:2]
8[m] [See ver. 7 above]
9[n] Nah. 3:2; [Judg. 5:22] [o] Ezek. 27:10 [p] Isa. 66:19
10[q] Isa. 13:9; Joel 1:15 [r] ch. 50:15 [s] Isa. 1:24 [t] [ver. 14; Isa. 34:5] [u] [Isa. 34:6] [v] ver. 6 [w] ver. 2
11[x] [ch. 8:22] [y] [Ezek. 30:21]
12[z] ver. 6
13[a] ch. 43:10, 11; 44:30; [Isa. 19:4; Ezek. 29:10]
14[b] See ch. 44:1 [c] [ver. 3, 4] [d] [ver. 10]
16[f] Lev. 26:37 [g] ch. 50:16
17[h] [Isa. 30:7]

46:10–13 Jeremiah 46–51 contains a series of judgment oracles against those nations that are part of Israel's world. Such prophetic oracles against the nations (cf. Isaiah 13–24; Ezekiel 25–32) show the rule of God over the whole of humanity. He is not a parochial deity. All nations are guilty before God even though they have not had the blessings of election and God's covenant word that are Israel's peculiar possession. All humans are without excuse because they have rejected the revelation of God in creation and in their own consciences (Rom. 1:18–32).

Jeremiah refers to the day of the Lord as a day of vengeance, a theme no more palatable in our own day than in his. The day of the Lord is the day on which he will act in judgment and salvation to bring in his kingdom (Isa. 13:6, 9, 13; Joel 1:15; 2:1–11). The New Testament takes up the theme as the day of the coming of the Son of Man (Matt. 24:29–36; 1 Thess. 5:1–11; 2 Pet. 3:10–13; Rev. 6:12–17). The vengeance of God is an aspect of this day (Heb. 10:26–31).

18[i] See ch. 4:2 [j] ch. 48:15; 51:57; Isa. 47:4; 48:2 [k] Judg. 4:6 [l] 1 Kgs. 18:42, 44 **19**[m] [Ezek. 12:3] [n] [ch. 48:18] [o] See ch. 44:1 [p] See ch. 4:7 **20**[q] [Hos. 10:11] [r] ver. 6, 10, 24; See ch. 1:13 **21**[s] Amos 6:4; Mal. 4:2 [t] ch. 50:27

22 “She makes [u]a sound like a serpent gliding away;
for her enemies march in force
and come against her with axes
[v]like those who fell trees.
23 [v]They shall cut down her forest,
declares the LORD,
though it is impenetrable,
because [w]they are more numerous than locusts;
they are without number.
24 The daughter of Egypt shall be put to shame;
she shall be delivered into the hand of
[r]a people from the north.”

25 The LORD of hosts, the God of Israel, said:
“Behold, I am bringing punishment upon
[x]Amon of [y]Thebes, and Pharaoh and Egypt
[z]and her gods and her kings, upon Pharaoh
and those who trust in him. 26 [a]I will deliver
them into the hand of those who seek their
life, into the hand of Nebuchadnezzar king
of Babylon and his officers. [b]Afterward Egypt
shall be inhabited [c]as in the days of old,
declares the LORD.

27 [d]“But fear not, O Jacob my servant,
nor be dismayed, O Israel,
for behold, I will save you from far away,
and your offspring from the land of their captivity.
Jacob shall return and have quiet and ease,
and none shall make him afraid.
28 [d]Fear not, O Jacob my servant,
declares the LORD,
for I am with you.
I will make a full end of all the nations
to which I have driven you,
but of you I will not make a full end.
[e]I will discipline you in just measure,
and I will by no means leave you unpunished.”

Judgment on the Philistines

47 The word of the LORD that came to
Jeremiah the prophet [f]concerning
the Philistines, before Pharaoh struck down
[g]Gaza.

2 “Thus says the LORD:
[h]Behold, waters are rising [i]out of the north,
[h]and shall become an overflowing torrent;
they shall overflow [j]the land and all that fills it,
the city and those who dwell in it.
Men shall cry out,
and every inhabitant of the land shall wail.
3 At the noise of the stamping of the hoofs of his stallions,
[l]at the rushing of his chariots, at the rumbling of their wheels,
the fathers [m]look not back to their children,
so feeble are their hands,

46:27–28 In this oracle, set amid the oracles against the nations, the Lord gives a wonderful assurance of salvation for his people. “Fear not” is a typical introductory formula to a prophetic word of assurance of salvation (e.g., 30:10; Isa. 41:10, 13–14; 43:2, 5; 44:2, 8; 54:4; Joel 2:21; Zeph. 3:16–17; Hag. 2:4–9).

In a similar way the challenge to “fear not” comes in the New Testament context of salvation in Christ (Luke 2:10; 8:50; 12:7, 32; John 12:14–15; Rev. 1:17–18). Despite all appearances of chaos as judgment overtakes whole nations in warfare, the remnant of God’s elect are reassured of their safety and final salvation. God’s faithfulness to his covenant ensures that his people will enjoy the blessings of the covenant. They will be delivered from captivity, from turmoil, and from fear. This can happen only through the conquest of their enemies. But it will also be accompanied by disciplining of the faithful (Jer. 46:28; Heb. 12:3–11). The prophetic hope is fulfilled by Christ’s coming (Luke 1:68–75). His coming, heralded by John the Baptist, assures us “that we, being delivered from the hand of our enemies, might serve him without fear, in holiness and righteousness before him all our days” (Luke 1:74–75).

47:1–49:39 Throughout these chapters the Lord continues to declare the judgment that will befall idolatrous foreign nations. Such judgments are horrific in what they detail, and are difficult to read.

One truth that is hammered home in these chapters is the awful reality of sin. The horror over divine judgment is not an overreaction. The heinousness of human

22 [u][Isa. 29:4] [v][Isa. 10:34; 14:8]
23 [v][See ver. 22 above] [w][Judg. 6:5; 7:12]
24 [r][See ver. 20 above]
25 [x][Nah. 3:8] [y]Ezek. 30:14, 15, 16 [z]See ch. 43:12
26 [a]ch. 44:30; Ezek. 30:4; 32:11 [b]Ezek. 29:13, 14; See Isa. 19:22-25 [c]Isa. 51:9
27 [d]See ch. 30:10, 11; Isa. 43:5
28 [d][See ver. 27 above] [e]ch. 10:24

Chapter 47
1 [f]ch. 25:20; Ezek. 25:15, 16; Zeph. 2:5 [g]Amos 1:6, 7; Zeph. 2:4
2 [h][ch. 46:7, 8; Isa. 8:7] [i]See ch. 1:13 [j][ch. 8:16]
3 [l]Nah. 3:2 [m]ch. 46:5

4 because of the day that is coming to
destroy
all [f]the Philistines,
to cut off from [n]Tyre and Sidon
every helper that remains.
For the LORD is destroying the Philistines,
[o]the remnant of the coastland of
[p]Caphtor.
5 [q]Baldness has come upon Gaza;
[r]Ashkelon has perished.
O remnant of their valley,
[s]how long will you gash yourselves?
6 [t]Ah, sword of the LORD!
How long till you are quiet?
Put yourself into your scabbard;
rest and be still!
7 How can it[1] be quiet
[u]when the LORD has given it a charge?
Against [v]Ashkelon and against the seashore
[w]he has appointed it."

Judgment on Moab

48 [x]Concerning Moab.
Thus says the LORD of hosts, the God
of Israel:

"Woe to [y]Nebo, for it is laid waste!
[z]Kiriathaim is put to shame, it is taken;
the fortress is put to shame [a]and broken
down;
2 the renown of Moab is no more.
In [b]Heshbon they planned disaster
against her:
'Come, let us cut her off [c]from being a
nation!'
You also, O [d]Madmen, shall be brought
to silence;
the sword shall pursue you.
3 "A voice! A cry from [e]Horonaim,
'Desolation and great destruction!'
4 Moab is destroyed;
her little ones have made a cry.
5 [e]For at the ascent of Luhith
they go up weeping;[2]
for [e]at the descent of Horonaim
they have heard the distressed cry[3] of
destruction.
6 Flee! Save yourselves!
You will be like [f]a juniper in the desert!
7 For, [g]because you trusted in your works
and your treasures,
you also shall be taken;
and [h]Chemosh [i]shall go into exile
with [j]his priests and his officials.
8 [k]The destroyer shall come upon every city,
and no city shall escape;
the valley shall perish,
and [l]the plain shall be destroyed,
as the LORD has spoken.

9 "Give wings to Moab,
for she would fly away;
her cities shall become a desolation,
with no inhabitant in them.

10 [m]"Cursed is he who does [n]the work of the
LORD with slackness, and cursed is he who
keeps back his sword from bloodshed.

11 "Moab has been at ease from his youth
and has [o]settled on his dregs;
he has not been emptied from vessel to
vessel,
nor has he gone into exile;
so his taste remains in him,
and his scent is not changed.

12 "Therefore, behold, the days are coming,
declares the LORD, when I shall send to him
pourers who will pour him, and empty his vessels and break his[4] jars in pieces.
13 Then [p]Moab
shall be ashamed of Chemosh, as [q]the house of
Israel was ashamed of [r]Bethel, their confidence.

[1] Septuagint, Vulgate; Hebrew *you* [2] Hebrew *weeping goes up with weeping* [3] Septuagint (compare Isaiah 15:5) *heard the cry* [4] Septuagint, Aquila; Hebrew *their*

4[f] [See ver. 1 above] [n] Isa. 23:1, 2; Joel 3:4; See ch. 25:22 [o] Amos 1:8 [p] Gen. 10:14; Amos 9:7
5[q] [ch. 48:37; Isa. 3:24] [r] ch. 25:20; [Judg. 1:18] [s] [ch. 48:37]
6[t] Deut. 32:41; See Ezek. 21:3-5
7[u] [Ezek. 14:17] [v] ch. 25:20; [Judg. 1:18] [w] Mic. 6:9

rebellion against an infinitely beautiful Creator merits consonant retribution. Such sober reminders of the awfulness of sin also, however, drive further home the wonder of the gospel. While the day of the Lord and the judgment on that day will be incomparably horrific, the magnificence of God's restoration of all those from every nation who put their trust in Christ will be an incomparable wonder.

For believers in Christ, the day of the Lord is a judgment that has already fallen on Christ. Our punishment is behind us. For those in Christ, justice has already been satisfied.

Chapter 48 **1**[x] ch. 25:21; 2 Kgs. 24:2; See Isa. 15–16; Ezek. 25:8-11; Amos 2:1-3; Zeph. 2:8, 9 [y] ver. 22; Num. 32:3 [z] ver. 23; Num. 32:37; Josh. 13:19; Ezek. 25:9 [a] ver. 20, 39 **2**[b] ver. 34, 45; ch. 49:3; Num. 32:37; Isa. 15:4 [c] [ch. 31:36] [d] [Isa. 10:31] **3**[e] Isa. 15:5; [ver. 34] **5**[e] [See ver. 3 above] **6**[f] ch. 17:6 **7**[g] ch. 49:4 [h] Num. 21:29 [i] [Isa. 46:2] [j] ch. 49:3 **8**[k] ch. 6:26 [l] ver. 21; Josh. 13:9, 17, 21; [Deut. 3:10] **10**[m] Judg. 5:23; [1 Sam. 15:3, 9; 1 Kgs. 20:42] [n] [1 Cor. 15:58] **11**[o] Zeph. 1:12 **13**[p] [Num. 21:29; Isa. 16:14] [q] [Hos. 10:6] [r] [1 Kgs. 12:29]

14 "How do you say, 'We are heroes
and mighty men of war'?
15 The destroyer of [s]Moab and his cities has
come up,
and the choicest of his young men
have [t]gone down to slaughter,
declares [u]the King, [u]whose name is the
LORD of hosts.
16 The calamity of Moab is near at hand,
and his affliction hastens swiftly.
17 [v]Grieve for him, all you who are around
him,
and all who know his name;
say, [w]'How the mighty scepter is broken,
the glorious staff.'

18 [x]"Come down from your glory,
and sit on the parched ground,
O inhabitant of [y]Dibon!
For the destroyer of Moab has come up
against you;
he has destroyed your strongholds.
19 [z]Stand by the way [z]and watch,
O inhabitant of [a]Aroer!
Ask him who flees and her who escapes;
say, 'What has happened?'
20 Moab is put to shame, for it is broken;
[v]wail and cry!
Tell it beside [b]the Arnon,
that [s]Moab is laid waste.

21 "Judgment has come upon [c]the tableland,
upon Holon, and [d]Jahzah, and Mephaath,
22 and [y]Dibon, and [e]Nebo, and Beth-
diblathaim, 23 and [f]Kiriathaim, and Beth-
gamul, and [g]Beth-meon, 24 and [h]Kerioth, and
[i]Bozrah, and all the cities of the land of Moab,
far and near. 25 [j]The horn of Moab is cut off,
and [k]his arm is broken, declares the LORD.
26 [l]"Make him drunk, [m]because he magnified
himself against the LORD, so that Moab shall
[l]wallow in his vomit, [n]and he too shall be held
in derision. 27 [o]Was not Israel a derision to you?
[p]Was he found among thieves, that whenever
you spoke of him [q]you wagged your head?

28 [r]"Leave the cities, and dwell in the rock,
O inhabitants of Moab!
Be [s]like the dove that nests
in the sides of the mouth of a gorge.
29 [t]We have heard of the pride of Moab—
he is very proud—
of his loftiness, his pride, and his arrogance,
and the haughtiness of his heart.
30 I know his insolence, declares the LORD;
[u]his boasts are false,
his deeds are false.
31 [v]Therefore I wail for Moab;
I cry out for all Moab;
for the men of [w]Kir-hareseth I mourn.
32 More than for [x]Jazer I weep for you,
[y]O vine of [z]Sibmah!
[a]Your branches passed over the sea,
reached to the Sea of [x]Jazer;
on your summer fruits and your grapes
the destroyer has fallen.
33 [b]Gladness and joy have been taken away
from the fruitful land of Moab;
I have made the wine cease from the
winepresses;
no one treads them with shouts of joy;
the shouting is not the shout of joy.

34 [c]"From the outcry at Heshbon even
to Elealeh, as far as Jahaz they utter their
voice, from Zoar to [d]Horonaim and Eglath-
shelishiyah. For the waters of Nimrim also
have become desolate. 35 And I will bring
to an end in Moab, declares the LORD, him
who offers sacrifice in [e]the high place and
makes offerings to his god. 36 Therefore my
heart moans for Moab like a flute, and my
heart moans like a flute for the men of [f]Kir-
hareseth. [g]Therefore the riches they gained
have perished.
37 [h]"For every head is shaved and every beard
cut off. [i]On all the hands are gashes, and
[j]around the waist is sackcloth. 38 On all the
housetops of Moab and in the squares there
is nothing but lamentation, for I have broken
Moab like [k]a vessel for which no one cares,
declares the LORD. 39 How it is broken! How
they wail! [l]How Moab has turned his back in
shame! So Moab [m]has become a derision and
a horror to all that are around him."

40 For thus says the LORD:
"Behold, [n]one shall fly swiftly like an eagle
[o]and spread his wings against Moab;

15[s] ver. 8, 18, 20; Isa. 15:1 [t] ch. 50:27 [u] See ch. 46:18 **17**[v] [Isa. 15:4, 5; 16:7] [w] [Isa. 9:4; 14:5] **18**[x] [Isa. 47:1] [y] Num. 21:30; Isa. 15:2 **19**[z] [1 Sam. 4:13, 16; Nah. 2:1] [a] Deut. 2:36; Josh. 13:9 **20**[v] [See ver. 17 above] [b] Isa. 16:2 [s] [See ver. 15 above] **21**[c] ver. 8; Num. 21:23 [d] Josh. 13:18 **22**[y] [See ver. 18 above] [e] Num. 33:46; Isa. 15:2 **23**[f] See ver. 1 [g] [Josh. 13:17; 1 Chr. 5:8] **24**[h] Amos 2:2 [i] ch. 49:13, 22; Isa. 63:1 **25**[j] [Ps. 75:10] [k] [Ezek. 30:21] **26**[l] ch. 25:27; 51:39; Isa. 19:14 [m] ver. 42 [n] ver. 39 **27**[o] Zeph. 2:8; [Ezek. 25:8] [p] [ch. 2:26] [q] Ps. 64:8; Lam. 2:15; Matt. 27:39 **28**[r] ver. 9 [s] Ps. 55:6, 7; Song 2:14 **29**[t] Isa. 16:6 **30**[u] [ch. 50:36] **31**[v] Isa. 15:5; 16:7, 11 [w] [2 Kgs. 3:25] **32**[x] Num. 21:32 [y] Isa. 16:8, 9 [z] Josh. 13:19 [a] [Ps. 80:11] **33**[b] Isa. 16:10 **34**[c] See Isa. 15:4-6 [d] ver. 3 **35**[e] [Isa. 15:2; 16:12; Ezek. 20:29] **36**[f] See ver. 31 [g] Isa. 15:7 **37**[h] Isa. 15:2, 3 [i] [ch. 47:5] [j] ch. 49:3; Lam. 2:10; See ch. 4:8 **38**[k] [ch. 22:28] **39**[l] [ver. 6] [m] ver. 26 **40**[n] ch. 49:22; [Deut. 28:49; Ezek. 17:3] [o] [Isa. 8:8]

41 [p]the cities shall be taken
and the strongholds seized.
[q]The heart of the warriors of Moab shall
be in that day
like the heart of [r]a woman in her birth
pains;
42 Moab shall be [s]destroyed and be no
longer a people,
because [t]he magnified himself against
the LORD.
43 [u]Terror, pit, and snare
are before you, O inhabitant of Moab!
declares the LORD.
44 He who flees from the terror
shall fall into the pit,
and he who climbs out of the pit
shall be caught in the snare.
[v]For I will bring these things upon Moab,
the year of their punishment,
declares the LORD.

45 "In the shadow of Heshbon
fugitives stop without strength,
for fire came out from Heshbon,
flame from the house of Sihon;
it has destroyed [w]the forehead of Moab,
the crown of [w]the sons of tumult.
46 [x]Woe to you, O Moab!
The people of [y]Chemosh are undone,
for your sons have been taken captive,
and your daughters into captivity.
47 [z]Yet I will restore the fortunes of Moab
in the latter days, declares the LORD."
Thus far is the judgment on Moab.

Judgment on Ammon

49 [a]Concerning the Ammonites.
Thus says the LORD:

"Has Israel no sons?
Has he no heir?
Why then has [b]Milcom [c]dispossessed Gad,
and his people settled in its cities?
2 Therefore, behold, the days are coming,
declares the LORD,
when I will cause [d]the battle cry to be
heard
against [e]Rabbah of the Ammonites;
it shall become a desolate [f]mound,
and its villages shall be burned with
fire;
then Israel shall dispossess those who
dispossessed him,
says the LORD.

3 "Wail, O [g]Heshbon, for Ai is laid waste!
Cry out, O daughters of [e]Rabbah!
[h]Put on sackcloth,
lament, and run to and fro among the
hedges!
For [i]Milcom shall go into exile,
[j]with his priests and his officials.
4 Why do you boast of your valleys,[1]
[k]O faithless daughter,
[l]who trusted in her treasures, saying,
'Who will come against me?'
5 Behold, [m]I will bring terror upon you,
declares the Lord GOD of hosts,
from all who are around you,
and you shall be driven out, every man
straight before him,
with none to gather the fugitives.

6 "But [n]afterward I will restore the fortunes
of the Ammonites, declares the LORD."

Judgment on Edom

7 Concerning [o]Edom.
Thus says the LORD of hosts:

[p]"Is wisdom no more in [p]Teman?
[q]Has counsel perished from the prudent?
[q]Has their wisdom vanished?
8 [r]Flee, turn back, dwell in the depths,
O inhabitants of [s]Dedan!
For I will bring the calamity of Esau
upon him,
[t]the time when I punish him.
9 [u]If grape gatherers came to you,
would they not leave [v]gleanings?
[u]If thieves came by night,
would they not destroy only enough
for themselves?
10 [w]But I have stripped Esau bare;
[u]I have uncovered his hiding places,
and he is not able to conceal himself.
His children are destroyed, and his
brothers,
and his neighbors; and [x]he is no more.
11 [y]Leave your fatherless children; I will
keep them alive;
[y]and let your widows trust in me."

[1] Hebrew *boast of your valleys, your valley flows*

41[p] ver. 24 [q][Isa. 13:7, 8] [r]See ch. 6:24 **42**[s][Isa. 7:8] [t]ver. 26 **43**[u]Isa. 24:17, 18; Lam. 3:47 **44**[v][ch. 11:23] **45**[w]Num. 24:17 **46**[x]See ver. 1 [y]ver. 13 **47**[z][ch. 46:27; 49:39] **Chapter 49** **1**[a]ch. 25:21; [Ezek. 21:28; 25:2] [b][1 Kgs. 11:5, 33; 2 Kgs. 23:13] [c][Amos 1:13] **2**[d]ch. 4:19 [e]Ezek. 21:20; 25:5; Amos 1:14 [f]ch. 30:18 **3**[g]ch. 48:2 [e][See ver. 2 above] [h]ch. 48:37; See ch. 4:8 [i][1 Kgs. 11:5, 33; 2 Kgs. 23:13] [j]ch. 48:7 **4**[k]ch. 3:14 [l]ch. 48:7 **5**[m][ch. 48:43] **6**[n][ver. 39; ch. 48:47] **7**[o]ch. 25:21; Isa. 34:5; Amos 1:11; Obad. 1; [Mal. 1:2]; See Ezek. 25:12-14 [p]ver. 20; Obad. 9 [q][Isa. 19:11, 12] **8**[r]ver. 30 [s]ch. 25:23; Gen. 25:3 [t]ch. 50:27, 31; [ch. 46:21; 50:27] **9**[u]Obad. 5, 6 [v][Judg. 8:2] **10**[w]Mal. 1:3 [u][See ver. 9 above] [x]ch. 31:15; Isa. 17:14 **11**[y][Ps. 10:14, 18; 68:5]

12 For thus says the LORD: [z]"If those who
did not deserve to drink the cup must drink
it, [a]will you go unpunished? You shall not
go unpunished, but you must drink. 13 [b]For
I have sworn by myself, declares the LORD,
that [c]Bozrah shall become [d]a horror, a taunt,
a waste, and a curse, and all her cities shall be
perpetual wastes."

14 [e]I have heard a message from the LORD,
and an envoy has been sent among
the nations:
[f]"Gather yourselves together and come
against her,
and rise up for battle!
15 For behold, I will make you small
among the nations,
despised among mankind.
16 The horror you inspire has deceived you,
and the pride of your heart,
you who live in the clefts of the rock,[1]
who hold the height of the hill.
Though you [g]make your nest as high as
the eagle's,
I will bring you down from there,
declares the LORD.

17 [h]"Edom shall become a horror. [i]Everyone
who passes by it will be horrified [i]and will hiss
because of all its disasters. 18 [j]As when Sodom
and Gomorrah and their [k]neighboring cities were overthrown, says the LORD, [l]no man
shall dwell there, [l]no man shall sojourn in her.
19 [m]Behold, [n]like a lion coming up from [o]the
jungle of the Jordan against a perennial pasture, I will suddenly make him[2] run away from
her. And I will appoint over her whomever
I choose. [p]For who is like me? [q]Who will summon me? [r]What shepherd can stand before
me? 20 Therefore hear the plan that the LORD
has made against [s]Edom and the purposes
that he has formed against the inhabitants of
[t]Teman: [u]Even the little ones of the flock shall
be dragged away. Surely their fold shall be
appalled at their fate. 21 At the sound of their
fall [v]the earth shall tremble; the sound of their
cry shall be heard at the Red Sea. 22 Behold,
[w]one shall mount up and fly swiftly like an
eagle and spread his wings against [x]Bozrah,
and the heart of the warriors of Edom shall
be in that day like the heart [y]of a woman in
her birth pains."

Judgment on Damascus

23 Concerning [z]Damascus:

[a]"Hamath and [b]Arpad are confounded,
for they have heard bad news;
they melt in fear,
[c]they are troubled like the sea that cannot be quiet.
24 [z]Damascus has become feeble, [d]she
turned to flee,
and panic seized her;
anguish and sorrows have taken hold of
her,
as [y]of a woman in labor.
25 How is [e]the famous city not forsaken,
the city of my joy?
26 [f]Therefore her young men shall fall in
her squares,
and all her soldiers shall be destroyed
in that day,
declares the LORD of hosts.
27 And [g]I will kindle a fire in the wall of
[z]Damascus,
and it shall devour the strongholds of
[h]Ben-hadad."

Judgment on Kedar and Hazor

28 Concerning [i]Kedar and the kingdoms of
Hazor that Nebuchadnezzar king of Babylon
struck down.

Thus says the LORD:
[j]"Rise up, advance against [i]Kedar!
Destroy [k]the people of the east!
29 [l]Their tents and their flocks shall be
taken,
their [l]curtains and all their goods;
their camels shall be led away from them,
and men shall cry to them: [m]'Terror
on every side!'
30 [n]Flee, wander far away, dwell in the
depths,
O inhabitants of Hazor!
declares the LORD.
For Nebuchadnezzar king of Babylon
has made a plan against you
and formed a purpose against you.

[1] Or *of Sela* [2] Septuagint, Syriac *them*

12 [z]ch. 25:28; [Obad. 16] [a]ch. 25:29 **13** [b]See ch. 22:5 [c]ver. 22; See ch. 48:24 [d]See ch. 24:9 **14** [e]See Obad. 1-4 [f][Isa. 13:4] **16** [g][ch. 48:28] **17** [h]Ezek. 35:3, 7, 9 [i][ch. 50:13] **18** [j]See Isa. 13:19 [k][Deut. 29:23] [l]ver. 33 **19** [m]For ver. 19-21, see ch. 50:44-46 [n]See ch. 4:7 [o]See ch. 12:5 [p]See ch. 10:6 [q]Job 9:19 [r][ch. 30:21] **20** [s]Ezek. 35:3, 7, 9 [t]See ver. 7 [u]ch. 50:45 **21** [v]ch. 8:16; 50:46; [Ezek. 26:15] **22** [w]See ch. 48:40 [x]ver. 13 [y]ver. 24; See ch. 6:24 **23** [z]Isa. 17:1; Amos 1:3 [a]1 Kgs. 8:65; Zech. 9:2 [b]2 Kgs. 18:34 [c]Zech. 9:4 **24** [z][See ver. 23 above] [d][ch. 46:5] [y][See ver. 22 above] **25** [e][ch. 33:9] **26** [f]ch. 50:30 **27** [g]See ch. 17:27 [z][See ver. 23 above] [h]1 Kgs. 15:18; 20:1; 2 Kgs. 6:24; 8:7; 13:3 **28** [i]Isa. 21:16; 60:7 [j]ver. 14, 31 [k]Isa. 11:14; Ezek. 25:4, 10; See Judg. 6:3 **29** [l]Ps. 120:5; Song 1:5 [m]See ch. 6:25 **30** [n]ver. 8

31 [j]"Rise up, advance against a nation [o]at ease,
[p]that dwells securely,
declares the LORD,
[p]that has no gates or bars,
that dwells alone.
32 [q]Their camels shall become plunder,
their herds of livestock a spoil.
[r]I will scatter to every wind
[s]those who cut the corners of their hair,
and I will bring their calamity
from every side of them,
declares the LORD.
33 Hazor shall become [t]a haunt of jackals,
an everlasting waste;
[u]no man shall dwell there;
[u]no man shall sojourn in her."

Judgment on Elam

34 The word of the LORD that came to
Jeremiah the prophet concerning [v]Elam, in
the beginning of the reign of [w]Zedekiah king
of Judah.
35 Thus says the LORD of hosts: "Behold,
I will break [x]the bow of [v]Elam, the mainstay of
their might. 36 And I will bring upon [v]Elam the
four winds from the four quarters of heaven.
And I will scatter them to all those winds, and
there shall be no nation to which those driven
out of [v]Elam shall not come. 37 I will [y]terrify
[v]Elam before their enemies and before those
who seek their life. I will bring disaster upon
them, [z]my fierce anger, declares the LORD. [a]I
will send the sword after them, until I have
consumed them, 38 and I will set my throne
in [v]Elam and destroy their king and officials,
declares the LORD.
39 "But in the latter days [b]I will restore the
fortunes of [v]Elam, declares the LORD."

Judgment on Babylon

50 The word that the LORD spoke concerning [c]Babylon, concerning the land
of the Chaldeans, [d]by Jeremiah the prophet:

2 "Declare among the nations and proclaim,
set up a banner and proclaim,
conceal it not, and say:
[e]'Babylon is taken,
[f]Bel is put to shame,
Merodach is dismayed.
[e]Her images are put to shame,
her idols are dismayed.'

3 "For [g]out of the north a nation has come
up against her, [h]which shall make her land a
desolation, and none shall dwell in it; [i]both
man and beast shall flee away.

4 [j]"In those days and in that time, declares the
LORD, [j]the people of Israel and the people of
Judah shall come together, [k]weeping as they
come, and they [l]shall seek the LORD their God.
5 [m]They shall ask the way to Zion, with faces
turned toward it, [n]saying, 'Come, let us join
ourselves to the LORD in an [o]everlasting covenant that will never be forgotten.'

31[j] [See ver. 28 above] [o] Job 16:12 [p] Ezek. 38:8, 11
32[q] [Ezek. 38:12] [r] ver. 36 [s] See ch. 9:26
33[t] See ch. 9:11 [u] ver. 18
34[v] ch. 25:25; Gen. 14:1; Isa. 11:11; 21:2; Ezek. 32:24; Dan. 8:2 [w] 2 Kgs. 24:17, 18
35[x] Isa. 22:6 [v] [See ver. 34 above]
36[v] [See ver. 34 above]
37[y] [ch. 1:17] [v] [See ver. 34 above] [z] See ch. 12:13 [a] See ch. 9:16
38[v] [See ver. 34 above]
39[b] [ch. 48:47] [v] [See ver. 34 above]

Chapter 50
1[c] See Isa. 13:1–14:27; 21:1-10 [d] [ch. 51:59, 60]
2[e] Isa. 21:9 [f] See Isa. 46:1
3[g] See ch. 1:14 [h] ver. 13, 23; ch. 51:29 [i] ch. 51:62; [Ps. 135:8]
4[j] See ch. 3:18 [k] ch. 31:9, 18; Ezra 8:21; Ps. 126:6 [l] Hos. 3:5
5[m] [ch. 31:21] [n] [Isa. 2:3] [o] See ch. 32:40

50:1–5 Babylon is a special case to the Lord, since it is the nation that brought destruction and deprivation to his people. Although Jeremiah had been entrusted to proclaim that God was giving Judah and Jerusalem, with its temple, into the hands of the Babylonians, these destroyers would, in God's time, meet their own destruction. Isaiah speaks of Cyrus the Persian, destroyer of Babylon and liberator of Judah, as his anointed one (messiah) (Isa. 45:1–4). Cyrus's edict of return (538 B.C.) led to the return of the exiles as recorded in Ezra–Nehemiah. "In those days and in that time" (Jer. 50:4) refers to the day of the Lord. These terms are not merely saying that one day God will act; they proclaim God's lordship over history. He has determined the rise and fall of nations and has set the day for the first advent of Jesus. This "fullness of time" speaks of God's purposes revealed in his Word being fulfilled when and how he determines (Gal. 4:4–5; Eph. 1:9–10; cf. Mark 1:14–15;).

Jeremiah's prophecy foreshadows that event when the final return is achieved, as the saints come to Zion through faith in Jesus (Heb. 12:22–24). He sees the faithful returning in repentance and seeking the Lord (Jer. 50:4). They will desire God, not in some self-generated religious feeling, but as a desire to know the God of the covenant. They will seek the way to Zion, the throne of God, so that they might find everlasting acceptance in his covenant (v. 5). Here we learn again that the humble way of salvation is not an undefined god-feeling. That all religions lead to the same god is the lie of the Devil. The covenant God made with Abraham to bless the nations through his Seed is the path of salvation. Jesus said, "I am the way, and the truth, and the life. No one comes to the Father except through me" (John 14:6).

6 [p]"My people have been lost sheep. [q]Their
shepherds have led them astray, turning them
away on the mountains. From mountain to
hill they have gone. They have forgotten their
fold. 7 All who found them have devoured
them, [r]and their enemies have said, 'We are
not guilty, for [s]they have sinned against the
LORD, [t]their habitation of righteousness, the
LORD, [u]the hope of their fathers.'

8 [v]"Flee from the midst of Babylon, [v]and go
out of the land of the Chaldeans, and be as
male goats before the flock. 9 For behold, I am
stirring up and bringing against Babylon [w]a
gathering of great nations, from the north
country. And they shall array themselves
against her. From there she shall be taken.
Their arrows are like a skilled warrior who
does not return empty-handed. 10 [x]Chaldea
shall be plundered; all who plunder her shall
be sated, declares the LORD.

11 [y]"Though you rejoice, though you exult,
O plunderers of my heritage,
though you frolic like a heifer in the pasture,
and neigh like stallions,
12 your mother shall be utterly shamed,
and she who bore you shall be disgraced.
Behold, she shall be the last of the nations,
[z]a wilderness, a dry land, and a desert.
13 [a]Because of the wrath of the LORD she shall not be inhabited
but shall be an utter desolation;
[b]everyone who passes by Babylon shall be appalled,
[b]and hiss because of all her wounds.
14 [c]Set yourselves in array against Babylon all around,
[d]all you who bend the bow;
shoot at her, spare no arrows,
[e]for she has sinned against the LORD.
15 [f]Raise a shout against her all around;
she has surrendered;
her bulwarks have fallen;
[g]her walls are thrown down.
For [h]this is the vengeance of the LORD:
take vengeance on her;
[i]do to her as she has done.
16 Cut off from Babylon the sower,
and the one who handles the sickle in time of harvest;
[j]because of the sword of the oppressor,
[k]every one shall turn to his own people,
and every one shall flee to his own land.

17 [l]"Israel is a hunted sheep [m]driven away
by lions. [n]First the king of Assyria [o]devoured
him, and now at last [p]Nebuchadnezzar king of
Babylon [q]has gnawed his bones. 18 Therefore,
thus says the LORD of hosts, the God of Israel:
Behold, [r]I am bringing punishment on the
king of Babylon and his land, [s]as I punished
the king of Assyria. 19 [t]I will restore Israel to
his pasture, and [t]he shall feed on [u]Carmel and
in [u]Bashan, and his desire shall be satisfied on
the hills of Ephraim and in [u]Gilead. 20 In those
days and in that time, declares the LORD, [v]iniquity shall be sought in Israel, and there shall
be none, and sin in Judah, and none shall be
found, for [w]I will pardon those whom I leave
as a remnant.

21 "Go up against the land of Merathaim,[1]
and against the inhabitants of Pekod.[2]
Kill, [x]and devote them to destruction,[3]
declares the LORD,
and do all that I have commanded you.
22 [y]The noise of battle is in the land,
and great destruction!
23 [z]How the hammer of the whole earth
is cut down and broken!
[a]How Babylon [b]has become
a horror among the nations!

[1] *Merathaim* means *double rebellion* [2] *Pekod* means *punishment* [3] That is, set apart (devote) as an offering to the Lord (for destruction)

50:6–7, 17–20 The lost sheep of Israel, led astray by false shepherds (23:1–4), will be restored (50:19). God's remnant will be pardoned and cleansed (v. 20). This will happen through the true and final Shepherd. This Good Shepherd comes to seek and to save his sheep (Matt. 9:36; John 10:11–18; Heb. 13:20–21; 1 Pet. 2:21–25). Christians need to understand that naming Jesus "the Good Shepherd" is more (though not less) than a metaphor for a tender, caring Savior. The term has its roots in the imagery of the Old Testament that speaks of the mighty, ruling, messiah-king. Our eternal security is in the mighty Lord who is exalted on high and rules over all.

6 [p] ver. 17; Isa. 53:6; [Matt. 18:12; Luke 15:4] [q] Zech. 10:2; See Ezek. 34:1-6
7 [r] [ch. 40:2, 3] [s] [ver. 14] [t] ch. 31:23 [u] See ch. 14:8
8 [v] ch. 51:6, 45; See Isa. 48:20
9 [w] See ch. 25:14
10 [x] [ch. 25:12]
11 [y] [Lam. 4:21]
12 [z] ch. 51:43
13 [a] ver. 39 [b] See ch. 18:16
14 [c] ver. 9; ch. 51:11; Isa. 21:2 [d] ver. 29; [ch. 51:3] [e] [ver. 7] **15** [f] [Josh. 6:16] [g] ch. 51:58 [h] ch. 46:10; 51:6, 11 [i] ver. 29; ch. 51:56 **16** [j] ch. 46:16 [k] [ch. 51:9]; See Isa. 13:14 **17** [l] See ver. 6 [m] ch. 2:15; 4:7; Isa. 5:29 [n] 2 Kgs. 17:6; 18:13 [o] ch. 51:34 [p] 2 Kgs. 24:10, 14; See 2 Kgs. 25:1-11 [q] [ch. 51:34] **18** [r] Isa. 10:12; 24:21; [Ps. 76:12] [s] Isa. 14:24, 25 **19** [t] Ezek. 34:13, 14 [u] Mic. 7:14 **20** [v] [Isa. 40:2] [w] Isa. 33:24; See ch. 31:34 **21** [x] ver. 26; [ch. 51:3] **22** [y] ch. 51:54 **23** [z] Isa. 14:6 [a] [Rev. 18:19, 21] [b] ver. 3, 13

24 [c]I set a snare for you and you were taken,
O Babylon,
and [d]you did not know it;
you were found and caught,
because you opposed the LORD.
25 The LORD has opened his armory
and brought out [e]the weapons of his
wrath,
for the Lord GOD of hosts has a work
to do
in the land of the Chaldeans.
26 Come against her from every quarter;
open her granaries;
[f]pile her up like heaps of grain, and
devote her to destruction;
let nothing be left of her.
27 Kill all [g]her bulls;
let them go down to the slaughter.
Woe to them, for their day has come,
[h]the time of their punishment.

28 "A voice! They [i]flee and escape from the land
of Babylon, [j]to declare in Zion the vengeance of
the LORD our God, vengeance for [k]his temple.

29 [l]"Summon archers against Babylon, all
those who bend the bow. [l]Encamp around
her; let no one escape. [m]Repay her according
to her deeds; do to her according to all that
she has done. For she has [n]proudly defied the
LORD, the Holy One of Israel. 30 [o]Therefore
her young men shall fall in her squares, and
all her soldiers shall be destroyed on that day,
declares the LORD.

31 "Behold, I am against you, O [n]proud one,
declares the Lord GOD of hosts,
[p]for your day has come,
the time when I will punish you.
32 [n]The proud one shall stumble and fall,
with none to raise him up,
[q]and I will kindle a fire in his cities,
and it will devour all that is around
him.

33 "Thus says the LORD of hosts: [r]The people of Israel are oppressed, and the people of
Judah with them. All who took them captive
have held them fast; [s]they refuse to let them
go. 34 [t]Their Redeemer is strong; [u]the LORD of

24[c] [Ps. 141:9] [d] [ch. 51:31; Dan. 5:30]
25[e] Isa. 13:5
26[f] [Neh. 4:2]
27[g] [Ps. 22:12; Isa. 34:7, 8] [h] ch. 46:21
28[i] [ver. 8] [j] ch. 51:10; Ps. 64:9 [k] [ch. 51:11; 52:13; Dan. 5:3, 23]
29[l] [ver. 14; Job 16:13] [m] ch. 25:14 [n] Isa. 47:10
30[o] ch. 49:26
31[n] [See ver. 29 above] [p] ver. 27; ch. 49:8
32[n] [See ver. 29 above] [q] See ch. 17:27
33[r] [ver. 17] [s] [Isa. 14:17]
34[t] See Isa. 43:14 [u] See ch. 10:16

50:25–28 The theme of God the warrior is repeated. Babylon was his unwitting agent of judgment, but Babylon is also culpable for all its evils. So reprehensible were its practices that it became a byword of evil. Thus John speaks of the fall of Babylon to refer to the overthrow of all the evil, godless powers of mankind (Revelation 18). Whatever the turmoil of our time, and however intractable the corruption of societies on earth, God will overthrow all powers and dominions that oppose his kingdom. The resurrection and ascension of Christ mean that we join the heavenly chorus: "The kingdom of the world has become the kingdom of our Lord and of his Christ, and he shall reign forever and ever" (Rev. 11:15).

God will wreak vengeance for the destruction of his temple (Jer. 50:28). God's temple or sanctuary is where he dwells with his people. Originally it was the garden of Eden, then the tabernacle in the wilderness. A sanctuary was built at Shiloh and then, eventually, in Jerusalem. The Babylonians' destruction of this temple could never go unpunished. The prophets also look forward to a new temple in a new Eden (Isa. 2:2–4; Ezekiel 40–47; Zechariah 4), and a new creation (Isa. 65:17–25). Jesus is shown to be that dwelling place of God with us: Immanuel (Isa. 7:14; Matt. 1:21–23). The destruction of *that* temple is doubly culpable, for wicked people crucified the Lord of glory (John 2:19–22; Acts 2:23–28; 1 Cor. 2:8). By coming to the true temple, Christians themselves are built into a spiritual house as God dwells with us by his Spirit (1 Cor. 3:16–17; Eph. 2:19–22; 1 Pet. 2:4–6).

The final biblical word regarding the temple is in Revelation 21:22: "And I saw no temple in the city, for its temple is the Lord God the Almighty and the Lamb."

50:33–34 The oppression of God's people in the Old Testament is the outward expression of the captivity of Adam's fallen race to sin, Satan, and death. A strong Redeemer pleads their cause. This advocacy indicates that their oppression is self-inflicted and they are guilty. "We have an advocate with the Father, Jesus Christ the righteous" (1 John 2:1). God is on the side of his people, and this is the winning side! That Jesus makes intercession for us (Rom. 8:31–34; Heb. 7:25) means that a strong Savior has conquered our foe to redeem us, and none can condemn us before God.

Reflecting on this great deliverance, we follow our Savior out of a heart transformed by his mercy rather than out of mere obligation or joyless duty.

hosts is his name. [v]He will surely plead their
cause, that he may give rest to the earth, but
unrest to the inhabitants of Babylon.

35 "A sword against the Chaldeans, declares the LORD,
and against the inhabitants of Babylon,
and against [w]her officials and her [x]wise men!
36 A sword against the diviners,
that they may become fools!
A sword against her [y]warriors,
that they may be destroyed!
37 A sword against her horses and against her chariots,
and against all [z]the foreign troops in her midst,
that [a]they may become women!
[b]A sword against all her treasures,
that they may be plundered!
38 [c]A drought against her waters,
that they may be dried up!
[d]For it is a land of images,
and they are mad over idols.

39 [e]"Therefore wild beasts shall dwell with
hyenas in Babylon, and ostriches shall dwell in
her. She shall never again have people, nor be
inhabited for all generations. 40 [f]As when God
overthrew Sodom and Gomorrah and their
neighboring cities, declares the LORD, [g]so no
man shall dwell there, and no son of man shall
sojourn in her.

41 [h]"Behold, a people comes from the north;
a mighty nation and many kings
are stirring from the farthest parts of the earth.
42 They lay hold of bow and spear;
they are cruel and have no mercy.
The sound of them is like the roaring of the sea;
they ride on horses,
arrayed as a man for battle
against you, O daughter of Babylon!
43 "The king of Babylon heard the report of them,
and his hands fell helpless;
anguish seized him,
pain as of a woman in labor.

44 [i]"Behold, like a lion coming up from
the thicket of the Jordan against a perennial pasture, I will suddenly make them run
away from her, and I will appoint over her
whomever I choose. For who is like me? Who
will summon me? What shepherd [j]can stand
before me? 45 Therefore hear [k]the plan that
the LORD has made against Babylon, [k]and
the purposes that he has formed against the
land of the Chaldeans: [l]Surely the little ones
of their flock shall be dragged away; surely
their fold shall be appalled at their fate. 46 [m]At
the sound of the capture of Babylon the earth
shall tremble, and her cry shall be heard
among the nations."

The Utter Destruction of Babylon

51 Thus says the LORD:
"Behold, I will stir up [n]the spirit of a destroyer
against Babylon,
against the inhabitants of Leb-kamai,[1]
2 and I will send to Babylon winnowers,
and [o]they shall winnow her,
and they shall empty her land,
when they come against her from every side
[p]on the day of trouble.
3 [q]Let not the archer bend his bow,
and let him not stand up in his armor.
Spare not her young men;
[r]devote to destruction[2] all her army.
4 They shall fall down slain in the land of the Chaldeans,
[s]and wounded in her streets.
5 [t]For Israel and Judah have not been forsaken
by their God, the LORD of hosts,
but the land of the Chaldeans[3] is full of guilt
against the Holy One of Israel.
6 [u]"Flee from the midst of Babylon;
let every one save his life!

[1] A code name for Chaldea [2] That is, set apart (devote) as an offering to the Lord (for destruction) [3] Hebrew *their land*

51:6, 45 The time would come, with Babylon's impending doom, that God's exiled people would have to come away from her (Isa. 48:20). There will be an end to the assurances of Jeremiah 29 that God's purposes for good lie in Babylon. God's plan is

34[v] ch. 51:36; Isa. 51:22 **35**[w] ch. 51:57; Dan. 5:30 [x] Dan. 4:6 **36**[y] ch. 51:57

37[z] See ch. 25:20 [a] ch. 51:30 [b] [Isa. 45:3] **38**[c] Isa. 44:27; [ch. 51:36] [d] ver. 2; ch. 51:47, 52 **39**[e] Isa. 13:21, 22 **40**[f] Gen. 19:25; See Isa. 13:19 [g] ch. 51:43 **41**[h] For ver. 41-43, see ch. 6:22-24 **44**[i] For ver. 44-46, see ch. 49:19-21 [j] Job 41:10 **45**[k] ch. 51:11, 12, 29; Isa. 14:24 [l] ch. 49:20 **46**[m] See ch. 49:21 **Chapter 51** **1**[n] [ch. 4:11; Isa. 21:1] **2**[o] [Matt. 3:12]; See ch. 15:7 [p] [ch. 2:28] **3**[q] [ch. 50:14, 29] [r] [ch. 50:21] **4**[s] ch. 49:26 **5**[t] See Isa. 54:5-7 **6**[u] ver. 45; ch. 50:8

[v]Be not cut off in her punishment,
[w]for this is the time of the LORD's vengeance,
the repayment he is rendering her.
7 Babylon was [x]a golden cup in the LORD's hand,
[y]making all the earth drunken;
[z]the nations drank of her wine;
therefore the nations went mad.
8 [a]Suddenly Babylon has fallen and been broken;
[b]wail for her!
[c]Take balm for her pain;
perhaps she may be healed.
9 We would have healed Babylon,
but she was not healed.
[d]Forsake her, and [e]let us go
each to his own country,
for [f]her judgment has reached up to heaven
and has been lifted up even to the skies.
10 [g]The LORD has brought about our vindication;
[h]come, let us declare in Zion
the work of the LORD our God.

11 [i]"Sharpen the arrows!
Take up the shields!

[j]The LORD has stirred up the spirit of the kings
of [k]the Medes, because [l]his purpose concerning Babylon is to destroy it, [m]for that is the
vengeance of the LORD, the vengeance for [m]his
temple.

12 [n]"Set up a standard against the walls of Babylon;
[o]make the watch strong;
set up watchmen;
prepare the ambushes;
[l]for the LORD has both planned and done
what he spoke concerning the inhabitants of Babylon.
13 [p]O you who dwell by many waters,
rich in treasures,
your end has come;
the thread of your life is cut.
14 [q]The LORD of hosts has sworn by himself:
Surely I will fill you with men, [r]as many as locusts,
[s]and they shall raise the shout of victory over you.

15 [t]"It is he who made the earth by his power,
who established the world by his wisdom,
and by his understanding stretched out the heavens.
16 When he utters his voice there is a tumult of waters in the heavens,
and he makes the mist rise from the ends of the earth.

6[v] [Gen. 19:15] [w]ch. 50:15
7[x] [Ps. 75:8; Rev. 17:4] [y]Rev. 14:8 [z]See ch. 25:15, 16
8[a] See Isa. 21:9 [b]Isa. 13:6; Rev. 18:9, 11, 19; [ch. 48:20] [c][ch. 46:11]
9[d] ver. 6, 45; ch. 50:8 [e][ch. 50:16]; See Isa. 13:14 [f]Rev. 18:5
10[g] Ps. 37:6; [ch. 23:6] [h]ch. 50:28
11[i] ch. 46:4 [j]See Isa. 13:17 [k]2 Kgs. 17:6; Dan. 5:31 [l][ch. 50:45] [m]ch. 50:28
12[n] ver. 27; ch. 50:2; [Isa. 13:2] [o][Isa. 21:5; Nah. 2:1] [l][See ver. 11 above]
13[p] Rev. 17:1, 15; [ver. 36]
14[q] See ch. 22:5 [r][Ps. 105:34; Joel 1:4; 2:25] [s]Isa. 16:9
15[t] For ver. 15-19, see ch. 10:12-16

to save his people out of the evil world, and the return of the exiles to the Promised Land would foreshadow the ultimate release from exile. Paul alludes to these words of Jeremiah in calling on Christians to avoid the uncleanness of the present age (2 Cor. 6:14–18; see also Rev. 18:4).

51:8–11 There will be a time of sudden destruction for Babylon (v. 8). Words of this passage have a familiar ring for New Testament believers who know that judgment comes like a thief in the night (Matt. 24:43–44). But the destruction of Babylon also set up providential events that resulted in the return of God's people to the Promised Land (see Dan. 5:30; 6:28; 2 Chron. 36:22–23; Ezra 1:1–3). Thus, we are also reminded of another pattern: the vindication (justification) of God's people is the "flip side" of judgment (Jer. 51:10). Not only is evil overthrown, but God's people are freed from their tribulation at the hands of their enemies. So also when Jesus conquered our enemies, he "led a host of captives" but gave "gifts" of salvation, edification, and witness to his people (Eph. 4:8).

For Jeremiah, the focal point of judgment on sin is the destruction of the temple, yet God appointed godless Babylon to do it. In the same way it was by "the definite plan and foreknowledge of God" that lawless people crucified Jesus (Acts 2:23), who would rise as the new temple (John 2:19–22). God's vengeance for his temple (Jer. 51:11) is yet to come in its fullness (Rev. 11:15–19; 15:5–8).

51:15–19 God's wisdom and power are seen in creation (v. 15; see Job 38:1–11; Prov. 8:22–36). By contrast, worldly wisdom, by which people create their idols, is stupidity (Jer. 51:17). Wisdom in Israel flowered when Solomon's kingdom was at its height (1 Kings 3–10). But it also was corrupted along with true religion (Jer. 18:18; Isa. 29:13–14; 47:10). Worldly wisdom is actually the height of folly, while it deems God's

He makes lightning for the rain,
and he brings forth the wind from his storehouses.
17 Every man is stupid and without knowledge;
every goldsmith is put to shame by his idols,
for his images are false,
and there is no breath in them.
18 They are worthless, a work of delusion;
at the time of their punishment they shall perish.
19 Not like these is he who is the portion of Jacob,
for he is the one who formed all things,
and Israel is the tribe of his inheritance;
the LORD of hosts is his name.

20 "You are my hammer and weapon of war:
with you I [u]break nations in pieces;
with you I destroy kingdoms;
21 with you I break in pieces the horse and his rider;
with you I break in pieces the chariot and the charioteer;
22 with you I break in pieces man and woman;
with you I break in pieces [v]the old man and the youth;
with you I break in pieces [v]the young man and the young woman;
23 with you I break in pieces the shepherd and his flock;
with you I break in pieces the farmer and his team;
with you I break in pieces [w]governors and commanders.

24 [x]"I will repay Babylon and all the inhabitants of Chaldea before your very eyes for all the evil that they have done in Zion, declares the LORD.

25 "Behold, I am against you, O destroying mountain,
declares the LORD,
which destroys the whole earth;
I will stretch out my hand against you,
and roll you down from the crags,
[y]and make you a burnt mountain.
26 No [z]stone shall be taken from you for a corner
and no stone for a foundation,
but you shall be [a]a perpetual waste,
declares the LORD.

27 [b]"Set up a standard on the earth;
[c]blow the trumpet among the nations;
[d]prepare [e]the nations for war against her;
summon against her [f]the kingdoms,
[g]Ararat, Minni, and [h]Ashkenaz;
appoint a [i]marshal against her;
[j]bring up horses like bristling locusts.
28 [d]Prepare [e]the nations for war against her,
the kings of [k]the Medes, [l]with their governors [l]and deputies,
and every [m]land under their dominion.
29 [n]The land trembles and writhes in pain,
[o]for the LORD's purposes against Babylon stand,
to make the land of Babylon a desolation,
without inhabitant.
30 The warriors of Babylon have ceased fighting;
they remain in their strongholds;
their strength has failed;
[p]they have become women;
[q]her dwellings are on fire;
[r]her bars are broken.
31 One [s]runner runs to meet another,
and one messenger to meet another,
to tell the king of Babylon
that his city is taken on every side;
32 the fords have been [t]seized,
the marshes are burned with fire,
and the soldiers are in panic.
33 For thus says the LORD of hosts, the God of Israel:
[u]The daughter of Babylon is like [u]a threshing floor
at the time when it is trodden;
yet a little while
and [v]the time of her harvest will come."

wisdom to be foolishness (1 Cor. 1:18–31). In 1 Corinthians 1:31, Paul cites Jeremiah 9:23–24 and applies it to the Christian. We boast in the Lord, for we find true wisdom in Christ who is our wisdom.

20[u] [Dan. 7:7, 19, 23]
22[v] 2 Chr. 36:17; [Isa. 13:16, 18]
23[w] ver. 28, 57
24[x] ch. 50:15, 29; [Ps. 137:8]

25[y] Rev. 8:8; [Rev. 18:8, 9] **26**[z] [Ps. 118:22; Isa. 28:16] [a] ver. 62; ch. 25:12 **27**[b] See ver. 12 [c] See ch. 4:5 [d] See ch. 6:4 [e] See ch. 25:14 [f] [ch. 50:41] [g] Gen. 8:4; 2 Kgs. 19:37 [h] Gen. 10:3; 1 Chr. 1:6 [i] Nah. 3:17 [j] See ver. 14 **28**[d] [See ver. 27 above] [e] [See ver. 27 above] [k] See ver. 11 [l] ver. 23, 57 [m] [ch. 34:1] **29**[n] See ch. 8:16 [o] ch. 50:45 **30**[p] ch. 50:37; [Isa. 19:16] [q] Isa. 47:14 [r] Lam. 2:9; Nah. 3:13 **31**[s] [2 Chr. 30:6] **32**[t] ver. 41 **33**[u] See Isa. 21:10 [v] [Isa. 17:5; Joel 3:13; Rev. 14:15]

34 “Nebuchadnezzar the king of Babylon
[w]has devoured me;
he has crushed me;
he has made me an empty vessel;
[x]he has swallowed me like [y]a monster;
he has filled his stomach with my delicacies;
he has rinsed me out.[1]
35 The violence done to me and to my kinsmen be upon Babylon,”
let the inhabitant of Zion say.
“My blood be upon the inhabitants of Chaldea,”
let Jerusalem say.
36 Therefore thus says the LORD:
“Behold, [z]I will plead your cause
and take vengeance for you.
[a]I will dry up her sea
and [b]make her fountain dry,
37 and Babylon shall become [c]a heap of ruins,
[d]the haunt of jackals,
[e]a horror [e]and a hissing,
without inhabitant.

38 [f]“They shall roar together [g]like lions;
they shall growl like lions’ cubs.
39 [h]While they are inflamed [h]I will prepare them a feast
and [i]make them drunk, that they may become merry,
[i]then sleep a perpetual sleep
and not wake, declares the LORD.
40 I will bring them down like lambs to the slaughter,
like rams and male goats.

41 “How [j]Babylon[2] is taken,
[k]the praise of the whole earth [l]seized!
How Babylon has become
a horror among the nations!
42 [m]The sea has come up on Babylon;
she is covered with its tumultuous waves.
43 Her cities have become a horror,
[n]a land of drought and a desert,
[o]a land in which no one dwells,
and through which no son of man passes.
44 And I will punish [p]Bel in Babylon,
and [q]take out of his mouth [r]what he has swallowed.
[s]The nations shall no longer flow to him;
[t]the wall of Babylon has fallen.

45 “Go out of the midst of her, [u]my people!
Let every one save his life
from [v]the fierce anger of the LORD!
46 Let not your heart faint, and be not fearful
[w]at the report heard in the land,
[x]when a report comes in one year
and afterward a report in another year,
and violence is in the land,
[x]and ruler is against ruler.

47 “Therefore, behold, the days are coming
when [y]I will punish the images of Babylon;
[z]her whole land shall be put to shame,
and all her slain shall fall in the midst of her.
48 [a]Then the heavens and the earth,
and all that is in them,
shall sing for joy over Babylon,
[b]for the destroyers shall come against them out of the north,
declares the LORD.
49 Babylon must fall for the slain of Israel,
[c]just as for Babylon have fallen the slain of all the earth.

50 [d]“You who have escaped from the sword,
go, do not stand still!
Remember the LORD from far away,
and let Jerusalem come into your mind:
51 [e]‘We are put to shame, for we have heard reproach;
[e]dishonor has covered our face,
[f]for foreigners have come
into the holy places of the LORD’s house.’

52 “Therefore, behold, the days are coming,
declares the LORD,
when [y]I will execute judgment upon her images,
[g]and through all her land
the wounded shall groan.

[1] Or *he has expelled me* [2] Hebrew *Sheshach*, a code name for Babylon

34[w] ch. 50:17 [x] ver. 44 [y] Ps. 74:13 **36**[z] ch. 50:34 [a] Isa. 44:27; [ch. 50:38] [b] [ver. 13] **37**[c] Isa. 25:2 [d] Isa. 13:22 [e] See ch. 18:16 **38**[f] [Amos 3:4] [g] Nah. 2:11, 12 **39**[h] [Isa. 21:5] [i] ver. 57 **41**[j] ch. 25:26 [k] [Isa. 13:19] [l] ver. 32 **42**[m] [ver. 55; Isa. 8:7, 8] **43**[n] ch. 50:12 [o] ch. 50:40 **44**[p] ch. 50:2; See Isa. 46:1 [q] ver. 34; [Ezra 1:7, 8] [r] ver. 34 [s] [ch. 31:12; Isa. 2:2] [t] ver. 58 **45**[u] See ver. 6 [v] See ch. 12:13 **46**[w] [Isa. 37:7] [x] Matt. 24:6, 7 **47**[y] [ch. 50:2] [z] [ch. 50:12] **48**[a] [Rev. 18:20]; See Isa. 44:23 [b] ch. 50:3 **49**[c] [ver. 24] **50**[d] [ch. 44:28] **51**[e] ch. 7:19; Ps. 44:15, 16 [f] Lam. 1:10 **52**[y] [See ver. 47 above] [g] Job 24:12; Ezek. 26:15

53 Though Babylon should [h]mount up to heaven,
and though she should [i]fortify her strong height,
yet destroyers would come from me against her,
declares the LORD.

54 [j]"A voice! A cry from Babylon!
The noise of great destruction from the land of the Chaldeans!
55 For the LORD is laying Babylon waste
and stilling her mighty voice.
[k]Their waves roar like many waters;
the noise of their voice is raised,
56 for a destroyer has come upon her,
upon Babylon;
her warriors are taken;
their bows are broken in pieces,
[l]for the LORD is a God of recompense;
he will surely repay.
57 [m]I will make drunk her officials and her wise men,
[n]her governors, her commanders, and her warriors;
they shall sleep a perpetual sleep and not wake,
declares [o]the King, whose name is the LORD of hosts.

58 "Thus says the LORD of hosts:
The broad [p]wall of Babylon
shall be leveled to the ground,
[q]and her high gates
shall be burned with fire.
[r]The peoples labor for nothing,
and [s]the nations weary themselves
only for fire."

59 The word that Jeremiah the prophet
commanded Seraiah [t]the son of Neriah, son
of Mahseiah, when he went with Zedekiah
king of Judah to Babylon, [u]in the fourth year
of his reign. Seraiah was the quartermaster.
60 [v]Jeremiah wrote in a book all the disaster
that should come upon Babylon, [w]all these
words that are written concerning Babylon.
61 And Jeremiah said to Seraiah: "When you
come to Babylon, see that you read all these
words, 62 and say, 'O LORD, you have said concerning this place that you will cut it off, so
[x]that nothing shall dwell in it, neither man
nor beast, and it shall be [y]desolate forever.'
63 When you finish reading this book, [z, a]tie
a stone to it [z]and cast it into the midst of the
Euphrates, 64 and say, [z]'Thus shall Babylon
sink, to rise no more, because of the disaster
that I am bringing upon her, [b]and they shall
become exhausted.'"

Thus far are the words of Jeremiah.

The Fall of Jerusalem Recounted

52 [c]Zedekiah was twenty-one years old
when he became king, and he reigned
eleven years in Jerusalem. His mother's name
was Hamutal the daughter of Jeremiah of
Libnah. 2 And he did what was evil in the sight
of the LORD, [d]according to all that Jehoiakim
had done. 3 For because of the anger of the
LORD it came to the point in Jerusalem and
Judah that he cast them out from his presence.
And Zedekiah rebelled against the king of
Babylon. 4 [e]And in the ninth year of his reign,
in the tenth month, on the tenth day of the
month, Nebuchadnezzar king of Babylon
came with all his army against Jerusalem, and
laid siege to it. And they built siegeworks all
around it. 5 So the city was besieged till the
eleventh year of King Zedekiah. 6 On the ninth
day of the fourth month the famine was so
severe in the city that there was no food for the
people of the land. 7 Then a breach was made in
the city, and all the men of war fled and went
out from the city by night by the way of a gate
between the two walls, by the king's garden,
and the Chaldeans were around the city. And

52:1–34 The last chapter of Jeremiah contains a summary of the history of Judah and Jerusalem as the axe falls. The only reference to God's acting in this chapter is in verse 3. But the whole chapter is an account of the judgment of the Lord in action as the Babylonians bring total destruction even to the Lord's house (v. 13). We are reminded here, as in the rest of the book, that human rebellion may flourish for a time even in the context of God's covenant mercies, but that flourishing will have an end. As in Moses' day (1 Cor. 10:1–5), and in Jeremiah's day, so it was in the time of Jesus: evil had its day. But God always has the final say over the course of human events. There is no greater evidence of his sovereign superintendence than in Jesus. For in him we see supremely that when God's greatest gift was despised and rejected, as people sought to forge their own history, God was at the same time providing for his people's eternal destiny.

53 [h][ver. 25]; See Isa. 14:13 [i][ch. 49:16]
54 [j]ch. 50:22
55 [k][ver. 42]; See ch. 5:22
56 [l]ch. 50:15; Isa. 59:18
57 [m]ver. 39 [n]ver. 23, 28 [o]See ch. 46:18
58 [p]ver. 44; ch. 50:15 [q][Isa. 45:2] [r]Hab. 2:13 [s]ver. 64
59 [t][ch. 32:12] [u][ch. 28:1]
60 [v][ch. 36:2] [w]See ver. 1-58; ch. 50:1-46
62 [x]ch. 50:3 [y]ver. 26
63 [z][ch. 19:10, 11] [a][Rev. 18:21]
64 [z][See ver. 63 above] [b]ver. 58

Chapter 52 **1** [c]For ver. 1-27, see 2 Kgs. 24:18–25:21 **2** [d]2 Kgs. 23:37; See ch. 22:13-17 **4** [e]For ver. 4-16, see ch. 39:1-10

they went in the direction of the Arabah. 8 But
the army of the Chaldeans pursued the king
and overtook Zedekiah in the plains of Jericho,
and all his army was scattered from him.
9 Then they captured the king and brought
him up to the king of Babylon at Riblah in
the land of Hamath, and he passed sentence
on him. 10 The king of Babylon slaughtered
the sons of Zedekiah before his eyes, and also
slaughtered all the officials of Judah at [f]Riblah.
11 [g]He put out the eyes of Zedekiah, and bound
him in chains, and the king of Babylon took
him to Babylon, and put him in prison [g]till the
day of his death.

The Temple Burned

12 [h]In the fifth month, on [i]the tenth day of
the month—that was [j]the nineteenth year
of King Nebuchadnezzar, king of Babylon—
Nebuzaradan the captain of the bodyguard,
who [k]served the king of Babylon, entered
Jerusalem. 13 And he burned the house of the
LORD, and the king's house and all the houses
of Jerusalem; every great house he burned
down. 14 And all the army of the Chaldeans,
who were with the captain of the guard, broke
down all the walls around Jerusalem. 15 And
Nebuzaradan the captain of the guard carried
away captive some of the poorest of the people and the rest of the people who were left in
the city and [l]the deserters who had deserted
to the king of Babylon, together with the
rest of the artisans. 16 But Nebuzaradan the
captain of the guard left some of the poorest
of the land to be vinedressers and plowmen.

17 And the [m]pillars of bronze that were in
the house of the LORD, and the stands and
the [n]bronze sea that were in the house of the
LORD, the Chaldeans broke in pieces, and [o]car-
ried all the bronze to Babylon. 18 And they
took away [p]the pots and the shovels and the
snuffers and the basins and the dishes for
incense and all the vessels of bronze used in
the temple service; 19 [q]also the small bowls
and the fire pans and the basins and the
pots and [r]the lampstands and [s]the dishes for
incense [s]and the bowls for drink offerings.
What was of gold the captain of the guard
took away as gold, and what was of silver, as
silver. 20 As for the two pillars, the one sea, [t]the
twelve bronze bulls that were under the sea,[1]
and the stands, which Solomon the king had
made for the house of the LORD, the bronze
of all these things was beyond weight. 21 As
for the pillars, the height of the one pillar
was eighteen cubits,[2] [u]its circumference was
twelve cubits, and its thickness was four fingers, and it was hollow. 22 On it was a capital of
bronze. The height of the one capital was [v]five
cubits. A network and pomegranates, all of
bronze, were around the capital. And the second pillar had the same, with pomegranates.
23 There were ninety-six pomegranates on the
sides; all the pomegranates were a hundred
upon the network all around.

The People Exiled to Babylon

24 And the captain of the guard took
[w]Seraiah the chief priest, and [x]Zephaniah
the second priest and the three keepers of
the threshold; 25 and from the city he took an
officer who had been in command of the men
of war, and [y]seven men of the king's council,
who were found in the city; and the secretary
of the commander of the army, who mustered the people of the land; and sixty men
of the people of the land, who were found in
the midst of the city. 26 And Nebuzaradan the
captain of the guard took them and brought
them to the king of Babylon at [z]Riblah. 27 And
the king of Babylon struck them down and
put them to death at [z]Riblah in the land of
Hamath. So Judah was taken into exile out
of its land.

28 This is the number of the people whom
Nebuchadnezzar carried away captive: [a]in the

[1] Hebrew lacks *the sea* [2] A *cubit* was about 18 inches or 45 centimeters

10 [f]ver. 26, 27
11 [g][Ezek. 12:13]
12 [h]ch. 1:3 [i][2 Kgs. 25:8] [j][ver. 29] [k]ch. 40:10
15 [l]See ch. 37:13
17 [m]ch. 27:19; See 2 Chr. 4:12-15 [n]2 Chr. 4:2, 10 [o]See ch. 27:22
18 [p]2 Kgs. 25:14
19 [q]1 Kgs. 7:50; 2 Kgs. 25:15 [r]1 Kgs. 7:49 [s]Ex. 25:29; 37:16
20 [t]1 Kgs. 7:25, 44

Jeremiah reminds us that we need a history and a destiny built on the one whose name is "The LORD is our righteousness" (Jer. 23:5–6; 33:14–16). Jesus came to live a new personal history for each of his own—a history that is presentable before God as our righteousness. He came also to pay the penalty for our failed, rebellious histories, so that our destiny would be eternally with him. The histories of the last kings of Judah limp to their ignominious endings. So will our personal histories crumble before the wrath to come without a Mediator. Only the righteousness of God applied to our lives through faith in Jesus Christ, which we receive as a gift, will survive on that day (Rom. 3:21–26).

21 [u]1 Kgs. 7:15 **22** [v]1 Kgs. 7:16; [2 Kgs. 25:17] **24** [w][1 Chr. 6:14, 15] [x][ch. 29:25] **25** [y][Esth. 1:14] **26** [z]ver. 9, 10 **27** [z][See ver. 26 above] **28** [a][2 Kgs. 24:12, 14]

seventh year, 3,023 Judeans; 29 [b]in the eighteenth year of Nebuchadnezzar he carried
away captive from Jerusalem 832 persons;
30 in the twenty-third year of Nebuchadnezzar,
Nebuzaradan the captain of the guard carried
away captive of the Judeans 745 persons; all
the persons were 4,600.

Jehoiachin Released from Prison

31 [c]And in the thirty-seventh year of the exile
of Jehoiachin king of Judah, in the twelfth
month, on the twenty-fifth day of the month,
Evil-merodach king of Babylon, in the year
that he began to reign, graciously freed[1]
[d]Jehoiachin king of Judah and brought him
out of prison. 32 And he spoke kindly to him
and gave him a seat above the seats of [e]the
kings who were with him in Babylon. 33 So
Jehoiachin put off his prison garments. And
every day of his life he dined regularly at the
king's table, 34 and for his allowance, a regular
allowance was given him by the king, according to his daily needs, until the day of his
death, as long as he lived.

[1] Hebrew *king, lifted up the head of*

29[b] [ver. 12] **31**[c] For ver. 31-34, see 2 Kgs. 25:27-30 [d] ch. 37:1; See ch. 22:24-30 **32**[e] [ch. 27:3]

Introduction to Lamentations

Author and Date

The author of this literary masterpiece is unknown. Lamentations provides eyewitness testimony in vivid, poetic detail of Babylon's destruction of Jerusalem in 586 B.C. It was likely written between 586 and 516 B.C.

The Gospel in Lamentations

The Old Testament is dominated by the covenant of grace established with sinners in a fallen world. Aspects of this covenant received initial expression prior to and including the time of Noah, but the most explicit communication of its nature and benefits was given to Abraham (Gen. 12:1–3; 15:1–6; 17:1–21; cf. Ex. 2:24–25). The covenant's redemptive grace was demonstrated in Israel's exodus from Egypt. The administration of the covenant at Sinai added instruction for the redeemed nation's life with God. This covenant administration required faithful obedience for blessings to flow, but warned of covenant curses and judgment if the people forsook the Lord (e.g., Deuteronomy 27–28). Later, possession of the Promised Land was crowned with the establishment of the kingship of David. Through him God extended a covenant promise of an eternal throne, and the building of a permanent temple in the holy city of Zion (Jerusalem) signified God's abiding presence among his people.

The culmination of covenant promises relating to Zion resulted in the city being regarded as sacred and inviolable (e.g., Psalms 46; 48; 87; Isaiah 37). Yet the history recorded from 1 Kings 11 to 2 Kings 25 tells of the relentless decline of Judah into apostasy and covenant unfaithfulness. The historical record relates the awful judgment of God through the destruction of the nation, the city, the temple, and the kingship. In 586 B.C. every outward and visible symbol of God's presence with Judah was reduced to rubble. Out of the smoking ruins came cries of lamentation and confession, and the daring hope of restoration.

Lamentations focuses on the suffering of Judah, Jerusalem, and the Jews at the hands of the Babylonians. Its five poems form a specific response to this particular event. Lamentations is, nevertheless, applicable at all times and in all places because of how it relates to the covenant developments that continue to touch all believers.

The book of Lamentations shows that God is a fierce enemy to those who trample on his word and despise his grace. But he is also rich in mercy and unfailingly faithful to his covenant promises. Somewhere, somehow, restoration will come. Not until the advent of Jesus Christ do we find the full resolution of the questions posed by this book.

Israel was chosen as a special people to bring redress to humanity's exile from Eden. The Promised Land and its focus in the city, the temple, and the kingship all reflect the original human story of Adam and Eve ruling in Eden with God and spreading that rule across the globe (Gen. 1:26–28). Jerusalem's destruction and the exile echo humankind's exile from Eden. Because of its own sin, Israel as God's servant could not put matters right. Thus, the divine remedy required the last Adam, the true Israel. Unlike the first Adam and first Israel, this One was without sin. He suffered vicariously an exile on the cross and in the grave so that he might demonstrate the faithfulness and righteousness of God toward those made in his image.

Lamentations is a confronting book, showing us the seriousness of rebellion against God. It spares no detail in revealing the radical sinfulness of sin and its awful consequences. But it also points beyond itself to the mercy of the God of the new covenant in Christ who, despite everything, fulfills God's covenant promises to his people, wayward though they are. For ultimately, this biblical book must be seen as Christ's cry from the cross, as he suffers for the sin Lamentations mourns.

Outline

I. How Lonely Sits the City (1:1–22)

II. God Has Set Zion under a Cloud (2:1–22)

III. I Am the Man Who Has Seen Affliction (3:1–66)

IV. How the Gold Has Grown Dim (4:1–22)

V. Restore Us to Yourself, O Lord (5:1–22)

Lamentations

How Lonely Sits the City

1 [a]How lonely sits the city
that was full of people!
How like [b]a widow has she become,
she who was great among the nations!
She who was [c]a princess among the provinces
has become [d]a slave.

2 [e]She weeps bitterly in the night,
with tears on her cheeks;
[f]among all her lovers
she has [g]none to comfort her;
[h]all her friends have dealt treacherously with her;
they have become her enemies.

3 [i]Judah has gone into exile because of affliction
and hard servitude;
[j]she dwells now among the nations,
[k]but finds no resting place;
her pursuers have all overtaken her
in the midst of her distress.[1]

4 The roads to Zion mourn,
for none come to [l]the festival;
[m]all her gates are desolate;
her priests [n]groan;
her virgins have been afflicted,[2]
and she herself suffers bitterly.

5 [o]Her foes have become the head;
her [p]enemies prosper,

[1] Or *in the narrow passes* [2] Septuagint, Old Latin *dragged away*

1:1–22 Lamentations consists of five distinct poems, corresponding to the five chapters in our English Bibles. The first four poems (chs. 1–4) are in acrostic form: the verses begin with successive letters of the Hebrew alphabet. Although the writer is close to the situation he describes, and writes with emotional intensity, the acrostic form provides bounds to his expression of grief and expresses the orderly comprehensiveness of his laments. This is suffering "from A to Z" (*aleph* to *tav* in Hebrew; cf. the form of Psalm 119).

The imagery of a widow, enslaved, comfortless, without dignity, taunted, exiled and desolate, paints a picture that is as bad as it can be (Lam. 1:1–5). In this humiliation there is no comfort such as that announced in Isaiah 40:1 or by Lamentations' contemporaries, the prophets Jeremiah, Ezekiel, and Daniel (Lam. 1:2, 9, 16, 17, 21). What is worse, it is the Lord himself who has afflicted Zion (vv. 5, 12, 14, 15, 17).

As to judgment, the writer shares the perspective of Deuteronomy 27–28 and 1 Kings 11 to 2 Kings 25. At this point, however, he seems oblivious to the promises of God. There is a lesson in this. It is necessary at times to contemplate the unmitigated horror of being forsaken by God and coming under his wrath. This in turn should bring us, as it would have brought the faithful few of Judah, to reflect on the utter sinfulness of our sin and our desperate need for repentance and rescue (Lam. 1:9, 11, 20).

The metaphors of uncleanness and nakedness (vv. 8, 9, 17) portray the radical nature of our moral revolt against God. The terrible reversal of fortune is a warning against ingratitude and against embracing other alliances in idolatry (v. 19). In the New Testament the notion of idolatry is extended to mean allegiance to anything detrimental to our relationship to Jesus—for example, covetousness (1 Cor. 5:9–11; Eph. 5:5; Col. 3:5; 1 John 5:20–21).

But is there a solution to this sense that God's promises are fragile and that there is no hope for redemption? Lamentations will point us to it later on. In the meantime, the writer's grief signifies a necessary stage in coming to embrace the prophetic hope

Chapter 1
1[a] [Jer. 7:34] [b] [Jer. 15:8] [c] [ch. 5:16; Ezra 4:20; Eccles. 2:8] [d] Isa. 31:8
2[e] Ps. 6:6; Jer. 9:1; 13:17 [f] ver. 19; Jer. 22:22; 30:14 [g] ver. 9, 16, 17, 21; Eccles. 4:1 [h] See Ezek. 23:22-26
3[i] Jer. 52:27 [j] [ch. 2:9; Deut. 28:64, 65] [k] Jer. 45:3
4[l] See ch. 2:6 [m] Jer. 14:2 [n] ver. 8, 11, 21, 22
5[o] [Deut. 28:13, 44; Jer. 13:21] [p] Jer. 12:1

because [q]the LORD has afflicted her
[r]for the multitude of her transgressions;
[s]her children have gone away,
captives before the foe.

6 From the daughter of Zion
all her majesty has departed.
Her princes have become like deer
[t]that find no pasture;
they fled without strength
before the pursuer.

7 Jerusalem remembers
in the days of her affliction and wandering
[u]all the precious things
that were hers from [v]days of old.
When her people fell into the hand of the foe,
and there was none to help her,
her foes gloated over her;
they [w]mocked at her downfall.

8 [x]Jerusalem sinned grievously;
therefore she became filthy;
all who honored her despise her,
[y]for they have seen her nakedness;
she herself [z]groans
and turns her face away.

9 Her uncleanness was [a]in her skirts;
[b]she took no thought of her future;[1]
therefore her fall is terrible;
[c]she has no comforter.
"O LORD, behold my affliction,
for the enemy has [d]triumphed!"

10 The enemy has stretched out his hands
over all her [e]precious things;
for she has seen [f]the nations
enter her sanctuary,
those whom you [g]forbade
to enter your congregation.

11 All her people [z]groan
as [h]they search for bread;
they trade their [e]treasures for [i]food
to revive their strength.
"Look, O LORD, and see,
for I am despised."

12 "Is it nothing to you, all [j]you who pass by?
[k]Look and see
if there is any sorrow like my sorrow,
which was brought upon me,
which [l]the LORD inflicted
on [m]the day of his fierce anger.

13 "From on high he [n]sent fire;
into my bones[2] he made it descend;
[o]he spread a net for my feet;
he turned me back;
[p]he has left me stunned,
faint all the day long.

14 "My transgressions were bound[3] into [q]a yoke;
by his hand they were fastened together;
they were set upon my neck;
he caused my strength to fail;
the Lord gave me into the hands
of those whom I cannot withstand.

15 "The Lord rejected
all my mighty men in my midst;
he summoned an assembly against me
to crush my young men;
[r]the Lord has trodden as in a winepress
the virgin daughter of Judah.

16 "For these things [s]I weep;
my eyes flow with tears;

[1] Or *end* [2] Septuagint; Hebrew *bones and* [3] The meaning of the Hebrew is uncertain

5[q] ver. 12; ch. 3:33 [r] Jer. 30:14, 15; Dan. 9:16 [s] 2 Chr. 36:17, 20; See Jer. 52:28-30
6[t] [Jer. 14:6]
7[u] ver. 10, 11 [v] ch. 2:17; Jer. 46:26 [w] Obad. 12, 13; [Ps. 119:51]
8[x] [Zech. 13:1] [y] [Ezek. 16:37] [z] ver. 4, 21, 22
9[a] [Jer. 13:22] [b] [Deut. 32:29; Isa. 47:7] [c] ver. 2 [d] Jer. 48:26
10[e] ver. 7 [f] Ps. 79:1; Jer. 51:51 [g] [Deut. 23:3; Neh. 13:1]
11[z] [See ver. 8 above] [h] ch. 2:12; 4:4; [Jer. 38:9; 52:6] [e] [See ver. 10 above] [i] ver. 19
12[j] Job 21:29; Ps. 80:12 [k] [Dan. 9:12] [l] ver. 5 [m] See Jer. 12:13
13[n] Ps. 102:3 [o] Ps. 9:15; Ezek. 12:13; 17:20 [p] ch. 3:11; See Jer. 8:18 **14**[q] Deut. 28:48 **15**[r] [Isa. 63:2, 3] **16**[s] See Jer. 13:17

that is fulfilled in Christ's suffering on the cross. The purpose of such grief is to lead us to true repentance and faith.

Ultimately, we see the seriousness of our rebellion against God when we see what he had to do in order to remedy the situation. The suffering of Zion foreshadows the suffering of Jesus on our behalf. Jesus' cry of desolation on the cross, "My God, my God, why have you forsaken me?" (Matt. 27:46; quoting Ps. 22:1), expresses the burden of our sin standing between him and the Father. We cannot fully understand the undeserved suffering of the sinless Son of the Father. But Lamentations shows us something of the horror of separation from God.

Grief, or a sense of spiritual deadness, can rob us of the realization of God's presence. But Jesus' disciples' feeling of disillusionment—"But we had hoped that he was the one to redeem Israel" (Luke 24:21)—was replaced by the joy of Christ's presence: "Did not our hearts burn within us while he talked to us on the road, while he opened to us the Scriptures?" (Luke 24:32).

for [t]a comforter is far from me,
one to [u]revive my spirit;
my children are desolate,
for the enemy has prevailed."

17 [v]Zion stretches out her hands,
but [t]there is none to comfort her;
the LORD has commanded against Jacob
that his neighbors should be his foes;
Jerusalem has become
a filthy thing among them.

18 [w]"The LORD is in the right,
[x]for I have rebelled against his word;
but hear, all you peoples,
and see my suffering;
[y]my young women and my young men
have gone into captivity.

19 "I called to [z]my lovers,
but they deceived me;
my priests and elders
perished in the city,
while [a]they sought food
to revive their strength.

20 "Look, O LORD, for I am in distress;
[b]my stomach churns;
my heart is wrung within me,
because I have been very rebellious.
[c]In the street the sword bereaves;
in the house it is like death.

21 "They heard[1] [d]my groaning,
yet [e]there is no one to comfort me.
All my enemies have heard of my trouble;
[f]they are glad that you have done it.
You have brought[2] the day you announced;
[f]now let them be as I am.

22 [g]"Let all their evildoing come before you,
and deal with them
as [h]you have dealt with me
because of all my transgressions;
for [d]my groans are many,
and [i]my heart is faint."

The Lord Has Destroyed Without Pity

2 How the Lord in his anger
has set the daughter of Zion [j]under a cloud!
[k]He has cast down from heaven to earth
the splendor of Israel;
he has not remembered [l]his footstool
in the day of his anger.

2 The Lord [m]has swallowed up [n]without mercy
all the habitations of Jacob;
in his wrath [o]he has broken down
the strongholds of the daughter of Judah;
he has brought [p]down to the ground [p]in dishonor
the kingdom [q]and its rulers.

3 He has cut down in [r]fierce anger
all [s]the might of Israel;
[t]he has withdrawn from them his right hand
in the face of the enemy;
[u]he has burned like a flaming fire in Jacob,
consuming all around.

[1] Septuagint, Syriac *Hear* [2] Syriac *Bring*

2:1–22 The unrelieved horror of this poem centers again on the theme of the reversal of fortune. But this time there is an added terrifying dimension. Whereas God had shown himself to Israel as the Warrior God who fought for his people to bring salvation and rest (Exodus 15; Deut. 20:4; 31:7–8; Ps. 24:8; Isa. 59:15b–20), now he has become Judah's enemy, the destroyer of the kingdom (Lam. 2:1–3). Here is the divine warrior fighting against his own people (vv. 4–5).

The writer reflects on the downfall of every tangible aspect of God's presence with his people: the land, the city (vv. 5, 8–9, 15–18), the temple (vv. 6–7), the nation (vv. 10–13, 19–22), and the kingship (vv. 6, 9). Furthermore, the official prophets have been false and have failed to speak God's word (vv. 9, 14). Even worse, the Lord has stopped revealing himself to them (v. 9; cf. Amos 8:11).

The emphasis on God's role in the destruction of Judah is seen especially in Lamentations 2:1–8, where he is the subject of almost every verb in this catalog of catastrophes. Similarly, Jesus was "delivered up according to the definite plan and foreknowledge of God" (Acts 2:23). In Lamentations 2:11–22, significantly, the writer identifies himself with Zion's suffering and describes his anguish at what he sees happening (vv. 11–17). The apostle Paul expresses something of this anguish as he contemplates the mystery of Jewish unbelief in the gospel (Rom. 9:1–5; 10:1–4).

16 [t]ver. 2, 21 [u][ver. 11]
17 [v]Isa. 1:15; Jer. 4:31 [t][See ver. 16 above]
18 [w]See Jer. 12:1 [x]1 Sam. 12:14, 15 [y][Deut. 28:41]
19 [z]See ver. 2 [a]ver. 11
20 [b]ch. 2:11; Job 30:27; Isa. 16:11 [c]Deut. 32:25; Ezek. 7:15; See Jer. 15:2
21 [d]ver. 4, 8, 11 [e]ver. 2, 16, 17 [f][ch. 4:21; Jer. 50:11]
22 [g]Ps. 109:14, 15 [h]ver. 12; ch. 2:20 [d][See ver. 21 above] [i]See Jer. 8:18

Chapter 2
1 [j][ch. 3:44] [k][Matt. 11:23]; See Isa. 14:15 [l]1 Chr. 28:2
2 [m]ver. 16; [Ps. 35:25; 56:2; Ezek. 36:3] [n]ver. 17, 21; ch. 3:43; [Ezek. 9:5, 10] [o]Ps. 89:40 [p]Ps. 74:7 [q]Isa. 43:28
3 [r]See Jer. 12:13 [s]1 Sam. 2:1 [t]Ps. 74:11 [u]Ps. 79:5; 89:46

4 [v]He has bent his bow like an enemy,
with his right hand set [w]like a foe;
and he has killed all who were delightful in our eyes
in the tent of the daughter of Zion;
he has poured out his fury like fire.

5 [w]The Lord has become like an enemy;
[x]he has swallowed up Israel;
[y]he has swallowed up all its palaces;
he has laid in ruins its strongholds,
and he has multiplied in the daughter of Judah
[z]mourning and lamentation.

6 He has laid waste his booth like a garden,
laid in ruins [a]his meeting place;
[a]the LORD has made Zion forget
festival and [b]Sabbath,
and in his fierce indignation has
spurned king and priest.

7 [c]The Lord has scorned his altar,
[d]disowned his sanctuary;
[e]he has delivered into the hand of the enemy
the walls of her palaces;
[f]they raised a clamor in the house of the LORD
as on the day of festival.

8 [g]The LORD determined to lay in ruins
[h]the wall of the daughter of Zion;
[i]he stretched out the measuring line;
he did not restrain his hand from destroying;
[j]he caused rampart and wall to lament;
[j]they languished together.

9 Her gates have sunk into the ground;
[k]he has ruined [k]and broken her bars;
[l]her king and princes are among the nations;
the law is no more,
and [m]her prophets find
no vision from the LORD.

10 The elders of the daughter of Zion
[n]sit on the ground [o]in silence;
[p]they have thrown dust on their heads
and [q]put on sackcloth;
the young women of Jerusalem
have bowed their heads to the ground.

11 [r]My eyes are spent with weeping;
[s]my stomach churns;
[t]my bile is poured out to the ground
[u]because of the destruction of the daughter of my people,
[v]because infants and babies [w]faint
in the streets of the city.

12 They cry to their mothers,
[x]"Where is bread and wine?"
[w]as they faint like a wounded man
in the streets of the city,
as their life is poured out
on their mothers' bosom.

13 What can I say for you, [y]to what compare you,
O daughter of Jerusalem?
[y]What can I liken to you, that I may comfort you,
O virgin daughter of Zion?
[z]For your ruin is vast as the sea;
who can heal you?

14 [a]Your prophets have seen for you
false and deceptive visions;
[b]they have not exposed your iniquity
to [c]restore your fortunes,
[d]but have seen for you [e]oracles
that are false and misleading.

15 All who pass along the way
clap their hands at you;
[f]they hiss and wag their heads
at the daughter of Jerusalem:
"Is this the city that was called
[g]the perfection of beauty,
[g]the joy of all the earth?"

4[v]ch. 3:12 [w]See Jer. 30:14
5[w][See ver. 4 above] [x]ver. 16; [Ps. 35:25; 56:2; Ezek. 36:3] [y][2 Kgs. 25:9] [z]Isa. 29:2
6[a]ch. 1:4; Isa. 1:13; Zeph. 3:18 [b]Isa. 1:13
7[c][Ps. 89:38] [d][Ezek. 24:21] [e]Deut. 32:30 [f]Ps. 74:4
8[g][Jer. 5:10] [h]ver. 18 [i]See 2 Kgs. 21:13 [j]Jer. 14:2
9[k]Jer. 51:30; Nah. 3:13 [l][Hos. 3:4] [m]Ps. 74:9

The climax of this complaint in Lamentations is that the entire debacle is what God had determined and had revealed in his words of warning to his people (Lam. 2:17). To be sure, the Babylonian was the destroyer, but only as the agent of Yahweh. It is God himself who alone determines the course of world history. The principle character in the drama of Scripture is God, who "works all things according to the counsel of his will" (Eph. 1:11). Our poet longs for his people to turn back to God (Lam. 2:18–19) and, in doing so, he foreshadows the grief of Jesus as he weeps over Jerusalem (Matt. 23:37–39; Luke 23:28). But he sees the day of the Lord only as the day of his anger (Lam. 2:21–22).

10[n]ch. 1:1; 3:28; Isa. 3:26 [o]Ezek. 3:15 [p]See Josh. 7:6 [q]Jer. 48:37; Ezek. 7:18; Amos 8:10; See Jer. 4:8 **11**[r][ver. 18; ch. 5:17; Ps. 6:7] [s]See ch. 1:20 [t][Job 16:13] [u]ch. 3:48 [v][ch. 4:4; Jer. 44:7] [w]ver. 19; [Isa. 51:20] **12**[x]See ch. 1:11 [w][See ver. 11 above] **13**[y][ch. 1:12] [z]2 Sam. 5:20; [Ezek. 26:3] **14**[a]See Jer. 5:31 [b][Isa. 58:1] [c]See Jer. 30:3 [d]See Jer. 5:31 [e][Jer. 23:33, 34] **15**[f]See 2 Chr. 29:8 [g]Ps. 48:2; Ezek. 16:14

16 [h]All your enemies
rail against you;
they hiss, they gnash their teeth,
they cry: "We [i]have swallowed her!
Ah, this is the day we longed for;
now we have it; [j]we see it!"

17 The LORD has done what he purposed;
he has carried out [k]his word,
which he commanded [l]long ago;
[m]he has thrown down [n]without pity;
[o]he has made the enemy rejoice over you
and exalted the [p]might of your foes.

18 Their heart cried to the Lord.
O [q]wall of the daughter of Zion,
[r]let tears stream down like a torrent
[s]day and night!
[t]Give yourself no rest,
[u]your eyes no respite!

19 "Arise, [v]cry out in the night,
at the beginning of the night
watches!
[w]Pour out your heart like water
before the presence of the Lord!
[x]Lift your hands to him
for the lives of your children,
[y]who faint for hunger
at the head of every street."

20 Look, O LORD, and see!
[z]With whom have you dealt thus?
[a]Should women eat the fruit of their
womb,
the children of [b]their tender care?
Should [c]priest and prophet be killed
in the sanctuary of the Lord?

21 In the dust of the streets
[d]lie the young and the old;
[d]my young women and my young men
have fallen by the sword;
[e]you have killed them in the day of your
anger,
slaughtering [f]without pity.

22 You summoned as if to [g]a festival day
[h]my terrors on every side,
[i]and on the day of the anger of the LORD
no one escaped or survived;
[j]those whom I held and raised
my enemy destroyed.

Great Is Your Faithfulness

3 [k]I am the man who has seen affliction
under the [l]rod of his wrath;
2 he has driven and brought me
[m]into darkness without any light;
3 surely against me he turns his hand
again and again the whole day long.

4 He has made my flesh and my skin waste
away;
[n]he has broken my bones;
5 [o]he has besieged and enveloped me
with [p]bitterness and tribulation;
6 [q]he has made me dwell in darkness
like the dead of long ago.

7 [r]He has walled me about so that [s]I cannot
escape;
he has made my chains heavy;
8 though [t]I call and cry for help,
he shuts out my prayer;
9 [r]he has blocked my ways with blocks of
stones;
he has made my paths crooked.

10 [u]He is a bear lying in wait for me,
a lion in hiding;
11 [v]he turned aside my steps and [u]tore me to
pieces;
[w]he has made me desolate;
12 [x]he bent his bow [y]and set me
as a target for his arrow.

3:1–20 Chapter 3 stands not only as the center of the book but as the heart of its theology. There is a progression from the poet's personal expression of grief and admission of guilt to a focus on the Lord's mercy and faithfulness. Then follows a community lament, and a return to contemplating God's mercy.

In this first section it is as if the poet has accepted upon himself the weight of Judah's guilt. He has personalized the problem to the extent that the faithlessness of Judah and its idolatry are his own (cf. Rom. 9:1–3; 10:1). He echoes the role of the servant of the Lord in Isaiah (Isa. 42:1–4; 49:1–6; 50:4–9; 52:13–53:12). Both foreshadow the truly sinless servant of the Lord who was made sin for us, so that "in him we might become the righteousness of God" (2 Cor. 5:21).

16[h] ch. 3:46; [Job 16:9, 10] [i] See ver. 2 [j] [Ps. 35:21]
17[k] See Lev. 26:14-45; Deut. 28:15-68 [l] ch. 1:7; Jer. 46:26 [m] See ver. 2 [n] ver. 2, 21 [o] [Ps. 38:16; 89:42] [p] [ver. 3]
18[q] ver. 8 [r] See ver. 11 [s] Ps. 32:4; 42:3 [t] Ps. 77:2 [u] Ps. 17:8
19[v] Ps. 119:147, 148 [w] Ps. 62:8; [1 Sam. 7:6] [x] [1 Tim. 2:8] [y] See ver. 11, 12
20[z] ch. 1:22 [a] ch. 4:10; See Jer. 19:9 [b] ver. 22 [c] [ch. 4:13]
21[d] [2 Chr. 36:17] [e] ch. 3:43

[f] ver. 2, 17 **22**[g] [ver. 6] [h] See Jer. 6:25 [i] [Jer. 42:17; 44:14] [j] ver. 20 **Chapter 3** **1**[k] Jer. 20:18 [l] Ps. 2:9 **2**[m] Isa. 5:30 **4**[n] Ps. 51:8; Isa. 38:13; Jer. 50:17 **5**[o] [Job 19:12] [p] ver. 19; Deut. 29:18 **6**[q] Ps. 143:3 **7**[r] Job 19:8 [s] Ps. 88:8 **8**[t] Job 19:7; 30:20; Ps. 22:2 **9**[r] [See ver. 7 above] **10**[u] See Hos. 13:8 **11**[v] [Jer. 18:15] [u] [See ver. 10 above] [w] ch. 1:13 **12**[x] ch. 2:4 [y] [Job 16:12]

13 He drove into my kidneys
[z]the arrows of his quiver;
14 [a]I have become the laughingstock of all peoples,
[b]the object of their taunts all day long.
15 [c]He has filled me with bitterness;
he has sated me with [d]wormwood.

16 [e]He has made my teeth grind on gravel,
and [f]made me cower in ashes;
17 my soul is bereft of peace;
I have forgotten what happiness[1] is;
18 [g]so I say, "My endurance has perished;
so has my hope from the LORD."

19 [h]Remember my affliction and my wanderings,
[d]the wormwood and [i]the gall!
20 My soul continually remembers it
[j]and is bowed down within me.
21 But this I call to mind,
and [k]therefore I have hope:

22 [l]The steadfast love of the LORD never ceases;[2]
[l]his mercies never come to an end;
23 they are new [m]every morning;
[n]great is your faithfulness.
24 [o]"The LORD is my portion," says my soul,
[k]"therefore I will hope in him."

25 The LORD is good to those who [p]wait for him,
to the soul who seeks him.
26 [q]It is good that one should wait quietly
for the salvation of the LORD.
27 [r]It is good for a man that he bear
the yoke [s]in his youth.

28 Let him [t]sit alone in silence
when it is laid on him;
29 [u]let him put his mouth in the dust—
there may yet be hope;
30 [v]let him give his cheek to the one who strikes,
and let him be filled with insults.

31 [w]For the Lord will not
cast off forever,
32 but, though he [x]cause grief, [y]he will have compassion
[z]according to the abundance of his steadfast love;
33 [a]for he does not afflict from his heart
or [b]grieve the children of men.

34 To crush underfoot
all [c]the prisoners of the earth,
35 [d]to deny a man justice
in the presence of the Most High,
36 to subvert a man in his lawsuit,
[d]the Lord does not approve.

37 [e]Who has spoken and it came to pass,
unless the Lord has commanded it?
38 [f]Is it not from the mouth of the Most High
that good and bad come?
39 [g]Why should a living man complain,
a man, about the punishment of his sins?

40 Let us test and examine our ways,
[h]and return to the LORD!

[1] Hebrew *good* [2] Syriac, Targum; Hebrew *Because of the steadfast love of the LORD, we are not cut off*

13[z] Job 6:4; Ps. 38:2
14[a] See Jer. 20:7 [b] ver. 63; Job 30:9; Ps. 69:12
15[c] [Isa. 51:17, 21] [d] Jer. 9:15
16[e] [Prov. 20:17] [f] See Jer. 6:26
18[g] [Ps. 9:18]
19[h] [ch. 1:9, 11, 20] [d] [See ver. 15 above] [i] ver. 5
20[j] Ps. 42:6; 44:25
21[k] [Ps. 42:5, 11]
22[l] [Mal. 3:6]
23[m] Job 7:18 [n] Ps. 36:5
24[o] Ps. 16:5; 73:26 [k] [See ver. 21 above]
25[p] Ps. 130:6; [Isa. 30:18]
26[q] Ps. 130:5, 7; Mic. 7:7
27[r] [Matt. 11:29] [s] [Eccles. 12:1]
28[t] ch. 1:1; 2:10; Isa. 3:26
29[u] Job 42:6
30[v] Isa. 50:6; Matt. 5:39
31[w] Ps. 103:9
32[x] ch. 1:5 [y] Ps. 103:8 [z] Ps. 106:45
33[a] [Heb. 12:6, 10] [b] [Heb. 12:11]
34[c] [Ps. 107:10]

3:21–39 In verse 18 the author seems to have simply given up both in endurance and in hope. But then hope revives (v. 21). His lamenting has had a cathartic effect. Grief is important even for Christians, but with this proviso: we should not grieve as those without hope (1 Thess. 4:13). And here hope is reborn out of grief; the basis of this hope is the steadfast covenant love of God (Lam. 3:22–24). God is indeed rich in mercy (Eph. 2:4), and his mercies are ever new.

Hope is a much-devalued word in our time, often expressing our desire for an uncertain outcome. In the Bible it is a strong word to express certainty in God's future provision based on his truth and faithfulness (Rom. 5:3–5; Gal. 5:5; Eph. 1:18–23; 1 Thess. 5:8–11; Titus 2:13–14; 3:4–7).

Though God has cast his people off, he will not do so forever (Lam. 3:31–39). "Steadfast love" (vv. 22, 32) translates the Hebrew word *hesed*, which links God's love to his covenant faithfulness. This covenant was never conditioned on human faithfulness, and it leads straight to the new covenant established solely by the sovereign mercy of God and ultimately sealed in Jesus' blood (Luke 22:20; 1 Cor. 11:25). God will never cast his people off, because he did cast off his own Son in their place (Rom. 8:32).

35[d] [Hab. 1:13] **36**[d] [See ver. 35 above] **37**[e] [Ps. 33:9] **38**[f] Isa. 45:7; Amos 3:6 **39**[g] Prov. 19:3 **40**[h] Joel 2:12, 13

41 [i]Let us lift up our hearts and hands
to God in heaven:
42 [j]"We have transgressed and [k]rebelled,
and you have not forgiven.

43 "You have wrapped yourself with anger
and pursued us,
[l]killing without pity;
44 [m]you have wrapped yourself with a cloud
so that no prayer can pass through.
45 [n]You have made us scum and garbage
among the peoples.

46 [o]"All our enemies
open their mouths against us;
47 [p]panic and pitfall have come upon us,
devastation and [q]destruction;
48 [r]my eyes flow with rivers of tears
because of the destruction of the
daughter of my people.

49 [r]"My eyes will flow without ceasing,
without respite,
50 [s]until the LORD from heaven
looks down and sees;
51 my eyes cause me grief
at the fate of all the daughters of my
city.

52 [t]"I have been hunted [u]like a bird
by those who were my enemies [v]without cause;
53 [w]they flung me alive into the pit
[x]and cast stones on me;
54 [y]water closed over my head;
I said, [z]'I am lost.'

55 [a]"I called on your name, O LORD,
from the depths of the pit;
56 [b]you heard my plea, 'Do not close
your ear to my cry for help!'
57 [c]You came near when I called on you;
you said, [d]'Do not fear!'

58 "You have [e]taken up my cause, [f]O Lord;
you have [e]redeemed my life.
59 You have seen the wrong done to me, [g]O
LORD;
judge my cause.
60 You have seen all their vengeance,
all [h]their plots against me.

61 [i]"You have heard their taunts, O LORD,
all [h]their plots against me.
62 The lips and thoughts [j]of my assailants
are against me all the day long.
63 [k]Behold their sitting and their rising;
[l]I am the object of their taunts.

64 [m]"You will repay them,[1] O LORD,
[n]according to the work of their hands.
65 You will give them[2] dullness of heart;
your curse will be[3] on them.
66 You will pursue them[4] in anger and
[o]destroy them
from under [p]your heavens, O LORD."[5]

The Holy Stones Lie Scattered

4 [q]How the gold has grown dim,
how the pure gold is changed!
The holy stones lie scattered
[r]at the head of every street.

[1] Or *Repay them* [2] Or *Give them* [3] Or *place your curse* [4] Or *Pursue them* [5] Syriac (compare Septuagint, Vulgate); Hebrew *the heavens of the LORD*

3:40–66 The poet exhorts the people to return to covenant faithfulness (vv. 40–42) before revisiting his grief over the present devastation (vv. 43–54). Finally, hope is revived and the Lord is extolled not as the enemy but as Savior (v. 57) and Redeemer (vv. 58–66). "If God is for us, who can be against us?" (Rom. 8:31). God will repay Judah's enemies (Lam. 3:64–66).

The rescue God ultimately provides for his sinful people reminds us that the real enemies of God's people are Satan, sin, and death, which are overthrown by Jesus' death on the cross (Luke 10:17–18; Rom. 6:6–14, 23; Rom. 8:37–39; Rom. 16:20; 1 Cor. 15:50–58; 2 Cor. 5:21; Rev. 12:7–11).

4:1–22 This poem is similar in tone to chapter 2, but announces the completion of Jerusalem's punishment. Central to its teaching is the common suffering of all the people of Judah. Yet it is suffering that is self-inflicted. The Christian doctrine of original sin does not relieve us of our responsibility as sinners. We sin because we want to, and because it is our nature to hate God until his Spirit draws us to himself through the gospel (Rom. 1:28–32; 5:12). God's grace is so profound that it gets deep down inside us, even to the level of *desire* (Rom. 8:5–15).

41 [i] Ps. 25:1; 119:48
42 [j] See Dan. 9:5 [k] Ps. 78:17
43 [l] ch. 2:2, 17, 21
44 [m] ver. 8; [ch. 2:1]
45 [n] [1 Cor. 4:13]
46 [o] ch. 2:16, 17
47 [p] Isa. 24:17; Jer. 48:43 [q] Isa. 51:19
48 [r] ch. 1:16; See Jer. 13:17
49 [r] [See ver. 48 above]
50 [s] Ps. 14:2; Isa. 63:15
52 [t] ch. 4:18 [u] Ps. 11:1 [v] See Ps. 35:19
53 [w] Jer. 37:16; 38:6, 9, 10 [x] [Dan. 6:17]
54 [y] Ps. 69:2 [z] Ps. 88:5; [Ezek. 37:11]
55 [a] Ps. 130:1
56 [b] [Ps. 130:2]
57 [c] [James 4:8] [d] See Josh. 1:9
58 [e] Ps. 119:154 [f] [1 Sam. 24:15]
59 [g] Ps. 35:22, 23
60 [h] See Jer. 11:19
61 [i] ch. 5:1 [h] [See ver. 60 above]
62 [j] Ps. 18:39, 48
63 [k] [Ps. 139:2] [l] See ver. 14 **64** [m] See Jer. 11:20 [n] Ps. 28:4; [2 Tim. 4:14] **66** [o] [Deut. 25:19; Jer. 10:11] [p] Ps. 8:3 **Chapter 4** **1** [q] [Isa. 1:22; Jer. 6:30] [r] ch. 2:19

2 The precious sons of Zion,
worth their weight in [s]fine gold,
how they are regarded as [t]earthen pots,
the work of a potter's hands!

3 Even jackals offer the breast;
they nurse their young,
but the daughter of my people has
become cruel,
like the ostriches in the wilderness.

4 The tongue of the nursing infant [u]sticks
to the roof of its mouth for thirst;
[v]the children beg for food,
but no one gives to them.

5 Those who once feasted on delicacies
perish in the streets;
[w]those who were brought up in purple
embrace ash heaps.

6 [x]For the chastisement[1] of the daughter of
my people has been greater
than the punishment[2] of Sodom,
[y]which was overthrown in a moment,
and no hands were wrung for her.[3]

7 Her princes were purer than snow,
whiter than milk;
their bodies were more ruddy than coral,
the beauty of their form[4] was like sapphire.[5]

8 [z]Now their face is blacker than soot;
they are not recognized in the streets;
their skin has shriveled on their bones;
it has become as dry as wood.

9 Happier were the victims of the sword
than the victims of hunger,
who wasted away, pierced
by lack of the fruits of the field.

10 [a]The hands of [b]compassionate women
[c]have boiled their own children;
[d]they became their food
during the destruction of the daughter of my people.

11 [e]The LORD gave full vent to his wrath;
he poured out his hot anger,
and [f]he kindled a fire in Zion
that consumed its foundations.

12 [g]The kings of the earth did not believe,
nor any of the inhabitants of the world,
that foe or enemy could enter
the gates of Jerusalem.

13 This was for [h]the sins of her prophets
and [h]the iniquities of her priests,
who shed in the midst of her
the blood of the righteous.

14 [i]They wandered, blind, through the
streets;
they were so defiled with blood
[j]that no one was able to touch
their garments.

15 "Away! [k]Unclean!" people cried at them.
"Away! Away! Do not touch!"
So they became fugitives and wanderers;
people said among the nations,
"They shall stay with us no longer."

[1] Or *iniquity* [2] Or *sin* [3] The meaning of the Hebrew is uncertain [4] The meaning of the Hebrew is uncertain [5] Hebrew *lapis lazuli*

2[s] Ps. 19:10 [t] See Jer. 19:11
4[u] Ps. 22:15 [v] [ch. 2:11]
5[w] [2 Sam. 1:24]
6[x] Matt. 10:15; Luke 10:12 [y] Gen. 19:25; 2 Pet. 2:6; Jude 7
8[z] ch. 5:10; Job 30:30; [Ps. 119:83]
10[a] See Jer. 19:9 [b] [1 Kgs. 3:26; Isa. 49:15] [c] [2 Kgs. 6:29] [d] Deut. 28:57
11[e] Ezek. 5:13 [f] See Jer. 17:27
12[g] [Isa. 52:15; 53:1]
13[h] [ch. 2:20]; See Jer. 5:31; 23:21
14[i] [Isa. 59:10] [j] [Num. 19:16]
15[k] [Lev. 13:45]

Zion's inviolability is a myth when used as a cloak for rebellion against Zion's God (Lam. 4:12–13). The status of leaders does not cover their sin and its consequences (vv. 13–16). Nevertheless, the word of comfort cannot be suppressed. Out of exile shall come redemption, and Zion will be comforted (v. 22; cf. Isa. 40:1–5; 51:3; 2 Cor. 1:4; 1 Thess. 4:16–18).

"The punishment of your iniquity, O daughter of Zion, is accomplished" (Lam. 4:22). With these words God promises that the punishment of his people will end—it has a terminus, as opposed to what will happen to Edom. But despite the merciful contrast being expressed, we still must ask, "How could it be that the punishment of the covenant people will end?" Israel has proven horribly rebellious time and time again, and all against a righteous and holy God. On top of that, as the writer to the Hebrews reminds us, "it is impossible for the blood of bulls and goats to take away sins" (Heb. 10:4). So how can a just God end the punishment of an unceasingly sinful people?

The answer is that the punishment of God's people is accomplished only in the perfect sacrifice of "the LORD's anointed" who was promised to provide an everlasting kingdom for his people (Lam. 4:20). He and he alone atones for sin. We must trust him and fall down in gratitude at his feet. He is worthy of all our praise. He is the sinless Anointed One who sacrificially took punishment he did not deserve to end *our* punishment for all time.

16 [l]The LORD himself[1] has scattered them;
he will regard them no more;
[m]no honor was shown to the priests,
[n]no favor to the elders.

17 [o]Our eyes failed, ever watching
[o]vainly for help;
in our watching we watched
for [p]a nation which could not save.

18 [q]They dogged our steps
so that we could not walk in our
streets;
[r]our end drew near; our days were numbered,
for our end had come.

19 Our pursuers were [s]swifter
than the eagles in the heavens;
they chased us on the mountains;
they lay in wait for us in the wilderness.

20 [t]The breath of our nostrils, [u]the LORD's
anointed,
was captured [v]in their pits,
of whom we said, [w]"Under his shadow
we shall live among the nations."

21 [x]Rejoice and be glad, O daughter of Edom,
you who dwell in [y]the land of Uz;
but to you also [z]the cup shall pass;
you shall become drunk and strip
yourself bare.

22 [a]The punishment of your iniquity,
O daughter of Zion, is accomplished;
he will keep you in exile no longer;[2]
but [b]your iniquity, O daughter of Edom,
he will punish;
he will uncover your sins.

Restore Us to Yourself, O LORD

5 [c]Remember, O LORD, what has befallen
us;
look, and see [d]our disgrace!
2 [e]Our inheritance has been turned over to
strangers,
our homes to foreigners.
3 We have become orphans, fatherless;
our mothers are like widows.
4 We must pay for the water we drink;
the wood we get must be bought.
5 [f]Our pursuers are at our necks;[3]
we are weary; we are given no rest.
6 We have given the hand to [g]Egypt, and
to [g]Assyria,
to get bread enough.
7 Our fathers sinned, and are no more;
[h]and we bear their iniquities.
8 [i]Slaves rule over us;
there is none to deliver us from their
hand.
9 [j]We get our bread at the peril of our lives,
because of the sword in the wilderness.

[1] Hebrew *The face of the LORD* [2] Or *he will not exile you again* [3] Symmachus *With a yoke on our necks*

5:1–22 As chapter 4 mirrors chapter 2, so chapter 5 returns to the desolation of chapter 1. But there is a significant difference, for here hope is a constant theme. This hope grows out of the realization of guilt, the confession of which leads to hope in God's mercy (5:1–18). The plea that God should remember (v. 1) becomes a plea for restoration (v. 21). The author realizes that Israel's sin is not momentary. The reference to the sins of the fathers (v. 7) only demonstrates this people's continuing lineage of sin and in no sense diminishes their guilt (vv. 16–18; see note on 4:1–22).

Though Lamentations focuses on one particular horrifying event, it becomes relevant for all time. Its darkness reveals the utter lostness of sinful humanity. But through the storm clouds streams a bright beam of hope that stems from God's mercy. This hope in the covenant faithfulness of God finds its full realization in Christ as he takes the weight of our rebellion upon himself on the cross of Calvary.

Lamentations guides our lips and our hearts in how to relate to this world. On the one hand, we are to take the horrors of this fallen world with utter seriousness. Christians of all people should not be frivolous or trite, given our doctrine of creation, the fall, and original sin. Yet on the other hand, the redemptive purposes of God in his grace get down even underneath the weight of sin and fallenness. Christ has himself gone through suffering and death and has come out on the other side. He has conquered every final reason for us to throw our hands up in the air. In him, kindness appeared in tangible, human form, yet not kindness that ignores evil and sadness. This was a steely kindness that came for the very purpose of overcoming all evil and sadness.

16[l] ch. 2:17 [m] [Isa. 24:2] [n] ch. 5:12
17[o] Ps. 119:82, 123; [Jer. 3:23] [p] Jer. 37:7, 8
18[q] ch. 3:52 [r] Ezek. 7:2, 3, 6; Amos 8:2
19[s] Jer. 4:13; [2 Sam. 1:23; Hab. 1:8]
20[t] [Gen. 2:7] [u] [ch. 2:9; 2 Kgs. 25:5, 6] [v] [Ezek. 12:13; 17:20; 19:4, 8] [w] [Judg. 9:15; Ezek. 31:6, 17]
21[x] [ch. 1:21] [y] Job 1:1; Jer. 25:20 [z] See Jer. 25:15, 16
22[a] [Isa. 40:2] [b] Obad. 10
Chapter 5
1[c] Ps. 89:50 [d] ch. 3:61
2[e] Ps. 79:1
5[f] [Josh. 10:24]
6[g] [Hos. 12:1]
7[h] Jer. 31:29; Ezek. 18:2
8[i] [Prov. 30:21, 22]
9[j] [Jer. 6:25]

10 [k]Our skin is hot as an oven
with [l]the burning heat of famine.
11 Women are raped in Zion,
young women in the towns of Judah.
12 [m]Princes are hung up by their hands;
[n]no respect is shown to the elders.
13 Young men are compelled to [o]grind at
the mill,
and boys stagger [p]under loads of wood.
14 [n]The old men have left the city gate,
the young men [q]their music.
15 [q]The joy of our hearts has ceased;
[r]our dancing has been turned to
mourning.
16 [s]The crown has fallen from our head;
woe to us, for we have sinned!
17 For this [t]our heart has become sick,
for these things [u]our eyes have grown
dim,
18 for Mount Zion which lies desolate;
[v]jackals prowl over it.
19 [w]But you, O LORD, reign forever;
your throne endures to all generations.
20 [x]Why do you forget us forever,
why do you forsake us for so many
days?
21 [y]Restore us to yourself, O LORD, that we
may be restored!
Renew our days as of old—
22 [z]unless you have utterly rejected us,
and you remain exceedingly angry
with us.

10[k] See ch. 4:8 [l][Deut. 32:24]
12[m] See 2 Kgs. 25:19-21 [n]ch. 4:16
13[o][Judg. 16:21] [p][Josh. 9:27]
14[n][See ver. 12 above] [q][Isa. 24:8]
15[q][See ver. 14 above] [r][Amos 8:10]
16[s]Ps. 89:39; Jer. 13:18; [ch. 1:1]
17[t]Isa. 1:5 [u]See ch. 2:11

The writer of Lamentations says, "The joy of our hearts has ceased; our dancing has been turned to mourning" (5:15). Such is the state of the soul that many of us will find ourselves experiencing at various seasons of life. Yet this state is not our final status. One day all joy will be restored, and mourning will turn to dancing. Jesus Christ, who underwent the ultimate mourning in Gethsemane as he prepared to be abandoned by the Father, has secured our eternal joy. His abandonment means our acceptance. This is the great exchange of the gospel. Look the horrors of this world and of your own soul square in the face, and trust *him*.

18[v][Isa. 34:13] **19**[w]Ps. 9:7; 102:12; 145:13 **20**[x]Ps. 13:1 **21**[y]Jer. 31:18; [Ps. 80:3, 7, 19] **22**[z]Jer. 14:19

Introduction to Ezekiel

Author and Date

The book of Ezekiel records the preaching and message of the sixth-century Hebrew prophet of the same name. Ezekiel's name literally means "God strengthens," appropriate for a man whose call was to prophesy to a people who had been carried into exile by a foreign power.

Ezekiel prophesied in the years following the exile of the Israelite people to Babylon that began in 597 B.C. In fact, Ezekiel himself was one of those carried from Jerusalem to Babylon and settled along the Chebar canal. Many of Ezekiel's prophecies are explicitly dated, with the earliest coming in the summer of 593 B.C., about four or five years after the exile, and the latest about 22 years after that.

Audience

Ezekiel prophesied to a people in exile, who were tempted to doubt both the power and the justice of their God. His messages, therefore, stress God's universal reign and the absolute rightness of his judgment of his own people. Ezekiel's message is not all about judgment, though. Grace shines through, as he also gives the exiled Israelites a series of beautiful messages about God's ability and determination to restore them, to bring them out of exile, and to give them life where there has been only death. Most of all, however, he reveals to God's people that even though they are currently in exile, God has determined that one day he will dwell among them forever. Thus the book ends with a description of God's city, and the name of it is "The LORD Is There."

The Gospel in Ezekiel

Many Christians approach the book of Ezekiel and see little more than an obscure mass of judgment oracles, within which are a few random passages that speak of God's grace. Compared to the other Major Prophets—Isaiah, Jeremiah, and Daniel—Ezekiel has probably the fewest obvious messianic passages anticipating Christ, so it is not the first book that comes to mind when one wants to see the gospel expounded in the Old Testament.

Understood rightly, however, Ezekiel contains and continues a beautiful story of God's grace to his undeserving people. It is a compelling Old Testament witness to the gospel of Jesus Christ.

The whole structure of the book, in fact, points to God's grace to his people in spite of their sin. In the first 24 chapters, the book contains a succession of oracles that promise judgment against the people of Israel. Jerusalem will be placed under siege and destroyed, Ezekiel warns, and this will happen because of the people's sin. The exile has not happened by accident, and neither will the destruction of Jerusalem. All of it comes from the hand of God in response to the people's rebellion against him.

In chapters 24–33, the focus changes as God turns his attention to judging the nations around Israel. He is sovereign not only over his people but over all the nations of the world. None of them will be excused for their rebellion.

In chapter 33, the focus of the book changes again. With God's judgment against Jerusalem carried out in full, and with judgment pronounced against Israel's enemies, God now begins to promise his people that they will be restored. Life will reign where there has been only death. God will pour out his Spirit on the people. The destroyed temple, the central symbol of God's presence among his people, will be restored. God will once again dwell with his people.

Not only does Ezekiel promise God's presence, he also indicates over and over again that God will accomplish this restoration of his people through the work of a king of Israel who will sit yet again on David's throne. This was an extraordinary prophecy, because Jehoiachin—the last of the Davidic line of kings—had himself been carried away into exile. The throne, therefore, was empty. God promises through Ezekiel, however, that it will not remain so forever. One day, God will restore his people and a new ruler will sit on David's throne. This king will not only reign for eternity but will also make atonement for his people's sins and bring them back into God's presence.

In all this, Ezekiel points powerfully both to the coming of Jesus Christ and to the grace of God in forgiving sinners. All human beings—not just Israel—are sinners who deserve God's judgment. Therefore the first 32 chapters of the book are not without relevance to us. We learn from them about God's holiness, the wickedness and consequences of rebellion against him, and the divine wrath such sin deserves. At the same time, though, we learn also of God's love for his people despite their rebellion, and of his promise to send a Savior who would restore them, give them life, and bring them to live in his presence forever.

Outline

I. Inaugural Vision (1:1–3:27)

II. Judgment on Jerusalem and Judah (4:1–24:27)

III. Oracles against Foreign Nations (25:1–32:32)

IV. After the Fall of Jerusalem, Visions of Restoration (33:1–48:35)

Ezekiel

Ezekiel in Babylon

1 [a]In the thirtieth year, in the fourth month,
on the fifth day of the month, as I was
among the exiles by [b]the Chebar canal, [c]the
heavens were opened, and I saw [d]visions of
God.[1] 2 On the fifth day of the month (it was
[e]the fifth year of [f]the exile of King Jehoiachin),
3 the word of the LORD came to Ezekiel [g]the
priest, the son of Buzi, in the land of the
Chaldeans by [b]the Chebar canal, and [h]the hand
of the LORD was upon him there.

The Glory of the LORD

4 As I looked, behold, [i]a stormy wind came
[j]out of the north, and a great cloud, with
[k]brightness around it, and fire flashing forth
continually, and in the midst of the fire, [l]as it
were gleaming metal.[2] 5 And from the midst of
it came the likeness of [m]four living creatures.
[n]And this was their appearance: they had a
human likeness, 6 [o]but each had four faces,
and each of them had four wings. 7 Their legs
were straight, and the soles of their feet were
like the sole of a calf's foot. And they sparkled
[p]like burnished bronze. 8 Under their wings
[q]on their four sides [r]they had human hands.
And the four had their faces and their wings
thus: 9 their wings touched one another. [s]Each
one of them went straight forward, [q]without
turning as they went. 10 As for the likeness of

[1] Or *from God* [2] Or *amber*; also verse 27

1:1–3:27 The first three chapters of Ezekiel describe the vision given to the prophet as he sat on the banks of the Chebar canal in Babylon. As he stood looking toward the north (1:4), Ezekiel witnessed a storm that evolved into a magnificent vision of God and his throne. The message, delivered even in the very details of the vision, was clear: though God had exiled his people to Babylon, he had not abandoned them entirely. He still reigned over all, even the Israelites' Babylonian captors.

The fact that God comes out of the north is significant (1:4). Though Babylon was situated far to the east, its invading army had arrived from the north—forced to march in a northward curve around the massive desert between the two lands. Ezekiel's vision thus shows God coming to Babylon along the same route, arriving from the north. When God moves to save his people, he does so in a way directly counter to the evil that has beset them.

1:5–14 Ezekiel first sees, coming out of the fiery storm, four living creatures, which are the attendants of God's throne. Each of the creatures has four faces—that of a human, a lion, an ox, and an eagle. Those faces represent the "rulers" of the various spheres of God's creation—the eagle as the greatest of the birds, the ox as the greatest of the domesticated animals, the lion as the greatest of the wild animals, and the human as the one given dominion over all. In the faces of the living creatures, all creation assembles to attend its Creator.

Ezekiel calls these four creatures "cherubim," a Hebrew word identifying heavenly beings or messengers. Cherubim appear multiple times in the Bible, and their function seems to be to prevent anything unholy from entering the presence of God. Thus the cherubim guard the way to the tree of life after Adam and Eve sin, they guard the mercy seat within the tabernacle (Exodus 25), and they match the description of those who stand before God's throne in the book of Revelation. These are the fearsome guardians of God's throne, and they remind us of our predicament: we are unholy sinners, unworthy to come into the presence of a holy God and deeply in need of a Savior to forgive us and make us righteous.

Chapter 1

1 [a][ver. 3; Num. 4:3] [b]ch. 3:15, 23; 10:15, 20, 22; 43:3 [c][Matt. 3:16; Mark 1:10; Luke 3:21; John 1:51; Acts 7:56; 10:11; Rev. 19:11] [d]ch. 8:3; 40:2; [ch. 11:24; Num. 12:6]
2 [e][ch. 8:1]; See ch. 20:1 [f]2 Kgs. 24:12, 15; [ch. 17:12; 19:8; 33:21; 40:1]
3 [g][ver. 1] [b][See ver. 1 above] [h]ch. 3:22; 8:1; 33:22; 37:1; 40:1; [1 Kgs. 18:46; 2 Kgs. 3:15]
4 [i]Jer. 23:19; 25:32; 30:23; [ch. 3:12] [j]See Jer. 1:14 [k]ver. 27 [l]ver. 27; ch. 8:2
5 [m]See Rev. 4:6-8 [n]ch. 10:14, 21
6 [o]ch. 10:21
7 [p]ch. 40:3; Rev. 1:15; 2:18
8 [q]ver. 17; ch. 10:11 [r]ch. 10:8, 21
9 [s]ch. 10:22 [q][See ver. 8 above]

their faces, [t]each had a human face. The four
had the face of a lion on the right side, the four
had the face of an ox on the left side, and the
four had the face of an eagle. 11 Such were their
faces. And their wings were spread out above.
Each creature had two wings, each of which
touched the wing of another, while [u]two covered their bodies. 12 [s]And each went straight
forward. [v]Wherever the spirit[1] would go, they
went, without turning as they went. 13 As
for the likeness of the living creatures, their
appearance was [w]like burning coals of fire, [w]like
the appearance of torches moving to and fro
among the living creatures. [x]And the fire was
bright, and out of the fire went forth lightning.
14 And the living creatures [y]darted to and fro,
[z]like the appearance of a flash of lightning.

15 [a]Now as I looked at the living creatures,
I saw a wheel on the earth beside the living
creatures, one for each of the four of them.[2]
16 [a]As for the appearance of the wheels and
their construction: their appearance was like
[b]the gleaming of beryl. [c]And the four had the
same likeness, their appearance and construction being as it were a wheel within a wheel.
17 [d]When they went, they went [e]in any of their
four directions[3] [f]without turning as they went.
18 And their rims were tall and awesome, [g]and
the rims of all four were full of eyes all around.
19 [h]And when the living creatures went, the
wheels went beside them; [i]and when the living creatures rose from the earth, the wheels
rose. 20 [j]Wherever the spirit wanted to go, they
went, and the wheels rose along with them,
[j]for the spirit of the living creatures[4] was in
the wheels. 21 [h]When those went, these went;
and when those stood, these stood; [i]and when
those rose from the earth, the wheels rose
along with them, [j]for the spirit of the living
creatures was in the wheels.

22 Over the heads of the living creatures there
was [k]the likeness of an expanse, shining like
awe-inspiring [l]crystal, spread out above their
heads. 23 And under the expanse their wings
were [m]stretched out straight, one toward
another. [n]And each creature had two wings covering its body. 24 And when they went, I heard
the sound of their wings [o]like the sound of

[1] Or *Spirit*; also twice in verse 20 and once in verse 21 [2] Hebrew *of their faces* [3] Hebrew *on their four sides* [4] Or *the spirit of life*; also verse 21

10[t] ch. 10:14, 21
11[u] ver. 23; [Isa. 6:2]
12[s] [See ver. 9 above] [v] ch. 10:17
13[w] [Ps. 104:4] [x] [Ps. 97:3, 4]
14[y] [Zech. 4:10] [z] [Matt. 24:27; Luke 17:24]
15[a] ch. 10:9; [Dan. 7:9]
16[a] [See ver. 15 above] [b] [Dan. 10:6] [c] ch. 10:10
17[d] ch. 10:11 [e] ver. 8 [f] ver. 9
18[g] ch. 10:12; [Rev. 4:8]
19[h] ch. 10:16 [i] [ch. 10:19; 11:22]
20[j] ch. 10:17
21[h] [See ver. 19 above] [i] [See ver. 19 above] [j] [See ver. 20 above]
22[k] [ver. 25, 26; ch. 10:1] [l] [Rev. 4:6]
23[m] ver. 7 [n] ver. 11
24[o] ch. 43:2; [Rev. 1:15]

1:15–21 Here Ezekiel describes perhaps the most perplexing aspect of his vision—the "wheels" that stand beside the four living creatures. Tall and awesome and made of some crystalline stone, the interwoven wheels are able to go in all directions (the four wings of the cherubim enable them to go in any direction without turning). The wheels are also covered with eyes, combining symbols of God's omnipotence and omniscience. Strange as they are, though, the wheels provide the best clue as to what Ezekiel is actually seeing in this vision. He is witnessing the arrival of God's throne-chariot, the kind of royal seat a king would ride in when he went into battle. God has come to his exiled people girded for war.

He would do so again five centuries later, not as a conquering king but as a suffering king.

1:22–27 As Ezekiel's gaze continues upward, he sees first a shimmering platform—the floor of the chariot—and then a throne made of sapphire with a blindingly bright figure sitting on it, surrounded by a rainbow. The sapphire throne (v. 26) is probably lapis lazuli, a blue stone considered enormously valuable in the ancient world, and a symbol of the wealth of both Babylon and Egypt. For God to be seated on a throne of lapis lazuli was to assert his supreme royalty, reigning even over these powerful empires and their greatest symbol of wealth. The rainbow surrounding the throne reminds us of God's promise to keep his covenants. He is a God of unfailing faithfulness, and he reminds his people of that fact as he comes to them in their exile.

The cumulative effect of this vision was terrifying and astonishing to Ezekiel. Notice how, throughout the first chapter, words seem to fail him. His description is full of phrases such as "seems like," "as it were," and "what looked like."

Terrifying though it was, the vision also would have been deeply comforting. God had arrived in power in a counter-invasion of Israel's enemy. No other god could stand before him, and no distance or geographical limitation could keep him away from his people. That is a truth we as Christians should remember in our own lives. No matter our circumstances, no matter our trials, God reigns over all. Indeed, the supreme invasion against the Enemy of God's people has taken place in the life, death, and resurrection of Jesus Christ (Col. 2:15).

many waters, like [p]the sound of the [q]Almighty,
a sound of tumult [r]like the sound of an army.
When they stood still, they let down their
wings. 25 And there came a voice from above
[s]the expanse over their heads. When they stood
still, they let down their wings.

26 And above the expanse over their heads
there was [t]the likeness of a throne, [t]in appearance [u]like sapphire;[1] and seated above the likeness of a throne was [v]a likeness with a human
appearance. 27 And [w]upward from what had
the appearance of his waist I saw as it were
[x]gleaming metal, like the appearance of fire
enclosed all around. And downward from
what had the appearance of his waist I saw as
it were the appearance of fire, and [y]there was
brightness around him.[2] 28 Like the appearance of [z]the bow that is in the cloud on the day
of rain, so was the appearance of the brightness all around.

Such was the appearance of the likeness of
[a]the glory of the LORD. And when I saw it, [b]I
fell on my face, and I heard the voice of one
speaking.

Ezekiel's Call

2 And he said to me, [c]"Son of man,[3] [d]stand
on your feet, and I will speak with you."
2 And as he spoke to me, [e]the Spirit entered
into me and [f]set me on my feet, and I heard
him speaking to me. 3 And he said to me, "Son
of man, I send you to the people of Israel, to
[g]nations of rebels, who have rebelled against
me. [h]They and their fathers have transgressed
against me to this very day. 4 The descendants
also are [i]impudent and stubborn: I send you
to them, and you shall say to them, 'Thus
says the Lord GOD.' 5 And [j]whether they hear
or refuse to hear (for they are [g]a rebellious
house) [k]they will know that a prophet has
been among them. 6 And you, son of man,
[l]be not afraid of them, nor be afraid of their
words, [m]though briers and thorns are with
you and you sit on [n]scorpions.[4] Be not afraid
of their words, nor be dismayed at their
looks, for they are a rebellious house. 7 And
you shall speak my words to them, [j]whether
they hear or refuse to hear, for they are a
rebellious house.

[1] Or *lapis lazuli* [2] Or *it* [3] Or *Son of Adam*; so throughout Ezekiel [4] Or *on scorpion plants*

1:28 The vision climaxes in an unexpected way. Ezekiel falls on his face at the glory of what he sees, but the high point of the vision is actually nothing visible at all—it is a sound: "I heard the voice of one speaking."

Throughout the Bible, it is the fact that God speaks that sets him apart from all other gods. That is part of the reason why Israel was to make no image of God; what mattered, finally, was not what God *looked like*, but what he *said*. Thus the high point of Ezekiel's vision was not the awesome visual scene, but rather the word of God.

For believers today, too, what matters preeminently is what God has said in the gospel. Our lives are not determined by personal failure, moral lapse, financial disaster, relational dysfunction, physical ailment, but by the word of grace that hangs like a banner over all of that and injects hope into all of life. Whatever happens, God has spoken. A word has come. The gospel defies what we deserve on our own merit. God has pronounced his forgiveness, acceptance, and ultimate rule. And he has done it through *the* Word, his own Son, Jesus Christ (John 1:1, 14).

2:1–3:27 These chapters recount God's instructions to Ezekiel. They essentially contain two main ideas woven together. First, God tells Ezekiel that his message will not be received well by the Israelites. Second, God makes the point forcefully that Ezekiel is a bound man. He is not free to say whatever he wishes, but must speak God's word precisely to his people. The same two truths were embodied in the ultimate and final Prophet, Jesus Christ. He too was rejected by his people (Matt. 13:57; Luke 9:22) and was bound to say what God said (John 12:49; 15:15).

2:1–7; 3:4–11 In these two sections, God tells Ezekiel that the people of Israel are hard-hearted and rebellious. Because of that, they will not respond to his message in the correct way. Nevertheless, Ezekiel must preach to them anyway. He must not be afraid of them (2:6–7) because, God says, he will make Ezekiel as hard-headed as *they* are (3:8–9). As is true for all human beings, the Israelites were dead in their transgressions. It would take an act of supernatural, life-giving mercy to bring them to repentance.

24 [p] Ps. 29:3, 4; 68:33 [q] See Gen. 17:1 [r] Dan. 10:6; [Rev. 19:6]
25 [s] [ver. 22]
26 [t] ch. 10:1; [1 Kgs. 22:19] [u] Ex. 24:10 [v] Dan. 8:15; [Rev. 1:13]
27 [w] ch. 8:2; [ver. 4] [x] See ver. 4 [y] ver. 4
28 [z] Gen. 9:13; [Rev. 4:3; 10:1] [a] ch. 3:23; 8:4; 9:3; 10:4, 18, 19; 11:22, 23; 43:4, 5; 44:4; [Ex. 24:16] [b] ch. 3:23; 43:3; 44:4; [Gen. 17:3, 17; Josh. 5:14; Dan. 8:17; Acts 9:4; Rev. 1:17]

Chapter 2
1 [c] ch. 3:1, 3, 4, 17, 25; 4:1, 16; 5:1 [d] Dan. 10:11
2 [e] ch. 3:24 [f] ch. 3:24; Dan. 8:18
3 [g] [ver. 5, 6, 8; ch. 3:26; 24:3; 44:6] [h] ch. 20:16, 18, 21
4 [i] [ch. 3:7]
5 [j] ch. 3:11; [ch. 3:27; 17:12] [g] [See ver. 3 above] [k] ch. 33:33
6 [l] ch. 3:9; Jer. 1:8 [m] [ch. 28:24; 2 Sam. 23:6; Mic. 7:4] [n] [Deut. 8:15]
7 [j] [See ver. 5 above]

8 “But you, son of man, hear what I say to
you. [o]Be not rebellious like that rebellious
house; open your mouth and [p]eat what I give
you.” 9 And when I looked, behold, [q]a hand was
stretched out to me, and behold, [r]a scroll of a
book was in it. 10 And he spread it before me.
And it had writing [s]on the front and on the
back, and there were written on it words of
lamentation and mourning and woe.

3 And he said to me, [c]“Son of man, eat whatever you find here. [t]Eat this scroll, and go,
speak to the house of Israel.” 2 So I opened my
mouth, and he gave me this scroll to eat. 3 And
he said to me, “Son of man, feed your belly
with this scroll that I give you and fill your
stomach with it.” [u]Then I ate it, and it was in
my mouth [v]as sweet as honey.

4 And he said to me, [w]“Son of man, go to the
house of Israel and speak with my words to
them. 5 For you are not sent to a people of foreign speech and a hard language, but to the
house of Israel— 6 not to many peoples of foreign speech and a hard language, whose words
you cannot understand. [x]Surely, if I sent you to
such, they would listen to you. 7 [y]But the house
of Israel will not be willing to listen to you, for
they are not willing to listen to me: because all
the house of Israel [z]have a hard forehead and
a stubborn heart. 8 [a]Behold, I have made your
face as hard as their faces, and your forehead
as hard as their foreheads. 9 Like [b]emery harder
than flint have I made your forehead. [c]Fear
them not, nor be dismayed at their looks, for
they are a rebellious house.” 10 Moreover, he
said to me, “Son of man, [d]all my words that
I shall speak to you receive [e]in your heart, and
hear with your ears. 11 And go to the exiles,
[f]to your people, and speak to them and say
to them, [g]‘Thus says the Lord GOD,’ [h]whether
they hear or refuse to hear.”

12 [i]Then the Spirit[1] lifted me up, and I heard
behind me the voice[2] of [j]a great earthquake:
“Blessed be the glory of the LORD from its
place!” 13 It was the sound of the wings of [k]the
living creatures as they touched one another,
and the sound of the wheels beside them, and
the sound of [l]a great earthquake. 14 [m]The Spirit
lifted me up and took me away, and I went in
bitterness in the heat of my spirit, the [n]hand of
the LORD being strong upon me. 15 [o]And I came
to the exiles at Tel-abib, who were dwelling
[o]by the Chebar canal, and I sat where they
were dwelling.[3] And [p]I sat there [q]overwhelmed
among them [r]seven days.

A Watchman for Israel

16 [s]And at the end of seven days, the word
of the LORD came to me: 17 [t]“Son of man, [u]I
have made you a watchman for the house of
Israel. Whenever you hear a word from my
mouth, you shall [v]give them warning from me.
18 [w]If I say to the wicked, [x]‘You shall surely die,’
[v]and you give him no warning, nor speak to
warn the wicked from his wicked way, in order
to save his life, that wicked person [y]shall die

[1] Or *the wind*; also verse 14 [2] Or *sound* [3] Or *Chebar, and to where they dwelt*

8 [o][Isa. 50:5] [p]Rev. 10:9; [ch. 3:1, 3]
9 [q]ch. 8:3; Dan. 10:10; Rev. 10:2 [r]Jer. 36:2
10 [s]Rev. 5:1
Chapter 3
1 [c][See ch. 2:1 above] [t][ch. 2:8]
3 [u]Jer. 15:16; Rev. 10:9, 10 [v][Ps. 19:10; 119:103]
4 [w]See ch. 2:1
6 [x][Matt. 11:21, 23]
7 [y][John 15:20] [z][ch. 2:4]
8 [a]See Jer. 1:18
9 [b][Isa. 50:7] [c]ch. 2:6
10 [d]Jer. 26:2 [e][ver. 3]
11 [f]ch. 33:2, 12, 17, 30 [g]ver. 27 [h]ch. 2:7
12 [i]ch. 8:3; 11:1, 24; 43:5; [ch. 37:1] [j][ch. 1:24]
13 [k]ch. 1:5, 15 [l][ch. 1:24]
14 [m]ch. 8:3; 11:1, 24; 43:5; [ch. 37:1] [n]See ch. 1:3
15 [o]See ch. 1:1 [p]Job 2:13; Ps. 137:1; Lam. 2:10 [q]ch. 4:17; Isa. 52:14; Jer. 14:9 [r][Gen. 50:10; 1 Sam. 31:13]
16 [s][Jer. 42:7]
17 [t]See ch. 2:1 [u]ch. 33:7; Isa. 52:8; 56:10; Jer. 6:17; [Heb. 13:17] [v]2 Chr. 19:10; [2 Kgs. 6:10]; See ver. 18-21; ch. 33:4-6 **18** [w]ch. 33:8 [x]Gen. 2:17 [v][See ver. 17 above] [y]ch. 18:18; Jer. 31:30; [John 8:21, 24]

We should not miss also God’s amazing grace to the Israelites. Despite their rebellion and hard-heartedness, God still speaks to them. Though he would have been justified in abandoning them in their exile, he determines in his covenant-keeping love not to do that. “You shall speak my words to them,” he tells Ezekiel, “whether they hear or refuse to hear, for they are a rebellious house” (2:7). Yes, God is angry with his people for their disobedience, but it is a display of amazing grace that he does not leave them in silence.

God shows the same grace to us. Even when we were dead in our sin, he did not leave us in silent condemnation. Rather, he spoke to us through his Son, revealed himself to us, and acted in amazing grace and mercy to save us.

2:8–3:3; 3:16–27 God makes clear to Ezekiel that he is a bound man; he is to speak the word of God accurately and precisely. Ezekiel’s eating of the scroll in 2:8 symbolizes his internalizing of God’s word. He takes it as his own and assumes responsibility for it. In 3:16–17, God makes the same point with a different image, telling Ezekiel that he is a “watchman” for the house of Israel. This, too, points to his taking on of responsibility to warn Israel about the coming judgment. Finally, and perhaps most pointedly, God shuts Ezekiel in his house, binds him with cords, and takes away his power of speech (3:22–26). In only one circumstance will Ezekiel’s tongue be loosed and he be able to speak (3:27)—that will be when God speaks through him!

for[1] his iniquity, [z]but his blood I will require
at your hand. 19 [a]But if you warn the wicked,
and he does not turn from his wickedness, or
from his wicked way, he shall die for his iniquity, [b]but you [c]will have delivered your soul.
20 [d]Again, if a righteous person turns from his
righteousness and commits injustice, [e]and
I lay a stumbling block before him, he shall
die. [v]Because you have not warned him, he
shall die for his sin, [d]and his righteous deeds
that he has done shall not be remembered,
[z]but his blood I will require at your hand.
21 But if you warn the righteous person not to
sin, and he does not sin, he shall surely live,
because he took warning, and you will have
delivered your soul."

22 [f]And the hand of the LORD was upon me
there. And he said to me, "Arise, go out into
[g]the valley,[2] and [h]there I will speak with you."
23 So I arose and went out into the valley, and
behold, [i]the glory of the LORD stood there, like
the glory that I had seen [j]by the Chebar canal,
[i]and I fell on my face. 24 [k]But the Spirit entered
into me and set me on my feet, and he spoke
with me and said to me, "Go, shut yourself
within your house. 25 And you, O son of man,
behold, [l]cords will be placed upon you, and
you shall be bound with them, so that you
cannot go out among the people. 26 And I will
make your tongue cling to the roof of your
mouth, so that [m]you shall be mute and unable
to reprove them, [n]for they are a rebellious
house. 27 [o]But when I speak with you, I will
open your mouth, and you shall say to them,
[p]'Thus says the Lord GOD.' [q]He who will hear,
let him hear; and he who will refuse to hear,
let him refuse, for they are a rebellious house.

The Siege of Jerusalem Symbolized

4 "And you, [r]son of man, [s]take a brick and
lay it before you, and engrave on it a city,
even Jerusalem. 2 [t]And put siegeworks against
it, [u]and build a siege wall against it, [v]and cast
up a mound against it. Set camps also against
it, [w]and plant battering rams against it all
around. 3 And you, take an iron griddle, and
place it as an iron wall between you and the
city; [x]and set your face toward it, [y]and let it be
in a state of siege, and press the siege against
it. This is [z]a sign for the house of Israel.

4 "Then lie on your left side, and place the
punishment[3] of the house of Israel upon it.
For the number of the days that you lie on it,
[a]you shall bear their punishment. 5 For I assign
to you a number of days, [b]390 days, [c]equal to
the number of the years of their punishment.
[a]So long shall you bear [d]the punishment of
the house of Israel. 6 And when you have
completed these, you shall lie down a second

[1] Or *in*; also verses 19, 20 [2] Or *plain*; also verse 23 [3] Or *iniquity*; also verses 5, 6, 17

4:1–24:27 For 21 chapters, God uses his prophet Ezekiel to lay out his case against his people. In a series of oracles and visions, he condemns the Israelites, showing them the judgments that are about to come against them and telling them *why* those judgments will come. Above all, these chapters show the justice and rightness of God's wrath against his people. He is holy, they have rebelled against him, and therefore they have earned his judgment.

This universe has a moral structure built into it, created as it is by a holy and righteous God. We are reminded throughout these chapters that sin infects not only people "out there" but also God's own people. Only God himself, of his own initiative of grace, can rectify this hopeless situation. He promises such restoration as a consequence of his faithfulness to his covenant. In Christ, this is precisely what he provided.

4:1–17 The alarm of God's impending judgment begins to sound against Jerusalem. As is common throughout this book, Ezekiel does not just *speak* his message to Israel; he acts it out. God tells Ezekiel to carve a model of the city of Jerusalem on a brick, and then to build miniature siegeworks around it. Worse, though, God tells Ezekiel to place an iron cooking grate between himself and the city. In this prophetic drama, Ezekiel plays the part of God; his face is turned away from the city, and the iron grate symbolizes God's refusal to be turned from his decision. Though the Babylonian army is physically laying this siege, God is the heavenly director of the unfolding drama.

The coming judgment on Israel would be terrible, a fact illustrated by God's instructions to Ezekiel. For 430 days, he laid bound on his side and ate almost nothing—the equivalent of about a quarter of a slice of bread a day, which he cooked over cow dung. The people of Israel were filthy, God was saying, and his judgment against their sin would be severe.

18 [z]ver. 20; ch. 33:6, 8; 34:10; [ch. 18:13; Acts 18:6; 20:26]
19 [a]ch. 33:9 [b][1 Tim. 4:16] [c]ch. 14:14, 20
20 [d]See ch. 18:24 [e]Jer. 6:21 [v][See ver. 17 above] [z][See ver. 18 above]
22 [f]See ch. 1:3 [g]ch. 8:4; 37:1; Gen. 11:2 [h][Acts 9:6; 22:10]
23 [i]See ch. 1:28 [j]See ch. 1:1
24 [k]See ch. 2:2
25 [l]ch. 4:8
26 [m][Isa. 8:16] [n][ch. 2:3]
27 [o][ch. 24:27; 29:21] [p]ver. 11 [q][Rev. 22:11]

Chapter 4
1 [r]See ch. 2:1 [s][ver. 3; Jer. 13:1, 2]
2 [t][2 Kgs. 25:1] [u]ch. 17:17; 21:22; 26:8 [v]Luke 19:43 [w]ch. 21:22; 26:9
3 [x]See ch. 21:2 [y][Isa. 29:3] [z]ch. 12:6, 11; 24:24, 27; [Isa. 8:18; 20:3]
4 [a]ch. 44:10, 12; [Lev. 16:22; Isa. 53:11, 12]
5 [b]ver. 9 [c][Num. 14:34] [a][See ver. 4 above] [d][ch. 23:4, 9, 10]

time, but on your right side, and [e]bear [f]the
punishment of the house of Judah. [g]Forty
days I assign you, a day for each year. 7 [h]And
you shall set your face toward the siege of
Jerusalem, [i]with your arm bared, and you
shall prophesy against the city. 8 And behold,
[j]I will place cords upon you, so that you cannot
turn from one side to the other, till you have
completed [k]the days of your siege.

9 "And you, take wheat and barley, beans and
lentils, millet and emmer,[1] and put them into a
single vessel and make your [l]bread from them.
[m]During the number of days that you lie on
your side, [n]390 days, you shall eat it. 10 And
your food that you eat shall be [o]by weight,
[p]twenty shekels[2] a day; from day to day[3] you
shall eat it. 11 And water you shall drink [o]by
measure, the sixth part of a hin;[4] from day
to day you shall drink. 12 And you shall eat it
as a barley cake, baking it [q]in their sight on
human dung." 13 And the LORD said, "Thus
shall the people of Israel eat [r]their bread
unclean, among the nations where I will drive
them." 14 Then I said, [s]"Ah, Lord GOD! Behold,
I have never defiled myself.[5] [t]From my youth
up till now I have never eaten [u]what died of
itself or was torn by beasts, nor has [v]tainted
meat come into my mouth." 15 Then he said
to me, "See, I assign to you cow's dung instead
of human dung, on which you may prepare
your bread." 16 Moreover, he said to me, [w]"Son
of man, behold, [x]I will break the supply[6] of
bread in Jerusalem. They shall eat bread [o]by
weight and with anxiety, and they shall drink
water [o]by measure and in dismay. 17 I will do
this that they may lack bread and water, and
[y]look at one another in dismay, and [z]rot away
because of their punishment.

Jerusalem Will Be Destroyed

5 "And you, [a]O son of man, take a [b]sharp
sword. Use it as [c]a barber's razor and [d]pass
it over your head and your beard. Then take
balances for weighing and divide the hair. 2 [e]A
third part you shall burn in the fire [f]in the
midst of the city, [g]when the days of the siege
are completed. And a third part you shall take
and strike with the sword all around the city.
[h]And a third part you shall scatter to the wind,
and [i]I will unsheathe the sword after them.
3 [j]And you shall take from these a small number and bind them in the skirts of your robe.
4 [k]And of these again you shall take some and
cast them into the midst of the fire and burn
them in the fire. From there a fire will come
out into all the house of Israel.

[1] A type of wheat [2] A *shekel* was about 2/5 ounce or 11 grams [3] Or *at a set time daily*; also verse 11 [4] A *hin* was about 4 quarts or 3.5 liters [5] Hebrew *my soul* (or *throat*) *has never been made unclean* [6] Hebrew *staff*

6 [e] ch. 44:10, 12; [Lev. 16:22; Isa. 53:11, 12] [f] [ch. 23:11, 12] [g] [Num. 14:34]
7 [h] See ch. 21:2 [i] Isa. 52:10
8 [j] ch. 3:25 [k] [ver. 9; ch. 5:2]; See 2 Kgs. 25:1-3; Jer. 39:1, 2; 52:4-6
9 [l] [1 Kgs. 22:27] [m] See ver. 8 [n] ver. 5
10 [o] ch. 12:19; [Jer. 37:21] [p] ch. 45:12
11 [o] [See ver. 10 above]
12 [q] See ch. 12:3
13 [r] Hos. 9:3; [Dan. 1:8]
14 [s] ch. 9:8; 11:13; 20:49 [t] [Acts 10:14] [u] ch. 44:31; [Lev. 7:24] [v] Isa. 65:4; [Lev. 7:18]
16 [w] See ch. 2:1 [x] ch. 5:16; 14:13; Lev. 26:26 [o] [See ver. 10 above]
17 [y] See ch. 3:15 [z] ch. 24:23; 33:10; Lev. 26:39

Chapter 5
1 [a] See ch. 2:1 [b] Ps. 57:4; Isa. 49:2 [c] [Isa. 7:20] [d] [ch. 1:3; 44:20; Lev. 21:5]
2 [e] See ver. 12 [f] [ver. 5; ch. 4:1] [g] See ch. 4:8 [h] [ver. 10] [i] ver. 12; ch. 12:14; [Jer. 9:16]
3 [j] [Jer. 40:6; 52:16]
4 [k] [Jer. 42:18; 44:14]

At the climax of human history, however, in an astounding act of mercy, God turned his face not from his people but from his own Son (Mark 15:33–34; Gal 3:13). Though not filthy in himself, Jesus bore the filth and judgment of his people in their place. As a result, all those who trust that Christ took their sin upon himself on the cross are at peace with God. We can—we *must*—leave our moral resumes at home. Through the provision of the gospel, we base our status before God on Christ alone.

5:1–17 Ezekiel cuts off his hair and uses it to symbolize the fates of the people of Israel. A third of the people, he shows, will die by fire in the siege; another third by the sword; and the last third will be scattered to the winds among the nations. Ezekiel's description of the wrath of God against his people (vv. 5–17) is one of the darkest and most terrifying passages in the book.

In communicating the filth of sin and the horror of God's judgment, Ezekiel is echoing the teaching of the entire Bible. Though we often minimize and rationalize our sin, the Bible teaches that it is unspeakably evil and deserving of the severest punishment. As Hebrews 10:31 says, "It is a fearful thing to fall into the hands of the living God." Understanding the horror of our sin grants understanding of the magnificence of the grace that rescues us from it and from its consequences. All of this helps us understand why Jesus had to suffer so terribly to save us from our sin. God's judgment is not a trivial, easily endured thing. It is terrible. When Jesus cried out on the cross, "My God, my God, why have you forsaken me?" (Matt. 27:46), he was himself experiencing the terrible wrath of God on our behalf.

Even here, however, God does not fail to show mercy to his people. He instructs Ezekiel to rescue a few of the hairs—symbolizing the people—from the destruction and to "bind them in the skirts of [his] robe" (Ezek. 5:3). These are the people of the remnant whom God will save from the calamity.

5 “Thus says the Lord GOD: [l]This is Jerusalem.
I have set her [m]in the center of the nations,
with countries all around her. **6** And she has
rebelled against my rules by doing wickedness [n]more than the nations, and against my
statutes more than [m]the countries all around
her; for they have rejected my rules and have
not walked in my statutes. **7** Therefore thus
says the Lord GOD: Because you are [o]more turbulent than the nations that are all around
you, [p]and have not walked in my statutes or
obeyed my rules, [q]and have not[1] even acted
according to the rules of the nations that are
all around you, **8** therefore thus says the Lord
GOD: Behold, I, even I, [r]am against you. [s]And
I will execute judgments[2] in your midst [t]in
the sight of the nations. **9** And because of all
your abominations I will do with you [u]what
I have never yet done, and the like of which
I will never do again. **10** Therefore [v]fathers shall
eat their sons in your midst, and sons shall
eat their fathers. [s]And I will execute judgments on you, [w]and any of you who survive
I will scatter to all the winds. **11** Therefore, [x]as
I live, declares the Lord GOD, surely, [y]because
you have defiled my sanctuary [z]with all your
detestable things and with all your [a]abomina-
tions, [b]therefore I will withdraw.[3] [c]My eye will
not spare, and I will have no pity. **12** [d]A third
part of you shall die of pestilence and be consumed with famine in your midst; [d]a third
part shall fall by the sword all around you;
[d]and a third part I will scatter to all the winds
and will unsheathe the sword after them.
13 [e]“Thus shall my anger spend itself, and
I will vent my fury upon them and satisfy
myself. And they shall know that [f]I am the
LORD—that I have spoken in my jealousy—
[e]when I spend my fury upon them. **14** Moreover,
I will make you [g]a desolation and [h]an object
of reproach among [i]the nations all around
you and in the sight of all who pass by. **15** You
shall be[4] a reproach and a taunt, a warning
[j]and a horror, to [i]the nations all around you,
[k]when I execute judgments on you in anger
and fury, and [l]with furious rebukes—I am the
LORD; I have spoken— **16** when I send against
you[5] [m]the deadly arrows of famine, arrows for
destruction, which I will send to destroy you,
and when I bring more and more famine upon
[n]you and break your supply[6] of bread. **17** I will
send famine and [o]wild beasts against you, [p]and
they will rob you of your children. Pestilence
and [q]blood shall pass through you, and I will
bring the sword upon you. I am the LORD;
I have spoken.”

Judgment Against Idolatry

6 The word of the LORD came to me: **2** [r]“Son
of man, [s]set your face toward [t]the mountains of Israel, and [u]prophesy against them,
3 and say, [v]You mountains of Israel, hear the
word of the Lord GOD! Thus says the Lord
GOD to [w]the mountains and [x]the hills, to [y]the
ravines and the valleys: Behold, I, even I, will
bring a sword upon you, [z]and I will destroy
your high places. **4** [z]Your altars shall become
desolate, and your [a]incense altars shall be broken, and I will cast down your slain before
your idols. **5** [z]And I will lay the dead bodies of
the people of Israel before their idols, [b]and
I will scatter your bones around your altars.

[1] Some Hebrew manuscripts and Syriac lack *not* [2] The same Hebrew expression can mean *obey rules*, or *execute judgments*, depending on the context [3] Some Hebrew manuscripts *I will cut you down* [4] Dead Sea Scroll, Septuagint, Syriac, Vulgate, Targum; Masoretic Text *And it shall be* [5] Hebrew *them* [6] Hebrew *staff*

6:1–7:27 Ezekiel pronounces judgment against both the mountains (ch. 6) and the low-lying land (ch. 7) of Israel. *Nothing* escapes God’s judgment. The city, the people, and now the very rocks and dirt will fall under it.

When Adam and Eve plunged humanity into sin, it was not only humanity that was affected. The entire cosmos was thrown into upheaval. The creation itself, therefore, groans, awaiting its day of release, of final redemption—which will come when humanity is redeemed (Rom. 8:18–23). And in counter-parallel to the events of the original fall, when humanity is restored, so too will be all of creation.

In Christ, who has already come once and who will one day come again, this restoration is sure. For he has been raised from the dead, the “firstfruits” of the dawning new creation. The risen Christ is the first installment of one great harvest, in which all believers, united to Christ, are invincibly included in a renewed creation.

5 [l][ver. 2; ch. 4:1] [m][ch. 38:12]
6 [n]See ch. 16:47, 48 [m][See ver. 5 above]
7 [o]Ps. 2:1; 46:6 [p]ch. 16:47 [q][ch. 11:12]
8 [r]See ch. 13:8 [s]ch. 11:9; 16:41; 23:10 [t]ch. 22:16
9 [u][2 Kgs. 21:12, 13; Lam. 1:12; Dan. 9:12]
10 [v]See Jer. 19:9 [s][See ver. 8 above] [w]ch. 12:14; 17:21; 22:15; 36:19; Deut. 28:64; Jer. 9:16; 15:4; Zech. 2:6; [ver. 2; ch. 36:19]
11 [x]See ch. 16:48 [y]ch. 8:3, 5, 6; 23:39; 2 Chr. 36:14; Jer. 7:30 [z]ch. 11:18 [a]ch. 7:20; 11:18, 21 [b]ch. 16:27 [c]ch. 7:4, 9; 8:18; 9:5, 10; [Jer. 21:7]

12 [d][ver. 2; ch. 6:11, 12; Jer. 15:2] **13** [e]ch. 6:12; 7:8; 20:8, 21; Lam. 4:11; [ch. 39:25] [f]ch. 36:5, 6; 38:19 **14** [g]ch. 6:6; See Jer. 22:5 [h]ch. 22:4; Neh. 2:17; Ps. 79:4; Jer. 24:9 [i]ver. 5, 6 **15** [j]ch. 14:8; Deut. 28:37 [i][See ver. 14 above] [k][ch. 14:21] [l]ch. 25:17 **16** [m]Deut. 32:23, 24 [n]See ch. 4:16 **17** [o]ch. 14:15; 33:27; 34:25; Deut. 32:24; [2 Kgs. 17:25] [p][ch. 36:12] [q]ch. 38:22 **Chapter 6** **2** [r]See ch. 2:1 [s]ch. 13:17; 20:46; 21:2; 25:2; 28:21; 29:2; 35:2; 38:2; [Luke 9:51] [t]ch. 19:9; 33:28; 34:13, 14; 35:12; 36:1, 4, 8; 37:22; 38:8; 39:2, 4, 17 [u]ch. 37:4, 9; 38:2 **3** [v]ch. 36:1, 4 [w]ch. 36:4, 6 [x][ver. 13] [y][ch. 31:12; Isa. 57:5, 6] [z]Lev. 26:30 **4** [z][See ver. 3 above] [a]See 2 Chr. 14:5 **5** [z][See ver. 3 above] [b][2 Kgs. 23:14, 16]

6 Wherever you dwell, [c]the cities shall be waste and [d]the high places ruined, so that your altars will be waste and ruined,[1] your idols broken and destroyed, your [a]incense altars cut down, and your works wiped out. 7 And the slain shall fall in your midst, and you shall know that I am the LORD.

8 [e]"Yet I will leave some of you alive. When you have among the nations [f]some who escape the sword, and when you are scattered through the countries, 9 then those of you who escape [g]will remember me among the nations where they are carried captive, how [h]I have been broken over their whoring heart that has departed from me and over their eyes [i]that go whoring after their idols. [g]And they will be loathsome in their own sight for the evils that they have committed, for all their abominations. 10 And they shall know that I am the LORD. [j]I have not said in vain that I would do this evil to them."

11 Thus says the Lord GOD: [k]"Clap your hands [l]and stamp your foot and say, Alas, because of all the evil abominations of the house of Israel, [m]for they shall fall by the sword, by famine, and by pestilence. 12 [n]He who is far off shall die of pestilence, and he who is near shall fall by the sword, and he who is left and is preserved shall die of famine. [o]Thus I will spend my fury upon them. 13 And you shall know that I am the LORD, [p]when their slain lie among their idols around their altars, [q]on every high hill, [r]on all the mountaintops, [s]under every green tree, and under [t]every leafy oak, wherever [u]they offered pleasing aroma to all their idols. 14 And [v]I will stretch out my hand against them and [w]make the land desolate and waste, [x]in all their dwelling places, from the wilderness to [y]Riblah.[2] Then [z]they will know that I am the LORD."

The Day of the Wrath of the LORD

7 The word of the LORD came to me: 2 "And you, [a]O son of man, thus says the Lord GOD to the land of Israel: [b]An end! The end has come upon the four corners of the land.[3] 3 Now [b]the end is upon you, and [c]I will send my anger upon you; [d]I will judge you according to your ways, and I will punish you for all your abominations. 4 [e]And my eye will not spare you, nor will I have pity, but [f]I will punish you for your ways, while your abominations are in your midst. [g]Then you will know that I am the LORD.

5 "Thus says the Lord GOD: Disaster [h]after disaster![4] Behold, it comes. 6 [b]An end has come; the end has come; it has awakened against you. Behold, it comes. 7 [i]Your doom[5] has come to you, O inhabitant of the land. [j]The time has come; the day is near, a day of tumult, and not [k]of joyful shouting on the mountains. 8 Now I will soon [l]pour out my wrath upon you, and [m]spend my anger against you, [d]and judge you according to your ways, and I will punish you for all your abominations. 9 [e]And my eye will not spare, nor will I have pity. I will punish you according to your ways, while your abominations are in your midst. [n]Then you will know that I am the LORD, who strikes.

10 [o]"Behold, the day! Behold, it comes! [p]Your doom has come; [q]the rod has blossomed; pride has budded. 11 [r]Violence has grown up into [q]a rod of wickedness. [s]None of them shall remain, nor their abundance, nor their wealth; neither shall there be preeminence among them.[6] 12 [j]The time has come; the day has arrived. Let not [t]the buyer rejoice, nor [t]the seller mourn, [u]for wrath is upon all their multitude.[7] 13 For [v]the seller shall not return to what he has sold, while they live. [w]For the vision concerns all their multitude; it shall not turn back; and because of his iniquity, none can maintain his life.[8]

14 "They have blown the trumpet and made everything ready, but none goes to battle, [x]for my wrath is upon all their multitude. 15 [y]The sword is without; pestilence and famine are within. [z]He who is in the field dies by the sword, [z]and him who is in the city famine and pestilence devour. 16 [a]And if any survivors escape, they will be on the mountains, like [b]doves of the valleys, all of them moaning, each one over his iniquity. 17 [c]All hands are

[1] Or *and punished* [2] Some Hebrew manuscripts; most Hebrew manuscripts *Diblah* [3] Or *earth* [4] Some Hebrew manuscripts (compare Syriac, Targum); most Hebrew manuscripts *Disaster! A unique disaster!* [5] The meaning of the Hebrew word is uncertain; also verse 10 [6] The meaning of this last Hebrew sentence is uncertain [7] Or *abundance*; also verses 13, 14 [8] The meaning of this last Hebrew sentence is uncertain

6 [c] ch. 12:20; [Isa. 27:10] [d] [ver. 3, 4] [a] [See ver. 4 above] **8** [e] ch. 12:16; 14:22 [f] ch. 7:16 **9** [g] ch. 16:61; 20:43; 36:31; Lev. 26:39, 40 [h] [Jer. 23:9] [i] See Ex. 34:15 **10** [j] [Num. 23:19] **11** [k] [ch. 21:14, 17] [l] [ch. 25:6] [m] See ch. 5:12 **12** [n] [ch. 7:15] [o] See ch. 5:13 **13** [p] [ver. 4, 5] [q] [ch. 20:28] [r] Hos. 4:13 [s] Jer. 2:20 [t] Isa. 1:29 [u] ch. 16:19; 20:28; Gen. 8:21 **14** [v] ch. 25:7, 13, 16; 35:3; Isa. 5:25 [w] ch. 33:28 [x] [ver. 6] [y] [Num. 34:11] [z] See ver. 7 **Chapter 7** **2** [a] See ch. 2:1 [b] Lam. 4:18; [Isa. 10:23] **3** [b] [See ver. 2 above] [c] See ver. 8 [d] See ch. 18:30 **4** [e] See ch. 5:11 [f] ch. 9:10; 11:21; 16:43; 22:31 [g] See ch. 6:7 **5** [h] [ch. 5:9] **6** [b] [See ver. 2 above] **7** [i] ver. 10 [j] Zeph. 1:14, 15; [ch. 12:23] [k] [Jer. 25:30] **8** [l] ch. 9:8; 14:19; 20:8, 13, 21, 33, 34; 22:22; 36:18 [m] See ch. 5:13 [d] [See ver. 3 above] **9** [e] [See ver. 4 above] [n] [ch. 6:7] **10** [o] [ver. 2] [p] ver. 7 [q] [Isa. 10:5; 14:5] **11** [r] [ver. 23] [q] [See ver. 10 above] [s] [ch. 17:13] **12** [j] [See ver. 7 above] [t] [Isa. 24:2; 1 Cor. 7:29, 30] [u] ver. 14 **13** [v] Lev. 25:13, 14 [w] See ch. 9:8-10 **14** [x] ver. 12 **15** [y] [ch. 6:12; Lam. 1:20] [z] Jer. 14:18 **16** [a] ch. 6:8 [b] [Isa. 38:14] **17** [c] ch. 21:7; Isa. 13:7; Jer. 6:24

feeble, and all knees turn to water. 18 [d]They
put on sackcloth, and [e]horror covers them.
Shame is on all faces, and [f]baldness on all their
heads. 19 They cast their silver into the streets,
and their gold is like an unclean thing. [g]Their
silver and gold are not able to deliver them in
the day of the wrath of the LORD. They cannot satisfy their hunger or fill their stomachs
with it. [h]For it was [i]the stumbling block of
their iniquity. 20 [j]His beautiful ornament they
used for pride, and [k]they made their abominable images and their detestable things of it.
Therefore [l]I make it an unclean thing to them.
21 And I will give it into the hands of [m]foreign-
ers for prey, [n]and to the wicked of the earth for
spoil, and [l]they shall profane it. 22 I will turn
my face from them, and [l]they shall profane
my treasured[1] place. Robbers shall enter [l]and
profane it.

23 [o]"Forge a chain![2] [p]For the land is full of
bloody crimes [q]and the city is full of violence.
24 I will bring [r]the worst of the nations to take
possession of their houses. [s]I will put an end
to the pride of the strong, [t]and their holy
places[3] shall be profaned. 25 [u]When anguish
comes, [v]they will seek peace, but there shall be
none. 26 [w]Disaster comes upon disaster; [x]rumor
follows rumor. [y]They seek a vision from the
prophet, while [z]the law[4] perishes from the
priest and [a]counsel from the elders. 27 The king
mourns, the prince is wrapped in despair, and
the hands of the people of the land are paralyzed by terror. According to their way [b]I will
do to them, and according to their judgments
I will judge them, [c]and they shall know that
I am the LORD."

Abominations in the Temple

8 [d]In the sixth year, in the sixth month, on
the fifth day of the month, [e]as I sat in my
house, with [f]the elders of Judah sitting before
me, [g]the hand of the Lord GOD fell upon me
there. 2 Then I looked, and behold, [h]a form that
had the appearance of a man.[5] [h]Below what
appeared to be his waist was fire, and above his
waist was something like the appearance of

[1] Or *secret* [2] Probably refers to an instrument of captivity [3] By revocalization (compare Septuagint); Hebrew *and those who sanctify them* [4] Or *instruction* [5] By revocalization (compare Septuagint); Hebrew *of fire*

8:1–9:11 To show the unimpeachable rightness of God's judgment against his people, Ezekiel is taken in a vision to the temple in Jerusalem, where the people's idolatries are exposed in excruciating detail. No one is sure precisely what the "image of jealousy" was (8:3), but it was a flagrant offense against the one true God. Digging through the outer wall of the temple, Ezekiel sees idolatrous images engraved on the walls, and the elders of Israel engaged in pagan worship. The abhorrent idolatry of Israel is deep and shocking. The people even turn their backs on the Lord so that they may worship the sun (8:16).

In response (ch. 9), God executes his judgment against the city, appointing six angels to kill the people. It was not a random judgment, however. God was meticulous in his execution of punishment, instructing another angel to mark those who "sigh and groan over all the abominations that are committed" in Jerusalem (9:4).

All this drives home the truth that God's punishment of Israel is neither arbitrary nor haphazard. On the contrary, it is fully deserved and it is carried out with utmost care. The people have been disobedient to God's law (5:6–8). They have committed violence and oppression (7:23; 9:9). They have committed gross idolatry, and through it all they have been marked by a high-handed arrogance and pride (7:19; 11:1–3). Thus, as in the rest of the Bible, God's anger is not an out-of-control lashing out. It is a settled, intense, and even meticulous opposition to sin. The impression left by the execution of punishment against Jerusalem is not one of chaos but rather of God's determined and scrupulous judgment against Israel for her sin. That should be a sobering thought for anyone who knows themselves to a be a sinner before God. The God who made us and judges us does not take sin lightly, and he does not overlook sin. He judges it, carefully and unfailingly.

Many people think that grace is a matter of God simply turning his eyes away from sin—ignoring it or "sweeping it under the rug." Nothing could be further from the truth. Grace is something entirely different; it is God pouring out his full judgment against sin, but doing so on his Son rather than on the sinner. God does not ignore our sin, even as he saves us. He punishes his Son in our place. In this way he shows supreme mercy while upholding perfect justice (Rom. 3:26). "Oh, the depth of the riches and wisdom and knowledge of God!" (Rom. 11:33).

18 [d]Isa. 15:2, 3; Lam. 2:10 [e]Ps. 55:5 [f]See Isa. 3:24
19 [g]Prov. 11:4; Zeph. 1:18 [h][1 Tim. 6:10] [i]ch. 14:3, 4, 7; 44:12
20 [j][Isa. 64:11] [k][ch. 16:17]; See ch. 8:5-16 [l][ch. 9:7; 24:21; 25:3]
21 [m]See ch. 28:7 [n][ver. 24; ch. 23:46] [l][See ver. 20 above]
22 [l][See ver. 20 above]
23 [o][Jer. 27:2] [p]ch. 8:17; 9:9; 11:6; 22:3, 4; Jer. 6:7 [q][ver. 11]
24 [r][ver. 21; Hab. 1:6, 13] [s][ver. 11] [t]See ver. 20
25 [u][ver. 2] [v][Jer. 6:14; 8:15; 1 Thess. 5:3]
26 [w][Jer. 4:20] [x]See Job 1:16-19 [y][ch. 20:1, 3; Ps. 74:9] [z][Mal. 2:7] [a][1 Kgs. 12:6]
27 [b][ver. 4] [c]See ch. 6:7
Chapter 8
1 [d][ch. 1:2]; See ch. 20:1 [e][2 Kgs. 6:32] [f]ver. 11, 12; ch. 14:1; 20:1, 3 [g]See ch. 1:3
2 [h]ch. 1:27

brightness, like [i]gleaming metal.[1] 3He [j]put out
the form of a hand and took me by a lock of
my head, and the Spirit lifted me up [k]between
earth and heaven and [l]brought me in [m]visions
of God to Jerusalem, [n]to the entrance of the
gateway of the inner court that faces north,
[o]where was the seat of the [p]image of jealousy,
[q]which provokes to jealousy. 4And behold, [r]the
glory of the God of Israel was there, like the
vision that I saw [s]in the valley.

5Then he said to me, [t]"Son of man, lift up your
eyes now toward the north." So I lifted up my
eyes toward the north, and behold, north of
[u]the altar gate, in the entrance, was this [p]image
of jealousy. 6And he said to me, "Son of man, [v]do
you see what they are doing, [w]the great abominations that the house of Israel are committing
here, [x]to drive me far from my sanctuary? But
you will see still greater abominations."

7And he brought me to the entrance of the
court, and when I looked, behold, there was a
hole in the wall. 8Then he said to me, "Son of
man, [y]dig in the wall." So I dug in the wall, and
behold, there was an entrance. 9And he said
to me, "Go in, and see [z]the vile abominations
that they are committing here." 10So I went in
and saw. And there, [a]engraved on the wall all
around, was [b]every form of [c]creeping things
and loathsome beasts, and all the idols of the
house of Israel. 11And before them stood [d]sev-
enty men of [e]the elders of the house of Israel,
with Jaazaniah the son of [f]Shaphan standing
among them. Each had his censer in his hand,
and [g]the smoke of the cloud of incense went
up. 12Then he said to me, "Son of man, have
you seen what the elders of the house of Israel
are doing [h]in the dark, each [i]in his room of
pictures? For they say, [j]'The LORD does not see
us, the LORD has forsaken the land.'" 13He said
also to me, [k]"You will see still greater abominations that they commit."

14Then he brought me to [l]the entrance of
the north gate of the house of the LORD,
and behold, there sat women weeping for
Tammuz. 15Then he said to me, "Have you
seen this, O [t]son of man? [k]You will see still
greater abominations than these."

16And he brought me into [m]the inner court
of the house of the LORD. And behold, at the
entrance of the temple of the LORD, [n]between
the [o]porch and [p]the altar, were about twenty-
five men, [q]with their backs to the temple of
the LORD, and their faces toward the east, worshiping [r]the sun toward the east. 17Then he
said to me, "Have you seen this, O [s]son of man?
Is it too light a thing for the house of Judah to
commit [t]the abominations that they commit
here, that [u]they should fill the land with violence and [v]provoke me still further to anger?
Behold, they put the branch to their[2] nose.
18Therefore [w]I will act in wrath. [x]My eye will
not spare, nor will I have pity. [y]And though
they cry in my ears with a loud voice, I will
not hear them."

Idolaters Killed

9 Then he cried in my ears with a loud voice,
saying, "Bring near the executioners of
the city, [z]each with his destroying weapon in
his hand." 2And behold, six men came from
the direction of [a]the upper gate, which faces
north, each with his weapon for slaughter in
his hand, and with them was [b]a man clothed
in linen, with a writing case at his waist. And
they went in and stood beside [c]the bronze
altar.

3Now [d]the glory of the God of Israel had gone
up from the cherub on which it rested to [e]the
threshold of the house. And he called to [b]the
man clothed in linen, who had the writing
case at his waist. 4And the LORD said to him,
"Pass through the city, through Jerusalem, and
[f]put a mark on the foreheads of the men who
[g]sigh and groan over all the abominations that
are committed in it." 5And to [h]the others he
said in my hearing, "Pass through the city after
him, and strike. [i]Your eye shall not spare, and
you shall show no pity. 6[j]Kill old men outright,
young men and maidens, little children and
women, but [k]touch no one on whom is the
mark. And [l]begin at my sanctuary." So they
began with the elders who were before the
house. 7Then he said to them, [m]"Defile the
house, and fill the courts with the slain. Go
out." So they went out and struck in the city.

[1] Or *amber* [2] Or *my*

2[i]ch. 1:4, 27 **3**[j][Dan. 5:5]; See ch. 2:9 [k][2 Cor. 12:2, 4] [l]ch. 11:1, 24; 40:2 [m]See ch. 1:1 [n]ver. 14 [o][ch. 5:11] [p][Deut. 4:16] [q]Deut. 32:16, 21 **4**[r]See ch. 1:28 [s]See ch. 3:22 **5**[t]See ch. 2:1 [u]See ver. 16 [p][See ver. 3 above] **6**[v][ch. 47:6] [w]See ch. 5:11 [x][ch. 10:18, 19] **8**[y][ch. 12:5] **9**[z]See ch. 5:11 **10**[a]ch. 23:14 [b]See Ex. 20:4 [c]Lev. 11:20; Rom. 1:23 **11**[d][Ex. 24:1; Num. 11:16] [e]See ver. 1 [f]2 Chr. 34:8 [g][ch. 6:13] **12**[h][ver. 7] [i][ver. 10] [j]ch. 9:9; Ps. 10:11; Isa. 29:15 **13**[k]ver. 6 **14**[l]ver. 3 **15**[t][See ver. 5 above] [k][See ver. 13 above] **16**[m]ch. 10:3; 40:28; 43:5; 45:19; 46:1; 1 Kgs. 6:36 [n]Joel 2:17 [o]1 Kgs. 6:3 [p]ver. 5; ch. 40:47; Ex. 40:6, 29; [ch. 9:2] [q][Jer. 2:27; 32:33] [r]See Jer. 8:2 **17**[s]See ch. 2:1 [t]See ch. 5:11 [u][ch. 7:11, 23] [v]Jer. 7:18, 19; [ch. 20:28] **18**[w]ch. 5:13 [x]See ch. 5:11 [y]Prov. 1:28; Isa. 1:15; Mic. 3:4 **Chapter 9** **1**[z][ch. 43:3] **2**[a]2 Kgs. 15:35; Jer. 20:2 [b]ch. 10:2, 6, 7; Dan. 10:5; 12:6, 7 [c][ch. 8:16] **3**[d]See ch. 1:28 [e]ch. 10:4, 18; 46:2; 47:1 [b][See ver. 2 above] **4**[f]Rev. 3:12; 7:3; 9:4; 14:1; 22:4; [Ex. 12:7; Rev. 13:16, 17; 14:9; 20:4] [g][Ps. 119:53, 136, 158] **5**[h][ver. 2] [i]See ch. 5:11 **6**[j][2 Chr. 36:17] [k][Rev. 9:4] [l]See Jer. 25:29 **7**[m]ch. 7:21, 22

8 And while they were striking, and I was left
alone, [n]I fell upon my face, and cried, [o]"Ah,
Lord GOD! [p]Will you destroy all the remnant
of Israel [q]in the outpouring of your wrath on
Jerusalem?"
9 Then he said to me, [r]"The guilt of the
house of Israel and Judah is exceedingly
great. [s]The land is full of blood, and the city
full of injustice. For [t]they say, 'The LORD has
forsaken the land, and the LORD does not
see.' 10 As for me, [u]my eye will not spare, nor
will I have pity; [v]I will bring their deeds upon
their heads."
11 And behold, [w]the man clothed in linen,
with the writing case at his waist, brought
back word, saying, "I have done as you commanded me."

The Glory of the LORD Leaves the Temple

10 Then I looked, and behold, [x]on the
expanse that was over the heads of the
cherubim there appeared above them something [y]like a sapphire,[1] in appearance like a
throne. 2 And he said to [z]the man clothed in
linen, "Go in among [a]the whirling wheels
underneath the cherubim. Fill your hands
with [b]burning coals from between the cherubim, and [c]scatter them over the city."
And he went in [d]before my eyes. 3 Now the
cherubim were standing [e]on the south side
of the house, when the man went in, and [f]a
cloud filled [g]the inner court. 4 And [h]the glory
of the LORD [i]went up from the cherub to the
threshold of the house, and the house [f]was
filled with the cloud, and the court was filled
with [j]the brightness of the glory of the LORD.
5 And [k]the sound of the wings of the cherubim
was heard as far as the outer court, [k]like the
voice of God Almighty when he speaks.
6 And when he commanded [l]the man clothed
in linen, [m]"Take fire from between [n]the whirling wheels, from between the cherubim," he
went in and stood beside a wheel. 7 And a
cherub stretched out his hand from between
the cherubim to the fire that was between the
cherubim, and took some of it and put it into
the hands of the man clothed in linen, who
took it and went out. 8 The cherubim appeared
to have [o]the form of a human hand under their
wings.

[1] Or *lapis lazuli*

10:3–11:25 At the moment of judgment, Ezekiel is shown again the vision of God's throne-chariot which he saw by the Chebar canal. This time, however, God is leaving his temple, abandoning it in its idolatry and sin. God's departure from his temple and from Jerusalem happens in stages. First, he moves from the Most Holy Place to the threshold of the sanctuary (10:3–5). Then he moves out to the east gate of the temple complex (10:18–19). Finally, the glory of the Lord departs from the city and goes out to the mountain on the east side of the city (11:22–23).

The departure of God's glory from the temple is a heartrending vision. This is the glory of God that led the nation from slavery in Egypt, remained with them in their wilderness wanderings, and settled among them in tabernacle and temple to declare God's covenant faithfulness and abiding care for his people. Even here in the account of the glory's departure, however, God's love for his people is evident. The departure does not happen quickly. At each stage—at the threshold of the sanctuary, at the east gate, even on the mountain outside the city—God lingers before he moves further away, giving his people every opportunity to repent. Indeed he is a God of great mercy, slow to anger and abounding in love!

Most strikingly, it is at the last moment that God answers Ezekiel's wrenching question in 11:13—"Ah, Lord GOD! Will you make a full end of the remnant of Israel?" The answer is no! In the first of many notes of grace sounded amid national moral catastrophe, God tells his people in 11:14–21 that he would not leave them in exile forever. There would come a day when he would gather them together again in their land, remove their hearts of stone, give them hearts of flesh, and give them a new spirit that would delight to obey him (cf. 36:22–32). From the inside out, God would renew his people. They would be wholly cleansed. Sin may abound, and judgment because of sin, but grace abounds all the more!

All this would happen ultimately through the saving work of God's Son, Jesus Christ. In Christ the new covenant is fulfilled. The long-awaited kingdom of God is inaugurated (Mark 1:15). In the coming of the Holy Spirit, the hearts of God's people are transformed from the inside out, and Ezekiel's prophecy is fulfilled (John 16:13; 2 Cor. 3:3–6).

8 [n] ch. 11:13; [Num. 14:5] [o] See ch. 4:14 [p] ch. 11:13 [q] See ch. 7:8
9 [r] See 2 Chr. 36:14-16 [s] See ch. 7:23 [t] See ch. 8:12
10 [u] See ch. 5:11 [v] See ch. 7:4
11 [w] ch. 10:2, 6, 7; Dan. 10:5; 12:6, 7

Chapter 10

1 [x] [ch. 1:22] [y] See ch. 1:26
2 [z] See ch. 9:2 [a] ver. 6, 13 [b] ch. 1:13 [c] [Rev. 8:5] [d] ver. 19
3 [e] [Luke 1:11] [f] See 1 Kgs. 8:10 [g] See ch. 8:16
4 [h] See ch. 1:28 [i] ver. 18, 19 [f] [See ver. 3 above] [j] [ch. 43:2]
5 [k] ch. 1:24
6 [l] See ch. 9:2 [m] [ver. 2] [n] ver. 2
8 [o] [ver. 21; ch. 1:8; 8:3]

9 [p]And I looked, and behold, there were four
wheels beside the cherubim, one beside each
cherub, and [q]the appearance of the wheels
was [r]like sparkling [s]beryl. 10 And as for their
appearance, the four had the same likeness, as
if a wheel were within a wheel. 11 [t]When they
went, they went in any of their four directions[1] [u]without turning as they went, [v]but in
whatever direction the front wheel[2] faced,
the others followed without turning as they
went. 12 [w]And their whole body, their rims,
and their spokes, their wings,[3] and the wheels
were full of eyes all around—the wheels that
the four of them had. 13 As for the wheels,
they were called in my hearing [n]"the whirling wheels." 14 [x]And every one had four faces:
[y]the first face was the face of the cherub, and
the second face was [z]a human face, and the
third the face of a lion, and the fourth the
face of an eagle.

15 [a]And the cherubim mounted up. These
were [b]the living creatures that I saw by [c]the
Chebar canal. 16 [d]And when the cherubim went,
the wheels went beside them. And [d]when the
cherubim lifted up their wings to mount up
from the earth, the wheels did not turn from
beside them. 17 [e]When they stood still, these
stood still, and when they mounted up, these
mounted up with them, for the spirit of the
living creatures[4] was in them.

18 [f]Then [g]the glory of the LORD went out
from the threshold of the house, and stood
over the cherubim. 19 [h]And the cherubim lifted
up their wings and mounted up from the
earth [i]before my eyes as they went out, with
the wheels beside them. And they stood at the
entrance of the [j]east gate of the house of the
LORD, and [k]the glory of the God of Israel was
over them.

20 [l]These were the living creatures that I saw
[m]underneath the God of Israel by [n]the Chebar
canal; and I knew that they were cherubim.
21 [o]Each had four faces, and each four wings,
and underneath their wings [p]the likeness of
human hands. 22 [q]And as for the likeness of
their faces, they were the same faces whose
appearance I had seen by the Chebar canal.
[r]Each one of them went straight forward.

Judgment on Wicked Counselors

11 [s]The Spirit lifted me up and brought
me to [t]the east gate of the house of the
LORD, which faces east. And behold, at the
entrance of the gateway there were [u]twenty-
five men. And I saw among them Jaazaniah
[v]the son of Azzur, and [w]Pelatiah the son of
Benaiah, princes of the people. 2 And he said
to me, [x]"Son of man, these are the men who
devise iniquity and who give wicked counsel
in this city; 3 [y]who say, [z]'The time is not near[5]
to build houses. [a]This city is the cauldron, and
we are the meat.' 4 Therefore prophesy against
them, prophesy, O son of man."

5 And [b]the Spirit of the LORD fell upon me,
and he said to me, "Say, Thus says the LORD:
So you think, O house of Israel. [c]For I know
the things that come into your mind. 6 [d]You
have multiplied your slain in this city and
have filled its streets with the slain. 7 Therefore
thus says the Lord GOD: [e]Your slain whom
you have laid in the midst of it, [a]they are the
meat, and [a]this city is the cauldron, but you
shall be brought out of the midst of it. 8 [f]You
have feared the sword, and I will bring the
sword upon you, declares the Lord GOD. 9 And
I will bring you out of the midst of it, and [g]give
you into the hands of foreigners, and [h]execute
judgments upon you. 10 [i]You shall fall by the
sword. I will judge you at the border of Israel,
[j]and you shall know that I am the LORD. 11 [k]This
city shall not be your cauldron, nor shall you
be the meat in the midst of it. I will judge you
at the border of Israel, 12 and you shall know
that I am the LORD. For you have not walked
in my statutes, nor obeyed my rules, [l]but have
acted according to the rules of the nations that
are around you."

13 And it came to pass, while I was prophesying, [m]that [n]Pelatiah the son of Benaiah died.
[o]Then I fell down on my face and cried out with
a loud voice and said, [o]"Ah, Lord GOD! [p]Will
you make a full end of the remnant of Israel?"

Israel's New Heart and Spirit

14 And the word of the LORD came to me:
15 [q]"Son of man, your brothers, even your
brothers, your kinsmen,[6] the whole house

[1] Hebrew *to their four sides* [2] Hebrew *the head* [3] Or *their whole body, their backs, their hands, and their wings* [4] Or *spirit of life* [5] Or *Is not the time near . . . ?* [6] Hebrew *the men of your redemption*

9 [p][ch. 1:15] [q]ch. 1:16 [r][ch. 1:4] [s][ch. 1:16; Dan. 10:6] **11** [t]ch. 1:17 [u]ch. 1:9 [v][ver. 22] **12** [w][ch. 1:18] **13** [n][See ver. 6 above] **14** [x][ch. 1:6] [y][ch. 1:10] [z][ch. 1:5, 10; 41:19] **15** [a]ver. 17, 19 [b]ch. 1:5 [c]See ch. 1:1 **16** [d]ch. 1:19 **17** [e]ch. 1:20 **18** [f][ver. 4] [g]ch. 43:2; See ch. 1:28 **19** [h]ch. 11:22 [i]ver. 2 [j]ch. 11:1 [k]ch. 43:2; See ch. 1:28 **20** [l]ch. 1:5 [m]ch. 1:22, 26 [n]See ch. 1:1 **21** [o][ch. 1:6] [p][ver. 8] **22** [q]ch. 1:10 [r][ver. 11] **Chapter 11** **1** [s]ver. 24; See ch. 3:12 [t]ch. 10:19 [u]ch. 8:16 [v]Jer. 28:1 [w]ver. 13 **2** [x]See ch. 2:1 **3** [y][Jer. 29:28] [z][ch. 12:22, 27] [a]ch. 24:3, 6 **5** [b]See ch. 2:2 [c]ch. 20:32; 38:10; [Isa. 29:15] **6** [d][ch. 7:23] **7** [e]ch. 24:7 [a][See ver. 3 above] **8** [f]Jer. 42:16 **9** [g]ch. 7:21 [h]See ch. 5:8 **10** [i]Jer. 39:6; See 2 Kgs. 25:18-21 [j]See ch. 6:7 **11** [k][ver. 3, 7] **12** [l][ch. 8:10, 14, 16] **13** [m][Acts 5:5] [n]ver. 1 [o]ch. 9:8 [p][ch. 20:17] **15** [q]See ch. 2:1

of Israel, all of them, are those of whom the
inhabitants of Jerusalem have said, [r]'Go far
from the LORD; to us this land is given for a
possession.' 16 Therefore say, 'Thus says the
Lord GOD: Though I removed them far off
among the nations, and though I scattered
them among the countries, yet [s]I have been
a sanctuary to them for a while[1] in the countries where they have gone.' 17 Therefore say,
'Thus says the Lord GOD: [t]I will gather you
from the peoples and assemble you out of the
countries where you have been scattered, [t]and
I will give you the land of Israel.' 18 And when
they come there, [u]they will remove from it all
its [v]detestable things and all its abominations.
19 [w]And I will give them one heart, and [x]a new
spirit I will put within them. [y]I will remove
the heart of stone from their flesh [z]and give
them a heart of flesh, 20 [a]that they may walk
in my statutes and keep my rules and obey
them. [b]And they shall be my people, and I will
be their God. 21 [c]But as for those whose heart
goes after their detestable things and their
abominations, [d]I will[2] bring their deeds upon
their own heads, declares the Lord GOD."
22 [e]Then the cherubim lifted up their wings,
with the wheels beside them, [e]and the glory
of the God of Israel was over them. 23 And the
glory of the LORD went up from the midst of
the city and [f]stood on the mountain that is
on the east side of the city. 24 [g]And the Spirit
lifted me up and brought me [h]in the vision by
the Spirit of God [i]into Chaldea, to the exiles.
Then the vision that I had seen went up from
me. 25 And I told the exiles all the things that
the LORD had shown me.

Judah's Captivity Symbolized

12 The word of the LORD came to me:
2 [j]"Son of man, you dwell in the midst of
[k]a rebellious house, [l]who have eyes to see, but
see not, who have ears to hear, but hear not, for
they are [k]a rebellious house. 3 As for you, son
of man, prepare for yourself [m]an exile's baggage, and go into exile by day [n]in their sight.
You shall go like an exile from your place to
another place [n]in their sight. [o]Perhaps they
will understand, though[3] they are a rebellious
house. 4 You shall bring out your baggage by
day in their sight, as baggage for exile, and
you shall go out yourself [p]at evening in their
sight, as those do who must go into exile. 5 In
their sight [q]dig through the wall, and bring
your baggage out through it. 6 In their sight
you shall lift the baggage upon your shoulder
and carry it out at dusk. You shall cover your
face that you may not see the land, for I have
made you [r]a sign for the house of Israel."
7 [s]And I did as I was commanded. [t]I brought
out my baggage by day, as baggage for exile,
and in the evening I dug through the wall
with my own hands. I brought out my baggage at dusk, carrying it on my shoulder in
their sight.
8 In the morning the word of the LORD
came to me: 9 [u]"Son of man, has not the house
of Israel, [v]the rebellious house, said to you,
[w]'What are you doing?' 10 Say to them, 'Thus

[1] Or *in small measure* [2] Hebrew *To the heart of their detestable things and their abominations their heart goes; I will* [3] Or *will see that*

12:8–13 Ezekiel makes a very specific prophecy about the fate of "the prince in Jerusalem" (v. 10). The prophecy concerns Zedekiah, the last king of Israel, who had been installed by the king of Babylon as a puppet ruler. Reflecting this, Ezekiel pointedly refuses to call him "king," preferring instead the term "prince."

Though the prophecy is dated several years before the actual siege of Jerusalem, God reveals in detail what would happen to Zedekiah, the history of which is recorded in 2 Kings 25:1–7. The breach in the wall and the secret flight of Zedekiah are prophesied here, and even Zedekiah's infamous blinding at the hands of the Babylonians seems to be prophesied obliquely by the covering of his face in Ezekiel 12:12, as well as the cryptic promise in verse 13 that he will be brought to Babylon but will never see it. Once again, God's judgment against sin is not haphazard. It is meticulous in its detail. The God of the Bible is not ambiguous or fuzzy about sin. He is crystal clear. Sin is evil. It must be punished—or God would not be God.

This note of exacting judgment is sobering to us, as fallen humans. Yet it is also profoundly hope-giving. What if God did not abhor evil? What if the Creator had no moral compass? For one thing, we could have no sure hope that injustices committed against us would ever be put right. This life under the sun would appear to be the only sphere in which justice could be carried out, and we would be a fiercely vengeful people—unless we knew of God's final vindication of all goodness and

15 [r][1 Sam. 26:19]
16 [s][ch. 37:26, 28; Isa. 8:14; Rev. 21:22]
17 [t]ch. 20:41; 28:25; 34:13; 36:24; 37:21; [ch. 38:8; 39:27; Isa. 11:12]
18 [u]ch. 37:23 [v]ch. 5:11
19 [w]Jer. 32:39; [Acts 4:32] [x]ch. 36:26; [ch. 18:31; Ps. 51:10; Jer. 31:33] [y][Zech. 7:12] [z][2 Cor. 3:3]
20 [a]Ps. 105:45 [b]ch. 14:11; 36:28; Lev. 26:12; See Jer. 30:22; 31:33
21 [c]See ch. 9:4-6 [d]See ch. 7:4
22 [e]ch. 10:19
23 [f]Zech. 14:4; [ch. 43:2]
24 [g]ver. 1; See ch. 3:12 [h]See ch. 1:1 [i][ch. 1:3]

Chapter 12
2 [j]See ch. 2:1 [k]See ch. 2:3, 5 [l]Isa. 42:18; Matt. 13:13
3 [m]ver. 4, 7 [n]ch. 4:12; 21:6; 37:20; 43:11 [o]See Jer. 36:3
4 [p][2 Kgs. 25:4; Jer. 39:4; 52:7]
5 [q][ch. 8:8]
6 [r]See ch. 4:3

7 [s]ch. 24:18; 37:7 [t][ver. 3] **9** [u]See ch. 2:1 [v]See ch. 2:3, 5 [w][ch. 17:12; 24:19; 37:18]

says the Lord GOD: This oracle concerns[1] [x]the
prince in Jerusalem and all the house of Israel
who are in it.'[2] 11 Say, [y]'I am a sign for you: [z]as
I have done, so shall it be done to them. They
shall go into exile, into captivity.' 12 [a]And the
prince who is among them shall lift his baggage upon his shoulder at dusk, and shall go
out. [b]They shall dig through the wall to bring
him out through it. [c]He shall cover his face,
that he may not see the land with his eyes.
13 [d]And I will spread my net over him, and he
shall be taken in my snare. And [e]I will bring
him to Babylon, the land of the Chaldeans,
[e]yet he shall not see it, and he shall die there.
14 [f]And I will scatter toward every wind all who
are around him, his helpers and all his troops,
[g]and I will unsheathe the sword after them.
15 [h]And they shall know that I am the LORD,
when I disperse them among the nations and
scatter them among the countries. 16 [i]But I will
let a few of them escape from the sword, from
famine and pestilence, that they may declare all
their abominations among the nations where
they go, [j]and may know that I am the LORD."

17 And the word of the LORD came to me:
18 [k]"Son of man, [l]eat your bread with quaking,
and drink water with trembling and with
anxiety. 19 And say to the people of the land,
Thus says the Lord GOD concerning the inhabitants of Jerusalem in the land of Israel: [m]They
shall eat their bread with anxiety, [m]and drink
water in dismay. In this way [n]her land will be
stripped of all it contains, [o]on account of the
violence of all those who dwell in it. 20 [p]And
the inhabited cities shall be laid waste, and
the land shall become a desolation; and you
shall know that I am the LORD."

21 And the word of the LORD came to me:
22 "Son of man, [q]what is this proverb that
you[3] have about the land of Israel, saying,
[r]'The days grow long, and every vision comes
to nothing'? 23 Tell them therefore, 'Thus says
the Lord GOD: I will put an end to this proverb, and they shall no more use it as a proverb
in Israel.' But say to them, [s]The days are near,
and the fulfillment[4] of every vision. 24 [t]For
there shall be no more any [u]false vision or flattering divination within the house of Israel.
25 For I am the LORD; I will speak [v]the word
that I will speak, and it will be performed. [w]It
will no longer be delayed, but in your days,
[x]O rebellious house, I will speak the word and
perform it, declares the Lord GOD."

26 And the word of the LORD came to me:
27 "Son of man, behold, they of the house of
Israel say, [y]'The vision that he sees is [z]for many
days from now, and he prophesies of times far
off.' 28 Therefore say to them, Thus says the
Lord GOD: [w]None of my words will be delayed
any longer, [v]but the word that I speak will be
performed, declares the Lord GOD."

False Prophets Condemned

13 The word of the LORD came to me:
2 [a]"Son of man, prophesy against the
prophets of Israel, who are prophesying, and
say to those [b]who prophesy from their own

[1] Or *This burden is* [2] Hebrew *in the midst of them* [3] The Hebrew for *you* is plural [4] Hebrew *word*

10 [x][ch. 21:25]; See 2 Chr. 36:11-13
11 [y][ver. 6] [z][ch. 24:24]
12 [a][2 Kgs. 25:4] [b][ver. 5] [c][ver. 6]
13 [d]ch. 17:20; 19:8; 32:3; [Hos. 7:12] [e][2 Kgs. 25:7; Jer. 32:4, 5; 52:11]
14 [f][2 Kgs. 25:5]; See ch. 5:10 [g]See ch. 5:2
15 [h]See ch. 6:7
16 [i]ch. 6:8, 9; 14:22 [j]See ch. 6:7
18 [k]See ch. 2:1 [l][ch. 4:10, 11]
19 [m]ch. 4:16 [n][ch. 32:15; Zech. 7:14] [o]ch. 7:11, 23
20 [p]ch. 6:6
22 [q][ch. 16:44; 18:2, 3] [r][ver. 27; ch. 11:3; 2 Pet. 3:4]
23 [s][ch. 7:7, 12]
24 [t]ch. 13:23 [u]ch. 13:6, 7
25 [v]Isa. 55:11 [w]Isa. 13:22 [x]See ch. 2:3, 5
27 [y][ver. 22; Amos 6:3] [z]ch. 38:8; Dan. 8:26; 10:14; [2 Pet. 3:4]
28 [w][See ver. 25 above] [v][See ver. 25 above]
Chapter 13
2 [a]See ch. 2:1 [b]ver. 17; Jer. 23:16, 26

judgment of all wickedness. The cross of Christ is tangible proof that God is a God who punishes sin. And most amazing of all, we find that at the cross it is his people's sin, not Christ's, that is punished.

12:21–28 The Israelites make excuses for their disbelief of Ezekiel's warnings. First, in verse 22, they sing a jingle about how visions never come to pass and prophecies always come to nothing. Then in verses 26–28, they promise themselves that even if this prophecy comes true, it will not happen for a very long time. In both cases, God rejects their foolishness. The visions *will* come true, he promises, and it will be *soon*.

Fallen human beings are masters at concocting reasons not to listen to God's word and not to respond to it. Our excuses, however, are as empty and as foolish as those of the people of Israel. God always keeps his promises, and he does not delay long to do so.

The supreme "word of God" to be proclaimed is the gospel itself, and the supreme folly is to resist its free offer of salvation to those who will penitently bow the knee, confess their guilt, and trust in Christ. This "word" that is heard is given flesh-and-blood reality in the "Word" that is seen—Jesus himself (John 1:1, 14; Heb. 1:1–3).

13:1–14:23 In these two chapters, God details several ways in which the Israelites have deliberately and grossly violated his law. In 13:1–8 he describes them as a nation overrun with people pretending to be prophets but who are in reality simply speaking

hearts: 'Hear the word of the LORD!' 3 Thus
says the Lord GOD, Woe to the foolish prophets who follow their own spirit, and have
seen nothing! 4 Your prophets have been like
jackals among ruins, O Israel. 5 [c]You have not
gone up into the breaches, or built up a wall
for the house of Israel, that it might stand in
battle in the day of the LORD. 6 [d]They have seen
false visions and lying divinations. They say,
'Declares the LORD,' [e]when the LORD has not
sent them, and yet they expect him to fulfill
their word. 7 Have you not seen a false vision
and uttered a lying divination, [f]whenever you
have said, 'Declares the LORD,' although I have
not spoken?"
8 Therefore thus says the Lord GOD: "Because
you have uttered falsehood and seen lying
visions, therefore behold, [g]I am against you,
declares the Lord GOD. 9 My hand will be
against the prophets who see false visions
and who give lying divinations. They shall
not be in the council of my people, [h]nor be
enrolled in the register of the house of Israel,
[i]nor shall they enter the land of Israel. [j]And you
shall know that I am the Lord GOD. 10 Precisely
because they have misled my people, [k]saying,
'Peace,' when there is no peace, and because,
when the people build a wall, [l]these prophets smear it with whitewash,[1] 11 say to those
who smear it with whitewash that it shall
fall! [m]There will be a deluge of rain, and you,
O great hailstones, will fall, and a stormy wind
break out. 12 And when the wall falls, will it not
be said to you, 'Where is the coating with which
you smeared it?' 13 Therefore thus says the Lord
GOD: [m]I will make a stormy wind break out in
my wrath, [m]and there shall be a deluge of rain
in my anger, and great hailstones in wrath to
make a full end. 14 And I will break down the
wall that you have smeared with whitewash,
and bring it down to the ground, so that its
foundation will be laid bare. When it falls,
you shall perish in the midst of it, [n]and you
shall know that I am the LORD. 15 Thus will
I spend my wrath upon the wall and upon
those who have smeared it with whitewash,
and I will say to you, The wall is no more, nor
those who smeared it, 16 the prophets of Israel
who prophesied concerning Jerusalem [k]and
saw visions of peace for her, when there was
no peace, declares the Lord GOD.
17 "And you, son of man, [o]set your face against
[p]the daughters of your people, [q]who prophesy out of their own hearts. Prophesy against
them 18 and say, Thus says the Lord GOD: Woe
to the women [r]who sew magic bands upon all
wrists, and [s]make veils for the heads of persons
of every stature, in [t]the hunt for souls! Will
you hunt down souls belonging to my people
and keep your own souls alive? 19 You have
profaned me among my people [u]for handfuls
of barley [v]and for pieces of bread, putting to
death souls who should not die and keeping
alive souls who should not live, by your lying
to my people, who listen to lies.
20 "Therefore thus says the Lord GOD:
Behold, [w]I am against [x]your magic bands
with which you hunt the souls like birds, and
I will tear them from your arms, and I will let
the souls whom you hunt go free, the souls
like birds. 21 Your veils also I will tear off and
[y]deliver my people out of your hand, and they
shall be no more in your hand as prey, [z]and
you shall know that I am the LORD. 22 [a]Because
you have disheartened the righteous falsely,
although I have not grieved him, and [b]you
have encouraged the wicked, that [c]he should
not turn from his evil way to save his life,
23 [d]therefore you shall no more see false visions
nor practice divination. I will deliver my people out of your hand. And you shall know that
I am the LORD."

[1] Or *plaster*; also verses 11, 14, 15

their own opinions and their own messages—words that are spoken in the name of the Lord but are not really from him. God had warned them in Deuteronomy 18:20 that such false prophets were an abomination. In Ezekiel 13:17–23 he also condemns prophetesses who were engaged in pagan religion and divination, a violation of God's law in Deuteronomy 18:9–14. In a systematic fashion, Ezekiel lays out the people's offenses against God. They are exposed and have no excuse for their sin.

What the people needed was a true prophet, a prophet who would speak no falsehood, who would offer no cover for sin, and who would only have the people's best interests in mind. Indeed, they needed a prophet who would not only diagnose and identify sin but would bear it. In Jesus this prophet arrives (Luke 24:19; Acts 3:20–23).

5 [c] ch. 22:30; Ps. 106:23; [Ps. 80:12; Isa. 5:5; 58:12]
6 [d] ver. 23; ch. 12:24; 21:29; 22:28; Jer. 5:31 [e] See Jer. 14:14
7 [f] Jer. 23:21
8 [g] ch. 5:8; 21:3; 26:3; 28:22; 29:3; 30:22; 34:10; 35:3; 38:3; Jer. 21:13
9 [h] [Ezra 2:59, 62; Neh. 7:5; Ps. 69:28; 87:6] [i] ch. 20:38 [j] See ch. 6:7
10 [k] ver. 16; Jer. 6:14; Mic. 3:5 [l] ch. 22:28
11 [m] ch. 38:22; Isa. 28:2, 17; [Isa. 30:13] **13** [m] [See ver. 11 above] **14** [n] See ch. 6:7 **16** [k] [See ver. 10 above] **17** [o] See ch. 6:2 [p] [Ex. 15:20; Judg. 4:4; 2 Kgs. 22:14] [q] ver. 2 **18** [r] ver. 20 [s] ver. 21 [t] ver. 20 **19** [u] [Mic. 3:5] [v] [Prov. 28:21] **20** [w] See ver. 8 [x] ver. 18 **21** [y] [ch. 34:10] [z] See ch. 6:7 **22** [a] [Jer. 14:14]; See Jer. 28:15 [b] Jer. 23:14 [c] See ch. 18:21 **23** [d] See ver. 6, 7, 9

Idolatrous Elders Condemned

14 Then certain of the [e]elders of Israel
came to me [e]and sat before me. 2 And
the word of the LORD came to me: 3 [f]“Son of
man, these men have taken their idols into
their hearts, and set [g]the stumbling block
of their iniquity before their faces. [h]Should
I indeed let myself be consulted by them?
4 Therefore speak to them and say to them,
Thus says the Lord GOD: Any one of the house
of Israel who takes his idols into his heart and
sets the stumbling block of his iniquity before
his face, and yet comes to the prophet, [i]I the
LORD will answer him as he comes with the
multitude of his idols, 5 [j]that I may lay hold of
the hearts of the house of Israel, [k]who are all
estranged from me through their idols.
6 “Therefore say to the house of Israel, Thus
says the Lord GOD: [l]Repent and turn away
from your idols, and turn away your faces
from all your abominations. 7 For any one of
the house of Israel, or of the strangers who
sojourn in Israel, [k]who separates himself from
me, taking his idols into his heart and putting
the stumbling block of his iniquity before his
face, and yet comes to a prophet to consult me
through him, [m]I the LORD will answer him
myself. 8 And [n]I will set my face against that
man; I [o]will make him a sign and a byword
[n]and cut him off from the midst of my people,
[p]and you shall know that I am the LORD. 9 And
if the prophet is deceived and speaks a word,
[q]I, the LORD, have deceived that prophet,
and I will stretch out my hand against him
and will destroy him from the midst of my
people Israel. 10 And they shall bear their punishment[1]—the punishment of the prophet
and the punishment of the inquirer shall be
alike— 11 that the house of Israel may no more
go astray from me, nor [r]defile themselves anymore with all their transgressions, [s]but that
they may be my people and I may be their God,
declares the Lord GOD.”

Jerusalem Will Not Be Spared

12 And the word of the LORD came to me:
13 [t]“Son of man, when a land sins against me
[u]by acting faithlessly, and I stretch out my
hand against it and [v]break its supply[2] of
bread and send famine upon it, and [w]cut off
from it man and beast, 14 [x]even if these three
men, [y]Noah, [z]Daniel, and [a]Job, were in it, [b]they
would deliver but their own lives by their
righteousness, declares the Lord GOD.
15 [c]“If I cause wild beasts to pass through the
land, and they ravage it, [d]and it be made desolate, so that no one may pass through because
of the beasts, 16 even if these three men were in
it, [e]as I live, declares the Lord GOD, they would
deliver neither sons nor daughters. They alone
would be delivered, but [f]the land would be
desolate.
17 “Or [g]if I bring a sword upon that land and
say, Let a sword pass through the land, [h]and
I cut off from it man and beast, 18 [x]though these
three men were in it, as I live, declares the Lord
GOD, they would deliver neither sons nor
daughters, but they alone would be delivered.
19 “Or [i]if I send a pestilence into that land
and pour out my wrath upon it with blood, to
cut off from it man and beast, 20 even if Noah,
Daniel, and Job were in it, as I live, declares the
Lord GOD, they would deliver neither son nor
daughter. They would deliver but their own
lives by their righteousness.
21 “For thus says the Lord GOD: How much

[1] Or *iniquity*; three times in this verse [2] Hebrew *staff*

14:2–3 Ezekiel uses an arresting and convicting phrase here. The elders of Israel “have taken their idols into their hearts!” (v. 3). Sin and idolatry are never content to be trifled with. We may think we can stop our idolatries at any point, but the reality is that when we toy with sin, we take our idols into our very hearts. We give them residence in our lives. Indeed, we *become* what we worship (Ps. 115:8). James describes this same reality in James 1:14–15 when he speaks of the way we are enticed and dragged into sin by our desires.

Ezekiel’s warning against “taking their idols into their hearts” helps us see just how insidious sin really is, even though we are tempted to take it lightly. It also helps us see that salvation from our idolatry and sin is not just a matter of new resolve or fresh effort. It is a matter of receiving a new heart—made possible for us by our being united to Jesus Christ and being given new life by the power of his Spirit. Instead of taking idols into our hearts, we receive into our hearts the Spirit of Christ (Rom. 2:28–29).

Chapter 14
1 [e]See ch. 8:1
3 [f]See ch. 2:1 [g]ch. 7:19; 44:12 [h]ch. 20:3, 31; 2 Kgs. 3:13; [ch. 36:37]
4 [i][ver. 7]
5 [j][2 Thess. 2:11, 12] [k]Isa. 1:4
6 [l][ch. 18:30, 32]
7 [k][See ver. 5 above] [m][ver. 4]
8 [n]ch. 15:7; Lev. 17:10; Jer. 44:11 [o]ch. 5:15; Deut. 28:37 [p]See ch. 6:7
9 [q][1 Kgs. 22:23]
11 [r]ch. 37:23 [s]See ch. 11:20
13 [t]See ch. 2:1 [u]ch. 15:8; 17:20; 18:24; 20:27; 2 Chr. 36:14 [v]See ch. 4:16 [w]ver. 17, 19, 21
14 [x][Jer. 15:1] [y]See Gen. 6:9 [z]ch. 28:3; Dan. 9:23 [a]Job 1:1 [b]ch. 3:19
15 [c]See ch. 5:17 [d]ch. 6:6; 12:20
16 [e]See ch. 5:11 [f]ch. 6:14
17 [g]ch. 21:3, 4, 9; Lev. 26:25; [Jer. 47:6, 7] [h]ver. 13
18 [x][See ver. 14 above]
19 [i]ch. 38:22; [2 Sam. 24:15]

more [j]when I send upon Jerusalem my four
disastrous acts of judgment, [k]sword, [l]famine,
[m]wild beasts, and [n]pestilence, to cut off from
it man and beast! 22 But behold, [o]some survivors will be left in it, sons and daughters who
will be brought out; behold, when they come
out to you, and [p]you see their ways and their
deeds, you will be consoled for the disaster
that I have brought upon Jerusalem, for all
that I have brought upon it. 23 They will console you, when you see their ways and their
deeds, and you shall know that I have not
done without cause all that I have done in it,
declares the Lord GOD."

Jerusalem, a Useless Vine

15 And the word of the LORD came to me:
2 [q]"Son of man, how does [r]the wood of
the vine surpass any wood, the vine branch
that is among the trees of the forest? 3 Is wood
taken from it to make anything? Do people
take [s]a peg from it to hang any vessel on it?
4 [t]Behold, it is given to the fire for fuel. When
the fire has consumed both ends of it, and the
middle of it is charred, is it useful for anything? 5 [u]Behold, when it was whole, it was
used for nothing. How much less, when the
fire has consumed it and it is charred, can it
ever be used for anything! 6 Therefore thus
says the Lord GOD: [v]Like the wood of the vine
among the trees of the forest, [t]which I have
given to the fire for fuel, so have I given up the
inhabitants of Jerusalem. 7 [w]And I will set my
face against them. Though [x]they escape from
the fire, the fire shall yet consume them, [y]and
you will know that I am the LORD, [w]when I set
my face against them. 8 [z]And I will make the
land desolate, because [a]they have acted faithlessly, declares the Lord GOD."

The LORD's Faithless Bride

16 Again the word of the LORD came
to me: 2 [b]"Son of man, [c]make known
to Jerusalem her abominations, 3 and say,
Thus says the Lord GOD to Jerusalem: Your
origin and your birth are of the land of the
Canaanites; your father was an [d]Amorite and
your mother a [e]Hittite. 4 And as for your birth,
[f]on the day you were born your cord was not
cut, nor were you washed with water to cleanse
you, nor rubbed with salt, nor wrapped in
swaddling cloths. 5 No eye pitied you, to do
any of these things to you out of compassion
for you, [g]but you were cast out on the open
field, for you were abhorred, [f]on the day that
you were born.

6 "And when I passed by you and saw you
wallowing [h]in your blood, I said to you [h]in
your blood, 'Live!' I said to you [h]in your blood,
'Live!' 7 [i]I made you flourish like a plant of the
field. And you grew up and became tall [j]and
arrived at full adornment. Your breasts were
formed, and your hair had grown; yet [k]you
were naked and bare.

8 "When I passed by you again and saw
you, behold, you were at the age for love,

15:1–16:63 Many times in Scripture, Israel is compared to a vine. Usually, however, the image is of a grapevine that produces fruit. Here in chapter 15, Ezekiel twists that image in a new direction to show Israel's fruitlessness. She is not a grapevine but rather a vine twisted around a tree and burned, useless in every way.

In chapter 16, Ezekiel brings his indictment of Israel to a climax with a long and detailed story of how God cared for her and poured kindness on her only to have her spit in his face. At the end of the chapter, beginning in verse 44, he even casts Israel together with Sodom and Gomorrah. "You are the same!" he says to them. "You are sisters! In fact, Sodom and Gomorrah find comfort in comparing themselves to your wickedness."

Like the Israelites, we are often tempted to think that our own sin is not that bad, or that it does not deserve punishment, or that God will not take it seriously. These chapters of Ezekiel, however, show us that God *always* takes sin seriously. When God judges our lives, there will be no doubt about the righteousness of his judgment. Like Israel, we are hopelessly and inarguably guilty before him, and therefore deserving of his punishment.

Yet at just the right time in human history, a new Vine appeared on the scene. This Vine represented Israel as she was meant to be. Those who trust in this One are united to the life-giving provision of the Vine (John 15:1–8). Indeed, those united to Christ are not living by their own strength or withering from a life of separation from him but are enabled to experience the vibrant flourishing of true life in Christ (John 7:37–38).

21 [j]ch. 5:17; Rev. 6:8; [ch. 33:27] [k]ver. 17 [l]ver. 13 [m]ver. 15 [n]ver. 19
22 [o]ch. 6:8; 12:16 [p]ver. 23; ch. 20:43; [ch. 16:54]

Chapter 15
2 [q]See ch. 2:1 [r]See ver. 6
3 [s][Isa. 22:23, 24]
4 [t][John 15:6]
5 [u][ver. 3]
6 [v][ch. 17:6; Ps. 80:8; Isa. 5:1]; See ch. 19:10-14 [t][See ver. 4 above]
7 [w]See ch. 14:8 [x][2 Kgs. 25:9] [y]See ch. 6:7
8 [z]ch. 6:14 [a]See ch. 14:13

Chapter 16
2 [b]See ch. 2:1 [c]ch. 22:2
3 [d]ver. 45; Gen. 15:16; Deut. 7:1 [e]ver. 45; Deut. 7:1; Judg. 1:26
4 [f][Hos. 2:3]
5 [g][Deut. 32:10] [f][See ver. 4 above]
6 [h]ver. 22
7 [i][Ex. 1:7] [j][ver. 11, 13] [k]ver. 22, 39; ch. 23:29

and [l]I spread the corner of my garment over you and covered your nakedness; I made my vow to you [m]and entered into a covenant with you, declares the Lord GOD, [n]and you became mine. 9 Then I bathed you with water and washed off your blood from you and [o]anointed you with oil. 10 [p]I clothed you also with embroidered cloth and shod you with fine leather. I wrapped you in fine linen and covered you with silk.[1] 11 [q]And I adorned you with ornaments and [r]put bracelets on your wrists and a chain on your neck. 12 And I put a ring on your nose and earrings in your ears and a beautiful crown on your head. 13 Thus you were adorned with gold and silver, and your clothing was of fine linen and silk and embroidered cloth. [s]You ate fine flour and honey and oil. [t]You grew exceedingly beautiful and advanced to royalty. 14 And [u]your renown went forth among the nations because of your beauty, for it was perfect through the splendor that I had bestowed on you, declares the Lord GOD.

15 [v]"But you trusted in your beauty [w]and played the whore[2] because of your renown [x]and lavished your whorings[3] on any passerby; your beauty[4] became his. 16 You took some of your garments and made for yourself colorful shrines, and on them played the whore. The like has never been, nor ever shall be.[5] 17 You also took [y]your beautiful jewels of my gold and of my silver, which I had given you, and [z]made for yourself images of men, and with them played the whore. 18 And you took your embroidered garments to cover them, [a]and set my oil and my incense before them. 19 [b]Also my bread that I gave you—[s]I fed you with fine flour and oil and honey—you set before them for [c]a pleasing aroma; and so it was, declares the Lord GOD. 20 [d]And you took your sons and your daughters, whom you had borne to me, and [e]these you sacrificed to them to be devoured. Were your whorings so small a matter 21 that you slaughtered my children and delivered them up as an offering by fire to them? 22 And in all your abominations and your whorings you did not remember [f]the days of your youth, [g]when you were naked and bare, wallowing in your blood.

23 "And after all your wickedness (woe, woe to you! declares the Lord GOD), 24 you built yourself [h]a vaulted chamber and made yourself a lofty place in every square. 25 At the head of every street [i]you built your lofty place and made [j]your beauty an abomination, [k]offering yourself[6] to any passerby and multiplying your whoring. 26 [w]You also played the whore [l]with the Egyptians, your lustful neighbors, [m]multiplying your whoring, [n]to provoke me to anger. 27 Behold, therefore, I stretched out my hand against you [o]and diminished your allotted portion [p]and delivered you to the greed of your enemies, [q]the daughters of the Philistines, who were ashamed of your lewd behavior. 28 [w]You played the whore also [r]with the Assyrians, because you were not satisfied; yes, you played the whore with them, and still you were not satisfied. 29 You multiplied your whoring also with the trading land [t]of Chaldea, and even with this you were not satisfied.

30 "How sick is your heart,[7] declares the Lord GOD, because you did all these things, the deeds of a brazen prostitute, 31 building your vaulted chamber at the head of every street, and making your lofty place in every square. Yet you were not like a prostitute, [u]because you scorned payment. 32 Adulterous wife, who receives strangers instead of her husband! 33 Men give gifts to all prostitutes, [v]but you gave your gifts to all your lovers, bribing them to come to you from every side with your whorings. 34 So you were different from other women in your whorings. No one solicited you to play the whore, and [v]you gave payment, while no payment was given to you; therefore you were different.

35 "Therefore, O prostitute, hear the word of the LORD: 36 Thus says the Lord GOD, Because your lust was poured out and your nakedness uncovered in your whorings with your lovers, and with all your abominable idols, [w]and because of the blood of your children that you gave to them, 37 therefore, behold, [x]I will gather all your lovers with whom you took pleasure,

[1] Or *with rich fabric* [2] Or *were unfaithful*; also verses 16, 17, 26, 28 [3] Or *unfaithfulness*; also verses 20, 22, 25, 26, 29, 33, 34, 36 [4] Hebrew *it* [5] The meaning of this Hebrew sentence is uncertain [6] Hebrew *spreading your legs* [7] Revocalization yields *How I am filled with anger against you*

8 [l]Ruth 3:9; [Jer. 2:2] [m][Ex. 24:7, 8] [n]See Ex. 19:5 **9** [o]Ruth 3:3; [Ps. 23:5] **10** [p]ver. 13, 18; [ch. 26:16; 27:7, 16; Ex. 26:36] **11** [q][ch. 23:40] [r][ch. 23:42; Gen. 24:22, 30, 47] **13** [s]Deut. 32:13, 14 [t][ver. 15, 25; Ps. 48:2] **14** [u]Lam. 2:15; [ch. 23:10] **15** [v][ver. 13] [w]ch. 23:3, 8, 11, 12; Lev. 17:7; Isa. 1:21; 57:8; Jer. 2:20; 3:2, 6, 20; Hos. 1:2 [x][ver. 25] **17** [y][ver. 11] [z][ch. 7:20; 23:14] **18** [a]ch. 23:41 **19** [b][Hos. 2:8] [s][See ver. 13 above] [c]See ch. 6:13 **20** [d][ver. 21, 36] [e]ch. 20:26, 31; 23:37 **22** [f]ver. 43, 60 [g]ver. 6, 7 **24** [h]ver. 39 **25** [i]ver. 31; [Isa. 57:7; Jer. 2:20; 3:2] [j][ver. 14] [k][ver. 15] **26** [w][See ver. 15 above] [l]ch. 20:7, 8; 23:19-21 [m]ch. 23:14, 19 [n]Jer. 7:18, 19 **27** [o][ch. 5:10, 11] [p][ver. 37] [q]ver. 57; [2 Sam. 1:20] **28** [w][See ver. 15 above] [r]ch. 23:12; Jer. 2:18, 36; See 2 Kgs. 16:7-18; 2 Chr. 28:16-21 **29** [t]See ch. 23:14-16 **31** [u][ver. 33, 34] **33** [v][ver. 41; Hos. 8:9] **34** [v][See ver. 33 above] **36** [w][ver. 20, 21, 38] **37** [x]Hos. 8:10

all those you loved and [y]all those you hated. [z]I will gather them against you from every side [a]and will uncover your nakedness to them, that [b]they may see all your nakedness. 38 [c]And I will judge you [d]as women who commit adultery and [e]shed blood are judged, and bring upon you the blood of wrath and jealousy. 39 And I will give you into their hands, and they shall throw down your [f]vaulted chamber and break down [g]your lofty places. [h]They shall strip you of your clothes and take [i]your beautiful jewels and leave you [j]naked and bare. 40 [k]They shall bring up a crowd against you, [l]and they shall stone you and cut you to pieces with their swords. 41 [l]And they shall [m]burn your houses and [n]execute judgments upon you in the sight of many women. [o]I will make you stop playing the whore, and [p]you shall also give payment no more. 42 [q]So will I satisfy my wrath on you, and my jealousy shall depart from you. I will be calm and will no more be angry. 43 Because you have not remembered [r]the days of your youth, but have enraged me with all these things, therefore, behold, [s]I have returned your deeds upon your head, declares the Lord GOD. Have you not [t]committed lewdness in addition to all your abominations?

44 "Behold, everyone [u]who uses proverbs will use this proverb about you: 'Like mother, like daughter.' 45 You are the daughter of your mother, who loathed her husband and her children; and you are the sister of [v]your sisters, who loathed their husbands and their children. [w]Your mother was a Hittite and [w]your father an Amorite. 46 And [x]your elder sister is Samaria, who lived with her daughters to the north of you; and [y]your younger sister, who lived to the south of you, is Sodom with her daughters. 47 [z]Not only did you walk in their ways and do according to their abominations; within a very little time [a]you were more corrupt than they in all your ways. 48 [b]As I live, declares the Lord GOD, your sister [c]Sodom and her daughters have not done as you and your daughters have done. 49 Behold, this was the guilt of your sister Sodom: she and her daughters had pride, [d]excess of food, and prosperous ease, but did not aid the poor and needy. 50 They were haughty and [e]did an abomination before me. So [f]I removed them, when I saw it. 51 [g]Samaria has not committed half your sins. You have committed more abominations than they, and [h]have made your sisters appear righteous by all the abominations that you have committed. 52 [i]Bear your disgrace, you also, for you have intervened on behalf of your sisters. Because of your sins in which you acted more abominably than they, they are more in the right than you. So be ashamed, you also, and bear your disgrace, for you have made your sisters appear righteous.

53 [j]"I will restore their fortunes, both the fortunes of Sodom and her daughters, and the fortunes of Samaria and her daughters, and I will restore your own fortunes in their midst, 54 that you may bear your disgrace [k]and be ashamed of all that you have done, [l]becoming a consolation to them. 55 As for your sisters, Sodom and her daughters shall return to their former state, [j]and Samaria and her daughters shall return [m]to their former state, [j]and you and your daughters shall return [m]to your former state. 56 Was not your sister Sodom a byword in your mouth [n]in the day of your pride, 57 before your wickedness was uncovered? Now you have become [o]an object of reproach for the daughters of Syria[1] and all those around her, and for [p]the daughters of the Philistines, [q]those all around who despise you. 58 [r]You bear the penalty of your lewdness and your abominations, declares the LORD.

The LORD's Everlasting Covenant

59 "For thus says the Lord GOD: I will deal with you as you have done, you [s]who have despised the oath in breaking the covenant,

[1] Some manuscripts (compare Syriac) *of Edom*

16:59–63 In light of God's unrelenting indictment of the Israelites, verse 60 comes as a shock to the reader. Verse 59 sounds like a continuation of judgment, but then—completely unexpectedly—God declares, "yet I will remember my covenant with you . . . and I will establish for you an everlasting covenant." Why does God show this grace to the Israelites, especially in light of their sin against him? It is not because they deserve his kindness. Verse 61 makes that clear. No, it is simply because he loves

37 [y][ver. 27; ch. 23:28] [z]ch. 23:22 [a]ch. 23:10, 29; Hos. 2:10; Rev. 17:16; [ver. 39] [b]Lam. 1:8 **38** [c]ch. 21:30 [d]ch. 23:45; Lev. 20:10; Deut. 22:22 [e]Gen. 9:6; [ch. 18:10; 23:37, 45] **39** [f]ver. 24 [g]ver. 25 [h]ch. 23:26; [Hos. 2:3] [i]ver. 11, 12 [j]ver. 7 **40** [k]ch. 23:46 [l]ch. 23:47; [Josh. 7:24, 25] **41** [l][See ver. 40 above] [m]2 Kgs. 25:9; Jer. 39:8; 52:13 [n]See ch. 5:8 [o]ch. 23:27, 48 [p][ver. 33, 34] **42** [q]See ch. 5:13 **43** [r]ver. 22, 60 [s]See ch. 7:4 [t]ch. 22:9 **44** [u][ch. 12:22; 18:2, 3] **45** [v][ver. 46] [w]See ver. 3 **46** [x]ver. 51, 53, 55; [ch. 23:4, 33] [y]ver. 48, 49, 53, 55; [Isa. 1:10] **47** [z]ch. 5:7 [a]ver. 48, 51, 52; ch. 5:6; [2 Kgs. 21:9; 2 Chr. 33:9; Jer. 2:10, 11] **48** [b]ch. 5:11; 14:16, 18, 20; 17:16, 19; 18:3; 20:3, 33; Isa. 49:18; Zeph. 2:9 [c]ver. 47; [Matt. 10:15; 11:24] **49** [d][Gen. 13:10] **50** [e]See Gen. 13:13 [f]See Gen. 19:24 **51** [g]ver. 46, 47 [h]ver. 52; Jer. 3:11 **52** [i]See ch. 32:24 **53** [j][ch. 29:14; 39:25; Zeph. 2:7; 3:20] **54** [k]ver. 61 [l][ch. 14:22, 23] **55** [j][See ver. 53 above] [m]ch. 36:11 **56** [n]See Isa. 2:6-11 **57** [o]See 2 Kgs. 16:5-7; Isa. 7:1, 2 [p]ver. 27; [2 Chr. 28:18] [q]ch. 28:24, 26 **58** [r][ch. 14:10; 23:35, 49] **59** [s][ch. 17:15, 16, 18, 19]

60 yet [t]I will remember my covenant with you [u]in the days of your youth, [v]and I will establish for you an everlasting covenant. 61 [w]Then you will remember your ways [x]and be ashamed when you take [y]your sisters, both your elder and your younger, and I give them to you [z]as daughters, but not on account of[1] the covenant with you. 62 I will establish my covenant with you, [a]and you shall know that I am the LORD, 63 that you may remember and be confounded, and [b]never open your mouth again because of your shame, when I atone for you for all that you have done, declares the Lord GOD."

Parable of Two Eagles and a Vine

17 The word of the LORD came to me: 2 [c]"Son of man, [d]propound a riddle, and speak a parable to the house of Israel; 3 say, Thus says the Lord GOD: [e]A great eagle [f]with great wings and long pinions, [f]rich in plumage of many colors, came [g]to Lebanon [h]and took the top of the cedar. 4 He broke off the topmost of its young twigs and carried it to a land of trade and set it in a city of merchants. 5 Then he took of the seed of the land [i]and planted it in fertile soil.[2] He placed it beside abundant waters. [j]He set it like a willow twig, 6 and it sprouted and became a [k]low [l]spreading vine, and its branches turned toward him, and its roots remained where it stood. So it became a vine and produced branches and put out boughs.

7 [m]"And there was another great eagle with great wings and much plumage, [m]and behold, this vine bent its roots toward him and shot forth its branches toward him from [n]the bed where it was planted, that he might water it. 8 [i]It had been planted on good soil by abundant waters, that it might produce branches and bear fruit and become a noble vine.

9 "Say, Thus says the Lord GOD: [m]Will it thrive? Will he not pull up its roots and cut off its fruit, so that it withers, so that all its fresh sprouting leaves wither? It will not take a strong arm or many people to pull it from its roots. 10 Behold, it is planted; will it thrive? [o]Will it not utterly wither when the east wind strikes it—wither away on the bed where it sprouted?"

11 Then the word of the LORD came to me: 12 "Say now to [p]the rebellious house, [q]Do you not know what these things mean? Tell them, behold, [r]the king of Babylon came to

[1] Or *not apart from* [2] Hebrew *in a field of seed*

60[t] See Lev. 26:42 [u] ver. 8, 22, 43 [v] Jer. 32:40; 50:5
61[w] See ch. 6:9 [x] ver. 54 [y] [ver. 45, 46] [z] [Isa. 54:1]
62[a] See ch. 6:7
63[b] [Rom. 3:19]
Chapter 17
2[c] See ch. 2:1 [d] [ch. 20:49; 24:3]
3[e] Jer. 48:40 [f] ver. 7 [g] [Jer. 22:23] [h] ver. 22; ch. 31:3, 4, 10
5[i] See Deut. 8:7-10 [j] [Isa. 44:4]
6[k] [ver. 14] [l] ch. 15:6
7[m] [ver. 15] [n] [ch. 31:4]
8[i] [See ver. 5 above]
9[m] [See ver. 7 above]
10[o] ch. 19:12; [Hos. 13:15]
12[p] See ch. 2:3-5 [q] See ch. 12:9-11 [r] 2 Kgs. 24:11, 12

them, and therefore he determines to maintain his faithfulness to his covenant by everlasting commitment to his people in spite of their faithlessness.

The word "yet" in verse 60 defibrillates our hearts with gospel grace. Following everything God has said to this point in the book, the word "yet" is not a rational word. It is not logical. It does not come because of a considered argument, but rather solely and completely because of love. There is no reason for God to save and restore Israel, no reason for him to establish his covenant into eternity with them. And yet he does so anyway!

The same is true of the good news that Jesus saves sinners. Not one of us deserves God's love. Rather, "God shows his love for us in that *while we were still sinners*, Christ died for us" (Rom. 5:8). Our entire eternity rests on the fact that God—in inexplicable and astonishing love for us—looked on our sin and said, "Yet!" (cf. Rom. 3:21; Eph. 2:4; Titus 3:4).

17:1–20:49 In these chapters, the falling of God's judgment is looming very close and so the sense of drama in Ezekiel's prophecy is heightening. Before the blow falls, however, the people of Israel try to find refuge in a series of self-assured lies. In these chapters, Ezekiel dismantles those lies one by one.

17:1–21 Ezekiel tells a parable of two eagles and a vine, which is meant to assault the lie that, "There is no need to worry! We have our alliances!" Israel had a long history of allying with pagan nations, even though God had told them from the beginning not to do so. Ezekiel therefore tells this parable to show the futility of looking for help from pagans. God asks a burning question: "Will it thrive?" (v. 9). That is, will Israel thrive under the protection of Egypt? And the answer is "No, it will not."

God's point to the Israelites is that they should not comfort themselves with the things of this world, and that message is important for us as well. Just as Israel trusted in her alliance with Egypt, we tend to trust in life's comforts and convince ourselves that there is nothing to worry about. But just as it was folly for Israel to trust in Egypt,

Jerusalem, and took her king and her princes
and brought them to him to Babylon. 13 [s]And
he took one of the royal offspring[1] [t]and made
a covenant with him, [u]putting him under
oath ([v]the chief men of the land he had taken
away), 14 that the kingdom might be humble
and not lift itself up, and keep his covenant
that it might stand. 15 [w]But he rebelled against
him by sending his ambassadors [x]to Egypt,
that they might give him horses and a large
army. [y]Will he thrive? Can one escape who does
such things? Can he [z]break the covenant and
yet escape?

16 [a]"As I live, declares the Lord GOD, surely [b]in
the place where the king dwells [c]who made
him king, whose oath he despised, and whose
covenant with him he broke, in Babylon he
shall die. 17 [d]Pharaoh with his mighty army
and great company will not help him in war,
[e]when mounds are cast up and siege walls
built to cut off many lives. 18 He despised the
oath in breaking the covenant, and behold,
he gave his hand and did all these things; he
shall not escape. 19 Therefore thus says the
Lord GOD: As I live, surely it is my oath that
he despised, and my covenant that he broke.
I will return it upon his head. 20 [f]I will spread
my net over him, and he shall be taken in my
snare, and I will bring him to Babylon [g]and
enter into judgment with him there [h]for
the treachery he has committed against me.
21 And all the pick[2] of his troops shall fall by the
sword, [i]and the survivors shall be scattered to
every wind, and you shall know that [j]I am the
LORD; I have spoken."

22 Thus says the Lord GOD: [k]"I myself will
take a sprig from the lofty top of the cedar and
will set it out. [l]I will break off from the topmost of its young twigs a tender one, and [m]I
myself will plant it on a high and lofty mountain. 23 [n]On the mountain height of Israel will
I plant it, that it may bear branches and produce fruit and become a noble cedar. [o]And
under it will dwell every kind of bird; in the
shade of its branches birds of every sort will
nest. 24 And all the trees of the field shall know
that I am the LORD; [p]I bring low the high tree,
and make high the low tree, dry up [q]the green
tree, and make [q]the dry tree flourish. [r]I am the
LORD; I have spoken, and I will do it."

The Soul Who Sins Shall Die

18 The word of the LORD came to me:
2 "What do you[3] mean [s]by repeating this
proverb concerning the land of Israel, [t]'The
fathers have eaten sour grapes, and the children's teeth are set on edge'? 3 [u]As I live, declares
the Lord GOD, [v]this proverb shall no more be

[1] Hebrew *seed* [2] Some Hebrew manuscripts, Syriac, Targum; most Hebrew manuscripts *all the fugitives* [3] The Hebrew for *you* is plural

it is folly for us to think that we can trust in anyone or anything besides Jesus Christ the Son of God for our salvation. "There is salvation in no one else, for there is no other name under heaven given among men by which we must be saved" (Acts 4:12).

17:22–24 In the parable of the two eagles and the vine, David's dynasty had been plucked up and planted in a foreign land. Here, however, God promises to take "a sprig" and plant it "on a high and lofty mountain," where it will thrive and become a haven for every kind of bird.

Ezekiel prophesies here about the coming of the Messiah. Jesus perhaps alludes to this passage when he says that the kingdom of God is like a mustard seed which becomes a great tree in which all the birds of the air make their nests (Matt. 13:32). There is a principle at work here that lies close to the heart of the gospel itself—namely, that God works not through human cleverness or ingenuity but through small things, through insignificance, even through weakness (1 Cor. 1:18–2:5; 2 Cor. 12:9–10; 13:4). In Ezekiel 17:24 the Lord says, "I bring low the high tree, and make high the low tree." This principle of inversion resounds through the teaching of Jesus, who drives home to his disciples that the way to greatness is through service (Matt. 20:26; Mark 10:43–44); the way to life is through death (Luke 9:24). This was true for Jesus (Mark 10:45). It is true for us as well.

18:1–32 In chapter 18, God takes aim at another lie: the Israelites' assurance to themselves that "We don't deserve this!" The proverb repeated by the people in verses 1–2 contains their challenge to God: "It was our forefathers who sinned," they say, "and yet you are punishing us!"

So convinced are they of their own innocence, in fact, that in verse 25 the people of God actually accuse God of injustice. God takes the challenge head on. Yes, he tells

13 [s]2 Kgs. 24:17 [t]ver. 15, 16, 18; 2 Chr. 36:13 [u][ch. 21:23] [v]2 Kgs. 24:14, 15
15 [w][ver. 7; ch. 23:27; 2 Kgs. 24:20; 2 Chr. 36:13; Jer. 37:5-7] [x]Deut. 17:16; [Isa. 31:1, 3]; 36:6, 9 [y][ver. 9, 10] [z]ch. 16:59; [ver. 13]
16 [a]See ch. 16:48 [b][ch. 12:13] [c]ver. 13
17 [d]ver. 15; See Jer. 37:5-8 [e]See ch. 4:2
20 [f]See ch. 12:13 [g][ch. 20:35; 38:22] [h]See ch. 14:13
21 [i]See ch. 5:10 [j]ch. 21:17, 32; 26:5, 14; 28:10; 30:12; 34:24; 39:5; [ver. 24]
22 [k]ver. 3 [l]ver. 4 [m][Ps. 2:6]
23 [n]ch. 20:40; 34:14 [o]ch. 31:6; Dan. 4:12; Matt. 13:32
24 [p][ch. 21:26, 27] [q]ch. 20:47; [Luke 23:31] [r]ch. 22:14; 24:14; 36:36; 37:14
Chapter 18
2 [s][ch. 12:22; 16:44] [t]Jer. 31:29
3 [u]See ch. 16:48 [v]Jer. 31:29, 30

used by you in Israel. 4 Behold, all souls are
mine; the soul of the father as well as the soul
of the son is mine: [w]the soul who sins shall die.
5 "If a man is righteous and does [x]what is
just and right— 6 if he [y]does not eat upon the
mountains or [z]lift up his eyes to the idols of
the house of Israel, [a]does not defile his neighbor's wife [b]or approach [c]a woman in her time
of menstrual impurity, 7 [d]does not oppress anyone, but [e]restores to the debtor his pledge,
[f]commits no robbery, [g]gives his bread to the
hungry [g]and covers the naked with a garment,
8 [h]does not lend at interest [h]or take any profit,[1]
withholds his hand from injustice, [i]executes
true justice between man and man, 9 [j]walks
in my statutes, and keeps my rules by acting
faithfully—he is righteous; [k]he shall surely
live, declares the Lord GOD.
10 "If he fathers a son who is violent, [l]a shed-
der of blood, who does any of these things
11 (though he himself did none of these things),
[m]who even eats upon the mountains, [n]defiles
his neighbor's wife, 12 oppresses the poor and
needy, [o]commits robbery, [o]does not restore the
pledge, [p]lifts up his eyes to the idols, [q]commits
abomination, 13 [r]lends at interest, and takes
profit; shall he then live? He shall not live.
He has done all these abominations; he shall
surely die; [s]his blood shall be upon himself.
14 "Now suppose this man fathers a son who
sees all the sins that his father has done; he
sees, and does not do likewise: 15 he does not
eat upon the mountains or lift up his eyes to
the idols of the house of Israel, does not defile
his neighbor's wife, 16 does not oppress anyone,
[t]exacts no pledge, [u]commits no robbery, [v]but
gives his bread to the hungry [v]and covers the
naked with a garment, 17 withholds his hand
from iniquity,[2] takes no interest or profit,
obeys my rules, [w]and walks in my statutes; he
shall not die for his father's iniquity; [x]he shall
surely live. 18 As for his father, because he practiced extortion, robbed his brother, and did
what is not good among his people, [y]behold,
he shall die for his iniquity.
19 "Yet you say, [z]'Why should not the son suffer for the iniquity of the father?' When the
son has done [a]what is just and right, and has
been careful to observe all my statutes, [b]he
shall surely live. 20 [c]The soul who sins shall die.
[d]The son shall not suffer for the iniquity of the
father, nor the father suffer for the iniquity of
the son. [e]The righteousness of the righteous
shall be upon himself, [f]and the wickedness of
the wicked shall be upon himself.
21 [g]"But if a wicked person turns away from
all his sins that he has committed and keeps all
my statutes and does [h]what is just and right,
[i]he shall surely live; he shall not die. 22 [j]None of
the transgressions that he has committed shall
be remembered against him; for the righteousness that he has done he shall live. 23 [k]Have
I any pleasure in the death of the wicked,
declares the Lord GOD, and not rather that
he should turn from his way and live? 24 [l]But
when a righteous person turns away from his
righteousness and does injustice and does the
same abominations that the wicked person
does, shall he live? [m]None of the righteous
deeds that he has done shall be remembered;
for [n]the treachery of which he is guilty and the
sin he has committed, for them he shall die.
25 [o]"Yet you say, 'The way of the Lord is not
just.' Hear now, O house of Israel: Is my way

[1] That is, profit that comes from charging interest to the poor; also verses 13, 17 (compare Leviticus 25:36) [2] Septuagint; Hebrew *from the poor*

them, their fathers sinned and deserved punishment for it, but the important point is that the current generation did not repent of those sinful ways but actually repeated them in even greater measure. Thus the punishment God is pouring out against them is unquestionably deserved. The judgment of the Lord is unassailably just.

Believers today inherit a sin nature and the righteous wrath of God due to their forefather, Adam. Some object that it is not fair that we, Adam's children, should be affected by the failures of our forefather. Yet what is more astounding than our inheriting the consequences of sin committed by another is that we would inherit the eternal blessings of free *grace* earned by another, Jesus Christ. If Adam's curse is due to what he has done (and we, in him), how much more is Christ's blessing due not to what we have done but what he has done for us (Rom. 5:15–19)!

For indeed, as just as he is, God has "no pleasure in the death of anyone . . . so turn, and live" (Ezek. 18:32). God must be just. But his heart is always bent toward expressing love and offering life. Turn to him. He is not reluctant to shower his mercy upon you!

4 [w]ver. 20
5 [x]ver. 19, 21, 27
6 [y]ver. 11, 15; ch. 22:9 [z]ch. 33:25 [a]ver. 11, 15; [ch. 22:11] [b]Lev. 18:19 [c]ch. 22:10
7 [d]ver. 12, 16; Ex. 22:21 [e]ver. 12; ch. 33:15; Ex. 22:26 [f]ver. 12, 16, 18 [g]ver. 16; Isa. 58:7; [Matt. 25:35, 36]
8 [h]ver. 13, 17; ch. 22:12; Ex. 22:25; Ps. 15:5 [i]Deut. 1:16; Zech. 8:16
9 [j]ver. 17 [k]ver. 17, 19, 21; ch. 20:11; Amos 5:4
10 [l]See ch. 16:38
11 [m]See ver. 6 [n]ver. 6; [Lev. 18:20]
12 [o]ver. 7 [p]ver. 6 [q]ch. 8:6, 17
13 [r]See ver. 8 [s]ch. 33:4; Lev. 20:9, 11; See ch. 3:18
16 [t][ver. 7, 12] [u]ver. 7 [v]See ver. 7 **17** [w]ver. 9 [x]See ver. 9 **18** [y]See ch. 3:18 **19** [z]Ex. 20:5; [ver. 2] [a]ver. 5, 21, 27 [b]See ver. 9 **20** [c]ver. 4 [d]See 2 Kgs. 14:6 [e]Isa. 3:10, 11 [f][Rom. 2:9] **21** [g]See ver. 27 [h]ver. 5, 19 [i]ver. 9 **22** [j]ch. 33:16 **23** [k]ver. 32; ch. 33:11; 1 Tim. 2:4, 6; 2 Pet. 3:9; [Titus 2:11] **24** [l]ch. 3:20; 33:12, 13, 18 [m][2 Pet. 2:20, 21] [n]See ch. 14:13 **25** [o]ch. 33:17, 20

not just? Is it not your ways that are not just?
26 [l]When a righteous person turns away from
his righteousness and does injustice, he shall
die for it; for the injustice that he has done he
shall die. 27 Again, [p]when a wicked person turns
away from the wickedness he has committed
and does what is just and right, he shall save
his life. 28 Because he considered and turned
away from all the transgressions that he had
committed, he shall surely live; he shall not die.
29 Yet the house of Israel says, 'The way of the
Lord is not just.' O house of Israel, are my ways
not just? Is it not your ways that are not just?
30 "Therefore [q]I will judge you, O house
of Israel, every one according to his ways,
declares the Lord GOD. [r]Repent and turn from
all your transgressions, [s]lest iniquity be your
ruin.[1] 31 [t]Cast away from you all the transgressions that you have committed, and [u]make
yourselves a new heart and a new spirit! [v]Why
will you die, O house of Israel? 32 [w]For I have
no pleasure in the death of anyone, declares
the Lord GOD; [r]so turn, and live."

A Lament for the Princes of Israel

19 And you, [x]take up a lamentation for the
princes of Israel, 2 and say:

What was your mother? [y]A lioness!
Among lions she crouched;
in the midst of young lions
she reared her cubs.
3 And she brought up one of her cubs;
[z]he became a young lion,
[a]and he learned to catch prey;
he devoured men.
4 The nations heard about him;
[b]he was caught in their pit,
[c]and they brought him with hooks
to the land of Egypt.
5 When she saw that she waited in vain,
that her hope was lost,
[d]she took another of her cubs
and made him a young lion.
6 He prowled among the lions;
he became a young lion,
and he learned to catch prey;
he devoured men,
7 and seized[2] their widows.
He laid waste their cities,
and the land was appalled and all who were in it
at the sound of his roaring.
8 [e]Then the nations set against him
from provinces on every side;
[f]they spread their net over him;
[b]he was taken in their pit.
9 With hooks [e]they put him in a cage[3]
and [g]brought him to the king of Babylon;
they brought him into custody,
that his voice should no more be heard
on [h]the mountains of Israel.
10 Your mother was [i]like a vine in a vineyard[4]
planted by the water,
[j]fruitful and full of branches
[k]by reason of abundant water.
11 Its strong stems became
rulers' scepters;
it towered aloft
among the thick boughs;[5]
it was seen in its height
with the mass of its branches.
12 But the vine was plucked up in fury,
cast down to the ground;

[1] Or *lest iniquity be your stumbling block* [2] Hebrew *knew* [3] Or *in a wooden collar* [4] Some Hebrew manuscripts; most Hebrew manuscripts *in your blood* [5] Or *the clouds*

19:1–14 Chapter 19 contains God's answer to another empty self-assurance: the Israelites' certainty that God would never let the Davidic kingship fall. The poem in these verses traces the downfall of three kings of Israel, each more tragic than the one before. Verses 1–4 trace the fall of Jehoahaz, who was carried away as a captive to Egypt. Verses 5–9 probably refer to Jehoiachin, exiled to Babylon. Most interestingly, verses 10–14 speak of the "mother" of these kings, that is, the Davidic dynasty as a whole. Far from being a strong tree flourishing in the Land of Promise, now the Davidic kingship has been plucked up and "cast down to the ground" (v. 12), "so that there remains in it no strong stem, no scepter for ruling" (v. 14). Instead of taking pride in the Davidic throne and assuring themselves that it stands as a barrier against God's judgment of their sin, the Israelites should see that dynasty's ruin as a sign of God's wrath against them.

Yet even from the rubble of this royal ruin hope would rise. One day, without any pomp but in humble guise, a king from the line of David would indeed arise (Matt. 1:1; Mark 12:35–37).

26 [l][See ver. 24 above]
27 [p]ver. 21; ch. 33:19; [ch. 13:22; 33:11, 12]
30 [q]ch. 7:3, 8; 33:20; 36:19; [ch. 39:24] [r][ch. 14:6; Hos. 14:1] [s][Isa. 3:8]
31 [t][ch. 20:7] [u]See ch. 11:19 [v]ch. 33:11
32 [w]See ver. 23 [r][See ver. 30 above]

Chapter 19
1 [x]ch. 26:17; 27:2, 32; 28:12; 32:2; Amos 5:1; [Jer. 7:29]
2 [y][Gen. 49:9]
3 [z][ch. 22:25; 32:2; 2 Kgs. 23:30, 31] [a]ch. 22:25, 27
4 [b]Lam. 4:20 [c][2 Kgs. 23:33, 34; Jer. 22:11, 12]
5 [d]2 Kgs. 23:34, 36
8 [e][2 Chr. 36:6] [f]See ch. 12:13 [b][See ver. 4 above]

9 [e][See ver. 8 above] [g][Jer. 22:26, 27] [h]See ch. 6:2 **10** [i]See ch. 15:6 [j][Ps. 80:9] [k][Deut. 8:7]

[l]the east wind dried up its fruit;
they were stripped off and withered.
As for its strong stem,
fire consumed it.
13 [m]Now it is planted in the wilderness,
in a dry and thirsty land.
14 [n]And fire has gone out from the stem of its shoots,
has consumed its fruit,
[o]so that there remains in it no strong stem,
no scepter for ruling.

This is [p]a lamentation and has become a
lamentation.

Israel's Continuing Rebellion

20 [q]In the seventh year, in the fifth month,
on the tenth day of the month, certain
of [r]the elders of Israel came to inquire of the
LORD, [s]and sat before me. 2 And the word of
the LORD came to me: 3 [t]"Son of man, speak
to the elders of Israel, and say to them, Thus
says the Lord GOD, Is it to inquire of me
that you come? [u]As I live, declares the Lord
GOD, [v]I will not be inquired of by you. 4 [w]Will
you judge them, son of man, will you judge
them? [x]Let them know the abominations of
their fathers, 5 and say to them, Thus says the
Lord GOD: [y]On the day when I chose Israel, [z]I
swore[1] to the offspring of the house of Jacob,
[a]making myself known to them in the land
of Egypt; [z]I swore to them, saying, I am the
LORD your God. 6 On that day I swore to them
that [b]I would bring them out of the land of
Egypt into a land that I had searched out for
them, a land [b]flowing with milk and honey,
[c]the most glorious of all lands. 7 And I said to
them, [d]Cast away the detestable things [e]your
eyes feast on, every one of you, and do not
defile yourselves with [f]the idols of Egypt; [g]I
am the LORD your God. 8 [h]But they rebelled
against me and were not willing to listen to
me. [i]None of them cast away the detestable
things their eyes feasted on, nor did they forsake the idols of Egypt.

"Then I said I would pour out my wrath
upon them [j]and spend my anger against them
in the midst of the land of Egypt. 9 [k]But I acted
[l]for the sake of my name, [m]that it should not
be profaned in the sight of the nations among
whom they lived, [n]in whose sight I made
myself known to them in bringing them out
of the land of Egypt. 10 [o]So I led them out of
the land of Egypt and brought them into the
wilderness. 11 [p]I gave them my statutes and
made known to them my rules, [q]by which, if
a person does them, he shall live. 12 Moreover,
I gave them [r]my Sabbaths, as a sign between
me and them, [s]that they might know that
I am the LORD who sanctifies them. 13 [t]But
the house of Israel rebelled against me in the
wilderness. [u]They did not walk in my statutes
but rejected my rules, by which, if a person
does them, he shall live; [v]and my Sabbaths
they greatly profaned.

[t]"Then I said I would pour out my wrath
upon them in the wilderness, to make a full
end of them. 14 But I acted for the sake of my
name, that it should not be profaned in the
sight of the nations, [w]in whose sight I had
brought them out. 15 Moreover, [x]I swore to
them in the wilderness [y]that I would not bring

[1] Hebrew *I lifted my hand*; twice in this verse; also verses 6, 15, 23, 28, 42

20:1–32 Here Israel seems to take comfort in her history. "We have a glorious history," she seems to tell herself. "The exodus, the Mosaic law, the conquest of the Promised Land! Surely God will not underestimate those triumphs!" Again, God wipes away their self-assurance, telling them that actually their history is one of repeated rebellion against him. In fact, God says, it was due to nothing but sheer mercy that he did not destroy them long ago. Their glorious history was due to his grace, not their own righteousness (cf. Deut. 9:4–12).

Israel's tendency to take comfort in such lies is not unique to them. Deep in every human heart is a settled inclination toward self-justification and self-assurance, a willingness to lie to ourselves or others in a futile effort to avoid the reality of our sin and its consequences. What kind of assurances do you give yourself about your sin? How well do those assurances hold up in light of God's assault on such excuses in Ezekiel 17–20? Acknowledge your failures, and find hope. In your contrition, God draws near (Isa. 66:2).

12 [l]ch. 17:10; [Hos. 13:15]
13 [m][ch. 1:1; Hos. 2:3; See 2 Kgs. 24:12-16]
14 [n][2 Kgs. 24:20]; See ch. 17:15-19 [o][ver. 11, 12] [p]See ver. 1

Chapter 20
1 [q][ch. 1:2; 8:1; 24:1; 26:1; 29:1, 17; 30:20; 31:1; 32:1, 17; 33:21; 40:1] [r]See ch. 8:1 [s]ch. 14:1
3 [t]See ch. 2:1 [u]See ch. 16:48 [v]See ch. 14:3
4 [w]ch. 22:2; 23:36 [x]ch. 16:2; 22:2
5 [y]See Ex. 6:7 [z]ver. 15, 23, 28, 42; ch. 36:7; 47:14; [Gen. 14:22] [a][Ex. 3:8; 4:31; 6:2]
6 [b]ver. 15; See Ex. 3:8 [c]ver. 15; [Jer. 3:19; Zech. 7:14]
7 [d][ver. 8; ch. 18:31] [e][ver. 24] [f][ver. 18; Lev. 18:3] [g]ver. 19; See Ex. 20:2 **8** [h]ver. 21 [i][ver. 7] [j]See ch. 5:13 **9** [k]ver. 22, 44 [l]Ps. 106:8 [m][Isa. 48:11] [n]ver. 14 **10** [o]Ex. 13:18, 20 **11** [p]Deut. 4:8; [Neh. 9:13, 14; Ps. 147:19, 20] [q]Lev. 18:5; Rom. 10:5; Gal. 3:12; See ch. 18:9 **12** [r][ver. 13, 16, 21, 24]; See Ex. 20:8-11; Deut. 5:12-15 [s]ch. 37:28; [Lev. 21:23] **13** [t]ver. 21 [u]ver. 21, 24 [v]ver. 21, 24; ch. 22:8; 23:38 **14** [w]ver. 9 **15** [x]See ver. 5 [y]Ps. 95:11; See Num. 14:28-30

them into the land that I had given them, a
land [z]flowing with milk and honey, [z]the most
glorious of all lands, 16 because they rejected
my rules and did not walk in my statutes,
and profaned my Sabbaths; [a]for their heart
went after their idols. 17 Nevertheless, [b]my eye
spared them, and I did not destroy them or
[c]make a full end of them in the wilderness.

18 "And I said to [d]their children in the wilderness, Do not walk [e]in the statutes of
your fathers, nor keep their rules, [f]nor defile
yourselves with their idols. 19 [g]I am the
LORD your God; [h]walk in my statutes, and
be careful to obey my rules, 20 and [i]keep my
Sabbaths holy that [j]they may be a sign between
me and you, that you may know that I am the
LORD your God. 21 [k]But the children [l]rebelled
against me. [m]They did not walk in my statutes and were not careful to obey my rules,
by which, if a person does them, he shall live;
they profaned my Sabbaths.

[n]"Then I said I would pour out my wrath
upon them and spend my anger against them
in the wilderness. 22 [o]But I withheld my hand
[p]and acted for the sake of my name, [q]that it
should not be profaned in the sight of the
nations, in whose sight I had brought them
out. 23 [r]Moreover, [s]I swore to them in the wilderness [t]that I would scatter them among the
nations and disperse them through the countries, 24 because they had not obeyed my rules,
but had rejected my statutes and profaned
my Sabbaths, [u]and their eyes were set on their
fathers' idols. 25 [v]Moreover, I gave them statutes that were not good and rules by which
they could not have life, 26 and I defiled them
through [w]their very gifts [w]in their offering
up all their firstborn, that I might devastate
them. I did it [x]that they might know that I am
the LORD.

27 "Therefore, [y]son of man, speak to the
house of Israel and say to them, Thus says
the Lord GOD: In this also your fathers blasphemed me, by [z]dealing treacherously with
me. 28 For when I had brought them into the
land that [a]I swore to give them, then wherever
they saw [b]any high hill or any leafy tree, there
they offered their sacrifices and there they presented [c]the provocation of their offering; there
they sent up their pleasing aromas, and there
they poured out their drink offerings. 29 (I said
to them, [d]What is the high place to which you
go? So its name is called Bamah[1] to this day.)

30 "Therefore say to the house of Israel, Thus
says the Lord GOD: [e]Will you defile yourselves
after the manner of your fathers and go [f]whor-
ing after their detestable things? 31 When you
present your gifts and [g]offer up your children
in fire,[2] you defile yourselves with all your
idols to this day. And [h]shall I be inquired of
by you, O house of Israel? [i]As I live, declares
the Lord GOD, I will not be inquired of by you.

32 [j]"What is in your mind shall never happen—the thought, [k]'Let us be like the nations,
like the tribes of the countries, [l]and worship
wood and stone.'

The LORD Will Restore Israel

33 [i]"As I live, declares the Lord GOD, [m]surely
with a mighty hand and an outstretched arm
and [n]with wrath poured out I will be king over
you. 34 [o]I will bring you out from the peoples
and gather you out of the countries where
you are scattered, with a mighty hand and an

[1] *Bamah* means *high place* [2] Hebrew *and make your children pass through the fire*

20:33–44 Even amid his warnings about coming judgment, God gives Israel several glimpses of his future grace to them. At the end of chapter 11, for example, he had promised to give them a new heart. In chapter 16, he promised to establish his everlasting covenant with them. Now in 20:40–44 we see a similar beautiful picture of restoration. Notice the reason for God's restoration of Israel, though. It is not because of anything they have done (v. 44), but rather simply because of his purposes of mercy to them. In other words, it is not for their own sake that he saves them, but for the sake of *his* own name.

This truth—that God will save his people for his own sake, and not because they deserve it—is taught over and over again in Ezekiel, and especially here in chapter 20. Throughout this chapter God's message to his people could not be clearer (vv. 7–10, 13–14, 21–22, 44). Salvation does not come to us because we in any way deserve it. On the contrary, it comes to us in spite of our deserving to be destroyed. God saves not because of who we are but in spite of who we are, out of his own purposes of grace.

15 [z]ver. 6; See Ex. 3:8
16 [a][ver. 24; Num. 15:39; Ps. 78:37]
17 [b]See ch. 5:11 [c][ch. 11:13]
18 [d]ver. 21; [ch. 2:3] [e]Josh. 24:14; 1 Pet. 1:18 [f][ver. 7]
19 [g]ver. 5; See Ex. 20:2 [h]Deut. 5:32, 33
20 [i]Jer. 17:22 [j]ver. 12; [Gen. 9:12; 17:11]
21 [k]Deut. 31:27 [l]ver. 8, 13 [m]ver. 13, 16 [n]ver. 8
22 [o]ver. 14 [p]ver. 9, 14, 44 [q]ver. 9
23 [r]ver. 15 [s]See ver. 5 [t]Deut. 28:64
24 [u][ver. 16]
25 [v]Ps. 81:12; Acts 7:42; Rom. 1:24, 28; 2 Thess. 2:11, 12; [ver. 39]
26 [w][ver. 31; ch. 16:20, 21] [x]See ch. 6:7

27 [y]See ch. 2:1 [z]See ch. 14:13 **28** [a]See ver. 5 [b][ch. 6:13] [c][ch. 8:17] **29** [d][ver. 40] **30** [e][ver. 7] [f]Ps. 106:39 **31** [g][ver. 26] [h]See ch. 14:3 [i]See ch. 16:48
32 [j]See ch. 11:5 [k][Jer. 44:17] [l]Deut. 4:28; 2 Kgs. 19:18; Dan. 5:4, 23; Rev. 9:20 **33** [i][See ver. 31 above] [m]See Jer. 21:5 [n][ver. 8] **34** [o][Jer. 31:8]

outstretched arm, and with wrath poured out.
35 [p]And I will bring you into the wilderness of
the peoples, [q]and there I will enter into judgment with you [r]face to face. 36 [s]As I entered into
judgment with your fathers in the wilderness
of the land of Egypt, so I will enter into judgment with you, declares the Lord GOD. 37 I will
make you [t]pass under the rod, and I will bring
you into the bond of the covenant. 38 [u]I will
purge out the rebels from among you, and
those who transgress against me. [v]I will bring
them out of the land where they sojourn, [w]but
they shall not enter the land of Israel. [x]Then
you will know that I am the LORD.

39 "As for you, O house of Israel, thus says the
Lord GOD: [y]Go serve every one of you his idols,
now and hereafter, if you will not listen to me;
[z]but my holy name you shall no more profane
with your gifts and your idols.

40 [a]"For on my holy mountain, the mountain height of Israel, declares the Lord GOD,
there [b]all the house of Israel, all of them, shall
serve me in the land. [c]There I will accept them,
and there I will require your contributions
and the choicest of your gifts, with all your
sacred offerings. 41 As a pleasing aroma I will
accept you, when [d]I bring you out from the
peoples and gather you out of the countries
where you have been scattered. And [e]I will
manifest my holiness among you in the sight
of the nations. 42 [f]And you shall know that I am
the LORD, when I bring you into the land of
Israel, the country that [g]I swore to give to your
fathers. 43 [h]And there you shall remember your
ways and all your deeds with which you have
defiled yourselves, [h]and you shall loathe yourselves for all the evils that you have committed. 44 And you shall know that I am the LORD,
[i]when I deal with you for my name's sake, [j]not
according to your evil ways, nor according to
your corrupt deeds, O house of Israel, declares
the Lord GOD."

45 [1] And the word of the LORD came to me:
46 [k]"Son of man, [l]set your face toward the
southland;[2] [m]preach against the south, and
prophesy against the forest land in the Negeb.
47 Say to the forest of the Negeb, Hear the word
of the LORD: Thus says the Lord GOD, Behold,
[n]I will kindle a fire in you, and it shall devour
every [o]green tree in you and every [o]dry tree.
The blazing flame shall not be quenched, and
[p]all faces from south to north shall be scorched
by it. 48 [q]All flesh shall see that I the LORD have
kindled it; it shall not be quenched." 49 Then
I said, [r]"Ah, Lord GOD! They are saying of me,
[s]'Is he not a maker of parables?'"

The LORD Has Drawn His Sword

21 [3] The word of the LORD came to me:
2 [t]"Son of man, [u]set your face toward
Jerusalem and [v]preach against the sanctuaries.[4] Prophesy against the land of Israel 3 and
say to the land of Israel, Thus says the LORD:
[w]Behold, I am against you and will draw [x]my
sword from its sheath and [y]will cut off from
you both righteous and wicked. 4 Because

[1] Ch 21:1 in Hebrew [2] Or *toward Teman* [3] Ch 21:6 in Hebrew [4] Some Hebrew manuscripts, compare Septuagint, Syriac *against their sanctuary*

35 [p] [ver. 10; Hos. 2:14] [q] [ch. 17:20] [r] [Deut. 5:4]
36 [s] See Num. 14:20-23, 28-30
37 [t] Lev. 27:32
38 [u] ch. 34:17, 20, 22; [Matt. 25:32, 33] [v] [ver. 35] [w] ch. 13:9 [x] See ch. 6:7
39 [y] [ver. 25, 26; Judg. 10:14] [z] ch. 39:7; 43:7; [Jer. 44:25, 26]
40 [a] ch. 17:23; [ch. 28:14; Isa. 56:7] [b] ch. 39:25 [c] ch. 43:27; Isa. 60:7; [Mal. 3:4; Rom. 12:1]
41 [d] ver. 34 [e] ch. 36:23; 39:27; [ch. 28:22; 38:16, 23; Num. 20:12; Isa. 8:13]
42 [f] See ch. 6:7 [g] See ver. 5
43 [h] See ch. 6:9
44 [i] ver. 9, 14, 22 [j] [Ps. 103:10]
46 [k] See ch. 2:1 [l] [ch. 21:2] [m] Amos 7:16; [Isa. 55:10, 11]
47 [n] Jer. 21:14 [o] ch. 17:24; [Luke 23:31] [p] ch. 21:4
48 [q] Isa. 40:5; [Isa. 30:33]
49 [r] See ch. 4:14 [s] [ch. 17:2; 24:3]
Chapter 21
2 [t] See ch. 2:1 [u] [ch. 20:46]

We as Christians have been swept up in something infinitely larger than our own lives and our own significance. We have been caught up into God's determination to glorify himself and his Son Jesus by saving a people who do not deserve it at all. God magnifies his grace by saving those who least deserve it.

21:1–24:27 With Israel's false self-assurances now exposed and eliminated, these chapters contain a dramatic, slow-motion depiction of God's righteous deathblow against Jerusalem.

21:1–23 The Lord draws his sword against Jerusalem in three stages. In verses 1–7, Ezekiel describes in terrifying language how the sword is drawn from its scabbard. Then in verses 8–17, we see the Lord sharpening the sword and then swinging it, as a warrior might do in preparation for battle—or for an execution.

It is fascinating that in verse 19 the sword of the Lord is shown to be King Nebuchadnezzar of Babylon. He is the instrument by which God will execute his judgment against Jerusalem (cf. Hab. 1:5–6). Ezekiel watches in a vision as Nebuchadnezzar pauses at a fork in his road, deciding whether to attack Jerusalem or to turn north and attack Rabbah, another rebellious city under the control of the Ammonites. Nebuchadnezzar uses pagan divination to make the decision (Ezek. 21:21), but God takes control of all the signs and sends him against Jerusalem (v. 22).

[v] See ch. 20:46 **3** [w] See ch. 13:8 [x] ver. 19, 30; [Deut. 32:41; Jer. 47:6] [y] [ch. 20:47; Job 9:22]

I will cut off from you both righteous and
wicked, therefore my sword shall be drawn
from its sheath against all flesh from south to
north. 5 [z]And all flesh shall know that I am the
LORD. I have drawn [x]my sword from its sheath;
[a]it shall not be sheathed again.

6 "As for you, son of man, [b]groan; with breaking heart and bitter grief, [c]groan before their
eyes. 7 [d]And when they say to you, 'Why do
you groan?' you shall say, 'Because of the news
[e]that it is coming. [f]Every heart will melt, and
[g]all hands will be feeble; every spirit will faint,
and [g]all knees will be weak as water. [h]Behold,
it is [e]coming, and it will be fulfilled,'" declares
the Lord GOD.

8 And the word of the LORD came to me:
9 [t]"Son of man, prophesy and say, Thus says
the Lord, say:

> [i]"A sword, a sword is sharpened
>   and also polished,
> 10 [j]sharpened for slaughter,
>   [j]polished to flash like lightning!

(Or [k]shall we rejoice? You have despised the
rod, my son, [l]with everything of wood.)[1] 11 So
the sword is given to be polished, that it may
be grasped in the hand. It is sharpened and
polished [m]to be given into the hand of the
slayer. 12 [n]Cry out and wail, son of man, for it is
against my people. It is against all the princes
of Israel. They are delivered over to the sword
with my people. [o]Strike therefore upon your
thigh. 13 For it will not be a testing—what
could it do if you despise [p]the rod?"[2] declares
the Lord GOD.

14 "As for you, [q]son of man, prophesy. [r]Clap
your hands and let the sword come down
twice, [s]yes, three times,[3] the sword for those
to be slain. It is the sword for the great slaughter, which surrounds them, 15 that their hearts
may melt, and many stumble.[4] At all their
gates I have given the glittering sword. Ah,
it is made like lightning; [t]it is taken up[5] for
slaughter. 16 Cut sharply to the right; set yourself to the left, wherever your face is directed.
17 I also will [r]clap my hands, [u]and I will satisfy
my fury; [v]I the LORD have spoken."

18 The word of the LORD came to me again:
19 "As for you, son of man, mark two ways for
[w]the sword of the king of Babylon to come.
Both of them shall come from the same land.
And make [x]a signpost; make it [x]at the head of
the way to a city. 20 Mark a way [y]for the sword
to come to Rabbah of the Ammonites and to
Judah, into Jerusalem the fortified. 21 For the
king of Babylon stands [z]at the parting of the
way, at the head of the two ways, to use divination. He shakes the arrows; he consults [a]the
teraphim;[6] he looks at the liver. 22 Into his right
hand comes the divination for Jerusalem, [b]to
set battering rams, to open the mouth with
murder, to lift up the voice with shouting, to
set battering rams against the gates, [c]to cast up
mounds, to build siege towers. 23 But to them
it will seem like a false divination. [d]They have
sworn solemn oaths, but he brings their guilt
to remembrance, [e]that they may be taken.

24 "Therefore thus says the Lord GOD:
Because you have made your guilt to be
remembered, in that your transgressions
are uncovered, so that in all your deeds your
sins appear—because you have come to
remembrance, [f]you shall be taken in hand.
25 And you, O profane[7] [g]wicked one, prince of
Israel, [h]whose day has come, [i]the time of your
final punishment, 26 thus says the Lord GOD:
Remove the turban and take off the crown.
Things shall not remain as they are. [j]Exalt
that which is low, and bring low that which
is exalted. 27 A ruin, ruin, ruin I will make it.

[1] Probable reading; Hebrew *The rod of my son despises everything of wood* [2] Or *For it is a testing; and what if even the rod despises? It shall not be!* [3] Hebrew *its third* [4] Hebrew *many stumbling blocks* [5] The meaning of the Hebrew word rendered *taken up* is uncertain [6] Or *household idols* [7] Or *slain*; also verse 29

21:24–27 As Nebuchadnezzar is about to plunge into the heart of Jerusalem, God addresses Zedekiah, the last king of Israel. He speaks to him about the fall of the Davidic dynasty (see also 19:10–14). In the midst of the cataclysm, however, comes one wholly unexpected spark of hope. Yes, the Davidic crown is fallen and is now "a ruin, ruin, ruin"—but only "*until he comes*, the one to whom judgment belongs" (21:27). Ultimately, that one to whom judgment belongs is Jesus. It is through Jesus, the Son of David, that God will save his people from the judgment they deserve. And in union with Jesus, believers themselves will join him in judging the world, including even the angels (1 Cor. 6:2–3).

5 [z][ch. 20:48] [x][See ver. 3 above] [a][ver. 30]
6 [b][ch. 6:11; 12:18] [c]See ch. 12:3
7 [d][ch. 12:9] [e][ch. 7:5, 6] [f]See Josh. 2:11 [g]See ch. 7:17 [h]ch. 39:8
9 [t][See ver. 2 above] [i]See ver. 3
10 [j][ver. 15, 28] [k][James 5:5] [l][ch. 20:47]
11 [m][ver. 19]
12 [n][ver. 6] [o]Jer. 31:19

13 [p][ver. 10] **14** [q]See ch. 2:1 [r]ch. 22:13; Num. 24:10 [s][2 Kgs. 24:1, 10; 25:1] **15** [t]ver. 10 **17** [r][See ver. 14 above] [u]See ch. 5:13 [v]See ch. 17:24 **19** [w]ver. 11 [x][ver. 21] **20** [y]See ch. 25:1-5; Jer. 49:1-6; Amos 1:13-15 **21** [z][ver. 19] [a]See Gen. 31:19 **22** [b]ch. 4:2; 26:9 [c]See ch. 4:2 **23** [d][ch. 17:13] [e][ch. 17:20] **24** [f][ch. 17:20] **25** [g][ch. 17:19; 2 Chr. 36:13; Jer. 52:2] [h]ver. 29; ch. 22:3, 4 [i]ch. 35:5 **26** [j][ch. 17:24; Luke 1:52]

[k]This also shall not be, [l]until he comes, the
one to whom judgment belongs, and I will
give it to him.
28 "And you, [m]son of man, prophesy, and
say, Thus says the Lord GOD [n]concerning the
Ammonites and concerning their reproach;
say, [o]A sword, a sword [p]is drawn for the slaughter. [o]It is polished to consume and to flash like
lightning— 29 while [q]they see for you false
visions, while they divine lies for you—to
place you on the necks of the profane wicked,
[r]whose day has come, the time of their final
punishment. 30 [p]Return it to its sheath. In the
place where you were created, in the land of
your origin, [s]I will judge you. 31 And [t]I will
pour out my indignation upon you; [u]I will
blow upon you with the fire of my wrath, and
I will deliver you into the hands of [v]brutish
men, skillful to destroy. 32 You shall be fuel for
the fire. Your blood shall be in the midst of the
land. [w]You shall be no more remembered, [x]for
I the LORD have spoken."

Israel's Shedding of Blood

22 And the word of the LORD came to
me, saying, 2 "And you, [y]son of man,
[z]will you judge, will you judge [a]the bloody
city? [b]Then declare to her all her abominations. 3 You shall say, Thus says the Lord GOD:
A city that sheds blood in her midst, so that
[c]her time may come, and that makes idols to
defile herself! 4 You have become guilty [a]by
the blood that you have shed, and defiled by
the idols that you have made, and you have
brought [c]your days near, the appointed time
of[1] your years has come. [d]Therefore I have
made you a reproach to the nations, and a
mockery to all the countries. 5 Those who
are near and those who are far from you will
mock you; [e]your name is defiled; [f]you are full
of tumult.
6 "Behold, [g]the princes of Israel in you, every
one according to his power, have been bent
on shedding blood. 7 Father and mother [h]are
treated with contempt in you; the sojourner
[i]suffers extortion in your midst; the fatherless and the widow [i]are wronged in you.
8 [j]You have despised my holy things and
[k]profaned my Sabbaths. 9 [l]There are men in
you who slander to shed blood, and people in
you [m]who eat on the mountains; [n]they commit lewdness in your midst. 10 In you [o]men
uncover their fathers' nakedness; in you they
violate women who are unclean in their menstrual impurity. 11 [p]One commits abomination with his neighbor's wife; [q]another lewdly
defiles his daughter-in-law; [r]another in you
violates his sister, his father's daughter. 12 In
you [s]they take bribes to shed blood; [t]you take
interest and profit[2] and make gain of your
neighbors by extortion; but [u]me you have
forgotten, declares the Lord GOD.
13 "Behold, [v]I strike my hand at [w]the dishonest gain that you have made, and at [x]the blood
that has been in your midst. 14 [y]Can your courage endure, or can your hands be strong, in the
days that I shall deal with you? [z]I the LORD
have spoken, and I will do it. 15 [a]I will scatter you among the nations and disperse you
through the countries, and [b]I will consume
your uncleanness out of you. 16 And [c]you shall
be profaned by your own doing [d]in the sight
of the nations, [e]and you shall know that I am
the LORD."
17 And the word of the LORD came to me:
18 [f]"Son of man, the house of Israel has become
[g]dross to me; all of them are [h]bronze and tin
and iron and lead in the furnace; they are

[1] Some Hebrew manuscripts, Septuagint, Syriac, Vulgate, Targum; most Hebrew manuscripts *until* [2] That is, profit that comes from charging interest to the poor (compare Leviticus 25:36)

22:1–23:49 As the sword plunges toward Israel's heart, the Lord gives one last accounting of her sin, as if to put an end to any question about whether his decision to punish her is right. Chapter 22 paints a picture of a society that is corrupt from top to bottom. Every part of the society is affected—economics, family relationships, politics, law—and every strata of society is involved—prophets (22:25, 28), priests (22:26), princes (22:27), and finally all "the people of the land" (22:29).

Chapter 23 then gives a stomach-turning and sexually explicit portrayal of Israel's adultery against God, especially in her alliances with Egypt and Assyria. Here we are shocked awake to the deeply profound covenant relationship into which God

27[k] [ver. 13] [l] Gen. 49:10; Zech. 6:12, 13; John 1:49; [Rev. 17:14]
28[m] See ch. 2:1 [n] See ver. 20 [o] [ver. 9, 10] [p] [ver. 5]
29[q] See ch. 13:6 [r] ver. 25
30[p] [See ver. 28 above] [s] ch. 16:38
31[t] See ch. 7:8 [u] ch. 22:20, 21 [v] See Ps. 49:10
32[w] ch. 25:10 [x] See ch. 17:24

Chapter 22
2[y] See ch. 2:1 [z] See ch. 20:4 [a] [ch. 16:38; 23:37; 24:6; 2 Kgs. 21:16]; See ch. 7:23 [b] ch. 16:2; 20:4 **3**[c] ch. 21:25, 29 **4**[a] [See ver. 2 above] [c] [See ver. 3 above] [d] See ch. 5:14 **5**[e] [Isa. 1:21] [f] Isa. 22:2 **6**[g] ver. 27 **7**[h] Deut. 27:16; [Eph. 6:2]; See Ex. 20:12 [i] Ex. 22:21, 22 **8**[j] [ver. 26] [k] See ch. 20:13 **9**[l] Lev. 19:16; [1 Sam. 22:9-19] [m] See ch. 18:6 [n] ch. 16:43 **10**[o] Lev. 18:7, 8; 20:11 **11**[p] Lev. 18:20; Jer. 5:8; [ch. 18:6] [q] Lev. 18:15; 20:12; [Amos 2:7] [r] Lev. 18:9; 20:17 **12**[s] Deut. 27:25 [t] See ch. 18:8 [u] ch. 23:35; See Jer. 2:32 **13**[v] ch. 21:14, 17 [w] ver. 27 [x] See ver. 2 **14**[y] [ch. 21:7] [z] See ch. 17:24 **15**[a] See ch. 5:10 [b] ch. 24:11; [ver. 21, 22] **16**[c] [ver. 26; ch. 7:24] [d] ch. 5:8 [e] See ch. 6:7 **18**[f] See ch. 2:1 [g] Ps. 119:119; Isa. 1:22, 25 [h] Jer. 6:28

[i]dross of silver. 19 Therefore thus says the Lord
GOD: Because you have all become dross,
therefore, behold, I will gather you into the
midst of Jerusalem. 20 As one gathers silver
and bronze and iron and lead and tin into a
furnace, [j]to blow the fire on it in order to melt
it, so I will gather you [k]in my anger and in my
wrath, and I will put you in and melt you. 21 I
will gather you and blow on you with the fire
of my wrath, and you shall be melted in the
midst of it. 22 As silver is melted in a furnace, so
you shall be melted in the midst of it, and you
shall know that I am the LORD; [l]I have poured
out my wrath upon you."

23 And the word of the LORD came to me:
24 "Son of man, say to her, You are a land that
is [m]not cleansed [n]or rained upon in the day of
indignation. 25 [o]The conspiracy of her prophets in her midst is [p]like a roaring lion [q]tear-
ing the prey; they have devoured human lives;
they have taken treasure and precious things;
they have made many widows in her midst.
26 [r]Her priests [s]have done violence to my law
and [t]have profaned my holy things. [u]They have
made no distinction between the holy and the
common, neither have they taught the difference between the unclean and the clean,
and [v]they have disregarded my Sabbaths,
[w]so that I am profaned among them. 27 [x]Her
princes in her midst are like wolves [y]tearing
the prey, [z]shedding blood, destroying lives to
get dishonest gain. 28 And [a]her prophets have
smeared whitewash for them, [b]seeing false
visions and divining lies for them, saying,
'Thus says the Lord GOD,' when the LORD has
not spoken. 29 The people of the land [c]have
practiced extortion and committed robbery.
They have oppressed the poor and needy, and
[c]have extorted from the sojourner without
justice. 30 [d]And I sought for a man among
them [e]who should build up the wall [e]and
stand in the breach before me for the land,
that I should not destroy it, but I found none.
31 Therefore [f]I have poured out my indignation
upon them. I have consumed them with the
fire of my wrath. I have returned [g]their way
upon their heads, declares the Lord GOD."

Oholah and Oholibah

23 The word of the LORD came to me:
2 [h]"Son of man, there were [i]two
women, the daughters of one mother. 3 [j]They
played the whore in Egypt; [j]they played the
whore [k]in their youth; there their breasts
were pressed and their virgin bosoms[1] handled. 4 Oholah was the name of the elder and
Oholibah the name of her sister. [l]They became
mine, and they [m]bore sons and daughters.
As for their names, Oholah is [n]Samaria, and
Oholibah is Jerusalem.

5 "Oholah played the whore [o]while she was
mine, and [p]she lusted after her lovers [q]the
Assyrians, warriors 6 clothed in purple, [r]gov-
ernors and commanders, [s]all of them desirable young men, [t]horsemen riding on horses.
7 She bestowed her whoring upon them, the
choicest men of Assyria all of them, and she
defiled herself with all the idols of everyone
after whom she lusted. 8 She did not give up
her whoring [u]that she had begun in Egypt;
for in her youth men had lain with her and
handled her virgin bosom and poured out
their whoring lust upon her. 9 Therefore [v]I
delivered her into the hands of her lovers,
into the hands of the Assyrians, after whom
she lusted. 10 [w]These uncovered her nakedness;
[x]they seized her sons and her daughters; and
as for her, they killed her with the sword; and
she became [y]a byword among women, [z]when
judgment had been executed on her.

11 [a]"Her sister Oholibah saw this, and she
became [b]more corrupt than her sister[2] in her

[1] Hebrew *nipples*; also verses 8, 21 [2] Hebrew *than she*

has entered with his people. To turn from him, to flirt with idols, to trust and delight in anything more than God himself, is spiritual adultery. It is more than this: it is whoredom (23:44).

Yet at the pinnacle of history God became one of us, in order to win adulterous sinners back to himself. For this reason Christ is portrayed throughout the New Testament as the bridegroom who gives himself for the sake of his defiled, impure bride (Matt. 9:15; John 3:29; Rev. 21:2, 9). The contaminated are cleansed; the filthy are washed clean (1 Cor. 6:11). Because Jesus has made us pure and holy through his work on the cross (Eph. 5:25–26), we delight to love and trust him with all our hearts.

18 [i]Isa. 1:25
20 [j]ch. 21:31; [Mal. 3:3] [k]Jer. 33:5
22 [l]See ch. 7:8
24 [m]See ver. 2-4 [n][ch. 34:26]; See 1 Kgs. 8:35, 36
25 [o]See Jer. 11:9 [p]See ch. 19:3 [q]ver. 27
26 [r][Mal. 2:8] [s]Zeph. 3:4 [t][ver. 8] [u]See Lev. 10:10 [v][Jer. 17:22, 24, 27] [w]See ch. 36:20
27 [x]ver. 6; Mic. 3:1, 2; Zeph. 3:3; [Matt. 7:15] [y]ver. 25 [z][ver. 13] **28** [a]ch. 13:10 [b]See ch. 13:6 **29** [c][ver. 7] **30** [d]Isa. 59:16; Jer. 5:1 [e]See ch. 13:5 **31** [f][ver. 21] [g]See ch. 7:4 **Chapter 23** **2** [h]See ch. 2:1 [i][ch. 16:45, 46] **3** [j]See ch. 16:15 [k][ch. 16:22] **4** [l]ch. 16:8 [m][ver. 37] [n][ch. 16:46] **5** [o]Num. 5:19, 20 [p][Hos. 2:5] [q]2 Kgs. 15:19; 17:3; Hos. 8:9 **6** [r]ver. 23 [s]ver. 23 [t]ch. 38:15; [Isa. 5:28] **8** [u][ver. 3, 19] **9** [v][2 Kgs. 15:29]; See 2 Kgs. 17:4-6, 23; 18:9-11 **10** [w]ver. 29; See ch. 16:37 [x]ver. 25 [y][ch. 16:14] [z]See ch. 5:8 **11** [a]Jer. 3:8, 9 [b]Jer. 3:11; See ch. 16:47

lust and in her whoring, which was worse than that of her sister. 12 She lusted after the Assyrians, governors and commanders, warriors clothed in full armor, horsemen riding on horses, [s]all of them desirable young men. 13 And I saw that she was defiled; they both took the same way. 14 But she carried her whoring further. She saw men [c]portrayed on the wall, the [d]images of [e]the Chaldeans portrayed in vermilion, 15 wearing belts on their waists, with flowing turbans on their heads, all of them having the appearance of officers, a likeness of Babylonians whose native land was Chaldea. 16 When she saw them, she lusted after them and [f]sent messengers to them [e]in Chaldea. 17 And the Babylonians came to her [g]into the bed of love, and they defiled her with their whoring lust. And after she was defiled by them, [h]she turned from them in disgust. 18 When she carried on her whoring so openly and flaunted her nakedness, I turned in disgust from her, as I had turned in disgust from her sister. 19 Yet she increased her whoring, [i]remembering the days of her youth, when she played the whore in the land of Egypt 20 and lusted after her lovers there, whose members were like those of donkeys, and whose issue was like that of horses. 21 Thus you longed for the lewdness of your youth, when the Egyptians handled your bosom and pressed[1] your young breasts."

22 Therefore, O Oholibah, thus says the Lord GOD: "Behold, I will stir up against you your lovers [h]from whom you turned in disgust, [j]and I will bring them against you from every side: 23 the Babylonians and all the Chaldeans, [k]Pekod and Shoa and Koa, and all the Assyrians with them, [l]desirable young men, [l]governors and commanders all of them, officers and men of renown, all of them riding on horses. 24 And they shall come against you from the north[2] with chariots and wagons and a host of peoples. [m]They shall set themselves against you on every side with buckler, shield, and helmet; and [n]I will commit the judgment to them, and [o]they shall judge you according to their judgments. 25 And I will direct my jealousy against you, [p]that they may deal with you in fury. They shall cut off your nose and your ears, and your survivors shall fall by the sword. [q]They shall seize your sons and your daughters, and your survivors shall be devoured by fire. 26 [r]They shall also strip you of your clothes and take away your beautiful jewels. 27 [s]Thus I will put an end to your lewdness and [t]your whoring begun in the land of Egypt, so that you shall not lift up your eyes to them or remember Egypt anymore.

28 "For thus says the Lord GOD: [u]Behold, I will deliver you into the hands of those whom you hate, [v]into the hands of those from whom you turned in disgust, 29 and [w]they shall deal with you in hatred and take away all the fruit of your labor [x]and leave you naked and bare, and [y]the nakedness of your whoring shall be uncovered. Your lewdness and your whoring 30 have brought this upon you, because [z]you played the whore with the nations and defiled yourself with their idols. 31 You have gone the way of your sister; [a]therefore I will give [b]her cup into your hand. 32 Thus says the Lord GOD:

"You shall drink your sister's cup
  that is deep and large;
you shall be laughed at and held in derision,
  for it contains much;
33 you will be filled with [c]drunkenness and sorrow.
[c]A cup of horror and desolation,
  the cup of [d]your sister Samaria;
34 [e]you shall drink it and drain it out,
  and gnaw its shards,
  and tear your breasts;

for I have spoken, declares the Lord GOD. 35 Therefore thus says the Lord GOD: Because [f]you have forgotten me and [g]cast me behind your back, you yourself [h]must bear the consequences of your lewdness and whoring."

36 The LORD said to me: [i]"Son of man, [j]will you judge Oholah and Oholibah? Declare to them their abominations. 37 For [k]they have committed adultery, [l]and blood is on their hands. With their idols they have committed adultery, and they have even [m]offered up[3] to them for food the children whom they had borne to me. 38 Moreover, this they have done to me: [n]they have defiled my sanctuary on the

[1] Vulgate, Syriac; Hebrew *bosom for the sake of* [2] Septuagint; the meaning of the Hebrew word is unknown [3] Or *have even made pass through the fire*

12 [s] [See ver. 6 above] **14** [c] ch. 8:10 [d] [ch. 16:17] [e] ch. 16:29; [2 Kgs. 20:12, 13; 24:1] **16** [f] [ver. 40; Isa. 57:9] [e] [See ver. 14 above] **17** [g] [ver. 41; Isa. 57:7, 8] [h] ver. 22, 28; [ch. 17:15] **19** [i] [ver. 3]; See ch. 16:15 **22** [h] [See ver. 17 above] [j] ch. 16:37 **23** [k] Jer. 50:21 [l] ver. 6, 12 **24** [m] [2 Kgs. 19:32] [n] [ch. 9:5, 6] [o] 2 Kgs. 25:6 **25** [p] ver. 29 [q] ver. 10 **26** [r] ch. 16:39 **27** [s] ver. 48; ch. 16:41 [t] ver. 3, 19 **28** [u] ch. 16:37 [v] ver. 17, 22 **29** [w] ver. 25 [x] ch. 16:7, 22, 39 [y] ver. 10; See ch. 16:37 **30** [z] ch. 6:9; See Ex. 34:15 **31** [a] [ver. 9, 10] [b] [Jer. 25:15] **33** [c] Isa. 51:17; Jer. 13:13; [Rev. 14:10] [d] [ver. 4] **34** [e] Ps. 75:8 **35** [f] ch. 22:12; See Jer. 2:32 [g] 1 Kgs. 14:9 [h] [ver. 49; ch. 14:10; 16:58] **36** [i] See ch. 2:1 [j] [ch. 20:4; 22:2] **37** [k] See ch. 16:38 [l] [ch. 22:2] [m] ch. 16:20, 21; [ch. 7:23] **38** [n] See ch. 5:11

same day and [o]profaned my Sabbaths. 39 For when [p]they had slaughtered their children in sacrifice to their idols, on the same day [q]they came into my sanctuary to profane it. And behold, [r]this is what they did in my house. 40 They even sent for men to come from afar, [s]to whom a messenger was sent; and behold, they came. For them you bathed yourself, [t]painted your eyes, [u]and adorned yourself with ornaments. 41 You sat on [v]a stately couch, with a table spread before it [w]on which you had placed my incense and [x]my oil. 42 The [y]sound of a carefree multitude was with her; and with men of the common sort, drunkards[1] were brought from the wilderness; and they put [z]bracelets on the hands of the women, and [a]beautiful crowns on their heads.

43 "Then I said of her who was worn out by adultery, Now they will continue to use her for a whore, even her![2] 44 For they have gone in to her, as men go in to a prostitute. Thus they went in to Oholah and to Oholibah, lewd women! 45 But righteous men [b]shall pass judgment on them with the sentence of adulteresses, and with the sentence of women who shed blood, because they are adulteresses, and blood is on their hands."

46 For thus says the Lord GOD: [c]"Bring up a vast host against them, and make them [d]an object of terror and [e]a plunder. 47 [f]And the host shall stone them and cut them down with their swords. [g]They shall kill their sons and their daughters, and [h]burn up their houses. 48 [i]Thus will I put an end to lewdness in the land, that all women may take warning and not commit lewdness as you have done. 49 And they shall return your lewdness upon you, and [j]you shall bear the penalty for your sinful idolatry, and [k]you shall know that I am the Lord GOD."

The Siege of Jerusalem

24 [l]In the ninth year, in the tenth month, on the tenth day of the month, the word of the LORD came to me: 2 [m]"Son of man, write down the name of this day, this very day. The king of Babylon has laid siege to Jerusalem this very day. 3 And [n]utter a parable to [o]the rebellious house and say to them, Thus says the Lord GOD:

"Set on [p]the pot, set it on;
pour in water also;
4 put in it the pieces of meat,
all the good pieces, [q]the thigh and the shoulder;
fill it with choice bones.
5 Take the choicest one of the flock;
pile the logs[3] under it;
boil it well;
seethe also its bones in it.

6 "Therefore thus says the Lord GOD: [r]Woe to the bloody city, to [p]the pot whose corrosion is in it, and whose corrosion has not gone out of it! Take out of it piece after piece, without making any choice.[4] 7 For the blood she has shed is in her midst; she put it on [s]the bare

[1] Or *Sabeans* [2] The meaning of the Hebrew verse is uncertain [3] Compare verse 10; Hebrew *the bones* [4] Hebrew *no lot has fallen upon it*

24:1–2 The sword pierces. Nebuchadnezzar, king of Babylon, lays siege to Jerusalem. As Ezekiel's precise dating of the event indicates, this is a major turning point in the book. The judgment about which God has been warning for the entire first half of the book has finally fallen, and Ezekiel is told about it in a prophetic vision.

24:3–14 Immediately following the piercing of the sword in Nebuchadnezzar's siege of Jerusalem, Ezekiel's book shifts to an almost hallucinatory image of the people of Israel dancing around a boiling pot, laughing, celebrating, and singing a cooking song. Apparently, the Israelites are thinking of themselves in this vision (vv. 3–5) as choice pieces of meat who are safe in the "pot" of the city of Jerusalem. Their celebration, however, quickly turns to terror as the pot is shown to be filled with filth and uncleanness. Logs are piled high, the pot is overturned, and all its contents are burned in the fire. Again, self-deluded honor turns to horrifying destruction. Blind confidence that judgment would never fall turns to terror as God executes his wrath against sin.

This text reminds us that the gospel of grace is no gospel at all without a sobering realization of divine wrath: God's holy and righteous fury and indignation against sin. It is only as we grasp how evil sin truly is that we begin to grasp the wonder of what God in his great love has done to undo it and restore sinners to himself through the work of his Son (Rom. 5:8; 1 Tim. 1:12–16). Those who believe themselves to be righteous by their own will and deeds do not see themselves as being in need of the grace they require (Luke 5:32).

38 [o]See ch. 20:13
39 [p]ver. 37; ch. 16:20, 21, 36 [q]ch. 44:7 [r][2 Kgs. 21:4]; See Jer. 23:11
40 [s][ver. 16] [t][2 Kgs. 9:30; Jer. 4:30] [u][ch. 16:11, 12]
41 [v][Esth. 1:6] [w]ch. 16:18; [Prov. 7:17] [x][Hos. 2:8]
42 [y][Isa. 22:2] [z][ch. 16:11] [a][ch. 16:12]
45 [b][ver. 24]; See ch. 16:38
46 [c]ch. 16:40 [d]Deut. 28:25 [e]ch. 7:21
47 [f]ch. 16:40, 41; [Josh. 7:24, 25] [g]ch. 24:21; See 2 Chr. 36:17 [h]2 Chr. 36:19
48 [i]ver. 27; [ch. 16:41]
49 [j][ver. 35] [k][See ch. 6:7]

Chapter 24
1 [l]See ch. 20:1
2 [m]See ch. 2:1
3 [n][ch. 17:2; 20:49] [o]See ch. 2:5 [p]ch. 11:3, 7, 11; 2 Kgs. 4:38
4 [q]See 1 Sam. 9:24
6 [r]ch. 22:2; [Nah. 3:1] [p][See ver. 3 above]
7 [s]ch. 26:4, 14

rock; [t]she did not pour it out on the ground
to cover it with dust. 8 To rouse my wrath, to
take vengeance, I have set on the bare rock
the blood she has shed, that it may not be
covered. 9 Therefore thus says the Lord GOD:
Woe to the bloody city! [u]I also will make the
pile great. 10 Heap on the logs, kindle the fire,
boil the meat well, mix in the spices,[1] and let
the bones be burned up. 11 Then set it empty
upon the coals, that it may become hot, and
its copper may burn, [v]that its uncleanness
may be melted in it, its corrosion consumed.
12 [w]She has wearied herself with toil;[2] its abundant corrosion does not go out of it. Into the
fire with its corrosion! 13 On account of your
unclean lewdness, because I would have
cleansed you and you were not cleansed from
your uncleanness, [x]you shall not be cleansed
anymore till [y]I have satisfied my fury upon
you. 14 [z]I am the LORD. I have spoken; it shall
come to pass; I will do it. I will not go back; [a]I
will not spare; [b]I will not relent; [c]according to
your ways and your deeds you will be judged,
declares the Lord GOD."

Ezekiel's Wife Dies

15 The word of the LORD came to me: 16 [d]"Son
of man, behold, I am about to take the delight
of your eyes away from you at a stroke; yet
you shall not mourn or weep, nor shall your
tears run down. 17 Sigh, but not aloud; make
no mourning for the dead. [e]Bind on your turban, and [f]put your shoes on your feet; do not
cover your lips, [g]nor eat the bread of men." 18 So
I spoke to the people in the morning, and [h]at
evening my wife died. And on the next morning I did [i]as I was commanded.

19 And [j]the people said to me, "Will you not
tell us what these things mean for us, that
you are acting thus?" 20 Then I said to them,
"The word of the LORD came to me: 21 'Say to
the house of Israel, Thus says the Lord GOD:
[k]Behold, I will profane my sanctuary, the pride
of your power, the delight of your eyes, and
the yearning of your soul, and [l]your sons and
your daughters whom you left behind shall
fall by the sword. 22 And [m]you shall do as I have
done; [m]you shall not cover your lips, [g]nor eat
the bread of men. 23 [m]Your turbans shall be
on your heads and your shoes on your feet;
you shall not mourn or weep, but [n]you shall
rot away in your iniquities and groan to one
another. 24 Thus shall Ezekiel be to you [o]a sign;
[m]according to all that he has done you shall do.
When this comes, then [p]you will know that
I am the Lord GOD.'

25 "As for you, [q]son of man, surely on the day
when I take from them [r]their stronghold,
their joy and glory, the delight of their eyes
and their soul's desire, and also their sons and
daughters, 26 [s]on that day a fugitive will come
to you to report to you the news. 27 On that day
your mouth [t]will be opened to the fugitive,
and you shall speak and be no longer mute.
[u]So you will be a sign to them, and [v]they will
know that I am the LORD."

Prophecy Against Ammon

25

The word of the LORD came to me:
2 [w]"Son of man, [x]set your face toward
[y]the Ammonites and prophesy against them.
3 Say to the Ammonites, Hear the word of the
Lord GOD: [z]Thus says the Lord GOD, Because
you said, [a]'Aha!' over my [b]sanctuary when it
was profaned, and over the land of Israel when
it was made desolate, and over the house of
Judah when they went into exile, 4 therefore
behold, I am handing you over to [c]the people
of the East for a possession, and they shall set
their encampments among you and make
their dwellings in your midst. They shall eat
your fruit, and they shall drink your milk.

[1] Or *empty out the broth* [2] The meaning of the Hebrew is uncertain

7[t] [Lev. 17:13; Deut. 12:16, 24]
9[u] Isa. 30:33
11[v] ch. 22:15
12[w] [Jer. 2:22]
13[x] Isa. 22:14 [y] See ch. 5:13
14[z] See ch. 17:24 [a] See ch. 5:11 [b] [Num. 23:19; 1 Sam. 15:29] [c] [ch. 20:43; 23:45]
16[d] See ch. 2:1
17[e] See Lev. 10:6 [f] [2 Sam. 15:30; Isa. 20:2] [g] Hos. 9:4; See Jer. 16:5-7
18[h] [ver. 16] [i] ch. 12:7; 37:7
19[j] See ch. 12:9
21[k] [Jer. 7:14]; See ch. 7:21

25:1–32:32 This is the second major section of Ezekiel's prophecy. The first section (chs. 1–24) contained repeated warnings about God's judgment of Israel's sin. It ended in chapter 24 when Ezekiel was told in a vision that King Nebuchadnezzar, acting as God's sword, has laid siege to Jerusalem. The third section will begin in chapter 33, when a fugitive from the ruined Jerusalem arrives in Babylon to tell the exiles that the city is fallen. From chapters 33–48, then, Ezekiel's message changes from one of warning and judgment to one of hope and restoration.

This second section (chs. 25–32) represents the time when the fugitive is making his way from Jerusalem to Babylon. In dramatic fashion, the "camera" spins out from the besieged Jerusalem—and the fugitive beginning his journey to Babylon—to a

[l] ch. 23:47; See 2 Chr. 36:17 **22**[m] [ver. 17; ch. 12:11] [g] [See ver. 17 above] **23**[m] [See ver. 22 above] [n] See ch. 4:17 **24**[o] ver. 27; See ch. 4:3 [m] [See ver. 22 above] [p] See ch. 6:7 **25**[q] See ch. 2:1 [r] [ver. 21] **26**[s] See ch. 33:21, 22 **27**[t] ch. 29:21; [ch. 3:26, 27] [u] ver. 24; See ch. 4:3 [v] See ch. 6:7 **Chapter 25** **2**[w] See ch. 2:1 [x] See ch. 6:2 [y] ch. 21:20, 28; See Jer. 49:1-6 **3**[z] ch. 2:4; 3:11, 27 [a] ch. 26:2; 36:2 [b] See ch. 7:22 **4**[c] Judg. 6:3

5 I will make [d]Rabbah a [e]pasture for camels
and Ammon[1] [e]a fold for flocks. [v]Then you will
know that I am the LORD. 6 For thus says the
Lord GOD: Because [f]you have clapped your
hands [g]and stamped your feet and [h]rejoiced
with all the [i]malice within your soul against
the land of Israel, 7 therefore, behold, [j]I have
stretched out my hand against you, and [k]will
hand you over as plunder to the nations. And
I will cut you off from the peoples and will
make you perish out of the countries; I will
destroy you. Then you will know that I am
the LORD.

Prophecy Against Moab and Seir

8 "Thus says the Lord GOD: Because [l]Moab
and [m]Seir[2] said, 'Behold, the [n]house of Judah
is like all the other nations,' 9 therefore [l]I will
lay open the flank of Moab from the cities,
from its cities on its frontier, the glory of the
country, [o]Beth-jeshimoth, [p]Baal-meon, and
[q]Kiriathaim. 10 I will give it [r]along with the
Ammonites [s]to the people of the East as a possession, [t]that the Ammonites may be remembered no more among the nations, 11 [l]and I will
execute judgments upon Moab. [u]Then they
will know that I am the LORD.

Prophecy Against Edom

12 "Thus says the Lord GOD: Because [v]Edom
acted revengefully against the house of Judah
and has grievously offended [w]in taking vengeance on them, 13 therefore thus says the Lord
GOD, [x]I will stretch out my hand against Edom
and cut off from it man and beast. And I will
make it desolate; from [y]Teman even to [z]Dedan
they shall fall by the sword. 14 And I will lay
my vengeance upon Edom [a]by the hand of
my people Israel, and they shall do in Edom
according to my anger and according to my
wrath, and [b]they shall know my vengeance,
declares the Lord GOD.

Prophecy Against Philistia

15 "Thus says the Lord GOD: Because [c]the
Philistines [d]acted revengefully and took
vengeance [e]with malice of soul to destroy in
never-ending enmity, 16 therefore thus says the
Lord GOD, [x]Behold, I will stretch out my hand
against the Philistines, and I will cut off [f]the
Cherethites and destroy the rest of the seacoast. 17 I will execute great vengeance on them
[g]with wrathful rebukes. [h]Then they will know
that I am the LORD, when I lay my vengeance
upon them."

[1] Hebrew *and the Ammonites* [2] Septuagint lacks *and Seir*

kaleidoscopic vision of God pouring out judgment on the nations of the world who have oppressed and belittled his people.

Even as the divine sword pierces into Jerusalem's heart—before word of the city's fall has even reached the ears of the exiles—God's heart turns with ferocious love to defend and restore his people. In these eight chapters, he asserts his authority over all the nations of the world, and indeed takes up his sword on behalf of his afflicted people.

We see the same ferocious, defending love of God for his people when Jesus endures the temptations of Satan in the wilderness (Matt. 4:1–11). He is not simply acting as an individual man there but rather as the pioneering champion of his people. He succeeds where they failed; he defeats Satan even as they were defeated by him (Col. 2:15). At the cross of Christ, God not only takes up the sword on behalf of his people; he aims it against his own Son. Such love arrests us. It changes us. We cannot remain as we are.

25:1–17 This chapter names the first four of seven nations against whom God pronounces judgment. Ammon, Moab, Edom, and Philistia suffer God's wrath. As we read such extended pronouncements of judgment against godless nations, it is at first difficult to see how all this connects to the grace and love shown by God in sending Jesus Christ. Yet upon further reflection we remember that it is the wrath deserved not only by pagan nations but by all of humanity that Jesus came to assuage. The punishment falling on the foreign nations throughout Ezekiel is the very punishment from which the work of Christ delivers us. As our King, he ultimately restrains and conquers all his and our enemies. He demonstrates that he can accomplish this by these accounts of his judgment upon the enemies of the covenant people.

As we read these denouncements, our hearts are sobered and softened. We are reminded, once more, that Jesus stood in for us. "In our place condemned he stood." We are also reminded that God will not overlook the wrongs done to his people (e.g.,

5 [d]2 Sam. 11:1; 12:26; See ch. 21:20 [e][Zeph. 2:15] [v][See ch. 24:27 above]
6 [f]Ps. 98:8; Isa. 55:12 [g][ch. 6:11] [h][Zeph. 2:8, 10] [i]ver. 15; ch. 36:5
7 [j]See ch. 6:14 [k][ver. 4; ch. 7:21]
8 [l]See Isa. 15:1-9; Jer. 48:1-47 [m]See ver. 12 [n]See Jer. 25:17-26
9 [l][See ver. 8 above] [o]Josh. 12:3 [p]1 Chr. 5:8 [q]See Jer. 48:1
10 [r]ver. 2 [s]ver. 4 [t]ch. 21:32
11 [l][See ver. 8 above] [u]See ch. 6:7
12 [v]ver. 8; ch. 32:29; 35:2, 5; 2 Chr. 28:17; Ps. 137:7; Isa. 21:11; 34:5; Amos 1:11, 12; See Jer. 49:7-22; Obad. 1-21 [w]ver. 15
13 [x]See ch. 6:14 [y]1 Chr. 1:45; Amos 1:12 [z]ch. 27:15, 20; 38:13; Isa. 21:13
14 [a]Amos 9:12; Obad. 18 [b][ver. 17]
15 [c]Jer. 25:20; 47:1; Joel 3:4; Amos 1:6; Zeph. 2:4; See Isa. 14:29-31 [d]ver. 12 [e]ver. 6; ch. 36:5
16 [x][See ver. 13 above] [f]See 1 Sam. 30:14
17 [g]ch. 5:15 [h][ver. 14]

Prophecy Against Tyre

26 [i]In the eleventh year, on the first day of
the month, the word of the LORD came
to me: 2 [j]"Son of man, because [k]Tyre said concerning Jerusalem, [l]'Aha, the gate of the peoples
is broken; it has swung open to me. I shall be
replenished, now that she is laid waste,' 3 therefore thus says the Lord GOD: [m]Behold, I am
against you, O Tyre, and will bring up [n]many
nations against you, [o]as the sea brings up its
waves. 4 They shall destroy the walls of Tyre
and break down her towers, and I will scrape
her soil from her and [p]make her a bare rock.
5 She [q]shall be in the midst of the sea a place
for the spreading of nets, [r]for I have spoken,
declares the Lord GOD. And she shall become
plunder for the nations, 6 and her daughters
on the mainland shall be killed by the sword.
[s]Then they will know that I am the LORD.

7 "For thus says the Lord GOD: [t]Behold,
I will bring against Tyre [u]from the north
Nebuchadnezzar[1] king of Babylon, [v]king of
kings, with horses and chariots, and with
horsemen and a host of many soldiers. 8 He
will kill with the sword [w]your daughters on
the mainland. [x]He will set up a siege wall
against you and throw up a mound against
you, and raise [y]a roof of shields against you.
9 [z]He will direct the shock of his battering rams
against your walls, and with his axes he will
break down your towers. 10 His horses will be
so many that their dust will cover you. Your
walls will shake at the noise of the horsemen
and wagons and chariots, when he enters
your gates as men enter a city that has been
breached. 11 With the hoofs of his horses he
will trample all your streets. He will kill your
people with the sword, and your mighty pillars will fall to the ground. 12 They will plunder [a]your riches and loot [a]your merchandise.
They will break down your walls and destroy
your pleasant houses. Your stones and timber
and [b]soil they will cast into the midst of the
waters. 13 [c]And I will stop the music of your
songs, and [d]the sound of your lyres shall be
heard no more. 14 [p]I will make you a bare rock.
[q]You shall be a place for the spreading of nets.
You shall never be rebuilt, [r]for I am the LORD;
I have spoken, declares the Lord GOD.

15 "Thus says the Lord GOD to Tyre: Will not
[e]the coastlands shake at the sound of your fall,
[f]when the wounded groan, when slaughter is
made in your midst? 16 Then all [g]the princes of
the sea will step down from their thrones and
[h]remove their robes and strip off their embroidered garments. They will clothe themselves
with trembling; [i]they will sit on the ground
and [j]tremble every moment and [k]be appalled
at you. 17 And they will [l]raise a lamentation
over you and say to you,

"'How you have perished,
you who were inhabited from the seas,
O city renowned,
[m]who was mighty on the sea;
she and her inhabitants [n]imposed their
terror
on all her inhabitants!
18 Now the coastlands tremble
on the day of your fall,
and the coastlands that are on the sea
are dismayed at your passing.'

19 "For thus says the Lord GOD: When I make
you a city laid waste, like the cities that are not
inhabited, [o]when I bring up the deep over you,
and the great waters cover you, 20 then [p]I will
make you go down with those who go down
to the pit, to the people of old, and I will make
you to dwell in the world below, among ruins
from of old, [p]with those who go down to the
pit, so that you will not be inhabited; but I will
set beauty [q]in the land of the living. 21 I will
bring you [r]to a dreadful end, and you shall be
no more. [s]Though you be sought for, you will
never be found again, declares the Lord GOD."

[1] Hebrew *Nebuchadrezzar*; so throughout Ezekiel

vv. 6–7). The clock is ticking; all wrongs will one day be put right. God's people will be vindicated. Penitent sinners are forgiven; impenitent sinners are not. On both counts, we praise and hope in God.

26:1–28:26 The fifth nation to suffer God's wrath is Tyre, a wealthy and beautiful coastal trading city. Chapters 26–27 describe Tyre's beauty, and then chapter 28 contains two prophecies against the king of Tyre. Ezekiel 28:20–24 describes God's judgment against Sidon, a sister city of Tyre and the sixth nation to fall under God's wrath.

Chapter 26
1 [i]See ch. 20:1
2 [j]See ch. 2:1 [k]See Isa. 23:1-18 [l]ch. 25:3; 36:2
3 [m]See ch. 13:8 [n][ch. 32:3; Jer. 34:1] [o][Lam. 2:13]
4 [p]ch. 24:7
5 [q]ch. 47:10 [r]See ch. 17:24
6 [s]See ch. 6:7
7 [t][ch. 29:18] [u]See Jer. 1:14 [v]Ezra 7:12; Dan. 2:37; [Hos. 8:10] **8** [w]ver. 6 [x]See ch. 4:2 [y][2 Kgs. 19:32] **9** [z]ch. 4:2; 21:22 **12** [a]See ch. 27:12-24 [b]ver. 4 **13** [c][Isa. 24:8; Jer. 7:34; 16:9] [d][Isa. 5:12; 23:16] **14** [p][See ver. 4 above] [q][See ver. 5 above] [r][See ver. 5 above] **15** [e]ch. 27:35 [f]Jer. 51:52 **16** [g][Isa. 23:8] [h][Jonah 3:6] [i]Isa. 3:26 [j]ch. 32:10 [k]ch. 27:35 **17** [l]ch. 19:1; 27:2, 32; [Rev. 18:9] [m][Isa. 23:4] [n]See ch. 32:23 **19** [o][ver. 3; ch. 27:34] **20** [p][ch. 31:14, 16; 32:18, 24] [q]ch. 32:23, 27, 32; Ps. 27:13 **21** [r]ch. 27:36; 28:19 [s][Ps. 37:36]

A Lament for Tyre

27 The word of the LORD came to me:
2 "Now you, [t]son of man, [u]raise a lamentation over Tyre, 3 and say to Tyre, who
dwells at [v]the entrances to the sea, [w]merchant
of the peoples to many coastlands, thus says
the Lord GOD:

"O Tyre, you have said,
'I am [x]perfect in beauty.'
4 Your borders are [y]in the heart of the seas;
your builders made perfect your
beauty.
5 They made all your planks
of fir trees from [z]Senir;
they took [a]a cedar from Lebanon
to make a mast for you.
6 Of [b]oaks of Bashan
they made your oars;
they made your deck of pines
from [c]the coasts of Cyprus,
inlaid with ivory.
7 [d]Of fine embroidered linen from Egypt
was your sail,
serving as your banner;
blue and purple from [c]the coasts of
Elishah
was your awning.
8 The inhabitants of Sidon and [e]Arvad
were your rowers;
your skilled men, O Tyre, were in you;
they were [f]your pilots.
9 The elders of [g]Gebal and her skilled men
were in you,
[h]caulking your seams;
all the ships of the sea with their mariners were in you
to barter for your wares.

10 [i]"Persia and [j]Lud and [j]Put were in your
army as your men of war. [k]They hung the
shield and helmet in you; they gave you
splendor. 11 Men of [e]Arvad and Helech were
on your walls all around, and men of Gamad
were in your towers. They hung their shields
on your walls all around; they made [x]perfect
your beauty.
12 [l]"Tarshish did [m]business with you because
of your great wealth of every kind; silver, iron,
tin, and lead they exchanged for your [n]wares.
13 [o]Javan, [p]Tubal, and [p]Meshech traded with
you; they exchanged human beings and vessels of bronze for your merchandise. 14 From
[q]Beth-togarmah they exchanged horses, war
horses, and mules [r]for your wares. 15 The men
of [s]Dedan[1] traded with you. Many coastlands
were your own special markets; they brought
you in payment ivory tusks and ebony. 16 Syria
[t]did business with you because of your abundant goods; they exchanged for your wares
[u]emeralds, [u]purple, [v]embroidered work, [w]fine
linen, coral, and [x]ruby. 17 Judah and the land
of Israel traded with you; they exchanged
for your merchandise [y]wheat of [z]Minnith,
meal,[2] honey, oil, and [a]balm. 18 [b]Damascus did
business with you for your abundant goods,
because of your great wealth of every kind;
wine of Helbon and [c]wool of Sahar 19 and
casks of wine[3] from Uzal they exchanged for
your wares; wrought iron, [d]cassia, and [e]cala-
mus were bartered for your merchandise.
20 Dedan traded with you in saddlecloths for
riding. 21 Arabia and all the princes of [f]Kedar
were your favored dealers [f]in lambs, rams, and
goats; in these they did business with you.
22 The traders of [g]Sheba and [g]Raamah traded
with you; they exchanged [h]for your wares
[i]the best of all kinds of spices and all precious
stones and gold. 23 [j]Haran, Canneh, [j]Eden,
traders of Sheba, [k]Asshur, and Chilmad traded
with you. 24 In your market these traded with
you in choice garments, in clothes of [l]blue and
[l]embroidered work, and in carpets of colored
material, bound with cords and made secure.
25 [m]The ships of [n]Tarshish traveled for you
with your merchandise. So you were filled and
heavily laden [o]in the heart of the seas.

26 "Your rowers have brought you out
into the high seas.
[p]The east wind has wrecked you
in the heart of the seas.
27 Your riches, your wares, your merchandise,
your mariners and [q]your pilots,
[r]your caulkers, your dealers in merchandise,
and all your men of war who are in
you,

[1] Hebrew; Septuagint *Rhodes* [2] The meaning of the Hebrew word is unknown [3] Probable reading; Hebrew *wool of Sahar, Vedan, and Javan*

Chapter 27 **2** [t]See ch. 2:1 [u]See ch. 19:1 **3** [v][Isa. 23:1] [w][Isa. 23:3] [x]ch. 28:12 **4** [y]ver. 25, 27 **5** [z]Deut. 3:9 [a]Judg. 9:15 **6** [b]See Isa. 2:13 [c]See Gen. 10:4 **7** [d]See ch. 16:10 [c][See ver. 6 above] **8** [e]Gen. 10:18 [f]ver. 27, 29 **9** [g]1 Kgs. 5:18; Ps. 83:7 [h]ver. 27 **10** [i]ch. 38:5 [j]ch. 30:5; [Isa. 66:19; Jer. 46:9] [k][2 Sam. 8:7; Song 4:4] **11** [e][See ver. 8 above] [x][See ver. 3 above] **12** [l]ver. 25; ch. 38:13; See 1 Kgs. 10:22 [m]ver. 16, 18, 21 [n]ver. 14, 16, 19, 22 **13** [o]Gen. 10:2 [p]ch. 32:26; 38:2; 39:1 **14** [q]ch. 38:6; Gen. 10:3 [r]ver. 12 **15** [s]Gen. 10:7; See ch. 25:13 **16** [t]ver. 12 [u]ch. 28:13 [v]ver. 7 [w]1 Chr. 15:27; Job 28:18 [x]Isa. 54:12 **17** [y]See 1 Kgs. 5:9, 11 [z]Judg. 11:33 [a]See Gen. 37:25 **18** [b]Isa. 7:8; [ver. 16] [c]Rev. 1:14 **19** [d]Ex. 30:24 [e][Ex. 30:23] **21** [f]Isa. 60:7 **22** [g]ch. 38:13; Gen. 10:7 [h]ver. 12 [i]Ex. 30:23 **23** [j]2 Kgs. 19:12 [k]Gen. 10:22 **24** [l]ver. 7 **25** [m]Ps. 48:7; Isa. 2:16; 23:14 [n]See ver. 12 [o]ver. 4 **26** [p]See Jer. 18:17 **27** [q]ver. 8 [r]ver. 9

with all your crew
that is in your midst,
sink into the heart of the seas
[s]on the day of your fall.
28 At the sound of the cry of your pilots
[t]the countryside shakes,
29 and down from their ships
[u]come all who handle the oar.
The mariners and all the pilots of the sea
stand on the land
30 [u]and shout aloud over you
and cry out bitterly.
[v]They cast dust on their heads
[w]and wallow in ashes;
31 they [x]make themselves bald for you
and put sackcloth on their waist,
and they weep over you in bitterness of soul,
with bitter mourning.
32 In their wailing they [y]raise a lamentation for you
and lament over you:
[z]'Who is like Tyre,
like one destroyed in the midst of the sea?
33 When your wares came from the seas,
[a]you satisfied many peoples;
with your abundant wealth and merchandise
[a]you enriched the kings of the earth.
34 Now [b]you are wrecked by the seas,
in the depths of the waters;
your merchandise and all your crew in your midst
have sunk with you.
35 [c]All the inhabitants of the coastlands
are appalled at you,
and [d]the hair of their kings bristles with horror;
their faces are convulsed.
36 [e]The merchants among the peoples [f]hiss at you;
[g]you have come to a dreadful end
and shall be no more forever.'"

Prophecy Against the Prince of Tyre

28 The word of the LORD came to me:
2 [h]"Son of man, say to [i]the prince of
Tyre, Thus says the Lord GOD:

[j]"Because your heart is proud,
and [k]you have said, 'I am a god,
I sit in the seat of the gods,
in the heart of the seas,'
yet [l]you are but a man, and no god,
[m]though you make your heart like the heart of a god—
3 [n]you are indeed wiser [o]than [p]Daniel;
no secret is hidden from you;
4 by your wisdom and your understanding
[q]you have made wealth for yourself,
and have gathered gold and silver
into your treasuries;
5 by your great wisdom in your trade
you have increased your wealth,
and [j]your heart has become proud in your wealth—
6 therefore thus says the Lord GOD:
[r]Because you make your heart
like the heart of a god,
7 therefore, behold, I will bring [s]foreigners upon you,
the most ruthless of the nations;
and they shall draw their swords against
[t]the beauty of your wisdom
and defile [t]your splendor.
8 [u]They shall thrust you down into the pit,
[v]and you shall die the death of the slain
in the heart of the seas.
9 [w]Will you still say, 'I am a god,'
in the presence of those who kill you,
though [l]you are but a man, and no god,
in the hands of those who slay you?
10 [x]You shall die the death of the uncircumcised
by the hand of foreigners;
[y]for I have spoken, declares the Lord GOD."

A Lament over the King of Tyre

11 Moreover, the word of the LORD came to
me: 12 [z]"Son of man, [a]raise a lamentation over

27[s] [ch. 26:18; 32:10]
28[t] [ch. 45:2; 48:15, 17]
29[u] [Rev. 18:17, 18]
30[u] [See ver. 29 above] [v] Lam. 2:10; Rev. 18:19 [w] See Jer. 6:26

28:11–19 Chapter 28 consists of two poems against the ruler of Tyre. The first (vv. 1–10) is addressed against "the prince of Tyre," and the second (vv. 11–19) against "the king of Tyre." Though the words are different, these two poems are probably addressed to the same person, one who goes by both titles, "king" and "prince." The second

31[x] See Isa. 3:24 **32**[y] See ch. 19:1 [z] [Rev. 18:18] **33**[a] [Rev. 18:15, 19] **34**[b] [ch. 26:19] **35**[c] ch. 26:15, 16 [d] [ch. 32:10] **36**[e] Rev. 18:11 [f] See Jer. 18:16 [g] ch. 26:21; 28:19 **Chapter 28** **2**[h] See ch. 2:1 [i] [ver. 12] [j] [Rev. 18:7] [k] [ver. 9] [l] Isa. 31:3 [m] ver. 6 **3**[n] [ver. 12; Zech. 9:2] [o] Dan. 1:17 [p] ch. 14:14 **4**[q] [Zech. 9:3] **5**[j] [See ver. 2 above] **6**[r] ver. 2 **7**[s] ver. 10; ch. 7:21; 30:12; 31:12 [t] [ver. 17] **8**[u] [ch. 32:18, 19] [v] [ch. 32:20] **9**[w] [ver. 2] [l] [See ver. 2 above] **10**[x] ch. 31:18; 32:19, 21, 24, 25 [y] See ch. 17:24 **12**[z] See ch. 2:1 [a] See ch. 19:1

[b]the king of Tyre, and say to him, Thus says
the Lord GOD:

"You were the signet of perfection,[1]
[c]full of wisdom and [d]perfect in beauty.
13 You were in [e]Eden, the garden of God;
[f]every precious stone was your covering,
[g]sardius, topaz, and diamond,
beryl, onyx, and jasper,
sapphire,[2] [f]emerald, and carbuncle;
and crafted in gold were your settings
and your engravings.[3]
[i]On the day that you were created
they were prepared.
14 You were an anointed [j]guardian cherub.
I placed you;[4] you were on [k]the holy
mountain of God;
in the midst of the stones of fire you
walked.
15 You were blameless in your ways
[l]from the day you were created,
till unrighteousness was found in you.
16 In the abundance of [m]your trade
you were filled with violence in your
midst, and you sinned;
so I cast you as a profane thing from [k]the
mountain of God,
and I destroyed you,[5] [j]O guardian
cherub,
from the midst of the stones of fire.
17 [n]Your heart was proud because of [o]your
beauty;
you corrupted your wisdom for the
sake of your splendor.
I cast you to the ground;
I exposed you before kings,
to feast their eyes on you.
18 By the multitude of your iniquities,
in the unrighteousness of your trade
you profaned your sanctuaries;
so [p]I brought fire out from your midst;
it consumed you,
and I turned you to ashes on the earth
[q]in the sight of all who saw you.
19 All who know you among the peoples
are appalled at you;
[r]you have come to a dreadful end
and shall be no more forever."

Prophecy Against Sidon

20 The word of the LORD came to me: 21 [s]"Son
of man, [t]set your face toward [u]Sidon, and
[t]prophesy against her 22 and say, Thus says
the Lord GOD:

"Behold, [v]I am against you, O Sidon,
and [w]I will manifest my glory in your
midst.
And [x]they shall know that I am the LORD
[y]when I execute judgments in her
and [z]manifest my holiness in her;
23 for I will send [a]pestilence into her,
and blood into her streets;
and the slain shall fall in her midst,
by the sword that is against her on
every side.
Then they will know that I am the LORD.

24 "And for the house of Israel [b]there shall
be no more a brier to prick or [c]a thorn to hurt

[1] The meaning of the Hebrew phrase is uncertain [2] Or *lapis lazuli* [3] The meaning of the Hebrew phrase is uncertain [4] The meaning of the Hebrew phrase is uncertain [5] Or *banished you*

poem, however, dramatically shows who ultimately stands behind all opposition to God and his people. In 28:11–15, it becomes clear that while we are still seeing the king of Tyre, something else is happening as well. Flickering in and out with the face of the king of Tyre is the face of Satan, the great Enemy of God's people who pursues and harasses them with temptation and despair. When God therefore destroys this "king of Tyre" in verses 16–19, the reader is meant to understand that the one whom God is defeating is the Evil One who stands behind this human king.

This passage is ultimately fulfilled in Revelation 20:7–10, when King Jesus commands that Satan be destroyed in the lake of fire and sulfur. Just as Ezekiel prophesies here, his doom and humiliation before God are total. Yet Ezekiel's prophecy is fulfilled in an inaugurated (i.e., decisively begun) way on the cross of Calvary, where Satan was defanged and his accusing voice silenced toward those who are in Christ (Col. 2:13–15). The destruction Satan effects now is only the angry lashings of a doomed and dying foe.

28:24–26 Why does God act in this way against all these nations? It is on behalf of his people, so that they can live in peace. God's passionate love for his people in this section of Ezekiel is palpable. It is a no-holds-barred defense of them, like a father roused to protect his children when they are being threatened.

12[b] [ver. 2] [c][ver. 3] [d]ch. 27:3
13[e]ch. 31:8, 9; See Isa. 51:3 [f][ch. 27:16] [g]Rev. 4:3; 21:19, 20 [i]ver. 15
14[j]Ex. 25:20; 1 Kgs. 8:7 [k][ch. 20:40]
15[l]ver. 13
16[m][ver. 5] [k][See ver. 14 above] [j][See ver. 14 above]
17[n]ver. 2, 5 [o][ver. 7]
18[p][ch. 30:8, 14, 16; Rev. 18:8] [q][ver. 17]
19[r]ch. 26:21; 27:36
21[s]See ch. 2:1 [t]See ch. 6:2 [u]See Isa. 23:2
22[v]See ch. 13:8 [w]ch. 39:13; [Ex. 14:4, 17, 18] [x]See ch. 6:7 [y]ver. 26 [z]See ch. 20:41
23[a]ch. 38:22
24[b]Num. 33:55; Josh. 23:13 [c][2 Cor. 12:7]

them among all their neighbors [d]who have treated them with contempt. Then they will know that I am the Lord GOD.

Israel Gathered in Security

25 "Thus says the Lord GOD: [e]When I gather the house of Israel from the peoples among whom they are scattered, and [z]manifest my holiness in them in the sight of the nations, [f]then they shall dwell in their own land that I gave to my servant Jacob. 26 [g]And they shall dwell securely in it, and they shall build houses and plant vineyards. They shall dwell securely, [h]when I execute judgments upon all their neighbors [d]who have treated them with contempt. [x]Then they will know that I am the LORD their God."

Prophecy Against Egypt

29 [i]In the tenth year, in the tenth month, on the twelfth day of the month, the word of the LORD came to me: 2 [j]"Son of man, [k]set your face against [l]Pharaoh king of Egypt, [m]and prophesy against him and [n]against all Egypt; 3 speak, and say, Thus says the Lord GOD:

[o]"Behold, I am against you,
Pharaoh king of Egypt,
[p]the great dragon that lies
in the midst of his streams,
[q]that says, 'My Nile is my own;
I made it for myself.'
4 I will [r]put hooks in your jaws,
and make the fish of your streams
stick to your scales;
and I will draw you up out of the midst
of your streams,
with all the fish of your streams
that stick to your scales.
5 [s]And I will cast you out into the wilderness,
you and all the fish of your streams;
you shall fall [t]on the open field,
and [u]not be brought together or gathered.
To the beasts of the earth and to the
birds of the heavens
[s]I give you as food.

6 Then all the inhabitants of Egypt [v]shall know that I am the LORD.

"Because you[1] have been [w]a staff of reed to the house of Israel, 7 [x]when they grasped you with the hand, you broke and tore all their shoulders; and when they leaned on you, you broke and made all their loins to shake.[2] 8 Therefore thus says the Lord GOD: [y]Behold, I will bring a sword upon you, and will cut off from you man and beast, 9 and the land of Egypt shall

[1] Hebrew *they* [2] Syriac (compare Psalm 69:23); Hebrew *to stand*

24 [d]ch. 16:57
25 [e]See ch. 11:17 [z][See ver. 22 above] [f]ch. 36:28; 37:25
26 [g]Jer. 23:6; 32:37 [h]ver. 22 [d][See ver. 24 above] [x][See ver. 22 above]

Chapter 29
1 [i]See ch. 20:1
2 [j]See ch. 2:1 [k]See ch. 6:2 [l]ch. 32:2 [m]See ch. 6:2 [n]See Isa. 19:1
3 [o]See ch. 13:8 [p]ch. 32:2; Ps. 74:13, 14; Isa. 27:1; 51:9 [q]ver. 9
4 [r]ch. 19:9; 38:4; 2 Kgs. 19:28
5 [s][ch. 32:4, 5] [t]Jer. 9:22 [u]See Jer. 8:2
6 [v]See ch. 6:7 [w]2 Kgs. 18:21; Isa. 36:6
7 [x][ch. 17:17; Isa. 20:5; 30:3, 5; Jer. 2:36; 37:5, 7]
8 [y]See ch. 14:17

29:1–32:32 These chapters contain prophecies against Egypt, the seventh nation God judges in chapters 25–32. God's point in all this is to assert his utter supremacy and authority over all the nations of the world, and especially to make known the foolishness of human pride before him. Each of these nations in turn asserted that what they had and what they were was the result of their own work, that it came from their own hand. Again and again, they exalt themselves against the Lord and against his people (25:1–3, 6, 8, 12, 15; 27:1–9; 28:11–16; 30:4). God promises to confront them and bring them low.

The Bible teaches frequently that pride is the most deadly attitude to have in God's presence. We as Christians should be careful never to think that what we have has come from our own hand or that we have won it for ourselves. What we have, in every particular, is given to us by God, and we should always remember that he could take it all away with a mere whisper. "What do you have that you did not receive?" (1 Cor. 4:7). Even our faith itself is a gift of God (Eph. 2:8).

Conversely, those who humble themselves before God, contritely trusting in Christ as their supreme refuge, have the greatest treasure in the universe (Phil. 3:8). It can never be taken away (John 10:28).

29:1–3 Not only does God confront and destroy these seven nations that have set themselves against him and his people, but he also metaphorically confronts and overthrows those nations' gods, proving in the process that they are no gods at all, and that he is the one true God.

These verses are a good example of God's confrontation with pagan deities. On the surface, verses 1–3 are simply an oracle against the pharaoh of Egypt in which he is pictured as a crocodile, the dragon of the Nile. But there also was an ancient pagan idea that this dragon symbolized a god who creates chaos in the world. This repre-

be a desolation and a waste. [y]Then they will
know that I am the LORD.
[z]"Because you[1] said, 'The Nile is mine, and
I made it,' 10 therefore, [z]behold, I am against
you and [a]against your streams, and [a]I will
make the land of Egypt an utter waste and
desolation, [b]from Migdol to Syene, as far as
the border of Cush. 11 [c]No foot of man shall
pass through it, and no foot of beast shall
pass through it; it shall be uninhabited forty
years. 12 [d]And I will make the land of Egypt
a desolation in the midst of desolated countries, and her cities shall be a desolation forty
years among cities that are laid waste. [e]I will
scatter the Egyptians among the nations, and
disperse them through the countries.
13 "For thus says the Lord GOD: At the end
of forty years [f]I will gather the Egyptians
from the peoples among whom they were
scattered, 14 and [g]I will restore the fortunes
of Egypt and bring them back to [h]the land of
Pathros, the land of their origin, and there
they shall be a lowly kingdom. 15 It shall be the
most lowly of the kingdoms, [i]and never again
exalt itself above the nations. And I will make
them so small that they will never again rule
over the nations. 16 And it shall never again
be [j]the reliance of the house of Israel, recalling their iniquity, when they turn to them
for aid. [k]Then they will know that I am the
Lord GOD."
17 [l]In the twenty-seventh year, in the first
month, on the first day of the month, the
word of the LORD came to me: 18 [m]"Son of
man, [n]Nebuchadnezzar king of Babylon
made his army labor hard against Tyre. Every
head was made bald, and every shoulder was
rubbed bare, yet neither he nor his army got
anything from Tyre to pay for the labor that
he had performed against her. 19 Therefore
thus says the Lord GOD: [o]Behold, I will give
the land of Egypt to Nebuchadnezzar king
of Babylon; [p]and he shall carry off its wealth[2]
[q]and despoil it and plunder it; and it shall be
the wages for his army. 20 [r]I have given him
the land of Egypt as his payment for which he
labored, because they worked for me, declares
the Lord GOD.
21 "On that day [s]I will cause a horn to spring
up for the house of Israel, and [t]I will open your
lips among them. [u]Then they will know that
I am the LORD."

A Lament for Egypt

30 The word of the LORD came to me:
2 [v]"Son of man, prophesy, and say, Thus
says the Lord GOD:

[w]"Wail, 'Alas for the day!'
3 [w]For the day is near,
[x]the day of the LORD is near;
it will be [y]a day of clouds,
a time of doom for[3] the nations.
4 [z]A sword shall come upon Egypt,
[a]and anguish shall be in [b]Cush,

[1] Hebrew *he* [2] Or *multitude* [3] Hebrew lacks *doom for*

sented a fundamentally dualistic worldview, with two equal deities forever in conflict. Of course, Yahweh will have none of this; he alone created and rules the world, and he brooks no rival gods, including the dragon. In these verses, then, God makes the point strongly. He hooks the dragon in the jaw, and drags him onto the land and out into the desert to die. There is no doubt who rules and reigns: Yahweh, not this Leviathan.

29:17–20 God's dominion over the nations' "gods" is also obvious in the way he controls those nations, their kings, and their armies. In this extraordinary passage, God says that he will soon give Egypt to Babylon as wages for their hard labor against Tyre.

The Babylonians believed they were serving their own gods; that their own gods were in control of their national destiny. But Yahweh turns the tables: he will give the Babylonians the wealth of Egypt in exchange for their labor against Tyre. And for whom was that labor performed? "They worked for me, declares the Lord GOD" (v. 20).

God "works all things according to the counsel of his will" (Eph. 1:11). And, for those who have sought refuge in Christ from the judgment they too deserve, "all things work together for good" (Rom. 8:28).

29:21 "Horn" here is simply a common symbol of power, but the phrase "spring up" comes from the Hebrew word "branch," a word fraught with messianic significance (see Isa. 11:1; Jer. 23:5; 33:15). As God confronts and overthrows these evil rival powers, he sets up a new power in their place who will reign as king forever. That king, ultimately, is Jesus Christ.

9 [y][See ver. 6 above] [z]ver. 3; See ch. 13:8
10 [z][See ver. 9 above] [a][ch. 30:12] [b]ch. 30:6
11 [c]ch. 32:13; [ch. 35:7]
12 [d]ch. 30:7 [e]ch. 30:23, 26; [Jer. 46:19]
13 [f][Isa. 19:22, 23; Jer. 46:26]
14 [g][ch. 39:25] [h]ch. 30:14; See Isa. 11:11
15 [i][ch. 30:13]
16 [j][Isa. 30:2, 3; 36:4, 6; Lam. 4:17] [k]ver. 6; See ch. 6:7
17 [l]See ch. 20:1
18 [m]See ch. 2:1 [n][ch. 26:7]
19 [o]ch. 30:10, 24, 25; 32:11; Jer. 46:13 [p]ch. 30:4 [q]ch. 32:12
20 [r][Isa. 43:3]
21 [s]Ps. 132:17; [Luke 1:69] [t]ch. 24:27; 33:22; [ch. 16:63] [u]See ch. 6:7

Chapter 30
2 [v]See ch. 2:1 [w]See Isa. 13:6
3 [w][See ver. 2 above] [x]ch. 7:7, 12; Joel 1:15; 2:1; Zeph. 1:7 [y]ch. 34:12
4 [z]ch. 29:8 [a][Isa. 21:3] [b][Isa. 43:3]

when the slain fall in Egypt,
and [c]her wealth[1] is carried away,
and [d]her foundations are torn down.

5 [b]Cush, and [e]Put, and Lud, and [f]all Arabia,
and Libya,[2] and the people of the land that is
in league,[3] shall fall with them by the sword.

6 "Thus says the LORD:
[g]Those who support Egypt shall fall,
and [h]her proud might shall come
down;
[i]from Migdol to Syene
they shall fall within her by the sword,
declares the Lord GOD.
7 [j]And they shall be desolated in the midst
of desolated countries,
and their cities shall be in the midst
of cities that are laid waste.
8 [k]Then they will know that I am the LORD,
when [l]I have set fire to Egypt,
and [g]all her helpers are broken.

9 "On that day [m]messengers shall go out from
me in ships to terrify the unsuspecting [b]people
of Cush, and [a]anguish shall come upon them
on the day of Egypt's doom;[4] for, behold, it
comes!
10 "Thus says the Lord GOD:

[n]"I will put an end to the wealth of Egypt,
by the hand of Nebuchadnezzar king
of Babylon.
11 He and his people with him, [o]the most
ruthless of nations,
shall be brought in to destroy the land,
[z]and they shall draw their swords against
Egypt
and fill the land with the slain.
12 And [p]I will [q]dry up the Nile
and will sell the land into the hand of
[r]evildoers;
[s]I will bring desolation upon the land
and everything in it,
by the hand of [t]foreigners;
[u]I am the LORD; I have spoken.

13 "Thus says the Lord GOD:

[v]"I will destroy the idols
and put an end to the images in
[w]Memphis;
[x]there shall no longer be a prince from
the land of Egypt;
so [y]I will put fear in the land of Egypt.
14 I will make [z]Pathros a desolation
and will set fire to [a]Zoan
[b]and will execute judgments on
[c]Thebes.
15 And I will pour out my wrath on
Pelusium,
the stronghold of Egypt,
and cut off the multitude[5] of Thebes.
16 And I will set fire to Egypt;
Pelusium shall be in great agony;
Thebes shall be breached,
and [w]Memphis shall face enemies[6] by
day.
17 The young men of On and of Pi-beseth
shall fall by the sword,
and the women[7] shall go into captivity.
18 At [d]Tehaphnehes [e]the day shall be dark,
when I break there the yoke bars of
Egypt,
and [f]her proud might shall come to an
end in her;
she shall be covered by a cloud,
and her daughters shall go into captivity.
19 Thus [g]I will execute judgments on Egypt.
[h]Then they will know that I am the
LORD."

Egypt Shall Fall to Babylon

20 [i]In the eleventh year, in the first month,
on the seventh day of the month, the word
of the LORD came to me: 21 [j]"Son of man, [k]I
have broken the arm of Pharaoh king of
Egypt, and behold, [l]it has not been bound
up, to heal it by binding it with a bandage,
so that it may become strong to wield the
sword. 22 Therefore thus says the Lord GOD:
Behold, I am against Pharaoh king of Egypt
and [m]will break his arms, both the strong
arm and the one that was broken, and I will
make the sword fall from his hand. 23 [n]I will
scatter the Egyptians among the nations
and disperse them through the countries.
24 And [o]I will strengthen the arms of the king
of Babylon and put [p]my sword in his hand,

[1] Or *multitude*; also verse 10 [2] With Septuagint; Hebrew *Cub* [3] Hebrew *and the sons of the land of the covenant* [4] Hebrew *the day of Egypt* [5] Or *wealth* [6] Or *distress* [7] Or *the cities*; Hebrew *they*

4 [c] ch. 29:19 [d] [ver. 6] **5** [b] [See ver. 4 above] [e] See ch. 27:10 [f] See Jer. 25:20 **6** [g] [ch. 32:21] [h] ver. 18; [ch. 33:28] [i] ch. 29:10 **7** [j] ch. 29:12 **8** [k] ch. 29:6; See ch. 6:7 [l] [ch. 28:18] [g] [See ver. 6 above] **9** [m] [Isa. 18:1, 2] [b] [See ver. 4 above] [a] [See ver. 4 above] **10** [n] See ch. 29:19 **11** [o] See ch. 28:7 [z] [See ver. 4 above] **12** [p] Isa. 19:5, 6; [ch. 29:10] [q] [ch. 29:3] [r] [Isa. 19:4] [s] [ch. 29:10] [t] See ch. 28:7 [u] See ch. 17:24 **13** [v] See Jer. 43:12 [w] Isa. 19:13 [x] [ch. 29:15; Zech. 10:11] [y] [Isa. 19:16] **14** [z] ch. 29:14; See Isa. 11:11 [a] See Num. 13:22 [b] ver. 19 [c] Jer. 46:25 **16** [w] [See ver. 13 above] **18** [d] See Jer. 2:16 [e] [Jer. 15:9; Amos 8:9] [f] ver. 6 **19** [g] ver. 14 [h] See ch. 6:7 **20** [i] See ch. 20:1 **21** [j] See ch. 2:1 [k] [Jer. 48:25] [l] [Jer. 30:13; 46:11] **22** [m] See ver. 21 **23** [n] ch. 29:12 **24** [o] ver. 10 [p] See ch. 21:3

but I will break the arms of Pharaoh, and he
will groan before him [q]like a man mortally
wounded. 25 I will strengthen the arms of the
king of Babylon, but the arms of Pharaoh
shall fall. [r]Then they shall know that I am the
LORD, [s]when I put my sword into the hand
of the king of Babylon and he stretches it out
against the land of Egypt. 26 And I will scatter
the Egyptians among the nations and disperse
them throughout the countries. Then they
will know that I am the LORD."

Pharaoh to Be Slain

31 [t]In the eleventh year, in the third
month, on the first day of the month,
the word of the LORD came to me: 2 [u]"Son of
man, say to Pharaoh king of Egypt and to [v]his
multitude:

[w]"Whom are you like in your greatness?
3 Behold, [x]Assyria was a [y]cedar in
[z]Lebanon,
with beautiful branches and [a]forest shade,
[b]and of towering height,
its top among the clouds.[1]
4 The waters nourished it;
the deep made it grow tall,
making [c]its rivers flow
around the place of its planting,
sending forth its streams
to all the trees of the field.
5 So [d]it towered high
above all the trees of the field;
its boughs grew large
and its branches long
from [e]abundant water in its shoots.
6 [f]All the birds of the heavens
made their nests in its boughs;
under its branches all the beasts of the
field
gave birth to their young,
and under its shadow
lived all great nations.
7 It was [g]beautiful in its greatness,
in the length of its branches;
[e]for its roots went down
to abundant waters.
8 [h]The cedars [i]in the garden of God could
not rival it,
nor the fir trees equal its boughs;
neither were the plane trees
like its branches;
no tree [i]in the garden of God
was its equal in beauty.
9 I made it beautiful
in the mass of its branches,
and all the trees of [j]Eden envied it,
that were in the garden of God.

10 "Therefore thus says the Lord GOD:
Because [k]it[2] towered high and set its top
among the clouds, and [l]its heart was proud
of its height, 11 I will give it into the hand of
a mighty one of the nations. He shall surely
deal with it as its wickedness deserves. I have
cast it out. 12 [m]Foreigners, [m]the most ruthless of
nations, have cut it down and left it. [n]On the
mountains and in all the valleys its branches
have fallen, and its boughs have been broken in all [o]the ravines of the land, and [p]all
the peoples of the earth have gone away from
its shadow and left it. 13 [q]On its fallen trunk
dwell all the birds of the heavens, and on its
branches are all the beasts of the field. 14 [r]All
this is in order that no trees by the waters
may grow to towering height or set their tops
among the clouds, and that no trees that drink
water may reach up to them in height. For
they are all given over to death, [s]to the world
[t]below, among the children of man,[3] with
those who go down to the pit.

15 "Thus says the Lord GOD: On the day [u]the
cedar[4] went down to Sheol I caused mourning;
I closed the deep over it, and restrained its rivers, and many waters were stopped. I clothed
Lebanon in gloom for it, and all the trees of
the field fainted because of it. 16 [v]I made the
nations quake at the sound of its fall, [u]when
I cast it down to Sheol with those who go
down to the pit. [w]And all the trees of Eden,
the choice and best of Lebanon, all that drink
water, [x]were comforted in the world below.
17 They also went down to Sheol with it, [y]to
those who are slain by the sword; yes, [z]those
who were its arm, [a]who lived under its shadow
among the nations.

18 [b]"Whom are you thus like in glory and
in greatness [w]among the trees of Eden? [c]You
shall be brought down with [w]the trees of Eden
to the world below. [d]You shall lie among the

[1] Or *its top went through the thick boughs*; also verses 10, 14 [2] Syriac, Vulgate; Hebrew *you* [3] Or *of Adam* [4] Hebrew *it*

24 [q] Job 24:12 **25** [r] See ch. 6:7 [s] [ver. 8] **Chapter 31** **1** [t] See ch. 20:1 **2** [u] See ch. 2:1 [v] [ch. 29:19; 30:4; 32:12, 16, 20, 31, 32] [w] [ver. 18; ch. 32:19] **3** [x] [Isa. 10:34]; See Dan. 4:10, 20-22 [y] See Judg. 9:15 [z] [ver. 15, 16] [a] [ch. 17:23] [b] [Isa. 10:33] **4** [c] [ch. 17:7] **5** [d] [Dan. 4:11] [e] ch. 17:5; [Ps. 1:3] **6** [f] ch. 17:23; Dan. 4:12, 21 **7** [g] [ver. 2] [e] [See ver. 5 above] **8** [h] [Amos 2:9] [i] ch. 28:13; [ver. 16, 18] **9** [j] See Isa. 51:3 **10** [k] [ver. 3] [l] Dan. 5:20; [Isa. 10:12] **12** [m] See ch. 28:7 [n] [ch. 32:5] [o] [ch. 6:3] [p] [Dan. 4:14] **13** [q] ch. 32:4 **14** [r] [ver. 5] [s] [ver. 16, 18; ch. 26:20; 32:18, 24] [t] Ps. 63:9 **15** [u] [ch. 32:18, 21; Isa. 14:9, 10] **16** [v] [ch. 26:15] [u] [See ver. 15 above] [w] ver. 9; [Isa. 14:8] [x] [ch. 32:31] **17** [y] ch. 32:20, 21; 35:8 [z] [ch. 30:5, 6, 8] [a] [ver. 6] **18** [b] [ver. 2] [w] [See ver. 16 above] [c] [Matt. 11:23; Luke 10:15] [d] ch. 28:10; 32:19, 21, 24, 25, 28

uncircumcised, [y]with those who are slain by
the sword.
[b]“This is Pharaoh and all his multitude,
declares the Lord GOD.”

A Lament over Pharaoh and Egypt

32 [e]In the twelfth year, in the twelfth
month, on the first day of the month,
the word of the LORD came to me: 2 [f]“Son of
man, [g]raise a lamentation over [h]Pharaoh king
of Egypt and say to him:

“You consider yourself [i]a lion of the
nations,
but you are like [j]a dragon [k]in the seas;
[l]you burst forth in your rivers,
trouble the waters with your feet,
and foul their rivers.
3 Thus says the Lord GOD:
[m]I will throw my net over you
with a host of [n]many peoples,
and [o]they will haul you up in my
dragnet.
4 And [p]I will cast you on the ground;
on the open field I will fling you,
and will cause all the birds of the heavens to settle on you,
and I will gorge the beasts of the
whole earth with you.
5 I will strew your flesh [q]upon the mountains
and fill the valleys with your carcass.[1]
6 I will drench the land even to the mountains
with your flowing blood,
and the ravines will be full of you.
7 [r]When I blot you out, [s]I will cover the
heavens
and make their stars dark;
I will cover the sun with a cloud,
and the moon shall not give its light.
8 All the bright lights of heaven
will I make dark over you,
and [t]put darkness on your land,
declares the Lord GOD.

9 “I will trouble the hearts of many peoples,
when I bring your destruction among the
nations, into the countries that you have not
known. 10 [u]I will make many peoples appalled
at you, and the hair of their kings shall bristle
with horror because of you, when [v]I brandish
my sword before them. [w]They shall tremble
every moment, every one for his own life, on
the day of your downfall.
11 “For thus says the Lord GOD: [x]The sword
of the king of Babylon shall come upon you.
12 I will cause [y]your multitude to fall by the
swords of mighty ones, all of them [z]most ruthless of nations.

[a]“They shall bring to ruin the pride of
Egypt,
and all its multitude[2] shall perish.
13 I will destroy all its beasts
from beside many waters;
[b]and no foot of man shall trouble them
anymore,
nor shall the hoofs of beasts trouble
them.
14 Then [c]I will make their waters clear,
and cause their rivers to run like oil,
declares the Lord GOD.
15 When I make the land of Egypt desolate,
and when the land [d]is desolate of all
that fills it,
when I strike down all who dwell in it,
then [e]they will know that I am the
LORD.

16 [f]This is a lamentation that shall be chanted;
the daughters of the nations shall chant it;
over Egypt, and over [g]all her multitude, shall
they chant it, declares the Lord GOD.”
17 [h]In the twelfth year, in the twelfth month,[3]
on the fifteenth day of the month, the word
of the LORD came to me: 18 [i]“Son of man,
[j]wail over [g]the multitude of Egypt, and [k]send
them down, her and the daughters of majestic
nations, [l]to the world below, to those who have
gone down to the pit:

[1] Hebrew *your height* [2] Or *wealth* [3] Hebrew lacks *in the twelfth month*

18[y] [See ver. 17 above]
Chapter 32
1[e] See ch. 20:1
2[f] See ch. 2:1 [g] See ch. 19:1 [h] ch. 29:2 [i] ch. 19:3, 5, 6; 38:13 [j] ch. 29:3 [k] [Isa. 18:2] [l] [ver. 14; Jer. 46:8]
3[m] See ch. 12:13 [n] [ch. 26:3]

32:18–32 Ezekiel paints a grotesque picture of Pharaoh’s corpse (representing all Egypt) being thrown down to sheol to rest with the other mighty nations who exalted themselves against God. With bitter irony, Ezekiel notes that the pharaoh of Egypt “will be comforted” when he sees this great multitude, for he will be able to see that he was not alone in falling in his pride before God. Everyone who raises an arm against Yahweh will be destroyed.

[o] [ch. 29:4] **4**[p] [ch. 29:5] **5**[q] [ch. 31:12] **7**[r] [Isa. 14:12] [s] [Isa. 13:10; Joel 2:31; Matt. 24:29; Mark 13:24, 25] **8**[t] [Ex. 10:21; Isa. 5:30] **10**[u] [ch. 27:35] [v] [1 Chr. 21:16] [w] ch. 26:16; [Deut. 28:66] **11**[x] [ch. 29:8, 19]; See Jer. 46:26 **12**[y] See ch. 31:2 [z] See ch. 28:7 [a] ch. 29:19 **13**[b] ch. 29:11 **14**[c] [ver. 2] **15**[d] [ch. 12:19] [e] [Ex. 7:5]; See ch. 6:7 **16**[f] [ver. 2] [g] See ch. 31:2 **17**[h] See ch. 20:1 **18**[i] See ch. 2:1 [j] [ver. 2] [g] [See ver. 16 above] [k] [ch. 26:20; 31:16] [l] See ch. 31:14

19 [m]'Whom do you surpass in beauty?
Go down and [n]be laid to rest with the
uncircumcised.'

20 They shall fall amid those [o]who are slain by
the sword. Egypt[1] is delivered to the sword;
drag her away, and [p]all her multitudes. 21 The
mighty chiefs [q]shall speak of them, [r]with their
helpers, out of the midst of Sheol: 'They have
come down, they lie still, [s]the uncircumcised,
[o]slain by the sword.'
22 [t]"Assyria is there, and all her company, [u]its
graves all around it, all of them slain, fallen
by the sword, 23 whose graves are set in [v]the
uttermost parts of the pit; and her company
is all around her grave, all of them slain, fallen
by the sword, [w]who spread terror [x]in the land
of the living.
24 [y]"Elam is [z]there, and all her multitude
around her grave; all of them [a]slain, fallen by
the sword, who went down uncircumcised
into [b]the world below, who spread their terror in the land of the living; and [c]they bear
their shame [b]with those who go down to the
pit. 25 [d]They have made her a bed among the
slain with all her multitude, [e]her graves all
around it, all of them uncircumcised, slain by
the sword; for terror of them was spread in the
land of the living, and they bear their shame
with those who go down to the pit; they are
placed among the slain.
26 [f]"Meshech-Tubal is [e]there, and all her multitude, [e]her graves all around it, all of them
uncircumcised, slain by the sword; for they
spread their terror in the land of the living.
27 And [g]they do not lie with the mighty, the
fallen from among the uncircumcised, who
went down to Sheol with their weapons of
war, whose swords were laid under their
heads, and whose iniquities are upon their
bones; for the terror of the mighty men was
in the land of the living. 28 But as for you, you
shall be broken [h]and lie among the uncircumcised, with those who are slain by the sword.
29 [i]"Edom is [j]there, her kings and all her
princes, who for all their might are laid with
those who are killed by the sword; they lie
with the uncircumcised, with those who go
down to the pit.
30 "The princes [k]of the north are there, all of
them, and all the [l]Sidonians, who have gone
down in shame with the slain, [m]for all the terror that they caused by their might; they lie
uncircumcised with those who are slain by
the sword, and [n]bear their shame with those
who go down to the pit.
31 "When Pharaoh sees them, he [o]will be comforted for [p]all his multitude, Pharaoh and all
his army, slain by the sword, declares the Lord
GOD. 32 [q]For I spread terror [r]in the land of the
living; and he shall be laid to rest among [s]the
uncircumcised, with those who are slain by
the sword, Pharaoh and all his multitude,
declares the Lord GOD."

Ezekiel Is Israel's Watchman

33 The word of the LORD came to me:
2 [t]"Son of man, speak to [u]your people
and say to them, If [v]I bring the sword upon
a land, and the people of the land take a
man from among them, and make him their
[w]watchman, 3 and if he sees the sword coming

[1] Hebrew *She*

The ultimate point of God's doing all this, of course, is so that "they will know that I am the LORD" (v. 15). That phrase is used 19 times in this center section of Ezekiel. When God fully and finally asserts his rule, then the knowledge of the Lord—his character, his holiness, his authority—will be universal. For Tyre and Sidon and Egypt, of course, that will not be a happy knowledge; it will be a knowledge born of judgment. Those peoples go to their graves finally realizing that they have exalted themselves against the God of the universe.

For God's people, though, it will be an exhilarating, resplendent knowledge. For they will know that their Savior has taken up the sword on their behalf, that he has defeated their Enemy, forgiven them of their sin, and made his dwelling among them forever.

33:1–33 In chapter 33 we come finally to the moment of the great reversal. It is here that the third major division of Ezekiel begins. For the past eight chapters, 25–32, we have seen God's judgment against other nations and their false gods. Now the focus of the book returns to God's own people, besieged in Jerusalem by Babylon. Ezekiel sits in his house in Babylon bound up, still giving the same prophetic messages he

19[m] [ch. 31:2, 18] [n] ver. 32; See ver. 28-30
20[o] ch. 31:17, 18 [p] See ch. 31:2
21[q] Isa. 14:9, 10 [r] [ch. 30:6, 8] [s] ch. 28:10; 31:18 [o] [See ver. 20 above]
22[t] [ver. 24, 26, 29, 30] [u] ver. 25, 26
23[v] Isa. 14:15 [w] ver. 24, 25, 26, 27; [ch. 26:17] [x] Ps. 27:13
24[y] Isa. 11:11; See Jer. 49:34-39 [z] [ver. 22] [a] ver. 20 [b] ver. 18; See ch. 31:14 [c] ver. 25, 30; ch. 16:52, 54; 36:7; 44:13; [ch. 34:29; 36:6; 39:26]
25[d] [Isa. 30:33] [e] [ver. 22]
26[f] See ch. 27:13 [e] [See ver. 25 above]
27[g] [Isa. 14:18, 19]
28[h] ch. 28:10; 31:18
29[i] See ch. 25:12-14 [j] [ver. 22]
30[k] [ch. 38:6; 39:2] [l] ch. 28:21; See Isa. 23:2 [m] ver. 23 [n] See ver. 24
31[o] [ch. 31:16] [p] See ch. 31:2

32[q] [ver. 10] [r] ver. 23 [s] ver. 21, 27 **Chapter 33** **2**[t] See ch. 2:1 [u] ver. 12, 17, 30; ch. 3:11; 37:18 [v] See ch. 14:17 [w] [Mic. 7:4]

upon the land and [x]blows the trumpet and
warns the people, 4 then if anyone who hears
the sound of the trumpet does not take warning, and the sword comes and takes him away,
[y]his blood shall be upon his own head. 5 [z]He
heard the sound of the trumpet and did not
take warning; his blood shall be upon himself.
But if he had taken warning, he would have
saved his life. 6 [a]But if the watchman sees the
sword coming and does not blow the trumpet,
so that the people are not warned, and the
sword comes and takes any one of them, [a]that
person is taken away in his iniquity, but his
blood I will require at the watchman's hand.

7 [b]"So you, [t]son of man, I have made a watchman for the house of Israel. [b]Whenever you
hear a word from my mouth, you shall give
them warning from me. 8 [c]If I say to the
wicked, O wicked one, you shall surely die,
[c]and you do not speak to warn the wicked to
turn from his way, [c]that wicked person shall
die in his iniquity, but his blood I will require
at your hand. 9 [d]But if you warn the wicked to
turn from his way, and he does not turn from
his way, [d]that person shall die in his iniquity,
[e]but you will have delivered your soul.

Why Will You Die, Israel?

10 "And you, [f]son of man, say to the house of
Israel, Thus have you said: 'Surely our transgressions and our sins are upon us, and [g]we
rot away because of them. [h]How then can we
live?' 11 Say to them, [i]As I live, declares the Lord
GOD, [j]I have no pleasure in the death of the
wicked, but that the wicked turn from his way
and live; [k]turn back, turn back from your evil
ways, [k]for why will you die, O house of Israel?

12 [t]"And you, son of man, say to [l]your people,
[m]The righteousness of the righteous shall not
deliver him when he transgresses, [n]and as for
the wickedness of the wicked, he shall not
fall by it when he turns from his wickedness,
[m]and the righteous shall not be able to live
by his righteousness[1] when he sins. 13 Though
I say to the righteous that he shall surely live,
yet [m]if he trusts in his righteousness and does
injustice, none of his righteous deeds shall be
remembered, but in his injustice that he has
done he shall die. 14 Again, [o]though I say to the
wicked, [p]'You shall surely die,' yet [q]if he turns
from his sin and does what is just and right,
15 if the wicked [r]restores the pledge, [s]gives back
what he has taken by robbery, and walks [t]in
the statutes of life, not doing injustice, he shall
surely live; he shall not die. 16 [u]None of the sins
that he has committed shall be remembered
against him. He has done what is just and
right; he shall surely live.

17 "Yet [l]your people say, [v]'The way of the Lord
is not just,' when it is their own way that is not
just. 18 [w]When the righteous turns from his
righteousness and does injustice, he shall die
for it. 19 And [x]when the wicked turns from his
wickedness and does what is just and right, he
shall live by this. 20 Yet you say, 'The way of the
Lord is not just.' O house of Israel, [y]I will judge
each of you according to his ways."

Jerusalem Struck Down

21 In the [z]twelfth year [a]of our exile, in the
tenth month, on the fifth day of the month,
[b]a fugitive from Jerusalem came to me and
said, [c]"The city has been struck down." 22 [d]Now
[e]the hand of the LORD had been upon me the
evening before the fugitive came; and he
had opened my mouth by the time the man
came to me in the morning, so my mouth was
opened, and I was no longer mute.

23 The word of the LORD came to me: 24 [f]"Son
of man, the inhabitants of these [g]waste places

[1] Hebrew *by it*

3[x] [Amos 3:6]
4[y] ch. 18:13; See ch. 3:18
5[z] [ch. 3:19]
6[a] [ch. 3:18]
7[b] See ch. 3:17 [t] [See ver. 2 above]
8[c] ver. 6
9[d] [ver. 4] [e] ch. 3:19; [1 Tim. 4:16]
10[f] See ch. 2:1 [g] See ch. 4:17 [h] [ch. 37:11; Isa. 49:14]
11[i] See ch. 16:48 [j] See ch. 18:23 [k] ch. 18:31
12[t] [See ver. 2 above] [l] See ver. 2 [m] [ver. 18]; See ch. 18:24 [n] [2 Chr. 7:14]

has been giving since the beginning of the book. He knows through a prophetic vision (24:1–2) that Nebuchadnezzar has laid siege to Jerusalem, but he and the exiles have not received word yet that the city has fallen; the fugitive who escaped the battle will not arrive until 33:21. Until then, it is as if the melody of the first 24 chapters of the book continues uninterrupted. Ezekiel 33:1–9 returns to the theme of Ezekiel as a watchman for Israel, and 33:10–20 sounds the familiar note of God's call for the Israelites to repent instead of blaming God for their plight.

Then, in 33:21, it happens—the fugitive arrives with word that Jerusalem has fallen. Everything changes. Immediately, Ezekiel is released from his bonds and his tongue is loosed (v. 22; cf. 3:27). It is as if the prophet's time of bearing the sin of Israel is finally over. The judgment has fallen; the great reversal now begins.

13[m] [See ver. 12 above] **14**[o] ch. 3:18 [p] [Gen. 2:17] [q] See ch. 18:27 **15**[r] ch. 18:7 [s] Lev. 6:2, 4, 5; [Luke 19:8] [t] See ch. 20:11 **16**[u] ch. 18:22 **17**[l] [See ver. 12 above] [v] ch. 18:25, 29 **18**[w] [ver. 12, 13; See ch. 18:26] **19**[x] ch. 18:27; [ver. 11, 12] **20**[y] See ch. 18:30 **21**[z] See ch. 20:1 [a] ch. 40:1; See ch. 1:2 [b] ch. 24:26 [c] ch. 40:1; [ch. 26:2]; See 2 Kgs. 25:2-11 **22**[d] ch. 24:26, 27 [e] See ch. 1:3 **24**[f] See ch. 2:1 [g] [ch. 36:4]

in the land of Israel keep saying, [h]'Abraham
was only one man, yet he got possession of
the land; but [i]we are many; the land is surely
given us to possess.' 25 Therefore say to them,
Thus says the Lord GOD: [j]You eat flesh with
the blood and [k]lift up your eyes to your idols
and [l]shed blood; shall you then possess the
land? 26 [m]You rely on the sword, [n]you commit abominations, and [n]each of you defiles
his neighbor's wife; shall you then possess
the land? 27 Say this to them, Thus says the
Lord GOD: [o]As I live, surely those who are in
[p]the waste places shall fall by [q]the sword, and
whoever is in the open field I will give to [q]the
beasts to be devoured, and those who are in
[r]strongholds and in caves shall die by [q]pesti-
lence. 28 [s]And I will make the land a desolation
and a waste, and [t]her proud might shall come
to an end, and [u]the mountains of Israel shall
be so desolate that none will pass through.
29 [v]Then they will know that I am the LORD,
when I have made the land a desolation and
a waste because of all their abominations that
they have committed.

30 "As for you, [f]son of man, [w]your people who
talk together about you by the walls and at
the doors of the houses, say to one another,
each to his brother, 'Come, and hear what the
word is that comes from the LORD.' 31 [x]And
they come to you as people come, and they sit
before you as my people, and they hear what
you say but they will not do it; for [y]with lustful talk in their mouths they act; their heart
is set on their gain. 32 And behold, you are to
them like one who sings lustful songs with a
beautiful voice and [z]plays[1] well on an instrument, for [a]they hear what you say, but they will
not do it. 33 [b]When this comes—and come it
will!—[c]then they will know that a prophet
has been among them."

Prophecy Against the Shepherds of Israel

34 The word of the LORD came to me:
2 [d]"Son of man, prophesy against the
shepherds of Israel; prophesy, and say to
them, even to the shepherds, Thus says the
Lord GOD: [e]Ah, shepherds of Israel [f]who have
been feeding yourselves! [g]Should not shepherds feed the sheep? 3 [h]You eat the fat, you
clothe yourselves with the wool, [i]you slaughter the fat ones, but you do not feed the sheep.
4 [j]The weak you have not strengthened, the
sick you have not healed, [h]the injured you
have not bound up, [h]the strayed you have not
brought back, [k]the lost you have not sought,
and with force and [l]harshness you have ruled
them. 5 [m]So they were scattered, because there
was no shepherd, and [n]they became food for
all the wild beasts. 6 My sheep were scattered;
they wandered over all the mountains and on
every high hill. My sheep were scattered over
all the face of the earth, [o]with none to search
or seek for them.

7 "Therefore, you shepherds, hear the word

[1] Hebrew *like the singing of lustful songs with a beautiful voice and one who plays*

34:1–31 Chapter 34 is where we begin to see the magnitude of God's change of heart toward his people. Instead of judgment, the Lord now begins to effect a series of amazing reversals in the life of his people (chs. 34–39). He gives them care in the face of abuse, life in the face of death, and victory in the face of defeat.

In 34:1–10, God condemns the shepherds of Israel for exploiting the people—using them for their own gain and for their own pleasure instead of caring for them as they should have. In verses 11–16, God takes matters into his own hands, saying that he will shepherd his sheep. He will care for his people in all the ways their leaders have not.

Verses 23–24 of chapter 34 contain another promise that God will restore the throne of David, even after it has been thrown down by the Babylonians. What is more, verses 25–31 promise that God will make a covenant of peace with his people, providing "showers of blessing" for their land, security from enemies, and his own presence. This is all reflective of his promises for an everlasting covenant in 16:59–63.

In Jesus, this everlasting peace is secured. It is secured by the greatest reversal of all, the climactic reversal of life out of death and victory out of defeat. On the cross, by all appearances, hell had won. Satan looked decisively victorious. Yet it was precisely that moment of ignominious shame and tragedy that achieved the release of God's people—restoration, forgiveness, invincible joy (Rom. 16:20; Col. 2:13–15). Through his great love and care for his people, God has indeed shepherded them (Ezek. 34:11–16)—Jesus is the Good Shepherd who laid down his life for the sheep (John 10:11; 1 Pet. 2:25; 5:4).

24 [h]Isa. 51:2; [Acts 7:5] [i][Matt. 3:9; Luke 3:8]
25 [j][Gen. 9:4; Lev. 3:17] [k]ch. 18:6 [l]See ch. 22:3
26 [m][Gen. 27:40] [n]ch. 22:11
27 [o]See ch. 16:48 [p][ch. 36:4] [q][ch. 14:21] [r][1 Sam. 23:29]
28 [s][ch. 35:3, 9; Jer. 44:2, 6, 22] [t][ch. 7:24; 30:6] [u]See ch. 6:2
29 [v]See ch. 6:7
30 [f][See ver. 24 above] [w]See ver. 2
31 [x]See ch. 8:1 [y]Ps. 78:36, 37; Isa. 29:13; Jer. 12:2; 1 John 3:18
32 [z][1 Sam. 16:17] [a][Matt. 7:26; Luke 6:49]
33 [b][ver. 29] [c]ch. 2:5
Chapter 34
2 [d]See ch. 2:1 [e]See Jer. 23:1 [f][ver. 8, 10; Jude 12] [g][2 Cor. 12:14]
3 [h]Zech. 11:16 [i]Zech. 11:4, 5; [Mic. 3:2, 3]
4 [j][ver. 16, 21] [h][See ver. 3 above] [k][Matt. 18:12; Luke 15:4] [l]Ex. 1:13, 14; [1 Pet. 5:3]
5 [m]1 Kgs. 22:17; Matt. 9:36 [n][Jer. 50:7, 17]
6 [o][ver. 11]

of the LORD: 8 [p]As I live, declares the Lord GOD, surely because [q]my sheep have become a prey, and my sheep have become food for all the wild beasts, since there was no shepherd, and because my shepherds have not searched for my sheep, but the shepherds have fed themselves, and have not fed my sheep, 9 therefore, you shepherds, hear the word of the LORD: 10 Thus says the Lord GOD, [r]Behold, I am against the shepherds, and [s]I will require my sheep at their hand and [t]put a stop to their feeding the sheep. [u]No longer shall the shepherds feed themselves. [v]I will rescue my sheep from their mouths, that they may not be food for them.

The Lord GOD Will Seek Them Out

11 "For thus says the Lord GOD: [w]Behold, I, I [x]myself will search for my sheep and will seek them out. 12 As a shepherd seeks out his flock when he is among his sheep that have been scattered, so will I seek out my sheep, and I will rescue them from all places where they have been scattered on [y]a day of clouds and [z]thick darkness. 13 And I will bring them out from the peoples [a]and gather them from the countries, and will bring them into their own land. And I will feed them on [b]the mountains of Israel, by the ravines, and in all the inhabited places of the country. 14 [c]I will feed them with good pasture, and on the mountain heights of Israel shall be their grazing land. [d]There they shall lie down in good grazing land, and on rich pasture they shall feed on the mountains of Israel. 15 [e]I myself will be the shepherd of my sheep, [d]and I myself will make them lie down, declares the Lord GOD. 16 [f]I will seek the lost, [g]and I will bring back the strayed, and I will bind up the injured, and I will strengthen the weak, and [h]the fat and the strong I will destroy.[1] I will feed them in justice.

17 "As for you, my flock, thus says the Lord GOD: [i]Behold, I judge between sheep and sheep, between rams and [j]male goats. 18 Is it not enough for you to feed on the good pasture, that you must tread down with your feet the rest of your pasture; and to drink of [k]clear water, that you must muddy the rest of the water with your feet? 19 And must my sheep eat what you have trodden with your feet, and drink what you have muddied with your feet?

20 "Therefore, thus says the Lord GOD to them: Behold, I, I myself will judge between the fat sheep and the lean sheep. 21 Because you push with side and shoulder, and [l]thrust at all the [m]weak with your horns, till you have scattered them abroad, 22 I will rescue[2] my flock; [n]they shall no longer be a prey. And I will judge between sheep and sheep. 23 And [o]I will set up over them one shepherd, [p]my servant David, and he shall feed them: he shall feed them and be their shepherd. 24 And [q]I, the LORD, will be their God, and my servant David shall be prince among them. [r]I am the LORD; I have spoken.

The LORD's Covenant of Peace

25 [s]"I will make with them a covenant of peace and [t]banish wild beasts from the land, [u]so that they may dwell securely in the wilderness and sleep in the woods. 26 And I will make them and the places all around my hill [v]a blessing, and [w]I will send down the showers in their season; they shall be [x]showers of blessing. 27 [y]And the trees of the field shall yield their fruit, and the earth shall yield its increase, [u]and they shall be secure in their land. And [z]they shall know that I am the LORD, when [a]I break the bars of their yoke, and [a]deliver them from the hand of those who enslaved them. 28 [n]They shall no more be a prey to the nations, [t]nor shall the beasts of the land devour them. [u]They shall dwell securely, and none shall make them afraid. 29 And I will provide for them [b]renowned plantations so that [c]they shall no more be consumed with hunger in the land, and no longer [d]suffer the reproach of the nations. 30 And they shall know that [q]I am the LORD their God with them, and that they, the house of Israel, are my people, declares the Lord GOD. 31 And you are my sheep, [e]human sheep of my pasture, and I am your God, declares the Lord GOD."

[1] Septuagint, Syriac, Vulgate *I will watch over* [2] Or *save*

8 [p] See ch. 16:48 [q] [ver. 22] **10** [r] See ch. 13:8 [s] [Heb. 13:17]; See ch. 3:18 [t] [Zech. 11:8] [u] [ver. 2, 8] [v] [ch. 13:21] **11** [w] [Luke 19:10; John 10:11] [x] [Mic. 4:6, 7] **12** [y] ch. 30:3 [z] Joel 2:2; Zeph. 1:15 **13** [a] See ch. 11:17 [b] See ch. 6:2 **14** [c] Ps. 23:2; [John 10:9] [d] [Isa. 32:18; Jer. 33:12] **15** [e] [ver. 23; Isa. 40:11] [d] [See ver. 14 above] **16** [f] [ver. 4] [g] Mic. 4:6 [h] [ver. 20; Isa. 10:16; Amos 4:1] **17** [i] ver. 20, 22; [ch. 20:38; Matt. 25:32, 33] [j] Zech. 10:3 **18** [k] [ch. 32:14] **21** [l] Deut. 33:17; Dan. 8:4 [m] [ver. 4] **22** [n] [ver. 8] **23** [o] ch. 37:22, 24; Jer. 23:4, 5; Mic. 5:4; 7:14; [ver. 15; John 10:11, 16] [p] ch. 37:24, 25; [2 Sam. 5:2; Ps. 78:71, 72] **24** [q] See ch. 37:27; Ex. 29:45; Lev. 26:12 [r] See ch. 17:24 **25** [s] ch. 37:26; See Isa. 54:10 [t] Lev. 26:6; Hos. 2:18; [Isa. 35:9]; See Isa. 11:6-9 [u] ch. 38:8, 14; 39:26 **26** [v] Gen. 12:2; Isa. 19:24; Zech. 8:13 [w] Lev. 26:4; [ch. 22:24] [x] Mal. 3:10 **27** [y] ch. 36:30; Lev. 26:4 [u] [See ver. 25 above] [z] See ch. 6:7 [a] Jer. 30:8 **28** [n] [See ver. 22 above] [t] [See ver. 25 above] [u] [See ver. 25 above] **29** [b] Isa. 60:21; 61:3 [c] ch. 36:29 [d] See ch. 32:24 **30** [q] [See ver. 24 above] **31** [e] Ps. 74:1; 100:3; John 10:16

Prophecy Against Mount Seir

35 The word of the LORD came to me:
2 [f]"Son of man, [g]set your face [h]against
[i]Mount Seir, and prophesy against it, 3 and say
to it, Thus says the Lord GOD: [j]Behold, I am
against you, Mount Seir, and [k]I will stretch out
my hand against you, [l]and I will make you a
desolation and a waste. 4 [m]I will lay your cities
waste, and you shall become a desolation, and
you shall know that I am the LORD. 5 Because
[n]you cherished perpetual enmity and gave
over the people of Israel to the power of the
sword [o]at the time of their calamity, [p]at the
time of their final punishment, 6 therefore,
[q]as I live, declares the Lord GOD, I will prepare
you for blood, and blood shall pursue you;
[r]because you did not hate bloodshed, therefore
blood shall pursue you. 7 [l]I will make Mount
Seir a waste [m]and a desolation, and I will cut
off from it [s]all who come and go. 8 And I will
fill [t]its mountains with the slain. On your hills
and in your valleys and in all [t]your ravines
[u]those slain with the sword shall fall. 9 [l]I will
make you a perpetual desolation, and [m]your
cities shall not be inhabited. Then [v]you will
know that I am the LORD.

10 "Because you said, [w]'These two nations
and these two countries shall be mine, and
[x]we will take possession of them'—although
the [y]LORD was there— 11 therefore, [q]as I live,
declares the Lord GOD, I will deal with you
[z]according to the anger and [z]envy that you
showed because of your hatred against them.
And [a]I will make myself known among them,
when I judge you. 12 And you shall know that
I am the LORD.

[b]"I have heard all the revilings that you
uttered against the mountains of Israel, saying, 'They are laid desolate; [c]they are given us
to devour.' 13 And [b]you magnified yourselves
against me [d]with your mouth, and multiplied
your words against me; I heard it. 14 Thus says
the Lord GOD: [e]While the whole earth rejoices,
I will make you desolate. 15 As you [f]rejoiced
over the inheritance of the house of Israel,
because it was desolate, so I will deal with
you; you shall be desolate, [g]Mount Seir, and
all Edom, all of it. Then [h]they will know that
I am the LORD.

Prophecy to the Mountains of Israel

36 "And you, [i]son of man, prophesy to [j]the
mountains of Israel, and say, O mountains of Israel, hear the word of the LORD.
2 Thus says the Lord GOD: Because [k]the enemy
said of you, [l]'Aha!' and, 'The ancient [m]heights
have become our possession,' 3 therefore
prophesy, and say, Thus says the Lord GOD:
Precisely because [n]they made you desolate and
crushed you from all sides, so that you became
the possession of the rest of the nations, and
[o]you became the talk and evil gossip of the
people, 4 therefore, O mountains of Israel,
hear the word of the Lord GOD: Thus says the
Lord GOD to [p]the mountains and the hills, the
ravines and the valleys, [q]the desolate wastes
and the deserted cities, which have become
[r]a prey and derision to the rest of the nations
all around, 5 therefore thus says the Lord
GOD: Surely I have spoken in [s]my hot jealousy
against the rest of the nations and [t]against all
Edom, who [u]gave my land to themselves as a
possession [v]with wholehearted joy and [w]utter
contempt, that they might make its pasturelands a prey. 6 Therefore prophesy concerning
the land of Israel, and say to [j]the mountains
and hills, to the ravines and valleys, Thus says
the Lord GOD: [x]Behold, I have spoken in my

35:1–37:28 In these next three chapters God shows his people that he is able to grant them life out of certain and seemingly irreversible death. The note is first struck in chapters 35–36, which form a pair of prophecies to two mountains, first Mount Seir in the land of Edom and then the mountains of Israel. Edom has every reason to believe that she has defeated Israel. You can see her confidence in 35:10–12, and again in 36:2–3. For Israel, the situation seems hopeless; she has no army and no king. She is all but dead. And yet, once again, God steps in and reverses the situation. He rescues Israel, gives her a new heart, and makes her desolate mountains explode with life (36:22–38).

A pattern that resounds throughout the Bible is that it is when God's people are at their lowest, their weakest, their most despairing, that grace steps in. God is drawn to the needy, the hopeless, and the perplexed. This is his way. "The Son of Man came to seek and to save the lost" (Luke 19:10).

Chapter 35
2 [f]See ch. 2:1 [g]See ch. 6:2 [h]ch. 25:12; Isa. 21:11, 12; Amos 1:11; Mal. 1:4 [i]ch. 25:8; Gen. 32:3
3 [j]See ch. 13:8 [k]See ch. 6:14 [l][ch. 33:28]
4 [m][Isa. 17:9; 27:10]
5 [n][Ps. 137:7; Amos 1:11] [o]Obad. 13 [p]ch. 21:25
6 [q]See ch. 16:48 [r]See Gen. 9:6
7 [l][See ver. 3 above] [m][See ver. 4 above] [s]ch. 29:11
8 [t][ch. 31:12] [u]ch. 31:17, 18; 32:20, 21
9 [l][See ver. 3 above] [m][See ver. 4 above] [v]See ch. 6:7

10 [w][ch. 37:22] [x][ch. 36:2, 3, 5; Ps. 83:6, 12] [y]See ch. 48:35 **11** [q][See ver. 6 above] [z][ver. 15; Matt. 7:2] [a][ver. 9] **12** [b][2 Kgs. 19:4, 28] [c][ver. 10] **13** [b][See ver. 12 above] [d][1 Sam. 2:3] **14** [e][Isa. 65:13, 14] **15** [f]ch. 36:5; Ps. 137:7 [g]ver. 2 [h]See ch. 6:7 **Chapter 36** **1** [i]See ch. 2:1 [j]See ch. 6:2 **2** [k]ver. 5; ch. 35:10, 12 [l]ch. 25:3; 26:2 [m]Deut. 32:13 **3** [n][ch. 6:3, 4] [o][Lam. 2:15, 16] **4** [p]ch. 6:3 [q][ch. 33:24, 27] [r][ch. 7:21] **5** [s]Deut. 4:24 [t]ch. 35:15 [u][ver. 3; ch. 35:10] [v]ch. 35:15 [w]ch. 25:6 **6** [j][See ver. 1 above] [x][ver. 5]

jealous wrath, because you have suffered [y]the
reproach of the nations. 7 Therefore thus says
the Lord GOD: [z]I swear that the nations that
are all around you [y]shall themselves suffer
reproach.
8 "But you, O mountains of Israel, [a]shall
shoot forth your branches and yield your
fruit to my people Israel, for [b]they will soon
come home. 9 For [c]behold, I am for you, and
I will turn to you, and [d]you shall be tilled and
sown. 10 And [e]I will multiply people on you,
the whole house of Israel, all of it. [f]The cities
shall be inhabited and the waste places rebuilt.
11 And I will multiply on you [g]man and beast,
and [h]they shall multiply and be fruitful. And
I will cause you to be inhabited as in [i]your former times, and [j]will do more good to you than
ever before. [k]Then you will know that I am the
LORD. 12 I will let people walk on you, even my
people Israel. [l]And they shall possess you, and
you shall be their inheritance, and you shall
no longer [m]bereave them of children. 13 Thus
says the Lord GOD: Because they say to you,
[n]'You devour people, and you bereave your
nation of children,' 14 therefore you shall no
longer devour people and no longer bereave
your nation of children, declares the Lord
GOD. 15 And I will not let you hear anymore
[y]the reproach of the nations, and you shall no
longer bear the disgrace of the peoples and no
longer cause your nation to stumble, declares
the Lord GOD."

The LORD's Concern for His Holy Name

16 The word of the LORD came to me: 17 [o]"Son
of man, when the house of Israel lived in their
own land, [p]they defiled it by their ways and
their deeds. Their ways before me were [q]like
the uncleanness of a woman in her menstrual
impurity. 18 So [r]I poured out my wrath upon
them [s]for the blood that they had shed in the
land, for the idols [t]with which they had defiled
it. 19 [u]I scattered them among the nations, and
they were dispersed through the countries. [v]In
accordance with their ways and their deeds
I judged them. 20 But when they came to the
nations, wherever they came, [w]they profaned
my holy name, in that people said of them,
'These are the people of the LORD, and yet they
had to go out of his land.' 21 But I had concern
[x]for my holy name, which the house of Israel
had profaned among the nations to which
they came.

I Will Put My Spirit Within You

22 "Therefore say to the house of Israel, Thus
says the Lord GOD: [y]It is not for your sake,
O house of Israel, that I am about to act, but
for the sake of my holy name, [w]which you
have profaned among the nations to which
you came. 23 [z]And I will vindicate the holiness
of my great name, which has been profaned
among the nations, and which you have
profaned among them. [a]And the nations
will know that I am the LORD, declares the
Lord GOD, when through you I vindicate my
holiness before their eyes. 24 [b]I will take you
[c]from the nations and gather you from all
the countries and [d]bring you into your own
land. 25 [e]I will sprinkle clean water on you,
and you shall be clean from [f]all your uncleannesses, and [g]from all your idols [h]I will cleanse

36:25–27 This is a powerful image of the new life that God gives to his people when they come to him in faith. What is needed is not simply a new ethical direction or a decision to live a better life. What is needed is "a new heart, and a new spirit"—and not a new heart created in some self-generated way, but one given by God: "I will give you a new heart" (v. 26).

We are people whose hearts are naturally made of stony rebellion toward God. None are exempt from this. Our only hope of salvation is for God, by the power of his Holy Spirit, to perform the miracle of removing those stony hearts and giving us "hearts of flesh" instead (v. 26)—that is, hearts that respond to him and love him and desire to know him. We are dead in our transgressions, and we need to be brought from death to life (Eph. 2:1–7). As Jesus said, we need to be born again (John 3:1–8).

The new life that the gospel brings is not a new set of clever strategies, or spiritual rehabilitation, or fresh resolve to live in a new way out of our old resources. It is an utterly new and foreign importation of divine power that changes us at the very core of who we are. We are changed from the inside out. It is a transformation so profound that even our very desires are changed. The Bible calls this regeneration, or new birth (Titus 3:5). Here in Ezekiel 36 we see one of the Old Testament's most beautiful and clearest anticipations of this inside-out change.

6 [y] See ch. 32:24
7 [z] See ch. 20:5 [y] [See ver. 6 above]
8 [a] See ch. 17:23 [b] ch. 12:23; [Isa. 56:1]
9 [c] [ch. 5:8] [d] [ver. 34]
10 [e] ver. 37; ch. 37:26; Jer. 30:19 [f] [ver. 33, 35]
11 [g] Jer. 31:27; [Jer. 33:12] [h] [Gen. 1:28] [i] [ch. 16:55] [j] [Job 42:12] [k] See ch. 6:7
12 [l] Obad. 17 [m] [ch. 5:17]
13 [n] [Num. 13:32]
15 [y] [See ver. 6 above]
17 [o] See ch. 2:1 [p] See Lev. 18:25 [q] See Lev. 18:19
18 [r] See ch. 7:8 [s] ch. 16:36; 22:3 [t] See ch. 5:11
19 [u] See ch. 5:10 [v] See ch. 18:30
20 [w] Isa. 52:5; [ch. 22:26; Rom. 2:24]
21 [x] [ch. 20:9; Isa. 43:25; 48:11]
22 [y] ver. 32; [Deut. 9:5] [w] [See ver. 20 above]
23 [z] See ch. 20:41 [a] [ch. 30:19, 26; 38:23; 39:7, 21]; See ch. 6:7
24 [b] See ch. 11:17 [c] See Ps. 44:11 [d] ch. 37:12, 21 **25** [e] [Isa. 52:15; Heb. 10:22] [f] Isa. 4:4; [ver. 17] [g] ch. 37:23 [h] Jer. 33:8

you. **26** And I will give you [i]a new heart, and [i]a
new spirit I will put within you. [i]And I will
remove the heart of stone from your flesh and
give you a heart of flesh. **27** [j]And I will put my
Spirit within you, [i]and cause you to walk in
my statutes and [k]be careful to obey my rules.[1]
28 [l]You shall dwell in the land that I gave to
your fathers, and [m]you shall be my people,
and I will be your God. **29** And [n]I will deliver
you from all your uncleannesses. And [o]I will
summon the grain and make it abundant and
[p]lay no famine upon you. **30** [q]I will make the
fruit of the tree and the increase of the field
abundant, [o]that you may never again suffer
the disgrace of famine among the nations.
31 Then [r]you will remember your evil ways,
and your deeds that were not good, and you
will loathe yourselves for your iniquities and
your abominations. **32** [y]It is not for your sake
that I will act, declares the Lord GOD; let that
be known to you. Be ashamed and confounded
for your ways, O house of Israel.

33 "Thus says the Lord GOD: On the day that
[s]I cleanse you from all your iniquities, [t]I will
cause the cities to be inhabited, and the waste
places shall be rebuilt. **34** And the land that was
desolate shall be tilled, instead of being the
desolation that it was in the sight of all who
passed by. **35** And they will say, 'This land that
was desolate has become like [u]the garden of
Eden, and the waste and desolate and ruined
cities are now fortified and inhabited.' **36** Then
[v]the nations that are left all around you shall
know that I am the LORD; I have rebuilt the
ruined places and [w]replanted that which was
desolate. [x]I am the LORD; I have spoken, and
I will do it.

37 "Thus says the Lord GOD: This also [y]I will
let the house of Israel ask me to do for them:
[z]to increase their people like [a]a flock. **38** Like the
flock for sacrifices,[2] [b]like the flock at Jerusalem
during her appointed feasts, so [t]shall the waste
cities be filled with flocks of people. [c]Then
they will know that I am the LORD."

The Valley of Dry Bones

37 [d]The hand of the LORD was upon me,
and [e]he brought me out in the Spirit
of the LORD and set me down in the middle
of the valley;[3] it was full of bones. **2** And he led
me around among them, and behold, there
were very many on the surface of the valley,
and behold, they were very dry. **3** And he said to
me, [f]"Son of man, [g]can these bones live?" And
[h]I answered, "O Lord GOD, you know." **4** Then
he said to me, [i]"Prophesy over these bones,
and say to them, [j]O dry bones, hear the word
of the LORD. **5** Thus says the Lord GOD to these
bones: Behold, I will cause [k]breath[4] to enter
you, and you shall live. **6** [l]And I will lay sinews
upon you, and will cause flesh to come upon
you, and [l]cover you with skin, and put breath
in you, and you shall live, [m]and you shall know
that I am the LORD."

7 So I prophesied [n]as I was commanded. And
as I prophesied, there was a sound, and behold,
[o]a rattling,[5] and the bones came together, bone
to its bone. **8** And I looked, and behold, there

[1] Or *my just decrees* [2] Hebrew *flock of holy things* [3] Or *plain*; also verse 2 [4] Or *spirit*; also verses 6, 9, 10 [5] Or *an earthquake* (compare 3:12, 13)

37:1–10 Ezekiel's vision of the valley of dry bones is perhaps the most famous passage in the book. Coming after God's promise in chapter 36 to give his people new hearts and a new spirit, the dry bones illustrate the magnitude of the miracle that will be required if God's people are to be saved. The bones Ezekiel sees are "very dry" (37:2), emphasizing the fact that there is no life whatsoever in them. The chance that they will ever live again is zero.

Nevertheless, God asks Ezekiel a shocking question: "Son of man, can these bones live?" (v. 3). The obvious answer is no, and yet Ezekiel has learned never to presume on God's power and intentions. So he answers, "O Lord GOD, you know."

God's next instructions to Ezekiel would be comical if it were not the life-giving God who gave them. He tells Ezekiel to "prophesy over these bones" (v. 4)—in other words, to preach to them! God wants Ezekiel and the whole nation of Israel to know that it is his word that brings life. In the most hopeless of situations—even in a valley full of death—God's word is powerful to bring resurrection life.

We as Christians can take heart, even in our darkest struggles with sin. Just as God spoke the creation into existence, just as Jesus called Lazarus out of the tomb with only a word, just as Ezekiel preached to the dry bones, God's word gives life. The supreme word from God, the gospel message itself, tells us not what we must do to earn life but what God has done, in Christ, to give life.

26 [i] See ch. 11:19, 20
27 [j] ch. 37:14 [i] [See ver. 26 above] [k] ch. 37:24
28 [l] ch. 28:25 [m] See ch. 11:20
29 [n] ch. 37:23; [Matt. 1:21] [o] Joel 2:19; [Zech. 9:17] [p] ch. 34:29
30 [q] ch. 34:27 [o] [See ver. 29 above]
31 [r] See ch. 6:9
32 [y] [See ver. 22 above]
33 [s] [ver. 25] [t] [ver. 9, 10]
35 [u] See Isa. 51:3
36 [v] [Ps. 126:2] [w] [ch. 34:29] [x] See ch. 17:24
37 [y] [ch. 14:3] [z] See ver. 10 [a] [ch. 34:31]
38 [b] [2 Chr. 35:7] [t] [See ver. 33 above] [c] See ch. 6:7

Chapter 37

1 [d] See ch. 1:3 [e] See ch. 3:12
3 [f] See ch. 2:1 [g] [1 Cor. 15:35] [h] [Deut. 32:39; John 5:21]
4 [i] [ch. 6:2] [j] [John 5:28]
5 [k] [Gen. 2:7]
6 [l] [ver. 8] [m] See ch. 6:7
7 [n] ch. 12:7; 24:18 [o] [1 Kgs. 19:11]

were sinews on them, and flesh had come upon them, and skin had covered them. But [p]there was no breath in them. 9 Then he said to me, [i]"Prophesy to the breath; prophesy, [f]son of man, and say to the breath, Thus says the Lord GOD: Come from [q]the four winds, O breath, and breathe on these slain, that they may live." 10 So I prophesied [n]as he commanded me, and [r]the breath came into them, and they lived and stood on their feet, an exceedingly great army.

11 Then he said to me, [f]"Son of man, these bones are the whole house of Israel. Behold, they say, 'Our bones are dried up, and [s]our hope is lost; [t]we are indeed cut off.' 12 Therefore [i]prophesy, and say to them, Thus says the Lord GOD: Behold, [u]I will open your graves and raise you from your graves, O my people. And [v]I will bring you into the land of Israel. 13 And [w]you shall know that I am the LORD, when I open your graves, and raise you from your graves, O my people. 14 And [x]I will put my Spirit within you, and you shall live, and I will place you in your own land. Then you shall know that I am the LORD; [y]I have spoken, and I will do it, declares the LORD."

I Will Be Their God, They Shall Be My People

15 The word of the LORD came to me: 16 [z]"Son of man, [a]take a stick[1] and write on it, 'For [b]Judah, and [c]the people of Israel associated with him'; then take another stick and write on it, 'For [b]Joseph (the stick of [d]Ephraim) and all the house of Israel associated with him.' 17 And [e]join them one to another into one stick, that [f]they may become [g]one in your hand. 18 And when [h]your people say to you, [i]'Will you not tell us what you mean by these?' 19 say to them, Thus says the Lord GOD: Behold, I am about to take [j]the stick of Joseph (that is in the hand of Ephraim) and the tribes of Israel associated with him. And I will join with it the [j]stick of Judah,[2] and [k]make them one stick, [g]that they may be one in my hand. 20 When the sticks on which you write are in your hand [l]before their eyes, 21 then say to them, Thus says the Lord GOD: Behold, [m]I will take the people of Israel from the nations among which they have gone, and will gather them from all around, and [m]bring them to their own land. 22 And [n]I will make them one nation in the land, on [o]the mountains of Israel. And [p]one king shall be king over them all, and they shall be no longer [q]two nations, and no longer divided into two kingdoms. 23 [r]They shall not [s]defile themselves anymore [t]with their idols and their detestable things, or with any of their transgressions. But [u]I will save them from all the backslidings[3] in which they have sinned, and will cleanse them; and [v]they shall be my people, and I will be their God.

24 "My servant [w]David [x]shall be king over them, and they shall all have [y]one shepherd.

[1] Or *one piece of wood*; also verses 17, 19, 20 [2] Hebrew *And I will place them on it, the stick of Judah* [3] Many Hebrew manuscripts; other Hebrew manuscripts *dwellings*

8 [p] [ver. 5]
9 [i] [See ver. 4 above] [f] [See ver. 3 above] [q] Dan. 7:2; 11:4; Rev. 7:1
10 [n] [See ver. 7 above] [r] Rev. 11:11
11 [f] [See ver. 3 above] [s] [ch. 33:10; Isa. 49:14] [t] Lam. 3:54
12 [i] [See ver. 4 above] [u] [Isa. 26:19; Hos. 13:14] [v] ver. 21, 25; ch. 36:24
13 [w] See ch. 6:7
14 [x] ch. 36:27 [y] See ch. 17:24
16 [z] See ch. 2:1 [a] [Num. 17:2] [b] [Zech. 10:6] [c] 2 Chr. 11:12, 13, 16; 15:9; 30:11, 18 [d] Gen. 48:13, 14, 19; [Hos. 5:3, 5]
17 [e] [ver. 22, 24] [f] [Isa. 11:13] [g] [ch. 35:10]
18 [h] See ch. 33:2 [i] See ch. 12:9
19 [j] [ver. 16] [k] [ver. 17] [g] [See ver. 17 above]
20 [l] See ch. 12:3
21 [m] ver. 25; ch. 36:24; See ch. 11:17
22 [n] [ver. 17; Jer. 50:4] [o] See ch. 6:2 [p] [ver. 24, 25; ch. 34:24] [q] [ch. 35:10]
23 [r] [ch. 36:25] [s] ch. 14:11 [t] ch. 36:25 [u] ch. 36:29 [v] ch. 34:24, 30; 2 Cor. 6:16; Rev. 21:3; See Ex. 29:45; Lev. 26:12
24 [w] See ch. 34:23 [x] See Jer. 23:5 [y] [ver. 22]

37:11–14 Beginning in verse 11, God explains the vision of the dry bones. It is not simply that God gives *physical* life; it is that he gives *spiritual* life in the midst of death. That, in its essence, is the message of the gospel of Jesus Christ. Christianity is not at its heart about ethical teaching or social engagement; it is the message that though we are dead in our sins, Jesus gives us life through his own life, death, and resurrection on our behalf (Rom. 6:1–4; Eph. 2:8–10; 1 Thess. 5:9–10; Titus 3:4–7).

This passage should also be encouraging to Christians who may have given up hope that God can bring restoration and renewal to certain areas of their lives. Whether a long struggle with sin, or broken relationships, or even hard affliction, life's circumstances can often blind us to God's life-giving power. The vision of the dry bones, however, should remind us that our God truly is in the business of giving life where everything seems hopelessly dead.

37:15–28 God gives Ezekiel another vision of broken Israel being restored. In verse 22, two sticks representing the divided kingdom are made one again. Verse 24 promises yet again a single king, a descendant of David, to rule over God's people, and verse 26 reiterates God's promise to make a new covenant of peace with his people. (See also Jer. 31:31–34.)

"But I will save them from all the backslidings in which they have sinned, and will cleanse them; and they shall be my people, and I will be their God" (Ezek. 37:23). This is God's settled, covenantally bound determination. In Jesus, this saving, this cleansing, this restoration of his people to himself, is decisively achieved (Col. 1:21–22).

[z]They shall walk in my rules and be careful to
obey my statutes. 25 [a]They shall dwell in the
land that I gave to my servant Jacob, where
your fathers lived. They and their children
and their children's children shall dwell there
[b]forever, and David my servant shall be their
prince [c]forever. 26 [d]I will make a covenant of
peace with them. It shall be [e]an everlasting
covenant with them. And I will set them in
their land[1] and [f]multiply them, and will [g]set
my sanctuary in their midst forevermore.
27 [h]My dwelling place shall be with them,
[v]and I will be their God, and they shall be my
people. 28 Then [i]the nations will know that [j]I
am the LORD who sanctifies Israel, when [g]my
sanctuary is in their midst forevermore."

Prophecy Against Gog

38 The word of the LORD came to me:
2 [k]"Son of man, [l]set your face toward
[m]Gog, of the land of [n]Magog, the [o]chief prince
of [p]Meshech[2] and [p]Tubal, and [q]prophesy
against him 3 and say, Thus says the Lord GOD:
Behold, [r]I am against you, O Gog, chief prince
of Meshech[3] and Tubal. 4 [s]And I will turn you
about and [t]put hooks into your jaws, and I will
bring you out, and [u]all your army, horses and
horsemen, all of them clothed in full armor, a
great host, all of them with buckler and shield,
wielding swords. 5 [v]Persia, [w]Cush, and [v]Put are
with them, all of them with shield and helmet;
6 [x]Gomer and all his [y]hordes; [z]Beth-togarmah
from [a]the uttermost parts of the north with
all his hordes—[u]many peoples are with you.
7 [b]"Be ready and keep ready, you and all your
hosts that are assembled about you, and be a
guard for them. 8 [c]After many days you will
be mustered. [d]In the latter years you will go
against [d]the land that is restored from war, the
land whose people [e]were gathered from many
peoples upon [f]the mountains of Israel, which
had been a continual waste. Its people were
brought out from the peoples and [g]now dwell
securely, all of them. 9 You will advance, coming on [h]like a storm. You will be [i]like a cloud
covering the land, you and all your [y]hordes,
and many peoples with you.
10 "Thus says the Lord GOD: On that day,
[j]thoughts will come into your mind, and you
will devise an evil scheme 11 and say, 'I will go
up against [k]the land of unwalled villages. I will
fall upon [l]the quiet people who dwell securely,
all of them dwelling without walls, and having no bars or gates,' 12 to seize spoil and carry
off plunder, to turn your hand against [m]the
waste places that are now inhabited, and [m]the
people who were gathered from the nations,
who have acquired livestock and goods, [n]who

[1] Hebrew lacks *in their land* [2] Or *Magog, the prince of Rosh, Meshech* [3] Or *Gog, prince of Rosh, Meshech*

38:1–39:29 Interpretation of these chapters has given Christians enormous difficulty. The main point of them is clear enough: God's people will be put under dire threat by the powers of this world, but God will rescue them in the end. Exactly who is described here, however, or what historical event might be in view is hard to determine. One of the most important truths to realize, though, is that this great battle between God's people and their enemies is instigated and orchestrated by God himself. In 38:3–4, God tells Gog, the ruler of the enemy army, that he will decisively defeat Gog. This, in fact, seems to be the purpose for which God incites Gog against his people in the first place.

Scholars have not been able to agree about who Gog actually is. Several ancient kings had names that suggest possible parallels—Gugu, Guges, Gagu—but none of those kings quite fit the historical bill. One intriguing possibility is that the kingdom of Gog represents Babylon, the nation in which the Israelites were suffering exile. This possibility is commended by the fact that, strangely, Babylon does not make an appearance in chapters 25–32, where God is meting out judgment against his people's enemies. It may be that these chapters (chs. 38–39) are the crowning act of that universal judgment—Babylon, too, is destroyed under God's righteous wrath.

If, however, Gog does represent Babylon, it would not be simply sixth-century-B.C. Babylon in view. It would be Babylon standing as a symbol of humanity in rebellion against God. This would not be the only time in the Bible that Babylon plays that symbolic role. The very founding of the city took place with the hubristic act of building the Tower of Babel (= Babylon), and in the book of Revelation, the fall of Babylon represents God's overthrowing of all human pride and rebellion (e.g., Rev. 17:5; 18:2). Adding weight to this interpretation—that Gog ultimately represents all of rebellious humanity—is the fact that in Revelation, Gog and Magog represent all the nations of the world being led by Satan in one final battle against Jesus' people (Rev. 20:8).

24 [z]ch. 36:27
25 [a]ch. 28:25 [b]Isa. 60:21; Joel 3:20; Amos 9:15 [c][John 12:34]
26 [d]ch. 34:25 [e]See Isa. 55:3 [f]See ch. 36:10 [g]ver. 28; ch. 43:7; See ch. 11:16
27 [h]Lev. 26:11; Rev. 21:3 [v][See ver. 23 above]
28 [i]See ch. 36:23 [j]See ch. 20:12 [g][See ver. 26 above]
Chapter 38
2 [k]See ch. 2:1 [l]See ch. 6:2 [m]ch. 39:1, 11; Rev. 20:8 [n]ch. 39:6; Gen. 10:2; Rev. 20:8 [o]ch. 39:1 [p]See ch. 27:13 [q][ver. 4, 9]
3 [r]See ch. 13:8
4 [s]ch. 39:2 [t]See ch. 29:4 [u][ver. 15]
5 [v]ch. 27:10 [w]Gen. 10:8
6 [x]Gen. 10:2 [y]ver. 22 [z]Gen. 10:3; See ch. 27:14 [a]ch. 39:2; [ch. 32:30] [u][See ver. 4 above]
7 [b][Isa. 8:9, 10]
8 [c]Isa. 24:22 [d][ver. 16] [e]See ch. 11:17 [f]See ch. 6:2 [g]ch. 34:25, 27, 28
9 [h][Isa. 28:2] [i][Jer. 4:13] [y][See ver. 6 above]
10 [j]See ch. 11:5
11 [k][Zech. 2:4, 5] [l][Jer. 49:31]
12 [m][ver. 8] [n][ch. 5:5, 7, 14, 15]

dwell at the center of the earth. 13 [o]Sheba and
[p]Dedan and the merchants of Tarshish and all
[q]its leaders[1] will say to you, 'Have you come to
seize spoil? Have you assembled your hosts
to carry off plunder, to carry away silver and
gold, to take away livestock and goods, to seize
great spoil?'

14 "Therefore, [r]son of man, prophesy, and say
to [s]Gog, Thus says the Lord GOD: On that day
when my people Israel are [g]dwelling securely,
[t]will you not know it? 15 You will come from
your place out of [u]the uttermost parts of the
north, you and [v]many peoples with you, [w]all of
them riding on horses, a great host, a mighty
army. 16 You will come up against my people
Israel, [i]like a cloud covering the land. [x]In the
latter days I will bring you against my land,
that the nations may know me, when through
you, O Gog, [y]I vindicate my holiness before
their eyes.

17 "Thus says the Lord GOD: Are you [z]he of
whom I spoke in former days by my servants
the prophets of Israel, who in those days
prophesied for years that I would bring you
against them? 18 But on that day, the day that
Gog shall come against the land of Israel,
declares the Lord GOD, [a]my wrath will be
roused in my anger. 19 For [b]in my jealousy and
in my blazing wrath I declare, On that day
[c]there shall be a great earthquake in the land
of Israel. 20 [d]The fish of the sea and the birds
of the heavens and the beasts of the field and
all creeping things that creep on the ground,
and all the people who are on the face of
the earth, [e]shall quake at my presence. And
[f]the mountains shall be thrown down, and the
cliffs shall fall, and every wall shall tumble to
the ground. 21 [g]I will summon a sword against
Gog[2] on all my mountains, declares the Lord
GOD. [h]Every man's sword will be against his
brother. 22 With pestilence and bloodshed [i]I
will enter into judgment with him, and [j]I will
rain upon him and [k]his hordes and the many
peoples who are with him [l]torrential rains and
hailstones, [m]fire and sulfur. 23 So I will show
my greatness and my [n]holiness and [o]make
myself known in the eyes of many nations.
Then [p]they will know that I am the LORD.

39 "And you, [q]son of man, [r]prophesy
against [s]Gog and say, Thus says the
Lord GOD: Behold, [t]I am against you, O Gog,
[u]chief prince of [v]Meshech[3] and [v]Tubal. 2 [w]And
I will turn you about and drive you forward,
and bring you up from [x]the uttermost parts
of the north, and lead you against the [y]moun-
tains of Israel. 3 Then [z]I will strike your bow
from your left hand, and [z]will make your
arrows drop out of your right hand. 4 [a]You
shall fall on [y]the mountains of Israel, you
and all your [b]hordes and the peoples who are
with you. [c]I will give you to birds of prey of
every sort and to the beasts of the field to be
devoured. 5 You shall fall in the open field, for
[d]I have spoken, declares the Lord GOD. 6 [e]I will
send fire on [f]Magog and on those [g]who dwell
securely in [h]the coastlands, and [i]they shall
know that I am the LORD.

7 "And [j]my holy name I will make known in
the midst of my people Israel, and [k]I will not
let my holy name be profaned anymore. And
[l]the nations shall know that I am [m]the LORD,
the Holy One in Israel. 8 [n]Behold, it is coming
and it will be brought about, declares the Lord
GOD. That is the day [o]of which I have spoken.

9 "Then those who dwell in the cities of Israel
will go out and [p]make fires of the weapons
and burn them, shields and bucklers, bow and
arrows, [q]clubs[4] and spears; and they will make

[1] Hebrew *young lions* [2] Hebrew *against him* [3] Or *Gog, prince of Rosh, Meshech* [4] Or *javelins*

13 [o]ch. 27:22 [p]ch. 25:13; 27:15 [q][ch. 32:2; Ps. 17:12]
14 [r]See ch. 2:1 [s]ver. 2, 3 [g][See ver. 8 above] [t][ver. 11]
15 [u]ver. 6; ch. 39:2 [v][ver. 6, 9, 22] [w]ch. 23:6
16 [i][See ver. 9 above] [x][ver. 8] [y]ver. 23; [ch. 39:13]; See ch. 20:41
17 [z][Jer. 6:22, 23]
18 [a][Ps. 18:8]
19 [b]See ch. 5:13 [c][Hag. 2:6, 7; Rev. 16:18]
20 [d][Hos. 4:3] [e][Ps. 114:7] [f]Jer. 4:24
21 [g]Jer. 25:29 [h][Judg. 7:22]
22 [i][ch. 17:20] [j]Ps. 11:6

These chapters are not merely symbolic, however. As prophecy so often does, they describe while also pointing beyond their immediate historical circumstances. In Ezekiel, the vision points to the opposition Israel will continue to face from the nations once God resettles them in their land. But by the time the Bible's story reaches its culmination in Revelation, Gog and Magog—the symbols of human rebellion against God—are said to have "marched up over the broad plain of the earth and surrounded the camp of *the saints*" (Rev. 20:9), that is, the people of Jesus. Thus, what Ezekiel saw in seed form, Revelation gives us more fully. The people of God—embodied by national Israel in Ezekiel's vision, but shown to be Jesus' people in Revelation—are brought to the brink of destruction until God himself comes spectacularly to their defense.

In Jesus, he has.

[k]ver. 6, 9 [l]ch. 13:11, 13 [m]Ps. 11:6; [ch. 39:6; Rev. 20:9] **23** [n]See ver. 16 [o]ch. 36:23; 37:28 [p]See ch. 6:7 **Chapter 39** **1** [q]See ch. 2:1 [r]ch. 38:2, 3 [s]ch. 38:2 [t]ch. 38:3; See ch. 13:8 [u]ch. 38:2, 3 [v]ch. 38:2 **2** [w]ch. 38:4 [x]ch. 38:6, 15; [ch. 32:30] [y]See ch. 6:2 **3** [z][Ps. 76:3] **4** [a][ch. 38:21] [y][See ver. 2 above] [b]ch. 38:6, 9, 22 [c][ver. 17] **5** [d]See ch. 17:21 **6** [e][ch. 28:18; 30:8, 14, 16; 38:22] [f]ch. 38:2 [g]ch. 38:8, 14 [h]ch. 27:3, 6, 7, 15 [i]See ch. 6:7 **7** [j][ver. 22] [k]See ch. 20:39 [l]See ch. 36:23 [m]Isa. 45:11 **8** [n]ch. 21:7 [o]ch. 38:17 **9** [p][Ps. 46:9; Isa. 9:5] [q][1 Sam. 17:40]

fires of them for seven years, 10 so that they
will not need to take wood out of the field or
cut down any out of the forests, for [p]they will
make their fires of the weapons. [r]They will
seize the spoil of those who despoiled them,
and plunder those who plundered them,
declares the Lord GOD.

11 "On that day I will give to [s]Gog a place for
burial in Israel, the Valley of the Travelers, east
of the sea. It will block the travelers, for there
Gog and all his multitude will be buried. It
will be called the Valley of [t]Hamon-gog.[1] 12 For
[u]seven months the house of Israel will be burying them, in order [v]to cleanse the land. 13 All
the people of the land will bury them, and
it will bring them renown on the day that [w]I
show my glory, declares the Lord GOD. 14 They
will set apart men to travel through the land
regularly and bury those travelers remaining
on the face of the land, so as [v]to cleanse it. At[2]
the end of [x]seven months they will make their
search. 15 And when these travel through the
land and anyone sees a human bone, then
he shall set up a sign by it, till the buriers
have buried it in the Valley of [y]Hamon-gog.
16 (Hamonah[3] is also the name of the city.) Thus
shall they cleanse the land.

17 "As for you, [z]son of man, thus says the Lord
GOD: [a]Speak to [b]the birds of every sort and to
[b]all beasts of the field, 'Assemble and come,
gather from all around to [c]the sacrificial feast
that I am preparing for you, a great sacrificial
feast on the mountains of Israel, and you shall
eat flesh and drink blood. 18 [d]You shall eat the
flesh of the mighty, and drink the blood of the
princes of the earth—of rams, of lambs, and
of he-goats, of bulls, all of them [e]fat beasts
of Bashan. 19 And you shall eat fat till you are
filled, and drink blood till you are drunk, at
the sacrificial feast that I am preparing for
you. 20 And you shall be filled at my table with
horses and charioteers, with mighty men and
all kinds of warriors,' declares the Lord GOD.

21 "And [f]I will set my glory among the nations,
and all the nations shall see [g]my judgment
that I have executed, and [g]my hand that I have
laid on them. 22 [h]The house of Israel shall know
that I am the LORD their God, from that day
forward. 23 And [i]the nations shall know that
the house of Israel went into captivity for their
iniquity, because they dealt so treacherously
with me that [j]I hid my face from them and
[k]gave them into the hand of their adversaries,
and they all fell by the sword. 24 I dealt with
them [l]according to their uncleanness and their
transgressions, and hid my face from them.

The LORD Will Restore Israel

25 "Therefore thus says the Lord GOD: Now
[m]I will restore the fortunes of Jacob and have
mercy on [n]the whole house of Israel, and [o]I
will be jealous for my holy name. 26 They shall
[p]forget their shame and all the treachery they
have practiced against me, when [q]they dwell
securely in their land with [r]none to make them
afraid, 27 [s]when I have brought them back
from the peoples and gathered them from
their enemies' lands, [t]and through them have
vindicated my holiness in the sight of many
nations. 28 [h]Then they shall know that I am
the LORD their God, because I sent them into
exile among the nations and then assembled
them into their own land. I will leave none of
them remaining among the nations anymore.
29 [u]And I will not hide my face anymore from
them, when [v]I pour out my Spirit upon the
house of Israel, declares the Lord GOD."

Vision of the New Temple

40 [w]In the twenty-fifth year [x]of our exile,
at the beginning of the year, on the
tenth day of the month, [y]in the fourteenth
year after the city was struck down, on that
very day, [z]the hand of the LORD was upon me,
and he brought me to the city.[4] 2 In [a]visions of
God he brought me to the land of Israel, and
set me down on [b]a very high mountain, on

[1] *Hamon-gog* means *the multitude of Gog* [2] Or *Until* [3] *Hamonah* means *multitude* [4] Hebrew *brought me there*

40:1–48:35 To most modern readers, these last nine chapters of Ezekiel are exasperating. Filled with exquisite detail about an ideal, rebuilt temple, they seem almost impenetrable to us. To the Israelites, however, this description would have been exhilarating. Exiled from their land, and with their temple destroyed, they had little hope that they would ever return home. Yet in these chapters, God gives them a tour of a place they loved with all their hearts, promising that he would bring them back

10 [p][See ver. 9 above] [r][Isa. 33:1]
11 [s]ch. 38:2 [t]ver. 15
12 [u][ver. 14] [v][Deut. 21:23]
13 [w]ch. 28:22
14 [v][See ver. 12 above] [x][ver. 12]
15 [y]ver. 11
17 [z]See ch. 2:1 [a][Rev. 19:17]
[b]ver. 4; [Jer. 12:9] [c][Isa. 34:6; Zeph. 1:7] **18** [d][Rev. 19:18] [e][Ps. 22:12] **21** [f]ver. 7, 13; [ch. 28:22; 37:28; 38:23]; See ch. 36:23 [g][Ex. 7:4] **22** [h]ver. 28; Joel 2:27; See ch. 6:7 **23** [i]See Deut. 29:24-28 [j]Deut. 31:17 [k][Lev. 26:25] **24** [l][See ch. 18:30] **25** [m]See Jer. 30:3 [n]ch. 20:40 [o][ch. 20:9]; See ch. 5:13 **26** [p]See ch. 32:24 [q]ch. 34:25, 27, 28; 38:8 [r]ch. 34:28 **27** [s]ch. 28:25; See ch. 11:17 [t]See ch. 20:41 **28** [h][See ver. 22 above] **29** [u][ver. 23] [v][Joel 2:28] **Chapter 40**
1 [w]See ch. 20:1 [x]ch. 33:21; See ch. 1:2 [y][ch. 26:1, 2] [z]See ch. 1:3 **2** [a]See ch. 1:1 [b][ch. 43:12; Rev. 21:10]

which was a structure like a city to the south.
3 When he brought me there, behold, there was
[c]a man whose appearance was [d]like bronze,
with [e]a linen cord and [f]a measuring reed in
his hand. And he was standing in the gateway. 4 And the man said to me, [g]"Son of man,
[h]look with your eyes, and [h]hear with your ears,
and set your heart upon all that I shall show
you, for you were brought here in order that
I might show it to you. [i]Declare all that you see
to the house of Israel."

The East Gate to the Outer Court

5 And behold, there was [j]a wall all around
the outside of the temple area, and the length
of the measuring reed in the man's hand
was six long cubits, [k]each being a cubit and
a handbreadth[1] in length. So he measured
the thickness of the wall, one reed; and the
height, one reed. 6 Then he went into [l]the
gateway facing east, [m]going up its steps, and
measured the threshold of the gate, one reed
deep.[2] 7 And [n]the side rooms, one reed long
and one reed broad; and the space between
the side rooms, five cubits; and the threshold of the gate by the vestibule of the gate at
the inner end, one reed. 8 Then he measured
the vestibule of the gateway, on the inside,
one reed. 9 Then he measured the vestibule
of the gateway, eight cubits; [o]and its jambs,
two cubits; and the vestibule of the gate was
at the inner end. 10 And there were three side
rooms on either side of the east gate. [p]The
three were of the same size, and the jambs
on either side were of the same size. 11 Then
he measured the width of the opening of the
gateway, ten cubits; and the length of the
gateway, thirteen cubits. 12 There was a barrier before the side rooms, one cubit on either
side. And the side rooms were six cubits on
either side. 13 Then he measured the gate
from the ceiling of the one side room to the
ceiling of the other, a breadth of twenty-five
cubits; the openings faced each other. 14 He
measured also [q]the vestibule, twenty cubits.
And around the vestibule of the gateway was
the court.[3] 15 From the front of the gate at
the entrance to the front of the inner vestibule of the gate was fifty cubits. 16 And the
gateway had [r]windows all around, narrowing
inwards toward the side rooms and toward
their [s]jambs, and likewise the vestibule had
windows all around inside, and on the jambs
were [t]palm trees.

The Outer Court

17 Then he brought me into [u]the outer court.
And behold, there were [v]chambers and a
[w]pavement, all around the court. [x]Thirty
chambers faced the pavement. 18 And the pavement ran along the side of the gates, corresponding to the length of the gates. This was
the lower pavement. 19 Then he measured the
distance from the inner front of the lower
gate to the outer front of the inner court,[4] a
hundred cubits on the east side and on the
north side.[5]

The North Gate

20 As for [y]the gate that faced toward the
north, belonging to [u]the outer court, he measured its length and its breadth. 21 Its [n]side
rooms, three on either side, and its jambs and

[1] A *cubit* was about 18 inches or 45 centimeters; a *handbreadth* was about 3 inches or 7.5 centimeters [2] Hebrew *deep, and one threshold, one reed deep* [3] Text uncertain; Hebrew *And he made the jambs sixty cubits, and to the jamb of the court was the gateway all around* [4] Hebrew *distance from before the low gate before the inner court to the outside* [5] Or *cubits. So far the eastern gate; now to the northern gate.*

3 [c] ch. 43:6; 47:3; See ch. 9:2 [d] See ch. 1:7 [e] [ch. 47:3] [f] [Rev. 11:1]; See ch. 42:16-19
4 [g] See ch. 2:1 [h] ch. 44:5 [i] ch. 43:10
5 [j] ch. 42:20 [k] [ch. 41:8; 43:13]
6 [l] See ch. 43:1 [m] [ver. 22]
7 [n] ver. 29, 33, 36
9 [o] ch. 41:1
10 [p] [ver. 7]
14 [q] ver. 9, 16
16 [r] ch. 41:16, 26; [1 Kgs. 6:4] [s] ver. 9, 14 [t] ch. 41:18
17 [u] ch. 42:1; [Rev. 11:2] [v] ver. 38, 44, 45, 46; ch. 41:10; See 2 Kgs. 23:11 [w] [2 Chr. 7:3] [x] ch. 41:6; [ch. 45:5]
20 [y] [ver. 6] [u] [See ver. 17 above]
21 [n] [See ver. 7 above]

home to a restored temple. Despite the people's sin, despite their rebellion, despite God's righteous wrath having been executed against them, he still wants to dwell among them, and he will make that happen.

The "tour" may be roughly divided into three parts. Chapters 40–42 are a tour of the temple grounds. Chapters 43–46 showcase the work of the priests in the temple, and then 47–48 provide a fly-over tour of the entire Promised Land. All this would have been deeply comforting to the Israelites, because it meant that God had not abandoned them forever. He would bring them back to their land and, more importantly, into his presence. The temple represented God's presence, and therefore to regain the temple was to regain restored communion with God.

At the climax of history, the true temple would come, and true communion with God would be restored (John 1:14). For God would come not in a temple of wood and stone but in a temple of flesh and blood (John 2:19–22). Jesus said that "everything written about me in . . . the Prophets . . . must be fulfilled" (Luke 24:44). Ezekiel 40–48 is not exempt from that.

its vestibule were of the same size as those of [z]the first gate. Its length was [a]fifty cubits, and its breadth [b]twenty-five cubits. 22 And [c]its windows, its vestibule, and [c]its palm trees were of the same size as those of the gate that faced toward the east. And by seven steps [d]people would go up to it, and find its vestibule before them. 23 And opposite the gate on the north, as on the east, was a gate to [e]the inner court. And [f]he measured from gate to gate, a hundred cubits.

The South Gate

24 And he led me toward the south, and behold, there was a gate on the south. And [g]he measured its jambs and its vestibule; they had the same size as the others. 25 Both it and its vestibule [h]had windows all around, like the windows of the others. Its length was fifty cubits, and its breadth twenty-five cubits. 26 And there were seven steps leading up to it, and its vestibule was before them, and it had [i]palm trees on its jambs, one on either side. 27 And there was a gate on the south of [j]the inner court. And he measured from gate to gate toward the south, a hundred cubits.

The Inner Court

28 Then he brought me to [j]the inner court through the south gate, and [k]he measured the south gate. It was of the same size as the others. 29 Its [l]side rooms, its jambs, and its vestibule were of the same size as the others, and both it and its vestibule [m]had windows all around. [m]Its length was fifty cubits, and its breadth twenty-five cubits. 30 And there were vestibules all around, twenty-five cubits long and five cubits broad. 31 Its vestibule faced the outer court, and [i]palm trees were on its jambs, and [n]its stairway had eight steps.

32 Then he brought me to the inner court on the east side, and [o]he measured the gate. It was of the same size as the others. 33 Its side rooms, its jambs, and its vestibule were of the same size as the others, and both it and its vestibule had windows all around. Its length was fifty cubits, and its breadth twenty-five cubits. 34 [p]Its vestibule faced the outer court, and it had palm trees on its jambs, on either side, and its stairway had eight steps.

35 Then he brought me to [q]the north gate, and [r]he measured it. It had the same size as the others. 36 Its side rooms, its jambs, and its vestibule were of the same size as the others,[1] and it had windows all around. Its length was fifty cubits, and its breadth twenty-five cubits. 37 Its vestibule[2] faced the outer court, and it had palm trees on its jambs, on either side, and its stairway had eight steps.

38 There was [s]a chamber with its door in the vestibule of the gate,[3] [t]where the burnt offering was to be washed. 39 And in the vestibule of the gate were two [u]tables on either side, on which the [v]burnt offering and the [w]sin offering and the [x]guilt offering were to be slaughtered. 40 And off to the side, on the outside as one goes up to the entrance of the north gate, were two tables; and off to the other side of the vestibule of the gate were two tables. 41 [y]Four tables were on either side of the gate, eight tables, [z]on which to slaughter. 42 And there were four tables [a]of hewn stone for the burnt offering, a cubit and a half long, and a cubit and a half broad, and one cubit high, on which the instruments were to be laid with which the [v]burnt offerings and the sacrifices were slaughtered. 43 And hooks,[4] a handbreadth long, were fastened all around within. And on the tables the flesh of the offering was to be laid.

Chambers for the Priests

44 On the outside of the inner gateway there were two [b]chambers[5] in the [c]inner court, one[6] at the side of the north gate facing south, the other at the side of the south[7] gate facing north. 45 And he said to me, "This chamber that faces south is for the priests [d]who have charge of the temple, 46 and the chamber that faces north is for the priests [e]who have charge of the altar. These are [f]the sons of Zadok, who alone[8] among the sons of Levi may come [g]near to the LORD to minister to him." 47 And he measured the court, [h]a hundred cubits long and [h]a hundred cubits broad, a square. And [i]the altar was in front of the temple.

[1] One manuscript (compare verses 29 and 33); most manuscripts lack *were of the same size as the others* [2] Septuagint, Vulgate (compare verses 26, 31, 34); Hebrew *jambs* [3] Hebrew *at the jambs, the gates* [4] Or *shelves* [5] Septuagint; Hebrew *were chambers for singers* [6] Hebrew lacks *one* [7] Septuagint; Hebrew *east* [8] Hebrew lacks *alone*

21 [z][ver. 6] [a][ver. 15] [b][ver. 13] **22** [c][ver. 16] [d][ver. 6] **23** [e]ver. 28; [ch. 8:3] [f]ver. 27 **24** [g][ver. 21] **25** [h]ver. 22 **26** [i][ver. 16] **27** [j]ver. 23; ch. 8:16
28 [j][See ver. 27 above] [k][ver. 24] **29** [l]See ver. 7 [m][ver. 25] **31** [i][See ver. 26 above] [n][ver. 22] **32** [o][ver. 21] **34** [p]ver. 31 **35** [q]ch. 47:2 [r]ver. 32, 33
38 [s][ver. 17] [t][ch. 46:2; 2 Chr. 4:6] **39** [u][ver. 42] [v][ch. 46:2]; See Lev. 1:3, 4 [w]ch. 42:13; See Lev. 4:2, 3 [x]ch. 42:13; 46:20; See Lev. 5:1-6 **41** [y][ver. 39, 40]
[z][ver. 38] **42** [a][Ex. 20:25] [v][See ver. 39 above] **44** [b][ver. 17, 38] [c]1 Chr. 6:31, 32 **45** [d]1 Chr. 9:23; [ch. 44:8, 14, 15, 16; 48:11]; See Lev. 8:35; Num. 1:53
46 [e][Num. 3:31]; See Num. 18:5 [f]ch. 43:19; 44:15; [1 Kgs. 2:35; 1 Chr. 24:3, 6] [g]ch. 42:13; 45:4 **47** [h]See ch. 41:13-15 [i][ch. 43:13; Ex. 40:29; Matt. 23:35]

The Vestibule of the Temple

48 Then he brought me to [j]the vestibule of the temple and measured the [k]jambs of the vestibule, five cubits on either side. And the breadth of the gate was fourteen cubits, and the sidewalls of the gate[1] were three cubits on either side. **49** [l]The length of the vestibule was twenty cubits, and the breadth twelve[2] cubits, and people would go up to it by ten steps.[3] And there were pillars beside the jambs, one on either side.

The Inner Temple

41 Then he brought me to [m]the nave and measured the [n]jambs. On each side six cubits[4] was the breadth of the jambs.[5] **2** And the breadth of the entrance was ten cubits, and the sidewalls of the entrance were five cubits on either side. And he measured the length of the nave,[6] [o]forty cubits, and its breadth, [p]twenty cubits. **3** Then he went [q]into the inner room and measured the jambs of the entrance, two cubits; and the entrance, six cubits; and the sidewalls on either side[7] of the entrance, seven cubits. **4** And he measured [r]the length of the room, twenty cubits, and its breadth, twenty cubits, across [s]the nave. And he said to me, "This is [t]the Most Holy Place."

5 Then he measured the wall of the temple, six cubits thick, and the breadth of [u]the side chambers, four cubits, [u]all around the temple. **6** And the side chambers were in three stories, one over another, [v]thirty in each story. There were offsets[8] all around the wall of the temple to serve as supports for the side chambers, [w]so that they should not be supported by the wall of the temple. **7** And it became broader as it wound upward to the side chambers, because the temple was enclosed upward all around the temple. Thus the temple had a broad area upward, and [x]so one went up from the lowest story to the top story through the middle story. **8** I saw also that the temple had a raised platform all around; the foundations of the side chambers measured a full reed of [y]six long cubits. **9** The thickness of the outer wall of the side chambers was five cubits. [z]The free space between the side chambers of the temple and the **10** [a]other chambers was a breadth of [b]twenty cubits all around the temple on every side. **11** And the doors of the [c]side chambers opened on [d]the free space, one door toward the north, and another door toward the south. And the breadth of the free space was five cubits all around.

12 The building that was facing [e]the separate yard on the west side was seventy cubits broad, and the wall of the building was five cubits thick all around, and its length ninety cubits.

13 Then he measured the temple, [f]a hundred cubits long; and the yard and the building with its walls, a hundred cubits long; **14** also the breadth of the east front of the temple and the yard, a hundred cubits.

15 Then he measured the length of [g]the building facing the yard that was at the back and [h]its galleries[9] on either side, a hundred cubits.

The inside of the nave and the vestibules of the court, **16** [i]the thresholds and [j]the narrow windows and the galleries all around the three of them, opposite the threshold, were paneled with wood all around, from the floor up to the windows (now the windows were covered), **17** to the space above the door, even to the inner room, and on the outside. And on all the walls all around, inside and outside, was a measured pattern.[10] **18** It was carved of [k]cherubim and [l]palm trees, a palm tree between cherub and cherub. Every cherub had two faces: **19** [m]a human face toward the palm tree on the one side, and the face of a young lion toward the palm tree on the other side. They were carved on the whole temple all around.

[1] Septuagint; Hebrew lacks *was fourteen cubits, and the sidewalls of the gate* [2] Septuagint; Hebrew *eleven* [3] Septuagint; Hebrew *and by steps that would go up to it* [4] A *cubit* was about 18 inches or 45 centimeters [5] Compare Septuagint; Hebrew *tent* [6] Hebrew *its length* [7] Septuagint; Hebrew *and the breadth* [8] Septuagint, compare 1 Kings 6:6; the meaning of the Hebrew word is uncertain [9] The meaning of the Hebrew term is unknown; also verse 16 [10] Hebrew *were measurements*

41:18–26 The description of the idealized temple here as including carved palm trees and cherubim draws the careful reader's mind back to the garden of Eden, where God first dwelt with mankind in unbroken harmony, and which also included lush trees and cherubim. We see Eden microcosmically regained in the first temple, built by Solomon (1 Kings 6:18, 29, 32, 35; 7:18–19). And Eden is truly and finally regained in the new earth, which likewise is filled with flourishing trees, cherubim, and the "templing" presence of God (Rev. 21:22–22:2).

48 [j] ch. 41:25, 26 [k] [ver. 9]
49 [l] 1 Kgs. 6:3

Chapter 41
1 [m] ver. 21, 23; ch. 42:8 [n] ver. 3; ch. 40:9
2 [o] 1 Kgs. 6:17 [p] 1 Kgs. 6:2
3 [q] ch. 40:16
4 [r] 1 Kgs. 6:20; 2 Chr. 3:8 [s] 1 Kgs. 6:5 [t] ver. 21, 23; ch. 45:3; See 1 Kgs. 6:16 **5** [u] 1 Kgs. 6:5, 8; See ver. 6-9 **6** [v] ch. 40:17 [w] 1 Kgs. 6:6 **7** [x] 1 Kgs. 6:8 **8** [y] [ch. 40:5; 43:13] **9** [z] [ver. 11] **10** [a] See ch. 40:17 [b] ch. 42:3 **11** [c] [ver. 5] [d] [ver. 9] **12** [e] ch. 42:1, 10, 13; See ver. 13-15 **13** [f] ch. 40:47 **15** [g] ver. 12; ch. 42:1 [h] ch. 42:3, 5 **16** [i] Isa. 6:4 [j] ver. 26; ch. 40:16, 25; [1 Kgs. 6:4] **18** [k] ver. 20, 25; 1 Kgs. 6:29, 32, 35; 7:36 [l] ch. 40:16, 22, 26, 31, 34, 37; 2 Chr. 3:5 **19** [m] [ch. 1:10; 10:14]

20 From the floor to above the door, cherubim
and palm trees were carved; similarly the wall
of the nave.

21 The doorposts of [n]the nave were squared,
and in front of [o]the Holy Place was something
resembling 22 [p]an altar of wood, three cubits
high, two cubits long, and two cubits broad.[1]
Its corners, its base,[2] and its walls were of
wood. He said to me, "This is [q]the table that
is before the LORD." 23 The nave and the Holy
Place had each [r]a double door. 24 The double
doors had two leaves apiece, [s]two swinging
leaves for each door. 25 And on the doors of
the nave were carved cherubim and palm
trees, [t]such as were carved on the walls. And
there was [u]a canopy[3] of wood in front of [v]the
vestibule outside. 26 And there were [j]narrow
windows and palm trees on either side, on the
sidewalls of the vestibule, [w]the side chambers
of the temple, and the [u]canopies.

The Temple's Chambers

42 Then he led me out into [x]the outer
court, [y]toward the north, and he
brought me to [x]the chambers that were opposite [z]the separate yard and opposite [a]the building on the north. 2 The length of the building
whose door faced north was [b]a hundred
cubits,[4] and [c]the breadth fifty cubits. 3 Facing
[d]the twenty cubits that belonged to the inner
court, and facing [e]the pavement that belonged
to the outer court, was [f]gallery[5] against gallery
in three stories. 4 And [g]before the chambers
was a passage inward, ten cubits wide and [h]a
hundred cubits long,[6] and [g]their doors were
on the north. 5 Now the upper chambers were
narrower, for the galleries took more away
from them than from the lower and middle
chambers of the building. 6 For they were in
three stories, and they had no pillars like the
pillars of the courts. Thus the upper chambers
were set back from the ground more than the
lower and the middle ones. 7 And [i]there was a
wall outside parallel to the chambers, toward
the outer court, opposite the chambers, [j]fifty
cubits long. 8 For the chambers on the outer
court were fifty cubits long, while those opposite [k]the nave[7] were [l]a hundred cubits long.
9 Below these chambers was [m]an entrance on
the east side, as one enters them from the
outer court.

10 In the thickness of [n]the wall of the court,
on the south[8] also, opposite [o]the yard and
opposite [o]the building, there were [p]chambers
11 with [q]a passage in front of them. They were
similar to the chambers on the north, of the
same length and breadth, with the same exits[9]
and arrangements and [q]doors, 12 as were the
entrances of the chambers on the south. There
was an entrance at the beginning of the passage, the passage before [n]the corresponding
wall on the east as one enters them.[10]

13 Then he said to me, "The north chambers
and the south chambers opposite [o]the yard
are the holy chambers, [r]where the priests who
approach the LORD [s]shall eat the [t]most holy
offerings. There they shall put the most holy
offerings—[t]the grain offering, [u]the sin offering, and [u]the guilt offering—for the place is
holy. 14 When the priests enter the Holy Place,
they shall not go out of it into the outer court
[v]without laying there the garments in which
they minister, for these are holy. [v]They shall
put on other garments before they go near to
that which is for the people."

15 Now when he had finished measuring the
interior of the temple area, he led me out by
[w]the gate that faced east, and measured the
temple area all around. 16 He measured the east
side with [x]the measuring reed, 500 cubits by
the measuring reed all around. 17 He measured
the north side, 500 cubits by the measuring
reed all around. 18 He measured the south side,
500 cubits by the measuring reed. 19 Then he
turned to the west side and measured, 500
cubits by the measuring reed. 20 He measured it
on the four sides. It had [y]a wall around it, [z]500
cubits long and [z]500 cubits broad, [a]to make a
separation between the holy and the common.

[1] Septuagint; Hebrew lacks *two cubits broad* [2] Septuagint; Hebrew *length* [3] The meaning of the Hebrew word is unknown; also verse 26 [4] A *cubit* was about 18 inches or 45 centimeters [5] The meaning of the Hebrew word is unknown; also verse 5 [6] Septuagint, Syriac; Hebrew *and a way of one cubit* [7] Or *temple* [8] Septuagint; Hebrew *east* [9] Hebrew *and all their exits* [10] The meaning of the Hebrew verse is uncertain

42:20 The wall of this idealized temple is there "to make a separation between the holy and the common." Such a distinction is tacitly sensible to us, for we know that God is *other* than us—he is pure; we are not. Yet in Jesus this distinction was overcome.

21 [n] ver. 1 [o] See ver. 4 **22** [p] Rev. 11:1; See Ex. 30:1 [q] ch. 44:16; [ch. 23:41; Mal. 1:7, 12]

23 [r] See 1 Kgs. 6:31-33 **24** [s] [1 Kgs. 6:34] **25** [t] ver. 18, 20 [u] 1 Kgs. 7:6 [v] ch. 40:48 **26** [j] [See ver. 16 above] [w] See ver. 5-9 [u] [See ver. 25 above] **Chapter 42** **1** [x] ch. 40:17 [y] ch. 40:20 [z] ver. 10, 13; ch. 41:12, 13 [a] ch. 41:12, 15 **2** [b] [ch. 41:13] [c] [ver. 8] **3** [d] ch. 41:10 [e] ch. 40:17 [f] [ver. 5; ch. 41:15, 16] **4** [g] [ch. 46:19] [h] [ver. 11] **7** [i] [ver. 10, 12] [j] [ver. 2] **8** [k] ch. 41:1, 21, 23 [l] [ch. 41:13, 14] **9** [m] ch. 44:5; 46:19 **10** [n] [ver. 7] [o] [ver. 1] [p] See ch. 40:17 **11** [q] [ver. 4] **12** [n] [See ver. 10 above] **13** [o] [See ver. 10 above] [r] ch. 40:46 [s] Lev. 6:16, 26; 10:13; 24:9 [t] Num. 18:9 [u] ch. 40:39 **14** [v] ch. 44:19; Lev. 6:11 **15** [w] See ch. 43:1 **16** [x] [ch. 40:3] **20** [y] ch. 40:5 [z] [ch. 45:2; Rev. 21:16] [a] [ch. 22:26; 43:12; 44:23; 48:15]

The Glory of the LORD Fills the Temple

43 Then he led me to [b]the gate, the gate
facing east. 2 And behold, [c]the glory of
the God of Israel was coming from the east.
And [d]the sound of his coming was like the
sound of many waters, and [e]the earth shone
with his glory. 3 And [f]the vision I saw was just
like the vision that I had seen [g]when he[1] came
to destroy the city, and just like [h]the vision that
I had seen [i]by the Chebar canal. And [j]I fell on
my face. 4 As [c]the glory of the LORD [k]entered
the temple by the gate facing east, 5 [l]the Spirit
lifted me up and brought me into [m]the inner
court; and behold, [n]the glory of the LORD filled
the temple.
6 [o]While the man was standing beside me, [p]I
heard one speaking to me out of the temple,
7 and he said to me, [q]"Son of man, this is [r]the
place of my throne and [s]the place of the soles
of my feet, [t]where I will dwell in the midst of
the people of Israel forever. And the house
of Israel shall no more [u]defile my holy name,
neither they, nor their kings, by their whoring and by the dead bodies[2] of their kings at
their high places,[3] 8 by setting their threshold
by my threshold and their doorposts beside
my doorposts, with [v]only a wall between me
and them. They have [w]defiled my holy name
by their abominations that they have committed, so I have consumed them in my anger.
9 Now let them put away their whoring and
the dead bodies of their kings far from me,
[t]and I will dwell in their midst forever.
10 "As for you, [q]son of man, [x]describe to the
house of Israel the temple, that they may be
ashamed of their iniquities; and they shall
measure the plan. 11 And if they are ashamed
of all that they have done, [x]make known to
them the design of the temple, its arrangement, [y]its exits and its entrances, that is, its
whole design; and make known to them as
well all its statutes and its whole design and
all its laws, and write it down [z]in their sight,
so that they may observe all its laws and all its
statutes and carry them out. 12 This is the law
of the temple: the whole territory on the top of
[a]the mountain [b]all around shall be most holy.
Behold, this is the law of the temple.

The Altar

13 "These are the measurements of [c]the altar
by cubits (the cubit being [d]a cubit and a handbreadth):[4] its base shall be one cubit high[5]
and one cubit broad, with a rim of one span[6]

[1] Some Hebrew manuscripts and Vulgate; most Hebrew manuscripts *when I* [2] Or *the monuments*; also verse 9 [3] Or *at their deaths* [4] A *cubit* was about 18 inches or 45 centimeters; a *handbreadth* was about 3 inches or 7.5 centimeters [5] Or *its gutter shall be one cubit deep* [6] A *span* was about 9 inches or 22 centimeters

Chapter 43
1 [b]ver. 4; ch. 10:19; 11:1; 40:6; 42:15; 44:1
2 [c]ch. 10:18, 19; 11:23; [Rev. 21:11] [d]ch. 1:24; [Rev. 1:15] [e][ch. 10:4; Rev. 18:1]
3 [f]See ch. 1:28 [g][ch. 9:1, 2, 5] [h]See ch. 1:4-28 [i]See ch. 1:1 [j]See ch. 1:28
4 [c][See ver. 2 above] [k][ch. 44:2]
5 [l]See ch. 3:12 [m]See ch. 8:16 [n]ch. 10:4; 44:4; 1 Kgs. 8:10, 11; [Isa. 6:1]
6 [o]See ch. 40:3 [p][Ex. 25:22]
7 [q]See ch. 2:1 [r][Ps. 99:1] [s][1 Chr. 28:2; Isa. 60:13] [t]See ch. 37:26, 28 [u][ver. 8]; See ch. 20:39
8 [v][ch. 42:20] [w][ver. 7]
9 [t][See ver. 7 above]
10 [q][See ver. 7 above] [x]ch. 40:4
11 [x][See ver. 10 above] [y][ch. 44:5] [z]See ch. 12:3
12 [a][ch. 40:2] [b]See ch. 42:15-20
13 [c][ch. 40:47; 47:1]; See Ex. 27:1-8 [d]ch. 40:5; [ch. 41:8]

Jesus, the true and final temple, brought together the holy and the common, the clean and the unclean. When Jesus walked the earth and touched an unclean person, the unclean one became clean; Jesus did not become unclean (e.g., Mark 1:41–42).

But the greatest demonstration of the eradication of distinction between the holy and the common among God's people occurred when the veil between the Most Holy Place and the outer chamber of the temple was torn at the crucifixion of Christ. At that moment, Scripture made it forever plain that wretched sinners were given access to a holy God by Christ's cleansing blood (Rom. 5:2; Eph. 3:12).

43:1–9 In chapter 10, God's presence had slowly and sadly left the temple and the city of Jerusalem. That reality was worse even than destruction; it meant that God had abandoned them. The temple *was* God's presence among his people. Here, though, grace abounds as God returns to the temple!

But how could he, given the people's intractable waywardness? The answer was that God chose to condescend—to climb down from heaven to his people—to clean them up, rather than waiting for his people to climb up to heaven by cleaning themselves up. In Christ, this is precisely what God did (John 1:51; Heb. 2:14).

43:13–27 Joy further pervades this part of the temple tour, where Ezekiel is shown the work of the priests. God is now accepting the sacrifices of his people; their sin is atoned for. Verse 27 puts the point beautifully: "When they have completed these days, then from the eighth day onward the priests shall offer on the altar your burnt offerings and your peace offerings, *and I will accept you*, declares the Lord GOD."

How are we to understand the fulfillment of this prophecy? Is it pointing to a future time when the temple will be rebuilt in Jerusalem and animal sacrifices will be resumed? Probably not. For one thing, these chapters are full of hints that we should

around its edge. And this shall be the height of the altar: 14 from the base on the ground to the lower ledge, two cubits, with a breadth of one cubit; and from the smaller ledge to the larger ledge, four cubits, with a breadth of one cubit; 15 and the altar hearth, four cubits; and from the altar hearth projecting upward, [e]four horns. 16 The altar hearth shall be [f]square, twelve cubits long by twelve broad. 17 The ledge also shall be square, fourteen cubits long by fourteen broad, with a rim around it half a cubit broad, and its base one cubit all around. [g]The steps of the altar shall face east."

18 And he said to me, [h]"Son of man, thus says the Lord GOD: These are the ordinances for the altar: On the day when it is erected for offering burnt offerings upon it and [i]for throwing blood against it, 19 you shall give to [j]the Levitical priests [k]of the family of Zadok, who draw near to me to minister to me, declares the Lord GOD, [l]a bull from the herd for a sin offering. 20 And [m]you shall take some of its blood and put it on [e]the four horns of the altar and on the four corners of the ledge and upon [n]the rim all around. [o]Thus you shall purify the altar and make atonement for it. 21 You shall also take the bull of the sin offering, and [p]it shall be burned in the appointed place belonging to the temple, outside the sacred area. 22 And on the second day you shall offer a male goat without blemish for a sin offering; and the altar shall be purified, as it was purified with the bull. 23 When you have finished [o]purifying it, you shall offer a bull from the herd without blemish and [q]a ram from the flock without blemish. 24 You shall present them before the LORD, and the priests [r]shall sprinkle salt on them and offer them up as a burnt offering to the LORD. 25 [s]For seven days you shall provide daily a male goat for a sin offering; also, a bull from the herd and a ram from the flock, without blemish, shall be provided. 26 Seven days shall they make atonement for the altar and cleanse it, and so consecrate it.[1] 27 And when they have completed these days, then [t]from the eighth day onward the priests shall offer on the altar your burnt offerings and your [u]peace offerings, and [v]I will accept you, declares the Lord GOD."

The Gate for the Prince

44 Then he brought me [w]back to the outer gate of the sanctuary, [x]which faces east. And it was shut. 2 And the LORD said to me, "This gate shall remain shut; it shall not be opened, and no one shall enter by it, for [y]the LORD, the God of Israel, has entered by it. Therefore it shall remain shut. 3 Only [z]the

[1] Hebrew *fill its hand*

not expect this temple or this division of the land *actually* to take place. Perhaps the most obvious hint is that the division of the land in chapters 47–48 makes no real geographical sense. The various allotments cut across the land in straight lines, like pizza slices, with no obvious awareness of any geographical markers. The point therefore does not seem to be an actual geographical allotment of the land to the tribes, but rather an idealized presentation of the beauty of the everlasting covenant that God will establish—a presentation made in terms that the ancient Israelites would understand but still expressed in ways too wonderful for them fully to comprehend.

More importantly, in order to read this chapter as promising a rebuilt temple and reconstituted sacrifices, one has to overlook the rest of the Bible's story line. Hebrews, for example, has no concept at all of animal sacrifices being valuable or necessary ever again. For Jesus has provided the final sacrifice "once for all" (Heb. 7:27; 9:12, 26; 10:10). Moreover, John 2:13–22 makes it clear that God's presence is no longer to be found in the temple, but in Jesus himself. And Revelation 21:22 says that in the beautiful new Jerusalem, there is no temple. Sinners meet God now not in a building of any kind, but in a person—in Jesus himself. He is present within us (Gal. 2:20), and we are the temple of his Holy Spirit wherever we are (1 Cor. 6:19).

By his priestly sacrifice and intercession, Jesus is the ultimate reason God can say in Ezekiel 43:27, "I will accept you."

44:1–3 In these verses, the gate of the temple is closed forever. Never again will God depart from his people. The vision of Ezekiel 40–48 continues to anticipate a time when God will dwell in the midst of his people, "templing" among them. Eden must be restored. This happens through the Holy Spirit, who dwells in us so that, united to Christ, we ourselves become the final temple (Eph. 2:19–22).

15 [e] See Ex. 27:2
16 [f] [ch. 40:47; Ex. 27:1]
17 [g] [Ex. 20:26]
18 [h] See ch. 2:1 [i] See Lev. 1:5
19 [j] ch. 44:15; Deut. 17:9; 18:1; 24:8; 27:9 [k] See ch. 40:46 [l] ch. 45:18; Ex. 29:1, 10
20 [m] ch. 45:19; Ex. 29:12; Lev. 8:15 [e] [See ver. 15 above] [n] [ver. 13, 17] [o] Ex. 29:36; [ch. 45:18]
21 [p] Ex. 29:14
23 [o] [See ver. 20 above] [q] [Ex. 29:1]
24 [r] Lev. 2:13
25 [s] Ex. 29:35, 36; Lev. 8:33, 35
27 [t] Lev. 9:1 [u] See Lev. 3:1 [v] See ch. 20:40

Chapter 44
1 [w] [ch. 43:5] [x] See ch. 43:1
2 [y] [ch. 43:4]
3 [z] ch. 34:24; 37:25; 45:7; 46:2

prince may sit in it [a]to eat bread before the
LORD. He [b]shall enter by way of the vestibule
of the gate, and shall go out by the same way."
4 Then he brought me by way of [c]the north
gate to the front of the temple, and I looked,
and behold, [d]the glory of the LORD filled the
temple of the LORD. And [e]I fell on my face.
5 And the LORD said to me, [f]"Son of man, mark
well, [g]see with your eyes, [g]and hear with your
ears all that I shall tell you concerning [h]all
the statutes of the temple of the LORD and all
its laws. And mark well [h]the entrance to the
temple and all the exits from the sanctuary.
6 And say to [i]the rebellious house,[1] to the [j]house
of Israel, Thus says the Lord GOD: O house
of Israel, [k]enough of all your abominations,
7 in [l]admitting foreigners, [m]uncircumcised in
heart and flesh, to be in my sanctuary, [n]pro-
faning my temple, when you offer to me my
food, the fat and the blood. You[2] have broken
my covenant, in addition to all your abominations. 8 And [o]you have not kept charge of my
holy things, but you have set others to keep
my charge for you in my sanctuary.
9 "Thus says the Lord GOD: [p]No foreigner,
uncircumcised in heart and flesh, of all the
foreigners who are among the people of Israel,
shall enter my sanctuary. 10 But [q]the Levites
who went far from me, going astray from me
after their idols [r]when Israel went astray, [s]shall
bear their punishment.[3] 11 They shall be [t]min-
isters in my sanctuary, having oversight [u]at
the gates of the temple and ministering in the
temple. They shall slaughter the burnt offering
and the sacrifice for the people, and [v]they shall
stand before the people, to minister to them.
12 Because they ministered to them before their
idols and became [w]a stumbling block of iniquity to the house of Israel, therefore I have
[x]sworn concerning them, declares the Lord
GOD, and they shall bear their punishment.
13 They [y]shall not come near to me, to serve me
as priest, nor come near any of my holy things
and the things that are most holy, but [z]they
shall bear their shame and the abominations
that they have committed. 14 Yet I will appoint
them to keep [a]charge of the temple, [b]to do all
its service and all that is to be done in it.

Rules for Levitical Priests

15 "But [c]the Levitical priests, [c]the sons of
Zadok, who kept [a]the charge of my sanctuary
[r]when the people of Israel went astray from
me, shall come near to me [d]to minister to me.
And they shall stand before me to offer me
[e]the fat and the blood, declares the Lord GOD.
16 They shall enter my sanctuary, and they shall
approach [f]my table, to minister to me, and
they shall keep my charge. 17 When they enter
the gates of the inner court, they shall wear
[g]linen garments. They shall have nothing of
wool on them, while they minister at the gates
of the inner court, and within. 18 They shall
have linen turbans on their heads, and linen
undergarments around their waists. They
shall not bind themselves with anything that
causes sweat. 19 And when they go out into the
outer court to the people, they shall put off the
garments in which they have been ministering
[h]and lay them in the holy chambers. And [i]they
shall put on other garments, [j]lest they transmit
holiness to the people with their garments.
20 [k]They shall not shave their heads or [l]let their
locks grow long; they shall surely trim the hair
of their heads. 21 [m]No priest shall drink wine
when he enters the inner court. 22 [n]They shall
not marry a widow or a divorced woman, but
only virgins of the offspring of the house of
Israel, or a widow who is the widow of a priest.
23 [o]They shall teach my people the difference
between the holy and the common, and [o]show
them how to distinguish between the unclean
and the clean. 24 [p]In a dispute, they shall act as
judges, and they shall judge it according to
my judgments. They shall keep my laws and
my statutes in all my appointed feasts, and
[q]they shall keep my Sabbaths holy. 25 [r]They
shall not defile themselves by going near to a
dead person. However, for father or mother,
for son or daughter, for brother or unmarried
sister they may defile themselves. 26 [s]After he[4]
has become clean, they shall count seven days
for him. 27 And on the day that he goes into the
Holy Place, [t]into the inner court, to minister in
the Holy Place, [u]he shall offer his sin offering,
declares the Lord GOD.
28 [v]"This shall be their inheritance: I am

[1] Septuagint; Hebrew lacks *house* [2] Septuagint, Syriac, Vulgate; Hebrew *They* [3] Or *iniquity*; also verse 12 [4] That is, a priest

3 [a] [Gen. 31:54] [b] ch. 46:2, 12 **4** [c] ch. 40:20 [d] See ch. 43:5 [e] See ch. 1:28 **5** [f] See ch. 2:1 [g] ch. 40:4 [h] [ch. 43:11] **6** [i] See ch. 2:3 [j] ch. 40:4 [k] ch. 45:9; [1 Pet. 4:3] **7** [l] [ver. 9; Neh. 7:64, 65; Acts 21:28] [m] [Jer. 9:26; Acts 7:51] [n] ch. 23:39 **8** [o] [ch. 22:26] **9** [p] [ver. 7] **10** [q] [ver. 15; ch. 48:11] [r] ch. 48:11 [s] See ch. 4:4 **11** [t] ch. 46:24 [u] [1 Chr. 26:1] [v] Num. 16:9 **12** [w] ch. 7:19; 14:3, 4, 7; [Mal. 2:8] [x] Ps. 106:26 **13** [y] Num. 18:3; 2 Kgs. 23:9 [z] See ch. 32:24 **14** [a] See ch. 40:45 [b] 1 Chr. 23:28, 32 **15** [c] See ch. 43:19 [a] [See ver. 14 above] [r] [See ver. 10 above] [d] [ver. 11; Deut. 10:8] [e] [ver. 7] **16** [f] See ch. 41:22 **17** [g] Ex. 28:39; 39:27 **19** [h] ch. 42:14 [i] Lev. 6:11 [j] [ch. 46:20; Ex. 29:37; 30:29; Lev. 6:27] **20** [k] Lev. 21:5; [ch. 5:1] [l] [Num. 6:5] **21** [m] Lev. 10:9 **22** [n] Lev. 21:7, 13, 14 **23** [o] [ch. 22:26]; See Lev. 10:10, 11 **24** [p] Deut. 17:8, 9; [2 Chr. 19:8] [q] [ch. 22:26] **25** [r] See Lev. 21:1-3 **26** [s] Num. 19:11, 12 **27** [t] ver. 17, 21 [u] ch. 40:39; 42:13; Lev. 4:2, 3 **28** [v] See Num. 18:20

their inheritance: and [w]you shall give them
no possession in Israel; I am their possession.
29 [x]They shall eat the grain offering, the sin
offering, and the guilt offering, and [y]every
devoted thing in Israel shall be theirs. 30 [z]And
the first of all the firstfruits of all kinds, and
every offering of all kinds from all your offerings, shall belong to the priests. [a]You shall
also give to the priests the first of your dough,
[b]that a blessing may rest on your house. 31 [c]The
priests shall not eat of [d]anything, whether bird
or beast, that has died of itself or is torn by
wild animals.

The Holy District

45 "When [e]you allot the land as an inheritance, [f]you shall set apart for the LORD
a portion of the land as a holy district, 25,000
cubits[1] long and 20,000[2] cubits broad. It shall
be holy throughout its whole extent. 2 [g]Of this
a square plot of 500 by 500 cubits shall be for
the sanctuary, with fifty cubits for [h]an open
space around it. 3 And [i]from this measured district you shall measure off a section 25,000
cubits long and 10,000 broad, [j]in which shall
be the sanctuary, [k]the Most Holy Place. 4 [l]It
shall be the holy portion of the land. It shall
be for the priests, who minister in the sanctuary and approach the LORD to minister to him,
and it shall be a place for their houses and a
holy place for the sanctuary. 5 [m]Another section,
25,000 cubits long and 10,000 cubits broad,
shall be for the Levites who minister at the
temple, as their possession for cities to live in.[3]
6 "Alongside the portion set apart as the holy
district [n]you shall assign for the property of
the city an area 5,000 cubits broad and 25,000
cubits long. [o]It shall belong to the whole house
of Israel.

The Portion for the Prince

7 [p]"And to [q]the prince shall belong the land
on both sides of the holy district and the
property of the city, alongside the holy district and the property of the city, on the west
and on the east, corresponding in length to
one of the tribal portions, and extending from
the western to the eastern boundary 8 of the
land. It is to be his property in Israel. And [r]my
princes shall no more oppress my people, but
[s]they shall let the house of Israel have the land
according to their tribes.
9 "Thus says the Lord GOD: [t]Enough,
O princes of Israel! Put away violence and
oppression, and execute justice and righteousness. Cease [u]your evictions of my people,
declares the Lord GOD.
10 [v]"You shall have just balances, a just
ephah, and a just bath.[4] 11 The ephah and
the bath shall be [w]of the same measure, [x]the
bath containing one tenth of a homer,[5] and
the ephah one tenth of a homer; the homer
shall be the standard measure. 12 [y]The shekel
shall be twenty gerahs;[6] twenty shekels plus
twenty-five shekels plus fifteen shekels shall
be your mina.[7]
13 [z]"This is the offering that you shall make:
one sixth of an ephah from each homer of
wheat, and one sixth of an ephah from each
homer of barley, 14 and as the fixed portion
of oil, measured in baths, one tenth of a bath
from each cor[8] (the cor, like the homer, contains [a]ten baths).[9] 15 And one sheep from every
flock of two hundred, from the watering places

[1] A *cubit* was about 18 inches or 45 centimeters [2] Septuagint; Hebrew *ten* [3] Septuagint; Hebrew *as their possession, twenty chambers*
[4] An *ephah* was about 3/5 of a bushel or 22 liters; a *bath* was about 6 gallons or 22 liters [5] A *homer* was about 6 bushels or 220 liters
[6] A *shekel* was about 2/5 ounce or 11 grams; a *gerah* was about 1/50 ounce or 0.6 gram [7] A *mina* was about 1 1/4 pounds or 0.6 kilogram
[8] A *cor* was about 6 bushels or 220 liters [9] See Vulgate; Hebrew *(ten baths are a homer, for ten baths are a homer)*

45:13–17 One of the most interesting things to notice about chapters 40–48 is the recurring appearance of this shadowy figure Ezekiel calls "the prince." In all likelihood, this prince is the culmination of a series of Davidic, messianic images that have appeared throughout the book. In 34:24, for example, God promised, "And I, the LORD, will be their God, and my servant David shall be prince among them." And in 37:25, Ezekiel said, "They shall dwell in the land that I gave to my servant Jacob, where your fathers lived. They and their children and their children's children shall dwell there forever, and David my servant shall be their prince forever."

It makes sense to think that this "prince" is another vision of that same person—a prophecy of the Davidic Messiah who will oversee the worship of God's people, have authority over them, and rule in righteousness and peace. It is also interesting to see what this prince does with reference to the sacrifices the priests are performing. In

28 [w][ch. 45:4, 5]
29 [x]See Lev. 6:14-18, 25-29; 7:1-6 [y]Lev. 27:21, 28; Num. 18:14
30 [z]See Ex. 23:19 [a]See Num. 15:20 [b]Mal. 3:10
31 [c]Lev. 22:8; [Ex. 22:31]; See Lev. 7:24 [d]ch. 4:14
Chapter 45
1 [e][ch. 48:29]; See ch. 47:21, 22 [f]See ch. 48:8-10
2 [g]See ch. 42:16-20 [h][ch. 27:28; 48:15, 17]; See Lev. 25:34
3 [i][ver. 1] [j]ch. 48:10 [k]See ch. 41:4
4 [l][ch. 48:11, 12]
5 [m]ch. 48:13

6 [n]ch. 48:15 [o][ch. 48:18, 19] **7** [p]ch. 48:21 [q]See ch. 44:3 **8** [r][ch. 22:27; 46:18] [s]ch. 47:13, 21; See ch. 48:1-7, 23-28 **9** [t]ch. 44:6 [u][ch. 46:18] **10** [v]See Lev. 19:35, 36 **11** [w][Deut. 25:14, 15] [x][Isa. 5:10] **12** [y]See Ex. 30:13 **13** [z]ch. 44:30 **14** [a]ver. 11

of Israel for grain offering, burnt offering, and peace offerings, [b]to make atonement for them, declares the Lord GOD. 16 All the people of the land shall be obliged to give this offering to the prince in Israel. 17 [c]It shall be the prince's duty to furnish the burnt offerings, grain offerings, and drink offerings, at the feasts, the new moons, and the Sabbaths, all the appointed feasts of the house of Israel: he shall provide the sin offerings, grain offerings, burnt offerings, and peace offerings, to make atonement on behalf of the house of Israel.

18 "Thus says the Lord GOD: In the first month, [d]on the first day of the month, you shall take a bull from the herd without blemish, and [e]purify the sanctuary. 19 [f]The priest shall take some of the blood of the sin offering and put it [g]on the doorposts of the temple, the four corners of the ledge of the altar, and the posts of the gate of the inner court. 20 You shall do the same on the seventh day of the month for anyone who has sinned through error or ignorance; so you shall make atonement for the temple.

21 [h]"In the first month, on the fourteenth day of the month, you shall celebrate the Feast of the Passover, and for seven days unleavened bread shall be eaten. 22 On that day the prince [i]shall provide for himself and all the people of the land a young bull for a sin offering. 23 And on [j]the seven days of the festival he shall provide as a burnt offering to the LORD seven young bulls and seven rams without blemish, on each of the seven days; and [k]a male goat daily for a sin offering. 24 And [l]he shall provide as [m]a grain offering an ephah for each bull, an ephah for each ram, and a hin[1] of oil to each ephah. 25 [n]In the seventh month, on the fifteenth day of the month and for the seven days of the feast, [o]he shall make the same provision for sin offerings, burnt offerings, and grain offerings, and for the oil.

The Prince and the Feasts

46 "Thus says the Lord GOD: [p]The gate of [q]the inner court that faces east shall be shut on the six working days, but on the Sabbath day it shall be opened, and [r]on the day of the new moon it shall be opened. 2 [s]The prince shall enter by the vestibule of the gate from outside, and shall take his stand by [t]the post of the gate. [u]The priests shall offer his burnt offering and his peace offerings, and he shall worship at [v]the threshold of the gate. Then he shall go out, but the gate shall not be shut until evening. 3 [w]The people of the land shall bow down at the entrance of that gate before the LORD on the Sabbaths and on the new moons. 4 [x]The burnt offering that the prince offers to the LORD [y]on the Sabbath day shall be six lambs without blemish and a ram without blemish. 5 And [z]the grain offering with the ram shall be an ephah,[2] and the grain offering with the lambs shall be [a]as much as he is able, together with a hin[3] of oil to each ephah. 6 On the day of the new moon he shall offer a bull from the herd without blemish, and six lambs and a ram, which shall be without blemish. 7 As a grain offering he shall provide an ephah with the bull and an ephah with the ram, and with the lambs [b]as much as he is able, together with a hin of oil to each ephah. 8 [c]When the prince enters, he shall enter by the vestibule of the gate, and he shall go out by the same way.

9 [d]"When the people of the land [e]come before the LORD at the appointed feasts, he who enters by the north gate to worship shall go out by the south gate, and he who enters by the south gate shall go out by the north gate: no one shall return by way of the gate by which he entered, but each shall go out straight ahead. 10 When they enter, [f]the prince shall enter with them, and when they go out, he shall go out.

11 "At the feasts and the appointed festivals, [z]the grain offering with a young bull shall

[1] A *hin* was about 4 quarts or 3.5 liters [2] An *ephah* was about 3/5 bushel or 22 liters [3] A *hin* was about 4 quarts or 3.5 liters

15[b] See Lev. 1:4
17[c] [2 Chr. 30:24; 35:7]; See ch. 46:4-7
18[d] [ch. 46:1, 3, 6] [e] Lev. 16:16; [ch. 43:20, 22, 23]
19[f] See ch. 43:20 [g] [Ex. 12:7]
21[h] See Lev. 23:5
22[i] [ver. 17]
23[j] Lev. 23:8 [k] Num. 28:15
24[l] ch. 46:5, 7 [m] See Lev. 2:1
25[n] See Lev. 23:34 [o] See ver. 22-24

these verses (45:13–17), it is the prince's duty "to furnish the burnt offerings, grain offerings, and drink offerings!" It is all still shadowy and mysterious, even blurry, but it is nonetheless there—a King, a descendant of David, who himself provides a sacrifice and makes atonement for God's people.

When Jesus came, he gathered up all the various threads that run through the Old Testament that anticipate a day of final release, of true and pure leadership, of restoration to the pristine beauty of Eden. In Jesus' first coming this day dawned. Upon his second coming it will be perfectly consummated.

Chapter 46 **1**[p] ch. 45:19 [q] See ch. 8:16 [r] [ch. 45:18] **2**[s] See ch. 44:3 [t] [ch. 45:19] [u] [ch. 40:38, 39] [v] [ch. 9:3] **3**[w] ver. 9 **4**[x] ch. 45:17 [y] [Num. 28:9, 10] **5**[z] ver. 14; ch. 45:24 [a] [Deut. 16:17] **7**[b] ver. 5 **8**[c] [ver. 2] **9**[d] ver. 3 [e] [Deut. 16:16]; See Ex. 23:14-17 **10**[f] [Ps. 42:4] **11**[z] [See ver. 5 above]

be an ephah, and with a ram an ephah, and with the lambs [b]as much as one is able to give, together with a hin of oil to an ephah. 12 When the prince provides [g]a freewill offering, either a burnt offering or peace offerings as a freewill offering to the LORD, [h]the gate facing east shall be opened for him. And he shall offer his burnt offering or his peace offerings [i]as he does on the Sabbath day. Then he shall go out, and after he has gone out the gate shall be shut.

13 [j]"You shall provide a lamb a year old without blemish for a burnt offering to the LORD daily; morning by morning you shall provide it. 14 And [k]you shall provide a grain offering with it morning by morning, one sixth of an ephah, and one third of a hin of oil to moisten the flour, as a grain offering to the LORD. This is a perpetual statute. 15 Thus the lamb and the meal offering and the oil shall be provided, morning by morning, for [l]a regular burnt offering.

16 "Thus says the Lord GOD: If the prince makes a gift to any of his sons as his inheritance, it shall belong to his sons. It is their property by inheritance. 17 But if he makes a gift [m]out of his inheritance to one of his servants, it shall be his to [n]the year of liberty. Then it shall revert to the prince; surely it is his inheritance—it shall belong to his sons. 18 [o]The prince shall not take any of the inheritance of the people, [p]thrusting them out of their property. He shall give his sons their inheritance out of his own property, so that none of my people shall be [q]scattered from his property."

Boiling Places for Offerings

19 Then he brought me through the entrance, which was [r]at the side of the gate, to the north row of [s]the holy chambers for the priests, and behold, a place was there at the extreme western end of them. 20 And he said to me, "This is the place where the priests [t]shall boil the guilt offering and the sin offering, and where [u]they shall bake the grain offering, in order not to bring them out into the outer court and so [v]transmit holiness to the people."

21 Then he brought me out to the outer court and led me around to the four corners of the court. And behold, in each corner of the court there was another court— 22 in the four corners of the court were small[1] courts, forty cubits[2] long and thirty broad; the four were of the same size. 23 On the inside, around each of the four courts was a row of masonry, with hearths made at the bottom of the rows all around. 24 Then he said to me, "These are the kitchens where those who [w]minister at the temple [t]shall boil the sacrifices of the people."

Water Flowing from the Temple

47 Then he brought me back to [x]the door of the temple, and behold, [y]water was issuing from below [z]the threshold of the temple toward the east (for the temple faced east). The water was flowing down from below the south end of the threshold of the temple, south of [a]the altar. 2 Then he brought me out by way of [b]the north gate and led me around on the outside to [c]the outer gate that faces toward the east; and behold, the water was trickling out on the south side.

3 Going on eastward with a measuring line in his hand, [d]the man measured a thousand cubits,[3] and then led me through the water, and it was ankle-deep. 4 Again he measured a thousand, and led me through the water, and it was knee-deep. Again he measured a

[1] Septuagint, Syriac, Vulgate; the meaning of the Hebrew word is uncertain [2] A *cubit* was about 18 inches or 45 centimeters [3] A *cubit* was about 18 inches or 45 centimeters

47:1–12 In one of the most curious parts of this vision of an eschatological temple, water flows from it. The water flows toward the east, nourishing the part of the world most in need of it (v. 1). Ezekiel is brought outside and led along the water, which gradually gets deeper and deeper (vv. 2–6). Eventually the water becomes "a river that could not be passed through" (v. 5). Drawing on the language of creation in Genesis 1–2, the text here goes on to describe the lush vegetation, trees, and teeming wildlife (vv. 7–9).

This vision of a river flowing from the temple goes not only back, however, but also forward. The influence of these fruitful waters are picked up in Zechariah 14:8, which speaks of the coming day of the Lord by saying, "On that day living waters shall flow out from Jerusalem." Jesus picks up the theme, saying that the Old Testament speaks of rivers of living water flowing out from the heart of the one who believes in him—yet not identifying or making transparently clear which Old Testament text

11 [b] [See ver. 7 above]
12 [g] Lev. 7:16; 22:23; Deut. 23:23 [h] [ver. 1] [i] [ver. 2]
13 [j] Ex. 29:38; Num. 28:3, 4
14 [k] ver. 5
15 [l] Num. 23:15, 17
17 [m] [ch. 45:7] [n] See Lev. 25:10
18 [o] [1 Sam. 8:14; 1 Kgs. 21:3, 7] [p] [ch. 45:8] [q] [ch. 34:4, 5]
19 [r] [ver. 1] [s] [ch. 42:4]
20 [t] 2 Chr. 35:13 [u] [Lev. 2:4] [v] See ch. 44:19
24 [w] ch. 44:11 [t] [See ver. 20 above]
Chapter 47
1 [x] [ch. 43:1, 2] [y] Ps. 46:4; Joel 3:18; [Zech. 14:8; Rev. 22:1] [z] See ch. 9:3 [a] See ch. 43:13
2 [b] ch. 40:35 [c] [ch. 40:6]
3 [d] [ch. 40:3]

thousand, and led me through the water, and it was waist-deep. 5 Again he measured a thousand, and it was a river that I could not pass through, for the water had risen. It was deep enough to swim in, a river that could not be passed through. 6 And he said to me, [e]"Son of man, [f]have you seen this?"

Then he led me back to the bank of the river. 7 As I went back, I saw on the bank of the river [g]very many trees on the one side and on the other. 8 And he said to me, "This water flows toward the eastern region and goes down into [h]the Arabah, and enters the sea;[1] when the water flows into [i]the sea, the water will become fresh.[2] 9 And wherever the river goes,[3] every living creature that swarms will live, and there will be very many fish. For this water goes there, that the waters of the sea[4] may become fresh; so everything will live where the river goes. 10 Fishermen will stand beside the sea. From [j]Engedi to [k]Eneglaim it will be a place for the spreading of nets. Its fish will be of very many kinds, like the fish of [l]the Great Sea.[5] 11 But its swamps and marshes will not become fresh; they are to be left for salt. 12 And on the banks, [m]on both sides of the river, there will grow [n]all kinds of trees for food. [o]Their leaves will not wither, nor their fruit fail, [p]but they will bear fresh fruit every month, because the water for them flows from the sanctuary. Their fruit will be for food, and [p]their leaves for healing."

Division of the Land

13 Thus says the Lord GOD: "This is the boundary[6] by which [q]you shall divide the land for inheritance among the twelve tribes of Israel. [r]Joseph shall have two portions. 14 And you shall divide equally what [s]I swore [t]to give to your fathers. [u]This land shall fall to you as your inheritance.

15 "This shall be the boundary of the land: On the north side, from [l]the Great Sea [v]by way of Hethlon to Lebo-hamath, and on to [w]Zedad,[7] 16 [x]Berothah, Sibraim (which lies on the border between [y]Damascus and [v]Hamath), as far as Hazer-hatticon, which is on the border of Hauran. 17 So the boundary shall run from the sea to [z]Hazar-enan, which is on the northern border of Damascus, with the border of Hamath to the north.[8] This shall be the north side.[9]

18 "On the east side, the boundary shall run between Hauran and Damascus; along the Jordan between [a]Gilead and the land of Israel; to [b]the eastern sea and as far as Tamar.[10] This shall be the east side.

19 "On the south side, it shall run from [c]Tamar as far as [d]the waters of Meribah-kadesh, from there along [e]the Brook of Egypt[11] to [f]the Great Sea. This shall be the south side.

20 "On the west side, the Great Sea shall be the boundary to a point [v]opposite Lebo-hamath. This shall be the west side.

21 [g]"So you shall divide this land among you according to the tribes of Israel. 22 [h]You shall allot it as an inheritance for yourselves and [i]for the sojourners who reside among you and have had children among you. [j]They shall be to you as native-born children of Israel. With you they shall be allotted an inheritance among the tribes of Israel. 23 In whatever tribe the sojourner resides, there you shall assign him his inheritance, declares the Lord GOD.

48 "These are the names of the tribes: Beginning at the northern extreme, beside [k]the way of Hethlon [l]to Lebo-hamath, as

[1] That is, the Dead Sea [2] Hebrew *will be healed*; also verses 9, 11 [3] Septuagint, Syriac, Vulgate, Targum; Hebrew *the two rivers go* [4] Hebrew lacks *the waters of the sea* [5] That is, the Mediterranean Sea; also verses 15, 19, 20 [6] Probable reading; Hebrew *The valley of the boundary* [7] Septuagint; Hebrew *the entrance of Zedad, Hamath* [8] The meaning of the Hebrew is uncertain [9] Probable reading; Hebrew *and as for the north side* [10] Compare Syriac; Hebrew *to the eastern sea you shall measure* [11] Hebrew lacks *of Egypt*

he is speaking of (John 7:38). And at the end of all things we see Ezekiel's watering temple in the new earth (Rev. 22:1–2). Just as in Ezekiel 47:7, 12, in Revelation 22:2 a river (now flowing from the throne of God instead of the temple, since no more sacrifice for sin needs to be made) produces trees growing on both sides of the river, bearing leaves "for the healing of the nations."

In every case, the waters point to the true refreshment that comes ultimately only in Jesus (John 7:37–39; cf. Isa. 41:17–20; 43:18–21). And, as these life-giving waters flow from the place of atonement (the temple and the throne of the Redeemer), they grow wider and deeper, making eternal life possible for the worst of sinners and for all the nations of the world.

6 [e] See ch. 2:1 [f] [ch. 8:6]
7 [g] ver. 12; [Rev. 22:2]
8 [h] See Deut. 1:1 [i] Deut. 3:17; 4:49; Josh. 3:16
10 [j] See 1 Sam. 23:29 [k] Isa. 15:8 [l] See Josh. 15:12
12 [m] [ver. 7] [n] [Gen. 2:9] [o] Ps. 1:3; [Jer. 17:8] [p] [Rev. 22:2]
13 [q] ch. 45:8; See ch. 48:1-7, 23-28 [r] [ch. 48:4, 5]; See Josh. 17:14-18
14 [s] See ch. 20:5 [t] See Gen. 12:7 [u] [ch. 48:29]
15 [l] [See ver. 10 above] [v] ch. 48:1 [w] Num. 34:8

16 [x] 2 Sam. 8:8 [y] ch. 48:1; Isa. 7:8 [v] [See ver. 15 above] **17** [z] [ch. 48:1] **18** [a] Josh. 13:11 [b] Joel 2:20 **19** [c] Gen. 14:7; 2 Chr. 20:2 [d] Num. 20:13 [e] Num. 34:5 [f] See Josh. 15:12 **20** [v] [See ver. 15 above] **21** [g] ver. 13 **22** [h] ch. 45:1; 48:29 [i] Isa. 14:1; [Eph. 3:6] [j] Ex. 12:19, 48, 49; [Rom. 10:12; Gal. 3:28; Col. 3:11] **Chapter 48** **1** [k] ch. 47:15 [l] ch. 47:20; See 1 Kgs. 8:65

far as [m]Hazar-enan (which is on the northern border of [n]Damascus over against Hamath), and[1] extending from the east side to the west,[2] [o]Dan, one portion. 2 Adjoining the territory of Dan, from the east side to the west, [o]Asher, one portion. 3 Adjoining the territory of Asher, from the east side to the west, [o]Naphtali, one portion. 4 Adjoining the territory of Naphtali, from the east side to the west, Manasseh, one portion. 5 Adjoining the territory of Manasseh, from the east side to the west, Ephraim, one portion. 6 Adjoining the territory of Ephraim, from the east side to the west, Reuben, one portion. 7 Adjoining the territory of Reuben, from the east side to the west, Judah, one portion.

8 "Adjoining the territory of Judah, from the east side to the west, shall be [p]the portion which you shall set apart, 25,000 cubits[3] in breadth, and in length equal to one of the tribal portions, from the east side to the west, with [q]the sanctuary in the midst of it. 9 The portion that you shall set apart for the LORD shall be 25,000 cubits in length, and 20,000[4] in breadth. 10 [r]These shall be the allotments of the holy portion: the priests shall have an allotment measuring 25,000 cubits on the northern side, 10,000 cubits in breadth on the western side, 10,000 in breadth on the eastern side, and 25,000 in length on the southern side, with the sanctuary of the LORD in the midst of it. 11 This shall be for [s]the consecrated priests, [t]the sons of Zadok, who kept my charge, who did not go astray when the people of Israel went astray, [u]as the Levites did. 12 And it shall belong to them as a special portion from the holy portion of the land, a most holy place, adjoining the territory of the Levites. 13 [v]And alongside the territory of the priests, the Levites shall have an allotment 25,000 cubits in length and 10,000 in breadth. The whole length shall be 25,000 cubits and the breadth 20,000.[5] 14 They [w]shall not sell or exchange any of it. They shall not alienate [x]this choice portion of the land, for it is holy to the LORD.

15 [y]"The remainder, 5,000 cubits in breadth and 25,000 in length, shall be [z]for common use for the city, for dwellings and for [a]open country. In the midst of it shall be the city, 16 and these shall be its measurements: [b]the north side 4,500 cubits, the south side 4,500, the east side 4,500, and the west side 4,500. 17 And the city shall have open land: on the north 250 cubits, on the south 250, on the east 250, and on the west 250. 18 The remainder of the length alongside the holy portion shall be 10,000 cubits to the east, and 10,000 to the west, and it shall be alongside the holy portion. [c]Its produce shall be food for the workers of the city. 19 And the workers of the city, from all the tribes of Israel, shall till it. 20 The whole portion that [d]you shall set apart shall be 25,000 cubits square, that is, the holy portion together with the property of the city.

21 [e]"What remains on both sides of the holy portion and of the property of the city shall belong to the prince. Extending from the 25,000 cubits of the holy portion to the east border, and westward from the 25,000 cubits to the west border, parallel to the tribal portions, it shall belong to the prince. [f]The holy portion with the sanctuary of the temple shall be in its midst. 22 It shall be separate from the property of the Levites and the property of the city, which are in the midst of that which belongs to the prince. The portion of the prince shall lie between the territory of Judah and the territory of Benjamin.

23 "As for the rest of the tribes: from the east side to the west, Benjamin, one portion. 24 Adjoining the territory of Benjamin, from the east side to the west, Simeon, one portion. 25 Adjoining the territory of Simeon, from the east side to the west, Issachar, one portion. 26 Adjoining the territory of Issachar, from the east side to the west, Zebulun, one portion. 27 Adjoining the territory of Zebulun, from the east side to the west, Gad, one portion. 28 And adjoining the territory of Gad to the south, the boundary shall run [g]from Tamar to the waters of [g]Meribah-kadesh, from there along the Brook of Egypt[6] to [h]the Great Sea.[7] 29 This is the land that [i]you shall allot as an inheritance among the tribes of Israel, and these are their portions, declares the Lord GOD.

[1] Probable reading; Hebrew *and they shall be his* [2] Septuagint (compare verses 2–8); Hebrew *the east side the west* [3] A *cubit* was about 18 inches or 45 centimeters [4] Compare 45:1; Hebrew *ten* [5] Septuagint; Hebrew *10,000* [6] Hebrew lacks *of Egypt* [7] That is, the Mediterranean Sea

1[m] [ch. 47:17] [n] ch. 47:16, 17, 18 [o] Num. 2:25-31 **2**[o] [See ver. 1 above] **3**[o] [See ver. 1 above] **8**[p] See ch. 45:1-6 [q] ver. 21 **10**[r] ch. 45:4 **11**[s] ch. 44:15 [t] See ch. 40:46 [u] ch. 44:10 **13**[v] ch. 45:5 **14**[w] [Lev. 27:10, 28, 33] [x] [ch. 44:30] **15**[y] ch. 45:6 [z] See ch. 42:20 [a] [ch. 27:28; 45:2] **16**[b] [ver. 20; Rev. 21:16] **18**[c] [ch. 45:6] **20**[d] [ch. 40:47] **21**[e] ch. 45:7 [f] ver. 8, 10 **28**[g] ch. 47:19 [h] ch. 47:10; See Josh. 15:12 **29**[i] ch. 47:22

The Gates of the City

30 "These shall be [l]the exits of the city: On
the north side, which is to be [k]4,500 cubits by
measure, 31 [l]three gates, the gate of [m]Reuben,
the gate of [m]Judah, and the gate of [m]Levi, the
gates of the city being named after the tribes of
Israel. 32 On the east side, which is to be 4,500
cubits, three gates, the gate of Joseph, the gate
of Benjamin, and the gate of Dan. 33 On the
south side, which is to be 4,500 cubits by measure, three gates, the gate of Simeon, the gate
of Issachar, and the gate of Zebulun. 34 On the
west side, which is to be 4,500 cubits, three
gates,[1] the gate of Gad, the gate of Asher, and
the gate of Naphtali. 35 The circumference of
the city shall be 18,000 cubits. And [n]the name
of the city from that time on shall be, [o]The
LORD Is There."

[1] One Hebrew manuscript, Syriac (compare Septuagint); most Hebrew manuscripts *their gates three*

30 [j]Num. 34:4, 5, 8, 9, 12; Josh. 15:4, 7, 11 [k][ver. 16]
31 [l][Rev. 21:12, 13] [m]See Deut. 33:6-8
35 [n]Isa. 60:14; [Jer. 23:6; 33:16] [o]ch. 35:10; Jer. 3:17; Joel 3:21; [Zech. 2:10; Rev. 21:3]

48:30–35 How far we have come since the beginning of the book of Ezekiel! In chapter 4, the prophet built siegeworks around a model of the city and set his face against it, even putting an iron barrier between it and himself to symbolize God's determination to destroy the city in his righteous wrath.

Now, by the close of the book, all is reversed. Wrath has given way to grace. The city is safe and secure, and the horrifying image of God's glory departing from the temple is replaced by the glorious new name of the city, in the very last words of Ezekiel—"The LORD Is There" (48:35).

This journey from exile from God's presence to gracious return through the Messiah traces the story of the entire Bible. Because of their sin, human beings were banished from God's presence, cast out of the garden of Eden and barred from returning. By his grace and because of his love, however, God acted through the Messiah Jesus Christ to reconcile his people to himself and bring them back into his presence. Thus the Bible ends with John's vision of a new Jerusalem, and the beautiful description in Revelation 21:2–3: "And I saw the holy city, new Jerusalem, coming down out of heaven from God, prepared as a bride adorned for her husband. And I heard a loud voice from the throne saying, 'Behold, the dwelling place of God is with man. He will dwell with them, and they will be his people, and God himself will be with them as their God.'"

What better name for this city than the one Ezekiel gives it? "The LORD Is There."

Introduction to Daniel

Author and Date

Daniel wrote this book in the sixth century B.C. It records the events of Daniel's life and the visions he saw from the time of his exile in 605 B.C. (1:1) until 536 B.C., the third year of King Cyrus (10:1).

The Gospel in Daniel

The "gospel according to Daniel" comes in glowing revelations of the power of God to redeem his people, overcome their enemies, and plan their future. We will not see these gospel truths clearly if we fall into two common but erroneous approaches to the book: (1) making Daniel the object of our worship; or, (2) making Daniel the subject of our debates.

We are tempted to make Daniel the object of our worship in the first half of the book, which is largely a biography of his life. Daniel's courage and faithfulness in a land of cruelty and captivity can easily tempt us to make him the primary hero of the text. In doing so we neglect Daniel's own message: God is the hero.

God saves a sinful and weak people; he preserves young men from impurity and old men from lions; he answers prayer and interprets dreams; he exalts the humble and humbles the proud; he vindicates the faithful and vanquishes the profane; and he rescues covenant-forsaking people by returning them to the land of the covenant. Daniel acts on the grace God repeatedly provides, but God is always the One who first provides the opportunity, resources, and rescue needed for Daniel's faithfulness. If we reverse the order, and make God's grace dependent on Daniel's goodness, then we forsake the gospel message Daniel is telling and produce the hero-worship of adventure tales, rather than the divine worship of the gospel according to Daniel.

The second half of the book, which contains most of the prophetic content, can make us susceptible to the second error: making Daniel primarily the subject of our debates about eschatology (the end times). This book contains some of the most amazing and detailed prophecies in all of Scripture. Centuries in advance, Daniel predicts events as momentous as the succession of vast empires, and he relates details as precise as the symptoms of a disease that will slay a future king. Daniel also speaks about the future of the people of God in visions that are hard to understand and that relate to some events still future to us.

These are important prophecies, but we can become so stressed and combative about the interpretation of particular aspects of the prophecies that we neglect the central message: God will rescue his people from their sin and misery by the work of a Messiah. The righteous will be vindicated, evil will be destroyed, and the covenant blessings will prevail because Jesus will reign. All this occurs *not* because humans control their fate or deserve God's redemption, but because the God of grace uses his sovereign power to maintain his covenant mercy forever. This, too, is the gospel according to Daniel that should give us courage against our foes, hope in our distress, and perseverance in our trials.

Outline

I. Daniel and the Three Friends at the Babylonian Court (1:1–6:28)

- A. Prologue (1:1–21)
- B. Nebuchadnezzar's dream of a great statue (2:1–49)
- C. Nebuchadnezzar builds a great statue (3:1–30)
- D. Nebuchadnezzar's dream of a toppled tree (4:1–37)
- E. Belshazzar's feast (5:1–31)
- F. The lions' den (6:1–28)

II. The Visions of Daniel (7:1–12:13)

- A. The vision of the four great beasts and the heavenly court (7:1–28)
- B. The vision of the ram, the goat, and the little horn (8:1–27)
- C. Daniel's prayer and its answer (9:1–27)
- D. Daniel's vision of the final conflict (10:1–12:13)

Daniel

Daniel Taken to Babylon

1 In the third year of [a]the reign of Jehoiakim
king of Judah, Nebuchadnezzar king of
Babylon came to Jerusalem and besieged it.
2 And the Lord gave Jehoiakim king of Judah
into his hand, with some of [b]the vessels of
the house of God. And he brought them to
[c]the land of Shinar, to the house of his god,
[d]and placed the vessels in the treasury of his
god. 3 Then the king commanded Ashpenaz,
[e]his chief eunuch, to bring some of the people of Israel, both of the royal family[1] and
of [f]the nobility, 4 youths without [g]blemish,
of good appearance and [h]skillful in all wisdom, endowed with knowledge, understanding learning, and competent to stand in the
king's palace, and to [i]teach them the literature
and language of the [j]Chaldeans. 5 The king
assigned them a daily portion of [k]the food
that the king ate, and of [l]the wine that he
drank. They were to be educated for [m]three
years, and at the end of that time they were
to [n]stand before the king. 6 Among these were
[o]Daniel, [p]Hananiah, [p]Mishael, and [p]Azariah
of the tribe of Judah. 7 And [e]the chief of the
eunuchs [q]gave them names: [r]Daniel he called
Belteshazzar, Hananiah he called Shadrach,
Mishael he called Meshach, and Azariah he
called Abednego.

Daniel's Faithfulness

8 But Daniel [s]resolved that he would not
[t]defile himself with [k]the king's food, or with
[l]the wine that he drank. Therefore he asked
the chief of the eunuchs to allow him not to
[t]defile himself. 9 [u]And God gave Daniel favor
and compassion in the sight of the chief of
the eunuchs, 10 and the chief of the eunuchs
said to Daniel, "I fear my lord the king, who
assigned your food and your drink; for why

[1] Hebrew *of the seed of the kingdom*

1:1–3 The opening words of Daniel remind us that God is faithful to his word and to his people. In Leviticus 26:33, 39, the Lord warned his people that faithlessness would result in exile. Now, after a lengthy history of disobedience, Nebuchadnezzar is the instrument of God's discipline. The discipline includes the details that the "vessels of the house of God" and members of the "royal family" (Dan. 1:2–3) were taken from Jerusalem in accord with previous prophecies from Isaiah (2 Kings 20:12–19; Isaiah 39) that came in response to King Hezekiah's arrogant display of Israel's treasures to Babylonian representatives.

The discipline shows God's faithfulness to his people in three ways. First, the discipline turns Israel from spiritually destructive disobedience to renewed blessing according to God's long-term plan. Second, the warning of discipline indicates a divine heart that takes no delight in his people's suffering. If God did not care, he would not warn. Third, the discipline itself demonstrates God's persevering love—because he is faithful to his covenant with his people, God does not destroy them but maintains a remnant (that includes the royal line of David) in exile, through whom the Messiah will eventually come.

1:8–16 Daniel acts faithfully, but God provides the protection and provision necessary for such righteousness. "God gave" the young man favor from the chief of the eunuchs (vv. 9–10). God also gives better health to the four young men who do not eat the better food. God is working prior to, through, and beyond Daniel's own resolve to act righteously. Such care reminds us to act righteously and let God take care of the rest that is needed for his purposes to be fulfilled.

Chapter 1

1 [a]2 Kgs. 24:1, 2; 2 Chr. 36:6
2 [b]ch. 5:2; 2 Kgs. 24:13; 2 Chr. 36:7, 10; [Jer. 27:18] [c]Gen. 11:2; Zech. 5:11 [d]2 Chr. 36:7; Ezra 5:14
3 [e][2 Kgs. 20:18; Isa. 39:7] [f]Esth. 1:3
4 [g][Lev. 24:19, 20; 2 Sam. 14:25] [h][ver. 17; ch. 9:22] [i][Isa. 47:10] [j]ch. 2:2, 4, 5, 10; 3:8; 4:7; 5:7, 11
5 [k]ch. 11:26 [l]ver. 8, 16 [m][ver. 18] [n][ch. 2:2; 1 Kgs. 10:8]; See Gen. 41:46
6 [o]Ezek. 14:14, 20; Matt. 24:15 [p]ch. 2:17
7 [e][See ver. 3 above] [q][2 Kgs. 23:34; 24:17] [r]ch. 2:26; 4:8, 9, 18, 19; 5:12; 10:1
8 [s]2 Cor. 9:7 [t][Lev. 3:17; Ezek. 4:13; Hos. 9:3] [k][See ver. 5 above] [l][See ver. 5 above]
9 [u][Gen. 39:21; Ps. 106:46; Prov. 16:7]

should he see that you were in worse condition
than the youths who are of your own age? So
you would endanger my head with the king."
11 Then Daniel said to the steward whom the
chief of the eunuchs had assigned over Daniel,
Hananiah, Mishael, and Azariah, 12 "Test your
servants for [v]ten days; let us be given vegetables to eat and water to drink. 13 Then let
our appearance and the appearance of the
youths who eat [k]the king's food be observed
by you, and deal with your servants according
to what you see." 14 So he listened to them in
this matter, and tested them for ten days. 15 At
the end of ten days it was seen that they were
better in appearance and fatter in flesh than
all the youths who ate [k]the king's food. 16 [w]So
the steward took away their food and the wine
they were to drink, and gave them [x]vegetables.
17 As for these four youths, [y]God gave them
learning and [z]skill in all literature and wisdom, and Daniel had [a]understanding in all
visions and dreams. 18 At the end of [b]the time,
when the king had commanded that they
should be brought in, the chief of the eunuchs
brought them in before Nebuchadnezzar.
19 And the king spoke with them, and among
all of them none was found like Daniel,
Hananiah, Mishael, and Azariah. Therefore
[c]they stood before the king. 20 And in every
matter of wisdom and understanding about
which the king inquired of them, he found
them ten times better than all [d]the magicians
and [e]enchanters that were in all his kingdom.
21 And Daniel [f]was there until the first year of
[g]King Cyrus.

Nebuchadnezzar's Dream

2 In the second year of the reign of Nebuchadnezzar, Nebuchadnezzar had dreams;
[h]his spirit was troubled, and [i]his sleep left him.
2 Then the king commanded that [d]the magicians, [e]the enchanters, the [j]sorcerers, and [k]the
Chaldeans be summoned to tell the king his
dreams. So they came in and [l]stood before
the king. 3 And the king said to them, "I had
a dream, and [h]my spirit is troubled to know
the dream." 4 Then [k]the Chaldeans said to the
king in Aramaic,[1] [m]"O king, live forever! Tell
your servants the dream, and we will show the
interpretation." 5 The king answered and said
to [k]the Chaldeans, "The word from me is firm:
if you do not make known to me the dream
and its interpretation, you shall be [n]torn limb
from limb, [n]and your [o]houses shall be laid in
ruins. 6 But if you show the dream and its
interpretation, [p]you shall receive from me gifts
and rewards and great honor. [q]Therefore show
me the dream and its interpretation." 7 They
answered a second time and said, "Let the
king tell his servants the dream, and we will
show its interpretation." 8 The king answered
and said, "I know with certainty that you are
trying to [r]gain time, because you see that the
word from me is firm— 9 if you do not make
the dream known to me, [s]there is but one
sentence for you. You have agreed to speak
lying and corrupt words before me till [t]the
times change. [u]Therefore tell me the dream,
and I shall know that you can show me its
interpretation." 10 [v]The Chaldeans answered
the king and said, "There is not a man on earth
who can meet the king's demand, for no great
and powerful king has asked such a thing of
any magician or enchanter or [v]Chaldean. 11 The
thing that the king asks is difficult, and no
one can show it to the king except [w]the gods,
whose dwelling is not with flesh."
12 Because of this the king was angry and
[x]very furious, and [y]commanded that all [z]the
wise men of Babylon be destroyed. 13 So the

[1] The text from this point to the end of chapter 7 is in Aramaic

12[v] [Rev. 2:10]
13[k] [See ver. 5 above]
15[k] [See ver. 5 above]
16[w] ver. 11 [x] ver. 12
17[y] [ch. 2:20, 23; Job 32:8; James 1:5] [z] ver. 4 [a] ch. 5:12; [ch. 9:23; 10:1, 11, 12]
18[b] [ver. 5]
19[c] ch. 2:2
20[d] [ch. 2:27; Gen. 41:8, 24; Ex. 7:11, 22; 8:7, 18, 19; 9:11] [e] ch. 2:2, 10, 27; 4:7; 5:7, 11, 15
21[f] [ch. 6:28; 10:1] [g] See ch. 6:28
Chapter 2
1[h] [ch. 4:5; 5:9; Gen. 41:8] [i] [ch. 6:18; Esth. 6:1] **2**[d] [See ch. 1:20 above] [e] [See ch. 1:20 above] [j] Deut. 18:10, 11; 2 Chr. 33:6; Isa. 47:9, 12 [k] See ch. 1:4 [l] See ch. 1:5 **3**[h] [See ver. 1 above] **4**[k] [See ver. 2 above] [m] ch. 3:9; 5:10; 6:6, 21; See 1 Kgs. 1:31 **5**[k] [See ver. 2 above] [n] ch. 3:29 [o] Ezra 6:11; [2 Kgs. 10:27] **6**[p] [ch. 5:7, 16] [q] [ver. 7, 9] **8**[r] Eph. 5:16; Col. 4:5 **9**[s] Esth. 4:11 [t] [ver. 21; ch. 7:25] [u] ver. 6; [ver. 7] **10**[v] See ch. 1:4 **11**[w] [ch. 5:11, 14] **12**[x] [ch. 3:19] [y] [ver. 24] [z] ch. 4:6

1:17–21 God supernaturally preserved Daniel and his friends, and then "God gave" supernatural insight into present and future events (v. 17). Though Daniel and his people are helpless before the earthly and spiritual powers holding them captive, God is working powerfully to provide them hope in that age and in the ages to come. The final words of the chapter mention King Cyrus, the future ruler who will allow Daniel's people to return to Israel (v. 21; cf. 2 Chron. 36:22–23; Ezra 1:1–3).

God's faithfulness through the ages and his promises *for* the ages to come give us abundant hope to act faithfully in present difficulties.

2:1–16 The inability of Nebuchadnezzar's wise men to provide the content and interpretation of his dream reminds us of the limitations of even the greatest human wisdom.

decree went out, and the wise men were
about to be killed; and they sought [a]Daniel
and his companions, to kill them. 14 Then
Daniel replied with prudence and discretion
to [b]Arioch, the [c]captain of the king's guard,
who had gone out to kill the wise men of
Babylon. 15 He declared[1] to Arioch, the king's
captain, "Why is the decree of the king [d]so
urgent?" Then Arioch made the matter known
to Daniel. 16 And Daniel went in and requested
the king to appoint him a time, that he might
show the interpretation to the king.

God Reveals Nebuchadnezzar's Dream

17 Then Daniel went to his house and made
the matter known to [e]Hananiah, [e]Mishael, and
[e]Azariah, his companions, 18 [f]and told them
to seek mercy from the [g]God of heaven concerning this mystery, so that Daniel and his
companions might not [h]be destroyed with the
rest of the wise men of Babylon. 19 Then the
mystery was revealed to Daniel in [i]a vision of
the night. Then Daniel [j]blessed the [g]God of
heaven. 20 Daniel answered and said:

[k]"Blessed be the name of God forever and
ever,
[l]to whom belong wisdom and might.
21 [m]He changes times and seasons;
[n]he removes kings and sets up kings;
[o]he gives wisdom to the wise
[o]and knowledge to those who have
understanding;
22 [p]he reveals deep and hidden things;
[p]he knows what is in the darkness,
[q]and the light dwells with him.
23 To you, O [r]God of my fathers,
[s]I give thanks and praise,
for [t]you have given me wisdom and
might,
and have now made known to me
what [u]we asked of you,
for you have made known to us the
king's matter."

24 Therefore Daniel went in to [v]Arioch, whom
the king had appointed to destroy the wise
men of Babylon. He went and said thus to
him: "Do not destroy the wise men of Babylon;
bring me in before the king, and I will show
the king the interpretation."

25 Then [v]Arioch brought in Daniel before the
king [w]in haste and said thus to him: "I have
found [x]among the exiles from Judah a man
who will make known to the king the interpretation." 26 The king declared to Daniel,
[y]whose name was Belteshazzar, [z]"Are you
able to make known to me the dream that
I have seen and its interpretation?" 27 Daniel
answered the king and said, "No wise men,
[a]enchanters, [a]magicians, or [b]astrologers can
show to the king the mystery that the king
has asked, 28 but [c]there is a God in heaven who
reveals mysteries, and he has made known to
King Nebuchadnezzar [d]what will be in the
latter days. Your dream and [e]the visions of
your head as you lay in bed are these: 29 To
you, O king, as you lay in bed came thoughts
of what would be after this, [f]and he who
reveals mysteries made known to you what
is to be. 30 But [g]as for me, this mystery has
been revealed to me, not because of any wisdom that I have more than all the living, but
in order that the interpretation may be made
known to the king, and that [h]you may know
the thoughts of your mind.

[1] Aramaic *answered and said*; also verse 26

2:17–30 Daniel does two things that demonstrate his dependence on God's gracious provision: (1) he urges that God be sought for needed answers (vv. 17–18), and (2) he gives God credit—in private and in public—for the revelation of the king's dream (vv. 20–23, 27–28).

2:31–45 The superiority of Daniel's God over the pagan deities is evident not only in the revelation of the dream but also in the revelation that Daniel's God will be the final and eternal victor over the successive kingdoms of humanity (vv. 44–45).

This vision coheres with the gospel promises that Christ will ultimately reign over all (2 Sam. 7:11–16; Isa. 9:7; Luke 1:32–33; Eph. 1:20–23). This kingdom reign of Jesus dawned decisively in his first coming (Mark 1:15), and his full and uncontested reign will be perfectly completed at his second coming (Rev. 20:6). Faith in Christ's ultimate rule over matters present and future is the basis for our abiding peace and unshakable hope amid present trials.

13[a] See ch. 1:4-7
14[b] ver. 24, 25 [c][Gen. 37:36]
15[d] ch. 3:22
17[e] ch. 1:6
18[f][Matt. 18:19] [g] ver. 19, 28, 37, 44; Rev. 11:13 [h][ver. 12, 24]
19[i][Num. 12:6; Job 33:15, 16] [j] See Josh. 22:33 [g][See ver. 18 above]
20[k] 1 Chr. 29:10; Ps. 72:18; 113:2; 115:18; Luke 1:68 [l][Isa. 28:29]
21[m][ver. 9; ch. 7:25] [n][ch. 4:17; 5:20; Job 12:18; Ps. 75:7; Rom. 13:1] [o] See ch. 1:17
22[p] Job 12:22; [Ps. 25:14; 139:12; Amos 4:13; Heb. 4:13] [q] 1 Tim. 6:16; James 1:17; 1 John 1:5; [John 1:4, 5] **23**[r] Deut. 26:7; 1 Chr. 12:17; 29:18 [s][ch. 6:10] [t][ver. 20]; See ch. 1:17 [u][ver. 18] **24**[v] ver. 14, 15 **25**[v][See ver. 24 above] [w] ch. 3:24 [x] ch. 5:13; Ezra 4:1; 6:16, 19, 20; 10:7, 16 **26**[y] See ch. 1:7 [z][ch. 5:16] **27**[a] See ch. 1:20 [b] ch. 4:7; 5:7 **28**[c] See ver. 22 [d] ch. 10:14; Hos. 3:5 [e] ch. 4:5; 7:15 **29**[f] ver. 45 **30**[g][Gen. 41:16; Acts 3:12] [h][Eccles. 3:18]

Daniel Interprets the Dream

31 "You saw, O king, and behold, a great image. This image, mighty and of exceeding brightness, stood before you, and its appearance was frightening. 32 [i]The head of this image was of fine gold, [j]its chest and arms of silver, its middle and [j]thighs of bronze, 33 [k]its legs of iron, its feet partly of iron and partly of clay. 34 As you looked, a stone was cut out [l]by no human hand,[1] and it struck the image on its feet of iron and clay, and [m]broke them in pieces. 35 Then the iron, the clay, the bronze, the silver, and the gold, all together were broken in pieces, and became [n]like the chaff of the summer threshing floors; and the wind carried them away, so that [o]not a trace of them could be found. But the stone that struck the image became [p]a great mountain [q]and filled the whole earth.

36 "This was the dream. Now we will tell the king its interpretation. 37 You, O king, [r]the king of kings, to whom [s]the God of heaven [t]has given the kingdom, the power, and the might, and the glory, 38 and into whose hand he has given, wherever they dwell, the children of man, [u]the beasts of the field, and the birds of the heavens, making you rule over them all—you are [v]the head of gold. 39 [w]Another kingdom inferior to you shall arise after you, and yet a third kingdom [v]of bronze, [x]which shall rule over all the earth. 40 And [y]there shall be a fourth kingdom, strong as iron, because iron [z]breaks to pieces and shatters all things. And like iron that crushes, it shall [z]break and crush all these. 41 And as you saw [a]the feet and toes, partly of potter's clay and partly of iron, it shall be a divided kingdom, but some of the [y]firmness of iron shall be in it, just as you saw iron mixed with the soft clay. 42 And as the toes of the feet were partly iron and partly clay, so the kingdom shall be partly strong and partly brittle. 43 As you saw the iron mixed with soft clay, so they will mix with one another in marriage,[1] but they will not hold together, just as iron does not mix with clay. 44 And in the days of those kings [b]the God of heaven will set up [c]a kingdom that shall never be destroyed, nor shall the kingdom be left to another people. [d]It shall break in pieces all these kingdoms and bring them to an end, and [c]it shall stand forever, 45 just as [e]you saw that [f]a stone was cut from a mountain by no human hand, and that [d]it broke in pieces the iron, the bronze, the clay, the silver, and the gold. A [g]great God has made known to the king what shall be after this. The dream is certain, and its interpretation sure."

Daniel Is Promoted

46 Then King Nebuchadnezzar [h]fell upon his face and [i]paid homage to Daniel, and commanded that [j]an offering and [k]incense be offered up to him. 47 The king answered and said to Daniel, "Truly, your [l]God is God of gods and [m]Lord of kings, and [n]a revealer of mysteries, for you have been able to reveal this mystery." 48 Then the king gave Daniel high honors and many great [o]gifts, and made him ruler over the whole [p]province of Babylon and [q]chief prefect over all the wise men of Babylon. 49 Daniel made a request of the king, and he [r]appointed [s]Shadrach, Meshach, and Abednego over the affairs of [p]the province of Babylon. But Daniel [t]remained at the king's court.

Nebuchadnezzar's Golden Image

3 King Nebuchadnezzar made an image of gold, whose height was sixty cubits[2] and its breadth six cubits. He set it up on [u]the plain of Dura, in [v]the province of Babylon. 2 Then King Nebuchadnezzar sent to gather [w]the satraps, the prefects, and [x]the governors, the counselors, the treasurers, the justices, the magistrates,

[1] Aramaic *by the seed of men* [2] A *cubit* was about 18 inches or 45 centimeters

32[i] [ver. 38] [j] [ver. 39]
33[k] [ver. 40]
34[l] [ch. 8:25; Job 34:20; Lam. 4:6; 2 Cor. 5:1] [m] ver. 35, 40, 44, 45; Isa. 8:9; [Matt. 21:44; Luke 20:18]
35[n] Ps. 1:4 [o] [Rev. 20:11] [p] [Isa. 2:2] [q] [Ps. 80:9]
37[r] Ezra 7:12; Ezek. 26:7 [s] ver. 19 [t] ch. 5:18; [Ezra 1:2]; See ver. 21
38[u] ch. 4:21; Jer. 27:6 [v] [ver. 32]

2:46–49 The superiority of Daniel's God is shown to the people of his time by the fact that their most powerful king pays homage both to God's representatives (vv. 46, 48–49) and to God himself (v. 49).

3:1–15 Daniel puts his friends, Shadrach, Meshach, and Abednego, in the spotlight to indicate that God is able to deliver all who trust in him from the powers of evil. This is supremely true for those who have been united by faith to Christ, who delivers his people from the ultimate powers of evil (Col. 2:15) and works all things together for good even now (Rom. 8:28).

39[w] [ver. 32; ch. 5:28, 31] [v] [See ver. 38 above] [x] [ch. 7:6] **40**[y] [ch. 7:7, 23] [z] See ver. 34 **41**[a] [ver. 33] [y] [See ver. 40 above] **44**[b] ver. 19 [c] ch. 4:3, 34; 6:26; 7:14, 27; Mic. 4:7; [Matt. 3:2; Luke 1:33; John 18:36] [d] [Isa. 60:12]; See ver. 34 **45**[e] [ver. 34] [f] [Isa. 28:16] [d] [See ver. 44 above] [g] ver. 28 **46**[h] [2 Sam. 14:22] [i] [Matt. 8:2; Acts 10:25] [j] [Acts 14:13] [k] [Ezra 6:10] **47**[l] Deut. 10:17 [m] [1 Tim. 6:15; Rev. 17:14; 19:16] [n] See ver. 22 **48**[o] [ver. 6] [p] ch. 3:1, 12, 30; [Esth. 1:1] [q] ch. 5:11; [ch. 4:9] **49**[r] ch. 3:12 [s] [ch. 1:7] [p] [See ver. 48 above] [t] Esth. 2:19 **Chapter 3** **1**[u] [Gen. 11:2] [v] ver. 12, 30; ch. 2:48, 49 **2**[w] ver. 27; ch. 6:1, 2, 3, 4, 6, 7; [Ezra 8:36] [x] ch. 2:48

and all the officials of the provinces to come to
the dedication of the image that King Nebuchadnezzar had set up. 3 Then [w]the satraps, the
prefects, and the governors, the counselors, the
treasurers, the justices, the magistrates, and all
the officials of the provinces gathered for the
dedication of the image that King Nebuchadnezzar had set up. And they stood before the
image that Nebuchadnezzar had set up. 4 And
the herald [y]proclaimed aloud, "You are commanded, O [z]peoples, nations, and languages,
5 that when you hear the [a]sound of the horn,
pipe, lyre, trigon, harp, bagpipe, and every kind
of music, you [b]are to fall down and worship the
golden image that King Nebuchadnezzar has
set up. 6 And whoever does not fall down and
worship shall immediately [c]be cast into a burning fiery furnace." 7 Therefore, as soon as all the
peoples heard the sound of the horn, pipe, lyre,
trigon, harp, bagpipe, and every kind of music,
all [z]the peoples, nations, and languages fell
down and worshiped the golden image that
King Nebuchadnezzar had set up.

The Fiery Furnace

8 Therefore at that time certain [d]Chaldeans
[e]came forward and maliciously accused the
Jews. 9 They declared[1] to King Nebuchadnezzar,
"O king, live forever! 10 You, O king, [f]have
made a decree, that every man who [g]hears
the sound of the horn, pipe, lyre, trigon, harp,
bagpipe, and every kind of music, [g]shall fall
down and worship the golden image. 11 And
whoever does not fall down and worship [c]shall
be cast into a burning fiery furnace. 12 There
are certain Jews whom you have [h]appointed
over the affairs of [v]the province of Babylon:
[i]Shadrach, Meshach, and Abednego. These
men, O king, [j]pay no attention to you; they
do not serve your gods or worship the golden
image that you have set up."

13 Then Nebuchadnezzar [k]in furious rage
commanded that [i]Shadrach, Meshach, and
Abednego be brought. So they brought these
men before the king. 14 Nebuchadnezzar
answered and said to them, "Is it true,
O Shadrach, Meshach, and Abednego, that
you do not serve my gods or worship the
golden image that I have set up? 15 Now if you
are ready when [l]you hear the sound of the
horn, pipe, lyre, trigon, harp, bagpipe, and
every kind of music, to fall down and worship
the image that I have made, well and good.[2]
But if you do not worship, [c]you shall immediately be cast into a burning fiery furnace.
And [m]who is the god who will deliver you out
of my hands?"

16 [i]Shadrach, Meshach, and Abednego
answered and said to the king, "O Nebuchadnezzar, we have no need to answer you
in this matter. 17 If this be so, [n]our God whom
we serve is able to deliver us from the burning fiery furnace, and he will deliver us out of
your hand, O king.[3] 18 But if not, be it known to
you, O king, that we will not serve your gods
or worship the golden image that you have
set up."

19 Then Nebuchadnezzar was [o]filled with
fury, and the expression of his face [p]was
changed against [i]Shadrach, Meshach, and
Abednego. He ordered the furnace heated
seven times more than it was usually heated.
20 And he ordered some of the mighty men
of his army [q]to bind [i]Shadrach, Meshach, and
Abednego, and to cast them into the burning
fiery furnace. 21 Then these men were [q]bound
in their cloaks, their tunics,[4] their hats, and
their other garments, and they were thrown
into the burning fiery furnace. 22 Because
the king's order was [r]urgent and the furnace
overheated, the flame of the fire killed those
men who took up [s]Shadrach, Meshach, and

[1] Aramaic *answered and said*; also verses 24, 26 [2] Aramaic lacks *well and good* [3] Or *If our God whom we serve is able to deliver us, he will deliver us from the burning fiery furnace and out of your hand, O king.* [4] The meaning of the Aramaic words rendered *cloaks* and *tunics* is uncertain; also verse 27

3:16–18 The three young men acknowledge that God is *able* to deliver them, regardless of what the king threatens. "But if not . . ." (v. 18) indicates a willingness to bow before God's sovereign wisdom and will. Whether God delivers them from the king's present threats or ushers them into eternal bliss in heaven, the young men will not serve the false idols of Nebuchadnezzar. They do not demand that God deliver them in the way that they think is best but trust that he will deliver as he knows is best. God's deliverance may come in this life or in the life to come, but his grace is always operating to provide what is best for our eternal good.

3[w] [See ver. 2 above]
4[y] ch. 4:14; 5:7; [Rev. 18:2] [z] ver. 29; ch. 4:1; 5:19; 6:25; 7:14; [Rev. 5:9]
5[a] ver. 7, 10, 15 [b] [ch. 2:46]
6[c] [Jer. 29:22; Ezek. 23:25]
7[z] [See ver. 4 above]
8[d] See ch. 1:4 [e] ch. 6:12
10[f] ver. 29; ch. 4:6; 6:26 [g] ver. 5, 7, 15
11[c] [See ver. 6 above]

12[h] ch. 2:49 [v] [See ver. 1 above] [i] [ch. 1:7] [j] ch. 6:13 **13**[k] ch. 2:12 [i] [See ver. 12 above] **15**[l] ver. 5, 7, 10 [c] [See ver. 6 above] [m] [ch. 6:20; Ex. 5:2; 2 Kgs. 18:35] **16**[i] [See ver. 12 above] **17**[n] [ver. 15] **19**[o] [ver. 13; Esth. 7:7] [p] [ch. 2:49] [i] [See ver. 12 above] **20**[q] [ver. 24, 25] [i] [See ver. 12 above] **21**[q] [See ver. 20 above] **22**[r] ch. 2:15 [s] [ch. 1:7]

Abednego. 23 And these three men, Shadrach, Meshach, and Abednego, fell [q]bound into the burning fiery furnace.

24 Then King Nebuchadnezzar was [t]astonished and rose up [u]in haste. He declared to his [v]counselors, "Did we not cast three men [w]bound into the fire?" They answered and said to the king, "True, O king." 25 He answered and said, "But I see four men unbound, [x]walking in the midst of the fire, and they [y]are not hurt; and the appearance of the fourth is like [z]a son of the gods."

26 Then Nebuchadnezzar came near to the door of the burning fiery furnace; he declared, [s]"Shadrach, Meshach, and Abednego, servants of the [a]Most High God, come out, and come here!" Then [s]Shadrach, Meshach, and Abednego came out from the fire. 27 And the [b]satraps, the prefects, the governors, and [v]the king's counselors gathered together and saw that [c]the fire had not had any power over the bodies of those men. The hair of their heads was not singed, their [d]cloaks were not harmed, and no smell of fire had come upon them. 28 Nebuchadnezzar answered and said, "Blessed be the God of [s]Shadrach, Meshach, and Abednego, who [e]has sent his angel and [f]delivered his servants, who [g]trusted in him, and set aside[1] the king's command, and yielded up their bodies rather than [h]serve and worship any god except their own God. 29 Therefore [i]I make a decree: Any [j]people, nation, or language that speaks anything against the God of [s]Shadrach, Meshach, and Abednego [k]shall be torn limb from limb, and their houses laid in ruins, for there is no other god who is able to rescue in this way." 30 Then the king promoted [s]Shadrach, Meshach, and Abednego in [l]the province of Babylon.

Nebuchadnezzar Praises God

4 [2] King Nebuchadnezzar to all [m]peoples, nations, and languages, [n]that dwell in all the earth: [o]Peace be multiplied to you! 2 It has seemed good to me to show the [p]signs and wonders that the [q]Most High God has done for me.

3 How great are [p]his signs,
how mighty his [p]wonders!
[r]His kingdom is an everlasting kingdom,
[r]and his dominion endures from generation to generation.

Nebuchadnezzar's Second Dream

4 [3] I, Nebuchadnezzar, was at ease in my house and prospering in my palace. 5 I saw a dream that made me afraid. As I lay in bed the fancies and [s]the visions of my head alarmed me. 6 So [t]I made a decree that [u]all the wise men of Babylon should be brought before me, that they might make known to me the interpretation of the dream. 7 Then [v]the magicians, the

[1] Aramaic *and changed* [2] Ch 3:31 in Aramaic [3] Ch 4:1 in Aramaic

23[q] [See ver. 20 above]
24[t] ch. 4:19 [u] ch. 2:25 [v] ch. 4:36; 6:7 [w] ver. 20, 21, 23
25[x] [Isa. 43:2] [y] [ch. 6:23] [z] [ver. 28; Job 1:6]
26[s] [See ver. 22 above] [a] ch. 4:2; 5:18, 21
27[b] ver. 2 [v] [See ver. 24 above] [c] [Heb. 11:34] [d] ver. 21
28[s] [See ver. 22 above] [e] ch. 6:22 [f] [ver. 15, 17; Ps. 34:7] [g] [Ps. 25:2] [h] [Ex. 20:3]
29[i] See ver. 10 [j] See ver. 4 [s] [See ver. 22 above] [k] ch. 2:5
30[s] [See ver. 22 above] [l] ver. 1, 12; ch. 2:48, 49

Chapter 4
1[m] See ch. 3:4 [n] ch. 6:25 [o] 1 Pet. 1:2; 2 Pet. 1:2
2[p] ch. 6:27; [John 4:48] [q] ch. 3:26
3[p] [See ver. 2 above] [r] See ch. 2:44
5[s] ch. 2:28; 7:15
6[t] See ch. 3:10 [u] ch. 2:12
7[v] See ch. 2:2

3:25 The presence in the furnace of one who "is like a son of the gods" may be a Christophany (i.e., an Old Testament appearance of Christ), but it is unquestionably an indication of the presence of a heavenly emissary from God. Such a presence reminds us of the saving nature of God, who will ultimately appear as Immanuel ("God with us") in the person of Jesus Christ (Isa. 7:14; Matt. 1:23). Then as now, Christ often meets his people most profoundly in the "furnace experiences" of life.

3:26–30 As he previously did with Daniel (see 2:46–49), Nebuchadnezzar gives homage and promotion to God's representatives and to God himself (3:26, 28–29). The absence of any singeing or smell of smoke indicates how thorough was God's protection and deliverance of his people. Sadly, Nebuchadnezzar does not yet acknowledge this God as his own; he only honors "the God of Shadrach, Meshach, and Abednego" (vv. 28–29). The words remind us of the importance of trusting Christ personally, not just acknowledging him as a religious icon or concept that others accept.

4:1–3 At the end of chapter 3, Nebuchadnezzar praises the God of Shadrach, Meshach, and Abednego but does not honor their God as his own. As chapter 4 begins, Nebuchadnezzar honors God for what "the Most High God has done for me" (4:2). The rest of the chapter explains why.

4:4–18 Nebuchadnezzar again turns to Daniel, believing the Israelite prophet's insight is superior to that of the wise men who serve the Babylonian gods. At this point, however, Nebuchadnezzar still speaks of the Babylonian deity as "my god" (v. 8); this king has not yet acknowledged the King.

enchanters, the Chaldeans, and the astrologers
came in, and I told them the dream, but [w]they
could not make known to me its interpretation. 8 At last Daniel came in before me—he
who was named [x]Belteshazzar after the name
of my god, and in whom is [y]the spirit of the
holy gods[1]—and I told him the dream, saying, 9 "O Belteshazzar, [z]chief of the magicians,
because I know that [y]the spirit of the holy gods
is in you and that no [a]mystery is too difficult
for you, tell me [s]the visions of my dream that
I saw and their interpretation. 10 [s]The visions
of my head as I lay in bed were these: I saw, and
[b]behold, a tree in the midst of the earth, and its
height was great. 11 [c]The tree grew and became
strong, and its top reached to heaven, and it
was visible to the end of the whole earth. 12 [d]Its
leaves were beautiful and its fruit abundant,
and in it was food for all. [e]The beasts of the
field found shade under it, and [e]the birds of
the heavens lived in its branches, and all flesh
was fed from it.

13 "I saw in [s]the visions of my head as I lay in
bed, and behold, [f]a watcher, [g]a holy one, came
down from heaven. 14 He [h]proclaimed aloud
and said thus: [i]'Chop down the tree and [j]lop
off its branches, [j]strip off its leaves and scatter
its fruit. [j]Let the beasts flee from under it and
the birds from its branches. 15 But leave the
stump of its roots in the earth, bound with
a band of iron and bronze, amid the tender
grass of the field. Let him be wet with the dew
of heaven. Let his portion be with the beasts
in the grass of the earth. 16 Let his mind be
changed from a man's, and let a beast's mind
be given to him; [k]and let seven periods of
time [l]pass over him. 17 The sentence is by the
decree of [f]the watchers, the decision by the
word of [g]the holy ones, to the end that the living may know that the Most High [m]rules the
kingdom of men [n]and gives it to whom he will
and [o]sets over it the lowliest of men.' 18 This
dream I, King Nebuchadnezzar, saw. And you,
O [p]Belteshazzar, tell me the interpretation,
because [q]all the wise men of my kingdom are
not able to make known to me the interpretation, but you are able, for [r]the spirit of the holy
gods is in you."

Daniel Interprets the Second Dream

19 Then Daniel, whose name was [p]Belte-
shazzar, was [s]dismayed for a while, and [t]his
thoughts alarmed him. The king answered
and said, "Belteshazzar, let not the dream or
the interpretation alarm you." Belteshazzar
answered and said, "My lord, [u]may the dream
be for those who hate you [u]and its interpretation for your enemies! 20 [v]The tree you saw,
which grew and became strong, so that its top
reached to heaven, and it was visible to the end
of the whole earth, 21 [w]whose leaves were beautiful and its fruit abundant, and in which was
food for all, under which beasts of the field
found shade, and in whose branches the birds
of the heavens lived— 22 [x]it is you, O king, who
have grown and become strong. [y]Your greatness has grown and reaches to heaven, [y]and
your dominion to the ends of the earth. 23 And
because the king saw [z]a watcher, a holy one,
coming down from heaven and saying, [a]'Chop
down the tree and destroy it, but leave the
stump of its roots in the earth, bound with a
band of iron and bronze, in the tender grass
of the field, and let him be wet with the dew
of heaven, and let his portion be with the
beasts of the field, till [b]seven periods of time
pass over him,' 24 this is the interpretation,
O king: It is a decree of the Most High, which
has come upon my lord the king, 25 [c]that you
shall be driven from among men, and your
dwelling shall be with the beasts of the field.
You shall be made [d]to eat grass like an ox,
and you shall be wet with the dew of heaven,

[1] Or *Spirit of the holy God*; also verses 9, 18

4:19–27 Daniel interprets the dream as a prediction of a great fall for the proud Nebuchadnezzar. Yet, in his grace, God provides opportunity for repentance and shows his heart of mercy by calling upon Nebuchadnezzar to show the same (v. 27). God's justice is not at odds with his delight to show mercy to those who will receive it. At the cross of Christ, we see this divine justice and mercy beautifully meet.

Jesus picks up the image of a giant tree whose branches provide shade for the birds of the air (v. 21) to speak of the kingdom of God (Mark 4:30–32). This kingdom displays not the proud military might of Nebuchadnezzar but the characteristics of its King, Jesus Christ, who is caring, humble, and invincible!

7 [w] [ver. 18; ch. 2:27; 5:8, 15]
8 [x] See ch. 1:7 [y] ver. 18; ch. 2:11; 5:11; Gen. 41:38; [Isa. 63:14]
9 [z] ch. 5:11; [ch. 2:48] [y] [See ver. 8 above] [a] ch. 2:18 [s] [See ver. 5 above]
10 [s] [See ver. 5 above] [b] [Ezek. 31:3]
11 [c] [Ps. 37:35]
12 [d] Ezek. 31:7 [e] Ezek. 31:6
13 [s] [See ver. 5 above] [f] ver. 23 [g] [Deut. 33:2; Zech. 14:5; Jude 14]

14 [h] See ch. 3:4 [i] ver. 23; [Matt. 3:10; Luke 3:9] [j] [Ezek. 31:12] **16** [k] [ver. 23, 25] [l] [1 Chr. 29:30] **17** [f] [See ver. 13 above] [g] [See ver. 13 above] [m] ver. 25, 32; ch. 5:21 [n] Jer. 27:5 [o] See 1 Sam. 2:8 **18** [p] See ch. 1:7 [q] [ver. 7; ch. 5:8, 15; Gen. 41:8] [r] See ver. 8 **19** [p] [See ver. 18 above] [s] ch. 3:24 [t] ch. 5:6 [u] [1 Sam. 25:26; 2 Sam. 18:32] **20** [v] [ver. 10, 11] **21** [w] [ver. 12] **22** [x] [Ezek. 31:3] [y] See Jer. 27:6-8 **23** [z] ver. 13 [a] ver. 14, 15 [b] ver. 16 **25** [c] ver. 32, 33; [ch. 5:21] [d] [Ps. 106:20]

and [b]seven periods of time shall pass over
you, till [e]you know that the Most High rules
the kingdom of men and gives it to whom
he will. 26 And as it was commanded [f]to leave
the stump of the roots of the tree, your kingdom shall be confirmed for you from the time
that you know that Heaven rules. 27 Therefore,
O king, let my counsel be acceptable to you:
break off your sins by [g]practicing righteousness, [h]and your iniquities by showing mercy
to the oppressed, [i]that there may perhaps be
a lengthening of your prosperity."

Nebuchadnezzar's Humiliation

28 All this came upon King Nebuchadnezzar.
29 At the end of twelve months he was
walking on the roof of the royal palace of
Babylon, 30 and the king answered and said,
[j]"Is not this great Babylon, which I have
built by [k]my mighty power as a royal residence and for [k]the glory of my majesty?"
31 [l]While the words were still in the king's
mouth, there fell a voice from heaven, "O
King Nebuchadnezzar, to you it is spoken:
The kingdom has departed from you, 32 [m]and
you shall be driven from among men, and
your dwelling shall be with the beasts of the
field. And you shall be made to eat grass like
an ox, and seven periods of time shall pass
over you, [m]until you know that the Most
High rules the kingdom of men and gives it
to whom he will." 33 Immediately the word
was fulfilled against Nebuchadnezzar. [m]He
was driven from among men and ate grass
like an ox, and his body was wet with the dew
of heaven till his hair grew as long as eagles'
feathers, and his nails were like birds' claws.

Nebuchadnezzar Restored

34 [n]At the end of the days I, Nebuchadnezzar,
lifted my eyes to heaven, and [o]my reason
returned to me, and I blessed the Most High,
and praised and honored [p]him who lives
forever,

[q]for his dominion is an everlasting
dominion,
and [q]his kingdom endures from generation to generation;
35 [r]all the inhabitants of the earth are
accounted as nothing,
and [s]he does according to his will
among the host of heaven
and among the inhabitants of the
earth;
[t]and none can stay his hand
or [u]say to him, "What have you
done?"

36 At the same time [v]my reason returned to
me, and for [w]the glory of my kingdom, [w]my
majesty and splendor returned to me. [x]My
counselors and [y]my lords sought me, and
I was established in my kingdom, and still
more greatness was [z]added to me. 37 Now I,
Nebuchadnezzar, [a]praise and extol and honor
the [b]King of heaven, [c]for all his works are right
and his ways are just; and [d]those who walk in
pride he is able to humble.

The Handwriting on the Wall

5 [e]King Belshazzar [f]made a great feast for a
thousand of his [g]lords and drank wine in
front of the thousand.
2 [e]Belshazzar, when he tasted the wine, commanded that [h]the vessels of gold and of silver

25[b] [See ver. 23 above] [e]ver. 17, 32
26[f] ver. 15, 23
27[g] Matt. 6:1 [h]Prov. 16:6; [Matt. 25:35, 36; Luke 11:41] [i][Jer. 18:8; Jonah 3:10; Acts 8:22; 2 Tim. 2:25]
30[j] [ch. 5:20] [k][ver. 36; ch. 2:37]
31[l] [ch. 5:5; Luke 12:20]
32[m] ver. 17, 25; ch. 5:21
33[m] [See ver. 32 above]
34[n] [ver. 26] [o]ver. 36 [p]ch. 6:26; 12:7; Rev. 4:10 [q][Ps. 10:16]; See ch. 2:44
35[r] Isa. 40:17 [s][Ps. 115:3; Heb. 1:13, 14] [t][Isa. 14:27] [u]Job 9:12; [Isa. 45:9; Rom. 9:20]
36[v] ver. 34 [w][ver. 30; ch. 5:18] [x]ch. 3:24; 6:7 [y]ch. 5:1; 6:17 [z][Job 42:12; Matt. 6:33]
37[a] ver. 34 [b][ch. 5:23] [c][Deut. 32:4; Ps. 33:4; Rev. 15:3] [d][ch. 5:20; Prov. 20:23]

4:28–33 A year passes from the time of Daniel's interpretation, providing opportunity for Nebuchadnezzar's repentance (v. 29). Instead, as he looks down upon his kingdom, the king's pride puffs him up (v. 30) and, at the zenith of his pride, God humbles him (vv. 31–33).

4:34 In his state of abject humiliation, Nebuchadnezzar lifts his eyes to heaven and is restored by God. As long as he looks down on others, God is distant; but when Nebuchadnezzar looks up in desperation, God provides his grace. The words remind us not only that "God opposes the proud, but gives grace to the humble" (James 4:6), but also that there are none so evil or so destitute that the grace of God cannot reach them (Dan. 4:37).

4:34–37 Daniel testified of his Lord for 40 years before Nebuchadnezzar finally claimed the true God as his own. Accordingly, we should not give up on God's grace regardless of the degree or duration of spiritual failure in others—or in ourselves.

5:1–3 In the previous chapter, Daniel used King Nebuchadnezzar's confession to affirm that the repentant can know God's grace however bleak their pasts. In this chapter,

Chapter 5 1[e] ver. 22, 29, 30; ch. 7:1; 8:1 [f]See Esth. 1:3 [g]ch. 4:36; 6:17 2[e] [See ver. 1 above] [h]ver. 23; See ch. 1:2

that Nebuchadnezzar his father[1] had taken
out of the temple in Jerusalem be brought,
that the king and his lords, his wives, and his
concubines might drink from them. 3 Then
they brought in [h]the golden vessels that had
been taken out of the temple, the house of
God in Jerusalem, and the king and his lords,
his wives, and his concubines drank from
them. 4 They drank wine and [i]praised the
[j]gods of gold and silver, bronze, iron, wood,
and stone.

5 [k]Immediately [l]the fingers of a human
hand appeared and wrote on the plaster of
the wall of the king's palace, opposite the
lampstand. And the king saw [m]the hand as it
wrote. 6 [n]Then the king's color changed, [o]and
his thoughts alarmed him; [p]his limbs gave
way, and [q]his knees knocked together. 7 [r]The
king called loudly to bring in [r]the enchanters, the [s]Chaldeans, and [t]the astrologers. The
king declared[2] to the wise men of Babylon,
[u]"Whoever reads this writing, and shows
me its interpretation, shall be clothed with
purple and have a chain of gold around his
neck and [v]shall be the third ruler in the kingdom." 8 Then all the king's wise men came
in, but [w]they could not read the writing or
make known to the king the interpretation.
9 Then King Belshazzar was greatly [x]alarmed,
and his [n]color changed, and his [y]lords were
perplexed.

10 The queen,[3] because of the words of the
king and his lords, came into the banqueting hall, and the queen declared, [z]"O king,
live forever! Let not your thoughts alarm
you [a]or your color change. 11 There is a man
in your kingdom [b]in whom is the spirit of
the holy gods.[4] In the days of your father,
[c]light and understanding and wisdom like
the wisdom of the gods were found in him,
and King Nebuchadnezzar, your father—
your father the king—[d]made him chief of
the magicians, [r]enchanters, Chaldeans, and
astrologers, 12 [e]because an excellent spirit,
knowledge, and [f]understanding [f]to interpret
dreams, explain riddles, and [g]solve problems
were found in this Daniel, [h]whom the king
named Belteshazzar. Now let Daniel be called,
and he will show the interpretation."

Daniel Interprets the Handwriting

13 Then Daniel was brought in before the
king. The king answered and said to Daniel,
"You are that Daniel, one of [i]the exiles of
Judah, whom the king my father brought from
Judah. 14 I have heard of you that [b]the spirit of
the gods[5] is in you, and that [c]light and understanding and excellent wisdom are found in
you. 15 Now [j]the wise men, the [k]enchanters,
have been brought in before me to read this
writing and make known to me its interpretation, but [l]they could not show the interpretation of the matter. 16 [m]But I have heard that you
can give interpretations and [n]solve problems.
[o]Now if you can read the writing and make
known to me its interpretation, [o]you shall be
clothed with purple and have a chain of gold
around your neck and [p]shall be the third ruler
in the kingdom."

17 Then Daniel answered and said before the
king, [q]"Let your gifts be for yourself, and give
your rewards to another. Nevertheless, I will
read the writing to the king and make known

[1] Or *predecessor*; also verses 11, 13, 18 [2] Aramaic *answered and said*; also verse 10 [3] Or *queen mother*; twice in this verse [4] Or *Spirit of the holy God* [5] Or *Spirit of God*

Daniel uses King Belshazzar's sacrilege to warn that the rebellious will reap God's wrath however secure their present. Where is the grace in such warning? If God did not love, he would not warn. Though this account was written about a pagan king, it is written to turn the people of God from sin to him.

5:4 Belshazzar praised the gods of silver, gold, bronze, iron, and wood—gods of his own making (cf. v. 23)—and believed he was secure behind the man-made walls of his palace. He trusted the work of human hands to protect him from pain or harm. Modern people may trust money, reputation, power, sex, or escapism to protect them from this world's pain and trials, but these products of human effort are just as undependable as Belshazzar's idols.

5:5–17 Israel's God provides what no other god can. Thus, Daniel refuses gifts, making sure that God alone is honored for the interpretation (v. 17).

3 [h] [See ver. 2 above]
4 [i] ver. 23; [Judg. 16:24] [j] ver. 23; [Rev. 9:20]; See Ps. 115:4-7
5 [k] [ch. 4:31] [l] [Ezek. 8:3] [m] ver. 24
6 [n] [ver. 10; ch. 7:28] [o] [ch. 4:5, 19; 7:28] [p] [Ps. 69:23; Isa. 45:1] [q] Nah. 2:10
7 [r] [ch. 2:2; 4:6] [s] See ch. 1:4 [t] ch. 2:27 [u] ver. 16, 29; [ch. 2:6] [v] ver. 16, 29
8 [w] ver. 15; ch. 4:7, 18; [ch. 2:27; Gen. 41:8]
9 [x] [ch. 2:1] [n] [See ver. 6 above] [y] ver. 1
10 [z] See ch. 2:4 [a] [ver. 6, 9]
11 [b] See ch. 4:8 [c] [ch. 1:20] [d] ch. 4:9; [ch. 2:48] [r] [See ver. 7 above]
12 [e] ch. 6:3 [f] See ch. 1:17

[g] ver. 16 [h] See ch. 1:7 **13** [i] See ch. 2:25 **14** [b] [See ver. 11 above] [c] [See ver. 11 above] **15** [j] ver. 7 [k] [ch. 2:2; 4:6] [l] See ver. 8 **16** [m] [ch. 2:26] [n] ver. 12 [o] ver. 7, 29 [p] ver. 7, 29 **17** [q] [2 Kgs. 5:16]

to him the interpretation. 18 O king, the [r]Most
High God [s]gave [t]Nebuchadnezzar your father
[u]kingship and greatness and glory and majesty. 19 And because of the greatness that he
gave him, [v]all peoples, nations, and languages
[w]trembled and feared before him. Whom he
would, he killed, and whom he would, he
kept alive; whom he would, he raised up,
and whom he would, he humbled. 20 But
[x]when his heart was lifted up and his spirit
was hardened so that he dealt proudly, [y]he
was brought down from his kingly throne,
and his glory was taken from him. 21 [z]He was
driven from among the children of mankind,
and his mind was made like that of a beast,
and his dwelling was with the wild donkeys.
He was fed grass like an ox, and his body was
wet with the dew of heaven, [z]until he knew
that the [r]Most High God rules the kingdom
of mankind and sets over it whom he will.
22 And you his son,[1] [a]Belshazzar, [b]have not
humbled your heart, though you knew all
this, 23 but you have lifted up yourself against
[c]the Lord of heaven. And [d]the vessels of his
house have been brought in before you, and
you and your lords, your wives, and your
concubines have drunk wine from them.
[e]And you have praised the gods of silver and
gold, of bronze, iron, wood, and stone, which
do not see or hear or know, [f]but the God in
whose hand is your breath, and [g]whose are all
your ways, [h]you have not honored.
24 "Then from his presence [i]the hand was
sent, and this writing was inscribed. 25 And
this is the writing that was inscribed: MENE,
MENE, TEKEL, and PARSIN. 26 This is the interpretation of the matter: MENE, God has numbered[2] the days of your kingdom and brought
it to an end; 27 TEKEL, [j]you have been weighed[3]
in the balances and found wanting; 28 PERES,
your kingdom is divided and given to [k]the
Medes and [l]Persians."[4]
29 Then [a]Belshazzar gave the command, and
Daniel [m]was clothed with purple, a chain of
gold was put around his neck, and a proclamation was made about him, that he should be
the third ruler in the kingdom.
30 [n]That very night [a]Belshazzar the [o]Chaldean
king was killed. 31[5] And [p]Darius [k]the Mede
received the kingdom, being about sixty-two
years old.

Daniel and the Lions' Den

6 It pleased Darius to set over the kingdom
[q]120 [r]satraps, to be throughout the whole
kingdom; 2 and over them [s]three high offi-

[1] Or *successor* [2] *MENE* sounds like the Aramaic for *numbered* [3] *TEKEL* sounds like the Aramaic for *weighed* [4] *PERES* (the singular of *Parsin*) sounds like the Aramaic for *divided* and for *Persia* [5] Ch 6:1 in Aramaic

18[r] ch. 3:26; 4:2 [s] [ch. 2:37; 4:22] [t] ver. 2 [u] [ch. 4:36]
19[v] See ch. 3:4 [w] [ch. 6:26]
20[x] [ch. 4:30, 31; Ezek. 31:10, 11] [y] See ch. 2:21
21[z] [ch. 4:25, 32] [r] [See ver. 18 above]
22[a] See ver. 1 [b] [2 Chr. 33:23]
23[c] [ch. 4:37] [d] ver. 3; See ch. 1:2 [e] ver. 4 [f] Job 12:10 [g] Jer. 10:23 [h] [Acts 12:23; Rev. 16:9]
24[i] ver. 5
27[j] Job 31:6; Ps. 62:9
28[k] ver. 31; [ch. 9:1; Isa. 13:17; 21:2; Jer. 51:28] [l] See ch. 6:28
29[a] [See ver. 22 above] [m] [ver. 7, 16]
30[n] Jer. 50:24; 51:31, 39, 57 [a] [See ver. 22 above] [o] ch. 9:1
31[p] ch. 9:1 [k] [See ver. 28 above]
Chapter 6
1[q] [Esth. 1:1] [r] See ch. 3:2
2[s] [ch. 5:7, 16, 29]

5:18–23 Four times in chapter 5 the text reminds us that Nebuchadnezzar was the "father" of Belshazzar's rule. While the term signifies "predecessor" more than an actual father, its repeated appearance implies something more profound. Daniel repeatedly directs his audience's attention to the spiritual victory in Nebuchadnezzar's life in contrast to Belshazzar's subsequent surrender to wickedness. The message is that sin can re-infect a people, but the primary audience of this message is not Babylon; it is the people of God. God is pointedly warning Israel (and us) that sin results in judgment and that every generation must seek him anew.

5:24–28 Daniel interprets the writing as God's judgment against Belshazzar. If grace is amazing, then it must rescue us from something; and that something is defined in this passage by the words Mene, Tekel, and Peres. The unrepentant will be identified, weighed, and judged; but the repentant are saved by grace.

5:29–31 Belshazzar makes a vain declaration that Daniel will be a ruler over the kingdom that we learn will be lost that very night. Belshazzar also conspicuously fails to give one word of honor to God for the miraculous interpretation. Through these events the prophet says to every person, "Beware, because there is no idol so fulfilling, no fortress so secure, and no activity so hidden that it can protect sin from the judgment of God." All must seek the grace of God. In Christ, that grace is abundantly available.

6:1–3 A new king from another nation now sits on Babylon's throne. He also recognizes Daniel's talents and fulfills the fallen King Belshazzar's vain promise to promote Daniel. Daniel's distinguished service is also evidence that he heeded an earlier prophet's instruction to seek the welfare of the city of his captors (Jer. 29:7). We are to bring the righteousness, grace, and rule of our God to all dimensions of our lives. Paul writes, "So, whether you eat or drink, or whatever you do, do all to the glory of God" (1 Cor. 10:31).

cials, of whom Daniel was one, to whom these
[r]satraps should give account, so that the king
might suffer no loss. 3 Then this Daniel became
[t]distinguished above all [s]the other high officials and [r]satraps, because [u]an excellent spirit
was in him. And the king planned [v]to set him
over the whole kingdom. 4 Then [s]the high officials and [r]the satraps [w]sought to find a ground
for complaint against Daniel with regard to
the kingdom, [x]but they could find no ground
for complaint or any fault, because he was
faithful, [x]and no error or fault was found in
him. 5 Then these men said, "We shall not find
any ground for complaint against this Daniel
unless we find it in connection with the law
of his God."
6 Then these [s]high officials and [r]satraps came
by agreement[1] to the king and said to him,
"O [y]King Darius, live forever! 7 All the [s]high
officials of the kingdom, the prefects and the
satraps, the [z]counselors and the governors
are agreed that the king should establish an
ordinance and enforce an [a]injunction, that
whoever makes petition to any god or man for
thirty days, except to you, O king, shall be cast
into the den of lions. 8 Now, O king, establish
[a]the injunction and sign the document, so that
it cannot be changed, according to [b]the law of
[c]the Medes and the Persians, [d]which cannot be
revoked." 9 Therefore King Darius signed the
document and [a]injunction.
10 When Daniel knew that the document
had been signed, he went to his house where
[e]he had windows in his upper chamber open
[f]toward Jerusalem. He got down on his knees
[g]three times a day and prayed and [h]gave
thanks before his God, as he had done previously. 11 Then these men came by agreement
and found Daniel making petition and plea
before his God. 12 Then they [i]came near and
said before the king, concerning the injunction, "O king! Did you not sign [j]an injunction, that anyone who makes petition to any
god or man within thirty days except to you,
O king, shall be cast into the den of lions?" The
king answered and said, "The thing stands
fast, according to the law of [c]the Medes and
Persians, [d]which cannot be revoked." 13 Then
they answered and said before the king,
[k]"Daniel, who is one [l]of the exiles [k]from
Judah, [m]pays no attention to you, O king, or
[j]the injunction you have signed, but makes
his petition [g]three times a day."
14 Then [n]the king, when he heard these words,
[n]was much distressed and set his mind to
deliver Daniel. And he labored till the sun went
down to rescue him. 15 Then these men came
by agreement to the king and said to the king,

[1] Or *came thronging*; also verses 11, 15

6:4–9 The new plot to destroy the aging Daniel (near his ninetieth year) indicates the world's continuous opposition to the people of God. Daniel's challenges remind us of our need of God's grace at every stage of life. Today's trials are preparation for tomorrow's battles.

6:7 The text says that "all" the officials of the king turned against Daniel. For all his wisdom and integrity, Daniel is an old man facing the jealousy of peers, the arrogance of a king, isolation from his people, and a lions' den. Such circumstances remind us to trust God on the basis of his character, not on the basis of our circumstances. God has been gracious to his people in the past, and has promised to be gracious in the future. These are sufficient reasons for Daniel (and us) to trust God. And yet, God provides us even more: the central act of divine grace that evokes our trust today is the sending of his own Son on our behalf.

6:10–13 When devotion seemed only to promote disaster, Daniel remained prayerfully dependent on the grace of God rather than on his own wisdom or work. Daniel encouraged similar prayer in the face of Nebuchadnezzar's earlier threats (2:18). Daniel's practice reminds us of the words of the apostle Paul: "In everything by prayer and supplication with thanksgiving let your requests be made known to God" (Phil. 4:6). Spiritual devotion may be risky, but knowing that we are depending on the God who saved Daniel makes such risks truly wise.

6:14–15 Even the king could not change a law of the Medes and Persians that had entrapped Daniel. What could one man do against such overwhelming evil? We can be tempted to believe that, "Because it will make no difference what I do, it does not matter what I do." Daniel teaches us that our duty to God remains even when evil

2 [r][See ver. 1 above]
3 [t][Esth. 3:1] [s][See ver. 2 above] [r][See ver. 1 above] [u]ch. 5:12 [v][Gen. 41:40; Esth. 10:3]
4 [s][See ver. 2 above] [r][See ver. 1 above] [w][Eccles. 4:4] [x][Ezek. 14:14, 20]
6 [s][See ver. 2 above] [r][See ver. 1 above] [y]ver. 21; See ch. 2:4
7 [s][See ver. 2 above] [z]ch. 3:24; 4:36 [a]ver. 12, 13, 15
8 [a][See ver. 7 above] [b]ver. 12, 15; Esth. 1:19 [c][ch. 8:20] [d][ver. 15; Esth. 8:8]
9 [a][See ver. 7 above]
10 [e][Ps. 137:5] [f][Ps. 28:2; 138:2]; See 1 Kgs. 8:48 [g]Ps. 55:17 [h][ch. 2:23]
12 [i]ch. 3:8 [j]ver. 7, 8, 9 [c][See ver. 8 above] [d][See ver. 8 above]
13 [k]ch. 1:6 [l]See ch. 2:25 [m]ch. 3:12 [j][See ver. 12 above] [g][See ver. 10 above]
14 [n][Matt. 14:9; Mark 6:26]

"Know, O king, that it is a law of the Medes and
Persians that no [l]injunction or ordinance that
the king establishes can be changed."
16 Then the king commanded, and Daniel
was brought and cast into the den of lions.
The king declared[1] to Daniel, "May [o]your
God, whom you serve continually, deliver
you!" 17 [p]And a stone was brought and laid on
the mouth of the den, [q]and the king sealed
it [r]with his own signet and with the signet
of his [s]lords, that nothing might be changed
concerning Daniel. 18 Then the king went to
his palace and spent the night fasting; [t]no
diversions were brought to him, and [u]sleep
fled from him.
19 Then, at break of day, the king arose and
went in haste to the den of lions. 20 As he came
near to the den where Daniel was, he cried
out in a tone of anguish. The king declared to
Daniel, "O Daniel, servant of [v]the living God,
[o]has your God, whom you serve continually,
[w]been able to deliver you from the lions?"
21 Then Daniel said to the king, [x]"O king, live
forever! 22 My God [y]sent his angel [z]and shut the
lions' mouths, and they have not harmed me,
because I was found blameless [a]before him;
[a]and also before you, O king, I have done no
harm." 23 Then the king was exceedingly glad,
and commanded that Daniel be taken up out
of the den. So Daniel was taken up out of the
den, and [b]no kind of harm was found on him,
because he had trusted in his God. 24 And the
king commanded, and [c]those men who had
maliciously accused Daniel were brought and
cast into the den of lions—they, their children,
and their wives. And before they reached the
bottom of the den, the lions overpowered
them and broke all their bones in pieces.
25 Then King Darius wrote to all [d]the peoples,
nations, and languages [e]that dwell in all the
earth: [f]"Peace be multiplied to you. 26 [g]I make
a decree, that in all my royal dominion [h]peo-
ple are to tremble and fear before the God of
Daniel,

for [i]he is [j]the living God,
enduring forever;
his kingdom shall never be destroyed,
[j]and his dominion shall be [k]to the end.
27 He delivers and rescues;
he works [l]signs and wonders
in heaven and on earth,
he who has [m]saved Daniel
from the power of the lions."

28 So this Daniel prospered during the reign
of Darius and [n]the reign of [o]Cyrus the Persian.

Daniel's Vision of the Four Beasts

7 In the first year of [p]Belshazzar king of
Babylon, [q]Daniel saw a dream and [r]visions
of his head as he lay in his bed. Then he wrote
down the dream and told the sum of the matter. 2 Daniel declared,[2] "I saw in my vision by
night, and behold, [s]the four winds of heaven
were stirring up the great sea. 3 And four great

[1] Aramaic *answered and said*; also verse 20 [2] Aramaic *answered and said*

15 [l][See ver. 12 above]
16 [o][Acts 27:23]
17 [p][Lam. 3:53] [q]Matt. 27:66; Rev. 20:3 [r][Esth. 3:12] [s]ch. 4:36; 5:1
18 [t][Prov. 25:20] [u]Esth. 6:1; [ch. 2:1]
20 [v]ver. 26 [o][See ver. 16 above] [w][ch. 3:15]
21 [x]See ch. 2:4
22 [y]ch. 3:28 [z]Heb. 11:33; [Ps. 22:21; 2 Tim. 4:17] [a][ver. 4]
23 [b][ch. 3:25]
24 [c][Deut. 19:19]
25 [d]See ch. 3:4 [e]ch. 4:1 [f]See ch. 4:1
26 [g]See ch. 3:10 [h][ch. 5:19; Ps. 99:1; Eccles. 12:13] [i]ver. 20 [j]See ch. 4:34 [k]ch. 7:26
27 [l]ch. 4:2 [m][ch. 3:28, 29]
28 [n][ch. 1:21] [o]2 Chr. 36:22, 23; Ezra 1:2; 4:3, 5; 6:3, 14; Isa. 44:28; 45:1; [ch. 1:21; 10:1]

Chapter 7
1 [p]See ch. 5:1 [q][ch. 1:17] [r]ver. 15; ch. 2:28; 4:5
2 [s]ch. 8:8; 11:4; [Ezek. 37:9; Zech. 2:6; Rev. 7:1]

seems immovable. We remain faithful to God in the face of overwhelming opposition because we believe in the grace of an overpowering God.

6:19–24 God miraculously delivers his prophet and destroys his opponents. Daniel gives God the glory for the deliverance (v. 22).

6:25–28 The king from yet another nation honors the God of Daniel (cf. 4:34–35). The "nations" are bowing before Israel's God, as prophesied (Gen. 27:29). And, as prophesied, Israel will return to her homeland and the birthplace of the coming Messiah due to the influence of Daniel on Babylon's rulers (Dan. 6:28; see note on 1:17–21). Cyrus the Persian, the last ruler under whom Daniel served, will begin to return the people of Israel to their homeland. Thus, the account of the lions' den ends with a poignant reminder that events have been set in motion for the coming of a Savior who will defeat forever the Enemy who prowls the earth "like a roaring lion, seeking someone to devour" (1 Pet. 5:8).

7:1–8 In chapter 4, King Nebuchadnezzar dreamed of successive world empires represented in a great statue with a head of gold, shoulders of silver, belly of bronze, and legs of iron. Then, a rock—representing the coming messianic King—came and struck the statue's feet of iron and clay, causing the entire form to topple. In this parallel dream, Daniel sees four beasts rise out of a churning sea: a lion with wings, representing Babylon (an image still prevalent in modern Iraq); a bear, representing Persia, the nation that would defeat Babylon in Daniel's lifetime and allow the Israelites

beasts [t]came up out of the sea, different from
one another. 4 The first was like a lion and
had eagles' wings. Then as I looked its wings
were plucked off, and it was lifted up from the
ground and made to stand on two feet like
a man, and the mind of a man was given to
it. 5 And behold, [u]another beast, a second one,
like a bear. It was raised up on one side. It had
three ribs in its mouth between its teeth; and it
was told, 'Arise, devour much flesh.' 6 After this
I looked, and behold, another, like a [v]leopard,
with four wings of a bird on its back. And the
beast had four heads, and [w]dominion was given
to it. 7 After this I saw in the night visions, and
behold, a fourth beast, [x]terrifying and dreadful
and exceedingly strong. It had great iron teeth;
[x]it devoured and broke in pieces [x]and stamped
what was left with its feet. It was different from
all the beasts that were before it, and [y]it had
ten horns. 8 I considered the horns, and behold,
[z]there came up among them another horn, a
little one, [z]before which three of the first horns
were plucked up by the roots. And behold, in
this horn were eyes like the eyes of a man, and
[a]a mouth speaking great things.

The Ancient of Days Reigns

9 "As I looked,

[b]thrones were placed,
and the [c]Ancient of Days took his seat;
[d]his clothing was white as snow,
and [e]the hair of his head like pure
wool;
his throne was fiery flames;
[f]its wheels were burning fire.
10 [g]A stream of fire issued
and came out from before him;
[h]a thousand thousands [i]served him,
[h]and ten thousand times ten thousand
[j]stood before him;
the [k]court sat in judgment,
and [l]the books were opened.

11 "I looked then because of the sound of
[a]the great words that the horn was speaking.
And as I looked, [m]the beast was killed, and its
body destroyed [m]and given over to be burned
with fire. 12 As for the rest of the beasts, [n]their
dominion was taken away, but their lives were
prolonged for a season and a time.

The Son of Man Is Given Dominion

13 "I saw in the night visions,

and [o]behold, with the clouds of heaven
there came one like a son of man,
and he came to the [c]Ancient of Days
and was presented before him.
14 [p]And to him was given dominion
and glory and a kingdom,
that all [q]peoples, nations, and languages
should serve him;
[r]his dominion is an everlasting dominion,
which shall not pass away,
and his kingdom one
that shall not be destroyed.

to return home; a leopard, representing Greece, the nation that would conquer the civilized world with amazing speed under Alexander the Great; and a final beast, not identified except to say that it has five times the normal number of animal horns—a powerful beast with teeth of iron, probably representing the Roman Empire. This last empire would become the most powerful of Israel's ancient opponents and would contain her most vicious nemesis: the "little" horn (v. 8), which most commentators identify as Antiochus IV Epiphanes, a Seleucid ruler who came under Roman control and did great harm to God's people, from 175–164 B.C.

Daniel's expansive vision reassures us that God knows all that will occur and has not lost control over any of it. God's sovereign will rules over all kingdoms, leaders, and events with utter authority and divine wisdom. He is worthy of our praise—and our trust.

7:9–12 The four beasts are brought before the judgment seat of God (the "Ancient of Days"), who destroys the dreaded little horn (v. 11; cf. v. 8) but allows the rest of the beasts to live for a season (v. 12). Commentators will debate the details, but no one questions the message of the big picture: God calls every nation that opposes him into judgment and destroys them, although he may allow his purposes to be fulfilled by them for a time.

7:13–14 The grand purpose of the Ancient of Days is to give dominion over "all peoples, nations, and languages" (v. 14) to one "like a son of man," who comes "with

3[t] [Rev. 13:1]
5[u] [ch. 2:39]
6[v] [Hab. 1:8; Rev. 13:2] [w] [ch. 11:5]
7[x] ver. 19, 23 [y] ver. 20; [Rev. 12:3; 13:1; 17:12]
8[z] [ver. 20, 21, 24; ch. 8:9] [a] ver. 20; [Rev. 13:5, 6]
9[b] Rev. 20:4; [Matt. 19:28]; See 1 Kgs. 22:19 [c] ver. 22; [Ps. 90:2] [d] Matt. 28:3 [e] Rev. 1:14 [f] [Ezek. 1:16; 10:2]
10[g] [Ps. 21:9] [h] Ps. 68:17; Heb. 12:22; Rev. 5:11 [i] Ps. 103:21 [j] [Zech. 3:4] [k] ver. 22, 26; Rev. 11:18; 20:4 [l] Rev. 20:12
11[a] [See ver. 8 above] [m] Rev. 19:20; [Rev. 20:10]
12[n] [ver. 14, 26]
13[o] Matt. 26:64; Mark 14:62; Rev. 1:7; 14:14 [c] [See ver. 9 above]
14[p] Ps. 110:1, 2; Isa. 9:6, 7; Rev. 11:15 [q] See ch. 3:4 [r] See ch. 2:44

Daniel's Vision Interpreted

15 "As for me, Daniel, my spirit within me[1]
was anxious, and [s]the visions of my head
alarmed me. 16 I approached one of those who
stood there and asked him the truth concerning all this. So he told me and made known to
me the interpretation of the things. 17 [t]"These
four great beasts are four kings who shall arise
out of the earth. 18 But [u]the saints of the Most
High shall receive the kingdom and possess
the kingdom forever, forever and ever.'

19 "Then I desired to know the truth about
[v]the fourth beast, which was different from
all the rest, exceedingly terrifying, with its
teeth of iron and claws of bronze, and which
devoured and broke in pieces and stamped
what was left with its feet, 20 [w]and about the
ten horns that were on its head, and the other
horn that came up and before which three of
them fell, the horn that had eyes and a mouth
that spoke great things, and that seemed
greater than its companions. 21 As I looked,
this horn [x]made war with the saints and prevailed over them, 22 until the [y]Ancient of Days
came, and [u]judgment was given for the saints
of the Most High, and the time came when
[u]the saints possessed the kingdom.

23 "Thus he said: 'As for [v]the fourth beast,

there shall be a fourth kingdom on
earth,
which shall be different from all the
kingdoms,
and it shall devour the whole earth,
and trample it down, and break it to
pieces.
24 As for the ten horns,
out of this kingdom ten kings shall
arise,
and another shall arise after them;
he shall be different from the former
ones,
and shall put down three kings.
25 [z]He shall speak words against the Most
High,
and shall wear out the saints of the
Most High,
and shall think to [a]change the times
and the law;
and they shall be given into his hand
for [b]a time, times, and half a time.
26 [c]But the court shall sit in judgment,
and [d]his dominion shall be taken
away,
to be consumed and destroyed [e]to the
end.
27 [f]And the kingdom and the dominion
and the greatness of the kingdoms
under the whole heaven
shall be given to the people of [f]the
saints of the Most High;
[g]his kingdom shall be an everlasting
kingdom,
and all dominions shall serve and
obey him.'[2]

28 "Here is the end of the matter. [h]As for me,
Daniel, my [i]thoughts greatly alarmed me, [j]and
my color changed, but [k]I kept the matter in
my heart."

Daniel's Vision of the Ram and the Goat

8 In the third year of the reign of [l]King
Belshazzar a vision appeared to me,
Daniel, [m]after that which appeared to me [m]at

[1] Aramaic *within its sheath* [2] Or *their kingdom shall be an everlasting kingdom, and all dominions shall serve and obey them*

15[s] See ver. 1
17[t] [ver. 3]
18[u] ver. 22, 27; Matt. 25:34; [1 Cor. 6:2; Rev. 2:26; 20:4]
19[v] ver. 7
20[w] ver. 8
21[x] [ch. 8:24]
22[y] ver. 9, 13 [u] [See ver. 18 above]
23[v] [See ver. 19 above]
25[z] [ch. 11:36] [a] ch. 2:9, 21 [b] ch. 12:7; Rev. 12:14
26[c] See ver. 10 [d] [ver. 12, 14] [e] ch. 6:26
27[f] See ver. 18 [g] See ch. 2:44
28[h] ver. 15; [ch. 8:27; 10:8, 16; Jer. 23:9] [i] ch. 4:5, 19; 5:6 [j] [ch. 5:6, 10] [k] [Luke 2:19, 51]
Chapter 8
1[l] See ch. 5:1 [m] [ch. 7:1]

the clouds of heaven" (v. 13) in the establishment of an eternal kingdom "that shall not be destroyed" (v. 14). The image so closely parallels Christ's description of himself (Matt. 24:30; 26:64; cf. Acts 1:11) that we must conclude Daniel here is seeing the ultimate victory of the messianic kingdom that gives every believer hope in a world often dominated by great evil.

7:15–28 Daniel remains "anxious" (v. 15) and "alarmed" (v. 28) because his vision allows for the enemy kingdoms to have their season (v. 12). Moreover, the vicious little horn (v. 8) that "made war with the saints and prevailed over them" (v. 21) succeeds "until the Ancient of Days came" and "the saints possessed the kingdom" (v. 22). One of the heavenly hosts seeks to calm Daniel with two truths: (1) the ultimate demise of four evil empires (vv. 17–18), including the dreaded fourth beast and its little horn (vv. 19–26); and (2) the ultimate and eternal rule of God's people (vv. 18, 27).

Alarming aspects of Daniel's vision are yet future to him, but our peace comes from knowing of the ultimate victory of our Savior and our eternal rule with him (cf. v. 27 and 2 Tim. 2:12; Rev. 20:6).

the first. 2 And I saw in the vision; and when
I saw, I was in [n]Susa the citadel, which is in the
province of [o]Elam. And [p]I saw in the vision,
[p]and I was at the [q]Ulai canal. 3 I raised my eyes
and saw, and behold, [r]a ram standing on the
bank of the canal. It had two horns, and both
horns were high, but one was higher than the
other, and the higher one came up last. 4 I saw
[s]the ram charging westward and northward
and southward. No [t]beast [u]could stand before
him, [v]and there was no one who could rescue
from his power. [w]He did as he pleased and
[x]became great.

5 As I was considering, behold, a [y]male goat
came from the west across the face of the
whole earth, without touching the ground.
And the goat had [y]a conspicuous horn
between his eyes. 6 He came to [z]the ram with
the two horns, which I had seen standing on
the bank of the canal, [a]and he ran at him in
his powerful wrath. 7 I saw him come close
to the ram, [b]and he was enraged against him
and struck the ram and broke his two horns.
[c]And the ram had no power to stand before
him, but he [d]cast him down to the ground and
trampled on him. And there was no one who
could rescue the ram from his power. 8 Then
[y]the goat [e]became exceedingly great, but when
he was strong, the great horn was broken, and
instead of it there came up four [f]conspicuous
horns toward [f]the four winds of heaven.

9 Out of one of them came [g]a little horn,
which grew exceedingly great toward [h]the
south, toward the east, and toward [i]the glorious land. 10 [j]It grew great, [k]even to the host of
heaven. And some of the host [k]and some[1] of
[l]the stars it threw down to the ground and
[m]trampled on them. 11 [n]It became great, even as
great as [o]the Prince of the host. [p]And the regular burnt offering was taken away from him,
and the place of his sanctuary was overthrown.
12 And a host will be given over to it together
with the regular burnt offering because of
transgression,[2] and it will throw truth to the
ground, and [q]it will act and prosper. 13 Then
I heard [r]a holy one speaking, and another
holy one said to the one who spoke, [s]"For
how long is the vision concerning the regular
burnt offering, [t]the transgression that makes
desolate, and the giving over of the sanctuary
and host to be trampled underfoot?" 14 And he
said to me,[3] "For 2,300 [u]evenings and mornings. Then the sanctuary shall be restored to
its rightful state."

The Interpretation of the Vision

15 When I, Daniel, had seen the vision,
I [v]sought to understand it. And behold, there
stood before me one having [w]the appearance
of a man. 16 [x]And I heard a man's voice [x]between
the banks of the [y]Ulai, and it called, [z]"Gabriel,
make this man understand the vision." 17 So he
came near where I stood. And when he came,
[a]I was frightened [b]and fell on my face. But he
said to me, "Understand, [c]O son of man, that
the vision is for [d]the time of the end."

18 And when he had spoken to me, [e]I fell
into a deep sleep with my face to the ground.
But [f]he touched me and made me stand up.
19 He said, "Behold, I will make known to
you what shall be at the latter end of [g]the
indignation, for it refers to [h]the appointed
time of the end. 20 As for [i]the ram that you
saw with the two horns, these are the kings

[1] Or *host, that is, some* [2] Or *in an act of rebellion* [3] Hebrew; Septuagint, Theodotion, Vulgate *to him*

8:1 Daniel says that he is writing in the third year of King Belshazzar's reign. This means the Jews are still captive to the Babylonians, the writing on the wall (ch. 5) has not yet occurred, and the conquering Persians have not yet come. Thus, Daniel's future revelations in this chapter are a special gift from God.

8:2–17 Daniel envisions a battle between a raging ram and a victorious goat, whose horn is broken, then multiplies, and finally produces another horn responsible for greater havoc. One "having the appearance of a man" has Gabriel explain the vision to Daniel (vv. 15–17), which reminds us of how our Lord has graciously provided his Word for our understanding.

8:18–26 Understanding the vision is not difficult; accepting it is. Gabriel explains that the ram with the two horns is the Median and Persian Empires. Then he says that the goat is Greece. The level of detail provided for these successive reigns defies natural explanation. Readers are able to discern the direction of the empires' campaigns, the

2 [n]See Neh. 1:1 [o]See Isa. 11:11 [p]See Ezek. 1:1 [q]ver. 16
3 [r][ver. 20]
4 [s][Deut. 33:17; Ezek. 34:21] [t][ch. 7:17] [u][ver. 7] [v][ch. 3:15] [w][ch. 11:3, 16, 36] [x]ver. 8
5 [y][ver. 21]
6 [z][ver. 20] [a][Job 15:26]
7 [b]ch. 11:11 [c][ver. 4] [d][Ps. 7:5]
8 [y][See ver. 5 above] [e]ver. 4 [f][ver. 5]; See ch. 7:2, 3
9 [g]ch. 7:8 [h][ch. 11:25] [i]ch. 11:16, 41; [Ps. 48:2; Ezek. 20:6, 15]
10 [j][ch. 11:28] [k]Isa. 14:13 [l][Rev. 12:4] [m]ver. 7
11 [n]ver. 25; See ch. 11:36 [o]Josh. 5:14 [p]ch. 11:31; 12:11
12 [q]ver. 24; ch. 11:28, 30
13 [r]See ch. 4:13 [s]ch. 12:6; [Rev. 6:10]; See ch. 9:21-27 [t]See ch. 11:31 **14** [u][ver. 26] **15** [v][1 Pet. 1:10, 11] [w]ch. 7:13; 10:16, 18; Ezek. 1:26; Rev. 1:13 **16** [x]See ch. 12:5-7 [y]ver. 2 [z]ch. 9:21; Luke 1:19, 26 **17** [a][Luke 1:12] [b]Ezek. 1:28 [c]See Ezek. 2:1 [d][ver. 19; ch. 11:27, 35, 40; 12:4, 9] **18** [e]ch. 10:9; [Luke 9:32] [f]ch. 9:21; 10:10, 18 **19** [g]ch. 11:36 [h][Ps. 102:13]; See ver. 17 **20** [i][ver. 3]

of [j]Media and Persia. 21 And [k]the goat[1] is the
king of Greece. And [k]the great horn between
his eyes is [l]the first king. 22 [m]As for the horn
that was broken, in place of which four others arose, four kingdoms shall arise from his[2]
nation, [n]but not with his power. 23 And at the
latter end of their kingdom, when the transgressors have reached their limit, a king of
bold face, one who understands riddles, shall
arise. 24 His power shall be great—[o]but not
by his own power; and he shall cause fearful destruction [p]and shall succeed in what
he does, [q]and destroy mighty men and the
people who are the saints. 25 [r]By his cunning
he shall make deceit prosper under his hand,
and in his own mind [s]he shall become great.
[t]Without warning he shall destroy many. And
he [s]shall even rise up against the Prince of
princes, and he shall be broken—but [u]by no
human hand. 26 The vision of [v]the evenings
and the mornings that has been told [w]is true,
but [x]seal up the vision, [y]for it refers to many
days from now."

27 And [z]I, Daniel, was overcome and lay sick
for some days. Then I rose and went about
the king's business, but I was appalled by the
vision [a]and did not understand it.

Daniel's Prayer for His People

9 [b]In the first year of [c]Darius the son of
Ahasuerus, by descent a [d]Mede, who was
made king over the realm of the [e]Chaldeans—
2 in the first year of his reign, I, Daniel, perceived in the books the number of years
that, according to [f]the word of the LORD to
Jeremiah the prophet, must pass before the
end of the desolations of Jerusalem, namely,
seventy years.

3 Then I turned my face to the Lord God,
seeking him by [g]prayer and pleas for mercy
with fasting and sackcloth and ashes. 4 I prayed
to the LORD my God and [h]made confession,
saying, [i]"O Lord, the [i]great and awesome God,
who [j]keeps covenant and steadfast love with
those who love him and keep his commandments, 5 [k]we have sinned and done wrong and
acted wickedly [l]and rebelled, turning aside
from your commandments and rules. 6 [m]We
have not listened to [n]your servants the prophets, who spoke in your name to [o]our kings,
our princes, and our fathers, and to all the
people of the land. 7 To you, [p]O Lord, belongs
righteousness, but to us open shame, as at this
day, to the men of Judah, to the inhabitants
of Jerusalem, and to all Israel, [q]those who are

[1] Or *the shaggy goat* [2] Theodotion, Septuagint, Vulgate; Hebrew *the*

20 [j][ch. 6:8]
21 [k][ver. 5] [l]ch. 10:20; 11:3
22 [m]ver. 8 [n]ver. 24
24 [o]Rev. 17:17 [p]ver. 12; ch. 11:28, 30 [q][ch. 7:21]
25 [r][ch. 11:23] [s]ver. 11 [t][ch. 11:21, 24] [u]See ch. 2:34
26 [v][ver. 14] [w][ch. 10:1] [x][ch. 12:4, 9] [y]ch. 10:14
27 [z][ch. 7:28] [a][ver. 16]
Chapter 9
1 [b]ch. 11:1 [c]See ch. 5:31 [d][ch. 8:20] [e]ch. 5:30
2 [f][Ezra 1:1; Jer. 25:12]
3 [g]ver. 17, 18, 23; [Neh. 1:4]
4 [h]ver. 20; [Ezra 10:1; Neh. 1:6] [i]Neh. 1:5; 9:32 [j]Deut. 7:9
5 [k]ver. 15 [l]Lam. 3:42
6 [m]2 Chr. 36:15, 16 [n]Ezra 9:11; Zech. 1:6 [o]Ezra 9:7; Neh. 9:34
7 [p][ver. 14; Lam. 1:18] [q][Esth. 9:20]

length of their occupation, and the specific details of their evil. To believe Daniel is writing prophecy, as he claims, and not merely an interpretation of events already past, as skeptics of the Bible claim, requires acceptance of supernatural inspiration. Since God so speaks to his people in his Word (2 Tim. 3:16–17), we have the gift of his abiding voice in the church and the great responsibility of listening and obeying.

8:27 After the vision is explained, Daniel is sickened by the revelation and struggles to understand. We similarly struggle when we learn that, even in God's great plan, evil may have its day—as Babylon, Persia, and Greece did. But Daniel arose and went about the king's business with this further assurance from his vision: God will have the final say. Of the most destructive horn that rises up against "the Prince of princes," Gabriel says, "he shall be broken—but by no human hand" (v. 25).

God will ultimately prevail over the worst of evil, giving us the grace needed faithfully to serve God's purposes even in trying circumstances. The clearest example of God working his redemptive purposes through adversity and pain is the cross of Christ, where acute suffering secured unfathomable grace.

9:1–20 Daniel learns by reading Jeremiah that the 70 years of captivity will soon end. He begins to pray in preparation, confessing his own sin and the sin of his people (v. 20). Daniel includes himself as a sinner needing the grace of God because he knows how righteous (vv. 7, 14) and holy (v. 20) God is. Daniel's words remind us that, in light of God's holiness, "all have sinned and fall short of the glory of God" (Rom. 3:23).

9:4–20 Daniel repeatedly acknowledges the abiding mercy of God (vv. 4, 9, 15). Yahweh (i.e., the LORD), the name for God that designates his covenant relationship with his people, though not used elsewhere in Daniel, is used seven times in this chapter. The people have been faithless, and yet Daniel counts on God's covenant faithfulness, saying, "For we do not present our pleas before you because of our righteousness, but

near and [q]those who are far away, in [r]all the
lands to which you have driven them, because
of [s]the treachery that they have committed
against you. 8 To us, O LORD, belongs open
shame, to our kings, to our princes, and to
our fathers, because [k]we have sinned against
you. 9 [t]To the Lord our God belong mercy and
forgiveness, for we have rebelled against him
10 [m]and have not obeyed the voice of the LORD
our God by walking in his laws, which he set
before us by [n]his servants the prophets. 11 [u]All
Israel has transgressed your law and turned
aside, [v]refusing to obey your voice. [w]And the
curse and oath [x]that are written in the Law of
[y]Moses the servant of God have been poured
out upon us, because [k]we have sinned against
him. 12 He has confirmed his words, which he
spoke against us and against [z]our rulers who
ruled us,[1] by [a]bringing upon us a great calamity. [b]For under the whole heaven there has not
been done anything like what has been done
against Jerusalem. 13 [x]As it is written in the Law
of Moses, all this calamity has come upon us;
yet we have not entreated the favor of the LORD
our God, [c]turning from our iniquities and
gaining insight by your truth. 14 [d]Therefore
the LORD has kept ready the calamity and has
brought it upon us, [e]for the LORD our God is
righteous in all the works that he has done,
and [f]we have not obeyed his voice. 15 And now,
O Lord our God, who brought your people out
of the land of Egypt [g]with a mighty hand, and
[h]have made a name for yourself, as at this day,
[i]we have sinned, we have done wickedly.

16 "O Lord, [j]according to all your righteous
acts, let your anger and your wrath turn away
from your city Jerusalem, [k]your holy hill,
[l]because for our sins, and for [m]the iniquities of
our fathers, [n]Jerusalem and your people have
become [o]a byword among all who are around
us. 17 Now therefore, O our God, listen to the
prayer of your servant and to his pleas for
mercy, and for your own sake, O Lord,[2] [p]make
your face to shine upon [q]your sanctuary, which
is desolate. 18 [r]O my God, incline your ear and
hear. Open your eyes and see [s]our desolations,
and [t]the city that is called by your name. For
we do not present our pleas before you because
of our righteousness, but because of your great
mercy. 19 O Lord, hear; O Lord, forgive. O Lord,
pay attention and act. [u]Delay not, [v]for your
own sake, O my God, because [t]your city and
[w]your people are called by your name."

Gabriel Brings an Answer

20 [x]While I was speaking and praying, confessing my sin and the sin of my people Israel,
and presenting my plea before the LORD my
God for [y]the holy hill of my God, 21 while I was
speaking in prayer, the man [z]Gabriel, whom
I had seen in the vision at the first, [a]came to
me in swift flight at [b]the time of the evening
sacrifice. 22 [c]He made me understand, speaking
with me and saying, "O Daniel, I have now
come out to give you [d]insight and understanding. 23 [e]At the beginning of your pleas for
mercy a word went out, [f]and I have come to tell
it to you, for [g]you are greatly loved. Therefore
consider the word [h]and understand the vision.

The Seventy Weeks

24 [i]"Seventy weeks[3] are decreed about your
people and [j]your holy city, to finish [k]the transgression, to put an end to sin, [l]and to atone

[1] Or *our judges who judged us* [2] Hebrew *for the Lord's sake* [3] Or *sevens*; also twice in verse 25 and once in verse 26

because of your great mercy" (v. 18). Forgiveness comes not on the basis of human deserving but on the basis of God's gracious character.

9:20–23 Gabriel, the Lord's representative, responds swiftly (v. 21), personally (v. 22), and lovingly (v. 23) to Daniel's confession, reminding us how God responds to humility (cf. Isa. 66:2).

9:24 Gabriel promises rescue for this sinful people. There are varying views of the timing of the rescue (see the *ESV Study Bible* notes on this passage), but the mysteries should not obscure the obvious gospel truths.

First, God will rescue. Second, while the timing of the rescue is difficult to understand, the nature of the rescue is not. The events will "finish the transgression," "put an end to sin," "atone for iniquity," "bring in everlasting righteousness," "seal [i.e., confirm] both vision and prophet," and "anoint a most holy place [or Holy One]."

7 [q][Esth. 9:20] [r]See Jer. 8:3 [s]Lev. 26:40
8 [k][See ver. 5 above]
9 [t]Neh. 9:17; Ps. 86:15
10 [m][See ver. 6 above] [n][See ver. 6 above]
11 [u]See Isa. 1:4-6 [v][Jer. 40:3; 44:23] [w]Jer. 44:22 [x]See Lev. 26:14-45; Deut. 28:15-68 [y]1 Chr. 6:49; 2 Chr. 24:9; Neh. 10:29 [k][See ver. 5 above]
12 [z][Ps. 82:2, 3] [a]Jer. 39:16 [b]Ezek. 5:9; [Lam. 1:12]
13 [x][See ver. 11 above] [c]Hos. 7:10
14 [d][Jer. 1:12] [e]Neh. 9:33; See ver. 7 [f]ver. 10
15 [g]Ex. 32:11; [Ex. 6:1; Neh. 1:10] [h]Ex. 14:18; Neh. 9:10

[i]See ver. 5 **16** [j]Ps. 31:1; 71:2 [k]ver. 20; ch. 11:45; Jer. 31:23; Zech. 8:3 [l]Lam. 1:5 [m][Ex. 20:5] [n]Lam. 2:15, 16 [o]Ps. 44:13; 79:4; Ezek. 36:4; Mic. 6:16 **17** [p]Num. 6:25 [q]Lam. 5:18 **18** [r]2 Kgs. 19:16; Isa. 37:17 [s]ver. 26; See ver. 27 [t]Jer. 25:29 **19** [u]Ps. 40:17; 70:5 [v]Ps. 25:11; 79:9 [t][See ver. 18 above] [w]Jer. 14:9 **20** [x]Isa. 65:24 [y]See ver. 16 **21** [z]See ch. 8:16 [a]See ch. 8:18 [b]Ex. 29:39; [1 Kgs. 18:36; Ezra 9:4, 5] **22** [c][ch. 8:16] [d][ch. 1:4, 17] **23** [e][ver. 20] [f][ch. 10:12, 14] [g]ch. 10:11, 19 [h][Matt. 24:15; Mark 13:14] **24** [i][Ezek. 4:6] [j]Neh. 11:1 [k]ch. 8:13 [l][Ps. 78:38; Heb. 2:17]; See Jer. 31:34

for iniquity, [m]to bring in everlasting righteousness, to seal both vision and prophet,
and [n]to anoint a most holy place.[1] 25 [o]Know
therefore and understand that [p]from the
going out of the word to restore and [q]build
Jerusalem to the coming of an [r]anointed one,
a [s]prince, there shall be seven weeks. Then for
sixty-two weeks it shall be built again[2] with
squares and moat, [t]but in a troubled time.
26 And after the sixty-two weeks, an anointed
one shall [u]be cut off and shall have nothing.
And the people of the prince who is to come
[v]shall destroy the city and the sanctuary. [w]Its[3]
end shall come with a flood, [x]and to the end
there shall be war. [y]Desolations are decreed.
27 And he shall make a strong covenant with
many for one week,[4] and for half of the week
he shall put an end to sacrifice and offering.
[z]And on the wing of abominations shall come
one who makes desolate, until [a]the decreed
end is poured out on the desolator."

Daniel's Terrifying Vision of a Man

10 [b]In the third year of Cyrus king of
Persia a word was revealed to Daniel,
[c]who was named Belteshazzar. And [d]the word
was true, and it was a great conflict.[5] And [e]he
understood the word and [e]had understanding
of the vision.
2 In those days I, Daniel, was mourning for
[f]three weeks. 3 I ate no delicacies, no meat or
wine entered my mouth, nor did I [g]anoint
myself at all, for [f]the full three weeks. 4 On
the twenty-fourth day of the first month, as
I was standing [h]on the bank of the great river
([i]that is, the Tigris) 5 [j]I lifted up my eyes and
looked, and behold, [k]a man clothed in linen,
[l]with a belt of fine [m]gold from Uphaz around
his waist. 6 His body was like [n]beryl, his face
[o]like the appearance of lightning, [p]his eyes like
flaming torches, his arms and [q]legs like the
gleam of burnished bronze, and [q]the sound
of his words like the sound of a multitude.
7 [r]And I, Daniel, alone saw the vision, for the
men who were with me did not see the vision,
but a great trembling fell upon them, and they
fled to hide themselves. 8 So I was left alone
and saw this great vision, and [s]no strength was
left in me. My radiant appearance was fearfully changed,[6] [t]and I retained no strength.
9 Then I heard the sound of his words, [u]and
as I heard the sound of his words, I fell on my
face in deep sleep [u]with my face to the ground.
10 And behold, [v]a hand touched me and set
me trembling on my hands and knees. 11 And
he said to me, "O Daniel, [w]man greatly loved,
[x]understand the words that I speak to you,

[1] Or *thing*, or *one* [2] Or *there shall be seven weeks and sixty-two weeks. It shall be built again* [3] Or *His* [4] Or *seven*; twice in this verse
[5] Or *and it was about a great conflict* [6] Hebrew *My splendor was changed to ruin*

24 [m]Rom. 3:25, 26; See Jer. 23:5, 6 [n][Ps. 45:7; Isa. 61:1; Acts 4:26, 27]
25 [o][ver. 23] [p][2 Chr. 36:23; Ezra 1:3; 4:24; 6:15; Neh. 6:15] [q][Ps. 51:18] [r]John 1:41 [s]Isa. 55:4 [t]See Neh. 4:7, 8, 16-18
26 [u]Isa. 53:8; [Mark 9:12; Luke 24:26] [v][Matt. 24:2; Mark 13:2; Luke 19:43, 44] [w]Nah. 1:8; [ch. 11:10, 22, 26, 40] [x]Matt. 24:6, 14 [y]ver. 18; See ver. 27
27 [z]Matt. 24:15; Mark 13:14; [Luke 21:20] [a]Isa. 10:23

Chapter 10
1 [b][ch. 1:21]; See ch. 6:28 [c]See ch. 1:7 [d][ch. 8:26] [e]See ch. 1:17
2 [f][ver. 13]
3 [g][Amos 6:6; Matt. 6:17] [f][See ver. 2 above]
4 [h][ch. 12:5] [i]Gen. 2:14
5 [j][Josh. 5:13] [k]Ezek. 9:2 [l][Rev. 1:13; 15:6] [m]Jer. 10:9
6 [n][Ezek. 1:16; 10:9] [o]Ezek. 1:14; Matt. 28:3 [p]Rev. 1:14 [q]Rev. 1:15
7 [r][Acts 9:7]
8 [s][ch. 7:28] [t]ver. 16
9 [u]ch. 8:18
10 [v]See Ezek. 2:9
11 [w]ver. 19; ch. 9:23 [x]See ch. 1:17

Daniel's vision is, unquestionably, ultimately about Christ's gracious work in behalf of his people.

9:25–26 Jerusalem and the temple will be restored, followed by a time of trouble, culminating in the appearance of the Messiah, who himself will be cut off before Jerusalem and its sanctuary are destroyed. These details align with Cyrus's release of the captives, Jerusalem's rebuilding, Christ's coming, his crucifixion, and the subsequent destruction of Jerusalem by the future Roman emperor Titus in 70 A.D.

9:27 This verse is extremely difficult to translate, and analyses should be set forth humbly. Legitimate interpretations allow that the "he" could be Christ, who by his death ended the need for temple sacrifice, or the Roman leader Titus, who by his conquest destroyed the place of temple sacrifice. It may well be that these events are also meant to establish a recognizable pattern of future, end-time events (as the exodus set a pattern for subsequent divine rescues), but a natural first reference is to the events surrounding Christ's first incarnation. God does not give the vision in order to puzzle us, but to comfort sinful people with the assurances of triumphant grace.

10:1–12:13 Chapters 10–12 form a single vision. Chapter 10 shows that the challenges to God's people on earth are paralleled by battles in the spiritual realms (cf. Eph. 6:12). This reality would overwhelm us were it not for the assurance given to us and to Daniel that the prevailing hosts of heaven are with us (Dan. 10:18–21).

10:2–14 Daniel is in mourning for the plight of his people when an angelic messenger of great glory appears in a way only Daniel can see (vv. 2–9). With a highly symbolic expression of gracious care, the angel touches Daniel, assures him of love, stands him upright, and offers understanding in response to the prophet's humility (vv. 10–14).

and [y]stand upright, for [z]now I have been sent
to you." And when he had spoken this word
to me, I stood up trembling. 12 Then he said to
me, [a]"Fear not, Daniel, for from the first day
that you [b]set your heart to understand and
[b]humbled yourself before your God, [c]your
words have been heard, [d]and I have come
because of your words. 13 [e]The prince of the
kingdom of Persia withstood me [f]twenty-one
days, but [g]Michael, one of the chief princes,
came to help me, for I was left there with
the kings of Persia, 14 [d]and came to make you
understand what is to happen to your people
[h]in the latter days. For [i]the vision is for days
yet to come."

15 When he had spoken to me according to
these words, [j]I turned my face toward the
ground [k]and was mute. 16 And behold, [l]one in
the likeness of the children of man [m]touched
my lips. Then I opened my mouth and spoke.
I said to him who stood before me, "O my lord,
by reason of the vision pains have come upon
me, and [n]I retain no strength. 17 How can my
lord's servant talk with my lord? For now no
strength remains in me, and no breath is left
in me."

18 Again [l]one having the appearance of a man
[m]touched me and strengthened me. 19 And he
said, [o]"O man greatly loved, [p]fear not, peace
be with you; be strong and of good courage."
And as he spoke to me, I was strengthened
and said, "Let my lord speak, for you have
strengthened me." 20 Then he said, "Do you
know why I have come to you? But now I will
return to fight against the [q]prince of Persia;
and when I go out, behold, the prince of
[r]Greece will come. 21 But I will tell you [s]what
is inscribed in the book of truth: there is none
who contends by my side against these except
[t]Michael, your prince.

The Kings of the South and the North

11 "And as for me, [u]in the first year of
[u]Darius the Mede, I stood up to confirm
and strengthen him.

2 "And now I will show you [v]the truth.
Behold, three more kings shall arise in
Persia, and a fourth shall be far richer than
all of them. And when he has become strong
through his riches, he shall stir up all against
the kingdom of Greece. 3 Then [w]a mighty king
shall arise, who shall rule with great dominion and [x]do as he wills. 4 And as soon as he
has arisen, [y]his kingdom shall be broken and
divided [y]toward the [z]four winds of heaven,
but [a]not to his posterity, nor according to the
authority with which he ruled, for his kingdom shall be plucked up and go to others
besides these.

5 "Then the king of the south shall be strong,
but one of his princes shall be stronger than
he [b]and shall rule, and his authority shall
be a great authority. 6 After some years [c]they
shall make an alliance, and the daughter of
the king of the south shall come to the king
of the north to make an agreement. But she
shall not retain the strength of her arm, and he
and his arm shall not endure, but she shall be

10:15–19 Daniel is awestruck that a being of such heavenly power would deign to draw near to him. Daniel's ability to express his sense of awe is enabled by the touch of the angel (v. 16), as also are his strength to stand and his breath to speak (vv. 17–18). Each touch is a mark of enabling grace that allows the humble to know God's love, peace, and strength (cf. vv. 11, 19).

10:20–21 These last verses of chapter 10 reiterate the truth earlier revealed (see v. 13): there are battles in the spiritual realm that parallel and affect the affairs of humanity. The last two words of the chapter are our great assurance against spiritual opposition. The angelic messenger indicates that his ally against evil is "Michael, *your* prince" (v. 21). Thus Daniel learns that he has a champion in heaven who fights for him—as do we (cf. Jer. 1:18–19; Heb. 12:2; Rev. 19:11–16).

11:1 With the insight and strength with which he had been strengthened in chapter 10, Daniel now strengthens another. Grace received is ours to share. We are channels, not dams, of God's love (Eph. 5:2).

11:2–28 As a result of the vision in chapter 10, Daniel here reveals a future succession of empires and rulers with incredible detail. Specifics are better studied elsewhere (see the notes in the *ESV Study Bible*), but the inescapable conclusion is that our God knows and directs the affairs of this world for his ultimate glory and our ultimate good.

11 [y]Ezek. 2:1 [z][Heb. 1:14]
12 [a]ver. 19; [Judg. 6:23; Rev. 1:17] [b][ch. 9:3] [c][Acts 10:4] [d][ch. 9:23]
13 [e]ver. 20 [f][ver. 2, 3] [g]ver. 21; ch. 12:1; Jude 9; Rev. 12:7
14 [d][See ver. 12 above] [h]ch. 2:28 [i]ch. 8:26; [Hab. 2:3]
15 [j]ver. 9; ch. 8:18 [k]Ps. 39:2, 9
16 [l]See ch. 8:15 [m]Isa. 6:7 [n]ver. 8
18 [l][See ver. 16 above] [m][See ver. 16 above]
19 [o]ver. 11; ch. 9:23 [p]See ver. 12
20 [q]ver. 13 [r]ch. 8:21
21 [s]ch. 12:1, 4; [Ex. 32:32] [t]See ver. 13

Chapter 11
1 [u]ch. 9:1
2 [v]ch. 10:21
3 [w][ch. 7:6; 8:5, 21] [x]ver. 16, 36; [ch. 8:4]
4 [y][ch. 8:8, 22] [z]See ch. 7:2 [a]Ps. 109:13
5 [b][ch. 7:6]
6 [c][ver. 23]

given up, and her attendants, he who fathered
her, and he who supported[1] her in those times.
7 "And from a branch from her roots one shall
arise in his place. He shall come against the
army and enter the [d]fortress of the king of the
north, and he shall deal with them and shall
prevail. 8 He shall also carry off to Egypt their
gods with their metal images and their precious [e]vessels of silver and gold, and for some
years he shall refrain from attacking the king
of the north. 9 Then the latter shall come into
the realm of the king of the south but shall
return to his own land.

10 "His sons shall wage war and assemble a
multitude of great forces, which shall keep
coming [f]and overflow and pass through, and
again shall carry the war as far as his [d]for-
tress. 11 Then the king of the south, [g]moved
with rage, shall come out and fight against the
king of the north. [h]And he shall raise a great
multitude, but it shall be given into his hand.
12 And when the multitude is taken away, his
heart shall be exalted, and he shall cast down
tens of thousands, but he shall not prevail.
13 For the king of the north shall again [i]raise
a multitude, greater than the first. And [j]after
some years[2] he shall come on with a great army
and abundant supplies.

14 "In those times many shall rise against the
king of the south, and the violent among your
own people shall lift themselves up in order
to fulfill the vision, but [k]they shall fail. 15 Then
the king of the north shall come and [l]throw
up siegeworks and take a well-fortified city.
And the forces of the south shall not stand,
or even his best troops, for there shall be no
strength to stand. 16 But he who comes against
him shall [m]do as he wills, and [n]none shall stand
before him. And he shall stand in [o]the glorious land, with destruction in his hand. 17 He
shall [p]set his face to come with the strength of
his whole kingdom, and he shall bring terms
of an agreement and perform them. He shall
give him the daughter of women to destroy
the kingdom,[3] but it shall not stand or be to
his advantage. 18 Afterward he shall turn his
face to the coastlands and shall capture many
of them, but a commander shall put an end
to his insolence. Indeed,[4] he [q]shall turn his
insolence back upon him. 19 Then he shall turn
his face back toward the [r]fortresses of his own
land, but he shall [s]stumble and fall, [t]and shall
not be found.

20 "Then shall arise in his place one who shall
send an [u]exactor of tribute for the glory of
the kingdom. But within a few days he shall
be broken, neither in anger nor in battle. 21 In
his place shall arise a contemptible person to
whom royal majesty has not been given. [v]He
shall come in without warning and obtain
the kingdom [w]by flatteries. 22 Armies shall be
[x]utterly swept away before him and broken,
even the prince of the covenant. 23 And from
the time that an alliance is made with him
he shall act deceitfully, and he shall become
strong with a small people. 24 [y]Without warning he shall come into [z]the richest parts[5] of
the province, and he shall do what neither
his fathers nor his fathers' fathers have done,
scattering among them plunder, spoil, and
goods. He shall devise plans against strongholds, but only for a time. 25 And he shall stir
up his power and his heart against [a]the king
of the south with a great army. And the king of
the south shall wage war with an exceedingly
great and mighty army, but he shall not stand,
for plots shall be devised against him. 26 Even
those who eat his food shall break him. His
army shall be [b]swept away, and many shall fall
down slain. 27 And as for the two kings, their
hearts shall be bent on doing evil. They shall
speak lies at the same table, but to no avail,
for [c]the end is yet to be at the time appointed.
28 And he shall return to his land with great
wealth, but his heart shall be set against the
holy covenant. And he shall work his will and
return to his own land.

29 "At the time appointed he shall return and
come into the south, but it shall not be this
time as it was before. 30 For ships of [d]Kittim

[1] Or *obtained* [2] Hebrew *at the end of the times* [3] Hebrew *her*, or *it* [4] The meaning of the Hebrew is uncertain [5] Or *among the richest men*

7[d] [ver. 10, 19, 38, 39]
8[e] [ver. 43]
10[f] ver. 26, 40; Isa. 8:8 [d] [See ver. 7 above]
11[g] ch. 8:7 [h] ver. 13
13[i] ver. 11 [j] [ch. 4:16]
14[k] ver. 19, 33, 34

11:29–45 The people of God are swept up in the tide and trials of these world events. Of special concern to Israel is the prediction that a future despot will "profane the temple" and "take away the regular burnt offering" (v. 31). The wise (presumably the covenant people who still honor God), with others who join them, will resist at the cost of their lives (vv. 32–35). Most commentators believe these details refer

15[l] See Ezek. 4:2 **16**[m] ver. 3, 36 [n] [Josh. 10:8] [o] ver. 41; See ch. 8:9 **17**[p] See Jer. 42:15 **18**[q] [Hos. 12:14] **19**[r] [ver. 7, 10, 38, 39] [s] Jer. 46:6 [t] Job 20:8; Ps. 37:36; Ezek. 26:21 **20**[u] [Isa. 60:17; Zech. 9:8] **21**[v] ver. 24 [w] [ver. 34] **22**[x] [ver. 10; Jer. 46:7] **24**[y] ver. 21 [z] [Gen. 27:28, 39] **25**[a] [ch. 8:9] **26**[b] ver. 10, 40 **27**[c] [ver. 35] **30**[d] Gen. 10:4; Num. 24:24

shall come against him, and he shall be afraid
and withdraw, and shall turn back and [e]be
enraged and [e]take action against the holy
covenant. He shall turn back and pay attention to those who forsake the holy covenant.
31 Forces from him shall appear and [f]profane
the temple and fortress, and shall take away
the regular burnt offering. And [g]they shall
set up the abomination that makes desolate.
32 He shall seduce with flattery those who violate the covenant, but the people who know
their God shall stand firm and take action.
33 [h]And the wise among the people shall make
many understand, though for some days they
shall stumble by sword and flame, by captivity and plunder. 34 When they stumble, they
shall receive a little help. And many shall join
themselves to them with flattery, 35 and some
of the wise shall stumble, so that they may
be refined, [i]purified, and [j]made white, until
[k]the time of the end, [k]for it still awaits the
appointed time.
36 "And the king shall [l]do as he wills. [m]He
shall exalt himself and magnify himself
above every god, [n]and shall speak astonishing things against [o]the God of gods. [p]He shall
prosper [q]till the indignation is accomplished;
for what is decreed shall be done. 37 He shall
pay no attention to the gods of his fathers, or
to the one beloved by women. He shall not
pay attention to any other god, for [m]he shall
magnify himself above all. 38 He shall honor
the god of fortresses instead of these. A god
whom his fathers did not know he shall honor
[r]with gold and silver, with precious stones and
costly gifts. 39 He shall deal with the strongest fortresses with the help of a foreign god.
Those who acknowledge him he shall load
with honor. He shall make them rulers over
many and [s]shall divide the land for a price.[1]
40 [t]"At the time of the end, the king of the
south shall attack[2] him, but the king of the
north shall rush upon him [u]like a whirlwind,
with chariots and horsemen, and with many
ships. And he shall come into countries and
[v]shall overflow and pass through. 41 He shall
come into [w]the glorious land. And tens of thousands shall fall, but these shall be delivered out
of his hand: [x]Edom and [x]Moab and the main
part of the [x]Ammonites. 42 He shall stretch out
his hand against the countries, and the land of
Egypt shall not escape. 43 He shall become ruler
of the treasures of gold and of silver, and all the
precious things of Egypt, and the [y]Libyans and
the [z]Cushites shall follow in his train. 44 But
news from the east and the north shall alarm
him, and he shall go out with great fury to
destroy and devote many to destruction. 45 And
he shall pitch his palatial tents between the sea
and the glorious holy mountain. Yet he shall
come to his end, with none to help him.

The Time of the End

12 "At that time shall arise [a]Michael, the
great prince who has charge of your
people. And [b]there shall be a time of trouble,
such as never has been since there was a nation
till that time. But at that time your people

[1] Or *land as payment* [2] Hebrew *thrust at*

to the Maccabean Revolt (167–164 B.C.) against Antiochus IV Epiphanes (see note on 7:1–8). This evil Seleucid king sets himself against "the God of gods" (11:36), but he is ultimately isolated and defeated (vv. 40–45).

As Daniel was strengthened by knowledge of this ultimate triumph over evil, so we are strengthened in the face of national and global evils by the knowledge that our God's purposes will ultimately prevail.

12:1–13 Chapters 10–12 are a single vision that begins with the assurance of God's love (ch. 10), continues with a revelation of world empire succession that will include great trials and martyrdom for God's people (ch. 11), and now concludes with a promise of resurrection and heavenly rest for the faithful (ch. 12). Some commentators place the events of chapter 12 entirely at the end times. The events more likely are primarily a continuation of chapter 11's description of the period associated with Antiochus IV Epiphanes, but are conflated with details of the final days when all believers will enter their eternal rest.

12:1–4 After a time of great suffering, God will send Michael to deliver his people (10:1). The deliverance includes resurrection to "everlasting life" (12:2) for all whose names are written in the book of life (cf. 7:10; 10:2–3). Those not in the book of life are raised to "everlasting contempt" (12:2). Daniel is to seal this knowledge in a book

30 [e] See ver. 28
31 [f] [ch. 12:11] [g] Matt. 24:15; Mark 13:14; [ch. 8:13; 12:11]
33 [h] ch. 12:3, 10
35 [i] [Mal. 3:3, 4] [j] [Rev. 7:14] [k] [ver. 27, 40]
36 [l] ver. 3, 16 [m] [ch. 7:25; 2 Thess. 2:4] [n] [ch. 7:25; Rev. 13:5, 6] [o] Deut. 10:17 [p] [ch. 8:12] [q] [Isa. 10:25]; ch. 9:27
37 [m] [See ver. 36 above]
38 [r] [Joel 3:5]
39 [s] [Lam. 5:2, 6]
40 [t] [ver. 27, 35] [u] Zech. 9:14 [v] ver. 10, 26
41 [w] ver. 16; See ch. 8:9 [x] [Isa. 11:14]
43 [y] [2 Chr. 12:3] [z] 2 Chr. 12:3; Ezek. 30:4, 5; Nah. 3:9

Chapter 12
1 [a] See ch. 10:13 [b] Jer. 30:7; Matt. 24:21; Mark 13:19; [Rev. 16:18]

shall be delivered, [c]everyone whose name shall
be found written in the book. 2 And many of
those who [d]sleep in [e]the dust of the earth shall
[e]awake, [f]some to everlasting life, and [f]some to
shame and everlasting contempt. 3 [g]And those
who are wise [h]shall shine like the brightness
of the sky above;[1] and [i]those who turn many
to righteousness, like the stars forever and
ever. 4 But you, Daniel, [j]shut up the words
and [k]seal the book, until [l]the time of the end.
[m]Many shall run to and fro, and knowledge
shall increase."

5 Then I, Daniel, looked, and behold, two others stood, one on [n]this bank of the stream and
one on that bank of the stream. 6 And someone
said to [o]the man clothed in linen, who was
above the waters of the stream,[2] [p]"How long
shall it be till the end of these wonders?" 7 And
I heard [o]the man clothed in linen, who was
above the waters of the stream; [q]he raised his
right hand and his left hand toward heaven
and [r]swore by him who lives forever that it
would be for a [s]time, times, and half a time,
and that when the shattering of [t]the power
of [t]the holy people comes to an end all these
things would be finished. 8 I heard, [u]but I did
not understand. Then I said, "O my lord, what
shall be the outcome of these things?" 9 He
said, [v]"Go your way, Daniel, [w]for the words
are shut up and sealed until the time of the
end. 10 [x]Many shall purify themselves and
make themselves white and be refined, but
[y]the wicked shall act wickedly. And none of
the wicked shall understand, [g]but those who
are wise shall understand. 11 And from the time
that [z]the regular burnt offering is taken away
and [a]the abomination that makes desolate is
set up, there shall be 1,290 days. 12 [b]Blessed is
he who waits and arrives at the 1,335 days.
13 [c]But go your way till the end. [d]And you shall
rest and shall stand in your allotted place at
[e]the end of the days."

[1] Hebrew *the expanse*; compare Genesis 1:6–8 [2] Or *who was upstream*; also verse 7

1 [c] Ex. 32:32, 33; [Ezek. 13:9; Luke 10:20; Rev. 20:12]
2 [d] [Ps. 17:15; John 11:11] [e] [Isa. 26:19]; See Ezek. 37:1-10 [f] Matt. 25:46; John 5:28, 29; Acts 24:15; Rev. 20:12, 13
3 [g] ch. 11:33 [h] Matt. 13:43 [i] [Mal. 2:6]
4 [j] [ver. 9; ch. 8:26] [k] Isa. 8:16; 29:11; Rev. 5:1; 10:4; 22:10 [l] [ver. 13]; See ch. 8:17 [m] Amos 8:12
5 [n] [ch. 10:4]
6 [o] ch. 10:5; Ezek. 9:2 [p] ch. 8:13
7 [o] [See ver. 6 above] [q] See Gen. 14:22 [r] [Rev. 10:6] [s] ch. 7:25 [t] [ch. 8:24]
8 [u] [ch. 8:15]
9 [v] ver. 13 [w] [ver. 4]
10 [x] [ch. 11:35] [y] [Rev. 9:20; 22:11] [g] [See ver. 3 above]
11 [z] ch. 11:31 [a] See ch. 11:31
12 [b] [Matt. 10:22]
13 [c] ver. 9 [d] Isa. 57:2; [Rev. 6:11] [e] [Matt. 13:39]

until the end comes and there is sufficient basis for its full understanding. By these words God tells his people all they need to know to endure the trials and martyrdom many will face; i.e., life everlasting awaits those who depend on him rather than their own wisdom or ways.

This is a key Old Testament text undergirding the more explicit New Testament teaching of the resurrection of the dead. The New Testament is so much clearer on this gospel doctrine because it is written on the other side of the life, teaching, death, and resurrection of Jesus himself (e.g., cf. Matt. 22:29–32). Paul explains that Christ is "the firstfruits" of the end-time resurrection from the dead (1 Cor. 15:20–23). That is, Jesus' resurrected body is the first installment of the coming great harvest of the redeemed (restored in body and spirit)—in which all those united to Christ will inevitably be included.

12:5–13 Daniel asks how long the time of great suffering will take to be completed. A heavenly messenger clothed in linen says the span will be three and a half years (i.e., "times" [v. 7]). Even Daniel does not understand precisely what this means (v. 8), but the messenger urges him to be content with the fact that God has determined the time, despite the future need for some to "be refined" by suffering and death (v. 10).

To give Daniel further confidence that God remains in control despite the trials to come, the messenger refines the time frame (1,290 days) between the ending of temple sacrifices and the profaning of the temple (cf. 11:31). Then the angel adds another 45 days to the 1,290 (totaling 1,335 days) that God's people will have to persevere before their deliverance (12:12). The specificity indicates God's comprehensive knowledge of what will come, and is the basis for Daniel's (and our) perseverance through trials because of the certainty that we "shall rest and shall stand in [our] allotted place at the end of the days" (v. 13).

We follow a crucified Savior to a heavenly rest. The path has inescapable pain, but the end is eternal, blessed, and sure.

Introduction to
Hosea

Author and Date

Hosea prophesied during the latter half of the eighth century B.C. (c. 753–722 B.C.). This period was an extremely difficult time in Israel's history, just before the northern kingdom went into exile.

The Gospel in Hosea

The message of the prophets is based squarely on earlier Scripture, and particularly significant are passages such as Leviticus 26, Deuteronomy 4:25–31, and Deuteronomy 28–32. In those passages Moses prophesied that Israel would enter the Promised Land, break the covenant, and be driven into exile under the curse of the covenant. From exile, however, they would seek the Lord, finding him faithful to his covenant when they sought him once more with all their hearts (cf. Deut. 5:29). The basic message of the prophets is that what Moses prophesied will indeed come to pass. As they point forward to the restoration after exile, they compare God's future deliverance of his people to the exodus from Egypt. This new exodus from exile will be followed by a return to the Promised Land, a new conquest of the land, and a new covenant between God and his people, who are themselves a new Adam, figuratively speaking, in a new Eden with a new David as their king.

This is the basic fund of Old Testament theology and imagery from which the authors of the New Testament draw to explain how the salvation God has accomplished in Messiah Jesus is the fulfillment of all that was prophesied in the Old Testament (see note on Hos. 12:1–14).

One particularly poignant way in which these salvation themes are seen in Hosea involves the covenant between God and Israel initiated at Sinai being treated as a marriage. This analogy sees all the indictments of Israel's idolatry as spiritual adultery. In addition, when God promises to save his people after he judges them (ch. 2), he depicts their future salvation as a new marriage ceremony at a new Sinai (cf. esp. 2:14–23). Jesus later came calling himself the bridegroom of God's people (e.g., Matt. 9:15), and Paul strikingly states that the great mystery of marriage "refers to Christ and the church" (Eph. 5:32). Jesus comes to initiate the new covenant, which is like the new betrothal prophesied in Hosea 2:14–23 (cf. 2 Cor. 11:2), and it will culminate in "the marriage of the Lamb" (Rev. 19:7), when "the Bride, the wife of the Lamb," comes "down out of heaven from God, having the glory of God" (Rev. 21:9–11).

Hosea also prophesies of the sinful nation of Israel being struck down by Yahweh, who comes at them like a lion (Hos. 5:14). But, with striking echoes of future salvation events, the prophet says that this death of the nation will happen when the people are driven into exile. Then, after the exile, Yahweh will raise his people from the dead on the third day (6:2–3).

These redemptive themes in Hosea's prophecy are supremely fulfilled in Jesus Christ. Jesus came as Israel's representative, and in his death he became the one who bore the curse of the covenant (Gal. 3:13). He was struck down under the wrath of God, and "he was raised on the third day in accordance with the Scriptures" (1 Cor. 15:4; cf. Hos. 5:14–6:3). Jesus laid down his life for his bride, the church (Eph. 5:25), buying her back from slavery to sin (cf. Hos. 3:1–5). He ransomed her as God had ransomed Israel at the exodus, and in his resurrection he justifies her (Rom. 4:25), accomplishing the prophesied new exodus and setting the return from exile in motion. The great consummation will be celebrated at the marriage feast of the Lamb, in fulfillment of all the prophets, not least Hosea.

This prophetic book sobers us and fills us with renewed hope. As ugly as Israel's adulterous faithlessness has been, it cannot extinguish God's resilient redemptive love that defies human calculation or annulment.

Outline

Chapters 1–3 use Hosea's own marriage as a parable for the relationship between God and Israel. The dominant image is of Israel as an unfaithful wife. Chapters 4–14 detail the comparison, with its series of accusations, warnings, appeals, and motivations for God's people to return.

I. Biographical: Hosea's Family (1:1–3:5)

II. Accusations, Warnings, and Promises for Israel (4:1–14:9)

Hosea

1 The word of the LORD that came to Hosea,
the son of Beeri, [a]in the days of Uzziah,
Jotham, Ahaz, and Hezekiah, kings of Judah,
and in the days of [b]Jeroboam the son of Joash,
king of Israel.

Hosea's Wife and Children

2 When the LORD first spoke through Hosea,
the LORD said to Hosea, [c]"Go, take to yourself
a wife of whoredom and have [d]children of
whoredom, for [e]the land commits great whoredom by forsaking the LORD." 3 So he went and
took Gomer, the daughter of Diblaim, and she
conceived and bore him a son.
4 And the LORD said to him, "Call his name
Jezreel, for in just a little while [f]I will punish
the house of Jehu for the blood of Jezreel, and
[g]I will put an end to the kingdom of the house
of Israel. 5 And on that day [h]I will break the
bow of Israel [i]in the Valley of Jezreel."
6 She conceived again and bore a daughter.
And the LORD said to him, [j]"Call her name No
Mercy,[1] for [k]I will no more have mercy on the
house of Israel, to forgive them at all. 7 But [l]I
will have mercy on the house of Judah, and
I will save them by the LORD their God. I [m]will
not save them by bow or by sword or by war
or by horses or by horsemen."
8 When she had weaned No Mercy, she conceived and bore a son. 9 And the LORD said,
[n]"Call his name Not My People,[2] for [o]you are
not my people, and I am not your God."[3]
10[4] Yet [p]the number of the children of Israel
shall be [q]like the sand of the sea, which cannot
be measured or numbered. [r]And [s]in the place
where it was said to them, [o]"You are not my

[1] Hebrew *Lo-ruhama*, which means *she has not received mercy* [2] Hebrew *Lo-ammi*, which means *not my people* [3] Hebrew *I am not yours*
[4] Ch 2:1 in Hebrew

1:1–2:1 God commissions Hosea to take "a wife of whoredom" because the people have committed whoredom by forsaking the Lord (1:2). Referring to the nation's sin as whoredom assumes that the covenant between Yahweh and Israel is a marriage. In the enacted parable of the relationship between Yahweh and Israel, Hosea represents the Lord and Gomer, his wife, represents Israel.

The children born to Hosea and Gomer have symbolic names, the first being Jezreel, apparently referring to the punitive slaughter that took place there as a consequence of Israel's previous unfaithfulness (Hos. 1:4–5; cf. 2 Kings 10:11). At the very least, nothing like what was required at Jezreel should be a part of the history of the people of God. "Breaking the bow" is apocalyptic language (cf. Ps. 46:9), and this imagery points forward to the future salvation the Lord will accomplish for his people in the latter days. There is a logical relationship between the names of the children. The sin brought to mind by the name "Jezreel" is followed by judgment echoed in the name "No Mercy" (Hos. 1:6–7); mercy to Israel is over, yet Yahweh will save Judah in his own way. Following "No Mercy" comes "Not My People" (vv. 8–9), a name made of terms that are a shocking reversal of the covenant language instituted in Exodus 6:7. The names reflect Israel's renunciation of the covenant, and as coming verses show, justify a divine declaration of divorce.

This is not the end of Israel's hope, however. For Hosea 1:10–2:1 declares that, after the exile, the glorious eschatological restoration will result in the fulfillment of the promise to Abraham: note the reference in 1:10 to the number of the children being immeasurable, "like the sand of the sea" (cf. Gen. 22:17; 13:16). We also see the realization of the covenant declaration of Exodus 6:7, in which Israel will be God's people and he, showing mercy, will be their God (cf. Hos. 2:1, 23; Ex. 4:22; Deut. 14:1).

Chapter 1
1 [a]Isa. 1:1; Amos 1:1; Mic. 1:1 [b]2 Kgs. 14:23; 15:1
2 [c][ch. 3:1] [d]ch. 2:4 [e][ch. 2:5]; See Ezek. 16:15
4 [f][2 Kgs. 10:11] [g][Amos 7:9]
5 [h][2 Kgs. 15:29] [i]Josh. 17:16; Judg. 6:33
6 [j][ver. 9; ch. 2:1, 23; Rom. 9:25; 1 Pet. 2:10] [k]ch. 2:4; 2 Kgs. 17:6, 23
7 [l][ch. 11:12; 2 Kgs. 19:35] [m][ch. 2:18; Zech. 4:6; 9:10]
9 [n]ver. 4, 6 [o]ch. 2:23; [Lev. 26:12]
10 [p][Ezek. 36:10, 37] [q]Gen. 22:17; See Gen. 13:16 [r]Cited Rom. 9:26 [s]Isa. 62:4 [o][See ver. 9 above]

people," it shall be said to them, [t]"Children[1] of
[u]the living God." 11 And [v]the children of Judah
and the children of Israel shall be gathered
together, and [w]they shall appoint for themselves
one head. And they shall go up from
the land, for great shall be the day of Jezreel.

Israel's Unfaithfulness Punished

2 [2] Say to your brothers, [x]"You are my people,"[3] and to your sisters, [y]"You have received mercy."[4]

2 "Plead with your mother, plead—
for [z]she is not my wife,
and I am not her husband—
that she put away [a]her whoring from her face,
and her adultery from between her breasts;
3 lest [b]I strip her naked
and make her as [c]in the day she was born,
and [d]make her like a wilderness,
and make her like a parched land,
and kill her with thirst.
4 [e]Upon her children also I will have no mercy,
[f]because they are children of whoredom.
5 For [g]their mother has played the whore;
she who conceived them has acted shamefully.
For [h]she said, 'I will go after my lovers,
who [i]give me my bread and my water,
my wool and my flax, my oil and my drink.'
6 Therefore [j]I will hedge up her[5] way with thorns,
and [k]I will build a wall against her,
so that she cannot find her paths.
7 She shall pursue her lovers
but not overtake them,
and she shall seek them
but shall not find them.
[l]Then she shall say,
'I will go and return to [m]my first husband,
[l]for it was better for me then than now.'
8 And [n]she did not know
that it was [o]I who gave her
[p]the grain, the wine, and the oil,
and who lavished on [q]her silver and gold,
[r]which they used for Baal.
9 Therefore [s]I will take back
my grain in its time,
and my wine in its season,
and [s]I will take away my wool and my flax,
which were to cover her nakedness.
10 Now [t]I will uncover her lewdness
in the sight of her lovers,
and no one shall rescue her out of my hand.
11 [u]And I will put an end to all her mirth,
her feasts, her [v]new moons, her [v]Sabbaths,
and all her [w]appointed feasts.
12 And [x]I will lay waste her vines and her fig trees,
[y]of which she said,

[1] Or *Sons* [2] Ch 2:3 in Hebrew [3] Hebrew *ammi*, which means *my people* [4] Hebrew *ruhama*, which means *she has received mercy* [5] Hebrew *your*

10[t] Deut. 14:1; [2 Cor. 6:18] [u] Ps. 42:2; See Josh. 3:10
11[v] Isa. 11:12, 13; Jer. 3:18; 50:4; Ezek. 34:23; Zech. 10:6; See Ezek. 37:16-24 [w] [ch. 3:5]
Chapter 2
1[x] [ch. 1:9] [y] [ch. 1:6]
2[z] [Isa. 50:1] [a] [ch. 4:12; Ezek. 16:25]
3[b] [Ezek. 16:39] [c] [Ezek. 16:4] [d] [ver. 9; Ezek. 19:13]
4[e] ch. 1:6 [f] ch. 1:2
5[g] [ch. 1:2] [h] [ver. 12, 13] [i] [ver. 8, 9; Jer. 44:17]
6[j] Job 3:23 [k] [Job 19:8; Lam. 3:7, 9]
7[l] [Luke 15:17, 18] [m] [Isa. 54:5, 6]
8[n] [ver. 20; Isa. 1:3] [o] [Ezek. 16:19] [p] Deut. 7:13 [q] ch. 13:2 [r] [Ezek. 16:17, 18]
9[s] [ver. 3; Joel 1:10]
10[t] Lam. 1:8; Ezek. 16:37; 23:29
11[u] [Jer. 7:34; Amos 8:10] [v] [Amos 8:5] [w] [ch. 9:5; Isa. 1:13, 14]
12[x] [Isa. 5:5] [y] [ver. 5]

Beyond this we hear of a new leader ("one head"; Hos. 1:11; cf. 3:5) and a new exodus ("they shall go up from the land" in 1:11 echoes "escape from the land" in Ex. 1:10).

Israel has horribly sinned. But she is being renewed. God's covenant love will not falter.

2:2–23 In verses 2–3 the Lord pleads that the people turn from their sin lest he exile them from the land. They ignore the pleas, so in verses 4–13 the Lord announces that he will exile Israel in order to stop their idolatry and turn them back to himself. Israel has sinned, they will be exiled, and in the future the Lord will save them as he saved them in the past.

Israel will experience a new exodus ("as at the time when she came out of the land of Egypt"; v. 15). Their conquest of the land will be renewed (the Lord will "make the Valley of Achor [where Achan was cursed; Josh. 7:25–26] a door of hope"; Hos. 2:15). They will enter into a new covenant as a new Adam in a new Eden (v. 18). And all this will be like a new, divine-human wedding (vv. 19–20).

In short, the judgments symbolized in the names of Hosea's three children (vv. 22–23) are outstripped by the restored glories the Lord will give. Truly this is a God "merciful and gracious, slow to anger, and abounding in steadfast love and faithfulness" (Ex. 34:6).

'These are [z]my wages,
which my lovers have given me.'
I will make them a forest,
[a]and the beasts of the field shall devour them.
13 And [b]I will punish her for [c]the feast days of the Baals
when she burned offerings to them
and [d]adorned herself with her ring and jewelry,
and went after her lovers
and forgot me, declares the LORD.

The LORD's Mercy on Israel

14 "Therefore, behold, I will allure her,
and [e]bring her into the wilderness,
and [f]speak tenderly to her.
15 And there I will give her her vineyards
and make the Valley of Achor[1] a door of hope.
And there she shall answer [g]as in the days of her youth,
as at the time when she came out of the land of Egypt.

16 "And [h]in that day, declares the LORD, you
will call me 'My Husband,' and no longer
will you call me 'My Baal.' 17 For [i]I will remove
the names of the Baals from her mouth, and
they shall be remembered by name no more.
18 And [j]I will make for them a covenant on that
day with the beasts of the field, the birds of
the heavens, and the creeping things of the
ground. And [k]I will abolish[2] the bow, the
sword, and war from the land, and I will make
you lie down in [l]safety. 19 And I will betroth
you to me [m]forever. [n]I will betroth you to me
in righteousness and in justice, in steadfast
love and in mercy. 20 [n]I will betroth you to me
in faithfulness. And [o]you shall know the LORD.

21 "And [p]in that day [q]I will answer, declares the LORD,
I will answer the heavens,
and they shall answer the earth,
22 and the earth shall answer the grain, the wine, and the oil,
and they shall answer [r]Jezreel,[3]
23 and [s]I will sow her for myself in the land.
And [t]I [u]will have mercy on No Mercy,[4]
and [v]I will say to Not My People,[5]
[w]'You are my people';
and he shall say, 'You are my God.'"

Hosea Redeems His Wife

3 And the LORD said to me, [x]"Go again,
love a woman who is loved by another
man and is an adulteress, even as the LORD
loves the children of Israel, though they turn
to other gods and love cakes of raisins." 2 So
I bought her for fifteen shekels of silver
and a [y]homer and a lethech[6] of barley. 3 And
I said to her, "You must [z]dwell as mine for
many days. You shall not play the whore, or
belong to another man; so will I also be to
you." 4 For the children of Israel [z]shall dwell
many days [a]without king or prince, [b]without
sacrifice or [c]pillar, without [d]ephod or [e]house-
hold gods. 5 Afterward [f]the children of Israel
shall return and [g]seek the LORD their God,
and [h]David their king, [i]and they shall come
in fear to the LORD and to his goodness in
the [j]latter days.

The LORD Accuses Israel

4 [k]Hear the word of the LORD, O children of Israel,
for [l]the LORD has a controversy with the inhabitants of the land.

[1] *Achor* means *trouble*; compare Joshua 7:26 [2] Hebrew *break* [3] *Jezreel* means *God will sow* [4] Hebrew *Lo-ruhama* [5] Hebrew *Lo-ammi*
[6] A *shekel* was about 2/5 ounce or 11 grams; a *homer* was about 6 bushels or 220 liters; a *lethech* was about 3 bushels or 110 liters

3:1–5 The comparison between Hosea's love for his sinful wife, Gomer, and Yahweh's love for Israel is directly stated in verse 1, one of the most beautiful verses in Scripture regarding God's faithfulness toward the unfaithful. In further reflection of God's steadfast love, Hosea buys Gomer back from adultery but does not immediately resume conjugal relations (vv. 3–4). There is a renewal of the marriage, but a delay in its consummation. This appears to correspond to the way that Israel was restored to the land, inaugurating the fulfillment of promises whose consummation would await the coming(s) of Jesus (see note on 12:1–14).

4:1–19 The people know neither God's character nor his person (cf. "faithfulness," "steadfast love," "knowledge of God" in 4:1b with Ex. 34:6–7). They break the commandments

12 [z][Mic. 1:7] [a][ch. 13:8]
13 [b][ch. 4:9] [c][ch. 11:2; 13:1, 2] [d]Ezek. 23:40; [Isa. 61:10]
14 [e][Ezek. 20:35] [f]Isa. 40:2
15 [g][ch. 9:10; 11:1; Jer. 2:2; Ezek. 16:22, 60]
16 [h]ver. 18, 21
17 [i]Zeph. 1:4; Zech. 13:2; [Ex. 23:13]
18 [j]Ezek. 34:25; [Job 5:23] [k]Ps. 46:9; Isa. 2:4; 9:5; Ezek. 39:9, 10 [l]Lev. 26:5; Jer. 23:6
19 [m][Ezek. 43:7] [n][ver. 7, 16; Jer. 3:14, 15; 2 Cor. 11:2]

20 [n][See ver. 19 above] [o]Jer. 31:34; John 17:3 **21** [p]ver. 16 [q][Zech. 8:12] **22** [r][ch. 1:4, 11] **23** [s][ch. 1:10]; See Ezek. 36:9-11 [t]Cited Rom. 9:25, 26 [u]ch. 1:6 [v]ch. 1:9; 1 Pet. 2:10 [w]ver. 1; Zech. 13:9; See Lev. 26:12; Jer. 31:33 **Chapter 3** **1** [x][ch. 1:2, 3] **2** [y]Lev. 27:16; [Ezek. 45:11] **3** [z]Deut. 21:13 **4** [z][See ver. 3 above] [a]ch. 10:3, 7 [b][ch. 9:4] [c][ch. 10:1, 2] [d]See Judg. 8:27 [e]See Gen. 31:19 **5** [f][ch. 14:1] [g]Jer. 29:13; 50:4 [h]Ezek. 34:23; [ch. 1:11]; See Jer. 23:5 [i][Mic. 7:17] [j]Isa. 2:2; See Mic. 4:1-3 **Chapter 4** **1** [k]See ch. 5:1 [l]Isa. 3:13, 14; Jer. 25:31; Mic. 6:2

There is no faithfulness or steadfast love,
and [m]no knowledge of God in the land;
2 [n]there is swearing, lying, murder, stealing, and committing adultery;
they break all bounds, and [o]bloodshed follows bloodshed.
3 Therefore [p]the land mourns,
and all who dwell in it languish,
[q]and also the beasts of the field
and the birds of the heavens,
[r]and even the fish of the sea are taken away.

4 [s]Yet let no one contend,
and let none accuse,
for with you is [t]my contention,
O priest.[1]
5 You shall stumble by day;
the prophet also shall stumble with you by night;
and I will destroy [u]your mother.
6 My people are destroyed [v]for lack of knowledge;
[w]because you have rejected knowledge,
I reject you [x]from being a priest to me.
And since you have forgotten the law of your God,
[y]I also will forget your children.

7 [z]The more they increased,
the more they sinned against me;
[a]I will change their glory into shame.
8 [b]They feed on the sin[2] of my people;
they are greedy for their iniquity.
9 [c]And it shall be like people, like priest;
I will punish them for their ways
and repay them for their deeds.
10 [d]They shall eat, but not be satisfied;
they shall play the whore, but not multiply,
because they have forsaken the LORD
to cherish 11 whoredom, wine, and new wine,
which [e]take away the understanding.
12 My people [f]inquire of a piece of wood,
and their walking staff gives them oracles.
For [g]a spirit of whoredom has led them astray,
and they have left their God to play the whore.
13 [h]They sacrifice on the tops of the mountains
and burn offerings on the hills,
[i]under oak, poplar, and terebinth,
because their shade is good.
Therefore your daughters play the whore,
and your brides commit adultery.
14 I will not punish your daughters when they play the whore,
nor your brides when they commit adultery;
for [j]the men themselves go aside with prostitutes
and sacrifice with [k]cult prostitutes,
and a people [l]without understanding shall come to ruin.

15 Though you play the whore, O [m]Israel,
let not [m]Judah become guilty.
[n]Enter not into [o]Gilgal,
nor go up to [p]Beth-aven,
and swear not, "As the LORD lives."
16 Like a stubborn heifer,
Israel is stubborn;

[1] Or *for your people are like those who contend with the priest* [2] Or *sin offering*

1[m] [ver. 6, 14; Jer. 4:22; 5:4]
2[n] [ch. 7:1] [o] [ch. 6:9; 12:14; Mic. 3:10; 7:2]
3[p] Isa. 24:4; Jer. 4:28; Joel 1:10 [q] [Joel 1:18; Zeph. 1:3] [r] [Ezek. 38:20]
4[s] [ver. 17] [t] [Deut. 17:12]
5[u] ch. 2:2
6[v] [ver. 1; Isa. 5:13] [w] [Prov. 1:29] [x] [Ex. 19:6] [y] [Jer. 23:39]
7[z] [ch. 13:6] [a] 1 Sam. 2:30; Mal. 2:9
8[b] [Lev. 6:25, 26; 10:17]
9[c] Isa. 24:2
10[d] Lev. 26:26; Mic. 6:14; Hag. 1:6
11[e] [1 Kgs. 11:4; Prov. 20:1]
12[f] [Judg. 18:5] [g] ch. 5:4; [ch. 2:2]
13[h] Ezek. 6:13 [i] [Isa. 1:29]

(Hos. 4:2), which causes the land, its inhabitants, and the animals of creation to suffer (v. 3; cf. Gen. 1:28). The devastating effects of sin are the blackness in which gospel light shines, radiating with the knowledge of God that results in gratitude and worship. Hosea 4:4–19 is a poetic description of why covenant-breaking Israel will go into exile.

Hosea often uses Ephraim (the most prominent tribe in Israel) to personify both the sin of Israel and the undeserved deliverance the nation will receive—even as Ephraim's original blessing was undeserved (cf. v. 17 and Gen. 48:15–17). This literary tie to the nation's origins reminds us that the grace of God is never out of sight even when Hosea cites the nation for her sin and prophesies coming judgment. The unrest in our hearts caused by the prophet's disturbing allusions to Israel's sin (and our similar patterns of unfaithfulness) can be settled only by the grace of God glimmering in the Old Testament and fulfilled in the ministry of Christ, to whom Hosea points. The accusing voice of the Lord in Hosea 4, so right in its denunciation, will ultimately be directed toward God's own Son, on behalf of those who trust in him.

14[j] [ch. 9:10] [k] Deut. 23:17 [l] [ver. 1, 6] 15[m] See ch. 6:4 [n] Amos 4:4, 5; 5:5 [o] ch. 9:15; 12:11 [p] ch. 5:8; 10:5; [ch. 10:8; 1 Kgs. 12:29; Amos 1:5]

can the LORD now feed them
like a lamb in a broad pasture?
17 [q]Ephraim is joined to idols;
[r]leave him alone.
18 When their drink is gone, they give
themselves to whoring;
[s]their rulers[1] dearly love shame.
19 [t]A wind has wrapped them[2] in its wings,
and they shall [u]be ashamed because of
their sacrifices.

Punishment Coming for Israel and Judah

5 [v]Hear this, O priests!
Pay attention, O house of Israel!
Give ear, O house of the king!
For the judgment is for you;
for [w]you have been a snare at Mizpah
and a net spread upon [x]Tabor.
2 And [y]the revolters [z]have gone deep into
slaughter,
but [a]I will discipline all of them.

3 [b]I know Ephraim,
and Israel is not hidden from me;
for now, O Ephraim, you have played the
whore;
Israel is defiled.
4 [c]Their deeds do not permit them
to return to their God.
For [d]the spirit of whoredom is within
them,
and they know not the LORD.
5 [e]The pride of Israel testifies to his face;[3]
Israel and [f]Ephraim shall stumble in
his guilt;
[f]Judah also shall stumble with them.
6 [g]With their flocks and herds they shall go
to seek the LORD,
[g]but they will not find him;
[h]he has withdrawn from them.
7 [i]They have dealt faithlessly with the LORD;
for they have borne alien children.
Now the new moon shall devour
them with their fields.

8 [j]Blow the horn in [k]Gibeah,
the trumpet in [l]Ramah.
Sound the alarm at [m]Beth-aven;
we follow you,[4] O Benjamin!
9 Ephraim shall become a desolation
in the day of punishment;
among the tribes of Israel
I make known what is sure.
10 The princes of Judah have become
like [n]those who move the landmark;
upon them I will pour out
my wrath like water.
11 Ephraim is [o]oppressed, crushed in judgment,
because he was determined to go after
filth.[5]
12 But I am [p]like a moth to Ephraim,
and [p]like dry rot to the house of Judah.

13 When Ephraim saw his sickness,
and Judah [q]his wound,

[1] Hebrew *shields* [2] Hebrew *her* [3] Or *in his presence* [4] Or *after you* [5] Or *to follow human precepts*

5:1–6:11 Hosea 5:4 explains that the actions the people have cultivated are not those that result in repentance. They do not have a humble and faithful spirit but the spirit of whoredom. They seek other gods and "know not the LORD."

In 5:13–6:3, God asserts that he will bring judgment on Israel because of the people's sin. Rather than repent of sin and trust in Yahweh, Israel seeks help from Assyria (5:13). In response to this, Yahweh speaks of how he will exile Israel from the land: the Lord casts himself as a lion and the nation is personified as an individual man. The Lord (the lion) will tear apart the man, Israel, and walk away from him (5:14). That is, Assyria will conquer and exile the nation of Israel.

Like Adam and Eve before them, God's people will be exiled from the Lord's presence in the land of life. Israel will languish in the unclean realm of the dead, like dead bones in a dry valley (cf. Ezekiel 37), until they seek the Lord (Hos. 5:15; cf. Deut. 4:29). Yet Israel's unhappy fate is not the last word. The Lord has judged them so that he can save them (Hos. 6:1), and the restoration of Israel to the land is figuratively described as the man (Israel) who was struck down by the lion (the Lord) being raised from the dead after two days. The new exodus and return from exile are thus depicted as resurrection from the dead on the third day (6:2). Israel's problem is that they have forgotten God (2:13; 4:10, 12); they do not know him (4:1, 6; 5:4). But the Lord promised that at the second exodus and return from exile, when he remarried his people and entered into a new covenant with them, they would know him (2:20).

17[q] [ver. 12; ch. 5:3] [r] [Matt. 15:14]
18[s] [ch. 9:10]
19[t] ch. 13:15; Jer. 4:11; 51:1; [Zech. 5:9] [u] [Isa. 1:29]
Chapter 5
1[v] ch. 4:1; Joel 1:2; Amos 3:1; Mic. 1:2 [w] [ch. 6:9; 9:8] [x] Judg. 4:6
2[y] [ch. 9:15] [z] [ch. 9:9; Isa. 29:15] [a] [Ps. 50:21]
3[b] [Amos 3:2; 5:12]
4[c] [Isa. 59:2] [d] ch. 4:12
5[e] ch. 7:10 [f] See ch. 6:4
6[g] ch. 6:6; Isa. 1:11 [h] ch. 9:12
7[i] ch. 6:7
8[j] ch. 8:1; Jer. 4:5 [k] ch. 9:9; 10:9 [l] Josh. 18:25 [m] See ch. 4:15
10[n] Deut. 19:14
11[o] Deut. 28:33; Amos 4:1
12[p] [Job 13:28]
13[q] [Isa. 1:5, 6]

then Ephraim went [r]to Assyria,
and sent to the great king.[1]
[s]But he is not able to cure you
or heal [q]your wound.
14 For I will be [t]like a lion to [u]Ephraim,
and like a young lion to the house of
[u]Judah.
[v]I, even I, will tear and go away;
I will carry off, and no one shall rescue.

15 [w]I will return again to my place,
until they acknowledge their guilt
and seek my face,
and [x]in their distress earnestly seek
me.

Israel and Judah Are Unrepentant

6 "Come, let us [y]return to the LORD;
for [z]he has torn us, that he may heal us;
he has struck us down, and [a]he will
bind us up.
2 After two days [b]he will revive us;
on the third day he will raise us up,
that we may live before him.
3 [c]Let us know; [c]let us press on to know the
LORD;
[d]his going out is sure as the dawn;
he will come to us [e]as the showers,
[f]as the spring rains that water the
earth."

4 What shall I do with you, [g]O [h]Ephraim?
What shall I do with you, O [h]Judah?
Your love is [i]like a morning cloud,
[i]like the dew that goes early away.
5 Therefore I have hewn them by the
prophets;
I have slain them [j]by the words of my
mouth,
and my judgment goes forth as the
light.
6 For [k]I desire steadfast love[2] and not sacrifice,
[l]the knowledge of God rather than
burnt offerings.

7 But [m]like Adam they [n]transgressed the
covenant;
[o]there they dealt faithlessly with me.
8 [p]Gilead is a city of evildoers,
[q]tracked with blood.
9 As robbers [r]lie in wait for a man,
so the priests band together;
they murder on the way to [s]Shechem;
they commit villainy.
10 In the house of Israel I have seen a horrible thing;
[t]Ephraim's whoredom is there; [u]Israel
is defiled.

11 For you also, O [u]Judah, [v]a harvest is
appointed,
when [w]I restore the fortunes of my
people.

7 [x]When I would heal Israel,
the iniquity of Ephraim is revealed,
and the evil deeds of [y]Samaria;
for [z]they deal falsely;
the thief breaks in,
and the bandits raid outside.

[1] Or *to King Jareb* [2] Septuagint *mercy*

13[r] ch. 7:11; 8:9; 12:1; 2 Kgs. 15:19 [s] ch. 14:3
14[t] ch. 13:7 [u] See ch. 6:4 [v] [Mic. 5:8]
15[w] [Jer. 29:10-12; Ezek. 6:9]; See Lev. 26:40-42 [x] Isa. 26:16
Chapter 6
1[y] ch. 14:1; [ch. 3:5] [z] ch. 5:14; [ch. 13:7, 8] [a] [Isa. 30:26]
2[b] Ps. 71:20; [Luke 24:27, 44; John 2:22; 20:9; 1 Cor. 15:4]
3[c] [ch. 4:6] [d] Mic. 5:2 [e] [ch. 14:5] [f] Joel 2:23
4[g] [ch. 11:8] [h] ver. 10, 11; ch. 4:15; 5:5; 8:14; 10:11; 11:12; 12:1, 2; See ch. 5:9-14 [i] ch. 13:3
5[j] Jer. 23:29; [Heb. 4:12]
6[k] Cited Matt. 9:13; 12:7; [1 Sam. 15:22] [l] [ch. 2:20]
7[m] [Gen. 3:11; Job 31:33; Rom. 5:14] [n] ch. 8:1; Deut. 17:2 [o] ch. 5:7
8[p] [ch. 12:11] [q] See ch. 4:2
9[r] [ch. 5:1; 7:6] [s] Josh. 24:1
10[t] ch. 5:3; 7:4; [ch. 4:2, 12, 14; 9:10] [u] See ver. 4
11[u] [See ver. 10 above] [v] See Joel 3:13 [w] Ps. 126:1; [Job 42:10] **Chapter 7** **1**[x] [ch. 6:4] [y] [Jer. 23:13] [z] [ch. 4:2]

Having spoken of the return from exile as a metaphorical resurrection from the dead (6:2), Hosea calls for pressing on to know the Lord (6:3). He asserts that the Lord's going forth is as sure as the sun rising and as nourishing as showers and spring rains (6:3). Hosea 6:6 then repudiates sacrifices offered without steadfast love and true knowledge of God, showing that sacrifice is not God's final goal, but rather a relationship where there is mutual knowledge and loyal love.

Hosea 6:7 likens Israel's sin to that of Adam, because both broke their covenant with God, for which Adam was and Israel will be driven from God's presence (cf. 8:1). The restoration to which Hosea points is restoration not merely to the land but to fellowship with God. The relationships of Eden will be restored. In Christ, all that Hosea anticipates with hope dawns on the stage of human history.

7:1–16 Hosea 7 shows the people failing to cry out to Yahweh for salvation. They do not consider that Yahweh remembers all their evil. Yet their deeds, Yahweh declares, are before his face (v. 2). In spite of their need, Yahweh can assert that "none of them calls upon me" (v. 7); they neither return to him nor seek him (v. 10); they have strayed from and rebelled against him (vv. 13–14).

The opposite of all this is what people must do if they are to experience the Lord's salvation: they must consider the evil of their deeds, realize their guilt, call upon the

2 But they do not consider
that [a]I remember all their evil.
Now [b]their deeds surround them;
[c]they are before my face.
3 By their evil [d]they make [d]the king glad,
and the princes by their treachery.
4 [e]They are all adulterers;
they are like a heated oven
whose baker ceases to stir the fire,
from the kneading of the dough
until it is leavened.
5 On the day of [f]our king, the princes
became sick with the heat of wine;
he stretched out his hand with mockers.
6 For with hearts like an oven [g]they
approach their intrigue;
all night their anger smolders;
in the morning it blazes like a flaming fire.
7 All of them are hot as an oven,
and they devour their rulers.
All [h]their kings [i]have fallen,
and none of them calls upon me.

8 Ephraim [j]mixes himself with the peoples;
Ephraim is a cake not turned.
9 [k]Strangers devour his strength,
and [l]he knows it not;
gray hairs are sprinkled upon him,
and [l]he knows it not.
10 [m]The pride of Israel testifies to his face;[1]
[n]yet they do not return to the LORD
their God,
nor seek him, for all this.

11 Ephraim is like a dove,
[o]silly and without sense,
calling to [p]Egypt, going to [q]Assyria.
12 As they go, [r]I will spread over them my net;
I will bring them down like birds of the heavens;
[s]I will discipline them [t]according to the report made to their congregation.
13 [u]Woe to them, for they have strayed from me!
Destruction to them, for they have rebelled against me!
[v]I would redeem them,
but [w]they speak lies against me.

14 [x]They do not cry to me from the heart,
but [y]they wail upon their beds;
for grain and wine they gash themselves;
they rebel against me.
15 Although [z]I trained and strengthened their arms,
yet they devise evil against me.
16 They [a]return, but not upward;[2]
they are [b]like a treacherous bow;
their princes shall fall by the sword
because of [c]the insolence of their tongue.
This shall be their derision [d]in the land of Egypt.

Israel Will Reap the Whirlwind

8 Set [e]the trumpet to your lips!
One [f]like a vulture is over the house of the LORD,
because [g]they have transgressed my covenant
and rebelled against my law.
2 To me they cry,
[h]"My God, we—Israel—know you."
3 Israel has spurned the good;
the enemy shall pursue him.

[1] Or *in his presence* [2] Or *to the Most High*

Lord, and submit to him, trusting him to show mercy. Those today who find themselves in similar straits, having realized their rebellion and desperate situation, are called to respond likewise—with two differences. First, unlike the situation in Hosea, now all nations are to call upon the Lord (Rom. 1:5). Second, they are specifically to call upon the Lord Jesus Christ (1 Cor. 1:2), the incarnate Savior whom Hosea anticipated but could only vaguely perceive (cf. 1 Pet. 1:10–11).

8:1–14 Hosea 8 continues to lay out the reasons that Israel will be exiled from the land. They have rebelled against the law (v. 1), a law that the Lord speaks of having written himself (v. 12). In keeping with the curses of the covenant, therefore, strangers will devour the produce of the land (v. 7; cf. Deut. 28:49–51). The people of Israel may claim to know God (Hos. 8:2), but their man-made kings (v. 4) and man-made idolatrous golden calves (vv. 5–6) show that they have in fact forgotten their Maker even as they built "palaces" (v. 14; a term that also refers to temples).

2[a] [ch. 5:3] [b] Ps. 9:16; Prov. 5:22 [c] Ps. 90:8
3[d] ver. 5; [Rom. 1:32]
4[e] See ch. 6:10
5[f] ver. 3
6[g] ch. 6:9
7[h] ch. 8:4 [i] 2 Kgs. 15:10, 14, 25, 30
8[j] Ps. 106:35
9[k] [ch. 8:7] [l] Isa. 42:25
10[m] ch. 5:5 [n] Isa. 9:13
11[o] ch. 4:11 [p] [ch. 12:1; 2 Kgs. 17:4] [q] See ch. 5:13
12[r] See Ezek. 12:13 [s] ch. 10:10 [t] See Lev. 26:14-39; Deut. 28:15-68
13[u] ch. 9:12 [v] ch. 13:14 [w] [ch. 11:12; 12:1; Mic. 6:12]
14[x] Ps. 78:36, 37 [y] [Amos 6:4, 5]
15[z] [ch. 11:3]
16[a] [ch. 6:1] [b] Ps. 78:57 [c] Ps. 73:9 [d] ch. 9:3 **Chapter 8** **1**[e] ch. 5:8 [f] See Deut. 28:49 [g] ch. 6:7 **2**[h] See Matt. 7:21-23

4 [i]They made kings, [j]but not through me.
They set up princes, but I knew it not.
With their silver and gold they made idols
for their own destruction.
5 [k]I have[1] spurned your calf, O Samaria.
My anger burns against them.
[l]How long will they be incapable of innocence?
6 For it is from Israel;
a craftsman made it;
it is not God.
[k]The calf of Samaria
[m]shall be broken to pieces.[2]

7 For [n]they sow the wind,
and they shall reap the whirlwind.
The standing grain has no heads;
it shall yield no flour;
if it were to yield,
[o]strangers would devour it.
8 [p]Israel is swallowed up;
already they are among the nations
as [q]a useless vessel.
9 For [r]they have gone up to Assyria,
[s]a wild donkey wandering alone;
Ephraim has hired lovers.
10 Though they hire allies among the nations,
I will soon gather them up.
And [t]the king and princes [u]shall soon writhe
because of the tribute.

11 Because Ephraim [v]has multiplied altars for sinning,
they have become to him altars for sinning.
12 [w]Were I to write for him my laws by the ten thousands,
they would be regarded as a strange thing.
13 As for my sacrificial offerings,
[x]they sacrifice meat and eat it,
but the LORD does not accept them.
[y]Now he will remember their iniquity
and punish their sins;
[z]they shall return to Egypt.
14 For [a]Israel has forgotten [b]his Maker
and [c]built palaces,
and [a]Judah has multiplied fortified cities;
so [d]I will send a fire upon his cities,
and it shall devour her strongholds.

The LORD Will Punish Israel

9 Rejoice not, O Israel!
Exult not like the peoples;
[e]for you have played the whore, forsaking your God.
[f]You have loved a prostitute's wages
on all threshing floors.
2 [g]Threshing floor and wine vat shall not feed them,
and [g]the new wine shall fail them.
3 They shall not remain in [h]the land of the LORD,
but [i]Ephraim shall return to Egypt,
and [j]they shall eat unclean food in Assyria.

4 [k]They shall not pour drink offerings of wine to the LORD,
[l]and their sacrifices shall not please him.

[1] Hebrew *He has* [2] Or *shall go up in flames*

4[i] ch. 7:7; 1 Kgs. 12:20 [j] [2 Chr. 13:5]
5[k] ch. 10:5, 6; [1 Kgs. 12:28] [l] [Jer. 13:27]
6[k] [See ver. 5 above] [m] [Mic. 1:6, 7]
7[n] [ch. 10:12, 13] [o] [ch. 7:9]
8[p] 2 Kgs. 17:6 [q] Jer. 22:28
9[r] See ch. 5:13 [s] [Jer. 2:24]
10[t] See Ezek. 26:7 [u] [ch. 4:7, 10]
11[v] ch. 10:1; 12:11
12[w] [Deut. 4:6, 8]
13[x] Jer. 7:21; [Amos 4:4] [y] ch. 9:9; Amos 8:7 [z] ch. 9:3; Deut. 28:68; [ch. 11:5]
14[a] See ch. 6:4 [b] Isa. 17:7 [c] [Amos 5:11] [d] Amos 2:5
Chapter 9
1[e] ch. 1:2 [f] ch. 2:5; Jer. 44:17
2[g] [ch. 2:9]
3[h] Jer. 2:7; 16:18; See Lev. 25:23 [i] See ch. 8:13 [j] Ezek. 4:13; Dan. 1:8
4[k] [ch. 3:4] [l] [ch. 8:13]

Israel's worship is unacceptable. Judgment must fall (v. 13). Such judgment will indeed befall not only God's people who rebel against him but also those from *any* people who reject him. But those who look to his Son Jesus Christ in contrition for deliverance find the cross of Calvary to be the location of their judgment—what they deserve at the end of history has befallen Christ in the middle of history (1 Pet. 3:18).

9:1–17 Whereas to know God is to know life and blessing, in Hosea 9 Israel is indicted for forsaking God (v. 1). Thus, they will not remain in the land (v. 3). Because they do not trust and love God, "their sacrifices shall not please him" (v. 4) and "he will remember their iniquity" (v. 9). Rather than consecrate themselves as Nazirites to the Lord, they have consecrated themselves to the "thing of shame" (v. 10), and they will experience the curses of the covenant rather than its blessings (vv. 12–17).

A chapter like this is an indirect witness to true gospel hope as Israel is indicted for trusting idols and other means of their own making rather than the Lord who had redeemed them. God's people are not offering sacrifices in faith, and they are choosing idols rather than their God. In the same way that the chapter shows the opposite of gospel faith, it shows the opposite of gospel life: idolatry and corruption, along with the judgment that awaits those who live in unrepentant sin.

It shall be like [m]mourners' bread to them;
all who eat of it shall be defiled;
for their bread shall be for their hunger only;
[n]it shall not come to the house of the LORD.

5 [o]What will you do on the day of the appointed festival,
and on the day of the feast of the LORD?
6 For behold, they are going away from destruction;
but [p]Egypt shall gather them;
Memphis shall bury them.
Nettles shall possess [q]their precious things of silver;
[r]thorns shall be in their tents.

7 [s]The days of punishment have come;
the days of recompense have come;
Israel shall know it.
[t]The prophet is a fool;
the man of the spirit is mad,
because of your great iniquity
and great hatred.
8 The prophet is [u]the watchman of Ephraim with my God;
yet [v]a fowler's snare is on all his ways,
and hatred in the house of his God.
9 [w]They have deeply corrupted themselves
as [x]in the days of Gibeah:
[w]he will remember their iniquity;
he will punish their sins.

10 Like grapes in the wilderness,
[y]I found Israel.
Like the first fruit on the fig tree
in its first season,
I saw your fathers.
But [z]they came to Baal-peor
and [a]consecrated themselves to the thing of shame,
and [b]became detestable like the thing they loved.
11 Ephraim's [c]glory shall fly away like a bird—
[d]no birth, no pregnancy, no conception!
12 [e]Even if they bring up children,
I will bereave them till none is left.
[f]Woe to them
when [g]I depart from them!
13 Ephraim, [h]as I have seen, was like a young palm[1] planted in a meadow;
but [e]Ephraim must lead his children out to slaughter.[2]
14 Give them, O LORD—
what will you give?
Give them [i]a miscarrying womb
and dry breasts.

15 Every evil of theirs is in [j]Gilgal;
there I began to hate them.
Because of the wickedness of their deeds
I will drive them out of my house.
I will love them no more;
all [k]their princes are [l]rebels.

16 Ephraim is stricken;
[m]their root is dried up;
they shall bear no fruit.
Even [n]though they give birth,
[e]I will put their beloved children to death.
17 [o]My God will reject them
because they have not listened to him;
[p]they shall be wanderers among the nations.

10

1 [q]Israel is a luxuriant vine
that yields its fruit.
The more his fruit increased,
[r]the more altars he built;
as his country improved,
he improved his pillars.
2 Their heart is false;
now they must bear their guilt.
The LORD[3] will break down their altars
and destroy their pillars.

[1] Or *like Tyre* [2] Hebrew *to him who slaughters* [3] Hebrew *He*

10:1–15 The theme sounded in verse 1—of Israel as a flourishing vine, planted by the Lord—reminds readers of the Promised Land, which itself was a reestablishment of Eden (cf. Gen. 2:8–10; Ps. 80:8; Isaiah 5; Jer. 2:21; Ezek. 15:1–8).

Rather than enjoy God's goodness, Israel used God's gifts to increase their corruption and sin (Hos. 10:1–5). Their idols will not save them but will be destroyed and taken captive (vv. 6–8). The Israelites have reaped what they have sown (cf. 8:7), but

4[m] Deut. 26:14; Ezek. 24:17 [n][Hag. 2:13] **5**[o][Isa. 10:3] **6**[p] See ch. 8:13 [q][ch. 10:8; Isa. 2:20] [r][ch. 10:8] **7**[s] See Isa. 10:3 [t] Ezek. 13:3 **8**[u] Ezek. 3:17 [v] Ps. 91:3; [ch. 5:1] **9**[w][ch. 5:2] [x] ch. 10:9; Judg. 19:22 **10**[y][Ps. 80:8; Isa. 5:1] [z] Num. 25:3; Ps. 106:28 [a][ch. 4:14] [b][Rom. 1:28, 29] **11**[c] ch. 10:5; [ch. 4:7] [d][Isa. 26:18] **12**[e] ch. 13:16 [f] ch. 7:13 [g] ch. 5:6; 1 Sam. 28:15, 16; Ezek. 10:18 **13**[h][Ezek. 27:3] [e][See ver. 12 above] **14**[i][Luke 23:29] **15**[j] ch. 4:15; 12:11 [k] ch. 8:4 [l][ch. 5:2] **16**[m][ver. 11] [n][ver. 12, 13] [e][See ver. 12 above] **17**[o][ch. 8:5] [p] Deut. 28:64, 65 **Chapter 10** **1**[q] See Ps. 80:8-11 [r] ch. 8:11

3 For now they will say:
[s]"We have no king,
for we do not fear the LORD;
and a king—what could he do for us?"
4 They utter [t]mere words;
with empty oaths they make covenants;
so [u]judgment springs up like poisonous weeds
[v]in the furrows of the field.
5 The inhabitants of Samaria tremble
for [w]the calf[1] of [x]Beth-aven.
Its people mourn for it, and so do its idolatrous priests—
those who rejoiced over it and [y]over its glory—
for it has departed[2] from them.
6 [z]The thing itself shall be carried to Assyria
as tribute to [a]the great king.[3]
Ephraim shall be put to shame,
and Israel shall be ashamed [b]of his idol.[4]

7 [c]Samaria's king shall perish
like a twig on the face of the waters.
8 The high places of [x]Aven, [d]the sin of Israel,
shall be destroyed.
[e]Thorn and thistle shall grow up
on their altars,
and [f]they shall say to the mountains, "Cover us,"
and to the hills, "Fall on us."

9 From [g]the days of Gibeah, you have sinned, O Israel;
there they have continued.
Shall not the war against the unjust[5] overtake them in Gibeah?
10 [h]When I please, [i]I will discipline them,
and nations shall be gathered against them
when they are bound up for [j]their double iniquity.
11 Ephraim was a trained calf
that [k]loved to thresh,
and I spared her fair neck;
but I will put [l]Ephraim to the yoke;
[l]Judah must plow;
Jacob must harrow for himself.
12 [m]Sow for yourselves righteousness;
reap steadfast love;
[n]break up your fallow ground,
for it is the time to seek the LORD,
that he may come and [o]rain righteousness upon you.

13 [p]You have plowed iniquity;
you have reaped injustice;
you have eaten the fruit of lies.
Because you have trusted in your own way
and in the multitude of your warriors,
14 therefore [q]the tumult of war shall arise among your people,
and all your fortresses shall be destroyed,
as [r]Shalman destroyed Beth-arbel on the day of battle;
[s]mothers were dashed in pieces with their children.
15 Thus it shall be done to you, O [t]Bethel,
because of your great evil.
At dawn [a]the king of Israel
shall be utterly cut off.

The LORD's Love for Israel

11 [u]When Israel was a child, [v]I loved him,
and out of Egypt I [w]called [x]my son.
2 [y]The more they were called,
the more they went away;
[z]they kept sacrificing to the Baals
and burning offerings to idols.

[1] Or *calves* [2] Or *has gone into exile* [3] Or *to King Jareb* [4] Or *counsel* [5] Hebrew *the children of injustice*

if they will sow righteousness they will reap steadfast love (10:12a). This is not works-based righteousness but a simple statement that the Lord will rain righteousness on those who seek him (v. 12b; note also Gal. 6:7–8). God delivered Israel at the exodus and gave them the opportunity to walk with him. If they will walk with him, they will be blessed. Because they have plowed iniquity instead, they have reaped injustice (Hos. 10:13). When the enemy army comes, the king of Israel shall be utterly cut off (v. 15; cf. v. 7). This means that when the walls are broken down in the northern kingdom, in Samaria, the demise of the nation will include the demise of its king.

Yet once again—as supremely seen in the message of the gospel—the word of justly deserved divine judgment is not the last word. In 11:1 Hosea will allude to Israel's past salvation at the exodus as a way of pointing forward to future salvation at the promised new exodus.

3[s] [ver. 7, 15, 1 Sam. 12:12]
4[t] [ch. 4:2] [u] Amos 5:7; 6:12 [v] ch. 12:11
5[w] See 1 Kgs. 12:28 [x] See ch. 4:15 [y] ch. 9:11; [1 Sam. 4:21, 22]
6[z] [Isa. 46:2] [a] ch. 5:13 [b] ch. 11:6
7[c] [ver. 3]
8[x] [See ver. 5 above] [d] 1 Kgs. 12:30; Amos 8:14 [e] [ch. 9:6] [f] Luke 23:30; Rev. 6:16; [Isa. 2:19]
9[g] ch. 9:9
10[h] [Ex. 32:34] [i] ch. 7:12 [j] [1 Kgs. 12:28]
11[k] [Deut. 25:4; 1 Cor. 9:9; 1 Tim. 5:18] [l] See ch. 6:4

12[m] [ch. 8:7; Gal. 6:8] [n] Jer. 4:3 [o] Isa. 45:8 **13**[p] [ch. 8:7] **14**[q] [ch. 1:5] [r] 2 Kgs. 17:3 [s] [ch. 13:16] **15**[t] [ver. 5] [a] [See ver. 6 above] **Chapter 11** **1**[u] [ch. 2:15] [v] Deut. 7:8; [ch. 14:4] [w] Cited Matt. 2:15 [x] Ex. 4:22; [Mal. 1:6] **2**[y] [ver. 7] [z] [ch. 2:13; 13:1, 2]

3 Yet it was [a]I who taught Ephraim to walk;
I took them up by their arms,
but they did not know that [b]I healed them.
4 [c]I led them with cords of kindness,[1]
with the bands of love,
and [d]I became to them as one who eases the yoke on their jaws,
and [e]I bent down to them and fed them.

5 [f]They shall not[2] return to the land of Egypt,
but [g]Assyria shall be their king,
[h]because [i]they have refused to return to me.
6 [j]The sword shall rage against their cities,
consume the bars of their gates,
and devour them [k]because of their own counsels.
7 My people are bent [l]on turning away from me,
and though [m]they call out to the Most High,
he shall not raise them up at all.

8 How can I give you up, O Ephraim?
How can I hand you over, O Israel?
[n]How can I make you [o]like Admah?
How can I treat you [o]like Zeboiim?
[p]My heart recoils within me;
my compassion grows warm and tender.
9 I will not execute my burning anger;
I will not again destroy Ephraim;
[q]for I am God and not a man,
[r]the Holy One in your midst,
and I will not come in wrath.[3]

10 [s]They shall go after the LORD;
[t]he will roar like a lion;
when he roars,
his children shall come trembling [u]from the west;
11 they shall come trembling like birds [v]from Egypt,
and [w]like doves [x]from the land of Assyria,
and I will return them to their homes,
declares the LORD.
12[4] Ephraim [y]has surrounded me with lies,
and the house of Israel with deceit,
but Judah still walks with God
and is faithful to the Holy One.

[1] Or *humaneness*; Hebrew *man* [2] Or *surely* [3] Or *into the city* [4] Ch 12:1 in Hebrew

11:1–7, 10–12 Implicit and explicit comparisons to earlier Old Testament events inform both what Hosea says in chapter 11 and the way that Matthew understands Hosea 11:1 and claims fulfillment for it in Matthew 2:15.

The sin of Israel that will lead to exile from the land has been compared to the sin of Adam that led to exile from the garden (Hos. 6:7). When God brings judgment on Israel it will be like the judgment he visited on Sodom and Gomorrah (11:8; cf. Gen. 10:19). The sojourn in Egypt prior to the exodus will be matched by exile to Assyria prior to the new exodus (Hos. 11:5). The exodus from Egypt, invoked in 11:1, is the paradigm for the new act of salvation, the new exodus, which will result in the return from exile (vv. 10–11). Having mentioned the king being cut off at dawn in 10:15, Hosea points back to the exodus from Egypt in 11:1 because mention of the exodus recalls God's past deliverance of his people (whom he identifies as "my son" in Ex. 4:22–23) and serves as a guarantee for the future deliverance of his people. The exodus is the pattern of salvation that Hosea uses to describe what God will do in the future (cf. Hos. 2:14–23).

So the good news that Hosea proclaims here is that in the future God will bring his people back from exile by means of a new act of redemption like the exodus from Egypt. When Matthew quotes Hosea 11:1, he is asserting that the pattern of the exodus and the prophesied return from exile are fulfilled in Jesus (see also note on Hos. 12:1–14).

11:8–9 This passage is one of the most moving statements in the Bible portraying the Lord's love for his people. With deeply emotive language, God declares that he simply cannot forsake his people. What can he do but love them! They are his. His "compassion grows warm and tender" (v. 8).

Such unfailing love is the only explanation for why, centuries after Hosea's prophecy, God would send his own Son to vindicate his justice while securing sinful people as his own beloved (John 3:16).

3[a] [ch. 7:15; Deut. 1:31] [b] Ex. 15:26
4[c] Jer. 31:3; [John 6:44; 12:32] [d] Lev. 26:13 [e] See Ps. 78:24-29
5[f] [ch. 8:13] [g] [ch. 10:3] [h] [2 Kgs. 17:13, 14] [i] [ch. 4:16; 7:16]
6[j] [ch. 10:14] [k] ch. 10:6
7[l] ch. 14:4 [m] [ver. 2]
8[n] [Gen. 19:24, 25; Jer. 49:18; 50:40; Amos 4:11; Jude 7] [o] Gen. 14:8; Deut. 29:23 [p] [Deut. 32:36]
9[q] See Num. 23:19 [r] See Isa. 12:6
10[s] [ch. 3:5] [t] Isa. 31:4; Jer. 25:30; Joel 3:16; Amos 1:2 [u] Isa. 11:11; Zech. 8:7
11[v] See ch. 8:13 [w] Isa. 60:8 [x] Zech. 10:6, 10; [ch. 9:3]
12[y] [ch. 7:13]

12 Ephraim feeds on the wind
and pursues [z]the east wind all day long;
they multiply [y]falsehood and violence;
[a]they make a covenant with Assyria,
and [b]oil is carried to Egypt.

The LORD's Indictment of Israel and Judah

2 [c]The LORD has an indictment against Judah
and will punish Jacob according to his ways;
he will repay him according to his deeds.
3 [d]In the womb he took his brother by the heel,
and in his manhood he strove with God.
4 He strove with the angel and prevailed;
he wept and sought his favor.
[e]He met God[1] at Bethel,
and there God spoke with us—
5 the LORD, the God of hosts,
[f]the LORD is his memorial name:
6 "So you, [g]by the help of your God, return,
[h]hold fast to love and justice,
and wait continually for your God."
7 A merchant, in whose hands are [i]false balances,
he loves [j]to oppress.
8 Ephraim has said, "Ah, but [k]I am rich;
I have found wealth for myself;
in all my labors [l]they cannot find in me iniquity or sin."
9 [m]I am the LORD your God
from the land of Egypt;
I will again make you [n]dwell in tents,
as in the days of the appointed feast.

10 [o]I spoke to the prophets;
it was I who multiplied [p]visions,
and through the prophets gave parables.
11 [q]If there is iniquity in Gilead,
they shall surely come to nothing:
[r]in Gilgal they sacrifice bulls;
[s]their altars also are like stone heaps
[t]on the furrows of the field.
12 [u]Jacob fled to the land of Aram;
there Israel [v]served for a wife,
and for a wife he guarded sheep.
13 By [w]a prophet [x]the LORD brought Israel up from Egypt,
and by a prophet he was guarded.

[1] Hebrew *him*

Chapter 12
1 [z][ch. 13:15; Jer. 18:17] [y][See ch. 11:12 above] [a]See ch. 5:13 [b][ch. 7:11; 2 Kgs. 17:4]
2 [c]See ch. 4:1
3 [d]Gen. 25:26; [Gen. 27:36]
4 [e]Gen. 28:12, 19; 35:9, 10, 15
5 [f]Ex. 3:15
6 [g]ch. 14:1, 2; Joel 2:12, 13 [h][Mic. 6:8]
7 [i]Amos 8:5; Mic. 6:11; [Prov. 11:1; 20:23] [j]Mic. 2:2
8 [k]Zech. 11:5; Rev. 3:17 [l][Deut. 29:19]
9 [m]ch. 13:4 [n]See Lev. 23:39-43; Neh. 8:14-18
10 [o][2 Kgs. 17:13] [p][Joel 2:28]
11 [q]ch. 6:8 [r]ch. 4:15; 9:15 [s]ch. 8:11 [t]ch. 10:4
12 [u]Gen. 28:5 [v]Gen. 29:20, 28
13 [w][Deut. 18:15] [x]Ex. 12:50, 51; Ps. 77:20; See Isa. 63:11-14

12:1–14 As comparisons informed Hosea's statements in chapter 11, so in chapter 12 Hosea seems to be working with patterns in Israel's history that he regards as types of the exile and return from exile.

Hosea appears to be comparing Jacob's experience to the experience of the nation descended from him at the exodus, and then to the experience of Hosea's own generation that faces exile and hopes for the return Hosea prophesies. This would explain why Hosea says the Lord has an indictment against Judah and will punish Jacob (v. 2) and then states that, "In the womb he took his brother by the heel" (v. 3). The sin of the nation that culminates in the exile of Hosea's day was prefigured and typified by the sin of Jacob grasping at Esau's heel for what God had already determined to give him. Hosea seems to regard Jacob's flight from the land as a kind of precursor of the exile (v. 12). Just as Jacob met God, wept, and sought his favor (v. 4), the expectation is that when God visits judgment on Israel and drives them from the land, like Jacob, they will meet God, repent of their sin, and seek the Lord (cf. v. 6). As things stand in Hosea's day, the nation is an unjust merchant growing wealthy by crooked business practices (vv. 7–8), but the Lord will make them dwell once more in tents after the prophesied new exodus that will set in motion the return from exile (v. 9). This helps explain the reference to the way Moses led Israel out of Egypt (v. 13).

In summary, the comparisons seem to work like this: Jacob was a sinner in the land (v. 3), met God in his flight from the land (v. 4), served another to gain a wife (v. 12) outside the land, and then was restored to the land knowing God (vv. 4b–5). This also corresponds to the way the nation later went down to Egypt (through the events and legacy of Jacob's son, Joseph), multiplied there, then met God at Sinai, and was shepherded through the wilderness by Moses (cf. vv. 9–10, 13). This pattern is being repeated in Hosea's day as, like Jacob, Ephraim (the largest tribe of Israel, used by Hosea to represent the nation) sins in the land (vv. 2–3, 7–8), will be driven into exile and sustained there by the Lord, and then, as at the exodus from Egypt, will meet God and return to the land to dwell there with him (cf. vv. 5, 11–14).

14 [y]Ephraim has given bitter provocation;
so his Lord [z]will leave his bloodguilt on him
[a]and will repay him for his disgraceful deeds.

The LORD's Relentless Judgment on Israel

13 When Ephraim spoke, there was trembling;
[b]he was exalted in Israel,
but he incurred guilt [c]through Baal and died.
2 And now they sin more and more,
and [d]make for themselves metal images,
idols skillfully made of their silver,
[e]all of them the work of craftsmen.
It is said of them,
"Those who offer human sacrifice [f]kiss calves!"
3 Therefore they shall be [g]like the morning mist
or [g]like the dew that goes early away,
[h]like the chaff that swirls from the threshing floor
or [i]like smoke from a window.

4 But [j]I am the LORD your God
from the land of Egypt;
[k]you know no God but me,
and [l]besides me there is no savior.
5 [m]It was I who knew you in the wilderness,
in the land of drought;
6 [n]but when they had grazed,[1] they became full,
[o]they were filled, and their heart was lifted up;
[o]therefore they forgot me.
7 So [p]I am to them like a lion;
[q]like a leopard I will lurk beside the way.
8 I will fall upon them [r]like a bear robbed of her cubs;
I will tear open their breast,
and there I will devour them like a lion,
[s]as a wild beast would rip them open.

9 He destroys[2] you, O Israel,
for you are against me, against [t]your helper.
10 [u]Where now is your king, to save you in all your cities?
Where are all your rulers—
those of whom [v]you said,
"Give me a king and princes"?
11 [w]I gave you a king in my anger,
and [x]I took him away in my wrath.

[1] Hebrew *according to their pasture* [2] Or *I will destroy*

These patterns are fulfilled in Jesus. Not only did he have a sojourn in Egypt (see Matt. 2:13–15), he also became the Passover Lamb (1 Cor. 5:7) in fulfillment of the exodus pattern to redeem his people (1 Cor. 6:20; 7:23), provided a place of rest for them by making them the temple of the Holy Spirit (1 Cor. 6:19), and gives them a new law for a new and continuing relationship with God (1 Cor. 9:20; 2 John 5–6). It is Christ himself who provides God's people with spiritual food and drink for their sojourn through the wilderness (cf. 1 Cor. 10:1–13; 11:17–34), on the way to the new and better heavens and earth, the kingdom of God (Rom. 14:17), where righteousness dwells (2 Pet. 3:13).

13:1–16 The northern kingdom of Israel is personified with the name Ephraim (the most prominent tribe of Israel, according to Jacob's unexpected blessing in Gen. 48:10–20). Others once trembled before the power of Ephraim, but "he" (the tribe represented by this son of Joseph) turned to idolatry, resulting in what God promised Adam would happen if he ate the forbidden fruit in Genesis 2:17: he died (Hos. 13:1).

When the Lord again identifies himself as Israel's God from the land of Egypt, asserting that beside himself "there is no savior" (v. 4), the idea is reinforced that God will save his people in the future as he did in the past. As with 5:14–6:3, where the exile and new exodus and return from exile are figuratively depicted in terms of the Lord tearing Israel as a lion, so in 13:7–13 the Lord will be like a lion, punishing Israel's sin (v. 12). Then he will overcome the death he has visited upon the nation, and the new exodus is described with terms reminiscent of the exodus from Egypt: ransom, death, plagues (v. 14; cf. 1 Cor. 15:54–55).

The New Testament presents the salvation Jesus accomplished as fulfilling the promised new exodus and return from exile (see note on Hos. 12:1–14). As in the exodus

14[y]2 Kgs. 17:17 [z]See ch. 4:2 [a]ver. 2
Chapter 13
1[b][Amos 6:13] [c]See ch. 11:2
2[d]ch. 2:8 [e][Ps. 115:4; Isa. 40:19, 20] [f][1 Kgs. 19:18; Job 31:26, 27]
3[g]ch. 6:4 [h]See Ps. 1:4 [i]See Ps. 68:2
4[j]ch. 12:9 [k]See Ex. 20:3 [l]Isa. 43:11; 45:21
5[m]Deut. 2:7; Amos 3:2
6[n][ch. 4:7] [o]Deut. 8:12, 14; [Deut. 32:15]
7[p]ch. 5:14 [q]Jer. 5:6
8[r]2 Sam. 17:8; Prov. 17:12 [s][ch. 2:12]
9[t][Deut. 33:26]
10[u][ch. 8:4; 10:3] [v]1 Sam. 8:5, 19
11[w][1 Sam. 8:22] [x][1 Sam. 15:23]

12 The iniquity of Ephraim is [y]bound up;
his sin is [y]kept in store.
13 [z]The pangs of childbirth come for him,
but he is an unwise son,
for at the right time he does not present
himself
[a]at the opening of the womb.

14 [b]Shall I ransom them from the power of
Sheol?
[b]Shall I redeem them from Death?
[c]O [d]Death, where are your plagues?
[c]O [d]Sheol, where is your sting?
[e]Compassion is hidden from my eyes.

15 Though [f]he may flourish among his
brothers,
[g]the east wind, the wind of the LORD,
shall come,
rising from the wilderness,
[h]and his fountain shall dry up;
his spring shall be parched;
it shall strip [i]his treasury
of every precious thing.
16[1] Samaria [j]shall bear her guilt,
because [k]she has rebelled against her
God;
they shall fall by the sword;
[l]their little ones shall be dashed in
pieces,
and their [m]pregnant women ripped
open.

A Plea to Return to the LORD

14 [n]Return, O Israel, to the LORD your
God,
for [o]you have stumbled because of
your iniquity.
2 Take with you words
and return to the LORD;
say to him,
"Take away all iniquity;
accept [p]what is good,
and we will pay with bulls
[q]the vows[2] of our lips.
3 [r]Assyria shall not save us;
[s]we will not ride on horses;
and [t]we will say no more, 'Our God,'
to the work of our hands.
[u]In you the orphan finds mercy."

4 I [v]will heal their apostasy;
[w]I will love them freely,
for my anger has turned from them.
5 [x]I will be like the dew to Israel;
[y]he shall blossom like the lily;
he shall take root like the trees [z]of
Lebanon;
6 his shoots shall spread out;
his beauty shall be [a]like the olive,
and his fragrance like Lebanon.
7 They shall return and [b]dwell beneath
my[3] shadow;
they shall flourish like the grain;

[1] Ch 14:1 in Hebrew [2] Septuagint, Syriac *pay the fruit* [3] Hebrew *his*

12[y] Job 14:17
13[z] Isa. 13:8; 1 Thess. 5:3 [a] [2 Kgs. 19:3]
14[b] Isa. 25:8; 26:19; Ezek. 37:12 [c] [1 Cor. 15:55] [d] [Ezek. 14:21] [e] [Ezek. 9:10]
15[f] [Gen. 41:52] [g] [Ezek. 19:12; Jonah 4:8; Hab. 1:9] [h] [Ezek. 17:10] [i] [ch. 12:8]
16[j] [Hab. 1:11] [k] 2 Kgs. 18:12 [l] [ch. 9:12; 10:14] [m] [2 Kgs. 8:12; 15:16; Amos 1:13]
Chapter 14
1[n] ch. 6:1; 12:6; [ch. 3:5] [o] [ch. 13:9]
2[p] [ch. 5:15] [q] Heb. 13:15; [Ps. 50:13, 14; 69:30, 31]
3[r] ch. 5:13 [s] [Isa. 30:16; 31:1] [t] [ver. 8] [u] See Ps. 10:14
4[v] Jer. 3:22; [ch. 6:1] [w] [ch. 11:1]
5[x] [ch. 6:3] [y] Isa. 27:6 [z] [Ps. 92:12; Isa. 35:2]
6[a] Ps. 52:8
7[b] Ps. 91:1

and the return from exile, New Testament believers have come home—not just to a plot of land but to Jesus (Matt. 11:28–30; John 14:23; 1 Pet. 2:25).

14:1–9 Hosea knows that Moses prophesied in Deuteronomy 4:29 that once Israel had experienced the Lord's wrath against their covenant-breaking sin (Deut. 4:25), once they had been exiled from the land (Deut. 4:26–28), from exile they would seek the Lord and return to him with all their hearts and would find him. And then in the latter days they would obey the voice of the Lord (Deut. 4:29–30). In Hosea 14:1–3, Hosea instructs Israel on how they should return to the Lord in that day, after they have experienced his wrath. Hosea then depicts the Lord's explanation of how he will save Israel, change their hearts so that their apostasy is healed (v. 4), and cause them to be like a tree planted by streams of water (vv. 5–6), bearing fruit in season (v. 7; cf. Psalm 1; Jer. 17:7–8). Hosea calls once more for rejection of idolatry (Hos. 14:8) before calling the wise to understand what he has prophesied in verse 9.

The basic message of Hosea is what Moses prophesied in Leviticus 26, Deuteronomy 4:25–31, and Deuteronomy 28–32: the northern kingdom of Israel has broken the covenant and will be exiled, and this is likened to a man being struck dead by the Lord. Yet after the judgment of the exile is poured out, God will save his people in the future as he saved them in the past, and this is likened to that man who was struck dead being resurrected (cf. Hos. 5:14–6:3). An apt image—not only of God's people then, but of God's people today. For in the death and resurrection of Jesus, these things are fulfilled (Rom. 6:5).

they shall blossom like the vine;
their fame shall be like the wine of Lebanon.

8 O [c]Ephraim, what have I to do with idols?
It is I who answer and look after you.[1]
I am like an evergreen cypress;
[d]from me comes your fruit.

9 [e]Whoever is wise, let him understand these things;
whoever is discerning, let him know them;
for the ways of the LORD are right,
and [f]the upright walk in them,
[f]but transgressors stumble in them.

[1] Hebrew *him*

8[c] [ver. 3; Isa. 30:22] [d] [ch. 2:8, 23; John 15:4, 5] **9**[e] Ps. 107:43; Jer. 9:12; Dan. 12:10; John 8:47; 18:37 [f] [Prov. 10:29; Luke 2:34; 2 Cor. 2:16]

Introduction to Joel

Author and Date

Little is known about Joel, a prophet from Judah (perhaps Jerusalem). Most scholars date the book of Joel after the exile to Babylon (586 B.C.).

The Gospel in Joel

In typical prophetic form, Joel gives his readers both the bad news of God's judgment and the good news of his promised deliverance. The book contains a description of a dramatic judgment on God's people through a devastating plague of locusts. This serves as a warning of the great "day of the Lord" at the end of time. Joel also includes one of the Old Testament's most significant promises regarding the future coming of the Holy Spirit.

Both the judgment and the promise remind us of our desperate need for God's help. The judgment that our sins deserve is far worse than a plague of locusts. The promise of the Spirit reminds us that the help we need is nothing less than supernatural. Through the ministry of Jesus Christ, the requirements of judgment and of supernatural provision have both been met. Jesus took upon himself the plague of judgment for our sins (2 Cor. 5:21; 1 Pet. 2:24) and then promised (John 14:16) and provided (Acts 2) the gift of the Holy Spirit. Preaching at Pentecost, the apostle Peter explains that in Jesus the "day of the Lord" prophesied by Joel has taken place—not at the end of history but in the middle of history (Acts 2:16–21). For believers, the end-time judgment has been carried out already—at the cross of Christ. The Spirit not only enables us to believe and receive this free gift but also empowers us to live a new, gospel-shaped life (Rom. 8:11).

Outline

I. The Judgment against Judah and the Day of the Lord (1:1–2:17)
   - A. Locust invasion: forerunner of the day of the Lord (1:1–20)
   - B. Army invasion: the arrival of the day of the Lord (2:1–17)

II. The Mercy of the Lord and Judgment against the Nations (2:18–3:21)
   - A. Mercy: the Lord responds by restoring his people (2:18–32)
   - B. Judgment: the Lord's judgment against the nations and his dwelling with his people (3:1–21)

Joel

1 The word of the LORD that came to Joel, the son of Pethuel:

An Invasion of Locusts

2 [a]Hear this, [b]you elders;
give ear, [b]all inhabitants of the land!
[c]Has such a thing happened in your days,
or in the days of your fathers?
3 [d]Tell your children of it,
and let your children tell their children,
and their children to another generation.
4 What [e]the cutting locust left,
[f]the swarming locust has eaten.
What the swarming locust left,
[g]the hopping locust has eaten,
and what the hopping locust left,
[h]the destroying locust has eaten.
5 Awake, you drunkards, and weep,
and [i]wail, all you drinkers of wine,
because of [j]the sweet wine,
for it is cut off from your mouth.
6 For [k]a nation has come up against my land,
[k]powerful and beyond number;
[l]its teeth are lions' teeth,
and it has the fangs of a lioness.
7 It has laid waste my vine
and splintered my [m]fig tree;

1:1–3 The first chapter describes the destruction brought by a plague of locusts. Joel opens with an urgent call to his listeners to recognize what has just happened. The leaders (elders) are told to pay attention (v. 2) and to teach their children (v. 3). The judgment of God is serious business.

How often do we fail to communicate this to our children and others in the rising generation? As we see in the Scriptures, we are only one generation away from forgetting the seriousness of the fear of the Lord (Judg. 2:8–10) as well as the scandalous good news of the gospel (2 Tim. 2:1–2). Just as the Israelites were to pass down to their children the mighty deeds of the Lord on their behalf (e.g., Psalm 106), so should we. Most importantly, we should tell the next generation of the mighty deeds of the life, death, and resurrection of Jesus Christ.

1:4–12 Here is a vivid picture of the destruction brought by the locusts. The descriptions are reminiscent of the locust plagues brought upon the Egyptians at the time of Israel's exodus (Ex. 10:12–19). The difference here is that the plague comes as judgment not upon some foreign oppressor but upon the people of God themselves.

This might seem strange, but the Scriptures are clear that "the Lord disciplines the one he loves" (Heb. 12:6). While we should be careful not to interpret every hardship or trial as discipline from the Lord—the mistake of the Pharisees in John 9—we should not forget that God may chastise us as he knows is best for the sake of our souls. Through the revelation that comes through his prophet Joel, it is clear that this plague comes as judgment upon God's people (see Joel 2:12–13). Yet the fact that God wants everyone (elders and children, rulers and workers, drunkards and priests) to know of this judgment makes it clear that he is also wanting to claim the attention and reclaim the hearts of his people.

It may take significant prayer and discernment to know whether our trials are for our discipline or for our development, but we can always be sure that the sovereign

Chapter 1
2[a][Hos. 5:1] [b]ver. 14 [c][ch. 2:2]
3[d][Ps. 78:4]
4[e]ch. 2:25; Amos 4:9 [f][Amos 7:1]; See Ex. 10:4 [g]ch. 2:25; Ps. 105:34; Nah. 3:15 [h]ch. 2:25; Ps. 78:46
5[i][Isa. 24:11] [j]ch. 3:18; Isa. 49:26; Amos 9:13
6[k]ch. 2:2 [l][Rev. 9:7, 8]
7[m][ver. 12]

it has stripped off their bark and thrown
it down;
their branches are made white.

8 Lament like a virgin[1] [n]wearing sackcloth
for the bridegroom of her youth.
9 [o]The grain offering and the drink offering are cut off
from the house of the LORD.
[p]The priests mourn,
[p] the ministers of the LORD.
10 The fields are destroyed,
[q] the ground mourns,
because [r]the grain is destroyed,
[r] the wine dries up,
the oil languishes.

11 [s]Be ashamed,[2] O tillers of the soil;
wail, O vinedressers,
for the wheat and the barley,
[t]because the harvest of the field has
perished.
12 The vine dries up;
[u] the fig tree languishes.
Pomegranate, palm, and apple,
all the trees of the field are dried up,
and [v]gladness dries up
from the children of man.

A Call to Repentance

13 [w]Put on sackcloth and lament, [p]O priests;
[x]wail, O ministers of the altar.
Go in, [w]pass the night in sackcloth,
[p] O ministers of my God!
[y]Because grain offering and drink offering
are withheld from the house of your
God.

14 [z]Consecrate a fast;
[z] call a solemn assembly.
Gather [a]the elders
and [a]all the inhabitants of the land
to the house of the LORD your God,
and cry out to the LORD.

15 Alas for the day!
[b]For the day of the LORD is near,
and as destruction from the
Almighty[3] it comes.
16 Is not the food cut off
before our eyes,
[c]joy and gladness
from the house of our God?

17 [d]The seed shrivels under the clods;[4]
the storehouses are desolate;
the granaries are torn down
because [e]the grain has dried up.
18 How [f]the beasts groan!
The herds of cattle are perplexed
because there is no pasture for them;
even the flocks of sheep suffer.[5]

19 To you, [g]O LORD, I call.
[h]For fire has devoured
the pastures of the wilderness,
[h] and flame has burned
all the trees of the field.
20 Even the beasts of the field [i]pant for
you
because the water brooks are dried
up,
[h]and fire has devoured
the pastures of the wilderness.

[1] Or *young woman* [2] The Hebrew words for *dry up* and *be ashamed* in verses 10–12, 17 sound alike [3] *Destruction* sounds like the Hebrew for *Almighty* [4] The meaning of the Hebrew line is uncertain [5] Or *are made desolate*

8[n] [ver. 13]; See 2 Sam. 3:31
9[o] ver. 13; ch. 2:14 [p] ch. 2:17; [Isa. 61:6; Ezek. 45:4]
10[q] See Hos. 4:3 [r] [Hos. 2:9]
11[s] [Jer. 14:4] [t] ver. 17
12[u] [ver. 7] [v] Isa. 24:11; Jer. 48:33
13[w] [ver. 8; Jer. 4:8] [p] [See ver. 9 above] [x] [ver. 8; Mic. 1:8] [y] ver. 9; ch. 2:14
14[z] ch. 2:15, 16; See 2 Chr. 20:3 [a] ver. 2
15[b] ch. 2:1, 11, 31; 3:14; Isa. 13:6, 9; Jer. 46:10; Ezek. 30:2, 3; Amos 5:18; Obad. 15; Zeph. 1:14, 15; Zech. 14:1; 2 Pet. 3:10
16[c] [Deut. 12:6, 7; 16:14, 15]
17[d] [Mal. 2:3] [e] ver. 11
18[f] ch. 2:22; [Jer. 12:4; Hos. 4:3]
19[g] Ps. 50:15 [h] Jer. 9:10
20[i] [Job 38:41; Ps. 104:21; 145:15] [h] [See ver. 19 above]

Lord is accomplishing his good purposes, not only in the world at large but in our life—as he was ultimately doing for Israel here (cf. 2:25–27 and Rom. 8:28).

1:13–20 The proper response to God's judgment is contrite repentance. Sackcloth (v. 13) was a very itchy and uncomfortable fabric that was a symbol of humility before the Lord. To "wail" or cry out was another clear expression of sorrow.

And yet the Lord is not mainly concerned with outward evidences of penitence but rather with genuine repentance from the heart. The fact that God is more desirous of fasts from the contrite than rich offerings from the wayward signifies his priority on genuine repentance and authentic relationship (vv. 13–14). Such priorities compel us to discern whether we are more sorry about the consequences of our sin (in this case, the destroyed crops and flocks) or about the fact that we have offended our holy God (2 Cor. 7:9–10). The latter is the evidence of true repentance.

The good news is that God does not give up on his people but is determined to be faithful to his promises and to finish what he started in their lives (Phil. 1:6). His purifying fires, for those united to Christ, are ultimately for our good.

The Day of the LORD

2 [j]Blow a trumpet in [k]Zion;
sound an alarm on [k]my holy mountain!
Let all the inhabitants of the land tremble,
for [l]the day of the LORD is coming; it is near,
2 [m]a day of darkness and gloom,
[m]a day of clouds and thick darkness!
Like blackness there is spread upon the mountains
[n]a great and powerful people;
[o]their like has never been before,
nor will be again after them
through the years of all generations.

3 [p]Fire devours before them,
and behind them a flame burns.
The land is like [q]the garden of Eden before them,
but [r]behind them a desolate wilderness,
and nothing escapes them.
4 [s]Their appearance is like the appearance of horses,
and like war horses they run.
5 [t]As with the rumbling of chariots,
they leap on the tops of the mountains,
like the crackling of [u]a flame of fire
devouring the stubble,
[n]like a powerful army
drawn up for battle.
6 Before them peoples are in anguish;
[v]all faces grow pale.
7 Like warriors they charge;
like soldiers they scale the wall.
They march each on his way;
they do not swerve from their paths.
8 They do not jostle one another;
[w]each marches in his path;
they burst through the weapons
and are not halted.
9 [x]They leap upon the city,
they run upon the walls,
[y]they climb up into the houses,
[y]they enter through the windows [z]like a thief.

10 [a]The earth quakes before them;
the heavens tremble.
[b]The sun and the moon are darkened,
and the stars withdraw their shining.
11 [c]The LORD utters his voice
before [d]his army,
for his camp is exceedingly great;
[e]he who executes his word is powerful.
[f]For the day of the LORD is [g]great and very awesome;
[h]who can endure it?

Return to the LORD

12 "Yet even now," declares the LORD,
[i]"return to me with all your heart,

2:1–11 In chapter 2 Joel reminds his listeners that the plague of locusts is not the worst thing that could happen. Another cataclysm is coming that should be of greater concern. The "day of the LORD" (vv. 1, 11) points us to the ultimate judgment spoken of in many other biblical texts (e.g., Isa. 13:6; Amos 5:18–20; Zeph. 1:14–17). Joel's language might seem to suggest another plague of locusts or even the attack of a human army, but he is describing the army of the Lord of hosts coming with our messianic King at the final judgment. God's people have proven faithless. God's people must reap the consequences.

The cosmic imagery of Joel 2:10 reminds us of the words of Jesus as he describes the same event (Matt. 24:29–31). He describes everything from the last trumpet to signs in the heavens to the army of angels who will accompany him at his return. It is the prospect of this final judgment day that should cause people to tremble. Jesus makes it clear, however, that for his people the final day is a day of deliverance—because he has already taken their judgment upon himself on the cross (also Mark 13:26–27).

Not only on the final day of history, but also on the final day of Christ's earthly ministry, the sun and sky were darkened (Mark 15:33). He died in the middle of history amid darkened skies so that we can know that our own personal darkened skies are not meant to punish us. Rather, such trials are preparing us for that final day when Christ will come in glory to receive and finally release his people into light and joy (Rev. 1:5–8).

2:12–17 Once again, in light of the coming of the day of the Lord, the call is to repent. Joel says "return" to the Lord (vv. 12–13). The Hebrew word means "turn." True

Chapter 2
1 [j]ver. 15; Isa. 58:1; Hos. 5:8; Amos 3:6 [k]See ch. 3:17 [l]See ch. 1:15
2 [m]Amos 5:18, 20; Zeph. 1:15 [n]ch. 1:6; [ver. 11, 25] [o][ch. 1:2]
3 [p]ch. 1:19, 20 [q]Gen. 2:8, 9; See Isa. 51:3 [r]Zech. 7:14
4 [s]Rev. 9:7
5 [t]Rev. 9:9; [Nah. 3:2] [u]Isa. 5:24; 47:14; Obad. 18; Nah. 1:10 [n][See ver. 2 above]
6 [v]Nah. 2:10
8 [w]Prov. 30:27
9 [x]Isa. 33:4 [y][Jer. 9:21] [z][John 10:1]
10 [a]ch. 3:16; [Ps. 18:7; Amos 8:8] [b]ch. 3:15; Isa. 13:10; Ezek. 32:7; Matt. 24:29; [Rev. 9:2]
11 [c]ch. 3:16; [1 Thess. 4:16] [d]ver. 25 [e]Rev. 18:8 [f]See ch. 1:15 [g]ver. 31 [h]Mal. 3:2; [Num. 24:23]
12 [i]Deut. 4:30; 1 Sam. 7:3; Jer. 4:1; Hos. 12:6

[j]with fasting, with weeping, and with mourning;
13 and [k]rend your hearts and not [l]your garments."
Return to the LORD your God,
[m]for he is gracious and merciful,
slow to anger, and abounding in steadfast love;
[n]and he relents over disaster.
14 [o]Who knows whether he will not turn and relent,
and [p]leave a blessing behind him,
[q]a grain offering and a drink offering
for the LORD your God?

15 [r]Blow the trumpet in Zion;
[s]consecrate a fast;
call a solemn assembly;
16 gather the people.
[t]Consecrate the congregation;
assemble the elders;
[u]gather the children,
even nursing infants.
[v]Let the bridegroom leave his room,
and the bride her chamber.

17 [w]Between the [x]vestibule and the [y]altar
[z]let the priests, the ministers of the LORD, weep
and say, "Spare your people, O LORD,
and make not your heritage a reproach,
a byword among the nations.[1]
[a]Why should they say among the peoples,
'Where is their God?'"

The LORD Had Pity

18 [b]Then the LORD became jealous for his land
[c]and had pity on his people.
19 The LORD answered and said to his people,
"Behold, [d]I am sending to you
grain, wine, and oil,
[d]and you will be satisfied;
and I will no more make you
a reproach among the nations.

20 "I will remove the northerner far from you,
and drive him into a parched and desolate land,
his vanguard[2] into [e]the eastern sea,
and his rear guard[3] into [f]the western sea;
[g]the stench and foul smell of him will rise,
for he has done great things.

21 "Fear not, O land;
be glad and rejoice,
for [h]the LORD has done great things!
22 Fear not, [i]you beasts of the field,
for [j]the pastures of the wilderness are green;
[k]the tree bears its fruit;
the fig tree and [k]vine give their full yield.

[1] Or *reproach, that the nations should rule over them* [2] Hebrew *face* [3] Hebrew *his end*

12[j][1 Sam. 7:6]
13[k][Ps. 34:18] [l]See Gen. 37:29 [m]Ex. 34:6; Ps. 86:5, 15; Jonah 4:2 [n][Num. 23:19; Ezek. 24:14]
14[o]Jonah 3:9 [p]Hag. 2:19; Mal. 3:10 [q]ch. 1:9, 13
15[r]See ver. 1 [s]See ch. 1:14
16[t]See Josh. 3:5 [u][2 Chr. 20:13] [v][Deut. 24:5; Eccles. 3:5; Zech. 12:12-14; 1 Cor. 7:5]
17[w]Ezek. 8:16 [x]1 Kgs. 6:3; 2 Chr. 3:4 [y]2 Chr. 4:1 [z]See ch. 1:9 [a]Ps. 42:3; 79:10; 115:2
18[b]Zech. 1:14; 8:2 [c][Ps. 103:13]
19[d][ch. 1:10; Ps. 4:7]; See Mal. 3:10-12
20[e]Ezek. 47:18; Zech. 14:8 [f]Zech. 14:8 [g]Isa. 34:3; [Amos 4:10]
21[h]Ps. 126:2, 3
22[i]See ch. 1:18 [j][ch. 1:19] [k][Zech. 8:12]

repentance is not only sorrow that we sinned against the Lord but a determination to change direction in our lives—turning from the sin to God, in love and dependence. You can tell that you have truly repented if you are determined to turn your back on sin and walk with the Lord in loving obedience, through the power he provides.

Our motive for heartfelt "returning" to the Lord is his own character: "gracious and merciful, slow to anger, and abounding in steadfast love" (v. 13; quoting Ex. 34:6). The apostle Paul will later echo these truths, saying, "God's kindness is meant to lead you to repentance" (Rom. 2:4).

2:18–27 These verses mark not only the halfway point of the book but also its turning point as Joel announces the covenant faithfulness of the Lord. Despite the sins of his people, the Lord's purpose will not be frustrated as he promises provision (vv. 19, 24, 26) and protection (v. 20).

What is at stake is not merely the well-being of God's people but the glory of his own holy name. The foundation of God's grace shines through in his promises despite the sins of his people. In Jesus we see the fulfillment of God's promise of both protection and provision. He protects us from the greatest of all dangers: condemnation for our sin (Rom. 8:1). And he promises to provide "every need of yours according to his riches in glory in Christ Jesus" (Phil. 4:19). When the Lord is your God, you have nothing to fear (Joel 2:21–22). When the Lord is your God, you have every reason to be glad (v. 23).

23 [l]"Be glad, O children of Zion,
and [l]rejoice in the LORD your God,
for he has given [m]the early rain for your
vindication;
he has poured down for you abundant rain,
[m]the early and [n]the latter rain, as before.
24 "The threshing floors shall be full of grain;
the vats shall overflow with wine and
oil.
25 I will restore[1] to you the years
that [o]the swarming locust has eaten,
[o]the hopper, [o]the destroyer, and [o]the cutter,
[p]my great army, which I sent among
you.
26 [q]"You shall eat in plenty and be satisfied,
and praise the name of the LORD your
God,
who has dealt wondrously with you.
And my people [r]shall never again be put
to shame.
27 [s]You shall know that I am [t]in the midst
of Israel,
and that [u]I am the LORD your God
[v]and there is none else.
And my people [r]shall never again be put
to shame.

The LORD Will Pour Out His Spirit

28[2] [w]"And it shall come to pass afterward,
that [x]I will pour out my Spirit on all
flesh;
[y]your sons and [z]your daughters shall
prophesy,
your old men shall dream dreams,
and your young men shall see visions.
29 [a]Even on the male and female servants
in those days I will pour out my Spirit.

30 "And I will show [b]wonders in the heavens
and [b]on the earth, blood and fire and columns
of smoke. 31 [c]The sun shall be turned to darkness, [d]and the moon to blood, [e]before the great
and awesome day of the LORD comes. 32 And
it shall come to pass that [f]everyone who calls
on the name of the LORD shall be saved. [g]For
in Mount Zion and in Jerusalem there shall be
those who escape, as the LORD has said, and
among [h]the survivors shall be those whom
the LORD calls.

The LORD Judges the Nations

3 [3] "For behold, [i]in those days and at that
time, when I restore the fortunes of
Judah and Jerusalem, 2 [j]I will gather all the
nations and bring them down to the Valley of
Jehoshaphat. And [k]I will enter into judgment

[1] Or *pay back* [2] Ch 3:1 in Hebrew [3] Ch 4:1 in Hebrew

2:28–32 The Lord promises not only provision and protection but the pervasive power and presence of the Holy Spirit. In the Old Testament narratives, the Spirit was primarily depicted as an instrument or expression of God's power that visited only certain people at specific times to accomplish certain divine purposes. Moses longed for the day when there would be a pervasive presence of this Spirit among all the Lord's people (Num. 11:29). These verses in Joel speak of the day when that longing will be fulfilled as a result of the great work of redemption of the coming Lord.

The fulfillment of this prophecy was made apparent on the day of Pentecost, as God made plain his eternal Trinitarian nature and the blessing of his Spirit upon all who believe in Christ (Acts 2:14–28). On that day and for the sake of the expanding church, God revealed fully the Spirit of God that indwells everyone who believes in Jesus—men and women, young and old, insider and outsider. Because the role of the Spirit is to testify of Jesus and minister him to our hearts (John 14:16–20; 16:7–15), Jesus is always present with believers through his Spirit—to comfort (John 14:25–27), transform (Gal. 5:22–23), teach (John 14:26), assure (Rom. 8:16–17), and intercede (Rom. 8:26). Joel 2:32 assures us that this grace and these gifts are available to *all* who will call on the Lord in faith and repentance.

3:1–16 In chapter 3 Joel reveals the Lord not only as the deliverer of his people but also as the judge of the nations who have harassed his people. "Jehoshaphat" (vv. 2, 12) means "the Lord is judge." Sometime we forget that the grace of God includes the defeat and judgment of the spiritual enemies of his people. Despite the efforts of these enemies of God to disrupt his plan and to destroy his people, *they* are the ones who will be judged. What they have sown they will reap. As the sovereign ruler of the universe, God's plans for his people cannot be disrupted. In verse 10 the imagery found elsewhere (Isa. 2:4) is turned around. "Beat your

23 [l]Ps. 100:1, 2; Hab. 3:18; Zech. 10:7 [m]Deut. 11:14; Jer. 5:24 [n]Hos. 6:3
25 [o]ch. 1:4 [p]ver. 11
26 [q]Lev. 25:19 [r][Isa. 49:23]
27 [s]ch. 3:17 [t]Hos. 11:9; See Ezek. 37:26 [u]See Ex. 20:2 [v][Isa. 44:8] [r][See ver. 26 above]
28 [w]ver. 28-32, cited Acts 2:17-21 [x]Isa. 32:15; Ezek. 39:29; Zech. 12:10; John 7:39 [y][Acts 2:39] [z][Acts 21:9]
29 [a][1 Cor. 12:13]
30 [b][Matt. 24:30; Luke 21:11]
31 [c]See ver. 10 [d]Rev. 6:12 [e]Mal. 4:5
32 [f]Cited Rom. 10:13 [g]Isa. 46:13; 59:20; Obad. 17 [h]Jer. 31:7; Mic. 4:7; Zech. 8:12
Chapter 3
1 [i]Jer. 30:3
2 [j][Zeph. 3:8]; See Zech. 14:2-4 [k]Isa. 66:16; Jer. 25:31

with them there, on behalf of my people and
my heritage Israel, because they have scattered
them among the nations and have divided up
my land, 3 and [l]have cast lots for my people,
and have traded a boy for a prostitute, and
have sold a girl for wine and have drunk it.
4 "What are you to me, [m]O Tyre and Sidon,
and all [n]the regions of Philistia? Are you paying me back for something? If you are paying
me back, [o]I will return your payment on your
own head swiftly and speedily. 5 For [p]you have
taken my silver and my gold, and have carried my rich treasures into your temples.[1] 6 You
have sold [q]the people of Judah and Jerusalem
to the Greeks in order to remove them far from
their own border. 7 Behold, I will stir them up
from the place to which you have sold them,
and [o]I will return your payment on your own
head. 8 I will sell your sons and your daughters
into the hand of the people of Judah, and they
will sell them to the [r]Sabeans, to a nation far
away, for the LORD has spoken."

9 Proclaim this among the nations:
[s]Consecrate for war;[2]
stir up the mighty men.
Let all the men of war draw near;
let them come up.
10 [t]Beat your plowshares into swords,
and [t]your pruning hooks into spears;
let the weak say, "I am a warrior."

11 [u]Hasten and come,
all you surrounding nations,
and gather yourselves there.
[v]Bring down your warriors, O LORD.
12 Let the nations stir themselves up
and come up to [w]the Valley of
Jehoshaphat;
[x]for there I will sit to judge
all the surrounding nations.

13 [y]Put in the sickle,
[z]for the harvest is ripe.
[a]Go in, tread,
[a]for the winepress is full.
The vats overflow,
for their evil is great.

14 Multitudes, multitudes,
in the valley of decision!
For [b]the day of the LORD is near
in the valley of decision.
15 [c]The sun and the moon are darkened,
and the stars withdraw their shining.

16 [d]The LORD roars from Zion,
and [d]utters his voice from Jerusalem,
[e]and the heavens and the earth quake.
But the LORD is [f]a refuge to his people,
a stronghold to the people of Israel.

The Glorious Future of Judah

17 [g]"So you shall know that I am the LORD
your God,
[h]who dwells in Zion, [i]my holy mountain.
And Jerusalem shall be holy,
and [j]strangers shall never again pass
through it.

18 "And in that day
[k]the mountains shall drip sweet wine,
and the hills shall flow with milk,
and [l]all the streambeds of Judah
shall flow with water;
[m]and a fountain shall come forth from the
house of the LORD
and water the Valley of [n]Shittim.

[1] Or *palaces* [2] Or *Consecrate a war*

3[l] Obad. 11; Nah. 3:10
4[m] Isa. 23:1, 2; Jer. 47:4; Amos 1:9 [n] [Ezek. 25:15, 16] [o] [Obad. 15]
5[p] [2 Chr. 21:16, 17]
6[q] [ver. 3]
7[o] [See ver. 4 above]
8[r] See 1 Kgs. 10:1
9[s] [Mic. 3:5]
10[t] [Isa. 2:4]
11[u] [Isa. 54:15] [v] [Zech. 14:5]
12[w] ver. 2 [x] Ps. 96:13; 98:9; 110:6; Isa. 2:4; 3:13; Mic. 4:3
13[y] Rev. 14:15 [z] [Jer. 51:33; Hos. 6:11; Matt. 13:30, 39; Mark 4:29; John 4:35; Rev. 14:15, 18] [a] Rev. 14:20; [Isa. 63:2, 3]
14[b] See ch. 1:15
15[c] See ch. 2:10

plowshares into swords, and your pruning hooks into spears." The nations are challenged to bring everything they've got—but it still won't be enough to frustrate God's purpose (cf. Ps. 2:4).

The Lord is the guarantor of his plan and the champion of his people. "If God is for us, who can be against us?" (Rom. 8:31). All this is secured through Christ, the ultimate "refuge to his people" (Joel 3:16).

3:17–21 These final verses of the book show the glorious result of God's gracious provision for his people in terms that would be paradise for an ancient people, including a dwelling place with him (v. 17), a never-ending supply of wine, milk, and flowing water (v. 18), and eternal security as well (v. 20). All of these blessings find their fulfillment in Jesus, who is always present with his people (Heb. 13:5), a never-ending spring of spiritual refreshment (John 4:14), and the giver of eternal life (John 3:16). In brief,

16[d] ch. 2:11; Amos 1:2; [Jer. 25:30] [e] ch. 2:10 [f] Isa. 4:6; 25:4 **17**[g] ch. 2:27; [Ezek. 6:7] [h] ver. 21; [Ezek. 43:7] [i] ch. 2:1; Ps. 48:1; Isa. 65:11; Jer. 31:23 [j] Isa. 52:1; Nah. 1:15; Zech. 14:21; [Rev. 21:27; 22:15] **18**[k] Jer. 31:12; Amos 9:13 [l] Isa. 30:25 [m] Ezek. 47:1 [n] See Num. 25:1

19 [o]"Egypt shall become a desolation
and [p]Edom a desolate wilderness,
[q]for the violence done to the people of Judah,
because they have shed innocent blood in their land.

20 [r]But Judah shall be inhabited forever,
and Jerusalem to all generations.

21 [s]I will avenge their blood,
blood I have not avenged,[1]
[h]for the LORD dwells in Zion."

[1] Or *I will acquit their bloodguilt that I have not acquitted*

Jesus restores Eden. In him, the new creation has dawned, even as the old age of sin and death continues. One day, he will come again and bring even this old age to a close, and Eden will be restored perfectly, forever, for his people.

19[o] See Isa. 19:1-17 [p] See Isa. 34:5 [q] Obad. 10
20[r] Ps. 125:1, 2; Ezek. 37:25
21[s] Isa. 4:4; Ezek. 36:25, 29 [h] [See ver. 17 above]

Introduction to Amos

Author and Date

Amos was not a prophet by profession (1:1; 7:14–15) but nevertheless was entrusted with bringing a message from the Lord to the northern kingdom of Israel. He prophesied sometime between 793–739 B.C.

The Gospel in Amos

In four ways, the Old Testament book of Amos is essential for a robust understanding of the gospel. First, Amos was written with God's people in mind. While Amos 1:2–2:3 includes judgments against the nations surrounding Israel, the bulk of the book is directed at Israel (with Judah, the southern kingdom, included). Importantly, the restoration of all the nations called by God's name in 9:11–15 brings the book full circle, as those once judged are ultimately blessed under a new affiliation. As such, the audience is both particular and universal. New Testament quotations from Amos refer to both of these groups. When quoted by Stephen in Acts 7, the words of Amos anticipate the covenant family of Israel as the audience. Yet eight chapters later (Acts 15:16–17), James will reference the book of Amos in terms of what God is saying to all the families of the earth (i.e., the Gentiles). Thus, Amos has something to say to ancient Israel as well as to the whole world—even to us.

Second, Amos was written with practicality in view. Christians often quote Amos for its emphasis on social justice, and rightly so. Yet we must learn to handle this emphasis properly. Amos's condemnation of Israel's life of luxury and laziness at the expense of the poor should not be treated in a way that reduces the heart of Christianity merely to social ethics. The heart of Christianity is the gospel. The necessary societal implications of the gospel must not be confused with the gospel itself. Both are crucial; our challenge is to understand how mercy is integral to the Christian's identity without reducing the entirety of the Christian message to doing acts of mercy. To see the gospel as a call merely to extend mercy to others without rooting this in the gospel's call to receive God's mercy toward us as sinners is to lose the gospel itself.

Third, the apostles' use of the concept of *place* in Amos reveals God's mission to the world. Place signifies more than mere geography. Amos uses a variety of terms for place (e.g., house, tent, city) to represent the people's relational proximity to or distance from God. For Amos, place becomes a way of addressing the people's orientation toward God as well as God's orientation toward them. From the opening verses to the book's closing, God announces and executes a ministry of justice and mercy from particular places: from Zion and Jerusalem (Amos 1:2), and from the altar (9:1). Once we grasp its importance in Amos, the concept of place will help us better understand the book's message and our mission in the world. Both times that Amos is directly quoted in the New Testament, the concept of place relating to God's family is in play. In Acts 7, Stephen uses Amos to vindicate God's judgment of his household when its members put their own well-being above his kingdom and rule. Later, in Acts 15, James references Amos, and *place* is again significant. This time, however, the message of Amos is used to validate God's plan for rebuilding his household from among all the nations of the earth.

Fourth, Amos's use of poetry reveals the intensity of God's relationship with the world. The book is largely a blistering declaration of God's impending judgment on Israel and the world. In fact, Amos uses a phrase for eschatological (end-time) judgment—"the day of the LORD" (Amos 5:18–20)—that the New Testament repeatedly echoes. That this judgment is expressed in poetry surprises many readers. And this raises the question: why did God give us Amos in poetic verse rather than in legal arguments? After all, in our day, poetry is often the language of love and not lawsuit. Yet poetic language can also express anger, disdain, or lament. As such, it is the genre best suited to convey the idea of God as a divine warrior, driven on by an emotive sense of justice that is at the same time grounded in love.

Outline

I. Superscription (1:1)

II. Oracles of Judgment (1:2–6:14)

III. Visions of Judgment (7:1–9:15)

Amos

1 The words of Amos, who was among the
[a]shepherds[1] of [b]Tekoa, which he saw concerning Israel [c]in the days of [d]Uzziah king of
Judah and in the days of [e]Jeroboam the son
of Joash, king of Israel, two years[2] before [f]the
earthquake.

Judgment on Israel's Neighbors

2 And he said:

[g]"The LORD roars from Zion
and utters his voice from Jerusalem;
[h]the pastures of the shepherds mourn,
and the [i]top of [j]Carmel withers."

3 Thus says the LORD:

[k]"For three transgressions of [l]Damascus,
and for four, [l]I will not revoke the
punishment,[3]
because they have threshed [m]Gilead
with threshing sledges of iron.
4 [n]So I will send a fire upon the house of
[o]Hazael,
and it shall devour the strongholds of
[o]Ben-hadad.
5 I will [p]break the gate-bar of [l]Damascus,
and cut off the inhabitants from the
Valley of [q]Aven,[4]

[1] Or *sheep breeders* [2] Or *during two years* [3] Hebrew *I will not turn it back*; also verses 6, 9, 11, 13 [4] Or *On*

1:1–2:3 After a brief historical introduction of the prophet (1:1), the book of Amos opens with six sermons of judgment against six nations, delivered from the roaring mouth of the Lord. God roars as a lion. This lion metaphor brackets the first two sections of the book (see also 3:8, 12). This portrayal of God as a divine predator appears elsewhere (Joel 3:16) and ultimately anticipates Jesus (Rev. 5:5; 10:3).

The totality and severity of judgment is captured in the image of impending fire (Amos 1:4, 7, 10, 12, 14; 2:2). Fire is often associated with punishment (Gen. 19:24; Rev. 19:20) or refinement (Mal. 3:2; 4:1). For Amos, fire seems primarily to represent looming judgment. As we will see, however, the idea of refinement is never completely absent (Amos 2:5; 5:6; 7:4; 9:8, 11–15).

Jesus picks up on this judging and refining motif in Luke 12:49 as a reason he has come: "I came to cast fire on the earth, and would that it were already kindled!" The context indicates that he understands his death and resurrection as being the time when this refining judgment is accomplished. According to the New Testament, then, Israel's response to Jesus' death and resurrection determines their outcome in the final day of fire. The people of Israel either will be consumed in fiery wrath or will become the products of fiery refinement.

What is true for Israel is also true for the nations. All of humanity is subject to the fire of divine wrath. And yet even here mercy is extended. The poetic structure of Amos lays out a distinct view of mercy. The patterned statement of indictment—"For three transgressions . . . and for four . . ."—becomes the basis for the repeated statement of judgment: "I will not revoke the punishment" (Amos 1:3, 6, 9, 11, 13; 2:1; see also 2:4, 6). Yes, God has decided to judge the world for repeated sin, but his gavel falls only after a season of patient endurance of repeated and unrepented sin. So, in the end, Amos holds out great hope for the nations (9:12) because the prophecy demonstrates that God is "slow to anger" (cf. Ex. 34:6; Ps. 145:8; Joel 2:13).

Finally, the impending judgment of God is focused squarely on how the people of the world behave toward one another. The sins in this passage are transgressions of the most basic laws of justice. Notice what God speaks against: border skirmishes (Amos 1:3), enslavement (1:6, 9), betrayal (1:9, 11), greed (1:13), and brutality (1:11, 13;

Chapter 1

1 [a]ch. 7:14, 15 [b]2 Sam. 14:2 [c]See Hos. 1:1 [d]2 Kgs. 15:1, 13, 30; 2 Chr. 26:1 [e]ch. 7:10; 2 Kgs. 14:23 [f]Zech. 14:5; [Isa. 29:6]
2 [g]See Joel 3:16 [h][Ps. 65:12] [i]ch. 9:3 [j]See Josh. 19:26
3 [k]ver. 9, 11, 13; ch. 2:1, 4, 6; Prov. 30:15, 18, 21, 29 [l][Isa. 8:4] [m]ver. 13; [2 Kgs. 10:33; Isa. 21:10]
4 [n]Jer. 49:27 [o]2 Kgs. 13:24, 25
5 [p]Jer. 51:30 [l][See ver. 3 above] [q]See Hos. 4:15

and him who holds the scepter from
[r]Beth-eden;
and the people of [s]Syria shall go into
exile to [t]Kir,"
says the LORD.

6 Thus says the LORD:

[k]"For three transgressions of [u]Gaza,
and for four, I will not revoke the
punishment,
because [v]they carried into exile a whole
people
to deliver them up to Edom.
7 So I will send a fire upon the wall of
[u]Gaza,
and it shall devour her strongholds.
8 I will cut off the inhabitants from [w]Ash-
dod,
and him who holds the scepter from
Ashkelon;
I will turn my hand against Ekron,
and the remnant of the Philistines
shall perish,"
says the Lord GOD.

9 Thus says the LORD:

[k]"For three transgressions of [x]Tyre,
and for four, I will not revoke the
punishment,
because they delivered up a whole people to Edom,
and did not remember the covenant
of brotherhood.
10 So I will send a fire upon the wall of [x]Tyre,
and it shall devour her strongholds."

11 Thus says the LORD:

[k]"For three transgressions of [y]Edom,
and for four, I will not revoke the
punishment,
[y]because he pursued his brother with the
sword
[z]and cast off all pity,
[a]and his anger tore perpetually,
[a]and he kept his wrath forever.
12 So I will send a fire upon [b]Teman,
and it shall devour the strongholds of
[c]Bozrah."

13 Thus says the LORD:

[k]"For three transgressions of the [d]Am-
monites,
and for four, I will not revoke the
punishment,
because [e]they have ripped open pregnant women in [f]Gilead,
that they might enlarge their border.
14 So I will kindle a fire in the wall of
[g]Rabbah,
[h]and it shall devour her strongholds,
with shouting on the day of battle,
[h]with a tempest in the day of the
whirlwind;
15 and [i]their king shall go into exile,
he and his princes[1] together,"
says the LORD.

2 Thus says the LORD:

[k]"For three transgressions of [j]Moab,
and for four, I will not revoke the
punishment,[2]
because [k]he burned to lime
the bones of the king of Edom.

[1] Or *officials* [2] Hebrew *I will not turn it back*; also verses 4, 6

5[r] 2 Kgs. 19:12 [s] ch. 9:7; [2 Kgs. 16:9] [t] ch. 9:7; 2 Kgs. 16:9
6[k] [See ver. 3 above] [u] Jer. 47:1, 5; Zeph. 2:4; Zech. 9:5 [v] 2 Chr. 28:18; See Joel 3:4-6
7[u] [See ver. 6 above]
8[w] ch. 3:9; 1 Sam. 5:1
9[k] [See ver. 3 above] [x] See Joel 3:4
10[x] [See ver. 9 above]
11[k] [See ver. 3 above] [y] [2 Chr. 28:17] [z] Ps. 137:7; [Joel 3:19; Mal. 1:4] [a] Ezek. 35:5
12[b] Obad. 9; See 1 Chr. 1:45 [c] Isa. 63:1; See 1 Chr. 1:44
13[k] [See ver. 3 above] [d] Jer. 49:1, 2; Zeph. 2:8, 9 [e] See Hos. 13:16 [f] ver. 3
14[g] 2 Sam. 11:1; 12:26; See Ezek. 21:20 [h] [Ezek. 21:28, 29]
15[i] Jer. 49:3

2:2). Because all humanity bears the image of God, this opportunistic and hateful behavior is an affront to God (cf. the sins described in Rom. 1:18–3:20). So, how are we to understand this universal punishment in light of God's mercy? We ought not to delight in the world getting what they deserve. The proper response for us is like that of creation in Amos 1:2: bowing low, mourning, and pleading "Lord, have mercy." God has had mercy, after all, on *us*.

2:4–3:15 God's judgment is not limited to the nations. It extends to Judah (2:4) and Israel (2:6)—to "the whole family" (3:1) of God. That God would judge his own people is a testament to his impartiality (2:9–16; cf. Rom. 2:6–3:20).

In these verses, two primary sins are listed as the reason for judgment. First, God's people have rejected God's Word (Amos 2:4, 12). Second, they harbor an inappropriate love of material possessions and illicit sexual pleasure at the expense of people and propriety (2:6–8; 3:10, 15). To capture the nature of this judgment, Amos returns to the lion motif (3:7–8). In a horrifying image, Amos envisions God as predator and his people as the tiny bits of prey left behind after being devoured (3:12).

Chapter 2 **1**[k] [See ch. 1:3 above] [j] Zeph. 2:8, 9; See Isa. 15 [k] [2 Kgs. 3:27]

2 So I will send a fire upon Moab,
and it shall devour the strongholds of [l]Kerioth,
and Moab shall die amid uproar,
amid shouting and the sound of the trumpet;
3 [m]I will cut off the ruler from its midst,
and will kill [m]all its princes[1] with him,"
says the LORD.

Judgment on Judah

4 Thus says the LORD:

[n]"For three transgressions of Judah,
and for four, I will not revoke the punishment,
because [o]they have rejected the law of the LORD,
and have not kept his statutes,
but [p]their lies have led them astray,
those after which their fathers walked.
5 So [q]I will send a fire upon Judah,
and it shall devour the strongholds of Jerusalem."

Judgment on Israel

6 Thus says the LORD:

[n]"For three transgressions of Israel,
and for four, I will not revoke the punishment,
because [r]they sell the righteous for [s]silver,
and the needy for a pair of sandals—
7 those who trample the head of the poor
[t]into the dust of the earth
and [u]turn aside the way of the afflicted;
[v]a man and his father go in to the same girl,
so that my holy name is profaned;
8 they lay themselves down beside every altar
on garments [w]taken in pledge,
and in the house of their God they drink
the wine of those who have been fined.

9 "Yet [x]it was I who destroyed the Amorite before them,
[y]whose height was like the height of the cedars
and who was as strong as the oaks;
[z]I destroyed his fruit above
and his roots beneath.
10 [a]Also it was I who brought you up out of the land of Egypt
[b]and led you forty years in the wilderness,
[x]to possess the land of the Amorite.
11 And I raised up some of your sons for prophets,
and some of your young men for [c]Nazirites.
Is it not indeed so, O people of Israel?"
declares the LORD.

12 "But you made the Nazirites [d]drink wine,
and commanded the prophets,
saying, [e]'You shall not prophesy.'
13 "Behold, I will press you down in your place,
as a cart full of sheaves presses down.
14 [f]Flight shall perish from the swift,
[f]and the strong shall not retain his strength,
[g]nor shall the mighty save his life;

[1] Or *officials*

When he arrived some 800 years later, Jesus denounced the people of God for the very same things (Matt. 23:1–38). The consistency of this judgment becomes instructive for us. First, in the face of the lion's roar, we should soberly revere, or "fear" God (Amos 3:8). As the church, we have a special relationship with God and therefore should be committed to repentance or turning from our rebellion. Second, just as obedience to God's Word was needed in Amos's day, the same is true for us. When we reject God's Word we should anticipate the teeth of God's discipline—not, however, as punishment of his enemies but as loving chastising of his children. Third, as in Amos's day, we need to uphold God's standards of sexual purity and social justice. When we live to advance our own pleasures and, by negligence or intent, oppress others, then we should expect that God's hand will soon be against us (cf. 1:8).

As Christians we should be thankful that Jesus came not only to denounce sin but to battle the powers that held us fast in it. He came as God's warrior King to defeat Satan and our sin at the cross (Col. 2:14–15), even as Israel's judgment fell on him. Jesus revered God perfectly, as we do not. He obeyed perfectly, as we cannot. He was sexually pure, materially selfless, and compassionate, as we are not.

2 [l]Jer. 48:24, 41
3 [m][Jer. 48:7]
4 [n]See ch. 1:3 [o]Lev. 26:14, 15; Neh. 1:7; Ezek. 20:13, 16, 24; [Dan. 9:11] [p]Jer. 16:19, 20; Rom. 1:25
5 [q]Jer. 17:27; Hos. 8:14
6 [n][See ver. 4 above] [r][Lev. 25:39; 2 Kgs. 4:1] [s]ch. 8:6
7 [t]Lam. 2:10 [u]ch. 5:12; Job 24:4; Isa. 10:2 [v][1 Cor. 5:1]; See Ezek. 22:11
8 [w]See Ex. 22:26
9 [x]Deut. 2:31; Josh. 24:8; See Num. 21:21-25 [y][Num. 13:32, 33; Isa. 10:33] [z][Job 18:16]
10 [a]ch. 3:1; Ex. 12:17, 51 [b]See Deut. 8:2 [x][See ver. 9 above]
11 [c]Num. 6:2
12 [d][Num. 6:3] [e]ch. 7:13, 16; Isa. 30:10; Mic. 2:6
14 [f][ch. 9:1; Eccles. 9:11] [g][Ps. 33:16]

15 he who handles the bow shall not stand,
and he who is [h]swift of foot shall not
save himself,
[i]nor shall he who rides the horse save
his life;
16 and he who is stout of heart among the
mighty
shall flee away naked in that day,"
declares the LORD.

Israel's Guilt and Punishment

3 [j]Hear this word that the LORD has spoken
against you, O people of Israel, against the
whole family that I brought up out of the land
of Egypt:

2 [k]"You only have I known
of all the families of the earth;
[l]therefore I will punish you
for all your iniquities.

3 "Do two walk together,
unless they have agreed to meet?
4 Does a lion roar in the forest,
when he has no prey?
Does a young lion cry out from his den,
if he has taken nothing?
5 Does a bird fall in a snare on the earth,
when there is no trap for it?
Does a snare spring up from the ground,
when it has taken nothing?
6 [m]Is a trumpet blown in a city,
and the people are not afraid?
[n]Does disaster come to a city,
unless the LORD has done it?
7 "For the Lord GOD does nothing
[o]without revealing his secret
to his servants the prophets.
8 The lion has roared;
who will not fear?
[p]The Lord GOD has spoken;
who can but prophesy?"
9 Proclaim to the strongholds in [q]Ashdod
and to the strongholds in the land of
Egypt,
and say, "Assemble yourselves on [r]the
mountains of Samaria,
and see the great tumults within her,
and [s]the oppressed in her midst."
10 "They do not know how to do right,"
declares the LORD,
[t]"those who store up violence and robbery in their strongholds."

11 Therefore thus says the Lord GOD:

[u]"An adversary shall surround the land
and bring down[1] your defenses from
you,
and [v]your strongholds shall be plundered."

12 Thus says the LORD: [w]"As the shepherd rescues from the mouth of the lion two legs, or
a piece of an ear, [x]so shall the people of Israel
[y]who dwell in Samaria be rescued, with the
corner of a couch and part[2] of a bed.

13 "Hear, [z]and testify against the house of
Jacob,"
declares the Lord GOD, [a]the God of
hosts,
14 "that on the day I punish Israel for his
transgressions,
[b]I will punish the altars of Bethel,
and [c]the horns of the altar shall be cut off
and fall to the ground.
15 [d]I will strike [e]the winter house along
with [f]the summer house,
and [g]the houses of ivory shall perish,
and the great houses[3] shall come to an
end,"
declares the LORD.

4 "Hear this word, [h]you cows of Bashan,
who are [i]on the mountain of Samaria,
[j]who oppress the poor, [j]who crush the
needy,
who say to your husbands, 'Bring,
that we may drink!'
2 [k]The Lord GOD has sworn by his holiness
that, behold, the days are coming
upon you,

[1] Hebrew *An adversary, one who surrounds the land—he shall bring down* [2] The meaning of the Hebrew word is uncertain [3] Or *and many houses*

15[h] [2 Sam. 2:18] [i] [Ps. 33:17]
Chapter 3
1[j] ch. 7:16; [ch. 2:10]

4:1–6:14 Chapters 4–6 place us squarely in the main section of Amos. The roar of impending judgment has been heard (chapters 1–3). The frightful visions of the execution of divine judgment are still to come (chapters 7–9). Thus, we expect these middle

2[k] Deut. 7:6; 10:15; Ps. 147:19, 20; [Hos. 5:3; 13:5; Mic. 2:3] [l] [Matt. 10:15; 11:21, 22; Luke 10:13, 14; 12:47; Rom. 2:9] **6**[m] Ezek. 33:4; See Joel 2:1 [n] [Isa. 45:7; Lam. 3:38; Mic. 1:12] **7**[o] Gen. 18:17; [Jer. 15:1] **8**[p] [Num. 22:38] **9**[q] ch. 1:8 [r] ch. 4:1; 6:1; [1 Kgs. 16:24] [s] Ps. 94:5, 6; 103:6; See 1 Kgs. 21:1-16 **10**[t] [ch. 6:3; Isa. 3:14, 15]; See Mic. 6:10-12 **11**[u] [2 Kgs. 17:5, 6]; See 2 Kgs. 18:9-12 [v] [Isa. 39:6] **12**[w] [Ex. 22:13] [x] See Jer. 31:8, 9 [y] [ch. 6:4] **13**[z] [Ps. 50:7; 81:8] [a] ch. 4:13; Ps. 80:4, 7, 14 **14**[b] [Hos. 10:15]; See 1 Kgs. 13:1-3 [c] [2 Kgs. 23:15] **15**[d] [ch. 6:11] [e] Jer. 36:22 [f] Judg. 3:20 [g] 1 Kgs. 22:39; Ps. 45:8 **Chapter 4** **1**[h] Ps. 22:12 [i] ch. 3:9; 6:1 [j] Hos. 5:11 **2**[k] Ps. 89:35

[l]when they shall take you away with
hooks,
[l]even the last of you with fishhooks.
3 [m]And you shall go out through the
breaches,
each one straight ahead;
and you shall be cast out into Harmon,"
declares the LORD.

4 [n]"Come to Bethel, and transgress;
to [o]Gilgal, and multiply transgression;
[n]bring your [p]sacrifices every morning,
your tithes every three days;
5 offer a sacrifice of thanksgiving of [q]that
which is leavened,
and proclaim [r]freewill offerings, publish them;
[s]for so you love to do, O people of
Israel!"
declares the Lord GOD.

Israel Has Not Returned to the LORD

6 "I gave you cleanness of teeth in all your
cities,
and [t]lack of bread in all your places,
[u]yet you did not return to me,"
declares the LORD.

7 "I also [v]withheld the rain from you
when there were yet three months to
the harvest;
[w]I would send rain on one city,
and send no rain on another city;
one field would have rain,
and the field on which it did not rain
would wither;
8 so two or three cities [x]would wander to
another city
to drink water, and would not be satisfied;
[u]yet you did not return to me,"
declares the LORD.

chapters to make the case for judgment. And in doing so, these chapters reveal to us the book's central themes.

In Amos 4–6, God's judgment on his own "house of Israel" is due to their setting aside of his Word (4:1; 5:1, 10), superficial worship (4:4–5; 5:21–24; cf. 5:7, 11–13; 6:12), and selfishness in social ethics (4:1; 5:11, 12, 15, 24; 6:4, 6). Simply put, in this time of blessing and affluence, God's people did not pursue God's house but rather their own. Even so, they thought that God would always look upon Zion as his place, and the people as heirs of his kingdom and members of his household—regardless of how they lived. Israel was presumptuous.

The fact that *house* (or place, tent, or kingdom) is a dominant theme in Amos is signaled by a change in the form of address in 3:13: "Hear, and testify against the house of Jacob." Amos uses a variety of terms for place (e.g., house, tent, city) to represent the people's relational proximity to or distance from God (see Introduction). For Amos, *place* becomes a way of addressing the people's orientation toward God as well as his orientation toward them. In this section, Israel is refered to as *house* seven times (5:1, 3, 4, 6, 25; 6:1, 14), and this is done as an emblem for Israel's rebellion and its consequences. For example, "you have built houses of hewn stone, but you shall not dwell in them" (5:11; cf. 3:15; 6:9, 10, 11). Amos uses other *place* terms 15 times (e.g., "beds," "place," "city," "gate" in 4:6, 8; 5:2, 3, 10, 12, 15, 16; 6:1, 2, 4, 8). Amos is about more than just social ethics. Amos is about God's *house*. In particular, the message of Amos vindicates God's judgment of his household when its members put their own well-being above his kingdom and rule.

Israel as God's *house* (or tent) becomes a prominent image the first time Amos is directly quoted in the New Testament. In Acts 7:42–43, Stephen quotes from Amos 5 in order to show how God's people traded in his *place* (i.e., the tent where God resided) for that of the pagans (i.e., "the tent of Moloch"). Stephen cites this to show that when the "day of the Lord" came in the death and resurrection of Jesus, it signaled judgment for the idolatrous people who had been chosen to be a dwelling place for God.

Stephen's understanding is part of a larger shift in the concept of *place* that had occurred since the writing of Amos, for Zion was replaced by a better dwelling: Jesus' very own person. With Christ's death, the geography of Jerusalem has been replaced by the topography of the cross, now planted by grace and through faith in the human heart (John 4:23). Those who respond to the work of Christ become the very *dwelling* of God. We are his house, his tent, his temple (1 Cor. 3:16; Eph. 2:17–22).

2 [l][Jer. 16:16; Hab. 1:15]; See 2 Kgs. 19:28
3 [m][Ezek. 12:5, 12]
4 [n][ch. 5:5; Ezek. 20:39; Matt. 23:32] [o][ch. 5:5; Hos. 4:15; 9:15; 12:11] [p]Num. 28:3, 4; [Jer. 7:21]
5 [q]Lev. 7:13 [r]Ex. 35:29; Lev. 22:18, 21; Deut. 12:6 [s][Ps. 81:11, 12]
6 [t][Deut. 28:57; Lam. 2:12] [u]Jer. 15:7; Hag. 2:17
7 [v]Jer. 3:3; [Joel 2:23] [w][Ex. 9:26]
8 [x][ch. 8:12] [u][See ver. 6 above]

9 [y]"I struck you with blight and mildew;
your many gardens and your vineyards,
your fig trees and your olive trees [z]the locust devoured;
[u]yet you did not return to me,"
declares the LORD.

10 "I sent among you a pestilence [a]after the manner of Egypt;
I killed your young men with the sword,
and [b]carried away your horses,[1]
and [c]I made the stench of your camp go up into your nostrils;
[u]yet you did not return to me,"
declares the LORD.

11 "I overthrew some of you,
[d]as when God overthrew Sodom and Gomorrah,
and you were [e]as a brand[2] plucked out of the burning;
[u]yet you did not return to me,"
declares the LORD.

12 "Therefore thus I will do to you, O Israel;
because I will do this to you,
prepare to meet your God, O Israel!"

13 For behold, [f]he who forms the mountains and creates the wind,
and [g]declares to man what is his thought,
[h]who makes the morning darkness,
and [i]treads on the heights of the earth—
[j]the LORD, the God of hosts, is his name!

Seek the LORD and Live

5 Hear this word that I [k]take up over you in
lamentation, O house of Israel:

2 "Fallen, no more to rise,
is [l]the virgin Israel;
forsaken on her land,
with none to raise her up."

3 For thus says the Lord GOD:

"The city that went out a thousand
shall have a hundred left,
and that which went out a hundred
shall have ten left
to the house of Israel."

4 For thus says the LORD to the house of Israel:

[m]"Seek me and live;
5 but do not seek [n]Bethel,
and do not enter into [n]Gilgal
or cross over to [o]Beersheba;
for [n]Gilgal shall surely go into exile,
and [n]Bethel shall come to nothing."

6 [m]Seek the LORD and live,
[p]lest he break out like fire in the house of Joseph,
and it devour, with none to quench it for [n]Bethel,
7 O [q]you who turn justice to wormwood[3]
and cast down righteousness to the earth!

8 He who made the [r]Pleiades and Orion,
and turns deep darkness into the morning
and [s]darkens the day into night,
who [t]calls for the waters of the sea
[t]and pours them out on the surface of the earth,
[u]the LORD is his name;
9 [v]who makes destruction flash forth against the strong,
so that destruction comes upon the fortress.

10 [w]They hate him who reproves [x]in the gate,
and they [y]abhor him who speaks the truth.
11 Therefore because you [z]trample on[4] the poor
and you exact taxes of grain from him,
[a]you have built houses of hewn stone,
but you shall not dwell in them;
[a]you have planted pleasant vineyards,
but you shall not drink their wine.
12 For I know how many are your transgressions
and how great are your sins—
you who afflict the righteous, who [b]take a bribe,
and [c]turn aside the needy [x]in the gate.

[1] Hebrew *along with the captivity of your horses* [2] That is, a burning stick [3] Or *to bitter fruit* [4] Or *you tax*

9[y] Deut. 28:22; Hag. 2:17 [z] Joel 1:4 [u] [See ver. 6 above] **10**[a] Deut. 28:27, 60; [Ex. 12:29; Ps. 78:50; Isa. 10:24, 26] [b] 2 Kgs. 13:7 [c] [Joel 2:20] [u] [See ver. 6 above] **11**[d] [Isa. 13:19] [e] Zech. 3:2; [Jude 23] [u] [See ver. 6 above] **13**[f] [Ps. 102:25] [g] [Ps. 139:2] [h] [ch. 5:8; 8:9] [i] Isa. 58:14; Mic. 1:3 [j] ch. 3:13; 5:8; 9:6; See Jer. 10:16 **Chapter 5** **1**[k] Ezek. 19:1 **2**[l] Lam. 2:1; [Isa. 47:1] **4**[m] 2 Chr. 15:2; Isa. 55:6; Zeph. 2:3 **5**[n] See ch. 4:4 [o] ch. 8:14 **6**[m] [See ver. 4 above] [p] [Isa. 9:18, 19] [n] [See ver. 5 above] **7**[q] [ch. 6:12] **8**[r] Job 9:9; 38:31 [s] Ps. 104:20; [ch. 4:13; 8:9] [t] ch. 9:6; [Gen. 6:17; Ps. 104:6, 7] [u] See ch. 4:13 **9**[v] [Jer. 50:32] **10**[w] Isa. 29:21; [Prov. 15:5, 10] [x] See Ruth 4:1 [y] [1 Kgs. 22:8] **11**[z] [James 2:6] [a] Deut. 28:30, 39; Mic. 6:15; Zeph. 1:13 **12**[b] 1 Sam. 8:3; 12:3; [Ps. 26:10] [c] ch. 2:7; Isa. 29:21 [x] [See ver. 10 above]

13 Therefore he who is prudent will [d]keep silent in such a time,
[e]for it is an evil time.

14 [f]Seek good, and not evil,
that you may live;
and so the LORD, [g]the God of hosts, will be with you,
as you have said.
15 [h]Hate evil, and love good,
and establish justice [x]in the gate;
[i]it may be that the LORD, the God of hosts,
will be gracious to the remnant of Joseph.

16 Therefore thus says the LORD, [g]the God of hosts, the Lord:

"In all the squares [j]there shall be wailing,
and in all the streets they shall say,
'Alas! Alas!'
They shall call the farmers to mourning
and [j]to wailing those who are skilled in lamentation,
17 and in all vineyards there shall be wailing,
for [k]I will pass through your midst,"
says the LORD.

Let Justice Roll Down

18 Woe to you who desire [l]the day of the LORD!
Why would you have the day of the LORD?
[m]It is darkness, and not light,
19 [n]as if a man fled from a lion,
and a bear met him,
or went into the house and leaned his hand against the wall,
and a serpent bit him.
20 [m]Is not the day of the LORD darkness, and not light,
and gloom with no brightness in it?

21 [o]"I hate, I despise your feasts,
and I take no delight in your solemn assemblies.
22 [p]Even though you offer me your burnt offerings and grain offerings,
I will not accept them;
and the peace offerings of your fattened animals,
I will not look upon them.
23 Take away from me the noise of your songs;
to [q]the melody of your harps I will not listen.
24 But let justice roll down like waters,
and righteousness like an ever-flowing stream.

25 [r]"Did you bring to me sacrifices and offerings during the forty years in the wilderness, O house of Israel? 26 [s]You [t]shall take up
Sikkuth your king, and Kiyyun your star-
god—your images that you made for yourselves, 27 [u]and I will send you into exile beyond
Damascus," says the LORD, whose name is [g]the
God of hosts.

Woe to Those at Ease in Zion

6 [w]"Woe to those who are at ease in Zion,
and to those who feel secure on [x]the mountain of Samaria,
[y]the notable men of [z]the first of the nations,
to whom the house of Israel comes!

5:18–24 The "day of the LORD" rises to the surface in this passage (see also 2:16; 3:14; 4:2; 8:3, 9, 10, 11, 13; 9:11, 13). For the Israelites of Amos's day, the meaning of the "day of the LORD" would be the dawning of an age of God's complete victory over all the nations. It was expected to be a day when God's people inherited all of God's promised and long anticipated blessings (see, e.g., Jer. 46:10; Ezek. 30:3; Obad. 15).

And yet, shockingly, this day turned out to be one of judgment on God's own people! Assyria swooped down and "the day of the LORD" arrived with all the unmitigated force of God's wrath. This transformed meaning of "the day" takes center stage in Amos 5:18–20. Only later, in chapter 9, will the "day of the LORD" be used as a term of future hope (see note on 9:11–15).

In the New Testament, the meaning of the "day of the Lord" becomes clearer (Acts 2:16–17; 1 Pet. 4:17). The day is already quietly underway through Jesus Christ, though not yet in final perfected form (1 Thess. 5:1–11; 2 Pet. 3:8–10). We have the advantage of living with a more complete understanding than the people of Amos's day. What we make of Jesus' death and resurrection will determine how we enter into and come through the final "day of the Lord." Knowing this, we should give ourselves to gospel-fueled social ethics even as we commit ourselves to speaking the gospel message in fulfillment of Christ's mission (see, e.g., Matt. 28:18–20).

13 [d][Eccles. 3:7] [e]Mic. 2:3
14 [f][Deut. 30:15, 19; Zeph. 2:3] [g]ch. 3:13
15 [h]Ps. 97:10; Rom. 12:9 [x][See ver. 10 above] [i]Joel 2:14; [Ex. 32:30]
16 [g][See ver. 14 above] [j][Jer. 9:17, 18]
17 [k]Ex. 12:12
18 [l]See Joel 1:15 [m]See Joel 2:1, 2
19 [n][Isa. 24:18; Jer. 48:44]
20 [m][See ver. 18 above]
21 [o]Isa. 1:14; [Jer. 6:20]
22 [p]Ps. 51:16, 17; Isa. 1:11
23 [q][ch. 6:5; 8:3; Isa. 5:12]
25 [r]Cited Acts 7:42, 43
26 [s][Deut. 32:17; Ezek. 20:16, 24] [t][Isa. 46:7]
27 [u]2 Kgs. 17:6 [g][See ver. 14 above]

Chapter 6

1 [w]Isa. 32:9; Zeph. 1:12; Luke 6:24; James 5:1 [x]ch. 3:9; 4:1 [y][Ezek. 22:6] [z]See Ex. 19:5

2 Pass over to [a]Calneh, and see,
and from there go to [b]Hamath the great;
then go down to [c]Gath of the Philistines.
[d]Are you better than these kingdoms?
Or is their territory greater than your territory,
3 [e]O you who put far away the day of disaster
[f]and bring near the seat of violence?

4 "Woe to those [g]who lie on [h]beds of ivory
[g] and stretch themselves out on their couches,
and eat lambs from the flock
[i]and calves from the midst of the stall,
5 [j]who sing idle songs to the sound of the harp
and like David [j]invent for themselves instruments of music,
6 [k]who drink wine in bowls
and [l]anoint themselves with the finest oils,
but are not grieved over the ruin of Joseph!
7 [m]Therefore they shall now be the first of those who go into exile,
and the revelry of those who stretch themselves out shall pass away."

8 [n]The Lord GOD has sworn by himself, declares the LORD, the God of hosts:

"I abhor [o]the pride of Jacob
and hate his strongholds,
[p]and I will deliver up the city and all that is in it."

9 And [q]if ten men remain in one house, they
shall die. 10 And when one's relative, [r]the one
who anoints him for burial, shall take him up
to bring the bones out of the house, and shall
say to him who is in the innermost parts of
the house, "Is there still anyone with you?"
he shall say, "No"; and he shall say, [s]"Silence!
We must not mention the name of the LORD."

11 For behold, the LORD commands,
and [t]the great house shall be struck down into fragments,
and the little house into bits.
12 Do horses run on rocks?
Does one plow there[1] with oxen?
[u]But you have turned justice into [v]poison
[u] and the fruit of righteousness into wormwood[2]—
13 you who rejoice in Lo-debar,[3]
who say, [w]"Have we not by our own strength
captured Karnaim[4] for ourselves?"
14 "For behold, [x]I will raise up against you a nation,
O house of Israel," declares the LORD, the God of hosts;
"and they shall oppress you from [y]Lebo-hamath
to the Brook of [z]the Arabah."

Warning Visions

7 [a]This is what the Lord GOD showed me:
behold, [b]he was forming locusts when the
latter growth was just beginning to sprout,
and behold, it was the latter growth after the
king's mowings. 2 When they had finished eating the grass of the land, I said,

"O Lord GOD, please forgive!
[c]How can Jacob stand?
He is so small!"
3 [d]The LORD relented concerning this:
"It shall not be," said the LORD.

4 [a]This is what the Lord GOD showed me:
behold, the Lord GOD was calling [e]for a judgment by fire, and it devoured the great deep
and was eating up the land. 5 Then I said,

[1] Or *the sea* [2] Or *into bitter fruit* [3] *Lo-debar* means *nothing* [4] *Karnaim* means *horns* (a symbol of strength)

7:1–17 With the case for judgment complete, Amos now pivots to the execution of it in the form of five visions (beginning with v. 1; cf. vv. 4, 7; 8:1; 9:1). God shows Amos what "the day of the LORD" will look like for the house of Israel. Interestingly, while the reader has been led to expect swift and total judgment, the first two visions show the Lord relenting from such obliterating action. Like Moses, the great prophet before him, Amos intercedes on Israel's behalf (7:3, 6) and secures a commitment that God will not make Israel so small that it could never recover (vv. 2–3, 5–6). Yet, after the content of the third vision was heard and subsequently rejected by Amaziah, Israel's compromised priest, God indicates that judgment is certain (vv. 10–13). At least three gospel lessons emerge.

2 [a] Gen. 10:10; Isa. 10:9 [b] 1 Kgs. 8:65; 2 Kgs. 18:34; Isa. 10:9 [c] See 1 Sam. 17:4 [d] [Nah. 3:8]
3 [e] [ch. 9:10; Ezek. 12:27] [f] See ch. 3:10
4 [g] [ch. 3:12] [h] [Esth. 1:6] [i] [James 5:5]
5 [j] See ch. 5:23
6 [k] [Isa. 5:12] [l] [Dan. 10:3]
7 [m] ch. 7:11, 17
8 [n] Jer. 22:5; 51:14 [o] ch. 8:7; [Ps. 47:4] [p] [Jer. 17:3]
9 [q] [ch. 3:3]
10 [r] See 1 Sam. 31:12
[s] [ch. 5:13; 8:3] **11** [t] [ch. 3:15] **12** [u] [ch. 5:7] [v] Deut. 29:18 **13** [w] [1 Kgs. 22:11; Mic. 4:13] **14** [x] [Jer. 5:15] [y] 2 Kgs. 14:25 [z] See Deut. 1:1 **Chapter 7** **1** [a] ch. 8:1 [b] [Joel 1:4]; See Ex. 10:4 **2** [c] [Ps. 130:3] **3** [d] [Deut. 32:36; Joel 2:13] **4** [a] [See ver. 1 above] [e] [Rev. 8:7, 8]

"O Lord GOD, please cease!
[c]How can Jacob stand?
He is so small!"
6 [d]The LORD relented concerning this:
"This also shall not be," said the Lord
GOD.

7 [a]This is what he showed me: behold, the
Lord was standing beside a wall built with
[f]a plumb line, with a plumb line in his hand.
8 And the LORD said to me, [g]"Amos, what do
you see?" And I said, "A plumb line." Then the
Lord said,

"Behold, I am setting [f]a plumb line
in the midst of my people Israel;
[g]I will never again pass by them;
9 [h]the high places of Isaac shall be made
desolate,
and the sanctuaries of Israel shall be
laid waste,
and I will rise against [i]the house of
Jeroboam with the sword."

Amos Accused

10 Then Amaziah [j]the priest of Bethel sent
to [k]Jeroboam king of Israel, saying, "Amos
has [l]conspired against you in the midst of the
house of Israel. The land is not able to bear all
his words. 11 For thus Amos has said,

"'Jeroboam shall die by the sword,
and [m]Israel must go into exile
away from his land.'"

12 And Amaziah said to Amos, [n]"O seer, go, flee
away [o]to the land of Judah, and [p]eat bread
there, and prophesy there, 13 but [q]never again
prophesy at Bethel, for [r]it is the king's sanctuary, and it is a temple of the kingdom."
14 Then Amos answered and said to Amaziah,
[s]"I was[1] no prophet, nor a prophet's son, but [t]I
was a herdsman and a dresser of sycamore figs.
15 [u]But the LORD took me from following the
flock, and the LORD said to me, 'Go, prophesy
to my people Israel.' 16 [v]Now therefore hear the
word of the LORD.

"You say, [n]'Do not prophesy against Israel,
and [w]do not preach against the house
of [x]Isaac.'
17 [y]Therefore thus says the LORD:

"'Your wife shall be a prostitute in the city,
and your sons and your daughters
shall fall by the sword,
and your land [z]shall be divided up
with a measuring line;
you yourself shall die in an unclean land,
and [m]Israel shall surely go into exile
away from its land.'"

The Coming Day of Bitter Mourning

8 [a]This is what the Lord GOD showed me:
behold, a basket of summer fruit. 2 And
he said, [b]"Amos, what do you see?" And I said,
[c]"A basket of summer fruit." Then the LORD
said to me,

[d]"The end[2] has come upon my people Israel;
I will never again pass by them.

[1] Or *am*; twice in this verse [2] The Hebrew words for *end* and *summer fruit* sound alike

First, if we are tempted to push aside a message of a final day of reckoning because it seems outdated, we can be assured: it will come. A wrath-free gospel is no gospel at all (vv. 14–17). If grace rescues us from nothing, then it is not really grace.

Second, the God of Amos is merciful. He is gracious, slow to anger, and executes wrath in a way that salvages a hope and a remnant among his covenant people (cf. 5:15). At its core, the gospel, like the book of Amos, is a message of mercy.

Third, just as judgment was dismissed by Amaziah the priest, so too a later priesthood rejected Jesus' rebukes and lament (Matt. 23:13–38; 26:3). Jesus' sad song should have been recognized by the priesthood of his day. God was signaling that the time of his justice had come. Ironically, though, Jesus is more than a mere successor to Amos as God's prophet. Jesus is not only *a* prophet; he is *the* ultimate prophet, embodying the message he proclaims (John 6:14; 7:40). For he not only represents God's message to his people but also stands as the representative of God's people before heaven's judgment throne. His death completes the priestly act of making sacrifice for sin, lest we all be sent to an eternal spiritual wasteland of exile. He is not only the final Prophet, speaking judgment, but also the final Priest, bearing that very judgment for us.

8:1–9:10 That wrath remains in view for Amos is beyond doubt (8:3, 9, 10, 11, 13; 9:11, 13). The reasons for this judgment are manifold, including exploitation of the poor (8:4, 6) and a superficial adherence to the Sabbath (8:5). And this exploitation

5 [c][See ver. 2 above]
6 [d][See ver. 3 above]
7 [a][See ver. 1 above] [f][ver. 17]; See 2 Kgs. 21:13
8 [g]ch. 8:2 [f][See ver. 7 above]
9 [h]Gen. 26:23, 25 [i]See 2 Kgs. 15:8-12
10 [j]1 Kgs. 12:32 [k]ch. 1:1 [l][Jer. 38:4]
11 [m]ch. 6:7
12 [n]See 1 Sam. 9:9 [o][ch. 1:1] [p][Mic. 3:5, 11]
13 [q]See ch. 2:12 [r]See 1 Kgs. 12:29–13:1
14 [s]ch. 1:1; [Zech. 13:5] [t]ch. 1:1
15 [u][Ps. 78:71]
16 [v]ch. 3:1 [n][See ver. 12 above] [w]Ezek. 20:46; 21:2; Mic. 2:6 [x][ver. 9]
17 [y][Jer. 28:16; 29:21, 31, 32] [z][ver. 7, 8] [m][See ver. 11 above]

Chapter 8
1 [a]ch. 7:1
2 [b]ch. 7:8 [c][Jer. 24:1; Mic. 7:1] [d]Lam. 4:18

3 [e]The songs of the temple[1] [f]shall become
wailings[2] in that day,"
declares the Lord GOD.
[g]"So many dead bodies!"
"They are thrown everywhere!"
[h]"Silence!"

4 Hear this, [i]you who trample on the needy
and bring the poor of the land to an
end,
5 saying, "When will [j]the new moon be
over,
that we may sell grain?
And [k]the Sabbath,
that we may offer wheat for sale,
that we may make [l]the ephah small and
the shekel[3] great
and deal deceitfully with false balances,
6 that we may buy the poor for [m]silver
and the needy for a pair of sandals
and sell the chaff of the wheat?"

7 The LORD has sworn by [n]the pride of
Jacob:
"Surely [o]I will never forget any of their
deeds.
8 [p]Shall not the land tremble on this
account,
and everyone mourn who dwells in it,
[q]and all of it rise like the Nile,
and be tossed about [r]and sink again,
like the Nile of Egypt?"

9 "And on that day," declares the Lord GOD,
[s]"I will make the sun go down at noon
and darken the earth in broad day-
light.
10 [t]I will turn your feasts into mourning
and all your songs into lamentation;
[u]I will bring sackcloth on every waist
[u]and baldness on every head;
[v]I will make it like the mourning for an
only son
and the end of it like a bitter day.

11 "Behold, the days are coming," declares
the Lord GOD,
"when [w]I will send a famine on the
land—
not a famine of bread, nor a thirst for
water,
[x]but of hearing the words of the LORD.

[1] Or *palace* [2] Or *The singing women of the palace shall wail* [3] An *ephah* was about 3/5 bushel or 22 liters; a *shekel* was about 2/5 ounce or 11 grams

3[e] [ch. 5:23] [f] [Jer. 47:2] [g] [ch. 6:9] [h] [ch. 6:10; Jer. 16:4, 6]
4[i] [Ps. 14:4]
5[j] See Num. 28:11 [k] [Neh. 13:15, 16] [l] Ezek. 45:10; Mic. 6:10, 11; See Hos. 12:7
6[m] ch. 2:6
7[n] ch. 6:8 [o] Hos. 8:13; 9:9
8[p] [Hos. 4:3] [q] ch. 9:5 [r] [Zech. 10:11]
9[s] Jer. 15:9; Mic. 3:6; Matt. 24:29; [ch. 4:13; 5:8]
10[t] [Jer. 7:34; 16:9; Hos. 2:11] [u] Isa. 3:24 [v] Jer. 6:26; Zech. 12:10
11[w] [Isa. 8:20, 21] [x] [Ps. 74:9; Prov. 29:18; Mic. 3:7]

and superficiality are the products of a brazen commitment to greed (8:6). As a result, a pronouncement of judgment upon God's people comes in two forms. In a sentence of physical death, their very lives will be taken away (9:1–4). And in a sentence of spiritual drought, God's very word, which they had rejected (4:1; 5:1, 10), will disappear (8:11–12).

Given this verdict and sentence, an important question emerges: why is God's displeasure with Israel based on her unmerciful treatment of *others*? Or to put it in our terms, why should I treat my neighbor as myself (Mark 12:31)? The answer is clear: because all humanity bears the image of God (Gen. 1:26–27) and because he treasures the helpless who depend entirely on him (Ps. 74:21), mistreatment of others is an affront to God. His gracious care of those least able to obtain it exhibits and glorifies his nature. Therefore when God's people in Amos's day treated the underprivileged poorly, judgment came. For sins against other people, God "strikes" the people (Amos 9:1), fixes his "eyes upon them for evil and not for good" (9:4), and brings them to "utter destruction" (9:8).

And yet even here we find God's mercy. Describing the dreadful "day of the LORD" (8:2), we find the language of covenant relationship. The "house of Israel," long destined for exile, is once again called "my people Israel" by God (8:2; cf. 7:8, 15; 9:10, 14). While God punishes the evil deeds of his people, he will not utterly destroy or abandon them (9:8). Hope remains.

This hope is prefigured in the judgment described in 8:9–10. The details are strikingly similar to the moment when Christ won our freedom from judgment on the cross. The day darkens at high noon (8:9; cf. Joel 3:15; Mark 15:33; Rev. 6:12), and the feasts are turned into "mourning for an only son" (Amos 8:10; cf. Rev. 19:6–21). For Amos, the mourning for an only son spoke of divine judgment—what a surprise, however, when this day of judgment turned out to be a judgment that fell on God's only Son, in our place.

Because of the death and resurrection of God's only Son, Jesus Christ, we who are united to him by faith have no reason to fear the final day.

12 [x]They shall wander from sea to sea,
and from north to east;
they shall run to and fro, to seek the
word of the LORD,
[y]but they shall not find it.

13 [z]"In that day the lovely virgins and the
young men
shall [a]faint for thirst.
14 Those who swear by [b]the Guilt of
Samaria,
and say, 'As your god lives, O Dan,'
and, 'As [c]the Way of [d]Beersheba lives,'
they shall fall, and never rise again."

The Destruction of Israel

9 I saw the Lord standing beside[1] the altar,
and he said:

[e]"Strike the capitals until [e]the thresholds
[f]shake,
[g]and shatter them on the heads of all
the people;[2]
and those who are left of them I will kill
with the sword;
[h]not one of them shall flee away;
not one of them shall escape.

2 [i]"If they dig into Sheol,
from there shall my hand take them;
[i]if they climb up to heaven,
from there I will bring them down.
3 If they hide themselves on [j]the top of
Carmel,
from there I will search them out and
take them;
[k]and if they hide from my sight at the
bottom of the sea,
there I will command the serpent,
and it shall bite them.
4 [l]And if they go into captivity before their
enemies,
there I will command the sword, and
it shall kill them;
[m]and I will fix my eyes upon them
for evil and not for good."

5 The Lord GOD of hosts,
he who touches the earth and [n]it melts,
and all who dwell in it mourn,
[o]and all of it rises like the Nile,
[o]and sinks again, like the Nile of
Egypt;
6 [p]who builds his upper chambers in the
heavens
and founds his vault upon the earth;
[q]who calls for the waters of the sea
and pours them out upon the surface
of the earth—
[r]the LORD is his name.

7 "Are you not like [s]the Cushites to me,
O people of Israel?" declares the LORD.
[t]"Did I not bring up Israel from the land
of Egypt,
and [u]the Philistines from [v]Caphtor
and the Syrians from [w]Kir?
8 Behold, [x]the eyes of the Lord GOD are
upon the sinful kingdom,
and I will destroy it from the surface
of the ground,
[y]except that I will not utterly destroy
the house of Jacob,"
declares the LORD.

9 "For behold, I will command,
[z]and shake the house of Israel among
all the nations
as one shakes with a sieve,
but no pebble shall fall to the earth.
10 All the sinners of my people shall die by
the sword,
who say, [a]'Disaster shall not overtake
or meet us.'

The Restoration of Israel

11 "In that day [b]I will raise up
the booth of David that is fallen

[1] Or *on* [2] Hebrew *all of them*

9:11–15 The final verses of Amos offer promises from God that turn the book into one of hope. The "day of the LORD" has, to this point, been one of utter destruction. But a great reversal seems to have arrived. "In that day" (v. 11), God promises to raise up the "booth" of David, "rebuild it as in the days of old," unite the nations to himself by his name (v. 12), and restore the fortunes of his people and his place.

The question is—when? When do we see the house of David restored (v. 11), representatives from the nations called by God's name (v. 12), and the fortunes of God's people restored (vv. 13–15)?

12[x] [See ver. 11 above] [y] [ch. 4:8]
13[z] Isa. 51:20 [a] [Jonah 4:8]
14[b] Deut. 9:21; 1 Kgs. 12:29, 30; Hos. 10:8 [c] [Acts 9:2] [d] ch. 5:5

Chapter 9
1[e] Zeph. 2:14 [f] [Isa. 6:4] [g] See Judg. 16:26-30 [h] [ch. 2:14]
2[i] [Ps. 139:8-10]
3[j] ch. 1:2 [k] [Job 26:5]
4[l] [Deut. 28:65]

[m] See Jer. 21:10 **5**[n] Ps. 46:6 [o] ch. 8:8 **6**[p] [Ps. 104:3, 5] [q] See ch. 5:8 [r] See ch. 4:13 **7**[s] [Zeph. 3:10] [t] Ex. 20:2 [u] Jer. 47:4 [v] Gen. 10:14 [w] ch. 1:5 **8**[x] [ver. 4] [y] Jer. 30:11; [Obad. 17] **9**[z] [Jer. 15:7; Matt. 3:12; Luke 3:17] **10**[a] [ch. 6:3] **11**[b] Cited Acts 15:16

and repair its breaches,
and raise up its ruins
and rebuild it as in the days of old,
12 [c]that they may possess the remnant of Edom
and [d]all the nations who are called by my name,"[1]
declares the LORD who does this.

13 "Behold, the days are coming," declares the LORD,
[e]"when the plowman shall overtake the reaper
and the treader of grapes him who sows the seed;
[f]the mountains shall drip sweet wine,
and all the hills shall flow with it.
14 [g]I will restore the fortunes of my people Israel,
and [h]they shall rebuild the ruined cities and inhabit them;
[i]they shall plant vineyards and drink their wine,
and they shall make gardens and eat their fruit.
15 [j]I will plant them on their land,
[k]and they shall never again be uprooted
out of the land [l]that I have given them,"
says the LORD your God.

[1] Hebrew; Septuagint (compare Acts 15:17) *that the remnant of mankind and all the nations who are called by my name may seek the Lord*

12[c][Obad. 19] [d]Cited Acts 15:17, 18
13[e]Lev. 26:5 [f]Joel 3:18
14[g]Jer. 30:3 [h]Isa. 61:4 [i]Jer. 31:5
15[j]Jer. 24:6; Ezek. 34:29 [k][Joel 3:20] [l][Jer. 3:18]

The ten northern tribes, led off to Assyria in 722 B.C. (4:2), never return from exile. That is, they never return to the land in a way that even approximates the fulfillment of these promises. And this absence of fulfillment remains today—unless, of course, the fulfillment was intended to represent what God accomplished for Israel and all the nations in the gospel of his Son. We must be clear on this interpretive shift. Where Amos understood these promises to concern place (see note on 1:1–2:3) and prosperity in the material sense, we understand place and prosperity in the book of Amos to be—and always to have been—symbols pointing to the end of the exile that comes with Christ. This is not to deny the historical reality of the restoration promised in Amos (nor to deny God's intentions for a remnant of ethnic Israel; see Rom. 11:23–29), but to recognize the dimension it takes on for the Christian. Israel's exile ultimately ended when Jesus ascended to the Father and sent the promised Spirit to take his place in the hearts of men and women who put their faith in him. Now the One who tabernacled among us in his own Son, Jesus (John 1:14), unites us to Christ and makes us part of that eternal temple (1 Cor. 7:17–19; 2 Cor. 6:16).

Significantly, this is precisely how the apostles understood this text. And as a church built on a "foundation of the apostles and prophets" (Eph. 2:20), our interpretation of Amos should follow theirs. When the Jerusalem council convened in Acts 15 to settle a dispute over how Gentiles could be saved without adherence to all the obligations of the law, James appealed to Amos 9:11–13 as proof that God was fulfilling in the church his promises to Amos. The message of Amos validates God's plan for rebuilding his household from among all the nations of the earth. Significant is the prophet's inclusion of a remnant of Edom—the nation descended from Esau and the constant antagonist of historic Israel—among the nations called by the name of the Lord (v. 12). By this inclusion, Amos makes the expansiveness of God's grace and our mission clear. Our happy privilege is to proclaim the gospel to the ends of the earth that God will claim by his grace for his glory.

Introduction to Obadiah

Author and Date

The book of Obadiah is an oracle of judgment pronounced in the mid-sixth century B.C., predicting God's destruction of Edom, Judah's neighbor comprised of the descendants of Jacob's brother Esau (Genesis 36). Little is known about Obadiah himself, although he is probably not any of those who share that name, mentioned elsewhere in the Old Testament.

Audience

Obadiah is directed explicitly at Edom (v. 1), with whom Israel (later Judah) had many conflicts. His message—that Edom would taste God's wrath for its hostility toward Judah—is not his alone (cf. Num. 24:18; Ps. 137:7; Jer. 25:21; 49:7–22; Lam. 4:21–22; Ezek. 25:12–14; ch. 35; Amos 1:11–12; Mal. 1:2–5).

The fulfillment of Obadiah's prophecy began with Babylonian attacks against Edom in 553 B.C. and continued with the north Arabian Nabatean destruction of Edom in the early fifth century. The ultimate fulfillment of Obadiah's prophecy will come when remnants of Edom are gathered with those of all the nations worshiping Israel's God in and through Jesus Christ.

Implicitly, as part of the Hebrew Scriptures, the audience of the prophecy is also Israel. God's public declaration that he would punish the oppressors of his people would be an oracle of hope to his people (see notes on Nahum). Obadiah's prophecy teaches us that an aspect of God's mercy is his ultimate restraining and conquering of the enemies of the people he loves. Grace is God's provision of what we need but cannot provide for ourselves, and this provision includes overcoming the efforts and punishing the evil of opponents of his covenant purposes. This provision may not come in the time of our choosing, but the prophets assure us of the certainty of God's ultimate victory. The dimensions of this victory in Obadiah's prophecy include: defeat of the enemy, preservation of God's people, removal of evil threats to God's people, and even the salvation of a remnant of the enemy—all dimensions of a grace beyond human expectation or ability.

The Gospel in Obadiah

As an oracle of judgment, Obadiah presents unique challenges for gospel application. For more on the general subject of meeting these challenges, see the introductory notes to Nahum which, along with Obadiah, consists entirely of such an oracle—though Obadiah makes more explicit mention of salvation and hope (vv. 17–21). Furthermore, there are indications that a remnant of Edom will be saved and ruled over by God as part of his people.

This hope is reflected in various ways. First, Obadiah may be an extended elaboration on Amos 9:11–12, the passage immediately preceding Obadiah in the Bible. The restoration of David's kingship through Israel's Messiah would not only restore the fortunes of Judah but would include a remnant of Edom (Deut. 28:9–10; Amos 9:11–12). The similarity between the two passages would implicitly remind the reader that a remnant of Edom will be among those from all nations who will worship the Lord in his consummated kingdom.

Second, Obadiah underscores God's grace from a redemptive-historical perspective. For the Judah-Edom relationship must be read against its origins in the Jacob-Esau relationship. The two strove against each other even before birth, but God sovereignly chose the younger to be served by the older (Gen. 25:22ff.). This sovereign act of God came to epitomize his electing grace in both the Old Testament (Mal. 1:2–3) and the New Testament (Rom. 9:13).

Jacob was designated heir of the covenant God made with Abraham—that God would bless him and, *through* him, bless the nations (Gen. 12:2–3; Ex. 2:24; Lev. 26:42). Nevertheless Jacob strove to obtain those promises unethically and self-reliantly—and his receiving them despite his conniving is a vivid demonstration of God's grace. For his part Esau, rather than living by faith in the promises God made to and *through* Jacob, lived by his appetites and chose rivalry with his brother instead. This pattern of antipathy repeatedly characterized the historic relations between the descendants of the two brothers (e.g., Num. 20:14–21; 2 Kings 16:6; Ezek. 25:12–13) and established the trajectory of the Judah-Edom relationship seen in Obadiah. But even though the "house" (nation and kingship) of Esau will be no more (Obad. 18), God will also graciously save a remnant of Edom for his kingdom (see above). For both the house of Jacob and the house of Esau, the blessings experienced are due only to the grace of God.

There are two general ways in which the New Testament takes up the Jacob-Edom dynamic. First, the descendants of Abraham, and therefore the rightful heirs to the promises to Abraham, are those who do the works of Abraham by believing in Jesus Christ (John 8:39–47). As such, followers of Jesus inherit the promises continued through Jacob/Israel (Gal. 3:7; Rom. 2:28; 9:6–18; cf. Heb. 12:15–17). Second, and foundational to the first, is that Jesus Christ himself is the promised Seed of Abraham (Gal. 3:16). Through him every divine promise has been, is being, and will be fulfilled (2 Cor. 1:20). The blessings of the Abrahamic covenant come to believers in Christ (Gal. 3:14). Even though he was harassed by his brothers (Mark 3:21), he has led free a host of captives (Eph. 4:8) and restored the fortunes of Judah.

Outline

I. The Announcement of Edom's Destruction (vv. 1–4)

II. The Extent of Edom's Destruction (vv. 5–9)

III. The Occasion of Edom's Destruction (vv. 10–14)

IV. The Day of the Lord Is Near (vv. 15–18)

V. The Extent of the Lord's Reign (vv. 19–21)

Obadiah

1The vision of Obadiah.

Edom Will Be Humbled

Thus says the Lord GOD [a]concerning Edom:
[b]We have heard a report from the LORD,
and a messenger has been sent among the nations:
"Rise up! Let us rise against her for battle!"
2 Behold, I will make you small among the nations;
you shall be utterly despised.[1]
3 [c]The pride of your heart has deceived you,
you who live in the clefts of the rock,[2]
in your lofty dwelling,
[d]who say in your heart,
"Who will bring me down to the ground?"
4 Though you soar aloft like the eagle,
though your nest is set among the stars,
from there I will bring you down,
declares the LORD.
5 If [e]thieves came to you,
if plunderers came by night—
how you have been destroyed!—
would they not steal only enough for themselves?
If [e]grape gatherers came to you,
would they not leave gleanings?

[1] Or *Behold, I have made you small among the nations; you are utterly despised* [2] Or *Sela*

1[a] See Jer. 49:7-22; Ezek. 25:12-14 [b] For ver. 1-4, see Jer. 49:14-16
3[c] [Num. 24:21, 22] [d] [Isa. 14:13-15]
5[e] Jer. 49:9

1–4 News of judgment will be broadcast among the nations so that the whole world will witness God's salvation of Judah (Ps. 98:2). This has now begun in the proclamation of the gospel. Edom had preyed upon Judah's weakness (likely by joining the Babylonians in the pillage of Jerusalem, as indicated in Ps. 137:7–9, though scholars vary over identification of the precise circumstances to which Obadiah refers). Yet, despite its initial triumph, Edom would become "despised" (Obad. 2), trading places with the once-despised nation of Israel because the proud Edomites did not understand that those things despised in the eyes of man are chosen by God to shame those who consider themselves powerful, mighty, and wise (Zech. 4:10; Matt. 5:6). The gospel, in which the weak are made strong through the strength of another, is the ultimate instance of this counterintuitive principle (1 Cor. 1:18–31; 2 Cor. 13:4).

The "pride of your heart" (Obad. 3), which is at the root of all fraternal violence (cf. Gen. 4:5–7), was what caused Edom's violence against Judah. Apart from repentance, such pride will inevitably lead to a fall (Prov. 16:18; James 4:6; 1 Pet. 5:5), but those who humble themselves will be exalted by God (1 Pet. 5:6), following in the pattern experienced by their Savior (Phil. 2:5–11).

5–9 The attacks awaiting Edom would be excessive, pointing toward divine justice as the purpose behind them (vv. 5–7). Such utter destruction is not inconsistent with but rather required by the fulfillment of God's promises in Christ. For the cross of Christ is the supreme display not only of God's mercy but also of his justice: sin must be judged. And yet, in the marvel of grace, for those who are in Christ, their end-time judgment has already taken place at the cross of Christ.

The Lord draws particular attention to the vaunted wisdom of his enemies, saying he will "destroy the wise men out of Edom" (v. 8). The gospel of a crucified Savior is the ultimate example in human history of God confounding the world's wisdom in the supreme display of grace (1 Cor. 1:18–21; cf. Isa. 29:14).

6 [f]How Esau has been pillaged,
his treasures sought out!
7 All your allies have driven you to your border;
those at peace with you have deceived you;
they have prevailed against you;
[g]those who eat your bread[1] have set a trap beneath you—
[h]you have[2] no understanding.

8 [i]Will I not on that day, declares the LORD,
destroy the wise men out of Edom,
and understanding out of [j]Mount Esau?
9 And your mighty men shall be dismayed, [k]O Teman,
so that every man from [j]Mount Esau
will be cut off by slaughter.

Edom's Violence Against Jacob

10 [l]Because of the violence done to your brother Jacob,
shame shall cover you,
[m]and you shall be cut off forever.
11 [n]On the day that you stood aloof,
[o]on the day that strangers carried off his wealth
and foreigners entered his gates
[p]and cast lots for Jerusalem,
you were like one of them.
12 [q]But do not gloat over the day of your brother
in the day of his misfortune;
[r]do not rejoice over the people of Judah
in the day of their ruin;
[s]do not boast[3]
in the day of distress.
13 [t]Do not enter the gate of my people
in the day of their calamity;
[t]do not gloat over his disaster
in the day of his calamity;
[u]do not loot his wealth
in the day of his calamity.
14 [v]Do not stand at the crossroads
to cut off his fugitives;
do not hand over his survivors
in the day of distress.

The Day of the LORD Is Near

15 For [w]the day of the LORD is near upon all the nations.
[x]As you have done, it shall be done to you;
your deeds shall return on your own head.
16 [y]For as you have drunk on [z]my holy mountain,
so all the nations shall drink continually;
they shall drink and swallow,
and shall be as though they had never been.
17 [a]But in Mount Zion there shall be those who escape,
and it shall be holy,
[b]and the house of Jacob shall possess their own possessions.
18 [c]The house of Jacob shall be a fire,
and the house of Joseph a flame,
and the house of Esau [d]stubble;
they shall burn them and consume them,
[e]and there shall be no survivor for the house of Esau,
for the LORD has spoken.

[1] Hebrew lacks *those who eat* [2] Hebrew *he has* [3] Hebrew *do not enlarge your mouth*

6[f] [Jer. 49:10]
7[g] [Ps. 41:9] [h] [Jer. 49:7]
8[i] [Isa. 29:14] [j] [Ezek. 35:2]
9[k] Amos 1:12; See 1 Chr. 1:45 [j] [See ver. 8 above]
10[l] Num. 20:20, 21 [m] [Ezek. 35:9]
11[n] Ps. 137:7; [Jer. 12:14] [o] See 2 Kgs. 25:10-20 [p] Joel 3:3
12[q] [Ps. 22:17] [r] [Mic. 4:11; 7:8] [s] [1 Sam. 2:3]
13[t] [Prov. 17:5] [u] [Ezek. 35:10]
14[v] [Ezek. 21:21]
15[w] See Joel 1:15 [x] Jer. 50:29; Ezek. 35:15; Hab. 2:8
16[y] See Jer. 25:27, 28 [z] See Joel 3:17
17[a] [Amos 9:8]; See Joel 2:32 [b] [Amos 9:12]
18[c] Zech. 12:6; [Isa. 10:17; Jer. 5:14] [d] See Joel 2:5 [e] Ezek. 25:14

10–14 Edom, rather than believing God's promises to Jacob and hoping in their fulfillment, instead sided with the enemy of God's people and celebrated Judah's suffering. This drew God's righteous wrath and secured their demise.

From the perspective of the whole Bible, this pattern of cruelly celebrating the unjust suffering of another is fulfilled in the religious authorities of Jesus' day. They sought to preserve their position rather than to identify with the suffering servant who would secure all of the blessings promised to Abraham. As a result, the kingdom of God was taken away from them and given to those who would humble themselves by looking outside themselves to the rejected cornerstone, Jesus Christ (Matt. 21:33–44).

15–18 While Edom had celebrated Judah's suffering (v. 16), the same fate awaited Edom at the hands of others (cf. Prov. 22:8). As the forerunner to Jesus, John the Baptist announced that the axe of God's judgment was laid at the root of those who failed to produce the fruit of righteousness. They would become chaff like Edom, no matter their ethic lineage (Matt. 3:10–12). It is a whole-Bible gospel principle that God looks at the heart (e.g., 1 Sam. 16:7).

The Kingdom of the Lord

19 Those of [f]the Negeb [b]shall possess
[g]Mount Esau,
and those of the Shephelah shall possess [h]the land of the Philistines;
they shall possess the land of Ephraim
and the land of [i]Samaria,
and Benjamin shall possess Gilead.
20 The exiles of this host of the people of Israel
shall possess the land of the Canaanites as far as [j]Zarephath,
and the exiles of Jerusalem who are in Sepharad
shall possess the cities of the Negeb.
21 [k]Saviors shall go up to Mount Zion
to rule [g]Mount Esau,
and [l]the kingdom shall be the Lord's.

19–21 The day of the Lord will culminate in the full extent of God's reign over the whole Promised Land (vv. 19–21). Mount Esau will be ruled from Mount Zion (vv. 18–19, 21).

This triumphant and hopeful ending to Obadiah's prophecy highlights the great theme of reversal that runs right through the whole Bible. God's humbled people will reign with him in the consummation of his kingdom in Christ, while those who have resisted his rule will be humiliated (Deut. 28:13, 44; Luke 2:34; 1 Pet. 5:6).

Those sites described in Obadiah, while encircling the boundaries of Old Testament Israel, will be transcended in the worldwide dominion of Jesus Christ (Ps. 72:9; Hab. 2:14; Rev. 11:15; ch. 21). A remnant of Edom who would repent could, like us, live by faith—walking in God's ways, showing humility, kindness, and mercy to others, and leaving final judgment in God's hands (Rom. 12:19; Heb. 10:30).

The kingdom of the Lord, anticipated by Obadiah, finds its true and final fulfillment in Jesus Christ. He came "proclaiming the gospel of God, and saying, 'The time is fulfilled, and the kingdom of God is at hand; repent and believe in the gospel'" (Mark 1:14–15). In Jesus the long anticipated new creation reign of God is inaugurated. We today live in the light of the dawning of God's eternal kingdom.

19[f] [Josh. 10:40; Judg. 1:9] [b] [See ver. 17 above] [g] ver. 8 [h] Jer. 17:26 [i] See Jer. 23:13
20[j] 1 Kgs. 17:9; [Luke 4:26]
21[k] [2 Kgs. 13:5; Isa. 19:20; 1 Tim. 4:16; James 5:20] [g] [See ver. 19 above] [l] Ps. 22:28; Dan. 2:44; 7:14, 27; Zech. 14:9; Luke 1:33; 1 Cor. 15:24; Rev. 11:15; 19:6

Introduction to Jonah

Author and Date

Jonah prophesied during the peaceful and prosperous time of Jeroboam II (2 Kings 14:23–28), who ruled in Israel (the northern kingdom) from 782 to 753 B.C.

The Gospel in Jonah

On the surface, the story of Jonah lends itself to a moralistic interpretation: God sends Jonah to the notoriously evil city of Nineveh (1:1–2), but Jonah runs away instead (1:3). So God sends a storm and a fish to rescue Jonah from his disobedience (ch. 2), he tells Jonah to go a second time (3:1–2), and finally Jonah gives in and obeys (3:3). Then God rewards Jonah's obedience by bringing him surprising success among the Ninevites (3:6–10).

But this interpretation leaves us with a number of problematic questions: Why is chapter 4 included? Why isn't our hero, Jonah, a better model of obedience in the end? Why is he still angry *after* his success in Nineveh? Once we begin to pull back the layers of the story, we discover that it is not really about what Jonah is doing for God, but what God is doing for Jonah.

Jonah is about the disturbing possibility that, having pledged our life to God, we could end up spending much of that life avoiding the God we set out to serve. You may have already discovered this strange contradiction that lies at the heart of all Christian experience: while loving Christ, you find yourself turning from him; while trusting Christ, you often battle fear and anxiety; while serving Christ, you sometimes struggle with disappointment about certain events in your life. You are not alone!

Some people teach us by their example; Jonah teaches us by his weakness. By confessing his own failures, Jonah holds up a mirror for us to see the struggles and enigmas of our Christian lives (1 Cor. 10:11). He wants us to discover the grace of God—which, once we see it, is stronger than all our fears, anxieties, and disappointments. The real hero in the story is God. We catch glimpses of God's extraordinary patience with weak people like Jonah (Jonah 3:1–2; 4:4, 9–10), his relentless pursuit of lost people like the Ninevites (1:2; 4:11), and the ultimate victory of his love (2:9; 3:10).

Outline

The story of Jonah includes seven episodes, with the first three paralleled by the second three. The final episode stands alone as the climax of the story:

A. Jonah's Commissioning and Flight (1:1–3)

B. Jonah and the Pagan Sailors (1:4–16)

C. Jonah's Grateful Prayer (1:17–2:10)

A′. Jonah's Recommissioning and Compliance (3:1–3a)

B′. Jonah and the Pagan Ninevites (3:3b–10)

C′. Jonah's Angry Prayer (4:1–4)

D. Jonah's Lesson about Compassion (4:5–11)

Jonah

Jonah Flees the Presence of the Lord

1 Now the word of the LORD came to [a]Jonah
the son of Amittai, saying, 2 "Arise, go to
[b]Nineveh, that [c]great city, and call out against
it, [d]for their evil[1] has come up before me." 3 But
Jonah [e]rose to flee to [f]Tarshish from the presence of the LORD. He went down to [g]Joppa and
found a ship going to [f]Tarshish. So he paid the
fare and went down into it, to go with them
to [f]Tarshish, [h]away from the presence of the
LORD.

4 But [i]the LORD hurled a great wind upon the
sea, and there was a mighty tempest on the sea,
so that the ship threatened [j]to break up. 5 Then
the mariners were afraid, and [k]each cried out
to his god. And [l]they hurled the cargo that was
in the ship into the sea to lighten it for them.
But Jonah had gone down into the inner part
of the ship and had lain down and was fast
asleep. 6 So the captain came and said to him,
"What do you mean, you sleeper? Arise, [k]call
out to your god! [m]Perhaps the god will give a
thought to us, that we may not perish."

Jonah Is Thrown into the Sea

7 And they said to one another, "Come, let us
[n]cast lots, that we may know on whose account
this evil has come upon us." So they cast lots,
and the lot fell on Jonah. 8 Then they said to
him, "Tell us on whose account this evil has
come upon us. What is your occupation? And
where do you come from? What is your country? And of what people are you?" 9 And he said
to them, "I am a Hebrew, and I fear [o]the LORD,
the God of heaven, [p]who made the sea and the
dry land." 10 Then the men were exceedingly
afraid and said to him, "What is this that you
have done!" For the men knew that [h]he was
fleeing from the presence of the LORD, because
he had told them.

11 Then they said to him, "What shall we
do to you, that the sea may quiet down for
us?" For the sea grew more and more tempestuous. 12 He said to them, "Pick me up
and hurl me into the sea; then the sea will
quiet down for you, [q]for I know it is because
of me that this great tempest has come upon

[1] The same Hebrew word can mean *evil* or *disaster*, depending on the context; so throughout Jonah

1:1–3 When God calls us to something new, he is always up to something good. However difficult the call may be, it is one of grace and it is for our ultimate joy. Reflect for a moment on the contrast between Jonah and Jesus.

Jonah was in a good place, doing good work, enjoying a good life. Then God said, "Jonah, I want you to go to another place, and do a different work for the sake of people I love; people who are facing an imminent judgment." Jonah said "No."

Jesus was in heaven, ruling the universe by the word of his power. Adored by angels, he was in the best place, doing the best work, and enjoying the best life. Then the Father said, "Go to another place, where you will be utterly rejected. You will live a life that will lead to torture, crucifixion, and death. You will become an atoning sacrifice for people I love, who are facing an eternal judgment." Jesus said "Yes."

Recognizing that Jesus did all this on our behalf moves us from being the kind of people who care about our own comfort, reputation, and success, to caring more about the people all around us whom we are called to love and serve. Loved much, we are freed to love much (Luke 7:47).

1:11–16 Imagine the scene: God had revealed, through his prophet, a way for the entire crew to be delivered from the storm of judgment. Safety would come through the sacrifice of one man who was willing to lay down his life (v. 12). But these men wanted to survive the storm without the sacrifice. They turned again to their own means to

Chapter 1

1 [a]2 Kgs. 14:25
2 [b]Gen. 10:11, 12; 2 Kgs. 19:36; Nah. 1:1; Zeph. 2:13; Matt. 12:41; Luke 11:30, 32 [c]ch. 3:3; 4:11 [d]Rev. 18:5
3 [e]ch. 4:2 [f]See 1 Kgs. 10:22 [g]See Josh. 19:46 [h]Gen. 4:16; [Ps. 139:9, 10]
4 [i][Ps. 107:25] [j]1 Kgs. 22:48; Ps. 48:7
5 [k][Ps. 107:28] [l][Acts 27:18, 19, 38]
6 [k][See ver. 5 above] [m][ch. 3:9]
7 [n][Judg. 20:9]
9 [o]Rev. 11:13 [p]Ps. 146:6
10 [h][See ver. 3 above]
12 [q][Josh. 7:20]

you." 13 Nevertheless, the men rowed hard[1] to
get back to dry land, but they could not, for
the sea grew more and more tempestuous
against them. 14 Therefore they called out to
the LORD, "O LORD, let us not perish for this
man's life, and [r]lay not on us innocent blood,
[s]for you, O LORD, have done as it pleased you."
15 So they picked up Jonah and hurled him
into the sea, [t]and the sea ceased from its raging. 16 Then the men feared the LORD exceedingly, [u]and they offered a sacrifice to the LORD
[v]and made vows.

A Great Fish Swallows Jonah

17[2] And the LORD appointed[3] a great fish to
swallow up Jonah. [w]And Jonah was in the belly
of the fish three days and three nights.

Jonah's Prayer

2 Then Jonah prayed to the LORD his God
from the belly of the fish, 2 saying,

[x]"I called out to the LORD, out of my distress,
and he answered me;
[y]out of the belly of Sheol I cried,
[z]and you heard my voice.
3 [a]For you cast me into the deep,
into the heart of the seas,
and the flood surrounded me;
[b]all your waves and your billows
passed over me.
4 [c]Then I said, 'I am driven away
from your sight;
[d]yet I shall again look
upon your holy temple.'
5 [e]The waters closed in over me [f]to take my life;
the deep surrounded me;
weeds were wrapped about my head
6 at the roots of the mountains.
I went down to the land
whose bars closed upon me forever;
yet you brought up my life from the pit,
O LORD my God.
7 When my life was fainting away,
I remembered the LORD,
[g]and my prayer came to you,
into your holy temple.
8 [h]Those who pay regard to vain idols
[i]forsake their hope of steadfast love.

[1] Hebrew *the men dug in* [their oars] [2] Ch 2:1 in Hebrew [3] Or *had appointed*

14[r] Deut. 21:8 [s] [Ps. 115:3]
15[t] Ps. 65:7; Luke 8:24
16[u] [Gen. 8:20; 31:54] [v] See ch. 2:9
17[w] Matt. 12:40; 16:4; [Luke 11:30]
Chapter 2
2[x] Ps. 3:4; 120:1; Lam. 3:55 [y] Ps. 118:5 [z] Lam. 3:56
3[a] Ps. 88:6, 7 [b] Ps. 42:7
4[c] Ps. 31:22 [d] [1 Kgs. 8:35, 38]
5[e] [Lam. 3:54] [f] Ps. 69:1
7[g] [2 Chr. 30:27]
8[h] Ps. 31:6; [2 Kgs. 17:15; Jer. 2:5] [i] [Jer. 2:13]

save themselves (v. 13). There's great courage in that, but there's also extraordinary resistance to God's revealed will. This impulse to depend on our own resources and refuse God's means of deliverance is deeply embedded within the human heart.

"But they could not . . ." (v. 13). These four words are the turning point in the story. When the crew realized they could not beat the storm, they turned in desperation and staked their lives on the sacrifice of Jonah. The storm of God's judgment is stronger than we are. We do not have the ability to escape such a storm, no matter how hard we try. The storm of God's judgment will wreck us, unless we depend upon his means of escape.

The means that God provides to deliver us from our sin and a fallen world is the sacrifice of his Son. On the cross, Jesus gave his life to deliver his people from God's righteous judgment against our sin. Cast out by men and forsaken by the Father (Matt. 27:46), Jesus offered himself as the sacrifice that would placate the wrath of God on our behalf (1 Thess. 1:10). God's storms that teach us our true dependence, and Christ's sacrifice that provides for our eternal deliverance, lie at the heart of the gospel. Christ was thrown into the storm of God's judgment so that, through faith in his sacrifice, we would be saved.

2:1–2 Jonah cried out when all hope was lost. His life seemed over. Yet such is often the way of the Lord with his children. That despairing moment when we throw our hands up in the air and say, "My life is over"—that moment is when God can really get to work. All through the Bible we see the truth that life comes not by avoiding death but *through* death (John 12:24–25); strength comes not despite weakness but *in* weakness (2 Cor. 12:7–10); comfort comes not by eliminating all affliction but *through* affliction (2 Cor. 1:3–7).

The supreme instance of this is Jesus himself, who "was crucified in weakness, but lives by the power of God" (2 Cor. 13:4). This lesson of gaining life by dying to self (Matt. 16:25) is what Jonah begins to learn here in chapter 2, as he sits, miserable, in the belly of the fish, having saved others by sacrificing himself.

9 [j]But I with the voice of thanksgiving
will sacrifice to you;
what I have vowed I will pay.
[k]Salvation belongs to the LORD!"

10 And the LORD spoke to the fish, and it vomited Jonah out upon the dry land.

Jonah Goes to Nineveh

3 Then the word of the LORD came to Jonah
the second time, saying, 2 "Arise, go to
[l]Nineveh, that great city, and call out against
it the message that I tell you." 3 So Jonah arose
and went to Nineveh, according to the word of
the LORD. Now [l]Nineveh was an exceedingly
great city,[1] three days' journey in breadth.[2]
4 Jonah began to go into the city, going a day's
journey. And he called out, "Yet forty days, and
Nineveh shall be overthrown!" 5 [m]And the people of Nineveh believed God. [n]They called for
a fast and [o]put on sackcloth, from the greatest
of them to the least of them.

The People of Nineveh Repent

6 The word reached[3] the king of Nineveh,
and [p]he arose from his throne, removed his
robe, covered himself with sackcloth, [q]and sat
in ashes. 7 And he issued a proclamation and
published through Nineveh, [r]"By the decree

[1] Hebrew *a great city to God* [2] Or *a visit was a three days' journey* [3] Or *had reached*

9 [j]Ps. 50:14; [Hos. 14:2; Heb. 13:15] [k]Ps. 3:8
Chapter 3
2 [l]See ch. 1:2
3 [l][See ver. 2 above]
5 [m][Matt. 12:41; Luke 11:32] [n]See 2 Chr. 20:3 [o]See 2 Sam. 3:31
6 [p][Job 1:20; Ezek. 26:16] [q]Job 2:8
7 [r][Dan. 6:26]

2:9 "Salvation belongs to the LORD!" God's dramatic intervention in the life of Jonah is full of hope—not only for those who seek God, but also for those who, like Jonah, have determined to shut him out. Many people believe God opens the door of salvation and then stands back, leaving it up to us to decide if we want to come in. But if God made salvation possible and then stepped back, refusing to interfere with our choice, then the entire life of believers would be about *us*—our believing, our serving, our following, and our choices to live a good life. In the case of Jonah, imprisoned in the whale's belly, God was claiming someone who was quite incapable of performing any redeeming work to compensate for his sin. God was not relying on Jonah to save Jonah. The message remains the same for each of us today: if you have trusted God for salvation, he has done more than simply make salvation possible; he has actually *saved* you.

Consider what lies behind our faith. Even before the creation of the world, we were "on God's horizon." God set his love on us and formed his plans for us even before we were born (Ps. 139:16; Eph. 1:4–5). When Jesus came into the world, he came to save real people with real names and faces. If we are in Christ, we are among them. The sins he carried to the cross were our sins. The hell he endured was our hell. God did all this for us before we were born, but it didn't end there. He brought salvation to us, opening our eyes to see our sin, and drawing our hearts to find hope in the Savior.

Each Christian has a unique story of how this took place. The times, the places, and the people involved vary, but behind each story, however simple, is the same amazing miracle of God's grace (Eph. 2:8–9). Once you see that God has come after you and has laid hold of you, it will open up a new sense of worship and wonder, a new awareness of his love, and a new confidence in what God can do for others.

3:1–2 This is a remarkable statement of God's grace to Jonah, which rings true also for each of us. God does not give us one shot at responding in faithfulness to his call. He is the God of second chances. Indeed, because of the work of Christ, God will never give up and quit on us. God's grace led Jonah not only to repentance but to useful ministry. Along with forgiveness came restoration. Jonah's experience of God's mercy then became the backdrop to his ministry in Nineveh.

3:3–10 People in the great cities of the world tend to live hectic lives, consumed with the pressing needs of the moment: running a business, raising a family, or enjoying some sport. Jonah walked right into the bustling city and said, "Yet forty days, and Nineveh shall be overthrown!" (v. 4).

God's word always engages people with eternal issues. It lifts our horizons from the immediate interests of our lives to the imminent and overwhelming reality of either everlasting destruction or eternal life. "Whatever you are doing now," Jonah was saying, "you need to realize that you will soon face the judgment of God—and that day is nearer than you think."

Surprisingly, the people of Nineveh responded in heartfelt belief (v. 5). They gave up their evil ways. The proclaimed word of God brought belief (v. 5), ignited prayer

of the king and his nobles: Let neither man
nor [s]beast, herd nor flock, taste anything. Let
them not feed or drink water, 8 but let man and
[s]beast be covered with sackcloth, and let them
call out mightily to God. [t]Let everyone turn
from his evil way and from [u]the violence that
is in his hands. 9 [v]Who knows? God may turn
and relent [w]and turn from his fierce anger, so
that we may not perish."

10 When God saw what they did, [x]how they
turned from their evil way, [x]God relented of
the disaster that he had said he would do to
them, and he did not do it.

Jonah's Anger and the LORD's Compassion

4 But it displeased Jonah exceedingly,[1] and
[y]he was angry. 2 And he prayed to the LORD
and said, "O LORD, is not this what I said when
I was yet in my country? [z]That is why I made
haste to flee to Tarshish; for I knew that you
are a [a]gracious God and merciful, slow to
anger and abounding in steadfast love, and
[a]relenting from disaster. 3 [b]Therefore now,
O LORD, please take my life from me, [c]for it
is better for me to die than to live." 4 And the
LORD said, [d]"Do you do well to be angry?"

5 Jonah went out of the city and sat to the
east of the city and [e]made a booth for himself there. He sat under it in the shade, till he
should see what would become of the city.
6 Now the LORD God appointed a plant[2] and
made it come up over Jonah, that it might be
a shade over his head, to save him from his
discomfort.[3] So Jonah was exceedingly glad
because of the plant. 7 But when dawn came
up the next day, God appointed a worm that
attacked the plant, so that it withered. 8 When
the sun rose, God appointed a scorching [f]east

[1] Hebrew *it was exceedingly evil to Jonah* [2] Hebrew *qiqayon*, probably the castor oil plant; also verses 7, 9, 10 [3] Or *his evil*

7 [s][ch. 4:11; Ps. 36:6; Joel 1:18, 20]
8 [s][See ver. 7 above] [t]Jer. 18:11; 36:3 [u]Isa. 59:6
9 [v]2 Sam. 12:22; Joel 2:14 [w]Ps. 85:3
10 [x][Jer. 18:8]
Chapter 4
1 [y][ver. 4, 9]
2 [z]ch. 1:3 [a]See Joel 2:13
3 [b][1 Kgs. 19:4] [c][Eccles. 7:1]
4 [d][ver. 1, 9]
5 [e][Neh. 8:15]
8 [f]Jer. 18:17

(v. 8), and produced repentance (v. 10) in people who had expressed no prior interest in God. Again, we learn from the converted hearts of these cruel pagans that true faith requires a supernatural work of God to change hearts.

Repentance and faith are two sides of the same coin. Neither can exist without the other. Repentance is possible only when faith is present; and where there is faith, repentance will also be found. Faith comes from a spiritual awakening to our own need and to God's glory. Repentance is a gift from God (Acts 11:18) that flows from faith; it is the evidence of genuine faith.

The three days and three nights that Jonah spent in the belly of a fish was for Nineveh the "sign" of God's great mercy for sinners; in the same way, Jesus' death and his resurrection three days later is a sign for us (Matt. 12:39–40; Luke 11:29–30). The good news of the gospel is that God has poured out on Jesus the wrath that we deserve, so that we may not perish. The death and resurrection of Jesus give us every reason to hope in the mercy of God!

4:5–9 The story of Jonah is peppered with testimonies of God's providence—his intricate care over every detail of life. God "appointed" the great fish by which Jonah's life was spared (1:17). He also "appointed" the vine, the worm, and the wind here in chapter 4. God's hand is at work in all the events of our lives—both the good and the bad.

The vine was a good gift from God—bringing joy, comfort, and blessing. But then God sent the worm—bringing sorrow, disappointment, and loss. On top of that, God sent the wind, which brought pain, affliction, and distress. It's easy to see how God can use the vine, but how does God use the worm and the wind? God used the worm and the wind to save Jonah from a "vine-centered" life. A vine-centered person is one who is so taken up with the joy of God's good gifts that he or she ends up loving the gifts more than the Giver. The Bible calls this *idolatry*. If we feel that without a certain person, or position, or achievement, our life would not be worth living, we may be deeper into idolatry than we think. Friends, family, money, ministry, and success are good gifts from God that can be very gratifying. But they are not the purpose of life. Christ died so that "those who live might no longer live for themselves but for him who for their sake died and was raised" (2 Cor. 5:15).

Jonah indicated the priorities of his heart when he became angry at the salvation of the Ninevites (Jonah 4:1–4). If we truly love the Lord, we will love whom and what he loves. God showed his love to Nineveh by sending that pagan city the message of salvation. When Jonah reacted negatively to news that the Ninevites had been saved, he showed that he actually had little regard for God. So also today, if we allow

wind, [g]and the sun beat down on the head of
Jonah so that he [h]was faint. And he asked that
he might die and said, [c]"It is better for me to
die than to live." 9 But God said to Jonah, [i]"Do
you do well to be angry for the plant?" And he
said, "Yes, I do well to be angry, angry enough
to die." 10 And the LORD said, "You pity the
plant, for which you did not labor, nor did
you make it grow, which came into being in
a night and perished in a night. 11 And should
not I pity [j]Nineveh, that great city, in which
there are more than 120,000 persons who do
not know their right hand from their left, and
also much [k]cattle?"

our differences with others to dampen our zeal for their salvation, then we may be disregarding those for whom Christ died. And simultaneously, we may be indicating our lack of regard for him.

4:11 People "who do not know their right hand from their left" have lost their moral compass and will soon lose their way and become hopelessly lost. God's pity is drawn out by the moral bankruptcy of the Ninevites. The Bible tells us that every one of us is born blind (2 Cor. 4:4), bound (John 8:34), and dead (Eph. 2:1). A robust and biblical doctrine of sin, properly applied, will help us to grow in compassion. Any softheartedness or virtue we have cultivated is, after all, a gift of God's grace (1 Cor. 4:7; 2 Cor. 8:1–2).

Jonah saw the moral bankruptcy of the Ninevites, and it led him to harshness and condemnation. He despised the evil people of Nineveh and felt that they deserved destruction. He identified outsiders as sinners, but, viewing himself as an insider, he did not see himself as a sinner. There were people like Jonah in Jesus' day (Matthew 23; John 9:41), and in ours as well. This deficient doctrine of sin erodes compassion. But God sees evil more comprehensively than we do, and he has pity on all kinds of people (1 Tim. 2:1–4). While we were still sinners—not just when we had "cleaned ourselves up"—Christ died for us (Rom. 5:8). Grasping the effect of sin on the human soul helps us grow in the kind of compassion that reflects the compassionate heart of God (Ex. 34:6–7).

8[g] [Ps. 121:6] [h] [Amos 8:13]
[c] [See ver. 3 above]
9[i] [ver. 1, 4]
11[j] See ch. 1:2 [k] [ch. 3:7]

Introduction to Micah

Author and Date

Micah prophesied during the reigns of the Judean kings Jotham (750–735 B.C.), Ahaz (735–715), and Hezekiah (715–687). This was about the same time as Hosea and Isaiah.

The Gospel in Micah

God deals with sinners in one of two ways: deserved justice, or undeserved grace. In Micah's day, both Samaria and Judah clearly deserved God's judgment for their oppression, idolatry, and corruption. They lived out this wickedness right alongside the motions of offering sacrifice, expecting that because they had the covenant promises and the temple in their midst, God would accept and protect them.

In his great grace, however, God sent the prophet Micah to confront their sin, warn them of judgment, and call them to repentance. Micah prophesied of the coming judgment, when God would abandon them (for a time) to the invading enemies of Assyria and Babylon, who would trample their cities and carry their people off to exile.

But while God is a righteous Judge who carries out deserved judgment, he is also a merciful Savior who gives undeserved grace and full forgiveness to those who turn to him in repentance. The specific hope Micah presented was the promise of a Shepherd-King who would gather his faithful remnant back in the land, tenderly care for them, and defeat their great enemy. The result would be that people from many nations would come to worship Israel's God. To God's people who had suffered under a line of failed kings and oppressive foreign regimes, Micah announced the coming of a Shepherd-King who would arise from Bethlehem, saying, "He shall be their peace" (Mic. 5:2–5).

Ultimately, Jesus himself is the long-anticipated Shepherd-King who has made peace with God. He has done it, however, not through the raw power of military deliverance but through "the blood of his cross" (Col. 1:20). He did not come to destroy but to be destroyed, laying down his life for his sheep (John 10:15). He now rules over his people in perfect justice and abundant mercy, empowering his people, by his Spirit, to walk humbly in his just and merciful ways (1 John 2:6)—the very life Israel in Micah's day had abandoned.

Because of this Shepherd-King, all those who look to Christ in trusting faith experience his kindness instead of his anger. They can expect that God will "pass over transgression for the remnant of his inheritance" (Mic. 7:18) because the prophet who confesses, "I have sinned against him [the Lord]," also proclaims, "he pleads my cause and executes judgment for me. He will bring me out to the light; I shall look upon his vindication" (v. 9).

Ultimately the transgression of all such persons has been put upon God's firstborn, Jesus Christ (Rom. 3:24–26). Christ will "bear the indignation of the LORD" on their behalf (Mic. 7:9). Though we may suffer and fall in our life's battle with evil, we shall rise, as the prophet believed he himself would, due to the Lord's vindication (vv. 8–9)—and, as indeed will all those who are united to Christ by faith (Rom. 6:5). This is the wonder of the gospel in Micah.

Outline

I. Superscription (1:1)

II. The Announcement of Judgment on Israel and Judah (1:2–2:13)

III. The Present Injustice and the Future Prospect of Just Rule in Jerusalem (3:1–5:15)

IV. The Lord's Indictment and Restoration of His People (6:1–7:20)

Micah

1 The word of the LORD that came to Micah [a]of Moresheth [b]in the days of Jotham, Ahaz, and Hezekiah, kings of Judah, which he saw [c]concerning [d]Samaria and Jerusalem.

The Coming Destruction

2 [e]Hear, you peoples, all of you;[1]
[f]pay attention, O earth, and all that is in it,
and [g]let the Lord GOD be a witness against you,
[h]the Lord from his holy temple.
3 For behold, [i]the LORD is coming out of [j]his place,
and will come down and [k]tread upon the high places of the earth.
4 And [l]the mountains will melt under him,
and the valleys will split open,
like wax before the fire,
like waters poured down a steep place.
5 All this is for [m]the transgression of Jacob
and for the sins of the house of Israel.
[n]What is the transgression of Jacob?
Is it not [d]Samaria?
And what is [o]the high place of Judah?
Is it not Jerusalem?
6 Therefore I will make [d]Samaria [p]a heap in the open country,
a place for planting vineyards,
and I will pour down her stones [q]into the valley
and [r]uncover her foundations.
7 All [s]her carved images shall be beaten to pieces,
[t]all her wages shall be burned with fire,
and all her idols I will lay waste,
for from [t]the fee of a prostitute she gathered them,
and to the fee of a prostitute they shall return.

8 [u]For this I will lament and wail;
I will go [v]stripped and naked;
I will make lamentation [w]like the jackals,
and mourning [x]like the ostriches.
9 [y]For her wound is incurable,
and it has come to Judah;
it has reached to the gate of my people,
to Jerusalem.

10 [z]Tell it not in [a]Gath;
weep not at all;
in Beth-le-aphrah
[b]roll yourselves in the dust.
11 Pass on your way,
inhabitants of Shaphir,
[c]in nakedness and shame;
the inhabitants of Zaanan
do not come out;
the lamentation of Beth-ezel
shall take away from you its standing place.
12 For the inhabitants of Maroth
wait anxiously for good,

[1] Hebrew *all of them*

1:1–16 Micah calls the peoples of the earth (v. 2), Israel's corrupt leaders (3:1), and God's covenant people (6:1) to hear the word of the Lord and repent of their sin. Israel faces judgment due to her unwillingness to hear and repent. Micah's response to the well-deserved, punitive destruction coming upon God's people was therefore to lament. This lament anticipates that of Jesus, who, even as he prophesied impending destruction, lamented that Jerusalem would not listen and repent (Luke 19:41–44). The mark of God's true people in every age is that they hear his voice and obey it, trusting in him (Luke 11:28; John 5:24).

Chapter 1
1[a] [ver. 14] [b] Isa. 1:1 [c] Amos 1:1 [d] Isa. 7:9; Jer. 23:13
2[e] ch. 3:1, 9; 6:1, 2; See Hos. 5:1 [f] See Isa. 1:2 [g] Mal. 3:5 [h] Ps. 11:4; Jonah 2:7; Hab. 2:20
3[i] Isa. 26:21 [j] Ps. 115:3 [k] Amos 4:13; [Deut. 32:13]
4[l] Ps. 97:5; [Judg. 5:5; Amos 9:5, 13; Nah. 1:5]

5[m] See ch. 3:8 [n] [ver. 13] [d] [See ver. 1 above] [o] [2 Chr. 28:4] **6**[d] [See ver. 1 above] [p] [ch. 3:12] [q] [1 Kgs. 16:24] [r] Ezek. 13:14 **7**[s] [Hos. 8:6] [t] [Hos. 2:12; 9:1] **8**[u] [Isa. 22:4] [v] See Isa. 20:2-4 [w] Job 30:29; Ps. 44:19 [x] Isa. 13:21 **9**[y] [Hos. 5:13] **10**[z] 2 Sam. 1:20 [a] See 1 Sam. 17:4 [b] [Jer. 6:26] **11**[c] [Isa. 20:4; 47:3]

because disaster has come down [d]from
the LORD
to the gate of Jerusalem.
13 Harness the steeds to the chariots,
inhabitants of [e]Lachish;
it was the beginning of sin
to the daughter of Zion,
for in you were found
[f]the transgressions of Israel.
14 Therefore you shall give parting gifts[1]
to [g]Moresheth-gath;
the houses of [h]Achzib shall be a deceitful
thing
to the kings of Israel.
15 I will again bring [i]a conqueror to you,
inhabitants of [h]Mareshah;
the glory of Israel
shall come to [j]Adullam.
16 [k]Make yourselves bald and cut off your
hair,
for the children of your delight;
[k]make yourselves as bald as the eagle,
for they shall go from you into exile.

Woe to the Oppressors

2 [l]Woe to those who devise wickedness
and work evil [m]on their beds!
When the morning dawns, they perform
it,
because it is in the power of their hand.
2 They covet fields and [n]seize them,
and houses, and take them away;
they oppress a man and his house,
a man and his inheritance.
3 Therefore thus says the LORD:
behold, against [o]this family I am devising disaster,[2]
from which you cannot remove your
necks,
and you [p]shall not walk haughtily,
[q]for it will be a time of disaster.
4 In that day [r]they shall take up a taunt
song against you
and moan bitterly,
and say, "We are utterly ruined;
[s]he changes the portion of my people;
[s]how he removes it from me!
[t]To an apostate he allots our fields."
5 Therefore you will have none [u]to cast the
line by lot
in the assembly of the LORD.

6 [v]"Do not preach"—thus they preach—
[w]"one should not preach of such things;
[x]disgrace will not overtake us."
7 Should this be said, O house of Jacob?
[v]Has the LORD grown impatient?[3]
Are these his deeds?
Do not my words do good
to him who walks uprightly?
8 But lately [y]my people have risen up as an
enemy;
you strip the rich robe from those who
pass by trustingly
with no thought of war.[4]
9 The women of my people you drive out
from their delightful houses;
from their young children you take away
my splendor forever.
10 [z]Arise and go,
for this is no [a]place to rest,

[1] Or *give dowry* [2] The same Hebrew word can mean *evil* or *disaster*, depending on the context [3] Hebrew *Has the spirit of the LORD grown short?* [4] Or *returning from war*

12[d] See Amos 3:6
13[e] Josh. 10:3; 2 Kgs. 18:14, 17; 2 Chr. 32:9 [f] [ver. 5; Hos. 13:1]
14[g] [ver. 1] [h] Josh. 15:44
15[i] [ch. 2:4; Jer. 6:12] [h] [See ver. 14 above] [j] See 1 Sam. 22:1, 2
16[k] See Isa. 22:12
Chapter 2
1[l] [Isa. 10:1, 2] [m] [Ps. 36:4]
2[n] [Isa. 5:8]
3[o] [Jer. 8:3; Amos 3:1, 2] [p] [Isa. 2:11, 17] [q] Amos 5:13
4[r] Hab. 2:6; See Num. 23:7 [s] [ch. 1:15] [t] [Ps. 68:6]
5[u] Deut. 32:8, 9; [Josh. 14:1, 2]
6[v] See Amos 2:12 [w] [Amos 8:11, 12] [x] [Amos 8:10]
7[v] [See ver. 6 above]
8[y] [2 Chr. 28:8]
10[z] [ch. 1:11, 16] [a] Deut. 12:9; [Heb. 13:14]

2:1–5 Micah pronounces woe on oppressors who covet, plot, and seize the property of the poor. He is warning that they will be excluded from the "assembly" of those who are allotted an inheritance in the land when the faithful remnant returns from exile.

His warning extends beyond Micah's day to all who persist in unrepentant wickedness and wrongly presume they will have an inheritance in the eternal kingdom of God (1 Cor. 6:8–10; Gal. 5:19–21). To the presumptuous, the gospel pronounces judgment. To the penitent, the gospel pronounces deliverance.

2:6–11 Unprincipled prophets told those who corrupted justice and oppressed the poor that, because they were Israelites, God would bless rather than judge them. Jesus, the true Prophet of God, pronounces blessing on those who reveal by their kindness and generosity toward the "least of these" that they belong to him; and he pronounces judgment on those who reveal by their lack of Christlike love for the needy that they have no real relationship to him (Matt. 25:31–46).

What we do reveals what we are. The outside reveals the inside (Matt. 7:17–18). The gospel of grace, when received with faith, does not just modify our behavior; it transforms our hearts.

because of [b]uncleanness that destroys
with a grievous destruction.
11 If a man should go about and [c]utter
wind and lies,
saying, "I will preach to you [d]of wine
and strong drink,"
he would be the preacher for this people!
12 I will surely assemble all of you, O Jacob;
[e]I will gather [f]the remnant of Israel;
I will set them together
like sheep in a fold,
[h]like a flock in its pasture,
a noisy multitude of men.
13 [i]He who opens the breach goes up before
them;
they break through and pass the gate,
[j]going out by it.
Their king passes on before them,
[k]the LORD at their head.

Rulers and Prophets Denounced

3 And I said:
[l]Hear, you heads of Jacob
and rulers of the house of Israel!
[m]Is it not for you to know justice?—
2 you [n]who hate the good and love the
evil,
[o]who tear the skin from off my people[1]
and their flesh from off their bones,
3 [p]who eat the flesh of my people,
and flay their skin from off them,
and break their bones in pieces
and chop them up like meat in a pot,
like flesh in a cauldron.

4 [q]Then they will cry to the LORD,
but he will not answer them;
[r]he will hide his face from them at that
time,
because they have made their deeds
evil.

5 Thus says the LORD concerning [s]the
prophets
who lead my people astray,
[t]who cry "Peace"
when they have something to eat,
but declare war against him
who puts nothing into their mouths.

[1] Hebrew *from off them*

2:12–13 The hope Micah presents in the face of Israel's coming destruction is a Shepherd who will gather his people safely to himself (v. 12; cf. John 10:11–16). This Shepherd is also identified as a King who will go before his people in battle against their enemies, a King who is the Lord (Mic. 2:13; cf. Col. 2:15; 1 John 3:8). This is a promise of sure deliverance and protection for the harassed people of God. In Christ, the fulfillment of this hope for an unfailing Shepherd-King is decisively accomplished.

Yet he delivers his harassed people not from a position of might and power but by being harassed himself by those who should have welcomed him (Mark 14:1; John 5:17; 7:1). He was the Shepherd who gave his life for his sheep (John 10:11). Ultimately this led to death on a cross to suffer the judgment we deserve, and resurrection from the powers of sin and death to provide the victory we need. Through this Shepherd's death, there is hope for the oppressed who trust in him to save—as well as for oppressors who turn away from injustice, looking to Christ for forgiveness and deliverance (1 Thess. 1:10).

3:1–4 The civil leaders of Judah were responsible to execute justice as a declaration and demonstration of Yahweh's justice, but their cannibalistic exploitation of the poor and powerless revealed that they had no interest in walking in his ways. Their refusal to listen to God or to the cries of his people meant that God would not hear their own cries for help. Those who demonstrate by their refusal to trust and revere God that they are not his children cannot expect him to answer their prayers (Ps. 66:18; 1 Pet. 3:7; James 5:13).

Ultimately, through our sins and failures, we all give God reason not to listen to us. Yet there was One who had no sins or failures, who deserved to be heard by God—and wasn't (Matt. 26:39). The sinless One's prayer was unanswered, so that the penitent sinner's prayer *can* be answered.

3:5–8 Rather than calling the rulers to repentance, these "prophets-for-pay" falsely assured them of peace with God. But Micah confronted the rulers regarding their sin in order that they might confess and repent and thereby enjoy true peace with God. This peace would ultimately be made possible by Christ's reconciling work on the cross (Rom. 5:1; Eph. 2:14).

10[b] Lev. 18:25
11[c] Jer. 5:13 [d][Amos 2:12]
12[e][2 Kgs. 25:11] [f]See ch. 4:7 [h][Jer. 31:10]
13[i][2 Kgs. 25:10] [j][ch. 4:10] [k][Isa. 52:12]
Chapter 3
1[l]See ch. 1:2 [m]Jer. 5:5; [Ezek. 22:6, 27]
2[n][ver. 9] [o][Ezek. 34:3]
3[p][Ps. 14:4; Isa. 3:15]
4[q]See Prov. 1:28 [r]Isa. 1:15; See Deut. 31:17
5[s]Jer. 23:13, 32; Ezek. 13:10 [t][Jer. 6:14]

6 Therefore [u]it shall be night to you, without vision,
and darkness to you, without divination.
[v]The sun shall go down on the prophets,
and the day shall be black over them;
7 [w]the seers shall be disgraced,
and the diviners put to shame;
[x]they shall all cover their lips,
for [y]there is no answer from God.
8 But as for me, [z]I am filled with power,
with the Spirit of the LORD,
and with justice and might,
to declare to Jacob [a]his transgression
and to Israel his sin.

9 [b]Hear this, you heads of the house of Jacob
and rulers of the house of Israel,
[c]who detest justice
and make crooked all that is straight,
10 [d]who build Zion with blood
and Jerusalem with iniquity.
11 [e]Its heads give judgment for a bribe;
[f]its priests teach for a price;
[g]its prophets practice divination for money;
[h]yet they lean on the LORD and [i]say,
"Is not the LORD in the midst of us?
[j]No disaster shall come upon us."
12 Therefore because of you
[k]Zion shall be plowed as a field;
Jerusalem [l]shall become a heap of ruins,
and [m]the mountain of the house [n]a wooded height.

The Mountain of the LORD

4 It shall come to pass [o]in the latter days
that the mountain of the house of the LORD
shall be established as the highest of the mountains,
and it shall be lifted up above the hills;
and peoples shall flow to it,
2 and many nations shall come, and say:
"Come, let us go up to the mountain of the LORD,
to the house of the God of Jacob,
that he may teach us his ways
and that we may walk in his paths."
For out of Zion shall go forth the law,[1]
and the word of the LORD from Jerusalem.
3 He shall judge between many peoples,
and shall decide for strong nations far away;
and they shall [p]beat their swords into plowshares,
and their spears into pruning hooks;

[1] Or *teaching*

6[u] Ezek. 12:24; 13:23 [v] See Amos 8:9
7[w] Zech. 13:4; [Jer. 37:19] [x] [Lev. 13:45] [y] See Amos 8:11
8[z] [Jer. 6:11] [a] ch. 1:5; Isa. 58:1; [Ezek. 23:36]
9[b] See ch. 1:2 [c] [ver. 2]
10[d] Jer. 22:13; Ezek. 22:27; Hab. 2:12
11[e] ch. 7:3; Isa. 1:23 [f] See Jer. 6:13 [g] [ver. 5; Ezek. 22:25] [h] Isa. 48:2 [i] Jer. 7:4; [Amos 5:14] [j] [Jer. 23:17; Amos 9:10]
12[k] Cited Jer. 26:18 [l] [ch. 1:6] [m] ch. 4:2 [n] [Luke 13:35]
Chapter 4
1[o] For ver. 1-3, see Isa. 2:2-4
3[p] [Joel 3:10]

3:9–12 Judah's crooked rulers, priests, and prophets led the people to wrongly assume that, because they had the covenant promises and the temple, they were safe from judgment. But those who truly trust the Lord demonstrate their trust by keeping God's commands and turning toward him in repentance when they fail, rather than persisting in unrepentant disobedience (Heb. 10:26; 1 John 2:4–6).

3:12–4:1 At one level, the coming destruction of Jerusalem and its temple because of Israel's sin, followed by the city and temple being restored and drawing people of many nations, anticipates what will occur at the second coming of Christ (see also Isa. 2:2). At another level, Micah's words prefigured what would happen to the true Israel, Christ himself. On the cross, Jesus was "plowed as a field" and became "a heap of ruins" (Mic. 3:12) as he took upon himself the judgment for his people's sins. But his death was followed by resurrection and being lifted up to God's right hand, from where he draws people from every nation to himself (John 2:19; 12:32). By his atoning work, believers in Christ from every nation are set free.

4:1–5 Micah envisions the "latter days" when Jerusalem will be raised up so that people from many nations will flow into it to be taught by God and to walk in his ways (cf. Isa. 2:1–2). In that day there will be abundant provision and restful security instead of war. This is the peace, safety, and abundance that believers experience in part even now through faith in Christ (Rom. 5:1; 15:13) and that they will experience in full in the new Jerusalem (Rev. 21:2–4, 25–27).

Ultimately, the Old Testament prophets can anticipate all nations flowing to Jerusalem because, in the New Testament, Jesus sends believers out from Jerusalem "to the end of the earth" (Acts 1:8) to gather them into his kingdom.

nation shall not lift up sword against
nation,
neither shall they learn war anymore;
4 [q]but they shall sit every man under his
vine and under his fig tree,
[r]and no one shall make them afraid,
[s]for the mouth of the LORD of hosts
has spoken.
5 For [t]all the peoples walk
each in the name of its god,
but [u]we will walk in the name of the
LORD our God
forever and ever.

The LORD Shall Rescue Zion

6 [v]In that day, declares the LORD,
[w]I will assemble the [x]lame
and gather those who have been driven
away
and those whom I have afflicted;
7 and the lame I will make [y]the remnant,
and those who were cast off, a strong
nation;
and [z]the LORD will reign over them [a]in
Mount Zion
from this time forth and forevermore.
8 And you, O tower of the flock,
hill of the daughter of Zion,
to you shall it come,
the former dominion shall come,
kingship for the daughter of
Jerusalem.

9 Now why do you cry aloud?
[b]Is there no king in you?
[c]Has your counselor perished,
that [d]pain seized you like a woman in
labor?
10 [e]Writhe and groan,[1] O daughter of Zion,
like a woman in labor,
for [f]now you shall go out from the city
and dwell in the open country;
you [g]shall go to Babylon.
There you shall be rescued;
[h]there the LORD will redeem you
from the hand of your enemies.

11 Now [i]many nations
are assembled against you,
saying, "Let her be defiled,
and [j]let our eyes gaze upon Zion."
12 But [k]they do not know
the thoughts of the LORD;
they do not understand his plan,
that [l]he has gathered them as sheaves
to the threshing floor.
13 Arise and thresh,
O daughter of Zion,
for I will make your horn iron,
and I will make your hoofs bronze;
you shall beat in pieces many peoples;
and [m]shall devote[2] [n]their gain to the
LORD,
their wealth to [o]the Lord of the whole
earth.

The Ruler to Be Born in Bethlehem

5[3] Now muster your troops, O daughter[4]
of troops;
siege is laid against us;
with a rod [p]they strike the judge of
Israel
on the cheek.
2[5] [q]But you, O Bethlehem Ephrathah,
who are too little to be among the
clans of [r]Judah,
from you shall come forth for me
one who is to be [s]ruler in Israel,
[t]whose coming forth is [u]from of old,
from ancient days.
3 Therefore he shall give them up [v]until
the time
when she who is in labor has given
birth;
then [w]the rest of his brothers shall return
to the people of Israel.

[1] Or *push* [2] Hebrew *devote to destruction* [3] Ch 4:14 in Hebrew [4] That is, city [5] Ch 5:1 in Hebrew

4:6–5:3 Though their enemies are coming to destroy their cities, defile their temple, and humiliate their king, God is going to raise up for himself a King in Israel. This ruler will be born, not in a place of power but in the unimpressive town of Bethlehem. He will be the fulfillment of the ancient promises—the seed (or "offspring") of the woman (Gen. 3:15), the blessing for all of the families of the earth (Gen. 12:3), the son of David (2 Sam. 7:12–13). Yet while born in obscurity and killed in ignominy, this King has been raised in glory (Heb. 8:1; 12:2) and will one day return in decisive triumph as a conquering and victorious King (Rev. 19:11–21).

4[q] See 1 Kgs. 4:25 [r] Isa. 17:2 [s] See Isa. 1:20
5[t] [Jer. 2:11] [u] [Zech. 10:12]
6[v] [ver. 1] [w] See Ezek. 11:17 [x] Ezek. 34:16; Zeph. 3:19
7[y] ch. 2:12; 5:7, 8; Joel 2:32; Zeph. 2:7 [z] Isa. 24:23; [Dan. 7:14; Luke 1:33] [a] Ps. 2:6; Heb. 12:22
9[b] Jer. 8:19 [c] [Isa. 3:3] [d] Jer. 6:24
10[e] [John 16:20, 21] [f] [ch. 2:13]

[g] Isa. 39:6, 7 [h] See Isa. 44:22, 23 **11**[i] Zech. 12:3 [j] ch. 7:10; Obad. 12 **12**[k] [Isa. 10:7] [l] [Joel 3:13; Hab. 3:12; Matt. 3:12; Luke 3:17] **13**[m] Lev. 27:28 [n] Isa. 23:18 [o] Ps. 97:5 **Chapter 5** **1**[p] See 1 Kgs. 22:24 **2**[q] Cited Matt. 2:6; [John 7:42] [r] [Heb. 7:14] [s] [Gen. 49:10; Isa. 9:6, 7; Jer. 30:21; Zech. 9:9] [t] Hos. 6:3 [u] Ps. 90:2; [Prov. 8:22, 23; John 1:1] **3**[v] [ch. 4:9, 10] [w] [ch. 4:7]

4 And he shall stand [x]and shepherd his
flock [y]in the strength of the LORD,
in the majesty of the name of the
LORD his God.
And they shall dwell secure, for now [z]he
shall be great
to the ends of the earth.
5 And he shall be [a]their peace.

[b]When the Assyrian comes into our land
and treads in our palaces,
then we will raise against him seven
[c]shepherds
and eight princes of men;
6 they shall shepherd the land of Assyria
with the sword,
and the land of [d]Nimrod at its
entrances;
and he shall deliver us from the Assyrian
[b]when he comes into our land
and treads within our border.

A Remnant Shall Be Delivered

7 Then [w]the remnant of Jacob shall be
in the midst of many peoples
like dew from the LORD,
like showers on the grass,
which delay not for a man
nor wait for the children of man.
8 And [w]the remnant of Jacob shall be
among the nations,
in the midst of many peoples,
like a lion among the beasts of the forest,
like a young lion among the flocks of
sheep,
[e]which, when it goes through, treads
down
and tears in pieces, and there is none
to deliver.
9 Your hand shall [f]be lifted up over your
adversaries,
and all your enemies shall be cut off.

10 And [g]in that day, declares the LORD,
[h]I will cut off your horses from among
you
and will destroy your chariots;
11 [i]and I will cut off the cities of your land
and throw down all your strongholds;
12 and I will cut off [j]sorceries from your
hand,
and [k]you shall have no more tellers of
fortunes;
13 and [l]I will cut off your carved images
and [m]your pillars from among you,
[n]and you shall bow down no more
to the work of your hands;
14 and I will root out your [o]Asherah images
from among you
[i]and destroy your cities.
15 And in anger and wrath [p]I will execute
vengeance
on the nations that did not obey.

4[x] Isa. 40:11; [ch. 7:14] [y] See Isa. 11:3-5 [z] Ps. 72:8; Isa. 52:13; Luke 1:32
5[a] [Isa. 9:6; Zech. 9:10; Eph. 2:14] [b] [2 Kgs. 18:13] [c] [Isa. 3:2, 3]
6[d] Gen. 10:8, 10, 11 [b] [See ver. 5 above]
7[w] [See ver. 3 above]
8[w] [See ver. 3 above] [e] [Hos. 5:14]
9[f] Isa. 26:11
10[g] [ch. 4:1, 6] [h] Zech. 9:10; [Isa. 2:7; Hag. 2:22]
11[i] ver. 14; Isa. 17:9; 27:10; [Hos. 8:14; Zech. 2:4]
12[j] [2 Kgs. 9:22] [k] Deut. 18:10; [Isa. 2:6]
13[l] Zech. 13:2 [m] Hos. 3:4 [n] [Isa. 17:8]
14[o] Ex. 34:13; See Deut. 16:21 [i] [See ver. 11 above]
15[p] [ver. 8; Ps. 149:7; 2 Thess. 1:8]

5:4 In his ultimate victory, this King will rule over all as a Shepherd who gathers, tends, and protects his flock in the power and authority of God himself. We have already seen the nature of this King as Jesus, the Good Shepherd, who came to gather his sheep to himself (John 10:27), feed them the bread of heaven (John 6:35), and give them living water (John 4:14). He heals their wounds (1 Pet. 2:24–25) and protects them by laying down his life for them (John 10:15). They are forever secure, for he will never cast them out, and they cannot be snatched from his hand (John 6:37; 10:28). He is a Savior worthy to be trusted. Bank everything on this Good Shepherd, who is our coming King!

5:5–6 False prophets spoke peace while ignoring the sins of the people. Assyria threatened with overwhelming military brutality. Yet Micah speaks of the peace to come when the Shepherd-King deals decisively with the people's sins (cf. Eph. 2:14) by canceling sin's debt and defeating the only powers that can really harm us in this world (Col. 2:14–15). The victory against Assyria foreshadows the Shepherd-King's victory over the greater enemies of sin and death (Rom. 5:8–11).

5:7–15 God intends Judah's exile to be a time of purification from their dependence on worldly power, occult knowledge, and false idols. He will preserve a remnant through this time of purification. Likewise, God intends to purify and sanctify believers during their time of exile in the world (Titus 2:14; 1 Pet. 2:11). Our journey through this fallen world is filled with joys but also with sorrows and pain (Acts 14:22; 2 Tim. 3:14). But our hope is sure. Our true home is in heaven (Phil. 3:20). And one day that true home will come to earth and reinstate Eden, without the trials and burdens we currently bear (Rev. 21:1–4).

The Indictment of the Lord

6 [q]Hear what the LORD says:
Arise, plead your case before the mountains,
and let the hills hear your voice.
2 [r]Hear, you mountains, [s]the indictment of the LORD,
and you enduring foundations of the earth,
for the LORD has an indictment against his people,
and he will contend with Israel.

3 "O my people, [t]what have I done to you?
[u]How have I wearied you? Answer me!
4 For [v]I brought you up from the land of Egypt
and [w]redeemed you from the house of slavery,
and I sent before you Moses,
Aaron, and [x]Miriam.
5 O my people, remember [y]what Balak king of Moab devised,
and what Balaam the son of Beor answered him,
and what happened from [z]Shittim to Gilgal,
that you may know [a]the righteous acts of the LORD."

What Does the Lord Require?

6 [b]"With what shall I come before the LORD,
and bow myself before [c]God on high?
Shall I come before him with burnt offerings,
with calves a year old?
7 [d]Will the LORD be pleased with[1] thousands of rams,
with ten thousands of rivers of oil?
[e]Shall I give my firstborn for my transgression,
the fruit of my body for the sin of my soul?"
8 He has told you, O man, what is good;
and [f]what does the LORD require of you
but to do justice, and to love kindness,[2]
and to [g]walk humbly with your God?

Destruction of the Wicked

9 The voice of the LORD cries to the city—
and it is sound wisdom to fear [h]your name:
"Hear of [i]the rod and of him who appointed it![3]
10 Can I forget any longer the treasures[4] of wickedness in the house of the wicked,
and the scant measure that is accursed?

[1] Or *Will the LORD accept* [2] Or *steadfast love* [3] The meaning of the Hebrew is uncertain [4] Or *Are there still treasures*

Chapter 6
1[q] See ch. 1:2
2[r] Ps. 50:1, 4; Ezek. 36:4 [s] Isa. 1:18; See Hos. 4:1
3[t] Isa. 5:4; [Jer. 2:5, 31] [u] Isa. 43:22, 23; [Mal. 1:13]
4[v] Ex. 12:51; Hos. 12:13; Amos 2:10 [w] 2 Sam. 7:23 [x] Ex. 15:20; Num. 12:1, 2
5[y] See Num. 22:5 [z] Num. 25:1 [a] [Judg. 5:11]
6[b] [Hos. 5:6; Heb. 10:4] [c] Isa. 57:15
7[d] See 1 Sam. 15:22 [e] 2 Kgs. 3:27; 16:3; 21:6; 23:10; [Lev. 18:21]
8[f] [Deut. 10:12] [g] [Gen. 5:22]
9[h] Isa. 30:27 [i] Isa. 10:5; 30:32

6:6–7 Micah speaks for people in every age, asking what God wants from sinners. Escalating from less costly to more costly sacrifices, the prophet proposes even the unthinkable: human sacrifice. God does require "human sacrifice," but he did not ultimately force us to pay for our sin with our own sons. What God requires is that we rest in the all-sufficient sacrifice of his own Son. What a scandal of mercy: God did not ask us to give our firstborn for our transgression; rather, he gives us *his* firstborn! (Rom. 4:25).

6:8 This text is a frequently quoted summary of godly living, and rightly so. This is the godly life, the beautiful life. To it we are called. Let us strive to embody Micah 6:8 in our lives. And let us do so in a way that gladly acknowledges that we will never "do justice" and "love kindness" and "walk humbly" with God as we should. Only Jesus lived this way perfectly. But the wonder of the gospel is that he did it in our place and transfers his record of perfect righteousness to all those joined to him by faith. As he indwells his people by his Spirit, they are empowered to do justice and love kindness, walking humbly in his ways (James 1:27).

In a remarkable way, this verse also foreshadows the gospel. It expresses first our obligation to the law ("to do justice"); then it compels us "to love kindness" (i.e., steadfast love or mercy), since none of us can fully keep the requirements of the law; and finally it calls us "to walk humbly with your God," because we depend upon our relationship with him to provide the justice and steadfast love required of us.

6:9–16 The following sentences of judgment are rendered for deceitful business practices that take advantage of the poor and weak: desolation, dissatisfaction, hissing, and scorn. These sentences have been placed upon all who have sinned, yet for those who confess and repent, this liberating truth is brought home: Christ became desolate for us. He experienced the hunger and thirst, and bore the mockery, hissing, and scorn that we rightly deserve, so that we can enjoy God's abundant blessing and glad welcome.

11 Shall I acquit the man[j] with wicked scales
and with a bag of deceitful weights?
12 Your[1] rich men are [k] full of violence;
your inhabitants [l] speak lies,
and [m] their tongue is deceitful in their
mouth.
13 Therefore I strike you with a grievous
blow,
[n] making you desolate because of your
sins.
14 [o] You shall eat, but not be satisfied,
and there shall be hunger within you;
you shall put away, but not preserve,
and what you preserve I will give to
the sword.
15 [p] You shall sow, but not reap;
you shall tread olives, but not anoint
yourselves with oil;
you shall tread grapes, but not drink
wine.
16 For you have kept the statutes of [q] Omri,[2]
and all the works of the house of [r] Ahab;
and you have walked in their counsels,
that I may make you [s] a desolation, and
your[3] inhabitants [s] a hissing;
so you shall bear [t] the scorn of my people."

Wait for the God of Salvation

7 Woe is me! For I have become
[u] as when the summer fruit has been
gathered,
as when the grapes have been gleaned:
there is no cluster to eat,
no [v] first-ripe fig that my soul desires.
2 [w] The godly has perished from the earth,
and [x] there is no one upright among
mankind;
[y] they all lie in wait for blood,
and [z] each hunts the other with a net.
3 [a] Their hands are on what is evil, to do it
well;
[b] the prince and [c] the judge ask for a
bribe,
and the great man utters the evil desire
of his soul;
thus they weave it together.
4 The best of them is [d] like a brier,
the most upright of them a thorn
hedge.
The day of [e] your watchmen, of your
punishment, has come;
[f] now their confusion is at hand.
5 [g] Put no trust in a neighbor;
have no confidence in a friend;
guard [h] the doors of your mouth
from her who lies in your arms;[4]
6 for [i] the son treats the father with contempt,
the daughter rises up against her
mother,
the daughter-in-law against her mother-
in-law;
[j] a man's enemies are the men of his
own house.
7 But as for me, I will look to the LORD;
[k] I will wait for the God of my salvation;
my God will hear me.
8 [l] Rejoice not over me, O [m] my enemy;
[n] when I fall, I shall rise;
[o] when I sit in darkness,
the LORD will be a light to me.
9 [p] I will bear the indignation of the LORD
because I have sinned against him,

[1] Hebrew *whose* [2] Hebrew *For the statutes of Omri are kept* [3] Hebrew *its* [4] Hebrew *bosom*

7:8–10 Micah expresses confidence that though the "city" of God's people (6:9; most likely Jerusalem) will fall to her enemies, she will rise again from the rubble. Enemies who taunted and trampled her will themselves be trampled. These promises will ultimately be fulfilled in Christ, as the city from which his kingdom is established becomes a beacon of hope to the nations despite its past destruction for sin.

To bear the indignation of the Lord is to recognize the weight of the offense of sin toward a holy God, and the cost of atonement for that sin (1 Pet. 1:19). Today, if we recognize God's right to indignation, then we mourn over how our sin offends his holiness. We long to approach him in genuine contrition, confident that Christ is our "advocate" pleading our cause before the Father, and that his grace is greater than our sin (1 John 2:1; cf. Rom 5:20). For though Micah expressed confidence that God would plead his cause and execute judgment *for* him (Mic. 7:9), he could not have seen how radically and truly God would do this—by sending his own Son to have judgment executed *upon* him.

11[j] See Hos. 12:7
12[k] Amos 3:10; Hab. 1:2, 3 [l] Hos. 7:13 [m] Jer. 9:8
13[n] ch. 7:13
14[o] Hos. 4:10
15[p] [Zeph. 1:13; Hag. 1:6]
16[q] 1 Kgs. 16:25, 26; [ch. 1:13] [r] See 1 Kgs. 16:30-33; 21:25, 26 [s] See 2 Chr. 29:8 [t] Isa. 25:8
Chapter 7
1[u] Isa. 24:13; [Isa. 17:6] [v] Hos. 9:10
2[w] [Ps. 12:1; Isa. 57:1] [x] Ps. 14:1, 3 [y] [Ps. 10:9; Hos. 6:8, 9] [z] Isa. 9:19
3[a] [Zeph. 3:7] [b] [Ps. 82:1, 2] [c] ch. 3:11
4[d] [2 Sam. 23:6, 7; Nah. 1:10]; See Ezek. 2:6 [e] See Ezek. 33:2 [f] [ch. 3:6, 7; Isa. 22:5]
5[g] Jer. 9:4 [h] [Ps. 141:3]
6[i] Ezek. 22:7; [Matt. 10:21, 35; Luke 12:53] [j] Cited Matt. 10:36 **7**[k] [Lam. 3:26] **8**[l] [Jer. 50:11; Lam. 4:21] [m] ver. 10 [n] Ps. 37:24 [o] Ps. 112:4 **9**[p] [Jer. 10:19]

until [q]he pleads my cause
and executes judgment for me.
[r]He will bring me out to the light;
I shall look upon his vindication.
10 Then [s]my enemy will see,
and shame will cover her who [t]said to me,
"Where is the LORD your God?"
[u]My eyes will look upon her;
now she will be trampled down
[v]like the mire of the streets.

11 [w]A day for the building of your walls!
In that day the boundary shall be far extended.
12 In that day they[1] will come to you,
[y]from Assyria and the cities of Egypt,
and from Egypt to [z]the River,
[a]from sea to sea and from mountain to mountain.
13 But [b]the earth will be desolate
because of its inhabitants,
for the fruit of their deeds.

14 [c]Shepherd your people [d]with your staff,
the flock of your inheritance,
who dwell alone in a forest
[e]in the midst of [f]a garden land;[2]
let them graze in Bashan and Gilead
as in the days of old.
15 [g]As in the days when you came out of the land of Egypt,
I will show them[3] marvelous things.
16 [h]The nations shall see and be ashamed of all their might;
[i]they shall lay their hands on their mouths;
their ears shall be deaf;
17 [j]they shall lick the dust like a serpent,
like the crawling things of the earth;
[k]they shall come trembling out of their strongholds;
[l]they shall turn in dread to the LORD our God,
and they shall be in fear of you.

God's Steadfast Love and Compassion

18 [m]Who is a God like you, [n]pardoning iniquity
and passing over transgression
[n]for the remnant of his inheritance?
[o]He does not retain his anger forever,
because he delights in steadfast love.
19 He will [p]again have compassion on us;
[q]he will tread our iniquities underfoot.
[r]You will cast all our[4] sins
into the depths of the sea.
20 [s]You will show faithfulness to Jacob
and steadfast love to Abraham,
[t]as you have sworn to our fathers
from the days of old.

[1] Hebrew *he* [2] Hebrew *of Carmel* [3] Hebrew *him* [4] Hebrew *their*

7:14–17 Micah prays on behalf of his people, asking God to shepherd them with the loving authority of his staff, to feed them, to work marvelous things among them, and to defeat their enemies as he did when they came out of Egypt. Micah's prayer was answered when the "great shepherd" (Heb. 13:20) appeared, spoke with authority (Matt. 7:29), fed his sheep with food that endures (John 6:27), worked miracles among them (John 20:30), and defeated their greatest Enemy (Heb. 2:14). We look forward to his second coming and triumphant reign, when "the Lamb in the midst of the throne will be their shepherd" (Rev. 7:17).

7:18–20 Micah offers ultimate hope to a people deserving judgment because of God's promises of steadfast love and compassion. We now understand that a holy God can pardon and pass over the transgression of those who put their faith in him only because those sins were put upon Christ (Rom. 3:24–26). God's wrath against the sin of those who belong to him was exhausted at the cross. Just as decisively as he dealt with the Egyptian army, so has God dealt with the sins of his people, through Christ (Rom. 8:1–4).

The exultant closing of Micah's prophecy is the hope-filled confidence of every believer. Have you grown bored with the gospel? Or do you wonder, as Micah does, "Who is a God like you, pardoning iniquity?" (Mic. 7:18). The apostle Peter tells us that these gospel matters, anticipated all through the Old Testament (1 Pet. 1:10–11), are "things into which angels long to look" (1 Pet. 1:12). The gospel explodes our categories for how God must deal with us in light of all our failures. Trust him. Christ's record is yours because your sinful record has been removed by his suffering on the cross. God has "cast all our sins into the depths of the sea" (Mic. 7:19). This is who God is.

9[q]See 1 Sam. 24:15 [r]Ps. 37:6
10[s]ver. 8 [t]See Joel 2:17 [u]ch. 4:11 [v]Ps. 18:42; See 2 Sam. 22:43
11[w][Ps. 102:13]
12[y][Isa. 11:11, 16; 19:23, 24; 27:13; Hos. 11:11; Zech. 10:10] [z]See Gen. 31:21 [a]Zech. 9:10
13[b]ch. 6:13
14[c]Ps. 28:9; [ch. 5:4] [d]Ps. 23:4 [e]Jer. 50:19; [Zech. 10:10] [f]See Josh. 19:26
15[g]Ps. 78:12; See Isa. 11:16
16[h][Isa. 26:11; 52:15] [i]See Judg. 18:19
17[j]Ps. 72:9; Isa. 49:23 [k]Ps. 18:45 [l][ch. 4:1]
18[m]See Ex. 15:11 [n]Jer. 50:20; See Ex. 34:7 [o]Ps. 103:9
19[p]Ps. 80:14 [q][Rom. 6:14] [r][Isa. 38:17]
20[s][Luke 1:72, 73] [t]Ps. 105:9, 10

Introduction to Nahum

Author and Date

Nahum is a series of judgment oracles and taunts against the Assyrian Empire and its capital city of Nineveh, given by God in a vision to the prophet Nahum, whose name means "comfort." The prophecies were made sometime between 660–630 B.C. from Elkosh, an unidentified locale in the southern kingdom of Judah.

Audience

Nineveh, capital of the Assyrian Empire, is the explicit audience of Nahum's announcement of God's impending judgment. The regional superpower of the eighth century, Assyria had been used by God to chasten the unfaithful northern kingdom of Israel, resulting in the exile and captivity of 722 B.C. (2 Kings 17). Nineveh had repented from its wickedness several years before Nahum through the warnings of Jonah, but this repentance was short-lived as Assyria added abuse to God's purpose for his just chastisement of Israel (Zech. 1:15) and exhibited the characteristic hubris of great earthly empires.

But Nahum is a prophet of Israel, and his prophecies are part of Israel's Scriptures. The *implicit* audience is the people of God, those already in exile or afraid they would be soon. "Overhearing" God's warning to Nineveh would have comforted those doubting God's power, justice, or faithfulness as well as providing hope that oppression would end.

The Gospel in Nahum

In a variety of ways, the prophecy of Nahum brings home the gospel and carries along the redemptive story that culminates in Jesus Christ.

First, there are explicit gospel promises in Nahum—promises of good news and peace (1:15) and an end to the Lord's discipline (v. 12) and to the power of the oppressors (v. 13). God is a stronghold and refuge for those in trouble (v. 7). God's saving character is made clear at numerous points.

Second, as God's excellencies are proclaimed in judgment (1:2–7), the repentant hear and receive grace. Even though Nahum does not explicitly call Nineveh to repent, repentance is always in order even if hope is not explicit (cf. Jer. 18:7–10). An oracle of judgment is a means of grace to the listening believer (Heb. 4:11; 6:1–8), and of gospel proclamation. Truth is being spoken. This is one manifestation of God's goodness to humanity.

Third, we are comforted in knowing that judgment upon wickedness will inevitably come. All will be set right. We can be hopeful and patient. The gospel frees us not only from God's just claims against us but from the dominion of the world, the flesh, and the Devil. In saving, God overthrows and destroys dominions that are opposed to his rule and oppress his people. This is why Jesus Christ would lift up some and overthrow others

(Luke 2:34), feed some and send others away (Luke 1:53). The good news is not good news for all. In his death and resurrection, Jesus brings an end to empires and puts to shame the powers who oppress (Psalm 2; Luke 20:43; John 12:31; Col. 2:14–15; Heb. 10:13).

Fourth, and supremely, our focus is drawn to the severity of judgment that Jesus Christ bore for us in his suffering in our place. The taunts deserved by evil (Nah. 3:5–7) were ultimately borne by him (Ps. 22:7; Luke 23:37). But for his extravagant act of mercy, our fate would be the same as Nineveh. Instead, we now stand in God's presence blameless, with great joy (Jude 24).

The whole Bible is about the grace of God ultimately revealed in Jesus (Luke 24:27, 44; John 5:39, 46). The whole Bible is about the gospel (Rom. 1:1–2; 1 Pet. 1:10–12). That includes Nahum. Reading Nahum, we see the judgment to fall on the wicked, and the trajectory that culminates in Jesus continues—a trajectory that clarifies how any wicked person can be fully and freely forgiven.

Outline

I. Introduction (1:1)

II. A Song of Praise to God the Divine Warrior (1:2–11)

III. Good News for the Afflicted (1:12–15)

IV. God's Marches against the Oppressor (2:1–13)

V. A Song of Woe toward the Doomed City (3:1–17)

VI. The Calm after the Storm (3:18–19)

Nahum

1 [a]An oracle concerning [b]Nineveh. The book of the vision of Nahum of Elkosh.

God's Wrath Against Nineveh

2 [c]The LORD is a jealous and avenging God;
the LORD is avenging and wrathful;
[d]the LORD takes vengeance on his adversaries
and [e]keeps wrath for his enemies.
3 [f]The LORD is slow to anger and [g]great in power,
and [h]the LORD will by no means clear the guilty.
[i]His way is in whirlwind and storm,
and the clouds are the dust of his feet.
4 [j]He rebukes the sea and makes it dry;
he dries up all the rivers;
[k]Bashan and [l]Carmel wither;
the bloom of [k]Lebanon withers.
5 [m]The mountains quake before him;
[n]the hills melt;
the earth heaves before him,
[o]the world and all who dwell in it.
6 [p]Who can stand before his indignation?
Who can endure the heat of his anger?
His wrath [q]is poured out like fire,
and [r]the rocks are broken into pieces by him.
7 [s]The LORD is good,
[t]a stronghold in the day of trouble;
[u]he knows those who take refuge in him.
8 But [v]with an overflowing flood
he will make a complete end of the adversaries,[1]
and [w]will pursue his enemies into darkness.

[1] Hebrew *of her place*

1:2–11 Like Babylon, Nineveh comes to stand for those who have hardened themselves to God and oppose both the Lord and his people. God's people can rejoice in God's justice only because they have themselves been humbled and chastened, having been brought to repentance through his great patience (v. 3). God's patience manifests his love and his desire that all would repent and turn to him, but this patience should not be mistaken for approval of the unrepentant (Rom. 8:22; 2 Pet. 3:8–10). Divine jealousy is a corollary of divine love and the complement to divine wrath (Nah. 1:2). God's justice and power are exhibited in judgment on Nineveh, but even more so in his only Son who, while we were enemies of God (Rom. 5:10), bore final judgment for us (Rom. 8:1), fully satisfying the penalty for our sin (John 19:30).

God is here presented in the imagery of a warrior, riding down upon the whirlwind and storm as if in a chariot (Nah. 1:3). Nature's elements as part of his weaponry strike fear and terror in his enemies (Exodus 14–15; Ps. 46:9; Isa. 66:15; Rev. 6:2; 14:14; 19:11). The storm-like warrior God of the Old Testament is the very same one who commanded the wind and the waves to be still, instilling fear in those who witnessed it, but who united himself to fallen humanity to bear the brunt of the storm as well (Mark 4:40–41; Heb. 2:9–11).

God's goodness (Nah. 1:7), once known in exile (Hos. 2:14), now came in salvation. Yet his ultimate goodness is manifested in Christ, so that we can hope in future salvation from every aspect of the fall (Rom. 8:32).

God is a refuge (Nah. 1:7; Ps. 46:1) who, in Jesus Christ, bids us come to him for rest (Matt. 11:28–30). God's kingdom has been decisively inaugurated in Christ to save his people and overthrow his and our enemies, so that there is an end to bondage and fear (Nah. 1:15; Luke 2:10, 14; Heb. 2:14).

Chapter 1
1 [a]See Isa. 13:1 [b]ch. 2:8; 3:7; See Jonah 1:2
2 [c]See Ex. 20:5 [d][Ps. 92:9] [e][Ps. 103:9]
3 [f]See Ex. 34:6 [g]Job 9:4; Ps. 147:5 [h]See Ex. 34:7 [i][Ps. 97:2]; See Ps. 18:9-13
4 [j]Ps. 106:9; [Isa. 50:2] [k]Isa. 33:9 [l]See Josh. 19:26
5 [m][Jer. 4:24; Hab. 3:6] [n]Amos 9:13 [o]Ps. 98:7
6 [p][Mal. 3:2] [q]2 Chr. 34:21; [Ps. 79:6] [r]Ezek. 38:20
7 [s]Jer. 33:11; See Ps. 100:5 [t]Ps. 46:1; Isa. 25:4 [u]Ps. 1:6; John 10:14, 27; 1 Cor. 8:3; 2 Tim. 2:19
8 [v][Isa. 30:28] [w]Isa. 8:22

9 What [x]do you plot against the LORD?
[y]He will make a complete end;
trouble will not rise up a second time.
10 For they are [z]like entangled thorns,
like drunkards as they drink;
[a]they are consumed like stubble fully dried.
11 From you came one
[b]who plotted evil against the LORD,
a worthless counselor.

12 Thus says the LORD,
"Though they are at full strength and many,
[c]they will be cut down and pass away.
[d]Though I have afflicted you,
I will afflict you no more.
13 And now [e]I will break his yoke from off you
and will burst your bonds apart."

14 The LORD has given commandment about you:
[f]"No more shall your name be perpetuated;
from [g]the house of your gods I will cut off
the carved image and the metal image.
[h]I will make your grave, [i]for you are vile."

15[1] [j]Behold, upon the mountains, [k]the feet of him
who brings good news,
who publishes peace!
[l]Keep your feasts, O Judah;
[m]fulfill your vows,
[n]for never again shall the worthless pass through you;
he is utterly cut off.

The Destruction of Nineveh

2 [o]The scatterer has come up against you.
[p]Man the ramparts;
watch the road;
dress for battle;[2]
collect all your strength.

2 For [q]the LORD is restoring the majesty of Jacob
as the majesty of Israel,
for plunderers have plundered them
and [r]ruined their branches.

3 The shield of his mighty men is red;
[s]his soldiers are clothed in scarlet.
The chariots come with flashing metal
on the day he musters them;
the cypress spears are brandished.
4 [t]The chariots race madly through the streets;
they rush to and fro through the squares;
they gleam like torches;
they dart like lightning.
5 He remembers [u]his officers;
[v]they stumble as they go,
they hasten to the wall;
the siege tower[3] is set up.
6 [w]The river gates are opened;
the palace [x]melts away;
7 its mistress[4] is [y]stripped;[5] she is carried off,
her slave girls [z]lamenting,

[1] Ch 2:1 in Hebrew [2] Hebrew *gird your loins* [3] Or *the mantelet* [4] The meaning of the Hebrew word rendered *its mistress* is uncertain
[5] Or *exiled*

9[x] [Isa. 10:7] [y] [Jer. 4:27]
10[z] See Mic. 7:4 [a] See Joel 2:5
11[b] [ver. 9; 2 Kgs. 19:22, 23]
12[c] Isa. 10:33, 34; [Isa. 37:36] [d] ver. 9; [Isa. 9:1]
13[e] [Isa. 9:4; 10:27; 14:25]
14[f] [Ps. 109:13] [g] [2 Kgs. 19:37] [h] [Isa. 30:33]; See Ezek. 32:21-23 [i] [ch. 3:6]
15[j] See Isa. 52:7 [k] [Rom. 10:15] [l] [Isa. 30:29] [m] See Num. 30:2 [n] [ver. 12]; See Joel 3:17

Chapter 2
1[o] [Jer. 51:20] [p] [Jer. 51:12]
2[q] [Isa. 37:31] [r] See Ps. 80:8-13; Isa. 5:1-7
3[s] [Ezek. 23:14, 15]
4[t] [ch. 3:2]
5[u] ch. 3:18 [v] Jer. 46:12
6[w] [Isa. 45:1] [x] [Isa. 14:31]
7[y] [Isa. 22:8] [z] Isa. 38:14

1:12–15 Judgment accompanies salvation (vv. 12–13). In Christ we see the ultimate manifestation of this truth, as the mighty will be brought down from their thrones (Luke 2:34, 51–52) and the imperial powers will be overthrown (Col. 2:15). Affliction by God, like Israel's at the hands of Assyria (Nah. 1:12), serves God's gracious purpose of conquering evil (or turning his people from it) and is always under his wise control. Our affliction has fallen upon Christ (Isa. 53:5; 1 Pet. 2:24), so that what we suffer is not toward final judgment but toward fatherly discipline (Heb. 12:5–11) and for our own good (2 Cor. 1:3–6).

The gospel is "good news" brought by one who "publishes peace" (Nah. 1:15a; cf. Isa. 52:7; Rom. 10:15). The good news is not only peace and restoration from exile for God's people but also judgment of oppressors (Nah. 1:15b). Final vindication and justice is coming. We can be patient in hope (cf. Rom. 12:12).

2:1–13 The unexpected calamity falling upon wicked Nineveh produces anguish. Such is the state of all who experience the curse of the fall—loss of hope, fear, anguish, and terror are constant companions of those who see their worldly fortresses of security melt away (v. 6).

moaning like doves
and beating their breasts.
8 [b]Nineveh is like a pool
whose waters run away.[1]
"Halt! Halt!" they cry,
but [c]none turns back.
9 Plunder the silver,
plunder the gold!
There is no end of the treasure
or of the wealth of all precious things.

10 [d]Desolate! Desolation and ruin!
[e]Hearts melt and [f]knees tremble;
[g]anguish is in all loins;
[h]all faces grow pale!
11 Where is the lions' den,
the feeding place of [i]the young lions,
where the lion and lioness went,
where his cubs were, with [j]none to disturb?
12 [k]The lion tore enough for his cubs
and [l]strangled prey for his lionesses;
he filled his caves with prey
and his dens with torn flesh.

13 [m]Behold, I am against you, declares the
LORD of hosts, and [n]I will burn your[2] chariots
in smoke, and the sword shall devour your
young lions. I will cut off your prey from the
earth, and [o]the voice of your messengers shall
no longer be heard.

Woe to Nineveh

3 Woe to [p]the bloody city,
all full of lies and plunder—
[q]no end to the prey!
2 The crack of the whip, and [r]rumble of the wheel,
[s]galloping horse and [t]bounding chariot!
3 Horsemen charging,
flashing sword and [u]glittering spear,
[v]hosts of slain,
heaps of corpses,
dead bodies without end—
they stumble over the bodies!
4 And all for the countless whorings of the [w]prostitute,
[x]graceful and of deadly charms,
who betrays nations with her whorings,
and peoples with her charms.

5 [m]Behold, I am against you,
declares the LORD of hosts,
and [y]will lift up your skirts over your face;
and I will make nations look at [z]your nakedness
and kingdoms at your shame.
6 I will throw filth at you
and [a]treat you with contempt
and make you [b]a spectacle.
7 And all who look at you [c]will shrink
from you and say,

[1] Compare Septuagint; the meaning of the Hebrew is uncertain [2] Hebrew *her*

In the midst of this punishing disaster, the majesty of God's people would be restored (v. 2), a restoration that ultimately climaxes in and is secured by Christ (Luke 2:32). The shame of exile and captivity would be borne away in the restoring work of the cross. The sudden and climactic fall of all that seemed unconquerable shocks and confuses those who put their trust in the sandy strongholds of this life for their security (Nah. 2:10; Matt. 7:26–27; Luke 1:51). But the one who trusts on the foundation of God's word in Christ will never be put to shame (Heb. 11:16; Rom. 5:5; 9:33; 10:11; 1 Pet. 2:6). God will vindicate us openly through Jesus Christ at his second coming.

"I am against you," God says to Nineveh (Nah. 2:13). So it is for all who refuse to bow the knee in trusting contrition. But for those who do, God is no longer against us—in Christ, he is for us. And "if God is for us, who can be against us?" (Rom. 8:31).

3:1–17 The final list of charges against Nineveh include "whorings" (v. 4). A shocking metaphor for idolatry, it is the giving away of affection that rightfully belongs to another. While literal fornication and adultery are sins in their own right, used metaphorically in this way the term reveals the deepest roots of sin, which is adulterous unfaithfulness to our Creator.

Nineveh will become a proverb for the ultimate catastrophe: human autonomy (vv. 8–17). Jesus warns us not to build on any foundation other than God's word, or our end will be the same (Matt. 7:24–27). Imperial power is no power before God's (Nah. 3:17), as Jesus would one day tell Pilate (John 19:11).

Throughout this passage the major theme is shame. Nineveh, famous for its brazen shaming of other nations through its might and wickedness, will have the tables turned on it. Continuing the adultery metaphor, God says he will expose Nineveh in

8[b] See ch. 1:1 [c] Jer. 46:5
10[d] See Zeph. 2:13-15 [e] Ps. 22:14; Isa. 13:7 [f] Dan. 5:6 [g] Isa. 21:3 [h] Joel 2:6
11[i] Isa. 5:29; Jer. 2:15 [j] See Isa. 17:2
12[k] [Ezek. 19:3] [l] [ver. 9; ch. 3:1]
13[m] ch. 3:5; [Zeph. 2:5]; See Ezek. 13:8 [n] [Ps. 46:9] [o] [2 Kgs. 19:9, 23]
Chapter 3
1[p] Ezek. 24:9; [Hab. 2:12] [q] [ch. 2:12]
2[r] [ch. 2:4] [s] [Judg. 5:22] [t] [Joel 2:5]
3[u] Hab. 3:11 [v] [2 Kgs. 19:35]
4[w] [Rev. 17:2; 18:3] [x] [Isa. 47:9, 12]
5[m] [See ch. 2:13 above] [y] Jer. 13:22, 26; [Isa. 3:17; 47:3] [z] Hab. 2:16
6[a] Mal. 2:9; [ch. 1:14] [b] Heb. 10:33; [1 Cor. 4:9]
7[c] Jer. 51:9; Rev. 18:10

"Wasted is [d]Nineveh; [e]who will grieve for
her?"
[f]Where shall I seek comforters for
you?

8 [g]Are you better than [h]Thebes[1]
that sat [i]by the Nile,
with water around her,
her rampart a sea,
and water her wall?
9 [j]Cush was her strength;
Egypt too, and that without limit;
[k]Put and the [l]Libyans were her[2] helpers.

10 [m]Yet she became an exile;
she went into captivity;
[n]her infants were dashed in pieces
at the head of every street;
for her honored men [o]lots were cast,
[p]and all her great men were bound in
chains.
11 [q]You also will be drunken;
you will go into hiding;
[r]you will seek a refuge from the enemy.
12 All your fortresses are [s]like fig trees
with first-ripe figs—
if shaken they fall
into the mouth of the eater.
13 Behold, your troops
[t]are women in your midst.
The gates of your land
are wide open to your enemies;
fire has devoured your bars.

14 [u]Draw water for the siege;
[r]strengthen your forts;
go into the clay;
tread the mortar;
take hold of the brick mold!
15 There will the fire devour you;
the sword will cut you off.
It will [v]devour you [w]like the locust.
Multiply yourselves [w]like the locust;
multiply [w]like the grasshopper!
16 You increased [x]your merchants
more than the stars of the heavens.
[w]The locust spreads its wings and flies
away.

17 Your [z]princes are [w]like grasshoppers,
[a]your scribes[3] like clouds of locusts
settling on the fences
in a day of cold—
when the sun rises, they fly away;
no one knows where they are.

18 Your shepherds [b]are asleep,
O king of Assyria;
[c]your nobles slumber.
Your people [d]are scattered on the mountains
with none to gather them.
19 There is no easing your hurt;
[e]your wound is grievous.
All who hear the news about you
[f]clap their hands over you.
For [g]upon whom has not come
your unceasing evil?

[1] Hebrew *No-amon* [2] Hebrew *your* [3] Or *marshals*

7[d] [Zeph. 2:13]; See ch. 1:1 [e] Isa. 51:19; Jer. 15:5 [f] Lam. 1:2, 9, 16, 17, 21
8[g] [Amos 6:2] [h] Jer. 46:25 [i] [Ezek. 29:3]
9[j] See Dan. 11:43 [k] Gen. 10:6 [l] See 2 Chr. 12:3
10[m] Isa. 20:4 [n] Isa. 13:16 [o] Joel 3:3; Obad. 11 [p] [Ps. 149:8]
11[q] Jer. 25:17, 27; [Ps. 75:8; Isa. 51:17; Obad. 16] [r] [Jer. 4:5, 6]
12[s] [Rev. 6:13]
13[t] Isa. 19:16; Jer. 51:30
14[u] [Isa. 22:11] [r] [See ver. 11 above]
15[v] [Joel 2:3] [w] [Joel 1:4, 6]
16[x] [Ezek. 27:23, 24] [w] [See ver. 15 above]
17[z] [Isa. 10:8] [w] [See ver. 15 above] [a] Jer. 51:27
18[b] [Ps. 76:5] [c] ch. 2:5 [d] [1 Kgs. 22:17]
19[e] Jer. 10:19; Mic. 1:9 [f] Lam. 2:15; [Zeph. 2:15] [g] [Isa. 37:18]

all its shame for the whole world to see (Nah. 3:5–6). In a fallen world, we too today know what it is to be ashamed. Sometimes it is because of our own sin. Other times we have been sinned against, causing shame. Our great Savior, however, "endured the cross, despising the shame" (Heb. 12:2)—so that all those who look to him can be assured of the end, someday very soon, of all shame.

3:18–19 Nineveh's fall is one of the numerous biblical witnesses to the reliability of God's word and the certainty of his purposes (see also Zeph. 2:13–15). Earthly powers, today as then, ignore or oppose God in various ways.

Jesus Christ, in his death and resurrection, has brought the ultimate end of every human authority opposed to God. He conquered not by killing but by being killed. The result is that one day every knee will bow, either in worship or under his rod of iron (Ps. 2:9, 12; Phil. 2:9–10). For those who have taken refuge in him, we don't know the answer to how long we have to wait (Rev. 6:10), but we know that salvation has come and is coming in Jesus.

Introduction to Habakkuk

Author and Date

Habakkuk is unusual as a prophetic book. It never addresses the people of Judah directly. Rather it is a dialogue between the prophet and God. The prophet Habakkuk was probably a contemporary of Zephaniah and Jeremiah. He probably prophesied no later than the end of Josiah's reign (640–609 B.C.).

The Gospel in Habakkuk

Like the book of Job, this book presents important gospel truths for people who encounter difficulties that seem incomprehensible. Like many of us today, the prophet Habakkuk asked God two fundamental questions amid God's apparent absence and the world's growing animosity toward God's people: (1) Where are you? (2) Why are you doing this? As this man of God observed the chaos of idolatry and immorality that was consuming those who ought to know better, he cried out in two complaints, beseeching God to act with justice against evildoers and to provide mercy for those who were faithful to God.

God responds to both of these complaints in ways that shock and surprise the prophet. First, God declares he will use an enemy nation (Babylon) to bring justice to the evildoers in Judah. Second, God will reveal to Israel his unsearchable wisdom and providence by judging not just Judah but all his enemies. This message finally instills in the prophet a deepened, resilient faith amid perplexing bewilderment.

The gospel shines forth in these themes of justice, mercy, wisdom, and providential provision. Whereas God seemed absent and inactive amid Habakkuk's doubt and distress, this book fits within the context of the Bible's larger story that, in the fullness of time, God himself, through the person and work of Jesus Christ, would come in the flesh to bring justice and mercy for all (Luke 24:27, 44; John 5:39, 46; 1 Pet. 1:10–12). At the cross, Jesus receives justice for *our* sins of idolatry and immorality. Moreover, at the cross, Jesus secures the mercy of forgiveness to all who trust in his substitutionary work. Thus it is on the cross at Calvary that justice and mercy meet.

This gospel shines forth in Habakkuk, as the prophet recounts God's faithful deliverance of Israel during the wilderness wanderings and calls God's people to renewed faith in his provision. As Israel experienced deliverance from Egypt and establishment in the Promised Land, so also Christ's followers today experience a much greater deliverance, a deliverance toward which every earthly Old Testament deliverance pointed—deliverance from sin, with the promise of a heavenly home. The New Testament proclaims the good news that in God's wise and purposeful providence, God himself has come in Jesus Christ to deliver his people from the bondage of sin through the life, death, and resurrection of his Son.

The gospel response that the prophet finally realized and that every generation must discover afresh is this: the righteous live by faith (Hab. 2:4). Habakkuk helps get us there.

Outline

I. Superscription (1:1)

II. First Cycle (1:2–11)

- A. Habakkuk's lament (1:2–4)
- B. God's response (1:5–11)

III. Second Cycle (1:12–2:20)

- A. Habakkuk's lament (1:12–2:1)
- B. God's response (2:2–20)

IV. Habakkuk's Prayer (3:1–19)

Habakkuk

1 [a]The oracle that Habakkuk the prophet
saw.

Habakkuk's Complaint

2 O LORD, [b]how long shall I cry for help,
and you will not hear?
Or cry to you [c]"Violence!"
and you will not save?
3 [d]Why do you make me see iniquity,
and why do you idly look at wrong?
Destruction [c]and violence are before me;
strife and contention arise.
4 [e]So the law is paralyzed,
and justice never goes forth.
[f]For the wicked surround the righteous;
so justice goes forth perverted.

The LORD's Answer

5 [g]"Look among the nations, and see;
wonder and be astounded.
[h]For I am doing a work in your days
that you would not believe if told.
6 For behold, [i]I am raising up the
Chaldeans,
that bitter and hasty nation,
[j]who march through the breadth of the
earth,
[k]to seize dwellings not their own.
7 They are dreaded and fearsome;
[l]their justice and dignity go forth
from themselves.
8 [m]Their horses are swifter than leopards,
more fierce than [n]the evening wolves;
their horsemen press proudly on.
Their horsemen come from afar;
[o]they fly like an eagle swift to devour.
9 They all come [p]for violence,
all their faces forward.
They gather captives [r]like sand.
10 At kings they scoff,
and at rulers they laugh.
[s]They laugh at every fortress,
for [t]they pile up earth and take it.
11 Then they sweep by like the wind and
go on,
[u]guilty men, [v]whose own might is
their god!"

1:2–11 The book begins with the prophet Habakkuk's first of two complaints (1:2–4) and God's unexpected response (1:5–11). As he sees the sins of immorality, lawlessness, and idolatry all around him, Habakkuk questions God and wonders, "Why do you idly look at wrong?" (v. 3). Amid Israel's internal spiritual corruption and external political pressure, the prophet begins to doubt whether there will be justice against evil and mercy for the faithful. Throughout the ages God's children, like Habakkuk, have often expressed this complaint. Job wondered why God seemed absent amid his difficult circumstances (Job 3), and Israel cried out during its wilderness wanderings, "Is the LORD among us or not?" (Ex. 17:7).

God's response was not what the prophet ever imagined or desired: God is surely among his people, will help them, and will bring them justice. But he will do it through the violent and haughty nation of Babylon ("the Chaldeans"; Hab. 1:6).

Through this perplexing response God challenges not only Habakkuk's faith but ours as well. That God can bring about good from evil is a theme that echoes down through the whole Bible, such as in Joseph's statement to his brothers: "As for you, you meant evil against me, but God meant it for good" (Gen. 50:20). God's response to Habakkuk also foreshadows the ultimate good—eternal salvation—that would come through the ultimate evil—execution of the sinless Son of God upon a cross.

Yet in the unfathomable wisdom of God, on that cross justice and mercy meet. Jesus receives the penalty that the justice of God requires for sin; and we receive,

Chapter 1
1[a] See Nah. 1:1
2[b] Ps. 13:1; 89:46 [c] Mic. 6:12
3[d] See Jer. 9:2-6 [c] [See ver. 2 above]
4[e] [Mic. 7:3] [f] [Job 21:7; Jer. 12:1]
5[g] Cited Acts 13:41 [h] [Isa. 28:21; 29:14]
6[i] See Jer. 5:15 [j] [ch. 2:5] [k] [ch. 2:6]
7[l] [ver. 10, 11]
8[m] Jer. 4:13 [n] Jer. 5:6; Zeph. 3:3 [o] See Deut. 28:49
9[p] [ch. 2:17] [r] See Josh. 11:4
10[s] [Nah. 3:12] [t] [Ezek. 4:2]
11[u] [Hos. 13:16] [v] [ver. 7]

Habakkuk's Second Complaint

12 Are you not [w]from everlasting,
O LORD my God, my Holy One?
[x]We shall not die.
O LORD, [y]you have ordained them as a judgment,
and you, O [z]Rock, have established them for reproof.
13 You who are [a]of purer eyes than to see evil
and cannot look at wrong,
[b]why do you idly look at traitors
and [c]remain silent when the wicked swallows up
the man more righteous than he?
14 You make mankind like the fish of the sea,
like crawling things that have no ruler.
15 [d]He[1] brings all of them up [e]with a hook;
he drags them out with his net;
he gathers them in his dragnet;
so he rejoices and is glad.
16 [f]Therefore he sacrifices to his net
and makes offerings to his dragnet;
for by them he lives in luxury,[2]
and his food is rich.
17 Is he then to keep on emptying his net
[g]and mercilessly killing nations forever?

2 I will [h]take my stand at my watchpost
and station myself on the tower,
and [i]look out to see [j]what he will say to me,
and what I will answer concerning my complaint.

The Righteous Shall Live by His Faith

2 And the LORD answered me:

[k]"Write the vision;
make it plain on tablets,
so he may run who reads it.
3 For still [l]the vision awaits its appointed time;
it hastens to the end—it will not lie.
If it seems slow, [m]wait for it;
[n]it will surely come; it will not delay.

4 "Behold, his soul is puffed up; it is not upright within him,
but [o]the righteous shall live by his faith.[3]

5 "Moreover, wine[4] is [p]a traitor,
an arrogant man who is never at rest.[5]
His greed is as wide as Sheol;
like death [q]he has never enough.
[r]He gathers for himself all nations
and collects as his own all peoples."

[1] That is, the wicked foe [2] Hebrew *his portion is fat* [3] Or *faithfulness* [4] Masoretic Text; Dead Sea Scroll *wealth* [5] The meaning of the Hebrew of these two lines is uncertain

12[w] Deut. 33:27; Ps. 90:2; 93:2 [x] [Mal. 3:6] [y] See Isa. 10:5-7 [z] See Deut. 32:4
13[a] [Ps. 5:5] [b] Jer. 12:1 [c] Ps. 35:22
15[d] Jer. 16:16; Amos 4:2 [e] [Isa. 19:8]
16[f] [ver. 11]
17[g] [ch. 2:10]
Chapter 2
1[h] Isa. 21:8 [i] Jer. 6:17; Ezek. 33:2 [j] Ps. 85:8
2[k] Isa. 8:1; 30:8; [Rev. 1:19]
3[l] [Dan. 10:14]; See Ezek. 7:5-7 [m] Zeph. 3:8; See Isa. 8:17 [n] Cited Heb. 10:37; [2 Pet. 3:9]
4[o] Cited Rom. 1:17; Gal. 3:11; Heb. 10:38; [John 3:36]
5[p] ch. 1:13; Isa. 21:2 [q] [Prov. 27:20] [r] Jer. 27:7; [ch. 1:6; Dan. 2:37, 38]

through faith, God's mercy in forgiveness of sin and the promise of eternal life (Rom. 3:21–26). This is why we can continue to have faith amid frustration: God's providential use of people and events is both purposeful and personal.

1:12–2:20 These verses record Habakkuk's second complaint (1:12–2:1) and God's response (2:2–20). Having heard of God's plan to use Babylon to bring justice, the prophet is even more perplexed: How can a good God use evil Babylon to punish his own people? Habakkuk finds it difficult to reconcile God's character with his actions. He correctly affirms the many attributes of God—eternality, holiness, and power (1:12)—but he cannot understand why God would use the more evil nation of Babylon to punish the seemingly less evil nation of Judah, God's own people.

God reminds Habakkuk that evil will never ultimately prosper, because God is providentially orchestrating history for his own righteous purposes. Though the timing of God's just purposes may seem slow, "it will surely come; it will not delay" (2:3; cf. 2 Pet. 3:8–9). The five woes pronounced upon Babylon (Hab. 2:6–20) reveal God's judgment upon any human power that sets itself against his reign and rule. From the tower builders of Babel to the empire builders of Rome, every generation will see kingdoms that achieve a measure of temporal earthly success. God's righteousness, however, will triumph in the end, and his glory will cover the earth (2:14)—a promise ultimately fulfilled in Christ, before whom "every knee should bow, in heaven and on earth and under the earth, and every tongue confess that Jesus Christ is Lord, to the glory of God the Father" (Phil. 2:10–11). It is in Christ's sinless life, sacrificial death, victorious resurrection, and vindicating reign that God's righteousness is finally revealed to all humanity over all the earth.

Woe to the Chaldeans

6 Shall not all these [s]take up their taunt against him, with scoffing and riddles for him, and say,

[t]"Woe to him [u]who heaps up what is not his own—
for [v]how long?—
and [w]loads himself with pledges!"
7 [x]Will not your debtors suddenly arise,
and those awake who will make you tremble?
Then you will be spoil for them.
8 [y]Because you have plundered many nations,
all the remnant of the peoples shall plunder you,
[z]for the blood of man and [y]violence to the earth,
to cities and all who dwell in them.

9 [t]"Woe to him who gets evil gain for his house,
[a]to [b]set his nest on high,
to be safe from the reach of harm!
10 You have devised shame for your house
[c]by cutting off many peoples;
you have forfeited your life.
11 For [d]the stone will cry out from the wall,
and the beam from the woodwork respond.

12 [t]"Woe to him [e]who builds a town with blood
and founds a city on iniquity!
13 Behold, is it not from the LORD of hosts
that [f]peoples labor merely for fire,
and nations weary themselves for nothing?
14 [g]For the earth will be filled
with the knowledge of [h]the glory of the LORD
as the waters cover the sea.

15 [t]"Woe to him [i]who makes his neighbors drink—
you pour out your wrath and make them drunk,
in order to gaze [j]at their nakedness!
16 You will have your fill [k]of shame instead of glory.
[l]Drink, yourself, and show your uncircumcision!
[l]The cup in the LORD's right hand
will come around to you,
and [m]utter shame will come upon your glory!
17 [n]The violence [o]done to Lebanon will overwhelm you,
as will the destruction of the beasts that terrified them,
[n]for the blood of man and violence to the earth,
to cities and all who dwell in them.

18 [p]"What profit is an idol
when its maker has shaped it,
a metal image, [q]a teacher of lies?
For its maker trusts in his own creation
when he makes [r]speechless idols!
19 [s]Woe to him [t]who says to a wooden thing, Awake;
to a silent stone, Arise!
Can this teach?
Behold, it is overlaid with gold and silver,
and [u]there is no breath at all in it.

Therefore, God's people are called to live by faith (Hab. 2:4). This call to trusting faith is an important notice to all believers in all ages of the path by which we may know and embrace the grace of God that is ultimately revealed in Christ (cf. Rom. 1:17; Gal. 3:11; Eph. 2:8). This is not a path of blind faith but a deep-rooted trust in the eternal, providential, ever-present God who resides in the holy temple provided for his people's atonement (Hab. 2:20). He unfolds all things—even the difficult and inexplicable—according to his wise and compassionate purposes. Like the psalmist who struggled to reconcile the wicked's unhindered prosperity and God's apparent inactivity, we are assured of God's providential rule over all things when we encounter God's presence in his temple (cf. Ps. 73:17), especially as we look to the One it prefigured: Jesus, God's ultimate temple. When Jesus stated, "Destroy this temple, and in three days I will raise it up" (John 2:19), he was foreshadowing God's provision through the cross and the empty tomb. Faith in the God who provided these is the foundation for living with confidence and hope in a fallen world filled with many trials and tears. As the hymn states so well, our faith is "built on nothing less than Jesus' blood and righteousness."

6 [s]Mic. 2:4; See Num. 23:7 [t]ver. 19; Isa. 5:8 [u][ch. 1:6] [v]See Zech. 1:12 [w][Ezek. 18:7]
7 [x]See Isa. 21:5-9
8 [y][Isa. 33:1] [z]ver. 17
9 [t][See ver. 6 above] [a][Isa. 14:13] [b]Jer. 49:16; [Num. 24:21]
10 [c][ch. 1:17]
11 [d][Luke 19:40]
12 [t][See ver. 6 above] [e]See Mic. 3:10
13 [f]Jer. 51:58
14 [g]Isa. 11:9 [h]Ps. 72:19
15 [t][See ver. 6 above] [i][ver. 5; Jer. 51:7] [j]Lam. 4:21; [Gen. 9:22]
16 [k]Nah. 3:5 [l]Jer. 25:15, 26 [m][Nah. 3:6]
17 [n]ver. 8 [o][Isa. 14:8; Jer. 22:23]
18 [p]Isa. 44:10 [q]Jer. 10:8, 14; Zech. 10:2 [r]Ps. 115:5; 1 Cor. 12:2
19 [s]ver. 6, 9, 12, 15 [t]See 1 Kgs. 18:26, 27 [u]Ps. 135:17; Jer. 10:14

20 But [v]the LORD is in his holy temple;
[w]let all the earth keep silence before him."

Habakkuk's Prayer

3 A prayer of Habakkuk the prophet, according to Shigionoth.

2 O LORD, [x]I have heard the report of you,
and [y]your work, O LORD, do I fear.
In the midst of the years [z]revive it;
in the midst of the years make it known;
[a]in wrath remember mercy.
3 God came from [b]Teman,
[c]and the Holy One from Mount Paran. *Selah*
His splendor covered the heavens,
and the earth was full of his praise.
4 [d]His brightness was like the light;
rays flashed from his hand;
and there he veiled his power.
5 [e]Before him went pestilence,
and plague followed [f]at his heels.[1]
6 He stood [g]and measured the earth;
he looked and shook the nations;
then the [h]eternal mountains [i]were scattered;
the everlasting hills sank low.
His were [j]the everlasting ways.
7 I saw the tents of [k]Cushan in affliction;
[l]the curtains of the land of Midian did tremble.
8 [m]Was your wrath against the rivers, O LORD?
Was your anger against the rivers,
[m]or your indignation against the sea,
[n]when you rode on your horses,
[n]on your chariot of salvation?
9 You stripped the sheath from your bow,
calling for many arrows.[2] *Selah*
[p]You split the earth with rivers.
10 [q]The mountains saw you and writhed;
the raging waters swept on;
[r]the deep gave forth its voice;
[s]it lifted its hands on high.
11 [t]The sun and moon stood still in their place
[u]at the light of your arrows as they sped,
at the flash of your glittering spear.
12 [v]You marched through the earth in fury;
[w]you threshed the nations in anger.
13 [v]You went out for the salvation of your people,
for the salvation of [x]your anointed.
[y]You crushed the head of the house of the wicked,
laying him bare from thigh to neck.[3] *Selah*
14 You pierced with his own arrows the heads of his warriors,
who came like a whirlwind to scatter me,
rejoicing as if to devour the poor in secret.

[1] Hebrew *feet* [2] The meaning of the Hebrew line is uncertain [3] The meaning of the Hebrew line is uncertain

20[v] Ps. 11:4; Mic. 1:2 [w] [Zeph. 1:7; Zech. 2:13]
Chapter 3
2[x] ver. 16; [Ps. 44:1] [y] Ps. 90:16 [z] Ps. 85:6 [a] [Ps. 77:9]
3[b] See 1 Chr. 1:45 [c] See Deut. 33:2
4[d] See Ezek. 1:27
5[e] [2 Kgs. 19:35]; See Ex. 12:29, 30; 1 Chr. 21:11-15 [f] [Job 18:11]
6[g] [Ps. 60:6] [h] Gen. 49:26; Deut. 33:15 [i] Mic. 1:4; Nah. 1:5 [j] [Isa. 51:9]
7[k] Judg. 3:8 [l] See Judg. 8:19-21
8[m] [Ps. 114:5] [n] Deut. 33:26, 27; Ps. 18:10; 68:4, 17; 104:3; Isa. 19:1; 66:15
9[p] Ps. 78:15, 16
10[q] Ex. 19:18; See Judg. 5:5 [r] Ps. 93:3 [s] [Ex. 14:22; 15:8]
11[t] See Josh. 10:12, 13 [u] [ver. 5]; See 2 Sam. 22:15
12[v] [Josh. 10:42] [w] [Mic. 4:12, 13]
13[v] [See ver. 12 above] [x] 1 Chr. 16:22; Ps. 105:15 [y] Ps. 68:21; 110:6

3:1–15 After Habakkuk's two complaints and God's corresponding responses, this last chapter reveals the transformation that has occurred in the depths of the prophet's soul. Habakkuk's prayer of praise, petition, recollection, and thanksgiving have much to teach us about the nature of prayer.

Consider verse 2. As he stands before God, the prophet reverently recognizes the holy and righteous purposes of God ("your work, O LORD, do I fear") but also the grace of God ("in [your] wrath remember mercy"). Then, despite the struggles that he is experiencing, Habakkuk asks that God's perfect will would be done ("In the midst of the years revive it; in the midst of the years make it known"). The prophet recognizes God's unsearchable plan for establishing his kingdom and offers to God a prayer of trust and confidence, with reverence and awe, knowing that God is a consuming fire (cf. Heb. 12:28–29).

Many prayers of trust found in the Bible begin by recounting God's faithfulness in the past (e.g., Psalm 90) and reveal steadfast hope in God's promises for the future (e.g., Psalm 121). Because of God's past faithfulness and future promises, we can pray with faith in the present without losing heart (Luke 18:1). In Habakkuk's prayer, he remembers God's faithfulness in Israel's history, recalling deliverance from Egypt's bondage (Hab. 3:5), safe passage through the Red Sea (v. 8), defeat of Canaanite enemies (v. 11), and establishment in the Promised Land. "Your anointed" (v. 13) referred to the Davidic king and the people he represented, but the word used there is the Hebrew word from which we get "Messiah." The final Davidic heir, representing God's people, was yet to come.

15 [z]You trampled the sea with your horses,
the surging of mighty waters.

16 [a]I hear, and [b]my body trembles;
my lips quiver at the sound;
[c]rottenness enters into my bones;
my legs tremble beneath me.
Yet [d]I will quietly wait for the day of trouble
to come upon people who invade us.

Habakkuk Rejoices in the LORD

17 Though the fig tree should not blossom,
nor fruit be on the vines,
the produce of the olive fail
and the fields yield no food,
the flock be cut off from the fold
and there be no herd in the stalls,
18 [e]yet I will rejoice in the LORD;
[f]I will take joy in the God of my salvation.
19 GOD, the Lord, is my strength;
[g]he makes my feet like the deer's;
he makes me [h]tread on my [i]high places.

[j]To the choirmaster: with [k]stringed[1] instruments.

[1] Hebrew *my stringed*

In reviewing God's faithfulness in Israel's history, Habakkuk can face his fears with faith and trust in the God of all history. For at the climax of all human history, the Messiah did come. God truly did "in wrath remember mercy" (v. 2). At the cross of Christ, God's wrath was poured out on his own Son, so that we who trust in Christ might be washed clean in an astounding act of mercy.

3:16–19 The recounting of God's faithfulness in Israel's past (vv. 1–15) draws our minds to the great and mighty deeds of the Lord on behalf of his people down through history. And all these deliverances and provisions foreshadow the ultimate mighty deed of history: the coming of Christ "when the fullness of time had come" (Gal. 4:4). The ultimate fulfillment of God's covenant promises to his people is found in Jesus (2 Cor. 1:20). Through his life, death, and resurrection, he delivers us from sin's bondage, brings us safely through death to life, and thus defeats our greatest enemies—Satan, sin, and death. And at the end of history, Christ will establish us in the eternal promised land of heaven.

This is why, even amid many difficulties and uncertainties, we can continue to "quietly wait" (Hab. 3:16) and "rejoice in the LORD" (v. 18) in prayer, looking to him as the "God of my salvation" (v. 18). When life crumbles all around us (v. 17), we need not despair. God has not abandoned his purposes. He remains with us, even in the trials and struggles. Jesus Christ has brought us to himself. We are restored to God. Hell cannot touch us, for we say, "GOD, the Lord, is my strength" (v. 19). We will rejoice in God.

15[z] [Ps. 77:19]
16[a] ver. 2 [b] Jer. 4:19 [c] [Prov. 12:4] [d] [Ps. 94:13; Isa. 14:3, 4]
18[e] [Job 13:15] [f] Ps. 9:14; 13:5; 21:1; 35:9; Luke 1:47; See Joel 2:23
19[g] See 2 Sam. 2:18 [h] Amos 4:13; Mic. 1:3 [i] Deut. 32:13; 33:29 [j] See Ps 4 [k] Isa. 38:20

Introduction to Zephaniah

Author and Date

Zephaniah prophesied during the reign of Josiah (640–609 B.C.), a Judean king who sought to reestablish acceptable worship practices (2 Kings 22:1–23:30).

The Gospel in Zephaniah

During his reign, King Manasseh brought Judah into idolatry, even going so far as setting up altars to the pagan god Baal. Amon, his son, was no better, and was assassinated two years into his reign. That meant Josiah, who became king at age 8, inherited a country that had long rebelled against God. But at age 16, he discovered the scroll of the Law in the temple and initiated a massive countrywide reform to return his people to faithfulness to God's law.

Zephaniah prophesied during these times (see Zeph. 1:1). While we don't know exactly when the book was written, it appears to have been part of the reform effort. Zephaniah rebuked the people for their sins, pride, and false worship, describing the Lord's judgment in vivid detail.

But the promise of judgment is preparation for the word of grace (3:9–20), where Zephaniah exhorts Judah to sing because God has taken her judgments away. At the climax of the book we hear one of the Bible's deepest assurances of God's invincible love for his people:

> "Fear not, O Zion;
> let not your hands grow weak.
> The LORD your God is in your midst,
> a mighty one who will save;
> he will rejoice over you with gladness;
> he will quiet you by his love." (3:16–17)

Zephaniah's prophecy, taken as a whole, points to Jesus. We learn from this prophet of the steadfast love of a just God. Such a love would ultimately provide the One who took the punishment for his people's sins to satisfy divine justice. For those who trust in him, the "day of the Lord" foretold in Zephaniah has already taken place, on Christ's cross (1 John 2:2). In Immanuel, "God with us" (Matt. 1:23), we see just how true the Lord's words are that he is "in our midst" and is "a mighty one who will save."

Zephaniah's exhortation to Judah has clear application to us today. On the one hand, he exhorts us to repent of our sins and idolatry because of the purity of God's holiness and the fierceness of his jealousy. Yet we also rejoice, with overflowing praise, because the God who judges is the very God who redeems. Then as now, he rejoices over his people with gladness. Zephaniah's prophecy is rich in the grace of God that ultimately climaxes with the coming of Jesus and the preaching of the gospel.

Outline

I. Heading (1:1)

II. Judgment Coming against Judah (1:2–6)

III. The Day of the Lord (1:7–3:20)

   A. Day of sacrifice and punishment (1:7–9)

   B. The coming wrath (1:10–18)

   C. Repentance is still possible (2:1–3)

   D. Nations warned (2:4–3:8)

   E. Anticipation of hope (3:9–20)

Zephaniah

1 The word of the LORD that came to Zephaniah the son of Cushi, son of Gedaliah,
son of Amariah, son of Hezekiah, [a]in the days
of [b]Josiah the son of Amon, king of Judah.

The Coming Judgment on Judah

2 [c]"I will utterly sweep away everything
from the face of the earth," declares
the LORD.
3 "I will sweep away [d]man and beast;
I will sweep away the birds of the
heavens
and [d]the fish of the sea,
and [e]the rubble[1] with the wicked.
I will [f]cut off mankind
from the face of the earth," declares
the LORD.
4 "I will stretch out my hand against Judah
and against all the inhabitants of
Jerusalem;
[g]and I will cut off from this place the
remnant of Baal
and the name of the idolatrous priests
along with the priests,
5 [h]those who bow down on the roofs
to the host of the heavens,
[i]those who bow down and swear to the
LORD
and yet swear by [j]Milcom,
6 [k]those who have turned back from following the LORD,
[l]who do not seek the LORD or inquire
of him."

The Day of the LORD Is Near

7 [m]Be silent before the Lord GOD!
For [n]the day of the LORD is near;
[o]the LORD has prepared a sacrifice
and [p]consecrated his guests.
8 And on the day of the LORD's sacrifice—
[q]"I will punish the officials and the king's
sons
and [r]all who array themselves in foreign attire.
9 On that day I will punish
everyone [s]who leaps over the threshold,
and those who fill their master's[2] house
with violence and fraud.

[1] Or *stumbling blocks* (that is, idols) [2] Or *their Lord's*

1:1–6 After a brief opening, Zephaniah begins the announcement of God's judgment. The "sweeping away" (v. 2) of all people and animals is reminiscent of the flood, a moment of God's judgment on sin (cf. Genesis 6–9). The judgment God warns about is total: all living things are included in it, not just humans. And its cause is religious: Zephaniah singles out the priests and false worship as the cause of God's judgment. The Judeans had become captive to the fundamental problem of idolatry, worshiping created things as if they were the Creator. This is a constant theme throughout the Bible (see Rom. 1:25). Worship is unavoidable—the only question is, what we will worship?

The proclamation of judgment that precedes the gospel, then, demands that we examine our lives and discern the falsehood of our worship and the implications—even the cosmic implications—of our sin. And we do so mindful of the redemption—cosmic in scope—that God is working out through Jesus Christ (Rom. 8:19–23).

1:7–16 This section is consumed by "the day of the LORD" (vv. 7, 8, 9, 10, 14), a day of wrath and judgment. Zephaniah exhorts God's people to "Be silent before the Lord GOD" because of it (v. 7). While sometimes in the Old Testament the "day of the LORD" is a day of salvation and blessing (Joel 2:31; cf. Isa. 35:1–10), here it is framed as a day of judgment, a day when God will "punish the men who are complacent" (Zeph. 1:12).

Chapter 1
1[a] Jer. 1:2 [b] 2 Kgs. 22:1
2[c] Jer. 8:13; [ver. 18; 2 Kgs. 22:16, 17]
3[d] Hos. 4:3 [e] See Ezek. 7:19 [f] Ezek. 14:17
4[g] See 2 Kgs. 23:4
5[h] Jer. 19:13 [i] [1 Kgs. 18:21; 2 Kgs. 17:33, 41] [j] 1 Kgs. 11:5, 33
6[k] Jer. 2:13, 17; 15:6 [l] [Jer. 5:24; Heb. 11:6]
7[m] [Hab. 2:20] [n] [ver. 14]; See Joel 1:15 [o] Isa. 34:6; Jer. 46:10; Ezek. 39:17, 19 [p] 1 Sam. 16:5
8[q] 2 Kgs. 24:12, 14; 25:7 [r] [Matt. 22:11]
9[s] [1 Sam. 5:5]

10 "On that day," declares the LORD,
"a cry will be heard from [t]the Fish Gate,
[u]a wail from [v]the Second Quarter,
a loud crash from the hills.
11 [w]Wail, O inhabitants of the Mortar!
For all the traders[1] are no more;
all who weigh out silver are cut off.
12 At that time [x]I will search Jerusalem
with lamps,
and I will punish the men
[y]who are complacent,[2]
[z]those who say in their hearts,
'The LORD will not do good,
nor will he do ill.'
13 Their goods shall be [a]plundered,
and their houses laid waste.
[b]Though they build houses,
they shall not inhabit them;
[c]though they plant vineyards,
they shall not drink wine from them."

14 [d]The great day of the LORD is near,
near and hastening fast;
the sound of the day of the LORD is bitter;
[e]the mighty man cries aloud there.
15 [f]A day of wrath is that day,
a day of distress and anguish,
a day of [g]ruin and devastation,
[h]a day of darkness and gloom,
[h]a day of clouds and thick darkness,
16 [i]a day of trumpet blast and battle cry
[j]against the fortified cities
and against the lofty battlements.

17 [k]I will bring distress on mankind,
so that they shall walk [l]like the blind,
because they have sinned against the
LORD;
[m]their blood shall be poured out like dust,
and their flesh [n]like dung.
18 [o]Neither their silver nor their gold
shall be able to deliver them
on the day of the wrath of the LORD.
[p]In the fire of his jealousy,
[q]all the earth shall be consumed;
[r]for a full and sudden end
he will make of all the inhabitants of
the earth.

Judgment on Judah's Enemies

2 Gather together, yes, gather,
O [s]shameless nation,
2 [t]before the decree takes effect[3]
—before the day passes away [u]like
chaff—
[v]before there comes upon you
the burning anger of the LORD,
before there comes upon you
the day of the anger of the LORD.

[1] Or *all the people of Canaan* [2] Hebrew *are thickening on the dregs* [of their wine] [3] Hebrew *gives birth*

10[t] See 2 Chr. 33:14 [u] Zech. 11:3 [v] 2 Kgs. 22:14
11[w] Zech. 11:2; James 5:1
12[x] Amos 9:3 [y] Jer. 48:11; [Amos 6:1] [z] Ps. 94:7; Ezek. 8:12; Mal. 2:17; 3:14, 15
13[a] Isa. 42:22 [b] See Amos 5:11 [c] See Mic. 6:15
14[d] [ver. 7; Ezek. 7:7, 12] [e] [Isa. 33:7]
15[f] See Joel 1:15 [g] Job 30:3 [h] See Joel 2:2
16[i] [Jer. 4:19] [j] [Isa. 2:15]
17[k] Jer. 10:18 [l] Deut. 28:29; Isa. 59:10 [m] Ps. 79:3 [n] [Ps. 83:10]
18[o] Ezek. 7:19; [Prov. 11:4] [p] [ch. 3:8] [q] Ezek. 36:5 [r] [ver. 2, 3]

Chapter 2
1[s] Jer. 6:15
2[t] [ch. 3:8] [u] Ps. 1:4 [v] [2 Kgs. 23:26]

The "sound of the day of the LORD is bitter," for a "day of wrath is that day, a day of distress and anguish" (vv. 14, 15).

The idea of the "day of the LORD" is an outgrowth of the reality that God is holy and just. All that is wrong, all that denies the reality of God's lordship, will be judged accordingly. However, God's judgment on sin is not meant to be the last word. The certainty and severity of God's judgment should be a catalyst for repentance. In 2 Peter 3:10, Peter describes "the day of the Lord" when "the works that are done on [the earth] will be exposed." But this is presented as a reason to pursue holiness relentlessly: "Since all these things are thus to be dissolved, what sort of people ought you to be in lives of holiness and godliness!" (2 Peter 3:11).

As harsh as Zephaniah 1:7–16 is, it is not devoid of hope. The section begins with a reminder that "the LORD has prepared a sacrifice and consecrated his guests" (v. 7). In the context of the judgment themes surrounding it, this verse probably indicates that the "guests" are the sacrifice God is preparing to vindicate his holiness through the judgments coming upon Judah. But the only reason these words make sense is that the people understand the nature of the atoning sacrifice that God has established as the means for turning aside his just wrath. Thus, though the words are threatening here, they are meant to turn the people in penitence back to the God who makes a way for them to come to him.

For those who remain impenitent, God's holiness and justice will be a fierce and terrifying reality on the day of the Lord. Yet those who trust in God's merciful way of salvation by grace through his own Son, Jesus, are given the confidence that their judgment day has already taken place—on the day when Jesus died on the cross. Jesus himself endured "a day of distress and anguish" in our place (v. 15; cf. 2 Cor. 5:21). Be at peace. In Christ, sinners are forgiven and secure.

3 [w]Seek the LORD, [x]all you humble of the land,
who do his just commands;[1]
[y]seek righteousness; seek humility;
[y]perhaps [z]you may be hidden
on the day of the anger of the LORD.
4 [a]For Gaza shall be deserted,
and Ashkelon shall become a desolation;
Ashdod's people shall be driven out at noon,
and Ekron shall be uprooted.

5 Woe to [b]you inhabitants of the seacoast,
you nation of [c]the Cherethites!
[d]The word of the LORD is against you,
[e]O Canaan, land of the Philistines;
and I will destroy you [f]until no inhabitant is left.
6 [g]And you, O seacoast, [h]shall be pastures,
with meadows[2] for shepherds
and folds for flocks.
7 [i]The seacoast shall become the possession
of [j]the remnant of the house of Judah,
[h]on which they shall graze,
and in the houses of Ashkelon
they shall lie down at evening.
For the LORD their God [k]will be mindful of them
and [l]restore their fortunes.
8 "I have heard [m]the taunts of Moab
and [n]the revilings of the Ammonites,
how they have taunted my people
and made boasts [o]against their territory.
9 Therefore, [p]as I live," declares the LORD of hosts,
the God of Israel,
"Moab shall become [q]like Sodom,
and the Ammonites [q]like Gomorrah,
a land possessed by nettles and salt pits,
and a waste forever.
The remnant of my people shall plunder them,
and the survivors of my nation shall possess them."
10 This shall be their lot in return [r]for their pride,
because they taunted and boasted
against the people of the LORD of hosts.
11 The LORD will be awesome against them;
[s]for he will famish all the gods of the earth,
and [t]to him shall bow down,
each in its place,
all [u]the lands of the nations.

12 [v]You also, O Cushites,
shall be slain by my sword.

13 And he will stretch out his hand against the north
[w]and destroy Assyria,
and he [x]will make Nineveh a desolation,
a dry waste like the desert.
14 [y]Herds shall lie down in her midst,
all kinds of beasts;[3]

[1] Or *who carry out his judgment* [2] Or *caves* [3] Hebrew *beasts of every nation*

2:1–15 Chapter 2 opens with a direct appeal for Israel to gather and humble themselves (vv. 1–4). Where God's judgment had been against those "who do not seek the LORD or inquire of him" (1:6), the exhortation comes in 2:3 to "Seek the LORD, all you humble of the land," with the hope that they would be "hidden on the day of the anger of the LORD." Zephaniah goes on to foretell God's judgment on the other nations, in order to warn Judah if they do not repent.

In a sense, the divine judgment against the other nations—Philistines (v. 5), Moabites and Ammonites (v. 8), Cushites (v. 12), Assyrians (v. 13)—empties the need for any retribution against them to be made by Judah, and this overcoming of Judah's enemies is a sign of God's faithfulness to his people. A remnant of Judah will "lie down" in the houses of the Philistines (v. 7) and plunder the land of the Moabites (v. 9). Even amid judgment, God offers hope of restoration (v. 7) and provision (v. 9) to those who humbly renew their loyalty to him (v. 3).

God is the one who judges our enemies. When wronged, we can endure, as our Savior did (1 Pet. 2:20–23). A day of vindication is coming. But we ourselves will also be judged—and rightly so, if we will not humble ourselves before the Lord. The heart of God is drawn to those who bow before him, whatever their failures (Isa. 57:15; 66:2). It is contrition despite failure, not feigned perfection, that brings the mercy of God raining down on sinners. Jesus himself said, "I have not come to call the righteous but sinners to repentance" (Luke 5:32).

3[w] See Amos 5:6 [x] Ps. 76:9; Isa. 11:4 [y] [Amos 5:14, 15] [z] [Isa. 2:10; 26:20, 21]
4[a] Zech. 9:5, 6; [Jer. 47:5]; See Amos 1:6-8
5[b] Jer. 47:7; Ezek. 25:16 [c] See 1 Sam. 30:14 [d] [Nah. 2:13] [e] [Josh. 13:3] [f] ch. 3:6
6[g] ver. 7 [h] Isa. 65:10
7[i] [Josh. 19:29] [j] [ch. 3:13; Obad. 19] [h] [See ver. 6 above] [k] Zech. 10:3; Luke 1:68 [l] ch. 3:20
8[m] [Jer. 48:27] [n] Ezek. 25:3, 6 [o] [Jer. 49:1]
9[p] Isa. 49:18; See Ezek. 16:48 [q] Deut. 29:23; See Isa. 13:19
10[r] Isa. 16:6
11[s] [Isa. 17:4] [t] Ps. 22:27 [u] See Gen. 10:5
12[v] [ch. 3:10]
13[w] [Isa. 10:12] [x] Nah. 3:7
14[y] Isa. 13:21, 22; 34:14

[z]even the owl and the hedgehog[1]
shall lodge in her capitals;
a voice shall hoot in the window;
devastation will be on the threshold;
for [a]her cedar work will be laid bare.
15 This is the exultant city
[b]that lived securely,
that said in her heart,
"I am, and there is no one else."
What a desolation she has become,
[c]a lair for wild beasts!
[d]Everyone who passes by her
hisses and [e]shakes his fist.

Judgment on Jerusalem and the Nations

3 Woe to her who is rebellious and defiled,
[f]the oppressing city!
2 She listens to no voice;
[g]she accepts no correction.
[h]She does not trust in the LORD;
she does not draw near to her God.

3 [i]Her officials within her
are roaring lions;
her judges are [j]evening wolves
that leave nothing till the morning.
4 [k]Her prophets are fickle, treacherous men;
[k]her priests [l]profane what is holy;
they do violence to the law.
5 The LORD within her [m]is righteous;
he does no injustice;
every morning he shows forth his justice;
each dawn he does not fail;
but [n]the unjust knows no shame.

6 [o]"I have cut off nations;
their battlements are in ruins;
I have laid waste their streets
[p]so that no one walks in them;
their cities have been made desolate,
without a man, without an inhabitant.
7 [q]I said, 'Surely you will fear me;
[r]you will accept correction.
Then your[2] dwelling would not be cut off
according to all that I have appointed against you.'[3]
But [s]all the more they were eager
to make all their deeds corrupt.

8 "Therefore [t]wait for me," declares the LORD,
"for the day when I rise up to seize the prey.
For my decision is [u]to gather nations,
to assemble kingdoms,
to pour out upon them my indignation,
all my burning anger;
for in the fire of my jealousy
[v]all the earth shall be consumed.

The Conversion of the Nations

9 "For at that time I will change the speech of the peoples
to [w]a pure speech,
that all of them may call upon the name of the LORD
and serve him with one accord.

[1] The identity of the animals rendered *owl* and *hedgehog* is uncertain [2] Hebrew *her* [3] Hebrew *her*

14[z] Isa. 34:11 [a] [Jer. 22:14, 15]
15[b] Isa. 47:8 [c] [Ezek. 25:5] [d] Jer. 19:8 [e] [Nah. 3:19]

Chapter 3
1[f] Jer. 6:6
2[g] Jer. 5:3 [h] [ver. 12]
3[i] Ezek. 22:27; [Mic. 3:9, 10] [j] Hab. 1:8
4[k] Jer. 23:11; Hos. 9:7 [l] Ezek. 22:26
5[m] [Jer. 12:1] [n] [ch. 2:1]
6[o] See ch. 2:4-15 [p] [Zech. 7:14; 9:8]
7[q] [Jer. 36:3] [r] [ver. 2] [s] [Mic. 7:3]
8[t] Hab. 2:3; See Isa. 8:17 [u] Joel 3:2 [v] [ch. 1:18]
9[w] Isa. 19:18

3:1–8 God's heart is fierce in its protectiveness of his own holiness and unyielding in his demand that his people be faithful to him. In this passage God declares the destruction that is coming upon not only the nations (vv. 6–8) but also his own people (vv. 1–5).

Because the Lord is unswervingly righteous (v. 5), he cannot let the guilty go free. To do so would undo the moral order of the universe. It is axiomatic that God "will not acquit the wicked" (Ex. 23:7). Yet in sending his own Son as a propitiation, satisfying God's righteous wrath toward all those who receive his Son's work as a free gift, a way out from the horror of the judgment of Zephaniah 3:1–8 is provided. The scandal of the gospel is that God "justifies the ungodly," if the ungodly will put their faith in Christ (Rom. 4:5). And just as judgment will come upon the impenitent both of God's own people and of the nations, so too does his salvation flow freely not only to his own people but also to the nations (Zeph. 3:9–10; Rom. 4:9–12).

3:9–13 Despite the nations' and Judah's record of evil, Zephaniah foretells a day when their arrogance would be expelled and they would be a humble people who worship God alone. The transformation is all God's doing, first for the nations: "For at that time I will change the speech of the peoples to a pure speech," declares the Lord, in order that they may call upon his name (v. 9); then, the children of Israel who have been dispersed by God's judgment will also be allowed to return to true worship, bringing God's offering to him (v. 10).

10 [x]From beyond the rivers [y]of Cush
my worshipers, the daughter of my
dispersed ones,
shall bring my offering.

11 [z]"On that day [a]you shall not be put to
shame
because of the deeds by which you
have rebelled against me;
for then [b]I will remove from your midst
your proudly exultant ones,
and [c]you shall no longer be haughty
in my holy mountain.
12 But I will leave in your midst
a people [d]humble and lowly.
[e]They shall seek refuge in the name of
the LORD,
13 [f]those who are left in Israel;
they [g]shall do no injustice
and speak no lies,
[h]nor shall there be found in their mouth
a deceitful tongue.
[i]For they shall graze and lie down,
and none shall make them afraid."

Israel's Joy and Restoration

14 [j]Sing aloud, O daughter of Zion;
shout, O Israel!
Rejoice and exult with all your heart,
O daughter of Jerusalem!
15 The LORD has taken away the judgments
against you;
he has cleared away your enemies.
[k]The King of Israel, [l]the LORD, is in your
midst;
you shall never again fear evil.
16 [z]On that day it shall be said to Jerusalem:
"Fear not, O Zion;
[m]let not your hands grow weak.
17 [l]The LORD your God is in your midst,
[n]a mighty one who will save;
[o]he will rejoice over you with gladness;
he will quiet you by his love;
he will exult over you with loud singing.
18 I will gather those of you who mourn
[p]for the festival,
so that you will no longer suffer
reproach.[1]

[1] The meaning of the Hebrew is uncertain

Those who then engage in true worship "shall not be put to shame," despite their past rebellion (v. 11), because the proud will be removed and the "humble and lowly" will "seek refuge in the name of the LORD" (v. 12). Thus, Zephaniah teaches us fundamental truths about a true relationship with the Lord. Having the benefits of his provision and blessing requires becoming "a people humble and lowly," who do not proudly seek to distinguish themselves but find their identity and security "in the name of the LORD."

Such persons reflect the grace they have received from God in their community as they "do no injustice" and "speak no lies" (v. 13). Philippians 2:3 similarly describes how those who know the grace and character of Christ are to "in humility count others more significant" than ourselves, and goes on to describe how Jesus models that humility for us and makes it available to us through his sacrifice on the cross. As Paul says to the Colossians, Christ is our life (Col. 3:4), and he provides all the blessings that Zephaniah promises. United to him and indwelt by the Spirit, we begin to manifest, from the inside out, the fruit of such a radical internal transformation—not least as we become "a people humble and lowly" who "seek refuge in the name of the LORD" (Zeph. 3:12).

3:14–20 Zephaniah's closing exhortation begins by calling Judah to sing in triumph because God's mercy has delivered his people from judgment. This is a marked contrast to 1:7, where Zephaniah had told them to "Be silent before the Lord GOD" because of his wrath that would be poured out on the "day of the LORD." The gospel of forgiveness, of cleansing and healing, is a gospel that turns us from a people who shake our fist in the face of God to those who seek the face of God.

The people of Judah sing because God first sang over them (3:17), just as we are able to love because God first loved us (1 John 4:19). The Lord rejoices in his people, delights in them, and cares for them. The majesty and the mystery of this passage is heightened by the severity of the judgment message that reverberates throughout the preceding sections of Zephaniah's prophecy. That God's wrath is so clearly on display in the book heightens our sense of wonder at his astonishing mercy.

10[x] Ps. 68:31; Isa. 11:11; 60:4 [y][ch. 2:12]
11[z] Isa. 2:11 [a][Isa. 54:4] [b][Mal. 4:1] [c] Jer. 7:4; [Matt. 3:9]
12[d] Isa. 14:32; [Matt. 5:3] [e][ver. 2]
13[f][ch. 2:7] [g] Isa. 60:21 [h][Rev. 14:5] [i] See Mic. 5:4
14[j] Isa. 12:6; 54:1; Zech. 2:10; 9:9
15[k] Matt. 27:42; John 1:49 [l] Ps. 46:5; Zech. 2:10; [Rev. 21:3]
16[z][See ver. 11 above] [m][Isa. 35:3; Heb. 12:12]
17[l][See ver. 15 above] [n][Isa. 63:1] [o] Isa. 62:5; Jer. 32:41
18[p] Lam. 1:4; 2:6

19 Behold, at that time [q]I will deal
with all your oppressors.
And [r]I will save the lame
and gather the outcast,
and I will change [s]their shame into [t]praise
and renown in all the earth.

20 [u]At that time I will bring you in,
at the time when I gather you together;
for I will make you renowned and praised
among all the peoples of the earth,
[v]when I restore your fortunes
before your eyes," says the LORD.

19[q][Isa. 60:14] [r]Mic. 4:6, 7 [s]Isa. 61:7 [t][Jer. 13:11; 33:9]
20[u]Isa. 11:12; Jer. 32:37; Ezek. 11:17 [v]ch. 2:7

Zephaniah's final word points us toward the gospel of grace: God's people can live in freedom, in joy, because of the good news that their judgments have been removed by God's merciful provision and not earned or achieved by them. In Zephaniah we see the severity of God's judgment against sin, the passionate wrath that he is willing to pour out, and the "fire of his jealousy" (Zeph. 1:18). Yet as the book closes we see God's equally fierce love for his covenant people. He delights over them. He rejoices in them. He loves them. He saves them (3:17). In Christ, we ultimately see this great love and provision in flesh and blood.

Introduction to
Haggai

Author and Date

The book of Haggai contains messages delivered by the prophet Haggai, and thus it is reasonable to consider Haggai its author. Little is known about Haggai's personal background. The specific mention of the "second year of Darius" (1:1) places the book in the year 520 B.C. Haggai ministered among the Jews who had returned to Judea after some 70 years of exile in Babylon. The Persian ruler Cyrus the Great captured Babylon in 539 B.C., and in 538 he permitted the Jews to return to Jerusalem to rebuild the temple (Ezra 1–2). The work of rebuilding stalled, however, when opposition arose (Ezra 3:1–4:5). Haggai encouraged the people to renew the work of restoration.

The Gospel in Haggai

With its focus on rebuilding the house of the Lord, the book of Haggai would be easy to apply moralistically, especially in the midst of a church building program. The key to applying the book in a gospel-centered way is to see that the temple, like the tabernacle before it, was the visible symbol of God dwelling in the midst of his people, and therefore it foreshadows Christ, the one in whom the Word became flesh and "tabernacled" in our midst (see John 1:14).

Christ himself is the new temple in the New Testament (John 2:19). As his body, the church is also the new temple (Eph. 2:16–22). The message of this book for Christians is thus not primarily about restoring a building in Jerusalem, or about constructing a contemporary building: Haggai is all about the ongoing work of building up the people of God, a work that is primarily God's (Matt. 16:18), but a work in which he, by his Spirit, invites us to participate (1 Cor. 3:10–17).

The other prominent link to the gospel is through Zerubbabel, the faithful descendant of David who leads the people in restoring the temple. Though Zerubbabel's grandfather, Jehoiachin (also known as Coniah), was earlier discarded by the Lord like an unwanted signet ring, in Zerubbabel the chosen status of the Davidic line was restored (Hag. 2:19–23). Zerubbabel was one of the ancestors of Christ (Matt. 1:12) and foreshadowed his faithful zeal to build God's house (John 2:17).

Outline

I. Introduction: Reluctant Rebuilders (1:1–2)

II. Consider Your Ways: Fruitless Prosperity (1:3–12)

III. Promise and Progress (1:13–15a)

IV. The Former and Latter Glory of This House (1:15b–2:9)

V. Consider Your Ways: Holiness and Defilement; Repentance and Blessing (2:10–19)

VI. Zerubbabel: The Signet Ring (2:20–23)

Haggai

The Command to Rebuild the Temple

1 [a]In the second year of Darius the king, in
the sixth month, on the first day of the
month, the word of the LORD came by the
hand of Haggai the prophet to [b]Zerubbabel
the son of [c]Shealtiel, governor of Judah, and
to [d]Joshua the son of [e]Jehozadak, the high
priest: 2 "Thus says the LORD of hosts: These
people say the time has not yet come to rebuild
the house of the LORD." 3 Then the word of
the LORD came [f]by the hand of Haggai the
prophet, 4 [g]"Is it a time for you yourselves
to dwell in your paneled houses, while [h]this
house lies in ruins? 5 Now, therefore, thus says
the LORD of hosts: [i]Consider your ways. 6 [j]You
have sown much, and harvested little. [k]You
eat, but you never have enough; you drink, but
you never have your fill. You clothe yourselves,
but no one is warm. And he who [l]earns wages
does so to put them into a bag with holes.

7 "Thus says the LORD of hosts: [i]Consider
your ways. 8 Go up to the hills and bring wood
and build the house, that [m]I may take pleasure in it and that [n]I may be glorified, says the
LORD. 9 [j]You looked for much, and behold, it
came to little. And when you brought it home,
[o]I blew it away. Why? declares the LORD of
hosts. Because of my house [h]that lies in ruins,
while each of you busies himself with his
own house. 10 Therefore [p]the heavens above
you have withheld the dew, and the earth
has withheld its produce. 11 And [q]I have called
for a drought on the land and the hills, on
[r]the grain, the new wine, the oil, on what the
ground brings forth, on man and beast, and
[s]on all their labors."

The People Obey the LORD

12 [t]Then [u]Zerubbabel the son of Shealtiel,
and [u]Joshua the son of Jehozadak, the high
priest, with all [v]the remnant of the people,
obeyed the voice of the LORD their God,
and the words of Haggai the prophet, as the
LORD their God had sent him. And the people
feared the LORD. 13 Then Haggai, the messenger of the LORD, spoke to the people with the

1:1–11 In difficult economic times, the people were saying, "The time has not yet come to rebuild the house of the LORD" (v. 2), though they were finding ways to build their own houses (v. 4). God promised that if they rebuilt his temple, he would be with them (Hag. 1:13; 2:4). He would turn the world upside down and bring the long-desired Messiah (2:6–7, 21–23).

We too need to repent of our focus on building our own houses, not the Lord's. We need to pour our energies into building God's house (i.e., pursuing his purposes), while remembering that the visible symbol of his presence in the midst of his people is no longer a building but Jesus Christ himself (John 2:19). As Immanuel, Jesus physically represented God's presence among his people. When he cleansed the temple (John 2), Jesus showed the true zeal for God's house that we often lack, and at the cross he took upon himself the punishment we deserve for our self-centered focus on our own houses. Now that Jesus has ascended back to heaven, God's presence in the world is represented by his people. As the body of Christ, the church is now the new temple (Eph. 2:16–22; 2 Cor. 6:16–7:1).

1:12–14 The people obeyed the voice of the Lord (v. 12) because the Lord stirred up their spirits (v. 14). God builds his new temple by stirring our spirits to work through the indwelling power of his Spirit (Jude 20–21). We are thereby called and empowered to glorify God with our bodies (1 Cor. 6:19–20). God will establish his kingdom in this world in and through us; we, in turn, are called to seek his kingdom first (Matt. 6:33).

Chapter 1

1 [a]ver. 15; ch. 2:10; Ezra 4:24; 5:1; Zech. 1:1, 7 [b]See 1 Chr. 3:19 [c]See 1 Chr. 3:17 [d]See Ezra 3:2 [e]1 Chr. 6:15
3 [f]Ezra 5:1
4 [g][2 Sam. 7:2]; See Ps. 132:3-5 [h]Neh. 2:3, 17; Isa. 64:11; Jer. 33:10, 12
5 [i][ch. 2:15, 18]
6 [j]See Mic. 6:15 [k]Hos. 4:10 [l][Zech. 8:10]
7 [i][See ver. 5 above]
8 [m][Ps. 132:13, 14] [n][ch. 2:9]
9 [j][See ver. 6 above] [o][ch. 2:17] [h][See ver. 4 above]
10 [p][Jer. 5:24, 25; Zech. 8:12]; See 1 Kgs. 8:35
11 [q]2 Kgs. 8:1; [Ps. 105:16] [r]Hos. 2:9 [s]ch. 2:17; Ps. 128:2
12 [t]Ezra 5:2 [u]ver. 1 [v]ch. 2:2

LORD's message, [w]"I am with you, declares the
LORD." 14 And [x]the LORD stirred up the spirit
of [u]Zerubbabel the son of Shealtiel, governor
of Judah, and the spirit of [y]Joshua the son of
Jehozadak, the high priest, and the spirit of all
[z]the remnant of the people. And they came and
[a]worked on the house of the LORD of hosts,
their God, 15 [b]on the twenty-fourth day of the
month, in the sixth month, in the second year
of Darius the king.

The Coming Glory of the Temple

2 [c]In the seventh month, on the twenty-first
day of the month, the word of the LORD
came by the hand of Haggai the prophet,
2 "Speak now to [d]Zerubbabel the son of Shealtiel, governor of Judah, and to [d]Joshua the
son of Jehozadak, the high priest, and to all
the remnant of the people, and say, 3 [e]'Who
is left among you who saw this house [f]in its
former glory? How do you see it now? [g]Is it
not as nothing in your eyes? 4 Yet now [h]be
strong, O [d]Zerubbabel, declares the LORD. [h]Be
strong, O [d]Joshua, son of Jehozadak, the high
priest. [h]Be strong, all you people of the land,
declares the LORD. [i]Work, for [j]I am with you,
declares the LORD of hosts, 5 [k]according to the
covenant that I made with you when you came
out of Egypt. [l]My Spirit remains in your midst.
[m]Fear not. 6 For thus says the LORD of hosts:
[n]Yet once more, in a little while, [o]I will shake
the heavens and the earth and the sea and the
dry land. 7 And I will shake all nations, so that
the treasures of all nations shall come in, and
[p]I will fill this house with glory, says the LORD
of hosts. 8 [q]The silver is mine, and the gold is
mine, declares the LORD of hosts. 9 [r]The latter
glory of this house shall be greater than the former, says the LORD of hosts. And [s]in this place
I will give peace, declares the LORD of hosts.'"

Blessings for a Defiled People

10 [t]On the twenty-fourth day of the ninth
month, [u]in the second year of Darius, the word
of the LORD came by Haggai the prophet,
11 "Thus says the LORD of hosts: [v]Ask the priests
about the law: 12 'If someone carries [w]holy meat
in the fold of his garment and touches with his
fold bread or stew or wine or oil or any kind
of food, does it become holy?'" The priests
answered and said, [x]"No." 13 Then Haggai said,
[y]"If someone who is unclean by contact with
a dead body [z]touches any of these, does it
become unclean?" The priests answered and
said, "It does become unclean." 14 Then Haggai
answered and said, [a]"So is it with this people,
and with this nation before me, declares the
LORD, and so with every work of their hands.
And what they offer there is unclean. 15 Now
then, [b]consider from this day onward.[1] Before

[1] Or *backward*; also verse 18

13 [w] ch. 2:4; [Isa. 43:5]
14 [x] [2 Chr. 36:22; Ezra 1:1] [u] [See ver. 12 above] [y] ver. 1 [z] ch. 2:2 [a] [ch. 2:4; Ezra 5:8]
15 [b] [ver. 1]
Chapter 2
1 [c] [Lev. 23:34, 36]
2 [d] ch. 1:1
3 [e] [Ezra 3:12] [f] [ver. 9] [g] [Zech. 4:10]
4 [h] Zech. 8:9; [Zech. 4:6, 7] [d] [See ver. 2 above] [i] [ch. 1:14] [j] ch. 1:13
5 [k] See Ex. 29:45 [l] Neh. 9:20 [m] Zech. 8:13, 15
6 [n] Cited Heb. 12:26 [o] ver. 21
7 [p] [Isa. 60:1]
8 [q] [1 Chr. 29:14, 16]
9 [r] [ch. 1:8] [s] [Zech. 6:13; Eph. 2:14]
10 [t] ver. 18, 20 [u] ch. 1:1
11 [v] See Lev. 10:10, 11
12 [w] Jer. 11:15 [x] [ver. 14]
13 [y] Lev. 22:4, 6 [z] [Num. 19:22]
14 [a] [Isa. 64:6]
15 [b] [ch. 1:5]

2:1–9 Haggai called the people to "Be strong . . . [and] work" (v. 4) on the basis of the Lord's past faithfulness and presence with them. This combination of hard work and dependence on God is God's plan for transformed lives (Phil. 2:12–13). The people of Haggai's day longed to see God "fill this house with glory" (Hag. 2:7), which continues to be God's purpose in the church (Eph. 1:5–6). At Jesus' birth, angels sang of God's glory bringing peace on earth (Luke 2:13). When the infant Jesus made his first trip to the temple, Simeon recognized him as the Promised One and declared that the glory of God had now returned to the temple (Luke 2:32).

This oracle in Haggai was delivered during the Feast of Tabernacles, in the seventh month (Hag. 2:1), which was a time to look back to God's past deliverance and forward to anticipate the fulfillment of God's promises. Whenever we celebrate the Lord's Supper, we look back to the cross where God accomplished our salvation and forward to the time when God will bring all of history to its consummation at Christ's return (1 Cor. 11:26).

2:10–19 The holy can be profaned through contact with something defiled, yet the defiled does not become holy in the same way. Even God-ordained obedience cannot make the unclean holy, since whatever defiled hands offer is itself defiled (v. 14). Even when a sinner does something otherwise good, he sins because the motives of his heart are corrupt.

Our salvation must therefore necessarily come to us from outside us, through an act of God. As the reestablishment of the temple was the turning point from curse to blessing in Haggai's day, so the coming of Christ is the turning point from curse to blessing for the world. This is how God brings peace on earth among those on whom his favor rests (v. 9; Luke 2:14).

stone was placed upon stone in the temple
of the LORD, 16 how did you fare? [c]When[1] one
came to a heap of twenty measures, there were
but ten. When one came to the wine vat to
draw fifty measures, there were but twenty.
17 [d]I struck you and all the products of your
toil with blight and with mildew and with
hail, [e]yet you did not turn to me, declares
the LORD. 18 [b]Consider from this day onward,
[f]from the twenty-fourth day of the ninth
month. Since [g]the day that the foundation of
the LORD's temple was laid, [b]consider: 19 [h]Is
the seed yet in the barn? Indeed, the vine, the
fig tree, the pomegranate, and the olive tree
have yielded nothing. But from this day on
[i]I will bless you."

Zerubbabel Chosen as a Signet

20 The word of the LORD came a second time
to Haggai [f]on the twenty-fourth day of the
month, 21 "Speak to [j]Zerubbabel, governor of
Judah, saying, [k]I am about to shake the heavens and the earth, 22 and [l]to overthrow the
throne of kingdoms. I am about to destroy
the strength of the kingdoms of the nations,
and [m]overthrow the chariots and their riders.
And the horses and their riders shall go down,
[n]every one by the sword of his brother. 23 On
that day, declares the LORD of hosts, I will take
you, O [j]Zerubbabel [o]my servant, the son of
[p]Shealtiel, declares the LORD, and make you
[q]like a[2] signet ring, [o]for I have chosen you,
declares the LORD of hosts."

[1] Probable reading (compare Septuagint); Hebrew *LORD, since they were. When* [2] Hebrew *the*

2:20–23 Haggai describes the Lord's future intervention to transform the world in the language of God's past acts to judge the wicked and deliver his people. He turns the minds of his hearers back to God's intervention in Israel's past, against the Egyptians and during the conquest, and declares that God will do it again.

This future intervention is foreshadowed in the person of Zerubbabel. He seemed an insignificant government official in an obscure province, the heir of a cast-off royal line (Jer. 22:24–25). Yet God had chosen Zerubbabel for a significant task, which he fulfilled faithfully. As a faithful son of David, Zerubbabel was a sign of hope for the whole community that God's choice of David and his offspring was restored (Hag. 2:23).

Jesus is the Greater Son of Zerubbabel (Matt. 1:13). He came in a position that would grant him no respect in the world, humbling himself and taking the form of a servant, being faithful unto death (Phil. 2:5–8). On the cross, Jesus looked more like a new Jehoiachin, cast off by God, than a new Zerubbabel, God's chosen servant. But underneath God's temporary rejection of his Anointed was an eternal promise that could not be broken. Just as the sins of the Davidic kings brought exile and destruction on their subjects, so now the righteous death of this Davidic King brings life to those who trust in him.

16 [c][ch. 1:6]
17 [d]Amos 4:9; [ch. 1:9; Deut. 28:22] [e]Jer. 5:3; Amos 4:6
18 [b][See ver. 15 above] [f]ver. 10 [g]Ezra 3:10; Zech. 8:9
19 [h][Zech. 8:12] [i]Joel 2:14
20 [f][See ver. 18 above]
21 [j]ch. 1:1; [Zech. 4:6] [k]ver. 6
22 [l]Dan. 2:44; Zech. 12:9; [Matt. 24:7] [m][Mic. 5:10] [n][Zech. 14:13]
23 [j][See ver. 21 above] [o][Isa. 43:10] [p]ch. 1:1 [q]Jer. 22:24

Introduction to Zechariah

Author and Date

Zechariah was a prophet and a priest. He began his ministry in 520 B.C., shortly after Haggai had begun his prophetic work. Nearly 20 years after returning from the Babylonian exile in the time of Cyrus (538 B.C.), God's people were discouraged. The foundation of the temple had been laid shortly after the initial return, in 536 B.C., but powerful opposition had prevented further progress on rebuilding it.

The Gospel in Zechariah

Zechariah's prophecy begins with a cycle of vivid and complex visions, and it would be easy to get lost trying to explain all of the intricate details. Yet we are not left alone to try to understand these visions: the Lord sent an interpreting angel to Zechariah (and to us), and we can find the meaning of the visions explained in the angel's comments. He repeatedly points us to the coming of "the Branch" (3:8; 6:12), the messianic offspring of David promised in Jeremiah 23:5 and 33:15, who combines in himself the offices of king and priest (Zech. 6:13). This Branch will purify his people and remove their sin in one day (3:9).

Writing to people who were discouraged by living, after the exile, in a "day of small things" (4:10), when there seemed to be little progress toward the glorious future promised in the earlier prophets, Zechariah encouraged them to look forward to the day when the Lord would act once again. The righteous King was coming to bring salvation and to bring to an end to war and suffering (9:9–17).

That coming would, strikingly, result in the piercing of God himself, which would be the means by which a cleansing fountain would be opened for sin (12:10–13:1). The Good Shepherd would be struck for his sheep, who would continue to endure great suffering until the time of the end (13:7–14:5). Yet the outcome of that time of suffering and pain would be the final victory of God and the vindication of his people (14:9). Given all of these messianic themes, it is not surprising that the book of Zechariah is one of the Old Testament books most frequently quoted in the New Testament.

Outline

- I. Oracles and Visions (1:1–8:23)
  - A. Introduction: return to me and I will return to you (1:1–6)
  - B. Eight night visions and a sign-act (1:7–6:15)
  - C. From fasts to feasts (7:1–8:23)

II. The Return of the King (9:1–14:21)

   A. The first oracle: leaders and their people (9:1–11:17)

   B. The second oracle: the people and their leaders (12:1–14:21)

Zechariah

A Call to Return to the LORD

1 In the eighth month, [a]in the second year of
Darius, the word of the LORD came to the
prophet [b]Zechariah, the son of [c]Berechiah, son
of [d]Iddo, saying, 2 [e]"The LORD was very angry
with your fathers. 3 Therefore say to them,
Thus declares the LORD of hosts: [f]'Return to
me, says the LORD of hosts, and [g]I will return
to you, says the LORD of hosts. 4 [h]Do not be
like your fathers, [i]to whom the former prophets cried out, 'Thus says the LORD of hosts,
[f]Return from your evil ways and from your
evil deeds.' But [j]they did not hear or pay attention to me, declares the LORD. 5 Your fathers,
where are they? And [k]the prophets, do they
live forever? 6 [l]But my words and my statutes,
which I commanded [m]my servants the prophets, did they not [n]overtake your fathers? So
they repented and said, [o]'As the LORD of hosts
purposed to deal with us for [p]our ways and
[p]deeds, so has he dealt with us.'"

A Vision of a Horseman

7 On the twenty-fourth day of the eleventh
month, which is the month of Shebat, in the
second year of Darius, the word of the LORD
came to the prophet [b]Zechariah, the son of
[c]Berechiah, son of [d]Iddo, saying, 8 "I saw in
the night, and behold, [q]a man riding on a red
horse! He was standing among the myrtle
trees in the glen, and behind him were [r]red,
sorrel, and white horses. 9 Then I said, 'What
are these, my lord?' [s]The angel who talked
with me said to me, 'I will show you what
they are.' 10 So [q]the man who was standing
among the myrtle trees answered, [t]'These are
they whom the LORD has sent to [u]patrol the
earth.' 11 And they answered [s]the angel of the
LORD who was standing among the myrtle
trees, and said, [u]'We have patrolled the earth,
and behold, all the earth [v]remains at rest.'
12 Then [s]the angel of the LORD said, [w]'O LORD
of hosts, [w]how long will you [x]have no mercy
on Jerusalem and the cities of Judah, against
which you have been angry these [y]seventy
years?' 13 And the LORD answered [z]gracious
and comforting words to [s]the angel who
talked with me. 14 So [s]the angel who talked
with me said to me, 'Cry out, Thus says the

1:1–6 Zechariah describes two generations who respond to God's word in different ways. The "fathers" prior to the exile heard God's word repeatedly but did not respond and were therefore buried by God's wrath (v. 4). The present generation, however, responded positively to Zechariah's call to turn to God and would therefore see God turn to them (v. 6). If that was true for God's word delivered through the prophets, how much more sinful is it for us to refuse to hear the climactic Word of God, now delivered to us in the gospel and revealed as the very Son of God (Heb. 1:1–2)?

1:7–17 Zechariah's hearers found life after exile an intense struggle. They wondered whether God noticed them and cared. The horsemen depict God's "special operations forces," concealed in the dark among the bushes but going throughout the world providing accurate intelligence (vv. 8–10). The 70 years of exile were nearly complete, and it was the Lord's purpose to bless Jerusalem again.

We too struggle when things are not as we wish. Yet God sees and cares about us, and he will answer our cries for help as he knows is best for the sake of Jesus, his Chosen One. Pain does not indicate the absence of God. Pain invites us into communion with Jesus and greater dependence on him, as we yearn for his coming while sharing in his sufferings (Phil. 3:10).

Chapter 1

1 [a]See Hag. 1:1 [b]Ezra 6:14; Matt. 23:35 [c]1 Chr. 6:39 [d]Neh. 12:4, 16
2 [e][Jer. 2:5]
3 [f]Isa. 31:6; Jer. 3:1, 22; Ezek. 18:30; Mal. 3:7 [g]Jer. 12:15; Mic. 7:19
4 [h][Ps. 78:8] [i]See 2 Chr. 36:15 [f][See ver. 3 above] [j]ch. 7:11; 2 Chr. 36:16; See Jer. 35:15
5 [k][John 8:52]
6 [l][Isa. 40:8; Matt. 24:35] [m]See Dan. 9:6 [n]Deut. 28:2, 15 [o]Lam. 2:17 [p][Ezek. 36:31]
7 [b][See ver. 1 above] [c][See ver. 1 above] [d][See ver. 1 above]
8 [q][Rev. 6:4] [r][Rev. 6:4, 5, 8]; See ch. 6:2-7
9 [s][Rev. 22:6]
10 [q][See ver. 8 above] [t][Heb. 1:14] [u]ch. 6:7; [Job 1:7]
11 [s][See ver. 9 above] [u][See ver. 10 above] [v][ver. 15]
12 [s][See ver. 9 above] [w]Ps. 80:4; 89:46; Hab. 2:6; Rev. 6:10 [x]Ps. 102:13 [y]ch. 7:5; Jer. 25:11; 29:10
13 [z]See Jer. 29:10, 11 [s][See ver. 9 above]
14 [s][See ver. 9 above]

LORD of hosts: [a]I am exceedingly jealous for
Jerusalem and for Zion. 15 [b]And I am exceedingly angry with the nations that are [c]at ease;
[d]for while I was angry but a little, [e]they fur-
thered the disaster. 16 Therefore, thus says
the LORD, [f]I have returned to Jerusalem with
mercy; [g]my house shall be built in it, declares
the LORD of hosts, and [h]the measuring line
shall be stretched out over Jerusalem. 17 Cry
out again, Thus says the LORD of hosts: [i]My
cities shall again overflow with prosperity,
[j]and the LORD will again comfort Zion and
again [k]choose Jerusalem.'"

A Vision of Horns and Craftsmen

18[1] And I lifted my eyes and saw, and behold,
[l]four horns! 19 And I said to [s]the angel who
talked with me, "What are these?" And he said
to me, [l]"These are the horns that have scattered Judah, Israel, and Jerusalem." 20 Then
the LORD showed me four craftsmen. 21 And
I said, "What are these coming to do?" He said,
[l]"These are the horns that scattered Judah, so
that no one raised his head. And these have
come [m]to terrify them, to cast down the horns
of the nations [n]who lifted up their horns
against the land of Judah to scatter it."

A Vision of a Man with a Measuring Line

2 [2] And I lifted my eyes and saw, and behold,
[o]a man with a measuring line in his hand!
2 Then I said, "Where are you going?" And he
said to me, [p]"To measure Jerusalem, to see
what is its width and what is its length." 3 And
behold, [q]the angel who talked with me came
forward, and another angel came forward to
meet him 4 and said to him, "Run, say to that
young man, [r]'Jerusalem shall be inhabited [s]as
villages without walls, because of [t]the multitude of people and livestock in it. 5 And I will
be to her [u]a wall of fire all around, declares the
LORD, and I will be the glory in her midst.'"
6 Up! Up! [v]Flee from the land of the north,
declares the LORD. For I have [w]spread you
abroad as the four winds of the heavens,
declares the LORD. 7 [x]Up! Escape to Zion, you
who dwell with the daughter of Babylon. 8 For
thus said the LORD of hosts, after his glory sent
me[3] to the nations who plundered you, [y]for he
who touches you touches [z]the apple of his eye:
9 "Behold, [a]I will shake my hand over them,
[b]and they shall become plunder for those who
served them. Then [c]you will know that the
LORD of hosts has sent me. 10 [d]Sing and rejoice,
O daughter of Zion, for [e]behold, I come [f]and
I will dwell in your midst, declares the LORD.
11 [g]And many nations shall join themselves to
the LORD in that day, and shall be my people.
[f]And I will dwell in your midst, and [c]you shall
know that the LORD of hosts has sent me to
you. 12 [h]And the LORD will inherit Judah as
his portion in the holy land, and will again
[i]choose Jerusalem."
13 Be silent, all flesh, before the LORD, for he
has roused himself from his holy dwelling.

[1] Ch 2:1 in Hebrew [2] Ch 2:5 in Hebrew [3] Or *he sent me after glory*

14[a] ch. 8:2; Joel 2:18
15[b] [Joel 3:2] [c] [ver. 11] [d] [Isa. 54:7, 8] [e] [Isa. 47:6]
16[f] ch. 8:3 [g] [ch. 4:9; Ezra 6:14] [h] Jer. 31:39; Ezek. 40:3; 47:3
17[i] ch. 2:4 [j] Isa. 40:1; 51:3 [k] ch. 2:12
18[l] [1 Kgs. 22:11]
19[s] [See ver. 9 above] [l] [See ver. 18 above]
21[l] [See ver. 18 above] [m] Deut. 28:26; Jer. 7:33 [n] [Ps. 75:4, 5]

Chapter 2
1[o] Ezek. 40:3; Rev. 11:1
2[p] [ch. 1:16]
3[q] ch. 1:9, 19
4[r] [ch. 12:6; 14:10, 11] [s] See Esth. 9:19 [t] Isa. 49:19; Jer. 31:27
5[u] Isa. 4:5; [ch. 9:8; Ps. 125:2]
6[v] Isa. 48:20 [w] [ch. 7:14; Ezek. 5:10; 17:21]
7[x] [Isa. 52:11]
8[y] Jer. 12:14 [z] See Deut. 32:10
9[a] Isa. 11:15; 19:16 [b] Ezek. 39:10 [c] ch. 4:9; 6:15; Ezek. 33:33
10[d] See Zeph. 3:14 [e] Ps. 40:7 [f] ch. 8:3; Isa. 12:6; Ezek. 37:27; Zeph. 3:15; 2 Cor. 6:16; See Lev. 26:12
11[g] ch. 8:22; See Isa. 2:2 [f] [See ver. 10 above] [c] [See ver. 9 above]
12[h] See Deut. 32:9 [i] ch. 1:17; [Hab. 2:20]

1:18–21 This vision demonstrates God's care for his people negatively. God will raise up nations to punish those who scattered Judah, Israel, and Jerusalem. Those who assault God's people should tremble. The threats of the Abrahamic covenant are not empty (Gen. 12:1–3). Even today, the Lord watches over his people and judges those who assault them. One day all will be put right. We need not seek vengeance now. God will settle all accounts in his own good time (Rom. 12:19).

2:1–13 God's plan is not just to destroy his enemies but to restore the world by dwelling in the midst of a holy people. The father of John the Baptist, also named Zechariah, speaks of the Christ who is coming both to destroy the wicked and to raise a horn of salvation for his people (Luke 1:69–75). God's people are called to join in the song of praise on Mount Zion, while his enemies will be silenced before him. And this holy people will be drawn from many nations—a "ransomed people for God from every tribe and language and people and nation" (Rev. 5:9).

3:1–10 Joshua the high priest is the defendant in court, with the Accuser eager to press charges. The priest's clothing is defiled, representing the sin that makes him unfit to stand before God and unable to remove his people's iniquity through the sacrifices. Yet God rules Satan's case out of order, and throws it out of court before he can present it. No charge can be brought, because Joshua has been chosen and rescued by God. Indeed, God himself clothes Joshua in clean garments (v. 5).

A Vision of Joshua the High Priest

3 Then he showed me [j]Joshua the high
priest standing before the angel of the
LORD, and [k]Satan[1] standing at his right hand
to accuse him. 2 And the LORD said to Satan,
[l]"The LORD rebuke you, O Satan! The LORD
who has [m]chosen Jerusalem rebuke you! Is
not this [n]a brand[2] plucked from the fire?"
3 Now [j]Joshua was standing before the angel,
[o]clothed with filthy garments. 4 And the angel
said to [p]those who were standing before him,
[q]"Remove the filthy garments from him." And
to him he said, "Behold, [r]I have taken your
iniquity away from you, and [s]I will clothe you
with pure vestments." 5 And I said, [t]"Let them
put a clean turban on his head." So they put
a clean turban on his head and clothed him
with garments. And the angel of the LORD was
standing by.

6 And the angel of the LORD solemnly assured
[j]Joshua, 7 "Thus says the LORD of hosts: If you
will walk in my ways and [u]keep my charge,
then you shall [v]rule my house and have charge
of my courts, and I will give you the right of
access among [w]those who are standing here.
8 Hear now, O Joshua the high priest, you and
your friends who sit before you, for [x]they are
men who are a sign: behold, I will bring [y]my
servant [z]the Branch. 9 For behold, on [a]the stone
that I have set before Joshua, on a single stone
with [b]seven eyes,[3] I will [c]engrave its inscription, declares the LORD of hosts, and [d]I will
remove the iniquity of this land in a single
day. 10 In that day, declares the LORD of hosts,
every one of you will invite his neighbor to
come [e]under his vine and under his fig tree."

A Vision of a Golden Lampstand

4 And [f]the angel who talked with me came
again [g]and woke me, like a man who is
awakened out of his sleep. 2 And he said to me,
"What do you see?" I said, "I see, and behold, [h]a
lampstand all of gold, with a bowl on the top
of it, and [i]seven lamps on it, with seven lips
on each of the lamps that are on the top of it.
3 And there are [j]two olive trees by it, one on
the right of the bowl and the other on its left."
4 And I said to [f]the angel who talked with me,
"What are these, my lord?" 5 Then the angel
who talked with me answered and said to me,

[1] Hebrew *the Accuser* or *the Adversary* [2] That is, a burning stick [3] Or *facets*

We too are defiled and unfit to appear before God. By his grace, God justifies us (declares us perfectly righteous), reclothing us in borrowed robes of righteousness that enable us to approach the throne of grace (Isa. 61:10; Phil. 3:9; Heb. 4:16). Since we are justified through the merit of Christ, there can be no condemnation for us (Rom. 8:1). Satan's charges against us are inadmissible. Ephesians 4:24 picks up the imagery of reclothing to show that God also sanctifies sinners, turning them into saints who are fit to serve.

Fulfillment of Zechariah's vision awaits the coming of the Messiah, "the Branch" (Zech. 3:8). Everything Joshua received would be enabled by Jesus making the opposite move: In place of Joshua's clean turban, Jesus was crowned with thorns. Instead of Joshua's festival garments, Jesus was stripped of his clothing, which was divided among his crucifiers. Joshua was found *not guilty* of defilement that was really his; Jesus was found *guilty* and crucified for the sin of others (2 Cor. 5:21). This is the wonder of the gospel. The cross is the means by which God "will remove the iniquity of this land in a single day" (Zech. 3:9).

4:1–14 In a day of small things (v. 10) there can be great temptation either to trust in human power and skill or to despair of ever seeing anything significant happen. God promised that Zerubbabel would complete the temple that he started and that God's omniscient blessing would be restored to their midst. This would not happen through human might or power, but by the unstoppable work of God's Spirit. The same principles hold true for us. When we face a day of small things, we may trust that the Spirit is still capable of doing his work. Indeed, the day of small things is often the very moment when the Spirit is most active.

Jesus established the foundation of the new temple through his death and resurrection. He is building his church, and the gates of hell shall not prevail against it (Matt. 16:18). As fellow-builders with Christ, we are called to build faithfully on that foundation (1 Cor. 3:11–13). Our work will be tested by fire, but what is true will remain, for God does the work, not us. He has begun a good work in our hearts and will bring it to completion in the day of great things when Christ returns (Phil. 1:6).

Chapter 3
1 [j]ch. 6:11; See Ezra 3:2 [k][1 Chr. 21:1; Ps. 109:6]
2 [l]Jude 9 [m]ch. 1:17; [Rom. 8:33] [n]Amos 4:11
3 [j][See ver. 1 above] [o][Isa. 64:6; Jude 23]
4 [p][ver. 7; Luke 1:19] [q]Rev. 7:14 [r][ver. 9; Isa. 6:7] [s]Isa. 61:10; Luke 15:22; Rev. 19:8
5 [t]Job 29:14; [ch. 6:11]
6 [j][See ver. 1 above]
7 [u]Gen. 26:5; Mal. 3:14; See Lev. 8:35 [v][Deut. 17:9; Mal. 2:7] [w][ver. 4]
8 [x][Ezek. 12:11] [y]See Isa. 42:1 [z]ch. 6:12; Isa. 11:1; See Jer. 23:5
9 [a]Ps. 118:22; Isa. 28:16; [ch. 4:7]; See Ezra 3:9-11 [b]ch. 4:10; Rev. 5:6 [c][2 Tim. 2:19] [d][ver. 4]
10 [e]See 1 Kgs. 4:25

Chapter 4
1 [f]ch. 1:9, 19 [g]Dan. 8:18; 10:9, 10
2 [h]See Ex. 25:31 [i]Ex. 25:37; [Rev. 1:12; 4:5]
3 [j][ver. 11; Rev. 11:4]
4 [f][See ver. 1 above]

[k]"Do you not know what these are?" I said,
"No, my lord." 6 Then he said to me, "This is
the word of the LORD to [l]Zerubbabel: [m]Not by
might, nor by power, but by my Spirit, says the
LORD of hosts. 7 Who are you, [n]O great mountain? Before [l]Zerubbabel [o]you shall become
a plain. And he shall bring forward [p]the top
stone amid shouts of 'Grace, grace to it!'"

8 Then the word of the LORD came to me,
saying, 9 [q]"The hands of [l]Zerubbabel have laid
the foundation of this house; his hands shall
also [r]complete it. [s]Then you will know that
the LORD of hosts has sent me to you. 10 [t]For
whoever has despised the day of small things
shall rejoice, and shall see [u]the plumb line in
the hand of Zerubbabel.

[v]"These seven [v]are the eyes of the LORD,
[w]which range through the whole earth." 11 Then
I said to him, "What are these [j]two olive trees
on the right and the left of the lampstand?"
12 And a second time I answered and said to
him, "What are these [j]two branches of the
olive trees, which are beside the two golden
pipes from which the golden oil[1] is poured
out?" 13 He said to me, [x]"Do you not know what
these are?" I said, "No, my lord." 14 Then he
said, [y]"These are the two anointed ones[2] who
stand by [z]the Lord of the whole earth."

A Vision of a Flying Scroll

5 Again I lifted my eyes and saw, and behold,
a flying [a]scroll! 2 And he said to me, "What
do you see?" I answered, "I see a flying [a]scroll.
Its length is twenty cubits, and its width
ten cubits."[3] 3 Then he said to me, "This is
[b]the curse that goes out over the face of the
whole land. For everyone who [c]steals shall be
cleaned out according to what is on one side,
and everyone who [d]swears falsely[4] shall be
cleaned out according to what is on the other
side. 4 I will send it out, declares the LORD of
hosts, and it shall enter the house of the thief,
and the house of [e]him who swears falsely by
my name. And [f]it shall remain in his house and
[g]consume it, both timber and stones."

A Vision of a Woman in a Basket

5 [h]Then the angel who talked with me came
forward and said to me, [i]"Lift your eyes and
see what this is that is going out." 6 And I said,
"What is it?" He said, "This is [j]the basket[5] that
is going out." And he said, "This is their iniquity[6] in all the land." 7 And behold, the leaden
cover was lifted, and there was a woman sitting in the basket! 8 And he said, "This is
Wickedness." And he thrust her back into the
basket, and thrust down [j]the leaden weight
on its opening.

9 Then I lifted my eyes and saw, and behold,
two women coming forward! [k]The wind
was in their wings. They had wings like the
wings of a stork, and they lifted up the basket
between earth and heaven. 10 Then I said to the
angel who talked with me, "Where are they
taking the basket?" 11 He said to me, "To the
[l]land of Shinar, to build a house for it. And
when this is prepared, they will set the basket
down there on its base."

[1] Hebrew lacks *oil* [2] Hebrew *two sons of new oil* [3] A *cubit* was about 18 inches or 45 centimeters [4] Hebrew lacks *falsely* (supplied from verse 4) [5] Hebrew *ephah*; also verses 7–11. An *ephah* was about 3/5 bushel or 22 liters [6] One Hebrew manuscript, Septuagint, Syriac; most Hebrew manuscripts *eye*

5 [k]ver. 12
6 [l]See 1 Chr. 3:19 [m][Hos. 1:7]
7 [n][Jer. 51:25] [l][See ver. 6 above] [o]Isa. 40:4 [p]See ch. 3:9
9 [q][Ezra 3:10] [l][See ver. 6 above] [r][ch. 1:16] [s]See ch. 2:9
10 [t][Hag. 2:3] [u][ch. 1:16] [v]ch. 3:9 [w]2 Chr. 16:9; [Prov. 15:3]
11 [j][See ver. 3 above]
12 [j][See ver. 3 above]
13 [x]ver. 5
14 [y]Rev. 11:4 [z]ch. 6:5

Chapter 5
1 [a]Jer. 36:2, 28
2 [a][See ver. 1 above]
3 [b][Jer. 29:18; Ezek. 2:9, 10]; See Deut. 29:27 [c]See Ex. 20:15 [d]Ex. 20:7; [Eccles. 5:2]
4 [e]ch. 8:17; Lev. 19:12; Mal. 3:5 [f]Prov. 3:33 [g][Lev. 14:45]
5 [h]ch. 1:9 [i][ver. 1, 9; ch. 6:1]
6 [j][Ezek. 45:11]
8 [j][See ver. 6 above]
9 [k][Hos. 4:19]
11 [l]See Gen. 11:2

5:1–11 These visions deal with the comprehensive removal of sin in two distinct ways—through the execution and exile of sinners. Sin cannot be ignored by God; it must be dealt with effectively. If this is not done through the sinner coming to Christ in faith and receiving salvation (see Zechariah 3), it must be done through the death of the sinner or his banishment into the uttermost darkness.

The removal of the impure from the midst of God's people also points to the transformation of what remains into a purified remnant. It is good news that the idolater and the thief will no longer be in the land, because it points to the certainty and completeness of God's sanctifying work. His restored people will become a holy nation, fit to receive the blessings of the covenant, not its curse. The future for God's people lies in the new, holy Jerusalem, not in defiled Babylon, which is destined for destruction (Revelation 18). "Sin will have no dominion over you" (Rom. 6:14) is a promise that encourages us eagerly to pursue lives of new obedience.

6:1–8 The idolaters who were driven out of God's land and transported to Babylon in the previous vision will not remain there forever, as an ongoing threat to God's people. God will send out his powerful forces, depicted as horsemen and chariots, to conquer the furthest reaches of the earth, extending his reign into every idolatrous corner of the world.

A Vision of Four Chariots

6 Again I lifted my eyes and saw, and behold, four chariots came out from between two mountains. And the mountains were mountains of [m]bronze. 2 The first chariot had [n]red horses, the second [o]black horses, 3 the third [p]white horses, and the fourth chariot dappled horses—all of them strong.[1] 4 Then I answered and said to [q]the angel who talked with me, "What are these, my lord?" 5 And the angel answered and said to me, [r]"These are going out to the four winds of heaven, after [s]presenting themselves before [t]the Lord of all the earth. 6 The chariot with the black horses goes toward [u]the north country, the white ones go after them, and the dappled ones go toward [v]the south country." 7 When the strong horses came out, they were impatient to go and [w]patrol the earth. And he said, "Go, [w]patrol the earth." [w]So they patrolled the earth. 8 Then he cried to me, "Behold, those who go toward [u]the north country have set my Spirit at rest in [u]the north country."

The Crown and the Temple

9 And the word of the LORD came to me: 10 "Take from the exiles [x]Heldai, Tobijah, and [y]Jedaiah, who have arrived from Babylon, and go the same day to the house of Josiah, the son of [z]Zephaniah. 11 Take from them silver and gold, and make a crown, [a]and set it on the head of [b]Joshua, the son of Jehozadak, the high priest. 12 And say to him, 'Thus says the LORD of hosts, "Behold, the man whose name is [c]the Branch: for he shall branch out from his place, and [d]he shall build the temple of the LORD. 13 [d]It is he who shall build the temple of the LORD [e]and shall bear royal honor, and shall sit and rule on his throne. And there shall be a [f]priest on his throne, [g]and the counsel of peace shall be between them both."' 14 And the crown shall be in the temple of the LORD as [h]a reminder to [i]Helem,[2] [i]Tobijah, [i]Jedaiah, and Hen [j]the son of Zephaniah.

15 [k]"And those who are far off shall come and [l]help to build the temple of the LORD. [m]And you shall know that the LORD of hosts has sent me to you. [n]And this shall come to pass, if you will diligently obey the voice of the LORD your God."

A Call for Justice and Mercy

7 [o]In the fourth year of King Darius, the word of the LORD came to Zechariah on the fourth day of the ninth month, which is [p]Chislev. 2 Now the people of Bethel had sent Sharezer and Regem-melech and their men [q]to entreat the favor of the LORD, 3 [r]saying to the priests of the house of the LORD of hosts and [s]the prophets, "Should I weep and [t]abstain in [u]the fifth month, as I have done for so many years?"

4 Then the word of the LORD of hosts came to me: 5 "Say to all the people of the land and

[1] Or *and the fourth chariot strong dappled horses* [2] An alternate spelling of *Heldai* (verse 10)

6:9–15 The complete destruction of Babylon awaits the coming of the Branch, the Messiah (v. 12). Meanwhile, the returned exiles are to join those already in Jerusalem in a symbolic coronation of Joshua the high priest, looking forward to the coming of the one who will build the temple of the Lord and bear royal honor. The crown will be kept in the temple as a memorial, a "reminder" to the Lord of his promise (v. 14).

Ultimately, Jesus is the promised Branch, who will establish the new temple in his own body. He unites in his person the two offices of king and priest, like Melchizedek (Hebrews 7), thereby making his people kings and priests to God (Rev. 5:10). The result of his coming is peace between us and God (Rom. 5:1) and ultimately throughout the cosmos (Eph. 1:21–23). This leaves no room for despair, even if our personal corner of time and space seems to be a day of small things (Zech. 4:10). For as king, Jesus represents God to us, and as priest he represents us to God.

7:1–14 What lies at the heart of our religious actions, whether fasting, going to church, reading the Bible, or praying? These are all good things, but if we are doing them for ourselves, they are a waste of time. We cannot rely on religious rituals when there is no matching evidence of true life change (see James 1:27). God's command is searching: keep the Law and the Prophets; love your neighbor, whom you see on a daily basis, as evidence that you truly love God, whom you do not see (cf. 1 John 4:20). Without obedience, there can be no fellowship with the Lord. The focus of Zechariah 7 is primarily law rather than gospel. To find hope, we need to look ahead into chapter 8, where the command of chapter 7 is placed in the context of God's faithfulness to his covenant promise (8:1–3), which will ultimately turn our fasting to feasting.

Chapter 6
1 [m]Dan. 2:39
2 [n]ch. 1:8; Rev. 6:4 [o]Rev. 6:5
3 [p]ch. 1:8; Rev. 6:2
4 [q]ch. 1:9
5 [r]Ps. 104:4; Heb. 1:7 [s]ch. 3:4 [t]ch. 4:14
6 [u]ver. 8; ch. 2:6; Jer. 1:13 [v][ch. 9:14]
7 [w][ch. 1:10]
8 [u][See ver. 6 above]
10 [x][ver. 14] [y]Neh. 7:39 [z]2 Kgs. 25:18
11 [a][ch. 3:5] [b]ch. 3:1
12 [c]See ch. 3:8 [d][Matt. 16:18; Heb. 3:3]; See Eph. 2:20-22
13 [d][See ver. 12 above] [e]Ps. 21:5; Ezek. 21:27 [f]Ps. 110:4; Heb. 3:1 [g][Hag. 2:9]
14 [h]Ex. 12:14; [Matt. 26:13; Mark 14:9] [i][ver. 10] [j]ver. 10
15 [k]Isa. 57:19; [Eph. 2:13, 19] [l]Isa. 60:10 [m]See ch. 2:9 [n]See Deut. 30:1-3

Chapter 7
1 [o][ch. 1:1, 7] [p]Neh. 1:1
2 [q]ch. 8:21, 22; 1 Sam. 13:12; Mal. 1:9
3 [r]Mal. 2:7 [s]ch. 8:9; [Ezra 5:1; 6:14] [t][ch. 12:12] [u]ch. 8:19; [2 Kgs. 25:8]

the priests, When you fasted and mourned in
[u]the fifth month and in [v]the seventh, for these
[w]seventy years, [x]was it [x]for me that you fasted?
6 [y]And when you eat and when you drink, do
you not eat for yourselves and drink for yourselves? 7 [z]Were not these the words that the
LORD proclaimed [a]by the former prophets,
when Jerusalem was inhabited and prosperous, [b]with her cities around her, and the
[b]South and the [b]lowland were inhabited?"
8 And the word of the LORD came to Zechariah, saying, 9 "Thus says the LORD of hosts,
[c]Render true judgments, show kindness and
mercy to one another, 10 [d]do not oppress the
widow, the fatherless, the sojourner, [e]or the
poor, and [f]let none of you devise evil against
another in your heart." 11 But [g]they refused to
pay attention [h]and turned a stubborn shoulder
and stopped their ears that they might not
hear.[1] 12 [i]They made their hearts diamond-hard
[j]lest they should hear the law and the words
that the LORD of hosts had sent [j]by his Spirit
through [k]the former prophets. [l]Therefore
great anger came from the LORD of hosts.
13 [m]"As I[2] called, and they would not hear, [m]so
they called, and I would not hear," says the
LORD of hosts, 14 [n]"and I scattered them with
a whirlwind among all [o]the nations that they
had not known. [p]Thus the land they left was
desolate, [q]so that no one went to and fro, [r]and
the pleasant land was made desolate."

The Coming Peace and Prosperity of Zion

8 And the word of the LORD of hosts came,
saying, 2 "Thus says the LORD of hosts:
[s]I am jealous for Zion with great jealousy, and
I am jealous for her with great wrath. 3 Thus
says the LORD: [t]I have returned to Zion and
[u]will dwell in the midst of Jerusalem, [v]and
Jerusalem shall be called the faithful city,
[w]and the mountain of the LORD of hosts, the
holy mountain. 4 Thus says the LORD of hosts:
[x]Old men and old women shall again sit in the
streets of Jerusalem, each with staff in hand
because of great age. 5 And the streets of the
city shall be full of boys and girls playing in
its streets. 6 Thus says the LORD of hosts: [y]If
it is marvelous in the sight of the remnant of
this people in those days, [z]should it also be
marvelous in my sight, declares the LORD of
hosts? 7 Thus says the LORD of hosts: Behold,
[a]I will save my people [b]from the east country
and from the west country, 8 and I will bring
them to dwell in the midst of Jerusalem. [c]And
they shall be my people, and I will be their
God, [d]in faithfulness and in righteousness."
9 Thus says the LORD of hosts: [e]"Let your
hands be strong, you who in these days have
been hearing these words from the mouth of
[f]the prophets who were present on [g]the day
that the foundation of the house of the LORD
of hosts was laid, that the temple might be
built. 10 For before those days [h]there was no
wage for man or any wage for beast, neither
was there any safety from the foe for him
who went out or came in, for I set every man
against his neighbor. 11 But now I will not deal
with the remnant of this people as in the former days, declares the LORD of hosts. 12 [i]For
there shall be a sowing of peace. The vine shall
give its fruit, and the ground shall give its produce, [j]and the heavens shall give their dew.
[k]And I will cause the remnant of this people
to possess all these things. 13 And as [l]you have

[1] Hebrew *and made their ears too heavy to hear* [2] Hebrew *he*

5[u] [See ver. 3 above] [v] [2 Kgs. 25:25] [w] See ch. 1:12 [x] [Isa. 58:4, 5]
6[y] [1 Cor. 11:20, 21]
7[z] [ch. 1:5, 6] [a] ver. 12 [b] Jer. 17:26
9[c] Isa. 1:17; Jer. 21:12; Mic. 6:8; [Matt. 23:23]
10[d] Isa. 1:23; Jer. 5:28; See Ex. 22:21, 22 [e] Prov. 22:22 [f] ch. 8:17
11[g] ch. 1:4 [h] Neh. 9:29
12[i] [Ezek. 11:19; 36:26] [j] [Neh. 9:30] [k] ver. 7 [l] [2 Chr. 36:16; 1 Thess. 2:16]
13[m] [Isa. 1:15; Jer. 11:11]; See Prov. 1:24-28
14[n] [ch. 2:6] [o] See Deut. 28:33 [p] Ezek. 12:19 [q] ch. 9:8; [Zeph. 3:6] [r] [Jer. 7:34]

Yet even as we reflect on Zechariah 7, we are drawn to remember that we can "show kindness and mercy to one another" (v. 9) only as we enjoy the kindness and mercy God has shown to us in Christ (Eph. 4:29–5:2).

8:1–23 The motivation for the self-denial of fasting was God's curse of exile on a nation of covenant breakers. Now that the temple had been rebuilt, was it time to stop fasting? God's faithfulness in bringing judgment on those who broke the covenant provided assurance that he would be similarly faithful in fulfilling his purpose in choosing Zion. He would return to Jerusalem and dwell among his people again, resulting in the covenantal blessings of happy youth and peaceful old age. Eden would be restored.

We too live in a fallen world that is under the curse of God, and we feel its effects in sickness, pain, and broken relationships. If God were to treat us as we deserve, our suffering would be overwhelming. In recognition of the sin within us and around us, it is appropriate for us to fast to express personal sorrow for sin and its bitter fruits.

Chapter 8 2[s] ch. 1:14 3[t] ch. 1:16 [u] See ch. 2:10 [v] [Isa. 1:26] [w] See Isa. 2:3 4[x] [Ps. 128:6; Prov. 10:27] 6[y] [Ps. 118:23] [z] See Gen. 18:14 7[a] ch. 10:6 [b] Ps. 107:3; Isa. 43:5; [Isa. 49:12; Ezek. 37:21] 8[c] ch. 13:9; See Jer. 31:33 [d] Jer. 4:2 9[e] 2 Sam. 16:21; [Hag. 2:4] [f] ch. 7:3; Ezra 5:1, 2 [g] Hag. 2:18 10[h] [Hag. 1:6] 12[i] Hos. 2:21, 22; Hag. 2:19 [j] [Hag. 1:10] [k] See Jer. 3:18 13[l] [Isa. 43:28; 65:15]

been a byword of cursing among the nations,
O house of Judah and house of Israel, [m]so will
I save you, and [n]you shall be a blessing. [o]Fear
not, but [e]let your hands be strong."
14 For thus says the LORD of hosts: [p]"As I
purposed to bring disaster to you when your
fathers provoked me to wrath, and I did not
relent, says the LORD of hosts, 15 so again have
I purposed in these days to bring good to
Jerusalem and to the house of Judah; [o]fear
not. 16 These are the things that you shall do:
[q]Speak the truth to one another; [r]render in
your gates judgments [s]that are true and make
for peace; 17 [t]do not devise evil in your hearts
against one another, and [u]love no false oath,
for all these things I hate, declares the LORD."
18 And the word of the LORD of hosts came
to me, saying, 19 "Thus says the LORD of hosts:
The fast of the [v]fourth month and the fast of
the [w]fifth and the fast of the [x]seventh and the
fast of the [y]tenth shall be to the house of Judah
[z]seasons of joy and gladness and cheerful
feasts. Therefore love [a]truth and peace.
20 "Thus says the LORD of hosts: Peoples shall
yet come, even the inhabitants of many cities. 21 The inhabitants of one city shall go to
another, saying, [b]'Let us go at once [c]to entreat
the favor of the LORD and to seek the LORD of
hosts; I myself am going.' 22 [b]Many peoples and
strong nations shall come to seek the LORD of
hosts in Jerusalem and [c]to entreat the favor
of the LORD. 23 Thus says the LORD of hosts:
In those days [d]ten men [e]from the nations of
every tongue shall take hold of the robe of a
Jew, saying, 'Let us go with you, for [f]we have
heard that God is with you.' "

Judgment on Israel's Enemies

9 The oracle of the word of the LORD is
against the land of Hadrach
and [g]Damascus is its resting place.
For the LORD has an eye on mankind
and on all the tribes of Israel,[1]
2 [h]and on Hamath also, which borders on it,
[i]Tyre and [i]Sidon, though [j]they are very
wise.
3 Tyre has built herself [k]a rampart
and [l]heaped up silver like dust,
and fine gold like the mud of the
streets.
4 But behold, the Lord will strip her of her
possessions
and strike down [m]her power on the
sea,
and [n]she shall be devoured by fire.

5 [o]Ashkelon shall see it, and be afraid;
Gaza too, and shall writhe in anguish;
Ekron also, because its hopes are confounded.
The king shall perish from Gaza;
Ashkelon shall be uninhabited;
6 [p]a mixed people[2] shall dwell in Ashdod,
and I will cut off the pride of Philistia.
7 I will take away [q]its blood from its
mouth,
and [r]its abominations from between
its teeth;
[s]it too shall be a remnant for our God;
it shall be like [t]a clan in Judah,
and Ekron shall be like the Jebusites.
8 Then [u]I will encamp at my house as a
guard,
[v]so that none shall march to and fro;

[1] Or *For the eye of mankind, especially of all the tribes of Israel, is toward the* LORD [2] Or *a foreign people*; Hebrew *a bastard*

Most fundamentally, however, the curse of sin is trumped by God's electing grace through Christ's perfect covenant keeping in our place. Nothing can prevent God's purpose for his chosen ones from triumphing (Rom. 8:37). God will bring to completion his sanctifying work in our hearts and the hearts of all of his people, so that our fasting will be turned into feasting at the marriage supper of the Lamb (Rev. 19:9). The peace and promises God provides for those who deny themselves in pursuit of his purposes will ultimately be a cause of others longing to know the God of Israel (Zech. 8:23).

9:1–17 The coming King is humble and righteous, bringing salvation to his people and breaking the battle bow of his enemies (v. 9). This passage forms the backdrop to Jesus' triumphal entry into Jerusalem. The crowds saw the coming King and thought there would be a straightforward road to victory. Yet the night before he died, Jesus said, "This is my blood of the covenant, which is poured out for many for the forgiveness of sins" (Matt. 26:28). His shed blood would bring us peace. The righteous King had to die in place of his unrighteous followers.

13 [m]ch. 10:6 [n]See Gen. 12:2, 3 [o]Hag. 2:5 [e][See ver. 9 above]
14 [p][Jer. 31:28; 32:42]
15 [o][See ver. 13 above]
16 [q]Cited Eph. 4:25; See Ps. 15:2 [r]See ch. 7:9 [s]ver. 19
17 [t]ch. 7:10 [u]See ch. 5:4
19 [v][Jer. 39:2] [w]ch. 7:3 [x]ch. 7:5 [y]2 Kgs. 25:1 [z]Isa. 35:10 [a]ver. 16
21 [b][ch. 2:11; 14:16; Isa. 2:3] [c]See ch. 7:2
22 [b][See ver. 21 above] [c][See ver. 21 above]
23 [d]See Gen. 31:7 [e][Isa. 66:18; Rev. 5:9] [f][1 Cor. 14:25]

Chapter 9
1 [g]See Isa. 17:1
2 [h]Jer. 49:23; See 1 Kgs. 8:65 [i]Josh. 19:28, 29; Isa. 23:1, 2 [j]See Ezek. 28:3-5
3 [k][Josh. 19:29] [l]Ezek. 28:4, 5

4 [m]Ezek. 26:17 [n]Ezek. 28:18 **5** [o]See Zeph. 2:4 **6** [p][Deut. 23:2] **7** [q]See Lev. 3:17 [r][Isa. 66:17] [s][Isa. 14:1] [t]ch. 12:5, 6 **8** [u][ch. 2:5] [v]ch. 7:14

[w]no oppressor shall again march over
them,
[x]for now I see with my own eyes.

The Coming King of Zion

9 [y]Rejoice greatly, O daughter of Zion!
Shout aloud, O daughter of Jerusalem!
[z]Behold, [a]your king is coming to you;
righteous and having salvation is he,
[b]humble and mounted on a donkey,
on a colt, the foal of a donkey.
10 [c]I will cut off the chariot from Ephraim
and [d]the war horse from Jerusalem;
and the battle bow shall be cut off,
and [e]he shall speak peace to the
nations;
[f]his rule shall be from sea to sea,
and from [g]the River to the ends of the
earth.
11 As for you also, because of [h]the blood of
my covenant with you,
[i]I will set your prisoners free from [j]the
waterless pit.
12 Return to your stronghold, O [k]prisoners
of hope;
today I declare that [l]I will restore to
you double.
13 For [m]I have bent Judah as my bow;
I have made Ephraim its arrow.
I will stir up your sons, O Zion,
against your sons, [n]O Greece,
and wield you like a warrior's sword.

The LORD Will Save His People

14 Then the LORD will appear over them,
and [o]his arrow will go forth like lightning;
[p]the Lord GOD will sound the trumpet
and will march forth in [q]the whirlwinds [r]of the south.
15 The LORD of hosts [s]will protect them,
and [t]they shall devour, [u]and tread
down the sling stones,
and [v]they shall drink and roar as if
drunk with wine,
and be full like a bowl,
drenched [w]like the corners of the
altar.
16 On that day the LORD their God will
save them,
as [x]the flock of his people;
for [y]like the jewels of a crown
they shall shine on his land.
17 [z]For how great is his goodness, and how
great his beauty!
[a]Grain shall make the young men
flourish,
and new wine the young women.

The Restoration for Judah and Israel

10 Ask rain [b]from the LORD
in the season of [c]the spring rain,
from the LORD [d]who makes the storm
clouds,
and [e]he will give them showers of
rain,
to everyone the vegetation in the
field.
2 For [f]the household gods [g]utter nonsense,
and the diviners see lies;
[h]they tell false dreams
and give empty consolation.

8[w]ch. 10:4; [Isa. 60:17] [x][ch. 12:4]
9[y]See Zeph. 3:14 [z]Cited Matt. 21:5; [John 12:15] [a]See Jer. 23:5 [b][Matt. 11:29]
10[c]See Hos. 1:7 [d]See Mic. 5:10 [e]See Mic. 5:5 [f]Ps. 72:8 [g]See Ex. 23:31
11[h]Ex. 24:8 [i]Isa. 42:7; 51:14; 61:1 [j][Gen. 37:24; Jer. 38:6]
12[k][Jer. 31:17] [l]Isa. 61:7
13[m][ch. 10:3, 4] [n]Gen. 10:2; Ezek. 27:13
14[o]See 2 Sam. 22:15 [p][Isa. 27:13] [q]Isa. 21:1 [r][ch. 6:6]
15[s]ch. 12:8; [ch. 10:5] [t]ch. 12:6 [u][ch. 10:5] [v]ch. 10:7 [w][Lev. 4:18, 25]
16[x]Ps. 100:3 [y]Isa. 62:3; [Mal. 3:17]
17[z][Isa. 62:3, 4] [a][Isa. 62:8, 9; Jer. 31:12]
Chapter 10
1[b]Jer. 14:22 [c]See Deut. 11:14 [d]Ps. 135:7 [e]Ezek. 34:26
2[f]See Gen. 31:19 [g]Hab. 2:18 [h]Jer. 23:25

The same King will return, not seated on a donkey but riding a war horse (Rev. 19:11–16). He will come to smash his enemies once for all—including the last enemy, death itself—and to set all of his people free. Meanwhile, as we experience a world of hostile foes and waterless pits (Zech. 9:10–11), we are called to wait with hope, confident that our King will return victoriously to bring about our full salvation.

10:1–12 Rain was the most basic (and unpredictable) necessity for life in Judah, so the God (or gods) from whom the people sought rain was a key indicator of their spiritual health (v. 1). For us, there are many things we view as essential to our lives, such as a fulfilling career or a loving relationship. Are we willing to entrust the most precious aspects of our lives to the Lord, and wait patiently for him to provide them, or do we turn to the idols of our own wiles, works, and superstitions?

The Lord would judge the false shepherds and provide the flock with the godly leaders they needed. Yet even these either failed or died eventually. None of them lasted. Jesus Christ is the Good Shepherd appointed by the Father to take care of his flock (John 10). He is the true cornerstone upon which his church is built (Acts 4:11; Eph. 2:20). God also gives pastors and teachers to shepherd his flock, under Christ (Eph. 4:11–13; 1 Pet. 5:1–4). In Jesus Christ we have been blessed with every spiritual

Therefore [i]the people wander like sheep;
they are afflicted for lack of a shepherd.
3 [j]"My anger is hot against the shepherds,
and [k]I will punish the leaders;[1]
for [l]the LORD of hosts cares for his flock,
the house of Judah,
and will make them like his majestic steed in battle.
4 From him shall come [m]the cornerstone,
from him [n]the tent peg,
from him the battle bow,
from him every ruler—[o]all of them together.
5 They shall be like mighty men in battle,
[p]trampling the foe in the mud of the streets;
they shall fight because the LORD is with them,
and they shall put to shame [q]the riders on horses.
6 [r]"I will strengthen the house of Judah,
and [s]I will save the house of Joseph.
[t]I will bring them back [u]because I have compassion on them,
and they shall be as though I had not rejected them,
for [v]I am the LORD their God and I will answer them.
7 Then Ephraim shall become like a mighty warrior,
and [w]their hearts shall be glad as with wine.
Their children shall see it and be glad;
their hearts shall rejoice in the LORD.
8 [x]"I will whistle for them and [y]gather them in,
for I have redeemed them,
and [z]they shall be as many as they were before.
9 [a]Though I scattered them among the nations,
yet in far countries [b]they shall remember me,
and with their children they shall live and return.
10 [c]I will bring them home from the land of Egypt,
and gather them from Assyria,
and [d]I will bring them to the land of Gilead and to Lebanon,
[e]till there is no room for them.
11 [f]He shall pass through the sea of troubles
and strike down the waves of the sea,
[g]and all the depths of the Nile shall be dried up.
The pride of Assyria shall be laid low,
and [h]the scepter of Egypt shall depart.
12 [i]I will make them strong in the LORD,
and [j]they shall walk in his name,"
declares the LORD.

The Flock Doomed to Slaughter

11 Open your doors, [k]O Lebanon,
that the fire may devour your cedars!
2 Wail, O cypress, for the cedar has fallen,
for the glorious trees are ruined!
Wail, [k]oaks of Bashan,
for the thick forest has been felled!
3 The sound of [l]the wail of [l]the shepherds,
for their glory is ruined!

[1] Hebrew *the male goats*

blessing (Eph. 1:3). One day he will bring us home (Zech. 10:10). Why should we feel the need to seek anything we need from any other source?

11:1–17 By raising up Zerubbabel, the Lord gave his people a fresh start under a shepherd who cared for their welfare. The people apparently rejected Zerubbabel, however, a choice that would have dire consequences. Jesus likewise came to earth to shepherd a flock otherwise destined to destruction. His own flock, the Jews, refused to receive him (John 1:11). His disciples abandoned him and fled, while Judas betrayed him for thirty pieces of silver (Matt. 26:14). When Judas later took his wages and tried to return them to the religious authorities, they used the money to buy a piece of ground known as "the potter's field" in which to bury foreigners (Matt. 27:9–10; cf. Zech. 11:12–13).

As the Good Shepherd, Jesus now unites Jews, Samaritans, and Gentiles into his new flock through his own death for the sheep. Yet those who reject Jesus, whether Jews or Gentiles, will hear God say, "I will not be your shepherd" (11:9). Such a rejection of the Messiah by the Jews of Jesus' day led to the destruction of Jerusalem in A.D. 70 by the Romans. Yet the Lord will not abandon his promise to have a flock of his own.

2 [i]Ezek. 34:5, 6
3 [j][Ezek. 34:10] [k][Ezek. 34:17] [l]Zeph. 2:7
4 [m][Ps. 118:22] [n]Isa. 22:23 [o][ch. 9:8]
5 [p][ch. 9:15] [q][Ps. 20:7]
6 [r][ver. 12] [s]ch. 8:7, 13 [t][Jer. 3:18] [u]Isa. 14:1 [v]ch. 13:9
7 [w]ch. 9:15
8 [x]Isa. 5:26 [y]Jer. 31:10, 11; See Hos. 1:11 [z]Ezek. 36:10, 11, 37
9 [a][Hos. 2:23] [b]Ezek. 6:9; See Deut. 30:1-3
10 [c]Isa. 11:11; 27:13; Hos. 11:11 [d][Mic. 7:14] [e]Isa. 49:20
11 [f]Isa. 11:15 [g][Amos 8:8] [h]Ezek. 30:13
12 [i][ver. 6] [j]Mic. 4:5
Chapter 11
1 [k][Isa. 2:12, 13]
2 [k][See ver. 1 above]
3 [l]Jer. 25:34

The sound of the roar of [m]the lions,
  [n]for the thicket of the Jordan is ruined!

4 Thus said the LORD my God: [o]"Become shepherd of the flock doomed to slaughter. 5 [p]Those who buy them slaughter them and go unpunished, and those who sell them say, 'Blessed be the LORD, [q]I have become rich,' and their own shepherds have no pity on them. 6 For [r]I will no longer have pity on the inhabitants of this land, declares the LORD. Behold, I will cause each of them to fall into the hand of his neighbor, and each into the hand of his king, and they shall crush the land, and I will deliver none from their hand."

7 [s]So I became the shepherd of the flock doomed to be slaughtered by the sheep traders. And I took two staffs, one I named [u]Favor, the other I named [v]Union. [s]And I tended the sheep. 8 In one month [w]I destroyed the three shepherds. But I became impatient with them, and they also detested me. 9 So I said, "I will not be your shepherd. [x]What is to die, let it die. What is to be destroyed, let it be destroyed. And let those who are left devour the flesh of one another." 10 And I took [y]my staff Favor, and I broke it, annulling the covenant that I had made with all the peoples. 11 So it was annulled on that day, and the sheep traders, who were watching me, knew that it was the word of the LORD. 12 Then I said to them, "If it seems good to you, give me my wages; but if not, keep them." And they weighed out as my wages [z]thirty pieces of silver. 13 Then the LORD said to me, "Throw it to the potter"—[a]the lordly price at which I was priced by them. So I took the [z]thirty pieces of silver and threw them into the house of the LORD, to the potter. 14 Then I broke [b]my second staff Union, annulling the brotherhood between Judah and Israel.

15 Then the LORD said to me, "Take once more the equipment of [c]a foolish shepherd. 16 For behold, I am raising up in the land a shepherd [d]who does not care for those being destroyed, or seek the young or heal the maimed or nourish the healthy, but [e]devours the flesh of the fat ones, tearing off even their hoofs.

17 [f]"Woe to my worthless shepherd,
  [g]who deserts the flock!
May the sword strike his arm
  and [h]his right eye!
Let his arm be wholly withered,
  his right eye utterly blinded!"

The LORD Will Give Salvation

12 [i]The oracle of the word of the LORD concerning Israel: Thus declares the LORD, [j]who stretched out the heavens and [k]founded the earth and [l]formed the spirit of man within him: 2 "Behold, I am about to make Jerusalem [l]a cup of staggering to [m]all the surrounding peoples. The siege of Jerusalem [n]will also be against Judah. 3 [o]On that day I will make Jerusalem a heavy stone for all the peoples. [p]All who lift it will surely hurt themselves. And [m]all the nations of the earth will gather against it. 4 [o]On that day, declares the LORD, [q]I will strike every horse [r]with panic, and its rider [r]with madness. But for the sake of the house of Judah I will keep my eyes open, when I strike every horse of the peoples [r]with blindness. 5 Then the clans of Judah shall say to themselves, 'The inhabitants of Jerusalem have strength through the LORD of hosts, their God.'

6 [o]"On that day I will make the clans of Judah

3[m] See Ezek. 19:1-3 [n][Jer. 12:5]
4[o][ver. 7]
5[p] Ezek. 34:3 [q] Hos. 12:8
6[r] Jer. 13:14
7[s][ver. 4] [u] ver. 10 [v] ver. 14
8[w][ver. 3, 16; ch. 10:3; Jer. 22:11, 18, 24]
9[x] Jer. 15:2
10[y] ver. 7
12[z][Ex. 21:32; Matt. 26:15]
13[a][Matt. 27:9, 10] [z][See ver. 12 above]
14[b] ver. 7
15[c] See 2 Kgs. 24:18-20
16[d][Ezek. 34:4; John 10:13] [e] Ezek. 34:3
17[f] Jer. 23:1 [g] John 10:12 [h][2 Kgs. 25:7]
Chapter 12
1[i] See Nah. 1:1 [j] See Isa. 42:5 [k] Isa. 48:13 **2**[l] Isa. 51:17, 22, 23 [m][ch. 14:2] [n][ch. 14:14] **3**[o] ch. 13:1, 2, 4; 14:4, 6, 8; Isa. 2:11 [p][Matt. 21:44; Luke 20:18] [m][See ver. 2 above] **4**[o][See ver. 3 above] [q][Ps. 76:6] [r][Deut. 28:28] **6**[o][See ver. 3 above]

12:1–9 God's purpose for Israel was that they would be a blessing to the nations (Gen. 12:1–3). Yet the Abrahamic covenant also warned that if the nations attacked his people, these nations would find themselves under the Lord's curse. The Lord is able to defend his people against all threats.

This message is relevant for God's people in all times and ages, even though the earthly city of Jerusalem is no longer the center of our hope. God no longer dwells in a particular location in the Middle East; now he dwells by his Spirit in the midst of his people, wherever they gather for worship (Matt. 18:20). The promises made to Jerusalem and Judah have continuing significance for us as Christians because trials and tribulations are a universal part of our experience (Acts 14:22). No matter how intense our trials, they should not cause us to despair, for the Lord is committed to deliver his people and judge our enemies. However weak we are in ourselves, the Lord is able to strengthen us to stand, giving us a glory far beyond anything that comes from ourselves (2 Corinthians 4).

[s]like a blazing pot in the midst of wood, like a
flaming torch among sheaves. And [t]they shall
devour to the right and to the left all the surrounding peoples, while [u]Jerusalem shall
again be inhabited in its place, in Jerusalem.
7 "And the LORD will give salvation to the
tents of Judah first, that the glory of the house
of David and the glory of the inhabitants of
Jerusalem may not surpass that of Judah. 8 [o]On
that day [v]the LORD will protect the inhabitants
of Jerusalem, so that [w]the feeblest among them
on that day shall be like David, and the house
of David shall be like God, [x]like the angel of
the LORD, going before them. 9 [o]And on that
day [y]I will seek to destroy all the nations that
come against Jerusalem.

Him Whom They Have Pierced

10 "And [z]I will pour out on the house of David
and the inhabitants of Jerusalem a spirit of
grace and [z]pleas for mercy, so that, [a]when they
look on me, on him whom they have pierced,
[b]they shall mourn for him, [c]as one mourns for
an only child, and weep bitterly over him, as
one weeps over a firstborn. 11 [o]On that day [d]the
mourning in Jerusalem will be as great [e]as the
mourning for Hadad-rimmon in the plain of
Megiddo. 12 The land shall mourn, [f]each family[1] by itself: the family of the house of David
by itself, and their wives by themselves; the
family of the house of [g]Nathan by itself, and
their wives by themselves; 13 the family of the
house of Levi by itself, and their wives by
themselves; the family of [h]the Shimeites by
itself, and their wives by themselves; 14 and
all the families that are left, each by itself, and
their wives by themselves.

13 [i]"On that day there shall be [j]a fountain
opened for the house of David and the
inhabitants of Jerusalem, to cleanse them
from sin and uncleanness.

Idolatry Cut Off

2 "And [i]on that day, declares the LORD of
hosts, [k]I will cut off the names of the idols from
the land, so that [l]they shall be remembered no
more. And also [m]I will remove from the land
the prophets and the spirit of uncleanness.
3 And if anyone again prophesies, his father
and mother who bore him will say to him,
[n]'You shall not live, for you speak lies in the
name of the LORD.' And his father and mother
who bore him shall pierce him through when
he prophesies.
4 "On that day [o]every prophet will be
ashamed of his vision when he prophesies.
He will not put on a hairy cloak in order to
deceive, 5 but he will say, [p]'I am no prophet,
I am a worker of the soil, for a man sold me
in my youth.'[2] 6 And if one asks him, 'What are
these wounds on your back?'[3] he will say, 'The
wounds I received in the house of my friends.'

The Shepherd Struck

7 "Awake, O sword, against [q]my shepherd,
against the man who stands next to
me,"
declares the LORD of hosts.

[1] Or *clan*; also verses 13, 14 [2] Or *for the land has been my possession since my youth* [3] Or *on your chest*; Hebrew *wounds between your hands*

12:10–13:9 Mourning for sin comes through a pouring out of God's grace and spirit (12:10). Repentance is a gift from God, worked by his Spirit, not an attitude that we drum up. Our sins have pierced the Lord not just metaphorically but literally, as our sin was paid for at the cross. That reality should make us weep over our personal sin, as well as the sins of others in our community. Yet the cross denotes not merely the sad reality of what we have done to God but also the triumphant reality of what he has done for us. At the cross, my sins pierced Christ, but the blood which flowed from his wounds forms a cleansing fountain that washes away all of my transgressions (13:1). As we confess our sins in true repentance, the blood of Christ purifies us from all our unrighteousness (1 John 1:9). For that reason, when we fix our eyes on the cross, we not only mourn for our sins, but we also glory in the grace of God that saved us and which will ultimately renew all creation.

The Good Shepherd that the Lord provided would be struck down (Zech. 13:7), resulting in difficult times of testing and purification for the flock. This prophecy is fulfilled in the death of Christ and the scattering of the disciples that followed (Matt. 26:31). The Christian life is a constant experience of trials and difficulties, yet these afflictions are God's means of refining his people and setting our hearts firmly on our heavenly home. And through it all, we know that our trials are not to punish us in anger but to train us in love. For Jesus was punished on our behalf, so that every trial can only be from a heavenly Father (not a detached Judge), for our good.

6[s] [Jer. 5:14; Obad. 18] [t] ch. 9:15 [u] ch. 2:4; 14:10, 11
8[o] [See ver. 3 above] [v] ch. 9:15 [w] [Isa. 60:22] [x] [1 Sam. 29:9; 2 Sam. 14:17, 20; 19:27]
9[o] [See ver. 3 above] [y] [ch. 14:3]
10[z] [Jer. 31:9] [a] Cited John 19:37; [Rev. 1:7] [b] Jer. 50:4 [c] Jer. 6:26; Amos 8:10
11[o] [See ver. 3 above] [d] [Acts 2:37] [e] [2 Chr. 35:24]
12[f] [ch. 7:3] [g] 2 Sam. 5:14; Luke 3:31
13[h] Num. 3:18
Chapter 13
1[i] See ch. 12:3 [j] [Ezek. 36:25]
2[i] [See ver. 1 above] [k] Mic. 5:13; [Jer. 10:11; Ezek. 30:13] [l] Ex. 23:13 [m] [ch. 10:2]
3[n] See Deut. 13:1-11
4[o] [Mic. 3:7]
5[p] Amos 7:14
7[q] [Isa. 40:11; Heb. 13:20]

[r]“Strike the shepherd, and the sheep will
be scattered;
I will turn my hand against the little
ones.
8 In the whole land, declares the LORD,
two thirds shall be cut off and perish,
[s]and one third shall be left alive.
9 And [t]I will put this third into the fire,
and refine them as one refines silver,
and test them as gold is tested.
[u]They will call upon my name,
and [v]I will answer them.
[w]I will say, ‘They are my people’;
and they will say, ‘The LORD is my
God.’ ”

The Coming Day of the LORD

14 Behold, [x]a day is coming for the LORD,
when the spoil taken from you will
be divided in your midst. 2 For [y]I will gather
all the nations against Jerusalem to battle,
and [z]the city shall be taken [a]and the houses
plundered [b]and the women raped. [c]Half of
the city shall go out into exile, but the rest
of the people shall not be cut off from the city.
3 [d]Then the LORD will go out and fight against
those nations as when he fights on a day of
battle. 4 [e]On that day his feet shall stand [f]on
[g]the Mount of Olives that lies before Jerusalem
on the east, and [g]the Mount of Olives shall
be split in two from east to west by [h]a very
wide valley, so that one half of the Mount
shall move northward, and the other half
southward. 5 And you shall flee to the valley
of my mountains, for the valley of the mountains shall reach to Azal. And you shall flee
as you fled from [i]the earthquake in the days
of Uzziah king of Judah. Then the LORD my
God will come, and all the holy ones with him.
6 [e]On that day [j]there shall be [j]no light, cold,
or frost.[1] 7 [k]And there shall be a unique[2] day,
[l]which is known to the LORD, neither day
nor night, but [m]at evening time there shall
be light.
8 [e]On that day [n]living waters shall flow out
from Jerusalem, half of them to [o]the eastern
sea[3] and half of them to [o]the western sea.[4] [p]It
shall continue in summer as in winter.
9 And [q]the LORD will be king over all the
earth. [r]On that day the LORD will be [s]one and
[t]his name one.
10 [u]The whole land shall be turned into
a plain from [v]Geba to [w]Rimmon south of
Jerusalem. But [x]Jerusalem shall remain aloft
[y]on its site from [z]the Gate of Benjamin to the
place of the former gate, to [a]the Corner Gate,
and from [b]the Tower of Hananel to the king’s
winepresses. 11 And it shall be inhabited, for
[c]there shall never again be a decree of utter
destruction.[5] [d]Jerusalem shall dwell in security.
12 And this shall be [e]the plague with which
the LORD will strike all the peoples that wage
war against Jerusalem: their flesh will rot
while they are still standing on their feet, their
eyes will rot in their sockets, and their tongues
will rot in their mouths.
13 And [f]on that day a great panic from the
LORD shall fall on them, so that [g]each will

[1] Compare Septuagint, Syriac, Vulgate, Targum; the meaning of the Hebrew is uncertain [2] Hebrew *one* [3] That is, the Dead Sea [4] That is, the Mediterranean Sea [5] The Hebrew term rendered *decree of utter destruction* refers to things devoted (or set apart) to the Lord (or by the Lord) for destruction

7[r] [Matt. 26:31; Mark 14:27]
8[s] [ch. 14:2]
9[t] Ps. 66:10, 12; Isa. 48:10; Mal. 3:2, 3; 1 Pet. 1:7 [u] [Ps. 50:15] [v] ch. 10:6 [w] ch. 8:8; See Ezek. 11:20
Chapter 14
1[x] See Joel 1:15
2[y] Joel 3:2 [z] [Luke 21:24] [a] Isa. 13:16 [b] Lam. 5:11 [c] ch. 13:8; [Matt. 24:40, 41]
3[d] [ch. 12:9]
4[e] [ver. 1]; See ch. 12:3 [f] [Ezek. 11:23] [g] 2 Sam. 15:30 [h] [ver. 10]
5[i] Amos 1:1
6[e] [See ver. 4 above] [j] [Isa. 60:19; Rev. 21:23]
7[k] Rev. 21:25 [l] Matt. 24:36 [m] [Isa. 30:26]
8[e] [See ver. 4 above] [n] John 4:10; Rev. 22:1; [Isa. 33:21; Ezek. 47:1; Joel 3:18] [o] Joel 2:20 [p] [Isa. 33:16]

14:1–21 The prophet warns people already struggling to remain faithful in difficult circumstances that there were far greater trials yet to come. And yet, even trials as horrific as those he describes in this chapter cannot destroy the Lord’s people, for God will certainly deliver them in the end. The persecutors of God’s people are more to be pitied than the martyrs whom they slaughter, for they will be victims of divine judgment of truly terrible proportions. On the last day, every knee will bow before the Lord and his Anointed, either willingly or unwillingly. How much better to bow willingly, no matter the cost, than to be found holding out against the Lord when time finally runs out.

Meanwhile, all of life is raised to the level of the sacred for those who have been redeemed (vv. 20–21). We are all called to exhibit supreme holiness, as living stones in God’s temple and members of a holy priesthood (1 Pet. 2:5). As temples of the Holy Spirit, we are to be separate from all uncleanness so that we can be wholly devoted to God’s service (2 Cor. 6:16–7:1). None of our acts are trivial, and none of our duties secular: in light of God’s supreme love for us in the gospel, our whole lives are to be placed on the altar as living sacrifices, holy to the Lord (Rom. 12:1).

9[q] Ps. 47:7; [ver. 16, 17; Mal. 1:14] [r] [ver. 1]; See ch. 12:3 [s] Eph. 4:5, 6 [t] [ch. 13:2] 10[u] [ver. 4; Isa. 40:4] [v] Josh. 18:24 [w] Josh. 15:32 [x] Isa. 2:2 [y] ch. 12:6; [ch. 2:4] [z] See Jer. 37:13 [a] Jer. 31:38 [b] Neh. 3:1; Jer. 31:38 11[c] Rev. 22:3 [d] [Jer. 23:6] 12[e] [ver. 15, 18] 13[f] See ch. 12:3 [g] Hag. 2:22; [1 Sam. 14:20]

seize the hand of another, and the hand of
the one will be raised against the hand of the
other. [14] Even [h]Judah will fight at Jerusalem.
And [i]the wealth of all the surrounding nations
shall be collected, gold, silver, and garments
in great abundance. [15] And [j]a plague like this
plague shall fall on the horses, the mules, the
camels, the donkeys, and whatever beasts may
be in those camps.

[16] Then everyone who survives of all the
nations that have come against Jerusalem
[k]shall go up year after year to worship [l]the
King, the LORD of hosts, and [m]to keep [n]the
Feast of Booths. [17] And if [o]any of the families of
the earth do not go up to Jerusalem to worship
[l]the King, the LORD of hosts, [p]there will be
no rain on them. [18] And if the family of Egypt
does not go up and present themselves, then
on them there shall be no rain;[1] there shall be
[j]the plague with which the LORD afflicts the
nations that do not go up [m]to keep the Feast
of Booths. [19] This shall be the punishment to
Egypt and the punishment to all the nations
that do not go up [m]to keep the Feast of Booths.

[20] And [q]on that day there shall be inscribed
on the bells of the horses, [r]"Holy to the LORD."
And the pots in the house of the LORD shall be
as the bowls before the altar. [21] And every pot
in Jerusalem and Judah shall be [r]holy to the
LORD of hosts, so that all who sacrifice may
come and take of them and boil the meat
of the sacrifice in them. And [s]there shall no
longer be [t]a trader[2] in the house of the LORD
of hosts [q]on that day.

[1] Hebrew lacks *rain* [2] Or *Canaanite*

14[h] [ch. 12:2] [i] [Ezek. 39:10] **15**[j] [ver. 12] **16**[k] See ch. 8:21 [l] [ver. 9] [m] [Nah. 1:15]; See Lev. 23:34 [n] See Lev. 23:39-43 **17**[o] Isa. 60:12 [l] [See ver. 16 above] [p] See 1 Kgs. 17:1 **18**[j] [See ver. 15 above] [m] [See ver. 16 above] **19**[m] [See ver. 16 above] **20**[q] See ch. 12:3 [r] Ex. 28:36; Isa. 23:18; Mic. 4:13 **21**[r] [See ver. 20 above] [s] Ezek. 44:9; See Joel 3:17 [t] [Deut. 7:1, 2] [q] [See ver. 20 above]

Introduction to Malachi

Author and Date

The prophet Malachi (whose name means "my messenger") probably lived at the same time as Ezra and Nehemiah, around 460 B.C.

The Gospel in Malachi

The book of Malachi contains six oracles (or disputations) that each begin with a saying of the people, to which the Lord responds through his prophet. Most of these oracles are searching rebukes. It is striking, however, that before the Lord rebukes the people, he begins by affirming his electing love for them, which is the reason they continue to exist after the judgment of the exile (1:2). He didn't choose their forefather Jacob to be the ancestor of his people because of his good works but in spite of his sin. So too, their sin cannot make God cease loving them. The non-elect, however, will be judged for their sin without hope, as the fate of the descendants of Esau (Edom) makes clear.

We too were chosen to belong to God, not based on our works but simply out of God's electing grace in Christ (Eph. 1:4–6). We therefore cannot sin our way out of God's love. Yet at the same time, we were chosen to be holy and blameless (Eph. 1:4), not only positionally but also practically. So God rebukes our sin through his Word, and calls us to repent sincerely and turn to him for forgiveness.

And yet the ultimate remedy for our sin is not our repentant obedience, but the Lord's coming to his temple (Mal. 3:1). Our own righteousness cannot stand the exposure that that day will bring any more than dross could survive the refiner's fire or dirt could endure the launderer's soap (3:2). We need the righteousness of another, if we are going to stand on that day—which is precisely what God gives us in the gospel. As a result, the day of the Lord's coming for believers is not a fiery, destructive furnace that we need to fear but rather a warming sun of righteousness that rises on us for our healing (4:1–2). For in Jesus, God does come to his temple—not the temple building, but the temple of Christ's own body—which we are. There, humans can once more meet with God.

Outline

I. Title (1:1)

II. Disputation 1 (1:2–5)

III. Disputation 2 (1:6–2:9)

IV. Disputation 3 (2:10–16)

V. Disputation 4 (2:17–3:5)

VI. Disputation 5 (3:6–12)

VII. Disputation 6 (3:13–4:3)

VIII. Summary (4:4–6)

Malachi

1 The oracle of the word of the LORD to
Israel by Malachi.[1]

The LORD's Love for Israel

2 [a]"I have loved you," says the LORD. [b]But you
say, "How have you loved us?" "Is not Esau
[c]Jacob's brother?" declares the LORD. "Yet
[d]I have loved Jacob 3 but Esau I have hated.
[e]I have laid waste his hill country and left his
heritage to jackals of the desert." 4 If Edom
says, "We are shattered but we will rebuild
the ruins," the LORD of hosts says, "They may
build, but I will tear down, and they will be
called 'the wicked country,' and 'the people
with whom the LORD is angry forever.'" 5 [f]Your
own eyes shall see this, and you shall say, "Great
is the LORD beyond the border of Israel!"

The Priests' Polluted Offerings

6 [g]"A son honors his father, and a servant
his master. If then I am [h]a father, where is my
honor? And if I am [i]a master, where is my fear?
says the LORD of hosts to you, O priests, who
despise my name. [b]But you say, 'How have we
despised your name?' 7 [j]By offering polluted
food upon my altar. [b]But you say, 'How have
we polluted you?' By saying that [k]the LORD's
table may be despised. 8 [l]When you offer blind
animals in sacrifice, is that not evil? And when
you offer those that are lame or sick, is that
not evil? Present that to your governor; will he
accept you or show you favor? says the LORD
of hosts. 9 And now [m]entreat the favor of God,
that he may be gracious to us. With such a
gift from your hand, [n]will he show favor to

[1] *Malachi* means *my messenger*

1:1–5 God's grace is not based on our works but on his sovereign, predestining love, as demonstrated in his choice of Jacob over Esau (vv. 1–4). This explains God's continuing undeserved grace to Israel, while Edom was deservedly cut off for their sins. Initially, the assurance that this covenant love extends to Israel may seem good for Jews yet limiting for others, but Malachi hints at a grander consequence (vv. 5, 11). What is more, since God is sovereign in election, he can extend his mercy more expansively upon whomever he chooses, Jew or Gentile, as the apostle Paul will make plain using this same example (Rom. 9:1–24). God's faithful commitment to his people (from the ranks of both Jew and Gentile) is possible because the destruction that all his chosen ones deserve for their sins has been poured out on Christ. Ethnicity is not the issue; faith in Christ is the banner under which people can gather from all nations.

Malachi reaffirms God's love for his people, before he begins to condemn their sins and failures. When we forget God's love and faithfulness to us, we lose our motivation to obey him and may blame God's perceived unfaithfulness or unfairness for our sin.

1:6–14 Malachi shows how God's people can go through the motions of orthodox worship and yet be wasting their time and wearying the Lord (cf. 2:17) with insincerity and selfishness. The message remains the same for us: True worship comes as our hearts are stirred afresh by God's amazing grace in sending Christ to be the perfect worshiper in our place. He gave the perfect and undefiled offering for us, and his merit is now credited to us by faith.

The result of Jesus' offering is that God's own people are restored to worship, and true worship is extended around the world. Jesus came to be a light not just to Israel but to the Gentiles as well (Luke 2:32). Because of his ministry, the incense of believing prayers and the worship of devoted hearts is offered not just in Jerusalem but to the ends of the earth (Acts 1:8).

Chapter 1
2 [a]Deut. 7:8; Jer. 31:3 [b][ch. 2:14, 17; 3:7, 8, 13] [c][Amos 1:11; Obad. 10] [d]Cited Rom. 9:13
3 [e]Isa. 34:13; Jer. 49:10, 18; Ezek. 35:3, 4; Joel 3:19
5 [f]Ps. 91:8
6 [g]See Ex. 20:12 [h]Ex. 4:22; Hos. 11:1 [i][Luke 6:46] [b][See ver. 2 above]
7 [j][ver. 8; ch. 2:12; 3:3] [b][See ver. 2 above] [k][ver. 12]
8 [l][ver. 13]; See Lev. 22:22
9 [m]See Zech. 7:2 [n]See Deut. 10:17

any of you? says the LORD of hosts. 10 [o]Oh that
there were one among you who would shut
the doors, that you might not kindle fire on
my altar in vain! I have no pleasure in you,
says the LORD of hosts, [p]and I will not accept
an offering from your hand. 11 For from the
rising of the sun to its setting my name [q]will
be[1] great among the nations, and in every place
incense will be offered to my name, and a pure
offering. For my name [q]will be great among
the nations, says the LORD of hosts. 12 But you
profane it when you say that [r]the Lord's table is
polluted, and its fruit, that is, its food may be
despised. 13 But you say, [s]'What a weariness this
is,' and you snort at it, says the LORD of hosts.
[t]You bring what has been taken by violence
or is lame or sick, and this you bring as your
offering! Shall I accept that from your hand?
says the LORD. 14 Cursed be the cheat who has
[u]a male in his flock, and [v]vows it, and yet sacrifices to the Lord what is blemished. For [w]I am
a great King, says the LORD of hosts, and my
name [x]will be feared among the nations.

The LORD Rebukes the Priests

2 "And now, [y]O priests, [z]this command is for
you. 2 [a]If you will not listen, if you will not
take it to heart to give honor to my name, says
the LORD of hosts, then I will send [b]the curse
upon you and I will curse [c]your blessings.
Indeed, I have already cursed them, because
you do not lay it to heart. 3 Behold, [d]I will
rebuke your offspring,[2] and [e]spread dung on
your faces, the [f]dung of your offerings, and
you shall be taken away with it.[3] 4 So shall you
know that I have sent [g]this command to you,
that [h]my covenant with Levi may stand, says
the LORD of hosts. 5 My covenant with him was
one of life and [i]peace, and I gave them to him.
[j]It was a covenant of fear, and he feared me. He
stood in awe of my name. 6 [k]True instruction[4]
was in his mouth, and no wrong was found
on his lips. He walked with me in peace and
uprightness, and he [l]turned many from iniquity. 7 For [m]the lips of a priest should guard
knowledge, and people[5] should seek instruction from his mouth, for he is the messenger
of the LORD of hosts. 8 But you have turned
aside from the way. [n]You have caused many
to stumble by your instruction. You have corrupted [o]the covenant of Levi, says the LORD
of hosts, 9 and so [p]I make you despised and
abased before all the people, inasmuch as you
do not keep my ways but [q]show partiality in
your instruction."

Judah Profaned the Covenant

10 Have we not all [r]one Father? Has not [s]one
God created us? Why then are we [t]faithless to
one another, profaning the covenant of our

[1] Or *is* (three times in verse 11; also verse 14) [2] Hebrew *seed* [3] Or *to it* [4] Or *law*; also verses 7, 8, 9 [5] Hebrew *they*

10 [o][Isa. 1:13] [p][Isa. 1:11; Jer. 6:20; Amos 5:21]
11 [q][Isa. 2:2; 56:7; 60:3; 66:19]
12 [r][ver. 7]
13 [s]Isa. 43:23; [ch. 3:14; Mic. 6:3] [t][ver. 8; Lev. 22:20]
14 [u]See Ex. 12:5 [v][Lev. 22:21] [w]See Zech. 14:9 [x]Ps. 47:2; 76:12

Chapter 2
1 [y]ch. 1:6 [z]ver. 4
2 [a]Lev. 26:14; See Deut. 28:15 [b][ch. 3:9] [c][Ps. 69:22]
3 [d][Joel 1:17; Hag. 2:17] [e]Nah. 3:6 [f][Ex. 29:14]
4 [g]ver. 1 [h]ver. 8; Num. 25:12, 13; Neh. 13:29; [Num. 3:45]
5 [i]See Isa. 54:10 [j][Lev. 16:2]
6 [k][Deut. 33:10] [l][Dan. 12:3; James 5:20]
7 [m]Deut. 17:9; See Lev. 10:11
8 [n][1 Sam. 2:17; Jer. 18:15; Ezek. 22:26] [o]See ver. 4
9 [p][1 Sam. 2:30] [q]Deut. 1:17; 16:19
10 [r]1 Cor. 8:6; Eph. 4:6 [s]Acts 17:26 [t][Isa. 21:2; 24:16; 33:1]

2:1–9 The duty of priests was faithful performance of their duties in behalf of God's people and in honor of God. We are part of a new priesthood (1 Pet. 2:9), with a duty to declare God's word to our neighbors and the nations. If we fail to declare that message faithfully because we fear people more than we fear the living God, we are guilty of the same offense as the priests of Malachi's day.

Yet God is determined to maintain the covenant with Levi. God's desire to grant his people life and peace will not be frustrated by the failures of their earthly representatives. His people need a perfect priest who will offer right sacrifices on their behalf and teach them the law accurately and fairly. That is why Jesus had to come as our Great High Priest and just Lawgiver (Matthew 5). The work of the Levitical priesthood has come to an end because it has fulfilled its purpose of pointing us to, and preparing the way for, Christ (Heb. 7:11–28).

2:10–16 Marriage is a primary metaphor for the relationship between God and his people in the Old Testament (e.g., v. 11), and of Christ and his church in the New Testament (Eph. 5:22–33). Marriage is also, of course, the way holy seed is raised up, the next generation of faith. Marrying an unbeliever or divorcing your spouse without biblical grounds (Mal. 2:14–15; cf. Matt. 19:1–12 and 1 Cor. 7:1–40) is therefore an assault on the Lord's plan of redemption.

Yet while divorce under most circumstances is sin, it is not unforgivable. Our hope rests in God's faithfulness, which always trumps our unfaithfulness. Israel was an unfaithful wife, who regularly strayed from her covenant commitments. She deserved to be divorced and abandoned, yet God pursued his wandering bride and wooed her back to himself (see Hosea 1–3). Jesus himself is the great bridegroom who pursued his people at great personal cost (Eph. 5:25–26).

fathers? [11]Judah has been [t]faithless, and abomination has been committed in Israel and in
Jerusalem. For [u]Judah has profaned the sanctuary of the LORD, which he loves, and has
married the daughter of a foreign god. [12]May
the LORD cut off from the tents of Jacob any
descendant[1] of the man who does this, who
[v]brings an offering to the LORD of hosts!

[13]And this second thing you do. [w]You cover
the LORD's altar with tears, with weeping and
groaning because he no longer regards the
offering or accepts it with favor from your
hand. [14][x]But you say, "Why does he not?"
Because the LORD [y]was witness between you
and the wife of your youth, [z]to whom [t]you
have been faithless, though she is your companion and your wife by covenant. [15][a]Did he
not make them one, with a portion of the
Spirit in their union?[2] And what was the one
God[3] seeking?[4] [b]Godly offspring. So guard
yourselves[5] in your spirit, and let none of
you be [t]faithless to the wife of your youth.
[16]"For [c]the man who does not love his wife
but divorces her,[6] says the LORD, the God of
Israel, covers[7] his garment with violence, says
the LORD of hosts. So guard yourselves in your
spirit, and [t]do not be faithless."

The Messenger of the LORD

[17][d]You have wearied the LORD with your
words. [x]But you say, "How have we wearied
him?" [e]By saying, "Everyone who does evil is
good in the sight of the LORD, and he delights
in them." Or by asking, [f]"Where is the God of
justice?"

3 [g]"Behold, I send [h]my messenger, and [i]he
will prepare the way before me. And the
Lord [j]whom you seek will suddenly come to
his temple; and [k]the messenger of the covenant in whom you delight, behold, he is
coming, says the LORD of hosts. [2]But [l]who
can endure the day of his coming, and who
can stand when he appears? For [m]he is like
a refiner's fire and like fullers' soap. [3]He will
sit [n]as a refiner and purifier of silver, and he
will purify the sons of Levi and refine them
like gold and silver, and they will bring [o]offer-
ings in righteousness to the LORD.[8] [4][p]Then
the offering of Judah and Jerusalem will be
pleasing to the LORD as in the days of old and
as in former years.

[5]"Then I will draw near to you for judgment.
I will be [q]a swift witness against the sorcerers, against the adulterers, against those who
swear falsely, against those [r]who oppress the
hired worker in his wages, [s]the widow and
the fatherless, against those who thrust aside
the sojourner, and do not fear me, says the
LORD of hosts.

Robbing God

[6]"For [t]I the LORD do not change; [u]therefore
you, O children of Jacob, are not consumed.
[7][v]From the days of your fathers you have

[1] Hebrew *any who wakes and answers* [2] Hebrew *in it* [3] Hebrew *the one* [4] Or *And not one has done this who has a portion of the Spirit. And what was that one seeking?* [5] Or *So take care*; also verse 16 [6] Hebrew *who hates and divorces* [7] Probable meaning (compare Septuagint and Deuteronomy 24:1–4); or *"The LORD, the God of Israel, says that he hates divorce, and him who covers* [8] Or *and they will belong to the LORD, bringers of an offering in righteousness*

2:17–3:5 Why does God allow evildoers to prosper? Surely if God is just, he should intervene immediately and give them what they deserve. Yet the Lord warns us to be careful about seeking his intervention glibly (2:17). God's judgment is coming against all kinds of sin (3:5), yet who can endure the day of his coming (3:2)? Strict justice would condemn us all.

The good news comes from Jacob's personal experience with God (3:6). He couldn't have survived justice: it would have destroyed him. Instead, Jacob received God's grace because God had chosen him in the beginning (see 1:1–5). We too are fickle and unfaithful, undeserving of God's love. God remains faithful, however, because he cannot deny himself (2 Tim. 2:12–13). The refiner's fire purifies us because it first burned Jesus; the launderer's soap washes us clean because its painful sting was borne by Christ. Only when we understand that can we truly rejoice to see holy Jesus coming to take possession of his temple.

3:6–12 God promises to bless (as he knows is best) generous giving to his purposes, and also to bring consequences upon the miserly (vv. 8–12). As an annual obligation to give the Lord 10 percent of the produce of the land, the tithe belongs to the Sinai covenant. It teaches us general principles of giving, but the obligation is transformed in key ways with the coming of Christ. Christianity radicalizes the source of the tithe: now the whole of life, not just agricultural produce, is explicitly under the lordship of God. Christian giving should still be proportional (1 Cor. 16:2), willing, and generous

11[t] [See ver. 10 above] [u] See Ezra 9:2
12[v] [ch. 1:7]
13[w] [Zech. 7:3]
14[x] [ch. 1:2] [y] ch. 3:5 [z] [ver. 11; Isa. 54:6] [t] [See ver. 10 above]
15[a] Matt. 19:4, 5; See Gen. 2:24 [b] [Ezra 9:2] [t] [See ver. 10 above]
16[c] Matt. 5:32; Mark 10:9, 11; Luke 16:18; 1 Cor. 7:10 [t] [See ver. 10 above]
17[d] Isa. 43:24 [x] [See ver. 14 above] [e] [ch. 3:15; Isa. 5:20] [f] [ch. 3:1; 2 Pet. 3:4]

Chapter 3
1[g] Cited Matt. 11:10; Mark 1:2; Luke 7:27; [ch. 4:5; Luke 1:76] [h] See ch. 2:7 [i] See Isa. 40:3 [j] [ch. 2:17] [k] [ch. 4:5]
2[l] Joel 2:11 [m] Isa. 4:4
3[n] Isa. 1:25; Zech. 13:9 [o] [ch. 1:7]
4[p] Ezek. 20:40
5[q] ch. 2:14; Jer. 29:23 [r] See Lev. 19:13 [s] See Deut. 24:17
6[t] Ps. 102:27; See Num. 23:19 [u] Lam. 3:22
7[v] Acts 7:51

turned aside from my statutes and have not
kept them. [w]Return to me, and I will return
to you, says the LORD of hosts. [x]But you say,
'How shall we return?' 8 Will man rob God?
Yet you are robbing me. [x]But you say, 'How
have we robbed you?' [y]In your tithes and contributions. 9 [z]You are cursed with a curse, for
you are robbing me, the whole nation of you.
10 [a]Bring the full tithe into the storehouse, that
there may be food in my house. And thereby
[b]put me to the test, says the LORD of hosts, if
I will not open [c]the windows of heaven for you
and pour down for you a blessing until there
is no more need. 11 I will rebuke [d]the devourer[1]
for you, so that it will not destroy the fruits of
your soil, and your vine in the field shall not
fail to bear, says the LORD of hosts. 12 Then [e]all
nations will call you blessed, for you will be [f]a
land of delight, says the LORD of hosts.

13 [g]"Your words have been hard against me,
says the LORD. [h]But you say, 'How have we spoken against you?' 14 You have said, [i]'It is vain to
serve God. [j]What is the profit of our keeping
his charge or of walking as in mourning before
the LORD of hosts? 15 And now we call [k]the arrogant blessed. [k]Evildoers not only prosper but
[l]they put God to the test and they escape.'"

The Book of Remembrance

16 Then those who feared the LORD [m]spoke
with one another. The LORD paid attention
and heard them, and [n]a book of remembrance
was written before him of those who feared
the LORD and esteemed his name. 17 "They
shall be mine, says the LORD of hosts, [o]in the
day when I make up [p]my treasured possession,
and I will spare them as a man spares his son
who serves him. 18 Then once more you shall
[q]see the distinction between the righteous and
the wicked, between one who serves God and
one who does not serve him.

The Great Day of the LORD

4 [2] "For behold, [r]the day is coming, [s]burning
like an oven, when [t]all the arrogant and
[t]all evildoers [u]will be stubble. The day that is
coming [u]shall set them ablaze, says the LORD
of hosts, so that it will leave them neither root
nor branch. 2 But for you [v]who fear my name,
[w]the sun [x]of righteousness shall rise [y]with
healing in its wings. You shall go out [z]leap-
ing like calves from the stall. 3 And you shall
tread down the wicked, for they will be ashes
under the soles of your feet, [a]on the day when
I act, says the LORD of hosts.

[1] Probably a name for some crop-destroying pest or pests [2] Ch 4:1–6 is ch 3:19–24 in Hebrew

7 [w]See Zech. 1:3 [x][ch. 1:2]
8 [x][See ver. 7 above] [y][Neh. 13:10]
9 [z][ch. 2:2]
10 [a][Prov. 3:9, 10] [b]See 2 Cor. 9:6-8 [c]See Gen. 7:11
11 [d][Joel 1:4]
12 [e]Zeph. 3:19 [f][Isa. 62:4]
13 [g][ch. 2:17] [h][ch. 1:2]
14 [i][Zeph. 1:12] [j][Job 21:15]
15 [k][ch. 4:1] [l][Ps. 95:9]
16 [m][Deut. 6:6, 7] [n]See Ex. 32:32
17 [o][ch. 4:3; Acts 17:31] [p]Ex. 19:5; 1 Pet. 2:9
18 [q][ch. 4:1]

Chapter 4
1 [r][ver. 5; ch. 3:2] [s][2 Thess. 1:7, 8] [t]ch. 3:15 [u]Isa. 47:14; [Matt. 3:12; Luke 3:17]
2 [v]ch. 3:16 [w]Ps. 84:11; Luke 1:78; John 1:4; 8:12; 9:5; 12:46 [x][Jer. 23:6] [y]Isa. 53:5 [z][Jer. 50:11]
3 [a]See ch. 3:17

(2 Cor. 9:7). A particular proportion is not specified in the New Testament, but it would be strange to give less in the new age of the gospel, this side of Christ's coming.

Our giving is also a diagnostic window into how we view God. If we see God as the gracious giver of all good gifts, we will desire to excel in the "grace" of giving (cf. 2 Cor. 8:7). If we view him as a hard taskmaster whose service is a burden, however, it will be visible in our reluctant giving. The issue is our attitude, not the amount (Luke 24:1–4).

Through it all, we remember Jesus, who "though he was rich, yet for your sake he became poor, so that you by his poverty might become rich" (2 Cor. 8:9). We are cheerfully generous not in order to pay God back, but in light of his great and lavish generosity toward us. What else could we do?

3:13–4:6 Unbelievers think serving God is worthless. Believers may be tempted to think likewise because of the difficulty of their circumstances. Yet God views the two groups differently. Those who fear the Lord are his treasured possession (Ex. 19:6). Because the Lord knows them, their final destiny is peace. However, the destiny of the wicked is to be stubble for the fire. When God finally acts, the difference between the righteous and the wicked will be clear to all (Mal. 3:1–3).

Yet if we are all sinners, how is a different destiny for the righteous and the wicked possible? Echoing this prophecy from Malachi, the Lord sent John the Baptist as his prophet Elijah to call people to repentance in preparation for Christ's public ministry (Matt. 11:14). John was merely the forerunner: in Christ, the door is opened for all who repent to receive spiritual healing through his sufferings (Matt. 17:12). Jesus was burned in the oven of God's wrath for our iniquity. He was crushed underfoot for our restoration. He is the Son on whom the Father did not show compassion, even though he served him faithfully, so that we might receive adoption as God's sons through his blood. No one serves God and loses, just as no one ultimately tests God and escapes. Those who mock the gospel will go to utter destruction, but those who trust in the Lord receive eternal life and wholeness in Christ.

4 [b]"Remember [c]the law of my servant Moses,
the statutes and rules[1] that I commanded him
at Horeb for all Israel.
5 [d]"Behold, I will send you [e]Elijah the
prophet [f]before the great and awesome day
of the LORD comes. 6 And he will [g]turn the
hearts of fathers to their children and the
hearts of children to their fathers, lest I come
and [h]strike the land with a decree of utter
destruction."[2]

[1] Or *and just decrees* [2] The Hebrew term rendered *decree of utter destruction* refers to things devoted (or set apart) to the Lord (or by the Lord) for destruction

4 [b][Deut. 4:9, 10] [c]See Ex. 20:3-17; Deut. 4:10
5 [d][ch. 3:1] [e][Matt. 11:14; Mark 9:11; Luke 1:17] [f]Joel 2:31
6 [g][Luke 1:17] [h]Isa. 11:4; [Zech. 5:3]

The Old Testament closes, then, with a word of promise ringing in the minds of its readers concerning the two greatest prophets of old: Moses (Mal. 4:4) and Elijah (4:5). When God determined to show the significance of Jesus' earthly ministry, he had these two men appear on a mountain with our Savior in the transfiguration (Mark 9:4). Moses represented the Law and Elijah represented the Prophets. Their appearance in Christ's time indicated that he was the apex of their messages, fulfilling and transcending them both, as demonstrated by his resplendent radiance (Mark 9:3). He is the One whom the Law and the Prophets ultimately anticipated—as he said to his disciples, "everything written about me in the Law of Moses and the Prophets and the Psalms must be fulfilled" (Luke 24:44).

In Jesus the entire Bible clicks into place. The whole Bible is, at its heart, the word of God's grace that culminates in his Son (Rom. 1:1–2; 2 Tim. 3:15).

The New Testament

Introduction to Matthew

Author and Date

Matthew was probably written in the late 50s or early 60s A.D. The author is Matthew (also called Levi), the former tax collector who became Jesus' disciple.

The Gospel in Matthew

Matthew's Gospel is focused on explaining what the gospel is and how it should be applied in the lives of Jesus' disciples. For Matthew, the gospel is the good news that God has inaugurated the final stage of his plan to reclaim the world from the destruction of sin and establish his just and merciful reign over it (4:23; 9:35; 11:5). God has given the central role in this final stage of his work to Jesus, his long-awaited and specially designated King (2:2; 21:5; 25:34). Where Jesus is present in Matthew's Gospel, God and his kingdom are present (1:23; 12:28). The reign of God is evident when Jesus banishes demons; heals the sick, the lame, and the blind; and gathers together a group of people whose lives are to demonstrate God's just and merciful character (4:23; 5:16; 9:35; 11:4–5; 12:28).

All this is cause for celebration to those who know they need deliverance from sin—to the poor in spirit (5:3), the grieving (5:4), those who long to see justice done (5:6, 10–11), those who know they need forgiveness for their sins (6:12; 9:10–13; 11:19), and those laboring under the burden of religious rule-keeping (11:28–30). When Jesus, like his predecessor John the Baptist, preaches the need to turn from sin and follow Jesus in light of God's coming kingdom (3:1–17; 4:17), these people embrace this message of deliverance without hesitating (4:20, 22) and with joy (13:44).

Matthew also paints a sobering picture of those who reject Jesus and his message. Surprisingly, Jesus' most energetic opponents are religious leaders who value so highly the recognition that comes from their positions of leadership and their clever interpretations of Scripture (23:1–7; see also 6:2, 5, 16) that they have become blind to its more basic principles (23:23). They would rather talk about the fine points of blasphemy, Sabbath, and tithing law than show compassion to the needy (9:1–7; 12:1–14; 23:23). They would rather find subtle ways around the fundamental principles of God's law, such as honoring parents, than make the sacrifices necessary for keeping it (15:3–9). This radical contrast between the evil that is in their hearts and their outward piety and concern for God's law shows that they are moving toward eternal destruction (23:15, 33).

Even more disturbing, however, is Matthew's portrait of those who claim to be followers of Jesus but whose claims will be found empty on the day of judgment. Like Jesus' real disciples they will have done much in his name, but Jesus will order them to depart from him because they were lawless (7:21–23; 22:11–14; 25:11–12) and because they neglected his disciples who needed food, clothing, medical attention, and support while in prison (25:41–46).

This does not mean that Matthew sees good works as the basis for entering God's kingdom. Instead, the condition of the heart will determine who enters God's kingdom on the day of judgment, and one's deeds will be the outward manifestation of that condition. The healthy tree bears good fruit and the diseased tree bears bad fruit (7:17–20; 12:33–37). The condition of the heart defiles a person, says Jesus, and the heart's condition is revealed in the evil thoughts, words, and actions that come out of it (15:10–20). This is why Jesus can say that, on the day of judgment, people will be either justified or condemned by their words: these words reveal their heart condition (12:36–37).

How can one's heart be in the right condition? Those for whom following Jesus is more important than anything else in life can be sure they are on the road to eternal life (16:24–27). This is what Jesus means when he insists on perfection from his disciples (5:48; 19:21). They certainly are not capable of being morally perfect in this life. Indeed, Jesus has deep compassion for sinners who need his forgiveness (9:9–13; 11:19). He demonstrates this in the restoration of his disciples after their miserable failure during his arrest and execution (28:7, 10, 18–20). As a consequence, Jesus' disciples become perfect in the sense that their desires and affections belong to him. They recognize that they must entirely depend upon him to provide what they most need—him. Like the merchant in the parable (13:45–46), they have found the one person who gives value to life, and they have put everything they have at his disposal (see also 4:20, 22; 13:44; 16:24–26; 19:21–22, 27–30; 26:6–13). Certainly they will fail, but, unlike Judas, recognition of their failure will send them to Jesus, who blesses the poor in spirit, promises rest to the weary, and gave his own life so that their sins might be forgiven (5:3; 11:28; 26:28).

Outline

I. The Arrival of Jesus the Messiah (1:1–2:23)

II. John the Baptist Prepares for the Messianic Kingdom (3:1–17)

III. Jesus the Messiah Begins to Advance the Messianic Kingdom (4:1–25)

IV. The Authoritative Message of the Messiah: Kingdom Life for His Disciples (5:1–7:29)

V. The Authoritative Power of the Messiah: Kingdom Power Demonstrated (8:1–9:38)

VI. The Authoritative Mission of the Messiah's Messengers (10:1–42)

VII. Opposition to the Messiah Increases (11:1–12:50)

VIII. The Messianic Kingdom Revealed in Parables (13:1–53)

IX. The Identity of the Messiah Revealed (13:54–16:20)

X. The Suffering of the Messiah Revealed (16:21–17:27)

XI. The Community of the Messiah Revealed (18:1–20:34)

XII. The Messiah Asserts His Authority over Jerusalem (21:1–23:39)

XIII. The Delay, Return, and Judgment of the Messiah (24:1–25:46)

XIV. The Crucified Messiah (26:1–27:66)

XV. The Resurrection and Commission of the Messiah (28:1–20)

The Gospel According to

Matthew

The Genealogy of Jesus Christ

1 [a]The book of the genealogy of Jesus Christ,
[b]the son of David, [c]the son of Abraham.
2 [d]Abraham was the father of Isaac, and [e]Isaac
the father of Jacob, and [f]Jacob the father of
Judah and his brothers, 3 and [g]Judah the father
of Perez and Zerah by Tamar, and Perez the
father of Hezron, and Hezron the father of
Ram,[1] 4 and Ram the father of Amminadab,
and Amminadab the father of Nahshon, and
Nahshon the father of Salmon, 5 and Salmon
the father of Boaz by [h]Rahab, and Boaz the
father of Obed by Ruth, and Obed the father of
Jesse, 6 and [i]Jesse the father of David the king.
And [j]David was the father of Solomon by
[k]the wife of Uriah, 7 and [l]Solomon the father of
Rehoboam, and Rehoboam the father of Abijah,
and Abijah the father of Asaph,[2] 8 and Asaph
the father of Jehoshaphat, and Jehoshaphat
the father of Joram, [m]and Joram the father of
Uzziah, 9 and Uzziah the father of Jotham, and
Jotham the father of Ahaz, and Ahaz the father
of Hezekiah, 10 and Hezekiah the father of
Manasseh, and Manasseh the father of Amos,[3]
and Amos the father of Josiah, 11 and [n]Josiah the
father of [o]Jechoniah and his brothers, at the
time of the deportation to Babylon.
12 And after the deportation to Babylon:
[p]Jechoniah was the father of [q]Shealtiel,[4] and
[r]Shealtiel the father of Zerubbabel, 13 and
Zerubbabel the father of Abiud, and Abiud
the father of Eliakim, and Eliakim the father

[1] Greek *Aram*; also verse 4 [2] *Asaph* is probably an alternate spelling of *Asa*; some manuscripts *Asa*; also verse 8 [3] *Amos* is probably an alternate spelling of *Amon*; some manuscripts *Amon*; twice in this verse [4] Greek *Salathiel*; twice in this verse

1:1–17 Matthew begins his Gospel with a genealogy, echoing the genealogies of the Old Testament. He thought of his work as a continuation of the Old Testament story of God's gracious redemption of his wayward people. His genealogy begins and ends with three great names in Israelite history: Abraham, David, and Jesus (vv. 1, 17). Interspersed with the names of the great patriarchs that recount the progression from Abraham to Jesus are reminders of God's acceptance of the sinful and marginalized.

Five women appear in the genealogy: Tamar, Rahab, Ruth, "the wife of Uriah" (Bathsheba), and Mary, all of whom faced great social difficulty in life, but all of whom God treated mercifully and used to carry forward his saving purposes for his people. Tamar, Rahab, and Bathsheba were involved in sexual sin (Genesis 38; Joshua 2; 2 Sam. 11:1–12:23), a point that Matthew especially emphasizes when he calls Bathsheba "the wife of Uriah." This phrase recalls the sordid story of adultery and murder that blighted Bathsheba's relationship with David (2 Sam. 11:26–27; 12:9). Ruth was a desperately poor immigrant field-worker (Ruth 2:2), and Mary, although innocent of sexual wrongdoing, was thought to have been unfaithful to her fiancé, Joseph (Matt. 1:19).

Despite lives made difficult by poverty and sin (whether their own or others'), God aided these women and gave them important places in his plan to "save his people from their sins" (v. 21). This reminds believers that "the power of God for salvation" comes "to everyone who believes" (Rom. 1:16) and that "God shows no partiality" (Rom. 2:11). God "justifies the ungodly" (Rom. 4:5) and uses for his saving purposes those whom the powerful institutions of the unbelieving world have oppressed and marginalized (1 Cor. 1:26–30; 2 Cor. 12:9). The way in which God helps the needy person is most often through the generosity of those among his people who have themselves experienced his grace and who have the resources to help those in need (Ex. 22:21; 23:9; Deut. 10:19; Acts 20:35; 2 Cor. 8:1–6; Eph. 4:28).

Chapter 1
1 [a][Luke 3:23-38] [b]2 Sam. 7:12-16; Ps. 132:11; Isa. 11:1; Jer. 23:5; Luke 1:32, 69; John 7:42; Acts 2:30; 13:23; Rom. 1:3; 2 Tim. 2:8; Rev. 22:16 [c]Gen. 22:18; Gal. 3:16
2 [d]Gen. 21:3 [e]Gen. 25:26 [f]Gen. 29:35
3 [g][Ruth 4:18-22; 1 Chr. 2:1-15]
5 [h]Josh. 6:25
6 [i]1 Sam. 16:1; 17:12 [j]2 Sam. 12:24 [k]2 Sam. 12:10
7 [l]For ver. 7-10, see 1 Chr. 3:10-14
8 [m][2 Kgs. 15:1; 1 Chr. 3:11, 12]
11 [n]1 Chr. 3:15, 16 [o]Esth. 2:6; Jer. 24:1; 27:20
12 [p]1 Chr. 3:17-19 [q]Luke 3:27 [r]Ezra 3:2

of Azor, 14 and Azor the father of Zadok, and Zadok the father of Achim, and Achim the father of Eliud, 15 and Eliud the father of Eleazar, and Eleazar the father of Matthan, and Matthan the father of Jacob, 16 and Jacob the father of [s]Joseph the husband of Mary, of whom Jesus was born, who is called Christ.

17 So all the generations from Abraham to David were fourteen generations, and from David to the deportation to Babylon fourteen generations, and from the deportation to Babylon to [t]the Christ fourteen generations.

The Birth of Jesus Christ

18 Now the birth of [u]Jesus Christ[1] took place in this way. [v]When his mother Mary had been betrothed[2] to Joseph, before they came together she was found to be with child [w]from the Holy Spirit. 19 And her husband Joseph, being a just man and unwilling [x]to put her to shame, resolved to divorce her quietly. 20 But as he considered these things, behold, [y]an angel of the Lord appeared to him in a dream, saying, "Joseph, son of David, do not fear to take Mary as your wife, for that which is conceived in her is from the Holy Spirit. 21 She will bear a son, and [z]you shall call his name Jesus, [a]for he will save his people from their sins." 22 [b]All this took place [c]to fulfill what the Lord had spoken by the prophet:

23 [d]"Behold, the virgin shall conceive and
bear a son,
and they shall call his name
[e]Immanuel"

(which means, God [f]with us). 24 When Joseph woke from sleep, he did as the angel of the Lord commanded him: he took his wife, 25 but knew her not until she had given birth to a son. And [g]he called his name Jesus.

The Visit of the Wise Men

2 Now [h]after Jesus was born in [i]Bethlehem of Judea [j]in the days of Herod the king, behold, wise men[3] from [k]the east came to Jerusalem, 2 saying, "Where is he who has been born [l]king of the Jews? For we saw [m]his star when it rose[4] and have come to [n]worship him." 3 When Herod the king heard this, he was troubled, and all Jerusalem with him; 4 and assembling all the chief priests and scribes of the people, he inquired of them where [o]the Christ was to be born. 5 They told him, "In Bethlehem of Judea, for so it is written by the prophet:

6 [p]" 'And you, O Bethlehem, in the land of
Judah,
are by no means least among the rulers
of Judah;
for from you shall come a ruler
who will [q]shepherd my people Israel.' "

[1] Some manuscripts *of the Christ* [2] That is, legally pledged to be married [3] Greek *magi*; also verses 7, 16 [4] Or *in the east*; also verse 9

16[s] Luke 3:23
17[t] ch. 2:4; 11:2; 16:16; 22:42; 23:10; Mark 8:29; Luke 3:15; [John 1:41; 4:25]
18[u] ver. 1; Mark 1:1; John 1:17; 17:3; [ver. 16] [v] Luke 1:27 [w] Luke 1:35
19[x] [Deut. 24:1]
20[y] ch. 2:13, 19; [ch. 2:12, 22]
21[z] ver. 25; Luke 1:31; 2:21 [a] Luke 2:11; Acts 4:12; 5:31; 13:23, 38; [Acts 3:26]
22[b] ch. 21:4; 26:56; John 19:36 [c] ch. 2:15, 23; 4:14; Mark 14:49
23[d] Cited from Isa. 7:14 [e] Isa. 8:8, 10 [f] See ch. 28:20
25[g] ver. 21

Chapter 2
1[h] Luke 2:4-7 [i] Luke 2:15; John 7:42 [j] Luke 1:5 [k] [Gen. 25:6; 1 Kgs. 4:30]
2[l] ch. 27:11, 37; Jer. 23:5; 30:9; Zech. 9:9 [m] [Num. 24:17; Rev. 22:16] [n] See ch. 8:2
4[o] See ch. 1:17
6[p] Cited from Mic. 5:2 [q] Ezek. 34:23; John 21:15-17; [2 Sam. 5:2; Rev. 7:17]

1:21–23 The angel's message to Joseph is good news. Jesus, as the meaning of his Hebrew name "Joshua" indicates, brings the salvation of the Lord. He will save people not merely in the physical sense (8:25; 10:22) but in the most fundamental sense because he will bring salvation from sins. Everyone has sinned against God, failing to give him the thanks he deserves and creating chaos within human society (Rom. 1:18–32; 3:9–20, 23), but in Jesus God has displayed with great clarity the merciful and forgiving character that he also exhibited in the Old Testament (Ps. 130:3–4, 7–8).

When Jesus came, he could be described as the fulfillment of Isaiah 7:14 because he was God, and so when he was among his people, God was with them (Matt. 8:23–27). God dwelling with his people was the climactic and greatest blessing in the Old Testament (Ex. 29:46; Lev. 26:11–12), but a blessing hindered by their rebellion against him. In Jesus, God has provided for salvation from sin and has healed the broken relationship between himself and his people, making it possible for God, in Jesus, to be "with" his disciples "always, to the end of the age" (Matt. 28:20).

2:1–12 The "wise men" who saw what they called the "star" of the "king of the Jews" and came searching for him would have been pagan astrologers from regions to the east of Israel. The journey of these non-Israelites to Jerusalem to worship the King of the Jews recalls the vision expressed in the Prophets of "all nations" and "many peoples" converging on Mount Zion in the future and seeking to learn God's "ways" and "walk in his paths" (Isa. 2:3; Mic. 4:2; see also Isa. 19:19–25; 66:18–21).

The Wise Men stand as a reminder that there is only one God, the Creator of the universe (Rom. 1:18–21; 3:30; 1 Cor. 8:6), and that he desires all people to worship him from the heart (John 4:23). Although God chose Abraham's descendants as his special people, they were to serve as a kingdom of priests mediating to the rest of the world

7 Then Herod summoned the wise men
secretly and ascertained from them what time
the star had appeared. 8 And he sent them to
Bethlehem, saying, "Go and search diligently
for the child, and when you have found him,
bring me word, that I too may come and worship him." 9 After listening to the king, they
went on their way. And behold, the star that
they had seen when it rose went before them
until it came to rest over the place where the
child was. 10 When they saw the star, they
rejoiced exceedingly with great joy. 11 And
going into the house they saw the child with
Mary his mother, and they fell down and worshiped him. Then, opening their treasures,
[r]they offered him gifts, [s]gold and [t]frankincense
and [u]myrrh. 12 And [v]being warned [w]in a dream
not to return to Herod, they departed to their
own country by another way.

The Flight to Egypt

13 Now when they had departed, behold,
[x]an angel of the Lord appeared to Joseph in a
dream and said, "Rise, take the child and his
mother, and flee to Egypt, and remain there
until I tell you, for Herod is about to search for
the child, to destroy him." 14 And he rose and
took the child and his mother by night and
departed to Egypt 15 and remained there until
the death of Herod. [y]This was to fulfill what
the Lord had spoken by the prophet, [z]"Out of
Egypt I called my son."

Herod Kills the Children

16 Then Herod, when he saw that he had been
tricked by the wise men, became furious, and
he sent and killed all the male children in
Bethlehem and in all that region who were
two years old or under, according to the time
that he had ascertained from the wise men.
17 [a]Then was fulfilled what was spoken by the
prophet Jeremiah:

18 [b]"A voice was heard in Ramah,
weeping and loud lamentation,
Rachel weeping for her children;
she refused to be comforted, because
they [c]are no more."

The Return to Nazareth

19 But when Herod died, behold, an angel
of the Lord appeared in a dream to Joseph in
Egypt, 20 saying, "Rise, take the child and his
mother and go to the land of Israel, for [d]those
who sought the child's life are dead." 21 And he
rose and took the child and his mother and
went to the land of Israel. 22 But when he heard
that Archelaus was reigning over Judea in
place of his father Herod, he was afraid to go
there, and [e]being warned in a dream he withdrew to the district of Galilee. 23 And he went
and lived in a city called [f]Nazareth, [g]so that
what was spoken by the prophets might be
fulfilled, that he would be called a Nazarene.

John the Baptist Prepares the Way

3 [h]In those days [i]John the Baptist came
preaching in [j]the wilderness of Judea,
2 [k]"Repent, for [l]the kingdom of heaven is at
hand." 3 For this is he who was spoken of by
the prophet Isaiah when he said,

[m]"The voice of one crying in the wilderness:
[n]'Prepare[1] the way of the Lord;
make his paths straight.'"

[1] Or *crying: Prepare in the wilderness*

God's identity as creator and his character as a merciful and forgiving God (Ex. 19:6). Here Matthew hints that this multinational blessing has started to be fulfilled. As the church reaches out with the gospel to a wide variety of social and ethnic groups, it fulfills the plan of God for his creation and works for the defeat of the forces of evil ranged against God and his people (Eph. 3:7–10).

The three steps in the religious quest of the Wise Men are all significant: God took the initiative, meeting the Wise Men in their own context and communicating with them in a way they could understand (Matt. 2:2, 9). Once the Wise Men found Jesus, they spontaneously and freely worshiped him as the object of their religious quest. The offerings they gave to Jesus were likewise free and natural expressions of the overwhelming joy they experienced at finding someone worthy of their worship (vv. 10–11).

3:1–12 John the Baptist's preaching provides a picture of what is entailed in repentance or conversion. Repentance involves a heart-change in perspective that leads to a change in the fundamental direction of one's life. Those who repent, confess their sin (v. 6). In other words, they admit they have not been obedient to the law of God, failing to love and worship him as he deserves and failing to love others as

11 [r][1 Sam. 9:7; Ps. 72:10] [s]Isa. 60:6 [t]Rev. 18:13 [u]Ex. 30:23; Ps. 45:8; John 19:39
12 [v]ver. 22; [ver. 13, 19] [w][ch. 27:19; Gen. 20:6; 31:11; Num. 12:6; Job 33:15]
13 [x]ver. 19; ch. 1:20; [ver. 12, 22]
15 [y]See ch. 1:22 [z]Cited from Hos. 11:1
17 [a]ch. 27:9; [ch. 1:22]
18 [b]Cited from Jer. 31:15 [c]Gen. 42:13, 36; Lam. 5:7
20 [d][Ex. 4:19]
22 [e]See ver. 12
23 [f]ch. 4:13; Mark 1:9; Luke 1:26; 2:39; 4:16; John 1:45 [g]See ch. 1:22

Chapter 3
1 [h]For ver. 1-12, see Mark 1:2-8; Luke 3:2-17 [i]John 1:6, 7 [j]Josh. 15:61; [Judg. 1:16]
2 [k]ch. 4:17; Mark 1:15 [l]ch. 10:7; Dan. 2:44; [ch. 6:10]
3 [m]John 1:23; Cited from Isa. 40:3 [n]Luke 1:76

4 Now John wore [o]a garment of camel's hair and a leather belt around his waist, and his food was [p]locusts and [q]wild honey. 5 Then Jerusalem and all Judea and all the region about the Jordan were going out to him, 6 and they were baptized by him in the river Jordan, [r]confessing their sins.

7 But when he saw many of [s]the Pharisees and [t]Sadducees coming to his baptism, he said to them, [u]"You brood of [v]vipers! Who warned you to flee from [w]the wrath to come? 8 Bear fruit [x]in keeping with repentance. 9 And do not presume to say to yourselves, [y]'We have Abraham as our father,' for I tell you, God is able from [z]these stones to raise up children for Abraham. 10 Even now the axe is laid to the root of the trees. [a]Every tree therefore that does not bear good fruit is cut down and thrown into the fire.

11 [b]"I baptize you with water [c]for repentance, but [d]he who is coming after me is mightier than I, whose sandals I am not worthy to carry. He will baptize you [e]with the Holy Spirit and [f]fire. 12 His [g]winnowing fork is in his hand, and he will clear his threshing floor and [h]gather his wheat into the barn, [i]but the chaff he will burn with [j]unquenchable fire."

The Baptism of Jesus

13 [k]Then Jesus came [l]from Galilee to the Jordan to John, to be baptized by him. 14 [m]John would have prevented him, saying, "I need to be baptized by you, and do you come to me?" 15 But Jesus answered him, "Let it be so now, for thus it is fitting for us to fulfill all righteousness." Then he consented. 16 And when Jesus was baptized, immediately he went up from the water, and behold, [o]the heavens were opened to him,[1] and he [p]saw the Spirit of God descending like a dove and coming to rest on him; 17 and behold, [q]a voice from heaven said, [r]"This is my beloved Son,[2] with whom I am well pleased."

The Temptation of Jesus

4 [s]Then Jesus was led up by the Spirit into the wilderness [t]to be tempted by the devil. 2 And after fasting [u]forty days and forty nights, he [v]was hungry. 3 And [w]the tempter came and said to him, "If you are [x]the Son of God, command [y]these stones to become loaves of bread." 4 But he answered, [z]"It is written,

> [a]" 'Man shall not live by bread alone,
> but by every word that comes from
> the mouth of God.' "

[1] Some manuscripts omit *to him* [2] Or *my Son, my* (or *the*) *Beloved*

4 [o]2 Kgs. 1:8; Zech. 13:4; [Heb. 11:37] [p]Lev. 11:22 [q]1 Sam. 14:26
6 [r]Acts 19:18
7 [s]ch. 23:13, 15 [t]ch. 22:23 [u]ch. 12:34; 23:33 [v]Ps. 140:3 [w]Rom. 5:9; Eph. 5:6; Col. 3:6; 1 Thess. 1:10
8 [x]Acts 26:20
9 [y]John 8:39 [z][ch. 4:3]
10 [a]ch. 7:19; Luke 13:7, 9; John 15:2, 6
11 [b]John 1:26; Acts 1:5 [c]Acts 13:24; 19:4 [d]John 1:15, 27; 3:30, 31; Acts 13:25 [e]John 1:33; Acts 11:16 [f][Isa. 4:4; Mal. 3:2, 3; Acts 2:3]
12 [g]Isa. 30:24 [h]ch. 13:30 [i]Mal. 4:1 [j]Mark 9:43, 48
13 [k]For ver. 13-17, see Mark 1:9-11; Luke 3:21, 22; [John 1:32-34] [l]ch. 2:22
14 [m][John 13:6]
16 [o]Acts 7:56 [p]John 1:32, 33; [Luke 4:18, 21; Acts 10:38]
17 [q]John 12:28 [r]ch. 17:5; 2 Pet. 1:17; [Ps. 2:7; Isa. 42:1; Eph. 1:6; Col. 1:13; 1 John 5:9]
Chapter 4
1 [s]For ver. 1-11, see Mark 1:12, 13; Luke 4:1-13 [t][Heb. 2:18; 4:15]
2 [u][Deut. 9:9, 18; 1 Kgs. 19:8] [v][John 4:6, 7]
3 [w]1 Thess. 3:5 [x]See ch. 14:33 [y][ch. 3:9]
4 [z]ver. 7, 10; Eph. 6:17 [a]Cited from Deut. 8:3; [John 4:34]

God desires. Those who repent also understand that they deserve God's punishment for their sins (vv. 2, 7, 10–12). Therefore they come to God not relying on anything in themselves, such as their prestigious family or their national or tribal affiliation (v. 9), but trusting only in the mercy of God. Furthermore, repentance leads to a change in the pattern of one's life from sinful behavior to behavior that honors God and deals lovingly with others (vv. 8, 10).

People often misunderstand the order of these elements. Repentance does not begin with changed behavior that in turn brings God's acceptance. It begins with a change in one's perspective on oneself, on God, and on the consequences of one's rejection of God. The change in one's perspective then brings about a change in behavior (cf. Rom. 12:2; Eph. 4:23–24).

3:13–4:11 Here Matthew emphasizes the sinlessness of Jesus. John was surprised to see Jesus coming to him for baptism because, as John has just said, he was baptizing those who needed to repent (3:11). The words "Let it be so now" (3:15) show that Jesus knew John was correct: Jesus knew he was sinless. But Jesus also knew that he needed to be baptized for another important reason. That reason is obliquely stated as "to fulfill all righteousness" (3:15), by which Jesus indicates he needed to show others the importance of submitting to this sign of identification with God's kingdom.

Because 3:13–17 emphasizes Jesus' sinlessness, it forms a fitting introduction to the temptation of Jesus in the wilderness (4:1–11), where Jesus refuses Satan's attempts to persuade him to rebel against God. The geographical location of the temptation—in the wilderness—recalls Israel's experience in the wilderness after their exodus from Egypt. Israel rebelled against God through their idolatry (Exodus 32), their complaining (Ex. 14:11; 15:24; 16:2; 17:3; Num. 11:1–3; 21:5), and their refusal to submit to the leaders whom God had appointed (Numbers 16). As a result of their sin, God punished his people. Unlike Israel, however, Jesus succeeded in obeying God in the wilderness.

5 [b]Then the devil took him to [c]the holy city and
set him on the pinnacle of the temple 6 and
said to him, "If you are the Son of God, throw
yourself down, for it is written,

> [d]" 'He will command his angels concerning
> you,'

and

> " 'On their hands they will bear you up,
> lest you strike your foot against a
> stone.' "

7 Jesus said to him, "Again [e]it is written, [f]'You
shall not [g]put the Lord your God to the test.' "
8 [h]Again, the devil took him to a very high
mountain and showed him all the kingdoms
of the world and their glory. 9 And he said to
him, "All these I will give you, if you will fall
down and worship me." 10 Then Jesus said to
him, "Be gone, [i]Satan! For [j]it is written,

> [k]" 'You shall worship the Lord your God
> and [l]him only shall you serve.' "

11 Then the devil left him, and behold, [m]angels
came and were ministering to him.

Jesus Begins His Ministry

12 Now when he heard that [n]John had been
arrested, [o]he withdrew into Galilee. 13 And leaving [p]Nazareth he went and lived in [q]Capernaum
by [r]the sea, in the territory of [s]Zebulun and
Naphtali, 14 [t]so that what was spoken by the
prophet Isaiah might be fulfilled:

> 15 [u]"The land of Zebulun and the land of
> Naphtali,
> the way of the sea, beyond the Jordan,
> Galilee of the Gentiles—
> 16 [v]the people dwelling in darkness
> have seen a great light,
> and for those dwelling in the region and
> [w]shadow of death,
> on them a light has dawned."

17 [x]From that time Jesus began to preach, saying, [z]"Repent, for the kingdom of heaven is
at hand."

Jesus Calls the First Disciples

18 [a]While walking by [b]the Sea of Galilee, he
saw two brothers, Simon (who is called Peter)
and Andrew his brother, casting a net into the
sea, for they were fishermen. 19 And he said to
them, "Follow me, and I will make you [c]fishers
of men."[1] 20 Immediately they left their nets
and followed him. 21 And going on from there
he saw two other brothers, James the son of
Zebedee and John his brother, in the boat with
Zebedee their father, mending their nets, and
he called them. 22 Immediately they left the
boat and their father and followed him.

[1] The Greek word *anthropoi* refers here to both men and women

The whole passage helps believers to appreciate the substitutionary nature of Jesus' death. Toward the end of Matthew, Jesus will explain that the Lord's Supper signifies the outpouring of his blood as a sacrifice for the forgiveness of sins (Matt. 26:28). Jesus' sacrifice could bring about the forgiveness of sin by a just God, however, only if Jesus himself were without sin (Rom. 3:21–26; 2 Cor. 5:21; Heb. 9:11–28; 1 Pet. 3:18; see also Isa. 53:9, 12). Understanding the implications of Jesus' sinlessness should encourage believers both to avoid repeating the idolatrous, ungrateful sinfulness of Israel in the wilderness and to be profoundly grateful to Jesus for his willing sacrifice on their behalf.

4:12–17 Jesus fulfills the expectation of Isaiah that the most northern part of Israel, the section of the country that first experienced God's judgment in the invasion of the Assyrians in the eighth century B.C. (Isa. 8:1–10; 2 Kings 15:29), would also be the first part of the country to experience God's climactic act of redemption as Jesus began his ministry there. Darkness and death (Matt. 4:16) were appropriate metaphors for the horrors of enemy invasion, the consequence of human rebellion against God. Now, in the preaching of Jesus in this same geographical region, God shines the light of his truth on his people and urges them to choose life. God would have been just to reject his people and leave them to the darkness and death they had chosen for themselves in the eighth century, but he is a "merciful and gracious" God, "slow to anger, and abounding in steadfast love and faithfulness" (Ex. 34:6; cf. Num. 14:18; Neh. 9:17; Ps. 86:15; 103:1–16).

Jesus' call to repent in advance of the coming kingdom, then, is part of God's continuing mercy toward those who had previously rejected him. His proclamation of the coming kingdom remains a merciful reminder that the heavenly kingdom will one day arrive in all its glory and bring light and life *only* to the repentant.

5 [b] Luke 4:9 [c] ch. 27:53; Neh. 11:18; Isa. 48:2; 52:1; Rev. 11:2; [Ps. 46:4; 48:1; Rev. 21:2; 22:19]
6 [d] Cited from Ps. 91:11, 12
7 [e] ver. 4, 10 [f] Cited from Deut. 6:16 [g] [Isa. 7:12]
8 [h] Luke 4:5
10 [i] See 1 Chr. 21:1 [j] ver. 4, 7 [k] Cited from Deut. 6:13 [l] 1 Sam. 7:3
11 [m] ch. 26:53; Luke 22:43
12 [n] ch. 14:3; Mark 1:14; Luke 3:19, 20; [John 3:24] [o] Luke 4:14
13 [p] See ch. 2:23 [q] [ch. 9:1] [r] John 6:1 [s] Josh. 19:32-34
14 [t] See ch. 1:22
15 [u] Cited from Isa. 9:1, 2
16 [v] Isa. 42:7; Luke 1:79 [w] Job 3:5; Ps. 23:4; Amos 5:8
17 [x] Mark 1:14 [z] ch. 3:2
18 [a] For ver. 18-22, see Mark 1:16-20; [Luke 5:2-11; John 1:40-42] [b] ver. 13
19 [c] ch. 13:47

Jesus Ministers to Great Crowds

23 [d]And he went throughout all Galilee,
[e]teaching in their synagogues and [f]proclaim-
ing the gospel of the kingdom and [g]healing
every disease and every affliction among
the people. 24 So his fame spread throughout all [h]Syria, and [g]they brought him all the
sick, those afflicted with various diseases
and [i]pains, [j]those oppressed by demons,
[k]epileptics, and [l]paralytics, and he healed
them. 25 [m]And great crowds followed him
from Galilee and the [n]Decapolis, and from
Jerusalem and Judea, and from beyond the
Jordan.

The Sermon on the Mount

5 Seeing the crowds, [o]he went up on the
mountain, and when he [p]sat down, his
disciples came to him.

The Beatitudes

2 And [q]he opened his mouth and taught
them, saying:
3 [r]"Blessed are [s]the poor in spirit, for [u]theirs
is the kingdom of heaven.
4 "Blessed are [v]those who mourn, for they
shall be comforted.
5 "Blessed are the [w]meek, for they [w]shall
inherit the earth.

23 [d]Mark 1:39 [e]ch. 9:35; 13:54; Mark 1:21; Luke 4:15; John 18:20 [f]ch. 24:14; Luke 4:43; [ch. 13:19] [g]ch. 8:16; 14:35, 36; Mark 1:34; 6:55, 56
24 [h]Luke 2:2 [g][See ver. 23 above] [i]ch. 8:6 [j][John 10:21] [k]ch. 17:15 [l]ch. 9:2, 6
25 [m]Mark 3:7, 8; Luke 6:17 [n]Mark 5:20

Chapter 5

1 [o]ch. 15:29 [p]Luke 4:20
2 [q]Ps. 78:2
3 [r]For ver. 3-12, [Luke 6:20-23] [s][Isa. 61:1; 66:2] [u][Luke 12:32]
4 [v]Isa. 61:2, 3; John 16:20; 2 Cor. 1:7; 7:10; Rev. 21:4; [James 4:9, 10]
5 [w]Ps. 37:11

4:23–25 Everywhere Jesus goes, he brings the kingdom of God with him, and the nature of God is evident in the goodness that results from Jesus' ministry. In the presence of Jesus, disease, affliction, pain, demonic oppression, and disability all begin to disappear. Moreover, Jesus does good to people from many lands (v. 25), not merely to his own people. In these ways, Jesus fulfills ancient promises regarding the Messiah who will heal his people as well as make them a light to the nations (Isa. 19:16–24; 35:5–6; 49:6).

The church today is similarly called to be a place where people do good to the needy. We do this in the name of our all-gracious God, breaking through social barriers by extending mercy to people of every social group and expressing Christ's mercy to those of all backgrounds and nations. For we are ourselves recipients of mercy.

5:1 Jesus has just called his first disciples to follow him (4:19, 21), and they have enthusiastically responded to his call to join him in gathering people into the kingdom in the same way they once gathered fish from the sea (4:19; 13:47). Now Jesus begins to teach his disciples how their own lives can serve as examples to others of what the kingdom of God will look like when it comes (5:1–7:29).

"The Sermon on the Mount" (chs. 5–7) is structurally similar to the Mosaic law. Like the Mosaic law, it begins with a reminder of God's blessing and grace. The first five beatitudes (5:3–7) emphasize that God's blessing comes to those who understand their need of his mercy, just as the Mosaic law begins with a reminder of God's gracious rescue of his people from slavery in Egypt (Ex. 19:4; 20:2). Also like the Mosaic law, the Sermon on the Mount describes the way of life that God calls his people to display as a means of showing the world the character of its Creator. Israel was to be a kingdom of priests, mediating God's character and will for the rest of humanity to all the earth (Ex. 19:5–6). Jesus' followers are to be salt and light in the world so that it might see their good works and glorify God (Matt. 5:13–16). In addition, both the Mosaic law and the Sermon on the Mount end with a description of the blessing that comes to those who follow their teaching and the trouble that comes to those who disobey (Leviticus 26; Deuteronomy 28–30; cf. Matt. 7:24–27).

It is important to avoid two errors in interpreting the "Sermon on the Mount." First, it is not a description of the requirements for *entering* the kingdom of God. Jesus taught this material to those who had already responded to his call to follow him (4:18–22; 5:1). Second, it is not an idealistic description of the way life will function after God has fully established his kingdom in the future. In that day, there will be no need to turn the other cheek (5:39). Rather, these teachings are a description of what life looks like for followers of Jesus as they try to be faithful to him and to the values of God's kingdom in a world that God has not yet fully transformed. They are about living as ambassadors of God's kingdom in a foreign land. In short, the Sermon shows us what life should look like for a heart that has been melted and transformed by the gospel of grace, while also making clear the true nature of God's standards of righteousness—high standards which mean that our right standing with God is ultimately dependent on the grace of the One who tells us of them.

6 "Blessed are those who hunger and [x]thirst
[y]for righteousness, for they shall be satisfied.
7 "Blessed are [z]the merciful, for they shall
receive mercy.
8 "Blessed are [a]the pure in heart, for [b]they
shall see God.
9 "Blessed are [c]the peacemakers, for [d]they
shall be called [e]sons[1] of God.
10 [f]"Blessed are those who are persecuted for
righteousness' sake, for [u]theirs is the kingdom
of heaven.
11 [g]"Blessed are you when others revile you
and persecute you and utter all kinds of evil
against you falsely [h]on my account. 12 [i]Rejoice
and be glad, for your reward is great in heaven,
for [j]so they persecuted the prophets who were
before you.

Salt and Light

13 "You are the salt of the earth, [k]but if salt
has lost its taste, how shall its saltiness be
restored? It is no longer good for anything
except to be thrown out and trampled under
people's feet.
14 [l]"You are the light of the world. A city set
on a hill cannot be hidden. 15 [m]Nor do people
light a lamp and put it under a basket, but on
a stand, and it gives light to all in the house.
16 In the same way, let your light shine before
others, so [n]that[2] they may see your good works
and [o]give glory to your Father who is in heaven.

Christ Came to Fulfill the Law

17 [p]"Do not think that I have come to abolish
[q]the Law or the Prophets; I have not come to
abolish them but [r]to fulfill them. 18 For truly,
I say to you, [s]until heaven and earth pass away,
not an iota, not a dot, will pass from the Law
until all is accomplished. 19 [t]Therefore whoever
relaxes [u]one of the least of these commandments and teaches others to do the same will
be called least [v]in the kingdom of heaven, but
whoever does them and teaches them will
be called great [v]in the kingdom of heaven.

[1] Greek *huioi*; see Preface [2] Or *house.* **16** *Let your light so shine before others that*

5:3–7 These first five blessings affirm an important principle for understanding the Sermon on the Mount. The Sermon is not an instruction manual for winning God's favor. Rather, it describes how God wants those to live who have already been transformed by his grace because they have understood their weakness and need for his mercy. The "poor in spirit" (v. 3) are those who know that they, as sinners, do not have the spiritual resources necessary to carry out God's demands. "Those who mourn" and who "hunger and thirst for righteousness" (vv. 4, 6) have experienced the disaster that disobedience to God has brought to the world. Because they understand their true position of weakness before God, the "meek" (v. 5) have a humility that translates into treating others with kindness. The "merciful" are those who understand their own need for God's mercy (v. 7).

5:13–16 The Sermon on the Mount describes how those who have already decided to follow Jesus (4:18–22; 5:1) are called to demonstrate the character of God and his kingdom through the character of their lives.

5:17–48 The Mosaic law is God's truthful, eternal word that continues to stand as a witness to his character and his gracious, redemptive work among his people (Ps. 19:7–11; Psalm 119; Rom. 7:12). This does not mean, however, that it is to be observed by God's people after Jesus' coming in the same way that it was observed among his people before Jesus came. When Jesus says that he came to "fulfill" the Law and the Prophets (Matt. 5:17), he means that both the Law and the Prophets pointed forward to his teaching. They brought the purposes of God to a certain point in the story of God's redemptive work among his people, and Jesus' teaching then picked up their message and completed it.

The Mosaic law was intended to govern Israelite society during the time when it functioned as a nation-state. It had to include legislation for governing all those who lived within the boundaries of political Israel, whether their hearts had been transformed by God or not, and thus whether they were part of the people of God or not (vv. 21, 27, 31, 33, 38). So, for example, on the question of divorce, the Mosaic law had to make provision for people whose hearts were hard and who were unconcerned about God's original purposes for marriage (19:8).

In contrast, the Sermon on the Mount shows what the eternal principles that undergird the Mosaic law look like in a society of people who have turned away from

6 [x]Ps. 42:2; Isa. 55:1, 2; John 7:37 [y]2 Tim. 2:22; [ch. 6:33]
7 [z]ch. 18:33; 25:34-36; Prov. 19:17; Luke 6:36; 2 Tim. 1:16; Heb. 6:10
8 [a]Ps. 24:4; 2 Tim. 2:22; [1 Pet. 1:22] [b]Heb. 12:14; 1 John 3:2, 3; Rev. 22:4; [1 Cor. 13:12]
9 [c]James 3:18 [d]1 John 3:1 [e]Rom. 8:14
10 [f]2 Tim. 2:12; James 5:11; 1 Pet. 3:14 [u][See ver. 3 above]
11 [g]Heb. 11:26; 1 Pet. 4:14 [h]John 15:21
12 [i]Acts 5:41; Rom. 5:3; 2 Cor. 12:10; Col. 1:11, 24; Heb. 10:34; James 1:2; 1 Pet. 4:13 [j]See ch. 21:35
13 [k]Mark 9:50; Luke 14:34
14 [l]Eph. 5:8; Phil. 2:15; [John 8:12]
15 [m]Mark 4:21; Luke 8:16; 11:33
16 [n]Philem. 6; 1 Pet. 2:12 [o]John 15:8; 2 Cor. 9:13; Phil. 1:11; [ch. 9:8]
17 [p]Rom. 3:31 [q]ch. 7:12 [r][Rom. 10:4; 13:8; Gal. 3:24]
18 [s]Luke 16:17; [ch. 24:35]
19 [t][1 Cor. 3:12-15] [u][Gal. 3:10; James 2:10] [v]ch. 11:11; 18:1-4

20 For I tell you, unless your righteousness exceeds [w]that of the scribes and Pharisees, you [x]will never enter the kingdom of heaven.

Anger

21 [y]"You have heard that it was said to those of old, [z]'You shall not murder; and whoever murders will be liable [a]to judgment.' 22 But I say to you that [b]everyone who is angry with his brother[1] will be liable [a]to judgment; whoever insults[2] his brother will be liable to the council; and whoever says, 'You fool!' will be liable to [c]the hell[3] of fire. 23 [d]So if [e]you are offering your gift at the altar and there remember that your brother has something against you, 24 leave your gift there before the altar and go. First be reconciled to your brother, and then come and offer your gift. 25 [f]Come to terms quickly with your accuser while you are going with him to court, lest your accuser hand you over to the judge, and the judge to the guard, and you be put in prison. 26 Truly, I say to you, [g]you will never get out until you have paid the last penny.[4]

Lust

27 [h]"You have heard that it was said, [i]'You shall not commit adultery.' 28 But I say to you that [j]everyone who looks at a woman with lustful intent has already committed adultery with her in his heart. 29 [k]If your right eye [l]causes you to sin, tear it out and throw it away. For it is better that you lose one of your members than that your whole body be thrown into [m]hell. 30 [k]And if your right hand [l]causes you to sin, cut it off and throw it away. For it is better that you lose one of your members than that your whole body go into [m]hell.

Divorce

31 [h]"It was also said, [n]'Whoever divorces his wife, let him give her a certificate of divorce.' 32 [o]But I say to you that everyone who divorces his wife, except on the ground of sexual immorality, makes her commit adultery, and [p]whoever marries a divorced woman commits adultery.

Oaths

33 "Again [h]you have heard that it was said to those of old, [q]'You shall not swear falsely, but [r]shall perform to the Lord what you have sworn.' 34 But I say to you, [s]Do not take an oath at all, either by heaven, for [t]it is the throne of God, 35 or by the earth, for it is his footstool, or by Jerusalem, for it is [u]the city of the great King. 36 And do not take an oath by your head, for you cannot make one hair white or black. 37 Let what you say be simply 'Yes' or 'No'; [v]anything more than this comes from evil.[5]

Retaliation

38 [h]"You have heard that it was said, [y]'An eye for an eye and a tooth for a tooth.' 39 But I say to you, [z]Do not resist the one who is evil. But

[1] Some manuscripts insert *without cause* [2] Greek *says Raca to* (a term of abuse) [3] Greek *Gehenna*; also verses 29, 30 [4] Greek *kodrantes*, Roman copper coin (Latin *quadrans*) worth about 1/64 of a *denarius* (which was a day's wage for a laborer) [5] Or *the evil one*

the attractions of sin and have decided to follow Jesus. The Sermon on the Mount, then, does not describe how governments should seek to establish a just society, but how believers in Jesus Christ should live within a sinful world.

5:20 The "scribes and Pharisees" encounter severe criticism from Jesus throughout Matthew's Gospel (12:38–45; 15:1–14; 23:1–39). Their basic problem lies in the contradiction between the condition of their hearts and their outward professions and acts of piety (15:8; 23:3–7). This contradiction was revealed especially in their neglect of the law's fundamental concern with justice, mercy, and faithfulness in favor of demonstrating to others their superior expertise in the law's minutia (23:23).

Exceeding the righteousness of the scribes and the Pharisees, then, is a matter of obeying God from a fundamentally changed heart. This is a heart that reaches beyond the legalistic boundaries of the law to its compassionate purposes, while simultaneously recognizing its own spiritual poverty apart from God's mercy (5:3, 6–7).

5:29–30 Jesus often used hyperbole in his teaching to make a point with color and force (cf. 7:5; 17:20; 19:24; 21:21; 23:15; Luke 14:26). The point here is that those whose hearts have been transformed by the gospel should be willing to make significant sacrifices in order to avoid becoming ensnared by sexual sin that will do them greater damage in spiritual terms (see also Matt. 18:8–9).

20 [w][Rom. 10:3; Phil. 3:9] [x]John 3:5
21 [y]ver. 33; [ver. 27, 31, 38, 43] [z]Cited from Ex. 20:13; Deut. 5:17; [ch. 19:18; Mark 10:19; Luke 18:20; Rom. 13:9; James 2:11] [a][Deut. 16:18]
22 [b]1 John 3:15 [a][See ver. 21 above] [c]ch. 18:9; Mark 9:43; James 3:6; [ver. 29]
23 [d][ch. 6:15; Mark 11:25] [e]ch. 8:4; 23:18
25 [f]Luke 12:58, 59
26 [g][ch. 18:34, 35]
27 [h]See ver. 21 [i]Cited from Ex. 20:14; Deut. 5:18
28 [j]Job 31:1; Prov. 6:25; [2 Sam. 11:2]
29 [k]ch. 18:8, 9; Mark 9:43-48 [l][ch. 13:41; Luke 17:1] [m]ch. 10:28; 23:15, 33; Luke 12:5; [ver. 22]
30 [k][See ver. 29 above] [l][See ver. 29 above] [m][See ver. 29 above]
31 [h][See ver. 27 above] [n]ch. 19:7; Jer. 3:1; Cited from Deut. 24:1
32 [o]ch. 19:9; Mark 10:11, 12; Luke 16:18; [1 Cor. 7:10, 11] [p]Rom. 7:3 **33** [h][See ver. 27 above] [q]Lev. 19:12; 1 Tim. 1:10 [r]Num. 30:2; Deut. 23:21; Eccles. 5:4 **34** [s]James 5:12 [t]ch. 23:22; Isa. 66:1; Acts 7:49; See Rev. 4:2 **35** [u]Ps. 48:2 **37** [v][Prov. 10:19] **38** [h][See ver. 27 above] [y]Cited from Ex. 21:24; Lev. 24:20; Deut. 19:21 **39** [z]1 Pet. 2:23

[a]if anyone [b]slaps you on the right cheek, turn to him the other also. 40 And [z]if anyone would sue you and take your tunic,[1] let him have your cloak as well. 41 And if anyone [c]forces you to go one mile, go with him two miles. 42 [d]Give to the one who begs from you, and [e]do not refuse the one who would borrow from you.

Love Your Enemies

43 [f]"You have heard that it was said, [g]'You shall love your neighbor and hate your enemy.' 44 But I say to you, [i]Love your enemies and [j]pray for those who persecute you, 45 [k]so that you may be sons of your Father who is in heaven. For he makes his sun rise on the evil and on the good, and [l]sends rain on the just and on the unjust. 46 [m]For if you love those who love you, what reward do you have? Do not even the tax collectors do the same? 47 And if you greet only your brothers,[2] what more are you doing than others? Do not even [n]the Gentiles do the same? 48 [o]You therefore must be [p]perfect, [q]as your heavenly Father is perfect.

Giving to the Needy

6 "Beware of [r]practicing your righteousness before other people in order [s]to be seen by them, for then you will have no reward from your Father who is in heaven.

2 [t]"Thus, when you give to the needy, sound no trumpet before you, as the hypocrites do in the synagogues and in the streets, that they may [u]be praised by others. Truly, I say to you, they have [v]received their reward. 3 But when you give to the needy, do not let your left hand know what your right hand is doing, 4 so that your giving may be in secret. [w]And your Father who sees in secret will reward you.

The Lord's Prayer

5 "And when you pray, you must not be like the hypocrites. For they love [x]to stand and pray in the synagogues and at the street corners, that they may be seen by others. [y]Truly, I say to you, they have received their reward. 6 But when you pray, [z]go into your room and shut the door and pray to your Father who is in secret. [a]And your Father who sees in secret will reward you.

7 "And when you pray, do not heap up empty phrases as [b]the Gentiles do, for [c]they think that they will be heard [d]for their many words. 8 Do not be like them, [e]for your Father knows what you need before you ask him. 9 [f]Pray then like this:

> [g]"Our Father in heaven,
> [h]hallowed be [i]your name.[3]

[1] Greek *chiton*, a long garment worn under the cloak next to the skin [2] Or *brothers and sisters*. The plural Greek word *adelphoi* (translated "brothers") refers to siblings in a family. In New Testament usage, depending on the context, *adelphoi* may refer either to *brothers* or to *brothers and sisters* [3] Or *Let your name be kept holy*, or *Let your name be treated with reverence*

5:48 The word "perfect" here refers to completeness and maturity. It is possible to do many good things in an outward sense and still not be "perfect" in this sense. Jesus speaks here of the heartfelt devotion of oneself to God, of finding one's ultimate satisfaction in him rather than in something else, such as wealth. Such perfection is required by a holy God, but is only discovered by humble dependence on this same God's provision.

This is the sort of perfection that the rich young man lacked (19:21), but that Abraham exhibited, according to Paul, when he became "fully convinced that God was able to do what he had promised," and God counted his faith as righteousness (Rom. 4:21–22; Gen. 15:5–6). The believer is to be "perfect" in the sense that his or her satisfaction and complete trust are in God. In light of the outrageous love of Christ shown in his suffering and death on our behalf, we are free to bank all our hopes on this Savior.

6:1–34 Here Jesus discusses two areas of life that tend to reveal where one's ultimate loyalties lie: religious practice (vv. 1–18) and the use of wealth (vv. 19–34). In both areas, Jesus urges his followers to find their satisfaction and security in God rather than in anything else. First, in the area of religious practice, whether almsgiving (vv. 1–4), praying (vv. 5–14), or fasting (vv. 16–18), Jesus encourages his disciples to avoid outward displays that bring praise to oneself (vv. 1–4, 16–18) and to steer clear of mechanical efforts to manipulate God (vv. 5–13). Almsgiving, prayer, and fasting should arise out of trust in God's fatherly affection, and performing them in secret is symptomatic of a healthy trust in and reliance on God. The public display of these religious practices,

39 [a]For ver. 39-42, see Luke 6:29, 30; [Rom. 12:17] [b]ch. 26:67; Isa. 50:6; Lam. 3:30
40 [z][See ver. 39 above]
41 [c]ch. 27:32
42 [d]Ps. 37:21; Prov. 21:26 [e]Deut. 15:8; Ps. 37:26; 112:5; Luke 6:34, 35
43 [f]See ver. 21 [g]Cited from Lev. 19:18; See ch. 19:19
44 [i]Luke 6:27, 28; Rom. 12:20; [Ex. 23:4; Job 31:29, 30; Ps. 7:4] [j]Luke 23:34; Acts 7:60; 2 Tim. 4:16; 1 Pet. 3:9
45 [k]Luke 6:35; [Eph. 5:1; Phil. 2:15] [l]Acts 14:17
46 [m]Luke 6:32
47 [n]ch. 6:7, 32
48 [o][Luke 6:36] [p]ch. 19:21; 1 Cor. 2:6 (Gk.); Phil. 3:15 (Gk.); Col. 1:28; 4:12 (Gk.); James 1:4; 3:2; See Gen. 17:1 [q][Lev. 19:2; 1 Pet. 1:15]
Chapter 6
1 [r]1 John 2:29 [s]ver. 16; ch. 23:5
2 [t][1 Cor. 13:3] [u]John 5:44 [v]Luke 6:24
4 [w]ver. 6, 18
5 [x]Mark 11:25; Luke 18:11 [y]ver. 2, 16
6 [z]2 Kgs. 4:33; Isa. 26:20 [a]ver. 4, 18
7 [b]ver. 32; ch. 5:47 [c]1 Kgs. 18:26 [d]Prov. 10:19; Eccles. 5:2 **8** [e]ver. 32 **9** [f]For ver. 9-13, [Luke 11:2-4] [g]ver. 1 [h]Isa. 29:23; [Luke 1:49; 1 Pet. 3:15] [i]John 17:6

10 [j] Your kingdom come,
[k] your will be done,[1]
[l] on earth as it is in heaven.
11 [m] Give us [n] this day our daily bread,[2]
12 and forgive us our debts,
as we also have forgiven our debtors.
13 And [o] lead us not into temptation,
but [p] deliver us from [q] evil.[3]

14 [r] For if you forgive others their trespasses, your
heavenly Father will also forgive you, 15 [s] but if
you do not forgive others their trespasses, neither will your Father forgive your trespasses.

Fasting

16 "And [t] when you fast, do not look gloomy
like the hypocrites, for they disfigure their
faces that their fasting may be seen by others.
[u] Truly, I say to you, they have received their
reward. 17 But when you fast, [v] anoint your
head and wash your face, 18 that your fasting
may not be seen by others but by your Father
who is in secret. [w] And your Father who sees in
secret will reward you.

Lay Up Treasures in Heaven

19 [x] "Do not lay up for yourselves treasures
on earth, where [y] moth and rust[4] destroy and
where thieves [z] break in and steal, 20 [x] but lay up
for yourselves treasures in heaven, where neither moth nor rust destroys and where thieves
do not break in and steal. 21 For where your
treasure is, there your heart will be also.
22 [a] "The eye is the lamp of the body. So, if your
eye is healthy, your whole body will be full of
light, 23 [a] but if [b] your eye is bad, your whole
body will be full of darkness. If then the light
in you is darkness, how great is the darkness!
24 [c] "No one can serve two masters, for either
he will hate the one and love the other, or he
will be devoted to the one and despise the
other. You cannot serve God and [d] money.[5]

Do Not Be Anxious

25 [e] "Therefore I tell you, [f] do not be anxious
about your life, what you will eat or what you
will drink, nor about your body, what you will
put on. Is not life more than food, and the
body more than clothing? 26 [g] Look at the birds
of the air: they neither sow nor reap nor gather
into barns, and yet your heavenly Father feeds
them. [h] Are you not of more value than they?
27 And which of you by being anxious can add
a single hour to his [i] span of life?[6] 28 And why
are you anxious about clothing? Consider the
lilies of the field, how they grow: they neither
toil nor spin, 29 yet I tell you, [j] even Solomon in
all his glory was not arrayed like one of these.
30 But if God so clothes the grass of the field,
which today is alive and tomorrow is thrown
into the oven, will he not much more clothe
you, [k] O you of little faith? 31 Therefore do not
be anxious, saying, 'What shall we eat?' or
'What shall we drink?' or 'What shall we wear?'
32 For [l] the Gentiles seek after all these things,
and [m] your heavenly Father knows that you
need them all. 33 But [n] seek first [o] the kingdom

[1] Or *Let your kingdom come, let your will be done* [2] Or *our bread for tomorrow* [3] Or *the evil one*; some manuscripts add *For yours is the kingdom and the power and the glory, forever. Amen* [4] Or *worm*; also verse 20 [5] Greek *mammon*, a Semitic word for money or possessions [6] Or *a single cubit to his stature*; a *cubit* was about 18 inches or 45 centimeters

10 [j] [ch. 3:2; 4:17] [k] ch. 26:42; Luke 22:42; Acts 21:14; [ch. 12:50; Heb. 13:21] [l] Ps. 103:20, 21; Dan. 4:35
11 [m] Prov. 30:8 [n] [ver. 34]
13 [o] ch. 26:41; Mark 14:38; Luke 22:40, 46; [1 Cor. 10:13] [p] John 17:15; 2 Thess. 3:3; [2 Tim. 4:18] [q] See ch. 13:19
14 [r] Mark 11:25; Luke 6:37; Eph. 4:32; Col. 3:13
15 [s] ch. 18:35; See James 2:13
16 [t] Isa. 58:5 [u] ver. 2, 5
17 [v] Ruth 3:3; 2 Sam. 12:20
18 [w] ver. 4, 6
19 [x] ch. 19:21; Luke 12:21, 33, 34; 18:22; 1 Tim. 6:9, 10, 17-19; Heb. 13:5 [y] James 5:2, 3 [z] ch. 24:43
20 [x] [See ver. 19 above]
22 [a] Luke 11:34, 35
23 [a] [See ver. 22 above] [b] ch. 20:15; Deut. 15:9; Prov. 28:22
24 [c] Luke 16:13; [Rom. 6:16; James 4:4] [d] Luke 16:9, 11, 13

or a concern to use the right formulas in performing them, can easily be motivated by self-absorption and greed.

Second, Jesus recognizes how easy it is to seek for ultimate security in money (vv. 19–34). When food, clothing, and shelter are scarce, people become understandably anxious about how they will find these basic necessities. But this anxiety can become so overwhelming that people begin hoarding wealth. They create ever-widening margins between themselves and the scarcity that they dread, in the process becoming less dependent on God and more dependent on themselves. Money itself can become their god (v. 24).

Jesus urges his followers to find their ultimate security not in wealth but in God who will meet their needs. God meets the needs of his followers largely through the generosity of those among his people who have more than others. In verse 3 Jesus assumes that his disciples give to the needy ("*when* you give to the needy"); and in 25:31–46, acts of generosity and compassion toward those in need are the mark of a genuine relationship with Jesus (see also Acts 20:35; 2 Cor. 8:1–5; Eph. 4:28). We have been given so much in Christ. It is our glad privilege to give to others, honoring and reflecting his own compassion.

25 [e] For ver. 25-33, see Luke 12:22-31 [f] ver. 27, 28, 31, 34; ch. 10:19; 13:22 (Gk.); 1 Cor. 7:32 (Gk.); Phil. 4:6; 1 Pet. 5:7 **26** [g] [Job 38:41; Ps. 147:9] [h] ch. 10:31 **27** [i] Luke 2:52 **29** [j] 1 Kgs. 10:4-7 **30** [k] ch. 8:26; 14:31; 16:8; [ch. 17:20] **32** [l] ver. 7 [m] ver. 8 **33** [n] [ch. 5:6, 20] [o] ver. 10

of God and his righteousness, [p]and all these
things will be added to you.
34 [q]"Therefore do not be anxious about
tomorrow, for tomorrow will be anxious for
itself. Sufficient for the day is its own trouble.

Judging Others

7 [r]"Judge not, that you be not judged. 2 [s]For
with the judgment you pronounce you
will be judged, and [t]with the measure you use
it will be measured to you. 3 Why do you see
the speck that is in your brother's eye, but
[u]do not notice the log that is in your own eye?
4 Or how can you say to your brother, 'Let me
take the speck out of your eye,' when there is
the log in your own eye? 5 You hypocrite, first
take the log out of your own eye, and then you
will see clearly to take the speck out of your
brother's eye.
6 [v]"Do not give [w]dogs what is holy, and do not
throw your [x]pearls before pigs, lest they trample them underfoot and turn to attack you.

Ask, and It Will Be Given

7 [y]"Ask, [z]and it will be given to you; [a]seek, and
you will find; [b]knock, and it will be opened
to you. 8 For everyone who asks receives, and
the one who seeks finds, and to the one who
knocks it will be opened. 9 Or which one of
you, if his son asks him for [c]bread, will give
him [c]a stone? 10 Or if he asks for a fish, will
give him a serpent? 11 If you then, [d]who are evil,
know how to give good gifts to your children,
how much more will [z]your Father who is in
heaven give good things to those who ask him!

The Golden Rule

12 "So [e]whatever you wish that others would
do to you, do also to them, for this is [f]the Law
and the Prophets.
13 [g]"Enter by the narrow gate. For the gate is
wide and the way is easy[1] that leads to destruction, and those who enter by it are many. 14 For
the gate is narrow and [h]the way is hard that
leads to life, and [i]those who find it are few.

A Tree and Its Fruit

15 [j]"Beware of false prophets, who come to you
in sheep's clothing but inwardly are [k]ravenous
wolves. 16 You will recognize them [l]by their
fruits. Are grapes gathered from thornbushes,
or figs from thistles? 17 So, [m]every healthy tree
bears good fruit, but the diseased tree bears
bad fruit. 18 A healthy tree cannot bear bad
fruit, nor can a diseased tree bear good fruit.
19 [n]Every tree that does not bear good fruit is
cut down and thrown into the fire. 20 Thus you
will recognize them [l]by their fruits.

I Never Knew You

21 [o]"Not everyone who [p]says to me, 'Lord,
Lord,' will [q]enter the kingdom of heaven, but
the one who [r]does the will of my Father who
is in heaven. 22 [s]On that day [t]many will say to
me, 'Lord, Lord, did we not [u]prophesy in your
name, and cast out demons [v]in your name, and

[1] Some manuscripts *For the way is wide and easy*

7:1–5 The Scriptures frequently warn believers against passing judgment on others (Luke 6:37; Rom. 14:10–13; 1 Cor. 4:5; James 4:11–12). Because they are sinful, human beings tend to excuse in themselves the sin they readily condemn in others (Rom. 2:1, 21–23). Here Jesus goes even further to say that people often excuse sins in themselves that are far worse than the sins they identify in others (Matt. 7:3–5; see also 18:21–35). The remedy to a judgmental attitude is an understanding of one's own need for spiritual healing, for righteousness, and for mercy (5:3, 6–7). The pride that feeds the hypocrisy Jesus criticizes here may be the "log" in one's own eye to which he refers (7:5).

God has judged Jesus in our place. If we are united to Christ through his cross, our end-time judgment is already behind us. We are therefore liberated from judging others, because of our lavish exoneration through the free grace of Christ.

7:15–23 The mere claim to be a follower of Jesus, and the mere possession of the outward trappings of a commitment to him (vv. 15, 21–22), do not indicate whether one's relationship with him is real. Christian discipleship is genuine when it arises from a heart and mind transformed by God's grace, and this inner transformation, which Matthew calls repentance, will inevitably bear good fruit (3:8).

33 [p][1 Kgs. 3:11-14; Mark 10:29, 30; 1 Tim. 4:8; 1 Pet. 3:9]
34 [q][James 4:13, 14]
Chapter 7
1 [r]For ver. 1-5, see Luke 6:37, 38, 41, 42; [Rom. 14:13; 1 Cor. 4:5; James 5:9]
2 [s]Rom. 2:1, 3; 14:10; James 2:13; 4:11, 12 [t]Mark 4:24; [Judg. 1:7]
3 [u][John 8:7-9]
6 [v]ch. 15:26; [Prov. 9:7, 8; 23:9] [w][Phil. 3:2; Rev. 22:15] [x]ch. 13:46
7 [y]For ver. 7-11, see Luke 11:9-13 [z]ch. 18:19; 21:22; Mark 11:24; John 14:13; 15:7, 16; 16:23, 24; James 1:5, 6, 17; 1 John 3:22; 5:14, 15 [a]1 Chr. 28:9; 2 Chr. 15:2; Prov. 8:17; Jer. 29:13; [Isa. 55:6] [b][Rev. 3:20]
9 [c]ch. 4:3
11 [d]ch. 12:34; Gen. 6:5; 8:21 [z][See ver. 7 above]
12 [e]Luke 6:31 [f]See ch. 22:40
13 [g]Luke 13:24
14 [h]Ps. 16:11; [ch. 18:8; John 14:6] [i][Luke 13:23] **15** [j]ch. 24:11, 24; Deut. 13:1-3; Jer. 14:14; 23:16; Mark 13:22; Luke 6:26; Acts 13:6; 2 Pet. 2:1; 1 John 4:1 [k]Ezek. 22:27; Acts 20:29; [Mic. 3:5; John 10:12] **16** [l]Luke 6:43, 44; James 2:18 **17** [m]ch. 12:33-35 **19** [n]See ch. 3:10 **20** [l][See ver. 16 above] **21** [o]Luke 6:46; Rom. 2:13; James 1:22 [p][Hos. 8:2] [q][John 3:3, 5] [r]ch. 12:50 **22** [s]ch. 25:11, 12; Luke 13:25-27 [t]Mal. 3:17, 18 [u][Num. 24:4; John 11:51; 1 Cor. 13:2] [v]See Mark 9:38

do many mighty works in your name?' 23 [t]And then will I declare to them, 'I [w]never knew you; [x]depart from me, [y]you workers of lawlessness.'

Build Your House on the Rock

24 [z]"Everyone then who hears these words of mine and does them will be like [a]a wise man who built his house on the rock. 25 And the rain fell, and the floods came, and the winds blew and beat on that house, but it did not fall, because it had been founded on the rock. 26 And everyone who hears these words of mine and does not do them will be like [a]a foolish man who built his house on the sand. 27 And the rain fell, and the floods came, and the winds blew and beat against that house, and it fell, and great was the fall of it."

The Authority of Jesus

28 And when Jesus finished these sayings, [b]the crowds were astonished at his teaching, 29 [c]for he was teaching them as one who had authority, and not as their scribes.

Jesus Cleanses a Leper

8 When he came down from the mountain, [d]great crowds followed him. 2 [e]And behold, a leper[1] came to him and [f]knelt before him, saying, "Lord, if you will, you can make me clean." 3 And Jesus[2] stretched out his hand and touched him, saying, "I will; be clean." And immediately his leprosy was cleansed. 4 And Jesus said to him, [g]"See that you say nothing to anyone, but go, [h]show yourself to the priest and [i]offer the gift that Moses commanded, [j]for a proof to them."

The Faith of a Centurion

5 [k]When he had entered Capernaum, a centurion came forward to him, appealing to him, 6 "Lord, my servant is lying paralyzed at home, suffering terribly." 7 And he said to him, "I will come and heal him." 8 But the centurion replied, "Lord, I am not worthy to have you come under my roof, but [l]only say the word, and my servant will be healed. 9 For I too am a man under authority, with soldiers under me. And I say to one, 'Go,' and he goes, and to another, 'Come,' and he comes, and to my servant,[3] 'Do this,' and he does it." 10 When Jesus heard this, [m]he marveled and said to those who followed him, "Truly, I tell you, with [n]no one in Israel[4] have I found such faith. 11 I tell you, [o]many will come from east and west and recline at table with Abraham, Isaac, and Jacob in the kingdom of heaven, 12 [p]while the sons of the kingdom [q]will be thrown into the outer darkness. In that place [r]there will be weeping and gnashing of teeth." 13 And to the centurion Jesus said, "Go; let it be done for you [s]as you have believed." [t]And the servant was healed at that very moment.

Jesus Heals Many

14 [u]And when Jesus entered Peter's house, he saw [v]his mother-in-law lying sick with a fever. 15 He [w]touched her hand, and the fever left her, and she rose and began to serve him. 16 That evening they brought to him many who were [x]oppressed by demons, and he cast out the spirits [y]with a word and healed all who were sick. 17 [z]This was to fulfill what was spoken by the prophet Isaiah: [a]"He took our illnesses and bore our diseases."

The Cost of Following Jesus

18 Now [b]when Jesus saw a crowd around him, [c]he gave orders to go over to the other side. 19 [d]And a scribe came up and said to him, "Teacher, I will follow you wherever you go." 20 And Jesus said to him, "Foxes have holes, and birds of the air have nests, but the Son of Man has nowhere to lay his head." 21 Another of the disciples said to him, "Lord, let me first go and bury my father." 22 And Jesus said to him, "Follow me, and leave [e]the dead to bury their own dead."

[1] *Leprosy* was a term for several skin diseases; see Leviticus 13 [2] Greek *he* [3] Greek *bondservant* [4] Some manuscripts *not even in Israel*

8:5–13 Just as with Rahab and Ruth (1:5), and the Wise Men from the east (2:1–2, 10–11), now the centurion demonstrates that the kingdom of God is not limited by social and ethnic boundaries (see also 12:18, 21, 38–42; and 15:28). This centurion was a commanding officer within the pagan army that occupied Judea, but he was as welcome in the kingdom as any Israelite. The critical criterion for entry into the kingdom is not the ethnic group to which one belongs but one's faith in Jesus (8:10).

23 [t][See ver. 22 above] [w]ch. 10:33; [Ps. 101:4] [x]ch. 25:41; Ps. 6:8 [y]ch. 13:41; Ps. 5:5
24 [z]For ver. 24-27, see Luke 6:47-49 [a]ch. 25:2; [Ezek. 13:10-14]
26 [a][See ver. 24 above]
28 [b]ch. 13:54; 22:33; Mark 1:22; 6:2; 11:18; Luke 4:32; [Acts 13:12] **29** [c]John 7:46 **Chapter 8** **1** [d]ch. 4:25 **2** [e]For ver. 2-4, see Mark 1:40-44; Luke 5:12-14 [f][ch. 18:26; Acts 10:25] **4** [g]ch. 9:30; 17:9; Mark 1:34; 5:43; 7:36; 8:26; See ch. 12:16 [h]Luke 17:14 [i]Lev. 14:2-32 [j]ch. 10:18; 24:14; Mark 6:11; Luke 9:5; James 5:3 **5** [k]For ver. 5-13, see Luke 7:1-10 **8** [l]Ps. 107:20; [ver. 16] **10** [m][Mark 6:6] [n]See ch. 9:2 **11** [o]Luke 13:29; Eph. 3:6; [Isa. 59:19; Mal. 1:11] **12** [p]Luke 13:28; [ch. 19:30; 21:41, 43] [q]ch. 22:13; 25:30 [r]ch. 13:42, 50; 22:13; 24:51; 25:30; Luke 13:28 **13** [s]ch. 9:29 [t]John 4:53; [ch. 9:22] **14** [u]For ver. 14-16, see Mark 1:29-34; Luke 4:38-41 [v]1 Cor. 9:5 **15** [w][ch. 9:25] **16** [x]ver. 28, 33; See ch. 4:24 [y][ver. 8] **17** [z]See ch. 1:22 [a]Cited from Isa. 53:4 **18** [b][ch. 14:22; John 6:15-17] [c]Mark 4:35; Luke 8:22 **19** [d]For ver. 19-22, see Luke 9:57-60 **22** [e][John 5:25]

Jesus Calms a Storm

23 [f]And when he got into the boat, his disciples
followed him. 24 And behold, there arose a great
storm on the sea, so that the boat was being
swamped by the waves; but [g]he was asleep.
25 And they went and woke him, saying, [h]"Save
us, Lord; we are perishing." 26 And he said to
them, "Why are you [i]afraid, [j]O you of little
faith?" Then he rose and [k]rebuked the winds
and the sea, and [l]there was a great calm. 27 And
the men [m]marveled, saying, "What sort of man
is this, that even [n]winds and sea obey him?"

Jesus Heals Two Men with Demons

28 [o]And when he came to the other side, to
the country of the Gadarenes,[1] two [p]demon-
possessed[2] men met him, coming out of the
tombs, so fierce that no one could pass that
way. 29 And behold, they [q]cried out, "What have
you to do with us, [r]O Son of God? Have you
come here to torment us [s]before the time?"
30 Now a herd of many pigs was feeding at
some distance from them. 31 And the demons
begged him, saying, "If you cast us out, send
us away into the herd of pigs." 32 And he said
to them, "Go." So they came out and went into
the pigs, and behold, the whole herd rushed
down the steep bank into the sea and drowned
in the waters. 33 The herdsmen fled, and going
into the city they told everything, especially
what had happened to the [t]demon-possessed
men. 34 And behold, all the city came out to
meet Jesus, and when they saw him, [u]they
begged him to leave their region.

Jesus Heals a Paralytic

9 And getting into a boat he crossed over
and came to [v]his own city. 2 [w]And behold,
some people brought to him a paralytic, lying
on a bed. And when Jesus [x]saw their faith, he
said to the paralytic, [y]"Take heart, my son;
[z]your sins are forgiven." 3 And behold, some
of the scribes said to themselves, [a]"This man
is blaspheming." 4 But Jesus, [b]knowing[3] their
thoughts, said, "Why do you think evil in your
hearts? 5 For which is easier, to say, 'Your sins
are forgiven,' or to say, 'Rise and walk'? 6 But
that you may know that the Son of Man has
authority on earth to forgive sins"—he then
said to the paralytic—"Rise, pick up your bed
and go home." 7 And he rose and went home.
8 When the crowds saw it, [c]they were afraid,
and [c]they glorified God, who had [d]given such
authority to men.

[1] Some manuscripts *Gergesenes*; some *Gerasenes* [2] Greek *daimonizomai*; also verse 33; elsewhere rendered *oppressed by demons*
[3] Some manuscripts *perceiving*

8:27 The disciples' question has already been answered by Jesus' stilling of the winds and the sea. Jesus is God himself (1:23): he can bring order to the chaos of the sea, as occurred at creation (Gen. 1:2); he can still the waves of a present storm, whenever his people cry out in distress (Ps. 107:23–32); and ultimately he will relieve all their distress, as seen in the promise of an eternal kingdom with no more chaotic sea (Rev. 21:1). As powerful as the Creator is, he stoops to the weakness of his people, heals their suffering (Matt. 8:17), and rescues them from peril despite their lack of faith (v. 26). This is who he *is*.

8:28–34 Wherever Jesus goes he brings the reign of God, and where God reigns, the invisible powers of the universe in rebellion against him are banished and left powerless to do anyone ultimate harm (see also 4:23–24; 12:28). As the demons recognize, they will someday be completely destroyed, and at this moment in the lives of these two demon-oppressed men, the time of the demons' final destruction is brought forward into the present (8:29, 32).

Demons still exist, are still in rebellion against God, and can still promote evil and create hardship (Eph. 2:2; 6:12, 16; Rev. 12:7–17). But God has already conquered and subdued them by means of Jesus' death, resurrection, and ascension to heaven (Luke 10:18; Eph. 1:20–22; Col. 2:15; 1 Pet. 3:18–22; Rev. 12:1–11). Since believers are united with Christ, they share Christ's victory over evil (Eph. 2:6; Rev. 12:11). Equipped with the armor that God supplies (Eph. 6:10–17), and engaged in prayer (Eph. 6:18–20), believers have nothing to fear from Satan and the demonic powers he controls.

9:1–8 Just as the reign of God brings victory over demons, so it brings forgiveness of sins. Eventually, when the heavens and earth are fully healed from the destruction of sin, all death, mourning, crying, and pain will be gone forever (Rev. 21:4). Here, for this moment, Jesus brings the future kingdom of God into the present. He graciously forgives this paralyzed man's sins on the basis of his faith, and he restores him to health.

23 [f]For ver. 23-27, see Mark 4:36-41; Luke 8:22-25; [John 6:16-21]
24 [g][John 4:6, 7]
25 [h][ch. 14:30]
26 [i]John 14:27 [j]See ch. 6:30 [k]Ps. 104:6, 7; [Luke 4:39] [l]Job 38:11; Ps. 65:7; [ch. 14:32]
27 [m][Mark 1:27] [n][Luke 5:9]
28 [o]For ch. 8:28-9:1, see Mark 5:1-21; Luke 8:26-40 [p]ver. 16; [Rev. 18:2]
29 [q]Mark 1:23, 24, 26; Luke 4:34; Acts 8:7 [r][ch. 4:3, 6]; See ch. 14:33 [s][Rev. 12:12]
33 [t]ver. 16
34 [u][1 Kgs. 17:18; Luke 5:8; Acts 16:39]

Chapter 9
1 [v]ch. 4:13; [Mark 2:1]
2 [w]For ver. 2-8, see Mark 2:3-12; Luke 5:18-26 [x]ver. 22, 29; ch. 8:10, 13; 15:28; Mark 10:52; Luke 7:9, 50; 17:19; 18:42; Acts 3:16; 14:9; James 5:15 [y]ver. 22 [z]Luke 7:48; [John 5:14]
3 [a]ch. 26:65; John 10:36
4 [b]ch. 12:25; John 2:24, 25
8 [c]See Luke 7:16 [d]ch. 28:18

Jesus Calls Matthew

9 [e]As Jesus passed on from there, he saw a
man called [f]Matthew sitting at the tax booth,
and he said to him, "Follow me." And he rose
and followed him.
10 And as Jesus[1] reclined at table in the house,
behold, many [g]tax collectors and sinners came
and were reclining with Jesus and his disciples. 11 And when the Pharisees saw this, they
said to his disciples, [h]"Why does your teacher
eat with [g]tax collectors and sinners?" 12 But
when he heard it, he said, "Those who are well
have no need of a physician, but those who are
sick. 13 Go and learn [i]what this means, [j]'I desire
mercy, and not sacrifice.' For [k]I came not to call
the righteous, [l]but sinners."

A Question About Fasting

14 Then [m]the disciples of John came to him,
saying, [n]"Why do we and [o]the Pharisees
fast,[2] but your disciples do not fast?" 15 And
Jesus said to them, [p]"Can the wedding
guests mourn as long as the bridegroom is
with them? [q]The days will come when the
bridegroom is taken away from them, and
[r]then they will fast. 16 No one puts a piece of
unshrunk cloth on an old garment, for the
patch tears away from the garment, and a
worse tear is made. 17 Neither is new wine
put into old [s]wineskins. If it is, the skins
burst and the wine is spilled and the skins
are destroyed. But new wine is put into fresh
wineskins, and so both are preserved."

A Girl Restored to Life and a Woman Healed

18 [t]While he was saying these things to them,
behold, a ruler came in and [u]knelt before him,
saying, "My daughter has just died, but come
and lay your hand on her, and she will live."
19 And Jesus rose and followed him, with his
disciples. 20 And behold, a woman [v]who had
suffered from a discharge of blood for twelve
years came up behind him and touched [w]the
fringe of his garment, 21 for she said to herself,
"If I only touch his garment, I will be made
well." 22 Jesus turned, and seeing her he said,
[x]"Take heart, daughter; your faith has made
you well." [y]And instantly[3] the woman was
made well. 23 And when Jesus came to the ruler's house and saw [z]the flute players and the
crowd making a commotion, 24 he said, "Go
away, for [a]the girl is not dead but [b]sleeping."
And they laughed at him. 25 But [c]when the
crowd had been put outside, he went in and
[d]took her by the hand, and the girl arose. 26 And
the report of this went through all that district.

Jesus Heals Two Blind Men

27 [e]And as Jesus passed on from there, two
blind men followed him, crying aloud,
"Have mercy on us, [f]Son of David." 28 When
he entered the house, the blind men came to
him, and Jesus said to them, "Do you believe
that I am able to do this?" They said to him,
"Yes, Lord." 29 [g]Then he touched their eyes,
saying, [h]"According to your faith be it done to
you." 30 And their eyes were opened. And Jesus

[1] Greek *he* [2] Some manuscripts add *much*, or *often* [3] Greek *from that hour*

9[e] For ver. 9-17, see Mark 2:14-22; Luke 5:27-38 [f] ch. 10:3; Mark 3:18; Luke 6:15; Acts 1:13
10[g] ch. 11:19; See ch. 5:46
11[h] [Luke 15:2] [g] [See ver. 10 above]
13[i] ch. 12:7 [j] Cited from Hos. 6:6; [ch. 23:23; Mark 12:33] [k] [Luke 15:7; John 9:39] [l] 1 Tim. 1:15
14[m] ch. 11:2; 14:12; Luke 11:1; John 1:35; 3:25; 4:1; [Acts 18:25; 19:3] [n] [ch. 15:2] [o] Luke 18:12
15[p] John 3:29 [q] See Luke 17:22 [r] [John 16:20]
17[s] Josh. 9:4
18[t] For ver. 18-26, see Mark 5:22-43; Luke 8:41-56 [u] See ch. 8:2
20[v] Lev. 15:25 [w] ch. 14:36; 23:5; [Num. 15:38, 39; Deut. 22:12]
22[x] ver. 2; See Luke 7:50 [y] ch. 15:28; 17:18; [ch. 8:13]
23[z] Rev. 18:22
24[a] [Acts 20:10] [b] John 11:4, 11
25[c] Acts 9:40 [d] Mark 9:27; Acts 3:7; 9:41

9:9–13 The gracious nature of God's reign is clear in Jesus' invitation to the tax collector Matthew to follow him, and in his table fellowship with other tax collectors and sinners. The coupling of tax collectors with sinners demonstrates how unsavory the business of tax collection was in Jesus' time (see also 5:46; 11:19; 21:31–32; Luke 18:11). It frequently involved extortion of money from people who were already very poor (Luke 3:12–13; 19:8). God is merciful to the sinner, however, who knows that he or she is unrighteous (Matt. 9:13), and who turns away from sin to the salvation that Jesus brings (Luke 5:32; 19:5–10).

9:18–34 Once again, wherever Jesus goes the kingdom of God goes with him, demonstrating that God is merciful and gracious. He gives life to the dead, heals the sick, restores the disabled, and banishes demonic powers.

The religious leaders' opposition to Jesus (v. 34; see also vv. 3, 11) is a sobering reminder that religious scholarship, professions of religious conviction, and observance of religious ritual do not make one a follower of Jesus. One can do all of this and yet so strongly resist the implications of Jesus' call for repentance and faith that one attributes the works of Jesus to the forces of evil. The hardheartedness of the Pharisees against Jesus demonstrates how deep human sin runs, and that religious people are not exempt from its destructive power.

27[e] [ch. 20:30-34] [f] ch. 12:23; 15:22; 20:30, 31; 22:42; See ch. 1:1 **29**[g] Mark 8:25; John 9:6 [h] See ver. 2

sternly warned them, [i]"See that no one knows
about it." 31[j]But they went away and spread his
fame through all that district.

Jesus Heals a Man Unable to Speak

32 As they were going away, behold, a
[k]demon-oppressed man who was mute [l]was
brought to him. 33 And when the demon
had been cast out, the mute man spoke. And
the crowds [m]marveled, saying, "Never was
anything like this seen in Israel." 34 But the
Pharisees said, "He casts out demons by the
prince of demons."

The Harvest Is Plentiful, the Laborers Few

35 [n]And Jesus went throughout all the cities and villages, teaching in their synagogues
and proclaiming the gospel of the kingdom
and healing every disease and every affliction.
36 [o]When he saw the crowds, [p]he had compassion for them, because they were harassed
and helpless, [q]like sheep without a shepherd.
37 [r]Then he said to his disciples, "The harvest is
plentiful, but the laborers are few; 38 therefore
[s]pray earnestly to the Lord of the harvest to
[t]send out laborers into his harvest."

The Twelve Apostles

10 [u]And he called to him his twelve disciples and gave them authority over
unclean spirits, to cast them out, and to heal
every disease and every affliction. 2 [v]The names
of the twelve apostles are these: first, Simon,
[w]who is called Peter, and [x]Andrew his brother;
[x]James the son of Zebedee, and John his
brother; 3 Philip and Bartholomew; Thomas
and [y]Matthew the tax collector; James the
son of Alphaeus, and Thaddaeus;[1] 4 Simon the
Zealot,[2] and Judas Iscariot, who betrayed him.

Jesus Sends Out the Twelve Apostles

5 [u]These twelve Jesus sent out, instructing
them, "Go nowhere among the Gentiles and
enter no town of [z]the Samaritans, 6 [a]but go
rather to [b]the lost sheep of [c]the house of Israel.
7 And proclaim as you go, saying, [d]'The kingdom of heaven is at hand.' 8 [e]Heal the sick, raise
the dead, cleanse lepers,[3] cast out demons.
[f]You received without paying; give without
pay. 9 [g]Acquire no gold or silver or copper for
your belts, 10 no bag for your journey, or two
tunics[4] or sandals or a staff, for [h]the laborer
deserves his food. 11 And whatever town or
village you enter, find out who is worthy in
it and stay there until you depart. 12 As you
enter the house, [i]greet it. 13 And if the house
is [j]worthy, let [j]your peace come upon it, but
if it is not worthy, let [j]your peace return to
you. 14 And if anyone will not receive you or
listen to your words, [l]shake off the dust from
your feet when you leave that house or town.
15 Truly, I say to you, [m]it will be more bearable
on the day of judgment for [n]the land of Sodom
and Gomorrah than for that town.

Persecution Will Come

16 [o]"Behold, I am sending you out as sheep
in the midst of wolves, so be [p]wise as serpents
and [q]innocent as doves. 17 Beware of men, for
[r]they will deliver you over to courts and flog

[1] Some manuscripts *Lebbaeus*, or *Lebbaeus called Thaddaeus* [2] Greek *kananaios*, meaning *zealot* [3] *Leprosy* was a term for several skin diseases; see Leviticus 13 [4] Greek *chiton*, a long garment worn under the cloak next to the skin

9:35–10:42 Jesus commissioned his disciples to help him in his work. This work was motivated by "compassion" for the "harassed and helpless" (9:36) and was to be done without any cost to those who benefited from it, just as the disciples' relationship with Jesus came to them without any cost (10:8). The disciples' ministry, then, was to imitate Jesus' ministry and to communicate the life-giving, restorative, utterly free grace of God so clearly displayed in Jesus' ministry. Like Jesus, the disciples would encounter rejection (10:14) and opposition (10:24–25), even from their own families (10:21–22, 35–37).

Jesus' disciples today are also called to live and minster in this way. The character of their lives and the practical methods they use in ministering to others in the name of Jesus should always bear the stamp of God's joyful, gracious, and utterly free forgiveness and restoration of his creatures. At the same time, no matter how good the news, how honest their methods, and how winsome their appeal, the message of the gospel will sometimes meet with harsh, even violent, rejection—as was true for Jesus himself.

30 [i]See ch. 8:4
31 [j]Mark 1:45; 7:36
32 [k][ch. 12:22-24; Luke 11:14, 15] [l]See ch. 4:24
33 [m][Mark 1:27]
35 [n]See ch. 4:23, 24
36 [o][ch. 14:14] [p]Mark 6:34 [q]Num. 27:17; 1 Kgs. 22:17; Ezek. 34:5
37 [r]Luke 10:2; John 4:35
38 [s][2 Thess. 3:1] [t]ch. 20:2; [Mark 1:12]

Chapter 10
1 [u]Mark 3:13-15; 6:7-13; Luke 6:13; 9:1, 2
2 [v]For ver. 2-4, see Mark 3:16-19; Luke 6:14-16; Acts 1:13 [w]ch. 16:18; John 1:42 [x]ch. 4:18, 21
3 [y]ch. 9:9
5 [u][See ver. 1 above] [z]2 Kgs. 17:24; Ezra 4:10; Luke 9:52; 10:33; 17:16; John 4:9, 39, 40; 8:48; Acts 8:25; [Acts 1:8] **6** [a]ch. 15:24; [Acts 3:25, 26; 13:46] [b]Ps. 119:176; Isa. 53:6; Jer. 50:6; [ch. 9:36; 18:12] [c]Acts 2:36; 7:42; Heb. 8:8, 10 **7** [d]ch. 3:2; 4:17; Luke 10:9 **8** [e][ch. 11:5] [f][Isa. 55:1; Acts 3:6; 20:33, 35] **9** [g]For ver. 9-15, see Mark 6:8-11; Luke 9:3-5; [Luke 10:4-12; 22:35] **10** [h]1 Tim. 5:18; [1 Cor. 9:4, 7-14] **12** [i][1 Sam. 25:6; 1 Chr. 12:18] **13** [j][ch. 8:8; Acts 16:15] [j][See ver. 12 above] **14** [l]Acts 13:51; [Neh. 5:13; Acts 18:6] **15** [m]ch. 11:24 [n]Gen. 18:20; 19:28; 2 Pet. 2:6 **16** [o]Luke 10:3; [John 17:18] [p]Gen. 3:1 [q]Rom. 16:19 (Gk.); Phil. 2:15; [1 Cor. 14:20] **17** [r]See Mark 13:9, 11; Luke 12:11, 12

you [s]in their synagogues, 18 [r]and you will be
dragged before governors and kings for my
sake, [t]to bear witness before them and the
Gentiles. 19 [r]When [u]they deliver you over, [v]do
not be anxious how you are to speak or what
you are to say, for [w]what you are to say will
be given to you in that hour. 20 [x]For it is not
you who speak, but [y]the Spirit of your Father
speaking through you. 21 [z]Brother will deliver
brother over to death, and the father his child,
and children will rise against parents and have
them put to death, 22 [a]and you will be hated
by all for my name's sake. [b]But the one who
endures to the end will be saved. 23 When they
[c]persecute you in one town, [d]flee to the next,
for truly, I say to you, you will not have gone
through all the towns of Israel [e]before the Son
of Man comes.

24 [f]"A disciple is not above his teacher, nor a
servant[1] above his master. 25 It is enough for
the disciple to be like his teacher, and the servant like his master. [g]If they have called the
master of the house Beelzebul, how much
more will they malign[2] those of his household.

Have No Fear

26 "So have no fear of them, [i]for nothing is
covered that will not be revealed, or hidden
that will not be known. 27 What I tell you in
the dark, say in the light, and what you hear
whispered, proclaim on [j]the housetops. 28 And
[k]do not fear those who kill the body but cannot kill the soul. Rather fear him [l]who can
destroy both soul and body in hell.[3] 29 Are not
two sparrows sold for a penny?[4] And not one
of them will fall to the ground apart from your
Father. 30 But [m]even the hairs of your head are
all numbered. 31 Fear not, therefore; [n]you are of
more value than many sparrows. 32 [o]So everyone who acknowledges me before men, I also
will acknowledge before my Father who is in
heaven, 33 but [p]whoever denies me before men,
[q]I also will deny before my Father who is in
heaven.

Not Peace, but a Sword

34 [r]"Do not think that I have come to bring
peace to the earth. [s]I have not come to bring
peace, but a sword. 35 [r]For I have come [t]to set a
man against his father, and a daughter against
her mother, and a daughter-in-law against her
mother-in-law. 36 [u]And a person's enemies will
be those of his own household. 37 [v]Whoever
loves father or mother more than me is not
worthy of me, and whoever loves son or
daughter more than me is not worthy of me.
38 And [w]whoever does not take his cross and
[x]follow me is not worthy of me. 39 [y]Whoever
finds his life will lose it, and whoever loses his
life for my sake will find it.

Rewards

40 [z]"Whoever receives you receives me, and
[a]whoever receives me receives him who sent
me. 41 [b]The one who receives a prophet because
he is a prophet will receive a prophet's reward,
and the one who receives a righteous person
because he is a righteous person will receive
a righteous person's reward. 42 And [c]whoever
gives one of [d]these little ones even a cup of
cold water because he is a disciple, truly, I say
to you, he will by no means lose his reward."

Messengers from John the Baptist

11 When Jesus had finished instructing his
twelve disciples, he went on from there
to teach and preach in their cities.

2 [e]Now when John heard [f]in prison about the
deeds of [g]the Christ, he sent word by [h]his disciples 3 and said to him, "Are you [i]the one who
is to come, or shall we [j]look for another?" 4 And
Jesus answered them, "Go and tell John what
you hear and see: 5 [k]the blind receive their

[1] Greek *bondservant*; also verse 25 [2] Greek lacks *will they malign* [3] Greek *Gehenna* [4] Greek *assarion*, Roman copper coin (Latin *quadrans*) worth about 1/16 of a *denarius* (which was a day's wage for a laborer)

17 [s]See ch. 23:34
18 [r][See ver. 17 above] [t]See ch. 8:4
19 [r][See ver. 17 above] [u]For ver. 19-22, [Mark 13:11-13; Luke 21:12-19; 2 Tim. 4:16, 17]

11:4–6 John began to doubt that Jesus was "the Christ" (11:2), the unique future King of Israel whom God had designated to bring in his universal reign of justice and blessing (Ps. 2:2, 7–12). Jesus' answer echoes the events of his own ministry up to this point. He has healed blind men (Matt. 9:27–31), a lame man (9:1–8), and a leper

[v]See ch. 6:25 [w]Deut. 18:18; [Num. 23:5]; See Ex. 4:12 **20** [x]Luke 12:12; Acts 4:8; 6:10; 13:9; 1 Cor. 15:10; 2 Cor. 13:3; [ver. 40; 1 Thess. 2:13; Heb. 1:1] [y][John 15:26] **21** [z]ver. 35, 36 **22** [a]ch. 24:9; John 15:18-21 [b]ch. 24:13; Mark 13:13; [Dan. 12:12, 13; James 5:11; Rev. 2:10]; See Heb. 3:6 **23** [c]ch. 23:34 [d][ch. 12:15; Acts 8:1; 9:25, 30; 14:6; 17:10, 14] [e]ch. 16:28 **24** [f]Luke 6:40; John 13:16; 15:20; [Heb. 12:3] **25** [g]ch. 9:34; 12:24; Mark 3:22; Luke 11:15; See John 7:20 **26** [i]Mark 4:22; Luke 8:17; [1 Tim. 5:25]; For ver. 26-33, see Luke 12:2-9 **27** [j]See Luke 5:19 **28** [k]Isa. 8:12, 13; 51:12, 13; Jer. 1:8; 1 Pet. 3:14 [l]James 4:12 **30** [m]See 1 Sam. 14:45 **31** [n]ch. 6:26; 12:12 **32** [o][Rom. 10:9, 10; Heb. 10:35; Rev. 3:5] **33** [p]2 Tim. 2:12; 2 Pet. 2:1; 1 John 2:23; [Mark 8:38] [q]ch. 7:23; 25:12; Luke 13:25 **34** [r]See Luke 12:51-53 [s][Rev. 6:4] **35** [r][See ver. 34 above] [t]ver. 21; [Mic. 7:6] **36** [u]Cited from Mic. 7:6; [Ps. 41:9; 55:12, 13; John 13:18] **37** [v]Luke 14:26 **38** [w]ch. 16:24; Mark 8:34; Luke 9:23; 14:27 [x]ch. 9:9; John 8:12; 12:26; 21:19 **39** [y]ch. 16:25; Mark 8:35; Luke 9:24; 17:33; John 12:25 **40** [z]Luke 10:16; John 13:20; Gal. 4:14; [ver. 20; ch. 18:5; 25:40] [a]Mark 9:37; Luke 9:48; [John 12:44, 45] **41** [b]1 Kgs. 17:10-15; 18:4; 2 Kgs. 4:8; [3 John 5-8] **42** [c]ch. 25:35, 40; Mark 9:41; Heb. 6:10 [d]ch. 18:10 **Chapter 11** **2** [e]For ver. 2-19, see Luke 7:18-35 [f]ch. 14:3; [ch. 4:12] [g]See ch. 1:17 [h]See ch. 9:14 **3** [i]John 4:25; 6:14; 11:27 [j][Luke 3:15] **5** [k]See Luke 7:22

sight and the lame walk, lepers[1] are cleansed
and the deaf hear, and the dead are raised
up, and [l]the poor have good news preached
to them. 6 And blessed is the one who [m]is not
offended by me."
7 As they went away, Jesus began to speak to
the crowds concerning John: "What did you go
out [n]into the wilderness to see? [o]A reed shaken
by the wind? 8 What then did you go out to see?
A man[2] dressed in soft clothing? Behold, those
who wear soft clothing are in kings' houses.
9 What then did you go out to see? [p]A prophet?[3]
Yes, I tell you, and more than a prophet. 10 This
is he of whom it is written,

[q]"'Behold, I send my messenger before
your face,
who will prepare your way before you.'

11 Truly, I say to you, among those born of
women there has arisen no one greater than
John the Baptist. Yet the one who is least in
the kingdom of heaven is greater than he.
12 [r]From the days of John the Baptist until
now the kingdom of heaven has suffered violence,[4] and the violent take it by force. 13 [r]For
all the Prophets and the Law prophesied until
John, 14 and if you are willing to accept it, he is
[s]Elijah who is to come. 15 [t]He who has ears to
hear,[5] let him hear.
16 "But to what shall I compare this generation? It is like children sitting in the marketplaces and calling to their playmates,

17 "'We played the flute for you, and you did
not dance;
we sang a dirge, and you did not
mourn.'

18 For John came [u]neither eating [v]nor drinking, and they say, 'He has a demon.' 19 The Son
of Man came [w]eating and drinking, and they
say, 'Look at him! A glutton and a drunkard,
[x]a friend of [y]tax collectors and sinners!' Yet
wisdom is justified by her deeds."[6]

Woe to Unrepentant Cities

20 [z]Then he began to denounce the cities
where most of his mighty works had been
done, because they did not repent. 21 [a]"Woe to
you, Chorazin! Woe to you, Bethsaida! For if
the mighty works done in you had been done
in [b]Tyre and Sidon, they would have repented
long ago in sackcloth and ashes. 22 [c]But I tell
you, it will be more bearable on [d]the day of
judgment for [b]Tyre and Sidon than for you.
23 And you, [e]Capernaum, will you be exalted to
heaven? You will be brought down to [f]Hades.
For if the mighty works done in you had been
done in Sodom, it would have remained until
this day. 24 [c]But I tell you that [g]it will be more
tolerable on [d]the day of judgment for the land
of Sodom than for you."

Come to Me, and I Will Give You Rest

25 [h]At that time Jesus declared, "I thank you,
Father, [i]Lord of heaven and earth, that [j]you

[1] *Leprosy* was a term for several skin diseases; see Leviticus 13 [2] Or *Why then did you go out? To see a man . . .* [3] Some manuscripts *Why then did you go out? To see a prophet?* [4] Or *has been coming violently* [5] Some manuscripts omit *to hear* [6] Some manuscripts *children* (compare Luke 7:35)

(8:2–3). He has restored a girl to life who was thought to be dead (9:18–26), and he has given the poor in spirit the good news that they are blessed (5:3).

Jesus' answer also echoes passages in the Prophets that describe the future restoration of God's people and of the entire world to wholeness and peace. In that day, says Isaiah, the deaf will hear, the blind will see, the meek will rejoice, and the poor will praise God (Isa. 29:17–19; 35:6; 61:1–3; Mic. 4:6–7).

Jesus, then, is the expected King whose reign establishes the compassionate, restorative rule of God. Some took offense at Jesus, however, because he established his reign by befriending tax collectors and sinners (Matt. 11:19), something they did not expect (v. 6). It is precisely those who know their need of a relationship with God through repentance and faith who are welcomed into his kingdom. The church today is to continue to be a refuge for sinners who understand their need for the forgiveness and restoration that God freely offers in the gospel.

11:25–26 The scribes and Pharisees who rejected Jesus would have been recognized as "wise and understanding" (v. 25; see also Isa. 29:18) according to the prevailing standards of their society. Paradoxically, the metaphorical "little children"—people whom society considered unimportant—were more responsive to God's revelation of his merciful and gracious character than the learned. Later in Matthew's Gospel, Jesus will say that unless a person turns and becomes like a little child, he or she cannot enter the kingdom of heaven (Matt. 18:3). Entry into the kingdom involves

5 [l] Luke 4:18; [ch. 5:3; James 2:5]
6 [m] Isa. 8:14, 15; John 6:61
7 [n] ch. 3:1; Luke 1:80 [o] [Eph. 4:14; James 1:6]
9 [p] ch. 14:5; 21:26; Luke 1:76
10 [q] Mark 1:2; Cited from Mal. 3:1
12 [r] Luke 16:16
13 [r] [See ver. 12 above]
14 [s] ch. 17:10-13; Mal. 4:5; Mark 9:11-13; Luke 1:17; [John 1:21]
15 [t] ch. 13:9, 43; Luke 8:8; 14:35
18 [u] ch. 3:4; Mark 1:6 [v] Luke 1:15
19 [w] ch. 9:10; Luke 7:36; 14:1; John 2:1; 12:2 [x] ch. 9:11; Luke 15:2; 19:7 [y] ch. 18:17
20 [z] [Ps. 81:11-13; Isa. 1:2-5]
21 [a] For ver. 21-24, see Luke 10:12-15 [b] ch. 15:21; Mark 3:8; [Isa. 23; Ezek. 28:2-24; Amos 1:9, 10]
22 [c] [Luke 12:47, 48] [d] See Acts 17:31 [b] [See ver. 21 above]
23 [e] Cited from Isa. 14:13-15 [f] ch. 16:18 (Gk.); Luke 16:23; Acts 2:27
24 [c] [See ver. 22 above] [g] ch. 10:15 [d] [See ver. 22 above]
25 [h] For ver. 25-27, see Luke 10:21, 22 [i] See Acts 17:24 [j] Job 37:24; 1 Cor. 1:19-27; 2 Cor. 3:14

have hidden these things from the wise and
understanding and [k]revealed them to little
children; 26 yes, Father, for such was your [l]gra-
cious will.[1] 27 [m]All things have been handed
over to me by my Father, and no one knows
the Son [n]except the Father, and no one knows
the Father except the Son and anyone [o]to
whom the Son chooses to reveal him. 28 [p]Come
to [q]me, all who labor and are [r]heavy laden, and
I will give you rest. 29 Take my yoke upon you,
and [s]learn from me, for I am [t]gentle and lowly
in heart, and [u]you will find rest for your souls.
30 For [v]my yoke is easy, and my burden is light."

Jesus Is Lord of the Sabbath

12 At that time [w]Jesus went through the
grainfields on the Sabbath. His disciples were hungry, and [x]they began to pluck
heads of grain and to eat. 2 But when the
Pharisees saw it, they said to him, [y]"Look, your
disciples are doing [z]what is not lawful to do
on the Sabbath." 3 He said to them, [a]"Have you
not read what David did when he was hungry, and those who were with him: 4 how he
entered the house of God and ate [b]the bread
of the Presence, which it was not lawful for
him to eat nor for those who were with him,

[1] Or *for so it pleased you well*

25 [k]ch. 21:16; Ps. 8:2; [ch. 13:11; 16:17]
26 [l]Luke 12:32; Gal. 1:15
27 [m]See ch. 28:18 [n][John 1:18; 6:46; 7:29; 8:19; 10:15; 17:25] [o][John 17:26]
28 [p]John 7:37; [John 6:37] [q][ver. 3] [r][ch. 23:4; Luke 11:46]
29 [s]John 13:15; Eph. 4:20; Phil. 2:5; 1 Pet. 2:21; 1 John 2:6 [t]Zech. 9:9; 2 Cor. 10:1; Phil. 2:7, 8; [ch. 5:5] [u]Jer. 6:16
30 [v]1 John 5:3

Chapter 12
1 [w]For ver. 1-8, see Mark 2:23-28; Luke 6:1-5 [x]Deut. 23:25
2 [y][ver. 10; Luke 13:14; 14:3; John 5:10; 7:23; 9:16] [z][Ex. 20:9-11]
3 [a]1 Sam. 21:1-6; See ch. 21:16
4 [b]Ex. 25:30; Lev. 24:5-9

understanding that one is wholly dependent upon God for salvation, just as a little child is wholly dependent for life and health upon loving adults.

Paul makes the same point with respect to the cross of Christ in 1 Corinthians 1:18–2:8. God used the cross to bring atonement for the sins of those who believe the gospel (Rom. 3:21–26; 2 Cor. 5:19–21; Gal. 3:13), but society viewed the cross as an instrument of pain, death, and defeat. The idea of saving people through the crucifixion of Jesus seemed like folly to those too fascinated with sinful worldly wisdom to accept the humbling truth that they were sinners in need of the atonement provided by this shameful death (1 Cor. 1:18, 21; 2:8). It was mainly those who were not "wise according to worldly standards" or "powerful" or "of noble birth"—the "foolish in the world"—who embraced the gospel when Paul preached it (1 Cor. 1:26–30).

11:28–30 Jesus now invites all who hear or read his words to experience the refreshment of being his disciple. His metaphor is drawn from the world of field work, where the labor is hard and the loads difficult for man and beast. Within the context of Matthew's Gospel, this imagery probably refers to the heavy load of religious observances that the scribes and Pharisees had bundled together and placed on people's backs (23:4).

The Mosaic law itself was not intended to be burdensome to keep (Deut. 30:11) but a delight and a blessing to the humble person who trusted God (Ps. 19:7–11; 119). The scribes and the Pharisees, however, had twisted God's law into a means of self-congratulation and showing off, by observing it in unnecessarily ostentatious ways devised by "learned" calculation (Matt. 23:5, 16, 18, 23, 25, 29–30). Those who were not learned—the "little children" to whom Jesus referred in 11:25—would likely have experienced the teaching of the scribes and Pharisees on these matters as burdensome.

Jesus offers relief to his disciples from the burden of religious observance as a means of attaining self-worth. Learning from Jesus is more like rest than work because Jesus, unlike the scribes and Pharisees, is meek and humble. This passage is the only place in all four Gospel accounts where Jesus tells us about his heart—and he says it is "gentle and lowly" (v. 29). He is ready to help all those who are themselves humble enough to admit their need of his mercy and grace. Indeed, he delights to do so.

12:1–14 Matthew gives two examples of how Jesus' yoke is easy and his burden light (11:30). In both examples, Jesus opposes the Pharisees' imposition on others of their burdensome way of observing the fourth commandment (Ex. 20:8–11; Deut. 5:12–15). The purpose of the Sabbath law was to show mercy to human beings and their farm animals by mandating regular rest from the hard labor of agrarian life (Matt. 12:8; Ex. 23:12). If its "observance" somehow made hungry people more miserable by forbidding them from obtaining food, or required a disabled person to remain disabled longer than necessary, then the purpose of the law itself had been violated (Matt. 12:7, 12; Hos. 6:6; Mic. 6:6–8).

Christians of every age and culture have formulated ideas about how the moral teaching of Scripture should be obeyed in their own time and place. Often these ideas

but only for the priests? 5 Or have you not read
[c]in the Law how on the Sabbath the priests in
the temple profane the Sabbath and are guiltless? 6 I tell you, [d]something greater than the
temple is here. 7 And if you had known [e]what
this means, [f]'I desire mercy, and not sacrifice,'
you would not have condemned the guiltless.
8 For [g]the Son of Man is lord of the Sabbath."

A Man with a Withered Hand

9 He went on from there and [h]entered their
synagogue. 10 And a man was there with a
withered hand. And they asked him, [i]"Is it
lawful to heal on the Sabbath?"—[j]so that they
might accuse him. 11 He said to them, "Which
one of you who has a sheep, [k]if it falls into a
pit on the Sabbath, will not take hold of it and
lift it out? 12 [l]Of how much more value is a man
than a sheep! So [m]it is lawful to do good on the
Sabbath." 13 Then he said to the man, "Stretch
out your hand." And [n]the man stretched it out,
and it was restored, healthy like the other.
14 But the Pharisees went out and conspired
against him, how to destroy him.

God's Chosen Servant

15 Jesus, aware of this, [o]withdrew from there.
And [p]many followed him, and he healed them
all 16 and [q]ordered them not to make him
known. 17 [r]This was to fulfill what was spoken
by the prophet Isaiah:

18 [s]"Behold, my [t]servant whom I have chosen,
my beloved with whom my soul is
well pleased.
[u]I will put my Spirit upon him,
and he will proclaim justice to the
Gentiles.
19 He will not quarrel or cry aloud,
nor will anyone hear his voice in the
streets;
20 a bruised reed he will not break,
and a smoldering wick he will not
quench,
until he brings justice to victory;
21 [v]and in his name the Gentiles will
hope."

Blasphemy Against the Holy Spirit

22 [w]Then a demon-oppressed man who was
blind and mute was brought to him, and he
healed him, so that the man spoke and saw.
23 [x]And all the people were amazed, and said,
[x]"Can this be the Son of David?" 24 But when
the Pharisees heard it, they said, [y]"It is only by
Beelzebul, the prince of demons, that this man
casts out demons." 25 [z]Knowing their thoughts,
[a]he said to them, "Every kingdom divided
against itself is laid waste, and no city or house
divided against itself will stand. 26 And if Satan
casts out Satan, he is divided against himself.
How then will his kingdom stand? 27 And if
I cast out demons by Beelzebul, [b]by whom do
[c]your sons cast them out? Therefore they will
be your judges. 28 But if it is [d]by the Spirit of
God that I cast out demons, then [e]the kingdom of God has come upon you. 29 Or [f]how can
someone enter a strong man's house and plunder his goods, unless he first binds the strong
man? Then indeed [g]he may plunder his house.
30 [h]Whoever is not with me is against me, and
whoever does not gather with me scatters.
31 [i]Therefore I tell you, every sin and blasphemy
will be forgiven people, but [j]the blasphemy
against the Spirit will not be forgiven. 32 And

become translated into rules for avoiding temptation in basic areas where Christians must interact with a non-Christian culture, whether over clothing, food, speech, or entertainment. Matthew 12:1–14 cautions believers as they engage in such rule-making to understand what they are doing: they are not formulating authoritative Scripture but giving fallible human advice, however prudent (5:29–30; 18:8–9), on how best to obey Scripture in particular circumstances. Whenever the tendency of these rules hinders the basic concern of Scripture for mercy, justice, and kindness, the rules have themselves become a hindrance to obeying God and need to be set aside.

12:31–32 Jesus speaks alarmingly here of a sin that cannot be forgiven (see also 1 John 5:16–17). It is important to consider this statement within its broader context in order to understand what it means. Jesus is responding to the claim of the Pharisees that he casts out demons by means of demonic power instead of the power of God's Spirit (Matt. 12:24; Mark 3:28–30). This is the second time in the Gospel that the Pharisees have said this (cf. Matt. 9:34; see also 10:25), and between the first and the second

5[c] Num. 28:9, 10; [1 Chr. 9:32; John 7:22, 23]
6[d] ver. 41, 42; [ver. 8; Hag. 2:9; Mal. 3:1]
7[e] ch. 9:13 [f] Cited from Hos. 6:6; [Mic. 6:6-8]
8[g] [ch. 9:6]
9[h] For ver. 9-14, see Mark 3:1-6; Luke 6:6-11
10[i] [Luke 14:3]; See ver. 2 [j] [Luke 11:54; 20:20; John 8:6]
11[k] [Ex. 23:4, 5; Deut. 22:4]
12[l] ch. 6:26; 10:31 [m] [John 5:16, 17]
13[n] [1 Kgs. 13:4]
15[o] Mark 3:7; John 10:39; See ch. 10:23 [p] ch. 19:2
16[q] Mark 1:25 (Gk.); 3:12; 8:30; Luke 4:41 (Gk.); 9:21; See ch. 8:4
17[r] See ch. 1:22

18[s] Cited from Isa. 42:1-3 [t] Acts 4:27, 30 [u] [Isa. 61:1; Luke 4:18; John 3:34; Acts 10:38] **21**[v] Isa. 42:4 (Gk.); [Isa. 11:10; Rom. 15:12] **22**[w] For ver. 22-24, see Luke 11:14, 15; [ch. 9:32-34] **23**[x] John 4:29; 7:26, 31; See ch. 9:27 **24**[y] Mark 3:22; See ch. 10:25 **25**[z] See ch. 9:4 [a] For ver. 25-29, see Mark 3:23-27; Luke 11:17-22 **27**[b] [Acts 19:13] **27**[c] [2 Kgs. 2:7] **28**[d] [ver. 18] [e] ch. 19:24; 21:31, 43; Luke 17:21 **29**[f] Isa. 49:24 [g] [Isa. 53:12] **30**[h] Luke 11:23; [Mark 9:40; Luke 9:50] **31**[i] For ver. 31, 32, see Mark 3:28-30; [Luke 12:10; Heb. 6:4-6; 10:26; 1 John 5:16] [j] [Acts 7:51; Heb. 10:29]

whoever speaks a word [k]against the Son of
Man [l]will be forgiven, but [j]whoever speaks
against the Holy Spirit will not be forgiven,
either in [m]this age or in the age to come.

A Tree Is Known by Its Fruit

33 [n]"Either make the tree good and its fruit
good, or make the tree bad and its fruit bad,
[o]for the tree is known by its fruit. 34 [p]You brood
of vipers! How can you speak good, [q]when you
are evil? [r]For out of the abundance of the heart
the mouth speaks. 35 [r]The good person out
of his good treasure brings forth good, and
the evil person out of his evil treasure brings
forth evil. 36 I tell you, [s]on the day of judgment
[t]people will give account for [u]every careless
word they speak, 37 for [v]by your words you
will be justified, and by your words you will
be condemned."

The Sign of Jonah

38 Then some of the scribes and Pharisees
answered him, saying, "Teacher, [w]we wish
to see a sign from you." 39 But he answered
them, [x]"An evil and [y]adulterous generation
seeks for a sign, but no sign will be given to
it except the sign of the prophet Jonah. 40 For
[z]just as Jonah was three days and three nights
in the belly of the great fish, [a]so will the Son
of Man be three days and three nights in the
heart of the earth. 41 [b]The men of Nineveh will
rise up at the judgment with this generation
and [c]condemn it, for [d]they repented at the
preaching of Jonah, and behold, [e]something
greater than Jonah is here. 42 [f]The queen of
the South will rise up at the judgment with
this generation and condemn it, for she came
from the ends of the earth to hear the wisdom
of Solomon, and behold, [e]something greater
than Solomon is here.

Return of an Unclean Spirit

43 "When [g]the unclean spirit has gone out of
a person, it passes through [h]waterless places
seeking rest, but finds none. 44 Then it says,
'I will return to my house from which I came.'
And when it comes, it finds the house empty,
swept, and put in order. 45 Then it goes and
brings with it seven other spirits more evil than
itself, and they enter and dwell there, and [i]the

32 [k]ch. 11:19; John 7:12; 9:24 [l]1 Tim. 1:12, 13 [j][See ver. 31 above] [m][Eph. 1:21]
33 [n]ch. 7:16-20 [o]Luke 6:43, 44
34 [p]ch. 3:7; 23:33 [q]ch. 7:11 [r]ch. 15:18, 19; Luke 6:45; [ch. 13:52; Eph. 4:29]
35 [r][See ver. 34 above]
36 [s][Eph. 5:4, 11; 2 Pet. 1:8] [t]Eccles. 12:14; Rom. 14:12; 1 Pet. 4:5 [u]See Acts 17:31
37 [v][ch. 5:22; James 3:2-12]
38 [w]ch. 16:1; Mark 8:11, 12; Luke 11:16; 23:8; John 2:18; 4:48; 6:30; 1 Cor. 1:22
39 [x]ch. 16:4; For ver. 39-42, see Luke 11:29-32; [Mark 8:11, 12] [y]Isa. 57:3; Mark 8:38; James 4:4
40 [z]Jonah 1:17 [a][ch. 17:22, 23]
41 [b]Jonah 1:2 [c]Heb. 11:7; [Jer. 3:11; Ezek. 16:51, 52; Rom. 2:27] [d]Jonah 3:5 [e]ver. 6
42 [f]1 Kgs. 10:1; 2 Chr. 9:1 [e][See ver. 41 above]
43 [g]For ver. 43-45, see Luke 11:24-26 [h][Ps. 63:1; Jer. 2:6]
45 [i]2 Pet. 2:20-22; [John 5:14]

occurrences of this verdict on Jesus' exorcisms, they have hatched a conspiracy to kill him (12:14). Their "blasphemy against the Spirit," then, is not an impulsive action or statement. It is rather a determined course of godlessness arising from a settled conviction that God's chosen servant, on whom God has put his Spirit (v. 18), is an agent of the very demonic powers Jesus came to defeat.

Blasphemy against the Holy Spirit is the unchanging conviction that Jesus is evil. In essence, the only "unforgivable" sin is a conclusive rejection of Christ rather than a contrite reception of him.

12:33–37 A person's inner spiritual condition becomes clear in his or her speech. The Pharisees, who have conspired to kill Jesus (v. 14) and have attributed his ability to cast out demons to the *influence* of demons (v. 24), have spoken words that arise from the "evil" condition of their hearts (v. 34). Unless they repent, they and others like them will be condemned on the day of judgment. The evidence of their hardheartedness, and therefore of their just condemnation, will be the unsupported, worthless words that they have spoken about Jesus.

The Pharisees' worthless words are a good example of the kind of "corrupting talk" that Paul says should not characterize the believer's speech. As people who have been transformed by God's grace, believers should instead engage in speech that gives "grace to those who hear" (Eph. 4:29; Col. 4:6). For that is precisely what the gospel does to *us*.

12:41–42 As the hostility of the intellectual leadership of the Jews rises to a crescendo, Jesus reminds them that there is precedent in Scripture for non-Jews having as much or more spiritual discernment than the Jews themselves. The pagan Ninevites repented when Jonah told them of God's coming judgment (Jonah 3:1–10), and the queen of the South (from the southern Arabian peninsula) praised the Lord for what she learned about him from Solomon (1 Kings 10:9).

People should not assume that their formal affiliation with the people of God or their expertise in the Scriptures somehow makes them acceptable to God or automatically makes them part of his true people (see also Matt. 3:9; 8:10–12; 11:25). Only those who have responded to Jesus' call to turn from their sins, trust his wonderful message of forgiveness, and follow him have a place within the people of God.

last state of that person is worse than the first.
So also will it be with this [j]evil generation."

Jesus' Mother and Brothers

46 While he was still speaking to the people,
behold, [k]his mother and his [l]brothers stood
outside, asking to speak to him.[1] 48 But he
replied to the man who told him, "Who is my
mother, and who are my brothers?" 49 And
stretching out his hand toward his disciples,
he said, "Here are my mother and my brothers!
50 For [m]whoever [n]does the will of my Father in
heaven is my brother and sister and mother."

The Parable of the Sower

13 That same day Jesus went out of the
house [o]and sat beside the sea. 2 And
great crowds gathered about him, [p]so that
he got into a boat and sat down. And the
whole crowd stood on the beach. 3 And [q]he
told them many things in parables, saying:
[r]"A sower went out to sow. 4 And as he sowed,
some seeds fell along the path, and the birds
came and devoured them. 5 Other seeds fell on
rocky ground, where they did not have much
soil, and immediately they sprang up, since
they had no depth of soil, 6 but [s]when the sun
rose they were scorched. And since they had
no root, [t]they withered away. 7 Other seeds fell
among [u]thorns, and the thorns grew up and
choked them. 8 Other seeds fell on good soil
and produced grain, some [v]a hundredfold,
some sixty, some thirty. 9 [w]He who has ears,[2]
let him hear."

The Purpose of the Parables

10 Then the disciples came and said to him,
"Why do you speak to them in parables?"
11 And he answered them, [x]"To you it has been
given to know [y]the secrets of the kingdom
of heaven, but to them it has not been given.
12 [z]For to the one who has, more will be given,
and he will have an abundance, but from the
one who has not, [a]even what he has will be
taken away. 13 This is why I speak to them in
parables, because [b]seeing they do not see, and
hearing they do not hear, [c]nor do they understand. 14 Indeed, in their case the prophecy of
Isaiah is fulfilled that says:

[d]"'You will indeed hear but never understand,
and you will indeed see but never perceive."
15 For this people's heart has grown dull,
and with their ears [e]they can barely
hear,
and [f]their eyes they have closed,
lest they should see with their eyes
and hear with their ears
and [g]understand with their heart
and [h]turn, and I would heal them.'

16 But [i]blessed are your eyes, for they see, and
your ears, for they hear. 17 [i]For truly, I say to

[1] Some manuscripts insert verse 47: *Someone told him, "Your mother and your brothers are standing outside, asking to speak to you"*
[2] Some manuscripts add here and in verse 43 *to hear*

13:1–52 In these eight parables Jesus describes both the hidden nature of the kingdom of God in the present and the mixed response of people who hear about it. The final chapter in God's plan to restore the universe to what it should be after the destruction of sin (17:11) has started in a way so small and seemingly insignificant that many people pay no attention to it or reject it. Like the seed that a farmer sows (13:3–9, 18–23, 31–32), a small amount of leaven (v. 33), a buried or hidden treasure (vv. 44, 52), or an elusive pearl (vv. 45–46), the beginning of the kingdom is not obvious.

The intellectual elites of Judaism did not recognize the arrival of the kingdom, despite their knowledge of the Scriptures (23:2; see also 1 Cor. 1:23; 2:8). The close-knit community in which Jesus grew up rejected it, thinking that the Jesus they knew was unimpressive (Matt. 13:53–58). Even those who at first embraced Jesus' message of the kingdom enthusiastically sometimes failed to persevere in their initial commitment to it (vv. 19–22; see also 10:4).

Others, however, responded with joy to the kingdom and devoted their lives to it without holding back (13:23, 44, 46). The genuineness of their commitment was evident in the way they lived (v. 23). Still, the parable of the sower makes it plain to us that, until the final day of judgment, the institutional church we can see with human eyes will always have some who are not truly believers (see also vv. 24–30, 36–43, 47–50; see also 1 Cor. 4:5).

45 [j]ver. 39
46 [k]For ver. 46-50, see Mark 3:31-35; Luke 8:19-21 [l]ch. 13:55; Mark 6:3; John 2:12; 7:3, 5, 10; Acts 1:14; 1 Cor. 9:5; Gal. 1:19
50 [m][John 15:14; Heb. 2:11] [n]ch. 7:21; [Luke 11:28]
Chapter 13
1 [o]For ver. 1-15, see Mark 4:1-12; Luke 8:4-10
2 [p][Mark 3:9; Luke 5:1-3]
3 [q]ver. 34 [r][Isa. 55:10; Amos 9:13]
6 [s]James 1:11 [t]John 15:6
7 [u]Jer. 4:3
8 [v]ver. 23; Gen. 26:12
9 [w]See ch. 11:15
11 [x]ch. 19:11; Col. 1:27; [1 Cor. 2:6-10; 1 John 2:20, 27]; See ch. 11:25 [y]See Rom. 16:25
12 [z]ch. 25:29; Mark 4:25; Luke 8:18; 19:26; [John 15:2; James 4:6] [a][Rev. 2:5]
13 [b]Deut. 29:4; Jer. 5:21; Ezek. 12:2; Rom. 11:8; 2 Cor. 3:14; 4:4; [Isa. 42:19, 20] [c]ver. 19, 51; ch. 15:10; 16:12; Mark 8:21
14 [d]John 12:40; Acts 28:26, 27; Cited from Isa. 6:9, 10

15 [e][Heb. 5:11] [f][John 9:39, 41] [g][Rom. 10:10] [h]See Luke 22:32 **16** [i]Luke 10:23, 24; [ch. 16:17] **17** [i][See ver. 16 above]

you, [j]many prophets and righteous people
longed to see what you see, and did not see it,
and to hear what you hear, and did not hear it.

The Parable of the Sower Explained

18 [k]"Hear then the parable of the sower:
19 When anyone hears the word of [l]the kingdom and [m]does not understand it, [n]the evil
one comes and snatches away what has been
sown in his heart. This is what was sown along
the path. 20 As for what was sown on rocky
ground, this is the one who hears the word
and immediately [o]receives it with joy, 21 yet
he has no root in himself, but [p]endures for a
while, and when tribulation or persecution
arises on account of the word, immediately
[q]he falls away.[1] 22 As for what was sown among
thorns, this is the one who hears the word,
but [r]the cares of [s]the world and [t]the deceitfulness of riches choke the word, and it proves
unfruitful. 23 As for what was sown on good
soil, this is the one who hears the word and
[m]understands it. He indeed [u]bears fruit and
yields, in one case [v]a hundredfold, in another
sixty, and in another thirty."

The Parable of the Weeds

24 He put another parable before them, saying, [w]"The kingdom of heaven may be compared to a man who sowed good seed in his
field, 25 but while his men were sleeping, his
enemy came and sowed weeds[2] among the
wheat and went away. 26 So when the plants
came up and bore grain, then the weeds
appeared also. 27 And the servants[3] of the
master of the house came and said to him,
'Master, did you not sow good seed in your
field? How then does it have weeds?' 28 He said
to them, 'An enemy has done this.' So the servants said to him, 'Then do you want us to go
and gather them?' 29 But he said, [x]'No, lest in
gathering the weeds you root up the wheat
along with them. 30 Let both grow together
until the harvest, and at harvest time I will tell
the reapers, [y]Gather the weeds first and bind
them in bundles to be burned, but gather the
wheat into my barn.'"

The Mustard Seed and the Leaven

31 He put another parable before them, saying, [z]"The kingdom of heaven is like [a]a grain of
mustard seed that a man took and sowed in his
field. 32 It is the smallest of all seeds, but when
it has grown it is larger than all the garden
plants and becomes a tree, so that the birds of
the air come and make nests in its branches."
33 He told them another parable. [b]"The kingdom of heaven is like leaven that a woman
took and hid in [c]three measures of flour, till
it was [d]all leavened."

Prophecy and Parables

34 [e]All these things Jesus said to the crowds
in parables; indeed, he said nothing to them
without a parable. 35 This was to fulfill what
was spoken by the prophet:[4]

[f]"I will open my mouth in parables;
[g]I will utter what has been hidden [h]since
the foundation of the world."

[1] Or *stumbles* [2] Probably *darnel*, a wheat-like weed [3] Greek *bondservants*; also verse 28 [4] Some manuscripts *Isaiah the prophet*

17 [j]Heb. 11:13; 1 Pet. 1:10-12; [John 8:56]
18 [k]For ver. 18-23, see Mark 4:13-20; Luke 8:11-15
19 [l]ver. 38; ch. 4:23; 8:12 [m]See ver. 13 [n]John 17:15; Eph. 6:16; 2 Thess. 3:3; 1 John 2:13, 14; 3:12; 5:18, 19
20 [o][Isa. 58:2; Ezek. 33:31, 32; Mark 6:20; John 5:35]
21 [p]Gal. 1:6; [Hos. 6:4; Gal. 5:7] [q]See ch. 11:6
22 [r]See ch. 6:25 [s]2 Tim. 4:10 [t]1 Tim. 6:9, 10, 17; [ch. 19:23; Mark 10:23; Acts 5:1-11; Heb. 3:13]
23 [m][See ver. 19 above] [u]Hos. 14:8; John 15:5, 16; Phil. 1:11; Col. 1:6 [v]ver. 8
24 [w]ver. 37-42; [Mark 4:26-29]
29 [x][1 Cor. 4:5]
30 [y]ch. 3:12
31 [z]For ver. 31, 32, see Mark 4:30-32; Luke 13:18, 19 [a]ch. 17:20; Luke 17:6
33 [b]Luke 13:20, 21 [c]Gen. 18:6

Although the gospel is much better known around the world now than when Jesus uttered these parables in the first century, these characteristics are still true of the proclamation of God's kingdom. Believers should not be discouraged by the rejection with which the faithful proclamation of the gospel is sometimes met, even among those thought at first to be believers. To genuine believers, the kingdom of God—with its message of forgiveness, restoration, and a living relationship with a loving Father—will always be good and joyful news.

The parable of the weeds (Matt. 13:24–30 and 36–43) is especially important for explaining why God does not root out all evil from our world immediately. Jesus pictures the wisdom of a farmer who will not damage his crop by pulling up weeds growing near the roots of good plants. So also God wisely delays judgment that would remove all of Satan's instruments, so that the followers of Christ and the purposes of God may reach maturity. Were God in this moment to root out all evil from the world, then not only would all institutions that are designed for human commerce, security, and health collapse, but so also would the cause of God's mission in the world for the millions who have yet to claim our Redeemer as their own. Patience in judgment is a significant grace of God.

[d]1 Cor. 5:6; Gal. 5:9 **34** [e]ver. 3; Mark 4:33, 34; [John 16:25, 29] **35** [f]Cited from Ps. 78:2 [g][ver. 11; Rom. 16:25, 26; 1 Cor. 2:7] [h]ch. 25:34; Luke 11:50; [John 17:24; Eph. 1:4; 1 Pet. 1:20]

The Parable of the Weeds Explained

36 Then he left the crowds and went into [i]the house. And his disciples came to him, saying, [j]"Explain to us the parable of the weeds of the field." 37 He answered, "The one who sows the good seed is the Son of Man. 38 The field is the world, and the good seed is [k]the sons of the kingdom. The weeds are [l]the sons of the evil one, 39 and the enemy who sowed them is the devil. [m]The harvest is [n]the end of the age, and the reapers are angels. 40 Just as the weeds [o]are gathered and burned with fire, so will it be at [n]the end of the age. 41 [p]The Son of Man will send his angels, and they will gather out of his kingdom all [q]causes of sin and [r]all law-breakers, 42 [s]and throw them into the fiery furnace. In that place [t]there will be weeping and gnashing of teeth. 43 Then [u]the righteous will shine like the sun [v]in the kingdom of their Father. [w]He who has ears, let him hear.

The Parable of the Hidden Treasure

44 "The kingdom of heaven [x]is like treasure hidden in a field, which a man found and covered up. Then in his joy [y]he goes and sells all that he has and [z]buys that field.

The Parable of the Pearl of Great Value

45 "Again, the kingdom of heaven is like a merchant in search of fine pearls, 46 who, on finding [a]one pearl of great value, [y]went and sold all that he had and [z]bought it.

The Parable of the Net

47 "Again, the kingdom of heaven is [b]like a net that was thrown into the sea and [c]gathered fish of every kind. 48 When it was full, [d]men drew it ashore and sat down and sorted the good into containers but threw away the bad. 49 So it will be at [e]the end of the age. The angels will come out and [f]separate the evil from the righteous 50 [g]and throw them into the fiery furnace. In that place [g]there will be weeping and gnashing of teeth.

New and Old Treasures

51 [h]"Have you understood all these things?" They said to him, "Yes." 52 And he said to them, "Therefore every [i]scribe [j]who has been trained for the kingdom of heaven is like a master of a house, who [k]brings out of his treasure what is new and what is old."

Jesus Rejected at Nazareth

53 And when Jesus had finished these parables, he went away from there, 54 [l]and coming to [m]his hometown [n]he taught them in their synagogue, so that [o]they were astonished, and said, "Where did this man get this wisdom and these mighty works? 55 [p]Is not this [q]the carpenter's son? Is not his mother called Mary? And are not [r]his brothers James and Joseph and Simon and Judas? 56 And are not all his sisters with us? Where then did this man get all these things?" 57 And [s]they took offense at him. But Jesus said to them, [t]"A prophet is not without honor except in his hometown and in his own household." 58 And he did not do many mighty works there, [u]because of their unbelief.

The Death of John the Baptist

14 [v]At that time [w]Herod the tetrarch heard about the fame of Jesus, 2 and he said to his servants, [x]"This is John the Baptist. He has been raised from the dead; that is why these miraculous powers are at work in him." 3 For [y]Herod had seized John and bound him and [z]put him in prison for the sake of Herodias, his brother Philip's wife,[1] 4 because John had been saying to him, [a]"It is not lawful for you to have her." 5 And though he wanted to put him to death, [b]he feared the people, because they held him to be [c]a prophet. 6 But when Herod's [d]birthday came, the daughter of Herodias danced before the company and pleased

[1] Some manuscripts *his brother's wife*

14:1–36 Jesus demonstrates here the power and compassion of God as he is revealed in the Old Testament. God fed his people in the wilderness (Ex. 16:1–17:7), and did so mercifully despite their ungrateful and complaining attitude (Ex. 16:3, 7, 12; 17:2–3, 7). Here Jesus heals the sick because of his compassion on them and provides miraculous food for them in a desolate place (Matt. 14:13–21; see also 15:32).

36 [i] ver. 1 [j] ver. 24-30; [ch. 15:15]
38 [k] [ver. 43] [l] John 8:44; Acts 13:10; 1 John 3:10; [ch. 23:15]; See ver. 19
39 [m] Joel 3:13; Rev. 14:15 [n] ver. 49; ch. 24:3; 28:20; [Dan. 12:13; Heb. 9:26]
40 [o] John 15:6; [ch. 3:12]

[n] [See ver. 39 above] **41** [p] ch. 24:31 [q] ch. 18:7; [Zeph. 1:3] [r] ch. 7:23 **42** [s] ver. 50; Rev. 9:2; [Rev. 19:20; 20:10] [t] See ch. 8:12 **43** [u] Prov. 4:18; Dan. 12:3; [1 Cor. 15:41, 42] [v] [ver. 38; ch. 25:34; 26:29; Luke 12:32] [w] See ch. 11:15 **44** [x] Prov. 2:4 [y] [ch. 25:9; Prov. 23:23; Phil. 3:7, 8] [z] [Isa. 55:1; Rev. 3:18] **46** [a] ch. 7:6 [y] [See ver. 44 above] [z] [See ver. 44 above] **47** [b] ch. 4:19 [c] [ver. 38; ch. 22:10; 25:2] **48** [d] John 21:11 **49** [e] See ver. 39 [f] ch. 25:32; [ver. 41] **50** [g] See ver. 42 **51** [h] ver. 10-16; [John 10:6; 16:29] **52** [i] ch. 23:34 [j] ch. 28:19 [k] [ch. 12:35] **54** [l] For ver. 54-58, see Mark 6:1-6; [Luke 4:16-30] [m] ch. 2:23; Luke 4:23 [n] See ch. 4:23 [o] See ch. 7:28 **55** [p] [Luke 4:22; John 6:42] [q] [Mark 6:3] [r] See ch. 12:46 **57** [s] See ch. 11:6 [t] Luke 4:24; John 4:44; [Jer. 11:21; 12:6; John 7:5] **58** [u] [ch. 17:20] **Chapter 14** **1** [v] For ver. 1-12, see Mark 6:14-29; Luke 9:7-9 [w] Luke 3:1; Acts 13:1 **2** [x] ch. 16:14 **3** [y] Luke 3:19, 20 [z] ch. 11:2; John 3:24 **4** [a] Lev. 18:16; 20:21 **5** [b] ch. 21:26; [ch. 21:46] [c] See ch. 11:9 **6** [d] Gen. 40:20

Herod, 7 so that he promised with an oath to
give her whatever she might ask. 8 Prompted
by her mother, she said, "Give me the head of
John the Baptist here on a platter." 9 And the
king was sorry, but because of his oaths and his
guests he commanded it to be given. 10 He sent
and had John beheaded in the prison, 11 and
his head was brought on a platter and given
to the girl, and she brought it to her mother.
12 And [e]his disciples came and took the body
and buried it, and they went and told Jesus.

Jesus Feeds the Five Thousand

13 Now when Jesus heard this, [f]he withdrew
from there in a boat to a desolate place by
himself. But when the crowds heard it, they
followed him on foot from the towns. 14 When
he went ashore he [g]saw a great crowd, and [g]he
had compassion on them and healed their sick.
15 Now when it was evening, the disciples came
to him and said, "This is a desolate place, and
the day is now over; [h]send the crowds away to
go into the villages and buy food for themselves." 16 But Jesus said, "They need not go
away; [i]you give them something to eat." 17 They
said to him, "We have only five loaves here and
two fish." 18 And he said, "Bring them here to
me." 19 Then he ordered the crowds to sit down
on the grass, and taking the five loaves and the
two fish, [j]he looked up to heaven and [k]said a
blessing. Then he broke the loaves and gave
them to the disciples, and the disciples gave
them to the crowds. 20 And they all ate and
were satisfied. And they took up twelve baskets full of the broken pieces left over. 21 And
those who ate were about five thousand men,
besides women and children.

Jesus Walks on the Water

22 [l]Immediately he [m]made the disciples get
into the boat and go before him to the other
side, while he dismissed the crowds. 23 And
after he had dismissed the crowds, [n]he went
up on the mountain by himself to pray. When
[o]evening came, he was there alone, 24 but the
boat by this time was a long way[1] from the
land,[2] beaten by the waves, for the wind was
against them. 25 And [l]in the fourth watch of
the night he came to them, walking on the sea.
26 But when the disciples saw him walking on
the sea, [p]they were terrified, and said, "It is a
ghost!" and they cried out in fear. 27 But immediately Jesus spoke to them, saying, [q]"Take
heart; it is I. [q]Do not be afraid."
28 And Peter answered him, "Lord, if it is you,
command me to come to you on the water."
29 He said, "Come." So Peter got out of the boat
and [r]walked on the water and came to Jesus.
30 But when he saw the wind,[3] he was afraid,
and beginning to sink he cried out, [s]"Lord,
save me." 31 Jesus immediately reached out his
hand and took hold of him, saying to him,
[t]"O you of little faith, why did you [u]doubt?"
32 And when they got into the boat, [s]the wind
ceased. 33 And [v]those in the boat [w]worshiped
him, saying, [x]"Truly you are [y]the Son of God."

Jesus Heals the Sick in Gennesaret

34 [z]And when they had crossed over, they came
to land at [a]Gennesaret. 35 And when the men
of that place recognized him, they sent around
to all that region and [b]brought to him all who
were sick 36 and implored him that they might
only touch [c]the fringe of his garment. And [d]as
many as touched it were made well.

[1] Greek *many stadia*, a *stadion* was about 607 feet or 185 meters [2] Some manuscripts *was out on the sea* [3] Some manuscripts *strong wind*

12 [e] See ch. 9:14
13 [f] For ver. 13-21, see Mark 6:32-44; Luke 9:10-17; John 6:1-13; [ch. 15:32-38; 16:9; Mark 8:2-9]
14 [g] [ch. 9:36]
15 [h] ver. 22; [ch. 15:23]
16 [i] [2 Kgs. 4:42-44]
19 [j] Mark 7:34; John 11:41; 17:1 [k] ch. 26:26; 1 Sam. 9:13; Mark 8:7; 14:22; Luke 24:30; [1 Cor. 14:16]
22 [l] For ver. 22-33, see Mark 6:45-51; John 6:15-21 [m] [ch. 8:18]
23 [n] Luke 6:12; 9:28; [Mark 1:35; Luke 5:16] [o] [Mark 13:35]
25 [l] [See ver. 22 above]
26 [p] [Luke 24:37]
27 [q] ch. 17:7; [Deut. 31:6; Isa. 41:13; 43:1, 2; John 16:33]

In the Old Testament, God controls the wind and the waves, and rescues those who call to him for help during storms at sea (Ps. 107:23–32; see also Matt. 8:27). Here Jesus does the same with his disciples (14:22–33), and particularly with Peter, who calls out, "Lord, save me," perhaps remembering Psalm 69:1–2.

God continues to help his people at their points of need, not because of anything within themselves that makes them worthy of his help but because he is a gracious and merciful God who delights in helping the needy (Eph. 1:18–23).

15:1–20 The Mosaic law nowhere mandated that people "wash their hands when they eat" (v. 2), but the Pharisees believed that it was important to follow an ancient tradition that viewed such washing as necessary, probably for purposes of ritual purity. Jesus probably regarded an insistence on observing such customs as an example of burdening people with rules that scholars had decided were necessary (23:4). The scribes and the Pharisees had become so enthralled with their own wisdom and

29 [r] [John 21:7] 30 [s] [ch. 8:25, 26] 31 [t] See ch. 6:30 [u] [James 1:6] 32 [s] [See ver. 30 above] 33 [v] ver. 22 [w] See ch. 8:2 [x] [John 6:14] [y] ch. 16:16; 26:63; Ps. 2:7; Mark 1:1; Luke 1:35; 4:41; John 1:49; 10:36; 11:27; 20:31; [ch. 3:17] 34 [z] For ver. 34-36, see Mark 6:53-56; [John 6:24, 25] [a] Luke 5:1 35 [b] ch. 4:24 36 [c] See ch. 9:20 [d] Mark 3:10; Luke 6:19; [Acts 5:15]

Traditions and Commandments

15 [e]Then Pharisees and [f]scribes came to
Jesus [f]from Jerusalem and said, 2 [g]"Why
do your disciples break [h]the tradition of the
elders? [i]For they do not wash their hands when
they eat." 3 He answered them, "And why do
you break the commandment of God for the
sake of your tradition? 4 For God commanded,
[k]'Honor your father and your mother,' and,
[l]'Whoever reviles father or mother must surely
die.' 5 But you say, 'If anyone tells his father
or his mother, "What you would have gained
from me is given to God,"[1] 6 he need not honor
his father.' So for the sake of your tradition
you have [m]made void the word[2] of God. 7 [n]You
hypocrites! Well did Isaiah prophesy of you,
when he said:

8 [o]" 'This people honors me with their lips,
but their heart is far from me;
9 in vain do they worship me,
teaching as [p]doctrines the commandments of men.' "

What Defiles a Person

10 And he called the people to him and said to
them, [q]"Hear and understand: 11 [r]it is not what
goes into the mouth that defiles a person, but
what comes out of the mouth; this defiles a
person." 12 Then the disciples came and said
to him, "Do you know that the Pharisees were
[s]offended when they heard this saying?" 13 He
answered, [t]"Every plant that my heavenly
Father has not planted [u]will be rooted up. 14 Let
them alone; [v]they are blind guides.[3] And [w]if
the blind lead the blind, both will fall into a
pit." 15 But Peter said to him, [x]"Explain the parable to us." 16 And he said, [y]"Are you also still
without understanding? 17 Do you not see that
[z]whatever goes into the mouth passes into the
stomach and is expelled?[4] 18 But [a]what comes
out of the mouth proceeds from the heart,
and this defiles a person. 19 For out of the heart
come [b]evil thoughts, [c]murder, adultery, sexual immorality, theft, false witness, [d]slander.
20 [e]These are what defile a person. But [f]to eat
with unwashed hands does not defile anyone."

The Faith of a Canaanite Woman

21 [g]And Jesus went away from there and
withdrew to the district of Tyre and Sidon.
22 And behold, [h]a Canaanite woman from that
region came out and was crying, [i]"Have mercy
on me, O Lord, Son of David; my daughter
is severely oppressed by a demon." 23 But
he did not answer her a word. And his disciples came and begged him, saying, [j]"Send
her away, for she is crying out after us." 24 He
answered, [k]"I was sent only to the lost sheep of
the house of Israel." 25 But she came and [l]knelt
before him, saying, "Lord, help me." 26 And he

[1] Or *is an offering* [2] Some manuscripts *law* [3] Some manuscripts add *of the blind* [4] Greek *is expelled into the latrine*

understanding in deriving, observing, and enforcing such rules that they did not realize the evil condition of their own hearts. The state of their hearts became especially clear in the example of their practice that Jesus mentions in 15:3–6. They were so greedy that they do not see the clear contradiction between the way they observed one of the traditions of the elders and the critically important fifth commandment of the Decalogue.

This way of disguising a heart in rebellion against God by means of outward forms of piety was precisely what, according to Isaiah, God would remedy among his people when he restored them to himself (Isa. 29:13–14, 18–19). Jesus proclaims that this time of restoration has begun (Matt. 11:5; 15:8–9).

Few things are more spiritually harmful than the outward practice of religion apart from the repentance and faith that characterize the true follower of Jesus. The person who teaches and practices religious rules without the inner transformation of the heart often becomes self-deceived, or "blind," as Jesus calls this condition (v. 14a). Since these people sometimes occupy positions of teaching authority, they can in turn lead others astray (v. 14b). By contrast, the secret practice of piety is a useful indicator that one's heart is in the right condition: for example, giving to the poor without anyone else's knowledge, and praying secretly and sincerely when no one else is looking (6:1–18).

15:21–39 This passage is an example of the expansion of Jesus' ministry to non-Jews (see also 1:5; 2:1–2, 10–11; 8:5–13; 12:18, 21, 38–42; 15:28). Although Jesus makes clear to this non-Jewish woman that he came first as the Shepherd of Israel, called to gather the sheep of God's people who were dispersed in exile because of their

Chapter 15
1 [e]For ver. 1-20, see Mark 7:1-23 [f]Mark 3:22
2 [g][ch. 9:11] [h]Gal. 1:14; Col. 2:8 [i]Luke 11:38
4 [k]Cited from Ex. 20:12 [l]Cited from Ex. 21:17
6 [m]Gal. 3:17 (Gk.); [Rom. 2:23]
7 [n]ch. 23:13
8 [o]Cited from Isa. 29:13; [Ezek. 33:31]
9 [p]Col. 2:22; Titus 1:14
10 [q]ch. 13:51
11 [r]See Acts 10:14, 15
12 [s][ch. 13:57; Luke 7:23]
13 [t][Isa. 60:21; 61:3; John 15:1, 2; 1 Cor. 3:9] [u]Jude 12
14 [v]ch. 23:16, 24; [Isa. 56:10; Mal. 2:8] [w]Luke 6:39
15 [x][ch. 13:36]
16 [y]ch. 16:9
17 [z][1 Cor. 6:13]
18 [a]ch. 12:34; James 3:6
19 [b]James 2:4 [c]ch. 5:22, 28; See Ex. 20:13-16 [d]Eph. 4:31; Col. 3:8; 1 Tim. 6:4
20 [e]1 Cor. 6:9, 10 [f]Mark 7:2, 5
21 [g]For ver. 21-28, see Mark 7:24-30
22 [h]Gen. 10:15, 19; Judg. 1:30-33 [i]See ch. 9:27
23 [j][ch. 14:15]
24 [k]Rom. 15:8; See ch. 10:5, 6
25 [l]See ch. 8:2

answered, "It is not right to take the children's
bread and [m]throw it to the dogs." 27 She said,
"Yes, Lord, yet even the dogs eat [n]the crumbs
that fall from their masters' table." 28 Then
Jesus answered her, "O woman, [o]great is your
faith! [p]Be it done for you as you desire." [q]And
her daughter was [p]healed instantly.[1]

Jesus Heals Many

29 [r]Jesus went on from there and walked
[s]beside the Sea of Galilee. And he [t]went up
on the mountain and sat down there. 30 And
great crowds came to him, bringing with them
[u]the lame, the blind, the crippled, the mute,
and many others, and they put them at his
feet, and he healed them, 31 [v]so that the crowd
wondered, when they saw the mute speaking,
[w]the crippled healthy, the lame walking, and
the blind seeing. And [x]they glorified [y]the God
of Israel.

Jesus Feeds the Four Thousand

32 [z]Then Jesus called his disciples to him
and said, [a]"I have compassion on the crowd
because they have been with me now three
days and have nothing to eat. And I am unwilling to send them away hungry, lest they faint
on the way." 33 And the disciples said to him,
"Where are we to get enough bread in such a
desolate place to feed so great a crowd?" 34 And
Jesus said to them, "How many loaves do you
have?" They said, [b]"Seven, and a few small
fish." 35 And directing the crowd to sit down
on the ground, 36 he took the seven loaves and
the fish, and [c]having given thanks he broke
them and gave them to the disciples, and the
disciples gave them to the crowds. 37 And [d]they
all ate and were satisfied. And they took up
seven baskets full of the broken pieces left
over. 38 Those who ate were four thousand
men, besides women and children. 39 And after
sending away the crowds, he got into the boat
and went to the region of [e]Magadan.

The Pharisees and Sadducees Demand Signs

16 [f]And the Pharisees and Sadducees came,
and [g]to test him [h]they asked him to
show them [i]a sign from heaven. 2 He answered
them,[2] [j]"When it is evening, you say, 'It will
be fair weather, for the sky is red.' 3 And in the
morning, 'It will be stormy today, for the sky is
red and threatening.' [k]You know how to interpret the appearance of the sky, but you cannot
interpret [l]the signs of the times. 4 [m]An evil and
adulterous generation seeks for a sign, but
no sign will be given to it except the sign of
Jonah." So [n]he left them and departed.

The Leaven of the Pharisees and Sadducees

5 When the disciples reached the other side,
they had forgotten to bring any bread. 6 Jesus
said to them, "Watch and [o]beware of [p]the leaven
of the Pharisees and Sadducees." 7 And they
began discussing it among themselves, saying,
"We brought no bread." 8 But [q]Jesus, aware of
this, said, [r]"O you of little faith, why are you
discussing among yourselves the fact that you
have no bread? 9 [s]Do you not yet perceive? Do
you not remember [t]the five loaves for the five
thousand, and how many baskets you gathered? 10 Or [u]the seven loaves for the four thousand, and how many baskets you gathered?
11 How is it that you fail to understand that I did
not speak about bread? [o]Beware of the leaven
of the Pharisees and Sadducees." 12 [v]Then they
understood that he did not tell them to beware
of the leaven of bread, but of [w]the teaching of
the Pharisees and Sadducees.

[1] Greek *from that hour* [2] Some manuscripts omit the following words to the end of verse 3

sin (Ezek. 34:6, 10–16), he nevertheless shows compassion to her and heals her daughter as she requested. He then shows the same compassion to the predominantly non-Jewish crowds in the regions east of the Sea of Galilee that he had shown to the predominantly Jewish crowds on the western side (where Magadan was located; Matt. 15:39). This vision of the inclusion within God's saving purposes of all kinds of people is also present in the Old Testament (Ps. 22:27–28; 86:9; Isa. 2:2–4; 66:18–23; Mic. 4:1–5).

Jesus brings good news to everyone, and makes no distinction between people on the basis of ethnic background, social status, or economic bracket. Christians personally, and the church generally, are also called to demonstrate in their attitudes, their actions, and the social institutions they put in place this same level of acceptance of all kinds of people.

26 [m] ch. 7:6
27 [n] [Luke 16:21]
28 [o] See ch. 9:2 [p] [ch. 8:13] [q] ch. 9:22; 17:18; [John 4:52, 53]
29 [r] For ver. 29-31, [Mark 7:31-37] [s] ch. 4:18; John 6:1 [t] ch. 5:1
30 [u] See ch. 11:5
31 [v] See ch. 9:33 [w] ch. 18:8; Mark 9:43 [x] ch. 9:8 [y] Isa. 29:23; Luke 1:68; Acts 13:17
32 [z] For ver. 32-39, see Mark 8:1-10; [ch. 14:14-21] [a] [ch. 9:36]
34 [b] ch. 16:10
36 [c] ch. 26:27; Mark 14:23; Luke 22:17, 19; John 6:11, 23; Acts 27:35; Rom. 14:6; 1 Cor. 10:30; 11:24; 14:16; 1 Tim. 4:3, 4 **37** [d] [2 Kgs. 4:42-44] **39** [e] [Mark 8:10] **Chapter 16** **1** [f] For ver. 1-12, see Mark 8:11-21 [g] John 8:6 [h] 1 Cor. 1:22; See ch. 12:38 [i] Luke 11:16; 21:11 **2** [j] [Luke 12:54, 55] **3** [k] Luke 12:56 [l] [ch. 12:28; Luke 19:44] **4** [m] See ch. 12:39 [n] ch. 4:13; 21:17 **6** [o] Luke 12:1 [p] 1 Cor. 5:6-8; Gal. 5:9 **8** [q] ch. 26:10 [r] See ch. 6:30 **9** [s] ch. 15:16 [t] ch. 14:17-21 **10** [u] ch. 15:34-38 **11** [o] [See ver. 6 above] **12** [v] ch. 17:13 [w] [ch. 5:20; 23:3]

Peter Confesses Jesus as the Christ

13 [x]Now when Jesus came into the district
of Caesarea Philippi, he asked his disciples,
"Who do people say that the Son of Man is?"
14 And they said, "Some say [y]John the Baptist,
others say [z]Elijah, and others Jeremiah or one
of the prophets." 15 He said to them, "But who
do you say that I am?" 16 Simon Peter replied,
[a]"You are [b]the Christ, [c]the Son of [d]the living
God." 17 And Jesus answered him, [e]"Blessed
are you, [f]Simon Bar-Jonah! For [g]flesh and
blood has not revealed this to you, [h]but my
Father who is in heaven. 18 And I tell you, [i]you
are Peter, and [j]on this rock[1] I will build my
church, and [k]the gates of [l]hell[2] shall not prevail against it. 19 I will give you [m]the keys of
the kingdom of heaven, and [n]whatever you
bind on earth shall be bound in heaven, and
whatever you loose on earth shall be loosed[3]
in heaven." 20 [o]Then he strictly charged the
disciples to tell no one that he was the Christ.

Jesus Foretells His Death and Resurrection

21 [p]From that time Jesus began to show
his disciples that [q]he must go to Jerusalem
and [r]suffer many things from the elders and
chief priests and scribes, and be killed, and
on [s]the third day be raised. 22 And Peter took
him aside and began to rebuke him, saying,
"Far be it from you, Lord![4] This shall never
happen to you." 23 But he turned and said
to Peter, [t]"Get behind me, Satan! You are [u]a
hindrance[5] to me. For you [v]are not setting
your mind on the things of God, but on the
things of man."

Take Up Your Cross and Follow Jesus

24 Then Jesus told his disciples, "If anyone
would come after me, let him [w]deny himself
and [x]take up his cross and follow me. 25 For
[x]whoever would save his life[6] will lose it, but
whoever loses his life for my sake will find it.
26 For [y]what will it profit a man if he gains the
whole world and forfeits his soul? Or [z]what
shall a man give in return for his soul? 27 [a]For
the Son of Man is going to come with [b]his
angels in the glory of his Father, and [c]then
he will repay each person according to what
he has done. 28 Truly, I say to you, there are
some standing here who will not [d]taste death
[e]until they see the Son of Man [f]coming in his
kingdom."

[1] The Greek words for *Peter* and *rock* sound similar [2] Greek *the gates of Hades* [3] Or *shall have been bound . . . shall have been loosed* [4] Or "[May God be] *merciful to you, Lord!*" [5] Greek *stumbling block* [6] The same Greek word can mean either *soul* or *life*, depending on the context; twice in this verse and twice in verse 26

16:21–28 Entrance into the reign of God is a valuable treasure and a great joy to those who experience it (13:44–46), but it involves the hardship of living in a way that is out of step with a sin-ravaged world. For Jesus, this meant experiencing the shame of rejection from the intellectual elites of his own culture, and a form of death—crucifixion (16:21)—reserved for the least valued and least powerful members of his society. From the perspective of a world in rebellion against God, to choose a life leading to such a death seemed like "folly" (1 Cor. 1:18–25). Despite the profound insight Peter has just had into Jesus' identity, and despite the Savior's promise to build his church upon that truth (Matt. 16:13–20), Peter is not yet sufficiently transformed by the gospel to understand just how dramatic is the conflict between Jesus and the sinful world (vv. 22–23) and how pivotal will be the role of the church in binding hearts to heaven (vv. 18–19).

Jesus therefore instructs Peter and all of his disciples (including, through this written account, disciples today) that entering God's kingdom by following him entails putting oneself at odds with the values and goals of the sinful world (vv. 24–28). Living in a way so dramatically different from the unbelieving world can feel shameful today, just as it did for the early Christians (v. 24; cf. 1 Cor. 1:18–25; 2:1–5; Gal. 6:14; Heb. 12:2).

Jesus encourages his disciples not to believe the world's lie that following him is shameful. What the world believes to be "life" is not life at all but really the loss of life, while the disciple of Jesus has chosen the path of true life that leads to lasting joy (Matt. 16:25–26; Eph. 2:1–3; 4:17–19). The believer may not experience the fullness of that joy until eternity, when the true nature of a life spent gaining the whole world versus a life spent following Jesus will become clear (Matt. 16:27). But we can experience the joy of the gospel even now, as we live with the assurance of God's constant presence, eternal care, and plans for our ultimate good (11:28–30; 13:44–46).

13 [x] For ver. 13-16, see Mark 8:27-29; Luke 9:18-20
14 [y] ch. 14:2; Mark 6:14; Luke 9:7 [z] Mark 6:15; Luke 9:8; [ch. 17:10; Mark 9:11; John 1:21]
16 [a] John 11:27 [b] See ch. 1:17 [c] See ch. 14:33 [d] Deut. 5:26; Josh. 3:10; Ps. 42:2; Jer. 10:10; Dan. 6:20; Hos. 1:10; Acts 14:15; 2 Cor. 3:3; 1 Tim. 4:10
17 [e] [ch. 13:16] [f] [John 1:42; 21:15-17] [g] 1 Cor. 15:50; Gal. 1:16 (Gk.); Eph. 6:12; Heb. 2:14 [h] 1 Cor. 2:10; 12:3; [ch. 11:25; John 6:45]
18 [i] [ch. 10:2; John 1:42] [j] Eph. 2:20; Rev. 21:14; [ch. 7:24] [k] Job 38:17; Isa. 38:10 [l] See ch. 11:23
19 [m] [Isa. 22:22; Rev. 1:18; 3:7] [n] [ch. 18:18; John 20:23]
20 [o] Mark 8:30; Luke 9:21; [ch. 17:9]; See ch. 12:16
21 [p] For ver. 21-28, see Mark 8:31–9:1; Luke 9:22-27; [ch. 17:12, 22, 23; 20:17-19] [q] ch. 20:18; [Luke 13:33] [r] ch. 17:12, 22, 23; Luke 24:7 [s] See ch. 27:63; John 2:19
23 [t] [ch. 4:10] [u] See ch. 13:41 [v] Rom. 8:5; Phil. 3:19; Col. 3:2; [Phil. 2:5]
24 [w] [2 Tim. 2:12, 13] [x] See ch. 10:38, 39
25 [x] [See ver. 24 above]
26 [y] [Luke 12:20] [z] [Ps. 49:7, 8]
27 [a] ch. 24:30; 25:31; 26:64; Dan. 7:10, 13; Zech. 14:5; John 1:51; Acts 1:11; 1 Thess. 1:10; 4:16; Jude 14; Rev. 1:7; [Deut. 33:2] [b] ch. 13:41 [c] Rom. 2:6; 14:12; 2 Cor. 5:10; Heb. 9:27; 1 Pet. 1:17; Rev. 2:23; 20:12; 22:12; See Acts 10:42; 1 Cor. 3:8 **28** [d] John 8:52; Heb. 2:9 [e] [ch. 10:23; 23:36; 24:34] [f] Luke 23:42

The Transfiguration

17 [g]And after six days Jesus took with
him [h]Peter and James, and John his
brother, and led them up a high mountain by
themselves. 2 And he was [i]transfigured before
them, and [j]his face shone like the sun, and [k]his
clothes became white as light. 3 And behold,
there appeared to them Moses and Elijah, talking with him. 4 And Peter said to Jesus, "Lord,
it is good that we are here. If you wish, I will
make three tents here, one for you and one for
Moses and one for [l]Elijah." 5 He was still speaking when, behold, [m]a bright cloud overshadowed them, and [m]a voice from the cloud said,
[n]"This is my beloved Son,[1] with whom I am
well pleased; [o]listen to him." 6 When [p]the disciples heard this, [q]they fell on their faces and
were terrified. 7 But Jesus came and [r]touched
them, saying, "Rise, and [s]have no fear." 8 And
when they lifted up their eyes, they saw no
one but Jesus only.

9 [t]And as they were coming down the mountain, Jesus commanded them, [u]"Tell no one the
vision, until the Son of Man is raised from the
dead." 10 And the disciples asked him, "Then
why do the scribes say [v]that first Elijah must
come?" 11 He answered, "Elijah does come, and
[w]he will restore all things. 12 But I tell you that
Elijah has already come, and they did not recognize him, but [x]did to him whatever they
pleased. [y]So also the Son of Man will certainly
suffer at their hands." 13 [z]Then the disciples
understood that he was speaking to them of
John the Baptist.

Jesus Heals a Boy with a Demon

14 [a]And when they came to the crowd, a man
came up to him and, kneeling before him,
15 said, "Lord, have mercy on my son, for he
is [b]an epileptic and he suffers terribly. For
often he falls into the fire, and often into the
water. 16 And I brought him to your disciples,
and [c]they could not heal him." 17 And Jesus
answered, "O faithless and [d]twisted generation, how long am I to be with you? [e]How
long am I to bear with you? Bring him here
to me." 18 And Jesus [f]rebuked the demon,[2] and
it[3] came out of him, and [g]the boy was healed
instantly.[4] 19 Then the disciples came to Jesus
privately and said, "Why could we not cast it
out?" 20 He said to them, [h]"Because of your
little faith. For [i]truly, I say to you, [j]if you have

[1] Or *my Son, my* (or *the*) *Beloved* [2] Greek *it* [3] Greek *the demon* [4] Greek *from that hour*

Chapter 17
1 [g]For ver. 1-8, see Mark 9:2-8; Luke 9:28-36 [h]ch. 26:37; Mark 5:37
2 [i][2 Cor. 3:18 (Gk.)] [j]Rev. 1:16; 10:1 [k]Dan. 7:9; [ch. 28:3; Ps. 104:2]
4 [l][Mal. 4:5]
5 [m]2 Pet. 1:17; [Ex. 24:15, 16] [n]See ch. 3:17 [o]Acts 3:22
6 [p]2 Pet. 1:18 [q][Gen. 17:3; Ezek. 1:28; Rev. 1:17]
7 [r]Dan. 8:18; 10:10, 18 [s]ch. 14:27
9 [t]For ver. 9-13, see Mark 9:9-13 [u]See ch. 8:4; 12:16
10 [v]See ch. 11:14; Mal. 4:5, 6
11 [w]Luke 1:16, 17; [Acts 1:6; 3:21]
12 [x]ch. 14:3, 10 [y]ch. 16:21
13 [z]ch. 16:12
14 [a]For ver. 14-19, see Mark 9:14-28; Luke 9:37-42
15 [b]ch. 4:24
16 [c][ch. 10:1; Mark 6:7; Luke 10:17]
17 [d]Phil. 2:15; [John 20:27] [e][John 14:9]
18 [f]ch. 8:26; Zech. 3:2; Mark 1:25; Luke 4:35, 39; Jude 9 [g]See ch. 9:22
20 [h][John 11:40]; See ch. 6:30 [i]ch. 21:21, 22; Mark 11:23 [j]Luke 17:6; [ch. 13:31]

17:1–13 Moses and Elijah appear with Jesus on the Mount of Transfiguration. Moses represents the Law and Elijah represents the Prophets, indicating that all that has preceded in God's Word and redemptive history leads to Christ. He is thus shown to be the apex of redemptive history and the fulfillment of God's promises of redemption. The Christ-centrality of all the Scripture is most evident visually in this text as the transcendent glory of the incarnate Word of God is confirmed by the witness of the most significant representatives of the inscripturated Word of God.

17:14–20 While Jesus, Peter, James, and John were on the Mount of Transfiguration (vv. 1–13), the other disciples were down below, attempting to drive out a demon that had produced in a boy the symptoms of epilepsy. Because of their "little faith," however, they were unable to help the boy (v. 20). It was not the intensity of their faith that was the problem, but its quality. Only a little of the *right* kind of faith is necessary to accomplish the work of the kingdom (v. 20; see also 4:24; 7:22; 8:16, 28–34; 9:32–34; 10:8; 12:22–23, 28; 15:22). The work of the kingdom depends on the power of God, not on the power or intensity of believers. The disciples' faith was probably faulty because it lay more in themselves (perhaps in using the right technique) than in God.

When believers today seek to accomplish seemingly impossible tasks in the advancement of God's kingdom, God will come to their aid, enabling them to do more and greater things than they thought possible. This passage cautions believers to rely on God rather than on themselves to accomplish the kingdom's goals, but it also encourages them not to be timid in their expectation of what God can do. After all, God has done the hardest thing—he has atoned for the sins of his people, in Jesus Christ.

The two incidents recorded in 17:1–20 provide a striking example for all believers: Having just had his glory revealed on the Mount of Transfiguration (vv. 1–13), Jesus did not hesitate to then immediately become involved in our world of pain and shame as he focused on the diseased child (vv. 14–20). Glory did not distract Jesus from compassion. Rather, compassion for the hurting became an expression of his glory.

faith like a grain of mustard seed, [k]you will say
to this mountain, 'Move from here to there,'
and it will move, and [l]nothing will be impossible for you."[1]

Jesus Again Foretells Death, Resurrection

22 [m]As they were gathering[2] in Galilee, Jesus
said to them, "The Son of Man is about to be
delivered into the hands of men, 23 and they
will kill him, and he will be raised on [n]the
third day." And they were greatly distressed.

The Temple Tax

24 [o]When they came to Capernaum, the collectors of [p]the two-drachma tax went up to Peter
and said, "Does your teacher not pay the tax?"
25 He said, "Yes." And when he came into the
house, Jesus spoke to him first, saying, [q]"What
do you think, Simon? From whom do kings
of the earth take toll or [r]tax? From their sons
or from others?" 26 And when he said, "From
others," Jesus said to him, "Then the sons are
free. 27 However, not to give offense to them, go
to the sea and cast a hook and take the first fish
that comes up, and when you open its mouth
you will find a shekel.[3] Take that and give it to
them for me and for yourself."

Who Is the Greatest?

18 [t]At that time the disciples came to
Jesus, saying, "Who is the greatest in
the kingdom of heaven?" 2 And calling to him
a child, he put him in the midst of them 3 and
said, "Truly, I say to you, unless you [u]turn and
[v]become like children, you [w]will never enter
the kingdom of heaven. 4 [x]Whoever humbles
himself like this child is the [w]greatest in the
kingdom of heaven.

5 [y]"Whoever receives one such child in my
name receives me, 6 but [z]whoever causes one
of these [a]little ones who believe in me to sin,[4]
it would be better for him to have a great
millstone fastened around his neck and to be
drowned in the depth of the sea.

Temptations to Sin

7 "Woe to the world for [b]temptations to sin![5]
[c]For it is necessary that temptations come,
[d]but woe to the one by whom the temptation
comes! 8 [e]And if your hand or your foot causes
you to sin, cut it off and throw it away. It is better for you to enter life crippled or lame than
with two hands or two feet to be thrown into
[f]the eternal fire. 9 [e]And if your eye causes you
to sin, tear it out and throw it away. It is better
for you to enter life with one eye than with
two eyes to be thrown into the [f]hell[6] of fire.

The Parable of the Lost Sheep

10 "See that you do not despise [g]one of these
little ones. For I tell you that in heaven [h]their
angels always [i]see the face of my Father who is
in heaven.[7] 12 [j]What do you think? [k]If a man has
a hundred sheep, and one of them has gone
astray, does he not leave the ninety-nine on
the mountains and go in search of the one that
went astray? 13 And if he finds it, truly, I say
to you, he rejoices over it more than over the
ninety-nine that never went astray. 14 So [l]it is
not the will of my[8] Father who is in heaven
that one of these little ones should perish.

If Your Brother Sins Against You

15 [m]"If your brother sins against you, [n]go
and tell him his fault, between you and him
alone. If he listens to you, you have [o]gained
your brother. 16 But if he does not listen, take
one or two others along with you, that every
charge may be established [p]by the evidence of
two or three witnesses. 17 If he refuses to listen

[1] Some manuscripts insert verse 21: *But this kind never comes out except by prayer and fasting* [2] Some manuscripts *remained* [3] Greek *stater*, a silver coin worth four drachmas or approximately one shekel [4] Greek *causes . . . to stumble*; also verses 8, 9 [5] Greek *stumbling blocks* [6] Greek *Gehenna* [7] Some manuscripts add verse 11: *For the Son of Man came to save the lost* [8] Some manuscripts *your*

18:1–35 The theme that binds this section together is God's concern for the spiritually needy: the powerless, those victimized by sin, and sinners who have victimized others. The kingdom of heaven is a place where everyone recognizes their dependence on God, just as children know they are dependent on loving adults to care for them (vv. 1–4; see also 11:25; 19:13–15). It is a place where the powerless are cared for (18:5, 12–14), and abuse of them is not tolerated (vv. 6–10). The kingdom of heaven is a place where sinners are mercifully restored (vv. 15–20), and where people are quick to forgive and to seek reconciliation, knowing that God in his grace has forgiven them (vv. 21–35; see also 6:12, 14–15; Mark 11:25; Eph. 4:32; Col. 3:13).

20 [k]ver. 9; [1 Cor. 13:2] [l]Mark 9:23
22 [m]For ver. 22, 23, see Mark 9:30-32; Luke 9:43-45; [ch. 16:21-28; 20:17-19]
23 [n]See Mark 8:31
24 [o]Mark 9:33 [p]Ex. 30:13; 38:26
25 [q]ch. 18:12; 21:28 [r]ch. 22:17, 19; Mark 12:14; Rom. 13:7

Chapter 18
1 [t]ch. 17:24; For ver. 1-5, see Mark 9:33-37; Luke 9:46-48; [ch. 20:20-28] **3** [u]See Luke 22:32 [v]ch. 19:14; Mark 10:15; Luke 18:17; [Ps. 131:2; 1 Cor. 14:20; 1 Pet. 2:2] [w][ch. 5:19, 20] **4** [x]ch. 20:27; 23:11, 12 [w][See ver. 3 above] **5** [y][ch. 10:40, 42] **6** [z]Mark 9:42 [a]Luke 17:2; [1 Cor. 8:12] **7** [b]See ch. 13:41 [c]Luke 17:1; See 1 Cor. 11:19 [d]ch. 26:24 **8** [e]ch. 5:29, 30; Mark 9:43-48 [f]See ch. 25:41 **9** [e][See ver. 8 above] [f][See ver. 8 above] **10** [g][ch. 6:29; 25:40, 45; Luke 15:7, 10] [h]Acts 12:15; [Ps. 34:7; 91:11; Heb. 1:14] [i]Luke 1:19; Rev. 8:2; [Esth. 1:14] **12** [j]ch. 17:25; 21:28 [k]For ver. 12-14, [Luke 15:4-7] **14** [l]John 6:39; 10:28; [John 17:12] **15** [m]Luke 17:3 [n]2 Thess. 3:15; [Titus 3:10; James 5:19]; See Lev. 19:17 [o]1 Cor. 9:19-22; 1 Pet. 3:1 **16** [p]Deut. 19:15; 2 Cor. 13:1; [Num. 35:30; John 8:17; 1 Tim. 5:19; Heb. 10:28]

to them, [q]tell it to the church. And if he refuses
to listen even to the church, [r]let him be to you
as [s]a Gentile and [s]a tax collector. 18 Truly, I say
to you, [t]whatever you bind on earth shall be
bound in heaven, and whatever you loose on
earth shall be loosed[1] in heaven. 19 Again I say
to you, if two of you [u]agree on earth about
anything they ask, [v]it will be done for them
by my Father in heaven. 20 For where two or
three are [w]gathered in my name, [x]there am
I among them."

The Parable of the Unforgiving Servant

21 Then Peter came up and said to him, "Lord,
how often [y]will my brother sin against me,
and I forgive him? [z]As many as seven times?"
22 Jesus said to him, "I do not say to you seven
times, but seventy-seven times.

23 "Therefore the kingdom of heaven may
be compared to a king who wished [a]to settle
accounts with his servants.[2] 24 When he began
to settle, one was brought to him who owed
him [b]ten thousand [c]talents.[3] 25 [d]And since he
could not pay, his master ordered him [e]to be
sold, with his wife and [f]children and all that
he had, and payment to be made. 26 So the servant[4] [g]fell on his knees, imploring him, 'Have
patience with me, and I will pay you everything.' 27 And out of pity for him, the master
of that servant released him and [d]forgave him
the debt. 28 But when that same servant went
out, he found one of his fellow servants who
owed him a hundred [h]denarii,[5] and seizing
him, he began to choke him, saying, 'Pay what
you owe.' 29 So his fellow servant fell down and
pleaded with him, 'Have patience with me,
and I will pay you.' 30 He refused and went
and put him in prison until he should pay
the debt. 31 When his fellow servants saw what
had taken place, they were greatly distressed,
and they went and reported to their master
all that had taken place. 32 Then his master
summoned him and said to him, 'You wicked
servant! I forgave you all that debt because you
pleaded with me. 33 [i]And should not you have
had mercy on your fellow servant, as I had
mercy on you?' 34 [j]And in anger his master
delivered him to the jailers,[6] [k]until he should
pay all his debt. 35 [l]So also my heavenly Father
will do to every one of you, if you do not forgive your brother [m]from your heart."

Teaching About Divorce

19 Now when Jesus had finished these
sayings, he went away from [n]Galilee
and [o]entered [p]the region of Judea beyond the
Jordan. 2 And [q]large crowds followed him, and
he healed them there.

3 And Pharisees came up to him and [r]tested
him by asking, [s]"Is it lawful to divorce one's
wife for any cause?" 4 He answered, [t]"Have you
not read that he who created them from the
beginning made them male and female, 5 and
said, [u]'Therefore a man shall leave his father
and his mother and hold fast to his wife, and
[v]the two shall become one flesh'? 6 So they are
no longer two but one flesh. [w]What therefore
God has joined together, let not man separate."
7 They said to him, [x]"Why then did Moses command one to give a certificate of divorce and
to send her away?" 8 He said to them, "Because
of your [y]hardness of heart Moses allowed you
to divorce your wives, but from the beginning it was not so. 9 [z]And I say to you: whoever
divorces his wife, except for sexual immorality, and marries another, commits adultery."[7]

10 The disciples said to him, "If such is the
case of a man with his wife, it is better not
to marry." 11 But he said to them, [a]"Not everyone can receive this saying, but only [b]those to
[c]whom it is given. 12 For there are eunuchs who
have been so from birth, and there are eunuchs
who have been made eunuchs by men, and
there are eunuchs who have made themselves eunuchs [d]for the sake of the kingdom
of heaven. Let the one who is able to receive
this receive it."

Let the Children Come to Me

13 [e]Then children were brought to him that
he might lay his hands on them and pray. The
disciples [f]rebuked the people, 14 but Jesus said,

[1] Or *shall have been bound . . . shall have been loosed* [2] Greek *bondservants*; also verses 28, 31 [3] A *talent* was a monetary unit worth about twenty years' wages for a laborer [4] Greek *bondservant*; also verses 27, 28, 29, 32, 33 [5] A *denarius* was a day's wage for a laborer [6] Greek *torturers* [7] Some manuscripts add *and whoever marries a divorced woman commits adultery*; other manuscripts *except for sexual immorality, makes her commit adultery, and whoever marries a divorced woman commits adultery*

17 [q] [1 Cor. 5:4, 5; 6:1-6] [r] [Rom. 16:17; 1 Cor. 5:9-13; 2 Thess. 3:6, 14; 2 John 10] [s] ch. 5:46, 47 **18** [t] [ch. 16:19; John 20:23] **19** [u] [Acts 12:5, 12; Philem. 22] [v] See ch. 7:7 **20** [w] [Acts 4:30, 31; 1 Cor. 5:4] [x] [ch. 28:20; John 12:26; 20:20, 26] **21** [y] ver. 15 [z] Luke 17:3, 4; [Col. 3:13] **23** [a] ch. 25:19 **24** [b] Esth. 3:9 [c] ch. 25:15 **25** [d] [Luke 7:42] [e] Ex. 21:2; Lev. 25:39 [f] 2 Kgs. 4:1; Neh. 5:5 **26** [g] Acts 10:25; See ch. 8:2 **27** [d] [See ver. 25 above] **28** [h] ch. 20:2; 22:19; Mark 6:37; 14:5; Luke 7:41; 10:35; John 6:7 **33** [i] [ch. 6:12; Eph. 4:32; Col. 3:13; 1 John 4:11] **34** [j] See James 2:13 [k] ver. 30; [ch. 5:25, 26] **35** [l] ch. 6:15; [Prov. 21:13] [m] 1 Pet. 1:22; [Rom. 6:17] **Chapter 19** **1** [n] ch. 17:24 [o] For ver. 1-9, see Mark 10:1-12 [p] Luke 9:51; 17:11; John 10:40; [ch. 4:25] **2** [q] ch. 12:15 **3** [r] John 8:6 [s] ch. 5:31 **4** [t] Gen. 1:27; 2:18, 21-23; 5:2; [ch. 21:16] **5** [u] Eph. 5:31; Cited from Gen. 2:24 [v] 1 Cor. 6:16; [Mal. 2:15] **6** [w] 1 Cor. 7:10 **7** [x] Deut. 24:1-4 **8** [y] Mark 16:14; [Mark 3:5; 6:52; Heb. 3:8] **9** [z] See ch. 5:32 **11** [a] 1 Cor. 7:2, 7-9, 17 [b] [ch. 20:23] [c] ch. 13:11 **12** [d] [1 Cor. 7:32] **13** [e] For ver. 13-15, see Mark 10:13-16; Luke 18:15-17 [f] Mark 10:48

[g]"Let the little children [h]come to me and do
not hinder them, for to such belongs the kingdom of heaven." 15 And he laid his hands on
them and went away.

The Rich Young Man

16 [i]And behold, a man came up to him, saying, "Teacher, what good deed must I do to
[j]have [k]eternal life?" 17 And he said to him, "Why
do you ask me about what is good? There is
only one who is good. [l]If you would enter life,
keep the commandments." 18 He said to him,
"Which ones?" And Jesus said, [m]"You shall not
murder, You shall not commit adultery, You
shall not steal, You shall not bear false witness,
19 Honor your father and mother, and, [n]You
shall love your neighbor as yourself." 20 The
young man said to him, [o]"All these I have kept.
What do I still lack?" 21 Jesus said to him, "If
you would be [p]perfect, go, [q]sell what you possess and give to the poor, and you will have
[r]treasure in heaven; and come, follow me."
22 [s]When the young man heard this he went
away sorrowful, for he had great possessions.
23 And Jesus said to his disciples, "Truly, I say
to you, [t]only with difficulty will a rich person
enter the kingdom of heaven. 24 [u]Again I tell
you, it is easier for a camel to go through the
eye of a needle than for a rich person to enter
[v]the kingdom of God." 25 When the disciples
heard this, they were greatly astonished, saying, "Who then can be saved?" 26 But Jesus
[w]looked at them and said, [x]"With man this
is impossible, but with God all things are

19:16–22 The rich young man asked a question of ultimate importance: he wanted to have eternal life, and wanted to know how this was possible. He assumed that he had to do something, and that Jesus would know what that something was (v. 16). But Jesus immediately shifted the conversation from what an individual must do to have eternal life to *the God who gives* eternal life (v. 17). Jesus' question encouraged the young man to think about the relationship between Jesus and God, and if the man had been paying attention to Jesus' ministry, it would have been natural for him to conclude that Jesus himself was God, and that to "enter the kingdom of heaven" (v. 23), or to "enter life" (v. 17), he should follow Jesus (v. 21b).

One crucial element of the man's life, however, hindered him from following Jesus, and Jesus wanted to help him identify that hindrance. If the man wanted to enter life, he had to keep the commandments (v. 17b), and these begin with, "You shall have no other gods before me" (Ex. 20:3). But Jesus bypassed this first commandment, the other three that go with it (Ex. 20:3–11), and the Decalogue's tenth commandment, "you shall not covet" (Ex. 20:17). Instead, he moved immediately to the commandments that concern one's relationship to other people (Ex. 20:12–16; summarized in Lev. 19:18). The man thought that he had kept all these commandments, but correctly understood that he still lacked something (Matt. 19:18–20). He lacked the one "good deed" (literally, "good thing"; v. 16) from which all other good things flow: a heartfelt devotion to God. To put his obedience to commandments five, six, seven, eight, and nine in their proper place (and perhaps to understand why he had not obeyed the tenth commandment), the rich man had to first obey the great and first commandment, loving God above all else (cf. 22:37–38). Obedience to that commandment involves a commitment to follow Jesus as life's highest priority (19:21). God does not call all people everywhere to give everything they have to the poor, but he does call all to put nothing above loyalty to him. And in the example of this young man, God reminds us all to examine whether we have depended on anything more than Jesus for our satisfaction and hope.

19:23–30 Throughout Matthew, Jesus has identified greed as a hindrance to embracing the gospel (6:19–34; 13:22; 15:5–6), and, in contrast, a willingness to give up everything to follow him as a sign of true discipleship (19:20, 22, 27; cf. 13:44–46). A rich person can enter the kingdom of God only with difficulty, because riches can so easily take the place of God in one's life. This is why, when Jesus talked about the impossibility of serving two masters (6:24), the two masters in view were God and money. Placing money before God explains why the Pharisees thought up loopholes in the law about honoring one's parents, in order to keep their own money (15:5–6). It is why the tenants in Jesus' parable imagined that they would inherit the vineyard if they killed the vineyard owner's son (21:38). It is why Judas betrayed Jesus for thirty pieces of silver (26:15; see also John 12:6).

14 [g]ch. 18:3 [h][Mark 9:39]
16 [i]For ver. 16-29, see Mark 10:17-30; Luke 18:18-30; [Luke 10:25-28] [j][ver. 29] [k]ch. 25:46; [ch. 18:8]
17 [l]Lev. 18:5; Neh. 9:29; Ezek. 20:11, 13, 21; Rom. 10:5; Gal. 3:12
18 [m]Rom. 13:9; Cited from Ex. 20:12-16; Deut. 5:16-20; [ch. 5:21, 27]
19 [n]ch. 5:43; 22:39; Mark 12:31; Luke 10:27; Gal. 5:14; James 2:8; Cited from Lev. 19:18
20 [o][Phil. 3:6]
21 [p]See ch. 5:48 [q]Luke 12:33; [Luke 16:9; 19:8; Acts 2:45; 4:34, 35; 1 Tim. 6:18, 19] [r]ch. 6:19, 20
22 [s][Ezek. 33:31]
23 [t][1 Cor. 1:26]; See ch. 13:22
24 [u][Mark 10:24] [v]See ch. 12:28
26 [w]Mark 10:21; Luke 22:61 [x]Gen. 18:14; Job 42:2; Jer. 32:17, 27; Zech. 8:6; Mark 14:36; Luke 1:37

possible." 27 Then Peter said in reply, "See, [y]we have left everything and followed you. What then will we have?" 28 Jesus said to them, "Truly, I say to you, in the new world,[1] [z]when the Son of Man will sit on his glorious throne, you who have followed me [a]will also sit on twelve thrones, [b]judging the twelve tribes of Israel. 29 [c]And everyone who has left houses or brothers or sisters or father or mother or children or lands, for my name's sake, will receive a hundredfold[2] and will [d]inherit eternal life. 30 But [e]many who are [f]first will be last, and the last first.

Laborers in the Vineyard

20 "For the kingdom of heaven is like a master of a house who went out early in the morning to hire laborers for his vineyard. 2 After agreeing with the laborers for a denarius[3] a day, he sent them into his vineyard. 3 And going out about the third hour he saw others standing idle in the marketplace, 4 and to them he said, 'You go into the vineyard too, and whatever is right I will give you.' 5 So they went. Going out again about the sixth hour and the ninth hour, he did the same. 6 And [g]about the eleventh hour he went out and found others standing. And he said to them, 'Why do you stand here idle all day?' 7 They said to him, 'Because no one has hired us.' He said to them, 'You go into the vineyard too.' 8 And [h]when evening came, the owner of the vineyard said to his [i]foreman, 'Call the laborers and pay them their wages, beginning with the last, up to the first.' 9 And when those hired about the eleventh hour came, each of them received a denarius. 10 Now when those hired first came, they thought they would receive more, but each of them also received a denarius. 11 And on receiving it they grumbled at the master of the house, 12 saying, 'These last worked only one hour, and you have made them equal to us who have borne the burden of the day and [j]the scorching heat.' 13 But he replied to one of them, [k]'Friend, I am doing you no wrong. Did you not agree with me for a denarius? 14 Take [l]what belongs to you and go. I choose to give to this last worker as I give to you. 15 [m]Am I not allowed to do what I choose with what belongs to me? Or [n]do you begrudge my generosity?'[4] 16 So [o]the last will be first, and the first last."

[1] Greek *in the regeneration* [2] Some manuscripts *manifold* [3] A *denarius* was a day's wage for a laborer [4] Or *is your eye bad because I am good?*

27 [y] ch. 4:20, 22; Mark 1:18, 20
28 [z] See ch. 16:27 [a] Luke 22:30; Rev. 3:21 [b] [1 Cor. 6:2]
29 [c] [Luke 14:26] [d] [ver. 16]; See ch. 25:34
30 [e] ch. 20:16; Mark 10:31; Luke 13:30 [f] [ch. 21:31, 32]
Chapter 20
6 [g] [1 Cor. 15:8]
8 [h] Lev. 19:13; Deut. 24:15 [i] Luke 8:3; [ch. 24:45]
12 [j] Luke 12:55; James 1:11 (Gk.)
13 [k] ch. 22:12; 26:50
14 [l] ch. 25:25
15 [m] [Rom. 9:15-24] [n] ch. 6:23; Deut. 15:9; Prov. 23:6
16 [o] See ch. 19:30

Money easily offers tangible forms of security and prestige that are incompatible with dependence upon God's grace. It is not merely a neutral tool that can be used for good or ill but something that adopts almost personal characteristics and demands one's service (Matt. 6:24), a powerful force that tends to pull people away from God. Jesus recognized that the best way for one to control money rather than to be controlled by it was to give it away. For the follower of Jesus, this giving should be done with the specific purpose of helping the needy (19:21, 27–30). And it is done in the powerful, happy motivation of what Jesus has done for us needy sinners.

20:1–16 The Old Testament prophets sometimes spoke of Israel as God's vineyard (Isa. 5:1–7; 27:2–11; Jer. 12:10–11). Thus, when Jesus spoke of a landowner hiring idle day-laborers for his vineyard, his listeners probably would have thought of God urging individuals—perhaps especially those on the margins of society—to join his people (Matt. 8:1–17; 9:10–13, 20–22, 32–34; 11:5; 12:9–14; 15:21–31; 17:14–21). This parable demonstrates that God's criterion for becoming a part of his people is very different from the criteria of the unbelieving world for acceptance into the ranks of the powerful and successful.

The world's way of thinking was well illustrated by the disciples' response to Jesus' interaction with the rich young man: if rich people can only enter God's kingdom with difficulty, then who can be saved? (19:25). Surely the rich deserve to be included, runs the logic, so if entering the kingdom is difficult even for them, then how can the rest of us be saved? Jesus' answer implies that entry into the kingdom and salvation are impossible for *anyone* on the basis of their own efforts, but God makes it possible (19:26).

Here, in the parable of the laborers in the vineyard (20:1–16), we learn that God makes entry into his kingdom possible for all types of people, with no distinction on the basis of their abilities, efforts, or social standing. Joining the people of God, entering the kingdom, and experiencing salvation come by God's power, through his

Jesus Foretells His Death a Third Time

17 [p]And as Jesus was going up to Jerusalem,
he took the twelve disciples aside, and on the
way he said to them, 18 "See, [q]we are going up
to Jerusalem. And the Son of Man will be delivered over to the chief priests and scribes, and
they will [r]condemn him to death 19 and [s]deliver
him over to the Gentiles [t]to be mocked and
flogged and [u]crucified, and he will be raised
on [v]the third day."

A Mother's Request

20 [w]Then [x]the mother of the sons of Zebedee
came up to him with her sons, and [y]kneel-
ing before him she asked him for something.
21 And he said to her, "What do you want?"
She said to him, "Say that these two sons of
mine [z]are to sit, one at your right hand and
one at your left, [a]in your kingdom." 22 Jesus
answered, [b]"You do not know what you are
asking. Are you able [c]to drink the cup that
I am to drink?" They said to him, "We are able."
23 He said to them, [d]"You will drink [e]my cup,
but to sit at my right hand and at my left is
not mine to grant, [f]but it is for those for whom
it has been [g]prepared by my Father." 24 And
when the ten heard it, they were indignant at
the two brothers. 25 But Jesus called them to
him and said, [h]"You know that the rulers of
the Gentiles [i]lord it over them, and their great
ones exercise authority over them. 26 [j]It shall
not be so among you. But whoever would be
great among you must be your servant,[1] 27 and
whoever would be first among you must be
your slave,[2] 28 even as the Son of Man came not
to be served but [k]to serve, and [l]to give his life
as a ransom for [m]many."

Jesus Heals Two Blind Men

29 [n]And as they went out of Jericho, a great
crowd followed him. 30 And behold, there were
two blind men sitting by the roadside, and
when they heard that Jesus was passing by,
they cried out, "Lord,[3] have mercy on us, [o]Son
of David!" 31 The crowd [p]rebuked them, telling
them to be silent, but they cried out all the
more, "Lord, have mercy on us, Son of David!"
32 And stopping, Jesus called them and said,
"What do you want me to do for you?" 33 They
said to him, "Lord, let our eyes be opened."
34 And Jesus in pity touched their eyes, and
immediately they recovered their sight and
followed him.

The Triumphal Entry

21 [q]Now when they drew near to Jerusalem and came to Bethphage, to [r]the
Mount of Olives, then Jesus [s]sent two disciples, 2 saying to them, "Go into the village in
front of you, and immediately you will find a
donkey tied, and a colt with her. Untie them
and bring them to me. 3 If anyone says anything to you, you shall say, 'The Lord needs
them,' and he will send them at once." 4 This
took place [t]to fulfill what was spoken by the
prophet, saying,

[1] Greek *diakonos* [2] Greek *bondservant* (*doulos*) [3] Some manuscripts omit *Lord*

grace, apart from anything that can be done to earn them. Because of this, many whom the unbelieving world's system of values would assign to the lowest place in any system of government or culture will occupy the highest place when God fully establishes his rule. This is the logic of the gospel.

20:20–28 The two "sons of Zebedee" (James and John; 4:21), their mother, and the rest of Jesus' disciples were still, at this point in their discipleship, substantially under the influence of the unbelieving world's system of values (20:20–21, 25). They did not understand what Jesus had taught in the parable of the laborers in the vineyard (vv. 1–16). Positions of leadership in God's kingdom belong to those who have been so transformed by the grace of God that they are willing to be despised and even persecuted by the unbelieving world (vv. 22–23) and are willing to lead by serving others rather than being served by them (vv. 26–28; see also 23:11).

Believers serve and forgive one another not to earn prestige or God's favor for themselves, but because they have experienced God's selfless love and forgiveness through their union with Christ Jesus (20:28). God's compassionate character is clear in the Old Testament (Ex. 2:23–25; 34:6–7; Num. 14:18; Neh. 9:17; Ps. 86:15; 103:1–14; Joel 2:12–14; Jonah 4:2) but appears preeminently in Jesus' life, teachings, and ministry (Phil. 2:1–11; see also Gal. 6:2–3; Eph. 4:32–5:2; Col. 2:13).

17 [p]For ver. 17-19, see Mark 10:32-34; Luke 18:31-33; [ch. 16:21-28; 17:12, 22, 23]
18 [q]See ch. 16:21 [r]ch. 26:66; John 19:7
19 [s]ch. 27:2; John 18:30, 31; Acts 3:13; [Acts 2:23; 4:27; 21:11] [t]ch. 27:26-31 [u]ch. 26:2; Luke 24:7; John 12:32, 33; 18:32 [v]ch. 16:21; 27:63
20 [w]For ver. 20-28, see Mark 10:35-45 [x]ch. 4:21; 27:56 [y]See ch. 8:2
21 [z][ch. 19:28] [a]ch. 16:28; 25:31, 34; Luke 23:42
22 [b][Luke 9:33; 23:34] [c]ch. 26:29, 42; Mark 14:36; Luke 22:42; John 18:11; [Isa. 51:22]
23 [d][Rom. 8:17; Phil. 3:10] [e]Acts 12:2; Rev. 1:9 [f][ch. 19:11] [g]ch. 25:34
25 [h]For ver. 25-28, [ch. 18:1-4; Luke 22:25-27] [i]1 Pet. 5:3
26 [j]ch. 23:11; [Luke 9:48]
28 [k]John 13:4, 13-15; Phil. 2:7; [2 Cor. 8:9] [l]Isa. 53:10; Dan. 9:26; John 10:15; 11:51, 52; Rom. 4:25; Gal. 1:4; 2:20; 1 Tim. 2:6; Titus 2:14; 1 Pet. 1:18, 19 [m]ch. 26:28; Isa. 53:11, 12; Heb. 2:10; 9:28; [Rom. 5:15; Rev. 5:9] **29** [n]For ver. 29-34, see Mark 10:46-52; Luke 18:35-43; [ch. 9:27-31] **30** [o]ch. 21:9; 22:42; See ch. 1:1 **31** [p]ch. 19:13 **Chapter 21** **1** [q]For ver. 1-9, see Mark 11:1-10; Luke 19:29-38; John 12:12-15 [r]ch. 24:3; 26:30; Zech. 14:4; [John 8:1]; [Acts 1:12] [s][Mark 14:13] **4** [t]See ch. 1:22

5 [u]"Say to the daughter of Zion,
'Behold, your king is coming to you,
[v]humble, and mounted on a donkey,
on a colt,[1] the foal of a beast of burden.'"

6 The disciples went and did as Jesus had
directed them. 7 They brought the donkey and
the colt and put on them their cloaks, and he
sat on them. 8 Most of the crowd [w]spread their
cloaks on the road, and others cut branches
from the trees and spread them on the road.
9 And the crowds that went before him and
that followed him were shouting, [x]"Hosanna
to [y]the Son of David! [z]Blessed is he who comes
in the name of the Lord! Hosanna [a]in the
highest!" 10 And [b]when he entered Jerusalem,
the whole city was stirred up, saying, "Who
is this?" 11 And the crowds said, "This is [c]the
prophet Jesus, [d]from Nazareth of Galilee."

Jesus Cleanses the Temple

12 [e]And Jesus entered the temple[2] and drove
out all who sold and bought in the temple,
and he overturned the tables of [f]the money-
changers and the seats of those who sold
[g]pigeons. 13 He said to them, "It is written, [h]'My
house shall be called a house of prayer,' but
[i]you make it a den of robbers."

14 [j]And the blind and the lame came to him in
the temple, and he healed them. 15 [k]But when
the chief priests and the scribes saw the wonderful things that he did, and the children
crying out in the temple, [x]"Hosanna to the
Son of David!" they were indignant, 16 and they
said to him, "Do you hear what these are saying?" And Jesus said to them, "Yes; [l]have you
never read,

[m]"'Out of the mouth of [n]infants and nursing babies
you have prepared praise'?"

17 And [o]leaving them, he [p]went out of the city
to [q]Bethany and lodged there.

Jesus Curses the Fig Tree

18 [r]In the morning, as he was returning to
the city, [s]he became hungry. 19 [t]And seeing a fig
tree by the wayside, he went to it and found
nothing on it but only leaves. And he said to
it, "May no fruit ever come from you again!"
And the fig tree withered at once.

20 When the disciples saw it, they marveled,
saying, "How did the fig tree wither at once?"
21 And Jesus answered them, [u]"Truly, I say to
you, [v]if you have faith and [w]do not doubt, you
will not only do what has been done to the
fig tree, but even if you say to this mountain,
[x]'Be taken up and thrown into the sea,' it will
happen. 22 And [v]whatever you ask in prayer,
you will receive, [y]if you have faith."

The Authority of Jesus Challenged

23 [z]And when he entered the temple, the chief
priests and the elders of the people came up to
him [a]as he was teaching, and said, [b]"By what
authority are you doing these things, and who
gave you this authority?" 24 Jesus answered
them, "I also will ask you one question, and if
you tell me the answer, then I also will tell you
by what authority I do these things. 25 The baptism of John, [c]from where did it come? [d]From

[1] Or *donkey, and on a colt,* [2] Some manuscripts add *of God*

5[u] Cited from Zech. 9:9; [Isa. 62:11] [v] ch. 11:29
8[w] 2 Kgs. 9:13
9[x] [Rev. 7:10]; See Ps. 118:25 (Heb.) [y] ch. 20:30 [z] ch. 23:39; Cited from Ps. 118:26 [a] Luke 2:14; [Ps. 148:1]
10[b] Mark 11:11
11[c] ver. 46; Luke 7:16; 13:33; 24:19; John 4:19; 6:14; 7:40; 9:17; [Mark 6:15; Luke 9:8, 19; John 1:21] [d] See ch. 2:23
12[e] For ver. 12-16, see Mark 11:15-18; Luke 19:45-47; [John 2:14-16] [f] [Ex. 30:13] [g] Lev. 1:14; 5:7; 12:8; Luke 2:24
13[h] Cited from Isa. 56:7 [i] Jer. 7:11
14[j] ch. 11:5; 15:31
15[k] [Luke 19:39, 40] [x] [See ver. 9 above]
16[l] ver. 42; ch. 12:3, 5; 19:4; 22:31

21:18–22 This teaching of Jesus on faith and prayer should be interpreted in terms of what he has already said on these topics in 17:14–20. There Jesus emphasized that the power of prayer lies not in the power of the believer but in the power of God. In addition, in 17:14–20 the context of Jesus' teaching made clear that Jesus was talking about prayer for the accomplishment of God's purposes, such as the defeat of the demonic world.

Here, then, when Jesus speaks of faith versus doubt, he also refers to trusting in the power of God, and the subject of the believer's request in prayer is not just anything imaginable but something that furthers God's purposes. Jesus' example of ordering a mountain to throw itself into the sea uses hyperbole to illustrate colorfully how powerful God is (for other examples of how Jesus used hyperbole in his teaching, see note on 5:29–30).

Believers who pray unselfishly for the things they think will advance God's merciful and saving purposes should also pray boldly. They should have faith that God will either do what they ask or will work in some other way that he knows will accomplish his purposes more perfectly (cf. 1 John 5:14–15).

[m] Cited from Ps. 8:2 (Gk.) [n] ch. 11:25 **17**[o] ch. 16:4 [p] Mark 11:19; [Luke 21:37] [q] Mark 11:1; Luke 19:29; 24:50; John 11:18 **18**[r] For ver. 18-22, see Mark 11:12-14, 20-24 [s] ch. 4:2 **19**[t] [Luke 13:6-9] **21**[u] ch. 17:20 [v] [John 14:12] [w] Acts 10:20; Rom. 4:20; 14:23; James 1:6 [x] [Ps. 46:2; 1 Cor. 13:2; Rev. 8:8] **22**[v] [See ver. 21 above] [y] See ch. 7:7 **23**[z] For ver. 23-27, see Mark 11:27-33; Luke 20:1-8 [a] See ch. 26:55 [b] [Ex. 2:14; John 1:25; Acts 4:7] **25**[c] [ch. 13:54] [d] Luke 15:18, 21; John 3:27

heaven or from man?" And they discussed it
among themselves, saying, "If we say, 'From
heaven,' he will say to us, [e]'Why then did you
not believe him?' 26 But if we say, 'From man,'
[f]we are afraid of the crowd, for they all hold
that John was [g]a prophet." 27 So they answered
Jesus, "We do not know." And he said to them,
"Neither will I tell you by what authority I do
these things.

The Parable of the Two Sons

28 [h]"What do you think? A man had two
sons. And he went to the first and said, 'Son,
go and work in [i]the vineyard today.' 29 And
he answered, 'I will not,' but afterward he
[j]changed his mind and went. 30 And he went
to the other son and said the same. And he
answered, 'I go, sir,' but did not go. 31 Which of
the two did the will of his father?" They said,
"The first." Jesus said to them, "Truly, I say to
you, [k]the tax collectors and [l]the prostitutes go
into [m]the kingdom of God before you. 32 For
John came to you [n]in the way of righteousness,
and [o]you did not believe him, but [p]the tax collectors and the prostitutes believed him. And
even when you saw it, you did not afterward
[j]change your minds and believe him.

The Parable of the Tenants

33 [q]"Hear another parable. There was a master
of a house who planted [r]a vineyard [s]and put
a fence around it and dug a winepress in it
and built a tower and [t]leased it to tenants, and
[u]went into another country. 34 When the season for fruit drew near, he sent his servants[1] to
the tenants [t]to get his fruit. 35 [v]And the tenants
took his servants and beat one, killed another,
and [w]stoned another. 36 [x]Again he sent other
servants, more than the first. And they did
the same to them. 37 Finally he sent his son
to them, saying, 'They will respect my son.'
38 But when the tenants saw the son, they said
to themselves, [y]'This is the heir. Come, [z]let us
kill him and have his inheritance.' 39 And they
took him and [a]threw him out of the vineyard
and killed him. 40 [b]When therefore the owner
of the vineyard comes, what will he do to those
tenants?" 41 They said to him, [c]"He will put
those wretches to a miserable death and [d]let
out the vineyard to other tenants who will
give him the fruits in their seasons."

42 Jesus said to them, [e]"Have you never read
in the Scriptures:

[f]"'The stone that the builders rejected
has become the cornerstone;[2]
this was the Lord's doing,
and it is marvelous in our eyes'?

43 Therefore I tell you, the kingdom of God
[g]will be taken away from you and given to a
people [h]producing its fruits. 44 And [i]the one
who falls on this stone will be broken to
pieces; and [j]when it falls on anyone, it will
crush him."[3]

45 When the chief priests and the Pharisees
heard his parables, they perceived that he was
speaking about them. 46 And [l]although they
were seeking to arrest him, [m]they feared the
crowds, because they held him to be [n]a prophet.

[1] Greek *bondservants*; also verses 35, 36 [2] Greek *the head of the corner* [3] Some manuscripts omit verse 44

21:28–22:14 Much of Jesus' teaching in Matthew's Gospel addresses the question, "Who belongs to the people of God?" or, to put it another way, "Who will enter the kingdom of God?" These three parables reveal that entering the kingdom involves responding in faith to the message of repentance that John the Baptist and Jesus preached (21:28–32), recognizing Jesus as the One who brings in God's kingdom (21:33–46), and living in a way consistent with this recognition (22:1–14). All three parables communicate the sad message that the leadership of Israel (21:23, 45; 22:15) had met none of these requirements for participation in God's kingdom (see also Isa. 5:1–7). Instead, "the tax collectors and the prostitutes" (Matt. 21:32), and others who respond to Jesus in repentance and faith, will comprise the new vineyard tenants and wedding feast guests (22:8–9).

The final paragraph of the section (22:11–14) is a sobering reminder that the warning Jesus issued to the leadership of Israel in these parables is still valid for the people of God today. People are attracted to the church for a variety of reasons: it offers a place to socialize, opportunities to meet people of one's own age and interests, and organizational structures for helping the needy. As a result, people whose hearts have never been transformed by God can find themselves associating with the church.

25 [e]ver. 32; Luke 7:30
26 [f]ver. 46; ch. 14:5 [g][John 5:35]; See ch. 11:9
28 [h]ch. 17:25; 18:12 [i]ver. 33; ch. 20:1
29 [j]ver. 32; ch. 27:3; Heb. 7:21
31 [k]Luke 7:29 [l]Luke 7:37-50 [m]See ch. 12:28
32 [n][ch. 3:8-12, 15; Prov. 8:20; 2 Pet. 2:21] [o]ver. 25; ch. 11:18 [p]Luke 3:12, 13 [j][See ver. 29 above]
33 [q]For ver. 33-46, see Mark 12:1-12; Luke 20:9-19 [r]ver. 28; Ps. 80:8; Isa. 5:1 [s]Isa. 5:2 [t]Song 8:11, 12 [u]ch. 25:14, 15; [Mark 13:34]
34 [t][See ver. 33 above]
35 [v]ch. 5:12; 22:6; 23:34, 37; [2 Chr. 24:19; 36:15, 16; Neh. 9:26; Jer. 37:15; 38:6; Acts 7:52; 2 Cor. 11:24-26; 1 Thess. 2:15; Heb. 11:36, 37] [w][2 Chr. 24:21; John 10:31-33; Acts 7:59]

36 [x]ch. 22:4 **38** [y]Heb. 1:2; [John 1:11; Rom. 8:17] [z][1 Kgs. 21:19] **39** [a]Heb. 13:12 **40** [b][ch. 24:50; 25:19] **41** [c]Luke 19:27 [d]ver. 43; Acts 13:46; 18:6; 28:28; [ch. 8:11, 12] **42** [e]ver. 16 [f]Acts 4:11; 1 Pet. 2:7; Cited from Ps. 118:22, 23 **43** [g][Luke 14:24] [h][ch. 3:10; Isa. 5:4, 7] **44** [i]Isa. 8:14, 15; Rom. 9:32, 33; 1 Pet. 2:8 [j]Dan. 2:34, 35, 44, 45 **46** [l]Mark 11:18; Luke 19:47, 48; John 7:25, 30, 44; [ch. 26:4] [m]ver. 26 [n][ver. 11]

The Parable of the Wedding Feast

22 And again Jesus [o]spoke to them in parables, saying, 2 [p]“The kingdom of heaven
may be compared to a king who gave [q]a wedding feast for his son, 3 and [r]sent his servants[1]
to call those who were invited to the wedding
feast, but they would not come. 4 [s]Again he
sent other servants, saying, ‘Tell those who
are invited, “See, I have prepared my [t]dinner,
[u]my oxen and my fat calves have been slaughtered, and everything is ready. Come to the
wedding feast.”’ 5 But [v]they paid no attention
and went off, one to his farm, another to his
business, 6 while the rest seized his servants,
[w]treated them shamefully, and [x]killed them.
7 The king was angry, and he sent his troops
and [y]destroyed those murderers and burned
their city. 8 Then he said to his servants, ‘The
wedding feast is ready, but those invited were
not [z]worthy. 9 Go therefore to the main roads
and invite to the wedding feast as many as
you find.’ 10 And those servants went out into
the roads and [b]gathered all whom they found,
both bad and good. So the wedding hall was
filled with guests.

11 “But when the king came in to look at the
guests, he saw there [c]a man who had no wedding garment. 12 And he said to him, [d]‘Friend,
how did you get in here without a wedding
garment?’ And he was speechless. 13 Then the
king said to the attendants, ‘Bind him hand
and foot and [e]cast him into the outer darkness. In that place [e]there will be weeping and
gnashing of teeth.’ 14 For many are [f]called, but
few are [f]chosen.”

Paying Taxes to Caesar

15 [g]Then the Pharisees went and plotted
how [h]to entangle him in his words. 16 And
they sent [i]their disciples to him, along with
[j]the Herodians, saying, “Teacher, [k]we know
that you are true and teach [l]the way of God
truthfully, and you do not care about anyone’s
opinion, for [m]you are not swayed by appearances.[2] 17 Tell us, then, what you think. Is it
lawful to pay [n]taxes to [o]Caesar, or not?” 18 But
Jesus, aware of their malice, said, “Why [p]put
me to the test, you hypocrites? 19 Show me
the coin for the tax.” And they brought him a
denarius.[3] 20 And Jesus said to them, “Whose
likeness and inscription is this?” 21 They said,
“Caesar’s.” Then he said to them, [q]“Therefore
render to Caesar the things that are Caesar’s,
and to God the things that are God’s.” 22 When
they heard it, they marveled. And they [r]left
him and went away.

Sadducees Ask About the Resurrection

23 The same day [s]Sadducees came to him,
[t]who say that there is no resurrection, and
they asked him a question, 24 saying, “Teacher,
Moses said, [u]‘If a man dies having no children,
his brother must marry the widow and raise
up offspring for his brother.’ 25 Now there were
seven brothers among us. The first married
and died, and having no offspring left his wife
to his brother. 26 So too the second and third,
down to the seventh. 27 After them all, the
woman died. 28 In the resurrection, therefore,
of the seven, whose wife will she be? For they
all had her.”

29 But Jesus answered them, “You are wrong,
[v]because you know neither the Scriptures nor
[w]the power of God. 30 For in the resurrection
they neither [x]marry nor [x]are given in marriage,
but are like angels in heaven. 31 And as for the
resurrection of the dead, [y]have you not read
what was said to you by God: 32 [z]‘I am the God
of Abraham, and the God of Isaac, and the God
of Jacob’? He is not God of the dead, but of the
living.” 33 And when the crowd heard it, [a]they
were astonished at his teaching.

The Great Commandment

34 [b]But when the Pharisees heard that he
had silenced [c]the Sadducees, they gathered
together. 35 [d]And one of them, [e]a lawyer, asked
him a question [f]to test him. 36 “Teacher, which

[1] Greek *bondservants*; also verses 4, 6, 8, 10 [2] Greek *for you do not look at people’s faces* [3] A *denarius* was a day’s wage for a laborer

This heart-transformation, evident in repentance, faith, and obedience to Jesus is the “wedding garment” that the guest in 22:11–14 lacked.

As Christians we are called to “examine” ourselves to see whether we are “in the faith” (2 Cor. 13:5; cf. Matt. 7:21–23; 13:24–30, 36–43, 47–50; 25:11–12, 44–46; 2 Pet. 1:10). Have we truly turned from our sin and turned to Jesus for forgiveness and direction?

Chapter 22
1 [o] ch. 13:34
2 [p] For ver. 2-14, [Luke 14:16-24] [q] See Rev. 19:7
3 [r] [Esth. 6:14; Prov. 9:3, 5]
4 [s] ch. 21:36 [t] Luke 11:38; John 21:12, 15 (Gk.) [u] Prov. 9:2

5 [v] [Heb. 2:3] **6** [w] Luke 18:32; Acts 14:5; 1 Thess. 2:2 [x] See ch. 21:35 **7** [y] ch. 21:41; Luke 19:27 **8** [z] ch. 10:11; Acts 13:46; Rev. 3:4; [Luke 20:35] **10** [b] See ch. 13:47 **11** [c] [Rev. 19:8; 22:14] **12** [d] ch. 20:13; 26:50 **13** [e] See ch. 8:12 **14** [f] Rev. 17:14 **15** [g] For ver. 15-32, see Mark 12:13-27; Luke 20:20-38 [h] [Luke 11:54] **16** [i] Mark 2:18 [j] Mark 3:6; [Mark 8:15] [k] [John 3:2] [l] Acts 18:26; [Acts 13:10] [m] See Acts 10:34 **17** [n] ch. 17:25 [o] Luke 2:1; 3:1 **18** [p] See John 8:6 **21** [q] Rom. 13:7 **22** [r] Mark 12:12 **23** [s] ver. 34; ch. 3:7; 16:1; Acts 4:1; 5:17; 23:6 [t] Acts 23:8; [Acts 4:2] **24** [u] [Deut. 25:5] **29** [v] John 20:9 [w] 1 Cor. 6:14 **30** [x] ch. 24:38; Luke 17:27 **31** [y] See ch. 21:16 **32** [z] Acts 7:32; Cited from Ex. 3:6 **33** [a] See ch. 7:28 **34** [b] For ver. 34-40, see Mark 12:28-33 [c] ver. 23 **35** [d] [Luke 10:25-28] [e] See Luke 7:30 [f] ver. 18

is the great commandment in the Law?" 37 And
he said to him, [g]"You shall love the Lord your
God with all your heart and with all your soul
and with all your mind. 38 This is the great and
first commandment. 39 And [h]a second is like
it: [i]You shall love your neighbor as yourself.
40 [j]On these two commandments depend [k]all
the Law and the Prophets."

Whose Son Is the Christ?

41 [l]Now while the Pharisees [m]were gathered
together, Jesus asked them a question, 42 saying,
"What do you think about [n]the Christ? Whose
son is he?" They said to him, [n]"The son of
David." 43 He said to them, "How is it then that
David, [o]in the Spirit, calls him Lord, saying,

44 [p]"'The Lord said to my Lord,
"Sit at my right hand,
until I put your enemies under your
feet"'?

45 If then David calls him Lord, [q]how is he his
son?" 46 [r]And no one was able to answer him a
word, [s]nor from that day did anyone dare to
ask him any more questions.

Seven Woes to the Scribes and Pharisees

23 Then Jesus [t]said to the crowds and to
his disciples, 2 [u]"The scribes and the
Pharisees [v]sit on Moses' seat, 3 so do and
observe whatever they tell you, [w]but not the
works they do. [x]For they preach, but do not
practice. 4 [y]They tie up heavy burdens, hard to
bear,[1] and lay them on people's shoulders, but
they themselves are not willing to move them
with their finger. 5 [t]They do all their deeds [z]to
be seen by others. For they make [a]their phy-
lacteries broad and [b]their fringes long, 6 and
they [c]love the place of honor at feasts and [d]the
best seats in the synagogues 7 and [d]greetings in
[e]the marketplaces and being called [f]rabbi[2] by
others. 8 [g]But you are not to be called rabbi, for
you have one teacher, and you are [h]all brothers.[3] 9 [i]And call no man your father on earth,
for [j]you have one Father, who is in heaven.
10 Neither be called instructors, for you have
one instructor, [k]the Christ. 11 [l]The greatest
among you shall be your servant. 12 [m]Whoever
exalts himself will be humbled, and whoever
humbles himself will be exalted.

[1] Some manuscripts omit *hard to bear* [2] *Rabbi* means *my teacher*, or *my master*; also verse 8 [3] Or *brothers and sisters*

22:34–40 The order of these two great commandments is important. Jesus did not teach that, in order to be in a loving relationship with God, his disciples must first love their neighbors. He taught instead that the "great and first commandment" is to love God with one's entire being, and elsewhere Scripture makes clear that this love for God is possible only because God loved believers first (1 John 4:19; see also Rom. 5:8). A loving commitment to God, initiated by God himself, results in love for one's neighbor. When we love God, we love what and whom *he* loves—because we desire to please and honor him.

In 2 Corinthians 8:1–7, Paul demonstrated how this works in practical terms. He used the Macedonian Christians as an example of unselfish generosity, to urge the Corinthian Christians toward the same kind of generosity. Although poor themselves, he says, the Macedonians gave beyond all expectation: "they gave themselves first to the Lord and then by the will of God to us" (2 Cor. 8:5). Jesus' disciples do not earn God's favor by loving their neighbors; they love God because he has shown them his grace and mercy through the sacrificial love of Jesus, and this love for God overflows in love for others (Eph. 4:32–5:2).

23:1–36 Why did Matthew include in his Gospel this discourse of Jesus against the scribes and the Pharisees? He may have wanted to issue a warning to them about their hardheartedness, in the hope that some of them would repent. He probably also wanted Christians to benefit from the Pharisees' negative example.

The scribes and Pharisees were positioned to do great damage to the Jewish people. They were learned in the Scriptures, and, because of their learning, occupied positions of authority and influence (vv. 2, 6–7). Yet they were blind to their own hardheartedness toward God (vv. 16, 17, 24). As a result, they were not only on the road to eternal destruction themselves but were leading others down the same road and leading astray those who were on the right road (vv. 13–15; see also 15:14). Their central problem was the disjunction between their inner condition and their outward appearance (23:25–28). To other people, they appeared devoted to God and worthy of respect (vv. 3–7), but they were motivated in their outward acts of piety by love

37 [g]Luke 10:27; Cited from Deut. 6:5
39 [h][1 John 4:21] [i]Cited from Lev. 19:18; See ch. 19:19
40 [j][Rom. 13:8, 10] [k]ch. 7:12; [Gal. 5:14]
41 [l]For ver. 41-45, see Mark 12:35-37; Luke 20:41-44 [m]ver. 34
42 [n]See ch. 1:1, 17
43 [o]Rev. 1:10; 4:2; [2 Sam. 23:2]
44 [p]Acts 2:34, 35; Heb. 1:13; Cited from Ps. 110:1; [1 Cor. 15:25; Heb. 10:13]
45 [q][Rom. 1:3, 4]
46 [r][Luke 14:6] [s]Mark 12:34; Luke 20:40
Chapter 23
1 [t]For ver. 1, 2, 5-7, see Mark 12:38, 39; Luke 20:45, 46; [Luke 11:43]
2 [u][Ezra 7:6, 10, 25; Neh. 8:4] [v][Deut. 17:10, 11; John 9:28, 29]
3 [w][ch. 5:20; 15:3-13] [x]Rom. 2:17-23
4 [y]Luke 11:46; [ch. 11:28-30; Acts 15:10]
5 [t][See ver. 1 above] [z]ch. 6:1, 16; [John 5:44] [a]Ex. 13:9; Deut. 6:8; 11:18 [b]See ch. 9:20
6 [c]Luke 14:7, 8 [d]Luke 11:43
7 [d][See ver. 6 above] [e]ch. 11:16; 20:3 [f]See John 1:38
8 [g]James 3:1 [h]Luke 22:32; John 21:23; See Philem. 16
9 [i][1 Cor. 1:12; 3:4] [j]ch. 6:9; Mal. 1:6; See ch. 7:11
10 [k]See ch. 1:17
11 [l]ch. 20:26
12 [m]Luke 14:11; 18:14; [ch. 18:4; Prov. 29:23; Ezek. 21:26; James 4:6, 10; 1 Pet. 5:5, 6]

13 “But woe [n]to you, scribes and Pharisees,
hypocrites! For you [o]shut the kingdom of
heaven in people’s faces. For you [p]neither enter
yourselves nor allow those who would enter
to go in.[1] 15 Woe to you, scribes and Pharisees,
hypocrites! For you travel across sea and land
to make a single [q]proselyte, and when he
becomes a proselyte, you make him twice as
much a [r]child of [s]hell[2] as yourselves.
16 “Woe to [t]you, [u]blind guides, who say, [v]‘If
anyone swears by the temple, it is nothing,
but if anyone swears by the gold of the temple,
he is bound by his oath.’ 17 You blind fools! For
which is greater, the gold or [w]the temple that
has made the gold sacred? 18 And you say, ‘If
anyone swears by the altar, it is nothing, but if
anyone swears by [x]the gift that is on the altar,
he is bound by his oath.’ 19 You blind men!
For which is greater, the gift or [y]the altar that
makes the gift sacred? 20 So whoever swears by
the altar swears by it and by everything on it.
21 And whoever swears by the temple swears by
it and by [z]him who dwells in it. 22 And whoever
swears by [a]heaven swears by [b]the throne of
God and by [c]him who sits upon it.
23 [d]“Woe to you, scribes and Pharisees, hypocrites! For [e]you tithe mint and dill and [f]cumin,
and have neglected the weightier matters
of the law: [g]justice and mercy and faithfulness. [h]These you ought to have done, without
neglecting the others. 24 You blind guides,
straining out a gnat and swallowing [i]a camel!
25 [j]“Woe to you, scribes and Pharisees, hypocrites! For [k]you clean the outside of [l]the cup
and the plate, but inside they are full of [m]greed
and self-indulgence. 26 You blind Pharisee!
First clean the inside of [l]the cup and the plate,
that the outside also may be clean.
27 [n]“Woe to you, scribes and Pharisees, hypocrites! For you are like [o]whitewashed tombs,
which outwardly appear beautiful, but
within are full of dead people’s bones and [p]all
uncleanness. 28 So you also [q]outwardly appear
righteous to others, but within you are full of
[r]hypocrisy and lawlessness.
29 [s]“Woe to you, scribes and Pharisees, hypocrites! For you build the tombs of the prophets
and decorate the monuments of the righteous,
30 saying, ‘If we had lived in the days of our
fathers, we would not have taken part with
them in shedding the blood of the prophets.’
31 Thus you witness against yourselves that you
are [t]sons of those who murdered the prophets.
32 [u]Fill up, then, the measure of your fathers.
33 You serpents, [v]you brood of vipers, how
are you to escape being sentenced to [w]hell?
34 [x]Therefore [y]I send you [z]prophets and wise
men and [a]scribes, [b]some of whom you will
kill and crucify, and [b]some you will [c]flog in
your synagogues and [d]persecute from town
to town, 35 so that on you may come all [e]the
righteous blood shed on earth, from the blood
of righteous [f]Abel to the blood of [g]Zechariah
the son of Barachiah,[3] whom you murdered
between [h]the sanctuary and [i]the altar. 36 Truly,
I say to you, [j]all these things will come upon
this generation.

Lament over Jerusalem

37 [k]“O Jerusalem, Jerusalem, the city that [l]kills
the prophets and stones those who are sent to
it! How often would I have [m]gathered [n]your

[1] Some manuscripts add here (or after verse 12) verse 14: *Woe to you, scribes and Pharisees, hypocrites! For you devour widows' houses and for a pretense you make long prayers; therefore you will receive the greater condemnation* [2] Greek *Gehenna*; also verse 33 [3] Some manuscripts omit *the son of Barachiah*

for the praise of others, pride in their technical cleverness, greed, and self-indulgence (vv. 5, 16–24, 25).

Throughout Matthew’s Gospel, Jesus provides several diagnostic tests for making sure that his disciples’ hearts are not hardened toward God. First, he urges them to be careful that their acts of devotion to God, such as giving to the needy, praying, and fasting, flow from the heart and not from a desire to win the approval of others. Secrecy is key here (6:1–18). Second, he encourages his disciples not to allow money and the temporary sense of security it can provide to replace God as their ultimate source of security (6:19–34; 13:22, 44–46; 19:16–30). Third, he encourages them to focus not on cleverly deduced methods and schemes for obeying God (15:5–9; 23:16–24), but on service to others (20:26–27; 23:11) and “the weightier matters of the law,” which he defines as “justice and mercy and faithfulness” (v. 23; see also Mic. 6:8; Hos. 6:6).

13 [n] Luke 11:52 [o] [ch. 16:19] [p] [ch. 5:20; 21:31; Luke 7:30]
15 [q] Acts 2:10; 6:5; 13:43 [r] [John 17:12; 2 Thess. 2:3] [s] See ch. 5:29
16 [t] See ch. 15:14 [u] ver. 17, 19, 26; John 9:39-41; Rom. 2:19; 2 Pet. 1:9; Rev. 3:17 [v] [ch. 5:33-35]
17 [w] Ex. 30:29
18 [x] ch. 5:23
19 [y] Ex. 29:37
21 [z] 1 Kgs. 8:13; 2 Chr. 6:2; Ps. 26:8; 132:14
22 [a] [ch. 21:25] [b] See ch. 5:34 [c] See Rev. 4:2
23 [d] Luke 11:42 [e] Deut. 14:22; [Luke 18:12] [f] Isa. 28:25, 27 [g] Ps. 33:5; Jer. 5:1; Mic. 6:8; Zech. 7:9 [h] [1 Sam. 15:22] **24** [i] ch. 19:24 **25** [j] For ver. 25-28, [ch. 15:11-20] [k] Luke 11:39, 40 [l] Mark 7:4 [m] Luke 16:14; 20:47 **26** [l] [See ver. 25 above] **27** [n] Luke 11:44 [o] [Acts 23:3] [p] Eph. 5:3; [Num. 19:16; 2 Kgs. 23:16] **28** [q] ver. 5 [r] Luke 12:1 **29** [s] Luke 11:47, 48 **31** [t] Acts 7:51, 52 **32** [u] Gen. 15:16; Dan. 8:23; 1 Thess. 2:15, 16 **33** [v] ch. 3:7; 12:34 [w] ver. 15 **34** [x] For ver. 34-36, [Luke 11:49-51] [y] ch. 10:16 [z] See Acts 13:1; 1 Cor. 12:28 [a] ch. 13:52 [b] See ch. 21:35 [c] ch. 10:17; Mark 13:9; Luke 21:12; Acts 22:19; 26:11; [Luke 12:11] [d] ch. 10:23 **35** [e] Rev. 18:24 [f] Gen. 4:4, 8; Heb. 11:4; 1 John 3:12 [g] [Zech. 1:1] [h] See Luke 1:9 [i] Ex. 40:6; 2 Kgs. 16:14; Ezek. 40:47 **36** [j] [ch. 10:23; 16:28; 24:34] **37** [k] For ver. 37-39, see Luke 13:34, 35; [Luke 19:41-44] [l] See ch. 21:35 [m] [Ps. 147:2; Prov. 1:24] [n] Luke 23:28

children together [o]as a hen gathers her brood
[p]under her wings, and [q]you were not willing!
38 See, [r]your house is left to you desolate. 39 For
I tell you, you will not see me again, until you
say, [s]'Blessed is he who comes in the name of
the Lord.'"

Jesus Foretells Destruction of the Temple

24 [t]Jesus left the temple and was going
away, when his disciples came to point
out to him the buildings of the temple. 2 But
he answered them, "You see all these, do you
not? Truly, I say to you, [u]there will not be left
here one stone upon another that will not be
thrown down."

Signs of the End of the Age

3 As he sat on [v]the Mount of Olives, the disciples came to him [w]privately, saying, "Tell us,
[x]when will these things be, and what will be
the sign of your [y]coming and of [z]the end of
the age?" 4 And Jesus answered them, [a]"See
that no one leads you astray. 5 For [b]many will
come in my name, saying, 'I am [c]the Christ,'
and they will lead many astray. 6 And you will
hear of wars and rumors of wars. See that you
[d]are not alarmed, for this [e]must take place, but
the end is not yet. 7 For [f]nation will rise against
nation, and [g]kingdom against kingdom, and
there will be [h]famines and earthquakes in various places. 8 All these are but the beginning of
[i]the birth pains.
9 "Then [j]they will deliver you up [k]to tribulation and [l]put you to death, and [m]you will
be hated by all nations for my name's sake.
10 And then many will fall away[1] and [n]betray
one another and hate one another. 11 And
many [o]false prophets will arise [p]and lead
many astray. 12 And because lawlessness will
be increased, [q]the love of many will grow cold.
13 [r]But the one who endures to the end will be
saved. 14 And this gospel of the kingdom [s]will
be proclaimed throughout the whole world
[t]as a testimony [u]to all nations, and [v]then the
end will come.

The Abomination of Desolation

15 "So when you see the abomination of
desolation [w]spoken of by the prophet Daniel,
standing in [x]the holy place ([y]let the reader
understand), 16 then let those who are in Judea
flee to the mountains. 17 [z]Let the one who is on
[a]the housetop not go down to take what is in
his house, 18 and let the one who is in the field
not turn back to take his cloak. 19 And [b]alas
for women who are pregnant and for those
who are nursing infants in those days! 20 Pray
that your flight may not be in winter or on a
Sabbath. 21 For then there will be [c]great tribulation, [d]such as has not been from the beginning
of the world until now, no, and never will be.
22 And if those days had not been cut short,
no human being would be saved. But for [e]the
sake of the elect those days will be cut short.
23 [f]Then if anyone says to you, 'Look, here is
the Christ!' or 'There he is!' do not believe it.
24 For [g]false christs and [h]false prophets will
arise and [i]perform great signs and wonders,
[h]so as to lead astray, if possible, even the elect.

[1] Or *stumble*

24:1–25:46 This long block of teaching emphasizes God's coming judgment of rebellion against him (24:1–41), the importance of being ready for this time of judgment (24:42–25:13), and what this readiness looks like for his disciples (25:14–46).

Jesus says that sin and the destruction it causes in society will go from bad to worse as the time of his coming approaches. Religious deception (24:4–5), war (24:6–7a), and natural disaster (24:7b) will continue to plague the world, but as the end of all things gets closer, persecution of Jesus' disciples will be added to this list of troubles (24:9–13). Jesus' followers will, nevertheless, continue to preach the gospel to the people groups of the world (24:14), and, after a final surge of societal evil (24:15–28), Jesus himself will break into the world's sinful routine, gather his people to himself, and end the world's rebellion against its Creator (24:29–31). While sin grows worse, most people will not even notice, including Jesus' disciples (24:37–39, 44, 50; 25:5, 19). The question then becomes, "How can Jesus' disciples be ready for his arrival?"

Jesus instructs his disciples to be ready for his coming at all times. This is the point of the parables in 24:43–25:13, all of which focus both on the uncertainty of the time of Jesus' coming (24:44, 50; 25:5, 19) and the importance of being busy about

37 [o][Deut. 32:11, 12] [p]Ruth 2:12 [q]John 5:40
38 [r][Isa. 64:11; Jer. 12:7; 22:5]
39 [s]ch. 21:9; Cited from Ps. 118:26

Chapter 24
1 [t][ch. 21:23]; For ver. 1-51, see Mark 13:1-37; Luke 21:5-36
2 [u]Luke 19:44
3 [v]See ch. 21:1 [w][Mark 4:34] [x][Acts 1:6, 7] [y]ver. 27, 37, 39; See 1 Thess. 2:19 [z]See ch. 13:39
4 [a]Jer. 29:8; Eph. 5:6; Col. 2:8; 2 Thess. 2:3; 1 John 3:7
5 [b]ver. 11, 24; Jer. 14:14; 1 John 2:18 [c]See ch. 1:17
6 [d]2 Thess. 2:2 [e]Rev. 1:1
7 [f]2 Chr. 15:6; [Rev. 6:4] [g]Isa. 19:2 [h]Acts 11:28; Rev. 6:8, 12
8 [i]John 16:21; Acts 2:24 (Gk.); Rom. 8:22
9 [j]ch. 10:17, 21 [k]ver. 21, 29; Rev. 2:10 [l]ch. 23:34; John 16:2 [m]See ch. 10:22 **10** [n]ch. 10:21 **11** [o]See ch. 7:15 [p]ver. 5, 24 **12** [q][Rev. 2:4] **13** [r]See ch. 10:22 **14** [s]Rom. 10:18; Col. 1:6, 23; [Mark 14:9] [t]ch. 10:18 [u]ch. 28:19 [v][ver. 6] **15** [w]Dan. 9:27; 11:31; 12:11 [x][John 11:48; Acts 6:13; 21:28] [y][Dan. 9:22, 23, 25; Rev. 1:3] **17** [z]Luke 17:31 [a]See Luke 5:19 **19** [b]Luke 23:29 **21** [c]ver. 29; Dan. 12:1; [Rev. 7:14] [d]Rev. 16:18 **22** [e]ver. 24, 31; Isa. 65:8, 9; Luke 18:7; [ch. 22:14] **23** [f]Luke 17:23; [ver. 5, 26] **24** [g][1 John 2:18] [h]ver. 11 [i]Deut. 13:1-3; 2 Thess. 2:9-11; Rev. 13:13, 14; 16:14; 19:20; [Acts 8:9]

25 See, [j]I have told you beforehand. 26 So, if they
say to you, 'Look, [k]he is in the wilderness,' do
not go out. If they say, 'Look, he is in the inner
rooms,' do not believe it. 27 [l]For as the lightning
comes from the east and shines as far as the
west, so will be [m]the coming of the Son of Man.
28 [n]Wherever the corpse is, there the vultures
will gather.

The Coming of the Son of Man

29 "Immediately after [o]the tribulation of
those days [p]the sun will be darkened, and the
moon will not give its light, and [q]the stars
will fall from heaven, and the powers of the
heavens will be shaken. 30 Then [r]will appear
in heaven [s]the sign of the Son of Man, and
then [t]all the tribes of the earth will mourn,
and [u]they will see the Son of Man coming on
the clouds of heaven [v]with power and great
glory. 31 And [w]he will send out his angels with
a loud [x]trumpet call, and they will [y]gather [z]his
elect from [a]the four winds, [b]from one end of
heaven to the other.

The Lesson of the Fig Tree

32 "From the fig tree learn its lesson: as soon
as its branch becomes tender and puts out its
leaves, you know that summer is near. 33 So
also, when you see all these things, you know
that he is near, [c]at the very gates. 34 [d]Truly,
I say to you, this generation will not pass away
until all these things take place. 35 [e]Heaven
and earth will pass away, but [f]my words will
not pass away.

No One Knows That Day and Hour

36 "But concerning that day and hour [g]no
one knows, not even the angels of heaven,
[h]nor the Son,[1] [i]but the Father only. 37 [j]For as
were the days of Noah, [k]so will be the coming of the Son of Man. 38 [j]For as in those days
before the flood they were eating and drinking, [l]marrying and giving in marriage, until
[m]the day when Noah entered the ark, 39 and
they were unaware until the flood came and
swept them all away, [k]so will be the coming
of the Son of Man. 40 Then two men will be
in the field; one will be taken and one left.
41 [n]Two women will be grinding [o]at the mill;
one will be taken and one left. 42 Therefore,
[p]stay awake, for you do not know on what day
[q]your Lord is coming. 43 [r]But know this, that
if the master of the house had known in what
part of the night [s]the thief was coming, he
would have stayed awake and would not have
let his house be broken into. 44 Therefore you
also must be [t]ready, for [u]the Son of Man is coming at an hour you do not expect.

45 "Who then is [v]the faithful and [w]wise servant,[2] whom his master has set over his household, to give them their food at the proper
time? 46 [x]Blessed is that servant whom his master will find so doing when he comes. 47 Truly,
I say to you, [y]he will set him over all his possessions. 48 But if that wicked servant says to
himself, 'My master [z]is delayed,' 49 and begins
to beat his fellow servants[3] and eats and drinks
with [a]drunkards, 50 the master of that servant
will come [b]on a day when he does not expect
him and at an hour he does not know 51 and
will cut him in pieces and put him with the
hypocrites. In that place [c]there will be weeping
and gnashing of teeth.

The Parable of the Ten Virgins

25 "Then the kingdom of heaven will be
like [d]ten virgins who took their lamps[4]
and went to meet [e]the bridegroom.[5] 2 Five of
them were foolish, and five were [w]wise. 3 For
when the foolish took their lamps, they took
no oil with them, 4 but the wise took flasks

[1] Some manuscripts omit *nor the Son* [2] Greek *bondservant*; also verses 46, 48, 50 [3] Greek *bondservants* [4] Or *torches* [5] Some manuscripts add *and the bride*

25 [j] John 13:19; 14:29; [2 Pet. 3:17]
26 [k] Acts 21:38
27 [l] Luke 17:24 [m] ver. 3, 37, 39
28 [n] Luke 17:37; [Job 39:30]
29 [o] ver. 21 [p] Isa. 13:10; 24:23; Ezek. 32:7; Joel 2:10, 31; 3:15; Acts 2:20; [Amos 5:20; 8:9; Zeph. 1:15; Rev. 6:12; 8:12] [q] Rev. 6:13;

doing his will (24:42, 46; 25:4, 16–17, 20–23, 27). The parable of the talents demonstrates that, despite the sometimes fearful imagery of the preceding parables (24:51), Christians are not to understand them as admonitions to live in fear of his coming (25:25). Instead, they are to make the most of the opportunities and resources God has given them (25:16–17, 20–23, 27; see also Eph. 5:15–17; Col. 4:5). The focus is not on one's level of performance (Matt. 25:21, 23) but on faithfully and thankfully responding to one's relationship with God (25:24–25).

[Isa. 14:12; 34:4] **30** [r] Dan. 7:13 [s] [ver. 3] [t] Rev. 1:7; [Zech. 12:12] [u] See ch. 16:27 [v] ch. 26:64; Mark 9:1; [ch. 25:31] **31** [w] ch. 13:41 [x] 1 Cor. 15:52; 1 Thess. 4:16 [y] [ch. 23:37; 2 Thess. 2:1] [z] ver. 22, 24 [a] Dan. 7:2; Zech. 2:6; Rev. 7:1 [b] Deut. 4:32; 30:4 **33** [c] James 5:9; Rev. 3:20 **34** [d] See ch. 16:28 **35** [e] Ps. 102:26; Isa. 51:6; 2 Pet. 3:10; [ch. 5:18; Heb. 12:27] [f] Ps. 119:89; Isa. 40:8; 1 Pet. 1:23, 25 **36** [g] ch. 25:13; 1 Thess. 5:1, 2 [h] [Phil. 2:6, 7] [i] [Zech. 14:7; Acts 1:7] **37** [j] Luke 17:26, 27 [k] ver. 27 **38** [j] [See ver. 37 above] [l] ch. 22:30 [m] Gen. 7:7-16 **39** [k] [See ver. 37 above] **41** [n] Luke 17:35 [o] Ex. 11:5; Isa. 47:2 **42** [p] Mark 14:34-38; Luke 12:37; 21:36; Acts 20:31; 1 Thess. 5:6 [q] John 13:13 **43** [r] For ver. 43-51, [Luke 12:39-46] [s] [1 Thess. 5:2; 2 Pet. 3:10; Rev. 3:3] **44** [t] ch. 25:10 [u] ver. 27 **45** [v] ch. 25:21; 1 Cor. 4:2; Heb. 3:5 [w] ch. 7:24; 10:16; 25:2 **46** [x] John 13:17; Rev. 16:15 **47** [y] ch. 25:21, 23 **48** [z] ch. 25:5 **49** [a] 1 Thess. 5:7 **50** [b] 2 Pet. 3:12; [ch. 25:13] **51** [c] See ch. 8:12 **Chapter 25** **1** [d] Luke 19:13 [e] ch. 9:15; John 3:29; Rev. 19:7; 21:2, 9 **2** [w] [See ch. 24:45 above]

of oil with their lamps. 5 As the bridegroom
[f]was delayed, they all became drowsy and
slept. 6 But [g]at midnight there was a cry, 'Here
is the bridegroom! Come out to meet him.'
7 Then all those virgins rose and [h]trimmed
their lamps. 8 And the foolish said to the wise,
'Give us some of your oil, for our lamps are
going out.' 9 But the wise answered, saying,
'Since there will not be enough for us and for
you, go rather to the dealers and buy for yourselves.' 10 And while they were going to buy,
the bridegroom came, and [i]those who were
ready went in with him to [j]the marriage feast,
and [k]the door was shut. 11 Afterward the other
virgins came also, saying, [l]'Lord, lord, open
to us.' 12 [l]But he answered, 'Truly, I say to you,
[m]I do not know you.' 13 [n]Watch therefore, for
you [o]know neither the day nor the hour.

The Parable of the Talents

14 [p]"For [q]it will be like a man [r]going on a journey, who called his servants[1] and entrusted to
them his property. 15 To one he gave five [s]tal-
ents,[2] to another two, to another one, [t]to each
according to his ability. Then he [r]went away.
16 He who had received the five talents went at
once and traded with them, and he made five
talents more. 17 So also he who had the two
talents made two talents more. 18 But he who
had received the one talent went and [u]dug in
the ground and hid his master's money. 19 Now
[v]after a long time the master of those servants
came and [w]settled accounts with them. 20 And
he who had received the five talents came
forward, bringing five talents more, saying,
'Master, you delivered to me five talents; here
I have made five talents more.' 21 His master
said to him, 'Well done, good and [x]faithful
servant.[3] [y]You have been faithful over a little;
[z]I will set you over much. Enter into [a]the joy
of your master.' 22 And he also who had the
two talents came forward, saying, 'Master,
you delivered to me two talents; here I have
made two talents more.' 23 His master said to
him, 'Well done, good and faithful servant.
You have been faithful over a little; I will set
you over much. Enter into the joy of your
master.' 24 He also who had received the one
talent came forward, saying, 'Master, I knew
you to be [b]a hard man, reaping [c]where you
did not sow, and gathering where you scattered no seed, 25 so I was afraid, and I went and
hid your talent in the ground. Here [d]you have
what is yours.' 26 But his master answered him,
'You [e]wicked and [e]slothful servant! You knew
that I reap where I have not sown and gather
where I scattered no seed? 27 Then you ought
to have invested my money with the bankers,
and at my coming I should have received what
was my own with interest. 28 So take the talent
from him and give it to him who has the ten
talents. 29 [f]For to everyone who has will more
be given, and he will have an abundance. But
from the one who has not, even what he has
will be taken away. 30 And [g]cast [h]the worthless
servant into the outer darkness. In that place
[g]there will be weeping and gnashing of teeth.'

The Final Judgment

31 [i]"When the Son of Man comes in his glory,
and all the angels with him, [j]then he will sit
on his glorious throne. 32 Before him [k]will be
gathered [l]all the nations, and [m]he will separate
people one from another as a shepherd separates [n]the sheep from the goats. 33 And he will
place the sheep on his right, but the goats on
the left. 34 Then [o]the King will say to [p]those
on his right, 'Come, you [q]who are blessed by
my Father, [r]inherit [s]the kingdom [t]prepared
for you [u]from the foundation of the world.

[1] Greek *bondservants*; also verse 19 [2] A *talent* was a monetary unit worth about twenty years' wages for a laborer [3] Greek *bondservant*; also verses 23, 26, 30

What does life look like for those who are handling their Master's resources faithfully and wisely? Jesus teaches in 25:31–46 that such a life is busy with helping the needy among Jesus' disciples, "the least of these my brothers" to whom Jesus refers in 25:40. It seems likely that these disciples had been impoverished, lonely, sick, and imprisoned (25:35–36, 42–43) because of their faithfulness in carrying on Jesus' mission (5:11–12; 10:16–25, 40–42; 24:9). The good works envisioned here are not works by which the righteous have earned a place in God's kingdom; they are instead the works that arise from a commitment to follow Jesus—the "good fruit" that every "healthy tree" bears (7:17–18).

5 [f]ch. 24:48; [ver. 19; Heb. 10:37; 2 Pet. 3:4, 9]
6 [g]Mark 13:35
7 [h][Luke 12:35]
10 [i]ch. 24:44 [j]ch. 22:2 [k]For ver. 10-12, [Luke 13:25-27]
11 [l][ch. 7:22, 23]
12 [l][See ver. 11 above] [m]ch. 10:33; [2 Tim. 2:19]
13 [n]ch. 24:42 [o][ch. 24:50]
14 [p]For ver. 14-30, [Luke 19:12-27] [q][Mark 13:34] [r]ch. 21:33
15 [s]ch. 18:24 [t][Rom. 12:6; 1 Cor. 12:11; Eph. 4:7; 1 Pet. 4:10] [r][See ver. 14 above] **18** [u][ch. 13:44] **19** [v][ver. 5] [w]ch. 18:23; Rom. 14:12; [Luke 16:2] **21** [x]ver. 23; ch. 24:45 [y]Luke 16:10; 1 Cor. 4:2; [1 Tim. 3:13] [z]ch. 24:47 [a]Heb. 12:2; [John 15:11] **24** [b]1 Sam. 25:3 [c][2 Cor. 8:12] **25** [d]ch. 20:14 **26** [e]ch. 18:32; Prov. 20:4; Rom. 12:11 **29** [f][Luke 12:48]; See ch. 13:12 **30** [g]See ch. 8:12 [h][Luke 17:10] **31** [i]See ch. 16:27, 28 [j]ch. 19:28 **32** [k][ch. 24:31] [l]Joel 3:12; [ch. 24:14; 28:19] [m]ch. 13:49 [n]Ezek. 34:17 **34** [o]ver. 40; Luke 19:38; Rev. 17:14; 19:16; [Isa. 6:5] [p]1 Kgs. 2:19; Ps. 45:9; 110:1 [q][Ps. 37:22; Isa. 65:23; Eph. 1:3] [r]ch. 19:29; Rev. 21:7 [s]Luke 12:32; 22:29 [t]ch. 20:23; [1 Cor. 2:9; Heb. 11:16] [u]See ch. 13:35

35 For [v]I was hungry and you gave me food, I was thirsty and you [w]gave me drink, [x]I was a stranger and you welcomed me, 36 [v]I was naked and you clothed me, [y]I was sick and you [z]visited me, [a]I was in prison and you came to me.' 37 Then the righteous will answer him, saying, 'Lord, when did we see you hungry and feed you, or thirsty and give you drink? 38 And when did we see you a stranger and welcome you, or naked and clothe you? 39 And when did we see you sick or in prison and visit you?' 40 And [b]the King will answer them, [c]'Truly, I say to you, as you did it to one of the least of these [d]my brothers,[1] you did it to me.'

41 "Then he will say to those on his left, [e]'Depart from me, you [f]cursed, into [g]the eternal fire prepared for [h]the devil and his angels. 42 For [i]I was hungry and you gave me no food, I was thirsty and you gave me no drink, 43 I was a stranger and you did not welcome me, naked and you did not clothe me, sick and in prison and you did not visit me.' 44 Then they also will answer, saying, 'Lord, when did we see you hungry or thirsty or a stranger or naked or sick or in prison, and did not minister to you?' 45 Then he will answer them, saying, 'Truly, I say to you, as you did not do it to one of the least of these, [j]you did not do it to me.' 46 And these will go away [k]into eternal punishment, but the righteous [k]into [l]eternal life."

The Plot to Kill Jesus

26 When Jesus had finished all these sayings, he said to his disciples, 2 [m]"You know that after two days [n]the Passover is coming, and [o]the Son of Man [p]will be delivered up to be crucified."

3 [q]Then the chief priests and the elders of the people gathered in [r]the palace of the high priest, whose name was [s]Caiaphas, 4 [t]and plotted together in order to arrest Jesus by stealth and kill him. 5 But they said, "Not during the feast, [u]lest there be an uproar among the people."

Jesus Anointed at Bethany

6 [v]Now when Jesus was at [w]Bethany in the house of Simon the leper,[2] 7 a woman came up to him with an alabaster flask of very expensive ointment, and she poured it on his head as he reclined at table. 8 And when the disciples saw it, they were indignant, saying, "Why this waste? 9 For this could have been sold for a large sum and [x]given to the poor." 10 But [y]Jesus, aware of this, said to them, "Why do you trouble the woman? For she has done a beautiful thing to me. 11 For [z]you always have the poor with you, but [a]you will not always have me. 12 In pouring this ointment on my body, she has done it [b]to prepare me for burial. 13 Truly, I say to you, wherever [c]this gospel is proclaimed in the whole world, what she has done will also be told [d]in memory of her."

Judas to Betray Jesus

14 [e]Then one of the twelve, whose name was [f]Judas Iscariot, went to the chief priests 15 and said, "What will you give me if I deliver him over to you?" And they [g]paid him [h]thirty pieces

[1] Or *brothers and sisters* [2] *Leprosy* was a term for several skin diseases; see Leviticus 13

35[v] Isa. 58:7; Ezek. 18:7, 16; [James 2:15, 16] [w] ch. 10:42 [x] Job 31:32; Rom. 12:13; Heb. 13:1, 2; 3 John 5
36[v] [See ver. 35 above] [y] [Luke 10:33, 34] [z] James 1:27 [a] 2 Tim. 1:16; [Heb. 10:34; 13:3]
40[b] ver. 34 [c] See ch. 10:40, 42 [d] ch. 28:10; John 20:17; Rom. 8:29; Heb. 2:11; [ch. 12:50]
41[e] ch. 7:23 [f] [Heb. 6:8] [g] ch. 13:40, 42; 18:8; Mark 9:43, 48; Jude 7; [Luke 16:24]; See 2 Thess. 1:8 [h] 2 Pet. 2:4; Jude 6; Rev. 12:7
42[i] Job 22:7
45[j] [Luke 10:16; Acts 9:5; 1 Cor. 8:12]
46[k] Dan. 12:2; [John 5:29; Acts 24:15] [l] Rom. 2:7; 5:21; 6:23

26:6–16 The woman's extravagant generosity in pouring out her "very expensive ointment" on Jesus stands in stark contrast to the greed that drove Judas to betray Jesus for thirty pieces of silver. The condition of one's heart will reveal itself in one's actions.

John's Gospel explains that it was Judas who voiced the disciples' objection to the woman's "waste" (John 12:4–5). John then adds that Judas objected because he was a thief, who stole out of the money bag, apparently the common fund that supported Jesus and the disciples and from which they gave to the poor (John 12:6). Given the choice between serving God or money, Judas had chosen money. He proved the truth of Jesus' teaching that the person who tries to serve two masters "will hate the one and love the other" (Matt. 6:24).

In contrast, the woman of 26:6–13, whom John's Gospel identifies as Mary of Bethany (John 12:3), the sister of Martha and Lazarus, made a costly sacrifice to express her devotion to Jesus. She illustrated the truth of the parables of the hidden treasure and the pearl of great value (Matt. 13:44–46), and offered a contrast to the rich young ruler (19:22). Jesus, to her, was more valuable than her personal property or financial security.

Chapter 26 **2**[m] For ver. 2-5, see Mark 14:1, 2; Luke 22:1, 2 [n] See John 6:4 [o] ver. 24 [p] See ch. 20:18, 19 **3**[q] [Ps. 2:2; John 11:47; Acts 4:27] [r] ver. 58, 69; Luke 11:21; John 18:15; [Rev. 11:2] [s] ver. 57; Luke 3:2; John 11:49; 18:13; Acts 4:6 **4**[t] John 11:53; See ch. 21:46 **5**[u] ch. 27:24 **6**[v] For ver. 6-13, see Mark 14:3-9; John 12:1-8; [Luke 7:37-39] [w] ch. 21:17; John 11:18 **9**[x] [John 13:29] **10**[y] ch. 16:8 **11**[z] Deut. 15:11 [a] ch. 9:15; See John 7:33 **12**[b] John 19:40 **13**[c] [ch. 24:14] [d] Acts 10:4 **14**[e] For ver. 14-16, see Mark 14:10, 11; Luke 22:3-6; [John 13:2, 27, 30] [f] ch. 10:4; 27:3; Acts 1:16; [John 6:71; 12:4] **15**[g] Zech. 11:12; [Gen. 23:16; Jer. 32:9] [h] ch. 27:3, 9; Ex. 21:32

of silver. 16 And from that moment he sought
an opportunity [i]to betray him.

The Passover with the Disciples

17 [j]Now on [k]the first day of Unleavened Bread
the disciples came to Jesus, saying, “Where
will you have us prepare for you to eat the
Passover?” 18 He said, “Go into the city to a certain man and say to him, [l]‘The Teacher says,
[m]My time is at hand. I will keep the Passover
at your house with my disciples.’ ” 19 And the
disciples did as Jesus had directed them, and
they prepared the Passover.
20 [n]When it was evening, he reclined at table
with the twelve.[1] 21 And as they were eating, [o]he
said, “Truly, I say to you, one of you will betray
me.” 22 And they were very sorrowful and
began to say to him one after another, “Is it I,
Lord?” 23 He answered, [p]“He who has dipped
his hand in the dish with me will betray me.
24 The Son of Man goes [q]as it is written of him,
but [r]woe to that man by whom the Son of Man
is betrayed! [s]It would have been better for that
man if he had not been born.” 25 Judas, who
would betray him, answered, “Is it I, [t]Rabbi?”
He said to him, [u]“You have said so.”

Institution of the Lord’s Supper

26 [v]Now as they were eating, Jesus took
bread, and [w]after blessing it broke it and gave
it to the disciples, and said, “Take, eat; [x]this
is my body.” 27 And he took a cup, and when
he [y]had given thanks he gave it to them, saying, “Drink of it, all of you, 28 for [x]this is my
[z]blood of the[2] covenant, which is poured out
for [a]many [b]for the forgiveness of sins. 29 I tell
you I will not drink again of this fruit of the
vine until that day when I drink it new with
you [c]in my Father’s kingdom.”

Jesus Foretells Peter’s Denial

30 [d]And when they had sung a hymn, [e]they
went out to [f]the Mount of Olives. 31 Then Jesus
said to them, “You will all fall away because of
me this night. For it is written, ‘I will [g]strike
the shepherd, and the sheep of the flock will
be scattered.’ 32 But after I am raised up, [h]I will
go before you to Galilee.” 33 [i]Peter answered
him, “Though they all fall away because of
you, I will never fall away.” 34 [j]Jesus said to him,
“Truly, I tell you, this very night, [k]before the
rooster crows, you will deny me three times.”
35 [l]Peter said to him, “Even if I must die with

[1] Some manuscripts add *disciples* [2] Some manuscripts insert *new*

26:17–29 The first Lord’s Supper was a Passover meal, the meal that, according to the Mosaic law, God’s people should celebrate annually as a reminder that God had delivered them from slavery in Egypt. This was the great act of redemption that initiated God’s covenant with Israel through Moses (Ex. 19:4–6). The Lord’s Supper redefined the Passover meal as a celebration of God’s second and greatest act of redemption, through the sacrificial death of Christ on the cross. Christ’s death atoned for the sins of God’s people up to the time of his coming (Rom. 3:25), and the sins of all those who would trust him for salvation since his coming (Rom. 3:26).

Because Jesus was innocent of any wrongdoing, his willing sacrifice allowed God both to forgive sinners of their transgressions and to remain just even as he did this (Matt. 26:28; Rom. 3:21–26; 4:25; Gal. 3:13; Heb. 9:28; 1 Pet. 3:18). Jesus’ death, then, established a new covenant between God and his people, a covenant whose central focus was the forgiveness of sins and a right relationship with God (Matt. 26:28; Luke 22:20; 1 Cor. 11:25; 2 Cor. 3:6, 11; see also Jer. 31:31–34).

For believers, God’s establishment of this new covenant of forgiveness and acquittal from sin should result in a joyful freedom from sin’s destructive influence. “Christ, our Passover lamb, has been sacrificed” for us, says Paul. “Let us therefore celebrate the festival, not with the old leaven, the leaven of malice and evil, but with the unleavened bread of sincerity and truth” (1 Cor. 5:7–8; see also Ex. 12:1–28). In the gospel, we have been freed!

26:30–27:10 The story of Jesus’ arrest, trial, and crucifixion is also the story of the failure of his disciples to be faithful to him during this immensely difficult time. When the religious and civic leaders came to arrest Jesus, not only Judas but all the disciples eventually abandoned him. Despite Peter’s protests of willingness to die for Jesus—protests which all the disciples affirmed (26:33, 35)—he failed miserably along with them all. They did not have enough compassion toward Jesus even to stay awake with him during the stressful night of his arrest (26:36–46), and when the crowd arrived to arrest him, Matthew tells us that all Jesus’ disciples “left him and

16 [i]See ch. 20:18, 19
17 [j]For ver. 17-19, see Mark 14:12-16; Luke 22:7-13 [k]Ex. 12:18
18 [l]See John 11:28 [m][ver. 45; John 7:6, 8, 30; 8:20; 13:1; 17:1]
20 [n]For ver. 20-24, see Mark 14:17-21; [Luke 22:14, 21-23; John 13:21-26]
21 [o][John 6:70, 71]
23 [p][John 13:18]
24 [q]ver. 54, 56; Mark 9:12; Luke 18:31; 24:25-27, 46; Acts 17:2, 3; 26:22, 23; 1 Cor. 15:3; 1 Pet. 1:10, 11 [r]ch. 18:7 [s]John 17:12
25 [t]ver. 49; See John 1:38 [u]ver. 64; See Luke 22:70
26 [v]For ver. 26-29, see Mark 14:22-25; Luke 22:18-20; 1 Cor. 11:23-25 [w]See ch. 14:19 [x]1 Cor. 10:16; [John 6:53]
27 [y]See ch. 15:36
28 [x][See ver. 26 above] [z]Ex. 24:8; [Zech. 9:11; Heb. 13:20] [a]See ch. 20:28 [b]Mark 1:4; [Luke 1:77]
29 [c][ch. 13:43]
30 [d]For ver. 30-35, see Mark 14:26-31 [e]Luke 22:39; John 18:1 [f]See ch. 21:1
31 [g]Cited from Zech. 13:7; [John 16:32]
32 [h]ch. 28:7, 10, 16; Mark 16:7
33 [i][Luke 22:31, 33]
34 [j]Luke 22:34; John 13:38 [k]ver. 75
35 [l]Luke 22:33; John 13:37

you, I will not deny you!" And all the disciples
said the same.

Jesus Prays in Gethsemane

36 [m]Then Jesus went with them [e]to a place
called Gethsemane, and he said to his disciples, "Sit here, while I go over there and pray."
37 And taking with him [n]Peter and [o]the two
sons of Zebedee, he began to be sorrowful and
troubled. 38 Then he said to them, [p]"My soul
is very sorrowful, even to death; remain here,
and [q]watch[1] with me." 39 And going a little
farther he fell on his face [r]and prayed, saying,
"My Father, if it be possible, let [s]this cup pass
from me; [t]nevertheless, not as I will, but as
you will." 40 And he came to the disciples and
found them sleeping. And he said to Peter,
"So, could you not watch with me one hour?
41 [q]Watch and [u]pray that you [v]may not enter
into temptation. The spirit indeed is willing,
but the flesh is weak." 42 Again, for the second
time, he went away and prayed, "My Father, if
this cannot pass unless I drink it, [w]your will
be done." 43 And again he came and found
them sleeping, for [x]their eyes were heavy.
44 So, leaving them again, he went away and
prayed for [y]the third time, saying the same
words again. 45 Then he came to the disciples
and said to them, "Sleep and take your rest
later on.[2] See, [z]the hour is at hand, and [a]the
Son of Man is betrayed into the hands of sinners. 46 Rise, let us be going; see, my betrayer
is at hand."

Betrayal and Arrest of Jesus

47 [b]While he was still speaking, [c]Judas came,
one of the twelve, and with him a great crowd
with swords and clubs, from the chief priests
and the elders of the people. 48 Now the
betrayer had given them a sign, saying, "The
one I will kiss is the man; seize him." 49 And he
came up to Jesus at once and said, "Greetings,
[d]Rabbi!" And he kissed him. 50 Jesus said to
him, [e]"Friend, [f]do what you came to do."[3]
Then they came up and laid hands on Jesus
and seized him. 51 And behold, one of those
who were with Jesus stretched out his hand
and drew his [g]sword and struck the servant[4]
of the high priest and cut off his ear. 52 Then
Jesus said to him, "Put your sword back into
its place. For [h]all who take the sword will perish by the sword. 53 [i]Do you think that I cannot appeal to my Father, and he will at once
send me [j]more than twelve [k]legions of angels?
54 [l]But how then should the Scriptures be
fulfilled, that it must be so?" 55 At that hour
Jesus said to the crowds, "Have you come out
as against a robber, with swords and clubs to
capture me? Day after day [m]I sat in the temple
[n]teaching, and you did not seize me. 56 But [l]all
this has taken place that the Scriptures of the
prophets might be fulfilled." [o]Then all the disciples left him and fled.

Jesus Before Caiaphas and the Council

57 [p]Then [q]those who had seized Jesus led
him to [r]Caiaphas the high priest, where the

[1] Or *keep awake*; also verses 40, 41 [2] Or *Are you still sleeping and taking your rest?* [3] Or *Friend, why are you here?* [4] Greek *bondservant*

36 [m]For ver. 36-46, see Mark 14:32-42; Luke 22:40-46 [e][See ver. 30 above]
37 [n]ch. 17:1 [o]ch. 4:21
38 [p][Ps. 42:5, 6; John 12:27] [q]See ch. 24:42
39 [r]Heb. 5:7 [s]See ch. 20:22 [t]ver. 42; John 5:30; 6:38; Phil. 2:8
41 [q][See ver. 38 above] [u]1 Pet. 4:7 [v]ch. 6:13
42 [w]ver. 39; See ch. 6:10
43 [x]Luke 9:32
44 [y][2 Cor. 12:8]
45 [z]John 12:23, 27; 13:1; 17:1; [ver. 18; Luke 22:53] [a]ch. 17:22; 20:18
47 [b]For ver. 47-56, see Mark 14:43-50; Luke 22:47-53; John 18:3-11 [c]ver. 14; Acts 1:16
49 [d]ver. 25
50 [e]ch. 20:13; 22:12 [f][John 13:27]
51 [g][Luke 22:38]
52 [h]Rev. 13:10; [Gen. 9:6; Ezek. 35:6]
53 [i][John 10:18] [j][ch. 4:11; 2 Kgs. 6:17; Dan. 7:10; Luke 22:43; John 18:36] [k]Luke 8:30
54 [l]See ver. 24; ch. 1:22
55 [m][John 8:2]; [Luke 2:46; John 18:20] [n]ch. 21:23; [ch. 4:23]
56 [l][See ver. 54] [o]ver. 31; [Ps. 88:8, 18; John 16:32]
57 [p]Luke 22:54 [q]For ver. 57-68, see Mark 14:53-65; [John 18:12, 13, 19-24] [r]ver. 3

fled" (26:56). Even Peter, who at least put up an ill-conceived effort to protect Jesus (26:51), and followed "at a distance" behind those who had arrested him (26:58), eventually denied that he even knew Jesus (26:72, 74).

Jesus knew that his disciples would be faithless (26:31–35), but he offered them the hope of forgiveness and restoration in his comment that, after his resurrection, he would go before them to Galilee (26:32). The death to which their unfaithfulness had consigned him was a death for the forgiveness of this sin also (26:28). Both Peter and Judas were sorry for their faithlessness to Jesus (26:75; 27:3–4), but whereas Judas's sorrow led to despair, Peter and the other disciples sought refuge in Jesus' offer of restored fellowship (28:7, 10) and his renewed call to service in the kingdom (28:16–20).

There is great hope for sinners in Matthew's account of Jesus' death, resurrection, and ascension, and that hope is not only for new disciples of Jesus but for his seasoned followers also. The proper response to sin, however grave it may be, is not despair. It is instead trust in Jesus' willingness to forgive and restore the sinner to full fellowship with himself and to useful service in the kingdom. What rich hope for those who want their lives to count for Christ, yet who are painfully aware of their inadequacy and failures.

scribes and the elders had gathered. 58 And
[s]Peter was following him at a distance, as far
as [r]the courtyard of the high priest, and going
inside he sat with [t]the guards to see the end.
59 Now the chief priests and the whole council[1]
[u]were seeking false testimony against Jesus
that they might put him to death, 60 but they
found none, [v]though many false witnesses
came forward. At last [w]two came forward 61 and
said, "This man said, [x]'I am able to [y]destroy
the temple of God, and to rebuild it in three
days.'" 62 And the high priest stood up and
said, "Have you no answer to make? What is
it that these men testify against you?"[2] 63 [z]But
Jesus remained silent. [a]And the high priest
said to him, [b]"I adjure you by [c]the living God,
[d]tell us if you are [e]the Christ, [f]the Son of God."
64 Jesus said to him, [g]"You have said so. But
I tell you, from now on [h]you will see the Son
of Man [i]seated at the right hand of Power and
[h]coming on the clouds of heaven." 65 Then the
high priest [j]tore his robes and said, [k]"He has
uttered blasphemy. What further witnesses do
we need? You have now heard his blasphemy.
66 What is your judgment?" They answered,
[l]"He deserves death." 67 Then [m]they spit in his
face [n]and [o]struck him. And some slapped him,
68 saying, "Prophesy to us, you [p]Christ! Who is
it that struck you?"

Peter Denies Jesus

69 [q]Now Peter was sitting outside [r]in the courtyard. And a servant girl came up to him and
said, "You also were with Jesus the Galilean."
70 But he denied it before them all, saying,
"I do not know what you mean." 71 And when
he went out to the entrance, another servant
girl saw him, and she said to the bystanders,
"This man was with Jesus [s]of Nazareth." 72 And
again he denied it with an oath: "I do not know
the man." 73 After a little while the bystanders
came up and said to Peter, "Certainly you too
are one of them, for [t]your accent betrays you."
74 Then he began to invoke a curse on himself
and to swear, "I do not know the man." And
immediately the rooster crowed. 75 And Peter
remembered the saying of Jesus, [u]"Before the
rooster crows, you will [v]deny me three times."
And he went out and wept bitterly.

Jesus Delivered to Pilate

27 [w]When morning came, all the chief
priests and the elders of the people
[x]took counsel against Jesus to put him to
death. 2 And they bound him and [y]led him
away and [z]delivered him over to [a]Pilate the
governor.

Judas Hangs Himself

3 Then when [b]Judas, his betrayer, saw that
Jesus[3] was condemned, [c]he changed his mind
and brought back [d]the thirty pieces of silver
to the chief priests and the elders, 4 saying,
"I have sinned by betraying innocent blood."
They said, "What is that to us? [e]See to it yourself." 5 And throwing down the pieces of silver
into the temple, [f]he departed, and he went and
hanged himself. 6 But the chief priests, taking
the pieces of silver, said, "It is not lawful to
put them into [g]the treasury, since it is blood
money." 7 So they took counsel and bought
with them the potter's field as a burial place
for strangers. 8 Therefore [h]that field has been
called the Field of Blood [i]to this day. 9 [j]Then
was fulfilled what had been spoken by the
prophet Jeremiah, saying, [k]"And they took
the thirty pieces of silver, the price of him on
whom a price had been set by some of the sons
of Israel, 10 and they gave them for the potter's
field, as the Lord directed me."

Jesus Before Pilate

11 [l]Now Jesus stood before the governor, and
the governor asked him, "Are you [m]the King
of the Jews?" Jesus said, [n]"You have said so."
12 [o]But when he was accused by the chief priests
and elders, he gave no answer. 13 Then Pilate
said to him, [p]"Do you not hear how many
things they testify against you?" 14 But he gave
him no answer, not even to a single charge, so
that the governor was greatly amazed.

The Crowd Chooses Barabbas

15 [q]Now at the feast the governor was accustomed to release for the crowd any one

[1] Greek *Sanhedrin* [2] Or *Have you no answer to what these men testify against you?* [3] Greek *he*

58 [s][John 18:15] [r][See ver. 57 above] [t]John 7:32; 18:3 **59** [u]See Acts 6:11 **60** [v]Ps. 27:12; 35:11 [w]Deut. 19:15 **61** [x][Acts 6:14]; See John 2:19 [y]ch. 27:40 **63** [z]ch. 27:12, 14; Isa. 53:7; John 19:9 [a]For ver. 63-66, [Luke 22:67-71] [b][Lev. 5:1; 1 Sam. 14:24, 26; Mark 5:7] [c]See ch. 16:16 [d]John 10:24 [e][ch. 22:42-45]; See ch. 1:17 [f]See ch. 14:33 **64** [g]ver. 25 [h]See ch. 16:27; 24:30 [i]Ps. 110:1; Heb. 1:3; [Mark 16:19] **65** [j]Num. 14:6; Acts 14:14 [k]ch. 9:3; John 10:36 **66** [l]See Lev. 24:16 **67** [m]ch. 27:30; Isa. 50:6; Mark 10:34 [n][Luke 22:63-65; John 18:22] [o]ch. 5:39; Acts 23:2 **68** [p]ver. 63 **69** [q]For ver. 69-75, see Mark 14:66-72; Luke 22:55-62; John 18:16-18, 25-27 [r]ver. 3 **71** [s]ch. 2:23 **73** [t][Judg. 12:6] **75** [u]ver. 34 [v][Acts 3:13, 14] **Chapter 27** **1** [w]Mark 15:1; Luke 22:66 [x]See ch. 26:4 **2** [y]Luke 23:1; John 18:28 [z]See ch. 20:19 [a]Luke 3:1; 13:1; Acts 3:13; 4:27; 1 Tim. 6:13 **3** [b]See ch. 26:14 [c]ch. 21:29 [d]ch. 26:15 **4** [e]ver. 24 **5** [f][2 Sam. 17:23; Acts 1:18] **6** [g]Mark 12:41, 43; Luke 21:1; John 8:20 **8** [h]Acts 1:19 [i]ch. 28:15 **9** [j]See ch. 1:22 [k]Cited from Zech. 11:13 **11** [l]For ver. 11-14, see Mark 15:2-5; Luke 23:2, 3; John 18:29-38 [m]ver. 29, 37; ch. 2:2; John 18:39; 19:3; [ver. 42] [n][1 Tim. 6:13]; See Luke 22:70 **12** [o]See ch. 26:63 **13** [p]John 19:10 **15** [q]For ver. 15-26, see Mark 15:6-15; Luke 23:18-25; John 18:39, 40; 19:16

prisoner whom they wanted. 16 And they had then a notorious prisoner called Barabbas. 17 So when they had gathered, Pilate said to them, "Whom do you want me to release for you: Barabbas, or [r]Jesus who is called Christ?" 18 For he knew that it was out [s]of envy that they had delivered him up. 19 Besides, while he was sitting on [t]the judgment seat, his wife sent word to him, "Have nothing to do with [u]that righteous man, for I have suffered much because of him today [v]in a dream." 20 Now the chief priests and the elders persuaded the crowd to [w]ask for Barabbas and destroy Jesus. 21 The governor again said to them, "Which of the two do you want me to release for you?" And they said, "Barabbas." 22 Pilate said to them, "Then what shall I do with Jesus who is called Christ?" [x]They all said, "Let him be crucified!" 23 And he said, "Why, [y]what evil has he done?" But they shouted all the more, "Let him be crucified!"

Pilate Delivers Jesus to Be Crucified

24 So when Pilate saw that he was gaining nothing, but rather that [z]a riot was beginning, he took water and [a]washed his hands before the crowd, saying, "I am innocent of [b]this man's blood;[1] [c]see to it yourselves." 25 And all the people answered, [d]"His blood be on us and [e]on our children!" 26 Then he released for them Barabbas, and having [f]scourged[2] Jesus, delivered him to be crucified.

Jesus Is Mocked

27 [g]Then the soldiers of the governor took Jesus into the [h]governor's headquarters,[3] and they gathered the whole [i]battalion[4] before him. 28 And they stripped him and put [j]a scarlet robe on him, 29 and twisting together a crown of thorns, they put it on his head and put a reed in his right hand. And kneeling before him, they [k]mocked him, saying, "Hail, [l]King of the Jews!" 30 And [m]they spit on him and took the reed and struck him on the head. 31 And when they had mocked him, they stripped him of the robe and put his own clothes on him and [n]led him away to crucify him.

The Crucifixion

32 [o, p]As they went out, they found a man of Cyrene, Simon by name. They compelled this man to [o]carry his cross. 33 [q]And when they came to a place called Golgotha (which means Place of a Skull), 34 [r]they offered him wine to drink, mixed with [s]gall, but when he tasted it, he would not drink it. 35 And when they had crucified him, [t]they divided his garments among them by casting lots. 36 Then they sat down and [u]kept watch over him there. 37 And over his head they put the charge against him, which read, "This is Jesus, [v]the King of the Jews." 38 Then two [w]robbers were crucified with him, [x]one on the right and one on the left. 39 And [y]those who passed by [z]derided him, [a]wagging their heads 40 and saying, [b]"You who would destroy the temple and rebuild it in three days, save yourself! [c]If you are [d]the Son of God, come down from the cross." 41 So also the chief priests, with the scribes and elders, mocked him, saying, 42 [e]"He saved others; [f]he cannot save himself. [g]He is the King of Israel; let him come down now from the cross, and we will believe in him. 43 [h]He trusts in God; let God deliver him now, if he desires him. For he said, 'I am the Son of God.'" 44 [i]And the robbers who were crucified with him also reviled him in the same way.

The Death of Jesus

45 Now from the sixth hour[5] there was darkness over all the land[6] until the ninth hour.[7] 46 And about the ninth hour Jesus [j]cried out with a loud voice, saying, [k]"Eli, Eli, lema sabachthani?" that is, "My God, my God, why have you forsaken me?" 47 And some of the bystanders, hearing it, said, "This man is calling Elijah." 48 And one of them at once ran and took a sponge, filled it with [l]sour wine, and put it on a reed and [m]gave it to him to drink. 49 But the others said, "Wait, let us see whether Elijah will come to save him." 50 And

[1] Some manuscripts *this righteous blood*, or *this righteous man's blood* [2] A Roman judicial penalty, consisting of a severe beating with a multi-lashed whip containing imbedded pieces of bone and metal [3] Greek *the praetorium* [4] Greek *cohort*; a tenth of a Roman legion, usually about 600 men [5] That is, noon [6] Or *earth* [7] That is, 3 P.M.

17 [r] ver. 22 **18** [s] [John 12:19] **19** [t] John 19:13 [u] ver. 24; [Luke 23:47] [v] See ch. 2:12 **20** [w] Acts 3:14 **22** [x] Acts 13:28 **23** [y] [Luke 23:41; John 8:46] **24** [z] ch. 26:5 [a] [Deut. 21:6-8; Ps. 26:6; 73:13] [b] ver. 19 [c] ver. 4 **25** [d] [ch. 23:35, 36; Josh. 2:19; Acts 5:28] [e] [Ex. 20:5; Lam. 5:7] **26** [f] ch. 20:19; Isa. 50:6; 53:5; [Luke 23:16; John 19:1] **27** [g] For ver. 27-31, see Mark 15:16-20; John 19:2, 3 [h] John 18:28, 33; 19:9; Acts 23:35; Phil. 1:13 (Gk.) [i] See Acts 10:1 (Gk.) **28** [j] Rev. 18:12, 16; [Luke 23:11] **29** [k] ch. 20:19 [l] See ver. 11 **30** [m] See ch. 26:67 **31** [n] Isa. 53:7 **32** [o] Mark 15:21; Luke 23:26; [John 19:17] [p] Heb. 13:12; [ch. 21:39; Num. 15:35] **33** [q] For ver. 33-51, see Mark 15:22-38; Luke 23:32-38, 44-46; John 19:17-19, 23, 24, 28-30 **34** [r] [Ps. 69:21] [s] Acts 8:23 **35** [t] Ps. 22:18 **36** [u] ver. 54; [Ps. 22:17] **37** [v] ver. 11, 29 **38** [w] [John 18:40] [x] [ch. 20:21] **39** [y] Ps. 22:7; 109:25; [Lam. 1:12] [z] Luke 22:65; 23:39; [James 2:7] [a] Job 16:4; Isa. 37:22; Jer. 18:16; Lam. 2:15 **40** [b] ch. 26:61 [c] ch. 4:3, 6 [d] ver. 43; ch. 26:63; See ch. 14:33 **42** [e] [Luke 4:23] [f] [ch. 26:53, 54; John 10:18] [g] John 1:49; 12:13; [ver. 37] **43** [h] Cited from Ps. 22:8 **44** [i] [Luke 23:39-43] **46** [j] [Heb. 5:7] [k] Cited from Ps. 22:1 **48** [l] Ruth 2:14 [m] Ps. 69:21

Jesus [n]cried out again with a loud voice and [o]yielded up his spirit.

51 And behold, [p]the curtain of the temple was torn in two, from top to bottom. And [q]the earth shook, and the rocks were split. 52 The tombs also were opened. And many bodies of [r]the saints [s]who had fallen asleep were raised, 53 and coming out of the tombs after his resurrection they went into [t]the holy city and appeared to many. 54 [u]When the centurion and those who were with him, [v]keeping watch over Jesus, saw the earthquake and what took place, they were filled with awe and said, [w]"Truly this was the Son[1] of God!"

55 There were also [x]many women there, looking on [y]from a distance, who had followed Jesus from Galilee, [z]ministering to him, 56 among whom were [z]Mary Magdalene and Mary the mother of James and Joseph and [a]the mother of the sons of Zebedee.

Jesus Is Buried

57 [b]When it was evening, there came a rich man from Arimathea, named Joseph, who also was a disciple of Jesus. 58 He went to Pilate and asked for the body of Jesus. Then Pilate ordered it to be given to him. 59 And Joseph took the body and wrapped it in a clean linen shroud 60 and [c]laid it in his own new tomb, [d]which he had cut in the rock. And he rolled [e]a great stone to the entrance of the tomb and went away. 61 Mary Magdalene and [f]the other Mary were there, sitting opposite the tomb.

The Guard at the Tomb

62 The next day, that is, after the day of [g]Preparation, the chief priests and the Pharisees gathered before Pilate 63 and said, "Sir, we remember how [h]that impostor said, while he was still alive, [i]'After three days I will rise.' 64 Therefore order the tomb to be made secure until the third day, [j]lest his disciples go and steal him away and tell the people, 'He has risen from the dead,' and the last fraud will be worse than the first." 65 Pilate said to them, "You have [k]a guard[2] of soldiers. Go, make it as secure as you can." 66 So they went and made the tomb secure by [l]sealing the stone and setting a guard.

The Resurrection

28 [m]Now after the Sabbath, toward the dawn of the first day of the week, Mary Magdalene and [n]the other Mary went to see the tomb. 2 And behold, there was a great earthquake, for [o]an angel of the Lord descended from heaven and came and rolled back the stone and sat on it. 3 [p]His appearance was like lightning, and [q]his clothing white as snow. 4 And for fear of him the guards trembled and [r]became like dead men. 5 But the angel said to the women, "Do not be afraid, for I know that you seek Jesus who was crucified. 6 He is not here, for he has risen, [s]as he said. Come, see the place where he[3] lay. 7 Then go quickly and tell his disciples that he has risen from the dead, and behold, [t]he is going before you to Galilee; there you will see him. See, I have told you." 8 So they departed quickly from the tomb [u]with fear and great joy, and ran to tell his disciples. 9 And behold, Jesus [v]met them and said, "Greetings!" And they came up and [w]took hold of his feet and [x]worshiped him. 10 Then Jesus said to them, "Do not be afraid; [y]go and tell [z]my brothers to go to Galilee, and there they will see me."

The Report of the Guard

11 While they were going, behold, some of [a]the guard went into the city and told the chief priests all that had taken place. 12 And when they had assembled with the elders and taken counsel, they gave a sufficient sum of money to the soldiers 13 and said, "Tell people, [b]'His disciples came by night and stole him away while we were asleep.' 14 And if this comes to [c]the governor's ears, we will [d]satisfy him and keep you out of trouble." 15 So they took the money and did as they were directed. And this story has been spread among the Jews [e]to this day.

The Great Commission

16 Now the eleven disciples [f]went to Galilee, to the mountain to which Jesus had directed

[1] Or *a son* [2] Or *Take a guard* [3] Some manuscripts *the Lord*

50[n] ver. 46 [o] [John 10:18] **51**[p] Ex. 26:31-33; 2 Chr. 3:14 [q] ver. 54 **52**[r] [Dan. 7:18, 22] [s] John 11:11-13; Acts 7:60; 13:36; 1 Cor. 15:6, 18, 20; 1 Thess. 4:13-15; 2 Pet. 3:4 **53**[t] See ch. 4:5 **54**[u] For ver. 54-56, see Mark 15:39-41; Luke 23:47, 49 [v] ver. 36 [w] ver. 43 **55**[x] John 19:25 [y] Ps. 38:11 [z] See Luke 8:2, 3 **56**[z] [See ver. 55 above] [a] ch. 20:20; [Mark 15:40] **57**[b] For ver. 57-61, see Mark 15:42-47; Luke 23:50-56; John 19:38-42 **60**[c] [Isa. 53:9] [d] Isa. 22:16 [e] Mark 16:4; [John 11:38] **61**[f] ver. 56; ch. 28:1 **62**[g] Mark 15:42; Luke 23:54; John 19:14, 31, 42 **63**[h] [ver. 64; John 7:12] [i] ch. 16:21; 17:23; 20:19; 28:6; Mark 8:31; 10:34; Luke 9:22; 18:33; 24:6, 7; [ch. 26:61; John 2:19] **64**[j] [ch. 28:13] **65**[k] ch. 28:11 **66**[l] Dan. 6:17 **Chapter 28** **1**[m] For ver. 1-8, see Mark 16:1-8; Luke 24:1-10; John 20:1 [n] ch. 27:56, 61 **2**[o] [John 20:12] **3**[p] Dan. 10:6 [q] [Dan. 7:9; Mark 9:3; John 20:12; Acts 1:10] **4**[r] [Rev. 1:17] **6**[s] ch. 27:63 **7**[t] ver. 10, 16; ch. 26:32 **8**[u] [Ps. 2:11] **9**[v] [Mark 16:9; John 20:14] [w] 2 Kgs. 4:27 [x] ver. 17; Luke 24:52 **10**[y] See John 20:18 [z] John 20:17; [Ps. 22:22; Rom. 8:29; Heb. 2:11, 12, 17] **11**[a] ch. 27:65, 66 **13**[b] [ch. 27:64] **14**[c] ch. 27:2 [d] See Acts 12:20 (Gk.) **15**[e] ch. 27:8 **16**[f] ver. 7

them. 17 And when they saw him they
[g]worshiped him, but some doubted. 18 And
Jesus came and said to them, [h]"All authority [i]in heaven and on earth has been given to
me. 19 [j]Go therefore and [k]make disciples of [l]all
nations, [j]baptizing them [m]in[1] [n]the name of the
Father and of the Son and of the Holy Spirit,
20 teaching them [o]to observe all that [p]I have
commanded you. And behold, [q]I am with you
always, to [r]the end of the age."

[1] Or *into*

17 [g] ver. 9
18 [h] ch. 11:27; Dan. 7:13, 14; John 3:35; 13:3; 17:2; Acts 2:36; Rom. 14:9; 1 Cor. 15:27; Eph. 1:10, 20-22; Phil. 2:9, 10; Col. 2:10; Heb. 1:2; 2:8; 1 Pet. 3:22; [ch. 9:6; John 5:27] [i] [ch. 6:10; Luke 2:14]
19 [j] Mark 16:15, 16 [k] ch. 13:52 [l] Luke 24:47; [ch. 24:14; Mark 11:17; Rom. 1:5] [m] See Acts 8:16 [n] [2 Cor. 13:14]
20 [o] John 14:15 [p] [Acts 1:2] [q] [ch. 1:23; 18:20; John 12:26; 14:3; 17:24; Acts 18:10] [r] See ch. 13:39

28:18–20 Jesus' disciples (v. 16) are now commissioned to make disciples in all people groups (v. 19). Matthew has shown throughout his Gospel that the kingdom of God crosses all social boundaries (1:3, 5; 2:1–12; 4:15; 8:1–13; 9:9–13; 12:38–42; 15:21–39), so it is not surprising that Jesus sends his disciples to "all nations." Jesus' royal authority extends to the whole universe, and the disciples, through their disciple making, are to extend Jesus' authority everywhere (see also Rom. 15:8–15; Eph. 2:11–22; 3:7–10; Rev. 5:6–14; 7:9–12; 21:23–26).

Disciple making involves two basic tasks: baptizing and teaching. Baptizing includes the proclamation of the gospel of God's kingdom and the call to repentance from sin and faith in Christ (Matt. 3:6, 11). Water baptism symbolizes the inward cleansing that God effects when people turn from their sins and turn in faith to God for forgiveness of their sins in Christ (3:14–15; see also Luke 3:3; Acts 2:38; 22:16; Rom. 6:3; 1 Pet. 3:21). "Teaching" involves instructing people to follow Jesus' commandments concerning how God wants his people to live, commandments such as he gives in the Sermon on the Mount (Matt. 5:1–7:29; see also Rom. 6:17–18).

The order of these two elements of discipleship is important. People do not become disciples of Jesus by obeying his commandments in order to win his acceptance. They have his acceptance as a free gift, if they come to him in faith (Rom. 3:21–22, 24; 5:1–2). Jesus' disciples joyfully do what Jesus has commanded them to do as a result of God's transformation of their hearts through the proclamation of the gospel (Rom. 6:12–14).

Introduction to Mark

Author, Date, and Recipients

John Mark wrote this Gospel, probably from Rome in the 50s or 60s A.D. Mark wrote to help people from all kinds of backgrounds understand the coming of Jesus as the culmination of God's work with Israel and the entire world.

The Gospel in Mark

The Gospel of Mark is presented in a way that demonstrates the fulfillment of Old Testament promises. This is clear right from the start, as Mark begins his account by focusing on the fulfillment of Isaiah 40:3 in John the Baptist, who prepares Israel for the comforting arrival of Yahweh to his people (cf. Mal. 3:1). Yahweh will come to pardon—and to rule over—his people (Isa. 40:1–11).

John the Baptist's preparatory ministry marks the continuation of God's long-standing gracious pursuit of his people (Mark 12:1–6; cf. Heb. 1:1). The origin of this pursuit goes back to God's establishment of his good creation, as he places Adam, Eve, and their offspring in a relationship with himself that is creational (living in God's creation), covenantal (living in light of God's faithfulness and commands), and kingly (living under God's rule and in pursuit of the cultural mandate) (Gen. 1:28; 2:16, 18). After the fall of mankind, God pursues his purposes especially by means of his redemptive call of Abraham as the father of his people. Trust in God's provisions will mark the pattern of progressive redemption, including Israel's exodus from Egyptian slavery (Exodus 13–19) and the giving of the Mosaic law (Exodus 20–23). God's pursuit also takes the shape of temporary mediators (judges and kings).

God keeps his promise alive that he will purify a people for himself (see note on Mark 14:53–65) by establishing and ruling over a holy nation (Israel; see Isa. 40:10–11). That nation repeatedly fails in its calling and experiences the disciplines of division and exile, but God never abandons his people. Centuries after the return from Babylonian exile (cf. Ezra and Nehemiah), John the Baptist announces in the desert—a place of preparation, purification, and testing—the great intervention of Yahweh promised by the prophets. Thus, while Isaiah 40 initially points to Israel's return from exile (Isa. 40:1–2), Mark makes it clear that the prophet was ultimately pointing to the coming of Jesus (Mark 1:1–13).

As Mark continues his account, Yahweh surprisingly "comes in sandals" in Jesus, through whom we ultimately see the divinity the prophets had promised (e.g., 2:5–12; 9:2–13; 12:1–12). Yahweh thus comes in the earthly presence of the eternal Son to begin fulfilling the messianic kingdom expectations of the Old Testament (Isa. 40:10–11). Jesus, the eternal Son of God, initially proclaims the kingdom of God, then later inaugurates it through his death and resurrection. Through these actions that ultimately conquer sin and the effects of the fall, Jesus turns out to be the eternally ruling, messianic King (2 Sam. 7:16).

The ultimate purpose of Mark in the context of God's unfolding redemptive-historical pursuit of his people is to testify to Jesus' summons of grace—that is, his summons to discipleship. Discipleship in Mark represents nothing less than God's ultimate restoration of his universal people to the original creation-design and purpose—namely, to "walk with God" (Gen. 5:22–24) and to be restored as true image-bearers of God (Rom. 8:29; 1 Cor. 15:49; 2 Cor. 3:18; Col. 3:10). This restoration gradually overcomes the marks of the fall, based on Christ's substitutionary atonement, healing, example, and teaching. Jesus' sovereign call to surrendered discipleship redresses Adam's sinful independence and disobedience. Discipleship is not merely a certain code of conduct for the disciples. Being a disciple of Christ means joining the people of God in God's creation, coming under his eternal covenant and kingly rule, and living in dependence on God rather than independence from him. We ultimately see that discipleship in Mark flows from dependence upon the Master's captivating and exemplary person, formative teaching, and atoning work.

In short, the Gospel of Mark shows that Jesus comes as the fulfillment of Old Testament hopes and promises that God would graciously restore his wayward people. Mark's Gospel is just that—*gospel*. It is good news.

Outline

Mark displays a two-part structure. Part 1 concerns the expansive presentation of Jesus' authority, while Part 2 narrates the severe test and ultimate affirmation of Jesus' authority, as well as the salvific necessity of his suffering.

- I. Introduction (1:1–15)
- II. (Part 1) Demonstration of Jesus' Authority (1:16–8:26)
  - A. Work in Galilee (1:16–3:12)
  - B. Climax in Galilee (3:13–6:6)
  - C. Work beyond Galilee (6:7–8:26)
- III. (Part 2) Testing Jesus' Authority in Suffering and the Necessity of His Death (8:27–16:8 [9–20])
  - A. Caesarea Philippi—journey to Jerusalem (8:27–10:52)
  - B. Work in Jerusalem (11:1–13:37)
  - C. Passion and resurrection in Jerusalem (14:1–16:8)
  - [D. Resurrection appearances / ascension (16:9–20)]

The Gospel According to

Mark

John the Baptist Prepares the Way

1 The beginning of the gospel of Jesus
Christ, [a]the Son of God.[1]
2 [b]As it is written in Isaiah the prophet,[2]

> [c]"Behold, I send my messenger before
> your face,
> who will prepare your way,
> 3 [d]the voice of one crying in the wilderness:
> [e]'Prepare[3] the way of the Lord,
> make his paths straight,'"

4 [f]John appeared, baptizing in [g]the wilderness
and proclaiming [h]a baptism of [i]repentance [j]for
the forgiveness of sins. 5 And all the country
of Judea and all Jerusalem were going out
to him and were being baptized by him in
the river Jordan, [k]confessing their sins. 6 Now
John was [l]clothed with camel's hair and [l]wore
a leather belt around his waist and ate [m]locusts
and [n]wild honey. 7 And he preached, saying,
[o]"After me comes he who is mightier than I,

[1] Some manuscripts omit *the Son of God* [2] Some manuscripts *in the prophets* [3] Or *crying: Prepare in the wilderness*

1:1–15 John the Baptist fulfills the prediction of a messenger who announces—and prepares for—the "one who is to come" (Matt. 11:2–15; cf. Isa. 40:3), namely Yahweh ("prepare the way of the LORD"). John the Baptist calls for radical repentance, while other Jewish groups of the time simply call for stricter performance of the Mosaic law. John's call echoes the Old Testament prophets who exhort Israel away from self-centered ways to God-dependence (Neh. 9:6–38). At the Jordan, many Jewish people undergo a "baptism of repentance" (i.e., "a baptism of returning to God"), which is usually required for repentant Gentiles converting to Judaism; thus the people of God prepare for Yahweh's coming.

Surprisingly, Jesus joins this movement of radical repentance. Since we will learn that he is without sin (cf. Mark 2:5–12; 7:14–23; 10:45; 14:22–25), we are immediately confronted with the question of why he joins the crowd in this ritual of repentance.

In his baptism, Jesus turns to and identifies with the long-prophesied and anticipated purposes of God, the eternal Father, who equips Jesus uniquely with the Holy Spirit for his unprecedented and universally significant work. By the unique circumstances of this baptism, we learn that Jesus is the unique Son of God the Father, and specially blessed by the Holy Spirit (1:11; 9:7; 12:1–6). The appearance of each member of the godhead at Christ's baptism advances believers' understanding that God eternally exists in three persons, namely as Father, Son, and Holy Spirit (the Trinity).

Jesus is tempted in the desert because Satan, a powerful fallen angel of light (2 Cor. 11:14), seeks to obstruct God's purposes of working redemption and reconciliation. Satan seeks to maintain power over human beings and over that part of God's good creation which persists in autonomy and enmity against God (Rom. 16:20). This signals a power struggle between God and Satan, in which God's kingdom grows as Jesus' power is extended (Mark 1:14–15; 14:25; Acts 2:30–32; Phil. 2:9–11; Col. 1:13, 18; 1 Cor. 15:25). Throughout the life of Jesus, he overcomes Satan by relying on his eternal Father's will, even in his greatest hour of trial, in Gethsemane.

The message of Mark 1:1–13 is that God brings his long-standing, redemptive work throughout the ages to a culmination by sending his eternal Son (Mark 1:11; Heb. 1:1). The grace that he has been working out through the ages comes to a decisive climax with Christ. In this way God achieves what human beings cannot achieve by themselves: forgiveness of rebellious sin against God and restoration to a reconciled relationship with God. Since the fall of Adam and Eve, mankind has anticipated this culmination, which

Chapter 1
1 [a]See Matt. 14:33
2 [b]For ver. 2-8, see Matt. 3:1-11; Luke 3:2-16 [c]Matt. 11:10; Luke 1:17, 76; 7:27; Cited from Mal. 3:1
3 [d]John 1:23; Cited from Isa. 40:3 [e]Luke 1:76
4 [f]John 1:6, 7 [g]Josh. 15:61; [Judg. 1:16] [h]Acts 2:38 [i]ver. 15 [j]Matt. 26:28; [Luke 1:77]
5 [k]Acts 19:18
6 [l][2 Kgs. 1:8; Zech. 13:4; Heb. 11:37] [m]Lev. 11:22 [n]1 Sam. 14:26
7 [o]John 1:15, 27; 3:30, 31; Acts 13:25

the strap of whose sandals I am not worthy
to stoop down and untie. 8 [p]I have baptized
you with water, but [q]he will baptize you with
the Holy Spirit."

The Baptism of Jesus

9 [r]In those days Jesus [s]came from Nazareth
of Galilee and was baptized by John in the
Jordan. 10 And when he came up out of the
water, immediately he [t]saw [u]the heavens being
torn open [v]and the Spirit descending on him
like a dove. 11 And [w]a voice came from heaven,
[x]"You are my beloved Son;[1] with you I am well
pleased."

The Temptation of Jesus

12 [y]The Spirit immediately drove him out into
the wilderness. 13 [y]And he was in the wilderness
forty days, being [z]tempted by [a]Satan. And he
was with the wild animals, and [b]the angels
were ministering to him.

Jesus Begins His Ministry

14 [c]Now after John was arrested, Jesus [d]came
into Galilee, proclaiming the gospel of God,
15 and saying, [e]"The time is fulfilled, and
[f]the kingdom of God is at hand; [g]repent and
believe in the gospel."

Jesus Calls the First Disciples

16 [h]Passing alongside the Sea of Galilee, he
saw Simon and Andrew the brother of Simon
casting a net into the sea, for they were fishermen. 17 And Jesus said to them, "Follow me,
and I will make you become [i]fishers of men."[2]
18 And immediately they left their nets and
followed him. 19 And going on a little farther,
he saw James the son of Zebedee and John his
brother, who were in their boat mending the
nets. 20 And immediately he called them, and
they left their father Zebedee in the boat with
the hired servants and followed him.

Jesus Heals a Man with an Unclean Spirit

21 [j]And they went into Capernaum, and
immediately [k]on the Sabbath [l]he entered the
synagogue and was teaching. 22 And [m]they
were astonished at his teaching, [m]for he taught
them as one who had authority, and not as the
scribes. 23 And immediately there was in their
synagogue a man with an unclean spirit. And
he cried out, 24 [n]"What have you to do with us,
Jesus of Nazareth? Have you come to destroy
us? [o]I know who you are—[p]the Holy One of
God." 25 But Jesus [q]rebuked him, saying, "Be
silent, and come out of him!" 26 And the unclean

[1] Or *my Son, my* (or *the*) *Beloved* [2] The Greek word *anthropoi* refers here to both men and women

8 [p]John 1:26; Acts 1:5; 11:16 [q]See John 1:33
9 [r]For ver. 9-11, see Matt. 3:13-17; Luke 3:21, 22; [John 1:32-34] [s]Matt. 2:23
10 [t]Acts 7:56 [u]Isa. 64:1 [v]John 1:32, 33; [Luke 4:18, 21; Acts 10:38]
11 [w]John 12:28 [x][ch. 9:7; Ps. 2:7; Isa. 42:1; Eph. 1:6; Col. 1:13; 2 Pet. 1:17; 1 John 5:9]
12 [y]See Matt. 4:1-11; Luke 4:1-13
13 [y][See ver. 12 above] [z][Heb. 2:18; 4:15] [a]See 1 Chr. 21:1 [b]Matt. 26:53; Luke 22:43
14 [c]Matt. 4:12; 14:3; Luke 3:20; [John 3:24] [d]Matt. 4:17, 23
15 [e]Dan. 9:25; Gal. 4:4; Eph. 1:10; [Luke 21:8; John 7:8] [f]See Matt. 3:2 [g]Acts 19:4; 20:21; Heb. 6:1
16 [h]For ver. 16-20, see Matt. 4:18-22; [Luke 5:2-11; John 1:40-42]
17 [i]Matt. 13:47
21 [j]Matt. 4:13; For ver. 21-28, see Luke 4:31-37 [k]See ch. 6:2 [l]ver. 39; See Matt. 4:23
22 [m]See Matt. 7:28, 29
24 [n]See Matt. 8:29 [o][ver. 34; Acts 19:15; James 2:19] [p]John 6:69; Acts 3:14; Rev. 3:7; [Luke 1:35; Heb. 7:26; 1 John 2:20]
25 [q]See Matt. 12:16

arrives in a surprising manner. No matter how accomplished or how broken a human being's life might look from a human perspective, from God's perspective the effect of the fall on human beings is so profound that it cannot be redressed by human effort. In God's holy love and righteousness, he relentlessly pursues human beings to reconcile them with himself through Jesus' life and atonement. Being placed into a God-given, righteous, and lasting relationship with him lies at the heart of God's love and grace.

1:16–8:26 The first half of Mark's Gospel describes Jesus' expanding authority over sickness, laws of nature, and the demonic world. His authority is also expressed by his calling, appointing, and sending out his disciples, while consistently teaching in a unique and authoritative way. The question of "who is he?" becomes increasingly urgent. The entire Gospel of Mark will answer this question by testifying to the following: (1) Jesus represents the coming Yahweh, according to Isaiah 40:3; (2) he is the messianic Lord of David (Mark 12:35–37; Ps. 110:1, 5); (3) he is the majestic and messianic Son of Man (Mark 8:38; 14:62; Dan. 7:13); (4) as the Son of Man, he is also the suffering servant of Isaiah 53:1–12 (Mark 10:45; 14:22–25); (5) he is God, who forgives sins (2:7; Neh. 9:17; Isa. 43:25; Ps. 103:2–3; 130:4; Jer. 31:34; Dan. 9:9); and (6) he is the eternal Son of God (Mark 1:11; 9:2–8; 12:1–12; Psalm 2).

Discipleship is defined in the context of the eminent authority of Jesus. Who Jesus is and what he does directly affect discipleship. Ultimately, Jesus teaches, exemplifies, and facilitates, through his atoning work, Christlikeness among his disciples as members of God's eternal and covenantal kingdom. This is the call of the gospel.

1:16–45 The initial calling of the disciples (cf. 1 Kings 19:19–21) displays the unusual kingdom authority of Jesus. He has a profoundly character-shaping impact on the disciples and brings decimation to the powers of darkness. Discipleship is marked by the identity of Jesus. His divine power over natural and spiritual forces supports his unique authority to call his disciples to radical discipleship. In Christ, God calls people

spirit, [r]convulsing him and [s]crying out with a
loud voice, came out of him. 27 And they were
all [t]amazed, so that they questioned among
themselves, saying, "What is this? [u]A new teaching with authority! He commands even the
unclean spirits, and they obey him." 28 And at
once his fame spread everywhere throughout
all the surrounding region of Galilee.

Jesus Heals Many

29 [v]And immediately he[1] [w]left the synagogue
and entered the house of Simon and Andrew,
with James and John. 30 Now [x]Simon's mother-
in-law lay ill with a fever, and immediately
they told him about her. 31 And he came and
[y]took her by the hand and lifted her up, and
the fever left her, and she began to serve them.
32 That evening at sundown they brought
to him all who were sick or [z]oppressed by
demons. 33 And the whole city was gathered
together at the door. 34 [a]And he healed many
who were sick with various diseases, and cast
out many demons. And [b]he would not permit
the demons to speak, because they knew him.

Jesus Preaches in Galilee

35 [c]And rising very early in the morning,
while it was still dark, he departed and went
out to a desolate place, and [d]there he prayed.
36 And Simon and those who were with him
searched for him, 37 and they found him and
said to him, [e]"Everyone is looking for you."
38 And he said to them, "Let us go on to the
next towns, that I may preach there also, for
[f]that is why I came out." 39 [g]And [h]he went
throughout all Galilee, preaching in their
synagogues and casting out demons.

Jesus Cleanses a Leper

40 [i]And a leper[2] came to him, imploring him,
and [j]kneeling said to him, [k]"If you will, you
can make me clean." 41 Moved with pity, he
stretched out his hand and touched him and
said to him, "I will; be clean." 42 And immediately the leprosy left him, and he was made
clean. 43 And [l]Jesus[3] sternly charged him and
sent him away at once, 44 and said to him,
[m]"See that you say nothing to anyone, but
go, [n]show yourself to the priest and [o]offer
for your cleansing what Moses commanded,
[p]for a proof to them." 45 [q]But he went out and
began to talk freely about it, and to spread
the news, so that Jesus could no longer openly
enter [r]a town, but was out in [r]desolate places,
and [s]people were coming to him from every
quarter.

Jesus Heals a Paralytic

2 And when he returned to [t]Capernaum after
some days, it was reported that he was at
home. 2 And many were gathered together, so
that there was no more room, not even at the
door. And he was preaching the word to them.
3 [u]And they came, bringing to him a paralytic

[1] Some manuscripts *they* [2] *Leprosy* was a term for several skin diseases; see Leviticus 13 [3] Greek *he*; also verse 45

to return to "walking with God"—the creational design of human beings in the first place. Jesus' call to discipleship is God calling human beings back to himself as the foundation of true and dignified human existence.

This is the rhythm of grace. God does not respond to our wayward rebellion with disgust, throwing his hands up in the air. He pursues us in love. This is who he is.

2:1–12 Jesus continues to display his authority in the spiritual and physical spheres of our world by directly forgiving the sins of a paralytic, as well as healing him. This act introduces early in Mark the theme of opposition to Jesus on the part of the spiritual and political leadership of Israel (see esp. v. 7). The theme of human opposition will continue in Mark: the Pharisees, Sadducees, and Herodians pursue a policy of preserving their political, economic, and religious power (3:6, 22–30; 6:4; 8:11–15). Jesus' own natural family will resist him (3:20–21, 31–35). Judas will oppose Jesus on account of Judas's openness to Satan and his political disappointment over Jesus (14:3–11; Luke 22:3–6; John 6:70). Peter will deny Jesus in order to preserve his own life (Mark 14:30, 66–72). Throughout the various forms of opposition to Jesus, the constant theme is self-preservation versus Jesus.

As disciples, we learn that Jesus' authority to forgive sins is unique, since only God has such authority (2:7; Neh. 9:17; Isa. 43:25; Ps. 103:2–3; 130:4; Jer. 31:34; Dan. 9:9). And this gospel of forgiveness, which Jesus ultimately accomplishes through being punished as our substitute on the cross (Mark 10:45), is of greater value to human existence than anything else. The gospel serves as the basis for personal healing, with the call to live in reconciled relationships in all areas of personal and corporate life.

26 [r]ch. 9:26 [s]ch. 5:7; Acts 8:7
27 [t][Matt. 8:27] [u]Acts 17:19
29 [v]For ver. 29-34, see Matt. 8:14-16; Luke 4:38-41 [w]ver. 21, 23
30 [x]1 Cor. 9:5
31 [y]ch. 9:27; Acts 3:7; 9:41
32 [z]See Matt. 4:24
34 [a]See Matt. 4:23 [b]ch. 3:11, 12; [Acts 16:17, 18]
35 [c]For ver. 35-38, see Luke 4:42, 43 [d]Luke 5:16; See Matt. 14:23
37 [e][John 12:19]
38 [f]Isa. 61:1
39 [g][Luke 4:44] [h]ver. 21
40 [i]For ver. 40-44, see Matt. 8:2-4; Luke 5:12-14 [j]ch. 10:17; Matt. 17:14; 27:29 [k][ch. 9:22, 23; Matt. 9:28]
43 [l]Matt. 9:30
44 [m]ver. 34; ch. 5:43; 7:36; 8:26; Matt. 9:30; 17:9; See Matt. 12:16 [n]Luke 17:14 [o]Lev. 14:2-32 [p]ch. 6:11; Luke 9:5; James 5:3
45 [q]ch. 7:36; Matt. 9:31; [Luke 5:15, 16] [r]2 Cor. 11:26 [s]ch. 2:2, 13; 3:7; [John 6:2]

Chapter 2
1 [t][Matt. 9:1]
3 [u]For ver. 3-12, see Matt. 9:2-8; Luke 5:18-26

carried by four men. 4 And when they could
not get near him because of the crowd, [v]they
removed the roof above him, and when they
had made an opening, they let down the bed
on which the paralytic lay. 5 And when Jesus
[w]saw their faith, he said to the paralytic, "Son,
[x]your sins are forgiven." 6 Now some of the
scribes were sitting there, questioning in
their hearts, 7 "Why does this man speak like
that? [y]He is blaspheming! [z]Who can forgive
sins but God alone?" 8 And immediately Jesus,
[a]perceiving in his spirit that they thus questioned within themselves, said to them, "Why
do you question these things in your hearts?
9 Which is easier, to say to the paralytic, 'Your
sins are forgiven,' or to say, 'Rise, take up your
bed and walk'? 10 But that you may know that
[b]the Son of Man has authority on earth to forgive sins"—he said to the paralytic— 11 "I say
to you, rise, pick up your bed, and go home."
12 And he rose and immediately picked up his
bed and went out before them all, so that they
were all amazed and [c]glorified God, saying,
"We never saw anything like this!"

Jesus Calls Levi

13 He went out again beside the sea, and [d]all
the crowd was coming to him, and he was
teaching them. 14 [e]And as he passed by, he saw
[f]Levi the son of Alphaeus sitting at the tax
booth, and he said to him, "Follow me." And
he rose and followed him.
15 And as he reclined at table in his house,
many [g]tax collectors and sinners were reclining with Jesus and his disciples, for there were
many who followed him. 16 And [h]the scribes
of[1] the Pharisees, when they saw that he was
eating with sinners and tax collectors, said to
his disciples, [g]"Why does he eat[2] with tax collectors and sinners?" 17 And when Jesus heard
it, he said to them, "Those who are well have
no need of a physician, but those who are sick.
[i]I came not to call the righteous, [j]but sinners."

A Question About Fasting

18 Now [k]John's disciples and the Pharisees
were fasting. And people came and said to
him, [l]"Why do John's disciples and [m]the disciples of the Pharisees fast, but your disciples
do not fast?" 19 And Jesus said to them, [n]"Can
the wedding guests fast while the bridegroom
is with them? As long as they have the bridegroom with them, they cannot fast. 20 [o]The
days will come when the bridegroom is taken
away from them, and [p]then they will fast in
that day. 21 No one sews a piece of unshrunk
cloth on an old garment. If he does, the patch
tears away from it, the new from the old,
and a worse tear is made. 22 And no one puts
new wine into old [q]wineskins. If he does, the

[1] Some manuscripts *and* [2] Some manuscripts add *and drink*

4 [v] [Luke 5:19]
5 [w] ch. 10:52; Matt. 8:10, 13; 9:22, 29; 15:28; Luke 7:9, 50; 17:19; 18:42; Acts 3:16; 14:9; James 5:15 [x] Luke 7:48; [John 5:14]
7 [y] ch. 14:64; John 10:36 [z] Ps. 32:5; Isa. 43:25
8 [a] See John 2:25
10 [b] [ver. 28]
12 [c] See Luke 7:16
13 [d] See ch. 1:45
14 [e] For ver. 14-22, see Matt. 9:9-17; Luke 5:27-38 [f] [Matt. 9:9]
15 [g] Matt. 11:19; Luke 15:2
16 [h] Acts 4:5; 23:9 [g] [See ver. 15 above]
17 [i] [Luke 15:7; John 9:39] [j] 1 Tim. 1:15
18 [k] Matt. 11:2; 14:12; Luke 11:1; John 1:35; 3:25; 4:1; [Acts 18:25; 19:3] [l] [ch. 7:5] [m] Luke 18:12
19 [n] John 3:29
20 [o] See Luke 17:22 [p] [John 16:20]
22 [q] Josh. 9:4

2:13–17 Jesus boldly challenges the cultural and religious convention of his day by intentionally associating with despised tax collectors and outcasts ("sinners"). In this way Jesus brings to fulfillment the Old Testament hopes that God would one day heal the broken and forgive the sinful among his people (Isa. 61:1–2; Joel 2:26–29).

God's pursuit of his people is not based on merit. It is based on our need and is grace-driven. Jesus' entire mission proceeds on this foundation. It assumes that human beings are not capable of restoring their broken relationship with God, including the destructive personal and communal consequences of sinfully striving to live independently of God.

Discipleship means becoming Christlike through ongoing dependence on him. This dependence involves more than just imitating Christ's actions. It means trusting in his forgiveness and letting the impact of that forgiveness and loving commitment to us blossom and bear fruit. Changed hearts result in changed lives. Christ's example serves as a guidepost to his followers for the paths we should walk in this changed life. This desire to follow Christ arises in part from the realization that a person reconciled with God is, and remains, a recipient of undeserved grace.

True followers of Christ are called to reflect Christ's compassion and holiness to other human beings, irrespective of their race, religious affiliation, sexual orientation, ethnicity, or any other mark of distinction. For Christ has shown such grace to us.

2:18–3:6 Far from ignoring spiritual disciplines such as fasting or Sabbath keeping, Jesus restores a God-centered and God-dependent dimension to those two disciplines. Both involve surrender to God and a trusting rest in his presence. A follower of Christ will fast from time to time, and will seek to honor the Sabbath day of rest. Such a follower will do this not as a means of meriting favor before God but as a consequence

wine will burst the skins—and the wine is
destroyed, and so are the skins. But new wine
is for fresh wineskins."[1]

Jesus Is Lord of the Sabbath

23 [r]One Sabbath he was going through the
grainfields, and as they made their way, his
disciples [s]began to pluck heads of grain. 24 And
the Pharisees were saying to him, "Look, [t]why
are they doing [u]what is not lawful on the
Sabbath?" 25 And he said to them, [v]"Have you
never read [w]what David did, when he was in
need and was hungry, he and those who were
with him: 26 how he entered the house of God,
in the time of[2] [x]Abiathar the high priest, and
ate [y]the bread of the Presence, which it is not
lawful for any but the priests to eat, and also
gave it to those who were with him?" 27 And
he said to them, [z]"The Sabbath was made for
man, [a]not man for the Sabbath. 28 So [b]the Son
of Man is lord even of the Sabbath."

A Man with a Withered Hand

3 [c]Again [d]he entered the synagogue, and a
man was there with a withered hand. 2 And
[e]they watched Jesus,[3] to see whether he would
heal him on the Sabbath, so that they might
accuse him. 3 And he said to the man with the
withered hand, "Come here." 4 And he said to
them, [f]"Is it lawful on the Sabbath to do good
or to do harm, to save life or to kill?" But they
were silent. 5 And he [g]looked around at them
with anger, grieved at [h]their hardness of heart,
and said to the man, "Stretch out your hand."
[i]He stretched it out, and his hand was restored.
6 [j]The Pharisees went out and immediately
[l]held counsel with [k]the Herodians against him,
how to destroy him.

A Great Crowd Follows Jesus

7 [l]Jesus withdrew with his disciples to the sea,
and [m]a great crowd followed, from Galilee and
Judea 8 and Jerusalem and [n]Idumea and from
beyond the Jordan and from around [o]Tyre
and Sidon. When the great crowd heard all
that he was doing, they came to him. 9 And he
told his disciples to [p]have a boat ready for him
because of the crowd, lest they [q]crush him,
10 for [r]he had healed many, so that all who had
[s]diseases pressed around him [t]to touch him.
11 [u]And whenever the unclean spirits saw him,
they [v]fell down before him and cried out, "You
are [w]the Son of God." 12 And [x]he strictly ordered
them not to make him known.

The Twelve Apostles

13 [y]And he went up on the mountain and
called to him those [z]whom he desired, and

[1] Some manuscripts omit *But new wine is for fresh wineskins* [2] Or *in the passage about* [3] Greek *him*

of living in the healing presence of Jesus, communicated by the Holy Spirit. Fasting is a particular, prayerful form of surrender to God, combined with acts of mercy (cf. Isa. 58:1–12). Honoring the Sabbath is reorientation before God (Mark 2:28; Isa. 58:13–14; cf. Heb. 4:9). Both practices are based on trust in God's provision and both spring from deep gratitude for having found rest in God through Jesus.

A first veiled prediction of Jesus' violent death arises in the metaphor of the bridegroom who is "taken away" (Mark 2:20; cf. Isa. 53:8), thus providing a Christ-centered cause for fasting when he is no longer physically present. Such spiritual disciplines do not earn God's love. Rather, they signal that we have ceased to seek our own pleasure and are resting in dependence on God's provision (Isa. 58:3, 13). Peace through God's grace is not the end but the beginning of maturing as a follower of Christ. Fasting as well as honoring the Sabbath day of rest are important elements of such maturing.

3:7–12 Jesus' bold actions and teachings arouse astonishment among some and increasing opposition among others, leading some to seek his death (v. 6). Yet Jesus was doing what the Old Testament predicted would happen (Isa. 61:1–2). He was restoring people to the way they were supposed to be. Jesus came not to tell us to try harder or dig deeper in our moral efforts. He came to set us free from human striving. This is why the crowds thronged around him (Mark 3:10).

3:13–19 A new stage in Jesus' active pursuit of his disciples is reached when he calls a distinct group of 12 to be his constant followers. The Twelve are to be with Jesus (v. 14), to help spread the message of the gospel and the kingdom of God (1:14–15), and to exorcise demons, thus following his example in word and deed (3:13–19). Key foundations for the eternal people of God are thus laid as Christ's disciples learn to be with him, pursuing his mission in his strength.

23 [r]For ver. 23-28, see Matt. 12:1-8; Luke 6:1-5 [s]Deut. 23:25
24 [t][Matt. 9:11] [u][Ex. 20:9-11]
25 [v]See Matt. 21:16 [w]1 Sam. 21:1-6
26 [x]1 Chr. 24:6; [1 Sam. 21:1; 2 Sam. 8:17] [y]Ex. 25:30; Lev. 24:5-9
27 [z]Ex. 23:12; Deut. 5:14 [a]Col. 2:16
28 [b][ver. 10]

Chapter 3

1 [c]For ver. 1-6, see Matt. 12:9-14; Luke 6:6-11 [d]ch. 1:29
2 [e]Luke 14:1; 20:20; [Luke 11:54; John 8:6]
4 [f][Luke 14:3]
5 [g]ver. 34; ch. 5:32; 10:23; [ch. 10:21] [h]ch. 6:52; Rom. 11:25; Eph. 4:18 [i][1 Kgs. 13:4]
6 [j]See Matt. 12:14 [k]ch. 12:13; Matt. 22:16; [ch. 8:15]
7 [l]Matt. 12:15 [m]Matt. 4:25; Luke 6:17
8 [n]Isa. 34:5; Ezek. 35:15 [o]See Matt. 11:21
9 [p]ch. 6:32, 45 (Gk.); 8:10 (Gk.) [q]ch. 5:24, 31
10 [r]See Matt. 4:23 [s]ch. 5:29, 34 [t]ch. 6:56; Matt. 9:20, 21; 14:36; Luke 6:19
11 [u]ch. 1:26, 34; Luke 4:41 [v]Luke 8:28 [w]See Matt. 14:33
12 [x]See Matt. 12:16
13 [y]Matt. 10:1; Luke 6:12, 13; [ch. 6:7-13; Luke 9:1, 2] [z]John 13:18; 15:16, 19

they came to him. 14 [y]And he appointed twelve
(whom he also named apostles) so that they
might be with him and he might send them
out to preach 15 [y]and have authority to cast out
demons. 16 He appointed the twelve: [a]Simon
(to whom [b]he gave the name Peter); 17 [c]James
the son of Zebedee and John the brother of
James (to whom he gave the name Boanerges,
that is, Sons of Thunder); 18 Andrew, and
Philip, and Bartholomew, and [d]Matthew,
and Thomas, and James the son of Alphaeus,
and Thaddaeus, and Simon the Zealot,[1] 19 and
Judas Iscariot, who betrayed him.

20 Then he went [e]home, and the crowd gathered again, [f]so that they could not even eat.
21 [g]And when [h]his family heard it, they went
out to seize him, for they were saying, "He [i]is
out of his mind."

Blasphemy Against the Holy Spirit

22 And [j]the scribes who came down from
Jerusalem were saying, [k]"He is possessed by
Beelzebul," and "by the prince of demons he
casts out the demons." 23 [l]And he called them
to him and said to them in parables, "How
can Satan cast out Satan? 24 If a kingdom is
divided against itself, that kingdom cannot
stand. 25 And if a house is divided against itself,
that house will not be able to stand. 26 And
if Satan has risen up against himself and is
divided, he cannot stand, but is coming to an
end. 27 But [m]no one can enter a strong man's
house and plunder his goods, unless he first
binds the strong man. [n]Then indeed he may
plunder his house.

28 [o]"Truly, I say to you, all sins will be forgiven
the children of man, and whatever blasphemies they utter, 29 but whoever [p]blasphemes
against the Holy Spirit never has forgiveness,
but is guilty of an eternal sin"— 30 for they
were saying, "He has an unclean spirit."

Jesus' Mother and Brothers

31 [q]And his mother and his [r]brothers came,
and standing outside they sent to him and
called him. 32 And a crowd was sitting around
him, and they said to him, "Your mother and
your brothers[2] are outside, seeking you."
33 And he answered them, "Who are my mother
and my brothers?" 34 And [s]looking about at
those who sat around him, he said, "Here are
my mother and my brothers! 35 [t]For whoever
[u]does the will of God, he is my brother and
sister and mother."

The Parable of the Sower

4 Again [v]he began to teach beside the sea.
And a very large crowd gathered about
him, [w]so that he got into a boat and sat in it on
the sea, and the whole crowd was beside the sea
on the land. 2 And [x]he was teaching them many
things in parables, and in his teaching he said
to them: 3 "Listen! [y]Behold, a sower went out
to sow. 4 And as he sowed, some seed fell along
the path, and the birds came and devoured it.
5 Other seed fell on rocky ground, where it did

[1] Greek *kananaios*, meaning *zealot* [2] Other early manuscripts add *and your sisters*

14[y] [See ver. 13 above]
15[y] [See ver. 13 above]
16[a] For ver. 16-19, see Matt. 10:2-4; Luke 6:14-16; Acts 1:13 [b] Matt. 16:18; John 1:42
17[c] Matt. 4:21
18[d] Matt. 9:9
20[e] ch. 7:17; 9:28 [f] ch. 6:31
21[g] [John 7:5] [h] [ver. 31] [i] 2 Cor. 5:13; [John 10:20; Acts 26:24]
22[j] ch. 7:1; Matt. 15:1 [k] Matt. 9:34; 12:24; Luke 11:15; [Matt. 10:25]; See John 7:20
23[l] For ver. 23-27, see Matt. 12:25-29; Luke 11:17-22
27[m] Isa. 49:24 [n] [Isa. 53:12]
28[o] For ver. 28-30, see Matt. 12:31, 32; [Luke 12:10; Heb. 6:4-6; 10:26; 1 John 5:16]
29[p] [Acts 7:51; Heb. 10:29]
31[q] For ver. 31-35, see Matt. 12:46-50; Luke 8:19-21 [r] ch. 6:3; Matt. 13:55; John 2:12; 7:3, 5, 10; Acts 1:14; 1 Cor. 9:5; Gal. 1:19
34[s] ver. 5
35[t] [John 15:14; Heb. 2:11] [u] Matt. 7:21; [Luke 11:28]

The initial disciples will be involved in unique aspects of Jesus' earthly ministry—for example, going out in pairs to the cities of Israel, with specific instructions for what they should take with them. And yet every follower of Christ is called to be with Jesus, now mediated through the promised presence of the Holy Spirit, and to live, work, and testify in the world as Christlike followers, dependent on him.

3:20–35 Strong opposition comes from Jesus' natural family (vv. 20–21, 31–35) and from the spiritual leadership of Israel (vv. 22–30). Both parties pursue their own interests; they do not acknowledge God's purposes expressed by and through Jesus.

Jesus never calls his followers to sever ties with their natural families (as do some cults and sectarian movements). He does, however, exhort each follower to place the call of Christ above all ties to the natural family. The hyperbolic language of Matthew 10:35 and Luke 14:26 should not be interpreted as a call to family antipathy but as a clear reminder of the priority of Christ's claim upon his disciples—his purposes must outweigh all other loyalties. This requires a sober assessment of loyalties toward one's natural family. While honoring parents is very important, Jesus does question absolute subservience to the natural family (see Mark 7:10–13 with 10:29–31). Focus on the will of God (3:35), as ascertained by means of prayer, humility, and in consultation with other believers, is central to defining one's relationship with his or her natural family. Having been delivered by Christ in a work of sheer grace, our fundamental loyalty is to him.

Chapter 4 1[v] For ver. 1-12, see Matt. 13:1-15; Luke 8:4-10 [w] [ch. 3:9; Luke 5:1-3] 2[x] ver. 33 3[y] [Isa. 55:10; Amos 9:13]

not have much soil, and immediately it sprang
up, since it had no depth of soil. 6 And [z]when
the sun rose, it was scorched, and since it had
no root, [a]it withered away. 7 Other seed fell
among [b]thorns, and the thorns grew up and
choked it, and it yielded no grain. 8 And other
seeds fell into good soil and produced grain,
growing up and increasing and yielding thir-
tyfold and sixtyfold and [c]a hundredfold." 9 And
he said, [d]"He who has ears to hear, let him hear."

The Purpose of the Parables

10 And [e]when he was alone, those around him
with the twelve asked him about the parables. 11 And he said to them, [f]"To you has been
given [g]the secret of the kingdom of God, but
for [h]those outside everything is in parables,
12 [i]so that

> "they [j]may indeed see but not perceive,
> and may indeed hear but not under-
> stand,
> lest they [k]should turn and be forgiven."

13 [l]And he said to them, "Do you not understand this parable? How then will you understand all the parables? 14 [m]The sower sows [n]the
word. 15 And these are the ones along the path,
where the word is sown: when they hear, Satan
immediately comes and takes away the word
that is sown in them. 16 And these are the ones
sown on rocky ground: the ones who, when
they hear the word, immediately receive it
[o]with joy. 17 And they have no root in themselves, but [p]endure for a while; then, when
tribulation or persecution arises on account of
the word, immediately [q]they fall away.[1] 18 And
others are the ones sown among thorns. They
are those who hear the word, 19 but [r]the cares
of [s]the world and [t]the deceitfulness of riches
and the desires for other things enter in and
choke the word, and it proves unfruitful.
20 But those that were sown on the good soil
are the ones who hear the word and accept it
and [u]bear fruit, [v]thirtyfold and sixtyfold and
a hundredfold."

A Lamp Under a Basket

21 [w]And he said to them, [x]"Is a lamp brought
in to be put under a basket, or under a bed,
and not on a stand? 22 [y]For nothing is hidden
except to be made manifest; nor is anything
secret except to come to light. 23 [z]If anyone
has ears to hear, let him hear." 24 And he said to
them, "Pay attention to what you hear: [a]with
the measure you use, it will be measured to
you, and still more will be added to you. 25 [b]For
to the one who has, more will be given, and
from the one who has not, even what he has
will be taken away."

The Parable of the Seed Growing

26 And he said, [c]"The kingdom of God is as if
a man should scatter seed on the ground. 27 He
sleeps and rises night and day, and the seed
sprouts and grows; [d]he knows not how. 28 The
earth produces by itself, first the blade, then
the ear, then the full grain in the ear. 29 But
when the grain is ripe, at once [e]he puts in the
sickle, because the harvest has come."

The Parable of the Mustard Seed

30 [f]And he said, "With what can we compare
the kingdom of God, or what parable shall we

[1] Or *stumble*

4:1–34 In response to the entrapping motives and hard hearts of those "outside" his followers (Isa. 6:9–10), *and* as a means of instructing his disciples, Jesus speaks in parables. Jesus' parables describe the new life God grants to those who belong to his kingdom. This new life stands in direct contrast to the powerful and established principles of a God-opposing life. The growth of this new messianic rule appears outwardly unremarkable, at least initially. But the influence of the kingdom develops progressively to reflect the visible glory of God.

Followers of Christ can easily grow discouraged by the fact that many of the powers and established structures in this world seem to overshadow the emerging kingdom of God. Jesus encourages all followers to trust that God's purposes, which grow slowly, will be accomplished, despite all setbacks (cf. Dan. 2:44–45).

The counterintuitive nature of God's kingdom should not surprise us. After all, the gospel of grace is itself a message that confounds our expectations and tells us that things are not as they seem: though sinful, we are forgiven; though broken, we are redeemed.

6 [z] James 1:11 [a] John 15:6
7 [b] Jer. 4:3
8 [c] ver. 20; Gen. 26:12
9 [d] See Matt. 11:15
10 [e] ver. 34
11 [f] Matt. 19:11; Col. 1:27; [1 Cor. 2:6-10; 1 John 2:20, 27]; See Matt. 11:25 [g] See Rom. 16:25 [h] 1 Cor. 5:12, 13; Col. 4:5; 1 Thess. 4:12; 1 Tim. 3:7
12 [i] Isa. 6:9, 10 [j] Deut. 29:4; Jer. 5:21; Ezek. 12:2; Rom. 11:8; 2 Cor. 3:14; 4:4; [Isa. 42:19, 20] [k] See Luke 22:32
13 [l] For ver. 13-20, see Matt. 13:18-23; Luke 8:11-15
14 [m] [Matt. 13:37; John 4:36, 37] [n] ver. 33; ch. 2:2; Luke 1:2; Acts 8:4; James 1:21
16 [o] [ch. 6:20; Isa. 58:2; Ezek. 33:31, 32; John 5:35]
17 [p] Gal. 1:6; [Hos. 6:4; Gal. 5:7] [q] See Matt. 11:6

19 [r] See Matt. 6:25 [s] 2 Tim. 4:10 [t] 1 Tim. 6:9, 10, 17; [ch. 10:23; Matt. 19:23; Acts 5:1-11; Heb. 3:13] **20** [u] Hos. 14:8; John 15:5, 16; Phil. 1:11; Col. 1:6 [v] ver. 8 **21** [w] For ver. 21-25, see Luke 8:16-18 [x] Matt. 5:15; Luke 11:33 **22** [y] Matt. 10:26; Luke 12:2; [1 Tim. 5:25] **23** [z] ver. 9 **24** [a] Matt. 7:2; Luke 6:38 **25** [b] See Matt. 13:12 **26** [c] [Matt. 13:24-30] **27** [d] [Eccles. 11:5, 6] **29** [e] Joel 3:13; Rev. 14:15 **30** [f] For ver. 30-32, see Matt. 13:31, 32; Luke 13:18, 19

use for it? 31 It is like [g]a grain of mustard seed, which, when sown on the ground, is the smallest of all the seeds on earth, 32 yet when it is sown it grows up and becomes larger than all the garden plants and puts out large branches, so that the birds of the air can make nests in its shade."

33 [h]With many such parables he spoke [i]the word to them, [j]as they were able to hear it. 34 He did not speak to them [k]without a parable, but [l]privately to his own disciples he [m]explained everything.

Jesus Calms a Storm

35 [n]On that day, when evening had come, he said to them, "Let us go across to the other side." 36 And leaving the crowd, they took him with them in the boat, just as he was. And other boats were with him. 37 And a great windstorm arose, and the waves [o]were breaking into the boat, so that the boat was already filling. 38 But he was in the stern, asleep on the cushion. And they woke him and said to him, "Teacher, do you not care that we are perishing?" 39 And he awoke and [p]rebuked the wind and said to the sea, "Peace! Be still!" And the wind ceased, and [q]there was a great calm. 40 He said to them, "Why are you [r]so afraid? Have you still no faith?" 41 And they were filled with great fear and said to one another, [s]"Who then is this, that even [t]the wind and the sea obey him?"

Jesus Heals a Man with a Demon

5 [u]They came to the other side of the sea, to the country of the Gerasenes.[1] 2 And when Jesus[2] had stepped out of the boat, immediately there met him out of the tombs a man with an unclean spirit. 3 [v]He lived among the tombs. And no one could bind him anymore, not even with a chain, 4 for he had often been bound with shackles and chains, but he wrenched the chains apart, and he broke the shackles in pieces. No one had the strength to subdue him. 5 Night and day among the tombs and on the mountains he was always crying out and cutting himself with stones. 6 And when he saw Jesus from afar, he ran and [w]fell down before him. 7 And [x]crying out with a loud voice, he said, "What have you to do with me, Jesus, [y]Son of [z]the Most High God? [a]I adjure you by God, do not torment me." 8 For he was saying to him, "Come out of the man, you unclean spirit!" 9 And Jesus asked him, "What is your name?" He replied, "My name is [b]Legion, for we are many." 10 And he begged him earnestly not to send them out of the country. 11 Now a great herd of pigs was feeding there on the hillside, 12 and they begged him, saying, "Send us to the pigs; let us enter them." 13 So he gave them permission. And the unclean spirits came out and entered the pigs; and the herd, numbering about two thousand, rushed down the steep bank into the sea and drowned in the sea.

14 The herdsmen fled and told it in the city and in the country. And people came to see what it was that had happened. 15 And they came to Jesus and saw the demon-possessed[3] man, the one who had had [c]the legion, sitting there, [d]clothed and in his right mind, and they were afraid. 16 And those who had seen it described to them what had happened to the demon-possessed man and to the pigs. 17 And

[1] Some manuscripts *Gergesenes*; some *Gadarenes* [2] Greek *he*; also verse 9 [3] Greek *daimonizomai*; also verses 16, 18; elsewhere rendered *oppressed by demons*

31 [g] Matt. 17:20; Luke 17:6
33 [h] Matt. 13:34 [i] See ver. 14 [j] John 16:12; 1 Cor. 3:2; Heb. 5:12
34 [k] [John 16:25] [l] ver. 10; [ch. 13:3] [m] [2 Pet. 1:20]
35 [n] For ver. 35-41, see Matt. 8:18, 23-27; Luke 8:22-25; [John 6:16-21]
37 [o] [Acts 27:14]
39 [p] Ps. 104:7; [Luke 4:39] [q] Job 38:11; Ps. 65:7; [ch. 6:51; Matt. 14:32]
40 [r] John 14:27
41 [s] [ch. 1:27] [t] [Luke 5:9]
Chapter 5
1 [u] For ver. 1-21, see Matt. 8:28-9:1; Luke 8:26-40
3 [v] [Rev. 18:2]
6 [w] See Matt. 8:2
7 [x] ch. 1:26; Acts 8:7 [y] [Matt. 4:3, 6]; See Matt. 14:33 [z] Gen. 14:18; Num. 24:16; Ps. 57:2; Dan. 3:26; Luke 1:32; 6:35; Acts 16:17 [a] Matt. 26:63; Acts 19:13; [James 2:19]
9 [b] Matt. 26:53
15 [c] [Luke 8:27] [d] ver. 9

4:35–5:43 Jesus continues to display his expanding range of power in every sphere of creation: power over the laws and forces of nature (4:35–41), power over the spiritual and demonic world (5:1–20), and power over human illness and death (5:21–43).

Jesus is not merely a political messiah along the lines of a Davidic king (cf. 2 Sam. 7:12–15). Rather, this Messiah is God, the eternal Son (see Psalm 2; 110:1, 5; Dan. 7:13–14; cf. 2 Sam. 7:16). He is Yahweh, come in the flesh (Isa. 40:3). It is crucial to realize this, since only God has the power to deliver and to save from the brokenness of our world and the bondage of sinful rebellion against him (e.g., Isa. 25:9; 33:22; 35:4; 37:20; 38:20; Jer. 17:14; Zech 8:7; 9:16; Heb. 7:25).

It is a great source of encouragement for followers of Jesus to remember who they serve: the triune Creator of this universe. The power of the eternal Son protects and guides with utter reliability, even in great distress. Since Jesus has paid the price for our sinful rebellion and has overcome the powers of Satan and the grip of death, his followers are in good hands—whether at any given moment this results in life or in death (Phil. 1:20–23). For in the gospel we know that because Christ has died and

[e]they began to beg Jesus[1] to depart from their region. 18 As he was getting into the boat, the man who had been possessed with demons begged him that he might be with him. 19 And he did not permit him but said to him, "Go home to your friends and [f]tell them how much the Lord has done for you, and how he has had mercy on you." 20 And he went away and began to proclaim in [g]the Decapolis how much Jesus had done for him, and everyone marveled.

Jesus Heals a Woman and Jairus's Daughter

21 And when Jesus had crossed again in the boat to the other side, a great crowd gathered about him, and he was beside the sea. 22 [h]Then came one of [i]the rulers of the synagogue, Jairus by name, and seeing him, he fell at his feet 23 and implored him earnestly, saying, "My little daughter is at the point of death. Come and [j]lay your hands on her, so that she may be made well and live." 24 And he went with him.

And a great crowd followed him and [k]thronged about him. 25 And there was a woman [l]who had had a discharge of blood for twelve years, 26 and who had suffered much under many physicians, and had spent all that she had, and was no better but rather grew worse. 27 She had heard the reports about Jesus and came up behind him in the crowd and touched his garment. 28 For she said, "If I touch even his garments, I will be made well." 29 [m]And immediately the flow of blood dried up, and she felt in her body that she was healed of her [n]disease. 30 And Jesus, perceiving in himself that [o]power had gone out from him, immediately turned about in the crowd and said, "Who touched my garments?" 31 And his disciples said to him, "You see the crowd pressing around you, and yet you say, 'Who touched me?'" 32 And he looked around to see who had done it. 33 But the woman, knowing what had happened to her, came in fear and trembling and fell down before him and told him the whole truth. 34 And he said to her, "Daughter, [p]your faith has made you well; [p]go in peace, and be healed of your [n]disease."

35 While he was still speaking, there came from [q]the ruler's house some who said, "Your daughter is dead. Why [r]trouble [s]the Teacher any further?" 36 But overhearing[2] what they said, Jesus said to [q]the ruler of the synagogue, "Do not fear, only believe." 37 And he allowed no one to follow him except [t]Peter and James and [u]John the brother of James. 38 They came to the house of the ruler of the synagogue, and Jesus[3] saw a commotion, people weeping and wailing loudly. 39 And when he had entered, he said to them, [v]"Why are you making a commotion and weeping? The child is not dead but [w]sleeping." 40 And they laughed at him. But he [x]put them all outside and took the child's father and mother and those who were with him and went in where the child was. 41 [y]Taking her by the hand he said to her, "Talitha cumi," which means, "Little girl, I say to you, [z]arise." 42 And immediately the girl got up and began walking (for she was twelve years of age), and they were immediately overcome with amazement. 43 And [a]he strictly charged them that no one should know this, and told them to give her something to eat.

Jesus Rejected at Nazareth

6 [b]He went away from there and came to [c]his hometown, and his disciples followed him. 2 And [d]on the Sabbath he began to teach in the synagogue, and [e]many who heard him were astonished, saying, "Where did this man get these things? What is the wisdom given to him? How are such mighty works done by his hands? 3 [f]Is not this [g]the carpenter, the son of Mary and [h]brother of James and Joses and Judas and Simon? And are not his sisters here with us?" And [i]they took offense at him. 4 And Jesus said to them, [j]"A prophet is not without

[1] Greek *him* [2] Or *ignoring*; some manuscripts *hearing* [3] Greek *he*

risen, and we are united to him, all that happens to us comes to us from the hand of a loving Father. All wrath has been removed. He does everything for our good.

6:1–6 Jesus' reputation in his hometown of Nazareth suffers on account of his perplexing claims and authority (vv. 1–6; cf. 3:6). The line of those who reject God's ways and his prophets is long (12:1–5; Neh. 9:16–19, 26–30, 34; Acts 7). It continues regarding John the Baptist (Mark 6:14–29) and culminates in the impending rejection of the

17[e] [Luke 5:8; Acts 16:39]
19[f] Ps. 66:16; [ch. 1:44]
20[g] ch. 7:31; Matt. 4:25
22[h] For ver. 22-43, see Matt. 9:18-26; Luke 8:41-56 [i] Luke 13:14; Acts 13:15; 18:8, 17
23[j] ch. 6:5; 7:32; 8:23, 25; 16:18; Matt. 9:18; Luke 4:40; 13:13; Acts 9:12, 17; 28:8
24[k] ver. 31; ch. 3:9

25[l] Lev. 15:25 **29**[m] Matt. 15:28; 17:18 [n] See ch. 3:10 **30**[o] Luke 5:17; 6:19; 8:46; [Acts 10:38] **34**[p] See Luke 7:50 [n] [See ver. 29 above] **35**[q] ver. 22 [r] Luke 7:6 [s] See John 11:28 **36**[q] [See ver. 35 above] **37**[t] ch. 9:2; 14:33 [u] ch. 3:17 **39**[v] [Acts 20:10] [w] John 11:4, 11 **40**[x] Acts 9:40 **41**[y] See ch. 1:31 [z] Luke 7:14, 22; [Matt. 11:5; John 11:43] **43**[a] ch. 9:9; See Matt. 8:4 **Chapter 6** **1**[b] For ver. 1-6, see Matt. 13:54-58; [Luke 4:16-30] [c] Matt. 2:23; Luke 4:23 **2**[d] ch. 1:21; Luke 4:31; 6:6; 13:10; [Acts 13:14]; See Matt. 4:23 [e] See Matt. 7:28 **3**[f] [Luke 4:22; John 6:42] [g] [Matt. 13:55] [h] See ch. 3:31 [i] See Matt. 11:6 **4**[j] Luke 4:24; John 4:44; [Jer. 11:21; 12:6; John 7:5]

honor, except in his hometown and among his relatives and in his own household." 5 And [k]he could do no mighty work there, except that [l]he laid his hands on a few sick people and healed them. 6 And [m]he marveled because of their unbelief.

[n]And he went about among the villages teaching.

Jesus Sends Out the Twelve Apostles

7 [o]And he called the twelve and began to send them out two by two, and gave them authority over the unclean spirits. 8 He charged them to take nothing for their journey except a staff—no bread, no bag, no money in their belts— 9 but to [p]wear sandals and not put on two tunics.[1] 10 And he said to them, "Whenever you enter a house, stay there until you depart from there. 11 And if any place will not receive you and they will not listen to you, when you leave, [q]shake off the dust that is on your feet [r]as a testimony against them." 12 [s]So they went out and [t]proclaimed [u]that people should repent. 13 [t]And they cast out many demons and [v]anointed with oil many who were sick and healed them.

The Death of John the Baptist

14 [w]King Herod heard of it, for Jesus'[2] name had become known. Some[3] said, [x]"John the Baptist[4] has been raised from the dead. That is why these miraculous powers are at work in him." 15 [x]But others said, "He is Elijah." And others said, "He is [y]a prophet, like one of the prophets of old." 16 But when Herod heard of it, he said, "John, whom I beheaded, has been raised." 17 [z]For it was Herod who had sent and seized John and [a]bound him in prison for the sake of Herodias, his brother Philip's wife, because he had married her. 18 [z]For John had been saying to Herod, [b]"It is not lawful for you to have your brother's wife." 19 And Herodias had a grudge against him and wanted to put him to death. But she could not, 20 for Herod [c]feared John, knowing that he was a righteous and holy man, and he kept him safe. When he heard him, he was greatly perplexed, and yet he [d]heard him gladly.

[1] Greek *chiton*, a long garment worn under the cloak next to the skin [2] Greek *his* [3] Some manuscripts *He* [4] Greek *baptizer*; also verse 24

5[k] [ch. 9:23; Gen. 19:22] [l] See ch. 5:23
6[m] [Matt. 8:10] [n] Matt. 9:35; 11:1; Luke 8:1; 13:22
7[o] ch. 3:13-15; For ver. 7-11, see Matt. 10:1, 5, 9-14; Luke 9:1, 3-5; [Luke 10:4-11; 22:35]
9[p] Acts 12:8
11[q] Acts 13:51; [Neh. 5:13; Acts 18:6] [r] See ch. 1:44
12[s] Luke 9:6 [t] Matt. 10:7, 8 [u] Matt. 3:2; 4:17
13[t] [See ver. 12 above] [v] James 5:14
14[w] For ver. 14-29, see Matt. 14:1-12; Luke 9:7-9 [x] ch. 8:28; Matt. 16:14
15[x] [See ver. 14 above] [y] See Matt. 21:11
17[z] Luke 3:19, 20 [a] Matt. 11:2; John 3:24
18[z] [See ver. 17 above] [b] Lev. 18:16; 20:21
20[c] [Matt. 14:5; 21:26] [d] ch. 12:37; [ch. 4:16]

eternal Son (12:6–8). To a degree, even the suffering of the followers of Christ (8:34; 10:39; Acts 4:3, 21; 5:17–18; 7:58; 12:1–5; 21:11, 30–33; 24:1–9; 26:6) continues the theme of opposition to God's purposes.

Just as Jesus is opposed by demonic darkness and human enemies, his followers will also be opposed by these same forces. Disciples of Christ should not blame God for the painful consequences of their own foolish decisions and actions, but they do need to remember, when they are opposed merely because of their obedience to Jesus, that Jesus himself suffered rejection (cf. Mark 10:30; 13:9, 13). We who follow a crucified Savior should not be surprised by the cruciform life that is thrust upon us as we seek to be faithful to him. And through it all, we walk with one who is "gentle and lowly in heart" (Matt. 11:29). We have a mighty Friend.

6:7–29 The death of John the Baptist, as yet another rejection of one of God's prophets (cf. 12:1–5), casts an ominous shadow on Jesus' own destiny (cf. 3:1–6; 6:1–6). Jesus' life is in danger, partly on account of his authoritative, miraculous deeds, and partly on account of his extraordinary claims. Human sin and Satan resist the claims and aims of God. We see here the clash between the "kingdom of self and Satan" and the kingdom of God (cf. Col. 1:13).

Jesus' discipleship-dynamic reaches another level as he sends his disciples out in pairs to preach repentance, to exorcise demons, and to heal (Mark 6:12–13; cf. v. 30). Discipleship begins to mature into Christ-empowered Christlikeness. Jesus invites his followers to be agents, under his own authority, who bring in the long-awaited kingdom of God.

Jesus' followers are being shaped by the character and will of the Master. He ultimately will enable them to express greater God-dependent Christlikeness as the result of his atonement for their sin. Through the cross and the empty tomb, toward which the entire Gospel of Mark is hurtling, Jesus decisively accomplishes the inauguration of the kingdom of God. The early manifestations of this kingdom, seen in healings, exorcisms, and miracles, anticipate the final and greatest "clinching" of the kingdom: Jesus' death and resurrection. There the kingdom of darkness is dealt its deathblow. Victory is secured. The outcome is certain.

21 But an opportunity came when Herod [e]on
his birthday [f]gave a banquet for his nobles and
military commanders and the leading men
of Galilee. 22 For when Herodias's daughter
came in and danced, she pleased Herod and
his guests. And the king said to the girl, "Ask
me for whatever you wish, and I will give it
to you." 23 And he vowed to her, "Whatever
you ask me, I will give you, [g]up to half of my
kingdom." 24 And she went out and said to
her mother, "For what should I ask?" And she
said, "The head of John the Baptist." 25 And she
came in immediately with haste to the king
and asked, saying, "I want you to give me at
once the head of John the Baptist on a platter." 26 And the king was exceedingly sorry, but
because of his oaths and his guests he did not
want to break his word to her. 27 And immediately the king sent an executioner with orders
to bring John's[1] head. He went and beheaded
him in the prison 28 and brought his head on
a platter and gave it to the girl, and the girl
gave it to her mother. 29 When his [h]disciples
heard of it, they came and took his body and
laid it in a tomb.

Jesus Feeds the Five Thousand

30 [i, j]The apostles returned to Jesus and told
him all that they had done and taught. 31 And
he said to them, "Come away by yourselves to
a desolate place and rest a while." For many
were coming and going, and [k]they had no lei-
sure even to eat. 32 [l]And they went away in [m]the
boat to a desolate place by themselves. 33 Now
many saw them going and [n]recognized them,
and they ran there on foot from all the towns
and got there ahead of them. 34 When he went
ashore he [o]saw a great crowd, and [o]he had
compassion on them, because they were like
sheep without a shepherd. And he began to
teach them many things. 35 And when it grew
late, his disciples came to him and said, "This
is a desolate place, and the hour is now late.
36 [p]Send them away to go into the surrounding
countryside and villages and buy themselves
something to eat." 37 But he answered them,
[q]"You give them something to eat." And [r]they
said to him, [s]"Shall we go and buy two hundred denarii[2] worth of bread and give it to
them to eat?" 38 And he said to them, "How
many loaves do you have? Go and see." And
when they had found out, they said, [t]"Five,
and two fish." 39 Then he commanded them
all to sit down in groups on the green grass.
40 So they sat down in groups, by hundreds
and by fifties. 41 And taking the five loaves and
the two fish he [u]looked up to heaven and [v]said
a blessing and broke the loaves and gave them
to the disciples to set before the people. And

[1] Greek *his* [2] A *denarius* was a day's wage for a laborer

6:30–56 The feeding of the 5,000 and walking on water continue Jesus' display of power (vv. 31–56). The feeding of the 5,000 (and later the 4,000; 8:1–10) echoes the feeding of manna to the people of Israel as they sojourned in the desert centuries before (Ex. 16:31; Deut. 8:16). Christ's power over wind and waves echoes the power God displayed on behalf of his people at the exodus. Jesus, the eternal Son of God, provides now what God provided then. Jesus is the one who restores abundance and joy.

More than this, Jesus is himself divine. When Jesus reveals himself to the disciples as he walks on the water, he says "It is I"—the very same phrase through which God revealed himself to Moses in Exodus 3:14, and the same phrase Jesus uses throughout John's Gospel to subtly underscore his own deity (e.g., John 8:58–59). God in the flesh is revealing himself to the disciples. This identification of Jesus as God is reinforced by the fact that the Old Testament speaks of Yahweh himself trampling on the waves of the sea (e.g., Job 9:8)—the very thing Jesus does here in Mark 6.

Today's disciple can trust in the power of Christ. But this may require faith in God's work beyond the boundaries of this life. For we must remember that immediately preceding this passage displaying the great power and provision of Christ is the account of the senseless execution of John the Baptist (Mark 6:14–29). God provides as he knows is best for eternal purposes. This provision might take the form of an opportunity to study, to work hard, to live a very modest life—or even to give one's life for the sake of the kingdom of God. Nothing is without divine purpose, and all will be made plain and vindicated in eternity, but we trust such things because we have already witnessed the divine power of God making provision for his people in the life of Christ. Understanding of the eternal purposes of Christ's provisions creates a radical transformation of the follower in terms of his or her attitude toward work, career, challenge, opposition, deprivation, sacrifice, future, and life itself.

21 [e]Gen. 40:20 [f]1 Kgs. 3:15; Esth. 1:3; 2:18
23 [g]Esth. 5:3; 7:2
29 [h]See Matt. 9:14
30 [i]Luke 9:10 [j]Matt. 10:2; Luke 6:13; 17:5; 22:14; 24:10
31 [k]ch. 3:20
32 [l]For ver. 32-44, see Matt. 14:13-21; Luke 9:10-17; John 6:1-13; [ch. 8:2-9] [m]See ch. 3:9
33 [n]ver. 54
34 [o][Matt. 9:36]
36 [p]ver. 45; [Matt. 15:23]
37 [q][2 Kgs. 4:42-44] [r][John 6:7] [s][Num. 11:13, 21, 22]
38 [t]ch. 8:19
41 [u]ch. 7:34; John 11:41; 17:1 [v]ch. 8:7; 14:22; 1 Sam. 9:13; Matt. 26:26; Luke 24:30; [1 Cor. 14:16]

he divided the two fish among them all. 42 And they all ate and were satisfied. 43 And they took up twelve baskets full of broken pieces and of the fish. 44 And those who ate the loaves were five thousand men.

Jesus Walks on the Water

45 [w]Immediately he [x]made his disciples get into [y]the boat and go before him to the other side, [z]to Bethsaida, while he dismissed the crowd. 46 And after he had taken leave of them, [a]he went up on the mountain to pray. 47 And when [b]evening came, the boat was out on the sea, and he was alone on the land. 48 And he saw that they were making headway painfully, for the wind was against them. And about [b]the fourth watch of the night[1] he came to them, walking on the sea. [c]He meant to pass by them, 49 but when they saw him walking on the sea they thought it was a ghost, and cried out, 50 for they all saw him and [d]were terrified. But immediately he spoke to them and said, [e]"Take heart; it is I. [e]Do not be afraid." 51 And he got into the boat with them, and the wind ceased. And they were utterly astounded, 52 for [f]they did not understand about the loaves, but their hearts [g]were hardened.

Jesus Heals the Sick in Gennesaret

53 [h]When they had crossed over, they came to land at [i]Gennesaret and moored to the shore. 54 And when they got out of the boat, the people immediately [j]recognized him 55 and ran about the whole region and began to bring [k]the sick people [l]on their beds to wherever they heard he was. 56 And wherever he came, in villages, cities, or countryside, [m]they laid the sick in the marketplaces and implored him that they might touch even [n]the fringe of his garment. And [o]as many as touched it were made well.

Traditions and Commandments

7 [p]Now when the Pharisees gathered to him, with some of the scribes [q]who had come from Jerusalem, 2 they saw that some of his disciples ate with hands that were [r]defiled, that is, unwashed. 3 (For the Pharisees and all the Jews do not eat unless they wash their hands properly,[2] holding to [s]the tradition of [t]the elders, 4 and when they come from the marketplace, they do not eat unless they wash.[3] And there are many other traditions that they observe, such as [u]the washing of [v]cups and pots and copper vessels and dining couches.[4]) 5 And the Pharisees and the scribes asked him, "Why do your disciples not walk according to [s]the tradition of [t]the elders, [w]but eat with [r]defiled hands?" 6 And he said to them, "Well did Isaiah prophesy of you [x]hypocrites, as it is written,

[y]" 'This people honors me with their lips,
but their heart is far from me;
7 in vain do they worship me,
teaching as [z]doctrines the commandments of men.'

8 You leave the commandment of God and hold to the tradition of men."

[1] That is, between 3 A.M. and 6 A.M. [2] Greek *unless they wash the hands with a fist*, probably indicating a kind of ceremonial washing [3] Greek *unless they baptize*; some manuscripts *unless they purify themselves* [4] Some manuscripts omit *and dining couches*

45 [w]For ver. 45-51, see Matt. 14:22-32; John 6:15-21 [x][Matt. 8:18] [y]ver. 32 [z]ch. 8:22; [Luke 9:10]
46 [a]Luke 6:12; 9:28; [ch. 1:35; Luke 5:16]
47 [b][ch. 13:35]
48 [b][See ver. 47 above] [c][Luke 24:28]
50 [d][Luke 24:37] [e]Matt. 17:7; [Deut. 31:6; Isa. 41:13; 43:1, 2; John 16:33]
52 [f]ch. 8:17-21 [g]John 12:40; Rom. 11:7; 2 Cor. 3:14; See ch. 3:5
53 [h]For ver. 53-56, see Matt. 14:34-36; [John 6:24, 25] [i]Luke 5:1
54 [j]ver. 33
55 [k]Matt. 4:24 [l]Luke 5:18
56 [m]Acts 5:15 [n]See Matt. 9:20 [o]ch. 3:10; Luke 6:19
Chapter 7
1 [p]For ver. 1-30, see Matt. 15:1-28 [q]ch. 3:22

7:1–23 Jesus encounters opposition over the proper interpretation of the law of Moses. Jesus arises as the new Moses (the Prophet like Moses; Deut. 18:15, 18). According to Jesus, focus on the ceremonial laws of cleanliness at the expense of a renewed heart or mercy distorts the purpose of the law and of God himself. On account of the profound defilement of the heart, even the Word of God gets reinterpreted or annulled for personal gain. The law cannot be fully or perfectly kept (Rom. 7:13). Without renewed hearts, pursuing the law and a pure life is in vain (Mark 7:1–23). Our sinful hearts inevitably twist God's good law toward selfish, self-excusing, self-justifying, or proud purposes.

Jesus is the fulfillment of the Mosaic law (Matt. 5:17). As such, he enables his followers to live out the moral aims of the Mosaic law by purifying their hearts. Such faithful living is the fruit of dependence on Christ.

The ceremonial and judicial aspects of the Mosaic law have essentially been brought to completion in Christ (Rom. 10:4; Heb. 10:16–23). Matthew 5–7 describes especially the refinement of the moral elements of Mosaic law, which Jesus now brings to fruition in the hearts of his followers.

2 [r][Acts 10:14; Rom. 14:14 (Gk.)] 3 [s]Gal. 1:14; Col. 2:8 [t]Heb. 11:2 4 [u]Heb. 9:10; [John 2:6] [v]Matt. 23:25; Luke 11:39 5 [s][See ver. 3 above] [t][See ver. 3 above] [w]Luke 11:38 [r][See ver. 2 above] 6 [x]Matt. 23:13 [y]Cited from Isa. 29:13; [Ezek. 33:31] 7 [z]Col. 2:22; Titus 1:14

9 And he said to them, "You have a fine way of [a]rejecting the commandment of God in order to establish your tradition! 10 For Moses said, [b]'Honor your father and your mother'; and, [c]'Whoever reviles father or mother must surely die.' 11 But you say, 'If a man tells his father or his mother, "Whatever you would have gained from me is Corban"' (that is, given to God)[1]— 12 then you no longer permit him to do anything for his father or mother, 13 thus [d]making void the word of God by your tradition that you have handed down. And many such things you do."

What Defiles a Person

14 And he called the people to him again and said to them, [e]"Hear me, all of you, and understand: 15 [f]There is nothing outside a person that by going into him can defile him, but the things that come out of a person are what defile him."[2] 17 And when he had entered [g]the house and left the people, [h]his disciples asked him about the parable. 18 And he said to them, "Then [i]are you also without understanding? Do you not see that whatever goes into a person from outside cannot defile him, 19 since it enters not his heart [j]but his stomach, and is expelled?"[3] ([k]Thus he declared all foods clean.) 20 And he said, [l]"What comes out of a person is what defiles him. 21 For from within, out of the heart of man, come evil thoughts, sexual immorality, theft, [m]murder, adultery, 22 coveting, wickedness, deceit, [n]sensuality, [o]envy, [p]slander, [q]pride, [r]foolishness. 23 [s]All these evil things come from within, and they defile a person."

The Syrophoenician Woman's Faith

24 And from there he arose and went away to the region of Tyre and Sidon.[4] And he entered a house and did not want anyone to know, yet he could not be hidden. 25 But immediately a woman whose little daughter had an unclean spirit heard of him and came and fell down at his feet. 26 [t]Now the woman was a [u]Gentile, [v]a Syrophoenician by birth. And she begged him to cast the demon out of her daughter. 27 And he said to her, "Let the children be [w]fed first, for it is not right to take the children's bread and [x]throw it to the dogs." 28 But she answered him, "Yes, Lord; yet even the dogs under the table eat the children's [y]crumbs." 29 And he said to her, "For this statement you may [z]go your way; the demon has left your daughter." 30 And she went home and found the child lying in bed and the demon gone.

Jesus Heals a Deaf Man

31 [a]Then he returned from the region of Tyre and went through Sidon to [b]the Sea of Galilee, in the region of the [c]Decapolis. 32 And they brought to him [d]a man who was deaf and [d]had a speech impediment, and they begged him to [e]lay his hand on him. 33 And [f]taking him aside from the crowd privately, he put his fingers

[1] Or *an offering* [2] Some manuscripts add verse 16: *If anyone has ears to hear, let him hear* [3] Greek *goes out into the latrine*
[4] Some manuscripts omit *and Sidon*

7:24–30 Jesus' ministry is one of both word and deed. His authoritative teaching runs parallel to the continuing display of his power to cast out demons, to heal, and to multiply food (7:24–8:10). Initially, his call goes out to the people of Israel, but Jesus already hints at a future work of the disciples among Gentiles (7:24–30; cf. 13:10; Isa. 42:1, 4, 6, 10–12 and 49:1, 6, 22).

The follower of Christ is above all being transformed as a person in fellowship and union with God. Only then does a disciple have the additional call of going to the ends of the earth with a holistic witness of proclaiming and living out the mission of God's redemption. This redemption includes evangelism, service of mercy, and living as "salt" and "light" in the economic, political, and cultural spheres of our societies.

7:31–8:10 The healing of the deaf man who is also unable to speak is a messianic deed of mercy (Isa. 61:1–2). It also serves to confront the disciples with their "deafness" of heart (see notes on Mark 8:11–21 and 8:22–26).

When Jesus heals people such as this deaf man, we tend to view these miracles in the Gospels as interruptions of the natural order. Yet given the promises of the Old Testament to restore the world to the way it was at the very beginning, miracles are not an interruption of the natural order but the *restoration* of the natural order. We are so used to a fallen world that sickness, disease, pain, and death seem natural. In fact, *they* are the interruption. Jesus' *super*natural miracles are a return to the truly natural.

9[a] Luke 7:30; Gal. 2:21 (Gk.); Heb. 10:28 (Gk.)
10[b] Cited from Ex. 20:12 [c] Cited from Ex. 21:17
13[d] Gal. 3:17 (Gk.); [Rom. 2:23]
14[e] Matt. 13:51
15[f] See Acts 10:14, 15
17[g] ch. 9:28 [h] [Matt. 13:36; 15:15]
18[i] ch. 8:17, 18
19[j] [1 Cor. 6:13] [k] [Luke 11:41; Acts 10:15; 11:9]
20[l] Matt. 12:34; James 3:6
21[m] Matt. 5:22, 28; See Ex. 20:13, 14, 17
22[n] 2 Cor. 12:21; Gal. 5:19; Eph. 4:19; 2 Pet. 2:7; Jude 4 [o] See Matt. 6:23 (Gk.) [p] Eph. 4:31; Col. 3:8; 1 Tim. 6:4 [q] See Luke 1:51 [r] [Eph. 5:17]
23[s] 1 Cor. 6:9, 10
26[t] [John 12:20, 21] [u] [1 Cor. 12:13] [v] [Acts 21:2, 3]
27[w] [Acts 3:26; Rom. 1:16] [x] Matt. 7:6
28[y] [Luke 16:21]
29[z] John 4:50
31[a] For ver. 31-37, [Matt. 15:29-31] [b] Matt. 4:18; John 6:1 [c] ch. 5:20; Matt. 4:25
32[d] Isa. 35:5, 6 [e] See ch. 5:23 **33**[f] ch. 8:23

into his ears, and [f]after spitting touched his
tongue. 34 And [g]looking up to heaven, [h]he
sighed and said to him, "Ephphatha," that
is, "Be opened." 35 [d]And his ears were opened,
his tongue was released, and he spoke plainly.
36 And [i]Jesus[1] charged them to tell no one. But
[j]the more he charged them, the more zealously
they proclaimed it. 37 And they were [k]aston-
ished beyond measure, saying, "He has done
all things well. He even makes the deaf hear
and the mute speak."

Jesus Feeds the Four Thousand

8 [l]In those days, when again a great crowd
had gathered, and they had nothing to eat,
he called his disciples to him and said to them,
2 [m]"I have compassion on the crowd, because
they have been with me now three days and
have nothing to eat. 3 And if I send them away
hungry to their homes, they will faint on the
way. And some of them have come from far
away." 4 And his disciples answered him, "How
can one feed these people with bread here in
this desolate place?" 5 And he asked them,
"How many loaves do you have?" They said,
[n]"Seven." 6 And he directed the crowd to sit
down on the ground. And he took the seven
loaves, and [o]having given thanks, he broke
them and gave them to his disciples to set
before the people; and they set them before
the crowd. 7 And they had a few small fish. And
[p]having blessed them, he said that these also
should be set before them. 8 And [q]they ate and
were satisfied. And they took up the broken
pieces left over, [n]seven baskets full. 9 And there
were about four thousand people. And he sent
them away. 10 And immediately he got into [r]the
boat with his disciples and went to the district
of [s]Dalmanutha.[2]

The Pharisees Demand a Sign

11 [t]The Pharisees came and began to argue
with him, [u]seeking from him [v]a sign from
heaven [w]to test him. 12 And [x]he sighed deeply
[y]in his spirit and said, "Why does this generation seek a sign? Truly, I say to you, no sign
will be given to this generation." 13 And [z]he
left them, got into the boat again, and went
to the other side.

The Leaven of the Pharisees and Herod

14 Now they had forgotten to bring bread,
and they had only one loaf with them in the
boat. 15 And he cautioned them, saying, "Watch
out; [a]beware of [b]the leaven of the Pharisees
and the leaven of [c]Herod."[3] 16 And they began
discussing with one another the fact that
they had no bread. 17 And [d]Jesus, aware of
this, said to them, "Why are you discussing
the fact that you have no bread? [e]Do you not
yet perceive [f]or understand? [f]Are your hearts
hardened? 18 [g]Having eyes do you not see, and
having ears do you not hear? And do you not
remember? 19 When I broke [h]the five loaves for
the five thousand, how many baskets full of
broken pieces did you take up?" They said to
him, "Twelve." 20 "And [i]the seven for the four
thousand, how many baskets full of broken
pieces did you take up?" And they said to him,
"Seven." 21 And he said to them, "Do you not
yet understand?"

Jesus Heals a Blind Man at Bethsaida

22 And they came [j]to Bethsaida. And some
people brought to him a blind man and
begged him to touch him. 23 And [k]he took the
blind man by the hand and led him out of the
village, and when [k]he had [l]spit on his eyes and
[m]laid his hands on him, he asked him, "Do

[1] Greek *he* [2] Some manuscripts *Magadan*, or *Magdala* [3] Some manuscripts *the Herodians*

33[f] ch. 8:23
34[g] See ch. 6:41 [h] ch. 8:12; [John 11:33]
35[d] [See ver. 32 above]
36[i] ch. 9:9; See Matt. 8:4 [j] ch. 1:45; Matt. 9:31
37[k] ch. 10:26
Chapter 8
1[l] For ver. 1-10, see Matt. 15:32-39; [ch. 6:32-44]
2[m] [Matt. 9:36]
5[n] Matt. 16:10
6[o] ch. 14:23; Matt. 26:27; Luke 22:17, 19; John 6:11, 23; Acts 27:35; Rom. 14:6; 1 Cor. 10:30; 11:24; 14:16; 1 Tim. 4:3, 4

8:11–21 The settled unbelief of the Jewish leaders (vv. 11–13) becomes an object lesson and a serious warning for the disciples by means of the metaphor of "leaven" (v. 15), which points to malicious self-sufficiency and hypocritical self-righteousness (cf. Luke 12:1; 1 Cor. 5:8). But the disciples neither understand (Mark 8:17, 21) nor "see" or "hear" (v. 18) properly. Jesus takes up Old Testament figures of speech (blindness and deafness) to describe the hard heart of the disciples (see 3:5; 6:52; Isa. 6:9–10; 42:18–19; 43:8; Jer. 5:21; Ezek. 12:2).

Without radical, personal transformation by the gospel of grace, beginning with Jesus' exposure of our own hearts, followers of Christ have nothing of substance to convey to others (cf. Eph. 1:18). God has spoken grace to us; we speak in grace to others. Loved, we love. This is the pattern of gospel life.

7[p] See Matt. 14:19 **8**[q] [2 Kgs. 4:42-44] [n] [See ver. 5 above] **10**[r] See ch. 3:9 [s] [Matt. 15:39] **11**[t] For ver. 11-21, see Matt. 16:1-12 [u] 1 Cor. 1:22; See Matt. 12:38 [v] Luke 11:16; 21:11 [w] John 8:6 **12**[x] ch. 7:34 [y] John 11:33 **13**[z] Matt. 4:13; 21:17 **15**[a] Luke 12:1 [b] 1 Cor. 5:6-8; Gal. 5:9 [c] [ch. 3:6; 12:13] **17**[d] Matt. 26:10 [e] ch. 7:18 [f] ch. 6:52 **18**[g] Jer. 5:21; Ezek. 12:2; [Isa. 42:18, 19; 43:8; Matt. 13:13] **19**[h] ch. 6:41, 44 **20**[i] ver. 6, 9 **22**[j] See ch. 6:45 **23**[k] ch. 7:33 [l] John 9:6 [m] See ch. 5:23

you see anything?" 24 And he looked up and
said, "I see people, but they look like trees,
walking." 25 Then Jesus[1] laid his hands on his
eyes again; and he opened his eyes, his sight
was restored, and he saw everything clearly.
26 And he sent him to his home, saying, [n]"Do
not even enter the village."

Peter Confesses Jesus as the Christ

27 [o]And Jesus went on with his disciples to
the villages of Caesarea Philippi. And on the
way he asked his disciples, "Who do people say
that I am?" 28 And they told him, [p]"John the
Baptist; and others say, [q]Elijah; and others, one
of the prophets." 29 And he asked them, "But
who do you say that I am?" Peter answered
him, [r]"You are [s]the Christ." 30 [t]And he strictly
charged them to tell no one about him.

Jesus Foretells His Death and Resurrection

31 [u]And he began to teach them that [v]the Son
of Man must [w]suffer many things and [x]be
rejected by the elders and the chief priests
and the scribes and be killed, and [y]after three
days rise again. 32 And he said this [z]plainly.
And Peter took him aside and began to rebuke

[1] Greek *he*

8:22–26 Jesus' rebuke of his disciples in verses 14–21 is reinforced by the contextual echoes of the healing of the deaf and mute man (7:32–35) and the two-stage healing of the blind man in this passage (8:22–26). These healings both represent messianic acts of mercy (cf. Isa. 61:1–2) and, in combination with Jesus' direct warnings (Mark 8:15, 17–18, 21), serve as prophetic acts that expose the hard hearts of the disciples.

Even in Jesus' presence, the disciples' alertness is at best like that of the half-healed blind man, who "perceives people as trees moving about" (see v. 24). This dull perception of themselves and of Jesus extends to Peter's divinely inspired confession of him (Matt. 16:17) as Messiah (Mark 8:29), since it is mixed with human misconceptions (v. 33). The deeply ingrained and virtually exclusive focus on the messianic expectation of a political, Davidic king, devoid of the characteristics of the suffering servant/ Son of Man (v. 31; 10:45; Isa. 53:1–12), exposes the disciples' partial blindness. At this point they fail to see who Jesus really is: One whose humility is integral to his divine splendor. Consequently, though the disciples see that Jesus is the coming King, they do not understand that he must be a suffering King.

To grasp reality from God's perspective, we must recognize that the path for Jesus, and the path for his disciples, does not make sense to our natural, intuitive ways of thinking.

8:27–16:8 The second half of Mark's Gospel narrates the divine necessity of Jesus' atoning suffering as well as the cost of following the Master. Jesus' path of suffering does not invalidate his authority or his claims. Rather, the impending events of crucifixion and divine vindication by physical resurrection from death constitute the ultimate test and final proof of Jesus' astonishing claims and authority. Jesus must both suffer and rule because both are necessary for the salvation of his people.

The severe events surrounding Jesus' passion will mark the disciples in their fundamental self-understanding and in their grasp of the mission of the triune God: protected by Jesus' substitutionary atonement, they are secure in his love. They too will be tested and opposed by Satan and by human hostility. Yet no one can snatch them out of God's hand (cf. John 10:28–29). In an ultimate sense, those who are united to Christ are invincible.

8:27–10:52 Three times in this portion of Mark's Gospel, Jesus predicts his death and resurrection (8:31; 9:31; 10:32–34). Each time, what he says is followed by instruction on the cost and nature of discipleship (8:34–37; 9:35–50; 10:35–44). Jesus is radically changing the disciples' perception of him and of what his fate as Messiah must be if God's people are to be restored. Jesus expands their narrow political perception of the expected Messiah: Jesus, the true Messiah, will endure suffering and humiliation (e.g., 8:31; cf. Isa. 53:1–12), will be the atoning Son of Man (Mark 10:45; Isa. 53:4–6, 8, 10–12), and will also be the exalted, divine Son of Man (Mark 8:38; 14:62; Dan. 7:13–14).

The disciples were right to understand the Messiah to be one who came to restore God's people. But they failed to see that this restoration would not be as they expected but as they most deeply needed—not political but spiritual. They wanted rescue from the Romans; they needed rescue from their sins.

26 [n]ver. 23; [Matt. 8:4]
27 [o]For ver. 27-29, see Matt. 16:13-16; Luke 9:18-20
28 [p]ch. 6:14; Matt. 14:2; Luke 9:7 [q]Luke 9:8; [ch. 9:11; Matt. 17:10; John 1:21]
29 [r]John 11:27 [s]ch. 14:61, 62; See Matt. 1:17
30 [t]Matt. 16:20; Luke 9:21; See Matt. 12:16
31 [u]For ch. 8:31-9:1, see Matt. 16:21-28; Luke 9:22-27 [v]ch. 10:33; [Luke 13:33] [w]ch. 9:30, 31; Matt. 17:12, 22, 23; Luke 24:7 [x]Luke 17:25; 1 Pet. 2:4; [ch. 12:10] [y]ch. 10:34; Matt. 27:63; [Matt. 12:40]; See John 2:19
32 [z]John 16:25

him. 33 But turning and seeing his disciples, he rebuked Peter and said, [a]"Get behind me, Satan! For you [b]are not setting your mind on the things of God, but on the things of man."

34 And calling the crowd to him with his disciples, he said to them, "If anyone would come after me, let him [c]deny himself and [d]take up his cross and follow me. 35 For [d]whoever would save his life[1] will lose it, but whoever loses his life for my sake [e]and the gospel's will save it. 36 [f]For what does it profit a man to gain the whole world and forfeit his soul? 37 For [g]what can a man give in return for his soul? 38 For [h]whoever is ashamed of me and of my words in this [i]adulterous and sinful generation, of him will the Son of Man also be ashamed [j]when he comes in the glory of his Father with [k]the holy angels."

9 And he said to them, "Truly, I say to you, there are some standing here who will not [l]taste death [m]until they see the kingdom of God after it has come [n]with power."

The Transfiguration

2 [o]And after six days Jesus took with him [p]Peter and James and John, and led them up a high mountain by themselves. And he was [q]transfigured before them, 3 and [r]his clothes became radiant, intensely white, as no one[2] on earth could bleach them. 4 And there appeared to them Elijah with Moses, and they were talking with Jesus. 5 And Peter said to Jesus, [s]"Rabbi,[3] it is good that we are here. Let us make three [t]tents, one for you and one for Moses and one for Elijah." 6 For [u]he did not know what to say, for they were terrified. 7 And [v]a cloud overshadowed them, and [v]a voice came out of the cloud, [w]"This is my beloved Son;[4] [x]listen to him." 8 And suddenly, looking around, they no longer saw anyone with them but Jesus only.

9 [y]And as they were coming down the mountain, [z]he charged them to tell no one what they had seen, [a]until the Son of Man had risen from the dead. 10 [b]So they kept the matter

[1] The same Greek word can mean either *soul* or *life*, depending on the context; twice in this verse and once in verse 36 and once in verse 37 [2] Greek *launderer (gnapheus)* [3] *Rabbi* means *my teacher*, or *my master* [4] Or *my Son, my* (or *the*) *Beloved*

33 [a][Matt. 4:10] [b]Rom. 8:5; Phil. 3:19; Col. 3:2; [Phil. 2:5]
34 [c][2 Tim. 2:12, 13] [d]See Matt. 10:38, 39
35 [d][See ver. 34 above] [e]ch. 10:29; [1 Cor. 9:23; 2 Tim. 1:8; Philem. 13]
36 [f][Luke 12:20]
37 [g][Ps. 49:7, 8]
38 [h]Rom. 1:16; 2 Tim. 1:8, 12, 16; Heb. 11:16; 1 John 2:28; [Matt. 10:33] [i]Isa. 57:3; Matt. 12:39; James 4:4 [j]Dan. 7:10, 13; Zech. 14:5; Matt. 24:30; 25:31; 26:64; Acts 1:11; 1 Thess. 1:10; 4:16; Jude 14; Rev. 1:7; [Deut. 33:2] [k]Acts 10:22; Rev. 14:10; [Matt. 13:41; 16:27]

Chapter 9
1 [l]John 8:52; Heb. 2:9 [m][ch. 13:30; Matt. 10:23; 23:36; 24:34] [n]ch. 13:26; 14:62; [Matt. 25:31]
2 [o]For ver. 2-8, see Matt. 17:1-8; Luke 9:28-36 [p]ch. 5:37; 14:33 [q][2 Cor. 3:18 (Gk.)]
3 [r]Dan. 7:9; [Ps. 104:2; Matt. 28:3]
5 [s]See John 1:38 [t][Neh. 8:15]
6 [u][ch. 14:40; Luke 9:33]
7 [v]2 Pet. 1:17; [Ex. 24:15, 16] [w]ch. 12:6; See Matt. 3:17 [x]Acts 3:22
9 [y]For ver. 9-13, see Matt. 17:9-13 [z]ch. 5:43; See Matt. 8:4 [a]ch. 8:31
10 [b]Luke 9:36

8:34–37 Jesus calls his disciples to let go of self-interest and self-reliance in order to be at Jesus' disposal. As was the case in the call of Elisha (1 Kings 19:19–21), letting go of self-sufficiency is necessary in order to follow Jesus and his purposes. This radical call is fueled by the gospel, in which all our sins are forgiven and we are reconciled to God through Christ (objectively). And yet our ongoing growth in Christ should continue the process of reversing our profound alienation from God (subjectively), since such a surrendered "walking with God" is the original design for human beings.

The follower of Christ realizes the enabling love of him who calls to such radical discipleship, recognizes the impurity in his own heart, and receives the reconciling and purifying work of Jesus on his or her behalf. Thus equipped, the disciple surrenders willingly small and large decisions, wishes, dreams, and so on, about marriage, work, and other aspirations. Such surrender includes the challenge of learning to bear responsibilities while keeping his or her will and thought in a guidable, non-controlling, and prayerful attitude before God.

This type of surrender does not end with self-abasement but requires assumption of the status and duties now assigned by our Lord. A disciple must remember: the One he or she surrenders to is good, trustworthy, wise, and powerful. The Master loves his followers and enables their faithfulness.

8:38–9:8 Jesus' transfiguration (9:2–8) affords a glimpse into his enduring divine nature (cf. Phil. 2:6). Jesus' radiance exceeds that of Moses (cf. Ex. 34:35), who merely reflected the radiance of God on his face. Jesus *himself* radiates in purity and glory. The disciple of Christ follows and trusts him who shares divine glory with the Father (Col. 2:9) and the Holy Spirit (see Isa. 42:1, in contrast to Isa. 42:8). This facilitates trusting surrender to him. Unlike any other religious leader, Jesus Christ is himself divine.

The appearance of Moses (representing the Law) and Elijah (representing the Prophets) with Jesus as his earthly ministry now turns toward passion and resurrection indicates that this is a culminating moment in redemptive history. The Law and the Prophets have led to this great provision of God's Son for his people. The passion is preceded by glory that assures Christ and his disciples of God's abiding purpose, and the consequence will be an even greater glory.

to themselves, [c]questioning what this rising
from the dead might mean. 11 And they asked
him, "Why do the scribes say [d]that first Elijah
must come?" 12 And he said to them, "Elijah
does come first [e]to restore all things. And [f]how
is it written of the Son of Man that he should
[g]suffer many things and [h]be treated with contempt? 13 But I tell you that Elijah has come,
and [i]they did to him whatever they pleased,
as it is written of him."

Jesus Heals a Boy with an Unclean Spirit

14 [j]And when they came to the disciples, they
saw a great crowd around them, and scribes
arguing with them. 15 And immediately all
the crowd, when they saw him, [k]were greatly
amazed and ran up to him and greeted him.
16 And he asked them, "What are you arguing
about with them?" 17 And someone from the
crowd answered him, "Teacher, I brought
my son to you, for he has [l]a spirit that makes
him mute. 18 And whenever it seizes him, it
throws him down, and he foams and grinds
his teeth and becomes rigid. So I asked your
disciples to cast it out, and [m]they were not
able." 19 And he answered them, "O [n]faithless
generation, [n]how long am I to be with you?
How long am I to bear with you? Bring him
to me." 20 And they brought the boy to him.
And when the spirit saw him, immediately it
[o]convulsed the boy, and he fell on the ground
and rolled about, foaming at the mouth. 21 And
Jesus asked his father, "How long has this been
happening to him?" And he said, "From childhood. 22 And it has often cast him into fire and
into water, to destroy him. But [p]if you can do
anything, have compassion on us and help
us." 23 And Jesus said to him, [p]"'If you can'!
[q]All things are possible for one who believes."
24 Immediately the father of the child cried
out[1] and said, "I believe; [r]help my unbelief!"
25 And when Jesus saw that [s]a crowd came
running together, he rebuked the unclean
spirit, saying to it, [t]"You mute and deaf spirit,
I command you, come out of him and never
enter him again." 26 And after crying out and
[o]convulsing him terribly, it came out, and the
boy was like a corpse, so that most of them
said, "He is dead." 27 But Jesus [u]took him by the
hand and lifted him up, and he arose. 28 And
when he had [v]entered the house, his disciples
asked him privately, "Why could we not cast it
out?" 29 And he said to them, "This kind cannot be driven out by anything but prayer."[2]

[1] Some manuscripts add *with tears* [2] Some manuscripts add *and fasting*

9:9–13 Jesus' command to silence (v. 9) is necessary, since his disciples still hold to a narrow, political, Davidic-royal expectation of the Messiah. While Peter has confessed Jesus as Messiah (8:29) by divine revelation (Matt. 16:17), he does not yet (Mark 8:32–33) grasp the true nature of Jesus as eternal Son of God (12:6; cf. Psalm 2) and as the Son of Man (Mark 8:38; Dan. 7:13–14) who must suffer to atone for our sins (Mark 10:45; Isa. 53:1–12).

As disciples of Christ, we must grow and mature in our hearts, wills, and minds toward concretely reflecting who Christ is, if we wish to have something to say and to give to others around us. Christlikeness in character is one way toward that end. Through the gospel, we are beckoned into such a life.

9:14–29 Jesus continues to struggle against evil demons and human opposition. The weapons against such things are prayer and faith. While his miracles are less emphasized in the second half of Mark, Jesus still undergirds his teaching by means of exorcism and healing (vv. 14–29; 10:46–52). Even though the divine nature of Jesus has now become apparent to the disciples, the struggle against opposition continues. The nature of the coming of the kingdom rule of God is thereby revealed. It does not arrive suddenly and fully but grows progressively, developing from inconspicuous weakness yet with certainty and determined invincibility (see the kingdom parables in 4:1–34).

Disciples are not necessarily protected from various effects of the fall, including sickness, oppression, suffering, and the various other difficulties of life. Prayer and even faith are gifts of God, through which Christ's disciples draw near to God in trust and surrender. We depend on our Lord, knowing that the struggle against spiritual and human opposition to his reconciling purposes has by no means ceased in our own day. A disciple's own physical well-being may (e.g., Acts 27:44) or may not (e.g., Acts 7:59–60) be sustained. But whatever happens to us, we remember that Christ has died and risen again, and we are eternally united to him who now sits at God's right hand. Our final glory and rest are assured.

10 [c] [John 16:17]
11 [d] See Matt. 11:14
12 [e] Mal. 4:6; Luke 1:16, 17; [Acts 1:6; 3:21] [f] Ps. 22:6, 7; Isa. 53:2, 3; Dan. 9:26; Zech. 13:7; [Phil. 2:7]; See Matt. 26:24 [g] See ch. 8:31 [h] Luke 23:11; Acts 4:11
13 [i] ch. 6:17, 27
14 [j] For ver. 14-28, see Matt. 17:14-19; Luke 9:37-42
15 [k] [ch. 10:32]
17 [l] ver. 25; Luke 11:14
18 [m] [ch. 6:7; Matt. 10:1; Luke 10:17]
19 [n] [John 14:9; 20:27]
20 [o] ch. 1:26
22 [p] [ch. 1:40; Matt. 9:28]
23 [p] [See ver. 22 above] [q] [ch. 6:5, 6; Matt. 17:20]
24 [r] [Luke 17:5]
25 [s] ver. 15 [t] ver. 17
26 [o] [See ver. 20 above]
27 [u] See ch. 1:31
28 [v] ch. 7:17

Jesus Again Foretells Death, Resurrection

30 [w]They went on from there and passed through Galilee. And he did not want anyone to know, 31 for he was teaching his disciples, saying to them, "The Son of Man is going to be delivered into the hands of men, and they will kill him. And when he is killed, [x]after three days he will rise." 32 [y]But they did not understand the saying, and were afraid to ask him.

Who Is the Greatest?

33 And [z]they came to Capernaum. And when he was in the house [a]he asked them, "What were you discussing on the way?" 34 But they kept silent, for on the way [b]they had argued with one another about who was the greatest. 35 And he sat down and called the twelve. And he said to them, [c]"If anyone would be first, he must be last of all and servant of all." 36 And he took a child and put him in the midst of them, and [d]taking him in his arms, he said to them, 37 [e]"Whoever receives one such child in my name receives me, and [e]whoever receives me, receives not me but him who sent me."

Anyone Not Against Us Is for Us

38 [f]John said to him, "Teacher, we saw someone [g]casting out demons in your name,[1] and [h]we tried to stop him, because he was not following us." 39 But Jesus said, "Do not stop him, for no one who does a mighty work in my name will be able soon afterward to speak evil of me. 40 [i]For the one who is not against us is for us. 41 For truly, I say to you, [j]whoever gives you a cup of water to drink because you belong to Christ will by no means lose his reward.

Temptations to Sin

42 [k]"Whoever causes one of [l]these little ones who believe in me to sin,[2] [m]it would be better for him if a great millstone were hung around his neck and he were thrown into the sea. 43 [n]And if your hand causes you to sin, cut it off. It is better for you to enter life crippled than with two hands to go to [o]hell,[3] to [p]the unquenchable fire.[4] 45 [q]And if your foot causes you to sin, cut it off. It is better for you to enter life lame than with two feet to be thrown into [o]hell. 47 [r]And if your eye causes you to sin, tear it out. It is better for you to enter the kingdom of God with one eye than with two eyes to be thrown into [s]hell, 48 'where [t]their worm does not die and the fire is not quenched.' 49 For everyone will be salted with fire.[5] 50 [v]Salt is good, [w]but if the salt has lost its saltiness, how will you make it salty again? [x]Have salt in yourselves, and [y]be at peace with one another."

Teaching About Divorce

10 [z]And he left there and went [a]to the region of Judea and beyond the Jordan, and crowds gathered to him again. And again, as was his custom, he taught them.

2 And Pharisees came up and in order [b]to test him asked, [c]"Is it lawful for a man to divorce his wife?" 3 He answered them, "What did Moses

[1] Some manuscripts add *who does not follow us* [2] Greek *to stumble*; also verses 43, 45, 47 [3] Greek *Gehenna*; also verse 47
[4] Some manuscripts add verses 44 and 46 (which are identical with verse 48) [5] Some manuscripts add *and every sacrifice will be salted with salt*

9:30–50 The crucial kingdom marks of humility and childlike trust are prominently featured throughout this section of Mark (vv. 35–50; 10:35–44). The disciples are to pursue a style of servant leadership which stands in sharp contrast to the oppressive approach of the political and religious leaders around them that is so natural to every human mind apart from the gospel.

Jesus does not encourage a follower to be childish; rather, he emphasizes that a follower must be *childlike* in trust and humble simplicity. The power of humility lies in the fact that it does not boast in or rely on its own strength, but trusts instead in him who is powerful and infinitely resourceful (cf. 2 Cor. 1:8–9). Humility is not self-seeking; rather, it seeks to pursue God's purposes in God's way. Though it feels like weakness, therefore, humility is in fact deeply powerful. Servant leadership is one expression of humility. It is the path Jesus himself took in suffering and dying for us.

10:1–12 The Pharisees brought up an ethical question concerning marriage, in an attempt to brand Jesus as an opponent of the law of Moses (v. 2). If Jesus' opponents succeeded, Jesus would be known as a man who spoke against God's revealed Word. Instead, Jesus once more exposes the hard-heartedness (v. 5) of those who sought to live out the law in only an external way.

30 [w]For ver. 30-32, see Matt. 17:22, 23; Luke 9:43-45; [ch. 8:31; 10:32-34]
31 [x]See ch. 8:31
32 [y]ch. 6:52; Luke 2:50; 18:34; 24:25; John 10:6; 12:16; 16:17-19; [ver. 10]
33 [z]Matt. 17:24 [a]For ver. 33-37, see Matt. 18:1-5; Luke 9:46-48; [ch. 10:35-45]
34 [b]Luke 22:24; [ver. 50]
35 [c]ch. 10:43, 44; Matt. 20:26, 27; 23:11, 12; Luke 22:26
36 [d]ch. 10:16
37 [e][Matt. 10:40, 42]
38 [f]For ver. 38-40, see Luke 9:49, 50 [g]ch. 16:17; Matt. 7:22; Luke 10:17; Acts 19:13; [Matt. 12:27] [h][Num. 11:28]
40 [i][Matt. 12:30; Luke 11:23]
41 [j]See Matt. 10:42
42 [k]Matt. 18:6; Luke 17:2; [1 Cor. 8:12] [l][Zech. 13:7] [m][ch. 14:21]
43 [n]Matt. 5:30; 18:8 [o]See Matt. 5:22, 29 [p]ver. 48; Matt. 3:12; See Matt. 25:41 **45** [q]Matt. 18:8 [o][See ver. 43 above] **47** [r]Matt. 5:29; 18:9 [s]See Matt. 5:22, 29 **48** [t]Isa. 66:24 **50** [v]Luke 14:34 [w]Matt. 5:13 [x]Ezek. 43:24; Col. 4:6; [Eph. 4:29] [y]Rom. 12:18; 2 Cor. 13:11; 1 Thess. 5:13; [ver. 34]; See Rom. 14:19 **Chapter 10** **1** [z]For ver. 1-12, see Matt. 19:1-9 [a]Luke 9:51; 17:11; John 10:40; [Matt. 4:25] **2** [b]See John 8:6 [c]Matt. 5:31

command you?" 4 They said, [d]"Moses allowed a
man to write a certificate of divorce and to send
her away." 5 And Jesus said to them, "Because
of your [e]hardness of heart he wrote you this
commandment. 6 But [f]from the beginning of
creation, 'God made them [g]male and female.'
7 [h]'Therefore a man shall leave his father and
mother and hold fast to his wife,[1] 8 and [i]the two
shall become one flesh.' So they are no longer
two but one flesh. 9 [j]What therefore God has
joined together, let not man separate."

10 And in the house the disciples asked him
again about this matter. 11 And he said to them,
[k]"Whoever divorces his wife and marries
another commits adultery against her, 12 and [l]if
she divorces her husband and marries another,
she commits adultery."

Let the Children Come to Me

13 [m]And they were bringing children to him
that he might touch them, and the disciples
[n]rebuked them. 14 But when Jesus saw it, he
was indignant and said to them, [o]"Let the children come to me; [p]do not hinder them, for to
such belongs the kingdom of God. 15 [q]Truly,
I say to you, whoever does not [r]receive the
kingdom of God like a child shall not enter it."
16 And [s]he took them in his arms and blessed
them, [t]laying his hands on them.

The Rich Young Man

17 [u]And as he was setting out on his journey, a man ran up and [v]knelt before him and
asked him, "Good Teacher, what must I do
to [w]inherit eternal life?" 18 And Jesus said to
him, "Why do you call me good? No one is
good except God alone. 19 You know the commandments: [x]'Do not murder, Do not commit adultery, Do not steal, Do not bear false
witness, Do not defraud, Honor your father
and mother.'" 20 And he said to him, "Teacher,
[y]all these I have kept from my youth." 21 And
Jesus, [z]looking at him, [a]loved him, and said
to him, "You lack one thing: go, [b]sell all that
you have and give to the poor, and you will
have [c]treasure in heaven; and come, follow
me." 22 [d]Disheartened by the saying, he went
away sorrowful, for he had great possessions.

[1] Some manuscripts omit *and hold fast to his wife*

The follower of Christ is, above all, a person whose heart is not self-seeking or self-defensive. Rather, the inner being of a disciple of Christ has been so softened that the need for a radical change is recognized—which affects his or her attitude (in this context) toward marriage and divorce. While there are many painful circumstances in marriage, the grace of God can manifest itself in the softening of one or both parties toward God and thus toward each other. Christ's disciples are empowered to live in such a way, laying down what feels to them to be their rights, because Jesus himself laid down his rights on their behalf to purchase them as his own bride.

10:13–16 The mercy of God's purposes extends to all people, including those who are not esteemed in a given society. As a deliberate example of this, Jesus loves and blesses children. He reminds us that it is childlike simplicity and trust that marks those who belong to God's kingdom. Intellectual sophistication, physical abilities, social popularity, or any of the world's ways of assessing worth are not the scale by which God measures significance and welcomes people into his presence.

A follower of Christ must search his heart regarding human beings who are ill-regarded in the prevailing ethnic, racial, or social environment. The kingdom of God opposes such "profiling." Every human being is made in the image of God and therefore has innate dignity, and thus ought not to be undervalued; and every Christian is still a fallen person and therefore ought not to *overvalue* himself.

10:17–22 Jesus highlights the serious conflict of interests between the pursuit of material wealth and entry into God's kingdom (v. 23). As Jesus puts it in Matthew's Gospel, no one can serve both God and money (Matt. 6:24). Our ultimate allegiance funnels down into one thing only.

Material wealth (e.g., Ps. 39:6; 49:6; Prov. 23:4; 28:22) can give a false and delusionary sense of security whereby trust in and dependence on God seems unnecessary. The young man was strictly obedient to the law of Moses. Yet his great wealth came to blind him to the idolatry that was in his life; while he kept the horizontal commandments (having to do with loving one's neighbor), he had failed to keep the vertical commandments (having to do with loving God). The fact that he had broken the very first vertical commandment ("You shall have no other gods before

4 [d] Deut. 24:1-4
5 [e] ch. 16:14; [ch. 3:5; 6:52; Heb. 3:8]
6 [f] ch. 13:19; 2 Pet. 3:4; [Rom. 1:20] [g] Cited from Gen. 1:27; 5:2
7 [h] Eph. 5:31; Cited from Gen. 2:24
8 [i] 1 Cor. 6:16; [Mal. 2:15]
9 [j] 1 Cor. 7:10
11 [k] See Matt. 5:32
12 [l] 1 Cor. 7:11, 13
13 [m] For ver. 13-16, see Matt. 19:13-15; Luke 18:15-17 [n] ver. 48
14 [o] Matt. 18:3 [p] [ch. 9:39]
15 [q] [John 3:3, 5] [r] [Luke 8:13; James 1:21]
16 [s] ch. 9:36 [t] Rev. 1:17
17 [u] For ver. 17-30, see Matt. 19:16-29; Luke 18:18-30; [Luke 10:25-28] [v] See ch. 1:40 [w] [Matt. 19:16]; See Matt. 25:34
19 [x] Rom. 13:9; Cited from Ex. 20:12-16; Deut. 5:16-20; [Matt. 5:21, 27]
20 [y] [Phil. 3:6]
21 [z] ver. 27; Luke 22:61; John 1:42; [ch. 3:5] [a] [John 11:5; 13:23] [b] Luke 12:33; [Luke 16:9; 19:8; Acts 2:45; 4:34, 35; 1 Tim. 6:18, 19] [c] Matt. 6:19, 20
22 [d] [Ezek. 33:31]

23 And Jesus [e]looked around and said to his
disciples, [f]"How difficult it will be for those
who have wealth to enter [g]the kingdom of
God!" 24 And the disciples [h]were amazed at
his words. But Jesus said to them again,
[i]"Children, [j]how difficult it is[1] to enter [g]the
kingdom of God! 25 It is easier for a camel to go
through the eye of a needle than for a rich person to enter [g]the kingdom of God." 26 And they
were exceedingly astonished, and said to him,[2]
"Then who can be saved?" 27 Jesus [k]looked at
them and said, [l]"With man it is impossible,
but not with God. For all things are possible
with God." 28 Peter began to say to him, "See,
[m]we have left everything and followed you."
29 Jesus said, "Truly, I say to you, [n]there is no
one who has left house or brothers or sisters or
mother or father or children or lands, for my
sake and [o]for the gospel, 30 who will not receive
a hundredfold [p]now in this time, houses and
brothers and sisters and mothers and children
and lands, [q]with persecutions, and in [r]the age
to come eternal life. 31 But [s]many who are first
will be last, and the last first."

Jesus Foretells His Death a Third Time

32 [t]And they were on the road, going up to
Jerusalem, and [u]Jesus was walking ahead of
them. And [v]they were amazed, and those who
followed were afraid. And taking the twelve
again, he began to tell them what was to
happen to him, 33 saying, "See, [w]we are going
up to Jerusalem, and the Son of Man will be
delivered over to the chief priests and the
scribes, and they will [x]condemn him to death
and [y]deliver him over to the Gentiles. 34 And
they will [z]mock him and [a]spit on him, and
flog him and kill him. And [b]after three days
he will rise."

The Request of James and John

35 [c]And James and John, [d]the sons of Zebedee,
came up to him and said to him, "Teacher, we
want you to do for us [e]whatever we ask of
you." 36 And he said to them, [f]"What do you
want me to do for you?" 37 And they said to
him, "Grant us [g]to sit, one at your right hand
and one at your left, [h]in your glory." 38 Jesus
said to them, [i]"You do not know what you
are asking. Are you able [j]to drink the cup that
I drink, or [k]to be baptized with the baptism
with which I am baptized?" 39 And they said
to him, "We are able." And Jesus said to them,
[l]"The cup that I drink [m]you will drink, and
with the baptism with which I am baptized,
[n]you will be baptized, 40 but to sit at my right

[1] Some manuscripts add *for those who trust in riches* [2] Some manuscripts *to one another*

23 [e] See ch. 3:5 [f] [1 Cor. 1:26]; See Matt. 13:22 [g] See Matt. 12:28
24 [h] ver. 32 [i] ch. 2:5 (Gk.); [John 13:33; 21:5] [j] Job 31:24; Ps. 49:6; 52:7; Prov. 11:28; 1 Tim. 6:17 [g] [See ver. 23 above]
25 [g] [See ver. 23 above]
27 [k] ver. 23 [l] ch. 14:36; Gen. 18:14; Job 42:2; Jer. 32:17, 27; Luke 1:37
28 [m] ch. 1:18, 20; Matt. 4:20, 22
29 [n] [Luke 14:26] [o] See ch. 8:35
30 [p] [Matt. 6:33] [q] 2 Cor. 12:10; 2 Thess. 1:4; 2 Tim. 3:11, 12; [John 15:20; Acts 14:22] [r] Matt. 12:32; Eph. 1:21; [Luke 20:35]
31 [s] See Matt. 19:30
32 [t] For ver. 32-34, see Matt. 20:17-19; Luke 18:31-33 [u] Luke 9:51; 19:28 [v] ver. 24
33 [w] See Matt. 16:21 [x] Matt. 26:66; John 19:7 [y] Matt. 27:2; John 18:30, 31; Acts 3:13; [Acts 2:23; 4:27; 21:11]
34 [z] Matt. 27:26-31 [a] ch. 14:65; 15:19; See Matt. 26:67 [b] See ch. 8:31
35 [c] For ver. 35-45, see Matt. 20:20-28 [d] ch. 1:19 [e] [Matt. 18:19]
36 [f] ver. 51
37 [g] [Matt. 19:28] [h] [Luke 9:26]
38 [i] [Luke 9:33; 23:34] [j] ch. 14:36; Matt. 26:29, 42; Luke 22:42; John 18:11; [Isa. 51:22] [k] Luke 12:50
39 [l] [Rom. 8:17; Phil. 3:10] [m] Acts 12:2; Rev. 1:9 [n] [Rom. 6:3]

me"; Ex. 20:3) becomes evident in two ways. First, the young man gives himself the status of God, claiming to be good, when Jesus has just told him, "No one is good except God alone" (cf. Mark 10:18, 20). Second, the young man makes it clear, when asking for God's blessing, that his real god is money. If he would turn his worship and trust from that god to the true God, the way would be open for him to be welcomed into the kingdom of God as a disciple of Jesus. While not every believer is called to give up all of his or her money, we are all called to put God's priorities above all else.

10:23–31 The disciples are "exceedingly astonished" by Jesus (v. 26) because, in first-century Judaism, wealth was associated with the blessing of God (cf. Job 1:1–3). If it was impossible for the rich to enter the kingdom, then, what hope could there be for anyone?

Once again Jesus turns upside down the natural assumptions of his disciples about the way the kingdom works. Because it is childlike trust (Mark 10:13–16) and not outward "blessings" such as wealth that qualifies one for the kingdom, the entrance into God's favor is effectively inverted from what is naturally expected. As Jesus puts it, "many who are first will be last, and the last first" (v. 31). All this is true because Jesus himself—the "first" if ever there was one—made himself "last" by going to a cross, so that those who simply acknowledge they are "last" can receive the grace of being "first"—forgiven and restored to fellowship with God as part of his kingdom.

10:32–45 Jesus again focuses on humility and servant leadership, which would be uniquely exemplified in his impending substitutionary atonement (v. 45). Jesus describes his own death and resurrection by means of the metaphors of the "cup" (cf. Isa. 51:17–23; Jer. 25:15–28) and of "baptism" (cf. Job 22:11). Both describe a severe though temporary judgment of God. In Isaiah and Jeremiah, the judgment of God begins with Jerusalem and then extends to the nations that oppress Judah (see Isa. 51:22–23; Jer. 25:29). Surprisingly, Jesus is the first to take the cup of judgment

hand or at my left is not mine to grant, [o]but it
is for those for whom it has been [p]prepared."
41 And when the ten heard it, they began to
be indignant at James and John. 42 [q]And Jesus
called them to him and said to them, "You
know that those who are considered rulers of
the Gentiles [r]lord it over them, and their great
ones exercise authority over them. 43 But [s]it
shall not be so among you. But whoever would
be great among you must be your servant,[1]
44 and whoever would be first among you must
be [t]slave[2] of all. 45 For even the Son of Man
came not to be served but [u]to serve, and [v]to
give his life as a ransom for [w]many."

Jesus Heals Blind Bartimaeus

46 [x]And they came to Jericho. And [y]as he
was leaving Jericho with his disciples and a
great crowd, Bartimaeus, [z]a blind beggar, the
son of Timaeus, was sitting by the roadside.
47 And when he heard that it was [a]Jesus of
Nazareth, he began to cry out and say, "Jesus,
Son of David, have mercy on me!" 48 And many
[b]rebuked him, telling him to be silent. But
he cried out all the more, "Son of David, have
mercy on me!" 49 And Jesus stopped and said,
"Call him." And they called the blind man, saying to him, [c]"Take heart. Get up; he is calling
you." 50 And throwing off his [d]cloak, he sprang
up and came to Jesus. 51 And Jesus said to him,
[e]"What do you want me to do for you?" And
the blind man said to him, [f]"Rabbi, let me
recover my sight." 52 And Jesus said to him,
"Go your way; [g]your faith has [h]made you well."
And immediately he recovered his sight and
followed him on the way.

The Triumphal Entry

11 [i]Now when they drew near to Jerusalem,
to [j]Bethphage and Bethany, at [k]the
Mount of Olives, Jesus[3] sent [l]two of his disciples 2 and said to them, "Go into the village in front of you, and immediately as you
enter it you will find a colt tied, [m]on which
no one has ever sat. Untie it and bring it. 3 If
anyone says to you, 'Why are you doing this?'

[1] Greek *diakonos* [2] Greek *bondservant* (*doulos*) [3] Greek *he*

(Luke 12:50), thereby protecting his followers who will drink the cup and receive the baptism after him. Their judgment is thus converted into a purifying fire (Luke 3:16: "He will baptize you with the Holy Spirit and fire"; see also 1 Pet. 4:17). On account of the substitutionary atonement of him who drank the cup and underwent the baptism first (Mark 10:45), judgment of his followers has been averted.

A significant mark of discipleship is that of Christlike humility, which arises from purification in and through suffering. Based on the substitutionary atonement of Christ (v. 45), God works purity into the lives of his followers by means of purifying chastisement and discipline—as an expression of his love.

Servant leadership grows out of such God-surrendered humility, whereby the disciple intentionally serves those around him or her, seeking to employ his or her gifts for the sake of others. Christlike humility, especially in leadership, is neither oppressive (like the Gentile leaders; v. 42) nor spineless. The inner strength and power of humility lies in the fact that the follower of Christ relies fully on God: on his power, his purposes, and his resources. Such a humble person will be strong and persistent in God-dependent character and "weak" in self-reliance.

10:46–52 The healing of blind Bartimaeus echoes the two-stage healing of the blind man in 8:22–26. It also continues the theme that Jesus reaches toward the outcast as one who is equally invited to follow him, receive his saving atonement, and thus enter the kingdom of God. No matter who we are, Jesus' immense grace is sufficient. A future follower of Jesus must only call out as Bartimaeus did: "Son of David, have mercy on me!" (10:48).

We also see the gospel of grace in the subtle contrast of James and John with blind Bartimaeus. To both parties Jesus asks, "What do you want me to do for you?" (vv. 36, 51). Yet while James and John request glory, Bartimaeus requests mercy. James and John, though physically seeing, were spiritually blind. Bartimaeus, though physically blind, was spiritually seeing. It is on those who know their need, not those who assume their superiority, that God pours out mercy.

11:1–11 Jesus' entry into Jerusalem fuels messianic expectations (v. 10). Note the messianic but also divine overtones of Zechariah 9:9 (Yahweh as King): "Rejoice greatly, O daughter of Zion! . . . Behold, your king is coming to you; righteous and

40 [o][Matt. 19:11] [p]Matt. 25:34
42 [q]For ver. 42-45, [ch. 9:33-36; Luke 22:25-27] [r]1 Pet. 5:3
43 [s]Matt. 23:11; [Luke 9:48]
44 [t]2 Cor. 4:5
45 [u]John 13:4, 13-15; Phil. 2:7; [2 Cor. 8:9] [v]Isa. 53:10; Dan. 9:26; John 10:15; 11:51, 52; Rom. 4:25; Gal. 1:4; 2:20; 1 Tim. 2:6; Titus 2:14; 1 Pet. 1:18, 19 [w]ch. 14:24; Isa. 53:11, 12; Heb. 2:10; 9:28; [Rom. 5:15; Rev. 5:9]
46 [x]For ver. 46-52, see Matt. 20:29-34; Luke 18:35-43 [y][Luke 18:35; 19:1] [z]John 9:1, 8
47 [a]ch. 1:24
48 [b]Matt. 19:13
49 [c]John 16:33
50 [d]ch. 13:16 (Gk.)
51 [e]ver. 36 [f]John 20:16
52 [g]ch. 5:34; Matt. 9:22; Luke 7:50; 8:48; 17:19 [h]ch. 5:23, 28; 6:56

Chapter 11
1 [i]For ver. 1-10, see Matt. 21:1-9; Luke 19:29-38; John 12:12-15; [Zech. 9:9] [j]Matt. 21:17; Luke 24:50; John 11:18 [k]Zech. 14:4; Matt. 24:3; 26:30; John 8:1; [Acts 1:12] [l][ch. 14:13]
2 [m][Luke 23:53]

say, 'The Lord has need of it and will send
it back here immediately.' " 4 And they went
away and found a colt tied at a door outside
in the street, and they untied it. 5 And some
of those standing there said to them, "What
are you doing, untying the colt?" 6 And they
told them what Jesus had said, and they let
them go. 7 And they brought the colt to Jesus
and threw their cloaks on it, and he sat on
it. 8 And many [n]spread their cloaks on the
road, and others spread leafy branches that
they had cut from the fields. 9 And those who
went before and those who followed were
shouting, [o]"Hosanna! [p]Blessed is he who
comes in the name of the Lord! 10 Blessed is
[q]the coming [r]kingdom of [s]our father [r]David!
[o]Hosanna [t]in the highest!"

11 [u]And he entered Jerusalem and went into
the temple. And when he had looked around
at everything, as it was already late, [v]he went
out to Bethany with the twelve.

Jesus Curses the Fig Tree

12 [w]On the following day, when they came
from Bethany, [x]he was hungry. 13 [y]And seeing in
the distance a fig tree in leaf, he went to see if
he could find anything on it. When he came to
it, he found nothing but leaves, for [z]it was not
the season for figs. 14 And he said to it, "May
no one ever eat fruit from you again." And his
disciples heard it.

Jesus Cleanses the Temple

15 [a]And they came to Jerusalem. And he
entered the temple and began to drive out
those who sold and those who bought in the
temple, and he overturned the tables of [b]the
money-changers and the seats of those who
sold [c]pigeons. 16 And he would not allow anyone to carry anything through the temple.
17 And he was teaching them and saying to
them, "Is it not written, [d]'My house shall be
called a house of prayer for all the nations'?
But [e]you have made it a den of robbers." 18 And
the chief priests and the scribes heard it and
[f]were seeking a way to destroy him, for they
feared him, because [g]all the crowd was astonished at his teaching. 19 [h]And when evening
came they[1] went out of the city.

[1] Some manuscripts *he*

8 [n]2 Kgs. 9:13
9 [o]See Ps. 118:25 (Heb.) [p]Matt. 23:39; Cited from Ps. 118:26
10 [q]See Luke 1:32 [r][Ezek. 37:24, 25] [s][Acts 2:29] [o][See ver. 9 above] [t]Luke 2:14; [Ps. 148:1]
11 [u]Matt. 21:10 [v]ver. 19; Matt. 21:17
12 [w]For ver. 12-14, see Matt. 21:18, 19 [x]Matt. 4:2
13 [y][Luke 13:6-9] [z]ch. 13:28
15 [a]For ver. 15-18, see Matt. 21:12-16; Luke 19:45-47; [John 2:14-16] [b][Ex. 30:13] [c]Lev. 1:14; 5:7; 12:8; Luke 2:24
17 [d]Cited from Isa. 56:7 [e]Jer. 7:11
18 [f]See Matt. 21:46 [g]See Matt. 7:28
19 [h]Luke 21:37; [ver. 11]

having salvation is he, humble and mounted on a donkey . . . ." Jesus visits Jerusalem in humility and zeal for true worship of God from people of all nations. Given the fact that Jesus already displayed his divine nature (esp. Mark 2:5–12; 9:2–7), the entry into Jerusalem and the cleansing of the temple (11:15–19) must be seen as God visiting the center of Israel: the city and its temple.

The infinite God comes to be with his people, both where they live and where they worship. But in both he finds a rejection of his ways that he must cleanse and correct.

11:12–25 Jesus juxtaposes the fruitless temple, signified by cursing the fig tree and cleansing the temple, with sincere trust in God (v. 22). Only through faith in God and his work do followers bear acceptable fruit of worship, prayer, and godliness (vv. 12–25).

Jesus is serious about true worship and prayer in—and among—his people (see Isa. 61:11), since they are becoming the new and eternal temple of God (Mark 12:10–11; 14:58; 15:29, 38; 1 Cor. 3:16–17; 6:19; 2 Cor. 6:16; Eph. 2:21; 1 Pet. 2:5; cf. Ps. 118:22; Matt. 12:6; John 2:19; Rev. 21:22). Because God's chosen people of ethnic Israel had proven to be a fruitless fig tree, God is extending his kingdom to every corner of the globe, to any who will receive the gospel in childlike trust in Christ.

11:12–14 The untimely cursing of the fig tree, which cannot bear fruit out of season, makes sense only if it is seen as representing the fruitless temple, which should bear fruit at any time. What befalls the fig tree will befall the fruitless temple (in A.D. 70; see 13:2).

The disciples of Christ are called to bear the fruit of godliness (e.g., worship and prayer) in all areas of life, as well as to give holistic testimony to others.

11:15–19 Jesus cleanses the temple (cf. 2 Chron. 29:16) because the temple is meant to display the fruit of true worship, not corrupt commerce and personal gain (1 Chron. 29:10–19; 2 Chron. 6:14–42). The temple is meant to draw people from all nations to the purity of God (cf. 2 Chron. 7:1–3).

The Lesson from the Withered Fig Tree

20 [i]As they passed by in the morning, they saw the fig tree withered away to its roots. 21 And Peter remembered and said to him, [j]"Rabbi, look! The fig tree that you cursed has withered." 22 And Jesus answered them, "Have [k]faith in God. 23 [l]Truly, I say to you, whoever says to this mountain, [m]'Be taken up and thrown into the sea,' and does not [n]doubt in his heart, but [o]believes that what he says will come to pass, it will be done for him. 24 Therefore I tell you, [p]whatever you ask in prayer, [o]believe that you [q]have received[1] it, and it will be yours. 25 And whenever [r]you stand praying, [s]forgive, [t]if you have anything against anyone, so that [u]your Father also who is in heaven may forgive you your trespasses."[2]

The Authority of Jesus Challenged

27 [v]And they came again to Jerusalem. And as he was walking in the temple, the chief priests and the scribes and the elders came to him, 28 and they said to him, [w]"By what authority are you doing these things, or who gave you this authority to do them?" 29 Jesus said to them, "I will ask you one question; answer me, and I will tell you by what authority I do these things. 30 Was the baptism of John [x]from heaven or from man? Answer me." 31 And they discussed it with one another, saying, "If we say, 'From heaven,' he will say, [y]'Why then did you not believe him?' 32 But shall we say, 'From man'?"—[z]they were afraid of the people, for they all held that John really was [a]a prophet. 33 So they answered Jesus, "We do not know." And Jesus said to them, "Neither will I tell you by what authority I do these things."

The Parable of the Tenants

12 [b]And he began to speak to them in parables. "A man planted [c]a vineyard [d]and put a fence around it and dug a pit for the winepress and built a tower, and [e]leased it to tenants and [f]went into another country. 2 When the season came, he sent a servant[3] to the tenants to get from them some of the fruit of the vineyard. 3 [g]And they took him and beat him and sent him away empty-handed. 4 [g]Again [h]he sent to them another servant, and [i]they struck him on the head and [j]treated him shamefully. 5 [g]And he sent another, and him they killed. And so with many others: some they beat, and some they killed. 6 He had still one other, [k]a beloved son. [l]Finally he sent him to them, saying, 'They will respect my son.' 7 But those tenants said to one another, [m]'This is the heir. Come, [n]let us kill him, and the inheritance will be ours.' 8 And they took him and killed him and [o]threw him out of the vineyard. 9 What will the owner of the vineyard do? [p]He will [q]come and destroy the tenants and [r]give the vineyard to others. 10 [s]Have you not read [t]this Scripture:

> [u]"'The stone that the builders rejected
> has become the cornerstone;[4]
> 11 this was the Lord's doing,
> and it is marvelous in our eyes'?"

12 And [v]they were seeking to arrest him [w]but feared the people, for they perceived that he

[1] Some manuscripts *are receiving* [2] Some manuscripts add verse 26: *But if you do not forgive, neither will your Father who is in heaven forgive your trespasses* [3] Greek *bondservant*; also verse 4 [4] Greek *the head of the corner*

God gives his disciples the Spirit of fire (cf. Luke 3:17). The mercy and grace of God has a purifying effect in their lives as living stones of his eternal temple (Eph. 2:21; 1 Pet. 2:4–5).

11:22–25 True worship of God is foundational to a healthy, God-designed life. Above all, it is the right response to the character and nature of God. Followers of Christ can pray boldly and confidently (with faith) toward the end that God would remove all hindrances (the figurative meaning of "mountain") to true worship of the triune God. However, this boldness can never be manipulative or coercive toward other human beings. We are to trust God. Jesus commands having "faith in God," not in the plans and priorities of finite human wisdom. Christ's focus lies always on surrendered trust in God's sovereign power, ability, and will. Surprisingly, lack of forgiveness is the first "mountain" to be removed in order for true worship to flourish.

20 [i]For ver. 20-24, see Matt. 21:19-22
21 [j]See John 1:38
22 [k]Eph. 3:12; Phil. 3:9
23 [l]Matt. 17:20 [m][Ps. 46:2; 1 Cor. 13:2; Rev. 8:8] [n]Rom. 4:20; 14:23; James 1:6 [o][ch. 16:17; John 14:12]
24 [p]See Matt. 7:7 [o][See ver. 23 above] [q][Isa. 65:24; Matt. 6:8]
25 [r]Matt. 6:5; Luke 18:11 [s]See Matt. 6:14 [t]Col. 3:13; [Matt. 5:23; 6:15] [u]Matt. 7:11
27 [v]For ver. 27-33, see Matt. 21:23-27; Luke 20:1-8
28 [w][Ex. 2:14; John 1:25; Acts 4:7]

30 [x]Luke 15:18, 21; John 3:27 **31** [y]Matt. 21:32; Luke 7:30 **32** [z]Matt. 14:5; 21:46 [a][John 5:35]; See Matt. 11:9 **Chapter 12** **1** [b]For ver. 1-12, see Matt. 21:33-46; Luke 20:9-19 [c]Ps. 80:8; Isa. 5:1; Matt. 21:28 [d]Isa. 5:2 [e]Song 8:11, 12 [f]ch. 13:34; Matt. 25:14, 15 **3** [g]Matt. 5:12; 22:6; 23:34, 37; [2 Chr. 24:19; 36:15, 16; Neh. 9:26; Jer. 37:15; 38:6; Acts 7:52; 2 Cor. 11:24-26; 1 Thess. 2:15; Heb. 11:36, 37] **4** [g][See ver. 3 above] [h]Matt. 22:4 [i][Acts 14:19] [j]Acts 5:41 (Gk.) **5** [g][See ver. 3 above] **6** [k]See Matt. 3:17 [l][Heb. 1:1] **7** [m]Heb. 1:2; [John 1:11; Rom. 8:17] [n][1 Kgs. 21:19] **8** [o]Heb. 13:12 **9** [p][Luke 19:27] [q][Matt. 24:50; 25:19] [r]Matt. 21:43; Acts 13:46; 18:6; 28:28; [Matt. 8:11, 12] **10** [s]See Matt. 21:16 [t]Luke 4:21; Acts 8:35 [u]Acts 4:11; 1 Pet. 2:7; Cited from Ps. 118:22, 23 **12** [v]ch. 11:18; Luke 19:47, 48; John 7:25, 30, 44; [Matt. 26:4] [w]ch. 11:32

had told the parable against them. So they [x]left him and went away.

Paying Taxes to Caesar

13 [y]And they sent to him some of [z]the Pharisees and some of [z]the Herodians, to [a]trap him in his talk. 14 And they came and said to him, "Teacher, [b]we know that you are true and do not care about anyone's opinion. For [c]you are not swayed by appearances,[1] but truly teach [d]the way of God. Is it lawful to pay [e]taxes to [f]Caesar, or not? Should we pay them, or should we not?" 15 But, knowing [g]their hypocrisy, he said to them, "Why [h]put me to the test? Bring me [i]a denarius[2] and let me look at it." 16 And they brought one. And he said to them, "Whose likeness and inscription is this?" They said to him, "Caesar's." 17 Jesus said to them, [j]"Render to Caesar the things that are Caesar's, and to God the things that are God's." And they marveled at him.

The Sadducees Ask About the Resurrection

18 And [k]Sadducees came to him, [l]who say that there is no resurrection. And they asked him a question, saying, 19 "Teacher, Moses wrote for us that [m]if a man's brother dies and leaves a wife, but leaves no child, the man[3] must take the widow and raise up offspring for his brother. 20 There were seven brothers; the first took a wife, and when he died left no offspring. 21 And the second took her, and died, leaving no offspring. And the third likewise. 22 And the seven left no offspring. Last of all the woman also died. 23 In the resurrection, when they rise again, whose wife will she be? For the seven had her as wife."

24 Jesus said to them, "Is this not the reason you are wrong, because [n]you know neither the Scriptures nor [o]the power of God? 25 For when they rise from the dead, they neither [p]marry nor [p]are given in marriage, but are like angels in heaven. 26 And as for the dead being raised, [q]have you not read in [r]the book of Moses, in [s]the passage about the bush, how God spoke to him, saying, [t]'I am the God of Abraham, and the God of Isaac, and the God of Jacob'? 27 He is not God of the dead, but of the living. You are quite wrong."

The Great Commandment

28 [u]And one of the scribes came up and heard them disputing with one another, and seeing that he answered them well, asked him, "Which commandment is the most important of all?" 29 Jesus answered, "The most important is, [v]'Hear, O Israel: The Lord our God, [w]the Lord is one. 30 And you shall love the Lord your God with all your heart and with all your soul and with all your mind and with all your strength.' 31 [x]The second is this: [y]'You shall love your neighbor as yourself.' There is no other commandment [z]greater than these." 32 And the scribe said to him, "You are right, Teacher. You have truly said that [w]he is one, and [a]there is no other besides him. 33 And to love him with all the heart and with all [b]the understanding and with all the strength, and to love one's neighbor as oneself, [c]is much more than all [d]whole burnt offerings and sacrifices." 34 And when Jesus saw that he answered wisely, he said to him, "You are not far from the kingdom of God." [e]And after that no one dared to ask him any more questions.

[1] Greek *you do not look at people's faces* [2] A *denarius* was a day's wage for a laborer [3] Greek *his brother*

12:13–37 Opposition to Jesus grows despite the fact that he cannot be convicted of breaking the law of Moses. Contrary to breaking the law, Jesus exposes hard-heartedness with regard to the proper interpretation of the law, here regarding taxes and divorce. He also challenges his opponents regarding the proper understanding of the Messiah of God, namely as the Lord of David (and not primarily a son of David; cf., however, 10:48). Jesus does not undercut the law of Moses; rather, his opponents reject or misinterpret it ("because you know neither the Scriptures nor the power of God"; 12:24). When a scribe displays a proper view of the chief commandments (see vv. 28–34, regarding Deut. 6:4–5 and Lev. 19:18), Jesus affirms him. Jesus thus arises as the Prophet-like-Moses, as the messianic interpreter of the law (cf. Matt. 5:17–20).

A disciple realizes that without the purification of the heart, other matters of life, such as a proper understanding of the law of Moses, ethics, and social issues, etc., cannot be addressed in a sustainable way. The eternal Son of God must effect such purification for there to be hope of lasting personal and social change.

12 [x] Matt. 22:22
13 [y] For ver. 13-27, see Matt. 22:15-32; Luke 20:20-38 [z] ch. 3:6; [ch. 8:15] [a] Luke 11:54
14 [b] [John 3:2] [c] See Acts 10:34 [d] Acts 18:25, 26; [Acts 13:10] [e] Matt. 17:25 [f] Luke 2:1; 3:1
15 [g] Matt. 23:28; Luke 12:1 [h] See John 8:6 [i] See Matt. 18:28
17 [j] Rom. 13:7
18 [k] Matt. 3:7; 16:1; 22:34; Acts 4:1; 5:17; 23:6 [l] Acts 23:8; [Acts 4:2]
19 [m] [Deut. 25:5]
24 [n] John 20:9 [o] 1 Cor. 6:14
25 [p] Matt. 24:38; Luke 17:27
26 [q] See Matt. 21:16 [r] [Luke 3:4; 20:42; Acts 1:20; 7:42] [s] Ex. 3:1-4, 17 [t] Acts 7:32; Cited from Ex. 3:6

28 [u] For ver. 28-34, see Matt. 22:34-40, 46; [Luke 10:25-28] **29** [v] Luke 10:27; Cited from Deut. 6:4, 5 [w] Rom. 3:30; 1 Cor. 8:4, 6; Gal. 3:20; Eph. 4:6; 1 Tim. 1:17; 2:5; James 2:19; 4:12; Jude 25; [Matt. 19:17; 23:9] **31** [x] [1 John 4:21] [y] Cited from Lev. 19:18; See Matt. 19:19 [z] [Matt. 23:23] **32** [w] [See ver. 29 above] [a] Cited from Deut. 4:35 (Gk.) **33** [b] Deut. 4:6; Luke 2:47; Col. 1:9; 2:2 [c] 1 Sam. 15:22; Hos. 6:6; Mic. 6:6-8; Matt. 9:13; 12:7 [d] Ps. 40:6; Heb. 10:6, 8 **34** [e] Luke 20:40

Whose Son Is the Christ?

35 [f]And as [g]Jesus taught in the temple, he said,
"How can the scribes say that [h]the Christ is the
son of David? 36 David himself, [i]in the Holy
Spirit, declared,

> [j]"'The Lord said to my Lord,
> "Sit at my right hand,
> until I put your enemies [k]under your
> feet."'

37 David himself calls him Lord. So [l]how is he
his son?" And the great throng [m]heard him
gladly.

Beware of the Scribes

38 [n]And in his teaching he said, "Beware of
the scribes, who like to walk around in long
robes and like greetings in the marketplaces
39 and have the best seats in the synagogues
and [o]the places of honor at feasts, 40 [p]who
devour widows' houses and [q]for a pretense
make long prayers. They will receive the
greater condemnation."

The Widow's Offering

41 [r]And he sat down opposite [s]the treasury
and watched the people [t]putting money into
the offering box. Many rich people put in large
sums. 42 And a poor widow came and put in
two [u]small copper coins, which make a penny.[1]
43 And he called his disciples to him and said
to them, "Truly, I say to you, [v]this poor widow
has put in more than all those who are contributing to the offering box. 44 For they all
contributed out of their abundance, but she
out of her [w]poverty has put in everything she
had, all [x]she had to live on."

Jesus Foretells Destruction of the Temple

13 [y]And as he came out of the temple,
one of his disciples said to him, "Look,
Teacher, what wonderful stones and what
wonderful buildings!" 2 And Jesus said to him,
"Do you see these great buildings? [z]There will
not be left here one stone upon another that
will not be thrown down."

Signs of the Close of the Age

3 And as he sat on [a]the Mount of Olives opposite the temple, [b]Peter and James and John
and [c]Andrew asked him [d]privately, 4 "Tell us,
[e]when will these things be, and what will be
the sign when all these things are about to
be accomplished?" 5 And Jesus began to say
to them, [f]"See that no one leads you astray.
6 [g]Many will come in my name, saying, [h]'I am
he!' and they will lead many astray. 7 And when
you hear of wars and rumors of wars, [i]do not
be alarmed. This [j]must take place, but the end
is not yet. 8 For [k]nation will rise against nation,
and [l]kingdom against kingdom. There will be
[m]earthquakes in various places; there will be
[n]famines. These are but the beginning of the
birth pains.
9 [o]"But [p]be on your guard. For they will
deliver you over to councils, and you will be

[1] Greek *two lepta*, which make a *kodrantes*; a *kodrantes* (Latin *quadrans*) was a Roman copper coin worth about 1/64 of a *denarius* (which was a day's wage for a laborer)

12:38–44 In sharp contrast to his proud and exploiting opponents, "who devour widows' houses" (v. 40), Jesus praises the sacrificial devotion of a poor widow. Her singular trust in God serves as a powerful example and as a penetrating window into God's opinion of true greatness and significance. The widow's devotion exposes the exploiting self-interest of those officials who handle temple taxes and tithes. Her devotion also indicates complete dependence on God. She gives all that she has, expecting him to provide all that she needs. Her willingness to put God's honor above all other priorities applies to us all, even as we carry out our biblical responsibilities to provide for the welfare of our families and communities.

Jesus does not separate belief from action. Authentic faith always bears the fruit of sincere and godly action. Vibrant faith cannot sit still; it must act in love (cf. James 2:14–26).

13:1–37 Jesus concludes his instructions with a look to the future, and warns his disciples to be alert to God's will and ways. Jesus points to imminent (regional) and future (cosmic) calamitous events. Disciples today need not speculate unnecessarily about specific future events. What is instead crucial is alertness regarding the essential mission of God, readiness to suffer, and trust in God's power to overcome all evil.

35 [f]For ver. 35-37, see Matt. 22:41-45; Luke 20:41-44 [g]See Matt. 26:55 [h]See Matt. 1:1, 17
36 [i][Luke 10:21; 1 Cor. 12:3] [j]Acts 2:34, 35; Heb. 1:13; Cited from Ps. 110:1; [1 Cor. 15:25; Heb. 10:13] [k][Acts 7:49]
37 [l][Rom. 1:3, 4] [m]ch. 6:20
38 [n]For ver. 38, 39, see Matt. 23:1, 2, 5-7; Luke 20:45, 46; [Luke 11:43]
39 [o]Luke 14:7, 8
40 [p][Luke 11:39; 16:14] [q][Matt. 6:5, 7]
41 [r]For ver. 41-44, see Luke 21:1-4 [s]Matt. 27:6; John 8:20 [t]2 Kgs. 12:9
42 [u]Luke 12:59
43 [v][2 Cor. 8:2, 12]
44 [w]Phil. 4:11 [x]Luke 8:43
Chapter 13
1 [y]For ver. 1-37, see Matt. 24:1-51; Luke 21:5-36
2 [z]Luke 19:44
3 [a]See Matt. 21:1 [b]Matt. 17:1 [c]ch. 1:16, 29 [d][ch. 4:34]

4 [e][Acts 1:6, 7] **5** [f]ver. 9, 23, 33; Jer. 29:8; Eph. 5:6; Col. 2:8; 1 Thess. 2:3; 1 John 3:7 **6** [g]ver. 22; Jer. 14:14; 1 John 2:18 [h]See John 8:24 **7** [i]2 Thess. 2:2 [j]Rev. 1:1 **8** [k]2 Chr. 15:6; [Rev. 6:4] [l]Isa. 19:2 [m]Rev. 6:12 [n]Acts 11:28; Rev. 6:8 **9** [o]For ver. 9, 11-13, [Matt. 10:17-22; Luke 12:11, 12] [p]ver. 5; 2 John 8

beaten [q]in synagogues, and you will stand
before [r]governors and [s]kings for my sake, [t]to
bear witness before them. 10 And the gospel
must first be proclaimed [u]to all nations. 11 And
when they bring you to trial and deliver you
over, [v]do not be anxious beforehand what you
are to say, but say [w]whatever is given you in
that hour, [x]for it is not you who speak, but
the Holy Spirit. 12 [y]And brother will deliver
brother over to death, and the father his child,
and children will rise against parents and have
them put to death. 13 [z]And you will be hated
by all for my name's sake. [a]But the one who
endures to the end will be saved.

The Abomination of Desolation

14 "But when you see [b]the abomination of
desolation standing where he ought not to be
([c]let the reader understand), then let those who
are in Judea flee to the mountains. 15 [d]Let the
one who is on [e]the housetop not go down, nor
enter his house, to take anything out, 16 and let
the one who is in the field not turn back to take
his cloak. 17 And [f]alas for women who are pregnant and for those who are nursing infants in
those days! 18 Pray that it may not happen in
winter. 19 For in those days there will be [g]such
[h]tribulation as has not been [i]from the beginning of the creation that [j]God created until
now, and never will be. 20 And if the Lord had
not cut short the days, no human being would
be saved. But for [k]the sake of the elect, whom
[l]he chose, he shortened the days. 21 And [m]then
if anyone says to you, 'Look, here is the Christ!'
or 'Look, there he is!' do not believe it. 22 [n]For
false christs and false prophets will arise and
[o]perform signs and wonders, [p]to lead astray, if
possible, [q]the elect. 23 But [r]be on guard; [s]I have
told you all things beforehand.

The Coming of the Son of Man

24 "But in those days, after [t]that tribulation,
[u]the sun will be darkened, and the moon will
not give its light, 25 and [v]the stars will be falling from heaven, and the powers in the heavens will be shaken. 26 And then they will see
[w]the Son of Man coming in clouds [x]with great
power and glory. 27 And then [y]he will send out
the angels and [z]gather [a]his elect from [b]the four
winds, from [c]the ends of the earth [d]to the ends
of heaven.

The Lesson of the Fig Tree

28 "From the fig tree learn its lesson: as soon
as its branch becomes tender and puts out its
leaves, you know that summer is near. 29 So
also, when you see these things taking place,
you know that he is near, [e]at the very gates.
30 [f]Truly, I say to you, this generation will not
pass away until all these things take place.
31 [g]Heaven and earth will pass away, but [h]my
words will not pass away.

No One Knows That Day or Hour

32 "But concerning that day or that hour, [i]no
one knows, not even the angels in heaven, [j]nor
the Son, [k]but only the Father. 33 [l]Be on guard,
[m]keep awake.[1] For you do not know when the
time will come. 34 [n]It is like a man [o]going on
a journey, when he leaves home and puts his
servants[2] in charge, [p]each with his work, and
commands [q]the doorkeeper to stay awake.
35 [r]Therefore stay awake—for you do not
know when the master of the house will come,
[s]in the evening, or [s]at midnight, or [t]when the
rooster crows,[3] or [u]in the morning— 36 lest [v]he
come suddenly and [w]find you asleep. 37 And
what I say to you I say to all: [r]Stay awake."

The Plot to Kill Jesus

14 [x]It was now two days before [y]the Passover and the Feast of Unleavened Bread.
And the chief priests and the scribes [z]were
seeking how to arrest him by stealth and kill
him, 2 for they said, "Not during the feast, [a]lest
there be an uproar from the people."

Jesus Anointed at Bethany

3 [b]And while he was at [c]Bethany in the house
of Simon the leper,[4] as he was reclining at

[1] Some manuscripts add *and pray* [2] Greek *bondservants* [3] That is, the third watch of the night, between midnight and 3 A.M. [4] *Leprosy* was a term for several skin diseases; see Leviticus 13

9 [q]See Matt. 23:34 [r]Acts 17:6; 18:12; 24:1; 25:6 [s][Acts 27:24] [t]See Matt. 8:4 **10** [u]Matt. 28:19; Rom. 10:18; Col. 1:6, 23; [ch. 14:9] **11** [v]See Matt. 6:25 [w]Deut. 18:18; [Num. 23:5]; See Ex. 4:12 [x]Acts 4:8; 6:10; 13:9; 1 Cor. 15:10; 2 Cor. 13:3; [1 Thess. 2:13; Heb. 1:1] **12** [y]Matt. 10:35, 36 **13** [z]John 15:18-21; [Luke 6:22] [a][Dan. 12:12, 13; James 5:11; Rev. 2:10]; See Heb. 3:6 **14** [b]Dan. 9:27; 11:31; 12:11 [c][Dan. 9:23, 25; Rev. 1:3] **15** [d]Luke 17:31 [e]See Luke 5:19 **17** [f]Luke 23:29 **19** [g]Rev. 16:18 [h]ver. 24; Dan. 12:1; [Rev. 7:14] [i]See ch. 10:6; [Deut. 4:32] [j]Gen. 1:1 **20** [k]ver. 22, 27; Isa. 65:8, 9; Luke 18:7; [Matt. 22:14] [l]John 13:18; 15:19; Eph. 1:4 **21** [m]Luke 17:23; [ver. 6] **22** [n][1 John 2:18] [o]Deut. 13:1-3; 2 Thess. 2:9-11; Rev. 13:13, 14; 16:14; 19:20; [Acts 8:9] [p]ver. 6 [q]ver. 20, 27 **23** [r]ver. 5 [s]John 13:19; 14:29; [2 Pet. 3:17] **24** [t]ver. 19 [u]Isa. 13:10; 24:23; Ezek. 32:7; Joel 2:10, 31; 3:15; Acts 2:20; [Amos 5:20; 8:9; Zeph. 1:15; Rev. 6:12; 8:12] **25** [v]Rev. 6:13; [Isa. 14:12; 34:4] **26** [w]See Dan. 7:13 [x]ch. 9:1; Matt. 26:64; [Matt. 25:31] **27** [y]Matt. 13:41 [z][Matt. 23:37; 2 Thess. 2:1] [a]ver. 20, 22 [b]Dan. 7:2; Zech. 2:6; Rev. 7:1 [c][Acts 1:8] [d]Deut. 4:32; 30:4 **29** [e][James 5:9; Rev. 3:20] **30** [f]See ch. 9:1 **31** [g]Ps. 102:26; Isa. 51:6; 2 Pet. 3:10; [Matt. 5:18; Heb. 12:27] [h]Ps. 119:89; Isa. 40:8; 1 Pet. 1:23, 25 **32** [i]Matt. 25:13; 1 Thess. 5:1, 2 [j][Phil. 2:6, 7] [k][Zech. 14:7; Acts 1:7] **33** [l]ver. 5 [m]Eph. 6:18; Heb. 13:17; [ch. 14:38] **34** [n][Matt. 25:14] [o][ch. 12:1; Matt. 21:33] [p][Rom. 12:6-8] [q]Ezek. 44:11; John 10:3; [Luke 12:36] **35** [r]ch. 14:34-38; Matt. 25:13; 26:41; Luke 12:37; 21:36; Acts 20:31; 1 Cor. 16:13; 1 Thess. 5:6; 1 Pet. 5:8 [s]ch. 1:32; Luke 12:38 [t]ch. 14:30, 68, 72 [u][ch. 6:48; Ex. 14:24] **36** [v][1 Thess. 5:1-6] [w]ch. 14:40 **37** [r][See ver. 35 above]
Chapter 14 **1** [x]For ver. 1, 2, see Matt. 26:2-5; Luke 22:1, 2 [y]See John 6:4 [z]John 11:53; See Matt. 21:46 **2** [a]Matt. 27:24 **3** [b]For ver. 3-9, see Matt. 26:6-13; John 12:1-8; [Luke 7:37-39] [c]Matt. 21:17; John 11:18

table, a woman came with an alabaster flask
of ointment of pure nard, very costly, and she
broke the flask and poured it over his head.
4 There were some who said to themselves
indignantly, "Why was the ointment wasted
like that? 5 For this ointment could have been
sold for more than three hundred denarii[1]
and [d]given to the poor." And they [e]scolded her.
6 But Jesus said, "Leave her alone. Why do you
trouble her? She has done a beautiful thing to
me. 7 For [f]you always have the poor with you,
and whenever [g]you want, you can do good for
them. But [h]you will not always have me. 8 [i]She
has done what she could; she has anointed my
body beforehand [j]for burial. 9 And truly, I say
to you, wherever [k]the gospel is proclaimed in
the whole world, what she has done will be
told [l]in memory of her."

Judas to Betray Jesus

10 [m]Then [n]Judas Iscariot, who was one of the
twelve, [n]went to the chief priests in order to
betray him to them. 11 And when they heard
it, they were glad and promised to give him
money. And he sought an opportunity to
[o]betray him.

The Passover with the Disciples

12 [p]And on [q]the first day of Unleavened Bread,
when they [r]sacrificed the Passover lamb, his
disciples said to him, "Where will you have
us go and prepare for you to eat the Passover?"
13 And he sent [s]two of his disciples and said to
them, "Go into the city, and a man carrying a
jar of water will meet you. Follow him, 14 and
wherever he enters, say to the master of the
house, [t]'The Teacher says, Where is [u]my guest
room, where I may eat the Passover with my
disciples?' 15 And he will show you [v]a large
upper room furnished and ready; there prepare for us." 16 And the disciples set out and
went to the city and found it just as he had
told them, and they prepared the Passover.
17 [w]And when it was evening, he came with

[1] A *denarius* was a day's wage for a laborer

14:1–15:37 Jesus has displayed his power in multiple ways. He now faces the ultimate test of his claims and actions. The Old Testament themes of the "suffering of the righteous one" and the betrayal by friends (Ps. 34:19; 37:12); the rejection of the messenger of God (Mark 12:1–12; see note on 6:1–6); and the necessity that the Messiah of God must suffer (8:31; 9:31; 10:32–34; cf. Isa. 53:1–12) and give himself as a substitutionary atonement for rebellious human beings (Mark 10:45; cf. Isa. 53:12) all converge in the event of Jesus' betrayal and death.

The follower of Christ will benefit from pondering the question of why Jesus had to pursue this painful path of suffering (Mark 8:31). Jesus goes alone to accomplish that which his followers could not accomplish (10:45). Here we see the great value of the scandal of the grace of God. God sent his Son to do what we never could do, and to suffer what we deserved to suffer.

14:1–11 The Messiah must be "cut off" (Dan. 9:26; cf. Isa. 53:8; Mark 3:6). While this is the intent of the opponents of Jesus, they inadvertently play into the hand of God, the Father, who called his eternal Son to atone for human sinfulness. Ultimately, God's will and purpose is accomplished, for it was through even the wickedness of Christ's enemies that God's great plan of redemption came to its climax and fulfillment.

We can trust in God's sovereign and overriding wisdom and power (Rom. 8:28), even though we must be careful not to be simplistic in applying this truth mechanically to our lives. God's ways, especially in our suffering, are often inexplicable. But we can trust that he is always good. Nothing can come to God's children out of divine wrath, for God's wrath has been exhausted on the cross. All that happens to disciples of Christ is from God's great heart of love for his own. We do not trust him because of what we can prove from our circumstances, but from what is revealed about his character at the cross. There we learn that even when circumstances are awful and inexplicable, God will ultimately bring about the good he intends.

14:12–25 The setting of a Passover meal indicates that Jesus intends his disciples to view the impending event of deliverance from sin, Satan, and judgment against the background of the Passover Feast which marks Israel's deliverance from Egyptian slavery. Both deliverances are accomplished by means of God's judgment (then of Egypt, and now of his eternal Son, who provides a substitutionary atonement). In the Passover, God's people are protected from judgment by the shedding of animal

5 [d][John 13:29] [e]John 11:33, 38 (Gk.)
7 [f]Deut. 15:11 [g][2 Cor. 9:7] [h]ch. 2:20; See John 7:33
8 [i][ch. 12:43; Luke 21:3; 2 Cor. 8:12] [j]John 19:40
9 [k][Matt. 24:14] [l]Acts 10:4
10 [m]For ver. 10, 11, see Matt. 26:14-16; Luke 22:3-6; [John 13:2, 27, 30] [n]ch. 3:19; Matt. 27:3; Acts 1:16; [John 6:71; 12:4]
11 [o]See Matt. 20:18, 19
12 [p]For ver. 12-16, see Matt. 26:17-19; Luke 22:7-13 [q]Ex. 12:18 [r]1 Cor. 5:7
13 [s][ch. 11:1]
14 [t]See John 11:28 [u]Luke 2:7 (Gk.)
15 [v][Acts 1:13]
17 [w]For ver. 17-21, see Matt. 26:20-24; [Luke 22:14, 21-23; John 13:21-26]

the twelve. 18 And as they were reclining at
table and eating, [x]Jesus said, "Truly, I say to
you, one of you will betray me, [y]one who is
eating with me." 19 They began to be sorrowful and to say to him one after another, "Is it
I?" 20 He said to them, "It is [z]one of the twelve,
[y]one who is dipping bread into the dish with
me. 21 For the Son of Man goes [a]as it is written
of him, but [b]woe to that man by whom the
Son of Man is betrayed! [c]It would have been
better for that man if he had not been born."

Institution of the Lord's Supper

22 [d]And as they were eating, he took bread,
and after [e]blessing it broke it and gave it to
them, and said, "Take; [f]this is my body." 23 And
he took a cup, and when he had [g]given thanks
he gave it to them, and they all drank of it.
24 And he said to them, [f]"This is my [h]blood of
the[1] covenant, which is poured out for [i]many.
25 Truly, I say to you, I will not drink again
of the fruit of the vine until that day when
I drink it new in the kingdom of God."

Jesus Foretells Peter's Denial

26 [j]And when they had sung a hymn, [k]they
went out to [l]the Mount of Olives. 27 And Jesus
said to them, "You will all fall away, for it is
written, 'I will [m]strike the shepherd, and the
sheep will be scattered.' 28 But after I am raised
up, [n]I will go before you to Galilee." 29 [o]Peter
said to him, "Even though they all fall away,
I will not." 30 And [p]Jesus said to him, "Truly,
I tell you, this very night, before [q]the rooster
crows twice, you will deny me three times."
31 But [r]he said emphatically, "If I must die with
you, I will not deny you." And they all said
the same.

Jesus Prays in Gethsemane

32 [s]And they went [k]to a place called Gethsemane. And he said to his disciples, "Sit
here while I pray." 33 And he took with him
[t]Peter and James and John, and began [u]to be
greatly distressed and troubled. 34 And he said
to them, [v]"My soul is very sorrowful, even
to death. Remain here and [w]watch."[2] 35 And
going a little farther, he fell on the ground
[x]and prayed that, if it were possible, [y]the hour
might pass from him. 36 And he said, [z]"Abba,
Father, [a]all things are possible for you. Remove
[b]this cup from me. [c]Yet not what I will, but
what you will." 37 And he came and found
them sleeping, and he said to Peter, "Simon,
are you asleep? Could you not watch one hour?

[1] Some manuscripts insert *new* [2] Or *keep awake*; also verses 37, 38

18[x] [John 6:70, 71] [y] [Ps. 41:9; John 13:18]
20[z] ver. 10 [y] [See ver. 18 above]
21[a] ver. 49; ch. 9:12; Luke 18:31; 24:25, 27, 46; Acts 17:2, 3; 26:22, 23; 1 Cor. 15:3; 1 Pet. 1:10, 11 [b] Matt. 18:7 [c] [See John 17:12]
22[d] For ver. 22-25, see Matt. 26:26-29; Luke 22:18-20; 1 Cor. 11:23-25 [e] See Matt. 14:19 [f] 1 Cor. 10:16; [John 6:53]
23[g] See Matt. 15:36
24[f] [See ver. 22 above] [h] Ex. 24:8; [Zech. 9:11; Heb. 13:20] [i] See Matt. 20:28
26[j] For ver. 26-31, see Matt. 26:30-35 [k] Luke 22:39; John 18:1 [l] See Matt. 21:1
27[m] Cited from Zech. 13:7; [John 16:32]
28[n] ch. 16:7; Matt. 28:7, 10, 16
29[o] [Luke 22:31, 33]
30[p] Luke 22:34; John 13:38 [q] ver. 68, 72
31[r] John 13:37
32[s] For ver. 32-42, see Matt. 26:36-46; Luke 22:40-46 [k] [See ver. 26 above]
33[t] ch. 5:37; 9:2 [u] [Matt. 17:23]
34[v] [Ps. 42:5, 6; John 12:27] [w] See Matt. 24:42
35[x] Heb. 5:7 [y] ver. 41; John 12:23, 27; 13:1; 17:1; [Luke 22:53; John 16:4]
36[z] Rom. 8:15; Gal. 4:6 [a] See Matt. 19:26 [b] See ch. 10:38 [c] John 5:30; 6:38; Phil. 2:8

blood; now they are "passed over" because of the blood of Christ (Lev. 17:11; Heb. 9:22). The eating of unleavened bread is now echoed by eating the bread to which Jesus extends the significance of his body, which is to be broken. While drinking of the Passover cup, Jews anticipate the coming of the Messiah; Jesus now pronounces the following words over the cup: "This is my blood of the covenant, which is poured out for many" (Mark 14:24).

Doubtless, the Passover Feast in Egypt (together with the Day of Atonement) serves as a blueprint for this ultimate Passover and exodus of liberation from the slavery of sin, Satan, and judgment (cf. Luke 9:31), as well as the entry into the ultimate Canaan, namely the "kingdom of his beloved Son" (Col. 1:13), which Jesus came preaching (Mark 1:14–15).

When followers of Christ celebrate the Lord's Supper, they come into the particular presence of the triune God. By eating the bread and drinking the wine, Christ reaffirms his followers in the redemptive efficacy of the once-and-for-all, covenantal shedding of his blood at Golgotha. The gospel is tangibly remembered. Believers are spiritually nourished. The disciples of Christ can trust in his real, spiritual presence, in his forgiveness, and in his purifying love. He has given his body and his blood for us.

14:26–42 As Jesus proceeds to give his life for "many" (10:45; Isa. 53:11), he prays in the garden of Gethsemane (Mark 14:32–42). Readers of Mark's Gospel are here given a unique window into the nature of Christ's suffering and his heart. In utter loneliness and exposed to the full judgment of his Father for the rebellion of humankind, Jesus begins to feel the full weight of what it will mean to be forsaken by the Father. Jesus cries out that he might be delivered from this cup of wrath, if that would be his Father's will (v. 36; cf. Heb. 5:7). Jesus knows that only the Father can effect ultimate deliverance from the cup of judgment. But he also knows that his heavenly Father knows what is best, and our Savior submits himself to that redemptive design.

38 [w]Watch and [d]pray that you may not [e]enter
into temptation. The spirit indeed is willing,
but the flesh is weak." 39 And again he went
away and prayed, [f]saying the same words.
40 And again he came and found them sleeping, for [g]their eyes were very heavy, and [h]they
did not know what to answer him. 41 And he
came the third time and said to them, "Are
you still sleeping and taking your rest? [i]It is
enough; [j]the hour has come. [k]The Son of Man
is betrayed into the hands of sinners. 42 Rise,
let us be going; see, my betrayer is at hand."

Betrayal and Arrest of Jesus

43 [l]And immediately, while he was still speaking, [m]Judas came, one of the twelve, and with
him a crowd with swords and clubs, from the
chief priests and the scribes and the elders.
44 Now the betrayer had given them a sign,
saying, "The one I will kiss is the man. Seize
him and lead him away under guard." 45 And
when he came, he went up to him at once and
said, [n]"Rabbi!" And he [o]kissed him. 46 And they
laid hands on him and seized him. 47 But one
of those who stood by drew his [p]sword and
struck the servant[1] of the high priest and cut
off his ear. 48 And Jesus said to them, "Have
you come out as against a robber, with swords
and clubs to capture me? 49 [q]Day after day I was
with you in the temple [r]teaching, and you did
not seize me. But [s]let the Scriptures be fulfilled." 50 [t]And they all left him and fled.

A Young Man Flees

51 And a young man followed him, with nothing but [u]a linen cloth about his body. And they
seized him, 52 but he left the linen cloth and
ran away naked.

Jesus Before the Council

53 [v]And [w]they led Jesus to the high priest.
And all the chief priests and the elders and the
scribes came together. 54 [w]And [x]Peter had followed him at a distance, [y]right into [z]the courtyard of the high priest. And he was sitting with
[a]the guards and [b]warming himself at the fire.
55 Now the chief priests and the whole council[2] were seeking testimony against Jesus to
put him to death, but they found none. 56 [c]For
many bore false witness against him, but their
testimony [d]did not agree. 57 And some stood
up and bore false witness against him, saying,
58 [e]"We heard him say, [f]'I will destroy this temple [g]that is made with hands, and in three days
I will build another, [h]not made with hands.' "
59 Yet even about this their testimony did not
agree. 60 And the high priest stood up in the
midst and asked Jesus, "Have you no answer to
make? What is it that these men testify against
you?"[3] 61 But [i]he remained silent and made no
answer. [j]Again the high priest asked him, "Are
you [k]the Christ, the Son of [l]the Blessed?" 62 And
Jesus said, "I am, and [m]you will see the Son of
Man [n]seated at the right hand of Power, and
[m]coming with the clouds of heaven." 63 And

[1] Greek *bondservant* [2] Greek *Sanhedrin* [3] Or *Have you no answer to what these men testify against you?*

The cup is not removed from Jesus. He intentionally goes to the place where we belong. There the Lord exacts judgment on the utterly alone Christ on behalf of his still largely clueless disciples, whom he loves. Indeed, the atoning work of that weekend long ago was the decisive moment of all of human history. There the wrath of God over all the sin of all of his people came crashing down on his only Son. There sin was forgiven, heaven was secured, joy was restored, and peace was won for sinners who trust in Christ.

14:43–52 The brutal reality of Christ's abandonment by God, his Father, means that he is handed into the violent and ungodly hands of men (cf. 9:31) for our sake. Jesus endured the hands of evil men so that the hand of the Evil One himself, Satan, might never have authority over us.

14:53–65 Jesus stands before the council and is accused. In this moment we are reminded of the accusation which we ourselves justly deserve. Yet Jesus remained silent before the religious leaders here so that ever after he might speak for us. We deserve the judgment he received, yet he did not defend himself, even though he rightfully could have. As the hymn says, "In our place condemned he stood." The heart of the gospel is being exposed here: substitution. God in Christ took our place of condemnation, and we receive freely the gift of acquittal. Reflecting on the magnanimous love of God shown in the gospel, our hearts are moved with fresh wonder.

38 [w][See ver. 34 above] [d]1 Pet. 4:7 [e]Matt. 6:13
39 [f]ver. 36
40 [g]Luke 9:32 [h][ch. 9:6; Luke 9:33]
41 [i][Luke 22:38] [j]See ver. 35 [k]ch. 9:31; 10:33
43 [l]For ver. 43-50, see Matt. 26:47-56; Luke 22:47-53; John 18:3-11 [m]ver. 10; Acts 1:16
45 [n]See John 1:38 [o]Luke 7:38, 45; 15:20; Acts 20:37 (Gk.)
47 [p][Luke 22:38]
49 [q][John 8:2]; [Luke 2:46; John 18:20] [r]Matt. 21:23; [Matt. 4:23] [s]See ver. 21; Matt. 1:22
50 [t]ver. 27; [Ps. 88:8, 18; John 16:32]
51 [u]ch. 15:46; Judg. 14:12; Prov. 31:24
53 [v]For ver. 53-65, see Matt. 26:57-68; [John 18:12, 13, 19-24] [w]Luke 22:54, 55
54 [w][See ver. 53 above] [x][John 18:15] [y][ver. 68] [z]See Matt. 26:3 [a]John 7:32; 18:3 [b]ver. 67; John 18:18
56 [c]Ps. 27:12; 35:11 [d][Deut. 17:6; 19:15] **58** [e][Acts 6:14] [f]ch. 15:29; See John 2:19 [g]Acts 7:48; 17:24; Heb. 9:11, 24 [h]2 Cor. 5:1 **61** [i]ch. 15:4, 5; Isa. 53:7; John 19:9 [j]For ver. 61-63, [Luke 22:67-71] [k]ch. 8:29; See Matt. 1:17 [l][Rom. 1:25] **62** [m]See Matt. 16:27; 24:30 [n]Ps. 110:1; Heb. 1:3; [ch. 16:19]

the high priest [o]tore his garments and said, "What further witnesses do we need? 64 You have heard [p]his blasphemy. What is your decision?" And they [q]all condemned him as [r]deserving death. 65 [s]And some began [t]to spit on him and [u]to cover his face and to strike him, saying to him, "Prophesy!" And the guards received him [v]with blows.

Peter Denies Jesus

66 [w]And as Peter was below in the courtyard, one of the servant girls of the high priest came, 67 and seeing Peter [x]warming himself, she looked at him and said, "You also were with the Nazarene, Jesus." 68 But he denied it, saying, "I neither know nor understand what you mean." And he went out into the gateway[1] and [y]the rooster crowed.[2] 69 And the servant girl saw him and began again to say to the bystanders, "This man is one of them." 70 But again he denied it. And after a little while the bystanders again said to Peter, "Certainly you are one of them, for you are a Galilean." 71 But he began to invoke a curse on himself and to swear, "I do not know this man of whom you speak." 72 And immediately the rooster crowed [z]a second time. And Peter remembered how Jesus had said to him, [a]"Before the rooster crows twice, you will [b]deny me three times." And he broke down and wept.[3]

Jesus Delivered to Pilate

15 [c]And as soon as it was morning, the chief priests [d]held a consultation with the elders and scribes and the whole council. And [e]they bound Jesus and [f]led him away and [g]delivered him over to [h]Pilate. 2 [i]And Pilate asked him, [j]"Are you the King of the Jews?" And he answered him, [k]"You have said so." 3 And the chief priests accused him of many things. 4 And Pilate again asked him, [l]"Have you no answer to make? See how many charges they bring against you." 5 But Jesus [l]made no further answer, so that Pilate was amazed.

Pilate Delivers Jesus to Be Crucified

6 [m]Now at the feast he used to release for them one prisoner for whom they asked. 7 And among the rebels in prison, who had [n]committed murder [o]in the insurrection, there was a man called Barabbas. 8 And the crowd came up and began to ask Pilate to do as he usually did for them. 9 And he answered them, saying, "Do you want me to release for you the King of the Jews?" 10 For he perceived that [p]it was out of envy that the chief priests had delivered him

[1] Or *forecourt* [2] Some manuscripts omit *and the rooster crowed* [3] Or *And when he had thought about it, he wept*

63[o] Num. 14:6; Acts 14:14
64[p] Matt. 9:3; John 10:36 [q] [Luke 23:50, 51] [r] See Lev. 24:16
65[s] Luke 22:63, 64 [t] ch. 10:34; 15:19; Isa. 50:6 [u] [Esth. 7:8] [v] Matt. 5:39; [Acts 23:2]
66[w] For ver. 66-72, see Matt. 26:69-75; Luke 22:55-62; John 18:16-18, 25-27
67[x] ver. 54
68[y] ver. 30, 72
72[z] ver. 68 [a] ver. 30 [b] [Acts 3:13, 14]

Chapter 15
1[c] Matt. 27:1; Luke 22:66 [d] ch. 3:6 [e] Matt. 27:2 [f] Luke 23:1; John 18:28 [g] See ch. 10:33 [h] Luke 3:1; 13:1; Acts 3:13; 4:27; 1 Tim. 6:13
2[i] For ver. 2-5, see Matt. 27:11-14; Luke 23:2, 3; John 18:29-38 [j] ver. 9, 12, 18, 26; Matt. 2:2; John 18:39; 19:3; [ver. 32] [k] [1 Tim. 6:13]; See Luke 22:70
4[l] [John 19:10]; See Matt. 26:63
5[l] [See ver. 4 above]
6[m] For ver. 6-15, see Matt. 27:15-26; Luke 23:18-25; John 18:39, 40; 19:16
7[n] Acts 3:14 [o] [Acts 5:36, 37]
10[p] [John 12:19]

14:66–72 Peter denies Christ because he fears for his life (cf. vv. 27–31). Later, Peter is graciously restored in his relationship with Jesus and affirmed in his calling as a shepherd (John 21:15–19).

The mercy of Jesus toward Peter is an encouragement to other followers: while they may stumble, deny, and sin, Jesus gives the gift of repentance, restores with reconciliation, and provides affirmation (1 Pet. 5:10). When such grace is truly and deeply apprehended, we are moved to love and honor our Savior (Rom. 5:20–6:1; 1 John 4:19). His grace compels us toward godliness, not licentiousness (cf. 2 Cor. 6:1). His grace transforms us (Titus 2:11–12).

15:1–20 Having been accused before the religious authorities, Jesus is now brought before the *irreligious* authorities. Both Jew and Greek alike condemn him. In the presence of Pilate, Jesus does not defend himself; he is like an innocent lamb being slaughtered (Isa. 53:7; Acts 8:32; 1 Pet. 1:19). The crowd demands that the criminal Barabbas be released, instead of Jesus. In Barabbas we see a sobering depiction of ourselves: guilty, released from judgment as Jesus is judged in our place.

Yet pain was not only the path for Jesus; it is also the path for his disciples. While at the ultimate level Jesus' suffering was in our place, at another level Jesus' suffering blazes a trail that we follow. With what attitudes should we then endure suffering?

First, we become more grateful for our salvation, by being reminded that Jesus' sacrificial atonement on our behalf is unique and secures a reconciled relationship with God. Second, as forgiven followers, we learn that purity of heart, which is the fruit of Christ's love for us, is crucial to enduring such suffering with godliness. Third, we humbly acknowledge that God's people are being purified in suffering, so that they may better know and reflect their Savior (Mark 10:39). Finally, we trust God amid suffering, knowing that he who gave up his own Son for us will only do what is best for our and others' eternities (Rom. 8:32).

up. 11 But the chief priests stirred up the crowd
to have him release for them Barabbas instead.
12 And Pilate again said to them, "Then what
shall I do with [q]the man you call the King of
the Jews?" 13 And they cried out again, "Crucify
him." 14 And Pilate said to them, "Why, [r]what
evil has he done?" But they shouted all the
more, "Crucify him." 15 So Pilate, wishing to
satisfy the crowd, released for them Barabbas,
and having [s]scourged[1] Jesus, he delivered him
to be crucified.

Jesus Is Mocked

16 [t]And the soldiers led him away inside [u]the
palace (that is, [v]the governor's headquarters),[2]
and they called together the whole [w]battalion.[3]
17 And they clothed him in [x]a purple cloak, and
twisting together a crown of thorns, they put
it on him. 18 And they began to salute him,
[y]"Hail, King of the Jews!" 19 And they were
striking his head with a reed and [z]spitting on
him and [a]kneeling down in homage to him.
20 And when they had [b]mocked him, they
stripped him of [x]the purple cloak and put his
own clothes on him. And they [c]led him out to
crucify him.

The Crucifixion

21 [d]And they compelled a passerby, Simon of
Cyrene, who was coming in from the country,
the father of Alexander and Rufus, to carry his
cross. 22 [e]And they brought him to the place
called Golgotha (which means Place of a Skull).
23 And they offered him wine mixed with
[f]myrrh, but he did not take it. 24 And they crucified him and [g]divided his garments among
them, casting lots for them, to decide what
each should take. 25 And [h]it was the third hour[4]
when they crucified him. 26 And the inscription of the charge against him read, [i]"The King
of the Jews." 27 And with him they crucified
two [j]robbers, [k]one on his right and one on his
left.[5] 29 And [l]those who passed by derided him,
[m]wagging their heads and saying, [n]"Aha! [o]You
who would destroy the temple and rebuild it
in three days, 30 save yourself, and come down
from the cross!" 31 So also the chief priests with
the scribes mocked him to one another, saying,
[p]"He saved others; [q]he cannot save himself.
32 Let [r]the Christ, [s]the King of Israel, come
down now from the cross that we may [t]see
and believe." [u]Those who were crucified with
him also reviled him.

The Death of Jesus

33 And when the sixth hour[6] had come, there
was darkness over the whole land until the
ninth hour.[7] 34 And at the ninth hour Jesus
[v]cried with a loud voice, [w]"Eloi, Eloi, lema
sabachthani?" which means, "My God, my
God, why have you forsaken me?" 35 And some
of the bystanders hearing it said, "Behold, he is
calling Elijah." 36 And someone ran and filled a
sponge with [x]sour wine, put it on a reed [y]and
gave it to him to drink, saying, "Wait, let us see
whether Elijah will come to take him down."
37 And Jesus [z]uttered a loud cry and [a]breathed
his last. 38 And [b]the curtain of the temple was
torn in two, from top to bottom. 39 [c]And when
the centurion, who stood facing him, saw

[1] A Roman judicial penalty, consisting of a severe beating with a multi-lashed whip containing imbedded pieces of bone and metal [2] Greek *the praetorium* [3] Greek *cohort*; a tenth of a Roman legion, usually about 600 men [4] That is, 9 A.M. [5] Some manuscripts insert verse 28: *And the Scripture was fulfilled that says, "He was numbered with the transgressors"* [6] That is, noon [7] That is, 3 P.M.

15:21–38 The crucifixion and death of Jesus are told in very terse terms. The death of Jesus (v. 37) and the tearing of the temple curtain (v. 38) are narrated in unison to indicate that the atoning death of Jesus gives his followers direct access to the Most Holy Place—that is, into the very presence of God (Heb. 9:24). Jesus is indeed the temple that is not made with human hands (Mark 14:58), for in him people of all nations (cf. 11:17; 15:39) are welcomed into restored fellowship with God—the very thing the temple was meant to facilitate.

Followers of Christ must ponder Jesus' substitutionary death as divine judgment for their sin. We are humbled. For the severity of sin—nothing less than the torture and murder of God's own divine Son—exposes the seriousness of our intellectual, moral, and emotional sickness and the depth of our human rebellion against God. Reflecting on what this all means, we are changed from the inside out; we become once again the humanity God first intended, approaching our responsibilities in life in trusting dependence on him and faithful devotion to him.

12[q] [John 19:15]
14[r] [Luke 23:41; John 8:46]
15[s] ch. 10:34; Isa. 50:6; 53:5; [Luke 23:16; John 19:1]
16[t] For ver. 16-20, see Matt. 27:27-31; John 19:2, 3 [u] See Matt. 26:3 [v] John 18:28, 33; 19:9; Acts 23:35; Phil. 1:13 (Gk.) [w] See Acts 10:1
17[x] Rev. 18:12, 16; [Luke 23:11]
18[y] See ver. 2
19[z] See ch. 14:65 [a] See Matt. 8:2
20[b] ch. 10:34 [x] [See ver. 17 above] [c] Isa. 53:7
21[d] Matt. 27:32; Luke 23:26; [John 19:17]
22[e] For ver. 22-38, see Matt. 27:33-51; Luke 23:32-38, 44-46; John 19:17-19, 23, 24, 28-30

23[f] Matt. 2:11; See John 19:39 **24**[g] Ps. 22:18 **25**[h] [John 19:14] **26**[i] ver. 2 **27**[j] [John 18:40] [k] [ch. 10:37] **29**[l] Ps. 22:7; 109:25; [Lam. 1:12] [m] Job 16:4; Jer. 18:16; Lam. 2:15 [n] Ps. 35:25; 40:15 [o] ch. 14:58 **31**[p] [Luke 4:23] [q] [Matt. 26:53, 54; John 10:18] **32**[r] See Matt. 1:17 [s] John 1:49; 12:13; [ver. 26] [t] John 20:29 [u] [Luke 23:39-43] **34**[v] [Heb. 5:7] [w] Cited from Ps. 22:1 **36**[x] Ruth 2:14 [y] Ps. 69:21 **37**[z] ver. 34 [a] [John 10:18] **38**[b] Ex. 26:31-33; 2 Chr. 3:14 **39**[c] For ver. 39-41, see Matt. 27:54-56; Luke 23:47, 49

that in this way he[1] breathed his last, he said,
[d]"Truly this man was the Son[2] of God!"
40 There were also [e]women looking on
[f]from a distance, among whom were [g]Mary
Magdalene, and Mary the mother of James the
younger and of Joses, and [i]Salome. 41 When he
was in Galilee, they followed him and [g]minis-
tered to him, and there were also many other
women who [j]came up with him to Jerusalem.

Jesus Is Buried

42 [k]And when evening had come, since it
was [l]the day of Preparation, that is, the day
before the Sabbath, 43 Joseph of Arimathea,
[m]a respected member of the council, who [n]was
also himself looking for the kingdom of God,
took courage and went to Pilate and asked for
the body of Jesus. 44 Pilate was surprised to
hear that he should have already died.[3] And
summoning [o]the centurion, he asked him
whether he was already dead. 45 And when
he learned from [o]the centurion that he was
dead, he granted the corpse to Joseph. 46 And
Joseph[4] bought [p]a linen shroud, and taking
him down, wrapped him in the linen shroud
and [q]laid him in a tomb [r]that had been cut
out of the rock. And he rolled [s]a stone against
the entrance of the tomb. 47 [t]Mary Magdalene
and Mary the mother of Joses saw where he
was laid.

The Resurrection

16 [u, v]When the Sabbath was past, [w]Mary
Magdalene, [w]Mary the mother of James,
and [i]Salome [x]bought spices, so that they might
go and anoint him. 2 And very early on the first
day of the week, when the sun had risen, they
went to the tomb. 3 And they were saying to
one another, "Who will roll away [y]the stone
for us from the entrance of the tomb?" 4 And
looking up, they saw that the stone had been
rolled back—[z]it was very large. 5 And [a]entering
the tomb, they saw a young man sitting on the
right side, [b]dressed in [c]a white robe, and [d]they
were alarmed. 6 And he said to them, [d]"Do not
be alarmed. You seek Jesus of Nazareth, who
was crucified. He has risen; he is not here. See
the place where they laid him. 7 But go, tell
his disciples and Peter that [e]he is going before
you to Galilee. There you will see him, [e]just
as he told you." 8 And they went out and fled
from the tomb, for trembling and astonishment had seized them, and they said nothing
to anyone, for they were afraid.

[SOME OF THE EARLIEST MANUSCRIPTS
DO NOT INCLUDE 16:9–20.][5]

Jesus Appears to Mary Magdalene

9 [[Now when he rose early on the first
day of the week, [f]he appeared first to [g]Mary
Magdalene, [g]from whom he had cast out seven

[1] Some manuscripts insert *cried out and* [2] Or *a son* [3] Or *Pilate wondered whether he had already died* [4] Greek *he* [5] Some manuscripts end the book with 16:8; others include verses 9–20 immediately after verse 8. At least one manuscript inserts additional material after verse 14; some manuscripts include after verse 8 the following: *But they reported briefly to Peter and those with him all that they had been told. And after this, Jesus himself sent out by means of them, from east to west, the sacred and imperishable proclamation of eternal salvation.* These manuscripts then continue with verses 9–20

15:40–41 As is so often the case in the Gospels, it is those who are socially marginalized—in this case, women—who prove to be most acutely aware of who Jesus is and the supreme worth of following him.

15:42–47 Jesus is buried. Though at one level this seems like a mundane fact of the narrative, it is a crucial part of the gospel and the salvation that is ours by grace. Jesus was not simply mocked or insulted or wounded on our behalf; he was killed. Jesus underwent the death that is unavoidable for every one of us since Adam's fall. Though each of us must pass through the awful experience of death, Jesus' own death, with his subsequent resurrection, means that our death, while awful, is no longer a dead end. It is a new beginning. Death for the follower of Christ is an entrance ramp, not an exit.

16:1–8 While none of the actual resurrection appearances (e.g., Matt. 28:9–10, 16–20; Luke 24:15–31; John 21:14–22; 1 Cor. 15:4–8) are recorded in Mark, the messenger of God speaks unmistakably of Jesus' physical resurrection to the women who had followed him (". . . Jesus of Nazareth, who was crucified. He has risen . . ."; Mark 16:6). The empty tomb is part of the fulfillment of Jesus' prediction of his resurrection (e.g., 8:31).

He who was punished and died on our behalf overcame judgment and death by divine vindication and physical resurrection. Discipleship now takes on a new dimension: Christ, as the living Master, will no longer be challenged by any satanic, human,

39[d] Matt. 27:43
40[e] John 19:25 [f] Ps. 38:11 [g] See Luke 8:2, 3 [i] ch. 16:1; [Matt. 27:56]
41[g] [See ver. 40 above] [j] Luke 2:4
42[k] For ver. 42-47, see Matt. 27:57-61; Luke 23:50-56; John 19:38-42 [l] See Matt. 27:62
43[m] Acts 13:50; 17:12 [n] Luke 2:25, 38
44[o] ver. 39
45[o] [See ver. 44 above]
46[p] See ch. 14:51 [q] [Isa. 53:9] [r] Isa. 22:16 [s] ch. 16:4; [John 11:38]
47[t] ver. 40

Chapter 16
1[u] For ver. 1-8, see Matt. 28:1-8; Luke 24:1-10; John 20:1 [v] [ch. 1:32] [w] ch. 15:40 [i] [See ch. 15:40 above] [x] Luke 23:56; [John 19:39, 40]
3[y] ch. 15:46
4[z] Matt. 27:60
5[a] [John 20:11, 12] [b] [ch. 9:3; Dan. 7:9; John 20:12; Acts 1:10] [c] Rev. 6:11; 7:9 [d] ch. 9:15 (Gk.)

6[d] [See ver. 5 above] **7**[e] ch. 14:28 **9**[f] John 20:14; [Matt. 28:9] [g] Luke 8:2

demons. 10 [h]She went and told those who had
been with him, [i]as they [j]mourned and wept.
11 But when they heard that he was alive and
had been seen by her, they [k]would not believe it.

Jesus Appears to Two Disciples

12 [l]After these things [m]he appeared in [n]another
form to two of them, as they were walking into
the country. 13 [o]And they went back and told
the rest, but they did not believe them.

The Great Commission

14 Afterward [m]he appeared [p]to the eleven
themselves as they were reclining at table, and
he rebuked them for their [q]unbelief and [r]hard-
ness of heart, because [s]they had not believed
those who saw him after he had risen. 15 And
he said to them, [t]"Go into all the world and
[u]proclaim the gospel to [v]the whole creation.
16 [w]Whoever believes and is [x]baptized [y]will be
saved, but [z]whoever [w]does not believe will be
condemned. 17 And [a]these signs will accompany those who believe: [b]in my name they
will cast out demons; [c]they will speak in new
tongues; 18 [d]they will pick up serpents with
their hands; and if they drink any deadly poison, it will not hurt them; [e]they will lay their
hands [f]on the sick, and they will recover."
19 So then the Lord Jesus, [g]after he had spoken
to them, [h]was taken up into heaven and [i]sat
down at the right hand of God. 20 And they
went out and preached everywhere, while [j]the
Lord worked with them and confirmed [k]the
message [l]by accompanying signs.]]

or physical power (Col. 1:15–17). The follower can be assured of what Paul says: "For I am sure that neither death nor life, . . . nor anything else in all creation, will be able to separate us from the love of God in Christ Jesus our Lord" (Rom. 8:38–39). For Christ has been raised. In him, the final age, the new creation, has dawned. Joy is invincibly washing over this fallen world, for Jesus has been raised.

16:9–20 This "longer ending" of Mark, missing from many of the earliest Greek manuscripts and unlikely a part of the original Gospel account, contains reports of Jesus' post-resurrection appearances. It also narrates his Great Commission and speaks of faith, miracles, and evangelism. Though these verses were likely added to Scripture, the underlying message fits with what we see elsewhere in Scripture: our God will enable the followers of Christ to fulfill his purposes in their lives.

10 [h] John 20:18; [Matt. 28:10; Luke 24:10] [i] John 16:20 [j] Luke 6:25
11 [k] Luke 24:11; [ver. 16]
12 [l] Luke 24:13-31 [m] ver. 14; [John 21:1, 14] [n] Luke 9:29 (Gk.)
13 [o] Luke 24:33-35
14 [m] [See ver. 12 above] [p] Luke 24:36; 1 Cor. 15:5 [q] [Luke 24:41] [r] See ch. 10:5 [s] ver. 11, 13
15 [t] Matt. 28:19 [u] Col. 1:23; [ch. 13:10; Acts 1:8; Rom. 10:18] [v] Rom. 8:22
16 [w] [John 3:18] [x] John 3:5 [y] Acts 16:31; Rom. 10:9; 1 Pet. 3:21 [z] ver. 11; Luke 24:11, 41; Acts 28:24; 1 Pet. 2:7; [2 Thess. 2:12] **17** [a] [ch. 11:23] [b] Acts 5:16; 8:7; 16:18; 19:12; See ch. 9:38 [c] Acts 2:4; 10:46; 19:6; 1 Cor. 12:10, 28, 30; 13:1; 14:2, 4 **18** [d] Luke 10:19; Acts 28:3-5 [e] See ch. 5:23 [f] Acts 5:15, 16; 8:7; 9:12, 17; 28:8; James 5:14, 15; [John 14:12] **19** [g] Acts 1:3 [h] Luke 9:51; 24:51; John 6:62; Acts 1:2; 1 Tim. 3:16; [John 20:17; Eph. 4:8-10; Heb. 4:14] [i] Acts 7:55, 56; Rom. 8:34; Eph. 1:20; Col. 3:1; Heb. 1:3; 8:1; 10:12; 12:2; 1 Pet. 3:22; Rev. 3:21; See Matt. 22:44; Acts 2:33 **20** [j] Heb. 2:3, 4; See 1 Cor. 3:9 [k] See ch. 4:14 [l] See Acts 5:12

Introduction to Luke

Author, Date, and Recipients

Luke was a physician and a travel companion of the apostle Paul (Col. 4:14). He wrote this Gospel and its sequel, the book of Acts. The earliest possible date of Luke–Acts is immediately after the events that Luke recorded in Acts 28, which would have been c. A.D. 62. Both Luke and Acts are addressed to "Theophilus" (Luke 1:3; Acts 1:1), about whom nothing more is known. Luke's broader audience consisted primarily of Gentile Christians like Theophilus.

The Gospel in Luke

Luke informs us from the beginning (1:1–4) that his is not the only Gospel to have been written nor the only Gospel account that could be written (cf. John 21:25). Nevertheless, the church has always recognized the great gift that the third Gospel is to us. There are many beautiful and essential teachings of Jesus and pictures of the gospel that come to us from Luke alone.

While the historical and theological witness of all four Gospels contains many consistent themes, Luke describes for us the gospel and its application in several specific and important ways. At the broadest level we learn from this Gospel account that the gospel is multi-faceted and full-orbed. That is, the gospel is explained and applied as being about our whole lives, physically and spiritually, externally and internally, for now and for the future, in our relationship with God and with others. The gospel is not simply a message about religion and the "religious" portion of our lives. Rather, Luke's presentation helps us see clearly that the gospel of Jesus is about the comprehensive *blessedness* of God available to us through Jesus Christ.

At a more specific level Luke retells the stories and teachings of Jesus in a way that consistently emphasizes that the gospel is a matter of the heart, the inner person, not mere external religion. Jesus constantly reveals the heart motivations behind our actions and pushes us toward opening our hearts in humility toward God. As a result, the gospel in Luke is often presented as a call to reevaluate everything in the world according to God's perspective, not ours. This means valuing humility over prestige, mercy over justice, favor with God over favor with people, and—especially challenging to us—valuing a rich relationship with God over the power of money.

To emphasize this comprehensive understanding of the gospel, Luke uses a variety of complementary images to describe it. The gospel includes the message of peace, the offer of forgiveness of sins through repentance, the promise of inheriting eternal life, the invitation to enter the kingdom of God, and the joy of being with Jesus as a disciple. In all of this, the gospel is *good news* because it announces the grace and peace that have now come to sinners in Jesus Christ.

Outline

I. The Prologue (1:1–4)

II. The Infancy Narrative (1:5–2:52)

III. Preparation for the Ministry of Jesus (3:1–4:15)

IV. The Ministry of Jesus in Galilee (4:16–9:50)

V. The Journey to Jerusalem (9:51–19:27)

VI. The Ministry of Jesus in Jerusalem (19:28–21:38)

VII. The Suffering and Death of Jesus (22:1–23:56)

VIII. The Resurrection of Jesus (24:1–53)

The Gospel According to

Luke

Dedication to Theophilus

1 Inasmuch as many have undertaken to
compile a narrative of the things that
[a]have been accomplished among us, 2 [b]just as
those who [c]from the beginning were [d]eyewit-
nesses and [e]ministers of [f]the word [g]have delivered them to us, 3 it seemed good to me also,
having followed all things closely for some
time past, to write [h]an orderly account for you,
[i]most excellent [j]Theophilus, 4 that you may
have [k]certainty concerning the things [l]you
have been taught.

Birth of John the Baptist Foretold

5 [m]In the days of Herod, king of Judea,
there was a priest named Zechariah,[1] [n]of [o]the
division of Abijah. And he had a wife from
the daughters of Aaron, and her name was
Elizabeth. 6 And they were both [p]righteous
before God, walking [q]blamelessly in all the
commandments and statutes of the Lord. 7 But
they had no child, because [r]Elizabeth was barren, and [s]both were advanced in years.
8 Now [t]while he was serving as priest before
God when [u]his division was on duty, 9 according to the custom of the priesthood, he was
chosen by lot [v]to enter [w]the temple of the Lord
and burn incense. 10 And the whole multitude
of the people [x]were praying [y]outside at the
hour of incense. 11 And there appeared to him
an angel of the Lord standing on the right
side of [z]the altar of incense. 12 And Zechariah
was troubled when he saw him, and [a]fear fell
upon him. 13 But the angel said to him, "Do
not be afraid, Zechariah, for [b]your prayer has
been heard, and your wife Elizabeth will bear
you a son, and [c]you shall call his name John.
14 And you will have joy and gladness, and

[1] Greek *Zacharias*

1:5–25 This historical story addresses key heart issues. It is a story of human suffering and sadness, coming from the brokenness of infertility. Like Sarah and Abraham of old, Zechariah and Elizabeth are advanced in age but without children, even though they were righteous followers of God (v. 6). This barrenness is a deep sadness for them and is even viewed as a reproach among others in their community (v. 25).

Yet from the bird's eye perspective that we are given, we learn that even in the midst of this decades-long trial for two godly people, God is working out a perfect plan of grace. He is using this couple's barrenness and brokenness to show forth his miraculous power and to witness to the world that his final plan of redemption is now at hand in Jesus Christ. The story of this couple's suffering turned to joy reminds us that in the pain of our own trials our limited perspective is not able to grasp the good plans that our kind God is perfecting for us (Rom. 8:18–28; 1 Cor. 2:9). We are called by this story to renew our active trust in God's will, even through our veil of tears.

Overlapping with this lesson, this story also shows the gospel's real call on us to believe and trust in God's words. While God is gracious from beginning to end in this story, with the miracle of barrenness broken there is also a message of the danger of hardness of heart. Zechariah, righteous and godly though he is (Luke 1:6), fails to believe God's message delivered through the angel Gabriel (v. 18). This is likely because of a natural jadedness that comes from years of trial, difficulty, and disappointment. Zechariah can only see the obstacles of his age and his wife's closed womb. The result is a gracious but real discipline from the Lord. God does not condemn Zechariah, though he does experience a new trial of muteness. Yet even in this God is perfecting a greater and more robust faith in Zechariah, who will soon be not just a priest but also a prophet (vv. 67–79).

Chapter 1
1 [a]2 Tim. 4:5, 17 (Gk.); [Acts 3:18]
2 [b][Heb. 2:3] [c]John 15:27; 16:4; [Mark 1:1; Acts 11:15] [d]2 Pet. 1:16; 1 John 1:1, 3; [Acts 4:20; 1 Pet. 5:1] [e]Acts 26:16; 1 Cor. 4:1 [f]See Mark 4:14 [g]1 Cor. 11:2, 23
3 [h]Acts 11:4 [i]Acts 23:26; 24:3; 26:25 [j]Acts 1:1
4 [k]Acts 2:36 (Gk.); [2 Pet. 1:16, 19] [l]Acts 18:25; Rom. 2:18; 1 Cor. 14:19; Gal. 6:6 (Gk.)
5 [m]Matt. 2:1 [n]1 Chr. 24:10 [o]ver. 8
6 [p]ch. 2:25 [q]Phil. 2:15; 3:6; 1 Thess. 2:10; 3:13; 5:23; [Acts 23:1; 24:16]
7 [r]ver. 36; [Judg. 13:2; 1 Sam. 1:2] [s][Gen. 18:11; Heb. 11:11, 12]
8 [t]1 Chr. 24:19; 2 Chr. 8:14; 31:2; [ver. 23] [u]ver. 5
9 [v]Ex. 30:7, 8; 1 Sam. 2:28; 1 Chr. 23:13; 2 Chr. 29:11 [w]ver. 21, 22; Rev. 11:2, 19; [Heb. 9:2, 3]
10 [x]Ps. 141:2; [Rev. 5:8; 8:3, 4] [y][Lev. 16:17]
11 [z]Ex. 30:1-10; 40:26, 27
12 [a]Acts 19:17
13 [b][Acts 10:4, 31] [c]ver. 60, 63

many will [d]rejoice at his birth, 15 for he will be
[e]great before the Lord. And [f]he must not drink
wine or strong [g]drink, and [g]he will be [h]filled
with the Holy Spirit, [i]even from his mother's
womb. 16 And he will turn many of the children
of Israel to the Lord their God, 17 and [j]he will go
before him [k]in the spirit and power of Elijah, [l]to
turn the hearts of the fathers to the children,
and [m]the disobedient to the wisdom of the just,
[n]to make ready for the Lord a people prepared."
18 And Zechariah said to the angel, [o]"How
shall I know this? For I am an old man, and
my wife is advanced in years." 19 And the angel
answered him, "I am [p]Gabriel. [q]I stand in the
presence of God, and I was sent to speak to you
and to bring you this good news. 20 And behold,
[r]you will be silent and unable to speak until
the day that these things take place, because
you did not believe my words, which will be
fulfilled in their time." 21 And the people were
waiting for Zechariah, and they were wondering at his delay in [s]the temple. 22 And when he
came out, he was unable to speak to them, and
they realized that he had seen a vision in [s]the
temple. And [t]he kept making signs to them
and remained mute. 23 And [u]when his time of
[v]service was ended, he went to his home.
24 After these days his wife Elizabeth conceived, and for five months she kept herself
hidden, saying, 25 "Thus the Lord has done for
me in the days when he looked on me, [w]to take
away my reproach among people."

Birth of Jesus Foretold

26 In the sixth month the angel [x]Gabriel
was sent from God to a city of Galilee named
[y]Nazareth, 27 [z]to a virgin betrothed[1] to a man
whose name was Joseph, [a]of the house of
David. And the virgin's name was Mary. 28 And
he came to her and said, "Greetings, [b]O favored
one, [c]the Lord is with you!"[2] 29 But [d]she was
greatly troubled at the saying, and tried to discern what sort of greeting this might be. 30 And
the angel said to her, "Do not be afraid, Mary,
for [e]you have found favor with God. 31 And
behold, [f]you will conceive in your womb and
bear a son, and [g]you shall call his name Jesus.
32 He will be great and will be called the Son of
[h]the Most High. And the Lord God [i]will give to
him the throne of [j]his father David, 33 and he
will reign over the house of Jacob [k]forever, and
of his kingdom there will be no end."
34 And Mary said to the angel, "How will this
be, since I am a virgin?"[3]
35 And the angel answered her, [l]"The Holy
Spirit will come upon you, and the power
of [h]the Most High will overshadow you;
therefore the child to be born[4] will be called
[m]holy—[n]the Son of God. 36 And behold, your
relative Elizabeth in her old age has also conceived a son, and this is the sixth month with
her [o]who was called barren. 37 For [p]nothing
will be impossible with God." 38 And Mary
said, "Behold, I am the servant[5] of the Lord;
let it be to me according to your word." And
[q]the angel departed from her.

Mary Visits Elizabeth

39 In those days Mary arose and went with
haste into [r]the hill country, to a town in Judah,
40 and she entered the house of Zechariah and
greeted Elizabeth. 41 And when Elizabeth
heard the greeting of Mary, the baby leaped
in her womb. And Elizabeth [s]was filled with

[1] That is, legally pledged to be married [2] Some manuscripts add *Blessed are you among women!* [3] Greek *since I do not know a man* [4] Some manuscripts add *of you* [5] Greek *bondservant*; also verse 48

1:26–38 This story is the next stop on the angel Gabriel's mission from God to prepare God's people for the coming Savior (v. 17). The engaged virgin Mary receives a message even more shocking than that given to Zechariah: she is going to give birth to the Son of God, who will reign as King forever (v. 32), even though she is still a virgin! Unlike Zechariah (v. 18), Mary exhibits the childlike faith that always brings joy to our Father God (18:16–17). Despite some lingering confusion and uncertainty and probably no small amount of fear, she responds to God's gracious provision with faith: "I am the servant of the Lord; let it be to me according to your word" (1:38).

All of this happens because God has set his favor upon Mary (v. 30). Such initiating and reassuring grace from God toward us finds fullest expression in Christ, who enables us to respond with this kind of faith, which itself brings great pleasure and glory to God (Eph. 2:1–10).

14[d] [ver. 58]
15[e] ch. 7:28; Matt. 11:11 [f] ch. 7:33; Num. 6:3; Judg. 13:4, 7, 14; Matt. 11:18 [g] [Acts 2:15, 17; Eph. 5:18] [h] ver. 41, 67; See Acts 2:4 [i] Isa. 49:1, 5; Jer. 1:5; Gal. 1:15
17[j] ver. 76; John 3:28 [k] See Matt. 11:14 [l] Cited from Mal. 4:6 [m] Rom. 10:21 [n] ch. 7:27; Mal. 3:1; Matt. 11:10; Mark 1:2
18[o] Gen. 15:8; [Gen. 17:17]
19[p] ver. 26; Dan. 8:16; 9:21 [q] Rev. 8:2; [1 Kgs. 17:1; Job 1:6; Isa. 63:9; Matt. 18:10]
20[r] [Ezek. 3:26; 24:27]
21[s] See ver. 9
22[s] [See ver. 21 above] [t] ver. 62

23[u] 2 Chr. 23:8; [ver. 8; 2 Kgs. 11:5; 1 Chr. 9:25] [v] Heb. 10:11 **25**[w] [Gen. 30:23; 1 Sam. 1:6; Ps. 113:9; Isa. 4:1] **26**[x] ver. 19 [y] See Matt. 2:23 **27**[z] Matt. 1:16, 18 [a] ch. 2:4; Matt. 1:20 **28**[b] [Ps. 45:2; Dan. 9:23] [c] Judg. 6:12 **29**[d] See ver. 12 **30**[e] Acts 7:46 **31**[f] Isa. 7:14 [g] ch. 2:21; Matt. 1:21, 25 **32**[h] ver. 76; ch. 6:35; Acts 7:48; See Mark 5:7 [i] ver. 69; 2 Sam. 7:11-13, 16; Ps. 89:4; 132:11; Isa. 9:6, 7; 16:5; Acts 2:30; [Rev. 3:7] [j] See Matt. 1:1 **33**[k] Dan. 2:44; 7:14, 18, 27; Heb. 1:8; Rev. 11:15; [John 12:34] **35**[l] Matt. 1:18, 20 [h] [See ver. 32 above] [m] John 6:69 [n] See Matt. 14:33 **36**[o] ver. 7 **37**[p] Cited from Gen. 18:14 (Gk.); See Matt. 19:26 **38**[q] [Judg. 6:21; Acts 12:10] **39**[r] ver. 65; Josh. 20:7; 21:11 **41**[s] ver. 15, 67

the Holy Spirit, 42 and she exclaimed with a
loud cry, [t]"Blessed are you among women, and
[u]blessed is [v]the fruit of your womb! 43 And why
is this granted to me that the mother of [w]my
Lord should come to me? 44 For behold, when
the sound of your greeting came to my ears,
the baby in my womb leaped for joy. 45 And
[x]blessed is she who believed that there would
be[1] a fulfillment of what was spoken to her
from the Lord."

Mary's Song of Praise: The Magnificat

46 And Mary said,

[y]"My [z]soul [a]magnifies the Lord,
47 [b]and my [z]spirit rejoices in [c]God my Savior,
48 for [d]he has looked on the humble estate of his servant.
For behold, from now on all generations [e]will call me blessed;
49 for [f]he who is mighty [g]has done great things for me,
and [h]holy is his name.
50 And [i]his mercy is for those who fear him from generation to generation.
51 [j]He has shown strength with his arm;
[k]he has scattered the proud in the thoughts of their hearts;
52 [j]he has brought down the mighty from their thrones
[l]and exalted those of humble estate;
53 he has filled [m]the hungry with good things,
and the rich [n]he has sent away empty.
54 He has [o]helped [p]his servant Israel,
[q]in remembrance of his mercy,
55 [r]as he spoke to our fathers,
[q]to Abraham and to his offspring forever."

56 And Mary remained with her about three
months and returned to her home.

The Birth of John the Baptist

57 Now the time came for Elizabeth to give
birth, and she bore a son. 58 And her neighbors and relatives heard that the Lord [s]had
shown great mercy to her, and they rejoiced
with her. 59 And [t]on the eighth day they came
to circumcise the child. And they would have
called him Zechariah after his father, 60 but
his mother answered, "No; [u]he shall be called
John." 61 And they said to her, "None of your
relatives is called by this name." 62 And [v]they
made signs to his father, inquiring what he
wanted him to be called. 63 And he asked for [w]a
writing tablet and wrote, [u]"His name is John."
And they all wondered. 64 [x]And immediately
his mouth was opened and his tongue [y]loosed,
and he spoke, [z]blessing God. 65 And [a]fear came
on all their neighbors. And all these things
were talked about through all [b]the hill country of Judea, 66 and all who heard them [c]laid
them up in their hearts, saying, "What then
will this child be?" For [d]the hand of the Lord
was with him.

Zechariah's Prophecy

67 And his father Zechariah [e]was filled with
the Holy Spirit and [f]prophesied, saying,

68 [g]"Blessed be the Lord [h]God of Israel,
for he has [i]visited and [j]redeemed his people

[1] Or *believed, for there will be*

1:67–79 This Spirit-inspired proclamation from Zechariah gives us a beautiful and powerful picture of the gospel. We often think of the gospel as the message of God legally forgiving our sins ("justifying" us) because of Jesus' work on the cross. While this is true, Zechariah's song (along with many other Bible passages) shows us that the gospel is even more comprehensive.

The gospel is explained here as God visiting and staying with his people (v. 68), saving us from our enemies (v. 71), fulfilling his ancient promises for us (vv. 72–73), delivering us so that we might serve him without fear (v. 75), forgiving our sins (v. 77), shining light on our darkness (v. 79), and guiding us into a life of peace (v. 79). The gospel is full of mercy (God *not* giving us what our sin deserves), but even more, it is full of grace, with God giving us countless gifts and his own presence!

When we begin to grasp the breadth and depth of the gracious, comprehensive work of God through Jesus as described here, our hearts are engaged with devotion

42[t] [Judg. 5:24] [u] [Deut. 28:4] [v] Ps. 127:3 **43**[w] ch. 20:42; John 20:28; [ch. 2:11] **45**[x] John 20:29; [ver. 20] **46**[y] For ver. 46-53, [1 Sam. 2:1-10] [z] 1 Thess. 5:23 [a] Ps. 34:2, 3; 69:30; Acts 10:46; 19:17 **47**[b] Ps. 35:9; Isa. 61:10; Hab. 3:18; [Acts 16:34] [z] [See ver. 46 above] [c] Ps. 106:21; 1 Tim. 1:1; 2:3; Titus 1:3; 2:10; 3:4; Jude 25; [2 Tim. 1:9] **48**[d] 1 Sam. 1:11; Ps. 138:6; [ch. 9:38] [e] ch. 11:27; Ps. 72:17; [Mal. 3:12] **49**[f] Ps. 89:8; Zeph. 3:17 [g] Ps. 71:19; 126:2, 3 [h] Ps. 99:3; 111:9; Isa. 57:15 **50**[i] Deut. 5:10; 7:9; Ps. 89:1, 2; 103:17 **51**[j] Ps. 89:10; 98:1; 118:16; Isa. 51:9 [k] Dan. 4:37; See James 4:6 **52**[j] [See ver. 51 above] [l] Job 5:11; Ps. 75:7; 107:40, 41; 113:7, 8; 147:6; Ezek. 21:26; [James 4:10] **53**[m] Ps. 34:10; 107:9; [ch. 6:21, 24, 25] [n] Job 22:9 **54**[o] Isa. 41:8, 9; Heb. 2:16 [p] Isa. 44:21; 49:3 [q] Ps. 98:3; Mic. 7:20; [ver. 72, 73] **55**[r] Gen. 17:19; Ps. 132:11; Gal. 3:16 [q] [See ver. 54 above] **58**[s] Gen. 19:19 **59**[t] ch. 2:21; Gen. 17:12; Lev. 12:3; Phil. 3:5 **60**[u] ver. 13 **62**[v] ver. 22 **63**[w] Isa. 8:1; 30:8 [u] [See ver. 60 above] **64**[x] ver. 20 [y] Mark 7:35 [z] ch. 2:28; 24:53 **65**[a] ch. 7:16 [b] See ver. 39 **66**[c] [ch. 2:19, 51] [d] Acts 11:21; 13:11 **67**[e] ver. 15, 41 [f] Joel 2:28 **68**[g] 1 Kgs. 1:48; 1 Chr. 29:10; Ezra 7:27; Ps. 41:13; 72:18; 106:48 [h] Isa. 29:23; Matt. 15:31; Acts 13:17 [i] ch. 7:16; Ex. 4:31; [ver. 78; Acts 15:14; Heb. 2:6] [j] ch. 2:38; Ps. 111:9; 130:7, 8; [ch. 24:21; Isa. 43:1; 59:20]

69 and [k]has raised up [l]a horn of salvation
for us
[m]in the house of his servant David,
70 [n]as [o]he spoke by the mouth of his holy
prophets from of old,
71 [p]that we should be saved from our enemies
and from the hand of all who hate us;
72 [q]to show the mercy promised to our
fathers
and [r]to remember his holy [s]covenant,
73 [t]the oath that he swore to our father
Abraham, to grant us
74 that we, being delivered from the
hand of our enemies,
might serve him [u]without fear,
75 [v]in holiness and righteousness before
him [w]all our days.
76 And you, child, will be called [x]the
prophet of [y]the Most High;
for [z]you will go before the Lord to prepare his ways,
77 to give knowledge of salvation to his
people
[a]in the forgiveness of their sins,
78 because of the [b]tender mercy of our God,
whereby [c]the sunrise shall [d]visit us[1]
[e]from on high
79 to [f]give light to [g]those who sit in darkness and in the shadow of death,
to guide our feet into [h]the way of
[i]peace."

80 [j]And the child grew and became strong in
spirit, and he was [k]in the wilderness until the
day of his public appearance to Israel.

The Birth of Jesus Christ

2 In those days [l]a decree went out from
[m]Caesar Augustus that all the world should
be [n]registered. 2 This was the first [n]registration
when[2] Quirinius [o]was governor of Syria. 3 And
all went to be registered, each to his own town.
4 And Joseph also went up [p]from Galilee, from
the town of [q]Nazareth, to Judea, to [r]the city of
David, which is called [s]Bethlehem, [t]because
he was of the house and lineage of David, 5 to
be registered with Mary, his betrothed,[3] who
was with child. 6 And [t]while they were there,
the time came for her to give birth. 7 And she
gave birth to her firstborn son and [u]wrapped
him in swaddling cloths and [v]laid him in a
manger, because there was no place for them
in [w]the inn.

The Shepherds and the Angels

8 And in the same region there were shepherds out in the field, keeping watch over
their flock by night. 9 And an angel of the Lord
[x]appeared to them, and [y]the glory of the Lord
shone around them, and they were filled with
great fear. 10 And the angel said to them, "Fear
not, for behold, I bring you good news of great
joy that will be for all [z]the people. 11 For [a]unto
you is born this day in [b]the city of David [c]a
Savior, who is [d]Christ [e]the Lord. 12 And [f]this
will be a sign for you: you will find a baby
[g]wrapped in swaddling cloths and lying in a

[1] Or *when the sunrise shall dawn upon us*; some manuscripts *since the sunrise has visited us* [2] Or *This was the registration before* [3] That is, one legally pledged to be married

to God. We begin to get a vision of all that God is for us. Understanding the gospel in this broader way makes Jesus not just the "religious" part of our lives but the focus of all our hopes. We should meditate regularly on the fullness of our salvation!

2:8–14 This familiar Christmastime story contains a depth of gospel meaning that we may not see at first glance. Rather than bringing fear, which is the appropriate response to seeing the glory and greatness of God, the gospel (the "good news") is described by the angels as "great joy that will be for all the people" (v. 10). It is a message of joy because a Savior and Lord has arrived to save and reign over us, including even those not born of Jewish descent. It is a message of joy because this Savior and Lord is the One who brings peace and acceptance from God himself (v. 14).

To receive the good news of the gospel is to come to understand that, despite our background and failures, God reaches out to us with the loving message of peace. Receiving the gospel is not just understanding an abstract idea but it is believing by faith that the glorious God of the universe is now pleased with us and speaks peace into our personal lives. The result is release from fear (v. 10) and entry into freedom, joy, and an eager seeking after this Lord (v. 15).

69[k] 1 Sam. 2:1, 10; Ps. 132:17; Ezek. 29:21 [l] 2 Sam. 22:3; Ps. 18:2 [m] ver. 32
70[n] Rom. 1:2; [Jer. 23:5, 6] [o] Acts 3:21
71[p] Ps. 106:10
72[q] Mic. 7:20 [r] Lev. 26:42; Ps. 105:8, 9; [ver. 54, 55] [s] See Rom. 9:4
73[t] Gen. 22:16-18; 26:3; Heb. 6:13, 14
74[u] Zeph. 3:15
75[v] Eph. 4:24; [1 Thess. 2:10; Titus 2:12] [w] [Jer. 32:39 (Heb.); Matt. 28:20 (Gk.)]
76[x] ch. 7:26; 20:6; Matt. 11:9; 14:5 [y] See ver. 32 [z] ver. 17; ch. 3:4; 7:27; Mal. 3:1; Matt. 3:3; Mark 1:2, 3
77[a] [Matt. 26:28; Mark 1:4]
78[b] Col. 3:12 (Gk.) [c] Mal. 4:2; Eph. 5:14; 2 Pet. 1:19 [d] See ver. 68 [e] ch. 24:49
79[f] Isa. 9:2; Matt. 4:16; [Acts 26:18]; See John 8:12

[g] Ps. 107:10; Isa. 42:7 [h] Rom. 3:17 [i] See ch. 2:14 **80**[j] ch. 2:40 [k] Matt. 3:1; 11:7 **Chapter 2** **1**[l] Acts 17:7 [m] [ch. 3:1] [n] [Acts 5:37] **2**[n] [See ver. 1 above] [o] ch. 3:1 **4**[p] ch. 1:26 [q] See Matt. 2:23 [r] ver. 11; John 7:42; [1 Sam. 16:1] [s] Matt. 2:1 [t] ch. 1:27 **6**[t] [See ver. 4 above] **7**[u] ver. 12 [v] ver. 16 [w] ch. 22:11 (Gk.) **9**[x] ch. 24:4; Acts 12:7 [y] ch. 9:31; Acts 7:55; 2 Cor. 3:18 **10**[z] ver. 32; John 11:50; [Zech. 9:9] **11**[a] Isa. 9:6 [b] ver. 4 [c] Matt. 1:21; John 4:42 [d] Acts 2:36; 10:36; [ch. 23:2]; See Matt. 1:17 [e] [ch. 1:43] **12**[f] 1 Sam. 2:34; 2 Kgs. 19:29; 20:8, 9; Isa. 7:11, 14 [g] ver. 7

manger." 13 And suddenly there was with the angel [h]a multitude of the heavenly host praising God and saying,

14 [i]"Glory to God [j]in the highest,
[j]and on earth [k]peace [l]among those
with whom he is pleased!"[1]

15 When the angels went away from them into heaven, the shepherds said to one another, "Let us go over to Bethlehem and see this thing that has happened, which the Lord has made known to us." 16 And they went with haste and found Mary and Joseph, and the baby [m]lying in a manger. 17 And when they saw it, they made known the saying that had been told them concerning this child. 18 And all who heard it wondered at what the shepherds told them. 19 But [n]Mary treasured up all these things, pondering them in her heart. 20 And the shepherds returned, [o]glorifying and praising God for all they had heard and seen, as it had been told them.

21 And [p]at the end of eight days, when he was circumcised, [q]he was called Jesus, the name given by the angel before he was conceived in the womb.

Jesus Presented at the Temple

22 And [r]when the time came for their purification according to the Law of Moses, they brought him up to Jerusalem [s]to present him to the Lord 23 (as it is written in [t]the Law of the Lord, [u]"Every male who first opens the womb shall be called holy to the Lord") 24 and to offer a sacrifice according to what is said in [t]the Law of the Lord, [v]"a pair of turtledoves, or two young pigeons." 25 Now there was a man in Jerusalem, whose name was Simeon, and this man was [w]righteous and [x]devout, [y]waiting for [z]the consolation of Israel, and the Holy Spirit was upon him. 26 And it had been revealed to him by the Holy Spirit that he would not [a]see death before he had seen [b]the Lord's Christ. 27 And he came in the Spirit into the temple, and when [c]the parents brought in the child Jesus, to do for him according to the custom of the Law, 28 he took him up in his arms and [d]blessed God and said,

29 "Lord, now you are letting your servant[2]
depart [e]in peace,
[f]according to your word;
30 for [g]my eyes have seen your [h]salvation
31 [i]that you have prepared in the presence of all peoples,
32 [j]a light for revelation to the Gentiles,
and [k]for glory to [l]your people Israel."

33 And [m]his father and his mother marveled at what was said about him. 34 And Simeon blessed them and said to Mary his mother, "Behold, this child is appointed [n]for the fall and rising of many in Israel, and for a sign [o]that is opposed 35 (and a sword will pierce through your own soul also), so that thoughts from many hearts may be revealed."

36 And there was [p]a prophetess, Anna, the daughter of Phanuel, of the tribe of Asher. She was advanced in years, having lived with her husband seven years from when she was a virgin, 37 and then as a widow until she was eighty-four.[3] She did not depart from the temple, [q]worshiping with [r]fasting and prayer night and day. 38 And coming up at that very hour she began to give thanks to God and to speak of him to all who were [s]waiting for the redemption of Jerusalem.

[1] Some manuscripts *peace, good will among men* [2] Greek *bondservant* [3] Or *as a widow for eighty-four years*

2:29–35 In Simeon's words we see the universal scope of the gospel. Now in Jesus, God's plan from the beginning of creation is being accomplished—the spreading of his grace to all the earth, to Jew and Gentile (vv. 31–32).

Yet this gospel which corporately unites all people together also divides all people at the level of the heart (vv. 34–35). Because Jesus is God himself in the flesh, to face the gospel of Jesus is to face God. And to face God is to have our thoughts and hearts opened and revealed (Heb. 4:12). This will result in a fall for any who are proud or opposed to Jesus (Luke 2:34). But for those like Simeon who see Jesus and respond to him with hope, there is great news! This story invites us to see Jesus rightly and receive him at the level of the heart as Savior and Lord, holding back nothing because God sees and knows all things, even what is in our hearts (Ps. 139:1–6).

13 [h]Gen. 28:12; 32:1, 2; 1 Kgs. 22:19; 2 Chr. 18:18; Ps. 103:21; 148:2; Dan. 7:10; Rev. 5:11
14 [i]ch. 19:38; [Ps. 148:1; Matt. 21:9] [j][ch. 10:21; Matt. 6:10; 28:18; John 17:4; Acts 7:49; Eph. 3:15; Col. 1:16, 20; Rev. 5:13] [k]ch. 1:79; Ps. 85:10; Isa. 9:6, 7; Hag. 2:9; Acts 10:36; Rom. 5:1; Eph. 2:14, 17; Col. 1:20 [l][ch. 3:22; 12:32; Eph. 1:5, 9; Phil. 2:13]
16 [m]ver. 7, 12
19 [n]ver. 51; [ch. 1:66; Gen. 37:11]

20 [o]See ch. 7:16 **21** [p]See ch. 1:59 [q]ch. 1:31; Matt. 1:21, 25 **22** [r]Lev. 12; [ver. 21, 27; Gal. 4:4] [s][1 Sam. 1:22, 24] **23** [t]ver. 39; Ex. 13:9; 2 Chr. 31:3 [u][Ex. 13:2, 12] **24** [t][See ver. 23 above] [v]Cited from Lev. 12:8 **25** [w]ch. 1:6 [x]Acts 2:5; 8:2; 22:12 [y]ver. 38; ch. 23:51; Isa. 25:9; Mark 15:43; [Gen. 49:18] [z]Isa. 40:1; 57:18 **26** [a]Ps. 89:48; John 8:51; Heb. 11:5; [Acts 2:27] [b][ch. 9:20; 23:35; 1 Sam. 24:6] **27** [c]ver. 33, 41, 43, 48-51 **28** [d]ch. 1:64 **29** [e]Gen. 15:15 [f]ver. 26 **30** [g]Isa. 52:10 [h]See ch. 3:6 **31** [i]Ps. 98:2; See ch. 24:47 **32** [j]Isa. 42:6; 49:6; 52:10; 60:3; John 8:12; Acts 13:47; 26:23 [k][Isa. 45:25; 46:13] [l]ver. 10 **33** [m]ver. 27 **34** [n][Isa. 8:14; Matt. 21:44; John 9:39; 1 Cor. 1:23, 24; 2 Cor. 2:16; 1 Pet. 2:8, 9] [o]Acts 28:22 **36** [p]See Ex. 15:20 **37** [q]1 Tim. 5:5 [r]ch. 5:33; Matt. 6:16-18; Acts 13:2; 14:23; 2 Cor. 6:5; 11:27 **38** [s]ver. 25; See ch. 1:68

The Return to Nazareth

39 And when they had performed everything according to [t]the Law of the Lord, they
returned into Galilee, to their own town of
[u]Nazareth. 40 [v]And the child grew and became
strong, filled with wisdom. And the favor of
God was upon him.

The Boy Jesus in the Temple

41 Now [w]his parents went [x]to Jerusalem every
year at [y]the Feast of the Passover. 42 And when
he was twelve years old, [z]they went up according to custom. 43 And when the feast [a]was
ended, as they were returning, the boy Jesus
stayed behind in Jerusalem. [w]His parents did
not know it, 44 but supposing him to be in the
group they went a day's journey, but then they
began to search for him among their relatives
and acquaintances, 45 and when they did not
find him, they returned to Jerusalem, searching for him. 46 After three days they found him
in the temple, [b]sitting among [c]the teachers,
listening to them and asking them questions.
47 And all who heard him were amazed at his
understanding and his answers. 48 And when
his parents[1] saw him, they were astonished.
And his mother said to him, "Son, why have
you treated us so? Behold, [d]your father and
I have been searching for you in great distress."
49 And he said to them, "Why were you looking for me? Did you not know that [e]I must be
in [f]my Father's house?"[2] 50 And [g]they did not
understand the saying that he spoke to them.
51 And he went down with them and came to
Nazareth and was submissive to them. And
[h]his mother treasured up all these things in
her heart.

52 And Jesus [i]increased in wisdom and in stature[3] and in [i]favor with God and man.

John the Baptist Prepares the Way

3 In the fifteenth year of the reign of
[j]Tiberius Caesar, [k]Pontius Pilate [l]being
governor of Judea, and [m]Herod being tetrarch
of Galilee, and his brother Philip tetrarch of
the region of Ituraea and Trachonitis, and
Lysanias tetrarch of Abilene, 2 during [n]the high
priesthood of Annas and [o]Caiaphas, [p]the word
of God came to [q]John the son of Zechariah
in [r]the wilderness. 3 And he went into all the
region around the Jordan, proclaiming [s]a baptism of repentance [t]for the forgiveness of sins.
4 As it is written in [u]the book of the words of
Isaiah the prophet,

[v]"The voice of one crying in the wilderness:
[w]'Prepare the way of the Lord,[4]
make his paths straight.
5 [x]Every valley shall be filled,
[y]and every mountain and hill shall be
made low,
[z]and the crooked shall become straight,
and the rough places shall become
level ways,
6 [a]and all flesh shall see [b]the salvation of
God.'"

7 He said therefore to the crowds that came
out to be baptized by him, [c]"You brood of
[d]vipers! Who warned you to flee from [e]the
wrath to come? 8 Bear fruits [f]in keeping with
repentance. And do not begin to say to yourselves, [g]'We have Abraham as our father.' For
I tell you, God is able from [h]these stones to

[1] Greek *they* [2] Or *about my Father's business* [3] Or *years* [4] Or *crying, Prepare in the wilderness the way of the Lord*

39[t] ver. 23 [u] ver. 4
40[v] ch. 1:80
41[w] ver. 27 [x] [1 Sam. 1:3] [y] Ex. 23:15; Deut. 16:1; John 2:13
42[z] John 11:55
43[a] Ex. 12:15; Lev. 23:8; Deut. 16:3 [w] [See ver. 41 above]
46[b] See Matt. 26:55 [c] ch. 5:17
48[d] ver. 27; [ver. 49]
49[e] See ch. 13:33 [f] John 2:16; 14:2
50[g] [ch. 18:34]; See Mark 9:32
51[h] See ver. 19
52[i] [1 Sam. 2:26]
Chapter 3
1[j] [ch. 2:1] [k] See Matt. 27:2 [l] ch. 2:2 [m] ver. 19; ch. 8:3; 9:7, 9; 13:31; 23:7; Matt. 14:1; Acts 4:27; 13:1; [Mark 6:14]
2[n] John 18:13, 24; Acts 4:6 [o] See Matt. 26:3

3:3 Experiencing the forgiveness of sins, which is a foundational part of the gospel, comes to us through repentance. John offered a baptism that was not a magical ritual but represented a turning from sin on the part of the one being baptized. This is a matter of the heart. It is bad news for those who wish to earn God's favor by religious actions. It is good news if we are willing to receive and experience the gospel at the level of the heart, turning away from our sins toward God.

3:7–9 John's command to bear fruits that correspond with repentance shows that there is both a true and a false kind of repentance. The false kind of repentance has some appearance of good but comes from an unhealthy, non-fruit-bearing tree and from those who may be called a "brood of vipers." These images both speak of the inner person. This is a heart issue, not just a behavioral one. The viperous people who have a false repentance are trusting in their heritage, standing, and past acts ("we have Abraham as our father"; v. 8). There is a real gospel warning here—not against weak faith or imperfect piety, but against a false repentance based on self-reliance.

[p] For ver. 2-17, see Matt. 3:1-12; Mark 1:2-8 [q] John 1:6, 7 [r] ch. 1:80; Josh. 15:61; [Judg. 1:16] **3**[s] Acts 2:38 [t] Matt. 26:28; [ch. 1:77] **4**[u] ch. 4:17; [Acts 8:28] [v] John 1:23; Cited from Isa. 40:3-5 [w] ch. 1:76 **5**[x] [Isa. 57:14] [y] Isa. 49:11; Zech. 4:7 [z] Isa. 42:16; 45:2 **6**[a] Isa. 52:10; [Ps. 98:2, 3] [b] ch. 2:30; Acts 28:28; [ch. 1:69, 71, 77; Titus 2:11] **7**[c] Matt. 12:34; 23:33 [d] Ps. 140:3 [e] Rom. 5:9; Eph. 5:6; Col. 3:6; 1 Thess. 1:10 **8**[f] Acts 26:20 [g] John 8:39 [h] [ch. 4:3]

raise up children for Abraham. [9]Even now the
axe is laid to the root of the trees. [i]Every tree
therefore that does not bear good fruit is cut
down and thrown into the fire."
[10]And the crowds asked him, [j]"What then
shall we do?" [11]And he answered them,
[k]"Whoever has two tunics[1] is to share with
him who has none, and whoever has food is
to do likewise." [12][l]Tax collectors also came
to be baptized and said to him, "Teacher,
[j]what shall we do?" [13]And he said to them,
[m]"Collect no more than you are authorized to
do." [14]Soldiers also asked him, "And we, [j]what
shall we do?" And he said to them, [m]"Do not
extort money from anyone by threats or by
false accusation, and be content with your
[n]wages."
[15]As the people were in expectation, and
all were questioning in their hearts concerning John, [o]whether he might be [p]the Christ,
[16][q]John answered them all, saying, "I baptize you with water, but [r]he who is mightier
than I is coming, [s]the strap of whose sandals
I am not worthy to untie. He will baptize you
[t]with the Holy Spirit and [u]fire. [17]His [v]winnow-
ing fork is in his hand, to clear his threshing
floor and to [w]gather the wheat into his barn,
[x]but the chaff he will burn with [y]unquench-
able fire."
[18]So [z]with many other exhortations he
preached good news to the people. [19]But
[a]Herod the tetrarch, who had been reproved
by him for Herodias, his brother's wife, and
for all the evil things that Herod had done,
[20]added this to them all, that [b]he locked up
John in prison.
[21]Now when all the people were baptized,
and when [c]Jesus also had been baptized and
was praying, [d]the heavens were opened, [22]and
[e]the Holy Spirit descended on him in bodily
form, like a dove; and [f]a voice came from
heaven, [g]"You are my beloved Son;[2] with you
I am well pleased."[3]

The Genealogy of Jesus Christ

[23]Jesus, [h]when he began his ministry, was
about [i]thirty years of age, being [j]the son (as was
supposed) of Joseph, the son of Heli, [24]the son
of Matthat, the son of Levi, the son of Melchi,
the son of Jannai, the son of Joseph, [25]the son
of Mattathias, the son of Amos, the son of
Nahum, the son of Esli, the son of Naggai,
[26]the son of Maath, the son of Mattathias, the
son of Semein, the son of Josech, the son of
Joda, [27]the son of Joanan, the son of Rhesa,
[k]the son of Zerubbabel, the son [l]of Shealtiel,[4]
the son of Neri, [28]the son of Melchi, the son of
Addi, the son of Cosam, the son of Elmadam,
the son of Er, [29]the son of Joshua, the son of
Eliezer, the son of Jorim, the son of Matthat,
the son of Levi, [30]the son of Simeon, the son
of Judah, the son of Joseph, the son of Jonam,
the son of Eliakim, [31]the son of Melea, the
son of Menna, the son of Mattatha, the son
of [m]Nathan, the son of David, [32][n]the son of
Jesse, the son of Obed, the son of Boaz, the
son of Sala, the son of Nahshon, [33]the son of
Amminadab, the son of Admin, the son of
Arni, the son of Hezron, the son of Perez, the
son of Judah, [34][o]the son of Jacob, [p]the son of
Isaac, [q]the son of Abraham, [r]the son of Terah,
the son of Nahor, [35]the son of Serug, the son
of Reu, the son of Peleg, the son of Eber, the
son of Shelah, [36]the son of Cainan, the son of
Arphaxad, the son of Shem, the son of Noah,
the son of Lamech, [37]the son of Methuselah,
the son of Enoch, the son of Jared, the son of
Mahalaleel, the son of Cainan, [38]the son of
Enos, the son of Seth, the son of Adam, the
son of God.

[1] Greek *chiton*, a long garment worn under the cloak next to the skin [2] Or *my Son, my* (or *the*) *Beloved* [3] Some manuscripts *beloved Son; today I have begotten you* [4] Greek *Salathiel*

3:10–14 John's various instructions regarding repentance are very informative for applying the gospel to our lives. There is no cookie-cutter formula for what gospel application looks like for different people in different walks of life. What is consistent in these assorted instructions is a heart-level truthfulness and a treating of others as we would want to be treated (6:31). The considerations that form the second greatest command of the Old Testament law—to love our neighbor as ourselves (10:27; cf. Deut. 6:5)—also inform gospel application with regard to relating to one another, demonstrating the consistency of God's heart throughout the Bible.

9[i] ch. 13:7, 9; Matt. 7:19; John 15:2, 6
10[j] Acts 2:37; 16:30; 22:10
11[k] Isa. 58:7; Dan. 4:27; Eph. 4:28; James 2:15, 16; 1 John 3:17; [ch. 18:22]
12[l] ch. 7:29; Matt. 21:32 [j] [See ver. 10 above]
13[m] ch. 19:8
14[j] [See ver. 10 above] [m] [See ver. 13 above]

[n] 1 Cor. 9:7 (Gk.) **15**[o] John 1:19, 20 [p] See Matt. 1:17 **16**[q] John 1:26; Acts 1:5 [r] John 1:15, 27; 3:30, 31; Acts 13:25 [s] Isa. 5:27 [t] John 1:33; Acts 11:16 [u] [Mal. 3:2, 3; Acts 2:3] **17**[v] Isa. 30:24 [w] Matt. 13:30 [x] Mal. 4:1 [y] Mark 9:43, 48 **18**[z] [John 20:30; 21:25] **19**[a] Matt. 14:3; Mark 6:17, 18; See ver. 1 **20**[b] [John 3:24] **21**[c] For ver. 21, 22, see Matt. 3:13-17; Mark 1:9-11; [John 1:32-34] [d] Acts 7:56 **22**[e] [ch. 4:18, 21; Acts 10:38] [f] John 12:28 [g] [ch. 9:35; Ps. 2:7; Isa. 42:1; Eph. 1:6; Col. 1:13; 2 Pet. 1:17; 1 John 5:9] **23**[h] Matt. 4:17; Acts 1:1, 22 [i] [Num. 4:3] [j] ch. 4:22; Matt. 13:55; John 1:45; 6:42; For ver. 23-38, [Matt. 1:1-16] **27**[k] Matt. 1:12 [l] Ezra 3:2 **31**[m] 2 Sam. 5:14; 1 Chr. 3:5; 14:4; Zech. 12:12 **32**[n] 1 Sam. 16:1; 17:12; [Ruth 4:18-22; 1 Chr. 2:1-15] **34**[o] Gen. 29:35 [p] Gen. 25:26 [q] Gen. 21:3 [r] For ver. 34-38, see Gen. 5:3-32; 11:10-26; 1 Chr. 1:1-4, 24-27

The Temptation of Jesus

4 [s]And Jesus, [t]full of the Holy Spirit,
[u]returned from the Jordan and was led [v]by
the Spirit in the wilderness 2 for [w]forty days,
[x]being tempted by the devil. [w]And he ate nothing during those days. And when they were
ended, [y]he was hungry. 3 The devil said to him,
"If you are [z]the Son of God, command [a]this
stone to become bread." 4 And Jesus answered
him, [b]"It is written, [c]'Man shall not live by
bread alone.'" 5 [d]And the devil took him up and
showed him all the kingdoms of the world in
a moment of time, 6 and said to him, "To you
[e]I will give all this authority and their glory,
[e]for it has been delivered to me, and I give it
to whom I will. 7 If you, then, will worship me,
it will all be yours." 8 And Jesus answered him,
[f]"It is written,

[g]"'You shall worship the Lord your God,
and [h]him only shall you serve.'"

9 [i]And he took him to Jerusalem and set him on
the pinnacle of the temple and said to him, "If
you are [j]the Son of God, throw yourself down
from here, 10 for it is written,

[k]"'He will command his angels concerning you,
to guard you,'

11 and

[k]"'On their hands they will bear you up,
lest you strike your foot against a stone.'"

12 And Jesus answered him, "It is said, [l]'You
shall not [m]put the Lord your God to the test.'"
13 And when the devil had ended every temptation, he departed from him [n]until an oppor-
tune time.

Jesus Begins His Ministry

14 [o]And Jesus returned [p]in the power of the
Spirit to Galilee, and [q]a report about him went
out through all the surrounding country.
15 And [r]he taught in their synagogues, being
glorified by all.

Jesus Rejected at Nazareth

16 [s]And he came to [t]Nazareth, where he had
been brought up. And [u]as was his custom, [v]he
went to the synagogue on the Sabbath day, and
he stood up [w]to read. 17 And [x]the scroll of the
prophet Isaiah was given to him. He unrolled
the scroll and found the place where it was
written,

18 [y]"The Spirit of the Lord [z]is upon me,
because he has anointed me
to [a]proclaim good news to the poor.
[b]He has sent me to proclaim liberty to the captives
and [c]recovering of sight to the blind,
[d]to set at liberty those who are oppressed,
19 [e]to proclaim the year of the Lord's favor."

20 And he rolled up the scroll and gave it back
to the attendant and [f]sat down. And the eyes
of all in the synagogue were [g]fixed on him.

Chapter 4
1 [s]For ver. 1-13, see Matt. 4:1-11; Mark 1:12, 13 [t]ver. 18; ch. 3:22; John 1:33; 3:34; Acts 10:38; [ch. 1:15; Acts 6:5] [u]ch. 3:3, 21 [v]ver. 14
2 [w][Deut. 9:9, 18; 1 Kgs. 19:8] [x][Heb. 2:18; 4:15] [y][John 4:6, 7]
3 [z]See Matt. 14:33 [a][ch. 3:8]
4 [b]ver. 8, 10; Eph. 6:17 [c]Cited from Deut. 8:3; [John 4:34]
5 [d]Matt. 4:8
6 [e]Rev. 13:2
8 [f]ver. 4; [ver. 12] [g]Cited from Deut. 6:13 [h]1 Sam. 7:3
9 [i]Matt. 4:5 [j]ver. 3
10 [k]Cited from Ps. 91:11, 12
11 [k][See ver. 10 above]
12 [l]Cited from Deut. 6:16 [m][Isa. 7:12]
13 [n][ch. 22:53; John 14:30]
14 [o]Matt. 4:12 [p]ver. 1; [Acts 1:8] [q]ver. 37
15 [r]See Matt. 4:23
16 [s]For ver. 16-30, [Matt. 13:54-58; Mark 6:1-6] [t]ch. 2:39, 51 [u][Acts 17:2] [v]ver. 31; See Mark 6:2

4:1–12 Before Jesus' ministry can begin he must experience temptation so that he may fully commune with humanity as a true man (Heb. 4:15). Typically this passage is applied by exhorting the believer to follow Jesus' example of using Scripture when facing temptation. This is not wrong and is a wise course of action, but absolute Christlikeness in heart and action is beyond mere human accomplishment. So there is something deeper at work here as well. Jesus models for us what gospel faith looks like—trusting the Lord to provide rather than making decisions based on the urgencies of the situation. In each temptation the Devil presented a half-truth. But in each temptation Jesus sees the deeper principle at work, that the call of faith is the call to look to the Lord's provision and timing. This kind of gospel living brings glory to God alone and defeats temptation.

4:18–19 In these verses we have yet another way in which the message of the gospel is explained. It is good news for those afflicted and in need (the "poor"); it is new freedom and liberty for those in bondage and the oppressed; it is a restoration of sight to the blind; it is, in short, the time and place of God's favor upon those incapable of gaining it by their status or abilities. These images are first physical in meaning but they have a spiritual application as well. There is no inherent virtue in being poor or oppressed or in bondage, but these experiences typically correspond to and foster a certain condition of heart and soul. When we recognize our brokenness and bondage

[w]Acts 13:15, 27; 15:21 **17** [x]ch. 3:4; [Acts 8:28] **18** [y]Cited from Isa. 61:1, 2 [z]ver. 1; [Acts 1:2] [a]Matt. 11:5; [ch. 6:20] [b]Ps. 146:7, 8 [c][Isa. 42:7; John 9:39; Acts 26:18] [d]Isa. 58:6 **19** [e]Lev. 25:10; [Isa. 49:8; 2 Cor. 6:2] **20** [f]Matt. 26:55; [John 8:2]; [Matt. 5:1; 13:2] [g]Acts 3:4; [ch. 19:48]

21 And he began to say to them, "Today [h]this
Scripture [i]has been fulfilled in your hearing."
22 And all spoke well of him and marveled at
[j]the gracious words that were coming from his
mouth. And they said, [k]"Is not this [l]Joseph's
son?" 23 And he said to them, "Doubtless you
will quote to me this proverb, [m]'Physician,
heal yourself.' What we have heard you did
[n]at Capernaum, do here in your hometown as
well." 24 And he said, "Truly, I say to you, [o]no
prophet is acceptable in his hometown. 25 But
in truth, I tell you, there were many widows in
Israel in the days of Elijah, when [p]the heavens
were shut up three years and six months, and
a great famine came over all the land, 26 and
Elijah was sent to none of them [q]but only to
Zarephath, in the land of Sidon, to a woman
who was a widow. 27 And [r]there were many lepers[1] in Israel in the time of the prophet Elisha,
and none of them was cleansed, [s]but only
Naaman the Syrian." 28 When they heard these
things, all in the synagogue were filled with
wrath. 29 And they rose up and [t]drove him out
of the town and brought him to the brow of
the hill on which their town was built, so that
they could throw him down the cliff. 30 But
[u]passing through their midst, he went away.

Jesus Heals a Man with an Unclean Demon

31 [v]And he [w]went down to Capernaum, a city
of Galilee. And [x]he was teaching them [y]on the
Sabbath, 32 and [z]they were astonished at his
teaching, [z]for his word possessed authority.
33 And [x]in the synagogue there was a man
who had the spirit of an unclean demon, and
he cried out with a loud voice, 34 "Ha![2] [a]What
have you to do with us, Jesus of Nazareth?
Have you come to destroy us? [b]I know who
you are—[c]the Holy One of God." 35 But Jesus
[d]rebuked him, saying, "Be silent and come out
of him!" And when the demon had thrown
him down in their midst, he came out of him,
having done him no harm. 36 And [e]they were
all amazed and said to one another, "What is
this word? [e]For with authority and power he
commands the unclean spirits, and they come
out!" 37 And [f]reports about him went out into
every place in the surrounding region.

Jesus Heals Many

38 [g]And he arose and left the synagogue
and entered Simon's house. Now [h]Simon's
mother-in-law was ill with a high fever, and
they appealed to him on her behalf. 39 And he
stood over her and [i]rebuked the fever, and it
left her, and immediately she rose and began
to serve them.
40 Now when the sun was setting, all those
who had any who were sick with various diseases brought them to him, and [j]he laid his
hands on every one of them and healed them.
41 [k]And demons also came out of many, [l]crying,
"You are [m]the Son of God!" But he rebuked
them and [k]would not allow them to speak,
because they knew that he was [n]the Christ.

Jesus Preaches in Synagogues

42 [o]And when it was day, he departed and
went [p]into a desolate place. And [q]the people
sought him and came to him, and would have
kept him from leaving them, 43 but he said to
them, [r]"I must [s]preach the good news of the
kingdom of God to the other towns as well;
for I was sent for this purpose." 44 And he was
preaching [t]in the synagogues of Judea.[3]

Jesus Calls the First Disciples

5 On one occasion, while the crowd was
pressing in on him to hear the word
of God, he was standing by [u]the lake of
Gennesaret, 2 [v]and he saw two boats by the
lake, but the fishermen had gone out of them
and were [w]washing their nets. 3 Getting into

[1] *Leprosy* was a term for several skin diseases; see Leviticus 13 [2] Or *Leave us alone* [3] Some manuscripts *Galilee*

and blindness, the gospel meets us fully and restores us. The gospel applies to our lives at the level of our whole person, not only our need for sin-forgiveness. We apply this full gospel to ourselves by looking to Jesus for restoration in every area of our lives, not just in the "spiritual" realm, recognizing that full restoration may await heavenly fulfillment.

5:1–11 In this beautiful and powerful story we see Jesus use a physical miracle (the catch of fish) to bring about a spiritual one (the conversion of a man). Even as

21 [h]Mark 12:10; Acts 8:35 [i]See Matt. 1:22
22 [j]Ps. 45:2 [k][Matt. 13:55; John 6:42] [l]ch. 3:23
23 [m][ch. 23:39; Matt. 27:42] [n]Matt. 11:23; Mark 2:1-12; John 4:46-53
24 [o]See Matt. 13:57
25 [p]1 Kgs. 17:1; 18:1; James 5:17; [Rev. 11:6]
26 [q]1 Kgs. 17:9

27 [r][2 Kgs. 7:3] [s]2 Kgs. 5:1-14 **29** [t][Num. 15:35; Acts 7:58] **30** [u]John 8:59; 10:39 **31** [v]For ver. 31-37, see Mark 1:21-28 [w]Matt. 4:13 [x]ver. 15, 16; See Matt. 4:23 [y]See Mark 6:2 **32** [z]ver. 36; See Matt. 7:28, 29 **33** [x][See ver. 31 above] **34** [a]See Matt. 8:29 [b][Acts 19:15; James 2:19] [c]John 6:69; Acts 3:14; Rev. 3:7; [ch. 1:35; Heb. 7:26; 1 John 2:20] **35** [d]ver. 41; See Matt. 12:16 **36** [e]ver. 32; [Matt. 8:27] **37** [f]ver. 14 **38** [g]For ver. 38-41, see Matt. 8:14-16; Mark 1:29-34 [h]1 Cor. 9:5 **39** [i]ch. 8:24; 9:42; Matt. 8:26; 17:18; Mark 4:39; 9:25 **40** [j]See Mark 5:23 **41** [k]Mark 3:11, 12; [Acts 16:17, 18] [l]ver. 33 [m]See Matt. 14:33 [n]See Matt. 1:17 **42** [o]For ver. 42, 43, see Mark 1:35-38 [p]ch. 5:16 [q][Mark 1:36] **43** [r]See ch. 13:33 [s]ch. 8:1; 16:16; Matt. 4:23; 24:14; Acts 8:12 **44** [t][Mark 1:39]
Chapter 5 **1** [u]Num. 34:11; Deut. 3:17; Josh. 12:3; John 6:1; [Matt. 14:34] **2** [v]For ver. 2-11, [Matt. 4:18-22; Mark 1:16-20; John 1:40-42] [w][Mark 1:19]

one of the boats, which was Simon's, he asked
him to put out a little from the land. And [x]he
sat down and taught the people from the boat.
4 And when he had finished speaking, he said
to Simon, [y]"Put out into the deep and let down
your nets for a catch." 5 And Simon answered,
"Master, [z]we toiled all night and took nothing!
But at your word I will let down the nets." 6 And
when they had done this, [a]they enclosed a large
number of fish, and [a]their nets were breaking.
7 They signaled to their partners in the other
boat to come and help them. [b]And they came
and filled both the boats, so that they began
to sink. 8 But when Simon Peter saw it, he fell
down at Jesus' knees, saying, [c]"Depart from
me, for [d]I am a sinful man, O Lord." 9 For he
and all who were with him were astonished
at the catch of fish that they had taken, 10 and
so also were James and John, sons of Zebedee,
who were partners with Simon. And Jesus said
to Simon, "Do not be afraid; from now on you
will be catching men."[1] 11 And when they had
brought their boats to land, [e]they left everything and followed him.

Jesus Cleanses a Leper

12 While he was in one of the cities, [f]there
came a man full of leprosy.[2] And when he saw
Jesus, he [g]fell on his face and begged him,
"Lord, [h]if you will, you can make me clean."
13 And Jesus[3] stretched out his hand and
touched him, saying, "I will; be clean." And
immediately the leprosy left him. 14 And he
charged him [i]to tell no one, but "go and show
[j]yourself to the priest, and [k]make an offering
for your cleansing, as Moses commanded,
[l]for a proof to them." 15 [m]But now even more
the report about him went abroad, and great
crowds gathered to hear him and to be healed
of their infirmities. 16 But [n]he would withdraw
to desolate places and [n]pray.

Jesus Heals a Paralytic

17 On one of those days, as he was teaching,
Pharisees and [o]teachers of the law were sitting there, who had come from every village
of Galilee and Judea and from Jerusalem. And
[p]the power of the Lord was with him to heal.[4]
18 [q]And behold, some men were bringing [r]on a
bed a man who was paralyzed, and they were
seeking to bring him in and lay him before
Jesus, 19 but finding no way to bring him in,
because of the crowd, they went up on [s]the
roof and let him down with his bed [t]through
the tiles into the midst before Jesus. 20 And
[u]when he saw their faith, he said, "Man, [v]your

[1] The Greek word *anthropoi* refers here to both men and women [2] *Leprosy* was a term for several skin diseases; see Leviticus 13 [3] Greek *he*
[4] Some manuscripts *was present to heal them*

3[x] [Matt. 5:1]
4[y] [John 21:6]
5[z] [John 21:3]
6[a] [John 21:11]
7[b] See John 21:4-8
8[c] See Matt. 8:34 [d] Isa. 6:5
11[e] ch. 18:28; Matt. 19:27; [ver. 28]
12[f] For ver. 12-14, see Matt. 8:2-4; Mark 1:40-44 [g] See ch. 17:16 [h] [Matt. 9:28; Mark 9:22, 23]
14[i] Matt. 9:30; 17:9; Mark 1:34; 5:43; 7:36; 8:26; See Matt. 12:16 [j] ch. 17:14 [k] Lev. 14:2-32 [l] ch. 9:5; Mark 6:11; James 5:3
15[m] [Mark 1:45]
16[n] Mark 1:35; See Matt. 14:23
17[o] ch. 2:46; Acts 5:34; 1 Tim. 1:7 (Gk.); [Matt. 22:35] [p] See ch. 8:46
18[q] For ver. 18-26, see Matt. 9:2-8; Mark 2:3-12 [r] Mark 6:55
19[s] Deut. 22:8; 1 Sam. 9:25; Neh. 8:16; Matt. 10:27; 24:17; Acts 10:9 [t] [Mark 2:4]
20[u] ch. 7:9, 50; 17:19; 18:42; Matt. 8:10, 13; 9:22, 29; 15:28; Mark 10:52; Acts 3:16; 14:9; James 5:15 [v] ch. 7:48; [John 5:14]

promised beforehand (2:34), we see the raising up of a lowly one in Israel—from being a fisherman to becoming the Lord's disciple and a "fisher of men" (Matt. 4:19).

The two stages of receiving the gospel are wonderfully manifested in this story. First, it is necessary that we see ourselves clearly—as sinful and broken before the holy God—even as Peter did (Luke 5:8). But this alone will result in despair if the second stage is lacking—seeing Jesus as gracious, forgiving, and inviting us to follow (v. 10).

This story invites us daily to apply the gospel to our lives in the same way. We should ask God to enable us to understand our own sinful hearts and to enlighten our eyes to see him as he truly is (Isa. 6:1–13; Eph. 3:14–19), both in his majesty and in his kindness toward us. This vision alone will enable us to follow him and proclaim his greatness to others.

5:17–26 As Luke continues to unfold the message of the gospel, we see in this story the repeated centrality of the forgiveness of our sins (v. 20). Our reconciliation with God through Jesus is at the core of the gospel message (1:77). Yet it is also more than this, with the repeated emphasis on our restoration as people. The gospel has implications for the whole person, with the hope of our final restoration in the new creation (Rom. 8:18–25; 1 Cor. 15:50–57).

As this gospel goes forth it encounters two responses from two types of people, contrasted in this story. On the one hand are those like the grumbling Pharisees. Although they may be theologically astute and correct (Luke 5:21), they fail to see Jesus correctly and fail to have compassion on those in need. The other possible response to Jesus is to have faith to pursue him (v. 18), to trust him enough to obey (v. 25), and to glorify God for the works of Jesus (v. 26). This story calls us to apply the gospel to ourselves by this kind of believing response to Jesus.

sins are forgiven you." 21 And the scribes and the Pharisees began to question, saying, "Who is this who speaks [w]blasphemies? [x]Who can forgive sins but God alone?" 22 When Jesus [y]perceived their thoughts, he answered them, "Why do you question in your hearts? 23 Which is easier, to say, 'Your sins are forgiven you,' or to say, 'Rise and walk'? 24 But that you may know that [z]the Son of Man has authority on earth to forgive sins"—he said to the man who was paralyzed—"I say to you, rise, pick up your bed and go home." 25 And immediately he rose up before them and picked up what he had been lying on and went home, [a]glorifying God. 26 And amazement seized them all, and they [a]glorified God and were filled [a]with awe, saying, "We have seen extraordinary things today."

Jesus Calls Levi

27 [b]After this he went out and saw [c]a tax collector named [d]Levi, sitting at the tax booth. And he said to him, "Follow me." 28 And [e]leaving everything, he rose and followed him.

29 And Levi made him a great feast in his house, and there was a large company [f]of tax collectors and others reclining at table with them. 30 And the Pharisees and [g]their scribes grumbled at his disciples, saying, [h]"Why do you eat and drink with tax collectors and sinners?" 31 And Jesus answered them, "Those who are well have no need of a physician, but those who are sick. 32 [i]I have not come to call the righteous [j]but sinners [k]to repentance."

A Question About Fasting

33 And they said to him, [l]"The disciples of John [m]fast often and [m]offer prayers, [n]and so do the disciples of the Pharisees, but yours eat and drink." 34 And Jesus said to them, [o]"Can you make wedding guests fast while the bridegroom is with them? 35 [p]The days will come when the bridegroom is taken away from them, and [q]then they will fast in those days." 36 He also told them a parable: "No one tears a piece from a new garment and puts it on an old garment. If he does, he will tear the new, and the piece from the new will not match the old. 37 And no one puts new wine into old [r]wineskins. If he does, the new wine will burst the skins and it will be spilled, and the skins will be destroyed. 38 But new wine must be put into fresh wineskins. 39 And no one after drinking old wine desires new, for he says, 'The old is good.'"[1]

Jesus Is Lord of the Sabbath

6 [s]On a Sabbath,[2] while he was going through the grainfields, his disciples [t]plucked and ate some heads of grain, rubbing them in their hands. 2 But some of the Pharisees said, [u]"Why are you doing [v]what is not lawful to do on the Sabbath?" 3 And Jesus answered them, [w]"Have you not read [x]what David did when he was hungry, he and those who were with him: 4 how he entered the house of God and took and ate [y]the bread of the Presence, [y]which is not lawful for any but the priests to eat, and also gave it to those with him?" 5 And he said to them, [z]"The Son of Man is lord of the Sabbath."

A Man with a Withered Hand

6 On another Sabbath, [a]he entered the synagogue [b]and was teaching, and a man was there whose right hand was withered. 7 And the scribes and the Pharisees [c]watched him, to

[1] Some manuscripts *better* [2] Some manuscripts *On the second first Sabbath* (that is, on the second Sabbath after the first)

6:1–11 In both the old and new covenants God gives instructions for how his people are to live in faithful response to him. Observing the Sabbath rest is one such example from the law. Yet in both the old and new covenants human nature is the same in our tendency to take God's instruction and make it external rather than internal, religious rather than faithful, law rather than grace. These two Sabbath-conflict stories show this human tendency and speak directly against a legalistic, gospel-less way of living.

Jesus points us toward God and toward himself. On the one hand these stories show us that, as the true representation of God, Jesus must be the focus of our religious devotion. At the same time, Jesus shows us that gospel living entails compassion toward those in need, because this is God's heart as well. So, in both ways the gospel is shown to be a matter of the heart—a heart of faith toward God and a heart of compassion toward others. This is the true gospel life: living not merely according to rules but in faithful obedience to God's gracious purposes revealed in the law.

21 [w]Matt. 26:65; John 10:36 [x]Ps. 32:5; Isa. 43:25
22 [y]See John 2:25
24 [z][ch. 6:5]
25 [a]See ch. 7:16
26 [a][See ver. 25 above]
27 [b]For ver. 27-38, see Matt. 9:9-17; Mark 2:14-22 [c]Matt. 11:19; See Matt. 5:46 [d][Matt. 9:9]
28 [e][ver. 11]
29 [f][ch. 15:1, 2]
30 [g]Acts 4:5; 23:9 [h]ch. 15:2; Matt. 11:19
32 [i][ch. 15:7; John 9:39] [j]1 Tim. 1:15 [k]ch. 13:3, 5; 15:10; 24:47; Matt. 4:17; 11:20; Mark 1:15; Acts 5:31
33 [l]ch. 11:1; Matt. 11:2; 14:12; John 1:35; 3:25; 4:1; [Acts 18:25; 19:3] [m]ch. 2:37 [n]ch. 18:12 **34** [o]John 3:29 **35** [p]See ch. 17:22 [q][John 16:20] **37** [r]Josh. 9:4 **Chapter 6** **1** [s]For ver. 1-5, see Matt. 12:1-8; Mark 2:23-28 [t]Deut. 23:25 **2** [u][Matt. 9:11] [v][Ex. 20:9-11] **3** [w]See Matt. 21:16 [x]1 Sam. 21:1-6 **4** [y]Ex. 25:30; Lev. 24:5-9 **5** [z][ch. 5:24] **6** [a]For ver. 6-11, see Matt. 12:9-14; Mark 3:1-6 [b]See Mark 6:2 **7** [c]ch. 14:1; 20:20; [ch. 11:54]

see whether he would heal on the Sabbath, [d]so that they might find a reason to accuse him. 8 But [e]he knew their thoughts, and he said to the man with the withered hand, "Come and stand here." And he rose and stood there. 9 And Jesus said to them, "I ask you, [f]is it lawful on the Sabbath to do good or to do harm, to save life or to destroy it?" 10 And [g]after looking around at them all he said to him, "Stretch out your hand." And [h]he did so, and his hand was restored. 11 But they were filled with [i]fury and discussed with one another what they might do to Jesus.

The Twelve Apostles

12 In these days [j]he went out to the mountain to pray, and all night he continued in prayer to God. 13 And when day came, [k]he called his disciples [l]and [m]chose from them twelve, whom he named [n]apostles: 14 Simon, [o]whom he named Peter, and [p]Andrew his brother, and [p]James and John, and Philip, and Bartholomew, 15 and [q]Matthew, and Thomas, and James the son of Alphaeus, and Simon who was called [r]the Zealot, 16 and [s]Judas the son of James, and Judas Iscariot, who became a traitor.

Jesus Ministers to a Great Multitude

17 And [t]he came down with them and stood on a level place, with [u]a great crowd of his disciples and a great multitude of people from all Judea and Jerusalem and the seacoast of [v]Tyre and Sidon, 18 who came to hear him and to be healed of their diseases. [w]And those who were troubled with unclean spirits were cured. 19 And all the crowd [x]sought to touch him, for [y]power came out from him and healed them all.

The Beatitudes

20 And [z]he lifted up his eyes on his disciples, [a]and said:

"Blessed are you who are poor, for [b]yours is the kingdom of God.

21 [c]"Blessed are you who are hungry now, for you shall be satisfied.

[d]"Blessed are you who weep now, for you shall laugh.

22 "Blessed are you when [e]people hate you and when they [f]exclude you and revile you and [g]spurn your name as evil, [h]on account of the Son of Man! 23 [i]Rejoice in that day, and leap for joy, for behold, your reward is great in heaven; for [j]so their fathers did to the prophets.

Jesus Pronounces Woes

24 [k]"But woe to you who are rich, [l]for you [m]have received your consolation.

25 "Woe to you who are full now, for [n]you shall be hungry.

"Woe to [o]you who laugh now, [o]for you shall mourn and weep.

26 "Woe to you, [p]when all people speak well of you, for [q]so their fathers did to [r]the false prophets.

Love Your Enemies

27 "But I say to you who hear, [s]Love your enemies, [t]do good to those who hate you, 28 [u]bless those who curse you, [s]pray for those who abuse you. 29 [v]To one who [w]strikes you on the cheek, offer the other also, and from one

7[d] [John 8:6]
8[e] See Matt. 9:4
9[f] ch. 14:3
10[g] Mark 3:34; 5:32; 10:23; [Mark 10:21] [h] [1 Kgs. 13:4]
11[i] 2 Tim. 3:9 (Gk.)
12[j] See Matt. 14:23
13[k] ch. 9:1; Matt. 10:1; Mark 3:13; 6:7 [l] For ver. 13-16, see Matt. 10:2-4; Mark 3:16-19; Acts 1:13 [m] See John 13:18 [n] See Mark 6:30
14[o] Matt. 16:18; John 1:42 [p] Matt. 4:18, 21
15[q] Matt. 9:9 [r] [Acts 21:20]
16[s] John 14:22
17[t] [ver. 12; Matt. 5:1] [u] Matt. 4:25; Mark 3:7, 8 [v] See Matt. 11:21
18[w] Matt. 4:24
19[x] Matt. 14:36; Mark 3:10; [Acts 5:15] [y] See ch. 8:46
20[z] John 6:5 [a] For ver. 20-23, [Matt. 5:3-12] [b] [ch. 12:32]

6:20–26 Using a series of contrasts, Jesus boldly outlines God's surprising vision of people and the world. Just the opposite of our natural valuations, God's blessings rest upon the poor, not the rich; the hungry, not the full; the weeping, not the laughing; the persecuted, not the popular.

The gospel of Jesus truly brings blessedness and wholeness. But in this fallen, sin-ravaged world this blessedness will often look like poverty, hunger, weeping, and persecution.

This teaching calls us to apply the gospel to our lives by choosing by faith to rejoice and even exult in trials (v. 23; James 1:2–4; 1 Pet. 1:6–7). We can rejoice because such difficulties in this world can serve as confirmation that we are on the path of God and that in the coming heavenly kingdom we will be rewarded with riches, satisfaction, joy, and God's affirmation of us despite present suffering.

6:27–36 Few things in life are more difficult or counterintuitive than loving one's enemies, described by Jesus in deep and practical images (vv. 28–35). The gospel alone, with its staggering promises of great reward (v. 35), offers the resources we need

21[c] [ch. 1:53] [d] Isa. 25:8; 57:18; See Matt. 5:4 22[e] See Matt. 10:22 [f] [John 9:22; 12:42; 16:2] [g] Heb. 11:26; 1 Pet. 4:14 [h] John 15:21 23[i] See Matt. 5:12 [j] See Matt. 21:35 24[k] Amos 6:1; James 5:1; [ch. 12:21] [l] [ch. 16:25] [m] Matt. 6:2 25[n] Isa. 65:13 [o] Isa. 65:14; [Prov. 14:13; James 4:9] 26[p] [John 15:19; 17:14; James 4:4; 1 John 4:5] [q] Jer. 5:31; [Isa. 30:10; Mic. 2:11] [r] See Matt. 7:15 27[s] See Matt. 5:44 [t] Prov. 25:21, 22; Rom. 12:20, 21 28[u] 1 Pet. 3:9 [s] [See ver. 27 above]
29[v] For ver. 29, 30, see Matt. 5:39-42; [Rom. 12:17] [w] Isa. 50:6; Lam. 3:30; Matt. 26:67

who takes away your cloak do not withhold your tunic[1] either. 30 [x]Give to everyone who begs from you, and from one who takes away your goods do not demand them back. 31 And [y]as you wish that others would do to you, do so to them.

32 [z]"If you love those who love you, what benefit is that to you? For even sinners love those who love them. 33 And if you do good to those who do good to you, what benefit is that to you? For even sinners do the same. 34 And [a]if you [b]lend to those from whom you expect to receive, what credit is that to you? Even sinners lend to sinners, to get back the same amount. 35 But [c]love your enemies, and do good, and lend, expecting nothing in return, and your reward will be great, and [d]you will be sons of [e]the Most High, for [f]he is kind to the ungrateful and the evil. 36 [g]Be merciful, even as [h]your Father is merciful.

Judging Others

37 [i, j]"Judge not, and you will not be judged; condemn not, and you will not be condemned; [j]forgive, and you will be forgiven; 38 [k]give, and it will be given to you. Good measure, pressed down, shaken together, running over, will be put [l]into your lap. For [m]with the measure you use it will be measured back to you."

39 He also told them a parable: [n]"Can a blind man lead a blind man? Will they not both fall into a pit? 40 [o]A disciple is not above his teacher, but everyone when he is [p]fully trained will be like his teacher. 41 [i]Why do you see the speck that is in your brother's eye, but [q]do not notice the log that is in your own eye? 42 How can you say to your brother, 'Brother, let me take out the speck that is in your eye,' when you yourself do not see the log that is in your own eye? You hypocrite, first take the log out of your own eye, and then you will see clearly to take out the speck that is in your brother's eye.

A Tree and Its Fruit

43 "For [r]no good tree bears bad fruit, nor again does a bad tree bear good fruit, 44 for [s]each tree is known by its own fruit. For figs are not gathered from thornbushes, nor are grapes picked from a bramble bush. 45 [t]The good person out of the good treasure of his heart produces good, and the evil person out of his evil treasure produces [u]evil, [v]for out of the abundance of the heart his mouth speaks.

Build Your House on the Rock

46 [w]"Why [x]do you call me 'Lord, Lord,' and not do what I tell you? 47 [y]Everyone who comes to me and hears my words and does them, I will show you what he is like: 48 he is like a man building a house, who dug deep and laid the foundation on the rock. And when a flood arose, the stream broke against that house and could not shake it, because it had been well built.[2] 49 [z]But the one who hears and does not do them is like a man who built a house on the ground without a foundation. When the stream broke against it, immediately it fell, and [a]the ruin of that house was great."

Jesus Heals a Centurion's Servant

7 After he had finished all his sayings in the hearing of the people, [b]he entered Capernaum. 2 Now a centurion had a servant[3] who was sick and at the point of death, who was highly valued by him. 3 When the

[1] Greek *chiton*, a long garment worn under the cloak next to the skin [2] Some manuscripts *founded upon the rock* [3] Greek *bondservant*; also verses 3, 8, 10

for this Spirit-driven behavior. The Word of God informs us of these truths, so that by meditating on them we might grow in believing hope and, thereby, empowered actions.

In this love of enemy we are modeling God's own character, manifested fully in Jesus. For when we were God's enemies, he loved us back into fellowship with himself (Rom. 5:6–10). We love as we have been loved (1 John 4:11).

7:1–10 Like many other healing stories in the Gospels, this event shows God's compassion, power, and plan, all incarnated perfectly in Jesus. God cares for people and has compassion on us as we live in this broken and sinful world; he cares about the things that affect our hearts and grieve us (1 Pet. 5:6–7). We also see that, as Creator and Sustainer, God through Jesus can and does powerfully heal brokenness and sin, which is a foretaste of his final restoration of all things (1 Cor. 15:50–57). God's plan to restore people from *every* tongue, tribe, and nation is also shown in

30 [x]Ps. 37:21; Prov. 21:26
31 [y]Matt. 7:12
32 [z]Matt. 5:46
34 [a][ch. 14:12-14; Prov. 19:17; Matt. 5:42] [b]Ps. 37:26
35 [c]ver. 27 [d]Matt. 5:45 [e]ch. 1:32; See Mark 5:7 [f][James 1:5]
36 [g][Matt. 5:7, 48; Eph. 5:1, 2; James 3:17] [h]James 5:11
37 [i]For ver. 37, 38, 41, 42, see Matt. 7:1-5; [Rom. 14:13; 1 Cor. 4:5; James 5:9] [j][Matt. 6:14; 18:23-35]
38 [k]2 Cor. 9:6-8 [l]Ps. 79:12; Isa. 65:6, 7 [m]Mark 4:24; [Judg. 1:7]
39 [n]Matt. 15:14
40 [o]See Matt. 10:24

[p]2 Cor. 13:11; Heb. 13:21; 1 Pet. 5:10; [1 Cor. 1:10; 2 Tim. 3:17] **41** [i][See ver. 37 above] [q][John 8:7-9] **43** [r]For ver. 43, 44, see Matt. 7:16, 20 **44** [s]Matt. 12:33 **45** [t]Matt. 12:35; 15:18, 19; [Matt. 13:52; Eph. 4:29] [u][Matt. 5:37] [v]Matt. 12:34 **46** [w][Mal. 1:6]; See Matt. 7:21 [x]John 13:13 **47** [y]For ver. 47-49, see Matt. 7:24-27 **49** [z][Ezek. 13:10-16] [a]Amos 6:11 **Chapter 7** **1** [b]For ver. 1-10, see Matt. 8:5-13

centurion[1] heard about Jesus, [c]he sent to him
elders of the Jews, asking him to come and
heal his servant. 4 And when they came to
Jesus, they pleaded with him earnestly, saying, [d]"He is worthy to have you do this for
him, 5 for he loves our nation, and he is the
one who built us [e]our synagogue." 6 And Jesus
went with them. When he was not far from
the house, the centurion sent friends, saying
to him, "Lord, [f]do not trouble yourself, for
I am not worthy to have you come under my
roof. 7 Therefore I did not presume to come to
you. But [g]say the word, and let my servant be
healed. 8 For I too am a man set under authority, with soldiers under me: and I say to one,
'Go,' and he goes; and to another, 'Come,' and
he comes; and to my servant, 'Do this,' and he
does it." 9 When Jesus heard these things, [h]he
marveled at him, and turning to the crowd
that followed him, said, "I tell you, not even
in Israel have I found such [i]faith." 10 And
when those who had been sent returned to
the house, they found the servant well.

Jesus Raises a Widow's Son

11 Soon afterward[2] he went to a town called
Nain, and his disciples and a great crowd went
with him. 12 As he drew near to the gate of the
town, behold, a man who had died was being
carried out, [j]the only son of his mother, and
she was a widow, and a considerable crowd
from the town was with her. 13 And when the
Lord saw her, [k]he had compassion on her and
[l]said to her, "Do not weep." 14 Then he came
up and touched [m]the bier, and the bearers
stood still. And he said, "Young man, I say
to you, [n]arise." 15 And the dead man sat up
and began to speak, and Jesus[3] [o]gave him to
his mother. 16 Fear seized them all, and [p]they
glorified God, saying, [q]"A great prophet has
arisen among us!" and [r]"God has visited his
people!" 17 And this report about him spread
through the whole of Judea and all the surrounding country.

Messengers from John the Baptist

18 [s, t]The disciples of John reported all these
things to him. And John, 19 calling two of
his disciples to him, sent them to the Lord,
saying, "Are you the one [u]who is to come, or
[v]shall we look for another?" 20 And when the
men had come to him, they said, "John the
Baptist has sent us to you, saying, 'Are you
the one [u]who is to come, or [v]shall we look for
another?'" 21 In that hour [w]he healed many
people of diseases and plagues and evil spirits,
and [x]on many who were blind he bestowed
sight. 22 And he answered them, "Go and tell
John what you have seen and heard: [y]the blind
receive their sight, the lame walk, [z]lepers[4] are
cleansed, and [a]the deaf hear, [b]the dead are
raised up, [c]the poor have good news preached
to them. 23 And blessed is the one who is [d]not
offended by me."

24 When John's messengers had gone, Jesus[5]
began to speak to the crowds concerning John:
"What did you go out [e]into the wilderness to
see? [f]A reed shaken by the wind? 25 What then
did you go out to see? A man dressed in soft
clothing? Behold, those who are dressed in
splendid clothing and live in luxury are in
kings' courts. 26 What then did you go out to
see? [g]A prophet? Yes, I tell you, and more than
a prophet. 27 This is he of whom it is written,

> [h]"'Behold, I send my messenger before
> your face,
> who will prepare your way before you.'

28 I tell you, among those born of women none
is greater than John. Yet the one who is least
in the kingdom of God is greater than he."
29 ([i]When all the people heard this, and [j]the tax
collectors too, they declared God just,[6] [j]hav-
ing been baptized with [k]the baptism of John,
30 [l]but the Pharisees and [m]the lawyers [n]rejected
[o]the purpose of God for themselves, not having been baptized by him.)

31 "To what then shall I compare the people
of this generation, and what are they like?

[1] Greek *he* [2] Some manuscripts *The next day* [3] Greek *he* [4] *Leprosy* was a term for several skin diseases; see Leviticus 13 [5] Greek *he*
[6] Greek *they justified God*

3[c] [Matt. 8:5]
4[d] [Acts 10:22]
5[e] ch. 4:31, 33
6[f] ch. 8:49; Mark 5:35; [Matt. 9:36 (Gk.)] **7**[g] Ps. 107:20; [Matt. 8:16] **9**[h] [Mark 6:6] [i] See Matt. 9:2 **12**[j] [ch. 8:42; 9:38; Judg. 11:34; Heb. 11:17] **13**[k] Matt. 20:34 [l] ch. 8:52 **14**[m] 2 Sam. 3:31 [n] ch. 8:54; Mark 5:41; [ver. 22; Matt. 11:5; John 11:43; Acts 9:40] **15**[o] [1 Kgs. 17:23; 2 Kgs. 4:36; Heb. 11:35] **16**[p] ch. 2:20; Matt. 9:8; 15:31; Acts 11:18; 21:20; [Matt. 5:16]; See ch. 13:13 [q] ver. 39; See Deut. 18:15; Matt. 21:11 [r] See ch. 1:68 **18**[s] For ver. 18-35, see Matt. 11:2-19 [t] See Matt. 9:14 **19**[u] John 4:25; 6:14; 11:27 [v] [ch. 3:15] **20**[u] [See ver. 19 above] [v] [See ver. 19 above] **21**[w] Mark 1:34 [x] ch. 18:42; Matt. 9:30; 12:22; 15:31; 20:34; 21:14; Mark 8:25; John 9:7 **22**[y] Isa. 29:18; 35:5, 6; Matt. 15:30 [z] ch. 17:14 [a] Mark 7:35 [b] See ver. 14 [c] ch. 4:18; [Matt. 5:3; James 2:5] **23**[d] Isa. 8:14, 15; John 6:61 **24**[e] ch. 1:80; 3:2 [f] [Eph. 4:14; James 1:6] **26**[g] ch. 1:76; 20:6; Matt. 14:5 **27**[h] Mark 1:2; Cited from Mal. 3:1; [ch. 1:17, 76] **29**[i] [ch. 20:6] [j] ch. 3:12; Matt. 21:32 [k] Acts 18:25; 19:3 **30**[l] [Matt. 21:25, 32; 23:13] [m] ch. 10:25; 11:45, 46, 52; 14:3; Matt. 22:35 [n] See Mark 7:9 [o] Acts 2:23; 13:36

Jesus' commending of this Roman centurion's faith (Luke 7:9; Gal. 3:28; Rev. 5:9). The centurion serves as a model of what response to the gospel looks like: believing trust, and hope in Jesus' power and compassion toward us.

32 They are like children sitting in the marketplace and calling to one another,

"'We played the flute for you, and you did
not dance;
we sang a dirge, and you did not weep.'

33 For John the Baptist has come [p]eating no
bread and [q]drinking no wine, and you say, 'He
has a demon.' 34 The Son of Man has come [r]eat-
ing and drinking, and you say, 'Look at him!
A glutton and a drunkard, [s]a friend of tax collectors and sinners!' 35 Yet [t]wisdom is justified
by all her children."

A Sinful Woman Forgiven

36 [u]One of the Pharisees asked him to eat with
him, and he went into the Pharisee's house
and reclined at the table. 37 [v]And behold, a
woman of the city, who was a sinner, when she
learned that he was reclining at table in the
Pharisee's house, brought an alabaster flask
of ointment, 38 and standing behind him at
his feet, weeping, she began to wet his feet
with her tears and [w]wiped them with the hair
of her head and kissed his feet and anointed
them with the ointment. 39 Now when the
Pharisee who had invited him saw this, he
said to himself, "If [x]this man were [y]a prophet,
he [z]would have known who and what sort of
woman this is who is touching him, for she is
a sinner." 40 And Jesus answering said to him,
"Simon, I have something to say to you." And
he answered, "Say it, Teacher."

41 "A certain moneylender had two debtors. One owed five hundred [a]denarii, and
the other fifty. 42 [b]When they could not pay,
he [c]cancelled the debt of both. Now which
of them will love him more?" 43 Simon
answered, "The one, I suppose, for whom he
cancelled the larger debt." And he said to him,
"You have judged rightly." 44 Then turning
toward the woman he said to Simon, "Do you
see this woman? I entered your house; [d]you
gave me no water for my feet, but [e]she has
wet my feet with her tears and wiped them
with her hair. 45 [f]You gave me no kiss, but
from the time I came in she has not ceased
to [g]kiss my feet. 46 [h]You did not anoint my
head with oil, but she has anointed my feet
with ointment. 47 Therefore I tell you, her
sins, [i]which are many, are forgiven—for she
loved much. But he who is forgiven little,
loves little." 48 And he said to her, [j]"Your sins
are forgiven." 49 Then those who were at table
with him began to say among[1] themselves,
[k]"Who is this, who even forgives sins?" 50 And
he said to the woman, [l]"Your faith has saved
you; [m]go in peace."

Women Accompanying Jesus

8 Soon afterward he went on [n]through cities
and villages, proclaiming and [o]bringing
the good news of the kingdom of God. And the
twelve were with him, 2 and also [p]some women
who had been healed of evil spirits and infirmities: [q]Mary, called Magdalene, [r]from whom
seven demons had gone out, 3 and [s]Joanna, the
wife of Chuza, Herod's household manager,
and Susanna, and many others, who provided
for them[2] out of their means.

[1] Or *to* [2] Some manuscripts *him*

7:36–50 This rich story touches on many key issues of the gospel and our response to it. First, we see a stark contrast between two different kinds of people, revealed in their heart responses to Jesus and to others. Simon the Pharisee fails to honor the non-prestigious Jesus with even basic hospitality (vv. 45–46), while also condemning in his heart a humble and sinful woman in need of compassion (v. 39). Meanwhile the "sinner" of this story, the broken prostitute, responds with a great and open love for Jesus that overrides any fear of man.

Second, this story once again emphasizes that the gospel is about our forgiveness of sins through faith in Jesus (vv. 47–50). Jesus has come to forgive our sins and free us from sin's bondage, and he has the power to do so; our part is to believe and hope in the same.

Taken together, these gospel truths teach us that our response to Jesus and our love for him are directly connected to a proper view of ourselves and others. When we understand our brokenness and cast ourselves upon Jesus, the result is forgiveness of sin, love, and peace. If instead we lack compassion for others and love Jesus little, then, like Simon, we show that we do not understand ourselves or Christ's grace.

33 [p]Matt. 3:4; Mark 1:6 [q]ch. 1:15
34 [r]ver. 36; ch. 14:1; Matt. 9:10; John 2:1; 12:2 [s]ch. 15:2; 19:7; Matt. 9:11
35 [t][ch. 11:49; Prov. 8:1-36]
36 [u]ch. 11:37; 14:1
37 [v]For ver. 37-39, [Matt. 26:6-13; Mark 14:3-9; John 12:1-8]
38 [w]ver. 44; John 11:2
39 [x][ch. 15:2] [y]ver. 16; John 4:19 [z][ch. 22:64]
41 [a]See Matt. 18:28
42 [b]Matt. 18:25 [c][Rom. 8:32 (Gk.)]
44 [d]1 Tim. 5:10; See Gen. 18:4 [e]ver. 38
45 [f]2 Sam. 15:5; 19:39; 20:9 [g]ver. 38
46 [h]Ps. 23:5; 141:5; Eccles. 9:8; Matt. 6:17
47 [i][ver. 39]
48 [j]ch. 5:20; Matt. 9:2; Mark 2:5; James 5:15; 1 John 2:12; [John 20:23]
49 [k]ch. 5:21
50 [l]ver. 9; [ver. 47; 1 Tim. 1:14]; See Mark 10:52; Eph. 2:8 [m]ch. 8:48; 1 Sam. 1:17; Mark 5:34 **Chapter 8** **1** [n]See Mark 6:6 [o]See ch. 4:43 **2** [p]ch. 23:49, 55; Matt. 27:55; Mark 15:40, 41; Acts 1:14 [q]ch. 24:10; Matt. 27:56, 61; 28:1; John 19:25; 20:1, 18 [r]Mark 16:9 **3** [s]ch. 24:10

The Parable of the Sower

4 [t]And when a great crowd was gathering and people from town after town came to him, he said in a parable, 5 [u]"A sower went out to sow his seed. And as he sowed, some fell along the path and was trampled underfoot, and the birds of the air devoured it. 6 And some fell on the rock, and as it grew up, [v]it withered away, because it had no moisture. 7 And some fell among [w]thorns, and the thorns grew up with it and choked it. 8 And some fell into good soil and grew and yielded [x]a hundredfold." As he said these things, he called out, [y]"He who has ears to hear, let him hear."

The Purpose of the Parables

9 And when his disciples asked him what this parable meant, 10 he said, [z]"To you it has been given to know [a]the secrets of the kingdom of God, but for others they are in parables, so [b]that 'seeing they may not see, and hearing they may not understand.' 11 [c]Now the parable is this: The seed is [d]the word of God. 12 The ones along the path are those who have heard; then the devil comes and takes away the word from their hearts, so that they may not [e]believe and be saved. 13 And the ones on the rock are those who, when they hear the word, receive it [f]with joy. But these have no root; they [g]believe for a while, and in time of testing [h]fall away. 14 And as for what fell among the thorns, they are those who hear, but [i]as they go on their way they are choked by the [j]cares and riches and pleasures of life, and their fruit does not mature. 15 As for that in the good soil, they are those who, hearing the word, hold it fast in an honest and good heart, and [k]bear fruit [l]with patience.

A Lamp Under a Jar

16 [m, n]"No one after lighting a lamp covers it with a jar or puts it under a bed, but puts it on a stand, so that those who enter may see the light. 17 [o]For nothing is hidden that will not be made manifest, nor is anything secret that will not be known and come to light. 18 [p]Take care then how you hear, [q]for to the one who has, more will be given, and from the one who has not, even what he thinks that he has will be taken away."

Jesus' Mother and Brothers

19 [r]Then his mother and [s]his brothers came to him, but they could not reach him because of the crowd. 20 And he was told, "Your mother and your brothers are standing outside, desiring to see you." 21 But he answered them, "My mother and my brothers are those [t]who hear the word of God and do it."

Jesus Calms a Storm

22 [u]One day he got into a boat with his disciples, and he said to them, "Let us go across to the other side of [v]the lake." So they set out, 23 and as they sailed he fell asleep. And a windstorm came down on [v]the lake, and they were filling with water and were in danger. 24 And they went and woke him, saying, "Master, Master, we are perishing!" And he awoke and [w]rebuked the wind and the raging waves, and they ceased, [x]and there was a calm. 25 He said to them, "Where is your faith?" And they [y]were afraid, and they [z]marveled, saying to one another, "Who then is this, that [a]he commands even winds and water, and they obey him?"

Jesus Heals a Man with a Demon

26 [b]Then they sailed to the country of the Gerasenes,[1] which is opposite Galilee. 27 When Jesus[2] had stepped out on land, there met him a man from the city who had demons. For a long time he had worn no clothes, and he had not lived in a house [c]but among the tombs.

[1] Some manuscripts *Gadarenes*; others *Gergesenes*; also verse 37 [2] Greek *he*; also verses 38, 42

4 [t]For ver. 4-10, see Matt. 13:1-15; Mark 4:1-12
5 [u][Isa. 55:10; Amos 9:13]
6 [v]John 15:6
7 [w]Jer. 4:3
8 [x]Gen. 26:12 [y]See Matt. 11:15
10 [z]Matt. 19:11; Col. 1:27; [1 Cor. 2:6-10; 1 John 2:20, 27]; See Matt. 11:25 [a]See Rom. 16:25 [b]Isa. 6:9, 10; See Matt. 13:13
11 [c]For ver. 11-15, see Matt. 13:18-23; Mark 4:13-20

8:4–15 Jesus' famous parable describes the varied responses to the gospel as it goes forth throughout the world and over time. The fourfold classification of responses is a sobering call as it shows that only a portion of those who hear and (apparently) respond to the gospel will ultimately prove to be disciples of Jesus. The difference between this fourth, fruit-bearing soul and the others is that the person holds to the gospel with an honest and good heart (v. 15). This does not mean true disciples experience moral perfection or freedom from sin's effects; it means that the gospel profoundly affects the hearts of those who truly receive it. To respond to the gospel

[d]ch. 1:2; Mark 2:2; 4:33; Acts 8:4; James 1:21 **12** [e]See Mark 16:16 **13** [f][Isa. 58:2; Ezek. 33:31, 32; Mark 6:20; John 5:35] [g]Gal. 1:6; [Hos. 6:4; Gal. 5:7] [h]1 Tim. 4:1; Heb. 3:12 **14** [i][James 1:11] [j]See Matt. 6:25 **15** [k]Hos. 14:8; John 15:5, 6; Phil. 1:11; Col. 1:6 [l]James 5:7; See Heb. 10:36 **16** [m]For ver. 16-18, see Mark 4:21-25 [n]ch. 11:33; Matt. 5:15 **17** [o]ch. 12:2; Matt. 10:26; [1 Tim. 5:25] **18** [p][ver. 11-15] [q]See Matt. 13:12 **19** [r]For ver. 19-21, see Matt. 12:46-50; Mark 3:31-35 [s]Matt. 13:55; Mark 6:3; John 2:12; 7:3, 5, 10; Acts 1:14; 1 Cor. 9:5; Gal. 1:19 **21** [t]ch. 11:28; See James 1:22 **22** [u]For ver. 22-25, see Matt. 8:23-27; Mark 4:36-41; [John 6:16-21] [v]ver. 33; See ch. 5:1 **23** [v][See ver. 22 above] **24** [w]ch. 4:39; Ps. 104:7 [x]Ps. 65:7; [Matt. 14:32; Mark 6:51] **25** [y]John 14:27 [z][Mark 1:27] [a][ch. 5:9] **26** [b]For ver. 26-40, see Matt. 8:28–9:1; Mark 5:1-21 **27** [c][Rev. 18:2]

28 When he saw Jesus, he [d]cried out and fell
down before him and said [d]with a loud voice,
"What have you to do with me, Jesus, [e]Son of
[f]the Most High God? I beg you, do not torment
me." 29 For he had commanded the unclean
spirit to come out of the man. (For many a
time it had seized him. He was kept under
guard and bound with chains and shackles,
but he would break the bonds and be driven
by the demon [g]into the desert.) 30 Jesus then
asked him, "What is your name?" And he said,
[h]"Legion," for many demons had entered him.
31 And they begged him not to command them
to depart into [i]the abyss. 32 Now a large herd
of pigs was feeding there on the hillside, and
they begged him to let them enter these. So
he gave them permission. 33 Then the demons
came out of the man and entered the pigs, and
the herd rushed down the steep bank into [j]the
lake and drowned.

34 When the herdsmen saw what had happened, they fled and told it in the city and in
the country. 35 Then people went out to see
what had happened, and they came to Jesus
and found the man from whom the demons
had gone, sitting [k]at the feet of Jesus, [l]clothed
and in his right mind, and they were afraid.
36 And those who had seen it told them how
the demon-possessed[1] man had been healed.
37 Then all the people of the surrounding country of the Gerasenes [m]asked him to depart from
them, for they were seized with great fear. So
he got into the boat and returned. 38 The man
from whom the demons had gone begged that
he might be with him, but Jesus sent him away,
saying, 39 "Return to your home, and [n]declare
how much God has done for you." And he went
away, proclaiming throughout the whole city
how much Jesus had done for him.

Jesus Heals a Woman and Jairus's Daughter

40 Now when Jesus returned, the crowd [o]wel-
comed him, for they were all waiting for him.
41 [p]And there came a man named Jairus, who
was [q]a ruler of the synagogue. And falling at
Jesus' feet, he implored him to come to his
house, 42 for he had [r]an only daughter, about
twelve years of age, and she was dying.

As Jesus went, the people [s]pressed around
him. 43 And there was a woman [t]who had had a
discharge of blood for twelve years, and though
she had spent all her [u]living on physicians,[2]
she could not be healed by anyone. 44 She came
up behind him and touched [v]the fringe of his
garment, and [w]immediately her discharge of
blood ceased. 45 And Jesus said, "Who was it
that touched me?" When all denied it, Peter[3]
said, "Master, the crowds surround you and are
pressing in on you!" 46 But Jesus said, "Someone
touched me, for I perceive that [x]power has
gone out from me." 47 And when the woman
saw that she was not hidden, she came trembling, and falling down before him declared
in the presence of all the people why she had
touched him, and how she had been immediately healed. 48 And he said to her, "Daughter,
[y]your faith has made you well; [y]go in peace."

49 While he was still speaking, someone from
[z]the ruler's house came and said, "Your daughter is dead; [a]do not trouble [b]the Teacher any
more." 50 But Jesus on hearing this answered
him, "Do not fear; only believe, and she will
be well." 51 And when he came to the house,
he allowed no one to enter with him, except
[c]Peter and [d]John and James, and the father
and mother of the child. 52 And all were weeping and [e]mourning for her, but he [f]said, "Do
not weep, for [g]she is not dead but [h]sleeping."
53 And they laughed at him, knowing that

[1] Greek *daimonizomai*; elsewhere rendered *oppressed by demons* [2] Some manuscripts omit *and though she had spent all her living on physicians,* [3] Some manuscripts add *and those who were with him*

truly is to be open to the Lord searching the depths of our hearts (1 Sam. 16:7; Jer. 17:10), transforming us not just in the realm of behavior but through the power of the Spirit changing our inner person (Rom. 12:1–2; Eph. 3:16).

8:40–56 These two interwoven healing stories show Jesus' compassionate power and the central gospel theme of faith or belief in Jesus. In the case of the chronically ill woman and even more with the deceased child, Jesus reveals the heart of God who cares for our plight in this broken world and who gladly intervenes with healing power. At the same time, we see again the relentless gospel theme of our necessary response of faith (vv. 48, 50). Trusting belief in Jesus' ability and willingness to heal as he knows is best is a deep gospel call upon our lives.

28 [d]ch. 4:33, 34; Mark 1:23, 24, 26; Acts 8:7 [e][ch. 4:3, 9]; See Matt. 14:33 [f]ch. 1:32; 6:35; Gen. 14:18; Num. 24:16; Ps. 57:2; Isa. 14:14; Dan. 3:26; Acts 16:17
29 [g][ch. 11:24; Matt. 12:43]
30 [h]Matt. 26:53
31 [i]See Rev. 9:1
33 [j]ver. 22, 23
35 [k]ch. 10:39 [l][ver. 27]
37 [m][ch. 5:8; Acts 16:39]
39 [n]Ps. 66:16; [ch. 5:14]
40 [o]ch. 9:11
41 [p]For ver. 41-56, see Matt. 9:18-26; Mark 5:22-43

[q]ch. 13:14; Acts 13:15; 18:8, 17 **42** [r]See ch. 7:12 [s]ver. 45; Mark 3:9 **43** [t]Lev. 15:25 [u]ch. 21:4; Mark 12:44 **44** [v]Matt. 14:36; 23:5; [Num. 15:38, 39; Deut. 22:12] [w]Matt. 15:28; 17:18 **46** [x]ch. 5:17; 6:19; [Acts 10:38] **48** [y]See ch. 7:50 **49** [z]ver. 41 [a]ch. 7:6 [b]See John 11:28 **51** [c]ch. 9:28; Mark 14:33 [d]Mark 3:17 **52** [e]ch. 23:27; Matt. 11:17 [f]ch. 7:13 [g][Acts 20:10] [h]John 11:4, 11

she was dead. 54 But [i]taking her by the hand
he called, saying, "Child, [j]arise." 55 And [k]her
spirit returned, and she got up at once. And
he directed that something should be given
her to eat. 56 And her parents were amazed,
but [l]he charged them to tell no one what had
happened.

Jesus Sends Out the Twelve Apostles

9 [m]And he called the twelve together and
gave them power and authority over all
demons and to cure diseases, 2 [n]and he sent
them out to [o]proclaim the kingdom of God
and to heal. 3 [p]And he said to them, "Take
nothing for your journey, [q]no staff, nor bag,
nor bread, nor money; and do not have two
tunics.[1] 4 And whatever house you enter, stay
there, and from there depart. 5 And wherever they do not receive you, when you leave
that town [r]shake off the dust from your feet
[s]as a testimony [t]against them." 6 [u]And they
departed and went through the villages,
preaching the gospel and healing everywhere.

Herod Is Perplexed by Jesus

7 [v]Now [w]Herod the tetrarch heard about all
that was happening, and he was perplexed,
because it was said by some that [x]John had
been raised from the dead, 8 [x]by some that
Elijah had appeared, and [x]by others that one
of the prophets of old had risen. 9 Herod said,
"John I beheaded, but who is this about whom
I hear such things?" And [y]he sought to see him.

Jesus Feeds the Five Thousand

10 On their return [z]the apostles told him all
that they had done. [a]And he took them and
withdrew apart to a town called Bethsaida.
11 When the crowds learned it, they followed
him, and he [b]welcomed them and [c]spoke
to them of the kingdom of God and [c]cured
those who had need of healing. 12 Now [d]the
day began to wear away, and the twelve came
and said to him, [e]"Send the crowd away to
go into the surrounding villages and countryside to find lodging and get provisions,
for we are here in a desolate place." 13 But he
said to them, [f]"You give them something
to eat." They said, "We have no more than
[g]five loaves and two fish—unless we are to
go and buy food for all these people." 14 For
there were about five thousand men. And he
said to his disciples, "Have them sit down in
groups of about fifty each." 15 And they did so,
and had them all sit down. 16 And taking the
five loaves and the two fish, [h]he looked up to
heaven and [i]said a blessing over them. Then
he broke the loaves and gave them to the
disciples to set before the crowd. 17 And they
all ate and were satisfied. And what was
left over was picked up, twelve baskets of
broken pieces.

Peter Confesses Jesus as the Christ

18 [j]Now it happened that as he was praying
alone, the disciples were with him. And he
asked them, "Who do the crowds say that
I am?" 19 And they answered, [k]"John the
Baptist. But others say, [l]Elijah, and others,
that one of the prophets of old has risen."
20 Then he said to them, "But who do you say
that I am?" And Peter answered, [m]"The Christ
of God."

[1] Greek *chiton*, a long garment worn under the cloak next to the skin

54 [i]See Mark 1:31 [j]ch. 7:14, 22; [Matt. 11:5; John 11:43]
55 [k][Judg. 15:19; 1 Sam. 30:12]
56 [l]See Matt. 8:4
Chapter 9
1 [m]Matt. 10:1; Mark 3:13-15; 6:7
2 [n]Matt. 10:5, 7, 8; [ver. 11; ch. 10:1, 9] [o]ver. 11, 60; See ch. 4:43
3 [p]For ver. 3-5, see Matt. 10:9-14; Mark 6:8-11; [ch. 10:4-11; 22:35] [q][Mark 6:8]
5 [r]Acts 13:51; [Neh. 5:13; Acts 18:6] [s]See Mark 1:44 [t]James 5:3
6 [u]Mark 6:12
7 [v]For ver. 7-9, see Matt. 14:1-12; Mark 6:14-29 [w]ch. 3:1, 19; Acts 13:1 [x]ver. 19
8 [x][See ver. 7 above]

9:10–17 In this well-known story of the feeding of the five thousand we have a picture of God's provision and power. This wilderness meal not only refers to a past event (the feeding of the Israelites with manna; Ex. 16:1–36) but hints at God's continual provision for us and the promise that one day we will no longer be hungry in this broken world but satisfied in a renewed one (Luke 6:21). This is the forward-looking hope that is at the center of the gospel.

At the same time, this story shows that God's provision for us is sure and abundant despite our lack of faith and understanding. Jesus seeks to elicit a faithful response and action from his disciples in challenging them to look to God to provide the needed meal (9:13). After all, they had just experienced this when apart from him (vv. 1–6). But they do not yet have this faith or understanding. Nevertheless, the grace of the gospel shines forth in that Jesus still gladly and graciously provides what they cannot provide for themselves, modeling for us the God-ward faith and action that we should pursue as well.

9 [y]ch. 23:8 **10** [z]Mark 6:30 [a]For ver. 10-17, see Matt. 14:13-21; Mark 6:32-44; John 6:1-13; [Matt. 15:32-38; Mark 8:2-9] **11** [b]ch. 8:40 [c]ver. 2 **12** [d]ch. 24:29 (Gk.); Jer. 6:4 [e][Matt. 15:23] **13** [f][2 Kgs. 4:42-44] [g]Matt. 16:9; Mark 8:19 **16** [h]Mark 7:34; John 11:41; 17:1 [i]ch. 24:30; 1 Sam. 9:13; Matt. 26:26; Mark 8:7; 14:22; [1 Cor. 14:16] **18** [j]For ver. 18-20, see Matt. 16:13-16; Mark 8:27-29 **19** [k]ver. 7; Matt. 14:2; Mark 6:14 [l]ver. 8; Mark 6:15; [Matt. 17:10; Mark 9:11; John 1:21] **20** [m]ch. 23:35; Acts 3:18; Rev. 12:10; See Matt. 1:17

Jesus Foretells His Death

21 [n]And he strictly charged and commanded
them to tell this to no one, 22 [o]saying, [p]"The
Son of Man must [q]suffer many things and [r]be
rejected by the elders and chief priests and
scribes, and be killed, and on [s]the third day
be raised."

Take Up Your Cross and Follow Jesus

23 And he said to all, "If anyone would come
after me, let him [t]deny himself and [u]take up
his cross [v]daily and follow me. 24 For [u]whoever
would save his life will lose it, but whoever
loses his life for my sake will save it. 25 [w]For
what does it profit a man if he gains the whole
world and loses or forfeits himself? 26 For
[x]whoever is ashamed of me and of my words,
of him will the Son of Man be ashamed [y]when
he comes in [z]his glory and the glory of the
Father and of [a]the holy angels. 27 But I tell you
truly, there are some standing here who will
not [b]taste death [c]until they see the kingdom
of God."

The Transfiguration

28 [d]Now about eight days after these sayings
he took with him [e]Peter and John and James
and [f]went up on the mountain to pray. 29 And
as he was praying, the appearance of his face
was [g]altered, and [h]his clothing became dazzling white. 30 And behold, two men were
talking with him, Moses and Elijah, 31 who
appeared in glory and spoke of his departure,[1] which he was about to accomplish at
Jerusalem. 32 Now Peter and those who were
with him [i]were heavy with sleep, but when
they became fully awake [j]they saw his glory
and the two men who stood with him. 33 And
as the men were parting from him, Peter said
to Jesus, "Master, it is good that we are here.
Let us make three [k]tents, one for you and one
for Moses and one for Elijah"—[l]not knowing
what he said. 34 As he was saying these things,
[m]a cloud came and overshadowed them, and
they were afraid as they entered the cloud.
35 And [m]a voice came out of the cloud, saying,
"This is my Son, [n]my Chosen One;[2] [o]listen to
him!" 36 And when the voice had spoken, Jesus
was found alone. [p]And they kept silent and
told no one in those days anything of what
they had seen.

Jesus Heals a Boy with an Unclean Spirit

37 [q]On the next day, when they had come
down from the mountain, a great crowd met
him. 38 And behold, a man from the crowd
cried out, "Teacher, I beg you to look at my
son, for [r]he is my only child. 39 And behold, a
spirit seizes him, and he suddenly cries out. It
convulses him so that he foams at the mouth,
and shatters him, and will hardly leave him.
40 And I begged your disciples to cast it out,
but [s]they could not." 41 Jesus answered, "O
[t]faithless and twisted generation, [u]how long
am I to be with you and bear with you? Bring
your son here." 42 While he was coming, the
demon threw him to the ground and convulsed him. But Jesus [v]rebuked the unclean
spirit and healed the boy, and [w]gave him back
to his father. 43 And all were astonished at [x]the
majesty of God.

Jesus Again Foretells His Death

[y]But while they were all marveling at everything he was doing, Jesus[3] said [z]to his disciples, 44 "Let these words sink into your ears:

[1] Greek *exodus* [2] Some manuscripts *my Beloved* [3] Greek *he*

9:23–27 Jesus' call to his disciples here reveals a couple of important aspects of our brokenness and sin. His strong exhortation to lose our lives and not be ashamed of his cross-bearing way shows our natural inclination to do the opposite. We *do* seek to gain the things of this world while losing the only thing that will last for eternity, our souls. We *do* seek the praise of men, and this drives us to be ashamed of the suffering and shame-filled way of Jesus. In these ways we stand guilty. Yet the promise of the gospel is that if we will exchange our values for God's, embracing the life he offers as the most rich and fulfilling, then we will receive glory and security that will last eternally. Jesus appeals to us to embrace the wisdom of God's way, promising that through following his path of death to self we will find eternal life in him.

21 [n]Matt. 16:20; Mark 8:30; See Matt. 12:16 **22** [o]For ver. 22-27, see Matt. 16:21-28; Mark 8:31–9:1 [p]ch. 18:31; [ch. 13:33] [q]ch. 24:7; Matt. 17:12, 22, 23; Mark 9:30, 31 [r]ch. 17:25; 1 Pet. 2:4; [ch. 20:17] [s]ch. 18:33; 24:7, 46; See Matt. 27:63; John 2:19 **23** [t][2 Tim. 2:12, 13] [u]See Matt. 10:38, 39 [v]1 Cor. 15:31 **24** [u][See ver. 23 above] **25** [w][ch. 12:20] **26** [x]Rom. 1:16; 2 Tim. 1:8, 12, 16; Heb. 11:16; 1 John 2:28; [Matt. 10:33] [y]Dan. 7:10, 13; Zech. 14:5; Matt. 24:30; 25:31; 26:64; John 1:51; Acts 1:11; 1 Thess. 1:10; 4:16; Jude 14; Rev. 1:7; [Deut. 33:2] [z]Matt. 19:28; 25:31; Mark 10:37; John 17:24 [a]Acts 10:22; Rev. 14:10; [Matt. 13:41; 16:27] **27** [b]John 8:52; Heb. 2:9 [c][ch. 21:31, 32; Matt. 10:23; 23:36; 24:34; Mark 13:30] **28** [d]For ver. 28-36, see Matt. 17:1-8; Mark 9:2-8 [e]ch. 8:51; Mark 14:33 [f]See Matt. 14:23 **29** [g]Mark 16:12 (Gk.) [h]Dan. 7:9; [Ps. 104:2; Matt. 28:3] **32** [i]Dan. 8:18; Matt. 26:43 [j]See John 1:14 **33** [k][Neh. 8:15] [l][Mark 9:6; 14:40] **34** [m]2 Pet. 1:17; [Ex. 24:15, 16] **35** [m][See ver. 34 above] [n]ch. 23:35; Isa. 42:1; [Ps. 89:3; Isa. 49:7] [o]Acts 3:22 **36** [p]Matt. 17:9; Mark 9:9, 10 **37** [q]For ver. 37-42, see Matt. 17:14-19; Mark 9:14-28 **38** [r]See ch. 7:12 **40** [s][ver. 1; ch. 10:17; Matt. 10:1; Mark 6:7] **41** [t]Phil. 2:15; [John 20:27] [u][John 14:9] **42** [v]ch. 4:35, 39; Zech. 3:2; Matt. 8:26; Mark 1:25; Jude 9 [w]See ch. 7:15 **43** [x]2 Pet. 1:16 [y]For ver. 43-45, see Matt. 17:22, 23; Mark 9:30-32 [z]ver. 22

[z]The Son of Man is about to be delivered into the hands of men." 45 [a]But they did not understand this saying, and [b]it was concealed from them, so that they might not perceive it. And they were afraid to ask him about this saying.

Who Is the Greatest?

46 [c]An argument arose among them as to which of them was the greatest. 47 But Jesus, knowing the reasoning of their hearts, took a child and put him by his side 48 and said to them, [d]"Whoever receives this child in my name receives me, and [d]whoever receives me receives him who sent me. For [e]he who is least among you all is the one who is great."

Anyone Not Against Us Is For Us

49 [f]John answered, "Master, we saw someone [g]casting out demons in your name, and [h]we tried to stop him, because he does not follow with us." 50 But Jesus said to him, "Do not stop him, [i]for the one who is not against you is for you."

A Samaritan Village Rejects Jesus

51 When the days drew near for [j]him to be taken up, [k]he set his face [l]to go to Jerusalem. 52 And [m]he sent messengers ahead of him, who went and entered a village of [n]the Samaritans, to make preparations for him. 53 But [o]the people did not receive him, because [p]his face was set toward Jerusalem. 54 And when his disciples James and John saw it, they said, "Lord, do you want us to tell [q]fire to come down from heaven and consume them?"[1] 55 But he turned and rebuked them.[2] 56 And they went on to another village.

The Cost of Following Jesus

57 As they were going [r]along the road, [s]someone said to him, "I will follow you wherever you go." 58 And Jesus said to him, "Foxes have holes, and birds of the air have nests, but the Son of Man has nowhere to lay his head." 59 To another he said, "Follow me." But he said, "Lord, let me first go and bury my father." 60 And Jesus[3] said to him, "Leave [t]the dead to bury their own dead. But as for you, go and [u]proclaim the kingdom of God." 61 Yet another said, "I will follow you, Lord, [v]but let me first say farewell to those at my home." 62 Jesus said to him, [w]"No one who puts his hand to the plow and looks back is fit for the kingdom of God."

Jesus Sends Out the Seventy-Two

10 After this the Lord appointed [x]seventy-two[4] others and [y]sent them on ahead of him, two by two, into every town and place where he himself was about to go. 2 [z]And he said to them, "The harvest is plentiful, but the laborers are few. [a]Therefore pray earnestly to the Lord of the harvest to send out laborers into his harvest. 3 Go your way; [b]behold, I am sending you out as lambs in the midst of wolves. 4 [c]Carry no moneybag, no knapsack, no sandals, and [d]greet no one on the road. 5 Whatever house you enter, first say, [e]'Peace be to this house!' 6 And if a son of peace is there, your peace will rest upon him. But if not, [f]it will return to you. 7 And remain in the same house, eating and drinking what they provide, for [g]the laborer deserves his wages. Do not go from house to house. 8 Whenever you enter

[1] Some manuscripts add *as Elijah did* [2] Some manuscripts add *and he said, "You do not know what manner of spirit you are of; for the Son of Man came not to destroy people's lives but to save them"* [3] Greek *he* [4] Some manuscripts *seventy*; also verse 17

44[z] [See ver. 43 above]
45[a] ch. 2:50; 18:34; Mark 6:52; John 10:6; 12:16; 16:17-19; [Matt. 17:13; Mark 9:10] [b] ch. 18:34; [ch. 24:16]
46[c] For ver. 46-48, see Matt. 18:1-5; Mark 9:33-37; [Matt. 20:20-28; Mark 10:35-45]
48[d] [Matt. 10:40, 42] [e] ch. 22:26
49[f] For ver. 49, 50, see Mark 9:38-40 [g] ch. 10:17; Matt. 7:22; Mark 16:17; Acts 19:13; [Matt. 12:27] [h] [Num. 11:28]
50[i] [ch. 11:23; Matt. 12:30]
51[j] See Mark 16:19 [k] 2 Kgs. 12:17; Isa. 50:7; Jer. 42:15 [l] ch. 13:22; 17:11; 18:31; 19:11, 28
52[m] [ch. 10:1] [n] See Matt. 10:5
53[o] John 4:9; [ch. 10:33] [p] John 4:20

9:46–48 Once again Jesus' teaching to his disciples provides a mirror for us to see our own brokenness. Our sinful and petty values are revealed in the disciples' argument about who is the greatest among them. The gospel answer to this is the revelation of God's radically different perspective. It is the childlike, humble person who is the truly great one. The gospel—both provided and modeled ultimately in Jesus—calls us to fight against the self-promotion inherent in our sinful souls and embrace the lowly way of humility, buttressed with the visionary promise that God will exalt us in the proper way and at the proper time (1 Pet. 5:5–6).

9:57–62 The gospel includes Christ's call to follow after him, not just to believe certain truths and do certain moral actions. Luke's record of some assorted interactions between Jesus and potential followers shows that the call of the gospel does have a cost: it reveals our values and our hearts (recall 2:35). The call of Christ lays bare whether we are devoted to God's kingdom or whether we are split in our allegiance.

54[q] See Rev. 13:13 **57**[r] ver. 51 [s] For ver. 57-60, see Matt. 8:19-22 **60**[t] [John 5:25] [u] ver. 2 **61**[v] [1 Kgs. 19:20] **62**[w] [Phil. 3:13] **Chapter 10** **1**[x] Ex. 24:1, 9; Num. 11:16 [y] [ch. 9:2, 52] **2**[z] Matt. 9:37, 38; John 4:35 [a] [2 Thess. 3:1] **3**[b] Matt. 10:16; [John 17:18] **4**[c] For ver. 4-12, [ch. 9:1-5; 22:35; Matt. 10:9-15; Mark 6:8-11] [d] 2 Kgs. 4:29 **5**[e] 1 Sam. 25:6 **6**[f] [Ps. 35:13 (Heb.)] **7**[g] See 1 Tim. 5:18

a town and they receive you, eat what is set
before you. 9 Heal the sick in it and say to them,
[h]'The kingdom of God has come near to you.'
10 But whenever you enter a town and they
do not receive you, go into its streets and say,
11 [i]'Even the dust of your town that clings to
our feet we wipe off against you. Nevertheless
know this, that [j]the kingdom of God has come
near.' 12 I tell you, [k]it will be more bearable on
[l]that day for Sodom than for that town.

Woe to Unrepentant Cities

13 [m]"Woe to you, Chorazin! Woe to you,
Bethsaida! For if the mighty works done in
you had been done in [n]Tyre and Sidon, they
would have repented long ago, sitting in sackcloth and ashes. 14 [o]But it will be more bearable in the judgment for [n]Tyre and Sidon than
for you. 15 And you, Capernaum, [p]will you be
exalted to heaven? You shall be brought down
to [q]Hades.

16 [r]"The one who hears you hears me, and
[s]the one who rejects you rejects me, and [t]the
one who rejects me rejects him who sent me."

The Return of the Seventy-Two

17 [u]The seventy-two returned with joy, saying, "Lord, [v]even the demons are subject to
us in your name!" 18 And he said to them, [w]"I
saw Satan [x]fall like lightning from heaven.
19 Behold, I have given you authority [y]to tread
on serpents and scorpions, and over all the
power of [z]the enemy, and [a]nothing shall hurt
you. 20 [b]Nevertheless, do not rejoice in this,
that the spirits are subject to you, but rejoice
that [c]your names are written in heaven."

Jesus Rejoices in the Father's Will

21 [d]In that same hour [e]he rejoiced [f]in the Holy
Spirit and said, "I thank you, Father, [g]Lord of
heaven and earth, that [h]you have hidden these
things from the wise and understanding and
[i]revealed them to little children; yes, Father, for
[j]such was your gracious will.[1] 22 [k]All things have
been handed over to me by my Father, and no
one knows who the Son is [k]except the Father,
or who the Father is [k]except the Son and anyone [l]to whom the Son chooses to reveal him."
23 Then turning to the disciples he said privately, [m]"Blessed are the eyes that see what you
see! 24 For I tell you [n]that many prophets and
kings desired to see what you see, and did not
see it, and to hear what you hear, and did not
hear it."

The Parable of the Good Samaritan

25 [o]And behold, a [p]lawyer stood up to [q]put
him to the test, saying, "Teacher, what shall
I do to [r]inherit eternal life?" 26 He said to him,
"What is written in the Law? How do you read
it?" 27 And he answered, [s]"You shall love the
Lord your God with all your heart and with all
your soul and with all your strength and with
all your mind, and [t]your neighbor as yourself."
28 And he said to him, "You have answered correctly; [u]do this, and you will live."
29 But he, [v]desiring to justify himself, said
to Jesus, "And who is my neighbor?" 30 Jesus

[1] Or *for so it pleased you well*

10:25–37 Throughout the New Testament, the gospel is described with a variety of terms and concepts. Here it is described as inheriting eternal life rather than the more typical language of the "kingdom of God," as often found in the Synoptic Gospels. "Eternal life" is the way that the Gospel of John typically speaks, but a passage like this one shows that "entering the kingdom" and "inheriting eternal life" are overlapping ways of understanding the gospel (see Luke 18:18–25 and Mark 10:17–31, where the terms are interchangeable).

Jesus' response to the lawyer's question is summed up here (Luke 10:27) by the first and second greatest commandments (cf. Matt. 22:37), both of which are matters of the heart—that is, what we most truly love and value. Jesus uses this story of the "good Samaritan" to reveal this lawyer's defective heart. He claims to love God and others, but rather than embracing the gospel of Jesus he is "desiring to justify himself" (Luke 10:29).

The command to go and do likewise (v. 37)—that is, show mercy to others—is not an "entrance requirement" for eternal life. Rather, it is a call to follow Jesus' way of loving God and others from the heart. Indeed, it is simply a life mindful of the way *we* have been loved, instead of living out of self-justification (v. 29).

9 [h] ver. 11; See Matt. 3:2
11 [i] Acts 13:51; [Neh. 5:13; Acts 18:6] [j] ver. 9
12 [k] See Matt. 10:15 [l] Matt. 7:22
13 [m] For ver. 13-15, see Matt. 11:21-23 [n] [Isa. 23; Ezek. 28:2-24; Amos 1:9, 10]
14 [o] [ch. 12:47, 48] [n] [See ver. 13 above]
15 [p] Cited from Isa. 14:13-15 [q] ch. 16:23; Acts 2:27
16 [r] See Matt. 10:40 [s] John 12:48; 1 Thess. 4:8; [Matt. 25:45] [t] John 5:23
17 [u] ver. 1 [v] See Mark 16:17
18 [w] [John 12:31; 16:11; Col. 2:15; Rev. 12:8, 9] [x] [Isa. 14:12; Rev. 9:1]
19 [y] Ps. 91:13; Mark 16:18; Acts 28:5 [z] Matt. 13:39 [a] ch. 21:18; [Rom. 8:28, 39]
20 [b] [Matt. 7:22, 23] [c] Ex. 32:32, 33; Ps. 69:28; Isa. 4:3; Ezek. 13:9; Dan. 12:1; Phil. 4:3; Heb. 12:23
21 [d] For ver. 21, 22, see Matt. 11:25-27 [e] [Isa. 53:11] [f] [Mark 12:36] [g] See Acts 17:24 [h] Job 37:24; 1 Cor. 1:19-27; 2 Cor. 3:14 [i] Ps. 8:2; Matt. 21:16; [ch. 8:10; Matt. 16:17] [j] [ch. 12:32]
22 [k] John 1:18; 6:46; 7:29; 8:19; 10:15; 17:25; See Matt. 28:18 [l] [John 17:26] **23** [m] Matt. 13:16, 17; [Matt. 16:17] **24** [n] Heb. 11:13; 1 Pet. 1:10-12; [John 8:56]
25 [o] For ver. 25-28, [ch. 18:18-20; Matt. 19:16-19; 22:34-39; Mark 10:17-19] [p] See ch. 7:30 [q] See John 8:6 [r] Matt. 19:29; 25:34, 46 **27** [s] Matt. 22:37; Mark 12:30; Cited from Deut. 6:5 [t] Cited from Lev. 19:18; See Matt. 19:19 **28** [u] Lev. 18:5; Neh. 9:29; Ezek. 20:11; Rom. 10:5; Gal. 3:12 **29** [v] ch. 16:15

replied, "A man [w]was going down from Jerusalem to Jericho, and he fell among robbers, who stripped him and beat him and departed, leaving him half dead. 31 Now by chance a [x]priest was going down that road, and when he saw him he passed by on the other side. 32 So likewise [x]a Levite, when he came to the place and saw him, passed by on the other side. 33 But a [y]Samaritan, as he journeyed, came to where he was, and when he saw him, he had compassion. 34 He went to him and [z]bound up his wounds, pouring on [z]oil and wine. Then he set him on his own animal and brought him to an inn and took care of him. 35 And the next day he took out two [a]denarii[1] and gave them to the innkeeper, saying, 'Take care of him, and whatever more you spend, I will repay you when I come back.' 36 Which of these three, do you think, proved to be a neighbor to the man who fell among the robbers?" 37 He said, "The one who showed him mercy." And Jesus said to him, "You go, and do likewise."

Martha and Mary

38 Now as they went on their way, Jesus[2] entered a village. And a woman named [b]Martha [c]welcomed him into her house. 39 And she had a sister called [b]Mary, who [d]sat at the Lord's feet and listened to his teaching. 40 But Martha was distracted with much serving. And she went up to him and said, "Lord, do you not care that my sister has left me to serve alone? Tell her then to help me." 41 But the Lord answered her, "Martha, Martha, you are [e]anxious and troubled about many things, 42 but one thing is necessary.[3] Mary has chosen [f]the good portion, which will not be taken away from her."

The Lord's Prayer

11 Now Jesus[4] was praying in a certain place, and when he finished, one of his disciples said to him, "Lord, teach us to pray, [g]as John taught his disciples." 2 And he said to them, [h]"When you pray, say:

[i]"Father, [j]hallowed be [k]your name.
[l]Your kingdom come.
3 [m]Give us [n]each day our daily bread,[5]
4 and [o]forgive us our sins,
for we ourselves forgive everyone who is indebted to us.
And [p]lead us not into temptation."

5 And he said to them, "Which of you who has a friend will go to him at midnight and say to him, 'Friend, lend me three loaves, 6 for a friend of mine has arrived on a journey, and I have nothing to set before him'; 7 and he will answer from within, 'Do not bother me; the door is now shut, and my children are with me in bed. I cannot get up and give you anything'? 8 I tell you, though he will not get up and give him anything [q]because he is his friend, yet because of his impudence[6] he will

[1] A *denarius* was a day's wage for a laborer [2] Greek *he* [3] Some manuscripts *few things are necessary, or only one* [4] Greek *he* [5] Or *our bread for tomorrow* [6] Or *persistence*

30[w] [ch. 18:31; 19:28]
31[x] John 1:19; [Num. 8:19]
32[x] [See ver. 31 above]
33[y] See Matt. 10:5
34[z] Isa. 1:6
35[a] See Matt. 18:28
38[b] John 11:1, 19, 20; 12:2, 3 [c] ch. 19:6
39[b] [See ver. 38 above] [d] ch. 8:35; [Acts 22:3]
41[e] [1 Cor. 7:32-34]; See ch. 12:22
42[f] Ps. 16:5

Chapter 11
1[g] See ch. 5:33
2[h] For ver. 2-4, [Matt. 6:9-13] [i] John 20:17; 1 Pet. 1:17 [j] Isa. 29:23; [ch. 1:49; 1 Pet. 3:15] [k] John 17:6 [l] [Matt. 3:2; 4:17]
3[m] Prov. 30:8 [n] [Matt. 6:34]
4[o] See ch. 7:48 [p] ch. 22:40, 46; Matt. 26:41; Mark 14:38; [1 Cor. 10:13]
8[q] [ch. 18:1-6]

10:38–42 This short story reveals the ever-present temptation, even among believers, of substituting religion for the gospel. We could define religion as human activity pursued in an attempt to please God. The gospel, however, is the message of God's gracious love toward us and the invitation to orient our lives toward him. Rather than focusing on *doing*—even doing good things such as serving—the one thing that is "necessary" and the "good portion" (v. 42) is to sit at the Lord's feet and listen to him. We can in fact be "distracted with much serving" (v. 40). Before the gospel is a call to doing it is an invitation to the presence of the Lord. To follow Jesus as a disciple means to be with him and listen to him. This abiding with and depending on the Lord alone enables us to take up our cross daily and follow him (9:23).

11:1–13 This passage contains shorter versions of several of the teachings found in the Sermon on the Mount (Matthew 5–7). These verses give instruction in how to pray, providing both a model prayer (Luke 11:2–4) and the reason for our confidence in praying (vv. 5–13). Jesus' model prayer emphasizes simplicity in approaching God as our loving and providing Father. This is buttressed by a series of encouraging images of God's heart toward us. If we ask and seek and knock we will receive gifts from our Father, based not on our goodness or effort but on his nature as a loving Father.

This revelation of who God is for us in Christ is a warm invitation to cast our cares on him (1 Pet. 5:7), seeking him with confidence, not fear (Heb. 4:16). The God-honoring response to this revelation is worship and rejoicing in his gift.

rise and give him whatever he needs. 9 And
I tell you, [r]ask, and [s]it will be given to you;
[t]seek, and you will find; [u]knock, and it will
be opened to you. 10 For everyone who asks
receives, and the one who seeks finds, and to
the one who knocks it will be opened. 11 What
father among you, if his son asks for[1] a fish,
will instead of a fish give him a serpent; 12 or
if he asks for an egg, will give him a scorpion?
13 If you then, [w]who are evil, know how to give
good gifts to your children, how much more
will the heavenly Father [x]give the Holy Spirit
to those who ask him!"

Jesus and Beelzebul

14 [y]Now he was casting out a demon that
was mute. When the demon had gone out,
the mute man spoke, and the people marveled. 15 But some of them said, "He casts out
demons [z]by Beelzebul, the prince of demons,"
16 while others, [a]to test him, kept seeking from
him a sign from heaven. 17 [b]But he, [c]knowing
their thoughts, said to them, "Every kingdom divided against itself is laid waste, and
a divided household falls. 18 And if Satan also
is divided against himself, how will his kingdom stand? For you say that I cast out demons
by Beelzebul. 19 And if I cast out demons by
Beelzebul, [d]by whom do [e]your sons cast them
out? Therefore they will be your judges.
20 But if it is by [f]the finger of God that I cast
out demons, then [g]the kingdom of God has
come upon you. 21 When a strong man, fully
armed, guards his own palace, his goods are
safe; 22 [h]but when one stronger than he attacks
him and [i]overcomes him, he takes away his
[j]armor in which he trusted and [k]divides his
spoil. 23 [l]Whoever is not with me is against me,
and whoever does not gather with me scatters.

Return of an Unclean Spirit

24 [m]"When the unclean spirit has gone out of
a person, it passes through [n]waterless places
seeking rest, and finding none it says, 'I will
return to my house from which I came.' 25 And
when it comes, it finds the house swept and
put in order. 26 Then it goes and brings seven
other spirits more evil than itself, and they
enter and dwell there. And [o]the last state of
that person is worse than the first."

True Blessedness

27 As he said these things, [p]a woman in
the crowd raised her voice and said to him,
[q]"Blessed is the womb that bore you, and the
breasts at which you nursed!" 28 But he said,
[r]"Blessed rather are those [s]who hear the word
of God and [t]keep it!"

The Sign of Jonah

29 [u]When the crowds were increasing, he
began to say, [v]"This generation is an evil generation. [w]It seeks for a sign, but no sign will be
given to it except the sign of Jonah. 30 For as
[x]Jonah became a sign to the people of Nineveh,
so will the Son of Man be to this generation.
31 [y]The queen of the South will rise up at the
judgment with the men of this generation and
[z]condemn them, for she came from the ends
of the earth to hear the wisdom of Solomon,
and behold, [a]something greater than Solomon
is here. 32 [b]The men of Nineveh will rise up at
the judgment with this generation and [z]con-
demn it, for [c]they repented at the preaching
of Jonah, and behold, [a]something greater than
Jonah is here.

The Light in You

33 [d]"No one after lighting a lamp puts it in
a cellar or under a basket, but on a stand, so

[1] Some manuscripts insert *bread, will give him a stone; or if he asks for*

11:27–28 The gospel is the message of blessedness. This is not a statement about success or physical well-being, though these are also blessings from God. Rather, to be blessed means to have peace with God through Christ and peace within ourselves as well (1:79; 2:14; John 14:27; Rom. 5:1; Eph. 2:17).

In a way consistent with the whole Bible's message (see, e.g., Psalm 1), Jesus defines true blessedness as hearing and keeping the Word of God (Luke 11:28). This definition involves a "gospel ordering" that cannot be reversed: the gospel is not a call to perform in order to get God's favor; rather, it is a call first to hear—to receive the message of God's kindness and love—and then to be transformed by the Spirit's work. From this basis, and constantly buoyed by grace, we strive to follow after Jesus in keeping the Word: that is, we persevere in the faith.

9 [r]For ver. 9-13, see Matt. 7:7-11 [s]Matt. 18:19; 21:22; Mark 11:24; John 14:13; 15:7, 16; 16:23, 24; James 1:5, 6, 17; 1 John 3:22; 5:14, 15 [t]1 Chr. 28:9; 2 Chr. 15:2; Prov. 8:17; Jer. 29:13; [Isa. 55:6] [u][Rev. 3:20]
13 [w]Gen. 6:5; 8:21; Matt. 12:34 [x][John 4:10; Acts 2:38]
14 [y]For ver. 14, 15, see Matt. 12:22-24; [Matt. 9:32-34]
15 [z]See Matt. 10:25
16 [a]See John 8:6
17 [b]For ver. 17-22, see Matt. 12:25-29; Mark 3:23-27

[c]See Matt. 9:4 **19** [d][Acts 19:13] [e][2 Kgs. 2:7] **20** [f]Ex. 8:19; 31:18; Deut. 9:10; Ps. 8:3 [g]ch. 17:21; Matt. 19:24; 21:31, 43 **22** [h]Isa. 49:24-26 [i][John 16:33] [j]Eph. 6:11 [k][Isa. 53:12] **23** [l]Matt. 12:30; [ch. 9:50; Mark 9:40] **24** [m]For ver. 24-26, see Matt. 12:43-45 [n][Ps. 63:1; Jer. 2:6] **26** [o]2 Pet. 2:20-22; [John 5:14] **27** [p]ch. 12:13 [q][2 Chr. 9:7]; See ch. 1:48 **28** [r][Rev. 1:3; 22:7] [s]ch. 8:21; See James 1:22 [t]Lev. 22:31 **29** [u]ch. 12:1 [v]For ver. 29-32, see Matt. 12:39-42; [Mark 8:11, 12] [w]ver. 16; See Matt. 12:38 **30** [x]Jonah 1:17 **31** [y]1 Kgs. 10:1; 2 Chr. 9:1 [z]Heb. 11:7; [Jer. 3:11; Ezek. 16:51, 52; Rom. 2:27] [a][Matt. 12:6] **32** [b]Jonah 1:2 [z][See ver. 31 above] [c]Jonah 3:5 [a][See ver. 31 above] **33** [d]ch. 8:16; Matt. 5:15; Mark 4:21

that those who enter may see the light. 34 Your
eye is [e]the lamp of your body. When your eye
is healthy, your whole body is full of light,
but when it is [f]bad, your body is full of darkness. 35 [e]Therefore be careful lest the light in
you be darkness. 36 If then your whole body
is full of light, having no part dark, it will be
wholly bright, [g]as when a lamp with its rays
gives you light."

Woes to the Pharisees and Lawyers

37 While Jesus[1] was speaking, [h]a Pharisee
asked him to dine with him, so he went in and
reclined at table. 38 The Pharisee was astonished to see [i]that he did not first wash before
dinner. 39 And the Lord said to him, [j]"Now you
Pharisees cleanse the outside of the cup and
of the dish, but inside you are full of [k]greed
and wickedness. 40 [l]You fools! [j]Did not he who
made the outside make the inside also? 41 But
[m]give as alms those things that are within, and
behold, [n]everything is clean for you.

42 [o]"But woe to you Pharisees! For [p]you tithe
mint and rue and every herb, and neglect [q]jus-
tice and [r]the love of God. [s]These you ought
to have done, without neglecting the others.
43 Woe to you Pharisees! For [t]you love the best
seat in the synagogues and greetings in the
marketplaces. 44 Woe to you! [u]For you are like
unmarked graves, and people walk over them
without knowing it."

45 One of [v]the lawyers answered him,
"Teacher, in saying these things you insult
us also." 46 And he said, "Woe to you [w]lawyers
also! For [x]you load people with burdens hard
to bear, and you yourselves do not touch the
burdens with one of your fingers. 47 [y]Woe to
you! For you build the tombs of the prophets
whom your fathers killed. 48 [z]So you are witnesses and you [a]consent to the deeds of [b]your
fathers, for they killed them, and you build
their tombs. 49 Therefore also [c]the Wisdom
of God said, [d]'I will send them [e]prophets
and apostles, [f]some of whom they will [g]kill
and persecute,' 50 so that [h]the blood of all the
prophets, shed [i]from the foundation of the
world, may be [j]charged against this generation, 51 from the blood of [k]Abel to the blood
of [l]Zechariah, who perished between [m]the
altar and the sanctuary. Yes, I tell you, it will
be [j]required of this generation. 52 Woe to you
[n]lawyers! [o]For you have taken away the key of
[p]knowledge. You [q]did not enter yourselves,
and you hindered those who were entering."

53 As he went away from there, the scribes
and the Pharisees began to press him hard and
to provoke him to speak about many things,
54 [r]lying in wait for him, [s]to catch him in something he might say.

Beware of the Leaven of the Pharisees

12 In the meantime, [t]when so many
thousands of the people had gathered together that they were trampling one
another, he began to say to his disciples first,
[u]"Beware of [v]the leaven of the Pharisees,

[1] Greek *he*

34 [e] Matt. 6:22, 23 [f] Deut. 15:9
35 [e] [See ver. 34 above]
36 [g] [Matt. 5:16]
37 [h] ch. 7:36; 14:1
38 [i] Matt. 15:2; Mark 7:3, 4
39 [j] Matt. 23:25, 26; [ch. 20:47] [k] [ch. 16:14]
40 [l] ch. 12:20 [j] [See ver. 39 above]
41 [m] ch. 12:33; [ch. 16:9; Dan. 4:27] [n] [Titus 1:15]
42 [o] Matt. 23:23 [p] ch. 18:12; Deut. 14:22 [q] Ps. 33:5; Jer. 5:1; Mic. 6:8; Zech. 7:9 [r] [1 John 3:17] [s] [1 Sam. 15:22]
43 [t] ch. 20:46; Matt. 23:6, 7; Mark 12:38, 39; [ch. 14:7]
44 [u] Matt. 23:27
45 [v] ver. 46, 52; See ch. 7:30
46 [w] ver. 45, 52 [x] Matt. 23:4; [Matt. 11:28-30; Acts 15:10]
47 [y] Matt. 23:29, 30
48 [z] Matt. 23:31 [a] See Rom. 1:32 [b] Acts 7:51, 52
49 [c] [ch. 7:35; Prov. 8:12, 22, 23, 30; Matt. 11:19; 1 Cor. 1:24, 30; Col. 2:3] [d] For ver. 49-51, [Matt. 23:34-36] [e] See Acts 13:1; 1 Cor. 12:28 [f] See Matt. 21:35 [g] 1 Thess. 2:15 (Gk.) **50** [h] Rev. 18:24 [i] See Matt. 13:35 [j] Gen. 42:22; 2 Chr. 24:22; Ezek. 3:18 **51** [k] Gen. 4:4, 8; Heb. 11:4; 1 John 3:12 [l] 2 Chr. 24:20, 21 [m] Ex. 40:6; 2 Kgs. 16:14; Ezek. 40:47 [j] [See ver. 50 above]
52 [n] ver. 45, 46 [o] Matt. 23:13; [Mal. 2:7, 8] [p] Rom. 2:20 [q] [ch. 7:30; Matt. 5:20; 21:31] **54** [r] ch. 20:20; Mark 3:2; John 8:6; [Isa. 29:21] [s] Matt. 22:15; Mark 12:13
Chapter 12 **1** [t] ch. 11:29 [u] Matt. 16:6, 11, 12; Mark 8:15 [v] 1 Cor. 5:6-8; Gal. 5:9

11:37–44 One of the main reasons Jesus sometimes offended people in his own day (6:11; 11:45), even as he does today, is that he constantly pressed his gospel message to the level of the heart. God sees the heart of all humans and is not impressed with mere outward religion. There *are* good deeds and actions inspired by faith (v. 42b; Eph. 2:10), but we very easily and subtly substitute religious activities and duties for what God sees and values—a heart-orientation toward him (the greatest commandment; Matt. 22:37–38) and from this, love toward others (the second greatest commandment; Matt. 22:39).

Jesus points out three ways in which his gospel reveals our brokenness and sin—ways in which we may be no different than the Pharisees: having an outward appearance of cleanness but being full of greed on the inside (Luke 11:39); sacrificing a portion of our possessions while neglecting justice for others and love for God (v. 42); and doing good out of a love for the honor that it brings us (v. 43).

Jesus' teaching not only points out these deficiencies of our hearts. It also invites us through union with Jesus to die to such double-living and to live by the Spirit in the gospel way of wholeness, being transformed not just on the outside but on the inside as well (Matt. 5:48; Rom. 12:1–2; Col. 3:1–10). Indeed, to be transformed internally is the only way to be truly transformed externally.

[w]which is hypocrisy. 2 [x]Nothing is covered up
that will not be revealed, or hidden that will
not be known. 3 Therefore whatever you have
said in the dark shall be heard in the light, and
what you have whispered in [y]private rooms
shall be proclaimed on [z]the housetops.

Have No Fear

4 "I tell you, my friends, [a]do not fear those
who kill the body, and after that have nothing more that they can do. 5 But I will warn
you whom to fear: fear him [b]who, after he has
killed, has authority to cast into hell.[1] Yes, I tell
you, fear him! 6 Are not five sparrows sold for
two pennies?[2] And [c]not one of them is forgotten before God. 7 Why, [d]even the hairs of your
head are all numbered. Fear not; [e]you are of
more value than many sparrows.

Acknowledge Christ Before Men

8 "And I tell you, [f]everyone who acknowledges me before men, the Son of Man also
will acknowledge [g]before the angels of God,
9 but [h]the one who denies me before men
[i]will be denied [g]before the angels of God.
10 And [j]everyone who speaks a word [k]against
the Son of Man [l]will be forgiven, but the one
who [m]blasphemes against the Holy Spirit will
not be forgiven. 11 [n]And when they [o]bring you
before the synagogues and [p]the rulers and [p]the
authorities, [q]do not be anxious about how you
should defend yourself or what you should
say, 12 [r]for the Holy Spirit will teach you in that
very hour what you ought to say."

The Parable of the Rich Fool

13 [s]Someone in the crowd said to him,
"Teacher, tell my brother to divide the
inheritance with me." 14 But he said to him,
[t]"Man, [u]who made me a judge or arbitrator
over you?" 15 And he said to them, [v]"Take
care, and be on your guard against all covetousness, for one's life does not consist in
the abundance of his possessions." 16 And he
told them a parable, saying, [w]"The land of
a rich man produced plentifully, 17 and he
thought to himself, [x]'What shall I do, for
I have nowhere to store my crops?' 18 And he
said, 'I will do this: I will tear down my [y]barns
and build larger ones, and there I will store
all my grain and my goods. 19 And I will say to
my soul, "Soul, you have ample goods laid up
[z]for many years; relax, [a]eat, drink, be merry." '
20 But God said to him, [b]'Fool! [z]This night
[c]your soul is required of you, and the things

[1] Greek *Gehenna* [2] Greek *two assaria*; an *assarion* was a Roman copper coin worth about 1/16 of a *denarius* (which was a day's wage for a laborer)

12:4–7 This short saying of Jesus is a great example of his profound wisdom as God's Son. At first glance it appears schizophrenic, with its simultaneous command to fear God (vv. 4–5) and to not fear him (vv. 6–7). We have a sinful yet natural tendency to be afraid of those who have the power to end our lives (v. 4). Jesus shows how foolish this fear is, because the end of our physical lives is not the end of us; we should rather fear our Creator God, who has the power and authority to render ultimate judgment not just on our bodies but also on our souls (v. 5). Understanding God's place as sovereign Judge is essential to understanding his character and the gospel message (Acts 10:42; 2 Tim. 4:1; 1 Pet. 4:5).

Yet the kind of "fear" we should have of God should not be compared to our fear of other humans. Rather, our fear of God should be one of worshipful reverence *because* God knows us intimately and cares for us above all his creatures (Luke 12:7). This is the kind of fear that Jesus himself exhibits toward his heavenly Father (see Isa. 11:2–3).

If we think of God as grandfatherly, with no role as sovereign Judge, then our thinking must be corrected. But if we hold God at a distance out of fear, then we should learn to embrace in worshipful reverence his Fatherly care and love for us.

12:13–34 At first these two sections (vv. 13–21 and 22–34) seem to be separate stories and teachings. But closer inspection reveals that they are intimately related, hinging on the "therefore" in verse 22.

Jesus' warning here is to beware of the double danger of money. On the one hand, money easily generates greed and covetousness (vv. 13–21). On the other hand, the reality of money easily creates heart-deep anxiety in us (vv. 22–34). The gospel teaches us how to defeat both of these destructive sins. We must seek God's kingdom first (v. 31), which will often mean letting go of our goods and money (v. 33).

1 [w] Matt. 23:28; Mark 12:15
2 [x] ch. 8:17; Mark 4:22; [1 Tim. 5:25]; For ver. 2-9, see Matt. 10:26-33
3 [y] Matt. 6:6 [z] See ch. 5:19
4 [a] Isa. 8:12, 13; 51:12, 13; Jer. 1:8; 1 Pet. 3:14
5 [b] James 4:12
6 [c] [Ps. 50:11]
7 [d] See 1 Sam. 14:45 [e] Matt. 6:26; 12:12
8 [f] [Rom. 10:9, 10; Heb. 10:35; Rev. 3:5] [g] [ch. 15:10; Matt. 25:31; 1 Tim. 5:21; Rev. 3:5]
9 [h] 2 Tim. 2:12; 2 Pet. 2:1; 1 John 2:23; [Mark 8:38] [i] ch. 13:25; Matt. 7:23; 25:12 [g] [See ver. 8 above]
10 [j] [Matt. 12:31, 32; Mark 3:28-30; Heb. 6:4-6; 10:26; 1 John 5:16] [k] Matt. 11:19; John 7:12; 9:24 [l] 1 Tim. 1:12, 13 [m] [Acts 7:51; Heb. 10:29]
11 [n] Matt. 10:17, 19; [ch. 21:12, 14; Mark 13:11] [o] See Matt. 23:34 [p] Titus 3:1 [q] See ver. 22
12 [r] See Matt. 10:19, 20
13 [s] ch. 11:27
14 [t] Mic. 6:8; Rom. 2:1, 3; 9:20 [u] [Ex. 2:14; Acts 7:27]
15 [v] 1 Tim. 6:6-11; [Heb. 13:5]
16 [w] [Ps. 49:16-20]
17 [x] [Eccles. 5:10]
18 [y] ver. 24
19 [z] [Prov. 27:1; James 4:13-15] [a] Eccles. 2:24; 11:9; 1 Cor. 15:32; [ch. 15:23]
20 [b] Jer. 17:11; [Matt. 16:26] [z] [See ver. 19 above] [c] Job 27:8

you have prepared, [d]whose will they be?' 21 So
is the one [e]who lays up treasure for himself
and is not rich toward God."

Do Not Be Anxious

22 And he said to his disciples, [f]"Therefore
I tell you, [g]do not be anxious about your life,
what you will eat, nor about your body, what
you will put on. 23 For life is more than food,
and the body more than clothing. 24 [h]Consider
the ravens: they neither sow nor reap, they
have neither storehouse nor barn, and yet
God feeds them. [i]Of how much more value
are you than the birds! 25 And which of you
by being anxious can add a single hour to
his [j]span of life?[1] 26 If then you are not able
to do as small a thing as that, why are you
anxious about the rest? 27 Consider the lilies,
how they grow: they neither toil nor spin,[2]
yet I tell you, [k]even Solomon in all his glory
was not arrayed like one of these. 28 But if God
so clothes the grass, which is alive in the field
today, and tomorrow is thrown into the oven,
how much more will he clothe you, [l]O you of
little faith! 29 And do not seek what you are to
eat and what you are to drink, nor [m]be worried. 30 For [n]all the nations of the world seek
after these things, and [n]your Father knows
that you need them. 31 Instead, [o]seek [p]his[3]
kingdom, [q]and these things will be added
to you.

32 [r]"Fear not, little [s]flock, for [t]it is your
Father's good pleasure to give you [u]the kingdom. 33 [v]Sell your possessions, and [w]give to
the needy. [x]Provide yourselves with money-
bags that do not grow old, with [y]a treasure
in the heavens that does not fail, where no
thief approaches and no moth destroys. 34 [z]For
where your treasure is, there will your heart
be also.

You Must Be Ready

35 [a]"Stay dressed for action[4] and [b]keep your
lamps burning, 36 and be like men who are
[c]waiting for their master to come home from
the wedding feast, so that they may open
the door to him at once when he comes and
[d]knocks. 37 [e]Blessed are those servants[5] whom
the master finds [e]awake when he comes.
Truly, I say to you, [f]he will dress himself for
service and [g]have them recline at table, and
he will come and serve them. 38 If he comes in
the second watch, or in the third, and finds
them awake, blessed are those servants! 39 [h]But
know this, that if the master of the house had
known at what hour [i]the thief was coming,
he[6] would not have left his house to be broken
into. 40 You also must be [j]ready, for [k]the Son of
Man is coming at an hour you do not expect."

41 Peter said, "Lord, [l]are you telling this parable for us or for all?" 42 And the Lord said,
"Who then is [m]the faithful and [m]wise [n]man-
ager, whom his master will set over his household, to give them their portion of food at the
proper time? 43 [o]Blessed is that servant[7] whom
his master will find so doing when he comes.
44 Truly, I say to you, [p]he will set him over all
his possessions. 45 But if that servant says to
himself, 'My master [q]is delayed in coming,'
and begins to beat the male and female servants, and to eat and drink and [r]get drunk,
46 the master of that servant will come [s]on
a day when he does not expect him and [s]at
an hour he does not know, and will cut him
in pieces and put him with the unfaithful.
47 [t]And that servant who [u]knew his master's
will but [v]did not get ready [u]or act according to
his will, will receive a [w]severe beating. 48 [x]But
the one who did not know, and did what
deserved a beating, [y]will receive a light beat-

[1] Or *a single cubit to his stature*; a *cubit* was about 18 inches or 45 centimeters [2] Some manuscripts *Consider the lilies; they neither spin nor weave* [3] Some manuscripts *God's* [4] Greek *Let your loins stay girded*; compare Exodus 12:11 [5] Greek *bondservants* [6] Some manuscripts add *would have stayed awake and* [7] Greek *bondservant*; also verses 45, 46, 47

20 [d]Ps. 39:6; [Job 27:17-22; Eccles. 2:18, 21]
21 [e]Matt. 6:19, 20
22 [f]For ver. 22-31, see Matt. 6:25-33 [g]ver. 11; ch. 10:41; Matt. 10:19; 13:22 (Gk.); 1 Cor. 7:32 (Gk.); Phil. 4:6; 1 Pet. 5:7
24 [h][Job 38:41; Ps. 147:9] [i]See ver. 7

Jesus motivates us to this counterintuitive solution by showing us that when we do so, God our Father will provide for all of our needs (v. 31). He does so because as our perfect Father he knows our needs (v. 30). He cares for us deeply and considers us very valuable (v. 24), and it is his good pleasure to give us what we most need for eternal as well as earthly purposes (v. 32). Only this vision of our heavenly Father, combined with the promise of eternal riches (v. 33), can motivate us at the heart level to live free from the love of money (Heb. 13:5) and find eternal joy in following Christ.

25 [j]ch. 2:52 (Gk.) **27** [k]1 Kgs. 10:4-7 **28** [l]Matt. 8:26; 14:31; 16:8; [ch. 17:6] **29** [m][James 1:6] **30** [n]Matt. 6:8 **31** [o][Matt. 5:6, 20] [p]ch. 11:2 [q][1 Kgs. 3:11-14; Mark 10:29, 30; 1 Tim. 4:8; 1 Pet. 3:9] **32** [r]Isa. 41:14; 44:2 [s]Isa. 40:11; Matt. 26:31; John 10:16; 21:15-17; Acts 20:28, 29; 1 Pet. 5:2, 3 [t][ch. 10:21; Matt. 11:26; Eph. 1:5, 9; Phil. 2:13] [u]ch. 22:29; See Matt. 13:19 **33** [v]See Matt. 19:21 [w]ch. 11:41 [x][ch. 16:9] [y]Matt. 6:20; [ver. 21; 1 Pet. 1:4] **34** [z]Matt. 6:21 **35** [a]Eph. 6:14; 1 Pet. 1:13 [b][Matt. 25:7] **36** [c]See 2 Pet. 3:12 [d]Rev. 3:20 **37** [e]See Matt. 24:42, 46 [f]John 13:4; [ver. 35; ch. 17:8] [g][ch. 22:27] **39** [h]For ver. 39-46, [Matt. 24:43-51] [i][1 Thess. 5:2; 2 Pet. 3:10; Rev. 3:3] **40** [j]ver. 47; Matt. 25:10 [k]ch. 21:27 **41** [l][Mark 13:37] **42** [m]See Matt. 24:45 [n]ch. 16:1 **43** [o]John 13:17; Rev. 16:15 **44** [p]Matt. 25:21, 23 **45** [q]Matt. 25:5; [Heb. 10:37; 2 Pet. 3:4, 9] [r]1 Thess. 5:7 **46** [s]2 Pet. 3:12; [ver. 40] **47** [t][Matt. 11:24; John 15:22, 24] [u][James 4:17; 2 Pet. 2:21] [v]ver. 40 [w][Deut. 25:2, 3] **48** [x]Lev. 5:17; [Num. 15:29, 30] [y]Rom. 1:19, 20; 2:14, 15; [1 Tim. 1:13]

ing. [z]Everyone to whom much was given, of
him much will be required, and from him to
whom they entrusted much, they will demand
the more.

Not Peace, but Division

49 [a]"I came to cast fire on the earth, and would
that it were already kindled! 50 [b]I have a baptism to be baptized with, and how [c]great is
my distress until it is accomplished! 51 [d]Do you
think that I have come to give peace on earth?
[e]No, I tell you, but rather division. 52 For from
now on in one house there will be five divided,
three against two and two against three.
53 They will be divided, [f]father against son and
son against father, mother against daughter
and daughter against mother, mother-in-law
against her daughter-in-law and daughter-in-
law against mother-in-law."

Interpreting the Time

54 He also said to the crowds, [g]"When you see
[h]a cloud rising in the west, you say at once, 'A
shower is coming.' And so it happens. 55 And
[g]when you see the south wind blowing, you
say, 'There will be [i]scorching heat,' and it
happens. 56 You hypocrites! [j]You know how
to interpret the appearance of earth and sky,
but why do you not know how to interpret
the present time?

Settle with Your Accuser

57 "And why [k]do you not judge [l]for yourselves
what is right? 58 [m]As you go with your accuser
before the magistrate, make an effort to settle
with him on the way, lest he drag you to the
judge, and the judge hand you over to the officer, and the officer put you in prison. 59 I tell
you, [n]you will never get out until you have
paid the very last [o]penny."[1]

Repent or Perish

13 There were some present at that very
time who told him about the Galileans
whose blood [p]Pilate had mingled with their
sacrifices. 2 And he answered them, [q]"Do you
think that these Galileans were worse sinners
than all the other Galileans, because they suffered in this way? 3 No, I tell you; but unless
you [r]repent, you will all likewise perish. 4 Or
those eighteen on whom the tower in [s]Siloam
fell and killed them: do you think that they
were worse offenders than all the others who
lived in Jerusalem? 5 No, I tell you; but unless
you [r]repent, you will all likewise perish."

The Parable of the Barren Fig Tree

6 And he told this parable: "A man had [t]a fig
tree planted in his vineyard, and he came seeking fruit on it and found none. 7 And he said
to the vinedresser, 'Look, for three years now
I have come seeking fruit on this fig tree, and
I find none. [u]Cut it down. Why should it use
up the ground?' 8 And he answered him, 'Sir,
let it alone this year also, until I dig around it
and put on manure. 9 Then if it should bear
fruit next year, well and good; but if not, you
can cut it down.'"

[1] Greek *lepton*, a Jewish bronze or copper coin worth about 1/128 of a *denarius* (which was a day's wage for a laborer)

12:49–53 The message of the gospel throughout Luke emphasizes peace (1:79; 2:14; 19:38; 24:36), so Jesus' teaching here about his coming to create division at first appears confusing. The gospel that brings deep inner *peace* to those who hope in Christ (2:29; Rom. 5:1) *divides* all the peoples of the world into two realms—even within one's own family (Luke 12:52–53)—based on their reception of the gospel message. As we seek to follow Christ, we should expect to reside on this point of tension—we will have Christ's abiding peace within us yet we will experience division, conflict, and even persecution from those who reject him (1 Pet. 4:3–4).

13:1–9 Often in the Gospels, paragraphs that contain separate teachings also connect together into a broader point. This is the case with verses 1–5 and 6–9. By itself, 13:1–5 reminds us that the gospel message entails a necessary call to repentance. Repentance—turning from ourselves and our sins, toward God—is the avenue through which we receive forgiveness of sins, an essential part of the gospel that Jesus preaches (1:77; 3:3; 24:47; Acts 2:38). The only alternative to the path of repentance-forgiveness is perishing (Luke 13:5).

Yet lest this gospel message be misunderstood as merely a stern command from God, the following words from Jesus (vv. 6–9) put this call into the context of God's patient grace toward us. Repentance will result in fruit bearing, that is, heart-led deeds of love for God and neighbor. Yet God is patient with us and works in us to cause the growth (1 Cor. 3:6–7).

48 [z][Matt. 25:29]; See Matt. 13:12
49 [a][Matt. 3:11]
50 [b]Mark 10:38 [c]2 Cor. 5:14 (Gk.)
51 [d]For ver. 51-53, see Matt. 10:34, 35 [e][Rev. 6:4]
53 [f]Matt. 10:21; [Mic. 7:6]
54 [g][Matt. 16:2, 3] [h]1 Kgs. 18:43, 44
55 [g][See ver. 54 above] [i]See Matt. 20:12
56 [j]Matt. 16:3
57 [k]ch. 21:30 [l]John 7:24; 1 Cor. 11:13
58 [m]Matt. 5:25, 26; [Prov. 25:8]
59 [n][Matt. 18:34, 35] [o]ch. 21:2; Mark 12:42

Chapter 13
1 [p]ch. 3:1
2 [q][Job 4:7; John 9:2; Acts 28:4]
3 [r]See ch. 5:32
4 [s]John 9:7, 11
5 [r][See ver. 3 above]
6 [t]Matt. 21:19; Mark 11:13; [Isa. 5:2]
7 [u]ch. 3:9; Matt. 7:19

A Woman with a Disabling Spirit

10 Now [v]he was teaching in one of the synagogues on the Sabbath. 11 And behold, there
was a woman who had had [w]a disabling spirit
for eighteen years. She was bent over and
could not fully straighten herself. 12 When
Jesus saw her, he called her over and said to
her, "Woman, you are freed from your disability." 13 And he [x]laid his hands on her, and
immediately she was made straight, and she
[y]glorified God. 14 But [z]the ruler of the synagogue, indignant because Jesus [a]had healed
on the Sabbath, said to the people, [b]"There
are six days in which work ought to be done.
Come on those days and be healed, and not on
the Sabbath day." 15 Then the Lord answered
him, "You hypocrites! [c]Does not each of you
on the Sabbath untie his ox or his donkey
from the manger and lead it away to water it?
16 And ought not this woman, [d]a daughter of
Abraham whom [e]Satan bound for eighteen
years, be loosed from this bond on the Sabbath
day?" 17 As he said these things, [f]all his adversaries were put to shame, and [g]all the people
rejoiced at all the glorious things that were
done by him.

The Mustard Seed and the Leaven

18 [h]He said therefore, "What is the kingdom
of God like? And to what shall I compare it?
19 It is like [i]a grain of mustard seed that a man
took and sowed in his garden, and it grew and
became a tree, and the birds of the air made
nests in its branches."

20 And again he said, "To what shall I compare the kingdom of God? 21 [j]It is like leaven
that a woman took and hid in [k]three measures
of flour, until it was [l]all leavened."

The Narrow Door

22 [m]He went on his way through towns and
villages, teaching and [n]journeying toward
Jerusalem. 23 And someone said to him, "Lord,
[o]will those who are saved be few?" And he said
to them, 24 [p]"Strive [q]to enter through the narrow door. For many, I tell you, will seek to
enter and will not be able. 25 [r]When once the
master of the house has risen and shut the
door, and you begin to stand outside and to
knock at the door, saying, [s]'Lord, open to us,'
then he will answer you, [t]'I do not know where
you come from.' 26 Then you will begin to say,
[u]'We ate and drank in your presence, and you
taught in our streets.' 27 But he will say, 'I tell
you, [t]I do not know where you come from.
[v]Depart from me, all you workers of evil!' 28 [w]In
that place there will be weeping and gnashing
of teeth, when you see [w]Abraham and Isaac
and Jacob and all the prophets in the kingdom
of God but [w]you yourselves cast out. 29 And
[w]people will come from east and west, and
from north and south, and [x]recline at table in
the kingdom of God. 30 And behold, [y]some are
last who will be first, and some are first who
will be last."

Lament over Jerusalem

31 At that very hour some Pharisees came
and said to him, "Get away from [z]here, for
[a]Herod wants to kill you." 32 And he said to
them, "Go and tell that fox, 'Behold, I cast out
demons and perform cures today and tomorrow, and the third day [b]I finish my course.
33 Nevertheless, [c]I [d]must go on my way today
and tomorrow and the day following, for it
cannot be that [e]a prophet should perish away
from Jerusalem.' 34 [f]O Jerusalem, Jerusalem,
the city that [g]kills the prophets and stones
those who are sent to it! [h]How often would
I have [i]gathered [j]your children together [k]as a
hen gathers her brood [l]under her wings, and
[m]you were not willing! 35 Behold, [n]your house
is forsaken. And I tell you, you will not see me
until you say, [o]'Blessed is he who comes in the
name of the Lord!'"

Healing of a Man on the Sabbath

14 One Sabbath, [p]when he went to dine
at the house of a ruler of the Pharisees,
they were [q]watching him carefully. 2 And
behold, there was a man before him who had
dropsy. 3 And Jesus responded to [r]the lawyers
and Pharisees, saying, [s]"Is it lawful to heal
on the Sabbath, or not?" 4 But they remained
silent. Then he took him and healed him and
sent him away. 5 And he said to them, [t]"Which

10 [v] See Matt. 4:23; Mark 6:2 **11** [w] Acts 16:16; [ver. 16] **13** [x] See Mark 5:23 [y] ch. 5:25; 18:43; See ch. 7:16 **14** [z] See ch. 8:41 [a] See Matt. 12:2 [b] Ex. 20:9; Ezek. 46:1 **15** [c] ch. 14:5; [Matt. 12:11] **16** [d] ch. 19:9 [e] [ver. 11; Acts 10:38; 1 Cor. 5:5; 2 Cor. 12:7]; See 1 Chr. 21:1 **17** [f] Ps. 132:18; 1 Pet. 3:16 [g] ch. 18:43 **18** [h] For ver. 18, 19, see Matt. 13:31, 32; Mark 4:30-32 **19** [i] ch. 17:6; Matt. 17:20 **21** [j] Matt. 13:33 [k] Gen. 18:6 [l] 1 Cor. 5:6; Gal. 5:9 **22** [m] See Mark 6:6 [n] [ver. 33]; See ch. 9:51 **23** [o] Acts 2:47; 1 Cor. 1:18; 2 Cor. 2:15 **24** [p] 1 Tim. 4:10; Heb. 12:4; [1 Tim. 6:12 (Gk.)]; See 1 Cor. 9:25 [q] Matt. 7:13 **25** [r] For ver. 25-27, [Matt. 25:10-12] [s] Matt. 7:22, 23 [t] Matt. 10:33; 25:12; [2 Tim. 2:19] **26** [u] [Ex. 24:11] **27** [t] [See ver. 25 above] [v] See Ps. 6:8 **28** [w] See Matt. 8:11, 12 **29** [w] [See ver. 28 above] [x] [ch. 14:15; 22:30] **30** [y] See Matt. 19:30 **31** [z] [Matt. 19:1; Mark 10:1] [a] See ch. 3:1 **32** [b] [See Heb. 2:10; 5:9; 7:28] **33** [c] [John 11:9] [d] Acts 3:21; 17:3 [e] See Matt. 21:11 **34** [f] For ver. 34, 35, see Matt. 23:37-39; [ch. 19:41-44] [g] See Matt. 21:35 [h] [Matt. 26:55] [i] [Ps. 147:2; Prov. 1:24] [j] ch. 23:28 [k] [Deut. 32:11, 12] [l] Ruth 2:12 [m] John 5:40 **35** [n] [Isa. 64:11; Jer. 12:7; 22:5] [o] ch. 19:38; Cited from Ps. 118:26 **Chapter 14** **1** [p] ch. 7:36; 11:37 [q] ch. 20:20; Mark 3:2 **3** [r] See ch. 7:30 [s] ch. 13:14; Matt. 12:10 **5** [t] ch. 13:15; [Deut. 22:4; Matt. 12:11]

of you, having a son[1] or an ox that has fallen
into a well on a Sabbath day, will not immediately pull him out?" 6 [u]And they could not
reply to these things.

The Parable of the Wedding Feast

7 Now he told a parable to those who were
invited, when he noticed [v]how they chose the
places of honor, saying to them, 8 "When you
are invited by someone to a wedding feast, do
not sit down in a place of honor, lest someone
more distinguished than you be invited by
him, 9 and he who invited you both will come
and say to you, 'Give your place to this person,'
and then you will begin with shame to take
the lowest place. 10 But when you are invited,
go and sit in the lowest place, [w]so that when
your host comes he may say to you, 'Friend,
move up higher.' Then you will be honored in
the presence of all who sit at table with you.
11 For [x]everyone who exalts himself will be
humbled, and he who humbles himself will
be exalted."

The Parable of the Great Banquet

12 He said also to the man who had invited
him, "When you give [y]a dinner or a banquet,
do not invite your friends or your brothers[2]
or your relatives or rich neighbors, [z]lest they
also invite you in return and you be repaid.
13 But when you give a feast, [a]invite [b]the poor,
the crippled, the lame, the blind, 14 and you
will be blessed, because they cannot repay you.
For you will be repaid [c]at [d]the resurrection of
the just."

15 When one of those who reclined at table
with him heard these things, he said to him,
[e]"Blessed is everyone who will [f]eat bread in
the kingdom of God!" 16 But he said to him, [g]"A
man once [h]gave a great banquet and invited
many. 17 And at the time for the banquet he
[i]sent his servant[3] to say to those who had been
invited, 'Come, for everything is now ready.'
18 But they all alike began to make excuses.
The first said to him, 'I have bought a field,
and I must go out and see it. Please have me
excused.' 19 And another said, 'I have bought
five yoke of oxen, and I go to examine them.
Please have me excused.' 20 And another said,
[j]'I have married a wife, and therefore I cannot
come.' 21 So the servant came and reported these
things to his master. Then the master of the
house became angry and said to his servant,
'Go out quickly to the streets and lanes of the
city, and bring in [k]the poor and crippled and
blind and lame.' 22 And the servant said, 'Sir,
what you commanded has been done, and still
there is room.' 23 And the master said to the servant, 'Go out to the highways and hedges and
compel people to come in, that my house may
be filled. 24 For I tell you,[4] [m]none of those men
who were invited shall taste my banquet.'"

The Cost of Discipleship

25 Now great crowds accompanied him, and
he turned and said to them, 26 [n]"If anyone

[1] Some manuscripts *a donkey* [2] Or *your brothers and sisters*. The plural Greek word *adelphoi* (translated "brothers") refers to siblings in a family. In New Testament usage, depending on the context, *adelphoi* may refer either to *brothers* or to *brothers and sisters* [3] Greek *bondservant*; also verses 21, 22, 23 [4] The Greek word for *you* here is plural

14:7–11 Being honored and avoiding shame are universal human desires. Ever since the first sin of Adam and Eve we have borne guilt and shame (Gen. 3:6–10). As a result, much of our behavior is motivated by attempts to earn the praise of others and avoid their rejection. Jesus cuts through this by painting a powerful picture of the foolishness of seeking one's own honor. Rather than jockeying for position, Jesus teaches and models the way of wise joy—humbling ourselves so that God may exalt us in the proper time (Luke 14:11). The image of seating at a wedding feast easily transfers to every aspect of our lives. In all our interactions with others and in every situation we can choose the humble way of considering others as more important than ourselves (Phil. 2:1–11). This is counterintuitive until we get a proper vision of the ways of God's wise kingdom as modeled in Jesus himself. God is opposed to the proud but loves to bless the humble (James 4:6), and he is faithful to lift us up in his own timing.

14:25–33 At first glance verses 28–32 might be interpreted to mean that we must work very hard to be Jesus' disciples, making sure that we have in our own strength the ability to persevere in following after him. Anyone who has sought to live a godly life knows how impossible this is and knows that this message would not be gospel—"good news"—but defeat (Rom. 7:21–25).

Instead, Jesus' gospel message is a call to value everything else as worthless compared to him (Luke 14:33; Phil 3:7–8). This message is so radically against our natural

6[u] [Matt. 22:46]
7[v] See ch. 11:43
10[w] Prov. 25:6, 7
11[x] ch. 18:14; [Prov. 29:23; Ezek. 21:26; Matt. 18:4; James 4:6, 10; 1 Pet. 5:5, 6]
12[y] John 21:12 (Gk.) [z] [ch. 6:34]
13[a] [Neh. 8:10, 12; Esth. 9:22] [b] ver. 21
14[c] 1 Cor. 15:23; 1 Thess. 4:16; [John 11:24; Rev. 20:4, 5] [d] Acts 24:15
15[e] Rev. 19:9 [f] [ch. 13:29; 22:16, 30]
16[g] For ver. 16-24, [Matt. 22:2-14] [h] [Isa. 25:6]
17[i] [Esth. 6:14; Prov. 9:3, 5]
20[j] Deut. 24:5
21[k] ver. 13
24[m] Matt. 21:43; Acts 13:46
26[n] ver. 33; Matt. 10:37; [Deut. 33:9]

comes to me and [o]does not hate his own father and mother and wife and children and brothers and sisters, [p]yes, and even his own life, he cannot be my disciple. 27 [q]Whoever does not [r]bear his own cross and come after me cannot be my disciple. 28 For which of you, desiring to build a tower, does not [s]first sit down and count the cost, whether he has enough to complete it? 29 Otherwise, when he has laid a foundation and is not able to finish, all who see it begin to mock him, 30 saying, 'This man began to build and was not able to finish.' 31 Or what king, going out to encounter another king in war, will not [t]sit down first and deliberate whether he is able with ten thousand to meet him who comes against him with twenty thousand? 32 And if not, while the other is yet a great way off, he sends a delegation and asks for terms of peace. 33 [u]So therefore, any one of you who [v]does not renounce all that he has cannot be my disciple.

Salt Without Taste Is Worthless

34 [w]"Salt is good, [x]but if salt has lost its taste, how shall its saltiness be restored? 35 It is of no use either for the soil or for the manure pile. It is thrown away. [y]He who has ears to hear, let him hear."

The Parable of the Lost Sheep

15 Now [z]the tax collectors and sinners were all drawing near to hear him. 2 And the Pharisees and the scribes [a]grumbled, saying, [b]"This man receives sinners and [c]eats with them."

3 So he told them this parable: 4 [d]"What man of you, having a hundred sheep, [e]if he has lost one of them, does not leave the ninety-nine [f]in the open country, and [g]go after the one that is lost, until he finds it? 5 And when he has found it, [h]he lays it on his shoulders, rejoicing. 6 And when he comes home, he calls together his friends and his neighbors, saying to them, 'Rejoice with me, for [i]I have found my sheep that was lost.' 7 Just so, I tell you, there will be more joy in heaven over one sinner who [j]repents than over ninety-nine [k]righteous persons who need no repentance.

The Parable of the Lost Coin

8 "Or what woman, having ten silver coins,[1] if she loses one coin, does not light a lamp and sweep the house and seek diligently until she finds it? 9 And when she has found it, she calls together her friends and neighbors, saying, 'Rejoice with me, for I have found the coin that I had lost.' 10 Just so, I tell you, there is joy before [l]the angels of God over one sinner who repents."

The Parable of the Prodigal Son

11 And he said, "There was a man who had two sons. 12 And the younger of them said to his father, 'Father, give me [m]the share of property that is coming to me.' And he divided [n]his property between them. 13 Not many days later, the younger son gathered all he had and

[1] Greek *ten drachmas*; a *drachma* was a Greek coin approximately equal in value to a Roman *denarius*, worth about a day's wage for a laborer

26 [o]ch. 16:13 [p]John 12:25; Acts 20:24; Rev. 12:11
27 [q]ch. 9:23; Matt. 10:38; 16:24; Mark 8:34 [r]John 19:17
28 [s][Prov. 24:27]
31 [t]ver. 28
33 [u][Phil. 3:7] [v][ver. 26; ch. 18:28]
34 [w]Mark 9:50 [x]Matt. 5:13
35 [y]See Matt. 11:15
Chapter 15
1 [z]See Matt. 11:19
2 [a]ch. 19:7; [Ex. 16:2, 7, 8; Num. 14:2; Josh. 9:18] [b][ch. 7:39] [c]ch. 5:30; Matt. 9:11; 11:19; Mark 2:16; [Acts 11:3; 1 Cor. 5:11; Gal. 2:12]
4 [d]For ver. 4-7, [Matt. 18:12-14] [e]Ezek. 34:6; [1 Pet. 2:25] [f][Ex. 3:1; 1 Sam. 17:28] [g]Ezek. 34:4, 11, 12, 16; [ch. 19:10]
5 [h][Isa. 40:11; 49:22; 60:4; 66:12]
6 [i]1 Pet. 2:25
7 [j]ver. 10; See ch. 5:32 [k][ch. 5:32; Matt. 9:13]
10 [l]See ch. 12:8
12 [m]Deut. 21:17 [n]ver. 30; Mark 12:44

tendencies that Jesus must shock us with the language of "hating" one's loved ones and even one's own life (Luke 14:26). As we read these startling words, however, we must also bear in mind Jesus' consistent teaching that actual hatred of anyone made in God's image is antithetical to the gospel (see 6:27, 35).

So there *is* a cost to being a disciple of Jesus. It is not one of effort, however, but of reorientation of our values toward the greatest worth of being called into God's kingdom and warmly accepted into God's family, all by sheer grace. For Jesus himself bore the greatest cost, the ultimate cost, in our place—condemnation.

15:1–32 We have in this series of three interrelated parables a profound picture of God's heart and the invitation of the gospel. The consistent theme throughout these parables is rejoicing over the finding of what was lost (one sheep, one coin, one son). These are images of God's joy in the restoration of a sinner through repentance (vv. 7, 10).

The third parable deepens and expands this message. God is pictured as a patient and compassionate Father who welcomes our repentance with great rejoicing. Our repentance is also vividly depicted as coming to realize the foolishness and unsatisfying nature of living apart from the Father (vv. 17–19). The gospel is explained through this image as a call for us to turn away from all that does not truly satisfy and return to the welcoming grace of our Father God. This applies not only at our conversion but to every day of our life of faith in a broken and tempting world. It is important to

took a journey into a far country, and there he
squandered his property in [o]reckless living.
14 And when he had spent everything, a severe
famine arose in that country, and he began to
be in need. 15 So he went and hired himself out
to[1] one of the citizens of that country, who sent
him into his fields to feed pigs. 16 And he [p]was
longing to be fed with the pods that the pigs
ate, and no one gave him anything.

17 "But [q]when he [r]came to himself, he said,
'How many of my father's hired servants have
more than enough bread, but I perish here
with hunger! 18 I will arise and go to my father,
and I will say to him, "Father, [s]I have sinned
against [t]heaven and before you. 19 [u]I am no
longer worthy to be called your son. Treat
me as one of your hired servants."' 20 And he
arose and came to his father. But while he
was still a long way off, his father saw him
and felt compassion, and [v]ran and [w]embraced
him and [x]kissed him. 21 And the son said to
him, 'Father, I have sinned against heaven
and before you. [u]I am no longer worthy to be
called your son.'[2] 22 But the father said to his
servants,[3] 'Bring quickly [y]the best robe, and
put it on him, and put [z]a ring on his hand,
and [a]shoes on his feet. 23 And bring [b]the fattened calf and kill it, and [c]let us eat and celebrate. 24 For this my son [d]was dead, and is
alive again; he was lost, and is found.' And
they began to celebrate.

25 "Now his older son was in the field, and as
he came and drew near to the house, he heard
music and dancing. 26 And he called one of the
servants and asked what these things meant.
27 And he said to him, 'Your brother has come,
and your father has killed the fattened calf,
because he has received him back safe and
sound.' 28 But he was angry and refused to go
in. His father came out and entreated him,
29 but he answered his father, 'Look, these
many years I have served you, and I never disobeyed your command, yet you never gave me
a young goat, that I might [e]celebrate with my
friends. 30 But when this son of yours came,
[f]who has devoured [g]your property with prostitutes, you killed the fattened calf for him!'
31 And he said to him, 'Son, [h]you are always
with me, and all that is mine is yours. 32 It was
fitting [e]to celebrate and be glad, for this your
brother [i]was dead, and is alive; he was lost,
and is found.'"

The Parable of the Dishonest Manager

16 He also said to the disciples, "There
was a rich man who had [j]a manager,
and charges were brought to him that this
man was wasting his possessions. 2 And he
called him and said to him, 'What is this
that I hear about you? Turn in the account of
your [k]management, for you can no longer be
manager.' 3 And the manager said to himself,
'What shall I do, since my master is taking
the management away from me? I am not
strong enough to dig, and I am ashamed to
beg. 4 I have decided what to do, so that when
I am removed from management, people
may receive me into their houses.' 5 So, summoning his master's debtors one by one, he
said to the first, 'How much do you owe my
master?' 6 He said, 'A hundred measures[4] of
oil.' He said to him, 'Take your bill, and sit
down quickly and write fifty.' 7 Then he said
to another, 'And how much do you owe?' He
said, 'A hundred measures[5] of wheat.' He said
to him, 'Take your bill, and write eighty.' 8 The
master commended the dishonest manager
for his [l]shrewdness. For [m]the sons of this
world[6] are [l]more shrewd in dealing with
their own generation than [n]the sons of light.
9 And I tell you, [o]make friends for yourselves
by means of [p]unrighteous wealth,[7] so that

[1] Greek *joined himself to* [2] Some manuscripts add *treat me as one of your hired servants* [3] Greek *bondservants* [4] About 875 gallons or 3,200 liters [5] Between 1,000 and 1,200 bushels or 37,000 to 45,000 liters [6] Greek *age* [7] Greek *mammon*, a Semitic word for money or possessions; also verse 11; rendered *money* in verse 13

note that the father runs in welcome to his son before his son has made any confession—grace even precedes the needed repentance.

This third parable also adds an unexpected twist at the end of the story (vv. 25–32) that applies to us who may not thinking of ourselves as "prodigal." Even we who have known the grace of a heavenly Father can be stingy about that grace being applied to others. The image of the angry older brother challenges us to have God's heart of compassion toward other sinners. Our compassion toward others is a good indicator of how well we understand our own need for grace.

13[o] [Eph. 5:18; Titus 1:6; 1 Pet. 4:4]
16[p] [ch. 16:21]
17[q] [1 Kgs. 8:47] [r] [Acts 12:11]
18[s] [Ex. 10:16] [t] Matt. 21:25; John 3:27
19[u] [ch. 7:6, 7]
20[v] [James 4:8] [w] Gen. 33:4; Acts 20:37 [x] 2 Sam. 14:33
21[u] [See ver. 19 above]
22[y] Zech. 3:3-5 [z] Gen. 41:42; Esth. 3:10; 8:2 [a] Ezek. 16:10

23[b] [1 Sam. 28:24] [c] [ch. 12:19] **24**[d] ver. 32; [Rom. 11:15; Eph. 2:1; Col. 2:13; Rev. 3:1] **29**[e] ver. 23 **30**[f] Prov. 29:3 [g] ver. 12 **31**[h] John 8:35 **32**[e] [See ver. 29 above] [i] ver. 24 **Chapter 16** **1**[j] ch. 12:42 **2**[k] See 1 Cor. 9:17 **8**[l] See Matt. 25:2 [m] ch. 20:34; See ch. 10:6 [n] John 12:36; 1 Thess. 5:5; [Eph. 5:8] **9**[o] [ch. 12:33; Matt. 6:20; 19:21; 1 Tim. 6:10, 17-19] [p] ver. 11, 13; Matt. 6:24

when it fails they may receive you into the
eternal dwellings.
10 [q]“One who is [r]faithful in a very little is also
faithful in much, and one who is dishonest
in a very little is also dishonest in much. 11 If
then you have not been faithful in the unrighteous wealth, who will entrust to you the true
riches? 12 And if you have not been faithful in
[s]that which is another’s, who will give you that
which is your own? 13 [p]No servant can serve
two masters, for either he will hate the one
and love the other, or he will be devoted to the
one and despise the other. You cannot serve
God and money.”

The Law and the Kingdom of God

14 [t]The Pharisees, who were [u]lovers of
money, heard all these things, and they [v]ridi-
culed him. 15 And he said to them, “You are
those who [w]justify yourselves before men, but
[x]God knows your hearts. For what is exalted
among men [y]is an abomination in the sight
of God.
16 [z]“The Law and the Prophets were until
John; since then [a]the good news of the kingdom of God is preached, and [b]everyone forces
his way into it.[1] 17 But [c]it is easier for heaven
and earth to pass away than for one dot of the
Law to become void.

Divorce and Remarriage

18 [d]“Everyone who divorces his wife and marries another commits adultery, and he who
marries a woman divorced from her husband
commits adultery.

The Rich Man and Lazarus

19 “There was a rich man who was clothed
in [e]purple and fine linen and [f]who feasted
sumptuously every day. 20 And at his gate [g]was
laid a poor man named Lazarus, covered with
sores, 21 who desired to be fed with [h]what fell
from the rich man’s table. Moreover, even the
dogs came and licked his sores. 22 The poor
man died and was carried by [i]the angels [j]to
Abraham’s side.[2] The rich man also died and
was buried, 23 and in [k]Hades, being in torment,
he lifted up his eyes and [l]saw Abraham far
off and Lazarus [j]at his side. 24 And he called
out, [m]‘Father Abraham, have mercy on me,
and send Lazarus to dip the end of his finger in water and [n]cool my tongue, for [o]I am in
anguish in this flame.’ 25 But Abraham said,
‘Child, remember that [p]you in your lifetime
received your good things, and Lazarus in like
manner bad things; but now he is comforted
here, and you are in anguish. 26 And besides
all this, between us and you a great chasm has
been fixed, in order that those who would pass
from here to you may not be able, and none
may cross from there to us.’ 27 And he said,
‘Then I beg you, father, to send him to my
father’s house— 28 for I have five brothers[3]—
so that he may warn them, lest they also come
into this place of torment.’ 29 But Abraham
said, ‘They have [q]Moses and the Prophets; [r]let
them hear them.’ 30 And he said, ‘No, [s]father
Abraham, but if someone goes to them from
the dead, they will repent.’ 31 He said to him,
‘If they do not hear [q]Moses and the Prophets,

[1] Or *everyone is forcefully urged into it* [2] Greek *bosom*; also verse 23 [3] Or *brothers and sisters*

10 [q] Matt. 25:21, 23 [r] ch. 19:17
12 [s] [1 Chr. 29:14, 16]
13 [p] [See ver. 9 above]
14 [t] [ch. 11:39; 20:47] [u] 2 Tim. 3:2; [1 Tim. 6:10] [v] ch. 23:35
15 [w] ch. 10:29 [x] 1 Sam. 16:7; 1 Chr. 28:9; Prov. 21:2 [y] Prov. 16:5
16 [z] Matt. 11:12, 13 [a] See ch. 4:43 [b] [ch. 15:1]
17 [c] Matt. 5:18
18 [d] See Matt. 5:32
19 [e] Esth. 8:15; Rev. 18:16 [f] [James 5:5]
20 [g] [Acts 3:2]
21 [h] [Matt. 15:27]
22 [i] ch. 15:10; Matt. 18:10; Acts 12:15; Heb. 1:13, 14; See ch. 12:8 [j] [John 13:23 (Gk.)]
23 [k] See Matt. 11:23 [l] Matt. 8:11, 12 [j] [See ver. 22 above]
24 [m] ver. 30; John 8:33, 39, 53 [n] [Zech. 14:12] [o] [Isa. 66:24]; See Matt. 25:41
25 [p] [ch. 6:24; Job 21:13; Ps. 17:14]
29 [q] ver. 31; ch. 24:27; Acts 26:22; 28:23 [r] [John 5:45-47] **30** [s] ver. 24 **31** [q] [See ver. 29 above]

16:13 This pithy and memorable saying of Jesus speaks to the danger of double-mindedness—or, we might say, double-heartedness (cf. James 1:8; 4:8). We need to reorient our values to those of God’s kingdom. This kind of discipleship is not easy or popular (Luke 13:24) because it requires a heart-level openness and spiritual transformation. Following Christ is foundationally about what we love and worship. We cannot serve both God *and* the wealth this world offers.

16:14–15 All the teaching in chapter 16 touches in some way on the issue of wealth. Verses 14–15 continue the emphasis on the danger of money: it is a mis-valuing of what is truly valuable. The Pharisees are described here in a way that is true of all of us—we are “lovers of money” (v. 14). Money is valued and sought because of the pleasure and honor it brings. Jesus points out that even though wealth brings honor with other people, God sees and cares about our hearts (cf. 1 Sam. 16:7). Even more strongly, this human valuing of wealth and what it brings is actually despised by God (Luke 16:15). Once again the gospel calls us to an inner-person response of consciously adopting God’s kingdom values (Rom. 12:2) and turning away from what is perceived as significant in sinful human society. This is possible only as we ponder the great love with which we are loved by God in the gospel of grace.

[t]neither will they be convinced if someone should rise from the dead.' "

Temptations to Sin

17 And he said to his disciples, [u]"Temptations to sin[1] are [v]sure to come, but [w]woe to the one through whom they come! 2 [x]It would be better for him if a millstone were hung around his neck and he were cast into the sea than that he should cause one of these little ones to sin.[2] 3 Pay attention to yourselves! [y]If your brother sins, [z]rebuke him, and if he repents, [a]forgive him, 4 and if he sins against you [b]seven times in the day, and turns to you seven times, saying, 'I repent,' you must forgive him."

Increase Our Faith

5 [c]The apostles said to the Lord, [d]"Increase our faith!" 6 And the Lord said, [e]"If you had faith like [f]a grain of mustard seed, you could say to this [g]mulberry tree, 'Be uprooted and planted in the sea,' and it would obey you.

Unworthy Servants

7 "Will any one of you who has a servant[3] plowing or keeping sheep say to him when he has come in from the field, 'Come at once and recline at table'? 8 Will he not rather say to him, 'Prepare supper for me, and [h]dress properly,[4] and serve me while I eat and drink, and afterward you will eat and drink'? 9 Does he thank the servant because he did what was commanded? 10 So you also, when you have done all that you were commanded, say, 'We are [i]unworthy servants;[5] we have only done what was our duty.' "

Jesus Cleanses Ten Lepers

11 [j]On the way to Jerusalem [k]he was passing along between Samaria and Galilee. 12 And as he entered a village, he was met by ten lepers,[6] [l]who stood at a distance 13 and lifted up their voices, saying, "Jesus, Master, have mercy on us." 14 When he saw them he said to them, "Go and [m]show yourselves to the priests." And as they went they were cleansed. 15 Then one of them, when he saw that he was healed, turned back, [n]praising God with a loud voice; 16 and [o]he fell on his face at Jesus' feet, giving him thanks. Now he was [p]a Samaritan. 17 Then Jesus answered, "Were not [q]ten cleansed? Where are the nine? 18 Was no one found to return and [r]give praise to God except this [s]foreigner?" 19 And he said to him, "Rise and go your way; [t]your faith has [t]made you well."[7]

The Coming of the Kingdom

20 Being asked by the Pharisees [u]when the kingdom of God would come, he answered them, "The kingdom of God [v]is not coming in ways that can be observed, 21 nor [w]will they

[1] Greek *Stumbling blocks* [2] Greek *stumble* [3] Greek *bondservant*; also verse 9 [4] Greek *gird yourself* [5] Greek *bondservants* [6] *Leprosy* was a term for several skin diseases; see Leviticus 13 [7] Or *has saved you*

17:5–6 Jesus' disciples ask him for a good thing—more faith. But Jesus' response shows that it is not the *quantity* or greatness of our faith that matters, but the *object* of our faith. That is, if we believe in God's grace and power then even seemingly impossible things can become realities, despite the smallness of our faith ("like a . . . mustard seed"; v. 6). This is good news for our daily Christian lives. God does not base his blessings on whether we can muster up great and powerful or even persistent faith. Rather, we are to look to *God's* greatness, power, and consistency, believing in him, not ourselves. Such faith in God, rather than in the faith we can generate, is the foundation of spiritual victory and calm in the soul.

17:11–19 This story emphasizes that faith in Jesus (cf. vv. 5–6) results in powerful change *and* produces a humble, worshipful response to God. This is the difference between the one leper and the other nine. They all asked for God's mercy (v. 13) but only one was shown to have true *understanding* faith, as shown by his casting himself with thankfulness at Jesus' feet. So too for us. Our worshipful response—or lack thereof—reflects the depth of our understanding of God's mercy and goodness. The first and greatest response to the gospel of grace is thankful worship. This brings the greatest glory to God and brings wholeness to us as well.

We are also told, strikingly, that the one who returned to give thanks to Jesus was a Samaritan—a despised outsider. Here, as all through Luke, we see the upside-down reversal that the gospel brings. The kingdom of God inverts the world's values and welcomes anyone, if they will simply repent and believe the good news, relying on Jesus alone for a new and eternal life.

31 [t][Matt. 28:11-15; John 12:10, 11]

Chapter 17

1 [u]Matt. 18:7 [v]See Matt. 13:41 [w]ch. 22:22
2 [x]Matt. 18:6; Mark 9:42
3 [y]Matt. 18:15, 21, 22 [z]Lev. 19:17 [a]See Matt. 6:14
4 [b][Matt. 18:21]
5 [c]See Mark 6:30 [d][Mark 9:24]
6 [e]Matt. 17:20 [f]Matt. 13:31 [g][ch. 19:4 (Gk.)]
8 [h]John 13:4; [ch. 12:35, 37]
10 [i]Matt. 25:30; [Job 22:2, 3; 35:7; Rom. 11:35]
11 [j]See ch. 9:51 [k][John 4:3, 4]; See Matt. 19:1
12 [l]See Lev. 13:45, 46
14 [m]ch. 5:14; Lev. 13:2–14:32; Matt. 8:4
15 [n]See ch. 13:13
16 [o]ch. 5:12; Num. 16:22; [Matt. 26:39] [p]See Matt. 10:5
17 [q]ver. 12
18 [r]See John 9:24 [s]Isa. 66:5
19 [t]See Mark 10:52
20 [u]ch. 19:11; Acts 1:6 [v][ch. 12:39]
21 [w][ver. 23]

say, 'Look, here it is!' or 'There!' for behold, the kingdom of God is in the midst of you."[1]

22 And he said to the disciples, [x]"The days are coming when you will desire [y]to see one of the days of the Son of Man, and you will not see it. 23 [z]And they will say to you, 'Look, there!' or 'Look, here!' Do not go out or follow them. 24 [a]For as the lightning flashes and lights up the sky from one side to the other, so will the Son of Man be [b]in his day.[2] 25 But first [c]he must suffer many things and [c]be rejected by this generation. 26 [d]Just as it was in the days of [e]Noah, so will it be in the days of the Son of Man. 27 [f]They were eating and drinking and marrying and being given in marriage, until the day when Noah entered the ark, and the flood came and destroyed them all. 28 Likewise, just as it was in the days of [g]Lot—they were eating and drinking, buying and selling, planting and building, 29 [h]but on the day when Lot went out from Sodom, fire and sulfur rained from heaven and destroyed them all— 30 so will it be [i]on the day when the Son of Man is revealed. 31 On that day, [j]let the one who is on [k]the housetop, with his goods in the house, not come down to take them away, and likewise let the one who is in the field not turn back. 32 [l]Remember Lot's wife. 33 [m]Whoever seeks to preserve his life will lose it, but whoever loses his life will [n]keep it. 34 I tell you, in that night there will be two in one bed. One will be taken and the other left. 35 [o]There will be two women [p]grinding together. One will be taken and the other left."[3] 37 And they said to him, "Where, Lord?" He said to them, [q]"Where the corpse[4] is, there the vultures[5] will gather."

The Parable of the Persistent Widow

18 And he told them a parable to the effect that they ought [r]always to pray and not [s]lose heart. 2 He said, "In a certain city there was a judge who [t]neither feared God nor respected man. 3 And there was a widow in that city who kept coming to him and saying, 'Give me justice against my adversary.' 4 For a while he refused, but afterward he said to himself, [u]'Though I neither fear God nor respect man, 5 yet because this widow keeps bothering me, I will give her justice, so that she will not beat me down by her continual coming.'" 6 And the Lord said, "Hear what the unrighteous judge says. 7 And [v]will not God give justice to [w]his elect, [x]who cry to him day and night? [y], [z]Will he delay long over them? 8 I tell you, he will give justice to them [a]speedily. Nevertheless, when the Son of Man comes, [b]will he find faith on earth?"

The Pharisee and the Tax Collector

9 He also told this parable to some [c]who trusted [d]in themselves that they were righteous, [e]and treated others with contempt: 10 "Two men [f]went up into the temple to pray,

[1] Or *within you*, or *within your grasp* [2] Some manuscripts omit *in his day* [3] Some manuscripts add verse 36: *Two men will be in the field; one will be taken and the other left* [4] Greek *body* [5] Or *eagles*

22 [x] ch. 5:35; 21:6; Matt. 9:15; Mark 2:20; [ch. 19:43; 23:29; John 4:21] [y] John 8:56; [Amos 5:18]
23 [z] ch. 21:8; Matt. 24:23; Mark 13:21; [ver. 21]
24 [a] Matt. 24:27 [b] See 1 Cor. 1:8
25 [c] See ch. 13:33; Matt. 16:21; 17:22; Mark 8:31
26 [d] Gen. 6:5; 7:7; Matt. 24:37; [1 Thess. 5:3] [e] Heb. 11:7; 1 Pet. 3:20; 2 Pet. 2:5
27 [f] Matt. 24:38, 39
28 [g] 2 Pet. 2:7
29 [h] Gen. 19:16, 24; 2 Pet. 2:6
30 [i] 1 Cor. 1:7; 2 Thess. 1:7; 1 Pet. 1:7, 13; 4:13; [Matt. 16:27; 24:44]
31 [j] ch. 21:21; Matt. 24:17, 18; Mark 13:15, 16 [k] See ch. 5:19
32 [l] Gen. 19:26
33 [m] See Matt. 10:39 [n] Acts 7:19 (Gk.)
35 [o] Matt. 24:41 [p] Ex. 11:5; Isa. 47:2
37 [q] Matt. 24:28; [Job 39:30]
Chapter 18
1 [r] ch. 21:36; Rom. 12:12; Eph. 6:18; Col. 4:2; 1 Thess. 5:17; [ch. 11:5-9] [s] 2 Cor. 4:1, 16; 2 Thess. 3:13 (Gk.) **2** [t] [2 Cor. 8:21] **4** [u] [ch. 11:8] **7** [v] Rev. 6:10; [Isa. 63:4] [w] Rom. 8:33; Col. 3:12; Titus 1:1; See Mark 13:20 [x] Ps. 88:1 [y] James 5:7 (Gk.) [z] 2 Pet. 3:9 **8** [a] Heb. 10:37 [b] ch. 17:26-30; [Matt. 24:12] **9** [c] ch. 16:15; [Matt. 5:20] [d] 2 Cor. 1:9 [e] Prov. 30:12; Isa. 65:5; John 7:48, 49 **10** [f] 2 Kgs. 20:5, 8; Acts 3:1; [ver. 14]

18:1–8 Jesus' parable uses a comparison to reveal God's heart toward us. If even an unrighteous judge will eventually hear the needs of a persistent petitioner, how much more should we seek our Father God to come to our aid? He will not delay to bring justice to his own elect people (v. 7).

We need to be told this because our frailty and brokenness make us lose heart and cease to believe this about our God (v. 1). Our perspective is limited and our vision is clouded (1 Cor. 13:12). Holy Scripture continually reminds us that God is truly *for* us in Jesus (see Rom. 8:31–33). We need this constant reminder of God's kind heart and great power toward us as we fight against our inherent unbelief. We now belong to him. He is our advocate. He delights to care for us and to defend us.

18:9–14 This parable is one of the most important teachings in Luke, showing both what God values and the call of the gospel. Jesus presents a vivid contrast between self-righteous religion and the opposite, proper response to the gospel. The two men of the parable represent these two contrary responses to God. On the one hand we have a self-confident person whose outward life is apparently without fault. On the other we have a man who would be considered a sinner, even a traitor to his own people because of his being a tax collector for Rome. But Jesus shows clearly the difference between these two men: God loves and accepts the

one a Pharisee and the other a tax collector. 11 The Pharisee, [g]standing by himself, prayed[1] [h]thus: 'God, I thank you that I am not like other men, extortioners, unjust, adulterers, or even like this tax collector. 12 [i]I fast twice a week; [j]I give tithes of all that I get.' 13 But the tax collector, [g]standing far off, [k]would not even lift up his eyes to heaven, but [l]beat his breast, saying, 'God, [m]be merciful to me, a sinner!' 14 I tell you, this man went down to his house justified, rather than the other. For [n]everyone who exalts himself will be humbled, but the one who humbles himself will be exalted."

Let the Children Come to Me

15 [o]Now they were bringing even infants to him that he might touch them. And when the disciples saw it, they [p]rebuked them. 16 But Jesus called them to him, saying, [q]"Let the children come to me, and [r]do not hinder them, [q]for to such belongs the kingdom of God. 17 [s]Truly, I say to you, whoever does not [t]receive the kingdom of God like a child shall not enter it."

The Rich Ruler

18 [u]And a ruler asked him, "Good Teacher, what must I do to [v]inherit eternal life?" 19 And Jesus said to him, "Why do you call me good? No one is good except God alone. 20 You know the commandments: [w]'Do not commit adultery, Do not murder, Do not steal, Do not bear false witness, Honor your father and mother.'" 21 And he said, [x]"All these I have kept from my youth." 22 When Jesus heard this, he said to him, "One thing you still lack. [y]Sell all that you have and distribute to the poor, and you will have [z]treasure in heaven; and come, follow me." 23 [a]But when he heard these things, he became very sad, for he was extremely rich. 24 Jesus, seeing that he had become sad, said, [b]"How difficult it is for those who have wealth to enter [c]the kingdom of God! 25 For it is easier for a camel to go through the eye of a needle than for a rich person to enter [c]the kingdom of God." 26 Those who heard it said, "Then who can be saved?" 27 But he said, [d]"What is impossible with man is possible with God." 28 And Peter said, "See, [e]we have left our homes and followed you." 29 And he said to them, "Truly, I say to you, [f]there is no one who has left house or wife or brothers[2] or parents or children, for the sake of the kingdom of God, 30 who will not receive [g]many times more [h]in this time, and in [i]the age to come eternal life."

[1] Or *standing, prayed to himself* [2] Or *wife or brothers and sisters*

person who humbly looks for mercy, while he rejects those who exalt themselves (v. 14; recall 7:36–50; 14:7–11).

This is good news (gospel) indeed. Jesus is not calling us to a plan of moral improvement or a list of wrong behaviors to avoid (18:11), but rather to the one thing that we can all pursue, no matter our brokenness or failures: to humble ourselves before God and call upon his mercy. This alone will result in "justification" (v. 14)—which is another way to describe the gospel of freely entering the kingdom (vv. 24–25) and inheriting eternal life (10:25–28; 18:18).

18:18–27 Here we have the opportunity to overhear yet another interaction between Jesus and a potential disciple. Similar to the story in 10:25–37, we see Jesus explain the gospel as both inheriting eternal life and entering God's kingdom. Most importantly, we see again that the gospel is a matter of the values and affections of our hearts, not merely outward religious activity or obedience.

In his sovereign wisdom, Jesus always diagnoses the real soul ailment of each individual. He rightly perceives that this wealthy ruler is entrapped by the power of money. He thinks that he has obeyed God according to rules (18:19–20), while not really hearing or understanding what Jesus has just said: "No one is good except God alone" (v. 19). It would seem that he is depending on his righteousness to leverage God to give what he values most: more wealth. His words betray an idolatry of wealth and an absence of what is most important for life and eternity: love for God in the inner man. His wealth is an ever-ready rival for the kind of wholeheartedness the gospel calls us to. This is why Jesus calls him to sell everything he has. Jesus did not tell each and every person he encountered to sell all their possessions (cf. 10:25–28; 19:1–10), but in this case he knew that that was the way to address the man's heart condition.

11 [g]Matt. 6:5; Mark 11:25 [h][Rev. 3:17]
12 [i]Matt. 9:14 [j]ch. 11:42
13 [g][See ver. 11 above] [k]Ezra 9:6 [l]ch. 23:48 [m]Ps. 79:9; Ezek. 16:63; Dan. 9:19
14 [n]See ch. 14:11
15 [o]For ver. 15-17, see Matt. 19:13-15; Mark 10:13-16 [p]ver. 39
16 [q]Matt. 18:3 [r][Mark 9:39]
17 [s][John 3:3, 5] [t][ch. 8:13; James 1:21]
18 [u]For ver. 18-30, see Matt. 19:16-29; Mark 10:17-30; [ch. 10:25-28] [v][Matt. 19:16]; See Matt. 25:34
20 [w]Rom. 13:9; Cited from Ex. 20:12-16; Deut. 5:16-20; [Matt. 5:21, 27]
21 [x][Phil. 3:6]
22 [y]ch. 12:33; [ch. 16:9; 19:8; Acts 2:45; 4:34, 35; 1 Tim. 6:18, 19] [z]Matt. 6:19, 20
23 [a][Ezek. 33:31]
24 [b][1 Cor. 1:26]; See Matt. 13:22 [c]See Matt. 12:28
25 [c][See ver. 24 above]
27 [d]ch. 1:37; Gen. 18:14; Job 42:2; Jer. 32:17, 27
28 [e]Matt. 4:20, 22; Mark 1:18, 20
29 [f][ch. 14:26]
30 [g][Job 42:10] [h][Matt. 6:33] [i]Matt. 12:32; Eph. 1:21; [ch. 20:35]

Jesus Foretells His Death a Third Time

31[j]And taking the twelve, he said to them, "See, [k]we are going up to Jerusalem, and [l]everything that is written about the Son of Man by the prophets will be accomplished. 32 For he will be [m]delivered over to the Gentiles and will be [n]mocked and shamefully treated and [o]spit upon. 33 And after flogging him, they will kill him, and on [p]the third day he will rise." 34[q]But they understood none of these things. [r]This saying was hidden from them, and they did not grasp what was said.

Jesus Heals a Blind Beggar

35[s]As he drew near to Jericho, [t]a blind man was sitting by the roadside begging. 36 And hearing a crowd going by, he inquired what this meant. 37 They told him, [u]"Jesus of Nazareth is passing by." 38 And he cried out, "Jesus, [v]Son of David, have mercy on me!" 39 And those who were in front [w]rebuked him, telling him to be silent. But he cried out all the more, "Son of David, have mercy on me!" 40 And Jesus stopped and commanded him to be brought to him. And when he came near, he asked him, 41[x]"What do you want me to do for you?" He said, "Lord, let me recover my sight." 42 And Jesus said to him, "Recover your sight; [y]your faith has [z]made you well." 43 And immediately he recovered his sight and followed him, [a]glorifying God. And [b]all the people, when they saw it, gave praise to God.

Jesus and Zacchaeus

19 [c]He entered Jericho and was passing through. 2 And behold, there was a man named Zacchaeus. He was a chief tax collector and was rich. 3 And [d]he was seeking to see who Jesus was, but on account of the crowd he could not, because he was small in stature. 4 So he ran on ahead and climbed up into [e]a sycamore tree to see him, for he was about to pass that way. 5 And when Jesus came to the place, he looked up and said to him, "Zacchaeus, hurry and come down, for [f]I must stay at your house today." 6 So he hurried and came down and [g]received him joyfully. 7 And when they saw it, they all [h]grumbled, "He has gone in to be the guest of a man who is a sinner." 8 And Zacchaeus stood and said to the Lord, "Behold, Lord, the half of my goods [i]I give to the poor. And if I have [j]defrauded anyone of anything, I restore it [k]fourfold." 9 And Jesus said to him, "Today salvation has come to this house, since [l]he also is a son of Abraham. 10 For [m]the Son of Man came to seek and to save the lost."

31[j]For ver. 31-33, see Matt. 20:17-19; Mark 10:32-34 [k]See ch. 9:51 [l]Ps. 22; See Matt. 1:22; 26:24
32[m]Matt. 27:2; John 18:30, 31; Acts 3:13; [Acts 2:23; 4:27; 21:11] [n]Matt. 27:26-31 [o]Mark 14:65; 15:19; See Matt. 26:67
33[p]See ch. 9:22
34[q]See Mark 9:32 [r]ch. 9:45; [ch. 24:16]
35[s]For ver. 35-43, see Matt. 20:29-34; Mark 10:46-52 [t]John 9:1, 8
37[u]Matt. 2:23
38[v]See Matt. 1:1; 9:27
39[w]ver. 15
41[x]Mark 10:36
42[y]ch. 7:50; 8:48; 17:19; Matt. 9:22; Mark 5:34 [z]ch. 7:3; 8:36, 50
43[a]See ch. 7:16; 13:13 [b][ch. 19:37]
Chapter 19
1[c]ch. 18:35; [Matt. 20:29; Mark 10:46]
3[d][John 12:21]
4[e]1 Kgs. 10:27; 1 Chr. 27:28; Ps. 78:47; Isa. 9:10
5[f][ch. 13:33]
6[g]ch. 10:38
7[h]See ch. 15:2
8[i][ch. 18:22] [j]ch. 3:14 [k]Ex. 22:1; 2 Sam. 12:6
9[l]John 8:33; Rom. 4:11, 12, 16; Gal. 3:7
10[m]Ezek. 34:11, 16; [ch. 15:4; Matt. 9:13; 10:6; 15:24; 18:12]

How do we apply this passage to our own heart condition? First, we must be prepared to be laid bare before God. To be a disciple of Jesus means to follow him, leaving behind us whatever might hinder us (9:57–62). The specific call of the gospel in our lives will vary according to each individual, but it is consistently a call to repentance and absolute humility and honesty before God. This is costly and painful, but anything less is mere externalized religion. Second, we must beware of the power of wealth in particular. Few disciples are called to sell all they have, but fewer still are immune from the destructive power of the love of money, which is the root of all kinds of evil (1 Tim. 6:10). To be a follower of Jesus means to live aware of this danger and to fight against it by faith in God's provision for us (Luke 11:1–13).

19:1–10 This well-known story provides a beautiful example of the power and effect of the gospel. We know little of Zacchaeus except that he was a "chief tax collector" and that he was "small in stature." We also know that he became a zealous disciple of the Lord. But we do not know what other conversation took place between Jesus and Zacchaeus when Jesus was a guest in his house. We can assume it contained the same kind of teaching and kingdom discussion that we have seen thus far in Luke's Gospel account. Regardless, his response to Jesus' gospel teaching and presence was remarkable. Zacchaeus turned from dependence on his wiles and wealth to dependence on God's grace. He joyfully and openly repented of his past wrongdoing and adopted the way of God that Jesus taught him (v. 8). He was a "lost" man whom Jesus came to "seek and save" (v. 10).

As seen in 18:18–27, there is no set pattern or requirement regarding what a disciple does with his or her wealth. Some are called to give up all because their love of money is rooted so deeply. Others are led to give a significant portion of what they have, as Zaccheus does (19:8). Others give a portion of their wealth in property (see Barnabas's actions in Acts 4:36–37). The gospel in the new covenant does not specify what we should do with our financial resources, but it does call us to give

The Parable of the Ten Minas

11 As they heard these things, he proceeded to
tell a parable, because he was near to Jerusalem,
and because [n]they supposed that the kingdom
of God was to appear immediately. 12 He said
therefore, [o]"A nobleman went into a far country to receive for himself a kingdom and then
return. 13 Calling [p]ten of his servants,[1] he gave
them ten minas,[2] and said to them, 'Engage in
business [q]until I come.' 14 But [r]his citizens hated
him and sent a delegation after him, saying,
'We do not want this man to reign over us.'
15 When he returned, having received the kingdom, he ordered these servants to whom he
had given the money to be called to him, that
he might know what they had gained by doing
business. 16 The first came before him, saying,
'Lord, your mina has made ten minas more.'
17 And he said to him, 'Well done, good servant![3]
Because you have been [s]faithful in a very little,
[t]you shall have authority over ten cities.' 18 And
the second came, saying, 'Lord, your mina has
made five minas.' 19 And he said to him, 'And
you are to be over five cities.' 20 Then another
came, saying, 'Lord, here is your mina, which
I kept laid away in [u]a handkerchief; 21 for I was
afraid of you, because you are [v]a severe man.
You take [w]what you did not deposit, and reap
what you did not sow.' 22 He said to him, [x]'I
will condemn you with your own words, [y]you
wicked servant! You knew that I was [v]a severe
man, taking what I did not deposit and reaping
what I did not sow? 23 Why then did you not
put my money in the bank, and at my coming
I might have collected it with interest?' 24 And
he said to those who stood by, 'Take the mina
from him, and give it to the one who has the
ten minas.' 25 And they said to him, 'Lord, he
has ten minas!' 26 'I tell you that [z]to everyone
who has, more will be given, but from the one
who has not, even what he has will be taken
away. 27 But [r]as for these enemies of mine, who
did not want me to reign over them, bring
them here and [a]slaughter them before me.'"

The Triumphal Entry

28 And when he had said these things, [b]he
went on ahead, [c]going up to Jerusalem.
29 [d]When he drew near to Bethphage and
[e]Bethany, at [f]the mount that is called Olivet,
he sent [g]two of the disciples, 30 saying, "Go into
the village in front of you, where on entering you will find a colt tied, [h]on which no one
has ever yet sat. Untie it and bring it here. 31 If
anyone asks you, 'Why are you untying it?' you
shall say this: 'The Lord has need of it.'" 32 So
those who were sent went away and found it
[i]just as he had told them. 33 And as they were
untying the colt, its owners said to them,
"Why are you untying the colt?" 34 And they
said, "The Lord has need of it." 35 And they
brought it to Jesus, and throwing their cloaks
on the colt, they set Jesus on it. 36 And as he
rode along, they [j]spread their cloaks on the
road. 37 As he was drawing near—already on
the way down the Mount of Olives—[k]the
whole multitude of his disciples began to
rejoice and praise God with a loud voice [l]for all
the mighty works that they had seen, 38 saying,
[m]"Blessed is [n]the King who comes in the name
of the Lord! Peace in heaven and [o]glory in the
highest!" 39 [p]And some of the Pharisees in the

[1] Greek *bondservants*; also verse 15 [2] A *mina* was about three months' wages for a laborer [3] Greek *bondservant*; also verse 22

cheerfully from the heart (2 Cor. 9:7). Zacchaeus's giving is not an entrance requirement or necessary model for our own application of the gospel. But it is a model of the proper and natural response to God's saving grace toward us. Grace frees us to give freely and boldly as we trust in God to meet all our needs (Matt. 6:25–34).

19:28–40 Luke's account of Jesus' arrival in Jerusalem just before his crucifixion reveals Jesus as powerful, as God's King, and as worthy of praise and honor. In the presence of such divine greatness, the natural response is worship (vv. 38–39). Yet not all respond to Jesus with such joyful gratitude. As we have seen throughout Luke's account, there is often another, opposite reaction to Jesus: grumbling and disputing (5:17–26; 6:1–11; 7:39; 19:7, 39). Hardness of heart and sin-blindness cause such darkness that even creation's spontaneous worship of God (19:40) can be hindered. This passage contains a challenge for us in how we respond to Jesus. The same spiritual malady that made the Pharisees oppose God's work in Jesus can ironically be our problem as well, as followers of Jesus. We must constantly pray for God to open our eyes to see him truly and to work truth in our inner person (Ps. 51:1–19; Eph. 3:14–21).

11 [n][ch. 17:20; Acts 1:6]
12 [o]For ver. 12-27, [Matt. 25:14-30; Mark 13:34]
13 [p]Matt. 25:1 [q][John 21:22, 23]
14 [r][John 1:14]
17 [s]ch. 16:10; 1 Cor. 4:2; [1 Tim. 3:13] [t][Matt. 24:47]
20 [u]John 11:44; 20:7; Acts 19:12 (Gk.)
21 [v][1 Sam. 25:3] [w][2 Cor. 8:12]
22 [x]2 Sam. 1:16; Job 9:20; 15:6 [y]Matt. 18:32 [v][See ver. 21 above]
26 [z][ch. 12:48]; See Matt. 13:12
27 [r][See ver. 14 above] [a]ch. 20:16; Matt. 22:7; [1 Sam. 15:33]
28 [b]Mark 10:32 [c]See ch. 9:51; 10:30
29 [d]For ver. 29-38, see Matt. 21:1-9; Mark 11:1-10; John 12:12-15; [Zech. 9:9]
[e]ch. 24:50; Matt. 21:17; John 11:18 [f]Zech. 14:4; Matt. 24:3; 26:30; [John 8:1]; [Acts 1:12] [g][Mark 14:13] **30** [h][ch. 23:53] **32** [i]ch. 22:13 **36** [j]2 Kgs. 9:13
37 [k][ch. 18:43] [l][John 12:17, 18] **38** [m]ch. 13:35; Cited from Ps. 118:26 [n]See Matt. 25:34; John 1:49 [o]ch. 2:14; [Ps. 148:1] **39** [p][Matt. 21:15, 16]

crowd said to him, "Teacher, rebuke your disciples." 40 He answered, "I tell you, if these were silent, [q]the very stones would cry out."

Jesus Weeps over Jerusalem

41 [r]And when he drew near and saw the city, [s]he wept over it, 42 saying, [t]"Would that you, even you, had known on this day the things that make for peace! But now [u]they are hidden from your eyes. 43 For [v]the days will come upon you, when your enemies [w]will set up a barricade around you and [x]surround you and hem you in on every side 44 [y]and tear you down to the ground, you and your children within you. And [z]they will not leave one stone upon another in you, because you did not know [a]the time of your [b]visitation."

Jesus Cleanses the Temple

45 [c]And he entered the temple and began to drive out those who sold, 46 saying to them, "It is written, [d]'My house shall be a house of prayer,' but [e]you have made it a den of robbers."

47 [f]And he was teaching daily in the temple. [g]The chief priests and the scribes and the principal men of the people were seeking to destroy him, 48 but they did not find anything they could do, for all the people were hanging on his words.

The Authority of Jesus Challenged

20 [h]One day, [i]as Jesus[1] was teaching the people in the temple and preaching the gospel, [j]the chief priests and the scribes with the elders came up 2 and said to him, "Tell us [k]by what authority you do these things, or who it is that gave you this authority." 3 He answered them, "I also will ask you a question. Now tell me, 4 was the baptism of John [l]from heaven or from man?" 5 And they discussed it with one another, saying, "If we say, 'From heaven,' he will say, [m]'Why did you not believe him?' 6 But if we say, 'From man,' all the people will stone us to death, for they are convinced that John was [n]a prophet." 7 So they answered that they did not know where it came from. 8 And Jesus said to them, "Neither will I tell you by what authority I do these things."

The Parable of the Wicked Tenants

9 [o]And he began to tell the people this parable: "A man planted [p]a vineyard and [q]let it out to tenants and [r]went into another country for a long while. 10 When the time came, he sent a servant[2] to the tenants, so that [q]they would give him some of the fruit of the vineyard. [s]But the tenants beat him and sent him away empty-handed. 11 [t]And [s]he sent another servant. But they also beat and [u]treated him shamefully, and sent him away empty-handed. 12 [s]And he sent yet a third. This one also they wounded and cast out. 13 Then the owner of the vineyard said, 'What shall I do? I will send my [v]beloved son; perhaps they will respect him.' 14 But when the tenants saw him, they said to themselves, [w]'This is the heir. [x]Let us kill him, so that the inheritance may be ours.' 15 And they [y]threw him out of the vineyard and killed him. What then will the owner of the vineyard do to them? 16 [z]He will [a]come and destroy those tenants and [b]give the vineyard to others." When they heard this, they said, "Surely not!" 17 But he [c]looked directly at them and said, "What then is this that is written:

> [d]" 'The stone that the builders rejected
> has become the cornerstone'?[3]

18 [e]Everyone who falls on that stone will be broken to pieces, and when it falls [f]on anyone, it will crush him."

Paying Taxes to Caesar

19 [h]The scribes and the chief priests sought to lay hands on him at that very hour, for they perceived that he had told this parable against them, but they feared the people. 20 [i]So they

[1] Greek *he* [2] Greek *bondservant*; also verse 11 [3] Greek *the head of the corner*

20:19–26 Despite the crafty intention of the religious leaders, the great wisdom of God incarnate in Jesus is on clear display here. Jesus takes the politically charged question about paying taxes to Caesar and turns it into an opportunity to stump his opponents and to draw more people to marvel at God's ways.

40 [q]Hab. 2:11
41 [r]For ver. 41-44, [ch. 13:34, 35; 23:28-31] [s][John 11:35; Heb. 5:7]
42 [t][Deut. 32:29] [u][John 12:40] **43** [v]See ch. 17:22 [w]Isa. 29:3; 37:33; Jer. 6:6; Ezek. 4:2; 26:8 [x]ch. 21:20 **44** [y][Ps. 137:9; Hos. 13:16; Nah. 3:10] [z]ch. 21:6 [a][Dan. 9:24] [b]1 Pet. 2:12 **45** [c]For ver. 45-47, see Matt. 21:12-16; Mark 11:15-18; [John 2:14-16] **46** [d]Cited from Isa. 56:7 [e]Jer. 7:11 **47** [f]ch. 20:1; See Matt. 26:55 [g]See Matt. 21:46 **Chapter 20** **1** [h]For ver. 1-8, see Matt. 21:23-27; Mark 11:27-33 [i]ch. 19:47 [j]Acts 4:1; 6:12 **2** [k][Ex. 2:14; John 1:25; Acts 4:7] **4** [l]ch. 15:18, 21; John 3:27 **5** [m]ch. 7:30; Matt. 21:32 **6** [n][John 5:35]; See Matt. 11:9 **9** [o]For ver. 9-19, see Matt. 21:33-46; Mark 12:1-12 [p]Ps. 80:8; Isa. 5:1; Matt. 21:28 [q]Song 8:11, 12 [r]Matt. 25:14, 15; [Mark 13:34] **10** [q][See ver. 9 above] [s]Matt. 5:12; 22:6; 23:34, 37; [2 Chr. 24:19; 36:15, 16; Neh. 9:26; Jer. 37:15; 38:6; Acts 7:52; 2 Cor. 11:24-26; 1 Thess. 2:15; Heb. 11:36, 37] **11** [t]Matt. 22:4 [s][See ver. 10 above] [u]Acts 5:41 (Gk.) **12** [s][See ver. 10 above] **13** [v]See Matt. 3:17 **14** [w]Heb. 1:2; [John 1:11; Rom. 8:17] [x][1 Kgs. 21:19] **15** [y]Heb. 13:12 **16** [z][ch. 19:27] [a][Matt. 24:50; 25:19] [b]Matt. 21:43; Acts 13:46; 18:6; 28:28; [Matt. 8:11, 12] **17** [c]See Mark 10:21 [d]Acts 4:11; 1 Pet. 2:7; Cited from Ps. 118:22 **18** [e]Isa. 8:14, 15; Rom. 9:32, 33; 1 Pet. 2:8 [f]Dan. 2:34, 35, 44, 45 **19** [h]ch. 19:47, 48 **20** [i]For ver. 20-38, see Matt. 22:15-32; Mark 12:13-27

[j]watched him and sent spies, who [k]pretended to be sincere, that they might [l]catch him in something he said, so as to deliver him up to the authority and jurisdiction of [m]the governor. 21 So they asked him, "Teacher, we know that you speak and teach rightly, and [o]show no partiality,[1] but truly teach [p]the way of God. 22 Is it lawful for us to give [q]tribute to [r]Caesar, or not?" 23 But he perceived their [s]craftiness, and said to them, 24 "Show me [t]a denarius.[2] Whose likeness and inscription does it have?" They said, "Caesar's." 25 He said to them, "Then [u]render to Caesar the things that are Caesar's, and to God the things that are God's." 26 And they were not able in the presence of the people [v]to catch him in what he said, but marveling at his answer they became silent.

Sadducees Ask About the Resurrection

27 There came to him [w]some Sadducees, [x]those who deny that there is a resurrection, 28 and they asked him a question, saying, "Teacher, Moses wrote for us [y]that if a man's brother dies, having a wife but no children, the man[3] must take the widow and raise up offspring for his brother. 29 Now there were seven brothers. The first took a wife, and died without children. 30 And the second 31 and the third took her, and likewise all seven left no children and died. 32 Afterward the woman also died. 33 In the resurrection, therefore, whose wife will the woman be? For the seven had her as wife."

34 And Jesus said to them, [z]"The sons of this age [a]marry and [a]are given in marriage, 35 but those who are [b]considered worthy to attain to [c]that age and to the resurrection from the dead [d]neither marry [d]nor are given in marriage, 36 for [e]they cannot die anymore, because they are [f]equal to angels and [g]are [h]sons of God, being [i]sons[4] of the resurrection. 37 But that the dead are raised, [j]even Moses showed, in [k]the passage about the bush, where he calls [l]the Lord the God of Abraham and the God of Isaac and the God of Jacob. 38 Now he is not God of the dead, but of the living, for all [m]live to him." 39 Then some of the scribes [n]answered, "Teacher, you have spoken well." 40 For [o]they no longer dared to ask him any question.

Whose Son Is the Christ?

41 [p]But he said to them, "How can they say that [q]the Christ is [q]David's son? 42 For David himself says in the Book of Psalms,

[1] Greek *and do not receive a face* [2] A *denarius* was a day's wage for a laborer [3] Greek *his brother* [4] Greek *huioi*; see Preface

Jesus' answer also raises the matter of the Christian's experience of living as citizens of two very different kingdoms, the earthly and the heavenly (Phil. 3:20). This reality of our dual citizenship is the source of great conflict internally and externally. From within, we struggle to reorient our lives toward God's radically different present and coming kingdom, even while living in this world. From without, we encounter persecution and discomfort in this sinful and God-opposed world (2 Tim. 3:12). Jesus does not eliminate this dilemma of our existence, but he does give us a vision of how to approach these matters. All of the world is God's, but in this overlapping age we must acknowledge that there is an authority and order to society that must be obeyed (Rom. 13:1–7), even while our ultimate allegiance is to God.

20:27–40 Although the death and resurrection of Jesus has not yet occurred in Luke's account, we are here given a foretaste of what is going to take place. Those who respond to the gospel will someday enjoy an invincible resurrected life, impervious to death and decay (v. 36). Believers who have already died are now alive to God and in his presence, even as are Abraham, Isaac, and Jacob (vv. 27–28; 1 Cor. 15:20–26). Contrary to the Sadducees, who denied any resurrection from the dead, Jesus teaches here that the blessings of the gospel extend far beyond this short life in our fallen world.

Believers will one day be raised to life—not an ethereal, ghost-like existence but embodied, physical life. It is a restoration of the life given to Adam and Eve in Eden, only this time without any possibility of sin. All this is achieved through the resurrection of Christ (Luke 24:1–12), who is "the firstfruits" (1 Cor. 15:20–22). That is, Jesus is the first ingathering of the harvest of all those united to him. Our final destiny is one of a renewed, embodied, immortal life on this earth (Rev. 21:1–2).

20:41–44 Jesus' enemies have just tried to entrap him by asking him two difficult questions (vv. 19–26; vv. 27–40). He now ends their questioning by asking them a question about himself. By quoting Psalm 110 and applying it to himself, Jesus emphasizes

20 [j]ch. 14:1; Mark 3:2 [k][1 Kgs. 14:6] [l]ver. 26; ch. 11:54 [m]Matt. 27:2, 11; 28:14; See Acts 23:24
21 [o]See Acts 10:34 [p]Acts 18:25, 26; [Acts 13:10]
22 [q]Matt. 17:25 [r]ch. 2:1; 3:1
23 [s]1 Cor. 3:19; 2 Cor. 4:2; 11:3; Eph. 4:14; [2 Cor. 12:16]
24 [t]See Matt. 18:28
25 [u]Rom. 13:7
26 [v]ver. 20
27 [w]Matt. 3:7; 16:1; 22:34; Acts 4:1; 5:17; 23:6 [x]Acts 23:8; [Acts 4:2]
28 [y][Deut. 25:5]
34 [z]ch. 16:8; See ch. 10:6 [a]ch. 17:27; Matt. 24:38; [ver. 35]
35 [b]Acts 5:41; 2 Thess. 1:5, 11; See Matt. 22:8 [c][ch. 18:30]; See Mark 10:30 [d][ver. 34]
36 [e]1 Cor. 15:54, 55; Rev. 21:4 [f][Heb. 2:7, 9] [g][Gen. 1:26; Ps. 82:6] [h][Rom. 8:19, 23; 1 Cor. 15:52] [i]See ch. 10:6
37 [j]ver. 28 [k]Ex. 3:1–4:17 [l]Acts 7:32; Cited from Ex. 3:15; [Ex. 3:6]
38 [m]Rom. 6:11; 14:7, 8; 2 Cor. 5:15; Gal. 2:19; 1 Thess. 5:10; 1 Pet. 4:2; [Heb. 9:14]
39 [n]Mark 12:28; [Matt. 22:34]
40 [o]Matt. 22:46; Mark 12:34
41 [p]For ver. 41-44, see Matt. 22:41-45; Mark 12:35-37 [q]See Matt. 1:1, 17

[r]“ ‘The Lord said to my Lord,
“Sit at my right hand,
43 until I make your enemies [s]your footstool.” ’

44 David thus calls him Lord, so [t]how is he his
son?”

Beware of the Scribes

45 [u]And in the hearing of all the people he
said to his disciples, 46 “Beware of the scribes,
who like to walk around in long robes, and
love greetings in the marketplaces and the
best seats in the synagogues and [v]the places
of honor at feasts, 47 [w]who devour widows'
houses and [x]for a pretense make long prayers.
They will receive the greater condemnation.”

The Widow's Offering

21 [y]Jesus[1] looked up and saw the rich [z]putting their gifts into [a]the offering box,
2 and he saw a poor widow put in two [b]small
copper coins.[2] 3 And he said, “Truly, I tell you,
[c]this poor widow has put in more than all of
them. 4 For they all contributed out of their
abundance, but she out of her [d]poverty put in
all [e]she had to live on.”

Jesus Foretells Destruction of the Temple

5 [f]And while some were speaking of the temple, how it was adorned with noble stones and
offerings, he said, 6 “As for these things that
you see, [g]the days will come when there will
not be left here one stone upon another that

[1] Greek *He* [2] Greek *two lepta*; a *lepton* was a Jewish bronze or copper coin worth about 1/128 of a *denarius* (which was a day's wage for a laborer)

42[r] Acts 2:34, 35; Heb. 1:13; Cited from Ps. 110:1; [1 Cor. 15:25; Heb. 10:13]
43[s] [Acts 7:49]
44[t] [Rom. 1:3, 4]
45[u] For ver. 45, 46, see Matt. 23:1, 2, 5-7; Mark 12:38, 39; [ch. 11:43]
46[v] ch. 14:7, 8
47[w] [ch. 11:39; 16:14] [x] [Matt. 6:5, 7]
Chapter 21
1[y] For ver. 1-4, see Mark 12:41-44 [z] 2 Kgs. 12:9 [a] John 8:20 (Gk.)
2[b] ch. 12:59
3[c] [2 Cor. 8:2, 12]
4[d] [Phil. 4:11] [e] ch. 8:43
5[f] For ver. 5-36, see Matt. 24:1-51; Mark 13:1-37
6[g] ch. 19:43, 44; See ch. 17:22

that his coming is the fulfillment of God's great promise that an heir of King David would reign over God's people (2 Sam. 7:13–16; Jer. 33:17).

But he is not only the Son of David, thus fulfilling the kingdom promises. He is also something greater. He is not only David's son but also David's Lord. The Messiah is not only the human son of David but also the divine Son of God. While the Old Testament often refers to the Davidic king as the “son” of God, throughout the Old Testament a trajectory builds that increasingly indicates that the coming Messiah would be more than a mere human king (Psalm 2; 45; 89:27; 110; Isa. 9:6–7; Ezek. 34:10–15, 23–24). Jesus himself here reinforces that trajectory. The New Testament clarifies what the Old Testament hints at: that indeed the Messiah, Jesus Christ, is himself divine, the eternally preexistent Son of God (Matt. 11:27; Luke 10:22; John 1:1, 14; 5:23; 14:9; 17:1–8; Rom. 9:5; 1 Cor. 8:6; Phil. 2:6; Col. 1:15–19; Heb. 1:2–3; 1 John 5:20).

20:45–47 A recurrent theme of the gospel is that God cares about the inner person and wants our affections to be rightly ordered. That is, to receive Jesus' message is to gladly reorient our loves and values according to God's kingdom. Jesus' brief warning here about the religious scribes of his day reemphasizes this point. Here he addresses a crucial heart condition that will result in condemnation: performance for the sake of the praise of others.

While it is entirely natural to like positive attention, and while we should give honor where honor is due, there is a disastrous problem when *love* for these things supplants love for God and neighbor. We must “beware” of this heart habit of the scribes (v. 46) and take care that we don't imitate their ways. When we find ourselves tempted to live for the praise of others we must repent, remembering that this is the opposite of the gospel message of humility.

In the gospel, God has given us full and free approval in Christ. We are accepted, reconciled, justified (Rom. 5:1; 2 Cor 5:18; Gal. 1:10; 1 Thess. 2:4). We no longer need to seek the approval of people, because we are approved by God—the only approval that matters, and the only approval that satisfies.

21:1–4 More than any of the other Gospel writers, Luke focuses on teachings, parables, and stories about money and wealth. This short story of the widow's offering is a good example. At one level, the story reminds us about the deceptiveness of riches and how we over-evaluate the worth of money (Matt. 6:19–21; Luke 8:14; 1 Tim. 6:17). At a deeper level, we are reminded that in God's economy it is not the *quantity* of money given but the *quality*, as evaluated by the worshiping heart behind the gift. This story challenges us to give more radically and sacrificially, but it also encourages us that God is no respecter of persons when it comes to financial means. He cares about our faith and worshipful giving, regardless of our ability to give.

will not be thrown down." 7 And they asked him, "Teacher, [h]when will these things be, and what will be the sign when these things are about to take place?" 8 And he said, [i]"See that you are not led astray. For [j]many will come in my name, saying, [k]'I am he!' and, [l]'The time is at hand!' Do not go after them. 9 And when you hear of wars and tumults, do not be [m]terrified, for these things [n]must first take place, but the end will not be at once."

Jesus Foretells Wars and Persecution

10 Then he said to them, [o]"Nation will rise against nation, and [p]kingdom against kingdom. 11 There will be great [q]earthquakes, and in various places [r]famines and pestilences. And there will be [s]terrors and great [t]signs from heaven. 12 But before all this [u]they will lay their hands on you and persecute you, delivering you up to [v]the synagogues and [w]prisons, and you [x]will be brought before [y]kings and [z]governors for my name's sake. 13 [a]This will be your opportunity to bear witness. 14 Settle it therefore in your minds [b]not to meditate beforehand how to answer, 15 for [c]I will give you a mouth and [d]wisdom, which none of your adversaries will be able to withstand or [e]contradict. 16 You will be delivered up [f]even by parents and brothers[1] and relatives and friends, and some of you they will put to death. 17 [g]You will be hated by all for my name's sake. 18 But [h]not a hair of your head will perish. 19 By your [i]endurance you will gain your lives.

Jesus Foretells Destruction of Jerusalem

20 "But [j]when you see Jerusalem surrounded by armies, then know that [k]its desolation has come near. 21 Then let those who are in Judea flee to the mountains, and let those who are inside the city depart, and let not those who are out in the country enter it, 22 for these are [l]days of [m]vengeance, to fulfill [n]all that is written. 23 [o]Alas for women who are pregnant and for those who are nursing infants in those days! For there will be great distress upon the earth and [p]wrath against this people. 24 They will fall by the edge of the sword and [q]be led captive among all nations, and [r]Jerusalem will be trampled underfoot by the Gentiles, [s]until the times of the Gentiles are fulfilled.

The Coming of the Son of Man

25 "And [t]there will be signs in sun and moon [u]and stars, and on the earth [v]distress of nations in perplexity because of the roaring of the sea and the waves, 26 people fainting with fear and with foreboding of what is coming on the world. For [w]the powers of the heavens will be shaken. 27 And then they will see [x]the Son of Man coming in a cloud [y]with power and

[1] Or *parents and brothers and sisters*

21:16–19 Jesus' teaching here contains a paradox that is a basic part of the Christian experience. On the one hand, to be a disciple of Jesus means to experience persecution, division, conflict, hatred, and for some, even death (v. 16). Yet at the same time Jesus says that not a hair of our heads will perish and that by endurance we will gain our "lives"—or, as the word could be translated, our souls (v. 19). These seem like contradictory statements until one sees that the gospel promises of blessing and peace are statements about one's soul in relation to God, not necessarily of our experience in this world. We apply this to our lives by an adjustment of our expectations of what the Christian life will be like. If we expect God's favor and blessings to mean that all goes our way in this fallen world, then we will either become disappointed and bitter or else we will avoid living according to God's kingdom ways, to avoid the pain and suffering.

21:20–33 The proper perspective on pain and suffering that Jesus has just related (vv. 16–19) is a necessary prelude to these important words about the future destruction of Jerusalem (vv. 20–24). The catastrophic scene Jesus describes would be unthinkable to his disciples. Yet though modern commentators debate the timing and identification of these events, it is important for us to recognize that they are real and that Jesus speaks to his immediate audience and to us with assurance that he will ultimately come to rescue his people (including the Gentiles he intends to save; v. 24) from their distress (vv. 25–28). Thus, it is important that none despair and all remain vigilant for the signs of his certain appearing (vv. 28–33). Here grace is expressed in terms of Christ coming to establish a kingdom that rescues from evil and destruction.

7 [h] [Acts 1:6, 7]
8 [i] Jer. 29:8; Eph. 5:6; Col. 2:8; 2 Thess. 2:3; 1 John 3:7 [j] Jer. 14:14; 1 John 2:18 [k] See John 8:24 [l] [Matt. 3:2; 4:17; Mark 1:15]
9 [m] ch. 24:37 [n] Rev. 1:1
10 [o] 2 Chr. 15:6; [Rev. 6:4] [p] Isa. 19:2
11 [q] Rev. 6:12 [r] Acts 11:28; Rev. 6:8 [s] Isa. 19:17 [t] ch. 11:16; Matt. 16:1; Mark 8:11; [ver. 25; Rev. 12:1, 3; 13:13; 15:1]
12 [u] For ver. 12-17, [Matt. 10:17-22] [v] Acts 22:19; 26:11 [w] Acts 4:3; 5:18; 8:3; 12:4; 16:24; 24:27; 2 Cor. 11:23 [x] See Acts 16:19 [y] [Acts 27:24] [z] Acts 17:6; 18:12; 24:1; 25:6
13 [a] [Phil. 1:13, 14, 19]
14 [b] ch. 12:11
15 [c] [Ex. 4:12; Jer. 1:9] [d] Acts 6:10 [e] [Acts 4:14]
16 [f] [ch. 12:53; Matt. 10:35]
17 [g] John 15:18-21; [ch. 6:22]
18 [h] [ver. 16; John 10:28]; See 1 Sam. 14:45
19 [i] Rom. 5:3; [Matt. 10:22; 24:13]; See Heb. 10:36
20 [j] See ch. 19:43 [k] Dan. 9:27
22 [l] Isa. 34:8; 63:4; Hos. 9:7 [m] [ch. 18:7, 8] [n] See Matt. 1:22
23 [o] ch. 23:29 [p] 1 Thess. 2:16
24 [q] [Deut. 28:64] [r] Rev. 11:2; [Ps. 79:1; Isa. 63:3, 18; Dan. 8:13; Zech. 12:3] [s] [Dan. 12:7; Rom. 11:25]
25 [t] Isa. 13:10; 24:23; Ezek. 32:7; Joel 2:10, 31; 3:15; Acts 2:20; [Amos 5:20; 8:9; Zeph. 1:15; Rev. 6:12; 8:12] [u] Rev. 6:13; [Isa. 14:12; 34:4] [v] [Ps. 65:7]
26 [w] [Isa. 34:4]
27 [x] See Dan. 7:13 [y] Matt. 26:64; Mark 9:1; [Matt. 25:31]

great glory. 28 Now when these things begin to
take place, straighten up and [z]raise your heads,
because [a]your redemption is drawing near."

The Lesson of the Fig Tree

29 And he told them a parable: "Look at the
fig tree, and all the trees. 30 As soon as they
come out in leaf, you see [b]for yourselves and
know that the summer is already near. 31 So
also, when you see these things taking place,
you know that the kingdom of God is near.
32 [c]Truly, I say to you, this generation will not
pass away until all has taken place. 33 [d]Heaven
and earth will pass away, but [e]my words will
not pass away.

Watch Yourselves

34 "But watch yourselves [f]lest [g]your hearts be
weighed down with dissipation and drunkenness and [h]cares of this life, and [i]that day come
upon you suddenly [j]like a trap. 35 For it will
come upon all who dwell on the face of the
whole earth. 36 But [k]stay awake at all times,
[l]praying that you may [m]have strength to escape
all these things that are going to take place,
and [n]to stand before the Son of Man."
37 And [o]every day he was teaching in the temple, but [p]at night he went out and lodged on
[q]the mount called Olivet. 38 And early in the
morning [o]all the people came to him in the
temple to hear him.

The Plot to Kill Jesus

22 [r]Now the Feast of Unleavened Bread
drew near, which is called [s]the Passover.
2 And the chief priests and the scribes [t]were
seeking how to put him to death, for they
feared the people.

Judas to Betray Jesus

3 [u]Then [v]Satan entered into [w]Judas called
Iscariot, who was of the number of the twelve.
4 He went away and conferred with the chief
priests and [x]officers how he might betray him
to them. 5 And they were glad, and agreed to
give him money. 6 So he consented and sought
an opportunity to [y]betray him to them in the
absence of a crowd.

The Passover with the Disciples

7 [z]Then came [a]the day of Unleavened Bread,
on which the Passover lamb had to be sacrificed. 8 So Jesus[1] sent Peter and John, saying,
"Go and prepare the Passover for us, that we
may eat it." 9 They said to him, "Where will
you have us prepare it?" 10 He said to them,
"Behold, when you have entered the city, a
man carrying a jar of water will meet you.
Follow him into the house that he enters 11 and
tell the master of the house, [b]'The Teacher says
to you, Where is [c]the guest room, where I may
eat the Passover with my disciples?' 12 And he
will show you [d]a large upper room furnished;
prepare it there." 13 And they went and found
it [e]just as he had told them, and they prepared
the Passover.

Institution of the Lord's Supper

14 [f]And when the hour came, he reclined at
table, and the apostles with him. 15 And he said
to them, "I have earnestly desired to eat this
Passover with you before I suffer. 16 For I tell
you I will not eat it[2] [g]until it is fulfilled in the
kingdom of God." 17 And he took a cup, and
[h]when he had given thanks he said, "Take this,
and divide it among yourselves. 18 [i]For I tell
you that from now on I will not drink of the

[1] Greek *he* [2] Some manuscripts *never eat it again*

28 [z]Job 10:15 [a]Rom. 8:23; Eph. 4:30; [Rom. 13:11]; See ch. 1:68
30 [b]ch. 12:57; [Matt. 16:3]
32 [c]See ch. 9:27
33 [d]Ps. 102:26; Isa. 51:6; 2 Pet. 3:10; [Matt. 5:18; Heb. 12:27] [e]Ps. 119:89; Isa. 40:8; 1 Pet. 1:23, 25
34 [f][Rom. 13:13; 1 Thess. 5:6, 7; 1 Pet. 4:7] [g]James 5:5 [h][Matt. 13:22] [i]1 Thess. 5:3, 4; [ch. 12:40] [j]Eccles. 9:12; Isa. 24:17
36 [k]ch. 12:37; Matt. 25:13; 26:41; Mark 14:34-38; Acts 20:31; 1 Cor. 16:13; 1 Thess. 5:6; 1 Pet. 5:8 [l]See ch. 18:1 [m][Hos. 12:4] [n]See Rev. 6:17

21:34–36 The gospel should never be conceived of as merely a new religion of duty, self-sacrifice, and piety. The true gospel will at times involve each of these things, but these are not the gospel itself, nor are they a safe gauge of the gospel's effect on our lives. Yet at the same time we must not think of the gospel in a sloppy or ambivalent way. Because God's kingdom, ruled by King Jesus, is coming upon the earth to set things aright, the gospel calls us to be on guard against the deceptive pleasures and cares of this life (v. 34; 8:14). The gospel call to "stay awake" (21:36) is not a command to strive for a certain level of self-imposed piety, but a reminder that the deceitfulness of sin and the work of the Devil (1 Pet. 5:8) must be resisted as we travel on the road of discipleship.

22:14–23 The Last Supper is one of the most important events in the Gospels, and each of the Gospel writers tells the story in a slightly different way to emphasize

37 [o]See Matt. 26:55 [p]ch. 22:39; Matt. 21:17; Mark 11:19; [John 8:1; 18:2] [q]See Matt. 21:1 **38** [o][See ver. 37 above] **Chapter 22** **1** [r]For ver. 1, 2, see Matt. 26:2-5; Mark 14:1, 2 [s]See John 6:4 **2** [t]John 11:53; See Matt. 21:46 **3** [u]For ver. 3-6, see Matt. 26:14-16; Mark 14:10, 11; [John 13:2, 27, 30] [v][Acts 5:3] [w]ch. 6:16; Matt. 27:3; Acts 1:16; [John 6:71; 12:4] **4** [x]Acts 4:1; 5:24, 26 **6** [y]See Matt. 20:18, 19 **7** [z]For ver. 7-14, see Matt. 26:17-19; Mark 14:12-16 [a]Ex. 12:18; 1 Cor. 5:7 **11** [b]See John 11:28 [c]ch. 2:7 (Gk.) **12** [d][Acts 1:13] **13** [e]ch. 19:32 **14** [f]Matt. 26:20; Mark 14:17 **16** [g][ver. 30; ch. 14:15; Rev. 19:9] **17** [h]See Matt. 15:36 **18** [i]Matt. 26:29; Mark 14:25

fruit of the vine [g]until the kingdom of God
comes." 19 [j]And he took bread, and [h]when he
had given thanks, he broke it and gave it to
them, saying, [k]"This is my body, which is given
for you. Do this in remembrance of me." 20 And
likewise the cup after they had eaten, saying,
[k]"This cup that is poured out for you is [l]the
new [m]covenant in my blood.[1] 21 [n]But behold,
the hand of him who betrays me is [o]with me
on the table. 22 For the Son of Man goes [p]as it
has been determined, but woe to that man by
whom he is betrayed!" 23 And they began to
question one another, which of them it could
be who was going to do this.

Who Is the Greatest?

24 [q]A dispute also arose among them, as
to which of them was to be regarded as the
greatest. 25 [r]And he said to them, "The kings
of the Gentiles [s]exercise lordship over them,
and those in authority over them are called
benefactors. 26 [t]But not so with you. Rather,
let [s]the greatest among you become as the
youngest, and the leader as one who serves.
27 For who is the greater, [u]one who reclines at
table or one who serves? Is it not the one who
reclines at table? But [v]I am among you as the
one who serves.

28 "You are those who have stayed with me
[w]in my trials, 29 and [x]I assign to you, as my
Father assigned to me, a kingdom, 30 [y]that you
may eat and drink at my table in my kingdom
and [z]sit on thrones judging [a]the twelve tribes
of Israel.

Jesus Foretells Peter's Denial

31 "Simon, Simon, behold, [b]Satan demanded
to have you,[2] [c]that he might sift you like wheat,
32 but [d]I have prayed for you that your faith
may not fail. And when you have turned again,
[e]strengthen your brothers." 33 Peter[3] said to
him, "Lord, I am ready to go with you both
[f]to prison and [g]to death." 34 [h]Jesus[4] said, "I tell
you, Peter, the rooster will not crow this day,
until you deny three times that you know me."

Scripture Must Be Fulfilled in Jesus

35 And he said to them, [i]"When I sent you out
with no moneybag or knapsack or sandals,
did you lack anything?" They said, "Nothing."
36 He said to them, "But now let the one who

[1] Some manuscripts omit, in whole or in part, verses 19b-20 (*which is given . . . in my blood*) [2] The Greek word for *you* (twice in this verse) is plural; in verse 32, all four instances are singular [3] Greek *He* [4] Greek *He*

different aspects of its importance. In the Last Supper we see how the gospel is backward-looking, presently engaging, and forward-looking. The *backward-looking* aspect is our continual remembrance of how Jesus sacrificed his body and blood on our behalf. This conscious act of remembering Christ's past sacrifice and *presently* uniting our hearts in communion with him should be regularly practiced in the church, producing gratitude and allegiance. At the same time, there is an equally essential *forward-looking* element to the ongoing practice of the Lord's Supper. It is highlighted twice by Jesus in his reference to the future time when the kingdom of God comes (vv. 15, 18). To be a disciple of Jesus means not only looking back to the cross with gratitude but also engaging with him in present allegiance and looking forward with hope. It is especially this forward-looking hope in God's coming kingdom that provides resources for our endurance and willingness to live now in the radically different ways that Jesus calls us to.

22:24–27 Constantly throughout Luke the gospel message has shown that what God values is often in direct contradiction to our natural and sinful tendencies. Jesus continually explains the gospel as a call to follow his example in living according to the unexpected but blessed ways of God's coming kingdom. We must repent of our own broken conduct and reorient our lives to God.

The particular issue at hand here concerns how we relate to one another in authority relationships as kingdom-gospel people. This same dispute, about who is the greatest among the disciples, has arisen before (9:46–48). Jesus addresses the matter head-on and turns our values upside down. Human greatness is not found in having authority, receiving honor, or being a recognized leader. Rather, in God's kingdom, it is the servant and the lowly who are the true leaders and the "great" ones.

Jesus himself is the ultimate model of this paradoxical truth (Phil. 2:1–10). Following Jesus' example, our lives together as Christians—individually and corporately—should be measured by this test: Is our primary goal toward each other about serving or about being served?

18 [g][See ver. 16 above]
19 [j]For ver. 19, 20, see Matt. 26:26-28; Mark 14:22-24; 1 Cor. 11:23-25 [h][See ver. 17 above] [k]1 Cor. 10:16; [John 6:53]
20 [k][See ver. 19 above] [l]See 2 Cor. 3:6 [m]Ex. 24:8; [Zech. 9:11; Heb. 13:20]
21 [n]For ver. 21-23, see Matt. 26:21-24; Mark 14:18-21; [John 13:21-26] [o][Ps. 41:9; John 13:18]
22 [p]Acts 2:23
24 [q]ch. 9:46; Mark 9:34
25 [r]For ver. 25-27, [Matt. 18:1-4; 20:25-28; Mark 10:42-45] [s]1 Pet. 5:3
26 [t]ch. 9:48; [Matt. 23:11] [s][See ver. 25 above]
27 [u][ch. 12:37] [v]See Matt. 20:28
28 [w][See Heb. 2:18; 4:15]
29 [x]2 Tim. 2:12; [John 17:18]; See Matt. 25:34; 28:18; Acts 14:22; Rev. 1:6
30 [y][ver. 16; ch. 13:29; 14:15; Matt. 8:11] [z]See Matt. 19:28 [a]Acts 26:7; James 1:1; Rev. 21:12
31 [b]Job 1:6-12; 2:1-6; [2 Cor. 2:11; 1 Pet. 5:8]; See 1 Cor. 5:5 [c]Amos 9:9; [John 16:32]
32 [d]John 17:9, 11, 15 [e][Ps. 51:13; John 21:15-17]
33 [f][Acts 12:4] [g][John 21:19]
34 [h][Matt. 26:33-35; Mark 14:29-31; John 13:37, 38]
35 [i]ch. 9:3; 10:4; Matt. 10:9, 10; Mark 6:8

has a moneybag take it, and likewise a knapsack. And let the one who has no sword sell his cloak and buy one. 37 For I tell you that [j]this Scripture must be fulfilled in me: [k]'And he was numbered with the transgressors.' For [l]what is written about me has its fulfillment." 38 And they said, "Look, Lord, here are two [m]swords." And he said to them, [n]"It is enough."

Jesus Prays on the Mount of Olives

39 [o]And he came out and went, [p]as was his custom, to [q]the Mount of Olives, and the disciples followed him. 40 [r]And when he came to [s]the place, he said to them, [t]"Pray that you may not [u]enter into temptation." 41 And he withdrew from them about a stone's throw, and [v]knelt down and prayed, 42 saying, [w]"Father, if you are willing, remove [x]this cup from me. [y]Nevertheless, not my will, but yours, be done." 43 And there appeared to him [z]an angel from heaven, strengthening him. 44 And [w]being in an agony he prayed more earnestly; and his sweat became like great drops of blood falling down to the ground.[1] 45 And when he rose from prayer, he came to the disciples and found them sleeping for sorrow, 46 and he said to them, "Why are you sleeping? Rise and [a]pray that you may not enter into temptation."

Betrayal and Arrest of Jesus

47 [b]While he was still speaking, there came a crowd, and the man called [c]Judas, one of the twelve, was leading them. He drew near to Jesus to kiss him, 48 but Jesus said to him, "Judas, would you betray the Son of Man with a kiss?" 49 And when those who were around him saw what would follow, they said, "Lord, shall we strike [d]with the sword?" 50 And one of them struck the servant[2] of the high priest and cut off his right ear. 51 But Jesus said, "No more of this!" And he touched his ear and healed him. 52 Then Jesus said to the chief priests and [e]officers of the temple and elders, who had come out against him, "Have you come out as against a robber, with swords and clubs? 53 When [f]I was with you day after day in the temple, you did not lay hands on me. But this is [g]your hour, and [h]the power of darkness."

Peter Denies Jesus

54 [i]Then they seized him and led him away, bringing him into the high priest's house, [j]and Peter was following at a distance. 55 [k]And when they had kindled a fire in the middle of [l]the courtyard and sat down together, Peter sat down among them. 56 Then a servant girl, seeing him as he sat in the light and looking

[1] Some manuscripts omit verses 43 and 44 [2] Greek *bondservant*

37 [j][Acts 1:16]; See ch. 13:33; Matt. 1:22 [k]Cited from Isa. 53:12 [l][John 17:4; 19:30]
38 [m][ver. 49] [n][Deut. 3:26; Mark 14:41]
39 [o]Matt. 26:30; Mark 14:26; [John 18:1] [p]ch. 21:37; John 18:2 [q]See Matt. 21:1
40 [r]For ver. 40-46, see Matt. 26:36-46; Mark 14:32-42 [s]John 18:2 [t]1 Pet. 4:7 [u]Matt. 6:13
41 [v]See Acts 7:60
42 [w]Heb. 5:7 [x]See Matt. 20:22 [y]See Matt. 6:10
43 [z]Matt. 4:11; [Heb. 1:14]
44 [w][See ver. 42 above]
46 [a]ver. 40
47 [b]For ver. 47-53, see Matt. 26:47-56; Mark 14:43-50; John 18:3-11 [c]ver. 3
49 [d]ver. 38
52 [e]See ver. 4
53 [f][John 8:2]; [ch. 2:46; John 18:20] [g][Mark 14:35, 41; John 12:27; 16:4] [h]Eph. 6:12; [Acts 26:18]
54 [i]Matt. 26:57; Mark 14:53 [j]Matt. 26:58; Mark 14:54; John 18:15
55 [k]For ver. 55-62, see Matt. 26:69-75; Mark 14:66-72; John 18:16-18, 25-27 [l]See Matt. 26:3

22:42 Jesus has previously given his disciples (including us) instructions on praying (11:1–13; 18:1–8). Here he models one of the most important and universal truths about what our prayer life should be like. Jesus expresses his desires and even laments before the Father with full honesty and humility (22:44). He desires to be delivered from the pain and suffering he is facing (v. 42). Yet there is something in his prayer that is even more important than his requests. It is his acknowledgment of God's sovereignty and goodness in all situations and his glad submission to whatever God's greater plan might be: "Nevertheless, not my will, but yours, be done" (v. 42). This is the banner that should fly over all of our prayer requests. It is the heart of childlike faith that honors God and blesses us. We can pray bold prayers, knowing that God is our Father, through our adoption based on the work of Christ. Yet we can also rest in confidence that since he is our Father, even his denials of our requests can only be what is best for us—as can be his granting us "far more abundantly than all that we ask or think" (Eph. 3:20).

22:54–62 The tragic story of Peter's denial of Jesus is really the second part of a story that began in verses 31–34 with Jesus' prediction of Peter's failure and Peter's vehement reaction. Thankfully, it is not the end of Peter's story. Unlike Judas, who also failed to be faithful to Jesus (vv. 47–53), Peter repented and was restored (John 21:15–19). Peter is a model of a zealous and sincere heart, even though he fails morally. In this he stands in a long line of biblical men and women who despite their failings were people who sought God from the heart (for example, Abraham, Moses, David, and Rahab).

God uses these real-life, flawed people as pictures of his loving and merciful kindness toward us. God cares most about our hearts, and even when we fail out of fear and rebellion he restores us out of his abundant grace. Such stories reveal God's heart of acceptance and forgiveness. When we understand God properly in this way,

closely at him, said, "This man also was with him." 57 But he denied it, saying, "Woman, I do not know him." 58 And a little later someone else saw him and said, "You also are one of them." But Peter said, "Man, I am not." 59 And after an interval of about an hour still another [m]insisted, saying, "Certainly this man also was with him, for he too is a Galilean." 60 But Peter said, "Man, I do not know what you are talking about." And immediately, while he was still speaking, the rooster crowed. 61 And the Lord turned and [n]looked at Peter. And Peter remembered the saying of the Lord, how he had said to him, [o]"Before the rooster crows today, you will [p]deny me three times." 62 And he went out and wept bitterly.

Jesus Is Mocked

63 [q]Now the men who were holding Jesus in custody were mocking him as they beat him. 64 [q]They also blindfolded him and kept asking him, [r]"Prophesy! [r]Who is it that struck you?" 65 And they said many other things against him, [s]blaspheming him.

Jesus Before the Council

66 [t]When day came, [u]the assembly of the elders of the people gathered together, both chief priests and scribes. And they led him away to their [v]council, and they [w]said, 67 [x]"If you are [y]the Christ, tell us." But he said to them, "If I tell you, you will not believe, 68 and if I ask you, you will not answer. 69 But from now on the Son of Man shall be seated [z]at the right hand of the power of God." 70 So they all said, "Are you [a]the Son of God, then?" And he said to them, [b]"You say that I am." 71 Then they said, "What further testimony do we need? We have heard it ourselves from his own lips."

Jesus Before Pilate

23 [c]Then the whole company of them arose and brought him before Pilate. 2 And they began to accuse him, saying, "We found this man [d]misleading our nation and [e]forbidding us to give tribute to [f]Caesar, and saying that he himself is Christ, [g]a king." 3 [h]And Pilate asked him, [i]"Are you the King of the Jews?" And he answered him, [j]"You have said so." 4 Then Pilate said to the chief priests and the crowds, [k]"I find no guilt in this man." 5 But they were urgent, saying, "He stirs up the people, teaching throughout all Judea, [l]from Galilee even to this place."

Jesus Before Herod

6 When Pilate heard this, he asked whether the man was a Galilean. 7 And when he learned that he belonged to [m]Herod's jurisdiction, he sent him over to Herod, who was himself in Jerusalem at that time. 8 When Herod saw Jesus, he was very glad, [n]for he had long desired to see him, [o]because he had heard about him, and he was hoping [p]to see some sign done by him. 9 So he questioned him at some length, but he made no answer. 10 The chief priests and the scribes stood by, vehemently accusing him. 11 And Herod with his soldiers [q]treated him with contempt and [r]mocked him. Then, [s]arraying him in splendid clothing, he sent him back to Pilate. 12 And [t]Herod and Pilate became friends with each other that very day, for before this they had been at enmity with each other.

13 Pilate then called together the chief priests

it creates in us a freedom to be honest and open about our weaknesses and failures, which is precisely the humility needed to approach God. Our acceptance of God's acceptance of us—free from condemnation, because of Christ (Rom. 8:1)—woos and draws us near to God and frees us from shame and fear.

22:66–23:31 The authorities of the world collude to conquer the Prince of Heaven. They fail to recognize that they are actually fulfilling the divine purpose by which Christ's death will conquer death, the Lamb slain will overcome the reign of sin, and the "seed of the woman" will crush the seed of Satan in fulfillment of the most ancient of gospel promises (Gen. 3:15). Had we been there, we would have protested the wrong and urged God to stop it. But though Christ's adversaries meant the events of his passion for evil, God meant them for good (cf. Gen. 50:20). Jesus' suffering for our salvation should always remind us that, as the old hymn puts it, "though the wrong seems oft so strong, God is the ruler yet." His grace shall reign over all and in all things.

59 [m]Acts 12:15
61 [n]See Mark 10:21 [o]ver. 34 [p][Acts 3:13, 14]
63 [q][Matt. 26:67, 68; Mark 14:65; John 18:22, 23]
64 [q][See ver. 63 above] [r][ch. 7:39]
65 [s]See Matt. 27:39
66 [t]Matt. 27:1; Mark 15:1; John 18:28 [u]Acts 22:5 (Gk.) [v]See Matt. 5:22 [w]For ver. 67-71, [Matt. 26:63-66; Mark 14:61-64; John 18:19-21]
67 [x]John 10:24, 25 [y]See Matt. 1:17
69 [z]Mark 16:19; Acts 7:56; Heb. 1:3
70 [a]See Matt. 14:33 [b]ch. 23:3; Matt. 27:11; Mark 15:2; [Matt. 26:25]

Chapter 23 **1** [c]Matt. 27:2; Mark 15:1; John 18:28 **2** [d]ver. 14; [Acts 17:6, 7; 24:5] [e][ch. 20:25] [f]ch. 2:1; 3:1 [g]John 18:33, 36, 37; 19:12; [Acts 17:7] **3** [h]Matt. 27:11; Mark 15:2 [i]ver. 37, 38; Matt. 2:2; John 18:39; 19:3 [j]See ch. 22:70 **4** [k]ver. 14, 22; John 18:38; 19:4, 6; [Matt. 27:24; 1 Pet. 2:22] **5** [l]ch. 4:14; Matt. 4:12, 23; Mark 1:14; John 1:43; 2:11 **7** [m]See ch. 3:1 **8** [n]ch. 9:9 [o]Matt. 14:1; Mark 6:14 [p]See Matt. 12:38 **11** [q]Mark 9:12; Acts 4:11 [r]ch. 18:32 [s][Matt. 27:28; Mark 15:17] **12** [t]Acts 4:27; [Ps. 2:2]

and [u]the rulers and the people, 14 and said to
them, "You brought me this man [v]as one who
was misleading the people. And [w]after examining him before you, behold, I [x]did not find
this man guilty of any of your charges against
him. 15 Neither did Herod, for [y]he sent him
back to us. Look, nothing deserving death has
been done by him. 16 [z]I will therefore punish
and release him."[1]

Pilate Delivers Jesus to Be Crucified

18 [a]But they all cried out together, [b]"Away with
this man, and release to us Barabbas"— 19 a
man who had been thrown into prison for an
insurrection started in the city and [c]for murder. 20 Pilate addressed them once more, desiring to release Jesus, 21 but they kept shouting,
"Crucify, crucify him!" 22 A third time he said
to them, "Why, [d]what evil has he done? [e]I have
found in him no guilt deserving death. [f]I will
therefore punish and release him." 23 But they
were urgent, demanding with loud cries that
he should be crucified. And their voices prevailed. 24 So Pilate decided that their demand
should be granted. 25 He released the man who
had been thrown into prison [g]for insurrection
and murder, for whom they asked, [h]but he
delivered Jesus over to their will.

The Crucifixion

26 [i]And as they led him away, they seized one
Simon of Cyrene, who was coming in from
the country, and laid on him the cross, to carry
it behind Jesus. 27 And there followed him a
great multitude of the people and of women
who were [j]mourning and lamenting for him.
28 But turning to them Jesus said, "Daughters
of Jerusalem, do not weep for me, but weep
for yourselves and for your children. 29 For
behold, [k]the days are coming when they will
say, [l]'Blessed are the barren and the wombs that
never bore and the breasts that never nursed!'
30 [m]Then they will begin to say to the mountains, 'Fall on us,' and to the hills, 'Cover us.'
31 For [n]if they do these things when [o]the wood
is green, what will happen [o]when it is dry?"
32 [p]Two others, who were criminals, were
led away to be put to death with him. 33 [q]And
when they came to the place that is called
The Skull, there they crucified him, and the
criminals, [p]one on his right and one on his
left. 34 And Jesus said, "Father, [r]forgive them,
[s]for they know not what they do."[2] And they
cast lots [t]to divide his garments. 35 And [u]the
people stood by, watching, [v]but [w]the rulers
[x]scoffed at him, saying, [y]"He saved others; [z]let
him save himself, [a]if he is [b]the Christ of God,
[c]his Chosen One!" 36 The soldiers also mocked
him, coming up and [d]offering him sour wine
37 and saying, [e]"If you are [f]the King of the Jews,
save yourself!" 38 [g]There was also an inscription over him,[3] "This is [f]the King of the Jews."
39 [h]One of the criminals who were hanged
[i]railed at him,[4] saying, "Are you not [j]the Christ?

[1] Here, or after verse 19, some manuscripts add verse 17: *Now he was obliged to release one man to them at the festival*
[2] Some manuscripts omit the sentence *And Jesus . . . what they do* [3] Some manuscripts add *in letters of Greek and Latin and Hebrew*
[4] Or *blasphemed him*

13 [u]See ch. 24:20
14 [v]ver. 2 [w]Acts 3:13 [x]ver. 4
15 [y]ver. 11
16 [z]ver. 22; John 19:1; [Acts 5:40]
18 [a]For ver. 18-25, see Matt. 27:15-26; Mark 15:6-15; John 18:39, 40; 19:16 [b][Acts 21:36; 22:22]
19 [c]Acts 3:14
22 [d][ver. 41; John 8:46] [e]ver. 14, 15 [f]ver. 16
25 [g]ver. 19 [h]John 19:16
26 [i]Matt. 27:32; Mark 15:21; [John 19:17]
27 [j]ch. 8:52; Matt. 11:17
29 [k]See ch. 17:22 [l]ch. 21:23; Matt. 24:19; Mark 13:17
30 [m]Hos. 10:8; Rev. 6:16; [Isa. 2:19]
31 [n][Prov. 11:31; 1 Pet. 4:17] [o]Ezek. 20:47
32 [p]Matt. 27:38; Mark 15:27; John 19:18; [Matt. 20:21]
33 [q]Matt. 27:33; Mark 15:22; John 19:17

23:32–43 The backdrop of this story is the three crosses of crucifixion upon which the rightful King Jesus and the two criminals were hung to die. But in the forefront of the story is a pair of sharp contrasts given for our instruction. The first contrast is between the crucified Jesus and the ones who crucified him. The Jewish leaders and the Roman soldiers mock and ridicule Jesus, revealing their sinful and hateful hearts. In contrast, Jesus does not respond in kind but rather asks the Father to forgive them (v. 34).

The second contrast is between the two criminals who are crucified on either side of Jesus. They are examples of two different responses to Jesus. One of the criminals responds with rejection and mocking, like the other mockers watching Jesus die (v. 39). The other criminal's response provides a beautiful image of the gospel's call. This man's interaction with Jesus is marked by the humility that comes from seeing his own sinfulness and Jesus' purity. This criminal's repentance and his looking in faith to Jesus grant him entrance into God's kingdom (vv. 40–42). The result is Jesus' staggering and beautiful promise that the repentant man would be in paradise in the presence of the Lord that very day (v. 43).

No moral resume is required to be finally accepted into heaven. All that is required is open acknowledgment of sin and trusting faith in Christ.

[p][See ver. 32 above] **34** [r]Isa. 53:12; See Matt. 5:44 [s][Mark 10:38]; See Acts 3:17 [t]Ps. 22:18; Matt. 27:35; Mark 15:24; John 19:23 **35** [u]Ps. 22:7, 17 [v]Matt. 27:41, 42; Mark 15:31, 32 [w]See ch. 24:20 [x]ch. 16:14 [y][ch. 4:23] [z][Matt. 26:53, 54; John 10:18] [a][ch. 4:3, 9] [b]See ch. 9:20; Matt. 1:17 [c]ch. 9:35; Isa. 42:1; [Matt. 12:18; 1 Pet. 2:4] **36** [d][Ps. 69:21; Matt. 27:48; Mark 15:36; John 19:29] **37** [e]ver. 35 [f]See ver. 3 **38** [g]Matt. 27:37; Mark 15:26; John 19:19; [John 19:21, 22] [f][See ver. 37 above] **39** [h][Matt. 27:44; Mark 15:32] [i]See Matt. 27:39 [j]ver. 35, 37

Save yourself and us!" 40 But the other rebuked
him, saying, "Do you not fear God, since you
are under the same sentence of condemnation? 41 And we indeed justly, for we are
receiving the due reward of our deeds; but
this man has done nothing wrong." 42 And he
said, "Jesus, remember me [k]when you come
into your kingdom." 43 And he said to him,
"Truly, I say to you, today you will be with me
in [l]Paradise."

The Death of Jesus

44 [m]It was now about the sixth hour,[1] and
there was darkness over the whole land until
the ninth hour,[2] 45 while the sun's light failed.
And [n]the curtain of the temple was torn in
two. 46 Then Jesus, [o]calling out with a loud
voice, said, "Father, [p]into your hands I [q]com-
mit my spirit!" And having said this [r]he
breathed his last. 47 Now [s]when the centurion
saw what had taken place, [t]he praised God,
saying, "Certainly this man was innocent!"
48 And all the crowds that had assembled for
this spectacle, when they saw what had taken
place, returned home [u]beating their breasts.
49 And all [v]his acquaintances and [w]the women
who had followed him from Galilee [x]stood at
a distance watching these things.

Jesus Is Buried

50 [y]Now there was a man named Joseph,
from the Jewish town of Arimathea. He was
a member of the council, a good and righteous man, 51 who had not consented to their
decision and action; and he [z]was looking for
the kingdom of God. 52 This man went to
Pilate and asked for the body of Jesus. 53 Then
he took it down and wrapped it in a linen
shroud and [a]laid him in a tomb cut in stone,
[b]where no one had ever yet been laid. 54 It
was the day of [c]Preparation, and the Sabbath
was beginning.[3] 55 [d]The women [e]who had
come with him from Galilee followed and
saw the tomb and how his body was laid.
56 Then they returned and [f]prepared spices
and ointments.

On the Sabbath they rested [g]according to the
commandment.

The Resurrection

24 [h]But on the first day of the week, at
early dawn, they went to the tomb,
[i]taking the spices they had prepared. 2 And
they found [j]the stone rolled away from the
tomb, 3 but when they went in they did not
find the body of the Lord Jesus. 4 While they
were perplexed about this, behold, [k]two [l]men
stood by them in dazzling apparel. 5 And as
they were [m]frightened and bowed their faces
to the ground, the men said to them, "Why
do you seek the living among the dead? 6 He
is not here, but has risen. Remember how he
told you, [n]while he was still in Galilee, 7 [n]that
the Son of Man [o]must be delivered into the
hands of sinful men and [p]be crucified and on
[q]the third day rise." 8 And [r]they remembered
his words, 9 and returning from the tomb they
[s]told all these things to the eleven and to all
the rest. 10 Now it was [t]Mary Magdalene and
[u]Joanna and Mary the mother of James and the
other women with them who told these things
to the apostles, 11 but these words seemed to
them an idle tale, and [v]they did not believe
them. 12 But [w]Peter rose and ran to the tomb;
stooping and looking in, he saw [x]the linen
cloths by themselves; and he went home marveling at what had happened.

On the Road to Emmaus

13 That very day [y]two of them were going to
a village named Emmaus, about seven miles[4]
from Jerusalem, 14 and they were talking
with each other about all these things that
had happened. 15 While they were talking and
discussing together, Jesus himself drew near
and went with them. 16 [z]But their eyes were
kept from recognizing him. 17 And he said to
them, "What is this conversation that you are
holding with each other as you walk?" And
they stood still, looking sad. 18 Then one of
them, named Cleopas, answered him, "Are
you the only visitor to Jerusalem who does
not know the things that have happened there
in these days?" 19 And he said to them, "What
things?" And they said to him, "Concerning
Jesus of Nazareth, a man who was [a]a prophet
[b]mighty in deed and word before God and all

[1] That is, noon [2] That is, 3 P.M. [3] Greek *was dawning* [4] Greek *sixty stadia*; a *stadion* was about 607 feet or 185 meters

42 [k][Matt. 16:28] **43** [l]2 Cor. 12:3; Rev. 2:7 **44** [m]Matt. 27:45; Mark 15:33; [John 19:14] **45** [n]Ex. 26:31-33; 2 Chr. 3:14 **46** [o][Matt. 27:50; Mark 15:37; John 19:30] [p]Cited from Ps. 31:5; [Acts 7:59] [q]1 Pet. 4:19 [r][John 10:18] **47** [s]Matt. 27:54; Mark 15:39 [t]See ch. 7:16 **48** [u]ch. 18:13 **49** [v]Ps. 88:8 [w]ver. 55; John 19:25; See ch. 8:2 [x]Ps. 38:11 **50** [y]For ver. 50-56, see Matt. 27:57-61; Mark 15:42-47; John 19:38-42 **51** [z]ch. 2:25, 38 **53** [a][Isa. 53:9] [b][Mark 11:2] **54** [c]See Matt. 27:62 **55** [d]Matt. 28:1 [e]ver. 49 **56** [f]ch. 24:1; Mark 16:1; [John 19:39] [g]Ex. 20:10; Deut. 5:14 **Chapter 24** **1** [h]For ver. 1-10, see Matt. 28:1-8; Mark 16:1-8; John 20:1 [i]ch. 23:56 **2** [j]Matt. 27:60; Mark 15:46; [John 11] **4** [k]John 20:12 [l][Acts 1:10; 10:30] **5** [m]ver. 37 **6** [n]ch. 9:22, 44; Matt. 17:22, 23; Mark 9:30, 31; [ver. 44] **7** [n][See ver. 6 above] [o]See ch. 13:33 [p]See Matt. 20:19 [q]See ch. 9:22 **8** [r]John 2:22; 12:1 **9** [s][John 20:18] **10** [t]Matt. 27:56; Mark 15:40, 41 [u]ch. 8:3 **11** [v]Mark 16:11; See Mark 16:16 **12** [w]John 20:3-6 [x]John 19:40 **13** [y]Mark 16:12 **16** [z]John 20:14; 21:4; [ver. 31; ch. 9:45; 18:34] **19** [a]See Matt. 21:11 [b]Acts 2:22; [Acts 7:22]

the people, 20 and [c]how our chief priests and
[d]rulers delivered him up to be condemned to
death, and crucified him. 21 But we had hoped
that he was [e]the one to redeem Israel. Yes, and
besides all this, it is now [f]the third day since
these things happened. 22 Moreover, some
women of our company amazed us. [g]They
were at the tomb early in the morning, 23 and
[h]when they did not find his body, they came
back saying that [i]they had even seen a vision
of angels, who said that he was alive. 24 [j]Some
of those who were with us went to the tomb
and found it just as the women had said, but
him they did not see." 25 And he said to them,
"O foolish ones, and slow of heart to believe
all that the prophets have spoken! 26 [k]Was it
not necessary that [l]the Christ should suffer
these things and enter into [m]his glory?" 27 And
[n]beginning with [o]Moses and [p]all the Prophets,
he interpreted to them in all the Scriptures the
things concerning himself.

28 So they drew near to the village to which
they were going. [q]He acted as if he were going
farther, 29 but they urged him strongly, saying, "Stay with us, for it is toward evening and
[r]the day is now far spent." So he went in to
stay with them. 30 When he was at table with
them, he took the bread and [s]blessed and
broke it and gave it to them. 31 [t]And their eyes
were opened, and they recognized him. And
[u]he vanished from their sight. 32 They said to
each other, [v]"Did not our hearts burn within
us while he talked to us on the road, while he
[w]opened to us the Scriptures?" 33 And they rose
that same hour and returned to Jerusalem.
And they [x]found the eleven and [y]those who
were with them gathered together, 34 saying,
"The Lord has risen indeed, and [z]has appeared
to Simon!" 35 Then they told what had happened on the road, and [a]how he was known
to them in [b]the breaking of the bread.

Jesus Appears to His Disciples

36 As they were talking about these things,
[c]Jesus himself stood among them, and said to
them, "Peace to you!" 37 But they were [d]startled
and [e]frightened and [f]thought they saw a spirit.
38 And he said to them, "Why are you troubled, and why do doubts arise in your hearts?
39 See my hands and my feet, that it is I myself.
[g]Touch me, and see. For a spirit does not have
flesh and bones as you see that I have." 40 And
when he had said this, [h]he showed them his
hands and his feet. 41 And while they still disbelieved [i]for joy and were marveling, [j]he said
to them, "Have you anything here to eat?"
42 They gave him a piece of broiled fish,[1] 43 and
he took it and ate before them.

[1] Some manuscripts add *and some honeycomb*

20[c] Acts 2:23; 5:30; 13:27, 28; 1 Thess. 2:15 [d]ch. 23:13, 35; John 3:1; 7:26, 48; 12:42; Acts 3:17; 4:5, 8; 13:27; [1 Cor. 2:8]
21[e] See ch. 1:68; 1 Pet. 1:18 [f]ver. 7
22[g] ver. 1
23[h] ver. 3 [i]ver. 4, 5, 9
24[j] ver. 12; John 20:3
26[k] ver. 7, 44, 46; Heb. 2:10; 12:2; 1 Pet. 1:11; See Acts 3:18 [l]See Matt. 1:17 [m]See ch. 9:26
27[n] Acts 8:35 [o]Gen. 3:15; 12:3; 22:18; Num. 21:9; 24:17; [John 1:45; 5:46] [p]2 Sam. 7:12-16; Isa. 7:14; 9:6; 50:6; 52:13-53:12; 61:1; Jer. 23:5, 6; Dan. 7:13, 14; 9:24-27; Mic. 5:2; Zech. 6:12; 9:9; 12:10; 13:7; [Acts 13:27]
28[q] [Mark 6:48]
29[r] ch. 9:12 (Gk.)
30[s] See Matt. 14:19
31[t] [ver. 16] [u][ch. 4:30]
32[v] Ps. 39:3 [w]ver. 45
33[x] Mark 16:13; Acts 17:3 [y][Acts 1:14]
34[z] 1 Cor. 15:5
35[a] ver. 30, 31 [b]See Acts 2:42
36[c] Mark 16:14; John 20:19
37[d] ch. 21:9 [e]ver. 5 [f][Matt. 14:26; Mark 6:49]
39[g] 1 John 1:1; [John 20:27]
40[h] John 20:20
41[i] Acts 12:14; [Gen. 45:26] [j]John 21:5

24:25–27 These crucial verses help us understand the message of the whole Bible. We learn that the whole of Scripture points ultimately to Jesus (v. 27; see also v. 44). Holy Scripture is the Word of God, the record of God speaking (2 Tim. 3:16). God has spoken in many and various ways, but has now revealed himself fully through his Son, who can rightly be called the Word of God and who is the full image and representation of who God is (Heb. 1:1–3). *All* that God has spoken before ultimately relates to this final Word, Jesus Christ. Jesus himself provides this way of reading the Scriptures for these early disciples and we, like them, are meant to learn this same way of reading God's Word (see also John 5:39–47, and the Introduction to the *Gospel Transformation Bible*).

Yet, at the same time, we have a problem, not of interpretation but of heart. Like these early disciples we too are "slow of heart to believe" and have trouble accepting that glory comes through suffering (Luke 24:25–26; Matt. 16:21–23; Mark 8:31–33). We need to be taught by Jesus himself, who now instructs and guides us through the power of the Holy Spirit (Luke 24:49; John 14:25–26).

24:36–49 Jesus' disciples had every reason to be frightened and troubled. Their hopes for Jesus' promised kingdom seem to be dashed. Jesus' body has disappeared, and many of them have doubted his resurrection (v. 11) and even denied him (22:54–62). And now, suddenly, he appears before them—or at least what seems to be his ghost (24:37). We too would be frightened, and when we think of our own brokenness and failures we likewise are often full of shame before God. One would expect this to be Jesus' opportunity to rebuke and correct and maybe even condemn their faithlessness. But instead he speaks these good news words: "Peace to you!" (v. 36).

44 Then he said to them, [k]"These are my
words that I spoke to you while I was still
with you, [l]that everything written about me
in the Law of Moses and the Prophets and the
Psalms must be fulfilled." 45 Then [m]he opened
their minds to understand the Scriptures,
46 and said to them, "Thus [n]it is written, [o]that
the Christ should suffer and on the third day
[p]rise from the dead, 47 and that [q]repentance
and[1] forgiveness of sins should be proclaimed
[r]in his name [s]to all nations, [t]beginning from
Jerusalem. 48 [u]You are witnesses of these things.
49 And behold, I am sending [v]the promise of
my Father upon you. But stay in the city until
you [w]are clothed with [x]power [y]from on high."

The Ascension

50 Then [z]he led them out as far as [a]Bethany,
and lifting up his hands he blessed them.
51 While he blessed them, [b]he parted from them
and was carried up into heaven. 52 And they
[c]worshiped him and [z]returned to Jerusalem
[d]with great joy, 53 and [e]were continually in the
temple [f]blessing God.

[1] Some manuscripts *for*

We have in this story and these words a picture of the gospel of grace and God's heart toward us in Jesus. He knows our weaknesses and that we are but dust (Ps. 103:14), yet he joyfully welcomes us to be his children. Even more, he commissions us to be his witnesses and agents of the gospel message throughout the world (Luke 24:48). It is this Spirit-given understanding of God's love and grace in welcoming us that empowers and motivates us to proclaim his grace to others (v. 49).

24:50–53 The beginning of Luke's Gospel account emphasizes that all that happened with Jesus is "gospel" or good news. It is good news because through Jesus' life, death, resurrection, and ascension God is forgiving our sins, blessing us, and giving us his peace (1:67–79; 2:14).

Luke's account ends by likewise emphasizing Jesus' blessing of his disciples (24:50–51). The result of God's blessing of us is that we are free to worship and bless him with great joy (vv. 52–53). The story concludes in an open-ended way, even as our lives continue on in a state of awaiting Jesus' return from heaven. This conclusion rightly emphasizes the most proper and beautiful response to the gospel of Jesus—worship of the triune God for his grace and blessings.

44 [k] See ver. 6 [l] See ver. 27
45 [m] ver. 32; [Job 33:16; Ps. 119:18; Acts 16:14; 1 John 5:20]
46 [n] See Matt. 26:24 [o] See ver. 7, 26 [p] John 20:9
47 [q] Acts 5:31; See Acts 2:38 [r] See Acts 4:12 [s] ch. 2:32; Gen. 12:3; Ps. 22:27; Isa. 2:2; 49:6; Hos. 2:23; Mal. 1:11; Matt. 28:19 [t] Acts 10:37; Gal. 3:8
48 [u] Acts 1:8, 22; 2:32; 3:15; 5:32; 10:39, 41; 13:31; 1 Pet. 5:1; [John 15:27; 1 Cor. 15:15]
49 [v] John 14:26; Acts 1:4; [Acts 2:33; Eph. 1:13]; See Acts 2:16, 17 [w] Job 29:14; Ps. 132:9 [x] Acts 1:8 [y] ch. 1:78; Isa. 32:15
50 [z] Acts 1:12 [a] Matt. 21:17; John 11:18
51 [b] See Mark 16:19
52 [c] Matt. 28:9 [z] [See ver. 50 above] [d] See John 16:22
53 [e] Acts 2:46; 3:1; 5:21, 42 [f] ch. 1:64; 2:28

Introduction to John

Author, Date, and Recipients

John the son of Zebedee wrote this Gospel. He was a Jew, one of the original twelve disciples, and a member of Jesus' inner apostolic circle. He was referred to as the disciple "whom Jesus loved" (13:23). John also wrote 1–3 John and Revelation. He likely wrote his Gospel account between A.D. 70 (the date of the destruction of the temple) and A.D. 100 (the end of John's life). His original audience consisted of Jews and Gentiles living in the larger Greco-Roman world, in Ephesus and beyond, toward the close of the first century A.D.

The Gospel in John

Setting out to find a gospel-focus in John's Gospel might seem like the "challenge" of finding a mountain in a photo montage of the Swiss Alps—an exercise in the obvious. Yet there is a great difference between holding a travel brochure in your hand and actually standing at the base of the Alps. It is the difference between pleasant thoughts and soul-gripping wonder; a curious imagination and awe-fueled adoration; being well studied, and being knee-buckling stunned. John's Gospel is written not just to inform our minds but to inflame our hearts.

Think of John's Gospel not so much as a book but as a destination. John is a tour guide of the Alps of the gospel. He says to us, his readers, "You've got to see Jesus for yourself. There's so much more to Jesus, and what he's done for you, than you can possibly imagine or even hope."

Indeed, John didn't write merely to communicate trustworthy data (which he did), but to generate transforming doxology (which he does). As we meet Jesus in the text, John anticipates we will respond like the Samaritan woman whose story he shares with us: "Come, see a man who told me all that I ever did. Can this be the Christ?" (4:29). To see Jesus in John's Gospel is to discover Christ and, consequently, to be changed forever.

John speaks from a firsthand encounter with Jesus. He doesn't just tell about the One who came from "the Father's side" (1:18); he writes as one who felt close enough to Jesus to rest his own head against Jesus' side (13:23). This beloved disciple (20:2) wants us to discover what he discovered—that from Jesus' fullness we receive "grace upon grace" (1:16).

From his prologue to his epilogue, John sets out to answer two primary questions: "Who is Jesus?" and "What has Jesus come into this world to accomplish?" John fixes our eyes on Jesus himself, the very embodiment of the gospel. John begins his Gospel heralding the advent of the new creation story—positioning Jesus as the principal character and carrier of the whole narrative.

Unlike the other three Gospel writers (Matthew, Mark, and Luke), John did not structure his Gospel with a strict chronology in mind. His is both a selective and a strategic record. In fact, while all four Gospel writers focus their accounts ultimately on the death and resurrection of Jesus, John spends a full 40 percent of his account on this last week—the most crucial week of our Lord's life and of human history (John 12:1–20:25). Everything John tells us about Jesus leads us to his cross and his empty tomb—to his substitutionary death and glorious resurrection.

We don't have to guess about John's purpose and goal in writing his Gospel. John tells us that he chose particular stories and "signs" so that "you may believe that Jesus is the Christ, the Son of God, and that by believing you may have life in his name" (20:30–31).

Who is Jesus? He is the promised Messiah. Why did he come? Jesus has come to give us life—abundant life (10:10), eternal life, the life of "the age to come" (cf. Luke 18:30; Heb. 6:5). The gospel of God's grace is so much more than a story about life after death. It is also a story about life *before* death—how through Jesus' death and resurrection the kingdom of God has already arrived and has restored fallen creatures, and the fallen creation, to their right relationship with the Lord of life. And one day this kingdom will arrive in fullness, eradicating all remaining sin and sadness. Let's begin our journey. With John, we will discover that there's not more *than* the gospel to bring fulfillment to our lives, just more *of* the gospel.

Outline

I. Prologue: The Incarnate Word (1:1–18)

II. Signs of the Messiah, with Teaching about Life in Him (1:19–11:57)

III. The Farewell Teaching and the Passion Narrative (12:1–20:31)

IV. Epilogue: The Roles of Peter and of the Disciple Whom Jesus Loved (21:1–25)

The Gospel According to

John

The Word Became Flesh

1 [a]In the beginning was [b]the Word, and [c]the
Word was with God, and [d]the Word was
God. 2 He was in the beginning with God. 3 [e]All
things were made through him, and without
him was not any thing made that was made.
4 [f]In him was life,[1] and [g]the life was the light of
men. 5 [h]The light shines in the darkness, and
the darkness has not overcome it.

6 There was a man [i]sent from God, whose
name was [j]John. 7 He came as a [k]witness, to
bear witness about the light, [l]that all might
believe through him. 8 [m]He was not the light,
but came to bear witness about the light.

9 [n]The true light, which gives light to everyone, was coming into the world. 10 He was in
the world, and the world was made through
him, yet [o]the world did not know him. 11 He
came to [p]his own,[2] and [q]his own people[3] [r]did
not receive him. 12 But to all who did receive
him, [s]who believed in his name, [t]he gave the
right [u]to become [v]children of God, 13 who
[w]were born, [x]not of blood [y]nor of the will of
the flesh nor of the will of man, but of God.

[1] Or *was not any thing made. That which has been made was life in him* [2] Greek *to his own things*; that is, to his own domain, or to his own people [3] *People* is implied in Greek

1:1–18 The prologue of John's Gospel is like the opening movement of a grand symphony. It is meant to grab our attention and draw us into the story—the story of all stories. The apostle sets the stage for the presentation of the gospel by highlighting the main plotline and central themes of the entire Bible—creation (vv. 1–4), the fall (v. 5), and redemption (vv. 9–13), all of which point to the person and culminating work of Jesus (see also vv. 23, 29).

Who is Jesus? This is John's main question and the quest of discovery that he bids us enter. John's Gospel helps us understand how to look for Jesus in Moses, the Prophets, and all the Scriptures (5:39–47). He wants us to see how Jesus is the "Yes!" and "Amen!" to every promise God has made (2 Cor. 1:20) throughout the history of redemption.

Jesus is eternally one with the Father—the very Word of God (John 1:1–2), God's agent in creating all things (vv. 3–4). And as he spoke light and brought life into the dark void of pre-creation chaos, so Jesus brings light and life into the dark world of sin and death. His "new creation" order is none other than the long-promised epoch of redemption and restoration of which Israel's prophets spoke, and angels longed to see (1 Pet. 1:10–12).

To receive Jesus is to be born from above and to become a member of God's family, all of which comes to us as a gift of God's grace (John 1:9–13), not at all of our own doing.

Even as John's prologue affirms Jesus' deity, so also it celebrates his humanity. The Word became flesh—God became man, yet Jesus never ceased being God. He came to us as the greater Moses (Deut. 18:15–19), to bring a greater exodus. Moses provided the tabernacle; Jesus "dwelt" (the Greek word literally means "tabernacled") among us (John 1:14), revealing God's glory and grace.

The law, which came through Moses, necessitated the grace and truth which came through Jesus (vv. 14–17), for the law could never save us, only drive us to Christ (Gal. 3:23–24). While Moses hid his face from God, Jesus "exegetes"—that is, reveals—the Father to us, as only the only begotten Son could do (see John 1:18, where the Greek word for "has made known" is *exegeomai*).

Chapter 1

1 [a]Gen. 1:1; [Col. 1:17; 1 John 1:1; Rev. 1:4, 8, 17; 3:14; 21:6; 22:13] [b]Rev. 19:13; [Heb. 4:12; 1 John 1:1] [c]1 John 1:2; [ch. 17:5] [d]Phil. 2:6
3 [e]ver. 10; Ps. 33:6; 1 Cor. 8:6; Col. 1:16; Heb. 1:2
4 [f]ch. 5:26; 11:25; 1 John 1:2; 5:11 [g]ch. 8:12; 9:5; 12:46
5 [h][ch. 3:19]
6 [i]ver. 33; ch. 3:28; Mal. 3:1 [j]Matt. 3:1; Mark 1:4; Luke 3:2
7 [k]ch. 3:26; 5:33 [l]Acts 19:4
8 [m]ver. 20
9 [n]Isa. 49:6; 1 John 2:8
10 [o][ch. 16:3; 1 John 3:1]
11 [p]Matt. 21:38 [q]ch. 13:1 [r]ch. 5:43; [ch. 3:11, 32]
12 [s]See 1 John 5:13 [t]1 John 5:1 [u]1 John 3:1; [Matt. 5:45] [v][Gal. 3:26]; See ch. 11:52
13 [w]James 1:18; [ch. 3:3; 1 Pet. 1:3] [x]1 Pet. 1:23 [y]ch. 3:6

14 And [z]the Word [a]became flesh and [b]dwelt among us, [c]and we have seen his glory, glory as of the only Son from the Father, full of [d]grace and [e]truth. 15 ([f]John bore witness about him, and cried out, "This was he of whom I said, [g]'He who comes after me ranks before me, because he was before me.'") 16 For from [h]his fullness we have all received, [i]grace upon grace.[1] 17 For [j]the law was given through Moses; [k]grace and truth came through Jesus Christ. 18 [l]No one has ever seen God; [m]the only God,[2] who is at the Father's side,[3] [n]he has made him known.

The Testimony of John the Baptist

19 And this is the [o]testimony of John, when the Jews sent priests and Levites from Jerusalem to ask him, [p]"Who are you?" 20 [q]He confessed, and did not deny, but confessed, "I am not the Christ." 21 And they asked him, "What then? [r]Are you Elijah?" He said, "I am not." "Are you [s]the Prophet?" And he answered, "No." 22 So they said to him, "Who are you? We need to give an answer to those who sent us. What do you say about yourself?" 23 He said, "I am [t]the voice of one crying out in the wilderness, 'Make straight[4] the way of the Lord,' as the prophet Isaiah said."

24 (Now they had been sent from the Pharisees.) 25 They asked him, [u]"Then why are you baptizing, if you are neither the Christ, nor Elijah, nor the Prophet?" 26 John answered them, [v]"I baptize with water, but among you stands one you do not know, 27 even [w]he who comes after me, the strap of whose sandal I am not worthy to untie." 28 These things took place in Bethany across the Jordan, where John was baptizing.

Behold, the Lamb of God

29 The next day he saw Jesus coming toward him, and said, "Behold, [x]the Lamb of God, who [y]takes away the sin [z]of the world! 30 This is he of whom I said, [a]'After me comes a man who ranks before me, because he was before me.' 31 I myself did not know him, but [b]for this purpose I came baptizing with water, that he might be revealed to Israel." 32 And John

[1] Or *grace in place of grace* [2] Or *the only One, who is God*; some manuscripts *the only Son* [3] Greek *in the bosom of the Father* [4] Or *crying out, 'In the wilderness make straight*

14 [z]ver. 1 [a]Rom. 1:3; 8:3; Gal. 4:4; Phil. 2:7, 8; Col. 1:22; 1 Tim. 3:16; Heb. 2:14; 1 John 4:2; 2 John 7; [ch. 6:51] [b]Rev. 7:15; 21:3 [c]ch. 2:11; Luke 9:32; 2 Pet. 1:16, 17; 1 John 1:1; 4:14 [d]See ver. 7 [e][ch. 14:6]
15 [f]See ver. 7 [g]ver. 27, 30; See Matt. 3:11
16 [h]Eph. 1:23; 3:19; 4:13; Col. 1:19; 2:9 [i][Matt. 25:29]
17 [j]ch. 7:19; Ex. 20:1 [k]ver. 14; [Rom. 5:21]
18 [l]ch. 5:37; 6:46; Ex. 33:20; Col. 1:15; 1 Tim. 6:16; 1 John 4:12, 20; [ch. 12:45] [m]ver. 14; See ch. 3:16 [n][Matt. 11:27]; See ch. 3:32
19 [o]ch. 3:26 [p][ch. 8:25]
20 [q]ver. 8; ch. 3:28; Acts 13:25; [Luke 3:15]
21 [r][Matt. 11:14; 16:14] [s]See Deut. 18:15, 18
23 [t]Cited from Isa. 40:3; See Matt. 3:3
25 [u]Matt. 3:6; Mark 1:4; Luke 3:3, 7
26 [v]Matt. 3:11; Mark 1:7, 8; Luke 3:16; Acts 1:5; 13:25
27 [w]ver. 15, 30
29 [x]ver. 36; Ex. 12:3; Isa. 53:7; Acts 8:32; 1 Pet. 1:19; [Gen. 22:8; Rev. 5:6] [y]1 John 3:5; [Heb. 10:4, 11] [z][ch. 3:16, 17; 4:42; 12:47; 1 John 2:2; 4:14]
30 [a]ver. 15, 27
31 [b]Luke 1:17, 76, 77

1:19–28 John the Baptist is a central character in John's Gospel because of the unique role he played in the history of redemption. John straddled the Old and New Testaments, like a redemptive bridge. He was the last of the Old Testament prophets, and at the same time he was the first herald of the arrival of God's promised kingdom in Jesus (Isa. 40:3).

Elijah is mentioned by John not only because Israel expected someone to come in the "spirit of Elijah" before the day of the Lord (Mal. 4:5), but also because he is representative of all of Israel's prophets. This is why Moses and Elijah appeared together with Jesus on the Mount of Transfiguration (Matt. 17:1–5). The whole Old Testament (the Law, represented by Moses, and the Prophets, represented by Elijah) points toward and is fulfilled by Jesus.

1:29–34 Not only does Jesus fulfill the law of Moses and the hopes of the prophets, he also completes the worship of Israel. In Jesus, old covenant types give way to the new creation antitype—shadow is supplanted by substance. To "Behold, the Lamb of God" is to see in Jesus the arrival of the suffering servant of Isaiah's prophecy (Isa. 53:4–12), who took the punishment we deserve to give us the grace we could never earn.

To see Jesus is to celebrate the end of the sacrificial system, which was central to Israel's worship. For the blood of Jesus cleanses us from our sin, once and for all (Heb. 10:10). This good news is so central to John's message that he spends 40 percent of his Gospel describing one week—the most crucial week of our Lord's life, the week of his death and resurrection (John 12:1–20:25). John wants us to see Jesus not just as a moral model but, far more importantly, as the substitute sacrifice for our sin.

As the Messiah, Jesus was anointed with the Spirit without measure (cf. Isa. 61:1–3; Luke 4:14–19), and he gives his Spirit without reservation to his people. By the Spirit's baptism, Jesus unites us to himself and inaugurates us into life and service in his kingdom. With Jesus, eternal life begins before death; earthly death is not the final chapter for those united to Christ eternally. The new age has broken in on us, and all are welcomed into it, by resting upon Christ's provision and resisting the urge to make our way to God with the merit of our obedience.

[c]bore witness: [d]"I saw the Spirit descend from
heaven like a dove, and [e]it remained on him.
33 I myself did not know him, but [f]he who sent
me to baptize [g]with water said to me, 'He on
whom you see the Spirit descend and remain,
[h]this is he who baptizes [g]with the Holy Spirit.'
34 And I have seen and have borne witness that
this is the Son of God."

Jesus Calls the First Disciples

35 The next day again John was standing
with two of his disciples, 36 and he looked
at Jesus as he walked by and said, "Behold,
[i]the Lamb of God!" 37 The two disciples heard
him say this, and they followed Jesus. 38 Jesus
turned and saw them following and said to
them, [j]"What are you seeking?" And they
said to him, [k]"Rabbi" (which means Teacher),
"where are you staying?" 39 He said to them,
"Come and you will see." So they came and
saw where he was staying, and they stayed
with him that day, for it was about the tenth
hour.[1] 40 [l]One of the two who heard John
speak and followed Jesus[2] was Andrew,
Simon Peter's brother. 41 He first found his
own brother Simon and said to him, "We have
found [m]the Messiah" (which means Christ).
42 He brought him to Jesus. Jesus looked at
him and said, "You are Simon the son of
[n]John. You shall be called [o]Cephas" (which
means [p]Peter[3]).

Jesus Calls Philip and Nathanael

43 [q]The next day Jesus decided [r]to go to
Galilee. He found Philip and said to him,
"Follow me." 44 Now [s]Philip was from Bethsaida, the city of Andrew and Peter. 45 Philip
found [t]Nathanael and said to him, "We have
found him of whom [u]Moses in the Law and
also the prophets wrote, Jesus [v]of Nazareth,
[w]the son of Joseph." 46 Nathanael said to him,
[x]"Can anything good come out of Nazareth?"
Philip said to him, "Come and see." 47 Jesus
saw Nathanael coming toward him and said of
him, "Behold, [y]an Israelite indeed, [z]in whom
there is no deceit!" 48 Nathanael said to him,
"How [a]do you know me?" Jesus answered
him, "Before Philip called you, when you were
under the fig tree, I saw you." 49 Nathanael
answered him, [b]"Rabbi, [c]you are the Son of
God! You are the [d]King of Israel!" 50 Jesus
answered him, "Because I said to you, 'I saw
you under the fig tree,' do you believe? You
will see greater things than these." 51 And he
said to him, "Truly, truly, I say to you,[4] you
will see [e]heaven opened, and [f]the angels of
God ascending and descending on [g]the Son
of Man."

The Wedding at Cana

2 On [h]the third day there was a wedding
at [i]Cana in Galilee, and the mother of
Jesus was there. 2 Jesus also was invited to

[1] That is, about 4 P.M. [2] Greek *him* [3] *Cephas* and *Peter* are from the word for *rock* in Aramaic and Greek, respectively [4] The Greek for *you* is plural; twice in this verse

1:35–51 Like the other Gospel writers, John shows us the paradox of service in Jesus' kingdom. As his first disciples and trusted servants, Jesus chooses unlikely men, mostly fishermen, all of whom will fail him at one time or another. God chooses the weak in order to exalt his name (cf. 1 Cor. 1:26–27). This is good news for all of us who recognize our own weaknesses and sin. Our failings do not disqualify us from Christ's kingdom. Spiritual heroism is not what qualifies us for heaven. There is only one hero in the gospel story: Jesus himself.

The most important qualification for Jesus' disciples is to know his name—that is, to be absolutely clear in heart and mind about who he is and what he has done. Thus, the first disciples were given an immersion course in Christology. In the span of 16 verses, Jesus is identified as "the Lamb of God," "the Messiah," "the Son of God," "the King of Israel," and "Son of Man"—all messianic names that take on a fuller meaning throughout John's Gospel.

At the heart of all these names is the truth that Jesus has come to save—to be the ladder from heaven to earth of which Jacob dreamed (Gen. 28:12) and to which Jesus alludes in John 1:51. But we do not climb our way up to God; God in Christ came down to us.

2:1–12 The miracle of turning water into wine at the wedding in Cana of Galilee is the first of seven "sign" miracles that John chose to record in his Gospel. Also included are the healing of the royal official's son (4:46–54), the healing of the paralytic at the Bethesda pool (5:1–17), the feeding of the 5,000 (6:1–14), the walking on water (6:16–21), the healing of the man born blind (9:1–41), and the raising of Lazarus (11:1–46).

32 [c]See ver. 7 [d]Matt. 3:16; Mark 1:10; Luke 3:22 [e][Isa. 11:2; Acts 10:38]
33 [f]ver. 6; Luke 3:2 [g][ch. 3:5] [h]Matt. 3:11; Mark 1:8; Luke 3:16; Acts 1:5
36 [i]See ver. 29
38 [j]ch. 18:4, 7; 20:15 [k]ver. 49; ch. 3:2, 26; 6:25; [ch. 20:16; Mark 10:51]
40 [l]For ver. 40-42, [Matt. 4:18-22; Mark 1:16-20; Luke 5:2-11]
41 [m]ch. 4:25
42 [n]ch. 21:15-17 [o]1 Cor. 1:12; 3:22 [p]Matt. 16:18
43 [q][ver. 35; ch. 2:1] [r][ver. 28]
44 [s]ch. 12:21
45 [t]ch. 21:2 [u]See Luke 16:16; 24:27 [v]See Matt. 2:23 [w]ch. 6:42; Luke 3:23
46 [x][ch. 7:41, 52]
47 [y]Ps. 73:1; Rom. 9:4, 6 [z]Ps. 32:2; [Zeph. 3:13; Rev. 14:5]
48 [a]ch. 2:24, 25
49 [b]See ver. 38 [c][ch. 6:69; 11:27; 20:28] [d]ch. 12:13; Zeph. 3:15; Matt. 27:11, 42; [Zech. 9:9]
51 [e]Ezek. 1:1; Matt. 3:16; Luke 3:21 [f][Gen. 28:12] [g]See Dan. 7:13

Chapter 2
1 [h][ch. 1:29, 35, 43] [i]ch. 4:46; 21:2

the wedding with [j]his disciples. 3 When the
wine ran out, the mother of Jesus said to him,
“They have no wine.” 4 And Jesus said to her,
[k]“Woman, [l]what does this have to do with me?
[m]My hour has not yet come.” 5 His mother said
to the servants, “Do whatever he tells you.”
6 Now there were six stone water jars there
[n]for the Jewish rites of purification, each holding twenty or thirty [o]gallons.[1] 7 Jesus said to
the servants, “Fill the jars with water.” And
they filled them up to the brim. 8 And he said
to them, “Now draw some out and take it to
the master of the feast.” So they took it. 9 When
the master of the feast tasted [p]the water now
become wine, and did not know where it came
from (though the servants who had drawn
the water knew), the master of the feast called
the bridegroom 10 and said to him, “Everyone
serves the good wine first, and when people
have drunk freely, then the poor wine. But you
have kept the good wine until now.” 11 This, the
first of his signs, Jesus did at Cana in Galilee,
and manifested [q]his glory. And [r]his disciples
believed in him.
12 After this he went down to Capernaum,
with his mother and [s]his brothers[2] and his
disciples, and they stayed there for a few days.

Jesus Cleanses the Temple

13 [t]The Passover of the Jews was at hand, and
Jesus [u]went up to Jerusalem. 14 [v]In the temple
he found those who were selling oxen and
sheep and pigeons, and the money-changers
sitting there. 15 And making a whip of cords,
he drove them all out of the temple, with
the sheep and oxen. And he poured out the
coins of the money-changers and overturned
their tables. 16 And he told those who sold the
pigeons, “Take these things away; do not make
[w]my Father’s house a house of trade.” 17 His

[1] Greek *two or three measures* (*metrētas*); a *metrētēs* was about 10 gallons or 35 liters [2] Or *brothers and sisters*. The plural Greek word *adelphoi* (translated “brothers”) refers to siblings in a family. In New Testament usage, depending on the context, *adelphoi* may refer either to *brothers* or to *brothers and sisters*

2 [j]ch. 1:40-49
4 [k]ch. 19:26 [l]See 2 Sam. 16:10 [m]ch. 7:30; 8:20; 13:1
6 [n]ch. 3:25; [Mark 7:3, 4] [o]2 Chr. 4:5 (Gk.)
9 [p]ch. 4:46
11 [q]See ch. 1:14 [r]ver. 2
12 [s]See Matt. 12:46
13 [t]ch. 11:55; See ch. 6:4 [u]ver. 23; Deut. 16:1-6; Luke 2:41
14 [v]For ver. 14-17, [Matt. 21:12, 13; Mark 11:15-17; Luke 19:45, 46, with Mal. 3:1-3]
16 [w][ch. 14:2; Luke 2:49]

Signs, for John, answer the question, “Who is Jesus?” They do this in part by affirming one or more of the titles ascribed to Jesus in the prologue (1:1–18).

What is revealed about Jesus in this first sign? Through Christ all things were created; he has power over the material universe. Who is Jesus? He is the Messiah who has come in the fullness of time, to usher in the longed-for messianic age—in which wine (evidence of blessed fruitfulness and provision) will flow in overwhelming abundance and the mountains will drip with the best wine for the joy of God’s people (Joel 3:18; Amos 9:13–14; Jer. 31:12).

Who is Jesus? He is the One who takes what is meant for purification and provides blessing through it. In doing so, he shows that he transforms the daily Jewish purification rites by the power of his perfect life (cf. John 2:6–7 and Heb. 9:12; 10:10). Who is Jesus? He is not merely the guest at our weddings but the great eschatological bridegroom who makes us *his* bride, by the cost of his life (Eph. 5:22–33). He clothes us with the wedding garment of his own righteousness (Isa. 61:10) and prepares us for the great wedding banquet of the Lamb (Rev. 19:6–10).

Who is Jesus? He is the Lord of glory, who calls us to believe in him and to put our trust in him.

2:13–22 In Israel’s history, the temple represented God’s gracious dwelling among his covenant people. By his own initiative, he provided for a restored relationship with his sinful people (Ex. 25:8–9). Unfortunately, however, ritual replaced reality, and pride was more obvious than humility; the “worship of worship”—and, as seen here, the desire for financial gain—took precedence over the worship of God.

Jesus’ cleansing of the temple was much more than an act of moral outrage and judgment. It was also a sign of end-time fulfillment. The temple was never given as an end in itself. Like the tabernacle, the temple was essential but ultimately temporary, for its abuses exposed just how broken God’s worship and God’s worshipers had become through sin. Something better was promised, and that something arrived with Jesus, the true and final temple (John 2:19–21). As the embodiment of the temple (the place where God was present among his people in the Old Testament), Jesus is God with us—Immanuel—and God for us (Isa. 7:14; Matt. 1:18–25).

By Jesus’ death and resurrection, the temple-less worship of the garden of Eden will once again be realized in the perfected worship of the new heaven and new earth. On that day, God himself and the Lamb will be the temple forever (Rev. 21:22).

disciples remembered that it was written,
[x]"Zeal for your house will consume me."
18 So the Jews said to him, [y]"What sign do
you show us for doing these things?" 19 Jesus
answered them, [z]"Destroy this temple, and in
three days [a]I will raise it up." 20 The Jews then
said, "It has taken forty-six years to build this
temple,[1] and will you raise it up in three days?"
21 But he was speaking about [b]the temple of his
body. 22 When therefore he was raised from the
dead, [c]his disciples remembered that he had
said this, and they believed [d]the Scripture and
the word that Jesus had spoken.

Jesus Knows What Is in Man

23 Now when he was in Jerusalem at the Passover Feast, many believed in his name [e]when
they saw the signs that he was doing. 24 But
Jesus [f]on his part did not entrust himself
to them, because [g]he knew all people 25 and
needed no one to bear witness about man, for
[g]he himself knew what was in man.

You Must Be Born Again

3 Now there was a man of the Pharisees
named [h]Nicodemus, [i]a ruler of the Jews.
2 This man came to Jesus[2] [j]by night and said to
him, [k]"Rabbi, [l]we know that you are a teacher
come from God, for no one can do these signs
that you do [m]unless God is with him." 3 Jesus
answered him, "Truly, truly, I say to you,
unless one is [n]born [o]again[3] he cannot [p]see the
kingdom of God." 4 Nicodemus said to him,
"How can a man be born when he is old? Can
he enter a second time into his mother's womb
and be born?" 5 Jesus answered, "Truly, truly,
I say to you, unless one is born [q]of water and
the Spirit, he cannot enter the kingdom of
God. 6 [r]That which is born of the flesh is [s]flesh,
and that which is born of the Spirit is spirit.[4]
7 [t]Do not marvel that I said to you, 'You[5] must
be born [u]again.' 8 [v]The wind[6] blows [w]where it
wishes, and you hear its sound, but you do not
know where it comes from or where it goes. So
it is with everyone who is born of the Spirit."
9 Nicodemus said to him, [x]"How can these
things be?" 10 Jesus answered him, "Are you
the teacher of Israel [y]and yet you do not
understand these things? 11 Truly, truly, I say
to you, [z]we speak of what we know, and bear
witness to what we have seen, but [z]you[7] do
not receive our testimony. 12 If I have told you
earthly things and you do not believe, how
can you believe if I tell you heavenly things?
13 [a]No one has [b]ascended into heaven except

[1] Or *This temple was built forty-six years ago* [2] Greek *him* [3] Or *from above*; the Greek is purposely ambiguous and can mean both *again* and *from above*; also verse 7 [4] The same Greek word means both *wind* and *spirit* [5] The Greek for *you* is plural here [6] The same Greek word means both *wind* and *spirit* [7] The Greek for *you* is plural here; also four times in verse 12

2:23–25 Ultimately, the gospel is not about us establishing a relationship with Jesus; it is about Jesus establishing a relationship with us—not simply as a consequence of our believing information about him, but more by Jesus "entrusting" himself to us in his revelation of himself. Jesus never did "signs" to impress anyone but to reveal himself as the Messiah and to redeem those he came to save as they recognized who he was and received what he was doing for them.

We know God only because we are known by God (Gal. 4:9). Until God reveals his Son to us and in us (Gal. 1:15–16), we remain spiritually dead (Eph. 2:5). Salvation, from beginning to end, is all of grace. This becomes clear as John now records for us the coming-to-faith experiences of a wide range of people.

3:1–15 Under the cloak of darkness, Nicodemus learned of a birth from above. As an old man, he needed new life—eternal life, life in the kingdom of God. But apart from the work of Jesus, he (no different than we) could not even see the kingdom of God, much less enter it. Becoming a Christian is a supernatural act of God's generosity. We, like Nicodemus, are just as dependent upon God for our second birth as for our first birth. To be born of "water and the Spirit" is to receive the new heart and the sin-cleansing washing God promised for the age of the Messiah (Ezek. 36:24–35).

As someone steeped in the Old Testament, John had a great appreciation for the symbolism of water. Just as Jesus created the headwaters that flowed through the garden of Eden (Gen. 2:10–14), so he is the source of the life-giving river promised in Ezekiel's vision of the end-time temple (Ezekiel 47). At his second coming, Jesus will "un-dam" the river of life and it will course its way through the new Jerusalem forever (Rev. 22:1–3). But even now, at his first coming, Jesus offers the firstfruits of living water to those who will bring their thirsty hearts to him (John 4:3–42; 7:37–39).

17 [x]Cited from Ps. 69:9
18 [y]ch. 4:48; 6:30; [Ex. 4:1, 8; 7:9]; See Matt. 12:38
19 [z][Matt. 26:61; 27:40; Mark 14:58; 15:29] [a]ch. 10:18
21 [b][ch. 1:14; 1 Cor. 6:19; Col. 2:9]
22 [c]ch. 12:16; Luke 24:8 [d]ch. 20:9; Ps. 16:10
23 [e]ch. 11:45
24 [f][ch. 6:14, 15] [g]ch. 1:48; 5:42; 16:30; [ch. 6:61, 64]; See Matt. 9:4
25 [g][See ver. 24 above]
Chapter 3
1 [h]ch. 7:50; 19:39 [i]See Luke 24:20
2 [j][ch. 12:42] [k]See ch. 1:38 [l][ch. 9:29; Matt. 22:16] [m]Acts 10:38; [ch. 5:36; 9:33; Acts 2:22]
3 [n]See ch. 1:13 [o][2 Cor. 5:17; Gal. 6:15; 1 Pet. 1:3, 23] [p]ver. 36
5 [q][Ezek. 36:25-27; Mark 16:16; Acts 2:38; Eph. 5:26; Titus 3:5; Heb. 10:22]
6 [r]1 Cor. 15:50 [s]ch. 6:63
7 [t]ch. 5:28 [u]See ver. 3
8 [v][Eccles. 11:5; Ezek. 37:9] [w]1 Cor. 12:11
9 [x]ch. 6:52, 60
10 [y][ch. 9:30]
11 [z]See ver. 32
13 [a]Prov. 30:4; [Acts 2:34; Eph. 4:9] [b][ch. 7:34]

[c]he who descended from heaven, the Son of
Man.[1] 14 And [d]as Moses lifted up the serpent
in the wilderness, so must the Son of Man [e]be
lifted up, 15 that whoever believes [f]in him [g]may
have eternal life.[2]

For God So Loved the World

16 "For [h]God so loved [i]the world,[3] [j]that he
gave his only Son, that whoever believes
in him should not [k]perish but have eternal
life. 17 For [l]God did not send his Son into the
world [m]to condemn the world, but in order
that the world might be saved through him.
18 [n]Whoever believes in him is not condemned,
but whoever does not believe is condemned
already, because he has not [o]believed in the
name of the only Son of God. 19 [p]And this is
the judgment: [q]the light has come into the
world, and [r]people loved the darkness rather
than the light because [s]their works were evil.
20 [t]For everyone who does wicked things hates
the light and does not come to the light, [u]lest
his works should be exposed. 21 But whoever
[v]does what is true [w]comes to the light, so that
it may be clearly seen that his works have been
carried out in God."

John the Baptist Exalts Christ

22 After this Jesus and his disciples went into
the Judean countryside, and he remained there
with them and [x]was baptizing. 23 John also was
baptizing at Aenon near Salim, because water
was plentiful there, and people were coming
and being baptized 24 (for [y]John had not yet
been put in prison).

25 Now a discussion arose between some
of John's disciples and a Jew over [z]purifica-
tion. 26 And they came to John and said to
him, [a]"Rabbi, he who was with you across the
Jordan, [b]to whom you bore witness—look,
he is baptizing, and [c]all are going to him."
27 John answered, [d]"A person cannot receive
even one thing [e]unless it is given him [f]from
heaven. 28 You yourselves bear me witness, that
I said, [g]'I am not the Christ, but [h]I have been
sent before him.' 29 [i]The one who has the bride

[1] Some manuscripts add *who is in heaven* [2] Some interpreters hold that the quotation ends at verse 15 [3] Or *For this is how God loved the world*

13 [c] ver. 31; ch. 6:38, 42, 62; 1 Cor. 15:47; [Rom. 10:6]
14 [d] Num. 21:9 [e] ch. 8:28; 12:32, 34
15 [f] [ch. 15:4; 16:33; 1 John 5:12, 20] [g] ver. 36
16 [h] Rom. 5:8; Eph. 2:4; 2 Thess. 2:16; 1 John 3:1; 4:9, 10 [i] See ch. 1:29 [j] Rom. 8:32 [k] ch. 10:28
17 [l] ch. 5:36, 38; 6:29, 57; 7:29; 8:42; 10:36; 11:42; 17:3; 20:21; Rom. 8:3; 1 John 4:9, 10, 14 [m] ch. 5:45; 8:15; 12:47
18 [n] ch. 5:24; [Mark 16:16] [o] See 1 John 5:13
19 [p] [ch. 9:39] [q] See ch. 1:4, 5, 9 [r] [Isa. 30:10; Jer. 5:31] [s] ch. 7:7
20 [t] [Job 24:13; Rom. 13:12; Eph. 5:13] [u] Eph. 5:11, 13
21 [v] 1 John 1:6 [w] Ps. 139:23, 24
22 [x] ver. 26; ch. 4:1, 2
24 [y] [ch. 5:35]; See Matt. 4:12
25 [z] ch. 2:6
26 [a] ver. 2 [b] See ch. 1:7 [c] ch. 12:19
27 [d] 1 Cor. 4:7; Heb. 5:4 [e] ch. 6:65; [James 1:17] [f] See Matt. 21:25
28 [g] See ch. 1:20 [h] Mal. 3:1; Mark 1:2; Luke 1:17; Acts 19:4
29 [i] See Matt. 25:1

Jesus freely gives us new life by the supreme offering of his costly death—an event Nicodemus would witness firsthand (19:38–40). When Moses lifted the bronze serpent (representing God's punishment for his people's sin) in the wilderness (Num. 21:4–9), it was to rescue the Israelites from God's judgment as they looked in faith to God's provision for healing. When Jesus was lifted onto the cross (representing God's punishment for his people's sin), it was to enter the wilderness of God's judgment for us, and those who look to him in faith for spiritual healing will also experience God's provision.

3:16–21 The greatness of God's love is measured in terms of its unsearchable riches as well as in terms of its unimaginable reach. The "world" spoken of in verse 16 is the rebellious world of God's image-bearers. God loved rebels, fools, and idolaters so much that he gave his only Son, Jesus, to redeem them—to actually purchase a pan-national, trans-generational family for himself (Rev. 7:9–10). Everyone the Father gives to Jesus will be saved (John 6:37–40; 10:14–18). There is no other way. There is no greater love.

For John, eternal life is a *quality* of life before it is a *quantity* of life. Eternal life is defined in the Bible as knowing God and his Son (17:3)—a sharing of the life and intimacy of the Godhead. It is earthly entry into the everlasting and ever-blessed life of the age to come, the age of the Messiah—the fullness of covenant life. Through Jesus this promised age arrived, and at our rebirth we are ushered into the initial stages of that eternal life. Indeed, the movement from deservedly condemned sinner to perfectly justified believer is instantaneous and complete.

3:22–36 The transition from the era of anticipation to the age of fulfillment continued as John the Baptist helped his disciples shift their focus even more expressly onto Jesus. The apostle John cites John the Baptist's testimony in terms that will become one of the apostle's favorite metaphors for describing the rich relationship Jesus establishes with his people: as Messiah, Jesus is the perfect bridegroom who came from heaven to make a most unlikely, unworthy bride (the church) his wife. Jesus did this by taking upon himself the wrath we deserve in order to give us the favor we could never earn (Eph. 5:22–33).

It is important to note that those rescued from wrath are granted eternal life because they *believe*, while those who are condemned experience wrath because

is the bridegroom. [j]The friend of the bridegroom, who stands and hears him, [k]rejoices
greatly at the bridegroom's voice. Therefore
this joy of mine is now complete. 30 [l]He must
increase, but I must decrease."[1]

31 [m]He who comes from above [n]is above all.
He who is of the earth belongs to the earth
and [o]speaks in an earthly way. [p]He who comes
from heaven [n]is above all. 32 [q]He bears witness
to what he has seen and heard, [r]yet no one
receives his testimony. 33 Whoever receives his
testimony [s]sets his seal to this, [t]that God is
true. 34 For he whom [u]God has sent utters the
words of God, for he gives the Spirit [v]with-
out measure. 35 [w]The Father loves the Son and
[x]has given all things into his hand. 36 [y]Whoever
believes in the Son has eternal life; [z]whoever
does not obey the Son shall not [a]see life, but
the wrath of God remains on him.

Jesus and the Woman of Samaria

4 Now when Jesus learned that the Pharisees had heard that Jesus was making
and [b]baptizing more disciples than John
2 (although Jesus himself did not baptize,
but only his disciples), 3 he left Judea and
departed [c]again for Galilee. 4 [d]And he had to
pass through Samaria. 5 So he came to a town
of Samaria called Sychar, near the field [e]that
Jacob had given to his son Joseph. 6 Jacob's well
was there; so Jesus, [f]wearied as he was from
his journey, was sitting beside the well. It was
about the sixth hour.[2]

7 A woman from Samaria came to draw water.
Jesus said to her, [f]"Give me a drink." 8 (For his
disciples had gone away into the city to buy
food.) 9 The Samaritan woman said to him,
"How is it that you, a Jew, ask for a drink from
me, a woman of Samaria?" ([g]For Jews have no
dealings with Samaritans.) 10 Jesus answered
her, "If you knew the gift of God, and who
it is that is saying to you, 'Give me a drink,'
you would have asked him, and he would
have given you [h]living water." 11 The woman
said to him, "Sir, you have nothing to draw
water with, and the well is deep. Where do
you get that living water? 12 [i]Are you greater
than our father Jacob? [j]He gave us the well and
drank from it himself, as did his sons and his
livestock." 13 Jesus said to her, "Everyone who
drinks of this water will be thirsty again, 14 but
[k]whoever drinks of the water that I will give
him [l]will never be thirsty again.[3] The water
that I will give him will become [m]in him a
spring of water welling up to eternal life."
15 The woman said to him, "Sir, [n]give me this
water, so that I will not be thirsty or have to
come here to draw water."

16 Jesus said to her, "Go, [o]call your husband,
and come here." 17 The woman answered him,

[1] Some interpreters hold that the quotation continues through verse 36 [2] That is, about noon [3] Greek *forever*

they *disobey* (John 3:36). The basis of God's judgment is his just sentence for sin; the basis of our salvation is God's grace toward those who put their faith in his Son's provision for them. Disobedience alone results in wrath. Faith alone results in salvation.

4:1–15 The world of sinners loved by God includes not just respectable insiders seeking truth (Nicodemus) but broken outsiders running from the truth (the Samaritan woman). None of us are beyond the need of God's grace and none of us are beyond the reach of God's grace. Jesus has come to seek and to save both the "found," those who presume they already have a relationship with God, and the "lost," those who realize they don't.

This interchange between Jesus and the Samaritan woman shows us that eternal life isn't just about our life in heaven when we die; it is also about the life of heaven "welling up" (v. 14) in us while we live. Jesus' conversation is designed to help this woman see the realities of "heaven" despite the realities of her sin and shame, but he also intends for her discovery to affect her community and culture. The gospel is not ethereal or abstract; it concerns people and place. The woman was shocked that a Jewish man would speak openly to a Samaritan woman. Here Jesus confronts racism and sexism. He has come, as the old hymn says, to "make his blessings flow far as the curse is found."

4:16–26 The gospel is bad news before it is good news. The living water of grace is sweet only to those who know the bitter taste of their sin. Whether this woman literally had gone through several marriages or was just given over to a life of promiscuity (the specifics of her sin make no difference), she needed what Jesus alone can give. She had been a poor steward of her thirst—a thirst only Jesus can satisfy. She had

29 [j]Judg. 14:20; Song 5:1 [k]Matt. 9:15
30 [l]Matt. 3:11
31 [m]ch. 8:23 [n]Rom. 9:5; Eph. 1:21 [o][1 John 4:5] [p]See ver. 13
32 [q]ver. 11 [r][ver. 19; ch. 1:11; 5:43; 12:37]
33 [s][ch. 6:27; 2 Cor. 1:22; Eph. 1:13; Rev. 7:3-8] [t][1 John 5:10]
34 [u]See ver. 17 [v][Ezek. 4:11, 16]
35 [w]See ch. 5:20 [x]See Matt. 28:18
36 [y]ver. 15, 16; ch. 5:24; 6:40, 47, 54; 1 John 5:12, 13; [ch. 11:25, 26; 20:31]; See Matt. 19:16 [z][Rom. 2:8; Eph. 5:6; Col. 3:6] [a]ver. 3

Chapter 4
1 [b]ch. 3:22, 26
3 [c]ch. 2:11, 12
4 [d][Luke 13:33]
5 [e]ver. 12; Gen. 33:19; 48:22; Josh. 24:32
6 [f]ch. 19:28; [Matt. 4:2; 8:24; 21:18]
7 [f][See ver. 6 above]
9 [g]Luke 9:53; [ch. 8:48; Ezra 4:3, 10]; See Matt. 10:5
10 [h]ch. 7:38; Jer. 2:13; 17:13
12 [i][ch. 8:53] [j]ver. 5
14 [k][ch. 6:35, 51, 58; 7:37] [l][Isa. 49:10; Rev. 7:16] [m]ch. 7:38
15 [n][ch. 6:34]
16 [o]ch. 16:8

"I have no husband." Jesus said to her, "You are right in saying, 'I have no husband'; 18 for you have had five husbands, and the one you now have is not your husband. What you have said is true." 19 The woman said to him, "Sir, I perceive that [p]you are [q]a prophet. 20 [r]Our fathers worshiped on [s]this mountain, but you say that [t]in Jerusalem is [u]the place where people ought to worship." 21 Jesus said to her, [v]"Woman, believe me, [w]the hour is coming when [x]neither on this mountain nor in Jerusalem will you worship the Father. 22 [y]You worship what you do not know; [z]we worship what we know, for [z]salvation is [a]from the Jews. 23 But [b]the hour is coming, and is now here, when the true worshipers will worship the Father [c]in spirit and [d]truth, for the Father [e]is seeking such people to worship him. 24 God is spirit, and those who worship him must worship in spirit and truth." 25 The woman said to him, "I know that [f]Messiah is coming (he who is called Christ). When he comes, [g]he will tell us all things." 26 Jesus said to her, [h]"I who speak to you am he."

27 Just then [i]his disciples came back. They marveled that he was talking with a woman, but no one said, "What do you seek?" or, "Why are you talking with her?" 28 So the woman left her water jar and went away into town and said to the people, 29 "Come, see a man [j]who told me all that I ever did. Can this be the Christ?" 30 They went out of the town and were coming to him.

31 Meanwhile the disciples were urging him, saying, [k]"Rabbi, eat." 32 But he said to them, "I have food to eat that you do not know about." 33 So the disciples said to one another, [l]"Has anyone brought him something to eat?" 34 Jesus said to them, [m]"My food is [n]to do the will of him who sent me and [o]to accomplish his work. 35 Do you not say, 'There are yet four months, then comes the harvest'? Look, I tell you, lift up your eyes, and see that [p]the fields are white for harvest. 36 Already the one who reaps is receiving wages and gathering fruit for eternal life, so that [q]sower and [r]reaper [s]may rejoice together. 37 For here the saying holds true, [t]'One sows and another reaps.' 38 I sent you to reap [u]that for which you did not labor. Others have labored, [v]and you have entered into their labor."

39 Many Samaritans [w]from that town believed in him [x]because of [y]the woman's testimony, "He told me all that I ever did." 40 So when the Samaritans came to him, they asked him to stay with them, and he stayed there two days. 41 And many more believed [z]because of his word. 42 They said to the woman, "It is no longer because of what you said that we believe, for we have heard for ourselves, [a]and we know that this is indeed [b]the Savior [c]of the world."

19 [p]ch. 9:17; [ch. 6:14] [q]Luke 7:16, 39; See Matt. 21:11
20 [r]Gen. 12:6, 7; 33:18, 20; Deut. 11:29; 27:12; Josh. 8:33 [s]Judg. 9:7 [t]See Deut. 12:5 [u][ch. 11:48]
21 [v]ch. 2:4 [w]ver. 23; ch. 5:25, 28; 16:2, 25, 32 [x]Zeph. 2:11; Mal. 1:11; 1 Tim. 2:8
22 [y][2 Kgs. 17:28-34; Acts 17:23] [z]Ps. 147:19, 20; Isa. 2:3; Rom. 3:1, 2; 9:4, 5 [a]Matt. 2:4, 5; Acts 13:23; Rom. 11:26
23 [b]ver. 21 [c][Rom. 8:15; Eph. 2:18; 6:18; Phil. 3:3] [d]Ps. 145:18; [ch. 1:17] [e][ch. 6:44]
25 [f]See ch. 1:41 [g]Deut. 18:18; [ver. 29]
26 [h]ch. 9:35-37
27 [i]ver. 8
29 [j]ver. 17, 18; [ver. 25]
31 [k]See ch. 1:38
33 [l][ver. 11, 15; ch. 3:4; 6:34, 52]
34 [m][Job 23:12] [n]ch. 5:30; 6:38; 14:31 [o]ch. 5:36; 17:4
35 [p]Matt. 9:37; Luke 10:2; [ver. 25, 30]
36 [q][Matt. 13:37; Mark 4:14] [r]ver. 38 [s]Isa. 9:3; [Amos 9:13]
37 [t][Job 31:8]
38 [u]Josh. 24:13 [v][Acts 8:5-17, 25]

spent most of her life running to broken cisterns that hold no water (Jer. 2:13), now she is offered the only water that will satisfy her, and us—the grace of the gospel.

By nature, we are allergic to grace. We resist it. Like this woman, we look for ways to avoid Jesus. She turned Jesus' pursuit of her heart into an evasive conversation about different perspectives on worship. In his mercy Jesus met her right there, for ultimately, all of life is about worship. To what or whom do we give the attention, affection, and adoration which rightfully belong to God? We can make idols (substitute gods) out of anything—relationships, religion, anything. But even changing the subject to worship puts Jesus once more in the spotlight, for he himself is the only one worthy of our worship.

4:27–38 Nicodemus and the Samaritan woman were both part of the prepared harvest for which Jesus came. As disciples of Jesus, we follow him into a great grace story that has secured the salvation of men and women "from every nation, from all tribes and peoples and languages" (Rev. 7:9). All of history is bound up with God's commitment to redeem his covenant family through the work of Jesus.

4:39–43 The gospel comes to us in order that it might run through us. Having believed on Jesus, the Samaritan woman went back to her community to share the good news with her family and friends. In doing so, she gives us the paradigm of a good testimony. Jesus is the hero of her story. She drew attention to the One who exposed her sin and gave her life; and in doing so, she invited her friends to do the same. The gospel is personal, but it is not private.

39 [w]ver. 5, 8 [x][ch. 17:20] [y]ver. 29 41 [z]ch. 8:30 42 [a][1 John 5:20] [b]1 John 4:14; [ch. 3:17; 12:47; 1 Tim. 4:10] [c]See ch. 1:29

43 After [d]the two days he departed for Galilee. 44 (For Jesus himself had testified [e]that a prophet has no honor in his own hometown.) 45 So when he came to Galilee, the Galileans welcomed him, [f]having seen all that he had done in Jerusalem at the feast. For [g]they too had gone to the feast.

Jesus Heals an Official's Son

46 So he came again to [h]Cana in Galilee, [i]where he had made the water wine. And at Capernaum there was an official whose son was ill. 47 When this man heard that Jesus [j]had come from Judea to Galilee, he went to him and asked him to come down and heal his son, for he was at the point of death. 48 So Jesus said to him, [k]"Unless you[1] see signs and wonders you will not believe." 49 The official said to him, "Sir, come down [l]before my child dies." 50 Jesus said to him, "Go; your son will live." The man believed the word that Jesus spoke to him and went on his way. 51 As he was going down, his servants[2] met him and told him that his son was recovering. 52 So he asked them the hour when he began to get better, and they said to him, "Yesterday at the seventh hour[3] the fever left him." 53 The father knew that was the hour when Jesus had said to him, "Your son will live." And he himself believed, [m]and all his household. 54 [n]This was now the second sign that Jesus did when he had come from Judea to Galilee.

The Healing at the Pool on the Sabbath

5 After this there was a [o]feast of the Jews, and Jesus went up to Jerusalem.

2 Now there is in Jerusalem by [p]the Sheep Gate a pool, in Aramaic[4] called Bethesda,[5] which has five roofed colonnades. 3 In these lay a multitude of invalids—blind, lame, and [q]paralyzed.[6] 5 One man was there who had been an invalid for thirty-eight years. 6 When Jesus saw him lying there and knew that he had already been there a long time, he said to him, "Do you want to be healed?" 7 The sick man answered him, "Sir, I have no one to put me into the pool when the water is stirred up, and while I am going another steps down before me." 8 Jesus said to him, [r]"Get up, take up your bed, and walk." 9 [r]And at once the man was healed, and he took up his bed and walked.

[s]Now that day was the Sabbath. 10 So the Jews[7] said to the man who had been healed, "It is the Sabbath, and [t]it is not lawful for you to take up your bed." 11 But he answered them,

[1] The Greek for *you* is plural; twice in this verse [2] Greek *bondservants* [3] That is, at 1 P.M. [4] Or *Hebrew* [5] Some manuscripts *Bethsaida*
[6] Some manuscripts insert, wholly or in part, *waiting for the moving of the water;* **4** *for an angel of the Lord went down at certain seasons into the pool, and stirred the water: whoever stepped in first after the stirring of the water was healed of whatever disease he had*
[7] The Greek word *Ioudaioi* refers specifically here to Jewish religious leaders, and others under their influence, who opposed Jesus in that time; also verses 15, 16, 18

5:1–9 The further we move into John's Gospel, the wider he draws open the curtains on Jesus' identity and mission. His miracles grow bigger and his words grow bolder—all revealing Jesus to be the Messiah, the Son of God—even God the Son.

Isaiah envisioned the age of the Messiah in terms of a new exodus. The blind will see, the deaf will hear, the lame will leap, and the desert sand will become a pool of refreshing water (Isa. 35:1–10). The healing of the invalid by the pool of Bethesda is another declaration that the eschatological era of the Messiah has dawned—the "last days" of God's final, earthly revelation of his grace have begun (Heb. 1:2; Acts 2:17). In Jesus, the kingdom of God has come near (Matt. 3:2; 4:17; Mark 1:15).

5:10–17 The fact that Jesus healed the lame man on the Sabbath is both intentional and significant. Jesus has authority over Israel's Sabbath, for he is the Lord of the Sabbath (Luke 6:1–11; Mark 2:23–28). The Jerusalem temple had become a house of commercial business (John 2:16), but God meant it to be a "house of mercy" (the meaning of "Bethesda"; 5:2). Only through Jesus can we find God's mercy and grace, and enter into true Sabbath rest (Heb. 4:1–10)—ceasing from our futile efforts to save ourselves, as we trust in Jesus' perfect work on our behalf.

Though Jesus cares about our whole being, this man's greatest need was not healed legs but a redeemed heart. When Jesus pursued him and spoke the words, "Sin no more," he wasn't calling him to sinless perfection but to live in response to the mercy of a perfect Savior. The entire Christian life is a life of growing in grace (2 Pet. 3:18). Though we are perfectly forgiven, we await the perfection of eternity with Christ. And yet as those swept up into and toward the latter-day kingdom of God, we are called to "sin no more"—to live out our new, radically transformed identity.

43 [d] ver. 40
44 [e] See Matt. 13:57
45 [f] ch. 2:23; 3:2 [g] ver. 20
46 [h] ch. 2:1 [i] ch. 2:9
47 [j] ver. 3, 54
48 [k] ch. 2:18; 6:30; [ch. 20:29]
49 [l] [ch. 11:21, 32; Mark 5:35; Luke 8:49]
53 [m] Acts 16:34; 18:8; See Acts 11:14
54 [n] [ch. 2:11 with ver. 45, 46]

Chapter 5
1 [o] See ch. 6:4
2 [p] Neh. 3:1, 32; 12:39
3 [q] Matt. 12:10
8 [r] Matt. 9:6, 7; Mark 2:9, 11, 12; Luke 5:24, 25
9 [r] [See ver. 8 above] [s] ch. 9:14
10 [t] Ex. 20:10; Neh. 13:19; Jer. 17:21, 22; [ch. 7:23; 9:16; Matt. 12:2; Mark 2:24; 3:4; Luke 6:2; 13:14]

“The man who healed me, that man said to
me, ‘Take up your bed, and walk.’ ” 12 They
asked him, “Who is the man who said to you,
‘Take up your bed and walk’?” 13 Now the man
who had been healed did not know who it
was, for [u]Jesus had withdrawn, as there was
a crowd in the place. 14 Afterward Jesus found
him in the temple and said to him, “See, you
are well! [v]Sin no more, [w]that nothing worse
may happen to you.” 15 The man went away
and told the Jews that it was Jesus who had
healed him. 16 And this was why the Jews [x]were
persecuting Jesus, [y]because he was doing these
things on the Sabbath. 17 But Jesus answered
them, “My Father is working until now, and
I am working.”

Jesus Is Equal with God

18 This was why the Jews [z]were seeking all
the more to kill him, [a]because not only was he
[b]breaking the Sabbath, but he was even calling
God [c]his own Father, [d]making himself equal
with God.

The Authority of the Son

19 So Jesus said to them, “Truly, truly, I say
to you, [e]the Son [f]can do nothing of his own
accord, but only what he sees the Father doing.
For whatever the Father[1] does, that the Son
does likewise. 20 For [g]the Father loves the Son
and shows him all that he himself is doing.
And [h]greater works than these will he show
him, so that [i]you may marvel. 21 For as the
Father [j]raises the dead and [k]gives them life,
so [l]also the Son gives life [m]to whom he will.
22 [n]The Father judges no one, but [o]has given all
judgment to the Son, 23 that all may honor the
Son, just as they [p]honor the Father. [q]Whoever
does not honor the Son does not honor the
Father who sent him. 24 Truly, truly, I say to
you, [r]whoever hears my word and [s]believes
him who sent me has eternal life. He [t]does
not come into judgment, but [u]has passed from
death to life.

25 “Truly, truly, I say to you, [v]an hour is coming, and is now here, when [w]the dead will hear
[x]the voice of the Son of God, and those who
hear [w]will live. 26 [y]For as the Father has life
in himself, [z]so he has granted the Son also to
have life in himself. 27 And he [a]has given him
authority to execute judgment, because he is
the Son of Man. 28 Do not marvel at this, for [v]an
hour is coming when [b]all who are in the tombs
will hear his voice 29 and come out, [c]those who
have done good to the resurrection of life, and
those who have done evil to the resurrection
of judgment.

Witnesses to Jesus

30 [d]“I can do nothing on my own. As I hear,
I judge, and [e]my judgment is just, because
[f]I seek not my own will [g]but the will of him
who sent me. 31 [h]If I alone bear witness about
myself, my testimony is not true. 32 There is
[i]another who bears witness about me, and
[j]I know that the testimony that he bears
about me is true. 33 [k]You sent to John, and he
has borne witness to the truth. 34 Not that
[l]the testimony that I receive is from man, but
I say these things so that you may be saved.

[1] Greek *he*

5:18–47 The conflict intensifies between Jesus and the Jewish leaders—an antagonism that would eventually lead to his crucifixion. Why the enmity? It was not just because of Jesus’ Sabbath breaking, but because he made claims that gave him equal status with God—an affirmation we encountered in the first verse of John’s Gospel: “the Word was God” (1:1). Only God can save us, and Jesus, God incarnate, is the second member of the Trinity.

Jesus claimed a unique filial relationship with God as Father, an assertion which in that culture gave him divine status and amounted to blasphemy in the eyes of the Jews (5:18). But Jesus did not back down. He claimed the Father’s works as his own, including raising the dead—a boast he would prove by raising Lazarus from the dead (ch. 11), an act that not only created greater opposition from his religious antagonists but was also a preview of his own resurrection.

To honor Jesus is to honor the Father (5:23). In fact, we too can know God as our Father if we honor Jesus—that is, if we believe on him (1:12; 14:9). We pass from judgment to life because Jesus took our judgment on the cross (5:22–24; cf. 2 Cor. 5:21). Our adoption is secured by Jesus’ propitiating (turning away, satisfying) God’s wrath.

13 [u][ch. 6:15]
14 [v][ch. 8:11] [w][Ezra 9:14]
16 [x]ch. 15:20; [Acts 9:4, 5] [y]ch. 7:23; 9:16
18 [z]See ch. 7:1 [a]See ch. 10:33 [b]ver. 16 [c][Rom. 8:32] [d]Phil. 2:6
19 [e]See ver. 30 [f][ch. 16:13]
20 [g]ch. 3:35; 10:17; 15:9, 10; 17:23-26; [Matt. 3:17] [h][ch. 14:12] [i]ch. 7:21
21 [j][Deut. 32:39; 2 Cor. 1:9] [k]Rom. 4:17; 8:11 [l][ch. 6:33; 11:25]; See 1 Cor. 15:45 [m][Rom. 9:18]
22 [n][Acts 17:31] [o]ver. 27; ch. 9:39; Acts 10:42; [ch. 3:17]; See ch. 17:2
23 [p]ch. 8:49 [q]Luke 10:16; [ch. 15:23; 1 John 2:23]
24 [r][ch. 8:51] [s]ch. 20:31; 1 John 5:9-13; [ch. 3:15, 36; 12:44] [t]ch. 3:18; [ver. 29] [u]1 John 3:14
25 [v]See ch. 4:21, 23 [w]See Eph. 2:1, 5 [x][ch. 11:43] **26** [y][ch. 6:57] [z]See ch. 1:4; 17:2 **27** [a]ver. 22 **28** [v][See ver. 25 above] [b]ch. 11:24; 1 Cor. 15:52; [ch. 11:44, 45] **29** [c]See Dan. 12:2 **30** [d]ver. 19; ch. 8:28; 14:10 [e]ch. 8:16 [f]ch. 4:34; 6:38; [ch. 7:18; Rom. 15:3] [g]See Matt. 26:39 **31** [h][ch. 8:13, 14, 18, 54; 18:21] **32** [i]ver. 37 [j]ch. 7:28, 29 **33** [k]See ch. 1:7, 19 **34** [l]1 John 5:9

35 He was a burning and [m]shining lamp, and
[n]you were willing to rejoice for a while in his
light. 36 But [l]the testimony that I have is greater
than that of John. For [o]the works that the
Father has given me [p]to accomplish, the very
works that I am doing, [q]bear witness about
me that [r]the Father has sent me. 37 And the
Father who sent me [s]has himself borne witness about me. His voice you have never heard,
[t]his form you have never seen, 38 and [u]you do
not have his word abiding in you, for you do
not believe the one whom he has sent. 39 [v]You
search the Scriptures because you think that
in them you have eternal life; and [w]it is they
that bear witness about me, 40 yet [x]you refuse
to come to me that you may have life. 41 [y]I do
not receive glory from people. 42 But [z]I know
that you do not have [a]the love of God within
you. 43 I have come [b]in my Father's name, and
[c]you do not receive me. [d]If another comes in
his own name, you will receive him. 44 How
can you believe, when you receive glory from
one another and [e]do not seek the glory that
comes from [f]the only God? 45 Do not think that
I will accuse you to the Father. There is one
who accuses you: Moses, [g]on whom you have
set your hope. 46 For if you believed Moses, you
would believe me; for [h]he wrote of me. 47 But [i]if
you do not believe his writings, how will you
believe my words?"

Jesus Feeds the Five Thousand

6 After this [j]Jesus went away to the other
side of [k]the Sea of Galilee, which is [l]the
Sea of Tiberias. 2 And a large crowd was following him, because they saw the signs that
he was doing on the sick. 3 Jesus went up on
[m]the mountain, and there he sat down with his
disciples. 4 Now [n]the Passover, the [o]feast of the
Jews, was at hand. 5 [p]Lifting up his eyes, then,
and seeing that a large crowd was coming
toward him, Jesus said to [q]Philip, "Where are
we to buy bread, so that these people may eat?"
6 He said this to test him, for he himself knew
what he would do. 7 [r]Philip answered him,
"Two hundred denarii[1] worth of bread would
not be enough for each of them to get a little."
8 One of his disciples, [s]Andrew, Simon Peter's
brother, said to him, 9 "There is a boy here who
has five [t]barley loaves and two fish, but [t]what
are they for so many?" 10 Jesus said, "Have the
people sit down." [u]Now there was much grass
in the place. So the men sat down, about five
thousand in number. 11 Jesus then took the
loaves, and [v]when he had given thanks, he
distributed them to those who were seated.
So also the fish, as much as they wanted. 12 And
when they had eaten their fill, he told his disciples, "Gather up the leftover fragments, that
nothing may be lost." 13 So they gathered them
up and filled twelve baskets with fragments

[1] A *denarius* was a day's wage for a laborer

According to Jesus, the only way we can derive life *from* the Scriptures is to see Jesus *in* the Scriptures, for all the Scriptures bear witness to him (John 5:30–47; cf. Luke 24:27, 44–47). The entire Bible, Genesis to Revelation, is ultimately about Jesus. Throughout Scripture God is unfolding the grace that culminates in Christ (John 5:39–40). The Bible is therefore not fundamentally about what we do for God but what God does for us.

The Jews, tragically, preferred receiving glory from one another rather than seeking the glory of God (v. 44). No sin or idolatry is more insidious and destructive than living for the approval of people (Prov. 29:25). In the gospel of grace, we are liberated from the need to be approved by people because in Jesus we have been approved by the only One whose approval matters and the only One whose approval satisfies.

6:1–21 John 6 is the longest chapter in the New Testament. It provides a rich redemptive-historical perspective on Moses and the central saving act of God in Israel's history—the exodus. John wants us to see Jesus as the greater Moses and the gospel as the greatest exodus of all. Just as Moses led the Israelites out of bondage in Egypt into the Land of Promise, so Jesus came to lead the pan-national family of God on the ultimate exodus—a journey out of sin and death into the quintessential Promised Land—the new heaven and new earth (Rev. 21:1–5).

Just as the first exodus involved a crisis at sea and the need for supernatural deliverance (Ex. 13:17–14:29), so Jesus responded to his fear-filled disciples, walking to them on the Sea of Galilee, securing their safe delivery to the other side.

35 [m]2 Pet. 1:19 [n][Matt. 13:20; 21:26]
36 [l][See ver. 34 above] [o]ch. 10:25, 38; 14:11; 15:24; [ch. 2:23; Matt. 11:4] [p]See ch. 4:34 [q][ch. 3:2] [r]See ch. 3:17
37 [s]ch. 8:18; [Matt. 3:17] [t]See ch. 1:18
38 [u][1 John 2:14; 4:13, 14; 5:10]
39 [v][Acts 17:11; 2 Tim. 3:15] [w]See Luke 24:27
40 [x]ver. 43; ch. 3:19; 7:17; [Matt. 23:37; Luke 13:34]
41 [y]ver. 34; [Matt. 6:1, 2; 1 Thess. 2:6]
42 [z]See ch. 2:24, 25 [a]Luke 11:42; See Jude 21
43 [b]ch. 10:25; 12:13; 17:12 [c]ch. 1:11; 3:11, 32 [d][Matt. 24:5]
44 [e]Rom. 2:29 [f]ch. 17:3
45 [g][ch. 9:28, 29; Rom. 2:17]
46 [h]ver. 47; Num. 21:9; Deut. 18:15; Luke 24:27; [ch. 12:41]
47 [i][Luke 16:31]

Chapter 6
1 [j]For ver. 1-13, see Matt. 14:13-21; Mark 6:32-44; Luke 9:10-17 [k]See Matt. 4:18 [l]ch. 21:1
3 [m]ver. 15
4 [n]ch. 2:13; 11:55; See Ex. 12 [o]ch. 5:1; 7:2
5 [p]Luke 6:20 [q]ch. 1:44
7 [r][Mark 6:37]
8 [s]ch. 1:40, 44 **9** [t]2 Kgs. 4:42, 43 **10** [u][Mark 6:39] **11** [v]ver. 23; See Matt. 15:36

from the five barley loaves left by those who
had eaten. 14 When the people saw the sign
that he had done, they said, [w]"This is indeed
[x]the Prophet [y]who is to come into the world!"
15 [z]Perceiving then that they were about to
come and take him by force to make him king,
Jesus [a]withdrew again to [b]the mountain by
himself.

Jesus Walks on Water

16 When evening came, his disciples went
down to the sea, 17 got into a boat, and started
across the sea to Capernaum. It was now dark,
and Jesus had not yet come to them. 18 The
sea became rough because a strong wind was
blowing. 19 When they had rowed about three
or four miles,[1] they saw Jesus walking on the
sea and coming near the boat, and they were
frightened. 20 [c]But he said to them, "It is I; do
not be afraid." 21 Then they were glad to take
him into the boat, and immediately the boat
was at the land to which they were going.

I Am the Bread of Life

22 On the next day the crowd that remained
on the other side of the sea saw that there
had been only [d]one boat there, and that Jesus
had not entered the boat with his disciples,
but that his disciples had gone away alone.
23 Other boats from Tiberias came near the
place where they had eaten the bread after the
Lord [e]had given thanks. 24 [f]So when the crowd
saw that Jesus was not there, nor his disciples,
they themselves got into the boats and [g]went
to Capernaum, seeking Jesus.
25 When they found him on the other side
of the sea, they said to him, [h]"Rabbi, when
did you come here?" 26 Jesus answered them,
"Truly, truly, I say to you, [i]you are seeking me,
not because you saw [j]signs, but because you
ate your fill of the loaves. 27 [k]Do not work for
the food that perishes, but for [l]the food that
endures to eternal life, which [m]the Son of Man
will give to you. For on [n]him God the Father has
[o]set his seal." 28 Then they said to him, "What
must we do, to be doing [p]the works of God?"
29 Jesus answered them, "This is the work of
God, [q]that you believe in him whom [r]he has
sent." 30 So they said to him, [s]"Then what sign
do you do, that we may see and believe you?
What work do you perform? 31 [t]Our fathers ate
the manna in the wilderness; as it is written,
[u]'He gave them bread from heaven to eat.'"
32 Jesus then said to them, "Truly, truly, I say to
you, it was not Moses who gave you the bread
from heaven, but my Father gives you the true
bread from heaven. 33 For the bread of God is
[v]he who comes down from heaven and gives
life to the world." 34 They said to him, [w]"Sir,
give us this bread always."
35 Jesus said to them, [x]"I am the bread of
life; [y]whoever comes to me shall not hunger,
and whoever believes in me shall never thirst.
36 But I said to you that you have seen me and
yet do not believe. 37 [z]All that [a]the Father gives
me will come to me, and [b]whoever comes to
me I will never cast out. 38 For [c]I have come
down from heaven, not to do [d]my own will
but [d]the will of him [e]who sent me. 39 And [f]this
is the will of him who sent me, [g]that I should
lose nothing of [h]all that he has given me, but
[i]raise it up on the last day. 40 For this is the will
of my Father, that everyone who [j]looks on the

[1] Greek *twenty-five or thirty stadia*; a *stadion* was about 607 feet or 185 meters

14 [w]See ch. 4:19 [x]ch. 1:21; 7:40; See Matt. 21:11 [y]ch. 11:27; See Matt. 11:3
15 [z][ch. 12:12-15] [a]For ver. 15-21, see Matt. 14:22-33; Mark 6:45-51; [Matt. 8:18] [b]ver. 3
20 [c][Luke 24:38, 39]
22 [d]ch. 21:8
23 [e]ver. 11
24 [f]For ver. 24, 25, [Matt. 14:34-36; Mark 6:53-56] [g]ver. 17, 59
25 [h]See ch. 1:38
26 [i]ver. 24 [j]ver. 2
27 [k]Isa. 55:2 [l][ver. 35, 50, 51, 54, 58] [m]See Dan. 7:13 [n][ch. 5:36, 37; 10:36] [o][Ezek. 9:4; Rom. 4:11; 1 Cor. 9:2; 2 Tim. 2:19]; See ch. 3:33
28 [p]1 Cor. 15:58; Rev. 2:26
29 [q]1 John 3:23 [r]See ch. 3:17

The timing of the feeding of the 5,000 is not coincidental. It occurred just before Passover—the meal that inaugurated Israel's journey through the wilderness. Indeed, Jesus didn't come merely to provide elements for the Passover meal but to *be* the Passover meal himself. He is the Lamb of God who takes away the sin of the world (John 1:29). On him we feed and are nourished.

6:22–59 Neither manna on the journey to the Promised Land in Moses' time (Ex. 16:13–18) nor barley loaves in the Promised Land in Jesus' time could satisfy the core hunger he came to satisfy. Too readily, we seek satisfaction from the bread of this world. When huge crowds followed him to the other side of the Sea of Galilee, Jesus seized the moment to expose their self-centered motivation and to reveal more of his God-glorifying vocation.

Jesus provides a bread that leads to eternal life. But Jesus doesn't just provide this bread; he *is* this bread—the Bread of Life. This is the first of several "I am" statements

30 [s]See Matt. 12:38 **31** [t]ver. 49, 58; Ex. 16:15; Num. 11:7-9 [u]Cited from Neh. 9:15; [Ps. 78:24, 25; 105:40; 1 Cor. 10:3] **33** [v]ver. 50 **34** [w]See ch. 4:15, 33 **35** [x]ver. 41, 48, 51; [ver. 58] [y]ch. 4:14; 7:37; [ch. 5:40; Matt. 11:28; Rev. 7:16] **37** [z]ver. 39; ch. 17:2 [a]ch. 10:29; 17:6, 9, 24 [b]ch. 10:28; 17:12 **38** [c]See ch. 3:13 [d]See ch. 5:30 [e]See ch. 4:34 **39** [f]ch. 10:28, 29; Matt. 18:14 [g]ch. 17:12; 18:9 [h]ver. 37 [i]ver. 40, 44, 54; [ch. 11:25; 1 Cor. 6:14] **40** [j]ch. 12:45; 14:17, 19

Son and [k]believes in him [l]should have eternal
life, and I will raise him up on the last day."
41 So the Jews grumbled about him, because
he said, [m]"I am the bread that came down from
heaven." 42 They said, [n]"Is not this Jesus, [o]the
son of Joseph, whose father and mother [p]we
know? How does he now say, 'I have come
down from heaven'?" 43 Jesus answered them,
"Do not grumble among yourselves. 44 No one
can come to me unless the Father who sent me
[q]draws him. And [r]I will raise him up on the last
day. 45 It is written in the Prophets, [s]'And they
will all be [t]taught by God.' [u]Everyone who has
heard and learned from the Father comes to
me— 46 [v]not that anyone has seen the Father
except [w]he who is from God; he [x]has seen the
Father. 47 Truly, truly, I say to you, [y]whoever
believes has eternal life. 48 [z]I am the bread of
life. 49 [a]Your fathers ate the manna in the wilderness, and [b]they died. 50 [c]This is the bread
that comes down from heaven, so that one
may eat of it [d]and not die. 51 I am the living
bread [e]that came down from heaven. If anyone
eats of this bread, he will live forever. And the
bread that I will give [f]for the life of the world
is [g]my flesh."
52 The Jews then [h]disputed among themselves, saying, [i]"How can this man give us his
flesh to eat?" 53 So Jesus said to them, "Truly,
truly, I say to you, unless you eat the flesh of
[j]the Son of Man and drink his blood, you [k]have
no life in you. 54 Whoever feeds on my flesh
and drinks my blood [l]has eternal life, and
[m]I will raise him up on the last day. 55 For my
flesh is true food, and my blood is true drink.
56 Whoever feeds on my flesh and drinks my
blood [n]abides in me, and I in him. 57 As [o]the
living Father [p]sent me, and [q]I live because of
the Father, so whoever feeds on me, he also
will live because of me. 58 [r]This is the bread
that came down from heaven, not like the
bread[1] the fathers ate, and died. Whoever feeds
on this bread will live forever." 59 Jesus[2] said
these things in the synagogue, as he taught
[s]at Capernaum.

The Words of Eternal Life

60 [t]When many of his disciples heard it, they
said, "This is a hard saying; who can listen to
it?" 61 But Jesus, [v]knowing in himself that his
disciples were grumbling about this, said to
them, "Do you take offense at this? 62 Then
what if you were to see [w]the Son of Man
[x]ascending to [y]where he was before? 63 [z]It is the
Spirit who gives life; [a]the flesh is no help at all.
[b]The words that I have spoken to you are spirit
and life. 64 But [c]there are some of you who do
not believe." (For Jesus [v]knew from the beginning who those were who did not believe, and
[d]who it was who would betray him.) 65 And
he said, "This is why I told you [e]that no one
can come to me unless it is granted him by
the Father."

[1] Greek lacks *the bread* [2] Greek *He*

by Jesus throughout John's Gospel—each of which are reminiscent of the God who revealed his name to Moses as "I AM" (Ex. 3:14).

How can we acquire this life-giving bread? The only "work" that guarantees the possession of this redemptive manna is to believe in Jesus (John 6:29). The gospel sabotages any notion of legalism or performance-based acceptability with God. The only thing we bring to Jesus is our need. All we offer is the admission that we have nothing to offer.

Tragically, just as God's people grumbled over the provision of the first manna, so now, as he offered the eschatological bread from heaven, some in the crowd did the same (Num. 11:1–15; John 6:43). Oh, the patience and forbearance of our God!

6:60–71 That the crowds were offended by Jesus' scandalous words is not surprising, and Jesus warned that there would be even greater grounds for offense in the coming days. Jesus didn't come to win a popularity contest but to give his life as "a ransom for many" (Mark 10:45). The cross, resurrection, and ascension of Jesus are foolishness, even offensive to the natural mind (1 Cor. 1:18; Gal. 5:11). For the gospel reveals the depth of our need and our total inability to save ourselves. When we trust in our own cleverness or obedience or resources or abilities, we abhor God's grace. But when God kindly deconstructs our vaunted self-sufficiency, our hearts come alive again. The Father generously grants many to believe on Jesus (John 6:39–40), and the Spirit gives life to all who call on his name.

40 [k]ver. 47; ch. 3:15, 16 [l]ver. 27, 54; ch. 4:14
41 [m]ver. 33, 35, 38
42 [n]See Matt. 13:55 [o]See ch. 1:45 [p]ch. 7:27, 28
44 [q]ch. 12:32; Jer. 31:3; Hos. 11:4; [ver. 65; ch. 4:23] [r]ver. 39
45 [s]Cited from Isa. 54:13; [Jer. 31:33, 34; Heb. 8:10, 11] [t]1 Cor. 2:13; 1 Thess. 4:9; 1 John 2:20 [u][ver. 37]
46 [v]See ch. 1:18 [w]See ch. 7:29 [x][ch. 3:32; 8:38]
47 [y]See ch. 3:36
48 [z]See ver. 35
49 [a]See ver. 31 [b]ver. 58
50 [c]ver. 33 [d]ver. 51, 58
51 [e]ch. 3:13 [f]ver. 57; Luke 22:19 [g]ver. 53-56; [ch. 1:14]
52 [h]ch. 9:16; 10:19 [i]ver. 60; ch. 3:9
53 [j]ver. 27 [k]See ch. 20:31
54 [l]See ver. 40 [m]ver. 39
56 [n]ch. 15:4, 5; 1 John 3:24; 4:13, 15, 16
57 [o][ch. 5:26]; See Matt. 16:16 [p]See ch. 3:17 [q]ch. 11:25; Rev. 1:18
58 [r]ver. 31, 33, 49-51
59 [s]ver. 24

60 [t]ver. 66; [ver. 64] **61** [v][ch. 2:24, 25] **62** [w]ver. 27 [x]See Mark 16:19 [y][ch. 17:5]; See ch. 3:13 **63** [z][1 Cor. 15:45; 2 Cor. 3:6] [a]ch. 3:6 [b]ver. 68 **64** [c]ver. 66 [v][See ver. 61 above] [d]ver. 71; ch. 13:11 **65** [e]ver. 44, 45; ch. 3:27

66 [f]After this many of his disciples turned
back and no longer walked with him. 67 So
Jesus said to [g]the Twelve, "Do you want to go
away as well?" 68 Simon Peter answered him,
"Lord, to whom shall we go? You have [h]the
words of eternal life, 69 and [i]we have believed,
and have come to know, that [j]you are [k]the Holy
One of God." 70 Jesus answered them, [l]"Did
I not choose you, [g]the Twelve? And yet one of
you is [m]a devil." 71 He spoke of Judas [n]the son
of Simon Iscariot, for [o]he, one of the Twelve,
was going to betray him.

Jesus at the Feast of Booths

7 After this Jesus went about in Galilee.
He would not go about in Judea, because
[p]the Jews[1] were seeking to kill him. 2 Now
[q]the Jews' Feast of [r]Booths was at hand. 3 [s]So
his brothers[2] said to him, "Leave here and
go to Judea, that your disciples also may see
the works you are doing. 4 For no one works
in secret if he seeks to be known openly. If
you do these things, [t]show yourself to the
world." 5 [u]For not even [v]his brothers believed
in him. 6 Jesus said to them, [w]"My time has
not yet come, but your time is always here.
7 The world cannot hate you, but [x]it hates
me because I testify about it that [y]its works
are evil. 8 You go up to the feast. I am not[3]
going up to this feast, for [z]my time has not yet
fully come." 9 After saying this, he remained
in Galilee.

10 But after [a]his brothers had gone up to
the feast, then he also went up, not publicly
but in private. 11 [b]The Jews [c]were looking for
him at the feast, and saying, "Where is he?"
12 And there was much [d]muttering about him
among the people. [e]While some said, "He is a
good man," others said, "No, [f]he is leading the
people astray." 13 Yet [g]for fear of the Jews no one
spoke openly of him.

14 About the middle of the feast Jesus went
up [h]into the temple and began teaching.
15 The Jews therefore [i]marveled, saying, "How
is it that this man has learning,[4] when he has
never studied?" 16 So Jesus answered them,
[j]"My teaching is not mine, but his [k]who sent
me. 17 [l]If anyone's will is to do God's[5] will,
[m]he will know whether the teaching is from
God or whether I [n]am speaking on my own
authority. 18 The one who speaks on his own
authority [o]seeks his own glory; but the one
who seeks the glory of him who sent him is
true, and in him there is no falsehood. 19 [p]Has
not Moses given you the law? Yet none of you
keeps the law. [q]Why do you seek to kill me?"
20 The crowd answered, [r]"You have a demon!
Who is seeking to kill you?" 21 Jesus answered
them, "I did [s]one work, and you all marvel at
it. 22 [t]Moses gave you circumcision (not that

[1] Or *Judeans*; Greek *Ioudaioi* probably refers here to Jewish religious leaders, and others under their influence, in that time [2] Or *brothers and sisters*; also verses 5, 10 [3] Some manuscripts add *yet* [4] Or *this man knows his letters* [5] Greek *his*

7:1–13 In John 7–8, Jesus' Christological claims grow even more dramatic, and the response of the Jews grows increasingly hostile. Nothing is as disruptive as grace. The Jews wanted to put Jesus to death. Indeed, they did put him to death, but only at the appointed time (see 7:6) and only for God's saving purposes (Acts 2:23–24). God's sovereignty never sleeps. Even the most disastrous and inexplicable of events are under his wise, governing hand.

Even members of Jesus' own family struggled with their half brother's identity—coming to faith only after his resurrection (Mark 3:21; Acts 1:14; 1 Cor. 15:7). None of us can presume upon our relationship to Jesus. It comes by grace alone through faith alone. We too, like Nicodemus, must be born from above so that we might believe from within.

7:14–24 In dramatic fashion, Jesus moved into the temple courts and began to teach. His words generated astonishment and rage: astonishment because of the depth of knowledge he possessed as a seemingly untrained rabbi; rage because his teaching exposed the people's sin. At the same time his teaching further distinguished him, his earthly authority, and his heavenly status.

The gospel of grace that comes to us because of who Jesus is and what Jesus has done in our place does not land on people in a neutral way. It is either received with joy or rejected with contempt. The gospel is the aroma of life to some and the aroma of death to others (2 Cor. 2:15–16). There is no middle ground.

66 [f] ver. 60, 64
67 [g] ver. 70, 71
68 [h] Acts 5:20; [ch. 12:50; 17:8]
69 [i] [ch. 11:27; 1 John 4:16] [j] See ch. 1:49 [k] See Mark 1:24
70 [l] See ch. 13:18 [g] [See ver. 67 above] [m] ch. 13:2, 27; 17:12
71 [n] ch. 13:26 [o] ver. 64, 67

Chapter 7
1 [p] ch. 5:18; 8:37, 40; 11:53
2 [q] ch. 5:1; 6:4 [r] See Lev. 23:34
3 [s] ver. 5, 10; See Matt. 12:46
4 [t] [ch. 14:22; 18:20]
5 [u] [Matt. 13:57; Mark 3:21] [v] ver. 3, 10
6 [w] [ver. 8, 30]; See ch. 2:4
7 [x] ch. 15:18, 24 [y] ch. 3:19; [Col. 1:21; 1 John 3:12]
8 [z] See ch. 2:4
10 [a] ver. 3, 5
11 [b] ver. 1 [c] ch. 11:56
12 [d] ver. 32 [e] [ver. 40-43] [f] ver. 47
13 [g] ch. 19:38; 20:19; [ch. 9:22; 12:42]
14 [h] ver. 28
15 [i] [ver. 46; Luke 2:47; 4:22; Acts 4:13]
16 [j] ch. 8:28; 12:49; 14:10, 24; [ch. 3:34] [k] See ch. 3:17
17 [l] [ch. 8:31, 32; 14:21, 23] [m] [ch. 8:43; Ps. 25:9; Dan. 12:10; Phil. 3:15] [n] See ch. 5:30
18 [o] ch. 5:41; 8:50 **19** [p] ver. 23; See ch. 1:17 [q] ver. 1 **20** [r] ch. 8:48, 52; 10:20; [Matt. 11:18; Mark 3:22; Luke 7:33] **21** [s] ver. 23; ch. 5:2-9 **22** [t] Lev. 12:3

it is from Moses, but [u]from the fathers), and you circumcise a man on the Sabbath. 23 If on the Sabbath a man receives circumcision, so that the law of Moses may not be broken, [v]are you angry with me because on the Sabbath I made a man's whole body well? 24 [w]Do not judge by appearances, but judge with right judgment."

Can This Be the Christ?

25 Some of the people of Jerusalem therefore said, "Is not this the man whom [x]they seek to kill? 26 And here he is, [y]speaking openly, and they say nothing to him! Can it be that [z]the authorities really know that this is the Christ? 27 But [a]we know [b]where this man comes from, and when the Christ appears, [c]no one will know where he comes from." 28 So Jesus proclaimed, [d]as he taught in the temple, [a]"You know me, and you know where I come from. But [e]I have not come of my own accord. [f]He who sent me is true, [g]and him you do not know. 29 [h]I know him, for I come [i]from him, and [j]he sent me." 30 [k]So they were seeking to arrest him, but [l]no one laid a hand on him, [m]because his hour had not yet come. 31 Yet [n]many of the people believed in him. They said, [o]"When the Christ appears, will he do more signs than this man has done?"

Officers Sent to Arrest Jesus

32 The Pharisees heard the crowd [p]muttering these things about him, and the chief priests and Pharisees sent [q]officers to arrest him. 33 Jesus then said, [r]"I will be with you a little longer, and then [s]I am going to him who sent me. 34 [t]You will seek me and you will not find me. Where I am you cannot come." 35 The Jews said to one another, "Where does this man intend to go that we will not find him? [u]Does he intend to go to [v]the Dispersion among [w]the Greeks and teach the Greeks? 36 What does he mean by saying, [x]'You will seek me and you will not find me,' and, 'Where I am you cannot come'?"

Rivers of Living Water

37 [y]On the last day of the feast, the great day, Jesus stood up and cried out, [z]"If anyone thirsts, let him [a]come to me and drink. 38 Whoever believes in me, [b]as[1] the Scripture has said, [c]'Out of his heart will flow rivers of [d]living water.'" 39 Now [e]this he said about the Spirit, [f]whom those who believed in him were to receive, [g]for as yet the Spirit had not been [h]given, [i]because Jesus was not yet glorified.

Division Among the People

40 When they heard these words, [j]some of the people said, "This really is [k]the Prophet." 41 Others said, "This is [l]the Christ." But some said, [m]"Is the Christ to come from Galilee? 42 Has not the Scripture said that the Christ comes [n]from the offspring of David, and comes [o]from Bethlehem, the village [p]where David was?" 43 So there was [q]a division among the people over him. 44 [r]Some of them wanted to arrest him, but no one laid hands on him.

[1] Or *let him come to me, and let him who believes in me drink. As*

7:25–44 The Feast of Booths was a joyful celebration in Jerusalem. It commemorated the ingathering of the fall crops and the years the Israelites spent living in tents as they journeyed through the wilderness (Lev. 23:33–43; Num. 29:2–38). Two symbols—water and light—played a significant role in this high feast. During the course of the week, water was drawn from Siloam and poured upon the altar, in commemoration of the refreshing stream that had come forth miraculously out of the rock at Meribah (Ex. 17:1–7).

Jesus' loud invitation to the thirsty was a startling, even scandalous declaration. He was claiming to be the rock that Moses struck in the wilderness—the rock from which life-sustaining water flowed (see also 1 Cor. 10:1–4). But Jesus was also looking ahead to the day of Pentecost, when "in the last days" he would pour out his Spirit (Joel 2:28–29; Acts 2). After his ascension, the Father gave the Spirit to Jesus without limit (John 3:34), and Jesus gives us the Spirit without reservation (John 1:33)—both enabling us to believe and confirming that we do believe (Eph. 1:13–14).

22 [u]Gen. 17:10
23 [v]ch. 5:16; See Matt. 12:2
24 [w]ch. 8:15; [Isa. 11:3; 2 Cor. 10:7]; See Deut. 1:16, 17
25 [x]ver. 1
26 [y]ch. 18:20 [z]ver. 48
27 [a][ch. 6:42; 8:14, 19; 9:29] [b]ch. 19:9 [c][ver. 42]
28 [d]ver. 14 [a][See ver. 27 above] [e]ch. 8:42; [ch. 5:43] [f]See ch. 8:26 [g]ch. 8:19; 15:21; [ch. 4:22; 8:55]
29 [h]ch. 8:55; See Matt. 11:27 [i]ch. 6:46; 9:16, 33; [ch. 1:14] [j]See ch. 3:17
30 [k]ver. 44; ch. 10:39; [Matt. 21:46] [l]ch. 8:20 [m]ver. 6
31 [n]ch. 8:30; 10:42; 11:45; 12:11; [ch. 2:23; 12:42; Matt. 21:11] [o]Matt. 12:23
32 [p]ver. 12 [q]ver. 45, 46
33 [r]ch. 12:35; 13:33; 14:19; 16:16-19 [s]ch. 16:5
34 [t]ch. 8:21; 13:33

35 [u][ch. 8:22] [v]James 1:1; 1 Pet. 1:1; [Isa. 11:12; Zeph. 3:10] [w]ch. 12:20 **36** [x]ver. 34 **37** [y]Lev. 23:36; Num. 29:35; Neh. 8:18 [z]Isa. 55:1; See ch. 4:14 [a]See ch. 6:35 **38** [b][Isa. 12:3; Ezek. 47:1] [c]ch. 4:14; [Prov. 18:4] [d]See ch. 4:10 **39** [e]Isa. 44:3; [1 Cor. 12:13; Gal. 3:14] [f]Joel 2:28; Acts 2:16-18; [ch. 1:33; 20:22; Luke 24:49] [g]Acts 2:4, 33 [h]ch. 3:34; Luke 11:13 [i]ch. 14:16, 17; 16:7 **40** [j]See ver. 31 [k]ch. 1:21; 6:14; See Matt. 21:11 **41** [l]ver. 26 [m][ver. 52; ch. 1:46] **42** [n][Ps. 89:3, 4]; See Matt. 1:1 [o]Mic. 5:2; Matt. 2:1, 5; Luke 2:4 [p]1 Sam. 16:1 **43** [q]ch. 9:16; 10:19; [ver. 12] **44** [r]ver. 30

45 [s]The officers then came to the chief priests and Pharisees, who said to them, "Why did you not bring him?" 46 The officers answered, [t]"No one ever spoke like this man!" 47 The Pharisees answered them, [u]"Have you also been deceived? 48 [v]Have any of the authorities or the Pharisees believed in him? 49 But this crowd that does not know the law is accursed." 50 [w]Nicodemus, who had gone to him before, and who was one of them, said to them, 51 [x]"Does our law judge a man without first [y]giving him a hearing and learning what he does?" 52 They replied, [z]"Are you from Galilee too? Search and see that [a]no prophet arises from Galilee."

[THE EARLIEST MANUSCRIPTS DO NOT INCLUDE 7:53–8:11.][1]

The Woman Caught in Adultery

8 53 [[They went each to his own house, 1 but Jesus went to the Mount of Olives. 2 [b]Early in the morning he came again to the temple. All the people came to him, and [c]he sat down and taught them. 3 The scribes and the Pharisees brought a woman who had been caught in adultery, and placing her in the midst 4 they said to him, "Teacher, this woman has been caught in the act of adultery. 5 Now [d]in the Law Moses commanded us [e]to stone such women. So what do you say?" 6 This they said [f]to test him, [g]that they might have some charge to bring against him. Jesus bent down and wrote with his finger on the ground. 7 And as they continued to ask him, he stood up and said to them, [h]"Let him who is without sin among you [i]be the first to throw a stone at her." 8 And once more he bent down and wrote on the ground. 9 But when they heard it, they went away one by one, beginning with the older ones, and Jesus was left alone with the woman standing before him. 10 Jesus stood up and said to her, "Woman, where are they? Has no one condemned you?" 11 She said, "No one, Lord." And Jesus said, [j]"Neither do I condemn you; go, and from now on [k]sin no more."]]

I Am the Light of the World

12 [l]Again Jesus spoke to them, saying, [m]"I am the light of the world. Whoever [n]follows me will not [o]walk in darkness, but will have the light of life." 13 So the Pharisees said to him, [p]"You are bearing witness about yourself; your testimony is not true." 14 Jesus answered, "Even if I do bear witness about myself, [q]my testimony is true, for I know [r]where I came from and [s]where I am going, but [t]you do not know where I come from or where I am going. 15 [u]You judge according to the flesh; [v]I judge no one. 16 Yet even if I do judge, [w]my judgment is true, for [x]it is not I alone who judge, but I and

[1] Some manuscripts do not include 7:53–8:11; others add the passage here or after 7:36 or after 21:25 or after Luke 21:38, with variations in the text

45 [s] ver. 32
46 [t] See Matt. 7:29
47 [u] ver. 12
48 [v] 1 Cor. 1:20, 26; 2:8; [ch. 12:42]
50 [w] ch. 3:1; 19:39
51 [x] Deut. 17:6; 19:15; [Acts 23:3] [y] Deut. 1:16; Prov. 18:13
52 [z] ver. 41 [a] [2 Kgs. 14:25 with Josh. 19:13]

Chapter 8
2 [b] [Luke 21:38] [c] Matt. 5:1; Luke 4:20
5 [d] Lev. 20:10; Deut. 22:22 [e] Deut. 22:24; Ezek. 16:38, 40
6 [f] Matt. 16:1; 19:3; 22:18, 35; Mark 8:11; 10:2; 12:15; Luke 10:25; 11:16 [g] See Luke 11:54
7 [h] Rom. 2:1, 22 [i] Deut. 17:7
11 [j] ver. 15; [ch. 3:17; Luke 12:14] [k] ch. 5:14
12 [l] ch. 7:37, 38 [m] [Ps. 36:9; Isa. 42:6; 49:6; Mal. 4:2]; See ch. 1:4, 9 [n] ch. 12:26; 21:19 [o] See ch. 12:35
13 [p] ch. 5:31
14 [q] [Rev. 3:14] [r] ch. 13:3; 16:28 [s] ver. 21; ch. 7:33 [t] [ch. 7:28; 9:29]
15 [u] ch. 7:24; 1 Sam. 16:7; [Job 10:4] [v] ch. 12:47; [ver. 11]
16 [w] ch. 5:30 [x] ver. 29; ch. 16:32

7:45–52 Nicodemus, who earlier sought out Jesus in the darkness, now seems ready to become his defender. While not actually making declarations of Christ's true status, he at least tries to slow down the plans of Christ's enemies. Nicodemus is not yet ready fully to declare his loyalty to Christ, but there has been movement in his heart that will mature further in its dedication (cf. 19:39–42).

Though the change may come in stages, knowing Jesus ultimately changes everything about us. To borrow some phrases from an old hymn, the gospel "charms our fears" of rejection and "breaks the power" of our addiction to people's approval. For we have, in Christ, the approval of God himself. He is our Father who sings over us (Zeph. 3:17).

8:12–20 At the end of the first day of the Feast of Booths, four golden lamps were lit in the temple courts amid great rejoicing. Singing and celebration, with music and dancing, continued through the nights of the feast, and the entire city was illuminated by the temple lights. It is in this context that Jesus makes his startling claim to be the Light of the World.

Light is a rich Old Testament symbol. It was the first thing God created (Gen. 1:3). During the exodus, the people of God were led in their journey by a pillar of cloud and fire (Ex. 13:21–22). The psalmist taught that "the LORD is my light" (Ps. 27:1). The coming age of the kingdom would be a time when the servant of the Lord would be as "a light for the nations, that my salvation may reach to the end of the earth" (Isa. 49:6), and a time when God himself would be his people's light (Isa. 60:19–22; Rev. 22:5).

Jesus was boldly saying, "The promised day of light has arrived. I am the source of everlasting joy." He is the sun by which we see all things.

the Father[1] who sent me. 17 [y]In your Law it is
written that the testimony of two people is
true. 18 I am the one who bears witness about
myself, and [z]the Father who sent me bears witness about me." 19 They said to him therefore,
"Where is your Father?" Jesus answered, [a]"You
know neither me nor my Father. [b]If you knew
me, you would know my Father also." 20 These
words he spoke in [c]the treasury, as he taught in
the temple; but [d]no one arrested him, because
[e]his hour had not yet come.

21 So he said to them again, [f]"I am going away,
and [g]you will seek me, and [h]you will die in
your sin. Where I am going, you cannot come."
22 So the Jews said, [i]"Will he kill himself, since
he says, 'Where I am going, you cannot come'?"
23 He said to them, [j]"You are from below; I am
from above. [k]You are of this world; [l]I am not
of this world. 24 I told you that you [m]would die
in your sins, for [n]unless you believe that [o]I am
he you will die in your sins." 25 So they said
to him, [p]"Who are you?" Jesus said to them,
"Just what I have been telling you from the
beginning. 26 I have much to say about you
and much to judge, but [q]he who sent me is
true, and I declare [r]to the world [s]what I have
heard from him." 27 They did not understand
that [t]he had been speaking to them about the
Father. 28 So Jesus said to them, "When you
have [u]lifted up the Son of Man, [v]then you will
know that [w]I am he, and that [x]I do nothing on
my own authority, but [y]speak just as the Father
taught me. 29 And [z]he who sent me is with me.
[z]He has not left me alone, for [a]I always do the
things that are pleasing to him." 30 As he was
saying these things, [b]many believed in him.

The Truth Will Set You Free

31 So Jesus said to the Jews who had believed
him, [c]"If you abide in my word, you are truly
my disciples, 32 and you will [d]know the truth,
and the truth [e]will set you free." 33 They
answered him, [f]"We are offspring of Abraham
and have never been enslaved to anyone. How
is it that you say, 'You will become free'?"

34 Jesus answered them, "Truly, truly, I say
to you, [g]everyone who practices sin is a slave[2]
to sin. 35 [h]The slave does not remain in the
house forever; [i]the son remains forever. 36 So
if the Son sets you free, you will be free indeed.
37 I know that you are offspring of Abraham;
yet [j]you seek to kill me because my word finds
no place in you. 38 [k]I speak of what I have seen
with my Father, and you do what you have
heard [l]from your father."

You Are of Your Father the Devil

39 They answered him, [m]"Abraham is our
father." Jesus said to them, [n]"If you were
Abraham's children, you would be doing the
works Abraham did, 40 but now [o]you seek to
kill me, a man who has told you the truth
[p]that I heard from God. This is not what

[1] Some manuscripts *he* [2] Greek *bondservant*; also verse 35

8:21–30 The hostile reaction of the Pharisees to Jesus' words is understandable, but rather than backing down, Jesus intensifies his claims. The accused now becomes the accuser—the witness takes the role of prosecuting attorney. Jesus is from above, they are from below; they are of this world, Jesus is not of this world. They charged Jesus with sin; they will remain in their sins unless they believe on him.

The gospel is an unrelenting assault on graceless religion, on all the ways we try to avoid grace. It is also a powerful demonstration of the sovereignty of God. In that very unlikely moment, many believed in Jesus. God can save anyone, anytime, anywhere. He is not constrained by human intuitions about who is really "save-able." Grace confounds our law-saturated, self-accomplishing expectations of what activates divine mercy.

8:31–59 Jesus promises a freedom that no one else can give based on truth that he alone possesses. As the Messiah, he has come to set prisoners free (Luke 4:16–21; Isa. 61:1–3). True freedom can be found only in the "right paternity": not everyone who claims Abraham as their father has God as their Father, "for not all who are descended from Israel belong to Israel" (Rom. 9:6). None can claim God as their Father who won't have his Son as their Savior.

If our spiritual genealogy includes only our earthly heritage (as was true of the "children of Abraham" in this passage), we may be religious, but we are still spiritual orphans. True spiritual heritage requires a connection to one who existed long before

17 [y]See Num. 35:30
18 [z]ch. 5:37
19 [a]ver. 55; ch. 16:3 [b]ch. 14:7
20 [c]See Matt. 27:6 [d]ch. 7:30 [e]ch. 7:8
21 [f]ch. 14:28; [ch. 14:2, 3; 16:7] [g]See ch. 7:34 [h]ver. 24; Ezek. 3:18; 33:8
22 [i][ch. 7:35]
23 [j][ver. 44; ch. 3:31] [k]1 John 4:5 [l]ch. 17:14, 16
24 [m]ver. 21 [n]ch. 16:9 [o]Mark 13:6; Luke 21:8
25 [p][ch. 1:19]
26 [q]ch. 3:33; 7:28; Rom. 3:4 [r][ch. 18:20] [s]ver. 40; ch. 15:15; [ch. 3:32; Rev. 1:1]
27 [t]ver. 18, 26
28 [u]ch. 3:14; 12:32, 34 [v][ch. 16:8-11] [w]See ver. 24 [x]See ch. 5:30 [y]See ch. 7:16
29 [z]ver. 16; ch. 16:32; Acts 10:38; See ch. 10:38 [a]ch. 4:34; 5:30; 6:38; [1 John 3:22]
30 [b]See ch. 7:31
31 [c]ch. 15:7, 8; 2 John 9
32 [d]2 John 1 [e]ver. 36; Rom. 6:18, 22; 8:2; 1 Cor. 7:22; 2 Cor. 3:17; Gal. 5:1, 13; James 1:25; 2:12; 1 Pet. 2:16

33 [f]ver. 37, 39; Matt. 3:9; [Luke 19:9; Rom. 9:7] **34** [g]Rom. 6:16-20; Titus 3:3; 2 Pet. 2:19 **35** [h]Gen. 21:10; Gal. 4:30 [i]Luke 15:31 **37** [j]ver. 40; See ch. 7:1
38 [k]ch. 3:32; 5:19; 6:46 [l]ver. 41, 44 **39** [m]ver. 33, 56 [n][Gal. 3:7, 9] **40** [o]ver. 37 [p]ver. 26

Abraham did. 41 You are doing the works
your father did." They said to him, [q]"We were
not born of sexual immorality. We have [r]one
Father—even God." 42 Jesus said to them, [s]"If
God were your Father, you would love me, for
[t]I came from God and [u]I am here. [v]I came not
of my own accord, but [w]he sent me. 43 [x]Why do
you not understand what I say? It is because
you cannot [y]bear to hear my word. 44 [z]You are
of your father the devil, and your will is to
do your father's desires. [a]He was a murderer
from the beginning, and [b]does not stand in
the truth, because there is no truth in him.
[c]When he lies, he speaks out of his own character, for he is a liar and the father of lies. 45 But
because I tell the truth, you do not believe
me. 46 Which one of you convicts me of sin?
If I tell the truth, why do you not believe me?
47 [d]Whoever is of God hears the words of God.
[e]The reason why you do not hear them is that
[f]you are not of God."

Before Abraham Was, I Am

48 The Jews answered him, "Are we not right
in saying that you are a Samaritan and [g]have
a demon?" 49 Jesus answered, "I do not have a
demon, but [h]I honor my Father, and you dishonor me. 50 Yet [i]I do not seek my own glory;
there is One who seeks it, and he is the judge.
51 Truly, truly, [j]I say to you, if anyone keeps my
word, he will never [k]see death." 52 The Jews
said to him, "Now we know that you have a
demon! [l]Abraham died, as did the prophets,
yet [m]you say, 'If anyone keeps my word, he will
never [n]taste death.' 53 [o]Are you greater than our
father Abraham, who died? And the prophets
died! Who do you make yourself out to be?"
54 Jesus answered, [p]"If I glorify myself, my
glory is nothing. [q]It is my Father who glorifies me, [r]of whom you say, 'He is our God.'[1]
55 But [s]you have not known him. [t]I know
him. If I were to say that I do not know him,
I would be [u]a liar [v]like you, but I do know him
and I keep his word. 56 [w]Your father Abraham
[x]rejoiced [y]that he would see my day. [z]He saw it
and was glad." 57 So the Jews said to him, "You
are not yet fifty years old, and have you seen
Abraham?"[2] 58 Jesus said to them, "Truly, truly,
I say to you, before Abraham was, [a]I am." 59 So
[b]they picked up stones to throw at him, but
Jesus hid himself and went out of the temple.

Jesus Heals a Man Born Blind

9 As he passed by, he saw a man blind
from birth. 2 And his disciples asked
him, [c]"Rabbi, [d]who sinned, [e]this man or
[f]his parents, that he was born blind?" 3 Jesus
answered, "It was not that this man sinned,
or his parents, but [g]that the works of God
might be displayed in him. 4 We must [h]work

[1] Some manuscripts *your God* [2] Some manuscripts *has Abraham seen you?*

41 [q] [Hos. 2:4] [r] Deut. 32:6; Isa. 63:16; 64:8; [ver. 47]
42 [s] [1 John 5:1] [t] 1 John 5:20; [Heb. 10:9] [u] ch. 16:28; 17:8 [v] ch. 7:28 [w] See ch. 3:17
43 [x] ch. 7:17 [y] Jer. 6:10; [1 Cor. 2:14]
44 [z] 1 John 3:8, 12; [ver. 23]; See Matt. 13:38 [a] Gen. 4:8, 9; 1 John 3:12, 15; [Rom. 5:12] [b] [1 John 2:4] [c] Gen. 3:4; 2 Cor. 11:3; Rev. 12:9
47 [d] [ch. 18:37; 1 John 4:6] [e] [ch. 10:26] [f] [ver. 41]
48 [g] See ch. 7:20
49 [h] ch. 5:23; [ch. 7:18]
50 [i] ver. 54; ch. 5:41
51 [j] ch. 5:24; 11:26 [k] See Luke 2:26
52 [l] [Zech. 1:5] [m] ver. 51 [n] Matt. 16:28; Heb. 2:9
53 [o] [ch. 4:12]
54 [p] ver. 50 [q] ch. 13:32; 17:1; Acts 3:13; Heb. 5:5; 2 Pet. 1:17 [r] ver. 41
55 [s] ver. 19; ch. 7:28 [t] ch. 7:29; See Matt. 11:27 [u] 1 John 1:6 [v] ver. 44
56 [w] ver. 39 [x] See Matt. 13:17 [y] Luke 17:22 [z] [Heb. 11:13]
58 [a] See Ex. 3:14
59 [b] ch. 10:31

Chapter 9
2 [c] See ch. 1:38 [d] [Luke 13:2, 4] [e] [ver. 34] [f] Ex. 20:5 **3** [g] [ch. 11:4] **4** [h] See ch. 4:34

Abraham, namely, Jesus: "before Abraham was, I am" (John 8:58). Only through the gospel can we be rescued from the dominion of darkness (Col. 1:13), where Satan is father, and be brought into the family of God, where we are given the full rights and delights of the children of God (John 1:12; Gal. 4:5; 1 John 3:1–3).

9:1–7 Before Jesus healed the blind man, he challenged the prevailing notion that there is a one-to-one correlation between our physical maladies and our character. We live in a fallen world where even good people experience terrible loss and pain. But though the gospel of grace doesn't immediately negate the reality of painful consequences resulting from poor choices or a corrupted creation (Gal. 6:8; Rom. 8:22–23), it does place us in a larger story. We are not blind to our world's present brokenness, nor are we fatalists about our future. Rather, we are followers of Jesus, graciously incorporated into his redeeming purposes for our world.

Instead of asking, "Why did this happen to me? Who's to blame?" we begin to ask, "Where is God in this situation? What is he up to? How may his glory ultimately shine through this?" Grace leads us to ask more vertical questions and fewer horizontal ones. Only the gospel of eternal purposes and hope beyond this world can enable us to accept suffering as a normal part of the Christian life. For the ultimate suffering, condemnation, and separation from the Father in hell has been undergone by Jesus in our place. All current suffering in the lives of those who are in Christ can therefore only be by the loving hand of a caring Father, who is training us to walk with him—and enabling others touched by our lives to do so also, as they walk through this broken world with us.

the works of him who sent me [i]while it is day; night is coming, when no one can work. 5 As long as I am in the world, [j]I am the light of the world." 6 Having said these things, [k]he spit on the ground and made mud with the saliva. [l]Then he anointed the man's eyes with the mud 7 and said to him, "Go, wash in [m]the pool of Siloam" (which means Sent). So he went and washed and [n]came back seeing.

8 The neighbors and those who had seen him before as a beggar were saying, [o]"Is this not the man who used to sit and beg?" 9 Some said, "It is he." Others said, "No, but he is like him." He kept saying, "I am the man." 10 So they said to him, "Then how were your eyes opened?" 11 He answered, [p]"The man called Jesus made mud and anointed my eyes and said to me, 'Go to Siloam and wash.' So I went and washed and received my sight." 12 They said to him, "Where is he?" He said, "I do not know."

13 They brought to the Pharisees the man who had formerly been blind. 14 [q]Now it was a Sabbath day when Jesus made the mud and opened his eyes. 15 [r]So the Pharisees again asked him how he had received his sight. And he said to them, "He put mud on my eyes, and I washed, and I see." 16 Some of the Pharisees said, "This man is not [s]from God, [t]for he does not keep the Sabbath." But others said, [u]"How can a man who is a sinner do such signs?" And [v]there was a division among them. 17 So they said again to the blind man, "What do you say about him, since he has opened your eyes?" He said, [w]"He is a prophet."

18 [x]The Jews[1] did not believe that he had been blind and had received his sight, until they called the parents of the man who had received his sight 19 and asked them, "Is this your son, who you say was born blind? How then does he now see?" 20 His parents answered, "We know that this is our son and that he was born blind. 21 But how he now sees we do not know, nor do we know who opened his eyes. Ask him; he is of age. He will speak for himself." 22 (His parents said these things [y]because they feared the Jews, for [z]the Jews had already agreed that if anyone should [a]confess Jesus[2] to be Christ, [b]he was to be put out of the synagogue.) 23 Therefore his parents said, [c]"He is of age; ask him."

24 So for the second time they called the man who had been blind and said to him, [d]"Give glory to God. We know that [e]this man is a sinner." 25 He answered, "Whether he is a sinner I do not know. One thing I do know, that though I [f]was blind, now I see." 26 They said to him, "What did he do to you? How did he open your eyes?" 27 He answered them, [g]"I have told you already, and you would not listen. Why do you want to hear it again? Do you also want to become his disciples?" 28 And they reviled him, saying, "You are his disciple, but [h]we are disciples of Moses. 29 We know that God has spoken to Moses, but as for this man, [i]we do

[1] Greek *Ioudaioi* probably refers here to Jewish religious leaders, and others under their influence, in that time; also verse 22 [2] Greek *him*

9:8–12 He who said, "Let there be light!" now says, "Let there be sight!" The spit and clay used in this miracle echo the elements of the first creation (Genesis 1–2). Even more profoundly, they also announce that, in Jesus, the new creation order has arrived. He who created man from dust now uses dust to restore him. The "sent one" (Jesus), sent the healed one to the pool of "Sent" (Siloam). He who was sent into the world to lift the curse of sin is here. Superstition is trumped by the truly supernatural, and the saved are sent in witness.

Jesus' miracles are reminders of the day when there was no brokenness (Eden) and of the firstfruits of the day when all brokenness will be removed forever (the new heaven and new earth; Rev. 21:1). Miracles are not primarily for our comfort but for God's glory—for declaring the power present in and the praise due to the person and work of Jesus.

9:13–34 The conversation between the healed man and the Pharisees is filled with gospel irony. He who sees for the first time in his life reveals the long-standing blindness of the Pharisees. They only see the law, but the healed man sees the Messiah, to whom the law points. In their hubris, the Pharisees can only boast about Moses; in his humility, the healed man only boasts about Jesus. The Pharisees charge the healed man with walking in the darkness of sin; but he sees the Light of the World—the Son who made the sun and everything else. The Pharisees excommunicated him from the life of the temple; Jesus made him a living stone (1 Pet. 2:4–12) in the only true and lasting temple—Christ himself (John 2:19–22; Rev. 21:22).

4 [i] ch. 11:9; 12:35; [Rom. 13:12; Gal. 6:10]
5 [j] See ch. 1:4, 5, 9; 8:12
6 [k] Mark 7:33; 8:23 [l] See Matt. 9:29
7 [m] Luke 13:4 [n] ch. 11:37
8 [o] [Acts 3:2, 10]
11 [p] ver. 6, 7
14 [q] ch. 5:9
15 [r] ver. 10
16 [s] See ch. 7:29 [t] See Matt. 12:2 [u] ver. 33 [v] ch. 7:43; 10:19
17 [w] See ch. 4:19; 6:14
18 [x] ver. 22; [ver. 13]
22 [y] See ch. 7:13 [z] [ch. 7:45-52] [a] [Rom. 10:9] [b] ch. 12:42; 16:2
23 [c] ver. 21
24 [d] Josh. 7:19; Jer. 13:16; [1 Sam. 6:5; Isa. 42:12; Acts 12:23] [e] ver. 16
25 [f] ver. 18, 24
27 [g] ver. 15
28 [h] [ch. 5:45]
29 [i] See ch. 8:14

not know where he comes from.” 30 The man
answered, “Why, this is [j]an amazing thing!
[k]You do not know where he comes from, and
yet he opened my eyes. 31 We know that [l]God
does not listen to sinners, but [m]if anyone is a
worshiper of God and does his will, God listens to him. 32 Never since the world began has
it been heard that anyone opened the eyes of a
man born blind. 33 [n]If this man were not from
God, he could do nothing.” 34 They answered
him, [o]“You were born in utter sin, and would
you teach us?” And they [p]cast him out.

35 Jesus heard that they had cast him out, and
having found him he said, “Do you believe in
[q]the Son of Man?”[1] 36 He answered, [r]“And who
is he, sir, that I may believe in him?” 37 Jesus
said to him, “You have seen him, and [s]it is
he who is speaking to you.” 38 He said, “Lord,
I believe,” and he worshiped him. 39 Jesus said,
[t]“For judgment I came into this world, [u]that
those who do not see may see, and [v]those
who see may become blind.” 40 Some of the
Pharisees near him heard these things, and
said to him, [w]“Are we also blind?” 41 Jesus said
to them, “If you were blind, [x]you would have
no guilt;[2] but now that you say, ‘We see,’ your
guilt remains.

I Am the Good Shepherd

10 “Truly, truly, I say to you, he who does
not enter the sheepfold by the door but
climbs in by another way, that man is a thief
and a robber. 2 But he who enters by the door
is the shepherd of the sheep. 3 To him the gatekeeper opens. The sheep hear his voice, and he
calls his own sheep by name and leads them
out. 4 When he has brought out all his own, he
goes before them, and the sheep follow him,
for they know his voice. 5 [y]A stranger they will
not follow, but they will flee from him, for
they do not know the voice of strangers.” 6 This
figure of speech Jesus [z]used with them, but
they [a]did not understand what he was saying
to them.

7 So Jesus again said to them, “Truly, truly,
I say to you, [b]I am the door of the sheep. 8 All
who came before me are thieves and robbers,
but the sheep did not listen to them. 9 I am
the door. If anyone enters by me, [c]he will be
saved and will go in and out and [d]find pasture.

[1] Some manuscripts *the Son of God* [2] Greek *you would not have sin*

30 [j][ch. 12:37] [k][ch. 3:10]
31 [l]Job 27:9; Ps. 66:18; Prov. 28:9 [m]Ps. 34:15, 16; 145:19; Prov. 15:20; [James 5:16]
33 [n]ver. 16; [ch. 1:21; 3:2]
34 [o][ver. 2] [p][ver. 22]
35 [q]ch. 10:36
36 [r][Rom. 10:14]
37 [s]ch. 4:26
39 [t]See ch. 5:22 [u][Matt. 11:25; Luke 4:18] [v][Matt. 9:13; 13:13; Mark 4:12; 2 Cor. 2:16]
40 [w]Rom. 2:19
41 [x]ch. 15:22, 24; [ch. 19:11; 1 John 1:8]

Chapter 10
5 [y][ver. 12, 13]
6 [z]ch. 9:40 [a]See Mark 9:32
7 [b]ver. 9; [ch. 14:6; Eph. 2:18]
9 [c][ch. 5:34] [d]Ps. 23:2; Ezek. 34:14

9:35–41 The whole of the Christian life consists of getting to know Jesus better and better. Jesus sought out the healed man in order to confirm his saving faith. Once again for John, the prevailing question in his Gospel, and in our lives, is, “Who is Jesus?” Jesus is the promised Son of Man (Dan. 7:13–14; Matt. 26:64), who one day will rule over all nations (Rev. 11:15). The gifts of God must lead us to the true and final gift of God: Jesus himself.

10:1–21 The imagery of sheep, shepherd, and sheepfold was a central part of Israel’s heritage—both as a Bedouin people and, more significantly, as the people of God (Psalm 23). By choosing this symbol, Jesus accomplished two things. He drew a strong contrast between himself and the shepherds of Israel. He also declared himself to be the messianic Shepherd for whom Israel hoped (Zech. 13:7–9).

The sheepfold was commonly attached to the shepherd’s home. Thus, to enter the sheepfold was to come home. As the “door of the sheep,” Jesus is the only means of coming home to God—of becoming a member of the household of faith. Jesus is the merciful Shepherd who provides shelter, security, and pasture for his beloved sheep. The shepherds who preceded him in Israel’s history were mercenaries—fleeing the sheep quickly when under threat; and fleecing the sheep regularly for personal gain.

Jesus is the Good Shepherd, whose “goodness” cannot be overstated. Like David, the shepherd-king, Jesus risks his life to care for his sheep (cf. 1 Sam. 17:34–37). He knows his flock by name, and each of his sheep recognize and love his voice. Though the gospel is not a private story, it is most definitely a personal one. Jesus delights in his whole flock, and in each one of his sheep. Jesus’ flock and sheepfold is enormous, exceeding the borders of Israel. He has come for lost sheep from every tribe, language, people, and nation (Rev. 5:9).

But as the promised King, the greater David, Jesus literally laid down his life for the sheep on the cross. What a glorious paradox: The Good Shepherd became the Lamb of God to take away the sin of the world. Even throughout eternity, Jesus will be known as the Lamb who shepherds his people and guides them to “springs of living water” (Rev. 7:17).

10 The thief comes only to steal and [e]kill and
destroy. I came that they may have life and
have it abundantly. 11 [f]I am the good shepherd.
The good shepherd [g]lays down his life for the
sheep. 12 He who is [h]a hired hand and not a
shepherd, who does not own the sheep, sees
the wolf coming and [i]leaves the sheep and
flees, and the wolf snatches them and [j]scatters
them. 13 He flees because [k]he is a hired hand
and [l]cares nothing for the sheep. 14 [m]I am the
good shepherd. [n]I know my own and [o]my own
know me, 15 [p]just as the Father knows me and
I know the Father; and [q]I lay down my life
for the sheep. 16 And [r]I have other sheep that
are not of this fold. [s]I must bring them also,
and [t]they will listen to my voice. So there will
be [u]one flock, [v]one shepherd. 17 [w]For this reason the Father loves me, [x]because [y]I lay down
my life that I may take it up again. 18 [z]No one
takes it from me, but [y]I lay it down [a]of my
own accord. I have authority to lay it down,
and [b]I have authority to take it up again. [c]This
charge I have received from my Father."

19 [d]There was again a division among the
Jews because of these words. 20 Many of them
said, [e]"He has a demon, and [f]is insane; why
listen to him?" 21 Others said, "These are not
the words of one who is oppressed by a demon.
[g]Can a demon open the eyes of the blind?"

I and the Father Are One

22 At that time the Feast of Dedication took
place at Jerusalem. It was winter, 23 and Jesus
was walking in the temple, [h]in the colonnade
of Solomon. 24 So the Jews gathered around
him and said to him, "How long will you keep
us in suspense? If you are [i]the Christ, [j]tell us
plainly." 25 Jesus answered them, "I told you,
and you do not believe. [k]The works that I do
[l]in my Father's name bear witness about me,
26 but [m]you do not believe because you are not
among my sheep. 27 [n]My sheep hear my voice,
and I know them, and they follow me. 28 [o]I give
them eternal life, and [p]they will never perish,
and [q]no one will snatch them out of my hand.
29 My Father, [r]who has given them to me,[1] [s]is
greater than all, and no one is able to snatch
them out of [t]the Father's hand. 30 [u]I and the
Father are one."

31 [v]The Jews picked up stones again to stone
him. 32 Jesus answered them, "I have shown
you many good works from the Father; for
which of them are you going to stone me?"
33 The Jews answered him, "It is not for a good
work that we are going to stone you but [w]for
blasphemy, because you, being a man, [x]make
yourself God." 34 Jesus answered them, "Is
it not written in [y]your Law, [z]'I said, you are
gods'? 35 If he called them gods to whom the
word of God came—and Scripture cannot be
[a]broken— 36 do you say of him whom [b]the
Father consecrated and [c]sent into the world,
'You are blaspheming,' because [d]I said, 'I am
the Son of God'? 37 [e]If I am not doing the works
of my Father, then do not believe me; 38 but if
I do them, [f]even though you do not believe
me, believe the works, that you may know and
understand that [g]the Father is in me and I am
in the Father." 39 [h]Again they sought to arrest
him, but he escaped from their hands.

40 He went away again across the Jordan to
the place [i]where John had been baptizing at
first, and there he remained. 41 And many came
to him. And they said, "John did no sign, but
[j]everything that John said about this man was
true." 42 And [k]many believed in him there.

[1] Some manuscripts *What my Father has given to me*

10:22–41 The Lamb of God is God the Lamb. Could Jesus have been any more explicit about his identity and purpose as the Messiah? Apparently many Jews still felt he was veiling his identity. But the issue wasn't one of information but of illumination. Jesus' sheep hear his voice. They understand him because they know him.

But more glorious than knowing Jesus is being known *by* Jesus (Gal. 4:9). To be known by Jesus is to be held secure by the grip of his grace. No one can snatch believers from Jesus' hand or from the Father's hand. Why? Because Jesus and the Father are one—they are both divine, acting with power and purpose that human forces cannot negate. This is an affirmation both of Jesus' deity and of the biblical doctrine of the Trinity. The Jews certainly took it as such, because they wanted to stone Jesus for blasphemy.

10 [e][Jer. 23:1; Ezek. 34:3] **11** [f]Isa. 40:11; Ezek. 34:12, 23; 37:24; Zech. 13:7; Heb. 13:20; 1 Pet. 2:25; 5:4; [ch. 21:15-17; Ps. 23; Rev. 7:17] [g]ver. 15, 17; ch. 15:13; 1 John 3:16; [Matt. 20:28; Mark 10:45] **12** [h][Ezek. 34:2-6] [i]Zech. 11:17; 13:7 [j][Jer. 23:1-3] **13** [k][1 Pet. 5:2] [l]Zech. 11:16 **14** [m]See ver. 11 [n]ver. 27; Nah. 1:7; 2 Tim. 2:19 [o]ver. 4 **15** [p]See Matt. 11:27 [q]See ver. 11 **16** [r]Isa. 56:8 [s][Ezek. 34:11-13; Matt. 8:11, 12; Eph. 2:13-18; 1 Pet. 2:25] [t]ch. 5:25; 18:37; [Acts 28:28] [u][ch. 11:52; 12:32; 17:11, 21, 22] [v]Ezek. 34:23; 37:24 **17** [w]Phil. 2:9; See ch. 5:20 [x]Isa. 53:7, 8, 12; Heb. 2:9 [y]ver. 11 **18** [z][Matt. 26:53] [y][See ver. 17 above] [a][ch. 5:30] [b]ch. 2:19; [Phil. 2:7] [c]ch. 12:49; 14:31; 15:10 **19** [d]ch. 7:43; 9:16 **20** [e]See ch. 7:20 [f][Mark 3:21] **21** [g][Ex. 4:11; Ps. 146:8]; See ch. 9:33 **23** [h]Acts 3:11; 5:12 **24** [i]ch. 1:41 [j]Matt. 26:63; Luke 22:67 **25** [k]ver. 38; See ch. 5:36 [l]See ch. 5:43 **26** [m][ch. 8:47] **27** [n]ver. 14, 16 **28** [o][1 John 2:25; 5:11] [p]ch. 17:12; 18:9 [q]ch. 6:37 **29** [r]ch. 6:37; 17:2 [s][ch. 14:28] [t][Deut. 32:39; Isa. 49:2; 51:16] **30** [u]ch. 17:11, 22; [ch. 5:19; 14:9] **31** [v]ch. 8:59 **33** [w]See Lev. 24:16; Matt. 9:3 [x]ch. 5:18 **34** [y][ch. 12:34; 15:25; 1 Cor. 14:21] [z]Cited from Ps. 82:6 **35** [a][Matt. 5:17, 19] **36** [b][ch. 6:27] [c]See ch. 3:17 [d]ch. 5:17, 18; [ver. 30] **37** [e]ch. 15:24 **38** [f]ver. 25; [ch. 14:11] [g]ch. 14:10, 11, 20; 17:21, 23; [ch. 8:29] **39** [h]ch. 7:30, 44 **40** [i]ch. 1:28 **41** [j]ch. 1:7, 29-34; 3:27-30; 5:33 **42** [k]See ch. 7:31

The Death of Lazarus

11 Now a certain man was ill, Lazarus of Bethany, the village of [l]Mary and her sister Martha. 2 [m]It was Mary who anointed the Lord with ointment and wiped his feet with her hair, whose brother Lazarus was ill. 3 So the sisters sent to him, saying, "Lord, [n]he whom you love is ill." 4 But when Jesus heard it he said, [o]"This illness does not lead to death. It is for [p]the glory of God, so that the Son of God may be glorified through it."

5 Now [q]Jesus loved Martha and her sister and Lazarus. 6 So, when he heard that Lazarus[1] was ill, [r]he stayed two days longer in the place where he was. 7 Then after this he said to the disciples, [s]"Let us go to Judea again." 8 The disciples said to him, [t]"Rabbi, [u]the Jews were just now seeking to stone you, and are you going there again?" 9 Jesus answered, [v]"Are there not twelve hours in the day? [w]If anyone walks in the day, he does not stumble, because he sees the light of this world. 10 But [x]if anyone walks in the night, he stumbles, because the light is not [x]in him." 11 After saying these things, he said to them, "Our friend Lazarus [y]has fallen asleep, but I go to awaken him." 12 The disciples said to him, "Lord, if he has fallen asleep, he will recover." 13 Now Jesus had spoken of his death, but they thought that he meant taking rest in sleep. 14 Then Jesus told them plainly, "Lazarus has died, 15 and for your sake I am glad that I was not there, so that you may believe. But let us go to him." 16 [z]So Thomas, called the Twin,[2] said to his fellow disciples, "Let us also go, [a]that we may die with him."

I Am the Resurrection and the Life

17 Now when Jesus came, he found that Lazarus had already been in the tomb [b]four days. 18 Bethany was near Jerusalem, about two miles[3] off, 19 and many of the Jews had come to Martha and Mary [c]to console them concerning their brother. 20 [d]So when Martha heard that Jesus was coming, she went and met him, but Mary remained seated in the house. 21 Martha said to [e]Jesus, "Lord, [f]if you had been here, my brother would not have died. 22 But even now I know that whatever you ask from God, [g]God will give you." 23 Jesus said to her, "Your brother will rise again." 24 [h]Martha said to him, "I know that he will rise again in [i]the resurrection on the last day." 25 Jesus said to her, [j]"I am the resurrection and [k]the life.[4] Whoever believes in me, [l]though he die, [m]yet shall he live, 26 and everyone who lives and believes in me [n]shall never die. Do you believe this?" 27 She said to him, "Yes, Lord; [o]I believe that [p]you are the Christ, the Son of God, [q]who is coming into the world."

[1] Greek *he*; also verse 17 [2] Greek *Didymus* [3] Greek *fifteen stadia*; a *stadion* was about 607 feet or 185 meters [4] Some manuscripts omit *and the life*

Chapter 11
1 [l]See Luke 10:38, 39
2 [m]ch. 12:3
3 [n]ver. 5, 11, 36
4 [o][ver. 11; Matt. 9:24] [p]ver. 40; [ch. 9:3; 13:31]
5 [q]ver. 3
6 [r][ch. 2:4; 7:6, 8]
7 [s]ch. 10:40
8 [t]See ch. 1:38 [u]ch. 8:59; 10:31
9 [v][Luke 13:33] [w]See ch. 9:4; 1 John 2:10
10 [x]Jer. 13:16
11 [y]See Matt. 27:52
16 [z]ch. 14:5; 20:24, 26-28; 21:2; Matt. 10:3; Mark 3:18; Luke 6:15; Acts 1:13 [a][ch. 13:37]
17 [b]ver. 39
19 [c]ver. 31; Job 2:11
20 [d][Luke 10:38, 39]
21 [e]ver. 32 [f][ver. 37]
22 [g][ver. 42; ch. 9:31]
24 [h][ver. 39] [i]ch. 5:29; Luke 14:14; See ch. 6:39
25 [j][ch. 5:21; 6:40, 44; 1 Cor. 15:21] [k]ch. 14:6; [ch. 6:57; Col. 3:4]; See ch. 1:4 [l][ch. 12:25] [m]See ch. 3:36
26 [n]ch. 6:50, 51; 8:51
27 [o]ch. 6:69; 20:31; 1 John 5:1, 5; [ch. 8:24; 13:19; 1 John 4:16] [p]Matt. 16:16 [q]ch. 6:14; See Matt. 11:3

11:1–16 Jesus enjoyed a special relationship with Lazarus and his two sisters, Mary and Martha. This family gave him welcome and oasis in a world of conflict and escalating hostility (cf. Luke 10:38–42). Perhaps it was precisely because of Jesus' great love for this family that he entrusted to them a very difficult story, a hard providence: the sickness and death of Lazarus.

The gospel is a story of our God doing all things well, not all things easily. His name is Abba Father, but this does not mean that he leads his children in a life of complacent ease and comfort. Indeed, upon hearing about Lazarus's sickness, Jesus waited two days longer before responding—apparently so that his compassion could be revealed by a more glorious expression of divine power, expressed according to divine wisdom and timing. God's ways are not our ways (Isa. 55:8). They are much better.

11:17–27 Jesus delayed coming to his beloved friends until he was certain Lazarus was dead. Martha and Mary were incredulous about Jesus' decision to wait. "Lord, if you had been here . . ." (v. 21). The discipline of delay is one of the hardest lessons we must learn, as followers of Jesus, especially when it is God who does the delaying. Only grace can enable us to accept God's rich vocabulary of answers to our earnest prayers—"yes," "no," "not yet," or even "yes, but it's going to feel like no"—because we trust that he "is able to do far more abundantly than all that we ask or think" (Eph. 3:20).

The more deeply we know and walk with Jesus, the more readily we accept God's glory as our greatest good, even when it feels like such a momentary bad. As "the resurrection and the life," Jesus is always writing better stories than we could ever pen. Martha and Mary would soon find this to be true.

Jesus Weeps

28 When she had said this, she went and
called her sister Mary, saying in private, [r]"The
Teacher is here and is calling for you." 29 And
when she heard it, she rose quickly and went
to him. 30 Now Jesus had not yet come into the
village, but was still in the place where Martha
had met him. 31 When the Jews [s]who were with
her in the house, consoling her, saw Mary rise
quickly and go out, they followed her, supposing that she was going to the tomb to weep
there. 32 Now when Mary came to where Jesus
was and saw him, she fell at his feet, saying to
him, [t]"Lord, if you had been here, my brother
would not have died." 33 When Jesus saw her
weeping, and the Jews who had come with
her also weeping, he [u]was deeply moved[1] in
his spirit and [v]greatly troubled. 34 And he said,
"Where have you laid him?" They said to him,
"Lord, come and see." 35 [w]Jesus wept. 36 So the
Jews said, "See [x]how he loved him!" 37 But some
of them said, "Could not he [y]who opened the
eyes of the blind man [z]also have kept this man
from dying?"

Jesus Raises Lazarus

38 Then Jesus, [a]deeply moved again, came
to the tomb. It was [b]a cave, and [c]a stone lay
against it. 39 Jesus said, "Take away the stone."
Martha, the sister of the dead man, said to
him, "Lord, by this time there will be an odor,
for [d]he has been dead four days." 40 Jesus said
to her, [e]"Did I not tell you that if you believed
you would see [f]the glory of God?" 41 So they
took away the stone. And Jesus [g]lifted up his
eyes and said, "Father, I thank you that you
have heard me. 42 [h]I knew that you always hear
me, but I said this [i]on account of the people
standing around, [j]that they may believe that
you sent me." 43 When he had said these things,
he cried out with a loud voice, "Lazarus, come
out." 44 [k]The man who had died came out, [l]his
hands and feet bound with linen strips, and
[m]his face wrapped with a cloth. Jesus said to
them, "Unbind him, and let him go."

The Plot to Kill Jesus

45 [n]Many of the Jews therefore, [o]who had
come with Mary and [p]had seen what he did,
believed in him, 46 but some of them went to
the Pharisees and told them what Jesus had
done. 47 So the chief priests and the Pharisees
[q]gathered [r]the council and said, [s]"What are
we to do? For this man performs many signs.
48 If we let him go on like this, everyone will
believe in him, and [t]the Romans will come
and take away both our [u]place and our nation."
49 But one of them, [v]Caiaphas, [w]who was high

[1] Or *was indignant*; also verse 38

11:28–37 Jesus identifies with us in our pain and loss. He comes to us in our weakness and brokenness. Though he knew he was about to raise Lazarus from the dead, Jesus wept when he saw the tears of Mary and her companions. This is Jesus being truly human. As God incarnate, Jesus shows us what he, as God, created man to be—a whole-hearted lover of God and a compassionate lover of fellow image-bearers—summarized in the two great commandments (Matt. 22:34–40).

But as the incarnate God, Jesus' tears in front of Lazarus's tomb are of a different order. This is Jesus feeling the weight of the fall—the violation and disintegration of the way things were meant to be. His holy tears are those of the Creator grieving over the forfeiture of beauty through the intrusion of sin and death. Once again, in the incarnate Lord, we see the heart of the Lamb who would offer his life to overcome our sin and death.

11:38–44 The death and resurrection of Lazarus were a precursor of Jesus' impending death and resurrection. Jesus had already spoken of the day when "all who are in the tombs will hear his voice and come out" (5:28–29). Here we are given a "preview of coming attractions." The apostle Paul spells out the vital connection between Jesus' bodily resurrection and ours (1 Cor. 15:12–23). If the dead are not raised, Jesus wasn't raised, but *if* Jesus was raised, we too shall be raised. The real loser in view is death itself, and more expressly Satan, who holds the power of death (Heb. 2:14). The resurrection we presently enjoy through our union with Christ (Eph. 2:4–7; Col. 3:1) will one day segue into the resurrection of our bodies.

11:45–57 Here is another example of the use of irony in John's Gospel (cf. note on 9:13–34). Caiaphas, the high priest, unwittingly prophesied that Jesus' death would be a vicarious, substitutionary atonement. The God of all grace is sovereignly at work,

28 [r] Matt. 26:18; Mark 14:14; Luke 22:11; See ch. 13:13
31 [s] ver. 19
32 [t] ver. 21
33 [u] ver. 38; Mark 14:5 (Gk.) [v] ch. 12:27; 13:21
35 [w] [Luke 19:41]
36 [x] ver. 3
37 [y] ch. 9:6, 7 [z] [ver. 21, 32]
38 [a] ver. 33 [b] Isa. 22:16 [c] ch. 20:1; Matt. 27:60; Mark 15:46; Luke 24:2
39 [d] ver. 17
40 [e] ver. 25, 26 [f] ver. 4; [Rom. 6:4]
41 [g] ch. 17:1
42 [h] [ver. 22; Matt. 26:53] [i] ch. 12:29, 30 [j] ch. 17:8, 21; See ch. 3:17
44 [k] ch. 5:28, 29 [l] ch. 19:40 [m] [ch. 20:7]
45 [n] ch. 12:11; [Acts 9:42] [o] ver. 19 [p] ch. 2:23
47 [q] See Matt. 26:3 [r] See Matt. 5:22 [s] ch. 12:19; [Acts 4:16]
48 [t] [ch. 6:15; 18:36, 37] [u] Acts 21:28
49 [v] See Matt. 26:3 [w] ver. 51; ch. 18:13

priest that year, said to them, "You know nothing at all. 50 Nor do you understand that [x]it is
better for you that one man should die for the
people, not that the whole nation should perish." 51 He did not say this of his own accord,
but [y]being high priest that year [z]he prophesied
that Jesus would die for the nation, 52 and [a]not
for the nation only, but also [b]to gather into one
the children of God who are scattered abroad.
53 So from that day on they [c]made plans to put
him to death.

54 Jesus therefore [d]no longer walked openly
among the Jews, but went from there to the
region near the wilderness, to a town called
Ephraim, and there he stayed with the disciples.
55 Now [e]the Passover of the Jews was at
hand, and [f]many went up from the country
to Jerusalem before the Passover [g]to purify
themselves. 56 [h]They were looking for[1] Jesus
and saying to one another as they stood in
the temple, "What do you think? That he will
not come to the feast at all?" 57 Now the chief
priests and the Pharisees had given orders that
if anyone knew where he was, he should let
them know, so that they might arrest him.

Mary Anoints Jesus at Bethany

12 Six days before [i]the Passover, [j]Jesus
therefore came to Bethany, [k]where
Lazarus was, whom Jesus had raised from the
dead. 2 So they gave a dinner for him there.
[l]Martha served, and Lazarus was one of those
reclining with him at table. 3 [m]Mary therefore
took a pound[2] of expensive ointment made
from pure nard, and anointed the feet of Jesus
and wiped his feet with her hair. The house
was filled with the fragrance of the perfume.
4 But Judas Iscariot, one of his disciples (he
who was about to betray him), said, 5 "Why
was this ointment not sold for three hundred
denarii[3] and [n]given to the poor?" 6 He said
this, not because he cared about the poor, but
because he was a thief, and [n]having charge of
the moneybag he used to help himself to what
was put into it. 7 Jesus said, "Leave her alone, so
that she may keep it[4] for the day of my burial.
8 For the poor you always have with you, but
you do not always have me."

The Plot to Kill Lazarus

9 When the large crowd of the Jews learned
that Jesus[5] was there, they came, not only on
account of him but also to see Lazarus, [o]whom
he had raised from the dead. 10 [p]So the chief
priests made plans to put Lazarus to death as
well, 11 because [q]on account of him many of the
Jews were going away and believing in Jesus.

The Triumphal Entry

12 The next day [r]the large crowd that had
come to the feast heard that Jesus was coming to Jerusalem. 13 So they took branches of
[s]palm trees and went out to meet him, crying

[1] Greek *were seeking for* [2] Greek *litra*; a *litra* (or Roman pound) was equal to about 11 1/2 ounces or 327 grams [3] A *denarius* was a day's wage for a laborer [4] Or *Leave her alone; she intended to keep it* [5] Greek *he*

50[x] ch. 18:14
51[y] ver. 49 [z] [Ex. 28:30; Num. 27:21; 1 Sam. 23:9; 30:7; Ezra 2:63; Neh. 7:65]
52[a] Isa. 49:6; 1 John 2:2 [b] See ch. 10:16
53[c] See ch. 7:1
54[d] ch. 7:1, 4
55[e] See ch. 6:4 [f] Luke 2:42 [g] 2 Chr. 30:17, 18; [ch. 18:28; Acts 21:24]
56[h] See ch. 7:11
Chapter 12
1[i] ver. 12, 20; ch. 11:55 [j] For ver. 1-8, see Matt. 26:6-11; Mark 14:3-8 [k] ch. 11:1
2[l] Luke 10:38, 40
3[m] [Luke 7:37, 38]
5[n] ch. 13:29
6[n] [See ver. 5 above]
9[o] ch. 11:44
10[p] [Luke 16:31]
11[q] ver. 18; ch. 11:45
12[r] For ver. 12-15, see Matt. 21:4-9; Mark 11:7-10; Luke 19:35-38
13[s] [Rev. 7:9]

at all times and in all places. He sits in heaven and laughs derisively at those who plot and scheme against his saving purposes in his Son (Ps. 2:2–4).

12:1–8 The contrast between Mary and Judas could not be bolder. Mary reclines at Jesus' feet in adoring love, offering extravagant devotion—anointing him for his burial. Judas sits in condescending arrogance, not only questioning Mary's action but judging Jesus' willing acceptance of such a gift. One is a worshiper; one is a thief. One gives sacrificial honor; the other seeks personal gain (Matt. 26:15). One demonstrates the way of grace; the other, the way of sin.

This story should remind us of a similar scene recorded in Luke's Gospel, where an unnamed sinful woman washes Jesus' feet with her tears, while Simon, a self-righteous Pharisee, "murders" Jesus in his heart (Luke 7:36–50). Those who have been forgiven much love much. Those who are greedy for much are greedy for more.

12:12–19 Jesus is his own "public relations firm"—and his own interpreter. The choice to ride into Jerusalem on a young donkey wasn't just to fulfill prophecy but to contradict the prevailing notions about Israel's Messiah. The waving of palm branches wasn't just an act of enthusiastic praise; it was a statement of nationalistic pride. But Jesus didn't come into Jerusalem as a political, economic, and social advocate for Israel. He came to establish a kingdom reign over all nations, including Israel and Rome—a reign of grace in the hearts of his followers and a reign of peace over all he has made. Jesus makes us joyful prisoners of hope by rescuing us from the empty promises of hype (Zech. 8:9–12).

out, [t]"Hosanna! Blessed is [u]he who comes in
the name of the Lord, even [v]the King of Israel!"
14 And Jesus found a young donkey and sat on
it, just as it is written,

15 [w]"Fear not, daughter of Zion;
behold, your king is coming,
sitting on a donkey's colt!"

16 [x]His disciples did not understand these
things at first, but [y]when Jesus was glorified,
then [z]they remembered that these things had
been written about him and had been done
to him. 17 [a]The crowd that had been with him
when he called Lazarus out of the tomb and
raised him from the dead continued to bear
witness. 18 The reason why the crowd went
to meet him [b]was that they heard he had
done this sign. 19 So the Pharisees said to one
another, [c]"You see that you are gaining nothing. Look, [d]the world has gone after him."

Some Greeks Seek Jesus

20 Now [e]among those who went up to worship at the feast were some [f]Greeks. 21 So these
came to [g]Philip, who was from Bethsaida
in Galilee, and asked him, "Sir, we wish to
see Jesus." 22 Philip went and told [h]Andrew;
Andrew and Philip went and told Jesus. 23 And
Jesus answered them, [i]"The hour has come [j]for
the Son of Man to be glorified. 24 Truly, truly,
I say to you, [k]unless a grain of wheat falls into
the earth and dies, it remains alone; but if it
dies, it bears much fruit. 25 [l]Whoever loves his
life loses it, and [m]whoever [n]hates his life in this
world will keep it for eternal life. 26 If anyone
serves me, he must [o]follow me; and [p]where
I am, there will my servant be also. [q]If anyone
serves me, [r]the Father will honor him.

The Son of Man Must Be Lifted Up

27 [s]"Now is my soul troubled. And what shall
I say? 'Father, [t]save me from [u]this hour'? But
[v]for this purpose I have come to [u]this hour.
28 Father, glorify your name." Then [w]a voice
came from heaven: "I have glorified it, and
I will glorify it again." 29 The crowd that stood
there and heard it said that it had thundered.
Others said, [x]"An angel has spoken to him."
30 Jesus answered, [y]"This voice has come for
your sake, not mine. 31 [z]Now is the judgment
of this world; now will [a]the ruler of this world
[b]be cast out. 32 And I, [c]when I am lifted up from
the earth, [d]will draw [e]all people to myself."
33 He said this [f]to show by what kind of death
he was going to die. 34 So the crowd answered
him, "We have heard from the Law that [g]the
Christ remains forever. How can you say that
[h]the Son of Man must be lifted up? Who is
this Son of Man?" 35 So Jesus said to them,
[i]"The light is among you [j]for a little while
longer. [k]Walk while you have the light, lest
darkness [l]overtake you. [m]The one who walks

12:20–26 The "not yet" is over; the appointed hour has arrived. The time for Jesus' passion is at hand. The Pharisees lamented, "The world has gone after him" (12:19). They simply had no clue how fully their words would be fulfilled. With the arrival of the Greeks, we are given a preview of the enormous harvest of nations that has been secured by the death of Jesus—the eschatological kernel of kingdom wheat. In Jesus we see the promise to Abraham fulfilled that he would be the father of many nations (Gen. 12:1–3).

These Greeks were seeking Jesus because Jesus was seeking them. He came into the world to seek and to save the lost. Apart from the sovereign grace of God, the message of the cross is foolishness to the Greeks and a scandal to the Jews (1 Cor. 1:22–24), just as it is to us—but for the grace of God.

12:27–36 First and foremost, the gospel is the good news of how God reconciles sinners to himself through the life, death, and resurrection of Jesus. But it is also the story of Jesus' triumph over all evil and over Satan himself, "the ruler of this world." Jesus came into the world to destroy him who holds the power of death (that is, the Devil) and to free those "who through fear of death were subject to lifelong slavery" (Heb. 2:15; cf. 1 John 3:8). His "bruised heel" secured the "crushed head" of the Serpent—fulfilling the first gospel promise (Gen. 3:15).

Satan's defeat has already been secured, and the clock is ticking on his ultimate demise. His present flurry of fury is actually a sign that he knows his time is short (Rev. 12:12).

13 [t]Ps. 118:25, 26 [u][ch. 5:43] [v]See ch. 1:49
15 [w]Cited from Zech. 9:9
16 [x][ch. 13:7]; See Mark 9:32 [y]ver. 23; See ch. 7:39 [z]ch. 2:22
17 [a][Luke 19:37]
18 [b]ver. 9-11
19 [c]ch. 11:47 [d][ch. 3:26]
20 [e][1 Kgs. 8:41-43; Acts 8:27] [f]Acts 17:4; [Mark 7:26]; See ch. 7:35
21 [g]ch. 1:44
22 [h]See Mark 13:3
23 [i]ch. 17:1; [ver. 27; ch. 13:31, 32; Mark 14:41]; See ch. 2:4 [j]ver. 16
24 [k]1 Cor. 15:36
25 [l]See Matt. 10:39 [m][ch. 11:25] [n]See Luke 14:26
26 [o]ch. 8:12; 21:18 [p]ch. 14:3; 17:24; [2 Cor. 5:8; 1 Thess. 4:17] [q][ch. 14:21, 23; 16:27] [r]1 Sam. 2:30; Ps. 91:15
27 [s]ch. 11:33; 13:21; [Luke 22:44] [t]Mark 14:35; [Heb. 5:7] [u]ver. 23 [v][ch. 18:37]
28 [w]Matt. 3:17; 17:5; Mark 1:11; 9:7; Luke 3:22; 9:35; 2 Pet. 1:17
29 [x]Acts 23:9
30 [y]ch. 11:42
31 [z]ch. 16:11; [ch. 16:33]
[a]ch. 14:30; 2 Cor. 4:4; Eph. 2:2; 6:12; [Matt. 13:19; Luke 4:6; 1 John 4:4; 5:19] [b][Luke 10:18; Col. 2:15; 1 John 3:8] **32** [c]ch. 3:14; 8:28 [d]See ch. 6:44 [e]Rom. 5:18; 8:32; 2 Cor. 5:15; 1 Tim. 2:6; Heb. 2:9; 1 John 2:2 **33** [f]ch. 18:32 **34** [g]Ps. 89:4; 110:4; Isa. 9:7; Ezek. 37:25; Luke 1:33 [h]ver. 32 **35** [i]ver. 46; See ch. 1:4, 9; 8:12 [j]See ch. 7:33 [k]Jer. 13:16; Eph. 5:8 [l]1 Thess. 5:4 [m]Isa. 9:2; 1 John 1:6; 2:11; [ch. 11:10]

in the darkness does not know where he is
going. 36 While you have the light, believe in
the light, that you may become [n]sons of light."

The Unbelief of the People

When Jesus had said these things, he departed and hid himself from them. 37 Though
he had done so many signs before them, they
still did not believe in him, 38 [o]so that the
word spoken by the prophet Isaiah might be
fulfilled:

> [p]"Lord, who has believed what he heard
> from us,
> and to whom has the arm of the Lord
> been revealed?"

39 Therefore they [q]could not believe. For again
Isaiah said,

> 40 [r]"He has blinded their eyes
> and [s]hardened their heart,
> lest they see with their eyes,
> and understand with their heart, and
> turn,
> and I would heal them."

41 Isaiah said these things because [t]he saw
his glory and [u]spoke of him. 42 Nevertheless,
[v]many even of the authorities believed in him,
but [w]for fear of the Pharisees they did not [x]con-
fess it, so that they would not be [x]put out of
the synagogue; 43 [y]for they loved the glory that
comes from man more than the glory that
comes from God.

Jesus Came to Save the World

44 And Jesus cried out and said, [z]"Whoever
believes in me, believes not in me but [a]in him
who sent me. 45 And [b]whoever [c]sees me sees
him who sent me. 46 [d]I have come into the
world as light, so that whoever believes in
me may not remain in darkness. 47 If anyone
[e]hears my words and does not keep them, [f]I do
not judge him; for [g]I did not come to judge
the world but to save the world. 48 [h]The one
who rejects me and does not receive my words
has a judge; [i]the word that I have spoken will
judge him [j]on the last day. 49 For [k]I have not
spoken on my own authority, but the Father
[l]who sent me has himself given me [m]a commandment—what to say and what to speak.
50 And I know that his commandment is
eternal life. What I say, therefore, I say as the
Father has told me."

Jesus Washes the Disciples' Feet

13 Now [n]before [o]the Feast of the Passover,
when Jesus knew that [p]his hour had
come [q]to depart out of this world to the
Father, [r]having loved [s]his own who were in
the world, he loved them to the end. 2 During
supper, when [t]the devil had already put it
into the heart of Judas Iscariot, Simon's son,
to betray him, 3 Jesus, knowing [u]that the
Father had given all things into his hands,
and that [v]he had come from God and [w]was
going back to God, 4 rose from supper. He laid
aside his outer garments, and taking a towel,
[x]tied it around his waist. 5 Then he [y]poured
water into a basin and began to wash the disciples' feet and to wipe them with the towel
that was wrapped around him. 6 He came to
Simon Peter, who said to him, "Lord, do you
wash my feet?" 7 [z]Jesus answered him, "What
I am doing [a]you do not understand now, but
afterward you will understand." 8 [b]Peter said

13:1–11 As Jesus prepares the disciples for the crucible of his death and the pain of his departure, what will they need? The same thing every generation of disciples need: not a pep talk, but a deeper understanding and experience of the gospel.

Jesus loved these men "to the end" (v. 1)—that is, to the completion of his work as the last Adam (1 Cor. 15:45–49); "to the end" that God will be glorified in the redemption of ill-deserving sinners; "to the end"—to the fullest extent. No one loves us like Jesus, and nothing will ever separate us from his love (Rom. 8:31–39). And his compelling love propels us into faithful service (2 Cor. 5:14).

The water and towel, with which Jesus humbly washed the disciples' feet, clearly anticipate the humiliation of his cross and blood, by which he would wash their hearts. Peter's adamant refusal (literally "never to eternity"; John 13:8) demonstrates our innate resistance to God's grace. Peter wasn't being noble; he was being foolish, even self-destructive. Unless we submit to the criticism of our uncleanness indicated by our need of the washing of Christ's blood shed on the cross, we have no life in Jesus. Jesus is always more ready to meet us at the throne of grace than we are willing to meet him there.

36 [n]See Luke 10:6
38 [o][Matt. 1:22] [p]Rom. 10:16; Cited from Isa. 53:1
39 [q][ch. 5:44]
40 [r][Isa. 6:10]; See Matt. 13:14, 15 [s]See Mark 6:52
41 [t]Isa. 6:1 [u][ch. 5:46]
42 [v]ch. 3:1; [ch. 7:48] [w]See ch. 7:13 [x]See ch. 9:22
43 [y]ch. 5:44
44 [z][ch. 13:20]; See Matt. 10:40 [a]ch. 14:1; [ch. 5:24; 1 Pet. 1:21]
45 [b]ch. 14:9 [c]ch. 6:40
46 [d]ver. 35, 36; See ch. 1:4, 5, 9; 8:12
47 [e][ch. 3:36] [f]ch. 8:15 [g]See ch. 3:17; 4:42
48 [h]Luke 10:16 [i]Deut. 18:18, 19 [j][Rom. 2:16]
49 [k]See ch. 5:19, 30 [l]See ch. 3:17 [m]ch. 15:10
Chapter 13
1 [n]ch. 12:1 [o]See ch. 6:4 [p]See ch. 12:23 [q]ver. 3; ch. 16:28 [r]ver. 34 [s]ch. 1:11; 17:6, 9-11 **2** [t]ver. 11, 27; [Acts 5:3]; See ch. 6:70, 71 **3** [u]See ch. 17:2; Matt. 11:27; Rev. 2:27 [v]ch. 8:42; 16:28 [w]See ch. 14:12 **4** [x][ch. 21:7; Luke 22:27] **5** [y][2 Kgs. 3:11] **7** [z][ver. 36] [a]ver. 12; [ch. 12:16; 15:15] **8** [b][Matt. 16:22]

to him, "You shall never wash my feet." Jesus
answered him, [c]"If I do not wash you, you
have no share with me." 9 Simon Peter said
to him, "Lord, not my feet only but also my
hands and my head!" 10 Jesus said to him,
"The one who has bathed does not need to
wash, [d]except for his feet,[1] but is completely
clean. And [e]you[2] are clean, [f]but not every one
of you." 11 [g]For he knew who was to betray
him; that was why he said, "Not all of you
are clean."

12 When he had washed their feet and [h]put
on his outer garments and resumed his place,
he said to them, [i]"Do you understand what
I have done to you? 13 [j]You call me [k]Teacher
and Lord, and you are right, for so I am. 14 If
I then, your Lord and Teacher, have washed
your feet, [l]you also ought to wash one another's feet. 15 For I have given you an example,
[m]that you also should do just as I have done
to you. 16 Truly, truly, I say to you, [n]a servant[3]
is not greater than his master, nor is a messenger greater than the one who sent him.
17 If you know these things, [o]blessed are you
if you do them. 18 [p]I am not speaking of all of
you; I know [q]whom I have chosen. But [r]the
Scripture will be fulfilled,[4] [s]'He who ate my
bread has lifted his heel against me.' 19 [t]I am
telling you this now, before it takes place,
that when it does take place you may believe
that I am he. 20 Truly, truly, I say to you, [u]who-
ever receives the one I send receives me, and
whoever receives me receives the one who
sent me."

One of You Will Betray Me

21 After saying these things, [v]Jesus was
troubled in his spirit, and testified, [w]"Truly,
truly, I say to you, [x]one of you will betray
me." 22 [y]The disciples looked at one another,
uncertain of whom he spoke. 23 [z]One of his
disciples, whom Jesus loved, was reclining
at table [a]at Jesus' side,[5] 24 so Simon Peter
motioned to him to ask Jesus[6] of whom he
was speaking. 25 [b]So that disciple, [c]leaning
back against Jesus, said to him, "Lord, who
is it?" 26 Jesus answered, [d]"It is he to whom
I will give this morsel of bread [e]when I have
dipped it." So when he had dipped the morsel,
[f]he gave it to Judas, [g]the son of Simon Iscariot.
27 Then after he had taken the morsel, [h]Satan
entered into him. Jesus said to him, [i]"What
you are going to do, do quickly." 28 Now no
one at the table knew why he said this to him.
29 Some thought that, [j]because Judas had the
moneybag, Jesus was telling him, "Buy what
we need [k]for the feast," or that he should [l]give
something to the poor. 30 So, after receiving
the morsel of bread, he immediately went
out. [m]And it was night.

[1] Some manuscripts omit *except for his feet* [2] The Greek words for *you* in this verse are plural [3] Greek *bondservant* [4] Greek *But in order that the Scripture may be fulfilled* [5] Greek *in the bosom of Jesus* [6] Greek lacks *Jesus*

13:12–20 Jesus is our substitute before he is our example. The imperative to wash one another's feet flows out of the indicative of Jesus washing us by his grace. Are we free (and lovingly compelled) to wash one another's feet in our services of worship? Of course we are; but only as a gospel reenactment of the grace we have received, and when such an expression is accompanied by a lifestyle of servant love. Ritual without humble recognition of and response to the reality of grace is vanity, only fueling sentimentality and self-righteousness.

Jesus is the servant of Yahweh (cf. Isa. 52:13–53:12) who did for us what we could never do for ourselves. Through our union with Jesus, and the encouragement of his love, we are set free to honor one another above ourselves, and to serve each other in humility (Phil. 2:1–11).

13:21–30 The troubling of Jesus' spirit in the upper room (v. 21) was simply the firstfruits of the agony he would experience later that same evening in the garden of Gethsemane (Matt. 26:36–46). Earlier in his Gospel, John shared the legend of the healing waters of the pool of Bethesda (John 5:1–17). When the waters were "stirred up" (5:7; the same word translated "troubled" in 13:21), healing was reputedly given to the first person who stepped in (see ESV footnote on 5:3). With Jesus, salvation is not merely reputed but is guaranteed for all who trust in him. All who call on the name of the Lord will be saved.

Notice the stark contrast between John, the disciple who leans against Jesus' side (13:23), and Judas, the disciple who betrays him unto death. Only sovereign grace can explain the difference.

8 [c][1 Cor. 6:11; Eph. 5:26; Titus 3:5; Heb. 10:22]
10 [d]See Gen. 18:4 [e]ch. 15:3 [f]ver. 18
11 [g]ver. 2; ch. 6:64; See ch. 2:24, 25
12 [h]ver. 4 [i]ver. 7
13 [j]Luke 6:46 [k]Matt. 23:8, 10; 1 Cor. 8:6; 12:3; Phil. 2:11
14 [l]1 Tim. 5:10; [1 Pet. 5:5]
15 [m]See Matt. 11:29
16 [n]ch. 15:20; Matt. 10:24
17 [o]See Luke 11:28; James 1:22
18 [p]ver. 10, 11 [q]ch. 6:70; 15:16, 19; [Mark 3:13; Luke 6:13; Acts 1:2] [r][ch. 17:12]; See Matt. 1:22 [s]Cited from Ps. 41:9; [ver. 26; Matt. 26:23]
19 [t]ch. 14:29; 16:4
20 [u]See Matt. 10:40
21 [v]ch. 12:27 [w]Matt. 26:21; Mark 14:18; Luke 22:21 [x]Acts 1:17
22 [y]Luke 22:23
23 [z]ch. 19:26; 20:2; 21:7, 20 [a][Luke 16:22 (Gk.)]
25 [b]Mark 4:36 [c]ch. 21:20 (Gk.)
26 [d]Matt. 26:23; Mark 14:20 [e]Ruth 2:14 [f][Matt. 26:25] [g]ch. 6:71
27 [h]Luke 22:3; [ver. 2; 1 Cor. 11:27] [i][Luke 12:50]
29 [j]ch. 12:6 [k]ver. 1 [l]ch. 12:5
30 [m][1 Sam. 28:8]

A New Commandment

31 When he had gone out, Jesus said, [n]"Now is
the Son of Man glorified, and [o]God is glorified
in him. 32 If God is glorified in him, [p]God will
also glorify him in himself, and [q]glorify him at
once. 33 Little children, [r]yet a little while I am
with you. You will seek me, and just [s]as I said
to the Jews, so now I also say to you, 'Where
I am going you cannot come.' 34 [t]A new commandment [u]I give to you, [v]that you love one
another: [w]just as I have loved you, you also are
to love one another. 35 [x]By this all people will
know that you are my disciples, if you have
love for one another."

Jesus Foretells Peter's Denial

36 Simon Peter said to him, "Lord, where are
you going?" [y]Jesus answered him, "Where I am
going [z]you cannot follow me now, [a]but you
will follow afterward." 37 [b]Peter said to him,
"Lord, why can I not follow you now? I will
lay down my life for you." 38 Jesus answered,
"Will you lay down your life for me? Truly,
truly, I say to you, [c]the rooster will not crow
till you have denied me three times.

I Am the Way, and the Truth, and the Life

14 [d]"Let not your hearts be troubled.
[e]Believe in God;[1] believe also in me.
2 In [f]my Father's house are many rooms. If it
were not so, would I have told you that [g]I go
to prepare a place for you?[2] 3 And if I go and
prepare a place for you, I will come again and
will take you [h]to myself, that [i]where I am you
may be also. 4 And you know the way to where
I am going."[3] 5 [j]Thomas said to him, "Lord, [k]we
do not know where you are going. How can
we know the way?" 6 Jesus said to him, "I am
[l]the way, and [m]the truth, and [n]the life. No one
comes to the Father except through me. 7 [o]If
you had known me, you would have [p]known
my Father also.[4] From now on you do know
him and [q]have seen him."

8 [r]Philip said to him, "Lord, [s]show us the
Father, and it is enough for us." 9 Jesus said to
him, "Have I been with you so long, and you
still do not know me, Philip? [t]Whoever has
seen me has seen the Father. How can you say,
'Show us the Father'? 10 Do you not believe that
[u]I am in the Father and the Father is in me?
The words that I say to you [v]I do not speak on

[1] Or *You believe in God* [2] Or *In my Father's house are many rooms; if it were not so, I would have told you; for I go to prepare a place for you* [3] Some manuscripts *Where I am going you know, and the way you know* [4] Or *If you know me, you will know my Father also*, or *If you have known me, you will know my Father also*

31 [n]See ch. 7:39 [o]ch. 14:13; 15:8; 17:1, 4; 1 Pet. 4:11
32 [p]ch. 17:1, 5 [q]See ch. 12:23
33 [r]See ch. 7:33 [s]ch. 7:34; 8:21
34 [t]1 John 2:7, 8; 3:11; 2 John 5 [u]ch. 15:12, 17; 1 John 3:23; 4:21 [v]Lev. 19:18; Rom. 13:8; Col. 3:14; 1 Thess. 4:9; 1 Tim. 1:5; 1 Pet. 1:22 [w]ch. 15:12; Eph. 5:2; 1 John 4:10, 11
35 [x][1 John 3:14; 4:20]
36 [y][ver. 7] [z][ch. 7:34; 14:2] [a]ch. 21:18, 19; 2 Pet. 1:14
37 [b]Matt. 26:33-35; Mark 14:29-31; Luke 22:33, 34
38 [c]ch. 18:27
Chapter 14
1 [d]ver. 27; [ch. 16:22, 23; 1 Pet. 3:14] [e]See ch. 12:44
2 [f][ch. 2:16] [g]ch. 16:7; [ch. 8:21, 22; 13:33, 36]
3 [h]ver. 18, 28; [ch. 21:22, 23] [i]See ch. 12:26
5 [j]See ch. 11:16 [k]ch. 13:36
6 [l]Heb. 9:8; 10:20; [Eph. 2:18] [m]ch. 1:14, 17; [1 John 5:20] [n]See ch. 11:25
7 [o]ch. 8:19 [p]1 John 2:13, 14 [q][ch. 6:46]
8 [r]ch. 1:43, 44; 12:21 [s][Ex. 33:18]
9 [t]ch. 12:45; [ch. 10:30; 15:24; Col. 1:15; Heb. 1:3]
10 [u]See ch. 10:38 [v]See ch. 5:19, 20

13:31–35 The newness of the new commandment can be understood only in light of the finished work of Jesus. God has always called his people to a life of neighbor love (Lev. 19:18), reaffirmed by Jesus as the second great commandment (Matt. 22:36–40). But the new commandment presupposes a new paradigm. The greatness of Jesus' love for us is now the motivation for our loving others. If we love Jesus truly and deeply, we will love what and whom he loves—the unlovely, the oppressed, those very different from us, and those whose actions have damaged us.

This confirming sign of our discipleship is not a badge of our commitment to Jesus; it is rather the beauty of Jesus' commitment to us. Discipleship is not a program for which we sign up; it is a whole new way of life for which we have been raised up.

13:36–38 There is something comforting about seeing how slow the disciples were to understand Jesus' teaching and how reluctant they were to own their brokenness. If Jesus could care for such as these, then there is hope for frail and faulty people such as we. Jesus is a patient teacher, and a most wonderful and merciful Savior. As in Peter's life, Jesus not only foresees our betrayals; he also foresees our restoration.

14:1–11 Having withdrawn from the crowds of Jerusalem, Jesus pours his time and efforts into his band of apostles—whose lives and witness will be an extension of his own. In comforting his disciples, Jesus gives us an extraordinary summary of who he is and what he came from heaven to do on our behalf. Though most often read at funerals, these familiar words prepare us for life long before we face death. Present relationship, comfort, and security with Jesus is being stressed more so than our future place of residence.

Jesus is the way, the truth, and the life. By boldly affirming these three categories, we can see how Jesus fulfills the three main offices God provided for his covenant people: prophet, priest, and king. As prophet, Jesus is the truth of the Father—he is the Word made flesh, the final word God has spoken to his people (Heb. 1:2). As priest, Jesus is the way to the Father—he is both the sacrifice for our sins and the Mediator

my own authority, but the Father who dwells
in me does his works. 11 Believe me that [u]I am
in the Father and the Father is in me, or else
[w]believe on account of the works themselves.
12 "Truly, truly, I say to you, [x]whoever believes
in me will also do the works that I do; and
greater works than these will he do, because
I [y]am going to the Father. 13 [z]Whatever you ask
in my name, this I will do, that [a]the Father
may be glorified in the Son. 14 [z]If you ask me[1]
anything in my name, I will do it.

Jesus Promises the Holy Spirit

15 [b]"If you love me, you will [c]keep my commandments. 16 And I will ask the Father, and
he will give you another [d]Helper,[2] to be with
you forever, 17 even [e]the Spirit of truth, [f]whom
the world cannot receive, because it neither
sees him nor knows him. You know him, for
he dwells with you and [g]will be[3] in you.
18 "I will not leave you as orphans; [h]I will
come to you. 19 [i]Yet a little while and the world
will see me no more, but [j]you will see me.
[k]Because I live, you also will live. 20 [l]In that day
you will know that [m]I am in my Father, and
[n]you in me, and [o]I in you. 21 [p]Whoever has my
commandments and [q]keeps them, he it is who
loves me. And [r]he who loves me [s]will be loved
by my Father, and I will love him and [t]mani-
fest myself to him." 22 [u]Judas (not Iscariot) said
to him, "Lord, how is it [v]that you will manifest
yourself to us, and not to the world?" 23 Jesus
answered him, [w]"If anyone loves me, he will
keep my word, and my Father will love him,
and [x]we will come to him and [y]make our home
with him. 24 Whoever does not love me does
not keep my words. And [z]the word that you
hear is not mine but the Father's who sent me.
25 "These things I have spoken to you while
I am still with you. 26 But the [a]Helper, the
Holy Spirit, [b]whom the Father will send in
my name, [c]he will teach you all things and
[d]bring to your remembrance all that I have
said to you. 27 [e]Peace I leave with you; [f]my peace
I give to you. Not as the world gives do I give
to you. [g]Let not your hearts be troubled, neither [h]let them be afraid. 28 [i]You heard me say
to you, [j]'I am going away, and I will come to

[1] Some manuscripts omit *me* [2] Or *Advocate*, or *Counselor*; also 14:26; 15:26; 16:7 [3] Some manuscripts *and is*

of the new covenant (Heb. 12:24). As king, Jesus is the life from the sovereign giver of life, the eternal Father—who gives life now and in the coming age for eternity (Heb. 6:5). He is the King whom the Father has already installed in Zion (Ps. 2:6) and the ruler over the kings of the earth (Rev. 1:5).

14:12–14 The promise of "greater works" presupposes Jesus' ongoing work in the world, as prophet, priest, and king—by which his purposes will be amplified by his multiplying believers and expanding the church. As the head of the church and the reigning King, Jesus continues his work in the world through his people indwelt by his Spirit. Our work *for* Jesus is really our work *with* Jesus. He is the One making all things new, and he does so in us and through us. He has made us to be a "kingdom, priests to his God and Father" (Rev. 1:6)

14:15 Carefully note what Jesus actually says. If we love him, we will obey him. Jesus does not say, if we obey him, he will love us. The gospel turns everything right side up. We can do nothing to earn or maintain a relationship with God. Our obedience merits us nothing; but our obedience is an essential affirmation of our love for Jesus. It is by Jesus' obedience that we are saved, and it is by our obedience, compelled by love for Christ, that we express our gratitude for so great a salvation.

14:16–31 As Jesus continues instructing his disciples in advance of his ascension, we enter the most profound teaching about the Trinity to be found anywhere in the Bible. There is much mystery here, but let us affirm what is clearly in the text. The better we know Jesus, the more Trinitarian we will become. The gospel is the means by which we enter the fellowship, love, and joy shared by the Father, Son, and Holy Spirit throughout eternity—a staggering thought indeed.

Jesus is the perfect Son whose obedience is counted as our own—the basis upon which the Father adopts us as his beloved children. The Spirit comes into our hearts as the spirit of sonship (Rom. 8:15)—freeing us from our orphan-like ways, leading us into greater intimacy with the Father and the Son. It is astonishing: we are the room in which the Trinity takes up residence (John 14:17, 20), becoming the new temple among all nations.

11 [u] [See ver. 10 above] [w] See ch. 5:36
12 [x] [Matt. 17:20; 21:21; Mark 11:23; 16:17] [y] ver. 28; ch. 16:28; [ch. 7:33; 13:1, 3; 16:5, 10, 17; 17:11, 13; 20:17]
13 [z] ch. 15:16; 16:23, 24; See Matt. 7:7 [a] See ch. 13:31
14 [z] [See ver. 13 above]
15 [b] ver. 21, 23; ch. 15:10; 1 John 5:3; 2 John 6 [c] See 1 John 2:3
16 [d] ver. 26; ch. 15:26; 16:7
17 [e] ch. 15:26; 16:13; [1 Cor. 2:12-14; 1 John 2:27; 4:6; 5:6] [f] 1 Cor. 2:14 [g] Acts 2:4; [1 John 2:27; 2 John 2]; See Rom. 8:9
18 [h] ver. 3, 28
19 [i] See ch. 7:33 [j] [ch. 12:45; 16:16] [k] [Rom. 5:10; Eph. 2:5; Rev. 20:4]
20 [l] ch. 16:23, 26 [m] ver. 10 [n] [ch. 15:4-7]; See 1 John 2:28 [o] ch. 17:21, 23, 26
21 [p] [ch. 7:17; 8:31, 32] [q] ver. 15; 1 John 2:5 [r] ch. 16:27 [s] [ch. 12:26] [t] See ch. 7:4
22 [u] Luke 6:16; Acts 1:13 [v] [Acts 10:40, 41]
23 [w] See ver. 15, 21 [x] Rev. 3:20 [y] [2 Cor. 6:16; 1 John 2:24]
24 [z] [ver. 10]; See ch. 7:16
26 [a] See ver. 16 [b] [Luke 24:49; Acts 2:33, with ch. 15:26; 16:7] [c] ch. 16:13; 1 Cor. 2:10; 1 John 2:20, 27 [d] See ch. 2:22
27 [e] ch. 20:19, 21, 26; Luke 24:36 [f] ch. 16:33; Col. 3:15; [Eph. 2:17; Phil. 4:7] [g] ver. 1 [h] 2 Tim. 1:7
28 [i] ver. 2-4 [j] See ch. 8:21

you.' If you loved me, you would have rejoiced,
because I [k]am going to the Father, for [l]the
Father is greater than I. 29 And [m]now I have
told you before it takes place, so that when it
does take place you may believe. 30 I will no
longer talk much with you, for [n]the ruler of
this world is coming. [o]He has no claim on me,
31 but I do [p]as the Father has commanded me,
[q]so that the world may know that I love the
Father. Rise, let us go from here.

I Am the True Vine

15 "I am the [r]true vine, and my Father is
[s]the vinedresser. 2 [t]Every branch in me
that does not bear fruit [u]he takes away, and
every branch that does bear fruit he prunes,
[v]that it may bear more fruit. 3 Already [w]you
are clean [x]because of the word that I have spoken to you. 4 [y]Abide [z]in me, and I in you. As
the branch cannot bear fruit by itself, unless
it abides in the vine, neither can you, unless
you abide in me. 5 I am the vine; [a]you are the
branches. Whoever abides in me and I in him,
he it is that [b]bears much fruit, for apart from
me you can do nothing. 6 If anyone does not
abide in me [c]he is thrown away like a branch
and withers; [d]and the branches are gathered,
thrown into the fire, and burned. 7 If [e]you
abide in me, and my words abide in you, [f]ask
whatever you wish, and it will be done for you.
8 [g]By this my Father is glorified, that you [h]bear
much fruit and so prove to be my disciples.
9 [i]As the Father has loved me, [j]so have I loved
you. Abide in my love. 10 [k]If you keep my commandments, you will abide in my love, just as
[l]I have kept [m]my Father's commandments and
abide in his love. 11 These things I have spoken
to you, [n]that my joy may be in you, and that
[o]your joy may be full.

12 [p]"This is my commandment, that you love
one another as I have loved you. 13 [q]Greater love
has no one than this, [r]that someone lay down
his life for his friends. 14 You are [s]my friends
[t]if you do what I command you. 15 [u]No longer
do I call you servants,[1] for the servant[2] [w]does
not know what his master is doing; but I have
called you friends, for [x]all that I have heard
from my Father [y]I have made known to you.
16 You did not choose me, but [z]I chose you and
appointed you that you should go and [a]bear
fruit and that your fruit should abide, so that
[b]whatever you ask the Father in my name, he
may give it to you. 17 These things I command
you, [c]so that you will love one another.

[1] Greek *bondservants* [2] Greek *bondservant*; also verse 20

28 [k]See ver. 12 [l][ch. 10:29; Phil. 2:6]
29 [m]ch. 13:19; 16:4
30 [n]See ch. 12:31 [o][ch. 17:14; 18:36; Heb. 4:15]
31 [p]ch. 12:49, 50; Phil. 2:8; Heb. 5:8 [q]ch. 17:21, 23
Chapter 15
1 [r][Jer. 2:21] [s][1 Cor. 3:9]
2 [t]ver. 6; Matt. 3:10; 7:19; [Rom. 11:17; 2 Pet. 1:8] [u][Matt. 15:13; Rom. 11:22] [v][Matt. 13:12]
3 [w]ch. 13:10 [x]ch. 17:17; [ver. 7; Eph. 5:26]
4 [y]ver. 5-7; 1 John 2:6; [Phil. 1:11; Col. 1:23]; See ch. 6:56 [z]See ch. 3:15
5 [a]Rom. 6:5 [b]ver. 16; Col. 1:6, 10
6 [c]See ver. 2 [d]Matt. 13:40-42; [Ezek. 15:4]
7 [e]See ch. 8:31 [f]See ch. 14:13
8 [g]Isa. 61:3; Matt. 5:16; 2 Cor. 9:13; Phil. 1:11 [h]ver. 5
9 [i]See ch. 5:20 [j]See ch. 13:34
10 [k][ch. 14:15, 23] [l]ch. 8:55; 17:4; Phil. 2:8 [m]See ch. 10:18
11 [n][2 Cor. 2:3] [o]ch. 3:29; 16:24; 17:13; 1 John 1:4; 2 John 12
12 [p]See ch. 13:34
13 [q]Rom. 5:7, 8; Eph. 5:2 [r]See ch. 10:11
14 [s]Luke 12:4 [t][ver. 10; Matt. 12:50]
15 [u][ver. 20] [w][ch. 13:7, 12] [x]ch. 3:32; 8:26, 40; [ch. 16:13] [y]ch. 17:26; [Gen. 18:17; 1 Cor. 2:16; 13:9, 10]
16 [z]See ch. 13:18 [a][2 John 8] [b][ver. 7]; See ch. 14:13
17 [c]ver. 12

15:1–11 The metaphor of vine and branches underscores how our salvation, from beginning to end, is all of grace. Jesus is the faithful remnant of Israel—the true Vine and fruitful Vineyard (Ps. 80:8–16; Isa. 5:1–7; Ezek. 15:1–6). By the Spirit's presence in our lives, we have entered into an organic union with him—a union of branches to Vine (Rom. 11:24). We are, as the New Testament puts it time and again, "in Christ" (Eph. 1:3–14). We are engrafted into the true Israel. Our lives are hidden with Christ in God (Col. 3:3).

Here Jesus says that he chose his disciples to be his branches; they did not choose him (John 15:16). This reminds us that our calling, as Christ's present disciples, is not to trumpet our wise decisions but simply to abide—to dwell, to marinate, to go "deeper still" into Jesus. For apart from Jesus, we can do nothing and will bear no fruit. Failing to abide in Jesus does not suggest the possibility of losing one's salvation; rather it underscores that salvation can be found nowhere else. Continuance in Christ is a test of reality. The Bible teaches both the perseverance of the saints and that true saints will persevere. We strive ahead, yet even that striving is a gift of grace (1 Cor. 15:10; Phil. 2:12–13; Col. 1:29).

15:12–17 Jesus defines the life of abiding as a life of love. Just as the Father loves Jesus, so Jesus loves us. Jesus loves us just as much as the Father loves him. We cannot earn Jesus' love. Our obedience to Jesus merits nothing, but it profits greatly. Jesus' commands are not burdensome, for they are for our best, and he has fulfilled the demands and the judgment of God's law that could condemn us (Rom. 10:4; 2 Cor. 5:21).

The radical grace of the gospel transforms servanthood into friendship. Only grace can free us to obey Jesus out of friendship and worship, and no longer out of fear or self-interest.

The Hatred of the World

18 [d]"If the world hates you, know that it has hated me before it hated you. 19 [e]If you were of the world, the world would love you as its own; but because [f]you are not of the world, but I chose you out of the world, therefore the world hates you. 20 Remember the word that I said to you: [g]'A servant is not greater than his master.' If they persecuted me, [h]they will also persecute you. [i]If they kept my word, they will also keep yours. 21 But [j]all these things they will do to you [k]on account of my name, [l]because they do not know him who sent me. 22 If I had not come and spoken to them, [m]they would not have been guilty of sin,[1] but now they have no excuse for their sin. 23 [n]Whoever hates me hates my Father also. 24 [o]If I had not done among them the works that no one else did, [m]they would not be guilty of sin, but now they have [p]seen and hated both me and my Father. 25 But [q]the word that is written in their Law must be fulfilled: [r]'They hated me without a cause.'

26 "But [s]when the Helper comes, whom I will send to you from the Father, the Spirit of truth, who proceeds from the Father, [t]he will bear witness about me. 27 And [u]you also will bear witness, [v]because you have been with me [w]from the beginning.

16 "I have said all these things to you to keep you from falling away. 2 [x]They will put you out of the synagogues. Indeed, [y]the hour is coming when [z]whoever kills you will think he is offering service to God. 3 And they will do these things [a]because they have not known the Father, nor me. 4 But [b]I have said these things to you, that when [c]their hour comes you may remember that I told them to you.

The Work of the Holy Spirit

"I did not say these things to you from the beginning, [d]because I was with you. 5 But now [e]I am going to him who sent me, and [f]none of you asks me, 'Where are you going?' 6 But because I have said these things to you, [g]sorrow has filled your heart. 7 Nevertheless, I tell you the truth: it is to your advantage that I go away, for [h]if I do not go away, [i]the Helper will not come to you. But [j]if [k]I go, [l]I will send him to you. 8 [m]And when he comes, he will [n]convict the world concerning sin and righteousness and judgment: 9 concerning sin, [o]because they do not believe in me; 10 [p]concerning

[1] Greek *they would not have sin*; also verse 24

15:18–16:4 The more fully we give ourselves to a life of abiding in Jesus, the richer our fellowship will be with all three members of the Trinity; and intimacy with God will propel us into the mission of God. The more the gospel takes hold in our churches, the more we will be outward-facing in mission, not inward-facing in fear. Grace comes to us in order that it might flow through us. Thus, according to Jesus, we should not be surprised at growing opposition, even persecution, from the world.

Why does the gospel of grace elicit such violent opposition from both religious and non-religious segments of society? Grace is *disruptive* before it is redemptive. The gospel sabotages all forms of self-salvation. Our need is so great that it took the death of the Son of God to save people like us. The good news is that Jesus went willingly and gladly to the cross for us.

16:4–15 With his departure in view—within hours, now—Jesus encourages the disciples about the future ministry of the Holy Spirit. Jesus is the quintessential encourager. As did his apostles, we share great blessings through the permanent indwelling of the Holy Spirit, whom we received the moment we believed in Jesus (Rom. 8:9; Gal. 3:2).

The Spirit is the consummate Helper. He frees us from trying to live the Christian life in our own power. The gospel is not "do more and try harder"; rather, it is "see Jesus and surrender to the Spirit."

How can we have confidence that the writings of the New Testament are inspired and trustworthy? Because the Holy Spirit reminded the apostles of Jesus' words and teachings (John 16:13). The Holy Spirit constantly draws attention to Jesus—nestling the gospel into our hearts and applying the finished work of Jesus to our lives (Rom. 8:16). To see and enjoy grace is the supreme work of the Spirit, as he bears witness to the truth and comfort of God's Word in our hearts.

18 [d]ch. 7:7; 1 John 3:13; [ver. 23, 24]
19 [e][1 John 4:5] [f]ch. 17:14, 16; [Luke 6:26; Gal. 1:4; James 4:4]
20 [g]ch. 13:16; Matt. 10:24; [ver. 15] [h]ch. 16:33; 1 Cor. 4:12; 2 Cor. 4:9; 1 Thess. 2:15; 2 Tim. 3:12 [i][Ezek. 3:7]; See ch. 8:51
21 [j]ch. 16:3 [k]Matt. 10:22; 24:9; Rev. 2:3; [Acts 5:41; 1 Pet. 4:14, 16] [l]See Acts 3:17
22 [m][Matt. 11:22, 24; Luke 12:47, 48]; See ch. 9:41
23 [n]See ch. 5:23
24 [o]ch. 3:2; 7:31; 9:32; Matt. 9:33; [ch. 10:32, 37] [m][See ver. 22 above] [p]See ch. 14:9
25 [q]See ch. 10:34; 12:38 [r]Cited from Ps. 35:19 or 69:4
26 [s]See ch. 14:16, 17, 26 [t]1 Cor. 12:3; 1 John 5:7
27 [u]ch. 19:35; 21:24; 1 John 1:2; 4:14; [3 John 12]; See Luke 24:48 [v]See Acts 4:20 [w][Luke 1:2; Acts 1:21, 22; 1 John 2:7]

Chapter 16
2 [x]ch. 9:22; 12:42 [y]See ch. 4:21 [z]Acts 8:1; 9:1; 26:9-11
3 [a]ch. 8:19, 55; 15:21; 17:25
4 [b]ch. 13:19; 14:29 [c]See Luke 22:53 [d][Matt. 9:15]
5 [e]See ch. 14:12 [f][ch. 13:36; 14:5]
6 [g]ver. 22; ch. 14:1
7 [h]ch. 7:39 [i]ch. 15:26; [ch. 14:16] [j][Acts 2:33]
[k]ch. 14:2 [l]See ch. 14:26 **8** [m][ch. 8:28] [n][ch. 8:46] **9** [o]ch. 8:24; [Acts 2:36, 37; 1 Cor. 12:3] **10** [p][Acts 17:31]

righteousness, [q]because I go to the Father,
and you will see me no longer; 11 [r]concerning
judgment, because the ruler of this world [s]is
judged.
12 "I still have many things to say to you, but
you cannot bear them now. 13 When [t]the Spirit
of truth comes, [u]he will [v]guide you into all the
truth, for he will not speak on his own authority, but [w]whatever he hears he will speak, and
he will declare to you the things that are to
come. 14 He will [x]glorify me, for he will take
what is mine and declare it to you. 15 [y]All that
the Father has is mine; [z]therefore I said that
he will take what is mine and declare it to you.

Your Sorrow Will Turn into Joy

16 [a]"A little while, and you will see me no
longer; and [b]again a little while, and you will
see me." 17 So [c]some of his disciples said to
one another, "What is this that he says to us,
[d]'A little while, and you will not see me, and
again a little while, and you will see me'; and,
[e]'because I am going to the Father'?" 18 So they
were saying, "What does he mean by 'a little
while'? [f]We do not know what he is talking
about." 19 [g]Jesus knew that they wanted to ask
him, so he said to them, "Is this what you are
asking yourselves, what I meant by saying, 'A
little while and you will not see me, and again
a little while and you will see me'? 20 Truly,
truly, I say to you, [h]you will weep and lament,
but [i]the world will rejoice. You will be sorrowful, but [j]your sorrow will turn into joy.
21 [k]When a woman is giving birth, she has sorrow because her hour has come, but when she
has delivered the baby, she no longer remembers the anguish, for joy that a human being
has been born into the world. 22 [l]So also you
have sorrow now, but [m]I will see you again,
and [n]your hearts will rejoice, and no one will
take your joy from you. 23 [o]In that day you will
[p]ask nothing of me. Truly, truly, I say to you,
[q]whatever you ask of the Father in my name,
[r]he will give it to you. 24 Until now you have
asked nothing in my name. [s]Ask, and you will
receive, [t]that your joy may be full.

I Have Overcome the World

25 "I have said these things to you in figures
of speech. [u]The hour is coming when I will no
longer speak to you in figures of speech but
will tell you plainly about the Father. 26 In that
day you will ask in my name, and I do not say
to you that I will ask the Father on your behalf;
27 [v]for the Father himself loves you, because
[w]you have loved me and [x]have believed that
I came from God.[1] 28 [y]I came from the Father
and have come into the world, and now [z]I am
leaving the world and going to the Father."
29 His disciples said, "Ah, now you are speaking plainly and not [a]using figurative speech!
30 Now we know that [b]you know all things
and do not need anyone to question you; this
is why we believe that [c]you came from God."
31 Jesus answered them, "Do you now believe?
32 Behold, [d]the hour is coming, indeed it has

[1] Some manuscripts *from the Father*

10[q] ver. 16, 17, 19
11[r] See ch. 12:31 [s] [Col. 2:15; Heb. 2:14]
13[t] See ch. 14:17 [u] See ch. 14:26 [v] Acts 8:31; [ch. 1:17; 14:6; Ps. 25:5] [w] [ch. 15:15]
14[x] See ch. 7:39
15[y] ch. 17:10 [z] ver. 14
16[a] See ch. 7:33 [b] [ver. 22]
17[c] [Mark 9:10, 32] [d] ver. 16 [e] ver. 10
18[f] [ch. 14:5]
19[g] [ver. 30]; See ch. 2:24, 25
20[h] Matt. 9:15; Mark 16:10; Luke 23:27 [i] [Rev. 11:10] [j] Jer. 31:13; See Matt. 5:4
21[k] Isa. 26:17; [Ps. 48:6; Isa. 13:8; 1 Thess. 5:3; Rev. 12:2]
22[l] ver. 6; [2 Cor. 6:10] [m] [ver. 16] [n] Ps. 33:21; Isa. 66:14; Luke 24:52; Acts 2:46; 8:8, 39; 13:52
23[o] ver. 26; ch. 14:20 [p] ver. 19, 30 [q] See ch. 14:13 [r] ch. 15:16; [Eph. 1:3]
24[s] See Matt. 7:7 [t] See ch. 15:11
25[u] ver. 2
27[v] [ch. 14:21, 23; 17:23]

16:16–24 The gospel frees us from the need to pose and pretend. Jesus anticipated the disciples' sorrow, so he validated their forthcoming tears and lamenting. But he also promised the emergence of great joy—similar to the transformation of pain into joy when a mother gives birth to a child.

Years later, the apostle Paul used the same metaphor—of our world being "pregnant with glory"—to describe life in Christ (Rom. 8:18–25). Our salvation has been given to us, but its blessings are yet to be fully revealed. Life in the "already and not yet" is often filled with complexities, changes, and challenges similar to those experienced in pregnancy, but a full-term birth is guaranteed—for both God's children and his cosmos.

16:25–33 Jesus continues to prepare his disciples for his "double leaving"—through death to the grave, and by ascension to the Father. Before his return, followers of Jesus should anticipate tribulation in this world, but the promise of overcoming stands, because Jesus is the overcomer par excellence. Indeed, the theme of living as an "overcomer" must be anchored in the gospel of grace. We overcome by the blood of the Lamb and the word of our testimony (Rev. 12:11)—that is, by placing our faith in the finished work of Christ and our union with him (1 John 5:4–5, 11–12). Overcoming is not something we do *for* Jesus; it is something we do *by* Jesus.

[w] ch. 21:15-17; [1 Cor. 16:22] [x] ver. 30; ch. 17:8 28[y] ch. 8:14; 13:3 [z] See ch. 14:12 29[a] ver. 25 30[b] ch. 21:17; See ch. 2:24, 25 [c] [ver. 27, 28; ch. 3:2]
32[d] [ch. 4:21, 23]

come, when [e]you will be scattered, each to his
own home, and [f]will leave me alone. [g]Yet I am
not alone, for the Father is with me. 33 I have
said these things to you, that [h]in me you may
have peace. [i]In the world you will have [j]tribulation. But [k]take heart; [l]I have overcome the
world."

The High Priestly Prayer

17 When Jesus had spoken these words,
[m]he lifted up his eyes to heaven, and
said, "Father, [n]the hour has come; [o]glorify your
Son that the Son may [p]glorify you, 2 since [q]you
have given him authority over all flesh, [r]to give
eternal life to all [s]whom you have given him.
3 [t]And this is eternal life, [u]that they know you
[v]the only [w]true God, and [x]Jesus Christ whom
you have sent. 4 I [y]glorified you on earth, [z]having accomplished the work that you gave me
to do. 5 And now, Father, [a]glorify me in your
own presence with the glory [b]that I had with
you [c]before the world existed.
6 [d]"I have manifested your name to the people
[e]whom you gave me out of the world. [f]Yours
they were, and you gave them to me, and they
have kept your word. 7 Now they know that
everything [f]that you have given me is from
you. 8 For I have given them [g]the words that
you gave me, and they have received them and
have come to know in truth that [h]I came from
you; and [i]they have believed that you sent me.
9 I am praying for them. [j]I am not praying for
the world but for those [k]whom you have given
me, for [l]they are yours. 10 [m]All mine are yours,
and yours are mine, and [n]I am glorified in
them. 11 And I am no longer in the world, but
[o]they are in the world, and [p]I am coming to
you. [q]Holy Father, [r]keep them in your name,
[s]which you have given me, [t]that they may be
one, [u]even as we are one. 12 [v]While I was with
them, I kept them in your name, which you
have given me. I have [w]guarded them, and
[x]not one of them has been lost except [y]the
son of destruction, [z]that the Scripture might
be fulfilled. 13 But now [a]I am coming to you,
and these things I speak in the world, that

17:1–5 Jesus' appointed "hour" has finally arrived. Very soon he will travail in prayer over his impending cross; but now, he intercedes with joy over his beloved disciples. No earthly feasts can even faintly compare with the nourishment we are given in Jesus' "high priestly prayer."

Unlike Israel's high priest, Jesus didn't have to offer a sacrifice for his own sins as he came into the Father's presence. The final Day of Atonement involved this eschatological High Priest becoming the sacrifice for the sins of the people (Heb. 7:27). There is no greater love than this (John 15:13; Rom. 5:6–10).

The joy set before Jesus, as he prepared to endure the cross (Heb. 12:2), included at least two things. Jesus longed to return to the Father, to enjoy the life he shared with him before the world was created. But Jesus also felt great joy in anticipation of redeeming and cherishing his international bride. He now delights in us and rejoices over us, as a bridegroom over his bride (Isa. 62:5; Zeph. 3:17).

17:6–19 Having given himself for our sins once for all (Heb. 7:27; 1 Pet. 3:18), Jesus now prays for us without ceasing (Rom. 8:34; Heb. 7:25). Because the disciples were given permission to eavesdrop on this prayer, we know what Jesus thinks of us and what he is now praying for us.

Jesus counts us a love gift to him from the Father (John 17:6; see also v. 24). He treasures and cherishes us as a bridegroom treasures his bride, for that is what we are (Eph. 5:22–33). Should anyone ask, "Who gives these sinners to this Savior?" the Father responds enthusiastically, "I do!" Election is the most wonderful prearranged marriage imaginable.

Because we are already beloved by Jesus, he prays for the increase of our joy—the same joy that fills his own heart. He also prays for our protection in the world—a battlefield that is also our mission field. Jesus doesn't pray that we won't suffer (Phil. 1:29) but that we will be kept from the Evil One, our defeated foe who seeks to sabotage our worship and work in the world.

Jesus also prays for our sanctification by the truth of the Father's words. The Father's words will always point us to Jesus—who is our "wisdom from God," our "righteousness and sanctification and redemption" (1 Cor. 1:30). The same grace that justifies us is the grace that sanctifies us. All saving benefits come from our union with Christ.

32 [e]Matt. 26:31; Mark 14:27 [f][Isa. 63:5] [g]See ch. 8:16, 29
33 [h]See ch. 14:27; Col. 3:15 [i][ch. 15:18-21] [j]Rev. 1:9; See Acts 14:22 [k]ch. 14:1, 27 [l][Rom. 8:37; 1 John 4:4; 5:4, 5; Rev. 3:21; 12:11]

Chapter 17
1 [m]ch. 11:41 [n][ch. 7:30]; See ch. 12:23 [o]See ch. 7:39 [p]ver. 4
2 [q]See Matt. 28:18; Rev. 2:26, 27 [r]ch. 10:28; 1 John 2:25 [s]ver. 6, 9, 24; ch. 6:37, 39; 10:29; 18:9; Heb. 2:13
3 [t][1 John 5:20] [u]Hos. 2:20; 6:3; 2 Pet. 1:2, 3 [v]ch. 5:44 [w]1 Thess. 1:9; 1 John 5:20; [Jer. 10:10] [x]See ch. 3:17
4 [y]ver. 1; See ch. 13:31 [z][ch. 19:30; Luke 22:37]
5 [a]ch. 13:32 [b]ch. 1:1, 2; [Rev. 3:21] [c]ver. 24; Prov. 8:23; See ch. 8:58
6 [d]ver. 26; Ps. 22:22 [e]See ver. 2 [f]ver. 9
7 [f][See ver. 6 above]
8 [g]ver. 14; ch. 15:15; [ch. 8:26; 12:49] [h]ch. 8:42; 16:27 [i]ver. 21, 25; ch. 11:42; 16:30
9 [j][ver. 20, 21] [k]See ver. 2 [l]ver. 6
10 [m]ch. 16:15 [n]2 Thess. 1:10
11 [o]ch. 13:1 [p]See ch. 14:12 [q][ver. 25] [r]ver. 12, 15; Jude 1 [s][Ex. 23:21; Phil. 2:9; Rev. 19:12] [t]ver. 21, 22; [ch. 10:16; Rom. 12:5; Gal. 3:28; Eph. 1:10; 4:4] [u]ch. 10:30
12 [v]See ch. 14:25 [w]2 Thess. 3:3; Jude 24 [x]ch. 18:9; [ch. 6:39; 10:28] [y]2 Thess. 2:3 [z]Ps. 109:8; Acts 1:16-20; [ch. 13:18]
13 [a]See ch. 14:12

they may have [b]my joy fulfilled in themselves.
14 [c]I have given them your word, and [d]the
world has hated them [e]because they are not
of the world, [f]just as I am not of the world.
15 I [g]do not ask that you [h]take them out of the
world, but that you [i]keep them from [j]the evil
one.[1] 16 [k]They are not of the world, just as I am
not of the world. 17 [l]Sanctify them[2] in the truth;
[m]your word is truth. 18 [n]As you sent me into
the world, so I have sent them into the world.
19 And [o]for their sake [p]I consecrate myself,[3] that
they also [q]may be sanctified[4] in truth.

20 "I do not [r]ask for these only, but also for
those [s]who will believe in me through their
word, 21 [t]that they may all be one, just as you,
Father, are in me, and I in you, that [u]they also
may be in [v]us, so that the world [w]may believe
that you have sent me. 22 [x]The glory that you
have given me [y]I have given to them, [t]that
they may be one even as we are one, 23 [z]I in
them and you in me, [a]that they may become
perfectly one, [b]so that the world may know
that you sent me and [c]loved them even as
[d]you loved me. 24 Father, I desire that they
also, whom you have given me, may be [e]with
me [f]where I am, [g]to see my glory that you
have given me because you loved me [h]before
the foundation of the world. 25 [i]O righteous
Father, even though [j]the world does not know
you, I know you, and these know that you have
sent me. 26 [k]I made known to them your name,
and I will continue to make it known, that the
love [l]with which you have loved me may be in
them, and [m]I in them."

Betrayal and Arrest of Jesus

18 When Jesus had spoken these words,
[n]he went out with his disciples across
[o]the brook Kidron, where there was a garden,
which he and his disciples entered. 2 Now
Judas, who betrayed him, also knew [p]the place,
for [q]Jesus often met there with his disciples.
3 [r]So Judas, having procured a band of soldiers
and some officers from the chief priests and
the Pharisees, went there with lanterns and
torches and weapons. 4 Then Jesus, [s]knowing
all that would happen to him, came forward
and said to them, [t]"Whom do you seek?" 5 They
answered him, "Jesus of Nazareth." Jesus said
to them, "I am he."[5] Judas, who betrayed him,
was standing with them. 6 [u]When Jesus[6] said to
them, "I am he," they drew back and fell to the
ground. 7 So he asked them again, [t]"Whom do
you seek?" And they said, "Jesus of Nazareth."
8 Jesus answered, "I told you that I am he. So,
if you seek me, let these men go." 9 [v]This was
to fulfill the word that he had spoken: "Of
those whom you gave me I have lost not one."
10 Then Simon Peter, [w]having a sword, drew
it and struck the high priest's servant[7] and
cut off his right ear. (The servant's name was
Malchus.) 11 So Jesus said to Peter, "Put your
sword into its sheath; [x]shall I not drink the
cup that the Father has given me?"

[1] Or *from evil* [2] Greek *Set them apart* (for holy service to God) [3] Or *I sanctify myself*; or *I set myself apart* (for holy service to God) [4] Greek *may be set apart* (for holy service to God) [5] Greek *I am*; also verses 6, 8 [6] Greek *he* [7] Greek *bondservant*; twice in this verse

13 [b]See ch. 15:11
14 [c]ver. 3 [d]See ch. 15:19 [e]ver. 16 [f]ch. 8:23
15 [g]ver. 9 [h][1 Cor. 5:10] [i]ver. 11 [j]See Matt. 13:19
16 [k]ver. 14
17 [l][1 Thess. 5:23; 2 Thess. 2:13; 1 Pet. 1:22]; See ch. 15:3 [m]2 Sam. 7:28; Ps. 119:160
18 [n]ch. 20:21; [ch. 4:38; Matt. 10:5]
19 [o][Titus 2:14] [p]ch. 10:36 [q][1 Cor. 1:2, 30; 6:11; Heb. 2:11; 10:10]
20 [r]ver. 9 [s][ch. 4:39; Rom. 10:14; 1 Cor. 3:5]
21 [t]See ver. 11; [1 Cor. 6:17] [u]1 John 1:3; 3:24; 5:20 [v]ch. 14:23 [w]See ver. 8
22 [x]ver. 24; [ch. 1:14; Luke 9:26] [y]Rom. 8:30 [t][See ver. 21 above]
23 [z]ver. 26; ch. 14:20; Rom. 8:10; 2 Cor. 13:5 [a]1 John 2:5; [Col. 3:14; 1 John 4:12, 17] [b]ver. 21; ch. 14:31 [c]ch. 16:27

17:20–26 Jesus expands his prayer to include those who will—not *might*, but *will*—believe in him. The "Great Commission" isn't our job to get done, but God's promise to fulfill. We are privileged to live as characters in God's story of redemption and also as proclaimers of that story; but we must never forget, it is God's story.

Jesus prays for the unity, not the uniformity, of his believers. God is praised, and the world takes notice, when Christians demonstrate a Spirit-given unity—a unity we must be eager to maintain (Eph. 4:1–3). Our fallen instincts encourage us to build our identity on what distinguishes us even from other believers, but Jesus exposes the self-centeredness of such a mind-set. Our *union with* Christ brings a *unity in* Christ that transcends all secondary disagreements.

18:1–14 Earlier in the history of redemption, another king crossed the Kidron Valley, reeling in the pain of betrayal. King David, barefoot and weeping, went away from Jerusalem because his son, Absalom, had conspired to replace his father by force—enlisting a small army to assist him. David's dear friend and counselor, Ahithophel, was also a part of the conspiracy (2 Samuel 15–17). King David fled *from* their advances; but Jesus, the greater Shepherd-King promised in 2 Samuel 7, fled *into* the betrayal of those closest to him—Judas and Peter.

[d]ver. 24, 26; See ch. 5:20 **24** [e]2 Tim. 2:11, 12 [f]See ch. 12:26 [g]ch. 1:14; 2 Cor. 3:18; [1 John 3:2] [h]Eph. 1:4; 1 Pet. 1:20; See ver. 5 **25** [i]Jer. 12:1; [ver. 11; Rev. 16:5]; See 1 John 1:9 [j]See ch. 8:55; 10:15 **26** [k]ver. 6; ch. 15:15 [l]ver. 23; ch. 15:9 [m]See ver. 23 **Chapter 18** **1** [n]Matt. 26:30, 36; Mark 14:26, 32; Luke 22:39 [o]See 2 Sam. 15:23 **2** [p]Luke 22:40 [q][Luke 21:37; 22:39] **3** [r]For ver. 3-11, see Matt. 26:47-56; Mark 14:43-50; Luke 22:47-53 **4** [s]ch. 13:1 [t]ver. 7; ch. 1:38; 20:15 **6** [u][ch. 10:18; Matt. 26:53; Rev. 1:17] **7** [t][See ver. 4 above] **9** [v]ch. 17:12 **10** [w][Luke 22:38] **11** [x]Matt. 20:22; 26:39, 42; [Isa. 51:22]

Jesus Faces Annas and Caiaphas

12 So the band of soldiers and their captain
and the officers of the Jews[1] arrested Jesus and
bound him. 13 First they [y]led him to [z]Annas, for
he was the father-in-law of [a]Caiaphas, who was
high priest that year. 14 It was Caiaphas who
had advised the Jews [b]that it would be expedi-
ent that one man should die for the people.

Peter Denies Jesus

15 [c]Simon Peter followed Jesus, and so did
another disciple. Since that disciple was
known to the high priest, he entered with
Jesus into the courtyard of the high priest,
16 [d]but Peter stood outside at the door. So the
other disciple, who was known to the high
priest, went out and spoke to the servant girl
who kept watch at the door, and brought Peter
in. 17 [e]The servant girl at the door said to Peter,
"You also are not one of this man's disciples,
are you?" He said, "I am not." 18 Now the servants[2] and officers had made a charcoal fire,
because it was cold, and they were standing
and warming themselves. [f]Peter also was with
them, standing and warming himself.

The High Priest Questions Jesus

19 [g]The high priest then questioned Jesus
about his disciples and his teaching. 20 Jesus
answered him, "I have spoken [h]openly [i]to the
world. I have always taught in synagogues and
in the temple, where all Jews come together.
[j]I have said nothing in secret. 21 Why do you ask
me? Ask those who have heard me what I said
to them; they know what I said." 22 When he
had said these things, one of the officers standing by struck Jesus with his hand, saying, [k]"Is
that how you answer the high priest?" 23 Jesus
answered him, "If what I said is wrong, bear
witness about the wrong; but if what I said is
right, why do you strike me?" 24 [l]Annas then
sent him bound to [l]Caiaphas the high priest.

Peter Denies Jesus Again

25 [m]Now Simon Peter was standing and
warming himself. So they said to him, "You
also are not one of his disciples, are you?" He
denied it and said, "I am not." 26 One of the
servants of the high priest, a relative of [n]the
man whose ear Peter had cut off, asked, "Did
I not see you [o]in the garden with him?" 27 Peter
again denied it, and [p]at once a rooster crowed.

Jesus Before Pilate

28 [q]Then they led Jesus [r]from the house of
Caiaphas to [s]the governor's headquarters.[3] It
was early morning. They themselves did not
enter the governor's headquarters, [t]so that

[1] Greek *Ioudaioi* probably refers here to Jewish religious leaders, and others under their influence, in that time; also verses 14, 31, 36, 38
[2] Greek *bondservants*; also verse 26 [3] Greek *the praetorium*

No one could take Jesus' life from him; he freely laid it down for us (John 10:17–18). A large army of natural enemies, both Jews and Gentiles, tried; but Jesus spoke two words, "I am," and they fell back to the ground (18:6)—an echo of divine encounters in the past (Ex. 3:14) and a preview of the day when every knee will bow and every tongue will confess that Jesus is Lord—many to their coronation; many others to their condemnation (Phil. 2:1–11).

Not only was the glory of the Son of God revealed in Jesus' arrest, but also the compassion of a caring Savior. Peter's misguided action of cutting off Malchus's ear is superseded by Jesus' merciful action of reattaching the severed ear (Luke 22:51). Oh, how low our God stoops to show mercy to the ill-deserving!

18:15–18, 25–27 Peter's words of denial, "I am not," are the tragic counterpoint of Jesus' words of affirmation, "I am" (v. 6). But even as the rooster was crowing, Jesus was still loving Peter "to the end" (13:1). Our sins do not separate us from the love of Jesus; Jesus separates us from the love of our sin, and from sin's guilt and power. Peter's threefold denial of Jesus will be answered, in time, by Jesus' threefold restoration of Peter (21:15–19).

18:28–32 The unrighteousness of self-righteousness is placarded before our eyes in the ugly irony of these verses. The rulers of Israel refused to enter the governor's headquarters because of their scrupulous commitment to the demands of the law, not wanting to be defiled before eating the Passover. But they were unscrupulous in their commitment to rid the world of the One to whom the law points—the One who fulfills the demands of the law for us—the true Passover Lamb, Jesus. He took the defilement of the cross so that we might know the unhindered delight of our God (Zeph. 3:14–17).

13[y] [Matt. 26:57] [z] ver. 24; Luke 3:2; Acts 4:6 [a] ver. 24, 28; See Matt. 26:3
14[b] ch. 11:50
15[c] Matt. 26:58; Mark 14:54; Luke 22:54
16[d] For ver. 16-18, see Matt. 26:69, 70; Mark 14:66-68; Luke 22:55-57
17[e] Acts 12:13
18[f] ver. 25; Mark 14:54
19[g] For ver. 19-24, [Matt. 26:59-68; Mark 14:55-65; Luke 22:63-71]
20[h] ch. 7:26; [Matt. 26:55] [i] [ch. 8:26] [j] Isa. 45:19; 48:16; [ch. 7:4]
22[k] [Acts 23:4]
24[l] ver. 13
25[m] For ver. 25-27, see Matt. 26:71-75; Mark 14:69-72; Luke 22:58-62
26[n] ver. 10 [o] ver. 1
27[p] ch. 13:38
28[q] Matt. 27:2; Mark 15:1; Luke 23:1 [r] ver. 24 [s] ver. 33; ch. 19:9; See Matt. 27:27 [t] Acts 10:28; 11:3; [ch. 11:55]

they would not be defiled, [u]but could eat the
Passover. 29 [v]So Pilate went outside to them
and said, “What accusation do you bring
against this man?” 30 They answered him, “If
this man were not doing evil, we would not
have delivered him over to you.” 31 Pilate said
to them, [w]“Take him yourselves and judge him
by your own law.” The Jews said to him, “It
is not lawful for us to put anyone to death.”
32 [x]This was to fulfill the word that Jesus had
spoken [y]to show by what kind of death he was
going to die.

My Kingdom Is Not of This World

33 [z]So Pilate entered his headquarters again
and called Jesus and said to him, [a]“Are you
the King of the Jews?” 34 Jesus answered, “Do
you say this of your own accord, or did others
say it to you about me?” 35 Pilate answered,
“Am I a Jew? Your own nation and the chief
priests have delivered you over to me. What
have you done?” 36 Jesus answered, [b]“My kingdom [c]is not of this world. If my kingdom were
of this world, [d]my servants would have been
fighting, that [e]I might not be delivered over
to the Jews. But my kingdom is not from the
world.” 37 Then Pilate said to him, “So you are
a king?” Jesus answered, [f]“You say that I am a
king. [g]For this purpose I was born and for this
purpose [h]I have come into the world—[i]to bear
witness to the truth. [j]Everyone who is [k]of the
truth [l]listens to my voice.” 38 Pilate said to him,
“What is truth?”

After he had said this, [m]he went back outside
to the Jews and told them, [n]“I find no guilt in
him. 39 [o]But you have a custom that I should
release one man for you at the Passover. So do
you want me to release to you the King of the
Jews?” 40 They cried out again, [p]“Not this man,
but Barabbas!” Now Barabbas was a robber.[1]

Jesus Delivered to Be Crucified

19 Then Pilate took Jesus and [q]flogged
him. 2 [r]And the soldiers twisted together
a crown of thorns and put it on his head and
arrayed him in a purple robe. 3 They came up
to him, saying, “Hail, King of the Jews!” and
struck him with their hands. 4 Pilate went out
again and said to them, “See, I am bringing
him out to you that you may know that [s]I find
no guilt in him.” 5 So Jesus came out, wearing [t]the crown of thorns and the purple robe.
Pilate said to them, [u]“Behold the man!” 6 When
the chief priests and the officers saw him, they
cried out, “Crucify him, crucify him!” Pilate
said to them, [v]“Take him yourselves and crucify him, for [w]I find no guilt in him.” 7 The
Jews[2] answered him, “We have a law, and
[x]according to that law he ought to die because
[y]he has made himself the Son of God.” 8 When
Pilate heard this statement, [z]he was even more
afraid. 9 [a]He entered his headquarters again
and said to Jesus, [b]“Where are you from?” But
[c]Jesus gave him no answer. 10 So Pilate said to
him, “You will not speak to me? Do you not
know that I have authority to release you and

[1] Or *an insurrectionist* [2] Greek *Ioudaioi* probably refers here to Jewish religious leaders, and others under their influence, in that time; also verses 12, 14, 31, 38

28 [u][ch. 19:14]
29 [v]For ver. 29-38, see Matt. 27:11-14; Mark 15:2-5; Luke 23:2, 3
31 [w][ch. 19:6]
32 [x][ch. 13:18] [y]ch. 12:32, 33; Matt. 20:19; 26:2; Mark 10:33; Luke 18:32
33 [z]ch. 19:9 [a][ch. 19:12]
36 [b][ch. 6:15; Dan. 2:44; 7:14, 27; Luke 17:21] [c]ch. 8:23; [ch. 15:19; 17:14, 16; 1 John 2:16; 4:5] [d][Matt. 26:53] [e]ch. 19:16
37 [f]See Luke 22:70 [g][ch. 12:27; Rom. 14:9] [h]ch. 16:28 [i]ch. 3:11, 32; 5:31; 8:13, 14, 18 [j]1 John 4:6; [ch. 8:47] [k]1 John 2:21; 3:19 [l]ch. 10:16, 27
38 [m]ch. 19:4 [n]ch. 19:4, 6; See Luke 23:4
39 [o]For ver. 39, 40, see Matt. 27:15-18, 20-23; Mark 15:6-14; Luke 23:18-23
40 [p]Acts 3:14
Chapter 19
1 [q]Matt. 20:19; 27:26; Mark 15:15; Luke 23:16 2 [r]Matt. 27:27-30; Mark 15:16-19 4 [s]ver. 6; ch. 18:38 5 [t]ver. 2 [u][ver. 14] 6 [v][ch. 18:31] [w]ver. 4 7 [x]Lev. 24:16; [ch. 10:33] [y]ch. 5:17, 18; 10:36; Matt. 26:63; Luke 22:70 8 [z][Matt. 27:19] 9 [a]ch. 18:33 [b]ch. 7:27 [c][ch. 18:37]; See Matt. 26:63

18:33–40 When Jesus declared, “My kingdom is not of this world” (v. 36), he wasn’t implying that his kingdom has no implications for the earth and the world we now live in. Nothing could be further from the truth. Rather he was saying, “My kingdom is on another plane than the kingdoms erected in the fallen ways of humanity.” For in fact, Jesus’ kingdom is simultaneously *over* this world and very much *in* this world. He has come to make all things new.

19:1–16 John’s account of the crucifixion is filled with gospel paradox and glorious providence. On the surface, Jesus seems to be completely subject to the whims of an approval-seeking Pilate and a frenzied mob of Jews. But when Pilate labeled Jesus “King of the Jews,” he was saying more than he knew.

Jesus was never more sovereign than when he submitted to death on the cross. This is why the refrain “to fulfill the Scripture” runs through the entire crucifixion story (vv. 24, 28, 36). Nothing was left to chance. No enemies—even as they acted according to their own volition—did anything that was unanticipated or outside the purpose of God’s sovereign providence and redemptive plan (Isa. 53:10; Rev. 13:7–8). This was the climax of all of human history. Jesus is not only the main character in this doxological drama of redemptive history; he is its writer, director, and producer.

authority to crucify you?" 11 Jesus answered
him, [d]"You would have no authority over me
at all unless it had been given you from above.
Therefore [e]he who delivered me over to you
[f]has the greater sin."

12 From then on [g]Pilate sought to release him,
but the Jews cried out, "If you release this man,
you are not Caesar's friend. [h]Everyone who
makes himself a king opposes Caesar." 13 So
when Pilate heard these words, he brought
Jesus out and sat down on [i]the judgment seat
at a place called The Stone Pavement, and in
Aramaic[1] Gabbatha. 14 Now it was [j]the day of
Preparation of the Passover. It was about the
sixth hour.[2] He said to the Jews, [k]"Behold your
King!" 15 They cried out, [l]"Away with him, away
with him, crucify him!" Pilate said to them,
"Shall I crucify your King?" The chief priests
answered, "We have no king but Caesar." 16 [m]So
he [n]delivered him over to them to be crucified.

The Crucifixion

So they took Jesus, 17 and [o]he went out, [p]bear-
ing his own cross, to the place called The
Place of a Skull, which in Aramaic is called
Golgotha. 18 [q]There they crucified him, and
with him two others, one on either side, and
Jesus between them. 19 Pilate [r]also wrote an
inscription and put it on the cross. It read,
"Jesus of Nazareth, the King of the Jews."
20 Many of the Jews read this inscription,
for [s]the place where Jesus was crucified was
near the city, and it was written in Aramaic,
in Latin, and in Greek. 21 So the chief priests
of the Jews said to Pilate, "Do not write, 'The
King of the Jews,' but rather, 'This man said,
I am King of the Jews.'" 22 Pilate answered,
[t]"What I have written I have written."

23 [u]When the soldiers had crucified Jesus,
they took his garments and divided them into
four parts, one part for each soldier; also his
tunic.[3] But the tunic was seamless, woven in
one piece from top to bottom, 24 so they said to
one another, "Let us not tear it, but cast lots for
it to see whose it shall be." [v]This was to fulfill
the Scripture which says,

> [w]"They divided my garments among
> them,
> and for my clothing they cast lots."

So the soldiers did these things, 25 [x]but standing by the cross of Jesus were his mother and
his mother's sister, Mary the wife of Clopas,
and Mary Magdalene. 26 When Jesus saw his

[1] Or *Hebrew*; also verses 17, 20 [2] That is, about noon [3] Greek *chiton*, a long garment worn under the cloak next to the skin

19:17–27 Death by crucifixion is considered one of the most barbaric, torturous, and humiliating of deaths ever conceived by mankind. Yet Jesus' heart of care and compassion shone through even in those awful moments. At a time when the pain of crucifixion would have driven most into a self-absorbed survival mode, Jesus gave focused attention and affection to a small group gathered at the foot of his cross—specifically Mary, his mother, and John, his beloved disciple.

Jesus invites us to see ourselves in this familial community of compassion. Earlier in his ministry, Jesus identified all who do the will of his Father as his "brother and sister and mother" (Matt. 12:46–50). Only the gospel can create this kind of mutually devoted community.

19:28–37 Along with the sovereignty and compassion of Jesus, John makes the substitutionary atonement of Jesus unambiguously central in his narration of the passion. Jesus didn't just take Barabbas's place on the cross (18:40), he substituted himself for all those he came to save.

Jesus' thirst (19:28) was the thirst of the Messiah, anticipated in Psalm 22:15–18. But it was also *our* thirst. Jesus became thirsty for us so that we would never thirst again (cf. John 4:14). His bones remained unbroken because Jesus died as the Passover Lamb (Ex. 12.46; Num. 9:12). Jesus wasn't just crucified between criminals, but *for* criminals *as* a criminal. God "made him to be sin who knew no sin, so that in him we might become the righteousness of God" (2 Cor. 5:21).

Because Jesus cried, "It is finished," and gave up his spirit, we now shout, "Hallelujah!" and *receive* his Spirit. Everything promised—everything needful for our redemption and for the coming "new world" (Matt. 19:28), was accomplished. Nothing was left undone.

Jesus' garments were not torn, because, unlike the first Israel, his kingdom will never be divided (1 Kings 11:29–31). "The kingdom of the world has become the kingdom of our Lord and of his Christ, and he shall reign forever and ever" (Rev. 11:15).

11 [d][Rom. 13:1] [e][ch. 18:14, 28-32; Matt. 27:2] [f]See ch. 9:41
12 [g]Acts 3:13 [h]See Luke 23:2
13 [i]Matt. 27:19
14 [j][ch. 18:28]; See Matt. 27:62 [k][ver. 5]
15 [l]Luke 23:18; [Acts 21:36]
16 [m]Matt. 27:26; Mark 15:15; Luke 23:25 [n]ch. 18:36-40
17 [o]Matt. 27:33; Mark 15:22; Luke 23:33 [p]Luke 14:27; [Matt. 27:32; Mark 15:21; Luke 23:26]
18 [q]Matt. 27:38; Mark 15:24, 27; Luke 23:32, 33
19 [r][Matt. 27:37; Mark 15:26; Luke 23:38]
20 [s]ver. 17; [Num. 15:35, 36; Heb. 13:12]
22 [t][Gen. 43:14; Esth. 4:16]
23 [u]Matt. 27:35; Mark 15:24; Luke 23:34
24 [v]See ch. 13:18 [w]Cited from Ps. 22:18
25 [x]Matt. 27:55, 56; Mark 15:40, 41; Luke 23:49

mother and [y]the disciple whom he loved standing nearby, he said to his mother, [z]"Woman, behold, your son!" 27 Then he said to the disciple, "Behold, your mother!" And from that hour the disciple took her to [a]his own home.

The Death of Jesus

28 After this, Jesus, knowing that all was now [b]finished, said ([v]to fulfill the Scripture), [c]"I thirst." 29 A jar full of sour wine stood there, [d]so they put a sponge full of the sour wine on a hyssop branch and held it to his mouth. 30 When Jesus had received the sour wine, he said, [e]"It is finished," and he bowed his head and [f]gave up his spirit.

Jesus' Side Is Pierced

31 Since it was [g]the day of Preparation, and [h]so that the bodies would not remain on the cross on the Sabbath (for that Sabbath was [i]a high day), the Jews asked Pilate that their legs might be broken and that they might be taken away. 32 So the soldiers came and broke the legs of the first, and of the other [j]who had been crucified with him. 33 But when they came to Jesus and saw that he was already dead, they did not break his legs. 34 But one of the soldiers pierced his side with a spear, and at once there came out [k]blood and water. 35 [l]He who saw it has borne witness—[m]his testimony is true, and he knows that he is telling the truth—[n]that you also may believe. 36 [o]For these things took place that the Scripture might be fulfilled: [p]"Not one of his bones [q]will be broken." 37 And again another Scripture says, [r]"They will look on him whom they have pierced."

Jesus Is Buried

38 [s]After these things Joseph of Arimathea, who was a disciple of Jesus, but secretly [t]for fear of the Jews, asked Pilate that he might take away the body of Jesus, and Pilate gave him permission. So he came and took away his body. 39 [u]Nicodemus also, who earlier had come to Jesus[1] by night, came [v]bringing a mixture of [w]myrrh and aloes, about seventy-five pounds[2] in weight. 40 So they took the body of Jesus and [x]bound it in [y]linen cloths with the spices, as is the burial custom of the Jews. 41 Now in the place where he was crucified there was a [z]garden, and [a]in the garden a new tomb [b]in which no one had yet been laid. 42 So because of the Jewish [c]day of Preparation, [d]since the tomb was close at hand, they laid Jesus there.

The Resurrection

20 [e]Now on the first day of the week Mary Magdalene came to the tomb early, while it was still dark, and saw that [f]the stone had been taken away from the tomb. 2 So she ran and went to Simon Peter and the other disciple, [g]the one whom Jesus loved, and said to them, "They have taken the Lord out of the tomb, and [h]we do not know where they have laid him." 3 [i]So Peter went out with the other disciple, and they were going toward the tomb. 4 Both of them were running together, but the other disciple outran Peter and reached the tomb first. 5 And stooping to look in, he saw [j]the linen cloths lying there, but he did not go in. 6 Then Simon Peter came, following him, and went into the tomb.

[1] Greek *him* [2] Greek *one hundred litras*; a *litra* (or Roman pound) was equal to about 11 1/2 ounces or 327 grams

20:1–10 How appropriate that Mary Magdalene was the first follower of Jesus to arrive at his tomb on resurrection morning. The Light of the World (8:12) had driven the darkness of seven demons from her soul (Luke 8:2); and now she came, while it was still dark, to witness the dawning of the new creation era. "Light and life to all he brings," says the hymn, "risen with healing in his wings." In the culmination of a principle that courses through all of Scripture, we see the supreme instance of the truth that through death comes life, and through darkness shines light.

Peter and John's slowness to accept the reality and significance of Jesus' resurrection shouldn't surprise us. Like them, we too need the Holy Spirit to help us understand what the Scriptures (the whole Bible) reveal about the person and work of Jesus.

After John "saw and believed" (John 20:8), he and Peter went back to their homes to share the good news with their families. At Jesus' dedication as an infant, Simeon told Mary, Jesus' mother, that a sword would pierce her soul (Luke 2:35). Now, after Christ's resurrection, John got to tell her that Jesus had pierced death's soul and destroyed it (cf. 1 Cor. 15:26; Rev. 20:14).

26 [y]See ch. 13:23 [z]ch. 2:4
27 [a][ch. 16:32]
28 [b][ver. 30] [v][See ver. 24 above] [c]Ps. 69:21; See ch. 4:6, 7
29 [d]Matt. 27:48; Mark 15:36; [Luke 23:36]
30 [e][ver. 28; Acts 13:29]; See ch. 17:4 [f]Matt. 27:50; Mark 15:37; Luke 23:46
31 [g]ver. 14 [h]Deut. 21:23; Josh. 8:29; 10:26, 27 [i]Ex. 12:16
32 [j]ver. 18
34 [k]1 John 5:6, 8
35 [l]1 John 1:1-3; Rev. 1:2; See ch. 15:27 [m][ch. 21:24] [n][ch. 20:31]
36 [o]See Matt. 1:22 [p]Cited from Ex. 12:46; Num. 9:12; [1 Cor. 5:7] [q]Ps. 34:20
37 [r]Cited from Zech. 12:10; [Rev. 1:7]
38 [s]For ver. 38-42, see Matt. 27:57-61; Mark 15:42-47; Luke 23:50-56 [t]See ch. 7:13 **39** [u]ch. 3:1, 2; 7:50 [v][Mark 16:1; Luke 24:1] [w]Ps. 45:8; Prov. 7:17; Song 4:14 **40** [x]ch. 11:44; [2 Chr. 16:14; Acts 5:6] [y]ch. 20:5-7; Luke 24:12 **41** [z][ch. 20:15] [a]2 Kgs. 21:18, 26 [b]Luke 23:53; [Mark 11:2] **42** [c]ver. 14, 31 [d]ver. 41 **Chapter 20** **1** [e]Matt. 28:1; Mark 16:1, 2; Luke 24:1 [f]Matt. 27:60, 66; 28:2; Mark 15:46; 16:3, 4; Luke 24:2 **2** [g]See ch. 13:23 [h]ver. 13 **3** [i]Luke 24:12 **5** [j]ch. 19:40

He saw the linen cloths lying there, 7 and [k]the face cloth, which had been on Jesus'[1] head, not lying with the linen cloths but folded up in a place by itself. 8 Then the other disciple, [l]who had reached the tomb first, also went in, and he saw and believed; 9 for as yet [m]they did not understand the Scripture, [n]that he must rise from the dead. 10 Then the disciples went back to their homes.

Jesus Appears to Mary Magdalene

11 But Mary stood weeping outside the tomb, and as she wept she stooped to look into the tomb. 12 And [o]she saw [p]two angels in white, sitting where the body of Jesus had lain, one at the head and one at the feet. 13 They said to her, [q]"Woman, why are you weeping?" She said to them, [r]"They have taken away my Lord, and I do not know where they have laid him." 14 Having said this, she turned around and [s]saw Jesus standing, [t]but she did not know that it was Jesus. 15 Jesus said to her, [u]"Woman, why are you weeping? [v]Whom are you seeking?" Supposing him to be [w]the gardener, she said to him, "Sir, if you have carried him away, tell me where you have laid him, and I will take him away." 16 Jesus said to her, "Mary." She turned and said to him in Aramaic,[2] [x]"Rabboni!" (which means Teacher). 17 Jesus said to her, "Do not cling to me, for I have not yet ascended to the Father; but go to [y]my brothers and say to them, [z]'I am ascending to my Father and your Father, to [a]my God and your God.'" 18 Mary Magdalene [b]went and announced to the disciples, "I have seen the Lord"—and that he had said these things to her.

Jesus Appears to the Disciples

19 [c]On the evening [d]of that day, the first day of the week, [e]the doors being locked where the disciples were [f]for fear of the Jews,[3] Jesus came and stood among them and said to them, [g]"Peace be with you." 20 When he had said this, [h]he showed them his hands and his side. Then [i]the disciples were glad when they saw the Lord. 21 Jesus said to them again, "Peace be with you. As [j]the Father has sent me, [k]even so I am sending you." 22 And when he had said this, he [l]breathed on them and said to them, [m]"Receive the Holy Spirit. 23 [n]If you forgive the sins of any, they are forgiven them; if you withhold forgiveness from any, it is withheld."

Jesus and Thomas

24 Now [o]Thomas, one of the Twelve, called the Twin,[4] was not with them when Jesus came. 25 So the other disciples told him, "We have seen the Lord." But he said to them, [p]"Unless I see in his hands the mark of the nails, and place my finger into the mark of the nails, and place my hand into his side, I will never believe."

26 Eight days later, his disciples were inside

[1] Greek *his* [2] Or *Hebrew* [3] Greek *Ioudaioi* probably refers here to Jewish religious leaders, and others under their influence, in that time [4] Greek *Didymus*

20:11–18 Mary Magdalene returned to the tomb, and lingered in her grief. At first she thought Jesus was a gardener, and indeed, he is; for where the first Adam failed his work in the garden, the last Adam has wondrously succeeded. The grain of gospel wheat died, and was planted in a garden tomb, and now the grand harvest begins (cf. 12:24–25).

It wasn't until Jesus spoke her name that Mary recognized him. The Good Shepherd had laid down his life and taken it up again. Now he called one of his sheep by name and she recognized his life-giving voice (10:4). The gospel is no mere invitation; it is a summons to glory. Each of us must move from the general of John 3:16 (God's love for the world generally) to the personal of Galatians 2:20 (God's love for me specifically).

20:19–31 Jesus' encounter with the fearful, guilt-ridden disciples is a model of what should happen every time we gather together in Jesus' name to worship God. Jesus comes into our midst and speaks to us by his Word, and then applies the gospel of peace to our souls and breathes his Spirit upon us, commissioning us to go forth as servants of the gospel.

The authority Jesus gave the apostles to pronounce the forgiveness of sins is extended through the church by the preaching of the gospel. Where can we go, with certainty, for the assurance of pardon? Not to the works of our hands, nor to the idols of our hearts. Only by believing the gospel of God's grace can we expect to hear Jesus say to us, "Peace be with *you*."

7 [k] ch. 11:44
8 [l] ver. 4
9 [m] Matt. 22:29 [n] Ps. 16:10; Luke 24:46; Acts 2:25-31; 13:34, 35; 17:3; 1 Cor. 15:4
12 [o] [Mark 16:5] [p] Luke 24:4
13 [q] ver. 15; [ch. 2:4] [r] ver. 2
14 [s] Mark 16:9; [Matt. 28:9] [t] ch. 21:4; Luke 24:16, 31
15 [u] ver. 13 [v] ch. 1:38; 18:4, 7 [w] [ch. 19:41]
16 [x] See ch. 1:38
17 [y] See Matt. 28:10 [z] [Mark 16:19]; See ch. 14:12 [a] Matt. 27:46; Eph. 1:17; Rev. 3:2, 12; [1 Cor. 3:23]
18 [b] Mark 16:10; [Matt. 28:10; Luke 24:10, 22, 23]
19 [c] 1 Cor. 15:5; [ver. 26] [d] Luke 24:33, 36 [e] ver. 26 [f] See ch. 7:13 [g] See ch. 14:27
20 [h] Luke 24:40 [i] ch. 16:22
21 [j] ch. 17:18; See ch. 3:17 [k] ch. 13:20; See Acts 1:2
22 [l] Gen. 2:7 [m] [Acts 2:4]; See ch. 7:39
23 [n] [Matt. 16:19; 18:18; 1 Cor. 5:4, 5]
24 [o] See ch. 11:16
25 [p] ver. 20; [Ps. 22:16]

again, and Thomas was with them. [q]Although
the doors were locked, Jesus came and stood
among them and said, [q]"Peace be with you."
27 Then he said to Thomas, [r]"Put your finger
here, and see my hands; and put out your
hand, and place it in my side. Do not disbelieve, but believe." 28 Thomas answered him,
[s]"My Lord and my God!" 29 Jesus said to him,
"Have you believed because you have seen me?
[t]Blessed are those who have not seen and yet
have believed."

The Purpose of This Book

30 [u]Now Jesus did many other signs [v]in the
presence of the disciples, which are not written in this book; 31 [w]but these are written so
that you may [x]believe that Jesus is the Christ,
[y]the Son of God, and that by believing [z]you
may have life [a]in his name.

Jesus Appears to Seven Disciples

21 After this Jesus [b]revealed himself [c]again
to the disciples by [d]the Sea of Tiberias,
and he revealed himself in this way. 2 Simon
Peter, [e]Thomas (called the Twin), Nathanael of
[f]Cana in Galilee, [g]the sons of Zebedee, and two
others of his disciples were together. 3 Simon
Peter said to them, "I am going fishing." They
said to him, "We will go with you." They went
out and got into the boat, but [h]that night they
caught nothing.

4 Just as day was breaking, Jesus stood on the
shore; yet the disciples [i]did not know that it
was Jesus. 5 [j]Jesus said to them, "Children, do
you have any fish?" They answered him, "No."
6 [k]He said to them, "Cast the net on the right
side of the boat, and you will find some." So
they cast it, and now they were not able to haul
it in, because of the quantity of fish. 7 That disciple [l]whom Jesus loved therefore said to Peter,
"It is the Lord!" When Simon Peter heard that
it was the Lord, [m]he put on his outer garment,
for he was [n]stripped for work, and [o]threw himself into the sea. 8 The other disciples came
in the boat, dragging the net full of fish, for
they were not far from the land, but about a
hundred yards[1] off.

9 When they got out on land, they saw a
charcoal fire in place, with fish laid out on it,
and bread. 10 Jesus said to them, "Bring some
of the fish that you have just caught." 11 So
Simon Peter went aboard and hauled the net
ashore, full of large fish, 153 of them. And
although there were so many, the net was
not torn. 12 Jesus said to them, [p]"Come and
[q]have breakfast." Now [r]none of the disciples
dared ask him, "Who are you?" They knew
it was the Lord. 13 Jesus came and [s]took the
bread and gave it to them, and so with the fish.
14 [t]This was now the third time that Jesus was
revealed to the disciples after he was raised
from the dead.

[1] Greek *two hundred cubits*; a *cubit* was about 18 inches or 45 centimeters

26 [q]ver. 19
27 [r]ver. 20; 1 John 1:1; [Luke 24:39]
28 [s][ch. 1:1, 49]
29 [t]1 Pet. 1:8; [2 Cor. 5:7]
30 [u]ch. 21:25 [v]Acts 10:41
31 [w]1 John 5:13 [x]See ch. 11:27 [y]See Matt. 14:33 [z]ch. 3:15, 16; 5:40; 6:53; 10:10 [a][Acts 10:43; 1 Cor. 6:11]; See Acts 3:6

Chapter 21
1 [b]ver. 14; [Mark 16:12, 14]; See ch. 7:4 [c]ch. 20:19, 26 [d]ch. 6:1
2 [e]See ch. 11:16 [f]ch. 2:1; 4:46 [g]Matt. 4:21; Luke 5:10
3 [h][Luke 5:5]
4 [i]ch. 20:14
5 [j]Luke 24:41
6 [k][Luke 5:4, 6, 7]
7 [l]See ch. 13:23 [m]ver. 18; [ch. 13:4] [n]1 Sam. 19:24; Isa. 20:2; Mic. 1:8 [o][Matt. 14:29]
12 [p]Acts 10:41 [q]ver. 15 [r][ch. 4:27]
13 [s]ver. 9
14 [t]ver. 1; ch. 20:19, 26

20:30–31 John wrote his Gospel, choosing from a large body of material from the life of Jesus. This editorial note should remind us that the Bible is not an exhaustive account of all things, but a sufficient account of necessary things—the things that reveal Jesus to be the Son of God, the Savior of all who trust him.

21:1–8 After writing what appears to be the perfect ending for his Gospel (20:30–31), John adds an epilogue which demonstrates that we never really come to the end of the gospel. We will never outgrow our need for the grace of Jesus.

Just as the apostle Paul would continue to make tents, so the apostles who preceded him continued to be fishermen. Whatever our vocation, Jesus meets us there, but he doesn't leave what we do untouched. Fishers of fish are also called to be fishers of men (Matt. 4:19), and both require Jesus. Peter hauled 153 fish ashore only because Jesus filled the nets. Peter would see 3,000 conversions on the day of Pentecost (Acts 2:41) only because Jesus is filling his church. Without him we can do nothing (John 15:5).

21:9–14 Peter had felt freedom to move toward Jesus in his brokenness, and we see Jesus welcoming his beloved friend. Jesus provides for our every need, even our food. There are only two times when a charcoal fire is mentioned in the New Testament: here, and earlier in John's Gospel, when Peter, while warming himself, denied Jesus in the presence of Israel's high priest (18:15–27). Now, in the presence of heaven's Great High Priest, Peter experiences the reconciling and restorative power of the gospel.

Jesus and Peter

[15]When they had [u]finished breakfast, Jesus
said to Simon Peter, [v]"Simon, [w]son of John, [x]do
you love me more than these?" He said to him,
"Yes, Lord; you know that I love you." He said
to him, "Feed [y]my lambs." [16]He said to him a
second time, "Simon, son of John, do you love
me?" He said to him, "Yes, Lord; you know that
I love you." He said to him, [z]"Tend [y]my sheep."
[17]He said to him the third time, "Simon, son
of John, do you love me?" Peter was grieved
because he said to him [a]the third time, "Do
you love me?" and he said to him, "Lord, [b]you
know everything; you know that I love you."
Jesus said to him, "Feed [c]my sheep. [18][d]Truly,
truly, I say to you, when you were young, [e]you
used to dress yourself and walk wherever you
wanted, but when you are old, you will stretch
out your hands, and another will dress you
and carry you where you do not want to go."
[19](This he said to show [f]by what kind of death
he was to glorify God.) And after saying this
he said to him, [g]"Follow me."

Jesus and the Beloved Apostle

[20]Peter turned and saw [h]the disciple whom
Jesus loved following them, [i]the one who also
had leaned back against him during the supper and had said, "Lord, who is it that is going
to betray you?" [21]When Peter saw him, he said
to Jesus, "Lord, what about this man?" [22]Jesus
said to him, "If it is my will that he remain
[j]until [k]I come, what is that to you? [l]You follow
me!" [23]So the saying spread abroad among
[m]the brothers[1] that this disciple was not to die;
yet Jesus did not say to him that he was not to
die, but, "If it is my will that he remain until
I come, what is that to you?"

[24]This is the disciple [n]who is bearing witness about these things, and who has written
these things, and [o]we know [p]that his testimony is true.

[25]Now [q]there are also many other things that
Jesus did. Were every one of them to be written, I suppose that [r]the world itself could not
contain the books that would be written.

[1] Or *brothers and sisters*

21:15–19 Jesus didn't hurry the process of Peter's restoration. The Savior asked three times for affirmation of the apostle's love, reflecting Peter's three denials during Christ's passion. Gospel surgery is free, but not always easy. Grace produces redemptive pain, not punitive pain. But pain is still painful. Indeed, the gospel brings an end to all deadening worldly grief. But the gospel is the beginning of enlivening godly grief (2 Cor. 7:10–11). The law condemns, the gospel convicts; the law creates self-centered tears, the gospel creates God-centered tears.

"Do you love me more than these?" It would have been easier on Peter had Jesus asked him, "Do you promise not to fail me again?" But Jesus knew better than to ask that question, because, of course, Peter would fail again (e.g., Gal. 2:11–21). Jesus is more jealous for our love than zealous for our works. If he has our hearts, he'll have everything else.

21:20–25 Peter had just been told to expect a death similar to the one his Savior experienced, but his thoughts immediately shifted to John. A fully restored Peter is not a fully transformed Peter. How easy it is for us to become distracted and envious of one another's callings. But the Good Shepherd, who knows us by name, leads us by decree. Jesus gives us saving grace and he also gives us serving grace. There are no little people or little places in God's story.

All things necessary for our salvation are written in the Bible. But the gospel will continue to write stories of Jesus' glory and grace wherever it is preached.

15[u] ver. 12 [v] [Matt. 16:17; Luke 22:31] [w] ch. 1:42 [x] [Matt. 26:33; Mark 14:29] [y] ch. 10:11-16; [Isa. 40:11]
16[z] Acts 20:28; 1 Pet. 5:2; Rev. 7:17 (Gk.) [y] [See ver. 15 above]
17[a] [ch. 13:38] [b] See ch. 2:25 [c] ver. 16
18[d] [ch. 13:36] [e] ver. 7
19[f] 2 Pet. 1:14 [g] ver. 22; Matt. 16:24; [ch. 13:36]; See ch. 8:12
20[h] ver. 7 [i] ch. 13:25
22[j] Matt. 10:23; 16:28; 1 Cor. 4:5; 11:26; James 5:7; Rev. 2:25 [k] [ch. 14:3, 18, 28; Heb. 10:37; Rev. 2:5, 16; 3:3, 11; 16:15; 22:7, 12, 20]; See Matt. 16:27 [l] ver. 19
23[m] Acts 1:15; 9:30; 11:1; 12:17; 15:1; 16:2, 40; 21:7, 17; 1 John 3:14, 16
24[n] See ch. 15:27 [o] 1 John 3:2, 14; 5:15, 18-20; [ch. 19:35] [p] 3 John 12
25[q] ch. 20:30 [r] [Amos 7:10]

Introduction to Acts

Author and Date

Acts is a sequel to the Gospel of Luke. Both were written by Luke, a physician who traveled with the apostle Paul. Acts ends with Paul under house arrest, awaiting trial before Caesar, c. A.D. 62. Many scholars assume Acts was written then because it does not record Paul's defense, release, and further gospel preaching. Luke's purpose for writing his Gospel (see Luke 1:3–4) applies to Acts as well: to give an "orderly" account of the early church after Christ's resurrection.

The Gospel in Acts

Acts is the story of God's grace flooding out to the world, from the cross and resurrection of Jesus in Jerusalem to the ends of the earth. Nothing is more prominent in Acts than the spread of the gospel. Jesus promises a geographic expansion at the outset (1:8), and Acts follows the news of his death and resurrection as it spreads from Jerusalem to Judea, Samaria, and the faraway capital of Rome.

The preaching of Jesus' death and resurrection is central in Acts. The Greek verb for "preach the gospel" (*euangelizo*) occurs more in this book than in any other in the New Testament. About a third of the book of Acts consists of speeches, and most of these are speeches by Peter or Paul proclaiming the gospel. The good news of the salvation accomplished in Christ and applied by the Holy Spirit extends to the "ends of the earth" through preaching.

In Acts, "grace" is a parallel for "the gospel" or "salvation." Jesus' message is summarized as "the word of his grace" (20:32), believers are said to have received "grace" or to be "full of grace" (6:8), and they are challenged to continue in grace. The missionaries in Acts proclaim the grace of God, and it is through this grace that people are able to respond with faith.

Acts reveals God's passionate pursuit of his people, beginning with his followers in Jerusalem, expanding to Samaria, then to the rest of the world. By the end of the book we see Paul living in Rome, "proclaiming the kingdom of God and teaching about the Lord Jesus Christ with all boldness and without hindrance" (28:31). The gospel draws people in, constitutes them as the church centered on the grace of Jesus, and then sends them out in mission to the world. The new group of believers is marked by the Holy Spirit, who creates such a distinctive community that others are drawn in, experiencing God's grace. At the same time, they take the gospel message to new people and new lands, making God's grace known to the ends of the earth.

The gospel's expansion is the culmination of what God has been doing since the beginning. Luke consistently grounds salvation in the ancient purpose of God, which comes to fruition at God's own initiative. Acts shows that the new Christian movement is not a fringe sect but the culmination of God's plan of redemption. What was seen only as shadows in the Old Testament God reveals finally and fully through Jesus Christ. The book of Acts does not primarily provide human patterns to emulate or avoid. Instead, it repeatedly calls us to reflect upon the work of God, fulfilled in Jesus Christ, establishing the church by the power of the Holy Spirit. We are invited to enter and participate in a story that is much bigger than we are.

In Acts, the gospel expands not through human strength, but through weakness, opposition, and persecution. Demonic forces, worldly powers and authorities, governmental opposition, language and cultural barriers, intense suffering and bloody persecution, unjust imprisonment, unbelief, internal disunity, and even shipwrecks and snakes all threaten to slow down the gospel's advance. But opposition and suffering do not thwart the spread of Jesus' grace; rather, they fuel it.

The gospel spreads despite barriers of geography, ethnicity, culture, gender, and wealth. Many of these barriers appear so inviolable that when the gospel is preached to a new segment of society, riots ensue. But Luke makes clear that no one is beyond the scope of God's saving power, nor is anyone exempt from the need for God's redeeming grace.

All people receive the grace of God through one man, Jesus Christ. Jesus' gospel goes out to all places and all types of people, because Jesus is Lord of all.

Outline

I. Preparation for Witness (1:1–2:13)

II. The Witness in Jerusalem (2:14–5:42)

III. The Witness beyond Jerusalem (6:1–12:25)

IV. The Witness in Cyprus and Southern Galatia (13:1–14:28)

V. The Jerusalem Council (15:1–35)

VI. The Witness in Greece (15:36–18:22)

VII. The Witness in Ephesus (18:23–21:16)

VIII. The Arrest in Jerusalem (21:17–23:35)

IX. The Witness in Caesarea (24:1–26:32)

X. The Witness in Rome (27:1–28:31)

The

Acts

of the Apostles

The Promise of the Holy Spirit

1 In the first book, O [a]Theophilus, I have
dealt with all that Jesus began [b]to do and
teach, 2 until the day when [c]he was taken up,
after he [d]had given commands [e]through the
Holy Spirit to the apostles whom he had chosen. 3 [f]He presented himself alive to them after
his suffering by many proofs, appearing to
them during forty days and speaking about
the kingdom of God.
4 And while staying[1] with them [g]he ordered
them not to depart from Jerusalem, but to
wait for the promise of the Father, which, he
said, "you heard from me; 5 for [h]John baptized
with water, [h]but you will be baptized [i]with[2]
the Holy Spirit not many days from now."

The Ascension

6 So when they had come together, they
asked him, "Lord, [j]will you at this time [k]restore
the kingdom to Israel?" 7 He said to them, [l]"It
is not for you to know [m]times or seasons that
the Father has fixed by his own authority. 8 But
you will receive [n]power [o]when the Holy Spirit
has come upon you, and [p]you will be [q]my
witnesses in Jerusalem and in all Judea and
[r]Samaria, and [s]to the end of the earth." 9 And
when he had said these things, as they were
looking on, [t]he was lifted up, and [u]a cloud took
him out of their sight. 10 And while they were
gazing into heaven as he went, behold, [v]two
[w]men stood by them in [x]white robes, 11 and said,
[y]"Men of Galilee, why do you stand looking

[1] Or *eating* [2] Or *in*

1:1–11 Despite its title, "The Acts of the Apostles," the book of Acts is a book about Jesus. In his first volume, the Gospel that bears his name, Luke recounted "all that Jesus began to do and teach" (v. 1). What Jesus began in Luke, he continues in Acts, even after his ascension (v. 9). He is the primary character of the book and the focus of all its events. As Jesus himself said in Luke's Gospel, he is the primary character and focus of *all* of Scripture (Luke 24:27).

Acts depicts the continuing actions and teachings of Jesus in a way that no other book of the Bible does. Luke claims that as the budding Christian movement spreads, Jesus himself is at work (cf. Acts 1:8; 4:10, 30; 5:32; 7:55, 59–60; 9:5, 15–17). The church is Jesus' vehicle to continue his work in the world. This is true for us today as well: as Paul says, we who are in Christ are his body (1 Cor. 12:27).

There is an awesome responsibility here, but the responsibility rests on Christ. The church is Jesus' church, and what he began in his earthly ministry, he will finish (Phil. 1:6).

The book of Acts is a continuation of the Gospel of Luke. Luke "rewinds" a little, and the key event that he reviews is the resurrection. The resurrection is a key topic in the evangelistic speeches in Acts. The word "resurrection" (Greek *anastasis*) occurs more times in the book of Acts than in any other New Testament book (eleven times in Acts; the next highest is Luke with six). The first item on Jesus' mind, post-resurrection, is that the apostles wait for the power of the Holy Spirit. This power leads to their being a "witness" in four concentric circles, leading out from Jerusalem. The fact that Jesus notes Samaria shows that the gospel will transcend not just geography (Jerusalem and Judea), but ethnicity as well.

The primary task of the people of God is to bear witness to his great deeds. The first disciples were charged to bear witness to the risen Christ, whom they had seen with their eyes. This witness would begin in Jerusalem, but would move outward to "the end of the earth" (Acts 1:8). In these verses, Jesus did not command his disciples

Chapter 1
1 [a]Luke 1:3 [b]Luke 24:19
2 [c]See Mark 16:19 [d][ch. 10:42; Matt. 28:19, 20; Mark 16:15; Luke 24:47; John 20:21] [e][ch. 10:38; Luke 4:1, 18; John 20:22]
3 [f]ch. 10:40, 41; 13:31; Matt. 28:17; Mark 16:14; Luke 24:34, 36-51; John 20:19-29; 21; 1 Cor. 15:5-7
4 [g]Luke 24:49
5 [h]ch. 11:16; See Matt. 3:11 [i]ch. 2:1-4
6 [j]See Luke 17:20 [k][Mic. 4:8; Matt. 17:11; Mark 9:12; Luke 19:11]
7 [l][Matt. 24:36; Mark 13:32] [m]Dan. 2:21; 1 Thess. 5:1
8 [n]ch. 4:33; Luke 24:49; 1 Thess. 1:5; [ch. 10:38; Luke 4:14] [o]ver. 5 [p][ver. 22]; See Luke 24:48 [q][Isa. 43:12] [r]ch. 8:1, 14; [Matt. 10:5] [s]ch. 13:47; [Mark 16:15; Col. 1:23]
9 [t]ver. 2 [u]See 1 Thess. 4:17
10 [v][Luke 24:4] [w]Josh. 5:13; Dan. 9:21; 10:5; 12:6, 7; Zech. 1:8-11 [x]Matt. 28:3; Mark 16:5; John 20:12
11 [y]ch. 2:7; 13:31

into heaven? This Jesus, who was taken up
from you into heaven, [z]will [a]come in the same
way as you saw him go into heaven."

Matthias Chosen to Replace Judas

12 Then [b]they returned to Jerusalem from the
mount called Olivet, which is near Jerusalem,
a Sabbath day's journey away. 13 And when they
had entered, they went up to [c]the upper room,
where they were staying, [d]Peter and John
and James and Andrew, Philip and Thomas,
Bartholomew and Matthew, James the son of
Alphaeus and Simon [e]the Zealot and Judas the
son of James. 14 All these [f]with one accord [g]were
devoting themselves to prayer, together with
[h]the women and Mary the mother of Jesus,
and [i]his brothers.[1]

15 In those days Peter stood up among [j]the
brothers (the company of persons was in all
about 120) and said, 16 "Brothers, [k]the Scripture
had to be fulfilled, which the Holy Spirit spoke
beforehand by the mouth of David concerning Judas, [l]who became a guide to those who
arrested Jesus. 17 For [m]he was numbered among
us and was allotted his share in [n]this ministry."
18 (Now this man [o]acquired a field with [p]the
reward of his wickedness, and falling headlong[2] he burst open in the middle and all his
bowels gushed out. 19 And it became known
to all the inhabitants of Jerusalem, so that
the field was called [q]in their own language
Akeldama, that is, Field of Blood.) 20 "For it is
written in the Book of Psalms,

> [r]" 'May his camp become desolate,
> and let there be no one to dwell in it';

and

> [s]" 'Let another take his office.'

21 So one of the men who have accompanied us
during [t]all the time that the Lord Jesus [u]went
in and out among us, 22 [v]beginning from the
baptism of John until the day when [w]he was
taken up from us—one of these men must
become with us [x]a witness to his resurrection."
23 And they put forward two, Joseph called
[y]Barsabbas, who was also called [z]Justus, and
[a]Matthias. 24 And [b]they prayed and said, "You,
Lord, [c]who know the hearts of all, show which
one of these two you have chosen 25 to take
the place in [d]this ministry and [e]apostleship
from which Judas turned aside to go to his
own place." 26 And they cast lots for them, and
the lot fell on Matthias, and he was numbered
with the eleven apostles.

The Coming of the Holy Spirit

2 When [f]the day of Pentecost arrived, they
were all together in one place. 2 And suddenly there came from heaven a sound like
[g]a mighty rushing wind, and [h]it filled the

[1] Or *brothers and sisters*. The plural Greek word *adelphoi* (translated "brothers") refers to siblings in a family. In New Testament usage, depending on the context, *adelphoi* may refer either to men or to both men and women who are siblings (brothers and sisters) in God's family, the church; also verse 15 [2] Or *swelling up*

11 [z][Phil. 3:20; 1 Thess. 1:10]; See Matt. 16:27 [a]2 Thess. 1:10
12 [b]Luke 24:50, 52
13 [c]ch. 9:37, 39; 20:8 [d]See Matt. 10:2-4; Mark 3:16-19; Luke 6:14-16 [e][ch. 21:20]
14 [f]ch. 2:46; 4:24; 5:12; 15:25; Rom. 15:6 [g]ch. 2:42; 6:4; Rom. 12:12; Col. 4:2; [Eph. 6:18] [h]Luke 8:2, 3 [i]See Matt. 12:46
15 [j]See John 21:23
16 [k]Luke 24:44; [Luke 22:37] [l]Matt. 26:47; Mark 14:43; Luke 22:47; John 18:3
17 [m]John 6:71; 13:21 [n]ver. 25; ch. 20:24; 21:19; Rom. 11:13; 2 Cor. 4:1
18 [o][Matt. 27:5-8] [p][Matt. 26:14-16]
19 [q][ch. 21:40]
20 [r]Cited from Ps. 69:25 [s]Cited from Ps. 109:8
21 [t][John 15:27] [u]Num. 27:17; Deut. 31:2; 1 Sam. 18:13
22 [v]ch. 13:24; Mark 1:1-4 [w]ver. 2, 9 [x]ch. 4:33; [ver. 8; 1 Pet. 1:3]; See Luke 24:48
23 [y][ch. 15:22] [z][ch. 18:7; Col. 4:11] [a]ver. 26

to perform certain rituals, to act according to certain rules, or to refrain from certain activities. He promised them that they would testify to his power when the Holy Spirit came upon them.

This is not a concept unique to Acts or the New Testament. God has always been concerned that his people reflect on what he has done and tell others about it. God's people have always been primarily witnesses to his greatness. "I have redeemed you," God says in Isaiah. " 'You are my witnesses . . . and my servant whom I have chosen, that you may know and believe me and understand that I am he' " (Isa. 43:1, 10).

2:1–13 Since the time of Babel (Gen. 11:1–9), the nations of the earth were divided by language, unable to come together as a result of their rebellion against God. In God's Old Testament redemptive acts, he singled out the Jewish nation to mediate his blessing to the world, and therefore the good news of God's grace was communicated only in the Hebrew language. With the outpouring of the Holy Spirit at Pentecost, however, the curse of Babel begins to unravel. No longer is the gospel confined to Hebrew; it is available directly to all nations and all languages. The restored order of God's kingdom begins to break into the dark and confused world of sin. This gives us hope today. The gospel triumphs in a world still groaning under the curse of sin (Rom. 8:22). One day Christ's reign will be fully realized, and the effects of sin will fall away completely.

24 [b]ch. 6:6; 13:3 [c]See 1 Sam. 16:7; Rom. 8:27 **25** [d]See ver. 17 [e]Rom. 1:5; 1 Cor. 9:2; Gal. 2:8 **Chapter 2** **1** [f]ch. 20:16; 1 Cor. 16:8; [Lev. 23:15] **2** [g][1 Kgs. 19:11; Job 38:1; Ezek. 1:4] [h][ch. 4:31; 16:26]

entire house where they were sitting. 3 And
divided tongues [i]as of fire appeared to them
and rested[1] on each one of them. 4 And they
were all [j]filled with the Holy Spirit and began
[k]to speak in other tongues [l]as the Spirit gave
them utterance.

5 Now there were dwelling in Jerusalem
Jews, devout men from every nation under
heaven. 6 And [m]at this sound the multitude
came together, and they were bewildered,
because each one was hearing them speak in
his own language. 7 And [n]they were amazed
and astonished, saying, "Are not all these who
are speaking [o]Galileans? 8 And how is it that
we hear, each of us in his own native language?
9 Parthians and [p]Medes and [q]Elamites and residents of Mesopotamia, Judea and Cappadocia,
Pontus and Asia, 10 Phrygia and Pamphylia,
Egypt and the parts of Libya belonging to
Cyrene, and visitors from Rome, 11 both Jews
and [r]proselytes, Cretans and Arabians—we
hear them telling in our own tongues the
mighty works of God." 12 And [s]all were amazed
and perplexed, saying to one another, "What
does this mean?" 13 But others [t]mocking said,
"They are filled with new wine."

Peter's Sermon at Pentecost

14 But Peter, standing with the eleven, lifted
up his voice and addressed them: "Men of
Judea and all who dwell in Jerusalem, let this
be known to you, and give ear to my words.
15 For these people are not drunk, as you suppose, [u]since it is only the third hour of the day.[2]
16 But this is what was uttered through the
prophet Joel:

17 [v]" 'And in the last days it shall be, God
declares,
[w]that I will pour out my Spirit [x]on all
flesh,
and your sons and [y]your daughters shall
prophesy,
and your young men shall see visions,
and your old men shall dream
dreams;
18 even on my male servants[3] and female
servants
in those days I will pour out my
Spirit, and [z]they shall prophesy.
19 And I will show wonders in the heavens
above
and signs on the earth below,
blood, and fire, and vapor of smoke;

[1] Or *And tongues as of fire appeared to them, distributed among them, and rested* [2] That is, 9 A.M. [3] Greek *bondservants*; twice in this verse

3[i] Matt. 3:11
4[j] ch. 4:31; 13:52 [k] See Mark 16:17 [l] [1 Cor. 12:10, 11]
6[m] ver. 2
7[n] ver. 12 [o] ch. 1:11; [Matt. 26:73]
9[p] 2 Kgs. 17:6 [q] Gen. 14:1, 9; Isa. 11:11; Dan. 8:2
11[r] ch. 6:5; 13:43; Matt. 23:15
12[s] ver. 7
13[t] [ch. 17:32; 1 Cor. 14:23]
15[u] [1 Thess. 5:7]
17[v] Cited from Joel 2:28-32 [w] ver. 18, 33; Isa. 32:15; 44:3; Ezek. 36:27; See Rom. 5:5 [x] [ch. 10:45; Titus 3:6] [y] ch. 21:9
18[z] ch. 11:28; 21:10; 1 Cor. 12:10

The experience of the Spirit at Pentecost fulfills John the Baptist's prophecy of the one (Jesus) who would baptize in the Holy Spirit (Matt. 3:11; cf. Acts 1:5). The coming of the Spirit at Pentecost has a specific purpose in redemptive history: to show that God's salvation is now flowing out to people from every nation, tribe, and language. This is repeated in the three outpourings of the Spirit that follow in Acts 8; 10–11; and 19. Luke's focus in Acts 2 is on the fulfillment of prophecy, not on paradigms for personal experience. Luke is introducing the expanding gospel ministry of the Holy Spirit as the gospel is beginning to spread.

The story in Acts is also our story, because we are participating in God's story. The descent of the Spirit on these apostles is really the birth story of all who are in Christ. While we think of our lives in terms of our own births, upbringing, education, families, line of work, and so on, there is another story that has been happening parallel to these events—actually, it has woven its way through all of these things. And this interwoven story begins here with the descent of the Holy Spirit who fills these believers. If this had never happened, if God had not looked on Christ's work on the cross and said "It is good," raised him from the dead, and set him at his right side to pour out his Spirit on his people, then we would still be dead in our sins. We would still be without the spiritual life of the new birth, lost and without hope.

2:14–41 Peter begins his famous Pentecost sermon with an extensive reference to the Old Testament, a citation from the prophet Joel, who predicted that God's Spirit would be poured out in the last days, before the final judgment (the "day of the Lord"). According to Peter, the last days have begun. This "new religion" is actually the continuation of what God has been doing through Israel all along. Better yet, God made promises years ago that these "last days" would come, and at Pentecost God is demonstrating that he is faithful and powerful to keep his promises. As he promised, God is pouring out his Spirit on *all* flesh—men and women, young and old, Jew and Gentile. God is mercifully and joyfully calling all people to salvation.

20 [a]the sun shall be turned to darkness
and the moon to blood,
before [b]the day of the Lord comes, the
great and magnificent day.
21 And it shall come to pass that [c]everyone
who calls upon the name of the
Lord shall be saved.'

22 "Men of Israel, hear these words: Jesus of
Nazareth, [d]a man attested to you by God [e]with
[f]mighty works and wonders and signs that
[g]God did through him in your midst, as you
yourselves know— 23 this Jesus,[1] [h]delivered up
according to [i]the definite plan and [j]foreknowl-
edge of God, [k]you crucified and killed by the
hands of lawless men. 24 [l]God raised him up,
loosing the pangs of death, because [m]it was not
possible for him to be held by it. 25 For David
says concerning him,

[n]"'I saw the Lord always before me,
for he is at my right hand that I may
not be shaken;
26 therefore my heart was glad, and my
tongue rejoiced;
my flesh also will dwell [o]in hope.
27 For you will not abandon my soul to
[p]Hades,
[q]or let your [r]Holy One [s]see corruption.
28 You have made known to me the paths
of life;
you will make me full of gladness
with your presence.'

29 "Brothers, I may say to you with confidence
about [t]the patriarch David [u]that he both died
and [v]was buried, and [w]his tomb is with us to
this day. 30 [x]Being therefore a prophet, and
knowing that [y]God had sworn with an oath to
him that he would set one of his descendants
on his throne, 31 he foresaw and spoke about
the resurrection of the Christ, that [z]he was
not abandoned to Hades, nor did his flesh see
corruption. 32 This Jesus [a]God raised up, [b]and
of that we all are witnesses. 33 [c]Being therefore
[d]exalted at the right hand of God, and having received from [e]the Father [f]the promise of
the Holy Spirit, [g]he has poured out this that
you yourselves are seeing and hearing. 34 For
[h]David did not ascend into the heavens, but
he himself says,

[i]"'The Lord said to my Lord,
"Sit at my right hand,
35 until I make your enemies your footstool."'

36 Let all the house of Israel therefore know
for certain that [j]God has made him [k]both Lord
and Christ, this Jesus [l]whom you crucified."
37 Now when [m]they heard this they were cut
to the heart, and said to Peter and the rest of
the apostles, "Brothers, [n]what shall we do?"
38 And Peter said to them, [o]"Repent and [p]be
baptized every one of you [q]in the name of
Jesus Christ [r]for the forgiveness of your sins,
and you will receive [s]the gift of the Holy Spirit.

[1] Greek *this one*

20[a] See Matt. 24:29 [b] [1 Thess. 5:2; Rev. 16:14]
21[c] Rom. 10:13; [ch. 16:31]
22[d] See John 3:2 [e] ch. 10:38; Luke 24:19 [f] 2 Cor. 12:12; 2 Thess. 2:9; Heb. 2:4 [g] [Matt. 12:28]
23[h] Matt. 26:24; [ch. 3:13; Matt. 20:19]; See Luke 24:20 [i] Luke 22:22; [ch. 3:18; 4:28; 13:27] [j] 1 Pet. 1:2; [1 Pet. 1:20; Rev. 13:8] [k] See ch. 5:30
24[l] ver. 32; ch. 3:15; 4:10; 10:40; 13:30, 33, 34, 37; 17:31; Rom. 4:24; 6:4; 8:11; 10:9; 1 Cor. 6:14; 15:15; 2 Cor. 4:14; Gal. 1:1; Eph. 1:20; Col. 2:12; 1 Thess. 1:10; Heb. 13:20; 1 Pet. 1:21; [Eph. 2:5] [m] [Luke 24:5; John 10:18; 2 Tim. 1:10; Heb. 2:14; Rev. 1:17, 18]
25[n] Cited from Ps. 16:8-11
26[o] Rom. 4:18
27[p] ver. 31; See Matt. 11:23 [q] ch. 13:35 [r] See Heb. 7:26 [s] [Luke 2:26]

In Peter's first sermon, the essence of gospel proclamation is clear: Jesus is Lord (v. 36); he is the fulfillment of God's promise for an eternal Davidic kingdom (vv. 29–36). This simple statement of Christ's lordship poses a fundamental challenge both to the Jews (with their strict monotheism) and to the Romans (with their religious-political system founded on the supremacy of Caesar as lord).

The resurrection is also one of the core elements throughout the gospel presentations in Acts. Peter quotes from Psalm 16:8–11 to show that the resurrection was God's intention all along. Thus, the crucifixion of Christ was necessarily part of God's plan, and he followed it by raising Jesus from the dead. Peter shows that this gospel plan is all promised in Scripture. God's grace breaks through the walls of the worst of human rebellion.

Just as Jesus promised that the gospel would spread to the end of the earth, Peter proclaims that, "the promise is for you and for your children *and* for all who are far off" (Acts 2:39). The gospel is for immediate hearers and their covenant children but is not confined by ethnic or geographical boundaries. And it is universal in scope: "far off" is not just geographical. By his death and resurrection, Jesus Christ has reconciled to himself all of us who were formerly "far off" from God and one another (Eph. 2:17–19). No one is so far removed that God cannot redeem them.

29[t] ch. 7:8, 9; Heb. 7:4 [u] [ch. 13:36] [v] 1 Kgs. 2:10 [w] Neh. 3:16 **30**[x] [2 Sam. 23:2; Matt. 22:43; Heb. 11:32] [y] See Luke 1:32 **31**[z] ver. 27 **32**[a] ver. 24 [b] ch. 1:22; 4:33 **33**[c] ch. 5:31; Eph. 1:20; Phil. 2:9; Heb. 2:9; 1 Pet. 3:22 [d] Ex. 15:6; Ps. 98:1 [e] ch. 1:4; [John 16:7] [f] Gal. 3:14 [g] ver. 17 **34**[h] [John 3:13] [i] Cited from Ps. 110:1 **36**[j] See Matt. 28:18 [k] Rom. 14:9; 2 Cor. 4:5 [l] ver. 23 **37**[m] [ch. 5:33; 7:54] [n] ch. 16:30; Luke 3:10 **38**[o] ch. 3:19; 20:21; 26:18, 20; Luke 24:47 [p] ch. 22:16; [ch. 8:12]; See Mark 16:16 [q] ch. 10:48; See ch. 8:16 [r] See Mark 1:4 [s] ch. 10:45; [ch. 8:15, 20; 11:17]; See John 7:39

39 For [t] the promise is for you and [u] for your
children and for all [v] who are far off, everyone
[w] whom the Lord our God calls to himself."
40 And with many other words he bore witness
and continued to exhort them, saying, [x] "Save
yourselves from this [y] crooked generation."
41 So those who received his word were baptized, and [z] there were added that day about
three thousand souls.

The Fellowship of the Believers

42 And [a] they devoted themselves to the
apostles' [b] teaching and the [c] fellowship, to [d] the
breaking of bread and the prayers. 43 And awe[1]
came upon every soul, and [e] many wonders and
signs were being done through the apostles.
44 And all who believed were together and
[f] had all things in common. 45 And [f] they were
selling their possessions and belongings and
distributing the proceeds to all, as any had
need. 46 And day by day, [g] attending the temple
[h] together and [i] breaking bread in their homes,
they received their food [j] with glad and generous hearts, 47 praising God and [k] having favor
with all the people. And the Lord [l] added to
their number [m] day by day those who [n] were
being saved.

The Lame Beggar Healed

3 Now Peter and John were [o] going up to the
temple at [p] the hour of prayer, [q] the ninth
hour.[2] 2 And a man [r] lame from birth was being
carried, [s] whom they laid daily at the gate of
the temple that is called the Beautiful Gate [t] to
ask alms of those entering the temple. 3 Seeing
Peter and John about to go into the temple,
he asked to receive alms. 4 And Peter directed
his gaze at him, as did John, and said, "Look
at us." 5 And he fixed his attention on them,
expecting to receive something from them.
6 But Peter said, [u] "I have no silver and gold,
but what I do have I give to you. [v] In the name
of Jesus Christ of Nazareth, rise up and walk!"
7 And he took him by the right hand and raised
him up, and immediately his feet and ankles
were made strong. 8 And [w] leaping up he stood
and began to walk, and entered the temple
with them, walking and leaping and praising
God. 9 And [x] all the people saw him walking
and praising God, 10 and recognized him as

[1] Or *fear* [2] That is, 3 P.M.

2:42–47 The Holy Spirit brings forth a devotion to the apostles' teaching, fellowship, community, and prayer. Notice also the unity of mind and heart of these first believers. In what way these first Christians "had all things in common" (v. 44) is difficult to discern, since they retained rights over their property (cf. 5:4). What is clear is that when God is present by his Spirit, there is unity and mutual care. The Holy Spirit desires to work in us both individually and collectively. He brings forth love, joy, peace, patience, kindness, goodness, faithfulness, gentleness, and self-control in individuals and in the community of believers (Gal. 5:22–23).

The Spirit's ministry also brings forth conversions and numerical growth, as we see that "the Lord added to their number day by day those who were being saved" (Acts 2:47). The Spirit produces not only inward spiritual growth but also expansion and growth of the church (though we recognize in later chapters of Acts that these may come in stages and are not always without challenge, persecution, or seeming delay). Gospel-fueled, Spirit-empowered growth is a repeated theme that runs throughout the rest of Acts, as we see that "more than ever believers were added to the Lord, multitudes of both men and women" (5:14) and "the churches were strengthened in the faith, and they increased in numbers daily" (16:5; see also 6:7; 9:31; 12:24; 13:49; 19:20). The Spirit continued to testify through the church to the grace of God in Jesus, bringing about growth in love and in numbers. The grace of God was fruitful and effective, and we see God taking the initiative to spread his grace to ever-expanding numbers of people—even in the face of virulent hostility.

3:1–10 The first three chapters of Acts form a triad, focused on the Spirit and the empowerment for witnessing to the name of Jesus that the Spirit will bring. Chapter 1 showed the apostles waiting for the Spirit, chapter 2 marked the coming of the Spirit, and now chapter 3 shows the apostles being empowered with the Spirit (on being "filled" with the Holy Spirit, cf. 2:4; 4:8; 4:31).

The power of God's salvation not only creates generosity but also drives concern for the weak and afflicted, as seen in Peter and John's interaction with this beggar. He is not just a statistic to them but a person. There is no wealth required to be a

39 [t] Rom. 9:4 [u] ch. 3:25; Isa. 54:13; [Isa. 44:3] [v] ch. 22:21; Isa. 57:19; Eph. 2:13, 17 [w] Joel 2:32; Rom. 8:30
40 [x] [ver. 21, 47] [y] Deut. 32:5; Matt. 17:17; Phil. 2:15
41 [z] ver. 47
42 [a] [Heb. 10:25]; See ch. 1:14 [b] See 1 Cor. 14:6 [c] Gal. 2:9; Phil. 1:5; 1 John 1:3 [d] Luke 24:35; [ver. 46]; See ch. 20:7
43 [e] See Mark 16:20
44 [f] ch. 4:32, 34, 35; [Matt. 19:21]
45 [f] [See ver. 44 above]
46 [g] ch. 3:1; 5:21, 42; Luke 24:53 [h] See ch. 1:14 [i] [ver. 42] [j] [ch. 16:34]; See John 16:22
47 [k] ch. 5:13 [l] ver. 41; ch. 5:14; 11:24 [m] ch. 16:5 [n] 1 Cor. 1:18; [ver. 21, 40; ch. 16:31]

Chapter 3
1 [o] See Luke 18:10 [p] Ps. 55:17 [q] ch. 10:3, 30; Matt. 27:46; [1 Kgs. 18:29]
2 [r] ch. 14:8 [s] [Luke 16:20] [t] [John 9:8]
6 [u] 2 Cor. 6:10 [v] [ch. 9:34]
8 [w] ch. 14:10; Isa. 35:6
9 [x] ch. 4:16, 21

the one who sat at the Beautiful Gate of the temple, asking for alms. And they were filled with wonder and amazement at what had happened to him.

Peter Speaks in Solomon's Portico

11 [y]While he clung to Peter and John, all the
people, utterly astounded, ran together to
them in [z]the portico called Solomon's. 12 And
when Peter saw it he addressed the people:
"Men of Israel, why do you wonder at this, or
why do you stare at us, as though by our own
power or piety we have made him walk? 13 [a]The
God of Abraham, the God of Isaac, and the God
of Jacob, [b]the God of our fathers, [c]glorified his
servant[1] Jesus, whom [d]you delivered over and
[e]denied in the presence of Pilate, [f]when he had
decided to release him. 14 But you denied [g]the
Holy and [h]Righteous One, and [i]asked for a
murderer to be granted to you, 15 and you killed
[j]the Author of life, [k]whom God raised from
the dead. To this we are witnesses. 16 And [l]his
name—by [m]faith in his name—has made this
man strong whom you see and know, and the
faith that is [n]through Jesus[2] has given the man
this perfect health in the presence of you all.

[1] Or *child*; also verse 26 [2] Greek *him*

11 [y]ch. 4:14 [z]ch. 5:12; John 10:23
13 [a]Matt. 22:32 [b]ch. 5:30; 22:14; [ch. 7:32] [c]Isa. 55:5; [Isa. 52:13]; See John 8:54 [d]See Matt. 20:19 [e]ch. 13:28; John 19:7, 12, 15 [f]Luke 23:14, 16; John 19:12
14 [g][ch. 4:27, 30]; See Mark 1:24 [h]ch. 7:52; 22:14; 1 Pet. 3:18; 1 John 2:1; 3:7; [James 5:6] [i]Luke 23:18, 19, 25
15 [j]ch. 5:31 [k]See ch. 2:24
16 [l][ver. 6] [m][John 1:12] [n][1 Pet. 1:21]

channel for God's grace to transform this man's body and heart. While Peter and John have no money, neither does the beggar; he has nothing whatsoever to offer in exchange for healing, but that is no hindrance to the grace of Christ, who extends his power of healing to one who has no right or ability to claim it.

3:11–26 The power of Jesus Christ creates such amazement that it requires an explanation. This mirrors Jesus' own pattern, as he often followed miraculous healings with periods of teaching on the nature of the kingdom of God. The miracles in Scripture should be seen not so much as models that we should seek to repeat but as evidences of divine authority for God's special messengers.

As people marvel at the power of the apostles, Peter immediately renounces praise and redirects their gaze to Jesus Christ: everything is about Jesus, whom God has glorified (v. 13) by raising him from the dead. Peter insists that this miraculous healing is the work of the same God of Abraham, Isaac, and Jacob whom his fellow Jews were on their way to worship. Even though they have failed to honor God's Messiah and are filled with sin that deserves judgment, God nevertheless continues to call them back to rest in him.

Jesus is "the Holy and Righteous One" (v. 14). In Isaiah 53:11 the "servant" of the Lord, a messianic title, is called the "righteous one," and this is picked up later in Acts as well (cf. Acts 7:52; 22:14). Jesus is also the "Author of life" (3:15), and yet his own people have rejected him and killed him.

That the Christ would suffer and die was a surprise for most of the Jews, and a significant stumbling block to their believing in Jesus as the promised Messiah (1 Cor. 1:23). But Peter points out that the suffering of the Messiah was foretold by the prophets (Acts 3:18). Isaiah spoke of the Messiah as one who "was pierced for our transgressions" and "crushed for our iniquities" (Isa. 53:5). David foreshadowed the suffering of the Messiah in a psalm that Jesus quoted on the cross: "They have pierced my hands and feet . . . they divide my garments among them, and for my clothing they cast lots" (Ps. 22:16, 18; cf. Matt. 27:35, 46). God tends to work triumph through the paradoxical means of weakness. The suffering of Christ is not the finale, but a necessary prelude to his glorification (cf. Phil. 2:6–11).

Moses spoke of the promised Messiah as one who would be "a prophet like me" (Deut. 18:15, 18; cf. Acts 3:22). Jesus is a better and truer Moses, like him in many ways, but excelling him in others (Heb. 3:1–6). Like Moses, Jesus in his infancy must be rescued from a king who kills hundreds of infants in an attempt to find him (Matt. 2:1–21; cf. Ex. 1:8–2:10). Like Moses, Jesus delivers a law for the people of God from a mountaintop (Matthew 5–7; cf. Ex. 19:20). Like Moses, Jesus delivers his people from slavery; but whereas Moses' deliverance only saved the Israelites from physical peril, Jesus delivers us from the slavery of sin and death (Gal. 4:4–7; Heb. 2:15). Jesus' "exodus" beyond the cross to the resurrection (cf. Luke 9:31) allows us to follow him—as a prophet like Moses—to the promised land of eternal life.

Not only Moses, but "all the prophets who have spoken, from Samuel and those who came after him" had foretold the coming of Jesus in "these days" (Acts 3:24).

17 “And now, brothers, I know that [o]you
acted in ignorance, as did also your rulers.
18 But what God [p]foretold [q]by the mouth of
all the prophets, that [r]his Christ would [s]suf-
fer, he thus fulfilled. 19 [t]Repent therefore,
and [u]turn back, that [v]your sins may be blotted out, 20 that times of refreshing may come
from the presence of the Lord, and that he
may send the Christ [w]appointed for you, Jesus,
21 [x]whom heaven must receive until the time
for [y]restoring all the things about which [z]God
spoke by the mouth of his holy prophets long
ago. 22 Moses said, ‘The Lord God will raise up
for you [a]a prophet like me from your brothers. You shall listen [b]to him in whatever he
tells you. 23 And it shall be that every soul
who does not listen to that prophet [c]shall be
destroyed from the people.’ 24 And [d]all the
prophets who have spoken, from Samuel and
those who came after him, also proclaimed
these days. 25 [e]You are the sons of the prophets and of [f]the covenant that God made with
your fathers, saying to Abraham, [g]‘And in your
offspring shall all the families of the earth be
blessed.’ 26 [h]God, [i]having raised up his servant,
sent him to you first, [j]to bless you [k]by turning
every one of you from your wickedness.”

Peter and John Before the Council

4 And as they were speaking to the people,
the priests and [l]the captain of the temple
and [m]the Sadducees came upon them, 2 greatly
annoyed because they were teaching the people and proclaiming [n]in Jesus the resurrection
from the dead. 3 And they arrested them and
[o]put them in custody until the next day, for it
was already evening. 4 But many of those who
had heard the word believed, and [p]the number
of the men came to about five thousand.
5 On the next day their rulers and elders
and scribes gathered together in Jerusalem,
6 with [q]Annas the high priest and [r]Caiaphas
and John and Alexander, and all who were
of the high-priestly family. 7 And when they
had set them in the midst, they inquired,
[s]“By what power or [t]by what name did you
do this?” 8 Then Peter, [u]filled with the Holy
Spirit, said to them, “Rulers of the people and
elders, 9 if we are being examined today [v]con-
cerning a good deed done to a crippled man,
by what means this man has been healed, 10 let
it be known to all of you and to all the people
of Israel that [w]by the name of Jesus Christ of
Nazareth, whom you crucified, [x]whom God
raised from the dead—by him this man is

Peter makes it personal for his Jewish brothers and sisters, reminding them that “you are the sons of the prophets and of the covenant that God made with your fathers, saying to Abraham, ‘And in your offspring shall all the families of the earth be blessed’” (v. 25). Jesus is the culmination of God’s plan of salvation from the beginning, the fulfillment of the promises God made to the founder of the nation of Israel to bless the entire world through the offspring of Abraham. Now that promised descendant has come, as Peter says, “to bless you by turning every one of you from your wickedness” (v. 26). He urges them to respond by repenting so that they can receive “refreshing . . . from the presence of the Lord” (v. 20). Though they are guilty of killing the promised Messiah, God is not seeking to punish them but instead he wants to bless and restore them. Marvelous grace!

4:1–22 Chapter 4 marks the first persecution of the early followers of Christ, a topic that will continue in the next triad of chapters (4–6) and reach its culmination in the gospel message and stoning of Stephen (ch. 7). From this chapter on, Acts will illustrate the diametrically opposed system of the “world”—its thinking, motivation, and values—and the lordship of Jesus and the values of his kingdom.

Peter and John are known to be “uneducated” and common men, yet they speak with “boldness” (4:13). Credentials or eloquence in public speaking are not necessary to proclaim the gospel to others. The power of God is that much more astonishing when working through regular people. Our many flaws are not barriers to God’s work or love; instead, they glorify God all the more.

Peter points to Jesus fulfilling one of the Psalms: “the stone that the builders rejected has become the cornerstone” (Ps. 118:22; cf. Acts 2:25–28, 34–35; 4:11). Jesus himself mentioned this prophecy during his earthly ministry (Luke 20:17), and Peter elaborates on it in the first of his letters (1 Pet. 2:4–8). Though rejected by his own people and crucified, Jesus was vindicated when God raised him from the dead. He now occupies the chief position, the cornerstone, around which the entire church is built up.

17 [o]ch. 13:27; [ch. 26:9; Luke 23:34; John 16:3; 1 Cor. 2:8; 1 Tim. 1:13]
18 [p]See ch. 2:23 [q]ch. 17:3; 26:22, 23; [Heb. 2:10]; See Luke 24:26, 27 [r]See Luke 9:20 [s]Matt. 17:12; Luke 22:15; 24:46; Heb. 13:12
19 [t]See ch. 2:38 [u]See Luke 22:32 [v]Ps. 51:1, 9; Isa. 43:25; 44:22; Col. 2:14
20 [w]ch. 22:14; 26:16
21 [x][ch. 1:11; Luke 24:26] [y][Matt. 17:11; Rom. 8:21] [z]Luke 1:70
22 [a]ch. 7:37, cited from Deut. 18:15, 18, 19 [b]Matt. 17:5
23 [c]Lev. 23:29
24 [d]ch. 13:20; 1 Sam. 3:20; Heb. 11:32
25 [e]See ch. 2:39 [f]See Rom. 9:4, 5 [g]Cited from Gen. 22:18; See Gen. 12:3
26 [h]Rom. 1:16; 2:9; 15:8; [Mark 7:27] [i]ver. 22 [j]ver. 25 [k]Rom. 11:26; [Ezek. 3:19]; See Matt. 1:21

Chapter 4
1 [l]ch. 5:24, 26; Luke 22:4, 52; [1 Chr. 9:11; Neh. 11:11] [m]See Matt. 22:23
2 [n]ch. 17:18; [ch. 3:15]
3 [o]See Luke 21:12
4 [p][ch. 2:41]
6 [q]Luke 3:2; John 18:13, 24 [r]See Matt. 26:3
7 [s][Matt. 21:23] [t][ver. 10]
8 [u]See Matt. 10:20
9 [v]ch. 3:7, 8
10 [w]ch. 3:6 [x]See ch. 2:24

standing before you well. 11 [y]This Jesus[1] is the
stone that was [z]rejected by you, the builders,
which has become the cornerstone.[2] 12 And
there is [a]salvation [b]in no one else, for [c]there is
no other [d]name under heaven given among
men[3] by which we must be saved."

13 [e]Now when they saw the boldness of Peter
and John, and perceived that they were uneducated, common men, they were astonished.
And they recognized that they had been with
Jesus. 14 But seeing the man who was healed
[f]standing beside them, [g]they had nothing
to say in opposition. 15 But when they had
commanded them to leave the council, they
conferred with one another, 16 saying, [h]"What
shall we do with these men? For that [i]a notable
sign has been performed through them is evident to all the inhabitants of Jerusalem, and
we cannot deny it. 17 But in order that it may
spread no further among the people, let us
warn them [j]to speak no more to anyone in
this name." 18 So they called them and charged
them not to speak or teach at all in the name
of Jesus. 19 But Peter and John answered them,
[k]"Whether it is right in the sight of God to
listen to you rather than to God, you must
judge, 20 for [l]we cannot but speak of what [m]we
have seen and heard." 21 And when they had
further threatened them, they let them go,
finding no way to punish them, [n]because of
the people, for all were praising God [o]for what
had happened. 22 For the man on whom this
sign of healing was performed was more than
forty years old.

The Believers Pray for Boldness

23 When they were released, they went to
their friends and reported what the chief
priests and the elders had said to them. 24 And
when they heard it, they lifted their voices
[p]together to God and said, "Sovereign Lord,
[q]who made the heaven and the earth and the
sea and everything in them, 25 who through
the mouth of our father David, your servant,[4]
said by the Holy Spirit,

[r]"'Why did the Gentiles rage,
and the peoples plot in vain?
26 The kings of the earth set themselves,
and [s]the rulers were gathered
together,
against the Lord and against his
[t]Anointed'[5]—

27 for truly in this city there were gathered
together against your [u]holy servant Jesus,
[v]whom you anointed, both [w]Herod and
[x]Pontius Pilate, along [y]with the Gentiles and
[z]the peoples of Israel, 28 [a]to do whatever your
hand and [b]your plan had predestined to take
place. 29 And now, Lord, [c]look upon their
threats and grant to your servants[6] to continue
to speak your word with all [d]boldness, 30 while
[e]you stretch out your hand to heal, and signs
and wonders are performed [f]through the

[1] Greek *This one* [2] Greek *the head of the corner* [3] The Greek word *anthropoi* refers here to both men and women [4] Or *child*; also verses 27, 30 [5] Or *Christ* [6] Greek *bondservants*

11 [y]See Ps. 118:22 [z]Mark 9:12; Luke 23:11
12 [a]ch. 13:26; 28:28; John 4:22; Heb. 2:3; Jude 3 [b][1 Tim. 2:5] [c][Gal. 1:7] [d]ch. 10:43; Luke 24:47; John 20:31
13 [e][John 7:15]
14 [f]ch. 3:11 [g][Luke 21:15]
16 [h][John 11:47; 12:19] [i]ver. 21; ch. 3:9, 10
17 [j]ch. 5:28, 40
19 [k]ch. 5:29
20 [l][Amos 3:8; John 15:27; 1 Cor. 9:16] [m]ch. 22:15; 1 John 1:1, 3
21 [n]ch. 5:13, 26; [Matt. 21:26, 46; Mark 11:32; Luke 20:6, 19; 22:2] [o]ch. 3:7, 8
24 [p]See ch. 1:14 [q]Ex. 20:11; 2 Chr. 2:12; Neh. 9:6; Ps. 102:25; 124:8; 134:3; 146:6
25 [r]Cited from Ps. 2:1, 2
26 [s]ver. 5 [t]ch. 10:38; Luke 4:18; Heb. 1:9; [Dan. 9:24; Rev. 11:15]
27 [u]ver. 30 [v]ver. 26 [w]Luke 23:7-11 [x]Matt. 27:2 [y]See Matt. 20:19 [z]Matt. 26:3
28 [a][Isa. 46:10] [b]See ch. 2:23
29 [c][2 Kgs. 19:16] [d]ver. 13, 31; ch. 9:27, 29; 13:46; 14:3; 18:26; 19:8; 28:31; Eph. 6:19
30 [e][Ps. 138:7; Prov. 31:20; Isa. 1:25; Zeph. 1:4] [f]ch. 3:6; [Matt. 7:22; Mark 9:39; 16:17]

4:23–31 Paradoxical as it may seem, God's sovereignty, even in predetermining the crucifixion (vv. 24, 27–28), does not prevent prayer but rather encourages it (vv. 29–30). Since Jesus reigns supreme, he is the one to approach with our needs.

Here we see the prayer that God answers: the prayer for boldness to speak his word. In light of the threats from the established powers, it would be understandable for the believers to pray for relief from persecution. Instead they ask for renewed courage to proclaim the word of God. But if these Christians avoided prayers for protection, it was not because they believed God was unable to protect them. In fact, by quoting Psalm 2, they are claiming the truth that God is sovereign over kings and lords. Rulers oppose God in vain, not simply because he is stronger but because he orchestrates the plots of evil people to conform to his will. The believers can be bold because they know that the effects of evil are fleeting, and those who oppose the gospel are no threat to God, who is always in control. What others intend for evil, he will work for good (Gen. 50:20). The ultimate example of this was the crucifixion of Jesus, which seemed like the final triumph of evil over good but was in fact the very culmination of God's plan to redeem the world (Acts 4:27–28).

Knowing God's tendency to maneuver the plots of people to accomplish his redemptive purposes, we can be bold and trust God. "If God is for us, who can be against us?" (Rom. 8:31). Not even those who decide matters of life and death pose a true threat, for we know the One who has defeated death.

name of your [g]holy servant Jesus." 31 And when they had prayed, [h]the place in which they were gathered together was shaken, and [i]they were all filled with the Holy Spirit and [j]continued to speak the word of God with boldness.

They Had Everything in Common

32 Now the full number of those who believed were of [k]one heart and [l]soul, and no one said that any of the things that belonged to him was his own, but [m]they had everything in common. 33 And with great [n]power the apostles were giving their testimony to the resurrection of the Lord Jesus, and [o]great grace was upon them all. 34 [p]There was not a needy person among them, for [q]as many as were owners of lands or houses sold them and brought the proceeds of what was sold 35 and [r]laid it at the apostles' feet, and [s]it was distributed to each as any had need. 36 Thus Joseph, who was also called by the apostles Barnabas (which means [t]son of encouragement), a Levite, a native of Cyprus, 37 sold a field that belonged to him and brought the money and [u]laid it at the apostles' feet.

Ananias and Sapphira

5 But a man named Ananias, with his wife Sapphira, sold a piece of property, 2 and with his wife's knowledge [v]he kept back for himself some of the proceeds and brought only a part of it and [w]laid it at the apostles' feet. 3 But Peter said, "Ananias, why has [x]Satan filled your heart to lie [y]to the Holy Spirit and [z]to keep back for yourself part of the proceeds of the land? 4 While it remained unsold, did it not remain your own? And after it was sold, was it not at your disposal? Why is it that you have contrived this deed in your heart? You have not lied to man but [a]to God." 5 When Ananias heard these words, he [b]fell down and breathed his last. And [c]great fear came upon all who heard of it. 6 The young men rose and [d]wrapped him up and carried him out and buried him.

7 After an interval of about three hours his wife came in, not knowing what had happened. 8 And Peter said to her, "Tell me whether you[1] sold the land for so much." And she said, "Yes, for so much." 9 But Peter said to her, "How is it that you have agreed together [e]to test [f]the Spirit of the Lord? Behold, the feet of those who have buried your husband are at the door, and they will carry you out." 10 Immediately she fell down at his feet and breathed her last. When the young men came in they found her dead, and they carried her out and buried her beside her husband. 11 And [g]great fear came upon the whole church and upon all who heard of these things.

Many Signs and Wonders Done

12 Now many signs and wonders were regularly done among the people [h]by the hands of the apostles. And they were all [i]together in [j]Solomon's Portico. 13 None of the rest dared join them, but [k]the people held them in high esteem. 14 And [l]more than ever believers were added to the Lord, multitudes of both men

[1] The Greek for *you* is plural here

4:32–37 The verses repeat the encouraging "progress report" of 2:42–47 (see note).

5:1–11 The account of Ananias and Sapphira is one of the most disturbing texts in the New Testament. It reveals how essential unity within the church is to God, and how seriously God takes deceit that threatens that unity (see also note on 2:42–47). Thankfully, most do not receive immediate judgment for our sins like Ananias and Sapphira did. Such judgment is rare, even in Scripture.

However, we can be sure that sin will be dealt with, and the consequence of sin without Christ's atonement is always death (Rom. 6:23). Jesus did not choose to die for us because our sin was trivial. Our sin was great, but he chose to die for us because his love for us was greater. The God who punished Ananias and Sapphira is the same radically merciful God who offers grace even to those who arranged the crucifixion of his Son (Acts 2:23, 37–39; 3:13–20).

5:12–42 Persecution against those proclaiming the name of Jesus now begins in earnest. The jealousy among the priestly group against the apostles is so great that they are enraged to the point of wanting their deaths (v. 33). Here we see the beginning of the cosmic spiritual collision of this present world system with Jesus and his kingdom. This is not a battle of human strategy and weapons; rather, the Holy Spirit himself witnesses for and about Jesus (v. 32).

30 [g] ver. 27
31 [h] [ch. 2:2; 16:26; Ps. 77:18] [i] See ch. 2:4 [j] [Phil. 1:14]
32 [k] 2 Chr. 30:12; Ezek. 11:19 [l] Phil. 1:27 [m] ch. 2:44
33 [n] See ch. 1:8, 22 [o] [ch. 11:23]
34 [p] [2 Cor. 8:14, 15] [q] ch. 2:45
35 [r] ver. 37; ch. 5:2 [s] [ch. 6:1]
36 [t] [Mark 3:17]
37 [u] ver. 35

Chapter 5
2 [v] ver. 3 [w] ch. 4:35, 37
3 [x] [Luke 22:3; John 13:2, 27] [y] [ver. 4, 9] [z] ver. 2
4 [a] [ver. 3, 9]
5 [b] [Ezek. 11:13] [c] ver. 11
6 [d] [ch. 8:2; Ezek. 29:5; John 19:40]
9 [e] [ch. 15:10; 1 Cor. 10:9] [f] [ver. 3, 4]
11 [g] ver. 5
12 [h] ch. 2:43; 4:30; 14:3; 19:11; Mark 16:20; Rom. 15:19; 2 Cor. 12:12; Heb. 2:4 [i] See ch. 1:14 [j] ch. 3:11; John 10:23
13 [k] ver. 26; ch. 2:47; 4:21
14 [l] [ch. 6:1, 2]

and women, 15 [m]so that they even [n]carried out
the sick into the streets and laid them on cots
and mats, that as Peter came by [o]at least his
shadow might fall on some of them. 16 The
people also gathered from the towns around
Jerusalem, [p]bringing the sick and those
afflicted with unclean spirits, and they were
all healed.

The Apostles Arrested and Freed

17 But the high priest rose up, and all who
were with him (that is, the party of [q]the
Sadducees), and filled with [r]jealousy 18 they
arrested the apostles and [s]put them in the
public prison. 19 But during the night [t]an
angel of the Lord [u]opened the prison doors
and brought them out, and said, 20 "Go and
stand in the temple and speak to the people
all [v]the words of [w]this [x]Life." 21 And when they
heard this, [y]they entered the temple [z]at daybreak and began to teach.

Now when the high priest came, and those
who were with him, they called together the
council, all the senate of the people of Israel,
and sent to the prison to have them brought.
22 But when the officers came, they did not
find them in the prison, so they returned and
reported, 23 "We found the prison securely
locked and the guards standing at the doors,
but when we opened them we found no one
inside." 24 Now when [a]the captain of the temple and the chief priests heard these words,
they were greatly perplexed about them,
wondering what this would come to. 25 And
someone came and told them, "Look! The men
whom you put in prison [b]are standing in the
temple and teaching the people." 26 Then [c]the
captain with the officers went and brought
them, but not by force, for [d]they were afraid
of being stoned by the people.

27 And when they had brought them, they
set them before the council. And the high
priest questioned them, 28 saying, [e]"We
strictly charged you not to teach in this name,
yet here you have filled Jerusalem with your
teaching, and you [f]intend to bring this man's
blood upon us." 29 But Peter and the apostles
answered, [g]"We must obey God rather than
men. 30 [h]The God of our fathers [i]raised Jesus,
[j]whom you killed by hanging him on [k]a tree.
31 God exalted [l]him at his right hand as [m]Leader
and [n]Savior, [o]to give [p]repentance to Israel and
[o]forgiveness of sins. 32 And [q]we are witnesses to
these things, and [r]so is the Holy Spirit, [s]whom
God has given to those who obey him."

33 When they heard this, they [t]were enraged
and wanted to kill them. 34 But a Pharisee in
the council named [u]Gamaliel, [v]a teacher of the
law held in honor by all the people, stood up
and gave orders to put the men outside for
a little while. 35 And he said to them, "Men
of Israel, take care what you are about to do
with these men. 36 For [w]before these days
Theudas rose up, [x]claiming to be somebody,
and a number of men, about four hundred,
joined him. He was killed, and all who followed him were dispersed and came to nothing. 37 After him Judas the Galilean rose up in
the days of [y]the census and drew away some of
the people after him. He too perished, and all
who followed him were scattered. 38 So in the
present case I tell you, keep away from these
men and let them alone, for [z]if this plan or this
undertaking is of man, it will fail; 39 but [a]if it
is of God, you will not be able to overthrow
them. You [b]might even be found opposing
God!" So they took his advice, 40 and [c]when
they had called in the apostles, [d]they beat them
and charged them not to speak in the name
of Jesus, and let them go. 41 Then they left the
presence of the council, [e]rejoicing that they
were counted worthy [f]to suffer dishonor for
[g]the name. 42 And every day, [h]in the temple and
from house to house, they did not cease teaching and [i]preaching [j]that the Christ is Jesus.

Every time the gospel meets with opposition in Acts, God finds a way to advance the message. As the gospel triumphantly crosses geographical, linguistic, social, religious, cultural, and ethnic boundaries, Luke shows that God is vindicating his message. Some of the most overt attempts to squelch the movement—like the persecution of the church in Jerusalem—lead to a further expansion of the gospel (8:1–4). No one is able to overthrow the gospel, because it is the power of God for salvation, both here in Jerusalem and to the end of the earth (Rom. 1:16).

15 [m][ch. 19:12] [n]Mark 6:55, 56 [o][2 Kgs. 4:29; Matt. 14:36]
16 [p]Mark 16:17, 18
17 [q]See Matt. 22:23 [r]ch. 13:45; James 3:14, 16; [ch. 7:9; 17:5]
18 [s]See Luke 21:12
19 [t]See ch. 8:26 [u]ch. 12:10; 16:26
20 [v][John 6:63, 68; Phil. 2:16] [w][ch. 13:46; 22:4; 28:28] [x]ch. 3:15; 11:18 **21** [y]ver. 25, 42 [z][John 8:2] **24** [a]ver. 26; See ch. 4:1 **25** [b]ver. 21 **26** [c]ver. 24 [d]ver. 13; See ch. 4:21 **28** [e]ch. 4:18 [f]ch. 2:23, 36; 3:15; 4:10; 7:52; Matt. 27:25 **29** [g][ch. 4:19, 20] **30** [h]See ch. 3:13 [i]See ch. 2:24 [j]ch. 10:39; Gal. 3:13; See Luke 24:20 [k]ch. 13:29; 1 Pet. 2:24 **31** [l]See ch. 2:33 [m]See ch. 3:15 [n]See Luke 2:11 [o]Luke 24:47; See Luke 5:32 [p]ch. 11:18; 2 Tim. 2:25; [Rom. 2:4] **32** [q]See Luke 24:48 [r][ch. 15:28; John 15:26, 27; Heb. 2:4; 1 John 5:7] [s]See ch. 2:4 **33** [t]ch. 7:54; [ch. 2:37] **34** [u]ch. 22:3 [v]See Luke 5:17 **36** [w][ch. 21:38] [x]ch. 8:9; [Gal. 2:6; 6:3] **37** [y][Luke 2:2] **38** [z]Lam. 3:37 **39** [a]Prov. 21:30; Isa. 8:9, 10; Nah. 1:9 [b]2 Chr. 13:12; [ch. 11:17] **40** [c]ch. 4:18 [d][ch. 22:19; Mark 13:9; Luke 23:16] **41** [e]1 Pet. 4:13, 14, 16; See Matt. 5:12 [f]ch. 9:16; 21:13; [Rom. 1:5]; See John 15:21 [g]Lev. 24:11, 16; Phil. 2:9; 3 John 7 **42** [h]ch. 2:46 [i]ch. 8:35; 11:20; 17:18 [j]See ch. 18:5

Seven Chosen to Serve

6 Now in these days [k]when the disciples were increasing in number, a complaint by the Hellenists[1] arose against the Hebrews because their widows were being neglected in [l]the daily distribution. 2 And the twelve summoned the full number of the disciples and said, "It is not right that we should give up preaching the word of God to serve tables. 3 [m]Therefore, brothers,[2] pick out from among you seven men [n]of good repute, [o]full of the Spirit and of wisdom, whom we will appoint to this duty. 4 But [p]we will devote ourselves to prayer and to the ministry of the word." 5 And what they said pleased the whole gathering, and they chose Stephen, [q]a man full of faith and [r]of the Holy Spirit, and [s]Philip, and Prochorus, and Nicanor, and Timon, and Parmenas, and Nicolaus, [t]a proselyte of Antioch. 6 These they set before the apostles, and [u]they prayed and [v]laid their hands on them.

7 And [w]the word of God continued to increase, and the number of the disciples multiplied greatly in Jerusalem, and a great many of the priests [x]became obedient to [y]the faith.

Stephen Is Seized

8 And Stephen, full of grace and [z]power, was doing great wonders and signs among the people. 9 Then some of those who belonged to the synagogue of the Freedmen (as it was called), and of the Cyrenians, and of the Alexandrians, and of those from Cilicia and Asia, rose up and disputed with Stephen. 10 But [a]they could not withstand the wisdom and the Spirit with which he was speaking. 11 Then [b]they secretly instigated men who said, "We have heard him speak blasphemous words against Moses and God." 12 And they stirred up the people and the elders and the scribes, and they came upon him and seized him and brought him before the council, 13 and they [c]set up false [d]witnesses who said, "This man never ceases to speak words against [e]this holy place and the law, 14 for we have heard him say that this Jesus of Nazareth [f]will destroy this place and will [g]change [h]the customs that Moses delivered to us." 15 And gazing at him, all who sat in the council saw that his face [i]was like the face of an angel.

Stephen's Speech

7 And the high priest said, "Are these things so?" 2 And Stephen said:

[j]"Brothers and fathers, hear me. [k]The God [l]of glory appeared to our father Abraham when he was in Mesopotamia, [m]before he lived in Haran, 3 and said to him, [n]'Go out from your land and from your kindred and go into the land that I will show you.' 4 [m]Then he went out from the land of the Chaldeans and lived in Haran. And [o]after his father died, [p]God removed him from there into this land in which you are now living. 5 Yet he gave him no inheritance in it, not even a foot's length, but promised [q]to give it to him as a possession and to his offspring after him, [r]though he had no child. 6 And God spoke to this effect—that [s]his offspring would [t]be sojourners in a land belonging to others, who would enslave them and afflict them [u]four hundred years. 7 'But [v]I will judge the nation that they serve,' said God, 'and after that they shall come out

[1] That is, Greek-speaking Jews [2] Or *brothers and sisters*

6:1–7 The "priests" mentioned in verse 7 are significant. It was this very group up to this point that was the most vehemently opposed to the gospel. This reminds us of the scope of the gospel: it is to be preached to everyone, even those who hate Christians and desire their deaths. Priests and Pharisees were a major group of antagonists during the life and ministry of Jesus. They instigated and influenced his death, and Jesus reserved his strongest words for religious leaders. Their faith in Christ in Acts is a reflection of the power of the gospel and the grace of God to those who opposed Jesus.

7:1–53 In response to the charge that Jesus and his followers oppose the Mosaic law and aim both to abolish it and destroy the temple, Stephen retells the story of Israel to reveal Jesus as the fulfillment of God's dealings with Israel throughout history (just as Jesus himself claimed to be; Matt. 5:17). In Stephen's speech, God's redemptive plan starts with his promise of an inheritance to the offspring of Abraham. Throughout Israel's circuitous history of wandering, slavery in Egypt, the exodus, settling in the

Chapter 6
1 [k] ch. 2:41, 47; 4:4; 5:14; [ver. 7] [l] [ch. 4:35]
3 [m] [Deut. 1:13] [n] [1 Tim. 3:7] [o] ver. 5; ch. 7:55; 11:24; [Luke 1:15; 4:1]
4 [p] See ch. 1:14
5 [q] ch. 11:24 [r] ver. 3 [s] ch. 8:5; 21:8 [t] ch. 2:11; 13:43; Matt. 23:15
6 [u] ch. 1:24; 13:3 [v] 1 Tim. 4:14; 5:22; 2 Tim. 1:6; [ch. 8:17; 9:17; 19:6; Heb. 6:2]
7 [w] ch. 12:24; 19:20; [Col. 1:5, 6] [x] See Rom. 1:5 [y] ch. 13:8; 14:22; 16:5
8 [z] See ch. 1:8
10 [a] See Luke 21:14, 15
11 [b] [1 Kgs. 21:10, 13; Matt. 26:59, 60]

13 [c] ver. 11 [d] ch. 7:58 [e] [ch. 21:28; 25:8; Matt. 24:15] **14** [f] [Dan. 9:26; Matt. 26:61] [g] [Matt. 5:17] [h] ch. 15:1; 21:21 **15** [i] [Judg. 13:6; Eccles. 8:1] **Chapter 7** **2** [j] ch. 22:1 [k] [Gen. 15:7; Josh. 24:3; Neh. 9:7] [l] Ps. 29:3; [1 Cor. 2:8; James 2:1] [m] Gen. 11:31 **3** [n] Cited from Gen. 12:1 **4** [m] [See ver. 2 above] [o] Gen. 11:32 [p] Gen. 12:4, 5 **5** [q] Gen. 12:7; 13:15; 15:18; 17:8; 48:4; Heb. 11:8, 9 [r] Gen. 15:3; 18:10 **6** [s] Cited from Gen. 15:13, 14 [t] [Ex. 2:22; Heb. 11:9] [u] ver. 17; See Ex. 12:40 **7** [v] [Jer. 25:12; 30:20]

[w]and worship me in this place.' 8 And [x]he gave
him the covenant of circumcision. And [y]so
Abraham became the father of Isaac, and [z]cir-
cumcised him on the eighth day, and [a]Isaac
became the father of Jacob, and [b]Jacob of the
twelve patriarchs.

9 "And the patriarchs, [c]jealous of Joseph, [d]sold
him into Egypt; but [e]God was with him 10 and
rescued him out of all his afflictions and [f]gave
him favor and wisdom before Pharaoh, king of
Egypt, [g]who made him ruler over Egypt and
over all his household. 11 Now [h]there came a
famine throughout all Egypt and Canaan, and
great affliction, and our fathers could find no
food. 12 [i]But when Jacob heard that there was
grain in Egypt, he sent out our fathers on their
first visit. 13 And [j]on the second visit [k]Joseph
made himself known to his brothers, and
[l]Joseph's family became known to Pharaoh.
14 And [m]Joseph sent and summoned Jacob
his father and all his kindred, [n]seventy-five
persons in all. 15 And [o]Jacob went down into
Egypt, and [p]he died, he [q]and our fathers, 16 and
[r]they were carried back to Shechem and laid in
the tomb that [s]Abraham had bought for a sum
of silver from the sons of Hamor in Shechem.

17 "But [t]as the time of the promise drew near,
which God had granted to Abraham, [u]the people increased and multiplied in Egypt 18 until
there arose over Egypt another king [v]who
did not know Joseph. 19 [w]He dealt shrewdly
with our race and forced our fathers to expose
their infants, [x]so that they would not be kept
alive. 20 [y]At this time Moses was born; and
he was beautiful in God's sight. And he was
brought up for three months in his father's
house, 21 and [z]when he was exposed, Pharaoh's
daughter adopted him and brought him up as
her own son. 22 And Moses [a]was instructed in
[b]all the wisdom of the Egyptians, and he was
[c]mighty in his words and deeds.

23 "When he was forty years old, it came into
his heart [d]to visit his brothers, the children
of Israel. 24 And seeing one of them being
wronged, he defended the oppressed man and
avenged him by striking down the Egyptian.
25 He supposed that his brothers would understand that God was giving them salvation by
his hand, but they did not understand. 26 [e]And
on the following day he appeared to them as
they were quarreling and tried to reconcile
them, saying, 'Men, you are brothers. Why
do you wrong each other?' 27 But the man
who was wronging his neighbor thrust him
aside, saying, [f]'Who made you a ruler and a
judge over us? 28 Do you want to kill me as
you killed the Egyptian yesterday?' 29 At this
retort [g]Moses fled and became an exile in the
land of Midian, [h]where he became the father
of two sons.

30 "Now when forty years had passed, [i]an
angel appeared to him [j]in the wilderness

7 [w][Ex. 3:12]
8 [x]Gen. 17:9-12 [y]Gen. 21:2-4 [z]See Luke 1:59 [a]Gen. 25:26 [b]Gen. 29:31-35; 30:5-24; 35:18, 23-26
9 [c]Gen. 37:11 [d]Gen. 37:28; 45:4; Ps. 105:17 [e]Gen. 39:2, 21, 23
10 [f]Gen. 41:37-40 [g]Gen. 41:41, 43, 46; 42:6; Ps. 105:21
11 [h]Gen. 41:54, 55; 42:5; Ps. 105:16
12 [i]Gen. 42:1-3
13 [j]Gen. 43:2-15 [k]Gen. 45:1-4 [l]Gen. 45:16
14 [m]Gen. 45:9, 10, 27 [n][Gen. 46:26, 27; Ex. 1:5; Deut. 10:22]
15 [o]Gen. 46:5, 28; Ps. 105:23 [p]Gen. 49:33 [q]Ex. 1:6
16 [r]Gen. 50:25; Ex. 13:19; Josh. 24:32 [s][Gen. 23:16 with Gen. 33:19; Josh. 24:32]
17 [t]ver. 5-7 [u]ch. 13:17; Ex. 1:7, 12; Ps. 105:24
18 [v]Cited from Ex. 1:8
19 [w]Ex. 1:9, 10; Ps. 105:25 [x]Ex. 1:16-18, 22
20 [y]Ex. 2:2; Heb. 11:23
21 [z]Ex. 2:3-10
22 [a][Dan. 1:4, 17] [b]1 Kgs. 4:30; [Isa. 19:11] [c][Luke 24:19]
23 [d]Ex. 2:11, 12
26 [e]Ex. 2:13, 14
27 [f]ver. 35; [Luke 12:14]
29 [g]Ex. 2:15 [h]Ex. 2:22; 18:3, 4
30 [i]Ex. 3:2 [j][Ex. 3:1]

Promised Land, and the construction of the temple under Solomon, God was graciously orchestrating events to lead to the coming of the promised offspring, the Righteous One, Jesus.

As Stephen retells the story, he highlights the fact that God's chosen prophets—Abraham, Joseph, Moses, David—have always been mistreated by their own people. Jesus stands as the last in the long line of God's prophets, and he too was persecuted by his own, even to the point of death. The great difference between the prophets of old and Jesus is that *they* spoke of the Righteous One to come, whereas Jesus *is* that Righteous One. It was through the persecution and death of the Righteous One that our sin was removed and we can now share in his righteousness (2 Cor. 5:21).

Stephen then recalls the days of David and Solomon, showing how the Jews have mistakenly associated God's presence only with the temple. But even in the Old Testament, God was not limited by a structure made with human hands (Acts 7:49–50). God is near to all who call on him (Ps. 145:18), and he has drawn near to us most fully in Jesus.

Does the gospel "destroy Moses"? Is Christianity something new that breaks away from the Old Testament? These are the sorts of charges that Luke continually refutes in Acts. Christ's incarnation, ministry, death, and resurrection are the true fulfillment of the Old Testament promises of God. Jesus did not overrule and obliterate the revelation of God that had been entrusted to the Jews; he embodied and fulfilled it.

In the Old Testament, God made his dwelling among the Jews in the form of the tabernacle, a temporary tent that allowed Israel to say, "The glory of God is with us" (cf. Ex. 40:34–35). In the incarnation of Christ, God came to dwell among us, taking on flesh so that we may truly call him "Immanuel, . . . God with us" (Matt. 1:23; cf. John 1:14).

of Mount Sinai, in a flame of fire in a bush.
31 When Moses saw it, he was amazed at the
sight, and as he drew near to look, there
came the voice of the Lord: 32 [k]'I am the God
of your fathers, the God of Abraham and of
Isaac and of Jacob.' And Moses trembled and
did not dare to look. 33 Then the Lord said to
him, [l]"Take off the sandals from your feet,
for the place where you are standing is holy
ground. 34 [m]I have surely seen the affliction
of my people who are in Egypt, and [n]have
heard their groaning, and [o]I have come down
to deliver them. [p]And now come, I will send
you to Egypt.'

35 "This Moses, whom they rejected, [q]saying,
'Who made you a ruler and a judge?'—this
man God sent as both ruler and redeemer [r]by
the hand of the angel who appeared to him in
the bush. 36 [s]This man led them out, performing [t]wonders and signs [u]in Egypt and [v]at the
Red Sea and [w]in the wilderness for [x]forty years.
37 This is the Moses who said to the Israelites,
'God will raise up for you [y]a prophet like me
from your brothers.' 38 This is the one [z]who
was in the congregation in the wilderness with
[a]the angel who spoke to him at Mount Sinai,
and with our fathers. [b]He received [c]living [d]ora-
cles to give to us. 39 Our fathers refused to obey
him, but thrust him aside, and [e]in their hearts
they turned to Egypt, 40 saying to Aaron,
[f]'Make for us gods who will go before us. As
for this Moses who led us out from the land
of Egypt, we do not know what has become
of him.' 41 And [g]they made a calf in those days,
and offered a sacrifice to the idol and [h]were
rejoicing in [i]the works of their hands. 42 But
[j]God turned away and [k]gave them over to worship [l]the host of heaven, as it is written in the
book of the prophets:

[m]" 'Did you bring to me slain beasts and sacrifices,
[n]during the forty years in the wilderness, O house of Israel?
43 You took up the tent of [o]Moloch
and the star of your god Rephan,
the images that you made to worship;
and I will send you into exile beyond
Babylon.'

44 "Our fathers had [p]the tent of witness in
the wilderness, just as he who spoke to Moses
[q]directed him to make it, according to the pattern that he had seen. 45 Our fathers in turn
[r]brought it in with Joshua when they [s]dispos-
sessed the nations [t]that God drove out before
our fathers. So it was [u]until the days of David,
46 [v]who found favor in the sight of God and
[w]asked to find a dwelling place for [x]the God
of Jacob.[1] 47 But it was [y]Solomon who built
a house for him. 48 [z]Yet the Most High does
not dwell [a]in houses made by hands, as the
prophet says,

49 [b]" 'Heaven is my throne,
[c]and the earth is my footstool.

[1] Some manuscripts *for the house of Jacob*

In the Old Testament law, God revealed his concern for justice and his love for the weak and oppressed (Deut. 10:18–19; 15:7–11; etc.). In the ministry of Christ, God himself brought good news to the poor, recovery of sight to the blind, and liberty to the oppressed (Luke 4:18; cf. Isa. 61:1–2).

In the Old Testament, God required the lives of spotless lambs so that the curse of death would pass over his people (Ex. 12:5). In the death of Christ, God *became* the Lamb, whose sacrifice would once and for all defeat death (John 1:29; Heb. 7:27).

In the Old Testament, God brought life out of death, empowering barren women to give birth and bringing the dead back from the grave (Gen. 21:1; 25:21; 1 Sam. 2:21; 1 Kings 17:19–22; 2 Kings 4:34–35). In the resurrection of Christ, the Son of God walked out of the grave, triumphantly offering new life to those under the curse of sin and death (Rom. 6:4; 1 Pet. 1:3).

The God who raised Jesus is the same God who acted powerfully and faithfully throughout the Old Testament—indeed, the Christian gospel depends on this identification. People are not merely urged to join a new fad but are offered the undeserved gift of being grafted into God's own people by the blood of Christ (Rom. 11:17–24; Eph. 2:12–13). We were once slaves, but now we are adopted as sons and daughters (Gal. 4:1–7).

32 [k]Cited from Ex. 3:6
33 [l]Ex. 3:5; Josh. 5:15
34 [m]Ex. 3:7 [n]Ex. 2:24 [o]Ex. 3:8 [p]Ex. 3:10
35 [q]ver. 27 [r][Ex. 3:2; 14:19; 23:20; Num. 20:16]
36 [s]Ex. 12:41; 33:1; Heb. 8:9 [t]Ex. 7:3 [u]Ex. 7-12; Ps. 78:43-51; 105:27-36 [v]Ex. 14:21, 27-31; Ps. 78:53; 106:9 [w]Ex. 16:1, 35; 17:1-6; Ps. 78:15 [x]ver. 42; ch. 13:18; Ex. 16:35; Num. 14:33, 34; Ps. 95:10; Heb. 3:10, 17
37 [y]ch. 3:22; Cited from Deut. 18:15
38 [z]Ex. 19:3, 17, 18 [a][ver. 53; Isa. 63:9] [b]Deut. 5:27, 31; 33:4; See John 1:17 [c][Deut. 32:47] [d]Rom. 3:2; Heb. 5:12; 1 Pet. 4:11
39 [e]Ex. 16:3; Num. 11:4, 5; 14:3, 4; Ezek. 20:8, 24
40 [f]Cited from Ex. 32:1, 23
41 [g]Ex. 32:4-6, 35; Deut. 9:16; Ps. 106:19 [h]Amos 6:13 [i]Isa. 2:8; Jer. 1:16; 25:6, 7
42 [j][Josh. 24:20; Isa. 63:10] [k]Ps. 81:12; Ezek. 20:39; Rom. 1:28 [l]Deut. 4:19; 2 Kgs. 17:16; 21:3; 23:5; Jer. 19:13; Zeph. 1:5 [m]Cited from Amos 5:25-27 [n]See ver. 36 **43** [o]See 1 Kgs. 11:7
44 [p]Rev. 15:5; See Ex. 38:21 [q]See Ex. 25:40 **45** [r]Josh. 3:14-17 [s]Num. 32:5; Deut. 32:49 [t]ch. 13:19; Josh. 3:10; 23:9; 24:18; 2 Chr. 20:7 [u]2 Sam. 7:1 **46** [v]ch. 13:22; 1 Sam. 16:1; Ps. 89:19 [w]1 Kgs. 8:17; 1 Chr. 22:7; Ps. 132:5 [x][Gen. 49:24; Isa. 49:26] **47** [y]2 Sam. 7:13; 1 Kgs. 6:1, 2; 8:20; 2 Chr. 3:1 **48** [z][1 Kgs. 8:27; 2 Chr. 2:6] [a]ch. 17:24 **49** [b][Ps. 11:4] [c]Matt. 5:34, 35; Cited from Isa. 66:1, 2

What kind of house will you build for
me, says the Lord,
or what is the place of my rest?
50 Did not my hand make all these things?'

51[d]"You stiff-necked people, [e]uncircumcised
in heart and ears, you always resist the Holy
Spirit. [f]As your fathers did, so do you. 52[g]Which
of the prophets did your fathers not persecute? And they killed those who announced
beforehand the coming of [h]the Righteous One,
[i]whom you have now betrayed and murdered,
53 you who received the law [j]as delivered by
angels and [k]did not keep it."

The Stoning of Stephen

54 Now when they heard these things [l]they
were enraged, and they [m]ground their teeth at
him. 55 But he, [n]full of the Holy Spirit, gazed
into heaven and saw [o]the glory of God, and
Jesus standing [p]at the right hand of God.
56 And he said, "Behold, I see [q]the heavens
opened, and [r]the Son of Man standing [p]at
the right hand of God." 57 But they cried out
with a loud voice and stopped their ears and
rushed together[1] at him. 58 Then [s]they cast him
out of the city and [t]stoned him. And [u]the witnesses laid down their garments [v]at the feet of
a young man named Saul. 59 And as they were
stoning Stephen, [w]he called out, "Lord Jesus,
[x]receive my spirit." 60 And [y]falling to his knees
he cried out with a loud voice, [z]"Lord, do not
hold this sin against them." And when he had
said this, [a]he fell asleep.

Saul Ravages the Church

8 And [b]Saul [c]approved of his execution.
And there arose on that day a great persecution against the church in Jerusalem,
and [d]they were all scattered throughout the
regions of Judea and Samaria, except the
apostles. 2 Devout men buried Stephen and
made great lamentation over him. 3 But [e]Saul
was ravaging the church, and entering house
after house, he [f]dragged off men and women
and committed them to prison.

Philip Proclaims Christ in Samaria

4 Now [g]those who were scattered went about
preaching the word. 5[h]Philip went down to the
city[2] of Samaria and proclaimed to them the
Christ. 6[i]And the crowds with one accord paid
attention to what was being said by Philip
when they heard him [j]and saw the signs that

[1] Or *rushed with one mind* [2] Some manuscripts *a city*

51[d]Deut. 10:16; See Ex. 32:9 [e]Lev. 26:41; Jer. 6:10; 9:26; Ezek. 44:7, 9 [f]Mal. 3:7
52[g]1 Kgs. 19:10; 2 Chr. 36:16; Jer. 2:30; Matt. 23:31, 37; See Matt. 5:12; 21:35 [h]See ch. 3:14 [i]See ch. 5:28
53[j]Gal. 3:19; Heb. 2:2; [ver. 38; Deut. 33:2] [k]John 7:19
54[l]ch. 5:33; [ch. 2:37] [m]Job 16:9; Ps. 35:16; 37:12
55[n]ch. 6:5 [o]Ex. 24:16; Luke 2:9; John 12:41 [p]Ps. 110:1; See Mark 16:19
56[q]See John 1:51 [r]See Dan. 7:13 [p][See ver. 55 above]
58[s]Lev. 24:14-16; Num. 15:35; 1 Kgs. 21:13; [Luke 4:29; Heb. 13:12] [t]Matt. 21:35; 23:37; Heb. 11:37 [u]ch. 6:13; [Deut. 13:9, 10; 17:7] [v]ch. 8:1; 22:20; [ch. 22:4]
59[w]ch. 9:14 [x]Ps. 31:5; Luke 23:46
60[y]ch. 9:40; 20:36; 21:5; Luke 22:41; Eph. 3:14 [z]See Matt. 5:44 [a]See Matt. 27:52

Chapter 8
1[b]ch. 7:58; 22:20 [c]See Rom. 1:32 [d]ch. 11:19; See Matt. 10:23
3[e]ch. 9:1, 13, 21; 22:4, 19; 26:10, 11; 1 Cor. 15:9; Gal. 1:13; Phil. 3:6; 1 Tim. 1:13 [f][James 2:6]
4[g]ver. 1
5[h]ch. 6:5
6[i][John 4:39] [j]John 2:23

7:54–8:3 Amid the very worst incident of persecution in Acts, we meet briefly a person who later will be used by God to proclaim the gospel more widely than any other person in the early church: Saul of Tarsus (7:58). Here we receive a glimpse of the radical grace that God will show to and through Saul: God does not leave behind even the worst of sinners (1 Tim. 1:15). This offers hope to sinners who feel unforgivable: we must never write off either others or ourselves as beyond redemption.

7:60 The gospel has so permeated Stephen's life that, when faced with an unjust death at the hands of an angry mob, his dying breath is spent pleading with God to forgive them. His model here is Jesus, who prayed for the forgiveness of his persecutors, even as they crucified him (Luke 23:34, 46). It is difficult to imagine a more dramatic example of loving one's enemies (Luke 6:27–28).

Stephen's selfless love is motivated by the gospel. Christ died for Stephen while Stephen was yet a sinner, showering him with undeserved grace. As a response to this grace, Stephen extends a reflection of that grace to his persecutors. The grace of God motivates mercy in his followers. Such radical forgiveness jars a watching world, which has little motivation or power to forgive enemies.

Stephen's confidence in the face of death and his mercy toward his enemies must have made an impression on Saul. The persecutor of the church would soon become its most famous advocate, joining Stephen in experiencing the abundant grace of God and responding with grace to all around him.

8:1–8 Samaritans, though technically "half" Jewish, were considered non-Jewish, even of lower status than a Gentile. The Jews regarded them as not having any part in the promises of God to his people. In this chapter the gospel reaches Samaria (fulfilling Acts 1:8) and thus the first cross-cultural barrier is breached. Acts 8 begins the process of the gospel being preached to all people groups. Disciples are scattered not just into Judea but Samaria (v. 1). Thus Philip, one of the proto-deacons of chapter 6, goes to Samaria to proclaim Christ, and many people are healed.

he did. 7 For [k]unclean spirits, crying out with a
loud voice, came out of many who had them,
and many who were paralyzed or lame were
healed. 8 So [l]there was much joy in that city.

Simon the Magician Believes

9 But there was a man named Simon, [m]who
had previously practiced magic in the city
and amazed the people of Samaria, [n]saying
that he himself was somebody great. 10 They
all paid attention to him, from the least to
the greatest, saying, [o]"This man is the power
of God that is called [p]Great." 11 And they paid
attention to him because for a long time he
had [q]amazed them with his magic. 12 But when
[r]they believed Philip as he preached good news
[s]about the kingdom of God and the name of
Jesus Christ, [r]they were baptized, both men
and women. 13 Even Simon himself believed,
and after being baptized he continued with
Philip. And [t]seeing signs and [u]great miracles[1]
performed, [v]he was amazed.

14 Now when [w]the apostles at Jerusalem
heard that [x]Samaria had received the word of
God, they sent to them Peter and John, 15 who
came down and prayed for them [y]that they
might receive the Holy Spirit, 16 for [z]he had not
yet [a]fallen on any of them, but [b]they had only
been baptized in the name of the Lord Jesus.
17 Then [c]they laid their hands on them and
[d]they received the Holy Spirit. 18 Now when
Simon saw that the Spirit was given through
the laying on of the apostles' hands, he offered
them money, 19 saying, "Give me this power
also, so that anyone on whom I lay my hands
may receive the Holy Spirit." 20 But Peter said
to him, [e]"May your silver perish with you,
because you thought you could obtain the
gift of God [f]with money! 21 You have neither
part nor lot in this matter, for [g]your heart is
not right before God. 22 Repent, therefore, of
this wickedness of yours, and pray to the Lord
that, [h]if possible, the intent of your heart may
be forgiven you. 23 For I see that you are in [i]the
gall[2] of bitterness and in [j]the bond of iniquity."

[1] Greek *works of power* [2] That is, a bitter fluid secreted by the liver; bile

Here we see how God cares for the suffering. God's heart has always been with the afflicted. When Israel was enslaved in Egypt, God heard their cries, saw their affliction, and knew their suffering (Ex. 3:7). He was involved. After redeeming Israel from Egypt, he gave them the law, which was replete with instructions to protect the poor, the outsiders, orphans, and widows (Deut. 10:18–19; 15:7–11; etc.). God's suffering servants have always been sinners as well. While much of their pain was inflicted from without, their deepest pangs were self-inflicted. God's people often went after idols, forsaking him and enslaving themselves to gods that could not deliver them (Isa. 45:20; Jer. 2:13). Many of our greatest pains are still caused by the folly of idolatry (i.e., seeking fulfillment through means other than God's). But Christ was the obedient servant who suffered without any sin. He walked in obedience to the Father but still suffered greatly, allowing him to identify both with the Father in his perfection and with us in our weakness and pain (Heb. 4:15). This allows Jesus to be the unique Mediator between God and humanity.

In the next four chapters (8–11), the book of Acts moves from the topic of persecution to the gospel spreading across borders and boundaries: first to the Samaritans, then to the Gentiles. All but the apostles are forced to flee Jerusalem in the wake of intense persecution, and their scattering unintentionally produces a mobilized mission force. Saul intends to destroy what he believes is a heretical sect. Instead, he ends up disseminating the gospel across dozens of cities. What is intended to crush the movement turns into fuel for the gospel's advance.

8:14–17 The Samaritans were considered racial "half-breeds." Here, it appears that God withholds the giving of the Spirit until the apostles arrive, in order to underscore the connection between the Jerusalem church and the Samaritans. Otherwise, the Samaritans may have assumed that they were autonomous from Jerusalem, or the disciples in Jerusalem may not have accepted them as full brothers and sisters in the family of God. The important point is that even the Samaritans, whom the Jews usually avoided, were now filled with the Spirit. This extraordinary sign confirmed the truth of Christ's earlier message (1:8) by indicating that Samaritans were now to be included in the church as full members (see also note on 3:11–26). Again, the unity and the fellowship of believers as the people of God is highlighted in Acts as a continuing sign of the Spirit's presence and blessing.

7[k] See Mark 16:17, 18
8[l] ver. 39; See John 16:22
9[m] ver. 11; ch. 13:6 [n] See ch. 5:36
10[o] ch. 14:11; 28:6 [p] [ch. 19:27, 28]
11[q] ver. 9; [ver. 13; Gal. 3:1]
12[r] ch. 16:33, 34; 18:8; Mark 16:16 [s] ch. 1:3
13[t] ver. 6, 7 [u] ch. 19:11 [v] [ver. 9]
14[w] ver. 1 [x] ch. 1:8
15[y] ch. 2:38
16[z] [ch. 19:2] [a] ch. 10:44; 11:15 [b] ch. 19:5; [ch. 2:38; 10:47, 48; Matt. 28:19; 1 Cor. 1:13, 15; Gal. 3:27]
17[c] ch. 9:17; 19:6; [ch. 6:6; Heb. 6:2] [d] See ch. 2:4
20[e] [2 Kgs. 5:16; Dan. 5:17] [f] Isa. 55:1
21[g] 2 Kgs. 10:15; Ps. 78:37
22[h] Dan. 4:27; 2 Tim. 2:25
23[i] Deut. 29:18; 32:32; Heb. 12:15 [j] Isa. 58:6; [Eph. 4:3; Col. 3:14]

24 And Simon answered, [k]"Pray for me to the
Lord, that nothing of what you have said may
come upon me."

25 Now when they had testified and spoken the word of the Lord, they returned to
Jerusalem, [l]preaching the gospel to many villages of the Samaritans.

Philip and the Ethiopian Eunuch

26 Now [m]an angel of the Lord said to Philip,
"Rise and go toward the south[1] to the road that
goes down from Jerusalem to Gaza." This is
a desert place. 27 And he rose and went. And
there was an [n]Ethiopian, a [o]eunuch, a court
official of Candace, queen of the Ethiopians,
[p]who was in charge of all her treasure. [q]He
had come to Jerusalem to worship 28 and was
returning, seated in his chariot, and he was
reading the prophet Isaiah. 29 And the Spirit
said to Philip, "Go over and join this chariot."
30 So Philip ran to him and heard him reading
Isaiah the prophet and asked, "Do you understand what you are reading?" 31 And he said,
[r]"How can I, unless someone [s]guides me?" And
[t]he invited Philip to come up and sit with him.
32 Now the passage of the Scripture that he was
reading was this:

[u]"Like a sheep he was led to the slaughter
and like a lamb before its shearer is
silent,
so he opens not his mouth.
33 In his [v]humiliation justice was denied
him.
Who can describe his generation?
For his life is taken away from the earth."

34 And the eunuch said to Philip, "About
whom, I ask you, does the prophet say this,
about himself or about someone else?" 35 Then
Philip opened his mouth, and [w]beginning
with this Scripture [x]he told him the good
news about Jesus. 36 And as they were going
along the road they came to some water, and
the eunuch said, "See, here is water! [y]What
prevents me from being baptized?"[2] 38 And
he commanded the chariot to stop, and they
both went down into the water, Philip and the
eunuch, and he baptized him. 39 And when
they came up out of the water, [z]the Spirit of
the Lord [a]carried Philip away, and the eunuch
saw him no more, and went on his way rejoicing. 40 But Philip found himself at Azotus, and
as he passed through he preached the gospel
to all the towns until he came to Caesarea.

The Conversion of Saul

9 But Saul, [b]still [c]breathing threats and
murder against the disciples of the Lord,
went to [d]the high priest 2 and asked him for
letters [e]to the synagogues at Damascus, so
that if he found any belonging to [f]the Way,
men or women, he might bring them bound
to Jerusalem. 3 [g]Now as he went on his way, he
approached Damascus, and suddenly a light
from heaven shone around him. 4 And falling
to the ground he heard a voice saying to him,
"Saul, Saul, why are you persecuting [h]me?"
5 And he said, "Who are you, Lord?" And he
said, "I am Jesus, [h]whom you are persecuting.
6 But [i]rise and enter the city, and you will be
told [j]what you are to do." 7 [k]The men who were
traveling with him stood speechless, [l]hear-
ing the voice but seeing no one. 8 Saul rose
from the ground, and although his eyes were
opened, [m]he saw nothing. So they led him by

[1] Or *go at about noon* [2] Some manuscripts add all or most of verse 37: *And Philip said, "If you believe with all your heart, you may." And he replied, "I believe that Jesus Christ is the Son of God."*

24 [k] [Ex. 8:8; 9:28; 10:17]
25 [l] [ver. 6-8; John 4:39]
26 [m] ch. 5:19; 10:3; 11:13; 12:7, 23; 27:23; [Judg. 6:12; 13:3]
27 [n] Ps. 68:31; 87:4; Zeph. 3:10 [o] [Jer. 38:7] [p] Ezra 7:21 [q] [1 Kgs. 8:41, 42; John 12:20]
31 [r] See Rom. 10:14 [s] John 16:13 [t] [1 Kgs. 20:33; 2 Kgs. 10:15]
32 [u] Cited from Isa. 53:7, 8
33 [v] [Phil. 2:8]
35 [w] Luke 24:27; [ch. 17:2; 18:28] [x] See ch. 5:42
36 [y] ch. 10:47
39 [z] 1 Kgs. 18:12; 2 Kgs. 2:16; Ezek. 3:12, 14; 8:3; 11:1, 24; 43:5 [a] See 2 Cor. 12:2

9:1–9 In the book of Acts, God's gospel not only overcomes formidable ethnic and geographical barriers but also breaks through the most formidable barrier of all: human sin. Saul learns firsthand how closely Jesus identifies with his church, here described as "the Way." In persecuting those of the Way, Saul was persecuting Christ himself. In response to the question, "Who are you?" Saul would have preferred any response to the one he receives: "I am Jesus, *whom you are persecuting.*" In opposing God's people, Saul has opposed God himself (cf. 5:38–39).

Saul is blinded by the magnificence of this appearance of Christ, and his physical blindness allows him to see himself truly. He finally recognizes his own powerlessness and weakness, and accepts his blindness in humility. Before commissioning Saul to take the gospel to the Gentiles, God tears down his reliance on his religious zeal. Only after being brought to a position of abject humility is Saul ready for the uplifting gospel of Jesus Christ. "God opposes the proud, but gives grace to the humble" (James 4:6).

Chapter 9 **1** [b] ver. 13, 21; See ch. 8:3 [c] [Ps. 27:12] [d] ch. 22:5; 26:10 **2** [e] ch. 22:19; [Luke 12:11; 21:12] [f] ch. 19:9, 23; 24:14, 22; [ch. 16:17; 18:25, 26; 22:4; Isa. 30:21; 35:8; Amos 8:14] **3** [g] For ver. 3-8, see ch. 22:6-11; 26:12-18; [1 Cor. 15:8] **4** [h] [Isa. 63:9; Zech. 2:8] **5** [h] [See ver. 4 above] **6** [i] [Ezek. 3:22; Gal. 1:1] [j] ver. 16; [1 Cor. 9:16] **7** [k] [Dan. 10:7] [l] [ch. 22:9 with John 12:29] **8** [m] [ch. 22:11]

the hand and brought him into Damascus.
9 And for three days he was without sight, and
neither ate nor drank.

10 Now there was a disciple at Damascus
named [n]Ananias. The Lord said to him in a
vision, "Ananias." And he said, [o]"Here I am,
Lord." 11 And the Lord said to him, "Rise and go
to the street called Straight, and at the house
of Judas look for a man [p]of Tarsus named Saul,
for behold, he is praying, 12 and he has seen in a
vision a man named Ananias come in and [q]lay
his hands on him so that he might regain his
sight." 13 But Ananias answered, "Lord, I have
heard from many about this man, [r]how much
evil he has done to [s]your [t]saints at Jerusalem.
14 And here he has authority from [u]the chief
priests to bind all who [v]call on your name."
15 But the Lord said to him, "Go, for [w]he is a
chosen instrument of mine to carry my name
[x]before the Gentiles and [y]kings and the children of Israel. 16 For [z]I will show him how
much [a]he must suffer [b]for the sake of my
name." 17 So [c]Ananias departed and entered the
house. And [d]laying his hands on him he said,
"Brother Saul, the Lord Jesus who appeared
to you on the road by which you came has
sent me so that you may regain your sight
and [e]be filled with the Holy Spirit." 18 And
immediately something like scales fell from
his eyes, and [f]he regained his sight. Then [g]he
rose and was baptized; 19 and [h]taking food, he
was strengthened.

Saul Proclaims Jesus in Synagogues

For [i]some days he was with the disciples at
Damascus. 20 And immediately he proclaimed
Jesus in the synagogues, saying, [j]"He is the
Son of God." 21 And all who heard him were
amazed and said, "Is not this the man who
[k]made havoc [l]in Jerusalem of those who called
upon this name? And has he not come here for
this purpose, to bring them bound before the
chief priests?" 22 But Saul [m]increased all the
more in strength, and [n]confounded the Jews
who lived in Damascus by proving [o]that Jesus
was the Christ.

Saul Escapes from Damascus

23 [p]When many days had passed, the Jews[1]
plotted to kill him, 24 but their [q]plot became
known to Saul. [r]They were watching the gates
day and night in order to kill him, 25 but his
disciples took him by night and [s]let him down
through an opening in the wall,[2] lowering him
in a basket.

Saul in Jerusalem

26 And [t]when he had come to Jerusalem,
he attempted to join the disciples. And they
were all afraid of him, for they did not believe
that he was a disciple. 27 But [u]Barnabas took
him and [v]brought him to the apostles and
declared to them [w]how on the road he had
seen the Lord, who spoke to him, and [x]how
at Damascus he had [y]preached boldly in the
name of Jesus. 28 So he went [z]in and out among
them at Jerusalem, preaching boldly in the
name of the Lord. 29 And he spoke and disputed against [a]the Hellenists.[3] But [b]they were
seeking to kill him. 30 And when [c]the brothers learned this, they brought him down to
Caesarea and sent him off [d]to Tarsus.

31 So [e]the church throughout all Judea and
Galilee and Samaria had peace and was being
built up. And [f]walking in the fear of the Lord
and in the comfort of the Holy Spirit, [g]it
multiplied.

The Healing of Aeneas

32 Now [h]as Peter went here and there among
them all, he came down also to the saints who

[1] The Greek word *Ioudaioi* refers specifically here to Jewish religious leaders, and others under their influence, who opposed the Christian faith in that time [2] Greek *through the wall* [3] That is, Greek-speaking Jews

Saul was at his worst, overseeing the murder of men and women in the church, with no sign of repentance, when Jesus met him on the Damascus road. Here again we are admonished against condemning anyone as lost beyond hope, and this includes ourselves. God will reach to his farthest-out enemies, he will defeat the uttermost human rebellion, but in doing so he does not crush these rebels but loves and converts them into chosen instruments of the good news (Acts 9:15). In Saul we see a rebel against God, an enemy of the long-promised Messiah. Yet Saul is reconciled to God through Jesus and is called God's ambassador, through whom God makes his appeal to the entire world (2 Cor. 5:20).

10 [n] ch. 22:12 [o] Gen. 22:1; Isa. 6:8
11 [p] ch. 21:39; 22:3
12 [q] ver. 17; See Mark 5:23
13 [r] ver. 1, 2 [s] 1 Thess. 3:13; 2 Thess. 1:10 [t] Rom. 15:25, 26, 31
14 [u] ver. 21 [v] ch. 22:16; Rom. 10:13; 1 Cor. 1:2; [ch. 7:59; 2 Tim. 2:22]
15 [w] [ch. 13:2; Rom. 1:1; Gal. 1:15; Eph. 3:7] [x] Rom. 1:5 (Gk.); 11:13; 15:16; Gal. 1:16; 2:2, 7-9; Eph. 3:7, 8; 1 Tim. 2:7; 2 Tim. 4:17 [y] ch. 25:22, 23; 26:1, 32; 2 Tim. 4:16 **16** [z] ch. 20:23; 21:4, 11; 1 Thess. 3:3 [a] ver. 6; [ch. 14:22; 2 Cor. 6:4, 5; 11:23-28] [b] See ch. 5:41 **17** [c] ch. 22:12-14 [d] ver. 12 [e] See ch. 2:4 **18** [f] ch. 22:13 [g] ch. 22:16 **19** [h] [ver. 9] [i] ch. 26:20 **20** [j] [ver. 22] **21** [k] ver. 13, 14 [l] Gal. 1:13, 23 **22** [m] See 1 Tim. 1:12 [n] ch. 18:28 [o] [ver. 20] **23** [p] [Gal. 1:17, 18] **24** [q] ch. 20:3, 19; 23:30; [ch. 23:12; 25:3] [r] 2 Cor. 11:32 **25** [s] 2 Cor. 11:33; [Josh. 2:15; 1 Sam. 19:12] **26** [t] ch. 22:17-20; 26:20 **27** [u] ch. 4:36 [v] [Gal. 1:18, 19] [w] ver. 3-6 [x] ver. 19, 20, 22 [y] See ch. 4:29 **28** [z] ch. 1:21 **29** [a] See ch. 6:1 [b] [ch. 22:18] **30** [c] See John 21:23 [d] [ch. 11:25; Gal. 1:21] **31** [e] [ch. 8:1; 16:5] [f] [Neh. 5:9] [g] ver. 35, 42 **32** [h] [ch. 8:25]

lived at Lydda. 33 There he found a man named
Aeneas, bedridden for eight years, who was
paralyzed. 34 And Peter said to him, “Aeneas,
[i]Jesus Christ heals you; rise and make your
bed.” And immediately he rose. 35 [j]And all the
residents of Lydda and [k]Sharon saw him, and
[l]they turned to the Lord.

Dorcas Restored to Life

36 Now there was in [m]Joppa a disciple named
Tabitha, which, translated, means Dorcas.[1] She
was full of [n]good works and acts of charity.
37 In those days she became ill and died, and
when they had washed her, they laid her in [o]an
upper room. 38 Since Lydda was near Joppa, the
disciples, hearing that Peter was there, sent
two men to him, urging him, [p]“Please come
to us without delay.” 39 So Peter rose and went
with them. And when he arrived, they took
him to [q]the upper room. All the widows stood
beside him weeping and showing tunics[2] and
other garments that Dorcas made while she
was with them. 40 But Peter [r]put them all outside, and [s]knelt down and prayed; and turning
to the body [t]he said, “Tabitha, arise.” And she
opened her eyes, and when she saw Peter she
sat up. 41 And he gave her his hand and raised
her up. Then calling the saints and widows, he
presented her alive. 42 And it became known
throughout all Joppa, and [u]many believed in
the Lord. 43 And he stayed in Joppa for many
days [v]with one Simon, a tanner.

Peter and Cornelius

10 At Caesarea there was a man named
Cornelius, a centurion of [w]what was
known as the Italian Cohort, 2 a devout man
[x]who feared God with all his household, gave
alms generously to the people, and prayed
continually to God. 3 [y]About the ninth hour of
the day[3] [z]he saw clearly in a vision [a]an angel of
God come in and say to him, “Cornelius.” 4 And
he stared at him in terror and said, “What is
it, Lord?” And he said to him, “Your prayers
and your alms [b]have ascended [c]as a memorial before God. 5 And now send men to Joppa
and bring one Simon who is called Peter. 6 He
is lodging [d]with one Simon, a tanner, whose
house is by the sea.” 7 When the angel who
spoke to him had departed, he called two of
his servants and a devout soldier from among
those who attended him, 8 and having related
everything to them, he sent them to Joppa.

Peter's Vision

9 The next day, as they were on their journey and approaching the city, [e]Peter went up
[f]on the housetop about [g]the sixth hour[4] to
pray. 10 And he became hungry and wanted
something to eat, but while they were preparing it, he fell into [h]a trance 11 and saw [i]the

[1] The Aramaic name *Tabitha* and the Greek name *Dorcas* both mean *gazelle* [2] Greek *chiton*, a long garment worn under the cloak next to the skin [3] That is, 3 P.M. [4] That is, noon

34 [i][ch. 3:6]
35 [j][ver. 31, 42] [k]1 Chr. 5:16; 27:29; Song 2:1 [l]ch. 11:21; 2 Cor. 3:16
36 [m]See Josh. 19:46 [n]1 Tim. 2:10
37 [o]ver. 39; ch. 1:13; 20:8
38 [p]Num. 22:16 (Heb.; Gk.)
39 [q]ver. 37
40 [r]Matt. 9:25 [s]See ch. 7:60 [t][Mark 5:41; John 11:43]
42 [u][John 11:45; 12:11]
43 [v]ch. 10:6
Chapter 10
1 [w]Matt. 27:27; Mark 15:16; John 18:3, 12
2 [x]ver. 22; ch. 13:16, 26
3 [y]See ch. 3:1 [z]ver. 17, 19 [a]See ch. 8:26
4 [b]Rev. 8:4; [Ps. 141:2; Dan. 10:12] [c]Matt. 26:13; Mark 14:9; [ver. 31; Heb. 6:10]
6 [d]ch. 9:43
9 [e]For ver. 9-32, see ch. 11:5-14 [f][2 Kgs. 23:12; Jer. 19:13; 32:29; Zeph. 1:5]; See 1 Sam. 9:25 [g]Ps. 55:17
10 [h]ch. 22:17
11 [i]See John 1:51

10:1–48 The story of the conversion of Cornelius is the longest narrative in the book of Acts. It is a very significant moment in the gospel's advance, as God is showing that the gospel is for all people, not just the Jews (in accord with the purposes Jesus outlined by the expanding concentric circles of 1:8). In the gospel, the same God who chose Israel is doing a new thing, bringing Israel's vocation to be a “light for the nations” (Isa. 49:6) to its climax and fruition. This happens as God embraces the Gentiles through Jesus, the perfect Israelite, the Light of the World. He is the Light who shines in the darkness of a rebel people to create new men and women from all nations who will carry this light through the Spirit to the ends of the earth.

10:9–33 The expression “the heavens opened” (v. 11) would have reminded readers of other significant communications from God, such as the baptism of Jesus (Luke 3:21) and, in this same book of Acts, Stephen's vision of the exalted Christ just before his martyrdom (Acts 7:56). In Peter's vision, a key word is “all”: God shows him “all kinds of animals and reptiles and birds of the air” (10:12). This would clearly have included animals forbidden in the Old Testament dietary regulations (Leviticus 11; Deuteronomy 14), yet God tells Peter to “kill and eat” (Acts 10:13). As a faithful Jew, Peter reacts with horror at the prospect of eating “unclean” foods. The vision initially confuses him, but when the God-fearing Cornelius sends for Peter, he makes the connection. God is using a buffet of foods to show that he is able to make anyone clean, and he has chosen to bring cleansing and salvation through Christ to all the nations. Peter now understands that he “should not call any person common or unclean” (v. 28). Once again, salvation extends beyond a significant boundary, this time beyond the borders of Israel and into the Gentile world.

heavens opened and something like a great sheet descending, being let down by its four corners upon the earth. 12 In it were all kinds of animals and reptiles and birds of the air. 13 And there came a voice to him: "Rise, Peter; kill and eat." 14 But Peter said, "By no means, Lord; [j]for I have never eaten anything that is [k]common or [l]unclean." 15 And the voice came to him again a second time, [m]"What God has made clean, do not call common." 16 This happened three times, and the thing was taken up at once to heaven.

17 Now while Peter was inwardly perplexed as to what [n]the vision that he had seen might mean, behold, [o]the men who were sent by Cornelius, having made inquiry for Simon's house, stood at the gate 18 and called out to ask whether Simon who was called Peter was lodging there. 19 And while Peter was pondering [n]the vision, [p]the Spirit said to him, "Behold, three men are looking for you. 20 Rise and go down and [q]accompany them without hesitation,[1] for I have sent them." 21 And Peter went down to the men and said, "I am the one you are looking for. What is the reason for your coming?" 22 And they said, "Cornelius, a centurion, an upright and [r]God-fearing man, who is well spoken of by the whole Jewish nation, was directed by [s]a holy angel to send for you to come to his house and [t]to hear what you have to say." 23 So he invited them in to be his guests.

The next day he rose and went away with them, and [u]some of [v]the brothers from Joppa accompanied him. 24 And on the following day they entered Caesarea. Cornelius was expecting them and had called together his relatives and close friends. 25 When Peter entered, Cornelius met him and [w]fell down at his feet and [x]worshiped him. 26 But Peter lifted him up, saying, [y]"Stand up; I too am a man." 27 And as he talked with him, he went in and found many persons gathered. 28 And he said to them, "You yourselves know how unlawful it is for a Jew [z]to associate with or to visit anyone of another nation, but [a]God has shown me that I should not call any person common or unclean. 29 So when I was sent for, I came without objection. I ask then why you sent for me."

30 And Cornelius said, [b]"Four days ago, about this hour, I was praying in my house at [c]the ninth hour,[2] and behold, [d]a man stood before me in bright clothing 31 and said, 'Cornelius, [e]your prayer has been heard and your alms have been remembered before God. 32 Send therefore to Joppa and ask for Simon who is called Peter. He is lodging in the house of Simon, a tanner, by the sea.' 33 So I sent for you at once, and you have been kind enough to come. Now therefore we are all here in the presence of God to hear all that you have been commanded by the Lord."

[1] Or *accompany them, making no distinction* [2] That is, 3 P.M.

That this vision, and its connection to Cornelius, is highly significant is made clear by several indicators. The vision is given by God three times (v. 16). The command in the vision to "kill and eat" is concise and direct (v. 13). The Spirit speaks directly to Peter (vv. 19–20). And finally, an angel speaks directly to Cornelius (vv. 30–32). Why is Luke so intent to relate these specifics regarding the importance of the vision and its effects on different persons? In part, to show that God intends to save both individuals and people groups. Up to this time individual Gentiles have been saved (from Ruth and Rahab in the Old Testament to the Ethiopian in this book of Acts). But Cornelius has a household with him, and it is apparent that others outside his household are aware of this new kind of mercy as well (v. 24). The gospel will spread not only to individuals but to entire people groups, who will repent and be grafted into God's people. And, of course, it is important to note that these groups now extend to those formerly considered unclean. The gospel knows no ethnic boundaries.

Satan often tempts us to doubt God's salvation, reminding us of the unclean blemish of sin in our or others' lives. Peter's vision, however, reminds us that what God has called clean, we have no right to call unclean (v. 15). God see us as pure in Christ, and how God sees things is how they truly are. There is no condemnation for those in Christ (Rom. 8:1), for he has removed our sins as far as the east is from the west (Ps. 103:12); he has made our scarlet sins as white as snow (Isa. 1:18). We no longer regard others or ourselves by outward appearance. Instead we regard others and ourselves according to the Spirit, in which God has made us clean, pure, and whole (2 Cor. 5:16).

14 [j] Ezek. 4:14; Dan. 1:8 [k] ver. 28 [l] Lev. 11:2-47; 20:25; Deut. 14:4-20
15 [m] Rom. 14:2, 14, 20; 1 Tim. 4:4; Titus 1:15; [Matt. 15:11; Mark 7:15, 19; 1 Cor. 10:25]
17 [n] ver. 3 [o] ver. 7, 8
19 [n] [See ver. 17 above] [p] See ch. 8:29
20 [q] [ch. 15:7-9]
22 [r] See ver. 2 [s] See Mark 8:38 [t] ch. 11:14
23 [u] ver. 45; [ch. 11:12] [v] See John 21:23
25 [w] ch. 16:29; Dan. 2:46 [x] See Matt. 8:2
26 [y] Rev. 19:10; 22:8, 9; [ch. 14:15]
28 [z] [ch. 11:3; John 4:9; 18:28; Gal. 2:12] [a] [ver. 35]; See ver. 14, 15
30 [b] ver. 9, 23, 24 [c] See ch. 3:1 [d] [ch. 1:10]
31 [e] See ver. 4

Gentiles Hear the Good News

34 So Peter opened his mouth and said: "Truly I understand that [f]God [g]shows no partiality, 35 but [f]in every nation anyone who fears him and [h]does what is right is acceptable to him. 36 As for [i]the word that he sent to Israel, [j]preaching good news of [k]peace through Jesus Christ ([l]he is Lord of all), 37 you yourselves know what happened throughout all Judea, [m]beginning [n]from Galilee after the baptism that John proclaimed: 38 how [o]God anointed Jesus of Nazareth [p]with the Holy Spirit and with [q]power. He went about doing good and healing all [r]who were oppressed by the devil, [s]for God was with him. 39 And [t]we are witnesses of all that he did both in the country of the Jews and in Jerusalem. [u]They put him to death by hanging him on a tree, 40 but [v]God raised him on [w]the third day and made him to [x]appear, 41 [y]not to all the people but to us who had been chosen by God as [z]witnesses, who ate and drank with him after he rose from the dead. 42 And [a]he commanded us to preach to the people and to testify [b]that he is the one appointed by God to be judge [c]of the living and the dead. 43 [d]To him [e]all the prophets bear witness that [f]everyone who believes in him receives [g]forgiveness of sins [h]through his name."

The Holy Spirit Falls on the Gentiles

44 While Peter was still saying these things, [i]the Holy Spirit fell on all who heard the word. 45 And the believers from among [j]the circumcised who had come with Peter were amazed, because [k]the gift of the Holy Spirit [l]was poured out even on the Gentiles. 46 For they were hearing them [m]speaking in tongues and extolling God. Then Peter declared, 47 [n]"Can anyone withhold water for baptizing these people, who have received the Holy Spirit [o]just as we have?" 48 And he [p]commanded them [q]to be baptized in the name of Jesus Christ. Then they asked him to remain for some days.

Peter Reports to the Church

11 Now the apostles and [r]the brothers[1] who were throughout Judea heard that the Gentiles also had received the word of God. 2 So when Peter went up to Jerusalem, [s]the circumcision party[2] criticized him, saying, 3 [t]"You went to uncircumcised men and [u]ate with them." 4 But Peter began and explained it to them in order: 5 [v]"I was in the city of Joppa praying, and in a trance I saw a vision, something like a great sheet descending, being let down from heaven by its four corners, and it came down to me. 6 Looking

[1] Or *brothers and sisters* [2] Or *Jerusalem, those of the circumcision*

10:34–43 In his gospel presentation, Peter does not quote the Old Testament as on previous occasions (2:14–36; 3:11–26), but his message remains consistent: Jesus lived, died, and was raised; he has been appointed by God as Judge of the living and the dead; and everyone is called to repent and believe, to receive forgiveness of sins through the name of Jesus. This is the culmination of God's redemptive plan.

God shows no partiality, but freely receives all who believe in his Son, Jesus Christ. Both Jew and Gentile receive forgiveness through Jesus (15:11). The cross of Christ is the great equalizer: we are all humbled as we grasp the magnitude of our sin and guilt; yet at the cross, the offer of forgiveness is made to all without distinction. Because Jesus is Lord of all (10:36), his gospel is available to all.

10:44–48 The Jewish believers with Peter are shocked that the Holy Spirit is poured out even on the Gentiles (v. 45). They probably thought that Gentiles should become Jewish proselytes first, but they knew the Holy Spirit fell on the Gentiles when they began speaking in tongues and praising God (v. 46). Peter later uses this incident to answer the challenge of the Jerusalem church that a believer in Jesus had to first be a Jewish proselyte (11:15–17). Therefore, there was nothing to prevent the Gentiles from being baptized as Christians.

Acts 10:47 quotes Peter as saying that they "have received the Holy Spirit just as we have." The reference to Acts 2 is obvious. The same Holy Spirit who had been poured out on Jews had also been poured out on Gentiles. God can make all things clean. The conclusion embraced by Peter and by the Jerusalem church was that these Gentiles were fellow believers. Repentance and salvation had been granted even to those who had not been under the Mosaic covenant.

34 [f] [ver. 28; ch. 15:19; Deut. 1:17; Rom. 3:29]; See Deut. 10:17 [g] Prov. 24:23; James 2:1, 9; [Jude 16]
35 [f] [See ver. 34 above] [h] Isa. 64:5
36 [i] ch. 13:26; Ps. 107:20; 147:18, 19 [j] Isa. 52:7; Nah. 1:15; Eph. 2:17 [k] See Luke 2:14 [l] Rom. 10:12; [Rev. 17:14; 19:16]; See ch. 2:36; Matt. 28:18
37 [m] Luke 24:47 [n] Matt. 4:12; Mark 1:14
38 [o] [Matt. 3:16; John 1:32, 33]; See ch. 4:26 [p] [ch. 1:2; 2:22; Matt. 12:28; Luke 4:18; Rom. 1:4] [q] [Luke 6:19] [r] See Matt. 4:24; Luke 13:16 [s] See John 8:29; 10:38
39 [t] ver. 41; See ch. 2:32; Luke 24:48 [u] ch. 5:30
40 [v] See ch. 2:24 [w] See Luke 9:22 [x] ch. 1:3
41 [y] [John 14:21, 22] [z] ver. 39
42 [a] See ch. 1:2 [b] ch. 17:31; 24:25; John 5:22, 27; 2 Cor. 5:10; See Matt. 16:27 [c] 2 Tim. 4:1; 1 Pet. 4:5; [Rom. 14:9, 10; 1 Thess. 4:15, 17]
43 [d] ch. 26:22; Rom. 3:21; [Jer. 31:34] [e] ch. 3:18, 24; Luke 24:27 [f] ch. 11:17; 13:38; 15:9; Rom. 9:33; 10:11; Gal. 3:22 [g] ch. 5:31 [h] ch. 2:38; 4:12; John 20:31; 1 John 2:12

44 [i] ch. 11:15; 15:8; 1 Thess. 1:5; See ch. 2:4 **45** [j] ver. 23; [ch. 11:2] [k] See ch. 2:38 [l] See ch. 2:17 **46** [m] See Mark 16:17 **47** [n] ch. 8:36 [o] ch. 2:4; 11:17; 15:8 **48** [p] [1 Cor. 1:14–17] [q] ch. 2:38; See ch. 8:12, 16 **Chapter 11** **1** [r] ver. 29; See John 21:23 **2** [s] ch. 10:45; Gal. 2:12; Col. 4:11; Titus 1:10; [Rom. 4:12] **3** [t] Gal. 2:12, 14; [ch. 10:28] [u] [Luke 15:2] **5** [v] For ver. 5-14, see ch. 10:9-32

at it closely, I observed animals and beasts of prey and reptiles and birds of the air. 7 And I heard a voice saying to me, 'Rise, Peter; kill and eat.' 8 But I said, 'By no means, Lord; for nothing common or unclean has ever entered my mouth.' 9 But the voice answered a second time from heaven, 'What God has made clean, do not call common.' 10 This happened three times, and all was drawn up again into heaven. 11 And behold, at that very moment three men arrived at the house in which we were, sent to me from Caesarea. 12 And the Spirit told me to go with them, [w]making no distinction. [x]These six brothers also accompanied me, and we entered the man's house. 13 And he told us how he had seen the angel stand in his house and say, 'Send to Joppa and bring Simon who is called Peter; 14 [y]he will declare to you a message by which [z]you will be saved, you and all your household.' 15 As I began to speak, [a]the Holy Spirit fell on them [b]just as on us at the beginning. 16 And I remembered the word of the Lord, how he said, [c]'John baptized with water, but you will be baptized with the Holy Spirit.' 17 If then [d]God gave [e]the same gift to them as he gave to us [f]when we believed in the Lord Jesus Christ, [g]who was I [h]that I could stand in God's way?" 18 When they heard these things they fell silent. And they [i]glorified God, saying, [j]"Then to the Gentiles also God has [k]granted [l]repentance that leads to life."

The Church in Antioch

19 [m]Now those who were scattered because of the persecution that arose over Stephen traveled as far as Phoenicia and Cyprus and Antioch, speaking the word to no one except Jews. 20 But there were some of them, men of Cyprus and Cyrene, who on coming to Antioch spoke to the Hellenists[1] also, [n]preaching the Lord Jesus. 21 And [o]the hand of the Lord was with them, and a great number who believed [p]turned to the Lord. 22 The report of this came to the ears of the church in Jerusalem, and they sent Barnabas to Antioch. 23 When he came and saw [q]the grace of God, he was glad, and he exhorted them all to remain faithful to the Lord [r]with steadfast purpose, 24 for he was a good man, [s]full of the Holy Spirit and of faith. And a great many people [t]were added to the Lord. 25 So Barnabas went to [u]Tarsus to look for Saul, 26 and when he had found him, he brought him to Antioch. For a whole year they met with the church and taught a great many people. And in Antioch the disciples were first called [v]Christians.

27 Now in these days [w]prophets came down from Jerusalem to Antioch. 28 And one of them named [x]Agabus stood up and foretold [y]by the Spirit that there would be a great [z]famine over all the world (this took place in the days of [a]Claudius). 29 So the disciples determined, every one according to his ability, [b]to send relief to [c]the brothers[2] living in Judea. 30 [d]And they did so, sending it to [e]the elders by the hand of Barnabas and Saul.

James Killed and Peter Imprisoned

12 About that time Herod the king laid violent hands on some who belonged to the church. 2 He killed [f]James the brother of John [g]with the sword, 3 and when he saw [h]that it pleased the Jews, he proceeded to arrest Peter also. This was during [i]the days of Unleavened Bread. 4 And when he had seized him, he put him [j]in prison, delivering him over to four [k]squads of soldiers to guard him, intending after the Passover to bring him out to the people. 5 So Peter was kept in prison, but earnest [l]prayer for him was made to God by the church.

[1] Or *Greeks* (that is, Greek-speaking non-Jews) [2] Or *brothers and sisters*

11:19–21 The persecution following Stephen's death (7:58–8:3) continues to have the opposite of its intended effect, as God uses it to spread his gospel abroad. The triumphant march of the gospel expands to the Gentile city of Antioch, as it becomes clearer that the Way is not merely a Jewish sect but a multiethnic work of God.

12:1–24 Having executed James, Herod plans to put Peter to a similar end, before God intervenes and foils his plot (vv. 6–19). Here is a blatant opponent to the work of God, not motivated as Saul was by religious zeal but by the desire for acclaim (v. 3). This idolatrous desire proves to be Herod's undoing. Herod accepts the praises of the

12 [w]ch. 15:9 [x]ch. 10:23, 45
14 [y]ch. 10:22 [z]ch. 10:2; 16:15, 31-34; 18:8; John 4:53
15 [a]ch. 10:44 [b]ch. 2:4
16 [c]ch. 1:5; [ch. 19:2]; See Matt. 3:11
17 [d]See ch. 10:47 [e]See ch. 2:38 [f]Eph. 1:13; See ch. 10:43 [g][Rom. 9:20] [h]ch. 10:47; See ch. 5:39
18 [i]ch. 21:20 [j][ch. 13:47; Matt. 8:11]; See ch. 10:34, 35

[k]See ch. 5:31 [l][2 Cor. 7:10] **19** [m]ch. 8:1, 4 **20** [n]See John 7:35; See ch. 5:42 **21** [o]ch. 13:11; Luke 1:66; [Ps. 80:17; 89:21] [p]ch. 9:35 **23** [q]ch. 13:43; 14:26; 20:24, 32; Rom. 5:15; 2 Cor. 6:1; Eph. 3:2, 7; Col. 1:6; Titus 2:11; Heb. 12:15; 1 Pet. 5:12; [ch. 4:33; 15:40] [r]2 Tim. 3:10 **24** [s]ch. 6:5 [t]ch. 5:14; [ver. 26] **25** [u]ch. 9:30 **26** [v]ch. 26:28; 1 Pet. 4:16 **27** [w]See ch. 13:1 **28** [x]ch. 21:10 [y]See ch. 2:18; 8:29 [z]Matt. 24:7 [a]ch. 18:2 **29** [b][ch. 24:17; Rom. 15:26] [c]ver. 1 **30** [d]ch. 12:25 [e]ch. 14:23; 15:2, 4, 6; 16:4; 20:17; 21:18; 1 Tim. 5:17, 19; Titus 1:5; James 5:14; 2 John 1; 3 John 1 **Chapter 12** **2** [f]Matt. 4:21; 20:23 [g]Heb. 11:37 **3** [h][ch. 24:27; 25:9] [i]ch. 20:6; Ex. 12:14, 15; 23:15 **4** [j]See Luke 21:12 [k][John 19:23] **5** [l]2 Cor. 1:11; Eph. 6:18

Peter Is Rescued

6 Now when Herod was about to bring him out, on that very night, Peter was sleeping between two soldiers, [m]bound with two chains, and sentries before the door were guarding the prison. 7 And behold, [n]an angel of the Lord [o]stood next to him, and a light shone in the cell. [p]He struck Peter on the side and woke him, saying, "Get up quickly." And [q]the chains fell off his hands. 8 And the angel said to him, "Dress yourself and [r]put on your sandals." And he did so. And he said to him, "Wrap your cloak around you and follow me." 9 And he went out and followed him. He did not know that what was being done by the angel was real, but [s]thought he was seeing a vision. 10 When they had passed the first and the second guard, they came to the iron gate leading into the city. [t]It opened for them of its own accord, and they went out and went along one street, and immediately the angel left him. 11 When Peter [u]came to himself, he said, "Now I am sure that [v]the Lord has sent his angel and [w]rescued me from the hand of Herod and from all that the Jewish people were expecting."

12 When he realized this, he went to the house of Mary, the mother of [x]John whose other name was Mark, where many were gathered together and [y]were praying. 13 And when he knocked at the door of the gateway, [z]a servant girl named Rhoda came to answer. 14 Recognizing Peter's voice, [a]in her joy she did not open the gate but ran in and reported that Peter was standing at the gate. 15 They said to her, "You are out of your mind." But she kept insisting that it was so, and they kept saying, "It is [b]his angel!" 16 But Peter continued knocking, and when they opened, they saw him and were amazed. 17 But [c]motioning to them with his hand to be silent, he described to them how the Lord had brought him out of the prison. And he said, "Tell these things to [d]James and to [e]the brothers."[1] Then he departed and went to another place.

18 Now when day came, there was no little disturbance among the soldiers over what had become of Peter. 19 And after Herod searched for him and did not find him, he examined the sentries and [f]ordered that they should be put to death. Then he went down from Judea to Caesarea and spent time there.

The Death of Herod

20 Now Herod was angry with the people of Tyre and Sidon, and they came to him with one accord, and [g]having persuaded Blastus, the king's chamberlain,[2] they asked for peace, because [h]their country depended on the king's country for food. 21 On an appointed day Herod put on his royal robes, took his seat upon the throne, and delivered an oration to them. 22 And the people were shouting, "The voice of a god, and not of a man!" 23 Immediately [i]an angel of the Lord struck him down, because [j]he did not give God the glory, and he was eaten by worms and breathed his last.

24 But [k]the word of God increased and multiplied.

25 [l]And Barnabas and Saul returned from[3] Jerusalem when they had completed their service, bringing with them [m]John, whose other name was Mark.

[1] Or *brothers and sisters* [2] That is, trusted personal attendant [3] Some manuscripts *to*

6 [m]ch. 21:33
7 [n]See ch. 8:26 [o]Luke 2:9; 24:4 [p][1 Kgs. 19:7] [q]ch. 16:26
8 [r]Mark 6:9
9 [s]Ps. 126:1
10 [t]ch. 5:19; 16:26
11 [u][Luke 15:17] [v]Ps. 34:7; 91:11; Dan. 3:28; 6:22 [w]Ps. 33:18, 19; 2 Cor. 1:10
12 [x]ver. 25; ch. 13:5, 13; 15:37, 39; Col. 4:10; 2 Tim. 4:11; Philem. 24; 1 Pet. 5:13 [y]ver. 5
13 [z]John 18:16, 17
14 [a]Luke 24:41; [Gen. 45:26]
15 [b]Matt. 18:10; See Heb. 1:14
17 [c]ch. 13:16; 19:33; 21:40 [d]ch. 15:13; 21:18; [Gal. 1:19; 2:9, 12] [e]See John 21:23
19 [f][ch. 16:27; 27:42]
20 [g]Matt. 28:14 (Gk.) [h][1 Kgs. 5:9; Ezra 3:7; Ezek. 27:17]
23 [i][2 Sam. 24:16; 2 Kgs. 19:35]; See ch. 8:26 [j]Ps. 115:1 **24** [k]See ch. 6:7 **25** [l]ch. 11:29, 30 [m]See ver. 12

crowd, attributing to him divine eloquence. Compare this with Peter's swift denial when Cornelius seeks to worship him (10:26), or Paul's vehement protests when the people of Lystra mistake him for the god Hermes (14:11–15).

The Old Testament consistently teaches that when a person exalts himself, or allows others to exalt him, God will bring him down (Gen. 11:4; Isa. 14:12–15; Dan. 4:19–27). This is a large part of how God's wrath and justice work. Conversely, it is also how his mercy and grace work: the humble, lowly, and needy are lifted up! Such is the glorious paradox of the gospel.

With Herod's death, "the word of God increased and multiplied" (Acts 12:24). God directly intervenes to eliminate another obstacle to his plans, proving that no human can stand in the way of his redemptive work. The world may bring distress and mourning, but it cannot ultimately shake those who have been touched by the power and grace of the resurrected Christ. They pray fervently amid persecution, threat, and suffering, and God works beyond even what they can ask or imagine (v. 15).

Barnabas and Saul Sent Off

13 Now there were in the church at Antioch [n]prophets and [n]teachers, [o]Barnabas,
Simeon who was called Niger,[1] Lucius of
Cyrene, Manaen a lifelong friend of [p]Herod
the tetrarch, and Saul. 2 While they were worshiping the Lord and fasting, [q]the Holy Spirit
said, [r]"Set apart for me Barnabas and Saul [s]for
the work to which I have called them." 3 Then
after fasting and [t]praying they laid their hands
on them and [u]sent them off.

Barnabas and Saul on Cyprus

4 So, being sent out [v]by the Holy Spirit,
they went down to Seleucia, and from there
they sailed to Cyprus. 5 When they arrived at
Salamis, they proclaimed the word of God
[w]in the synagogues of the Jews. And they had
[x]John to [y]assist them. 6 When they had gone
through the whole island as far as Paphos,
they came upon a certain [z]magician, [a]a Jewish
false prophet named Bar-Jesus. 7 He was with
[b]the proconsul, Sergius Paulus, a man of intelligence, who summoned Barnabas and Saul
and sought to hear the word of God. 8 But
Elymas the [z]magician (for that is the meaning
of his name) [c]opposed them, seeking to turn
[d]the proconsul away from the faith. 9 But Saul,
who was also called Paul, [e]filled with the Holy
Spirit, looked intently at him 10 and said, "You
[f]son of the devil, you enemy of all righteousness, full of all deceit and [g]villainy, will you not
stop [h]making crooked [i]the straight paths of
the Lord? 11 And now, behold, [j]the hand of the
Lord is upon you, and you will be blind and
unable to see the sun for a time." Immediately
mist and darkness fell upon him, and he went
about seeking [k]people to lead him by the hand.
12 Then the proconsul believed, when he saw
what had occurred, for he was astonished at
[l]the teaching of the Lord.

Paul and Barnabas at Antioch in Pisidia

13 Now Paul and his companions set sail from
Paphos and came to Perga in Pamphylia. And
[m]John left them and returned [n]to Jerusalem,
14 but they went on from Perga and came to
Antioch in Pisidia. And [o]on the Sabbath day
[p]they went into the synagogue and sat down.
15 After [q]the reading from [r]the Law and the
Prophets, [s]the rulers of the synagogue sent
a message to them, saying, "Brothers, if you
have any [t]word of encouragement for the people, say it." 16 So Paul stood up, and [u]motioning
with his hand said:

"Men of Israel and [v]you who fear God, listen. 17 [w]The God of this people Israel [x]chose
our fathers and [y]made the people great [z]dur-
ing their stay in the land of Egypt, and [a]with
uplifted arm he led them out of it. 18 And for
about [b]forty years [c]he put up with[2] them in
the wilderness. 19 And [d]after destroying [e]seven
nations in the land of Canaan, [f]he gave them
their land as an inheritance. 20 All this took
about 450 years. And after that [g]he gave them
judges until [h]Samuel the prophet. 21 Then [i]they
asked for a king, and God gave them Saul [j]the
son of Kish, a man of the tribe of Benjamin, for
forty years. 22 And [k]when he had removed him,
[l]he raised up David to be their king, of whom
he testified and said, [m]'I have found in David
the son of Jesse [n]a man after my heart, [o]who
will do all my will.' 23 [p]Of this man's offspring
God has brought to Israel [q]a Savior, Jesus, [r]as
he promised. 24 Before his coming, [s]John had
proclaimed [t]a baptism of repentance to all the
people of Israel. 25 And as John was finishing
his course, [u]he said, 'What do you suppose that
I am? I am not he. No, but behold, after me one
is coming, the sandals of whose feet I am not
worthy to untie.'

26 "Brothers, sons of the family of Abraham,
and those among you [v]who fear God, to us

[1] *Niger* is a Latin word meaning *black*, or *dark* [2] Some manuscripts *he carried* (compare Deuteronomy 1:31)

13:26–39 With the coming of Christ, forgiveness of sins is now available (v. 38). The law of Moses gave temporary provision for forgiveness by instituting priests to mediate between God and his people, but the law could not lead to eternal and ultimate forgiveness (v. 39). The law serves only to heighten our *understanding* of our own sin, not to lessen its *reality* (Rom. 7:7–12). Through Christ we can avail ourselves of a power that the law never had. The law hung over us as a ministry of death, threatening to kill us for our sins; the Spirit of Christ delivers us from the bondage of sin, guilt, and

Chapter 13
1 [n] ch. 11:27; 15:32; 19:6; 21:9, 10; Rom. 12:6, 7; See 1 Cor. 12:28, 29 [o] ch. 11:22-26 [p] See Luke 3:1
2 [q] [ch. 20:28]; See ch. 8:29 [r] Rom. 1:1; Gal. 1:15 [s] See ch. 9:15
3 [t] See ch. 6:6 [u] ch. 14:26
4 [v] ver. 2; [ch. 16:6, 7]

5 [w] ver. 14; ch. 9:20; 14:1; 17:1, 2, 10, 17; 18:4, 19; 19:8; [ver. 46]; See Mark 6:2 [x] See ch. 12:12 [y] [ch. 19:22] **6** [z] ch. 8:9, 11 [a] See Matt. 7:15 **7** [b] ver. 8, 12; ch. 18:12; 19:38 **8** [z] [See ver. 6 above] [c] [Ex. 7:11; 2 Tim. 3:8] [d] ver. 7, 12 **9** [e] ch. 4:8 **10** [f] See Matt. 13:38 [g] [ch. 18:14] [h] Mic. 3:9 [i] Hos. 14:9; 2 Pet. 2:15; [ch. 18:25, 26] **11** [j] ch. 11:21; Ex. 9:3; 1 Sam. 5:6, 7, 11; Ps. 32:4; [Heb. 10:31; 1 Pet. 5:6] [k] [ch. 9:8; 22:11] **12** [l] [ver. 49; ch. 15:35] **13** [m] ver. 5 [n] ch. 12:12 **14** [o] ver. 42, 44; ch. 16:13; 17:2; 18:4 [p] See ver. 5 **15** [q] ch. 15:21 [r] See Luke 16:16 [s] See Mark 5:22 [t] Heb. 13:22 **16** [u] See ch. 12:17 [v] ver. 26; ch. 10:2, 22 **17** [w] See Matt. 15:31 [x] Deut. 7:6-8 [y] Num. 24:7 [z] ch. 7:17; Ex. 1:1, 7, 12; Ps. 105:23, 24 [a] Ex. 6:6; 13:14, 16 **18** [b] See ch. 7:36 [c] [Deut. 9:5-24] **19** [d] See ch. 7:45 [e] Deut. 7:1 [f] Josh. 14:1, 2; 19:51; Ps. 78:55; 136:21, 22 **20** [g] Judg. 2:16; 3:9 [h] See ch. 3:24 **21** [i] 1 Sam. 8:5; 10:1 [j] 1 Sam. 9:1, 2 **22** [k] 1 Sam. 15:23, 26, 28; 16:1; [Hos. 13:11] [l] 1 Sam. 16:13; 2 Sam. 2:4; 5:3 [m] Cited from Ps. 89:20 [n] ch. 7:46; Cited from 1 Sam. 13:14 [o] ver. 36 **23** [p] See Matt. 1:1 [q] See Luke 2:11 [r] Ps. 132:11; [ver. 32, 33] **24** [s] ch. 1:22; Matt. 3:1 [t] ch. 19:4; Mark 1:4; Luke 3:3; [ch. 2:38; Matt. 3:11] **25** [u] John 1:20, 27; [Matt. 3:11; Mark 1:7; Luke 3:16] **26** [v] ver. 16

has been sent [w]the message of [x]this salvation. 27 For those who live in Jerusalem and
their rulers, because [y]they did not recognize him nor understand [z]the utterances of
the prophets, which are read every Sabbath,
[a]fulfilled them by condemning him. 28 And
[b]though they found in him no guilt worthy of
death, [c]they asked Pilate to have him executed.
29 And when [d]they had carried out all that was
written of him, [e]they took him down from [f]the
tree and laid him in a tomb. 30 But [g]God raised
him from the dead, 31 and for many days [h]he
appeared to those [i]who had come up with him
[j]from Galilee to Jerusalem, [k]who are now [l]his
witnesses to the people. 32 And we bring you
the good news [m]that what God promised to
the fathers, 33 [n]this he has fulfilled to us their
children by raising Jesus, as also it is written
in the second Psalm,

> [o]"'You are my Son,
> today I have begotten you.'

34 And as for the fact that he raised him from
the dead, [p, q]no more to return to corruption,
he has spoken in this way,

> "'I will give you [r]the holy and sure blessings of David.'

35 Therefore he says also in another psalm,

> [s]"'You will not let your Holy One see corruption.'

36 For David, after he had [t]served the purpose
of God in his own generation, [u]fell asleep and
[v]was laid with his fathers and saw corruption,
37 but he whom [w]God raised up did not see
corruption. 38 Let it be known to you therefore, brothers, [x]that through this man [y]for-
giveness of sins is proclaimed to you, 39 and
by him [z]everyone who believes is freed[1] from
everything [a]from which you could not be
freed by the law of Moses. 40 Beware, therefore, lest what is said in the Prophets should
come about:

> 41 [b]"'Look, you scoffers,
> be astounded and perish;
> for I am doing a work in your days,
> a work that you will not believe, even
> if one tells it to you.'"

42 As they went out, the people begged that
these things might be told them the next
Sabbath. 43 And after the meeting of the synagogue broke up, many Jews and [c]devout [d]con-
verts to Judaism followed Paul and Barnabas,
who, as they spoke with them, urged them [e]to
continue in [f]the grace of God.
44 The next Sabbath almost the whole city
gathered to hear the word of the Lord. 45 [g]But
[h]when the Jews saw the crowds, they were
filled with [i]jealousy and began to contradict
what was spoken by Paul, [j]reviling him. 46 And
Paul and Barnabas spoke out boldly, saying, "It
was necessary that the word of God [k]be spoken
first to you. [l]Since you thrust it aside and judge
yourselves [m]unworthy of eternal life, behold,

[1] Greek *justified*; twice in this verse

death into new life (2 Cor. 3:6–7). What the law was powerless to do, because it was "weakened by the flesh," God did by "sending his own Son in the likeness of sinful flesh" to be a sin offering (Rom. 8:3).

God's grace is overflowing and abundant (Rom. 5:15, 17; 6:1; 2 Cor. 4:15; 8:9; 9:8, 14). It is also powerful: grace motivates changed lives, as Paul writes: "The love of Christ controls us!" (2 Cor. 5:14). The law threatens and demands, but in itself cannot produce the love true holiness requires (Matt. 22:37–38). This is not to discount the value of the law. The law of God is "perfect . . . true, and righteous altogether" (Ps. 19:7–9) and "holy and righteous and good" (Rom. 7:12). We live in accord with the law to demonstrate love for the One who gave it for our good and his glory. But the law has no inherent power to produce the life it requires. The apostle Paul writes, "If a law had been given that could give life, then righteousness would indeed be by the law" (Gal. 3:21). Law does not empower us to do what it mandates—only grace can do that (Matt. 10:8; Rom. 2:4; 6:14; Titus 2:11–12).

13:44–48 Repeatedly in Acts we see that God's grace plays the crucial role in the advance of the gospel. When the Gentiles hear the gospel, we read that "as many as were appointed to eternal life believed" (v. 48). Even belief in the gospel is a gift of God's grace.

26 [w]ch. 10:36; [Eph. 1:13] [x][ch. 5:20]; See ch. 4:12
27 [y][2 Cor. 3:14, 15]; See ch. 3:17 [z]ver. 15; [ch. 15:21] [a]See Luke 24:20, 26, 27, 44
28 [b][Mark 14:55; Luke 23:22] [c]ch. 2:23; 3:14, 15; Luke 23:23
29 [d]Luke 18:31; 24:44; John 19:28, 30, 36, 37 [e]Matt. 27:59, 60; Mark 15:46; Luke 23:53; John 19:38, 41, 42 [f]See ch. 5:30
30 [g]See ch. 2:24
31 [h]See ch. 1:3 [i]Mark 15:41 [j]ch. 1:11; 2:7 [k]See Luke 24:48 [l]See ch. 1:8
32 [m]ch. 26:6; Rom. 4:13; 15:8; Gal. 3:16; [Rom. 9:4]
33 [n][ver. 23; Luke 1:69-73] [o]Heb. 1:5; 5:5; Cited from Ps. 2:7
34 [p]Rom. 6:9; [Heb. 9:25-28] [q]ver. 35-37 [r]Cited from Isa. 55:3
35 [s]ch. 2:27; Cited from Ps. 16:10
36 [t]ver. 22; ch. 20:27 [u]2 Sam. 7:12; 1 Kgs. 2:10; [ch. 2:29] [v]Judg. 2:10 **37** [w]ver. 30 **38** [x]Luke 24:47; 1 John 2:12 [y]ch. 5:31 **39** [z]Rom. 3:28; See ch. 10:43 [a]Rom. 2:13; 3:20; 8:3; Gal. 2:16; 3:11; Eph. 2:9; 2 Tim. 1:9; Titus 3:5; [Heb. 7:19] **41** [b]Cited from Hab. 1:5; [Isa. 29:14] **43** [c]ver. 50; ch. 17:4, 17; [ch. 16:14] [d]ch. 2:11; 6:5; Matt. 23:15 [e][Jude 21] [f]Jude 4; See ch. 11:23 **45** [g][ch. 19:9] [h][1 Thess. 2:16] [i]See ch. 5:17 [j]ch. 18:6; 26:11; 1 Tim. 1:20 **46** [k]ver. 5, 14; See ch. 3:26 [l]See Matt. 21:43 [m]See Matt. 22:8

we [n]are turning to the Gentiles. 47 [o]For so the
Lord has commanded us, saying,

> [p]"'I have made you [q]a light for the
> Gentiles,
> that you may [r]bring salvation to the
> ends of the earth.'"

48 And when the Gentiles heard this, they
began rejoicing and [s]glorifying the word of
the Lord, and as many as were appointed to
eternal life believed. 49 And the word of the
Lord was spreading throughout the whole
region. 50 [t]But the Jews[1] incited the devout
[u]women of high standing and the leading men
of the city, [v]stirred up persecution against Paul
and Barnabas, and [w]drove them out of their
district. 51 But they [x]shook off the dust from
their feet against them and went to Iconium.
52 And the disciples were filled [y]with joy and
[z]with the Holy Spirit.

Paul and Barnabas at Iconium

14 Now at Iconium [a]they entered together
into the Jewish synagogue and spoke in
such a way that a great number of both Jews
and Greeks believed. 2 [b]But the [c]unbelieving
Jews stirred up the Gentiles and poisoned
their minds against [d]the brothers.[2] 3 So they
remained for a long time, speaking boldly for
[e]the Lord, who bore witness to [f]the word of
his grace, [g]granting signs and wonders to be
done by their hands. 4 But the people of the
city [h]were divided; [i]some sided with the Jews
and some with the apostles. 5 When an attempt
was made by both Gentiles and Jews, with
their rulers, [j]to mistreat them and [k]to stone
them, 6 they learned of it and [l]fled to [m]Lystra
and Derbe, cities of Lycaonia, and to the surrounding country, 7 and there they continued
to preach the gospel.

Paul and Barnabas at Lystra

8 Now at Lystra there was a man sitting who
could not use his feet. He was [n]crippled from
birth and had never walked. 9 He listened to
Paul speaking. And Paul, looking intently at
him and [o]seeing that he had faith to be made
well,[3] 10 said in a loud voice, "Stand upright on
your feet." And he [p]sprang up and began walking. 11 And when the crowds saw what Paul
had done, they lifted up their voices, saying in
Lycaonian, [q]"The gods have come down to us
in the likeness of men!" 12 Barnabas they called
[r]Zeus, and Paul, Hermes, because he was the
chief speaker. 13 And the priest of [r]Zeus, whose
temple was at the entrance to the city, brought
oxen and garlands to the gates and [s]wanted to
offer sacrifice with the crowds. 14 But when the
apostles Barnabas and Paul heard of it, they
[t]tore their garments and rushed out into the
crowd, crying out, 15 "Men, [u]why are you doing
these things? We also are men, [v]of like nature
with you, and we bring you good news, that
[w]you should turn from these [x]vain things to
[y]a living God, [z]who made the heaven and the
earth and the sea and all that is in them. 16 In
past generations he [a]allowed all the nations [b]to
walk in their own ways. 17 Yet [c]he did not leave
himself without witness, for he [d]did good by
[e]giving you rains from heaven and [f]fruitful
seasons, satisfying your hearts with [g]food
and [h]gladness." 18 Even with these words they
scarcely restrained the people from offering
sacrifice to them.

Paul Stoned at Lystra

19 [i]But Jews came from Antioch and Iconium,
and having persuaded the crowds, [j]they
stoned Paul and dragged him out of the city,
supposing that he was dead. 20 But when the
disciples gathered about him, he rose up and
entered the city, and on the next day he went

[1] Greek *Ioudaioi* probably refers here to Jewish religious leaders, and others under their influence, in that time [2] Or *brothers and sisters*
[3] Or *be saved*

The reference in verse 47 to Isaiah 49:6 shows that the gospel going to the Gentiles was God's plan all along. Acts 13:46 is perhaps the official marker of the apostles turning to the Gentiles.

14:14–15 Those who proclaim the gospel must realize that they are no more than rescued sinners, filled with the Holy Spirit, sharing the good news.

46 [n]ch. 18:6; 22:21; 26:17, 18, 20; 28:28; See ch. 9:15 **47** [o][ch. 11:18] [p]Cited from Isa. 49:6; [Isa. 45:22] [q]Isa. 42:6; Luke 2:32 [r][ver. 26; ch. 1:8] **48** [s][2 Thess. 1:12] **50** [t][ch. 14:2, 19; 17:5, 13; 18:12; 20:3, 19; 21:27] [u]ch. 17:12 [v]2 Tim. 3:11 [w]1 Thess. 2:15 **51** [x]Matt. 10:14; Mark 6:11; Luke 9:5; [ch. 18:6] **52** [y][1 Thess. 1:6]; See Matt. 5:12; John 16:22 [z]See ch. 2:4 **Chapter 14** **1** [a]See ch. 13:5 **2** [b]See ch. 13:50 [c]ch. 19:9; John 3:36; Rom. 15:31 [d]See John 21:23 **3** [e]ch. 15:8; Heb. 2:4; [Mark 16:20] [f]ch. 20:32 [g]ch. 4:29, 30 **4** [h][ch. 23:7] [i][ch. 17:4, 5; 19:9; 28:24] **5** [j]1 Thess. 2:2; [2 Cor. 12:10] [k][ver. 19] **6** [l]See Matt. 10:23 [m]2 Tim. 3:11 **8** [n]ch. 3:2 **9** [o]See Matt. 9:2 **10** [p]ch. 3:8; Isa. 35:6 **11** [q]ch. 8:10; 28:6 **12** [r][ch. 19:35; 28:11 (Gk.)] **13** [r][See ver. 12 above] [s][Dan. 2:46] **14** [t]See Gen. 37:29 **15** [u]See ch. 10:26 [v]James 5:17 [w]ch. 15:19; 26:18, 20; Luke 1:16; 1 Thess. 1:9; [ch. 15:3; James 5:19, 20]; See ch. 9:35 [x]Deut. 32:21; 1 Sam. 12:21; Jer. 14:22; [1 Cor. 8:4] [y]See Matt. 16:16 [z]ch. 17:24; Gen. 1:1; Ex. 20:11; Ps. 146:6; Rev. 4:11; 10:6; 14:7 **16** [a][ch. 17:30; 1 Pet. 4:3] [b][Ps. 81:13; Mic. 4:5] **17** [c][ch. 17:27; Rom. 1:19, 20] [d]Num. 10:32 [e]Lev. 26:4; Deut. 11:14; 28:12; Job 5:10; Ps. 65:10; 147:8, 18; Ezek. 34:26; Joel 2:23 [f]Ps. 67:6; 85:12; Ezek. 34:27; Joel 2:24; Zech. 8:12 [g]Ps. 104:27 [h]Ps. 104:15 **19** [i]See ch. 13:45, 50 [j]2 Cor. 11:25; [ver. 5; 2 Tim. 3:11]; See ch. 7:58

on with Barnabas to Derbe. 21 When they had
preached the gospel to that city and had [k]made
many disciples, they returned to Lystra and
to Iconium and to Antioch, 22 [l]strengthening
the souls of the disciples, encouraging them
[m]to continue in [n]the faith, and saying that
[o]through many tribulations we must enter
the kingdom of God. 23 And when they had
[p]appointed [q]elders for them in every church,
with prayer and fasting [r]they committed them
to the Lord in whom they had believed.

Paul and Barnabas Return to Antioch in Syria

24 Then they passed through Pisidia and came
to Pamphylia. 25 And when they had spoken
the word in Perga, they went down to Attalia,
26 and from there they sailed to Antioch, [s]where
they had been [t]commended to the grace of God
for the work that they had fulfilled. 27 And
when they arrived and gathered the church
together, [u]they declared all that God had done
with them, and [v]how he had [w]opened [x]a door
of faith to the Gentiles. 28 And they remained
no little time with the disciples.

The Jerusalem Council

15 [y]But some men came down from
Judea and were teaching [z]the brothers,
"Unless you are [a]circumcised [b]according to the
custom of Moses, you cannot be saved." 2 And
after Paul and Barnabas had no small dissension and [c]debate with them, Paul and Barnabas
and [d]some of the others were appointed to go
up to Jerusalem to [e]the apostles and the elders
about this question. 3 So, [f]being sent on their
way by the church, they passed through both
Phoenicia and Samaria, [g]describing in detail
the conversion of the Gentiles, and [h]brought
great joy to all [i]the brothers.[1] 4 [j]When they
came to Jerusalem, they were welcomed by
the church and [k]the apostles and the elders,
and [g]they declared all that God had done with
them. 5 But some believers who belonged to
[l]the party of the Pharisees rose up and said,
[m]"It is necessary [n]to circumcise them and to
order them to keep the law of Moses."

6 [o]The [k]apostles and the elders were gathered
together to consider this matter. 7 And after
there had been much [p]debate, Peter stood up

[1] Or *brothers and sisters*; also verse 22

21 [k] Matt. 28:19
22 [l] ch. 15:32, 41; [ch. 18:23; 1 Thess. 3:2, 13] [m] ch. 13:43; Col. 1:23 [n] See ch. 6:7 [o] John 15:20; 16:33; 1 Thess. 3:3; 2 Tim. 3:12; [ch. 9:16; Mark 10:30; Luke 22:28, 29; Rom. 8:17; Phil. 1:20; 2 Thess. 1:5; 2 Tim. 2:12; 1 Pet. 5:10; Rev. 1:9]
23 [p] [Titus 1:5] [q] See ch. 11:30 [r] ch. 20:32
26 [s] ch. 13:3 [t] ch. 15:40
27 [u] ch. 15:4; [ch. 15:3, 12; 21:19] [v] [ch. 11:18] [w] 1 Cor. 16:9; 2 Cor. 2:12; Col. 4:3; Rev. 3:8 [x] [Hos. 2:15]

Chapter 15
1 [y] ver. 24 [z] ver. 3, 22, 23, 36, 40; See John 21:23 [a] ver. 5; Gal. 5:2; [1 Cor. 7:18; Gal. 2:11, 14] [b] ch. 6:14; Lev. 12:3
2 [c] ver. 7 [d] [Gal. 2:1, 2] [e] ver. 4, 6, 22, 23; ch. 16:4; See ch. 5:12; 11:30
3 [f] ch. 21:5; Rom. 15:24; 1 Cor. 16:6, 11; 2 Cor. 1:16; Titus 3:13; 3 John 6; [ch. 17:15] [g] See ch. 14:27 [h] ch. 11:18 [i] ver. 1
4 [j] [ch. 21:17] [k] ver. 2 [g] [See ver. 3 above]
5 [l] See ch. 24:5 [m] ver. 1 [n] Gal. 5:3
6 [o] [ver. 12, 25] [k] [See ver. 4 above]
7 [p] ver. 2

14:27 Once again we see that faith in Christ comes as a result of God's gracious initiative, as Paul and Barnabas revel in the fact that God "had opened a door of faith to the Gentiles."

15:1–35 Along with the rising persecution from outside the church, there are some within the church who begin speaking against Gentile believers who do not adopt Jewish customs. The Jerusalem council is convened to decide whether non-Jewish believers must submit to all the requirements of the law of Moses, especially circumcision, in order to be accepted as members of the church.

After much debate, Peter stands up and asks, "Why are you putting God to the test by placing a yoke on the disciples that neither our fathers nor we have been able to bear?" (v. 10). The law informed God's followers about how to walk in integrity with him, but it never provided the power to obey it; instead, it only revealed the inability of God's people to live up to God's perfect righteousness.

In the Bible, graceless religion is presented as an intolerable burden that only brings discouragement and despair. When Peter refers to the law as a "yoke" that no one is able to carry, he is echoing the words of Jesus, who declared, "Come to me, all who labor and are heavy laden, and I will give you rest. Take my yoke upon you, and learn from me, for I am gentle and lowly in heart, and you will find rest for your souls. For my yoke is easy, and my burden is light" (Matt. 11:28–30). God favors the weak and burdened, not the spiritually proud. Jesus embraces the meek and the broken—the ones who feel swamped with heavy burdens. It is no small thing that he spent so much time with those considered the spiritual losers of his day.

Through their system of sacrifices, the people of Israel were to look forward to the sacrifice that was coming, the true spotless Lamb who would take away their sins forever (John 1:29). Instead, they attempted to attain righteousness through fulfilling the law's commands, which only served to place them under the yoke of guilt-driven slavery.

The law binds, but the grace of Jesus frees (Gal. 5:1). As long as we attempt to salve our conscience through acting right, we will find ourselves bound to the

and said to them, "Brothers, you know that
in the early days God made a choice among
you, [q]that by my mouth the Gentiles should
hear [r]the word of [s]the gospel and believe. 8 And
God, [t]who knows the heart, [u]bore witness to
them, [v]by giving them the Holy Spirit just as
he did to us, 9 and [w]he made no distinction
between us and them, [x]having cleansed their
hearts [y]by faith. 10 Now, therefore, why [z]are
you putting God to the test [a]by placing a yoke
on the neck of the disciples [b]that neither our
fathers nor we have been able to bear? 11 But we
[c]believe that we will be [d]saved through [e]the
grace of the Lord Jesus, [w]just as they will."

12 And all the assembly fell silent, and they
listened to Barnabas and Paul [f]as they related
what signs and wonders God had done
through them among the Gentiles. 13 After they
finished speaking, [g]James replied, "Brothers,
listen to me. 14 [h]Simeon has related how God
first visited the Gentiles, to take from them [i]a
people for his name. 15 And with this the words
of the prophets agree, just as it is written,

16 [j]"'After this I will return,
and I will rebuild the tent of David that has fallen;
I will rebuild its ruins,
and I will restore it,
17 that the remnant[1] of mankind [k]may seek the Lord,
and all the Gentiles [l]who are called by my name,
says the Lord, who makes these things
18 [m]known from of old.'

19 Therefore [n]my judgment is that we should
not trouble those of the Gentiles who [o]turn to
God, 20 but should write to them [p]to abstain
from [q]the things polluted by idols, and from
[r]sexual immorality, and from [s]what has
been strangled, and from [s]blood. 21 For from
ancient generations Moses has had in every
city those who proclaim him, [t]for he is read
every Sabbath in the synagogues."

The Council's Letter to Gentile Believers

22 Then it seemed good to [u]the apostles and
the elders, with the whole church, to choose
men from among them and send them to
Antioch with Paul and Barnabas. They sent
Judas called [v]Barsabbas, and [w]Silas, leading
men among [x]the brothers, 23 with the following letter: [x]"The brothers, both [u]the apostles
and the elders, to the brothers[2] who are of
the Gentiles in Antioch and Syria and Cilicia,
[y]greetings. 24 Since we have heard that [z]some
persons have gone out from us and [a]troubled
you[3] with words, unsettling your minds,
although we gave them no instructions, 25 it
has seemed good to us, having come [b]to one
accord, to choose men and send them to you
with our [c]beloved Barnabas and Paul, 26 [d]men

[1] Or *rest* [2] Or *brothers and sisters*; also verses 32, 33, 36 [3] Some manuscripts *some persons from us have troubled you*

taskmasters of guilt and fear: Have I done enough? Is God pleased with me now? True freedom from guilt comes only when we recognize the boundless and undeserved love that God has poured out on us through his Son. Jesus has done enough for God to be pleased with us.

Peter insists that both Jews and Gentiles are saved only by the grace of the Lord Jesus (Acts 15:11). Because God has clearly chosen to include people of all nations in the new community of Christ, the old restrictions that served to set Israel apart, such as circumcision and dietary laws, no longer apply.

If circumcision is unnecessary for salvation, then why are restrictions (vv. 20, 29) given at all? Here we see an example of the principle of respect for the "weaker" brother (cf. Romans 14; 1 Corinthians 8). The counsel to respect dietary restrictions was intended to demonstrate love and respect for the Jewish Christians. Because of their background, Jewish Christians would have struggled to share a meal with Gentiles who seemed to flaunt traditional Jewish dietary customs (cf. Acts 15:19–21). The Jerusalem council aims to avoid such potentially divisive offense by instructing the Gentiles not only to abstain from obvious sin ("sexual immorality") but also to accommodate the sensitivities of their Jewish brothers and sisters. The response of the Gentile believers—joy—shows that they hardly view these requirements as burdensome (v. 31). As Christ laid down his freedom for their sake, so they find joy in laying down their freedoms out of love for others.

7 [q]ch. 10:20 [r][Eph. 1:13; Col. 1:5; 1 Thess. 1:5] [s]ch. 20:24
8 [t]ch. 1:24 [u]ch. 14:3 [v]ch. 10:44, 47; 11:15, 17; [ver. 28; Gal. 3:2]
9 [w]ch. 11:12; Rom. 3:22-24; Eph. 3:6; [ch. 10:28, 34] [x]Ps. 51:10; [ch. 26:18; 2 Cor. 7:1; 1 Pet. 1:22] [y]See ch. 10:43
10 [z]Ps. 106:14; Isa. 7:12 [a]Gal. 5:1; [ver. 28] [b][Matt. 11:28; 23:4; Luke 11:46]
11 [c][ch. 16:31] [d]Eph. 2:5, 8; 2 Tim. 1:9; Titus 2:11; 3:7; [Rom. 3:24; 1 Thess. 5:9] [e]Rom. 5:15 [w][See ver. 9 above]
12 [f]ver. 4; See ch. 14:27
13 [g]See ch. 12:17
14 [h][ver. 7] [i][ch. 18:10; Deut. 7:6; Isa. 43:21; Rom. 9:24-26]
16 [j]Cited from Amos 9:11, 12; [Jer. 12:15]
17 [k][ch. 17:27] [l]Isa. 43:7; Jer. 14:9; Dan. 9:19
18 [m][Isa. 45:21]
19 [n][ver. 28] [o]See ch. 14:15
20 [p]ch. 21:25 [q][ver. 29; Ezek. 4:13, 14; Dan. 1:8; Mal. 1:7, 12] [r]1 Cor. 10:7, 8; Rev. 2:14, 20; See 1 Cor. 6:18 [s]See Lev. 3:17 **21** [t]ch. 13:15; 2 Cor. 3:14, 15; [ch. 13:27] **22** [u]ver. 2 [v][ch. 1:23] [w]See 1 Pet. 5:12 [x]ver. 1 **23** [x][See ver. 22 above] [u][See ver. 22 above] [y]ch. 23:26; James 1:1; [2 John 10, 11] **24** [z]ver. 1; [Gal. 2:4; 5:12; Titus 1:10] [a]Gal. 1:7; 5:10 **25** [b]See ch. 1:14 [c][2 Pet. 3:15] **26** [d]ch. 9:23-25; 14:19

who have [e]risked their lives for the name of
our Lord Jesus Christ. 27 We have therefore sent
[f]Judas and Silas, who themselves will tell you
the same things by word of mouth. 28 For it
has seemed good [g]to the Holy Spirit and [h]to
us [i]to lay on you no greater burden than these
requirements: 29 [j]that you abstain from [k]what
has been sacrificed to idols, and from blood,
and from what has been strangled, and from
sexual immorality. If you keep yourselves
from these, you will do well. Farewell."

30 So when they were sent off, they went
down to Antioch, and having gathered the
congregation together, they delivered the letter. 31 And when they had read it, they rejoiced
because of its encouragement. 32 And Judas
and Silas, who were themselves [l]prophets,
encouraged and [m]strengthened [n]the brothers
with many words. 33 And after they had spent
some time, they were sent off [o]in peace by [n]the
brothers to those who had sent them.[1] 35 But
[p]Paul and Barnabas remained in Antioch,
teaching and preaching the word of the Lord,
with many others also.

Paul and Barnabas Separate

36 And after some days Paul said to Barnabas,
"Let us return and visit [n]the brothers [q]in every
city where we proclaimed the word of the
Lord, and see how they are." 37 Now Barnabas
wanted to take with them [r]John called Mark.
38 But Paul thought best not to take with
them one [s]who had withdrawn from them
in Pamphylia and had not gone with them to
the work. 39 And there arose [t]a sharp disagreement, so that they separated from each other.
[u]Barnabas took Mark with him and sailed
away to Cyprus, 40 but Paul chose Silas and
departed, [v]having been commended by [w]the
brothers to [x]the grace of the Lord. 41 And he
went through Syria and Cilicia, [y]strengthen-
ing the churches.

Timothy Joins Paul and Silas

16 Paul[2] came also to Derbe and to Lystra.
A disciple was there, named [z]Timothy,
[a]the son of a Jewish woman who was a believer,
but his father was a Greek. 2 He was well spoken of by [b]the brothers[3] at Lystra and Iconium.
3 Paul wanted Timothy to accompany him, and
he [c]took him and circumcised him because of
the Jews who were in those places, for they all
knew that his father was a Greek. 4 As they
went on their way through the cities, they
delivered to them for observance [d]the decisions [e]that had been reached by [f]the apostles
and elders who were in Jerusalem. 5 [g]So the
churches were strengthened in [h]the faith, and
they increased in numbers [i]daily.

The Macedonian Call

6 And [j]they went through the region of
Phrygia and Galatia, having been forbidden
by the Holy Spirit to speak the word in Asia.
7 And when they had come up to Mysia, they
attempted to go into Bithynia, but [k]the Spirit
of Jesus did not allow them. 8 So, passing
by Mysia, they went down [l]to Troas. 9 And a
vision appeared to Paul in the night: a man
of Macedonia was standing there, urging
him and saying, "Come over to Macedonia
and help us." 10 And when Paul[4] had seen the
vision, immediately [m]we sought to go on into
Macedonia, concluding that God had called
us to preach the gospel to them.

[1] Some manuscripts insert verse 34: *But it seemed good to Silas to remain there* [2] Greek *He* [3] Or *brothers and sisters*; also verse 40
[4] Greek *he*

16:1–3 Though circumcision was not one of the four regulations set in writing by the Jerusalem council, Paul will be taking Timothy with him in delivering the news of those regulations. Paul therefore asks that Timothy be circumcised, not as a requirement for salvation or even an act of obedience to God, but to remove a significant barrier as both men minister to churches of Jewish and Gentile congregations. This was grace and love in practice to others on behalf of Paul and especially Timothy.

Context and motivation are critical to Paul. He argues strongly *against* being circumcised if those arguing for circumcision believe that it is necessary in order to please God (Gal. 5:1–6); yet if the motivation is to remove barriers to people hearing about the grace of God, Paul will gladly give up any number of cultural practices or preferences (1 Cor. 9:12–23).

26 [e] [ch. 20:24; 21:13; 2 Cor. 4:11; 1 John 3:16]
27 [f] ver. 22, 32
28 [g] [ver. 8; ch. 5:32; John 16:13; 1 Cor. 7:40] [h] [ver. 19] [i] [ver. 10; Rev. 2:24]
29 [j] See ver. 20 [k] ch. 21:25; 1 Cor. 8:1, 4, 7, 10; 10:19; Rev. 2:14, 20
32 [l] See ch. 13:1 [m] See ch. 14:22 [n] ver. 1
33 [o] Gen. 26:29; Heb. 11:31; [1 Cor. 16:11] [n] [See ver. 32 above]
35 [p] ch. 13:1
36 [n] [See ver. 32 above] [q] ch. 13:4, 13, 14, 51; 14:6, 24, 25 **37** [r] See ch. 12:12 **38** [s] ch. 13:13 **39** [t] [ch. 17:16 (Gk.)] [u] [Col. 4:10] **40** [v] ch. 14:26 [w] ver. 1 [x] ver. 11; [ch. 11:23]; See Rom. 16:20 **41** [y] ver. 32; ch. 16:5 **Chapter 16** **1** [z] ch. 17:14; 18:5; 19:22; 20:4; Rom. 16:21; 1 Cor. 4:17; Phil. 2:19; Col. 1:1; 1 Thess. 3:2; 2 Thess. 1:1; 1 Tim. 1:2, 18; 2 Tim. 1:2 [a] 2 Tim. 1:5; 3:15 **2** [b] See John 21:23 **3** [c] [Gal. 2:3] **4** [d] ch. 17:7 [e] ch. 15:28, 29 [f] See ch. 15:2 **5** [g] [ch. 9:31] [h] See ch. 6:7 [i] ch. 2:47 **6** [j] ch. 18:23; [Gal. 4:13] **7** [k] Rom. 8:9; Gal. 4:6; Phil. 1:19; 1 Pet. 1:11; [ver. 6; ch. 8:29] **8** [l] ch. 20:5, 6; 2 Cor. 2:12; 2 Tim. 4:13 **10** [m] ver. 11-17; ch. 20:5-8, 13-15; 21:1-18; 27:1–28:16

The Conversion of Lydia

11 So, setting sail from Troas, we [n]made a
direct voyage to Samothrace, and the following day to Neapolis, 12 and from there to
[o]Philippi, which is a leading city of the[1] district of Macedonia and [p]a Roman colony. We
remained in this city some days. 13 And [q]on the
Sabbath day we went outside the gate [r]to the
riverside, where we supposed there was a place
of prayer, and we [s]sat down and spoke to the
women who had come together. 14 One who
heard us was a woman named Lydia, from the
city of Thyatira, a seller of purple goods, [t]who
was a worshiper of God. The Lord [u]opened
her heart to pay attention to what was said
by Paul. 15 And after she was baptized, [v]and
her household as well, she urged us, saying,
"If you have judged me to be faithful to the
Lord, come to my house and stay." And she
[w]prevailed upon us.

Paul and Silas in Prison

16 As we were going to [x]the place of prayer,
we were met by a slave girl who had [y]a spirit
of [z]divination and [a]brought her owners much
gain by fortune-telling. 17 She followed Paul and
us, [b]crying out, "These men are [c]servants[2] of
[d]the Most High God, who proclaim to you [e]the
way of salvation." 18 And this she kept doing
for many days. Paul, having become greatly
annoyed, turned and said to the spirit, [f]"I command you [g]in the name of Jesus Christ to come
out of her." And [h]it came out that very hour.
19 But [i]when her owners saw that their hope
of gain was gone, they seized Paul and Silas
and [j]dragged them into the marketplace
before the rulers. 20 And when they had
brought them to the magistrates, they said,
"These men are Jews, and they are disturbing
our city. 21 They [k]advocate customs that are not
lawful for us [l]as Romans to accept or practice."
22 The crowd joined in attacking them, and the
magistrates tore the garments off them and
gave orders [m]to beat them with rods. 23 And
when they had inflicted many blows upon
them, they threw them into prison, ordering the jailer to keep them safely. 24 Having
received this order, he put them into the inner
[n]prison and fastened their feet in [o]the stocks.

The Philippian Jailer Converted

25 [p]About midnight Paul and Silas were
praying and singing hymns to God, and the
prisoners were listening to them, 26 and suddenly [q]there was a great earthquake, so that
the foundations of the prison were shaken.
And immediately [r]all the doors were opened,
and [s]everyone's bonds were unfastened.
27 When the jailer woke and saw that the
prison doors were open, he drew his sword
and [t]was about to kill himself, supposing that
the prisoners had escaped. 28 But Paul cried
with a loud voice, "Do not harm yourself, for
we are all here." 29 And the jailer[3] called for
lights and rushed in, and trembling with fear
he [u]fell down before Paul and Silas. 30 Then he
brought them out and said, "Sirs, [v]what must
I do to be [w]saved?" 31 And they said, [x]"Believe in
the Lord Jesus, and you will be saved, you [y]and

[1] Or *that* [2] Greek *bondservants* [3] Greek *he*

16:14 Yet again Luke emphasizes that God is the active agent in bringing believers to faith in Christ, this time with the example of Lydia. The Lord is the one who graciously opens hearts to repent and believe the gospel. Because God is powerful and does this, it encourages us to pray for those who do not yet believe.

16:25–34 This is one of the most moving episodes in Acts. Paul and Silas have been savagely beaten and imprisoned for rescuing a girl from a dishonorable and probably oppressive occupation. We then see the terror-ridden job of the Philippian jailer, one in which he faced death for any failure (see 12:19). He knows he has failed, he knows his fate, and he decides to take his own life. He has given up.

But, through Paul, God rescues this man. "What must I do to be saved?" the man asks (16:30). The response is stunning. Paul and Silas do not tell the jailer to clean up his life. They do not exhort him to forsake any particular sin. They do not tell him to *do* anything. Rather: "Believe in the Lord Jesus, and you will be saved, you and your household" (v. 31). Trusting faith in Christ, apart from anything we bring to the table, is all that is required to be saved from what we rightly deserve: condemnation and hell. This is the promise of grace to us, as individuals, and it extends to our households as well (see note on 2:14–41).

11 [n]ch. 21:1
12 [o]Phil. 1:1; 1 Thess. 2:2 [p][ver. 21]
13 [q]See ch. 13:14 [r][Ezra 8:15, 21; Ps. 137:1] [s]Matt. 5:1
14 [t]ch. 18:7 [u]See Luke 24:45
15 [v]See ch. 11:14 [w]Gen. 19:3; Luke 24:29
16 [x]ver. 13 [y]Luke 13:11 [z]See Lev. 19:31 [a]ver. 19
17 [b]See James 2:19 [c]Dan. 3:26 [d]See Mark 5:7 [e][ch. 9:2; Matt. 7:14]
18 [f][Mark 1:25, 34] [g]See Mark 9:38 [h][Matt. 17:18]
19 [i]ver. 16; [ch. 19:25, 26] [j]ch. 17:6-8; 21:30; James 2:6; [ch. 8:3; 18:12; Matt. 10:18]
21 [k][Esth. 3:8] [l][ver. 12]
22 [m]2 Cor. 6:5; 11:23-25; 1 Thess. 2:2
24 [n]See Luke 21:12 [o]Job 13:27; 33:11; Jer. 20:2, 3; 29:26
25 [p]Job 35:10; Ps. 42:8; 77:6; 119:62
26 [q]See ch. 4:31 [r]ch. 5:19; 12:10 [s]ch. 12:7
27 [t][ch. 12:19; 27:42; 1 Kgs. 20:39]
29 [u]ch. 10:25
30 [v]ch. 2:37; 22:10; Luke 3:10, 12, 14; [John 6:28, 29] [w][ver. 17]
31 [x]See Mark 16:16 [y]See ch. 11:14

your household." 32 And they spoke the word of the Lord to him and to all who were in his house. 33 And he took them [z]the same hour of the night and washed their wounds; and he [a]was baptized at once, he and all his family. 34 Then he brought them up into his house and set food before them. And he [b]rejoiced along with his entire household that he had believed in God.

35 But when it was day, the magistrates sent the police, saying, "Let those men go." 36 And the jailer reported these words to Paul, saying, "The magistrates have sent to let you go. Therefore come out now and go in peace." 37 But Paul said to them, "They have beaten us publicly, [c]uncondemned, men who are Roman citizens, and have thrown us into prison; and do they now throw us out secretly? No! Let them come themselves and take us out." 38 The police reported these words to the magistrates, and [c]they were afraid when they heard that they were Roman citizens. 39 So they came and apologized to them. And they took them out and [d]asked them to leave the city. 40 So they went out of the prison and visited [e]Lydia. And when they had seen [f]the brothers, they encouraged them and departed.

Paul and Silas in Thessalonica

17 Now when they had passed through Amphipolis and Apollonia, they came to [g]Thessalonica, where there was a synagogue of the Jews. 2 And Paul went in, [h]as was his custom, and on three Sabbath days he reasoned with them [i]from the Scriptures, 3 [j]explaining and proving that it was necessary for [k]the Christ to suffer and [l]to rise from the dead, and saying, "This Jesus, whom I proclaim to you, is the Christ." 4 And [m]some of them were persuaded and joined Paul and Silas, as did [n]a great many of the devout [o]Greeks and not a few of the leading women. 5 [p]But the Jews[1] [q]were jealous, and taking [r]some wicked men of the rabble, they formed a mob, set the city in an uproar, and attacked the house of Jason, seeking to bring them out to the crowd. 6 And when they could not find them, [s]they dragged Jason and some of the brothers before the city authorities, shouting, "These men who have turned the world upside down have come here also, 7 and Jason has received them, and they are all acting against [t]the decrees of Caesar, saying that there is [u]another king, Jesus." 8 And the people and the city authorities were disturbed when they heard these things. 9 And when they had taken money as security from Jason and the rest, they let them go.

Paul and Silas in Berea

10 [v]The brothers[2] immediately sent Paul and Silas away by night to Berea, and when they arrived they [w]went into the Jewish synagogue. 11 Now these Jews were more noble than those in Thessalonica; they received the word with all eagerness, [x]examining the Scriptures daily to see if these things were so. 12 [y]Many of them therefore believed, with not a few Greek [z]women of high standing as well as men. 13 But when the Jews from Thessalonica learned that the word of God was proclaimed by Paul at Berea also, they came there too, [a]agitating and stirring up the crowds. 14 Then the brothers [b]immediately sent Paul off on his way to the sea, but Silas and [c]Timothy remained there. 15 [d]Those who conducted Paul brought him as far as [e]Athens, and after receiving a command [f]for Silas and Timothy to come to him as soon as possible, they departed.

Paul in Athens

16 Now while Paul was waiting for them at Athens, his spirit was [g]provoked within him as he saw that the city was [h]full of idols. 17 So [i]he reasoned in the synagogue with the Jews and the devout persons, and in the marketplace every day with those who happened to be there. 18 Some of the Epicurean and Stoic philosophers also conversed with him. And some said, [j]"What does this babbler wish to say?" Others said, "He seems to be a preacher of foreign divinities"—because [k]he was preaching [l]Jesus and the resurrection. 19 And they took him and brought him to [m]the Areopagus, saying, "May we know what this [n]new teaching is that you are presenting? 20 For you bring some [o]strange things to our ears. We wish to know therefore what these

[1] Greek *Ioudaioi* probably refers here to Jewish religious leaders, and others under their influence, in that time; also verse 13 [2] Or *brothers and sisters*; also verse 14

33 [z] ver. 25 [a] See ch. 8:12 **34** [b] Ps. 9:14; 13:5; Isa. 25:9; Luke 1:47; 1 Pet. 1:6, 8; [ch. 2:46] **37** [c] ch. 22:25, 29 **38** [c] [See ver. 37 above] **39** [d] [Matt. 8:34] **40** [e] ver. 14 [f] See John 21:23 **Chapter 17** **1** [g] ch. 20:4; Phil. 4:16; 1 Thess. 1:1 **2** [h] See ch. 13:5 [i] See ch. 8:35 **3** [j] Luke 24:26, 32 [k] See ch. 3:18 [l] See John 20:9 **4** [m] [1 Thess. 2:1, 2]; See ch. 14:4 [n] ver. 12 [o] See John 7:35 **5** [p] 1 Thess. 2:14-16; See ch. 13:50 [q] See ch. 5:17 [r] [Judg. 9:4; 11:3; 2 Chr. 13:7] **6** [s] ch. 16:19-21 **7** [t] ch. 16:4; Luke 2:1 [u] See Luke 23:2 **10** [v] ver. 14; See John 21:23 [w] ver. 2 **11** [x] [Isa. 34:16; John 5:39] **12** [y] ver. 4 [z] ch. 13:50 **13** [a] ver. 8 **14** [b] ver. 10; See Matt. 10:23 [c] See ch. 16:1 **15** [d] [ch. 15:3] [e] ch. 18:1; 1 Thess. 3:1 [f] ch. 18:5 **16** [g] [2 Pet. 2:8] [h] [Isa. 2:8] **17** [i] See ch. 13:5 **18** [j] [1 Cor. 4:10] [k] See ch. 5:42 [l] ver. 31, 32; ch. 4:2; [1 Cor. 15:12] **19** [m] ver. 22; [ver. 34] [n] Mark 1:27; [John 7:16; Heb. 13:9] **20** [o] 1 Pet. 4:4, 12; [Hos. 8:12]

things mean." 21 Now all the Athenians and
the foreigners who lived there would spend
their time in nothing except telling or hearing
something new.

Paul Addresses the Areopagus

22 So Paul, standing in the midst of the
Areopagus, said: "Men of Athens, I perceive
that in every way you are very religious. 23 For
as I passed along and observed the objects of
your worship, I found also an altar with this
inscription, [p]'To the unknown god.' [p]What
therefore you worship [q]as unknown, this
I proclaim to you. 24 [r]The God who made the
world and everything in it, being [s]Lord of
heaven and earth, [t]does not live in temples
made by man,[1] 25 nor is he served by human
hands, [u]as though he needed anything, since
he himself [v]gives to all mankind [w]life and
breath and everything. 26 And [x]he made from
one man every nation of mankind to live [y]on
all the face of the earth, [z]having determined
allotted periods and [a]the boundaries of their
dwelling place, 27 [b]that they should seek God,
[c]and perhaps feel their way toward him and
find him. [d]Yet he is actually not far from each
one of us, 28 for

> [e]"'In him we live and move and have our
> being';[2]

as even some of [f]your own poets have said,

> "'For we are indeed his offspring.'[3]

29 [g]Being then God's offspring, [h]we ought not
to think that the divine being is like gold or
silver or stone, an image formed by the art and
imagination of man. 30 [i]The times of ignorance
[j]God overlooked, but [k]now he [l]commands all
people everywhere to repent, 31 because he
has fixed [m]a day on which [n]he will judge the
world [o]in righteousness by a man whom he
has appointed; and [p]of this he has given assurance to all [q]by raising him from the dead."

32 Now when they heard of [r]the resurrection
of the dead, [s]some mocked. But others said,
[t]"We will hear you again about this." 33 So Paul
went out from their midst. 34 But some men
joined him and believed, among whom also
were Dionysius [u]the Areopagite and a woman
named Damaris and others with them.

Paul in Corinth

18 After this Paul[4] left Athens and went to
Corinth. 2 And he found a Jew named
[v]Aquila, a native of Pontus, recently come from

[1] Greek *made by hands* [2] Probably from Epimenides of Crete [3] From Aratus's poem "Phainomena" [4] Greek *he*

17:22–34 The gospel has not changed, though Paul's presentation of it begins in a much different manner than usual. Proclaiming the gospel takes a variety of forms in the book of Acts. Paul "reasoned with them from the Scriptures" in Thessalonica (Acts 17:2). But here in Athens, Paul freely uses aspects of Greek culture as bridges to the gospel, while calling people influenced by that same culture to repent (vv. 23–24, 30). God is gracious to reach each culture where we are, even in the midst of our idolatry; he is too gracious, though, to allow us to remain there.

Paul's approach to the Greek elites of Athens is a contrast in preaching style to how he approaches the Jews in the synagogues, but it is the same gospel of the grace of God through Jesus Christ. Paul's outreach to the Gentiles, though it tends to stir up the Jews to jealousy, is simply a reflection of Jesus' gracious approach to outsiders.

Jesus' ministry was inclusive from its beginning. He ministered to the rich, the poor, the despised, the religious, the secular, men, and women (e.g., Matt. 8:1-13; 15:22–28; John 4:2–42). Jesus' ministry reached beyond Jerusalem to include Nazareth, Galilee, and Samaria.

Paul and the other apostles simply carried forward the inclusive approach set forth by Jesus. Paul insisted, "There is neither Jew nor Greek, there is neither slave nor free, there is no male and female, for you are all one in Christ Jesus" (Gal. 3:28), and he taught that the expansion of God's kingdom to other nations was at the very heart of God's plan to redeem the cosmos. The inclusiveness of the kingdom of God is artistically expressed in the book of Revelation, where we read that people from "every tribe and language and people and nation" (Rev. 5:9; 14:6) receive the gospel and are gathered in celebration of the Lamb.

18:1–11 God speaks directly to Paul, encouraging him to remain in Corinth despite his frustrations, because God apparently has many people to redeem there (v. 10).

23 [p][John 4:22; 1 Cor. 15:34] [q][ver. 30]
24 [r]Isa. 42:5; See ch. 14:15 [s]Matt. 11:25; [Deut. 10:14; Ps. 115:16] [t]See ch. 7:48
25 [u]Ps. 50:8-12; [1 Chr. 29:14, 16; Job 22:2] [v]1 Tim. 6:17; James 1:5, 17 [w]Gen. 2:7; 7:22; Job 33:4; [Job 27:3; Eccles. 12:7; Zech. 12:1]; See ver. 28
26 [x][Gen. 3:20; Mal. 2:10] [y]Gen. 11:8; Luke 21:35 [z][Job 12:23; 14:5] [a]Deut. 32:8; [Ps. 74:17]
27 [b][ch. 15:17] [c][Job 23:3, 8, 9] [d][Deut. 4:7; Ps. 145:18; Jer. 23:23, 24]; See ch. 14:17
28 [e]Job 12:10; Dan. 5:23; [Heb. 2:11] [f][Titus 1:12]
29 [g][Luke 3:38; Heb. 12:9] [h]Isa. 40:18, 19, 25; 46:5; [Rom. 1:23]
30 [i]Eph. 4:18; 1 Pet. 1:14; [ver. 23] [j][Rom. 3:25]; See ch. 14:16 [k][Mark 1:15; Titus 2:11, 12; 1 Pet. 4:3] [l]Mark 6:12
31 [m]Matt. 12:36; Rom. 2:16; 1 Cor. 3:13; 2 Pet. 2:9; 1 John 4:17; [Isa. 2:12] [n]2 Tim. 4:8; See ch. 10:42 [o]Ps. 9:8; 96:13; 98:9; 1 Pet. 2:23; [Rom. 3:6] [p][John 16:10, 11; Rom. 1:4] [q]See ch. 2:24
32 [r]Heb. 6:2; See ver. 18 [s][ch. 2:13; 26:8] [t]ch. 24:25
34 [u]ver. 19, 22

Chapter 18
2 [v]ver. 18, 26; Rom. 16:3; 1 Cor. 16:19; 2 Tim. 4:19

Italy with his wife [v]Priscilla, because [w]Claudius
had commanded all the Jews to leave Rome.
And he went to see them, 3 and [x]because he
was of the same trade he stayed with them
and worked, for they were tentmakers by
trade. 4 And [y]he reasoned in the synagogue
[y]every Sabbath, and tried to persuade Jews
and Greeks.

5 [z]When Silas and Timothy arrived from
Macedonia, Paul [a]was occupied with the
word, [b]testifying to the Jews that the Christ
was [c]Jesus. 6 And when they opposed and
reviled him, [d]he shook out his garments and
said to them, [e]"Your blood be on your own
heads! [f]I am innocent. [g]From now on I will go
to the Gentiles." 7 And he left there and went
to the house of a man named Titius [h]Justus,
[i]a worshiper of God. His house was next door
to the synagogue. 8 [j]Crispus, the ruler of the
synagogue, believed in the Lord, together
[k]with his entire household. And many of the
Corinthians hearing Paul believed and were
baptized. 9 And the Lord said to Paul [l]one
night in [m]a vision, [n]"Do not be afraid, but go
on speaking and do not be silent, 10 [n]for I am
with you, and [o]no one will attack you to harm
you, for [p]I have many in this city who are my
people." 11 And he stayed a year and six months,
teaching the word of God among them.

12 But when Gallio was [q]proconsul of Achaia,
[r]the Jews[1] made a united attack on Paul and
[s]brought him before the tribunal, 13 saying,
"This man is persuading people to worship
God contrary to [t]the law." 14 But when Paul
was about to open his mouth, Gallio said to
the Jews, "If it were a matter of wrongdoing
or vicious [u]crime, O Jews, I would have reason
to accept your complaint. 15 But [v]since it is a
matter of questions about words and names
and [w]your own law, see to it yourselves. I refuse
to be a judge of these things." 16 And he drove
them from the tribunal. 17 And they all seized
Sosthenes, the ruler of the synagogue, and
beat him in front of the tribunal. But Gallio
paid no attention to any of this.

Paul Returns to Antioch

18 After this, Paul stayed many days longer
and then took leave of [x]the brothers[2] and
set sail for Syria, and with him [y]Priscilla and
Aquila. At [z]Cenchreae [a]he had cut his hair,
for he was under a vow. 19 And they came to
[b]Ephesus, and he left them there, but [c]he himself went into the synagogue and reasoned
with the Jews. 20 When they asked him to stay
for a longer period, he declined. 21 But on taking leave of them he said, "I will return to you
[d]if God wills," and he set sail from Ephesus.

22 When he had landed at Caesarea, he [e]went
up and greeted the church, and then went
down to Antioch. 23 After spending some time
there, he departed and [f]went from one place
to the next through the region of Galatia and
Phrygia, [g]strengthening all the disciples.

Apollos Speaks Boldly in Ephesus

24 Now a Jew named [h]Apollos, a native of
Alexandria, came to Ephesus. He was an eloquent man, [i]competent in the Scriptures. 25 He
had been instructed in [j]the way of the Lord.
And [k]being fervent in spirit,[3] he spoke and
taught accurately the things concerning Jesus,
though he knew only [l]the baptism of John.
26 He began to speak boldly in the synagogue,
but when [m]Priscilla and Aquila heard him, they
took him aside and explained to him [n]the way

[1] Greek *Ioudaioi* probably refers here to Jewish religious leaders, and others under their influence, in that time; also verses 14 (twice), 28
[2] Or *brothers and sisters*; also verse 27 [3] Or *in the Spirit*

In the face of opposition, God steps in with faithful love to strengthen Paul's resolve. God promises (1) protection: despite the danger of Paul's opponents, God will ensure that they do not harm him; and (2) presence: God himself will be with Paul so that he need not doubt whether the hostility he experiences reflects God's displeasure.

Christ offers believers both of these promises. We are protected from the wrath of God through his death as our substitute. We also possess the promise of God's presence through the Holy Spirit as we partner in his mission (Matt. 28:18–20; John 14:18, 27). Knowing that God himself dwells within us allows us to press forward through adversity. It is God's presence ("I am with you"; Acts 18:10) that not only energizes believers but protects them in the midst of fear, anxiety, and doubt. This is a recurring theme in Scripture: God's presence casts out fear.

2 [v] ver. 18, 26; Rom. 16:3; 1 Cor. 16:19; 2 Tim. 4:19 [w] ch. 11:28 **3** [x] ch. 20:34; 1 Cor. 4:12; 9:15; 2 Cor. 11:7; 12:13; 1 Thess. 2:9; 2 Thess. 3:8 **4** [y] ch. 17:17; See ch. 13:5, 14 **5** [z] ch. 17:15; 1 Thess. 3:6 [a] 2 Cor. 5:14; [Job 32:18; Jer. 6:11; 20:9; Amos 3:8] [b] ch. 20:21 [c] ver. 28; ch. 2:36; 5:42; 17:3; [ch. 3:20; 8:5; 9:22] **6** [d] Neh. 5:13; [ch. 13:51] [e] Ezek. 18:13; 33:4; [2 Sam. 1:16; Matt. 27:25] [f] ch. 20:26 (Gk.); [Ezek. 3:18, 19] [g] See ch. 13:46 **7** [h] [ch. 1:23; Col. 4:11] [i] ch. 16:14 **8** [j] 1 Cor. 1:14 [k] See ch. 11:14 **9** [l] ch. 23:11; 27:23 [m] [ch. 26:16; 2 Cor. 12:1-4] [n] ch. 27:24; Josh. 1:5, 6; Jer. 1:8; Matt. 28:20 **10** [n] [See ver. 9 above] [o] [Luke 21:18; 2 Thess. 3:2] [p] [John 10:16] **12** [q] See ch. 13:7 [r] See ch. 13:50 [s] See ch. 16:19 **13** [t] ver. 15 **14** [u] [ch. 13:10] **15** [v] ch. 23:29; 25:19; [1 Tim. 6:4; 2 Tim. 2:14] [w] ver. 13 **18** [x] See John 21:23 [y] ver. 2 [z] Rom. 16:1 [a] [ch. 21:23, 24; Num. 6:2, 18] **19** [b] ch. 19:1; 20:16, 17; 1 Cor. 15:32; 16:8; Eph. 1:1; 1 Tim. 1:3; 2 Tim. 1:18 [c] ver. 4 **21** [d] 1 Cor. 4:19; 16:7; Heb. 6:3; James 4:15; [Rom. 15:32; 1 Pet. 3:17] **22** [e] ch. 11:2; 21:15 **23** [f] ch. 16:6 [g] See ch. 14:22 **24** [h] ch. 19:1; 1 Cor. 1:12; 3:5, 6; 4:6; 16:12; Titus 3:13 [i] [Ezra 7:6] **25** [j] See ch. 9:2 [k] Rom. 12:11 [l] ch. 19:3; Luke 7:29 **26** [m] See ver. 2 [n] Matt. 22:16; [ver. 25]

of God more accurately. 27 And when he wished
to cross to [o]Achaia, [p]the brothers encouraged
him and [q]wrote to the disciples to welcome
him. When he arrived, [r]he greatly helped those
who through grace had believed, 28 for he powerfully refuted the Jews in public, showing by
the Scriptures [s]that the Christ was Jesus.

Paul in Ephesus

19 And it happened that while [t]Apollos
was at Corinth, Paul passed [u]through
the inland[1] country and came to Ephesus.
There he found some disciples. 2 And he said
to them, [v]"Did you receive the Holy Spirit
when you believed?" And they said, "No,
[w]we have not even heard that there is a Holy
Spirit." 3 And he said, [x]"Into what then were
you baptized?" They said, "Into [y]John's baptism." 4 And Paul said, [y]"John baptized with
the baptism of repentance, telling the people
[z]to believe in the one who was to come after
him, that is, Jesus." 5 On hearing this, [a]they
were baptized in[2] the name of the Lord Jesus.
6 And [b]when Paul had laid his hands on them,
the Holy Spirit came on them, and [c]they began
speaking in tongues and [d]prophesying. 7 There
were about twelve men in all.
8 And [e]he entered the synagogue and for
three months spoke boldly, reasoning and
persuading them [f]about the kingdom of God.
9 [g]But when some became stubborn and [h]con-
tinued in unbelief, speaking evil of [i]the Way
before the congregation, he withdrew from
them and took the disciples with him, reasoning daily in the hall of Tyrannus.[3] 10 This continued for [j]two years, so that [k]all the residents
of Asia heard the word of the Lord, both Jews
and Greeks.

The Sons of Sceva

11 And [l]God was doing extraordinary miracles
by the hands of Paul, 12 [l]so that even handker-
chiefs or aprons that had touched his skin
were carried away to the sick, and their diseases left them and [m]the evil spirits came out
of them. 13 Then some of the itinerant Jewish
[n]exorcists [o]undertook to invoke the name of
the Lord Jesus over those who had evil spirits, saying, [p]"I adjure you by the Jesus whom
Paul proclaims." 14 Seven sons of a Jewish high
priest named Sceva were doing this. 15 But the
evil spirit answered them, [q]"Jesus I know, and
Paul I recognize, but who are you?" 16 And the
man in whom was the evil spirit leaped on
them, mastered all[4] of them and overpowered
them, so that they fled out of that house naked
and wounded. 17 And this became known to
all the residents of Ephesus, both Jews and
Greeks. And fear fell upon them all, and [r]the
name of the Lord Jesus was extolled. 18 Also
many of those who were now believers came,
[s]confessing and divulging their practices.
19 And a number of those who had practiced
magic arts brought their books together and
burned them in the sight of all. And they
counted the value of them and found it came

[1] Greek *upper* (that is, highland) [2] Or *into* [3] Some manuscripts add *from the fifth hour to the tenth* (that is, from 11 A.M. to 4 P.M.) [4] Or *both*

18:27 Apollos helped "those who through grace had believed." Belief is not something humans can manufacture; salvation, including faith, is completely the work of God's grace (Eph. 2:8–9). We are saved by grace, not by anything we have done. Salvation is completely a gift of God. We have done nothing to bring it about that could lead us to boast. And yet it is nearly impossible not to boast in the radical love of God when we grasp this reality.

19:1–7 Apollos and some Ephesians had become followers of John the Baptist and had received his baptism. They knew that John pointed beyond himself to Jesus. They apparently knew of Jesus' life and ministry, and his death and resurrection, but *not* about the coming of the Spirit at Pentecost and its significance for the new era. These believers were in a salvation-history "time-warp," as if they were still in Acts 1, before the unfolding of redemptive history at Pentecost. Their experience of tongues (19:6) served as the witness to the Ephesian believers themselves of the gift of the Spirit that transferred them as a group from the old era to the new one in which they should be living.

In Acts 2, Jewish believers are filled with the Holy Spirit. In Acts 8, Samaritans are filled with the Spirit after they believe the gospel preached by Philip. In Acts 10 and 11, Peter preaches to Gentiles, who believe and are filled with the Spirit. Here in Acts 19, Paul meets some followers of John the Baptist who didn't even know all that Jesus did

27 [o][ch. 19:1] [p]ver. 18 [q][2 Cor. 3:1] [r]1 Cor. 3:6; [ch. 11:21, 23; 15:11; Eph. 2:8]
28 [s]See ver. 5
Chapter 19
1 [t]See ch. 18:24 [u][ch. 18:23]
2 [v][ch. 11:16, 17] [w][ch. 8:16; John 7:39]
3 [x]See ch. 8:16 [y]ch. 18:25; [Heb. 6:2]; See ch. 13:24, 25
4 [y][See ver. 3 above] [z]John 1:7
5 [a]See ch. 8:12, 16
6 [b]See ch. 8:17 [c]ch. 10:46; See Mark 16:17 [d]See ch. 13:1
8 [e]See ch. 13:5 [f]ch. 1:3; 28:23
9 [g][ch. 13:45, 46; 1 Cor. 16:9] [h]See ch. 14:2 [i]ver. 23; See ch. 9:2
10 [j][ver. 8; ch. 20:31] [k][2 Tim. 1:15]
11 [l][ch. 5:15]; See ch. 5:12
12 [l][See ver. 11 above] [m]See Mark 16:17
13 [n][Matt. 12:27; Luke 11:19] [o]See Mark 9:38 [p]Matt. 26:63; Mark 5:7
15 [q]See James 2:19
17 [r][2 Thess. 1:12]

18 [s]Matt. 3:6; Mark 1:5; Rom. 14:11; James 5:16

to fifty thousand pieces of silver. 20 So the word of the Lord [t]continued to increase and prevail mightily.

A Riot at Ephesus

21 Now after these events Paul resolved in the Spirit [u]to pass through [v]Macedonia and Achaia and [w]go to Jerusalem, saying, "After I have been there, [x]I must also see Rome." 22 And having sent into Macedonia two of [y]his helpers, [z]Timothy and Erastus, he himself stayed in Asia [a]for a while.

23 About that time [b]there arose no little disturbance concerning [c]the Way. 24 For a man named Demetrius, a silversmith, who made silver shrines of Artemis, [d]brought no little business to the craftsmen. 25 [d]These he gathered together, with the workmen in similar trades, and said, "Men, you know that from this business we have our wealth. 26 And you see and hear that not only in Ephesus but in almost all of Asia this Paul has persuaded and turned away a great many people, [e]saying that [f]gods made with hands are not gods. 27 And there is danger not only that this trade of ours may come into disrepute but also that the temple of the [g]great goddess Artemis may be counted as nothing, and that she may even be deposed from her magnificence, she whom all Asia and the world worship."

28 When they heard this they were enraged and were crying out, [g]"Great is Artemis of the Ephesians!" 29 So the city was filled with the confusion, and they rushed together into the theater, dragging with them Gaius and [h]Aristarchus, Macedonians who were Paul's [i]companions in travel. 30 But when Paul wished to go in among the crowd, the disciples would not let him. 31 And even some of the Asiarchs,[1] who were friends of his, sent to him and were urging him not to venture into the theater. 32 [j]Now some cried out one thing, some another, for the assembly was in confusion, and most of them did not know why they had come together. 33 Some of the crowd prompted Alexander, whom the Jews had put forward. And Alexander, [k]motioning with his hand, wanted to make a defense to the crowd. 34 But when they recognized that he was a Jew, for about two hours they all cried out with one voice, [l]"Great is Artemis of the Ephesians!"

35 And when the town clerk had quieted the crowd, he said, "Men of Ephesus, who is there who does not know that the city of the Ephesians is temple keeper of the great Artemis, and of the sacred stone that fell from [m]the sky?[2] 36 Seeing then that these things cannot be denied, you ought to be quiet and do nothing rash. 37 For you have brought [n]these men here who are neither [o]sacrilegious nor blasphemers of our goddess. 38 If therefore Demetrius and the craftsmen with him have a complaint against anyone, the courts are open, and there are [p]proconsuls. Let them bring charges against one another. 39 But if you seek anything further,[3] it shall be settled in the regular assembly. 40 For we really are in danger of being charged with rioting today, since there is no cause that we can give to justify this commotion." 41 And when he had said these things, he dismissed the assembly.

Paul in Macedonia and Greece

20 After the uproar ceased, Paul sent for the disciples, and after encouraging them, he said farewell and [q]departed for Macedonia. 2 When he had gone through those regions and had given them much encouragement, he came to Greece. 3 There he spent three months, and when [r]a plot was made against him by the Jews[4] as he was about to set sail for Syria, he decided to return through Macedonia. 4 Sopater the Berean, son of Pyrrhus, accompanied him; and of the

[1] That is, high-ranking officers of the province of Asia [2] The meaning of the Greek is uncertain [3] Some manuscripts *seek about other matters* [4] Greek *Ioudaioi* probably refers here to Jewish religious leaders, and others under their influence, in that time; also verse 19

20 [t]ch. 6:7; 12:24
21 [u]1 Cor. 16:5; [ch. 20:1] [v]Rom. 15:26; 1 Thess. 1:7, 8 [w]ch. 20:16, 22; Rom. 15:25; 2 Cor. 1:16; [1 Cor. 16:3, 4] [x]Rom. 15:24, 28; [ch. 23:11; Rom. 1:13]
22 [y]Col. 4:7; 2 Tim. 1:18; 4:11; Philem. 13; [ver. 29; ch. 13:5] [z]See ch. 16:1 [a][1 Cor. 16:8, 9]
23 [b][2 Cor. 1:8] [c]ver. 9

and taught. So they believe and are filled (see earlier notes on 3:11–26 and 8:14–17). In this progression we see the ever-expanding scope of the gospel. God's mercy is poured out deep and wide. The Spirit's ministry is expansive, just as Jesus' ministry was—including those who previously were excluded or uninformed. The gospel-centered focus of Acts can be pictured by expanding concentric circles: the Holy Spirit brings Jesus' good news to a small group of disciples, to Jews, to Samaritans, to Gentiles, and to the entire world (see earlier notes on 1:1–11; 2:1–13; 10:1–48).

24 [d][ch. 16:16, 19] **25** [d][See ver. 24 above] **26** [e]ch. 14:15; 17:29; 1 Cor. 8:4 [f]Deut. 4:28; 2 Kgs. 19:18; Ps. 115:4; Isa. 44:10-20; Jer. 10:3-6; Rev. 9:20
27 [g][ch. 8:10] **28** [g][See ver. 27 above] **29** [h]ch. 20:4; 27:2; Col. 4:10; Philem. 24 [i]2 Cor. 8:19; [ver. 22; ch. 20:34] **32** [j]ch. 21:34 **33** [k]See ch. 12:17
34 [l]ver. 28 **35** [m][ch. 14:12] **37** [n]ver. 29 [o]Rom. 2:22 **38** [p]See ch. 13:7 **Chapter 20** **1** [q]See ch. 19:21 **3** [r]ver. 19; [ch. 13:50]; See ch. 9:24

Thessalonians, [s]Aristarchus and Secundus; and [s]Gaius of Derbe, and [t]Timothy; and the Asians, [u]Tychicus and [v]Trophimus. 5 These went on ahead and were waiting for [w]us at [x]Troas, 6 but we sailed away from Philippi after [y]the days of Unleavened Bread, and in five days we came to them at Troas, where we stayed for seven days.

Eutychus Raised from the Dead

7 [z]On the first day of the week, when we were gathered together [a]to break bread, Paul talked with them, intending to depart on the next day, and he prolonged his speech until midnight. 8 There were many lamps in [b]the upper room where we were gathered. 9 And a young man named Eutychus, sitting at the window, sank into a deep sleep as Paul talked still longer. And being overcome by sleep, he [c]fell down from the third story and was taken up dead. 10 But Paul went down and [d]bent over him, and taking him in his arms, said, [e]"Do not be alarmed, for his life is in him." 11 And when Paul had gone up and [f]had broken bread and eaten, he conversed with them a long while, until daybreak, and so departed. 12 And they took the youth away alive, and were not a little comforted.

13 But going ahead to the ship, we set sail for Assos, intending to take Paul aboard there, for so he had arranged, intending himself to go by land. 14 And when he met us at Assos, we took him on board and went to Mitylene. 15 And sailing from there we came the following day opposite Chios; the next day we touched at Samos; and[1] the day after that we went to Miletus. 16 For Paul had decided to sail past Ephesus, so that he might not have to spend time in Asia, for he was hastening [g]to be at Jerusalem, if possible, [h]on the day of Pentecost.

Paul Speaks to the Ephesian Elders

17 Now from Miletus he sent to Ephesus and called [i]the elders of the church to come to him. 18 And when they came to him, he said to them:

[j]"You yourselves know [k]how I lived among you the whole time [l]from the first day that I set foot in Asia, 19 [l]serving the Lord [m]with all humility and with [n]tears and with trials that happened to me through [o]the plots of the Jews; 20 how I [p]did not shrink from declaring to you anything that was profitable, and [q]teaching you in public and from house to house, 21 [r]testifying both to Jews and to Greeks of [s]repentance toward God and of [t]faith in our Lord Jesus Christ. 22 And now, behold, I am going to Jerusalem, constrained [u]by[2] the Spirit, not knowing what will happen to me there, 23 except that [v]the Holy Spirit testifies to me in every city that [w]imprisonment and [x]afflictions await me. 24 But [y]I do not account my life of any value nor as precious to myself,

[1] Some manuscripts add *after remaining at Trogyllium* [2] Or *bound in*

20:17–21 Some leaders of the world, as Jesus said, use their positions of power to maintain an advantage over their subjects (Matt. 20:25). Jesus modeled a different way. He placed himself in a position of weakness and was completely humble with his disciples, even calling them his friends (John 15:15). Paul exemplifies this humility as well (e.g., 2 Cor. 11:29–30).

Whereas Jesus was able to be completely open with his disciples because he had no fault within him to hide, Christians do not always have that same level of confidence. Our lives are often marked by failures and shame, by "tears and . . . trials" and "all humility" (Acts 20:19). Our strength to open ourselves up to others, to be vulnerable despite our failings, comes not as we drum up self-confidence but as we focus on Christ's finished work and rely on him. Paul was weak, yet he was confident in the strength of his Lord (2 Cor. 12:10). When our identity is found in Christ, we are free to be honest (James 5:16). If you have faith in Christ, your new identity is secure and robust. Your new identity in Christ is deeper than any of your wounds, sins, suffering, trials, and failures.

20:24–38 Paul reminds the Ephesians of how God has worked in him to testify to the gospel of the grace of God (v. 24). He expresses confidence not in human ability but in "the word of his grace, which is able to build you up and to give you the inheritance among all those who are sanctified" (v. 32). Paul knows that the grace of God is more powerful than any laws, commands, or threats to motivate and build up his people. Paul is concerned that they continue to live under the grace of God that has been poured out for them.

4 [s]ch. 14:6, 21; See ch. 19:29 [t]See ch. 16:1 [u]Eph. 6:21; Col. 4:7; 2 Tim. 4:12; Titus 3:12 [v]ch. 21:29; 2 Tim. 4:20
5 [w]ver. 6-8, 13-15 [x]ch. 16:8-11
6 [y]ch. 12:3; Ex. 12:14, 15; 23:15
7 [z]1 Cor. 16:2; [Mark 16:9; John 20:19; Rev. 1:10] [a]ver. 11; 1 Cor. 10:16; 11:23, 24; See ch. 2:42
8 [b]ch. 1:13; 9:37, 39
9 [c]2 Kgs. 1:2
10 [d][1 Kgs. 17:21; 2 Kgs. 4:34] [e][Matt. 9:23, 24; Mark 5:39]
11 [f]ver. 7
16 [g]ver. 22; ch. 24:11; [ver. 6; ch. 19:21; 1 Cor. 16:8] [h]ch. 2:1
17 [i]See ch. 11:30
18 [j]1 Thess. 1:5; [ver. 31, 34] [k]ch. 18:19; 19:1, 10
19 [l][Rom. 12:11; Col. 3:24] [m][1 Thess. 2:6, 7]; See Eph. 4:2 [n][ver. 31; 2 Cor. 2:4; Phil. 3:18] [o]See ver. 3
20 [p]ver. 27 [q][ver. 31]
21 [r]ver. 24; ch. 18:5 [s]Mark 1:15; Heb. 6:1; See ch. 2:38 [t][Eph. 1:15; Col. 1:4; 1 Tim. 3:13]
22 [u][ch. 17:16]
23 [v][ch. 21:4, 11]; See ch. 8:29; 9:16 [w]ch. 21:33 [x]ch. 14:22; 1 Thess. 3:3
24 [y]See ch. 21:13

if only [z]I may finish my course and [a]the ministry [b]that I received from the Lord Jesus, [c]to testify to [d]the gospel of [e]the grace of God. 25 And
now, behold, [f]I know that none of you among
whom I have gone about [g]proclaiming the
kingdom will see my face again. 26 Therefore
[h]I testify to you this day that [i]I am innocent of
the blood of all, 27 for [j]I did not shrink from
declaring to you [k]the whole counsel of God.
28 [l]Pay careful attention to yourselves and to
all [m]the flock, in which [n]the Holy Spirit has
made you [o]overseers, [p]to care for [q]the church
of God,[1] which he [r]obtained [s]with his own
blood.[2] 29 I [r]know that after my departure
[t]fierce wolves will come in among you, [u]not
sparing the flock; 30 and [v]from among your
own selves will arise men speaking twisted
things, to draw away the disciples after them.
31 Therefore [w]be alert, remembering that [x]for
three years I did not cease night or day [y]to
admonish every one [z]with tears. 32 And now
[a]I commend you to God and to [b]the word of
his grace, which is able to [c]build you up and
to give you [d]the inheritance among all those
who are sanctified. 33 [e]I coveted no one's silver
or gold or apparel. 34 [f]You yourselves know
that [g]these hands ministered to my necessities and [h]to those who were with me. 35 In all
things [i]I have shown you that [j]by working
hard in this way we must [k]help the weak and
[l]remember the words of the Lord Jesus, how
he himself said, 'It is more blessed [m]to give
than to receive.' "

36 And when he had said these things, [n]he
knelt down and prayed with them all. 37 And
[o]there was much weeping on the part of all;
[p]they embraced Paul and [p]kissed him, 38 being
sorrowful most of all because of [q]the word he
had spoken, that they would not see his face
again. And [r]they accompanied him to the ship.

Paul Goes to Jerusalem

21 And when [s]we had parted from them
and set sail, we [t]came by a straight
course to Cos, and the next day to Rhodes, and
from there to Patara.[3] 2 And having found a
ship crossing to Phoenicia, we went aboard
and set sail. 3 When we had come in sight of
Cyprus, leaving it on the left we sailed to Syria
and landed at Tyre, for there the ship was to
unload its cargo. 4 And having sought out the
disciples, we stayed there for seven days. And
[u]through the Spirit they were telling Paul
not to go on to Jerusalem. 5 When our days
there were ended, we departed and went on
our journey, and they all, with wives and children, [v]accompanied us until we were outside
the city. And [w]kneeling down on the beach,
we prayed 6 and said farewell to one another.
Then we went on board the ship, and they
returned home.

7 When we had finished the voyage from
Tyre, we arrived at Ptolemais, and we greeted
[x]the brothers[4] and stayed with them for one
day. 8 On the next day we departed and came
to Caesarea, and we entered the house of
[y]Philip [z]the evangelist, who was one of the
seven, and stayed with him. 9 He had four
unmarried daughters, [a]who prophesied.
10 While we were staying for many days, a
prophet named [b]Agabus came down from
Judea. 11 And coming to us, he [c]took Paul's
belt and bound his own feet and hands and
said, [d]"Thus says the Holy Spirit, [e]'This is
how the Jews[5] at Jerusalem will bind the man
who owns this belt and [f]deliver him into the
hands of the Gentiles.' " 12 When we heard this,
we and the people there [g]urged him not to
go up to Jerusalem. 13 Then Paul answered,
[g]"What are you doing, weeping and breaking my heart? For [h]I am ready not only to be
imprisoned but even to die in Jerusalem [i]for
the name of the Lord Jesus." 14 And since he
would not be persuaded, [j]we ceased and said,
[k]"Let the will of the Lord be done."

15 After these days we got ready and went
up to Jerusalem. 16 And some of the disciples
from Caesarea went with us, bringing us to the
house of Mnason of Cyprus, an early disciple,
with whom we should lodge.

[1] Some manuscripts *of the Lord* [2] Or *with the blood of his Own* [3] Some manuscripts add *and Myra* [4] Or *brothers and sisters*; also verse 17
[5] Greek *Ioudaioi* probably refers here to Jewish religious leaders, and others under their influence, in that time

24 [z] 2 Tim. 4:7 [a] ch. 1:17; 1 Tim. 1:12 [b] Gal. 1:1; 1 Thess. 2:4; [ch. 26:16; Titus 1:3] [c] ver. 21 [d] ch. 15:7 [e] [ver. 32; 1 Tim. 1:14]; See ch. 11:23 **25** [f] [Phil. 1:25] [g] See ch. 28:31 **26** [h] Deut. 8:19 [i] See ch. 18:6 **27** [j] ver. 20; [Jer. 26:2; Ezek. 33:8] [k] ch. 13:36; Luke 7:30; [ch. 2:23; Eph. 1:11; Heb. 6:17] **28** [l] [1 Tim. 4:16] [m] ver. 29; [Eph. 4:11]; See Luke 12:32 [n] [ch. 13:2; 1 Cor. 12:8-11] [o] Phil. 1:1; 1 Tim. 3:2; Titus 1:7; [ver. 17] [p] See John 21:16 [q] 1 Cor. 1:2; 10:32; 11:16; 15:9 [r] [2 Pet. 2:1] [s] Heb. 9:12, 14; [Eph. 1:7; 1 John 1:7]; See 1 Pet. 1:18, 19; Rev. 5:9 **29** [r] [See ver. 28 above] [t] See Matt. 7:15 [u] John 10:12; [Col. 2:8] **30** [v] [1 Cor. 11:19; 2 Cor. 11:13; 1 Tim. 1:19, 20; 1 John 2:18, 19] **31** [w] [Heb. 13:17]; See Matt. 24:42 [x] [ch. 19:8, 10; 24:17] [y] Col. 1:28 [z] [Heb. 13:17]; See ver. 19 **32** [a] ch. 14:23 [b] ch. 14:3; [ver. 24] [c] See Col. 2:7 [d] ch. 26:18; Eph. 1:14, 18; 5:5; Col. 1:12; 3:24; Heb. 9:15; [1 Pet. 1:4]; See Matt. 25:34; Rom. 8:17 **33** [e] 1 Cor. 9:12; 2 Cor. 7:2; 11:9; 12:17; [1 Sam. 12:3; Matt. 10:8; 1 Thess. 2:5] **34** [f] [ver. 18] [g] See ch. 18:3 [h] ch. 19:22, 29 **35** [i] 2 Thess. 3:7 [j] Eph. 4:28 [k] 1 Thess. 5:14; [1 Cor. 12:28] [l] ch. 11:16 [m] Matt. 10:8 **36** [n] See ch. 7:60 **37** [o] [2 Tim. 1:4] [p] See Luke 15:20 **38** [q] ver. 25 [r] See ch. 15:3 **Chapter 21** **1** [s] See ch. 16:10 [t] ch. 16:11 **4** [u] ver. 11; ch. 20:23 **5** [v] ch. 20:38 [w] ch. 20:36 **7** [x] See John 21:23 **8** [y] ch. 6:5; 8:5 [z] Eph. 4:11; 2 Tim. 4:5 **9** [a] ch. 2:17, 18; Luke 2:36; 1 Cor. 11:5; See ch. 13:1 **10** [b] ch. 11:28 **11** [c] [1 Sam. 15:27, 28; 1 Kgs. 11:30; Isa. 20:3; Jer. 13:1-11; 27:2] [d] See ch. 20:23 [e] [ver. 33]; See ch. 9:16 [f] [ver. 31-33; Matt. 20:19] **12** [g] [Matt. 16:21-23] **13** [g] [See ver. 12 above] [h] ch. 20:24; Rom. 8:36; 2 Cor. 4:16; 12:10; Phil. 2:17; [ch. 15:26] [i] See ch. 5:41 **14** [j] [Ruth 1:18] [k] See Matt. 6:10

Paul Visits James

17 When we had come to Jerusalem, [l]the
brothers received us gladly. 18 On the following day Paul went in with us to [m]James, and
all [n]the elders were present. 19 After greeting
them, [o]he related one by one [p]the things that
God had done among the Gentiles through
his [q]ministry. 20 And when they heard it, they
[r]glorified God. And they said to him, "You
see, brother, how many thousands there are
among the Jews of those who have believed.
They are all [s]zealous for the law, 21 and they
have been told about you that you teach all
[t]the Jews who are among the Gentiles to forsake Moses, [u]telling them [v]not to circumcise
their children or [w]walk according to [x]our
customs. 22 What then is to be done? They
will certainly hear that you have come. 23 Do
therefore what we tell you. We have four men
[y]who are under a vow; 24 take these men and
[z]purify yourself along with them and pay their
expenses, [y]so that they may shave their heads.
Thus all will know that there is nothing in
what they have been told about you, but that
you yourself also live in observance of the law.
25 But as for the Gentiles who have believed,
[a]we have sent a letter with our judgment that
they should abstain from what has been sacrificed to idols, and from blood, and from what
has been strangled,[1] and from sexual immorality." 26 Then Paul took the men, and the next
day [z]he purified himself along with them and
[b]went into the temple, giving notice when the
days of purification would be fulfilled and [c]the
offering presented for each one of them.

Paul Arrested in the Temple

27 When [c]the seven days were almost completed, [d]the Jews from Asia, [e]seeing him in the
temple, stirred up the whole crowd and laid
hands on him, 28 crying out, "Men of Israel,
help! This is the man who [f]is teaching everyone
everywhere against the people and [g]the law
and [g]this place. Moreover, he even brought
Greeks into the temple and [h]has defiled [g]this
holy place." 29 For they had previously seen
[i]Trophimus the Ephesian with him in the city,
and they supposed that Paul had brought him

[1] Some manuscripts omit *and from what has been strangled*

21:17–26 Paul's visit with James is another episode in the continuing struggle on the part of many Jewish Christians to comprehend the spread of the gospel to the Gentiles. With Paul at the forefront, the word about Jesus scandalizes many Jews because it brings Gentiles into the people of God without requiring them to abide by the law. We see Paul confronting this issue throughout his letters, most especially in Galatians and Romans.

Paul is unyielding about the obligation to spread the gospel to the Gentiles, and about their not having to keep the laws regarding Jewish ceremonies and traditions; however, we also see Paul doing all he can to demonstrate to the Jews that he values the law, even undergoing these rites of purification (v. 26). For the sake of spreading the message of God's grace, Paul insists that he can become "all things to all people," allowing a remarkable space for adaptation in nonessentials for the sake of mission (without compromising the gospel or his identity in Christ; see 1 Cor. 9:19–23). He also encourages others to this flexibility in nonessentials for the sake of harmony and humility in the church (see Romans 14).

21:20–26 The grace of the gospel frequently leads to the charge of antinomianism, or lawlessness—that if grace is free, people will feel free to sin all they want. The first to levy such charges are, as here, those who are zealous to keep religious commands and compel others to do the same. Paul goes to great lengths to satisfy the Jerusalem accusers (v. 25), even accommodating James by submitting to a ritual Mosaic cleansing (v. 26).

Paul's opponents believed that commands could only be kept out of fear of punishment, and that if that fear were removed, there would no longer be any motivation to live a righteous life. Into this situation comes news of the gospel, in which Jesus has removed the fear of punishment and freely reconciled us to God. Those zealous for the law can only see the potential danger: If Christians do not fear punishment, they will do whatever they want! Think of the anarchy! The book of Acts refutes such accusations, showing that those who have experienced grace are motivated by remembering God's grace; because of God's great love for them, they do whatever he wants (cf. John 14:15). They are compelled by the love of Christ (2 Cor. 5:14).

17 [l] ver. 7; [ch. 15:4]
18 [m] See ch. 12:17 [n] See ch. 11:30
19 [o] See ch. 14:27 [p] [Rom. 15:18, 19] [q] See ch. 1:17
20 [r] ch. 11:18 [s] ch. 22:3; Rom. 10:2; Gal. 1:14
21 [t] [James 1:1] [u] ver. 28 [v] [Rom. 2:28, 29; 1 Cor. 7:19] [w] [Mark 7:5; Gal. 2:14] [x] ch. 6:14; 15:1
23 [y] [ch. 18:18]
24 [z] ver. 26; ch. 24:18; [John 11:55] [y] [See ver. 23 above]
25 [a] See ch. 15:19, 20, 29
26 [z] [See ver. 24 above] [b] [Num. 6:13] [c] [Num. 6:9-12]
27 [c] [See ver. 26 above] [d] See ch. 13:50 [e] ch. 24:18; 26:21
28 [f] ver. 21 [g] See ch. 6:13 [h] ch. 24:6
29 [i] ch. 20:4

into the temple. 30 Then all the city was stirred
up, and the people ran together. They seized
Paul and [j]dragged him out of the temple, and
at once the gates were shut. 31 [j]And as they were
seeking to kill him, word came to the tribune
of [k]the cohort that all Jerusalem was in confusion. 32 [l]He at once took soldiers and centurions
and ran down to them. And when they saw the
tribune and the soldiers, they stopped beating
Paul. 33 Then the tribune came up and arrested
him and ordered him [m]to be bound [n]with two
chains. He inquired who he was and what he
had done. 34 [o]Some in the crowd were shouting one thing, some another. And as he could
not learn the facts because of the uproar, he
ordered him to be brought into [p]the barracks.
35 And when he came to the steps, he was actually carried by the soldiers because of the violence of the crowd, 36 for the mob of the people
followed, crying out, [q]"Away with him!"

Paul Speaks to the People

37 As Paul was about to be brought into the
barracks, he said to the tribune, "May I say
something to you?" And he said, "Do you know
Greek? 38 Are you not [r]the Egyptian, then, who
recently stirred up a revolt and led the four
thousand men of the Assassins out [s]into the
wilderness?" 39 Paul replied, [t]"I am a Jew, from
Tarsus in Cilicia, a citizen of no obscure city.
I beg you, permit me to speak to the people."
40 And when he had given him permission,
Paul, standing on the steps, [u]motioned with
his hand to the people. And when there was a
great hush, he addressed them in [v]the Hebrew
language,[1] saying:

22 [w]"Brothers and fathers, hear the
defense that I now make before you."
2 And when they heard that he was addressing them in [x]the Hebrew language,[2] they
became even more quiet. And he said:
3 [y]"I am a Jew, born in Tarsus in Cilicia, but
brought up in this city, educated [z]at the feet of
[a]Gamaliel[3] [b]according to the strict manner of
the law of our fathers, [c]being zealous for God
[d]as all of you are this day. 4 [e]I persecuted [f]this
Way [g]to the death, binding and delivering to
prison both men and women, 5 as [h]the high
priest and [i]the whole council of elders can bear
me witness. From them I received letters to [j]the
brothers, and I journeyed toward Damascus to
take those also who were there and bring them
in bonds to Jerusalem to be punished.
6 [k]"As I was on my way and drew near to
Damascus, about noon a great light from
heaven suddenly shone around me. 7 And
I fell to the ground and heard a voice saying
to me, 'Saul, Saul, why are you persecuting
me?' 8 And I answered, 'Who are you, Lord?'
And he said to me, 'I am [l]Jesus of Nazareth,
whom you are persecuting.' 9 [m]Now those who
were with me saw the light but did not understand[4] the voice of the one who was speaking
to me. 10 And I said, [n]'What shall I do, Lord?'
And the Lord said to me, 'Rise, and go into
Damascus, and there you will be told all that
is appointed for you to do.' 11 And since I could
not see because of the brightness of that light,
I was led by the hand by those who were with
me, and came into Damascus.
12 "And [o]one Ananias, a devout man [p]accord-
ing to the law, [q]well spoken of by all the Jews
who lived there, 13 [r]came to me, and standing
by me said to me, 'Brother Saul, receive your
sight.' And [s]at that very hour I received my
sight and saw him. 14 And he said, [t]'The God
of our fathers [u]appointed you to know his will,
[v]to see [w]the Righteous One and [x]to hear a voice
from his mouth; 15 for [y]you will be a witness for
him to everyone of what [z]you have seen and
heard. 16 And now why do you wait? [a]Rise and
be baptized and [b]wash away your sins, [c]calling
on his name.'
17 [d]"When I had returned to Jerusalem and
[e]was praying in the temple, I fell into [f]a trance
18 and saw him saying to me, [g]'Make haste and
get out of Jerusalem quickly, because they will
not accept your testimony about me.' 19 And
I said, 'Lord, they themselves know that in one
synagogue after another [h]I imprisoned and
[i]beat those who believed in you. 20 And when
the blood of Stephen [j]your witness was being
shed, [k]I myself was standing by and [l]approving
and [k]watching over the garments of those who

[1] Or *the Hebrew dialect* (probably Aramaic) [2] Or *the Hebrew dialect* (probably Aramaic) [3] Or *city at the feet of Gamaliel, educated*
[4] Or *hear with understanding*

30 [j] ch. 26:21; [2 Kgs. 11:15] **31** [j] [See ver. 30 above] [k] See ch. 10:1 **32** [l] [ch. 23:27] **33** [m] ch. 20:23; [ver. 11] [n] ch. 12:6; [ch. 22:29; 26:29; 28:20; Eph. 6:20; 2 Tim. 1:16] **34** [o] ch. 19:32 [p] ch. 22:24; 23:10 **36** [q] ch. 22:22; [Luke 23:18; John 19:15] **38** [r] [ch. 5:36] [s] Matt. 24:26 **39** [t] ch. 9:11; 22:3 **40** [u] See ch. 12:17 [v] ch. 22:2; 26:14 **Chapter 22** **1** [w] ch. 7:2 **2** [x] ch. 21:40 **3** [y] ch. 9:11; 21:39; Rom. 11:1; 2 Cor. 11:22; Phil. 3:5 [z] Deut. 33:3; 2 Kgs. 4:38; [Luke 10:39] [a] ch. 5:34 [b] ch. 26:5 [c] [John 16:2; Phil. 3:6]; See ch. 21:20 [d] Rom. 10:2 **4** [e] ver. 19; See ch. 8:3 [f] [ch. 5:20]; See ch. 9:2 [g] ch. 26:10; [ver. 20; ch. 8:1] **5** [h] ch. 9:1 [i] Luke 22:66 (Gk.); 1 Tim. 4:14 (Gk.) [j] ch. 28:21 **6** [k] For ver. 6-11, see ch. 9:3-8; 26:12-18 **8** [l] ch. 26:9 **9** [m] [Dan. 10:7]; See ch. 9:7 **10** [n] See ch. 16:30 **12** [o] ch. 9:10 [p] ch. 24:14 [q] ch. 10:22 **13** [r] ch. 9:17 [s] ch. 9:18 **14** [t] See ch. 3:13 [u] ch. 9:15; 26:16 [v] ver. 18; ch. 9:17; 26:16; 1 Cor. 9:1; 15:8; [ver. 15] [w] See ch. 3:14 [x] [Gal. 1:12] **15** [y] ch. 23:11 [z] ver. 14; ch. 4:20 **16** [a] ch. 9:18 [b] 1 Cor. 6:11; Heb. 10:22; [Ps. 51:2]; See ch. 2:38 [c] See ch. 9:14 **17** [d] ch. 9:26; 26:20 [e] ch. 3:1; Luke 18:10 [f] ch. 10:10; 11:5; [2 Cor. 12:1-4] **18** [g] [ch. 9:29] **19** [h] ver. 4 [i] ch. 26:11; See Matt. 10:17 **20** [j] [Rev. 2:13] [k] ch. 7:58 [l] ch. 8:1; [ch. 26:10]; See Rom. 1:32

killed him.' 21 And he said to me, 'Go, for I will
send you [m]far away to the Gentiles.' "

Paul and the Roman Tribune

22 Up to this word they listened to him. Then
they raised their voices and said, [n]"Away with
such a fellow from the earth! For [o]he should
not be allowed to live." 23 And as they were
shouting and throwing off their cloaks and
flinging dust into the air, 24 the tribune
ordered him to be brought into [p]the barracks, saying that he should be [q]examined by
flogging, to find out why they were shouting
against him like this. 25 But when they had
stretched him out for the whips,[1] Paul said
to the centurion who was standing by, "Is it
lawful for you to flog [r]a man who is a Roman
citizen and uncondemned?" 26 When the centurion heard this, he went to the tribune and
said to him, "What are you about to do? For
this man is a Roman citizen." 27 So the tribune came and said to him, "Tell me, are you
a Roman citizen?" And he said, "Yes." 28 The
tribune answered, "I bought this citizenship
for a large sum." Paul said, "But I am a citizen
by birth." 29 So those who were about [s]to examine him withdrew from him immediately, and
the tribune also [t]was afraid, [u]for he realized
that Paul was a Roman citizen and that [v]he
had bound him.

Paul Before the Council

30 But on the next day, [w]desiring to know
the real reason why he was being accused by
the Jews, he unbound him and commanded the
chief priests and all the council to meet, and he
brought Paul down and set him before them.

23 And looking intently at the council,
Paul said, "Brothers, [x]I have lived my
life before God in all good conscience up to
this day." 2 And the high priest [y]Ananias commanded those who stood by him [z]to strike him
on the mouth. 3 Then Paul said to him, "God is
going to strike you, you [a]whitewashed [b]wall!
Are you sitting to judge me according to the
law, and yet [c]contrary to the law you [c]order
me to be struck?" 4 Those who stood by said,
"Would you revile [d]God's high priest?" 5 And
Paul said, [e]"I did not know, brothers, that he
was the high priest, for it is written, [f]'You shall
not speak evil of a ruler of your people.' "
6 Now when Paul perceived that one part
were [g]Sadducees and the other Pharisees, he
cried out in the council, "Brothers, [h]I am a
Pharisee, a son of Pharisees. It is [i]with respect
to the [j]hope and the resurrection of the dead
that I am on trial." 7 And when he had said this,
a dissension arose between the Pharisees and
the Sadducees, and the assembly was divided.
8 For the Sadducees [k]say that there is no resurrection, nor angel, nor spirit, but the Pharisees
acknowledge them all. 9 Then a great clamor
arose, and some of [l]the scribes of the Pharisees'
party stood up and contended sharply, [m]"We
find nothing wrong in this man. What [n]if a
spirit or an angel spoke to him?" 10 And when
the dissension became violent, the tribune,
afraid that Paul would be torn to pieces by
them, commanded the soldiers to go down
and take him away from among them by force
and bring him into [o]the barracks.
11 [p]The following night [q]the Lord stood by
him and said, [r]"Take courage, for [s]as you have

[1] Or *when they had tied him up with leather strips*

22:21–23 The gospel Paul proclaims sometimes incites riots: it challenges the livelihood of some (Acts 19), it stirs up fears of antinomianism in others (Acts 21), and here the Jews of Jerusalem are offended that God is concerned with the Gentiles. As soon as Paul mentions God commissioning him to go to the Gentiles, they are infuriated and want to execute him.

This is the scandal of the gospel. The Jews treasured their status as God's people, and found it difficult to accept that God was "grafting in" those from outside their race (see Rom. 11:17–24). God's grace extends to those we assume are beyond his reach, even to those we despise.

22:22–29 Paul is living out the persecution that Jesus promised would come to some of his followers when he foresaw that families would be bitterly divided on account of his kingdom (Luke 12:51–53). Paul is convinced that God has called him to this vocation, despite the rejection he suffers. Enduring such suffering for the sake of the gospel involves greater love for the very ones who persecute him.

21 [m] See ch. 2:39; 9:15
22 [n] See ch. 21:36 [o] ch. 25:24
24 [p] ch. 21:34; 23:10 [q] ver. 29
25 [r] ch. 16:37
29 [s] ver. 24 [t] ch. 16:38 [u] [ch. 23:27] [v] ch. 21:33
30 [w] ver. 24; ch. 23:28

Chapter 23
1 [x] 2 Cor. 1:12; 2 Tim. 1:3; [ch. 24:16; Job 27:5, 6; 1 Cor. 4:4; 2 Cor. 4:2; 5:11; Heb. 13:18]
2 [y] ch. 24:1 [z] 1 Kgs. 22:24; Lam. 3:30; Mic. 5:1; 2 Cor. 11:20
3 [a] [Matt. 23:27] [b] [Isa. 30:13; Ezek. 13:10-14] [c] Deut. 25:1, 2; See John 7:51
4 [d] [1 Sam. 2:28; Ps. 106:16]
5 [e] [ch. 24:1] [f] Cited from Ex. 22:28
6 [g] See Matt. 22:23 [h] ch. 26:5; Phil. 3:5 [i] ch. 24:15, 21; 26:6-8; 28:20 [j] [ch. 2:26, 27]; See Col. 1:5 **8** [k] Luke 20:27; [1 Cor. 15:12] **9** [l] ch. 4:5; Mark 2:16; Luke 5:30 [m] [ver. 29] [n] [ch. 22:7, 17, 18; John 12:29] **10** [o] ver. 16, 32; ch. 21:34; 22:24 **11** [p] ch. 18:9; 27:23 [q] 1 Sam. 3:10 [r] [2 Tim. 4:17] [s] [ch. 19:21]

testified to the facts about me in Jerusalem, so
you must [t]testify also in Rome."

A Plot to Kill Paul

12 When it was day, [u]the Jews made a plot and
[v]bound themselves by an oath neither to eat
nor drink till they had killed Paul. 13 There
were more than forty who made this conspiracy. 14 They went to the chief priests and
elders and said, "We have strictly bound ourselves by an oath to taste no food till we have
killed Paul. 15 Now therefore you, along with
the council, give notice to the tribune to bring
him down to you, as though you were going
to determine his case more exactly. And we are
ready to kill him before he comes near."

16 Now the son of Paul's sister heard of their
ambush, so he went and entered [w]the barracks
and told Paul. 17 Paul called one of the centurions and said, "Take this young man to the
tribune, for he has something to tell him." 18 So
he took him and brought him to the tribune
and said, "Paul [x]the prisoner called me and
asked me to bring this young man to you, as
he has something to say to you." 19 The tribune
took him by the hand, and going aside asked
him privately, "What is it that you have to tell
me?" 20 And he said, [y]"The Jews have agreed
to ask you to bring Paul down to the council tomorrow, as though they were going to
inquire somewhat more closely about him.
21 But do not be persuaded by them, for more
than forty of their men are lying in ambush
for him, who [z]have bound themselves by an
oath neither to eat nor drink till they have
killed him. And now they are ready, waiting
for your consent." 22 So the tribune dismissed
the young man, charging him, "Tell no one
that you have informed me of these things."

Paul Sent to Felix the Governor

23 Then he called two of the centurions and
said, "Get ready two hundred soldiers, with
seventy horsemen and two hundred spearmen
to go as far as Caesarea at the third hour of the
night.[1] 24 Also provide mounts for Paul to ride
and bring him safely to [a]Felix [b]the governor."
25 And he wrote a letter to this effect:

26 "Claudius Lysias, to [c]his Excellency the
governor Felix, [d]greetings. 27 [e]This man was
seized by the Jews and [f]was about to be killed
by them [f]when I came upon them with the soldiers and rescued him, [g]having learned that he
was a Roman citizen. 28 And [h]desiring to know
the charge for which they were accusing him,
I brought him down to their council. 29 I found
that he was being accused [i]about questions of
their law, but [j]charged with nothing deserving
death or imprisonment. 30 [k]And when it was
disclosed to me [l]that there would be a plot
against the man, I sent him to you at once,
[m]ordering his accusers also to state before you
what they have against him."

31 So the soldiers, according to their instructions, took Paul and brought him by night
to Antipatris. 32 And on the next day they
returned to [n]the barracks, letting the horsemen go on with him. 33 When they had come to
Caesarea and delivered the letter to the governor, they presented Paul also before him. 34 On
reading the letter, he asked what [o]province
he was from. And when he learned [p]that he
was from Cilicia, 35 he said, "I will give you a
hearing [q]when your accusers arrive." And he
commanded him to be guarded in Herod's
[r]praetorium.

Paul Before Felix at Caesarea

24 And [s]after five days the high priest
[t]Ananias came down with some elders
and a spokesman, one Tertullus. They laid
before [u]the governor their case against Paul.
2 And when he had been summoned, Tertullus
began to accuse him, saying:

"Since through you we enjoy much peace,
and since by your foresight, [v]most excellent
Felix, reforms are being made for this nation,
3 in every way and everywhere we accept this
with all gratitude. 4 But, to detain[2] you no further, I beg you in your kindness to hear us
briefly. 5 For we have found this man a plague,
[w]one who stirs up riots among all the Jews
throughout the world and is a ringleader of
[x]the sect of the Nazarenes. 6 [y]He even tried to
profane the temple, but we seized him.[3] 8 By
examining him yourself you will be able to
find out from him about everything of which
we accuse him."

9 The Jews also joined in the charge, affirming that all these things were so.

[1] That is, 9 P.M. [2] Or *weary* [3] Some manuscripts add *and we would have judged him according to our law. 7But the chief captain Lysias came and with great violence took him out of our hands, 8commanding his accusers to come before you.*

11 [t]ch. 22:15 **12** [u]ver. 30 [v]ver. 14, 21 **16** [w]ver. 10, 32 **18** [x]See Eph. 3:1 **20** [y]ver. 14, 15 **21** [z]ver. 12, 14 **24** [a]ver. 26; ch. 24:2; 25:14 [b]ver. 33; ch. 24:1, 10; 26:30; See Luke 20:20 **26** [c]ch. 24:1 [d]See ch. 15:23 **27** [e]ch. 21:27 [f][ch. 21:32, 33] [g][ch. 22:25-29] **28** [h]ch. 22:30 **29** [i]ch. 18:15; 25:19 [j]ch. 25:25; 26:31; 28:18; [ver. 9] **30** [k]ver. 20 [l]ver. 12; See ch. 9:24 [m]ver. 35; [ch. 24:19; 25:16] **32** [n]ver. 10, 16 **34** [o]ch. 25:1 [p]ch. 21:39 **35** [q]ver. 30 [r]See Matt. 27:27
Chapter 24 **1** [s][ch. 21:18, 27, with ver. 11] [t]ch. 23:2 [u]ch. 23:24 **2** [v]ch. 23:26; Luke 1:3 **5** [w]See Luke 23:2 [x]ver. 14; ch. 5:17; 15:5; 26:5; 28:22 **6** [y]ch. 21:27-29

10 And when the governor had nodded to
him to speak, Paul replied:
"Knowing that for many years you have been
a judge over this nation, I cheerfully make my
defense. 11 You can verify that [z]it is not more
than twelve days since I [a]went up [b]to worship
in Jerusalem, 12 and [c]they did not find me disputing with anyone or stirring up a crowd,
either in the temple or in the synagogues or
in the city. 13 [d]Neither can they prove to you
what they now bring up against me. 14 But this
I confess to you, that according to [e]the Way,
which they call [f]a sect, [g]I worship [h]the God of
our fathers, believing everything [i]laid down by
the Law and written in the Prophets, 15 [j]having
[k]a hope in God, which these men themselves
accept, that there will be [l]a resurrection [m]of
both the just and the unjust. 16 So I always
[n]take pains to have a [o]clear conscience toward
both God and man. 17 Now [p]after several years
[q]I came to bring alms to [r]my nation and to
present [s]offerings. 18 While I was doing this,
they found me [t]purified in the temple, without any crowd or tumult. But [u]some Jews from
Asia— 19 [v]they ought to be here before you
and to make an accusation, should they have
anything against me. 20 Or else let these men
themselves say what wrongdoing they found
when I stood before the council, 21 other than
this one thing [w]that I cried out while standing
among them: 'It is with respect to the resurrection of the dead that I am on trial before
you this day.' "

Paul Kept in Custody

22 But Felix, having a rather accurate knowledge of [x]the Way, put them off, saying, "When
Lysias the tribune comes down, I will decide
your case." 23 Then he gave orders to the centurion that he [y]should be kept in custody but
have some liberty, and that [z]none of his friends
should be prevented from attending to his
needs.

24 After some days Felix came with his wife
Drusilla, who was Jewish, and he sent for Paul
and heard him speak about [a]faith [b]in Christ
Jesus. 25 And as he reasoned [c]about righteousness and self-control and the coming judgment, Felix was alarmed and said, "Go away for
the present. [d]When I get an opportunity I will
summon you." 26 At the same time he hoped
[e]that money would be given him by Paul. So
he sent for him often and conversed with him.
27 When two years had elapsed, Felix was succeeded by Porcius [f]Festus. And [g]desiring to do
the Jews a favor, [h]Felix left Paul in prison.

Paul Appeals to Caesar

25 Now three days after Festus had arrived
in [i]the province, he went up to Jerusalem from Caesarea. 2 And the chief priests
and the principal men of the Jews [j]laid out
their case against Paul, and they urged him,
3 asking as a favor against Paul[1] that he summon him to Jerusalem—because [k]they were
planning an ambush to kill him on the way.
4 Festus replied that Paul was being kept at
Caesarea and that he himself intended to go
there shortly. 5 "So," said he, "let the men of
authority among you go down with me, and
if there is anything wrong about the man, let
them bring charges against him."
6 After he stayed among them not more than
eight or ten days, he went down to Caesarea.
And the next day he took his seat on [l]the tribunal and ordered Paul to be brought. 7 When
he had arrived, the Jews who had come down
from Jerusalem stood around him, bringing many and serious charges against him
[m]that they could not prove. 8 Paul argued in
his defense, "Neither [n]against [o]the law of the
Jews, nor against the temple, nor [p]against
Caesar have I committed any offense." 9 But
Festus, [q]wishing to do the Jews a favor, said to
Paul, "Do you wish to go up to Jerusalem and
there be tried on these charges before me?"

[1] Greek *him*

24:10–21 Faced with the hatred of his accusers, Paul does not respond to hatred with hatred. Rather he sees each interaction, and even the whole ordeal of his arrest and imprisonment (of several years), as a chance to proclaim the gospel. He witnesses to the grace of God and warns of the consequences awaiting those who reject it.

25:9–12 Here we see a picture of God's creative sovereignty as he redirects injustice for his good purposes. Paul is embroiled in a legal squabble that has kept him

11 [z]See ver. 1 [a]ch. 8:27; John 12:20 [b]ch. 20:16
12 [c][ch. 25:8]
13 [d]ch. 25:7
14 [e]ver. 22; See ch. 9:2 [f]ver. 5 [g]2 Tim. 1:3; [ch. 27:23; Luke 1:74; Rom. 1:9; Heb. 9:14; 12:28] [h]See ch. 3:13; 22:3 [i]ch. 26:22; 28:23; [Rom. 3:21]

15 [j]See ch. 23:6 [k]Titus 2:13; [Gal. 5:5] [l]Luke 14:14 [m]See Dan. 12:2 **16** [n][1 Tim. 4:7, 15] [o]1 Cor. 10:32; Phil. 1:10; [Jude 24]; See ch. 23:1 **17** [p][ch. 20:31] [q]Rom. 15:25-28, 31; 1 Cor. 16:1-3; 2 Cor. 8:1-4; 9:1, 2, 12; [Gal. 2:10] [r]ch. 26:4; 28:19 [s][ver. 11; ch. 20:16] **18** [t]ch. 21:26; 26:21 [u]ch. 21:27 **19** [v]See ch. 23:30 **21** [w]See ch. 23:6 **22** [x]ver. 14; See ch. 9:2 **23** [y][ch. 28:16] [z][ch. 27:3] **24** [a]See ch. 20:21 [b]Gal. 2:16; [Rom. 3:24] **25** [c][Titus 2:12, 13] [d]ch. 17:32; [2 Tim. 4:2] **26** [e][ver. 17] **27** [f]ch. 25:1; 26:24 [g]ch. 25:9; [ch. 12:3; Mark 15:15] [h]ch. 25:14; See Luke 21:12 **Chapter 25** **1** [i]ch. 23:34 **2** [j]ver. 15 **3** [k]See ch. 9:24 **6** [l]ver. 10, 17; See Matt. 27:19 **7** [m]ch. 24:13 **8** [n][ch. 24:12; 28:17]; See ch. 6:13 [o]John 7:19; 19:7 [p]John 19:12 **9** [q]ch. 24:27

10 But Paul said, "I am standing before Caesar's
[r]tribunal, where I ought to be tried. To the
Jews I have done no wrong, as you yourself
know very well. 11 If then I am a wrongdoer and
have committed anything for which I deserve
to die, I do not seek to escape death. But if
there is nothing to their charges against me,
no one can give me up to them. [s]I appeal to
Caesar." 12 Then Festus, when he had conferred
with his council, answered, "To Caesar you
have appealed; to Caesar you shall go."

Paul Before Agrippa and Bernice

13 Now when some days had passed, Agrippa
the king and Bernice arrived at Caesarea and
greeted Festus. 14 And as they stayed there
many days, Festus laid Paul's case before the
king, saying, [t]"There is a man left prisoner
by Felix, 15 and when I was at Jerusalem, the
chief priests and the elders of the Jews laid out
their case [u]against him, asking for a sentence
of condemnation against him. 16 [v]I answered
them that it was not the custom of the Romans
to give up anyone [w]before the accused met the
accusers face to face and had opportunity to
make his defense concerning the charge laid
against him. 17 [x]So when they came together
here, I made no delay, but on the next day
took my seat on [y]the tribunal and ordered
the man to be brought. 18 When the accusers stood up, they brought no charge in his
case of such evils as I supposed. 19 Rather they
[z]had certain points of dispute with him about
their own religion and about [a]a certain Jesus,
who was dead, but whom Paul asserted to
be alive. 20 Being at a loss how to investigate
these questions, I [b]asked whether he wanted
to go to Jerusalem and be tried there regarding them. 21 But [c]when Paul had appealed to
be kept in custody for the decision of [d]the
emperor, I ordered him to be held until I could
send him to Caesar." 22 Then [e]Agrippa said to
Festus, "I would like to hear the man myself."
"Tomorrow," said he, "you will hear him."

23 So on the next day [f]Agrippa and Bernice
came with great pomp, and they entered the
audience hall with the military tribunes and
the prominent men of the city. Then, at the
command of Festus, Paul was brought in.
24 And Festus said, "King Agrippa and all who
are present with us, you see this man about
whom [g]the whole Jewish people petitioned
me, both in Jerusalem and here, [h]shouting that
he ought not to live any longer. 25 But I found
that [i]he had done nothing deserving death.
And [j]as he himself appealed to [k]the emperor,
I decided to go ahead and send him. 26 But
I have nothing definite to write to my lord
about him. Therefore I have brought him
before you all, and especially before you, King
Agrippa, so that, after we have examined him,
I may have something to write. 27 For it seems
to me unreasonable, in sending a prisoner, not
to indicate the charges against him."

Paul's Defense Before Agrippa

26 So [l]Agrippa said to Paul, "You have permission to speak for yourself." Then
Paul stretched out his hand and made his
defense:

2 "I consider myself fortunate that it is before
you, King Agrippa, I am going to make my
defense today [m]against all the accusations of the
Jews, 3 especially because you are familiar with
all the [n]customs and [o]controversies of the Jews.
Therefore I beg you to listen to me patiently.

4 [p]"My manner of life from my youth, spent
from the beginning among [q]my own nation
and in Jerusalem, is known by all the Jews.
5 They have known for a long time, if they

10 [r] ver. 6, 17
11 [s] ch. 26:32; 28:19
14 [t] ch. 24:27
15 [u] ver. 2, 3
16 [v] ver. 4, 5 [w] [John 7:51]; See ch. 23:30
17 [x] ver. 7, 24 [y] ver. 6, 10
19 [z] ch. 18:15; 23:29 [a] [ch. 17:18]
20 [b] ver. 9
21 [c] See ver. 11 [d] ver. 25
22 [e] See ch. 9:15
23 [f] ver. 13; ch. 26:30
24 [g] ver. 2, 7
24 [h] ch. 22:22
25 [i] See ch. 23:29 [j] ver. 11, 12 [k] ver. 21

Chapter 26
1 [l] See ch. 9:15
2 [m] ch. 25:7, 19; [ver. 7]
3 [n] See ch. 6:14 [o] See ch. 18:15
4 [p] [Gal. 1:13] [q] ch. 24:17; 28:19

imprisoned in Caesarea for two years (24:27), even while he yearns to bring the gospel to Rome (19:21). But in God's providence this convoluted legal squabble becomes the means for the gospel to reach Rome. When Festus attempts to transfer Paul out of his jurisdiction, Paul seizes the opportunity: taking advantage of his right as a Roman citizen, Paul appeals directly to the emperor, guaranteeing a journey to Rome.

It is unlikely that Paul ever imagined that his journey to Rome would occur in chains. But Paul was confident that God would fulfill his promise (23:11), and he knew that God's sovereignty works even through convoluted legal structures. Knowing that God is in control and that his gospel will ultimately triumph allows us, like Paul, to take creative risks for God and trust him in the times of confusion and suffering.

26:6–8 The central tenet of Paul's faith, and one that continually causes trouble throughout Acts, is Christ's resurrection. It was scorned in Athens (17:32) and fre-

are willing to testify, that [r]according to the
strictest [s]party of our [t]religion I have lived as
[u]a Pharisee. 6 And now I stand here on trial
because of my hope in [v]the promise made by
God to our fathers, 7 [w]to which [x]our twelve
tribes hope to [y]attain, as they earnestly worship
night and day. And for this hope [z]I am accused
by Jews, O king! 8 Why is it thought [a]incredible
by any of you that God raises the dead?

9 [b]"I myself was convinced that I ought to do
many things in opposing the name of [c]Jesus
of Nazareth. 10 [d]And I did so in Jerusalem. I not
only locked up many of the saints in prison
after receiving authority [e]from the chief
priests, but [f]when they were put to death I cast
my vote against them. 11 And [g]I punished them
often in all the synagogues and tried to make
them [h]blaspheme, and [i]in raging fury against
them I [j]persecuted them even to foreign cities.

Paul Tells of His Conversion

12 "In this connection [k]I journeyed to Damascus with the authority and commission
of the chief priests. 13 At midday, O king, I saw
on the way a light from heaven, brighter than
the sun, that shone around me and those who
journeyed with me. 14 And when we had all
fallen to the ground, I heard a voice saying
to me [l]in the Hebrew language,[1] 'Saul, Saul,
why are you persecuting me? It is hard for
you to kick against the goads.' 15 And I said,
'Who are you, Lord?' And the Lord said, 'I am
Jesus whom you are persecuting. 16 But rise
and [m]stand upon your feet, for I have appeared
to you for this purpose, [n]to appoint you as a
servant and witness to the things in which
you have seen me and to those in which I will
appear to you, 17 [o]delivering you from your
people and from the Gentiles—[p]to whom
I [q]am sending you 18 [r]to open their eyes, so
that they may turn from darkness to light and
from [s]the power of Satan to God, that they may
receive [t]forgiveness of sins and [u]a place among
those who are sanctified [v]by faith in me.'

19 "Therefore, O King Agrippa, I was not
disobedient to [w]the heavenly vision, 20 but
declared first [x]to those in Damascus, [y]then
in Jerusalem and throughout all the region
of Judea, and also [z]to the Gentiles, that they
should [a]repent and [b]turn to God, performing
deeds [c]in keeping with their repentance. 21 For
this reason [d]the Jews seized me in the temple
and tried to kill me. 22 [e]To this day I have had
the help that comes from God, and so [f]I stand
here testifying both to small and great, saying
nothing but what [g]the prophets and Moses
said would come to pass: 23 [h]that the Christ
[i]must suffer and that, [j]by being the first [k]to rise

[1] Or *the Hebrew dialect* (probably Aramaic)

quently called into question by the Jews. But Paul recognizes that the resurrection is the hope for which all of the Old Testament prophets waited and watched (Heb. 11:13, 39).

God has always been about the business of bringing life from the dead, whether by creating life out of nothing (Gen. 1:1; Heb. 11:3), by giving children to barren women (Gen. 21:1; 25:21; 1 Sam. 2:21; Heb. 11:12), or by using his prophets to literally raise the dead (1 Kings 17:19–22; 2 Kings 4:34–35). Why, Paul asks, is it thought incredible that God raises the dead, when he has always had the power to do so? In the resurrection of Christ, God's power to raise the dead has been clearly manifested. And by believing in him, we can share in his resurrection (Rom. 6:5; Phil. 3:10). This reality gives us a sure hope for eternity and therefore should permeate our lives even today.

26:12–18 Here Paul relates additional details about his conversion on the Damascus road. He recalls Jesus expressing the gospel message as a call to turn from darkness and the power of Satan to the light of God. God's light has overcome Satan's darkness (see John 1:5), even that darkness which inhabits each one of us. God offers defeat of the powers of darkness to those still under their control. He offers not merely self-help but the washing away of sins to all who will trust in him.

26:22–23 Paul bases his hope on God's raising of Jesus, which he sees as the culminating fulfillment of God's promises through the Law and the Prophets (see also vv. 6–8). For Paul, the resurrection of Jesus both confirms God's faithfulness and power to fulfill his promises, and provides the impetus for the spread of God's gospel and Spirit to Jews and Gentiles over all the earth (v. 23; cf. 1 Cor. 15:1–28).

5 [r]ch. 22:3 [s]See ch. 24:5 [t]James 1:26, 27 [u]ch. 23:6
6 [v]See ch. 13:32
7 [w][ch. 2:33; Heb. 10:36; 11:13, 39] [x]Matt. 19:28; Luke 22:30; James 1:1, Rev. 21:12; [Ezra 6:17] [y]Phil. 3:11 [z]ver. 2
8 [a][ch. 17:3; 1 Cor. 15:12]
9 [b]1 Tim. 1:13; [John 16:2]; See ch. 3:17 [c]ch. 22:8
10 [d]See ch. 8:3 [e]ver. 12; ch. 9:1, 2, 14, 21; 22:4, 5 [f]See ch. 22:20
11 [g]ch. 22:19 [h]See ch. 13:45 [i]ch. 9:1 [j]ch. 22:5
12 [k]For ver. 12-18, see ch. 9:3-8; 22:6-11
14 [l]ch. 21:40; 22:2
16 [m]Ezek. 2:1; Dan. 10:11 [n]See ch. 22:14, 15
17 [o][ch. 12:11; 1 Chr. 16:35; Jer. 1:8, 19; 15:20] [p]See ch. 9:15 [q][Rom. 11:13; 1 Tim. 2:7]
18 [r]Isa. 35:5; 42:7 [s]See Luke 22:53; 1 Cor. 5:5 [t]See ch. 5:31 [u]See ch. 20:32 [v][ch. 15:9; 2 Thess. 2:13]
19 [w]ver. 13
20 [x]ch. 9:19, 20 [y]ch. 9:26-29; 22:17-20 [z]See ch. 13:46 [a]See ch. 2:38 [b]See ch. 14:15 [c]Matt. 3:8; Luke 3:8
21 [d]ch. 21:27, 30, 31; 24:18
22 [e]2 Cor. 1:10; [Heb. 13:5, 6] [f][Eph. 6:13] [g]See ch. 10:43; 24:14
23 [h][Luke 24:26; Heb. 2:10]; See ch. 3:18 [i][John 12:34] [j]1 Cor. 15:20, 23; Col. 1:18; Rev. 1:5 [k]Rom. 1:4

from the dead, [l]he would proclaim [m]light both
to our people and to the Gentiles."
24 And as he was saying these things in his
defense, Festus said with a loud voice, "Paul,
[n]you are out of your mind; your great learning is driving you out of your mind." 25 But
Paul said, "I am not out of my mind, [o]most
excellent Festus, but I am speaking [p]true and
[q]rational words. 26 For [r]the king knows about
these things, and to him I speak boldly. For
I am persuaded that none of these things has
escaped his notice, for this has not been done
in a corner. 27 King Agrippa, do you believe
the prophets? I know that you believe." 28 And
Agrippa said to Paul, "In a short time would
you persuade me to be [s]a Christian?"[1] 29 And
Paul said, "Whether short or long, I would to
God that not only you but also all who hear me
this day [t]might become such as I am—except
for [u]these chains."
30 Then the king rose, and [v]the governor and
Bernice and those who were sitting with them.
31 And when they had withdrawn, they said
to one another, [w]"This man is doing nothing
to deserve death or imprisonment." 32 And
Agrippa said to Festus, [x]"This man could have
been set [y]free if he had not appealed [z]to Caesar."

Paul Sails for Rome

27 And when it was decided [a]that [b]we
should sail for Italy, they delivered
Paul and some other prisoners to a centurion
of the Augustan [c]Cohort named Julius. 2 And
embarking in a ship of Adramyttium, which
was about to sail to the ports along the coast
of Asia, we put to sea, accompanied by [d]Aris-
tarchus, a Macedonian from Thessalonica.
3 The next day we put in at Sidon. And [e]Julius
[f]treated Paul kindly and [g]gave him leave to go
to his friends and be cared for. 4 And putting
out to sea from there we sailed under the lee
of Cyprus, because the winds were against us.
5 And when we had sailed across the open sea
along the coast of Cilicia and Pamphylia, we
came to Myra in Lycia. 6 There the centurion
found [h]a ship of Alexandria sailing for Italy
and put us on board. 7 We sailed slowly for a
number of days and arrived with difficulty off
Cnidus, and as the wind did not allow us to
go farther, we sailed under the lee of Crete off
Salmone. 8 Coasting along it with difficulty, we
came to a place called Fair Havens, near which
was the city of Lasea.
9 Since much time had passed, and the voyage was now dangerous because even [i]the Fast[2]
was already over, Paul advised them, 10 saying,
"Sirs, I perceive that the voyage will be with
[j]injury and much loss, not only of the cargo
and the ship, but also of our lives." 11 But the
centurion paid more attention to [k]the pilot
and to the owner of the ship than to what Paul
said. 12 And because the harbor was not suitable
to spend the winter in, the majority decided to
put out to sea from there, on the chance that
somehow they could reach Phoenix, a harbor
of Crete, facing both southwest and north-
west, and spend the winter there.

The Storm at Sea

13 Now when the south wind blew gently, supposing that they had obtained their purpose,
they weighed anchor and sailed along Crete,
close to the shore. 14 But soon a tempestuous
wind, called the northeaster, [l]struck down
from the land. 15 And when the ship was caught
and could not face the wind, we gave way to it
and were driven along. 16 Running under the
lee of a small island called Cauda,[3] we managed
with difficulty to secure the ship's boat. 17 After
hoisting it up, they used supports to undergird
the ship. Then, fearing that they would [m]run
aground on the Syrtis, they lowered the gear,[4]
and thus they were driven along. 18 Since we
were violently storm-tossed, they began the

[1] Or *In a short time you would persuade me to act like a Christian!* [2] That is, the Day of Atonement [3] Some manuscripts *Clauda* [4] That is, the sea-anchor (or possibly the mainsail)

23 [l] [Eph. 2:17] [m] ver. 18; See Luke 2:32
24 [n] ch. 12:15; [ver. 8; ch. 17:32; 2 Kgs. 9:11; Jer. 29:26; Mark 3:21; John 10:20; 1 Cor. 1:23; 2:14; 4:10]
25 [o] See ch. 24:2 [p] [2 Pet. 1:16] [q] [2 Cor. 5:13]
26 [r] [ver. 3]
28 [s] ch. 11:26; 1 Pet. 4:16
29 [t] [1 Cor. 7:7] [u] See ch. 21:33

27:13–44 Compared to other parts of Paul's journeys in Acts, Luke goes into great detail about the storm at sea. This journey shows God's sovereign purposes and underscores that God can be trusted to fulfill his promises: God not only led and called Paul but protected him and was indeed an intricate part of every step of Paul's voyage. Paul announces to the other sailors and prisoners what was revealed to him, that despite an imminent shipwreck, they will reach Rome without loss of life (vv. 21–26). Sure enough, the ship crashes against an island, but no one dies (vv. 39–44). Paul had taken God at his word, even as the storm dragged on and the professional sailors despaired.

30 [v] See ch. 23:24 **31** [w] See ch. 23:29 **32** [x] ch. 28:18 [y] ch. 25:11; 28:19 [z] See ch. 9:15 **Chapter 27** **1** [a] ch. 25:12, 25 [b] See ch. 16:10 [c] See ch. 10:1 **2** [d] See ch. 19:29 **3** [e] ver. 43 [f] ch. 28:2 [g] [ch. 24:23; 28:16, 30] **6** [h] ch. 28:11 **9** [i] Lev. 16:29-31; 23:27-29; Num. 29:7 **10** [j] ver. 21 **11** [k] Rev. 18:17 (Gk.) **14** [l] [Mark 4:37] **17** [m] ver. 26, 29

next day [n]to jettison the cargo. 19 And on the
third day they threw the ship's tackle overboard with their own hands. 20 When neither
sun nor stars appeared for many days, and no
small tempest lay on us, all hope of our being
saved was at last abandoned.

21 Since they had been without food for a long
time, Paul stood up among them and said,
"Men, [o]you should have listened to me and
not have set sail from Crete and incurred this
[o]injury and loss. 22 Yet now I urge you to [p]take
heart, for there will be no loss of life among
you, but only of the ship. 23 For this very night
[q]there [r]stood before me [s]an angel of the God [t]to
whom I belong and [u]whom I worship, 24 and
he said, 'Do not be afraid, Paul; [v]you must
stand before Caesar. And behold, [w]God has
granted you all those who sail with you.' 25 So
take heart, men, for I have faith in God that it
will be exactly as I have been told. 26 But [x]we
must [y]run aground on some island."

27 When the fourteenth night had come, as
we were being driven across the Adriatic Sea,
about midnight the sailors suspected that they
were nearing land. 28 So they took a sounding
and found twenty fathoms.[1] A little farther on
they took a sounding again and found fifteen
fathoms.[2] 29 And fearing that we might [z]run
on the rocks, they let down four anchors from
the stern and prayed for day to come. 30 And
as the sailors were seeking to escape from the
ship, and had lowered [a]the ship's boat into the
sea under pretense of laying out anchors from
the bow, 31 Paul said to the centurion and the
soldiers, "Unless these men stay in the ship,
you cannot be saved." 32 Then the soldiers cut
away the ropes of the ship's boat and let it go.

33 As day was about to dawn, Paul urged
them all to take some food, saying, "Today is
the fourteenth day that you have continued
in suspense and without food, having taken
nothing. 34 Therefore I urge you to take some
food. For it will give you strength,[3] for [b]not
a hair is to perish from the head of any of
you." 35 And when he had said these things,
he took bread, and [c]giving thanks to God in
the presence of all he broke it and began to
eat. 36 Then they all [d]were encouraged and ate
some food themselves. 37 (We were in all 276[4]
[e]persons in the ship.) 38 And when they had
eaten enough, they lightened the ship, [f]throw-
ing out the wheat into the sea.

The Shipwreck

39 Now when it was day, [g]they did not recognize the land, but they noticed a bay with
a beach, on which they planned if possible
to run the ship ashore. 40 So they cast off the
anchors and left them in the sea, at the same
time loosening the ropes that tied the rudders. Then hoisting the foresail to the wind
they made for the beach. 41 But striking a reef,[5]
[h]they ran the vessel aground. The bow stuck
and remained immovable, and the stern was
being broken up by the surf. 42 [i]The soldiers'
plan was to kill the prisoners, lest any should
swim away and escape. 43 But the centurion,
[j]wishing to save Paul, kept them from carrying
out their plan. He ordered those who could
swim to jump overboard first and make for the
land, 44 and the rest on planks or on pieces of
the ship. And so it was that [k]all were brought
safely to land.

Paul on Malta

28 After we were brought safely through,
[l]we then learned that [m]the island was
called Malta. 2 [n]The native people[6] showed
us unusual [o]kindness, for they kindled a fire
and welcomed us all, because it had begun to
rain and was cold. 3 When Paul had gathered
a bundle of sticks and put them on the fire,
a viper came out because of the heat and fastened on his hand. 4 When [p]the native people
saw the creature hanging from his hand, they
said to one another, [q]"No doubt this man is a
murderer. Though he has escaped from the
sea, [r]Justice[7] has not allowed him to live." 5 He,
however, [s]shook off the creature into the fire

[1] About 120 feet; a fathom (Greek *orguia*) was about 6 feet or 2 meters [2] About 90 feet (see previous note) [3] Or *For it is for your deliverance* [4] Some manuscripts *seventy-six*, or *about seventy-six* [5] Or *sandbank*, or *crosscurrent*; Greek *place between two seas* [6] Greek *barbaroi* (that is, non-Greek speakers); also verse 4 [7] Or *justice*

God is the true actor behind the scenes. Paul acts as a messenger of God's promise, but he displays no power to quiet the storm, as Jesus did (Luke 8:22–25). Paul was first a recipient of God's grace, and now is an agent of grace to others, but God is the ultimate deliverer.

18[n] Jonah 1:5; [ver. 38]
21[o] ver. 10
22[p] ver. 25, 36
23[q] ch. 18:9; 23:11 [r] 2 Tim. 4:17 [s] See ch. 8:26 [t] Ps. 119:94; Dan. 5:23 [u] [Dan. 6:16]; See ch. 24:14 **24**[v] ch. 23:11 [w] [Gen. 18:26; 19:21, 29; Ezek. 14:14] **26**[x] ch. 28:1 [y] ver. 17, 29 **29**[z] ver. 17, 26 **30**[a] ver. 16 **34**[b] 1 Sam. 14:45; 2 Sam. 14:11; 1 Kgs. 1:52; Luke 21:18; [Matt. 10:30] **35**[c] See Matt. 15:36 **36**[d] ver. 22 **37**[e] ch. 2:41; 7:14; Rom. 13:1; 1 Pet. 3:20 **38**[f] [ver. 18] **39**[g] [ch. 28:1] **41**[h] [2 Cor. 11:25] **42**[i] [ch. 12:19] **43**[j] ver. 3 **44**[k] ver. 22 **Chapter 28** **1**[l] [ch. 27:39] [m] ch. 27:26 **2**[n] ver. 4; Rom. 1:14; 1 Cor. 14:11; Col. 3:11 [o] ch. 27:3 **4**[p] ver. 2 [q] [Job 4:7; Luke 13:2, 4; John 9:2] [r] [Num. 32:23; Amos 5:19; 9:3] **5**[s] Mark 16:18; Luke 10:19

and suffered no harm. 6 They were waiting for him to swell up or suddenly fall down dead. But when they had waited a long time and saw no misfortune come to him, [t]they changed their minds and [u]said that he was a god.

7 Now in the neighborhood of that place were lands belonging to the chief man of the island, named Publius, who received us and entertained us hospitably for three days. 8 It happened that the father of Publius lay sick with fever and dysentery. And Paul visited him and [v]prayed, and [w]putting his hands on him healed him. 9 And when this had taken place, the rest of the people on the island who had diseases also came and were cured. 10 They also honored us greatly,[1] and when we were about to sail, they put on board whatever we needed.

Paul Arrives at Rome

11 After three months we set sail in [x]a ship that had wintered in the island, a ship of Alexandria, with the twin gods[2] as a figurehead. 12 Putting in at Syracuse, we stayed there for three days. 13 And from there we made a circuit and arrived at Rhegium. And after one day a south wind sprang up, and on the second day we came to Puteoli. 14 There we found [y]brothers[3] and were invited to stay with them for seven days. And so we came to Rome. 15 And [y]the brothers there, when they heard about us, came as far as the Forum of Appius and Three Taverns to meet us. On seeing them, [z]Paul thanked God and took courage. 16 And when we came into Rome, [a]Paul was allowed to stay by himself, with the soldier who guarded him.

Paul in Rome

17 After three days he called together the local leaders of the Jews, and when they had gathered, he said to them, "Brothers, [b]though I had done nothing against our people or [c]the customs of our fathers, yet I was delivered as a prisoner from Jerusalem into the hands of the Romans. 18 When they had examined me, they [d]wished to set me at liberty, [e]because there was no reason for the death penalty in my case. 19 But because the Jews objected, I was compelled [f]to appeal to Caesar—though I had no charge to bring against [g]my nation. 20 For this reason, therefore, I have asked to see you and speak with you, since it is [h]because of [i]the hope of Israel that I am wearing [j]this [k]chain." 21 And they said to him, "We have received no letters from Judea about you, and none of [l]the brothers coming here has reported or spoken any evil about you. 22 But we desire to hear from you what your views are, for with regard to this [m]sect we know that everywhere [n]it is spoken against."

23 When they had appointed a day for him, they came to him at his lodging in greater numbers. From morning till evening [o]he expounded to them, testifying to [p]the kingdom of God and [q]trying to convince them about Jesus [r]both from the Law of Moses and from the Prophets. 24 And [s]some were convinced by what he said, but others disbelieved. 25 And disagreeing among themselves, they departed after Paul had made one statement: [t]"The Holy Spirit was right in saying to your fathers through Isaiah the prophet:

[1] Greek *honored us with many honors* [2] That is, the Greek gods Castor and Pollux [3] Or *brothers and sisters*; also verses 15, 21

6 [t][ch. 14:11, 19] [u][ch. 8:10; 14:11]
8 [v]ch. 9:40; [James 5:14, 15] [w]See Mark 5:23
11 [x]ch. 27:6
14 [y]See John 21:23
15 [y][See ver. 14 above] [z][Rom. 1:9-12]
16 [a][ch. 24:23; 27:3]
17 [b][ch. 25:8] [c]ch. 6:14; 15:1; 21:21
18 [d]ch. 26:31, 32 [e]See ch. 23:29
19 [f]ch. 25:11; 26:32 [g]ch. 24:17; 26:4
20 [h]See ch. 23:6 [i][Luke 2:25] [j]ch. 26:29 [k]Eph. 6:20; 2 Tim. 1:16; See ch. 21:33; Phil. 1:7
21 [l]ch. 22:5
22 [m]See ch. 24:5 [n]Luke 2:34; [1 Pet. 2:12; 3:16; 4:14, 16]
23 [o][ch. 17:2, 3] [p]ver. 31 [q][ch. 19:8] [r]ch. 8:35; 24:14; 26:22
24 [s][ch. 14:4; 17:4, 5; 19:9; 23:7]
25 [t]Matt. 15:7

28:23 As in John 5:39–47 and Luke 24:25–27, 44, we are once again encouraged to see that the entire Bible, even the parts that come before Christ's birth, are about Christ himself. He is the point of the Bible. The Bible is fundamentally a single book with a single message of God's redemption through his Son of lost and rebellious sinners. Everything in Scripture, from Genesis to Revelation, contributes to this overarching message.

28:30–31 Luke ends his account on a note of triumph, showing Paul in the capital of the world as he preaches the gospel "without hindrance" to all who will hear it.

Luke and Paul both knew that the mission that Christ had laid out was not fully accomplished. Paul mentions in his letters that he intended to travel beyond Rome to even more distant Spain (Rom. 15:24). In its early form, however, Jesus has fulfilled his promise (Acts 1:8): the message of salvation has begun to reach the "end of the earth," and because God has proven faithful to bring his gospel to Rome, we can trust that he will continue to spread it abroad. Acts is intentionally open-ended, inviting our participation in God's mission, as he overcomes opposition to bring his word of forgiveness to all people.

26 [u]"'Go to this people, and say,
[v]"You will indeed hear but never understand,
and you will indeed see but never perceive."
27 [w]For this people's heart has grown dull,
and with their ears they can barely hear,
and their eyes they have closed;
lest they should see with their eyes
and hear with their ears
and understand with their heart
and [x]turn, and I would heal them.'

28 Therefore let it be known to you that
[y]this [z]salvation of God [a]has been sent to the
Gentiles; [b]they will listen."[1]
30 He lived there two whole years at his own
expense,[2] and [c]welcomed all who came to
him, 31 [d]proclaiming [e]the kingdom of God and
teaching about the Lord Jesus Christ [f]with all
boldness and [g]without hindrance.

[1] Some manuscripts add verse 29: *And when he had said these words, the Jews departed, having much dispute among themselves*
[2] Or *in his own hired dwelling*

The book ends with Paul preaching the kingdom of God with "boldness and without hindrance." This is a fitting summary and conclusion to the book. The gospel of Jesus Christ goes from Jerusalem to the ends of the earth, not without trouble, but without hindrance. God's purposes will have their way. The book of Acts tells the story of Jesus building his church by his grace and gives us confidence that he will continue so to build it until he returns.

26 [u] Cited from Isa. 6:9, 10 [v] Matt. 13:14, 15; Mark 4:12; [Luke 8:10] **27** [w] [John 12:40; Rom. 11:8] [x] See Luke 22:32 **28** [y] ch. 13:26 [z] Ps. 67:2; Isa. 40:5; Luke 2:30; 3:6; [Rom. 11:11] [a] See ch. 13:46 [b] John 10:16; [ch. 13:48; Matt. 8:11; 21:43] **30** [c] [Phil. 1:13] **31** [d] [ch. 8:12; 20:25] [e] ver. 23; See Matt. 12:28; 13:19 [f] See ch. 4:29 [g] [Phil. 1:12, 13; 2 Tim. 2:9]

Introduction to Romans

Author, Recipients, and Date

The apostle Paul wrote to the Jewish and Gentile Christians in Rome. He probably did this while he was in Corinth on his third missionary journey, in A.D. 57 (Acts 20:1–3).

The Gospel in Romans

In the sweep of the New Testament, Romans is the first epistle encountered. This is fitting, as it builds on the Old Testament, explains the saving work of Jesus reported in the Gospels, and unpacks many of the teachings that were foundational to the churches that arose in Acts. In these respects, Romans flows naturally from the biblical books preceding it.

Yet the epistle to the Romans holds a prominent place among all other biblical writings. First, it played a direct role in the conversion of such key figures in church history as Augustine, Martin Luther, and John Wesley. John Calvin wrote that Romans is the doorway to the treasure of all of Scripture.

Second, Romans is widely regarded as the most complete summary of the gospel message and Christian doctrine found in any single biblical book. It is certainly Paul's most extended and concentrated presentation of God's saving work in Christ.

Third, its overarching theme is the gospel message. That message is not merely useful information: it is no less than "the power of God for salvation to everyone who believes" (1:16). As God's sovereign word created the world (Genesis 1), so by God's message about his Son a creative and renewing "righteousness of God is revealed from faith for faith" (Rom. 1:17). To read Romans is to encounter a message able to elicit "the obedience of faith" (1:5; 16:26) in Jesus Christ from start to finish. This brings the righteousness Jesus established by his life and saving death to the sinner, to the church, and by extension to the whole world. If the mission of Jesus' followers is to carry his good news to all places, Romans is a key biblical book to take to heart.

Is there any way to summarize such a revolutionary, rich, and wide-ranging epistle? One approach to discovering what is most central in Romans is to note which significant nouns are used most frequently. Paul used these three words most often in Romans (word counts based on the original Greek text):

> *God* (153 times). He is the subject around whom the entire epistle revolves. Romans lifts our gaze from the tyranny of our self-absorption to the grandeur of a God of kindness (2:4), faithfulness (3:3), truth (3:4), righteousness (3:5), and glory (3:7), to name just a few of his attributes. Yes, he is severe in judgment (11:22), yet through faith he is so dear

that his people know him as "Abba" (8:15), their caring heavenly Father. They have "peace with God," they stand in his grace, and they "rejoice in hope of the glory of God" (5:1–2).

Law (74 times). Cultures may be diverse, but Scripture views humans of all cultures as having one thing profoundly in common: "all have sinned and fall short of the glory of God" (3:23). We have all broken God's "holy and righteous and good" commandment (7:12). Yet Romans trumpets that in sending "his own Son," God fulfilled what the law demanded but we humans could not furnish (8:3–4). Believers are liberated "in Christ Jesus from the law of sin and death" (8:2).

Christ (65 times; see also *Lord*, 43 times; *Jesus*, 36 times). The author of Romans is a slave or servant of Christ (1:1). His readers are "called to belong to Jesus Christ" (1:6). Next to "Amen," "Christ" is the last word of Romans (16:27). Through him God will "graciously give . . . all things" he has promised to those who are changed by the gospel message (8:32).

Romans is not only about weighty words piling up into lofty teachings. It is also about ethics—how to live. No chapter is without gospel-informed implications for daily living, with chapters 12–15 most suggestive in this regard. Similarly, Romans testifies repeatedly to divine love. We are creatures of devotion, created to know and to love the God who made us. Through the love unleashed by the gospel, poured into our hearts by the Holy Spirit (5:5), we join in the doxologies that dot the epistle (see 1:25; 9:5; 11:36), such as this one at the close: "to the only wise God be glory forevermore through Jesus Christ! Amen" (16:27).

Outline

I. The Gospel as the Revelation of God's Righteousness (1:1–17)

II. God's Righteousness in His Wrath against Sinners (1:18–3:20)

III. The Saving Righteousness of God (3:21–4:25)

IV. Hope as a Result of Righteousness by Faith (5:1–8:39)

V. God's Righteousness to Israel and to the Gentiles (9:1–11:36)

VI. God's Righteousness in Everyday Life (12:1–15:13)

VII. The Extension of God's Righteousness through Paul's Mission (15:14–16:23)

VIII. Final Summary of the Gospel of God's Righteousness (16:25–27)

The Letter of Paul to the

Romans

Greeting

1 Paul,[a] a servant[1] of Christ Jesus,[b] called
to be an apostle,[c] set apart for the gospel
of God, 2 which[d] he promised beforehand
[e] through his prophets in the holy Scriptures,
3 concerning his Son,[f] who was descended
from David[2][g] according to the flesh 4 and[h] was
declared to be the Son of God[i] in power according to the Spirit of holiness by his resurrection
from the dead, Jesus Christ our Lord, 5 through
whom[j] we have received grace and[k] apostleship[l] to bring about the obedience of faith for
the sake of his name[m] among all the nations,
6 including you who are[n] called to belong to
Jesus Christ,

7 To all those in Rome who are loved by God
and called to be saints:

[o] Grace to you and peace from God our Father
and the Lord Jesus Christ.

Longing to Go to Rome

8 First,[p] I thank my God through Jesus Christ
for all of you,[q] because your faith is proclaimed
in all the world. 9[r] For God is my witness,
[s] whom I serve with my spirit in the gospel of
his Son,[t] that without ceasing I mention you
10 always in my prayers, asking that somehow
[u] by God's will I may now at last succeed in
coming to you. 11 For[v] I long to see you, that
I may impart to you some spiritual gift to
strengthen you— 12 that is, that we may be
mutually encouraged[w] by each other's faith,
both yours and mine. 13 I do not want you
to be unaware, brothers,[3] that[x] I have often
intended to come to you (but[y] thus far have
been prevented), in order that I may reap some
[z] harvest among you as well as among the rest
of the Gentiles. 14[a] I am under obligation both
to Greeks and to[b] barbarians,[4] both to the wise

[1] Or *slave* (for the contextual rendering of the Greek word *doulos*, see Preface) [2] Or *who came from the offspring of David* [3] Or *brothers and sisters*. The plural Greek word *adelphoi* (translated "brothers") refers to siblings in a family. In New Testament usage, depending on the context, *adelphoi* may refer either to men or to both men and women who are siblings (brothers and sisters) in God's family, the church [4] That is, non-Greeks

1:1–6 God fulfills his promises. In the polytheistic Roman world of hundreds of gods, there is One who sends "the gospel" (v. 1). This is the good news of a Savior who will destroy death and rescue creation from its bondage to decay (8:18–39). This gospel was promised in advance, as the Old Testament prophets and their writings attest (1:2). They pointed to David's Son, God's Son, whose heavenly favor was confirmed by his resurrection from the dead (v. 4). To get the message of salvation out, God in his grace set apart messengers (apostles) like Paul (vv. 1, 6). They announced a blessing to be received "among all the nations" (v. 5), an echo and fulfillment of God's promises to Abraham (see Gen. 12:1–3). That message and blessing continue to penetrate the world today.

1:8–15 The heartbeat of those who know God through faith in Christ is to make him known. Paul longs to visit Rome "to preach the gospel" there (v. 15) and through mutual encouragement (v. 12) to take the gospel to even more distant lands, like Spain (see 15:24). The gospel's proper application is for the benefit of those still unreached; those who receive it must battle the temptation to soak up its benefits solely for themselves.

At the same time, the gospel is not irrelevant for those already in Christ. Notice that Paul says he is "eager to preach the gospel" to the Roman church—those who already knew the gospel (1:15)! Paul viewed the gospel as the daily food for every human heart, since it is not just abstract truth but "the power of God" (v. 16).

Chapter 1
1[a] [Gal. 1:10] [b] 1 Cor. 1:1; [1 Cor. 9:1; Heb. 5:4]; See 2 Cor. 1:1 [c] See Acts 13:2
2[d] Titus 1:2 [e] ch. 3:21; 16:26; Luke 1:70
3[f] See Matt. 1:1 [g] Gal. 4:4
4[h] [Acts 13:33] [i] 2 Cor. 13:4; Eph. 1:19, 20; Phil. 3:10; [Acts 10:38; 26:23]
5[j] ch. 12:3; 15:15 [k] See Acts 1:25 [l] ch. 6:16; 16:26; 1 Pet. 1:2; [ch. 15:18; Acts 6:7] [m] See Acts 9:15
6[n] Rev. 17:14; [ch. 8:28, 30]
7[o] 1 Cor. 1:3
8[p] 1 Cor. 1:4; Eph. 1:15, 16; Phil. 1:3; Col. 1:3, 4; [ch. 6:17; Phil. 4:6; 2 Tim. 1:3] [q] ch. 16:19; [1 Thess. 1:8]
9[r] Phil. 1:8; 1 Thess. 2:5, 10; [ch. 9:1; 2 Cor. 1:23; 11:10, 31] [s] See Acts 24:14 [t] 2 Tim. 1:3
10[u] ch. 15:32; [1 Thess. 3:10]
11[v] ch. 15:22, 23; [Acts 19:21]
12[w] See 2 Pet. 1:1
13[x] ch. 15:22, 23; [Acts 19:21] [y] ch. 15:22; [1 Thess. 2:18] [z] Phil. 4:17; [John 4:36]
14[a] 1 Cor. 9:16 [b] See Acts 28:2

and to the foolish. 15 So I am eager to preach the
gospel to you also who are in Rome.

The Righteous Shall Live by Faith

16 For [d]I am not ashamed of the gospel, for it
is [e]the power of God for salvation to everyone
who believes, to the Jew [f]first and also to [g]the
Greek. 17 For in it [h]the righteousness of God is
revealed [i]from faith for faith,[1] [j]as it is written,
“The righteous shall live by faith.”[2]

God's Wrath on Unrighteousness

18 For [k]the wrath of God [l]is revealed from
heaven against all ungodliness and unrighteousness of men, who by their unrighteousness suppress the truth. 19 For what can be
[m]known about God is plain to them, because
God has shown it to them. 20 For his invisible attributes, namely, his eternal power and
divine nature, [n]have been clearly perceived,
ever since the creation of the world,[3] in the
things that have been made. So they are without excuse. 21 For although they knew God,
they did not honor him as God or give thanks
to him, but they [o]became futile in their thinking, and their foolish hearts were darkened.
22 [p]Claiming to be wise, they became fools,
23 and [q]exchanged the glory of [r]the immortal
God for images resembling mortal man and
birds and animals and creeping things.
24 Therefore [s]God gave them up in the lusts
of their hearts to impurity, to [t]the dishonoring
of their bodies among themselves, 25 because
they exchanged the truth about God for [u]a
lie and worshiped and served the creature
rather than the Creator, [v]who is blessed forever! Amen.
26 For this reason [w]God gave them up to
[x]dishonorable passions. For their women
exchanged natural relations for those that are
contrary to nature; 27 and the men likewise
gave up natural relations with women and
were consumed with passion for one another,
[y]men committing shameless acts with men
and receiving in themselves the due penalty
for their error.
28 And since they did not see fit to acknowledge God, [z]God gave them up to [a]a debased
mind to do [b]what ought not to be done. 29 They
were filled with all manner of unrighteousness, evil, covetousness, malice. They are full
of envy, murder, strife, deceit, maliciousness.
They are gossips, 30 slanderers, haters of God,
insolent, haughty, boastful, inventors of evil,
disobedient to parents, 31 foolish, faithless,
heartless, ruthless. 32 Though they know [c]God's
righteous decree that those who practice such
things [d]deserve to die, they not only do them
but [e]give approval to those who practice them.

God's Righteous Judgment

2 Therefore you have [f]no excuse, O man,
every one of you who judges. For [g]in passing judgment on another you condemn yourself, because you, the judge, practice the very
same things. 2 We know that the judgment of

[1] Or *beginning and ending in faith* [2] Or *The one who by faith is righteous shall live* [3] Or *clearly perceived from the creation of the world*

16[d] [Ps. 40:9, 10]; See Mark 8:38 [e] 1 Cor. 1:18, 24 [f] ch. 2:9; See Acts 3:26 [g] [Mark 7:26]; See John 7:35
17[h] ch. 3:21; [2 Cor. 5:21; Phil. 3:9] [i] See ch. 9:30 [j] Gal. 3:11; Heb. 10:38; Cited from Hab. 2:4
18[k] Eph. 5:6; Col. 3:6; [ch. 5:9] [l] [ch. 2:5]
19[m] ch. 2:14, 15; Acts 14:17; 17:24-27
20[n] [Ps. 19:1-6; Jer. 5:21, 22]
21[o] 2 Kgs. 17:15; Jer. 2:5; Eph. 4:17, 18
22[p] Jer. 10:14; 1 Cor. 1:20
23[q] Ps. 106:20; Jer. 2:11; [Deut. 4:16-18; Acts 17:29] [r] 1 Tim. 1:17
24[s] ver. 26, 28; [Eph. 4:19] [t] [1 Thess. 4:4]
25[u] Isa. 28:15; 44:19, 20; Jer. 10:14; Amos 2:4; [2 Thess. 2:11] [v] ch. 9:5
26[w] ver. 24, 28 [x] [Col. 3:5; 1 Thess. 4:5]
27[y] Lev. 18:22; 20:13
28[z] ver. 24, 26 [a] [Jer. 6:30] [b] [Eph. 5:4]
32[c] ch. 2:26; 8:4 [d] ch. 6:21

1:16–17 Announcing the epistle's theme, Paul speaks of the power of the good news of Jesus' coming, his life, his saving death, and his resurrection. Through proclamation, Jesus' words and work save “everyone who believes” (v. 16), whatever their identity, social location, ethnicity, or other human distinctives. This takes place as “the righteousness of God” (i.e., God satisfying his justice by putting the penalty of our sin on Christ) “is revealed” to those who confess faith in Christ so that they might live faithfully. Undergirding these truths is Old Testament Scripture, in this case Habakkuk 2:4, quoted in Romans 1:17.

1:18–32 The gospel gains urgency in the light of God's verdict on humanity. Transgression gives rise to divine wrath (v. 18). Examples of transgression are ingratitude (v. 21) and idolatry (v. 23). Homosexual behavior is also depicted as odious in God's sight (vv. 26–27). None of us is innocent of a number of the sins described (see vv. 28–31). Even if we do not practice every sinful deed found here, we may secretly approve and even envy when others cross God's moral boundaries. We thereby fail to love God (because we break his commandments) and to love our neighbor (because we support our neighbors in their folly). The outcome is judgment.

Behind the good news of the gospel lies the tough news that all people are implicated in acts and attitudes that God has promised to punish unless his means of grace are embraced. The gospel is the antidote, for through trust in Christ comes

[e] Luke 11:48; Acts 8:1; 22:20; [1 Cor. 13:6; 2 Thess. 2:12] **Chapter 2** **1**[f] ch. 1:20 [g] 2 Sam. 12:5-7; [John 8:7]; See Matt. 7:2

God rightly falls on those who practice such
things. 3 Do you suppose, O man—you who
judge those who practice such things and yet
do them yourself—that you will escape the
judgment of God? 4 Or do you presume on
[h]the riches of his kindness and [i]forbearance
and [j]patience, [k]not knowing that God's kindness is meant to lead you to repentance? 5 But
because of your hard and impenitent heart
you are [l]storing up [m]wrath for yourself on the
day of wrath when God's righteous judgment
will be revealed.

6 [n]He will render to each one according to
his works: 7 to those who [o]by patience in well-
doing seek for glory and honor and immortality, he will give eternal life; 8 but for those
who are self-seeking[1] and [p]do not obey the
truth, but obey unrighteousness, there will be
wrath and fury. 9 There will be tribulation and
distress [q]for every human being who does evil,
the Jew [r]first and also the Greek, 10 but glory
and honor and [s]peace for everyone who does
good, [t]the Jew first and also the Greek. 11 For
[u]God shows no partiality.

God's Judgment and the Law

12 For all who have sinned [v]without the law
will also perish without the law, and all who
have sinned under the law will be judged by
the law. 13 For [w]it is not the hearers of the law
who are righteous before God, but the doers
of the law who will be justified. 14 For when
Gentiles, who do not have the law, [x]by nature
do what the law requires, they are a law to
themselves, even though they do not have
the law. 15 They show that the work of the law
is [y]written on their hearts, while their conscience also bears witness, and their conflicting thoughts accuse or even excuse them 16 [z]on
that day when, [a]according to my gospel, God
judges [b]the secrets of men [c]by Christ Jesus.

17 But if you call yourself a Jew and [d]rely
on the law and boast in God 18 and know his
will and approve what is excellent, because
you are instructed from the law; 19 and if you
are sure that you yourself are [e]a guide to
the blind, a light to those who are in darkness, 20 an instructor of the foolish, a teacher
of children, having in the law [f]the embodiment of [g]knowledge and truth— 21 [h]you then

[1] Or *contentious*

"the obedience of faith," believing as God requires (1:5; 16:26). Our lives grow in the richness of knowing and being known by Christ.

2:1–10 Paul expands on the human plight. People condemn themselves by the way they judge others for things they themselves do (v. 1). Paul's rhetorical questions confirm the universality of human error (vv. 3–4). God kindly gives time for repentance and reform, but people presume on him and store up future woe, when God will act to vindicate his name (v. 5).

"According to his works" (v. 6) can be rendered "according to how a person lives." Some will seek God and receive eternal life (v. 7). From numerous other passages (e.g., 3:22) we know that this will be through faith in Christ's finished work. Others will spurn the call to follow Christ, to take up his cross. They will be "self-seeking" (2:8). One way (v. 9) or the other (v. 10), people's choices will position them before God in ways they will either rejoice in or bitterly regret, in this life and the next.

2:12–24 Paul continues to sketch the contours and consequences of humans' estrangement from God due to their sin. There are two classes of people on earth (v. 12): those "without the law," the Gentiles; and those "under the law," the Jews. Gentiles have an inner awareness of God's moral demands (v. 15) but do not live up to their own sense of right and wrong. Jews are descendants of Abraham and of Moses, who received the law from God. But God's standard is not merely to have Abrahamic ancestry and to hear the law: it is to fulfill the law by doing what it says (v. 13). Paul charges the Jews (his own people group; see 9:3; 10:1; 11:1) with dishonoring God by violating the law he gave them (2:23). This gives God a bad name among the Gentiles, all those who are not of Abrahamic ancestry (v. 24).

Paul will eventually turn (see 3:21) from his focus on sin and judgment to take up again the gospel, which he last mentioned in 1:16. But in God's wisdom this portion of Romans is devoted to a lengthy and stark depiction of the lost human condition. Readers and hearers of Romans can be confident that the wounds of this frank appraisal of human fallenness will provide a platform for the announcement of God's healing solution later in the epistle.

4 [h]ch. 9:23; 10:12 [i]ch. 3:25 [j]ch. 9:22; [Ex. 34:6] [k]Isa. 30:18; 2 Pet. 3:9, 15; Rev. 2:21
5 [l][Deut. 32:34]; See James 5:3 [m]Ps. 110:5
6 [n]Job 34:11; Ps. 62:12; Prov. 24:12; Jer. 17:10; 32:19; See Matt. 16:27
7 [o]See Luke 8:15
8 [p]2 Thess. 2:12
9 [q]Ezek. 18:20 [r]See 1 Pet. 4:17
10 [s]Isa. 57:19 [t]See ch. 1:16
11 [u]See Acts 10:34
12 [v]1 Cor. 9:21
13 [w]See James 1:22, 23
14 [x]See ch. 1:19
15 [y]Jer. 31:33
16 [z][ch. 3:6; 14:10; 1 Cor. 4:5]; See Acts 10:42; 17:31 [a]ch. 16:25; 2 Tim. 2:8; [Gal. 1:11; 1 Tim. 1:11] [b]Eccles. 12:14 [c]ch. 16:25; [1 Tim. 1:11; 2 Tim. 2:8]
17 [d]ver. 23; Mic. 3:11; [ch. 9:4; John 5:45]
19 [e][Job 29:15; Matt. 15:14; 23:16; John 9:39-41]
20 [f]2 Tim. 3:5; [Gal. 4:19; 2 Tim. 1:13] [g]Luke 11:52
21 [h]Matt. 23:3-28; [Ps. 50:16-21; Matt. 15:1-9]

who teach others, do you not teach yourself?
While you preach against stealing, do you
steal? 22 You who say that one must not commit adultery, do you commit adultery? You
who abhor idols, do you [i]rob temples? 23 You
who [j]boast in the law [k]dishonor God by breaking the law. 24 For, [l]as it is written, "The name
of God is blasphemed [m]among the Gentiles
because of you."

25 For circumcision indeed is of value [n]if you
obey the law, but if you break the law, your
circumcision becomes uncircumcision. 26 So, if
[o]a man who is uncircumcised keeps [p]the precepts of the law, will not his uncircumcision
be regarded[1] as circumcision? 27 Then he who
is physically[2] uncircumcised but keeps the law
[q]will condemn you who have [r]the written code[3]
and circumcision but break the law. 28 For [s]no
one is a Jew [t]who is merely one outwardly, nor
is circumcision outward and physical. 29 But
a Jew is one [u]inwardly, and [v]circumcision is a
matter of the heart, by the Spirit, not by the letter. [w]His praise is not from man but from God.

God's Righteousness Upheld

3 Then what advantage has the Jew? Or
what is the value of circumcision? 2 Much
in every way. To begin with, [x]the Jews were
entrusted with [y]the oracles of God. 3 [z]What if
some were unfaithful? [a]Does their faithlessness nullify the faithfulness of God? 4 By no
means! [b]Let God be true though [c]every one
were a liar, as it is written,

> [d]"That you may be justified in your words,
> and prevail when you [e]are judged."

5 But if our unrighteousness serves to show
the righteousness of God, what shall we say?
That God is unrighteous to inflict [f]wrath on
us? ([g]I speak in a human way.) 6 By no means!
For then how could [h]God judge the world?
7 But if through my lie God's truth abounds
to his glory, [i]why am I still being condemned
as a sinner? 8 And why not [j]do evil that good
may come?—as some people slanderously
charge us with saying. Their condemnation
is just.

No One Is Righteous

9 What then? Are we Jews[4] any better off?[5]
No, not at all. For we have already charged
that all, both [k]Jews and [l]Greeks, are [m]under
sin, 10 as it is written:

> [n]"None is righteous, no, not one;
> 11 no one understands;
> no one seeks for God.

[1] Or *counted* [2] Or *is by nature* [3] Or *the letter* [4] Greek *Are we* [5] Or *at any disadvantage?*

22 [i] Acts 19:37; [Mal. 3:8]
23 [j] See ver. 17; ch. 3:27 [k] [Mal. 1:6]
24 [l] Cited from Isa. 52:5 [m] [2 Sam. 12:14; Ezek. 36:20, 23; 2 Pet. 2:2]
25 [n] Gal. 5:3
26 [o] Eph. 2:11; [ch. 3:30] [p] ch. 1:32; 8:4
27 [q] See Matt. 12:41 [r] ver. 29; ch. 7:6; 2 Cor. 3:6
28 [s] ch. 9:6-8; [Gal. 6:15] [t] [ver. 17]
29 [u] See 1 Pet. 3:4 [v] [Deut. 10:16; 30:6; Jer. 4:4; Acts 7:51; Phil. 3:3; Col. 2:11] [w] 2 Cor. 10:18; 1 Thess. 2:4; [Gal. 1:10]

Chapter 3
2 [x] Deut. 4:8; Ps. 147:19, 20; See John 4:22 [y] See Acts 7:38
3 [z] ch. 10:16; Heb. 4:2 [a] [ch. 9:6; 2 Tim. 2:13]
4 [b] See John 8:26 [c] Ps. 62:9; 116:11; [ver. 7] [d] Cited from Ps. 51:4 (Gk.) [e] [Job 9:32]
5 [f] [ch. 2:5] [g] ch. 6:19; 1 Cor. 9:8; Gal. 3:15; [1 Cor. 15:32]
6 [h] [Gen. 18:25; Job 8:3]; See ch. 2:16
7 [i] [ch. 9:19]
8 [j] [ch. 6:1, 15]
9 [k] ch. 2:1-29 [l] ch. 1:18-32 [m] Gal. 3:22; [ver. 19, 23; ch. 11:32; Prov. 20:9]
10 [n] ver. 10-12, cited from Ps. 14:1-3; 53:1-3

2:25–29 Blessedness before God requires transformation of the heart. This insight is at least as old as Jeremiah (Jer. 4:4), Moses (Deut. 10:16; 30:6), and Abraham, whose circumcision (Genesis 17) confirmed, and did not substitute for, personal trust in the God who had spoken to him (Gen. 12:1–3; 15:6). God established his covenant through Abraham's faith before sealing it (i.e., pledging to honor the faith represented) through the sign of circumcision, which symbolized the removal of impurity (Rom. 4:11). In Romans 2:25–29, Paul chides his fellow Jews for equating ritual (circumcision) and ethnicity with blessedness. God's acceptance or "praise" (v. 29) comes through his work in the heart "by the Spirit" (v. 29). Paul (like Jesus' forerunner John the Baptist; Matt. 3:9) knew from experience that too many of his fellow Jews had lost sight of this truth.

The gospel of grace transforms us from the inside out. Changed at a heart level, we live differently; we cannot simply act in a certain way in order to become changed at a heart level. If the heart is not right with God, no ritual will supply the true righteousness he requires.

3:1–4 God's greatest gift to his people is his "oracles" (v. 2). This refers to what we call Scripture. For the Jews of Paul's day this was what we call the Old Testament. Since Christ's coming, "Scripture" is both Testaments, Old and New. Later Paul will remind us that "faith comes from hearing, and hearing through the word of Christ" (10:17); this has its counterpart in Moses' question to Israel: "And what great nation is there, that has statutes and rules so righteous as all this law that I set before you today?" (Deut. 4:8).

The word of God forms the people of God, and in all ages this is an incomparable gift. The refusal of some to acknowledge Scripture's words as divine in origin and substance does not alter the fact of who gave those words and what they are in God's sight (Rom. 3:3–4).

12 All have turned aside; together they
have become worthless;
no one does good,
not even one."
13 [o]"Their throat is [p]an open grave;
they use their tongues to deceive."
[q]"The venom of asps is under their lips."
14 [r]"Their mouth is full of curses and bitterness."
15 [s]"Their feet are swift to shed blood;
16 in their paths are ruin and misery,
17 and [t]the way of peace they have not
known."
18 [u]"There is no fear of God before their
eyes."

19 Now we know that whatever [v]the law says
it speaks to those who are under the law, [w]so
that every mouth may be stopped, and [x]the
whole world may be held accountable to God.
20 For [y]by works of the law no human being[1]
will be justified in his sight, since [z]through
the law comes knowledge of sin.

The Righteousness of God Through Faith

21 But now [a]the righteousness of God [b]has
been manifested apart from the law, although
[c]the Law and the Prophets bear witness to it—
22 the righteousness of God [d]through faith in
Jesus Christ for all who believe. [e]For there is no
distinction: 23 for [f]all have sinned and fall short
of the glory of God, 24 [g]and are justified [h]by his
grace as a gift, [i]through the redemption that
is in Christ Jesus, 25 whom God [j]put forward
as [k]a propitiation [l]by his blood, to be received
by faith. This was to show God's righteousness, because in [m]his divine forbearance he had
passed over [n]former sins. 26 It was to show his
righteousness at the present time, so that he
might be just and the justifier of the one who
has faith in Jesus.
27 [o]Then what becomes of our boasting? It
is excluded. By what kind of law? By a law of
works? No, but by the law of faith. 28 For we
hold that one is justified by faith [p]apart from
works of the law. 29 Or [q]is God the God of Jews

[1] Greek *flesh*

3:9–20 The human plight is that "the whole world" (v. 19), every single person, fails to live up to the moral standard God requires. Paul draws here on all he has said stretching back to 1:18. He marshals grim evidence from various Psalm passages—more "oracles of God" (see Rom. 3:2) that inform humans of the truth they seek to suppress (see 1:18). All mouths are stopped (3:19). Deep down, humans know sin and guilt, but they lack the means to evade divine judgment, which requires being "justified" in God's sight (v. 20).

3:21–26 If previous verses might lead to despair, Paul now sets forth grounds for rejoicing. What Abraham set his hope on by faith, so that God granted him a righteous standing (Gen. 15:6), Jesus Christ has accomplished "for all who believe" the gospel promise as Abraham did (Rom. 3:22). Yes, the sinful human condition is universal and terminal (v. 23). But believers "are justified" by God's "grace as a gift, through the redemption that is in Christ Jesus" (v. 24). The term "redemption" suggests a picture of slaves being purchased and freed. God sent his Son to be a "propitiation": he satisfied the demands of God's wrath by his death on the cross in the place of sinners. When he "passed over former sins" (v. 25) prior to Jesus' coming, God did not merely dismiss the charges against the guilty. Rather, God's righteous demands were met in Jesus' death. God proved to be "just" in not overlooking sin, and he also freely chose to act as "justifier" for "the one who has faith in Jesus" (v. 26).

Our hearts are moved as we marvel at the wisdom of God in providing a righteous way of rescue for guilty sinners that does not in any way compromise his justice and holiness. We marvel, too, at God's great love in sending his own Son to accomplish this salvation.

3:27–31 The outcome of God's saving act in Jesus includes the elimination of "boasting" (v. 27) or confidence in human self-sufficiency. There is no religious system or achievement through which any humans, Jew or Gentile, can meet the righteous standards of God's law. There is one God and accordingly one humanity (both Jew and Gentile) and one way of redemption: Jesus Christ's perfect work received by faith (v. 30). Yet far from canceling the Old Testament, saving faith in God through Christ vindicates the law in its truth, promises, and guidance (v. 31). The book of Romans confirms this conviction by its dozens of Old Testament citations and allusions. The church through the centuries has agreed with Paul in receiving the whole Bible, not just the New Testament, as God's inspired Word.

13 [o] Cited from Ps. 5:9 [p] Jer. 5:16 [q] Cited from Ps. 140:3
14 [r] Cited from Ps. 10:7 (Gk.)
15 [s] Cited from Prov. 1:16; ver. 15-17 cited from Isa. 59:7, 8
17 [t] Luke 1:79
18 [u] Cited from Ps. 36:1
19 [v] John 10:34; 15:25 [w] Job 5:16; Ps. 63:11; 107:42; Ezek. 16:63; [ch. 1:20; 2:1] [x] See ver. 9
20 [y] Gal. 2:16; [Ps. 143:2; Acts 13:39] [z] ch. 7:7; [ch. 4:15; 5:13, 20]
21 [a] See ch. 1:17 [b] ch. 16:26; 2 Tim. 1:10 [c] Acts 10:43; [ch. 1:2; John 5:46]
22 [d] ch. 4:5; [2 Tim. 3:15] [e] ch. 10:12; [Gal. 3:28; Col. 3:11]
23 [f] See ver. 9
24 [g] Titus 3:7 [h] ch. 4:4, 5, 16; See Acts 15:11 [i] Eph. 1:7; Col. 1:14; Heb. 9:15; [1 Cor. 1:30]
25 [j] Eph. 1:9 [k] See 1 John 2:2 [l] ch. 5:9; Eph. 2:13 [m] ch. 2:4 [n] [Acts 17:30]
27 [o] ch. 2:17, 23; 4:2; 1 Cor. 1:29-31; Eph. 2:9; 2 Tim. 1:9; See Acts 13:39
28 [p] See James 2:18
29 [q] ch. 9:24; 10:12; 15:9

only? Is he not the God of Gentiles also? Yes,
of Gentiles also, 30 since [r]God is one—who
will justify the circumcised by faith and [s]the
uncircumcised through faith. 31 Do we then
overthrow the law by this faith? By no means!
On the contrary, we uphold the law.

Abraham Justified by Faith

4 What then shall we say was gained by[1]
Abraham, [t]our forefather according to the
flesh? 2 For if Abraham was justified by works,
he has something to boast about, but [u]not
before God. 3 For what does the Scripture say?
[v]"Abraham believed God, and it was counted
to him as righteousness." 4 Now [w]to the one
who works, his wages are not counted as a gift
but as his due. 5 And to the one who does not
work but [x]believes in[2] him who justifies the
ungodly, his faith is counted as righteousness,
6 just as David also speaks of the blessing of
the one to whom God counts righteousness
apart from works:

7 [y]"Blessed are those whose lawless deeds
are forgiven,
and whose sins are covered;
8 blessed is the man against whom the
Lord will not [z]count his sin."

9 Is this blessing then only for [a]the circumcised, or also for the uncircumcised? [b]For we
say that faith was counted to Abraham as righteousness. 10 How then was it counted to him?
Was it before or after he had been circumcised?
It was not after, but before he was circumcised.
11 [c]He received the sign of circumcision as a
seal of the righteousness that he had by faith
while he was still uncircumcised. The purpose
was [d]to make him the father of all who believe
without being circumcised, so that righteousness would be counted to them as well, 12 and
to make him the father of the circumcised who
are not merely circumcised but who also walk
in the footsteps of the faith that our father
Abraham had before he was circumcised.

The Promise Realized Through Faith

13 For [e]the promise to Abraham and his offspring [f]that he would be heir of the world did
not come through the law but through the
righteousness of faith. 14 [g]For if it is the adherents of the law who are to be the heirs, faith
is null and the promise is void. 15 For [h]the law
brings wrath, but [i]where there is no law [j]there
is no transgression.
16 That is why it depends on faith, [k]in order
that the promise may rest on grace and [l]be
guaranteed to all his offspring—not only to
the adherent of the law but also to the one who
shares the faith of Abraham, [m]who is the father
of us all, 17 as it is written, [n]"I have made you
the father of many nations"—in the presence
of the God in whom he believed, [o]who gives
life to the dead and calls into existence [p]the
things that do not exist. 18 In hope he believed

[1] Some manuscripts *say about* [2] Or *but trusts*; compare verse 24

30 [r]Gal. 3:20; [ch. 10:12] [s]Gal. 3:8; [ch. 4:9]; See ch. 2:26
Chapter 4
1 [t]ver. 16
2 [u][1 Cor. 1:31]
3 [v]ver. 9, 22; Gal. 3:6; James 2:23; Cited from Gen. 15:6 (Gk.); [Titus 3:8]
4 [w][ch. 11:6; Deut. 9:4, 5]
5 [x]ch. 3:22; See John 6:29
7 [y]Cited from Ps. 32:1, 2
8 [z]2 Cor. 5:19
9 [a]ch. 3:30 [b]ver. 3
11 [c]Gen. 17:10, 11 [d]ver. 12, 16; [ch. 3:22]; See Luke 19:9
13 [e]Gal. 3:16; Heb. 6:15, 17; 7:6; 11:9, 17; [ch. 9:8]; See Acts 13:32 [f]Gen. 17:4-6
14 [g]Gal. 3:17, 18
15 [h]ch. 7:7, 10-25; 2 Cor. 3:7, 9; Gal. 3:10 [i][ch. 3:20] [j]Gal. 3:19
16 [k]See ch. 3:24 [l]Gal. 3:22; [ch. 15:8] [m][ch. 9:8]
17 [n]Cited from Gen. 17:5; [ver. 18] [o][Heb. 11:19]; See John 5:21 [p]1 Cor. 1:28; [Heb. 11:3]

4:1–12 Paul furnishes an example of how gospel faith is rooted in the good news which "the law" (3:31; here meaning the Old Testament) conveys. Both Abraham (long before Moses gave "the law" proper) and David (centuries after Moses) found earthly and eternal blessedness in God's sight. This came about through God granting them righteousness, despite their sin, through their faith in his promises—the promises that would be vindicated in Jesus' saving work. This action of God's part "covered" their sin (4:7) and headed off their condemnation on the day of judgment that all will face (v. 8).

While God is the heavenly Father of his people, Abraham serves as "the father of all who believe" (v. 11) in the sense that those who hear and receive the gospel message "walk in the footsteps of the faith that our father Abraham had" (v. 12). Just as Abraham did not earn a righteous standing through some meritorious act or some ritual like circumcision, Christ's followers know God's full acceptance apart from any merit they might try to earn through their own piety, moral achievement, or religious exercise.

4:16 Faith, promise, grace: this bundle of words encapsulates the point of Paul's story of Abraham in Romans 4. *Faith* (full personal trust) is the right posture for approaching God; *promise* (the centuries-old pledge to redeem those who are truly his) is God's invitation to exercise faith; *grace* is God's gift of acceptance and new life in full fellowship with him. All three words are powerful because they tap into Christ's work as related in 3:21–26 and restated in 4:24–25. "Faith" is not faith in or from itself but faith in and from God's saving act through Jesus. To constantly examine whether you have enough faith is to turn faith into its opposite; faith is not looking at yourself at all, but at Christ.

against hope, that he should become the father
of many nations, as he had been told, [q]"So shall
your offspring be." 19 He did not weaken in
faith when he considered his own body, which
was [r]as good as dead ([s]since he was about a
hundred years old), or when he considered
[t]the barrenness[1] of Sarah's womb. 20 No unbelief made him waver concerning the promise
of God, but he grew strong in his faith as he
gave glory to God, 21 fully convinced that [u]God
was able to do what he had promised. 22 That
is why his faith was "counted to him as righteousness." 23 But [v]the words "it was counted
to him" were not written for his sake alone,
24 but for ours also. It will be counted to us
[w]who believe in [x]him who raised from the dead
Jesus our Lord, 25 [y]who was delivered up for
our trespasses and raised [z]for our justification.

Peace with God Through Faith

5 [a]Therefore, since we have been justified by
faith, [b]we[2] have peace with God through
our Lord Jesus Christ. 2 Through him we have
also [c]obtained access by faith[3] into this grace
[d]in which we stand, and [e]we[4] rejoice[5] in hope
of the glory of God. 3 Not only that, but we
[f]rejoice in our sufferings, knowing that suffering [g]produces endurance, 4 and endurance
produces character, and character produces
hope, 5 and [h]hope does not put us to shame,
because God's love [i]has been poured into our
hearts through the Holy Spirit who has been
given to us.

6 For [j]while we were still weak, at the right
time [k]Christ died for the ungodly. 7 For one will
scarcely die for a righteous person—though
perhaps for a good person one would dare
even to die— 8 but [l]God shows his love for us
in that [m]while we were still sinners, Christ died
for us. 9 Since, therefore, [n]we have now been
justified by his blood, much more shall we be
saved by him from [o]the wrath of God. 10 For if
[p]while we were enemies [q]we were reconciled
to God by the death of his Son, much more,
now that we are reconciled, shall we be saved
by [r]his life. 11 More than that, we also rejoice in
God through our Lord Jesus Christ, through
whom we have now received [s]reconciliation.

[1] Greek *deadness* [2] Some manuscripts *let us* [3] Some manuscripts omit *by faith* [4] Or *let us*; also verse 3 [5] Or *boast*; also verses 3, 11

4:23–25 Abraham is not just a character in an ancient story: he carries world-changing weight for us too. As Abraham received a righteous standing through faith, so do we—not because of Abraham's greatness but because of "him who raised from the dead Jesus our Lord" (v. 24). Faith in him who died and rose results in "justification" (v. 25). This means God accounts Christ's righteousness to us who entrust our lives to him. His resurrection life (cleansed of sin and endued with the power of life-giving holiness) becomes our own, not only after this life but right now, as chapter 5 will make clear.

5:1–5 Previous chapters have majored on the gospel (1:16–17), our abject need for it (1:18–3:20), and Christ's centrality in it (3:21–26). Justification—God's reckoning or accounting of Christ's righteousness to sinners—is through faith alone (3:27–31). The only thing we contribute is our need. This is true for us who look back on Jesus' coming, as it was true for Old Testament figures (like Abraham and David; ch. 4) who looked ahead to God's fulfillment of his promises through his Son.

Now Paul begins to unpack what knowing Christ means in terms of daily life. He takes up sanctification, the work of God's grace to set us free from sin and make us joyful servants of God's righteousness (see 6:17–18). Believers in Christ have peace with God (5:1), a state of grace and rejoicing (v. 2), and a way of living that is both sobering and satisfying.

It is sobering that trusting in Christ brings sufferings (v. 3; see also 8:17). But it is satisfying that those sufferings produce endurance, which produces proven character, which produces a confident hope in God's enduring and eternal care (5:3–5). God's Spirit gives God's love in abundance. This is the normal yet glorious life of gospel faith.

5:6–11 Paul supports the assertions of 5:1–5 by drawing on what it means that "Christ died for the ungodly" (v. 6). It is as if Paul recalls Jesus' words: "For I came not to call the righteous, but sinners" (Matt. 9:13). All are sinners (Rom. 3:23), but Christ saves those who admit it and turn to him.

The mark of God's love is his regard for us who because of our transgressions were his enemies (5:10). Paul, who had been a persecutor of the church (Gal. 1:13), is a prime example of this (1 Tim. 1:15). Through Jesus' saving death "for us" (Rom. 5:8),

18 [q] Cited from Gen. 15:5
19 [r] Heb. 11:12 [s] Gen. 17:17 [t] Gen. 18:11
21 [u] Gen. 18:14; [Heb. 11:19]
23 [v] ch. 15:4; 1 Cor. 9:9, 10; 10:6, 11; 2 Tim. 3:16, 17; [Ps. 102:18]
24 [w] ch. 10:9; 1 Pet. 1:21 [x] See Acts 2:24
25 [y] ch. 5:6, 8; 8:32; Isa. 53:5, 6; Matt. 20:28; Gal. 1:4 [z] ch. 5:18; [1 Cor. 15:17]
Chapter 5
1 [a] ch. 3:28 [b] [ch. 15:13; Heb. 12:28]
2 [c] Eph. 2:18; 3:12; [Heb. 10:19, 20; 1 Pet. 3:18] [d] 1 Cor. 15:1 [e] ver. 11; Heb. 3:6; [ch. 12:12]
3 [f] See Matt. 5:12 [g] See Luke 21:19; James 1:3
5 [h] Ps. 119:116; Phil. 1:20 [i] Acts 2:17, 18, 33; Titus 3:6; [Gal. 4:6]
6 [j] ver. 8, 10; [Hos. 13:9; Eph. 2:5] [k] See ch. 4:25
8 [l] See John 3:16 [m] ver. 6, 10
9 [n] See ch. 3:25 [o] 1 Thess. 1:10; 2:16; See ch. 1:18
10 [p] ver. 6, 8; Col. 1:21; [ch. 8:32] [q] 2 Cor. 5:18-20; Eph. 2:16; Col. 1:20, 21 [r] 2 Cor. 4:10, 11
11 [s] ch. 11:15; 2 Cor. 5:18, 19

Death in Adam, Life in Christ

12 Therefore, just as [t]sin came into the world through one man, and [u]death through sin, and [v]so death spread to all men[1] because [w]all sinned— 13 for sin indeed was in the world before the law was given, but [x]sin is not counted where there is no law. 14 Yet death reigned from Adam to Moses, even over those whose sinning was not [y]like the transgression of Adam, [z]who was a type of [a]the one who was to come.

15 But the free gift is not like the trespass. For if many died through one man's trespass, much more have the grace of God and the free gift by the grace of that one man Jesus Christ abounded for [b]many. 16 And the free gift is not like the result of that one man's sin. For [c]the judgment following one trespass brought condemnation, but the free gift following many trespasses brought [d]justification. 17 For if, because of one man's trespass, death reigned through that one man, much more will those who receive the abundance of grace and the free gift of righteousness [e]reign in life through the one man Jesus Christ.

18 Therefore, as one trespass[2] led to condemnation for all men, so one act of righteousness[3] leads to justification and life for [f]all men. 19 For as by the one man's [g]disobedience the many were made sinners, so by the one man's [h]obedience the many will be made righteous. 20 Now [i]the law came in to increase the trespass, but where sin increased, [j]grace abounded all the more, 21 so that, [k]as sin reigned in death, [l]grace also might reign through righteousness leading to eternal life through Jesus Christ our Lord.

Dead to Sin, Alive to God

6 What shall we say then? [m]Are we to continue in sin that grace may abound? 2 By no means! How can [n]we who died to sin still live in it? 3 Do you not know that all of us [o]who have been baptized [p]into Christ Jesus were baptized into his death? 4 We were [q]buried therefore with him by baptism into death, in

[1] The Greek word *anthropoi* refers here to both men and women; also twice in verse 18 [2] Or *the trespass of one* [3] Or *the act of righteousness of one*

12 [t]Gen. 2:17; 3:6; 1 Cor. 15:21, 22; [ver. 15-17; ch. 6:9; Ps. 51:5] [u]ch. 6:23; James 1:15 [v][ver. 14, 21; 1 Cor. 15:22] [w]Eph. 2:3
13 [x]See ch. 3:20
14 [y]Hos. 6:7 [z]1 Cor. 15:45 [a][Matt. 11:3]
15 [b]ver. 19; Isa. 53:11
16 [c]1 Cor. 11:32 [d]ver. 18
17 [e]Rev. 22:5
18 [f]See John 12:32
19 [g][2 Cor. 10:6] [h]Heb. 5:8; [Phil. 2:8]
20 [i]Gal. 3:19; See ch. 3:20 [j]1 Tim. 1:14
21 [k][ver. 12, 14] [l]See John 1:17

Chapter 6
1 [m]ver. 15; [ch. 3:8]
2 [n]ver. 11; ch. 7:4, 6; Gal. 2:19; Col. 2:20; 3:3; 1 Pet. 2:24
3 [o]Gal. 3:27 [p]See Matt. 28:19
4 [q]Col. 2:12

there is release from fear of future condemnation (v. 9). Through our reconciliation with God as a result of Christ's resurrection life (v. 10), there is "now" (not just later, at the judgment or in the age to come) rejoicing. As we look back on God's great love for us when we were his enemies, we can be quietly confident that he will love and care for us now that we are his children.

5:12–14 Paul has just shown how Christ's death brings us peace with God through reconciliation. Now he sketches details of how Christ restores what was lost when Adam sinned.

Sin in Eden brought death into the world. Death "reigned" (5:14, 17) even before the law given to Moses specifically condemned it. The sin that leads to death has continued to ensnare all people ever since. Paul describes here both the sin of human choice *and* the natural bent to sinning (original sin) found in every human born since Adam (i.e., sin was present even before there was a formal law to break; cf. vv. 13, 18–19). Adam was a "type" of Christ in that his act would have wide-ranging consequences for the whole world, just as Jesus' life (and death) would have.

5:15–21 Every human being is either in Adam or in Christ. We are all born in Adam, but God by his grace brings many into Christ. Whereas Adam's trespass led to death and woe, God's grace abounds through the free gift offered "by the grace of that one man Jesus Christ" (v. 15). The word "grace" occurs 21 times in Romans—six times in Romans 5 alone. This chapter marks a high point of Romans' teaching about grace. By God's grace, the "free gift of righteousness" can be dominant in our lives (v. 17). Condemnation for "all men" because of Adam is universal, but the availability of "justification and life for all men" (v. 18) does not mean universal salvation, as the next verse makes clear. It is by grace—received through faith—that Christ's obedience makes righteous "the many" (not "all"; v. 19). In the end, grace reigns over and among God's people through the righteousness Christ won (v. 21). The result is eternal life through him—the strongest possible reversal of all the ills that came about through Adam.

God's glorious good news can be twisted and misconstrued. In 6:1–14 Paul deals with the first of three possible distortions of the gospel message he has been explaining (for the other two, see 6:15–7:6 and 7:7–25).

order that, just as [r]Christ was raised from the
dead by [s]the glory of the Father, we too might
walk in [t]newness of life.
5 For [u]if we have been united with him in
[v]a death like his, we shall certainly be united
with him in a resurrection like his. 6 We know
that [w]our old self[1] [x]was crucified with him in
order that [y]the body of sin might be brought
to nothing, so that we would no longer be
enslaved to sin. 7 For [z]one who has died [a]has
been set free[2] from sin. 8 Now [b]if we have died
with Christ, we believe that we will also live
with him. 9 We know that [c]Christ, being raised
from the dead, will never die again; [d]death
no longer has dominion over him. 10 For the
death he died he died to sin, [e]once for all, but
the life he lives he lives to God. 11 So you also
must consider yourselves [f]dead to sin and alive
to God in Christ Jesus.
12 Let not [g]sin therefore reign in your mortal
body, to make you obey its passions. 13 [h]Do not
present your members to sin as instruments
for unrighteousness, but [i]present yourselves
to God as those who have been brought from
death to life, and your members to God as
instruments for righteousness. 14 For [j]sin [k]will
have no dominion over you, since you are not
under law but under grace.

Slaves to Righteousness

15 What then? [l]Are we to sin [m]because we are
not under law but under grace? By no means!
16 Do you not know that if you present yourselves [n]to anyone as obedient slaves,[3] you are
slaves of the one whom you obey, either of
sin, which leads to death, or of obedience,
which leads to righteousness? 17 But [o]thanks
be to God, that you who were once slaves of

[1] Greek *man* [2] Greek *has been justified* [3] For the contextual rendering of the Greek word *doulos*, see Preface (twice in this verse and verse 19; also once in verses 17, 20)

6:1–11 The gospel message is not only for proclaiming and believing: it is for living. Grace and forgiveness do not mean we can "continue in sin that grace may abound" (v. 1). That notion is unthinkable (v. 2). Christian baptism signifies our unity with Christ in his death (v. 3); when he was crucified, we were present with him in that he bore our sins (see also 2 Cor. 5:21).

But this also means that when Jesus was raised from death "by the glory of the Father," a transformed way of living became possible for those who trust in him (Rom. 6:4). Although we will not experience bodily resurrection until Christ comes again, believers already, by virtue of their union with Christ, have been resurrected with him and possess the benefits of his new life (see also 8:10; Eph. 2:6; Col. 3:1). This co-resurrection with Christ has profound ethical implications. It is true that all of us fall short of God's glory (Rom. 3:23), but it is also true that Christ's resurrection brings change into our lives *now*, in this present life. Through faith, we are united with Christ both in his death and in his resurrection (6:5–6). God's goal in the gospel is for his people to "no longer be enslaved to sin" (v. 6). Jesus' death, and our union with him there, breaks sin's stranglehold (v. 7). Jesus' resurrection life infuses the lives of believers both now and in the age to come (vv. 8–9). Jesus defeated death and is alive in God's presence (v. 10). We as his followers can and should consider ourselves "dead to sin and alive to God in Christ Jesus" (v. 11).

6:12–14 The gospel message calls believers to humble defiance of sin's claim to "reign" in our physical bodies and everyday lives (v. 12). Because believers "have been brought from death to life" (v. 13), we can "present" ourselves and every part of our bodies to God. Eyes, ears, hands, feet, voices, minds—our entire bodies, once ravaged by sin (3:13–18), become tools "for righteousness." Sin's "dominion" is broken. The law's tyranny ended in Jesus' death. We do not groan under law, leading to sin; we are "under grace," which ushers us into God's "dominion" (6:14)—his own goodness and fullness. We become fully human again as intended at creation, before the effects of Adam's fall diminished us.

6:15–19 In 6:15–7:6 Paul deals with the second of three misunderstandings of gospel teaching (see also 6:1–14 and 7:7–25). Is it true that sin is now permissible, since we are "under grace" and not under law (6:15)?

No! Paul invokes what we might call "the presentation principle." You are the slave of the person to whom you present your life (v. 16), so, by all means, present yourself to God (see also 12:1–2)! The "standard of teaching" of the gospel calls forth

4 [r]ver. 9; ch. 8:11; See Acts 2:24 [s][John 11:40; 2 Cor. 13:4] [t]2 Cor. 5:17; Gal. 6:15; Eph. 4:23, 24; Col. 3:10; [ch. 7:6]
5 [u][2 Cor. 4:10] [v]Phil. 3:10, 11; [Col. 2:12; 3:1]
6 [w]Eph. 4:22; Col. 3:9 [x]Gal. 2:20; 5:24; 6:14 [y][ch. 7:24]
7 [z]1 Pet. 4:1 [a][ver. 18]
8 [b]2 Tim. 2:11; [2 Cor. 4:10; 13:4]
9 [c]Acts 13:34; Rev. 1:18 [d][ch. 5:14, 17]
10 [e]See Heb. 7:27
11 [f]See ver. 2
12 [g]ver. 14; Ps. 19:13; 119:133; Mic. 7:19; [2 Cor. 5:17]
13 [h]ch. 7:5; Col. 3:5 [i]ch. 12:1; 1 Pet. 2:24; 4:2
14 [j][ch. 8:2, 12] [k]See ver. 12
15 [l]ver. 1 [m][1 Cor. 9:21]
16 [n][ver. 20; Matt. 6:24]; See John 8:34
17 [o]See ch. 1:8

sin have become obedient from the heart to
the [p]standard of teaching to which you were
committed, 18 and, [q]having been set free from
sin, [r]have become slaves of righteousness.
19 [s]I am speaking in human terms, because of
your natural limitations. For [t]just as you once
presented your members as slaves to impurity
and to lawlessness leading to more lawlessness, so now present your members [u]as slaves
to righteousness leading to sanctification.

20 [v]For when you were slaves of sin, you were
free in regard to righteousness. 21 [w]But what
fruit were you getting at that time from the
things [x]of which you are now ashamed? [y]For
the end of those things is death. 22 But now
that you [z]have been set free from sin and [a]have
become slaves of God, [b]the fruit you get leads
to sanctification and [c]its end, eternal life. 23 [d]For
the wages of sin is death, but the free gift of
God is eternal life in Christ Jesus our Lord.

Released from the Law

7 Or do you not know, brothers[1]—for I am
speaking to those who know the law—
that the law is binding on a person only as
long as he lives? 2 For [e]a married woman is
bound by law to her husband while he lives,
but if her husband dies she is released from
the law of marriage.[2] 3 Accordingly, [f]she will be
called an adulteress if she lives with another
man while her husband is alive. But if her husband dies, she is free from that law, and if she
marries another man she is not an adulteress.

4 Likewise, my brothers, [g]you also have died
[h]to the law [i]through the body of Christ, so that
you may belong to another, to him who has
been raised from the dead, [j]in order that we
may bear fruit for God. 5 For while we were
living in the flesh, our sinful passions, aroused
by the law, were at work [k]in our members [l]to
bear fruit for death. 6 But now we are released
from the law, having died to that which held
us captive, so that we serve in the [m]new way
of [n]the Spirit and not in the old way of the
written code.[3]

The Law and Sin

7 What then shall we say? That the law is
sin? By no means! Yet if it had not been for
the law, [o]I would not have known sin. For
I would not have known what it is to covet if
[p]the law had not said, "You shall not covet."
8 But sin, [q]seizing an opportunity through the
commandment, produced in me all kinds of
covetousness. [r]For apart from the law, sin lies
dead. 9 I was once alive apart from the law,
but when the commandment came, sin came
alive and I died. 10 The very commandment
[s]that promised life proved to be death to me.
11 For sin, [t]seizing an opportunity through the

[1] Or *brothers and sisters*; also verse 4 [2] Greek *law concerning the husband* [3] Greek *of the letter*

17 [p][2 Tim. 1:13]
18 [q]ver. 22; ch. 8:2; [ver. 7]; See John 8:32 [r][ver. 22]
19 [s]See ch. 3:5 [t]See ver. 13 [u][1 Cor. 9:27]
20 [v]See ver. 16
21 [w]ch. 7:5; [Jer. 12:13] [x][2 Cor. 4:2] [y]ch. 1:32; 8:6, 13; Prov. 14:12; Gal. 6:8
22 [z]See ver. 18 [a]1 Cor. 7:22; 1 Pet. 2:16 [b]ch. 7:4 [c]1 Pet. 1:9
23 [d][ch. 2:7]; See ch. 5:12
Chapter 7
2 [e]1 Cor. 7:39
3 [f]Matt. 5:32
4 [g]ver. 6; See ch. 6:2 [h]ch. 8:2; Gal. 2:19; 5:18; Eph. 2:15; Col. 2:14 [i][Eph. 2:16; Col. 1:22] [j]ch. 6:22; Gal. 5:22; Eph. 5:9
5 [k]ch. 6:13 [l]See ch. 6:21, 23
6 [m]See ch. 6:4 [n]ch. 2:27, 29; 2 Cor. 3:6
7 [o]See ch. 3:20 [p]ch. 13:9; Ex. 20:17; Deut. 5:21
8 [q]ver. 11; [Gal. 5:13] [r]1 Cor. 15:56
10 [s]See ch. 10:5
11 [t]ver. 8

a dedication "from the heart" (6:17). Our very hearts have been changed. The gospel brings heart-transformation, not merely behavior modification. Sin is not inevitable, as it was before. We have been "set free" (v. 18). We are not miserably enveloped in impurity and lawlessness; rather, "righteousness leading to sanctification" is the promise of the gospel (v. 19). "Sanctification" here means progressive conformity to God in his holiness.

6:20–23 These brief verses give the "backstory" of the sanctification promised in the preceding verses. Before the gospel is received, sin has the upper hand (v. 20). There is no way out, and deep down we sense this (v. 21). The gospel makes God our Master, produces his fruit in our lives, and sets us on course for the age to come ("eternal life"; v. 22). We do not dread sin's bitter payoff. There is rejoicing in God's "free gift" (v. 23). All is of grace.

7:1–6 Paul makes a comparison between believers who have "died to the law" through Jesus' death (v. 4) and a married couple. While wife and husband both live, their marriage vows are binding (v. 1). But at death there is release from that binding relationship (v. 2). Just so, before receiving the gospel, we are "married" to sin because we have broken God's law and are chained to its verdict and mastery. Our desires are stirred up by the law. We "bear fruit for death" (v. 5). But through faith we died to sin and we now "belong to another," the One who rose, the One who makes us "bear fruit for God" (v. 4).

This is the Christ whom the gospel proclaims. He releases us from captivity to what could only condemn us, as "the new way of the Spirit" sets about its lifelong and life-changing activity. We have "died to that which held us captive" (v. 6). We are *free*.

commandment, [u]deceived me and through it
killed me. 12 So [v]the law is holy, and the commandment is holy and righteous and good.
13 Did that which is good, then, bring death
to me? By no means! It was sin, producing death in me through what is good, in
order that sin might be shown to be sin, and
through the commandment might become
sinful beyond measure. 14 For we know that
the law is spiritual, but I am of the flesh, [w]sold
under sin. 15 For I do not understand my own
actions. For [x]I do not do what I want, but I do
the very thing I hate. 16 Now if I do what I do
not want, I agree with [y]the law, that it is good.
17 So now [z]it is no longer I who do it, but sin
that dwells within me. 18 For I know that nothing good dwells [a]in me, that is, in my flesh. For
I have the desire to do what is right, but not
the ability to carry it out. 19 [b]For I do not do the
good I want, but the evil I do not want is what
I keep on doing. 20 Now if I do what I do not
want, [c]it is no longer I who do it, but sin that
dwells within me.
21 So I find it to be a law that when I want to
do right, evil lies close at hand. 22 For [d]I delight
in the law of God, [e]in my inner being, 23 but
I see in my members [f]another law waging
war against the law of my mind and making

7:7–12 In 7:7–25 Paul deals with the third of three possible distortions of gospel teaching (see also 6:1–14 and 6:15–7:6). Someone might charge that "the law is sin" (7:7), since it condemns and even arouses sinful passions (see v. 5). No, the law is God's gracious way of revealing to us our flaws. Paul uses the example of coveting (v. 7), the one commandment in the Ten Commandments that addresses only the heart. Our sin takes God's good command and produces in us the desire to do what God says not to do. It's like the boy whose mother says, "Stay out of the cookie jar!" All the boy can think of is cookies.

Paul describes a time "when the commandment came," which was when he became aware of his condemnation under the law (v. 9). He thought he would find life through his obedience to the law, but no (v. 10); sin was revealed by the commandment, and his self-sufficiency was dashed (v. 11). Above all this, God's law, his written command as found in all the Old Testament, remains "holy and righteous and good" (v. 12). The law is not our problem; we are! This is the sad truth that the gospel mercifully addresses.

7:13–20 Paul continues to commend God's good and perfect written Word. It is sin, not God's holy law, that brings death. God's word of conviction makes that painfully transparent (v. 13). Various theories try to account for just who the "I" is in these verses. Some see here an unconverted person (for example, a conscientious Pharisee, such as Paul once was, trying perfectly to honor the law). Some think Paul is focusing more abstractly on how the law does its work, and is not concerned with whether a converted or an unconverted person is in view. Many believe these verses describe the struggle of believers, even under grace, as we find that we often act against our own beliefs and will (v. 15). Each of these struggles confirms the goodness of the law (v. 16) and the persistence of sin's effects (v. 17). We must always acknowledge that, although the gospel has brought Christ's goodness into our lives *already*, we are *not yet* perfected in him (vv. 18–19). There remains still a despicable presence of sin in our actions despite our cleansed status through faith in Christ (v. 20).

Whichever interpretation we take, this passage drives home the profound and perplexing disorder that sin introduces into the human mind, a disorder that can be healed only by the even more profound grace of God in the gospel.

7:21–25 Even amid the working of divine grace, there is moral and spiritual struggle. The drive to do evil lurks alongside the will "to do right" and the inward delight in God's law (vv. 21–22). This is not a pleasant state, and it arouses a cry for deliverance (v. 24). Paul expresses gratitude to God, whose work in Christ is complete, but Paul also notes again the moral struggle amid which the gospel message sustains God's people (v. 25).

The struggle against sin is perplexing and, at times, overwhelming. We feel, as Paul puts it, "wretched" (v. 24). Yet with Paul, as we groan and cry out, "Who will deliver me?" we take refuge in the gospel of grace: "Thanks be to God through Jesus Christ our Lord!" (vv. 24, 25).

11 [u][Gen. 3:13; Heb. 3:13]
12 [v]Ps. 19:8, 9; 119:137; 2 Pet. 2:21; [ver. 16]
14 [w]1 Kgs. 21:20, 25; 2 Kgs. 17:17; Isa. 50:1; 52:3
15 [x]ver. 18, 19; [Gal. 5:17]
16 [y]1 Tim. 1:8; [ver. 12]
17 [z]ver. 20
18 [a]Gen. 6:5; 8:21; Job 14:4; 15:14; Ps. 51:5
19 [b]ver. 15
20 [c]ver. 17
22 [d]Ps. 1:2; 112:1; 119:35 [e]2 Cor. 4:16; Eph. 3:16; [1 Pet. 3:4]
23 [f]Gal. 5:17; [James 4:1]

me captive to the law of sin that dwells in my
members. 24 Wretched man that I am! Who
will deliver me from [g]this body of death?
25 Thanks be to God through Jesus Christ our
Lord! So then, I myself serve the law of God
with my mind, but with my flesh I serve the
law of sin.

Life in the Spirit

8 There is therefore now no condemnation
for those who are in Christ Jesus.[1] 2 For the
law of [h]the Spirit of life [i]has set you[2] free in
Christ Jesus from the law of sin and death.
3 For [j]God has done what the law, [k]weakened
by the flesh, [l]could not do. [m]By sending his
own Son [n]in the likeness of sinful flesh and [o]for
sin,[3] he condemned sin in the flesh, 4 in order
that [p]the righteous requirement of the law
might be fulfilled in us, [q]who walk not according to the flesh but according to the Spirit.
5 For [r]those who live according to the flesh set
their minds on [s]the things of the flesh, but
those who live according to the Spirit set their
minds on [t]the things of the Spirit. 6 For to set
[u]the mind on the flesh is death, but to set the
mind on the Spirit is life and peace. 7 For the
mind that is set on the flesh is [v]hostile to God,
for it does not submit to God's law; [w]indeed,
it cannot. 8 Those who are in the flesh cannot
please God.

9 You, however, are not in the flesh but in the
Spirit, if in fact [x]the Spirit of God dwells in
you. [y]Anyone who does not have [z]the Spirit of
Christ does not belong to him. 10 But if Christ
is in you, although the body is dead because
of sin, the Spirit is life because of righteousness. 11 If the Spirit of [a]him who raised Jesus
from the dead dwells in you, he who raised
Christ Jesus[4] from the dead will also give life
to your mortal bodies [b]through his Spirit who
dwells in you.

Heirs with Christ

12 So then, brothers,[5] we are debtors, [c]not to
the flesh, to live according to the flesh. 13 For
if you live according to the flesh you will die,
but if by the Spirit you [d]put to death the deeds
of the body, you will live. 14 For all who are [e]led
by the Spirit of God are [f]sons[6] of God. 15 For
[g]you did not receive [h]the spirit of slavery to

[1] Some manuscripts add *who walk not according to the flesh (but according to the Spirit)* [2] Some manuscripts *me* [3] Or *and as a sin offering* [4] Some manuscripts lack *Jesus* [5] Or *brothers and sisters*; also verse 29 [6] See discussion on "sons" in the Preface

24[g] [ch. 6:6; 8:23]
Chapter 8
2[h] 1 Cor. 15:45; 2 Cor. 3:6 [i] ver. 12; See ch. 6:14, 18; 7:4
3[j] Heb. 10:1, 2, 10, 14; See Acts 13:39 [k] Gal. 4:9; Heb. 7:18 [l] Heb. 10:6, 8 [m] 2 Cor. 5:21 [n] Phil. 2:7; See John 1:14 [o] Lev. 16:5; Heb. 10:6, 8; 13:11
4[p] ch. 1:32; 2:26 [q] Gal. 5:16, 25
5[r] [Gal. 6:8] [s] Gal. 5:19-21 [t] Gal. 5:22, 23, 25
6[u] ver. 13; [Col. 2:18]; See ch. 6:21
7[v] James 4:4 [w] 1 Cor. 2:14
9[x] ver. 11; 1 Cor. 3:16; 6:19; 2 Cor. 6:16; 2 Tim. 1:14 [y] Jude 19; [John 14:17] [z] See Acts 16:7
11[a] See Acts 2:24 [b] [2 Cor. 3:6]
12[c] See ver. 2
13[d] Col. 3:5
14[e] Gal. 5:18 [f] ver. 16, 19; ch. 9:8, 26; Deut. 14:1; Hos. 1:10; John 1:12
15[g] 1 Cor. 2:12 [h] 2 Tim. 1:7; [Gal. 2:4; Heb. 2:15; 1 John 4:18]

8:1–8 Having corrected mistaken impressions about the law and how the gospel relates to it (chs. 6–7), Paul explains how there is "now no condemnation" for believers "in Christ Jesus" (v. 1). Christians are "set free" from sin's guilt and power by the work of the Holy Spirit as he imparts spiritual life (v. 2). Neither the law nor human obedience could confer this life. Only the Son by his coming could, and did (v. 3).

By Christ's finished work, what the law calls for—living in harmony with God and his will—can actually take place through the work of God's Spirit (v. 4). But we all face a stark either/or: either we are oriented toward "the flesh" (the human inclination to sin), which leads to death; or the Spirit reorients us, so that our present possession and final destiny are "life and peace" (vv. 5–6). Without the Spirit, we "cannot please God" (vv. 7–8).

8:9–11 Believers live "in the Spirit" rather than "in the flesh" (v. 9). Physically speaking, in this life our bodies are mortal and sin is present. But God's "righteousness" through the gospel (see 1:16–17) means (among much else) that the Spirit brings life (8:10). The Spirit who raised Jesus transforms believers' everyday lives (v. 11) as he "dwells" among God's people and in their personal spheres. As in chapter 6, Paul teaches that the very resurrection life of Christ dwells in those who have been united to this risen Lord.

8:12–17 Paul discusses the payoff and implications of the Spirit's presence. Before we received the gospel, we could not do God's will freely nor please him fully. But now, through the Spirit, believers have new affections (vv. 5, 15) and can turn their back on sinful behavior (v. 13; for a description of "deeds of the body," see Gal. 5:19–21). God's Spirit leads (Rom. 8:14), grants a new status in God's sight, and prompts an outcry that is quite the opposite of the cry of "Wretched man!" in 7:24: believers, instead, call out, "Abba! Father!" (8:15)

God is not their stern judge but their confidant and helper as he makes them his children by adoption. There is an inward sense of sonship (v. 16). There is the promise

fall back into fear, but you have received the Spirit of [i]adoption as sons, by whom we cry, [j]"Abba! Father!" 16 [k]The Spirit himself bears witness with our spirit that we are children of God, 17 and if children, then [l]heirs—heirs of God and fellow heirs with Christ, [m]provided we suffer with him in order that we may also be glorified with him.

Future Glory

18 For I consider that the sufferings of this present time [n]are not worth comparing with the glory that is to be revealed to us. 19 For the creation waits with eager longing for [o]the revealing of the sons of God. 20 For the creation [p]was subjected to futility, not willingly, but [q]because of him who subjected it, in hope 21 that [r]the creation itself will be set free from its bondage to corruption and obtain the freedom of the glory of the children of God. 22 For we know that [s]the whole creation [t]has been groaning together in the pains of childbirth until now. 23 And not only the creation, but we ourselves, who have [u]the firstfruits of the Spirit, [v]groan inwardly as [w]we wait eagerly for adoption as sons, [x]the redemption of our bodies. 24 For [y]in this hope we were saved. Now [z]hope that is seen is not hope. For who hopes for what he sees? 25 But if we hope for what we do not see, we [a]wait for it with patience.

26 Likewise the Spirit helps us in our weakness. For [b]we do not know what to pray for as we ought, but [c]the Spirit himself intercedes for us with groanings too deep for words. 27 And [d]he who searches hearts knows what is [e]the mind of the Spirit, because[1] the Spirit [f]intercedes for the saints [g]according to the will of God. 28 And we know that for those who love God all things work together [h]for good,[2] for [i]those who are called according to his purpose. 29 For those whom he [j]foreknew he also [k]predestined [l]to be conformed to the image of his Son, in order that he might be [m]the firstborn among many brothers. 30 And those whom he predestined he also called, and those whom he called he also [n]justified, and those whom he justified he also [o]glorified.

God's Everlasting Love

31 What then shall we say to these things? [p]If God is for us, who can be[3] against us? 32 [q]He who did not spare his own Son but [r]gave him

[1] Or *that* [2] Some manuscripts *God works all things together for good*, or *God works in all things for the good* [3] Or *who is*

of present and future inheritance—on the condition that we receive the cross that the gospel calls for as well as the crown that it promises (v. 17). The way of the cross is the only path to the glory awaiting "fellow heirs with Christ." The gospel means strength for trials, not escape from them.

Through it all, however, we remain confident that we are God's own children. By grace, through faith, Christ is our elder brother and we are heirs of God.

8:18–25 Glory awaits the believer in Christ, but "this present time" brings "sufferings" in abundance (v. 18). All creation is "groaning" in anticipation of the "freedom" from "bondage" and "corruption" that God promises (8:19–23; see Gen. 3:16–19). Believers groan, too, as their full salvation lies in the future, which calls for patience (Rom. 8:24–25), a fruit the Spirit gives (see Gal. 5:22–23).

We see in these verses that one day God is going to renovate and restore not only our souls, and not only our physical bodies, but the entire cosmos. All will be put right. Eden will be restored. This globe will become what it was always meant to be.

8:26–30 The whole array of gospel benefits are glimpsed here: the Spirit's intercession (v. 26), combined with God's omniscience (v. 27), God's omnipotence in and over "all things" (v. 28), and the full, unbroken succession of God's savings acts so that believers are assured of their eternal security, and consequently can "be conformed" to the image of God's Son (vv. 29–30). Our salvation is utterly secure: those whom God has foreknown before the dawn of time will one day be glorified.

We could not be more secure. Reflecting on this, our hearts are calmed as we give glory to God for the utter stability of our deliverance.

8:31–39 Paul extolls the glories of "the love of God in Christ Jesus our Lord" (v. 39). No one can frustrate God's purposes (v. 31). Since he gave Jesus (the ultimate treasure of heaven) for us, we can be assured that his care and all his promises stand firm for our present time and for eternity (v. 32; cf. v. 28). Any accuser—Satan, circumstances, sins—shrivels in stature alongside the risen Christ who is interceding for us at God's

15 [i]ver. 23; Gal. 4:5; [ch. 9:4; Isa. 56:5; Jer. 31:9] [j]Gal. 4:6; [Mark 14:36]
16 [k]2 Cor. 1:22; 5:5; Eph. 1:13, 14; 1 John 3:24
17 [l]Gal. 3:29; 4:7; Titus 3:7 [m]2 Cor. 1:7; 2 Tim. 2:12; See Acts 14:22
18 [n]2 Cor. 4:17; [1 Pet. 1:5, 6]
19 [o]1 Pet. 4:13; 5:1; 1 John 3:2; [ch. 2:7]
20 [p]Gen. 3:18, 19; Eccles. 1:2 [q]Gen. 3:17
21 [r][Acts 3:21]
22 [s]Mark 16:15 [t]Jer. 12:4, 11
23 [u][2 Cor. 5:5; James 1:18] [v]2 Cor. 5:2, 4 [w]ver. 19, 25; Isa. 25:9; Gal. 5:5 [x]See ch. 7:24; Luke 21:28
24 [y][1 Thess. 1:3; 5:8] [z]2 Cor. 4:18; Heb. 11:1
25 [a][1 Thess. 1:3; 5:8]
26 [b][Matt. 20:22; James 4:3] [c]Zech. 12:10; Eph. 6:18; See John 14:16
27 [d]1 Sam. 16:7; 1 Chr. 28:9; Prov. 15:11; 17:3; Jer. 11:20; 17:10; Luke 16:15; 1 Thess. 2:4 [e]See ver. 6 [f][ver. 34] [g][1 John 5:14]
28 [h]Ezra 8:22; [Eccles. 8:12] [i]ch. 9:24; 1 Cor. 1:9; 7:15, 17; Gal. 1:15; 5:8; Eph. 4:1, 4; 2 Tim. 1:9
29 [j]ch. 11:2; 1 Pet. 1:2 [k]1 Cor. 2:7; Eph. 1:5, 11; [ch. 9:23] [l]Phil. 3:21; [1 Cor. 15:49; Col. 3:10]; See 1 John 3:2 [m]Col. 1:15, 18; Heb. 1:6; Rev. 1:5
30 [n]1 Cor. 6:11 [o]John 17:22; [Heb. 2:10]
31 [p]Num. 14:9; 2 Kgs. 6:16; Ps. 118:6; 1 John 4:4
32 [q]John 3:16 [r]See ch. 4:25

up for us all, how will he not also with him
graciously give us all things? 33 Who shall
bring any charge against God's elect? [s]It is God
who justifies. 34 [t]Who is to condemn? Christ
Jesus is the one who died—more than that,
who was raised—[u]who is at the right hand of
God, [v]who indeed is interceding for us.[1] 35 Who
shall separate us from the love of Christ? Shall
tribulation, or distress, or persecution, or famine, or nakedness, or danger, or sword? 36 As
it is written,

> [w]"For your sake [x]we are being killed all the
> day long;
> we are regarded as sheep to be slaugh-
> tered."

37 No, in all these things we are more than
[y]conquerors through [z]him who loved us.
38 For I am sure that neither death nor life,
nor angels nor rulers, nor things present nor
things to come, nor powers, 39 nor height nor
depth, nor anything else in all creation, will
be able to separate us from the love of God in
Christ Jesus our Lord.

God's Sovereign Choice

9 [a]I am speaking the truth in Christ—I am
not lying; my conscience bears me witness
in the Holy Spirit— 2 that I have great sorrow and unceasing anguish in my heart. 3 For
[b]I could wish that I myself were [c]accursed and
cut off from Christ for the sake of my brothers,[2] my kinsmen [d]according to the flesh.
4 They are [e]Israelites, and to them belong [f]the
adoption, [g]the glory, [h]the covenants, [i]the giving of the law, [j]the worship, and [k]the promises. 5 To them belong [l]the patriarchs, and from
their race, according to the flesh, is the Christ,
[m]who is God over all, [n]blessed forever. Amen.
6 But it is not as though the word of God has
failed. For not all who are descended from
Israel belong to Israel, 7 and not all are children
of Abraham [o]because they are his offspring,
but [p]"Through Isaac shall your offspring be
named." 8 This means that it is not the children
of the flesh who are the children of God, but
[q]the children of the promise are counted as
offspring. 9 For this is what the promise said:
[r]"About this time next year I will return, and
Sarah shall have a son." 10 And not only so, but
[s]also when Rebekah had conceived children by
one man, our forefather Isaac, 11 though they
were not yet born and had done nothing either
good or bad—in order that God's purpose of
election might continue, not because of works
but because of [t]him who calls— 12 she was told,
[u]"The older will serve the younger." 13 As it is
written, [v]"Jacob I loved, but Esau I hated."

[1] Or *Is it Christ Jesus who died . . . for us?* [2] Or *brothers and sisters*

33[s] Isa. 50:8, 9; [Rev. 12:10, 11]
34[t] ver. 1 [u] See Mark 16:19 [v] Heb. 7:25; 1 John 2:1; [ver. 27]
36[w] Cited from Ps. 44:22 [x] 1 Cor. 4:9; 15:30, 31; 2 Cor. 4:10, 11; See Acts 20:24
37[y] 1 Cor. 15:57; See John 16:33 [z] Gal. 2:20; Eph. 5:2; Rev. 1:5; 3:9
Chapter 9
1[a] 2 Cor. 11:10; 1 Tim. 2:7; [2 Cor. 12:19; Gal. 1:20]; See ch. 1:9
3[b] [Ex. 32:32] [c] 1 Cor. 12:3; 16:22; Gal. 1:8, 9 [d] [ch. 11:14]
4[e] [ver. 6; ch. 2:28, 29; Gal. 6:16] [f] [Ex. 4:22]; See ch. 8:15 [g] Ex. 40:34; 1 Sam. 4:21; 1 Kgs. 8:11 [h] Gen. 17:2; Deut. 29:14; Gal. 4:24; Eph. 2:12 [i] Deut. 4:14; [Ps. 147:19] [j] Heb. 9:1 (Gk.); [ch. 12:1] [k] [Eph. 2:12]; See John 4:22; Acts 13:32
5[l] ch. 11:28 [m] [Eph. 4:6; Col. 1:16-19] [n] ch. 1:25; John 1:1; 2 Cor. 11:31; Heb. 1:8
7[o] [Gal. 4:23]; See John 8:33 [p] Heb. 11:18; Cited from Gen. 21:12; [Gal. 3:29]
8[q] Gal. 4:23, 28
9[r] Cited from Gen. 18:10, 14; [Gen. 17:21]
10[s] Gen. 25:21
11[t] [ch. 4:17]; See ch. 8:28
12[u] Cited from Gen. 25:23 **13**[v] Cited from Mal. 1:2, 3

right hand (vv. 33–34). Paul makes the testimony of the psalmist his own (v. 36). "In all these things" (v. 37; see v. 35) that could seem to defeat God's people, God and the "elect" (v. 33) whom he loves remain united and inseparable, now and forever (vv. 38–39).

9:1–5 As an apostle "set apart for the gospel of God" (1:1), Paul agonizes (9:2) over his "kinsmen" (his fellow Jews; v. 3) just as Christ wept over Jerusalem (Matt. 23:37). Those who know the gospel feel a burden for helping others to know it, too; they have a painful sense of responsibility for their souls (cf. 2 Cor. 11:28; Heb. 13:17). Despite all the gifts and promises they received in former times, right up to and including "Christ, who is God over all" (Rom. 9:4–5), the majority of Jews in Paul's time did not acknowledge Jesus as God's promised Savior and King.

9:6–13 Paul anticipates a key objection to his gospel message: if Jesus is the Christ, and if he came in fulfillment of God's promises in his Word, and if God's chosen people reject the Christ, does that not mean that God's Word has somehow failed? After all, God's people the Jews did not rally to that Word.

Paul's answer is a clear no (v. 6), and across all of chapters 9–11 he gives a sustained response to this question. At the core of Paul's answer is that the gospel is a promise (for the key role that "promise" plays in Romans, see also 1:2; 4:13, 14, 16, 20, 21; 7:10; 9:4; 15:8). Gospel blessing is not a human entitlement based on ethnicity (9:7–8) or some other human achievement or qualification (see John 1:13). Paul bases his claim on the story of "God's purpose of election" seen in the case of Jacob and Esau (Rom. 9:9–13). God bestows his grace with utter sovereignty and wisdom. We bow before him in worship and wonder, knowing that our salvation is truly all of grace.

14 What shall we say then? [w]Is there injustice on God's part? By no means! 15 For he
says to Moses, [x]"I will have mercy on whom
I have mercy, and I will have compassion
on whom I have compassion." 16 So then it
depends not on human will or exertion,[1] but
on God, who has mercy. 17 For the Scripture
says to Pharaoh, [y]"For this very purpose
I have raised you up, that I might show my
power in you, and that my name might be
proclaimed in all the earth." 18 So then he has
mercy on whomever he wills, and he hardens
whomever he wills.

19 You will say to me then, "Why does he still
find fault? For [z]who can resist his will?" 20 But
who are you, O man, [a]to answer back to God?
[b]Will what is molded say to its molder, "Why
have you made me like this?" 21 [c]Has the potter no right over the clay, to make out of the
same lump [d]one vessel for honorable use and
another for dishonorable use? 22 What if God,
desiring to show his wrath and to make known
his power, has endured with much patience
[e]vessels of wrath [f]prepared for destruction,
23 in order to make known [g]the riches of his
glory for vessels of mercy, which he [h]has
prepared beforehand for glory— 24 even us
whom he [i]has called, [j]not from the Jews only
but also from the Gentiles? 25 As indeed he
says in Hosea,

> [k]"Those who were not my people I will
> call 'my people,'
> and her who was not beloved I will
> call 'beloved.'"
> 26 [l]"And in the very place where it was said
> to them, 'You are not my people,'
> there they will be called [m]'sons of the
> living God.'"

27 And Isaiah cries out concerning Israel:
[n]"Though the number of the sons of Israel[2] be
as the sand of the sea, [o]only a remnant of them
will be saved, 28 for the Lord will carry out his
sentence upon the earth fully and without
delay." 29 And as Isaiah predicted,

> [p,q]"If the Lord of hosts had not left us off-
> spring,
> [r]we would have been like Sodom
> and become like Gomorrah."

[1] Greek *not of him who wills or runs* [2] Or *children of Israel*

9:14–18 The God who offers his good news of redemption is certainly not unjust (v. 14; see also 3:4–6). He remains faithful to his own ways, purposes, and promises (9:15). Much depends here on whether God's Word is the measure of his actions, or whether human definition is the standard; Paul argues based on God's Word. God is the only possible ground and source of his mercy (v. 16), as the story of Pharaoh confirms (vv. 17–18). He is not indebted to human expectations or demands.

9:19–24 The objection of verse 19 carries in it a note of accusation against God. Certainly God is willing to "reason together" with humans (see Isa. 1:18). As Jesus was silent before his accusers (1 Pet. 2:23), however, so also Paul gives no explicit answer other than to remind his accusers of God's right to do as he will with those whom he has made (Rom. 9:20–21), in order to reveal his mercy to those whom he has chosen (vv. 22–23).

The answer does not satisfy all of our questions, but it is important to remember that Paul was not seeking here to address the concerns of unbelievers. In this section Paul is still fundamentally answering the earlier question of the concerned Jews in his audience: Has God's Word failed (see v. 6)? Paul asserts God's prerogative to act as he pleases (v. 20), to regard people in keeping with his eternal purposes (vv. 21–23), and so to constitute "his people" not only from Jews (many of whom rejected the gospel) but also from Gentiles (v. 24). In this sense, Paul is actually *expanding* his readers' understanding of those to whom the grace of God applies.

It is at first unsettling to be confronted with God's absolute sovereignty in our salvation. But ultimately this is our true security, for if there was nothing in us, but only God's good pleasure, that brought us *into* grace, then there is nothing in us that can take us *out of* grace.

9:25–29 Paul cites Scripture to verify his conception of God's free and untameable grace. Both Hosea and Isaiah show that God has a track record of confounding human expectations, dispersing his grace freely and uplifting the undeserving. He was never bound to limit the Abrahamic promise (see Rom. 9:7) strictly to bloodlines.

14 [w]Deut. 32:4; 2 Chr. 19:7; Job 8:3; 34:10; Ps. 92:15
15 [x]Cited from Ex. 33:19
17 [y]Cited from Ex. 9:16
19 [z]2 Chr. 20:6; Job 9:12; Dan. 4:35
20 [a]Job 33:13 [b]Isa. 29:16; 45:9
21 [c]Isa. 64:8; Jer. 18:6 [d]2 Tim. 2:20
22 [e][ver. 21, 23; Acts 9:15] [f][Prov. 16:4; 1 Pet. 2:8]
23 [g]Eph. 3:16; See ch. 2:4 [h][ch. 8:29]
24 [i]See ch. 8:28 [j]See ch. 3:29
25 [k]Cited from Hos. 2:23; [1 Pet. 2:10]
26 [l]Cited from Hos. 1:10 [m]See ch. 8:14; Matt. 16:16
27 [n]Cited from Isa. 10:22, 23; [Hos. 1:10] [o]ch. 11:5
29 [p]Cited from Isa. 1:9 [q]James 5:4 [r]Deut. 29:23; Isa. 13:19; Jer. 49:18; 50:40; Amos 4:11

Israel's Unbelief

30 What shall we say, then? [s]That Gentiles who did not pursue righteousness have attained it, that is, [t]a righteousness that is by faith; 31 but that Israel [u]who pursued a law that would lead to righteousness[1] [v]did not succeed in reaching that law. 32 Why? Because they did not pursue it by faith, but as if it were based on works. They have stumbled over the [w]stumbling stone, 33 as it is written,

> [x]"Behold, I am laying in Zion [y]a stone of
> stumbling, and a rock of offense;
> [z]and whoever believes in him will not
> be [a]put to shame."

10 Brothers,[2] my heart's desire and prayer to God for them is that they may be saved. 2 For I bear them witness that [b]they have a zeal for God, [c]but not according to knowledge. 3 For, being ignorant of [d]the righteousness of God, and seeking to establish their own, they did not submit to God's righteousness. 4 For [e]Christ is the end of the law for righteousness to everyone who believes.[3]

The Message of Salvation to All

5 For [f]Moses writes about the righteousness that is based on the law, that [g]the person who does the commandments shall live by them. 6 But [h]the righteousness based on faith says, [i]"Do not say in your heart, 'Who will ascend into heaven?'" (that is, to bring Christ down) 7 "or 'Who will descend into the [j]abyss?'" (that is, [k]to bring Christ up from the dead). 8 But what does it say? [l]"The word is near you, in your mouth and in your heart" (that is, the word of faith that we proclaim); 9 because, if [m]you confess with your mouth that Jesus is Lord and [n]believe in your heart [o]that God raised him from the dead, you will be saved. 10 For with the heart one believes and is justified, and with the mouth one confesses and is saved. 11 For the Scripture says, [p]"Everyone who believes in him will not be put to shame."

[1] Greek *a law of righteousness* [2] Or *Brothers and sisters* [3] Or *end of the law, that everyone who believes may be justified*

30 [s] [ch. 10:20] [t] ch. 1:17; 3:21, 22; 10:6; Gal. 2:16; 3:24; Phil. 3:9; Heb. 11:7
31 [u] [ch. 10:2, 3; 11:7] [v] [Gal. 5:4]
32 [w] See 1 Pet. 2:8
33 [x] 1 Pet. 2:6, 7; Cited from Isa. 28:16; [Ps. 118:22] [y] Isa. 8:14 [z] ch. 10:11 [a] Isa. 49:23; Joel 2:26, 27

Chapter 10
2 [b] See Acts 21:20 [c] [ch. 9:31]
3 [d] See ch. 1:17
4 [e] [Matt. 5:17; Gal. 3:24]
5 [f] Cited from Lev. 18:5 [g] Neh. 9:29; Ezek. 20:11, 13, 21; Matt. 19:17; Luke 10:28; Gal. 3:12; [ch. 7:10]
6 [h] See ch. 9:30 [i] [Deut. 30:12, 13]
7 [j] See Rev. 9:1 [k] Heb. 13:20
8 [l] Cited from Deut. 30:14
9 [m] Matt. 10:32; Luke 12:8; [1 Cor. 12:3; Phil. 2:11] [n] See Acts 16:31 [o] [1 Pet. 1:21]; See Acts 2:24
11 [p] See ch. 9:33

9:30–33 Paul draws this portion of his argument to a close. The gospel's saving effect, "a righteousness that is by faith" (see 1:17), has swept through Gentile populations in places like Rome (9:30). In contrast, "Israel" (meaning most of the millions of Jews in the Roman Empire), fell short of their own law (v. 31). That law reveals sin and points people to their need of Jesus, whom most of the Jews did not accept as their promised King and Savior. As had been true of Paul himself in his youth (see Gal. 1:14), their approach to God was faulty (Rom. 9:32), resulting in stumbling and offense (v. 33) rather than hearing, forgiveness, and new life.

Humanly generated "righteousness" is hollow and worthless. True righteousness is "by faith" (v. 30). This means that we come to God, sinners as we are, with the empty hands of faith, trusting only in Christ.

10:1–4 The question of whether God's Word has failed (9:6) is still on the table. So is Paul's distress that the judgment preached by John the Baptist and Jesus abides on unbelieving Israel in his day. He wants his fellow Jews to be saved from divine wrath (10:1; see 1:18; 2:9). He commends the moral and religious zeal which are his own roots as well (10:2). But this zeal is misguided, he says (v. 2). The Jews' conception of righteousness is flawed because they think it comes from them rather than from God (v. 3), and they will not submit to "God's righteousness" (v. 3)—the provision God makes for our sin to be forgiven and God's justice to be satisfied by faith in Christ (v. 4). Whether "end" in verse 4 means "goal" or "termination" or some of both, Christ is regarded as neither by most of Paul's kinsmen.

These verses are sobering. Evidently it is possible to be zealous for God and for righteousness (vv. 2–3) and yet to be unsaved (v. 1). The distinguishing line among all human beings is not between those who have zeal and those who do not, but between those who have faith and those who do not.

10:5–13 To show that God's Word has not failed (9:6), Paul continually explains his gospel message by appeal to God's Word, in this case Moses and other prophets.

Moses does teach that commandment keeping matters (10:5). But the righteousness based on faith which the gospel reveals (1:17) counsels against the error of replacing Christ's work with human striving or speculation (10:6–7). In verse 8, Paul quotes from Deuteronomy 30:14, seeing there a foreshadowing of the "word of faith" embodied in Christ. The heart of gospel response is acknowledgment of Jesus'

12 [q]For there is no distinction between Jew
and Greek; [r]for the same Lord is Lord of all,
[s]bestowing his riches on all who call on him.
13 For [t]"everyone who calls on the name of the
Lord will be saved."
14 How then will they call on him in whom
they have not believed? And how are they
to believe in him [u]of whom they have never
heard?[1] And how are they to hear [v]without
someone preaching? 15 And how are they to
preach unless they are sent? As it is written,
[w]"How beautiful are the feet of those who
preach the good news!" 16 But [x]they have not
all obeyed the gospel. For Isaiah says, [y]"Lord,
who has believed what he has heard from us?"
17 So [z]faith comes from hearing, and hearing
through the word of Christ.
18 But I ask, have they not heard? Indeed they
have, for

> [a]"Their voice has gone out [b]to all the earth,
> and their words to the ends of the
> world."

19 But I ask, did Israel not understand? First
Moses says,

> [c]"I will [d]make you jealous of those who are
> not a nation;
> with a [e]foolish nation I will make you
> angry."

20 Then Isaiah is so bold as to say,

> [f]"I have been found by those who did not
> seek me;
> I have shown myself to those who did
> not ask for me."

21 But of Israel he says, [g]"All day long I have
held out my hands to a disobedient and contrary people."

The Remnant of Israel

11 I ask, then, [h]has God rejected his people? By no means! For [i]I myself am an
Israelite, a descendant of Abraham,[2] a member of the tribe of Benjamin. 2 [j]God has not
rejected his people whom he [k]foreknew. Do

[1] Or *him whom they have never heard* [2] Or *one of the offspring of Abraham*

divinity, his status as Lord, along with personal trust in him as resurrected from the dead. This fulfills Scripture (Rom. 10:11) and is binding on Jew and Greek alike, for there is only one Lord, and he deals with all persons and ethnicities consistently (v. 12), as Scripture makes clear (v. 13).

10:14–17 These verses outline factors that help explain why so many of Paul's fellow Jews regard Jesus with disbelief. They also help justify Paul's concern for and appeal to Jews. To be saved, they must call on Jesus as Lord (vv. 9, 13). But without believing, which requires hearing, which implies preaching, what hope do they have (v. 14)? And there are no preachers unless they are sent (v. 15). Yet even when all these conditions are met, as in Paul's day when Jesus has come and the gospel message has gone forth to synagogues in many places, the Jews "have not all obeyed the gospel" (v. 16). In the end, it is not the Word of God that has failed (see again 9:6). The issue is rather that many Jews are not giving the Word of Christ a hearing, resulting in disbelief (10:17).

10:18–21 These verses are a reminder of why the book of Isaiah has often been called the fifth Gospel. In Romans 10:18 Paul quotes Isaiah to affirm that the good news has gone out everywhere. Jewish unbelief cannot be blamed on lack of opportunity to hear. In Romans 10:19 Paul quotes Isaiah to affirm that Gentile reception of the gospel should not be an offense to Jews; they should "understand" that what is happening is according to God's will because Isaiah foretells God's revealing himself in a saving way "to those who did not ask for me"—which refers to the Gentiles, as Isaiah makes clear in another passage (Rom. 10:20). In contrast, most of Paul's kinsmen have slammed the door in God's face (v. 21)—yet another gospel prediction and application of Isaiah.

Throughout this section, Paul's point is that the failure of most Jews to receive the gospel does not lie in God's Word (which foresees it happening) but in the refusal of his ancient covenant people to receive it. God himself is perfectly faithful; they, not God, are the faithless ones (cf. 2 Tim. 2:13). The same message applies to people today who reject the offer of the gospel from God's Word, but we ourselves also become faithless if we do not proclaim that Word regardless of the anticipated or actual results.

11:1–6 Romans 11 looks at the question "Has God's word failed?" (9:6) from a fresh vantage point. Paul has shown that God's Word has not failed (Romans 9–10). Perhaps, then, God has rejected his people (11:1). Paul rules out that notion categorically (vv. 1–2).

12 [q]See ch. 3:22, 29 [r]Acts 10:36 [s]See ch. 2:4
13 [t]Acts 2:21; Cited from Joel 2:32
14 [u]Eph. 4:21; [John 9:36; 17:20] [v][Acts 8:31; Titus 1:3]
15 [w]Cited from Isa. 52:7; [Nah. 1:15; Eph. 6:15]
16 [x]ch. 3:3; Heb. 4:2 [y]John 12:38; Cited from Isa. 53:1
17 [z]Gal. 3:2, 5
18 [a]Cited from Ps. 19:4; [1 Thess. 1:8] [b][Mark 16:15]; See Matt. 24:14
19 [c]Cited from Deut. 32:21 [d]ch. 11:11, 14 [e][Titus 3:3]
20 [f]Cited from Isa. 65:1; [ch. 9:30]
21 [g]Cited from Isa. 65:2
Chapter 11
1 [h]1 Sam. 12:22; Jer. 31:37; 33:24 [i]2 Cor. 11:22; Phil. 3:5
2 [j]Ps. 94:14 [k]ch. 8:29

you not know what the Scripture says of Elijah, how he appeals to God against Israel? 3 [l]"Lord, they have killed your prophets, they have demolished your altars, and I alone am left, and they seek my life." 4 But what is God's reply to him? [m]"I have kept for myself seven thousand men who have not bowed the knee to Baal." 5 So too at the present time there is [n]a remnant, chosen by grace. 6 [o]But if it is by grace, it is no longer on the basis of works; otherwise grace would no longer be grace.

7 What then? [p]Israel failed to obtain what it was seeking. The elect obtained it, but the rest [q]were hardened, 8 as it is written,

> [r]"God gave them a spirit of stupor,
> [s]eyes that would not see
> and ears that would not hear,
> down to this very day."

9 And David says,

> [t]"Let their table become a snare and a trap,
> a stumbling block and a retribution
> for them;
> 10 let their eyes be darkened so that they
> cannot see,
> and bend their backs forever."

Gentiles Grafted In

11 So I ask, did they stumble in order that they might fall? By no means! Rather through their trespass [u]salvation has come to the Gentiles, so as to make Israel jealous. 12 Now if their trespass means riches for the world, and if their failure means riches for the Gentiles, how much more will their full inclusion[1] mean!

13 Now I am speaking to you Gentiles. Inasmuch then as [v]I am an apostle to the Gentiles, I magnify my ministry 14 in order somehow to make my fellow Jews jealous, and [w]thus save some of them. 15 For if their rejection means [x]the reconciliation of the world, what will their acceptance mean but life from the dead? 16 [y]If the dough offered as firstfruits is holy, so is the whole lump, and if the root is holy, so are the branches.

17 But if [z]some of the branches were broken off, and you, [a]although a wild olive shoot, were grafted in among the others and now share in the nourishing root[2] of the olive tree, 18 do not be arrogant toward the branches. If you are, remember it is not you who support the root, but the root that supports you. 19 Then you will say, "Branches were broken off so that I might

[1] Greek *their fullness* [2] Greek *root of richness*; some manuscripts *richness*

3[l] Cited from 1 Kgs. 19:10, 14
4[m] Cited from 1 Kgs. 19:18
5[n] ch. 9:27; [Jer. 3:14; Zech. 13:8]
6[o] [ch. 4:4; Deut. 9:4, 5]
7[p] See ch. 9:31 [q] [ver. 25]
8[r] Isa. 29:10 [s] Deut. 29:4; [Isa. 43:8; Jer. 5:21; Ezek. 12:2; Eph. 4:18]; See Matt. 13:14
9[t] Cited from Ps. 69:22, 23
11[u] [Acts 28:28]
13[v] ch. 15:16; [Acts 26:17]; See Acts 9:15
14[w] 1 Cor. 7:16; 9:22; 1 Tim. 4:16; James 5:20
15[x] ch. 5:11
16[y] Num. 15:18-21; Neh. 10:37; Ezek. 44:30
17[z] Jer. 11:16; [Ps. 52:8; John 15:2] [a] [Eph. 2:12]

Once again he turns to Scripture to explain Jewish disbelief of the gospel: it was like that in Elijah's time. There was much rejection of God among Israel, and Elijah despaired (vv. 2–3). But things were not as hopeless as Elijah supposed (v. 4). God's redemptive purposes of grace cannot be thwarted, whatever appearances may be. So it is in Paul's own time: "there is a remnant [like Paul himself], chosen by grace" (v. 5). The mention of grace, not works (v. 6), echoes 9:32 and becomes a transition to 11:7. For grace to remain grace, works must be wholly excluded (v. 6). Grace plus works as a way to God's favor is no grace at all. Grace is all or nothing.

11:7–10 The gospel offers pardon and new life by grace. "Israel" throughout its history was often "hardened" (v. 7). In Paul's time this occurred because they "pursued a law that would lead to righteousness" (9:31). But there is no such law. "The elect obtained" (11:7) divine grace, but others came under divine disfavor, as Scripture describes (vv. 8–10). The gospel proclamation is not only a word of liberation; to those who refuse it, it is a word of judgment (cf. 2 Cor. 2:15–16).

11:11–16 God has not rejected his people, the Jews (vv. 1–6), even though they have stumbled (vv. 7–10). This stumbling (which Paul has already lamented; 9:2–3; 10:1) has a bright side. Gentile reception of the salvation Israel refused might make the latter jealous (11:11). Without question, Jewish disbelief of the gospel is sad, but in their "trespass" lies a backdoor benefit in the form of Gentile redemption (v. 12). By "full inclusion" (see also "their acceptance"; v. 15) Paul probably envisions a coming time when Jewish reception of the gospel will increase dramatically. The next few verses (vv. 13–16) restate and extend verses 11–12. "Dough" and "roots" (v. 16) refer to God's remnant people in Old Testament times, within whose heritage believing Gentiles now stand.

11:17–24 God has not uprooted his people; "the root" remains "holy" (v. 16). But he has broken off branches and grafted Gentiles into "the olive tree" of God's covenant people (v. 17; see also v. 24). Paul warns of arrogance in the form of Gentile disregard

be grafted in." 20 That is true. They were broken off because of their unbelief, but you
[b]stand fast through faith. So [c]do not become
proud, but [d]fear. 21 For if God did not spare the
natural branches, neither will he spare you.
22 Note then the kindness and the severity of
God: severity toward those who have fallen,
but God's kindness to you, [e]provided you
continue in his kindness. Otherwise [f]you too
will be cut off. 23 And [g]even they, if they do not
continue in their unbelief, will be grafted in,
for God has the power to graft them in again.
24 For if you were cut from what is by nature a
wild olive tree, and grafted, contrary to nature,
into a cultivated olive tree, how much more
will these, the natural branches, be grafted
back into their own olive tree.

The Mystery of Israel's Salvation

25 [h]Lest you be wise in your own sight, I do
not want you to be unaware of this mystery,
brothers:[1] [i]a partial hardening has come upon
Israel, [j]until the fullness of the Gentiles has
come in. 26 And in this way all Israel will be
saved, as it is written,

[k]"The Deliverer will come [l]from Zion,
he will banish ungodliness from Jacob";
27 "and this will be my [m]covenant with them
[n]when I take away their sins."

28 As regards the gospel, they are enemies for
your sake. But as regards election, they are
[o]beloved for the sake of their forefathers. 29 For
the gifts and [p]the calling of God are irrevocable. 30 For just as [q]you were at one time disobedient to God but now have received mercy
because of their disobedience, 31 so they too
have now been disobedient in order that by
the mercy shown to you they also may now[2]
receive mercy. 32 For God [r]has consigned all to
disobedience, that he may have mercy on all.

33 Oh, the depth of the riches and [s]wisdom
and knowledge of God! [t]How unsearchable are
his judgments and how inscrutable his ways!

34 "For [u]who has known the mind of the Lord,
or [v]who has been his counselor?"
35 "Or [w]who has given a gift to him
that he might be repaid?"

36 For [x]from him and through him and to him
are all things. [y]To him be glory forever. Amen.

[1] Or *brothers and sisters* [2] Some manuscripts omit *now*

for the Jews, or perhaps disdain for the church's Old Testament heritage (which he emphatically commends; 9:4–5).

Christian complacency has a long and shameful history, and Paul foresees it (11:19). He also warns of its consequences (v. 20). Those Gentiles who suppose they stand fast should not be proud, but should fear (v. 20). Gentiles who get cocky will find that God deals with them just as he dealt with hard-hearted Jews (v. 22). God is both kind and severe, depending on how we approach him; to approach him with presumption to is risk his judgment (v. 23). God can certainly pour out his blessing on those who might seem to have turned away forever (vv. 23–24), just as he can pull the rug out from under the prideful.

11:25–32 Paul hints at how he understands the big picture of the gospel's rejection (by most Jews) and acceptance (by many Gentiles). Jewish "hardening" is only partial. It will one day cease (v. 25). The statement that "all Israel will be saved" (vv. 26–27) may foretell a mass conversion of Jews, or it may assert the salvation of all the "remnant" (v. 5) of God's people, that is, "Israel" in the spiritual sense (see 2:29; 9:6–8). Whatever the case, the effects of God's "election" of Abraham's descendants—however they are defined—are permanent (11:28–29).

There is a mysterious symmetry and reciprocity in God's judgment and mercy to both Gentiles and Jews (vv. 30–32). The bottom line is that God desires to "have mercy on all" (both Jews and Gentiles). Mercy is his heart (cf. Matt. 11:28–30); it is *who he is*.

11:33–36 With high praise and lofty Scripture citations, these verses sum up Paul's arguments in Romans 9–11. God's Word has not failed (Romans 9–10); God has not abandoned his people (Romans 11). Not that humans, including Paul, can understand and explain everything—but at the limits of our understanding of the gospel, there can be awe and joy and hope and wonder. God is working things out despite any appearances to the contrary, and his glory will endure (v. 36). His people can rejoice and rest secure in his gospel promises. The end result of Romans 9–11 is not academic dissection or theological argument, but worship.

20 [b]1 Cor. 10:12; 2 Cor. 1:24 [c]ch. 12:3, 16; 1 Tim. 6:17 [d]Prov. 28:14; Isa. 66:2, 5; Jer. 44:10; Phil. 2:12
22 [e]1 Cor. 15:2; Heb. 3:6, 14 [f][John 15:2]
23 [g]2 Cor. 3:16
25 [h]ch. 12:16 [i]2 Cor. 3:14; [ver. 7] [j][Rev. 7:9]; See Luke 21:24
26 [k]Cited from Isa. 59:20, 21; [John 4:22; Heb. 8:8-12] [l]Ps. 14:7; 53:6
27 [m]See ch. 9:4 [n]Isa. 27:9; [Heb. 8:12]
28 [o]ch. 9:5; Deut. 7:8; 10:15
29 [p]See ch. 8:28
30 [q]Eph. 2:2, 3, 11, 13; Col. 1:21; 3:7; Titus 3:3
32 [r]See ch. 3:9
33 [s]Col. 2:3; [Ps. 139:6; Eph. 3:10] [t]Deut. 29:29
34 [u]Isa. 40:13; 1 Cor. 2:16; [Job 15:8] [v]Job 36:22, 23
35 [w]Job 35:7; 41:11
36 [x]1 Cor. 8:6; 11:12; Col. 1:16; [Heb. 2:10] [y]ch. 16:27; Eph. 3:21; Phil. 4:20; 1 Tim. 1:17; 1 Pet. 4:11; 2 Pet. 3:18; Jude 25; Rev. 1:6; 5:13

A Living Sacrifice

12 [z]I appeal to you therefore, brothers,[1] by
the mercies of God, [a]to present your
bodies [b]as a living sacrifice, holy and acceptable to God, which is your spiritual worship.[2]
2 [c]Do not be conformed to this world,[3] but be
transformed by [d]the renewal of your mind, that
by testing you may [e]discern what is the will of
God, what is good and acceptable and perfect.[4]

Gifts of Grace

3 For [f]by the grace given to me I say to everyone among you [g]not to think of himself more
highly than he ought to think, but to think
with sober judgment, [h]each according to [i]the
measure of faith that God has assigned. 4 For
[j]as in one body we have many members,[5] and
the members do not all have the same function, 5 so we, [k]though many, [l]are one body in
Christ, and individually [m]members one of
another. 6 [n]Having gifts that differ according to the grace given to us, let us use them:
if [o]prophecy, [p]in proportion to our faith; 7 if
[q]service, in our serving; the one who teaches,
in his teaching; 8 the one who exhorts, in his
exhortation; the one who contributes, in generosity; [r]the one who leads,[6] with zeal; the one
who does acts of mercy, with [s]cheerfulness.

Marks of the True Christian

9 [t]Let love be genuine. [u]Abhor what is evil;
hold fast to what is good. 10 [v]Love one another
with brotherly affection. [w]Outdo one another
in showing honor. 11 Do not be slothful in zeal,
[x]be fervent in spirit,[7] [y]serve the Lord. 12 [z]Rejoice
in hope, [a]be patient in tribulation, [b]be constant
in prayer. 13 [c]Contribute to the needs of the
saints and [d]seek to show hospitality.
14 [e]Bless those who persecute you; bless and
do not curse them. 15 [f]Rejoice with those who

[1] Or *brothers and sisters* [2] Or *your rational service* [3] Greek *age* [4] Or *what is the good and acceptable and perfect will of God* [5] Greek *parts*; also verse 5 [6] Or *gives aid* [7] Or *fervent in the Spirit*

Chapter 12
1 [z]1 Cor. 1:10; 2 Cor. 10:1; Eph. 4:1 [a]ch. 6:13, 16, 19; [Ps. 50:13, 14; 1 Cor. 6:20]; See 1 Pet. 2:5 [b]Heb. 10:20
2 [c]1 Pet. 1:14; [1 John 2:15] [d]Titus 3:5; [Ps. 51:10; 2 Cor. 4:16; Eph. 4:23; Col. 3:10] [e]Eph. 5:10; 1 Thess. 4:3
3 [f]See ch. 1:5 [g]ver. 16; ch. 11:20 [h]1 Cor. 7:17 [i]Eph. 4:7
4 [j]1 Cor. 12:12-14; Eph. 4:4, 16
5 [k]1 Cor. 10:17, 33 [l]1 Cor. 12:20; Eph. 4:13; See John 17:11 [m]Eph. 4:25; [1 Cor. 6:15; 12:27]
6 [n]1 Cor. 12:4; 1 Pet. 4:10, 11; [1 Cor. 7:7; 12:7-11] [o]1 Cor. 12:10; See Acts 13:1 [p][2 Tim. 2:15]
7 [q]See Acts 6:1
8 [r]1 Tim. 5:17; [1 Cor. 12:28] [s]2 Cor. 9:7
9 [t]2 Cor. 6:6; 1 Tim. 1:5; 1 Pet. 1:22 [u]Ps. 97:10; 101:3; Amos 5:15; [1 Thess. 5:21, 22]
10 [v]See Heb. 13:1 [w]ch. 13:7; Phil. 2:3; 1 Pet. 2:17
11 [x]Acts 18:25 [y]Acts 20:19
12 [z]See ch. 5:2 [a]See Heb. 10:36 [b]See Acts 1:14
13 [c]ch. 15:25; 1 Cor. 16:1, 15; 2 Cor. 9:1, 12; Heb. 6:10; 13:16; [1 Tim. 6:18] [d]See Matt. 25:35
14 [e]See Matt. 5:44; 1 Pet. 3:9
15 [f]1 Cor. 12:26; [Job 30:25; Heb. 13:3]

12:1–2 Following numerous and important doctrinal explorations of God's plan of redemption in previous chapters, Paul appeals to his readers "by the mercies of God" (mercies that make believers "holy and acceptable to God") to let all he has said about the gospel do its glorious work. The ethical vision of these later chapters of Romans flows from the grand vision of divine grace in the first 11 chapters. Giving glory to God (11:36) is worship, and that is what the gospel enables (12:1) as people present their whole selves and lives completely to God. Part of this is a break with "this world" in its negative aspects, allowing renewal and discernment (v. 2), resulting in life that is "good and acceptable and perfect" (that is, "complete," fulfilling God's purposes).

The aim of the gospel is not merely doctrinal truth but lives that connect with God, delight in his will, and further his interests in glad communion with him.

12:3–8 Faith in Christ brings humility, but it also brings an active resolve to live to the full measure of one's faith (v. 3). This is a growing and not static self-assessment, far removed from self-absorbed and passive piety. There is both unity and individuality in the household of faith that the gospel produces (vv. 4–5). We are indebted to the larger body—Christ's body, the church—and we owe our fellow believers the fruit of the grace God has given us (v. 6). Our God-given strengths (vv. 6–8) may involve gifts of a "public" nature (prophecy, teaching, exhorting), or we may find ourselves using our gifts in a more non-public way (serving, contributing, leading, showing mercy). In either case, God has assigned each believer a faith-capacity that begs for expression in serving God and others.

The gospel does not produce perpetual spectators but mobilizes hearers to make a difference for others as God has made a difference in them. We love as he has loved us (Eph. 4:32–5:2). We serve as he has served us (Mark 10:45).

12:9–13 "Let love be genuine" (v. 9) may be the heading under which to understand the rest of this chapter, and perhaps beyond. Love combines with faith and hope (see 1 Cor. 13:13) to describe the highest fulfillment of God's saving Word to his people (see Rom. 13:8–10). Genuine love, produced by the gospel through which God's love is "poured into our hearts" (5:5), detests evil and pursues good (12:9). It spawns mutual affection in the church and promotes others (v. 10). It is zealous, fervent, and selfless for the Lord's sake (v. 11). In the most difficult of circumstances, love overcomes through hope, steadfastness in suffering, and prayer (v. 12). It is openhanded and openhearted to others and their physical needs (v. 13).

rejoice, weep with those who weep. 16 [g]Live
in harmony with one another. [h]Do not be
haughty, but associate with the lowly.[1] [i]Never
be wise in your own sight. 17 [j]Repay no one
evil for evil, but [k]give thought to do what is
honorable in the sight of all. 18 If possible, so
far as it depends on you, [l]live peaceably with
all. 19 Beloved, [m]never avenge yourselves, but
leave it[2] to the wrath of God, for it is written, [n]"Vengeance is mine, I will repay, says
the Lord." 20 To the contrary, [o]"if your enemy
is hungry, feed him; if he is thirsty, give him
something to drink; for by so doing you will
heap burning coals on his head." 21 Do not be
overcome by evil, but overcome evil with good.

Submission to the Authorities

13 Let every person [p]be subject to the
governing authorities. For [q]there is no
authority except from God, and those that
exist have been instituted by God. 2 Therefore
whoever resists the authorities resists what
God has appointed, and those who resist will
incur judgment. 3 For rulers are not a terror
to good conduct, but to bad. Would you have
no fear of the one who is in authority? Then
do what is good, and you [r]will receive his
approval, 4 for [s]he is God's servant for your
good. But if you do wrong, be afraid, for he
does not bear the sword in vain. For he is the
servant of God, [t]an avenger who carries out
God's wrath on the wrongdoer. 5 Therefore one
must be in subjection, not only to avoid God's
wrath but also [u]for the sake of conscience.
6 For because of this you also pay taxes, for
the authorities are ministers of God, attending
to this very thing. 7 [v]Pay to all what is owed to
them: taxes to whom taxes are owed, revenue
to whom revenue is owed, respect to whom
respect is owed, honor to whom honor is owed.

Fulfilling the Law Through Love

8 [w]Owe no one anything, except to love each
other, for [x]the one who loves another has

[1] Or *give yourselves to humble tasks* [2] Greek *give place*

These things describe the love shown to us by the Lord Jesus himself in the gospel. To love genuinely is to live compassionately toward others in the way that Jesus himself has already treated us.

12:14–21 A catalog of loving acts and strategies continues. Much here echoes Jesus' teaching in the Gospels, as it also reflects the way he lived on earth. This includes love even for detractors or opponents (vv. 14, 20–21). Faith in Christ through the gospel message activates love full of empathy (v. 15), harmony (v. 16), and noble deference to others, even enemies (v. 17). Where conflict can possibly be avoided, the gospel mandates peaceable relations with others (v. 18), not rivalry, contention, or apathy. A strong sense of God's presence, faithfulness, and ultimate justice means that vengeance can be left in his sure hands (v. 19).

Those united to Christ imitate their Master not in dutiful, self-generated efforts but in light of the great love with which he himself has loved us.

13:1–7 This section continues to apply Paul's call for genuine love (see 12:9, and its restatement in 13:8–10). Love for God means respecting structures "instituted by God" (13:1), such as government. Paul speaks in general terms about government in its God-given functions such as deterring bad conduct (v. 2), approving good conduct (v. 3), and administering punishment to wrongdoers (v. 4).

There are plenty of examples in Scripture of God's servants making the difficult decision to "obey God rather than men" (Acts 5:29). The gospel does not endorse blind submission to every governmental presence or policy, especially where citizens have voting rights and must choose between candidates and ultimately between governments. For every election means a choice for one governmental option rather than another. Misguided citizenship, whether too little compliance with government or too much, can be harmful to the conscience (Rom. 13:5). Paying taxes is an expression of respect for government (v. 6).

Believers in Christ should have an open, honest, respectful, and affirming interface with governmental authorities and the forms their oversight of society takes (v. 7). Such an attitude was exemplified by our Lord (Matt. 22:21).

13:8–10 These verses conclude Paul's call for proactive love across the sweep of believers' lives that began back in 12:9. "Owe" in 13:8 refers back to verse 7. Believers

16 [g]ch. 15:5; 2 Cor. 13:11; Phil. 2:2; 4:2; 1 Pet. 3:8 [h]ver. 3; Ps. 131:1; Jer. 45:5 [i]ch. 11:25; Prov. 3:7
17 [j]Prov. 20:22; Matt. 5:39; [ch. 14:19] [k]2 Cor. 8:21; [ch. 14:16]
18 [l]See Mark 9:50
19 [m]Prov. 20:22; Matt. 5:39; [ch. 14:19] [n]Heb. 10:30; Cited from Deut. 32:35; [Ps. 94:1; 1 Thess. 4:6]
20 [o]Cited from Prov. 25:21, 22; [Ex. 23:4, 5; 2 Kgs. 6:22; Luke 6:27]

Chapter 13
1 [p]Titus 3:1; 1 Pet. 2:13 [q][John 19:11]; See Dan. 2:21
3 [r]1 Pet. 2:14
4 [s]2 Chr. 19:6 [t]1 Thess. 4:6
5 [u]1 Pet. 2:19; [Eccles. 8:2]
7 [v]Matt. 17:25; 22:21; Mark 12:17
8 [w][Lev. 19:13; Prov. 3:27, 28] [x]ver. 10; [Matt. 22:40; Col. 3:14]; See John 13:34

fulfilled the law. 9 For the commandments,
[y]"You shall not commit adultery, You shall
not murder, You shall not steal, You shall not
covet," and any other commandment, are
summed up in this word: [z]"You shall love your
neighbor as yourself." 10 Love does no wrong
to a neighbor; therefore [a]love is the fulfilling
of the law.

11 Besides this you know the time, that the
hour has come for you [b]to wake from sleep.
[c]For salvation is nearer to us now than when
we first believed. 12 [d]The night is far gone;
the day is at hand. So then let us [e]cast off [f]the
works of darkness and [g]put on the armor of
light. 13 [h]Let us walk properly as in the daytime,
[i]not in orgies and drunkenness, not in sexual
immorality and sensuality, [j]not in quarreling and jealousy. 14 But [k]put on the Lord Jesus
Christ, and make no provision for the flesh,
[l]to gratify its desires.

Do Not Pass Judgment on One Another

14 As for [m]the one who is weak in faith,
welcome him, but not to quarrel over
opinions. 2 [n]One person believes he may eat
anything, while the weak person eats only
vegetables. 3 Let not the one who eats despise
the one who abstains, and [o]let not the one who
abstains pass judgment on the one who eats,
for God has welcomed him. 4 [p]Who are you to
pass judgment on the servant of another? It is
before his own master[1] that he stands or falls.
And he will be upheld, for the Lord is able to
make him stand.

[1] Or *lord*

9 [y] Matt. 19:18; Cited from Ex. 20:13-17; Deut. 5:17-21 [z] Cited from Lev. 19:18
10 [a] [John 14:15]; See ver. 8
11 [b] 1 Cor. 15:34; Eph. 5:14; 1 Thess. 5:6 [c] [Isa. 56:1; Luke 21:28]
12 [d] [John 9:4] [e] Col. 3:8 [f] Eph. 5:11; [John 3:20] [g] 2 Cor. 6:7; Eph. 6:11, 13; 1 Thess. 5:8
13 [h] 1 Thess. 4:12 [i] Luke 21:34; Gal. 5:21; 1 Pet. 4:3 [j] James 3:14, 16
14 [k] Gal. 3:27; [Job 29:14; Ps. 132:9; Luke 24:49; Eph. 4:24; Col. 3:10] [l] Gal. 5:16; 1 Pet. 2:11

Chapter 14
1 [m] ch. 15:1; 1 Cor. 8:9-11; 9:22
2 [n] ver. 14
3 [o] Col. 2:16
4 [p] James 4:12

should not be in debt for back taxes or other forms of social irresponsibility. The gospel calls for more, and that is "to love each other" (v. 8).

Properly understood and applied, all God's commandments are good and important, as Paul already argued (see 3:31; 7:12). But together, they point to the expression of all laws combined: the embodiment of God's own nature (see 1 John 4:8, 16) in fond personal regard for others (Rom. 13:9). To break the commands mentioned in 13:9 would be to violate the love imperative; to "love your neighbor" is a form of living out in the Spirit what the law calls for (v. 10; see also 8:4). It should be observed how closely Paul connects Old Testament Scripture with what gospel belief means for Christians (see also 15:4).

Christians love. That is what we do. In this is our entire ethic summed up. Yet we love not to earn God's love for us, but in reflection of, and being assured of, his love.

13:11–14 If 12:9–13:10 gives applications of gospel-driven love, this section pictures gospel-driven hope. Knowing "the time" (13:11) was also a theme in Jesus' teaching (Luke 12:56). In these verses Paul applies insights from apostolic teaching on the end times (eschatology). Christ has come and has died and risen, and "the day is at hand" that his reign at God's right hand upholds (Rom. 13:12; cf. Heb. 1:3). Implied here is the vindication of the gospel at Christ's return. This calls for transformed living (Rom. 13:11), casting off certain behaviors and putting on the armor of Jesus' goodness and guidance (v. 12). Jesus spoke of people loving darkness (John 3:19); Paul gives examples of dark behaviors from which God's good news frees his people (Rom. 13:13; see 6:17–18). The overarching antidote to deeds that dishonor God is a union with Christ (13:14) that overwhelms sinful tendencies by satisfying the soul and filling the lives of God's people with his wonderful expectations, perfect will, and overcoming power (see 12:2).

This passage (specifically 13:13–14) is the passage God used to turn around the life of the great Christian leader Augustine (A.D. 354–430).

14:1–4 Paul takes up the matter of peaceful coexistence in church congregations. The faith of some may be mature, but others' faith may be weak (see 1 Cor. 8:7). Mutual acceptance is called for (Rom. 14:1). Diet was (and in places still is) a point of contention (vv. 2–3). Paul applies Jesus' teaching on misguided judgment of others (vv. 4, 10; cf. Matt. 7:1–5). Gospel communities should major in mutual support. Members should give God space to work with people whose devotion needs an upgrade (Rom. 14:5). In all our relationships with other believers, we are to embody the grace that God has shown us in Christ.

5 [q]One person esteems one day as better than another, while another esteems all days alike. [r]Each one should be fully convinced in his own mind. 6 The one who observes the day, observes it in honor of the Lord. The one who eats, eats in honor of the Lord, since [s]he gives thanks to God, while the one who abstains, abstains in honor of the Lord and gives thanks to God. 7 For [t]none of us lives to himself, and none of us dies to himself. 8 For if we live, we live to the Lord, and if we die, we die to the Lord. So then, [u]whether we live or whether we die, we are the Lord's. 9 For to this end Christ [v]died and lived again, that he might be Lord both [w]of the dead and of the living.

10 Why do you pass judgment on your brother? Or you, why do you despise your brother? For [w]we will all stand before [x]the judgment seat of God; 11 for it is written,

> [y]"As I live, says the Lord, every knee shall bow to me,
> and every tongue shall confess[1] to God."

12 So then [z]each of us will give an account of himself to God.

Do Not Cause Another to Stumble

13 [a]Therefore let us not pass judgment on one another any longer, but rather decide [b]never to put a stumbling block or hindrance in the way of a brother. 14 I know and am persuaded in the Lord Jesus [c]that nothing is unclean in itself, [d]but it is unclean for anyone who thinks it unclean. 15 For if your brother is grieved by what you eat, [e]you are no longer walking in love. [f]By what you eat, do not destroy the one for whom Christ died. 16 [g]So do not let what you regard as good be spoken of as evil. 17 [h]For the kingdom of God is not a matter of eating and drinking but [i]of righteousness and [j]peace and joy in the Holy Spirit. 18 Whoever thus serves Christ is [k]acceptable to God and approved by men. 19 So then let us [l]pursue what makes for peace and for [m]mutual upbuilding.

20 [n]Do not, for the sake of food, destroy the work of God. [o]Everything is indeed clean, but [p]it is wrong for anyone to make another stumble by what he eats. 21 [q]It is good not to eat meat or drink wine or do anything that causes your brother to stumble.[2] 22 The faith

[1] Or *shall give praise* [2] Some manuscripts add *or be hindered or be weakened*

14:5–9 Another example of potential conflict: various attitudes about the observance of "days" (v. 5). This may point to Jew-Gentile tensions in Roman congregations, as Jewish converts may have had a soft spot for continuing observance of feasts and occasions that Gentile converts felt no responsibility toward. An analogy today might be differing views on what kinds of activities one may engage in on Sundays. But since every congregation member is "the Lord's" (v. 8), we should work through these matters with mutual love and respect—serving one another with the priority of building up the church rather that enforcing our own preferences. Jesus' death and resurrection on behalf of all those in the church—i.e., the core of the gospel message—provides the foundation for Paul's reasoning in this entire section (v. 9).

14:10–12 Throughout 14:1–15:7, Paul speaks of matters involving legitimate differences of opinion, not issues of overt biblical commands such as stealing or idolatry or sexual misconduct, which are matters for congregational discipline (see 1 Cor. 5:9–13). Where there is personal latitude and freedom of choice, God's coming judgment should make believers hesitant to try to do his job for him. We act toward others mindful of God's supreme authority over us, as Jesus himself taught (cf. Matt. 7:1).

14:13–19 Paul is not calling for indifference toward other members, nor suspension of all objective standards. The idea is rather to avoid hindering others' spiritual growth (v. 13), and to realize that the same activity may or may not be appropriate for everyone in a congregation (v. 14). What does *not* vary is the gospel mandate to be "walking in love" (v. 15). Don't force God's expectations for you onto someone else (v. 16); the very highest considerations, drawing on God's own character and gifts, should rule (v. 17; see Col. 3:15). God's approval, human affirmation (where possible; see Rom. 12:18), and mutual promotion in the sight of God are the priorities (14:18–19).

14:20–23 The gospel message does "the work of God" in his people's lives (v. 20). Believers should not interfere with that. Jesus declared all foods "clean" (Mark 7:19; see Acts 10:15). There may still be need to restrain one's own liberty for the sake of not impeding or damaging others (Rom. 14:21). The goal is integrity in one's personal

5 [q]Gal. 4:10; [Zech. 7:5, 6] [r]ver. 23
6 [s]1 Cor. 10:30, 31; 1 Tim. 4:3, 4; See Matt. 15:36
7 [t]2 Cor. 5:15; Gal. 2:20; 1 Pet. 4:2; [1 Cor. 6:19; 1 Thess. 5:10]
8 [u]Phil. 1:20
9 [v]Rev. 1:18; 2:8 [w]See Acts 10:42; Rev. 20:12
10 [w][See ver. 9 above] [x]2 Cor. 5:10
11 [y]Phil. 2:10, 11; Cited from Isa. 45:23
12 [z]Matt. 12:36; 16:27; 1 Pet. 4:5; [Gal. 6:5]
13 [a]See Matt. 7:1 [b][1 Cor. 8:13]
14 [c]ver. 2, 20; See Acts 10:15 [d][1 Cor. 8:7, 10]
15 [e]Eph. 5:2 [f]1 Cor. 8:11; [ver. 20]
16 [g][ch. 12:17; 1 Cor. 10:29, 30]
17 [h]1 Cor. 8:8 [i][1 Cor. 6:9] [j]Gal. 5:22; [ch. 15:13]
18 [k][2 Cor. 8:21]
19 [l]Ps. 34:14; 1 Cor. 7:15; 2 Tim. 2:22 [m]ch. 15:2; 1 Cor. 14:12
20 [n]ver. 15 [o]Titus 1:15; See ver. 14 [p]1 Cor. 8:9-12
21 [q]1 Cor. 8:13

that you have, keep between yourself and God.
[r]Blessed is the one who has no reason to pass
judgment on himself for what he approves.
23 But whoever has doubts is condemned if he
eats, because the eating is not from faith. For
whatever does not proceed from faith is sin.[1]

The Example of Christ

15 [s]We who are strong [t]have an obligation
to bear with the failings of the weak,
and not to please ourselves. 2 [u]Let each of us
please his neighbor for his good, to build him
up. 3 For [v]Christ did not please himself, but as
it is written, [w]"The reproaches of those who
reproached you fell on me." 4 For [x]whatever
was written in former days was written for
our [y]instruction, that through endurance and
through [z]the encouragement of the Scriptures
we might have hope. 5 May the God of endurance and encouragement grant you [a]to live
in such harmony with one another, in accord
with Christ Jesus, 6 that together you may with
one voice glorify [b]the God and Father of our
Lord Jesus Christ. 7 Therefore welcome one
another as Christ has welcomed you, for the
glory of God.

Christ the Hope of Jews and Gentiles

8 For I tell you that Christ [c]became a servant
to the circumcised to show God's truthfulness, in order [d]to confirm the promises given
to the patriarchs, 9 and in order [e]that the
Gentiles might glorify God for his mercy. As
it is written,

> [f]"Therefore I will praise you among the
> Gentiles,
> and sing to your name."

10 And again it is said,

> [g]"Rejoice, O Gentiles, with his people."

11 And again,

> [h]"Praise the Lord, all you Gentiles,
> and let all the peoples extol him."

12 And again Isaiah says,

> [i,j]"The root of Jesse will come,
> even he who arises to rule the
> Gentiles;
> [k]in him will the Gentiles hope."

13 May the God of hope fill you with all [l]joy and
peace in believing, so that by the power of the
Holy Spirit you may abound in hope.

[1] Some manuscripts insert here 16:25–27

22 [r]1 John 3:21
Chapter 15
1 [s][Gal. 6:1] [t]1 Thess. 5:14; See ch. 14:1
2 [u]1 Cor. 10:33; [1 Cor. 9:19, 22; 10:24; Phil. 2:4]
3 [v]Phil. 2:5, 8; [John 5:30; 6:38] [w]Cited from Ps. 69:9
4 [x]ch. 4:23 [y]2 Tim. 3:16 [z]Ps. 119:50
5 [a]See ch. 12:16
6 [b]2 Cor. 1:3; Eph. 1:3; 1 Pet. 1:3; [John 20:17; Eph. 1:17; Rev. 1:6]
8 [c]Matt. 15:24; John 1:11; [Heb. 3:1]; See Acts 3:26 [d][ch. 4:16; 2 Cor. 1:20]
9 [e]See ch. 3:29 [f]Cited from 2 Sam. 22:50; Ps. 18:49
10 [g]Cited from Deut. 32:43
11 [h]Cited from Ps. 117:1
12 [i]Cited from Isa. 11:10 [j]Isa. 11:1; [Rev. 5:5; 22:16] [k]Matt. 12:21
13 [l][ch. 5:1, 2; 14:17]

life and avoidance of what does not please God (v. 22). Gospel faith is the means of embracing, and the measure of, what is acceptable in God's sight (v. 23). We sacrifice our own desires for the sake of others because that is precisely what Jesus has done for us.

15:1–7 This section continues the theme of Romans 14: gospel faith produces maximal regard for the good of others, not a relentless drive toward self-satisfaction through self-justification (15:1–2). Christ forwent his own rights and dignity so that salvation might come to others, in keeping with Old Testament prophecy (v. 3). These same Scriptures, the Bible upon which Jesus relied, are a primary source for Christian perseverance, direction, and resilience (v. 4). The Old Testament, Paul says, was written, ultimately, so that "we might have hope" (v. 4). The whole Bible is a message of hope, not, in the first instance, of demand. This section concludes with a glorious vision of the nature, activity, and agenda that can and should characterize every church (vv. 5–7).

15:8–13 These verses serve two purposes. They repeat that Jesus gave himself for the sake of others, even for "the circumcised" (v. 8)—his own people, who for the most part had rejected him (John 1:11). This shows believers how they should treat one another (see Rom. 15:7) even when they hold deep-seated and opposing personal opinions. These differences may be especially acute in the Roman church, where Jews and Gentiles of different ethnicities, backgrounds, and habits are gathering together for Christian worship. Thus, these verses also give a fourfold Scriptural proof of God's desire to bring Gentiles into the kingdom in order to fulfill his promises to the Jewish patriarchs (vv. 8–12). This epochal truth and fulfillment of prophecy is the ground for Paul's encouraging the Roman Christians toward mutual love: the multiethnic gathering of worshipers was always God's plan, and his past faithfulness to his plan and promises brings the hope of greater victories for the gospel in the future (v. 13). God's mission to the Gentiles in his Son will also be a main theme of the next section.

Paul the Minister to the Gentiles

14 [m]I myself am satisfied about you, my
brothers,[1] that you yourselves are full of goodness, filled with [n]all knowledge and able to
instruct one another. 15 But on some points
I have written to you very boldly by way of
reminder, [o]because of the grace given me by
God 16 to be [p]a minister of Christ Jesus to the
Gentiles [q]in the priestly service of the gospel
of God, so that [r]the offering of the Gentiles
may be acceptable, sanctified by the Holy
Spirit. 17 In Christ Jesus, then, I have [s]reason
to be proud of [t]my work for God. 18 For I will
not venture to speak of anything except
[u]what Christ has accomplished through me
[v]to bring the Gentiles to obedience—by word
and deed, 19 [w]by the power of signs and wonders, by the power of the Spirit of God—so
that [x]from Jerusalem and all the way around
[y]to Illyricum I have fulfilled the ministry of
the gospel of Christ; 20 and thus I make it my
ambition to preach the gospel, not where
Christ has already been named, [z]lest I build
on someone else's foundation, 21 but as it is
written,

> [a]"Those who have never been told of him
> will see,
> and those who have never heard will
> understand."

Paul's Plan to Visit Rome

22 This is the reason why [b]I have so often
been hindered from coming to you. 23 But
now, since I no longer have any room for work
in these regions, and [c]since I have longed for
many years to come to you, 24 I hope to see
you in passing as I go [d]to Spain, and [e]to be
helped on my journey there by you, once
I have enjoyed your company for a while. 25 At
present, however, [f]I am going to Jerusalem
bringing aid to the saints. 26 For [g]Macedonia
and Achaia have been pleased to make some
contribution for the poor among the saints
at Jerusalem. 27 For they were pleased to do
it, and indeed [h]they owe it to them. For if the
Gentiles have come to share in their spiritual
blessings, they ought also to be of service to
them in material blessings. 28 When therefore
I have completed this and have delivered to
them what has been collected,[2] I will leave
[i]for Spain by way of you. 29 I know that when
I come to you I will come in the fullness of the
blessing[3] of Christ.

30 I appeal to you, brothers, by our Lord Jesus
Christ and by [j]the love of the Spirit, [k]to strive
together with me in your prayers to God on
my behalf, 31 [l]that I may be delivered from the
unbelievers in Judea, and that [m]my service for
Jerusalem may be acceptable to the saints, 32 so
that by God's will I may come to you with joy

[1] Or *brothers and sisters*; also verse 30 [2] Greek *sealed to them this fruit* [3] Some manuscripts insert *of the gospel*

15:14–21 Paul's expectations are high (v. 14) because he knows these believers have received the gospel. But they need to be pushed (v. 15), because they play a part in Paul's spread of "the gospel of God" (v. 16). That gospel's work through Paul, "in Christ Jesus" (v. 17), has accomplished a great deal (v. 18), as it continues to do today, as Gentiles pour into the kingdom by "the Spirit of God" in fulfillment of the apostolic "ministry of the gospel of Christ" (v. 19). God has been true to his age-old gospel promises, as he will be to the end of the age (vv. 20–21; cf. Matt. 28:20). To abandon his promises would be to "de-God" himself; he cannot do it.

15:22–29 These verses help prepare for Paul's eventual, hoped-for arrival in Rome. They also demonstrate aspects of the gospel's work in Paul's own life. He longs for the Romans, whom he has never seen (vv. 22–23). He has continuing missionary zeal and desire to unite with the Romans in spreading the good news (v. 24). He shows the compassion for his Jewish kinsmen also expressed in chapters 9–11, as he speaks of the "contribution" which has been ongoing for years to alleviate suffering among Jewish believers in Judea (15:25–28; cf. 1 Cor. 16:1–3). He shows optimism that God will overcome all barriers to the gospel going forth (Rom. 15:29).

15:30–33 In gospel service, prayer is a primary key to fulfillment of God's call (v. 30; see Eph. 6:18–19). So is a frank acceptance of likely impediments and dangers, along with the courage to trust God despite them (Rom. 15:31), borne up by a lively sense of God's goodness and power to bestow refreshment and peace whatever may come (vv. 32–33).

14 [m][2 Pet. 1:12; 3:1; 1 John 2:21] [n]1 Cor. 1:5; 13:2; [1 Cor. 8:1, 7, 10; 12:8]
15 [o]See ch. 1:5
16 [p]See ch. 11:13 [q][Mal. 1:11] [r]Isa. 66:20; [Phil. 2:17]
17 [s]Phil. 3:3 [t]Heb. 2:17; 5:1
18 [u]Acts 15:12; 21:19; Gal. 2:8 [v]See ch. 1:5
19 [w]2 Cor. 12:12; [Acts 19:11] [x]Acts 22:17-21 [y][Acts 20:1, 2]
20 [z][2 Cor. 10:13, 15, 16]
21 [a]Cited from Isa. 52:15
22 [b]ch. 1:13; [1 Thess. 2:18]
23 [c]ver. 29, 32; ch. 1:10, 11; Acts 19:21
24 [d]ver. 28 [e]See Acts 15:3
25 [f]Acts 19:21; 20:22; 21:15; 24:17; [ver. 31]
26 [g]1 Cor. 16:1-4; 2 Cor. 8:1; 9:2, 13
27 [h]1 Cor. 9:11; [Gal. 6:6]
28 [i]ver. 24
30 [j][Phil. 2:1; Col. 1:8] [k]Col. 4:12; [2 Cor. 1:11; Col. 2:1, 2; Heb. 13:18]
31 [l]2 Thess. 3:2; [2 Tim. 3:11; 4:17] [m]2 Cor. 8:4

and [n]be refreshed in your company. [33]May [o]the
God of peace be with you all. Amen.

Personal Greetings

16 I commend to you our sister Phoebe,
a servant[1] of the church at [p]Cenchreae,
[2]that you [q]may welcome her in the Lord in
a way worthy of the saints, and help her in
whatever she may need from you, for she has
been a patron of many and of myself as well.
[3]Greet [r]Prisca and Aquila, my fellow workers in Christ Jesus, [4]who risked their necks
for my life, to whom not only I give thanks
but all the churches of the Gentiles give
thanks as well. [5]Greet also [s]the church in their
house. Greet my beloved Epaenetus, who was
[t]the first convert[2] to Christ in Asia. [6]Greet
Mary, who has worked hard for you. [7]Greet
Andronicus and Junia,[3] my kinsmen and
my [u]fellow prisoners. They are well known
to the apostles,[4] and they were in Christ
before me. [8]Greet Ampliatus, my beloved
in the Lord. [9]Greet Urbanus, our fellow
worker in Christ, and my beloved Stachys.
[10]Greet Apelles, who is approved in Christ.
Greet those [v]who belong to the family of
Aristobulus. [11]Greet my kinsman Herodion.
Greet those in the Lord who belong to the
family of Narcissus. [12]Greet those workers in
the Lord, Tryphaena and Tryphosa. Greet the
beloved Persis, who has worked hard in the
Lord. [13]Greet Rufus, chosen in the Lord; also
his mother, who has been a mother to me as
well. [14]Greet Asyncritus, Phlegon, Hermes,
Patrobas, Hermas, and the brothers[5] who are
with them. [15]Greet Philologus, Julia, Nereus
and his sister, and Olympas, and all the saints
who are with them. [16] [w]Greet one another
with a holy kiss. All the churches of Christ
greet you.

Final Instructions and Greetings

[17]I appeal to you, brothers, to watch out for
those who cause divisions and create obstacles
[x]contrary to the doctrine that you have been
taught; [y]avoid them. [18]For such persons do not
serve our Lord Christ, but [z]their own appetites,[6] and [a]by smooth talk and flattery they
deceive the hearts of the naive. [19]For [b]your obedience is known to all, so that I rejoice over
you, but I want you [c]to be wise as to what is
good and innocent as to what is evil. [20] [d]The

[1] Or *deaconess* [2] Greek *firstfruit* [3] Or *Junias* [4] Or *messengers* [5] Or *brothers and sisters*; also verse 17 [6] Greek *their own belly*

32[n] [1 Cor. 16:18; 2 Cor. 7:13; Philem. 7, 20]
33[o] ch. 16:20; 2 Cor. 13:11; Phil. 4:9; 1 Thess. 5:23; Heb. 13:20; [1 Cor. 14:33; 2 Thess. 3:16]
Chapter 16
1[p] Acts 18:18
2[q] Phil. 2:29
3[r] See Acts 18:2
5[s] 1 Cor. 16:19; [Col. 4:15; Philem. 2] [t] [1 Cor. 16:15]
7[u] Col. 4:10; Philem. 23
10[v] 1 Cor. 1:11
16[w] 1 Cor. 16:20; 2 Cor. 13:12; 1 Thess. 5:26; [1 Pet. 5:14]
17[x] 1 Tim. 1:3; 6:3 [y] See 2 John 10
18[z] Phil. 3:19; [2 Tim. 3:4; Titus 1:12] [a] Col. 2:4; 2 Pet. 2:3
19[b] ch. 1:8 [c] [Jer. 4:22]; See Matt. 10:16
20[d] See ch. 15:33

16:1–16 These verses show how the spreading of the gospel can prosper. First, there is prayer and love on the part of a leader, in this case Paul. His recollection of so many names and details is best explained by his sustained and systematic prayer for them.

Second, there is mutual trust and shared ministry. Phoebe (v. 1) has supported Paul and others (v. 2; she must have had some wealth); now she is carrying this letter to Rome. Like many others mentioned in this section, the gospel has gone forth in part due to her commitment and involvement.

Third, many have worked hard for the sake of the gospel: Mary (v. 6); Urbanus (v. 9); Tryphaena, Tryphosa, and Persis (v. 12). Some have risked their lives (Prisca and Aquila; v. 3).

Fourth and in sum, the gospel most frequently goes forth not by individual effort alone but through the shared labor and sacrifice of many, representing both genders, many backgrounds, different social classes, and varying locations. This section is, then, a wonderful illustration of the doctrine of the church expressed in 12:5.

16:17–20 There will always be opposition to Christ's followers and their mission. This typically takes the form of divisive behavior and skewed doctrine (v. 17). People use the church and Christ's name for their own ends (v. 18). The gospel calls for innocence but diligence to avoid being taken in (v. 19). God will vindicate his interests and bring down his enemies in the end, including their leader, Satan himself (v. 20). God will crush Satan under the feet of believers—fulfilling the ancient prophecy all the way back in the garden of Eden (Gen. 3:15).

16:21–23 Paul gives the names of his inner circle as he composes this letter during a layover in Corinth (see Acts 20:2–3). Paul has a unique grace given to him (Rom. 1:5; 12:3; 15:15), but effective Christian leadership is no place for hard-core loners. Paul led decisively but in interaction with others who built alongside him on the foundation he laid (see 15:20).

God of peace [e]will soon crush Satan under
your feet. [f]The grace of our Lord Jesus Christ
be with you.
21 [g]Timothy, my fellow worker, greets you;
so do Lucius and Jason and Sosipater, my
kinsmen.
22 I Tertius, [h]who wrote this letter, greet you
in the Lord.
23 [i]Gaius, who is host to me and to the whole
church, greets you. Erastus, the city treasurer,
and our brother Quartus, greet you.[1]

Doxology

25 [j]Now to him who is able to strengthen you
[k]according to my gospel and the preaching of
Jesus Christ, [l]according to the revelation of the
mystery [m]that was kept secret for [n]long ages
26 but [o]has now been disclosed and through
the prophetic writings has been made known
to all nations, according to the command of
the eternal God, [p]to bring about the obedience
of faith— 27 to [q]the only wise God [r]be glory
forevermore through Jesus Christ! Amen.

[1] Some manuscripts insert verse 24: *The grace of our Lord Jesus Christ be with you all. Amen.*

16:25–27 Gospel assurance lies in God's upholding strength through the preaching of Christ and truths divinely revealed (v. 25). These truths, enshrined in Scripture, are for all nations, as God has commanded, to establish and enhance a worldwide and eternal communion (v. 26). By the gospel Paul ministers and which this epistle explains, God in his matchless wisdom is forever glorified through his Son (v. 27). This closing doxology recalls almost all the main themes of the letter to the Romans, funneling it all down into praise and worship of God. This is where Romans brings us.

20 [e] Gen. 3:15; [Luke 10:17-19; Rev. 12:11] [f] 1 Cor. 16:23
21 [g] See Acts 16:1
22 [h] See 1 Cor. 16:21
23 [i] 1 Cor. 1:14; [Acts 19:29; 20:4; 3 John 1]
25 [j] Eph. 3:20; Jude 24 [k] See ch. 2:16 [l] 1 Cor. 2:1; 4:1; Eph. 1:9; 3:3-5; 5:32; 6:19 [m] [1 Cor. 2:7] [n] 2 Tim. 1:9; Titus 1:2
26 [o] Col. 1:26; 2 Tim. 1:10; Titus 1:3 [p] [Col. 1:6]; See ch. 1:5 **27** [q] 1 Tim. 1:17; 6:16 [r] See ch. 11:36

Introduction to 1 Corinthians

Author, Date, and Recipients

The apostle Paul wrote this letter to the Corinthian church in the spring of A.D. 53, 54, or 55. This was near the end of his three-year ministry in Ephesus.

The Gospel in 1 Corinthians

The gospel—the good news of what God has done for sinners through Jesus Christ—permeates 1 Corinthians. The letter opens with a celebration of the cross of Christ (1:18–31), closes with an emphasis on Christ's resurrection (15:3–58), and repeatedly presents Christ and the gospel as the essence of Paul's preaching (2:1–5; 3:10–11; 9:16; 15:1–8).

Despite these emphases, 1 Corinthians offers several challenges to gospel-focused interpretation. Because Paul addresses various practical problems confronting the Corinthians, it is easy to view the letter as a collection of unrelated topics. But such an approach misses larger patterns of gospel truth that run throughout Paul's instructions. To be sure, the epistle contains stern warnings about judgment, discipline, and the consequences of sin. Yet as we seek to hear such warnings within the framework of the gospel, we must take care that neither voice drowns out the other. First Corinthians discusses many hotly debated issues, including divorce and remarriage, gender roles in worship, and spiritual gifts such as speaking in tongues and prophecy. While we must acknowledge the complexity of the issues, we should not allow this to obscure gospel principles that are clearly expressed in the text.

Readers of 1 Corinthians should be alert for four pervasive gospel themes. First, human beings—including believers in Christ—desperately need God's grace. Every problem Paul addresses stems from the fact that we have profoundly flawed spiritual priorities. Our need is so great that only Christ, who is the very wisdom and power of God, can redeem us (1:22–25). Second, our hope is in Christ, and not in our own perfection. As clearly as any other portion of Scripture, 1 Corinthians demonstrates that God's people, both individually and in community, can develop serious spiritual "blind spots." Yet we need not despair, because the work of Christ makes genuine repentance and transformation possible. Third, where the grace of the gospel is at work, holiness will result. On the one hand, this means that we must not soften the book's radical demands for holy living, for these reflect the transforming power of the gospel. On the other hand, it means that we must not neglect the book's emphasis on the gospel as the power by which we fulfill these demands. Fourth, Christians are called to apply the gospel to everyday life. Where our faith intersects with culture, the potential for compromise abounds; where we disagree with other believers about Christian freedom, conflict can erupt. But whatever the problem, we must pursue the glory of God and the good of others, even at great cost to ourselves—in short, we must embody the priorities of the cross (10:31–11:1).

First Corinthians is addressed to people who desire spiritual maturity. Some seek maturity through displays of wisdom and eloquence, some through a complete break with the circumstances of their pre-Christian lives, and some in the exercise of personal freedom. But as Paul reminds us, the gospel is not, "I am wise, I am pure, I am free." Rather, the gospel boasts in nothing but "Jesus Christ and him crucified" (2:2). To the human mind it seems foolish to hope that we could be saved through the cross of Christ, with its associations of weakness and shame. But it is at the cross that God's wisdom, power, and glory are fully revealed—along with the true nature of self-sacrificial love. Because love never ends (13:8) and because we long to see God's power over all things displayed forever (15:28), we must never lose sight of the cross. True maturity will take us deeper into the gospel of Christ crucified, but never beyond it.

Outline

I. Introduction to the Letter's Main Themes (1:1–9)

II. Divisions over Christian Preachers (1:10–4:21)

III. A Report of Sexual Immorality and Lawsuits (5:1–6:20)

IV. Three Issues from the Corinthians' Letter (7:1–11:1)

V. Divisions over Corporate Worship (11:2–14:40)

VI. The Futility of Faith If the Dead Are Not Raised (15:1–58)

VII. The Collection for the Saints and Travel Plans (16:1–12)

VIII. Closing Admonitions and Greetings (16:13–24)

The First Letter of Paul to the Corinthians

1 Corinthians

Greeting

1 Paul, [a]called [b]by the will of God to be an
apostle of Christ Jesus, and our brother
Sosthenes,
2 To the church of God that is in Corinth, to
those [c]sanctified in Christ Jesus, [d]called to be
saints together with all those who in every
place [e]call upon the name of our Lord Jesus
Christ, both their Lord and ours:
3 [d]Grace to you and peace from God our
Father and the Lord Jesus Christ.

Thanksgiving

4 I [f]give thanks to my God always for you
because of the grace of God that was given
you in Christ Jesus, 5 that in every way [g]you
were enriched in him in all [h]speech and all
knowledge— 6 even as [i]the testimony about
Christ was confirmed among you— 7 so that
you are not lacking in any gift, as you [j]wait for
the revealing of our Lord Jesus Christ, 8 [k]who
will sustain you to the end, [l]guiltless [m]in the
day of our Lord Jesus Christ. 9 [n]God is faithful,
by whom you were called into the [o]fellowship
of his Son, Jesus Christ our Lord.

Divisions in the Church

10 I appeal to you, brothers,[1] by the name of
our Lord Jesus Christ, that all of you agree,
and that there be no [p]divisions among you, but
that you be united [q]in the same mind and the
same judgment. 11 For it has been reported to

[1] Or *brothers and sisters*. The plural Greek word *adelphoi* (translated "brothers") refers to siblings in a family. In New Testament usage, depending on the context, *adelphoi* may refer either to men or to both men and women who are siblings (brothers and sisters) in God's family, the church; also verses 11, 26

1:1–9 In 1 Corinthians, Paul addresses a church that, like many in our day, is both deeply flawed and greatly loved. To prepare his readers to confront the many challenges to their spiritual maturity, he reminds them that God's people possess the resources needed for spiritual growth and transformation. We are united to Christ ("in Christ Jesus"; vv. 2, 4). We share fellowship with him and with God as our Father (vv. 3, 9). As a result, we receive the blessings of grace, peace, and the gifts of the Spirit (vv. 3–7). Though we were once defiled by sin, God has now cleansed us and made us his holy people through Christ's perfect sacrifice ("sanctified," "saints," v. 2; "guiltless," v. 8). Confidence that we can grow in holiness rests not on ourselves but on the faithfulness of God and of his Son Jesus, who will "sustain [us] to the end" (vv. 8–9).

The logic of the epistle is therefore clear: the kind of repentance, holy living, and self-sacrificial love that should characterize believers in Christ can be realized only by the supply of, and dependence upon, gospel provisions.

1:10–2:16 Among the problems that have been reported to Paul about the church in Corinth (1:11) is that of division, as factions are forming around various leaders. His response in 1:10–2:16 exposes two powerful temptations that face the church in every era, and the ways he confronts the temptations provide some of the most moving summaries of the gospel in all of Scripture (1:18–25, 30; 2:1–4).

The first temptation involved boasting in leaders whose speech is eloquent (1:17; 2:1, 4), putting confidence in human wisdom and strength. But the gospel teaches us to boast only "in the Lord" (1:31), and particularly in "Christ crucified," who is "the power of God and the wisdom of God" (1:23–24). We rely not on human accomplishment but on that of Christ, who has become our "righteousness" (giving us right standing with God), our "sanctification" (cleansing us from the impurity of disobedience), and our "redemption" (liberating us from bondage to sin) (1:30). To access God's

Chapter 1
1 [a]See Rom. 1:1 [b]2 Cor. 1:1; Eph. 1:1; Col. 1:1; 2 Tim. 1:1
2 [c]ch. 6:11; [ver. 30]; See John 17:19 [d]See Rom. 1:7 [e]See Acts 9:14
3 [d][See ver. 2 above]
4 [f]See Rom. 1:8
5 [g]2 Cor. 9:11; [2 Cor. 6:10] [h]2 Cor. 8:7; [ch. 12:8]; See Rom. 15:14; 1 John 2:20
6 [i]2 Tim. 1:8; [2 Thess. 1:10; 1 Tim. 2:6; Rev. 1:2]
7 [j]Rom. 8:19; Phil. 3:20; Heb. 9:28; See Luke 17:30; 2 Pet. 3:12
8 [k][Phil. 1:6; 1 Thess. 3:13] [l]Col. 1:22 [m]ch. 5:5; 2 Cor. 1:14; Phil. 2:16; [Luke 17:24]
9 [n]ch. 10:13; Deut. 7:9; Isa. 49:7; 2 Cor. 1:18 [o]1 John 1:3
10 [p]ch. 11:18 [q][Phil. 1:27]

me by Chloe's people that there is [r]quarreling
among you, my brothers. 12 What I mean is
that [s]each one of you says, "I follow Paul," or
"I follow [t]Apollos," or "I follow [u]Cephas," or "I
follow Christ." 13 [v]Is Christ divided? Was Paul
crucified for you? Or were you [w]baptized in the
name of Paul? 14 I thank God that I baptized
none of you except [x]Crispus and [y]Gaius, 15 so
that no one may say that you were baptized
in my name. 16 (I did baptize also [z]the household of Stephanas. Beyond that, I do not know
whether I baptized anyone else.) 17 For Christ
did not send me to baptize but to preach the
gospel, and [a]not with words of eloquent wisdom, lest the cross of Christ be emptied of
its power.

Christ the Wisdom and Power of God

18 For the word of the cross is [b]folly to
[c]those who are perishing, but to us [d]who are
being saved it is [e]the power of God. 19 For it
is written,

> [f]"I will destroy the wisdom of the wise,
> and the discernment of the discern-
> ing I will thwart."

20 [g]Where is the one who is wise? Where is
the scribe? Where is the debater of this age?
[h]Has not God made foolish the wisdom of the
world? 21 For since, in the wisdom of God, the
world did not know God through wisdom,
it pleased God through the folly of what we
preach[1] to save those who believe. 22 For [i]Jews
demand signs and Greeks seek wisdom, 23 but
we preach Christ [j]crucified, a stumbling block
to Jews and folly to Gentiles, 24 but to those
who are called, both Jews and Greeks, Christ
[k]the power of God and [l]the wisdom of God.
25 For the foolishness of God is wiser than
men, and the weakness of God is stronger
than men.

26 For consider your calling, brothers: [m]not
many of you were wise according to worldly
standards,[2] not many were powerful, not
many were of noble birth. 27 But [n]God chose
what is foolish in the world to shame the
wise; [o]God chose what is weak in the world
to shame the strong; 28 God chose what is low
and despised in the world, even [p]things that
are not, to [q]bring to nothing things that are,
29 so [r]that no human being[3] might boast in
the presence of God. 30 And because of him[4]
you are in Christ Jesus, who became to us
[s]wisdom from God, [t]righteousness and [u]sanc-
tification and [v]redemption, 31 so that, as it is
written, [w]"Let the one who boasts, boast in
the Lord."

Proclaiming Christ Crucified

2 And I, when I came to you, brothers,[5] [x]did
not come proclaiming to you [y]the testimony[6] of God with lofty speech or wisdom.
2 For I decided to know nothing among you
except [z]Jesus Christ and him crucified. 3 And
[a]I was with you [b]in weakness and in fear and
much trembling, 4 and my speech and my
message were not in plausible words of wisdom, but in demonstration of [c]the Spirit and
of power, 5 so that your faith might not rest in
the wisdom of men[7] but [d]in the power of God.

[1] Or *the folly of preaching* [2] Greek *according to the flesh* [3] Greek *no flesh* [4] Greek *And from him* [5] Or *brothers and sisters*
[6] Some manuscripts *mystery* (or *secret*) [7] The Greek word *anthropoi* can refer to both men and women

transforming power, believers therefore do not need to focus on worldly measures of success (1:26–28); instead, we need only to keep "the word of the cross" at the heart of our faith and practice (1:17–18).

The second temptation involved believers trying to separate the *beginning* of the Christian life from the *living* of the Christian life. As Paul reminds the Corinthians, our lives as Christians begin with absolute dependence on God's powerful, saving work. We hear the gospel of Christ crucified and respond to it in faith (1:17; 2:1–5). This response is the result of the Spirit's work, who gives us true wisdom so that we can understand, rather than reject, the gospel (2:12–14). We are also baptized in the name of Christ, the only Savior and Lord (1:12–15). Yet this dependence on God's provision is not a temporary stage in our spiritual development, for the gospel is both the gracious gift by which we begin the Christian life and the source of ongoing power for living the Christian life (cf. 15:1–4). The truth about "Jesus Christ and him crucified" (2:2) is therefore not a basic teaching to be left behind as we mature but a lens through which to view all of Scripture (1:19, 31; 2:9, 16) and all of life.

11 [r]ch. 3:3
12 [s]ch. 3:4; [Matt. 23:9, 10] [t]See Acts 18:24 [u]See John 1:42
13 [v][ch. 12:5; 2 Cor. 11:4; Eph. 4:5] [w]See Acts 8:16
14 [x]Acts 18:8 [y]See Rom. 16:23
16 [z]ch. 16:15, 17
17 [a]ch. 2:1, 4, 13; [2 Cor. 10:10; 11:6; 2 Pet. 1:16]
18 [b]ver. 21, 23, 25; ch. 2:14 [c]2 Cor. 2:15; 4:3; 2 Thess. 2:10 [d]ch. 15:2; [Acts 2:47] [e]Rom. 1:16; [ver. 24]
19 [f]Cited from Isa. 29:14; [Job 5:12, 13; Jer. 8:9; Matt. 11:25]
20 [g]Isa. 19:12 [h]ch. 2:6; 3:19; Isa. 44:25; Rom. 1:22; [ver. 26]
22 [i]See Matt. 12:38
23 [j]Gal. 5:11; See 1 Pet. 2:8
24 [k][ver. 18] [l]ver. 30; Col. 2:3; [Luke 11:49]
26 [m]ch. 2:8; John 7:48; [ver. 20]; See Matt. 11:25 **27** [n]James 2:5 [o]Ps. 8:2 **28** [p]Rom. 4:17 [q]ch. 2:6; [Job 34:19, 24] **29** [r]Eph. 2:9; [Judg. 7:2] **30** [s][ver. 24] [t]Jer. 23:5, 6; 33:16; 2 Cor. 5:21; Phil. 3:9 [u][ver. 2] [v]Eph. 1:7; Col. 1:14; [Rom. 3:24] **31** [w]2 Cor. 10:17; [Jer. 9:23, 24] **Chapter 2** **1** [x]ver. 4, 13; [2 Cor. 1:12]; See ch. 1:17 [y]See Rom. 16:25 **2** [z]Gal. 6:14 **3** [a]Acts 18:1, 6, 12 [b]2 Cor. 11:30; 12:5, 9; 13:4, 9; Gal. 4:13 **4** [c]ch. 4:20; Rom. 15:13, 19; 1 Thess. 1:5; 2 Pet. 1:16 **5** [d]2 Cor. 4:7; 6:7; [Zech. 4:6; 2 Cor. 10:4; 12:9]

Wisdom from the Spirit

6 Yet among [e]the mature we do impart wisdom, although it is not [f]a wisdom of this age
or of the rulers of this age, [g]who are doomed to
pass away. 7 But we impart a secret and hidden
wisdom of God, [h]which God decreed before
the ages for our glory. 8 None of [i]the rulers of
this age understood this, for [j]if they had, they
would not have crucified [k]the Lord of glory.
9 But, as it is written,

[l]"What no eye has seen, nor ear heard,
nor the heart of man imagined,
what God has [m]prepared [n]for those who
love him"—

10 these things [o]God has revealed to us through
the Spirit. For the Spirit searches everything,
even [p]the depths of God. 11 For who knows a
person's thoughts [q]except the spirit of that
person, which is in him? So also no one comprehends the thoughts of God except the
Spirit of God. 12 Now [r]we have received not [s]the
spirit of the world, but the Spirit who is from
God, that we might understand the things
freely given us by God. 13 And we impart this
[t]in words not taught by human wisdom but
taught by the Spirit, [u]interpreting spiritual
truths to those who are spiritual.[1]
14 The natural person does not accept the
things of the Spirit of God, for they are [v]folly
to him, and [w]he is not able to understand
them because they are spiritually discerned.
15 The [x]spiritual person judges all things, but
is himself to be judged by no one. 16 [y]"For who
has understood the mind of the Lord so as to
instruct him?" But [z]we have the mind of Christ.

Divisions in the Church

3 But I, brothers,[2] could not address you
as [a]spiritual people, but as [b]people of the
flesh, as [c]infants in Christ. 2 [d]I fed you with
milk, not solid food, for [e]you were not ready
for it. And even now you are not yet ready,
3 for you are still of the flesh. For while there
is [f]jealousy and strife among you, are you not
of the flesh and behaving only in a human
way? 4 For [g]when one says, "I follow Paul," and
another, "I follow Apollos," [h]are you not being
merely human?
5 What then is Apollos? What is Paul?
[i]Servants through whom you believed, [j]as
the Lord assigned to each. 6 [k]I planted, [l]Apol-
los watered, [m]but God gave the growth. 7 So
[n]neither he who plants nor he who waters is
anything, but only God who gives the growth.
8 He who plants and he who waters are one,

[1] Or *interpreting spiritual truths in spiritual language*, or *comparing spiritual things with spiritual* [2] Or *brothers and sisters*

3:1–4:5 In this section of the letter, continuing his response to the problem of factions in the church, Paul contrasts the Christ-centered perspective which believers should embrace ("the mind of Christ"; 2:16) with the human-centered, worldly perspective so prominent in the Corinthian church (3:4, 19).

The text assumes three things about believers in Christ. First, we are God's holy temple, built on the foundation of Christ's work, and filled with God's Spirit (3:9–11, 16–17). Second, we are still capable of profound spiritual immaturity, and of living like "people of the flesh" (3:1–4). Third, because the Spirit is at work in us (2:14–15), we are capable of responding with repentance when confronted with our sin. Because of these truths, we neither deny our sin nor despair when it is revealed. Instead, knowing that we belong to Christ (3:23), we are free to take both sin and repentance seriously.

For the Corinthians, association with noteworthy and accomplished church leaders is a means of claiming superiority over other believers. By contrast, Paul exemplifies a perspective that honors divine provision over human accomplishment. He reminds the Corinthians that even the greatest leader is only a servant of the Lord Jesus, and human labor is fruitful only because God "gives the growth" (3:5–7). Because our gifts and service are "according to the grace of God" (3:10), we cannot take credit for the good he accomplishes through us. Further, since believers are "fellow heirs" with Christ (Rom. 8:17; cf. 8:14–30; 1 Cor. 3:22–23; 15:27), worldly measures of success and status (3:18–21) cannot enhance or diminish our standing before God. Finally, a Christ-centered perspective means that we need not fear how other people evaluate us, caring less about human praise or criticism than about faithfulness to the Lord who has bought us and made us his servants (4:1–5).

Within this framework of grace, Paul exhorts believers, all of whom have a part to play in the church's gospel-promoting mission, to prepare for a future evaluation of their service to Christ (3:10–17; 4:5). Love for Christ means that we should not depend

6 [e]Phil. 3:15; [ch. 3:1] [f][James 3:15] [g]ch. 1:28
7 [h]Rom. 16:25, 26; Eph. 3:5, 9; Col. 1:26; 2 Tim. 1:9
8 [i]Acts 13:27; See Luke 24:20 [j]See Acts 3:17 [k]James 2:1; [Ps. 24:7-10; Acts 7:2]
9 [l][Isa. 64:4] [m]See Matt. 25:34 [n]James 1:12
10 [o]Matt. 16:17; Gal. 1:12, 16; Eph. 3:3, 5; See John 14:26 [p][Rev. 2:24]
11 [q]Prov. 20:27
12 [r]Rom. 8:15 [s][1 John 4:4]
13 [t]ver. 1, 4; See ch. 1:17 [u]2 Cor. 10:12
14 [v]ch. 1:18 [w]Rom. 8:7
15 [x]ch. 3:1; 14:37; Gal. 6:1; [Prov. 28:5]
16 [y]Cited from Isa. 40:13; See Rom. 11:34 [z][John 15:15]

Chapter 3
1 [a]ch. 2:15; Rom. 7:14 [b][ch. 2:14] [c]Heb. 5:13; [ch. 2:6]
2 [d]Heb. 5:12, 13; 1 Pet. 2:2 [e]John 16:12
3 [f]Gal. 5:19, 20; [ch. 1:11; 11:18; Rom. 13:13]
4 [g]See ch. 1:12 [h][ver. 3]
5 [i]2 Cor. 6:4; Eph. 3:7; Col. 1:25; [2 Cor. 3:3] [j]See Rom. 12:6
6 [k]ch. 4:15; 9:1; 15:1; Acts 18:4-11; 2 Cor. 10:14, 15 [l]Acts 18:27 [m][ch. 15:10; Col. 1:18]
7 [n]2 Cor. 12:11; Gal. 6:3; [Gal. 2:6]

and each [o]will receive his wages according to his labor. 9 For we are [p]God's fellow workers. You are God's field, [q]God's building.

10 [r]According to the grace of God given to me, like a skilled master builder I laid a [s]foundation, and [t]someone else is building upon it. Let each one take care how he builds upon it. 11 For no one can lay a [u]foundation other [v]than that which is laid, [w]which is Jesus Christ. 12 Now if anyone builds on the foundation with gold, silver, precious stones, wood, hay, straw— 13 [x]each one's work will become manifest, for the Day will disclose it, because it will be revealed [y]by fire, and [z]the fire will test what sort of work each one has done. 14 If the work that anyone has built on the foundation survives, [a]he will receive a reward. 15 If anyone's work is burned up, he will suffer loss, though he himself will be saved, [b]but only as through fire.

16 [c]Do you not know that you[1] are God's temple and that God's Spirit dwells in you? 17 If anyone destroys God's temple, God will destroy him. For [d]God's temple is holy, and you are that temple.

18 [e]Let no one deceive himself. [f]If anyone among you thinks that he is wise in this age, let him become a fool that he may become wise. 19 For [g]the wisdom of this world is folly with God. For it is written, [h]"He catches the wise in their craftiness," 20 and again, [i]"The Lord knows the thoughts of the wise, that they are futile." 21 So [j]let no one boast in men. For [k]all things are yours, 22 whether Paul or Apollos or Cephas or the world or life or death or the present or the future—all are yours, 23 and [l]you are Christ's, and [m]Christ is God's.

The Ministry of Apostles

4 This is how one should regard us, as servants of Christ and [n]stewards of the mysteries of God. 2 Moreover, it is required of stewards that they be found faithful. 3 But with me it is a very small thing that I should be judged by you or by any human court. In fact, I do not even judge myself. 4 [o]For I am not aware of anything against myself, [p]but I am not thereby acquitted. It is the Lord who judges me. 5 Therefore [q]do not pronounce judgment before the time, [r]before the Lord comes, [s]who will bring to light the things now hidden in darkness and will disclose the purposes of the heart. [t]Then each one will receive his commendation from God.

6 I have applied all these things to myself and Apollos for your benefit, brothers,[2] that you may learn by us not to go beyond what is

[1] The Greek for *you* is plural in verses 16 and 17 [2] Or *brothers and sisters*

8 [o]ver. 14; ch. 15:58; 2 John 8; [ch. 4:5; Gal. 6:4, 5]; See Matt. 16:27; Rom. 2:6
9 [p]Mark 16:20; 2 Cor. 6:1 [q]Eph. 2:20-22; Col. 2:7; [ver. 16; Ps. 127:1]
10 [r][2 Pet. 3:15]; See Rom. 12:3 [s]ver. 11, 12; Rom. 15:20; [Rev. 21:14] [t][ch. 4:15]
11 [u]Isa. 28:16 [v][2 Cor. 11:4; Gal. 1:6, 7] [w][Eph. 2:20]
13 [x]ch. 4:5 [y]ver. 15; 2 Thess. 1:8 [z]1 Pet. 1:7
14 [a]See ver. 8
15 [b][Ps. 66:12; Isa. 43:2; Jude 23]
16 [c]ch. 6:19; 2 Cor. 6:16; Eph. 2:21
17 [d][2 Cor. 7:1]
18 [e][Isa. 5:21; Gal. 6:3] [f][ch. 8:2; Jer. 8:8, 9]
19 [g]See ch. 1:20 [h]Cited from Job 5:13
20 [i]Cited from Ps. 94:11
21 [j]ver. 4-6; ch. 1:12; 4:6 [k]Rom. 8:28
23 [l]2 Cor. 10:7; Gal. 3:29 [m][ch. 11:3]
Chapter 4
1 [n][ch. 9:17]; See 1 Pet. 4:10
4 [o]See Acts 23:1 [p]Job 9:2, 15; Ps. 130:3; 143:2; [1 John 3:21]
5 [q]Matt. 7:1; Rom. 2:1; [Matt. 13:29] [r]See John 21:22; Rom. 2:16 [s]ch. 3:13 [t]2 Cor. 10:18; See ch. 3:8

on ordinary building materials (such as worldly wisdom, boasting, or human strength) as we build on the "foundation" of his work; rather, Christ deserves the "gold, silver, [and] precious stones" of which temples are made—that is, a mind-set and lifestyle devoted to God's glory, wisdom, and power (1 Cor. 3:12). At the day of judgment, the Lord Jesus will wisely and justly remove from our work anything that honors human contributions above his own; though this discipline will be painful, we will be saved by his finished work (3:15; cf. 5:5). Despite its serious warning, the text displays several aspects of God's grace: (1) God not only reveals the threat of "loss" (3:15), but a path of repentance by which we may avoid such loss; (2) whatever "reward" (3:14) we receive in the end will honor "the grace of God" (3:10) by which we labored; and (3) ability for faithful labor comes from our new identity as "God's temple" (3:16).

4:6–21 Paul's final comments on the problem of factions in the church center on one admonition: "be imitators of me" (v. 16). The text reflects a cycle of gospel embrace (Paul's passion for the gospel), leading to gospel transformation (Paul's Christ-like character), and promoting gospel multiplication (Paul's desire to help others grow in Christ).

As Paul, the former persecutor of believers, knows from personal experience, his preaching of "Jesus Christ and him crucified" is not merely a matter of recited words; it is a testimony of the Spirit's transforming power (v. 20; 2:1–5). This power has made Paul an example of Christ-centered living for his spiritual children (4:14–17; cf. 10:32–11:1). Thus, rather than viewing leaders like him through a lens of human accomplishment and boasting, believers are to imitate their "ways in Christ" (4:17), which include: (1) delighting not when others recognize our wealth and power (v. 8), but when our foolishness, weakness, dishonor, and desperate need are put on display for all to see (vv. 9–12); and (2) enduring hardship with Christlike compassion, even praying for those who treat us like "scum" and "refuse" (vv. 12–13).

written, that none of you may [u]be puffed up
in favor of one against another. 7 For who sees
anything different in you? [v]What do you have
that you did not receive? If then you received
it, why do you boast as if you did not receive it?
8 Already you have all you want! Already
you have become rich! Without us you have
become kings! And would that you did reign,
so that we might share the rule with you! 9 For
I think that God has exhibited us apostles
as last of all, [w]like men sentenced to death,
because we [x]have become a spectacle to the
world, to angels, and to men. 10 [y]We are fools
for Christ's sake, but [z]you are wise in Christ.
[a]We are weak, but you are strong. You are
held in honor, but we in disrepute. 11 To the
present hour [b]we hunger and thirst, we are
poorly dressed and [c]buffeted and [d]homeless,
12 and we [e]labor, working with our own hands.
[f]When reviled, we bless; [g]when persecuted,
we endure; 13 when slandered, we entreat. [h]We
have become, and are still, like the scum of the
world, [i]the refuse of all things.
14 I do not write these things [j]to make you
ashamed, but to admonish you [k]as my beloved
children. 15 For [l]though you have countless[1]
guides in Christ, you do not have many
fathers. For [m]I became your father in Christ
Jesus through the gospel. 16 I urge you, then,
[n]be imitators of me. 17 That is why [o]I sent[2] you
Timothy, [p]my beloved and faithful child in
the Lord, to remind you of my ways in Christ,[3]
[q]as I teach them everywhere in every church.
18 Some are [r]arrogant, [s]as though I were not
coming to you. 19 But [t]I will come to you soon,
if the Lord wills, and I will find out not the
talk of these arrogant people but their power.
20 For [u]the kingdom of God does not consist in
talk but in power. 21 What do you wish? [v]Shall
I come to you with a rod, or with love in a
spirit of gentleness?

Sexual Immorality Defiles the Church

5 It is actually reported that there is [w]sexual
immorality among you, and of a kind that
is not tolerated even among pagans, [x]for a man
has his father's wife. 2 And [y]you are arrogant!
Ought you [z]not rather to mourn? Let him who
has done this be removed from among you.
3 For though [a]absent in body, I am present
in spirit; and as if present, I have already pronounced judgment on the one who did such a

[1] Greek *you have ten thousand* [2] Or *am sending* [3] Some manuscripts add *Jesus*

In short, more mature believers should model, and less mature believers should learn, the ways of the cross. This will increase our dependence on Christ, as the faithfulness of any human hero ultimately reflects and results from the Savior's faithfulness.

5:1–13 In chapter 5, Paul rebukes the church at Corinth for another problem that has been reported to him (v. 1; cf. 1:11): they are tolerating a sexually immoral relationship between a man and his stepmother. The chapter is a powerful, clear reminder that God's grace provides not permission to sin but power for holiness. During the Feast of Unleavened Bread, Old Testament believers diligently purged their homes of all "leaven" in honor of God's gracious deliverance of Israel from slavery in Egypt (see Ex. 12:17; 13:3; 23:15). Similarly, the work of Christ delivers Christians from bondage to sin, giving us joy and strength for purging our lives of "the old leaven" of disobedience (1 Cor. 5:7–8). Paul therefore bases his call to holy living on the redeeming death of Christ ("Christ, our Passover lamb, has been sacrificed"; v. 7) and the new, holy status it gives believers ("you really are unleavened"; v. 7).

This text reveals two fundamental principles for gospel application. First, where the gospel is at work, holiness will result. Those who profess faith in Christ are therefore not free to engage in immorality, sexual or otherwise (v. 11), and they must be disciplined when they persist in sin. The most severe form of discipline involves being cut off from the fellowship of the church (vv. 2, 9, 11). Yet the gospel offers hope that even such offenders may one day be restored to full fellowship and "saved in the day of the Lord" (v. 5).

Second, the kind of holiness God desires cannot be produced apart from the gospel. When the sinful patterns "of this world" (v. 10) surround us and tempt us to compromise, the proper response is to return to the unchanging grace of God, who made his saving mercies known in the Passover, and ultimately in Christ—acting as our Passover Lamb (v. 7). Christ was "sacrificed" in the past: "let us therefore celebrate the festival" (honoring Christ just as the Passover honored God) in the present by lives of sincere devotion and truth (v. 8).

6 [u]ver. 18, 19; ch. 5:2; 13:4
7 [v]John 3:27; [1 Chr. 29:14; James 1:17; 1 Pet. 4:10]
9 [w]See Rom. 8:36 [x]Heb. 10:33 (Gk.); [Isa. 20:3]
10 [y][Acts 17:18]; See ch. 1:18; Acts 26:24 [z]2 Cor. 11:19 [a]ch. 2:3; 2 Cor. 13:9
11 [b]Rom. 8:35; 2 Cor. 11:27; Phil. 4:12 [c]2 Cor. 11:20, 23 [d][Matt. 8:20]
12 [e]See Acts 18:3 [f]See 1 Pet. 3:9 [g]See John 15:20
13 [h][Isa. 30:22; 64:6] [i]Lam. 3:45
14 [j][ch. 6:5; 15:34] [k]2 Cor. 6:13; 1 Thess. 2:11; 3 John 4
15 [l][ch. 3:10] [m]Philem. 10; [Gal. 4:19]
16 [n]ch. 11:1; Phil. 3:17; 1 Thess. 1:6; [Phil. 4:9; 2 Thess. 3:9]
17 [o]ch. 16:10 [p]1 Tim. 1:2; 2 Tim. 1:2 [q]ch. 7:17
18 [r]See ver. 6 [s]ver. 21; [2 Cor. 10:2]
19 [t]ch. 11:34; 16:5, 6; Acts 19:21; 20:2; 2 Cor. 1:15, 16
20 [u]See ch. 2:4
21 [v]2 Cor. 1:23; 2:1, 3; 12:20; 13:2, 10

Chapter 5
1 [w]2 Cor. 12:21 [x]Lev. 18:8; Deut. 22:30; 27:20
2 [y]See ch. 4:6 [z][2 Cor. 7:7-10]
3 [a]Col. 2:5; [1 Thess. 2:17]

thing. 4 When you are assembled [b]in the name of the Lord Jesus and my spirit is present, with the power of our Lord Jesus, 5 you are [c]to deliver this man to Satan for the destruction of the flesh, so [d]that his spirit may be saved [e]in the day of the Lord.[1]

6 [f]Your boasting is not good. Do you not know that [g]a little leaven leavens the whole lump? 7 Cleanse out the old leaven that you may be a new lump, as you really are unleavened. For Christ, our Passover lamb, has been sacrificed. 8 Let us therefore celebrate the festival, [h]not with the old leaven, [i]the leaven of malice and evil, but with the unleavened bread of sincerity and truth.

9 I wrote to you in my letter [j]not to associate with sexually immoral people— 10 [k]not at all meaning [l]the sexually immoral of this world, or the greedy and swindlers, or idolaters, [m]since then you would need to go out of the world. 11 But now I am writing to you not to associate with anyone [n]who bears the name of brother if he is guilty of sexual immorality or greed, or is an idolater, reviler, drunkard, or swindler—not even to eat with such a one. 12 For what have I to do with judging [o]outsiders? [p]Is it not those inside the church[2] whom you are to judge? 13 God judges[3] those outside. [q]"Purge the evil person from among you."

Lawsuits Against Believers

6 When one of you has a grievance against another, does he dare go to law before the unrighteous [r]instead of the saints? 2 Or do you not know that [s]the saints will judge the world? And if the world is to be judged by you, are you incompetent to try trivial cases? 3 Do you not know that we are to judge angels? How much more, then, matters pertaining to this life! 4 So if you have such cases, [t]why do you lay them before those who have no standing in the church? 5 [u]I say this to your shame. Can it be that there is no one among you wise enough to settle a dispute between the brothers, 6 but brother goes to law against brother, and that before unbelievers? 7 To have lawsuits at all with one another is already a defeat for you. [v]Why not rather suffer wrong? Why not rather be defrauded? 8 But you yourselves wrong and defraud—even [w]your own brothers![4]

9 Or do you not know that the unrighteous[5] will not inherit the kingdom of God? Do not

[1] Some manuscripts add *Jesus* [2] Greek *those inside* [3] Or *will judge* [4] Or *brothers and sisters* [5] Or *wrongdoers*

4 [b] 2 Thess. 3:6; [Matt. 16:19; 18:18; John 20:23; 2 Cor. 13:3, 10; 1 Tim. 5:20]
5 [c] 1 Tim. 1:20; [Job 2:6; Acts 26:18] [d] [Prov. 23:14] [e] See ch. 1:8
6 [f] James 4:16; [ver. 2] [g] Gal. 5:9; [ch. 15:33]
8 [h] Ex. 12:15; Deut. 16:3 [i] [Matt. 16:6, 12; Mark 8:15; Luke 12:1]
9 [j] [2 Cor. 6:14; Eph. 5:11; 2 Thess. 3:6, 14]
10 [k] [ch. 10:27] [l] Eph. 5:5; Col. 3:5; [ch. 6:9] [m] [John 17:15]
11 [n] 2 Thess. 3:6
12 [o] See Mark 4:11 [p] [ch. 6:1-4]
13 [q] [Deut. 13:5; 17:7, 12; 21:21; 22:21, 22, 24; Judg. 20:13]

Chapter 6
1 [r] [Matt. 18:17]
2 [s] Dan. 7:22; [Matt. 19:28; Rev. 20:4]
4 [t] [ch. 5:12]
5 [u] ch. 15:34; [ch. 4:14]
7 [v] [Matt. 5:39, 40]
8 [w] 1 Thess. 4:6

6:1–20 Here Paul confronts two additional problems: some of the Corinthians are suing one another in secular courts (vv. 1–11), and others are engaging in sexual relations with prostitutes (vv. 12–20). Paul's response makes it clear that grace and holiness go hand in hand. As mutual heirs of God's kingdom, we are not free to bring lawsuits against fellow believers regarding property/financial disputes that can be settled in the church (vv. 1–7); we are not free to "wrong and defraud" our brothers (v. 8), or to engage in the various other forms of self-indulgence named in verses 9–10. Once we were mired in the filth of such sin, but now we are "washed," "sanctified" (made fit for God's holy purposes), and "justified" (made righteous in Christ, and therefore heirs of God's kingdom; vv. 9–11). God accomplishes this gracious work *for* us through "the Lord Jesus Christ," and *in* us "by the Spirit" (v. 11). When he does this work in us, we are given power for a new life, which includes the desire and ability to repent when we hear stern warnings about sin and its consequences.

Two additional gospel truths appear in Paul's rebuke concerning prostitution. First, gratitude for the redeeming death of Christ provides a powerful motive for physical devotion to God. "You were bought with a price," Paul says, "So glorify God in your body" (v. 20). Second, union with Christ gives us a new spiritual power for all of life. Believers in Christ are "joined to the Lord" (v. 17) so closely that even our bodies become "members of Christ" and temples of the Holy Spirit (vv. 15, 19). Because of this life-giving union (v. 14), we have both a responsibility to live all of life for Christ ("The body is . . . for the Lord") and the promise that Christ, by his Spirit, is always with us and providing for us ("and the Lord for the body"; v. 13).

The power of the cross pulses through the entire chapter. Only through such power can we surrender our rights, patiently "suffer wrong" (v. 7), and forgive those who harm us (Luke 6:27–36; 23:34). And because sin, sexual or otherwise, appeals to our desire for self-gratification, only something as powerful as Christ's self-sacrifice can produce the selfless devotion that will exercise Christ's power to release us from temptation's grip.

be deceived: [x]neither the sexually immoral,
nor idolaters, nor adulterers, nor men who
practice homosexuality,[1] 10 nor thieves, nor
the greedy, nor drunkards, nor revilers, nor
swindlers will inherit the kingdom of God.
11 And [y]such were some of you. But [z]you were
washed, [a]you were sanctified, [b]you were justified in the name of the Lord Jesus Christ and
by the Spirit of our God.

Flee Sexual Immorality

12 [c]"All things are lawful for me," but not
all things are helpful. "All things are lawful for me," but I will not be dominated by
anything. 13 [d]"Food is meant for the stomach
and the stomach for food"—and God will
destroy both one [e]and the other. The body is
not meant for sexual immorality, but [f]for the
Lord, and [g]the Lord for the body. 14 And [h]God
raised the Lord and [i]will also raise us up [j]by his
power. 15 Do you not know that [k]your bodies
are members of Christ? Shall I then take the
members of Christ and make them members
of a prostitute? Never! 16 Or do you not know
that he who is joined[2] to a prostitute becomes
one body with her? For, as it is written, [l]"The
two will become one flesh." 17 But he who is
joined to the Lord [m]becomes one spirit with
him. 18 [n]Flee from sexual immorality. Every
other sin[3] a person commits is outside the
body, but the sexually immoral person [o]sins
against his own body. 19 Or [p]do you not know
that your body is a temple of the Holy Spirit
within you, whom you have from God? [q]You
are not your own, 20 [r]for you were bought with
a price. [s]So glorify God in your body.

Principles for Marriage

7 Now concerning the matters about which
you wrote: [t]"It is good for a man not to
have sexual relations with a woman." 2 But
because of the temptation to sexual immorality, each man should have his own wife and
each woman her own husband. 3 [u]The husband
should give to his wife her conjugal rights,
and likewise the wife to her husband. 4 For
the wife does not have authority over her own
body, but the husband does. Likewise the husband does not have authority over his own
body, but the wife does. 5 [v]Do not deprive one
another, except perhaps by agreement for a
limited time, that you may devote yourselves
to prayer; but then come together again, [w]so
that Satan may not tempt you because of your
lack of self-control.
6 Now as a concession, [x]not a command, I say
this.[4] 7 [y]I wish that all were [z]as I myself am. But
[a]each has his own gift from God, [b]one of one
kind and one of another.
8 To the unmarried and the widows I say that
[c]it is good for them to remain single [d]as I am.
9 But if they cannot exercise self-control, [e]they
should marry. For it is better to marry than to
burn with passion.

[1] The two Greek terms translated by this phrase refer to the passive and active partners in consensual homosexual acts [2] Or *who holds fast* (compare Genesis 2:24 and Deuteronomy 10:20); also verse 17 [3] Or *Every sin* [4] Or *I say this:*

7:1–40 Having dealt with problems that had been reported to him, Paul now addresses various issues that the Corinthians had raised in a letter (7:1, 25; 8:1; 12:1). The first has to do with marriage and sexuality, as a group in Corinth is apparently arguing that Christians should avoid marriage, or at least avoid sexual activity within marriage. Paul's response in chapter 7 underscores two redemptive patterns that together point us to the incarnation of Christ.

First, the work of Christ fundamentally changes our identity and our priorities. The most significant thing about Christians is not our marital status, cultural background, psychological state, or economic activity (7:17, 29–30). Not even social conditions as extreme as slavery or freedom determine our identity (vv. 21–22). What is most important is that we belong to Christ: "You were bought with a price" (v. 23; cf. 6:20). Since we belong to him, our calling is not to follow human religious "wisdom" (like that of the anti-marriage party in Corinth), but to devote ourselves "to the Lord" with undivided hearts (7:35). This devotion can express itself in a variety of ways, depending on the gifts God gives (v. 7); thus Paul can commend single life to some, and married life to others.

Second, God uses our ordinary routines and relationships to bring about his redemptive purposes in a fallen world. Marriage, for example, brings about three such purposes. First, it provides appropriate means of sexual fulfillment, and therefore of

9 [x]ch. 15:50; Gal. 5:21; Eph. 5:5; 1 Tim. 1:9; Heb. 12:14; 13:4; Rev. 21:8; 22:15
11 [y]ch. 12:2; Eph. 2:2, 3; 4:22; 5:8; Col. 3:7; Titus 3:3 [z]Acts 22:16; Heb. 10:22; [Titus 3:5] [a]See ch. 1:2 [b]Rom. 8:30
12 [c]ch. 10:23
13 [d][Matt. 15:17] [e]Col. 2:22 [f]ver. 15, 19 [g][Eph. 5:23]
14 [h]See Acts 2:24 [i]ch. 15:22, 23; [John 6:39, 40] [j]Matt. 22:29; [Eph. 1:19, 20]
15 [k]ver. 13; Eph. 5:30; [ch. 12:27; Rom. 12:5]
16 [l]Matt. 19:5; Mark 10:8; Eph. 5:31; Cited from Gen. 2:24
17 [m]Eph. 4:4; [John 17:21-23]
18 [n]2 Cor. 12:21; Eph. 5:3 [o][Prov. 5:11]
19 [p][John 2:21]; See ch. 3:16 [q]See Rom. 14:7
20 [r]ch. 7:23; [Acts 20:28; Heb. 9:12, 14]; See 2 Pet. 2:1 [s][Phil. 1:20]

Chapter 7
1 [t]ver. 8, 26
3 [u]Ex. 21:10

5 [v][Ex. 19:15; 1 Sam. 21:4; Eccles. 3:5; Zech. 12:12-14] [w]1 Thess. 3:5 **6** [x]ver. 12, 25; 2 Cor. 8:8; [ver. 10, 40] **7** [y][Acts 26:29] [z]ver. 8; [ch. 9:5] [a]ch. 12:4, 11; 1 Pet. 4:10; [Rom. 12:6] [b]Matt. 19:11, 12 **8** [c]ver. 1, 26 [d]ver. 7 **9** [e][1 Tim. 5:14]

10 To the married [f]I give this charge (not I, but
the Lord): [g]the wife should not separate from
her husband 11 (but if she does, [h]she should
remain unmarried or else be reconciled to
her husband), and [g]the husband should not
divorce his wife.
12 To the rest I say (I, not the Lord) that if any
brother has a wife who is an unbeliever, and
she consents to live with him, he should not
divorce her. 13 If any woman has a husband
who is an unbeliever, and he consents to live
with her, she should not divorce him. 14 For
the unbelieving husband is made holy because
of his wife, and the unbelieving wife is made
holy because of her husband. [i]Otherwise your
children would be unclean, but as it is, they are
holy. 15 But if the unbelieving partner separates,
let it be so. In such cases the brother or sister
is not enslaved. God has called you[1] [j]to peace.
16 For how do you know, wife, [k]whether you
will save your husband? Or how do you know,
husband, whether you will save your wife?

Live as You Are Called

17 Only let each person lead the life[2] [l]that
the Lord has assigned to him, and to which
God has called him. [m]This is my rule in [n]all
the churches. 18 Was anyone at the time of his
call already circumcised? Let him not seek to
remove the marks of circumcision. Was anyone at the time of his call uncircumcised?
[o]Let him not seek circumcision. 19 [p]For neither circumcision counts for anything nor
uncircumcision, but [q]keeping the commandments of God. 20 [r]Each one should remain in
the condition in which he was called. 21 Were
you a bondservant[3] when called? Do not be
concerned about it. (But if you can gain your
freedom, avail yourself of the opportunity.)
22 For he who was called in the Lord as a bondservant is [s]a freedman of the Lord. Likewise he
who was free when called is [t]a bondservant of
Christ. 23 [u]You were bought with a price; [v]do
not become bondservants[4] of men. 24 So, brothers,[5] [w]in whatever condition each was called,
there let him remain with God.

The Unmarried and the Widowed

25 Now concerning[6] the betrothed,[7] [x]I have
no command from the Lord, but I give my
judgment as [y]one who by the Lord's mercy
is [z]trustworthy. 26 I think that in view of the
present[8] distress [a]it is good for a person to
remain as he is. 27 Are you bound to a wife? Do
not seek to be free. Are you free from a wife?
Do not seek a wife. 28 But if you do marry, you
have not sinned, and if a betrothed woman[9]
marries, she has not sinned. Yet those who
marry will have worldly troubles, and I would
spare you that. 29 This is what I mean, brothers: [b]the appointed time has grown very short.
From now on, let those who have wives live
as though they had none, 30 and those who
mourn as though they were not mourning,
and those who rejoice as though they were not
rejoicing, and those who buy [c]as though they
had no goods, 31 and those who deal with the
world as though they had no dealings with

[1] Some manuscripts *us* [2] Or *each person walk in the way* [3] Or *slave*; also twice in verse 22 (for the contextual rendering of the Greek word *doulos*, see Preface) [4] Or *slaves* (for the contextual rendering of the Greek word *doulos*, see Preface) [5] Or *brothers and sisters*; also verse 29 [6] The expression *Now concerning* introduces a reply to a question in the Corinthians' letter; see 7:1 [7] Greek *virgins* [8] Or *impending* [9] Greek *virgin*; also verse 34

10 [f] See ver. 6 [g] Mal. 2:16; See Matt. 5:32
11 [h] Mark 10:12 [g] [See ver. 10 above]
14 [i] Ezra 9:2; Mal. 2:15
15 [j] Col. 3:15; See Rom. 14:19
16 [k] 1 Pet. 3:1; See Rom. 11:14
17 [l] See Rom. 12:3 [m] ch. 4:17 [n] 2 Cor. 8:18; 11:28
18 [o] Acts 15:1, 5, 19, 24, 28; Gal. 5:2
19 [p] Gal. 3:28; 5:6; 6:15; Col. 3:11 [q] See 1 John 2:3
20 [r] ver. 24
22 [s] [Col. 3:24; Philem. 16]; See John 8:36 [t] [ch. 9:21; 1 Pet. 2:16]
23 [u] See ch. 6:20 [v] Lev. 25:42, 55
24 [w] ver. 20
25 [x] See ver. 6 [y] 2 Cor. 4:1; 1 Tim. 1:13, 16 [z] ch. 4:2
26 [a] ver. 1, 8
29 [b] See Rom. 13:11
30 [c] 2 Cor. 6:10

avoiding temptation and sin (vv. 2, 5, 9, 36). Second, it makes young children "holy" by bringing them into covenant relationship with God through the belief of at least one parent—whose belief apparently can cover the unholiness of an unbelieving spouse in terms of the child's covenant status before God (v. 14; cf. Acts 2:39; 16:31). Third, marriage sometimes leads to the salvation of unbelieving spouses (1 Cor. 7:16). God similarly calls and equips every believer (v. 17; cf. 1:8–9), whatever their circumstances (7:24), to advance his life-giving, loving purposes. (Note that Paul treats slavery differently, recommending that slaves seek freedom as they have opportunity [v. 21]. God's redemptive purpose is ultimately to eliminate such fundamentally unjust social structures. We see this redemptive ethic unfolding more in Gal. 3:28 and Philem. 15, 16.)

Ultimately, this chapter points to the incarnation of Christ, in which we see the perfect combination of involvement in the world without dependence on the world. Jesus lived a genuinely human life, bearing with all the difficulties and temptations of life in a fallen world. Yet he never let sinful priorities govern his mind-set or lifestyle. His coming has broken the power of this world (1 Cor. 7:31), so that as we await his return ("the appointed time"; v. 29), we too are able live faithfully before God.

it. For [d]the present form of this world is passing away.
32 I want you to be [e]free from anxieties. [f]The
unmarried man is anxious about the things
of the Lord, how to please the Lord. 33 But the
married man is anxious about worldly things,
how to please his wife, 34 and his interests are
divided. And the unmarried or betrothed
woman is anxious about the things of the
Lord, how to be holy in body and spirit. But
the married woman is anxious about worldly
things, how to please her husband. 35 I say this
for your own benefit, [g]not to lay any restraint
upon you, but to promote good order and to
secure your undivided devotion to the Lord.
36 If anyone thinks that he is not behaving
properly toward his betrothed,[1] if his[2] passions
are strong, and it has to be, let him do as he
wishes: let them marry—it is no sin. 37 But
whoever is firmly established in his heart,
being under no necessity but having his desire
under control, and has determined this in his
heart, to keep her as his betrothed, he will do
well. 38 So then he who marries his betrothed
[h]does well, and he who refrains from marriage
will do even better.
39 [i]A wife is bound to her husband as long as
he lives. But if her husband dies, she is free to
be married to whom she wishes, only [j]in the
Lord. 40 Yet [k]in my judgment she is happier if
she remains as she is. And I think [l]that I too
have the Spirit of God.

Food Offered to Idols

8 Now concerning[3] [m]food offered to idols:
we know that [n]"all of us possess knowledge." This "knowledge" [o]puffs up, [p]but love
builds up. 2 [q]If anyone imagines that he knows
something, [r]he does not yet know as he ought
to know. 3 But if anyone loves God, [s]he is
known by God.[4]
4 Therefore, as to the eating of food offered
to idols, we know that [t]"an idol has no real
existence," and that [u]"there is no God but one."
5 For although there may be [v]so-called gods in
heaven or on earth—as indeed there are many
"gods" and many "lords"— 6 yet [w]for us there
is one God, the Father, [x]from whom are all
things and for whom we exist, and [y]one Lord,
Jesus Christ, through whom are all things and
[z]through whom we exist.
7 However, not all possess this knowledge.
But some, [a]through former association with
idols, eat food as really offered to an idol,
and [b]their conscience, being weak, is defiled.
8 [c]Food will not commend us to God. We are no
worse off if we do not eat, and no better off if
we do. 9 But take care [d]that this right of yours
does not somehow become a stumbling block
[e]to the weak. 10 For if anyone sees you who have
knowledge eating[5] in an idol's temple, will he
not be encouraged,[6] if his conscience is weak,
to eat food offered to idols? 11 And so by your
knowledge this weak person is [f]destroyed, the
brother for whom Christ died. 12 Thus, sinning

[1] Greek *virgin*; also verses 37, 38 [2] Or *her* [3] The expression *Now concerning* introduces a reply to a question in the Corinthians' letter; see 7:1 [4] Greek *him* [5] Greek *reclining at table* [6] Or *fortified*; Greek *built up*

8:1–13 Chapters 8–10 of Paul's epistle address a second topic from the Corinthians' letter: food offered to idols, some of which was sold in public markets (10:25), and some of which was eaten in feasts at pagan temples (8:10; 10:20). Believers in different times, places, and cultures may not share the Corinthians' precise concerns. Still, the principles of the text are unchanging: in the everyday matters where Christian faith intersects with non-Christian culture, the gospel transforms us to pursue the glory of God (8:3; 10:31) and the good of our neighbor (8:1; 10:24) by laying aside our personal freedoms.

For the believer, it should be unthinkable to "sin against Christ" or against our brothers "for whom Christ died" (8:11–12). Rather, love for Christ will lead us to cherish those he cherishes. As a result, we will take care to avoid doing anything that would interrupt the progress of other believers toward maturity in Christ ("stumbling block/stumble"; vv. 9, 13). Instead, we will gladly give up our rights out of love for our brothers (v. 13)—even those who seem to us less mature ("the weak"). Like the Corinthians, we often ask, "What am I free to do?" But as believers in Christ, we are able to ask a different question: "What am I free to give up for the good of others?" Similarly, when we know spiritual truth as we ought, we will use it not to justify doing what we please, but to "build up" other people (vv. 1–2).

Only by the transforming power of the gospel can the good of our neighbor come to mean more to us than our own rights and privileges. For in the gospel, Jesus himself gave up his own rights and privileges for our sake.

31 [d]Ps. 39:6; James 1:10; 1 Pet. 1:24; 4:7; 1 John 2:17
32 [e]See Matt. 6:25; Luke 10:41 [f][1 Tim. 5:5]
35 [g][Prov. 22:25]
38 [h]Heb. 13:4
39 [i]Rom. 7:2 [j][2 Cor. 6:14]
40 [k]See ver. 6 [l][Acts 15:28]
Chapter 8
1 [m]ver. 4, 7, 10; See Acts 15:29 [n]See Rom. 15:14 [o]Rom. 14:3 [p]ch. 13:4-13
2 [q]Gal. 6:3; [ch. 3:18] [r][ch. 13:8, 9, 12; 1 Tim. 6:3, 4]
3 [s]Gal. 4:9; [Ex. 33:12, 17; Jer. 1:5; Nah. 1:7; 2 Tim. 2:19]
4 [t]ch. 10:19; Isa. 41:24; [Acts 14:15] [u]ver. 6; See Deut. 4:35, 39
5 [v]2 Thess. 2:4
6 [w]ver. 4; Mal. 2:10; Eph. 4:6 [x]See Rom. 11:36 [y]Eph. 4:5; [ch. 1:2; 1 Tim. 2:5]; See John 13:13 [z]John 1:3; Col. 1:16
7 [a][Rom. 14:14, 22, 23] [b]ch. 10:25, 28, 29
8 [c]Rom. 14:17
9 [d][ch. 10:23; Rom. 14:21; Gal. 5:13] [e]Rom. 14:1, 2
11 [f]Rom. 14:15, 20

against your brothers[1] and [g]wounding their
conscience when it is weak, [h]you sin against
Christ. 13 Therefore, [i]if food makes my brother
stumble, I will never eat meat, lest I make my
brother stumble.

Paul Surrenders His Rights

9 [j]Am I not free? [k]Am I not an apostle? [l]Have
I not seen Jesus our Lord? [m]Are not you my
workmanship in the Lord? 2 If to others I am
not an apostle, at least I am to you, for you are
[n]the seal of my apostleship in the Lord.

3 This is my defense to those who would
examine me. 4 [o]Do we not have the right to eat
and drink? 5 [p]Do we not have the right to take
along a believing wife,[2] as do the other apostles and [q]the brothers of the Lord and [r]Cephas?
6 Or is it only Barnabas and I who have no right
to refrain from working for a living? 7 [s]Who
serves as a soldier at his own expense? [t]Who
plants a vineyard without eating any of its
fruit? Or who tends a flock without getting
some of the milk?

8 Do I say these things on human authority? Does not the Law say the same? 9 For it is
written in the Law of Moses, [u]"You shall not
muzzle an ox when it treads out the grain."
Is it for oxen that God is concerned? 10 Does
he not certainly speak for our sake? It was
written [v]for our sake, because [w]the plowman
should plow in hope and the thresher thresh
in hope of sharing in the crop. 11 [x]If we have
sown spiritual things among you, is it too
much if we reap material things from you?
12 If others share this rightful claim on you, do
not we even more?

Nevertheless, [y]we have not made use of this
right, but we endure anything [z]rather than
put an obstacle in the way of the gospel of
Christ. 13 Do you not know that [a]those who
are employed in the temple service get their
food from the temple, and those who serve
at the altar share in the sacrificial offerings?
14 In the same way, the Lord commanded that
[b]those who proclaim the gospel should get
their living by the gospel.

15 But [c]I have made no use of any of these
rights, nor am I writing these things to secure
any such provision. For I would rather die than
have anyone [d]deprive me of my ground for
boasting. 16 For if I preach the gospel, that gives
me no ground for boasting. For [e]necessity is
laid upon me. Woe to me if I do not preach the
gospel! 17 For if I do this of my own will, I have
a reward, but if not of my own will, I am still
entrusted with [f]a stewardship. 18 What then
is my reward? That in my preaching [g]I may
present the gospel free of charge, so as not to
make full use of my right in the gospel.

19 For [h]though I am free from all, [i]I have made
myself a servant to all, that I might [j]win more
of them. 20 [k]To the Jews I became as a Jew, in
order to win Jews. To those under the law
I became as one under the law (though not
being myself under the law) that I might win
those under the law. 21 To [l]those outside the law
I became [m]as one outside the law (not being
outside the law of God but [n]under the law of

[1] Or *brothers and sisters* [2] Greek *a sister as wife*

12[g] [Zech. 2:8; Matt. 18:6] [h] [Matt. 25:45]
13[i] Rom. 14:13, 21; [2 Cor. 6:3; 11:29]
Chapter 9
1[j] ver. 19 [k] Acts 14:14; 2 Cor. 12:12; 1 Thess. 2:6; [2 Cor. 10:7; Rev. 2:2] [l] ch. 15:8; Acts 9:3, 17; 18:9; 22:14, 18; 23:11 [m] See ch. 3:6
2[n] [2 Cor. 3:2]
4[o] ver. 14; 1 Thess. 2:6, 9; 2 Thess. 3:8, 9
5[p] [ch. 7:7] [q] See Matt. 12:46 [r] Matt. 8:14; See John 1:42
7[s] 2 Cor. 10:4; 1 Tim. 1:18; 2 Tim. 2:3, 4 [t] [ch. 3:6-8; Deut. 20:6; Prov. 27:18; Song 8:12]
9[u] 1 Tim. 5:18; Cited from Deut. 25:4
10[v] See Rom. 4:24 [w] 2 Tim. 2:6
11[x] [Rom. 15:27; Gal. 6:6]
12[y] ver. 15, 18; See Acts 20:33 [z] [2 Cor. 6:3; 11:12]
13[a] Lev. 6:16, 26; 7:6; Num. 5:9, 10; 18:8-20; Deut. 18:1

9:1–27 1 Corinthians 9 illustrates what it means to give up our rights for the good of others. As an apostle, Paul has the right to financial support (vv. 4, 6–12). But love for Christ leads him to give up this right, so that others will understand that God's saving mercies are a free gift ("free of charge"; v. 18), not something obtained through human resources. In fact, though he has many rights ("I am free from all"), Paul lives as though he has none ("a servant to all"; v. 19). For the sake of the gospel (v. 23), he has become "all things to all people" (v. 22)—that is, he has adopted many customs and cultural practices that are not his own preferences, so that he might honor Christ and bless others by sharing the gospel with as many different kinds of people as possible. Even those of us who are not apostles are called to show such zeal for "building up" our neighbors (8:1; 10:23).

The source of such selflessness is the transforming power of love for Christ, who gave up so much to become a servant for our sake (Mark 10:45; Phil. 2:7; 2 Cor. 8:9). When we are gripped by such love, a focus on personal comfort gives way to a focus on advancing the gospel and the blessings it brings. As the athletic images in 1 Corinthians 9:24–26 remind us, passion for Christ fuels sustained, intense effort. The grace we have already received gives us strength and motive to complete our "race," where the final victory of resurrection life in Christ awaits us (v. 25; cf. 15:50–57).

14[b] ver. 4; Matt. 10:10 **15**[c] See Acts 18:3 [d] 2 Cor. 11:10 **16**[e] [Acts 4:20; 9:6; Rom. 1:14] **17**[f] ch. 4:1; Gal. 2:7; [Phil. 1:16] **18**[g] 2 Cor. 11:7; 12:13 **19**[h] ver. 1; [ch. 10:29] [i] [Gal. 5:13] [j] Matt. 18:15; 1 Pet. 3:1 **20**[k] Acts 16:3; 21:23-26 **21**[l] Rom. 2:12, 14 [m] [Gal. 2:3; 3:2] [n] See ch. 7:22

Christ) that I might win those outside the law. 22 [o]To the weak I became weak, that I might win the weak. [p]I have become all things to all people, that [q]by all means I might save some. 23 I do it all for the sake of the gospel, [r]that I may share with them in its blessings.

24 Do you not know that in a race all the runners run, but only one receives [s]the prize? So [t]run that you may obtain it. 25 Every [u]athlete exercises self-control in all things. They do it to receive a perishable wreath, but we [v]an imperishable. 26 So I do not run aimlessly; I [w]do not box as one [x]beating the air. 27 But I discipline my body and [y]keep it under control,[1] lest after preaching to others [z]I myself should be [a]disqualified.

Warning Against Idolatry

10 For I do not want you to be unaware, brothers,[2] that our fathers were all under [b]the cloud, and all [c]passed through the sea, 2 and all were baptized into Moses in the cloud and in the sea, 3 and [d]all ate the same [e]spiritual food, 4 and [f]all drank the same spiritual drink. For they drank from the spiritual Rock that followed them, and the Rock was Christ. 5 Nevertheless, with most of them God was not pleased, for [g]they were overthrown[3] in the wilderness.

6 Now these things took place as examples for us, that we might not desire evil as [h]they did. 7 [i]Do not be idolaters [j]as some of them were; as it is written, [k]"The people sat down to eat and drink and rose up to play." 8 [l]We must not indulge in sexual immorality [m]as some of them did, and [n]twenty-three thousand fell in a single day. 9 We must not put Christ[4] to the test, [o]as some of them did and [p]were destroyed by serpents, 10 nor grumble, [q]as some of them did and [r]were destroyed by [s]the Destroyer. 11 Now these things happened to them as an example, but [t]they were written down for our instruction, [u]on whom the end of the ages has come. 12 Therefore [v]let anyone who thinks that he stands take heed lest he fall. 13 No temptation has overtaken you that is not common to man. [w]God is faithful, and [x]he will not let you be tempted beyond your ability, but with the temptation he will also provide the way of escape, that you may be able to endure it.

14 Therefore, my beloved, [y]flee from idolatry. 15 I speak [z]as to sensible people; judge for yourselves what I say. 16 [a]The cup of blessing that we bless, is it not a participation in the blood of Christ? [b]The bread that we break, is it not a participation in the body of Christ? 17 Because there is one bread, we who are many are [c]one body, for we all partake of the one bread. 18 Consider [d]the people of Israel:[5] [e]are not those who eat the sacrifices participants in the altar? 19 What do I imply then? That food offered to

[1] Greek *I pummel my body and make it a slave* [2] Or *brothers and sisters* [3] Or *were laid low* [4] Some manuscripts *the Lord* [5] Greek *Consider Israel according to the flesh*

10:1–22 Paul's focus now shifts to the problem of idolatry. Here the question is not whether the Corinthians are free to eat meat purchased in the market, but whether they may participate in religious feasts at pagan temples.

Three truths stand out: (1) as Christians we are united to Christ, and therefore we share in the redeeming power of his death, as represented in the Lord's Supper (vv. 16–17); (2) the appropriate response to such mercy is to honor Christ as our only Lord, not sharing fellowship with him and with false gods (vv. 20–22); (3) when we do engage in idolatry, warnings of judgment give us opportunity to repent (vv. 12–14). In fact, no matter what sin confronts us, God faithfully provides a means to escape temptation—a promise that encourages us to resist to the utmost of our "ability" (v. 13).

Throughout the text, Paul interprets the Old Testament in a way that is centered on Christ. Christ is the "Rock" that accompanied and sustained Israel in her wilderness wanderings (vv. 1–4, 9). Christ's "table" (representing his death) fulfills the purpose of Israel's "altar" (representing the sacrifice of animals; vv. 16–21). And Christ, "into" whom believers are baptized (Acts 2:38; Rom. 6:3; Gal. 3:27), is the leader of a new exodus, a greater deliverance than the exodus led by Moses (1 Cor. 10:1–2). Thus the Old Testament provides Christians not only instructive examples (vv. 6, 11) but also rich reminders that God's Son has always been, and will always be, the only means by which sinners have access to God's saving mercies.

22 [o] 2 Cor. 11:29 [p] ch. 10:33 [q] ch. 7:16; Rom. 11:14
23 [r] [ch. 10:24]
24 [s] Phil. 3:14; Col. 2:18 [t] Gal. 2:2; 5:7; Phil. 2:16; Heb. 12:1; [2 Tim. 4:7]
25 [u] 1 Tim. 6:12; 2 Tim. 2:5; 4:7; [Jude 3] [v] See James 1:12
26 [w] [Heb. 12:4] [x] [ch. 14:9]
27 [y] [Rom. 6:19] [z] [Song 1:6] [a] [Jer. 6:30; Rom. 1:28; Heb. 6:8]

Chapter 10
1 [b] See Ex. 13:21 [c] See Ex. 14:22
3 [d] Ex. 16:15, 35; Deut. 8:3; Neh. 9:15, 20; Ps. 78:24 [e] Ps. 78:25; 105:40; John 6:31
4 [f] See Ex. 17:6
5 [g] Num. 14:29, 37; 26:64, 65; Ps. 106:26; Heb. 3:17; Jude 5
6 [h] Num. 11:4, 33, 34; Ps. 78:18; 106:14
7 [i] ver. 14 [j] Ex. 32:4 [k] Cited from Ex. 32:6
8 [l] See ch. 6:18; Acts 15:20 [m] Num. 25:1 [n] [Num. 25:9; Ps. 106:29]
9 [o] Num. 21:5; [Ex. 17:2, 7]; See Ps. 78:18 [p] See Num. 21:6 **10** [q] See Num. 14:2 [r] Num. 14:29-37 [s] Ex. 12:23; 2 Sam. 24:16; 1 Chr. 21:15; Ps. 78:49 **11** [t] See Rom. 4:23 [u] See Rom. 13:11 **12** [v] Rom. 11:20; [2 Pet. 3:17] **13** [w] See ch. 1:9 [x] [Dan. 3:17]; See 2 Pet. 2:9 **14** [y] ver. 7 **15** [z] [ch. 8:1] **16** [a] ch. 11:25; Matt. 26:27, 28 [b] ch. 11:23, 24; Matt. 26:26; See Acts 2:42; 20:7 **17** [c] ch. 12:12, 13, 20; Rom. 12:5; Eph. 4:4, 16; Col. 3:15 **18** [d] Rom. 1:3; 4:1; 9:5; 2 Cor. 11:18 [e] Lev. 3:3; 7:15; [Heb. 13:10]

idols is anything, or that [f]an idol is anything?
20 No, I imply that what pagans sacrifice [g]they
offer to demons and not to God. I do not want
you to be participants with demons. 21 [h]You
cannot drink the cup of the Lord and [i]the cup
of demons. You cannot partake of the table of
the Lord and [j]the table of demons. 22 [k]Shall we
provoke the Lord to jealousy? [l]Are we stronger
than he?

Do All to the Glory of God

23 [m]"All things are lawful," but not all things
are helpful. "All things are lawful," but not all
things build up. 24 [n]Let no one seek his own
good, but the good of his neighbor. 25 [o]Eat
whatever is sold in the meat market without
raising any question on the ground of conscience.
26 For [p]"the earth is the Lord's, and the
fullness thereof." 27 If one of the unbelievers
invites you to dinner and you are disposed
to go, [q]eat whatever is set before you without
raising any question on the ground of conscience.
28 But if someone says to you, "This has
been offered in sacrifice," then do not eat it,
for the sake of the one who informed you, and
for the sake of conscience— 29 I do not mean
[r]your conscience, but his. For [s]why should my
liberty be determined by someone else's conscience?
30 If I partake with thankfulness, why
am I denounced because of that [t]for which
I give thanks?

31 So, whether you eat or drink, or [u]whatever
you do, do all to the glory of God. 32 [v]Give
no offense to Jews or to Greeks or to [w]the
church of God, 33 just as [x]I try to please everyone
in everything I do, [y]not seeking my own
advantage, but that of many, that they may
be saved.

11 [z]Be imitators of me, as I am of Christ.

Head Coverings

2 Now I commend you [a]because you remember
me in everything and [b]maintain the traditions
[c]even as I delivered them to you. 3 But
I want you to understand that [d]the head of

19 [f]See ch. 8:4
20 [g]Deut. 32:17
21 [h][2 Cor. 6:15, 16] [i][Deut. 32:38] [j][Isa. 65:11]
22 [k]Deut. 32:21 [l]Eccles. 6:10; Ezek. 22:14
23 [m]ch. 6:12; See ch. 8:9
24 [n]ver. 33; ch. 13:5; Phil. 2:21; [ch. 9:23; 2 Cor. 12:14]; See Rom. 15:1
25 [o]ch. 8:7
26 [p]Cited from Ps. 24:1; [Ex. 9:29; 19:5; Deut. 10:14; Job 41:11; Ps. 50:12]
27 [q]Luke 10:8
29 [r][ch. 8:9-12] [s][ch. 9:19; Rom. 14:16]
30 [t]Rom. 14:6; 1 Tim. 4:3, 4
31 [u]Col. 3:17; 1 Pet. 4:11
32 [v]ch. 8:13; Rom. 14:13; 2 Cor. 6:3 [w][ch. 11:16]; See Acts 20:28
33 [x]ch. 9:22; [Gal. 1:10] [y]See ver. 24

Chapter 11
1 [z]See ch. 4:16
2 [a][ch. 4:17; 1 Thess. 3:6] [b]2 Thess. 2:15; 3:6 [c][1 Thess. 4:1, 2]
3 [d]Eph. 1:22; 4:15; 5:23; Col. 1:18

10:23–11:1 Here Paul returns to the topic of the Corinthians' freedom to eat meat sold in the market (10:25), concluding the section of the epistle that began in 8:1. In doing so, he underscores two principles that demonstrate the fruit of the gospel in our lives, and that ultimately point us to the work of Christ.

First, in matters of conscience, a Christian should not "seek his own good, but the good of his neighbor" (10:24). In Christ, our goal is to do not simply what is "lawful" but what is "helpful" for others (v. 23). Paul's own practice, presented in detail in chapter 9, is again summarized: he does not seek his own good, "but that of many, that they may be saved" (10:33). The apostle now states explicitly where he learned such a pattern: "Be imitators of me, as I am of Christ" (11:1; cf. the cycle of gospel embrace, gospel transformation, and gospel multiplication seen in the note on 4:6–21). As Christ gave up many freedoms to secure our salvation, we are called to give up many personal rights and preferences so that others may receive and enjoy that salvation. Paul will touch on this subject from the opposite perspective in other passages—urging Christians not to give up their freedom, due to the legalisms of others—but there as well as here the key principle is honoring what most promotes the gospel (2 Cor. 3:17; Gal. 2:4–5; 5:1).

Second, as Jesus honors his Father in all things (1 Cor. 11:3; 15:24–28), Christians are to seek "the glory of God" in everything we do (10:31). This is not easy, since sin tempts us to insist on our own rights at others' expense, and to compromise our loyalty to God. But the gospel offers us this hope: we who have received Christ as Savior also have strength to follow his example.

Indeed, the cross of Christ, where our salvation is accomplished, is the place where we learn to imitate Christ by doing costly things for God's glory and our neighbor's good. For Christ himself did the supremely costly thing for *our* good—dying in our place.

11:2–16 In the next major section of the letter (11:2–14:40), Paul addresses a series of problems related to worship in Corinth. In each case, self-promotion, a spirit of independence, and neglect of others' good are at work. Only through the power of the gospel can such patterns of sin be displaced by love (13:1–13).

The first such problem concerns women who are dishonoring their husbands by praying and prophesying without wearing head coverings (11:5). Interpreters debate

every man is Christ, [e]the head of a wife[1] is
her husband, and [f]the head of Christ is God.
4 Every man who prays or prophesies with his
head covered dishonors his head, 5 but every
wife[2] who prays or [g]prophesies [h]with her
head uncovered dishonors her head, since it
is the same [i]as if her head were shaven. 6 For
if a wife will not cover her head, then she
should cut her hair short. But since it is disgraceful for a wife to cut off her hair or shave
her head, let her cover her head. 7 For a man
ought not to cover his head, since [j]he is the
image and glory of God, but [k]woman is the
glory of man. 8 For [l]man was not made from
woman, but woman from man. 9 Neither was
man created for woman, but [m]woman for man.
10 That is why a wife ought to have a symbol of authority on her head, because of the
angels.[3] 11 Nevertheless, [n]in the Lord woman is
not independent of man nor man of woman;
12 for as woman was made from man, so man is
now born of woman. And [o]all things are from
God. 13 Judge for yourselves: is it proper for a
wife to pray to God with her head uncovered?
14 Does not nature itself teach you that if a man
wears long hair it is a disgrace for him, 15 but if
a woman has long hair, it is her glory? For her
hair is given to her for a covering. 16 [p]If anyone
is inclined to be contentious, we have no such
practice, nor do [q]the churches of God.

The Lord's Supper

17 But in the following instructions I do
not commend you, because when you come
together it is not for the better but for the
worse. 18 For, in the first place, when you come
together as a church, [r]I hear that there are divisions among you. And I believe it in part,[4] 19 for
[s]there must be factions among you in order
[t]that those who are genuine among you may
be recognized. 20 When you come together,
it is not the Lord's supper that you eat. 21 For
in eating, each one goes ahead with his own
meal. One goes hungry, [u]another gets drunk.

[1] Greek *gunē*. This term may refer to a *woman* or a *wife*, depending on the context [2] In verses 5–13, the Greek word *gunē* is translated *wife* in verses that deal with wearing a veil, a sign of being married in first-century culture [3] Or *messengers*, that is, people sent to observe and report [4] Or *I believe a certain report*

precisely how Paul's discussion of praying and prophesying with covered heads applies to today's church. Whatever the case, the apostle's instructions are rooted in two clear gospel principles.

First, Christ and his Father are bound to one another as closely as a head to a body ("the head of Christ is God"; v. 3). Within this relationship of love, Christ gladly honors his Father, and neither seeks to establish independence from the other. Therefore, when Scripture calls believers to unity, love, and the sharing of common life, it is calling us to respond to and reflect patterns of divine love. In marriage (vv. 3–6; cf. Eph. 5:21–33), this means that a wife should respect her husband's authority (as the Son honors the Father), and a husband should delight in his wife (as the Father delights in the Son). And while a spirit of mutual dependence should certainly characterize marriage (1 Cor. 11:11–12), the principle applies to all other relationships in the body of Christ as well.

Second, reflecting the love that exists within the Trinity has been God's purpose for his image-bearers since creation (vv. 7–9, 12). In the church, God is restoring relationships that have been distorted by sin, so that his unchanging character may be displayed. It is therefore crucial that believers' conduct in worship reflect the character of divine love.

11:17–34 Some in Corinth are treating the Lord's Supper as an opportunity for selfish indulgence, amplifying the divisions between rich and poor. Paul's strong language and stern warnings remind us that our worship of Christ must honor his sacrifice for us.

The text reflects patterns of sin that blind us, even in worship. Self-centeredness can turn "the Lord's" Supper into one that is the worshiper's "own" (vv. 20–21). And it is easy to humiliate those for whom Christ has died while we should be "proclaiming the Lord's death" (v. 26). Such sins are so serious that they call forth the Lord's judgment and discipline (vv. 29–34).

Yet the text also reminds us that the gospel has power to pardon sin and transform hardened hearts. Fulfilling the Old Testament promise of a "new covenant" (Jer. 31:31–34), Jesus has secured our forgiveness by giving his body and blood for us (1 Cor. 11:24–25; cf. Luke 22:17–20). When we "remember" him through the Lord's

3 [e] See Gen. 3:16 [f] [ch. 3:23]
5 [g] Luke 2:36; Acts 21:9; [ch. 14:34] [h] [Num. 5:18] [i] Deut. 21:12
7 [j] See Gen. 1:26 [k] [Prov. 12:4]
8 [l] Gen. 2:21-23; [1 Tim. 2:13]
9 [m] Gen. 2:18
11 [n] Gal. 3:28
12 [o] See Rom. 11:36
16 [p] 1 Tim. 6:3, 4 [q] 2 Thess. 1:4; [1 Thess. 2:14]; See ch. 7:17; 10:32
18 [r] ch. 1:10-12; [ch. 3:3]
19 [s] [Matt. 18:7; Luke 17:1; Acts 20:30; 1 Tim. 4:1; 2 Pet. 2:1] [t] 1 John 2:19; [Deut. 13:3]
21 [u] [2 Pet. 2:13; Jude 12]

22 What! Do you not have houses to eat and
drink in? Or do you despise [v]the church of
God and [w]humiliate those who have nothing?
What shall I say to you? Shall I commend you
in this? No, I will not.
23 For [x]I received from the Lord what I also
delivered to you, that [y]the Lord Jesus on the
night when he was betrayed took bread, 24 and
when he had given thanks, he broke it, and
said, "This is my body which is for[1] you. Do
this in remembrance of me."[2] 25 In the same
way also he took the cup, after supper, saying,
"This cup is the new covenant in my blood. Do
this, as often as you drink it, in remembrance
of me." 26 For as often as you eat this bread and
drink the cup, you proclaim the Lord's death
[z]until he comes.
27 [a]Whoever, therefore, eats the bread or
drinks the cup of the Lord [b]in an unworthy
manner will be guilty concerning [c]the body
and blood of the Lord. 28 [d]Let a person examine
himself, then, and so eat of the bread and drink
of the cup. 29 For anyone who eats and drinks
without discerning the body eats and drinks
judgment on himself. 30 That is why many of
you are weak and ill, and some [e]have died.[3]
31 [f]But if we judged[4] ourselves truly, we would
not be judged. 32 But when we are judged by
the Lord, [g]we are disciplined[5] so that we may
not be [h]condemned along with the world.
33 So then, my brothers,[6] when you come
together to eat, wait for[7] one another— 34 [i]if
anyone is hungry, [j]let him eat at home—so
that when you come together it will not be for
judgment. About the other things [k]I will give
directions [l]when I come.

Spiritual Gifts

12 Now [m]concerning[8] spiritual gifts,[9]
brothers,[10] I do not want you to be
uninformed. 2 You know that [n]when you were
pagans [o]you were led astray to [p]mute idols,
however you were led. 3 Therefore I want you
to understand that [q]no one speaking in the
Spirit of God ever says "Jesus is [r]accursed!" and
[s]no one can say "Jesus is Lord" except in the
Holy Spirit.
4 Now [t]there are varieties of gifts, but [u]the
same Spirit; 5 and [v]there are varieties of service,
but [u]the same Lord; 6 and there are varieties of
activities, but it is [u]the same God who empowers them all in everyone. 7 [w]To each is given the
manifestation of the Spirit for the common
good. 8 For to one is given through the Spirit

[1] Some manuscripts *broken for* [2] Or *as my memorial*; also verse 25 [3] Greek *have fallen asleep* (as in 15:6, 20) [4] Or *discerned* [5] Or *when we are judged we are being disciplined by the Lord* [6] Or *brothers and sisters* [7] Or *share with* [8] The expression *Now concerning* introduces a reply to a question in the Corinthians' letter; see 7:1 [9] Or *spiritual persons* [10] Or *brothers and sisters*

22 [v]See Acts 20:28 [w][Prov. 17:5; James 2:6]
23 [x]ch. 15:3; Gal. 1:12 [y]For ver. 23-25, see Matt. 26:26-28; Mark 14:22-24; Luke 22:19, 20
26 [z]See John 21:22
27 [a][Num. 9:10, 13] [b][John 13:27] [c]John 6:51, 53-56
28 [d][2 Cor. 13:5; Gal. 6:4]
30 [e]See Matt. 27:52
31 [f]See 1 John 1:9
32 [g]See Prov. 3:11 [h]Rom. 5:16
34 [i]ver. 21 [j]ver. 22 [k]ch. 7:17; Titus 1:5 [l]See ch. 4:19

Chapter 12
1 [m]ch. 14:1
2 [n]Eph. 2:11, 12; [1 Pet. 4:3]; See ch. 6:11 [o]1 Thess. 1:9 [p]Hab. 2:18, 19; [Ps. 115:5; Isa. 46:7; Jer. 10:5]
3 [q]1 John 4:2, 3 [r]See Rom. 9:3 [s]John 15:26; [Matt. 16:17]; See Rom. 10:9
4 [t][Heb. 2:4]; See Rom. 12:6 [u]Eph. 4:4-6
5 [v]Rom. 12:7; [Eph. 4:11] [u][See ver. 4 above]
6 [u][See ver. 4 above]
7 [w]Eph. 4:7; [ch. 14:26; Rom. 12:3]

Supper, we recall this great act of covenant love—and we proclaim that we need the power of the Lord's death to strengthen us "until he comes" (1 Cor. 11:26), just as we need food ("the bread") and drink ("the cup") to sustain our bodies. Only through such power are we able to give the highest honor to the least privileged ("those who have nothing"; v. 22) and to put the good of others before our own ("wait for one another"; v. 33).

Even the more challenging portions of this text reflect gospel principles. The warning of verse 27 presupposes a desire to honor (not profane) Christ's work by reflecting its worth as we participate in the Lord's Supper. In fact, when we examine ourselves (v. 28) and judge ourselves (v. 31) in light of Christ's saving work, we will find courage to repent more deeply than we otherwise could. Even the Lord's discipline will not lead to condemnation (v. 32) but to assurance that we are beloved children (Heb. 12:5–11; Prov. 3:11–12). Stern warnings and severe discipline indicate that our Savior desires our good even more than we do.

12:1–31 The next three chapters of the letter provide a framework for understanding spiritual gifts (chs. 12–13), followed by a discussion of two particular gifts that are causing problems in the Corinthians' worship (ch. 14). For Paul, the work of the Holy Spirit frees us from slavery to "mute idols" (12:2), enables us to confess Jesus as Lord (v. 3), and gives us gifts that move the church toward greater maturity. These opening verses on the Holy Spirit provide the foundation for the entire section.

Running throughout chapter 12 is the theme of unity-in-diversity, which reflects the nature and goodness of the triune God ("the same Spirit . . . the same Lord . . . the same God"; vv. 4–6). An overemphasis on diversity might lead us to a sinful spirit of independence from other believers; an undue stress on unity might lead to an arrogant insistence that all other believers be exactly like us.

the utterance of [x]wisdom, and to another the
utterance of [y]knowledge according to the
same Spirit, 9 to another [z]faith by the same
Spirit, to another [a]gifts of healing by the one
Spirit, 10 to another [b]the working of miracles,
to another [c]prophecy, to another [d]the ability to
distinguish between spirits, to another [e]vari-
ous kinds of tongues, to another [f]the interpretation of tongues. 11 All these are empowered
by one and the same Spirit, [g]who apportions
to each one individually [h]as he wills.

One Body with Many Members

12 For just as [i]the body is one and has many
members, and all the members of the body,
though many, are one body, [j]so it is with Christ.
13 For [k]in one Spirit we were all baptized into
one body—[l]Jews or Greeks, slaves[1] or free—
and [m]all were made to drink of one Spirit.

14 For the body does not consist of one
member but of many. 15 If the foot should say,
"Because I am not a hand, I do not belong to
the body," that would not make it any less a
part of the body. 16 And if the ear should say,
"Because I am not an eye, I do not belong to
the body," that would not make it any less
a part of the body. 17 If the whole body were
an eye, where would be the sense of hearing?
If the whole body were an ear, where would
be the sense of smell? 18 But as it is, [n]God
arranged the members in the body, each one
of them, [o]as he chose. 19 If all were a single
member, where would the body be? 20 As it is,
there are many parts,[2] yet one body.

21 The eye cannot say to the hand, "I have no
need of you," nor again the head to the feet,
"I have no need of you." 22 On the contrary,
the parts of the body that seem to be weaker
are indispensable, 23 and on those parts of
the body that we think less honorable we
bestow the greater honor, and our unpresent-
able parts are treated with greater modesty,
24 which our more presentable parts do not
require. But God has so composed the body,
giving greater honor to the part that lacked
it, 25 that there may be no division in the body,
but that the members may have the same care
for one another. 26 If one member suffers, all
suffer together; if one member is honored, [p]all
rejoice together.

27 Now [q]you are the body of Christ and
individually [r]members of it. 28 And [s]God has
appointed in the church first [t]apostles, second
[u]prophets, third teachers, then [v]miracles, then
[w]gifts of healing, [x]helping, [y]administrating,
and [v]various kinds of tongues. 29 Are all apostles? Are all prophets? Are all teachers? Do all
work miracles? 30 Do all possess gifts of healing? Do all speak with tongues? Do all interpret? 31 But [z]earnestly desire the higher gifts.

And I will show you a still more excellent way.

The Way of Love

13 If I speak in the tongues of men and of
angels, but have not love, I am a noisy
gong or a clanging cymbal. 2 And if I have [a]pro-
phetic powers, and understand all mysteries
and all knowledge, and if I have all faith, [b]so

[1] Or *servants*; Greek *bondservants* [2] Or *members*; also verse 22

Instead, God has given a diversity of gifts to his people, who together function as one body (vv. 12–27). We are to use these gifts "for the common good" (v. 7) and with no sense of envy, rivalry, superiority, or inferiority, because this is the kind of love shared among Father, Son, and Spirit. And just as the cross has a preeminent place in God's saving plan despite its associations with weakness and shame, special honor must be given to members of the body who seem "weaker" because their gifts are not as visible, celebrated, or developed (vv. 22–23).

The power to live according to God's design comes when we, the body, are united to Christ, our head ("the body of Christ"; v. 27), who shares his life with us. One mark of this life is grieving with those who suffer and rejoicing with those who are honored (v. 26). Another mark is "earnestly desiring" greater gifts (v. 31)—that is, gifts that bring the greatest benefit not to ourselves but to the church as a whole.

13:1–13 Paul now proceeds to a beautiful description of love, without which spiritual gifts are worthless. In its context, this chapter serves three purposes.

First, it shows us our great need of redemption, warning us that sin causes us to prize dramatic—but worthless—spiritual displays (like those listed in vv. 1–3) more than our neighbor's good. In fact, the text directly counters sins addressed elsewhere in the letter. Love "does not envy" and "is not arrogant," but the Corinthian church is full of jealousy (3:3), boasting (4:6), and arrogance (4:18–19; 5:2; 8:1). Love is "not

8 [x]ch. 2:6, 7 [y]See ch. 1:5
9 [z]ch. 13:2; 2 Cor. 4:13 [a]ver. 28, 30
10 [b]ver. 28, 29; [Gal. 3:5] [c]ch. 13:2, 8; 14:1 [d][ch. 14:29; 1 John 4:1] [e]See Mark 16:17 [f]ver. 30; ch. 14:26
11 [g][2 Cor. 10:13] [h]Heb. 2:4
12 [i]See ch. 10:17 [j]ver. 27
13 [k][Rom. 6:5; Eph. 2:18] [l]Gal. 3:28; Col. 3:11; [Eph. 2:13-17] [m][John 7:37-39]
18 [n]ver. 28 [o]ver. 11; [ch. 3:5; Rom. 12:3]
26 [p]Rom. 12:15
27 [q][Eph. 1:23; 4:12; 5:30; Col. 1:24] [r]See Rom. 12:5
28 [s]ver. 18 [t]Eph. 4:11 [u]Eph. 2:20; 3:5 [v]ver. 10 [w]ver. 9 [x][Acts 20:35] [y][Rom. 12:8; 1 Tim. 5:17; Heb. 13:7, 17, 24]
31 [z]ch. 14:1, 39

Chapter 13
2 [a][ch. 14:1, 39; Matt. 7:22]; See Acts 2:18 [b]Matt. 17:20; Mark 11:23; [Luke 17:6]

as to remove mountains, but have not love,
I am nothing. 3 [c]If I give away all I have, and [d]if
I deliver up my body to be burned,[1] but have
not love, I gain nothing.
4 [e]Love is patient and [f]kind; love [g]does not
envy or boast; it [h]is not arrogant 5 or rude.
It [i]does not insist on its own way; it [j]is not
irritable or resentful;[2] 6 it [k]does not rejoice
at wrongdoing, but [l]rejoices with the truth.
7 [m]Love bears all things, believes all things,
hopes all things, [e]endures all things.
8 Love never ends. As for prophecies, they
will pass away; as for tongues, they will cease;
as for knowledge, it will pass away. 9 For [n]we
know in part and we prophesy in part, 10 but
[o]when the perfect comes, the partial will pass
away. 11 When I was a child, I spoke like a child,
I thought like a child, I reasoned like a child.
When I became a man, I gave up childish ways.
12 For [p]now we see in a mirror dimly, but [q]then
face to face. Now I know in part; then I shall
know fully, even as [r]I have been fully known.
13 So now faith, hope, and love abide, these
three; but the greatest of these is love.

Prophecy and Tongues

14 [s]Pursue love, and [t]earnestly desire the
[u]spiritual gifts, especially that you may
[v]prophesy. 2 For [w]one who speaks in a tongue
speaks not to men but to God; for no one
understands him, but he utters mysteries in
the Spirit. 3 On the other hand, the one who
prophesies speaks to people for their upbuilding and encouragement and consolation. 4 The
one who speaks in a tongue builds up himself, but the one who prophesies builds up
the church. 5 Now I want you all to speak in
tongues, but [x]even more to prophesy. The one
who prophesies is greater than the one who
speaks in tongues, unless someone interprets,
so that the church may be built up.
6 Now, brothers,[3] if I come to you speaking in tongues, how will I benefit you unless
I bring you some [y]revelation or knowledge or
prophecy or [z]teaching? 7 If even lifeless instruments, such as the flute or the harp, do not
give distinct notes, how will anyone know
what is played? 8 And [a]if the bugle gives an
indistinct sound, who will get ready for bat-

[1] Some manuscripts *deliver up my body* [to death] *that I may boast* [2] Greek *irritable and does not count up wrongdoing* [3] Or *brothers and sisters*; also verses 20, 26, 39

3 [c][Matt. 6:2] [d]Dan. 3:28
4 [e][Prov. 10:12; 17:9; 1 Thess. 5:14; 2 Tim. 2:10; 1 Pet. 4:8] [f][2 Cor. 6:6; Gal. 5:22; Eph. 4:32; Col. 3:12] [g]Acts 7:9 [h]See ch. 4:6
5 [i]See ch. 10:24 [j][Rom. 4:6; 2 Cor. 5:19]
6 [k][Rom. 1:32; 2 Thess. 2:12] [l][2 John 4; 3 John 3, 4]
7 [m]ch. 9:12 [e][See ver. 4 above]
9 [n][ch. 8:2]
10 [o][John 15:15]
12 [p]James 1:23; [Num. 12:8; Job 36:26; 2 Cor. 3:18; 5:7] [q]1 John 3:2; See Matt. 5:8 [r]See ch. 8:3

Chapter 14
1 [s]ch. 16:14 [t]ch. 12:31 [u]ch. 12:1 [v]See ch. 11:4; 13:2
2 [w]ver. 18-23, 27, 28
5 [x][Num. 11:29]
6 [y]ver. 26; Eph. 1:17 [z]ver. 26; Acts 2:42; Rom. 6:17
8 [a][Num. 10:9; Isa. 58:1; Jer. 4:19; Ezek. 33:3-6; Joel 2:1]

rude," but Corinthian worship is shameful and indecent (11:5, 22; 14:40). No church is immune to such temptation; we therefore need God's pardoning, transforming, and sustaining grace so that we may follow the "more excellent way" of love (12:31).

Second, this chapter calls for a response of love. Those who have received the *gifts* of the Spirit must exercise them alongside the *fruit* of the Spirit, including love, patience, and kindness (Gal. 5:22). Wherever the gospel goes, it bears the fruit of faith, hope, and love (1 Cor. 13:13; Col. 1:4–5; 1 Thess. 1:3). Of these, love is the greatest, because unlike hope (which will be fulfilled at Christ's return) and faith (which will then become "sight"; 2 Cor. 5:7), love will never pass away. For all of eternity, love will be the appropriate response to the mercy we receive in the gospel.

Finally, this chapter motivates and enables such a response by deepening our appreciation for the love of God, given to us in Christ. Patience and kindness (1 Cor. 13:4) are not only marks of human love but key biblical descriptors of God's gracious character (see Ex. 34:6; Num. 14:18; Ps. 25:7–8; 69:16; 100:5; Jer. 33:11; Rom. 2:4; 11:22; Eph. 2:7; 1 Tim. 1:16). When love does not "insist on [lit., 'seek'] its own way" (1 Cor. 13:5), it mirrors the sacrifice of Christ, who did not "seek [his] own advantage, but that of many, that they may be saved" (10:33–11:1; cf. Phil. 2:4–11, 21). Similarly, love "is not . . . resentful" (1 Cor. 13:5; lit. does not "count evil") but forgives the evil things others do to us, just as in Christ God does not "count" our sins against us (2 Cor. 5:19; Rom. 4:8).

As we seek to grow in love, we must always keep Christ's saving work in clear view, since Scripture consistently treats this as the ultimate demonstration of love (John 3:16; 15:12–13; Rom. 5:8; Gal. 2:20; Eph. 2:4–7; 5:2, 25; 1 John 3:16; 4:9–10; Rev. 1:5).

14:1–40 Following his emphasis on love, Paul turns to a very specific problem: the Corinthian church's improper use of speaking in tongues (speaking of God's saving works in a language unknown to the speaker; Acts 2:1–11) and prophecy (spontaneous, Spirit-prompted proclamation and exhortation; Acts 11:27–28; 21:10–11). Some believe that these gifts continue to operate in the contemporary church; others believe that such gifts served to confirm the testimony of the apostles (Acts 2:43; Rom. 15:19;

tle? 9 So with yourselves, if with your tongue
you utter speech that is not intelligible, how
will anyone know what is said? For you will
be [b]speaking into the air. 10 There are doubtless many different languages in the world,
and none is without meaning, 11 but if I do not
know the meaning of the language, I will be
[c]a foreigner to the speaker and the speaker a
foreigner to me. 12 So with yourselves, since
you are eager for manifestations of the Spirit,
strive to excel in building up the church.

13 Therefore, one who speaks in a tongue
should pray that he may interpret. 14 For if
I pray in a tongue, my spirit prays but my
mind is unfruitful. 15 What am I to do? I will
pray with my spirit, but I will pray with
my mind also; [d]I will sing praise with my
spirit, but I will [e]sing with my mind also.
16 Otherwise, if you give thanks with your
spirit, how can anyone in the position of an
outsider[1] say [f]"Amen" to [g]your thanksgiving
when he does not know what you are saying?
17 For you may be giving thanks well enough,
but the other person is not being built up. 18 I
thank God that I speak in tongues more than
all of you. 19 Nevertheless, in church I would
rather speak five words with my mind in order
to instruct others, than ten thousand words
in a tongue.

20 Brothers, [h]do not be children in your thinking. [i]Be infants in evil, but in your thinking be
[j]mature. 21 [k]In the Law it is written, [l]"By people
of strange tongues and by the lips of foreigners
will I speak to this people, and even then they
will not listen to me, says the Lord." 22 Thus
tongues are a sign not for believers but for
unbelievers, while prophecy is a sign[2] not for
unbelievers but for believers. 23 If, therefore,
the whole church comes together and all speak
in tongues, and outsiders or unbelievers enter,
[m]will they not say that you are out of your
minds? 24 But if all prophesy, and an unbeliever or outsider enters, he is convicted by all,
he is called to account by all, 25 [n]the secrets of
his heart are disclosed, and so, [o]falling on his
face, he will worship God and [p]declare that
God is really among you.

Orderly Worship

26 What then, brothers? When you come
together, each one has [q]a hymn, [r]a lesson, [r]a
revelation, [s]a tongue, or [t]an interpretation.

[1] Or *of him that is without gifts* [2] Greek lacks *a sign*

2 Cor. 12:12) and were therefore unique to the apostolic era. Whatever we conclude, we must not miss Paul's gospel-saturated logic: believers' use of spiritual gifts should be governed by the same priorities we see in the work of Christ—namely, "the glory of God" (1 Cor. 10:31) and the "advantage . . . of many" (10:33).

Where spiritual gifts are exercised without concern for the good of other people, we dishonor the Spirit who provides the gifts. When God's gracious gifts are at work, we are satisfied not when we ourselves are "built up" (14:4) but when others around us—both Christians ("the church"; vv. 4–5) and non-Christians (the "outsider"; vv. 16, 23–25)—are also enabled to delight in God and the blessings he gives. This presupposes that the power of the gospel is transforming our hearts, so that concern for our neighbor's "encouragement and consolation" (v. 3) and understanding (vv. 5–18) replaces sinful preoccupation with displays that only benefit self. When Paul says that he would rather speak five words for others' benefit than ten thousand words that benefit only himself (v. 19; see also v. 6), we see proof that his heart has been gripped by the gospel.

Concern for God's glory comes to the fore in the latter part of the chapter. Hearts shaped by the gospel will long to see nonbelievers convicted of sin and brought to worship God (vv. 24–25). Likewise, when we know God's character (v. 33) we will desire to honor him in our worship. This will express itself in humility, as we defer to others (v. 27), submit to their evaluation of our words (v. 29), and sometimes remain silent—even when we have something worthwhile to say (vv. 28, 30). When the Spirit is truly at work in us (v. 37), we will bear the fruit of self-control, submitting our desires to God and to the authority and communication structures he has instituted (vv. 23, 27–29), including apostolic teaching (v. 37) and the husband-wife relationship (vv. 34–35; these verses likely apply only to the public evaluation of prophecy, since 11:5 does allow women to pray and prophesy).

The patterns Paul describes are all reflections of Christ, in whom the Spirit's power and God-honoring submission were perfectly combined.

9 [b][ch. 9:26]
11 [c]See Acts 28:2
15 [d][Eph. 5:19; Col. 3:16; James 5:13] [e]Ps. 47:7
16 [f]1 Chr. 16:36; Neh. 5:13; 8:6; Ps. 106:48; Jer. 11:5; 28:6; Rev. 5:14; 7:12; 19:4; [2 Cor. 1:20] [g]ch. 11:24
20 [h]Eph. 4:14; Heb. 5:12, 13 [i][Ps. 131:2; Isa. 28:9; Rom. 16:19]; See Matt. 18:3 [j]ch. 2:6
21 [k]See John 10:34 [l]Cited from Isa. 28:11, 12; [Deut. 28:49]
23 [m][Acts 2:13]
25 [n][Heb. 4:12] [o]Luke 17:16 [p]Isa. 45:14; Zech. 8:23
26 [q]Eph. 5:19 [r]See ver. 6 [s]ver. 18 [t]ver. 5, 13, 27, 28; ch. 12:10, 30

[u]Let all things be done for building up. 27 If any
speak in [s]a tongue, let there be only two or at
most three, and each in turn, and let someone
interpret. 28 But if there is no one to interpret,
let each of them keep silent in church and
speak to himself and to God. 29 Let two or three
prophets speak, and let the others [v]weigh what
is said. 30 If a revelation is made to another
sitting there, [w]let the first be silent. 31 For you
can all prophesy one by one, so that all may
learn and all be encouraged, 32 and the spirits
of prophets are subject to prophets. 33 For God
is not a God of [x]confusion but of peace.

As in [y]all the churches of the saints, 34 [z]the
women should keep silent in the churches. For
they are not permitted to speak, but [a]should
be in submission, as [b]the Law also says. 35 If
there is anything they desire to learn, let them
ask their husbands at home. For it is shameful
for a woman to speak in church.

36 Or was it from you that the word of God
came? Or are you the only ones it has reached?
37 [c]If anyone thinks that he is a prophet, or
spiritual, he should acknowledge that the
things I am writing to you are a command of
the Lord. 38 If anyone does not recognize this,
he is not recognized. 39 So, my brothers, [d]ear-
nestly desire to prophesy, and do not forbid
speaking in tongues. 40 [e]But all things should
be done decently and [f]in order.

The Resurrection of Christ

15 Now I would remind you, brothers,[1] of
the gospel [g]I preached to you, which
you received, [h]in which you stand, 2 and by
which [i]you are being saved, if you [j]hold fast
to the word I preached to you—[k]unless you
believed in vain.

3 For [l]I delivered to you as of first importance
what I also received: that Christ died [m]for our
sins [n]in accordance with the Scriptures, 4 that
he was buried, that he was raised [o]on the
third day [p]in accordance with the Scriptures,
5 and that [q]he appeared to Cephas, then [r]to
the twelve. 6 Then he appeared to more than
five hundred brothers at one time, most of
whom are still alive, though some have fallen
asleep. 7 Then he appeared to [s]James, then [t]to
all the apostles. 8 Last of all, as to one untimely
born, [u]he appeared also to me. 9 For [v]I am the

[1] Or *brothers and sisters*; also verses 6, 31, 50, 58

26[u] 2 Cor. 12:19; 13:10; [ch. 12:7]
27[s] [See ver. 26 above]
29[v] [ch. 12:10; Job 12:11; 1 John 4:1]
30[w] [1 Thess. 5:19, 20]
33[x] [ver. 40] [y] See ch. 7:17
34[z] [1 Tim. 2:11, 12] [a] See 1 Pet. 3:1 [b] [ver. 21]
37[c] [2 Cor. 10:7; 1 John 4:6]
39[d] ch. 12:31
40[e] [ver. 31, 33] [f] Col. 2:5

Chapter 15
1[g] [2 Tim. 2:8]; See ch. 3:6 [h] Rom. 5:2; [2 Cor. 1:24; 1 Pet. 5:12]
2[i] ch. 1:18 [j] ch. 11:2; [Heb. 3:6, 14] [k] Gal. 3:4
3[l] ch. 11:23; Gal. 1:12 [m] John 1:29; Gal. 1:4; Heb. 5:1, 3; 1 Pet. 2:24 [n] Isa. 53; Dan. 9:26; Zech. 13:7; [1 Pet. 1:11]
4[o] [Hos. 6:2; Matt. 12:40; John 2:22] [p] Ps. 16:10; Isa. 53:10; [Acts 2:25-32; 13:33-35; 26:22, 23]
5[q] Luke 24:34 [r] Mark 16:14; Luke 24:36; John 20:19, 26; Acts 10:41
7[s] See Acts 12:17 [t] Luke 24:50; Acts 1:3, 4
8[u] See ch. 9:1
9[v] 2 Cor. 12:11; Eph. 3:7, 8; 1 Tim. 1:13-16

15:1–11 Before addressing a final problem in verses 12–58, Paul gives a two-fold summary of the gospel—first in terms of its content (vv. 1–8) and then in terms of its transforming power in his own life and ministry (vv. 9–11). Once again we hear the rhythm of gospel transformation: for those united to Christ the truth of the gospel always produces a transformed life, which can be sustained in an ongoing way only by the power of the gospel. Thus the gospel is not only something we embrace at the beginning of the Christian life ("which you received"; v. 1), but the source of strength throughout the Christian life ("in which you stand"; v. 1; cf. 10:12–13; 16:13). It is remarkable that Paul sees a need to "remind" the Corinthians—already believers!—of the gospel (15:1). Evidently, the gospel message is not only for evangelism but also for discipleship; not only for unbelievers, but also for believers.

Paul summarizes the content of the gospel in terms of Christ's death, burial, resurrection, and post-resurrection appearances. The fact that Jesus died "for our sins" (v. 3) reminds us both of our need and of Jesus' atoning work, as nothing short of God's Son enduring divine judgment in our place could redeem us. The phrase "in accordance with the Scriptures" (vv. 3–4) teaches us that Christ's work fulfills God's saving purposes, implying that all of Scripture points us ultimately to the grace of God in Christ. Jesus' burial confirms that he really died, and his appearances to eyewitnesses confirm that he truly rose. Thus we are not building our lives on myth or legend when we look to him for grace to pardon our sins and empower holy living.

Paul's testimony in verses 8–10 allows us to see what effects "the grace of God" can have, even on those with hearts hardened toward Christ. These include humility ("least"; "unworthy"), honesty regarding past sin ("I persecuted the church"), and repentance ("I persecuted. . . . But . . ."). God's transforming grace gives us not only a new identity ("I am what I am"; in Paul's case, no longer a persecutor but an apostle) but the strength to labor diligently in God's service ("I worked harder"; see also Col. 1:29; 1 Tim. 4:10). Gratitude for God's grace means that we will rejoice to see its effects in our lives ("his grace . . . was not in vain"), but we will never take credit for those effects ("not I, but the grace of God"). God is the hero of Paul's story, and of every believer's story as well.

least of the apostles, unworthy to be called
an apostle, because [w]I persecuted the church
of God. 10 But by the grace of God I am what
I am, and his grace toward me was not in vain.
On the contrary, [x]I worked harder than any of
them, [y]though it was not I, but the grace of
God that is with me. 11 Whether then it was I or
they, so we preach and so you believed.

The Resurrection of the Dead

12 Now if Christ is proclaimed as raised from
the dead, [z]how can some of you say that there
is no resurrection of the dead? 13 But if there
is no resurrection of the dead, [a]then not even
Christ has been raised. 14 And if Christ has not
been raised, then our preaching is in vain and
your faith is in vain. 15 We are even found to
be misrepresenting God, because we testified
about God that [b]he raised Christ, whom he
did not raise if it is true that the dead are not
raised. 16 For if the dead are not raised, not even
Christ has been raised. 17 And if Christ has not
been raised, your faith is futile and [c]you are
still in your sins. 18 Then those also who [d]have
fallen asleep in Christ have perished. 19 If in
Christ we have hope[1] in this life only, [e]we are
of all people most to be pitied.

20 But in fact [f]Christ has been raised from
the dead, [g]the firstfruits of those who have
fallen asleep. 21 For as [h]by a man came death,
[i]by a man has come also the resurrection of the
dead. 22 For [j]as in Adam all die, so also in Christ
shall all be made alive. 23 But each in his own
order: Christ the firstfruits, then [k]at his coming [l]those who belong to Christ. 24 Then comes
the end, when he delivers [m]the kingdom to
God the Father after destroying [n]every rule
and every authority and power. 25 For he must
reign [o]until he has put all his enemies under
his feet. 26 The last enemy to be [p]destroyed is
death. 27 For [q]"God[2] has put all things in subjection under his feet." But when it says, "all
things are put in subjection," it is plain that he
is excepted who put all things in subjection
under him. 28 When [r]all things are subjected
to him, then the Son himself will also be subjected to him who put all things in subjection
under him, that [s]God may be all in all.

29 Otherwise, what do people mean by being
baptized on behalf of the dead? If the dead are
not raised at all, why are people baptized on
their behalf? 30 Why are we [t]in danger every
hour? 31 I protest, brothers, by [u]my pride in
you, which I have in Christ Jesus our Lord, [v]I
die every day! 32 What do I gain if, humanly
speaking, [w]I fought with beasts at Ephesus? If
the dead are not raised, [x]"Let us eat and drink,
for tomorrow we die." 33 [y]Do not be deceived:

[1] Or *we have hoped* [2] Greek *he*

15:12–58 Here Paul addresses a final problem, as some in Corinth accept Jesus' resurrection from the dead but deny that Christians will share in resurrection life with Jesus (vv. 12, 16). Paul's response emphasizes three gospel truths.

First, believers are united to Christ and will share in every benefit of his work. Apart from Christ, we are united to Adam ("in Adam"; v. 22) and share in the death sentence brought about by his work (v. 22). But if by faith we are "in Christ," then we will share in the victory by which he has defeated sin and death (vv. 54–57). Since Christ, the "firstfruits" (vv. 20, 23) has been raised, then we, the remainder of the harvest, will be raised also (cf. Lev. 23:10; Neh. 10:35–37; Col. 1:18).

Second, Christ's work addresses every level of human need. He removes our sin and guilt before God (1 Cor. 15:17); he gives us power to obey God's law, which we are unable to do while we are in our sins ("the power of sin is the law"; v. 56); and he will one day free us from the physical effects of sin such as death, disease, and disability ("imperishable"; "immortality"; "spiritual"—terms implying that our resurrection bodies will possess all the life-giving power of God's Spirit).

Third, Jesus fulfills all of God's purposes for humanity. According to Psalm 8 (cited in 1 Cor. 15:27), human beings were created to rule over creation in a way that displays God's glory. Sin and death have distorted this design, so that instead we live to display our own glory. Only in Jesus, who has conquered these powers, have we seen God's design faithfully expressed. At his return, we will witness two final acts of faithfulness: Jesus will demonstrate his complete power over death, the "last enemy" (vv. 20–26); and he will display God's glory by delivering "the kingdom to God the Father" (v. 24). As at the cross, we will once again see Christ's ultimate power joined to perfect humility—a pattern that should govern our lives as those who are part of the new humanity God is creating in Christ.

9 [w] See Acts 8:3
10 [x] 2 Cor. 11:23; 12:11; Col. 1:29 [y] [ch. 3:6; 2 Cor. 3:5; Phil. 2:13]; See Matt. 10:20
12 [z] [Acts 23:8; 2 Tim. 2:18]
13 [a] 1 Thess. 4:14
15 [b] See Acts 2:24
17 [c] See Rom. 4:25
18 [d] 1 Thess. 4:16; Rev. 14:13
19 [e] [ch. 4:9; 2 Tim. 3:12]
20 [f] 2 Tim. 2:8; 1 Pet. 1:3 [g] ver. 23; See Acts 26:23
21 [h] See Rom. 5:12 [i] John 11:25; Rom. 6:23
22 [j] [Rom. 5:14-18]
23 [k] See 1 Thess. 2:19 [l] ver. 52; 1 Thess. 4:16; See Luke 14:14
24 [m] [Dan. 7:14, 27] [n] Eph. 1:21
25 [o] See Ps. 110:1
26 [p] 2 Tim. 1:10; [Rev. 20:14; 21:4]
27 [q] Eph. 1:22; Cited from Ps. 8:6; See Matt. 11:27; 28:18
28 [r] Phil. 3:21 [s] [ch. 3:23; 11:3]
30 [t] 2 Cor. 11:26
31 [u] 1 Thess. 2:19 [v] Luke 9:23; See Rom. 8:36
32 [w] [2 Cor. 1:8] [x] Cited from Isa. 22:13; [Isa. 56:12; Luke 12:19]
33 [y] James 1:16

[z]"Bad company ruins good morals."[1] 34 [a]Wake up from your drunken stupor, as is right, and do not go on sinning. For [b]some have no knowledge of God. [c]I say this to your shame.

The Resurrection Body

35 But someone will ask, [d]"How are the dead raised? With what kind of body do they come?" 36 You foolish person! [e]What you sow does not come to life unless it dies. 37 And what you sow is not the body that is to be, but a bare kernel, perhaps of wheat or of some other grain. 38 But God gives it a body as he has chosen, and to each kind of seed its own body. 39 For not all flesh is the same, but there is one kind for humans, another for animals, another for birds, and another for fish. 40 There are heavenly bodies and earthly bodies, but the glory of the heavenly is of one kind, and the glory of the earthly is of another. 41 There is one glory of the sun, and another glory of the moon, and another glory of the stars; for star differs from star in glory.

42 [f]So is it with the resurrection of the dead. What is sown is perishable; what is raised is imperishable. 43 It is sown in dishonor; [g]it is raised in glory. It is sown in weakness; it is raised in power. 44 It is sown a natural body; it is raised a spiritual body. If there is a natural body, there is also a spiritual body. 45 Thus it is written, [h]"The first man Adam became a living being";[2] [i]the last Adam became a [j]life-giving spirit. 46 But it is not the spiritual that is first but the natural, and then the spiritual. 47 [k]The first man was from the earth, [l]a man of dust; [m]the second man is from heaven. 48 As was the man of dust, so also are those who are of the dust, and as is the man of heaven, [n]so also are those who are of heaven. 49 Just [o]as we have borne the image of the man of dust, [p]we shall[3] also bear the image of the man of heaven.

Mystery and Victory

50 I tell you this, brothers: [q]flesh and blood [r]cannot inherit the kingdom of God, nor does the perishable inherit the imperishable. 51 Behold! I tell you a mystery. [s]We shall not all sleep, [t]but we shall all be changed, 52 in a moment, in the twinkling of an eye, at the last trumpet. For [u]the trumpet will sound, and [v]the dead will be raised imperishable, and we shall be changed. 53 For this perishable body must put on the imperishable, and [w]this mortal body must put on immortality. 54 When the perishable puts on the imperishable, and the mortal puts on immortality, then shall come to pass the saying that is written:

[x]"Death is swallowed up in victory."
55 [y]"O death, where is your victory?
O death, where is your sting?"

56 The sting of death is sin, and [z]the power of sin is the law. 57 But thanks be to God, [a]who gives us the victory through our Lord Jesus Christ.

58 [b]Therefore, my beloved brothers, be steadfast, immovable, always abounding in [c]the work of the Lord, knowing that in the Lord [d]your labor is not in vain.

The Collection for the Saints

16 Now concerning[4] [e]the collection for the saints: as I directed the churches of Galatia, so you also are to do. 2 On [f]the first day of every week, each of you is to put something

[1] Probably from Menander's comedy *Thais* [2] Greek *a living soul* [3] Some manuscripts *let us* [4] The expression *Now concerning* introduces a reply to a question in the Corinthians' letter; see 7:1; also verse 12

33[z] [ch. 5:6]
34[a] See Rom. 13:11 [b] 1 Thess. 4:5 [c] ch. 6:5; [ch. 4:14]
35[d] [Ezek. 37:3]
36[e] John 12:24
42[f] Dan. 12:3; [Matt. 13:43]
43[g] Phil. 3:21; Col. 3:4
45[h] Cited from Gen. 2:7 [i] Rom. 5:14 [j] John 5:21; [John 6:33, 39, 40, 54, 57; Rom. 8:2, 10]
47[k] John 3:31 [l] [Gen. 2:7; 3:19] [m] John 3:13, 31
48[n] [Phil. 3:20]
49[o] Gen. 5:3 [p] See Rom. 8:29
50[q] See Matt. 16:17 [r] [John 3:3, 5]
51[s] 1 Thess. 4:15, 17 [t] Phil. 3:21
52[u] Matt. 24:31; 1 Thess. 4:16; [Isa. 27:13; Zech. 9:14] [v] John 5:25, 28; [Luke 20:36] **53**[w] [2 Cor. 5:2-4] **54**[x] Cited from Isa. 25:8; [Heb. 2:14, 15; Rev. 20:14; 21:4] **55**[y] Hos. 13:14 **56**[z] Rom. 4:15; 5:13; 7:5, 8, 13 **57**[a] [Rom. 8:37; 1 John 5:4] **58**[b] 2 Pet. 3:14 [c] ch. 16:10; Jer. 48:10; John 6:28 [d] [Gal. 6:9]; See ch. 3:8 **Chapter 16** **1**[e] See Acts 24:17 **2**[f] Acts 20:7; [Rev. 1:10]

These gospel truths lead to two major applications. First, rather than defining ourselves by the emptiness of "this life" and its pleasures (vv. 19, 32), we must cherish the promise that we will share in Christ's glory. Second, we must embrace this resurrection hope as a source of power by which we may endure hardship (vv. 30–32) and struggle against sin (vv. 33–34). Gratitude for the victory that God has given us through Christ must lead us to be "steadfast, immovable, always abounding in the work of the Lord" (vv. 57–58). The gospel therefore combats hopelessness and gives purpose to our daily endeavors: "in the Lord your labor is not in vain" (v. 58).

16:1–24 The concluding chapter of the letter features several practical expressions of believers' unity in Christ. Those who have received the Father's grace are members of one family ("brothers"; vv. 12, 15) and are therefore eager to gather for corporate worship (vv. 2, 19), to give generously to meet the needs of other believers (vv. 1–3), and to offer encouragement—including financial support—to those who labor in

aside and store it up, [g]as he may prosper, [h]so
that there will be no collecting when I come.
3 And when I arrive, I will send [i]those whom
you accredit by letter to carry your gift to
Jerusalem. 4 If it seems advisable that I should
go also, they will accompany me.

Plans for Travel

5 [j]I will visit you after passing through [k]Mace-
donia, for [l]I intend to pass through Macedonia,
6 and perhaps I will stay with you or even spend
the winter, so that you may [m]help me on my
journey, wherever I go. 7 For I do not want to
see you now [n]just in passing. I hope to spend
some time with you, [o]if the Lord permits. 8 But
I will stay in Ephesus until [p]Pentecost, 9 for [q]a
wide door for effective work has opened to me,
and [r]there are many adversaries.
10 [s]When Timothy comes, see that you put
him at ease among you, for [t]he is doing [u]the
work of the Lord, as I am. 11 So [v]let no one
despise him. [w]Help him on his way [x]in peace,
that he may return to me, for I am expecting
him with the brothers.

Final Instructions

12 Now concerning [y]our brother Apollos,
I strongly urged him to visit you with the other
brothers, but it was not at all his will[1] to come
now. He will come when he has opportunity.
13 [z]Be watchful, [a]stand firm in the faith, [b]act
like men, [c]be strong. 14 [d]Let all that you do be
done in love.
15 Now I urge you, brothers[2]—you know that
[e]the household[3] of Stephanas were [f]the first
converts in Achaia, and that they have devoted
themselves [g]to the service of the saints— 16 [h]be
subject to such as these, and to every fellow
worker and laborer. 17 I rejoice at the coming
of Stephanas and Fortunatus and Achaicus,
because they have made up for [i]your absence,
18 for they [j]refreshed my spirit as well as yours.
[k]Give recognition to such people.

Greetings

19 The churches of Asia send you greetings.
[l]Aquila and Prisca, together with [m]the church
in their house, send you hearty greetings in
the Lord. 20 All the brothers send you greetings. [n]Greet one another with a holy kiss.
21 I, Paul, write [o]this greeting with my own
hand. 22 If anyone has no love for the Lord,
let him be [p]accursed. Our Lord, come![4] 23 [q]The
grace of the Lord Jesus be with you. 24 My love
be with you all in Christ Jesus. Amen.

[1] Or *God's will for him* [2] Or *brothers and sisters*; also verse 20 [3] Greek *house* [4] Greek *Maranatha* (a transliteration of Aramaic)

spreading the gospel (vv. 5–11, 15–18). Here again we see how grace that captures the heart spurs the believer into selfless service rather than selfish indulgence.

In verse 13, Paul calls believers to be courageous and strong. The psalmist uses identical terms when he calls Israel to "wait for the LORD" for strength (Ps. 27:14; 130:5). As God strengthened Old Testament saints, he now enables Christians to "stand firm in the faith" (1 Cor. 16:13). In verse 14, we see that such courage goes hand in hand with loving relationships. Even here we may detect the power of Christ's cross, where courage and love perfectly met.

Paul's closing words (vv. 22–24) powerfully summarize four gospel themes: (1) only a relationship with Christ can provide freedom from the curse; (2) obedience to the instructions contained in 1 Corinthians is an expression of "love for the Lord"; (3) the life of the church is sustained by "the grace of the Lord Jesus"; and (4) this grace leads to love for all who are "in Christ Jesus." Like the Corinthians, our lives, our relationships, and our churches may be plagued by many problems. Yet the grace of the Lord and the fellowship of his people are available to anyone who is united to him by faith.

2 [g] 2 Cor. 8:3, 11 [h] 2 Cor. 9:3
3 [i] [2 Cor. 8:18, 19]
5 [j] See ch. 4:19 [k] See Acts 16:9 [l] Acts 19:21
6 [m] ver. 11; See Acts 15:3
7 [n] [2 Cor. 1:15, 16] [o] ch. 4:19; Acts 18:21; James 4:15
8 [p] See Acts 2:1
9 [q] See Acts 14:27 [r] Acts 19:9
10 [s] ch. 4:17; [2 Cor. 1:1] [t] Rom. 16:21; 1 Thess. 3:2; [Phil. 2:20, 22] [u] See ch. 15:58
11 [v] 1 Tim. 4:12; [Titus 2:15] [w] ver. 6 [x] Acts 15:33
12 [y] See Acts 18:24
13 [z] See Matt. 24:42 [a] Gal. 5:1; Phil. 1:27; 4:1; 1 Thess. 3:8; 2 Thess. 2:15; See ch. 15:1 [b] 1 Sam. 4:9; 2 Sam. 10:12; Isa. 46:8 [c] Eph. 3:16; [Eph. 6:10; Col. 1:11]
14 [d] ch. 14:1
15 [e] ch. 1:16 [f] [Rom. 16:5]
[g] See Rom. 15:31 **16** [h] 1 Thess. 5:12; Heb. 13:17 **17** [i] Phil. 2:30; [2 Cor. 11:9; Philem. 13] **18** [j] 2 Cor. 7:13; [Rom. 15:32; Philem. 7, 20] [k] Phil. 2:29; 1 Thess. 5:12
19 [l] See Acts 18:2 [m] See Rom. 16:5 **20** [n] See Rom. 16:16 **21** [o] Col. 4:18; 2 Thess. 3:17; [Rom. 16:22; Gal. 6:11; Philem. 19] **22** [p] See Rom. 9:3 **23** [q] Rom. 16:20

Introduction to
2 Corinthians

Author and Date

Based on the opening salutation (1:1), there is a clear consensus that the apostle Paul wrote 2 Corinthians. The historical setting suggests that Paul penned the epistle in Macedonia sometime after leaving Ephesus (Acts 20:1) but before returning to Corinth (Acts 20:2–3). This places the date for the letter around A.D. 55/56.

Audience

Paul wrote on several occasions "to the church of God that is at Corinth" (1:1; cf. 1 Cor. 1:1–2; 5:9; 2 Cor. 2:3–4). The Corinthian church rebelled against Paul and his teaching because they were being influenced by "super-apostles" who were proclaiming "a different gospel" (11:4–5). Paul writes this letter to demonstrate their error and to convince them to embrace the true gospel.

The Gospel in 2 Corinthians

Second Corinthians is filled with the astounding paradoxes of the gospel. Rather than a well-ordered theological treatise (like Romans or Ephesians), we find a letter that stylistically is somewhat free-flowing. Yet it is overflowing with the apostle's gospel-love for his readers. Though this can sometimes make the argument of the book difficult to follow, the unique historical setting of the book allows the modern reader to see how Paul applies the gospel *in the moment*. He is using the real-life situation of his audience in order to apply the truths of the gospel in real time. As a physician cleans and bandages a wound, Paul addresses the contamination of the Corinthians' foul hearts and applies the healing balm of the gospel.

The primary occasion for the book (false teaching) provides Paul an opportunity to demonstrate the contrast between the gospel and the prevailing cultural story of his day. Whereas the false apostles are concerned with external qualifications, Paul focuses on the internal heart change brought about by the Spirit (2 Cor. 3:1–4). Whereas his opponents are concerned with self-commendation by the use of rhetoric, Paul is characterized by a self-effacing, simple presentation of the truth of the gospel in word and deed (11:4–10). Similarly, the book is effective in unmasking our own cultural idols of wealth, power, and comfort.

The theme of gospel paradoxes appears frequently throughout the book: in Christ, we are comforted in affliction (1:3–13), rich in poverty (8:9), and strong in weakness (12:10). Gospel comparisons also provide needed encouragement: God's promises are more permanent than our momentary trials (4:7–18), and our future life is more certain than our present circumstances (5:1–10). We can boast in our suffering, knowing that God uses it as a crucible to produce humility and true strength (11:16–12:10).

We can reconcile because we have been undeservedly accepted and restored (5:18–21). We can give generously because we have received the self-giving love of Jesus (8:9–10).

Second Corinthians provides documentary evidence that the gospel works. By the grace of God, over time, the gospel is worked into our hearts so that we will recognize the deep implications of the gospel in every dimension of life. As you encounter God's Word, you can trust that God the Holy Spirit is operating *in the moment* to transform your heart and to reorganize your life around the promises of God which find their "Yes" in Jesus (1:20).

Outline

I. Introduction (1:1–11)
  A. Greeting (1:1–2)
  B. Thanksgiving for comfort in affliction (1:3–11)
II. Paul's Gospel-Driven Account of His Ministry (1:12–7:16)
  A. God's faithfulness in changed plans (1:12–2:4)
  B. Living the truth in love through restoration (2:5–11)
  C. The ironic glory of new covenant ministry (2:12–4:6)
  D. Apparent experiences eclipsed by actual realities (4:7–5:10)
  E. Unfashionable ambassadors of reconciliation (5:11–6:13)
  F. Undivided living in response to undeserved grace (6:14–7:1)
  G. The gospel applied in church relationships (7:2–16)
III. Paul's Christ-Centered Appeal for Sacrificial Giving (8:1–9:15)
IV. Paul's Upside-Down Apologetic for His Apostolic Ministry (10:1–13:10)
  A. Boasting only in that which is given by Christ (10:1–18)
  B. Uncovering the falsity of the "super-apostles" (11:1–15)
  C. Upside-down commendation of the apostolic call (11:16–12:13)
  D. Preparations for a future visit (12:14–13:10)
V. Concluding Greetings (13:11–14)

The Second Letter of Paul to the Corinthians

2 Corinthians

Greeting

1 Paul, [a]an apostle of Christ Jesus [b]by the will
of God, and [c]Timothy our brother,
To the church of God that is at Corinth, [d]with
all the saints who are in the whole of Achaia:
2 [e]Grace to you and peace from God our
Father and the Lord Jesus Christ.

God of All Comfort

3 [f]Blessed be the [g]God and Father of our Lord
Jesus Christ, the Father of mercies and [h]God
of all comfort, 4 [i]who comforts us in all our
affliction, so that we may be able to comfort
those who are in any affliction, with the comfort with which we ourselves are comforted by
God. 5 For as we share abundantly in [j]Christ's
sufferings, so through Christ we share abundantly in comfort too.[1] 6 [k]If we are afflicted, it
is for your comfort and salvation; and if we
are comforted, it is for your comfort, which
you experience when you patiently endure
the same sufferings that we suffer. 7 Our hope
for you is unshaken, for we know that as you
[l]share in our sufferings, you will also share in
our comfort.
8 For we do not want you to be unaware,
brothers,[2] of [m]the affliction we experienced in
Asia. For we were so utterly burdened beyond
our strength that we despaired of life itself.
9 Indeed, we felt that we had received the sentence of death. But that was to make us [n]rely
not on ourselves [o]but on God [p]who raises the
dead. 10 [q]He delivered us from such a deadly
peril, and he will deliver us. [r]On him we have
set our hope that he will deliver us again. 11 [s]You
also must help us by prayer, so that many will
give thanks on our behalf [t]for the blessing
granted us through the prayers of many.

Paul's Change of Plans

12 For our boast is this, [u]the testimony of
our conscience, that we behaved in the world

[1] Or *For as the sufferings of Christ abound for us, so also our comfort abounds through Christ* [2] Or *brothers and sisters*. The plural Greek word *adelphoi* (translated "brothers") refers to siblings in a family. In New Testament usage, depending on the context, *adelphoi* may refer either to men or to both men and women who are siblings (brothers and sisters) in God's family, the church

1:1–11 Paul is an afflicted leader (vv. 8–9; 11:23–33) who is writing to a congregation that is experiencing affliction. His response to their trials is to direct them to the "God of all comfort" (1:3). This understanding of God's nature is grounded in the person and work of Jesus, who experienced ultimate suffering and affliction on the cross, and who, in his resurrected rule, abundantly comforts his people.

Knowing this, and experiencing the comfort that he provides, we are able to understand our own afflictions as evidence of our solidarity with Christ. We can never suffer for the purpose of redemption, for we cannot add to the atoning work of Christ. However, our afflictions can serve as windows to the reality and benefits of our union with Christ. If we experience affliction as Christ did, we can expect to be comforted as Christ was (v. 5). If we undergo suffering, we can anticipate consolation. Even if we experience deadly peril, our hope has been set on a God who delivers us from death (v. 10).

The reason for our afflictions is "to make us rely not on ourselves but on God" (v. 9). This reliance translates into a life of patience (v. 6) and prayer (v. 11). As we experience the deep comforts of the gospel, which transcend circumstance and self-centeredness, we become comforters of the afflicted (v. 4; 2:7). Those who share in the comforts of the gospel are those who actively share the comforts of the gospel with those in need.

1:12–24 The apostle seeks to set things straight with the Corinthians, who have wrongly assumed that he is a person who goes back on his word (v. 17). Rather than

Chapter 1
1 [a]Eph. 1:1; Col. 1:1; 1 Tim. 1:1; 2 Tim. 1:1; Titus 1:1; [Rom. 1:1; Gal. 1:1] [b]See 1 Cor. 1:1 [c]See 1 Thess. 3:2 [d]Phil. 1:1; Col. 1:2
2 [e]See Rom. 1:7
3 [f]Eph. 1:3; 1 Pet. 1:3 [g]See Rom. 15:6 [h]Rom. 15:5
4 [i][Isa. 51:12; 66:13]
5 [j][ch. 4:10; Phil. 3:10; Col. 1:24]
6 [k]2 Tim. 2:10; [ch. 4:15; 12:15; Eph. 3:13]
7 [l]See Rom. 8:17
8 [m]Acts 19:23; 1 Cor. 15:32
9 [n]Luke 18:9 [o]Ps. 2:12; 25:2; 26:1 [p]ch. 4:14
10 [q]See Rom. 15:31 [r]1 Tim. 4:10
11 [s][Acts 12:5; Rom. 15:30; Phil. 1:19; Philem. 22] [t][ch. 4:15; 9:11, 12]
12 [u][1 Thess. 2:10]; See Acts 23:1

with simplicity[1] and [v]godly sincerity, [w]not by earthly wisdom but by the grace of God, and supremely so toward you. 13 For we are not writing to you anything other than what you read and understand and I hope you will fully understand— 14 just as you did [x]partially understand us—that [y]on the day of our Lord Jesus [z]you will boast of us as [a]we will boast of you.

15 Because I was sure of this, [b]I wanted to come to you first, so that you might have [c]a second [d]experience of grace. 16 I wanted to visit you [e]on my way to Macedonia, and to come back to you from Macedonia and have you send me on my way to Judea. 17 Was I vacillating when I wanted to do this? Do I make my plans [f]according to the flesh, ready to say "Yes, yes" and "No, no" at the same time? 18 As surely as [g]God is faithful, [h]our word to you has not been Yes and No. 19 For [i]the Son of God, Jesus Christ, whom we proclaimed among you, [j]Silvanus and Timothy and I, was not Yes and No, but [k]in him it is always Yes. 20 For [l]all the promises of God find their Yes in him. That is why it is through him that we utter our [m]Amen to God for his glory. 21 And it is God who establishes us with you in Christ, and [n]has anointed us, 22 and who has also [o]put his seal on us and [p]given us his Spirit in our hearts as a guarantee.[2]

23 But [q]I call God to witness against me—it was [r]to spare you that I refrained from coming again to Corinth. 24 Not that we [s]lord it over your faith, but we work with you for your joy, for you stand firm [t]in your faith.

2 For I made up my mind [u]not to make another painful visit to you. 2 For [v]if I cause you pain, who is there to make me glad but the one whom I have pained? 3 And I wrote as I did, so that when I came I might not suffer pain from those who should have made me rejoice, [w]for I felt sure of all of you, that my joy would be the joy of you all. 4 For [x]I wrote to you out of much affliction and anguish of heart and with many tears, not to cause you pain but to let you know the abundant love that I have for you.

[1] Some manuscripts *holiness* [2] Or *down payment*

12 [v]ch. 2:17; 4:2 [w]1 Cor. 2:4, 13
14 [x]ch. 2:5 [y]See 1 Cor. 1:8 [z][ch. 5:12; 9:3] [a]1 Cor. 9:15; Phil. 2:16; 4:1; 1 Thess. 2:19, 20
15 [b]See 1 Cor. 4:19 [c][Acts 18:1-18] [d][Rom. 1:11]
16 [e]Acts 19:21; [1 Cor. 16:5-7]
17 [f]ch. 10:2, 3
18 [g]See 1 Cor. 1:9 [h][ch. 2:17]
19 [i]See Matt. 14:33 [j]Acts 15:22 [k][Heb. 13:8]
20 [l][Rom. 15:8; Heb. 10:23] [m][Rev. 3:14]; See 1 Cor. 14:16
21 [n][1 John 2:20, 27]
22 [o]Eph. 1:13; 4:30 [p]ch. 5:5; Eph. 1:14; See Rom. 8:16
23 [q][Gal. 1:20]; See Rom. 1:9 [r]ch. 2:1, 3; See 1 Cor. 4:21
24 [s]1 Pet. 5:3; [ch. 4:5; Matt. 23:8-10] [t]Rom. 11:20; See 1 Cor. 15:1

Chapter 2
1 [u]ch. 1:23; [ch. 12:20, 21; 13:10]
2 [v][ch. 7:8]
3 [w]ch. 8:22; Gal. 5:10; 2 Thess. 3:4; [ch. 7:16]
4 [x]ch. 7:8, 12; See Acts 20:19

relying on his own authority, character, insight, or earthly wisdom, Paul appeals to that which is being done in him by the grace of God (v. 12). Paul's faithfulness finds its ultimate support in this truth, that God is faithful (v. 18).

The fullness of God's faithfulness is on display in Jesus Christ. Rather than having a duplicitous "Yes and No" posture, God has spoken a singular Yes in Jesus. In his life, death, and resurrection, Christ Jesus is the Yes to every one of God's promises. In the life of a believer, the confirmation of this Yes is the "Spirit in our hearts as a guarantee" (v. 22). Having this seal causes the believer to be far more concerned about the witness of God than the witness of men (v. 23). We no longer depend on the fickle approval of others because we have the final approval of God in Christ—a reality Paul asserts to explain why he had put off coming to Corinth sooner: he did so not for his own convenience but to spare the Corinthians the discipline they deserved. His concern was for them, not for himself, because he was confident of the approval of God.

As Paul exemplified in this situation, living in light of God's acceptance causes us to respond well to unwarranted or anticipated criticism. God's promises develop in us a paradoxical life of both confidence and meekness. We become humble rather than arrogant, faithful rather than doubtful. This in turn serves as a worshipful response—a means of uttering our "Amen to God for his glory" (v. 20).

2:1–11 The Corinthian church is known for its besetting sins. These sins have caused Paul graciously to delay his coming so as not to come in harsh judgment (vv. 1–4), although their actions warrant additional instruction. Paul's posture in the face of sin is one of abundant love (v. 4), which flows from the comfort that he himself has received through the death and resurrection of Christ (1:5).

How should Christians treat a fellow believer who has sinned? The way we have been treated by Christ. Forgiveness is offered as the unexpected means of breaking the cycle of sin and "un-grace." Comfort is offered in the face of affliction (2:7). Love is reaffirmed so that the guilty party will not be overwhelmed by excessive sorrow over brokenness in a relationship (v. 8). Even if we are called upon to administer consequences for sin or restorative discipline, these obligations do not remove the greater obligations of love and forgiveness.

Forgive the Sinner

5 Now [y]if anyone has caused pain, [z]he has
caused it not to me, but [a]in some measure—
not to put it too severely—to all of you. 6 For
such a one, [b]this punishment by the majority is
enough, 7 so [c]you should rather turn to forgive
and comfort him, or he may be overwhelmed
by excessive sorrow. 8 So I beg you to reaffirm
your love for him. 9 For this is why I wrote,
that I might [d]test you and know [e]whether you
are obedient in everything. 10 Anyone whom
you forgive, I also forgive. Indeed, what I have
forgiven, if I have forgiven anything, has been
for your sake in the presence of Christ, 11 so that
we would not be outwitted by Satan; for [f]we
are not ignorant of his designs.

Triumph in Christ

12 When [g]I came to Troas to preach the gospel
of Christ, even though [h]a door was opened
for me in the Lord, 13 my spirit [i]was not at
rest because I did not find my brother Titus
there. So I took leave of them and went on to
Macedonia.

14 But [j]thanks be to God, who in Christ
always [k]leads us in triumphal procession,
and through us spreads [l]the fragrance of the
knowledge of him everywhere. 15 For we are
the aroma of Christ to God among [m]those who
are being saved and among [n]those who are
perishing, 16 [o]to one a fragrance from death to
death, [o]to the other a fragrance from life to life.
[p]Who is sufficient for these things? 17 For we
are not, like so many, peddlers of God's word,
but as men of sincerity, as commissioned by
God, in the sight of God we speak in Christ.

Ministers of the New Covenant

3 [q]Are we beginning to commend ourselves
again? Or do we need, [r]as some do, [s]let-
ters of recommendation to you, or from you?
2 [t]You yourselves are our letter of recommendation, written on our[1] hearts, to be known
and read by all. 3 And you show that you are
a letter from Christ delivered by us, written
not with ink but with the Spirit of [u]the living
God, not on [v]tablets of stone but on [w]tablets
of [x]human hearts.[2]

[1] Some manuscripts *your* [2] Greek *fleshly hearts*

A heart that has been forgiven much is a heart that forgives much (Matt. 18:21–35). On the one hand, because we know the depths of our own sin, we do not take the sin of others lightly. Paul indicates that the sinner in this case has undergone some form of church discipline (2 Cor. 2:6). On the other hand, because we know the depths of forgiveness that we have in Christ, we do not require payment for the sins of others. In the community of faith, sin is never overlooked. Rather, sin is directly addressed, acknowledged, and forgiven. In this way, we outwit Satan, whose intentions are to keep us in unrepentant, unforgiving, and divisive sin (v. 11).

2:12–17 Paul is dealing with false apostles who have shaped the hearts of the Corinthians through artful rhetoric, power grabbing, and status seeking. His upside-down response is to show his insufficiency for the call to preach the gospel (vv. 12, 16b)! It is precisely in Paul's weakness and inadequacies that God is shown to be all-sufficient (3:6; 12:9). At the center of Paul's life stands the inverted, status-eschewing self-sacrifice of the Son of God. The result is a willingness to abandon wise words, exhibitions of strength, and prestige in favor of being led as a captive in the counterintuitive triumphal procession of Christ (2:14).

As believers live in sacrificial submission to God, their speech and actions serve as the "fragrance" and "aroma" of Christ (vv. 14–15). To those looking for worldly evidences of power, the upside-down nature of the gospel feels like death. To those in whom the Spirit of God is at work, however, the fragrance is one of life to life (v. 16). Because Christians are commissioned by God and follow the lead of Christ, our ministry need not be ostentatious, showy, or professional. Because victory in Christ actually refers to self-death and self-donation, we define our successes in terms of service and self-giving. Only the One whose death has secured our life can provide the resources for the radical reversal of all of our values.

3:1–6 The rhetorical (and ironic) questions in verse 1 reveal Paul's desire to challenge the false apostles' tendency toward one-upmanship. He says, essentially, "I don't need an external letter of recommendation or reintroduction, because the internal work of the Spirit in your hearts is all the endorsement that is required." The changed lives of the Corinthians are proof that Paul is a minister of the new covenant (cf. Jer. 31:31–33;

5 [y][1 Cor. 5:1, 2] [z][Gal. 4:12] [a]ch. 1:14
6 [b]1 Cor. 5:4, 5; [ch. 7:11]
7 [c]Gal. 6:1; [Eph. 4:32]
9 [d]Phil. 2:22 [e]ch. 7:15; 10:6
11 [f]See 1 Pet. 5:8
12 [g]Acts 16:8; 20:6 [h]See Acts 14:27
13 [i]ch. 7:5
14 [j]ch. 8:16; [ch. 9:15]; See Rom. 6:17 [k]Col. 2:15 (Gk.) [l]Eph. 5:2; Phil. 4:18; [Song 1:3]
15 [m]See 1 Cor. 1:18 [n]ch. 4:3
16 [o][Luke 2:34; John 9:39; 1 Pet. 2:7, 8] [p]ch. 3:5, 6

Chapter 3
1 [q]ch. 5:12; 10:12; 12:11 [r][ch. 11:4] [s][Acts 18:27; 1 Cor. 16:3]
2 [t][1 Cor. 9:2]
3 [u]See Matt. 16:16 [v]Ex. 24:12 [w]Prov. 3:3; 7:3; Jer. 17:1 [x]Ezek. 11:19; 36:26; [Jer. 31:33; Heb. 8:10]

4 [y]Such is the confidence that we have
through Christ toward God. 5 [z]Not that we
are sufficient in ourselves to claim anything
as coming from us, but [a]our sufficiency is from
God, 6 who has made us sufficient to be [b]min-
isters of [c]a new covenant, not of [d]the letter
but of the Spirit. For the letter kills, but [e]the
Spirit gives life.

7 Now if [f]the ministry of death, carved in letters on stone, came with such glory [g]that the
Israelites could not gaze at Moses' face because
of its glory, which was being brought to an
end, 8 will not the ministry of the Spirit have
even more glory? 9 For if there was glory in
[h]the ministry of condemnation, [i]the ministry
of righteousness must far exceed it in glory.
10 Indeed, in this case, what once had glory
has come to have no glory at all, because of
the glory that surpasses it. 11 For if what was
being brought to an end came with glory,
much more will what is permanent have glory.

12 Since we have such a hope, [j]we are very bold,
13 not like Moses, [k]who would put a veil over
his face so that the Israelites might not gaze
at the outcome of what was being brought to
an end. 14 But [l]their minds were [m]hardened. For
to this day, [n]when they read [o]the old covenant,
that same veil remains unlifted, because only
through Christ is it taken away. 15 Yes, to this
day whenever Moses is read a veil lies over
their hearts. 16 But when [p]one[1] turns to the
Lord, [q]the veil is removed. 17 Now the Lord[2] is
the Spirit, and where [r]the Spirit of the Lord is,
there is [s]freedom. 18 And we all, with unveiled
face, [t]beholding [u]the glory of the Lord,[3] [v]are
being transformed into the same image [w]from
one degree of glory to another. For this comes
from the Lord who is the Spirit.

[1] Greek *he* [2] Or *this Lord* [3] Or *reflecting the glory of the Lord*

4 [y] Eph. 3:12
5 [z] [Eph. 2:8] [a] See 1 Cor. 15:10
6 [b] Eph. 3:7; Col. 1:23, 25; [ch. 4:1; 5:18; 1 Tim. 1:12] [c] Jer. 31:31; Luke 22:20; 1 Cor. 11:25; Heb. 8:8, 13; [ver. 14; Heb. 9:15] [d] See Rom. 2:27 [e] [John 6:63; Rom. 8:2]
7 [f] ver. 9; See Rom. 4:15 [g] ver. 13; Ex. 34:29-35
9 [h] ver. 7; [Heb. 12:18-21] [i] ch. 11:15
12 [j] ch. 7:4; Eph. 6:19
13 [k] ver. 7
14 [l] [ch. 4:4; Rom. 11:25] [m] See Mark 6:52 [n] Acts 13:15; 15:21 [o] [ver. 6]
16 [p] Rom. 11:23; [Ex. 34:34] [q] [Isa. 25:7]
17 [r] Isa. 61:1, 2; [Gal. 4:6] [s] Gal. 5:1, 13; See John 8:32
18 [t] See 1 Cor. 13:12 [u] ch. 4:4, 6; 1 Tim. 1:11; See John 17:24 [v] Rom. 8:29; 1 Cor. 15:49 [w] [Ps. 84:7]

Ezek. 36:26–27). Under this new administration, the *internal* effects of the gospel upon the heart take precedence over one's *external* credentials.

Moralism and external religiosity are marked by the belief that change happens from the outside in (i.e., change your behavior, and you will experience the grace of God). In contrast, the gospel claims that, by the work of the Spirit, transformation happens from the inside out (i.e., because you have experienced the grace of God, you can be sure that the Spirit is working in your heart to bring about change). Because the believer's sufficiency/competence comes not from external achievements but from God (2 Cor. 3:5), we should not grasp after a secure position in life on the basis of outward performance. Rather, we can rest in our already established position before God, knowing that the inward "heart work" of the Spirit leads to genuine, visible change.

3:7–18 Unlike the ministry of Moses, which was limited, impermanent, veiled, and lacking transformative power, Paul's new covenant ministry is characterized by an all-surpassing, permanent, unveiled, transformative glory that is mediated by the Spirit of the Lord (vv. 10–11, 16–18). Moses had a remarkable encounter with the presence of God (Ex. 34:29–35), but the new covenant believer's access is even more astoundingly complete. While Israel could not even look at Moses' face without the aid of a veil (Ex. 34:33), Christians can now behold the glory of the Lord with an unveiled face. This experience is ours "through Christ" (2 Cor. 3:14). He himself is the answer to the question, how can we behold the glory of God? Jesus, the new temple, has given us full access to the presence of God "through his flesh" (Heb. 10:20), literally tearing the temple curtain that formerly acted as a barrier between a holy God and a sinful people (Matt. 27:51; Ex. 26:31–33).

The implications of this are profound. First, we have *unlimited access* to the very presence of God (2 Cor. 3:18). Second, in Christ we are given an *unashamed boldness* to enjoy our free and limitless access to God (v. 12). Third, this bold beholding of God's glory is the very means that the Spirit uses to bring about our *utter transformation* into the image of God's glory (v. 18). From start to finish, the believer is being transformed by God's glory, for God's glory, and into the image of God's glory.

4:1–6 Paul's reference to Genesis 1:3 shows that the work of God in revealing the light of the gospel in our hearts is a new creational act (2 Cor. 4:6; cf. 5:17). It is the means by which the veil is removed from our eyes (4:3) and we are transferred from darkness into his marvelous light (1 Pet. 2:9; cf. Col. 1:13–14). This new creational work is bound up with Christ's death and resurrection. Jesus, who is the Light of the World

The Light of the Gospel

4 Therefore, having [x]this ministry [y]by the
mercy of God,[1] we do not lose heart. 2 But
we have renounced [z]disgraceful, underhanded
ways. We refuse to practice[2] cunning or [a]to
tamper with God's word, but [b]by the open
statement of the truth [c]we would commend
ourselves to everyone's conscience in the sight
of God. 3 And even [d]if our gospel is veiled, [e]it
is veiled to [f]those who are perishing. 4 In their
case [g]the god of this world [d]has blinded the
minds of the unbelievers, to keep them from
seeing [h]the light of [i]the gospel of the glory of
Christ, [j]who is the image of God. 5 For what
[k]we proclaim is not ourselves, but Jesus Christ
as Lord, with [l]ourselves as your servants[3] for
Jesus' sake. 6 For God, who said, [m]"Let light
shine out of darkness," [n]has shone in our
hearts to give [o]the light of the knowledge of
the glory of God in the face of Jesus Christ.

Treasure in Jars of Clay

7 But we have this treasure in [p]jars of clay,
[q]to show that the surpassing power belongs
to God and not to us. 8 We are [r]afflicted in
every way, but not crushed; perplexed, but
not driven to despair; 9 persecuted, but [s]not
forsaken; [t]struck down, but not destroyed;
10 [u]always carrying in the body the death of
Jesus, [v]so that the life of Jesus may also be
manifested in our bodies. 11 For we who live
are always being given over to death for Jesus'
sake, so that the life of Jesus also may be manifested in our mortal flesh. 12 So [w]death is at
work in us, but life in you.

13 Since we have [x]the same spirit of faith
according to what has been written, [y]"I
believed, and so I spoke," we also believe, and
so we also speak, 14 knowing that [z]he who
raised the Lord Jesus [a]will raise us also with
Jesus and [b]bring us with you into his presence.

[1] Greek *as we have received mercy* [2] Greek *to walk in* [3] Greek *bondservants*

(John 8:12; 9:5), endures "the power of darkness" (Luke 22:53; cf. Matt. 27:45) in order to absorb and to rescue us from eternal outer darkness (Matt. 8:12; 25:30). And it is through his "being the first to rise from the dead" that he now "proclaims light" (Acts 26:23). The result is that our minds are no longer blinded by unbelief (2 Cor. 4:4). Instead, we are now creatures who are called to "walk as children of light" (Eph. 5:8).

The gospel is the ultimate source of light that puts all of life into proper perspective. Because we view life according to how we are seen in the sight of God, we are free to abandon underhanded ways in favor of a transparent, grace-dependent life. All other ways of seeing will lead to blindness; other light sources represent darkness (Luke 11:34–36). God graciously exposes this darkness and empowers us to live as "children of light" (1 Thess. 5:5) who are being transformed by the work of the Spirit (2 Cor. 3:18).

4:7–18 The Christian life is paradoxical because it is built upon the ultimate paradox, the death of Christ, where perfect divinity and beauty was horribly killed. Through that tragedy, life for sinners blossomed. We are comforted because of his affliction (see 1:3–11), accepted because of his rejection. We live because he died. When we taste life in light of the gospel, we begin to understand Paul's paradoxical logic:

	Momentary Experience	*Permanent Promise*
(v. 7)	jars of clay (as storage for . . .)	treasure
(v. 8)	afflicted	not crushed
(v. 8)	perplexed	not driven to despair
(v. 9)	persecuted	not forsaken
(v. 9)	struck down	not destroyed
(v. 10)	death of Jesus (carried in our bodies in order to manifest . . .)	the life of Jesus (in our bodies)
(v. 11)	given over to death (in order to manifest . . .)	the life of Jesus (in our bodies)
(v. 12)	death is at work	life is on display
(v. 16)	outer self is wasting away	inner self is being renewed
(v. 17)	present affliction (is "light and momentary" compared to . . .)	eternal weight of glory
(v. 18)	things that are seen	things that are unseen
(v. 18)	things that are transient	things that are eternal

The gospel enables us to deal with difficult momentary experiences because it assures us of the permanence of God's promises. When we are momentarily afflicted,

Chapter 4
1 [x]See ch. 3:6 [y]1 Cor. 7:25; 1 Tim. 1:13
2 [z]See Rom. 6:21 [a]ch. 2:17 [b]ch. 6:7; 7:14 [c]ch. 5:11, 12
3 [d][ch. 3:14] [e][Matt. 13:15] [f]ch. 2:15; 1 Cor. 1:18; 2 Thess. 2:10
4 [g]See John 12:31 [d][See ver. 3 above] [h]ver. 6; See Acts 26:18 [i]See ch. 3:18 [j]Col. 1:15; [Phil. 2:6; Heb. 1:3]
5 [k][1 Thess. 2:6] [l]1 Cor. 9:19; See ch. 1:24
6 [m]Gen. 1:3 [n]2 Pet. 1:19 [o]ver. 4
7 [p]2 Tim. 2:20; [ch. 5:1; Job 10:9; 13:12; Lam. 4:2; 1 Thess. 4:4; 1 Pet. 3:7] [q]1 Cor. 2:5; [Judg. 7:2]
8 [r]ch. 7:5; [Ps. 129:2]
9 [s]Heb. 13:5; [Deut. 4:31] [t]Ps. 37:24; Prov. 24:16; Mic. 7:8
10 [u]ch. 6:9; 1 Cor. 4:9; 15:31; [ch. 1:5, 9; Rom. 6:5; 8:36] [v]2 Tim. 2:11; [Rom. 5:10; 6:8]
12 [w][ch. 13:9]
13 [x]1 Cor. 12:9; 2 Pet. 1:1 [y]Cited from Ps. 116:10
14 [z]1 Thess. 4:14; See Acts 2:24 [a]ch. 1:9 [b][Jude 24]

15 For [c]it is all for your sake, so that as [d]grace extends to more and more people it may increase thanksgiving, [e]to the glory of God.

16 So we do not lose heart. [f]Though our outer self[1] is wasting away, [g]our inner self [h]is being renewed day by day. 17 For [i]this light momentary affliction is preparing for us an eternal weight of glory beyond all comparison, 18 [j]as we look not to the things that are seen but to the things that are unseen. For the things that are seen are transient, but the things that are unseen are eternal.

Our Heavenly Dwelling

5 For we know that if [k]the tent that is [l]our earthly home is destroyed, we have a building from God, [m]a house not made with hands, eternal in the heavens. 2 For in this tent [n]we groan, longing to [o]put on our heavenly dwelling, 3 if indeed by putting it on[2] we may not be found naked. 4 For while we are still in this tent, we groan, being burdened—not that we would be unclothed, but that we would be further clothed, so that what is mortal [p]may be swallowed up by life. 5 He who has prepared us for this very thing is God, [q]who has given us the Spirit as a guarantee.

6 So we are always of good courage. We know that [r]while we are at home in the body we are away from the Lord, 7 for [s]we walk by faith, not [t]by sight. 8 Yes, we are of good courage, and we [u]would rather be away from the body and at home with the Lord. 9 So whether we are at home or away, we make it our aim to [v]please him. 10 For [w]we must all appear before the judgment seat of Christ, [x]so that each one may receive what is due for what he has done in the body, whether good or evil.

The Ministry of Reconciliation

11 Therefore, knowing [y]the fear of the Lord, we persuade others. But [z]what we are is known to God, and I hope it is known also to your conscience. 12 [a]We are not commending ourselves

[1] Greek *man* [2] Some manuscripts *putting it off*

15[c][ch. 1:6]; See Rom. 8:28 [d][ch. 1:11; 9:11, 12] [e]ch. 8:19
16[f]See Acts 20:24 [g]See Rom. 7:22 [h][Isa. 40:30, 31]; See Rom. 12:2
17[i]Rom. 8:18; 1 Pet. 1:6; 5:10; [Ps. 30:5; Isa. 54:7]
18[j]ch. 5:7; Rom. 8:24; Heb. 11:1, 13
Chapter 5
1[k]2 Pet. 1:13, 14 [l]See ch. 4:7 [m]Mark 14:58
2[n]Rom. 8:23 [o][1 Cor. 15:53, 54]
4[p]1 Cor. 15:54
5[q][Rom. 8:23]; See ch. 1:22
6[r][Heb. 11:13, 14]
7[s][John 20:29]; See ch. 4:18 [t]1 Cor. 13:12
8[u][Phil. 1:23]
9[v][Col. 1:10; 1 Thess. 4:1]
10[w]Matt. 25:31, 32; [Rom. 14:10]; See Acts 10:42 [x]See Ps. 62:12
11[y][Job 31:23; Acts 9:31; Heb. 10:31; Jude 23] [z]ch. 4:2
12[a]See ch. 3:1

we are certain that we will not be crushed because Jesus was crushed on our behalf (Isa. 53:5). When we are persecuted, we know that God will not forsake us because Jesus was forsaken in our place (Mark 15:34). When we experience death we need not fear, for we know that we will experience resurrection life because Jesus bore the penalty of death on our behalf (2 Tim. 1:10).

Paul claims that these paradoxes exist to show that surpassing power—beyond human control or fathoming—belongs to God. Furthermore, the fruit of gospel faithfulness in momentary affliction is a picture of our witness. As we believe and speak the gospel (2 Cor. 4:13) during the most difficult times, the result is that grace extends to more and more people, and God is seen to be more glorious (v. 15).

5:1–10 Paul refers to the present, mortal body as a tent, whereas he speaks of the future resurrected body as a house (v. 1). Although we are presently clothed in our mortal flesh, we will one day be further clothed with a glorified body that will swallow up our mortality (v. 4). Gospel-believing Christians can experience the reality of this resurrection hope even now through the indwelling of the Spirit, who is "the guarantee of our inheritance until we acquire possession of it" (Eph. 1:14).

The doctrine of the resurrection of the dead is inextricably tied to the resurrection of Christ (2 Cor. 4:14), which ensures that death itself has been nullified. It is a gospel promise. The Christian does not need to fear death but can confidently know that it has been defeated (1 Cor. 15:55).

Whatever suffering, trial, burden, fear, or discouragement you may experience, it is not as tragic, painful, or final as death. Thus, to know that Christ has defeated death is to know that he has taken away the ultimate sting of all our present sufferings. Though we groan under our burdens (2 Cor. 5:4), we do so with good courage (vv. 6, 8), being content that "whether . . . at home or away" we can make it our aim to please him (v. 9). To believe that God's permanent, death-defeating promise is more defining than our momentary experiences is to walk by faith, not by sight (v. 7).

5:11–21 At the core of the good news of the gospel is what has often been called the "great exchange" or "imputation." Our sin is imputed (reckoned, accounted) to Christ as he is made to be sin for us; his righteousness is imputed to us as we receive his righteous status (v. 21). He takes our sin; he gives us his righteousness. This shocking transfer lies at the heart of the Christian faith and is as clear here in 2 Corinthians 5 as

to you again but [b]giving you cause to boast about us, so that you may be able to answer those who boast about outward appearance and not about what is in the heart. 13 For if we [c]are beside ourselves, it is for God; if we are in our right mind, it is for you. 14 For the love of Christ [d]controls us, because we have concluded this: that [e]one has died for all, therefore all have died; 15 and he died for all, [f]that those who live might no longer live for themselves but [g]for him who for their sake died and was raised.

16 From now on, therefore, [h]we regard no one according to the flesh. Even though we once regarded Christ according to the flesh, we regard him thus no longer. 17 Therefore, if anyone is [i]in Christ, he is [j]a new creation.[1] [k]The old has passed away; behold, the new has come. 18 All this is from God, [l]who through Christ reconciled us to himself and gave us [m]the ministry of reconciliation; 19 that is, in Christ God was reconciling[2] the world to himself, [n]not counting their trespasses against them, and entrusting to us [m]the message of reconciliation. 20 Therefore, [o]we are ambassadors for Christ, [p]God making his appeal through us. We implore you on behalf of Christ, be reconciled to God. 21 [q]For our sake he made him to be sin [r]who knew no sin, so that in him we might become [s]the righteousness of God.

6

[t]Working together with him, then, [u]we appeal to you [v]not to receive the grace of God in vain. 2 For he says,

> [w]"In a favorable time I listened to you,
> and in a day of salvation I have helped you."

Behold, [x]now is the [y]favorable time; behold, now is the day of salvation. 3 We [z]put no obstacle in anyone's way, so that no fault may be found with our ministry, 4 but [a]as servants of God we commend ourselves in every way: [b]by great endurance, [c]in afflictions, [d]hardships, calamities, 5 [e]beatings, imprisonments, [f]riots, labors, sleepless nights, hunger; 6 [g]by purity, [h]knowledge, patience, kindness, [i]the Holy Spirit, [j]genuine love; 7 by [k]truthful speech, and [l]the power of God; with [m]the weapons of righteousness for the right hand and for the left; 8 through honor and dishonor, [n]through slander and praise. We are treated

[1] Or *creature* [2] Or *God was in Christ, reconciling*

anywhere in the Bible. This transfer is not a dry, cold matter, however. An individual is reconciled to God (vv. 18, 20) and made a new creation in Christ (v. 17) on the basis of this exchange. Furthermore, this power leads the Christian to become a sacrificial minister of reconciliation (vv. 14–15, 18), as our love for Christ compels us to speak of him despite opposition and affliction.

We are connected vitally and legally through our union with Christ because he imputed his perfect, righteous life of obedience into our account. He imputed not only innocence but also righteousness, not only pardon but also perfection. He not only stood condemned in our place as a punishment bearer; he also stood in our place as our law keeper. Jesus not only died the death that we should have died; he also lived the life that we should have lived. All has been taken care of.

Things drastically change in light of the exchange of Christ's righteousness for our sin. Our legal *standing* before God has shifted from that of unrighteousness to righteousness. The *status* of our relationship with God has moved from conflict to reconciliation, ensuring peace and communion with God. Our very *being* is transferred from the impending death of this world to the promised life of God's new creational order, leading us to an increased appetite for that which pleases God and a growing distaste for that which does not please him. Finally, our *perspective* is altered so that we no longer focus on outward appearances but on a radical interior radiance (vv. 12, 16).

6:1–13 Paul wants the Corinthian Christians to open their hearts to him (v. 13) so that they can receive the grace of God immediately (vv. 1–2). To accomplish this, Paul commends himself by way of paradoxical inversion (also 2:12–17; 4:7–18). First, Paul's *circumstantial hardships* (6:4b–5) are evidence of the enduring strength he receives from Christ, who himself endured afflictions, beatings, and ultimately death. Second, Paul's *internal spiritual realities* (v. 6) stand in stark contrast to the external, "boasted mission" of the "super-apostles" who had captured the church's attention (11:5, 12). Third, even Paul's *external displays* (6:7) are spiritual in nature—all dependent upon

12 [b][ch. 1:14]
13 [c]ch. 11:1, 16, 17; 12:6, 11
14 [d]Acts 18:5 [e]Rom. 5:15
15 [f][Rom. 6:11, 12]; See Rom. 14:7 [g][ch. 12:10]
16 [h][Gal. 2:6; Phil. 3:7, 8; Col. 2:11; 1 Tim. 5:21]
17 [i]ch. 12:2; Rom. 16:7; Gal. 1:22 [j][John 3:3]; See Rom. 6:4 [k]Isa. 43:18, 19; Rev. 21:5; [Isa. 65:17; Eph. 2:15; 4:24; Heb. 8:13]
18 [l]Col. 1:20; See Rom. 5:10; 1 John 2:2 [m]Rom. 5:11
19 [n]Ps. 32:2; Rom. 4:8 [m][See ver. 18 above]
20 [o]Eph. 6:20; [Mal. 2:7; Gal. 4:14] [p]ch. 6:1
21 [q]Rom. 8:3; Gal. 3:13; See Rom. 4:25 [r]See 1 Pet. 2:22 [s]See Rom. 1:17; 1 Cor. 1:30

Chapter 6
1 [t]Mark 16:20; 1 Cor. 3:9; [Acts 15:4] [u]ch. 5:20 [v][Heb. 12:15]
2 [w]Cited from Isa. 49:8 [x][Ps. 32:6; 69:13; Isa. 55:6; Heb. 3:13] [y][Luke 4:19]
3 [z]See 1 Cor. 8:13; 9:12
4 [a][1 Thess. 3:2; 2 Tim. 2:24, 25]; See ch. 3:6 [b]ch. 12:12; 2 Tim. 3:10 [c]Acts 9:16 [d]ch. 12:10
5 [e]ch. 11:23-27; Acts 16:23 [f]Acts 17:5
6 [g]1 Thess. 2:10 [h]ch. 11:6 [i]Rom. 15:19; 1 Thess. 1:5 [j]Rom. 12:9; [James 3:17]
7 [k]Eph. 1:13; Col. 1:5 [l]See 1 Cor. 2:5 [m]ch. 10:4; Eph. 6:11-17
8 [n]Rom. 3:8

as impostors, and yet are true; 9 as unknown,
and [o]yet well known; [p]as dying, and behold,
we live; [q]as punished, and yet not killed; 10 [r]as
sorrowful, yet always rejoicing; [s]as poor, yet
making many rich; [t]as having nothing, [u]yet
possessing everything.
11 We have spoken freely to you,[1] Corinthians;
[v]our heart is wide open. 12 You are not restricted
by us, but [w]you are restricted in your own
affections. 13 [x]In return (I speak [y]as to children)
widen your hearts also.

The Temple of the Living God

14 [z]Do not be unequally yoked with unbelievers. For [a]what partnership has righteousness
with lawlessness? Or [b]what fellowship has
light with darkness? 15 [c]What accord has Christ
with Belial?[2] Or what portion does a believer
share with an unbeliever? 16 What agreement
has the temple of God with idols? For [d]we are
the temple of the living God; as God said,

> [e]"I will make my dwelling among them
> and [f]walk among them,
> and [g]I will be their God,
> and they shall be my people.
> 17 Therefore [h]go out from their midst,
> and be separate from them, says the
> Lord,
> and touch no unclean thing;
> then I will welcome you,
> 18 [i]and I will be a father to you,
> and you shall be sons and daughters
> to me,
> says the Lord Almighty."

7 Since we have these promises, beloved,
[j]let us cleanse ourselves from every defilement of body[3] and spirit, bringing holiness to
completion in the fear of God.

Paul's Joy

2 [k]Make room in your hearts[4] for us. [l]We have
wronged no one, we have corrupted no one,

[1] Greek *Our mouth is open to you* [2] Greek *Beliar* [3] Greek *flesh* [4] Greek lacks *in your hearts*

9 [o][ch. 11:6] [p]See ch. 4:10 [q]Ps. 118:18
10 [r]John 16:22; [ch. 7:4] [s][ch. 8:9; Prov. 13:7; 1 Cor. 1:5] [t]Acts 3:6 [u]1 Cor. 7:30
11 [v]ch. 7:3; [ch. 11:11; 12:15; Ps. 119:32]
12 [w]ch. 7:2
13 [x][Gal. 4:12] [y]1 Cor. 4:14
14 [z]Deut. 7:3; Josh. 23:12; Ezra 9:2; Neh. 13:25; [1 Cor. 7:39] [a]Eph. 5:7, 11; 1 John 1:6 [b]See Acts 26:18
15 [c][1 Cor. 10:21]
16 [d][Eph. 2:22]; See 1 Cor. 3:16 [e]Cited from Lev. 26:12; See Ex. 29:45 [f][Rev. 2:1; 21:3] [g]Ex. 6:7; Jer. 31:33; Ezek. 11:20
17 [h]Cited from Isa. 52:11; [ch. 7:1; Ezek. 20:34, 41; Zeph. 3:20; Rev. 18:4]
18 [i][Ex. 4:22; 2 Sam. 7:8, 14; Isa. 43:6; Jer. 31:9; Hos. 1:10; Rev. 21:7]

Chapter 7
1 [j]1 Pet. 2:11; 1 John 3:3
2 [k]ch. 6:12, 13 [l]Acts 20:33; [ch. 11:20]

God's word and power. Finally, the *apparent tragedies* (vv. 8–10) are overshadowed by the actual victories that Paul is experiencing in the gospel.

No one wants to have "restricted" affections, but that is exactly what we find when we grow suspicious of the gospel (v. 12). The result is that our present circumstances overwhelm us, our internal spiritual life becomes dull, our attention shifts to external performance, and we live by what apparently seems true rather than by what actually *is* true. When we embrace the upside-down realities of the gospel by faith, all of this is set right. The gospel gives us wide-open hearts toward individuals who approach us with narrow, closed hearts (vv. 11–12). We should pray for heart-widening, upside-down, unrestricted gospel affections, as we "walk by faith, not by sight" (5:7).

6:14–7:1 We are the beneficiaries of God's new community. Through the crucified body of Christ, we have been given access to the presence of God along with other believers (see 3:7–18). By the work of the Spirit, we are all being gloriously transformed (3:18). Here, Paul calls us to live lives that are in accord with these new covenant realities (based not on external conformity to the law but on heart commitments that result in true holiness; see 3:6), particularly in our relationships with unbelievers (6:14–16a).

The image of being unequally yoked draws to mind two animals unsuited to work together. A large ox and a small mule are not meant to plow side by side; they will consistently be moving in opposing directions. Similarly, believers and unbelievers have different operating principles and aims. Just as Christ has nothing to do with Satan (6:15), and light has nothing to do with darkness (6:14), so the believer must not be intimately allied, yoked, and in partnership with an unbeliever. This does not mean that we are to have no relationships with unbelievers (or else evangelism would be impossible), but we are not to be in partnerships that allow principles or practices contrary to Christ to control us.

The basis for obedience to this command is not moralism (living morally in order to be loved by God) but the gospel (living morally because we are already loved by God). We are to be set apart (6:17) *since we have these promises* (7:1). The grounds for our obedience are God's new covenant promises that are fulfilled through Christ by the Spirit. We should refuse to identify and partner with idols because "we *are* the temple of the living God" (6:16), not because we are meritoriously becoming the temple of the living God. We ought not to touch any unclean thing because we *are*

we have taken advantage of no one. 3 I do not
say this to condemn you, for I said before that
[m]you are in our hearts, to die together and to
live together. 4 I am acting with [n]great boldness
toward you; [o]I have great pride in you; [p]I am
filled with comfort. In all our affliction, I am
overflowing with joy.

5 For even [q]when we came into Macedonia,
our bodies had no rest, but we were afflicted
at every turn—[r]fighting without and fear
within. 6 But [s]God, who comforts the downcast, [t]comforted us by the coming of Titus,
7 and not only by his coming but also by the
comfort with which he was comforted by you,
as he told us of your longing, your mourning,
your zeal for me, so that I rejoiced still more.
8 For [u]even if I made you grieve with my letter,
I do not regret it—though [v]I did regret it, for
I see that that letter grieved you, though only
for a while. 9 As it is, I rejoice, not because you
were grieved, but [w]because you were grieved
into repenting. For you felt a godly grief, so
that you suffered no loss through us.

10 For [x]godly grief produces a repentance
that leads to salvation without regret, whereas
[y]worldly grief produces death. 11 For see what
earnestness this godly grief has produced in
you, but also what eagerness to clear yourselves, what indignation, what fear, what longing, [z]what zeal, what punishment! At every
point you have proved yourselves innocent in
the matter. 12 So although I wrote to you, it was
not for the sake of the one [a]who did the wrong,
nor for the sake of the one who suffered the
wrong, but in order that your earnestness for
us might be revealed to you in the sight of
God. 13 Therefore [b]we are comforted.

And besides our own comfort, we rejoiced
still more at the joy of Titus, because his spirit
[c]has been refreshed by you all. 14 For [d]whatever
boasts I made to him about you, I was not put
to shame. But just as everything we said to you
[e]was true, so also our boasting before Titus
has proved true. 15 And his affection for you is
even greater, as he remembers [f]the obedience
of you all, how you received him with fear and
trembling. 16 I rejoice, because I have complete
[g]confidence in you.

Encouragement to Give Generously

8 We want you to know, brothers,[1] about the
grace of God that has been [h]given among
the churches of Macedonia, 2 for in a severe
test of affliction, their abundance of joy and
[i]their extreme poverty have overflowed in a

[1] Or *brothers and sisters*

God's sons and daughters, not because we are able by our own efforts to achieve access to his family (6:18). Grace is the fuel for our obedience.

7:2–16 Paul is comforted by the Corinthians' response to the gospel. His earlier descriptions of comfort in affliction (1:3–11) are true in his own life. It is the change that he sees in their lives that brings great comfort to Paul (7:7, 13). This transformation is characterized by their response of godly sorrow and repentance (vv. 9–10) to Paul's difficult letter (v. 8).

To see gospel transformation in action, consider these movements of grace: Paul receives comfort in his affliction from Christ (1:5). This gives him the confidence and grace to write a difficult letter to the Corinthians in which he speaks the truth in love (7:8; see 2:1–11). Their response is godly sorrow that leads to repentance (7:10). Their repentance leads to a renewed zeal for godliness (v. 11). As they are refreshed by the Spirit, they become a source of refreshment-bringing joy to their leaders through their obedience to the gospel (vv. 13b, 15). In turn, Titus experiences rejuvenation, which causes Paul to rejoice all the more (v. 13b). The gospel transformation is beautifully personal and interpersonal. When I pass on to my community the comfort I have received from Christ, the effect is a multiplication of the grace that I have received (v. 10), which is cause for both comfort and rejoicing (vv. 13, 16).

8:1–15 The Corinthians had started out eager to support fellow Christians in their financial need (vv. 10, 14) but have now lost the desire to give generously. Though Paul might legitimately appeal to his apostolic authority or to the obligation to give a tithe (Lev. 27:30–33), he knows that the Corinthians need a deeper motivation. And so he appeals to the gospel.

Jesus gave not just a tenth of himself, but all of his riches. He embraced poverty so that we might become rich (2 Cor. 8:9). His radical act of total self-giving is the

3 [m][ch. 6:11-13]
4 [n]ch. 3:12 [o]ch. 1:12; 8:24; 9:2 [p]ch. 1:4; Phil. 2:17; Col. 1:24; [ch. 6:10]
5 [q]ch. 2:13 [r][Deut. 32:25; Lam. 1:20]
6 [s]ch. 1:4 [t]ver. 13; [1 Thess. 3:6, 7]
8 [u][ch. 2:2] [v]ch. 2:4
9 [w]Ps. 38:18; [1 Cor. 5:2]
10 [x][2 Sam. 12:13; Acts 11:18] [y][Prov. 17:22]
11 [z][ch. 2:6]
12 [a][1 Cor. 5:1, 2]
13 [b]ver. 6 [c]See Rom. 15:32
14 [d]ch. 8:24; 9:2; 10:8; [2 Thess. 1:4] [e]ch. 4:2; 6:7
15 [f]ch. 2:9; 10:6
16 [g]See ch. 2:3

Chapter 8
1 [h]ver. 5
2 [i][Mark 12:44]

wealth of generosity on their part. 3 For they
gave[j] according to their means, as I can testify,
and beyond their means, of their own accord,
4 begging us earnestly[k] for the favor[1] of taking
part in [l]the relief of the saints— 5 and this,
not as we expected, but they [m]gave themselves
first to the Lord and then by the will of God
to us. 6 Accordingly, [n]we urged Titus that as he
had started, so he should complete among you
[o]this act of grace. 7 But as [p]you excel in everything—in faith, in speech, in knowledge, in
all earnestness, and in our love for you[2]—[q]see
that you excel in this act of grace also.
8 [r]I say this not as a command, but to prove
by the earnestness of others that your love
also is genuine. 9 For you know the grace of
our Lord Jesus Christ, that [s]though he was
rich, yet for your sake he became poor, so
that you by his poverty might become rich.
10 And in this matter [t]I give my judgment:
[u]this benefits you, who [v]a year ago started
not only to do this work but also to desire to
do it. 11 So now finish doing it as well, so that
your readiness in desiring it may be matched
by your completing it out of what you have.
12 For if the readiness is there, it is acceptable
[w]according to what a person has, not according to what he does not have. 13 For I do not
mean that others should be eased and you
burdened, but that as a matter of fairness
14 your abundance at the present time should
supply [x]their need, so that their abundance
may supply your need, that there may be fairness. 15 As it is written, [y]"Whoever gathered
much had nothing left over, and whoever
gathered little had no lack."

Commendation of Titus

16 But [z]thanks be to God, [a]who put into the
heart of Titus the same earnest care I have for
you. 17 For [b]he not only accepted our appeal,
but being himself very earnest he is going[3] to
you of his own accord. 18 With him we are sending[4] [c]the brother who is famous among [d]all the
churches for his preaching of the gospel. 19 And
not only that, but he has been [e]appointed by
the churches to travel with us as we carry out
this act of [f]grace that is being ministered by
us, [g]for the glory of the Lord himself and to
show our good will. 20 We take this course so
that no one should blame us about this generous gift that is being administered by us,
21 for [h]we aim at what is honorable [i]not only in
the Lord's sight but also in the sight of man.
22 And with them we are sending our brother
whom we have often tested and found earnest
in many matters, but who is now more earnest
than ever because of his great confidence in
you. 23 As for Titus, he is [j]my partner and fellow worker for your benefit. And as for our
brothers, they are messengers[5] of the churches,
the glory of Christ. 24 So give proof before the
churches of your love and of [k]our boasting
about you to these men.

The Collection for Christians in Jerusalem

9 Now [l]it is superfluous for me to write to
you about [m]the ministry for the saints,
2 for I know your readiness, [n]of which I boast

[1] The Greek word *charis* can mean *favor* or *grace* or *thanks*, depending on the context [2] Some manuscripts *in your love for us* [3] Or *he went*
[4] Or *we sent*; also verse 22 [5] Greek *apostles*

3[j] ver. 11; 1 Cor. 16:2
4[k] ch. 9:2; Rom. 15:25, 26; See Acts 24:17 [l] See Rom. 15:31
5[m] ver. 1
6[n] ver. 17; ch. 12:18 [o] ver. 19; [ver. 4]
7[p] See 1 Cor. 1:5 [q] ch. 9:8
8[r] 1 Cor. 7:6
9[s] Phil. 2:6, 7; [ch. 6:10; Matt. 20:28]
10[t] 1 Cor. 7:25 [u] Deut. 15:7, 8; Prov. 19:17; 28:27; 1 Tim. 6:18, 19; Heb. 13:16 [v] ch. 9:2
12[w] [ch. 9:7; Mark 12:43, 44; Luke 21:3]
14[x] ch. 9:12; [Acts 4:34]
15[y] Cited from Ex. 16:18
16[z] See ch. 2:14 [a] Rev. 17:17
17[b] ver. 6
18[c] ch. 12:18 [d] See 1 Cor. 7:17
19[e] [1 Cor. 16:3, 4] [f] ver. 6 [g] ch. 4:15
21[h] See Rom. 12:17 [i] [Rom. 14:18; Phil. 4:8; 1 Pet. 2:12]
23[j] [Philem. 17]

only thing that can consistently move us to give beyond the minimum. In essence, if we don't desire to respond to God's grace with sacrificial giving, then we have not yet fully understood the nature of the gospel. The answer to our motivation problem is not adherence to a new command but a more thoroughgoing knowledge and experience of the extravagant self-giving of Christ.

If we understand that all we have is a direct result of what Christ has given us, we will be moved to give out of our abundance, to carry others' burdens, and to seek after fairness and equity (vv. 13–14).

8:16–9:5 Here we see gospel priorities at work in the life of the church. First, the preaching of the gospel is essential for the ongoing health of the church (8:18). When Paul wants to see continued change in the Corinthians, he makes it a priority to send them someone who will faithfully and continually preach the gospel.

Second, Christian obedience is responsive gospel action. The giving of the Corinthians that was addressed in 8:1–15 is understood as an act of grace (8:19). In other words, our self-giving ought to be so organically connected to Christ's self-giving that the former is seen as a natural outgrowth of the latter.

24[k] ch. 7:4, 14; 9:2, 3 **Chapter 9** **1**[l] [1 Thess. 4:9] [m] See Rom. 15:25 **2**[n] ch. 8:24

about you to the people of Macedonia, saying
that Achaia has been ready [o]since last year. And
your zeal has stirred up most of them. 3 But
[p]I am sending[1] the brothers so that our boasting about you may not prove empty in this
matter, so that you may be ready, [q]as I said you
would be. 4 Otherwise, if some Macedonians
[r]come with me and find that you are not ready,
we would be humiliated—to say nothing of
you—for being so confident. 5 So I thought it
necessary to urge the brothers to go on ahead
to you and arrange in advance for the [s]gift[2]
you have promised, so that it may be ready [t]as
a willing gift, [u]not as an exaction.[3]

The Cheerful Giver

6 The point is this: [v]whoever sows sparingly
will also reap sparingly, and whoever sows
bountifully[4] will also reap bountifully. 7 Each
one must give as he has decided in his heart,
[w]not reluctantly or under compulsion, for
[x]God loves a cheerful giver. 8 And [y]God is able
to make all grace abound to you, so that having all sufficiency[5] in all things at all times,
you may abound in every good work. 9 As it
is written,

> [z]"He has distributed freely, he has given to
> the poor;
> his righteousness endures forever."

10 He who supplies [a]seed to the sower and
bread for food will supply and multiply your
seed for sowing and [b]increase the harvest of
your righteousness. 11 [c]You will be enriched in
every way to be generous in every way, which
[d]through us will produce thanksgiving to
God. 12 For the ministry of this service is not
only supplying [e]the needs of the saints but
is also overflowing in many thanksgivings
to God. 13 By their approval of this service,
[f]they[6] will glorify God because of your submission that comes from your [g]confession of
the gospel of Christ, and the generosity of
your contribution for them and for all others, 14 while they long for you and pray for
you, because of the surpassing grace of God
upon you. 15 [h]Thanks be to God for his inexpressible gift!

[1] Or *I have sent* [2] Greek *blessing*; twice in this verse [3] Or *a gift expecting something in return*; Greek *greed* [4] Greek *with blessings*; twice in this verse [5] Or *all contentment* [6] Or *you*

2 [o]ch. 8:10
3 [p]ch. 8:6, 17, 18, 22 [q]1 Cor. 16:2
4 [r][Acts 20:4]
5 [s]Gen. 33:11; Judg. 1:15; 1 Sam. 25:27 [t][Phil. 4:17] [u][ch. 12:17, 18]
6 [v]Prov. 11:24, 25; 22:9; Gal. 6:7, 9; [Mal. 3:10; Luke 6:38]
7 [w]Deut. 15:10; See ch. 8:12 [x]See Ex. 25:2
8 [y]Phil. 4:19; [Eph. 3:2]
9 [z]Cited from Ps. 112:9
10 [a]Isa. 55:10 [b][Hos. 10:12]
11 [c]1 Cor. 1:5 [d][ch. 1:11]
12 [e]ch. 8:14
13 [f]See Matt. 5:16; 1 Pet. 2:12 [g]1 Tim. 6:12, 13; Heb. 3:1; 4:14; 10:23
15 [h][John 3:16; Eph. 2:8]; See ch. 2:14

Third, external acts of grace are not to be seen as means to gain favor with God, but are to be understood as proof that the gospel is working in our lives (8:24). The honorable conduct of the messengers ensures that they are not getting in the way of the message (8:20–21).

Finally, because of the gospel, our obedience is never compulsory but is always a willing gift (9:5). Rather than giving out of obligation or compulsion, we give abundantly because God's grace is being irresistibly worked into our hearts. Grace becomes a fountain within us. We are not mercenary in our giving but are free to participate in one-way giving without expecting anything in return. This gospel logic undergirds the life of the church: the preaching of the gospel leads to changed hearts that compulsively act out the gospel as proof of God's radical generosity in Christ.

9:6–15 Paul is careful to ground his call for Christian obedience in the grace that we have been given in Christ. Obedience is an attempt to express our gratitude for the inexpressible gift that we have received (v. 15). Our abounding good works flow out of Christ's abounding grace (v. 8). The distribution of our resources flows out of his free distribution (v. 9). We supply others because he has supplied us with a multitude of blessings (v. 10). Yes, there is a sense in which all of this is submission, but it is a submission to an authority of grace—a compulsion of responsive love. It is something that is naturally flowing from our "confession of the gospel of Christ" (v. 13). The result is the production and overflowing of thanksgivings to God (vv. 11–12).

If you find yourself lacking the impulse to give to those in need, you are likely forgetting the surpassing grace that was given to you while you were in need (v. 6). If you are unable to forgive, you have lost sight of the forgiveness that is yours in Christ. A forgiving heart is a forgiven heart. If you are unable to give something up, there is lack of appreciation for all that Christ gave up on your behalf. When you identify the area where gospel growth is lacking, you are identifying the place where you are failing to believe the gospel. Ask the Holy Spirit to make Christ and the gospel real to you. This is what the Spirit delights to do.

Paul Defends His Ministry

10 [i]I, Paul, myself entreat you, by the [j]meek-
ness and gentleness of Christ—I who
am humble when face to face with you, but
bold toward you when I am away!— 2 I beg of
you [k]that when I am present I may not have
to show [l]boldness with such confidence as
I count on showing against some who suspect us of walking according to the flesh.
3 For though we walk in the flesh, we are not
waging war according to the flesh. 4 For the
[m]weapons of [n]our warfare are not of the flesh
but have [o]divine power [p]to destroy strongholds. 5 We destroy arguments and [q]every lofty
opinion raised against the knowledge of God,
and take every thought captive to [r]obey Christ,
6 [s]being ready to punish every disobedience,
[t]when your obedience is complete.

7 [u]Look at what is before your eyes. [v]If anyone
is confident that he is Christ's, let him remind
himself that just as [w]he is Christ's, [x]so also are
we. 8 For even if I boast a little too much of [y]our
authority, which the Lord gave for building
you up and not for destroying you, I will not
be ashamed. 9 I do not want to appear to be
frightening you with my letters. 10 For they
say, "His letters are weighty and strong, but
[z]his bodily presence is weak, and [a]his speech
of no account." 11 Let such a person understand
that what we say by letter when absent, we
do when present. 12 Not that we dare to clas-
sify or [b]compare ourselves with some of those
who [c]are commending themselves. But when
they measure themselves by one another and
compare themselves with one another, they
are [d]without understanding.

13 But we will not boast [e]beyond limits, but
will [f]boast only with regard to the area of
influence God assigned to us, [g]to reach even to
you. 14 For we are not overextending ourselves,
as though we did not reach you. [h]For we were
the first to come all the way to you with the
gospel of Christ. 15 We do not boast beyond
limit in the labors of others. But our hope is
that [i]as your faith increases, our area of influence among you may be [j]greatly enlarged, 16 so
that we may preach the gospel in lands beyond
you, without boasting of work already done in
another's area of influence. 17 "Let [k]the one who
boasts, boast in the Lord." 18 For it is [l]not the
one who commends himself who is approved,
but the one [m]whom the Lord commends.

Paul and the False Apostles

11 I wish you would bear with me in a little
foolishness. Do bear with me! 2 For I feel
a divine jealousy for you, since [n]I betrothed
you to one husband, [o]to present you [p]as a pure
virgin to Christ. 3 But I am afraid that [q]as the
serpent deceived Eve by his cunning, your
thoughts [r]will be led astray from a [s]sincere
and [t]pure devotion to Christ. 4 For if someone
comes and [u]proclaims another Jesus than the

Chapter 10
1 [i]See Rom. 12:1 [j]Zech. 9:9; Matt. 11:29; Phil. 2:7, 8
2 [k]ch. 13:2, 10; 1 Cor. 4:18, 21 [l]ver. 6
4 [m]ch. 6:7; [Eph. 6:11; 1 Thess. 5:8] [n]See 1 Cor. 9:7 [o]ch. 13:3, 4; See 1 Cor. 2:5 [p]Jer. 1:10
5 [q][Isa. 2:11, 12] [r]ch. 9:13; [Rom. 5:19]
6 [s]See ver. 2 [t]ch. 2:9; 7:15
7 [u][ch. 5:12; John 7:24] [v][1 Cor. 1:12; 14:37; 1 John 4:6] [w]1 Cor. 3:23 [x][ch. 11:23; 1 Cor. 9:1; Gal. 1:12]
8 [y]ch. 13:10
10 [z]ch. 11:21; [ch. 12:7] [a]See 1 Cor. 1:17
12 [b]1 Cor. 2:13 [c]ver. 18; ch. 3:1; 12:6; [Prov. 27:2] [d][Prov. 26:12]
13 [e]ver. 15 [f]See Rom. 12:3 [g][Rom. 15:20]
14 [h]1 Cor. 3:5; 4:15; 9:1
15 [i]2 Thess. 1:3 [j][Acts 5:13]
17 [k]1 Cor. 1:31; [Jer. 9:23, 24]
18 [l]See ver. 12 [m]Rom. 2:29; 1 Cor. 4:5

Chapter 11
2 [n][Hos. 2:19, 20] [o]Col. 1:22, 28 [p]Eph. 5:27; Rev. 14:4
3 [q]Gen. 3:4; 1 Tim. 2:14; [John 8:44; 1 Thess. 3:5] [r]Col. 2:4, 8 [s][Eph. 6:5] [t]ch. 6:6
4 [u][1 Cor. 3:11]

10:1–18 In the face of self-boasting false apostles (v. 12), Paul responds in a way that shows that he has been shaped by the gospel. The meekness and gentleness of Christ (cf. Matt. 11:29) causes Paul to avoid posturing and rhetorical one-upmanship (2 Cor. 10:1). His focus remains on the internal and the actual rather than on the external and apparent (vv. 3–6, 10–11). He boasts only about that which has been given to him by Christ. He views his apostolic authority and ministerial influence as gifts to be used in his service to the church (v. 8, 13–16).

All of this is possible because Paul finds the entirety of his identity in the Lord's approval and commendation (v. 18). He has no need to compare himself to others because he does not find his validation through other people's assessment of his value (v. 12).

The gospel saves us from the deadly trap of having to develop our own identity. It thereby frees us from false criticism (God has already handed down the final verdict of approval in Christ) and from foolish comparisons (we are nothing in ourselves but have received everything from Christ). A resulting fruit of the gospel is a faithful confidence that allows us to boast in the work of the Lord, but refuses to boast beyond limits (vv. 13, 17).

11:1–6 Christians understand themselves as betrothed to one husband (v. 2), awaiting the consummate marriage celebration at the bridegroom's return (Rev. 19:7–9). There is perhaps no greater illustration of gospel intimacy. God's deep and affectionate love for us moves us to worship, but it also reveals the darkness of our idolatry. Sin is adultery, as the Old Testament prophets made clear time and again. Though Paul wants to present the church as a pure virgin to Christ (2 Cor. 11:2), its people are deceived

one we proclaimed, or if you receive a different spirit from the one you received, or if you
accept [v]a different gospel from the one you
accepted, you put up with it readily enough.
5 Indeed, I consider that [w]I am not in the least
inferior to these super-apostles. 6 [x]Even if I am
unskilled in speaking, [y]I am not so in knowledge; indeed, in every way [z]we have made this
plain to you in all things.
7 Or [a]did I commit a sin in humbling
myself so that you might be exalted, because
[b]I preached God's gospel to you free of charge?
8 I robbed other churches by accepting support
from them in order to serve you. 9 And when
I was with you and was [c]in need, [d]I did not burden anyone, for the brothers who came from
Macedonia [e]supplied my need. So I refrained
and will refrain [f]from burdening you in any
way. 10 [g]As the truth of Christ is in me, this
boasting of mine [h]will not be silenced in the
regions of Achaia. 11 And why? [i]Because I do not
love you? [j]God knows I do!
12 And what I am doing I will continue to
do, [k]in order to undermine the claim of those
who would like to claim that in their boasted
mission they work on the same terms as we do.
13 For such men are [l]false apostles, [m]deceitful
workmen, [n]disguising themselves as apostles
of Christ. 14 And no wonder, for even Satan
disguises himself as [o]an angel of light. 15 So it is
no surprise if his servants, also, disguise themselves as [p]servants of righteousness. [q]Their end
will correspond to their deeds.

Paul's Sufferings as an Apostle

16 I repeat, [r]let no one think me foolish. But
even if you do, accept me as a fool, so that
I too may boast a little. 17 What I am saying

and defiled by false apostles. When God's redeemed people embrace other spirits, different gospels, and even a different Jesus (v. 4), they are committing adultery.

We ourselves commit spiritual adultery, and it's far more subtle than we think. When we fail to believe the gospel we not only suspect the truth and goodness of God; we place our faith in a different "good news." We ask something (or someone) to do what only the gospel is capable of doing.

What other "good news" do you sometimes believe? What other "husbands" captivate you? What other counterfeit hope captures your love? The key to gospel fidelity is to know that Christ's sincere and pure devotion to you is far stronger than yours to him (v. 3). When we were unacceptable and at our worst, he bound himself to us with his covenantal love. Christ's marital fidelity to his bride is on full display at the cross, and it moves his bride to an increasingly sincere and pure devotion.

11:7–15 Paul lives out the gospel, humbling himself so that others might be exalted, even as Christ did for him (v. 7). He follows Jesus' lead in loving the rebellious church, and is grieved by their disloyalty to him. Paul works on different terms than the false apostles (v. 12). While they are deceitful and disguised (v. 13), he is honest and open in his ministry (4:2).

The question is, if the Corinthians had a compelling gospel witness in the life and ministry of Paul, how were they deceived by the false apostles? The answer is, just as the cunning serpent who deceived Eve (11:3) disguises himself as an angel of light (v. 14), so the false apostles have disguised themselves as servants of righteousness. Temptations and false teachings dress in appealing clothing—they retell the prevailing cultural story. In a world where success was defined by rhetoric and pedigree, the false apostles tried to show that Paul was lacking both.

In our world—where success is defined by self-achieved wealth, power, and social capital—false gospels also tell us what we want to hear. To guard and proclaim the gospel, we must show that our culture's definition of success (i.e., money, control, and fame) lacks transformative power. The gospel claims that through the ministry of Christ in and for us poverty is wealth, weakness is power, and the interest of others is more important than my own self-interest. Christ's self-giving love leads us to live this kind of paradoxical life (cf. Phil. 2:5–11).

11:16–33 In 11:7–15, the false apostles dress up as angels of light to deceive the church. Here, Paul mockingly dresses up in the false apostles' rhetorical style to show how the church has been deceived. He is speaking as a fool to uncover the foolishness of triumphalistic boasting (v. 21). Counterintuitively, Paul commends himself by cataloging

4 [v] Gal. 1:6
5 [w] ch. 12:11; Gal. 2:6
6 [x] See 1 Cor. 1:17 [y] [Eph. 3:4] [z] ch. 4:2; 5:11; 12:12
7 [a] [ch. 12:13] [b] See Acts 18:3
9 [c] Phil. 4:12 [d] ch. 12:13, 14 [e] [1 Cor. 16:17; Phil. 4:15, 16] [f] ch. 12:16; 1 Thess. 2:6
10 [g] See Rom. 1:9; 9:1 [h] 1 Cor. 9:15
11 [i] See ch. 6:11 [j] ver. 31; ch. 12:2, 3
12 [k] [1 Cor. 9:12]
13 [l] Rev. 2:2; [Gal. 1:7; 2:4; 6:12; Phil. 1:15; 3:18; Titus 1:10, 12; 2 Pet. 2:1; 1 John 4:1] [m] [Phil. 3:2] [n] ver. 14, 15
14 [o] Gal. 1:8
15 [p] ch. 3:9 [q] Phil. 3:19
16 [r] ch. 12:6

[s]with this boastful confidence, [t]I say not as the
Lord would[1] but as a fool. 18 Since [u]many boast
according to the flesh, I too will boast. 19 For
you gladly bear with fools, [v]being wise yourselves! 20 For you bear it if someone [w]makes
slaves of you, or [x]devours you, or takes advantage of you, or puts on airs, or [y]strikes you in
the face. 21 To my shame, I must say, [z]we were
too weak for that!

But whatever anyone else dares to boast
of—I am speaking as a fool—I also dare to
boast of that. 22 Are they Hebrews? [a]So am I.
Are they Israelites? So am I. Are they offspring
of Abraham? So am I. 23 Are they [b]servants of
Christ? [c]I am a better one—I am talking like a
madman—with far greater labors, [d]far more
imprisonments, [e]with countless beatings, and
[f]often near death. 24 Five times I received at
the hands of the Jews the [g]forty lashes less
one. 25 Three times I was [h]beaten with rods.
[i]Once I was stoned. Three times I [j]was ship-
wrecked; a night and a day I was adrift at sea;
26 on frequent journeys, in danger from rivers, danger from robbers, [k]danger from my
own people, [l]danger from Gentiles, [m]danger
in the city, danger in the wilderness, danger
at sea, danger from false brothers; 27 [n]in toil
and hardship, through many a sleepless night,
[o]in hunger and thirst, often without food,[2] in
cold and exposure. 28 And, apart from other
things, there is the daily pressure on me of my
anxiety for [p]all the churches. 29 [q]Who is weak,
and I am not weak? Who is made to fall, and
I am not indignant?

30 [r]If I must boast, I will boast of the things
that show my weakness. 31 [s]The God and Father
of the Lord Jesus, [t]he who is blessed forever,
[u]knows that I am not lying. 32 At Damascus, the
governor under King Aretas [v]was guarding the
city of Damascus in order to seize me, 33 [w]but
I was let down in a basket through a window
in the wall and escaped his hands.

Paul's Visions and His Thorn

12 I must go on boasting. Though there
is nothing to be gained by it, I will go
on to visions and [x]revelations of the Lord.
2 I know a man [y]in Christ who fourteen years
ago was [z]caught up to [a]the third heaven—
whether in the body or out of the body I do
not know, [b]God knows. 3 And I know that this
man was caught up into [c]paradise—whether
in the body or out of the body I do not know,
[b]God knows— 4 and he heard things that cannot be told, which man may not utter. 5 On

[1] Greek *not according to the Lord* [2] Or *often in fasting*

17[s] ch. 9:4 [t][1 Cor. 7:12]
18[u] Phil. 3:3, 4
19[v] 1 Cor. 4:10
20[w] Gal. 2:4; [Gal. 4:3, 9; 5:1] [x][ch. 7:2] [y]1 Cor. 4:11
21[z] ch. 10:10
22[a] Rom. 11:1; Phil. 3:5
23[b] See ch. 3:6; 10:7 [c]See 1 Cor. 15:10 [d]ch. 6:5 [e]Acts 16:23 [f]ch. 1:9, 10; 4:11; 6:9; Rom. 8:36; 1 Cor. 15:30-32
24[g] Deut. 25:3
25[h] Acts 16:22 [i]Acts 14:19 [j][Acts 27:41]
26[k] Acts 9:23; 13:50; 14:5; 17:5; 1 Thess. 2:15; [Acts 18:12; 20:3, 19; 21:27; 23:10, 12; 25:3] [l]Acts 14:5; [Acts 19:23; 27:42] [m]Acts 21:31
27[n] 1 Thess. 2:9; 2 Thess. 3:8 [o]1 Cor. 4:11; Phil. 4:12
28[p] See 1 Cor. 7:17
29[q] See 1 Cor. 8:13; 9:22
30[r] ch. 10:10; 12:5, 9; See 1 Cor. 2:3
31[s] See Rom. 15:6 [t]See Rom. 9:5 [u]ver. 11
32[v] Acts 9:24
33[w] Acts 9:25
Chapter 12
1[x] Gal. 1:12; 2:2; Eph. 3:3
2[y] See ch. 5:17 [z]ver. 3; 1 Thess. 4:17; Rev. 12:5; [Ezek. 8:3; Acts 8:39] [a]See Ps. 148:4 [b]ch. 11:11
3[c] Luke 23:43; Rev. 2:7; [Gen. 2:8] [b][See ver. 2 above]

his sufferings for Christ (vv. 23–28, 32–33). He uses an ironic, upside-down paradigm to communicate the inverted, upside-down reality of the gospel of which he is a minister. As such, he is far more interested in the things that show his weakness than in his audience's definition of strength (v. 30; 10:17). For his weakness puts the power of Christ on display.

In the economy of the gospel, godly foolishness trumps worldly wisdom, and at the heart of Christian folly is the crucified Messiah (1 Cor. 1:20–23). Paul's catalog of sufferings is the greatest argument for his apostolic authority because it demonstrates his solidarity with God. Christ suffered; Paul, Christ's apostle, suffers. As we understand our own trials and sufferings in this light, we discover that, far from disqualifying us from experiencing and proclaiming the gospel, they actually qualify us for it. God uses the hardest and most shameful experiences of our lives to soften us and bring us to fuller understanding of his surpassing benefits. In our isolation from the world's provision, we learn that we are fully satisfied when he is our portion (Ps. 73:26). He uses our sufferings to demonstrate his sufficiency. And he uses our afflictions as the occasion for dispersing comfort and the deepest realities of his abiding care (2 Cor. 1:3–11).

12:1–10 Heavenly revelations and thorns in the flesh are the two extreme realities of Paul's apostolic experience (vv. 4, 7). Both have the potential to knock him off balance, but the gospel stabilizes him and provides proper perspective. While he might have become arrogant over receiving unutterable visions and revelations (vv. 1, 4), he refrains from divulging details because he doesn't want anyone to think more of him than is accurate (v. 6). Nothing, not even mysterious spiritual experiences, will muddy the waters of Paul's gospel witness.

Paul's thorn in the flesh was so painful that it could have crushed his spirit (v. 8). However, he has a gospel paradigm that assures him that when he is weak, then he

behalf of this man I will boast, but on my own
behalf I will not boast, [d]except of my weaknesses— 6 though if I should wish to boast,
[e]I would not be a fool, for I would be speaking
the truth; but I refrain from it, so that no one
may think more of me than he sees in me or
hears from me. 7 So [f]to keep me from becoming
conceited because of the surpassing greatness
of the revelations,[1] [g]a thorn was given me in
the flesh, [h]a messenger of Satan to harass me,
to keep me from becoming conceited. 8 [i]Three
times I pleaded with the Lord about this, that
it should leave me. 9 But he said to me, [j]"My
grace is sufficient for you, for [k]my power is
made perfect in weakness." Therefore I will
boast all the more gladly of my weaknesses,
so that [l]the power of Christ may rest upon me.
10 [m]For the sake of Christ, then, [n]I am content
with weaknesses, insults, hardships, persecutions, and calamities. For [o]when I am weak,
then I am strong.

Concern for the Corinthian Church

11 [p]I have been a fool! You forced me to it, for
I ought to have been commended by you. For
I was [q]not at all inferior to these super-apostles, [r]even though I am nothing. 12 [s]The signs
of a true apostle were performed among you
[t]with utmost patience, with signs and wonders and mighty works. 13 For in what were
you less favored than the rest of the churches,
except that [u]I myself did not burden you?
Forgive me this wrong!

14 Here [v]for the third time I am ready to come
to you. And I will not be a burden, for [w]I seek
not what is yours but you. For [x]children are
not obligated to save up for their parents, but
[y]parents for their children. 15 [z]I will most gladly
spend and be spent for your souls. If [a]I love
you more, am I to be loved less? 16 But granting
that [b]I myself did not burden you, I was crafty,
you say, and got the better of you by deceit.
17 Did I take advantage of you [c]through any of
those whom I sent to you? 18 [d]I urged Titus to
go, and sent [e]the brother with him. Did Titus
take advantage of you? Did we not act in the
same spirit? Did we not take the same steps?
19 Have you been thinking all along that
we have been defending ourselves to you?
It is [f]in the sight of God that we have been

[1] Or *hears from me, even because of the surpassing greatness of the revelations. So to keep me from becoming conceited*

is strong (v. 10). Nothing, not even mysterious painful experiences, will bring Paul to doubt his identity and calling in the gospel. His painful circumstances brought him to cherish the all-sufficient grace of God (v. 9a)—indeed, to *boast* in his weaknesses (v. 9b). Is this how you handle your own weaknesses? The gospel gives us a radical shift in thinking, one that is deeply liberating. For if weakness is something in which we can boast, nothing can ultimately overwhelm us.

We must also guard our hearts against both spiritual arrogance and situational sulking. Because we are defined by Christ and not by what we know or do, there should be no boasting about our theological experience or knowledge. Similarly, because Christ has already proven his unchanging love for us, our circumstances should never cause us to suspect his goodness. The gospel allows us to receive God's grace as an unmerited gift, and to understand our circumstances as opportunities for him to be proven all-sufficient and all-powerful (v. 9). When we are weak, we are strong.

12:11–21 The apostle seems nearly at the end of himself in trying to win over the Corinthians. But it is precisely at the point where Paul seems on the verge of lashing out at them that we find him overflowing in love. He makes himself a fool for the sake of those who have so quickly abandoned him (v. 11). By default, he must carry the burden that he chooses not to place on them (v. 14). Rather than ask them to cover his expenses, he is glad to spend and be spent for their souls (v. 15). He does not want to take advantage of those who have taken advantage of him (v. 17). He desires the upbuilding of the very people who have torn him down (vv. 18–19). This is nothing short of the sacrificial love of Christ working itself out in Paul's life. He is passing on to the Corinthians exactly what he has received from Jesus.

Like Paul, we are better able to see the paradoxes of the gospel when we have nothing to which we can cling. We are comforted in affliction, made strong through weakness, and become more concerned with the actual than with the apparent. When the gospel is at work in our hearts, we can respond to conflict with a sacrificial heart that seeks to carry the burdens of the burdened and build up those who have sought to demolish us.

5 [d]See 1 Cor. 2:3
6 [e]ch. 5:13; 11:16, 17; [ver. 11]
7 [f][ch. 10:10] [g][Num. 33:55; Ezek. 28:24] [h][Luke 13:16]; See 1 Cor. 5:5
8 [i][Matt. 26:44]
9 [j]Isa. 43:2 [k]Isa. 40:29-31; [Phil. 4:13] [l]See 1 Cor. 2:5
10 [m][ch. 5:15]; See Matt. 5:11, 12 [n]Rom. 5:3 [o][ch. 13:4]
11 [p][ver. 6] [q]See ch. 11:5; 1 Cor. 15:10 [r]See 1 Cor. 3:7; 15:9
12 [s]See Rom. 15:19; 1 Cor. 9:1 [t]ch. 6:4
13 [u]1 Cor. 9:12; See Acts 20:33
14 [v]ch. 13:1; [ch. 1:15; 13:2] [w]1 Cor. 10:24, 33 [x]1 Cor. 4:14, 15 [y][Prov. 19:14; Ezek. 34:2]
15 [z][ch. 1:6; Phil. 2:17; Col. 1:24; 1 Thess. 2:8; 2 Tim. 2:10] [a]See ch. 6:11
16 [b]ch. 11:9
17 [c][ch. 9:5]
18 [d]ch. 8:6 [e]ch. 8:18
19 [f]See Rom. 1:9; 9:1

speaking in Christ, and [g]all for your upbuilding, beloved. 20 For I fear that perhaps [h]when
I come I may find you not as I wish, and that
you may find me not as you wish—that perhaps there may be quarreling, jealousy, anger,
hostility, slander, gossip, conceit, and disorder. 21 I fear that when I come again my God
may humble me before you, and I may have
to mourn over many of those [i]who sinned earlier and have not repented of the impurity,
[j]sexual immorality, and sensuality that they
have practiced.

Final Warnings

13 [k]This is the third time I am coming to
you. Every charge must be established
[l]by the evidence of two or three witnesses.
2 [m]I warned [n]those who sinned before and all
the others, and I warn them now while absent,
as I did when present on my second visit, that
[o]if I come again I will not spare them— 3 since
you seek proof that Christ [p]is speaking in me.
He is not weak in dealing with you, but [q]is
powerful among you. 4 For [r]he was crucified
in weakness, but [s]lives by the power of God.
For [t]we also are weak in him, but in dealing
with you [u]we will live with him by the power
of God.

5 Examine yourselves, to see whether you
are in the faith. [v]Test yourselves. Or do you
not realize this about yourselves, that [w]Jesus
Christ is in you?—unless indeed you fail to
meet the test! 6 I hope you will find out that we
have not failed the test. 7 But we pray to God
that you may not do wrong—not that we may
appear to have met the test, but that you may
do what is right, though we may seem to have
failed. 8 For we cannot do anything against the
truth, but only for the truth. 9 For we are glad
when [x]we are weak and you are strong. Your
[y]restoration is what we pray for. 10 For this reason I write these things while I am away from
you, that when I come [z]I may not have to be
[a]severe in my use of [b]the authority that the
Lord has given me for building up and not
for tearing down.

Final Greetings

11 Finally, brothers,[1] rejoice. [c]Aim for restoration, comfort one another,[2] [d]agree with one
another, [e]live in peace; and the God of love and
[f]peace will be with you. 12 [g]Greet one another
with a holy kiss. 13 [h]All the saints greet you.
14 [i]The grace of the Lord Jesus Christ and [j]the
love of God and [k]the fellowship of the Holy
Spirit be with you all.

[1] Or *brothers and sisters* [2] Or *listen to my appeal*

19 [g]See 1 Cor. 14:26
20 [h][ch. 2:1-4]; See 1 Cor. 4:21
21 [i]ch. 13:2; [Rev. 2:21] [j]1 Cor. 5:1; See 1 Cor. 6:18
Chapter 13
1 [k]See ch. 12:14 [l]Cited from Deut. 19:15; See Num. 35:30
2 [m]ch. 10:2 [n]ch. 12:21 [o]ver. 10; See 1 Cor. 4:21
3 [p]See Matt. 10:20; 1 Cor. 5:4 [q]ch. 10:4
4 [r][Phil. 2:7, 8; 1 Pet. 3:18] [s]See Rom. 1:4; 6:4 [t][ch. 12:10] [u]See Rom. 6:8
5 [v][1 Cor. 11:28; Gal. 6:4] [w]Rom. 8:10; Gal. 4:19
9 [x]1 Cor. 4:10; [ch. 4:12; 12:5, 9, 10] [y]Eph. 4:12; 1 Thess. 3:10; [ver. 11]
10 [z][ch. 2:3] [a]Titus 1:13 [b]ch. 10:8
11 [c]See Luke 6:40 [d]See Rom. 12:16 [e]See Mark 9:50 [f]See Rom. 15:33
12 [g]See Rom. 16:16
13 [h]Phil. 4:22
14 [i]Rom. 16:20 [j]Jude 21 [k]Phil. 2:1

13:1–14 The apostle lovingly and sternly addresses the Corinthians' sin as he concludes his epistle (vv. 1–4). Because he is weak, a weakness into which the crucified Christ entered, he is confident to address sin with the power of the resurrected Christ (v. 4). Gospel-love never overlooks sin, but lovingly confronts it for the restoration of the erring brother (vv. 9–10; 12:19). Furthermore, gospel-love does not address sin for the sake of keeping up appearances but in order to be in accord with the truth (13:7–8).

Because we are prone to sin, it is our responsibility regularly to examine ourselves for evidence that the gospel is working itself out in our lives (v. 5). Am I experiencing and sharing the comfort of Christ in affliction (1:3–11)? Is the forgiveness I have experienced leading me to forgive others (2:1–11)? Are the permanent promises of God more important to me than momentary afflictions (4:7–18)? Are my affections for other Christians restricted by my sin (6:1–13)? Am I eager to give sacrificially in response to Christ's becoming poor for my sake (8:1–15)? Does the "one husband" who gave his life for me hold preeminence over all other suitors (11:1–6)? To the extent that we see the fruit of the gospel in our lives, we ought to rejoice (13:11). When we spot sin in our hearts, it is to a self-sacrificing God of love and peace that we can freely run (v. 11). For Christ was crucified for us (v. 4). This is the heart of the gospel, and the note on which Paul concludes his letter.

Introduction to Galatians

Author, Date, and Recipients

The apostle Paul wrote this letter in the late 40s A.D. The Galatians were probably members of the churches of the southern region of the Roman province of Galatia. Paul is more critical of his audience here than in any of his other letters, because they are allowing false teachers to obscure the gospel itself.

The Gospel in Galatians

Grace permeates Galatians. The letter is about protecting the truth of the gospel, which declares what God has done in Christ for sinners. The gospel cannot be supplemented by human effort or obedience. If human obedience is "dialed in" to any degree, salvation is impossible. Rescue from sin must be all of grace. And this is what God has done in Jesus.

Paul wrote the letter to a group of Christians whom false teachers had infiltrated. Among these newly established congregations, the false teachers (or "Judaizers") were teaching "a different gospel" (1:6) that required Gentiles to adopt Jewish works of the law in order to be justified before God. Paul reminds these congregations of the sufficiency of the gospel he preached among them. Any attempt to add to the gospel by human effort becomes a denial of grace and renders Christ's death pointless (2:21).

The Christian life from beginning to end is the result of God's grace and is empowered by the work of the Holy Spirit. We begin by grace and move on by grace (3:1–5). The supreme demonstration of God's provision for sinful humanity is seen in the death and resurrection of Jesus. When people try to *cooperate* with God for their salvation, with works of the law being "their part" and the cross being "God's part," the cross is emptied of its significance. There is nothing a Christian can do to add to what Christ has done to rescue us from the eternal consequences of sin, and any effort to supplement his saving work demonstrates a lack of understanding of the gospel. Human effort will not transform the heart of the sinner. Such internal transformation through the work of the Holy Spirit results in a new life conforming to Christ's character. The Spirit is given by God to indwell and enable the Christian to reflect more closely the moral character of our Savior (5:22–23).

Galatians is a declaration of freedom from the condemnation of sin and from a performance mind-set. Looking to Christ, the culmination of all the promises of the Old Testament, sinners can be freely counted righteous in him. Perhaps nowhere in the Bible is this clearer than in Paul's letter to the Galatians.

Outline

I. Opening (1:1–10)

II. Indirect Appeal: Paul's Ministry and the Gospel (1:11–2:21)

III. Direct Appeals to the Galatians (3:1–5:15)

IV. Life in the Spirit and Love (5:16–6:10)

V. Final Warning (6:11–18)

The Letter of Paul to the

Galatians

Greeting

1 Paul, an [a]apostle—[b]not from men nor
through man, but [c]through Jesus Christ
and God the Father, [d]who raised him from
the dead— 2 and all [e]the brothers[1] who are
with me,

To [f]the churches of Galatia:

3 [g]Grace to you and peace [h]from God our
Father and the Lord Jesus Christ, 4 [i]who gave
himself for our sins to deliver us from the
present [j]evil age, according to the will of [k]our
God and Father, 5 to whom be the glory forever
and ever. Amen.

No Other Gospel

6 I am astonished that you are [l]so quickly
deserting [m]him who called you in the grace of
Christ and are turning to [n]a different gospel—
7 [o]not that there is another one, but [p]there are
some who trouble you and want to distort the
gospel of Christ. 8 But even if we or [q]an angel
from heaven should preach to you a gospel
contrary to the one we preached to you, [r]let
him be accursed. 9 As we have said before, so
now I say again: If anyone is preaching to you
a gospel contrary to the one you received, [r]let
him be accursed.

[1] Or *brothers and sisters*. The plural Greek word *adelphoi* (translated "brothers") refers to siblings in a family. In New Testament usage, depending on the context, *adelphoi* may refer either to men or to both men and women who are siblings (brothers and sisters) in God's family, the church; also verse 11

1:1–5 Paul begins the letter by asserting his apostolic authority. False teachers were undermining Paul's authority by claiming that he was self-appointed, lacking the endorsement of the Jerusalem apostles. Paul refutes this charge by pointing out that his appointment is from the risen Lord Jesus (v. 1).

The introduction to Galatians does not include the normal Pauline prayer of thanksgiving. This omission may point to the severity of the issues in Galatia. Paul does, however, pray that God will bestow grace and peace upon his readers (v. 3). This is because of Jesus' crucifixion, through which peace is established with God as we are "delivered from the present evil age" and transferred into the dawning new age (v. 4; cf. Col. 1:13–14; 2 Cor. 5:17). This succinct statement of the gospel, centering on Christ's gracious self-giving on the cross, is explained more fully as the letter proceeds.

1:6–10 Paul passes to the major theme of the letter as he expresses astonishment that the Galatians are deserting the gospel. While Paul can begin with thanksgiving when he writes to the Corinthians despite the radical dysfunction in that church (1 Cor. 1:4–9), Paul views a loss of the pure grace of the gospel to be a more radical problem than what Corinth was dealing with. Though the Galatians would seem far more outwardly impressive and mature than the Corinthians, their spiritual peril was in fact far greater; hence Paul's scathing opening words in Galatians 1:6 and following.

God has called the Galatians in grace (v. 6), but they are distorting the gospel of grace (v. 7) by placing works as a requirement for salvation upon Gentile converts. This distortion is outlined in the remainder of the letter (5:2–6; 6:12–13; cf. 2:3–5), and Paul's condemnation of those who taught this is unambiguous (1:8). False teaching can take root in anyone, as is seen in Paul's rebuke of Peter and Barnabas (2:11–14). The truth of the gospel is not determined by the identity of the one who preaches but by the content of the message. Paul's desire is to please God, not people, even if, as a servant of Christ (1:10), faithfulness results in many hardships (5:11; 6:17).

Paul touches on something very profound for fallen humans when he speaks of "seeking the approval of man" (1:10). This need for approval is deeply wired into us. Yet

Chapter 1
1 [a]See 2 Cor. 1:1 [b]ver. 11, 12 [c]Acts 9:6; 20:24; 22:10, 15, 21; 26:16; [1 Tim. 1:1; Titus 1:3] [d]See Acts 2:24
2 [e]Phil. 4:21 [f]Acts 16:6; 1 Cor. 16:1
3 [g]Rom. 1:7; 1 Cor. 1:3 [h]1 Tim. 1:2
4 [i]See Matt. 20:28; Rom. 4:25; 1 Cor. 15:3 [j][Eph. 2:2; 1 John 5:19]; See John 15:19 [k]Phil. 4:20; 1 Thess. 1:3; 3:11, 13
6 [l][ch. 4:13; Acts 16:6; 18:23] [m]ch. 5:8 [n]2 Cor. 11:4; [1 Tim. 1:3]
7 [o][Acts 4:12; 1 Cor. 3:11] [p]ch. 5:10; Acts 15:24; See 2 Cor. 11:13
8 [q]2 Cor. 11:14 [r]See Rom. 9:3
9 [r][See ver. 8 above]

10 For am I now seeking the approval of man,
or of God? Or am I trying [s]to please man? If
I were still trying to please man, I would not
be a [t]servant[1] of Christ.

Paul Called by God

11 For [u]I would have you know, brothers, that
[v]the gospel that was preached by me is not
man's gospel.[2] 12 [w]For I did not receive it from
any man, nor was I taught it, but I received it
[x]through a revelation of Jesus Christ. 13 For you
have heard of [y]my former life in Judaism, how
[z]I persecuted the church of God violently and
tried to destroy it. 14 And I was advancing in
Judaism beyond many of my own age among
my people, so extremely [a]zealous was I for [b]the
traditions of my fathers. 15 But when he [c]who
had set me apart [d]before I was born,[3] and who
[e]called me by his grace, 16 was pleased to reveal
his Son to[4] me, in order [f]that I might preach
him among the Gentiles, I did not immediately consult with anyone;[5] 17 nor did I go up
to Jerusalem to those who were apostles before
me, but I went away into Arabia, and returned
again to Damascus.

18 Then [g]after three years I went up to Jerusalem to visit Cephas and remained with him
fifteen days. 19 But I saw none of the other
apostles except James [h]the Lord's brother.
20 (In what I am writing to you, [i]before God,
I do not lie!) 21 [j]Then I went into the regions
of Syria and Cilicia. 22 And I was still unknown
in person to [k]the churches of Judea that are in
Christ. 23 They only were hearing it said, "He
who used to persecute us is now preaching
the faith he once tried to destroy." 24 And they
glorified God because of me.

Paul Accepted by the Apostles

2 Then after fourteen years I went up again
to Jerusalem with Barnabas, taking Titus
along with me. 2 I went up because of a revelation and set before them (though privately
before those [l]who seemed influential) the

[1] Or *slave*; Greek *bondservant* [2] Greek *not according to man* [3] Greek *set me apart from my mother's womb* [4] Greek *in* [5] Greek *with flesh and blood*

10 [s]1 Thess. 2:4; [Rom. 2:29; 1 Cor. 10:33; Eph. 6:6; Col. 3:22] [t][Rom. 1:1]
11 [u]1 Cor. 15:1 [v]See Rom. 2:16
12 [w]ver. 1; 1 Cor. 11:23; 15:3; [Acts 22:14] [x]ver. 16; See 1 Cor. 2:10; 2 Cor. 12:1
13 [y][Acts 26:4] [z]See Acts 8:3
14 [a]Phil. 3:6; See Acts 21:20 [b][Jer. 9:14; 2 Tim. 1:3]; See Matt. 15:2
15 [c]Acts 13:2; Rom. 1:1 [d]Isa. 49:1, 5; Jer. 1:5; Luke 1:15 [e]ver. 6
16 [f]ch. 2:9; See Acts 9:15
18 [g][Acts 9:22, 23]
19 [h]See Matt. 12:46; Acts 12:17
20 [i]See Rom. 1:9; 9:1
21 [j][Acts 9:30; 11:25, 26; 13:1]
22 [k]1 Thess. 2:14
Chapter 2
2 [l]ver. 6, 9

the gospel has the power to calm the quest for human approval, for in the gospel we are freely given the full and free approval of God in Jesus. We are accepted and approved.

1:11–17 Paul insists that the gospel he proclaims is of divine origin; he received it on the Damascus Road (Acts 9:1–7), where he received a revelation of Jesus Christ. Subsequent to this, Paul did not meet with the Jerusalem apostles but went into Arabia (Gal. 1:17), east of the Jordan River. Prior to his encounter with Jesus, Paul, a Pharisee (Acts 26:5; Phil. 3:5), educated under Gamaliel (Acts 22:3), was zealous for the traditions of Judaism. This zeal led him to persecute the church, seeking to destroy it (Gal. 1:13). After Jesus revealed himself to Paul (vv. 15–16), Paul understood that the gospel is the fulfillment of Jewish law (4:4, 5; Rom. 10:4), and he was transformed from a church persecutor to a church planter. He was commissioned to declare this gospel of grace to the Gentiles, a task for which God had set him apart prior to his birth (Gal. 1:15).

Paul's pre-Christian zeal was not only insufficient; it blocked the way for him to see the need for Christ. Like many of his lost fellow Jews, who zealously sought to establish their own moral righteousness (Rom. 10:2–3), Paul had formerly been zealous "for the traditions of my fathers" (Gal. 1:14). What disrupted this, he says, was being called by *grace* (v. 15). Moral zeal is necessary (Titus 2:14) but is dangerous to the Christian life if pursued in human strength alone and for personal distinction (Gal. 1:14; Phil. 3:6; Rom. 10:2).

1:18–24 Paul presents the case that he is independent from the Jerusalem apostles (cf. vv. 1, 17). He did not meet Cephas (Peter) until three years after the Damascus Road encounter, and then only for two weeks. When he did meet Peter, it did not result in a new gospel in which the Gentiles needed to submit to the practices of the Jewish law. Paul proceeds to describe his itinerary through Syria and Cilicia (v. 21), which matches Acts 9:30 (Tarsus is in Cilicia). This is again a reference to his independence from the Jerusalem apostles.

Despite Paul's incredible experience of "a revelation of Jesus Christ" (Gal. 1:12), the event did not lead him to spiritual arrogance but rather the experience magnified God: "they glorified God because of me" (v. 24). This is what grace does. It glorifies the Giver.

gospel that [m]I proclaim among the Gentiles,
[n]in order to make sure I was not running or
had not [o]run in vain. 3 But even Titus, who was
with me, [p]was not forced to be circumcised,
though he was a Greek. 4 [q]Yet because of false
brothers secretly brought in—who [r]slipped
in to spy out [s]our freedom that we have in
Christ Jesus, [t]so that they might bring us into
slavery— 5 to them we did not yield in submission even for a moment, so that [u]the truth of
the gospel might be preserved for you. 6 And
from those [v]who seemed to be influential
(what they were makes no difference to me;
[w]God shows no partiality)—those, I say, who
seemed influential [x]added nothing to me. 7 On
the contrary, when they saw that I had been
[y]entrusted with [z]the gospel to the uncircumcised, just as Peter had been entrusted with the
gospel to the circumcised 8 (for he who worked
through Peter for his apostolic ministry to
the circumcised worked also through me for
mine to the Gentiles), 9 and when James and
Cephas and John, [v]who seemed to be [a]pillars,
perceived the [b]grace that was given to me, they
[c]gave the right hand of fellowship to Barnabas
and me, that we should go to the Gentiles and
they to the circumcised. 10 Only, they asked us
to remember the poor, [d]the very thing I was
eager to do.

Paul Opposes Peter

11 But [e]when Cephas came to Antioch, I
opposed him [f]to his face, because he stood condemned. 12 For before certain men came from
James, [g]he was eating with the Gentiles; but
when they came he drew back and separated
himself, fearing [h]the circumcision party.[1] 13 And
the rest of the Jews acted hypocritically along
with him, so that even Barnabas was led astray
by their hypocrisy. 14 But when I saw that their
[i]conduct was not in step with [j]the truth of the
gospel, I said to Cephas [k]before them all, "If

[1] Or *fearing those of the circumcision*

2:1–10 Paul returned to Jerusalem after 14 years, accompanied by Titus and Barnabas. This return to Jerusalem is recounted in Acts 11:27–30. During this visit Paul presented the gospel he proclaimed to the "pillars" of the Jerusalem church—James, Cephas (Peter), and John (Gal. 2:2, 9)—who accepted both Paul and his message. This affirmation of a gospel apart from observance of Jewish works of the law is seen as Titus (v. 3), an uncircumcised Greek, was not required to be circumcised. Paul's opponents taught that Gentiles needed to become Jews in order to become part of the people of God (v. 4). The juxtaposition of the freedom of the gospel and the slavery of the law becomes a major theme of Galatians (4:1, 7, 22–26, 31; 5:1, 13).

The Jerusalem apostles gave Paul the "right hand of fellowship" (2:9), not to establish his authority but to endorse his ministry in recognition of the grace he had received for his work among the Gentiles, just as Peter had been entrusted with gospel ministry to the Jews (vv. 7–8).

2:11–14 Paul furthers his argument of his independence from the Jerusalem apostles by relating how he had rebuked Peter, one of the "pillars" of the church (v. 9). When Peter arrived in Antioch he gladly ate with Gentiles, as had been his practice since he had received a vision prior to his visit with Cornelius (Acts 10:9–16) in which he had been told that all foods are clean (cf. Mark 7:14–19). Peter's subsequent withdrawal from table fellowship with Gentiles was a tacit but unmistakable denial of the truth of the gospel (Gal. 2:14), in which dietary laws have been fulfilled and are therefore not required for Christian fellowship. Peter's snub, which had the effect of forcing Gentiles to live like Jews with respect to food laws (v. 14), was akin to the false teachers forcing Gentiles to be circumcised (vv. 3–4). Consequently, Paul rebuked Peter as a hypocrite (v. 13). Later references in the New Testament to the relationship between Paul and Peter (e.g., 1 Cor. 1:12; 3:22; 9:5; 15:5; 2 Pet. 3:15) imply that Peter heeded Paul's rebuke.

Note that in his rebuke of Peter—a Christian—Paul invoked the gospel. Peter's racist ways were not fundamentally a failure to follow a particular rule but a failure to walk "in step with the truth of the gospel" (Gal. 2:14). For Paul, the gospel is not only something for Christians to pass on to non-Christians; it is also the daily bread for Christians themselves to feed on (cf. 3:3). Peter evidently had forgotten that he had already been justified by grace, and was seeking to be "justified" (cf. 2:15–16) by human approval—the very thing Paul had determined not to do (1:10), and from which the grace of God's eternal approval in Christ saves us.

2 [m]1 Tim. 3:16 [n]ch. 4:11; 1 Thess. 3:5 [o]Phil. 2:16
3 [p][Acts 16:3]
4 [q]Acts 15:24; 2 Cor. 11:26; [ch. 5:12] [r][2 Pet. 2:1; Jude 4] [s]See ch. 5:1 [t]ch. 4:3, 9, 24, 25; 2 Cor. 11:20; [Rom. 8:15]
5 [u]ver. 14; [ch. 4:16; 5:7; Titus 1:14; 2 John 1]
6 [v]ver. 2, 9; [ch. 6:3; Acts 5:36]; See 1 Cor. 3:7 [w]See Deut. 10:17 [x][2 Cor. 11:5; 12:11]
7 [y]1 Thess. 2:4; 1 Tim. 1:11; See 1 Cor. 9:17 [z]ch. 1:16; See Acts 9:15
9 [v][See ver. 6 above] [a]Jer. 1:18; Rev. 3:12 [b]See Rom. 1:5 [c][2 Pet. 3:15]
10 [d]See Acts 24:17
11 [e][Acts 15:1, 35] [f]Job 21:31
12 [g]Acts 11:3; [ver. 14; Acts 10:28]; See Luke 15:2 [h]See Acts 11:2
14 [i]Heb. 12:13 [j]See ver. 5 [k]1 Tim. 5:20

you, though a Jew, [l]live like a Gentile and not like a Jew, how can you force the Gentiles to live like Jews?"

Justified by Faith

15 We ourselves are Jews by birth and not [m]Gentile sinners; 16 yet we know that [n]a person is not justified[1] by works of the law [o]but through faith in Jesus Christ, so we also have believed in Christ Jesus, in order to be justified by faith in Christ and not by works of the law, [p]because by works of the law no one will be justified.

17 But if, in our endeavor to be justified in Christ, we too were found [q]to be sinners, is Christ then a servant of sin? Certainly not! 18 For if I rebuild what I tore down, I prove myself to be a transgressor. 19 For through the law I [r]died to the law, so that I might [s]live to God. 20 I have been [t]crucified with Christ. It is no longer I who live, but Christ who lives [u]in me. And the life I now live in the flesh I live by faith in the Son of God, [v]who loved me and [w]gave himself for me. 21 I do not nullify the grace of God, for [x]if righteousness[2] were through the law, [y]then Christ died for no purpose.

By Faith, or by Works of the Law?

3 O foolish Galatians! Who has bewitched you? [z]It was before your eyes that Jesus Christ was publicly [a]portrayed as crucified.

[1] Or *counted righteous* (three times in verse 16); also verse 17 [2] Or *justification*

14[l] See ver. 12
15[m] ver. 17; [Eph. 2:3, 12]
16[n] ch. 3:11; See Acts 13:39 [o] See Rom. 9:30 [p] Rom. 3:20; [Ps. 143:2]
17[q] ver. 15
19[r] See Rom. 6:2; 7:4 [s] Luke 20:38; Rom. 6:11; 14:7, 8; 2 Cor. 5:15; 1 Thess. 5:10; Heb. 9:14; 1 Pet. 4:2
20[t] ch. 5:24; 6:14; Rom. 6:6 [u] See John 17:23 [v] See Rom. 8:37 [w] See ch. 1:4
21[x] [ch. 3:21; Heb. 7:11] [y] [ch. 5:4]
Chapter 3
1[z] [Num. 21:9] [a] [1 Cor. 1:23]

2:15–21 Justification by faith apart from works of the law applies to Jews as well as to Gentiles (vv. 15–16). By justification, Paul means the acquittal of a guilty person before God's judgment seat. Because of Christ's death and resurrection in the middle of history, not only can Christians know that there is no present condemnation from God (Rom. 8:1); they also can look at the cross and see their final judgment—at the end of history—already carried out on Christ in their place. The expression "works of the law" (Gal. 2:16; 3:2, 5, 10; Rom. 3:20, 28) does not refer to any inherent defect in the law itself, which is "holy and righteous and good" (Rom. 7:12). Rather, these works are God's holy requirements, which we sinners cannot adequately meet (cf. Gal. 3:10–11). The problem is not the law but us.

By faith, believers are justified through the completed work of Jesus Christ. He kept the law that could not be kept even by those to whom it was given (2:15–16); he was faithful to his Father, was crucified, and then was raised to redeem people from the curse of the law (1:4; 3:1; 4:4–5). Jesus was born under the law (4:4) and kept it perfectly, and he died to redeem those who had transgressed it. Believers are united with Christ by faith (2:16, 20). As a consequence, we have been crucified with him and our past sinful identity is nailed to the cross with him at the same time that he indwells us with his resurrected life (v. 20). Thus, by faith, we are united both to the death and the life of Christ—free from our past sin by union with his death, and free to live for him by union with his life. The false teachers were nullifying God's love graciously provided in this union by seeking to supplement Christ's death and resurrection (v. 21) with works of the law.

3:1–5 The Galatians are in danger of making the same mistake of reverting to Jewish rites as Peter did in Antioch (2:11–14). False teachers were teaching that circumcision and adherence to the works of the law were necessary for membership in the people of God. Within Judaism, many Gentile God-fearers attended the synagogue but were not circumcised, probably due to the pain and medical risks associated with the operation. These people were seen as non-Jews, and the false teachers now applied the same principle to Gentile Christians.

Paul and Barnabas had taught the message of the crucifixion on their first missionary journey, and the Galatians had responded by "hearing with faith" (3:2, 5). This response resulted both in suffering (v. 4), which may have come from synagogues (cf. Acts 14:22), and in the gift of the Spirit, whose presence had resulted in miracles (Gal. 3:5). This mention of the Spirit shows that Paul is referring not just to membership in the local church but to acceptance before God (cf. Rom. 5:5; 8:9; 1 Cor. 2:14). If God has accepted people by faith alone, apart from circumcision, so too must the local church.

Faith is what fuels the Christian life. We "receive the Spirit" not "by works of the law" but rather "by hearing with faith" (Gal. 3:2)—and it is this faith that then not only begins but continues the Christian life (v. 3).

2 Let me ask you only this: [b]Did you receive
the Spirit by works of the law or by [c]hearing
with faith? 3 Are you so foolish? [d]Having begun
by the Spirit, are you now being perfected by[1]
the flesh? 4 [e]Did you suffer[2] so many things in
vain—if indeed it was in vain? 5 Does he who
supplies the Spirit to you and [f]works miracles among you do so [g]by works of the law,
or by hearing with faith— 6 just as [h]Abraham
"believed God, and it was counted to him as
righteousness"?

7 Know then that it is [i]those of faith who are
[j]the sons of Abraham. 8 And the Scripture, foreseeing that [k]God would justify[3] the Gentiles
by faith, preached the gospel beforehand to
Abraham, saying, [l]"In you shall all the nations
be blessed." 9 So then, those who are of faith are
blessed along with Abraham, the man of faith.

The Righteous Shall Live by Faith

10 For all who rely on works of the law are
[m]under a curse; for it is written, [n]"Cursed be
everyone who does not [o]abide by all things
written in the Book of the Law, and do them."
11 Now it is evident that [p]no one is justified
before God by the law, for [q]"The righteous
shall live by faith."[4] 12 But the law is not of
faith, rather [r]"The one who does them shall
live by them." 13 Christ [s]redeemed us from the
curse of the law by becoming a curse for us—
for it is written, [t]"Cursed is everyone who is
hanged [u]on a tree"— 14 so that in Christ Jesus
the blessing of Abraham might [v]come to the
Gentiles, so that [w]we might receive [x]the promised Spirit[5] through faith.

The Law and the Promise

15 [y]To give a human example, brothers:[6] [z]even
with a man-made covenant, no one annuls it
or adds to it once it has been ratified. 16 Now
[a]the promises were made [b]to Abraham and
to his offspring. It does not say, "And to off-
springs," referring to many, but referring to
one, [c]"And to your offspring," who is Christ.
17 This is what I mean: the law, which came
[d]430 years afterward, does not annul a cov-

[1] Or *now ending with* [2] Or *experience* [3] Or *count righteous*; also verses 11, 24 [4] Or *The one who by faith is righteous will live* [5] Greek *receive the promise of the Spirit* [6] Or *brothers and sisters*

3:6–9 Paul cites Genesis 15:6 in Galatians 3:6 as an example of Abraham being counted as righteous through faith. As Abraham was not circumcised until Genesis 17:24, this declaration is doubly significant: the physical ritual did not determine his spiritual status. Faith is the conduit by which grace flows to Abraham. This faith is mentioned three times in Galatians 3:8–9 as the sole determiner of present membership in God's covenant.

Furthermore, Paul alludes to Genesis 12:3 as an expression of God's intention from the beginning to bless the Gentiles who believe as Abraham did (Gal. 3:8–9). Old Testament believers looked forward on the basis of the work of the promised Messiah; New Testament believers look back to the death and resurrection of Jesus. Each are included by faith in the promises of God's covenant with Abraham.

3:10–14 Paul cites several Old Testament passages to show that believing Gentiles receive the blessing of Abraham in Christ. Deuteronomy 27:26 shows the universality of the curse for disobedience to the law. As people fail to live by the works of the law, they do not find life in the law but curse. Paul then cites Habakkuk 2:4 to show that the righteous will live by faith, and this faith is now directed toward the One who took the curse of the law through crucifixion.

Paul had previously persecuted the church because he could not conceive of a cursed Messiah (Deut. 21:23); the cross was a stumbling block to the Jews (1 Cor. 1:23). Through this curse of crucifixion Christ took on himself—even though he did not deserve it—the curse for disobedience (Gal. 3:13). He substituted his life for ours, ensuring that life, righteousness, and the Spirit would be received by all who believe in him.

3:15–25 The false teachers appear to be elevating the Mosaic law above the Abrahamic promise. Paul asserts that the Christians' inheritance comes by promise, not by the law (v. 18). The Abrahamic promise looks at what God will do; the Mosaic laws look at human response. The promise concerns Abraham's "offspring" (singular) in whom all the nations of the earth would be blessed (v. 8). All who are united to the offspring, Jesus the Messiah, are heirs of Abraham through faith—whether Jew or Gentile, slave or free, male or female (v. 28).

But if the law was subsequent to the Abrahamic promise, and if law does not lead to life, what was its purpose? It served particular purposes for a limited time.

2 [b] ver. 14; Eph. 1:13; Heb. 6:4; See Acts 15:8 [c] Rom. 10:17
3 [d] Phil. 1:6; [ch. 4:9]
4 [e] 1 Cor. 15:2; [Heb. 10:35; 2 John 8]
5 [f] [1 Cor. 12:10] [g] ver. 2
6 [h] Cited from Gen. 15:6; [Rom. 4:9, 21, 22]; See Rom. 4:3
7 [i] ver. 9 [j] See Luke 19:9
8 [k] See Rom. 3:30 [l] Cited from Gen. 12:3
10 [m] [ch. 5:4]; See Rom. 4:15 [n] Cited from Deut. 27:26; [Jer. 11:3; Ezek. 18:4] [o] [Matt. 5:19]
11 [p] See ch. 2:16 [q] Rom. 1:17; Heb. 10:38; Cited from Hab. 2:4
12 [r] Cited from Lev. 18:5; See Rom. 10:5
13 [s] ch. 4:5; [Rev. 22:3]; See 2 Pet. 2:1 [t] Cited from Deut. 21:23 [u] See Acts 5:30
14 [v] Rom. 4:9, 16; [ver. 28] [w] ver. 2 [x] Acts 2:33; [Isa. 32:15; 44:3; Joel 2:28; John 7:39; Eph. 1:13]
15 [y] See Rom. 3:5 [z] [Heb. 9:17]
16 [a] Rom. 4:13, 16; See Luke 1:55 [b] Gen. 12:7; Acts 13:32 [c] Acts 3:25
17 [d] Ex. 12:40, 41; [Gen. 15:13; Acts 7:6]

enant previously ratified by God, so as [e]to
make the promise void. 18 For if the inheritance
comes by the law, it no longer comes by promise; but [f]God gave it to Abraham by a promise.
19 Why then the law? [g]It was added because
of transgressions, [h]until the offspring should
come to whom the promise had been made,
and it was [i]put in place through angels [j]by an
intermediary. 20 Now [k]an intermediary implies
more than one, but [l]God is one.
21 Is the law then contrary to the promises
of God? Certainly not! For [m]if a law had been
given that could give life, then righteousness would indeed be by the law. 22 But the
Scripture [n]imprisoned everything under sin,
so that [o]the promise by faith in Jesus Christ
might be given [p]to those who believe.
23 Now before faith came, we were held captive under the law, [q]imprisoned until the coming faith would be revealed. 24 So then, [r]the law
was our [s]guardian until Christ came, [t]in order
that we might be justified by faith. 25 But now
that faith has come, we are no longer under
a guardian, 26 for in Christ Jesus [u]you are all
sons of God, through faith. 27 For as many
of you as [v]were baptized [w]into Christ have
[x]put on Christ. 28 [y]There is neither Jew nor
Greek, there is neither slave[1] nor free, [z]there
is no male and female, for you are all one in
Christ Jesus. 29 And [a]if you are Christ's, then
you are Abraham's offspring, [b]heirs according
to promise.

Sons and Heirs

4 I mean that the heir, as long as he is a child,
is no different from a slave,[2] though he
is the owner of everything, 2 but he is under
guardians and managers until the date set by

[1] Greek *bondservant* [2] Greek *bondservant*; also verse 7

17[e] Rom. 4:14
18[f] [Heb. 6:13, 14]
19[g] [Rom. 4:15] [h] ver. 16 [i] Acts 7:53; Heb. 2:2 [j] Ex. 20:19, 21, 22; Deut. 5:5, 22, 23, 27, 31; Acts 7:38
20[k] 1 Tim. 2:5; Heb. 8:6; 9:15; 12:24; [Heb. 6:17] [l] Rom. 3:30
21[m] See ch. 2:21
22[n] Rom. 11:32; See Rom. 3:9 [o] Rom. 4:16 [p] See Acts 10:43
23[q] [1 Pet. 1:5]
24[r] [Matt. 5:17; Rom. 10:4; Col. 2:17; Heb. 9:9, 10] [s] 1 Cor. 4:15 (Gk.) [t] ver. 11; See ch. 2:16
26[u] ch. 4:5, 6; [John 1:12]; See Rom. 8:14-16
27[v] Rom. 6:3 [w] See Acts 8:16 [x] See Rom. 13:14
28[y] [ver. 14; ch. 5:6; 6:15]; See Rom. 3:30; 1 Cor. 12:13 [z] 1 Cor. 11:11
29[a] See Rom. 9:7; 1 Cor. 3:23 [b] ch. 4:1, 7; Rom. 8:17; Eph. 3:6; [ch. 4:28; 2 Tim. 1:1; Titus 1:2; Heb. 9:15]

One purpose was to "imprison" God's people in the reality of their inability and sin, so that they would yearn for freedom by faith (vv. 22–23). The second purpose was to provide a "guardian" for God's people; i.e., one who would guard and guide the children of God in righteousness until they reached maturity. The image is of a guard who accompanies school children. Israel certainly needed guarding and guiding in its centuries-long journey toward rightly honoring God. But both a prison and a guardian are only required or desired for a limited time. Paul wants the Galatians to understand that the requirements of the law that imprisoned past generations in guilt and guided them away from self-trust were also leading them to faith in Christ. Faith in Jesus would not eliminate the moral requirements of the law, but would grant freedom from its condemnation and give hope of new life to those who had become aware of their inability to keep its holy standards.

3:26–29 Paul's references to being "in Christ Jesus" in verses 26 and 28 serve as bookends surrounding those identified in between: those who have been baptized into Christ (v. 27). Baptized Christians are incorporated into a community in which each member has put on a kind of clothing that covers differences that normally divide people, such as gender, ethnicity, and social status. On the basis of faith, by which anyone can be united to Christ, all Christians are included regardless of such apparent differences.

Paul neither directly condones nor condemns slavery, a common social institution of his day, but in the short book of Philemon he sets another trajectory for the Christian community as he encourages Philemon to receive back the runaway slave Onesimus and regard him not as a slave but as a brother (Philem. 16). Further, while Paul does not encourage people to deny their gender or ethnicity, he does encourage them to take their primary identity from being in Christ. So even though differences remain, unity and spiritual equality are respected and upheld. All who belong to Christ through faith are Abraham's true offspring and heirs of the promise of grace (Gal. 3:29). Roles and responsibilities may vary on earth, but value in heaven does not—and we should regard each other from this heavenly point of view (2 Cor. 5:16).

4:1–7 Paul returns to the metaphor of Israel being a child under a guardian (cf. 3:24–25). A son, though an heir, is no different than a slave in terms of his dependence on guardians. This slavery is seen by Israel being "under the law" (4:5) and, through their sinful disobedience to this law (3:22), being under a curse (3:10) and therefore needing a guardian (3:25). In the fullness of time (4:4), God redeemed his people (v. 5), gave them his Spirit, and adopted them as sons, enabling them to call

his father. 3 In the same way we also, when we
were children, [c]were enslaved to the elementary principles[1] of the world. 4 But [d]when the
fullness of time had come, God sent forth his
Son, [e]born [f]of woman, born [g]under the law,
5 [h]to redeem those who were under the law,
so that we might receive [i]adoption as sons.
6 And because you are sons, God has sent [j]the
Spirit of his Son into our hearts, crying, "Abba!
Father!" 7 So you are no longer a slave, but a
son, and if a son, then [k]an heir through God.

Paul's Concern for the Galatians

8 Formerly, when you [l]did not know God,
you [m]were enslaved to those that by nature
[n]are not gods. 9 But now that you have come
to know God, or rather [o]to be known by God,
[p]how can you turn back again to [q]the weak
and worthless elementary principles of the
world, whose slaves you want to be once more?
10 [r]You observe days and months and seasons
and years! 11 I am afraid [s]I may have labored
over you in vain.
12 Brothers,[2] [t]I entreat you, become as I am,
for I also have become as you are. [u]You did
me no wrong. 13 You know it was [v]because of
a bodily ailment that I preached the gospel to
you [w]at first, 14 and though my condition was
a trial to you, you did not scorn or despise me,
but received me [x]as an angel of God, [y]as Christ
Jesus. 15 What then has become of your blessedness? For I testify to you that, if possible, you
would have gouged out your eyes and given
them to me. 16 Have I then become your enemy
by [z]telling you the truth?[3] 17 They make much
of you, but for no good purpose. They want
to shut you out, that you may make much of
them. 18 It is always good to be made much of
for a good purpose, and [a]not only when I am
present with you, 19 [b]my little children, [c]for
whom I am again in the anguish of childbirth
until Christ [d]is formed in you! 20 I wish I could

[1] Or *elemental spirits*; also verse 9 [2] Or *Brothers and sisters*; also verses 28, 31 [3] Or *by dealing truthfully with you*

him "Abba! Father!" (v. 6). These gifts of God's grace (redemption, adoption, and the gift of the Spirit) are for all the offspring of Abraham, meaning all those who are in Christ (3:28, 29), whether Jew or Gentile.

Reflecting on these truths, our hearts cannot sit still. We are moved with wonder as we consider the great lengths to which God has gone to comfort his people. He has sent forth both his Son and his Spirit—the Son objectively to rescue us eternally from the penalty of sin, and the Spirit subjectively to apply that rescue to our attitudes and actions in daily life. The work of the Son is "outside in," an alien righteousness; the work of the Spirit is "inside out," an experience in which we cry out, "Abba! Father!"

4:8–11 Prior to God taking the initiative to make himself known to the Galatians, they had been enslaved to idols (vv. 8–9). The reference to days and months and seasons (v. 10) indicates that the Galatians had worshiped fertility gods connected to the movements of the sun and the moon. But Paul is not suggesting that the Galatians were now turning back to these idols; rather, they were turning to a *new* slavery expressed in Jewish annual feasts such as Passover and Booths, as well as new moon festivals and weekly Sabbaths.

It is hard to see why the Galatians would be attracted by slavery except that the perversity of the fallen human heart wants to do something itself to contribute to being justified before God. We have here in these verses not only a window into the Galatians' thinking but also a mirror into our own heart, for we too are strongly inclined to contribute something toward our justification. The scandalous freedom of the gospel rejects all such self-generated contribution. Christ has accomplished everything.

4:12–20 Paul mentions that he had first preached the gospel in Galatia because of a bodily ailment (v. 13), the exact nature of which we are not told. Paul frequently sees his suffering as God's means for the spread of the gospel (2 Cor. 1:3–11; 2:14–15; 4:7–12; 11:23–29; 13:4; Col. 1:24–29). The apostle's ministry among the Galatians was a great blessing (Gal. 4:15), but now they are turning away from the gospel to embrace the works of the law (3:2). They are thus putting themselves at odds with the gospel of grace (4:16).

Paul uses the metaphor of childbirth (v. 19) to emphasize that, having been born again by hearing the gospel of grace (cf. 1 Pet. 1:3), the Galatians are to continue in grace, walking by the Spirit (Gal. 5:16). Paul is writing this letter to them so that they

Chapter 4
3 [c]See ch. 2:4
4 [d][1 Tim. 2:6]; See Mark 1:15 [e]Phil. 2:7; See John 1:14 [f][1 Tim. 2:15]; See Gen. 3:15 [g][Luke 2:21, 22, 27]
5 [h]See ch. 3:13 [i]ch. 3:26; See Rom. 8:15
6 [j][Rom. 5:5; 2 Cor. 3:17]; See Acts 16:7
7 [k]See ch. 3:29
8 [l]1 Cor. 1:21; 1 Thess. 4:5; 2 Thess. 1:8; 1 John 4:8 [m][Eph. 2:11, 12; 1 Thess. 1:9] [n]2 Chr. 13:9; Isa. 37:19; Jer. 2:11; 5:7; 16:20; [1 Cor. 8:4]
9 [o]See 1 Cor. 8:3 [p][ch. 3:3] [q]Rom. 8:3; Heb. 7:18
10 [r]Rom. 14:5; Col. 2:16
11 [s]ch. 2:2; 5:2, 4; 1 Thess. 3:5
12 [t][2 Cor. 6:13] [u][2 Cor. 2:5]
13 [v]See 1 Cor. 2:3 [w][ch. 1:6]
14 [x]1 Sam. 29:9; [Mal. 2:7 (Gk.); 2 Cor. 5:20] [y]See Matt. 10:40
16 [z]See ch. 2:5
18 [a][ver. 13]
19 [b][1 Cor. 4:15; Philem. 10] [c][James 1:18] [d]Rom. 8:10

be present with you now and change my tone,
for I am perplexed about you.

Example of Hagar and Sarah

21 Tell me, you who desire to be under the
law, do you not listen to the law? 22 For it is
written that Abraham had two sons, [e]one by a
slave woman and [f]one by a free woman. 23 But
[g]the son of the slave was born according to
the flesh, while [h]the son of the free woman
was born through promise. 24 Now this may be
interpreted allegorically: these women are two
[i]covenants. [j]One is from Mount Sinai, bearing children for slavery; she is Hagar. 25 Now
Hagar is Mount Sinai in Arabia;[1] she corresponds to the present Jerusalem, for she is in
slavery with her children. 26 But [k]the Jerusalem
above is free, and she is our mother. 27 For it
is written,

[l]"Rejoice, O barren one who does not bear;
break forth and cry aloud, you who
are not in labor!
For the children of the desolate one will
be more
than those of the one who has a husband."

28 Now you,[2] brothers, [m]like Isaac, [n]are children
of promise. 29 But just as at that time he who
was born according to the flesh [o]persecuted
him who was born according to the Spirit, [p]so
also it is now. 30 But what does the Scripture
say? [q]"Cast out the slave woman and her son,
for the son of the slave woman shall not
inherit with the son of the free woman." 31 So,
brothers, we are not children of the slave but
[r]of the free woman.

Christ Has Set Us Free

5 For [s]freedom Christ has [t]set us free; [u]stand
firm therefore, and do not submit again to
[v]a yoke of [w]slavery.
2 Look: I, Paul, say to you that [x]if you accept
circumcision, [y]Christ will be of no advantage
to you. 3 I testify again to every man who
accepts circumcision that [z]he is obligated to
keep the whole law. 4 You are [a]severed from
Christ, [b]you who would be justified[3] by the
law; [c]you have fallen away from grace. 5 For
through the Spirit, by faith, we ourselves
eagerly [d]wait for the hope of righteousness.
6 For in Christ Jesus [e]neither circumcision nor
uncircumcision counts for anything, but [f]only
faith working through love.
7 [g]You were running well. Who hindered you
from obeying [h]the truth? 8 This persuasion is
not from [i]him who calls you. 9 [j]A little leaven

[1] Some manuscripts *For Sinai is a mountain in Arabia* [2] Some manuscripts *we* [3] Or *counted righteous*

22[e] Gen. 16:5 [f] Gen. 21:2
23[g] ver. 29; [Rom. 9:7] [h] ver. 28; Gen. 17:16-19; 18:10, 14; 21:1, 2; Heb. 11:11
24[i] See Rom. 9:4 [j] Deut. 33:2
26[k] [Heb. 12:22; Rev. 3:12; 21:2, 10]
27[l] Cited from Isa. 54:1
28[m] See ver. 23 [n] Rom. 9:8; See ch. 3:29
29[o] Gen. 21:9 [p] See ch. 5:11
30[q] Cited from Gen. 21:10; [John 8:35]
31[r] [1 Pet. 3:6]
Chapter 5
1[s] ver. 13; ch. 2:4; See James 1:25 [t] See John 8:32 [u] See 1 Cor. 16:13 [v] Acts 15:10 [w] See ch. 2:4
2[x] ver. 3, 11; Acts 15:1; 1 Cor. 7:18 [y] See ch. 4:11
3[z] Rom. 2:25
4[a] Rom. 7:6 (Gk.) [b] [ch. 2:21; 3:10; Rom. 9:31, 32] [c] [Heb. 12:15; 2 Pet. 3:17]
5[d] See Rom. 8:23, 25
6[e] ch. 6:15; 1 Cor. 7:19; Col. 3:11; See ch. 3:28 [f] [Eph. 6:23; 1 Thess. 1:3; James 2:18, 20, 22]
7[g] See 1 Cor. 9:24 [h] See ch. 2:5
8[i] ch. 1:6
9[j] 1 Cor. 5:6; [1 Cor. 15:33; Heb. 12:15]

will rediscover grace and not be lured by the flattery of those who are enticing them (v. 17) to believe that they can mature spiritually through more self-distinguishing observances of the law.

4:21–31 Paul compares slavery and freedom through the story of Hagar and Sarah and their respective sons, Ishmael and Isaac. The false teachers believed they were descendants of Isaac, but Paul identifies them as children of Hagar through Ishmael and thus in slavery. By contrast, Paul identifies himself with those who are of the line of Sarah, "our mother" (v. 26). Sarah's conceiving of Isaac is associated with the promise of God; the Galatian believers are children of that promise.

There is a further comparison between the present Jerusalem (v. 25), enslaved by the law, and the "Jerusalem above," which will bear more children among the Gentiles (v. 26). Paul concludes by quoting Sarah's words to Abraham, when she urged him to cast out the slave woman who was her rival (Gen. 21:10). The harsh words indicate the seriousness of Paul's concern for the Galatian Christians to cast out those who were advocating works of the law to strengthen their status before God.

5:1–6 This is the first time in the letter that the issue of circumcision is dealt with directly. Paul's point is clear: if someone requires one part of the law—circumcision—such a person is obligated to do all the works of the law (cf. James 2:10). The response to those who are seeking to be justified before God by the works of the law is the reminder that "faith working through love" is the manifestation of a life that knows it is saved by grace alone (Gal. 5:6). This is the first mention of love in the letter, and it now becomes a major theme (vv. 13–14, 22; cf. Rom. 13:8–10).

5:7–15 There appears to be a leader of these false teachers who is described as one who will bear the penalty (v. 10) for his actions, although the nature of the penalty is

leavens the whole lump. 10 [k]I have confidence
in the Lord that you will [l]take no other view,
and [m]the one who is troubling you will bear
the penalty, whoever he is. 11 But if I, brothers,[1]
still preach[2] circumcision, [n]why am I still being
persecuted? In that case [o]the offense of the
cross has been removed. 12 I wish [p]those who
unsettle you would emasculate themselves!

13 For you were called to freedom, brothers.
[q]Only do not use your freedom as an opportunity for the flesh, but through love [r]serve
one another. 14 For [s]the whole law is fulfilled
in one word: [t]"You shall love your neighbor
as yourself." 15 But if you [u]bite and devour one
another, watch out that you are not consumed
by one another.

Keep in Step with the Spirit

16 But I say, [v]walk by the Spirit, and you will
not gratify [w]the desires of the flesh. 17 For [x]the
desires of the flesh are against the Spirit, and
the desires of the Spirit are against the flesh,
for these are opposed to each other, [y]to keep
you from doing the things you want to do.
18 But if you are [z]led by the Spirit, [a]you are
not under the law. 19 Now [b]the works of the
flesh are evident: sexual immorality, impurity,
sensuality, 20 idolatry, sorcery, enmity, strife,
jealousy, fits of anger, rivalries, dissensions,
[c]divisions, 21 envy,[3] drunkenness, orgies, and
things like these. I warn you, as I warned you
before, that [d]those who do such things will
not inherit the kingdom of God. 22 But [e]the
fruit of the Spirit is [f]love, joy, peace, patience,
[g]kindness, goodness, faithfulness, 23 [h]gentle-
ness, [i]self-control; [j]against such things there
is no law. 24 And those who belong to Christ
Jesus [k]have crucified the flesh with its [l]pas-
sions and desires.

25 If we live by the Spirit, [m]let us also keep
in step with the Spirit. 26 [n]Let us not become
conceited, provoking one another, envying
one another.

[1] Or *brothers and sisters*; also verse 13 [2] Greek *proclaim* [3] Some manuscripts add *murder*

10 [k] See 2 Cor. 2:3 [l] [Phil. 3:15] [m] ch. 1:7; [ver. 12]
11 [n] ch. 4:29; 6:12 [o] 1 Cor. 1:23; See 1 Pet. 2:8
12 [p] [ver. 10]; See ch. 2:4
13 [q] 1 Pet. 2:16; Jude 4; [1 Cor. 8:9; 2 Pet. 2:19] [r] 1 Cor. 9:19
14 [s] [Matt. 7:12; 22:40] [t] Cited from Lev. 19:18; [ver. 22; ch. 6:2]; See Matt. 19:19; John 13:34
15 [u] [Phil. 3:2]
16 [v] ver. 24, 25; Rom. 8:4; See Rom. 13:14 [w] Eph. 2:3
17 [x] Rom. 7:23; 8:5-7 [y] Rom. 7:15, 18, 19
18 [z] Rom. 8:14 [a] See Rom. 7:4
19 [b] 1 Cor. 3:3; Eph. 5:3; Col. 3:5; James 3:14, 15; [Matt. 15:18-20]
20 [c] 1 Cor. 11:19
21 [d] [Col. 3:6]; See 1 Cor. 6:9
22 [e] [Rom. 7:4; 8:5; Eph. 5:9] [f] See Rom. 5:1-5; Col. 3:12-17 [g] 2 Cor. 6:6
23 [h] Eph. 4:2 [i] Acts 24:25 [j] 1 Tim. 1:9
24 [k] [ver. 16]; See Rom. 6:6 [l] Rom. 7:5
25 [m] [ver. 16]
26 [n] Phil. 2:3

not specified. Paul expresses confidence that the Galatians will return to gospel truth (v. 10): they will realize that justification by faith brings freedom, while the works of the law bring slavery.

Obedience is the fruit of faith (Rom. 10:16; 15:18; 1 Thess. 1:3); it is not the same as faith, nor is it a required addition to faith. Human effort cannot be added to grace; to attempt to do this brings Paul's sharpest condemnation (Gal. 5:12). The true gospel, when received with the empty hands of faith, makes us "obedient from the heart" (Rom. 6:17).

The freedom brought about by the gospel is not a license to sin but an opportunity for love and service. A true understanding of faith, working through love, is the antidote to self-oriented behavior, and results in service (Gal. 5:13). This service does not merit anything but is the outworking of faith.

5:16–26 Paul has mentioned the work of the Spirit several times in this letter (3:2, 3, 5, 14; 4:6, 29; 5:5, 16, 17, 18, 22, 25; 6:8) and he now exhorts the Galatians to walk "by the Spirit" (5:25). Unlike the requirements of the Mosaic law that were written on stone, God writes the requirements of the covenant of grace on the hearts of his people (Jer. 31:33) through the activity of the Spirit (Ezek. 36:26–27), transforming them to live according to God's requirements of loving regard for his name and for his people. The moral requirements do not vary, but the motivation to obey and the power to obey are entirely different. Now we live the life of love ("keep in step with the Spirit"; see Gal. 5:25) as we are guided by the character and care of God as reflected in his law. We do this to please our Redeemer rather than to distinguish ourselves, striving to please him in the power of his might rather than in the strength of our own resolve or resources.

The works of the flesh are evident (v. 19), for they do not prioritize others above self and God above all. Those who practice these works show that they have not encountered the transforming work of the Spirit. Paul has already taught that the Christian life begins when one receives the Spirit through hearing with faith (3:2; 4:6). The Spirit exercises a transforming work of grace in the life of the person who walks by the Spirit (5:25). This life produces fruit consistent with the character of the Spirit. Notice that Paul speaks of "fruit," not "fruits," of the Spirit—the fruit of the Spirit is not a checklist to work through but the unified blossoming of a heart liberated by the gospel of grace.

Bear One Another's Burdens

6 Brothers,[1] [o]if anyone is caught in any transgression, [p]you who are spiritual should
restore him in [q]a spirit of gentleness. Keep
watch on yourself, lest you too be tempted.
2 [r]Bear one another's burdens, and [s]so fulfill
[t]the law of Christ. 3 For [u]if anyone thinks he is
something, [v]when he is nothing, he deceives
himself. 4 But let each one [w]test his own work,
and then his reason to boast will be in himself
alone and not in his neighbor. 5 For [x]each will
have to bear his own load.

6 [y]Let the one who is taught the word share
all good things with the one who teaches.
7 [z]Do not be deceived: God is not mocked, for
[a]whatever one sows, that will he also reap. 8 For
[b]the one who sows to his own flesh [c]will from
the flesh reap corruption, but [d]the one who
sows to the Spirit will from the Spirit reap
eternal life. 9 And [e]let us not grow weary of
doing good, for in due season we will reap,
[f]if we do not give up. 10 So then, [g]as we have
opportunity, let us [h]do good to everyone, and
especially to those who are [i]of the household
of faith.

Final Warning and Benediction

11 See with what large letters I am writing
to you [j]with my own hand. 12 [k]It is those who
want to make a good showing in the flesh [l]who
would force you to be circumcised, and only
[m]in order that they may not be persecuted for
the cross of Christ. 13 For even those who are
circumcised do not themselves keep the law,
but they desire to have you circumcised that
they may boast in your flesh. 14 But far be it
from me to boast [n]except in the cross of our
Lord Jesus Christ, by which[2] the world [o]has
been crucified to me, and I to the world. 15 For
[p]neither circumcision counts for anything, nor
uncircumcision, but [q]a new creation. 16 And as
for all who walk by this rule, [r]peace and mercy
be upon them, and upon [s]the Israel of God.

17 From now on let no one cause me trouble,
for I bear on my body the marks of Jesus.

18 [t]The grace of our Lord Jesus Christ be [u]with
your spirit, brothers. Amen.

[1] Or *Brothers and sisters*; also verse 18 [2] Or *through whom*

Chapter 6
1 [o][Ps. 141:5; 2 Cor. 2:7; Heb. 12:13; James 5:19] [p][Rom. 15:1; 1 Cor. 10:15]; See 1 Cor. 2:15 [q]1 Cor. 4:21; [2 Tim. 2:25]
2 [r]Rom. 15:1; 1 Thess. 5:14 [s][ch. 5:14] [t]1 John 4:21; See John 13:34
3 [u][ch. 2:6]; See 1 Cor. 3:7, 18 [v]2 Cor. 12:11
4 [w][1 Cor. 11:28; 2 Cor. 13:5]
5 [x][Rom. 14:12]
6 [y][Rom. 15:27; 1 Cor. 9:11]
7 [z]1 Cor. 6:9; 15:33; James 1:16 [a]See 2 Cor. 9:6
8 [b][Hos. 8:7]; See Job 4:8 [c]See Rom. 6:21 [d]See James 3:18
9 [e]2 Thess. 3:13; [1 Cor. 15:58] [f]Heb. 12:3, 5; [Heb. 10:36]; See Matt. 10:22
10 [g]Prov. 3:27; John 9:4; 12:35 [h]Eph. 4:28; 1 Tim. 6:18; [1 Thess. 5:15] [i][Eph. 2:19; 1 Tim. 5:8; Heb. 3:6]
11 [j]See 1 Cor. 16:21
12 [k]See 2 Cor. 11:13 [l]ch. 2:3 [m]ch. 5:11
14 [n]1 Cor. 2:2; [Phil. 3:3, 7, 8] [o]See Rom. 6:6
15 [p][Rom. 2:28]; See ch. 5:6 [q][John 3:5, 7]; See Rom. 6:4
16 [r]Ps. 125:5; 128:6 [s]ch. 3:7, 9, 29; Rom. 2:29; 4:12; 9:6-8; Phil. 3:3
18 [t]Philem. 25; See Rom. 16:20 [u]2 Tim. 4:22

6:1–5 Paul's letter began with rebuke (1:6; 3:1) and with justification of his apostolic authority (1:1, 11–24); it now adopts a more familial tone as Paul addresses the Galatians as "brothers" (6:1).

The injunction to watch one's own life is prominent in this section. The fulfillment of the law is seen in the expression of love as fruit of a transformed life empowered by the Spirit. Grace does not negate the need for moral character; it empowers it. Evidence of this work of grace in the life of the Christian will be seen in bearing each other's burdens (v. 2) and in a true assessment of one's own life (vv. 3–4).

6:6–10 The warmth of Paul's relationship with the Galatians is seen as he instructs them to support their teachers, a theme repeated elsewhere in the apostle's writings (1 Cor. 9:14; 1 Tim. 5:17–18). The importance of teaching is underscored in Paul's agricultural illustration: that which is sown affects what is reaped. In Galatia, false teaching has impacted the churches (Gal. 5:7–9), but correct teaching enabled by the Spirit produces life (6:8) and good works (vv. 9–10). A true understanding of grace working through faith will result in good works.

6:11–18 Paul concludes Galatians by addressing a key issue of the letter: circumcision. Those who require circumcision are motivated by a desire to avoid persecution by appeasing Judaizers. Paul plays on the word "flesh" (v. 13), which refers both to the skin removed in circumcision and the "works of the flesh" as outlined in 5:19–21. The enforcement of circumcision is a denial of the gospel.

Paul concludes with the most appropriate word: grace (6:18). This is the message of Galatians for guilty sinners.

Introduction to Ephesians

Author, Date, and Recipients

The apostle Paul wrote this letter to the churches in Ephesus and the surrounding region c. A.D. 62 while imprisoned in Rome (Acts 28). During this time he also wrote Colossians and Philemon.

The Gospel in Ephesians

The book of Ephesians is full of gospel from start to finish. In fact, there may be no other book in all the Bible that packs in as much gospel per square inch. The first half of the book is almost nothing but gospel explanation, while the second half is almost entirely gospel application—mind-boggling indicatives followed by grace-filled (and grace-motivated) imperatives.

The good news of the first three chapters centers on the word "blessing," specifically all the blessings we have by virtue of union with Christ (1:3). We were chosen in him (1:4). We were adopted in him (1:5). We have redemption in him (1:7). We have our inheritance in him (1:11). And in Christ, God is bringing the entire universe to its fulfillment (1:10). Paul goes on to explain that in Christ, God is exercising his mighty power for us who believe (1:19). In him, we who were dead in trespasses have been made alive (2:4–5). In him we have been created for good works (2:10). In him we who were far away have been brought near (2:13). In him, long-time enemies can come together in peace (2:14). In him we are being built together into a dwelling place for God (2:22).

All of this is ours in Christ Jesus, which is why Paul prays twice that we may know Christ more and more (1:15–19; 3:14–21). In him, we find a love that is wide and long and high and deep (3:18), a love that will surprise, and a love that surpasses knowledge (3:19–20).

The glorious gospel in the first half of the book does not fade to the background in the second half. Instead, we see that the good news of chapters 1–3 makes possible, natural, and desirable the good commands of chapters 4–6. Therefore, as God's beloved ones, we put off falsehood, unrighteous anger, stealing, unwholesome talk, and bitterness. We put on truth-telling, righteous anger, hard work, edifying conversation, and compassion (4:17–32). Out of love for Christ, wives submit to their husbands (5:22), children honor their parents (6:1), and bondservants obey their masters (6:5). Husbands lay down their lives for their wives (5:25), fathers instruct their children in the Lord (6:4), and masters deal kindly with their servants (6:9). Taking our stand on the love of Christ, we stand our ground against the Devil and resist the schemes of the Evil One (6:10–18). In Christ we have become holy, and in Christ we can grow in holiness.

The message of Ephesians is that when we embrace the love of Christ, we will also embrace the way of life that Christ loves.

Outline

I. Introduction (1:1–14)

II. Paul's Prayer of Thanksgiving (1:15–23)

III. Salvation by Grace through Faith (2:1–10)

IV. Unity and the Peace of Christ (2:11–22)

V. Revelation of the Gospel Mystery (3:1–13)

VI. Paul's Prayer for Strength and Insight (3:14–21)

VII. Unity of the Body of Christ (4:1–16)

VIII. Paul's Testimony (4:17–24)

IX. Encouragement for a Holy Lifestyle (4:25–5:2)

X. New Life in Love (5:3–21)

XI. Submission to One Another (5:22–6:9)

XII. The Whole Armor of God (6:10–20)

XIII. Conclusion (6:21–24)

The Letter of Paul to the

Ephesians

Greeting

1 Paul, [a]an apostle of Christ Jesus [b]by the
will of God,
To the saints who are in Ephesus, and [c]are
faithful[1] in Christ Jesus:
2 [d]Grace to you and peace from God our
Father and the Lord Jesus Christ.

Spiritual Blessings in Christ

3 [e]Blessed be [f]the God and Father of our Lord
Jesus Christ, who has blessed us in Christ
with every spiritual blessing [g]in the heavenly
places, 4 [h]even as he [i]chose us in him [j]before
the foundation of the world, that we should
be [k]holy and blameless before him. In love 5 [l]he
predestined us[2] for [m]adoption as sons through
Jesus Christ, [n]according to the purpose of his
will, 6 [o]to the praise of his glorious grace, with
which he has blessed us in [p]the Beloved. 7 [q]In
him we have [r]redemption [s]through his blood,
[t]the forgiveness of our trespasses, [u]according
to the riches of his grace, 8 which he lavished
upon us, in all wisdom and insight 9 [v]making
known[3] to us the mystery of his will, [n]according
to his purpose, which he [w]set forth in
Christ 10 as a plan for [x]the fullness of time, [y]to
unite all things in him, things in heaven and
things on earth.
11 In him we have obtained [z]an inheritance,
[a]having been predestined [b]according to the

[1] Some manuscripts *saints who are also faithful* (omitting *in Ephesus*) [2] Or *before him in love, having predestined us* [3] Or *he lavished upon us in all wisdom and insight, making known . . .*

1:1–2 Paul uses two words to describe the Christians in Ephesus: saints and faithful. Every Christian is both. The word "saint" means holy ones. We have been sanctified, or set apart, unto God. We are saints because of what Christ did for us. He made us clean and makes us holy. In verse 1, the word "faithful" does not mean "dependable" as much as "full of faith in Jesus Christ." A Christian is a person made holy by God (a saint) and a person who trusts in Christ (faithful).

1:3–10 There may be no more glorious topic sentence in all the Bible than the one beginning this paragraph. Paul uses three prepositions to describe our great blessing. God has blessed us *in* the heavenly places *with* every spiritual blessing *in* Christ. Because we belong to Christ, we reside where he resides (heaven) and we receive what he deserves (unending blessing). All this is possible because of our union with Christ.

Paul uses the language of "in Christ" or "in him" or "in the Lord Jesus" roughly 40 times in Ephesians. The whole of our salvation can be summed up with reference to this reality. Union with Christ is not a single specific blessing we receive in our salvation. Rather it is the best phrase to describe *all* the blessings of salvation. We have unconditional election in Christ (v. 4), adoption in Christ (v. 5), redemption and forgiveness in Christ (v. 7), and the fulfillment of God's plan in Christ (v. 9), until the final uniting of all things in Christ (v. 10).

Our entire blessedness—our victory, our happiness, our hope—is bound up in our being bound to Christ. How foolish, and ultimately disappointed, are those who stoop to drink from any other fountain.

1:11–13 No eye has seen, no ear has heard, and no heart can possibly imagine all that God has stored up for those who love him (1 Cor. 2:9). Though this promise is for the next life, our inheritance was guaranteed before any of us had life. The elect were predestined for this privilege (Eph. 1:11) before the foundation of the world (v. 4), before we had done anything good or bad (Rom. 9:11). We can be confident of finally

Chapter 1
1 [a]See 2 Cor. 1:1 [b]See 1 Cor. 1:1 [c]Col. 1:2
2 [d]See Rom. 1:7
3 [e]2 Cor. 1:3; 1 Pet. 1:3 [f]See Rom. 15:6 [g]ver. 20; ch. 2:6; 3:10; 6:12
4 [h][ch. 2:10; 2 Thess. 2:13; 1 Pet. 1:2] [i]James 2:5; [Deut. 7:6; 26:18] [j][2 Tim. 1:9]; See Matt. 13:35 [k]ch. 5:27; Col. 1:22; 1 Thess. 4:7
5 [l]ver. 11; Rom. 8:29, 30 [m]See Rom. 8:15 [n]ver. 9; [Luke 2:14; Heb. 2:4]; See Luke 12:32
6 [o]ver. 12, 14 [p][John 3:35; 10:17; Col. 1:13]; See Matt. 3:17
7 [q]Col. 1:14 [r]Rom. 3:24; 1 Cor. 1:30; [ch. 4:30] [s]See Acts 20:28 [t]See Acts 2:38 [u][ch. 3:8, 16; Col. 1:27]; See Rom. 2:4
9 [v]See Rom. 16:25 [n][See ver. 5 above] [w][ver. 11; Rom. 8:28; 9:11]
10 [x]See Mark 1:15 [y]Col. 1:16, 20; [ch. 3:15; Phil. 2:9, 10]
11 [z]Deut. 4:20; 32:9; See ver. 14 [a]ver. 5 [b]ch. 3:11; [Rev. 4:11]; See Rom. 8:28

purpose of him who works all things according to [c]the counsel of his will, 12 so that we who
were the first to hope in Christ might be [d]to the
praise of his glory. 13 In him you also, when you
heard [e]the word of truth, the gospel of your
salvation, and believed in him, [f]were sealed
with the [g]promised Holy Spirit, 14 who is [h]the
guarantee[1] of our [i]inheritance until [j]we acquire
[k]possession of it,[2] [l]to the praise of his glory.

Thanksgiving and Prayer

15 For this reason, [m]because I have heard of
your faith in the Lord Jesus and your love[3]
toward all the saints, 16 I [n]do not cease to give
thanks for you, [o]remembering you in my
prayers, 17 that [p]the God of our Lord Jesus
Christ, the Father of glory, [q]may give you
the Spirit of wisdom and of revelation in the
knowledge of him, 18 [r]having the eyes of your
hearts enlightened, that you may know what
is [s]the hope to which he has called you, what
are [t]the riches of his glorious inheritance in
the saints, 19 and what is the immeasurable
greatness of his power toward us who believe,
[u]according to the working of [v]his great might
20 that he worked in Christ [w]when he raised
him from the dead and [x]seated him at his
right hand [y]in the heavenly places, 21 [z]far above
[a]all rule and authority and power and dominion, and above [b]every name that is named,
not only in [c]this age but also in the one to
come. 22 And [d]he put all things under his feet
and gave him as [e]head over all things to the
church, 23 [f]which is his body, [g]the fullness of
him [h]who fills [i]all in all.

[1] Or *down payment* [2] Or *until God redeems his possession* [3] Some manuscripts omit *your love*

11 [c][Acts 20:27]
12 [d]ver. 6, 14; [Phil. 1:11]
13 [e]2 Cor. 6:7; Col. 1:5; 2 Tim. 2:15; [Acts 13:26; 15:7] [f]ch. 4:30 [g]See Acts 1:4
14 [h]2 Cor. 1:22 [i]Acts 20:32; [ver. 18] [j]Titus 2:14; See ver. 7 [k]See 1 Pet. 2:9 [l]ver. 6, 12
15 [m]Col. 1:4; Philem. 5; See Rom. 1:8
16 [n]Col. 1:9 [o]Rom. 1:9; 2 Tim. 1:3
17 [p]See Rom. 15:6 [q][Col. 1:9]
18 [r][Heb. 6:4; 10:32; Rev. 3:17, 18]; See Acts 26:18 [s]ch. 4:4; [ch. 2:12] [t]ch. 3:8, 16; Col. 1:27; See ver. 7
19 [u]ch. 3:7; Phil. 3:21; Col. 1:29; 2:12 [v]ch. 6:10; [Dan. 4:30]
20 [w]See Acts 2:24 [x]See Mark 16:19; Acts 2:33; 1 Pet. 3:22 [y]See ver. 3
21 [z]ch. 4:10; Col. 2:10; See John 3:31 [a]1 Cor. 15:24 [b]ch. 3:15; Phil. 2:9; [Heb. 1:4] [c][Matt. 12:32]
22 [d]Cited from Ps. 8:6; See 1 Cor. 15:27 [e]ch. 4:15; 5:23; Col. 1:18; 2:19; [1 Cor. 11:3; Col. 2:10]
23 [f]ch. 4:12, 16; 5:30; Col. 1:18, 24; [ch. 5:23; 1 Cor. 12:27] [g]ch. 3:19; See John 1:16 [h]ch. 4:10 [i][Jer. 23:24; Col. 3:11]

receiving this inheritance because the One who planned it accomplishes whatever he purposes (Eph. 1:11; cf. Isa. 46:9–10).

We can also be confident because of the sealing of the Holy Spirit (Eph. 1:13). Just like our signature on the dotted line or an official seal on a government document, the seal of the Spirit (which is belief in the gospel of salvation through Christ; v. 13b) authenticates us as truly included in Christ (v. 13a). This seal secures our eternal safety (v. 14a) and marks us out as God's possession (v. 14b). Apart from the work of the Holy Spirit, we would neither believe in Christ (v. 13) nor have the eyes of our hearts opened to the realities and promises of his word (v. 18). Thus, we do not test the authenticity of our faith by the perfection of our performance but by our belief in the necessity and provision of Christ—concerns that we could not have apart from his Spirit in us. This authentication is an objective reality true of every Christian and also an experiential reality we can know more and more (vv. 17–18).

1:14 And why are we given such a torrential shower of blessing in verses 3–14? God's chief purpose is for the praise of his name (vv. 6, 12, 14). Every blessing for us in Christ, planned by the Father and sealed by the Spirit, is meant to make much of our triune God. Grace glorifies the Giver.

1:15–23 In addition to giving thanks (v. 16), Paul makes three petitions, all of which are instructive for our prayer lives. We should pray to know God better (v. 17). We should pray to know God's riches (v. 18). We should pray to know God's power (v. 19).

The anatomy of God's "for-us" power is remarkable. First, we are told that the One who is for us is at the right hand of God, the position of highest privilege given to Christ for all ages after his resurrection and ascension (vv. 20–21). Next, as Jesus is in that honored position, God places all things under his feet and gives him authority over all (vv. 21–22). Finally, we are told the purpose of Christ's dominion is for the church (v. 22), his body, which not only reflects him but ultimately "fills all in all" (v. 23).

These statements of the amazing privilege, power, and future for the church of which all believers are a part receive further explication as Paul's letter unfolds. He will go on to tell us that we can fulfill God's calling to fill all things with Christ's purposes because the risen Lord who is head over the church is the One who cares for the church (5:29), strengthens the church (4:15–16), and exercises authority over the church (5:22–24). And finally, Paul reminds us that we do this together because collectively we are the body of Christ, held together by him and made to be like him in every way (4:13). When we recall that all of this power is for us, it is no wonder that we should pray that our eyes might be opened to see it, marvel, and believe (1:18).

By Grace Through Faith

2 [j]And you were [k]dead in the trespasses and
sins 2 [l]in which you once walked, following the course of this world, following [m]the
prince of the power of the air, the spirit that
is now at work in [n]the sons of disobedience—
3 among whom we all once lived in [o]the passions of our flesh, carrying out the desires of
the body[1] and the mind, and [p]were by nature
[q]children of wrath, like the rest of mankind.[2]
4 But[3] God, being [r]rich in mercy, [s]because of
the great love with which he loved us, 5 even
[t]when we were dead in our trespasses, [u]made
us alive together with Christ—[v]by grace you
have been saved— 6 and raised us up with him
and [w]seated us with him in the heavenly places
in Christ Jesus, 7 so that in the coming ages he
might show the immeasurable [x]riches of his
grace in [y]kindness toward us in Christ Jesus.
8 For [z]by grace you have been saved [a]through
faith. And this is [b]not your own doing; [c]it is
the gift of God, 9 [d]not a result of works, [e]so that
no one may boast. 10 For [f]we are his workmanship, [g]created in Christ Jesus [h]for good works,
[i]which God prepared beforehand, [j]that we
should walk in them.

One in Christ

11 Therefore remember that at one time you
Gentiles in the flesh, called "the uncircumcision" by what is called [k]the circumcision,
which is made in the flesh by hands—
12 remember [l]that you were at that time
separated from Christ, [m]alienated from the
commonwealth of Israel and strangers to [n]the
covenants of promise, [o]having no hope and

[1] Greek *flesh* [2] Greek *like the rest* [3] Or *And*

2:4–5 The heart of the gospel pumps bright red in the first two words of verse 4. In verses 1–3 we see that mankind was dead, disobedient, demonic, and destined for destruction. We were prodigals, scoundrels, vile, impure, unholy, treacherous, lecherous, self-absorbed, self-exalting, out-and-out rebels. That's the bad news. And then this good news: "But God!" We were dead, but God made us alive in Christ. We were not strugglers in need of a helping hand or sinking swimmers in need of a raft; we were stone-cold dead—spiritually lifeless, without a religious pulse, without anything to please God. But he loves the loveless, gives life to the lifeless, and is merciful to those deserving no mercy.

2:8–9 The anti-gospel which runs through every false religion and every false heart is the "gospel" that says "can do" instead "is finished" by Christ. We are saved by faith alone, not because of any works. What's more, faith itself is a gift. Faith is not the ultimate good deed that saves us but the instrumental cause of our salvation—grace flows through the channel of faith, but the channel is itself of God's construction. We are saved by Christ; faith simply acknowledges and rests upon who he is and what he provides.

Because salvation is entirely by the grace of God, we ought never to boast of our spiritual insights or accomplishments. Instead we should rest in Christ our righteousness, our holiness, and our redemption (see 1 Cor. 1:30).

2:10 Faith alone justifies, but, the Reformers would say, the faith that justifies is never alone. Good works are not the root of our redemption, but they are the necessary fruit. If God has prepared good deeds beforehand, we must consider how and where we will walk today in order to fulfill his eternal purposes for us in Christ.

2:11–16 Throughout the Bible we see that the greatest privilege a people can have is to be near to God (Ex. 19:4–6; Rev. 21:3) and the greatest curse is to be banished from his presence (Gen. 3:23; Hos. 1:9).

In these verses Paul announces the seemingly impossible: the Gentiles who were excluded from the promises of God have been brought near by the blood of Christ. More than that, the hostility between Jew and Gentile has been broken down. The "dividing wall" may have reference to the barrier separating the Court of the Gentiles from the rest of the temple proper, but the most immediate allusion is to the abolition of the law. The ceremonies of circumcision, holy days, and kosher food which divided Jew from Gentile have been removed. The cross of Christ which brought together such disparate peoples can surely be the means of reconciliation for those presently divided by ethnicity, nationality, upbringing, economic status, or any other earthly distinctions that wrongly separate us.

Chapter 2
1 [j]Col. 2:13; [Col. 1:21] [k]ver. 5; [ch. 4:18]; See Luke 15:24
2 [l]ch. 4:17, 22; 5:8; Col. 3:7; See Rom. 11:30; 1 Cor. 6:11 [m][ch. 6:12; Rev. 9:11]; See John 12:31 [n]ch. 5:6; [1 Pet. 1:14]
3 [o]Gal. 5:16 [p]See Ps. 51:5; Rom. 5:12 [q][2 Pet. 2:14]
4 [r]ver. 7; Titus 3:5; See Rom. 2:4 [s]See John 3:16
5 [t]ver. 1; [Rom. 5:6, 8, 10] [u]Col. 2:12, 13; [John 14:19; Rev. 20:4] [v]ver. 8; See Acts 15:11
6 [w]See ch. 1:20
7 [x]ver. 4 [y]Titus 3:4
8 [z]ver. 5 [a]1 Pet. 1:5; [Rom. 4:16] [b][2 Cor. 3:5] [c][John 4:10; Heb. 6:4]
9 [d]2 Tim. 1:9; Titus 3:5; See Rom. 3:20, 28 [e]1 Cor. 1:29; [Judg. 7:2]
10 [f]Deut. 32:6, 15; Ps. 100:3 [g][ch. 3:9; 4:24; Col. 3:10] [h]ch. 4:24 [i][ch. 1:4] [j]Col. 1:10
11 [k]Rom. 2:26, 28; [Col. 2:11, 13]
12 [l]1 Cor. 12:2; [ch. 5:8; Col. 3:7] [m]ch. 4:18; Col. 1:21; [Ezek. 14:5; Gal. 2:15; 4:8] [n]See Rom. 9:4 [o]1 Thess. 4:13; See ch. 1:18

without God in the world. 13 But now in Christ
Jesus you who once were [p] far off have been
brought near [q] by the blood of Christ. 14 For
[r] he himself is our peace, [s] who has made us
both one and has broken down [t] in his flesh
the dividing wall of hostility 15 by abolish-
ing the law of commandments expressed in
[u] ordinances, that he might create in himself
one [v] new man in place of the two, so making
peace, 16 and might [w] reconcile us both to God
in one body through the cross, thereby killing
the hostility. 17 And he came and [x] preached
peace to you who were [y] far off and peace to
those who were [z] near. 18 For [a] through him we
both have [b] access in [c] one Spirit to the Father.
19 So then you are no longer [d] strangers and
aliens,[1] but you are [e] fellow citizens with the
saints and [f] members of the household of God,
20 [g] built on the foundation of the [h] apostles
and prophets, [i] Christ Jesus himself being [j] the
cornerstone, 21 [k] in whom the whole structure,
being joined together, grows into [l] a holy temple in the Lord. 22 In him [m] you also are being
built together [n] into a dwelling place for God
by[2] the Spirit.

The Mystery of the Gospel Revealed

3 For this reason I, Paul, [o] a prisoner for
Christ Jesus [p] on behalf of you Gentiles—
2 assuming that you have heard of [q] the stewardship of [r] God's grace that was given to me
for you, 3 [s] how the mystery was made known
to me [t] by revelation, [u] as I have written briefly.
4 [v] When you read this, you can perceive my
insight into [w] the mystery of Christ, 5 which
was not made known to the sons of men in
other generations as it has now been revealed
to his holy apostles and prophets by the Spirit.
6 This mystery is[3] that the Gentiles are [x] fellow
heirs, [y] members of the same body, and [z] partakers of the promise in Christ Jesus through
the gospel.

7 [a] Of this gospel I was made [b] a minister
according to the gift of [c] God's grace, which
was given me [d] by the working of his power.
8 To me, [e] though I am the very least of all the
saints, this grace was given, [f] to preach to the
Gentiles the [g] unsearchable [h] riches of Christ,
9 and [i] to bring to light for everyone what is
the plan of the mystery [j] hidden for ages in[4]
God [k] who created all things, 10 so that through

[1] Or *sojourners* [2] Or *in* [3] The words *This mystery is* are inferred from verse 4 [4] Or *by*

13 [p] ver. 17; Acts 2:39 [q] [Col. 1:20]; See Rom. 3:25
14 [r] Ps. 72:7; Mic. 5:5; Zech. 9:10; [Col. 3:15]; See Luke 2:14 [s] See Gal. 3:28 [t] Col. 1:21, 22; [Rom. 7:4]
15 [u] Col. 2:14, 20 [v] See Rom. 6:4
16 [w] Col. 1:20-22; [1 Cor. 12:13]
17 [x] Isa. 57:19 [y] ver. 13 [z] Deut. 4:7; Ps. 148:14
18 [a] [John 14:6] [b] ch. 3:12; [John 10:7, 9]; See Rom. 5:2 [c] ch. 4:4; 1 Cor. 12:13; [John 4:23]
19 [d] ver. 12; [Heb. 11:13; 13:14] [e] Phil. 3:20; [Heb. 12:22, 23] [f] See Gal. 6:10
20 [g] [Jer. 12:16]; See 1 Cor. 3:9 [h] Matt. 16:18; Rev. 21:14 [i] [1 Cor. 3:11] [j] Ps. 118:22; Isa. 28:16
21 [k] ch. 4:15, 16 [l] See 1 Cor. 3:16, 17
22 [m] 1 Pet. 2:5 [n] [ch. 3:17; 2 Cor. 6:16; 1 Tim. 3:15]

Chapter 3
1 [o] ch. 4:1; Acts 23:18; Phil. 1:7; [ch. 6:20] [p] ver. 13; Col. 1:24
2 [q] ch. 1:10; Col. 1:25; 1 Tim. 1:4 [r] ver. 7; ch. 4:7; See Acts 11:23; Rom. 1:5
3 [s] Acts 22:17, 21; 26:16-18 [t] [Dan. 2:29]; See Rom. 16:25; 2 Cor. 12:1 [u] [ch. 1:9, 10]
4 [v] [2 Cor. 11:6] [w] Col. 4:3
6 [x] See Gal. 3:29 [y] ch. 2:16 [z] ch. 5:7
7 [a] Col. 1:23, 25 [b] See 2 Cor. 3:6 [c] See ver. 2 [d] [ver. 20]; See ch. 1:19
8 [e] See 1 Cor. 15:9 [f] See Acts 9:15 [g] [Job 5:9; Rom. 11:33] [h] See ch. 1:18; Rom. 2:4
9 [i] See ver. 2, 3 [j] Col. 1:26 [k] Rev. 4:11; [ch. 2:10]

2:19–22 Paul mentions three metaphors for the church: God's people (fellow citizens), God's household, and God's temple.

The first two metaphors are important to communicate the relational security that we have, with increasing intimacy. We learn first that we have a place in the kingdom, and then we learn that we have a place at the King's table. These metaphors are of particular significance when we remember that those gathering in the Ephesian church were of different backgrounds and ethnicities. The work of the gospel not only breaks down barriers but unites hearts in profound ways.

The third metaphor is particularly rich in theological significance. The temple in the Old Testament was the physical representation of the divine manifestation. The sacrifices, the rituals, the festivals—these all took place at the temple because God dwelt there. God lived among his people and met with them through the temple to indicate his care and their preciousness to him. In the age of the new covenant we are the Holy Spirit's home and the temple of God (vv. 20–22; cf. 2 Cor. 6:16; 1 Pet. 2:5), to indicate his care for us wherever we are and to indicate our preciousness to him whatever our situation.

Temple imagery stretches from Genesis to Revelation—from Eden (the first place of God's presence) to the tabernacle (the portable temple) to Solomon's temple (designed to resemble a garden paradise) to Ezekiel's temple, to Jesus Christ the incarnated Son of God who "tabernacled" among us (John 1:14). The cubic dimensions of the new Jerusalem suggest that heaven is our final temple (Rev. 21:16).

What an indescribable privilege that we who have the Spirit of Christ should be counted as the temple of God. Living in light of this privilege leads to joy, gratitude, confidence, and holy living as God's holy people.

3:10 The magnitude of the effect of Christ's people coming together in the church across cultural and personal barriers gets unique expression here. The manifold wisdom of God evident in Christ's united body, the church, becomes a witness to the spiritual

the church the manifold [l]wisdom of God
[m]might now be made known to [n]the rulers and
authorities [o]in the heavenly places. 11 This was
[p]according to the eternal purpose that he has
realized in Christ Jesus our Lord, 12 in whom
we have [q]boldness and [r]access with [s]confidence
through our [t]faith in him. 13 So I ask you not to
lose heart over what I am suffering [u]for you,
[v]which is your glory.

Prayer for Spiritual Strength

14 For this reason I bow my knees before the
Father, 15 from whom [w]every family[1] in heaven
and on earth is named, 16 that according to [x]the
riches of his glory [y]he may grant you to be
strengthened with power through his Spirit
[z]in your inner being, 17 [a]so that Christ may
dwell in your hearts through faith—that you,
being [b]rooted and [c]grounded in love, 18 may
have strength to [d]comprehend with all the
saints what is the breadth and length and
[e]height and depth, 19 and to know the love of
Christ [f]that surpasses knowledge, that [g]you
may be filled with all [h]the fullness of God.

20 [i]Now to [j]him who is able to do far more
abundantly than all that we ask or think,
[k]according to the power at work within us,
21 [l]to him be glory in the church and in Christ
Jesus throughout all generations, forever and
ever. Amen.

[1] Or *fatherhood*; the Greek word *patria* is closely related to the word for *Father* in verse 14

hosts (some commentators identify these as the spiritual enemies of the gospel; see 6:12) of the greatness of the gospel's transformation of the human heart.

3:13 Paul goes through a lot of theology in verses 1–12 to get to his conclusion in verse 13. His concern is that the Ephesians not be overly concerned for him. He may be suffering for the gospel, but they should not lose heart—and Paul has not lost heart—because the glory of the gospel is weightier than his suffering. The mystery of the gospel (vv. 2–6), the ministry of the gospel (vv. 7–9), and the manifold wisdom of the gospel (vv. 10–12) makes "counting the cost" an easy calculation.

If presidential campaigns can raise millions of dollars, recruit thousands of volunteers, and make hundreds of speeches, all for a human leader and a human message, how much more should we press on in the face of suffering when we announce a divine message and serve a heavenly King. After all, the sufferings of Christians, following our crucified Savior, are preparing a weight of glory for us beyond all comparison (2 Cor. 4:16–18).

3:14–17 In Paul's second prayer for the Ephesians (cf. 1:15–19), he asks the Father for power through the Spirit so that Christ may dwell in their hearts through faith. This is one of the epistle's many references to the Trinity (cf. 1:13–14; 2:18, 20–22: 3:14–17; 4:4–6; 5:18–20; 6:10–18). Our lives would be richer if the doctrine of the Trinity did more to inform our prayers, our praise, and our Christian practice. We are saved from first to last by the triune God—the Father planning salvation, the Son accomplishing salvation, and the Spirit applying salvation.

3:18–19 Paul's main petition is for Spirit-given strength in our inner being (v. 16). The specific nature of this strength is the ability to comprehend the incomprehensible love of Christ (vv. 18–19). We will not be fully mature until this love is planted in our hearts. We will not live as God's holy ones until we know that we are first of all his beloved ones. We will not treat our neighbors with mercy until we apprehend Christ's mercy toward us. We do not know anything about Christianity until we know the love of Christ that surpasses knowledge.

3:20–21 Both prayers in the letter focus on power. In chapter 1 Paul asks that the Ephesians might know God's power *toward* them (1:19) and in chapter 3 he asks that they might know God's power at work *within* them (3:20).

The reason we doubt God's ability to do far more abundantly than "all that we ask or think" is that we grossly underestimate the power at work within us. We do not have a little 9-volt battery of spiritual power inside of us, but an entire nuclear power plant of divine might. The same power that raised Christ from the dead now indwells us by his presence and Spirit. We ought to anticipate, and request, that God will overcome big sins, change bad habits, and make us into better followers of Christ. As long as he desires to get glory through the church

10 [l]Rom. 11:33 [m][1 Pet. 1:12] [n]ch. 1:21; [ch. 6:12] [o]See ch. 1:3
11 [p]See ch. 1:11
12 [q]Heb. 4:16; 10:19 [r]See ch. 2:18 [s]2 Cor. 3:4 [t]Mark 11:22; Phil. 3:9
13 [u]ver. 1 [v][2 Cor. 1:6]
15 [w]See ch. 1:10, 21
16 [x]See ver. 8 [y]1 Cor. 16:13; [ch. 6:10; Phil. 4:13; Col. 1:11] [z]See Rom. 7:22
17 [a][ch. 2:22] [b]Col. 2:7 [c]Col. 1:23
18 [d][John 1:5] [e]Rom. 8:39; [Job 11:8, 9]
19 [f][Phil. 4:7] [g]Col. 2:10 [h]ch. 1:23
20 [i]Rom. 16:25; Jude 24 [j][2 Cor. 9:8] [k][ver. 7]
21 [l]See Rom. 11:36

Unity in the Body of Christ

4 I therefore, [m]a prisoner for the Lord, urge
you to [n]walk in a manner worthy of [o]the
calling to which you have been called, 2 with
all [p]humility and [q]gentleness, with [r]patience,
[s]bearing with one another in love, 3 eager to
maintain the unity of the Spirit in [t]the bond
of peace. 4 There is [u]one body and [v]one Spirit—
just as you were called to the one [w]hope that
belongs to your call— 5 [x]one Lord, [y]one faith,
[z]one baptism, 6 [a]one God and Father of all,
[b]who is over all and through all and in all. 7 But
[c]grace was given [d]to each one of us [e]according
to the measure of Christ's gift. 8 Therefore
it says,

> [f]"When he ascended on high [g]he led a host
> of captives,
> and he gave gifts to men."[1]

9 ([h]In saying, "He ascended," what does it mean
but that he had also descended into [i]the lower
regions, the earth?[2] 10 He who descended is the
one who also [j]ascended [k]far above all the heavens,
that he might [l]fill all things.) 11 And [m]he
gave the [n]apostles, the prophets, the [o]evangelists,
the [p]shepherds[3] and teachers,[4] 12 [q]to equip
the saints for the work of ministry, for [r]building
up [s]the body of Christ, 13 until we all attain
to [t]the unity of the faith and of the knowledge
of the Son of God, [u]to mature manhood,[5] to
the measure of the stature of [v]the fullness of
Christ, 14 so that we may no longer be children,
[w]tossed to and fro by the waves and carried
about by every wind of doctrine, by human
cunning, by craftiness in [x]deceitful schemes.
15 Rather, [y]speaking the truth in love, we are
to [z]grow up in every way into him who is [a]the
head, into Christ, 16 [b]from whom the whole

[1] The Greek word *anthropoi* can refer to both men and women [2] Or *the lower parts of the earth?* [3] Or *pastors* [4] Or *the shepherd-teachers*
[5] Greek *to a full-grown man*

Chapter 4
1 [m]See ch. 3:1 [n]Col. 1:10; 2:6; 1 Thess. 2:12; [Phil. 1:27] [o]See Rom. 8:28
2 [p]Acts 20:19; Phil. 2:3; Col. 3:12; 1 Pet. 3:8; 5:5; [Col. 2:18, 23] [q]Gal. 5:23 [r]Col. 1:11 [s]Col. 3:13
3 [t]Col. 3:14; [Acts 8:23]
4 [u]ch. 2:16 [v]See ch. 2:18 [w]ch. 1:18
5 [x]Zech. 14:9; See 1 Cor. 1:13; 8:6 [y][ver. 13; Jude 3] [z]See Gal. 3:27, 28
6 [a]1 Cor. 12:5, 6 [b]Rom. 9:5
7 [c]See ch. 3:2 [d][Matt. 25:15; 1 Cor. 12:7] [e]Rom. 12:3; [ver. 16]
8 [f]Cited from Ps. 68:18 [g]Judg. 5:12; [Col. 2:15]
9 [h]See John 3:13 [i]Ps. 63:9; Isa. 44:23
10 [j]See Mark 16:19 [k]Heb. 4:14; 7:26; 9:24 [l]ch. 1:23
11 [m][1 Cor. 12:5, 6] [n]See 1 Cor. 12:28 [o]Acts 21:8; 2 Tim. 4:5 [p]Jer. 3:15; [Acts 20:28]
12 [q]See 2 Cor. 13:9 [r]ver. 16, 29 [s]See 1 Cor. 12:27
13 [t][ver. 5] [u]Heb. 5:14 [v]ch. 1:23
14 [w][Matt. 11:7; Heb. 13:9; James 1:6; Jude 12] [x]ch. 6:11
15 [y]1 John 3:18; [ver. 25] [z]ch. 2:21 [a]See ch. 1:22
16 [b]Col. 2:19

and in Christ Jesus, we can be sure that God, in ways that are surprising and at times imperceptible, will magnificently exceed our expectations, to his everlasting honor and our everlasting joy.

4:1 The first three chapters were largely in the indicative: "God has done this for you. You were like this and have become that." The last three chapters are largely in the imperative: "Live this way. Do this; don't do that." God has called us by his grace and blessed us in Christ (chs. 1–3); therefore we must live out our calling in Christ as his holy and beloved people (chs. 4–6). The indicative fuels the imperative; the imperative does not earn the indicative.

4:2–6 The first set of imperatives concerns the unity of the Spirit. Paul urges the Ephesians to maintain the bond of peace by doing four things (vv. 2–3). They are to be humble, gentle, and patient, bearing with one another in love. How many relational problems could be avoided if only we waded into conflict more slowly and gave people the benefit of the doubt?

Having explained practically how to *maintain* the unity of the Spirit in the bond of peace, Paul goes on to mention seven theological propositions that speak to the reality of the unity the church in Ephesus already shares: (1) We are one body. (2) We have one Spirit. (3) We have one hope. (4) We have one Lord. (5) We have one faith. (6) We have one baptism. (7) We have one God and Father of all. The unity of the church—which given this doctrinal foundation does not require any sort of watered-down theology—is precious to Christ and should be precious to us (cf. John 17:20–23).

4:11–16 Because Paul makes so much of our positional holiness in Christ and our secure inheritance through the Spirit, believers sometimes make the mistake of thinking it is improper to speak of growth or of differing levels of attainment in the Christian life. But Paul clearly teaches the importance of Christian maturity and our need to grow into it.

This maturation, which is aided by gifted teachers and leaders (v. 11), is described in a variety of ways: as the fullness of Christ (v. 13), as doctrinal stability (v. 14), as growing up into Christ (v. 15), and as strengthening the body (v. 16). It is important to note that Paul is describing much of this growth corporately, not just individually. The church is Christ's instrument not only of world outreach and renewal but also of his sanctifying work in believers' own lives through Christian example, worship, and accountability. All of these contribute to our growth in grace. The good news of the gospel is not just that we can be saved by Christ but that we are being renewed into the image of Christ (v. 24; cf. Rom. 8:29; 2 Cor. 3:18; 4:4).

body, joined and held together by every joint
with which it is equipped, [c]when each part is
working properly, makes the body grow so
that it builds itself up in love.

The New Life

17 Now this I say and [d]testify in the Lord, [e]that
you must no longer walk as the Gentiles do,
[f]in the futility of their minds. 18 They [g]are
darkened in their understanding, [h]alienated
from the life of God because of the ignorance
that is in them, due to [i]their hardness of heart.
19 They [j]have become callous and [k]have given
themselves up to sensuality, greedy to practice
every kind of impurity. 20 But that is not the
way you [l]learned Christ!— 21 assuming that
[m]you have heard about him and [n]were taught
in him, as the truth is in Jesus, 22 to [o]put off
[p]your old self,[1] which belongs to your former
manner of life and is corrupt through [q]deceit-
ful desires, 23 and [r]to be renewed in the spirit
of your minds, 24 and to put on [s]the new self,
[t]created after the likeness of God in true righteousness and holiness.
25 Therefore, having put away falsehood,
let each one of you [u]speak the truth with his
neighbor, for [v]we are members one of another.
26 [w]Be angry and do not sin; do not let the sun
go down on your anger, 27 and [x]give no opportunity to the devil. 28 Let the thief no longer
steal, but rather [y]let him labor, [z]doing honest
work with his own hands, so [a]that he may have
something to share with anyone in need. 29 [b]Let
no corrupting talk come out of your mouths,
but only such as is good for building up, as fits
the occasion, that it may give [c]grace to those
who hear. 30 And [d]do not grieve the Holy Spirit
of God, [e]by whom you were sealed for the day
of [f]redemption. 31 [g]Let all bitterness and wrath
and anger and clamor and slander be put away
from you, along with all malice. 32 [h]Be kind
to one another, tenderhearted, [i]forgiving one
another, as God in Christ forgave you.

Walk in Love

5 [j]Therefore be imitators of God, as beloved
children. 2 And [k]walk in love, [l]as Christ
loved us and [m]gave himself up for us, a [n]fra-
grant [o]offering and sacrifice to God.
3 But [p]sexual immorality and all impurity or
covetousness [q]must not even be named among
you, as is proper among saints. 4 Let there be

[1] Greek *man*; also verse 24

4:20 When we embraced Christ and received him, it was not to continue on in the same futile ways of thinking. If our lives do not differ from the lives of unbelievers, we have not truly learned of Christ. When Christ calls us to himself it is always a call to leave the world, die to self, and live for God. Let us never accept a false gospel which says we can have Jesus as Savior without also having him as Lord. It must be both or neither.

4:22–24 What does it look like, then, to have genuinely "learned Christ"? Paul mentions three things (using three infinitive verbs). Learning Christ means we are renewed in the spirit of our minds (v. 23), we put off the old self (v. 22), and we put on the new (v. 24). These exhortations get to the heart of the New Testament view of sanctification. The moral imperative for the Christian is to "be who you now are." We are new creations in Christ, so let us turn away from the old ways of the world and live like new people of the Spirit. When we sin, we betray our new identity as sons and daughters of God. Our obedience does not create our holy status but reflects it, honors God by it, and aids others through our expression of it.

4:25–5:2 This section of seemingly random exhortations is much more structured than meets the eye. There are five areas of life which Paul highlights. Each topic contrasts two ways of living ("put off" and "put on") and then offers an underlying motivation for Christlikeness.

We must choose between truth or lies (4:25), sinful anger or righteous anger (4:26–27), stealing or hard work (4:28), rotten talk or wholesome talk (4:29–30), bitterness or compassion (4:31–32). In each case, the motivation for godliness is more than a simple "God said so." We pursue holiness for the good of our neighbor (4:25, 28–29), for the pleasure of God (4:30), and in imitation of and appreciation for God's work in Christ (4:32; 5:1–2).

5:3–14 Paul grounds this series of moral imperatives (chiefly regarding sexual purity) in two realities: our present identity in Christ, and the future judgment of Christ.

16 [c][ver. 7]
17 [d]1 Thess. 2:12 [e]ver. 22; ch. 2:1-3; Col. 3:7; 1 Pet. 4:3 [f]Rom. 1:21; 1 Pet. 1:18; [Col. 2:18; 2 Pet. 2:18]
18 [g][Rom. 11:10] [h]See ch. 2:12 [i]See Mark 3:5
19 [j][Prov. 23:35]; 1 Tim. 4:2 [k][1 Kgs. 21:25; Rom. 1:24, 26, 28]
20 [l]See Matt. 11:29
21 [m]ch. 1:13 [n]Col. 2:7
22 [o]Col. 3:8; Heb. 12:1; James 1:21; 1 Pet. 2:1 [p]Rom. 6:6; Col. 3:9 [q][Heb. 3:13]
23 [r]See Rom. 12:2
24 [s]See Rom. 6:4 [t]See ch. 2:10
25 [u]Zech. 8:16; Col. 3:9; [ver. 15] [v]Rom. 12:5
26 [w][Ps. 37:8]
27 [x]See James 4:7
28 [y]Acts 20:35; Gal. 6:10 [z]1 Thess. 4:11; 2 Thess. 3:8, 11, 12 [a][Prov. 21:26]
29 [b]ch. 5:4; Col. 3:8; [Matt. 12:34] [c]Col. 4:6; [Eccles. 10:12]
30 [d]Isa. 63:10; [1 Thess. 5:19] [e]ch. 1:13 [f]See ch. 1:7
31 [g]Col. 3:8, 19
32 [h]Col. 3:12, 13; 1 Pet. 3:8 [i][2 Cor. 2:7, 10]; See Matt. 6:14

Chapter 5
1 [j][ch. 4:32; Matt. 5:7, 48; Luke 6:36]
2 [k]Rom. 14:15; [Col. 3:14]; See John 13:34 [l]See Rom. 8:37 [m]See Rom. 4:25 [n]See Gen. 8:21 [o]Heb. 7:27; 9:14; 10:10, 12
3 [p]1 Cor. 6:18; See Gal. 5:19 [q][ver. 12; Ps. 16:4]

[r]no filthiness nor foolish talk nor crude joking, [s]which are out of place, but instead [t]let
there be thanksgiving. 5 For you may be sure of
this, that [u]everyone who is sexually immoral
or impure, or who is covetous ([v]that is, an
idolater), has no inheritance in the kingdom
of Christ and God. 6 [w]Let no one [x]deceive you
with empty words, for because of these things
[y]the wrath of God comes upon [z]the sons of
disobedience. 7 Therefore [a]do not become partners with them; 8 for [b]at one time you were
[c]darkness, but now you are light in the Lord.
[d]Walk as children of light 9 (for [e]the fruit of
light is found in all that is good and right and
true), 10 and [f]try to discern what is pleasing
to the Lord. 11 [g]Take no part in the [h]unfruit-
ful [i]works of darkness, but instead [j]expose
them. 12 For [k]it is shameful even to speak of
the things that they do in secret. 13 But when
[l]anything is exposed by the light, it becomes
visible, 14 for anything that becomes visible is
light. Therefore it says,

[m]"Awake, O sleeper,
and [n]arise from the dead,
and [o]Christ will shine on you."

15 [p]Look carefully then how you walk, not
as unwise but as wise, 16 [p]making the best
use of the time, because [q]the days are evil.
17 Therefore do not be foolish, but understand
what [r]the will of the Lord is. 18 And [s]do not
get drunk with wine, for that is [t]debauch-
ery, but [u]be filled with the Spirit, 19 addressing one another in [v]psalms and hymns and
spiritual songs, singing and making melody to the Lord with your heart, 20 [w]giving
thanks always and for everything to God the
Father [x]in the name of our Lord Jesus Christ,
21 [y]submitting to one another out of reverence
for Christ.

Wives and Husbands

22 [z]Wives, [a]submit to your own husbands, [b]as
to the Lord. 23 For [c]the husband is the head
of the wife even as [d]Christ is the head of the

4 [r]ch. 4:29; [Eccles. 10:13] [s][Rom. 1:28] [t]ver. 20
5 [u]See 1 Cor. 6:9 [v]Col. 3:5
6 [w]See Matt. 24:4 [x]Col. 2:8 [y]Rom. 1:18; Col. 3:6 [z]ch. 2:2; [1 Pet. 1:14]
7 [a]ch. 3:6
8 [b]See ch. 2:1, 2 [c]See Acts 26:18 [d]Isa. 2:5; See Luke 16:8; John 12:35, 36
9 [e][Gal. 5:22]; See Rom. 7:4
10 [f]1 Thess. 2:4; 5:21
11 [g]See 1 Cor. 5:9 [h]Rom. 6:21 [i]Rom. 13:12 [j]Lev. 19:17; 1 Tim. 5:20
12 [k][ver. 3]
13 [l]John 3:20, 21; [ver. 9]
14 [m][Isa. 51:17; 52:1; 60:1; Mal. 4:2]; See Rom. 13:11 [n]Isa. 26:19 [o]Luke 1:78, 79
15 [p]Col. 4:5; [Prov. 15:21]
16 [p][See ver. 15 above] [q]ch. 6:13; Eccles. 12:1; Amos 5:13; Gal. 1:4
17 [r]Rom. 12:2; 1 Thess. 4:3; 5:18
18 [s]Prov. 20:1; 23:20, 31; 1 Cor. 5:11 [t]Titus 1:6; 1 Pet. 4:4 [u][Luke 1:15]
19 [v]Acts 16:25; 1 Cor. 14:26; Col. 3:16; James 5:13
20 [w]Col. 3:17; 1 Thess. 1:2; 2 Thess. 1:3 [x]Heb. 13:15; [John 14:13]
21 [y][Phil. 2:3]
22 [z]For ch. 5:22–6:9, see Col. 3:18–4:1 [a]See Gen. 3:16 [b][ch. 6:5]
23 [c]1 Cor. 11:3 [d]See ch. 1:22, 23

Regarding the former, Paul tells the Ephesians to act as saints (v. 3) and to walk as children of light (v. 8). Concerning the latter, he admonishes them based on the coming wrath of God (v. 6) and the coming light of Christ (vv. 13–14). Both realities (present identity and future judgment) are connected to the gospel. The gospel connects to our present identity because it is the good news of our changed allegiance; the gospel connects to future judgment because it gives a gracious warning for those who profess the lordship of Christ with their mouths but deny him by their works (Matt. 7:21–23; Titus 1:16). Grace covers all the sin of those who trust in the finished work of Jesus upon the cross. Judgment does not await those who are united to Christ, but an unrepentant life turned from God has no assurance of that union.

5:15–18 Because we live in dark times, we need frequent reminders to wake up (v. 14) and to watch out (v. 15). This means discerning what is pleasing to the Lord (v. 10) and walking in countercultural obedience to him: not unwise, but wise (v. 15); not foolish, but understanding (v. 17); not drunk on wine, but filled with the Spirit (v. 18). The world wants to press us into its mold (Rom. 12:2), but we have been given a different pattern.

While the wrath of God is not in the future for any true believer, we should not presume that ungodly pursuits will have no effect upon us or our loved ones. God loves us enough to tell us of the safe path of godliness, and he loves us enough to warn us of the consequences of wandering from that path.

5:19–21 Paul explains the "filling" in verse 18 with four participles in verses 19–21. To be under the sway of the Spirit (instead of intoxicated by strong drink) leads to speaking in song, singing in your heart, giving thanks to God, and submitting to one another out of reverence for Christ. Not everyone submits to everyone, but all are called to submit to the proper authorities in their lives—and all are called to live sacrificially for the sake of others in their lives (v. 2), a theme that will get much expression in the following verses, even for those in authority. Being "Spirit-filled" has less to do with spontaneity and exuberance, and more to do with living a life marked by the ordinary and glorious fruit of the Spirit (cf. Gal. 5:22–23).

5:22–27 Jesus Christ is the focal point of history and the reference point for all our obedience. Husbands find in Christ a model for sacrificial, loving, strong, tender headship. Wives find in the church's submission to Christ a model for intelligent, gracious, trusting, respectful submission. Though these commands may be designed to reverse

church, his body, and is [e]himself its Savior.
24 Now as the church submits to Christ, so also
wives should submit [f]in everything to their
husbands.
25 [g]Husbands, love your wives, as Christ
loved the church and [h]gave himself up for her,
26 that he might sanctify her, having cleansed
her by [i]the washing of water [j]with the word,
27 so [k]that he might present the church to himself in splendor, [l]without spot or wrinkle or
any such thing, that she might be holy and
without blemish.[1] 28 In the same way [m]hus-
bands should love their wives as their own
bodies. He who loves his wife loves himself.
29 For no one ever hated his own flesh, but
nourishes and cherishes it, just as Christ does
the church, 30 because [n]we are members of
his body. 31 [o]"Therefore a man shall leave his
father and mother and hold fast to his wife,
and [p]the two shall become one flesh." 32 This
mystery is profound, and I am saying that it
refers to Christ and the church. 33 However,
[q]let each one of you love his wife as himself,
and let the wife see that she [r]respects her
husband.

Children and Parents

6 [s]Children, obey your parents in the Lord,
for this is right. 2 [t]"Honor your father and
mother" (this is the first commandment with
a promise), 3 "that it may go well with you and
that you may live long in the land." 4 Fathers,
do not provoke your children to anger, [u]but
bring them up in the discipline and instruction of the Lord.

Bondservants and Masters

5 [v]Bondservants,[2] obey your earthly masters[3]
with fear and trembling, [w]with a sincere heart,
[x]as you would Christ, 6 not by the way of eye-
service, as [y]people-pleasers, but as bondservants of Christ, doing the will of God from
the heart, 7 rendering service with a good will
as to the Lord and not to man, 8 [z]knowing
that whatever good anyone does, this he will
receive back from the Lord, [a]whether he is a
bondservant[4] or is free. 9 Masters, do the same
to them, [b]and stop your threatening, knowing
that [c]he who is both their Master[5] and yours
is in heaven, and that [d]there is no partiality
with him.

The Whole Armor of God

10 Finally, [e]be strong in the Lord and in [f]the
strength of his might. 11 [g]Put on [h]the whole
armor of God, that you may be able to stand
against [i]the schemes of the devil. 12 For [j]we
do not wrestle against flesh and blood, but
against [k]the rulers, against the authorities,
against [l]the cosmic powers over [m]this present

[1] Or *holy and blameless* [2] Or *slaves*; also verse 6 (for the contextual rendering of the Greek word *doulos*, see Preface) [3] Or *your masters according to the flesh* [4] Or *slave* (for the contextual rendering of the Greek word *doulos*, see Preface) [5] Greek *Lord*

the sin of Eden (where the woman usurped her husband's authority and the man relinquished his sacrificial leadership), the Bible never roots these gender roles in the fall, let alone in a certain cultural context. Instead, these roles are meant to be an expression of the unchanging gospel dynamics of Christ's relationship to the church and the church's relationship to him.

5:32 In Ephesians, "mystery" refers to an aspect of the gospel that was hidden and is now, with the coming of Christ, revealed. The full inclusion of the Gentiles is a mystery (3:6) and, given this hidden-to-revealed logic, so is marriage. God's covenant relationship as a husband to his (often wayward) bride is one of the recurring themes all through Scripture (Ezekiel 16; Hosea 1–3; Revelation 19). In Christ we see the full extent of God's love and marital faithfulness. Our marriages should point to the same. God does not exist to make much of marriage; marriage exists to show the world the glory of Christ and his church.

6:1–9 These household instructions, though common in the ancient world, are given a new gospel twist. Children obey parents because of gospel promises (v. 3); bondservants obey masters from a gospel heart (vv. 5–7); masters do not relinquish authority but use it (as should husbands, 5:25; and parents, 6:4) for the good of those needing gospel expression (v. 9); and believers do good deeds because of gospel hope (v. 8). There is no area of life too big or too mundane that the person and work of Christ cannot sanctify and empower it. The Christian gospel is not an ethereal formula unrelated to daily living. The gospel informs and transforms all of life.

23 [e][1 Cor. 6:13]
24 [f][Col. 3:20, 22; Titus 2:9]
25 [g]ver. 28, 33; [1 Pet. 3:7] [h]ver. 2
26 [i]Titus 3:5; [Rev. 7:14] [j]ch. 6:17; Heb. 6:5; See John 15:3
27 [k]2 Cor. 11:2; See ch. 1:4 [l]Song 4:7
28 [m]ver. 25, 33
30 [n][Gen. 2:23]; See 1 Cor. 6:15
31 [o]Matt. 19:5; Mark 10:7, 8; Cited from Gen. 2:24 [p]1 Cor. 6:16
33 [q]ver. 25, 28 [r]1 Pet. 3:2, 6
Chapter 6
1 [s]Prov. 1:8; 6:20; 23:22
2 [t]Cited from Ex. 20:12
4 [u]Gen. 18:19; Deut. 4:9; 6:7; 11:19; Ps. 78:4; Prov. 19:18; 22:6; 29:17; [2 Tim. 3:15]
5 [v]See 1 Pet. 2:18 [w][2 Cor. 11:3] [x][ch. 5:22]
6 [y]See Gal. 1:10
8 [z]See Ps. 62:12 [a]Gal. 3:28; Col. 3:11
9 [b]Lev. 25:43 [c]John 13:13; [Job 31:13-15] [d]See Deut. 10:17
10 [e]Rom. 4:20 (Gk.); 2 Tim. 2:1; [1 John 2:14]; See ch. 3:16 [f]ch. 1:19
11 [g]ver. 14; Job 29:14; See Rom. 13:12 [h]ver. 13; [2 Cor. 10:4] [i]ch. 4:14
12 [j]See 1 Cor. 9:25 [k]ch. 1:21 [l]See ch. 2:2 [m]Luke 22:53; Col. 1:13

darkness, against [n]the spiritual forces of evil
[o]in the heavenly places. 13 Therefore [p]take up
the whole armor of God, that you may be able
to withstand in [q]the evil day, and having done
all, to stand firm. 14 Stand therefore, [r]having
fastened on the belt of truth, and [s]having put
on the breastplate of righteousness, 15 and, [t]as
shoes for your feet, having put on the readiness given by the gospel of peace. 16 In all circumstances take up [u]the shield of faith, with
which you can extinguish all [v]the flaming
darts of [w]the evil one; 17 and take [s]the helmet of
salvation, and [x]the sword of the Spirit, which
is the word of God, 18 praying [y]at all times [z]in
the Spirit, [a]with all prayer and supplication.
To that end [b]keep alert with all perseverance,
making [c]supplication for all the saints, 19 and
[d]also for me, that words may be given to me
in opening my mouth [e]boldly to proclaim [f]the
mystery of the gospel, 20 for which I [g]am an
ambassador [h]in chains, that I may declare it
boldly, as I ought to speak.

Final Greetings

21 [i]So that you also may know how I am and
what I am doing, [j]Tychicus the beloved brother
and faithful minister in the Lord will tell you
everything. 22 I have sent him to you for this
very purpose, that you may know how we are,
and that he may [k]encourage your hearts.

23 [l]Peace be to the brothers,[1] and [m]love with
faith, from God the Father and the Lord Jesus
Christ. 24 Grace be with all who [n]love our Lord
Jesus Christ with love incorruptible.

[1] Or *brothers and sisters*

12[n][ch. 3:10] [o]See ch. 1:3
13[p][1 Pet. 4:1] [q]ch. 5:16
14[r]1 Pet. 1:13; [Isa. 11:5]; See Luke 12:35 [s]Isa. 59:17; 1 Thess. 5:8; [Isa. 61:10; 2 Cor. 6:7]
15[t]Isa. 52:7; Rom. 10:15; [Ex. 12:11]
16[u][1 John 5:4] [v][Ps. 120:4] [w]See Matt. 13:19
17[s][See ver. 14 above] [x]Heb. 4:12; [Isa. 49:2; Hos. 6:5; 2 Cor. 6:7]
18[y]Luke 18:1 [z]Jude 20; See Rom. 8:26 [a]Col. 4:2-4 [b]See Mark 13:33 [c]1 Tim. 2:1
19[d]Col. 4:3; 1 Thess. 5:25; 2 Thess. 3:1; [Isa. 50:4] [e]See Acts 4:29 [f]ch. 3:3
20[g]See 2 Cor. 5:20 [h]See Acts 28:20
21[i]Col. 4:7-9 [j]Acts 20:4; 2 Tim. 4:12; Titus 3:12
22[k]Col. 2:2
23[l]Gal. 6:16; 2 Thess. 3:16; 1 Pet. 5:14 [m][Gal. 5:6; 1 Thess. 5:8]
24[n][1 Cor. 16:22]

6:13–18 God does not send us into battle against Satan without divine assistance. In fact, he dresses us in his own armor. The imagery comes from the book of Isaiah, where the Lord and his Messiah are arrayed for battle (Isa. 11:4–5; 52:7; 59:17). We war against the Devil's lies and accusations with the truth of the gospel, fighting the fight of faith to believe that the cross brings us peace, our salvation is secure, and the Lord is our righteousness. Our posture is almost entirely defensive. We are told to "stand" (Eph. 6:11, 13, 14), knowing that Christ has already won the victory (cf. 1:7–10). Our one offensive weapon is the sword of the Spirit.

But all of this instruction for spiritual battle begins with the reminder to "be strong in the Lord and in the strength of his might" (6:10). We do not win any battle against evil in our own strength, but only with the spiritual resources provided by our Savior, the One who is "far above all rule and authority and power and dominion" (1:21). In the words of a hymn by Martin Luther, "The prince of darkness grim, we tremble not for him. His rage we can endure, for lo his doom is sure. One little word shall fell him."

6:24 Having already prayed for the Ephesians to know the love of Christ which surpasses knowledge (3:19), Paul concludes his letter with a reference to the Ephesians' incorruptible love for Christ. This impossible sounding love has already been fleshed out in many practical ways in chapters 4–6. To guard our tongues and protect our purity and honor our spouse and obey our parents and stand against the Devil—this is what it looks like to love Christ (John 14:15, 23–24). The God who blesses us in the Beloved is a God worthy to be loved.

Introduction to Philippians

Author, Date, and Recipients

The apostle Paul wrote this letter to the Christians in the city of Philippi, probably from Rome c. A.D. 62.

The Gospel in Philippians

If there ever was a clarion call to rejoice because of the gospel, it is Paul's epistle to the Philippians. Writing from his jail cell in Rome (1:12–16), Paul calls the Philippian readers to turn their gaze back to the power and joy of the gospel—and particularly their deep fellowship in it—and away from outward circumstances.

By outward appearances, as Paul writes, there is little reason for the Philippian believers to rejoice. Their beloved leader Paul is in jail; they face tremendous opposition from enemies; their church is experiencing rivalry and disunity; one of their key leaders, Epaphroditus, has nearly died twice; and some are subtly teaching confidence in the flesh rather than the cross of Christ. How can they rejoice?

Despite all these circumstances, Paul calls the Philippians to remember the power and joy of the gospel and their secure citizenship in heaven (1:27 [ESV footnote]; 3:20). What matters more than any earthly event is what God is doing as a result of his good news (1:6; 2:9–10). Because of the gospel, and their unity with Christ in it, the Philippians can stand firm (1:27) in the face of opposition. Paul himself, remembering his longstanding gospel partnership with the Philippians (1:7; 3:14–15), rejoices. Seen through the lens of the gospel, his imprisonment and their suffering are actually, counterintuitively, reasons to rejoice. For such hardships, painful as they are, serve to advance the gospel.

Furthermore, the key to retaining proper gospel perspective and avoiding getting caught up in petty conceit and rivalry is to look to Christ himself. If he humbled himself and made himself nothing, and if God has now exalted him above all, how much more should we be willing to humble ourselves as well? Jesus' example sets the model for servant-humility as a normal part of the Christian life.

Paul's own life (1:25–26; 2:17–18; 3:7–17), as well as the lives of Timothy and Epaphroditus (2:19–30), follow Christ's servant-model of prioritizing the gospel above all else. This prizing of the heavenly includes discounting the emphasis on "the flesh" (3:1–11) and pressing on to the heavenly prize (3:12–4:1). Two prime marks of standing firm in the gospel are unity (4:2–3) and joy (4:4–7). Paul concludes his letter with further rejoicing and thankfulness for the Philippians' partnership in the gospel (4:10–23).

Several sets of key words help us trace the emphases in Philippians. The most obvious are words related to *joy*, which occur 20 times (1:3–4, 18, 25;

2:2, 9, 17–18, 28–29; 3:1; 4:1, 4, 6, 10). A second key term in Philippians is *fellowship* (Greek *koinonia*), translated as "partnership" or "participation" (1:5, 7; 2:1; 3:10; 4:14–15), which can relate either to other believers (1:5; 4:14–15), the gospel of grace (1:7), or Christ himself (2:1; 3:10). A third key term is *citizenship*, which occurs only twice but is strategically placed (1:27 [ESV footnote]; 3:20). A fourth key expression, "in Christ," occurs in some form at least nine times, reflecting the spiritual union that gives us status and resources from the Savior in all of life's circumstances. Finally, of course, are the words for the good news itself: *grace*, which appears three times (1:2, 7; 4:23) and *gospel*, which occurs nine times (1:5, 7, 12, 16, 27 [2x]; 2:22; 4:3, 15).

Our union with and unity in Christ are the basis for joyful, humble service—no matter what the circumstances. Paul calls us to stand firm, rejoice, and humbly serve others even as Christ humbly served us through his redemptive work. May we "strain forward" (see 3:13) for the prize of citizenship with Christ—whom God has exalted for universal praise!

Outline

I. Greeting and Prayer (1:1–11)

II. Paul's Reflections on His Imprisonment (1:12–30)

III. Encouragement to Humble Service (2:1–30)

IV. Opponents of the Gospel: Where Does Righteousness Come From? (3:1–21)

V. Concluding Encouragement and Thanksgiving (4:1–23)

The Letter of Paul to the

Philippians

Greeting

1 Paul and Timothy, servants[1] of Christ Jesus,
To all the [a]saints in Christ Jesus who are at
Philippi, with the [b]overseers[2] and [c]deacons:[3]
2 [d]Grace to you and peace from God our
Father and the Lord Jesus Christ.

Thanksgiving and Prayer

3 [e]I thank my God [f]in all my remembrance of
you, **4** always in every prayer of mine for you
all making my prayer with joy, **5** [g]because of
your partnership in the gospel from the first
day until now. **6** And I am sure of this, that he
who began [h]a good work in you [i]will bring it
to completion at [j]the day of Jesus Christ. **7** It
is right for me to feel this way about you all,
because I hold you [k]in my heart, for you are
all [l]partakers with me of grace,[4] both [m]in my
imprisonment and in [n]the defense and confirmation of the gospel. **8** For [o]God is my witness,
[p]how I yearn for you all with the affection of
Christ Jesus. **9** And it is my prayer that [q]your
love may abound more and more, [r]with knowledge and all discernment, **10** so that you may

[1] Or *slaves* (for the contextual rendering of the Greek word *doulos*, see Preface) [2] Or *bishops*; Greek *episkopoi* [3] Or *servants*, or *ministers*; Greek *diakonoi* [4] Or *you all have fellowship with me in grace*

1:1–2 Paul's greeting to the Philippians sounds the theme of the gospel of grace immediately. That Paul could speak of himself as a servant of Christ Jesus testifies to God's grace in the life of a man who had been an arrogant and self-righteous persecutor of the church (Acts 9:1–2; Phil. 3:6). And since "saints" literally means "holy ones," Paul reminds us that in the gospel our identity has been fundamentally changed. Having been cleansed by the work of Christ once and for all, we are called to holy lives that reflect who we now are. The imperatives of the gospel are based on the indicatives of our relationship with Christ already established by his grace.

Grace and peace are more than mere greetings: they are two of God's greatest gifts through the gospel. Grace (God's unmerited favor or undeserved lavish blessing) and peace (restored, non-hostile relationship with God) come only through Christ's self-sacrificing work on the cross and his subsequent resurrection (2:1–11).

1:3–11 The remarkable prayer of Paul for the Philippians spills over with the thankfulness that meditation on the gospel of grace produces. The gospel brought tremendous joy to Paul (v. 3) not only because of the Philippians' partnership in the gospel (v. 5) but also because Paul is confident of God's continued work in their lives (v. 6).

The word Paul uses for "partnership" (v. 5) is the Greek term *koinonia*, often translated "fellowship." Used six times in Philippians (1:5, 7; 2:1; 3:10; 4:14–15; see Introduction), here in verse 5 and in 4:14–15 it includes the idea of working together for the advance of the gospel (as well as for financial support of the mission). The same word in verse 7 (translated "partakers") carries the idea of participating together in the grace of salvation.

Paul is thankful that the gospel produces (v. 6) not merely justification (God's righteous declaration of our right standing before him; see also 3:9) but also sanctification (progressive holiness; see also 3:12–16) that inevitably leads to our glorification (complete holiness; see also Rom. 8:17) when Christ returns.

Christians are called to live as a community marked by ongoing thankfulness and confidence in God's continued work among them. Relationships of partnership in the gospel with others ought to be celebrated, not only as an opportunity for the gospel to continue to grow but also as a challenge to grow in love, knowledge, and discernment.

Chapter 1
1 [a]2 Cor. 1:1; Col. 1:2 [b]See Acts 20:28 [c]1 Tim. 3:8, 12
2 [d]Rom. 1:7; 1 Cor. 1:3
3 [e]See Rom. 1:8 [f]Rom. 1:9; Eph. 1:16; 2 Tim. 1:3
5 [g][ch. 2:12; 4:15; Acts 16:12-40]
6 [h][1 Thess. 1:3] [i]Ps. 57:2 (Heb.); 138:8; [1 Thess. 5:24] [j]See 1 Cor. 1:8
7 [k]2 Cor. 7:3 [l][ch. 4:14] [m]Acts 20:23; 26:29; Col. 4:18; 2 Tim. 2:9; Philem. 10, 13; See Eph. 3:1 [n]ver. 16
8 [o]See Rom. 1:9; 9:1 [p][ch. 4:1; Rom. 1:11; 15:23; 1 Thess. 3:6; 2 Tim. 1:4]
9 [q]1 Thess. 3:12; 2 Thess. 1:3 [r]Col. 1:9; 3:10; Philem. 6

approve what is excellent, [s]and so be pure and
blameless [t]for the day of Christ, [11]filled [u]with
the fruit of righteousness that comes [v]through
Jesus Christ, [w]to the glory and praise of God.

The Advance of the Gospel

[12]I want you to know, brothers,[1] that what
has happened to me has really [x]served to
advance the gospel, [13]so that it has become
known throughout the whole imperial guard[2]
and [y]to all the rest that [z]my imprisonment is
for Christ. [14]And most of the brothers, having
become confident in the Lord by my imprisonment, are much more bold [a]to speak the word[3]
without fear.

[15][b]Some indeed preach Christ from envy
and rivalry, but others from good will. [16]The
latter do it out of love, [c]knowing that I am
put here for [d]the defense of the gospel. [17]The
former proclaim Christ [e]out of selfish ambition, not sincerely but thinking to afflict me
in my imprisonment. [18]What then? Only that
in every way, whether in pretense or in truth,
Christ is proclaimed, and in that I rejoice.

To Live Is Christ

Yes, and I will rejoice, [19]for I know that
[f]through your prayers and [g]the help of [h]the
Spirit of Jesus Christ this will turn out for my
deliverance, [20]as it is my eager expectation and
hope [i]that I will not be at all ashamed, but that
with full [j]courage now as always Christ [k]will
be honored in my body, [l]whether by life or by
death. [21]For to me [m]to live is Christ, and to die
is gain. [22]If I am to live in the flesh, that means
fruitful labor for me. Yet which I shall choose
I cannot tell. [23][n]I am hard pressed between
the two. My desire is [o]to depart and [p]be with

[1] Or *brothers and sisters.* The plural Greek word *adelphoi* (translated "brothers") refers to siblings in a family. In New Testament usage, depending on the context, *adelphoi* may refer either to men or to both men and women who are siblings (brothers and sisters) in God's family, the church; also verse 14 [2] Greek *in the whole praetorium* [3] Some manuscripts add *of God*

10[s] Acts 24:16; 1 Thess. 3:13; 5:23 [t] ver. 6
11[u] [Col. 1:6, 10]; See James 3:18 [v] [John 15:4, 5] [w] See Eph. 1:12, 14
12[x] ver. 25; 1 Tim. 4:15
13[y] [Acts 28:30, 31; 2 Tim. 2:9] [z] [Luke 21:13]; See ver. 7
14[a] [Acts 4:31]
15[b] See 2 Cor. 11:13
16[c] [1 Cor. 9:17] [d] ver. 7
17[e] ch. 2:3; See James 3:14
19[f] See 2 Cor. 1:11 [g] Gal. 3:5 [h] See Acts 16:7
20[i] Rom. 5:5; [Joel 2:27; 2 Tim. 2:15] [j] See Acts 4:13 [k] [1 Cor. 6:20] [l] Rom. 14:8
21[m] [Gal. 2:20]
23[n] [2 Cor. 5:8] [o] 2 Tim. 4:6 [p] See John 12:26

1:12–18 Paul continues his reflection on the gospel by explaining that God's work is not hindered by the persecution that has come to him. Quite the opposite. Rather than Paul's imprisonment being a barrier to the growth of the gospel, God is using it to advance the gospel. Paul can say he is imprisoned *for* Christ (v. 13). His imprisonment inspires boldness to proclaim Christ to others (v. 14). Paul even finds a reason to rejoice in those who preach Christ out of rivalry (vv. 15–16).

With Paul, our confidence and joy in the gospel must never be marginalized by trials. Hostility to Christians, when rightly viewed through the gospel, can embolden us to speak good news without fear, as it did for Paul and his colleagues. Just as Paul finds that he can rejoice in persecution and even in those who preach out of rivalry, we too are freed from fearing the suffering that comes because of our allegiance to Christ. After all, such suffering ushers us into profound communion with Christ, our suffering Savior (cf. 3:10).

1:19–30 Paul repeats the main theme of the letter: rejoicing in the gospel no matter what the circumstances. This is not a blind or naive rejoicing. Nor is it a pain-denying stoicism. It is confidence that God's purposes will triumph in the end (v. 19).

Personally, Paul faces a dilemma as he writes (v. 23). He contemplates the possibility of death by Roman execution, and wonders which is better: remaining on in the flesh or dying. Either way (v. 20), Paul wants Christ to be honored in his body. In one of the most famous and powerful statements in Philippians, Paul acknowledges that death is "gain" but that continued living is "Christ" (v. 21). This remarkable affirmation of the union of a believer with the once-suffering and now-risen Lord gives us important insight into our own relationship with the Savior. Ongoing ministry will further conform Paul to Christ, who already is his identity (cf. Gal. 2:20; Col. 3:4), especially as, through personal trial, Paul experientially learns more of Jesus' life of sacrificial servanthood (which Paul will soon describe in memorable terms; Phil. 2:1–11). The life that we now live in union with Christ furthers our understanding of the One who gives us his identity and resources despite our sin and weaknesses. The result is that we may be confident of God's care and purpose for each of us, as his precious child, united to all others who are in Christ.

Like Paul, the Philippians are called to live in a way that is worthy of the gospel of Jesus Christ (1:27–30). This involves standing firm through suffering (v. 29). Paul literally tells the Philippians to live as "citizens" worthy of the gospel (v. 27 [ESV footnote]; 3:20). They are citizens of heaven, even as they suffer in this world. Paul reminds

Righteousness Through Faith in Christ

3 Finally, my brothers,[1] [k]rejoice in the Lord.
[l]To write the same things to you is no
trouble to me and is safe for you.
2 Look out for [m]the dogs, look out for [n]the
evildoers, look out for those who mutilate
the flesh. 3 For [o]we are the circumcision, [p]who
worship [q]by the Spirit of God[2] and [r]glory in
Christ Jesus and put no confidence in the
flesh— 4 [s]though I myself have reason for confidence in the flesh also. If anyone else thinks
he has reason for confidence in the flesh, I have
more: 5 [t]circumcised on the eighth day, [u]of the
people of Israel, [v]of the tribe of Benjamin, [u]a
Hebrew of Hebrews; as to the law, [w]a Pharisee;
6 [x]as to zeal, [y]a persecutor of the church; [z]as to
righteousness under the law,[3] blameless. 7 But
[a]whatever gain I had, [b]I counted as loss for the
sake of Christ. 8 Indeed, I count everything
as loss because of [c]the surpassing worth of
[d]knowing Christ Jesus my Lord. For his sake
I [e]have suffered the loss of all things and
count them as rubbish, in order that I may
gain Christ 9 and be found in him, not having
[f]a righteousness of my own that comes from
the law, but [g]that which comes through faith
in Christ, the righteousness from God that
depends on faith— 10 [h]that I may know him
and [i]the power of his resurrection, and [j]may
share his sufferings, becoming like him in
his death, 11 that by any means possible I may
[k]attain the resurrection from the dead.

[1] Or *brothers and sisters*; also verses 13, 17 [2] Some manuscripts *God in spirit* [3] Greek *in the law*

"minister"—all in just one verse (v. 25). Paul's affection for Epaphroditus was so potent that his death would have caused "sorrow upon sorrow" (v. 27).

Christians need biblical teaching on godly self-sacrifice, but we also need models of those who have placed their faith and hope in Christ. He is the primary model of humble service. But let us also look around ourselves today for men and women who, like Timothy and Epaphroditus, set an example of humble, sacrificial service because they are living in gratitude for God's grace. People like Timothy and Epaphroditus should be honored (v. 29), commended, and unleashed for ministry (vv. 19, 25, 28) even as we rejoice in God for their lives. Living for Christ is not easy. It requires humility, service, and dependence on God's grace. A redemptive perspective on others that views them as examples not in place of Jesus but for the sake of Jesus encourages us in this grace.

3:1–11 One of the greatest obstacles to applying the gospel to ourselves is our human tendency to depend on our own resources. In these verses Paul demolishes any dependence on human ability for righteousness. The "dogs" who "mutilate the flesh" (v. 2) are Judaizers who taught that circumcision was necessary for salvation. Paul lists the reasons that he himself might put "confidence in the flesh" (vv. 4–6) only to claim that these trophies are nothing but rubbish (vv. 7–8a) in comparison with the righteousness that comes from God by faith (vv. 8b–9). Rather than taking pride in his own accomplishments, Paul says he "gains" Christ by the loss of all such things. His salvation comes not from his accomplishments but from depending on nothing but the Savior's provision. Paul aims to be found in Christ, to know him and the power of his resurrection, sharing (*koinonia*) in his suffering (v. 10) and his death so that he might attain (i.e., arrive at, or reach) the resurrection (v. 11). Sharing in suffering does not "earn" us the resurrection but enables us to identify more with Christ, to experience the power that gave him new life, and to understand more of the love of the Savior who had to endure immeasurable pain for his resurrection and ours.

When we take serious stock of our lives in light of the gospel, we realize that we must repent not only of our sins but also of the achievements that we would use to justify ourselves before God. But curiously and wonderfully, this descent from our pedestals identifies us with the risen Savior who gave up heaven's honor to suffer for our sin. God's righteousness comes by faith alone, in Christ alone (v. 9). God invites us to share, to fellowship (*koinonia*), not just in grace (1:7) but in Christ's sufferings as well (3:10) in order that we might grasp the greatness of his love and the power of his resurrection hope. Can we say with Paul that we consider the achievements of our lives to be "rubbish"? In Christ, we can not only say such things but also discover that the greater wonders of the resurrection are ours no matter what we face in this life.

Life under the gospel is an utter repudiation of our own moral resume—not only the bad but also the good. Christ is all. He alone has "surpassing worth" (v. 8).

Chapter 3
1 [k]ch. 4:4; 1 Thess. 5:16 [l][2 Pet. 1:12]
2 [m]Ps. 22:16, 20; Isa. 56:10, 11; Rev. 22:15; [Gal. 5:15] [n][2 Cor. 11:13]
3 [o]See Rom. 2:29 [p][John 4:23] [q][Gal. 5:25; Jude 20] [r]Rom. 15:17; [Gal. 6:14]
4 [s]2 Cor. 11:18
5 [t]See Gen. 17:12 [u]2 Cor. 11:22 [v]Rom. 11:1 [w]Acts 23:6; 26:5
6 [x]Acts 22:3, 4; Gal. 1:13, 14 [y]See Acts 8:3 [z][ver. 9]
7 [a][Luke 14:33] [b][Heb. 11:26]
8 [c][2 Cor. 5:15] [d]Isa. 53:11; Jer. 9:23, 24; John 17:3; 2 Pet. 1:3 [e]Luke 9:25 (Gk.)
9 [f]Rom. 10:5; [ver. 6] [g]See Rom. 9:30; 1 Cor. 1:30
10 [h][Eph. 4:13] [i][Rom. 1:4; 6:5] [j]1 Pet. 4:13; See 2 Cor. 1:5
11 [k]Acts 26:7

Straining Toward the Goal

12 Not that I have already [l]obtained this or [m]am already perfect, but I press on to make it my own, because Christ Jesus has made me his own. 13 Brothers, I do not consider that I have made it my own. But one thing I do: [n]forgetting what lies behind and straining forward to what lies ahead, 14 I press on toward the goal for [o]the prize of the upward [p]call of God in Christ Jesus. 15 Let those of us who are [q]mature think this way, and if in anything [r]you think otherwise, [s]God will reveal that also to you. 16 Only [t]let us hold true to what we have attained.

17 Brothers, [u]join in imitating me, and keep your eyes on those who walk [v]according to the example you have in us. 18 For [w]many, of whom I have often told you and now tell you [x]even with tears, walk as enemies of the cross of Christ. 19 [y]Their end is destruction, [z]their god is their belly, and [a]they glory in their shame, with [b]minds set on earthly things. 20 But [c]our citizenship is in heaven, and [d]from it we [e]await a Savior, the Lord Jesus Christ, 21 who will transform [f]our lowly body [g]to be like his glorious body, [h]by the power that enables him even [i]to subject all things to himself.

4 Therefore, my brothers,[1] whom I love and [j]long for, [k]my joy and [l]crown, [m]stand firm thus in the Lord, my beloved.

Exhortation, Encouragement, and Prayer

2 I entreat Euodia and I entreat Syntyche to [n]agree in the Lord. 3 Yes, I ask you also, true companion,[2] help these women, who have labored side by side with me in the gospel together with Clement and the rest of my fellow workers, [o]whose names are in the book of life.

4 [p]Rejoice in the Lord always; again I will say, rejoice. 5 Let your reasonableness be known to everyone. [q]The Lord is at hand; 6 [r]do not be anxious about anything, [s]but in everything by prayer and supplication [t]with thanksgiving let your requests be made known to God. 7 And [u]the peace of God, [v]which surpasses all understanding, will guard your hearts and your minds in Christ Jesus.

8 Finally, brothers, whatever is true, whatever is honorable, whatever is just, whatever

[1] Or *brothers and sisters*; also verses 8, 21 [2] Or *loyal Syzygus*; Greek *true yokefellow*

12 [l][1 Tim. 6:12, 19] [m]Heb. 11:40; 12:23; [Heb. 5:9]
13 [n][Ps. 45:10; Luke 9:62; Heb. 6:1]
14 [o]1 Cor. 9:24 [p][Heb. 3:1; 1 Pet. 5:10]; See Rom. 8:28
15 [q]1 Cor. 2:6; See Matt. 5:48 [r][Gal. 5:10] [s][John 7:17]
16 [t]Gal. 6:16
17 [u][ch. 4:9]; See 1 Cor. 4:16 [v]1 Pet. 5:3
18 [w]See 2 Cor. 11:13 [x][Acts 20:31]
19 [y]2 Cor. 11:15, [2 Thess. 1:9; 2 Pet. 2:1, 3] [z]See Rom. 16:18 [a][Hos. 4:7; 2 Cor. 11:12; Gal. 6:13; Jude 13] [b]Rom. 8:5; Col. 3:2
20 [c]See Eph. 2:19 [d]Acts 1:11 [e]See 1 Cor. 1:7
21 [f][1 Cor. 15:43-53] [g][ver. 10; Col. 3:4]; See Rom. 8:29 [h]See Eph. 1:19 [i]1 Cor. 15:28

Chapter 4
1 [j]See ch. 1:8 [k]ch. 1:4; 2:16; See 2 Cor. 1:14 [l]Prov. 16:31; 17:6 [m]ch. 1:27
2 [n]ch. 2:2
3 [o]See Luke 10:20
4 [p]ch. 3:1
5 [q]See James 5:8
6 [r]See Matt. 6:25 [s][Prov. 16:3] [t]See Rom. 1:8
7 [u][ver. 9; Isa. 26:3; Col. 3:15]; See John 14:27 [v][Eph. 3:19]

3:12–21 Paul returns to the imagery of heavenly citizenship (v. 20; cf. 1:27 [ESV footnote]) to depict the complete knowledge, rule, and righteousness of Christ that we will someday see. This future glory is something toward which Paul is "straining forward" to obtain (3:13–14). Paul forgets what lies behind and strains toward what lies ahead, pressing toward the prize in heaven. Paul wants the Philippians to imitate him (v. 17) and any who walk according to his example.

Tearfully, however, Paul points out that many are enemies of the cross (v. 18). They set their minds on earthly things (v. 19) and do not look forward to the return of Christ (v. 21). Their end is destruction (v. 19). This is the destiny of all those whose hearts are not transformed by the gospel.

As those who belong to Christ, we are not to grow too comfortable on earth. Nor are we to be distracted by the pleasures of the earth. Our citizenship is in heaven, where Christ has been exalted (2:9–11). With Paul, we eagerly strain toward our heavenly prize.

4:2–9 Paul further applies the gospel, first to two partners in ministry and then to the Philippian church as a whole. The ministry partners Euodia and Syntyche need to agree in the Lord. Their disunity contradicts the model of Christian servanthood and humility outlined in 2:1–11.

Paul climaxes his teaching on the joy in gospel unity with a two-fold call to rejoice (4:4; cf. 3:1). The reason for rejoicing is the proximity of the Lord's presence. God conquers anxiety that creates tensions in and among believers through (1) petition, with (2) thanksgiving, which (3) invites God's all-surpassing peace (4:7). In context, 4:8–9 is a reminder to meditate on all that is true—but particularly on what is honorable, pure, and lovely in the gospel.

Our Christian community, Paul reminds us once more, is to be marked by unity and joy. Relational discord and unappeased anxiety rob our gospel communities of joy. God's presence means that we can cultivate thankful, praying, peaceful hearts marked by a joyful reflection on what is good. Do you find yourself anxious? Take time to prayerfully memorize and meditate on Philippians 4:4–7.

is pure, whatever is lovely, whatever is commendable, if there is any excellence, if there is
anything worthy of praise, think about these
things. 9 What you have learned and [w]received
and heard and seen [x]in me—practice these
things, and [y]the God of peace will be with you.

God's Provision

10 I rejoiced in the Lord greatly that now at
length [z]you have revived your concern for me.
You were indeed concerned for me, but you
had no opportunity. 11 Not that I am speaking
of being in need, for I have learned in whatever situation I am to be [a]content. 12 I know
how to be brought low, and I know how to
abound. In any and every circumstance, I have
learned the secret of facing plenty and [b]hun-
ger, abundance and [c]need. 13 I can do all things
[d]through him who strengthens me.
14 Yet it was kind of you [e]to share[1] my trouble. 15 And you Philippians yourselves know
that [f]in the beginning of the gospel, when
I left Macedonia, [g]no church entered into
partnership with me in giving and receiving,
except you only. 16 Even in Thessalonica you
sent me help for my needs once and again.
17 [h]Not that I seek the gift, but I seek [i]the fruit
that increases to your credit.[2] 18 I have received
full payment, and more. I am well supplied,
[j]having received from Epaphroditus the gifts
you sent, [k]a fragrant offering, [l]a sacrifice
acceptable and pleasing to God. 19 And my
God [m]will supply every need of yours [n]accord-
ing to his riches in glory in Christ Jesus. 20 To
[o]our God and Father be [p]glory forever and
ever. Amen.

Final Greetings

21 Greet every saint in Christ Jesus. [q]The
brothers who are with me greet you. 22 [r]All the
saints greet you, especially those of Caesar's
household.
23 [s]The grace of the Lord Jesus Christ be with
your spirit.

[1] Or *have fellowship in* [2] Or *I seek the profit that accrues to your account*

4:10–20 As Paul concludes, he returns to the theme of rejoicing despite difficulty (v. 10). Cheered as he is by the Philippians' revived concern for him, his contentment lies elsewhere. He is not dependent on their support to find contentment (v. 11). He rejoices in the practical oneness that the gospel brings, but emphasizes practical humility. He has learned the secret of facing both plenty and hunger.

Our contentment as Christians, likewise, rests in the fruit of the gospel—including our oneness in Christ. Paul teaches us to look beyond our circumstances, whether we have much or little, and rejoice in Christ. In him, we have all we could ever need or desire.

4:21–23 Returning in verse 23 to the blessing of grace with which the apostle greeted them initially (1:2), and of which they are partakers (1:7), Paul re-centers a troubled Philippian church on the humble joy and fruit of the gospel. From first to last, the letter to the Philippians is a summons to grace—to receive it, to rest in it, and to work it out in one's life.

9 [w]1 Thess. 4:1 [x][ch. 3:17] [y][ver. 7]; See Rom. 15:33
10 [z][2 Cor. 11:9; ch. 2:30]
11 [a]1 Tim. 6:6, 8; [2 Cor. 9:8; Heb. 13:5]
12 [b]1 Cor. 4:11; 2 Cor. 11:27 [c]2 Cor. 11:9
13 [d][2 Cor. 12:9]; See Eph. 3:16; 1 Tim. 1:12
14 [e][ch. 1:7; Rev. 1:9]
15 [f]ch. 1:5 [g]2 Cor. 11:8, 9
17 [h][2 Cor. 9:5] [i]Rom. 1:13; [Titus 3:14]
18 [j]ch. 2:25 [k]See Gen. 8:21 [l]Heb. 13:16
19 [m]Ps. 23:1; 2 Cor. 9:8 [n]See Rom. 2:4
20 [o]Gal. 1:4; 1 Thess. 1:3; 3:11, 13 [p]Gal. 1:5; See Rom. 11:36
21 [q]Gal. 1:2
22 [r]2 Cor. 13:13
23 [s]See Rom. 16:20

Introduction to Colossians

Author, Date, and Recipients

The apostle Paul wrote this letter to Christians living in the small city of Colossae. It was probably written c. A.D. 62, while Paul was in prison in Rome (Acts 27–28). This was about the same time he wrote Ephesians and Philemon.

The Gospel in Colossians

Of all the books in the Bible, Colossians may rightly be considered the most Christ-centered. In this short letter Paul goes to great lengths to proclaim the supremacy and sufficiency of Christ in all things and for all people. The good news of Christ's lordship over creation as well as his redemption for his people rings forth from start to finish in this epistle.

Paul focuses on these themes because the world, both that of the early Christians and our own, undermines the truth of Christ's supremacy and sufficiency for all of life. In the hearts and minds of unsuspecting Christians, this can cause uncertainty about Christ truly being our all in all. This can lead to doubts about God's sovereignty and salvation, despair when life seems confusing and out of control, and outright destruction of the foundations of our faith.

Paul writes this letter as an effective antidote to these very real dangers. He strengthens our gospel defense by fixing our eyes on who Jesus is. We are strengthened to combat the temptations to capitulate to worldly ambitions and desires, reduce the gospel to mere religious maxims, or separate our belief in Christ from our behavior for Christ.

Throughout the entire letter Paul redirects Christians' often-distracted focus back to Christ, who is the Creator of all things, Savior of all peoples, and Victor over all enemies because of his life, death, resurrection, and exaltation. Knowing and focusing on Christ builds a strong defense and forms a strategic offense against enemies both inside and outside the church. As clearly as any book of the Bible, Colossians rivets us on who Christ is and what he has accomplished—the very motivation and power believers need to live by faith, walk in obedience, and glorify God.

Outline

I. Greeting (1:1–2)

II. Thanksgiving (1:3–8)

III. Prayer (1:9–14)

IV. Praise to Christ (1:15–20)

V. Reconciliation to God (1:21–23)

VI. Paul's Labor for the Gospel (1:24–2:5)

VII. The Dangerous Teaching at Colossae (2:6–23)

VIII. The Proper Focus: Christ and the Life Above (3:1–4)

IX. Instructions on Living the Christian Life (3:5–4:6)

X. Personal Greetings and Instructions (4:7–17)

XI. Closing (4:18)

The Letter of Paul to the

Colossians

Greeting

1 Paul, [a]an apostle of Christ Jesus [b]by the will
of God, and Timothy [c]our brother,
2 To the [d]saints and faithful brothers[1] in
Christ at Colossae:
[e]Grace to you and peace from God our Father.

Thanksgiving and Prayer

3 [f]We always thank God, the Father of our
Lord Jesus Christ, when we pray for you,
4 since we heard of [g]your faith in Christ Jesus
and of [g]the love that you have for all the
saints, 5 because of [h]the hope [i]laid up for you
in heaven. Of this you have heard before in
[j]the word of the truth, the gospel, 6 which has
come to you, as indeed [k]in the whole world it is
[l]bearing fruit and increasing—as it also does
among you, since the day you [m]heard it and
understood [n]the grace of God in truth, 7 just
as you learned it from [o]Epaphras our beloved
[p]fellow servant.[2] He is [p]a faithful minister of
Christ on your[3] behalf 8 and has made known
to us your [q]love in the Spirit.
9 And so, [r]from the day we heard, [s]we have
not ceased to pray for you, asking that [t]you
may be filled with the knowledge of his will
in all [u]spiritual wisdom and understanding,
10 so as [v]to walk in a manner worthy of the
Lord, [w]fully pleasing to him, [x]bearing fruit
in every good work and increasing in the
knowledge of God. 11 [y]May you be strengthened with all power, according to his glorious
might, for [z]all endurance and patience [a]with
joy, 12 [b]giving thanks[4] to the Father, who has
qualified you[5] to share in [c]the inheritance
of the saints in light. 13 He [d]has delivered us
from [e]the domain of darkness and transferred us to [f]the kingdom of [g]his beloved
Son, 14 [h]in whom we have redemption, the
forgiveness of sins.

[1] Or *brothers and sisters*. The plural Greek word *adelphoi* (translated "brothers") refers to siblings in a family. In New Testament usage, depending on the context, *adelphoi* may refer either to men or to both men and women who are siblings (brothers and sisters) in God's family, the church [2] Greek *fellow bondservant* [3] Some manuscripts *our* [4] Or *patience, with joy giving thanks* [5] Some manuscripts *us*

1:1–14 The apostle Paul begins his letter to the young Christians in Colossae with a greeting and a prayer. He gives thanks that the grace of the Father, the gospel of the Son, and the love of the Spirit have been made manifest to them so that they can experience and exemplify the faith, love, and hope of the Christ-centered life. These three Christian virtues that believers share (cf. 1 Cor. 13:13) are based on the objective word of grace and truth that was proclaimed in the good news of the gospel. With the help of faithful partners in ministry like Epaphras, Paul calls on the Colossian Christians to remember *who they are* and *what they have* because of Christ's wondrous work of grace and truth.

This work of grace and truth (Col. 1:6) is directly connected to what Christ has done in delivering all of his followers from the realm of darkness into light, from death to life (v. 13). Through Christ's work on the cross, they have been redeemed from and forgiven of their sins (v. 14). Because of this change in position from one realm to another, Paul calls on Christians to practice a new life in Christ that pleases God and bears good fruit (v. 10; cf. Matt. 7:17–19). With the knowledge, wisdom, and power that the God of "glorious might" will provide (Col. 1:9–11), believers can endure the inevitable trials and tribulations of the Christian life with patience, joy, and thanksgiving (vv. 11–12). For it is the gospel itself that causes fruit to be borne in the lives of God's people (v. 6). We do not "graduate" from the gospel of grace; rather, we move more deeply into it over time, as we continue to see how profoundly sinful we are, yet how much more profoundly gracious God is.

Chapter 1
1 [a]See 2 Cor. 1:1 [b]See 1 Cor. 1:1 [c]See 1 Thess. 3:2
2 [d]Eph. 1:1; See Phil. 1:1 [e]Rom. 1:7
3 [f]Eph. 1:15, 16; Philem. 4
4 [g]See 1 Thess. 1:3
5 [h]ver. 23; See Acts 23:6; Titus 1:2; Heb. 3:6 [i]2 Tim. 4:8; 1 Pet. 1:4 [j]See Eph. 1:13
6 [k][ver. 23; Ps. 98:3]; See Matt. 24:14 [l]John 15:5, 16; [Phil. 1:11] [m][Rom. 16:26; Eph. 4:21] [n]See Acts 11:23
7 [o]ch. 4:12; Philem. 23 [p]ch. 4:7
8 [q][Rom. 15:30]
9 [r]ver. 4 [s]2 Thess. 1:11 [t][Eph. 1:17] [u]ch. 4:5; Eph. 1:8; [1 Cor. 12:8]
10 [v][Ps. 1:1, 3]; See Eph. 4:1 [w][2 Cor. 5:9; Eph. 5:10; 1 Thess. 4:1] [x]ver. 6
11 [y]See Eph. 3:16 [z]Eph. 4:2 [a]See Matt. 5:12
12 [b]ch. 3:15; Eph. 5:20 [c]See Acts 26:18
13 [d]1 Thess. 1:10 [e]Luke 22:53; Eph. 6:12 [f]2 Pet. 1:11 [g][Eph. 1:6]
14 [h]See Eph. 1:7

The Preeminence of Christ

15 [i]He is the image of [j]the invisible God, [k]the firstborn of all creation. 16 For by[1] him all things were created, [l]in heaven and on earth, visible and invisible, whether [m]thrones or [n]dominions or rulers or authorities—all things were created [o]through him and for him. 17 And [p]he is before all things, and in him all things [q]hold together. 18 And [r]he is the head of the body, the church. He is [s]the beginning, [t]the firstborn from the dead, that in everything he might be preeminent. 19 For [u]in him all the [v]fullness of God was pleased to dwell, 20 and [w]through him to reconcile to himself all things, whether on earth or in heaven, [x]making peace [y]by the blood of his cross.

21 [z]And you, who once were alienated and hostile in mind, [a]doing evil deeds, 22 he has now reconciled [b]in his body of flesh by his death, [c]in order to present you holy and blameless and [d]above reproach before him, 23 [e]if indeed you continue in the faith, [f]stable and steadfast, not shifting from [g]the hope of the gospel that you heard, which has been proclaimed [h]in all creation[2] under heaven, [i]and of which I, Paul, became a minister.

Paul's Ministry to the Church

24 Now [j]I rejoice in my sufferings for your sake, and in my flesh [k]I am filling up [l]what is lacking in Christ's afflictions [m]for the sake of his body, that is, the church, 25 [n]of which I became a minister according to [o]the stewardship from God that was given to me for you, to make the word of God fully known, 26 [p]the mystery hidden for ages and generations but now revealed to his saints. 27 [q]To them God chose to make known how great among the Gentiles are [r]the riches of the glory of [p]this mystery, which is Christ in you, [s]the hope of glory. 28 Him we proclaim, warning everyone and teaching everyone with all wisdom, that [t]we may present everyone [u]mature in Christ. 29 For this [v]I toil, [w]struggling [x]with all his energy that he powerfully works within me.

2 For I want you to know [y]how great a [w]struggle I have for you and for those at Laodicea and for all who have not seen me face to face, 2 that [z]their hearts may be encouraged, being [a]knit together in love, to reach all the riches of full assurance of understanding and the knowledge of [b]God's mystery, which is Christ, 3 [c]in whom are hidden all the treasures

[1] That is, by means of; or *in* [2] Or *to every creature*

15 [i]See 2 Cor. 4:4 [j]See 1 Tim. 1:17 [k][Ps. 89:27]; See Rom. 8:29
16 [l]Eph. 1:10 [m][Ezek. 10:1] [n]Eph. 1:21 [o]Rom. 11:36; 1 Cor. 8:6
17 [p][John 8:58]; See John 1:1 [q][Heb. 1:3]
18 [r]See Eph. 1:22, 23 [s]Rev. 3:14 [t]Acts 26:23; 1 Cor. 15:20; Rev. 1:5
19 [u]ch. 2:9 [v]See John 1:16
20 [w]See 2 Cor. 5:18; Eph. 1:10 [x]See Eph. 2:14 [y][Eph. 2:13]
21 [z]See Eph. 2:1, 2, 12 [a][Titus 1:16]
22 [b][Rom. 7:4] [c]Jude 24; See Eph. 1:4; 5:27 [d]1 Cor. 1:8
23 [e]See John 15:4 [f]ch. 2:7; Eph. 3:17 [g]ver. 5, 6 [h]Mark 16:15; [Acts 2:5] [i]See 2 Cor. 3:6
24 [j]See 2 Cor. 7:4 [k][2 Tim. 1:8; 2:10] [l]See 2 Cor. 1:5 [m][Eph. 4:12]
25 [n]ver. 23 [o]See Eph. 3:2
26 [p]Eph. 3:9; See Rom. 16:25, 26
27 [q][ch. 2:2] [r]Eph. 1:18; 3:16 [p][See ver. 26 above] [s]1 Tim. 1:1
28 [t]See ver. 22, 23 [u]See Matt. 5:48
29 [v]1 Cor. 15:10; 1 Tim. 4:10 [w]ch. 4:12; [ch. 2:1] [x]See Eph. 1:19

Chapter 2
1 [y]Phil. 1:30 [w][See ch. 1:29 above]
2 [z]ch. 4:8; Eph. 6:22 [a][ch. 3:14] [b]See ch. 1:27
3 [c]Isa. 11:2; 45:3; 1 Cor. 1:24, 30; 2:6, 7; [Luke 11:49; Eph. 1:8]

1:15–23 In this moving passage that reads like a psalm, Paul declares the preeminence of Christ over all things, visible and invisible. To clear away confusion, the apostle states that from the creation of all things to the redemption of their souls, Christ is Lord of all. He is both transcendent Lord of all things far removed from them, and immanent Lord of all things near to them. The One through whom all things were created (v. 16) is also the One who provides peace with God through his blood on the cross (v. 20). He is the head of creation (vv. 15–17) and the head of the church (vv. 18–20).

Here is the awe-inspiring mystery of the God-man, Jesus Christ—he who threw out the stars with his hands also had nails driven through those hands to reconcile us who were once alienated, hostile, and evil (vv. 21–22). Now that we are considered holy and blameless before God through Christ's sinless life and sacrificial work on the cross, Christians are called by Paul to remember their hope in the Lord Jesus and to remain steadfast in their walk (v. 23; cf. Matt. 7:24–27). And once more Paul tells us that the gospel is our daily source of sustenance; we are to be "stable and steadfast, not shifting from the hope of the gospel that you heard" (Col. 1:23).

1:24–2:5 Here Paul transitions to explain the content, method, and goal of his labors. In doing so, he provides an exemplary model of Christian ministry.

He first unequivocally states that the only *content* of his ministry is Christ: "Him we proclaim" (1:28; cf. 1 Cor. 1:23; 2 Cor. 4:5). Paul asserts that this formerly hidden "mystery" is not some form of esoteric knowledge reserved for a select few, but is God's unfolding plan of redemption through Jesus Christ revealed to all. No longer exclusive to Israel, the content of this message (i.e., Christ, "the hope of glory"; Col. 1:27) is now accessible to all and must be preached to all. We preach not fundamentally an ethical code or a set of doctrines or right behavior, but *Christ*.

As for *method*, Paul continues the paradigm of seeing and preaching Christ from all the Scriptures that was made clear by Jesus himself on the road to Emmaus (Luke 24:27, 44). Paul knew that all of God's Word centers on Christ and what he has done to save sinners, not on what sinners must do for God. As Old Testament believers

of wisdom and knowledge. 4 I say this in order
[d]that no one may delude you with plausible
arguments. 5 For [e]though I am absent in body,
yet I am with you in spirit, rejoicing to see
your [f]good order and [g]the firmness of your
faith in Christ.

Alive in Christ

6 [h]Therefore, as you received Christ Jesus the
Lord, so walk in him, 7 [i]rooted and [j]built up
in him and [k]established in the faith, just [l]as
you were taught, abounding [m]in thanksgiving.
8 See to it that no one takes you captive by
[n]philosophy and [o]empty deceit, according to
[p]human tradition, according to the [q]elemen-
tal spirits[1] of the world, and not according to
Christ. 9 For [r]in him the whole fullness of deity
dwells [s]bodily, 10 and [t]you have been filled in
him, who is [u]the head of all rule and authority.
11 In him also [v]you were circumcised with a circumcision made without hands, by [w]putting
off the body of the flesh, by the circumcision
of Christ, 12 [x]having been buried with him in
baptism, in which [y]you were also raised with
him through faith in [z]the powerful working
of God, [z]who raised him from the dead. 13 [a]And
you, who were dead in your trespasses and the
uncircumcision of your flesh, God [b]made alive
together with him, having forgiven us all our
trespasses, 14 by [c]canceling [d]the record of debt
that stood against us with its legal demands.
This he set aside, nailing it to the cross. 15 [w]He
disarmed the rulers and authorities[2] and [e]put
them to open shame, by [f]triumphing over
them in him.[3]

Let No One Disqualify You

16 Therefore let no one [g]pass judgment
on you [h]in questions of food and drink, or
with regard to [i]a festival or [j]a new moon or a
Sabbath. 17 [k]These are a shadow of the things
to come, but [l]the substance belongs to Christ.
18 Let no one [m]disqualify you, [n]insisting on
asceticism and worship of angels, [o]going on in

[1] Or *elementary principles*; also verse 20 [2] Probably demonic rulers and authorities [3] Or *in it* (that is, the cross)

looked forward to the Christ whose coming was prophesied in Scripture, and as New Testament believers look back to the Christ whose coming was recorded in Scripture, so also are we to look to Christ in all of Scripture as we await his return. Thus he warns and teaches from all the Scriptures through this lens (Col. 1:28). Paul recognized that only Jesus fulfills all the redemptive themes in Scripture. So we too must grow in our understanding of Christ as the center of Scripture.

Lastly, Paul states that he labors tirelessly with this content and method toward a specific *goal*: to "present everyone mature in Christ" (1:28). He does this so that the Christians in the Colossian church would be encouraged and edified with the knowledge of all the blessings included in being united to Christ (2:1–3). Paul experienced the new life that occurs when Christ transforms the believer from the inside out (1 Tim. 1:12–16). As he presents the treasury of wisdom and knowledge that is Christ, he focuses on *maturity in* faith and not just *profession of* faith. He knows that many Christians face the temptation to give up their faith in Christ alone—especially through false teaching (Col. 2:4). But as they grow in their knowledge of Christ through the Word of God, Christians can combat heresy in whatever shape or form.

2:6–23 Paul tells Christians about the benefits available by virtue of being united to Christ in order to "walk in him" faithfully and wisely—especially in the face of false teaching. He calls on them to understand all the resources they have in Christ so as to utilize those resources to fight the good fight of faith (1 Tim. 6:12).

Through the use of the simple yet profound phrase "in him," Paul reveals all the resources available to combat falsehood. In union with Christ, Christians have been rooted, built up, and established in faith (Col. 2:7). In Christ they have been filled with the same authority that Christ possesses (v. 10). In Christ they have been spiritually "circumcised," or set apart from the realm of the flesh to that of the Spirit (v. 11). In him they have "died" to sin and have been "raised" to new life through Christ's baptism of death and resurrection (v. 12). In him they have been forgiven of all their spiritual debts because of the cross (v. 13). In him they have the certainty of victory over Satan and death (v. 15).

And in Christ, as Paul has said already numerous times in this letter, believers walk (vv. 6–7). In the same ways that we received Christ—through faith, by grace—we move forward. The gospel is for sanctification, not only justification; for growth, not

4 [d]Rom. 16:18; [Eph. 5:6; 2 Pet. 2:3]
5 [e]1 Cor. 5:3 [f]1 Cor. 14:40 [g]1 Pet. 5:9
6 [h]ch. 1:10; 1 Thess. 4:1
7 [i]Eph. 3:17 [j]Acts 20:32; Eph. 2:20; See 1 Cor. 3:9 [k]Heb. 13:9 [l]Eph. 4:21 [m]ch. 4:2; Eph. 5:20
8 [n][1 Tim. 6:20] [o]Eph. 5:6 [p]See Matt. 15:2 [q]ver. 20
9 [r]ch. 1:19; John 1:14 [s][ver. 17]
10 [t]Eph. 3:19 [u]See Eph. 1:21, 22
11 [v][Eph. 2:11]; See Rom. 2:29 [w]ver. 15; ch. 3:9
12 [x]Rom. 6:4 [y]ch. 3:1; [Rom. 6:5] [z][1 Cor. 6:14]; See Acts 2:24; Eph. 1:19
13 [a]See Eph. 2:1 [b]See Eph. 2:5
14 [c]See Acts 3:19 [d]See Rom. 7:4
15 [w][See ver. 11 above] [e][Gen. 3:15; Ps. 68:18; Isa. 53:12; Matt. 12:29; Luke 10:18; John 12:31; 16:11; Eph. 4:8; Heb. 2:14] [f]Eph. 2:16
16 [g]Rom. 14:3, 10, 13 [h]Rom. 14:17; Heb. 9:10; See Lev. 11:2 [i]Lev. 23:2; Rom. 14:5 [j][Mark 2:28]; See Num. 28:11
17 [k]Heb. 8:5; 10:1 [l][ver. 2]
18 [m]1 Cor. 9:24 [n]ver. 23 [o][Ezek. 13:7; 1 Tim. 1:7]

detail about visions,[1] [p]puffed up without reason by [q]his sensuous mind, **19** and [r]not [s]holding fast to the Head, from whom the whole body, nourished and knit together through its joints and ligaments, grows with a growth that is from God.

20 If with Christ [t]you died to the [u]elemental spirits of the world, [v]why, as if you were still alive in the world, do you submit to regulations— **21** [w]"Do not handle, Do not taste, Do not touch" **22** ([x]referring to things that all perish as they are used)—according to [y]human precepts and teachings? **23** These have indeed an appearance of wisdom in [z]promoting self-made religion and asceticism and severity to the body, but they are [a]of no value in stopping the indulgence of the flesh.

Put On the New Self

3 [b]If then you have been raised with Christ, seek [c]the things that are above, where Christ is, [d]seated at the right hand of God. **2** [e]Set your minds on things that are above, not on things that are on earth. **3** For [f]you have died, and your life is hidden with Christ in God. **4** When Christ [g]who is your[2] life [h]appears, then you also will appear with him [i]in glory.

5 [j]Put to death therefore [k]what is earthly in you:[3] [l]sexual immorality, impurity, [m]passion, evil desire, and covetousness, [n]which is idolatry. **6** [o]On account of these the wrath of God is coming.[4] **7** [p]In these you too once walked, when you were living in them. **8** But now [q]you must put them all away: [r]anger, wrath, malice, [s]slander, and obscene talk from your mouth. **9** [t]Do not lie to one another, seeing that [u]you have put off [v]the old self[5] with its practices **10** and [w]have put on [x]the new self, [y]which is being renewed in knowledge [z]after the image of [a]its creator. **11** [b]Here there is not Greek and Jew, circumcised and uncircumcised, barbarian, Scythian, slave,[6] free; but Christ is [c]all, and in all.

12 [d]Put on then, as [e]God's chosen ones, holy and beloved, [f]compassionate hearts, [g]kindness, [h]humility, meekness, and patience, **13** [h]bearing with one another and, [i]if one has a complaint against another, [g]forgiving each other; [g]as the Lord has forgiven you, so you also must forgive. **14** And above all these put on [j]love,

[1] Or *about the things he has seen* [2] Some manuscripts *our* [3] Greek *therefore your members that are on the earth* [4] Some manuscripts add *upon the sons of disobedience* [5] Greek *man*; also as supplied in verse 10 [6] Greek *bondservant*

18 [p] [Eph. 4:17] [q] [Rom. 8:7]
19 [r] See Eph. 4:15, 16 [s] Rev. 2:13; 3:11
20 [t] See Rom. 6:2 [u] ver. 8 [v] [Gal. 4:9]
21 [w] ver. 16; 1 Tim. 4:3
22 [x] 1 Cor. 6:13 [y] Isa. 29:13; Matt. 15:9; [Titus 1:14]
23 [z] ver. 18 [a] [1 Tim. 4:8]

Chapter 3
1 [b] ch. 2:12 [c] [Phil. 3:14] [d] See Eph. 1:20
2 [e] See Matt. 16:23
3 [f] ch. 2:20; See Rom. 6:2
4 [g] See John 11:25 [h] [Phil. 3:21; 1 Pet. 1:1, 7, 13; 1 John 2:28; 3:2] [i] 1 Cor. 15:43
5 [j] Rom. 8:13; [Gal. 5:24] [k] Rom. 6:13 [l] See Eph. 5:3, 5 [m] Rom. 1:26 [n] [Job 31:25, 26]
6 [o] See Eph. 5:6
7 [p] See Eph. 2:2, 11
8 [q] See Eph. 4:22 [r] Eph. 4:31 [s] See Eph. 4:29
9 [t] Lev. 19:11; See Eph. 4:25 [u] ch. 2:11 [v] Rom. 6:6; Eph. 4:22
10 [w] Eph. 4:24 [x] See Rom. 6:4 [y] See Rom. 12:2 [z] See Rom. 8:29 [a] [Eph. 2:10]
11 [b] [Rom. 10:12]; See 1 Cor. 12:13; Gal. 5:6 [c] Eph. 1:23
12 [d] ver. 10 [e] Rom. 8:33 [f] Phil. 2:1 [g] Eph. 4:32 [h] See Eph. 4:2
13 [h] [See ver. 12 above] [i] Mark 11:25 [g] [See ver. 12 above]
14 [j] [1 Thess. 5:8]; See Eph. 5:2

only conversion. We do what Jesus instructs in the confidence that he knows and will accomplish what is best for our lives, and we are motivated and enabled to do this as he instructs us by his grace.

Paul thus calls on believers who are united to Christ to utilize these promises and benefits and to not be led astray by any teaching that is contrary to the gospel that he taught them (v. 8). For fear that they may fall prey to humanly devised rules regarding true spirituality (vv. 16–18), Paul reminds them of all that they know about Christ and all that they possess in Christ (v. 19). Through faith, believers have the assurance of accessing the resources of the Word and Spirit to remain steadfast amid the storms of false teaching (cf. 1 John 2:26–27).

3:1–17 Having established the supremacy of Christ and salvation in Christ, in chapter 3 Paul turns his attention to the practical implications of living out what it means to be united to Christ by faith. He begins by describing the status of believers and then the servanthood that follows from that status. In this way the indicatives of the gospel (*who we are* by virtue of God's grace) drive the imperatives for our lives (*what we should do* in accordance with God's Word).

The new status that believers possess includes being raised and seated with Christ at the right hand of God in heaven (v. 1), having certainty of their future state of glory (v. 4), becoming equal heirs of God's kingdom with all other Christian believers (v. 11), and being forgiven by Christ (v. 13). Believers already possess many benefits tied to Christ's resurrection, ascension, intercession, and glorification. Some of these blessings, however, will not be fully realized until Christ's return. Thus, believers live in an already/not yet (or "eschatological") tension. The blessings of the final age have dawned right now, in the middle of history, becoming ours through union with Christ. We are therefore pilgrims who, though our destiny is secure, are called to journey through life with faith and obedience.

In light of these many gracious eschatological blessings, Paul calls on the Colossians to seek, out of gratitude to and love for God, the knowledge and wisdom that comes

which [k]binds everything together in [l]perfect
harmony. 15 And let [m]the peace of Christ rule in
your hearts, to which indeed you were called
[n]in one body. And [o]be thankful. 16 Let [p]the
word of Christ dwell in you richly, teaching
and admonishing one another in all wisdom,
[q]singing psalms and hymns and spiritual
songs, [r]with thankfulness in your hearts to
God. 17 And [s]whatever you do, in word or deed,
do everything in the name of the Lord Jesus,
[t]giving thanks to God the Father through him.

Rules for Christian Households

18 [u]Wives, submit to your husbands, as [v]is fitting in the Lord. 19 Husbands, love your wives,
and [w]do not be harsh with them. 20 Children,
obey your parents [x]in everything, for this
pleases the Lord. 21 Fathers, do not provoke
your children, lest they become discouraged.
22 Bondservants,[1] obey [x]in everything those
who are your earthly masters,[2] not by way of
eye-service, as people-pleasers, but with sincerity of heart, fearing the Lord. 23 [y]Whatever
you do, work heartily, [z]as for the Lord and not
for men, 24 knowing that from the Lord [a]you
will receive the inheritance as your reward.
[b]You are serving the Lord Christ. 25 For the
wrongdoer will be paid back for the wrong he
has done, and there is no partiality.

4 Masters, treat your bondservants justly
and fairly, knowing that you also have a
Master in heaven.

Further Instructions

2 [c]Continue steadfastly in prayer, being
watchful in it [d]with thanksgiving. 3 At the
same time, pray also for us, that God may
[e]open to us a door for the word, [f]to declare
the mystery of Christ, [g]on account of which
I am in prison— 4 that I may make it clear,
which is how I ought to speak.
5 [h]Walk in wisdom toward [i]outsiders, making the best use of the time. 6 Let your speech
always [j]be gracious, [k]seasoned with salt, [l]so
that you may know how you ought to answer
each person.

[1] Or *Slaves*; also 4:1 (for the contextual rendering of the Greek word *doulos*, see Preface) [2] Or *your masters according to the flesh*

from Christ alone (vv. 1–2). More than this, Paul summons them to serve others in a manner consistent with the characteristics of Christ's kingdom. He describes Christlike servanthood as both a "putting off" (vv. 5–11), no longer practicing the old vices that characterized their lives before Christ, and a "putting on" (vv. 12–17), practicing the virtues of love, joy, peace, patience, kindness, goodness, faithfulness, gentleness, and self-control (cf. Gal. 5:22–23). This ongoing process of becoming a Christlike servant (sanctification; cf. Phil. 2:12–14) occurs only because of the change in status (justification, etc.; cf. Rom. 3:21–31) that God has granted. It is as we learn of God's love for us that our hearts are changed and we are moved to obey him from the inside out.

3:18–4:1 Paul continues the exposition and application that he began in the previous section: Because our relationship with God has changed *through* Christ, our relationships with those around us must change *for* Christ.

Having spoken in general about our servanthood, Paul now focuses particular attention on how such service to Christ affects those relationships closest to us—in our homes and work. Note first how many times Paul reminds his readers that in each of these relationships "the Lord" is present. They must now treat others with a new perspective—one that includes the Lord Jesus' grace and righteousness. Then, since they have experienced the grace of Christ, Paul calls on them to be gracious to one another: wives submit fittingly (cf. Eph. 5:22–24), husbands love sacrificially (cf. Eph. 5:25–32), children obey rightly (cf. Eph. 6:1–3), parents discipline unprovokingly (cf. Eph. 6:4), workers work diligently (cf. Eph. 6:5–8), and bosses act justly (cf. Eph. 6:9). This is the beauty of the life into which the gospel of grace calls us.

4:2–18 In this final section of the letter, Paul encourages believers with several points that follow from his insistence that, since Christ is Lord and Savior of all, they have every spiritual blessing in their union with Christ. Here we see that the gospel fuels the Christian life in three ways: in prayer, partnership, and purpose.

First, we must cultivate a life of persistent prayer (4:2; cf. Mark 1:35; 14:32–39). As those who have been adopted into God's very family, we have full and free access to the Father and should seek him for his gracious blessing upon our lives, which he delights to give. We are liberated to come to him not tepidly or reluctantly but "with thanksgiving" (Col. 4:2).

14 [k]Eph. 4:3 [l]Heb. 6:1; [John 17:23]
15 [m]See Phil. 4:7 [n]Eph. 2:16 [o]ver. 17
16 [p]John 15:3 [q]See Eph. 5:19 [r]ch. 4:6
17 [s]ver. 23; 1 Cor. 10:31 [t]ch. 1:12; 4:2; See Eph. 5:20
18 [u]For ch. 3:18–4:1, see Eph. 5:22-6:9 [v]Eph. 5:4; Philem. 8
19 [w]Eph. 4:31
20 [x][Eph. 5:24; Titus 2:9]
22 [x][See ver. 20 above]
23 [y]ver. 17 [z][Philem. 16]
24 [a][Eph. 6:8] [b][1 Cor. 7:22]
Chapter 4
2 [c]For ver. 2-4, see Eph. 6:18-20 [d]ch. 2:7
3 [e]See Acts 14:27 [f]See Rom. 16:25 [g]ver. 18; Eph. 6:20; See Phil. 1:7
5 [h]See Eph. 5:15-17 [i]See Mark 4:11
6 [j]ch. 3:16 [k]See Mark 9:50 [l]1 Pet. 3:15

Final Greetings

[7]Tychicus will tell you [m]all about my activities. He is a beloved brother and faithful minister and fellow servant[1] in the Lord. [8]I have sent
him to you for this very purpose, that you may
know how we are and that he may encourage
your hearts, [9]and with him [n]Onesimus, our
faithful and [o]beloved brother, who is one of
you. They will tell you of everything that has
taken place here.
[10][p]Aristarchus my fellow prisoner greets you,
and Mark [q]the cousin of Barnabas (concerning whom you have received instructions—[r]if
he comes to you, welcome him), [11]and Jesus
who is called [s]Justus. [t]These are the only men
of the circumcision among my fellow workers for the kingdom of God, and [u]they have
been a comfort to me. [12][v]Epaphras, who is
one of you, a servant of Christ Jesus, greets
you, always [w]struggling on your behalf in
his prayers, that you may stand [x]mature and
fully assured in all the will of God. [13]For I bear
him witness that he has worked hard for you
and for those in Laodicea and in Hierapolis.
[14][y]Luke the beloved physician greets you,
as does [z]Demas. [15]Give my greetings to the
brothers[2] at Laodicea, and to Nympha and [a]the
church in her house. [16]And when [b]this letter
has been read among you, have it also read in
the church of the Laodiceans; and see that you
also read the letter from Laodicea. [17]And say to
[c]Archippus, "See that you fulfill [d]the ministry
that you have received in the Lord."
[18]I, Paul, [e]write this greeting with my own
hand. [f]Remember [g]my chains. [h]Grace be with
you.

[1] Greek *fellow bondservant*; also verse 12 [2] Or *brothers and sisters*

7[m] For ver. 7-9, see Eph. 6:21, 22
9[n] Philem. 10 [o] Philem. 16
10[p] Acts 19:29; 20:4; 27:2; Philem. 24; [Rom. 16:7] [q] See Acts 15:37, 39 [r] [2 Tim. 4:11]
11[s] [Acts 1:23; 18:7] [t] See Acts 11:2 [u] [Philem. 7]
12[v] ch. 1:7; Philem. 23 [w] See Rom. 15:30 [x] See Matt. 5:48
14[y] 2 Tim. 4:11; See Acts 16:10 [z] 2 Tim. 4:10; Philem. 24
15[a] See Rom. 16:5

Second, we must humbly partner with others for the sake of gospel ministry (vv. 3–4, 7–17; cf. Mark 3:13–19). Not all of us are preachers, but we are all invited into the adventure of spreading the preached gospel by praying for preachers in our community to have "a door for the word, to declare the mystery of Christ" (Col. 4:3).

Third, our lives must be purposeful, so that through the testimony of our conduct (words and deeds), Christ may be seen (vv. 5–6; cf. Eph. 4:29). We treat others in a "gracious" (Col. 4:6) way, as God in Christ has treated us.

The letter ends on a note that sums up the message of Paul's ministry to the Colossians: "Grace be with you" (v. 18).

16[b] 1 Thess. 5:27 **17**[c] Philem. 2 [d] 2 Tim. 4:5 **18**[e] See 1 Cor. 16:21 [f] [Heb. 13:3] [g] ver. 3; See Phil. 1:7 [h] 1 Tim. 6:21; 2 Tim. 4:22; [Titus 3:15]

Introduction to 1 Thessalonians

Author, Date, and Recipients

Paul wrote this letter to the church in Thessalonica. He probably wrote in A.D. 49–51 from Corinth, during his second missionary journey (Acts 18:1–18).

The Gospel in 1 Thessalonians

Paul's letters to the Thessalonians bear witness to the glorious reality that the gospel is "the power of God for salvation to everyone who believes" (see Rom. 1:16). In 1 Thessalonians, Paul cannot stop rejoicing that the gospel came to the Thessalonians in word, in power, and with full conviction by the Holy Spirit (1 Thess. 1:5). Paul and his companions labored diligently among the Thessalonians (Acts 17), and by God's grace they could glorify God as they witnessed the steadfast faithfulness of the body of Christ in Thessalonica. The Thessalonians were a congregation who genuinely loved one another as they followed the example of Christ and his apostles, and they lived each day in light of the promised return of Jesus Christ.

As the Thessalonian believers waited, Paul urged them to be steadfast in their faith in Christ, to continue to grow in love for one another, and to remain sexually pure according to God's holy calling. Such living, Paul explained, must be grounded in the daily heart-application of the gospel itself. In this way the Thessalonians would continue to manifest their genuine faith in the resurrected and returning Jesus Christ—living gratefully, prayerfully, and expectantly. The gospel promise is that we who are saved by God's grace alone through faith alone in the sinless life, sacrificial death, and victorious resurrection of Jesus Christ can eagerly look forward to his return that will come "like a thief in the night" to rescue us and unite us with his loved ones from all the world and from all ages (1 Thess. 4:13–5:11).

Outline

I. Opening (1:1)

II. Thanksgiving and Encouragement (1:2–3:13)

III. Instruction and Exhortation (4:1–5:28)

The First Letter of Paul to the Thessalonians

1 Thessalonians

Greeting

1 Paul, [a]Silvanus, and Timothy,
To the church of the [b]Thessalonians in
God the Father and the Lord Jesus Christ:
[c]Grace to you and peace.

The Thessalonians' Faith and Example

2 [d]We give thanks to God always for all of
you, constantly[1] [e]mentioning you in our
prayers, 3 remembering before [f]our God and
Father [g]your work of faith and labor of [h]love
and [i]steadfastness of hope in our Lord Jesus
Christ. 4 For we know, [j]brothers[2] loved by God,
[k]that he has chosen you, 5 because [l]our gospel came to you not only in word, but also in
power and [m]in the Holy Spirit and with full
[n]conviction. You know [o]what kind of men we
proved to be among you for your sake. 6 And
[p]you became imitators of us [q]and of the Lord,
for [r]you received the word in much affliction,

[1] Or *without ceasing* [2] Or *brothers and sisters*. The plural Greek word *adelphoi* (translated "brothers") refers to siblings in a family. In New Testament usage, depending on the context, *adelphoi* may refer either to men or to both men and women who are siblings (brothers and sisters) in God's family, the church

1:1–10 The apostle Paul was not put off by the reality that he was ministering to an imperfect church. He focused instead on the understanding that he was writing to the redeemed body and promised bride of Jesus Christ. Thus, each of his letters opens with a benediction (a "good word"). First Thessalonians is no exception.

Paul begins this letter with grace (v. 1), but he also concludes it with grace (5:28). God's grace is the foundation and fountain of the gospel message, and an underlying theme of Paul's letters to the Thessalonians (5:23–24; 2 Thess. 1:12; 2:16). This grace had produced in the Thessalonians a steadfast hope in Christ on account of the steadfastness of Christ himself. This hope sustained the Thessalonian believers in their work of faith and labor of love (2 Thess. 3:5).

Furthermore, God established the reason for their hope in his own sovereign work, having loved them, chosen them, and called them by the external call of the gospel through Paul's preaching and the internal call of the gospel in power and in the Holy Spirit (1 Thess. 1:4–5). Having received the gospel of Jesus Christ by the calling of the Holy Spirit in accord with the Father's sovereign plan, the Thessalonians became imitators of the apostles and of the Lord Jesus Christ (v. 6). Our imitation of Christ is a natural consequence of the Holy Spirit's work of regeneration. We seek, trust, pursue, and imitate Christ because Christ sought, found, pursued, and rescued us. Thus Paul rejoices in the Thessalonians' faithfulness as they serve as an example to believers (v. 7), sound forth the word of the Lord, possess a faith that goes forth everywhere as a shining light to a dark world (v. 8), show generous hospitality, and serve the living and true God, having repented and turned from serving idols (v. 9).

The Thessalonians know the gospel and live faithfully in light of it to such a degree that Paul admits that he and his companions "need not say anything" (v. 8). The Thessalonians' faith shines so brightly that people everywhere know who they are and the truth of the word they proclaim. From the very beginning, even amid much affliction, the Thessalonian church has been a gospel-centered church, reflecting the light of Christ and the gospel with the joy of the Holy Spirit (v. 6) and awaiting the return of the risen Christ who "delivers us from the wrath to come" (v. 10). The gospel story of Christ's life, death, and resurrection culminates in our final deliverance from the wrath of God (5:9). First Thessalonians is a message of good news from start to finish.

Chapter 1
1 [a]Acts 15:22; 2 Cor. 1:19; 2 Thess. 1:1; 1 Pet. 5:12 [b]See Acts 17:1 [c]Rom. 1:7
2 [d]ch. 2:13; See Rom. 1:8; Eph. 5:20 [e]Rom. 1:9; 2 Tim. 1:3
3 [f]See Gal. 1:4 [g]2 Thess. 1:11; [John 6:29; Gal. 5:6; Heb. 6:10; James 2:22] [h]2 Thess. 1:3, 4; [Col. 1:4; 1 Tim. 1:14; Rev. 2:19] [i]Rom. 8:25; 15:4
4 [j]2 Thess. 2:13 [k]2 Pet. 1:10
5 [l]2 Thess. 2:14 [m]2 Cor. 6:6; See 1 Cor. 2:4 [n]Col. 2:2; [Heb. 2:3] [o][ch. 2:10; Acts 20:18; 2 Thess. 3:7]
6 [p][ch. 2:14; 2 Thess. 3:7, 9]; See 1 Cor. 4:16 [q]1 Cor. 11:1 [r]Acts 17:5-10

[s]with the [t]joy of the Holy Spirit, 7 so that you
became an example to all the believers in
Macedonia and in Achaia. 8 For not only has
the word of the Lord [u]sounded forth from you
in Macedonia and Achaia, but your faith in
God has gone forth [v]everywhere, so that we
need not say anything. 9 For they themselves
report concerning us the kind of [w]reception
we had among you, and how [x]you turned to
God [y]from idols to serve the living and [z]true
God, 10 and [a]to wait for his Son [b]from heaven,
[c]whom he raised from the dead, Jesus [d]who
delivers us from [e]the wrath to come.

Paul's Ministry to the Thessalonians

2 For you yourselves know, brothers,[1] that
our [f]coming to you [g]was not in vain. 2 But
though we had already suffered and been
shamefully treated [h]at Philippi, as you know,
[i]we had boldness in our God [j]to declare to
you the gospel of God in the midst of much
[k]conflict. 3 For [l]our appeal does not spring
from [m]error or [n]impurity or [o]any attempt to
deceive, 4 but just as we have been approved
by God [p]to be entrusted with the gospel, so
we speak, not [q]to please man, but to please
God [r]who tests our hearts. 5 [s]For we never came
with words of flattery,[2] as you know, nor with
a pretext for greed—[t]God is witness. 6 [u]Nor
did we seek glory from people, whether from
you or from others, [v]though we could have
made [w]demands as [x]apostles of Christ. 7 But
we were [y]gentle[3] among you, [z]like a nursing
mother taking care of her own children. 8 So,
being affectionately desirous of you, we were
ready to share with you not only the gospel of
God [a]but also our own selves, because you had
become very dear to us.
9 For you remember, brothers, [b]our labor and
toil: we [c]worked night and day, that we might
not be a burden to any of you, while we proclaimed to you the gospel of God. 10 You are
witnesses, and [d]God also, [e]how holy and righteous and blameless was our conduct toward

[1] Or *brothers and sisters*; also verses 9, 14, 17 [2] Or *with a flattering speech* [3] Some manuscripts *infants*

6 [s] See Matt. 5:12 [t] Acts 13:52; Gal. 5:22
8 [u] [Rom. 10:18; 2 Thess. 3:1] [v] [Rom. 1:8; 16:19; 2 Thess. 1:4]
9 [w] ch. 2:1 [x] See Acts 14:15 [y] 1 Cor. 12:2; [Gal. 4:8] [z] See John 17:3
10 [a] See 1 Cor. 1:7 [b] ch. 4:16; [2 Thess. 1:10]; See Acts 1:11 [c] See Acts 2:24 [d] Col. 1:13 [e] ch. 2:16; 5:9; Matt. 3:7; Rom. 5:9

Chapter 2
1 [f] ch. 1:9 [g] [2 Thess. 1:10]
2 [h] Acts 16:22-24 [i] See Acts 4:13 [j] Acts 17:2-9 [k] Phil. 1:30
3 [l] [2 Cor. 2:17] [m] 2 Thess. 2:11 [n] ch. 4:7 [o] 2 Cor. 4:2
4 [p] See Gal. 2:7 [q] See Gal. 1:10 [r] Ps. 17:3; See Rom. 8:27
5 [s] See Acts 20:33 [t] ver. 10; See Rom. 1:9
6 [u] [2 Cor. 4:5]; See John 5:41 [v] 1 Cor. 9:4; 2 Thess. 3:9; [Philem. 8, 9] [w] [ver. 9; 2 Cor. 11:9] [x] See 1 Cor. 9:1
7 [y] 2 Tim. 2:24; [1 Cor. 14:20] [z] [ver. 11; Isa. 49:23; 60:16]
8 [a] See 2 Cor. 12:15
9 [b] 2 Thess. 3:8; [Phil. 4:16] [c] See Acts 18:3
10 [d] ver. 5 [e] See ch. 1:5

2:1–12 The gospel is a glorious announcement, a message of good news to be proclaimed to all nations. It takes boldness to declare news, especially news that initially offends sinners, but Paul's boldness is not a self-generated confidence. Instead, it is a confidence that is from God and in God. As Paul explained to the Corinthian church, we are not "sufficient in ourselves to claim anything as coming from us, but our sufficiency is from God" (2 Cor. 3:5). Our boldness in proclaiming the good news about what God has accomplished through Christ comes from God's sufficiency and strength, not our own. God-reliance rather than self-reliance is indeed a principle at the very heart of the gospel, for this is the very reflex of the heart that trusts in Christ's righteousness rather than its own.

Considering the conflict that Paul and his companions encountered while preaching the gospel at Philippi (Acts 16:19–24), Paul wants to make it clear that just as the gospel they preach does not come from mere humans, nor are they motivated in their ministry by a desire for human approval (1 Thess. 2:4; cf. Gal. 1:10). Apostolic messengers are servants of God, entrusted with the gospel of God and having the primary aim of God's approval. God does not evaluate faithfulness based on outward appearance; he sees and tests our hearts (1 Sam. 16:7). In the face of conflict or opposition, God calls his people to stand firm in faith (Isa. 7:1–9) because God's promises are sure, his gospel is his power unto salvation, and his Word never returns empty but always accomplishes his sovereign intent. It is precisely for these reasons that Paul will not compromise the content of the gospel. He never tried to deceive the Thessalonians with words of flattery or with any other message that would be a pretext for gaining money, fame, or glory from people, or to advance his own power over people (1 Thess. 2:3, 5–6).

When we trust God and his gospel to do the powerful work God promises, our gospel ministry will never be in vain (v. 1), for while we are responsible to plant and water, God brings the increase according to his own plan and timing (cf. 1 Cor. 3:5–9). Moreover, we will not feel the need to deceive, make demands, or be belligerent. On the contrary, we will feel the freedom to be gentle (1 Thess. 2:7) and respectful in our declaration and defense of the gospel (1 Pet. 3:15).

Although Paul sought to please God and not man, he also understood the importance of living in a Christlike way before the eyes of the watching world. For while God alone tests hearts, he has also called us to be holy and righteous and blameless, and even to have a good reputation with those outside the church (1 Tim. 3:7).

you believers. 11 For you know how, [f]like a
father with his children, 12 we exhorted each
one of you and encouraged you and [g]charged
[h]you to walk in a manner worthy of God, [i]who
calls you into his own kingdom and glory.
13 And [j]we also thank God constantly[1] for
this, that when you received [k]the word of God,
which you heard from us, you accepted it [l]not
as the word of men[2] but as what it really is,
the word of God, [m]which is at work in you
believers. 14 For you, brothers, [n]became imitators of [o]the churches of God in Christ Jesus
that are in Judea. For [p]you suffered the same
things from your own countrymen [q]as they
did from the Jews,[3] 15 [r]who killed both the Lord
Jesus and [s]the prophets, and drove us out, and
displease God and [t]oppose all mankind 16 [u]by
hindering us from speaking to the Gentiles
that they might be saved—so as always [v]to fill
up the measure of their sins. But [w]wrath has
come upon them at last![4]

Paul's Longing to See Them Again

17 But since we were torn away from you,
brothers, for a short time, [x]in person not in
heart, we endeavored the more eagerly and
with great desire [y]to see you face to face,
18 because we wanted to come to you—I, Paul,
again and again—but Satan [z]hindered us.
19 For what is our hope or [a]joy or crown of
boasting [b]before our Lord Jesus at his [c]coming?
Is it not you? 20 For you are our glory and joy.

3 Therefore when we could bear it no longer,
we were willing [d]to be left behind at Athens
alone, 2 and we [e]sent Timothy, [f]our brother
and God's coworker[5] in the gospel of Christ,
to establish and exhort you in your faith, 3 that
no one be moved by these afflictions. For you
yourselves know that [g]we are destined for this.
4 For when we were with you, we kept telling
you beforehand that we were to suffer affliction, [h]just as it has come to pass, and just as you
know. 5 For this reason, [i]when I could bear it no
longer, [j]I sent to learn about your faith, [j]for fear
that somehow [k]the tempter had tempted you
and [l]our labor would be in vain.

Timothy's Encouraging Report

6 But [m]now that Timothy has come to us
from you, and has brought us the good news
of [n]your faith and love and reported [o]that you
always remember us kindly and [p]long to see

[1] Or *without ceasing* [2] The Greek word *anthropoi* can refer to both men and women [3] The Greek word *Ioudaioi* can refer to Jewish religious leaders and others under their influence, who opposed the Christian faith in that time [4] Or *completely*, or *forever* [5] Some manuscripts *servant*

When we live as imitators of Christ (1 Thess. 1:6), manifesting the powerful work of the Holy Spirit within our hearts, we will not live hypocritically but authentically. We are representing the One we proclaim, after all, who never acted hypocritically. This is why Paul exhorts, encourages, and charges the Thessalonian believers as a loving father (2:11) and nursing mother (v. 7) to walk in a manner worthy of the God who has called us into his own kingdom and glory.

3:6–12 Paul and his companions proclaimed the gospel of Jesus Christ to the Thessalonians, and when the Holy Spirit plants the gospel in the hearts of his people, gospel fruit always abounds. Timothy's report of the Thessalonians' faith and love was good news that confirmed their authentic reception of the good news of Christ (v. 6). Their steadfastness in Christ is life-giving encouragement to Paul, who finds joy over the fact that the Thessalonians are standing fast in the Lord (v. 8), knowing that if they were not to stand fast amid persecution, there would be no evidence that they actually believed the gospel.

The Thessalonians' true reception of the gospel, however, was evident in their vibrant faith in Christ, expressing itself in love for Christ and all that Christ loves (cf. Gal. 5:6). Such love is reciprocal love, which not only receives but also extends Christ's love, manifesting itself before the world as the love of Christ's true disciples (cf. John 13:35). This beautiful love has been evident among the Thessalonians, and Paul rejoices in it, responding to their kind remembrance and their longing to see the apostles. Paul expresses his longing to see the Thessalonians face to face and to supply what is lacking in their faith (1 Thess. 3:10). Not that the Thessalonians lack what is necessary for saving faith, but due to the brevity of Paul's initial ministry among them (Acts 17), they still have much to learn about the implications of the gospel for Christian living and doctrine.

Here we see Paul's heart as a church-planting, disciple-making pastor of God's people. Throughout Paul's letters, we observe that his concern is to see sinners not only converted to Christ but growing in Christ and eagerly awaiting Christ's return.

11 [f] [ver. 7]; See 1 Cor. 4:14
12 [g] Eph. 4:17 [h] See Eph. 4:1 [i] ch. 5:24; 2 Thess. 2:14; 1 Pet. 5:10; See Rom. 8:28
13 [j] See ch. 1:2, 3 [k] [Rom. 10:17] [l] [Gal. 4:14]; See Matt. 10:20 [m] Heb. 4:12
14 [n] See ch. 1:6 [o] See 1 Cor. 7:17 [p] ch. 3:4; Acts 17:5; 2 Thess. 1:4, 5 [q] [Heb. 10:33, 34]
15 [r] See Luke 24:20 [s] Jer. 2:30; Matt. 23:29-34; See Matt. 5:12 [t] [Esth. 3:8]
16 [u] Acts 13:45, 50; 14:2, 19; 17:5, 13; 18:12; 22:21, 22 [v] See Gen. 15:16 [w] See ch. 1:10
17 [x] 1 Cor. 5:3; Col. 2:5 [y] ch. 3:10
18 [z] Rom. 15:22; [Rom. 1:13]
19 [a] See Phil. 4:1 [b] 1 Cor. 15:31; [2 Thess. 1:4]; See 2 Cor. 1:14 [c] ch. 3:13; 4:15; 5:23; Matt. 24:3; 1 Cor. 15:23; 2 Thess. 2:1, 8; James 5:7, 8; 2 Pet. 1:16; 3:4, 12; 1 John 2:28

Chapter 3
1 [d] Acts 17:15, 16
2 [e] See Phil. 2:19 [f] 2 Cor. 1:1; Col. 1:1; Philem. 1; Heb. 13:23
3 [g] See Acts 9:16; 14:22
4 [h] See ch. 2:14
5 [i] ver. 1, 2 [j] [1 Cor. 7:5; 2 Cor. 11:3] [k] Matt. 4:3 [l] See Phil. 2:16
6 [m] Acts 18:5; [2 Cor. 7:6, 9] [n] See ch. 1:3 [o] [1 Cor. 11:2] [p] See Phil. 1:8

us, as we long to see you— 7 for this reason,
brothers,[1] in all our distress and affliction [q]we
have been comforted about you through your
faith. 8 For now we live, if you [r]are standing
fast in the Lord. 9 For [s]what thanksgiving can
we return to God for you, for all the joy that
we feel for your sake before our God, 10 as we
pray most earnestly [t]night and day [u]that we
may see you face to face and [v]supply what is
lacking in your faith?
11 Now may [w]our God and Father himself,
and our Lord Jesus, [x]direct our way to you,
12 and may the Lord [y]make you increase and
abound in love [z]for one another and for all, as
we do for you, 13 so that he may [a]establish your
hearts blameless in holiness before [w]our God
and Father, at [b]the coming of our Lord Jesus
[c]with all his saints.

A Life Pleasing to God

4 Finally, then, brothers,[2] we ask and urge
you in the Lord Jesus, that as you [d]received
from us [e]how you ought to walk and [f]to please
God, just as you are doing, that you [g]do so
more and more. 2 For [h]you know what instructions we gave you through the Lord Jesus. 3 For
this is the will of God, [i]your sanctification:[3]
[j]that you abstain from sexual immorality;
4 that each one of you know how to control
his own [k]body[4] in holiness and [l]honor, 5 not
in [m]the passion of lust [n]like the Gentiles [o]who
do not know God; 6 that no one transgress and
[p]wrong his brother in this matter, because the
Lord is [q]an avenger in all these things, as we
told you beforehand and solemnly warned
you. 7 For [r]God has not called us for [s]impu-
rity, but in holiness. 8 Therefore [t]whoever

[1] Or *brothers and sisters* [2] Or *brothers and sisters*; also verses 10, 13 [3] Or *your holiness* [4] Or *how to take a wife for himself*; Greek *how to possess his own vessel*

7 [q] 2 Cor. 1:4
8 [r] See 1 Cor. 16:13
9 [s] [ch. 1:2]
10 [t] 2 Tim. 1:3 [u] ch. 2:17; [Rom. 1:10] [v] See 2 Cor. 13:9
11 [w] See Gal. 1:4 [x] 2 Thess. 3:5
12 [y] ch. 4:1, 10; Phil. 1:9; 2 Thess. 1:3 [z] ch. 4:9; 5:15
13 [a] James 5:8 [w] [See ver. 11 above] [b] See ch. 2:19 [c] Zech. 14:5; Jude 14

Chapter 4
1 [d] Phil. 4:9; Col. 2:6 [e] See Eph. 4:1 [f] See Col. 1:10 [g] See ch. 3:12
2 [h] [1 Cor. 11:2]
3 [i] Rom. 6:19, 22; 1 Cor. 1:30; 2 Thess. 2:13; 1 Tim. 2:15; Heb. 12:14; 1 Pet. 1:2 [j] See 1 Cor. 6:18
4 [k] 1 Pet. 3:7; [2 Cor. 4:7] [l] [Rom. 1:24]
5 [m] See Rom. 1:26 [n] Eph. 4:17 [o] Ps. 79:6; Jer. 9:3; 10:25; See Gal. 4:8
6 [p] 1 Cor. 6:8 [q] Rom. 13:4; [Rom. 12:19; Heb. 13:4]
7 [r] ver. 3; See 1 Pet. 1:15 [s] ch. 2:3
8 [t] [ch. 2:13]; See Luke 10:16

So it is that whenever we study the Word of God or hear it preached, we are seeking to be more fully supplied with what we need to grow in the grace and knowledge of Jesus Christ (2 Pet. 3:18). This is Paul's earnest desire for the Thessalonians, as it is for all the churches he planted. Paul thus reminds them that just as God establishes our holy status by declaring us righteous (forensic justification), he also increasingly enables us to live more righteously (progressive sanctification) (2 Thess. 2:17).

Therefore, Paul gives the Thessalonians a word of encouragement and a prayer of blessing before concluding with his final instructions in 1 Thessalonians 4 and 5. In light of the imminent return of Christ, Paul's desire is that the Thessalonians remain steadfast in Christ, not merely living out their days but growing as they increase and abound in love for one another and for all (3:12). The beauty of the gospel promise is that the Lord is the one ultimately responsible not only for our increase in love but also for establishing us in holiness before our God and Father (v. 13). Our entire salvation is of grace. We all will stand before God at the coming of our Lord Jesus, who is coming with all those he has declared and established in his holiness, namely, his saints ("holy ones").

4:1–12 Having referred to the Thessalonians as "saints" at the end of chapter 3, Paul urges them to walk as saints in chapter 4. This is the apostle's common theme in discipling believers: reminding them of who they are in Christ and urging them to walk accordingly (Gal. 5:25; Eph. 2:10; 5:8; Col. 2:6). Paul's doctrine of Christian living is established on, and motivated by, the very gospel through which we become Christians in the first place. The imperatives of the Christian life (what we should do) are built upon the indicatives of the gospel (who we are by virtue of Christ's work on our behalf). The inversion of this order is antithetical to the gospel, even if it promotes good behavior.

Paul's constant encouragement to believers is to live in accordance with our new, grace-given identity—to be what we are in Christ. This is why Paul in his instructions to the Thessalonians is careful to reiterate that all of his asking and urging and instructing is established on the fact that we have been taught by God (1 Thess. 4:9), in and through the Lord Jesus (vv. 1–2), who gives his Holy Spirit (v. 8). The Father, Son, and Holy Spirit each take part in our justification (enabling us to be declared righteous) and in our sanctification (enabling us to live righteously). In other words, "He who began a good work in you will bring it to completion at the day of Jesus Christ" (Phil. 1:6). Simply put, God finishes what he starts. He begins his good work in us by the power of the gospel of Jesus Christ through the regenerating work of the Holy Spirit. That same power creates in us the faith by which we are declared

disregards this, disregards not man but God,
[u]who gives his Holy Spirit to you.
9 Now concerning [v]brotherly love [w]you have
no need for anyone to write to you, for you
yourselves have been [x]taught by God [y]to love
one another, 10 for that indeed is what [z]you
are doing to all the brothers throughout
Macedonia. But we urge you, brothers, to [a]do
this more and more, 11 and to aspire [b]to live
quietly, and [c]to mind your own affairs, and
[d]to work with your hands, as we instructed
you, 12 so that you may [e]walk properly before
[f]outsiders and be dependent on no one.

The Coming of the Lord

13 But we do not want you to be uninformed,
brothers, about those who are asleep, [g]that
you may not grieve as others do [h]who have no
hope. 14 For [i]since we believe that Jesus died
and rose again, even so, through Jesus, God
will bring with him [j]those who have fallen
asleep. 15 For this we declare to you [k]by a word
from the Lord,[1] that [l]we who are alive, who
are left until [m]the coming of the Lord, will not
precede those who have fallen asleep. 16 For
[n]the Lord himself will descend [o]from heaven
[p]with a cry of command, with the voice of [q]an
archangel, and [r]with the sound of the trumpet
of God. And [s]the dead in Christ will rise first.
17 Then we who are alive, who are left, will be
[t]caught up together with them [u]in the clouds
to meet the Lord in the air, and so [v]we will
always be with the Lord. 18 Therefore encourage one another with these words.

The Day of the Lord

5 Now concerning [w]the times and the seasons, brothers,[2] [x]you have no need to have
anything written to you. 2 For you yourselves
are fully aware that [y]the day of the Lord will
come like a thief in the night. 3 While people
are saying, "There is peace and security," then

[1] Or *by the word of the Lord* [2] Or *brothers and sisters*; also verses 4, 12, 14, 25, 26, 27

righteous (i.e., justification) and by which he enables us to live more consistently with our righteous status (i.e., sanctification) by the indwelling power of the Holy Spirit (Rom. 1:16–17; 5:1–5).

This sanctification, Paul says to the Thessalonian church, is the will of God (1 Thess. 4:3). When we struggle to know the will of God in our lives, we can always rest assured in the glorious truth that his will is that we become increasingly holy—that we become like him. As believers, we cannot help but want to be more like our Lord and Savior, for he has given us new hearts and is renewing our minds so that we might have the mind of Christ (see also Rom. 12:1–2; Phil. 2:1–11).

The gospel has all-of-life-encompassing implications. Therefore, Paul urges the Thessalonians not to grow weary but to continue to walk with God and seek to please him more and more (1 Thess. 4:1), to abstain from sexual immorality (v. 3), to know how to control one's body in holiness and honor (v. 4), to walk properly before outsiders (v. 12), and not to transgress and wrong one's brother in this matter of sexual immorality (v. 6), which was as common a sin in the first century as it is in the twenty-first.

The motivating reason Paul gives the Thessalonians for their holiness is God's gracious calling (v. 7; cf. Eph. 1:4). God's own great love for us teaches us to love one another (1 Thess. 4:9), thereby showing the world that we are followers of Jesus Christ (John 13:35; cf. Eph. 5:1–2). His great grace toward us creates in us a compulsion to want to please him, honor him, and share his love with others.

4:13–5:11 Having mentioned the second coming of Christ only a few times up to this point (1:10; 2:19; 3:13), Paul now gives the Thessalonian believers a fuller explanation of the promise and practical implications of Christ's return. In providing them with some details surrounding Christ's return, Paul aims to comfort, encourage, and exhort the Thessalonians with words of hope. He encourages current faithfulness with the promises of Christ's eternal provisions—provisions that stimulate hope, endurance, and joy in the face of present trials and tragedies.

Paul does not want his readers to be uninformed about those who are asleep (i.e., fellow believers who have died), but to give the Thessalonians hope as they mourn these believers' deaths. For though we grieve in this life, we do not grieve "as others do who have no hope" (4:13). We have real hope that is rooted in Christ's bodily death and resurrection in the past, and in the promise of Christ's bodily return in the future (4:14). The heavenly promise Paul gives to the church is so certain that

8 [u]1 John 3:24; 4:13
9 [v]See Heb. 13:1 [w]ch. 5:1 [x]John 6:45; [1 John 2:27] [y]See John 13:34
10 [z]ch. 1:7 [a]See ch. 3:12
11 [b]Prov. 17:14; 20:3; 25:8; 2 Thess. 3:12 [c]2 Thess. 3:11; 1 Pet. 4:15 [d][Acts 18:3]; See Eph. 4:28
12 [e]Rom. 13:13; [Col. 4:5] [f]See Mark 4:11
13 [g][Lev. 19:28; Deut. 14:1; 2 Sam. 12:20-23; Mark 5:39] [h]Eph. 2:12
14 [i]1 Cor. 15:13; [2 Cor. 4:14; Rev. 1:18] [j]1 Cor. 15:18
15 [k]See 1 Kgs. 13:17 [l]1 Cor. 15:51 [m]See ch. 2:19
16 [n]See Matt. 16:27 [o]2 Thess. 1:7 [p][Joel 2:11] [q]Jude 9 [r]Matt. 24:31; 1 Cor. 15:52 [s]1 Cor. 15:23; [2 Thess. 2:1; Rev. 14:13]
17 [t]See 2 Cor. 12:2 [u][Dan. 7:13; Acts 1:9; Rev. 11:12] [v]See John 12:26

Chapter 5
1 [w]Dan. 2:21; Acts 1:7 [x]ch. 4:9
2 [y][2 Thess. 2:2]; See Matt. 24:43; Luke 17:24

[z]sudden destruction will come upon them [a]as
labor pains come upon a pregnant woman,
and they will not escape. 4 But you [b]are not
in darkness, brothers, for that day to surprise
you like a thief. 5 For you are all [c]children[1] of
light, children of the day. We are not of the
night or of the darkness. 6 So then [d]let us not
sleep, as others do, but let us [e]keep awake and
[f]be sober. 7 For those who sleep, sleep at night,
and those who get drunk, [g]are drunk at night.
8 But since we belong to the day, let us be sober,
[h]having put on the breastplate of [i]faith and
love, and for a helmet the hope of salvation.
9 For God has not destined us for [j]wrath, but
[k]to obtain salvation through our Lord Jesus
Christ, 10 [l]who died for us so that whether we
are awake or asleep we might live with him.
11 Therefore encourage one another and build
one another up, just as you are doing.

Final Instructions and Benediction

12 We ask you, brothers, [m]to respect those who
labor among you and [n]are over you in the Lord
and admonish you, 13 and to esteem them very
highly in love because of their work. [o]Be at
peace among yourselves. 14 And we urge you,
brothers, admonish [p]the idle,[2] [q]encourage the
fainthearted, [r]help the weak, [s]be patient with
them all. 15 See that [t]no one repays anyone evil
for evil, but always [u]seek to do good to one
another and to everyone. 16 [v]Rejoice always,
17 [w]pray without ceasing, 18 [x]give thanks in all
circumstances; for this is the will of God in
Christ Jesus for you. 19 [y]Do not quench the
Spirit. 20 Do not despise [z]prophecies, 21 but [a]test
everything; hold fast what is good. 22 Abstain
from every form of evil.

23 Now may [b]the God of peace himself [c]sanc-
tify you completely, and may your [d]whole
[e]spirit and soul and body be kept blameless
at [f]the coming of our Lord Jesus Christ. 24 [g]He
who calls you is faithful; [h]he will surely do it.

25 [i]Brothers, pray for us.

26 [j]Greet all the brothers with a holy kiss.

27 I put you under oath before the Lord to
have [k]this letter read to all the brothers.

28 [l]The grace of our Lord Jesus Christ be with
you.

[1] Or *sons*; twice in this verse [2] Or *disorderly*, or *undisciplined*

3 [z]Luke 21:34; [Ps. 35:8; Luke 17:26-30; 2 Thess. 1:9] [a]See Isa. 13:8
4 [b]1 John 2:8
5 [c]See Luke 16:8
6 [d][Mark 13:36]; See Rom. 13:11-13 [e]See Matt. 24:42 [f]See 1 Pet. 1:13
7 [g][Acts 2:15; 2 Pet. 2:13]
8 [h]Isa. 59:17; Eph. 6:14, 17 [i][Eph. 6:23]
9 [j]See ch. 1:10 [k]2 Thess. 2:13, 14; [Heb. 10:39]
10 [l]Rom. 14:9; [2 Tim. 2:11]
12 [m]1 Cor. 16:18; Phil. 2:29 [n]1 Cor. 16:16; Heb. 13:17
13 [o]See Mark 9:50
14 [p]2 Thess. 3:6, 7, 11 [q]Isa. 35:4; [Heb. 12:12] [r]Acts 20:35; See Rom. 15:1 [s]See 1 Cor. 13:4
15 [t]1 Pet. 3:9; See Rom. 12:17 [u][Rom. 12:9]; See Gal. 6:10
16 [v]Phil. 4:4
17 [w]See Luke 18:1
18 [x]See Eph. 5:20
19 [y][1 Cor. 14:30; Eph. 4:30; 1 Tim. 4:14; 2 Tim. 1:6]
20 [z]See 1 Cor. 11:4
21 [a]1 John 4:1; [Job 34:4]; See Eph. 5:10
23 [b]See Rom. 15:33 [c]Ex. 31:13; John 17:17 [d]2 Pet. 3:14; Jude 1 [e]Luke 1:46, 47; Heb. 4:12; [1 Cor. 14:14] [f]See ch. 2:19
24 [g]See 1 Cor. 1:9 [h][Phil. 1:6]
25 [i]2 Thess. 3:1; Heb. 13:18
26 [j]See Rom. 16:16
27 [k]Col. 4:16
28 [l]See Rom. 16:20

he is able to provide not simply a vague notion of the future but a concrete picture of what will come to pass: The day of the Lord will come "like a thief in the night," and "the dead in Christ will rise first," and then we "who are left" (5:2; 4:16, 17). So we who are alive in Christ along with our deceased loved ones in Christ "will always be with the Lord" (4:17).

Whether we live in Christ or die in Christ, we who are in Christ will live forever with him as children of light (5:5, 10). So, Paul admonishes us to "be sober, having put on the breastplate of faith and love, and for a helmet the hope of salvation" (5:8). All this is established in God's sovereign electing love, having "not destined us for wrath, but to obtain salvation through our Lord Jesus Christ" (5:9). This is our glorious hope through the gospel of Jesus Christ, who died in our place. The promise of the gospel is that Christ died as the certain guarantee of our inheritance and will return that we might live with him forever.

5:12–28 As is common for Paul, he concludes his letter to the Thessalonian church with a litany of exhortations established on the truths of the gospel he has set forth throughout his letter. The imperatives of the Christian life—what we are called to do as we follow Christ by faith—are founded on and flow from the indicatives of the Christian life—who we are in Christ by faith. Moreover, every imperative in the Christian life is provided to us as a gracious admonition from God so that we might glorify him and enjoy him as we live the free and abundant life we have in Christ—who is the way, the truth, and the life (John 14:6).

The commands of God are the Christian's duty and delight as we live by the indwelling power of the Holy Spirit to fulfill God's calling while we "rejoice always" (1 Thess. 5:16), "pray without ceasing" (v. 17), and "give thanks in all circumstances" (v. 18), resting in the hope that "the God of peace himself" will "sanctify [us] completely" (v. 23) because "he who calls [us] is faithful" and "will surely do it" (v. 24). We remain responsible to live the Christian life, even as we rest upon the faithfulness of the Lord and rely upon his power.

Introduction to
2 Thessalonians

Author, Date, and Recipients

Shortly after writing 1 Thessalonians, the apostle Paul received a report (2 Thess. 3:11) that the Thessalonian church had accepted the strange claim that "the day of the Lord has come" (2:1–2). Paul sent them this second letter in A.D. 49–51. He was probably in Corinth at the time.

The Gospel in 2 Thessalonians

Paul's second letter to the Thessalonians is a letter of comfort to those eagerly awaiting the promised return of Jesus Christ. Since receiving Paul's first letter, the Thessalonians' faith in Christ and their love for one another had continued to grow abundantly while they endured affliction for the sake of the gospel. Paul writes to encourage them to remain steadfast in their commitment to the gospel and the doctrine they had learned from the apostles. False prophets had been spreading rumors suggesting that the "day of the Lord" (2:2; cf. 1:10) had already come, and Paul writes to set the record straight by providing further details about the events surrounding the second coming of Christ.

Paul also deals with misbehavior that has been a consequence of the Thessalonians' misunderstanding. While awaiting the coming day of the Lord, some of the believers at Thessalonica had become unwilling to work. Paul urges the believers to continue to work and not to grow weary in doing good while waiting in hope for God's impending vengeance against the wicked and his salvation of his chosen people. Just as God called us through the gospel, so he is faithful to his promise to guard us and establish us in every good work until Jesus returns.

Outline

I. Opening (1:1–2)

II. Thanksgiving and Comfort for the Persecuted Thessalonians (1:3–12)

III. Disproving the False Claim about the Day of the Lord (2:1–17)

IV. Transition (3:1–5)

V. The Problem of Lazy Christians (3:6–15)

VI. Conclusion (3:16–18)

The Second Letter of Paul to the Thessalonians

2 Thessalonians

Greeting

1 [a]Paul, Silvanus, and Timothy,
To the church of the Thessalonians in God
our Father and the Lord Jesus Christ:
2 Grace to you and peace from God our Father
and the Lord Jesus Christ.

Thanksgiving

3 [b]We ought always to give thanks to God
for you, brothers,[1] as is right, because your
faith is growing abundantly, and the love of
every one of you for one another is increasing.
4 Therefore [c]we ourselves boast about you [d]in
the churches of God for your steadfastness
and faith [e]in all your persecutions and in the
afflictions that you are enduring.

The Judgment at Christ's Coming

5 This is [f]evidence of the righteous judgment of God, that you may be [g]considered
worthy of the kingdom of God, for which you
are also suffering— 6 since indeed God considers it [h]just [i]to repay with affliction those
who afflict you, 7 and to grant [j]relief to you
who are afflicted as well as to us, when [k]the
Lord Jesus is revealed from heaven [l]with his
mighty angels 8 [m]in flaming fire, inflicting
vengeance on those [n]who do not know God
and on those who [o]do not obey the gospel of
our Lord Jesus. 9 They will suffer the punishment of [p]eternal destruction, [q]away from[2] the
presence of the Lord and from the glory of
his might, 10 [r]when he comes on [s]that day [t]to
be glorified in his saints, and to be marveled
at among all who have believed, because our
[u]testimony to you [v]was believed. 11 To this end
we [w]always pray for you, that our God may
[x]make you worthy of his calling and may fulfill every resolve for good and every [y]work of
faith by his power, 12 so that the name of our
Lord Jesus [z]may be glorified in you, and you
in him, according to the grace of our God and
the Lord Jesus Christ.

[1] Or *brothers and sisters*. The plural Greek word *adelphoi* (translated "brothers") refers to siblings in a family. In New Testament usage, depending on the context, *adelphoi* may refer either to men or to both men and women who are siblings (brothers and sisters) in God's family, the church [2] Or *destruction that comes from*

1:3–12 Paul begins and concludes his second letter to the Thessalonian church as he did the first letter, with an apostolic blessing of grace and peace from God (v. 2; 3:18). Amid their persecutions and afflictions, the Thessalonians have continued growing in mutual love, steadfastness, and faith, and so Paul and his companions give thanks to God and boast about them (1:3–4). Paul continues encouraging the church along the same lines as in his previous letter, striving to give them confident hope in the imminent return of Jesus Christ.

When we face persecution and affliction in this world, we tend to lose our grasp on our assurance and hope. We may wonder whether our suffering indicates God's absence from our lives. We wonder if God will ever bring release or vindication from the assaults of enemies. Although we sometimes doubt God's gospel promises when afflictions and persecutions enter our lives, such trials are evidence that we belong to him (v. 5). Just as Jesus' own path to glory was through pain, so too is this true for his disciples in a world that is naturally opposed to our God and his gospel (cf. Mark 10:42–45).

Yet, precisely because we are called-out citizens of the kingdom of God, we will be persecuted by the unbelieving citizens of the kingdom of this earth—just as they persecuted Jesus. In the end, however, those who have opposed the Lord will suffer the punishment of eternal destruction (2 Thess. 1:9). We can also find hope in the promise of the gospel that Jesus will return to be worshiped, to be marveled at

Chapter 1
1[a] For ver. 1, 2, see 1 Thess. 1:1
3[b] ch. 2:13; See Eph. 5:20; 1 Thess. 1:2, 3
4[c] [2 Cor. 7:14]; See 1 Thess. 2:19 [d] [1 Thess. 1:8]; See 1 Cor. 7:17 [e] [Mark 10:30]; See 1 Thess. 2:14
5[f] [Phil. 1:28] [g] [Acts 14:22]; See Luke 20:35
6[h] [Rev. 6:10] [i] [Ex. 23:22; Joel 3:4, 7]
7[j] [Rev. 6:11; 11:18; 14:13] [k] See Luke 17:30 [l] See Jude 14
8[m] Isa. 66:15, 16; Matt. 25:41; 1 Cor. 3:13; Heb. 10:27; 12:29; 2 Pet. 3:7; [Mal. 4:1] [n] See Gal. 4:8 [o] Rom. 2:8
9[p] [Phil. 3:19; 1 Thess. 5:3] [q] Isa. 2:10, 19, 21; [ch. 2:8]
10[r] See 1 Thess. 1:10 [s] See 1 Cor. 3:13 [t] Ps. 89:7 (Gk.); Isa. 49:3; John 17:10 [u] [1 Cor. 1:6] [v] [1 Thess. 2:1, 13; 1 Tim. 3:16]
11[w] Col. 1:9 [x] [ver. 5] [y] 1 Thess. 1:3
12[z] [Isa. 66:5; Acts 13:48]

The Man of Lawlessness

2 Now concerning [a]the coming of our Lord
Jesus Christ and our [b]being gathered
together to him, we ask you, brothers,[1] 2 not
to be quickly shaken in mind or [c]alarmed,
either [d]by a spirit or a [e]spoken word, or [e]a letter seeming to be from us, to the effect that
[f]the day of the Lord has come. 3 [g]Let no one
deceive you in any way. For that day will not
come, [h]unless the rebellion comes first, and
[i]the man of lawlessness[2] is revealed, [j]the son of
destruction,[3] 4 who opposes and exalts himself
against every so-called god or object of worship, so that he takes his seat in the temple
of God, [k]proclaiming himself to be God. 5 Do
you not remember that when I was still with
you I told you these things? 6 And you know
what is restraining him now so that he may
be revealed in his time. 7 For [l]the mystery of
lawlessness [m]is already at work. Only he who
now restrains it will do so until he is out of
the way. 8 And then [n]the lawless one will be
revealed, whom the Lord Jesus [o]will kill with
[p]the breath of his mouth and bring to nothing
by [q]the appearance of his coming. 9 The coming of the lawless one is by the activity of Satan
[r]with all power and false signs and wonders,
10 and with all wicked deception for [s]those who
are perishing, because they refused to love the
truth and so be saved. 11 Therefore [t]God sends
them a strong delusion, so that they may
believe [u]what is false, 12 in order that all may
be condemned [v]who did not believe the truth
but [w]had pleasure in unrighteousness.

Stand Firm

13 But [x]we ought always to give thanks to God
for you, [y]brothers beloved by the Lord, because

[1] Or *brothers and sisters*; also verses 13, 15 [2] Some manuscripts *sin* [3] Greek *the son of perdition* (a Hebrew idiom)

Chapter 2
1 [a] See 1 Thess. 2:19 [b] [Matt. 24:31; 1 Thess. 4:15-17]
2 [c] Matt. 24:6; Mark 13:7 [d] [1 John 4:1] [e] ver. 15; [1 Thess. 5:2] [f] See 1 Cor. 1:8
3 [g] Eph. 5:6 [h] 1 Tim. 4:1 [i] [ver. 8; Dan. 7:25; 8:25; 11:36; Rev. 13:5, 6] [j] John 17:12; [Matt. 23:15]
4 [k] [Isa. 14:14; Ezek. 28:2]
7 [l] Rev. 17:5, 7 [m] 1 John 2:18; 4:3
8 [n] See ver. 3 [o] [Dan. 7:10, 11] [p] Isa. 11:4 [q] [1 Tim. 6:14; 2 Tim. 1:10; 4:1, 8; Titus 2:13]
9 [r] [Rev. 13:14]; See Matt. 24:24
10 [s] See 1 Cor. 1:18
11 [t] [1 Kgs. 22:22; Ezek. 14:9; Rev. 17:17] [u] [1 Thess. 2:3; 1 Tim. 4:2]; See Rom. 1:25
12 [v] Rom. 2:8 [w] See Rom. 1:32
13 [x] ch. 1:3 [y] 1 Thess. 1:4; [Deut. 33:12]

among all who have believed (v. 10). At Christ's return, we will worship the Lord Jesus because God declares us worthy to worship Christ by the worthiness *of* Christ. This same God will make us worthy of his calling for our eternal good and Christ's eternal glory—all according to his glorious grace (vv. 11–12).

2:1–15 The second coming of Christ is a foundational doctrine of the New Testament, though we often forget this truth amid the daily activity of life. Christ's return is meant to generate hope in the midst of present sin, affliction, and trials. The final prayer of Scripture is a prayer for this second coming: "Come, Lord Jesus!" (Rev. 22:20). Such prayer—made in the light of God's promise that our Savior will come to execute justice, vindicate the righteous, and make the world right—has the power to refresh and sustain us regardless of whatever pain may wash into our lives.

Paul's teaching about Christ's return is also aimed at encouraging the Thessalonians "not to be quickly shaken in mind or alarmed" about premature rumors of the Lord's return (2 Thess. 2:2). Therefore, to answer any looming questions about Christ's return and to allow no one to "deceive [us] in any way," Paul provides further details about "the day of the Lord," "the rebellion," the activity of Satan, and the false signs and wonders that will accompany the revealing of the "man of lawlessness" (vv. 3–4). Throughout Paul's vivid description of the day of the Lord is the resounding truth of Christ's victory and God's sovereignty over all that will come to pass. Jesus will kill the man of lawlessness "with the breath of his mouth," and God will send a "strong delusion" upon those who "refused to love the truth and so be saved" (vv. 8–12).

Paul is clear: only believing the truth of the gospel of the Lord Jesus Christ will save us from God's condemnation on the day of the Lord (cf. Rom. 8:1). God declares us righteous according to the finished work of Christ by faith alone. Such faith produces a life that is unlike the lives of the wicked, who take "pleasure in unrighteousness" (2 Thess. 2:12). Rather, because God chose us, loved us, gave us eternal comfort through grace, and called us through the gospel, we will "obtain the glory of our Lord Jesus Christ" (vv. 13–14).

Established in the glorious promise of the gospel, we are called to stand firm as we rest confidently in the sustaining work of sanctification by the Spirit, the Lord Jesus, and God our Father (v. 15). Our triune God is faithful to his gospel promise, a promise accompanied by his gracious commitment to comfort our hearts and establish them in every good work and word so that all might see our good works and glorify our Father in heaven (Matt. 5:16).

God chose you [z]as the firstfruits[1] [a]to be saved,
[b]through sanctification by the Spirit and belief
in the truth. 14 To this he called you through
[c]our gospel, [a]so that you may obtain the glory
of our Lord Jesus Christ. 15 So then, brothers,
[d]stand firm and hold to [e]the traditions that
you were taught by us, either [f]by our spoken
word or by [f]our letter.

16 Now may our Lord Jesus Christ himself,
and God our Father, [g]who loved us and gave
us eternal comfort and good [h]hope through
grace, 17 comfort your hearts and [i]establish
them in every good work and word.

Pray for Us

3 Finally, brothers,[2] [j]pray for us, that [k]the
word of the Lord may speed ahead and be
honored,[3] as happened among you, 2 and
[l]that we may be delivered from wicked and
evil men. For [m]not all have faith. 3 But [n]the
Lord is faithful. He will establish you and
[o]guard you against [p]the evil one.[4] 4 And [q]we
have confidence in the Lord about you, that
you are doing and will do the things that we
command. 5 May the Lord [r]direct your hearts
to the love of God and to the steadfastness
of Christ.

Warning Against Idleness

6 Now we command you, brothers, [s]in the
name of our Lord Jesus Christ, [t]that you keep
away from any [u]brother [v]who is walking in
idleness and not in accord with the tradition
that you received from us. 7 For you yourselves
know [w]how you ought to imitate us, because
[x]we were not idle when we were with you, 8 nor
did we eat anyone's bread without paying for
it, but [y]with toil and labor we worked night
and day, that we might not be a burden to any
of you. 9 It was [z]not because we do not have
that right, but to give you in ourselves [a]an
example to imitate. 10 For even when we were
with you, we would give you this command:
[b]If anyone is not willing to work, let him not
eat. 11 For we hear that some among you [c]walk
in idleness, not busy at work, but [d]busybodies.
12 Now such persons we command and encourage in the Lord Jesus Christ to do their work
quietly and to earn their own living.[5]

13 As for you, brothers, [e]do not grow weary in
doing good. 14 If anyone does not obey what we
say in this letter, take note of that person, and
[f]have nothing to do with him, that he may be
ashamed. 15 [g]Do not regard him as an enemy,
but [h]warn him as a brother.

[1] Some manuscripts *chose you from the beginning* [2] Or *brothers and sisters*; also verses 6, 13 [3] Or *glorified* [4] Or *evil* [5] Greek *to eat their own bread*

3:1–16 As they awaited the return of Christ, some of the professing believers at Thessalonica had fallen into the sin of laziness and were not willing to work (v. 6). Paul urges them not to be idle but to imitate him and his companions, who worked day and night when they ministered among the Thessalonians (vv. 7–9). Idleness is a serious matter; it affects not only the idle person himself but also his family and community. Most importantly, idleness dishonors the body of Christ and the name of Christ before the eyes of the watching world. Paul thus admonishes the Thessalonians to give brotherly warning to anyone who does not heed his words (vv. 14–15).

Paul's fundamental concern is the advance of the gospel of Jesus Christ. To that end, he has worked, prayed, and asked for prayer that the word of the Lord would speed ahead and be honored and that he and his companions would be delivered from wicked and evil men (vv. 1–2). Paul's prayer for deliverance is not motivated by concern about his own health or security but by his desire to advance the gospel. Knowing that his calling will lead to confrontation with those in Thessalonica or elsewhere who do not love Christ, Paul nevertheless boldly proclaims the truths and responsibilities of the gospel. He reminds his readers (and us) that the Lord is faithful and will establish and guard his people against the Evil One (v. 3). Established on these glorious gospel truths of God's faithfulness, Paul communicates his confidence that the Thessalonians and all true believers will do the things that Jesus Christ and his apostles command (v. 4).

Paul ends his letter with a final encouragement for believers facing the trials that will always be present until Christ returns. The trials are not to have the final word or controlling influence on our hearts, for the Lord of peace himself gives us peace "at all times in every way" (v. 16). Walking with and relying upon this God of such abundant compassion and grace, we are stabilized amid the storms of life as we await Christ's return in power and glory.

13 [z]Eph. 1:4 [a]1 Thess. 5:9; [2 Tim. 1:9] [b]See 1 Thess. 4:3
14 [c]1 Thess. 1:5 [a][See ver. 13 above]
15 [d]See 1 Cor. 16:13 [e]ch. 3:6; 1 Cor. 11:2 [f]ver. 2
16 [g]John 3:16; 1 John 4:10; Rev. 1:5 [h]1 Pet. 1:3
17 [i]ch. 3:3; 1 Thess. 3:13
Chapter 3
1 [j]See 1 Thess. 5:25 [k]Ps. 147:15; [1 Thess. 1:8]
2 [l]Rom. 15:31 [m][Deut. 32:20]
3 [n]See 1 Cor. 1:9 [o]Matt. 6:13; John 17:15 [p]See Matt. 13:19
4 [q]See 2 Cor. 2:3
5 [r]1 Thess. 3:11
6 [s]1 Cor. 5:4 [t]ver. 14; [Matt. 18:17; 2 Tim. 3:5]; See 1 Cor. 5:9; 2 John 10 [u]1 Cor. 5:11 [v]ver. 11; 1 Thess. 5:14
7 [w][Acts 20:35]; See 1 Thess. 1:6 [x]1 Thess. 1:5
8 [y]See 1 Thess. 2:9
9 [z]1 Cor. 9:4; 1 Thess. 2:6 [a]ver. 7; 1 Pet. 5:3
10 [b][Gen. 3:19]; See 1 Thess. 4:11
11 [c]ver. 6 [d]1 Tim. 5:13; 1 Pet. 4:15
13 [e]Gal. 6:9; [1 Cor. 15:58]
14 [f]See ver. 6
15 [g]See Lev. 19:17; Matt. 18:15 [h]1 Thess. 5:12, 14; [Titus 3:10]

Benediction

16 Now may [i]the Lord of peace himself [j]give
you peace at all times in every way. [k]The Lord
be with you all.

17 I, Paul, write [l]this greeting with my own
hand. This is the sign of genuineness in every
letter of mine; it is the way I write.
18 [m]The
grace of our Lord Jesus Christ be with you all.

16[i] See Rom. 15:33; Eph. 6:23 [j] Num. 6:26 [k] Ruth 2:4 **17**[l] See 1 Cor. 16:21 **18**[m] See Rom. 16:20

Introduction to 1 Timothy

Author, Date, and Recipient

The apostle Paul probably wrote this letter to Timothy in the mid-60s A.D., after his first release from imprisonment. Timothy was a pastor in Ephesus.

The Gospel in 1 Timothy

The thrust of 1 Timothy is that godliness is central to the Christian's continuing in the gospel and the church's proclamation of the gospel. Words relating to "godliness" occur ten times in this short book (2:2, 10; 3:16; 4:7, 8; 5:4; 6:3, 5, 6, 11), and throughout the letter Paul grounds godly behavior in Christ's gospel. Sadly, those whose behavior is contrary to the gospel of Christ deny the reality of their faith (1:6, 19–20; 4:1; 5:6, 8, 11–12; 6:9–10). Indeed, personal godliness (Christ-infused godliness) is not only indispensable to perseverance in faithfulness, but absolutely essential to the proclamation of the gospel to the lost world. In a nutshell, the theme of 1 Timothy is *Christ-centered godliness for the sake of the gospel.*

This gospel theme is explicit in 2:1–7, where Paul urges that prayers be made for all people so that believers may lead godly lives. He comments, "This is good, and it is pleasing in the sight of God our Savior, who desires all people to be saved and to come to the knowledge of the truth" (2:3–4). Paul follows this declaration of God's gospel heart with consecutive detailed directives for godliness to three groups: women (2:9–15), overseers (3:1–7), and deacons (3:8–13). These instructions are followed by what are the universally acknowledged key verses of the letter (3:14–16), calling the church to conduct that is radically Christ-centered and Christ-generated—which is to say, gospel-centered godliness.

Chapter 4 begins with a warning against pursuing godliness through man-centered asceticism, which Paul terms the "teaching of demons" (4:1–5). This is followed by the famous non-ascetic command to Timothy to "train yourself for godliness" and its accompanying array of applications and benefits (4:7–16). Chapter 5 flows into chapter 6 with directives regarding how the treatment of various groups in the church must be shaped by godliness: older men and women, younger men and women (5:1–2), widows (5:3–16), elders (5:17–25), and masters (6:1–2). In chapter 6 Paul warns against those who teach a different doctrine that "does not agree with the sound words of our Lord Jesus Christ and the teaching that accords with godliness" (6:3–5). Godliness and greed are juxtaposed (6:6–10). Paul closes by exhorting Timothy, "Pursue righteousness, godliness, faith, love, steadfastness, gentleness." And, in this Christlike spirit, "Fight the good fight of the faith" (6:11–16).

So we see that 1 Timothy is not simply a moralistic manual for church conduct. It is rather a call to Christ-centered, gospel-centered godliness for the sake of the church—and a lost world.

Outline

I. Greeting (1:1–2)

II. Confronting the False Teaching (1:3–20)

III. Descriptions of Gospel-Shaped Living (2:1–3:13)

IV. Purpose of Writing: Behavior in the Church (3:14–16)

V. Identifying the False Teaching (4:1–5)

VI. How Timothy Should Be Shaped by the Gospel (4:6–16)

VII. How Specific Groups in the Church Should Be Shaped by the Gospel (5:1–6:2)

VIII. Confronting the False Teaching Again (6:3–21)

The First Letter of Paul to Timothy

1 Timothy

Greeting

1 Paul, [a]an apostle of Christ Jesus [b]by command of [c]God our Savior and of Christ
Jesus [d]our hope,
2 To Timothy, [e]my true child in the faith:
[f]Grace, mercy, and peace from God the Father
and Christ Jesus our Lord.

Warning Against False Teachers

3 [g]As I urged you when I was going to Macedonia, remain at Ephesus so that you may
charge certain persons not [h]to teach any different doctrine, 4 nor [i]to devote themselves to
myths and endless [j]genealogies, which promote [k]speculations rather than the stewardship[1] from God that is by faith. 5 The aim of
our charge is love [l]that issues from a pure heart
and [m]a good conscience and [n]a sincere faith.
6 Certain persons, by [o]swerving from these,
have wandered away into [p]vain discussion,
7 desiring to be teachers of the law, [q]without
understanding either what they are saying or
the things about which they make confident
assertions.
8 Now we know that [r]the law is good, if one
uses it lawfully, 9 understanding this, that the
[s]law is not laid down for the just but for the
lawless and disobedient, for the ungodly and
sinners, for the unholy and profane, for those
who strike their fathers and mothers, for murderers, 10 the sexually immoral, men who practice homosexuality, enslavers,[2] liars, perjurers,
and whatever else is contrary to [t]sound[3] doctrine, 11 in accordance with [u]the gospel of the
glory of [v]the blessed God [w]with which I have
been entrusted.

[1] Or *good order* [2] That is, those who take someone captive in order to sell him into slavery [3] Or *healthy*

1:1–2 Three times Paul invokes the title "Christ [*Messiah*] Jesus" in his greeting to Timothy. Paul's placing of a reference to God the Father as "God our Savior" between the opening references to "Christ Jesus" is especially significant because the Messiah's work was the good work of the Father from eternity (cf. Luke 1:46–47; Phil. 2:8–11; Heb. 10:5–10). Here in 1 Timothy, Jesus' fulfillment of messianic prophecies is tellingly recurrent—the title appears 12 more times, for a total of 15 occurrences (1 Tim. 1:12, 14–16; 2:5; 3:13; 4:6; 5:21; 6:3, 13–14). The godly conduct that Paul will demand is possible only through trust in, dependence upon, and strength from the atoning death and resurrection of Messiah Jesus.

1:3–11 After urging Timothy to withstand the false teachers of the law and their vain speculations (vv. 3–7), Paul lays the groundwork for a glorious assertion of the gospel in verse 11 by first presenting a litany of the sins which the law exposed (vv. 8–10).

The list begins by naming six general sins, and then specifically refers to dark sins that break the fifth through ninth commandments—which have to do with the ways ungodly people sin against each other. But Paul caps the list with a summary reference that not only is intended to capture the nature of all unmentioned sins but that also is worded in terms that set up by contrast the bright hope of the gospel: "and whatever else is contrary to sound doctrine, in accordance with the gospel of the glory of the blessed God with which I have been entrusted" (vv. 10–11). "Sound doctrine" that is "in accordance with the gospel" is literally "healthy doctrine"—that is, life-giving doctrine.

The gospel, entrusted to Paul and to us, is the only answer to the dark, impossible, sin-sick pathology of the human heart. All healthy, life-giving theology accords with this glorious gospel of grace.

Chapter 1
1 [a]See 2 Cor. 1:1 [b]Titus 1:3; [Rom. 16:26] [c]See Luke 1:47 [d]Col. 1:27
2 [e]Titus 1:4 [f]2 Tim. 1:2; 2 John 3; [Jude 2]
3 [g][Titus 1:5] [h]ch. 6:3; [Gal. 1:6, 7]
4 [i]ch. 4:7; 2 Tim. 4:4; Titus 1:14; 2 Pet. 1:16 [j]Titus 3:9 [k]ch. 6:4
5 [l]2 Tim. 2:22 [m]1 Pet. 3:16, 21 [n]Rom. 12:9; 2 Tim. 1:5
6 [o]ch. 6:21 [p]Titus 1:10
7 [q][ch. 6:4; Col. 2:18]
8 [r]Rom. 7:16
9 [s]Gal. 5:23
10 [t]2 Tim. 4:3; [ch. 6:3; 2 Tim. 1:13; Titus 1:13; 2:2]
11 [u][2 Cor. 4:4] [v]ch. 6:15 [w]Titus 1:3; See Rom. 2:16; Gal. 2:7

Christ Jesus Came to Save Sinners

12 I thank him [x]who has given me strength,
Christ Jesus our Lord, because he judged
me faithful, [y]appointing me to his service,
13 though formerly I was a blasphemer, [z]per-
secutor, and insolent opponent. But [a]I received
mercy [b]because I had acted ignorantly in unbelief, 14 and [c]the grace of our Lord overflowed
for me with the [d]faith and love that are in
Christ Jesus. 15 The saying is [e]trustworthy and
deserving of full acceptance, that Christ Jesus
[f]came into the world to save sinners, [g]of whom
I am the foremost. 16 But I received mercy for
this reason, that in me, as the foremost, Jesus
Christ might display his perfect patience as
an example to those who were to believe in
him for eternal life. 17 To [h]the King of the ages,
[i]immortal, [j]invisible, [k]the only God, [l]be honor
and glory forever and ever.[1] Amen.

18 This charge [m]I entrust to you, Timothy,
my child, in accordance with [n]the prophecies
previously made about you, that by them you
may [o]wage the good warfare, 19 [p]holding faith
and a good conscience. By rejecting this, some
have [q]made shipwreck of their faith, 20 among
whom are [r]Hymenaeus and [s]Alexander, whom
I [t]have handed over to Satan that they may
learn not to [u]blaspheme.

Pray for All People

2 First of all, then, I urge that supplications,
prayers, intercessions, and thanksgivings
be made for all people, 2 [v]for kings and all who
are in high positions, that we may lead a peaceful and quiet life, godly and [w]dignified in every
way. 3 This is good, and [x]it is pleasing in the
sight of [y]God our Savior, 4 who desires [z]all people to be saved and [a]to come to [b]the knowledge

[1] Greek *to the ages of ages*

12 [x]Acts 9:22; Phil. 4:13 [y]See 2 Cor. 3:6
13 [z]See Acts 8:3 [a]1 Cor. 7:25; 2 Cor. 4:1 [b]See Acts 3:17
14 [c]Rom. 5:20 [d][Luke 7:47, 50]; See 1 Thess. 1:3
15 [e]ch. 3:1; 4:9; 2 Tim. 2:11; Titus 3:8; [Rev. 22:6] [f]Matt. 9:13; See John 3:17; Rom. 4:25 [g][1 Cor. 15:9]
17 [h][Ps. 10:16; Rev. 4:9, 10] [i]ch. 6:15, 16; Rom. 1:23 [j]John 1:18; Col. 1:15; Heb. 11:27; 1 John 4:12 [k]Jude 25 [l]1 Chr. 29:11
18 [m]2 Tim. 2:2 [n]ch. 4:14 [o]1 Cor. 9:7; 2 Cor. 10:4; 2 Tim. 2:3, 4; [ch. 6:12]
19 [p][ch. 3:9] [q][ch. 6:9]
20 [r]2 Tim. 2:17 [s]2 Tim. 4:14 [t]See 1 Cor. 5:5 [u]Acts 13:45

Chapter 2

2 [v]Ezra 6:10 [w]ch. 3:4
3 [x]ch. 5:4 [y]ch. 1:1
4 [z]ch. 4:10; Ezek. 18:23, 32 [a]2 Tim. 3:7 [b]2 Tim. 2:25; Titus 1:1; Heb. 10:26

1:12–17 Paul's mention of "the gospel of the glory of the blessed God" (v. 11) has paved the way to one of the greatest gospel texts in all of Scripture, an awesome expression of the magnitude of the gospel of grace.

This section is replete with gospel terminology: "Christ," four times; and "grace," bracketed by two occurrences of "mercy." The very center of the text reads, "The saying is trustworthy and deserving of full acceptance, that Christ Jesus came into the world to save sinners, of whom I am the foremost" (v. 15). Paul (then named Saul) appeared to be impossibly lost. He was a religious predator whose hands were stained with the blood of Christians—a callous, self-righteous, bigoted murderer hell-bent on a full-scale inquisition (Acts 9:1–2; 26:9–11). But on the Damascus road, he met the Lion of the tribe of Judah (Acts 9:3–6). There, while he did not deserve mercy, he was shown mercy—he "received mercy" (1 Tim. 1:13, 16). Literally, he "was mercied."

The result? In Paul's own words, "and the grace of our Lord overflowed for me with the faith and love that are in Christ Jesus" (v. 14). The words portray an overwhelming supply of mercy. This same Paul expressed it with careful precision at the conclusion of Romans 5: "Now the law came in to increase the trespass, but where sin increased, grace abounded all the more, so that, as sin reigned in death, grace also might reign through righteousness leading to eternal life through Jesus Christ our Lord" (Rom. 5:20–21). Oh, the magnitude of the overflowing, superabundant grace of the gospel! No one is beyond saving grace—this is the "glory of the blessed God."

2:1–2 Here Paul instructs Timothy and his church on how to pray and how to live so that the gospel would go out to the lost world. Their prayers were to be expansive—"for all people"—including kings and all those in high positions. Why the mention of kings and rulers? So that their rule might create a peaceful context conducive to these believers living "godly and dignified" lives, thus preparing the unbelieving world to hear the claims of the gospel. Clearly, expansive prayer and personal godliness are integral to sound preaching of the gospel.

2:3–4 Paul memorably asserts that the church's prayers for all people are consonant with God's evangelistic desire. "God our Savior . . . desires all people to be saved and to come to the knowledge of the truth."

The term "God our Savior" (cf. 4:10) locates the source of the gospel in the very heart of God the Father. This is God's eternal disposition. This is who God is. He does not delight in the destruction of the wicked. By articulating this, Paul was assaulting the exclusivism that was being taught by some of the false teachers in Ephesus (the city where Timothy ministered). Of course, the Scriptures explicitly

of the truth. 5For [c]there is one God, and there
is one mediator between God and men, the
man[1] Christ Jesus, 6[d]who gave himself as a
ransom for all, which is [e]the testimony given
[f]at the proper time. 7[g]For this I was appointed
a preacher and an apostle ([h]I am telling the
truth, I am not lying), [i]a teacher of the Gentiles
in faith and truth.
8I desire then that [j]in every place the men
should pray, [k]lifting [l]holy hands without

[1] *men* and *man* render the same Greek word that is translated *people* in verses 1 and 4

5[c] See Gal. 3:20
6[d] See Matt. 20:28 [e] See 1 Cor. 1:6 [f] ch. 6:15; Titus 1:3; [Gal. 4:4]
7[g] ch. 1:11; Eph. 3:7, 8; 2 Tim. 1:11 [h] See Rom. 9:1 [i] See Acts 9:15
8[j] [John 4:21] [k] Ps. 63:4; 119:48; [Isa. 1:15] [l] Job 17:9; Ps. 24:4

teach divine election (e.g., Matt. 11:25–27; John 6:37–44; Acts 13:48; Eph. 1:4–5; Rom. 8:30; 2 Thess. 2:13; 1 Pet. 1:1–2). But Scripture also teaches the complementary truth, clearly stated in our text, that God "desires all people to be saved" (1 Tim. 2:4). Some interpret this phrase simply to mean that God desires "all *kinds* of people" to be saved, or that Paul is abbreviating the Abrahamic promise, referencing God's blessings upon "all nations [i.e., people]" through the Messiah (e.g., Gen. 26:4). But such interpretations seem strained and designed more to maintain a theological perspective than to capture the apostle's immediate thought (cf. the "all people" for whom we are to pray; 1 Tim. 2:1–2). Paul seems to want us to understand that God retains love for all whom he has made, despite their rejection of him (cf. Ps. 145:9, 13, 17; John 3:19).

This does not mean that God ultimately *wills* everyone to be finally saved. If he did, all would be saved, because no one can resist God's will (Rom. 9:19). Yet, in the divine mysteries of salvation in which a sovereign God does no violence to the will of his creatures, there remains a merciful inclination toward all even as God allows the unrepentant to have their way (Rom. 1:24), while simultaneously using the consequences of their waywardness to direct the elect to his blessings (Rom. 9:22–23).

We have here in 1 Timothy an expression of the expansiveness of the divine desire that brought about Christ's incarnation and death on the cross—which was to be preached to the whole world (Matt. 24:14). "For God so loved the world, that he gave his only Son, that whoever believes in him should not perish but have eternal life" (John 3:16). This divine desire and the universal offer are meant to inform our world evangelism. It is not our responsibility or capability to solve the problem of divine sovereignty versus human responsibility. It is our task simply to preach the gospel to all the world.

2:5–6 Paul follows his teaching that God desires "all people to be saved" with the declaration that the saving gospel is all the work of God. There is one God, says Paul, and one Mediator, who sacrificed himself to ransom sinners.

Because he is the "one God," he is the God of every nation, tongue, and tribe—every soul. All must come to him for salvation. On top of this, the *one* God has *one* Mediator—"there is one mediator between God and men, the man Christ Jesus" (v. 5). Jesus is the only go-between. Because he is both God and man, he fully represents both sides. The apex of God's saving work is the blood ransom paid by the God-man Christ Jesus, "who gave himself as a ransom for all" (v. 6). So we see that everything in the gospel is of God; and the gospel can save any soul, anywhere, anytime. That is why Paul exultingly proclaims at the beginning of Romans, "I am not ashamed of the gospel, for it is the power of God for salvation to everyone who believes" (Rom. 1:16).

For us, as we follow the flow of thought here in 1 Timothy 2, it means that we are: (1) to pray for the gospel's outreach to all people, and (2) to live godly lives that promote the preaching of the gospel.

From 2:8 to the end of the letter, Paul will now turn his attention to calling Timothy and his church to *godly conduct for the sake of the gospel*. He begins by addressing four groups in sequence: men, women, overseers, and deacons.

2:8 Paul assumes that men will pray with upraised hands. His concern is not, however, about bodily posture but about the attitude with which they will pray. This instruction is in the context of the apostle's call for prayer for "all people" (v. 1), echoing his comments in 2:4 about God's desire that "all people" be saved. Paul exhorts that this prayer be conducted by "lifting holy hands without anger or quarreling." In other words, godly prayer comes from godly hearts—all rooted in the gospel.

anger or quarreling; [9]likewise also [m]that
women should adorn themselves in respectable apparel, with modesty and self-control,
not with braided hair and gold or pearls or
costly attire, [10][n]but with what is proper for
women who profess godliness—with good
works. [11]Let a woman learn quietly [o]with all
submissiveness. [12][p]I do not permit a woman
to teach or to exercise authority over a man;
rather, she is to remain quiet. [13][q]For Adam was
formed first, [r]then Eve; [14]and Adam was not
deceived, but [s]the woman was deceived and
became a transgressor. [15]Yet she will be saved
through [t]childbearing—if they continue in
[u]faith and love and holiness, with self-control.

Qualifications for Overseers

3 The saying is [v]trustworthy: If anyone
aspires to [w]the office of overseer, he desires
a noble task. [2]Therefore [x]an overseer[1] must be
above reproach, [y]the husband of one wife,[2]
[z]sober-minded, self-controlled, respectable,
[a]hospitable, [b]able to teach, [3]not a drunkard,
not violent but [c]gentle, not quarrelsome, [d]not
a lover of money. [4]He must manage his own
household well, with all dignity [e]keeping his
children submissive, [5]for if someone does not
know how to manage his own household, how
will he care for [w]God's church? [6]He must not
be a recent convert, or he may [f]become puffed
up with conceit and fall into the condemnation of the devil. [7]Moreover, he must be well
thought of by [g]outsiders, so that he may not
fall into disgrace, into [h]a snare of the devil.

Qualifications for Deacons

[8][i]Deacons likewise must be dignified, not
double-tongued,[3] [j]not addicted to much wine,
[k]not greedy for dishonest gain. [9]They must
[l]hold the mystery of the faith with [m]a clear
conscience. [10]And [n]let them also be tested
first; then let them serve as deacons if they
prove themselves blameless. [11][o]Their wives
likewise must[4] be dignified, not slanderers,

[1] Or *bishop*; Greek *episkopos*; a similar term occurs in verse 1 [2] Or *a man of one woman*; also verse 12 [3] Or *devious in speech* [4] Or *Wives, likewise, must*, or *Women, likewise, must*

9[m] 1 Pet. 3:3; [Isa. 3:18-23]
10[n] [1 Pet. 3:4]
11[o] Titus 2:5
12[p] [1 Cor. 14:34]
13[q] Gen. 1:27; 2:8 [r] Gen. 2:18, 22
14[s] Gen. 3:6, 13
15[t] [Gal. 4:4] [u] ch. 1:14
Chapter 3
1[v] See ch. 1:15 [w] See Acts 20:28
2[x] Titus 1:6-9 [y] [ch. 5:9] [z] ver. 11; Titus 2:2 [a] 1 Pet. 4:9 [b] 2 Tim. 2:24
3[c] Titus 3:2 [d] Heb. 13:5; [ch. 6:10]
4[e] [ver. 12]
5[w] [See ver. 1 above]
6[f] ch. 6:4; 2 Tim. 3:4
7[g] See Mark 4:11 [h] 2 Tim. 2:26; [ch. 6:9]
8[i] Phil. 1:1 [j] [ch. 5:23; Titus 2:3] [k] Titus 1:7; 1 Pet. 5:2
9[l] [ch. 1:19] [m] See Acts 23:1
10[n] [ch. 5:22]
11[o] Titus 2:3

2:9–15 As to the conduct of women, they should dress modestly—"with what is proper for women who profess godliness—with good works" (v. 10). Paul was concerned that the way women dressed and deported themselves would not detract from but would enhance the gospel mission.

Further, a woman was not to violate the creation order by teaching or exercising authority over a man in the church contexts Paul is addressing (vv. 11–14). Such role reversals are not consonant with godliness and are, implicitly, hindrances to the gospel.

Scholarly interpretations vary regarding the meaning of "she will be saved through childbearing" (v. 15). Some regard this as a general reference to the homemaking role of women, or even to women being kept safe in childbearing if they attend to home matters. More theologically sensitive interpretations see these words either (1) as indicating the opportunity for women who focus on family to counter the effects of Eve's sin by multiplying faithful believers in the home, or (2) as an oblique reference to the Edenic promise that from Eve would ultimately come a child who would rescue the world from sin (Gen. 3:15). What is undisputable, however, is that Paul is *not* saying that the spiritual salvation of any particular woman depends on her bearing children. Rather he is affirming that the witness of the gospel is best maintained as men and women live and worship together as God intends.

3:1–7 Turning his attention to overseers, Paul gives directives as to the godliness of church leaders. It is an ecclesial axiom that, as the years go by, what leaders are in microcosm the congregation will become in macrocosm. Paul wants a church that radiates the gospel to a dark world.

The contours of Paul's directives to the overseers in Ephesus include the overseer's reputation, marriage, self-mastery, ministry, temperance, temperament, money, family, maturity, and reputation (vv. 2–6). These graces cultivate a godly symmetry in the lives of overseers and the church as a whole. Consequently, the gospel is adorned beautifully before a lost world.

3:8–13 The reasoning that applies to overseers applies to deacons as well. Once more, the spiritual trajectories of leaders' lives are of paramount importance in

but sober-minded, [p]faithful in all things.
12 Let deacons each be [q]the husband of one
wife, [q]managing their children and their own
households well. 13 For [r]those who serve well
as deacons gain a good standing for themselves and also great confidence in the faith
that is in Christ Jesus.

The Mystery of Godliness

14 I hope to come to you soon, but I am writing
these things to you so that, 15 if I delay, you may
know how one ought to behave in the household of God, which is the church of the living
God, a pillar and buttress of the truth. 16 Great
indeed, we confess, is the mystery of godliness:

[s]He[1] was manifested in the flesh,
vindicated[2] by the Spirit,[3]
[t]seen by angels,
[u]proclaimed among the nations,
[v]believed on in the world,
[w]taken up in glory.

Some Will Depart from the Faith

4 Now [x]the Spirit expressly says that [y]in
later times some will depart from the
faith by devoting themselves to [z]deceitful
spirits and teachings of demons, 2 through
the insincerity of [a]liars whose consciences are
seared, 3 [b]who forbid marriage and [c]require
abstinence from foods [d]that God created [e]to
be received with thanksgiving by those who
believe and know the truth. 4 For [f]everything
created by God is good, and [g]nothing is to be
rejected if it is [e]received with thanksgiving,
5 for it is made holy [h]by the word of God and
prayer.

[1] Greek *Who*; some manuscripts *God*; others *Which* [2] Or *justified* [3] Or *vindicated in spirit*

regard to the furtherance of the gospel. Indeed, when it comes to the spread of the gospel, godliness is a matter of life and death. And such godliness is always the result of the gospel of grace, which is the only power that can transform the human heart.

3:14–16 Paul's mounting call to godly conduct culminates in what is the key text of 1 Timothy. The description of the church here pulses with vitality: "household" is metaphorical for "family" (cf. vv. 4, 5, 12). At the head of the family is the "living God." The church is the place where God most clearly manifests his living presence. As such it is a "pillar and buttress of the truth" (v. 15). The living church family has been appointed to uphold and undergird the truth that God has revealed through Christ. And how is this to be done? By conduct in the household of God that is consistent with, and springs from, the gospel of Jesus Christ—"the mystery of godliness" (v. 16).

Paul then offers the famous creedal confession in verse 16. Whenever Paul uses the word "mystery," he is referring to Christ as the revelation of the plan of salvation that had been hidden up to that point. The content of this creedal hymn confirms the deep theological meaning of "the mystery." But the phrase "the mystery of godliness" means more than the objective theological content of the gospel. In the context of 1 Timothy (cf. 2:2, 8–14; 3:1–7, 8–13, 14–15), it points to the pattern of life drawn forth from the gospel. Ultimately, it points to Christ himself as the essence and source of all godly conduct.

So the call to godly conduct is not a challenge to pursue a self-generated "bootstrap" godliness. Rather, it is a call to live out the dizzying realities of the gospel. The Lord Jesus Christ is the burning essence of godliness—its radiating nuclear core, so to speak. In his incarnation, death, and resurrection, the mystery of godliness was displayed before the universe. And by virtue of Christ's saving grace, all those who believe in him have been united to him so that they share in his godliness. His godly record becomes ours by grace, but in the thankful response of regenerated hearts, we also begin to live out personally the godliness Christ embodied. Paul's call to godliness is thus both gospel-generated and gospel-sustained. If you have Christ, you possess and are possessed by the very "mystery of godliness." And you can live out this mystery!

4:1–5 Having just presented Christ as the source and center of godliness, Paul excoriates those who teach that ascetic discipline is essential to godliness. Paul calls such teaching the "teachings of demons." Indeed, asceticism lays the axe to the gospel of grace. Our standing with God is based on Jesus' self-sacrifice, not ours.

11 [p][Titus 2:10]
12 [q]ver. 2, 4
13 [r]See Matt. 25:21
16 [s]John 1:14; 1 Pet. 1:20 [t]Luke 2:13; 24:4 [u]Gal. 2:2 [v]2 Thess. 1:10 [w]See Acts 1:2

Chapter 4

1 [x]See John 14:17 [y][2 Thess. 2:3-9; 2 Tim. 3:1]; See 1 Cor. 11:19 [z]1 John 4:6 (Gk.); See Matt. 7:15
2 [a][1 Thess. 2:3; 2 Thess. 2:11]
3 [b][Dan. 11:37; Heb. 13:4] [c]See Col. 2:16 [d]Gen. 1:29; 9:3 [e]See Rom. 14:6
4 [f]Gen. 1:31 [g]See Acts 10:15 [e][See ver. 3 above]
5 [h]Gen. 1:25, 31

A Good Servant of Christ Jesus

6 [i]If you put these things before the brothers,[1] you will be a good servant of Christ Jesus,
being trained in the words of the faith and
of the good doctrine that you have [j]followed.
7 Have nothing to do with irreverent, [k]silly
myths. Rather [l]train yourself for godliness;
8 for while [m]bodily training is of some value,
godliness [n]is of value in every way, as [o]it holds
promise for the present life and also for the
life to come. 9 The saying is [p]trustworthy and
deserving of full acceptance. 10 For to this end
we toil and strive,[2] because we have our hope
set on the living God, [q]who is the Savior of all
people, especially of those who believe.
11 Command and teach [r]these things. 12 [s]Let
no one despise you for your youth, but set the
believers [t]an example in speech, in conduct, in
love, in faith, in purity. 13 Until I come, devote
yourself to the public reading of Scripture,
to exhortation, to teaching. 14 [u]Do not neglect
the gift you have, which was given you [v]by
prophecy when the council of elders [w]laid their
hands on you. 15 Practice these things, immerse
yourself in them,[3] so that [x]all may see your
progress. 16 [y]Keep a close watch on yourself and
on the teaching. Persist in this, for by so doing
you will save [z]both yourself and [a]your hearers.

Instructions for the Church

5 [b]Do not rebuke an older man but encourage him as you would a father, [c]younger
men as brothers, 2 older women as mothers,
younger women as sisters, in all purity.
3 Honor widows [d]who are truly widows. 4 But
if a widow has children or grandchildren, let
them first learn [e]to show godliness to their own
household and to make some return to their
parents, for [f]this is pleasing in the sight of God.
5 She [g]who is truly a widow, left all alone, has set
her hope on God and [h]continues in supplications and prayers night and day, 6 but [i]she who
is self-indulgent is [j]dead even while she lives.
7 [k]Command these things as well, so that they

[1] Or *brothers and sisters*. The plural Greek word *adelphoi* (translated "brothers") refers to siblings in a family. In New Testament usage, depending on the context, *adelphoi* may refer either to men or to both men and women who are siblings (brothers and sisters) in God's family, the church [2] Some manuscripts *and suffer reproach* [3] Greek *be in them*

6 [i][2 Tim. 3:14, 15] [j]2 Tim. 3:10
7 [k]See ch. 1:4 [l]Heb. 5:14
8 [m][Col. 2:23] [n][ch. 6:6] [o]Ps. 37:4, 9, 11; 84:11; 112:2; 145:19; Prov. 19:23; 22:4; Matt. 6:33; Mark 10:30; 1 Pet. 3:9
9 [p]See ch. 1:15
10 [q]See ch. 2:4; John 4:42
11 [r]ch. 5:7; 6:2
12 [s]1 Cor. 16:11; [2 Tim. 2:22; Titus 2:15] [t]Titus 2:7; 1 Pet. 5:3
14 [u]See 1 Thess. 5:19 [v]ch. 1:18 [w]See Acts 6:6
15 [x]Phil. 1:12
16 [y][Acts 20:28] [z]Ezek. 33:9 [a]See Rom. 11:14

Chapter 5
1 [b][Lev. 19:32] [c]Titus 2:6
3 [d]ver. 5, 16
4 [e]Matt. 15:4-6; Mark 7:10-13; Eph. 6:1, 2; [Gen. 45:9-11] [f]ch. 2:3
5 [g]ver. 3, 16 [h][Luke 2:37; 18:1-5]
6 [i]James 5:5; [Ezek. 16:49] [j]Rev. 3:1
7 [k]ch. 4:11; 6:2

4:6–10 Paul was not, however, opposed to spiritual discipline for the purpose of godliness. In fact, he commands it, not to gain grace but to enjoy the blessings it offers now and in the life to come (vv. 7–8). Paul further emphasizes the command's importance by adding, "The saying is trustworthy and deserving of full acceptance" (v. 9).

To some ears, the command to "train [or discipline] yourself for godliness" (v. 7) may smack of legalism. But the difference is profound. Legalism imagines, "I will do this thing to gain merit, or standing before God," while godly training says, "I will do this because I love God and want to please him." Remember that this same Paul who commands spiritual discipline passionately opposed legalism and cursed it as a "different gospel" (cf. Gal. 1:6–8). Significantly, Paul had earlier told the Corinthians that it was grace that energized his gospel work (1 Cor. 15:10), thus combining grace and hard work. The apostle's incredibly hard-working, disciplined life was all of grace!

Paul's command to "train yourself for godliness" is not self-generated works-righteousness because it is Christ, "the mystery of godliness," who indwells and compels all true spiritual discipline. The entire command drips with grace. Paul then reminds the church in 1 Timothy 4:10 that godliness is crucial to the spread of the gospel. "For to this end [a life disciplined for godliness] we toil and strive, because we have our hope set on the living God" (cf. 2:1–3).

Paul's call to Christ-centered, gospel-centric, godly conduct—for the sake of the church and a lost world—then flows into chapters 5 and 6 with specific pastoral directives to various groups in the Ephesian church.

5:1–2 Paul provides the church godly relational wisdom that spans across age and gender. How beautiful are church members who know who they are, and then treat one another properly as fathers, mothers, brothers, and sisters. Such a graced family knows how to "behave in the household of God" (3:15). This is the gracious conduct that adorns the gospel.

5:3–16 Next follows extended advice regarding the care of widows. First, Paul discusses the care of widows who qualify by their poverty and godliness and childlessness (vv. 3–8). They are "truly widows" and, as such, are to receive "honor"—that is, they are to be cared for by the church.

may be without reproach. 8 But if anyone does
not provide for his relatives, and especially for
[l]members of his household, he has [m]denied the
faith and is worse than an unbeliever.
9 Let a widow be enrolled if she is not less
than sixty years of age, having been [n]the wife
of one husband,[1] 10 and having a reputation for
good works: if she has brought up children,
has [n]shown hospitality, [o]has washed the feet
of the saints, has [p]cared for the afflicted, and
has [q]devoted herself to every good work. 11 But
refuse to enroll younger widows, for when
[r]their passions draw them away from Christ,
they desire to marry 12 and so incur condemnation for having abandoned their former faith.
13 Besides that, they learn to be idlers, going
about from house to house, and not only idlers,
but also [s]gossips and [t]busybodies, saying what
they should not. 14 So I would have [u]younger
widows marry, bear children, [v]manage their
households, and [w]give the adversary no occasion for slander. 15 [x]For some have already
strayed after Satan. 16 If any believing woman
has relatives who are widows, let her care for
them. Let the church not be burdened, so that
it may care for those [y]who are truly widows.
17 Let the elders [z]who rule well be considered
worthy of [a]double honor, especially those
who labor in preaching and teaching. 18 For
the Scripture says, [b]"You shall not muzzle an
ox when it treads out the grain," and, [c]"The
laborer deserves his wages." 19 Do not admit
a charge against an elder except [d]on the evidence of two or three witnesses. 20 As for those
who persist in sin, [e]rebuke them in the presence of all, [f]so that the rest may stand in fear.
21 In the presence of God and of Christ Jesus
and of the elect angels [g]I charge you to keep
these rules without prejudging, [h]doing nothing from partiality. 22 [i]Do not be hasty in the
[j]laying on of hands, nor [k]take part in the sins of
others; keep yourself pure. 23 (No longer drink
only water, but [l]use a little wine [m]for the sake
of your stomach and your frequent ailments.)
24 The sins of some people are conspicuous,
going before them to judgment, but the sins
of others appear later. 25 So also good works
are conspicuous, and [n]even those that are not
cannot remain hidden.

6 [o]Let all who are under a yoke as bondservants[2] regard their own masters as worthy
of all honor, [p]so that the name of God and the
teaching may not be reviled. 2 Those who have
believing masters must not be disrespectful
on the ground that they are [q]brothers; rather
they must serve all the better since those who
benefit by their good service are believers and
beloved.

[1] Or *a woman of one man* [2] Or *slaves* (for the contextual rendering of the Greek word *doulos*, see Preface)

Second, regarding the care of widows who have children, Paul says, "But if a widow has children or grandchildren, let them first learn to show godliness [note that word] to their own household and to make some return to their parents, for this is pleasing in the sight of God" (v. 4). The purpose of Paul's carefully targeted advice was that, as the church body cared for its childless widows, and as children meanwhile shouldered their sacred responsibilities to their widowed mothers and grandmothers, the church's testimony brightened before the pagan world. In its essence, grace is God providing the spiritual rescue we cannot provide for ourselves. This care for those who truly cannot provide for themselves demonstrates the principles of the gospel for both those in and those outside of the church. This gospel testimony was further strengthened by the careful selection and enrollment of older widows to extend the caring ministries of the church (vv. 9–16). Such "godliness" radiated the gospel's light.

5:17–25 Paul addresses the care and maintenance of elders with explicit instructions as to their remuneration (vv. 17–18), their discipline (vv. 19–21), and their selection (vv. 22–25). Such counsel, prayerfully applied, helps keep the church centered on Christ.

6:1–2 Paul addresses Christian slaves, exhorting them to a work ethic that honors unbelieving masters in such a way that "the name of God and the teaching may not be reviled." This is, moreover, an ethic that respects and serves Christian masters all the more since those who benefit "are believers and beloved." Clearly, Paul is calling for godly conduct that elevates the name of Christ and generates praise for the gospel both in the church and in the world. He is also subtly undermining any unfair or unkind behavior of believing masters by reminding Christian slaves not to be slack in service or respect on the premise that the believing masters are merely "brothers," a designation that simultaneously reminds masters to treat their servants as "brothers" in Christ (cf. Eph. 6:9; Philem. 16, 20).

8 [l]See Gal. 6:10 [m]Rev. 2:13; [2 Tim. 3:5; Titus 1:16; 2 Pet. 2:1; Rev. 3:8]
9 [n][ch. 3:2]
10 [n][See ver. 9 above] [o]See Gen. 18:4 [p]ver. 16 [q][ch. 6:18]
11 [r][Rev. 18:3, 7, 9]
13 [s]3 John 10 (Gk.) [t]2 Thess. 3:11; 1 Pet. 4:15
14 [u][1 Cor. 7:9] [v][Titus 2:5] [w]ch. 6:1; Titus 2:5, 8
15 [x][ch. 1:20]
16 [y]ver. 3, 5
17 [z]Rom. 12:8; 1 Thess. 5:12; [1 Cor. 12:28] [a]Deut. 21:17
18 [b]1 Cor. 9:9; Cited from Deut. 25:4 [c]Matt. 10:10; Luke 10:7; [Lev. 19:13; Deut. 24:15; 1 Cor. 9:4, 7-14]
19 [d]See Deut. 19:15
20 [e]Titus 1:13; 2:15 [f]Deut. 13:11
21 [g]ch. 6:13; 2 Tim. 2:14; 4:1 [h]See 2 Cor. 5:16
22 [i][ch. 3:10] [j]See Acts 6:6 [k][2 John 11]
23 [l][ch. 3:8] [m]Ps. 104:15
25 [n][Ps. 37:6; Prov. 10:9]
Chapter 6
1 [o]See 1 Pet. 2:18 [p]Isa. 52:5; Rom. 2:24; Titus 2:5
2 [q]See Philem. 16

False Teachers and True Contentment

[r]Teach and urge these things. 3 If anyone [s]teaches a different doctrine and does not agree with [t]the sound[1] words of our Lord Jesus Christ and the teaching [u]that accords with godliness, 4 [v]he is puffed up with conceit and [w]understands nothing. He has an unhealthy craving for [x]controversy and for [y]quarrels about words, which produce envy, dissension, slander, evil suspicions, 5 and constant friction among people [z]who are depraved in mind and deprived of the truth, [a]imagining that godliness is a means of gain. 6 But [b]godliness [c]with contentment is great gain, 7 for [d]we brought nothing into the world, and[2] we cannot take anything out of the world. 8 But [e]if we have food and clothing, with these we will be content. 9 But [f]those who desire to be rich fall into temptation, [g]into a snare, into many senseless and harmful desires that [h]plunge people into ruin and destruction. 10 For the love of money is a root of [i]all kinds of evils. It is through this craving that some have wandered away from the faith and pierced themselves with many pangs.

Fight the Good Fight of Faith

11 But as for you, [j]O man of God, [k]flee these things. [l]Pursue righteousness, godliness, faith, love, steadfastness, gentleness. 12 [m]Fight the good fight of the faith. [n]Take hold of the eternal life [o]to which you were called and about which you made [p]the good confession in the presence of many witnesses. 13 [q]I charge you in the presence of God, who gives life to all things, and of Christ Jesus, [r]who in his testimony before[3] Pontius Pilate made [p]the good confession, 14 to keep the commandment unstained and free from reproach until [s]the appearing of our Lord Jesus Christ, 15 which he will display [t]at the proper time—he who is [u]the blessed and only Sovereign, [v]the King of kings and Lord of lords, 16 [w]who alone has immortality, [x]who dwells in [y]unapproachable light, [z]whom no one has ever seen or can see. To him be honor and eternal dominion. Amen.

17 As for the rich in [a]this present age, charge them [b]not to be haughty, nor [c]to set their hopes on [d]the uncertainty of riches, but on God, [e]who richly provides us with everything to enjoy. 18 They are to do good, [f]to be rich in good works, to be generous and [g]ready to share, 19 thus [h]storing up treasure for themselves as a good foundation for the future, so that they may [i]take hold of [j]that which is truly life.

20 O Timothy, guard the deposit entrusted to you. [k]Avoid the [l]irreverent babble and contradictions of what is falsely called "knowledge," 21 for by professing it some have swerved from the faith.

[m]Grace be with you.[4]

[1] Or *healthy* [2] Greek *for*; some manuscripts insert [it is] *certain* [that] [3] Or *in the time of* [4] The Greek for *you* is plural

6:3–5 Paul warns against anyone who teaches "a different doctrine and does not agree with the sound words of our Lord Jesus Christ and the teaching that accords with godliness" (v. 3). Doctrine that contravenes Christ's teaching will reveal its ugly self in ungodly behavior. It is axiomatic: where godliness, there the gospel; where the gospel, there godliness. The two are bound up with each other.

6:5–10 Paul concludes verse 5 by noting that the ungodly imagine that "godliness is a means of gain." Then he adds, "But godliness with contentment is great gain" (v. 6).

Thus, another warning: those who desire to be rich, who love money, will depart from the faith. The gospel and greed are mutually exclusive (vv. 9–10). This accords with Christ's maxim that, "You cannot serve God and money" (Luke 16:13). Let those who claim the gospel, and who revel in grace, and want to be rich—beware! The greatest riches in the universe are in Christ, and in the gospel that proclaims his grace to us.

6:11–16 Paul begins his closing words to Timothy with an eloquent charge toward godliness. Timothy is to "pursue" the virtues toward which God summons us. But this is not a godliness devoid of the gospel of grace. Rather, this is itself the life of faith: "Fight the good fight of the faith" (v. 12). There can be no fulfilling of the gospel ministry without godliness and its attendant virtues, all of which arise from the beauty of the gospel, as we behold Christ, the mystery of godliness (3:16).

2 [r] ch. 4:11, 13; 5:7
3 [s] ch. 1:3 [t] See ch. 1:10 [u] Titus 1:1
4 [v] ch. 3:6; 2 Tim. 3:4 [w] 1 Cor. 8:2; [ch. 1:7] [x] ch. 1:4; 2 Tim. 2:23; Titus 3:9 [y] 2 Tim. 2:14; [Acts 18:15]
5 [z] 2 Tim. 3:8; [Eph. 4:22; Titus 1:15] [a] Titus 1:11; 2 Pet. 2:3
6 [b] [ch. 4:8] [c] Ps. 37:16; Prov. 15:16; 16:8; Phil. 4:11; Heb. 13:5
7 [d] Job 1:21; Ps. 49:17; Eccles. 5:15
8 [e] Gen. 28:20; Prov. 30:8
9 [f] Prov. 15:27; 23:4; 28:20; Matt. 13:22 [g] [ch. 3:7] [h] [ch. 1:19]
10 [i] [Ex. 23:8; Deut. 16:19]
11 [j] 2 Tim. 3:17 [k] 2 Tim. 2:22 [l] See Prov. 15:9
12 [m] [ch. 1:18]; See 1 Cor. 9:25 [n] [Phil. 3:12] [o] 1 Pet. 5:10 [p] See 2 Cor. 9:13
13 [q] See ch. 5:21 [r] [Matt. 27:11; John 18:37; Rev. 1:5; 3:14] [p] [See ver. 12 above]
14 [s] See 2 Thess. 2:8
15 [t] See ch. 2:6 [u] ch. 1:11 [v] See Rev. 17:14
16 [w] See ch. 1:17 [x] [Ps. 104:2] [y] Job 37:23 [z] See John 1:18 **17** [a] 2 Tim. 4:10; Titus 2:12 [b] Rom. 11:20; 12:3, 16 [c] See Mark 10:24 [d] Prov. 23:5; [Matt. 13:22] [e] See Acts 14:17 **18** [f] Luke 12:21; Titus 3:8, 14 [g] See Rom. 12:13 **19** [h] See Matt. 6:19, 20 [i] ver. 12 [j] [2 Tim. 1:1] **20** [k] 2 Tim. 3:5; [Col. 2:8; 2 Tim. 4:4; Titus 1:14] [l] 2 Tim. 2:16
21 [m] See Col. 4:18

Introduction to 2 Timothy

Author, Date, and Recipient

Paul wrote this second letter to Timothy during his second imprisonment in Rome, shortly before his death. This imprisonment was after the one recorded in Acts 28. He probably wrote the letter in A.D. 64–65.

The Gospel in 2 Timothy

Paul's second letter to Timothy is a call to endurance amid opposition and suffering for the sake of the gospel. The theme of endurance is present throughout the letter through the use of Greek words that variously express the idea (2:10, 12, 24; 3:11; 4:5). Suffering for the gospel is explicitly stated in 1:8, 12 (cf. 2:3; 3:10–11).

Paul's exhortation to endure has shaped the very structure of the letter. After expressing his affectionate greetings to Timothy, his "beloved child," and recounting his fond remembrance of the young man's spiritual beginnings (1:1–5), Paul issues an extended exhortation to endurance (1:6–2:13). This exhortation begins with a powerful call to gospel-centered endurance (1:6–14), followed by contrasting real-life examples of two who failed to endure and one who did (1:15–18). Paul then resumes his call to gospel endurance (2:1–13), with directives to be strengthened by the grace that is in Christ Jesus (2:1–2), to share in suffering as a good soldier (2:3–7), to remember Jesus Christ as preached in Paul's gospel (2:8–9), and to endure through the work of Christ (2:10–13).

In the next section (2:14–3:9) Paul provides wisdom for enduring false teachers. Timothy is charged to rightly handle the word (2:14–19), remain an honorable vessel, be ready for every good work (2:20–21), avoid ignorant controversies (2:23), and correct opponents with gentleness (2:24–26). As Paul moves to the end of his letter (3:10–4:8), he issues a mounting, ascending call to endure for the gospel. Paul encourages Timothy to follow his own astonishing example of endurance (3:10–13), continuing in the God-breathed Scriptures that make souls wise for salvation through faith in Christ Jesus (3:14–17) and taking up the stunning call to preach the word (4:1–8).

The apostle closes with a moving example of enduring to the end in gospel ministry (4:9–22). Second Timothy is, so to speak, Paul's last will and testament and, as such, it bears power and soul-moving piquancy—all rooted in the beauty of the gospel of grace (1:8–11).

Outline

I. Opening (1:1–2)

II. Enduring for the Gospel (1:3–2:13)

III. Dealing with False Teachers (2:14–3:9)

IV. Contrasting Timothy with False Teachers (3:10–4:8)

V. Conclusion (4:9–22)

The Second Letter of Paul to Timothy

2 Timothy

Greeting

1 Paul, [a]an apostle of Christ Jesus [b]by the will
of God according to [c]the promise of the life
that is in Christ Jesus,
2 To Timothy, [d]my beloved child:
[e]Grace, mercy, and peace from God the
Father and Christ Jesus our Lord.

Guard the Deposit Entrusted to You

3 [f]I thank God [g]whom I serve, as did my ancestors, [h]with a clear conscience, as I remember
you [i]constantly in my prayers night and day.
4 [j]As I remember your tears, [k]I long to see you,
that I may be filled with joy. 5 I am reminded
of [l]your sincere faith, a faith that dwelt first
in your grandmother Lois and [m]your mother
Eunice and now, I am sure, dwells in you as
well. 6 For this reason I remind you [n]to fan into
flame the gift of God, which is in you through
the laying on of my hands, 7 for God gave us [o]a
spirit not of fear but [p]of power and love and
self-control.
8 Therefore [q]do not be ashamed of [r]the testimony about our Lord, nor of [s]me his prisoner,
but [t]share in suffering for the gospel by the
power of God, 9 [u]who saved us and [v]called us to[1]
a holy calling, [w]not because of our works but
because of [v]his own purpose and grace, which
he gave us in Christ Jesus [x]before the ages
began,[2] 10 and which now has [y]been manifested
through [z]the appearing of our Savior Christ
Jesus, [a]who abolished death and [b]brought life
and [c]immortality to light through the gospel,
11 [d]for which I was appointed a preacher and
apostle and teacher, 12 [e]which is why I suffer as
I do. But [f]I am not ashamed, for [g]I know whom
I have believed, and I am convinced that he is
able to guard until [h]that Day [i]what has been

[1] Or *with* [2] Greek *before times eternal*

1:1–2 The messianic title "Christ Jesus" is used three times in this brief, affectionate introduction, the last of which is "Christ Jesus our Lord"—apostolic shorthand for the gospel. As Paul says elsewhere, "For what we proclaim is not ourselves, but Jesus Christ as Lord" (2 Cor. 4:5; cf. 1 Cor. 15:1–4). The gospel is no gospel at all without the radiating person of Christ (the *Anointed One* promised to the nations) Jesus (the *deliverer* of his people) our Lord (the One who restrains and conquers all enemies to establish his blessed kingdom for our eternal reign with him) at its very center.

1:6–14 Paul's mighty opening call to endurance is utterly gospel-centered. Embedded in the very heart of the call is one of the grandest descriptions of the gospel in the New Testament. This description is bracketed at both ends by the very word "gospel," exquisitely encapsulating the grace of the gospel.

In Paul's description, we first see *sovereign grace*, because the ability to endure suffering and shame is rooted in God's grace: "Therefore do not be ashamed of the testimony about our Lord, nor of me his prisoner, but share in suffering for the gospel by the power of God, who saved us and called us to a holy calling, not because of our works but because of his own purpose and grace" (1:8–9a). As Paul puts it in Titus 3:5, "he saved us, not because of works done by us in righteousness, but according to his own mercy." As he stated it most famously in Ephesians 2:8–9, "For by grace you have been saved through faith. And this is not your own doing; it is the gift of God, not a result of works, so that no one may boast." All glory goes to God for his sovereign, omnipotent, empowering grace!

Sovereign grace is also *preexistent grace*, "grace, which he gave us in Christ Jesus before the ages began" (2 Tim. 1:9). Thus we understand that Christ existed before

Chapter 1

1 [a]See 2 Cor. 1:1 [b]See 1 Cor. 1:1 [c]Titus 1:2; Heb. 9:15
2 [d]1 Cor. 4:17; [ch. 2:1]; See 3 John 4 [e]See 1 Tim. 1:2
3 [f]See Rom. 1:8 [g]See Acts 22:3; 24:14 [h]1 Tim. 3:9; See Acts 23:1 [i]Rom. 1:9
4 [j][Acts 20:37] [k]Phil. 1:8; [ch. 4:9, 21]
5 [l]Rom. 12:9; 1 Tim. 1:5 [m]Acts 16:1; [ch. 3:15; Ps. 86:16; 116:16]
6 [n]1 Tim. 4:14; [1 Thess. 5:19]
7 [o]Rom. 8:15; [John 14:27; Rev. 21:8] [p]Luke 24:49; Acts 1:8
8 [q]See Mark 8:38 [r]See 1 Cor. 1:6 [s][ver. 16]; See Eph. 3:1 [t]ch. 2:3, 9; 4:5
9 [u]1 Tim. 1:1; Titus 3:4 [v][Heb. 3:1]; See Rom. 8:28 [w]Titus 3:5; See Rom. 3:27 [x]Titus 1:2; [Rom. 16:25]; See Eph. 1:4
10 [y]See Rom. 16:26 [z]See 2 Thess. 2:8 [a]1 Cor. 15:26; [1 Cor. 15:54, 55; Heb. 2:14, 15] [b][Job 33:30] [c]Rom. 2:7
11 [d]See 1 Tim. 2:7
12 [e]ch. 2:9 [f]ver. 8 [g][Ps. 10:14; 1 Pet. 4:19] [h]ver. 18; ch. 4:8; See 1 Cor. 3:13 [i]1 Tim. 6:20

entrusted to me.[1] 13 [j]Follow [k]the pattern of [l]the
sound[2] words [m]that you have heard from me,
in [n]the faith and love that are in Christ Jesus.
14 By the Holy Spirit [o]who dwells within us,
guard [i]the good deposit entrusted to you.
15 You are aware that [p]all who are in Asia
turned away from me, among whom are
Phygelus and Hermogenes. 16 May the Lord
grant mercy to [q]the household of Onesiphorus,
for he often [r]refreshed me and was not ashamed
of [s]my chains, 17 but when he arrived in Rome
[t]he searched for me earnestly and found me—
18 may the Lord grant him to find mercy from
the Lord on [u]that Day!—and you well know all
the service he [v]rendered at Ephesus.

A Good Soldier of Christ Jesus

2 You then, [w]my child, [x]be strengthened by
the grace that is in Christ Jesus, 2 and [y]what
you have heard from me in the presence of
many witnesses [z]entrust to faithful men[3] [a]who
will be able to teach others also. 3 [b]Share in suffering as [c]a good soldier of Christ Jesus. 4 No
soldier [d]gets entangled in civilian pursuits,
since his aim is to please the one who enlisted
him. 5 [e]An athlete is not [f]crowned unless he
competes according to the rules. 6 It is [g]the
hard-working farmer who ought to have the
first share of the crops. 7 Think over what I say,
for the Lord will give you understanding in
everything.
8 Remember Jesus Christ, [h]risen from the
dead, the [i]offspring of David, [j]as preached in
my gospel, 9 [k]for which I am suffering, [l]bound
with chains as a criminal. But [m]the word of
God is not bound! 10 Therefore [n]I endure everything for the sake of the elect, that they also
may obtain [o]the salvation that is in Christ
Jesus with [p]eternal glory. 11 The saying is [q]trust-
worthy, for:

[1] Or *what I have entrusted to him*; Greek *my deposit* [2] Or *healthy* [3] The Greek word *anthropoi* can refer to both men and women, depending on the context

13 [j][ch. 3:14; Titus 1:9; Rev. 3:3] [k][Rom. 2:20; 6:17] [l]See 1 Tim. 1:10 [m]ch. 2:2 [n]1 Tim. 1:14
14 [o]See Rom. 8:9 [i][See ver. 12 above]
15 [p]Acts 19:10; [ch. 4:10, 11, 16]
16 [q]ch. 4:19 [r]Philem. 7, 20 [s][ver. 8]; See Acts 28:20
17 [t]Matt. 25:36-40
18 [u]ver. 12 [v]Heb. 6:10
Chapter 2
1 [w]See ch. 1:2 [x]See Eph. 6:10
2 [y]ch. 1:13 [z]1 Tim. 1:18 [a][Titus 1:5]
3 [b]ch. 1:8; 4:5 [c]1 Tim. 1:18
4 [d]2 Pet. 2:20
5 [e]See 1 Cor. 9:25 [f][ch. 4:8]
6 [g]1 Cor. 9:10; [Heb. 6:7]
8 [h]1 Cor. 15:20 [i]See Matt. 1:1 [j]See Rom. 2:16
9 [k]ch. 1:8, 12 [l]See Phil. 1:7 [m][ch. 4:17]; See Phil. 1:13
10 [n]Eph. 3:13; Col. 1:24; [1 Cor. 13:7] [o]2 Cor. 1:6 [p]1 Pet. 5:10
11 [q]See 1 Tim. 1:15

the beginning of time and that grace preexisted in Christ. This thought is marvelously expanded in Ephesians 1:4–6. This sovereign, preexistent grace is wholly sufficient to save us and to impart gospel endurance.

Ultimately, God's sovereign grace, preexistent in Christ, became *visible grace* in the incarnation, death, and resurrection of Christ: "which [grace] now has been manifested through the appearing of our Savior Christ Jesus, who abolished death and brought life and immortality to light through the gospel" (2 Tim. 1:10). This gospel is all-powerful. It can save anyone who believes (Rom. 1:16). And, it can sustain any regenerate person amid the rigors of suffering and shame. As Paul says, "I am not ashamed, for I know whom I have believed, and I am convinced that he is able to guard until that Day what has been entrusted to me" (2 Tim. 1:12). The gospel-centered life will endure shame and suffering for the gospel.

2:1 As Paul continues his bold call to endurance, he applies what he has just explained about God's empowering grace to Timothy: "You then, my child, be strengthened by the grace that is in Christ Jesus."

As is true of all who are in Christ, Timothy already had the grace that claimed his heart, but that was not the end of God's provision. Grace was also a continual source of Timothy's (and our) power for Christian living. As John put it, "For from his fullness we have all received, grace upon grace" (John 1:16). As James remarked, "he gives more grace" (James 4:6). More grace was always there for Timothy, as it is for all believers. Indeed, it is grace itself that strengthens believers—"be strengthened *by* the grace . . ." This is true for all who are in Christ. We are not only converted but also strengthened in the grace of the gospel. Knowing that our God loves us, forgives us, purifies us, helps us, comforts us, enables us, and secures us—all because of his mercy rather than because of our merit—encourages and strengthens us for the calling he gives us.

2:8 Paul continues his call to endurance. The opening words of the command to "Remember Jesus Christ" call for the remembrance of two things: first, Jesus was "risen from the dead," and second, he was "the offspring of David." "Jesus" (his human name, given at birth, meaning "deliverer") aligns with "risen from the dead," the victory over sin that secures our salvation. "Christ" (Messiah) aligns with "offspring of David," a reminder of Christ's Davidic lineage in accord with God's promise and long-prophesied plan. Note that in the rest of 2 Timothy Paul uses the title "Christ

[r]If we have died with him, we will also
[s]live with him;
12 [t]if we endure, we will also reign with
him;
[u]if we deny him, he also will deny us;
13 [v]if we are faithless, [w]he remains faithful—
for [x]he cannot deny himself.

A Worker Approved by God

14 Remind them of these things, and [y]charge them before God[1] [z]not to quarrel about words, [a]which does no good, but only ruins the hearers. 15 Do your best to present yourself to God as one approved,[2] a worker [b]who has no need to be ashamed, rightly handling the word of truth. 16 But [c]avoid [d]irreverent babble, for it will lead people into more and more ungodliness, 17 and their talk will spread like gangrene. Among them are [e]Hymenaeus and Philetus, 18 who have swerved from the truth, [f]saying that the resurrection has already happened. They are upsetting the faith of some. 19 But God's firm foundation stands, bearing this seal: [g]"The Lord knows those who are his," and, "Let everyone [h]who names the name of the Lord depart from iniquity."

20 Now in [i]a great house there are not only vessels of gold and silver but also of wood and clay, [j]some for honorable use, some for dishonorable. 21 Therefore, [k]if anyone cleanses himself from what is dishonorable,[3] he will be a vessel for honorable use, set apart as holy, useful to the master of the house, [l]ready for every good work.

22 So [m]flee [n]youthful passions and pursue righteousness, faith, love, and peace, along with [o]those who call on the Lord [p]from a pure heart. 23 Have nothing to do with foolish, ignorant [q]controversies; you know that they breed quarrels. 24 And [r]the Lord's servant[4] must not be quarrelsome but [s]kind to everyone, [t]able to teach, patiently enduring evil, 25 correcting his opponents [u]with gentleness. God [v]may perhaps grant them repentance [w]leading to a knowledge of the truth, 26 and they may come to their senses and escape from [x]the snare of the devil, after being captured by him to do his will.

Godlessness in the Last Days

3 But understand this, that [y]in the last days there will come times of difficulty. 2 For people will be [z]lovers of self, [a]lovers of money, [b]proud, [b]arrogant, abusive, [b]disobedient to their parents, ungrateful, unholy, 3 [c]heartless, unappeasable, slanderous, without self-control, brutal, [d]not loving good, 4 treacherous, reckless, [e]swollen with conceit, [f]lovers of pleasure rather than lovers of God, 5 having

[1] Some manuscripts *the Lord* [2] That is, one approved after being tested [3] Greek *from these things* [4] Greek *bondservant*

Jesus," but here he says "Jesus Christ," to correspond to his order of emphases. By remembering Jesus' resurrection, we recall the gospel's awesome power (cf. Rom. 6:4; 1 Cor. 15:20–22; Eph. 1:19–20). By remembering Christ's messiahship, we recall God's awesome faithfulness, fulfilling all the Scriptures (Luke 24:26–27) and honoring the Davidic covenant (esp. 2 Sam. 7:12–16).

The Savior's resurrection and messiahship make up the essential gospel. Certainly there are other crucial elements in the gospel (Christ's atoning death, imputed righteousness that comes by faith alone through Christ alone, and so on), but this text is code for the whole thing. "Remember Jesus Christ, risen from the dead, the offspring of David, as preached in my gospel." "Remember" is a continuous command ("remember, and keep on remembering") because it is this theological remembrance of God's long but resolute and irresistible faithfulness that will steel every Christian to endure.

2:11–13 Paul caps his long call to gospel endurance (which began in 1:6) with an easy-to-remember four-stanza poem. Each stanza begins with an "if we . . ." phrase that introduces specific conduct, followed by a corresponding phrase that gives the response to the conduct. The first three stanzas record predictable (equitable) responses. But the fourth stanza, that begins with "if we are faithless," is followed by a surprise response, one that is gloriously inequitable: "he remains faithful." This is followed by the magnificent reason, "for he cannot deny himself."

Here is unforgettable comfort for all who attempt to endure for the gospel. Though we may sometimes waver and fall into unfaithfulness in our efforts to endure, God remains faithful. No one is always faithful; only Jesus is perfectly faithful. And yet in the beauty of the gospel, it is Jesus' own faithfulness that provides the very reason that God can be faithful to faithless sinners. How encouraging to all who desire to endure!

11 [r][1 Thess. 5:10]; See Rom. 6:8 [s]Rev. 20:4
12 [t][2 Thess. 1:4, 5]; See Rom. 8:17; Heb. 10:36; Rev. 20:4 [u]See Matt. 10:33
13 [v]See Rom. 3:3 [w]See 1 Cor. 1:9 [x]Num. 23:19; Titus 1:2
14 [y]1 Tim. 5:21; 6:13 [z]1 Tim. 6:4; [ver. 23] [a]Titus 3:9
15 [b][Phil. 1:20]
16 [c]Titus 3:9 [d]1 Tim. 6:20
17 [e]1 Tim. 1:20
18 [f][1 Cor. 15:12]
19 [g]Num. 16:5; Nah. 1:7; John 10:14, 27; [Luke 13:27]; See 1 Cor. 8:3 [h]Isa. 26:13
20 [i]See 1 Tim. 3:15 [j]Rom. 9:21
21 [k][Prov. 25:4; Isa. 52:11] [l]ch. 3:17; Titus 3:1; [1 Tim. 5:10]
22 [m]1 Tim. 6:11 [n][1 Tim. 4:12] [o]Acts 7:59; 9:14 [p]1 Tim. 1:5
23 [q]See 1 Tim. 6:4
24 [r][1 Tim. 3:3] [s]1 Thess. 2:7 [t]1 Tim. 3:2
25 [u]Gal. 6:1; Titus 3:2; [1 Tim. 6:11; 1 Pet. 3:15] [v]Dan. 4:27; Acts 8:22; See Acts 5:31 [w]See 1 Tim. 2:4
26 [x]1 Tim. 3:7
Chapter 3
1 [y]See 1 Tim. 4:1
2 [z][Phil. 2:21] [a]Luke 16:14; [1 Tim. 6:10] [b]Rom. 1:30
3 [c]Rom. 1:31 [d][Titus 1:8]
4 [e]1 Tim. 3:6; 6:4 [f]Phil. 3:19

the appearance of godliness, but [g]denying its
power. [h]Avoid such people. 6 For among them
are [i]those who creep into households and capture weak women, burdened with sins and led
astray by various passions, 7 always learning
and never able to [j]arrive at a knowledge of the
truth. 8 Just as [k]Jannes and Jambres [l]opposed
Moses, so these men also oppose the truth,
[m]men corrupted in mind and [n]disqualified
regarding the faith. 9 But they will not get very
far, for their folly will be plain to all, [o]as was
that of those two men.

All Scripture Is Breathed Out by God

10 [p]You, however, have followed my teaching, my conduct, my aim in life, my faith,
my patience, my love, my steadfastness,
11 my persecutions and sufferings that happened to me [q]at Antioch, [r]at Iconium, and [s]at
Lystra—which persecutions I endured; yet
[t]from them all [u]the Lord rescued me. 12 Indeed,
all who desire to [v]live a godly life in Christ
Jesus [w]will be persecuted, 13 while [x]evil people
and impostors will go on from bad to worse,
deceiving and [y]being deceived. 14 But as for
you, [z]continue in what you have learned and
have firmly believed, knowing from whom[1]
you learned it 15 and how [a]from childhood
you have been acquainted with [b]the sacred
writings, [c]which are able to make you wise for
salvation through faith in Christ Jesus. 16 [d]All
Scripture is breathed out by God and profitable for teaching, for reproof, for correction,
and for training in righteousness, 17 that [e]the

[1] The Greek for *whom* is plural

5 [g] See 1 Tim. 5:8 [h] 1 Tim. 6:20; [Titus 1:14]
6 [i] [Titus 1:11]
7 [j] 1 Tim. 2:4
8 [k] Ex. 7:11 [l] [Acts 13:8] [m] See 1 Tim. 6:5 [n] Titus 1:16
9 [o] Ex. 7:12; 8:18; 9:11
10 [p] [Phil. 2:22]
11 [q] Acts 13:14, 45, 50 [r] Acts 14:1, 2, 5 [s] Acts 14:6, 19 [t] Ps. 34:19 [u] ch. 4:17; [2 Cor. 1:10]
12 [v] Titus 2:12 [w] See Acts 14:22
13 [x] [Rev. 22:11] [y] Titus 3:3
14 [z] [1 Tim. 4:6]
15 [a] [Eph. 6:4]; See ch. 1:5 [b] [John 5:39] [c] Ps. 119:99
16 [d] Rom. 15:4; 2 Pet. 1:20, 21
17 [e] See 1 Tim. 6:11

3:10–4:8 After providing wisdom for dealing with false teachers (2:14–26), followed by a profile of false teachers (3:1–9), Paul issues a three-tiered call to endure for the gospel (3:10–4:8).

3:10–13 The first tier (see previous note) is an implicit call for Timothy to endure, as Paul reminds his young protégé that he has been a close observer of everything in Paul's life, culminating in Paul's endurance of multiple persecutions (vv. 10–11). This reminder was a gentle, fatherly prod for Timothy to shoulder the same noble mantle that comes with a life committed to the gospel. With this, Paul presents a universal truth regarding such a life: "Indeed, all who desire to live a godly life in Christ Jesus will be persecuted" (v. 12).

This is one of the great glories of the gospel, because suffering for the gospel is a palpable link to the suffering of our Messiah. This became part of Paul's spiritual DNA from the beginning of his spiritual life on the road to Damascus when, following a blinding flash, Jesus called to him, "Saul, Saul, why are you persecuting me?" (Acts 9:4). Saul's attack upon Christians (those *in* Christ) was an attack on Christ himself. Significantly, Ananias of Damascus was immediately commissioned to go to Saul, "For," as Christ explained, "I will show him how much he must suffer for the sake of my name" (Acts 9:16).

Indeed, Paul's sufferings were enough to break a thousand lesser men (cf. 2 Cor. 11:23–29). But the abiding glory of Paul's life, and of those who likewise endure suffering for the gospel, is that the Messiah suffers in and with them. Such suffering can only turn out for our glory and the advancement of his purposes (2 Cor. 4:16–18). By such suffering we not only learn more of how great was the love of the Prince of Heaven who gave himself for us, but also we identify with him, participate in his purposes for others in a world that opposes him, and fill up in our sufferings what is needed for Christ's mission in the world to continue until the day of his ultimate victory and return (Col. 1:24).

3:14–17 This section, the second tier in Paul's welling call to endure, ends with the famous declaration of the inspiration and usefulness of all of Scripture. The statement in full is foundational to understanding the inerrancy and sufficiency of Scripture. Volumes have been written on it.

However, as important as the text is in teaching us about the nature of Scripture, it actually serves to anchor Paul's overarching concern that Timothy endure in the gospel. Paul exhorts Timothy to give close attention to the Scriptures and to "continue in what you have learned and have firmly believed, knowing from whom you learned it and how from childhood you have been acquainted with the sacred writings, which are able to make you wise for salvation through faith in Christ Jesus" (vv. 14–15). The

man of God[1] may be complete, [f]equipped [g]for
every good work.

Preach the Word

4 [h]I charge you in the presence of God and
of Christ Jesus, [i]who is to judge the living
and the dead, and by [j]his appearing and his
kingdom: 2 preach the word; be ready in season and out of season; [k]reprove, rebuke, and
[l]exhort, with complete patience and teaching. 3 [m]For the time is coming when people
will not endure [n]sound[2] teaching, but having
itching ears they will accumulate for themselves teachers to suit their own passions, 4 and
[o]will turn away from listening to the truth and
[p]wander off into myths. 5 As for you, [q]always be
sober-minded, [r]endure suffering, do the work
of [s]an evangelist, [t]fulfill your ministry.
6 For [u]I am already being poured out as a
drink offering, and the time of my [v]depar-
ture has come. 7 [w]I have fought the good fight,
[x]I have finished the race, I have kept the faith.
8 Henceforth there is [y]laid up for me [z]the
crown of righteousness, which the Lord, [a]the
righteous judge, will award to me on [b]that
Day, and not only to me but also to all [c]who
have loved his appearing.

Personal Instructions

9 [d]Do your best to come to me soon. 10 For
[e]Demas, [f]in love with [g]this present world,
[h]has deserted me and gone to Thessalonica.

[1] That is, a messenger of God (the phrase echoes a common Old Testament expression) [2] Or *healthy*

"sacred writings" here primarily refer to the Old Testament, as does "All Scripture" in the statement that "All Scripture is breathed out by God" (which follows).

We learn, then, that the Old Testament Scriptures are key to understanding the gospel and who Messiah Jesus is. In fact, they are full of Messiah Jesus. Without him, the Old Testament does not make sense (cf. Luke 24:25–27, 44–47; John 5:39–40; 1 Cor. 15:1–4; Acts 10:42–43). That is why the Scriptures "are able to make you wise for salvation through faith in Christ Jesus"—and this ancient saving wisdom will help us endure suffering for the sake of the gospel.

The fact that these gospel-testifying Scriptures are "breathed out by God" gives us confidence that Scripture is trustworthy and authoritative for our lives, guiding us graciously into all that is good.

4:1–8 The final tier in Paul's call to bold gospel endurance begins with the ringing charge to "preach the word." Paul reminds Timothy that God and Christ, having first commissioned Timothy to preach, will also ultimately hold the preacher accountable for faithfulness to the message of the inspired Scriptures. In light of this heavenly commissioning, the charge is then immediately and appropriately coupled to a call to constancy despite the vagaries of earth: "be ready in season and out of season" (v. 2).

Paul gives two reasons for this awesome charge. The first is in verses 3–5: "For the time is coming when people will not endure sound teaching" (v. 3a). Timothy must persevere steadily, because people will be fickle. Paul therefore directs Timothy to gospel-centered endurance. "As for you, always be sober-minded, endure suffering, do the work of an evangelist [literally, one who speaks the gospel], fulfill your ministry" (v. 5).

The second reason Paul gives for carrying on his mighty charge to "preach the word" is his own example of endurance in the gospel enterprise. "For I am already being poured out as a drink offering, and the time of my departure has come. I have fought the good fight, I have finished the race, I have kept the faith" (vv. 6–7). Paul is passing the baton of faithful preaching, knowing that he is nearing the end of his earthly race.

In light of his own faithful example, could anything be more motivating than the throbbing, blood-earnestness of this last-will-and-testament appeal of Paul to his beloved child, Timothy? Only this: "Henceforth there is laid up for me the crown of righteousness, which the Lord, the righteous judge, will award me on that Day, and not only to me but also to all who have loved his appearing" (v. 8). To encourage Timothy, Paul does not merely point backward to his example but also forward to the day when earthly faithfulness will be recognized and rewarded by heaven's King. A comparison of the vocabulary here with that of verse 1 reveals that "the Lord, the righteous judge" is "Christ Jesus." It is Messiah Jesus, the source and center of the gospel, the one in whom "all the promises of God find their Yes" (2 Cor. 1:20)—this Messiah will award the crown of righteousness. What a day that will be!

17 [f][Luke 6:40] [g]See ch. 2:21
Chapter 4
1 [h]ch. 2:14; 1 Tim. 5:21; 6:13 [i]See Acts 10:42 [j]ver. 8; See 2 Thess. 2:8
2 [k]1 Tim. 5:20; Titus 1:13; 2:15 [l]1 Tim. 4:13
3 [m]ch. 3:1 [n]See 1 Tim. 1:10
4 [o]See 1 Tim. 6:20 [p]See 1 Tim. 1:4, 6
5 [q]1 Pet. 1:13 [r]ch. 1:8; 2:3, 9 [s]Acts 21:8; Eph. 4:11 [t]Col. 4:17
6 [u]Phil. 2:17 [v]Phil. 1:23; [2 Pet. 1:14]
7 [w]See 1 Tim. 6:12 [x]Acts 20:24
8 [y]Col. 1:5; 1 Pet. 1:4 [z]See James 1:12 [a]Ps. 7:11 [b]ch. 1:12 [c][Rev. 22:20]
9 [d]ch. 1:4
10 [e]Col. 4:14; Philem. 24 [f]See 1 John 2:15 [g]1 Tim. 6:17; Titus 2:12 [h][ch. 1:15]

Crescens has gone to Galatia,[1] [i]Titus to
Dalmatia. 11 [h]Luke alone is with me. Get [j]Mark
and bring him with you, for he is very useful
to me for ministry. 12 [k]Tychicus I have sent to
Ephesus. 13 When you come, bring the cloak
that I left with Carpus at Troas, also the books,
and above all the parchments. 14 [l]Alexander
the coppersmith did me great harm; [m]the
Lord will repay him according to his deeds.
15 Beware of him yourself, for he strongly
opposed our message. 16 At my first defense
no one came to stand by me, but all deserted
me. [n]May it not be charged against them! 17 But
[o]the Lord stood by me and [p]strengthened me,
so that through me the message might be fully
proclaimed and [q]all the Gentiles might hear it.
So [r]I was rescued [s]from the lion's mouth. 18 The
Lord will rescue me from every evil deed and
bring me safely into his heavenly kingdom.
[t]To him be the glory forever and ever. Amen.

Final Greetings

19 Greet [u]Prisca and Aquila, and [v]the household of Onesiphorus. 20 Erastus remained at
Corinth, and I left [w]Trophimus, who was ill, at
Miletus. 21 [x]Do your best to come before winter.
Eubulus sends greetings to you, as do Pudens
and Linus and Claudia and all the brothers.[2]
22 The Lord be [y]with your spirit. [z]Grace be
with you.[3]

[1] Some manuscripts *Gaul* [2] Or *brothers and sisters*. The plural Greek word *adelphoi* (translated "brothers") refers to siblings in a family. In New Testament usage, depending on the context, *adelphoi* may refer either to men or to both men and women who are siblings (brothers and sisters) in God's family, the church [3] The Greek for *you* is plural

10 [i][Titus 3:12] **11** [h][See ver. 10 above] [j]See Acts 12:12 **12** [k]Acts 20:4; Eph. 6:21; Col. 4:7; Titus 3:12 **14** [l]See 1 Tim. 1:20 [m]Ps. 62:12; Prov. 24:12; [Neh. 6:14; 13:29; Ps. 28:4; Rev. 18:6] **16** [n][Acts 7:60] **17** [o]Acts 23:11; 27:23; [Matt. 10:19] [p]See 1 Tim. 1:12 [q]See Acts 9:15 [r]ch. 3:11 [s]Ps. 22:21; [1 Sam. 17:37] **18** [t]See Rom. 11:36 **19** [u]See Acts 18:2 [v]ch. 1:16 **20** [w]Acts 20:4; 21:29 **21** [x]ver. 9 **22** [y]Gal. 6:18; Philem. 25 [z]See Col. 4:18

Introduction to Titus

Author, Date, and Recipient

The apostle Paul wrote this letter to his coworker Titus. The letter was probably written in the mid-60s A.D. between Paul's first imprisonment (Acts 28) and his second imprisonment, which is not mentioned in Acts.

The Gospel in Titus

The book of Titus is a letter from Paul to a young pastor, urging him to lead his people deeper into the gospel. Paul is concerned about the corrupting influence of false teachers in Crete, and this concern frames the book. He shows that the gospel presents a fundamentally different approach toward God than the false teachers do, one based on hope in God's grace and not on human accomplishments. Grace produces an entirely different kind of fruit in the lives of believers.

The church in Crete was plagued by two problems: licentiousness and legalism (1:10–16). Licentiousness is reckless, godless, rule-free living. Legalism is dutiful, strict, dry living. The first takes advantage of the grace of God, the latter seeks to earn it. Though very different in their expressions, Paul shows that licentiousness and legalism grow from the same root: hope in the flesh for personal fulfillment. The licentious person feeds on the lusts of the flesh; the legalist feeds on pride in his flesh. Both paths result in spiritual fatigue, strife, sin, and eventually, hatred of God.

Paul shows that the answer to both licentiousness and legalism is the gospel. The gospel alone gives the security, love, and joy that the human heart craves. The gospel frees us from captivity to the lusts of the flesh and the need to exalt ourselves above others, as the absolute approval of the only One whose opinion really matters has been given to us as a gift in Christ. He is all we need for everlasting joy.

Furthermore, the gospel creates in us something human religion is utterly unable to create: a "longing" for God. The gospel "trains our hearts" to pursue righteousness and to be zealous for good works (2:11–12). The good news does this not through threat of punishment or promise of reward but by making us stand in awe of the God who gave himself for us. Regulating the flesh cannot curb sinful desire any more than you can tame a wild animal by chaining it. Only a profound experience with God's grace transforms the heart. The gospel gives us the satisfaction in God that curbs our desire for sin and the security in God that no failures on our part can threaten (2:11–14; 3:3–7).

A proper understanding of the gospel therefore necessarily produces joyful, generous, holy living. Where these things are absent, Paul says, so is the power of the gospel. Paul urges the church, therefore, to strive for good works (2:4, 7, 10; 3:8, 14). When they do so with the motivations of grace, he says, the difference between the gospel and legalism will be made clear.

Paul believes that as the gospel grows deeper in believers, it will grow wider in the world (cf. Col. 1:5–6). Paul's prescription in this book is not, however, for the Cretan believers simply to try harder at being better. He wants them to believe the gospel more deeply. If they will focus on the roots of the gospel, they will produce the fruits of godliness (Titus 2:10; 3:14).

Outline

I. Opening (1:1–4)

II. The Occasion: The Need for Proper Leadership (1:5–9)

III. The Problem: False Teachers (1:10–16)

IV. Christian Living in Contrast to the False Teachers (2:1–3:8)

V. The Problem Restated: False Teachers (3:9–11)

VI. Closing Encouragement (3:12–15)

The Letter of Paul to

Titus

Greeting

1 Paul, a servant[1] of God and [a]an apostle of
Jesus Christ, for the sake of the faith of
God's elect and [b]their knowledge of the truth,
[c]which accords with godliness, 2 [d]in hope of
eternal life, which God, [e]who never lies, [f]prom-
ised [g]before the ages began[2] 3 and [h]at the proper
time manifested in his word [i]through the
preaching [j]with which I have been entrusted
[k]by the command of God our Savior;
4 To Titus, [l]my true child in [m]a common faith:
[n]Grace and peace from God the Father and
Christ Jesus our Savior.

Qualifications for Elders

5 [o]This is why I left you in Crete, so that you
might put what remained into order, and
[p]appoint elders in every town as I directed
you— 6 [q]if anyone is above reproach, the husband of one wife,[3] and his children are believers[4] and not open to the charge of [r]debauchery
or insubordination. 7 For an overseer,[5] [s]as God's
steward, must be above reproach. He must not
[t]be arrogant or quick-tempered or a drunkard
or violent [u]or greedy for gain, 8 but hospitable,
a lover of good, self-controlled, upright, holy,
[v]and disciplined. 9 He must [w]hold firm to the
trustworthy word as taught, so that he may
be able to give instruction in [x]sound[6] doctrine
and also to rebuke those who contradict it.
10 For there are many who are insubordinate,
[y]empty talkers and deceivers, especially those
of [z]the circumcision party.[7] 11 They must be
silenced, since [a]they are upsetting whole families by teaching [b]for shameful gain what they
ought not to teach. 12 [c]One of the Cretans,[8] a
prophet of their own, said, "Cretans are always
liars, evil beasts, lazy gluttons."[9] 13 This testimony is true. Therefore [d]rebuke them [e]sharply,
that they [f]may be sound in the faith, 14 [g]not
devoting themselves to Jewish myths and [h]the
commands of people [i]who turn away from the
truth. 15 [j]To the pure, all things are pure, but to
the defiled and [k]unbelieving, nothing is pure;

[1] Or *slave* (for the contextual rendering of the Greek word *doulos*, see Preface) [2] Greek *before times eternal* [3] Or *a man of one woman* [4] Or *are faithful* [5] Or *bishop*; Greek *episkopos* [6] Or *healthy*; also verse 13 [7] Or *especially those of the circumcision* [8] Greek *One of them* [9] Probably from Epimenides of Crete

1:5–9 Elders exist on account of the gospel. Paul instructs Titus to "appoint elders in every town" (v. 5) who are upright men. The final, culminating mark of an elder is that he is someone who cherishes "the trustworthy word as taught"—that is, the gospel, with all the "sound doctrine" (v. 9) that unpacks the gospel. Elders are gospel men.

1:10–16 Paul identifies fallen humanity's fundamental problem as a corrupted heart with distorted desires. Emphasizing ritual purity, food laws, and external conformity to the law does nothing to address the corruption of the heart. "To the defiled and unbelieving, nothing is pure"—that is, coercing a sinful heart into godly behavior does not make it pure (v. 15; cf. Matt. 15:11; Rom. 14:17–20). The external conformity urged by the legalizers merely papers over hearts of idolatry (seeking to gain God's benefits by human efforts).

Even worse, those with defiled hearts will try to use religious activities for their perverse ends, using religious accomplishment for self-justification, self-exultation, and self-indulgence. Such religion, Paul says, for all its lofty language, is "empty" and "deceptive" (Titus 1:10). Ironically, the false teachers share a fundamental union with the licentious in that both live in and by the flesh rather than through hope in God's grace (v. 16; cf. 3:3–7).

Chapter 1
1 [a]See 2 Cor. 1:1 [b]See 1 Tim. 2:4 [c]1 Tim. 6:3
2 [d]2 Tim. 1:1; Heb. 9:15; [ch. 2:13; 3:7] [e]Num. 23:19; 2 Tim. 2:13; Heb. 6:18 [f]Rom. 1:2 [g]See 2 Tim. 1:9
3 [h]See 1 Tim. 2:6 [i][Rom. 10:14] [j]See 1 Tim. 1:11 [k]1 Tim. 1:1
4 [l]See 3 John 4 [m]Jude 3; See 2 Pet. 1:1 [n]See 1 Tim. 1:2
5 [o][1 Tim. 1:3] [p][Acts 14:23; 2 Tim. 2:2]
6 [q]For ver. 6-8, see 1 Tim. 3:2-4 [r]See Eph. 5:18
7 [s]Luke 12:42; 1 Cor. 4:1; 1 Pet. 4:10 [t]2 Pet. 2:10 [u]1 Tim. 3:8; 1 Pet. 5:2
8 [v][1 Cor. 9:25]
9 [w][2 Thess. 2:13, 15]; See 1 Tim. 1:15; 2 Tim. 1:13 [x]See 1 Tim. 1:10
10 [y]1 Tim. 1:6 [z]See Acts 11:2
11 [a][2 Tim. 3:6] [b]1 Tim. 6:5; 2 Pet. 2:3

12 [c][Acts 17:28] **13** [d]ch. 2:15; 1 Tim. 5:20 [e]2 Cor. 13:10 [f]ch. 2:1, 2 **14** [g]See 1 Tim. 1:4 [h]See Col. 2:22 [i]See 1 Tim. 6:20 **15** [j][Luke 11:41; 1 Tim. 4:3]; See Acts 10:15 [k][Rom. 14:23]

but both [l]their minds and their consciences are defiled. 16 [m]They profess to know God, but they [n]deny him by their works. They are detestable, disobedient, [o]unfit for any good work.

Teach Sound Doctrine

2 But as for you, teach what accords with [p]sound[1] doctrine. 2 Older men are to be sober-minded, dignified, self-controlled, [p]sound in faith, in love, and in steadfastness. 3 [q]Older women likewise are to be reverent in behavior, [r]not slanderers [s]or slaves to much wine. They are to teach what is good, 4 and so train the young women to love their husbands and children, 5 to be self-controlled, [t]pure, [u]working at home, kind, and [v]submissive to their own husbands, [w]that the word of God may not be reviled. 6 Likewise, urge [x]the younger men to be self-controlled. 7 Show yourself in all respects to be [y]a model of good works, and in your teaching [z]show integrity, [a]dignity, 8 and [b]sound speech that cannot be condemned, [c]so that an opponent may be put to shame, having nothing evil to say about us. 9 [d]Bondservants[2] are to be submissive to their own masters [e]in everything; they are to be well-pleasing, not argumentative, 10 not pilfering, [f]but showing all good faith, [g]so that in everything they may adorn the doctrine of God our Savior.

11 For [h]the grace of God [i]has appeared, bringing salvation [j]for all people, 12 training us to renounce ungodliness and [k]worldly passions, and [l]to live self-controlled, upright, and godly lives in [m]the present age, 13 [n]waiting for our blessed [o]hope, the [p]appearing of the glory of our great [q]God and Savior Jesus Christ, 14 [r]who gave himself for us to [s]redeem us from all lawlessness and [t]to purify for himself [t]a people for his own possession who are [u]zealous for good works.

15 Declare these things; exhort and [v]rebuke with all authority. [w]Let no one disregard you.

Be Ready for Every Good Work

3 Remind them [x]to be submissive to rulers and authorities, [y]to be obedient, to be ready for every good work, 2 [z]to speak evil of

[1] Or *healthy*; also verses 2, 8 [2] Or *Slaves* (for the contextual rendering of the Greek word *doulos*, see Preface)

15 [l]See 1 Tim. 6:5
16 [m][1 John 2:4] [n]See 1 Tim. 5:8 [o]2 Tim. 3:8
Chapter 2
1 [p]See 1 Tim. 1:10
2 [p][See ver. 1 above]
3 [q][1 Tim. 2:9] [r]1 Tim. 3:11 [s][1 Tim. 3:8; 5:23]
5 [t]1 Pet. 3:2 [u][1 Tim. 5:14] [v]See Gen. 3:16 [w]See 1 Tim. 6:1
6 [x]1 Tim. 5:1
7 [y]1 Tim. 4:12; 1 Pet. 5:3 [z][2 Cor. 11:3] [a]1 Tim. 2:2
8 [b][1 Tim. 6:3] [c]Neh. 5:9; 1 Tim. 5:14; 1 Pet. 2:12; 3:16
9 [d]See 1 Pet. 2:18 [e][Col. 3:22]
10 [f][1 Tim. 3:11] [g]Matt. 5:16; Phil. 2:15
11 [h]ch. 3:7; See Acts 11:23 [i]ch. 3:4 [j][Ps. 67:2]; See 1 Tim. 2:4
12 [k]1 Pet. 4:2; 1 John 2:16 [l]2 Tim. 3:12; [Acts 24:25] [m]1 Tim. 6:17; 2 Tim. 4:10
13 [n]See 1 Cor. 1:7; 2 Pet. 3:12 [o]See ch. 1:2 [p]See 2 Thess. 2:8 [q]2 Pet. 1:1
14 [r]See Matt. 20:28 [s]Ps. 130:8; See 1 Pet. 1:18 [t]Ezek. 37:23; See Ex. 19:5 [u]ch. 3:8; Eph. 2:10
15 [v]ch. 1:13; 1 Tim. 5:20 [w]See 1 Tim. 4:12
Chapter 3
1 [x]Rom. 13:1; 1 Pet. 2:13 [y]See 2 Tim. 2:21
2 [z]Eph. 4:31

2:1–10 Gospel change is best evidenced not by flamboyant religious ritual but in integrity, humility, kindness, self-control, patience, and consistency of character. These are the fruits of abiding in the hope of the gospel. This section of Titus is intended to contrast the lives of true believers with those of the false teachers described in 1:10–16. Paul's list of gospel "fruit" here, combined with his lists in other epistles, such as Galatians 5:22–23 or 1 Corinthians 13:4–8, makes plain that grace is not an excuse for sin. Godliness is not merely an option for Christians; it is essential. The rules do not change, but the reasons do, as love for the God of grace becomes the primary motivation of the Christian life.

Gospel change is from the inside out, not from the outside in. If the heart is healthy, fruit will come.

2:10 Godly behavior adorns the gospel, putting on display the beauty of Jesus' character to the world. Godly behavior makes plain the difference between works-based "religion" that focuses on benefits for the practitioner and the gospel of grace that focuses on honoring (loving) the God who delivers from sin and its consequences.

2:11–14 These verses are arguably the most concise explanation of gospel-centered living found anywhere in Scripture. "Self-controlled, upright, and godly lives . . . zealous for good works" are produced by embracing the grace of God. Spiritual disciplines, Scriptural memorization, and accountability structures have their place. But a profound encounter with the grace of the gospel is the only thing that can produce change at the level of our *desires*. The gospel produces such loving and longing for our great God and Savior Jesus Christ that we desire to honor him with our lives (v. 13). When that love and longing are present, godly behaviors follow.

2:15 The pastor's role is constantly to hold up the good news of the gospel and to rebuke all beliefs or practices that contradict it. Because licentiousness and legalism are both at odds with the gospel, gospel preachers can expect resistance from both. After all, Jesus' crucifixion was a joint project between both pagan (Roman) and religious (Jewish) leaders.

3:1–3 Three often overlooked evidences of gospel change are submissiveness (v. 1), kindness in speech (v. 2), and humility (v. 3). These are qualities demonstrated more

no one, [a]to avoid quarreling, to be gentle, and
[b]to show perfect courtesy toward all people.
3 For [c]we ourselves were once foolish, disobedient, led astray, slaves to various passions
and pleasures, passing our days in malice and
envy, hated by others and hating one another.
4 But when [d]the goodness and loving kindness of God our Savior appeared, 5 he saved
us, [e]not because of works done by us in righteousness, but [f]according to his own mercy,
by [g]the washing of regeneration and [h]renewal
of the Holy Spirit, 6 whom he [i]poured out
on us richly through Jesus Christ our Savior,
7 so that [j]being justified by his grace we
might become [k]heirs [l]according to the hope
of eternal life. 8 The saying is [m]trustworthy,

in the home than they are on the stage. If the gospel has not transformed us in these areas, we cannot claim to know anything of its power (cf. 1 John 3:16–24; James 1:26–27; 3:6–12). Again Paul is making a direct contrast between the lives of true believers and false teachers (Titus 1:10–16; 3:9–11). Christ's disciples are "submissive" rather than "insubordinate"; "gentle" and "courteous" rather than "evil beasts" and "detestable"; "ready" for every good work rather than "unfit" for them; and they avoid "quarreling" rather than "quarreling about the law." This is the fruit produced by the gospel of grace.

3:4 Note Paul's use of the word "appeared" both here and in 2:11–14. Christ's appearance among his people to display "the goodness and loving kindness of God our Savior" is presented as the means by which his people are motivated "to devote themselves to good works" (3:8). Transformation comes from the "appearance" of the loving kindness of God our Savior to our hearts. He who saved us by a rich outpouring of his mercy and not according to our worthiness, becomes the passion of our endeavors. All true godliness is a consequence of understanding that God mercifully came and found us. He "appeared" to us. We did not, fundamentally, seek after him.

This "appearance" not only removes the penalty of our sin, it liberates our hearts from "slavery to various passions." Such a radical transformation fuels the good works that Paul so repeatedly calls for in this book. The point of Christ's coming was to make God's grace "appear" to the hearts of hearers. Apprehending the grace of God creates in us a stronger desire for God that brings all lesser desires into captivity, what Puritan Thomas Chalmers called "the expulsive power of a new affection." Standing in awe of what God has done for us will do more to transform our hearts than piling up good works in a subtle attempt to appease God.

3:5–7 Few passages in the New Testament better capture the totality of Christian salvation than these verses. We are reminded that God and God alone "saved us," not due to any contribution we make but solely due to his own mercy (v. 5). We learn that this mercy gives us new birth, or "regeneration," the total renewal of who we are by the Holy Spirit (v. 5). We learn that this regeneration *washes* us—messy sinners get clean not by washing themselves but by being washed by the Spirit, poured out on us (vv. 5–6); we are reminded of the way Jesus himself in his earthly ministry cleansed, with a touch of his hand, those deemed dirty by society (e.g., Matt. 8:3; Mark 1:41). We learn that justification—being declared acquitted and righteous in God's divine courtroom—is only "by his grace" and makes us not only righteous but heirs, with Christ, of all things through the hope of eternal life (Titus 3:7).

Salvation through the gospel is a total salvation, and is totally by God's own free grace, enabling us to live with a godly abandon—living for Christ without being intimidated by the world or enslaved by its motivations.

3:7–8 Throughout this letter Paul weaves together the indicative (the fact of our settled status in Christ) and the imperative (commands about what we should do for Christ in response). Paul does not merely tell believers to rest in grace; he urges them to strive for godliness. While our righteous standing before God has been settled, our sanctification is a lifelong struggle.

To be sure, exhorting believers to grow in godliness, as Paul does in his letter to Titus, can reinforce the Pharisee lurking in every human heart. Yet the answer to legalism is not to cease preaching Christian imperatives but to ground them in the indicatives of the gospel. While our victory over sin will not make us any more acceptable to God, an acute awareness of God's free acceptance of us in Christ transforms the

2 [a]1 Tim. 3:3 [b]See 2 Tim. 2:25
3 [c]See 1 Cor. 6:11
4 [d]See Rom. 2:4
5 [e]See Rom. 3:27 [f]Eph. 2:4; 1 Pet. 1:3 [g]See John 3:5; 1 Cor. 6:11; 1 Pet. 3:21 [h]See Rom. 12:2
6 [i]Joel 2:28; Acts 2:33; 10:45; Rom. 5:5
7 [j]ch. 2:11 [k]Rom. 8:17 [l]See ch. 1:2
8 [m]See 1 Tim. 1:15

and I want you to insist on these things, so that those who have believed in God may be careful [n]to devote themselves to good works. These things are excellent and profitable for people. 9 But [o]avoid foolish [p]controversies, [q]genealogies, dissensions, and quarrels about the law, for [r]they are unprofitable and worthless. 10 As for a person who stirs up division, [s]after warning him once and then twice, [t]have nothing more to do with him, 11 knowing that such a person is warped and sinful; he is self-condemned.

Final Instructions and Greetings

12 When I send Artemas or [u]Tychicus to you, do your best to come to me [v]at Nicopolis, for I have decided to spend the winter there. 13 Do your best to speed Zenas the lawyer and [w]Apollos on their way; see that they lack nothing. 14 And let our people learn [x]to devote themselves to good works, so as to help cases of urgent need, and not [y]be unfruitful.

15 All who are with me send greetings to you. Greet those who love us in the faith.

[z]Grace be with you all.

8 [n] ver. 14; ch. 2:14
9 [o] 2 Tim. 2:16 [p] See 1 Tim. 6:4 [q] 1 Tim. 1:4 [r] 2 Tim. 2:14
10 [s] See Matt. 18:15 [t] See 2 John 10
12 [u] See 2 Tim. 4:12 [v] [2 Tim. 4:10]
13 [w] See Acts 18:24
14 [x] ver. 8 [y] 2 Pet. 1:8; [Phil. 1:11; 4:17; Col. 1:10]
15 [z] See Col. 4:18

heart in such a way that we devote ourselves to godliness. Indeed, it is striking that Paul tells Titus to "insist on these things"—presumably the great salvation with all its dimensions outlined in 3:3–7—"*so that* those who have believed in God may be careful to devote themselves to good works" (v. 8). Gospel preaching leads to godly living.

3:8–10 Whereas the gospel produces humility, submissiveness, gentleness, and patience, religion (based on human motivations) produces quarreling, competitiveness, and division. Believers know they are not saved because of their righteousness but because of the unmerited kindness of God (v. 5). We need constant reminders of this unmerited grace in every age lest we turn the very doctrines God intended to humble our flesh into mechanisms for its exaltation. The doctrines of grace are not intended to fill us with pride in our knowledge or privileges. Paul tells us to avoid those with a divisive, contentious spirit. Such a spirit harms gospel work, even if the doctrines held are correct ones.

3:14 Paul ends the letter by again admonishing the Cretan believers to devote themselves to good works, a theme he has brought up repeatedly throughout this short book (2:7, 10, 14; 3:1, 8). The church is, as Francis Schaeffer put it, God's "demonstration community," his "final witness" to the lost world.

Godly, generous behavior within the church is the best "advertisement" for the gospel. The situation with Zenas and Apollos provides an immediate, practical opportunity for believers in Crete to engage in such works. We don't need to look far for opportunities for good works; God has placed them all around us—in our families, neighborhoods, churches, schools, and workplaces.

Introduction to Philemon

Author, Date, and Recipients

This is a personal letter from the apostle Paul to Philemon, a wealthy Christian from Colossae. It was also intended to be read to the entire church that met in Philemon's home. It was probably written c. A.D. 62, during Paul's first imprisonment in Rome (Acts 27–28).

The Gospel in Philemon

The central gospel themes in Paul's shortest letter are surprisingly substantial. Philemon teaches us simply yet profoundly that the gospel transforms us from the inside out. God's grace in the gospel therefore has the power to reconcile people and transform relationships. When a wealthy slave owner and his fugitive slave both encounter the gospel of grace, they are forever changed. Though they were both formerly slaves to sin, they have become prisoners of grace, each learning how to move from being self-centered to becoming other-oriented.

In this way Philemon and Onesimus were following the reconciling footsteps of their Master, the servant Jesus Christ, who "though he was in the form of God, did not count equality with God a thing to be grasped, but emptied himself, by taking the form of a servant" in his incarnation, humble and sinless life, and obedience to death on the cross (Phil. 2:5–8). This sacrificial service was predicted by Jesus himself, who told his disciples, "whoever would be great among you must be your servant, and whoever would be first among you must be slave of all. For even the Son of Man came not to be served but to serve, and to give his life as a ransom for many" (Mark 10:43–45).

Because of Jesus, the ultimate reconciler who made peace on the cross (Col. 1:20), we must let the peace of Christ rule in our hearts in all of our relationships, since we are one body with Christ who is our head (Col. 3:15). In this way, the gospel will transform us from the inside out, not by compelling us against our will to love one another, but by changing the will itself.

Outline

I. Greetings (vv. 1–3)

II. Thanksgiving and Prayer (vv. 4–7)

III. Paul's Appeal to Philemon for Onesimus (vv. 8–20)

IV. Personal Remarks and Greetings (vv. 21–25)

The Letter of Paul to

Philemon

Greeting

1 Paul, [a]a prisoner for Christ Jesus, and [b]Timothy our brother,

To Philemon our beloved fellow worker 2 and Apphia our sister and [c]Archippus our [d]fellow soldier, and [e]the church in your house:

3 [f]Grace to you and peace from God our Father and the Lord Jesus Christ.

Philemon's Love and Faith

4 [g]I thank my God always when I remember you in my prayers, 5 because I [h]hear of your love and [i]of the faith that you have toward the Lord Jesus and for all the saints, 6 and I pray that the sharing of your faith may become effective for the full [j]knowledge of every good thing that is in us for the sake of Christ.[1] 7 For I have derived much joy and [k]comfort from your love, my brother, because the hearts of the saints [l]have been refreshed through you.

Paul's Plea for Onesimus

8 Accordingly, [m]though I am bold enough in Christ to command you to do [n]what is required, 9 yet for love's sake I prefer to appeal to you—I, Paul, an old man and now [o]a prisoner also for Christ Jesus— 10 I appeal to you for [p]my child, [q]Onesimus,[2] [r]whose father I became in my imprisonment. 11 (Formerly he was useless to you, but now he is indeed useful to you and to me.) 12 I am sending him back to you, sending my very heart. 13 I would have been glad to keep him with me, in order that he might serve me [s]on your behalf [t]during my imprisonment for the gospel, 14 but I preferred to do nothing without your consent in order that your goodness might not be [u]by compulsion but of your own accord. 15 For this perhaps is why [v]he was parted from you for a while, that you might have him back forever, 16 [w]no longer as a bondservant[3] but more than

[1] Or *for Christ's service* [2] *Onesimus* means *useful* (see verse 11) or *beneficial* (see verse 20) [3] Or *slave*; twice in this verse (for the contextual rendering of the Greek word *doulos*, see Preface)

1–7 This opening greeting of Paul is full of thanksgiving and praise for what God has done in Philemon's life. Because of the work of Christ in his life, Philemon has become not only a "beloved fellow worker" of the apostle but also a gracious host for the church that was meeting in his home (vv. 1–2). Paul recognizes this and prays that the love, faith, witness, and hospitality that Philemon has already displayed will continue to grow and bear more fruit (vv. 5–7).

While details are sparse, it is clear that Philemon's life has changed radically because of the gospel. He now uses his time, talents, and treasures to serve his new Master, the Lord Jesus Christ, by ministering to others. The "hearts of the saints have been refreshed through" Philemon. This is what the gospel does—the love of Christ flows through us onto others.

8–16 Paul continues to build upon the gospel foundation he started in the opening greeting. Based on the transformation that Philemon experienced through faith in Christ, Paul appeals to Philemon regarding his runaway slave Onesimus.

Paul begins his plea by reminding Philemon of the status they both share as "prisoners . . . for Christ" (v. 9). He tells Philemon that Onesimus has now providentially become a fellow prisoner of grace through Paul's ministry in Rome. He wants Philemon now to view Onesimus through the lens of the gospel—as a penitent sinner who has turned to Christ in faith and whose faithful service to Paul was evidence of this transformation (vv. 11, 13). With tender language, Paul petitions Philemon

1 [a] ver. 9; See Eph. 3:1 [b] See 1 Thess. 3:2
2 [c] Col. 4:17 [d] Phil. 2:25 [e] See Rom. 16:5
3 [f] See Rom. 1:7
4 [g] See Rom. 1:8, 9
5 [h] Col. 1:4 [i] Eph. 1:15
6 [j] Phil. 1:9; Col. 1:9
7 [k] [2 Cor. 7:4, 13; Col. 4:11] [l] ver. 20; 2 Tim. 1:16; [Rom. 15:32; 2 Cor. 7:13]
8 [m] [1 Thess. 2:6] [n] Eph. 5:4
9 [o] ver. 1
10 [p] See 3 John 4 [q] Col. 4:9 [r] ver. 13; 1 Cor. 4:15; [Gal. 4:19]
13 [s] See 1 Cor. 16:17 [t] ver. 10; See Phil. 1:7
14 [u] [2 Cor. 9:7; 1 Pet. 5:2]
15 [v] [Gen. 45:5, 8]
16 [w] See 1 Cor. 7:22

a bondservant, as [x]a beloved brother—especially to me, but how much more to you, [y]both
in the flesh and in the Lord.
17 So if you consider me [z]your partner,
receive him as you would receive me. 18 If he
has wronged you at all, or owes you anything,
charge that to my account. 19 [a]I, Paul, write
this with my own hand: I will repay it—to
say nothing of your owing me even your own
self. 20 Yes, brother, I want some benefit from
you in the Lord. [b]Refresh my heart in Christ.
21 [c]Confident of your obedience, I write to
you, knowing that you will do even more than
I say. 22 At the same time, prepare a guest room
for me, for [d]I am hoping that [e]through your
prayers [f]I will be graciously given to you.

Final Greetings

23 [g]Epaphras, my [h]fellow prisoner in Christ
Jesus, sends greetings to you, 24 and so do
[i]Mark, [i]Aristarchus, [j]Demas, and [j]Luke, my
fellow workers.
25 [k]The grace of the Lord Jesus Christ be with
your spirit.

16[x] Matt. 23:8; Col. 4:9; 1 Tim. 6:2 [y] Col. 3:22, 23; [Eph. 6:5]
17[z] 2 Cor. 8:23
19[a] See 1 Cor. 16:21
20[b] See ver. 7
21[c] See 2 Cor. 2:3
22[d] Phil. 1:25; 2:24 [e] See 2 Cor. 1:11 [f] [Heb. 13:19]
23[g] See Col. 1:7 [h] Rom. 16:7
24[i] See Col. 4:10 [j] See Col. 4:14; 2 Tim. 4:10, 11
25[k] See Gal. 6:18

to consider Onesimus no longer as a runaway slave with a debt to repay, but as a "beloved brother" who will serve the Lord alongside him (v. 16).

In essence, Paul is appealing to Philemon from the inside out. While Paul could demand that Philemon do what the apostle says (v. 8), he appeals in love instead (v. 9). This is a profound gospel pattern; rather than coercing us against our will, the gospel transforms us from the inside out. As a peacemaker transformed by the reconciling power of the gospel, Paul's goal is that Philemon express "goodness" toward Onesimus not by "compulsion" but by "consent" (v. 14) based on the apostle's own love (v. 10, 12) and Onesimus's new status as a Christian "brother" (v. 16).

17–20 Note how Paul models the transforming love of the gospel as he asks Philemon to "charge that to my account" (v. 18) since Christ already paid the price for all of them. This gospel paradigm reminds us of the "charge it to my account" that Christ himself has said to us. Likewise, when Paul asks Philemon to "receive him as you would receive me" (v. 17), this request that Philemon regard Onesimus as he would Paul himself draws our minds to the gospel. For in the gospel, God regards us as he would his own Son. God receives us as he would receive Christ.

Ever so gently and subtly, then, Paul's words undermine the cultural norms that are contrary to the gospel by transforming worldly perspectives with the realities of grace. This grace is so powerful that it makes a slave not only a brother (v. 16) and a partner (v. 17) without debt (v. 18); the slave even becomes one to whom a master becomes indebted by the relational ties of the gospel (v. 19).

21–25 Paul concludes the letter in a confident tone, knowing that Philemon will receive Onesimus back unconditionally and wholeheartedly. Paul can do this because he knows that the unconditional and wholehearted love of God in Christ that has so transformed him has also transformed Philemon. Christ has not only paid the penalty for our sins; he now gives us the power, through grace supplied by his Spirit, to live changed lives—lives of reconciliation and peace, of unity and mutual servanthood.

Introduction to Hebrews

Author, Date, and Recipients

It is not clear who wrote Hebrews. The author knew Timothy (13:23). He also knew his readers and wanted to see them again (13:19). The letter was probably written before A.D. 70.

The Gospel in Hebrews

The book of Hebrews unfolds the gospel in at least five ways: it shows the connection between Christ's person and his work, shows his superiority to Old Testament persons and institutions, underscores humanity's need for redemption, warns of apostasy, and exhorts professed believers to persevere.

First, Hebrews remarkably combines the person and work of Christ. Chapter 1 teaches the deity of Christ as powerfully as any place in Scripture. Chapter 2 highlights Christ's humanity. Chapters 7–9 constitute the most extensive teaching on Christ's priesthood and atoning sacrifice. What is the point? The person of Christ as God and man constitutes the basis for his saving work. His identity undergirds his performing the unique saving deeds of dying for sinners and rising from the dead. Because he is God, *he is able* to save us, for only God can save. Because he became a man of flesh and blood, he is able *to save us*, for one of our human race died in our place and overcame death and the Devil in his resurrection.

Second, Hebrews shows Christ's superiority to Old Testament persons and institutions. He is the great and final Prophet, far surpassing Old Testament mediators of revelation—prophets and angels (ch. 1). Therefore, the gospel that he brought is even more important than the law that was given to Moses through angels (2:1–4; Acts 7:53; Gal. 3:19). He is superior to Moses, Aaron, and all Israel's subsequent high priests (Heb. 3:6; chs. 5; 7). This is because Jesus is a priest according to the order of Melchizedek who, unlike the sons of Aaron, lives forever and thus has a perpetual priesthood. He is the Great High Priest who presents himself as the final offering, bringing the end to sacrifice and saving to the uttermost those who come to God through him (chs. 9–10).

Third, Hebrews underscores humanity's need for redemption. As children of Adam we are fallen, and we do not exercise proper dominion over creation (2:8). We are held in bondage by the fear of death and by him who had the power of death, the Devil (2:14–15). Left to ourselves, like Israel of old, our hearts are unbelieving and rebellious (chs. 3–4). We are unclean and need Christ's purifying blood, his violent death, to be cleansed to serve the living God (9:14, 23; 10:22). Even as believers we are prone to wander from our first love and thus we need God's warnings, exhortations, and grace to persevere. In a word, we are needy sinners in need of a gracious and mighty Savior. And that is just what God has provided in his incarnate Son, Jesus Christ.

Fourth, as strongly as any place in the Bible, Hebrews warns of the danger of apostasy—in five passages: 2:1–4; 3:7–4:13; 5:11–6:12; 10:19–39; and 12:1–29. Plainly, the original readers of Hebrews were in danger of turning from the faith they had formerly professed. However, Hebrews also asserts that God not only saves his people from their sins but also keeps them saved to the end (6:13–20; 7:23–25). And one of the means that God employs to keep us is to warn of the folly of deserting him who saves us freely by his grace. There is nowhere else to turn.

Fifth, Hebrews exhorts professed believers to persevere (2:1; 4:14; 6:1–3; 10:23, 36; 12:1–2). It is true that God saves us once and for all. But that salvation is not static but dynamic. It is as dynamic as the living relationship between God and his people (made formal in the new covenant; ch. 8). The covenant is God's pledge to be God to us and to make us his own. Because he loves us, he not only assures us of his love with both promise and oath but also exhorts us to keep on living obediently in the faith, to keep on gathering with other believers for worship, and not to harden our hearts against him in rebellion.

While Hebrews clearly makes its own unique contribution, it joins other New Testament books in exulting in the same amazing grace in Jesus that forms the Bible's main message. The message of Hebrews is, at its core, the gospel: the good news of redemption for struggling sinners.

Outline

I. Jesus Is Superior to Angelic Beings (1:1–2:18)

II. Jesus Is Superior to the Mosaic Law (3:1–10:18)

III. Call to Faith and Endurance (10:19–12:29)

IV. Concluding Encouragements and Remarks (13:1–25)

The Letter to the

Hebrews

The Supremacy of God's Son

1 Long ago, at many times and [a]in many
ways, God spoke to our fathers by the
prophets, 2 but [b]in these last days [c]he has spoken to us by [d]his Son, whom he appointed
[e]the heir of all things, [f]through whom also
he created [g]the world. 3 He is the radiance of
the glory of God and [h]the exact imprint of his
nature, and he upholds the universe by the
word of his power. [i]After making purification
for sins, [j]he sat down [k]at the right hand of the
Majesty on high, 4 having become as much
superior to angels as the name [l]he has inherited is more excellent than theirs.
5 For to which of the angels did God ever
say,

[m]"You are my Son,
today I have begotten you"?

Or again,

1:1–2 The Son of God is the great and final Prophet whose revelation completes that of the Old Testament prophets, through whom God also spoke. In John 6:68, Peter, speaking for all believers, says to Jesus, "You have the words of eternal life." Therefore, we must pay attention (Heb. 2:1) to Jesus our Lord and Savior when he teaches us through his apostolic witness in the New Testament.

1:3 Hebrews 1 also presents the Son as Priest and King. What qualifies him to fulfill these Old Testament offices? His identity. He is the beginning and the end of all things: God's agent in creation and his heir (v. 2). And that is because he is almighty God. He shares the divine glory and is the "exact imprint of [God's] nature" (v. 3). He is of the very nature of God himself. He also performs works that only God performs, such as creating the universe (v. 10) and upholding it "by the word of his power" (v. 3).

All this introduces Hebrews' main message—that Jesus with divine power and prerogative has made "purification for sins" and has sat down at God's right hand. His sitting indicates that, unlike Old Testament priests who never sat when making sacrifices, Jesus has finished his work. There is no other sacrifice for sin besides Jesus' offering of himself to God on the cross. And because of where he sat—at God's right hand, the place of greatest honor and authority in the universe—his work is perfect. It cannot be improved upon. And because his work is finished and perfect, it is effective to forgive sins.

Even sinners who think they are beyond redemption can find forgiveness if they sincerely repent and believe in Jesus as their substitute. Christians sometimes do not act as if Christ's sacrifice were finished, perfect, and effective. When they sin, they sometimes beat themselves up spiritually and do a form of evangelical "penance," as if their extra prayers, promises, and tears can somehow atone for their sins. It is right to be displeased with ourselves when we sin. But there is no other antidote to the poison of sin than Christ's sacrifice. We dishonor him and his death if we act otherwise. Let us sincerely confess our sins and take forgiveness and cleansing from God's hand (1 John 1:9) based on the unique accomplishment of God's Son, our Savior.

1:4–14 Although this chapter mentions Christ's prophetic and priestly offices, its major idea is his royal office. He inherits the name of divine Son (King) when he sits at God's right hand (vv. 3–5). In this way he surpasses the angels who, as creatures and servants of God, worship the Son. His throne lasts forever and his rule is righteous. This means that he has the right to command and the power to rescue.

Chapter 1
1 [a][Num. 12:6, 8; Joel 2:28]
2 [b]1 Pet. 1:20; [ch. 9:26; Acts 2:17] [c]ch. 2:3 [d]See Matt. 14:33 [e]Ps. 2:8; Matt. 21:38; See Matt. 28:18 [f][ch. 3:3]; See John 1:3 [g]ch. 11:3
3 [h]See 2 Cor. 4:4 [i]See ch. 9:14 [j]See Mark 16:19 [k][Luke 22:69]
4 [l]Eph. 1:21; Phil. 2:9
5 [m]ch. 5:5; Acts 13:33; Cited from Ps. 2:7

[n]"I will be to him a father,
and he shall be to me a son"?

6 And again, when he brings [o]the firstborn into
the world, he says,

[p]"Let all God's angels worship him."

7 Of the angels he says,

[q]"He makes his angels winds,
and his ministers a flame of fire."

8 But of the Son he says,

[r]"Your throne, O God, is forever and ever,
the scepter of uprightness is the scepter of your kingdom.
9 You have loved righteousness and hated wickedness;
therefore God, your God, [s]has anointed you
with [t]the oil of gladness beyond your companions."

10 And,

[u]"You, Lord, laid the foundation of the earth in the beginning,
and the heavens are the work of your hands;
11 they will perish, but you remain;
they will all wear out like a garment,
12 like a robe you will roll them up,
like a garment they will be changed.[1]
But you are [v]the same,
and your years will have no end."

13 And to which of the angels has he ever said,

[w]"Sit at my right hand
[x]until I make your enemies a footstool for your feet"?

14 Are they not all ministering spirits [y]sent
out to serve for the sake of those who are to
[z]inherit salvation?

Warning Against Neglecting Salvation

2 Therefore we must pay much closer
attention to what we have heard, lest we
drift away from it. 2 For since [a]the message
declared by angels proved to be reliable, and
[b]every transgression or disobedience received
a just [c]retribution, 3 [d]how shall we escape if we
[e]neglect such a great salvation? It was [f]declared
at first by the Lord, and it was [g]attested to us
[h]by those who heard, 4 [g]while God also bore
witness [i]by signs and wonders and various
miracles and by [j]gifts of the Holy Spirit [k]distributed according to his will.

The Founder of Salvation

5 For it was not to angels that God subjected
the world [l]to come, of which we are speaking.
6 It has been testified somewhere,

[m]"What is man, that you are mindful of him,
or the son of man, that you care for him?
7 You made him for a little while lower than the angels;
you have crowned him with glory and honor,[2]
8 putting everything in subjection under his feet."

Now in putting everything in subjection to
him, he left nothing outside his control. At
present, [n]we do not yet see everything in subjection to him. 9 But we see him [o]who for a little

[1] Some manuscripts omit *like a garment* [2] Some manuscripts insert *and set him over the works of your hands*

5[n] Cited from 2 Sam. 7:14; [Ps. 89:26, 27]
6[o] See Rom. 8:29 [p] Cited from Deut. 32:43 (Gk.); [Ps. 97:7]
7[q] Cited from Ps. 104:4
8[r] Cited from Ps. 45:6, 7
9[s] Isa. 61:1 [t] Isa. 61:3
10[u] Cited from Ps. 102:25-27
12[v] ch. 13:8
13[w] Cited from Ps. 110:1 [x] ch. 10:13
14[y] Gen. 19:16; 28:12; 32:1, 2; Judg. 6:11; 13:3; Ps. 34:7; 91:11; 103:20, 21; Dan. 3:28; 6:22; 10:11; Matt. 18:10 [z] See Matt. 25:34

Chapter 2
2[a] See Acts 7:53 [b] [ch. 10:28; Num. 15:30, 31; Deut. 4:3; 17:2, 5, 12; 27:26] [c] ch. 10:35; 11:26

We, his people, saved freely by his grace, gladly submit to his righteous rule over us. We love him and keep his commandments because he first loved us (John 14:15, 21, 23; 1 John 4:19). His perfect love for us drives away our fear of God's wrath (1 John 4:18). He, our strong King, keeps us safe in his care. We have many reasons to thank him!

2:1–4 These verses apply chapter 1. Jesus as the Mediator of the new covenant excels the Old Testament mediators of revelation: prophets (1:1–2) and angels (1:4–14). When did angels bring revelation? The law was "delivered by angels" (Acts 7:53; Gal. 3:19). Because Jesus is a better Mediator we "must pay much closer attention" (Heb. 2:1) to his message than even to the Ten Commandments. We are not saved by obeying him, but, once saved, we obey him in eager and grateful response to his grace. Christ "gave himself for us to redeem us from all lawlessness and to purify for himself a people for his own possession who are zealous for good works" (Titus 2:14).

2:9–10 Adam and Eve disobeyed God and forfeited much of the glory and dominion that was theirs from creation (vv. 7–8). But God sent his Son to become "the last

3[d] [ch. 10:28, 29; 12:25] [e] Matt. 22:5 (Gk.) [f] ch. 1:2 [g] Mark 16:20; [Acts 5:32] [h] [Luke 1:2] **4**[g] [See ver. 3 above] [i] Acts 2:22, 43 [j] [1 Cor. 12:4, 11] [k] [Eph. 1:5]
5[l] ch. 6:5 **6**[m] Cited from Ps. 8:4-6 **8**[n] [1 Cor. 15:25] **9**[o] ver. 7

while was made lower than the angels, namely
Jesus, [p]crowned with glory and honor [q]because
of the suffering of death, so that by the grace
of God he might [r]taste death [s]for everyone.
10 For it [t]was fitting that he, [u]for whom and by
whom all things exist, in bringing many sons
[v]to glory, should make the [w]founder of their
salvation [x]perfect through suffering. 11 For [y]he
who sanctifies and [z]those who are sanctified
[a]all have one source.[1] That is why he is not
ashamed to call them [b]brothers,[2] 12 saying,

> [c]"I will tell of your name to my brothers;
> in the midst of the [d]congregation
> I will sing your praise."

13 And again,

> [e]"I will put my trust in him."

And again,

> [f]"Behold, I and the children [g]God has
> given me."

14 Since therefore the children share in flesh
and blood, he himself likewise [h]partook of
the same things, that [i]through death he
might [j]destroy [k]the one who has the power
of death, that is, the devil, 15 and deliver all
those who [l]through fear of death were subject
to lifelong slavery. 16 For surely it is not angels
that he helps, but he [m]helps the offspring of
Abraham. 17 Therefore he had [n]to be made like
his brothers in every respect, [o]so that he might
become a merciful and faithful high priest [p]in
the service of God, to make propitiation for
the sins of the people. 18 For because he himself
has suffered [q]when tempted, he is able to help
those who are being tempted.

Jesus Greater Than Moses

3 Therefore, holy brothers,[3] you who share
in [r]a heavenly calling, consider Jesus, [s]the
apostle and high priest of our confession,
2 who was faithful to him who appointed him,
[t]just as Moses also was faithful in all God's[4]
house. 3 For Jesus has been counted worthy of
more glory than Moses—as much more glory
as the builder of a house has more honor than
the house itself. 4 (For every house is built by
someone, but [u]the builder of all things is God.)
5 [v]Now Moses was faithful in all God's house
[w]as a servant, [x]to testify to the things that were
to be spoken later, 6 but Christ is faithful over

[1] Greek *all are of one* [2] Or *brothers and sisters.* The plural Greek word *adelphoi* (translated "brothers") refers to siblings in a family. In New Testament usage, depending on the context, *adelphoi* may refer either to men or to both men and women who are siblings (brothers and sisters) in God's family, the church; also verse 12 [3] Or *brothers and sisters*; also verse 12 [4] Greek *his*; also verses 5, 6

Adam" and "the second man" (1 Cor. 15:45, 47) to rectify the situation. The Son of God left heaven's glory and "for a little while was made lower than the angels" (Heb. 2:9). He became a man so that by God's grace he could die in order to ransom "people for God from every tribe and language and people and nation" (Rev. 5:9; cf. Heb. 2:9).

Consequently, he is now crowned with the "glory and honor" that our first parents lost. And amazingly, "he is not ashamed to call . . . brothers" all who believe in him, and he intends to bring them "to glory" (vv. 10–11). Because the Son of God shared our humanity, died, and rose again, he can and will usher us into heavenly glory. Such a bright prospect fills us with hope and purpose, even in days of trial and shame.

2:14–18 The plan of salvation was conceived by God in heaven. It involved his Son sharing "in flesh and blood," that is, becoming a human being. Why? So that he might live a sinless life and die as a perfect sacrifice for us. What does his death accomplish? First, he died to "destroy the one who has the power of death . . . the devil" (v. 14). When the Devil seduced our first parents to rebel against their Creator, he put them under the power of death that was the consequence of their sin. (Of course, the Devil is under God, who alone has absolute power.) By disobeying God, Adam and Eve, who were created to rule God's creation, instead became slaves to sin, Satan, and death. But we are grateful to God that One stronger than the Devil loved us and gave himself for us to destroy the Evil One and void his purposes. How comforting to know that "he who is in you is greater than he [Satan] who is in the world" (1 John 4:4)!

Second, Christ's death delivers "all those who through fear of death were subject to lifelong slavery" (Heb. 2:15). The "fear of death" here is not merely a fear of dying—that is perfectly natural. It is rather the "fear" that "has to do with punishment," a fear which "perfect love casts out" (1 John 4:18). God's love in Christ assures us that "there is therefore now no condemnation for those who are in Christ Jesus" (Rom. 8:1). God wants us to rejoice in our great Redeemer and as his loved sons and daughters to be unafraid of the wrath that will be manifested on the last day.

9 [p]Acts 3:13; 1 Pet. 1:21; See Acts 2:33 [q]Phil. 2:7-9; See John 10:17 [r]Matt. 16:28; John 8:52 [s]See John 12:32
10 [t][Luke 24:26] [u]Rom. 11:36 [v][ch. 3:1; Rom. 8:30] [w][ch. 5:9] [x]ch. 5:9; 7:28; Luke 13:32; [Phil. 3:12]
11 [y]ch. 13:12 [z]ch. 10:10, 14, 29 [a]Acts 17:28 [b]Matt. 25:40
12 [c]Cited from Ps. 22:22 [d]ch. 12:23
13 [e][Ps. 18:2; Isa. 8:17; 12:2] [f]Cited from Isa. 8:18 [g]See John 17:2
14 [h]See John 1:14 [i]See 1 Cor. 15:54-56 [j][Col. 2:15; 2 Tim. 1:10] [k]1 John 3:8; [John 16:11]
15 [l]See Rom. 8:15
16 [m]Isa. 41:8, 9; [ch. 8:9]
17 [n]Phil. 2:7 [o]ch. 4:15, 16; [ch. 5:2, 7, 8] [p]ch. 5:1; Rom. 15:17
18 [q]ch. 4:15; Luke 22:28

Chapter 3

1 [r]Eph. 4:1; Phil. 3:14 [s][John 20:21; Rom. 15:8]
2 [t]ver. 5
4 [u]Eph. 2:10; 3:9
5 [v]ver. 2; Cited from Num. 12:7 [w]Ex. 14:31; Deut. 34:5; Josh. 1:2; 8:31; Ps. 105:26; Rev. 15:3 [x]Deut. 18:15, 18, 19

God's house as [y]a son. And [z]we are his house if
indeed we [a]hold fast our confidence and our
boasting in our hope.[1]

A Rest for the People of God

7 Therefore, as the Holy Spirit says,

[b]"Today, if you hear his voice,
8 do not harden your hearts as in the rebellion,
on the day of testing in the wilderness,
9 where your fathers put me to the test
and saw my works for [c]forty years.
10 Therefore I was provoked with that generation,
and said, 'They always go astray in their heart;
they have not known my ways.'
11 [d]As I swore in my wrath,
'They shall not enter my rest.'"

12 Take care, brothers, lest there be in any of
you an evil, unbelieving heart, leading you to
fall away from [e]the living God. 13 But [f]exhort
one another every day, as long as it is called
"today," that none of you may be hardened by
[g]the deceitfulness of sin. 14 For we have come to
share in Christ, [h]if indeed we hold our original
confidence firm to the end. 15 As it is said,

[b]"Today, if you hear his voice,
do not harden your hearts as in the rebellion."

16 For [i]who were those who heard and yet
rebelled? Was it not [j]all those who left Egypt
led by Moses? 17 And with whom was he provoked for forty years? Was it not with those
who sinned, [k]whose bodies fell in the wilderness? 18 And to whom did he swear that [l]they
would not enter his rest, but to those who
were disobedient? 19 So we see that [m]they were
unable to enter because of unbelief.

4 Therefore, while the promise of entering
his rest still stands, let us fear lest any of
you should seem [n]to have failed to reach it.
2 For good news came to us just as to them,
but the message they heard did not benefit
them, because [o]they were not united by faith
with those who listened.[2] 3 For we who have
believed enter that rest, as he has said,

[p]"As I swore in my wrath,
'They shall not enter my rest,'"

although his works were finished from the
foundation of the world. 4 For he has somewhere spoken of the seventh day in this way:
[q]"And God rested on the seventh day from all
his works." 5 And again in this passage he said,

[r]"They shall not enter my rest."

6 Since therefore it remains for some to enter
it, and those who formerly received the good
news [s]failed to enter because of disobedience,
7 again he appoints a certain day, "Today," saying through David so long afterward, in the
words already quoted,

[t]"Today, if you hear his voice,
do not harden your hearts."

8 For if Joshua had given them rest, God[3]
would not have spoken of another day later
on. 9 So then, there remains a Sabbath rest for
the people of God, 10 for whoever has entered
God's rest has also [u]rested from his works as
God did from his.
11 Let us therefore strive to enter that rest, so
[v]that no one may fall by the same sort of dis-

[1] Some manuscripts insert *firm to the end* [2] Some manuscripts *it did not meet with faith in the hearers* [3] Greek *he*

6 [y]See ch. 1:2 [z]1 Cor. 3:16; 6:19; 2 Cor. 6:16; Eph. 2:21; 1 Tim. 3:15; 1 Pet. 2:5 [a]ver. 14; ch. 6:11; Ps. 119:33, 112; Matt. 10:22; Rev. 2:26
7 [b]ver. 15; ch. 4:7; Cited from Ps. 95:7-11
9 [c]See Acts 7:36
11 [d]ch. 4:3, 5
12 [e]See Matt. 16:16
13 [f][ch. 10:24, 25] [g][Isa. 44:20; Rom. 7:11; Eph. 4:22]
14 [h]ver. 6; ch. 10:23; 1 Cor. 15:2
15 [b][See ver. 7 above]
16 [i]Num. 14:2; Deut. 1:34, 35 [j][Num. 14:24, 30; Deut. 1:36, 38]
17 [k]Num. 14:29; See Jude 5
18 [l]Deut. 1:34, 35; [ch. 4:2]
19 [m]ch. 4:6; Ps. 78:22; 106:24

3:12–14 Those who are truly the Lord's do not fall away (apostatize) forever, but there is no assurance that we are truly the Lord's if we live contrary to him (cf. 10:14; Rom. 8:29–30; Eph. 2:6; Col. 3:1–3). So, these strong words call all professing Christians to a self-examination that would keep us from living in fear or rebellion (see also 2 Cor. 13:5). One evidence of truly knowing Christ is perseverance in faith. We must be on guard, therefore, that we do not develop "an evil, unbelieving heart." What is the antidote to the poison of unbelief? It is mutual accountability and daily encouragement of one another. Sin is deceitful and can harden our hearts.

Let us be watchful, then, and "hold our original confidence firm to the end" (Heb. 3:14). We thank God for faithful spouses and other friends who help us walk with Christ. And we should be on the lookout for those who name Christ's name yet do not continue with him. They need our prayers and maybe our help.

4:11–13 This is one of many exhortations in Hebrews to continue in faith and obedience until the culmination of our salvation ("to enter that rest"; v. 11). Next the writer

Chapter 4 **1** [n]ch. 12:15 **2** [o]Rom. 3:3 **3** [p]ch. 3:11; Cited from Ps. 95:11 **4** [q]Cited from Gen. 2:2; [Ex. 20:11; 31:17] **5** [r]ver. 3 **6** [s]See ch. 3:19 **7** [t]See ch. 3:7, 8 **10** [u][Rev. 14:13] **11** [v][ch. 3:12]

obedience. 12 For [w]the word of God is living and
[x]active, [y]sharper than any [z]two-edged sword,
piercing to the division of soul and of spirit,
of joints and of marrow, and [a]discerning the
thoughts and intentions of the heart. 13 And
[b]no creature is hidden from his sight, but all
are [c]naked and exposed to the eyes of him to
whom we must give account.

Jesus the Great High Priest

14 Since then we have [d]a great high priest
[e]who has passed through the heavens, Jesus,
the Son of God, [f]let us hold fast our confession. 15 For we do not have a high priest [g]who
is unable to sympathize with our weaknesses, but one who in every respect has been
[d]tempted as we are, [h]yet without sin. 16 [i]Let us
then with confidence draw near to the throne
of grace, that we may receive mercy and find
grace to help in time of need.

5 For every high priest chosen from among
men [j]is appointed to act on behalf of men
[k]in relation to God, [l]to offer gifts and sacrifices
for sins. 2 [m]He can deal gently with the ignorant and wayward, since he himself [n]is beset
with weakness. 3 Because of this he is obligated
to offer sacrifice for his own sins [o]just as he
does for those of the people. 4 And [p]no one
takes this honor for himself, but only when
called by God, [q]just as Aaron was.

5 So also Christ [r]did not exalt himself to be
made a high priest, but was appointed by him
who said to him,

> [s]"You are my Son,
> today I have begotten you";

6 as he says also in another place,

> [t]"You are a priest forever,
> after the order of Melchizedek."

7 In the days of his flesh, [u]Jesus[1] offered up
prayers and supplications, [v]with loud cries and
tears, to him [w]who was able to save him from
death, and [x]he was heard because of his reverence. 8 Although [y]he was a son, [z]he learned
obedience through what he suffered. 9 And

[1] Greek *he*

speaks of the Word of God. He describes it as dynamic, powerful, "sharp," cutting, and able to read our hearts (v. 12).

These descriptions point to the fact that God uses his Word to reveal unbelief and disobedience lurking in our hearts. All things are transparent to God; no one can hide from him (v. 13). He uses his living and piercing Word to search us deep within and to show us "thoughts and intentions" that are displeasing to him. Let us avail ourselves of this vital ministry of Scripture (cf. Ps. 19:11–14) through Bible reading, Bible study, and church attendance that deepens our understanding of God's Word. God gives us what we need if we use his means of grace.

4:14–16 This passage summarizes much that has gone before and anticipates much that will follow. Our Great High Priest is a human being who identifies with us. This is communicated through the human name, "Jesus," given him at birth (Matt. 1:25; Luke 2:21) and through the noteworthy statement of Hebrews 4:15: "For we do not have a high priest who is unable to sympathize with our weaknesses, but one who in every respect has been tempted as we are, yet without sin." Our Great High Priest is also divine—God himself. This is communicated through the author's saying that Jesus "has passed through the heavens"; no earthly high priest ever ascended to God's heavenly throne! Jesus' deity is also communicated through the divine title "the Son of God."

Consequently, our priest is both God and man. As a genuine human being he is able to sympathize with us in our weaknesses, since he shared them, including knowing temptation. But as the second Adam he never sinned. Therefore, as God himself who became the perfect man, he is able to give us mercy and grace when we come to God through him. We are to come boldly before God's awesome heavenly throne—which through Christ has become for us "the throne of grace"! And we do so assured that Jesus as a man understands our struggles and as God is able and willing to help us in our distress. This is a great incentive to prayer and praise.

5:7–10 Christ was appointed to be our High Priest according to the will of God (vv. 5–6). This office involved his being both God and man. Hebrews underscores Jesus' deity when it applies to him the divine designation "Son" (vv. 5, 8). Hebrews underscores the genuineness of his humanity when it speaks of Jesus' "flesh," his

12 [w]1 Pet. 1:23 [x][Jer. 23:29; 1 Thess. 2:13] [y]Isa. 49:2; Eph. 6:17 [z]Prov. 5:4; Rev. 1:16; 2:12 [a][1 Cor. 14:24, 25]
13 [b]2 Chr. 16:9; Job 34:21; Ps. 33:13-15 [c]Job 26:6
14 [d]ch. 2:17, 18; [ch. 10:21] [e]Eph. 4:10 [f]ch. 10:23
15 [g][ch. 5:2; Isa. 53:3] [d][See ver. 14 above] [h]ch. 9:28; 1 Pet. 2:22; 1 John 3:5; [ch. 7:26; John 8:46; 14:30]
16 [i]ch. 10:19; Eph. 3:12; [ch. 7:19, 25]

Chapter 5
1 [j]ch. 8:3 [k]ch. 2:17 [l]ch. 8:3, 4; 9:9; 10:11; 11:4
2 [m]ch. 2:18; 4:15 [n][ch. 7:28]
3 [o]ch. 7:27; 9:7; Lev. 4:3; 9:7; 16:6
4 [p]Num. 16:5, 40; 18:7; 2 Chr. 26:18 [q]Ex. 28:1; 1 Chr. 23:13
5 [r]John 8:54 [s]See ch. 1:5
6 [t]ch. 7:17, 21; Cited from Ps. 110:4
7 [u]Matt. 26:39, 44; Mark 14:36, 39; Luke 22:41, 44 [v]Ps. 22:1, 2; [Matt. 27:46, 50; Mark 15:34, 37; Luke 23:46] [w]Mark 14:36 [x]Ps. 22:24
8 [y]See ch. 1:2 [z]Phil. 2:8

[a]being made perfect, he became the source of
eternal salvation to all who obey him, 10 being
designated by God a high priest [b]after the
order of Melchizedek.

Warning Against Apostasy

11 About this we have much to say, and it is
[c]hard to explain, since you have become dull
of hearing. 12 For though by this time you
ought to be teachers, you need someone to
teach you again [d]the basic principles of the
oracles of God. You need [e]milk, not solid food,
13 for everyone who lives on milk is unskilled
in the word of righteousness, since he is [f]a
child. 14 But solid food is for [g]the mature, for
those who have their powers [h]of discernment
trained by constant practice to distinguish
good from evil.

6 Therefore [i]let us leave [j]the elementary
doctrine of Christ and go on to maturity,
not laying again a foundation of repentance
[k]from dead works and of faith toward God,
2 and of [l]instruction about washings,[1] [m]the
laying on of hands, [n]the resurrection of the
dead, and [o]eternal judgment. 3 And this we
will do [p]if God permits. 4 For it is impossible, in the case of those [q]who have once been
enlightened, who have tasted [r]the heavenly
gift, and [s]have shared in the Holy Spirit, 5 and
[t]have tasted the goodness of the word of God
and the powers of the age to come, 6 and [u]then
have fallen away, to restore them again to
repentance, since [v]they are crucifying once
again the Son of God to their own harm and
holding him up to contempt. 7 For [w]land that
has drunk the rain that often falls on it, and
produces a crop useful to those for whose
sake it is cultivated, receives a blessing from
God. 8 But [x]if it bears thorns and thistles, it is
worthless and near to being cursed, [y]and its
end is to be burned.

9 Though we speak in this way, yet in your
case, beloved, we feel sure of better things—
things that belong to salvation. 10 For [z]God is
not unjust so as to overlook [a]your work and
the love that you have shown for his name
in [b]serving the saints, as you still do. 11 And
we desire each one of you to show the same
earnestness to have the full assurance [c]of hope
until the end, 12 so that you may not be sluggish, but [d]imitators of those who through
faith and patience inherit the promises.

[1] Or *baptisms* (that is, cleansing rites)

9[a] See ch. 2:10
10[b] ver. 6; ch. 6:20
11[c] [2 Pet. 3:16]
12[d] ch. 6:1 [e] 1 Cor. 3:2
13[f] 1 Cor. 3:1; [1 Pet. 2:2]
14[g] Eph. 4:13 [h] Gen. 3:22; 1 Kgs. 3:9; Isa. 7:15

Chapter 6
1[i] [Phil. 3:12-14] [j] ch. 5:12 [k] ch. 9:14
2[l] Acts 19:4, 5 [m] Acts 8:17; 19:6 [n] Acts 17:31, 32 [o] See Acts 10:42
3[p] See 1 Cor. 16:7
4[q] ch. 10:32 [r] [John 4:10; Eph. 2:8] [s] ch. 2:4, 5; Gal. 3:2, 5
5[t] Ps. 34:8
6[u] [Matt. 19:26]; See 1 John 5:16 [v] [ch. 10:29]
7[w] Ps. 65:10
8[x] Isa. 5:1-7; [Gen. 3:17, 18; Deut. 29:22, 23; Jer. 44:22; Luke 13:6-9] [y] [Mal. 4:1; John 15:6]
10[z] Prov. 19:17; Matt. 10:42; 25:40; Mark 9:41 [a] 1 Thess. 1:3 [b] Rom. 15:31; 2 Cor. 8:4; 9:1, 12; 2 Tim. 1:18; Rev. 2:19
11[c] Rom. 5:2-5
12[d] ch. 13:7; [ch. 10:36]

"loud cries and tears," his learning "obedience," the fact that "he suffered," and his "being made perfect" completing all that was required of him (vv. 7–9). The eternal Son of God took to himself genuine humanity—"flesh"—in his incarnation. His "loud cries and tears" pertain to his whole earthly life as "a man of sorrows, and acquainted with grief" (Isa. 53:3), perhaps epitomized in Gethsemane. His learning "obedience through what he suffered" provides a clue to the meaning of the difficult expression that he was "made perfect" (Heb. 5:9). He was made "perfect" in the sense that he became perfectly qualified in experience to be "the source of eternal salvation" to all believers (v. 9).

Astonishingly, there were three qualifications for the position of Mediator between God and humanity: candidates must be God (only the three persons of the Godhead qualify!), they must have become human (only one qualifies), and they need "on the job" experience. Christ met the third qualification by learning obedience to God's will through suffering.

How the Son of God loved us to humble himself in such a way! Our lives must say "thank you" every day for such matchless grace.

6:9–12 These words follow what is perhaps the most famous warning passage in the Bible, in verses 4–8. Although the writer issues a strong warning to his hearers about the perils of falling away from Christ (see note on 3:12–14), he is confident that those he addresses will not fall away (6:9). Why? He knows that God is just and will not forget the Hebrew Christians' diligence, love, and service, all of which testify to their having truly received Christ as he is offered in the gospel.

Our subjective confidence (i.e., our human assessment) of our final salvation is based on three things: the Word of God, the inner witness of the Spirit, and a changed life. The author here highlights the third: he wants "each one" of his readers to persevere so as to "have the full assurance of hope until the end" (v. 11). This is not salvation by works but is perseverance in service and love that demonstrates that the readers "through faith and patience inherit the promises" of God (v. 12).

The Certainty of God's Promise

13 For when God made a promise to Abraham, since he had no one greater by whom to swear, [e]he swore by himself, 14 saying, [f]"Surely I will bless you and multiply you." 15 And thus Abraham,[1] [g]having patiently waited, obtained the promise. 16 For people swear by something greater than themselves, and in all their disputes [h]an oath is final for confirmation. 17 So when God desired to show more convincingly to [i]the heirs of the promise [j]the unchangeable character of his purpose, [k]he guaranteed it with an oath, 18 so that by two unchangeable things, in which [l]it is impossible for God to lie, we who have fled for refuge might have strong encouragement to hold fast to the hope [m]set before us. 19 We have this as a sure and steadfast anchor of the soul, a hope that enters into [n]the inner place behind the curtain, 20 where Jesus has gone [o]as a forerunner on our behalf, [p]having become a high priest forever after the order of Melchizedek.

The Priestly Order of Melchizedek

7 For this [q]Melchizedek, king of [r]Salem, priest of [s]the Most High God, met Abraham returning from the slaughter of the kings and blessed him, 2 and to him Abraham apportioned a tenth part of everything. He is first, by translation of his name, king of righteousness, and then he is also king of Salem, that is, king of peace. 3 He is without father or mother [t]or genealogy, having neither beginning of days nor end of life, but resembling the Son of God he continues a priest forever.

4 See how great this man was to whom Abraham [u]the patriarch gave a tenth of the spoils! 5 And [v]those descendants of Levi who receive the priestly office have a commandment in the law to take tithes from the people, that is, from their brothers,[2] though these also are descended from Abraham. 6 But this man [w]who does not have his descent from them received tithes from Abraham and blessed [x]him who had the promises. 7 It is beyond dispute that the inferior is blessed by the superior. 8 In the one case tithes are received by mortal men, but in the other case, by one [y]of whom it is testified that [z]he lives. 9 One might even say that Levi himself, who receives tithes, paid tithes through Abraham, 10 for he was still in the loins of his ancestor when Melchizedek met him.

Jesus Compared to Melchizedek

11 [a]Now if perfection had been attainable through the Levitical priesthood (for under it the people received the law), what further need would there have been for another priest to arise after the order of Melchizedek, rather than one named after the order of Aaron? 12 For when there is a change in the priesthood, there is necessarily a change in the law as well. 13 For the one of whom these things are spoken belonged to another tribe, from which no one has ever served at the altar. 14 For it is evident that our Lord was descended [b]from Judah, and in connection with that tribe Moses said nothing about priests.

15 This becomes even more evident when another priest arises in the likeness of Melchizedek, 16 who has become a priest, not on the basis of a legal requirement concerning bodily descent, but by the power of an indestructible life. 17 For it is witnessed of him,

> [c]"You are a priest forever,
> after the order of Melchizedek."

[1] Greek *he* [2] Or *brothers and sisters*

6:13–20 This chapter is famous for its strong warning passage (vv. 4–8), and rightly so. Unfortunately, its strong preservation ("eternal security") passage is not nearly as well known. God made promises to Abraham and fortified them with an oath (vv. 13–14). Abraham believed God and "obtained the promise" (v. 15) and the readers of this letter are to do the same. God stooped to meet us in our weakness; he added his oath to his promise (as if his Word were not enough!). Why? So that we, heirs of the promise made to Abraham and believers in Jesus, "might have strong encouragement" (v. 18). God does not want us to doubt our salvation.

At the same time he spurs us on so that we might "hold fast to the hope set before us" (v. 18). Our hope is secure as an "anchor of the soul" (v. 19) that Jesus took with him into the Most Holy Place when he returned to the Father's presence. He went to heaven "as a forerunner on our behalf" (v. 20); therefore, we will surely follow him there.

Such a hope inspires us to love him who loved us like this and to "seek first the kingdom of God and his righteousness" (Matt. 6:33).

13[e] Gen. 22:16
14[f] Cited from Gen. 22:17
15[g] ver. 12, 17; [ch. 7:6]; See Rom. 4:13
16[h] Ex. 22:11
17[i] ch. 11:9 [j] ver. 18; [Ps. 110:4; Prov. 19:21] [k] [Gal. 3:20]
18[l] See Titus 1:2 [m] ch. 12:1, 2
19[n] ch. 9:7; Lev. 16:15
20[o] ch. 4:14; 8:1; 9:24 [p] ch. 3:1; 5:6, 10; 7:17, 21

Chapter 7

1[q] Gen. 14:18-20 [r] Ps. 76:2 [s] Num. 24:16; Deut. 32:8
3[t] [ver. 6]
4[u] [Acts 2:29; 7:8, 9]
5[v] Num. 18:21, 26; 2 Chr. 31:4, 5
6[w] [ver. 3] [x] See Rom. 4:13
8[y] [ch. 5:6; 6:20] [z] [John 6:57; Rev. 1:17, 18]

11[a] ver. 18, 19; ch. 8:7; [Gal. 2:21] **14**[b] Isa. 11:1; Mic. 5:2; Matt. 1:3; Luke 3:33; Rev. 5:5 **17**[c] ver. 21; ch. 5:6; 6:20; Cited from Ps. 110:4

18 For on the one hand, a former commandment is set aside [d]because of its weakness and uselessness 19 (for [e]the law made nothing perfect); but on the other hand, [f]a better hope is introduced, through which [g]we draw near to God.

20 And it was not without an oath. For those who formerly became priests were made such without an oath, 21 but this one was made a priest with an oath by the one who said to him:

> [h]"The Lord has sworn
>   and will not change his mind,
> 'You are a priest forever.'"

22 This makes Jesus the guarantor of [i]a better covenant.

23 The former priests were many in number, because they were prevented by death from continuing in office, 24 but he holds his priesthood permanently, because he continues [j]forever. 25 Consequently, he is able to save to the uttermost[1] [k]those who draw near to God [l]through him, since he always lives [m]to make intercession for them.

26 For it was indeed fitting that we should have such a high priest, [n]holy, innocent, unstained, [o]separated from sinners, and [p]exalted above the heavens. 27 He has no need, like those high priests, to offer sacrifices daily, [q]first for his own sins and then for those of the people, since he did this [r]once for all when he offered up himself. 28 For the law appoints men [s]in their weakness as high priests, but the word of the oath, which came later than the law, appoints a Son who has been made [t]perfect forever.

Jesus, High Priest of a Better Covenant

8 Now the point in what we are saying is this: we have such a high priest, [u]one who is seated at the right hand of the throne of the Majesty in heaven, 2 a minister in the holy places, in [v]the true tent[2] that the Lord [w]set up, not man. 3 For [x]every high priest is appointed to offer gifts and sacrifices; thus [y]it is necessary for this priest also to have something to offer. 4 Now if he were on earth, he would not be a priest at all, since there are priests who offer gifts according to the law. 5 They serve [z]a copy and [a]shadow of the heavenly things. For when Moses was about to erect the tent, he was instructed by God, saying, [b]"See that you make everything according to the pattern that was shown you on the mountain." 6 But as it is, Christ[3] has obtained a ministry that is [c]as much more excellent than the old as [d]the covenant [e]he mediates is better, since it is enacted on better promises. 7 [f]For if that first covenant had been faultless, there would have been no occasion to look for a second.

8 For he finds fault with them when he says:[4]

> [g]"Behold, the days are coming, declares
>   the Lord,
>   when I will establish a new covenant
>   with the house of Israel
>   and with the house of Judah,

[1] That is, completely; or *at all times* [2] Or *tabernacle*; also verse 5 [3] Greek *he* [4] Some manuscripts *For finding fault with it he says to them*

18[d] Rom. 8:3; Gal. 4:9
19[e] ch. 9:9; 10:1; Lev. 16:16; See Acts 13:39 [f] ch. 6:18 [g] [ver. 25; Lev. 10:3]; See ch. 4:16
21[h] See ver. 17
22[i] ch. 8:6
24[j] ver. 21, 28
25[k] [ver. 19] [l] [John 14:6] [m] ch. 9:24; See Rom. 8:34
26[n] Ps. 16:10; Rev. 15:4; 16:5; [Mark 1:24] [o] See ch. 4:15 [p] [ch. 8:1]; See ch. 4:14
27[q] See ch. 5:3 [r] ch. 9:12; 10:10; [ch. 9:28]
28[s] [ch. 5:2] [t] ch. 2:10; 5:9
Chapter 8
1[u] See Mark 16:19
2[v] ch. 9:24; [ch. 9:11] [w] Ex. 33:7
3[x] See ch. 5:1 [y] ch. 9:12-14; 10:9-12; Eph. 5:2
5[z] ch. 9:23 [a] ch. 10:1; Col. 2:17 [b] Cited from Ex. 25:40
6[c] ch. 1:4; 2 Cor. 3:6-11 [d] ch. 7:22 [e] ch. 9:15; 12:24; [Gal. 3:19]
7[f] See ch. 7:11
8[g] Cited from Jer. 31:31-34

7:22–25 Jesus is superior to the Old Testament high priests. They were high priests in the order of Aaron, and it was impossible for Jesus to belong to that order because in his humanity he was descended from Judah, not Aaron. So what did God do? He established another priesthood, this one after Melchizedek, the mysterious figure who appears in Genesis 14 as a "priest of God Most High" (Gen. 14:18). Melchizedek receives a tithe from Abraham and then disappears until Psalm 110. Old Testament priests became such "on the basis of a legal requirement" (Heb. 7:16), but Christ became one by God's oath: "You are a priest forever, after the order of Melchizedek" (v. 17; cf. Ps. 110:4). Aaronic priests died and were succeeded in office by their sons. But Christ is a priest in the order of Melchizedek and as such needs no successor because he is a priest "by the power of an indestructible life," seen in his resurrection from the dead (Heb. 7:16).

All this and more "makes Jesus the guarantor of a better covenant" (v. 22). There had to be many Old Testament priests, "because they were prevented by death from continuing in office" (v. 23). But the Son of God "holds his priesthood permanently, because he continues forever," having been raised from the dead (v. 24). How does this affect us? It brings us great security of salvation because Jesus "is able to save to the uttermost those who draw near to God through him, since he always lives to make intercession for them" (v. 25). The living Christ, our Great High Priest, appears in the presence of God on our behalf and presents his finished sacrifice in intercession for us sinners "who draw near to God through him" (v. 25). The Father, then, will never reject us.

9 not like the covenant that I made with
their fathers
on the day when I took them by the
hand to bring them out of the
land of Egypt.
For they did not continue in my covenant,
and so I showed no concern for them,
declares the Lord.
10 [h]For this is the covenant that I will make
with the house of Israel
after those days, declares the Lord:
I will put my laws into their minds,
and [i]write them on their hearts,
and I will be their God,
and they shall be my people.
11 And they shall not teach, each one his
neighbor
and each one his brother, saying,
'Know the Lord,'
for they shall [j]all know me,
from the least of them to the greatest.
12 For I will be merciful toward their iniquities,
[k]and I will remember their sins no
more."

13 In speaking of a new covenant, he makes the
first one obsolete. And [l]what is becoming obsolete and growing old is ready to vanish away.

The Earthly Holy Place

9 Now even the first covenant had regulations for worship and [m]an earthly place of
holiness. 2 For [n]a tent[1] was prepared, the first
section, in which were [o]the lampstand and [p]the
table and [q]the bread of the Presence.[2] It is called
the Holy Place. 3 Behind [r]the second curtain
was a second section[3] called the Most Holy
Place, 4 having the golden [s]altar of incense and
[t]the ark of the covenant covered on all sides
with gold, in which was [u]a golden urn holding the manna, and [v]Aaron's staff that budded, and [w]the tablets of the covenant. 5 Above
it were [x]the cherubim of glory overshadowing
[y]the mercy seat. Of these things we cannot now
speak in detail.

6 These preparations having thus been made,
[z]the priests go regularly into the first section,
performing their ritual duties, 7 but into the
second only [a]the high priest goes, and he but
[a]once a year, and not without taking blood,
[b]which he offers for himself and for the unintentional sins of the people. 8 By this the Holy
Spirit indicates that [c]the way into the holy
places is not yet opened as long as the first
section is still standing 9 (which is symbolic for
the present age).[4] According to this arrangement, gifts and sacrifices are offered [d]that cannot perfect the conscience of the worshiper,
10 but deal only with [e]food and drink and
[f]various washings, regulations for the body
imposed until the time of reformation.

Redemption Through the Blood of Christ

11 But when Christ appeared as a high priest
[g]of the good things that have come,[5] then
through [h]the greater and more perfect tent

[1] Or *tabernacle*; also verses 11, 21 [2] Greek *the presentation of the loaves* [3] Greek *tent*; also verses 6, 8 [4] Or *which is symbolic for the age then present* [5] Some manuscripts *good things to come*

9:11–15 In contrast to Old Testament high priests who offered the blood of sacrificial animals in an earthly sanctuary, Christ presented his own blood in God's presence in heaven itself. What is the result? He secured "an eternal redemption" (v. 12). This is incredible. When we compare the millions of Old Testament sacrifices with the power and effects of Christ's single sacrifice, we are amazed at his. Unlike theirs, his sacrifice achieved an eternal redemption! The one sacrifice of the Son of God delivers forever all the redeemed.

Because of who Jesus is and what he has done, "he is the mediator of a new covenant" (v. 15). Old Testament prophets (such as Jeremiah and Ezekiel) prophesied that God would make a new covenant with his people in the last days (Jer. 31:31–34; Ezekiel 36–37). As his words at the Last Supper indicate, Jesus' death inaugurated the new covenant: "This cup . . . is the new covenant in my blood" (Luke 22:20). His sacrifice is so monumental that it saves Old Testament believers as well as New Testament ones: his death "redeems them from the transgressions committed under the first covenant" (Heb. 9:15)!

Christ's atonement is the work of the Trinity. Of course, only the Son became a man, died, and rose again. But Paul speaks of the Father when he writes that, "in Christ God was reconciling the world to himself" (2 Cor. 5:19); and Hebrews adds, "Christ . . . through the eternal Spirit offered himself without blemish to God" (Heb. 9:14). The author again distinguishes Christ's unique sacrifice from its Old Testament

10 [h]ch. 10:16; Rom. 11:27 [i][2 Cor. 3:3]
11 [j]Isa. 54:13; John 6:45; 1 John 2:27
12 [k]ch. 10:17; Rom. 11:27
13 [l][2 Cor. 5:17]

Chapter 9
1 [m]Ex. 25:8
2 [n]Ex. 26:1 [o]Ex. 25:31-39; 26:35; 40:4 [p]Ex. 25:23-29 [q]Ex. 25:30; Lev. 24:5-8
3 [r]Ex. 26:31-33; 40:3, 21
4 [s]Lev. 16:12, 13 [t]Ex. 25:10; 26:33; 40:3, 21; Rev. 11:19 [u]Ex. 16:33, 34 [v]Num. 17:10 [w]Ex. 25:16; 40:20; Deut. 10:2, 5; 1 Kgs. 8:9, 21; 2 Chr. 5:10
5 [x]Ex. 25:18-22; [1 Kgs. 8:6, 7] [y]Lev. 16:2
6 [z][Num. 28:3]
7 [a]Lev. 16:15, 34; [ch. 10:3; Ex. 30:10] [b]See ch. 5:3
8 [c]ch. 10:20; [John 14:6]
9 [d]See ch. 7:19
10 [e]See Lev. 11:2 [f]Mark 7:4, 8; See Lev. 11:25
11 [g]ch. 10:1 [h][ver. 24; ch. 8:2]

([i]not made with hands, that is, not of this creation) 12 he [j]entered [k]once for all into the holy
places, not by means of [l]the blood of goats
and calves but [m]by means of his own blood,
[n]thus securing an eternal redemption. 13 For if
[o]the blood of goats and bulls, and the sprinkling of defiled persons with [p]the ashes of
a heifer, sanctify[1] for the purification of the
flesh, 14 how much more will [q]the blood of
Christ, who through the eternal Spirit [r]offered
himself without blemish to God, [s]purify our[2]
conscience [t]from dead works [u]to serve the living God.

15 Therefore he is [v]the mediator of a new
covenant, so that [w]those who are called may
[x]receive the promised eternal inheritance,
[y]since a death has occurred that redeems
them from the transgressions committed
under the first covenant.[3] 16 For where a will
is involved, the death of the one who made it
must be established. 17 For [z]a will takes effect
only at death, since it is not in force as long
as the one who made it is alive. 18 Therefore
not even the first covenant was inaugurated
[a]without blood. 19 For when every commandment of the law had been declared by Moses
to all the people, he took [b]the blood of calves
and goats, [c]with water and scarlet wool and
hyssop, and sprinkled both the book itself and
all the people, 20 saying, [d]"This is the blood of
the covenant that God commanded for you."
21 And in the same way he sprinkled with the
blood both [e]the tent and all the vessels used
in worship. 22 Indeed, under the law almost
everything is purified with blood, and [f]with-
out the shedding of blood there is no forgiveness of sins.

23 Thus it was necessary for [g]the copies of
the heavenly things to be purified with these
rites, but the heavenly things themselves

[1] Or *For if the sprinkling of defiled persons with the blood of goats and bulls and with the ashes of a heifer sanctifies* [2] Some manuscripts *your* [3] The Greek word means both *covenant* and *will*; also verses 16, 17

11 [i]See Mark 14:58
12 [j]ver. 24 [k]ch. 7:27; 10:10 [l]ch. 10:4 [m]See Acts 20:28 [n]Job 33:24; [Dan. 9:24; 1 Cor. 6:20]
13 [o]Lev. 16:14-16 [p]Num. 19:2, 17, 18
14 [q]ver. 12; 1 John 1:7; Rev. 7:14 [r]ch. 7:27; 8:3 [s]ch. 1:3; 10:22 [t]ch. 6:1 [u]Rom. 6:13; 1 Pet. 4:2
15 [v]ch. 8:6; 12:24 [w][ch. 3:1]; See Rom. 8:28 [x][ch. 10:36; Ex. 32:13] [y]Rom. 3:24, 25; 5:6
17 [z][Gal. 3:15]
18 [a]Ex. 24:6, 8
19 [b]ver. 12 [c][Lev. 14:4, 7; Num. 19:6, 17]
20 [d]Cited from Ex. 24:8; [Matt. 26:28]
21 [e][Ex. 29:12, 36; Lev. 8:15, 19; 16:14, 16; 2 Chr. 29:22]
22 [f]Lev. 17:11
23 [g]ch. 8:5

precursors: the blood of sacrificed animals set apart God's Old Testament people as holy to the Lord. "How much more" will Christ's violent death (his "blood") "purify our conscience from dead works to serve the living God" (v. 14).

Christ's atonement frees us to serve God by cleansing our consciences. All human beings' consciences (except those hardened beyond feeling) act as internal sin detectors, sometimes "going off" when we do wrong. Only Christ's atoning death can wash our consciences and liberate us to serve God with the sincerity and zeal that he deserves. His cross work was "a labor of love" (if there ever was one!) that fuels our Christian lives by cleansing our consciences. He freed us to "love [him who] first loved us" (1 John 4:19). This means that by God's grace set forth in Jesus' death and resurrection we can now enjoy God, walk with him, and do his will.

9:23–28 Verse 23 is one of the most startling verses in all Scripture. It teaches that Christ's sacrifice cleansed heaven itself! The key to understanding this is found in the preceding verses. There we learn that the blood of sacrificial animals purified "almost everything" (v. 22) connected to the old covenant: the book of the covenant (the law), the people, the tabernacle, and its vessels (vv. 18–22). In fact, on the Day of Atonement, the sacrificial blood was applied to the Holy Place and the altar (Lev. 16:15–19). The high priest "shall make atonement for the Holy Place, because of the uncleannesses of the people of Israel and because of their transgressions, all their sins. . . . Then he shall go out to the altar that is before the LORD and make atonement for it. . . . and consecrate it from the uncleannesses of the people of Israel" (Lev. 16:16, 18–19).

Does this mean that God or his presence is intrinsically in need of purification? Of course not! Just as the passage quoted said twice— it is because of the sins ("uncleannesses") of God's people that atonement needed to be made for heaven. And the next verse in Hebrews confirms this interpretation by identifying the "heavenly things" of Heb. 9:23: Christ entered "heaven itself, now to appear in the presence of God on our behalf" (v. 24). The last three words are crucial—Christ cleansed heaven itself "on our behalf." Nothing was wrong with God and his heavenly dwelling place in themselves. But our sins stink to high heaven and, just as the Old Testament picture showed, they contaminate the very presence of God in whose presence all things exist (4:13; Col. 1:17).

All of this extols the greatness of Christ's sacrifice! It purifies heaven itself for us sinners. Surely this is a gigantic way of saying that salvation is all of God and all of

with better sacrifices than these. 24 For Christ
has entered, not into holy places [h] made with
hands, which are copies of the true things,
but into heaven itself, now to appear in the
presence of God [i] on our behalf. 25 Nor was it
to offer himself repeatedly, as [j] the high priest
enters [k] the holy places every year with blood
not his own, 26 for then he would have had
to suffer repeatedly since the foundation of
the world. But as it is, [l] he has appeared [m] once
for all [n] at the end of the ages to put away sin
by the sacrifice of himself. 27 And just as [o] it
is appointed for man to die once, and [p] after
that comes judgment, 28 so Christ, having been
offered once [q] to bear the sins of [r] many, will
appear [s] a second time, [t] not to deal with sin but
to save those who are eagerly [u] waiting for him.

Christ's Sacrifice Once for All

10 For since the law has but [v] a shadow [w] of
the good things to come instead of the
true form of these realities, [x] it can never, by
the same sacrifices that are continually offered
every year, make perfect those who draw near.
2 Otherwise, would they not have ceased to
be offered, since the worshipers, having once
been cleansed, would no longer have any consciousness of sins? 3 But [y] in these sacrifices
[z] there is a reminder of sins every year. 4 For [a] it
is impossible for the blood of bulls and goats
to take away sins.

5 Consequently, [b] when Christ[1] came into the
world, he said,

> [c] "Sacrifices and offerings you have not
> desired,
> but a body have you prepared for me;
> 6 in burnt offerings and sin offerings
> you have taken no pleasure.
> 7 Then I said, 'Behold, I have come to do
> your will, O God,
> as it is written of me in the scroll of
> the book.'"

8 When he said above, "You have neither
desired nor taken pleasure in [c] sacrifices and
offerings and burnt offerings and sin offerings" (these are offered according to the law),
9 then he added, [d] "Behold, I have come to do
your will." He does away with the first in order
to establish the second. 10 And by that will [e] we

[1] Greek *he*

grace. What should we say to such a truth? "Thank you, Jesus!" would be a very good beginning! And then, "Lord, give us your enabling grace so that we might live holy and loving lives that say 'thank you' every day for such remarkable love." God richly provides the motivation we his people need to dedicate our whole hearts to him—he sent his Son to make atonement for our sins and even to cleanse "heaven itself" (Heb. 9:24) by his blood. Hallelujah, what a Savior!

The writer points to more differences between the Old Testament high priest on the Day of Atonement and Christ. The former high priest entered the Most Holy Place "every year" to make atonement (v. 25). By contrast, Christ entered heaven itself "once for all at the end of the ages" (v. 26). The former high priest offered "blood not his own," but Christ offered "the sacrifice of himself" (vv. 25–26). The marvelous result of Jesus' unique self-sacrifice is that his death "put away sin" (v. 26). Human beings desperately need Christ's saving accomplishment because "it is appointed for man to die once, and after that comes judgment" (v. 27). Ever since Adam's fall, by divine appointment, death awaits human beings, and beyond that, there is "eternal judgment" (6:2). But Christ cancels for his people the inevitability of judgment following death. Although he too died, at his return he will bring final salvation, not judgment, for believers. The reason? Christ's death, unlike that of all others, was redemptive; he died to "bear . . . sins" (9:28). "So Christ, having been offered once to bear the sins of many, will appear a second time, not to deal with sin but to save those who are eagerly waiting for him" (v. 28).

Salvation is bigger and greater than many imagine. The Savior's death and resurrection not only suffice for past sins; they also save us now and until the second coming. Jesus "will appear a second time . . . to save" those who anticipate his return (v. 28). This gospel truth should infuse us with tremendous hope. Regardless of our successes and failures and our accomplishments or lack of them, if we know Jesus as Savior and Lord, he will surely come back for us, bringing the final installment of our great salvation. This is God's grand impetus for Christian living: to tell us over and over that "the Son of God . . . loved" us "and gave himself for" us (Gal. 2:20). What else can believing hearts do except love him in return and gladly obey him?

24 [h] ch. 8:2; [ver. 11] [i] ch. 7:25; See Rom. 8:34
25 [j] See ver. 7 [k] ch. 10:19
26 [l] 1 John 3:5 [m] ver. 12; ch. 7:27; 10:10; 1 Pet. 3:18 [n] [ch. 1:2; 1 Cor. 10:11]
27 [o] See Gen. 3:19 [p] See Matt. 16:27
28 [q] Isa. 53:12; 1 Pet. 2:24; 3:18 [r] Matt. 20:28; 26:28; Mark 10:45; Rev. 5:9 [s] Acts 1:11 [t] See ch. 4:15 [u] Titus 2:13; [Isa. 25:9]

Chapter 10
1 [v] ch. 8:5; Col. 2:17 [w] ch. 9:11 [x] [ch. 9:9]
3 [y] See ch. 9:7 [z] Lev. 16:21
4 [a] ver. 11
5 [b] [ch. 1:6] [c] Cited from Ps. 40:6-8
8 [c] [See ver. 5 above]
9 [d] ver. 7
10 [e] ch. 2:11; 13:12

have been sanctified through the offering of
[f]the body of Jesus Christ [g]once for all.
11 And every priest stands [h]daily at his service,
[i]offering repeatedly the same sacrifices, [j]which
can never take away sins. 12 But when Christ[1]
had offered for all time a single sacrifice for
sins, he [k]sat down at the right hand of God,
13 waiting from that time [l]until his enemies
should be made a footstool for his feet. 14 For
by a single offering [m]he has perfected for all
time those who are being sanctified.

15 And the Holy Spirit also bears witness to
us; for after saying,

16 [n]"This is the covenant that I will make
with them
after those days, declares the Lord:
I will put my laws on their hearts,
and write them on their minds,"

17 then he adds,

[o]"I will remember their sins and their lawless deeds no more."

[1] Greek *this one*

10[f] Matt. 26:26; Mark 14:22; Luke 22:19; 1 Cor. 11:24; [ver. 5] [g] ch. 7:27; 9:12
11[h] [Num. 28:3] [i] See ch. 5:1 [j] ver. 1, 4; [ch. 9:9]
12[k] ch. 1:3; See Mark 16:19
13[l] ch. 1:13; [1 Cor. 15:25-28]
14[m] ver. 1
16[n] ch. 8:10; Rom. 11:27; Cited from Jer. 31:33
17[o] ch. 8:12; Cited from Jer. 31:34

10:11–14 Once more Hebrews sharply contrasts Old Testament priests and Christ, to show his superiority. While ministering, the priests stood, indicating that their work was never done. Christ "sat down at the right hand of God" (v. 12), indicating that his priestly work was completely finished. Old Testament priests offered "repeatedly the same sacrifices, which can never take away sins" (v. 11). Christ's unique self-offering is effective and perfects believers forever (v. 14). Old Testament sacrifices were plural; Christ's was "a single sacrifice" (v. 12). All of this means that the former priests' ministries were earthly, provisional, temporary, and thus not effective. Over against Old Testament offerings, Christ's offering was heavenly (although accomplished on earth), final, permanent, and successful.

Because of the magnificence of Christ's atoning sacrifice, "by a single offering he has perfected for all time those who are being sanctified" (v. 14). This verse wonderfully summarizes the biblical doctrine of salvation applied. The basis for believers' acceptance by God is always and only Christ's "single offering." On good days and bad, in health and sickness, in wealth and poverty, in each and every circumstance, it is the unique Son of God's atonement that perfects us "for all time." But at the same time, God's people are recognizable; you can pick them out. They are "those who are being sanctified." They are not perfect and never will be in this life, but they are "on their way" to that eternal reality.

Those whom God has saved are not totally new in this life; their perfection awaits their resurrection and transformation on the last day. In the meantime, they are genuinely new—they are different than they were. They now love God and live for him, which includes confessing their sins every day and in a special communal way on Sundays (cf. 10:23–24; 1 John 1:8–10). God has not chosen to keep us in line by threatening to put us out of his family. But he expects us to show a family resemblance to our heavenly Father (Matt. 5:48; Eph. 4:32; 5:1; Heb. 10:16; 1 Pet. 1:15–17) and to Christ, our older Brother (John 15:12; Eph. 5:2; Phil. 2:5; 1 Pet. 2:21–23) by the power of the Holy Spirit (Gal. 5:16, 22, 25).

Christ our triumphant High Priest waits from the time of his death and resurrection "until his enemies should be made a footstool for his feet" (Heb. 10:13). His sacrifice should thus be viewed from both the past and the future. Seen from the past, his self-offering is the fulfillment and the completion and annulment of all of the Old Testament sacrifices (7:18–19; 8:13). Seen from the future, his death guarantees the defeat of his foes and ours and causes us to be "eagerly waiting" for his return (9:28). Some of us have been put off from biblical prophecy because of overly dogmatic opinions and date-setters. This is understandable but wrong. We are to be among those "who have loved his appearing" (2 Tim. 4:8) and who regard his return as "our blessed hope" (Titus 2:13).

As the author has taught (in Heb. 9:15), Christ's sacrifice was so great that it made the Old Testament sacrifices effective in their day. They truly brought forgiveness, not in themselves but as foreshadows of Christ, "the Lamb of God, who takes away the sin of the world!" (John 1:29, 36). Gratitude for such grace should transform us now into a people filled with love and mercy for others, both lost persons and wayward Christians (Matt. 18:21–35; Eph. 4:32).

18 Where there is forgiveness of these, there is
no longer any offering for sin.

The Full Assurance of Faith

19 [p]Therefore, brothers,[1] since we have confidence to enter [q]the holy places by the blood
of Jesus, 20 by [r]the new and living way that he
opened for us through [s]the curtain, that is,
through his flesh, 21 and since we have [t]a great
priest over the house of God, 22 let us draw
near with a true heart in full assurance of
faith, with our hearts [u]sprinkled clean [v]from
an evil conscience and our bodies [w]washed
with pure water. 23 [x]Let us hold fast the confession of our hope without wavering, for
[y]he who promised is faithful. 24 And [z]let us
consider how to stir up one another to love
and good works, 25 [a]not neglecting to meet
together, as is the habit of some, but encouraging one another, and [b]all the more as you
see [c]the Day drawing near.

26 For [d]if we go on sinning deliberately [e]after
receiving the knowledge of the truth, [f]there
no longer remains a sacrifice for sins, 27 [g]but a
fearful expectation of judgment, and [h]a fury of
fire that will consume the adversaries. 28 [i]Any-
one who has set aside the law of Moses dies
without mercy [j]on the evidence of two or three
witnesses. 29 How much worse punishment, do
you think, will be deserved by the one [k]who
has trampled underfoot the Son of God, and
has profaned [l]the blood of the covenant [m]by
which he was sanctified, and has [n]outraged
the Spirit of grace? 30 For we know him who
said, [o]"Vengeance is mine; I will repay." And
again, [p]"The Lord will judge his people." 31 [q]It
is a fearful thing to fall into the hands of the
living God.

[1] Or *brothers and sisters*

10:19–25 Most of Hebrews is gospel exposition from which it is not difficult to derive gospel application. But this passage is gospel application already. The writer himself applies his teaching concerning Christ's person and work to his readers and us. Three times he exhorts his audience with the words "Let us . . ." (vv. 22, 23, 24). These gospel-driven exhortations provide inspiration based on the self-offering of Jesus, the divine-human Mediator. And each time the writer refers to one of the three cardinal Christian virtues: "faith," "hope," and "love" (vv. 22, 23, 24).

First, he urges true knowledge and worship of God. The basis for this exhortation is that Christ, our Great High Priest, authorizes us to enter God's heavenly presence through his blood (vv. 19–21). "Let us draw near with a true heart in full assurance of faith," having experienced Christian conversion (pictured by hearts cleansed and bodies washed in baptism; v. 22). Because of Christ's priestly work we have the privilege of drawing near to God in worship, prayer, and faith.

Second, he urges perseverance. "Let us hold fast the confession of our hope without wavering, for he who promised is faithful" (v. 23). Once again the author, writing to Hebrew Christians, a minority of whom are tempted to turn from Christ to escape persecution, urges them to continue in the faith, "for he who promised is faithful." We have strong incentive to persevere in faith because our God is absolutely faithful and "it is impossible for God to lie" (6:18). We are to imitate Sarah, who "considered him faithful who had promised" (11:11). God will never fail us; therefore, we must be steadfast to the end in faith, holiness, and love.

Third, he urges love. "And let us consider how to stir up one another to love and good works" (10:24). Amid trials, believers are to show practical concern for one another. This expresses itself in "good works," such as those formerly done by the first readers of this letter (vv. 33–34). They are to continue caring for each other, whatever the cost. Such care is stimulated by meeting together for worship, fellowship, and mutual encouragement (vv. 24–25). Here the writer supplements the second coming of our heavenly High Priest to bring salvation (9:28) with the Old Testament idea of "the Day" of the Lord (10:25). He thereby offers both reassurance and a warning of the need to persevere until that Day. Verse 25 thus serves as a bridge to the severe warning that follows in verses 26–31.

God lavished his grace on his people for many wonderful purposes. Here the Lord assures us of our acceptance through Christ that leads us to know and worship God; to persevere in believing the gospel, even in difficult times; and to show practical care for one another. In short, by underscoring the grace of God in the work of Christ, our Great High Priest, Hebrews seeks to motivate us in faith, hope, and love.

19 [p]See ch. 4:16 [q]ch. 9:25
20 [r]ch. 9:8; [John 10:9; 14:6] [s]ch. 9:3
21 [t]Zech. 6:11-13; [ch. 4:14]; See ch. 2:17
22 [u]Ezek. 36:25; [ch. 12:24; 2 Cor. 7:1; 1 Pet. 1:2] [v]ch. 9:14 [w][1 Cor. 6:11]
23 [x]ch. 4:14 [y]ch. 11:11; See 1 Cor. 1:9
24 [z][ch. 3:13]
25 [a][Acts 2:42] [b]Rom. 13:11-13 [c]See 1 Cor. 3:13
26 [d]Num. 15:30; Deut. 17:12 [e]ch. 6:4; 2 Pet. 2:20, 21 [f][ch. 6:6; 1 John 5:16]
27 [g]ch. 2:3; 12:25 [h]Ps. 79:5; Isa. 26:11; Zeph. 1:18; 3:8; [Ezek. 36:5; Zech. 8:2]; See 2 Thess. 1:8
28 [i]Deut. 17:2-6 [j]See Num. 35:30
29 [k][ch. 6:6] [l]ch. 13:20; Zech. 9:11 [m]ch. 9:13, 14 [n][Matt. 12:31, 32; Eph. 4:30]
30 [o]Rom. 12:19; Cited from Deut. 32:35 [p]Ps. 50:4; 135:14; Cited from Deut. 32:36
31 [q]Isa. 33:14; Luke 12:5

32 But recall the former days when, after
[r]you were enlightened, you endured [s]a hard
struggle with sufferings, 33 sometimes being
[t]publicly exposed to reproach and affliction,
and sometimes being partners with those so
treated. 34 For [u]you had compassion on those
in prison, and [v]you joyfully accepted the plundering of your property, since you knew that
you yourselves had [w]a better possession and an
abiding one. 35 Therefore do not throw away
your confidence, which has [x]a great reward.
36 For [y]you have need of endurance, so that
[z]when you have done the will of God you may
[a]receive what is promised. 37 For,

[b]"Yet a little while,
and [c]the coming one will come and
will not delay;
38 [d]but my righteous one shall live by faith,
and if he shrinks back,
my soul has no pleasure in him."

39 But we are not of those who shrink back and
are destroyed, but of those who have faith and
preserve their souls.

By Faith

11 Now faith is the assurance of things
hoped for, the conviction of [e]things
not seen. 2 For by it the people of old received
their commendation. 3 By faith we understand
that the universe was created by [f]the word of
God, so that what is seen was not made out of
[g]things that are visible.

4 By faith [h]Abel offered to God [i]a more acceptable sacrifice than Cain, through which he was
commended as righteous, God commending
him by accepting his gifts. And [j]through his
faith, though he died, he [k]still speaks. 5 By faith
[l]Enoch was taken up so that he should not
see death, and he was not found, because God
had taken him. Now before he was taken he
was commended as having pleased God. 6 And
without faith it is impossible to please him,
for whoever would draw near to God [m]must
believe that he exists and [m]that he rewards
those who seek him. 7 By faith [n]Noah, being
warned by God concerning [o]events as yet
unseen, in reverent fear constructed an ark
for the saving of his household. By this he condemned the world and became an heir of [p]the
righteousness that comes by faith.

8 By faith [q]Abraham obeyed when he was
called to go out to a place [r]that he was to
receive as an inheritance. And he went out,
not knowing where he was going. 9 By faith
he went to live in [s]the land of promise, as in
a foreign land, [t]living in tents [u]with Isaac and
Jacob, heirs with him of the same promise.
10 For he was looking forward to [v]the city that
has [w]foundations, [x]whose designer and builder
is God. 11 By faith [y]Sarah herself received power
to conceive, even when she was past the age,
since she considered [z]him faithful who had
promised. 12 Therefore from one man, and [a]him
as good as dead, were born descendants [b]as

32[r] ch. 6:4 [s] See Phil. 1:30
33[t] 1 Cor. 4:9 (Gk.)
34[u] [ch. 13:3; Matt. 25:36; 2 Tim. 1:16] [v] See Matt. 5:12 [w] 1 Pet. 1:4
35[x] ch. 2:2; 11:26
36[y] ch. 12:1-7; Luke 21:19; Rom. 2:7; 12:12; See Matt. 10:22 [z] ch. 13:21; [1 John 2:17] [a] ch. 11:39
37[b] Isa. 26:20; Hag. 2:6; Luke 18:8 [c] Cited from Hab. 2:3, 4
38[d] Rom. 1:17; Gal. 3:11
Chapter 11
1[e] Rom. 8:24; 2 Cor. 4:18; 5:7; 1 Pet. 1:8
3[f] See Gen. 1:1 [g] [Rom. 4:17]
4[h] Gen. 4:4-8; 1 John 3:12 [i] Prov. 15:8 [j] Gen. 4:10 [k] ch. 12:24
5[l] Gen. 5:22-24; [2 Kgs. 2:11]
6[m] 1 Chr. 28:9; Jer. 29:12-14; [John 4:24]
7[n] Gen. 6:13-22; Luke 17:26; 1 Pet. 3:20 [o] ver. 1 [p] Rom. 4:13; [Gen. 6:9; Ezek. 14:14, 20]
8[q] Gen. 12:1-4; Acts 7:2-4 [r] Gen. 12:7
9[s] Acts 7:5 [t] Gen. 12:8; 13:3, 18; 18:1, 9 [u] Gen. 35:27
10[v] ch. 12:22; [ch. 13:14] [w] Ps. 87:1; Rev. 21:14 [x] Rev. 21:2, 10
11[y] Gen. 17:19; 18:11-14; 21:2 [z] ch. 10:23
12[a] Rom. 4:19 [b] Gen. 22:17; 32:12; See Gen. 15:5

11:1–40 We sometimes do not see the forest because we are intently looking at the trees. So it is with this great "faith chapter." It is easy to get lost in the details and to miss the big picture. The heroes and heroines of faith have much in common. Often their faith is directed to the future, which is unseen: "Now faith is the assurance of things hoped for, the conviction of things not seen" (v. 1). Why this emphasis? The answer lies in the historical occasion of the book. The writer motivates those who have professed Christ under the threat of persecution. He wants them to endure to obtain God's unseen, future promises. This is the accent when he introduces the concept of faith in 6:12: he wants his readers to be "imitators of those who through faith and patience inherit the promises." That is what Abraham did (11:15) and that is what the witnesses to faith in chapter 11 do too. "By faith Noah, being warned by God concerning events as yet unseen, in reverent fear constructed an ark for the saving of his household" (v. 7).

Because the original readers of Hebrews would not receive the full benefits of their faith in this life, the author focuses on heroes whose lives highlighted the future dimension of faith. Abraham, for example, "was looking forward to the city that has foundations, whose designer and builder is God" (v. 10). In fact, the writer summarizes the witnesses to faith up to and including Abraham in this way: "These all died in faith, not having received the things promised, but having seen them and greeted them from afar, and having acknowledged that they were strangers and exiles on the earth" (v. 13).

many as the stars of heaven and as many as the innumerable grains of sand by the seashore.

13 These all died in faith, [c]not having received the things promised, but [d]having seen them and greeted them from afar, and [e]having acknowledged that they were [f]strangers and exiles on the earth. 14 For people who speak thus make it clear that they are seeking a homeland. 15 If they had been thinking of that land from which they had gone out, [g]they would have had opportunity to return. 16 But as it is, they desire a better country, that is, a heavenly one. Therefore God is not ashamed [h]to be called their God, for [i]he has prepared for them a city.

17 By faith [j]Abraham, when he was tested, offered up Isaac, and he who had received the promises was in the act of offering up his only son, 18 of whom it was said, [k]"Through Isaac shall your offspring be named." 19 [l]He considered that God was able even to raise him from the dead, from which, figuratively speaking, he did receive him back. 20 By faith [m]Isaac invoked future blessings on Jacob and Esau. 21 By faith [n]Jacob, when dying, blessed each of the sons of Joseph, [o]bowing in worship over the head of his staff. 22 By faith [p]Joseph, at the end of his life, made mention of the exodus of the Israelites and gave directions concerning his bones.

23 By faith [q]Moses, when he was born, was hidden for three months by his parents, because they saw that the child was beautiful, and they were not afraid of [r]the king's edict. 24 By faith Moses, when he was grown up, [s]refused to be called the son of Pharaoh's daughter, 25 [t]choosing rather to be mistreated with the people of God than to enjoy [u]the fleeting pleasures of sin. 26 [v]He considered the reproach of Christ greater wealth than the treasures of Egypt, for he was looking to [w]the reward. 27 By faith he [x]left Egypt, [y]not being afraid of the anger of the king, for he endured [z]as seeing him who is invisible. 28 By faith [a]he kept the Passover and sprinkled the blood, so that the Destroyer of the firstborn might not touch them.

29 By faith [b]the people crossed the Red Sea as on dry land, but the Egyptians, when they attempted to do the same, were drowned. 30 By faith [c]the walls of Jericho fell down after they had been encircled for seven days. 31 By faith [d]Rahab the prostitute did not perish with those who were disobedient, because she [e]had given a friendly welcome to the spies.

32 And what more shall I say? For time would fail me to tell of [f]Gideon, [g]Barak, [h]Samson, [i]Jephthah, of [j]David and [k]Samuel and the prophets— 33 who through faith conquered kingdoms, enforced justice, obtained promises, [l]stopped the mouths of lions, 34 [m]quenched the power of fire, escaped the edge of the sword, were made strong out of

Another key dimension of faith extolled in chapter 11 is its firm, steadfast character, especially in light of present sufferings and future glory. So it is that Moses chose "rather to be mistreated with the people of God than to enjoy the fleeting pleasures of sin. He considered the reproach of Christ [i.e., being like Christ in suffering on behalf of God's people] greater wealth than the treasures of Egypt" (vv. 25–26). Hebrews combines the steadfastness of faith with its unseen reward when it says of Moses, "he endured as seeing him who is invisible" (v. 27).

If ever there was a biblical chapter that prosperity theology teachers should avoid, this is it! The heroines and heroes of faith hardly "named it and claimed it." To the contrary, "They were stoned, they were sawn in two, they were killed with the sword. They went about. . . . destitute, afflicted, mistreated—of whom the world was not worthy" (vv. 37–38). The chapter ends still focusing on the future promises of faith: "And all these, though commended through their faith, did not receive what was promised, since God had provided something better for us, that apart from us they should not be made perfect" (vv. 39–40). These words draw attention to the final salvation accomplished by Christ's priestly ministry. Old Testament saints looked forward to this ministry and, amazingly, Christians now enjoy its fruits, solely by God's grace.

Sometimes Hebrews 11 is referenced as the New Testament's "Hall of Heroes," but it is important to remember that the "heroes" identified were often quite fallible in character. They became heroic not by their abilities or advantages but by the eternal purposes of the One in whom they placed their faith. The strong medicine of chapter 11 is applied to hearers' needs in the first four verses of chapter 12.

13 [c]ver. 39 [d]ver. 27; John 8:56; [Matt. 13:17] [e]Gen. 23:4; 47:9; [1 Chr. 29:15; Ps. 39:12] [f]Eph. 2:19
15 [g][Gen. 24:6-8]
16 [h]Gen. 26:24; 28:13; Ex. 3:6; 4:5; [ch. 2:11] [i][ver. 10; Matt. 25:34; John 14:2]
17 [j]Gen. 22:1-10; James 2:21
18 [k]Rom. 9:7; Cited from Gen. 21:12
19 [l]Rom. 4:17-21
20 [m]Gen. 27:27-29, 39, 40
21 [n]Gen. 48:16, 20 [o][Gen. 47:31]
22 [p]Gen. 50:24, 25; Ex. 13:19
23 [q]Ex. 2:2, 3; Acts 7:20 [r]Ex. 1:16, 22
24 [s]Ex. 2:10, 11
25 [t][Job 36:21; Ps. 84:10] [u]1 John 2:17
26 [v]ch. 13:13; [Ps. 89:50, 51; Phil. 3:7, 8; 1 Pet. 4:14] [w]ch. 2:2; 10:35
27 [x]Ex. 12:37; 13:17, 18 [y]Ex. 10:28, 29 [z]ver. 13; See 1 Tim. 1:17
28 [a]Ex. 12:21-30
29 [b]Ex. 14:21-30
30 [c]Josh. 6:15, 16, 20
31 [d]Josh. 6:25; James 2:25 [e]Josh. 2:1, 8-13
32 [f]Judg. 6:11 [g]Judg. 4:6 [h]Judg. 13:24 [i]Judg. 11:1 [j]1 Sam. 16:1, 13 [k]1 Sam. 1:20
33 [l]Judg. 14:6; 1 Sam. 17:35; Dan. 6:22
34 [m]Dan. 3:25

weakness, [n]became mighty in war, [n]put foreign
armies to flight. 35 [o]Women received back their
dead by resurrection. Some were tortured,
refusing to accept release, so that they might
rise again to a better life. 36 Others suffered
mocking and flogging, and even [p]chains and
imprisonment. 37 [q]They were stoned, they
were sawn in two,[1] [r]they were killed with the
sword. [s]They went about in skins of sheep and
goats, destitute, afflicted, mistreated— 38 of
whom the world was not worthy—[t]wander-
ing about in deserts and mountains, and in
dens and caves of the earth.
39 And all these, [u]though commended
through their faith, [u]did not receive what was
promised, 40 since God had provided something better for us, [v]that apart from us they
should not be made perfect.

Jesus, Founder and Perfecter of Our Faith

12 Therefore, since we are surrounded by
so great a cloud of witnesses, let us also
lay aside every weight, and [w]sin which clings
so closely, and [x]let us run [y]with endurance the
race that is [z]set before us, 2 looking to Jesus, the
founder and perfecter of our faith, [a]who for
the joy that was set before him endured the
cross, despising [b]the shame, and [c]is seated at
the right hand of the throne of God.

Do Not Grow Weary

3 [d]Consider him who endured from sinners
such hostility against himself, so that you
may not grow weary or [e]fainthearted. 4 In
your struggle against sin you have not yet
resisted to the point of shedding your blood.
5 And have you forgotten the exhortation that
addresses you as sons?

> [f]"My son, [g]do not regard lightly the discipline of the Lord,
> nor be weary when reproved by him.
> 6 For [h]the Lord disciplines the one he loves,
> and chastises every son whom he receives."

7 It is for discipline that you have to endure.
[i]God is treating you as sons. For what son is
there whom his father does not discipline?
8 If you are left without discipline, [j]in which
all have participated, then you are illegitimate
children and not sons. 9 Besides this, we have
had earthly fathers who disciplined us and
we respected them. Shall we not much more
be subject to [k]the Father of spirits [l]and live?
10 For they disciplined us for a short time as
it seemed best to them, but he disciplines us
for our good, [m]that we may share his holiness.
11 [n]For the moment all discipline seems painful
rather than pleasant, but later it yields [o]the

[1] Some manuscripts add *they were tempted*

34[n] Judg. 7:21; 1 Sam. 17:51; 2 Sam. 12:29
35[o] 1 Kgs. 17:22; 2 Kgs. 4:35
36[p] Gen. 39:20; Jer. 20:2; 37:15
37[q] 1 Kgs. 21:13; 2 Chr. 24:21 [r] 1 Kgs. 19:10; Jer. 26:23 [s] 2 Kgs. 1:8
38[t] 1 Sam. 22:1; 1 Kgs. 18:4; 19:9
39[u] ver. 2, 13; [1 Pet. 1:12]
40[v] [Rev. 6:11]
Chapter 12
1[w] See Eph. 4:22 [x] See 1 Cor. 9:24 [y] See ch. 10:36 [z] ch. 6:18
2[a] Luke 24:26; Phil. 2:8; [Isa. 53:11] [b] Ps. 22:6, 7; 69:19; Isa. 53:3 [c] ch. 1:3
3[d] [Matt. 10:24; Rev. 2:3] [e] Gal. 6:9
5[f] Cited from Prov. 3:11, 12 [g] Job 5:17
6[h] Ps. 94:12; 119:67, 75; Rev. 3:19
7[i] Deut. 8:5; 2 Sam. 7:14; [Prov. 13:24; 19:18; 23:13]
8[j] [1 Pet. 5:9]
9[k] See Num. 16:22 [l] [Isa. 38:16]
10[m] [2 Pet. 1:4]; See Lev. 11:44
11[n] [1 Pet. 1:6] [o] James 3:17, 18

12:1–4 Missiologists teach us that the church in any one locale needs the church in the whole world in order to read the Bible correctly. So it is with this passage. Believers under persecution will find these words and their ensuing fellowship with Christ in his sufferings very precious. Those believers who have not known persecution will have more trouble identifying with the kind of suffering the writer of Hebrews wants to address. So, the writer appeals to the "hall of fame" of faith in chapter 11 to motivate his hearers and future generations: "Therefore, since we are surrounded by so great a cloud of witnesses . . . let us run with endurance the race that is set before us" (v. 1).

But Hebrews does not ultimately look to these old covenant heroes for motivation to run the race; rather, we are to run "looking to Jesus, the founder and perfecter of our faith, who for the joy that was set before him endured the cross, despising the shame, and is seated at the right hand of the throne of God" (v. 2). Jesus, as Mediator of the new covenant, is the supreme example of a faith that endures to the end. He suffered the ultimate martyrdom—the holy Son of God on a Roman cross—to save us from our sins. His struggle and victory are ours—he alone is "the founder and perfecter of our faith," the champion who brought faith to its complete expression and as such is also our ultimate example of bearing up steadfastly under unjust suffering (cf. 1 Pet. 2:19–23).

Perhaps it is shocking to us, when reading Hebrews 12:3–4, how tough biblical Christianity is. Yet even more shocking perhaps is how soft and untested many Christians are who have not faced persecution. The writer points his readers squarely to Jesus: "Consider him who endured from sinners such hostility against himself, so that you may not grow weary or fainthearted" (v. 3). We are to draw courage from Jesus' steadfast example of honoring God no matter the cost. And we too must be willing to pay the ultimate price: "In your struggle against sin you have not yet resisted to the point of shedding your blood" (v. 4).

peaceful fruit of righteousness to those who have been trained by it.

12 Therefore [p]lift your drooping hands and strengthen your weak knees, 13 and [q]make straight paths for your feet, so that what is lame may not be put out of joint [r]but rather be healed. 14 [s]Strive for peace with everyone, and for the [t]holiness [u]without which no one will see the Lord. 15 See to it that no one [v]fails to obtain the grace of God; that no [w]"root of bitterness" springs up and causes trouble, and by it many become defiled; 16 that no one is [x]sexually immoral or unholy like Esau, who sold his birthright for a single meal. 17 For you know that [y]afterward, when he desired to inherit the blessing, he was rejected, for he found no chance to repent, though he sought it with tears.

A Kingdom That Cannot Be Shaken

18 For you have not come to [z]what may be touched, a blazing fire and darkness and gloom and a tempest 19 and [a]the sound of a trumpet and a voice whose words [b]made the hearers beg that no further messages be spoken to them. 20 For they could not endure the order that was given, [c]"If even a beast touches the mountain, it shall be stoned." 21 Indeed, [d]so terrifying was the sight that Moses said, "I tremble with fear." 22 But you have come to [e]Mount Zion and to the city of the living God, [f]the heavenly Jerusalem, and to [g]innumerable angels in festal gathering, 23 and to [h]the assembly[1] of the firstborn who are [i]enrolled in heaven, and to [j]God, the judge of all, and to the spirits of the righteous made perfect, 24 and to Jesus, [k]the mediator of a new covenant, and to [l]the sprinkled blood [m]that speaks a better word than the blood of Abel.

25 See that you do not refuse him who is speaking. For [n]if they did not escape when they refused him who warned them on earth, much less will we escape if we reject him who warns from heaven. 26 At that time [o]his voice shook the earth, but now he has promised, [p]"Yet once more I will shake not only the earth but also the heavens." 27 This phrase, "Yet once more," indicates [q]the removal of things that are shaken—that is, things that have been made—in order that the things that cannot be shaken may remain. 28 Therefore let us be grateful for receiving [r]a kingdom that cannot be shaken, and thus [s]let us offer to God acceptable worship, with reverence and awe, 29 for our [t]God is a consuming fire.

Sacrifices Pleasing to God

13 Let [u]brotherly love continue. 2 [v]Do not neglect to show hospitality to strangers, for thereby [w]some have entertained angels unawares. 3 [x]Remember those who are in prison, as though in prison with them, and those who are mistreated, since you also are in the body. 4 [y]Let marriage be held in honor among all, and let the marriage bed be undefiled, for God will judge [z]the sexually immoral and adulterous. 5 Keep your life [a]free from love of money, and [b]be content with what you have, for he has said, [c]"I will never leave you nor forsake you." 6 So we can confidently say,

[d]"The Lord is my helper;
[e]I will not fear;
what can man do to me?"

7 Remember [f]your leaders, those who spoke to you the word of God. Consider the outcome of their way of life, and [g]imitate their faith. 8 Jesus Christ is [h]the same yesterday and today

[1] Or *church*

To contemporary sufferers and martyrs for Christ, all other believers should bow in admiration, with gratitude for their example and for the grace of Christ evident in their lives. It is they who know the deep privilege of suffering discipline as the children of God (vv. 5–11). "The Lord disciplines the one he loves, and chastises every son whom he receives. It is for discipline that you have to endure. God is treating you as sons" (vv. 6–7). May God use this passage to help those who face trials to see them as fatherly discipline toward "the peaceful fruit of righteousness" (v. 11). And may he move those who do not face persecution to pray for their brothers and sisters who do.

13:7–9 The readers are to remember their former leaders, who preached the gospel to them and have since died, and to follow their example of faith in life and death. These

12[p] Cited from Isa. 35:3; [Job 4:3, 4]
13[q] Prov. 4:26, 27 [r] James 5:16; [Gal. 6:1]
14[s] See Rom. 14:19 [t] 1 Thess. 4:7 [u] Matt. 5:8; [2 Cor. 7:1; Eph. 5:5; Rev. 21:27; 22:4]
15[v] ch. 4:1; [2 Cor. 6:1; Gal. 5:4] [w] Deut. 29:18
16[x] ch. 13:4; Gen. 25:33
17[y] Gen. 27:34, 36, 38
18[z] Ex. 19:18; 20:18; Deut. 4:11; 5:22; [2 Cor. 3:9]
19[a] Ex. 19:16, 19 [b] Ex. 20:19; Deut. 5:5; 18:16
20[c] Cited from Ex. 19:12, 13

21[d] [Ex. 19:16; Deut. 9:19] **22**[e] Rev. 14:1 [f] See Gal. 4:26 [g] Jude 14 **23**[h] [Ex. 4:22] [i] Luke 10:20 [j] Gen. 18:25 **24**[k] ch. 8:6; 9:15 [l] See ch. 10:22 [m] ch. 11:4; Gen. 4:10 **25**[n] See ch. 2:3 **26**[o] Ex. 19:18 [p] Cited from Hag. 2:6; [Hag. 2:21] **27**[q] See Ps. 102:26 **28**[r] Dan. 2:44 [s] ch. 13:15 **29**[t] Cited from Deut. 4:24; See 2 Thess. 1:8 **Chapter 13** **1**[u] Rom. 12:10; 1 Thess. 4:9; 1 Pet. 1:22; 2 Pet. 1:7; [1 Pet. 2:17; 3:8; 1 John 3:10; 4:7, 20, 21] **2**[v] See Matt. 25:35; 1 Pet. 4:9 [w] Gen. 18:3; 19:2 **3**[x] ch. 10:34; Matt. 25:36 **4**[y] 1 Cor. 7:38; [1 Tim. 4:3] [z] See 1 Cor. 6:9 **5**[a] 1 Tim. 3:3 [b] 1 Tim. 6:7, 8; [Phil. 4:11]; See Matt. 6:25 [c] Cited from Josh. 1:5; [Ps. 37:25; 2 Cor. 4:9] **6**[d] Cited from Ps. 118:6; [Ps. 27:1] [e] Ps. 56:4, 11 **7**[f] ver. 17, 24 [g] [ch. 6:12] **8**[h] ch. 1:12; John 8:58; Rev. 1:4, 8; [2 Cor. 1:19]

and forever. [9] Do not be [i]led away by diverse and strange teachings, for it is good for the heart to be strengthened by grace, [j]not by foods, which have not benefited those devoted to them. [10] We have an altar [k]from which those who serve the tent have no right to eat. [11] For [l]the bodies of those animals whose blood is brought into the holy places by the high priest as a sacrifice for sin are burned [m]outside the camp. [12] So Jesus also [n]suffered [o]outside the gate in order to sanctify the people [p]through his own blood. [13] Therefore let us go to him outside the camp and bear [q]the reproach he endured. [14] For [r]here we have no lasting city, but we seek the city that is to come. [15] [s]Through him then let us continually offer up [t]a sacrifice of praise to God, that is, [u]the fruit of lips that acknowledge his name. [16] Do not neglect to do good and [v]to share what you have, for such [w]sacrifices are pleasing to God.

[17] Obey [x]your leaders and submit to them, [y]for they are keeping watch over your souls, as those who will have to [z]give an account. [a]Let them do this with joy and not with groaning, for that would be of no advantage to you.

[18] [b]Pray for us, for we are sure that we have a clear conscience, desiring to act honorably in all things. [19] I urge you the more earnestly to do this in order [c]that I may be restored to you the sooner.

9 [i] Jude 12; See Eph. 4:14 [j] See Col. 2:16
10 [k] [1 Cor. 9:13; 10:18]
11 [l] See Ex. 29:14 [m] ver. 13
12 [n] ch. 9:12 [o] Matt. 21:39; 27:32; John 19:17, 20; [Acts 7:58] [p] [Rev. 14:20]
13 [q] ch. 11:26; 1 Pet. 4:14
14 [r] [ch. 11:10, 16; 12:28; Mic. 2:10]; See Eph. 2:19
15 [s] Eph. 5:20 [t] Lev. 7:12; Ps. 107:22; 116:17 [u] Isa. 57:19; Hos. 14:2; [Ps. 119:108]
16 [v] See Rom. 12:13 [w] Mic. 6:7, 8; Phil. 4:18
17 [x] ver. 7, 24 [y] See Ezek. 3:17 [z] Jer. 13:20; Ezek. 34:10 [a] [Acts 20:24, 31]
18 [b] 1 Thess. 5:25; 2 Thess. 3:1
19 [c] [Philem. 22]

leaders, similar to the examples of faith in chapter 11, displayed a faith that looked to the future. They remind us of Abel, who "through his faith, though he died . . . still speaks" (11:4). What message did the deceased leaders bear? In a word, the gospel! "Jesus Christ is the same yesterday and today and forever" (13:8). Leaders come and go, but the message about Christ, our Lord and Savior, remains the same. "So faith comes from hearing, and hearing through the word of Christ" (Rom. 10:17). And this is the word the church is to heed. We are not to "be led away by diverse and strange teachings," whatever they may be (Heb. 13:9). Verse 8, which extols Christ, is the bridge between verses 7 and 9. The leaders who have passed on to their reward preached Christ, our faithful High Priest. Any teaching which rejects him must itself be rejected.

In contrast to the false teaching, "it is good for the heart to be strengthened by grace" (v. 9). The author has implied this all along and now says it explicitly. God's grace is not only his love that saved us when we were estranged from him (Eph. 2:4–9); it is also God's power that enables us to live for him (1 Cor. 15:10). "My grace is sufficient for you, for my power is made perfect in weakness" (2 Cor. 12:9) is a key principle for the Christian life. We need God's grace once and for all to become his children. We also need it every day of our lives to walk as befits his children. That is why Paul prays that God would grant his readers grace both at the beginning and at the close of his letters. And that is why Hebrews ends this way too (Heb. 13:25; cf. 4:16). We must rely on God's matchless grace day by day.

13:20–21 The end of Hebrews combines a prayer with a benediction. The author prays that "the God of peace" may equip his readers to live for God and to please him. As we might expect, once more he exalts Christ, the theme of the book: "Now may the God of peace who brought again from the dead our Lord Jesus, the great shepherd of the sheep, by the blood of the eternal covenant . . ." (v. 20). Although Jesus' resurrection was implied earlier (7:16, 24–25), here alone in Hebrews is it explicit. God the Father raised his Son from the dead, ratifying his work on the cross and promising eternal life to all who trust in him. "The blood of the eternal covenant" (v. 20) speaks of Jesus' death; it refers to "the new covenant" that he ratified with his blood (Luke 22:20; 1 Cor. 11:25). As, in John's Gospel, Jesus is the Good Shepherd (John 10:11–18), so here he is "the great shepherd of the sheep" (Heb. 13:20). He is the Savior who on the basis of his death and resurrection leads his flock to eternal rest (4:9–11).

The writer prays that God the Father who raised Jesus will furnish believers with all they need to do God's will and to please him (13:21). It is important to see that God is at work here. As Paul says elsewhere, "Work out your own salvation . . . for it is God who works in you, both to will and to work for his good pleasure" (Phil. 2:12–13). God not only equips his people to obey and to honor him, he also works "in us that which is pleasing in his sight" (Heb. 13:21). Hebrews thus concludes with another reminder that the strength to please God is provided by God himself. We work hard in the Christian life. But it is not a self-help program. Paul succinctly summarizes, "I toil, struggling with all his energy that he powerfully works within me" (Col. 1:29).

Benediction

20 Now [d]may the God of peace [e]who brought
again from the dead our Lord Jesus, [f]the great
shepherd of the sheep, by [g]the blood of the
eternal covenant, 21 [h]equip you with everything
good that you may do his will, [i]working in us[1]
that which is pleasing in his sight, through
Jesus Christ, [j]to whom be glory forever and
ever. Amen.

Final Greetings

22 I appeal to you, brothers,[2] bear with my
word of exhortation, for [k]I have written to you
briefly. 23 You should know that [l]our brother
Timothy has been released, with whom I shall
see you if he comes soon. 24 Greet all [m]your
leaders and all the saints. Those who come
from Italy send you greetings. 25 [n]Grace be with
all of you.

[1] Some manuscripts *you* [2] Or *brothers and sisters*

The ultimate goal of all of this? As always, the glory of God. The prayer ends "... through Jesus Christ, to whom be glory forever and ever. Amen" (Heb. 13:21). To whom is glory ascribed here, the Father or the Son? Although "Jesus Christ" has just been named, the structure of the prayer/doxology (vv. 20–21) reveals that it is the Father who is to receive the glory. (Jesus himself is the subject of a doxology, however, in 2 Pet. 3:18.) Christian theology insists that the three persons of the Trinity uniquely deserve the praise of human beings and angels. Indeed, to God the holy Trinity "be glory forever and ever. Amen"!

20 [d]See Rom. 15:33 [e]See Acts 2:24 [f]Isa. 63:11; See John 10:11 [g]ch. 10:29; Zech. 9:11; [Isa. 54:10]
21 [h]2 Thess. 2:17; 1 Pet. 5:10 [i]ch. 10:36; [Phil. 2:13] [j]See Rom. 11:36
22 [k][1 Pet. 5:12]
23 [l]See 1 Thess. 3:2
24 [m]ver. 7, 17
25 [n]See Col. 4:18

Introduction to James

Author, Date, and Recipients

This letter was written by James, the brother of Jesus (Matt. 13:55; Gal. 1:19) and leader of the Jerusalem church (Acts 15). It was probably written about A.D. 40–45 to Jewish Christians living outside Palestine who were suffering persecution and living in poverty.

The Gospel in James

James is a beloved epistle, eminently practical and full of vivid exhortations to godly living. The author presents profound counsel on numerous essentials: trials, poverty, riches, justice, speech, worldliness, and prayer. His clarity and prophetic urgency call readers to action, but his assessment of our failures is almost too penetrating, as it exposes our inability to perform what he commands—driving us to the ever-present refuge of the gospel. Yet at the same time James stirs us to action, to the obedience that is a hallmark not of bare external conformity but of living faith: "Be doers of the word, and not hearers only" (1:22).

Since James demands what readers cannot render, we struggle to resolve the tension between those demands and our inability to attain them. We might expect James to discuss justification here, but he never mentions that or the cross, resurrection, or atonement. Indeed, the absence of these elements has prompted some to doubt the canonicity of James. Further, while he uses Jesus' name twice (1:1; 2:1), both are passing references, not expositions of his life and saving work.

With 59 commands in 108 verses, James declares King Jesus' royal law (2:8). He insists that obedience is a prime mark of true religion: "Whoever keeps the whole law but fails in one point has become accountable for all of it" (2:10; cf. 3:1; 4:17). The hasty reader could therefore miss the gospel in James. If James merely commands, his clarity is a burden and his commands ultimately condemn.

We will begin to understand the gospel intentions of the book by noting that James 1:26–27 structures the book when he declares that "anyone [who] thinks he is religious" will show it in three ways. He will "bridle his tongue," watch over "orphans and widows in their affliction," and keep himself "unstained" by the world. Remarkably, James next demonstrates that everyone fails to meet these standards. We must control the tongue, yet no one can tame the tongue (3:8). We must care for the needy—orphans and widows—yet we're willing to *wish them well and do nothing* (2:15–17). We must avoid the pollution of the world, yet our envy and quarrels prove our worldliness (4:1–4).

If no one has true religion, then all are liable to judgment. Still, James says "mercy triumphs over judgment" (2:13; 5:11). The climax of the epistle,

James 4:6, explains *how* mercy triumphs. No one controls the tongue, cares for the needy, or stays unstained, but God "gives more grace. Therefore it says 'God opposes the proud, but gives grace to the humble.'" Here "it" means all Scripture, which attests to God's grace for the humble. James reinforces the lesson in 4:10, commanding, "Humble yourselves before the Lord, and he will exalt you." That is the gospel according to James: No one is obedient, no one consistently demonstrates true religion. Therefore, the Father who gives good gifts (1:5, 17) gives the supreme gift of saving grace to the humble.

Further, the wisdom to understand such grace is from above (1:17–18), as God grants needed understanding generously and without reproach to whomever asks (1:5). We therefore understand that, though none can meet God's requirements, he grants the wisdom needed to navigate this world and the next to all who simply have faith to ask his aid (1:6)—this is undeniable grace.

Outline

I. Greeting (1:1)

II. The Testing of Faith (1:2–18)

III. Hearing and Doing the Word (1:19–27)

IV. The Sin of Favoritism (2:1–13)

V. Faith without Works Is Dead (2:14–26)

VI. The Sin of Dissension in the Community (3:1–4:12)

VII. The Sins of the Wealthy (4:13–5:12)

VIII. The Prayer of Faith (5:13–18)

IX. Concluding Admonition (5:19–20)

The Letter of

James

Greeting

1 [a]James, a servant[1] of God and [b]of the Lord
Jesus Christ,
To [c]the twelve tribes in [d]the Dispersion:
Greetings.

Testing of Your Faith

2 [e]Count it all joy, my brothers,[2] when you
meet trials [f]of various kinds, 3 for you know
that [g]the testing of your faith [h]produces steadfastness. 4 And let steadfastness have its full
effect, that you may be [i]perfect and complete,
lacking in nothing.
5 [j]If any of you lacks wisdom, [k]let him ask
God, [l]who gives generously to all without
reproach, and it will be given him. 6 But [m]let
him ask in faith, [n]with no doubting, for the
one who doubts is like [o]a wave of the sea that
is driven and tossed by the wind. 7 For that person must not suppose that he will receive anything from the Lord; 8 [p]he is a double-minded
man, [q]unstable in all his ways.
9 Let the lowly brother boast in his exaltation, 10 and [r]the rich in his humiliation,
because [s]like a flower of the grass[3] he will pass
away. 11 For the sun rises with its scorching heat
and [t]withers the grass; its flower falls, and its
beauty perishes. So also will the rich man fade
away in the midst of his pursuits.
12 [u]Blessed is the man who remains steadfast
under trial, for when he has stood the test he
will receive [v]the crown of life, [w]which God
has promised to those who love him. 13 Let
no one say when he is tempted, "I am being
tempted by God," for God cannot be tempted
with evil, and he himself tempts no one. 14 But

[1] Or *slave* (for the contextual rendering of the Greek word *doulos*, see Preface) [2] Or *brothers and sisters*. The plural Greek word *adelphoi* (translated "brothers") refers to siblings in a family. In New Testament usage, depending on the context, *adelphoi* may refer either to men or to both men and women who are siblings (brothers and sisters) in God's family, the church; also verses 16, 19 [3] Or *a wild flower*

1:1 Jesus graciously appeared to James, the half brother who once mocked him, after the resurrection. James believed and here calls himself Jesus' servant. That a family member of Jesus who once refused to believe in him would now be chosen to testify of Jesus' teachings through inspired Scripture is itself a witness to the grace of the gospel.

1:2–12 Life brings constant tests and trials. God designs them to bring us to maturity (vv. 2–4). Yet he doesn't leave us to strive alone but promises wisdom for the trial, which he gives "generously" and "without reproach" (v. 5). Yet we must ask sincerely for genuine faith that unites us to him (vv. 5–8). Before God, rich and poor, high and low, are the same—weak, mortal, humbled (vv. 9–11).

The provisions of the gospel are not based on human distinctions or accomplishments. God blesses the man who perseveres in trials, and he promises to crown that man with life, the resurrection life we receive through faith in Jesus (v. 12).

1:13–25 God intends trials to strengthen us, but some say trials tempt them to sin, and blame God for it. But temptation only entices us when we desire the sin (vv. 13–15). God wants to give gifts; his chief gift is new birth by "the word of truth" —that is, the gospel (v. 18; cf. Eph. 1:13; Col. 1:5–6).

Since humanity is prone to anger and proliferating moral filth, our hope lies with God's Word, which his Spirit plants in us. This implanted Word "is able to save your souls" and empower moral reform (James 1:20–21). Then we will hear the Word, see it as a mirror to our souls, remember it, and do what it says (vv. 22–25). Thus, the initiative and enabling for divine usefulness are from God. God provides for what he requires, and genuine obedience to God's Word also brings freedom and blessing (v. 25).

Chapter 1
1 [a]See Acts 12:17 [b]Rom. 1:1; 2 Pet. 1:1; Jude 1 [c]Luke 22:30; Acts 26:7 [d]1 Pet. 1:1; [Acts 2:9-11]; See John 7:35
2 [e]See Matt. 5:12 [f]1 Pet. 1:6
3 [g]1 Pet. 1:7 [h]Rom. 5:3; [ch. 5:11; Heb. 10:36; 2 Pet. 1:6]
4 [i]1 Thess. 5:23; See Matt. 5:48
5 [j]1 Kgs. 3:9-12; Prov. 2:3-6 [k]See Matt. 7:7 [l]Prov. 28:5
6 [m]Mark 11:24 [n]Matt. 21:21 [o][Isa. 57:20; Eph. 4:14]
8 [p]ch. 4:8 [q][2 Pet. 2:14; 3:16]
10 [r]Jer. 9:23 [s][Ps. 102:4, 11; 1 Cor. 7:31; 1 Pet. 1:24]
11 [t]Isa. 40:7
12 [u]ch. 5:11; Matt. 10:22; 1 Pet. 3:14; [Dan. 12:12] [v]Rev. 2:10; 3:11; [1 Cor. 9:25; 2 Tim. 4:8; 1 Pet. 5:4] [w]ch. 2:5

each person is tempted when he is lured and
enticed by his own desire. 15 Then desire [x]when
it has conceived gives birth to sin, and [y]sin
when it is fully grown brings forth death.
16 Do not be deceived, my beloved brothers.
17 [z]Every good gift and every perfect gift is from
above, coming down from [a]the Father of lights
[b]with whom there is no variation or shadow
due to change.[1] 18 [c]Of his own will he [d]brought
us forth by the word of truth, [e]that we should
be a kind of [f]firstfruits of his creatures.

Hearing and Doing the Word

19 [g]Know this, my beloved brothers: let every
person [h]be quick to hear, [i]slow to speak, [j]slow
to anger; 20 for the anger of man does not produce the righteousness of God. 21 Therefore
[k]put away all filthiness and rampant wickedness and receive with [l]meekness the implanted
word, [m]which is able to save your souls.
22 But be [n]doers of the word, and not hearers only, deceiving yourselves. 23 For if anyone
is a hearer of the word and not a doer, he is
like a man who looks intently at his natural
face in a mirror. 24 For he looks at himself and
goes away and at once forgets what he was
like. 25 But the one who looks into the perfect
law, [o]the law of liberty, and perseveres, being
no hearer who forgets but a doer who acts, [p]he
will be blessed in his doing.
26 If anyone thinks he is religious [q]and does
not bridle his tongue but deceives his heart,
this person's [r]religion is worthless. 27 Religion
that is pure and undefiled before God, the
Father, is this: [s]to visit [t]orphans and widows in their affliction, and [u]to keep oneself
[v]unstained from the world.

The Sin of Partiality

2 My brothers,[2] [w]show no partiality as you
hold the faith in our Lord Jesus Christ, [x]the
Lord of glory. 2 For if a man wearing a gold ring
and fine clothing comes into your assembly,
and a poor man in shabby clothing also comes
in, 3 and if you pay attention to the one who
wears the fine clothing and say, "You sit here
in a good place," [y]while you say to the poor
man, "You stand over there," or, "Sit down at
my feet," 4 have you not then made distinctions
among yourselves and become [z]judges with
evil thoughts? 5 Listen, my beloved brothers,
[a]has not God chosen those who are poor in the
world to be [b]rich in faith and heirs of [c]the kingdom, [d]which he has promised to those who
love him? 6 But you [e]have dishonored the poor
man. Are not the rich the ones who oppress
you, and the ones who [f]drag you [g]into court?
7 Are they not the ones who blaspheme the
honorable [h]name by which you were called?
8 If you really fulfill the royal law according
to the Scripture, [i]"You shall love your neighbor as yourself," you are doing well. 9 But if
you [j]show partiality, you are committing sin
and are convicted by the law as transgressors.
10 For whoever keeps the whole law but fails in
one point [k]has become accountable for all of it.
11 For he who said, [l]"Do not commit adultery,"
also said, [l]"Do not murder." If you do not commit adultery but do murder, you have become
a transgressor of the law. 12 So speak and so act
as those who are to be judged under [m]the law
of liberty. 13 For [n]judgment is without mercy to
one who has shown no mercy. Mercy triumphs
over judgment.

[1] Some manuscripts *variation due to a shadow of turning* [2] Or *brothers and sisters*; also verses 5, 14

1:26–2:7 The Word, received with genuine faith, brings obedience and true religion, but James knows true religion is elusive, even within the church, and so he proposes a test case. Two men, one poor and one rich, enter a gathering where just one seat remains. If the rich man gets the seat and the poor man gets the floor, that violates "pure" religion as defined in 1:27. The *world* invades the church and the *poor*, who hope that at least the church grants them equality, are put down once more.

2:8–13 Will someone object that partiality is a minor sin? Yet it violates the gospel principle that God shows no partiality. He judges all by the same law, and by the same grace, he redeems everyone whose faith rests in the Lord Jesus alone (v. 1). Further, all sins are major, for all violate the law of King Jesus, who spoke every commandment. The willful violation of even one law is transgression against the King and Lord of all. So everyone is liable to judgment "without mercy." Yet through Christ "mercy triumphs over judgment" (v. 13).

15 [x]Job 15:35; Ps. 7:14; Isa. 59:4 [y]Rom. 5:12; 6:23
17 [z]Ps. 85:12; John 3:27; 1 Cor. 4:7 [a]1 John 1:5 [b]Mal. 3:6
18 [c]John 1:13 [d][Gal. 4:19; 1 Pet. 1:3, 23] [e][Eph. 1:12] [f]Jer. 2:3; Rev. 14:4; [Rom. 8:19-23]
19 [g]1 John 2:21 [h][Eccles. 5:1, 2] [i]Prov. 10:19; 17:27 [j]See Prov. 14:29
21 [k]Col. 3:8 [l]ch. 3:13 [m]1 Cor. 15:2; Eph. 1:13
22 [n]Rom. 2:13; [ch. 2:14-20; Matt. 7:21, 24-27; Luke 8:21; John 13:17]
25 [o]ch. 2:12; [Gal. 2:4; 5:1, 13; 1 Pet. 2:16; 2 Pet. 2:19]; See John 8:32 [p]Ps. 1:1, 2; Luke 11:28

26 [q]ch. 3:2, 3; Ps. 39:1; [ch. 3:6; Ps. 34:13; 141:3] [r]Acts 26:5 **27** [s]Matt. 25:36 [t]Job 31:17, 18; Isa. 1:17, 23 [u]1 Tim. 5:22; 1 John 5:18 [v]2 Pet. 3:14 **Chapter 2** **1** [w]ver. 9; Lev. 19:15; Deut. 1:17; 16:19; Prov. 24:23; Rom. 2:11; Eph. 6:9 [x]1 Cor. 2:8; [Acts 7:2] **3** [y][Prov. 18:23] **4** [z]John 7:24 **5** [a]1 Cor. 1:27, 28; [Job 34:19] [b]2 Cor. 8:9; Rev. 2:9; See Luke 12:21 [c]Matt. 5:3; Luke 6:20; 12:32 [d]See ch. 1:12 **6** [e][1 Cor. 11:22] [f]Acts 16:19 [g]Acts 8:3; 17:6; 18:12; [ch. 5:6] **7** [h][Isa. 63:19; 65:1; Amos 9:12; Acts 15:17] **8** [i]Cited from Lev. 19:18 **9** [j]ver. 1 **10** [k]Matt. 5:19; Gal. 3:10 **11** [l]Cited from Ex. 20:14, 13 **12** [m]See ch. 1:25 **13** [n]Job 22:6-11; Ps. 18:25, 26; Prov. 21:13; Ezek. 25:11-14; Matt. 6:15; 18:32-35; Luke 6:38

Faith Without Works Is Dead

[14] What good is it, my brothers, if someone says he has faith [o]but does not have works? Can that faith save him? [15] [p]If a brother or sister is poorly clothed and lacking in daily food, [16] [q]and one of you says to them, "Go in peace, be warmed and filled," without giving them the things needed for the body, what good[1] is that? [17] So also faith by itself, if it does not have works, is dead.

[18] But someone will say, "You have faith and I have works." Show me your faith [r]apart from your works, and I will show you my faith [s]by my works. [19] [t]You believe that God is one; you do well. Even [u]the demons believe—and shudder! [20] Do you want to be shown, you foolish person, that faith apart from works is useless? [21] [v]Was not Abraham our father justified by works when he offered up his son Isaac on the altar? [22] You see that [w]faith was active along with his works, and faith was completed [x]by his works; [23] and the Scripture was fulfilled that says, [y]"Abraham believed God, and it was counted to him as righteousness"—and he was called a [z]friend of God. [24] You see that a person is justified by works and not by faith alone. [25] And in the same way was not also [a]Rahab the prostitute justified by works [b]when she received the messengers and sent them out by another way? [26] For as the body apart from the spirit is dead, so also faith apart from works is dead.

Taming the Tongue

3 [c]Not many of you should become teachers, my brothers, for you know that we who teach will be judged with greater strictness. [2] For [d]we all stumble in many ways. And if anyone does not stumble in what he says, [e]he is a perfect man, [f]able also to bridle his whole body. [3] If we put [g]bits into the mouths of horses so that they obey us, we guide their whole bodies as well. [4] Look at the ships also: though they are so large and are driven by strong winds, they are guided by a very small rudder wherever the will of the pilot directs. [5] So also the tongue is a small member, yet [h]it boasts of great things.

How great a forest is set ablaze by such a small fire! [6] And [i]the tongue is a fire, a world of unrighteousness. The tongue is set among our members, [j]staining the whole body, setting on fire the entire course of life,[2] and set on fire by hell.[3] [7] For every kind of beast and bird, of reptile and sea creature, can be tamed and has been tamed by mankind, [8] but no human

[1] Or *benefit* [2] Or *wheel of birth* [3] Greek *Gehenna*

2:14–26 James explores the nature of saving faith. There is a "faith" that cannot save. Such faith has kind words but no deeds, no aid for the naked and hungry. It is "dead" because it rests in ideas, not in a life dependent upon and reflective of Jesus (vv. 14–17). Orthodox theology "apart from works is useless" (v. 20). Demons prove this, since they hold to orthodox ideas about God yet live in terror since they don't trust him (v. 19).

Abraham's faith did *work* "when he offered up his son Isaac on the altar," and his "faith was completed by his works" (vv. 20–22). When James says Abraham was "justified by works" (v. 21) he means that his claim to believe was vindicated or validated, not that he earned his salvation. He knows that "Abraham believed God, and it was counted to him as righteousness" (v. 23). But again, faith proves itself real by works. We are not saved by our works, but faithful works flow from saving faith.

Rahab, a Gentile and a prostitute, contrasts with Abraham in every way except that her deeds also proved her faith. She claimed that she feared God and she called him Lord, and she proved it when she risked her life to hide Israel's spies (vv. 25–26).

James does not suggest, then, that faith plus works equals justification. He agrees with Paul that faith alone justifies. But he knows there is a so-called "faith" that is dangerous because it deludes but does not justify. He contrasts that with the faith that does justify—a living faith that by its very nature reflects the One on whom our faith rests, delighting to love others in concrete ways.

3:1–12 James indicts human sinfulness again, beginning with teachers. They know more, but like everyone, they stumble, notably in speech. Thus teachers, a verbose tribe, are most liable to judgment. If humans can control great horses and ships with small bits and rudders, we should be able to control our tiny tongues. The tongue's power to bless or curse, to start fires, makes mastery essential, but "no human . . . can tame the tongue" (v. 8).

14 [o][ch. 1:22]
15 [p][Job 31:19, 20]; See Luke 3:11
16 [q]1 John 3:17, 18
18 [r][Rom. 3:28; 4:6; Heb. 11:33] [s]Matt. 7:16, 17; Gal. 5:6
19 [t]Deut. 6:4; [Rom. 2:17-25] [u]Matt. 8:29; Mark 1:24; 5:7; Luke 4:33, 34; Acts 16:17; 19:15
21 [v]Gen. 22:9, 12, 16-18
22 [w]Heb. 11:17 [x]See 1 Thess. 1:3
23 [y]Rom. 4:3; Gal. 3:6; Cited from Gen. 15:6 [z]2 Chr. 20:7; Isa. 41:8
25 [a]Heb. 11:31 [b]Josh. 2:1-22; 6:23

Chapter 3
1 [c]Matt. 23:8; [Rom. 2:20, 21; 1 Tim. 1:7]
2 [d]1 Kgs. 8:46; Prov. 20:9; Eccles. 7:20; 1 John 1:8 [e][Matt. 12:37] [f]See ch. 1:26
3 [g]Ps. 32:9
5 [h][Ps. 12:3, 4; 73:8, 9]
6 [i]Ps. 120:2-4; Prov. 16:27 [j]Matt. 15:18

being can tame the tongue. It is a restless evil,
[k]full of deadly poison. 9 With it we bless our
Lord and Father, and with it we curse people
[l]who are made in the likeness of God. 10 From
the same mouth come blessing and cursing.
My brothers,[1] these things ought not to be
so. 11 Does a spring pour forth from the same
opening both fresh and salt water? 12 Can a fig
tree, my brothers, bear olives, or a grapevine
produce figs? Neither can a salt pond yield
fresh water.

Wisdom from Above

13 Who is wise and understanding among
you? [m]By his good conduct let him show his
works [n]in the meekness of wisdom. 14 But if
you have bitter [o]jealousy and selfish ambition
in your hearts, do not boast and be false to the
truth. 15 This is not [p]the wisdom that comes
down from above, but is earthly, unspiritual,
[q]demonic. 16 For where jealousy and selfish
ambition exist, there will be disorder and
every vile practice. 17 But [r]the wisdom from
above is first pure, then [s]peaceable, gentle,
open to reason, [t]full of mercy and good fruits,
[u]impartial and [v]sincere. 18 And [w]a harvest of
righteousness [x]is sown in peace by those who
make peace.

Warning Against Worldliness

4 What causes quarrels and what causes
fights among you? Is it not this, that your
passions[2] are [y]at war within you?[3] 2 You desire
and do not have, so you murder. You covet and
cannot obtain, so you fight and quarrel. You
do not have, because you do not ask. 3 You ask
and do not receive, because you ask [z]wrongly,
to spend it on your passions. 4 [a]You adulterous
people![4] Do you not know that friendship with
the world is enmity with God? [b]Therefore whoever wishes to be a friend of the world makes
himself an enemy of God. 5 Or do you suppose
it is to no purpose that the Scripture says, "He
yearns jealously over the spirit [c]that he has
made to dwell in us"? 6 But [d]he gives more grace.
Therefore it says, [e]"God opposes the proud, but
[d]gives grace to the humble." 7 Submit yourselves
therefore to God. [f]Resist the devil, and he will
flee from you. 8 [g]Draw near to God, and he will
draw near to you. [h]Cleanse your hands, you
sinners, and [i]purify your hearts, [j]you double-
minded. 9 [k]Be wretched and mourn and weep.
Let your laughter be turned to mourning and
your joy to gloom. 10 [l]Humble yourselves before
the Lord, and he will exalt you.
11 [m]Do not speak evil against one another,

[1] Or *brothers and sisters*; also verse 12 [2] Greek *pleasures*; also verse 3 [3] Greek *in your members* [4] Greek *You adulteresses!*

8[k] Ps. 140:3; Eccles. 10:11; Rom. 3:13
9[l] See Gen. 1:26
13[m] ch. 2:18 [n] ch. 1:21
14[o] ver. 16; Acts 5:17; Rom. 2:8; 2 Cor. 12:20; Gal. 5:20; Phil. 1:17; 2:3; [Rom. 13:13]
15[p] ch. 1:17 [q] [1 Kgs. 22:22; 2 Thess. 2:9, 10; 1 Tim. 4:1; Rev. 2:24]
17[r] [1 Cor. 2:6, 7] [s] Heb. 12:11 [t] [Luke 6:36] [u] ch. 2:4 (Gk.) [v] Rom. 12:9
18[w] Prov. 11:18; Isa. 32:17; Hos. 10:12; Amos 6:12; Phil. 1:11 [x] Matt. 5:9; Gal. 6:7, 8

Chapter 4
1[y] Rom. 7:23; 1 Pet. 2:11
3[z] [1 John 5:14]
4[a] Isa. 54:5; Jer. 2:2 [b] John 15:19; 1 John 2:15; [Matt. 6:24]
5[c] 1 Cor. 6:19; 2 Cor. 6:16
6[d] Isa. 54:7, 8; See Matt. 13:12 [e] 1 Pet. 5:5; Cited from Prov. 3:34 (Gk.)
7[f] 1 Pet. 5:8, 9; [Eph. 4:27; 6:11]
8[g] 2 Chr. 15:2; Lam. 3:57; Zech. 1:3; Mal. 3:7; [Luke 15:20] [h] Isa. 1:16 [i] Jer. 4:14 [j] ch. 1:8
9[k] [Matt. 5:4]
10[l] ver. 6; Isa. 57:15; [Luke 1:52]; See Matt. 23:12
11[m] 2 Cor. 12:20; 1 Pet. 2:1; [ch. 5:9]

This sounds like despair, yet if no *human* can tame the tongue, the One who created mankind still can. Indeed, if the same tongue praises God and curses people made in God's image, we should cry out for God's intervention. So the tongue, now speaking from a renewed heart, lays hold of God's grace as presented in the gospel (Rom. 10:9–10).

3:13–4:6 James presents two kinds of wisdom. Selfish ambition and jealousy drive the "earthly, unspiritual" wisdom that grasps for everything and resents all who have more (3:14–15). If there is no God, it is logical to seize all we can, even if it causes "every vile practice" (3:16). But God's wisdom is pure, peaceful, merciful, and righteous (3:17–18). As Jesus often did, James offers two choices, two ways of life. If God gives us wisdom (1:5), we will claim "the wisdom from above" (3:17). But earthly wisdom brings battles *between* people, since battles rage *within* people, as they long to possess things and fail to acquire all that they long for (4:1–3).

Ultimately, we must choose between love of God and love of the world (4:4). Alas, unaided human nature will choose the world. Yet God seeks us and "gives grace to the humble" (4:5–6).

4:7–10 If we live by God's grace, we draw near to God and we "cleanse [our] hands . . . and purify [our] hearts" (v. 8). That means we change both deeds and thoughts. Moreover, we "mourn and weep" over sin (v. 9). We rightly say that God humbles us, but James commands us to humble ourselves. Then God will exalt us (v. 10).

This principle lies at the heart of the gospel itself. When we humble ourselves, lay down our moral pride and achievements, and cast ourselves on Christ in faith, God exalts us (Luke 18:14). We become his children, accepted and reconciled to the Father.

4:11–5:6 James says this gospel-driven humility will be manifest in us as we turn from our prideful sins. First, heeding James's question, "Who are you to judge your

brothers.[1] The one who speaks against a brother or [n]judges his brother, speaks evil against the law and judges the law. But if you judge the law, you are not a doer of the law but a judge. 12 There is only [o]one lawgiver and [p]judge, he who is able to save and [q]to destroy. But [r]who are you to judge your neighbor?

Boasting About Tomorrow

13 Come now, you who say, [s]"Today or tomorrow we will go into such and such a town and spend a year there and trade and make a profit"— 14 yet you do not know what tomorrow will bring. What is your life? For [t]you are a mist that appears for a little time and then vanishes. 15 Instead you ought to say, [u]"If the Lord wills, we will live and do this or that." 16 As it is, you boast in your arrogance. [v]All such boasting is evil. 17 [w]So whoever knows the right thing to do and fails to do it, for him it is sin.

Warning to the Rich

5 Come now, [x]you rich, weep and howl for the [y]miseries that are coming upon you. 2 [z]Your riches have rotted and [z]your garments are moth-eaten. 3 Your gold and silver have corroded, and their corrosion will be evidence against you and will eat your flesh like fire. [a]You have laid up treasure [b]in the last days. 4 Behold, [c]the wages of the laborers who mowed your fields, which you kept back by fraud, are crying out against you, and [d]the cries of the harvesters have reached the ears of [e]the Lord of hosts. 5 [f]You have lived on the earth in luxury and [g]in self-indulgence. You have fattened your hearts in [h]a day of slaughter. 6 You have condemned and [i]murdered [j]the righteous person. He does not resist you.

Patience in Suffering

7 Be patient, therefore, brothers,[2] until the coming of the Lord. See how the farmer waits for the precious fruit of the earth, being patient about it, until it receives [k]the early and the late rains. 8 You also, be patient. [l]Establish your hearts, for the coming of the Lord [m]is at hand. 9 Do not grumble against one another, brothers, [n]so that you may not be judged; behold, [o]the Judge is standing [p]at the door. 10 As an example of suffering and patience, brothers, take [q]the prophets who spoke in the name of the Lord. 11 Behold, we consider those blessed who remained steadfast. You have heard of [r]the steadfastness of Job, and you have seen [s]the purpose of the Lord, how [t]the Lord is compassionate and merciful.

12 But above all, my brothers, [u]do not swear, either by heaven or by earth or by any other oath, but let your "yes" be yes and your "no" be no, so that you may not fall under condemnation.

[1] Or *brothers and sisters* [2] Or *brothers and sisters*; also verses 9, 10, 12, 19

neighbor?" we will leave judgment to the Judge—the Judge who can also save (4:11–12). Second, we will stop making grandiose plans. We will confess that God is sovereign, that we by comparison are like a mist, that all achievement depends on God's will and favor (4:13–16). Third, those who are rich will stop oppressing the poor (5:1–6; see note).

5:1–6 James has been addressing "brothers" (e.g., 4:11; 5:7, 9, 10), but in these verses he warns "you rich" that judgment is coming, for they have oppressed their laborers (v. 4) and have "fattened" themselves in "a day of slaughter" (v. 5). The counterintuitive reversal of this passage, here applied to money, picks up a whole-Bible theme. From Genesis to Revelation we see God inverting the world's natural standards of significance and strength (see also 1:9–10).

The supreme instance of this is the gospel itself, in which self-divesting contrition rather than self-resourced accomplishment brings divine favor and power flooding into one's life. This can be true ultimately only because Jesus Christ, the one truly strong and significant human who ever lived, allowed himself to be made weak and pitiable on behalf of pitiable sinners.

5:7–12 For now, believers must be patient through suffering and trial, "for the coming of the Lord" is near (v. 8). The Judge will soon deal with the impenitent, but we long for that day, since God is "compassionate and merciful" (v. 11). This great grace of an ultimate vindicating rescue from our difficulties keeps us from grumbling, judgmentalism, and capitulation to evil.

11 [n]See Matt. 7:1
12 [o]Isa. 33:22 [p]ch. 5:9 [q]Matt. 10:28 [r]Rom. 14:4
13 [s]Prov. 27:1; Luke 12:18-20
14 [t]Ps. 102:3; [Job 7:7]
15 [u]See Acts 18:21
16 [v][1 Cor. 5:6]
17 [w][Luke 12:47, 48; 2 Pet. 2:21]; See John 9:41

Chapter 5
1 [x]Luke 6:24; [Prov. 11:28; Amos 6:1; 1 Tim. 6:9] [y]Rom. 3:16
2 [z]Job 13:28; Isa. 50:9; Matt. 6:19, 20
3 [a]Matt. 6:19; Luke 12:21; Rom. 2:5 [b][ver. 8, 9]
4 [c]Job 24:10; See Lev. 19:13 [d]Deut. 24:15 [e]Rom. 9:29
5 [f][Job 21:13; Luke 16:19; 2 Pet. 2:13] [g]1 Tim. 5:6 [h]Jer. 12:3
6 [i]ch. 4:2 [j][Acts 3:14]
7 [k]See Deut. 11:14
8 [l]1 Thess. 3:13 [m]1 Pet. 4:7; [Rom. 13:11, 12; Phil. 4:5; Heb. 10:25, 37]
9 [n]Matt. 7:1 [o][1 Pet. 4:5; Rev. 22:12] [p]Matt. 24:33; Mark 13:29; [1 Cor. 4:5]
10 [q]Matt. 5:12; 23:34; Acts 7:52; Heb. 11:32-38
11 [r]Job 1:21, 22; 2:10 [s]Job 42:10, 12 [t]See Ex. 34:6
12 [u]Matt. 5:34

The Prayer of Faith

[13]Is anyone among you suffering? Let him pray. Is anyone cheerful? Let him [v]sing praise. [14]Is anyone among you sick? Let him call for the elders of the church, and let them pray over him, [w]anointing him with oil in the name of the Lord. [15]And the prayer of faith will save the one who is sick, and the Lord will raise him up. And [x]if he has committed sins, he will be forgiven. [16]Therefore, [y]confess your sins to one another and pray for one another, [z]that you may be healed. [a]The prayer of a righteous person has great power as it is working.[1] [17]Elijah was a man [b]with a nature like ours, and [c]he prayed fervently that it might not rain, and for [d]three years and six months it did not rain on the earth. [18][e]Then he prayed again, and heaven gave rain, and the earth bore its fruit.

[19]My brothers, [f]if anyone among you wanders from the truth and someone [g]brings him back, [20]let him know that whoever brings back a sinner from his wandering [h]will save his soul from death and [i]will cover a multitude of sins.

[1] Or *The effective prayer of a righteous person has great power*

13[v][Col. 3:16]
14[w]Mark 6:13; [Mark 16:18]
15[x]Isa. 33:24; Matt. 9:2; Mark 2:5; Luke 5:20
16[y]Acts 19:18 [z]Heb. 12:13 [a]Gen. 18:23-32; 20:17; Num. 11:2; 1 Kgs. 13:6; 17:22; 2 Kgs. 4:33; 19:15-20; 20:2-5; Job 42:8; Prov. 15:29
17[b]Acts 14:15 [c]1 Kgs. 17:1; 18:1 [d]Luke 4:25
18[e]1 Kgs. 18:42, 45
19[f][Matt. 18:15; Gal. 6:1] [g]Ps. 51:13; Dan. 12:3; Mal. 2:6; [Luke 1:16]
20[h]See Rom. 11:14 [i]1 Pet. 4:8; [Neh. 4:5; Ps. 32:1; 85:2; Prov. 10:12]

5:13–20 James exhorts us to praise the Lord for every blessing and petition him in every sorrow. In serious illness, we confess our sins and call the elders. He promises that, "the prayer of faith will save" the sick "and the Lord will raise him up" (probably an intentional double meaning, using resurrection language in reference to healing). That may happen in this life or in the next (v. 15). Elders are "righteous" men with powerful prayers.

James teaches us to doubt our righteousness, but the Lord grants and imputes righteousness by faith. So James cites Elijah, a prophet who prayed effectively even though he had "a nature like ours," stumbling as we do (vv. 17–18). James concludes pastorally, with a call to restore "anyone" who "wanders from the truth" (v. 19). From a human perspective, we "save" such a person's "soul from death," but from God's perspective we participate in the work of Christ, who covers sin and defeats it (v. 20).

Introduction to 1 Peter

Author, Date, and Recipients

The apostle Peter wrote this letter (1:1). He was once a fisherman but now was an apostle, having been "a witness of the sufferings of Christ" (5:1). He probably wrote the letter from Rome (5:13; "Babylon" probably refers to Rome) around A.D. 62–63, during Nero's reign. The letter is addressed to Christians scattered throughout what is modern-day Turkey (see 1:1).

The Gospel in 1 Peter

Hardship and holiness: these are the twin themes of Peter's first epistle, written to a church composed of Gentile converts from licentious hedonism on the one hand and Jewish converts with Old Testament traditions on the other hand. Together they experienced an alien and exile status in a hostile world. Persecution against and oppression of the church of Jesus Christ had already begun, and Peter writes to encourage this "mixed bag" of believers with dear but easily forgotten truths of the gospel of Jesus Christ.

Peter provides this encouragement through a combination of proclamation and exhortation, and curiously, one of the proclamations is that suffering is inevitable for followers of Jesus. Such brutal facts may be difficult to take initially. But as trials come, the understanding that such suffering can be the mark and measure of faithfulness helps these early Christians to see that affliction is one more means of Christlikeness and, indeed, one more avenue of true joy.

Peter's words on holiness and hardship are inextricably connected. Because of the way the Spirit conforms us to the image of Christ, Peter not only sees holiness as necessary for enduring hardship; he sees hardship as a way the Spirit makes us holy.

Peter is gracious to apply these truths generally at first, and then gradually more specifically to the practical challenges of everyday life. The connection between hardship and holiness is applicable for Christian citizenship (2:13–25), Christian families (3:1–7), and Christian churches (5:1–11).

From Peter's instructions, believers in Jesus are trained in seeing the role and even the value of suffering. Christians learn that hardship is not outside God's sovereign will and is used by God to fashion us according to Christ's image. Authentic holiness in this adversity-filled life is possible through the power of the Spirit in the gospel, and indeed it is this very adversity that trains us for godliness. Through it all, however, we remember that the hardships of the world are temporary blips on the radar of the joyful life of eternal glory that begins when our flesh gives way and we go to be with the Lord. And one day, Christ will return to avenge our persecution and vindicate our suffering.

Outline

I. Opening (1:1–2)

II. Called to Salvation as Exiles (1:3–2:12)

III. Living as Strangers to Bring Glory to God in a Hostile World (2:13–4:11)

IV. Enduring Suffering (4:12–5:11)

V. Concluding Words (5:12–14)

The First Letter of Peter

1 Peter

Greeting

1 Peter, an apostle of Jesus Christ,
To those who are elect exiles of [a]the Dispersion in Pontus, Galatia, Cappadocia, Asia,
and Bithynia, 2 according to [b]the foreknowledge of God the Father, [c]in the sanctification
of the Spirit, for obedience to Jesus Christ and
[d]for sprinkling with his blood:
May [e]grace and [f]peace be multiplied to you.

Born Again to a Living Hope

3 [g]Blessed be the God and Father of our Lord
Jesus Christ! [h]According to his great mercy,
[i]he has caused us to be born again to a living hope [j]through the resurrection of Jesus
Christ from the dead, 4 to [k]an inheritance
that is imperishable, undefiled, and [l]unfad-
ing, [m]kept in heaven for you, 5 who by God's
power are being guarded [n]through faith for a
salvation [o]ready to be revealed in the last time.
6 In this you rejoice, though now for a little
while, if necessary, you have been grieved by
[p]various trials, 7 so that [q]the tested genuineness
of your faith—more precious than gold that
perishes [r]though it is tested by [s]fire—may be
found to result in [t]praise and glory and honor
at the revelation of Jesus Christ. 8 [u]Though you
have not seen him, you love him. [v]Though you
do not now see him, you believe in him and

1:1–2 The apostle Peter's first epistle is a treasure trove of gospel richness, and his greeting is no exception. What appears at one glance to be a customary "hello," upon second glance reveals theological depth.

In verse 2 we see the Trinitarian shape of the gospel. We are reminded that all three persons of the triune Godhead are active in the salvation of sinners: the Father purposes the saving work for those whom he foreknows (cf. Rom. 8:29), the Son accomplishes the work by his blood, and the Spirit applies the work to the sinner. Here is how "practical" the doctrine of the Trinity can be: it is the Trinity that saves sinners, uniting them to Christ so that they will walk in obedience to him.

It is no wonder that Peter then says, "Grace and peace be multiplied" to us. The wonder of redemption worked out for us by the triune God does not grant tepid or mild grace and peace; grace and peace are multiplied, proliferated, abundantly provided.

1:3–9 In this letter, Peter primarily approaches two difficult subjects: holiness and suffering. Peter would agree with Paul that holiness and suffering are vitally connected (see Rom. 5:3–4). He knows that the holy will suffer and that the holy will be made more holy as they share in Christ's suffering (1 Pet. 1:7; Phil. 3:10). "But rejoice insofar as you share Christ's sufferings, that you may also rejoice and be glad when his glory is revealed," Peter will later write (1 Pet. 4:13).

To take his readers into the commands of holiness and the demands of hardship, however, he must first take them to the sovereign power and assurance necessary for both. This power is found only in the gospel. Consider how Peter exults in the gospel in this opening paragraph to the letter. We are "born again to a living hope" (1:3), "to an inheritance that is imperishable, undefiled, and unfading," that is "kept in heaven" for us (v. 4). This assurance of our enduring hope is important for believers to remember so that we neither despair of God's commands to obedience (which as sinners we will struggle with) nor despair of God's allowing of suffering (which as frail people we may break under). Instead, we are empowered to obey, knowing that we are forgiven for all eternity; and we are encouraged to hope in God through hardship, knowing that our souls are infinitely secure.

Chapter 1
1 [a]See James 1:1
2 [b]Acts 2:23; [Rom. 8:29; 11:2] [c]See 1 Thess. 4:3 [d]Heb. 10:22; 12:24 [e]2 Pet. 1:2 [f]Dan. 4:1; Jude 2
3 [g]2 Cor. 1:3; Eph. 1:3 [h]Titus 3:5 [i]ver. 23 [j]ch. 3:21; [1 Cor. 15:20]
4 [k]Rom. 8:17 [l][ch. 5:4] [m][Col. 1:5; 2 Tim. 4:8]
5 [n]Eph. 2:8 [o][ch. 5:10; Rom. 8:18; 2 Cor. 4:17; Heb. 12:11]
6 [p]James 1:2; [ch. 4:12]
7 [q]James 1:3 [r]Job 23:10; Ps. 66:10; Prov. 17:3; Isa. 48:10 [s]1 Cor. 3:13 [t]Rom. 2:7, 10; 1 Cor. 4:5; [2 Thess. 1:7-12]
8 [u][1 John 4:20] [v][Heb. 11:27]; See John 20:29

rejoice with joy that is inexpressible and filled with glory, 9 obtaining [w]the outcome of your faith, the salvation of your souls.

10 Concerning this salvation, [x]the prophets who prophesied about the grace that was to be yours searched and inquired carefully, 11 inquiring [y]what person or time [z]the Spirit of Christ in them was indicating [a]when he predicted [b]the sufferings of Christ and the subsequent glories. 12 [c]It was revealed to them that [d]they were serving not themselves but you, in the things that have now been announced to you through those who preached the good news to you [e]by the Holy Spirit sent from heaven, [f]things into which angels long to look.

Called to Be Holy

13 Therefore, [g]preparing your minds for action,[1] and [h]being sober-minded, set your hope fully on the grace that will be brought to you at the revelation of Jesus Christ. 14 As obedient children, [i]do not be conformed to the passions [j]of your former ignorance, 15 but [k]as he who called you is holy, you also be holy [l]in all your conduct, 16 since it is written, [m]"You shall be holy, for I am holy." 17 And if you [n]call on him as Father who [o]judges [p]impartially according to each one's deeds, conduct yourselves [q]with fear throughout the time of your exile, 18 knowing that you [r]were ransomed from [s]the futile ways inherited from your forefathers, not with perishable things such as silver or gold, 19 but [t]with the precious blood of Christ, like that of [u]a lamb [v]without blemish or spot. 20 He was foreknown before the foundation of the world but [w]was made manifest [x]in the last times for the sake of you 21 [y]who through him are believers in God, [z]who raised him from the dead and [a]gave him glory, so that your faith and hope are in God.

22 Having purified your souls by your obedience to the truth for [b]a sincere brotherly love, [c]love one another earnestly from a pure heart, 23 [d]since you have been born again, [e]not of perishable seed but of imperishable, through [f]the living and abiding word of God; 24 for

[g]"All flesh is like grass
and all its glory like the flower of grass.

[1] Greek *girding up the loins of your mind*

9 [w] Rom. 6:22
10 [x] 2 Pet. 1:19; [Dan. 8:15; Matt. 13:17; Luke 10:24]
11 [y] Dan. 9:24-26 [z] Rom. 8:9; [2 Pet. 1:21]; See Acts 16:7 [a] See Matt. 26:24 [b] Isa. 52:13-53:12; Luke 24:26; Acts 3:18
12 [c] Dan. 12:4, 9, 13 [d] [Matt. 13:17; Heb. 11:39, 40] [e] Acts 2:2-4 [f] [Dan. 8:13; 12:5-7; Eph. 3:10]
13 [g] See Luke 12:35 [h] ch. 4:7; 5:8; 1 Thess. 5:6, 8; 2 Tim. 4:5
14 [i] ch. 4:2, 3; Rom. 12:2; Titus 3:3 [j] Acts 17:30
15 [k] 1 John 3:3; [2 Cor. 7:1; 1 Thess. 4:7; Heb. 12:14] [l] James 3:13
16 [m] Cited from Lev. 11:44
17 [n] Jer. 3:19; Mal. 1:6; 2 Cor. 6:18; [Matt. 6:9] [o] See Ps. 62:12 [p] See James 2:1 [q] ch. 3:15; 2 Cor. 7:1; [Rom. 11:20]
18 [r] [Ps. 49:8; 130:8; 1 Cor. 6:20; Titus 2:14; 2 Pet. 2:1] [s] See Eph. 4:17
19 [t] See Acts 20:28 [u] See John 1:29 [v] Heb. 9:14; [Ex. 12:5]
20 [w] See Rom. 16:26 [x] Heb. 1:2
21 [y] John 12:44 [z] [Rom. 10:9]; See Acts 2:24 [a] Acts 3:13; Heb. 2:9; [ch. 3:22]; See John 7:39
22 [b] Rom. 12:9; See Heb. 13:1 [c] 1 Tim. 1:5
23 [d] ver. 3; [John 3:3; James 1:18] [e] John 1:13 [f] Heb. 4:12
24 [g] James 1:10, 11; Cited from Isa. 40:6, 8

1:10–12 The gospel of grace in which Peter exults (vv. 3–9) is the fulfillment of the prophetic hope throughout the Old Testament. The gospel is not a new idea as Peter is writing; the redemption accomplished by Christ is the pinnacle of all preceding human history. The prophets wrote of "the grace that was to be yours" (v. 10). The Old Testament, too, is a message of grace. The whole Bible is the unfolding story of God's redemption of human sinners—a redemption even the angels of heaven marvel to behold (v. 12).

1:13–23 Peter now enters the more practical matters of obedience and endurance under hardship. And yet the grounding of the gospel is his ever-present offering of help in these matters. Believers are first commanded not to set their hope on their own efforts or their own strength but "fully on the grace" that will be completely and finally manifested when Christ returns (v. 13). We are granted grace here and now; and yet this grace will be publicly displayed before the whole world upon Christ's second coming.

The commands of verses 14–17 flow from "knowing that you were ransomed" (v. 18). And what precious value is this grace! The "precious blood of Christ, like that of a lamb" (v. 19) makes "silver or gold" (v. 18) seem like rubbish. We have been ransomed by the imperishable blood of Christ, which affords for us eternal life. And eternal life is just what it says it is: eternal! Therefore, the entire set of instructions to holiness and love in verses 13–22 is sourced in verse 23's "since you have been born again."

This is the rhythm of Christian living. Having been redeemed, we are freed to live a life of glad obedience. This is our true joy. Having been loved so well, our delight is to love in return. We are not loved because we obey; we obey because we are loved: "knowing that you were ransomed" (v. 18).

1:24–25 Peter quotes the prophet Isaiah's words about the eternally enduring quality of the word of God (Isa. 40:6, 8). Most of us have heard these words quoted with respect to the enduring dependability of all Scripture, and it is certainly true that the entire revelation of God's written Word will endure forever. But notice that Peter says

The grass withers,
and the flower falls,
25 [h]but the word of the Lord remains forever."

And this word [i]is the good news that was
preached to you.

A Living Stone and a Holy People

2 [j]So put away all malice and all deceit and
hypocrisy and envy and all slander. 2 [k]Like
newborn infants, long for the pure spiritual
[l]milk, that by it you may grow up into salvation— 3 if indeed you have [m]tasted that the
Lord is good.
4 As you come to him, a living stone [n]rejected
by men but in the sight of God chosen and
precious, 5 [o]you yourselves like living stones
are being built up as [p]a spiritual house, to be
[q]a holy priesthood, [r]to offer spiritual sacrifices
[s]acceptable to God through Jesus Christ. 6 For
it stands in Scripture:

[t]"Behold, I am laying in Zion a stone,
a cornerstone chosen and precious,
[u]and whoever believes in him will not be
put to shame."

7 So the honor is for you who [v]believe, but for
those who [v]do not believe,

[w]"The stone that the builders rejected
has become the cornerstone,"[1]

8 and

[x]"A stone of stumbling,
and a rock of offense."

They stumble because they disobey the word,
[y]as they were destined to do.
9 But you are [z]a chosen race, [a]a royal [b]priest-
hood, [c]a holy nation, [d]a people for his own
possession, that you may proclaim the excellencies of him who called you [e]out of darkness
into [f]his marvelous light. 10 [g]Once you were not

[1] Greek *the head of the corner*

the word that remains forever is "the good news that was preached to you" (1 Pet. 1:25). It is the gospel itself that, according to Peter, "remains forever" (v. 25).

The gospel of grace is not a passing fad, not trendy, not temporary. It is the abiding hope of the world. Even though "the grass withers, and the flower falls" (v. 24), the gospel never will. The gospel that Christians believe in has no expiration date!

2:1–3 When we taste and see "that the Lord is good" (cf. Ps. 34:8), we "put away" the bitter fruit of unrepentance. It has been said that Christ will not taste sweet to us until sin tastes bitter, and the reverse is true as well. Christ and sin cannot both look beautiful to us; as the appeal of one rises, the other falls. When we are savoring the Bread of Life (or, as symbolized in v. 2, "pure spiritual milk"), we lose our taste and appetite for the dusty things of earth. Even the law becomes a delight when we obey it in our freedom from its curse (Ps. 40:8; 119:77).

Once we have tasted the goodness of Christ and his gospel, we will long for more (1 Pet. 2:2), and it is this longing that fuels our continued growth. By "the pure spiritual milk" of the Word of God and especially the gospel (cf. 1:25), believers "grow up into salvation." Gospel grace not only converts us at a single point in time; it also changes us over time so that we become by practice what Christ has already made us by grace. This truth is similar to Paul's words in Titus 2:11–12, where we learn that it is the grace of God that trains us to renounce ungodliness and worldly passions—grace leads to godliness as we are drawn by Christ's love to honor him more and more in Christian maturity.

2:4–5 Once more we see the pattern of gospel obedience: believers "offer spiritual sacrifices acceptable to God *through Jesus Christ*" (v. 5). Our sacrificial lives of devotion to the Lord are not what makes us acceptable to God. Jesus himself made the ultimate sacrifice on our behalf; in light of his great work of redemption, we devote ourselves wholeheartedly to the Lord of mercy.

2:9–12 In recalling prophecies like Hosea 2:23, Peter is likely referring to God's gracious inclusion of the Gentiles in his saving purposes. It is important for the harmony of the church that both Gentiles and former Jews know that God has made a new people that transcends old divisions. "A chosen race" and "a holy nation" (1 Pet. 2:9) specifically includes the consecration of sinners into new creations, but it also corporately involves the consecration of aliens and strangers into true Israel (cf. Rom. 9:6; 11:25; 1 Cor. 12:13; Gal. 3:28; Col. 3:11).

25 [h][Matt. 24:35] [i]Isa. 40:9
Chapter 2
1 [j]Eph. 4:22, 25, 31; Col. 3:8
2 [k]See Matt. 18:3 [l]1 Cor. 3:2; Heb. 5:12, 13
3 [m]Ps. 34:8; Heb. 6:5
4 [n]ver. 6, 7
5 [o]Eph. 2:20-22; [1 Cor. 3:9] [p]Heb. 3:4, 6 [q]ver. 9 [r]Isa. 56:7; Mal. 1:11; Rom. 12:1; Heb. 13:15 [s]Rom. 15:16; Phil. 4:18
6 [t]Cited from Isa. 28:16 [u]Rom. 9:33; 10:11
7 [v][2 Cor. 2:16] [w]Cited from Ps. 118:22
8 [x]Rom. 9:33; Cited from Isa. 8:14 [y][Rom. 9:22; Jude 4]
9 [z]Deut. 10:15; Isa. 43:20 [a]Ex. 19:6; Rev. 1:6; 5:10 [b]Isa. 61:6; 66:21 [c]Deut. 7:6 [d]Ex. 19:5; Deut. 7:6; Isa. 43:21; Mal. 3:17 [e][Isa. 42:16]; See Acts 26:18 [f]Ps. 36:9
10 [g]Hos. 1:6, 9, 10; 2:23; Rom. 9:25, 26; 10:19

a people, but now you are God's people; once
you had not received mercy, but now you have
received mercy.
11 Beloved, I urge you [h]as sojourners and
exiles [i]to abstain from the passions of the flesh,
[j]which wage war against your soul. 12 [k]Keep
your conduct among the Gentiles honorable,
so that when they speak against you as evildoers, [l]they may see your good deeds and glorify
God on [m]the day of visitation.

Submission to Authority

13 [n]Be subject for the Lord's sake to every
human institution,[1] whether it be to the
emperor[2] as supreme, 14 or to governors as
sent by him [o]to punish those who do evil and
[p]to praise those who do good. 15 For this is the
will of God, [q]that by doing good you should
put to silence the ignorance of foolish people.
16 [r]Live as people who are free, not using your
freedom as a cover-up for evil, but [s]living as
servants[3] of God. 17 [t]Honor everyone. [u]Love the
brotherhood. [v]Fear God. Honor the emperor.
18 [w]Servants, be subject to your masters with
all respect, not only to the good and gentle
but also to the unjust. 19 For this is a gracious
thing, when, [x]mindful of God, one endures
sorrows while suffering unjustly. 20 For what
credit is it if, when you sin and are beaten
for it, you endure? But [y]if when you do good
and suffer for it you endure, this is a gracious
thing in the sight of God. 21 For [z]to this you
have been called, [y]because Christ also suffered
for you, [a]leaving you an example, so that you
might follow in his steps. 22 [b]He committed
no sin, neither was deceit found in his mouth.
23 [c]When he was reviled, he did not revile in
return; when he suffered, he did not threaten,
[d]but continued entrusting himself to him who
judges justly. 24 [e]He himself bore our sins in
his body on the tree, that we [f]might die to sin
and [g]live to righteousness. [h]By his wounds you
have been healed. 25 For [i]you were straying like
sheep, but have now returned to [j]the Shepherd
and Overseer of your souls.

[1] Or *every institution ordained for people* [2] Or *king*; also verse 17 [3] Greek *bondservants*

11 [h]See Lev. 25:23 [i]Rom. 13:14; Gal. 5:24 [j]James 4:1
12 [k][ch. 3:16; 2 Cor. 8:21; Phil. 2:15; Titus 2:8] [l]Matt. 5:16; 2 Cor. 9:13; Gal. 1:24 [m]Isa. 10:3; Luke 19:44
13 [n]Rom. 13:1; Titus 3:1
14 [o]Rom. 13:4 [p]Rom. 13:3
15 [q]ver. 12
16 [r]See James 1:25 [s]1 Cor. 7:22; [Rom. 6:22]
17 [t]Rom. 12:10; 13:7 [u]See Heb. 13:1 [v]Prov. 24:21
18 [w]Eph. 6:5; Col. 3:22; 1 Tim. 6:1; Titus 2:9
19 [x]ch. 3:14, 17; [ch. 4:16]
20 [y]ch. 3:17, 18; 4:13, 16
21 [z]ch. 3:9; See Acts 14:22 [y][See ver. 20 above] [a]See Matt. 11:29
22 [b]Isa. 53:9; [2 Cor. 5:21; Heb. 4:15; 1 John 3:5]
23 [c]ch. 3:9; Isa. 53:7; Heb. 12:3 [d]Luke 23:46
24 [e]Isa. 53:4, 11; Matt. 8:17; Heb. 9:28 [f]Rom. 6:2, 11; 7:4, 6; Col. 2:20; 3:3 [g]Rom. 6:13 [h]Isa. 53:5
25 [i]Isa. 53:6; [Ps. 119:176; Ezek. 34:6; Luke 15:4] [j]See John 10:11

Now that through the gospel the church is inaugurated and growing, Peter urges God's people to exhibit their newness and freeness (1 Pet. 2:11–12) as a witness to their identity in Christ. In verses 9–12, Peter reminds Christians that holiness means not just being set apart *from* something (sin and its worldly systems) but being set apart *for* something (God's glory). God's "mercy" (v. 10) leads to a certain kind of "conduct" (v. 12).

2:13–17 Freedom in Christ to worship him as Lord does not preclude submission to earthly authorities. Rather, having been set free in Christ to trust him body and soul, we are now free to trust that earthly authorities are only in place by his permission (see also Rom. 13:1–7). When we sinfully rebel against earthly authorities, we unwittingly testify that our hope is in earthly things. Ironically enough, however, when we cling to Christ's sovereign lordship and eternal riches, we are free to submit to civil authorities, demonstrating that our hearts are not tuned to the world and its passing riches (cf. Mark 12:17). In other passages the Bible will help believers consider how to deal with unlawful authorities, or those who may be lawfully opposed. Here, however, the focus is on honoring the government (even one that may be antagonistic to Christians) that maintains a society's order, thus becoming God's instrument for facilitating the testimony and progress of the gospel.

Peter believes that holding to the gospel will make us not problematic revolutionaries but humble and honorable citizens. This underscores yet another distinction between Christians and those who trust only in the things of this world and who consequently are always seeking power and privilege (Ps. 20:7).

2:19–25 Why is it a "gracious thing" to suffer unjustly (vv. 19–20)? Because, when we refuse to react to suffering in sinful ways, it makes us like Jesus and testifies to our confidence in him. Peter helpfully reminds us that God will not ask of us anything his Son was not willing to undergo himself. By his redemptive suffering, we know that any injustice we suffer in this world is merely temporary. Our vindication is sure, promised by our God, to whom vengeance belongs (v. 23; cf. Deut. 32:35; Rom. 12:19; Heb. 10:30).

We also must keep God's gracious purposes in mind when we suffer so that we do not despair over our suffering as if it were God's punishment. "He himself bore our

Wives and Husbands

3 Likewise, wives, [k]be subject to your own husbands, so that [l]even if some do not obey the word, [m]they may be won without a word by the conduct of their wives, 2 when they see your [n]respectful and pure conduct. 3 [o]Do not let your adorning be external—the braiding of hair and the putting on of gold jewelry, or the clothing you wear— 4 but let your adorning be [p]the hidden person of the heart with the imperishable beauty of a gentle and quiet spirit, which in God's sight is very precious. 5 For this is how the holy women who hoped in God used to adorn themselves, by submitting to their own husbands, 6 as Sarah obeyed Abraham, [q]calling him lord. And you are her children, if you do good and [r]do not fear anything that is frightening.

7 Likewise, [s]husbands, live with your wives in an understanding way, showing honor to the woman as the weaker [t]vessel, since they are heirs with you[1] of the grace of life, so that your prayers may not be hindered.

Suffering for Righteousness' Sake

8 Finally, all of you, [u]have unity of mind, sympathy, [v]brotherly love, [w]a tender heart, and [x]a humble mind. 9 [y]Do not repay evil for evil or reviling for reviling, but on the contrary, [z]bless, for [a]to this you were called, that you may obtain a blessing. 10 For

[b]"Whoever desires to love life
and see good days,
let him keep his tongue from evil
and his lips from speaking deceit;
11 let him turn away from evil and do good;
let him seek peace and pursue it.
12 For the eyes of the Lord are on the righteous,
and his ears are open to their prayer.
But the face of the Lord is against those
who do evil."

[1] Some manuscripts *since you are joint heirs*

sins in his body on the tree" (1 Pet. 2:24) so that we do not have to. The punishment for our sin was taken by Christ in his crucifixion. It is profound consolation in our suffering to know that it is not a sign of God's wrath on us. As Paul reminds us, "There is therefore now no condemnation for those who are in Christ Jesus" (Rom. 8:1). As we suffer the wrath of those who revile us for our faith, our hearts can remain calm, for God has satisfied his own wrath in his own Son's death.

3:1–7 Peter transitions from outlining the duties of gospel-believers in wider society to outlining the duties of gospel-believers in their immediate "society"—their home. As Christians ought to trust God enough not to sinfully bristle under legal authority, Christian wives ought to trust God enough not to sinfully bristle under their husbands' authority (vv. 1–2). Peter is essentially telling wives of unbelieving husbands that faith without works is dead (James 2:17), and that constant "God-talk" without abundant godly witness is likely to have a negative effect on the marriage (cf. Prov. 21:19; 25:24).

The admonition in 1 Peter 3:3–4 is not so much a prohibition of hairdos and jewelry as it is a prohibition of superficial vanity—a problem in Peter's day and in ours as well. Women are constantly being bombarded with worldly ideals relating to beauty and identity. But while our human drives tend to fixate on appearances, God's chief concern is the quality of our hearts (1 Sam. 16:7). The gospel works from the inside out, resulting in humility and modesty precisely because of the inner security of a heart captivated by Christ.

Of course, the humble submission commanded of wives is complemented by the exhortation to husbands to exercise humble and gentle authority (1 Pet. 3:7). A husband's leadership of his wife is meant to be a picture of Christ's sacrificial lordship over us, driven by selfless love, full of grace, and aimed squarely at another's benefit and joy. Christ himself, the eternal Lord of the universe, is "gentle and lowly in heart" (Matt. 11:29). Christian husbands are called to this same heart. The word used to describe the "honor" they are to show their wives (1 Pet. 3:7) is from the same root as the word used to describe the "honor" emperors are to be afforded (cf. 2:17).

3:8–17 Whatever befalls us, as long as we are looking to Christ as Lord we cannot finally be harmed. The good life is the hard life of trusting Christ. In the gospel we have been promised an unfathomable inheritance, ours freely for the taking, all because of the grace of God. This is "the hope that is in [us]" (v. 15), through which we can

Chapter 3
1 [k]See Gen. 3:16 [l]1 Cor. 7:16 [m]Matt. 18:15; 1 Cor. 9:19-22
2 [n]Titus 2:5
3 [o]1 Tim. 2:9; [Isa. 3:18-23]
4 [p]Rom. 2:29; [Rom. 7:22; 2 Cor. 4:16; Eph. 3:16]
6 [q]Gen. 18:12 [r]Prov. 3:25
7 [s]Eph. 5:25; Col. 3:19 [t]See 1 Thess. 4:4
8 [u]See Rom. 12:16 [v]See Heb. 13:1 [w]Eph. 4:32 [x]See Eph. 4:2
9 [y]ch. 2:23; See Rom. 12:17 [z]Luke 6:28; Rom. 12:14; 1 Cor. 4:12 [a]ch. 2:21
10 [b]Cited from Ps. 34:12-16

13 Now [c]who is there to harm you if you are
zealous for what is good? 14 [d]But even if you
should suffer for righteousness' sake, you
will be blessed. [e]Have no fear of them, [f]nor be
troubled, 15 but [g]in your hearts honor Christ
the Lord as holy, [h]always being prepared to
make a defense to anyone who asks you for
a reason for the hope that is in you; yet do it
with gentleness and [i]respect, 16 [j]having a good
conscience, so that, [k]when you are slandered,
those who revile your good behavior in Christ
may be put to shame. 17 For [l]it is better to suffer for doing good, if that should be God's
will, than for doing evil.
18 For Christ also [m]suffered[1] [n]once for sins,
the righteous for the unrighteous, [o]that he
might bring us to God, being put to death
[p]in the flesh but made alive [q]in the spirit,
19 in which[2] he went and [q]proclaimed[3] to the
spirits in prison, 20 because[4] they formerly
did not obey, [r]when God's patience waited in
the days of Noah, [s]while the ark was being
prepared, in which a few, that is, [t]eight persons, were brought safely through water.
21 Baptism, which corresponds to this, [u]now
saves you, not as a removal of dirt from the
body but [v]as an appeal to God for a good
conscience, [w]through the resurrection of
Jesus Christ, 22 who has gone into heaven and
[x]is at the right hand of God, [y]with angels,
authorities, and powers having been subjected to him.

[1] Some manuscripts *died* [2] Or *the Spirit, in whom* [3] Or *preached* [4] Or *when*

13 [c][Prov. 16:7]
14 [d]ch. 2:19, 20; 4:14, 16; Matt. 5:10 [e]Isa. 8:12, 13; [ver. 6; Matt. 10:28] [f]John 14:1, 27
15 [g][Isa. 29:23; Matt. 6:9] [h]Col. 4:6; [2 Tim. 2:25] [i]See ch. 1:17
16 [j]Heb. 13:18 [k]ch. 2:12
17 [l]ch. 2:20; [ch. 4:15, 16]
18 [m]ch. 2:21; 4:1; See Rom. 4:25 [n]Heb. 9:26, 28 [o]Rom. 5:2 [p]ch. 4:1; Col. 1:22; [2 Cor. 13:4] [q]ch. 4:6
19 [q][See ver. 18 above]
20 [r]Gen. 6:3, 5, 13, 14 [s]Heb. 11:7 [t]Gen. 7:1, 7, 23; 8:18; 2 Pet. 2:5
21 [u]Mark 16:16; Acts 16:33; Rom. 6:3-6; Titus 3:5 [v][Rom. 10:10] [w]ch. 1:3
22 [x]Acts 2:33, 34; Rom. 8:34; Eph. 1:20; Col. 3:1; Heb. 1:3 [y]Rom. 8:38; 1 Cor. 15:24; Eph. 1:21

quietly endure all things. We await an eternal glory that will make the hardships of this life, though genuinely painful, ultimately have the significance of a scratch on the penny of a millionaire (Rom. 8:18; 2 Cor. 4:16–18). Our calling now is to "honor Christ the Lord as holy" in our hearts (1 Pet. 3:15), knowing that when eternity is secured by this commitment, all other concerns become slight in comparison.

3:18 Here is one of the richest, clearest, and briefest New Testament summaries of the work of Christ. Theologians describe the heart of the gospel as *penal substitutionary atonement*. Jesus paid the penalty for sins (*penal*) as a substitute in our place (*substitutionary*) to undo the effects of our sin and restore us to God (*atonement*, literally "at-one-ment"). This is precisely what we find in this verse: Christ "suffered once for sins [penal], the righteous for the unrighteous [substitutionary], that he might bring us to God [atonement]."

As beautiful as are these gospel truths, the work of Christ accomplished even more. For example, the Devil and his demons are once and for all disarmed. The caring and righteous work of Christ is also an example for us to follow, as Peter himself asserts (2:21). But penal substitution is the fundamental heart of the gospel. The other benefits of Christ's work all flow from this.

Because of the work of Christ proclaimed in the gospel of grace, we are restored to God. The wreckage we have introduced into our lives through sin and failure and error is canceled. All is forgiven, and one day we will be with Christ in the new earth, in perfect joy.

3:20–22 It is not the physical cleansing of water on the body in baptism that "saves," but the appeal in faith to God for the cleansing of conscience. We are saved by grace received through faith; our salvation is not the result of works (Eph. 2:8–9).

Baptism is a tangible sign of the grace that brings us through the spiritual perils of this life, just as Noah's family was brought through water to be saved by God's mercy (1 Pet. 3:20–21). God delights to give this sign to those in his church who put their faith in the death and resurrection of Jesus as the means of washing away sins and purifying believers for God. When a church administers baptism, it indicates God's pledge that the promises of grace secured by the risen Lord will apply when the condition of faith is met; the act does not accomplish salvation but rather indicates what God accomplishes through faith.

For the believers in Peter's time, the significance of this pledge was the knowledge that they were made eternally secure by Christ's work on their behalf. Faith linked them to the powerful working of Christ at God's right hand, regardless of the trials and difficulties they faced in the world (v. 22). These same assurances secured by faith are indicated by our baptisms today.

Stewards of God's Grace

4 Since therefore [z]Christ suffered in the
flesh,[1] [a]arm yourselves with the same way
of thinking, for [b]whoever has suffered in the
flesh [c]has ceased from sin, 2 [d]so as to live for
[e]the rest of the time in the flesh [f]no longer
for human passions but [g]for the will of God.
3 For the time that is past [h]suffices [i]for doing
what the Gentiles want to do, living in sensuality, passions, drunkenness, orgies, drinking
parties, and lawless idolatry. 4 With respect to
this they are surprised when you do not join
them in the same flood of [j]debauchery, and
[k]they malign you; 5 but they will give account
to him who is ready [l]to judge the living and
the dead. 6 For this is why [m]the gospel was
preached even to those who are dead, that
though judged in the flesh the way people are,
they might live in the spirit the way God does.
7 [n]The end of all things is at hand; therefore
[o]be self-controlled and sober-minded [p]for the
sake of your prayers. 8 Above all, keep loving
one another earnestly, since [q]love covers a
multitude of sins. 9 [r]Show hospitality to one
another without grumbling. 10 [s]As each has
received a gift, use it to serve one another, [t]as
good stewards of God's varied grace: 11 whoever speaks, as one who speaks [u]oracles of
God; whoever serves, as one who serves [v]by
the strength that God supplies—in order
that in everything [w]God may be glorified
through Jesus Christ. [x]To him belong glory
and [y]dominion forever and ever. Amen.

Suffering as a Christian

12 Beloved, do not be surprised at [z]the fiery
trial when it comes upon you to test you, as
though something strange were happening
to you. 13 But rejoice [a]insofar as you share
Christ's sufferings, that you may also rejoice
and be glad [b]when his glory is revealed. 14 [c]If
you are insulted [d]for the name of Christ, you
are blessed, because the Spirit of glory[2] and
of God rests upon you. 15 But [e]let none of you
suffer as a murderer or a thief or an evildoer
or [f]as a meddler. 16 Yet [e]if anyone suffers as a
[g]Christian, let him not be ashamed, but let
him glorify God [d]in that name. 17 For it is time
for judgment [h]to begin at the household of
God; and [i]if it begins with us, what will be the
outcome for those who [j]do not obey the gospel
of God? 18 And

[1] Some manuscripts add *for us*; some *for you* [2] Some manuscripts insert *and of power*

4:1–6 To suffer for belief in God's will is to follow in the footsteps of the sufferings of Christ. Peter wants believers to "arm" themselves (v. 1) with this reality, as they focus on "the will of God" rather than on "human passions." While such suffering may not lead to a ceasing from every sin, godly priorities establish a wholesome pattern of life (vv. 1–2).

Note that Peter speaks not simply of making better decisions but of *living for* something (v. 2). Only in the gospel of grace are we given the power to surrender all our rights and live for Christ (cf. Phil. 3:7–9). Peter also reminds those who suffer that to die having lived a life of holiness is no waste. God will judge unrepentant persecutors of his people and will vindicate his persecuted saints (1 Pet. 4:5–6).

4:8 The work of a Christian is simply this: love. This is the fulfillment of all the law (Rom. 13:8–10). Yet love is hard. How do we love others? And how do we do so "earnestly"? Only the gospel generates such inside-out affection and service of others, for Jesus Christ has loved us earnestly. As our hearts are armed by the love of Christ, we are changed. We delight to love others (cf. Eph. 4:32–5:2).

4:17–19 To "obey the gospel of God" is to set one's mind and heart on the truth of the finished work of Christ for the forgiveness of sins and eternal life. What many Christians today mean by "gospel-centeredness" is what Peter here means by "obeying the gospel." We are spurred on to worship God in holy living not by human-centered motivations but in grateful response to the good news that was given to us and that is sanctifying us. For this reason, Paul writes in Philippians 3:12, "Not that I have already obtained this or am already perfect, but I press on to make it my own, because Christ Jesus has made me his own." Our knowledge of our identity in Christ drives the way we live (cf. 1 Pet. 4:19).

Sadly, those who do not have this identity face God's judgment without the grace of Christ's righteousness to cover them (v. 18); it is a destiny that believers avoid since their judgment was carried out on Christ at the cross. This destiny is worked

Chapter 4
1 [z]ch. 3:18 [a][Eph. 6:13] [b]Rom. 6:2, 7; Gal. 5:24; Col. 3:3, 5 [c][2 Pet. 2:14]
2 [d]Rom. 6:14; 14:7; 2 Cor. 5:15 [e]ch. 1:14 [f]Titus 2:12; 1 John 2:16 [g]Rom. 6:11
3 [h]Ezek. 44:6; 45:9; Acts 17:30 [i]Eph. 4:17-19; 1 Thess. 4:5; [1 Cor. 12:2]
4 [j]See Eph. 5:18 [k]ch. 2:12; 3:16
5 [l][James 5:9]; See Acts 10:42
6 [m]ch. 3:19
7 [n]See James 5:8 [o]See ch. 1:13 [p]Matt. 26:41; Luke 21:36
8 [q][1 Cor. 13:5, 6]; See James 5:20
9 [r]Heb. 13:2; [1 Tim. 3:2; Titus 1:8]
10 [s]Rom. 12:6, 7; 1 Cor. 4:7; [Matt. 25:15] [t]Luke 12:42; 1 Cor. 4:1, 2; Titus 1:7
11 [u]Acts 7:38; Rom. 3:2; Heb. 5:12 [v]Rom. 12:3 [w]1 Cor. 10:31 [x]See Rom. 11:36 [y]ch. 5:11; Jude 25; Rev. 1:6; 5:13
12 [z]ch. 1:7
13 [a]Phil. 3:10, 11; See Acts 5:41 [b][ch. 1:5-7; 5:1; Rom. 8:17, 18; Jude 24]
14 [c]Ps. 89:51; Matt. 5:11 [d]John 15:21; [Heb. 11:26]
15 [e]ch. 2:19, 20; 3:14, 17 [f]1 Thess. 4:11; 2 Thess. 3:11; 1 Tim. 5:13
16 [e][See ver. 15 above] [g]See Acts 26:28 [d][See ver. 14 above]
17 [h]Jer. 25:29; Ezek. 9:6; Amos 3:2; Rom. 2:9 [i][Luke 23:31] [j][2 Thess. 1:8]

[k]"If the righteous is scarcely saved,
what will become of the ungodly and
the sinner?"[1]

19 Therefore let those who suffer according
to God's will [l]entrust their souls to a faithful
Creator while doing good.

Shepherd the Flock of God

5 So I exhort the elders among you, [m]as a fellow elder and [n]a witness of the sufferings
of Christ, as well as a partaker in the glory
that is going to be revealed: 2 [o]shepherd the
flock of God that is among you, exercising
oversight,[2] [p]not under compulsion, but willingly, as God would have you;[3] [q]not for shameful gain, but eagerly; 3 not [r]domineering over
those in your charge, but [s]being examples
to the flock. 4 And when [t]the chief Shepherd
appears, you will receive the [u]unfading [v]crown
of glory. 5 Likewise, you who are younger, be
subject to the elders. [w]Clothe yourselves, all
of you, with humility toward one another,
for [x]"God opposes the proud but gives grace
to the humble."

6 [x]Humble yourselves, therefore, under the
mighty hand of God so that at the proper
time he may exalt you, 7 [y]casting all your anxieties on him, because [z]he cares for you. 8 [a]Be
sober-minded; [b]be watchful. Your [c]adversary
the devil [d]prowls around [e]like a roaring lion,
seeking someone to devour. 9 [f]Resist him,
[g]firm in your faith, knowing that [h]the same
kinds of suffering are being experienced by
your brotherhood throughout the world.
10 And [i]after you have suffered a little while,
the God of all grace, [j]who has called you
to his [k]eternal glory in Christ, will himself
[l]restore, [m]confirm, strengthen, and establish

[1] Greek *where will the ungodly and sinner appear?* [2] Some manuscripts omit *exercising oversight* [3] Some manuscripts omit *as God would have you*

18 [k]Prov. 11:31
19 [l]Ps. 31:5; Luke 23:46; [Ps. 10:14; 2 Tim. 1:12]
Chapter 5
1 [m][2 John 1; 3 John 1] [n]See Luke 24:48
2 [o][Jude 12]; See John 21:16 [p][Philem. 14] [q]1 Tim. 3:8; Titus 1:7
3 [r]Ezek. 34:4; Matt. 20:25; Mark 10:42; 2 Cor. 1:24 [s]Phil. 3:17; 2 Thess. 3:9; 1 Tim. 4:12; Titus 2:7
4 [t]Heb. 13:20 [u][ch. 1:4] [v]1 Cor. 9:25; See James 1:12
5 [w][Matt. 20:26, 27; John 13:4, 5, 14] [x]See James 4:6, 10
6 [x][See ver. 5 above]
7 [y][Ps. 37:5; 55:22]; See Matt. 6:25 [z]Ps. 40:17
8 [a]See ch. 1:13 [b]See Matt. 24:42 [c]Eph. 4:27; 6:11; Rev. 12:9, 12; [Job 1:9-12; Luke 22:31; 2 Cor. 2:11] [d]Job 1:7; 2:2 [e][Ps. 22:21]
9 [f]James 4:7 [g]Col. 2:5 [h]Acts 14:22; 1 Thess. 3:3; 2 Tim. 3:12
10 [i]ch. 1:6 [j]1 Cor. 1:9; 1 Thess. 2:12; 1 Tim. 6:12 [k]2 Tim. 2:10 [l]Heb. 13:21 [m]Luke 22:32; Rom. 16:25

out practically today, as Peter says, by doing God's will and entrusting our souls to our faithful Creator (v. 19).

5:1–4 In 4:17, Peter may have been recalling Ezekiel 9 (esp. Ezek. 9:6) in saying that judgment will begin at the household of God, and now in 1 Peter 5 he surmises that this judgment will start with the leaders of the household. Peter's "gospel posture" in this passage is a beautiful comfort. He places the exhortations to pastoral holiness and love between two key proclamations regarding our identity and our reward.

First, in verse 1 Peter identifies himself as a witness of Christ's sufferings. Of course, Peter notoriously botched his witness to Christ's sufferings (Matt. 26:69–75). Yet he connects this sullied witness with the affirmation of his being a "fellow elder" and one who will partake in heavenly glory with other elders (1 Pet. 5:1). His witness to Christ gives him credentials of authority to instruct others but, at the same moment, does not separate him from the humanity of other church leaders that require the crucifixion Peter witnessed (v. 1). Thus, right with this authoritative exhortation to live for the gospel is Peter's acknowledgment that he *needs* it. The gospel is for sinners like Peter. Peter makes no admonition without acknowledging his own vulnerabilities.

After these pastoral exhortations, Peter reminds the elders of their reward (v. 4). The chief Shepherd will provide a crown of glory to those who serve in his own pattern of selfless leadership for his flock. Herein lies the power to obey: looking back to Jesus' sacrifice that justifies us and looking forward to Jesus' return that will glorify us. All is taken care of. And all is of grace, enabling us to live and lead with selfless confidence, for him and for his people.

5:6–11 Peter connects every command to a gospel promise. "Humble yourselves" because God will exalt you (v. 6). "[Cast] all your anxieties on him, because he cares for you" (v. 7). "Be sober-minded" and "watchful," because you have an Enemy who is out to get you (which presupposes that *we* are on the Lord's side; v. 8). "Resist" the Devil and stand "firm," because you are not alone: your Christian brothers and sisters throughout the world share that struggle with you (v. 9). Thus, the gospel becomes the motivation and compulsion for faithful living.

We are not left to wonder about the logic of gospel holiness. God is near to us, by his own initiative of grace. We live in light of this glorious reality. Peter thus concludes with a promise that Jesus himself will "restore, confirm, strengthen, and establish" us (v. 10). What a comfort to know we do not have an absentee Father, a distant Savior, or a "hands off" Spirit! The Lord who has eternal dominion over all things (v. 11) has

you. 11 [n]To him be the dominion forever and ever. Amen.

Final Greetings

12 By [o]Silvanus, a faithful brother as I regard
him, [p]I have written briefly to you, exhorting
and declaring that this is [q]the true grace of
God. [r]Stand firm in it. 13 She who is at Babylon,
who is likewise chosen, sends you greetings,
and so does [s]Mark, my son. 14 [t]Greet one
another with the kiss of love.

[u]Peace to all of you who are in Christ.

restored us and secured us to himself. We endure suffering and confidently live for him because he has provided such overwhelming, sustaining, eternal, and compelling grace for us.

11 [n]See ch. 4:11
12 [o]Acts 15:22; 2 Cor. 1:19; 1 Thess. 1:1; 2 Thess. 1:1 [p][Heb. 13:22] [q]See Acts 11:23 [r]See 1 Cor. 15:1 **13** [s]See Acts 12:12 **14** [t]See Rom. 16:16 [u]Eph. 6:23

Introduction to
2 Peter

Author, Date, and Recipients

Peter identifies himself as an "apostle of Jesus Christ" (1:1). He specifically mentions that he was an eyewitness of the transfiguration (1:16–18; see Matt. 17:1–8). Peter probably wrote this letter from prison in Rome (see 2 Pet. 1:12–15) not too long before his death by execution, sometime during A.D. 64–67. It is difficult to identify with certainty the churches Peter addresses.

The Gospel in 2 Peter

In his first letter, the apostle Peter writes largely about the relationship between holiness and hardship. In this letter, a follow-up to the previous one (3:1), he writes about the relationship between holiness and heresy—a "hardship" in its own right in the early church as well as in the church today. Similar to Paul in his letter to the Galatians, or Jude (who likely used 2 Peter as a reference point), Peter provides an abundant and unequivocal warning to believers about those who will infiltrate the church and teach seductive blasphemy. He cautions that some will even use the words of Scripture to support their perverted doctrines and lives (3:16).

Peter urges resistance to such distortions of grace. He reminds us about the importance of accurate knowledge of the truth (1:2, 3, 5–6, 8, 12; 2:2, 20; 3:18). And he shows us once more, as throughout the New Testament, that the faithfulness needed to combat such wickedness requires: an experience of God's powerful grace in the gospel (1:1–20); a diligence in repentant living (1:5–8; 3:14); a sober-minded awareness of and resistance to heresy (2:1–22; 3:1–4, 15–17); and a hopeful expectation of God's patience and faithfulness (3:8–18).

Outline

I. Initial Greeting (1:1–2)

II. God's Grace in Christ Is the Source of Godly Living (1:3–11)

III. Peter's Reminder to the Churches (1:12–21)

IV. Evaluation of False Teachers (2:1–22)

V. The Day of the Lord Will Surely Come (3:1–13)

VI. Concluding Encouragements (3:14–18)

The Second Letter of Peter

2 Peter

Greeting

1 Simeon[1] Peter, a servant[2] and apostle of
Jesus Christ,
To those who have obtained [a]a faith of equal
standing with ours [b]by the righteousness of
our [c]God and Savior Jesus Christ:
2 [d]May grace and peace be multiplied to you
[e]in the knowledge of God and of Jesus our Lord.

Confirm Your Calling and Election

3 His divine power has granted to us all
things that pertain to life and godliness,
through the knowledge of him [f]who called
us to[3] his own glory and excellence,[4] 4 by
which he has granted to us his precious and
very great promises, so that through them you
may become [g]partakers of the divine nature,

[1] Some manuscripts *Simon* [2] Or *slave* (for the contextual rendering of the Greek word *doulos*, see Preface) [3] Or *by* [4] Or *virtue*

1:1 Peter addresses his letter "to those who have obtained a faith of equal standing with ours by the righteousness of our God and Savior Jesus Christ," thus establishing the foundation of the gospel from which all else he writes will flow. This dynamic is reiterated in verses 3–5, in which the "effort" urged in verse 5 is "for the reason(s)" stated in verses 3–4.

The great message of the Bible is that God has himself provided a standing for sinners not through their own self-generated efforts but through a righteousness (a right standing) granted freely in grace, achieved by Christ on our behalf. "The righteousness of our God" here and in similar phrasing in the writings of Paul is best understood as the descriptor for God maintaining his own righteousness by providing Jesus to take the just penalty for the sin of those who place their faith in him.

1:2 Growing in grace (and peace, along with the other fruits of the Spirit) results from growing in our knowledge of Christ. As John writes, "For from his fullness we have all received, grace upon grace" (John 1:16). On this principle of growth in the gospel, Paul writes, "And we all, with unveiled face, beholding the glory of the Lord, are being transformed into the same image from one degree of glory to another" (2 Cor. 3:18). An increase in the apprehension of God's glory (cf. 2 Pet. 1:16) in Christ is how Christians change.

This, then, is how Peter begins his second letter, reminding his readers that grace is multiplied (made apparent and applicable in increasing dimensions of our lives) through the knowledge of Christ.

1:3–4 God has left nothing to chance. He knew he was calling messy sinners to himself, and so he has "granted to us all things that pertain to life and godliness" by the "divine power" that comes through "the knowledge of" (i.e., an informed relationship with) Jesus our Lord (v. 3). In Christ we have everything we need to live a life that honors God.

But how? How do we live such a life, given our proclivity toward sin and failure and the tendency of our hearts to wander? Peter tells us it is through "his precious and very great promises" that believers become "partakers of the divine nature" (v. 4). As we receive, believe, and are changed by the lavish promises of God, supremely the promise of the gospel, we are restored to the status of the sanctified and god-glorifying men and women we were created to be. This does not mean we become deity; but it does mean we share in Christ's nature derivatively, in that we become the "imagers of God" that we (unlike every other created thing) were created to be.

As partakers in the divine nature, we are freed from the bondage of sin and are now able to glorify our Lord in all that pertains to life and godliness.

Chapter 1
1 [a]Rom. 1:12; 2 Cor. 4:13; Titus 1:4 [b]Rom. 3:21-26 [c]Titus 2:13
2 [d]1 Pet. 1:2; Jude 2 [e]ver. 3, 8; ch. 2:20; [John 17:3; Phil. 3:8]
3 [f][1 Thess. 2:12; 2 Thess. 2:14; 2 Tim. 1:9; 1 Pet. 5:10]
4 [g][Eph. 4:24; Heb. 12:10; 1 John 3:2]

[h]having escaped from the corruption that is
in the world because of sinful desire. 5 For
this very reason, make every effort to supplement your faith [i]with virtue,[1] and virtue [j]with
knowledge, 6 and knowledge with self-control,
and self-control [k]with steadfastness, and steadfastness with godliness, 7 and godliness [l]with
brotherly affection, and brotherly affection
[m]with love. 8 For if these qualities[2] are yours
and are increasing, they keep you from being
ineffective or [n]unfruitful in the knowledge
of our Lord Jesus Christ. 9 For whoever lacks
these qualities is so nearsighted that he [o]is
blind, having forgotten that he was [p]cleansed
from his former sins. 10 Therefore, brothers,[3] be
all the more diligent to confirm your calling
and [q]election, for if you practice these qualities
[r]you will never fall. 11 For in this way there will
be richly provided for you [s]an entrance into
the eternal kingdom of our Lord and Savior
Jesus Christ.
12 Therefore I intend [t]always to remind you
of these qualities, though you know them and
are established in [u]the truth that you have.
13 I think it right, as long as I am in this [v]body,[4]
[w]to stir you up by way of reminder, 14 [x]since
I know that the putting off of my body will be
soon, [y]as our Lord Jesus Christ made clear to
me. 15 And I will make every effort so that after
my departure you may be able at any time to
recall these things.

Christ's Glory and the Prophetic Word

16 For we did not follow [z]cleverly devised
[a]myths when we made known to you [b]the
power and [c]coming of our Lord Jesus Christ,
but [d]we were eyewitnesses of his majesty. 17 For
when he received honor and glory from God
the Father, and the voice was borne to him by
the Majestic Glory, [e]"This is my beloved Son,[5]
with whom I am well pleased," 18 we ourselves
heard this very voice borne from heaven, for
we were with him on [f]the holy mountain.
19 And [g]we have the prophetic word more
fully confirmed, to which you will do well to
pay attention [h]as to a lamp shining in a dark
place, until [i]the day [j]dawns and the morning
star rises in your hearts, 20 knowing this first
of all, that no prophecy of Scripture comes
from someone's own interpretation. 21 For

[1] Or *excellence*; twice in this verse [2] Greek *these things*; also verses 9, 10, 12 [3] Or *brothers and sisters*. The plural Greek word *adelphoi* (translated "brothers") refers to siblings in a family. In New Testament usage, depending on the context, *adelphoi* may refer either to men or to both men and women who are siblings (brothers and sisters) in God's family, the church [4] Greek *tent*; also verse 14 [5] Or *my Son, my* (or *the*) *Beloved*

4 [h]ch. 2:18, 20
5 [i]Phil. 4:8 [j]1 Pet. 3:7
6 [k]See Heb. 10:36; James 1:3
7 [l]See Heb. 13:1 [m]1 Cor. 13; 1 John 4:16
8 [n]See John 15:2; Titus 3:14
9 [o]Job 5:14; 12:25; Isa. 59:10; Zeph. 1:17; [1 John 2:9-11] [p]Eph. 5:26; Titus 2:14; Heb. 9:14; 1 John 1:7; Rev. 7:14
10 [q]1 Thess. 1:4 [r][ch. 3:17; 1 John 2:10]
11 [s]Col. 1:13; [Acts 14:22]
12 [t]Jude 5; [Rom. 15:14, 15; Phil. 3:1; 1 John 2:21] [u]2 John 2
13 [v]2 Cor. 5:1, 4 [w]ch. 3:1
14 [x][Deut. 4:21, 22; 31:14; 2 Tim. 4:6] [y]John 21:18, 19
16 [z]See 1 Cor. 1:17 [a]See 1 Tim. 1:4 [b]1 Cor. 2:4 [c]See 1 Thess. 2:19 [d]Matt. 17:1, 2, 6; Mark 9:2; Luke 9:28, 29; John 1:14
17 [e]Matt. 17:5; Mark 9:7; Luke 9:35; [Matt. 3:17]
18 [f][Ex. 3:5; Josh. 5:15]
19 [g]See 1 Pet. 1:10 [h]Ps. 119:105; John 5:35 [i]Rev. 2:28; 22:16; [Mal. 4:2] [j]2 Cor. 4:6

1:5–10 Peter urges believers to "make every effort" (v. 5) to corroborate their faith with behavior consistent with the "qualities" (vv. 8–9) of those who are being sanctified by the Spirit. The gospel is not opposed to *effort* but to *earning*. Paul, too, could put grace and hard work side by side (1 Cor. 15:10). In contrast to the passions akin to animal instinct that Peter will condemn in the next chapter (2 Pet. 2:12), he urges believers to live in accordance with their transformed hearts. What we do should flow from who we are.

Jesus himself talked about defilement coming from the inside to the outside, instead of the other way around (Mark 7:14–15), and he narrowed down the source of murder and adultery to heart passions (Matt. 5:21–30). That is, he highlighted the roles of desire and objects of idolatrous worship in causing sin. He knew that unless a person's heart is changed, his or her behavior cannot really honor God (see his words to the Pharisees in Matt. 23:27). This is the difficult and deceptive reality that Peter will address in 2 Peter 2:20–22. Perhaps Peter is recalling a lesson learned as he walked side by side with Jesus for so long: a good tree produces good fruit (Matt. 7:17).

Note how Peter concludes his list of virtues: "whoever lacks these qualities" has "forgotten that he was cleansed from his former sins" (2 Pet. 1:9). The cultivation of godly virtue comes, according to Peter, as we *remember* the gospel cleansing of our sins. The gospel is not something we move past; it is something we remember and enjoy our whole lives long. It is grace that changes us from the inside out.

1:16–21 Peter highlights the power inherent in the Word of God (cf. Rom. 1:16; Eph. 3:7; 1 Thess. 1:5). The grace of God that justifies sinners through their faith is a "capital-S" Spiritual force embedded in the Word of God (2 Pet. 1:21). Peter speaks of the voice "borne to him by the Majestic Glory" (v. 17), consistent with Paul's teaching in Romans 10:17 that "faith comes from hearing, and hearing through the word of Christ." The prophetic word is a light shining "in a dark place" (2 Pet. 2:19) that will become like a sunrise over the world at the dawn of the age to come (cf. Mal. 4:2; Rev. 21:23; 22:16).

[k]no prophecy was ever produced by the will
of man, but men spoke from God [l]as they were
carried along by the Holy Spirit.

False Prophets and Teachers

2 But [m]false prophets also arose among the
people, [n]just as there will be false teachers among you, who will [o]secretly bring in
destructive heresies, even denying the Master
[p]who bought them, bringing upon themselves
swift destruction. 2 And many will follow their
sensuality, and because of them the way of
truth [q]will be blasphemed. 3 And [r]in their
greed they will exploit you [s]with false words.
[t]Their condemnation from long ago is not
idle, and their destruction is not asleep.
4 For if God did not spare [u]angels when they
sinned, but [v]cast them into hell[1] and committed them to chains[2] of gloomy darkness
[w]to be kept until the judgment; 5 if he did
not spare the ancient world, but [x]preserved
Noah, a herald of righteousness, with seven
others, when he brought [y]a flood upon the
world of the ungodly; 6 if by [z]turning the cities of Sodom and Gomorrah to ashes he condemned them to extinction, [a]making them an
example of [b]what is going to happen to the
ungodly;[3] 7 and [c]if he rescued righteous Lot,
greatly distressed by the sensual conduct of
the wicked 8 (for as that righteous man lived
among them day after day, [d]he was tormenting
his righteous soul over their lawless deeds that
he saw and heard); 9 then [e]the Lord knows how
to rescue the godly from trials,[4] and to keep
the unrighteous under punishment until the
day of judgment, 10 and especially [f]those who
indulge[5] in the lust of defiling passion and
[g]despise authority.
Bold and willful, they do not tremble [g]as they
blaspheme the glorious ones, 11 [h]whereas angels,
though greater in might and power, do not pronounce a blasphemous judgment against them
before the Lord. 12 [i]But these, like irrational animals, [j]creatures of instinct, born to be caught
and destroyed, blaspheming about matters of
which they are ignorant, will also be destroyed
in their destruction, 13 suffering wrong as [k]the
wage for their wrongdoing. They count it pleasure [l]to revel in the daytime. They are blots
and blemishes, reveling in their deceptions,[6]
while [m]they feast with you. 14 They have eyes
full of adultery, [n]insatiable for sin. They entice
unsteady souls. They have hearts [o]trained in
greed. [p]Accursed children! 15 Forsaking the
right way, [q]they have gone astray. They have
followed [r]the way of Balaam, the son of Beor,
who loved [s]gain from wrongdoing, 16 but was
rebuked for his own transgression; [t]a speechless donkey spoke with human voice and
restrained the prophet's madness.
17 [u]These are waterless springs and mists
driven by a storm. [v]For them the gloom of utter
darkness has been reserved. 18 For, [w]speaking
loud boasts of folly, they entice by sensual

[1] Greek *Tartarus* [2] Some manuscripts *pits* [3] Some manuscripts *an example to those who were to be ungodly* [4] Or *temptations* [5] Greek *who go after the flesh* [6] Some manuscripts *love feasts*

2:1–10 Notice the contrast between the gospel's authoritative power (1:16–20) and heresy's serpentine seduction. In these words about false teaching infiltrating the church, Peter makes two promises and therein one great encouragement.

The first promise is that God will not let the guilty go unpunished. What may seem like leniency or passivity about blasphemy and injustice is in fact sovereign patience (cf. 3:9; Rom. 2:4). But Peter minces no words: "Their condemnation from long ago is not idle, and their destruction is not asleep" (2 Pet. 2:3). The second promise is like the first: God is just. And so, just as his justice will result in condemnation for the wicked, his justice will also result in "rescue" (v. 9) for those whose sins were punished at the cross of Christ. These two promises—God will punish the wicked, and God will rescue the godly—are an encouragement to live holy, hopeful lives even amid trials and false accusations (v. 3; cf. Col. 2:4), and to remain firm in the faith when the seductive winds of heresy begin to blow.

2:17–22 This is a difficult passage, not least because it appears to imply the falling away of those who have been saved. But the careful reader will note that, as in Hebrews 6:4–9, whatever knowledge of the Lord (2 Pet. 2:20) those in question have obtained has not freed them from their enslavement to corruption (v. 19). Earlier Peter has called them "creatures of instinct," born "to be destroyed," speaking about things of which they are actually "ignorant" (v. 12). Rather than being transformed

21 [k]2 Tim. 3:16 [l]1 Pet. 1:11; [2 Sam. 23:2; Luke 1:70; Acts 1:16; 3:18]

Chapter 2

1 [m]Deut. 13:1; See Matt. 7:15 [n]Acts 20:30; 2 Cor. 11:13; 1 Tim. 4:1; [Matt. 24:11] [o]Jude 4; [Matt. 10:33; Gal. 2:4] [p]1 Cor. 6:20; 7:23; Gal. 3:13; 4:5; Rev. 5:9; [Ex. 15:16; 1 Pet. 1:18; Rev. 14:3, 4]
2 [q]Rom. 2:24
3 [r][2 Cor. 12:17, 18; 1 Tim. 6:5; Titus 1:11] [s]Rom. 16:18; Col. 2:4 [t][Deut. 32:35; Phil. 3:19]
4 [u]Jude 6 [v][Rev. 20:2, 3, 10] [w]Matt. 25:41
5 [x]See 1 Pet. 3:20 [y]ch. 3:6; Job 22:16
6 [z]See Gen. 19:24 [a][Num. 26:10] [b]Jude 15
7 [c]Gen. 19:16
8 [d]Ps. 119:136, 158; [Ezek. 9:4]
9 [e]1 Cor. 10:13; Rev. 3:10
10 [f]Jude 16, 18 [g]Jude 8; [Ex. 22:28]
11 [h]Jude 9
12 [i]Jude 10 [j][Jer. 12:3; Phil. 3:19]
13 [k]ver. 15 [l][Rom. 13:13; 1 Thess. 5:7]; See James 5:5 [m][1 Cor. 11:21] **14** [n][1 Pet. 4:1] [o]ver. 3; [1 Tim. 4:7] [p][Eph. 2:3] **15** [q]Ezek. 14:11 [r]Num. 22:5, 7; Deut. 23:4; Neh. 13:2; Jude 11; Rev. 2:14 [s]ver. 13 **16** [t]Num. 22:21, 23, 28 **17** [u]Jude 12 [v]Jude 13 **18** [w]Jude 16

passions of the flesh those who are barely
[x]escaping from those who live in error. 19 They
promise them [y]freedom, [z]but they themselves
are slaves[1] of corruption. For whatever overcomes a person, to that he is enslaved. 20 For if,
[a]after they have escaped the defilements of the
world [b]through the knowledge of our Lord and
Savior Jesus Christ, they are again entangled in
them and overcome, [c]the last state has become
worse for them than the first. 21 For [d]it would
have been better for them never to have known
the way of righteousness than after knowing
it to turn back from [e]the holy commandment
delivered to them. 22 What the true proverb
says has happened to them: "The [f]dog returns
to its own vomit, and the sow, after washing
herself, returns to wallow in the mire."

The Day of the Lord Will Come

3 This is now the second letter that I am
writing to you, beloved. In both of them
[g]I am stirring up your sincere mind by way of
reminder, 2 [h]that you should remember the
predictions of [i]the holy prophets and the commandment of the Lord and Savior through
your apostles, 3 knowing this first of all, that
scoffers will come [j]in the last days with scoffing, [k]following their own sinful desires. 4 [l]They
will say, "Where is the promise of [m]his coming? For ever since the fathers fell asleep, all
things are continuing as they were from the
beginning of creation." 5 For they deliberately
overlook this fact, that the heavens existed
long ago, and the earth [n]was formed out of
water and through water [o]by the word of God,
6 and that by means of these the world that
then existed [p]was deluged with water and
[q]perished. 7 But by the same word [r]the heavens and earth that now exist are stored up for
fire, being kept until the day of judgment and
[s]destruction of the ungodly.
8 But do not overlook this one fact, beloved,
that with the Lord one day is as a thousand

[1] Greek *bondservants*

18 [x]ver. 20; ch. 1:4
19 [y]Gal. 5:13; See James 1:25 [z]John 8:34; Rom. 6:16
20 [a]ver. 18 [b]See ch. 1:2 [c]Matt. 12:45
21 [d][Ezek. 18:24; Luke 12:47; Heb. 6:4-6; 10:26, 27; James 4:17] [e]Rom. 7:12
22 [f]Prov. 26:11
Chapter 3
1 [g]ch. 1:13
2 [h]Jude 17 [i]Luke 1:70; Acts 3:21
3 [j]Jude 18 [k]ch. 2:10
4 [l]Isa. 5:19; Jer. 17:15; Ezek. 11:3; 12:22, 27; Mal. 2:17 [m]See 1 Thess. 2:19
5 [n]Ps. 24:2; 136:6 [o]Gen. 1:6, 9; Ps. 33:6; [Heb. 11:3]
6 [p]ch. 2:5 [q]Gen. 7:11, 21
7 [r]ver. 10, 12 [s][2 Thess. 1:9]

by the power of the gospel as Peter described earlier (1:16–21), they have perhaps given the appearance of being a part of the church but have actually rejected the holy commandment (2:21). This becomes evident in their unrepentantly turning to their former defilements.

Evidently, then, those who ultimately "fall away" were never overcome by the gospel to be enslaved to Christ's life (vv. 19–20; cf. 1 John 2:19). Their "knowledge of our Lord and Savior Jesus Christ" is superficial, not able to release them fully from the entanglements of the world (2 Pet. 2:20). The gospel, when fully and truly grasped by a humbled heart, is a mighty force. It is "the power of God" (Rom. 1:16). Those who truly receive it are born again (1 Pet. 1:3, 23), and this supernatural change can never be reversed. Those who fall away, especially after they have lived in the ways of the Christian community for a time, show that they were never truly in Christ. More than this, they are actually more susceptible to the seductions of sin and more hardened to the appeal of the gospel because they think they have already tasted it and have found it wanting (2 Pet. 2:20–21). In making this pastoral observation, Peter does not use the precise language of our theological dictionaries but rather offers the practical wisdom gained from long experience in the church.

3:1–9 For good reason, the cry "How long, O Lord?" is a recurring refrain in the Psalms (e.g., Ps. 6:3; 13:1; 35:17; 79:1–5; 94:3) and in the Prophets (e.g., Isa. 6:11; Hab. 1:2; Zech. 1:12). It is the cry of a troubled heart tuned to God's glory. Those who hope in the Lord amid affliction are no less human than those who hurt apart from faith in the Lord. Like all people, believers cry for justice and deliverance; but unlike children of the world, they cry out to God as a loving Father. In 2 Peter 3, the apostle offers a unique comfort. What seems to us to take so long is but a moment to our transcendent God. He is neither slow nor forgetful. He is not faithless to us. What we see here is that "eternal weight of glory" up against the "light momentary affliction" that Paul writes about in 2 Corinthians 4:17–18. In 2 Peter 3:9, Peter assures us of God's faithfulness, and his commitment to finish what he's begun with us (cf. Phil. 1:6), so that none of his loved ones shall perish from his eternal purposes.

God's loving kindness is everlasting. He will ensure the perseverance of his saints—not ultimately because we are faithful but because *he* is. One day Christ will return, and while the wicked will then see that their scoffing was misplaced, the faithful will then see that their hope was true.

years, and [t]a thousand years as one day. 9 [u]The
Lord is not slow to fulfill his promise [v]as some
count slowness, but [w]is patient toward you,[1]
[x]not wishing that any should perish, but [y]that
all should reach repentance. 10 But [z]the day of
the Lord will come like a thief, and then [a]the
heavens will pass away with a roar, and [b]the
heavenly bodies[2] will be burned up and dissolved, and the earth and the works that are
done on it will be exposed.[3]

11 Since all these things are thus to be dissolved, [c]what sort of people ought you to be in
lives of holiness and godliness, 12 [d]waiting for
and hastening the coming of the day of God,
because of which the heavens will be set on
fire and dissolved, and [e]the heavenly bodies
will melt as they burn! 13 But according to his
promise we are waiting for [f]new heavens and
a new earth [g]in which righteousness dwells.

Final Words

14 [h]Therefore, beloved, since you are waiting for these, be diligent to be found by him
[i]without spot or [j]blemish, and [k]at peace. 15 And
count [l]the patience of our Lord as salvation,
just as [m]our beloved brother Paul also wrote
to you [n]according to the wisdom given him,
16 as he does in all his letters when he speaks
in them of these matters. [o]There are some
things in them that are hard to understand,
which the ignorant and unstable twist to
their own destruction, [p]as they do the other
Scriptures. 17 You therefore, beloved, [q]knowing
this beforehand, [r]take care that you are not
carried away with the error of lawless people
and lose your own stability. 18 But [s]grow in the
grace and knowledge of our Lord and Savior
Jesus Christ. [t]To him be the glory both now
and to the day of [u]eternity. Amen.

[1] Some manuscripts *on your account* [2] Or *elements*; also verse 12 [3] Greek *found*; some manuscripts *will be burned up*

3:10–13 God's vision for the world is that every square inch will be covered with the knowledge of his glory, like the waters cover the seas (Hab. 2:14). God's cleansing renewal will one day wash over this globe and restore all things.

We, along with all creation, groan inwardly for this restoration (Rom. 8:22–23). To this restorative conclusion of history Peter now turns. He knows it will be a great encouragement to those suffering spiritually from the corruption of the church and also suffering bodily from outside persecution and hardship. The destruction of the world to which Peter refers is not the final word about the fall of humanity and the resulting corruption; no, there is the promise of "new heavens and a new earth in which righteousness dwells" (2 Pet. 3:13; cf. Job 19:25; Isa. 65:17; 66:22; 1 Cor. 15:50–58). Perhaps recalling Jesus' words in Matthew 24:36–51, Peter writes that the reality of our future judgment, vindication, and transformation should encourage us to be holy and godly in the present age (2 Pet. 3:11).

3:14–17 In his concluding remarks, Peter reiterates the need to keep ourselves holy and blameless in these days of heresy and hardship (v. 14). He does not hold out these efforts as the means of salvation but as the natural result of salvation. Because there is a new world coming (v. 13), we are at peace in our spirits and diligent in our efforts. Because we have the truth of the gospel (v. 15), we are to resist the lure of false teaching and spiritual corruptions (v. 17). Peter knows that the Christian life is not lived on autopilot. Those who are born again fight to grow. But it is a fight they cannot lose. God's own power has provided all we need (1:3).

3:18 If we are in Christ, we will grow "in the grace and knowledge" of Christ (v. 18). The promise is as big as the possibilities. "From his fullness," John 1:16 tells us, "we have all received, grace upon grace." Peter has already reminded us of the "precious and very great promises" (2 Pet. 1:4) we received through the knowledge of Christ. Promises—plural—all of which are "Yes" and "Amen" in Christ Jesus (2 Cor. 1:20).

What an infinitude of blessings awaits the Christian who comes to see that we cannot wear out the gospel of Jesus! We do not and cannot graduate from the gospel, because once it promises our union with Christ, it announces God's making good on all the promises entailed in that promise. The same grace of Christ that empowers our saving knowledge of Christ will empower our growth in that knowledge, nurturing our relationship with the One with whom we have been united, until that final day when we meet him face to face.

8 [t]Ps. 90:4
9 [u]Hab. 2:3; Heb. 10:37 [v][Eccles. 8:11; Rev. 2:21] [w]Isa. 30:18; Luke 18:7 [x]Ezek. 18:23, 32; 33:11 [y]1 Tim. 2:4
10 [z]See Matt. 24:43 [a][Rev. 6:14; 20:11; 21:1]; See Matt. 24:35 [b]Isa. 34:4; [Isa. 24:19; Mic. 1:4; Nah. 1:5]
11 [c]1 Pet. 1:15
12 [d][Luke 12:36; 1 Cor. 1:7; 1 Thess. 1:10; Titus 2:13; Jude 21] [e]See ver. 10
13 [f]Isa. 65:17; 66:22; Rev. 21:1 [g]Isa. 60:21; Rev. 21:27
14 [h]1 Cor. 15:58 [i]James 1:27 [j]Phil. 2:15; [Phil. 1:10; 1 Thess. 3:13] [k][1 Thess. 5:23]
15 [l]See ver. 9 [m][Acts 15:25] [n]1 Cor. 3:10
16 [o][Heb. 5:11] [p][Isa. 28:13]
17 [q]ch. 1:12; [Mark 13:23] [r]ch. 1:10; 1 Cor. 10:12
18 [s]ch. 1:5; Eph. 4:15; Col. 1:10; 2:19; 1 Pet. 2:2 [t]See Rom. 11:36 [u][ver. 8]

Introduction to 1–3 John

Author, Date, and Recipients

John the son of Zebedee wrote these three letters, probably no later than the 90s A.D. He wrote from Ephesus (in present-day western Turkey), perhaps to churches like those mentioned in Revelation 2:8–3:22. John also wrote the Fourth Gospel and the book of Revelation.

The Gospel in 1–3 John

The word "gospel" never appears in the letters of John. Yet it is hard to imagine a book more intimately connected to the gospel of saving grace in Christ Jesus than John's first letter, and in each of his other two letters John deals with a practical issue arising directly out of a care for the integrity of the gospel in the life of the church.

In 1 John the themes of fellowshiping with God (1:3, 6; 2:6, 13; 3:1–2), genuinely believing in the unique person and work of Jesus (2:1–2, 22–24; 4:2–3, 10, 14–15; 5:1, 5–6), walking in the light (1:7; 2:9–11), practicing righteousness (2:4; 3:7–10; 5:3), loving other Christians (2:10; 3:11–17, 23; 4:7, 11, 20–21), and especially, being assured of eternal life (2:3, 5; 3:10, 14, 19, 24; 4:17; 5:13, 20) are all deeply rooted in gospel reality, especially its transformative power.

John writes his first letter to "you who believe in the name of the Son of God" so "that you may know that you have eternal life" (5:13). Two purposes are contained here: (1) that professing believers might test themselves to see the genuineness of their faith; and (2) that true believers would be assured of their right standing with God. In these purposes John helps all *professing* believers avoid a dangerous presumption and he helps all *genuine* believers avoid a debilitating uncertainty.

The bulk of John's first letter is taken up with three tests of genuine faith: (1) the moral test—do you obey God's commands? (2) the doctrinal test—do you believe Jesus is the Son of God? (3) the love test—do you love God and his children? Early in the letter these tests appear distinctly, but as John proceeds they are increasingly intertwined into a unified picture of the truly gospel-transformed life.

In his second letter John reiterates the same themes of truth, obedience, and love. But now he especially addresses the church regarding the danger of false teaching, and in particular teaching that denies that Jesus Christ has come in the flesh (v. 7). From the opening verse his emphasis is on "the truth" (vv. 1–4), and he clearly instructs the church to have nothing to do with those who have departed from the truth of the gospel (vv. 10–11). Agreement regarding Christ's person and work is necessary for church fellowship.

John's third letter is, to a large degree, addressing the opposite side of the issue raised in his second letter. Here the exhortation has to do with how to respond to faithful ministers of the gospel (as opposed to how to respond to the false teachers addressed in his second letter). John again emphasizes the priority of truth for the health of the church (vv. 3–4), but then proceeds to commend Gaius (and presumably those in fellowship with him) for actively supporting those in gospel ministry, and he encourages all believers to do the same (v. 8).

1 John Outline

I. God Is Light and Christ Is the Way (1:1–2:6)
II. The Unchanging Commandment in a Changing World (2:7–17)
III. Overcoming the Antichrist by Confessing the Son (2:18–3:10)
IV. Overcoming Evil by Listening to the Apostle (3:11–4:6)
V. The Assurance of God through the Love of God (4:7–21)
VI. Faith in the Son as the Way to Life (5:1–12)
VII. Final Call to Faith and Understanding (5:13–21)

2 John Outline

I. Greeting: The Elder's Love (vv. 1–3)
II. The Elder's Joy and Request (vv. 4–6)
III. The Elder's Concern (vv. 7–8)
IV. The Elder's Warning (vv. 9–11)
V. Closing: The Elder's Farewell (vv. 12–13)

3 John Outline

I. Greeting: The Elder's Joy at Gaius's Faithfulness (vv. 1–4)
II. Praise for Gaius's Support for Traveling Christian Workers (vv. 5–8)
III. Concern about Diotrephes (vv. 9–10)
IV. Advice and Commendation of Demetrius (vv. 11–12)
V. Closing: A Promise to Visit (vv. 13–15)

The First Letter of John

1 John

The Word of Life

1 [a]That which was [b]from the beginning,
[c]which we have heard, [d]which we have
seen with our eyes, [e]which we looked upon
and [f]have touched with our hands, concerning the word of life— 2 [g]the life [h]was made
manifest, and we have seen it, and [i]testify to
it and proclaim to you the eternal life, [a]which
was with the Father and [h]was made manifest
to us— 3 [c]that which we have seen and heard
we proclaim also to you, so that you too may
have fellowship with us; and indeed [j]our fellowship is with the Father and with his Son
Jesus Christ. 4 And we are writing these things
so [k]that our[1] joy may be complete.

Walking in the Light

5 [l]This is the message we have heard from him
and proclaim to you, that [m]God is light, and in
him is no darkness at all. 6 [n]If we say we have
fellowship with him while we walk in darkness, we lie and [o]do not practice the truth. 7 But
[p]if we walk in the light, [q]as he is in the light,
we have fellowship with one another, and [r]the
blood of Jesus his Son cleanses us from all sin.
8 [s]If we say we have no sin, we deceive ourselves,
and [t]the truth is not in us. 9 [u]If we confess our
sins, he is [v]faithful and just to forgive us our
sins and [r]to cleanse us from all unrighteousness. 10 If we say we have not sinned, [w]we make
him a liar, and [x]his word is not in us.

Christ Our Advocate

2 My little children, I am writing these
things to you so that you may not sin. But
if anyone does sin, [y]we have an advocate with
the Father, Jesus Christ the righteous. 2 [z]He is
the propitiation for our sins, and not for ours

[1] Some manuscripts *your*

1:1–4 John begins his letter by grounding his readers in the objective historical reality of the gospel. The Son, who existed "with the Father" (v. 2), "from the beginning" (v. 1), has entered human history as a real human being, the man Jesus. John attests to this as an "eye," "ear," and "hand" witness. This incarnation was essential to the eternal purpose of God so that the "life" that is in Christ Jesus might be "made manifest" (v. 2) and then "proclaimed" (vv. 2, 3), so that it might be received. The essence of that life is to be in "fellowship" with God the Father and with Jesus Christ (v. 3). This fellowship is exactly what Jesus prayed for when he was on earth (John 17:3).

Christianity is not a vague, abstract set of ideas or an ethical system. It is, above all, the good news of what God has done in our space-and-time history in the real, tangible experience of sending his Son to rescue us from the destruction that our own sins are bringing upon us, apart from him.

1:5–10 In these verses John introduces one of the great effects of the gospel, namely, the transformation of life that occurs in the genuine gospel-believer. John speaks of this transformation as one from "darkness" into "light." To "walk in darkness" means to pursue a pattern of life apart from God, who is light (vv. 5–6). "Walking in the light" means both fellowship with God (v. 6) and fellowship with other believers (v. 7). It does not mean that we will never sin. After all, in this very passage John reminds us that when we do sin, God has provided a trustworthy ground of forgiveness: "The blood of Jesus his Son cleanses us from all sin" (v. 7). When we base our confessions of sin on this fact, God is "faithful and just to forgive us our sins" and also to "cleanse us from all unrighteousness" (v. 9).

2:1–2 John refers here to both the "righteous" life of Christ and his "propitiating"

Chapter 1
1 [a]See John 1:1 [b][ch. 2:13, 14] [c]Acts 4:20 [d]John 19:35 [e]ch. 4:14; John 1:14; 2 Pet. 1:16 [f]Luke 24:39; John 20:27
2 [g]John 1:4; 11:25; 14:6 [h]ch. 3:5, 8; Rom. 16:26; 1 Tim. 3:16 [i]See John 15:27 [a][See ver. 1 above]
3 [c][See ver. 1 above] [j]John 17:21; 1 Cor. 1:9; [ch. 2:24]
4 [k]John 15:11; 16:24
5 [l]ch. 3:11 [m]James 1:17; [ch. 4:8; John 4:24]
6 [n]ch. 2:11; John 12:35; 2 Cor. 6:14 [o]John 3:21
7 [p][Isa. 2:5] [q][Ps. 104:2; 1 Tim. 6:16] [r]Eph. 1:7; Heb. 9:14; 1 Pet. 1:19; Rev. 5:9; 7:14; 12:11
8 [s][Job 15:14; Jer. 2:35]; See James 3:2 [t]ch. 2:4
9 [u]Ps. 32:5; 51:3; Prov. 28:13 [v][Ps. 143:1; Rom. 3:26] [r][See ver. 7 above]
10 [w]ch. 5:10 [x]John 5:38; 8:37
Chapter 2
1 [y]Rom. 8:34; 1 Tim. 2:5; Heb. 7:25
2 [z]ch. 4:10; Rom. 3:25; [2 Cor. 5:18, 19; Col. 1:20]

only but [a]also for the sins of the whole world.
3 And by this we know that we have come to
know him, if we [b]keep his commandments.
4 Whoever says "I know him" but does not keep
his commandments [c]is a liar, and [c]the truth is
not in him, 5 but whoever [d]keeps his word, in
him truly [e]the love of God is perfected. [f]By this
we may know that we are in him: 6 whoever
says he [g]abides in him [h]ought to walk in the
same way in which he walked.

The New Commandment

7 Beloved, I am writing you [i]no new commandment, but [j]an old commandment [k]that
you had from the beginning. The old commandment is the word that you have heard.
8 At the same time, it is [l]a new commandment
that I am writing to you, which is true in him
and in you, because[1] [m]the darkness is passing
away and [n]the true light is already shining.
9 Whoever says he is in the light and [o]hates his
brother is still in darkness. 10 Whoever loves
his brother abides in the light, and in him[2]
there is no [p]cause for stumbling. 11 But whoever hates his brother is in the darkness and
[q]walks in the darkness, and does not know
where he is going, because the darkness has
blinded his eyes.

[1] Or *that* [2] Or *it*

2 [a] ch. 4:14; John 1:29; 4:42; 11:51, 52; 12:32
3 [b] John 14:15; 15:10
4 [c] ch. 1:8; John 8:44
5 [d] ch. 5:3; John 14:23 [e] ch. 4:12 [f] ch. 3:24; 4:13; 5:2
6 [g] John 15:4, 5, 7 [h] See Matt. 11:29
7 [i] 2 John 5 [j] Lev. 19:18 [k] [ver. 24; ch. 3:11; 2 John 5, 6]
8 [l] See John 13:34 [m] Rom. 13:12; Eph. 5:8; 1 Thess. 5:4, 5 [n] John 1:9; 8:12
9 [o] ch. 4:20; [ch. 3:14, 15; Titus 3:3]
10 [p] John 11:10; [Prov. 4:19; 2 Pet. 1:10]
11 [q] See ch. 1:6

death, which together are the grounds of a believer's justification (cf. Rom. 3:24–26; 2 Cor. 5:21). It is on these grounds—his sinless life and substitutionary death—that Jesus stands as our "advocate" before the Father.

The word "propitiation" appears only rarely in the New Testament, but at crucial points (e.g., Rom. 3:25). Moreover, the reality expressed in the word "propitiation," with its profound gospel significance, reverberates throughout the whole Bible. This key term refers to a sacrifice which satisfies the just wrath of God for sin. As it is applied to Christ, we learn that through his death Jesus absorbed the just wrath of God toward us for our sin and thereby opened the way for God's full favor to be shown to all who believe. This profound change of our situation provided by Christ's propitiation for our sin produces in our hearts a deep gratitude, a note clearly sounded by John when he says, "See what kind of love the Father has given to us" (1 John 3:1).

How Christ's propitiation applies to the "sins of the whole world" (2:2) may be explained in three ways: (1) Christ's sacrifice is sufficient for all, though applicable only to those placing their faith in him; (2) Christ's sacrifice is the fulfillment of the Abrahamic promise to bless all the nations of the earth through the Messiah; (3) Christ's sacrifice is able to save believers from all the world, regardless of ethnicity or past loyalties. What is clear, however, is that John is clearly not arguing for some form of universalism (in which all persons will be saved regardless of their faith) because he says that "whoever does not have the Son of God does not have life" (5:12).

2:3–6 In verse 3 John explicitly introduces his main theme of assurance for the gospel-believer through his often repeated phrase "by this we know." (Forms of this phrase appear some 15 times in this brief letter.) The ground of assurance John presents here is our obedience to Christ's commands. This is often spoken of as the "moral test" of genuine belief. Whoever obeys Christ out of a genuine love for God (v. 5) finds, in that very obedience, the grounds for assurance that he is genuinely "in him" (v. 5).

John is not referring to faultless obedience, but to a new trajectory of life that springs from the radical transformation of having been born again (cf. 3:9). John is also not saying that our obedience merits or earns God's love (he has already established Christ's propitiating sacrifice as the basis of our salvation; see 2:1–2), but rather that those who have God's love show it, and this evidence of a life transformed by him is critical assurance of being united to him. Our obedience does not gain his love but evidences it. Our disobedience does not remove his love but does affect our assurance. We cannot confidently claim that his grace is ours if we show no evidence that our lives are his.

2:7–11 Having introduced the "moral" test of keeping Christ's commands, John now proceeds to highlight a particular command of Christ which genuine gospel-believers

12 I am writing to you, little children,
because [r]your sins are forgiven for his name's sake.
13 I am writing to you, fathers,
because you know [s]him who is from the beginning.
I am writing to you, young men,
because [t]you have overcome the evil one.
I write to you, children,
because [u]you know the Father.
14 I write to you, fathers,
because you know [s]him who is from the beginning.
I write to you, young men,
because [t]you are strong,
and the word of God abides in you,
and you have overcome the evil one.

Do Not Love the World

15 [v]Do not love the world or the things in the
world. [w]If anyone loves the world, the love
of the Father is not in him. 16 For all that is
in the world—[x]the desires of the flesh and
[y]the desires of the eyes and pride of life[1]—is
not from the Father but is from the world.
17 And [z]the world is passing away along with
its desires, but whoever does the will of God
abides forever.

Warning Concerning Antichrists

18 Children, [a]it is the last hour, and as you
have heard that [b]antichrist is coming, so now
[c]many antichrists have come. [d]Therefore we
know that it is the last hour. 19 [e]They went out
from us, but they were not of us; for [f]if they had
been of us, they would have continued with us.
But they went out, [g]that it might become plain
that they all are not of us. 20 But you have been
[h]anointed by [i]the Holy One, and [j]you all have
knowledge.[2] 21 I write to you, not because you
do not know the truth, but because you know
it, and because no lie is of the truth. 22 Who is
the liar but [k]he who denies that Jesus is the
Christ? This is [b]the antichrist, he who denies
the Father and the Son. 23 [l]No one who denies
the Son has the Father. Whoever confesses the
Son has the Father also. 24 Let [m]what you heard

[1] Or *pride in possessions* [2] Some manuscripts *you know everything*

are called to obey. The specific command John speaks of is to love our "brothers" (vv. 9, 10, 11). This is often spoken of as the "love test" of genuine belief.

This commandment is both "old" (v. 7), as it is grounded in the character of Christ who is "from the beginning" (v. 7; cf. 1:1); and "new" (v. 8), as it grows out of the dawning new age and the transformation brought about in a believer by the transforming power of the gospel. Note, then, that believers are not only called to obey this command but are also enabled to obey it: we love one another "*because* the darkness is passing away and the true light is already shining" (v. 8).

2:12–17 In a brief poetic interlude (vv. 12–14), John warmly relates to the various levels of spiritual maturity in his audience—"children," "fathers," "young men"—and provides a summary of the gospel realities they enjoy in Christ: forgiveness (v. 12), fellowship with God (vv. 13–14), and victory over the "evil one" (vv. 13–14). John then returns again to the moral implications of gospel transformation (vv. 15–17). His direct appeal to turn away from worldliness (poignantly described in terms of sensuality, materialism, and pride; v. 16) is based in part on a pragmatic realism (v. 17) but especially on our other-worldly love for God (v. 15).

2:18–29 John has already laid out the "moral" (vv. 3–6) and "love" (vv. 1–11) tests of genuine belief; he now presents the third, the "doctrinal test." If the truth about Christ "abides" in us (v. 24a), we will "abide" in God (v. 24b) and thus have full "confidence" that we are in a right relationship with him when Christ returns (v. 28). The specific truth we are called to "abide" in is "that Jesus is the Christ" (v. 22; John 15:4–7). There are, John warns, "antichrists" who deny this.

The word "antichrist" evokes John's apocalyptic vision (in the book of Revelation) of the end times and the great enemies of God's redemptive plan who appear there; and yet John says there are "antichrists" among us now. In one sense we are already in "the last hour" because the Christ, to whom the Old Testament prophets pointed as Israel's final hope, has already come (cf. Acts 2:17; Heb. 1:2; 1 Pet. 1:20). In this context the false teachers against whom John cautions believers are "antichrists." They are against Christ because they deny that Jesus is the Christ. These false teachers, by denying "the Son," also deny "the Father" (1 John 2:22), because of the full

12 [r]Luke 24:47; Acts 10:43; 13:38
13 [s][ch. 1:1] [t]Eph. 6:10; [ch. 5:4, 5] [u]John 14:7
14 [s][See ver. 13 above] [t][See ver. 13 above]
15 [v][Rom. 12:2; 2 Tim. 4:10] [w]See James 4:4
16 [x]Rom. 13:14; Eph. 2:3; 1 Pet. 4:2; 2 Pet. 2:18 [y]Eccles. 4:8; 5:11
17 [z]See 1 Cor. 7:31
18 [a][2 Tim. 3:1; James 5:3; 2 Pet. 3:3; Jude 18] [b]ver. 22; ch. 4:3; 2 John 7; [Matt. 24:5, 24] [c][ch. 4:1; Matt. 24:5] [d]1 Tim. 4:1
19 [e]Deut. 13:13; Acts 20:30 [f]See John 17:12 [g]1 Cor. 11:19
20 [h]ver. 27; [2 Cor. 1:21] [i]See Mark 1:24 [j]ver. 27; See John 14:26
22 [k]ch. 4:3; 2 John 7 [b][See ver. 18 above]
23 [l]ch. 4:15; 5:1; 2 John 9
24 [m]ch. 3:11; 2 John 6

from the beginning abide in you. If what you heard from the beginning abides in you, then [n]you too will abide in the Son and in the Father. 25 And this is the promise that he made to us[1]—[o]eternal life.

26 I write these things to you about [p]those who are trying to deceive you. 27 But [q]the anointing that you received from him abides in you, and [r]you have no need that anyone should teach you. But as his anointing teaches you about everything, and [s]is true, and is no lie—just as it has taught you, abide in him.

Children of God

28 And now, little children, abide in him, so that [t]when he appears [u]we may have confidence and not shrink from him in shame at his [v]coming. 29 If you know that [w]he is righteous, you may be sure that [x]everyone who practices righteousness has been born of him.

3 See [y]what kind of love the Father has given to us, that we should be called [z]children of God; and so we are. The reason why [a]the world does not know us is that [b]it did not know him. 2 Beloved, we are [z]God's children [c]now, and what we will be [d]has not yet appeared; but we know that [e]when he appears[2] [f]we shall be like him, because [g]we shall see him as he is. 3 And everyone who [h]thus hopes in him [i]purifies himself as he is pure.

4 Everyone who makes a practice of sinning also practices lawlessness; [j]sin is lawlessness. 5 You know that [k]he appeared in order to [l]take away sins, and [m]in him there is no sin. 6 No one who abides in him keeps on sinning; [n]no one who keeps on sinning has either seen him or known him. 7 Little children, [o]let no one deceive you. [p]Whoever practices righteousness is righteous, as he is righteous. 8 [q]Whoever makes a practice of sinning is of the devil, for the devil has been sinning from the beginning. The reason the Son of God appeared was [r]to destroy the works of the devil. 9 [s]No one born of God makes a practice of sinning, for God's[3] seed abides in him, and he cannot keep on sinning because he has been born of God. 10 By this it is evident who are the children of God, and who are the children of the devil: whoever does not practice righteousness is not of God, [t]nor is the one who [u]does not love his brother.

[1] Some manuscripts *you* [2] Or *when it appears* [3] Greek *his*

24[n] [John 14:23]; See ch. 1:3
25[o] John 17:2
26[p] ch. 3:7; 2 John 7
27[q] ver. 20 [r] Jer. 31:34; Heb. 8:11 [s] John 14:17
28[t] ch. 3:2; [Col. 3:4] [u] ch. 3:21; 4:17; 5:14 [v] See 1 Thess. 2:19
29[w] ch. 3:7 [x] ch. 3:9; 4:7; 5:1, 4, 18; 3 John 11

Chapter 3

1[y] ch. 4:10; John 3:16 [z] John 1:12 [a] [ch. 4:17] [b] John 16:3; 17:25
2[z] [See ver. 1 above] [c] Rom. 8:15; Gal. 3:26; Eph. 1:5 [d] [Rom. 8:18; 2 Cor. 4:17] [e] ch. 2:28 [f] Rom. 8:29; 2 Cor. 3:18; 4:11; Phil. 3:21; 2 Pet. 1:4 [g] John 17:24; 1 Cor. 13:12; Rev. 22:4
3[h] Rom. 15:12 [i] 2 Cor. 7:1
4[j] [ch. 5:17; Rom. 4:15]
5[k] Heb. 9:26; See ch. 1:2 [l] [Isa. 53:11, 12] [m] See 1 Pet. 2:22
6[n] ch. 2:4; 4:8; 3 John 11
7[o] ch. 2:26 [p] ch. 2:29
8[q] Matt. 13:38; John 8:44 [r] Heb. 2:14; [Gen. 3:15; Luke 10:18; John 16:11]
9[s] ch. 5:18
10[t] ch. 4:8 [u] ch. 4:20, 21

identity of life and purpose shared by the Father and Son (v. 23; cf. 1:2). This "life," shared by the Father and the Son, is the very life "manifested" to us in Christ (1:2), "proclaimed" to us in the gospel (1:3), and "promised" to all who believe (2:25). It is precisely because Jesus *is* the Christ that our belief in him assures us of eternal life (cf. John 3:36; 5:24). As John will say later in this letter, "God gave us eternal life, and this life is in his Son. Whoever has the Son has life" (5:11–12).

3:1–10 In these verses John sets forth, for the third time, the "moral" test of genuine gospel-belief. John speaks of true believers as "practicing righteousness" (v. 7) as opposed to "practicing sin" (vv. 4, 8). While we still sin as believers (cf. 1:8–2:1), a genuine believer does not "practice sinning" (i.e., have a life pattern of sinful pursuits without correction or remorse) because he has been "born of God" and therefore has a completely new identity (3:9; cf. Gal. 3:26; 2 Cor. 5:17). Anyone who does "practice sinning" not only has no grounds for assurance of being in a right relationship with God (1 John 3:10) but also is shown to be still in darkness and at enmity with God, being "of the devil" (v. 8).

The gospel holds out the only hope for those in such a condition. The good news is that Jesus "appeared in order to take away sins" (v. 5). He also "appeared . . . to destroy the works of the devil" (v. 8). As the gospel continues its transforming work in the lives of believers, they will increasingly bear resemblance to their heavenly Father (vv. 2–3; cf. Gen. 1:26). This is God's very purpose, that we should be "conformed to the image of his Son" (Rom. 8:29). And the ultimate blessing of being conformed to the image of God's Child is that we are also regarded as "children of God," loved by him as much as Jesus is loved by him (1 John 3:1).

What a prospect the genuine gospel-believer and child of God has to look forward to—that one day God's redemptive purpose will be brought to full completion and, seeing him, we shall completely and perfectly bear his likeness (v. 2). Such a hope motivates us all the more to "purify" ourselves through the "practice" of righteousness (vv. 3, 7).

Love One Another

11 For [v]this is the message that you have heard
from the beginning, [w]that we should love one
another. 12 We should not be like [x]Cain, who
was of the evil one and murdered his brother.
And why did he murder him? [y]Because his
own deeds were evil and his brother's righteous. 13 Do not be surprised, brothers,[1] [z]that
the world hates you. 14 We know that [a]we have
passed out of death into life, because we love
the brothers. Whoever does not love abides in
death. 15 [b]Everyone who hates his brother is a
murderer, and you know that [c]no murderer
has eternal life abiding in him.
16 By this we know love, that [d]he laid down
his life for us, and [e]we ought to lay down our
lives for the brothers. 17 But [f]if anyone has the
world's goods and sees his brother in need, yet
[g]closes his heart against him, [h]how does God's
love abide in him? 18 Little children, let us not
[i]love in word or talk but in deed and [j]in truth.
19 By this we shall know that we are of the
truth and reassure our heart before him;
20 for whenever our heart condemns us, God
is greater than our heart, and he knows everything. 21 Beloved, [k]if our heart does not condemn us, [l]we have confidence before God;
22 and [m]whatever we ask we receive from him,
because we keep his commandments and [n]do
what pleases him. 23 And this is his commandment, [o]that we believe in the name of his Son
Jesus Christ and [p]love one another, [q]just as
he has commanded us. 24 [r]Whoever keeps his
commandments abides in God,[2] and God[3] in
him. And [s]by this we know that he abides in
us, by the Spirit whom he has given us.

[1] Or *brothers and sisters*. The plural Greek word *adelphoi* (translated "brothers") refers to siblings in a family. In New Testament usage, depending on the context, *adelphoi* may refer either to men or to both men and women who are siblings (brothers and sisters) in God's family, the church; also verses 14, 16 [2] Greek *him* [3] Greek *he*

3:11–24 At the very end of the preceding section John once again transitions directly from the "moral" test to the "love" test (cf. 2:6–7), showing that our love for one another is an integral part of the total transformation of life brought about by God through the gospel.

John states explicitly that genuine love for other believers is a right ground for assurance of genuine belief (3:14), just as hate is a sure sign that one is "of the evil one" (v. 12) and is without the "eternal life" possessed by those who believe (v. 15). A believer's love flows out of and resembles the love he has received from God through Jesus Christ (vv. 16–18). This will make our love exceedingly practical (vv. 17–18). The presence of this love will provide right grounds for assurance in the face of uncertainty and feelings of condemnation, reminding us that what God knows to be true of us is what is right (vv. 19–21).

In verses 23–24 John begins to intertwine the three tests he has already laid out, speaking now of the connection between right belief (v. 23), genuine love (v. 23), and ongoing obedience (v. 24), all of which enable us to know that we "abide in him." While reference to the presence of the Holy Spirit in the life of the believer does not emerge with the same emphasis as these other grounds of assurance do in John's letter, here (v. 24) and again later (4:13; cf. 5:6) John speaks of the presence of the Spirit as another ground of assurance that God "abides in us" and that we abide in him. Similarly, the New Testament elsewhere speaks of the Spirit as a "guarantee" or down payment (2 Cor. 1:22; 5:5; Eph. 1:14) of our eternal salvation. The new belief, new behaviors, and new affections generated by the Spirit evidence his presence in us and grant assurance of our relationship with God (see also Rom. 8:5–7, 13–16).

In all this we remember the great consolation of 1 John 3:20: when we feel accused and condemned, we can look to Christ and know that all sin is forgiven. God's sentence of acquittal overrules our heart's sentence of condemnation. And that is not because God does not see all the facts or has overlooked some of our failures; quite the contrary, "he knows everything" (v. 20) but forgives us anyway! This is profound liberation to haunted consciences.

By a preeminent love for God, we are also liberated from selfishness so that "whatever we ask we receive from him" (v. 22). Such prayers are not for worldly priorities and selfish gain but for "what pleases him." God is thus willing to grant that which enables us to "keep his commandments" (vv. 22–23) and "abide in God"—the eternal priorities of heaven, not of earth (cf. 5:14).

11 [v]ch. 1:5; 2:24 [w]See John 13:34
12 [x]Gen. 4:4, 8; Heb. 11:4; Jude 11 [y]Ps. 38:20; Prov. 29:10
13 [z]John 15:18; 17:14
14 [a]John 5:24
15 [b]Matt. 5:21, 22 [c]Gal. 5:21; Rev. 21:8
16 [d]See John 15:13 [e][Phil. 2:17]
17 [f]James 2:15, 16 [g]Deut. 15:7 [h][ch. 4:20]
18 [i]Ezek. 33:31; Eph. 4:15 [j]2 John 1; 3 John 1
21 [k][1 Cor. 4:4] [l]ch. 5:14; [Job 11:15; 22:26; Rom. 14:22]
22 [m]See Matt. 7:7 [n]John 8:29
23 [o]John 6:29; [Acts 18:8] [p]ver. 11 [q][ch. 2:8]
24 [r][John 6:56; 14:20; 15:4, 5; 17:21] [s]ch. 4:13; Rom. 8:9

Test the Spirits

4 Beloved, [t]do not believe every spirit, but
[u]test the spirits to see whether they are
from God, for [v]many [w]false prophets [x]have
gone out into the world. 2 By this you know
the Spirit of God: [y]every spirit that confesses
that [z]Jesus Christ has come in the flesh is from
God, 3 and every spirit [a]that does not confess
Jesus is not from God. This is the spirit of the
antichrist, which you heard was coming and
[b]now is in the world already. 4 Little children,
you are from God and have overcome them,
for [c]he who is in you is greater than [d]he who is
in the world. 5 [e]They are from the world; therefore they speak from the world, and [f]the world
listens to them. 6 We are from God. [g]Whoever
knows God listens to us; whoever is not from
God does not listen to us. By this we know [h]the
Spirit of truth and [i]the spirit of error.

God Is Love

7 Beloved, [j]let us love one another, for love is
from God, and [k]whoever loves has been born
of God and knows God. 8 [l]Anyone who does
not love does not know God, because [m]God is
love. 9 In this the love of God was made manifest among us, that [n]God sent his only Son
into the world, so that we might live through
him. 10 In this is love, [o]not that we have loved
God [n]but that he loved us and sent his Son to
be [p]the propitiation for our sins. 11 Beloved,
if God so loved us, we also ought to love one
another. 12 [q]No one has ever seen God; if we
love one another, God abides in us and [r]his
love is perfected in us.

13 [s]By this we know that we abide in him
and he in us, because he has given us of his
Spirit. 14 And [t]we have seen and testify that
[u]the Father has sent his Son to be the Savior
of [v]the world. 15 [w]Whoever confesses that Jesus
is the Son of God, God abides in him, and he
in God. 16 So [x]we have come to know and to
believe the love that God has for us. [y]God
is love, and [z]whoever abides in love abides
in God, and God abides in him. 17 By this [a]is
love perfected with us, so that [b]we may have
confidence for the day of judgment, because
[c]as he is so also are we in this world. 18 There
is no fear in love, but [d]perfect love casts out
fear. For fear has to do with punishment,
and whoever fears has not [a]been perfected
in love. 19 [e]We love because he first loved us.
20 [f]If anyone says, "I love God," and [g]hates his
brother, he is a liar; for he who does not love

Chapter 4
1 [t]Jer. 29:8 [u]1 Thess. 5:21; [1 Cor. 12:10; 14:29; Rev. 2:2] [v]See ch. 2:18 [w]2 Pet. 2:1 [x]2 John 7
2 [y][1 Cor. 12:3] [z]2 John 7
3 [a]ch. 2:22; 2 John 7 [b]ch. 2:18; [2 Thess. 2:3-7]
4 [c]See Rom. 8:31 [d][1 Cor. 2:12]; See John 12:31
5 [e]John 3:31; 8:23 [f]John 15:19
6 [g][John 8:47; 10:16; 18:37; 1 Cor. 14:37] [h]John 14:17; 15:26; 16:13 [i][1 Cor. 2:12; 1 Tim. 4:1]
7 [j]ch. 3:11 [k]ch. 2:29
8 [l]ch. 3:10 [m]ver. 16; 2 Cor. 13:11; [ch. 1:5; John 4:24]
9 [n]See John 3:16
10 [o]Rom. 5:8, 10 [n][See ver. 9 above] [p]See ch. 2:2
12 [q]ver. 20; John 1:18; 1 Tim. 6:16 [r]ch. 2:5
13 [s]ch. 3:24
14 [t]ch. 1:1, 2 [u]See John 3:17 [v]See ch. 2:2
15 [w]ch. 5:5; [Rom. 10:9]; See Matt. 14:33
16 [x]John 6:69 [y]See ver. 8 [z]ver. 12; ch. 3:24
17 [a][ch. 2:5] [b]ch. 2:28; 3:21 [c][ch. 3:1]
18 [d][John 3:18; Rom. 8:15] [a][See ver. 17 above]
19 [e]ver. 10
20 [f]ch. 2:4; 3:17 [g]ch. 2:9, 11

4:1–6 Here, for the second time, John lays out the "doctrinal" test for genuine belief. He calls us to "test the spirits" (v. 1), referring to the spiritual presence behind teaching, whether true or false; we are to discern "whether they are from God" (vv. 1, 6).

The specific point of doctrine in question (as was the case in 2:18–27) is that "Jesus Christ has come in the flesh" (4:2) or, in other words, that "Jesus [the man] is the Christ" (2:22). Those who deny this are not "from God" (4:3). Those who do believe this are "from God" (vv. 2, 4, 6) and "know God" (v. 6). The added way of knowing what is from God is testing whether what is being taught is consistent with apostolic witness—that is, Scripture. John says, "whoever is not from God does not listen to us. By this we know the Spirit of truth and the spirit of error" (v. 6). Thus, we test whether others' teachings are correct based on their consistency with apostolic witness to (1) Christ's redemption and (2) Scripture's truth.

4:7–21 For the third time, John lays out the "love" test. The sheer volume of space dedicated to this in John's letter speaks of the importance of love for fellow believers in the gospel-transformed life (cf. 1 Cor. 13:13).

Jesus himself said that this is how *others* would know that we are true believers (John 13:35). John's point, here once again, is that this is how *we* can know with confidence we are true believers (1 John 4:7, 12, 16–17). Amid the encouragement to love one another that bookends this section (vv. 7, 21), John presents a moving summary of the gospel (vv. 9–10) as both model and motivation for our love for one another (v. 11).

John also refers to love being "perfected in/with us" (vv. 12, 17). By this John speaks of love being brought progressively to its full godlike character in us as the gospel continues its ongoing transformative work through God's abiding presence with us (v. 16). This will both "cast fear" out of us (v. 18) and produce "confidence" in us (v. 17) as we anticipate "the day of judgment." For genuine gospel-believers there need be no fear of judgment day; there will be no punishment for God's children (v. 18), because God "sent his Son to be the propitiation for our sins" (v. 10).

his brother whom he has seen cannot[1] love
God [h]whom he has not seen. 21 And [i]this com-
mandment we have from him: [j]whoever loves
God must also love his brother.

Overcoming the World

5 [k]Everyone who believes that [l]Jesus is the
Christ has been born of God, and [m]every-
one who loves the Father loves whoever has
been born of him. 2 [n]By this we know that we
love the children of God, when we love God
and obey his commandments. 3 For [o]this is
the love of God, that we [p]keep his commandments. And [q]his commandments are not burdensome. 4 For [r]everyone who has been born
of God overcomes the world. And this is the
victory that has overcome the world—[s]our
faith. 5 Who is it that overcomes the world
except the one who believes [t]that Jesus is the
Son of God?

Testimony Concerning the Son of God

6 This is he who came [u]by water and blood—
Jesus Christ; not by the water only but by the
water and the blood. And [v]the Spirit is the one
who testifies, because [w]the Spirit is the truth.
7 For there are three that testify: 8 the Spirit
and the water and the blood; and these three
agree. 9 [x]If we receive the testimony of men, the
testimony of God is greater, for this is the testimony of God [y]that he has borne concerning
his Son. 10 Whoever believes in the Son of God
[z]has the testimony in himself. Whoever does
not believe God [a]has made him a liar, [b]because
he has not believed in the testimony that God
has borne concerning his Son. 11 And this is the
testimony, that God gave us [c]eternal life, and
[d]this life is in his Son. 12 [e]Whoever has the Son
has life; whoever does not have the Son of God
does not have life.

That You May Know

13 I write [f]these things to you who [g]believe
in the name of the Son of God that you may
know that you have eternal life. 14 And this
is [h]the confidence that we have toward him,
that [i]if we ask anything according to his will
he hears us. 15 And if we know that he hears us
in whatever we ask, we know that we have the
requests that we have asked of him.

16 If anyone sees his brother committing a sin
not leading to death, he shall ask, and [j]God[2]
will give him life—to those who commit sins
that do not lead to death. [k]There is sin that
leads to death; [l]I do not say that one should
pray for that. 17 [m]All wrongdoing is sin, but
there is sin that does not lead to death.

18 We know that [n]everyone who has been born
of God does not keep on sinning, but [o]he who

[1] Some manuscripts *how can he* [2] Greek *he*

The ground for all of this love-based behavior and rejoicing is grace: "We love because he first loved us" (v. 19). Our obedience is not a fearful striving to please God but a thankful and joyous response to the love with which he has already embraced us and provided for us by the sacrifice of his Son. The gospel is indeed news of great comfort and joy!

5:1–12 As John approaches the end of his letter, he weaves the three strands of right belief (vv. 1, 5), godlike love for other believers (vv. 1–2), and glad obedience (vv. 2–3) into a strong cord of assurance. There is nothing here that provides new content beyond what John has already said. His purpose here is to show the interconnectedness of these three realities of gospel transformation. Belief, love, and obedience are all mutually reinforcing. The Christian life is one of head, heart, and hands. However, key for the right interpretation of this passage and later writings of John is the fact that the person who "overcomes the world" (i.e., is given ultimate victory over sin and its effects) is one marked by "our faith" (v. 4) and who "believes that Jesus is the Son of God" (v. 5; cf. Rev. 2:7ff.; 3:5ff.; 21:7). Eternal salvation is never gained by human effort but is granted to those who rest on Christ.

In 1 John 5:6–11, John speaks of the truth of the gospel being testified to both by historical fact ("by water and blood," perhaps referring to Christ's confirming baptism and sacrificial death) and by a divine, spiritual confirmation in the heart of the believer. Belief in this twin testimony brings us, by faith (v. 4), into the "eternal life" God gives us in his Son (vv. 11–12).

5:13–21 John brings his letter to a close, clearly announcing his purpose, namely, that his genuinely believing readers might have full assurance of the "eternal life" they have in Jesus Christ (v. 13). This confidence in eternal life should translate into

20 [h]ver. 12; [1 Pet. 1:8]
21 [i]Gal. 6:2 [j]ver. 7; ch. 3:11
Chapter 5
1 [k]John 1:12 [l]ch. 2:22 [m]John 8:42
2 [n]ch. 2:5; 3:24; 4:13
3 [o]2 John 6; See John 14:15 [p]See ch. 2:3 [q]Matt. 11:30
4 [r]ch. 3:9; 4:4; John 16:33 [s][1 Cor. 15:57; Eph. 6:16]
5 [t]ch. 4:15
6 [u][ver. 8] [v]John 15:26; [Acts 5:32] [w]John 14:17; 15:26; 16:13
9 [x]John 5:34, 36, 37; 8:17, 18 [y]See Matt. 3:17
10 [z][Rom. 8:16; Gal. 4:6; Rev. 12:17; 19:10] [a]ch. 1:10; [John 3:33] [b][John 5:38]
11 [c]ch. 2:25; [ch. 4:9] [d]See John 1:4
12 [e][John 3:15, 36; 5:24; 6:40, 47]
13 [f]John 20:31 [g]John 1:12
14 [h]ch. 2:28; 3:21; 4:17 [i]ch. 3:22; [Prov. 10:24]
16 [j][Job 42:8; James 5:15] [k]Matt. 12:31, 32; Mark 3:29; Luke 12:10; Heb. 6:4-6; 10:26 [l][Jer. 7:16; 14:11]
17 [m][ch. 3:4]
18 [n]ch. 3:9 [o]John 1:18

was born of God [p]protects him, and the evil
one does not touch him.
19 We know that we are from God, and [q]the
whole world lies in the power of the evil one.
20 And we know that the Son of God has
come and [r]has given us understanding, so that
we may know [s]him who is true; and we are in
him who is true, in his Son Jesus Christ. He is
the true God and [t]eternal life. 21 Little children,
[u]keep yourselves from idols.

18 [p] John 17:12
19 [q] [Luke 4:6; Gal. 1:4]
20 [r] [Luke 24:45] [s] See John 17:3; Rev. 3:7 [t] ver. 11-13
21 [u] 1 Cor. 10:7, 14

a daily confidence here and now, worked out in prayer that is "according to [God's] will" (cf. 3:22) for ourselves (5:14–15), and for others (vv. 16–17), with trust for spiritual protection (vv. 18–19), and in daily fellowship with God and in Christ (v. 20) that turns us from all earthly idols (v. 21).

The Second Letter of John

2 John

Greeting

1 [a]The elder to the elect lady and her children, [b]whom I love in truth, and not only I,
but also all who [c]know [d]the truth, 2 [e]because
of the truth that abides in us and will be with
us forever:

3 [f]Grace, mercy, and peace will be with us,
from God the Father and from Jesus Christ
the Father's Son, in truth and love.

Walking in Truth and Love

4 [g]I rejoiced greatly to find some of your
children walking in the truth, just as we
were commanded by the Father. 5 And now
I ask you, dear lady—[h]not as though I were
writing you a new commandment, but the
one we have had from the beginning—[i]that
we love one another. 6 And [j]this is love, that
we walk according to his commandments;
this is the commandment, just [k]as you have
heard from the beginning, so that you should
walk in it. 7 For [l]many deceivers [m]have gone
out into the world, [n]those who do not confess
the coming of Jesus Christ in the flesh. Such a
one is the deceiver and the antichrist. 8 Watch
yourselves, [o]so that you may not lose what we[1]
have worked for, but [p]may win a full reward.
9 Everyone who goes on ahead and does not
abide in the teaching of Christ, [q]does not have

[1] Some manuscripts *you*

1–3 It is impossible to miss John's emphasis on "truth" in these opening verses. As in his first letter, John is here concerned that the truth of the gospel be the foundation upon which all church life in general, and all relationships between professing believers specifically, be grounded.

While it is John's concern for the truth that emerges with greatest force, he makes a point to link it with love (vv. 1, 3; cf. v. 12), a connection that reverberates throughout 1 John too. Right from the start, John establishes the content of the gospel (the "truth" of "grace, mercy, and peace . . . from God the Father and from Jesus Christ the Father's Son") and one of the primary fruits of the gospel ("love"). The apostles Paul and Peter also joined truth with love (Eph. 4:15; 1 Pet. 1:22).

4–6 Virtually a remix of the major themes of John's first letter, these verses set forth the priorities of gospel soundness (v. 4), genuine love among believers (v. 5; cf. 1 John 2:7–10), and obedience to God's commands (2 John 6) for the health of the church. Of particular interest is John's claim that our obedience to God's commands is the very means by which we love one another, showing again that transformation is the inevitable result of a right response to God's word of grace in the gospel.

Having been loved so marvelously, all out of proportion to what we deserve, we are freed to love others—even when *they* do not deserve it. And the means of expressing that love is not hidden, but rather is demonstrated by living in accord with the commands of God that are an expression of his character and care.

7–11 Here is presented the primary burden of this letter. John warns his readers to be on the alert for anyone who in their teaching "does not abide in the teaching of Christ" (v. 9) and who thus teaches in a way that erodes both the content and the effect of the gospel. The doctrinal test for teaching is here the same as is seen in 1 John: whether or not someone confesses "the coming of Jesus Christ in the flesh" (2 John 7; cf. 1 John 4:2–3). Any attempt to change or replace the gospel will be tested by the unchanging truths of the gospel of Jesus, the Christ. Failure to detect and guard

1 [a]3 John 1; [1 Pet. 5:1] [b]1 John 3:18; 3 John 1 [c]John 8:32; [1 Tim. 2:4; Heb. 10:26] [d]John 1:17; 14:6; See Gal. 2:5
2 [e][1 Cor. 13:6]
3 [f]1 Tim. 1:2; 2 Tim. 1:2; [Jude 2]
4 [g]3 John 3, 4
5 [h]1 John 2:7 [i]See 1 John 3:11
6 [j]1 John 5:3; [1 John 2:5]; See John 14:15 [k]1 John 2:24
7 [l]See 1 John 2:18, 26 [m]1 John 4:1 [n]1 John 2:22; 4:2, 3
8 [o][Gal. 3:4; Heb. 10:35] [p]See 1 Cor. 3:8
9 [q]See 1 John 2:23

God. Whoever abides in the teaching [q]has both
the Father and the Son. 10 If anyone comes to
you and does not bring this teaching, [r]do not
receive him into your house or give him any
greeting, 11 for whoever greets him [s]takes part
in his wicked works.

Final Greetings

12 [t]Though I have much to write to you,
I would rather not use paper and ink. [u]Instead
I hope to come to you and talk face to face, [v]so
that our joy may be complete.
13 The children of your elect sister greet you.

9[q] See 1 John 2:23
10[r] [Rom. 16:17; Gal. 1:8, 9; 2 Thess. 3:6, 14; Titus 3:10]
11[s] [1 Tim. 5:22]
12[t] 3 John 13 [u] 3 John 14 [v] John 15:11; 17:13

against false teaching, including refusing all hospitality to the false teachers (2 John 10), will not only open the door to serious compromise in the church (v. 8) but will also render one guilty for participating in opposition to the gospel (v. 11).

We are never called to move past the gospel but rather to abide in it (v. 9). The gospel of God's great love for us, won by Another, is our daily meat and drink.

The Third Letter of John

3 John

Greeting

1 [a]The elder to the beloved Gaius, [b]whom
I love in truth.
2 Beloved, I pray that all may go well with
you and that you may be in good health, as
it goes well with your soul. 3 For [c]I rejoiced
greatly when the brothers[1] came and testified
to your truth, as indeed you are walking in the
truth. 4 I have no greater joy than to hear that
[d]my children are walking in the truth.

Support and Opposition

5 Beloved, it is a faithful thing you do in all
your efforts for [e]these brothers, [f]strangers as
they are, 6 who testified to your love before
the church. You will do well to send them
on their journey in a manner [g]worthy of God.
7 For they have gone out for the sake of [h]the
name, [i]accepting nothing from the Gentiles.
8 Therefore we ought to support people like
these, that we may be fellow workers for the
truth.
9 I have written something to the church,
but Diotrephes, who likes to put himself
first, does not acknowledge our authority. 10 So
if I come, I will bring up what he is doing,
talking wicked nonsense against us. And not

[1] Or *brothers and sisters*. The plural Greek word *adelphoi* (translated "brothers") refers to siblings in a family. In New Testament usage, depending on the context, *adelphoi* may refer either to men or to both men and women who are siblings (brothers and sisters) in God's family, the church; also verses 5, 10

1[a] 2 John 1 [b] 1 John 3:18; 2 John 1
3[c] 2 John 4
4[d] [1 Cor. 4:14, 15; Gal. 4:19; 1 Tim. 1:2; 2 Tim. 1:2; Titus 1:4; Philem. 10]
5[e] [Gal. 6:10; Heb. 13:1] [f] See Matt. 25:35
6[g] 1 Thess. 2:12; [Col. 1:10]
7[h] See Acts 5:41 [i] 1 Cor. 9:12, 15

1–4 Once again John's concern for the integrity of the truth of the gospel (explained in his previous letters; e.g., 1 John 1:1–3; 2:21–22; 2 John 3), held tightly by individual believers and controlling relationships between believers, emerges with clarity and force in the opening verses of his letter.

Four times in these opening verses the word "truth" appears, and each time it does so with clear emphasis. John is unapologetically communicating the importance of faithfulness to the objective content of the gospel for the health of both the individual believer and the local church (cf. 3 John 6, 9). By inference, we see John's passionate opposition to teaching that is false, both for its very falseness and for its effect. It should not go without notice that this passion for the truth is, as we have come to expect from John, suffused with a deep love for those to whom he writes (v. 1; cf. vv. 14–15). John rejoices in his spiritual "children" who are "walking in the truth" (v. 4; cf. 2 John 4).

There is no tension between loving truth and loving grace. After all, Jesus himself came, as John says in his Gospel account, "full of grace and truth" (John 1:14). In cherishing truth and earnestly loving others, we follow in the footsteps of the Savior.

5–8 John's burden in this letter is (1) the commendation of the church, and of Gaius in particular, for supporting faithful gospel ministers, and (2) encouragement that such support might continue. By such support, believers actually participate in faithful gospel ministry (v. 8). (This is exactly the opposite of the "participation" in wickedness that we see in 2 John 11.) Therefore, all genuine believers should be supporting (i.e., materially participating in) the ministry of the gospel as it goes forth.

It is striking that John speaks of those who "have gone out for the sake of the name" (3 John 7). This is, indeed, our impelling motive in all that we do: the name of Jesus. He laid down his life for our sake; we gladly respond by laying down our lives for his sake.

9–15 John gives an example of one who was refusing to support gospel-faithful ministry (vv. 9–11), evidently as a result of a desire to draw attention to himself and content with that, he refuses to welcome the brothers, and also stops those who want to and puts them out of the church.

[11]Beloved, [j]do not imitate evil but imitate good. [k]Whoever does good is from God; [l]whoever does evil has not seen God. [12]Demetrius [m]has received a good testimony from everyone, and from the truth itself. We also add our testimony, and [n]you know that our testimony is true.

Final Greetings

[13][o]I had much to write to you, but I would rather not write with pen and ink. [14]I hope to see you soon, and we will talk face to face.

[15]Peace be to you. The friends greet you. Greet the friends, [p]each by name.

11[j][Ps. 34:14; 37:27; Isa. 1:16, 17] [k]1 John 2:29 [l]See 1 John 3:6
12[m][1 Tim. 3:7] [n]John 21:24
13[o]2 John 12
15[p]John 10:3

to be independent of anyone else's authority. As such, Diotrephes demonstrates again how a failure to personally yield to the gospel will inevitably result in a life that betrays the gospel.

John encourages his readers rather to follow the example of those whose lives conform to God's truth and whose lives put on display for all to see the transforming power of the gospel (vv. 11–12). There is a fellowship in the gospel, and John calls his readers to purposefully engage in it, both for specific purposes (v. 8) and in daily life (v. 11; cf. vv. 14–15). He ends his letter with a reminder of the great promise of the gospel (peace), with an expression of hope concerning his plans for a future visit, and with expressions of personal fellowship (vv. 14–15).

Introduction to Jude

Author, Date, and Recipients

This book was written by Jude, the brother of James and Jesus (see Matt. 13:55; Mark 6:3; in Greek, "Judas" is the same as "Jude"). Jude was probably written in the mid-60s A.D. Jude's audience was probably Jewish Christians, or a mixture including Gentile Christians who were familiar with Jewish traditions.

The Gospel in Jude

Where is the gospel in Jude's epistle? In such a compact space, we actually receive a potent portrait of the gospel.

First and most pervasively, Jude displays the "photo negative" of the gospel, giving us a vivid and dark picture of those who twist the lavish grace of the gospel into a license to sin (e.g., vv. 12–13). Jude piles on the metaphors throughout his letter, making it abundantly clear that false teaching smuggles death into a church. And yet, by contrast, this bleak picture still reveals the reality of the good news of God's glory in Christ's atoning work.

Made in God's image to reflect his glory, we were created as mirrors at 45-degree angles, meant to reflect out to the world the unhindered radiance of God's glory. But in disobedience, we turn around to face the ground. And when you turn a mirror upside down, it does not reflect a light but casts a shadow on the ground. In the same way, we sinners tend to focus upon the shadow of self-centered, worldly priorities rather than on the glory emanating from God himself. Jude invites us to worship this God—"him who is able to keep you from stumbling and to present you blameless before the presence of his glory with great joy" (v. 24).

Second, Jude's persistent admonition to avoid false teachers, though sobering, is itself a gift of God's grace. God is loving us by warning us against false teaching. As our Father, God wants his people to be healthy, joyful witnesses to the gospel. He therefore instructs us—scathingly, at times, as in Jude's letter—out of his great love for us.

Third and finally, Jude reminds us of God's saving work in Christ that echoes across all of human history. Jude startlingly remarks in verse 5 that it was Jesus who brought God's people out of Egypt—centuries before the incarnation! Whatever Jude meant to convey here, at the least he is reminding us that Christ's saving work is not an isolated and disconnected historical event. Rather, Christ's work of redemption is the climax to all of God's mighty deeds on behalf of his people.

Outline

I. Initial Greeting (vv. 1–2)

II. Jude's Appeal: Contend for the Faith (vv. 3–4)

III. The Immoral Character and Resulting Judgment of the False Teachers (vv. 5–16)

IV. Concluding Exhortations (vv. 17–25)

The Letter of

Jude

Greeting

1 Jude, a servant[1] of Jesus Christ and brother of James,

[a]To those who are called, [b]beloved in God the Father and [c]kept for[2] Jesus Christ:

2 May [d]mercy, [e]peace, and love be multiplied to you.

Judgment on False Teachers

3 Beloved, although I was very eager to write to you about our [f]common salvation, I found it necessary to write appealing to you [g]to contend for the faith that was once for all delivered to the saints.
4 For [h]certain people [i]have crept in unnoticed [j]who long ago were designated for this condemnation, ungodly people, who pervert [k]the grace of our God into sensuality and [l]deny our only Master and Lord, Jesus Christ.

5 Now I want [m]to remind you, although you once fully knew it, that [n]Jesus, who saved[3]

[1] Or *slave* (for the contextual rendering of the Greek word *doulos*, see Preface) [2] Or *by* [3] Some manuscripts *although you fully knew it, that the Lord who once saved*

1[a] Rom. 1:7; 1 Cor. 1:24 [b] 1 Thess. 1:4; 2 Thess. 2:13 [c] John 17:11, 15; 1 Thess. 5:23
2[d] [2 John 3] [e] 1 Pet. 1:2; 2 Pet. 1:2
3[f] Titus 1:4 [g] 1 Tim. 6:12; 2 Tim. 4:7; [Luke 13:24; 1 Cor. 9:25; Phil. 1:27]
4[h] 2 Pet. 2:1 [i] [Gal. 2:4] [j] 1 Pet. 2:8 [k] See Acts 11:23 [l] Titus 1:16; 2 Pet. 2:1; 1 John 2:22
5[m] 2 Pet. 1:12; 3:17 [n] [1 Cor. 10:4, 5, 9]

1 There is a lot wrapped up in this simple greeting, the opening line of Jude's epistle. Jude is the brother of James, by which he means James the apostle, the brother of Jesus (not James the disciple of Jesus, who was killed by Herod; Acts 12:2). So Jude himself is the brother of Jesus. But he doesn't identify himself as such. He calls himself James's brother but Jesus' "servant."

The reason for Jude's humility is obvious: this brother of Jude is the incarnate Son of God (John 3:16). He is the head and "the beginning, the firstborn from the dead, that in everything he might be preeminent" (Col. 1:18). Jude says of the One who is not ashamed to call us his brothers (Heb. 2:11), "I am not worthy to call my brother my brother. I am his servant!" Yet, the one who is only worthy of being a "servant" addresses his readers as "beloved in God the Father and kept for Jesus Christ" (Jude 1). Thus, Jude grants believers his own family status. In doing so, he reminds us of the great gospel privilege of being children of God (1 John 3:1) even though we are deserving only of being his servants.

2 Since the gospel is true, this is how we are invited to begin every day: with the multiplication of "mercy, peace, and love." This is what is raining down on us every moment of the day by the grace of God. This is what is most deeply true of us.

3–4 Jude urges believers to resist those who pervert the promises of grace into an excuse for sensuality (cf. Titus 2:11–12). He urges believers to contend for the faith once for all delivered to them. In 1 Timothy 1:8–11 we learn that sensual sins, passions of the flesh, are contrary to "sound doctrine" and "the gospel of the glory of the blessed God." What we learn in this passage in Jude and others is that God's grace does not lead us away from our Master and Lord (Jude 4). Grace liberates us not only by forgiving us but also by freeing us from bondage to sin by instilling loyalty to Christ in our hearts. Because he has given himself for us, we give ourselves to him. The gospel transforms our desires from the inside out. We are led into righteousness by discovering that our life and joy are most full as we serve the One we most love.

5–7 Grace *forgives* disobedience but it does not *produce* disobedience, nor is it a free pass to disobey. Jude recalls God's mighty deeds in history to remind his readers of coming judgment for the wicked. We are given three sobering reminders in these verses.

a people out of the land of Egypt, [o]after-
ward destroyed those who did not believe.
6 And [p]the angels who did not stay within
their own position of authority, but left
their proper dwelling, he has kept in eternal chains under gloomy darkness until the
judgment of the great day— 7 just as [q]Sodom
and Gomorrah and [r]the surrounding cities,
which likewise indulged in sexual immorality and [s]pursued unnatural desire,[1] serve as
an example by undergoing a punishment of
eternal fire.

8 Yet in like manner these people also, relying on their dreams, defile the flesh, reject
authority, and [t]blaspheme the glorious ones.
9 But when [u]the archangel [v]Michael, contending with the devil, was disputing [w]about the
body of Moses, he did not presume to pronounce a blasphemous judgment, but said,
[x]"The Lord rebuke you." 10 [y]But these people
blaspheme all that they do not understand,
and they are destroyed by all that they, like
unreasoning animals, understand instinc-
tively. 11 Woe to them! For they walked in [z]the
way of Cain and abandoned themselves for the
sake of gain [a]to Balaam's error and [b]perished in
Korah's rebellion. 12 These are hidden reefs[2] [c]at
your love feasts, as they feast with you without
fear, [d]shepherds feeding themselves; [e]water-
less clouds, [f]swept along by winds; fruitless
trees in late autumn, twice dead, [g]uprooted;
13 [h]wild waves of the sea, casting up the foam
of [i]their own shame; [j]wandering stars, [k]for
whom the gloom of utter darkness has been
reserved forever.

14 It was also about these that Enoch, [l]the
seventh from Adam, prophesied, saying,
[m]"Behold, the Lord comes with ten thousands
of his holy ones, 15 [n]to execute judgment on
all and to convict all the ungodly of all their
deeds of ungodliness that they have [o]commit-
ted in such an ungodly way, and of all [p]the
harsh things that ungodly sinners have spoken against him." 16 These are grumblers, mal-
contents, [q]following their own sinful desires;
[r]they are loud-mouthed boasters, [s]showing
favoritism to gain advantage.

A Call to Persevere

17 But you must [t]remember, beloved, the
predictions of the apostles of our Lord Jesus
Christ. 18 They[3] said to you, [u]"In the last time
there will be scoffers, following their own
ungodly passions." 19 It is these who cause divisions, worldly people, [v]devoid of the Spirit.
20 But you, beloved, [w]building yourselves up in
your most holy faith and [x]praying in the Holy
Spirit, 21 [y]keep yourselves in the love of God,
[z]waiting for the mercy of our Lord Jesus Christ
that leads to eternal life. 22 And have mercy on
those who doubt; 23 save others by [a]snatching
them out of [b]the fire; to others show mercy
[c]with fear, hating even [d]the garment[4] stained
by the flesh.

[1] Greek *other flesh* [2] Or *are blemishes* [3] Or *Christ, because they* [4] Greek *chiton*, a long garment worn under the cloak next to the skin

First, hell is real. What is the effect of combining two earthly accounts of judgment (vv. 5, 7) with one heavenly account of the same (v. 6)? By equating the heavenly event with the two earthly events, Jude makes all spiritual spheres subject to the same historical reality. Condemnation for unrepented wickedness is not theoretical nor intended for only a portion of God's creation. The spiritual judgment of hell will be real—sadly and painfully real. Second, hell is eternal. Note Jude's language of "eternal chains" (v. 6) and "punishment of eternal fire" (v. 7). Third, there will be those participating in the spiritual communities of heaven and earth who are going to hell. Jude gives three examples: some Israelites, certain angels, and the cities surrounding Sodom and Gomorrah. A cursory connection to God's people is no guaranteed refuge from the punishment of sin. There are indeed "people who have crept in" to the community of faith (v. 4), who have gotten into the sheepfold in another way than that of true salvation (John 10:1). Peter refers to these in 2 Peter 2:1.

So where is the comfort amid all this gloom and doom? Jude gives it to us in verse 5. It is Jesus, who saved God's people out of bondage in Egypt. He was the active agent rescuing his covenant people from bondage and preparing them to be the means by which the nations of the earth would be blessed. Christ alone saves. He did it in the days of the exodus, and he does it today, for any sinner who turns trustingly to him.

14–16 The reality of coming judgment is sobering. Yet Christians can take comfort, for at least two reasons. First, all wrongs and injustices committed against God's people

5 [o]Num. 14:29, 37; 26:64, 65; Ps. 106:26; Heb. 3:17-19
6 [p]2 Pet. 2:4; [Rev. 20:2]
7 [q]See Gen. 19:24 [r]Deut. 29:23; Hos. 11:8 [s]2 Pet. 2:10
8 [t]2 Pet. 2:10
9 [u]1 Thess. 4:16; [2 Pet. 2:11] [v]Dan. 10:13; 12:1; Rev. 12:7 [w][Deut. 34:6] [x]Zech. 3:2
10 [y]2 Pet. 2:12
11 [z]See Gen. 4:5-8 [a]See 2 Pet. 2:15 [b]Num. 16:1-3, 31-35
12 [c]2 Pet. 2:13 [d]Ezek. 34:2, 8, 10 [e]Prov. 25:14; 2 Pet. 2:17 [f]Heb. 13:9 [g]Matt. 15:13
13 [h]Isa. 57:20 [i][2 Cor. 4:2; Phil. 3:19] [j][Isa. 14:12] [k]2 Pet. 2:17
14 [l]Gen. 5:18 [m]See Deut. 33:2; [Dan. 7:10; Mark 8:38; 1 Thess. 3:13; 2 Thess. 1:7]
15 [n][2 Pet. 2:5] [o]2 Pet. 2:6 [p]1 Sam. 2:3; Ps. 94:4; John 6:60
16 [q]2 Pet. 2:10 [r]2 Pet. 2:18 [s]Lev. 19:15; Deut. 10:17
17 [t]2 Pet. 3:2
18 [u]2 Pet. 3:3
19 [v][Rom. 8:9; Phil. 3:3]
20 [w]See Col. 2:7 [x]Eph. 6:18; [Rom. 8:26]
21 [y]2 Cor. 13:14; [Acts 13:43] [z]Titus 2:13; 2 Pet. 3:12 **23** [a]Amos 4:11; Zech. 3:2 [b]See 1 Cor. 3:15 [c][2 Cor. 5:11] [d]Rev. 3:4; [Zech. 3:4]

Introduction to Revelation

Author and Date

Jesus Christ is the divine author of this "revelation" (1:1). He describes coming events to his servant John. John, son of Zebedee, was the "beloved disciple" who also wrote the Fourth Gospel and 1, 2, and 3 John. Most scholars believe John recorded these visions while imprisoned on the island of Patmos in the mid-90s A.D.

Audience

The book of Revelation is addressed to the seven churches named in 1:11, and John presents the risen Christ addressing each church in Revelation 2–3. Each letter to a particular church, however, ends with the words "He who has an ear, let him hear what the Spirit says to the churches" (2:7, 11, 17, 29; 3:6, 13, 22), so with the number seven pointing to completion and with each letter calling all the churches to hear, in addressing seven churches John writes representatively to all churches. In their culture, the churches seem to be small, insignificant, and struggling against mounting persecution from the Roman Empire. John shows them the world as it really is.

The Gospel in Revelation

John has built the unique application of the gospel he provides in Revelation into the very structure of the book.

The opening (1:1–8) and closing (22:6–21) reveal things as they are and promise that Jesus is coming soon. Then the letters to the seven churches in the world (1:9–3:22) are matched by the concluding depiction of the church in glory in the new heaven and earth (21:1–22:5). In the midst of his tribulation and the struggles of the churches, John is given a throne-room vision that includes Christ conquering and opening the scroll (4:1–6:17). This is matched near the end of the book by his vision of Christ returning to conquer, set up his thousand-year kingdom, then open the scrolls for judgment (19:11–20:15). John's vision of the sealing of the 144,000 saints and the trumpets that bring plagues (7:1–9:21) is paralleled by his vision of the redemption of the 144,000 and the outpouring of the bowls of wrath (14:1–19:10). John is attested as a true prophet as he eats the scroll like Ezekiel (10:1–11), and the churches are warned against the deception of the false prophet (13:11–18).

The two complementary accounts of Satan's war on the church as it proclaims the gospel (11:1–14; 12:1–13:10) frame the centerpiece of the book, in which "the kingdom of the world" becomes "the kingdom of our Lord and of his Christ" at the blast of the seventh trumpet (11:15–19). This structure proclaims that Christ is Lord, so that though Satan is persecuting the churches and though they are small and beleaguered, they will yet hold fast the word of God and testimony of Jesus, with the expectation that their patient endurance will be rewarded.

Gospel faith makes people right with God and produces gospel faithfulness, which reaps gospel reward. The book of Revelation is a triumphant vision of God's final victory over all the forces of evil in the world. This final victory is secured because of the blood of the Lamb that purifies God's people for his ultimate reign. Revelation is filled with the gracious purposes of God, to strengthen his people.

Outline

I. Revelation, Blessing, and Epistolary Opening (1:1–8)

II. John's Vision on the Lord's Day (1:9–22:5)

  A. Jesus and the letters (1:9–3:22)

  B. The throne and the judgments (4:1–16:21)

    1. The throne room vision (4:1–5:14)
    2. Six seals (6:1–17)
    3. The sealing of the saints and their worship (7:1–17)
    4. The seventh seal (8:1–5)
    5. Six trumpets (8:6–9:21)
    6. Prophetic witness (10:1–11:14)
    7. The seventh trumpet (11:15–19)
    8. Conflict between the Seed of the woman and the seed of the Serpent (12:1–14:20)
    9. Seven bowls (15:1–16:21)

  C. The harlot, the king, and the bride (17:1–22:5)

III. Revelation, Blessing, and Epistolary Closing (22:6–21)

The

Revelation

to John

Prologue

1 The revelation of Jesus Christ, which God
[a]gave him [b]to show to his servants[1] the
things that must soon take place. [c]He made
it known by sending his angel to his servant[2]
John, **2** [d]who bore witness to the word of God
and to [e]the testimony of Jesus Christ, even [f]to
all that he saw. **3** [g]Blessed is the one who reads
aloud the words of this prophecy, and blessed
are those who hear, and who keep what is written in it, [h]for the time is near.

Greeting to the Seven Churches

4 John to the seven churches that are in Asia:
Grace to you and peace from [i]him [j]who is
and [k]who was and who is to come, and from
[l]the seven spirits who are before his throne,
5 and from Jesus Christ [m]the faithful witness,
[n]the firstborn of the dead, and [o]the ruler of
kings on earth.

To [p]him who loves us and [q]has freed us from
our sins by his blood **6** and made us [r]a kingdom, [r]priests to [s]his God and Father, to him

[1] Greek *bondservants* [2] Greek *bondservant*

1:1–3 John presents his book as the revelation of Jesus Christ (1:1); that is, the book comes from and is about Jesus. God gave the message to Jesus, who sent his angel to John with it, so that the servants of Jesus would be motivated to bear witness to the word of God and to Jesus (see comments on the "chain of revelatory disclosure" in the note on 10:1–11). John pronounces the first of seven beatitudes in the book on the one who reads aloud the words of this prophecy, on those who hear, and on those who keep what is written in it (1:3; cf. 14:13; 16:15; 19:9; 20:6; 22:7, 14). Because he died and rose again, Jesus now reigns and blesses those who are faithful to him to the end.

1:4–8 In Revelation, John is not so much teaching the gospel as he is building on it, encouraging Christians to endure because of it, and to be faithful to it even unto death. Consequently, he does not always refer to the gospel of Christ's atoning work to defeat the guilt and power of our sin explicitly. Here in verse 5, however, John refers to Jesus as "the firstborn of the dead" because his resurrection guarantees the general resurrection (cf. 1 Cor. 15:20–22). John also identifies Jesus as the one "who loves us and has freed us from our sins by his blood" (Rev. 1:5). Christ loves sinners and has freed us from our sins. This is the wonder of the gospel.

At many points, such as here, John presents the salvation Jesus has accomplished as the ultimate fulfillment of a rescue of God's covenant people analogous to Israel's exodus from Egypt. Jesus dies as the new and better Passover Lamb (cf. 5:6). Moreover, just as God made Israel a kingdom of priests (Ex. 19:6), so here, having redeemed us from sin and death, Jesus makes us "a kingdom, priests to his God and Father" (Rev. 1:6).

We receive John's worshipful response to this gospel message as he ascribes to Jesus glory and dominion forever and ever. Because of the salvation Jesus has accomplished, he is worthy of praise (cf. 5:5–14; 7:9–12; 14:2–3; 15:2–4). John refers to the death of Christ as he describes Jesus coming with the clouds (in fulfillment of Dan. 7:13) when at his second coming "every eye will see him, even those who pierced him" (Rev. 1:7). This piercing took place at the cross in fulfillment of Zechariah 12:10, which is itself reflecting the piercing of the Davidic servant in Isaiah 53. By citing Zechariah 12:10 and Daniel 7:13, John brings together the Old Testament themes of the suffering and conquering Messiah, identifying the former with Christ's first coming and the latter with his second.

Chapter 1

1 [a]John 17:7, 8; [John 8:26; 14:10] [b]ch. 22:6 [c]ch. 22:16
2 [d]John 19:35 [e]ch. 6:9; 12:17; 19:10; See 1 Cor. 1:6 [f]ver. 11, 19
3 [g]ch. 22:7; [Luke 11:28; John 8:51; 1 John 2:3] [h]ch. 22:10; [1 John 2:18]; See Rom. 13:11
4 [i]ver. 8; ch. 4:8; Heb. 13:8 [j]Ex. 3:14 (Gk.) [k]John 1:1 [l]ch. 3:1; 4:5; 5:6
5 [m]ch. 3:14; John 18:37; 1 Tim. 6:13; [ch. 2:13; Ps. 89:37; Isa. 55:4] [n]Col. 1:18; [Ps. 89:27; Acts 26:23; 1 Cor. 15:20] [o]ch. 17:14; 19:16; [Ps. 89:27] [p]John 13:34; 15:9 [q]1 Pet. 1:18, 19
6 [r]ch. 5:10; 20:6; 1 Pet. 2:9 [s]See Rom. 15:6

be [t]glory and [u]dominion forever and ever.
Amen. 7 Behold, [v]he is coming with the clouds,
and [w]every eye will see him, even those who
pierced him, and all tribes of the earth will
wail[1] on account of him. Even so. Amen.
8 [x]"I am the Alpha and the Omega," says the
Lord God, [y]"who is and who was and who is
to come, the Almighty."

Vision of the Son of Man

9 I, John, your brother and [z]partner in
[a]the tribulation and [b]the kingdom and [c]the
patient endurance that are in Jesus, was on
the island called Patmos [d]on account of the
word of God and the testimony of Jesus. 10 [e]I
was in the Spirit [f]on the Lord's day, and I heard
behind me a loud voice [g]like a trumpet 11 saying, [h]"Write what you see in a book and send
it to the seven churches, to Ephesus and to
Smyrna and to Pergamum and to Thyatira and
to Sardis and to Philadelphia and to Laodicea."
12 Then I turned to see the voice that was
speaking to me, and on turning I saw [i]seven
golden lampstands, 13 and in the midst of the
lampstands [j]one like [k]a son of man, [l]clothed
with a long robe and [m]with a golden sash
around his chest. 14 [n]The hairs of his head were
white, like white wool, like snow. [o]His eyes
were like a flame of fire, 15 [p]his feet were like
burnished bronze, refined in a furnace, and
[q]his voice was like the roar of many waters. 16 [r]In
his right hand he held seven stars, [s]from his
mouth came a sharp two-edged sword, and [t]his
face was like the sun shining [u]in full strength.
17 [v]When I saw him, I fell at his feet as though
dead. But [v]he laid his right hand on me, [w]say-
ing, "Fear not, [x]I am the first and the last, 18 and
the living one. [y]I died, and behold I am alive
forevermore, and [z]I have the keys of Death and
Hades. 19 [a]Write therefore [b]the things that you
have seen, those that are and those that are to
take place after this. 20 As for the mystery of
the seven stars that you saw in my right hand,
and [c]the seven golden lampstands, the seven
stars are the angels of the seven churches, and
[d]the seven lampstands are the seven churches.

To the Church in Ephesus

2 "To the angel of the church in Ephesus
write: 'The words of [e]him who holds the
seven stars in his right hand, [f]who walks
among the seven golden lampstands.
2 [g]" 'I know your works, your toil and your
patient endurance, and how you cannot bear
with those who are evil, but [h]have tested those
[i]who call themselves apostles and are not, and

[1] Or *mourn*

6 [t]See Rom. 11:36 [u]1 Pet. 4:11
7 [v]Dan. 7:13; See Matt. 16:27 [w]Zech. 12:10; John 19:37
8 [x]ch. 21:6; 22:13; [Isa. 41:4; 43:10; 44:6] [y]ver. 4
9 [z][Phil. 4:14] [a]John 16:33 [b]2 Tim. 2:12 [c]ch. 3:10 [d]See ver. 2
10 [e]ch. 4:2; [ch. 17:3; 21:10; 1 Kgs. 18:12; Ezek. 3:12; Matt. 22:43; 2 Cor. 12:2] [f]Acts 20:7; 1 Cor. 16:2 [g]ch. 4:1
11 [h]ver. 2, 19
12 [i]ver. 20; ch. 2:1; Ex. 25:37; 2 Chr. 4:20; Zech. 4:2; [ch. 11:4]
13 [j]Dan. 7:13 [k]ch. 14:14; Dan. 10:16 [l]Dan. 10:5 [m]ch. 15:6
14 [n]Dan. 7:9 [o]ch. 2:18; 19:12; [Dan. 10:6]
15 [p]Ezek. 1:7; Dan. 10:6 [q]ch. 14:2; 19:6; Ezek. 43:2
16 [r]ver. 20; ch. 2:1; 3:1 [s]ch. 19:15; [ch. 2:12, 16; Isa. 49:2; Eph. 6:17; Heb. 4:12] [t]Matt. 17:2 [u]Judg. 5:31
17 [v]Dan. 8:17, 18; 10:9, 10, 15; [Luke 24:37; John 21:12] [w]Matt. 17:7 [x]ch. 2:8; 22:13; Isa. 41:4; 44:6; 48:12
18 [y]Rom. 6:9; 14:9 [z][ch. 9:1; 20:1]
19 [a]ver. 2, 11 [b]ver. 12-16
20 [c]See ver. 12 [d][Matt. 5:14, 15]

Chapter 2

1 [e]ch. 1:16, 20 [f]ch. 1:13
2 [g]ver. 19; ch. 3:1, 8, 15 [h]See 1 John 4:1 [i]See 2 Cor. 11:13

1:9–20 John identifies with his audience as their brother and partner in both the tribulation and the kingdom, requiring patient endurance on the part of those who live between the two comings of Christ. One consistent New Testament theme related to the gospel is that those who embrace it will face tribulation (v. 9; cf. Matt. 5:11–12; Mark 10:29–30; Acts 14:22; 1 Thess. 2:4; 2 Tim. 3:12; 1 Pet. 2:21). The pattern of suffering-to-glory undergone by the Savior is the pattern for his disciples.

John himself has been exiled to Patmos because of "the word of God and the testimony of Jesus" (Rev. 1:9), likely a reference to the way that he has borne witness to the gospel. In the midst of his affliction, the risen Christ appears to him in glory (vv. 10–20), and the way that Jesus presents himself to John in his resurrection glory is applied to the churches in Revelation 2–3. John is not to fear, because Jesus is eternal (1:17), and also because of the victorious gospel: Jesus tells him in verse 18 that he died and yet is alive forever. This assertion means that even if those united to Christ are put to death, he can guarantee that death will not hold his followers just as death could not hold him, as the firstborn from the dead (v. 5). This is stated even more explicitly when Jesus declares that he has "the keys of Death and Hades" (v. 18). Death and hell cannot bind the followers of Jesus.

In Christ, death itself has been undone. Those who are in him have nothing to fear on earth. Our eternal future could not be more secure.

2:1–3:22 Jesus applies the results of his death and resurrection to the churches in threats of discipline and promises of reward. Because of what he accomplished and his consequent status as our heavenly enthroned Lord, he can guarantee both.

Jesus announces that he walks among the lampstands (2:1) as he threatens to remove the lampstand of the church in Ephesus (2:5; cf. 1:13). Jesus again asserts that he died and came to life (2:8; cf. 1:18), then he calls the church in Smyrna to be faithful unto death (2:10). Threatening to war against them with "the sword of my

found them to be false. 3 I know you are enduring patiently and bearing up [j]for my name's
sake, and you [k]have not grown weary. 4 But
I have this against you, that you have abandoned [l]the love you had at first. 5 Remember
therefore from where you have fallen; repent,
and do [m]the works you did at first. If not, [n]I will
come to you and remove your lampstand from
its place, unless you repent. 6 Yet this you have:
you hate the works of [o]the Nicolaitans, which
I also hate. 7 [p]He who has an ear, let him hear
what the Spirit says to the churches. [q]To the
one who conquers I will grant to eat of [r]the
tree of life, which is in [s]the paradise of God.'

To the Church in Smyrna

8 "And to the angel of the church in Smyrna
write: 'The words of [t]the first and the last,
[u]who died and came to life.
9 "'I know your tribulation and [v]your poverty
([v]but you are rich) and the slander[1] of [w]those
who say that they are Jews and are not, but are
a synagogue of Satan. 10 Do not fear what you
are about to suffer. Behold, the devil is about
to throw some of you into prison, [w]that you
may be tested, and for [x]ten days [y]you will have
tribulation. [z]Be faithful [a]unto death, and I will
give you [b]the crown of life. 11 [c]He who has an
ear, let him hear what the Spirit says to the
churches. [c]The one who conquers will not be
hurt by [d]the second death.'

To the Church in Pergamum

12 "And to the angel of the church in Pergamum write: 'The words of him who has [e]the
sharp two-edged sword.
13 "'I know where you dwell, [f]where Satan's
throne is. Yet you hold fast my name, and you
did not [g]deny my faith[2] even in the days of
Antipas [h]my faithful witness, who was killed
among you, where Satan dwells. 14 But I have
a few things against you: you have some there
who hold the teaching of [i]Balaam, who taught
Balak to put a stumbling block before the sons
of Israel, so that they might [j]eat food sacrificed
to idols and [k]practice sexual immorality. 15 So
also you have some who hold the teaching of
[l]the Nicolaitans. 16 Therefore repent. If not, [m]I
will come to you soon and [n]war against them
with [e]the sword of my mouth. 17 [c]He who has
an ear, let him hear what the Spirit says to the
churches. [c]To the one who conquers I will give
some of [o]the hidden manna, and I will give
him a white stone, with [p]a new name written
on the stone [q]that no one knows except the
one who receives it.'

To the Church in Thyatira

18 "And to the angel of the church in Thyatira
write: 'The words of the Son of God, [r]who has
eyes like a flame of fire, and whose feet are like
burnished bronze.
19 [s]"'I know your works, your love and faith

[1] Greek *blasphemy* [2] Or *your faith in me*

mouth" (i.e., his Word, 2:16; cf. Eph. 6:17; Rev. 19:15, 21; and for John, Christ is also the representation of that Word; cf. John 1:1), Jesus warns the church in Pergamum that he has the sharp two-edged sword (Rev. 2:12; cf. 1:16; Heb. 4:12). Jesus tells the church in Thyatira that he has eyes like a flame of fire (Rev. 2:18) and then warns that he searches mind and heart (2:23). The church in Sardis is dead and needs the one who has the seven spirits of God (3:1) to enable them to wake up, strengthen, remember, keep what they received, and repent (3:2–3). Because Jesus has the key of David (3:7), he can set before the church in Philadelphia an open door to God's eternal purposes (3:8), and because he is the faithful and true witness, the church in Laodicea should heed his counsel (3:18).

Because of the truth of the gospel, Ephesus should maintain its first love (2:4) and Laodicea should not be lukewarm (3:16); Smyrna and Philadelphia should stand fast against the persecution from the synagogue of Satan (2:9; 3:9), and Pergamum, Thyatira, and Sardis should avoid the kinds of compromises with false teaching (2:14, 20) that result in eating food sacrificed to idols and sexual immorality (2:14, 20). Perhaps hiding their compromise resulted in their false reputation of being alive, but those who do such things are dead (3:1). Those who are enduring patiently (2:3), being faithful unto death (2:10), are heeding what the Spirit says to the churches and obeying the call to repent (2:5, 16, 21; 3:3, 19) as they hold fast to the gospel (2:25; 3:11). They will eat from the tree of life (2:7), will not be hurt by the second death (2:11), will receive a new name (2:17), and will have authority over the nations (2:26).

Jesus promises the one who overcomes that he will never blot his name out of the book of life (3:5), and will make him a pillar in the temple (3:12). Overcomers will have clothing for their nakedness and salve for their eyes (3:18), and they will sit

3 [j] John 15:21 [k] [Heb. 12:3, 5]
4 [l] Jer. 2:2
5 [m] ver. 2; [Heb. 10:32] [n] ch. 3:3, 19
6 [o] ver. 15
7 [p] ver. 11, 17, 29; ch. 3:6, 13, 22; 13:9 [q] ch. 3:5; 21:7 [r] See Gen. 2:9 [s] Ezek. 28:13; 31:8 (Gk.)
8 [t] See ch. 1:17 [u] ch. 1:18
9 [v] James 2:5; [1 Tim. 6:18; Heb. 10:34; 11:26] [w] ch. 3:9, 10
10 [w] [See ver. 9 above] [x] [Gen. 24:55; Dan. 1:12, 14] [y] Matt. 24:9 [z] See Matt. 10:22; Heb. 3:6 [a] ch. 12:11 [b] See James 1:12
11 [c] See ver. 7 [d] ch. 20:6, 14; 21:8
12 [e] ver. 16; ch. 1:16
13 [f] ver. 9 [g] See 1 Tim. 5:8 [h] Acts 22:20
14 [i] See 2 Pet. 2:15 [j] ver. 20; Acts 15:29; 1 Cor. 8:10; 10:19 [k] Num. 25:1; 31:16; 1 Cor. 10:8
15 [l] ver. 6
16 [m] [ch. 22:7] [n] See 2 Thess. 2:8 [e] [See ver. 12 above]
17 [c] [See ver. 11 above] [o] [John 6:48-50] [p] ch. 3:12; Isa. 62:2; 65:15 [q] ch. 19:12; [ch. 14:3]
18 [r] ch. 1:14, 15
19 [s] ver. 2

and service and patient endurance, and that
your latter works exceed the first. 20 But I have
this against you, that you tolerate that woman
[t]Jezebel, who calls herself a prophetess and
is teaching and seducing my servants[1] [u]to
practice sexual immorality and [u]to eat food
sacrificed to idols. 21 I gave her time to repent,
but [v]she refuses to repent of her sexual immorality. 22 Behold, I will throw her onto a sickbed, and those who commit adultery with
her I will throw into great tribulation, unless
they repent of her works, 23 and I will strike
her children dead. And all the churches will
know that I am he [w]who searches mind and
heart, and [x]I will give to each of you according to your works. 24 But to the rest of you in
Thyatira, who do not hold this teaching, who
have not learned what some call [y]the deep
things of Satan, to you I say, I [z]do not lay on
you any other burden. 25 Only hold fast [a]what
you have until I come. 26 [b]The one who conquers and who keeps my works [c]until the end,
[d]to him I will give authority over the nations,
27 and [e]he will [f]rule them with a rod of iron,
[g]as when earthen pots are broken in pieces,
even as I myself have received authority from
my Father. 28 And I will give him [h]the morning
star. 29 [p]He who has an ear, let him hear what
the Spirit says to the churches.'

To the Church in Sardis

3 "And to the angel of the church in Sardis
write: 'The words of him [i]who has the
seven spirits of God and the seven stars.
"'I know your works. You have the reputation [j]of being alive, [k]but you are dead. 2 Wake
up, and strengthen what remains and is about
to die, for I have not found your works [l]com-
plete in the sight of my God. 3 [m]Remember,
then, what you received and heard. Keep it,
and repent. If you will not wake up, [n]I will
come [o]like a thief, and you will not know at
what hour I will come against you. 4 Yet you
have still a few names in Sardis, people who
have not [p]soiled their garments, and they will
walk with me [q]in white, for they are [r]worthy.
5 [s]The one who conquers will be clothed thus
in white garments, and I will never [t]blot his
name out of [u]the book of life. [v]I will confess his
name before my Father and before his angels.
6 [p]He who has an ear, let him hear what the
Spirit says to the churches.'

To the Church in Philadelphia

7 "And to the angel of the church in Philadelphia write: 'The words of [w]the holy one,
[x]the true one, [y]who has the key of David, [z]who
opens and no one will shut, who shuts and no
one opens.
8 "'I know your works. Behold, I have set
before you [a]an open door, which no one is able
to shut. I know that you have but little power,
and yet you have kept my word and have not
denied my name. 9 Behold, I will make those
of [b]the synagogue of Satan who say that they
are Jews and are not, but lie—behold, [c]I will
make them come and bow down before your
feet, and they will learn that [d]I have loved
you. 10 [e]Because you have kept my word about
patient endurance, I will keep you from the
hour of trial that is coming on the whole
world, to try [f]those who dwell on the earth. 11 [g]I
am coming soon. [h]Hold fast what you have, so
that no one may seize [i]your crown. 12 [j]The one
who conquers, I will make him [k]a pillar in the
temple of my God. Never shall he go out of it,
and I will write on him [l]the name of my God,
and [m]the name of the city of my God, [m]the new

[1] Greek *bondservants*

20 [t] 1 Kgs. 16:31; 21:25; 2 Kgs. 9:7 [u] See ver. 14
21 [v] [ch. 9:20, 21; 16:9, 11]; See Rom. 2:4
23 [w] Ps. 7:9; 26:2; Jer. 20:12; See Rom. 8:27 [x] See Matt. 16:27
24 [y] [1 Cor. 2:10] [z] [Acts 15:28]
25 [a] ch. 3:11
26 [b] See ver. 7 [c] See Heb. 3:6 [d] Ps. 2:8; [ch. 3:21; 20:4]
27 [e] Ps. 2:9 [f] ch. 12:5; 19:15 [g] Isa. 30:14; Jer. 19:11
28 [h] [2 Pet. 1:19]; See ch. 22:16
29 [p] [See ver. 7 above]

with Jesus on his throne, having conquered as he did (3:21). They endure, Jesus says, "for my name's sake" (2:3); as they do so, they hold fast Jesus' name (2:13) and have not denied that name (3:8). The identification of "overcomers" with those who are united to Christ is important for correct interpretation. Overcoming, for the apostle John, is not a consequence of human effort but a result of faith in the work of Christ Jesus (see 1 John 5:4–5).

Jesus identifies himself as the one who has brought good news, and on the basis of the way he has accomplished salvation, he (1) offers the rewards of the gospel to those who are faithful to his provision for them, (2) threatens judgment against those who stray from the gospel, and (3) asserts that those who maintain the gospel do so for the glory of his name.

Chapter 3 **1** [i] See ch. 1:4, 16 [j] 1 Tim. 5:6 [k] See Luke 15:24 **2** [l] Acts 14:26 **3** [m] [2 Tim. 1:13] [n] ch. 2:5 [o] ch. 16:15; Matt. 24:43; 1 Thess. 5:2, 4; 2 Pet. 3:10 **4** [p] Jude 23 [q] ch. 6:11; 7:9; [Eccles. 9:8] [r] [Luke 20:35] **5** [s] See ch. 2:7 [t] See Ex. 32:32 [u] ch. 13:8; 17:8; 20:12, 15; 21:27; Phil. 4:3 [v] Matt. 10:32; Luke 12:8 **6** [p] [See ch. 2:7 above] **7** [w] ch. 6:10 [x] ver. 14; ch. 19:11; 1 John 5:20 [y] Isa. 22:22; [Luke 1:32] [z] Job 12:14; [Matt. 16:19] **8** [a] Acts 14:27; 1 Cor. 16:9; 2 Cor. 2:12; Col. 4:3 **9** [b] ch. 2:9 [c] [Isa. 45:14; 49:23; 60:14] [d] Isa. 43:4 **10** [e] ch. 1:9; 2 Pet. 2:9 [f] ch. 6:10; 8:13; 11:10; 13:8, 14; 17:8 **11** [g] ch. 22:7, 12, 20 [h] ch. 2:25 [i] ch. 2:10 **12** [j] See ch. 2:7 [k] 1 Kgs. 7:21; 2 Chr. 3:17; Jer. 1:18; Gal. 2:9; [Ps. 23:6; 27:4] [l] ch. 14:1; 22:4 [m] ch. 21:2; Ezek. 48:35; [Gal. 4:26; Heb. 12:22]

Jerusalem, [n]which comes down from my God out of heaven, and my own [o]new name. 13 [p]He who has an ear, let him hear what the Spirit says to the churches.'

To the Church in Laodicea

14 "And to the angel of the church in Laodicea write: 'The words of the [p]Amen, [q]the faithful and true witness, [r]the beginning of God's creation.

15 "'I know your works: you are neither cold nor hot. [s]Would that you were either cold or hot! 16 So, because you are lukewarm, and neither hot nor cold, I will spit you out of my mouth. 17 [t]For you say, I am rich, I have prospered, and I need nothing, not realizing that you are wretched, pitiable, poor, [u]blind, and naked. 18 I counsel you [v]to buy from me gold refined by fire, so that you may be rich, and [w]white garments so that you may clothe yourself and [x]the shame of your nakedness may not be seen, and salve to anoint your eyes, [u]so that you may see. 19 [y]Those whom I love, I reprove and discipline, so be zealous and repent. 20 Behold, I stand at the door and [z]knock. [a]If anyone hears my voice and opens the door, [b]I will come in to him and eat with him, and he with me. 21 [c]The one who conquers, [d]I will grant him to sit with me on my throne, as [e]I also conquered and sat down with my Father on his throne. 22 [p]He who has an ear, let him hear what the Spirit says to the churches.'"

The Throne in Heaven

4 After this I looked, and behold, a door standing open in heaven! And the first voice, which I had heard speaking to me [f]like a trumpet, said, [g]"Come up here, and [h]I will show you what must take place after this." 2 At once [i]I was in the Spirit, and behold, [j]a throne stood in heaven, with one seated on the throne. 3 And he who sat there had the appearance of [k]jasper and carnelian, and around the throne was [l]a rainbow that had the appearance of an emerald. 4 Around the throne were [m]twenty-four thrones, and seated on the thrones were twenty-four elders, [n]clothed in white garments, with [o]golden crowns on their heads. 5 From the throne came [p]flashes of lightning, and rumblings[1] and peals of thunder, and before the throne were burning [q]seven torches of fire, [r]which are the seven spirits of God, 6 and before the throne there was [s]as it were a sea of glass, like crystal.

And around the throne, on each side of the throne, are [t]four living creatures, [u]full of eyes in front and behind: 7 [v]the first living creature like a lion, the second living creature like an ox, the third living creature with the face of a man, and the fourth living creature like an eagle in flight. 8 And the four living creatures, [w]each of them with six wings, are [x]full of eyes all around and within, and [y]day and night they never cease to say,

[z]"Holy, holy, holy, is the Lord God
Almighty,
[a]who was and is and is to come!"

9 And whenever the living creatures give glory and honor and thanks to him who is seated on the throne, [b]who lives forever and ever, 10 the twenty-four elders [c]fall down before him who is seated on the throne and worship him who lives forever and ever. They cast [d]their crowns before the throne, saying,

11 [e]"Worthy are you, our Lord and God,
to receive glory and honor and power,

[1] Or *voices*, or *sounds*

4:1–11 John writes to harassed churches facing persecution and tribulation (2:9–10; 3:9–10). He identifies with them, having been exiled to Patmos for the gospel, "the word of God," and "the testimony of Jesus" (1:9; cf. 1:2). In the midst of these difficult circumstances, John is invited into the heavenly throne room and sees the Lord God Almighty on the throne (4:2), reigning and being worshiped by the dignitaries of the heavenly court (vv. 6–10) for the exercise of his will in all things (v. 11).

The knowledge that God is seated on his heavenly throne, being worshiped as he rightly deserves, is given to encourage persecuted Christians who seem like a small, insignificant minority in the face of the wicked world. God in heaven rules. One day this rule will cover the earth and bring all evil and darkness to a final end. Christ's death and resurrection secure this.

12 [n]ch. 21:10 [o]ch. 2:17
13 [p][See ch. 2:7 above]
14 [p]2 Cor. 1:20 [q]ver. 7; ch. 1:5; 19:11; 22:6 [r]Col. 1:15, 18; [ch. 21:6; 22:13; Prov. 8:22]
15 [s][2 Pet. 2:21]
17 [t]Hos. 12:8; Zech. 11:5; 1 Cor. 4:8 [u]John 9:39-41; Eph. 1:18
18 [v]Isa. 55:1; Matt. 13:44; 25:9; [Prov. 8:19] [w][ch. 19:8]; See ver. 4 [x]ch. 16:15 [u][See ver. 17 above]
19 [y]See Heb. 12:6
20 [z][Song 5:2] [a]Luke 12:36 [b]John 14:23; [Luke 24:29, 30]

21 [c]See ch. 2:7 [d]ch. 20:4; [ch. 2:26; John 12:26; 2 Tim. 2:12]; See Matt. 19:28 [e]ch. 5:5; 6:2; 17:14; John 16:33 **22** [p][See ch. 2:7 above] **Chapter 4** **1** [f]ch. 1:10; [Ex. 19:19, 20] [g]ch. 11:12 [h]ch. 1:1, 19; 22:6 **2** [i]See ch. 1:10 [j]Ps. 11:4; 103:19; Isa. 66:1; Matt. 5:34; 23:22; See 1 Kgs. 22:19 **3** [k]ch. 21:11 [l]Ezek. 1:28; [ch. 10:1; Gen. 9:13-17] **4** [m]ch. 11:16 [n]See ch. 3:4 [o]ver. 10; See James 1:12 **5** [p]ch. 8:5; 11:19; 16:18; [Ex. 19:16] [q][Zech. 4:2] [r]See ch. 1:4 **6** [s]ch. 15:2; [ch. 21:18, 21; Ps. 77:19] [t]Ezek. 1:5 [u]Ezek. 10:12 **7** [v][Ezek. 1:10; 10:14] **8** [w]Isa. 6:2 [x]ver. 6 [y]ch. 14:11 [z]Isa. 6:3 [a]See ch. 1:4 **9** [b]ch. 1:18; 5:13; 15:7; Dan. 4:34; 12:7 **10** [c]ch. 5:8, 14; 7:11; 11:16; 19:4 [d]ver. 4 **11** [e]ch. 5:12

for [f]you created all things,
and [g]by your will they existed and
were created."

The Scroll and the Lamb

5 Then I saw in the right hand of him who
was seated on the throne [h]a scroll written within and on the back, [i]sealed with seven
seals. 2 And [j]I saw a mighty angel proclaiming with a loud voice, "Who is worthy to open
the scroll and break its seals?" 3 And no one
in heaven or on earth or under the earth was
able to open the scroll or to look into it, 4 and
I began to weep loudly because no one was
found worthy to open the scroll or to look into
it. 5 And one of the elders said to me, "Weep no
more; behold, [k]the Lion [l]of the tribe of Judah,
[m]the Root of David, has conquered, so that he
can open the scroll and its seven seals."
6 And between the throne and the four living
creatures and among the elders I saw [n]a Lamb
standing, as though it had been slain, with
seven horns and with [o]seven eyes, which are
[p]the seven spirits of God sent out into all the
earth. 7 And he went and took the scroll from
the right hand of him who was seated on the
throne. 8 And when he had taken the scroll,
the four living creatures and the twenty-four
elders [q]fell down before the Lamb, [r]each holding a harp, and [s]golden bowls full of incense,
[t]which are the prayers of the saints. 9 And they
sang [u]a new song, saying,

"Worthy are you to take the scroll
and to open its seals,
for [v]you were slain, and by your blood
[w]you ransomed people for God
from [x]every tribe and language and
people and nation,
10 and you have made them [y]a kingdom
and priests to our God,
and they shall reign on the earth."

11 [f]ch. 10:6; 14:7; Gen. 1:1; Acts 14:15 [g]Ps. 33:9-11; [Eph. 1:11]
Chapter 5
1 [h]Ezek. 2:9, 10 [i]Isa. 29:11; Dan. 12:4
2 [j][ch. 10:1; 18:21]
5 [k]Gen. 49:9 [l]Heb. 7:14 [m]ch. 22:16; Isa. 11:1, 10; Rom. 15:12
6 [n]ver. 9, 12; ch. 13:8; Isa. 53:7; John 1:29, 36; 1 Pet. 1:19 [o]Zech. 3:9; 4:10 [p]See ch. 1:4
8 [q]See ch. 4:10 [r]ch. 14:2; 15:2 [s][ch. 15:7] [t]ch. 8:3, 4; Ps. 141:2
9 [u]ch. 14:3; See Ps. 33:3 [v]ver. 6 [w]ch. 14:3, 4; See 2 Pet. 2:1 [x]ch. 7:9; 11:9; 14:6; See Dan. 3:4
10 [y]See ch. 1:6

5:1–8 Verses 1–4 dramatically depict the world's desperate need for Christ. God is seated on a throne, holding a scroll sealed with seven seals. No member of the heavenly entourage is worthy to open it; nor can anyone on or under the earth do so (vv. 2–3). John's response of weeping loudly (v. 4) indicates that the resolution of history—the defeat of evil, sin, and death—all depends on the opening of this scroll.

The elder's announcement in verse 5 identifies the Lion of the tribe of Judah (Gen. 49:8–12) with the Root of David (Isaiah 11) as he proclaims that Christ has conquered and is thus able to open the scroll. The nature of Christ's conquest is illustrated in Revelation 5:6, when John sees a Lamb standing, as though it had been slain. It is striking that the Lamb was slain and yet stands. This depicts the sacrificial death of Christ on the cross and his triumphant resurrection from the dead. Ironically, the sacrificial Lamb has seven horns, a symbol of absolute military power. Christ, who has all power, allowed himself to be slain for sinners.

Because of the way that he has brought the gospel to pass, in fulfillment of the scene in Daniel 7 when the son of man is presented before the Ancient of Days, Christ can now be presented before the Father, take the sealed scroll, and open it (Rev. 5:7). His conquest through his death and resurrection guarantees history's resolution. He has seized control of the world's destiny.

Once again John depicts an appropriate response to the gospel—appropriate and shocking at the same time. All heaven was worshiping God in Revelation 4, yet now Christ comes into the scene, takes the scroll from the Lord God Almighty (5:8), and the eyes of heaven turn from him who sits on the throne to the Son, as all creation joins the heavenly host in celebration of the Son! Perhaps nothing more clearly declares the deity of Jesus Christ than the fact that the focus of heaven's worship shifts to him in this way.

5:9–14 The content of the praise of Christ in these verses is instructive: none but Christ was found worthy (vv. 2–6), so the living creatures and the elders declare to him in verse 9, "Worthy are you." The praise also specifically states that he is worthy because by his death on the cross—communicated in the words "by your blood"—he ransomed people for God. This was not a ransom paid to Satan but a ransom from the wrath of God and his just punishment of sin. This is the true wonder of the gospel: we sinners, dead in our sin, could do nothing to extricate ourselves from our earthly dilemma. Our situation was hopeless. But God himself undertook to save us—the same God who had every right instead to punish us. And he did this through the provision

[11]Then I looked, and I heard around the throne
and the living creatures and the elders the
voice of many angels, numbering [z]myriads of
myriads and thousands of thousands, [12]saying
with a loud voice,

[a]"Worthy is the Lamb who was slain,
to receive power and wealth and wisdom
and might
and honor and glory and blessing!"

[13]And I heard [b]every creature in heaven and on
earth and under the earth and in the sea, and
all that is in them, saying,

"To him who sits on the throne and to
the Lamb
be blessing and honor and glory and
might forever and ever!"

[14]And the four living creatures [c]said, "Amen!"
and the elders [d]fell down and worshiped.

The Seven Seals

6 Now I watched when the Lamb opened
one of [e]the seven seals, and I heard [f]one of
the four living creatures say [g]with a voice like
thunder, [h]"Come!" [2]And I looked, and behold,
[i]a white horse! And [j]its rider had a bow, and
[k]a crown was given to him, and he came out
[l]conquering, and to conquer.
[3]When he opened the second seal, I heard
[m]the second living creature say, "Come!" [4]And
out came another horse, [n]bright red. Its rider
was permitted [o]to take peace from the earth,
so that people should slay one another, and he
was given a great sword.
[5]When he opened the third seal, I heard
the [m]third living creature say, "Come!" And
I looked, and behold, [p]a black horse! And its
rider had a pair of scales in his hand. [6]And
I heard what seemed to be a voice in the midst
of the four living creatures, saying, [q]"A quart[1]
of wheat for a denarius,[2] and three quarts of
barley for a denarius, and [r]do not harm the
oil and wine!"
[7]When he opened the fourth seal, I heard
the voice of [m]the fourth living creature say,
"Come!" [8]And I looked, and behold, [s]a pale
horse! And its rider's name was Death, and
Hades followed him. And they were given
authority over a fourth of the earth, to kill
[t]with sword and with famine and with pestilence and [u]by wild beasts of the earth.
[9]When he opened the fifth seal, I saw under

[1] Greek *choinix*, a dry measure equal to about a quart [2] A *denarius* was a day's wage for a laborer

of his own Son. God the Father sent God the Son to bear the wrath we deserved. What a wonder of mercy!

Again the fulfillment of the pattern of the exodus from Egypt is in view as Christ recapitulates and improves upon what happened there. At the exodus, Israel was redeemed from physical slavery, but Christ has redeemed and ransomed us from the power of sin and death and the just punishment of hell. At the exodus, Israel was redeemed and made a nation, but Christ has redeemed those "from every tribe and language and people and nation" (5:9) and, as in 1:6, he has made them "a kingdom and priests to our God" (5:10). Jesus is a king and a priest, and he makes his people, those united to him, who will conquer as he has conquered (cf. 12:11), like himself.

The book of Revelation consistently portrays those who enjoy the benefits of the gospel praising the one who made those benefits possible (5:9–14). Because of the way that Christ has laid down his life for others, he is worthy to receive everything (v. 12) from everyone (vv. 11, 13–14). We delight to praise him.

6:1–17 As Jesus opens the seals on the scroll he took from God's hand (ch. 5), the events that unfold broadly correspond to the events predicted by Jesus in the Olivet Discourse (e.g., Mark 13). Thus it seems that the rider on the white horse in Revelation 6:2 pretends to be what only Jesus is (cf. 19:11), just as Jesus said, "Many will come in my name, saying, 'I am he!'" (Mark 13:6). Jesus said there would be "wars and rumors of wars" (Mark 13:7), and this is exactly what results from the rider on the white horse who comes out to conquer (Rev. 6:2) and the rider on the red horse who is permitted to take peace from the earth (v. 4). Wars in the ancient world had devastating effects on crops and food supplies, so the wars caused by the first two riders are followed by the famines and plagues the second two bring (vv. 5–8).

Thus what John shows here reaffirms the teaching of Jesus and prepares his readers to hold fast the word of God and to follow the martyrs in the witness they had borne to complete the number of those to be killed for the gospel (vv. 9–11). John is

11 [z]Dan. 7:10; [Heb. 12:22]
12 [a]ch. 4:11
13 [b]Ps. 145:21; 150:6
14 [c]ch. 7:12; 19:4 [d]ver. 8; See ch. 4:10

Chapter 6
1 [e]ch. 5:1, 5-7 [f]ch. 4:7 [g]ch. 14:2; 19:6 [h]ch. 22:20
2 [i]Zech. 6:3; [ch. 19:11, 19, 21] [j][Ps. 45:4, 5; Hab. 3:8, 9; Zech. 9:13, 14] [k]ch. 14:14; [Zech. 6:11] [l]See ch. 3:21
3 [m]ch. 4:7
4 [n]Zech. 1:8; 6:2 [o][Matt. 10:34; 24:6, 7]
5 [m][See ver. 3 above] [p]Zech. 6:2
6 [q][Ezek. 4:10, 11; 5:10, 16] [r]ch. 7:3; 9:4
7 [m][See ver. 3 above]
8 [s][Zech. 6:3] [t]Ezek. 14:21 [u]Lev. 26:22; Deut. 32:24

[v]the altar [w]the souls of those who had been
slain [x]for the word of God and for [y]the witness they had borne. 10 They cried out with a
loud voice, "O Sovereign Lord, [z]holy and true,
[a]how long [b]before you will judge and [c]avenge
our blood on [d]those who dwell on the earth?"
11 Then they were each given [e]a white robe and
[f]told to rest a little longer, [g]until the number
of their fellow servants[1] and their brothers[2]
[h]should be complete, who were to be killed as
they themselves had been.

12 When he opened the sixth seal, I looked,
and behold, [i]there was a great earthquake, and
[j]the sun became black as [k]sackcloth, the full
moon became like blood, 13 and [l]the stars of
the sky fell to the earth [m]as the fig tree sheds its
winter fruit when shaken by a gale. 14 [n]The sky
vanished [m]like a scroll that is being rolled up,
and [o]every mountain and island was removed
from its place. 15 Then the kings of the earth
and the great ones and the generals and the
rich and the powerful, and everyone, slave[3]
and free, [p]hid themselves in the caves and
among the rocks of the mountains, 16 [q]calling
to the mountains and rocks, "Fall on us and
hide us from the face of [r]him who is seated on
the throne, and from the wrath of the Lamb,
17 for [s]the great day of their wrath has come,
and [t]who can stand?"

The 144,000 of Israel Sealed

7 After this I saw four angels standing at
the four corners of the earth, holding
back [u]the four winds of the earth, [v]that no
wind might blow on earth or sea or against
any tree. 2 Then I saw another angel ascending [w]from the rising of the sun, with [x]the seal
of the living God, and he called with a loud
voice to the four angels who had been given
power to harm earth and sea, 3 saying, [y]"Do not
harm the earth or the sea or the trees, until we
have sealed the servants[4] of our God [z]on their
foreheads." 4 And [a]I heard the number of the
sealed, 144,000, sealed from every tribe of the
sons of Israel:

5 12,000 from the tribe of Judah were sealed,
12,000 from the tribe of Reuben,
12,000 from the tribe of Gad,
6 12,000 from the tribe of Asher,
12,000 from the tribe of Naphtali,
12,000 from the tribe of Manasseh,
7 12,000 from the tribe of Simeon,
12,000 from the tribe of Levi,
12,000 from the tribe of Issachar,
8 12,000 from the tribe of Zebulun,
12,000 from the tribe of Joseph,
12,000 from the tribe of Benjamin were sealed.

[1] Greek *fellow bondservants* [2] Or *brothers and sisters*. The plural Greek word *adelphoi* (translated "brothers") refers to siblings in a family. In New Testament usage, depending on the context, *adelphoi* may refer either to men or to both men and women who are siblings (brothers and sisters) in God's family, the church [3] Or *servant*; Greek *bondservant* [4] Greek *bondservants*

9 [v]ch. 14:18; 16:7 [w]ch. 20:4 [x]ch. 1:9 [y]See ch. 1:2
10 [z]ch. 3:7 [a][Ps. 94:3; Zech. 1:12] [b]ch. 11:18; 19:2 [c]Ps. 79:10; 119:84; Luke 18:7, 8 [d]See ch. 3:10
11 [e]ch. 3:4; 7:9 [f]ch. 14:13 [g][Heb. 11:40] [h][Gen. 15:16]
12 [i]ch. 11:13; 16:18; [Heb. 12:26] [j]See Matt. 24:29 [k]Isa. 50:3
13 [l][ch. 8:10; 9:1] [m]Isa. 34:4
14 [n][ch. 20:11; 21:1] [m][See ver. 13 above] [o]ch. 16:20; [Isa. 54:10; Jer. 4:24; Ezek. 38:20; Nah. 1:5]
15 [p]Isa. 2:19, 21
16 [q]Hos. 10:8; Luke 23:30 [r]ch. 4:2
17 [s]Jer. 30:7; Joel 2:11, 31 [t]Ezra 9:15; Ps. 76:7; Mal. 3:2; Luke 21:36

Chapter 7

1 [u]Jer. 49:36; Dan. 7:2 [v][ver. 3]
2 [w]ch. 16:12 [x]ch. 9:4
3 [y]ch. 6:6; 9:4 [z]ch. 14:1; 22:4; Ezek. 9:4; [ch. 13:16; Ezek. 3:8, 9]
4 [a]ch. 9:16

preparing his audience not merely to reject the false gospels of the false messiahs but also to be faithful to the true gospel, even unto death (cf. 2:10).

The terrifying depiction in 6:12–17 of the great day of the wrath of the Lamb also encourages believers to hold fast the word of God and the testimony of Jesus, as it shows the wrath of the Lamb to be infinitely more terrible than the martyrs' deaths.

7:1–8 In verse 3 God "seals" his servants; that is, he marks them with a sign that they are his, as an ancient king would seal a document with his signet ring on wax. This seal preserves them from the visitation of his wrath (cf. 9:4), developing what Jesus said in 3:10, where he promised to keep those faithful to him through the hour of trial coming on the whole world.

In 13:16–18 Satan also "seals" his servants, the mark of the beast being a cheap imitation of what God does for his people. The "number" of the beast protects Satan's servants from his wrath but not from God's. In that context Satan also kills those who are faithful to God, but Revelation depicts God raising them from the dead (20:4–6). When John shows the sealing of God's servants and the mark of the beast, he is again preparing his audience for the persecution they will face. John assures them that it is not God's wrath that results in their death. Indeed, though Satan conquers them by killing them, *they* will conquer *him* by the blood of the Lamb (12:11) and will finally be raised from the dead.

The listing of the tribes as 144,000 (7:4–8) seems to give a whole, round number that depicts the same group as the innumerable multitude in verse 9. God will save all his people. Not one will be lost. And it will be a vast number of souls. John signals

A Great Multitude from Every Nation

9 After this I looked, and behold, [b]a great
multitude that no one could number, [c]from
every nation, from all tribes and peoples and
languages, standing before the throne and
before the Lamb, [d]clothed in white robes, with
[e]palm branches in their hands, 10 and crying
out with a loud voice, [f]"Salvation belongs to
our God who sits on the throne, and to the
Lamb!" 11 And all the angels were standing
around the throne and around the elders
and [g]the four living creatures, and they [h]fell
on their faces before the throne and worshiped God, 12 [i]saying, "Amen! Blessing and
glory and wisdom and thanksgiving and
honor and power and might be to our God
forever and ever! Amen."

13 Then one of the elders addressed me, saying, "Who are these, [d]clothed in white robes,
and from where have they come?" 14 I said
to him, "Sir, you know." And he said to me,
"These are the ones coming out of [j]the great
tribulation. [k]They have washed their robes and
[l]made them white [m]in the blood of the Lamb.

15 "Therefore they are before the throne of
God,
and [n]serve him day and night in his
temple;
and he who sits on the throne [o]will
shelter them with his presence.
16 [p]They shall hunger no more, neither
thirst anymore;
[q]the sun shall not strike them,
nor any scorching heat.

that the tribes are to be interpreted as a figurative depiction of the whole people of God by leaving out Dan and Ephraim and including Levi along with both Joseph and Manasseh. Joseph's sons Ephraim and Manasseh were usually listed instead of Joseph, so John seems to have replaced Ephraim with Joseph.

In any case, the message of this passage comes through clearly: God will bring *all* his people into his heavenly kingdom. His purposes of grace will prevail. The ancient promises to his people of old cannot fail. Christ, the Lamb, has secured their fulfillment.

7:9–17 As we saw in 5:9–14, in these verses the redeemed respond with praise to the Father and to Jesus for their work in accomplishing salvation. We are struck once more by the global scope of the gospel as those from every people group give praise to God for his salvation in Christ.

In 7:9, the redeemed wear white robes, and verse 14 says the robes have been washed white in the blood of the Lamb. This is a figurative description of the way that faith in Christ—believing that God put him forward as a sacrifice of propitiation (Rom. 3:25) and raised him from the dead (Rom 10:9)—cleanses the conscience (Heb. 9:14) and gives assurance of forgiveness and cleansing from sin (1 John 1:9).

The white-robed redeemed have palm branches in their hands, which recalls the Feast of Booths (Rev. 7:9; cf. Lev. 23:40). The Feast of Booths celebrated God's provision for and protection of Israel during the sojourn through the wilderness to the Promised Land. Wilderness/Booths imagery is invoked in Revelation 7:15–17, with language reminiscent of Isaiah 4:5–6. The booths built at the feast were reminders of the tents/tabernacles Israel used through the wilderness, and when Revelation 7:15 says he who sits on the throne will shelter them with his presence, the verb rendered "shelter" could be translated "tabernacle" (cf. John 1:14). As water was provided from the rock along with manna from heaven in the wilderness, so in Revelation 7:16 those who experience the fulfillment of God's protection and provision, which is the fulfillment of the booths (symbolically represented in the Feast of Booths), will neither hunger nor thirst, nor will the sun and its heat harm them. Moses shepherded Israel through the wilderness; and when the Lamb fulfills this in verse 17 he will be their Shepherd who, like the good shepherd in Psalm 23, will guide them to springs of living water (cf. John 4:10; 7:38). We saw the fulfillment of the exodus and Feast of Passover in the praise of Revelation 5:9–14. The praise of 7:9–17 presents the fulfillment of the wilderness sojourn and the Feast of Booths.

Just as the celebration of Booths was impossible without Passover, so here the fulfillment of the Feast of Booths is based on the fulfillment of Passover. Rightly, then, the declaration of verse 10 ascribes all glory in salvation to God and to the Lamb.

9 [b] [Rom. 11:25] [c] ch. 5:9 [d] ver. 14; See ch. 3:4 [e] [Lev. 23:40; John 12:13]
10 [f] ch. 12:10; 19:1; See Ps. 3:8
11 [g] ch. 4:6 [h] See ch. 4:10
12 [i] ch. 5:14; 19:4; [1 Chr. 29:10, 11]
13 [d] [See ver. 9 above]
14 [j] See Matt. 24:21 [k] ch. 22:14; [Isa. 1:18; Zech. 3:3-5] [l] [Dan. 12:10; 1 John 1:7] [m] ch. 1:5
15 [n] ch. 22:3 [o] ch. 21:3; [Isa. 4:5, 6]
16 [p] Isa. 49:10 [q] Ps. 121:6

17 For the Lamb in the midst of the throne
[r]will be their shepherd,
and he will guide them to springs of
[s]living water,
and [t]God will wipe away every tear from
their eyes."

The Seventh Seal and the Golden Censer

8 When the Lamb opened [u]the seventh seal,
there was silence in heaven for about half
an hour. 2 Then I saw the seven angels [v]who
stand before God, and seven trumpets were
given to them. 3 And another angel came
and stood [w]at the altar with a golden censer,
and he was given much incense to offer with
[x]the prayers of all the saints on [y]the golden
altar before the throne, 4 and [z]the smoke of
the incense, with the prayers of the saints,
rose before God from the hand of the angel.
5 Then the angel took the censer and [a]filled
it with fire from the altar and threw it on
the earth, and [b]there were peals of [c]thun-
der, rumblings,[1] flashes of lightning, and an
earthquake.

The Seven Trumpets

6 Now the seven angels who had the seven
trumpets prepared to blow them.

7 The first angel blew his trumpet, and there
followed [d]hail and [e]fire, mixed with blood,
and these were thrown upon the earth. And a
[f]third of the earth was burned up, and a third
of [g]the trees were burned up, and all green
grass was burned up.

8 The second angel blew his trumpet, and
something like [h]a great mountain, burning
with fire, was thrown into the sea, and a third
of the sea [i]became blood. 9 A third of the living
creatures in the sea died, and a third of [j]the
ships were destroyed.

10 The third angel blew his trumpet, and
[k]a great star fell from heaven, blazing like a
torch, and it fell on a third of the rivers and
on [l]the springs of water. 11 The name of the star
is Wormwood.[2] A third of the waters [m]became
wormwood, and many people died from the
water, [n]because it had been made bitter.

12 The fourth angel blew his trumpet, and a
third of [o]the sun was struck, and a third of the
moon, and a third of the stars, so that a third
of their light might be darkened, and a third
of the day might be kept from shining, and
likewise a third of the night.

13 Then I looked, and I heard an eagle crying
with a loud voice as it flew directly overhead,

[1] Or *voices*, or *sounds* [2] *Wormwood* is the name of a plant and of the bitter-tasting extract derived from it

17 [r]Ps. 23:1, 2; [Matt. 2:6]; See John 10:11 [s]ch. 22:1; [Ps. 36:8, 9; John 4:14] [t]ch. 21:4; Isa. 25:8
Chapter 8
1 [u]ch. 5:1; 6:1
2 [v]Luke 1:19
3 [w]Amos 9:1 [x]ch. 5:8 [y]ch. 9:13; Ex. 30:1, 3
4 [z][Ps. 141:2]
5 [a]Lev. 16:12 [b][Ps. 18:7, 8] [c]See ch. 4:5
7 [d]Ex. 9:23, 24; Ps. 18:13; Ezek. 38:22 [e]Joel 2:30 [f]ver. 8-12; ch. 9:15, 18; 12:4; [Zech. 13:8, 9] [g]ch. 9:4; Isa. 2:13
8 [h]Jer. 51:25; [Mark 11:23] [i]ch. 11:6; [Ex. 7:17, 19]
9 [j]Isa. 2:16
10 [k]ch. 9:1; [Isa. 14:12] [l]ch. 14:7; 16:4
11 [m]Deut. 29:18; Jer. 9:15; 23:15 [n][Ex. 15:23]
12 [o][Ex. 10:21-23; Isa. 13:10; 30:26]

The triune God alone works salvation, and Jesus is the one Mediator between God and man (1 Tim. 2:5).

The hosts of heaven worship God in response to the salvation he has achieved (Rev. 7:11–12), and then the redeemed are identified (vv. 13–14). These redeemed come out of the great tribulation (v. 14), in which John is their brother (1:9). This great tribulation seems to refer to the whole of church history, a period characterized by the messianic woes (cf. Dan. 7:25–27; 11:31–12:3; Matt. 24:8–13; John 16:33; Acts 14:22; Rom. 8:18; 2 Cor. 4:17; Col. 1:24; Rev. 2:10). Those redeemed by the death and resurrection of Jesus (in fulfillment of Passover) will be protected and provided for by the Good Shepherd through the wilderness sojourn (in fulfillment of the Feast of Booths) to the new heaven and earth (in fulfillment of the Feast of Weeks, which celebrated God's goodness in the Land of Promise).

8:1–9:21 This section of Revelation seems to present the future deliverance of the people of God at the end of history as the final fulfillment of the exodus pattern. The Lord heard the people's "cry for rescue" in Exodus 2:23–25 and delivered his people through the plague judgments at the exodus (Exodus 3–14). Similarly, the prayers of all the saints are presented before the Lord in Revelation 8:3 (cf. 6:9–11), and the Lord will deliver his people from their bondage to corruption through the trumpet (chs. 8–9) and bowl (ch. 16) judgments—which John describes in ways that recall the plagues on Egypt.

The judgment of the first trumpet, hail and fire (8:7) matches the seventh plague on Egypt (Ex. 9:23–25). The second and third trumpets result in the sea turning to blood (Rev. 8:8–9) and the rivers and springs being made bitter (8:10–11), recalling the first plague on Egypt (Ex. 7:19–21). The fourth trumpet results in darkness (Rev. 8:12), like the ninth plague (Ex. 10:21–29). The fifth trumpet is followed by

[p]"Woe, woe, woe to those who dwell on the
earth, at the blasts of the other trumpets that
the three angels are about to blow!"

9 And the fifth angel blew his trumpet, and
[q]I saw a star fallen from heaven to earth,
and he was given [r]the key to the shaft of [s]the
bottomless pit.[1] 2 He opened the shaft of the
bottomless pit, and from the shaft [t]rose smoke
like the smoke of a great furnace, and [u]the sun
and the air were darkened with the smoke
from the shaft. 3 Then from the smoke came
[v]locusts on the earth, and they were given
power like the power of scorpions of the earth.
4 They were told [w]not to harm [x]the grass of
the earth or any green plant or any tree, but
only those people who do not have [y]the seal of
God on their foreheads. 5 They were allowed to
torment them [z]for five months, but not to kill
them, and their torment was like the torment
of a scorpion when it stings someone. 6 And in
those days [a]people will seek death and will not
find it. They will long to die, but death will
flee from them.

7 [b]In appearance the locusts were like horses
prepared for battle: [c]on their heads were what
looked like crowns of gold; their faces were
[d]like human faces, 8 their hair like women's
hair, and [e]their teeth like lions' teeth; 9 they
had breastplates like breastplates of iron, and
the noise of their wings was [f]like the noise
of many chariots with [g]horses rushing into
battle. 10 They have tails and stings like scorpions, and their power to hurt people [h]for five
months is in their tails. 11 They have [i]as king
over them the angel of the bottomless pit. His
name in Hebrew is [j]Abaddon, and in Greek he
is called Apollyon.[2]

12 [k]The first woe has passed; behold, two woes
are still to come.

13 Then the sixth angel blew his trumpet,
and I heard a voice from [l]the four horns of
the golden altar before God, 14 saying to the
sixth angel who had the trumpet, "Release
[m]the four angels who are bound at [n]the great
river Euphrates." 15 So the four angels, who
had been prepared for the hour, the day, the
month, and the year, were released [o]to kill a
third of mankind. 16 The number of [p]mounted
troops was [q]twice ten thousand times ten
thousand; [r]I heard their number. 17 And this
is how I saw the horses in my vision and those
who rode them: they wore breastplates the
color of fire and of sapphire[3] and of sulfur,
and the heads of the horses were [s]like lions'
heads, and fire and smoke and sulfur came
out of their mouths. 18 By these three plagues
a third of mankind was killed, by the fire
and smoke and sulfur coming out of their
mouths. 19 For the power of the horses is in
their mouths and in their tails, for their tails
are like serpents with heads, and by means of
them they wound.

20 The rest of mankind, who were not killed
by these plagues, [t]did not repent of [u]the
works of their hands nor give up worshiping [v]demons [w]and idols of gold and silver and
bronze and stone and wood, which cannot see
or hear or walk, 21 nor did they repent of their
murders or their [x]sorceries or their sexual
immorality or their thefts.

[1] Greek *the abyss*; also verses 2, 11 [2] *Abaddon* means *destruction*; *Apollyon* means *destroyer* [3] Greek *hyacinth*

locust-like scorpions (Rev. 9:1–11), just as the eighth plague on Egypt was of locusts (Ex. 10:12–20). The sixth trumpet results in mounted troops who kill a third of humanity (Rev. 9:13–21), perhaps recalling the death angel who killed the Egyptian firstborn (Ex. 11:1–10; 12:29–32).

That John means for the trumpet judgments to echo the plagues on Egypt would seem to be supported by the mighty angel, who is wrapped in a cloud and has legs like pillars of fire (Rev. 10:1). Just as God led Israel out of Egypt through the wilderness with a pillar of fire and cloud (Ex. 13:21), so now that the plagues have been fulfilled in the trumpet judgments, God sends an angel of cloud and flame to give guidance to the people of God through his servant John.

We marvel, amid all this, at what God has accomplished in Jesus Christ on our behalf. We sinners, enslaved by sin and death, require nothing less than a new exodus out of slavery and into the Promised Land of restored fellowship with God. This is precisely what Christ has accomplished—by being himself the sacrificial Passover Lamb. God passes over us in mercy because he did *not* pass over his own Son.

13[p] [ch. 9:12; 11:14]

Chapter 9

1[q] ch. 8:10; [ch. 12:9; Luke 10:18] [r]See ch. 1:18 [s]ver. 2, 11; ch. 11:7; 17:8; 20:1, 3; Luke 8:31; Rom. 10:7
2[t] [Gen. 19:28; Isa. 34:10] [u][Joel 2:10]
3[v] See Ex. 10:4
4[w] ch. 6:6; 7:3 [x]ch. 8:7 [y]See ch. 7:2, 3
5[z] ver. 10
6[a] Job 3:21; 7:15, 16; Jer. 8:3
7[b] Joel 2:4 [c][Nah. 3:17] [d]Dan. 7:8
8[e] Joel 1:6
9[f] Joel 2:5 [g]Jer. 8:6; [Job 39:21-25]
10[h] ver. 5
11[i] [Job 18:14; Prov. 30:27; Eph. 2:2] [j]See Job 26:6
12[k] [ch. 8:13; 11:14]
13[l] Ex. 30:3
14[m] [ch. 7:1] [n]ch. 16:12

15[o] See ch. 8:7 **16**[p] Ezek. 38:4 [q][Ps. 68:17; Dan. 7:10] [r]ch. 7:4 **17**[s] [1 Chr. 12:8; Isa. 5:28, 29] **20**[t] See ch. 2:21 [u]Deut. 31:29; Jer. 1:16; 25:14 [v]See 1 Cor. 10:20 [w]Ps. 115:4-7; 135:15-17; Dan. 5:23 **21**[x] ch. 21:8; 22:15; Gal. 5:20

The Angel and the Little Scroll

10 Then I saw another mighty angel coming down from heaven, wrapped in a
cloud, with [y]a rainbow over his head, and [z]his
face was like the sun, and [a]his legs like pillars
of fire. 2 [b]He had a little scroll open in his hand.
And he set his right foot on the sea, and his left
foot on the land, 3 and called out with a loud
voice, [c]like a lion roaring. When he called out,
the seven thunders sounded. 4 And when the
seven thunders had sounded, I was about to
write, but I heard a voice from heaven saying,
[d]"Seal up what the seven thunders have said,
and do not write it down." 5 And the angel
whom I saw standing on the sea and on the
land [e]raised his right hand to heaven 6 and
swore by [f]him who lives forever and ever, [g]who
created heaven and what is in it, the earth and
what is in it, and the sea and what is in it, that
there would be no more delay, 7 but that [h]in the
days of the trumpet call to be sounded by the
seventh angel, the mystery of God would be
fulfilled, [i]just as he announced to his servants[1]
the prophets.
8 Then the voice that I had heard from
heaven spoke to me again, saying, "Go, take
the scroll that is open in the hand of the angel
who is standing on the sea and on the land."
9 So I went to the angel and told him to give
me the little scroll. And he said to me, [j]"Take
and [k]eat it; it will make your stomach bitter,
but in your mouth it will be sweet as honey."
10 And I took the little scroll from the hand of
the angel and ate it. It was sweet as honey in
my mouth, but when I had eaten it my stomach was made bitter. 11 And I was told, [l]"You
must again prophesy about many peoples and
nations and languages and kings."

The Two Witnesses

11 Then I was given [m]a measuring rod
like a staff, and I was told, "Rise and
measure the temple of God and the altar and
those who worship there, 2 but do not measure [n]the court outside the temple; leave that
out, for [o]it is given over to the nations, and
they will trample the holy city for [p]forty-two
months. 3 And I will grant authority to my two

[1] Greek *bondservants*

Chapter 10
1 [y]Ezek. 1:28 [z]ch. 1:16; Matt. 17:2 [a]ch. 1:15
2 [b]ver. 8-10
3 [c]Joel 3:16; Amos 1:2
4 [d]Dan. 8:26; 12:4, 9; [ch. 22:10]
5 [e]See Gen. 14:22
6 [f]See ch. 4:9 [g]See ch. 4:11
7 [h]ch. 11:15 [i][Amos 3:7]
9 [j]Ezek. 2:8; 3:1-3 [k][Jer. 15:16]
11 [l][Ezek. 37:4]

Chapter 11
1 [m]ch. 21:15, 16; Ezek. 40:3; Zech. 2:1
2 [n]Ezek. 40:17, 20 [o]See Luke 21:24 [p]ch. 12:6; 13:5

10:1–11 The appearance of the angel invokes not only the Lord leading the people by the pillar of cloud and flame after the exodus, but also the salvation of Noah: the angel has a rainbow over his head (v. 1). These past acts of salvation have led to and have been more fully fulfilled in Christ's death and resurrection. Jesus provides the final, climactic act of deliverance, the deliverance of which every other deliverance is an anticipation.

The angel now comes to provide guidance for the redeemed. Revelation 1:1 said "God gave" the "revelation" to Christ who "made it known by sending his angel to his servant John," who was to "show to [the Lord's] servants the things that must soon take place." That chain of revelatory disclosure is being enacted: Jesus took the scroll from the Father in chapter 5 and opened it in chapters 6–8; the angel brings it down in 10:2, and John will eat the scroll and prophesy in verses 8–11. The universal significance of the message of what Christ has done and will do is shown by the angel putting his right foot on the sea and his left foot on the land (v. 2).

John is authenticated as a true prophet in Revelation 10:8–11 as he reenacts a scene from Ezekiel 2:9–3:4. As John eats the scroll just as Ezekiel did, the people of God are given proof that he is a true prophet, like the Old Testament prophets, whom they can trust. The churches are confronted with false teachers (e.g., Rev. 2:14, 20), and a false prophet will soon enter the picture (13:11–18; 16:13). Those redeemed by the work of Christ are to trust the prophet (John), who makes known the contents of the scroll that Christ has opened. In 10:11 the message is sent to all peoples and nations and languages and kings, reminding us of the universal significance of what is unfolding throughout Revelation.

11:1–14 There is disagreement among faithful Christians over the best interpretation of the temple, the two witnesses, and the three-and-a-half-year period in these verses (see note on 12:1–6). Some see the events described as reflecting past and present realities leading to Christ's return; many see the referents as primarily future. Yet those who see them as future events are also divided over the sequence of events indicated.

Perhaps all can agree, however, on how John intended this passage to function for his audience. John sees the temple protected for 42 months (three and a half

witnesses, and they will prophesy for [p]1,260
days, [q]clothed in sackcloth."
4 These are [r]the two olive trees and the two
lampstands that stand before the Lord of the
earth. 5 And if anyone would harm them,
[s]fire pours from their mouth and consumes
their foes. If anyone would harm them, [t]this
is how he is doomed to be killed. 6 They have
the power [u]to shut the sky, that no rain may
fall during the days of their prophesying, and
they have power over the waters to turn them
into blood and [v]to strike the earth with every
kind of plague, as often as they desire. 7 And
when they have finished their testimony, [w]the
beast that rises from [x]the bottomless pit[1] [y]will
make war on them and conquer them and kill
them, 8 and their dead bodies will lie in the
street of the great city that symbolically[2] is
called [z]Sodom and [a]Egypt, where their Lord
was crucified. 9 For three and a half days some
from the peoples and tribes and languages
and nations will gaze at their dead bodies and
[b]refuse to let them be placed in a tomb, 10 and
[c]those who dwell on the earth will rejoice over
them and make merry and [d]exchange presents, because these two prophets [e]had been a
torment to those who dwell on the earth. 11 But
after the three and a half days [f]a breath of life
from God entered them, and they stood up
on their feet, and great fear fell on those who

[1] Or *the abyss* [2] Greek *spiritually*

years) in 11:1–2 and the two witnesses prophesying for the whole of their appointed time (1,260 days, another way to describe three and a half years) in verses 2–6. The two witnesses are killed in verse 7, but God vindicates them, and their resurrection is reminiscent of the valley of the dry bones in Ezekiel 37 (cf. "breath of life"; Rev. 11:11). On any interpretation of the temple, the witnesses, and the time period, John's description tells the churches that God is able to protect his people for the whole of the time he has appointed for them to preach the gospel. And even if their enemies kill them, God can raise the dead. This would encourage persecuted churches to continue to proclaim the gospel.

John seems to indicate that the temple that will be protected throughout the 42 months (vv. 1–2) is the church. This appears to be why John refers to those who worship there in verse 1 and identifies the dwelling of God with those who dwell in heaven in 13:6. In keeping with Paul's assertion that God's people are his temple and that the Holy Spirit dwells in them (1 Cor. 3:16), in the New Testament age the people of God, corporately represented in the church, are the temple.

Similarly, the two witnesses apparently symbolize the church proclaiming the gospel throughout the duration of church history (Rev. 11:3). They are identified as two lampstands (v. 4); the olive oil symbolizes the Holy Spirit's presence; and, in the imagery of Revelation, Christ stands among the lampstands (1:12–13). We see in 11:5–6 a correspondence to Elijah (fire consumes their foes, and they shut the sky; see 1 Kings 17:1; 2 Kings 1:10–12) and Moses (they turn waters to blood and strike the earth with plagues; see Ex. 7:14–25). We should remember that elsewhere in the Bible, Moses and Elijah represent the Law and the Prophets, which combine to give witness to and preparation for the ministry of Christ (Matt. 11:13; 17:1–5; Luke 24:27; John 1:45; Acts 28:23; Rom. 3:21–22). Thus, Revelation's descriptions signify these two witnesses' ability to demonstrate that there is only one living and true God (cf. Elijah's defeat of the prophets of Baal) and that God has fulfilled the pattern of the exodus in the salvation accomplished by Jesus, which is referenced in the symbolic identification of Jerusalem, where their Lord was crucified, with Sodom and Egypt (Rev. 11:8).

The 42-month period is likely a symbolic way of referring to the whole period of time between the two comings of Christ (see note on 12:1–6). The slaying of the two witnesses (11:7) and their resurrection a short time later (vv. 9–11), followed by their being called up to God in heaven (v. 12), appears to portend an almost total stamping out of Christianity right before the return of Christ and the resurrection described in 20:4–6. This would make sense of the placement of the seventh trumpet blast immediately after this narrative: the church will proclaim the gospel to all nations (Matt. 24:14), the full number of the Gentiles will come in (Rom. 11:25), the witnesses will finish their testimony (Rev. 11:7), and then the end will come. All of human history is being guided along under the wise and sovereign hand of God. We can trust him even through the great trials that must be endured by believers.

3 [p][See ver. 2 above] [q]Isa. 20:2
4 [r]Zech. 4:3, 11, 14; [Ps. 52:8; Jer. 11:16]
5 [s][2 Kgs. 1:10, 12; Jer. 5:14] [t][Num. 16:29, 35]
6 [u][1 Kgs. 17:1; Luke 4:25; James 5:17] [v][Ex. 7–10; 1 Sam. 4:8]
7 [w]ch. 17:8; [ch. 13:1] [x]See ch. 9:1 [y]Dan. 7:21
8 [z]Isa. 1:10; 3:9 [a][Ezek. 23:3, 8, 19, 27]
9 [b]Ps. 79:2, 3
10 [c][John 16:20]; See ch. 3:10 [d]Neh. 8:10, 12; Esth. 9:19, 22 [e][1 Kgs. 18:17]
11 [f]Gen. 2:7; Ezek. 37:5, 9, 10, 14

saw them. 12 Then they heard a loud voice from
heaven saying to them, [g]"Come up here!" And
[h]they went up to heaven [i]in a cloud, and their
enemies watched them. 13 And at that hour
there was [j]a great earthquake, and [k]a tenth
of the city fell. Seven thousand people were
killed in the earthquake, and the rest were
terrified and [l]gave glory to [m]the God of heaven.
14 [n]The second woe has passed; behold, the
third woe is soon to come.

The Seventh Trumpet

15 Then [o]the seventh angel blew his trumpet,
and [p]there were loud voices in heaven, saying,
[q]"The kingdom of the world has become the
kingdom of our Lord and of [r]his Christ, and
[s]he shall reign forever and ever." 16 And the
twenty-four elders [t]who sit on their thrones
before God [u]fell on their faces and worshiped
God, 17 saying,

"We give thanks to you, Lord God
Almighty,
[v]who is and who was,
for you have taken your great power
and [w]begun to reign.
18 The nations raged,
but [x]your wrath came,
and [y]the time for the dead to be
judged,
and for rewarding your servants,[1] the
prophets and saints,
and [z]those who fear your name,
both small and great,
and [a]for destroying the destroyers of the
earth."

19 Then [b]God's temple in heaven was opened,
and [c]the ark of his covenant was seen within
his temple. There were flashes of lightning,
rumblings,[2] peals of thunder, an earthquake,
and [d]heavy hail.

The Woman and the Dragon

12 And a great sign appeared in heaven:
a woman [e]clothed with [f]the sun, with
[f]the moon under her feet, and on her head a
crown of twelve stars. 2 She was pregnant and
[g]was crying out in birth pains and the agony
of giving birth. 3 And another sign appeared
in heaven: behold, a great [h]red dragon, [i]with
seven heads and [j]ten horns, and on his heads

[1] Greek *bondservants* [2] Or *voices*, or *sounds*

12 [g] ch. 4:1 [h] [ch. 12:5; 2 Kgs. 2:11] [i] [Acts 1:9]
13 [j] ch. 6:12 [k] [ch. 16:19] [l] ch. 14:7; 16:9; 19:7; Josh. 7:19 [m] 2 Chr. 36:23
14 [n] [ch. 8:13; 9:12]
15 [o] ch. 10:7 [p] ch. 16:17; 19:1; [Isa. 27:13] [q] ch. 12:10 [r] Ps. 2:2 (Gk.); Luke 9:20 [s] See Luke 1:33
16 [t] ch. 4:4 [u] See ch. 4:10
17 [v] ch. 16:5; [ch. 1:4, 8; 4:8] [w] ch. 19:6; Ps. 97:1
18 [x] Ps. 2:5; 110:5 [y] ch. 6:10; 20:12; [Dan. 7:10; 2 Thess. 1:6, 7] [z] ch. 19:5 [a] [ch. 13:10]
19 [b] ch. 15:5 [c] See Heb. 9:4 [d] ch. 16:21

Chapter 12
1 [e] [Ps. 104:2] [f] [Song 6:10]
2 [g] [Isa. 66:7-10; Mic. 4:10]
3 [h] [ch. 17:3; Isa. 27:1] [i] ch. 13:1; 17:9, 12 [j] Dan. 7:7

11:15–19 Leviticus 25:9 calls for the trumpet to be blown on the Day of Atonement in the Year of Jubilee. In language drawn from that passage, Isaiah prophesied that the new exodus would be marked by "a great trumpet" blast (Isa. 27:13). Now John shows the fulfillment of the pattern of the Year of Jubilee and the prophecy of Isaiah as the seventh angel blows his trumpet (Rev. 11:15). The "kingdom of the world" becomes "the kingdom of our Lord and of his Christ"; both "the Lord" and "Christ" are mentioned here, followed by the singular phrase "and he shall reign forever" (cf. Matt. 28:19).

Recalling Psalm 2:1–3, Revelation 11:18 says the nations raged—and the church was persecuted as a result—but God's wrath came, and his servants were rewarded and the wicked destroyed. There was an outpouring of wrath when the temple was destroyed, and the prophets described that day of the Lord with imagery similar to what we find in verse 19. There was also darkness and an earthquake when Christ died on the cross (Matt. 27:32–54), and the veil was torn when Christ died (Matt. 27:51). The wrath that should have fallen on us fell instead on God's Son, in our place. This is the message of the gospel, culminating in Revelation with trumpet blasts, but only after the crescendo has consistently built throughout the rest of the Bible.

12:1–6 Revelation 11:1–14 depicted witnesses proclaiming the gospel for the whole of church history. Another symbolic depiction of the same thing is presented in 12:1–13:10, this time with the focus on the outworking of Genesis 3:15 as the Serpent makes war on the offspring of the woman, both individually (Rev. 12:1–5) and collectively (v. 17; in this reference the "offspring" indicates all who are identified with Christ, i.e., his church; cf. Gal. 3:26, 29).

The woman (Rev. 12:1) seems to be a sign of (1) the mother of Jesus in particular, with her descriptions echoing aspects of Jesus' nativity (vv. 4–6) and of her child's being destined to rule all the nations with a rod of iron (v. 5); and (2) of the people of God in general (v. 17). The earthly life of Jesus' first coming is collapsed into one line in verse 5; only his birth and ascension are directly mentioned, with everything else, including his death and resurrection, being assumed. The flight into the wilderness (v. 6) seems to echo both the holy family's flight to Egypt for protection from Herod

[k]seven diadems. 4 His tail swept down [l]a third of the stars of heaven and [m]cast them to the earth. And the dragon stood before the woman who was about to give birth, so that when she bore her child [n]he might devour it. 5 She gave birth to a male child, [o]one who is to rule all the nations with a rod of iron, but her child was [p]caught up to God and to his throne, 6 and the woman fled into the wilderness, where she has a place prepared by God, in which she is to be nourished for [q]1,260 days.

Satan Thrown Down to Earth

7 Now war arose in heaven, [r]Michael and [s]his angels fighting against the dragon. And the dragon and his angels fought back, 8 but he was defeated, and there was no longer any place for them in heaven. 9 And [t]the great dragon was thrown down, [u]that ancient serpent, who is called the devil and Satan, [v]the deceiver of the whole world—[w]he was thrown down to the earth, and his angels were thrown down with him. 10 And I heard a loud voice in heaven, saying, "Now [x]the salvation and the power and the kingdom of our God and the authority of his Christ have come, for the accuser of our brothers[1] has been thrown down, [y]who accuses them day and night before our God. 11 And [z]they have conquered him by the blood of the Lamb and by the word of their testimony, for [a]they loved not their lives [b]even unto death. 12 Therefore, [c]rejoice, O heavens and you who dwell in them! But [d]woe to you, O earth and sea, for the devil has come down to you in great wrath, because [e]he knows that his time is short!"

13 And when the dragon saw that he had been thrown down to the earth, he pursued [f]the woman who had given birth to the male child. 14 But the woman was given the two [g]wings of the great eagle so that she might fly from the serpent [h]into the wilderness, to the place where she is to be nourished [i]for a time, and times, and half a time. 15 The serpent poured water [j]like a river out of his mouth after the woman, to sweep her away with a flood. 16 But the earth came to the help of the woman, and the earth opened its mouth

[1] Or *brothers and sisters*

and also Israel's wilderness experience prior to entering the Promised Land—both periods of spiritual preparation prior to blessing with which a persecuted church would want to identify (cf. Hos. 2:14).

The designation of 1,260 days echoes the three and a half years of the divided seventieth week of Daniel (Dan. 9:27), whose direct reference scholars debate (i.e., was this the period of Jewish persecution under Antiochus Epiphanes; or is it a period of future tribulation; or, on the analogy of previous persecutions, does it symbolize the persecution the church faces in all ages until Christ's return?). What is clear is that the days designated are symbolic of a time of trouble from which the woman and her child are sheltered in preparation for the great war described in following verses.

12:7–12 On the basis of what Christ accomplished in his death and resurrection (v. 5), Michael is enabled to drive Satan and his angels from the heavenly field of battle. The account echoes the description of heavenly warfare mentioned in Daniel 12:7, reminding us that we are not alone in the spiritual battles we fight on earth. They are paralleled in the heavenly realms with heavenly hosts as our advocates and champions.

We see what this means when Revelation 12:10 states that the "accuser of our brothers" has been thrown down. Formerly, Satan had been standing in heaven to accuse God's people (cf. Job 1–2; Zech. 3:1–2). Now that Christ has died and risen, however, Satan no longer has any standing before God to accuse us. His charges are thrown out, and he is thrown down to the earth (Rev. 12:9). On the basis of the blood of the Lamb, the people of Jesus can conquer the dragon by testifying to the gospel and being faithful unto death.

To lay down one's life to benefit others with the message of the gospel is to conquer in the same way that Jesus did (v. 11; cf. 5:5–6). For Christ and for us, life comes through death.

12:13–17 Just as the two witnesses prophesy for 1,260 days (11:3), the woman will be nourished in the wilderness for 1,260 days (12:6), which is also "a time, and times, and half a time" (v. 14; see note on 12:1–6). These references to three and a half years interpret the halving of Daniel's seventieth week (Dan. 9:27). Satan has failed to devour

3 [k][ch. 19:12]
4 [l]See ch. 8:7 [m]Dan. 8:10 [n][Matt. 2:16]
5 [o]Matt. 2:6; See ch. 2:27 [p]See 2 Cor. 12:2
6 [q]ch. 11:2; 13:5
7 [r]See Jude 9 [s]See Matt. 25:41
9 [t]Luke 10:18; John 12:31 [u]ch. 20:2; Gen. 3:1 [v]ch. 20:3, 10; [ch. 13:14; John 8:44] [w]See ch. 9:1
10 [x]ch. 7:10; 19:1 [y]Job 1:9; 2:5; Zech. 3:1
11 [z]ch. 15:2; [Rom. 16:20]; See John 16:33 [a]Luke 14:26; John 12:25 [b]ch. 2:10
12 [c]ch. 18:20; Ps. 96:11; Isa. 44:23; 49:13 [d]ch. 8:13 [e][Matt. 8:29]; See ch. 10:6
13 [f]ver. 5
14 [g]See Ex. 19:4 [h]ver. 6 [i]Dan. 7:25; 12:7; See ver. 6
15 [j][Isa. 59:19]

and swallowed the river that the dragon had
poured from his mouth. 17 Then the dragon
became furious with the woman and went off
[k]to make war on the rest of [l]her offspring, [m]on
those who keep the commandments of God
and hold to [n]the testimony of Jesus. And he
stood[1] on the sand of the sea.

The First Beast

13 And I saw a beast rising out of the sea,
[o]with ten horns and seven heads, with
ten diadems on its horns and [p]blasphemous
names on its heads. 2 And the beast that I saw
was [q]like a leopard; its feet were like [r]a bear's,
and its mouth was like [s]a lion's mouth. And to
it [t]the dragon gave his power and [u]his throne
and great authority. 3 One of its heads seemed
to have a mortal wound, but its mortal wound
was healed, and [v]the whole earth marveled as
they followed the beast. 4 And they worshiped
the dragon, for he had given his authority to
the beast, and they worshiped the beast, saying, [w]"Who is like the beast, and who can fight
against it?"

5 And the beast was given [x]a mouth uttering
haughty and blasphemous words, and it was
allowed to exercise authority for [y]forty-two
months. 6 It opened its mouth to utter blasphemies against God, blaspheming his name
and his dwelling,[2] that is, those who dwell in
heaven. 7 Also it was allowed [z]to make war on
the saints and to conquer them.[3] And authority
was given it over every tribe and people and
language and nation, 8 and all [a]who dwell on
earth will worship it, everyone whose name has
not been written before the foundation of the
world in [b]the book of life of [c]the Lamb [d]who
was slain. 9 [e]If anyone has an ear, let him hear:

10 [f]If anyone is to be taken captive,
to captivity he goes;
[g]if anyone is to be slain with the sword,
with the sword must he be slain.

[1] Some manuscripts *And I stood*, connecting the sentence with 13:1 [2] Or *tabernacle* [3] Some manuscripts omit this sentence

17[k] ch. 11:7; 13:7 [l] Gen. 3:15 [m] ch. 14:12; See 1 John 2:3 [n] ch. 1:2; 6:9; 19:10
Chapter 13
1[o] Dan. 7:3; See ch. 12:3 [p] ch. 17:3
2[q] Dan. 7:6 [r] Dan. 7:5 [s] Dan. 7:4 [t] ver. 4, 11; [Luke 4:6] [u] ch. 16:10
3[v] [ch. 17:8]
4[w] [ch. 18:18]
5[x] Dan. 7:8, 11, 20; 11:36; [2 Thess. 2:4] [y] ch. 11:2; 12:6
7[z] ch. 11:7; 12:17; Dan. 7:21
8[a] See ch. 3:10 [b] See ch. 3:5 [c] See ch. 5:6 [d] [Acts 2:23; 1 Pet. 1:19, 20]
9[e] See ch. 2:7
10[f] [Isa. 33:1; Jer. 15:2; 43:11] [g] See Gen. 9:6

the male child (Rev. 12:4–5), and God delivered the woman from him as well (vv. 6, 13–16), so Satan sets out to make war on the rest of her offspring (v. 17; see earlier comments on "offspring" in the note on 12:1–6).

We are reminded that our battle is not against flesh and blood (Eph. 6:10–20). Our lives are part of a great cosmic battle that has been raging since Genesis 3—but the outcome is certain.

13:1–10 Satan pursues his war on the collective offspring of the woman (12:17) by conjuring an imitation of the Christian gospel. This deceptive imitation intends to establish Satan himself in the place of God the Father (12:17; 16:13), the beast in the place of Christ (13:3), the false prophet in the place of the Holy Spirit (v. 12), and those with the mark of the beast in the place of those sealed by the Spirit (vv. 16–18). John equips those who believe the gospel to maintain their testimony to it in spite of Satan's war on them by pulling back the curtain on the satanic scheme. Those who view the descriptions of 12:6 (see earlier note) as entirely future will primarily look for future world events to be represented by the descriptions in this passage; those who view the earlier descriptions as representing the church's battles in all ages see this passage as analogous to the spiritual battles that believers will always face until Christ's final victory.

In this spiritual war, God has a Lamb (5:6), while Satan has a beast (13:1). The Lamb is the image of God. The beast is the image of the dragon, both having seven heads and ten horns (12:3; 13:1). The Lamb in 5:6 was "standing, as though it had been slain," and now Satan deceives the nations (12:9; 13:14) with a fake christ, this beast who "was wounded by the sword and yet lived." All the heavenly host and every creature in heaven and on earth worshiped the Lamb standing as though slain in 5:5–14, and in 13:3–8 the whole earth marveled at and worshiped the beast whose head "seemed to have a mortal wound, but its mortal wound was healed."

Words that should be spoken only of the living God are blasphemously spoken of Satan's beast (v. 4), and verse 7 is a close parallel with 11:7, both verses speaking of those who die for their fidelity to the gospel. God is able to keep those whom he has recorded for himself from Satan's deception (13:8), and one of the means for their preservation is John making Satan's ways known in this passage. John himself applies the message to his readers when he warns them that even their suffering is foreordained, and as he announces that his making it known is a call for the endurance and faith of the saints (v. 10).

[h]Here is a call for the endurance and faith of
the saints.

The Second Beast

11 Then [i]I saw another beast rising out of
the earth. It had two horns like a lamb and
it spoke like a dragon. 12 It exercises all the
authority of the first beast in its presence,[1]
and makes the earth and its inhabitants worship the first beast, [j]whose mortal wound was
healed. 13 [k]It performs great signs, even [l]mak-
ing fire come down from heaven to earth in
front of people, 14 and by the signs that it is
allowed to work in the presence of[2] the beast
[m]it deceives those who dwell on earth, telling
them to make an image for the beast [n]that was
wounded by the sword and yet lived. 15 And
it was allowed to give breath to the image
of the beast, so that the image of the beast
might even speak and might cause those who
would not [o]worship the image of the beast
[p]to be slain. 16 Also it causes all, both small
and great, both rich and poor, both free and
slave,[3] [q]to be marked on the right hand or
the forehead, 17 so that no one can buy or sell
unless he has the mark, that is, [r]the name of
the beast or [s]the number of its name. 18 [t]This
calls for wisdom: let the one who has understanding calculate the number of the beast,
for it is the number [u]of a man, and his number is 666.[4]

The Lamb and the 144,000

14 Then I looked, and behold, on [v]Mount
Zion [w]stood the Lamb, and with him
[x]144,000 who [y]had his name and his Father's
name written [z]on their foreheads. 2 And
I heard a voice from heaven [a]like the roar
of many waters and [b]like the sound of loud
thunder. The voice I heard was like the sound
of [c]harpists playing on their harps, 3 and
they were singing [d]a new song before the
throne and before the four living creatures
and before the elders. [e]No one could learn
that song except the 144,000 who had been
redeemed from the earth. 4 It is these who
have not defiled themselves with women,
for [f]they are virgins. It is these [g]who follow
the Lamb wherever he goes. These have been
redeemed from mankind as [h]firstfruits for
God and the Lamb, 5 and [i]in their mouth no
lie was found, for they are [j]blameless.

[1] Or *on its behalf* [2] Or *on behalf of* [3] Greek *bondservant* [4] Some manuscripts *616*

13:11–18 What John put in verbal form elsewhere (1 John 2:18) he puts in picture form here. The beast in Revelation 13:11 looks like a lamb, that is, like Jesus (cf. 5:6), but it speaks like a dragon, that is, like Satan (12:9).

This warns believers not to be deceived by those who dress "in sheep's clothing but inwardly are ravenous wolves" (Matt. 7:15). John is warning the churches against those who come claiming to present the Christian gospel but who in fact proclaim Satan's message. John warns that Satan's counterfeit might even do powerful signs that look like what the two prophets did in Revelation 11:5, making fire come down from heaven (13:13). Christians must be vigilant against false gospels and the imposters who peddle them, and this calls for wisdom (v. 18). Christians must see that they are not deceived. Satan and his false trinity (v. 14) deceive those who dwell on earth (12:9; 13:7), but one day Christ will come and put an end to their ability to deceive the nations (20:1–3).

Christians must endure until then, even if it means they cannot buy or sell (13:17) or must be slain (vv. 10, 15). For whatever happens, we have Christ, and he is everything.

14:1–5 Revelation 13:16–18 spoke of those with the mark of the beast on the right hand or the forehead, and Revelation 14:1 develops 7:1–4 by showing the 144,000 (see note on 7:1–8) with the name of the Lamb and his Father's name written on their foreheads. As in chapters 5 and 7, those who experience the gospel respond to it by praising God for it (14:2–3).

The statements in verses 4–5 that these are virgins and that in their mouth no lie was found do not mean these people were celibates or that they were perfectly sinless in what their lips uttered. Rather, these people lived the gospel by avoiding spiritual adultery with the world, and they told the truth about God. They did not engage in idolatry and the sexual immorality that accompanies it. The redeemed follow the Lamb and do not lie. They worship God and they tell the truth about how to be made right with him by grace through faith in Jesus. Redemption results in purity of action and speech.

10 [h]ch. 14:12
11 [i][ver. 1, 14; ch. 16:13]
12 [j]ver. 3
13 [k]ch. 16:14; 19:20; Deut. 13:1-3; Matt. 24:24; 2 Thess. 2:9-11 [l]ch. 20:9; 1 Kgs. 18:38; 2 Kgs. 1:10, 12; Luke 9:54
14 [m][ch. 12:9] [n]ver. 3, 12
15 [o]ch. 14:9, 11; 16:2; 19:20; 20:4 [p][ch. 16:6]
16 [q][ch. 7:3]; See Gal. 6:17
17 [r]ch. 14:11 [s]ch. 15:2
18 [t][ch. 17:9] [u][ch. 21:17]
Chapter 14
1 [v]Ps. 2:6; Heb. 12:22 [w]See ch. 5:6 [x]ch. 7:4 [y]ch. 3:12 [z]ch. 7:3
2 [a]See ch. 1:15 [b]ch. 6:1; 19:6 [c]ch. 5:8; 15:2
3 [d]ch. 5:9 [e][ch. 2:17; 19:12]
4 [f]2 Cor. 11:2 [g][ch. 3:4; 17:14] [h]James 1:18
5 [i]Zeph. 3:13; [Ps. 32:2; Isa. 63:8; John 1:47] [j]See Jude 24

The Messages of the Three Angels

6 Then I saw another angel [k]flying directly
overhead, with an eternal gospel to proclaim
to [l]those who dwell on earth, to every nation
and tribe and language and people. 7 And he
said with a loud voice, [m]"Fear God and [n]give
him glory, because the hour of his judgment
has come, and [o]worship him who made heaven
and earth, the sea and the [p]springs of water."
8 Another angel, a second, followed, saying,
[q]"Fallen, fallen is [r]Babylon the great, [s]she who
made all nations drink [t]the wine of the passion[1] of her sexual immorality."
9 And another angel, a third, followed them,
saying with a loud voice, "If anyone [u]worships
the beast and its image and receives [v]a mark
on his forehead or on his hand, 10 he also will
drink [w]the wine of God's wrath, [x]poured full
strength into the cup of his anger, and [y]he will
be tormented with fire and sulfur in the presence of the holy angels and in the presence of
the Lamb. 11 And [z]the smoke of their torment
goes up forever and ever, and [a]they have no
rest, day or night, these [u]worshipers of the
beast and its image, and whoever receives the
mark of its name."
12 [b]Here is a call for the endurance of the
saints, those who [c]keep the commandments
of God and their faith in Jesus.[2]
13 And I heard a voice from heaven saying,
"Write this: [d]Blessed are the dead [e]who die
in the Lord from now on." "Blessed indeed,"
says the Spirit, [f]"that they may rest from their
labors, for their deeds follow them!"

The Harvest of the Earth

14 Then I looked, and behold, a white cloud,
and seated on the cloud one [g]like a son of man,
[h]with a golden crown on his head, and a sharp
sickle in his hand. 15 And another angel [i]came
out of the temple, calling with a loud voice to
him who sat on the cloud, [j]"Put in your sickle,
and reap, for the hour to reap has come, for
[k]the harvest of the earth is fully ripe." 16 So he
who sat on the cloud swung his sickle across
the earth, and the earth was reaped.
17 Then another angel came out of the temple
in heaven, and he too had a sharp sickle. 18 And
another angel came out from the altar, [l]the
angel who has authority over the fire, and he
called with a loud voice to the one who had
the sharp sickle, "Put in your sickle and gather
the clusters from the vine of the earth, [m]for
its grapes are ripe." 19 So the angel swung his
sickle across the earth and gathered the grape
harvest of the earth and threw it into the great
[n]winepress of the wrath of God. 20 And [o]the
winepress was trodden [p]outside the city, and
blood flowed from the winepress, as high as
[q]a horse's bridle, for 1,600 stadia.[3]

The Seven Angels with Seven Plagues

15 Then [r]I saw another sign in heaven,
great and amazing, [s]seven angels with
seven plagues, which are the last, for with
them the wrath of God is finished.
2 And I saw [t]what appeared to be a sea of glass
mingled with fire—and also those [u]who had
conquered the beast and its image and [v]the

[1] Or *wrath* [2] Greek *and the faith of Jesus* [3] About 184 miles; a *stadion* was about 607 feet or 185 meters

6[k] ch. 8:13 [l][ch. 3:10]
7[m] ch. 15:4 [n] See ch. 11:13 [o] Neh. 9:6; See ch. 4:11 [p] ch. 8:10; 16:4
8[q] ch. 18:2; Isa. 21:9; Jer. 51:8 [r] ch. 16:19; 17:5; 18:10; [Dan. 4:30] [s] Jer. 51:7 [t] ch. 18:3
9[u] See ch. 13:15 [v] ch. 13:16
10[w] ch. 16:19; See Job 21:20 [x] [ch. 18:6; Isa. 1:22] [y] ch. 20:10
11[z] Isa. 34:10; [ch. 18:18; 19:3; Gen. 19:28] [a] ch. 4:8 [u] [See ver. 9 above]
12[b] ch. 13:10 [c] ch. 12:17
13[d] ch. 20:6; [Eccles. 4:2] [e] 1 Cor. 15:18; 1 Thess. 4:16 [f] ch. 6:11
14[g] See ch. 1:13 [h] ch. 6:2
15[i] [ch. 15:6; 16:17] [j] ver. 18; Joel 3:13; Mark 4:29; [Matt. 13:39] [k] Jer. 51:33
18[l] [ch. 16:8] [m] Joel 3:13
19[n] ch. 19:15
20[o] Isa. 63:3; Lam. 1:15 [p] [Heb. 13:12] [q] [ch. 19:14]

Chapter 15
1[r] [ch. 12:1, 3] [s] ch. 16:1; 17:1; 21:9
2[t] ch. 4:6; 21:18, 21 [u] ch. 12:11 [v] ch. 13:17

14:6–13 The call in verses 6–7 to fear, give glory to, and worship God is based on the certainty that he will establish justice in his creation, which is the blessed end result of the eternal gospel. Because of Christ's cross, God can show mercy, but those who refuse the mercy offered there will face his judgment. The declaration in verse 8 that Babylon is fallen is not explicitly called "gospel," but Nahum 1:15 calls the downfall of Assyria "good news."

It is good news that God acts in perfect justice, because otherwise evil would never be punished. The call of the third angel in Revelation 14:9–11 explains that not worshiping the beast equals not committing idolatry, and not receiving his mark equals not making peace with the world. John again applies the message in verse 12, explaining that the endurance of the saints means keeping the commandments of God not to commit idolatry or make friends with the world, and keeping faith in Jesus.

John recounts in verse 13 that he heard a voice from out of heaven declaring "rest" to those who "die in the Lord" (i.e., who are Christians). Those who oppose Christ, on the other hand, "have no rest, day or night" (v. 11). This is where the gospel finally takes us: *rest*. Jesus himself said that he came to give rest (Matt. 11:28–30), picking up a theme from the prophets (e.g., Isa. 30:15; Jer. 6:16).

15:1–8 The judgments that accompany the bowls of wrath are called plagues in verse 1 because the deliverance that will come through them fulfills the deliverance

number of its name, standing beside the sea of
glass [w]with harps of God in their hands. 3 And
they sing [x]the song of Moses, [y]the servant[1] of
God, and the song of the Lamb, saying,

[z]"Great and amazing are your deeds,
O Lord God the Almighty!
[a]Just and true are your ways,
O King of the nations![2]
4 [b]Who will not fear, O Lord,
and glorify your name?
For you alone are [c]holy.
[d]All nations will come
and worship you,
for your righteous acts have been
revealed."

5 After this I looked, and [e]the sanctuary of
[f]the tent[3] of witness in heaven was opened,
6 and out of the sanctuary came [g]the seven
angels with the seven plagues, clothed in pure,
bright [i]linen, [j]with golden sashes around their
chests. 7 And one of [k]the four living creatures
gave to the seven angels seven [l]golden bowls
full of the wrath of God [m]who lives forever
and ever, 8 and [n]the sanctuary was filled with
smoke from the glory of God and from his
power, and [o]no one could enter the sanctuary
until the seven plagues of the seven angels
were finished.

The Seven Bowls of God's Wrath

16 Then I heard a loud voice from the
temple telling [p]the seven angels, "Go
and [q]pour out on the earth [r]the seven bowls
of the wrath of God."
2 So the first angel went and poured out his
bowl on the earth, and harmful and painful
[s]sores came upon the people who bore [t]the
mark of the beast and worshiped its image.
3 The second angel poured out his bowl
into the sea, and [u]it became like the blood of
a corpse, and [v]every living thing died that was
in the sea.
4 The third angel poured out his bowl into
[w]the rivers and the springs of water, and [x]they
became blood. 5 And I heard the angel in
charge of the waters[4] say,

[y]"Just are you, [z]O Holy One, [a]who is and
who was,
for you brought these judgments.
6 For [b]they have shed the blood of [c]saints
and prophets,
and [d]you have given them blood to
drink.
It is what they deserve!"

7 And I heard [e]the altar saying,

"Yes, Lord God the Almighty,
[f]true and just are your judgments!"

[1] Greek *bondservant* [2] Some manuscripts *the ages* [3] Or *tabernacle* [4] Greek *angel of the waters*

of Israel from Egypt. Then in verse 3 the song of Moses has become the song of the Lamb because Jesus died as the Passover Lamb in the new exodus, fulfilling the exodus from Egypt.

This new exodus frees not just one nation but all, and verse 4 sings that all nations will come to worship the creating and redeeming God (cf. 5:9–10; 7:9–10). The reference in 15:5 to the tent of witness recalls the one in which Moses met with God, but this is the one in heaven of which the Mosaic was only a shadow. What was depicted in shadow at the completion of the tabernacle and the temple, when each was filled with the glory of God (Ex. 40:34; 1 Kings 8:10–11), is fulfilled in Revelation 15:8 as God prepares to fill the world with his glory.

16:1–21 The bowls match the trumpets in the literary structure of Revelation (see "The Gospel in Revelation"), and both are fulfillments of the plagues on Egypt. The sores of the first bowl (v. 2) match the sores of the sixth plague (Ex. 9:10). As with the first plague on Egypt (Ex. 7:17–21), the second and third bowls (Rev. 16:3–7) see waters turned to blood. The fifth brings darkness (vv. 10–11) like the ninth plague (Ex. 10:21–29), and the unclean spirits gathering for battle after the sixth (Rev. 16:12–15) may correspond to the death angel (Ex. 11:1–10; 12:29–32). The hail that accompanies the seventh bowl (Rev. 16:17–21) matches the hail of the seventh plague (Ex. 9:13–35).

Through the outpouring of these bowls, God is bringing the final fulfillment of the exodus pattern to completion. This pattern points forward to the final salvation of God's people through the judgment of their enemies in the everlasting glory of God. In this final salvation and judgment we take strong hope despite the trials and tribulations we face until that time.

2 [w]ch. 5:8; 14:2
3 [x]Ex. 15:1; Deut. 31:30 [y]See Heb. 3:5 [z]Deut. 32:3, 4; [Job 37:5; Ps. 111:2; 139:14; 145:17] [a]ch. 16:7; Hos. 14:9
4 [b]ch. 14:7; Mal. 2:2 [c]ch. 16:5; Heb. 7:26 [d]See Ps. 86:9
5 [e]ch. 11:19 [f]Ex. 38:21; Num. 1:50; Acts 7:44
6 [g]See ver. 1 [i]ch. 19:8 [j]ch. 1:13
7 [k]ch. 4:6 [l][ch. 5:8] [m]ch. 1:18; 4:9; 5:13
8 [n]Ex. 40:34; Isa. 6:4; Hag. 2:7; [1 Kgs. 8:10, 11; 2 Chr. 5:13, 14] [o]Ex. 40:35; 1 Kgs. 8:11

Chapter 16
1 [p]See ch. 15:1 [q]Ps. 79:6; Jer. 10:25; Zeph. 3:8 [r]ch. 15:7
2 [s]ver. 11; Ex. 9:9-11 [t]ch. 13:16
3 [u]ch. 8:8 [v]ch. 8:9
4 [w]ch. 8:10 [x]Ex. 7:17-20
5 [y]Jer. 12:1; John 17:25 [z]ch. 15:4 [a]ch. 11:17; [ch. 1:4, 8; 4:8]
6 [b]ch. 18:24; [ch. 13:15] [c]ch. 11:18 [d][Isa. 49:26; Luke 11:49, 50]
7 [e]ch. 6:9 [f]ch. 15:3; 19:2; [Ps. 119:137]

8 The fourth angel poured out his bowl on
the sun, and it was allowed to scorch people
[g]with fire. 9 They were scorched by the fierce
heat, and [h]they cursed[1] the name of God who
had power over these plagues. [i]They did not
repent [j]and give him glory.
10 The fifth angel poured out his bowl on
[k]the throne of the beast, and [l]its kingdom was
plunged into darkness. People gnawed their
tongues in anguish 11 and cursed [m]the God of
heaven for their pain and [n]sores. [o]They did not
repent of their deeds.
12 The sixth angel poured out his bowl on
[p]the great river Euphrates, and [q]its water was
dried up, [r]to prepare the way for the kings
[s]from the east. 13 And I saw, coming out of the
mouth of [t]the dragon and out of the mouth of
[u]the beast and out of the mouth of [v]the false
prophet, three [w]unclean spirits like [x]frogs.
14 For they are [y]demonic spirits, [z]performing
signs, who go abroad to the kings of the whole
world, [a]to assemble them for battle on [b]the
great day of God the Almighty. 15 ("Behold,
[c]I am coming like a thief! [d]Blessed is the one
who stays awake, keeping his garments on,
[e]that he may not go about naked and be seen
exposed!") 16 And [f]they assembled them at the
place that in Hebrew is called [g]Armageddon.

The Seventh Bowl

17 The seventh angel poured out his bowl
into [h]the air, and a loud voice came out of the
temple, from the throne, saying, [i]"It is done!"
18 And there were [j]flashes of lightning, rumblings,[2] peals of thunder, and [k]a great earthquake [l]such as there had never been since man
was on the earth, so great was that earthquake.
19 [m]The great city [n]was split into three parts,
and the cities of the nations fell, and God
[o]remembered [p]Babylon the great, [q]to make
her drain the cup of the wine of the fury of
his wrath. 20 And [r]every island fled away, and
no mountains were to be found. 21 And [s]great
hailstones, about one hundred pounds[3] each,
fell from heaven on people; and [t]they cursed
God for [u]the plague of the hail, because the
plague was so severe.

The Great Prostitute and the Beast

17 Then [v]one of the seven angels who
had [w]the seven bowls came and said to
me, "Come, I will show you the judgment of
[x]the great prostitute [y]who is seated on many
waters, 2 [z]with whom the kings of the earth
have committed sexual immorality, and
[a]with the wine of whose sexual immorality
[b]the dwellers on earth have become drunk."
3 And [c]he carried me away in the Spirit [d]into
a wilderness, and I saw a woman sitting on
[e]a scarlet beast that was full of [f]blasphemous
names, and [g]it had seven heads and ten horns.
4 The woman [h]was arrayed in purple and scarlet, and adorned [i]with gold and jewels and
pearls, holding in her hand [j]a golden cup
full of abominations and the impurities of
her sexual immorality. 5 And on her forehead
was written a name of [k]mystery: [l]"Babylon
the great, mother of prostitutes and of earth's
abominations." 6 And I saw the woman, drunk
[m]with the blood of the saints, the blood of [n]the
martyrs of Jesus.[4]
When I saw her, I marveled greatly. 7 But the
angel said to me, "Why do you marvel? I will
tell you [o]the mystery of the woman, and of the
beast with seven heads and ten horns that carries her. 8 The beast that you saw [p]was, and is
not, and [q]is about to rise from [r]the bottomless
pit[5] and [s]go to destruction. And [t]the dwellers

[1] Greek *blasphemed*; also verses 11, 21 [2] Or *voices*, or *sounds* [3] Greek *a talent in weight* [4] Greek *the witnesses to Jesus* [5] Greek *the abyss*

17:1–18 As in Revelation 13, chapter 17 presents a satanic parody of God. In 1:4 God was described as "him who is and who was and who is to come"; the beast is described in 17:8 as the one who was, and is not, and is about to rise from the bottomless pit. The beast tries to be God, but unlike God the beast goes to destruction.

Only the true gospel of the true God saves. As in 13:8, in 17:8 the dwellers on earth whose names have not been written in the book of life from the foundation of the world will worship the beast. Yet God is able to preserve his own from all satanic deception. This is what we see when the Lamb conquers (17:14), and those with him are called and chosen and faithful. Jesus has saved his own, chosen them, and called them to himself, enabling them to be faithful to him.

8 [g]ch. 9:17; [ch. 14:18]
9 [h]ver. 11, 21 [i][Dan. 5:22]; See ch. 2:21 [j][Dan. 5:23]; See ch. 11:13
10 [k]ch. 13:2 [l]ch. 9:2; Ex. 10:21
11 [m]ch. 11:13 [n]ver. 2 [o]See ch. 2:21
12 [p]ch. 9:14 [q]Isa. 11:15; 44:27; Jer. 50:38; 51:32, 36 [r][Isa. 41:2, 25; 46:11] [s]ch. 7:2
13 [t]ch. 12:3, 9 [u]ch. 13:1 [v]ch. 19:20; 20:10; [ch. 13:11, 14] [w]ch. 18:2 [x][Ex. 8:6]
14 [y][1 Tim. 4:1] [z]See ch. 13:13 [a]ch. 20:8; [ch. 17:14; 19:19; 1 Kgs. 22:20] [b]See ch. 6:17

15 [c]See ch. 3:3 [d]ch. 3:2, 3; See Matt. 24:42 [e]ch. 3:18 **16** [f]ch. 19:19 [g]Zech. 12:11; See Judg. 5:19 **17** [h][Eph. 2:2] [i]See ch. 10:6 **18** [j]ch. 4:5; 8:5; 11:19 [k]ch. 6:12; 11:13 [l]Dan. 12:1; Joel 2:2; Matt. 24:21 **19** [m]ch. 11:8 [n][ch. 11:13] [o]ch. 18:5; [Ps. 74:18] [p]See ch. 14:8 [q]See ch. 14:10 **20** [r]See ch. 6:14 **21** [s]ch. 11:19 [t]ver. 9, 11 [u]Ex. 9:23-25 **Chapter 17** **1** [v]ch. 21:9 [w]ch. 15:7 [x]ch. 19:2; Nah. 3:4; [Isa. 1:21; Jer. 2:20] [y]ver. 15; [Jer. 51:13] **2** [z]ch. 18:3, 9; [Isa. 23:17] [a]ch. 14:8; Jer. 51:7 [b]See ch. 3:10 **3** [c]ch. 21:10 [d]ch. 12:6, 14 [e][ch. 12:3] [f]ch. 13:1 [g]ver. 7, 9, 12 **4** [h]ch. 18:16 [i]Dan. 11:38 [j]Jer. 51:7; [ch. 18:6] **5** [k]ver. 7; 2 Thess. 2:7 [l]See ch. 14:8 **6** [m]ch. 16:6; [ch. 13:15] [n]ch. 2:13 **7** [o]ver. 5 **8** [p]ver. 11; [ch. 1:4; 13:3] [q]ch. 11:7 [r]See ch. 9:1 [s]ch. 13:10 [t]See ch. 3:10

on earth whose names have not been written
in [u]the book of life from the foundation of the
world will marvel to see the beast, because [p]it
was and is not and is to come. 9 [v]This calls for a
mind with wisdom: the seven heads are seven
mountains on which the woman is seated;
10 they are also seven kings, five of whom have
fallen, one is, the other has not yet come, and
when he does come he must remain only a
little while. 11 As for the beast [w]that was and is
not, it is an eighth but it belongs to the seven,
and it goes to destruction. 12 And [x]the ten horns
that you saw are ten kings who have not yet
received royal power, but they are to receive
authority as kings [y]for one hour, together with
the beast. 13 These are of one mind, and they
hand over their power and authority to the
beast. 14 They [z]will make war on the Lamb, and
[a]the Lamb will conquer them, for he is [b]Lord of
lords and [b]King of kings, and those with him
are [c]called and chosen and faithful."

15 And the angel[1] said to me, [d]"The waters
that you saw, where the prostitute is seated,
are peoples and multitudes and nations and
languages. 16 And [e]the ten horns that you saw,
they and the beast [f]will hate the prostitute.
They will make her [g]desolate and [h]naked, and
[i]devour her flesh and [j]burn her up with fire,
17 for [k]God has put it into their hearts to carry
out his purpose by being of one mind and
[l]handing over their royal power to the beast,
until the words of God are fulfilled. 18 And the
woman that you saw is [m]the great city that has
dominion over the kings of the earth."

The Fall of Babylon

18 After this I saw [n]another angel coming down from heaven, having great
authority, and [o]the earth was made bright
with his glory. 2 And he called out with a
mighty voice,

[p]"Fallen, fallen is Babylon the great!
She has become [q]a dwelling place for demons,
a haunt [r]for every unclean spirit,
a haunt [s]for every unclean bird,
a haunt for every unclean and detestable beast.
3 For all nations have drunk[2]
[t]the wine of the passion of her sexual immorality,
and [u]the kings of the earth have committed immorality with her,
and [v]the merchants of the earth have grown rich from the power of her luxurious living."

4 Then I heard another voice from heaven
saying,

[w]"Come out of her, my people,
lest you take part in her sins,
lest you share in her plagues;
5 for [x]her sins are heaped high as heaven,
and [y]God has remembered her iniquities.
6 [z]Pay her back as she herself has paid back others,
and repay her [a]double for her deeds;
mix a double portion for her [b]in the cup she mixed.
7 [c]As she glorified herself and lived in luxury,
so give her a like measure of torment and mourning,
since in her heart she says,
[d]'I sit as a queen,
I am no widow,
and mourning I shall never see.'
8 For this reason her plagues will come [e]in a single day,
death and mourning and famine,

[1] Greek *he* [2] Some manuscripts *fallen by*

18:1–24 When Old Testament Israel was in its captivity, the prophets often spoke of a new exodus that would result in the return of the people from their exile to Babylon. The words of verse 4, "Come out of her, my people," pick up the words of Isaiah 48:20, "Go out from Babylon, flee from Chaldea." This is because the fulfillment of the exodus initiated in the bowls of wrath is resulting in the fulfillment of the return from exile as the fall of Babylon is celebrated. God's people come out of Babylon (the representation of earth's evil; e.g., Rev. 18:5, 20, 24) to journey toward the new Jerusalem (cf. Revelation 21–22), and also so that they will neither take part in her sins nor share in her plagues (18:4).

8 [u]See ch. 3:5
9 [v][ch. 13:18]
11 [w]ver. 8; [ch. 11:17]
12 [x]ver. 16; Dan. 7:24; [ch. 13:1; Zech. 1:18-21] [y][ch. 18:10, 17, 19]
14 [z]See ch. 16:14 [a]See ch. 3:21 [b]ch. 19:16; Deut. 10:17; Ps. 136:3; Dan. 2:47; 1 Tim. 6:15; [ch. 1:5; Matt. 28:18; Acts 10:36] [c]See ch. 2:10; Luke 18:7 (Gk.); Rom. 1:6
15 [d]ver. 1; [Isa. 8:7]
16 [e]See ver. 12 [f][Jer. 50:41, 42]

[g]ch. 18:17, 19 [h]Ezek. 16:37, 39 [i][ch. 19:18] [j]ch. 18:8; [Lev. 21:9] **17** [k]2 Cor. 8:16 [l][2 Thess. 2:11] **18** [m]ch. 16:19 **Chapter 18** **1** [n]ch. 17:1, 7 [o]Ezek. 43:2 **2** [p]See ch. 14:8 [q]Isa. 13:21; 34:14; Jer. 50:39; 51:37; [Zeph. 2:14, 15] [r]ch. 16:13 [s]Isa. 14:23; 34:11 **3** [t]ch. 14:8 [u]ver. 9; ch. 17:2 [v]ver. 11, 15; Ezek. 27:33 **4** [w][2 Cor. 6:17]; See Isa. 48:20 **5** [x]Jer. 51:9; [Gen. 18:20, 21; Ezra 9:6; Jonah 1:2] [y]ch. 16:19 **6** [z]Ps. 137:8; Jer. 50:15, 29; 51:24, 49 [a]Jer. 16:18 [b][ch. 14:10; 16:19; 17:4] **7** [c][Ezek. 28:2-8] [d]Isa. 47:7, 8; Zeph. 2:15; [ch. 3:17] **8** [e]Isa. 47:9; [ver. 10]

and [f]she will be burned up with fire;
for [g]mighty is the Lord God who has
judged her."

[9]And [h]the kings of the earth, who committed
sexual immorality and lived in luxury with
her, [i]will weep and wail over her [j]when they
see the smoke of her burning. [10][k]They will
stand far off, in fear of her torment, and say,

"Alas! Alas! [l]You great city,
you mighty city, Babylon!
For [m]in a single hour your judgment has
come."

[11]And [n]the merchants of the earth weep and
mourn for her, since no one buys their cargo
anymore, [12]cargo of gold, silver, jewels, pearls,
fine linen, purple cloth, silk, scarlet cloth, all
kinds of scented wood, all kinds of articles
of ivory, all kinds of articles of costly wood,
bronze, iron and marble, [13]cinnamon, spice,
incense, myrrh, frankincense, wine, oil, fine
flour, wheat, cattle and sheep, horses and chariots, and slaves, that is, human souls.[1]

14 "The fruit for which your soul longed
has gone from you,
and all your delicacies and your splendors
are lost to you,
never to be found again!"

[15][o]The merchants of these wares, who gained
wealth from her, [p]will stand far off, in fear of
her torment, weeping and mourning aloud,

16 "Alas, alas, for the great city
[q]that was clothed in fine linen,
in purple and scarlet,
adorned with gold,
with jewels, and with pearls!
17 For [r]in a single hour all this wealth [s]has
been laid waste."

And [t]all shipmasters and seafaring men, sailors and all whose trade is on the sea, stood far
off [18]and [u]cried out [v]as they saw the smoke of
her burning,

[w]"What city was like the great city?"

[19]And they threw [x]dust on their heads as they
wept and mourned, crying out,

"Alas, alas, for the great city
[y]where all who had ships at sea
grew rich by her wealth!
For [z]in a single hour she has been laid
waste.
20 [a]Rejoice over her, O heaven,
and you saints and [b]apostles and
prophets,
for [c]God has given judgment for you
against her!"

[21]Then [d]a mighty angel [e]took up a stone like
a great millstone and threw it into the sea,
saying,

"So will Babylon [f]the great city be thrown
down with violence,
and will be found no more;
22 and [g]the sound of harpists and musicians, of flute players and trumpeters,
will be heard in you no more,
and a craftsman of any craft
will be found in you no more,
and [h]the sound of the mill
will be heard in you no more,
23 and the light of a lamp
will shine in you no more,
and [i]the voice of bridegroom and bride
will be heard in you no more,
for [j]your merchants were the great ones
of the earth,
and all nations were deceived [k]by your
sorcery.
24 And [l]in her was found the blood of
prophets and of saints,
and of [m]all who have been slain on
earth."

[1] Or *and slaves, and human lives*

8[f] ch. 17:16 [g] Jer. 50:34
9[h] ver. 3; ch. 17:2; [Ezek. 26:16, 17] [i] [Jer. 50:46] [j] ver. 18; ch. 19:3
10[k] ver. 15, 17 [l] See ch. 14:8 [m] ver. 17, 19; [ver. 8]
11[n] ver. 3, 15; [Ezek. 27:36]
15[o] ver. 3, 11 [p] ver. 10
16[q] ch. 17:4
17[r] ver. 10, 19 [s] ch. 17:16 [t] Ezek. 27:28, 29

God delivers those who believe the gospel from his wrath and from the sins that incur that wrath. Verses 9–24 show the obliteration of everything people choose over the gospel and holy living, and the visitation of God's justice gives way to the call in verse 20 for those who belong to God to rejoice in the triumph of God which entails their vindication. In verses 22–23 all joy is gone from the wicked world: the rejoicing will be done by God's people, not the world. Reflecting on this stable assurance, our hearts are moved with fresh confidence and trust in the Lord of heaven.

18[u] Ezek. 27:30 [v] ver. 9 [w] Ezek. 27:32; [ch. 13:4] **19**[x] See Josh. 7:6; Job 2:12 [y] ver. 3, 15 [z] ver. 10, 17 **20**[a] Deut. 32:43; Jer. 51:48; See ch. 12:12 [b] Luke 11:49, 50 [c] ch. 19:2 **21**[d] ch. 5:2; 10:1 [e] [Jer. 51:63, 64] [f] ver. 10 **22**[g] Isa. 14:11; 24:8; Ezek. 26:13 [h] Eccles. 12:4; Jer. 25:10 **23**[i] Jer. 7:34; 16:9; 33:11 [j] Isa. 23:8 [k] Nah. 3:4 **24**[l] ch. 17:6; [Matt. 23:35, 36] [m] [Jer. 51:49]

Rejoicing in Heaven

19 After this I heard [n]what seemed to be
the loud voice of a great multitude in
heaven, crying out,

"Hallelujah!
[o]Salvation and glory and power belong to
our God,
2 for [p]his judgments are true and just;
for he has judged [q]the great prostitute
who corrupted the earth with her
immorality,
and [r]has avenged on her the blood of his
servants."[1]

3 Once more they cried out,

"Hallelujah!
[s]The smoke from her goes up forever and
ever."

4 And [t]the twenty-four elders and the four living creatures fell down and worshiped God
who was seated on the throne, saying, "Amen.
Hallelujah!" 5 And from the throne came a
voice saying,

[u]"Praise our God,
all you his servants,
[v]you who fear him,
small and great."

The Marriage Supper of the Lamb

6 Then I heard what seemed to be [w]the voice
of a great multitude, like [x]the roar of many
waters and [y]like the sound of mighty peals of
thunder, crying out,

"Hallelujah!
For the Lord our God
the Almighty [z]reigns.
7 Let us rejoice and exult
and give him the glory,
for [a]the marriage of the Lamb has come,
and [b]his Bride has made herself ready;
8 [c]it was granted her to clothe herself
with fine linen, bright and pure"—

for the fine linen is [d]the righteous deeds of
the saints.
9 And the angel said[2] to me, "Write this:
[e]Blessed are those who are invited to the marriage supper of the Lamb." And he said to me,
[f]"These are the true words of God." 10 Then
[g]I fell down at his feet to worship him, [h]but
he said to me, "You must not do that! I am a
fellow servant[3] with you and your brothers
who hold to [i]the testimony of Jesus. Worship
God." For the testimony of Jesus is the spirit
of prophecy.

The Rider on a White Horse

11 Then I saw [j]heaven opened, and behold,
[k]a white horse! The one sitting on it is called
[l]Faithful and True, and [m]in righteousness he
judges and makes war. 12 [n]His eyes are like a
flame of fire, and on his head are [o]many diadems, and he has [p]a name written that no one
knows but himself. 13 He is clothed in [q]a robe
dipped in[4] blood, and the name by which he is
called is [r]The Word of God. 14 And the armies of
heaven, [s]arrayed in fine linen, white and pure,

[1] Greek *bondservants*; also verse 5 [2] Greek *he said* [3] Greek *fellow bondservant* [4] Some manuscripts *sprinkled with*

19:1–10 The redeemed have praised God for his work of saving them (chs. 5; 7; 14; and 15). Now the redeemed join the inhabitants of heaven to celebrate the visitation of God's justice through which the final deliverance has been wrought.

Marriage is ultimately about Christ and the church (cf. Ephesians 5). Now that the marriage of the Lamb has come, the people of God, figuratively called virgins in Revelation 14:4, are a pure bride clothed in fine linen, bright and pure. The fine linen symbolizes righteous deeds (19:7–8; cf. 7:9, 13–14). Such deeds in Revelation refer to faithfulness to "the word of God and to the testimony of Jesus" (1:2, 9; 6:9; 11:7; 12:11, 17; 14:12; 19:10; 20:4)—that is, the true gospel, and rejection of idolatry and sexual immorality.

19:11–21 At long last, Christ comes to save his people through the judgment of their enemies. Unlike every antichrist or satanic beast, Jesus is Faithful and True (v. 11).

Jesus is able to save because he knew no sin (2 Cor. 5:21), and he will reign in a way that is worthy of trust: in righteousness he judges and makes war (Rev. 19:11). He will slay his enemies with the sword that comes from his mouth (v. 21; cf. the power of the word of gospel truth represented in 1:16; 2:12, 16; 19:15). Because the battle has not yet begun, the description in verse 13 that he is clothed in a robe dipped in blood seems to refer to his own blood from his death on the cross rather than to the image of Isaiah 63:3, where the divine warrior wears a robe spattered with the blood of his enemies. People will either be saved by the blood of Jesus through faith in

Chapter 19
1 [n]See ch. 11:15 [o]ch. 4:11; 7:10; 12:10
2 [p]ch. 15:3; 16:7 [q]See ch. 17:1 [r]Deut. 32:43; 2 Kgs. 9:7; [ch. 16:6]; See ch. 6:10
3 [s]ch. 18:9, 18; Isa. 34:10; [ch. 14:11]
4 [t]ch. 4:4, 6, 10; 5:14
5 [u]Ps. 22:23; 113:1; 134:1; 135:1 [v]ch. 11:18
6 [w]Dan. 10:6; [ver. 1] [x]See ch. 1:15 [y]ch. 6:1; 14:2 [z]ch. 11:15, 17; Ps. 97:1
7 [a]Matt. 22:2; 25:10; Luke 12:36; 14:8; John 2:1; [Eph. 5:22-32] [b]ch. 21:2, 9; [Isa. 54:5; Hos. 2:19, 20]
8 [c][Ps. 45:13-15; Ezek. 16:10] [d][Ps. 132:9; Isa. 61:10]
9 [e]Luke 14:15; See ver. 7 [f][ch. 21:5; 22:6]
10 [g]ch. 22:8 [h]ch. 22:9; See Acts 10:26 [i]ch. 1:2; 6:9; 12:17
11 [j]See Ezek. 1:1 [k]See ch. 6:2 [l]See ch. 3:7, 14 [m][Ps. 96:13; Isa. 11:4]
12 [n]ch. 1:14; 2:18 [o][ch. 12:3] [p]ver. 16; ch. 2:17; [Prov. 30:4]
13 [q]Isa. 63:2, 3 [r]See John 1:1
14 [s]ch. 3:4; 7:9

[t]were following him on white horses. 15 [u]From
his mouth comes a sharp sword [v]with which to
strike down the nations, and [w]he will rule them
with a rod of iron. [x]He will tread the winepress
of the fury of the wrath of God the Almighty.
16 On his robe and on his thigh [y]he has a name
written, [z]King of kings and Lord of lords.
17 Then I saw an angel standing in the sun,
and with a loud voice he called to [a]all the birds
that fly directly overhead, [b]"Come, gather for
[c]the great supper of God, 18 [d]to eat the flesh of
kings, the flesh of captains, the flesh of mighty
men, the flesh of horses and their riders, and
the flesh of all men, both free and slave,[1] both
small and great." 19 And I saw [e]the beast and
the kings of the earth with their armies [f]gath-
ered to make war against him who was sitting on the horse and against his army. 20 And
the beast was captured, and with it [g]the false
prophet [h]who in its presence[2] had done the
signs by which he deceived those who had
received the mark of the beast and those who
[i]worshiped its image. These two were [j]thrown
alive into the lake of [k]fire that burns with sulfur. 21 And the rest were slain by the sword [l]that
came from the mouth of him who was sitting
on the horse, and [m]all the birds were gorged
with their flesh.

The Thousand Years

20 Then I saw an angel coming down from
heaven, [n]holding in his hand the key to
[o]the bottomless pit[3] and a great chain. 2 And
he seized [p]the dragon, that ancient serpent,
who is the devil and Satan, and [q]bound him
for a thousand years, 3 and threw him into [o]the
pit, and shut it and [r]sealed it over him, so that
[s]he might not deceive the nations any longer,
until the thousand years were ended. After
that he must be released for a little while.
4 Then I saw [t]thrones, and [u]seated on them
were those to whom the authority to judge
was committed. Also I saw [v]the souls of those
who had been beheaded for the testimony of
Jesus and for the word of God, and those [w]who
had not worshiped the beast or its image and
had not received its mark on their foreheads
or their hands. [x]They came to life and [y]reigned
with Christ for a thousand years. 5 The rest of
the dead did not come to life until the thousand years were ended. This is the first resurrection. 6 [z]Blessed and holy is the one who
shares in the first resurrection! Over such [a]the
second death has no power, but they will be
[b]priests of God and of Christ, and they [c]will
reign with him for a thousand years.

The Defeat of Satan

7 And when the thousand years are ended,
[d]Satan will be released from his prison 8 and
will come out [e]to deceive the nations that
are at the four corners of the earth, [f]Gog
and Magog, [g]to gather them for battle; their
number is like the sand of the sea. 9 And [h]they
marched up over the broad plain of the earth
and surrounded [i]the camp of the saints and

[1] Greek *bondservant* [2] Or *on its behalf* [3] Greek *the abyss*; also verse 3

him or they will be judged and will pay for their sins with their own blood. One way or another, all sin will be punished.

John is encouraging persecuted Christians to keep the faith, to reject the world-pleasing idolatry that would end their persecution, and to keep the commands of God and avoid sexual immorality. He has shown them how Satan, the beast, and the false prophet have used the wicked world as a prostitute to sell what could be had for free in covenant with God (Revelation 13 and 17). Now John shows the beast and false prophet captured and thrown alive into the lake of fire that burns with sulfur in 19:20. Strengthening believers in the conviction that the deceivers will one day be judged is a powerful argument to be vigilant against deception and to adhere to the truth.

20:1–10 The argument for vigilance against deception continues in verses 1–3, where Satan is seized and bound for a thousand years, so that he might not deceive the nations any longer (as he was doing in 12:9 and 13:14). During the thousand years in which Satan is bound, those slain while he was deceiving the nations (cf. 11:7; 13:7, 15) are raised from the dead to reign with Christ (20:4–6). These who believed the gospel and were faithful to it during the persecution (described in 11:1–14; 12:1–13:18; and 17:1–18) are now raised from the dead to receive their reward. The rewards received (chs. 20–22) correspond to the promises made to those who conquer (chs. 2–3), encouraging the churches to overcome and receive what has been promised.

14[t] [ch. 14:20]
15[u] ver. 21; See ch. 1:16 [v] [Isa. 11:4; 2 Thess. 2:8] [w] ch. 2:27; 12:5 [x] ch. 14:20; Isa. 63:3
16[y] ver. 12 [z] See ch. 17:14
17[a] ver. 21 [b] Jer. 12:9; Ezek. 39:17 [c] [Isa. 34:6; Jer. 46:10; Ezek. 39:19]
18[d] Ezek. 39:18, 20
19[e] ch. 11:7; 13:1 [f] ch. 16:16
20[g] ch. 16:13; 20:10 [h] ch. 13:11-14 [i] See ch. 13:15 [j] ch. 20:10, 14, 15; [Dan. 7:11] [k] ch. 14:10; 21:8; See 2 Thess. 1:8
21[l] ver. 15 [m] ver. 17
Chapter 20
1[n] See ch. 1:18 [o] See ch. 9:1
2[p] See ch. 12:9 [q] [2 Pet. 2:4; Jude 6]
3[o] [See ver. 1 above] [r] Dan. 6:17; [Matt. 27:66] [s] ver. 8, 10
4[t] Dan. 7:9; Matt. 19:28 [u] ch. 3:21; Dan. 7:22 [v] ch. 6:9 [w] ch. 13:12, 14-16 [x] [John 14:19; 2 Tim. 2:11] [y] ver. 6; ch. 5:10; 22:5; Dan. 7:18; Matt. 20:21, 27; 2 Tim. 2:12; [Ps. 45:16]
6[z] ch. 14:13 [a] ver. 14; ch. 2:11; 21:8 [b] See ch. 1:6 [c] ver. 4 **7**[d] ver. 2 **8**[e] ver. 3, 10 [f] Ezek. 38:2; 39:1 [g] See ch. 16:14 **9**[h] [Isa. 8:8; Ezek. 38:9, 16; Hab. 1:6] [i] Heb. 13:11, 13

[j]the beloved city, but [k]fire came down from
heaven[l] and consumed them, 10 and the devil
[l]who had deceived them was [m]thrown into the
lake of fire and sulfur where [n]the beast and the
false prophet were, and they will be tormented
day and night forever and ever.

Judgment Before the Great White Throne

11 Then I saw a great white throne and him
who was seated on it. From his presence
[o]earth and sky fled away, and [p]no place was
found for them. 12 And I saw the dead, great
and small, standing before the throne, and
[q]books were opened. Then another book was
opened, which is [r]the book of life. And [s]the
dead were judged by what was written in
the books, [t]according to what they had done.
13 And the sea gave up the dead who were in
it, [u]Death and Hades gave up the dead who
were in them, and they were judged, each one
of them, [t]according to what they had done.
14 Then [u]Death and Hades [v]were thrown into
the lake of fire. This is [w]the second death, the
lake of fire. 15 And if anyone's name was not
found written in the book of life, [x]he was
thrown into the lake of fire.

The New Heaven and the New Earth

21 Then I saw [y]a new heaven and a new
earth, for [z]the first heaven and the
first earth had passed away, and the sea was
no more. 2 And I saw [a]the holy city, [b]new
Jerusalem, [c]coming down out of heaven from
God, [d]prepared [e]as a bride adorned for her
husband. 3 And I heard a loud voice from the
throne saying, "Behold, [f]the dwelling place[2]
of God is with man. He will [g]dwell with them,
and they will be his people,[3] and God himself will be with them as their God.[4] 4 [h]He
will wipe away every tear from their eyes, and
[i]death shall be no more, [j]neither shall there be
mourning, nor crying, nor pain anymore, for
the former things have passed away."
5 And [k]he who was seated on the throne said,
"Behold, I [l]am making all things new." Also he
said, "Write this down, for [m]these words are
trustworthy and true." 6 And he said to me, [n]"It
is done! [o]I am the Alpha and the Omega, the

[1] Some manuscripts *from God, out of heaven,* or *out of heaven from God* [2] Or *tabernacle* [3] Some manuscripts *peoples* [4] Some manuscripts omit *as their God*

20:11–15 After the final rebellion (vv. 7–10), the dead are judged according to what they have done (v. 12). This judgment is in keeping with the moral order of God's universe, and is not in conflict with the gospel of grace. Indeed, the very same verse speaks of the book of life, which contains the names of those who are saved (v. 15; cf. 13:8; 17:8). God, then, who has written their names there, is ultimately responsible (rather than the believers' works) for their salvation. We are saved by grace through faith in "the word of God and the testimony of Jesus" (1:2, 9).

Those who are saved have "overcome" sin by faith in Christ (1 John 5:4–5). They have made white their heavenly robes by washing them in the blood of the Lamb (Rev. 7:14), so that the crowns of the best of these are cast at the feet of Jesus, who alone is to receive glory (4:10–11). At the same time, those who have been truly saved have clearly demonstrated their salvation by grace through a faithful and transformed life, even through tribulation (cf. 7:14).

21:1–8 The final two chapters of Revelation depict the consummation of the purposes of God in the gospel. Picking up the whole-Bible motif of marriage, the people of God (represented in the new Jerusalem; v. 2) are wedded to the Lamb (symbolizing our eternal reconciliation, union, and presence with Christ; vv. 2–3).

We also see here the fulfillment of God's creation agenda (vv. 1–4). The absence of sea (v. 1) reflects the absence of earthly disorder as was first accomplished by the Holy Spirit. It reminds us not only of the physical elements over which Christ had power but also of the peace he brought (Mark 4:39). The defeat of death is the good news realized in its fullness (Rev. 21:4), and those who conquer with Jesus are rewarded as Jesus himself has been rewarded in verse 7. Christ is now the eternal dwelling place of saved humanity, as the Old Testament tabernacle/temple promises reach their fulfillment (v. 3; cf. Ex. 29:44–46; Lev. 26:11–12; 2 Chron. 6:18).

In these final two chapters of the Bible, then, we see the final restoration and advancement of the creation introduced in the first two chapters of the Bible—only this time without any possibility of sin or its effects entering in, for Satan has been destroyed once and for all (Rev. 20:7–10).

9 [j][Ps. 132:13] [k]See ch. 13:13
10 [l]ver. 3, 8 [m]See ch. 19:20 [n]See ch. 16:13
11 [o]See Ps. 102:26 [p]ch. 12:8; Dan. 2:35
12 [q]Dan. 7:10 [r]See ch. 3:5 [s]Rom. 14:10; 2 Cor. 5:10; See ch. 11:18 [t]See Matt. 16:27
13 [u]ch. 6:8 [t][See ver. 12 above]
14 [u][See ver. 13 above] [v][ch. 21:4; Luke 20:36; 1 Cor. 15:26] [w]ver. 6
15 [x]Matt. 13:42, 50

Chapter 21

1 [y]Isa. 65:17; 66:22; 2 Pet. 3:13 [z]ch. 20:11
2 [a]ch. 11:2; 22:19; Isa. 52:1 [b]See ch. 3:12 [c][Heb. 11:10] [d]ch. 19:7; [John 14:3] [e]Isa. 61:10
3 [f]See Lev. 26:11, 12 [g][ch. 7:15]
4 [h]See ch. 7:17 [i][ch. 20:14; 1 Cor. 15:26] [j]Isa. 35:10; 51:11; 65:19
5 [k]ch. 4:2, 9; 5:1; 20:11 [l]See 2 Cor. 5:17 [m]ch. 22:6; [ch. 3:14; 19:11; 1 Tim. 1:15]
6 [n]See ch. 10:6 [o]ch. 1:8; 22:13

beginning and the end. [p]To the thirsty I will
give from the spring of the water of life without payment. 7 [q]The one who conquers will
have this heritage, and [r]I will be his God and
[s]he will be my son. 8 [t]But as for the cowardly,
the faithless, the detestable, as for murderers, the sexually immoral, sorcerers, idolaters,
and all liars, [u]their portion will be in [v]the lake
that burns with fire and sulfur, which is [w]the
second death."

The New Jerusalem

9 Then came [x]one of the seven angels who had
the seven bowls full of [y]the seven last plagues
and spoke to me, saying, "Come, I will show
you [z]the Bride, the wife of the Lamb." 10 And
[a]he carried me away in the Spirit to [b]a great,
high mountain, and showed me the holy city
Jerusalem coming down out of heaven from
God, 11 [c]having the glory of God, [d]its radiance
[e]like a most rare jewel, like a jasper, clear as
crystal. 12 It had a great, high wall, [f]with twelve
gates, and at the gates twelve angels, and on
the gates the names of the twelve tribes of the
sons of Israel were inscribed— 13 on the east
three gates, on the north three gates, on the
south three gates, and on the west three gates.
14 And the wall of the city had twelve [g]founda-
tions, and [h]on them were the twelve names of
the twelve apostles of the Lamb.
15 And the one who spoke with me [i]had a
measuring rod of gold to measure the city
and its gates and walls. 16 The city lies four-
square, its length the same as its width. And
he measured the city with his rod, 12,000
stadia.[1] Its length and width and height are
equal. 17 He also measured its wall, 144 cubits[2]
by [j]human measurement, which is also [k]an
angel's measurement. 18 The wall was built of
[l]jasper, while the city was pure gold, like [l]clear
glass. 19 [m]The foundations of the wall of the city
were adorned with every kind of jewel. The
first was jasper, the second sapphire, the third
agate, the fourth emerald, 20 the fifth onyx,
the sixth carnelian, the seventh chrysolite,
the eighth beryl, the ninth topaz, the tenth
chrysoprase, the eleventh jacinth, the twelfth
amethyst. 21 And the twelve gates were twelve
pearls, each of the gates made of a single pearl,
and [n]the street of the city was pure gold, like
transparent glass.
22 And [o]I saw no temple in the city, for its
temple is the Lord God the Almighty and the
Lamb. 23 And the city [p]has no need of sun or
moon to shine on it, for [q]the glory of God gives
it light, and its lamp is the Lamb. 24 By its light
[r]will the nations walk, and the kings of the
earth [s]will bring their glory into it, 25 and [t]its
gates will never be shut by day—and [u]there
will be no night there. 26 They will bring into
it the glory and the honor of the nations. 27 But
[v]nothing unclean will ever enter it, nor anyone
who does what is detestable or false, but only
those who are written in the Lamb's [w]book
of life.

The River of Life

22 Then the angel[3] showed me [x]the river
of [y]the water of life, bright as crystal,
flowing from the throne of God and of the
Lamb 2 through the middle of [z]the street of
the city; [a]also, on either side of the river, [b]the
tree of life[4] with its twelve kinds of fruit,
yielding its fruit each month. The leaves of
the tree were [c]for the healing of the nations.
3 [d]No longer will there be anything accursed,

[1] About 1,380 miles; a *stadion* was about 607 feet or 185 meters [2] A *cubit* was about 18 inches or 45 centimeters [3] Greek *he* [4] Or *the Lamb. In the midst of the street of the city, and on either side of the river, was the tree of life*

6 [p] ch. 22:17; See John 4:10; 7:37
7 [q] ch. 2:7 [r] ver. 3 [s] See 2 Cor. 6:18
8 [t] ch. 22:15; 1 Cor. 6:9, 10; Gal. 5:19-21; Eph. 5:5; 1 Tim. 1:9; Heb. 12:14 [u] Luke 12:46 [v] ch. 19:20 [w] ch. 2:11; 20:6, 14
9 [x] ch. 17:1 [y] ch. 15:1 [z] ver. 2
10 [a] ch. 17:3; [Ezek. 43:5] [b] Ps. 87:1; Ezek. 40:2
11 [c] ver. 23; [ch. 22:5; Ps. 84:11; Ezek. 43:2, 4] [d] [Matt. 5:14; Phil. 2:15] [e] ch. 4:3, 6
12 [f] Ezek. 48:31-34
14 [g] Heb. 11:10; [1 Cor. 3:11] [h] Matt. 16:18; Eph. 2:20
15 [i] See ch. 11:1

21:22–22:5 There is no temple in the new Jerusalem because there is no more need for a building in which humans can meet with God. We will meet with God himself directly in the person of the Lamb. When Adam and Eve fell into sin, the corruption of their hearts and our world created separation from our holy God. Throughout history, the tabernacle and then the temple provided microcosmic restorations of the fellowship enjoyed in Eden. In the new earth, we have unhindered access to the fellowship, goodness, and glory of our God (presented here in terms of a new and improved Paradise; 22:1–5), for all that is unclean is now outside the new Jerusalem (21:27; cf. 22:3, 15).

All this is because of the gospel. Jesus was the one clean person to ever walk the face of the earth, but he went to a cross. There he became "unclean" so that we unclean sinners can be fully and finally cleansed, all by grace (2 Cor. 5:21).

17 [j] Deut. 3:11; [ch. 13:18] [k] ver. 9 **18** [l] ver. 11 **19** [m] [Isa. 54:11, 12] **21** [n] ch. 22:2 **22** [o] [John 4:23] **23** [p] ch. 22:5; Isa. 60:19, 20; [ver. 25] [q] ver. 11 **24** [r] Isa. 60:3; [ch. 22:2] [s] ver. 26; [Isa. 60:5, 16] **25** [t] Isa. 60:11 [u] See ver. 23 **27** [v] [ch. 22:14, 15; Isa. 35:8; 52:1; Ezek. 44:9; Joel 3:17; Zech. 14:21] [w] See ch. 3:5 **Chapter 22** **1** [x] Ezek. 47:1; Zech. 14:8; [Ps. 46:4] [y] See ch. 21:6 **2** [z] ch. 21:21 [a] Ezek. 47:12 [b] ver. 14, 19; ch. 2:7; Gen. 2:9 [c] [ch. 21:24] **3** [d] Zech. 14:11; [Gen. 3:17]

but [e]the throne of God and of the Lamb will
be in it, and [f]his servants[1] will worship him.
4 [g]They will see his face, and [h]his name will
be on their foreheads. 5 And [i]night will be no
more. They will need no light of lamp [j]or sun,
for [k]the Lord God will be their light, and [l]they
will reign forever and ever.

Jesus Is Coming

6 And he said to me, [m]"These words are trustworthy and true. And the Lord, the God of [n]the
spirits of the prophets, [o]has sent his angel to
show his servants what must soon take place."
7 "And behold, [p]I am coming soon. [q]Blessed is
the one who keeps the words of the prophecy
of this book."
8 I, [r]John, am the one who heard and saw
these things. And when I heard and saw them,
[s]I fell down to worship at the feet of the angel
who showed them to me, 9 [s]but he said to me,
"You must not do that! I am a fellow servant[2]
with you and your brothers the prophets, and
with those [m]who keep the words of this book.
Worship God."
10 And he said to me, [t]"Do not seal up the
words of the prophecy of this book, for the
time is near. 11 [u]Let the evildoer still do evil, and
the filthy still be filthy, and the righteous still
do right, and the holy still be holy."
12 "Behold, [v]I am coming soon, [w]bringing my
recompense with me, [x]to repay each one for
what he has done. 13 [y]I am the Alpha and the
Omega, [z]the first and the last, [a]the beginning
and the end."
14 Blessed are those who [b]wash their robes,[3]
so that they may have the right to [c]the tree of
life and that [d]they may enter the city by the
gates. 15 [e]Outside are [f]the dogs [g]and sorcerers
and the sexually immoral and murderers and
idolaters, and everyone who loves and practices falsehood.
16 [h]"I, Jesus, have sent my angel to testify to
you about these things [i]for the churches. I am
[j]the root and [k]the descendant of David, [l]the
bright morning star."
17 The Spirit and [m]the Bride say, "Come." And
let the one who hears say, "Come." And [n]let
the one who is thirsty come; let the one who
desires take the [o]water of life without price.
18 I warn everyone who hears the words of the
prophecy of this book: [p]if anyone adds to them,
God will add to him the plagues described in
this book, 19 and if anyone takes away from the
words of the book of this prophecy, God will
take away his share in [q]the tree of life and in
[r]the holy city, which are described in this book.
20 He who testifies to these things says,
"Surely [s]I am coming soon." Amen. [t]Come,
Lord Jesus!
21 The grace of the Lord Jesus be with all.[4]
Amen.

[1] Greek *bondservants*; also verse 6 [2] Greek *fellow bondservant* [3] Some manuscripts *do his commandments* [4] Some manuscripts *all the saints*

22:6–21 We are moved with hope as we reflect on this final prayer for Jesus to come soon to make all things new and to bring his people home to himself. This great gospel of redemption is the hope of the world, and yet in the Bible's final words we are reminded one final time that it is free for the taking: "let the one who desires take the water of life *without price*" (v. 17; cf. Isa. 55:1–2).

How can this be? The answer is not that God is lenient toward sin or that fallen human beings deserve such grace. The answer is that Jesus Christ, the Lamb, has paid the price on our behalf. Our robes are made white and we have access to the tree of life eternally (Rev. 22:14) because of the provision of our Savior. Though he was the promised root and descendant of David, the bright morning star of an eternal kingdom (v. 16), Jesus was punished so that we could be delivered. He was forsaken so that we could be befriended. He was cast out so that we could be brought in. All for free. All God asks is that we lay down our insistence on contributing to God's estimation of our merits and embrace Christ's record as our own. Nothing is to be added or subtracted from this message of salvation in Christ Jesus our Lord (vv. 18–19).

From Genesis to Revelation, the Bible is a message of God's saving grace in Jesus, whose final glory is yet to come. Thus we pray for him to come quickly because we love him, trust him, and long for the fulfillment of our hope and his glory. He is our great hope and eternal treasure.

3 [e]ch. 21:3, 23; Ezek. 48:35 [f]ch. 7:15
4 [g]Matt. 5:8; 1 Cor. 13:12; 1 John 3:2 [h]ch. 3:12; 7:3; 14:1
5 [i]ch. 21:25 [j]See ch. 21:23 [k]Ps. 36:9; See ch. 21:11 [l]Dan. 7:18, 27; Rom. 5:17; 2 Tim. 2:12; See ch. 20:4
6 [m]See ch. 21:5 [n]1 Cor. 14:32 [o]ch. 1:1
7 [p]ver. 12, 20; ch. 3:11 [q]ch. 1:3
8 [r]ch. 1:1, 4, 9 [s]ch. 19:10
9 [s][See ver. 8 above] [m][See ver. 6 above]
10 [t][ch. 10:4]
11 [u]Ezek. 3:27; [Dan. 12:10; 2 Tim. 3:13]
12 [v]ver. 7, 20 [w]Isa. 40:10; 62:11 [x]See Matt. 16:27
13 [y]See ch. 1:8 [z]See ch. 1:17 [a]ch. 21:6
14 [b]See ch. 7:14 [c]ver. 2, 19 [d]Ps. 118:20; See ch. 21:27
15 [e][Gal. 5:19-21]; See Matt. 8:12 [f]See Phil. 3:2 [g]See ch. 21:8
16 [h]ch. 1:1 [i]ch. 1:4 [j]See ch. 5:5 [k]See Matt. 1:1 [l][ch. 2:28; Num. 24:17; Isa. 60:3; Matt. 2:2]

17 [m]ch. 21:2, 9 [n]ch. 21:6; Isa. 55:1; John 7:37 [o]See ch. 21:6 **18** [p]Deut. 4:2; 12:32; [Prov. 30:6] **19** [q]ver. 2, 14 [r]See ch. 21:2 **20** [s]ver. 7, 12 [t][2 Tim. 4:8]

Topical Index

The following index lists subjects that are touched upon in the *Gospel Transformation Bible* notes. The index can be used for a variety of purposes, but the overarching goal is to help readers of the Bible see the way themes are picked up and developed throughout the Bible. This index thus serves to underscore the unity of God's work in history on behalf of his people, culminating in Christ (Luke 24:27, 44).

Table of

Weights and Measures

and Monetary Units

The following table is based on the best generally accepted information available for biblical weights, measures, and monetary units. All equivalents are approximate. Weights and measures also varied somewhat in different times and places in the ancient world. Most weights, measures, and monetary units are also explained in footnotes on the pages where they occur in the ESV text.

Biblical Unit	Approximate American and Metric Equivalents	Biblical Equivalent
bath	A *bath* was about 6 gallons or 22 liters	1 ephah
beka	A *beka* was about 1/5 ounce or 5.5 grams	10 gerahs
cor	A *cor* was about 6 bushels or 220 liters	10 ephahs
cubit	A *cubit* was about 18 inches or 45 centimeters	6 handbreadths
daric	A *daric* was a coin of about 1/4 ounce or 8.5 grams	
denarius	A *denarius* was a day's wage for a laborer	
ephah	An *ephah* was about 3/5 bushel or 22 liters	10 omers
gerah	A *gerah* was about 1/50 ounce or 0.6 gram	1/10 beka
handbreadth	A *handbreadth* was about 3 inches or 7.5 centimeters	1/6 cubit
hin	A *hin* was about 4 quarts or 3.5 liters	1/6 bath
homer	A *homer* was about 6 bushels or 220 liters	10 ephahs
kab	A *kab* was about 1 quart or 1 liter	1/22 ephah
lethech	A *lethech* was about 3 bushels or 110 liters	5 ephahs
log	A *log* was about 1/3 quart or 0.3 liter	1/72 bath
mina	A *mina* was about 1 1/4 pounds or 0.6 kilogram	50 shekels
omer	An *omer* was about 2 quarts or 2 liters	1/10 ephah
pim	A *pim* was about 1/3 ounce or 7.5 grams	2/3 shekel
seah	A *seah* was about 7 quarts or 7.3 liters	1/3 ephah
shekel	A *shekel* was about 2/5 ounce or 11 grams	2 bekas
span	A *span* was about 9 inches or 22 centimeters	3 handbreadths
stadion	A *stadion* was about 607 feet or 185 meters	
talent	A *talent* was about 75 pounds or 34 kilograms	60 minas

Weights and Measures

Concordance

As an essentially literal translation, the ESV Bible is ideally suited for use with a concordance, as the ESV seeks to use the same English word, as far as possible and where appropriate to the meaning in each context, to translate important recurring words in the original languages. However, with a total of more than 757,000 words appearing in the ESV Bible, a shorter concordance such as this must be selective in the words it includes.

In choosing which words to list, the guiding principles were importance, familiarity, and breadth of coverage. Since the ESV is within the stream of English Bible translations that began with the King James Version of 1611, there was a special effort to include references to as many familiar Bible passages as possible. As to breadth of coverage, the goal has been to list key references for many different words rather than more lengthy listings for fewer words.

Passages appearing in more than one of the Synoptic Gospels usually have only one reference, most often to the book of Matthew.

Readers will find the functionality of this concordance greatly increased if, after locating a Bible passage, the cross-reference system is then utilized for further research.

Those desiring a more complete concordance for the ESV Bible should consult the *ESV Comprehensive Concordance of the Bible*, which has more than 300,000 verse listings for nearly 14,000 different words. Readers with internet access will find optimal word-search capability with the search engine at the ESV web site, www.esvbible.org.

OLD TESTAMENT ABBREVIATIONS

Genesis	Gn
Exodus	Ex
Leviticus	Lv
Numbers	Nm
Deuteronomy	Dt
Joshua	Jos
Judges	Jgs
Ruth	Ru
1 Samuel	1 Sm
2 Samuel	2 Sm
1 Kings	1 Kgs
2 Kings	2 Kgs
1 Chronicles	1 Chr
2 Chronicles	2 Chr
Ezra	Ezr
Nehemiah	Neh
Esther	Est
Job	Jb
Psalms	Ps
Proverbs	Prv
Ecclesiastes	Eccl
Song of Solomon	Sg
Isaiah	Is
Jeremiah	Jer
Lamentations	Lam
Ezekiel	Ezk
Daniel	Dn
Hosea	Hos
Joel	Jl
Amos	Am
Obadiah	Ob
Jonah	Jon
Micah	Mi
Nahum	Na
Habakkuk	Hab
Zephaniah	Zep
Haggai	Hg
Zechariah	Zec
Malachi	Mal

NEW TESTAMENT ABBREVIATIONS

Matthew	Mt
Mark	Mk
Luke	Lk
John	Jn
Acts	Acts
Romans	Rom
1 Corinthians	1 Cor
2 Corinthians	2 Cor
Galatians	Gal
Ephesians	Eph
Philippians	Phil
Colossians	Col
1 Thessalonians	1 Thes
2 Thessalonians	2 Thes
1 Timothy	1 Tm
2 Timothy	2 Tm
Titus	Ti
Philemon	Phlm
Hebrews	Heb
James	Jas
1 Peter	1 Pt
2 Peter	2 Pt
1 John	1 Jn
2 John	2 Jn
3 John	3 Jn
Jude	Jude
Revelation	Rv

AARON
Moses and he said, "Is there not **A**, ... Ex 4:14
So **A** said to them, "Take off the rings . . . . Ex 32:2
And the staff of **A** was among their . . . . . Nm 17:6
congregation saw that **A** had perished, Nm 20:29
saying to **A**, 'Make for us gods who . . . . Acts 7:40
called by God, just as **A** was. . . . . Heb 5:4

ABADDON
before God, and **A** has no covering. . . . . . . Jb 26:6
in the grave, or your faithfulness in **A**? . . Ps 88:11
Sheol and **A** lie open before the . . . . Prv 15:11
His name in Hebrew is **A**, and in Greek . . . Rv 9:11

ABANDON
For you will not **a** my soul to Sheol, ... Ps 16:10
The LORD will not **a** him to . . . . Ps 37:33
he will not **a** his heritage; . . . . Ps 94:14
For you will not **a** my soul to Hades, . . . Acts 2:27

ABANDONED
'It is because they **a** the covenant of the. . Dt 29:25
'Because they **a** the LORD their . . . . 1 Kgs 9:9
Christ, that he was not **a** to Hades,. . . . . Acts 2:31
for having **a** their former faith. . . . . 1 Tm 5:12
that you have **a** the love you had at first. . . Rv 2:4

ABBA
"**A**, Father, all things are possible for . . . Mk 14:36
sons, by whom we cry, "**A**! Father!" . . . . Rom 8:15
into our hearts, crying, "**A**! Father!" . . . . . . Gal 4:6

ABEL
A was a keeper of sheep, and Cain. . . . . . . Gn 4:2
"Where is **A** your brother?" He said, ... Gn 4:9
blood of righteous **A** to the blood of . . . . Mt 23:35
By faith **A** offered to God a more . . . . Heb 11:4
a better word than the blood of **A**.. . . . . Heb 12:24

ABHOR
they **a** him who speaks the truth. . . . . Am 5:10
A what is evil; hold fast to what is . . . . . Rom 12:9

ABHORS
statutes, and if your soul **a** my rules, ... Lv 26:15
LORD **a** the bloodthirsty and. . . . . Ps 5:6

ABIATHAR
A, escaped and fled after David. . . . . . 1 Sm 22:20
son of Zeruiah and with **A** the priest. . . . . 1 Kgs 1:7

ABIDE
His soul shall **a** in well-being, ... Ps 25:13
the Most High will **a** in the shadow. . . . . Ps 91:1
righteousness **a** in the fruitful field. . . . . . . Is 32:16
"If you **a** in my word, you are truly my . . . Jn 8:31
A in me, and I in you. As the branch . . . . . Jn 15:4
so have I loved you. **A** in my love.. . . . . Jn 15:9
a in him, so that when he appears we . . . 1 Jn 2:28
By this we know that we **a** in him and. . . 1 Jn 4:13
ahead and does not **a** in the teaching . . . . . 2 Jn 9

ABIDES
which cannot be moved, but **a** forever. . . . Ps 125:1
fruit by itself, unless it **a** in the vine, ... Jn 15:4
whoever says he **a** in him ought to walk . 1 Jn 2:6
No one who **a** in him keeps on sinning; . . 1 Jn 3:6
whoever **a** in love **a** in God, ... 1 Jn 4:16

ABIDING
are like a shadow, and there is no **a**. . . 1 Chr 29:15
had a better possession and an **a** one. Heb 10:34

ABIGAIL
When **A** saw David, she hurried and . . 1 Sm 25:23
Then David sent and spoke to **A**, ... 1 Sm 25:39
second, Daniel, by **A** the Carmelite, ... 1 Chr 3:1

ABIJAH
At that time **A** the son of Jeroboam . . . 1 Kgs 14:1
and **A** his son reigned in his place. . . . . 2 Chr 12:16

ABILITY
Spirit of God, with **a** and intelligence, ... Ex 31:3
According to their **a** they gave to the . . . Ezr 2:69
another one, to each according to his **a**. . Mt 25:15
is right, but not the **a** to carry it out. . . . Rom 7:18

ABIMELECH
prayed to God, and God healed **A**, ... Gn 20:17
At that time **A** and Phicol the . . . . Gn 21:22
A said, "What is this you have done to . Gn 26:10
Now **A** the son of Jerubbaal went to . . . . . Jgs 9:1

ABISHAI
and to Joab's brother **A** the son of. . . . 1 Sm 26:6
So Joab and **A** his brother killed Abner, . 2 Sm 3:30
And David said to **A**, "Now Sheba the . . 2 Sm 20:6
Zeruiah: **A**, Joab, and Asahel, three. . . . . 1 Chr 2:16

ABLE
Every man shall give as he is **a**, ... Dt 16:17
But who is **a** to build him a house, ... 2 Chr 2:6
silver and gold are not **a** to deliver. . . . . . Ezk 7:19
our God whom we serve is **a** . . . . Dn 3:17
"Do you believe that I am **a** to do this?" . Mt 9:28
Are you **a** to drink the cup that I am to. Mt 20:22
will be **a** to separate us from the love . . Rom 8:39
Now to him who is **a** to strengthen you . Rom 16:25
Now to him who is **a** to do far more . . . Eph 3:20
kind to everyone, **a** to teach, patiently. 2 Tm 2:24
him who was **a** to save him from death, . Heb 5:7
Now to him who is **a** to keep you from . . Jude 24
an open door, which no one is **a** to shut. . . Rv 3:8
under the earth was **a** to open the scroll . . Rv 5:3

ABNER
of his army was **A** the son of Ner, ... 1 Sm 14:50
sat opposite, and **A** sat by Saul's side, . . 1 Sm 20:25
A was making himself strong in the . . . . 2 Sm 3:6
And the king lamented for **A**, saying,. . 2 Sm 3:33

ABOLISH
I have not come to **a** them but to fulfill. . . Mt 5:17

ABOLISHED
Jesus, who **a** death and brought life . . . 2 Tm 1:10

ABOMINABLE
to practice any of these **a** customs that . Lv 18:30
learn to follow the **a** practices of those . . . Dt 18:9
and they made their **a** images and their . Ezk 7:20

ABOMINATION
devious person is an **a** to the LORD, ... Prv 3:32
Lying lips are an **a** to the LORD, ... Prv 12:22
the scoffer is an **a** to mankind. . . . . Prv 24:9
shall set up the **a** that makes desolate. . . . Dn 11:31
"So when you see the **a** of desolation . . . Mt 24:15
what is exalted among men is an **a** in . . . Lk 16:15

ABOMINATIONS
were before you, did all of these **a**, ... Lv 18:27
because of these **a** the LORD your. . . . . Dt 18:12
for there are seven **a** in his heart; . . . . . . Prv 26:25
on the wing of **a** shall come one who . . . Dn 9:27
golden cup full of **a** and the impurities . . . Rv 17:4

ABOUND
the LORD will make you **a** . . . . Dt 28:11
continue in sin that grace may **a**? . . . . Rom 6:1
of the Holy Spirit you may **a** in hope.. . . Rom 15:13
you may **a** in every good work. . . . . 2 Cor 9:8
make you increase and **a** in love for . . . 1 Thes 3:12

ABOUNDED
that one man Jesus Christ **a** for many. . Rom 5:15
sin increased, grace **a** all the more, ... Rom 5:20

ABOUNDING
LORD is slow to anger and **a**. . . . . Nm 14:18
slow to anger and **a** in steadfast love. . . . Ps 103:8
and **a** in steadfast love; and he . . . . Jl 2:13
slow to anger and **a** in steadfast love, ... Jon 4:2

ABOVE
LORD is God in heaven **a** . . . . Dt 4:39
Be exalted, O God, **a** the heavens! . . . . Ps 57:5
who sits **a** the circle of the earth, ... Is 40:22
He who comes from **a** is **a** all. . . . . Jn 3:31
"You are from below; I am from **a**. . . . . Jn 8:23
unless it had been given you from **a**. . . . . . Jn 19:11
far **a** all rule and authority and . . . . Eph 1:21
the name that is **a** every name, ... Phil 2:9
and every perfect gift is from **a**, ... Jas 1:17
A all, keep loving one another. . . . . 1 Pt 4:8

ABRAHAM
Abram, but your name shall be **A**, ... Gn 17:5
Then **A** took Ishmael his son and all. . . . . Gn 17:23
these things God tested **A** and said to . . . Gn 22:1
A breathed his last and died . . . . Gn 25:8
"I am the God of **A** your father.. . . . . Gn 26:24
Christ, the son of David, the son of **A**. . . . . . . Mt 1:1
yourselves, 'We have **A** as our father,' . . . . . Mt 3:9
to **A** and to his offspring forever." . . . . Lk 1:55
called out, 'Father **A**, have mercy on . . . . Lk 16:24
"**A** believed God, and it was counted. . . . Rom 4:3
just as **A** "believed God, and it was . . . . . . Gal 3:6
By faith **A** obeyed when he was called . . Heb 11:8

ABRAHAM'S
carried by the angels to **A** side.. . . . . Lk 16:22
"If you were **A** children, you. . . . . Jn 8:39
are Christ's, then you are **A** offspring, . . . Gal 3:29

ABRAM
LORD said to **A**, "Go from your. . . . . Gn 12:1
A heard that his kinsman had been taken. . Gn 14:14
vision: "Fear not, **A**, I am your shield;. . . . . Gn 15:1
LORD made a covenant with **A**, ... Gn 15:18

ABSALOM
Now **A**, David's son, had a beautiful. . . . 2 Sm 13:1
So **A** stole the hearts of the men of . . . 2 Sm 15:6
surrounded **A** and struck him and . . . . 2 Sm 18:15
"O my son **A**, O **A**, my son, ... 2 Sm 19:4

ABSTAIN
A from every form of evil. . . . . 1 Thes 5:22
to **a** from the passions of the flesh, ... 1 Pt 2:11

ABSTAINS
thanks to God, while the one who **a**, . . . Rom 14:6

ABUNDANCE
of heart, because of the **a** of all things, . . Dt 28:47
But I, through the **a** of your steadfast . . . . . Ps 5:7
according to the **a** of his steadfast love; Lam 3:32
will be given, and he will have an **a**, ... Mt 13:12
contributed out of their **a**, but she . . . . . Mk 12:44
for out of the **a** of the heart. . . . . Lk 6:45
so that their **a** may supply your need, . 2 Cor 8:14

ABUNDANT
Oh, how **a** is your goodness, which you . Ps 31:19
to let you know the **a** love that I have . . 2 Cor 2:4

ABUNDANTLY
may have life and have it **a**. . . . . Jn 10:10
For as we share **a** in Christ's sufferings, . 2 Cor 1:5
because your faith is growing **a**, ... 2 Thes 1:3

ABUSE
pray for those who **a** you. . . . . Lk 6:28

ABYSS
command them to depart into the **a**. . . . . . Lk 8:31
descend into the **a**?'" (that is, to bring . Rom 10:7

ACCENT
one of them, for your **a** betrays you." . . . Mt 26:73

ACCEPT
substance, and **a** the work of his hands; . . Dt 33:11
A my freewill offerings of praise, O . . . . Ps 119:108
Hear, my son, and **a** my words, ... Prv 4:10
to **a** his lot and rejoice in his toil— . . . . . . Eccl 5:19
hear the word and **a** it and bear fruit, . . . Mk 4:20
does not **a** the things of the Spirit . . . . . 1 Cor 2:14

ACCEPTABLE
meditation of my heart be **a** ... Ps 19:14
lips of the righteous know what is **a**, ... Prv 10:32
fast, and a day **a** to the LORD? ... Is 58:5
Your burnt offerings are not **a**, nor ... Jer 6:20
holy and **a** to God, which is ... Rom 12:1
it is **a** according to what a person has, 2 Cor 8:12
thus let us offer to God **a** worship, ... Heb 12:28

ACCEPTANCE
but the upright enjoy **a**. ... Prv 14:9
what will their **a** mean but life from ... Rom 11:15
is trustworthy and deserving of full **a**, ... 1 Tm 1:15

ACCEPTED
If you do well, will you not be **a**? ... Gn 4:7
the LORD **a** Job's prayer. ... Jb 42:9
and their sacrifices will be **a**. ... Is 56:7
a different gospel from the one you **a**, . 2 Cor 11:4
you **a** it not as the word of men but .. 1 Thes 2:13
and you joyfully **a** the plundering of .. Heb 10:34

ACCESS
we both have **a** in one Spirit ... Eph 2:18

ACCOMPLISH
but it shall **a** that which I purpose, ... Is 55:11
which he was about to **a** at Jerusalem. ... Lk 9:31
works that the Father has given me to **a**, . Jn 5:36

ACCOMPLISHED
all these things are about to be **a**?" ... Mk 13:4
Son of Man by the prophets will be **a**. ... Lk 18:31
having **a** the work that you gave me to ... Jn 17:4
except what Christ has **a** through me . Rom 15:18

ACCORD
I have not come of my own **a**. ... Jn 7:28
I lay it down of my own **a**. ... Jn 10:18
All these with one **a** were devoting ... Acts 1:14
being in full **a** and of one mind. ... Phil 2:2

ACCORDANCE
in **a** with all the curses of the covenant. . Dt 29:21
died for our sins in **a** with. ... 1 Cor 15:3

ACCORDS
teach what **a** with sound doctrine. ... Ti 2:1

ACCOUNT
"Tell us on whose **a** this evil has come. ... Jon 1:8
of evil against you falsely on my **a**. ... Mt 5:11
people will give **a** for every careless. ... Mt 12:36
to write an orderly **a** for you, ... Lk 1:3
Turn in the **a** of your management, ... Lk 16:2
But I do not **a** my life of any value ... Acts 20:24
each of us will give an **a** ... Rom 14:12
you anything, charge that to my **a**. ... Phlm 18
eyes of him to whom we must give **a**. ... Heb 4:13
but they will give **a** to him ... 1 Pt 4:5

ACCOUNTABLE
whole world may be held **a** to God. ... Rom 3:19
in one point has become **a** for all of it. .. Jas 2:10

ACCURSED
wish that I myself were **a** ... Rom 9:3
no love for the Lord, let him be **a**. ... 1 Cor 16:22
No longer will there be anything **a**, ... Rv 22:3

ACCUSATION
"What **a** do you bring against ... Jn 18:29

ACCUSE
me evil for good **a** me because I follow. . Ps 38:20
In return for my love they **a** me, ... Ps 109:4
Satan standing at his right hand to **a**. ... Zec 3:1
so that they might **a** him. ... Mt 12:10
their conflicting thoughts **a** ... Rom 2:15

ACCUSED
witness and has **a** his brother falsely, ... Dt 19:18
forward and maliciously **a** the Jews. ... Dn 3:8
who had maliciously **a** Daniel were. ... Dn 6:24
But when he was **a** by the chief priests. . Mt 27:12
And for this hope I am **a** by Jews, O ... Acts 26:7

ACCUSER
I must appeal for mercy to my **a**. ... Jb 9:15
let an **a** stand at his right hand. ... Ps 109:6
lest your **a** hand you over to the judge, ... Mt 5:25
go with your **a** before the magistrate, ... Lk 12:58
for the **a** of our brothers has been ... Rv 12:10

ACKNOWLEDGE
In all your ways **a** him, and he ... Prv 3:6
and you who are near, **a** my might. ... Is 33:13
We **a** our wickedness, O LORD, ... Jer 14:20
until they **a** their guilt and seek my face, . Hos 5:15
I also will **a** before my Father ... Mt 10:32
not see fit to **a** God, God gave them up. . Rom 1:28
the fruit of lips that **a** his name. ... Heb 13:15
himself first, does not **a** our authority. ... 3 Jn 9

ACKNOWLEDGED
I **a** my sin to you, and I did not cover ... Ps 32:5

ACQUAINTED
lying down and are **a** with all my ways. . Ps 139:3
a man of sorrows, and **a** with grief; ... Is 53:3

ACT
hear in heaven and **a** and judge your. . 1 Kgs 8:32
trust in him, and he will **a**. ... Ps 37:5
forgive. O Lord, pay attention and **a**. ... Dn 9:19
complete among you this **a** of grace. ... 2 Cor 8:6

ACTED
We have **a** very corruptly ... Neh 1:7
done wrong and **a** wickedly and ... Dn 9:5

ADAM
But for **A** there was not found a helper. . Gn 2:20
And to **A** he said, "Because you have ... Gn 3:17
Thus all the days that **A** lived ... Gn 5:5
But like **A** they transgressed the ... Hos 6:7
Yet death reigned from **A**. ... Rom 5:14
For as in **A** all die, so also. ... 1 Cor 15:22
"The first man **A** became a living ... 1 Cor 15:45
For **A** was formed first, then Eve; ... 1 Tm 2:13

ADD
You shall not **a** to the word that I ... Dt 4:2
a heavy yoke, I will **a** to your yoke. ... 1 Kgs 12:11
Do not **a** to his words, lest he ... Prv 30:6
I will **a** fifteen years to your life. ... Is 38:5
God will **a** to him the plagues ... Rv 22:18

ADMONISH
night or day to **a** every one with tears. Acts 20:31
but to **a** you as my beloved children. ... 1 Cor 4:14
a the idle, encourage the fainthearted, . 1 Thes 5:14

ADONIJAH
A the son of Haggith exalted himself, ... 1 Kgs 1:5
And **A** feared Solomon. So he arose ... 1 Kgs 1:50

ADOPTION
received the Spirit of **a** as sons, ... Rom 8:15
are Israelites, and to them belong the **a**, . Rom 9:4
law, so that we might receive **a** as sons. .. Gal 4:5
he predestined us for **a** as sons. ... Eph 1:5

ADORN
"**A** yourself with majesty and dignity; ... Jb 40:10
women should **a** themselves in ... 1 Tm 2:9
in everything they may **a** the doctrine. ... Ti 2:10
women who hoped in God used to **a**. ... 1 Pt 3:5

ADULTERERS
For the land is full of **a**; because of the. Jer 23:10
against the sorcerers, against the **a**, ... Mal 3:5
unjust, **a**, or even like this tax collector. ... Lk 18:11

ADULTERESS
both the adulterer and the **a** shall surely . . Lv 20:10
from the **a** with her smooth words, ... Prv 2:16
and embrace the bosom of an **a**? ... Prv 5:20
This is the way of an **a**: ... Prv 30:20

ADULTEROUS
A wife, who receives strangers instead . Ezk 16:32
my words in this **a** and sinful generation, . Mk 8:38
You **a** people! Do you not know that ... Jas 4:4

ADULTERY
"You shall not commit **a**. ... Ex 20:14
He who commits **a** lacks sense; ... Prv 6:32
it was said, 'You shall not commit **a**.' ... Mt 5:27
heart come evil thoughts, murder, **a**, ... Mt 15:19
marries another, commits **a**." ... Mt 19:9
been caught in the act of **a**. ... Jn 8:4
They have eyes full of **a**, insatiable for. . 2 Pt 2:14
and those who commit **a** with her I will . . Rv 2:22

ADVANTAGE
it is to your **a** that I go away, ... Jn 16:7
Then what **a** has the Jew? Or what is ... Rom 3:1
Christ will be of no **a** to you. ... Gal 5:2
boasters, showing favoritism to gain **a**. .. Jude 16

ADVERSARIES
of your majesty you overthrow your **a**; ... Ex 15:7
Give me not up to the will of my **a**; ... Ps 27:12
you will destroy all the **a** of my soul, ... Ps 143:12
LORD takes vengeance on his **a** ... Na 1:2
things, all his **a** were put to shame, ... Lk 13:17
which none of your **a** will be able. ... Lk 21:15
opened to me, and there are many **a**. .. 1 Cor 16:9
a fury of fire that will consume the **a**. . Heb 10:27

ADVERSARY
saying, 'Give me justice against my **a**.' ... Lk 18:3
and give the **a** no occasion for slander. . 1 Tm 5:14
Your **a** the devil prowls around like a ... 1 Pt 5:8

ADVERSITY
all times, and a brother is born for **a**. ... Prv 17:17
be joyful, and in the day of **a** consider: . Eccl 7:14
the Lord give you the bread of **a** ... Is 30:20

ADVICE
but a wise man listens to **a**. ... Prv 12:15
but with those who take **a** is wisdom. ... Prv 13:10
Listen to **a** and accept instruction, ... Prv 19:20
opposing God!" So they took his **a**, ... Acts 5:39

ADVOCATE
does sin, we have an **a** with the Father, ... 1 Jn 2:1

AFFECTION
Love one another with brotherly **a**. ... Rom 12:10
for you all with the **a** of Christ Jesus. ... Phil 1:8
and brotherly **a** with love. ... 2 Pt 1:7

AFFLICT
taskmasters over them to **a** them with ... Ex 1:11
he does not willingly **a** from his heart . . Lam 3:33
sincerely but thinking to **a** me in my ... Phil 1:17
repay with affliction those who **a** you, . 2 Thes 1:6

AFFLICTED
and they will be **a** for four hundred ... Gn 15:13
He delivers the **a** by their affliction. ... Jb 36:15
gracious to me, for I am lonely and **a**. ... Ps 25:16
glad for as many days as you have **a** us, . . Ps 90:15
Before I was **a** I went astray, but now I . Ps 119:67
him stricken, smitten by God, and **a**. ... Is 53:4
those **a** with various diseases and pains, . Mt 4:24
sick and those **a** with unclean spirits, ... Acts 5:16
If we are **a**, it is for your comfort ... 2 Cor 1:6
We are **a** in every way, but not ... 2 Cor 4:8
feet of the saints, has cared for the **a**, .. 1 Tm 5:10

AFFLICTION
"I have surely seen the **a** of my people ... Ex 3:7
Consider my **a** and my trouble, and ... Ps 25:18
love, because you have seen my **a**; ... Ps 31:7
This is my comfort in my **a**, that ... Ps 119:50
I have tried you in the furnace of **a**. ... Is 48:10
In all their **a** he was afflicted, and the ... Is 63:9
and healing every disease and every **a**. ... Mt 9:35
who comforts us in all our **a**, so that ... 2 Cor 1:4

light momentary **a** is preparing....... 2 Cor 4:17
In all our **a**, I am overflowing with joy... 2 Cor 7:4
all our distress and **a** we have been.... 1 Thes 3:7

AFFLICTIONS

Many are the **a** of the righteous, but .... Ps 34:19
that imprisonment and **a** await me.... Acts 20:23
by great endurance, in **a**, hardships,.... 2 Cor 6:4
what is lacking in Christ's **a** for the...... Col 1:24
that no one be moved by these **a**...... 1 Thes 3:3

AFRAID

and I was **a**, because I was naked, ... Gn 3:10
the people were **a** and trembled, ... Ex 20:18
LORD, and they shall be **a** of you. .... Dt 28:10
to them, "Do not be **a** or dismayed;.... Jos 10:25
of my life; of whom shall I be **a**?......... Ps 27:1
When I am **a**, I put my trust in you....... Ps 56:3
He is not **a** of bad news;................ Ps 112:7
She is not **a** of snow for her household, . Prv 31:21
Fear not, nor be **a**; have I not told .... Is 44:8
Do not be **a** of them, for I am with you.... Jer 1:8
And you, son of man, be not **a** of them, .. Ezk 2:6
"Why are you **a**, O you of little faith?"... Mt 8:26
"Take heart; it is I. Do not be **a**."........ Mt 14:27
Jesus said to them, "Do not be **a**;....... Mt 28:10
"Do not be **a**, Mary, for you have .... Lk 1:30
Jesus said to Simon, "Do not be **a**;....... Lk 5:10
be troubled, neither let them be **a**....... Jn 14:27
Paul one night in a vision, "Do not be **a**, .. Acts 18:9
But if you do wrong, be **a**, for he ...... Rom 13:4

AGABUS

a prophet named **A** came down .... Acts 21:10

AGE

Why do the wicked live, reach old **a**,..... Jb 21:7
They still bear fruit in old **a**; they are.... Ps 92:14
either in this **a** or in the **a** to .... Mt 12:32
The harvest is the end of the **a**, and..... Mt 13:39
your coming and of the end of the **a**?"... Mt 24:3
with you always, to the end of the **a**.".. Mt 28:20
and in the **a** to come eternal life....... Mk 10:30
"The sons of this **a** marry and are...... Lk 20:34
it is not a wisdom of this **a**........... 1 Cor 2:6
to deliver us from the present evil **a**, ... Gal 1:4
not only in this **a** but also in the one to.. Eph 1:21

AGES

renown, O LORD, throughout all **a**....... Ps 135:13
God decreed before the **a** for our glory. .1 Cor 2:7
the mystery hidden for **a** in God........ Eph 3:9
mystery hidden for **a** and generations... Col 1:26
us in Christ Jesus before the **a** began,... 2 Tm 1:9
never lies, promised before the **a** began.... Ti 1:2

AGONY

And being in an **a** he prayed more..... Lk 22:44

AGREE

if two of you **a** on earth about anything . Mt 18:19
Did you not **a** with me for a denarius?... Mt 20:13
him, but their testimony did not **a**...... Mk 14:56
a with one another, live in peace;..... 2 Cor 13:11
I entreat Syntyche to **a** in the Lord....... Phil 4:2
water and the blood; and these three **a**.. 1 Jn 5:8

AGREEMENT

What **a** has the temple of God with... 2 Cor 6:16

AGRIPPA

A the king and Bernice arrived at..... Acts 25:13
And **A** said to Paul, "In a short time... Acts 26:28

AHAB

A did more to provoke the LORD, ... 1 Kgs 16:33
So Elijah went to show himself to **A**.... 1 Kgs 18:2
rain. And **A** rode and went to Jezreel. 1 Kgs 18:45
after this **A** said to Naboth, "Give me .. 1 Kgs 21:2

AHASUERUS

A who reigned from India to Ethiopia..... Est 1:1
In the first year of Darius the son of **A**,.... Dn 9:1

AHAZ

A the son of Jotham, king of Judah, ... 2 Kgs 16:1
Again the LORD spoke to **A**,............... Is 7:10

AHAZIAH

A the son of Ahab began to reign over. .1 Kgs 22:51
Now **A** fell through the lattice in his.... 2 Kgs 1:2
A the son of Jehoram, king of Judah, . 2 Kgs 8:25
saying to **A**, "Treachery, O **A**!"........ 2 Kgs 9:23
searched for **A**, and he was captured.. 2 Chr 22:9

AHIMELECH

David came to Nob to **A** the priest...... 1 Sm 21:1
surely die, **A**, you and all your father's .. 1 Sm 22:16

AHITHOPHEL

for **A** the Gilonite, David's counselor, .. 2 Sm 15:12
Absalom said to **A**, "Give your counsel.. 2 Sm 16:20
When **A** saw that his counsel was not .. 2 Sm 17:23

AI

Joshua burned **A** and made it forever ... Jos 8:28

AIM

for we **a** at what is honorable not only .. 2 Cor 8:21
A for restoration, comfort one another, .. 2 Cor 13:11
The **a** of our charge is love that issues... 1 Tm 1:5
my teaching, my conduct, my **a** in life, . 2 Tm 3:10

AIR

and the birds of the **a** devoured it......... Lk 8:5
cloaks and flinging dust into the **a**,.... Acts 22:23
I do not box as one beating the **a**..... 1 Cor 9:26
to meet the Lord in the **a**, ... 1 Thes 4:17
angel poured out his bowl into the **a**, ... Rv 16:17

ALABASTER

him with an **a** flask of very expensive .... Mt 26:7

ALARMED

and the visions of my head **a** me......... Dn 4:5
rumors of wars. See that you are not **a**, . Mt 24:6
in a white robe, and they were **a**......... Mk 16:5
not to be quickly shaken in mind or **a**,. 2 Thes 2:2

ALERT

Therefore be **a**, remembering .... Acts 20:31
supplication. To that end keep **a**........ Eph 6:18

ALEXANDER

Some of the crowd prompted **A**,...... Acts 19:33

ALIENATED

a from the commonwealth of Israel..... Eph 2:12
a from the life of God because of....... Eph 4:18
who once were **a** and hostile in mind,.... Col 1:21

ALIVE

into the ark to keep them **a** with you..... Gn 6:19
LORD your God are all **a** today............ Dt 4:4
grass of the field, which today is **a** and .. Mt 6:30
heard that he was **a** and had been seen . Mk 16:11
He presented himself **a** to them after ... Acts 1:3
came, sin came **a** and I died............ Rom 7:9
so also in Christ shall all be made **a**. .. 1 Cor 15:22
made us **a** together with Christ— .... Eph 2:5
why, as if you were still **a** in the world, .. Col 2:20
I died, and behold I am **a** forevermore, ... Rv 1:18
You have the reputation of being **a**, but ... Rv 3:1
These two were thrown **a** into the lake .. Rv 19:20

ALMIGHTY

"I am God **A**; walk before me,........... Gn 17:1
God **A** bless you and make you fruitful .. Gn 28:3
"I am God **A**: be fruitful and............ Gn 35:11
to Isaac, and to Jacob, as God **A**,......... Ex 6:3
For the arrows of the **A** are in me;........ Jb 6:4
"Shall a faultfinder contend with the **A**? . Jb 40:2
High will abide in the shadow of the **A**..... Ps 91:1
many waters, like the sound of the **A**, ... Ezk 1:24
like the voice of God **A** when he........ Ezk 10:5
who was and who is to come, the **A**." ..... Rv 1:8
For the Lord our God the **A** reigns....... Rv 19:6
is the Lord God the **A** and the Lamb..... Rv 21:22

ALMS

give as **a** those things that are within,.... Lk 11:41
prayers and your **a** have ascended as .. Acts 10:4

ALONE

"It is not good that the man should be **a**; .. Gn 2:18
for you. You are not able to do it **a**...... Ex 18:18
you, O LORD, are God **a**."............. 2 Kgs 19:19
LORD, you **a**. You have made .... Neh 9:6
you **a**, O LORD, make me dwell............ Ps 4:8
For God **a** my soul waits in silence; ...... Ps 62:1
woe to him who is **a** when he falls and . Eccl 4:10
know that you **a** are the LORD."......... Is 37:20
good? No one is good except God **a**..... Mk 10:18
it happened that as he was praying **a**,.... Lk 9:18
I am not **a**, for the Father is with me..... Jn 16:32
justified by works and not by faith **a**..... Jas 2:24

ALPHA

"I am the **A** and the Omega,"............. Rv 1:8
I am the **A** and the Omega,............. Rv 21:6
I am the **A** and the Omega,............ Rv 22:13

ALPHAEUS

saw Levi the son of **A** sitting at the tax... Mk 2:14
James the son of **A** and Simon the...... Acts 1:13

ALTAR

Then Noah built an **a** to the LORD....... Gn 8:20
And Moses built an **a** and called........ Ex 17:15
"You shall make the **a** of acacia wood, ... Ex 27:1
for you on the **a** to make atonement for.. Lv 17:11
David built there an **a**.............. 2 Sm 24:25
And he repaired the **a** of the LORD ... 1 Kgs 18:30
and they built the **a** of the God.......... Ezr 3:2
Then I will go to the **a** of God, to God.... Ps 43:4
you say, 'If anyone swears by the **a**,..... Mt 23:18
perished between the **a** and the......... Lk 11:51
I found also an **a** with this inscription,. Acts 17:23
having the golden **a** of incense and the . Heb 9:4
I saw under the **a** the souls of those who. Rv 6:9
And I heard the **a** saying, "Yes, Lord ..... Rv 16:7

ALTARS

You shall tear down their **a** and break... Ex 34:13
prophets, they have demolished your **a**, .Rom 11:3

ALWAYS

delight; be intoxicated **a** in her love. .... Prv 5:19
I am with you **a**, to the end .... Mt 28:20
Christ **a** leads us in triumphal .... 2 Cor 2:14
So we are **a** of good courage.......... 2 Cor 5:6
giving thanks **a** and for everything..... Eph 5:20
Rejoice in the Lord **a**; again I will say, ... Phil 4:4
a being prepared to make a defense to.. 1 Pt 3:15

AMAZED

And all the people were **a**,............. Mt 12:23
they were all **a** and glorified God,........ Mk 2:12
And the disciples were **a** at his words.. Mk 10:24
heard him were **a** at his understanding... Lk 2:47
And her parents were **a**, but he charged. .Lk 8:56
And they were **a** and astonished,....... Acts 2:7

AMAZIAH

and **A** his son reigned in his place..... 2 Kgs 12:21
king of Israel captured **A** king of Judah, .. 2 Kgs 14:13
And **A** said to Amos, "O seer, go, flee ... Am 7:12

AMBASSADOR

for which I am an **a** in chains, that I.... Eph 6:20

AMBASSADORS

we are **a** for Christ, God .... 2 Cor 5:20

AMBITION

I make it my **a** to preach the gospel, .. Rom 15:20
jealousy and selfish **a** in your hearts,.... Jas 3:14

AMBUSH

son of Paul's sister heard of their **a**,... Acts 23:16
they were planning an **a** to kill him on.. Acts 25:3

ARMAGEDDON
at the place that in Hebrew is called **A**... Rv 16:16

ARMOR
Then Saul clothed David with his **a**.... 1 Sm 17:38
and put on the **a** of light............. Rom 13:12
Put on the whole **a** of God,............ Eph 6:11

ARMS
and underneath are the everlasting **a**.... Dt 33:27
snapped the ropes off his **a** like a thread. Jgs 16:12
he will gather the lambs in his **a**;........ Is 40:11
of fine gold, its chest and **a** of silver,.... Dn 2:32
midst of them, and taking him in his **a**,.. Mk 9:36
took them in his **a** and blessed them,... Mk 10:16
him up in his **a** and blessed God and..... Lk 2:28
over him, and taking him in his **a**,..... Acts 20:10

ARMY
was a great **a**, like an **a** of God........ 1 Chr 12:22
Though an **a** encamp against me, my.... Ps 27:3
The king is not saved by his great **a**;.... Ps 33:16
Hezekiah at Jerusalem, with a great **a**.... Is 36:2
on their feet, an exceedingly great **a**.... Ezk 37:10
Lord utters his voice before his **a**,........ Jl 2:11
sitting on the horse and against his **a**.... Rv 19:19

AROMA
Lord smelled the pleasing **a**,............ Gn 8:21
For we are the **a** of Christ to God..... 2 Cor 2:15

ARRAYED
it on his head and **a** him in a purple robe. Jn 19:2
the armies of heaven, **a** in fine linen,.... Rv 19:14

ARREST
together in order to **a** Jesus by stealth.. Mt 26:4
the Jews, he proceeded to **a** Peter also. Acts 12:3

ARRESTED
when he heard that John had been **a**,.... Mt 4:12
officers of the Jews **a** Jesus and bound... Jn 18:12
And they **a** them and put them in...... Acts 4:3
they **a** the apostles and put them in... Acts 5:18
came up and **a** him and ordered...... Acts 21:33

ARROGANCE
Pride and **a** and the way of evil......... Prv 8:13
who say in pride and in **a** of heart:........ Is 9:9
how proud he is!—of his **a**, his pride,...... Is 16:6
As it is, you boast in your **a**............. Jas 4:16

ARROGANT
Everyone who is **a** in heart is........... Prv 16:5
the speech of the **a** heart of the king..... Is 10:12
do not be **a** toward the branches....... Rom 11:18
love does not envy or boast; it is not **a**.. 1 Cor 13:4
reproach. He must not be **a** or............ Ti 1:7

ARROW
"The Lord's **a** of victory,............. 2 Kgs 13:17
The **a** cannot make him flee; for him.... Jb 41:28
night, nor the **a** that flies by day,........ Ps 91:5
he hid me; he made me a polished **a**;.... Is 49:2
Their tongue is a deadly **a**; it speaks..... Jer 9:8
bow and set me as a target for his **a**.... Lam 3:12

ARROWS
I will shoot three **a** to the side....... 1 Sm 20:20
"Take a bow and **a**." So he took a..... 2 Kgs 13:15
For the **a** of the Almighty are in me;...... Jb 6:4
For your **a** have sunk into me,........... Ps 38:2
who aim bitter words like **a**,............ Ps 64:3
against you the deadly **a** of famine,..... Ezk 5:16
from your bow, calling for many **a**....... Hab 3:9

ARTAXERXES
associates wrote to **A** king of Persia...... Ezr 4:7
Nisan, in the twentieth year of King **A**,... Neh 2:1
to the thirty-second year of **A** the king,. Neh 5:14

ARTEMIS
"Great is **A** of the Ephesians!"........ Acts 19:28

ASA
A did what was right in the eyes...... 1 Kgs 15:11
A cried to the Lord his God,......... 2 Chr 14:11

ASAHEL
And **A** pursued Abner, and as he...... 2 Sm 2:19
A the brother of Joab was one of the.. 2 Sm 23:24
A the brother of Joab was fourth,..... 1 Chr 27:7

ASCEND
'Who will **a** to heaven for us and bring.. Dt 30:12
Who shall **a** the hill of the Lord?......... Ps 24:3
If I **a** to heaven, you are there!.......... Ps 139:8
said in your heart, 'I will **a** to heaven;..... Is 14:13
For David did not **a** into the heavens,.. Acts 2:34
'Who will **a** into heaven?'" (that is,..... Rom 10:6

ASCENDED
You **a** on high, leading a host.......... Ps 68:18
Who has **a** to heaven and come down?.. Prv 30:4
No one has **a** into heaven except he..... Jn 3:13
for I have not yet **a** to the Father;....... Jn 20:17
"When he **a** on high he led a host of.... Eph 4:8

ASCENDING
the angels of God **a** and descending on... Jn 1:51
were to see the Son of Man **a** to where... Jn 6:62
I saw another angel **a** from the rising..... Rv 7:2

ASCETICISM
insisting on **a** and worship of angels,.... Col 2:18
self-made religion and **a** and severity... Col 2:23

ASCRIBE
Lord; **a** greatness to our God!........... Dt 32:3
A to the Lord the glory due............ Ps 29:2
A power to God, whose majesty is over Ps 68:34
A to the Lord the glory................ Ps 96:8

ASHAMED
were both naked and were not **a**........ Gn 2:25
All my enemies shall be **a** and........... Ps 6:10
radiant, and their faces shall never be **a**... Ps 34:5
that they may be **a** of their iniquities;.. Ezk 43:10
For whoever is **a** of me and of my...... Mk 8:38
For I am not **a** of the gospel, for it is.... Rom 1:16
things of which you are now **a**?....... Rom 6:21
to do with him, that he may be **a**..... 2 Thes 3:14
Therefore do not be **a** of the testimony.. 2 Tm 1:8
a worker who has no need to be **a**,.... 2 Tm 2:15
is why he is not **a** to call them brothers,. Heb 2:11
God is not **a** to be called their God,.... Heb 11:16
let him not be **a**, but let him glorify..... 1 Pt 4:16

ASHER
So she called his name **A**.............. Gn 30:13
of **A** he said, "Most blessed of sons..... Dt 33:24
12,000 from the tribe of **A**,.............. Rv 7:6

ASHERAH
of Baal and the 400 prophets of **A**,... 1 Kgs 18:19
had made a detestable image for **A**... 2 Chr 15:16
root out your **A** images from among..... Mi 5:14

ASHES
I who am but dust and **a**.............. Gn 18:27
his clothes and put on sackcloth and **a**,.... Est 4:1
to scrape himself while he sat in the **a**..... Jb 2:8
despise myself, and repent in dust and **a**.".. Jb 42:6
For I eat **a** like bread and mingle tears.. Ps 102:9
He feeds on **a**; a deluded heart has led.. Is 44:20
people, put on sackcloth, and roll in **a**;.. Jer 6:26
himself with sackcloth, and sat in **a**....... Jon 3:6
sprinkling of defiled persons with the **a**. Heb 9:13

ASIA
the Holy Spirit to speak the word in **A**.. Acts 16:6
of the affliction we experienced in **A**.... 2 Cor 1:8
to the seven churches that are in **A**:....... Rv 1:4

ASIDE
But you have turned **a** from the way...... Mal 2:8
He laid **a** his outer garments, and taking.. Jn 13:4
All have turned **a**; together they have.. Rom 3:12

each of you is to put something **a** and. 1 Cor 16:2

ASK
"Why is it that you **a** my name?" And.. Gn 32:29
"When your children **a** their fathers in... Jos 4:21
"**A** a sign of the Lord your God;.......... Is 7:11
They shall **a** the way to Zion, with faces. Jer 50:5
A rain from the Lord in the............ Zec 10:1
"**A**, and it will be given to you; seek,...... Mt 7:7
And whatever you **a** in prayer, you will.. Mt 21:22
the girl, "**A** me for whatever you wish,... Mk 6:22
the Holy Spirit to those who **a** him!"..... Lk 11:13
I know that whatever you **a** from God,... Jn 11:22
If you **a** me anything in my name, I..... Jn 14:14
a whatever you wish, and it will be done. Jn 15:7
A, and you will receive, that your joy.... Jn 16:24
let them **a** their husbands at home.... 1 Cor 14:35
abundantly than all that we **a** or think,. Eph 3:20
You do not have, because you do not **a**... Jas 4:2
that he hears us in whatever we **a**,...... 1 Jn 5:15

ASKS
For everyone who **a** receives,............ Mt 7:8
among you, if his son **a** for a fish,........ Lk 11:11
If anyone **a** you, 'Why are you untying.. Lk 19:31

ASLEEP
And he fell **a** and dreamed a second..... Gn 41:5
he is **a** and must be awakened."...... 1 Kgs 18:27
ship and had lain down and was fast **a**.... Jon 1:5
swamped by the waves; but he was **a**.... Mt 8:24
"Our friend Lazarus has fallen **a**,......... Jn 11:11
still alive, though some have fallen **a**... 1 Cor 15:6
we are awake or **a** we might live...... 1 Thes 5:10
For ever since the fathers fell **a**, all...... 2 Pt 3:4

ASSEMBLY
And all the **a** said "Amen" and praised.. Neh 5:13
consecrate a fast; call a solemn **a**;........ Jl 2:15
and to the **a** of the firstborn who are... Heb 12:23
and fine clothing comes into your **a**,..... Jas 2:2

ASSIGNED
as my Father **a** to me, a kingdom,...... Lk 22:29
to the area of influence God **a** to us,.. 2 Cor 10:13

ASSURANCE
all the riches of full **a** of understanding... Col 2:2
to have the full **a** of hope until the end,. Heb 6:11
with a true heart in full **a** of faith,..... Heb 10:22
Now faith is the **a** of things hoped for,... Heb 11:1

ASSYRIA
is opposite Egypt in the direction of **A**... Gn 25:18
the king of **A** captured Samaria,...... 2 Kgs 17:6
shall be carried to **A** as tribute to the... Hos 10:6
A shall not save us; we will not ride on.. Hos 14:3

ASTONISHED
many were **a** at you—his appearance..... Is 52:14
the crowds were **a** at his teaching,....... Mt 7:28
when his parents saw him, they were **a**... Lk 2:48
who were with him were **a** at the catch... Lk 5:9
all were **a** at the majesty of God. But..... Lk 9:43
uneducated, common men, they were **a**... Acts 4:13
I am **a** that you are so quickly deserting.. Gal 1:6

ASTRAY
make me understand how I have gone **a**.. Jb 6:24
are a people who go **a** in their heart,.... Ps 95:10
statutes, but their lies have led them **a**,.. Am 2:4
go in search of the one that went **a**?.... Mt 18:12
to lead **a**, if possible, the elect.......... Mk 13:22
"See that you are not led **a**.............. Lk 21:8
sins and led **a** by various passions,..... 2 Tm 3:6
'They always go **a** in their heart;........ Heb 3:10
the right way, they have gone **a**........ 2 Pt 2:15

ATE
one wise, she took of its fruit and **a**,..... Gn 3:6
Your words were found, and I **a** them,... Jer 15:16
I **a** it, and it was in my mouth as sweet... Ezk 3:3
I **a** no delicacies, no meat or wine....... Dn 10:3

And they all **a** and were satisfied........Mt 14:20
not like the bread the fathers **a**, and died. . Jn 6:58
and all **a** the same spiritual food,.......1 Cor 10:3
from the hand of the angel and **a** it. .....Rv 10:10

ATHALIAH
His mother's name was **A**; she.........2 Kgs 8:26
Thus they hid him from **A**, so..........2 Kgs 11:2

ATHENS
"Men of **A**, I perceive that in every.... Acts 17:22
willing to be left behind at **A** alone,....1 Thes 3:1

ATHLETE
Every **a** exercises self-control......... 1 Cor 9:25
a is not crowned unless he competes ...2 Tm 2:5

ATONE
you **a** for our transgressions.............Ps 65:3
a for our sins, for your name's sake!......Ps 79:9
put an end to sin, and to **a** for iniquity,.. Dn 9:24

ATONED
love and faithfulness iniquity is **a**....... Prv 16:6
guilt is taken away, and your sin **a** for.".... Is 6:7

ATONEMENT
shall offer a bull as a sin offering for **a**.. Ex 29:36
Aaron shall make **a** on its horns once a. .Ex 30:10
of this seventh month is the Day of **A**.. . Lv 23:27
for his God and made **a** for the people . Nm 25:13
And how shall I make **a**, that you ......2 Sm 21:3
the sin offerings to make **a** for Israel,.. Neh 10:33
days shall they make **a** for the altar... Ezk 43:26

ATTAIN
for me; it is high; I cannot **a** it........... Ps 139:6
are considered worthy to **a** to that age. .Lk 20:35
until we all **a** to the unity of the faith....Eph 4:13
possible I may **a** the resurrection from .. Phil 3:11

ATTAINED
did not pursue righteousness have **a** it,. .Rom 9:30
Only let us hold true to what we have **a**. . .Phil 3:16

ATTENTION
Give **a** to the sound of my cry, my........Ps 5:2
your flocks, and give **a** to your herds, . .Prv 27:23
But they paid no **a** and went off, ...Mt 22:5
said to them, "Pay **a** to what you hear: . . Mk 4:24
must pay much closer **a** to what we .....Heb 2:1
if you pay **a** to the one who wears the ... Jas 2:3
will do well to pay **a** as to a lamp.......2 Pt 1:19

ATTENTIVE
of all the people were **a** to the Book .... Neh 8:3
Let your ears be **a** to the voice of my ...Ps 130:2
making your ear **a** to wisdom and .... Prv 2:2

AUGUSTUS
a decree went out from Caesar **A**......... Lk 2:1

AUTHOR
and you killed the **A** of life, whom ..... Acts 3:15

AUTHORITIES
many even of the **a** believed in him,.....Jn 12:42
taxes, for the **a** are ministers of God,... Rom 13:6
be made known to the rulers and **a**.....Eph 3:10
but against the rulers, against the **a**, ...Eph 6:12
be submissive to rulers and **a**,.............Ti 3:1
right hand of God, with angels, **a**,........1 Pt 3:22

AUTHORITY
store up grain under the **a** of Pharaoh...Gn 41:35
and will commit your **a** to his hand........Is 22:21
teaching them as one who had **a**,........Mt 7:29
Son of Man has **a** on earth to forgive......Mt 9:6
and gave them **a** over unclean spirits,.... Mt 10:1
"All **a** in heaven and on earth has been . . Mt 28:18
I will give all this **a** and their glory,........Lk 4:6
For I too am a man set under **a**, with........Lk 7:8
"Tell us by what **a** you do these things,...Lk 20:2
has given him **a** to execute judgment,....Jn 5:27
that the Father has fixed by his own **a**... Acts 1:7
For there is no **a** except from God,......Rom 13:1
wife does not have **a** over her own .... 1 Cor 7:4
to have a symbol of **a** on her head, ... 1 Cor 11:10
after destroying every rule and every **a** . . 1 Cor 15:24
far above all rule and **a** and power...... Eph 1:21
lust of defiling passion and despise **a**....2 Pt 2:10
first, does not acknowledge our **a**.........3 Jn 9
be glory, majesty, dominion, and **a**, ... Jude 25
to him I will give **a** over the nations, ... Rv 2:26
And I will grant **a** to my two witnesses,... Rv 11:3
his power and his throne and great **a**..... Rv 13:2

AVENGE
may the Lord **a** me against you,......1 Sm 24:12
from my enemies and **a** myself on my.....Is 1:24
I will **a** their blood, blood I have not ......Jl 3:21
never **a** yourselves, but leave it to .... Rom 12:19
you will judge and **a** our blood on ....Rv 6:10

AVENGED
a on her the blood of his servants."...... Rv 19:2

AVENGER
shall be for you a refuge from the **a**, ... Nm 35:12
to them, but an **a** of their wrongdoings. . .Ps 99:8
an **a** who carries out God's wrath on... Rom 13:4
because the Lord is an **a** in all these .. 1 Thes 4:6

AVOID
not only to **a** God's wrath but also for. . Rom 13:5
A the irreverent babble...............1 Tm 6:20
denying its power. **A** such people. ......2 Tm 3:5

AWAKE
when I **a**, I shall be satisfied with ....Ps 17:15
My eyes are **a** before the watches of ...Ps 119:148
I **a**, and I am still with you............. Ps 139:18
I slept, but my heart was **a**. A sound!......Sg 5:2
A, **a**, put on strength, O arm ....Is 51:9
sleep in the dust of the earth shall **a**,.....Dn 12:2
stay **a**, for you do not know........... Mt 24:42
But stay **a** at all times, praying that you . Lk 21:36
"**A**, O sleeper, and arise from the dead,. .Eph 5:14
but let us keep **a** and be sober........ 1 Thes 5:6
that whether we are **a** or asleep we...1 Thes 5:10
Blessed is the one who stays **a**,......... Rv 16:15

AWE
the ends of the earth are in **a** at your ....Ps 65:8
of Jacob and will stand in **a** of the God. . Is 29:23
He stood in **a** of my name............... Mal 2:5
they were filled with **a** and said,........ Mt 27:54
glorified God and were filled with **a**, ...Lk 5:26
And **a** came upon every soul, ...Acts 2:43

AWESOME
"How **a** is this place! This is none other. .Gn 28:17
for it is an **a** thing that I will do with ....Ex 34:10
God is in your midst, a great and **a** ...... Dt 7:21
appearance of the angel of God, very **a**. . Jgs 13:6
God is clothed with **a** majesty...........Jb 37:22
"How **a** are your deeds! So great is ......Ps 66:3
When you did **a** things that we.......... Is 64:3
"O Lord, the great and **a** God,........... Dn 9:4
of the Lord is great and very **a**; .... Jl 2:11
great and **a** day of the Lord.............Mal 4:5

AXE
his **a** head fell into the water,...........2 Kgs 6:5
Shall the **a** boast over him who hews..... Is 10:15
Even now the **a** is laid to the root........Mt 3:10

AZARIAH
king of Israel, **A** the son of Amaziah, ...2 Kgs 15:1
the prophecy of **A** the son of Oded,.. 2 Chr 15:8

BAAL
So Israel yoked himself to **B** of Peor.....Nm 25:3
Thus Jehu wiped out **B** from Israel. . . 2 Kgs 10:28
Lord all the vessels made for **B**, ...2 Kgs 23:4
no longer will you call me 'My **B**.' ....Hos 2:16
who have not bowed the knee to **B**."... Rom 11:4

BAASHA
between Asa and **B** king of Israel.....1 Kgs 15:16
B king of Israel went up against ....2 Chr 16:1

BABEL
The beginning of his kingdom was **B**, ...Gn 10:10
Therefore its name was called **B**, ... Gn 11:9

BABY
the child, and behold, the **b** was crying....Ex 2:6
of Mary, the **b** leaped in her womb........Lk 1:41
you will find a **b** wrapped in swaddling... Lk 2:12

BABYLON
of Assyria brought people from **B**,... 2 Kgs 17:24
Nebuchadnezzar the king of **B** ....Ezr 2:1
By the waters of **B**, there we sat down ...Ps 137:1
fallen is **B**; and all the carved............Is 21:9
To **B** you shall go, and there ....Jer 20:6
carried into exile to **B** the rest of the.... Jer 39:9
Do not fear the king of **B**,..............Jer 42:11
"Is not this great **B**, which I .... Dn 4:30
"Fallen, fallen is **B** the great, she who ....Rv 14:8

BACK
But Lot's wife, behind him, looked **b**,....Gn 19:26
away my hand, and you shall see my **b**, .Ex 33:23
he brought the shadow **b** ten steps,.. 2 Kgs 20:11
cast your law behind their **b** and killed. . Neh 9:26
I gave my **b** to those who strike,......... Is 50:6
forgotten me and cast me behind your **b**,.. Ezk 23:35
to the plow and looks **b** is fit for the.....Lk 9:62
he saw that he was healed, turned **b**, ...Lk 17:15
"I am he," they drew **b** and fell to........ Jn 18:6
the disciples went **b** to their homes. .....Jn 20:10
that whoever brings **b** a sinner from ....Jas 5:20
a scroll written within and on the **b**,....... Rv 5:1

BACKSLIDING
but he went on **b** in the way of his....... Is 57:17
people turned away in perpetual **b**?...... Jer 8:5

BAD
"**B**, **b**," says the buyer, but .... Prv 20:14
but if your eye is **b**, your whole body ....Mt 6:23
"For no good tree bears **b** fruit, nor.......Lk 6:43
impostors will go on from **b** to worse,. . 2 Tm 3:13

BAG
transgression would be sealed up in a **b**, Jb 14:17
does so to put them into a **b** with holes... .Hg 1:6

BAKED
them a feast and **b** unleavened bread,....Gn 19:3
And they **b** unleavened cakes of the .... Ex 12:39
it was like the taste of cakes **b** with oil... .Nm 11:8

BAKER
the chief cupbearer and the chief **b**, ... Gn 40:2

BALAAM
And **B** said to the donkey, "Because ...Nm 22:29
They have followed the way of **B**, the ...2 Pt 2:15
some there who hold the teaching of **B**,. . Rv 2:14

BALAK
to God, "**B** the son of Zippor, king of... Nm 22:10

BALANCE
(Let me be weighed in a just **b**,.......... Jb 31:6
false **b** is an abomination to the .... Prv 11:1

BALANCES
You shall have just **b**, just weights,...... Lv 19:36
weighed in the **b** and found wanting; ... Dn 5:27

BALD
They shall not make **b** patches on .... Lv 21:5
they make themselves **b** for you and... Ezk 27:31
make yourselves as **b** as the eagle, ...Mi 1:16

BALM
a little **b** and a little honey,............. Gn 43:11
Is there no **b** in Gilead? Is there no...... Jer 8:22

BANISH
I will **b** from them the voice of mirth . . . Jer 25:10
he will **b** ungodliness from Jacob";. . . . Rom 11:26

BANNER
name of it, The LORD Is My **B**,. . . . . Ex 17:15
You have set up a **b** for those who fear. . Ps 60:4
and his **b** over me was love. . . . . .Sg 2:4

BANQUET
his birthday gave a **b** for his nobles . . . . . .Mk 6:21
"When you give a dinner or a **b**,. . . . . Lk 14:12

BAPTISM
The **b** of John, from where did it come? . Mt 21:25
proclaiming a **b** of repentance for . . . . .Mk 1:4
and with the **b** with which I am. . . . . Mk 10:39
been baptized with the **b** of John,. . . . . . . .Lk 7:29
I have a **b** to be baptized with,. . . . . .Lk 12:50
he knew only the **b** of John. . . . . Acts 18:25
therefore with him by **b** into death,. . . . . .Rom 6:4
one Lord, one faith, one **b**,. . . . . Eph 4:5
having been buried with him in **b**, ... Col 2:12
B, which corresponds to this,. . . . . 1 Pt 3:21

BAPTIST
"John the **B** has been raised from the . . . .Mk 6:14
"The head of John the **B**." . . . . Mk 6:24
For John the **B** has come eating no . . . . . .Lk 7:33

BAPTIZE
He will **b** you with the Holy Spirit. . . . . Mt 3:11
John answered them, "I **b** with water, ... Jn 1:26
he who sent me to **b** with water said. . . . . Jn 1:33
(although Jesus himself did not **b**,. . . . . .Jn 4:2
did not send me to **b** but to preach . . . . 1 Cor 1:17

BAPTIZED
to the Jordan to John, to be **b** by him. . . . Mt 3:13
Now when all the people were **b**,. . . . . Lk 3:21
been **b** with the baptism of John,. . . . . .Lk 7:29
and people were coming and being **b** . . . .Jn 3:23
for John **b** with water, but you will be . . . Acts 1:5
"Repent and be **b** every one of you in. . Acts 2:38
into Christ Jesus were **b** into his death? .Rom 6:3
Or were you **b** in the name of Paul?. . . . 1 Cor 1:13
and all were **b** into Moses in the . . . . . . .1 Cor 10:2
we were all **b** into one body— . . . . 1 Cor 12:13
people mean by being **b** on behalf of .1 Cor 15:29
of you as were **b** into Christ have put . . . Gal 3:27

BAPTIZING
b them in the name of the Father and. . . Mt 28:19
for this purpose I came **b** with water, ...Jn 1:31
Jesus was making and **b** more disciples . . . Jn 4:1
withhold water for **b** these people,. . . . Acts 10:47

BARABBAS
notorious prisoner called **B**. . . . . .Mt 27:16

BARAK
She sent and summoned **B** . . . . .Jgs 4:6
tell of Gideon, **B**, Samson, Jephthah, . . . Heb 11:32

BARE
world were laid **b** at your rebuke,. . . . . .Ps 18:15
LORD will lay **b** their secret . . . . Is 3:17
so that its foundation will be laid **b**. . . . . Ezk 13:14
the body that is to be, but a **b** kernel, .1 Cor 15:37

BARN
but gather the wheat into my **b**.'" . . . . . . .Mt 13:30
they have neither storehouse nor **b**,. . . . . Lk 12:24

BARNABAS
called by the apostles **B** (which means. .Acts 4:36
"Set apart for me **B** and Saul for the . . . Acts 13:2
B took Mark with him and sailed. . . . . . Acts 15:39
Or is it only **B** and I who have no . . . . . . 1 Cor 9:6
so that even **B** was led astray by their. . . Gal 2:13
the cousin of **B** (concerning whom. . . . . . Col 4:10

BARNS
the blessing on you in your **b** and in all. . .Dt 28:8
then your **b** will be filled with plenty,. . . . Prv 3:10
will tear down my **b** and build larger. . . . .Lk 12:18

BARREN
Sarai was **b**; she had no child. . . . . Gn 11:30
None shall miscarry or be **b** in your . . . . .Ex 23:26
The **b** has borne seven, but she who . . . . 1 Sm 2:5
He gives the **b** woman a home,. . . . . Ps 113:9
"Sing, O **b** one, who did not bear; . . . . .Is 54:1
had no child, because Elizabeth was **b**,. . . . Lk 1:7
'Blessed are the **b** and the wombs . . . . . .Lk 23:29
"Rejoice, O **b** one who does not bear; . . . Gal 4:27

BARTHOLOMEW
Philip and **B**; Thomas and Matthew . . . . . .Mt 10:3
Philip and Thomas, **B** and Matthew,. . . . . Acts 1:13

BARTIMAEUS
B, a blind beggar, the son of . . . . Mk 10:46

BARUCH
After him **B** the son of Zabbai repaired . .Neh 3:20
And **B** the son of Neriah did all that. . . . .Jer 36:8
Jeremiah the prophet and **B** the son of. . Jer 43:6

BARZILLAI
B the Gileadite from Rogelim,. . . . . .2 Sm 17:27
B was a very aged man, eighty . . . . . . .2 Sm 19:32

BASHAN
Og the king of **B** came out against. . . . . Nm 21:33
"Hear this word, you cows of **B**, who. . . . . Am 4:1
let them graze in **B** and Gilead as in the . . Mi 7:14

BASIN
"You shall also make a **b** of bronze,. . . . .Ex 30:18
four corners were supports for a **b**. . . . 1 Kgs 7:30
and removed the **b** from them,. . . . . . . .2 Kgs 16:17

BASKET
she took for him a **b** made of bulrushes . . .Ex 2:3
One **b** had very good figs, like first-ripe . Jer 24:2
"A **b** of summer fruit.". . . . . .Am 8:2
in the wall, lowering him in a **b**. . . . . . . .Acts 9:25

BASKETS
there were three cake **b** on my head,. . . Gn 40:16
they took up twelve **b** full of the broken . .Mt 14:20
the broken pieces left over, seven **b** full. . . Mk 8:8
filled twelve **b** with fragments from . . . . . . Jn 6:13

BATHSHEBA
David comforted his wife, **B**, ...2 Sm 12:24
"Call **B** to me." So she came into the . . .1 Kgs 1:28

BATTLE
For the **b** is the LORD's,. . . . . 1 Sm 17:47
Philistines for the **b** against Saul. . . . . . 1 Chr 12:19
for the **b** is not yours but God's. . . . . . 2 Chr 20:15
equipped me with strength for the **b**; . . . Ps 18:39
the LORD, mighty in **b**!. . . . . .Ps 24:8
not to the swift, nor the **b** to the strong, . . Eccl 9:11
all the nations against Jerusalem to **b**, . . Zec 14:2
sound, who will get ready for **b**? . . . . . .1 Cor 14:8
assemble them for **b** on the great day. . . Rv 16:14

BEAR
made the **B** and Orion, the Pleiades. . . . . . .Jb 9:9
On their hands they will **b** you up,. . . . . . .Ps 91:12
They still **b** fruit in old age; they. . . . . Ps 92:14
but a crushed spirit who can **b**? . . . . .Prv 18:14
and he shall **b** their iniquities. . . . . Is 53:11
like a **b**. It was raised up on one side. . . . . Dn 7:5
upon them like a **b** robbed of her cubs; . Hos 13:8
She will **b** a son, and you shall call his. . . . Mt 1:21
B fruit in keeping with repentance.. . . . . . . .Mt 3:8
to **b** witness about the light, ... Jn 1:7
in order that we may **b** fruit for God. . . . .Rom 7:4
b the image of the man of heaven. . . . 1 Cor 15:49
B one another's burdens, and so fulfill. . . . Gal 6:2
for I **b** on my body the marks of Jesus. . . Gal 6:17
offered once to **b** the sins of many, ... Heb 9:28

BEARS
but the root of the righteous **b** fruit. . . . .Prv 12:12
every healthy tree **b** good fruit, but . . . . . . Mt 7:17
he it is that **b** much fruit, for apart. . . . . . . Jn 15:5
Love **b** all things, believes all things, . . . 1 Cor 13:7
the Holy Spirit also **b** witness to us;. . . . Heb 10:15

BEAST
For every **b** of the forest is mine, ...Ps 50:10
has regard for the life of his **b**, ... Prv 12:10
his mind was made like that of a **b**,. . . . . . Dn 5:21
the **b** had four heads, and dominion . . . . . Dn 7:6
and they worshiped the **b**,. . . . . .Rv 13:4
had not worshiped the **b** or its image . . . Rv 20:4

BEASTS
And God made the **b** of the earth . . . . . . .Gn 1:25
I will remove harmful **b** from the land,. . . .Lv 26:6
He gives to the **b** their food, and to the . Ps 147:9
I fought with **b** at Ephesus?. . . . . .1 Cor 15:32

BEAT
up his eyes to heaven, but **b** his breast,. . .Lk 18:13
were mocking him as they **b** him. . . . . . . .Lk 22:63
they **b** them and charged them not to. .Acts 5:40

BEATING
and he saw an Egyptian **b** a Hebrew,. . . . . .Ex 2:11
and the soldiers, they stopped **b** Paul.. Acts 21:32
I do not box as one **b** the air.. . . . . 1 Cor 9:26

BEATINGS
b, imprisonments, riots, labors,. . . . . 2 Cor 6:5
imprisonments, with countless **b**, ...2 Cor 11:23

BEAUTIFUL
that you are a woman **b** in appearance, . .Gn 12:11
He has made everything **b** in its time. . . . Eccl 3:11
You are altogether **b**, my love;. . . . . .Sg 4:7
branch of the LORD shall be **b** . . . . Is 4:2
How **b** upon the mountains are the feet . . .Is 52:7
For she has done a **b** thing to me. . . . . . .Mt 26:10
that is called the **B** Gate to ask alms . . . . Acts 3:2
"How **b** are the feet of those who . . . . Rom 10:15

BEAUTY
You shall make them for glory and **b**. . . Ex 28:40
to gaze upon the **b** of the LORD. . . . . .Ps 27:4
Out of Zion, the perfection of **b**,. . . . . .Ps 50:2
strength and **b** are in his sanctuary. . . . . . .Ps 96:6
Charm is deceitful, and **b** is vain, ... Prv 31:30
no **b** that we should desire him. . . . . Is 53:2
with the imperishable **b** of a gentle . . . . . .1 Pt 3:4

BED
every night I flood my **b** with tears;. . . . . . .Ps 6:6
when I remember you upon my **b**,. . . . . . .Ps 63:6
its hinges, so does a sluggard on his **b**.. Prv 26:14
brought to him a paralytic, lying on a **b**. . . .Mt 9:2
"Get up, take up your **b**, and walk." . . . . . . .Jn 5:8
and let the marriage **b** be undefiled, ...Heb 13:4

BEDS
let them sing for joy on their **b**.. . . . . Ps 149:5
they rest in their **b** who walk in their. . . . . .Is 57:2
sick people on their **b** to wherever. . . . . . Mk 6:55

BEERSHEBA
So they made a covenant at **B**. . . . . .Gn 21:32
with all that he had and came to **B**,. . . . . .Gn 46:1
Israel and over Judah, from Dan to **B**." .2 Sm 3:10

BEES
b in the body of the lion, and honey. . . . . Jgs 14:8

BEFOREHAND
beginning, that we might know, and **b**, . . .Is 41:26
See, I have told you **b**.. . . . . Mt 24:25
do not be anxious **b** what you are to. . . . .Mk 13:11
which he promised **b** through his . . . . Rom 1:2
which he has prepared **b** for glory— . . .Rom 9:23
for good works, which God prepared **b**, .Eph 2:10

BEG
"Teacher, I **b** you to look at my son,......Lk 9:38
enough to dig, and I am ashamed to **b**.... Lk 16:3
the man who used to sit and **b**?".........Jn 9:8
So I **b** you to reaffirm your love for .... 2 Cor 2:8

BEGGAR
a great crowd, Bartimaeus, a blind **b**,... Mk 10:46
seen him before as a **b** were saying, ...Jn 9:8

BEGINNING
In the **b**, God created the heavens and .... Gn 1:1
latter days of Job more than his **b**.......Jb 42:12
The fear of the LORD is the **b**............ Prv 1:7
Better is the end of a thing than its **b**,... Eccl 7:8
In the **b** was the Word, and the Word ......Jn 1:1
He was in the **b** with God................ Jn 1:2
Jesus knew from the **b** who those were . .Jn 6:64
He is the **b**, the firstborn from the dead,. .Col 1:18
having neither **b** of days nor end of life,. Heb 7:3
That which was from the **b**, which we .... 1 Jn 1:1
first and the last, the **b** and the end." ...Rv 22:13

BEGOTTEN
"You are my Son; today I have **b** you. .....Ps 2:7
are my Son, today I have **b** you.'...... Acts 13:33
"You are my Son, today I have **b** you"?...Heb 1:5

BEGS
Give to the one who **b** from you, ...Mt 5:42

BEHALF
and plead with him on **b** of her people. .. Est 4:8
that I will ask the Father on your **b**;.....Jn 16:26
has gone as a forerunner on our **b**, ...Heb 6:20

BEHAVE
how one ought to **b** in the household . . 1 Tm 3:15

BEHAVED
but the man was harsh and badly **b**; . . .1 Sm 25:3
we **b** in the world with simplicity and . . 2 Cor 1:12

BEHAVIOR
So he changed his **b** before them......1 Sm 21:13
women likewise are to be reverent in **b**, ... Ti 2:3

BEHEADED
He sent and had John **b** in the prison,... Mt 14:10
Herod said, "John I **b**, but who is this......Lk 9:9
those who had been **b** for the testimony. . Rv 20:4

BEHEMOTH
B, which I made as I made you;.........Jb 40:15

BEHIND
turned and said to Peter, "Get **b** me, ...Mt 16:23
the boy Jesus stayed **b** in Jerusalem......Lk 2:43
on him the cross, to carry it **b** Jesus.....Lk 23:26
forgetting what lies **b** and straining ..... Phil 3:13
and I heard **b** me a loud voice like a ..... Rv 1:10

BEHOLD
"**B**, I am the servant of the Lord;......... Lk 1:38
"**B**, the Lamb of God, who takes away.... Jn 1:29
Pilate said to them, "**B** the man!" .... Jn 19:5
to his mother, "Woman, **b**, your son!" ... Jn 19:26
"**B**, the dwelling place of God is with..... Rv 21:3
"**B**, I am making all things new." .... Rv 21:5
"**B**, I am coming soon, bringing my ..... Rv 22:12

BEING
sing praise to my God while I have **b**. . . Ps 104:33
sing and make melody with all my **b**! ... Ps 108:1
praises to my God while I have my **b**. ... Ps 146:2
My inmost **b** will exult when your lips . . Prv 23:16
cut short, no human **b** would be saved.. Mt 24:22
joy that a human **b** has been born into . . .Jn 16:21
we live and move and have our **b**';.... Acts 17:28
for every human **b** who does evil,.......Rom 2:9
in the law of God, in my inner **b**,.......Rom 7:22
so that no human **b** might boast in .....1 Cor 1:29
through his Spirit in your inner **b**,.......Eph 3:16

BEL
B bows down; Nebo stoops; ....Is 46:1
And I will punish **B** in Babylon, ... Jer 51:44

BELIEVE
"that they may **b** that the LORD, ...Ex 4:5
how long will they not **b** in me,.........Nm 14:11
B in the LORD your God, ...2 Chr 20:20
I **b** that I shall look upon the goodness . . Ps 27:13
that you may know and **b** me ....Is 43:10
your days that you would not **b** if told.... Hab 1:5
"Do you **b** that I am able to do this?" ... Mt 9:28
or 'There he is!' do not **b** it........... Mt 24:23
at hand; repent and **b** in the gospel."..... Mk 1:15
"Do not fear, only **b**.".................. Mk 5:36
"I **b**; help my unbelief!"................ Mk 9:24
But these have no root; they **b** for a ..... Lk 8:13
unless you **b** that I am he you will die . . . .Jn 8:24
you do not **b** me, **b** the works, ...Jn 10:38
I **b** that you are the Christ,..............Jn 11:27
B in God; **b** also in me...................Jn 14:1
it in my side. Do not disbelieve, but **b**." . .Jn 20:27
"**B** in the Lord Jesus, and you will be. . .Acts 16:31
will be counted to us who **b** in him ....Rom 4:24
we **b** that we will also live with him. ....Rom 6:8
that Jesus is Lord and **b** in your heart . . Rom 10:9
greatness of his power toward us who **b**,. . Eph 1:19
For since we **b** that Jesus died and . . .1 Thes 4:14
all people, especially of those who **b**. . . 1 Tm 4:10
Though you do not now see him, you **b** . . 1 Pt 1:8

BELIEVED
And he **b** the LORD, and he.............Gn 15:6
and they **b** in the LORD and .... Ex 14:31
Who has **b** what he has heard from us? . . . Is 53:1
And the people of Nineveh **b** God........Jon 3:5
many **b** in his name when they saw......Jn 2:23
For not even his brothers **b** in him.........Jn 7:5
who have not seen and yet have **b**." ... Jn 20:29
And all who **b** were together and had . .Acts 2:44
receive the Holy Spirit when you **b**?"... Acts 19:2
nearer to us now than when we first **b**. . Rom 13:11
preached to you—unless you **b** in vain. . 1 Cor 15:2
just as Abraham "**b** God, and it was......Gal 3:6
I know whom I have **b**, ... 2 Tm 1:12
For we who have **b** enter that rest, ... Heb 4:3
"Abraham **b** God, and it was ....Jas 2:23

BELIEVER
son of a Jewish woman who was a **b**, . . .Acts 16:1
what portion does a **b** share with an . . 2 Cor 6:15

BELIEVERS
And more than ever **b** were added to . . Acts 5:14
by their good service are **b** and beloved. .1 Tm 6:2
and his children are **b** and not open to .....Ti 1:6

BELIEVES
All things are possible for one who **b**." . . Mk 9:23
not doubt in his heart, but **b** that what . . Mk 11:23
whoever **b** in him should not perish...... Jn 3:16
Whoever **b** in me, as the Scripture has . . .Jn 7:38
who lives and **b** in me shall never die.....Jn 11:26
b in him receives forgiveness of sins . . Acts 10:43
God for salvation to everyone who **b**, . . .Rom 1:16
not work but **b** in him who justifies .....Rom 4:5
b in him will not be put to shame." ....Rom 9:33
Everyone who **b** that Jesus is the Christ . . 1 Jn 5:1

BELIEVING
and that by **b** you may have life in his. . . Jn 20:31
the right to take along a **b** wife,....... 1 Cor 9:5
Those who have **b** masters must not. . . . 1 Tm 6:2

BELLY
on your **b** you shall go, and dust you. .....Gn 3:14
Jonah was in the **b** of the fish three......Jon 1:17
three nights in the **b** of the great fish,. . .Mt 12:40
end is destruction, their god is their **b**, . . Phil 3:19

BELONG
"The secret things **b** to the LORD.........Dt 29:29
The plans of the heart **b** to man, but.....Prv 16:1
It shall **b** to those who walk on the way;. . Is 35:8
Lord our God **b** mercy and forgiveness, . . Dn 9:9
to drink because you **b** to Christ will .....Mk 9:41
Spirit of Christ does not **b** to him. ......Rom 8:9
at his coming those who **b** to Christ. . .1 Cor 15:23
And those who **b** to Christ Jesus ....Gal 5:24
things that **b** to salvation................ Heb 6:9
To him **b** glory and dominion forever.... 1 Pt 4:11
and glory and power **b** to our God, ... Rv 19:1

BELONGS
I heard this: that power **b** to God,........Ps 62:11
For our shield **b** to the LORD,...........Ps 89:18
but the victory **b** to the LORD............Prv 21:31
Salvation **b** to the LORD!" ....Jon 2:9
to such **b** the kingdom of God..........Mk 10:14
"Salvation **b** to our God who sits ....Rv 7:10

BELOVED
That your **b** ones may be delivered,......Ps 60:5
My **b** is mine, and I am his; he...........Sg 2:16
Let me sing for my **b** my love song ....Is 5:1
"This is my **b** Son, with whom........... Mt 3:17
who was not **b** I will call '**b**.'"..........Rom 9:25
and all for your upbuilding, **b**.........2 Cor 12:19
he has blessed us in the **B**...............Eph 1:6
the Majestic Glory, "This is my **b** Son, ... 2 Pt 1:17
B, let us love one another, for love is.....1 Jn 4:7

BELSHAZZAR
King **B** made a great feast for a ....Dn 5:1

BELT
Righteousness shall be the **b** of his .... Is 11:5
of camel's hair and a leather **b** ....Mt 3:4
he took Paul's **b** and bound his own ... Acts 21:11
having fastened on the **b** of truth, ...Eph 6:14

BENJAMIN
but his father called him **B**. ....Gn 35:18
Of **B** he said, "The beloved of the....... Dt 33:12
of the people of Israel, of the tribe of **B**, . Phil 3:5

BENT
and I **b** down to them and fed them..... Hos 11:4
She was **b** over and could not fully ...... Lk 13:11
Jesus **b** down and wrote with his finger . . . Jn 8:6
But Paul went down and **b** over him,. . Acts 20:10

BEREA
Paul and Silas away by night to **B**, ...Acts 17:10

BEREAVE
Outdoors the sword shall **b**, and........Dt 32:25
and you **b** your nation of children,'..... Ezk 36:13
children, I will **b** them till none is left. ...Hos 9:12

BEREFT
repay me evil for good; my soul is **b**..... Ps 35:12
my soul is **b** of peace; I have forgotten . .Lam 3:17

BESIDES
LORD is God; there is no other **b** ....Dt 4:35
like the LORD: for there is none **b** ....1 Sm 2:2
and there is no God **b** you,...........1 Chr 17:20
And there is no other god **b** me, a.......Is 45:21
the ear, no eye has seen a God **b** you,.... Is 64:4
but me, and **b** me there is no savior.....Hos 13:4
he is one, and there is no other **b** him. . .Mk 12:32

BESIEGED
So the city was **b** till the eleventh year . . Jer 52:5
he has **b** and enveloped me with .... Lam 3:5
of Babylon came to Jerusalem and **b** it. ... Dn 1:1

BEST
his servants, 'Bring quickly the **b** robe, . . Lk 15:22
the marketplaces and the **b** seats in the . . Lk 20:46
outsiders, making the **b** use of the time. . . Col 4:5

BETHANY
out of the city to **B** and lodged there.... Mt 21:17
when Jesus was at **B** in the house of..... Mt 26:6
certain man was ill, Lazarus of **B**, ... Jn 11:1

Passover, Jesus therefore came to **B**, ... Jn 12:1

BETHEL

on the east of **B** and pitched his tent, ... Gn 12:8
He called the name of that place **B**, ... Gn 28:19

BETHLEHEM

man of **B** in Judah went to sojourn . . . . Ru 1:1
LORD commanded and came to **B**. . . . . . 1 Sm 16:4
O **B** Ephrathah, who are too little . . . . Mi 5:2
"In **B** of Judea, for so it is. . . . . Mt 2:5
city of David, which is called **B**,. . . . . Lk 2:4
offspring of David, and comes from **B**, . . . Jn 7:42

BETHSAIDA

B! For if the mighty works done in. . . . . . . Mt 11:21
and withdrew apart to a town called **B**.. . . Lk 9:10

BETRAY

many will fall away and **b** one another . . Mt 24:10
I say to you, one of you will **b** me, ... Mk 14:18
b the Son of Man with a kiss?" . . . . Lk 22:48
For he knew who was to **b** him; . . . . Jn 13:11
who is it that is going to **b** you?" . . . . Jn 21:20

BETRAYED

Judas Iscariot, who **b** him. . . . . Mt 10:4
The Son of Man is **b** into the hands of . . . Mk 14:41
the night when he was **b** took bread, . 1 Cor 11:23

BETROTHED

his mother Mary had been **b** to Joseph, . . Mt 1:18
to be registered with Mary, his **b**, who. . . . . Lk 2:5
Now concerning the **b**, I have no . . . . . . 1 Cor 7:25

BETTER

Behold, to obey is **b** than sacrifice,. . . . 1 Sm 15:22
your steadfast love is **b** than life, ... Ps 63:3
in your courts is **b** than a thousand . . . . . Ps 84:10
B is a little with the fear of the . . . . Prv 15:16
B is a dinner of herbs where love is . . . . . Prv 15:17
B is a dry morsel with quiet than a . . . . . . Prv 17:1
B is a neighbor who is near than a. . . . . Prv 27:10
good name is **b** than precious ointment,. . Eccl 7:1
For your love is **b** than wine; . . . . Sg 1:2
for it is **b** for me to die than to live." . . . . . Jon 4:3
For it is **b** that you lose one of . . . . Mt 5:29
It is **b** for you to enter life crippled. . . . . . Mk 9:43
It would be **b** for him if a millstone . . . . . . Lk 17:2
b for you that one man should die for . . . Jn 11:50
and be with Christ, for that is far **b**. . . . . . Phil 1:23
God had provided something **b** for us, . Heb 11:40
blood that speaks a **b** word than the. . . Heb 12:24
For it is **b** to suffer for doing good, ... 1 Pt 3:17
it would have been **b** for them never. . . . 2 Pt 2:21

BETWEEN

covenant that I make **b** me and you. . . . . . Gn 9:12
a flaming torch passed **b** these pieces. . . Gn 15:17
May the LORD judge **b** you . . . . Gn 16:5
It is a sign forever **b** me and the people . Ex 31:17
"The LORD will be witness **b** us,. . . . . Jgs 11:10
He shall judge **b** many peoples, ... Mi 4:3
see the distinction **b** the righteous and . . Mal 3:18
is no distinction **b** Jew and Greek; . . . . . Rom 10:12
there is one mediator **b** God and men, . . 1 Tm 2:5
And **b** the throne and the four living . . . . . . Rv 5:6

BEWARE

B lest you say in your heart, 'My power. . . Dt 8:17
"**B** of practicing your righteousness . . . . Mt 6:1
"**B** of false prophets, who come . . . . Mt 7:15
B of the leaven of the Pharisees . . . . Mt 16:11
"**B** of the scribes, who like to walk . . . . . . Mk 12:38

BEYOND

who does great things **b** searching out, . . Jb 9:10
I will send you into exile **b** Babylon.' . . . Acts 7:43
as I can testify, and **b** their means,. . . . . 2 Cor 8:3
advancing in Judaism **b** many of my . . . . . Gal 1:14

BILDAD

B the Shuhite, and Zophar the. . . . . Jb 2:11

BILHAH

And **B** conceived and bore Jacob a son. . Gn 30:5

BIND

forsake you; **b** them around your neck;. . . Prv 3:3
B up the testimony; seal the teaching . . . . . Is 8:16
and whatever you **b** on earth. . . . . Mt 16:19
'**B** him hand and foot and cast him . . . . . Mt 22:13

BINDS

For he wounds, but he **b** up; . . . . Jb 5:18
unless he first **b** the strong man.. . . . . Mk 3:27
which **b** everything together in perfect . . Col 3:14

BIRDS

the **b** of the heavens, and the . . . . Ps 8:8
Look at the **b** of the air: they. . . . . Mt 6:26
much more value are you than the **b**! . . . Lk 12:24

BIRTH

and to a stone, 'You gave me **b**.'. . . . . Jer 2:27
the **b** of Jesus Christ took place in . . . . Mt 1:18
but the beginning of the **b** pains. . . . . Mt 24:8
gladness, and many will rejoice at his **b**,. . . Lk 1:14
passed by, he saw a man blind from **b**. . . . . Jn 9:1

BIRTHRIGHT

Jacob said, "Sell me your **b** now.". . . . . . . Gn 25:31
Thus Esau despised his **b**.. . . . . Gn 25:34
firstborn according to his **b** and the. . . . Gn 43:33
Esau, who sold his **b** for a single meal. . Heb 12:16

BITTER

made their lives **b** with hard service, ... Ex 1:14
the water of Marah because it was **b**; . . . Ex 15:23
swords, who aim **b** words like arrows, ... Ps 64:3
But if you have **b** jealousy and selfish . . . Jas 3:14

BITTERNESS

The heart knows its own **b**, ... Prv 14:10
Let all **b** and wrath and anger and . . . . . . Eph 4:31
that no "root of **b**" springs up and . . . . . Heb 12:15

BLACK

and the day shall be **b** over them; . . . . Mi 3:6
And I looked, and behold, a **b** horse! . . . . . . Rv 6:5
the sun became **b** as sackcloth,. . . . . Rv 6:12

BLAMELESS

Almighty; walk before me, and be **b**, ... Gn 17:1
You shall be **b** before the LORD . . . . Dt 18:13
I shall be **b**, and innocent of great . . . . . . Ps 19:13
May my heart be **b** in your statutes,. . . . Ps 119:80
be holy and **b** before him. . . . . Eph 1:4
be pure and **b** for the day of . . . . Phil 1:10
that you may be **b** and innocent, ... Phil 2:15
holy and righteous and **b** . . . . 1 Thes 2:10
soul and body be kept **b** at the coming. . 1 Thes 5:23
present you **b** before the presence. . . . . . Jude 24
mouth no lie was found, for they are **b**. . . Rv 14:5

BLASPHEME

and tried to make them **b**, ... Acts 26:11
the ones who **b** the honorable name . . . . . Jas 2:7
and **b** the glorious ones. . . . . Jude 8

BLASPHEMED

name of God is **b** among the Gentiles . . Rom 2:24
of them the way of truth will be **b**.. . . . . . 2 Pt 2:2

BLASPHEMES

Whoever **b** the name of the LORD. . . . . . . Lv 24:16
but the one who **b** against the Holy. . . . . Lk 12:10

BLASPHEMING

knew, because his sons were **b** God, . . . 1 Sm 3:13
He is **b**! Who can forgive sins . . . . Mk 2:7
b about matters of which they are . . . . . . 2 Pt 2:12
God, **b** his name and his dwelling, ... Rv 13:6

BLASPHEMOUS

heard him speak **b** words against . . . . Acts 6:11
on its horns and **b** names on its heads. . . . Rv 13:1
a scarlet beast that was full of **b** names,. . Rv 17:3

BLASPHEMY

every sin and **b** will be forgiven people, . Mt 12:31
but the **b** against the Spirit will not be . . Mt 12:31
his robes and said, "He has uttered **b**. . . Mt 26:65
that we are going to stone you but for **b**,. . Jn 10:33

BLEMISH

lamb shall be without **b**, ... Ex 12:5
children of God without **b** in the midst . . Phil 2:15
like that of a lamb without **b** or spot. . . . 1 Pt 1:19
to be found by him without spot or **b**,. . 2 Pt 3:14

BLESS

and I will **b** you and make your name . . . . Gn 12:2
I will **b** those who **b** you, ... Gn 12:3
I will surely **b** you, and I . . . . Gn 22:17
The LORD **b** you and keep you; . . . . Nm 6:24
He will love you, **b** you, and multiply . . . . . Dt 7:13
I **b** the LORD who gives me. . . . . Ps 16:7
I will **b** the LORD at all times; . . . . Ps 34:1
B the LORD, O my soul, ... Ps 103:1
that I might **b** him and multiply him. . . . . . . Is 51:2
b those who curse you, pray for . . . . Lk 6:28
B those who persecute you;. . . . . Rom 12:14
When reviled, we **b**; when persecuted, . 1 Cor 4:12
"Surely I will **b** you and multiply you.". . . Heb 6:14

BLESSED

And God **b** them, saying, "Be fruitful . . . . . Gn 1:22
all the families of the earth shall be **b**." . . . Gn 12:3
shall all the nations of the earth be **b**, . . . Gn 22:18
B is the man who walks not in . . . . Ps 1:1
B be the LORD forever! Amen. . . . . Ps 89:52
B be the name of the LORD. . . . . Ps 113:2
Whoever has a bountiful eye will be **b**, . . Prv 22:9
"**B** are the poor in spirit, for. . . . . Mt 5:3
"**B** are those who mourn, for . . . . Mt 5:4
"**B** are the meek, for they shall . . . . Mt 5:5
"**B** are those who hunger and . . . . Mt 5:6
"**B** are the merciful, for they. . . . . Mt 5:7
"**B** are the pure in heart, for. . . . . Mt 5:8
"**B** are the peacemakers, for. . . . . Mt 5:9
"**B** are those who are persecuted for . . . . . Mt 5:10
"**B** are you when others revile you . . . . Mt 5:11
b is the one who is not offended by . . . . . Mt 11:6
"**B** are you among women,. . . . . Lk 1:42
'**B** is he who comes in the name of. . . . . . Lk 13:35
B are those who have not seen and yet Jn 20:29
shall all the families of the earth be **b**.' . Acts 3:25
more **b** to give than to receive.'". . . . . . Acts 20:35
b is the man against whom the Lord . . . . Rom 4:8
who has **b** us in Christ with every. . . . . Eph 1:3
waiting for our **b** hope, the appearing. . . . . Ti 2:13
B is the man who remains steadfast. . . . . . Jas 1:12
for righteousness' sake, you will be **b**. . . . 1 Pt 3:14
B are those who wash their robes, ... Rv 22:14

BLESSES

and blessed be everyone who **b** you!" . . Gn 27:29
sworn covenant, **b** himself in his heart, . . Dt 29:19
gates; he **b** your children within you. . . . Ps 147:13
but he **b** the dwelling of the righteous. . . Prv 3:33

BLESSING

name great, so that you will be a **b**. . . . . . . Gn 12:2
before you today a **b** and a curse: . . . . . . Dt 11:26
yet our God turned the curse into a **b**. . . Neh 13:2
Whoever brings **b** will be enriched, ... Prv 11:25
in the fullness of the **b** of Christ. . . . . . . Rom 15:29
were called, that you may obtain a **b**. . . . . 1 Pt 3:9
to the Lamb be **b** and honor and glory . . . Rv 5:13
B and glory and wisdom and. . . . . Rv 7:12

BLESSINGS

And all these **b** shall come upon you. . . . . Dt 28:2
A faithful man will abound with **b**, ... Prv 28:20
that I may share with them in its **b**. . . . 1 Cor 9:23

BLIND

anyone who misleads a **b** man on the . . . Dt 27:18
LORD opens the eyes of the **b**. . . . . Ps 146:8
Then the eyes of the **b** shall be opened, . . Is 35:5

to open the eyes that are **b**, to bring out . Is 42:7
the **b** receive their sight and the lame.... Mt 11:5
"Can a **b** man lead a **b** man?............Lk 6:39
a **b** man was sitting by the roadside .... Lk 18:35
that though I was **b**, now I see.".........Jn 9:25
that you yourself are a guide to the **b**, . Rom 2:19
wretched, pitiable, poor, **b**, and naked.... Rv 3:17

BLOOD

your brother's **b** is crying to me ....Gn 4:10
"Whoever sheds the **b** of man, by man... Gn 9:6
all the water in the Nile turned into **b**.....Ex 7:20
when I see the **b**, I will pass over .... Ex 12:13
"Behold the **b** of the covenant ....Ex 24:8
life of every creature is its **b**:............Lv 17:14
I do not delight in the **b** of bulls, ...Is 1:11
b of all the prophets, shed from .... Lk 11:50
not of **b** nor of the will of the flesh nor....Jn 1:13
flesh and drinks my **b** has eternal life,....Jn 6:54
we have now been justified by his **b**,....Rom 5:9
"This cup is the new covenant in my **b**...1 Cor 11:25
him we have redemption through his **b**, ..Eph 1:7
been brought near by the **b** of Christ....Eph 2:13
making peace by the **b** of his cross...... Col 1:20
sanctify the people through his own **b**.. Heb 13:12
Christ and for sprinkling with his **b**:.......1 Pt 1:2
and the **b** of Jesus his Son cleanses us...1 Jn 1:7
has freed us from our sins by his **b** .... Rv 1:5

BLOODSHED

ears from hearing of **b** and shuts his.....Is 33:15
because you did not hate **b**, ...Ezk 35:6
and **b** follows **b**....................... Hos 4:2

BLOT

"I will **b** out man whom I have created ... Gn 6:7
I will **b** out of my book.................Ex 32:33
and **b** out all my iniquities............... Ps 51:9
and I will never **b** his name out...........Rv 3:5

BLOTS

I am he who **b** out your transgressions.. Is 43:25

BLOTTED

I have **b** out your transgressions like a... Is 44:22
turn back, that your sins may be **b** out,. Acts 3:19

BLUSH

I am ashamed and **b** to lift my face to.... Ezr 9:6
and you shall **b** for the gardens that you ..Is 1:29
ashamed; they did not know how to **b**... Jer 6:15

BOAST

My soul makes its **b** in the Lord;.........Ps 34:2
Do not **b** about tomorrow, for.......... Prv 27:1
but let him who boasts **b** in this,........Jer 9:24
he has something to **b** about, ...Rom 4:2
the one who boasts, **b** in the Lord.".... 1 Cor 1:31
love does not envy or **b**;..............1 Cor 13:4
If I must **b**, I will **b** of the ....2 Cor 11:30
be it from me to **b** except in the cross... Gal 6:14
a result of works, so that no one may **b**.. Eph 2:9
do not **b** and be false to the truth....... Jas 3:14

BOASTFUL

The **b** shall not stand before your eyes;....Ps 5:5
I say to the **b**, 'Do not boast,'............Ps 75:4
insolent, haughty, **b**, inventors of evil, .. Rom 1:30
I am saying with this **b** confidence, ... 2 Cor 11:17

BOASTING

Then what becomes of our **b**? It is.....Rom 3:27
gospel, that gives me no ground for **b**. .1 Cor 9:16
arrogance. All such **b** is evil............. Jas 4:16

BOASTS

a man who **b** of a gift he does not give... Prv 25:14
yet it **b** of great things. How .... Jas 3:5
speaking loud **b** of folly, they...........2 Pt 2:18

BOAT

they left the **b** and their father ....Mt 4:22
Peter got out of the **b** and walked on ...Mt 14:29
the waves were breaking into the **b**, ... Mk 4:37
went away in the **b** to a desolate place.. Mk 6:32
down and taught the people from the **b**. ..Lk 5:3
on the sea and coming near the **b**,....... Jn 6:19

BOAZ

So **B** took Ruth, and she became his .....Ru 4:13
and **B** the father of Obed by Ruth,........ Mt 1:5

BODIES

dishonoring of their **b** among .... Rom 1:24
life to your mortal **b** through his Spirit ..Rom 8:11
you not know that your **b** are members. .1 Cor 6:15
There are heavenly **b** and earthly .....1 Cor 15:40
may also be manifested in our **b**...... 2 Cor 4:10
should love their wives as their own **b**.. Eph 5:28

BODILY

strong, but his **b** presence is weak,... 2 Cor 10:10
the whole fullness of deity dwells **b**, ... Col 2:9
for while **b** training is of some value,....1 Tm 4:8

BODY

"Take, eat; this is my **b**." .... Mt 26:26
when they did not find his **b**, they ......Lk 24:23
will deliver me from this **b**............Rom 7:24
For as in one **b** we have many......... Rom 12:4
though absent in **b**, I am present ....1 Cor 5:3
not know that your **b** is a temple of....1 Cor 6:19
we who are many are one **b**,..........1 Cor 10:17
"This is my **b** which is for you.........1 Cor 11:24
For just as the **b** is one and has ...... 1 Cor 12:12
Now you are the **b** of Christ..........1 Cor 12:27
There is one **b** and one Spirit— .... Eph 4:4
because we are members of his **b**...... Eph 5:30
will transform our lowly **b** to be like..... Phil 3:21
has now reconciled in his **b** of flesh..... Col 1:22
the offering of the **b** of Jesus Christ....Heb 10:10

BOLD

but the righteous are **b** as a lion........ Prv 28:1
we have such a hope, we are very **b**,...2 Cor 3:12
are much more **b** to speak the word .... Phil 1:14

BOLDLY

And Paul and Barnabas spoke out **b**,.. Acts 13:46
began to speak **b** in the synagogue, .. Acts 18:26
in chains, that I may declare it **b**, as I... Eph 6:20

BOLDNESS

to speak the word of God with **b**....... Acts 4:31
Christ with all **b** and without......... Acts 28:31
in whom we have **b** and access with .... Eph 3:12

BOND

bring you into the **b** of the covenant.. .Ezk 20:37
be loosed from this **b** on the Sabbath... Lk 13:16
unity of the Spirit in the **b** of peace. .... Eph 4:3

BONE

"This at last is **b** of my bones and flesh.. Gn 2:23
and a soft tongue will break a **b**. ...... Prv 25:15

BONES

the **b** of Joseph, which the people.....Jos 24:32
like water, and all my **b** are out of joint; . Ps 22:14
my **b** wasted away through my..........Ps 32:3
but a crushed spirit dries up the **b**........ Prv 17:22
dry **b**, hear the word of the Lord........Ezk 37:4
spirit does not have flesh and **b** as you. .Lk 24:39
"Not one of his **b** will be broken."....... Jn 19:36

BOOK

as a memorial in a **b** and recite it in the . Ex 17:14
"Take this **B** of the Law and........... Dt 31:26
This **B** of the Law shall not depart .... Jos 1:8
"I have found the **B** of the Law in the .2 Kgs 22:8
name shall be found written in the **b**. .... Dn 12:1
whose names are in the **b** of life.........Phil 4:3
not found written in the **b** of life, ...Rv 20:15
who are written in the Lamb's **b** of life... Rv 21:27

BOOKS

Of making many **b** there is no end, ... Eccl 12:12
sat in judgment, and the **b** were opened. .Dn 7:10
could not contain the **b** that would be .. Jn 21:25

BOOTHS

You shall dwell in **b** for seven days......Lv 23:42
palm, and other leafy trees to make **b**, ..Neh 8:15
Now the Jews' Feast of **B** was at hand.....Jn 7:2

BORE

yet he **b** the sin of many, and makes .....Is 53:12
took our illnesses and **b** our diseases."... Mt 8:17
He himself **b** our sins in his body on ....1 Pt 2:24

BORN

man is **b** to trouble as the sparks fly ......Jb 5:7
For unto you is **b** this day in the city of....Lk 2:11
unless one is **b** again he cannot ....Jn 3:3
this purpose I was **b** and for this........ Jn 18:37
Last of all, as to one untimely **b**, he....1 Cor 15:8
set me apart before I was **b**, ...Gal 1:15
servant, being **b** in the likeness of men. ..Phil 2:7
since you have been **b** again, not of..... 1 Pt 1:23
No one **b** of God makes a practice of ....1 Jn 3:9

BORNE

Surely he has **b** our griefs and........... Is 53:4
And I have seen and have **b** witness ..... Jn 1:34

BORROW

b vessels from all your neighbors, ...2 Kgs 4:3
not refuse the one who would **b** from you...Mt 5:42

BORROWER

the **b** is the slave of the lender.......... Prv 22:7

BOSOM

he will carry them in his **b**, and gently.... Is 40:11

BOTTOMLESS

given the key to the shaft of the **b** pit..... Rv 9:1
about to rise from the **b** pit and go to.... Rv 17:8
hand the key to the **b** pit and a great ....Rv 20:1

BOUGHT

went and sold all that he had and **b** it. ..Mt 13:46
you were **b** with a price. So glorify.... 1 Cor 6:20

BOUNTIFULLY

because he has dealt **b** with me.......... Ps 13:6
and whoever sows **b** will also reap..... 2 Cor 9:6

BOW

You shall not **b** down to them or serve .. Ex 20:5
let us worship and **b** down; let ....Ps 95:6
'To me every knee shall **b**, every........ Is 45:23
every knee shall **b** to me, ...Rom 14:11
the name of Jesus every knee should **b**, .Phil 2:10

BOWLS

on the earth the seven **b** of the wrath.... Rv 16:1

BRANCH

the **b** of the Lord shall be................ Is 4:2
and a **b** from his roots shall bear fruit.......Is 11:1
I will raise up for David a righteous **B**,... Jer 23:5
a righteous **B** to spring up for David,... Jer 33:15
behold, I will bring my servant the **B**. .....Zec 3:8
and every **b** that does bear fruit he ...... Jn 15:2

BRANCHES

the birds of the air made nests in its **b**.". Lk 13:19
I am the vine; you are the **b**. Whoever.... Jn 15:5
and if the root is holy, so are the **b**.....Rom 11:16

BREAD

king of Salem brought out **b** and wine... Gn 14:18
I am about to rain **b** from heaven........Ex 16:4
and the **b** of the Presence;............. Ex 35:13
that man does not live by **b** alone,........Dt 8:3
ravens brought him **b** and meat in .....1 Kgs 17:6
Man ate of the **b** of the angels;.........Ps 78:25
and gave them **b** from heaven in ......Ps 105:40
"'Man shall not live by **b** alone,.......... Mt 4:4
Jesus took **b**, and after blessing it ..... Mt 26:26
Give us each day our daily **b**,.............Lk 11:3
"I am the **b** of life; whoever.............Jn 6:35

CAIAPHAS
the high priest, whose name was **C**,......Mt 26:3

CAIN
C spoke to Abel his brother.............Gn 4:8
a more acceptable sacrifice than **C**,.....Heb 11:4
We should not be like **C**, who was of....1 Jn 3:12
the way of **C** and abandoned............Jude 11

CALAMITIES
from all your **c** and your distresses,...1 Sm 10:19
endurance, in afflictions, hardships, **c**,..2 Cor 6:4

CALAMITY
LORD relented from the **c** and ....2 Sm 24:16
who is glad at **c** will not go unpunished.. Prv 17:5
hardens his heart will fall into **c**........Prv 28:14

CALEB
But **C** quieted the people before Moses. .Nm 13:30
C, because he has a different spirit ....Nm 14:24
he gave Hebron to **C** the son of ....Jos 14:13

CALF
with a graving tool and made a golden **c**.. .Ex 32:4
You had made yourselves a golden **c**.....Dt 9:16
And bring the fattened **c** and kill it,.....Lk 15:23

CALL
people began to **c** upon the name of the..Gn 4:26
I **c** upon the LORD, who is..............Ps 18:3
to all who **c** on him in truth............Ps 145:18
c upon his name, make known his deeds ..Is 12:4
c upon him while he is near;............Is 55:6
Before they **c** I will answer; while they...Is 65:24
C to me and I will answer you, and will..Jer 33:3
and you shall **c** his name Jesus,.........Mt 1:21
I have not come to **c** the righteous but...Lk 5:32
How then will they **c** on him ....Rom 10:14
prize of the upward **c** of God in Christ...Phil 3:14
Here is a **c** for the endurance of the.....Rv 14:12

CALLED
God **c** the light Day, and the darkness.....Gn 1:5
And whatever the man **c** every living.....Gn 2:19
if my people who are **c** by my name ..2 Chr 7:14
I have **c** you in righteousness;...........Is 42:6
I have **c** you by name, you are mine.......Is 43:1
The LORD **c** me from the womb, ...Is 49:1
for they shall be **c** sons of God...........Mt 5:9
For many are **c**, but few are chosen."....Mt 22:14
and those whom he **c** he also justified,..Rom 8:30
For you were **c** to freedom,............Gal 5:13
just as you were **c** to the one hope .....Eph 4:4
who saved us and **c** us to a holy........2 Tm 1:9
For to this you have been **c**,...........1 Pt 2:21
c us to his own glory and excellence,.....2 Pt 1:3

CALLING
wash away your sins, **c** on his name.'..Acts 22:16
For the gifts and the **c** of God are ....Rom 11:29
For consider your **c**, brothers: not......1 Cor 1:26
in a manner worthy of the **c** to which....Eph 4:1
you worthy of his **c** and may fulfill....2 Thes 1:11
to confirm your **c** and election,.........2 Pt 1:10

CALLS
When he **c** to me, I will answer him; I ...Ps 91:15
There is no one who **c** upon your name,..Is 64:7
and he **c** his own sheep by name ....Jn 10:3
who **c** upon the name of the Lord shall. Acts 2:21
whom the Lord our God **c** to himself."..Acts 2:39
works but because of him who **c**—......Rom 9:11
For "everyone who **c** on the name of.. Rom 10:13
who **c** you into his own kingdom .....1 Thes 2:12
He who **c** you is faithful;............1 Thes 5:24

CAMEL
out a gnat and swallowing a **c**!........Mt 23:24
It is easier for a **c** to go through the eye..Mk 10:25

CAMP
"This is God's **c**!" So he called the ......Gn 32:2
and shall **c** around the tabernacle.......Nm 1:50
your God walks in the midst of your **c**,..Dt 23:14
to him outside the **c** and bear the .....Heb 13:13

CANA
day there was a wedding at **C**............Jn 2:1
So he came again to **C** in...............Jn 4:46

CANAAN
Abram settled in the land of **C**,.........Gn 13:12
"Send men to spy out the land of **C**,....Nm 13:2
I will give the land of **C**,.............1 Chr 16:18
a famine throughout all Egypt and **C**,...Acts 7:11

CANAANITE
not take a wife from the **C** women.......Gn 28:1
a **C** woman from that region came out ..Mt 15:22

CANAANITES
before you, and I will drive out the **C**,....Ex 33:2
the people of Israel lived among the **C**,...Jgs 3:5

CAPERNAUM
he went and lived in **C** by the sea,.......Mt 4:13
What we have heard you did at **C**, do....Lk 4:23
in the synagogue, as he taught at **C**......Jn 6:59

CAPTIVE
he carried the people **c** to Assyria....2 Kgs 15:29
of Babylon brought **c** to Babylon all. .2 Kgs 24:16
sword and be led **c** among all nations,..Lk 21:24
died to that which held us **c**,...........Rom 7:6
take every thought **c** to obey Christ,..2 Cor 10:5
we were held **c** under the law,..........Gal 3:23
no one takes you **c** by philosophy and ...Col 2:8

CAPTIVES
leading a host of **c** in your train ....Ps 68:18
to proclaim liberty to the **c**,..............Is 61:1
to proclaim liberty to the **c** and..........Lk 4:18
ascended on high he led a host of **c**,.....Eph 4:8

CAPTIVITY
not be yours, for they shall go into **c**. ...Dt 28:41
into **c** from Jerusalem to Babylon....2 Kgs 24:15
plead with you in the land of their **c**,..2 Chr 6:37
that time those who had come from **c**,..Ezr 8:35
until the **c** of Jerusalem in the fifth ....Jer 1:3
is to be taken captive, to **c** he goes;.....Rv 13:10

CARE
"Only take **c**, and keep your soul ....Dt 4:9
and the son of man that you **c** for him? ...Ps 8:4
him to an inn and took **c** of him.........Lk 10:34
Let each one take **c** how he builds.....1 Cor 3:10
have the same **c** for one another.......1 Cor 12:25
or the son of man, that you **c** for him? .. Heb 2:6

CAREFUL
O Israel, and be **c** to do them, that it......Dt 6:3
being **c** to do according to all the law ....Jos 1:7
Pay **c** attention to yourselves and to all..Acts 20:28
c to devote themselves to good works.....Ti 3:8

CARELESS
from evil, but a fool is reckless and **c**...Prv 14:16
account for every **c** word they speak, ...Mt 12:36

CARES
When the **c** of my heart are many,......Ps 94:19
remains to me; no one **c** for my soul....Ps 142:4
LORD of hosts **c** for his flock,...........Zec 10:3
a hired hand and **c** nothing for the......Jn 10:13
anxieties on him, because he **c** for you....1 Pt 5:7

CARMEL
the prophets together at Mount **C**....1 Kgs 18:20

CARPENTER
The **c** stretches a line; he marks it out....Is 44:13
Is not this the **c**, the son of Mary and ....Mk 6:3

CARPENTER'S
Is not this the **c** son? Is not his mother ..Mt 13:55

CARRIED
how the LORD your God **c** you,...........Dt 1:31
borne our griefs and **c** our sorrows;......Is 53:4
from them and was **c** up into heaven....Lk 24:51
God as they were **c** along by the Holy...2 Pt 1:21
And he **c** me away in the Spirit to a.....Rv 21:10

CARRY
I am not able to **c** all this people alone; .Nm 11:14
Be their shepherd and **c** them forever.....Ps 28:9

CARVED
On them he **c** cherubim and palm ....1 Kgs 6:35
to no other, nor my praise to **c** idols......Is 42:8
ministry of death, **c** in letters on stone,. 2 Cor 3:7

CASE
Any hard **c** they brought to Moses, but..Ex 18:26
and I desire to argue my **c** with God......Jb 13:3
one who states his **c** first seems right,...Prv 18:17
Set forth your **c**, says the LORD;..........Is 41:21
the governor their **c** against Paul.......Acts 24:1

CAST
them, and for my clothing they **c** lots....Ps 22:18
Why are you **c** down, O my soul, ...Ps 42:11
C me not away from your presence,......Ps 51:11
C your burden on the LORD,............Ps 55:22
You will **c** all our sins into the depths ....Mi 7:19
by the Spirit of God that I **c** out ....Mt 12:28
"How can Satan **c** out Satan?...........Mk 3:23
they **c** lots to divide his garments.......Lk 23:34
comes to me I will never **c** out...........Jn 6:37
let us **c** off the works of darkness......Rom 13:12

CASTING
his garments among them by **c** lots.....Mt 27:35
in their synagogues and **c** out demons....Mk 1:39
c all your anxieties on him, because he...1 Pt 5:7

CATCH
"Put out your hand and **c** it by the tail"—. .Ex 4:4
were astonished at the **c** of fish that ......Lk 5:9
to **c** him in something he might say.....Lk 11:54
that they might **c** him in something he . Lk 20:20

CATTLE
is mine, the **c** on a thousand hills........Ps 50:10
and the lowing of **c** is not heard; ....Jer 9:10

CAUGHT
that this man was **c** up into paradise—..2 Cor 12:3
will be **c** up together with ....1 Thes 4:17
but her child was **c** up to God and to ....Rv 12:5

CAUSE
and defend my **c** against an ungodly.....Ps 43:1
Who has wounds without **c**?..........Prv 23:29
to the fatherless, plead the widow's **c**.......Is 1:17
pleads my **c** and executes judgment ....Mi 7:9
fulfilled: 'They hated me without a **c**.' ....Jn 15:25
may have ample **c** to glory in Christ.....Phil 1:26

CAUSES
If your right eye **c** you to sin,...........Mt 5:29
but whoever **c** one of these little ones.....Mt 18:6
or do anything that **c** your brother to . Rom 14:21

CAVES
hid themselves in **c** and in holes.......1 Sm 13:6
people shall enter the **c** of the rocks......Is 2:19
hid themselves in the **c** and among the...Rv 6:15

CEASE
and winter, day and night, shall not **c**."..Gn 8:22
make our children **c** to worship the ....Jos 22:25
before my eyes; **c** to do evil,............Is 1:16
they never **c** to say, "Holy, holy, holy,......Rv 4:8

CEASES
love of the LORD never **c**;.............Lam 3:22

CEDAR
"See now, I dwell in a house of **c**,......2 Sm 7:2

love one another, just as he has c us.... 1 Jn 3:23

COMMANDER
I am the c of the army of the LORD...... Jos 5:14
a leader and c for the peoples........... Is 55:4
but a c shall put an end to his.......... Dn 11:18

COMMANDMENT
the c of the LORD is pure,............... Ps 19:8
For the c is a lamp and the teaching a .. Prv 6:23
This is the great and first c........... Mt 22:38
"This is my c, that you love one another .. Jn 15:12
Beloved, I am writing you no new c, ... 1 Jn 2:7

COMMANDMENTS
who love me and keep my c........... Ex 20:6
the words of the covenant, the Ten C... Ex 34:28
if you obey the c of the LORD........... Dt 11:27
I find my delight in your c,............ Ps 119:47
but let your heart keep my c, ... Prv 3:1
Fear God and keep his c, for this is .... Eccl 12:13
those who love him and keep his c, ... Dn 9:4
On these two c depend all the Law and .. Mt 22:40
but keeping the c of God............ 1 Cor 7:19
And his c are not burdensome.......... 1 Jn 5:3
those who keep the c of God and hold .. Rv 12:17

COMMANDS
He c even the unclean spirits, and they... Mk 1:27
that he c even winds and water,......... Lk 8:25

COMMEND
One generation shall c your works to ... Ps 145:4
Food will not c us to God............. 1 Cor 8:8

COMMENDATION
each one will receive his c from God.... 1 Cor 4:5

COMMENDED
A man is c according to his good sense,. Prv 12:8
The master c the dishonest manager for.. Lk 16:8
where they had been c to the grace of .. Acts 14:26
though c through their faith,.......... Heb 11:39

COMMIT
C your way to the LORD; trust .... Ps 37:5

COMMITS
He who c adultery lacks sense;......... Prv 6:32
wife and marries another c adultery, ... Lk 16:18

COMMITTED
lustful intent has already c adultery...... Mt 5:28
if he has c sins, he will be forgiven. ..... Jas 5:15
He c no sin, neither was deceit found in .. 1 Pt 2:22

COMMON
distinguish between the holy and the c, . Lv 10:10
were together and had all things in c... Acts 2:44
God has made clean, do not call c.' ..... Acts 11:9

COMPANION
who forsakes the c of her youth........ Prv 2:17
though she is your c and your wife ..... Mal 2:14

COMPANY
For the c of the godless is barren, ... Jb 15:34
with joy and be refreshed in your c.... Rom 15:32
"Bad c ruins good morals."........... 1 Cor 15:33

COMPARE
none can c with you! I will .... Ps 40:5
liken God, or what likeness c with him?.. Is 40:18

COMPASSION
As a father shows c to his children, ... Ps 103:13
everlasting love I will have c on you," .... Is 54:8
my c grows warm and tender........... Hos 11:8
he saw the crowds, he had c for them, .. Mt 9:36
his father saw him and felt c, and ran ... Lk 15:20
I will have c on whom I have c." .... Rom 9:15
For you had c on those in prison,..... Heb 10:34

COMPASSIONATE
if he cries to me, I will hear, for I am c... Ex 22:27
c hearts, kindness, humility,............ Col 3:12
how the Lord is c and merciful.......... Jas 5:11

COMPETENT
an eloquent man, c in the Scriptures... Acts 18:24

COMPLACENCY
and the c of fools destroys them;....... Prv 1:32
against me and your c has come to my.. Is 37:29

COMPLAINT
"Today also my c is bitter; my hand is.... Jb 23:2
I am restless in my c and I moan,........ Ps 55:2
I pour out my c before him; I........... Ps 142:2
find a ground for c against Daniel .... Dn 6:4
if one has a c against another,.......... Col 3:13

COMPLETE
For he will c what he appoints for me, .. Jb 23:14
c my joy by being of the same mind,..... Phil 2:2
that the man of God may be c,........ 2 Tm 3:17
that you may be perfect and c,.......... Jas 1:4
so that our joy may be c................ 1 Jn 1:4

COMPLETED
the house of the LORD was c.......... 2 Chr 8:16
works, and faith was c by his works; .... Jas 2:22

COMPLETELY
except for his feet, but is c clean........ Jn 13:10
God of peace himself sanctify you c,. 1 Thes 5:23

COMPLETION
bringing holiness to c in the fear of..... 2 Cor 7:1
work in you will bring it to c .... Phil 1:6

CONCEAL
he will c me under the cover of his tent;.. Ps 27:5
It is the glory of God to c things, but.... Prv 25:2

CONCEIT
slander, gossip, c, and disorder....... 2 Cor 12:20
Do nothing from selfish ambition or c, ... Phil 2:3
he is puffed up with c and understands .. 1 Tm 6:4

CONCEITED
Let us not become c, provoking one .... Gal 5:26

CONCEIVE
the virgin shall c and bear a son, ... Is 7:14
the virgin shall c and bear a son, ... Mt 1:23
you will c in your womb and bear a son,... Lk 1:31

CONCEIVED
for that which is c in her is from the ..... Mt 1:20
Elizabeth in her old age has also c a son,. Lk 1:36
Then desire when it has c gives birth..... Jas 1:15

CONDEMN
save him from those who c his soul.... Ps 109:31
c not, and you will not be condemned;... Lk 6:37
his Son into the world to c the world, ... Jn 3:17
And Jesus said, "Neither do I c you;....... Jn 8:11
Who is to c? Christ Jesus is the one.... Rom 8:34
if our heart does not c us, we .... 1 Jn 3:21

CONDEMNATION
C is ready for scoffers, and beating for.. Prv 19:29
They will receive the greater c." .... Mk 12:40
as one trespass led to c for all men,.... Rom 5:18
There is therefore now no c for those ... Rom 8:1
be no, so that you may not fall under c.. Jas 5:12
Their c from long ago is not idle, ... 2 Pt 2:3

CONDEMNED
and by your words you will be c."....... Mt 12:37
rulers delivered him up to be c to death, .. Lk 24:20
Whoever believes in him is not c,........ Jn 3:18
for sin, he c sin in the flesh,............ Rom 8:3
By this he c the world and became an .. Heb 11:7

CONDEMNS
for whenever our heart c us, God is.... 1 Jn 3:20

CONDUCT
but the c of the pure is upright......... Prv 21:8
For rulers are not a terror to good c,... Rom 13:3
By his good c let him show his works ... Jas 3:13
is holy, you also be holy in all your c,..... 1 Pt 1:15

CONFESS
c my transgressions to the LORD,"........ Ps 32:5
if you c with your mouth that Jesus is.. Rom 10:9
c your sins to one another............. Jas 5:16
If we c our sins, he is faithful and just .... 1 Jn 1:9
not c the coming of Jesus Christ in the flesh... 2 Jn 7
I will c his name before my Father........ Rv 3:5

CONFESSES
but he who c and forsakes them will... Prv 28:13
and with the mouth one c and is saved.. Rom 10:10
Whoever c that Jesus is the Son of God,.. 1 Jn 4:15

CONFESSION
Now then make c to the LORD,.......... Ezr 10:11
that comes from your c of the gospel . 2 Cor 9:13
you made the good c in the presence .. 1 Tm 6:12
us hold fast the c of our hope without.. Heb 10:23

CONFIDENCE
Is not your fear of God your c, ... Jb 4:6
for the LORD will be your c............. Prv 3:26
we have boldness and access with c .... Eph 3:12
And we have c in the Lord about you,.. 2 Thes 3:4
if indeed we hold fast our c............ Heb 3:6
Let us then with c draw near........... Heb 4:16
since we have c to enter the holy...... Heb 10:19
appears we may have c and not shrink . 1 Jn 2:28
not condemn us, we have c before God;. 1 Jn 3:21

CONFIRM
in order to c the promises given to .... Rom 15:8
will himself restore, c, strengthen, ... 1 Pt 5:10

CONFIRMED
with them and c the message by ...... Mk 16:20
about Christ was c among you—........ 1 Cor 1:6

CONFORMED
he also predestined to be c to the ..... Rom 8:29
Do not be c to this world, but be ...... Rom 12:2
do not be c to the passions of your..... 1 Pt 1:14

CONFUSE
go down and there c their language,..... Gn 11:7

CONGREGATION
and having gathered the c together, .. Acts 15:30
in the midst of the c I will sing your..... Heb 2:12

CONQUER
and he came out conquering, and to c..... Rv 6:2
the Lamb will c them, for he is Lord of .. Rv 17:14

CONQUERED
who through faith c kingdoms,........ Heb 11:33
also those who had c the beast and its... Rv 15:2

CONQUERORS
we are more than c through him....... Rom 8:37

CONSCIENCE
to have a clear c toward both God.... Acts 24:16
while their c also bears witness,....... Rom 2:15
their c, being weak, is defiled.......... 1 Cor 8:7
any question on the ground of c...... 1 Cor 10:25
testimony of our c, that we behaved ... 2 Cor 1:12
the mystery of the faith with a clear c... 1 Tm 3:9
but as an appeal to God for a good c,... 1 Pt 3:21

CONSCIENCES
insincerity of liars whose c are seared, .. 1 Tm 4:2
both their minds and their c are defiled.... Ti 1:15

CONSECRATE
"C to me all the firstborn................ Ex 13:2
C yourselves, therefore, and be holy,..... Lv 20:7
C a fast; call a solemn assembly........... Jl 1:14
And for their sake I c myself, that........ Jn 17:19

COVERED
is forgiven, whose sin is **c**. . . . . Ps 32:1
is trustworthy in spirit keeps a thing **c**. . . Prv 11:13
Nothing is **c** up that will not be. . . . . Lk 12:2
are forgiven, and whose sins are **c**;. . . . . .Rom 4:7
prophesies with his head **c** dishonors . . 1 Cor 11:4

COVERS
Whoever **c** an offense seeks love,. . . . . . . Prv 17:9
since love **c** a multitude of sins. . . . . .1 Pt 4:8

COVET
"You shall not **c** your neighbor's. . . . . Ex 20:17
They **c** fields and seize them,. . . . . Mi 2:2
You shall not **c**," and any other . . . . Rom 13:9
You **c** and cannot obtain, so you fight. . . . Jas 4:2

COVETOUSNESS
be on your guard against all **c**, ...Lk 12:15
produced in me all kinds of **c**. . . . . .Rom 7:8
all impurity or **c** must not even be . . . . . . Eph 5:3
impurity, passion, evil desire, and **c**,. . . . . . Col 3:5

CRAFTINESS
He catches the wise in their own **c**, ... Jb 5:13
"He catches the wise in their **c**," . . . . . . .1 Cor 3:19

CRAVES
soul of the sluggard **c** and gets nothing,. Prv 13:4
All day long he **c** and **c**, but. . . . . Prv 21:26

CREATE
C in me a clean heart, O God, ... Ps 51:10
I form light and **c** darkness, I make . . . . . . Is 45:7
I **c** new heavens and a new earth,. . . . . . . .Is 65:17
that he might **c** in himself one new man . .Eph 2:15

CREATED
God **c** the heavens and the earth.. . . . . Gn 1:1
So God **c** man in his own image,. . . . . .Gn 1:27
Male and female he **c** them, and he . . . . . . Gn 5:2
For he commanded and they were **c**.. . . . Ps 148:5
Lord, who **c** the heavens and . . . . Is 42:5
read that he who **c** them from the . . . . . . .Mt 19:4
of the creation that God **c** until now, ... Mk 13:19
Neither was man **c** for woman, but . . . . 1 Cor 11:9
c in Christ Jesus for good works, ...Eph 2:10
hidden for ages in God who **c** all things,. Eph 3:9
For by him all things were **c**, in heaven . . .Col 1:16
For everything **c** by God is good, ...1 Tm 4:4
the universe was **c** by the word of God, . Heb 11:3
honor and power, for you **c** all things, ... Rv 4:11
who **c** heaven and what is in it,. . . . . .Rv 10:6

CREATION
beginning of **c**, 'God made them male. . . Mk 10:6
For the **c** waits with eager longing. . . . . Rom 8:19
in Christ, he is a new **c**. The old has. . . .2 Cor 5:17
nor uncircumcision, but a new **c**.. . . . . . . Gal 6:15
the invisible God, the firstborn of all **c**. . . .Col 1:15
true witness, the beginning of God's **c**. . . . Rv 3:14

CREATOR
Remember also your **C** in the days of . . . Eccl 12:1
God, the **C** of the ends of the earth.. . . . . Is 40:28
served the creature rather than the **C**,. . Rom 1:25
in knowledge after the image of its **c**. . . . Col 3:10
souls to a faithful **C** while doing good. . .1 Pt 4:19

CREATURE
whatever the man called every living **c**,. . .Gn 2:19
For the life of every **c** is its blood: . . . . . . .Lv 17:14
Each **c** had two wings, each of which . . . . Ezk 1:11
And no **c** is hidden from his sight, but. . .Heb 4:13

CREATURES
bring forth living **c** according to their . . . .Gn 1:24
the earth is full of your **c**. . . . . .Ps 104:24
of it came the likeness of four living **c**. . . . Ezk 1:5
should be a kind of firstfruits of his **c**. . . . .Jas 1:18
c of instinct, born to be caught. . . . . .2 Pt 2:12
and the four living **c** fell down and. . . . . . .Rv 19:4

CRIED
I **c** to you for help, and you . . . . .Ps 30:2
left alone, I fell upon my face, and **c**, ...Ezk 9:8
the ninth hour Jesus **c** out with a loud . Mt 27:46
Once more they **c** out, "Hallelujah! . . . . Rv 19:3

CRIMINAL
suffering, bound with chains as a **c**. . . . 2 Tm 2:9

CRIMINALS
there they crucified him, and the **c**, ...Lk 23:33

CRIPPLED
saw the mute speaking, the **c** healthy,. . . Mt 15:31
better for you to enter life **c** . . . . Mt 18:8
a good deed done to a **c** man, ...Acts 4:9

CROOKED
they are a **c** and twisted generation. . . . . .Dt 32:5
The way of the guilty is **c**, ... Prv 21:8
the **c** shall become straight,. . . . . .Lk 3:5
without blemish in the midst of a **c** . . . . . Phil 2:15

CROPS
but abundant **c** come by the strength . . . Prv 14:4
for I have nowhere to store my **c**?' . . . . . . .Lk 12:17
ought to have the first share of the **c**. . . 2 Tm 2:6

CROSS
whoever does not take his **c** and follow . .Mt 10:38
let him come down now from the **c**,. . . . Mt 27:42
but standing by the **c** of Jesus were his . Jn 19:25
lest the **c** of Christ be emptied of its . . . 1 Cor 1:17
For the word of the **c** is folly to those . . 1 Cor 1:18
boast except in the **c** of our Lord . . . . Gal 6:14
point of death, even death on a **c**. . . . . . . .Phil 2:8
set aside, nailing it to the **c**. . . . . Col 2:14
that was set before him endured the **c**,. .Heb 12:2

CROWD
compassion on the **c** because they. . . . . .Mt 15:32
could not get near him because of the **c**, . Mk 2:4
And all the **c** sought to touch him, for. . . . Lk 6:19
withdrawn, as there was a **c** in the place. . Jn 5:13

CROWDS
Then he ordered the **c** to sit down on . . . Mt 14:19
and great **c** gathered to hear him and to . Lk 5:15

CROWN
you set a **c** of fine gold upon his head. . . . Ps 21:3
You shall be a **c** of beauty in the hand . . . Is 62:3
wearing the **c** of thorns and the purple. . . Jn 19:5
whom I love and long for, my joy and **c**, . Phil 4:1
laid up for me the **c** of righteousness, . . 2 Tm 4:8
the test he will receive the **c** of life, ...Jas 1:12
receive the unfading **c** of glory.. . . . . .1 Pt 5:4
and I will give you the **c** of life.. . . . . .Rv 2:10

CROWNED
heavenly beings and **c** him with glory . . . . .Ps 8:5
An athlete is not **c** unless he competes . .2 Tm 2:5
Jesus, **c** with glory and honor because . . Heb 2:9

CROWNS
who **c** you with steadfast love and. . . . . .Ps 103:4
They cast their **c** before the throne, ...Rv 4:10

CRUCIFIED
mocked and flogged and **c**, ...Mt 20:19
I know that you seek Jesus who was **c**. . . .Mt 28:5
is called The Skull, there they **c** him, ...Lk 23:33
of sinful men and be **c** and on the third . .Lk 24:7
There they **c** him, and with him two. . . . . Jn 19:18
this Jesus whom you **c**." . . . . .Acts 2:36
know that our old self was **c** with him. . .Rom 6:6
but we preach Christ **c**, ...1 Cor 1:23
For he was **c** in weakness, but lives . . . 2 Cor 13:4
I have been **c** with Christ. . . . . .Gal 2:20
by which the world has been **c** to me,. . . Gal 6:14
where their Lord was **c**.. . . . . Rv 11:8

CRUCIFY
him and led him away to **c** him. . . . . .Mt 27:31
"**C**, **c** him!" . . . . Lk 23:21
"Shall I **c** your King?" The chief . . . . .Jn 19:15

CRUCIFYING
since they are **c** once again the Son of . . Heb 6:6

CRUSH
They **c** your people, O Lord, ...Ps 94:5
the will of the Lord to **c** him;. . . . . .Is 53:10
who oppress the poor, who **c** the needy,. . Am 4:1
when it falls on anyone, it will **c** him." . . .Mt 21:44
The God of peace will soon **c** Satan. . . Rom 16:20

CRUSHED
brokenhearted and saves the **c** in spirit. . Ps 34:18
but by sorrow of heart the spirit is **c**.. . . .Prv 15:13
but a **c** spirit dries up the bones. . . . . . . Prv 17:22
but not **c**; perplexed, but not. . . . . 2 Cor 4:8

CRY
he inclined to me and heard my **c**. . . . . . . Ps 40:1
I rise before dawn and **c** for help;. . . . . .Ps 119:147
He will not **c** aloud or lift up his voice,. . . . Is 42:2
They do not **c** to me from the heart, ...Hos 7:14
He will not quarrel or **c** aloud,. . . . . Mt 12:19
Jesus uttered a loud **c** and breathed his. .Mk 15:37
silent, the very stones would **c** out.". . . . .Lk 19:40

CRYSTAL
expanse, shining like awe-inspiring **c**,. . . . Ezk 1:22
river of the water of life, bright as **c**, ... Rv 22:1

CUP
is my chosen portion and my **c**; . . . . Ps 16:5
head with oil; my **c** overflows. . . . . .Ps 23:5
my hand this **c** of the wine of wrath,. . . Jer 25:15
little ones even a **c** of cold water . . . . . . .Mt 10:42
you clean the outside of the **c**. . . . . .Mt 23:25
if it be possible, let this **c** pass . . . . Mt 26:39
shall I not drink the **c** that the Father . . . . Jn 18:11
"This **c** is the new covenant . . . . 1 Cor 11:25
full strength into the **c** of his anger, ... Rv 14:10

CURE
He would **c** him of his leprosy." . . . . .2 Kgs 5:3
he is not able to **c** you or heal your . . . . .Hos 5:13
over all demons and to **c** diseases,. . . . . Lk 9:1

CURED
troubled with unclean spirits were **c**. . . . . . Lk 6:18
had diseases also came and were **c**.. . . .Acts 28:9

CURSE
"I will never again **c** the ground . . . . .Gn 8:21
and him who dishonors you I will **c**, ...Gn 12:3
revile God, nor **c** a ruler of your people. .Ex 22:28
The Lord's **c** is on the house of. . . . . Prv 3:33
You are cursed with a **c**, for you are. . . . . .Mal 3:9
began to invoke a **c** on himself and to. . .Mt 26:74
of the law by becoming a **c** for us— . . . . . Gal 3:13
with it we **c** people who are made in. . . . . Jas 3:9

CURSED
c is the ground because of you; . . . . .Gn 3:17
The fig tree that you **c** has withered." . . . .Mk 11:21
"**C** is everyone who is hanged on a" . . . . . Gal 3:13
and they **c** the name of God who had . . . . Rv 16:9

CURSES
If one **c** his father or his mother, his. . . Prv 20:20
mouth is full of **c** and bitterness." . . . . . . Rom 3:14

CURTAIN
length of each **c** shall be twenty-eight . . .Ex 26:2
who stretches out the heavens like a **c**,. . Is 40:22
the **c** of the temple was torn in two, ... Mt 27:51
that he opened for us through the **c**,. . Heb 10:20

CUT
"I am **c** off from your sight." But you. . . . Ps 31:22
considered that he was **c** off out of the. . . Is 53:8
everlasting name that shall not be **c** off. . . Is 56:5
you to sin, **c** it off and throw it away. . . . Mt 5:30
of the high priest and **c** off his ear.. . . . . .Mt 26:51

they heard this they were **c** to the heart,. . Acts 2:37

CYMBAL

I am a noisy gong or a clanging **c**. . . . . . 1 Cor 13:1

CYRUS

"Thus says **C** king of Persia,. . . . . 2 Chr 36:23
In the first year of **C** king of Persia, ... Ezr 1:1
was there until the first year of King **C**. . . . Dn 1:21

DAGON

offer a great sacrifice to **D** their god . . . Jgs 16:23
it into the house of **D** and set it up . . . . . 1 Sm 5:2

DAILY

twice as much as they gather **d**." . . . . Ex 16:5
Blessed be the Lord, who **d** bears us up;. . Ps 68:19
Give us this day our **d** bread,. . . . . Mt 6:11
and take up his cross **d** and follow me. . . . Lk 9:23
examining the Scriptures **d** to see if. . . . Acts 17:11

DAMASCUS

him for letters to the synagogues at **D**,. . Acts 9:2

DAN

Therefore she called his name **D**. . . . . Gn 30:6
"**D** shall judge his people as one of the . Gn 49:16
And the people of **D** set up the carved . Jgs 18:30

DANCE

Praise him with tambourine and **d**;. . . . . . Ps 150:4
a time to mourn, and a time to **d**;. . . . . . . Eccl 3:4
for you, and you did not **d**; we sang a. . . . Mt 11:17

DANCED

And David **d** before the LORD. . . . . 2 Sm 6:14
daughter of Herodias **d** before the. . . . . . . Mt 14:6

DANCING

the camp and saw the calf and the **d**, . . . Ex 32:19
turned for me my mourning into **d**; . . . . . Ps 30:11
Let them praise his name with **d**, ... Ps 149:3
our **d** has been turned to mourning. . . . Lam 5:15

DANGER

The prudent sees **d** and hides himself,. . Prv 27:12
frequent journeys, in **d** from rivers,. . . . 2 Cor 11:26

DANIEL

even if Noah, **D**, and Job were in it, ... Ezk 14:20
D he called Belteshazzar, ... Dn 1:7
And God gave **D** favor and compassion . . . Dn 1:9
Then this **D** became distinguished . . . . Dn 6:3
D was brought and cast into the den. . . . . Dn 6:16
desolation spoken of by the prophet **D**, . Mt 24:15

DARE

good person one would **d** even to die— . Rom 5:7

DARIUS

even until the reign of **D** king of Persia. . . Ezr 4:5
And **D** the Mede received the kingdom, . . Dn 5:31
In the second year of **D** the king, in the . . . Hg 1:1

DARK

even the darkness is not **d** to you; . . . . . Ps 139:12
body is full of light, having no part **d**, . . . Lk 11:36
whatever you have said in the **d** shall . . . . Lk 12:3
to the tomb early, while it was still **d**, ... Jn 20:1

DARKENED

the whole land, so that the land was **d**,. . Ex 10:15
that tribulation, the sun will be **d**,. . . . . . . Mk 13:24
and their foolish hearts were **d**. . . . . Rom 1:21
They are **d** in their understanding, ... Eph 4:18

DARKNESS

was pitch **d** in all the land of Egypt . . . . . Ex 10:22
who walked in **d** have seen a great . . . . Is 9:2
The sun shall be turned to **d**,. . . . . Jl 2:31
the people dwelling in **d** have seen . . . . . . Mt 4:16
is bad, your whole body will be full of **d**. . Mt 6:23
will be thrown into the outer **d**. . . . . Mt 8:12
loved the **d** rather than the light. . . . . Jn 3:19
Whoever follows me will not walk in **d**, . . . Jn 8:12
Or what fellowship has light with **d**? . . 2 Cor 6:14
for at one time you were **d**, but now . . . . Eph 5:8
God is light, and in him is no **d** at all. . . . . 1 Jn 1:5
chains under gloomy **d** until the . . . . Jude 6
and its kingdom was plunged into **d**. . . . . Rv 16:10

DAUGHTER

"Please tell me whose **d** you are. . . . . . . Gn 24:23
shall transfer his inheritance to his **d**. . . . Nm 27:8
year to lament the **d** of Jephthah the . . Jgs 11:40
For the wound of the **d** of my people is . . Jer 8:21
about you: 'Like mother, like **d**.'. . . . . Ezk 16:44
Rejoice greatly, O **d** of Zion! Shout. . . . . . . Zec 9:9
"My **d** has just died, but come and. . . . . . . Mt 9:18
his father, and a **d** against her mother, . . Mt 10:35
"**D**, your faith has made you well;. . . . . . . Mk 5:34

DAUGHTERS

Jesus said, "**D** of Jerusalem, do not . . . . . Lk 23:28
and you shall be sons and **d** to me, . . . 2 Cor 6:18

DAVID

was the father of Jesse, the father of **D**. . . Ru 4:17
Spirit of the LORD rushed upon **D** . . . . . 1 Sm 16:13
and there they anointed **D** king over . . . 2 Sm 2:4
D said to Nathan, "I have sinned. . . . . . 2 Sm 12:13
And **D** built there an altar to the. . . . . 2 Sm 24:25
D said to Solomon, "My son, I had . . . . . 1 Chr 22:7
anointed, to **D** and his offspring forever. . Ps 18:50
covenant, my steadfast, sure love for **D**. . . Is 55:3
the son of **D**, the son of Abraham. . . . . Mt 1:1
"Have mercy on us, Son of **D**.". . . . . Mt 9:27
to the city of **D**, which is called. . . . . Lk 2:4
Christ comes from the offspring of **D**, ... Jn 7:42
risen from the dead, the offspring of **D**, . 2 Tm 2:8
of **D** and Samuel and the prophets— . . . Heb 11:32
of Judah, the Root of **D**, has conquered,. . . Rv 5:5
I am the root and the descendant of **D**,. . Rv 22:16

DAY

God called the light **D**, and the . . . . Gn 1:5
for it is a **D** of Atonement, to make . . . . . Lv 23:28
in a pillar of cloud by **d** and in a pillar . . Nm 14:14
There has been no **d** like it before or . . . Jos 10:14
This is the **d** that the LORD has . . . . Ps 118:24
you do not know what a **d** may bring. . . . Prv 27:1
for the **d** of the LORD is near;. . . . . Is 13:6
For the **d** of the LORD is great . . . . Jl 2:11
For the **d** of the LORD is near . . . . Ob 15
And there shall be a unique **d**, which is. . Zec 14:7
But who can endure the **d** of his coming, . Mal 3:2
do not know on what **d** your Lord is . . . Mt 24:42
given me, but raise it up on the last **d**. . . Jn 6:39
manifest, for the **D** will disclose it, ... 1 Cor 3:13
spirit may be saved in the **d** of the Lord. . . 1 Cor 5:5
were sealed for the **d** of redemption. . . . Eph 4:30
it to completion at the **d** of Jesus Christ. . Phil 1:6
d of the Lord will come like a thief. . . . . 1 Thes 5:2
that he is able to guard until that **D**. . . . 2 Tm 1:12
more as you see the **D** drawing near. . . Heb 10:25
with the Lord one **d** is as a thousand. . . . 2 Pt 3:8
battle on the great **d** of God the. . . . . Rv 16:14

DAYS

for he is flesh: his **d** shall be 120 years." . . Gn 6:3
he shall read in it all the **d** of his life,. . . . . Dt 17:19
in those **d** I will pour out my Spirit. . . . . . . Jl 2:29
be killed, and after three **d** rise again. . . . . Mk 8:31
use of the time, because the **d** are evil. . . Eph 5:16
that in the last **d** there will come times. . 2 Tm 3:1
but in these last **d** he has spoken to us. . . Heb 1:2
scoffers will come in the last **d** with. . . . . 2 Pt 3:3

DEACONS

at Philippi, with the overseers and **d**: . . . . . Phil 1:1
D likewise must be dignified, not . . . . 1 Tm 3:8
Let **d** each be the husband of one . . . . . 1 Tm 3:12

DEAD

he stood between the **d** and the living, . . Nm 16:48
I have been forgotten like one who is **d**; . . Ps 31:12
Your **d** shall live; their bodies shall rise. . . Is 26:19
leave the **d** to bury their own **d**." . . . . Mt 8:22
disciples that he has risen from the **d**, . . . Mt 28:7
He is not God of the **d**, but of the living. . Mk 12:27
do you seek the living among the **d**? . . . . . Lk 24:5
But God raised him from the **d**,. . . . . . . Acts 13:30
Christ to suffer and to rise from the **d**, . . Acts 17:3
who raised from the **d** Jesus our Lord,. . Rom 4:24
must consider yourselves **d** to sin. . . . . . . Rom 6:11
For if the **d** are not raised, ... 1 Cor 15:16
And you were **d** in the trespasses. . . . . Eph 2:1
may attain the resurrection from the **d**. . Phil 3:11
of God, who raised him from the **d**. . . . . . Col 2:12
And the **d** in Christ will rise first. . . . . . . 1 Thes 4:16
who is to judge the living and the **d**, ... 2 Tm 4:1
faith apart from works is **d**. . . . . Jas 2:26
ready to judge the living and the **d**. . . . . . . 1 Pt 4:5
And the **d** were judged by what was . . . . Rv 20:12

DEADLY

He delivered us from such a **d** peril,. . . . 2 Cor 1:10
tongue. It is a restless evil, full of **d** . . . . . . Jas 3:8

DEAF

Who makes him mute, or **d**, or seeing, . . . Ex 4:11
In that day the **d** shall hear the words. . . . Is 29:18
"You mute and **d** spirit, I command . . . . . Mk 9:25

DEAL

we will **d** kindly and faithfully with. . . . . . Jos 2:14
his prayer not to **d** with you according . . . Jb 42:8
children who will not **d** falsely.". . . . . Is 63:8
I will **d** with you as you have done, ... Ezk 16:59

DEATH

that I have set before you life and **d**, ... Dt 30:19
if anything but **d** parts me from you." . . . . Ru 1:17
through the valley of the shadow of **d**, . . . Ps 23:4
For you have delivered my soul from **d**, . Ps 56:13
the LORD is the **d** of his saints. . . . . Ps 116:15
Her feet go down to **d**; her steps follow . . Prv 5:5
to a man, but its end is the way to **d**. . . Prv 14:12
upon your arm, for love is strong as **d**, ... Sg 8:6
He will swallow up **d** forever;. . . . . Is 25:8
I have no pleasure in the **d** of anyone,. . Ezk 18:32
O **D**, where are your plagues? . . . . Hos 13:14
who will not taste **d** until they see the. . . Mt 16:28
but has passed from **d** to life. . . . . Jn 5:24
keeps my word, he will never see **d**." . . . . . Jn 8:51
reconciled to God by the **d** of his Son, . Rom 5:10
For the wages of sin is **d**, but the free . . Rom 6:23
Christ Jesus from the law of sin and **d**. . . Rom 8:2
I am sure that neither **d** nor life, ... Rom 8:38
"O **d**, where is your victory?. . . . . 1 Cor 15:55
point of **d**, even **d** on a cross. . . . . Phil 2:8
sufferings, becoming like him in his **d**, . . . Phil 3:10
Put to **d** therefore what is earthly in . . . . . Col 3:5
through **d** he might destroy the one . . . . Heb 2:14
when it is fully grown brings forth **d**. . . . . . Jas 1:15
we have passed out of **d** into life,. . . . . . . 1 Jn 3:14
There is sin that leads to **d**; . . . . 1 Jn 5:16
they loved not their lives even unto **d**. . . . Rv 12:11
Over such the second **d** has no power, . . Rv 20:6
This is the second **d**, the lake of fire. . . . . Rv 20:14
from their eyes, and **d** shall be no more,. . Rv 21:4

DEBASED

gave them up to a **d** mind to do what. . Rom 1:28

DEBAUCHERY

and not open to the charge of **d**. . . . . Ti 1:6
do not join them in the same flood of **d**,. 1 Pt 4:4

DEBORAH

Now **D**, a prophetess, the wife. . . . . Jgs 4:4

DEBT

I forgave you all that **d** because you . . . . Mt 18:32
by canceling the record of **d** that stood . Col 2:14

DEBTORS

"A certain moneylender had two **d**. . . . . . . Lk 7:41
summoning his master's **d** one by one, . . . Lk 16:5
we are **d**, not to the flesh, to live . . . . . . Rom 8:12

DEBTS
"Go, sell the oil and pay your **d**, ... 2 Kgs 4:7
and forgive us our **d**, as we also have . . . . Mt 6:12

DECEIT
and in whose spirit there is no **d**. . . . . Ps 32:2
D is in the heart of those who devise . . Prv 12:20
and there was no **d** in his mouth. . . . . Is 53:9
d, sensuality, envy, slander,. . . . . Mk 7:22
full of envy, murder, strife, **d**, ... Rom 1:29
neither was **d** found in his mouth. . . . . . . 1 Pt 2:22

DECEITFUL
Charm is **d**, and beauty is vain, but a. . . Prv 31:30
The heart is **d** above all things, ... Jer 17:9
false apostles, **d** workmen, disguising . 2 Cor 11:13

DECEITFULNESS
cares of the world and the **d** of riches. . . Mt 13:22
may be hardened by the **d** of sin. . . . . Heb 3:13

DECEIVE
d us, saying, 'We are very far from. . . . . . Jos 9:22
diviners who are among you **d** you, ... Jer 29:8
Let no one **d** himself. If anyone . . . . 1 Cor 3:18
Let no one **d** you with empty words, ... Eph 5:6
we **d** ourselves, and the truth . . . . 1 Jn 1:8
will come out to **d** the nations that are . . Rv 20:8

DECEIVED
"The serpent **d** me, and I ate.". . . . . Gn 3:13
Take care lest your heart be **d**, ... Dt 11:16
Do not be **d**: "Bad company ruins. . . . . 1 Cor 15:33
Do not be **d**: God is not mocked, ... Gal 6:7
not **d**, but the woman was **d** . . . . 1 Tm 2:14

DECEIVER
Such a one is the **d** and the antichrist.. . . . . 2 Jn 7
Satan, the **d** of the whole world— . . . . Rv 12:9

DECEIVERS
empty talkers and **d**, especially. . . . . Ti 1:10
For many **d** have gone out into the . . . . 2 Jn 7

DECEIVES
when he is nothing, he **d** himself. . . . . Gal 6:3
not bridle his tongue but **d** his heart, ... Jas 1:26
of the beast it **d** those who dwell on . . . . Rv 13:14

DECEIVING
his way, but the folly of fools is **d**. . . . . . . Prv 14:8
bad to worse, **d** and being deceived. . . . 2 Tm 3:13

DECISION
but its every **d** is from the LORD. . . . . Prv 16:33
the **d** by the word of the holy ones, ... Dn 4:17
LORD is near in the valley of **d**.. . . . . Jl 3:14
For my **d** is to gather nations, to . . . . Zep 3:8

DECLARE
The heavens **d** the glory of God, ... Ps 19:1
to **d** your steadfast love in the morning, . . Ps 92:2
D his glory among the nations, his. . . . . . . Ps 96:3
and new things I now **d**; before they . . . . . Is 42:9
d how much God has done for you." . . . . . Lk 8:39
D these things; exhort and rebuke . . . . Ti 2:15

DECREASE
He must increase, but I must **d**.". . . . . Jn 3:30

DECREED
Whatever is **d** by the God of heaven, ... Ezr 7:23
which God **d** before the ages for our. . . . 1 Cor 2:7

DEDICATION
celebrated the **d** of this house of God . . . Ezr 6:16
time the Feast of **D** took place at. . . . . . . Jn 10:22

DEED
God will bring every **d** into judgment, . . Eccl 12:14
what good **d** must I do to have eternal. . Mt 19:16
Lord will rescue me from every evil **d** . . 2 Tm 4:18
let us not love in word or talk but in **d** . . 1 Jn 3:18

DEEDS
awesome in glorious **d**, doing wonders? . . Ex 15:11
make known his **d** among the peoples! . . Ps 105:1
all our righteous **d** are like a polluted . . . . Is 64:6
They do all their **d** to be seen by . . . . Mt 23:5
are receiving the due reward of our **d**;. . . Lk 23:41
d in keeping with their repentance. . . . Acts 26:20
impartially according to each one's **d**, ... 1 Pt 1:17
may see your good **d** and glorify God. . . 1 Pt 2:12
linen is the righteous **d** of the saints. . . . . . Rv 19:8

DEEP
and darkness was over the face of the **d**. . . Gn 1:2
the fountains of the great **d** burst forth, . . Gn 7:11
He makes the **d** boil like a pot; he makes . . Jb 41:31
D calls to **d** at the roar of your . . . . Ps 42:7
he drew a circle on the face of the **d**, . . . Prv 8:27
to draw water with, and the well is **d**. . . . . Jn 4:11

DEER
As a **d** pants for flowing streams, ... Ps 42:1

DEFEND
For I will **d** this city to save it, for my . . 2 Kgs 19:34
d the rights of the poor and needy. . . . . . Prv 31:9
they do not **d** the rights of the needy. . . . Jer 5:28
how you should **d** yourself or what you . . Lk 12:11

DEFENSE
I am put here for the **d** of the gospel. . . . Phil 1:16
being prepared to make a **d** to anyone . . 1 Pt 3:15

DEFILE
resolved that he would not **d** himself. . . . . . Dn 1:8
These are what **d** a person. . . . . Mt 15:20

DEFILED
The earth lies **d** under its inhabitants; . . . . Is 24:5
you **d** my land and made my heritage. . . . Jer 2:7
and their conscience, being weak, is **d**. . 1 Cor 8:7

DEFRAUDED
And if I have **d** anyone of anything, I. . . . . Lk 19:8
suffer wrong? Why not rather be **d**? . . . . 1 Cor 6:7

DELAY
not far off, and my salvation will not **d**;. . . Is 46:13
Will he **d** long over them? . . . . Lk 18:7
upon the earth fully and without **d**." . . . Rom 9:28
coming one will come and will not **d**; . . Heb 10:37
that there would be no more **d**, ... Rv 10:6

DELAYED
people saw that Moses **d** to come down. . Ex 32:1
says to himself, 'My master is **d**,' . . . . Mt 24:48
As the bridegroom was **d**, they all . . . . Mt 25:5

DELIGHT
his **d** is in the law of the LORD, ... Ps 1:2
D yourself in the LORD, ... Ps 37:4
For you will not **d** in sacrifice, or I . . . . . . Ps 51:16
to me a joy and the **d** of my heart, ... Jer 15:16
For I **d** in the law of God, in my inner . . Rom 7:22

DELIGHTS
them drink from the river of your **d**.. . . . . Ps 36:8
you are, O loved one, with all your **d**! . . . . . Sg 7:6
my chosen, in whom my soul **d**; . . . . Is 42:1
forever, because he **d** in steadfast love. . . . Mi 7:18

DELILAH
So **D** said to Samson, "Please tell me. . . . Jgs 16:6

DELIVER
I have come down to **d** them out of the . . . Ex 3:8
there is none that can **d** out of my hand. . Dt 32:39
"He trusts in the LORD; let him **d** . . . . Ps 22:8
but **d** us from evil. . . . . Mt 6:13
He trusts in God; let God **d** him now, . . . Mt 27:43
gave himself for our sins to **d** us. . . . . Gal 1:4

DELIVERANCE
you surround me with shouts of **d**. . . . . . . Ps 32:7
Jesus Christ this will turn out for my **d**, . . Phil 1:19

DELIVERED
For you have **d** my soul from death, ... Ps 56:13
Son of Man will be **d** up to be crucified." Mt 26:2
who was **d** up for our trespasses . . . . . . Rom 4:25
He **d** us from such a deadly peril, ... 2 Cor 1:10
He has **d** us from the domain of . . . . Col 1:13
and that we may be **d** from wicked . . . 2 Thes 3:2

DELIVERER
the LORD raised up a **d** for the. . . . . Jgs 3:9
my rock and my fortress and my **d**, ... Ps 18:2
"The **D** will come from Zion, ... Rom 11:26

DELIVERS
the LORD hears and **d** them out. . . . . Ps 34:17
but righteousness **d** from death. . . . . Prv 10:2
when he **d** the kingdom to God . . . . . . 1 Cor 15:24
d us from the wrath to come. . . . . 1 Thes 1:10

DELUSION
breath; those of high estate are a **d**; . . . . . Ps 62:9
Behold, they are all a **d**; their works. . . . . . Is 41:29
God sends them a strong **d**, ... 2 Thes 2:11

DEMAND
away your goods do not **d** them back. . . . Lk 6:30

DEMON
And when the **d** had been cast out, ... Mt 9:33
daughter is severely oppressed by a **d**." . Mt 15:22
man who had the spirit of an unclean **d**, . Lk 4:33
he was casting out a **d** that was mute. . . . Lk 11:14
words of one who is oppressed by a **d**. . . Jn 10:21

DEMON-OPPRESSED
a **d** man who was mute was brought. . . . . Mt 9:32
Then a **d** man who was blind. . . . . Mt 12:22

DEMON-POSSESSED
two **d** men met him, coming out. . . . . Mt 8:28
what had happened to the **d** men. . . . . Mt 8:33

DEMONIC
above, but is earthly, unspiritual, **d**. . . . . . Jas 3:15
For they are **d** spirits, performing signs, . Rv 16:14

DEMONS
They sacrificed to **d** that were no gods, . Dt 32:17
sons and their daughters to the **d**; . . . . . Ps 106:37
And if I cast out **d** by Beelzebul, by . . . . . Mt 12:27
they cast out many **d** and anointed . . . . . . Mk 6:13
and authority over all **d** and to cure. . . . . . . Lk 9:1
they offer to **d** and not to God. . . . . . . 1 Cor 10:20
to deceitful spirits and teachings of **d**, . . . 1 Tm 4:1
Even the **d** believe—and shudder!. . . . . . . Jas 2:19

DEN
become a **d** of robbers in your eyes? . . . . . Jer 7:11
brought and cast into the **d** of lions. . . . . . Dn 6:16
but you make it a **d** of robbers." . . . . Mt 21:13

DENARIUS
agreeing with the laborers for a **d** a day, Mt 20:2
Bring me a **d** and let me look at it." . . . . . Mk 12:15

DENIED
Peter again **d** it, and at once a rooster . . Jn 18:27
he has **d** the faith and is worse than an. . 1 Tm 5:8
kept my word and have not **d** my name.. . . Rv 3:8

DENIES
but whoever **d** me before men, I also . . . Mt 10:33
No one who **d** the Son has the Father. . . 1 Jn 2:23

DENY
let him **d** himself and take up his cross . . . Lk 9:23
you will **d** me three times." . . . . Lk 22:61
if we **d** him, he also will **d** us;. . . . . 2 Tm 2:12
profess to know God, but they **d** him. . . . . . Ti 1:16
into sensuality and **d** our only Master . . . . Jude 4
my name, and you did not **d** my faith . . . . Rv 2:13

DENYING
and **d** the LORD, and turning. . . . . Is 59:13
of godliness, but **d** its power. Avoid . . . . . 2 Tm 3:5

even **d** the Master who bought them, ... 2 Pt 2:1

DEPART
lest they **d** from your heart all the days. . . . Dt 4:9
d from me, you workers of lawlessness.' . . Mt 7:23
say to those on his left, '**D** from me, ... Mt 25:41
"**D** from me, for I am a sinful man, ... Lk 5:8
later times some will **d** from the faith . . . 1 Tm 4:1

DEPARTURE
appeared in glory and spoke of his **d**, ... Lk 9:31
that after my **d** fierce wolves will . . . . . Acts 20:29
and the time of my **d** has come. . . . . 2 Tm 4:6
so that after my **d** you may be able . . . . . 2 Pt 1:15

DEPENDS
That is why it **d** on faith, in order . . . . . . Rom 4:16
righteousness from God that **d** on faith. . . Phil 3:9

DEPRAVED
are **d** in mind and deprived of the truth, . 1 Tm 6:5

DEPRAVITY
her nakedness; they are relatives; it is **d**. . Lv 18:17

DEPRIVE
wicked or to **d** the righteous of justice. . . Prv 18:5
a bribe, and **d** the innocent of his right! . . Is 5:23
Do not **d** one another, except perhaps. . . 1 Cor 7:5

DEPTH
sprang up, since they had no **d** of soil, . . . Mt 13:5
nor height nor **d**, nor anything else in . . Rom 8:39
Oh, the **d** of the riches and wisdom . . . . Rom 11:33

DEPTHS
they went down into the **d** like a stone. . . Ex 15:5
In his hand are the **d** of the earth; the . . . Ps 95:4
LORD, from the **d** of the pit; . . . . Lam 3:55
cast all our sins into the **d** of the sea. . . . . Mi 7:19
everything, even the **d** of God. . . . . 1 Cor 2:10

DESCEND
"I saw the Spirit **d** from heaven like a . . . . Jn 1:32
'Who will **d** into the abyss?'" (that is, . . . Rom 10:7

DESCENDANTS
All the **d** of Jacob were seventy . . . . Ex 1:5
LORD rejected all the **d** of Israel. . . . . . 2 Kgs 17:20
it forever to the **d** of Abraham your . . . 2 Chr 20:7
offspring, and my blessing on your **d**. . . . . Is 44:3
were born **d** as many as the stars of . . . Heb 11:12

DESCENDED
and the Holy Spirit **d** on him in bodily. . . . Lk 3:22
He who **d** is the one who also ascended. . Eph 4:10

DESCENDING
saw the Spirit of God **d** like a dove . . . . . . Mt 3:16
and something like a great sheet **d**, ... Acts 10:11

DESERT
He turns a **d** into pools of water, ... Ps 107:35
the **d** shall rejoice and blossom like the. . . . Is 35:1
in the wilderness, and streams in the **d**; . . Is 35:6

DESIRE
Its **d** is for you, but you must rule over . . . Gn 4:7
had sought him with their whole **d**, . . . 2 Chr 15:15
you hear the **d** of the afflicted; . . . . Ps 10:17
grant you your heart's **d** and fulfill all . . . . Ps 20:4
He fulfills the **d** of those who fear him; . Ps 145:19
and nothing you **d** can compare with . . . Prv 3:15
the **d** of the righteous will be granted. . Prv 10:24
A **d** fulfilled is sweet to the soul, ... Prv 13:19
D without knowledge is not good, ... Prv 19:2
I am my beloved's, and his **d** is for me. . . . Sg 7:10
and satisfy the **d** of the afflicted, ... Is 58:10
For I **d** steadfast love and not sacrifice, . . Hos 6:6
'I **d** mercy, and not sacrifice.' . . . . Mt 9:13
but having his **d** under control, ... 1 Cor 7:37
My **d** is to depart and be with Christ, ... Phil 1:23
d a better country, that is, a heavenly . . Heb 11:16
lured and enticed by his own **d**. . . . . Jas 1:14

DESIRED
More to be **d** are they than gold, ... Ps 19:10
And whatever my eyes **d** I did not keep . . Eccl 2:10
many prophets and kings **d** to see what . . Lk 10:24

DESIRES
he will give you the **d** of your heart. . . . . . Ps 37:4
For the **d** of the flesh are against . . . . Gal 5:17
world is passing away along with its **d**, . . 1 Jn 2:17
following their own sinful **d**; . . . . Jude 16
let the one who **d** take the water of life . Rv 22:17

DESOLATE
lest the land become **d** and the wild . . . . Ex 23:29
set up the abomination that makes **d**. . . . . Dn 11:31
went away in the boat to a **d** place . . . . . Mk 6:32
he would withdraw to **d** places and pray. . Lk 5:16

DESOLATION
they should become a **d** and a curse, . . 2 Kgs 22:19
see the abomination of **d** spoken of by . . Mt 24:15
then know that its **d** has come near. . . . . Lk 21:20

DESOLATIONS
how he has brought **d** on the earth. . . . . . . Ps 46:8
there shall be war. **D** are decreed. . . . . Dn 9:26

DESPAIR
broken my heart, so that I am in **d**. . . . . Ps 69:20
crushed; perplexed, but not driven to **d**; . . 2 Cor 4:8

DESPISE
therefore I **d** myself, and repent in dust. . . Jb 42:6
O priests, who **d** my name. . . . . Mal 1:6
Or do you **d** the church of God and . . . 1 Cor 11:22
Let no one **d** you for your youth, ... 1 Tm 4:12

DESPISED
d the word of the Holy One of Israel. . . . . Is 5:24
He was **d** and rejected by men; . . . . Is 53:3
chose what is low and **d** in the world, . . 1 Cor 1:28

DESPISES
Whoever **d** the word brings . . . . Prv 13:13
A fool **d** his father's instruction, ... Prv 15:5

DESTINED
know that we are **d** for this. . . . . 1 Thes 3:3
For God has not **d** us for wrath, ... 1 Thes 5:9

DESTITUTE
the right of the afflicted and the **d**. . . . . . . Ps 82:3
regards the prayer of the **d** . . . . Ps 102:17
d, afflicted, mistreated— . . . . Heb 11:37

DESTROY
Behold, I will **d** them with the earth. . . . . . Gn 6:13
Haman sought to **d** all the Jews, ... Est 3:6
fear him who can **d** both soul and . . . . . . Mt 10:28
thief comes only to steal and kill and **d**. . Jn 10:10
but have divine power to **d** strongholds. . 2 Cor 10:4
judge, he who is able to save and to **d**. . . Jas 4:12
was to **d** the works of the devil. . . . . 1 Jn 3:8

DESTROYED
set up a kingdom that shall never be **d**, . Dn 2:44
ark, and the flood came and **d** them all. . Lk 17:27
earthly home is **d**, we have a building . . . 2 Cor 5:1
of those who shrink back and are **d**, . . Heb 10:39

DESTROYER
will not allow the **d** to enter your . . . . Ex 12:23
did and were destroyed by the **D**. . . . . . 1 Cor 10:10
so that the **D** of the firstborn might . . . . Heb 11:28

DESTROYS
lacks sense; he who does it **d** himself. . . . Prv 6:32
but one sinner **d** much good. . . . . Eccl 9:18
no thief approaches and no moth **d**. . . . . Lk 12:33
If anyone **d** God's temple, God will. . . . . 1 Cor 3:17

DESTRUCTION
Pride goes before **d**, and a haughty . . . . . Prv 16:18
wide and the way is easy that leads to **d**, . Mt 7:13
vessels of wrath prepared for **d**, ... Rom 9:22
peace and security," then sudden **d** . . . . 1 Thes 5:3
suffer the punishment of eternal **d**, . . . 2 Thes 1:9

DETERMINED
Since his days are **d**, and the number . . . . Jb 14:5
"'Have you not heard that I **d** it long . . . . Is 37:26
of the earth, having **d** allotted periods. . Acts 17:26

DETESTABLE
Cast away the **d** things your eyes feast. . Ezk 20:7
and became **d** like the thing they loved. . Hos 9:10
They are **d**, disobedient, unfit for any . . . . . Ti 1:16
as for the cowardly, the faithless, the **d**, . . Rv 21:8

DEVICES
foolishly, and a man of evil **d** is hated. . . . Prv 14:17
upon this people, the fruit of their **d**, ... Jer 6:19

DEVIL
the wilderness to be tempted by the **d**. . . . . Mt 4:1
the enemy who sowed them is the **d**. . . . Mt 13:39
fire prepared for the **d** and his angels. . . . Mt 25:41
then the **d** comes and takes away . . . . Lk 8:12
And yet one of you is a **d**." . . . . Jn 6:70
You are of your father the **d**, and your. . . . Jn 8:44
the **d** had already put it into the heart . . . Jn 13:2
give no opportunity to the **d**. . . . . Eph 4:27
to stand against the schemes of the **d**. . . Eph 6:11
fall into disgrace, into a snare of the **d**. . . 1 Tm 3:7
Your adversary the **d** prowls around . . . . . 1 Pt 5:8
makes a practice of sinning is of the **d**, . . . 1 Jn 3:8
and the **d** who had deceived them was. . Rv 20:10

DEVIOUS
for the **d** person is an abomination . . . . . Prv 3:32
but he who is **d** in his ways despises . . . . Prv 14:2

DEVISE
to **d** artistic designs, to work in gold, ... Ex 31:4
Those who **d** good meet steadfast love. . Prv 14:22
Woe to those who **d** wickedness . . . . Mi 2:1

DEVOID
worldly people, **d** of the Spirit. . . . . Jude 19

DEVOTE
But we will **d** ourselves to prayer . . . . Acts 6:4
that you may **d** yourselves to prayer; . . . . 1 Cor 7:5
d yourself to the public reading of. . . . . 1 Tm 4:13

DEVOTED
every **d** thing is most holy to the . . . . Lv 27:28
that they have **d** themselves to the . . . 1 Cor 16:15

DEVOTION
"I remember the **d** of your youth, ... Jer 2:2
from a sincere and pure **d** to Christ. . . . . 2 Cor 11:3

DEVOUR
to Joab, "Shall the sword **d** forever? . . 2 Sm 2:26
But if you bite and **d** one another, ... Gal 5:15
when she bore her child he might **d** it. . . . Rv 12:4

DEVOURED
your own sword **d** your prophets like a . . Jer 2:30
fig trees and your olive trees the locust **d**; . . Am 4:9
path, and the birds came and **d** them. . . . . Mt 13:4

DEVOURING
glory of the LORD was like a **d** fire . . . . . . Ex 24:17
his nostrils, and **d** fire from his mouth; . . . Ps 18:8
in furious anger and a flame of **d** fire, . . . Is 30:30

DEVOUT
and this man was righteous and **d**, ... Lk 2:25
d men from every nation under heaven. . Acts 2:5

DEW
God give you of the **d** of heaven . . . . . . Gn 27:28
as the rain, my speech distill as the **d**, ... Dt 32:2
If there is **d** on the fleece alone, ... Jgs 6:37
upon him as the **d** falls on the. . . . . 2 Sm 17:12
I will be like the **d** to Israel; he shall . . . . . Hos 14:5

DISQUALIFIED
preaching to others I myself should be **d**. . 1 Cor 9:27
corrupted in mind and **d** regarding . . . . .2 Tm 3:8

DISSENSION
had no small **d** and debate with . . . . Acts 15:2
a **d** arose between the Pharisees and . . Acts 23:7

DISSENSIONS
fits of anger, rivalries, **d**, divisions, ...Gal 5:20
genealogies, **d**, and quarrels about. . . . . Ti 3:9

DISSOLVED
the heavens will be set on fire and **d**, . . .2 Pt 3:12

DISTINCTION
to make a **d** between the unclean and. . . .Lv 11:47
d between the holy and the common,. .Ezk 22:26
and he made no **d** between us and . . . . Acts 15:9
for all who believe. For there is no **d**:. . .Rom 3:22
For there is no **d** between Jew and . . . Rom 10:12

DISTINGUISH
d between the holy and the common,. . . Lv 10:10
the ability to **d** between spirits,. . . . . . .1 Cor 12:10
by constant practice to **d** good from evil. . .Heb 5:14

DISTORT
you and want to **d** the gospel of Christ. . . .Gal 1:7

DISTRESS
God who answers me in the day of my **d**. .Gn 35:3
In my **d** I called upon the LORD;. . . . . Ps 18:6
called out to the LORD, out of my **d**,. . . . . .Jon 2:2
will be great **d** upon the earth and. . . . . . Lk 21:23

DISTRIBUTE
Sell all that you have and **d** to the poor, . Lk 18:22

DISTRIBUTED
inheritances that Moses **d** in the plains . Jos 13:32
has **d** freely; he has given to the poor; . . Ps 112:9
and it was **d** to each as any had need. .Acts 4:35
"He has **d** freely, he has given to the . . . 2 Cor 9:9

DIVIDE
out your hand over the sea and **d** it, ... Ex 14:16
king said, "**D** the living child in two,. . . 1 Kgs 3:25
they cast lots to **d** his garments.. . . . . . . .Lk 23:34

DIVIDED
the sea dry land, and the waters were **d**. . Ex 14:21
"Every kingdom **d** against itself is laid. . . Mt 12:25
"They **d** my garments among them,. . . . . Jn 19:24
Is Christ **d**? Was Paul crucified . . . . 1 Cor 1:13

DIVINATION
who practices **d** or tells fortunes. . . . . Dt 18:10
For rebellion is as the sin of **d**, ... 1 Sm 15:23
to you a lying vision, worthless **d**,. . . . . . .Jer 14:14
had a spirit of **d** and brought her . . . . . .Acts 16:16

DIVINE
because in his **d** forbearance he had . . .Rom 3:25
not of the flesh but have **d** power to . . 2 Cor 10:4
His **d** power has granted to us all things. .2 Pt 1:3

DIVINERS
called for the priests and the **d** and said,. .1 Sm 6:2
the signs of liars and makes fools of **d**,. . Is 44:25
So do not listen to your prophets, your **d**,. . Jer 27:9

DIVISION
I will put a **d** between my people and . . . .Ex 8:23
No, I tell you, but rather **d**. . . . . .Lk 12:51
that there may be no **d** in the body,. . .1 Cor 12:25
As for a person who stirs up **d**, after . . . . . .Ti 3:10

DIVISIONS
watch out for those who cause **d** . . . . . Rom 16:17
and that there be no **d** among you,. . . . 1 Cor 1:10
It is these who cause **d**, worldly people,. Jude 19

DIVORCE
he writes her a certificate of **d** . . . . Dt 24:1
let him give her a certificate of **d**.' . . . . Mt 5:31
"Is it lawful to **d** one's wife for any. . . . . . . Mt 19:3
the husband should not **d** his wife.. . . . . 1 Cor 7:11
live with her, she should not **d** him. . . . . 1 Cor 7:13

DIVORCES
who does not love his wife but **d** her, . . . Mal 2:16
I say to you that everyone who **d** his . . . . .Mt 5:32
whoever **d** his wife, except for sexual . . . . Mt 19:9

DOCTRINE
'My **d** is pure, and I am clean. . . . . Jb 11:4
create obstacles contrary to the **d** . . . . Rom 16:17
carried about by every wind of **d**,. . . . . . .Eph 4:14
whatever else is contrary to sound **d**, . . .1 Tm 1:10
the good **d** that you have followed. . . . . .1 Tm 4:6
anyone teaches a different **d** . . . . .1 Tm 6:3
to give instruction in sound **d** . . . . .Ti 1:9
teach what accords with sound **d**. . . . . .Ti 2:1
d of Christ and go on to maturity, ...Heb 6:1

DOERS
the **d** of the law who will be justified. . . Rom 2:13
But be **d** of the word, and not hearers. . . Jas 1:22

DOG
Philistine said to David, "Am I a **d**, ... 1 Sm 17:43
"The **d** returns to its own vomit, ... 2 Pt 2:22

DOGS
"Do not give **d** what is holy,. . . . . .Mt 7:6
even the **d** eat the crumbs that fall . . . . . Mt 15:27

DOMINION
fill the earth and subdue it, and have **d**. . .Gn 1:28
You have given him **d** over the works . . . . .Ps 8:6
for his **d** is an everlasting **d**,. . . . . Dn 4:34
death no longer has **d** over him. . . . . .Rom 6:9
all rule and authority and power and **d**, . Eph 1:21
to him be glory and **d** forever and ever. . . . Rv 1:6

DONKEY
He shall be a wild **d** of a man, his hand. . Gn 16:12
And the **d** saw the angel of the. . . . . . . .Nm 22:23
humble and mounted on a **d**, ...Zec 9:9
humble, and mounted on a **d**, ... Mt 21:5
a speechless **d** spoke with human voice . . 2 Pt 2:16

DOOR
and do not go near the **d** of her house,. . . Prv 5:8
As a **d** turns on its hinges, so does a . . . Prv 26:14
the marriage feast, and the **d** was shut. .Mt 25:10
"Strive to enter through the narrow **d**. . . Lk 13:24
I am the **d**. If anyone enters by me, ... Jn 10:9
God may open to us a **d** for the word,. . . . Col 4:3
behold, the Judge is standing at the **d**. . . .Jas 5:9
Behold, I stand at the **d** and knock. If . . . Rv 3:20

DOORKEEPER
I would rather be a **d** in the house of. . . .Ps 84:10

DOORPOSTS
put it on the two **d** and the lintel of the . . Ex 12:7
write them on the **d** of your house. . . . . . . .Dt 6:9

DORCAS
Tabitha, which, translated, means **D**. . . .Acts 9:36

DOUBLE-MINDED
he is a **d** man, unstable in all his ways. . . . Jas 1:8
sinners, and purify your hearts, you **d**. . . . .Jas 4:8

DOUBT
"O you of little faith, why did you **d**?". . . Mt 14:31
to you, if you have faith and do not **d**,. . . Mt 21:21
and does not **d** in his heart,. . . . . Mk 11:23
And have mercy on those who **d**; . . . . Jude 22

DOUBTS
why do **d** arise in your hearts? . . . . .Lk 24:38
one who **d** is like a wave of the sea . . . . . . Jas 1:6

DOVE
And the **d** came back to him. . . . . Gn 8:11
"Oh, that I had wings like a **d**!. . . . . .Ps 55:6
Spirit of God descending like a **d** . . . . Mt 3:16

DOWNCAST
"Why are your faces **d** today?" . . . . Gn 40:7
But God, who comforts the **d**,. . . . . 2 Cor 7:6

DRAGON
and he will slay the **d** that is in the sea. . . . Is 27:1
and his angels fighting against the **d**. . . . . Rv 12:7
And they worshiped the **d**, for he. . . . . Rv 13:4
he seized the **d**, that ancient serpent, . . . Rv 20:2

DRAIN
wicked of the earth shall **d** it down to. . . .Ps 75:8
you shall drink it and **d** it out, and . . . . .Ezk 23:34
to make her **d** the cup of the wine of . . . Rv 16:19

DRAW
D near to my soul, redeem me; ransom. . Ps 69:18
a man of understanding will **d** it out. . . . .Prv 20:5
With joy you will **d** water from the wells. . . Is 12:3
the earth, will **d** all people to myself." . . . Jn 12:32
let us **d** near with a true heart in full . . Heb 10:22
for whoever would **d** near to God. . . . . . . Heb 11:6
D near to God, and he will **d** near. . . . . Jas 4:8

DRAWING
sinners were all **d** near to hear him. . . . . . . .Lk 15:1
because your redemption is **d** near." . . . . Lk 21:28
all the more as you see the Day **d** near. . Heb 10:25

DRAWS
My righteousness **d** near, my salvation . . . . Is 51:5
unless the Father who sent me **d** him. . . . .Jn 6:44

DREAD
the **d** of you shall be upon every beast. . . Gn 9:2
be your fear, and let him be your **d**. . . . . . . .Is 8:13
they shall turn in **d** to the LORD . . . . Mi 7:17

DREAM
Joseph had a **d**, and when he told . . . . . . Gn 37:5
appeared to Solomon in a **d** by night, . . 1 Kgs 3:5
Therefore show me the **d** and its . . . . Dn 2:6
Lord appeared to Joseph in a **d** . . . . Mt 2:13
and your old men shall **d** dreams;. . . . . . . Acts 2:17

DREAMER
to one another, "Here comes this **d**. . . . . .Gn 37:19

DREAMS
did not answer him, either by **d**, or by. .1 Sm 28:6
For when **d** increase and words grow . . . Eccl 5:7
relying on their **d**, defile the flesh, ... Jude 8

DRIED
the waters were **d** up from the earth. . . . . Gn 8:7
had **d** up the waters of the Jordan for. . . . Jos 5:1

DRINK
D water from your own cistern,. . . . . Prv 5:15
Wine is a mocker, strong **d** a brawler, . . . Prv 20:1
Jesus said to her, "Give me a **d**.". . . . . .Jn 4:7
thirsts, let him come to me and **d**. . . . . .Jn 7:37
shall I not **d** the cup that the Father. . . . . . Jn 18:11
and all were made to **d** of one Spirit. . . 1 Cor 12:13
being poured out as a **d** offering,. . . . . . 2 Tm 4:6

DRINKS
eats and **d** with drunkards,. . . . . Mt 24:49
whoever **d** of the water that I will give . . . Jn 4:14
who eats and **d** without discerning . . . 1 Cor 11:29

DRIVE
So you shall **d** them out and make them. . . Dt 9:3
they did not **d** out the Canaanites . . . . . Jos 16:10
D out a scoffer, and strife will go out, . . Prv 22:10
temple and began to **d** out those. . . . . . . .Mk 11:15

DROSS
of the earth you discard like **d**, ... Ps 119:119
Take away the **d** from the silver, ...Prv 25:4

DROVE
The Spirit immediately **d** him out into. . . . Mk 1:12

DROWNED
his neck and to be **d** in the depth of . . . . . Mt 18:6
the steep bank into the lake and **d**. . . . . . . Lk 8:33

DROWSY
delayed, they all became **d** and slept. . . . . Mt 25:5

DRUNK
"How long will you go on being **d**? . . . . . 1 Sm 1:14
Be **d**, but not with wine; . . . . Is 29:9
For these people are not **d**, as you. . . . . Acts 2:15
And do not get **d** with wine, for that. . . . Eph 5:18
those who get **d**, are **d** at night. . . . . 1 Thes 5:7

DRUNKARD
d and the glutton will come to poverty,. . Prv 23:21
d, or swindler—not even to eat with. . . . 1 Cor 5:11
not a **d**, not violent but gentle, not . . . . . 1 Tm 3:3

DRUNKARDS
Be not among **d** or among gluttonous . Prv 23:20
nor thieves, nor the greedy, nor **d**, ... 1 Cor 6:10

DRUNKENNESS
weighed down with dissipation and **d** . . . Lk 21:34
as in the daytime, not in orgies and **d**,. . Rom 13:13
d, orgies, and things like these. . . . . Gal 5:21
passions, **d**, orgies, drinking parties,. . . . . . 1 Pt 4:3

DRY
may go through the sea on **d** ground. . . . Ex 14:16
on **d** ground in the midst of the Jordan, . Jos 3:17
O **d** bones, hear the word of the LORD. . . Ezk 37:4

DUE
not pervert the justice **d** to your poor . . . . Ex 23:6
to give them their food in **d** season. . . . Ps 104:27
in themselves the **d** penalty for their . . . Rom 1:27
may receive what is **d** for what he . . . . 2 Cor 5:10

DULL
Make the heart of this people **d**, and . . . . . . Is 6:10
For this people's heart has grown **d**, ... Mt 13:15
since you have become **d** of hearing. . . . . Heb 5:11

DUST
LORD God formed the man of **d**. . . . . Gn 2:7
are **d**, and to **d** you shall return." . . . . Gn 3:19
he remembers that we are **d**. . . . . Ps 103:14
All are from the **d**, and to **d** all . . . . Eccl 3:20
town shake off the **d** from your feet as . . . . Lk 9:5
they shook off the **d** from their feet. . . . Acts 13:51
borne the image of the man of **d**,. . . . . 1 Cor 15:49

DUTY
for this is the whole **d** of man. . . . . Eccl 12:13
we have only done what was our **d**.'" . . . Lk 17:10
wisdom, whom we will appoint to this **d**. . . Acts 6:3

DWELL
"But will God indeed **d** with man on . . 2 Chr 6:18
and I shall **d** in the house of the . . . . Ps 23:6
I **d** in the midst of a people of unclean . . . . Is 6:5
will come upon all who **d** on the face of. Lk 21:35
so that Christ may **d** in your hearts . . . . . Eph 3:17
fullness of God was pleased to **d**, ... Col 1:19
the spirit that he has made to **d** in us"? . . Jas 4:5

DWELLING
The eternal God is your **d** place, ... Dt 33:27
And listen in heaven your **d** place, ... 1 Kgs 8:30
been our **d** place in all generations. . . . . . . Ps 90:1
longing to put on our heavenly **d**, ... 2 Cor 5:2
"I will make my **d** among them . . . . 2 Cor 6:16
built together into a **d** place for God . . . Eph 2:22
the **d** place of God is with man. . . . . Rv 21:3

DWELLS
He who **d** in the shelter of the Most. . . . . . . Ps 91:1
is exalted, for he **d** on high; . . . . Is 33:5
darkness, and the light **d** with him. . . . . Dn 2:22
but the Father who **d** in me does his. . . . Jn 14:10
if in fact the Spirit of God **d** in you. . . . . . Rom 8:9
temple and that God's Spirit **d** in you? . . 1 Cor 3:16
whole fullness of deity **d** bodily, ... Col 2:9
By the Holy Spirit who **d** within us, ... 2 Tm 1:14
a new earth in which righteousness **d**. . . 2 Pt 3:13

DWELT
Word became flesh and **d** among us,. . . . . . Jn 1:14

EAGLE
Like an **e** that stirs up its nest, that . . . . . . Dt 32:11
side, and the four had the face of an **e**. . . Ezk 1:10
A great **e** with great wings and long . . . . Ezk 17:3
fourth living creature like an **e** in flight. . . . Rv 4:7

EAGLE'S
so that your youth is renewed like the **e**. . Ps 103:5

EAGLES'
I bore you on **e** wings and brought you . . Ex 19:4

EAR
master shall bore his **e** through with an . . Ex 21:6
Give **e** to my words, O LORD; . . . . Ps 5:1
no one has heard or perceived by the **e**,. . Is 64:4
of the high priest and cut off his **e**. . . . . . Mt 26:51
And if the **e** should say, "Because I . . . 1 Cor 12:16

EARLY
And rising very **e** in the morning, ... Mk 1:35
And **e** in the morning all the people . . . . Lk 21:38
were at the tomb **e** in the morning, ... Lk 24:22

EARN
quietly and to **e** their own living. . . . . 2 Thes 3:12

EARNESTLY
O God, you are my God; **e** I seek you; . . . . Ps 63:1
my spirit within me **e** seeks you. . . . . Is 26:9
Therefore pray **e** to the Lord . . . . Lk 10:2
Above all, keep loving one another **e**, ... 1 Pt 4:8

EARS
He who has **e** to hear, let him hear. . . . . . . Mt 11:15
but having itching **e** they will . . . . 2 Tm 4:3
and his **e** are open to their prayer. . . . . . . 1 Pt 3:12

EARTH
God called the dry land **E**, ... Gn 1:10
Now the **e** was corrupt in God's sight, ... Gn 6:11
Everything that is on the **e** shall die. . . . . . Gn 6:17
Most High, Possessor of heaven and **e**; . . Gn 14:19
know that the **e** is the LORD's. . . . . Ex 9:29
is no God like you, in heaven or on **e**, . 2 Chr 6:14
the void and hangs the **e** on nothing. . . . . Jb 26:7
how majestic is your name in all the **e**! . . . . Ps 8:1
The **e** is the LORD's and the fullness . . . . . . Ps 24:1
He set the **e** on its foundations, so that. . Ps 104:5
LORD by wisdom founded the **e**; . . . . Prv 3:19
the whole **e** is full of his glory!". . . . . Is 6:3
I made the **e** and created man on it; . . . . . Is 45:12
heavens and the new **e** that I make shall. . Is 66:22
let all the **e** keep silence before him." . . Hab 2:20
until heaven and **e** pass away, not an iota, . Mt 5:18
your will be done, on **e** as it is in . . . . Mt 6:10
you, Father, Lord of heaven and **e**, ... Lk 10:21
For "the **e** is the Lord's, and the . . . . . . 1 Cor 10:26
descended into the lower regions, the **e**? . . Eph 4:9
heaven and on **e** and under the **e**, ... Phil 2:10

EARTHLY
I have told you **e** things and you do not . . Jn 3:12
if the tent that is our **e** home is. . . . . 2 Cor 5:1

EARTHQUAKE
but the LORD was not in the **e**. . . . . 1 Kgs 19:11
And behold, there was a great **e**, for an . . Mt 28:2
and suddenly there was a great **e**, so . Acts 16:26
and behold, there was a great **e**, ... Rv 6:12
thousand people were killed in the **e**, ... Rv 11:13

EARTHQUAKES
will be famines and **e** in various places. . . Mt 24:7
There will be great **e**, and in various . . . . . Lk 21:11

EASE
I was at **e**, and he broke me apart; . . . . . . Jb 16:12
Tremble, you women who are at **e**, ... Is 32:11
shall return and have quiet and **e**, ... Jer 30:10

EASIER
For which is **e**, to say, 'Your sins are . . . . . . Mt 9:5
Again I tell you, it is **e** for a camel to . . . . Mt 19:24
But it is **e** for heaven and earth to pass. . Lk 16:17

EAST
as far as the **e** is from the west, so far. . Ps 103:12
And people will come from **e** and west, . Lk 13:29
the way for the kings from the **e**. . . . . Rv 16:12
on the **e** three gates, on the north three. Rv 21:13

EASY
gate is wide and the way is **e** that leads . . Mt 7:13
For my yoke is **e**, and my burden is . . . . . Mt 11:30

EAT
day that you **e** of it you shall surely die." . Gn 2:17
E this scroll, and go, speak to the. . . . . Ezk 3:1
They shall **e**, but not be satisfied; they . . Hos 4:10
your life, what you will **e** or what . . . . Mt 6:25
But to **e** with unwashed hands does not . . Mt 15:20
"I have food to **e** that you do not know . . Jn 4:32
voice to him: "Rise, Peter; kill and **e**.". . . Acts 10:13
brother stumble, I will never **e** meat, . . . 1 Cor 8:13
e whatever is set before you without. . 1 Cor 10:27
is not willing to work, let him not **e**. . 2 Thes 3:10
I will come in to him and **e** with him, ... Rv 3:20

EATING
The Son of Man came **e** and drinking, ... Mt 11:19
kingdom of God is not a matter of **e** . . Rom 14:17
as to the **e** of food offered to idols, ... 1 Cor 8:4

EATS
man receives sinners and **e** with them." . . Lk 15:2
If anyone **e** of this bread, he will live . . . . . Jn 6:51
For anyone who **e** and drinks without . . 1 Cor 11:29

EBENEZER
and called its name **E**; . . . . 1 Sm 7:12

EDEN
LORD God planted a garden in **E**, ... Gn 2:8
settled in the land of Nod, east of **E**. . . . . . Gn 4:16
makes her wilderness like **E**, her desert. . . . Is 51:3
You were in **E**, the garden of God; . . . . . Ezk 28:13

EDOM
(Therefore his name was called **E**.). . . . . Gn 25:30
But **E** said to him, "You shall not pass . . Nm 20:18

EFFECT
the **e** of righteousness will be peace, ... Is 32:17
For a will takes **e** only at death, since . . . Heb 9:17
And let steadfastness have its full **e**, ... Jas 1:4

EFFORT
make an **e** to settle with him on the. . . . . Lk 12:58
make every **e** to supplement your faith. . . 2 Pt 1:5

EGYPT
They took Joseph to **E**. . . . . Gn 37:28
and came into **E**, Jacob and all his . . . . . . Gn 46:6
children of Israel, out of **E**." . . . . Ex 3:10
of Israel lived in **E** was 430 years. . . . . Ex 12:40
'Behold, a people has come out of **E**,. . . . Nm 22:11
out of **E** I called my son. . . . . Hos 11:1
the child and his mother, and flee to **E**, . . . Mt 2:13
"Out of **E** I called my son." . . . . Mt 2:15
By faith he left **E**, not being afraid of. . . Heb 11:27
symbolically is called Sodom and **E**, ... Rv 11:8

ELDER
the youth will be insolent to the **e**, ... Is 3:5
a charge against an **e** except on the . . . 1 Tm 5:19

ELDERS
and seventy of the **e** of Israel went up, . . . Ex 24:9
they had appointed **e** for them in. . . . . Acts 14:23
Let the **e** who rule well be considered. . 1 Tm 5:17
into order, and appoint **e** in every town . . . . Ti 1:5
Let him call for the **e** of the church, ... Jas 5:14

God of Israel, **e** above the cherubim, ... Is 37:16

ENTICE
My son, if sinners **e** you, do not . . . . Prv 1:10
insatiable for sin. They **e** unsteady . . . . . . 2 Pt 2:14

ENTREATED
he **e** the favor of the LORD his . . . . 2 Chr 33:12
yet we have not **e** the favor of the . . . . Dn 9:13

ENTRUST
who will **e** to you the true riches? . . . . Lk 16:11
on his part did not **e** himself to them, ... Jn 2:24
e to faithful people who will be able . . . . 2 Tm 2:2
suffer according to God's will **e** their . . . . 1 Pt 4:19

ENTRUSTED
Jews were **e** with the oracles of God. . . . Rom 3:2
saw that I had been **e** with the gospel. . . . Gal 2:7
approved by God to be **e** with the . . . . 1 Thes 2:4

ENVIOUS
For I was **e** of the arrogant when I saw . . . Ps 73:3
Be not **e** of evil men, nor desire to be . . . Prv 24:1

ENVY
but **e** makes the bones rot. . . . . Prv 14:30
Let not your heart **e** sinners, ... Prv 23:17
it was out of **e** that they had delivered . . Mt 27:18
e, slander, pride, foolishness. . . . . Mk 7:22
They are full of **e**, murder, strife, ... Rom 1:29
love does not **e** or boast; it . . . . 1 Cor 13:4
e, drunkenness, orgies, and things like. . . Gal 5:21
preach Christ from **e** and rivalry, ... Phil 1:15
and hypocrisy and **e** and all slander. . . . . . 1 Pt 2:1

EPHESUS
And they came to **E**, and he left them. . Acts 18:19
I fought with beasts at **E**? . . . . 1 Cor 15:32
"To the angel of the church in **E** write: . . . . Rv 2:1

EPHOD
"And they shall make the **e** of gold, ... Ex 28:6
And Gideon made an **e** of it. . . . . Jgs 8:27
Abiathar the priest, "Bring the **e** here." . . 1 Sm 23:9

EPHRAIM
The name of the second he called **E**, ... Gn 41:52
Joseph were two tribes, Manasseh and **E**. . Jos 14:4
near the wilderness, to a town called **E**, . . Jn 11:54

EPHRATHAH
you act worthily in **E** and be renowned . . . Ru 4:11
you, O Bethlehem **E**, who are too little . . . . Mi 5:2

EPICUREAN
Some of the **E** and Stoic philosophers. . Acts 17:18

EQUAL
will you liken me and make me **e**, ... Is 46:5
you have made them **e** to us who have. . Mt 20:12
are **e** to angels and are sons of God, . . . Lk 20:36
Father, making himself **e** with God. . . . . . . Jn 5:18
obtained a faith of **e** standing with ours . . 2 Pt 1:1

EQUALITY
form of God, did not count **e** with God . . . Phil 2:6

EQUIP
besides me there is no God; I **e** you, ... Is 45:5
to **e** the saints for the work of ministry, . . Eph 4:12
e you with everything good that you. . . Heb 13:21

EQUIPPED
the God who **e** me with strength and . . . Ps 18:32
may be complete, **e** for every good . . . . 2 Tm 3:17

EQUITY
David administered justice and **e** to all . 2 Sm 8:15
You have established **e**; you have . . . . Ps 99:4
dealing, in righteousness, justice, and **e**; . . Prv 1:3
and decide with **e** for the meek of the . . . . Is 11:4

ERROR
and no **e** or fault was found in him. . . . . . . Dn 6:4

escaping from those who live in **e**. . . . . . . 2 Pt 2:18
away with the **e** of lawless people . . . . . . 2 Pt 3:17
the Spirit of truth and the spirit of **e**. . . . . 1 Jn 4:6

ESAU
Thus **E** despised his birthright. . . . . Gn 25:34
But **E** ran to meet him and embraced . . . Gn 33:4
but **E** I have hated. I have laid waste . . . . . Mal 1:3
"Jacob I loved, but **E** I hated." . . . . Rom 9:13
unholy like **E**, who sold his birthright . . . Heb 12:16

ESCAPE
went into the ark to **e** the waters of the . . . Gn 7:7
how are you to **e** being sentenced to. . . . Mt 23:33
may have strength to **e** all these things. . Lk 21:36
that you will **e** the judgment of God? . . . Rom 2:3
he will also provide the way of **e**, ... 1 Cor 10:13
e from the snare of the devil, ... 2 Tm 2:26
how shall we **e** if we neglect such . . . . . . Heb 2:3
much less will we **e** if we reject him. . . . Heb 12:25

ESCAPED
We have **e** like a bird from the snare . . . . Ps 124:7
to arrest him, but he **e** from their hands. . Jn 10:39
of fire, **e** the edge of the sword, ... Heb 11:34

ESTABLISH
I will **e** his kingdom forever if he. . . . . . 1 Chr 28:7
and **e** the work of our hands upon us; . . . Ps 90:17
of God, and seeking to **e** their own, ... Rom 10:3
that he may **e** your hearts blameless . . 1 Thes 3:13
E your hearts, for the coming of the . . . . . Jas 5:8
confirm, strengthen, and **e** you. . . . . 1 Pt 5:10

ESTABLISHED
The steps of a man are **e** by the . . . . Ps 37:23
by understanding he **e** the heavens; . . . . . Prv 3:19
No one is **e** by wickedness, but the . . . . . Prv 12:3
Who has **e** all the ends of the earth? . . . . Prv 30:4
who **e** the world by his wisdom, ... Jer 10:12
and built up in him and **e** in the faith, ... Col 2:7
know them and are **e** in the truth that. . . 2 Pt 1:12

ESTABLISHES
but the LORD **e** his steps. . . . . Prv 16:9
no rest until he **e** Jerusalem and makes . . Is 62:7
And it is God who **e** us with you in . . . . 2 Cor 1:21

ESTHER
He was bringing up Hadassah, that is **E**, . . Est 2:7

ETERNAL
The **e** God is your dwelling place, ... Dt 33:27
because man is going to his **e** home, ... Eccl 12:5
but the righteous into **e** life." . . . . Mt 25:46
what must I do to inherit **e** life?" . . . . Mk 10:17
should not perish but have **e** life. . . . . Jn 3:16
a spring of water welling up to **e** life." . . . . Jn 4:14
believes him who sent me has **e** life. . . . . . Jn 5:24
as were appointed to **e** life believed. . . Acts 13:48
righteousness leading to **e** life through . Rom 5:21
This was according to the **e** purpose . . . . Eph 3:11
blood, thus securing an **e** redemption. . . Heb 9:12
you an entrance into the **e** kingdom . . . . . 2 Pt 1:11
may know that you have **e** life. . . . . 1 Jn 5:13

ETERNITY
he has put **e** into man's heart, yet . . . . . . Eccl 3:11
the glory both now and to the day of **e**. . 2 Pt 3:18

EUPHRATES
And the fourth river is the **E**. . . . . Gn 2:14
of Egypt to the great river, the river **E**, . . Gn 15:18
So I went and hid it by the **E**, as the . . . . . Jer 13:5
out his bowl on the great river **E**, ... Rv 16:12

EVANGELIST
we entered the house of Philip the **e**, . . Acts 21:8
endure suffering, do the work of an **e**, . . 2 Tm 4:5

EVANGELISTS
gave the apostles, the prophets, the **e**, . . Eph 4:11

EVE
The man called his wife's name **E**, ... Gn 3:20
as the serpent deceived **E** by his . . . . . . 2 Cor 11:3
For Adam was formed first, then **E**; . . . . 1 Tm 2:13

EVER
LORD will reign forever and **e**." . . . . Ex 15:18
"No one **e** spoke like this man!" . . . . Jn 7:46
to whom be the glory forever and **e**. . . . . . Gal 1:5
might be to our God forever and **e**! . . . . . . Rv 7:12
But nothing unclean will **e** enter it, nor . . Rv 21:27

EVERLASTING
see it and remember the **e** covenant . . . . . Gn 9:16
from **e** to **e** you are God. . . . . Ps 90:2
way in me, and lead me in the way **e**! . . Ps 139:24
the **e** God, the Creator of the ends. . . . . . Is 40:28
I will make with you an **e** covenant, ... Is 55:3
a double portion; they shall have **e** joy. . . . Is 61:7
I have loved you with an **e** love; . . . . Jer 31:3
I will make with them an **e** covenant, . . . Jer 32:40
His kingdom is an **e** kingdom, ... Dn 4:3
of the earth shall awake, some to **e** life, . . Dn 12:2

EVERY
He blotted out **e** living thing that was on . . Gn 7:23
E valley shall be lifted up, and **e** . . . . Is 40:4
bearing fruit in **e** good work and . . . . Col 1:10

EVERYONE
let **e** who is godly offer prayer . . . . Ps 32:6
e whose name shall be found written . . . . Dn 12:1
that **e** who calls on the name of the . . . . . Jl 2:32
Let **e** turn from his evil way and from . . . . Jon 3:8
"Not **e** who says to me, 'Lord, Lord,' . . . . . Mt 7:21
So it is with **e** who is born of the Spirit." . . . Jn 3:8
E who is of the truth listens to my . . . . . . Jn 18:37
e whose name has not been written . . . . . Rv 13:8

EVERYTHING
And God saw **e** that he had made, and . . . Gn 1:31
Let **e** that has breath praise the . . . . Ps 150:6
made **e** for its purpose, even the . . . . Prv 16:4
to land, they left **e** and followed him. . . . . . Lk 5:11
and **e** that is written about the Son of. . . Lk 18:31
as having nothing, yet possessing **e**. . . 2 Cor 6:10
in order that in **e** God may be glorified . . 1 Pt 4:11

EVIDENCE
On the **e** of two witnesses or of three . . . . Dt 17:6
be established by the **e** of two or three. . 2 Cor 13:1
This is **e** of the righteous judgment of. . 2 Thes 1:5
their corrosion will be **e** against you . . . . . Jas 5:3

EVIDENT
Now the works of the flesh are **e**: . . . . Gal 5:19
By this it is **e** who are the children . . . . . . 1 Jn 3:10

EVIL
will be like God, knowing good and **e**." . . . Gn 3:5
intention of man's heart is **e** from his. . . . . Gn 8:21
Turn away from **e** and do good; . . . . Ps 34:14
no **e** shall be allowed to befall you, ... Ps 91:10
an **e** person will not go unpunished, ... Prv 11:21
Woe to those who call **e** good and. . . . . . . Is 5:20
into temptation, but deliver us from **e**. . . . Mt 6:13
The weeds are the sons of the **e** one, . . . Mt 13:38
Depart from me, all you workers of **e**!' . . . Lk 13:27
the light because their works were **e**. . . . . Jn 3:19
but that you keep them from the **e** one. . . Jn 17:15
the good I want, but the **e** I do not . . . . Rom 7:19
Repay no one **e** for **e**, but. . . . . Rom 12:17
"Purge the **e** person from among . . . . . . 1 Cor 5:13
use of the time, because the days are **e**. . Eph 5:16
speak **e** of no one, to avoid quarreling, ... Ti 3:2
for God cannot be tempted with **e**, ... Jas 1:13
Do not speak **e** against one another, ... Jas 4:11
using your freedom as a cover-up for **e**, . 1 Pt 2:16
because you have overcome the **e** one. . . 1 Jn 2:13
and the **e** one does not touch him. . . . . . . 1 Jn 5:18
Beloved, do not imitate **e** but imitate . . . . . 3 Jn 11

Let not steadfast love and f forsake you; . Prv 3:3
belt of his waist, and f the belt of. . . . . Is 11:5
are new every morning; great is your f. . Lam 3:23
their faithlessness nullify the f of God? . . Rom 3:3

FAITHLESS
if we are f, he remains faithful— . . . . 2 Tm 2:13
But as for the cowardly, the f, the. . . . . Rv 21:8

FALL
though he f, he shall not be cast. . . . . Ps 37:24
For if they f, one will lift up his fellow. . . Eccl 4:10
"You will all f away because of me . . . . . . Mt 26:31
to say to the mountains, 'F on us,' . . . . . . Lk 23:30
all have sinned and f short of the glory . . Rom 3:23
that he stands take heed lest he f. . . . . 1 Cor 10:12
It is a fearful thing to f into the hands . . Heb 10:31
"F on us and hide us from the face of . . . . Rv 6:16

FALLEN
law; you have f away from grace. . . . . Gal 5:4
with him those who have f asleep. . . . . 1 Thes 4:14
have f away, to restore them again. . . . . . Heb 6:6
"F, f is Babylon the great, ... Rv 14:8

FALLING
to you to keep you from f away. . . . . Jn 16:1

FALLOW
year you shall let it rest and lie f, ... Ex 23:11
"Break up your f ground, and sow not. . . . Jer 4:3

FALSE
"You shall not bear f witness . . . . Ex 20:16
they tell f dreams and give empty . . . . . . Zec 10:2
And many f prophets will arise and . . . . . Mt 24:11
Do not steal, Do not bear f witness, ... Mk 10:19
For f christs and f prophets will . . . . Mk 13:22
For such men are f apostles, ... 2 Cor 11:13
all power and f signs and wonders, . . . 2 Thes 2:9
are from God, for many f prophets. . . . . . . 1 Jn 4:1
and out of the mouth of the f prophet, . . Rv 16:13

FALSEHOOD
him is true, and in him there is no f. . . . . . . Jn 7:18
Therefore, having put away f, let. . . . . . . Eph 4:25
everyone who loves and practices f. . . . . . Rv 22:15

FALSELY
adulterers, against those who swear f, ... Mal 3:5
all kinds of evil against you f on my. . . . . . Mt 5:11
to those of old, 'You shall not swear f, ... Mt 5:33

FAMILIES
in you all the f of the earth shall be . . . . . . Gn 12:3
offspring shall all the f of the earth be . Acts 3:25
are upsetting whole f by teaching for . . . . . . Ti 1:11

FAMILY
was baptized at once, he and all his f. . Acts 16:33
from whom every f in heaven and on . . . Eph 3:15

FAMINE
there will arise seven years of f, ... Gn 41:30
not a f of bread, nor a thirst for water, . . . Am 8:11
sword and with f and with pestilence . . . . Rv 6:8

FAMINES
and there will be f and earthquakes in. . . . Mt 24:7
in various places; there will be f. . . . . Mk 13:8

FAR
their lips, but their heart is f from me; . . . . Mt 15:8
"You are not f from the kingdom of . . . . . Mk 12:34
once were f off have been brought near . . Eph 2:13

FARMER
It is the hard-working f who ought to . . 2 Tm 2:6
how the f waits for the precious fruit. . . . . Jas 5:7

FAST
Consecrate a f; call a solemn assembly. . . . . Jl 1:14
"And when you f, do not look gloomy . . . . Mt 6:16
but your disciples do not f?" . . . . Mk 2:18
I f twice a week; I give tithes of all. . . . . . . Lk 18:12
test everything; hold f what is good. . . 1 Thes 5:21

FASTED
So we f and implored our God for . . . . . . Ezr 8:23
'Why have we f, and you see it not? . . . . . Is 58:3

FASTING
pleas for mercy with f and sackcloth . . . . . Dn 9:3
And after f forty days and forty nights, ... Mt 4:2
worshiping with f and prayer night and. . . Lk 2:37
they were worshiping the Lord and f, . . Acts 13:2

FATHER
shall be the f of a multitude of nations. . . . Gn 17:4
"Honor your f and your mother, that . . . . Ex 20:12
Is not he your f, who created you, ... Dt 32:6
how you left your f and mother and . . . . . Ru 2:11
For my f and my mother have forsaken . Ps 27:10
F of the fatherless and protector of . . . . . . Ps 68:5
As a f shows compassion to his . . . . Ps 103:13
He who loves wisdom makes his f glad, . Prv 29:3
you are our F; we are the clay, ... Is 64:8
son suffer for the iniquity of the f?' . . . . Ezk 18:19
If then I am a f, where is my honor? . . . . . . Mal 1:6
"Our F in heaven, hallowed be. . . . . Mt 6:9
acknowledge before my F who is in. . . . . Mt 10:32
Whoever loves f or mother more than. . . Mt 10:37
a man shall leave his f and his mother. . . . Mt 19:5
And call no man your f on earth, for . . . . . Mt 23:9
What f among you, if his son asks for . . . . Lk 11:11
They will be divided, f against son and . . Lk 12:53
his f saw him and felt compassion, ... Lk 15:20
And Jesus said, "F, forgive them, for . . . . Lk 23:34
"F, into your hands I commit my. . . . . Lk 23:46
I and the F are one." . . . . Jn 10:30
No one comes to the F except through. . . Jn 14:6
whatever you ask of the F in my name, . . Jn 16:23
to make him the f of all who believe . . . . Rom 4:11
For I became your f in Christ Jesus . . . . 1 Cor 4:15
and I will be a f to you, and you shall . 2 Cor 6:18
our hearts, crying, "Abba! F!" . . . . Gal 4:6
both have access in one Spirit to the F. . . Eph 2:18
"Honor your f and mother" (this. . . . . Eph 6:2
how, like a f with his children, ... 1 Thes 2:11
whom his f does not discipline? . . . . Heb 12:7
See what kind of love the F has given. . . . 1 Jn 3:1

FATHER'S
it new with you in my F kingdom." . . . . . Mt 26:29
know that I must be in my F house?" . . . . . Lk 2:49
to snatch them out of the F hand. . . . . . . Jn 10:29
In my F house are many rooms. If it. . . . . . Jn 14:2
his name and his F name written on . . . . . Rv 14:1

FATHERLESS
shall not mistreat any widow or f child. . Ex 22:22
He executes justice for the f and the . . . . Dt 10:18
Father of the f and protector of widows . . Ps 68:5
he upholds the widow and the f, ... Ps 146:9
or violence to the resident alien, the f, . . Jer 22:3

FATHERS
visiting the iniquity of the f on the. . . . . . Ex 20:5
and the glory of children is their f. . . . . . . Prv 17:6
our sins, and for the iniquities of our f, . . . Dn 9:16
turn the hearts of f to their children. . . . . . Mal 4:6
F, do not provoke your children, lest . . . . Col 3:21
have had earthly f who disciplined us . . . Heb 12:9

FAULT
sins against you, go and tell him his f, . . . Mt 18:15
to me then, "Why does he still find f? . . Rom 9:19

FAVOR
Noah found f in the eyes of the LORD. . . . . Gn 6:8
a moment, and his f is for a lifetime. . . . . . Ps 30:5
the LORD bestows f and honor. . . . . Ps 84:11
good man obtains f from the LORD, ... Prv 12:2
the year of the LORD's f, ... Is 61:2
And the f of God was upon him. . . . . Lk 2:40
to proclaim the year of the Lord's f." . . . . . Lk 4:19
praising God and having f with all the. . Acts 2:47

FAVORED
to her and said, "Greetings, O f one, ... Lk 1:28

FEAR
The f of you and the dread of you shall. . . Gn 9:2
the LORD your God you shall f. . . . . Dt 6:13
"Now therefore f the LORD . . . . Jos 24:14
Serve the LORD with f, ... Ps 2:11
the f of the LORD is clean, ... Ps 19:9
light and my salvation; whom shall I f? . . . Ps 27:1
f of the LORD is the beginning . . . . Prv 1:7
The f of man lays a snare, but . . . . Prv 29:25
F God and keep his commandments, . . . Eccl 12:13
F not, for I am with you; . . . . Is 43:5
And do not f those who kill the body . . . Mt 10:28
"Do not f, only believe." . . . . Mk 5:36
"F not, little flock, for it is your . . . . Lk 12:32
is no f of God before their eyes." . . . . . . Rom 3:18
So do not become proud, but f. . . . . . . Rom 11:20
no f of the one who is in authority? . . . . Rom 13:3
holiness to completion in the f of God. . . 2 Cor 7:1
God gave us a spirit not of f but of . . . . . 2 Tm 1:7
let us f lest any of you should seem. . . . . . Heb 4:1
F God. Honor the emperor. . . . . 1 Pt 2:17
no f of them, nor be troubled, ... 1 Pt 3:14
but perfect love casts out f. . . . . 1 Jn 4:18
"F God and give him glory, because. . . . . . Rv 14:7

FEARED
so the people f the LORD, ... Ex 14:31
greatly f the LORD and Samuel. . . . . 1 Sm 12:18
there is forgiveness, that you may be f. . Ps 130:4
Then the men f the LORD . . . . Jon 1:16
my name will be f among the nations. . . . . Mal 1:14
seeking to arrest him but f the people, . . Mk 12:12

FEARING
by walking in his ways and by f him. . . . . . . Dt 8:6
but with sincerity of heart, f the Lord. . . . Col 3:22

FEARS
and delivered me from all my f. . . . . Ps 34:4
Blessed is the one who f the LORD . . . . . Prv 28:14

FEAST
made them a f and baked unleavened. . . . Gn 19:3
shall observe the F of Unleavened . . . . . . Ex 12:17
king who gave a wedding f for his son, . . . Mt 22:2
every year at the F of the Passover. . . . . . . Lk 2:41
But when you give a f, invite the poor, . . Lk 14:13
The Jews were looking for him at the f, . . . Jn 7:11
their deceptions, while they f with you. . 2 Pt 2:13

FEASTS
of joy and gladness and cheerful f. . . . . . . Zec 8:19
place of honor at f and the best seats. . . . Mt 23:6
These are hidden reefs at your love f, ... Jude 12

FEEBLE
Samaria, "What are these f Jews doing? . Neh 4:2
and you have made firm the f knees. . . . . . Jb 4:4
weak hands, and make firm the f knees. . . Is 35:3

FEED
the ravens to f you there." . . . . 1 Kgs 17:4
The lips of the righteous f many, but . . . Prv 10:21
he shall f them and be their shepherd. . Ezk 34:23
desolate place to f so great a crowd?" . . Mt 15:33
when did we see you hungry and f you, . Mt 25:37
Jesus said to him, "F my sheep. . . . . Jn 21:17

FEET
you have put all things under his f, ... Ps 8:6
made my f like the f of a deer. . . . . Ps 18:33
miry bog, and set my f upon a rock, ... Ps 40:2
its f partly of iron and partly of clay. . . . . Dn 2:33
he makes my f like the deer's; . . . . Hab 3:19
until I put your enemies under your f"? . . Mt 22:44
she began to wet his f with her tears. . . . . Lk 7:38
he showed them his hands and his f. . . . Lk 24:40
wash the disciples' f and to wipe them . . . Jn 13:5
will soon crush Satan under your f. . . . Rom 16:20
all things in subjection under his f." . . . 1 Cor 15:27

he put all things under his f. . . . . Eph 1:22
I saw him, I fell at his f as though dead. . . Rv 1:17

FELLOW
found one of his f servants who owed. . . Mt 18:28
heirs of God and f heirs with Christ,. . . . Rom 8:17
I am a f servant with you and your. . . . . . Rv 22:9

FELLOWSHIP
you were called into the f of his Son,. . . . 1 Cor 1:9
the love of God and the f of the Holy . 2 Cor 13:14
the right hand of f to Barnabas and me,. . Gal 2:9
If we say we have f with him while we . . . 1 Jn 1:6
he is in the light, we have f with one . . . . . 1 Jn 1:7

FEMALE
male and f he created them. . . . . Gn 1:27
of any figure, the likeness of male or f,. . . Dt 4:16
creation, 'God made them male and f.' . . Mk 10:6

FESTIVAL
Let us therefore celebrate the f, not. . . . . 1 Cor 5:8
or with regard to a f or a new moon . . . . Col 2:16

FEVER
his mother-in-law lying sick with a f. . . . . . Mt 8:14
at the seventh hour the f left him.". . . . . . . Jn 4:52

FEW
Therefore let your words be f. . . . . Eccl 5:2
For many are called, but f are chosen." . . Mt 22:14
"Lord, will those who are saved be f?" . . Lk 13:23

FIELD
house to house, who add f to f, ... Is 5:8
The f is the world, and the good seed. . . Mt 13:38
Then two men will be in the f; one. . . . . Mt 24:40
You are God's f, God's building. . . . . 1 Cor 3:9

FIG
And they sewed f leaves together . . . . Gn 3:7
And seeing a f tree by the wayside, he . . Mt 21:19
"From the f tree learn its lesson: as . . . . Mt 24:32
"A man had a f tree planted in his . . . . Lk 13:6
Can a f tree, my brothers, bear olives,. . . Jas 3:12

FIGHT
The Lord will f for you,. . . . . Ex 14:14
Our God will f for us." . . . . Neh 4:20
F the good f of the faith. . . . . 1 Tm 6:12
I have fought the good f, ... 2 Tm 4:7

FIGHTS
Lord your God who f for you, ... Jos 23:10
and what causes f among you?. . . . . Jas 4:1

FIGS
baskets of f placed before the temple. . . . Jer 24:1
from thornbushes, or f from thistles?. . . . Mt 7:16

FILL
Do I not f heaven and earth?. . . . . Jer 23:24
in, and I will f this house with glory,. . . . . . Hg 2:7
"F the jars with water." . . . . Jn 2:7
the God of hope f you with all joy . . . . . Rom 15:13
the heavens, that he might f all things.) . . Eph 4:10

FILLED
of the Lord f the tabernacle. . . . . Ex 40:34
glory of the Lord f the house . . . . 1 Kgs 8:11
glory of the Lord f the temple. . . . . Ezk 43:5
and he will be f with the Holy Spirit, ... Lk 1:15
they were all f with the Holy Spirit. . . . . . Acts 2:4
is debauchery, but be f with the Spirit, . . Eph 5:18
f with the fruit of righteousness . . . . Phil 1:11

FILTHINESS
Let there be no f nor foolish talk nor. . . . Eph 5:4
Therefore put away all f and rampant . . . . Jas 1:21

FIND
and be sure your sin will f you out. . . . . Nm 32:23
your God and you will f him, ... Dt 4:29
loses his life for my sake will f it. . . . . . . Mt 16:25
you will f a baby wrapped in swaddling . . Lk 2:12
"I f no guilt in this man.". . . . . Lk 23:4

FINDS
Blessed is the one who f wisdom,. . . . . . . Prv 3:13
He who f a wife f a good . . . . Prv 18:22
and the one who seeks f, ... Mt 7:8
Whoever f his life will lose it, and. . . . . . . Mt 10:39
after the one that is lost, until he f it? . . . . Lk 15:4

FINGER
"This is the f of God." But Pharaoh's . . . . . Ex 8:19
of stone, written with the f of God. . . . . . Ex 31:18
and wrote with his f on the ground.. . . . . Jn 8:6
said to Thomas, "Put your f here, ... Jn 20:27

FINISH
began to build and was not able to f.' . . . Lk 14:30
So now f doing it as well, so that . . . . . . 2 Cor 8:11

FINISHED
And on the seventh day God f his work . . Gn 2:2
When Moses had f writing the words. . . . Dt 31:24
"It is f," and he bowed his head . . . . Jn 19:30
fought the good fight, I have f the race, . . 2 Tm 4:7
for with them the wrath of God is f.. . . . . . Rv 15:1

FIRE
night in a pillar of f to give them light, . . Ex 13:21
Lord your God is a consuming f,. . . . . Dt 4:24
Then the f of the Lord fell . . . . 1 Kgs 18:38
and chariots of f all around Elisha. . . . . 2 Kgs 6:17
can dwell with the consuming f?. . . . . Is 33:14
Is not my word like f, declares the . . . . . Jer 23:29
unbound, walking in the midst of the f, . . Dn 3:25
For he is like a refiner's f and like . . . . Mal 3:2
to be thrown into the hell of f. . . . . Mt 18:9
into the eternal f prepared for the devil . Mt 25:41
to go to hell, to the unquenchable f. . . . Mk 9:43
And divided tongues as of f appeared. . . Acts 2:3
f will test what sort of work each one . . 1 Cor 3:13
though it is tested by f—may be found . . . 1 Pt 1:7
earth that now exist are stored up for f, . 2 Pt 3:7
others by snatching them out of the f; . . Jude 23
but f came down from heaven and. . . . . . Rv 20:9
This is the second death, the lake of f. . . Rv 20:14

FIRM
said to the people, "Fear not, stand f, . . . Ex 14:13
heart is f, trusting in the Lord.. . . . . Ps 112:7
your joy, for you stand f in your faith. . 2 Cor 1:24
day, and having done all, to stand f.. . . . . Eph 6:13

FIRST
"I am the f and I am the last; . . . . Is 44:6
But seek f the kingdom of God . . . . Mt 6:33
But many who are f will be last, ... Mt 19:30
the f of his signs, Jesus did at Cana . . . . Jn 2:11
disciples were f called Christians. . . . . . . Acts 11:26
covenant, he makes the f one obsolete. . Heb 8:13
We love because he f loved us. . . . . 1 Jn 4:19
This is the f resurrection. . . . . Rv 20:5

FIRSTBORN
the Lord, Israel is my f son, ... Ex 4:22
every f in the land of Egypt shall die, ... Ex 11:5
"Consecrate to me all the f. . . . . Ex 13:2
gave birth to her f son and wrapped. . . . . . Lk 2:7
order that he might be the f among . . . Rom 8:29
the invisible God, the f of all creation. . . . . Col 1:15
the faithful witness, the f of the dead,. . . . . Rv 1:5

FIRSTFRUITS
the f of those who have fallen asleep. 1 Cor 15:20
God chose you as the f to be saved, . 2 Thes 2:13
should be a kind of f of his creatures. . . . . Jas 1:18
from mankind as f for God and. . . . . Rv 14:4

FISH
Or if he asks for a f, will give him a . . . . . . Mt 7:10
three nights in the belly of the great f, . . Mt 12:40
have only five loaves here and two f." . . . Mt 14:17
haul it in, because of the quantity of f. . . . Jn 21:6

FISHERS
and I will make you f of men.". . . . . Mt 4:19

FIVE
the f loaves for the f thousand,. . . . . Mt 16:9
F of them were foolish, and f. . . . . Mt 25:2
of the men came to about f thousand. . . Acts 4:4

FIXED
You have f all the boundaries . . . . Ps 74:17
day and night and the f order of heaven. . Jer 33:25
us and you a great chasm has been f, . . . Lk 16:26

FLAME
become a fire, and his Holy One a f, ... Is 10:17
tongue, for I am in anguish in this f.' . . . . Lk 16:24
you to fan into f the gift of God,. . . . . 2 Tm 1:6

FLATTERS
For he f himself in his own eyes . . . . Ps 36:2
A man who f his neighbor spreads a . . . . Prv 29:5

FLATTERY
shall seduce with f those who violate . . . Dn 11:32
and by smooth talk and f they deceive . . Rom 16:18
For we never came with words of f,. . . . 1 Thes 2:5

FLEE
where shall I f from your presence? . . . . . Ps 139:7
The wicked f when no one pursues,. . . . . Prv 28:1
F from sexual immorality. . . . . 1 Cor 6:18
my beloved, f from idolatry. . . . . 1 Cor 10:14
So f youthful passions and pursue . . . . . 2 Tm 2:22
Resist the devil, and he will f from you. . . Jas 4:7

FLEECE
let me test just once more with the f. . . Jgs 6:39

FLESH
bone of my bones and f of my f; . . . . Gn 2:23
wife, and they shall become one f. . . . . . . Gn 2:24
not abide in man forever, for he is f: . . . . . Gn 6:3
my covenant be in your f an everlasting . Gn 17:13
destroyed, yet in my f I shall see God,. . . Jb 19:26
not be afraid. What can f do to me? . . . . . Ps 56:4
"What shall I cry?" All f is grass,. . . . . Is 40:6
Be silent, all f, before the Lord,. . . . . Zec 2:13
So they are no longer two but one f. . . . . . Mt 19:6
willing, but the f is weak." . . . . Mt 26:41
all f shall see the salvation of God.'". . . . . . . Lk 3:6
That which is born of the f is f,. . . . . Jn 3:6
For my f is true food, and my blood is . . . Jn 6:55
For while we were living in the f, ... Rom 7:5
who are in the f cannot please God. . . . . Rom 8:8
and make no provision for the f,. . . . . . Rom 13:14
to Satan for the destruction of the f, ... 1 Cor 5:5
we regard no one according to the f. . . 2 Cor 5:16
you will not gratify the desires of the f. . . Gal 5:16
all once lived in the passions of our f, ... Eph 2:3
wife, and the two shall become one f." . . Eph 5:31
we do not wrestle against f and blood, . . Eph 6:12
put no confidence in the f— . . . . Phil 3:3
by putting off the body of the f,. . . . . Col 2:11
"All f is like grass and all its glory. . . . . . . 1 Pt 1:24
the desires of the f and the desires of. . . 1 Jn 2:16
Christ has come in the f is from God,. . . . . 1 Jn 4:2

FLOCK
You led your people like a f. . . . . Ps 77:20
gather the remnant of my f out of all . . . Jer 23:3
keeping watch over their f by night.. . . . . . . Lk 2:8
So there will be one f, one shepherd.. . . . Jn 10:16
shepherd the f of God that is among. . . . . 1 Pt 5:2

FLOG
some you will f in your synagogues. . . . Mt 23:34
spit on him, and f him and kill him. . . . . Mk 10:34
"Is it lawful for you to f a man who . . . Acts 22:25

FLOGGING
And after f him, they will kill him,. . . . . . . Lk 18:33
Others suffered mocking and f,. . . . . Heb 11:36

FLOOD
For behold, I will bring a f of waters . . . . . Gn 6:17
never again become a f to destroy all . . . . Gn 9:15
as in those days before the f they were . . Mt 24:38
when he brought a f upon the world . . . . 2 Pt 2:5

FLOODS
piled up; the f stood up in a heap; . . . . Ex 15:8
quench love, neither can f drown it . . . . Sg 8:7
And the rain fell, and the f came, ... Mt 7:25

FLOW
all vigilance, for from it f the springs . . . . Prv 4:23
living waters shall f out from Jerusalem, . . Zec 14:8
'Out of his heart will f rivers of . . . . Jn 7:38

FLOWER
he flourishes like a f of the field; . . . . Ps 103:15
The grass withers, the f fades, but . . . . Is 40:8
because like a f of the grass he will . . . . . . Jas 1:10
The grass withers, and the f falls, ... 1 Pt 1:24

FLOWING
a land f with milk and honey. . . . . Jos 5:6
The water was f down from below . . . . . . Ezk 47:1
f from the throne of God and of the . . . . . Rv 22:1

FLY
He will f away like a dream and not . . . . . . Jb 20:8
like a dove! I would f away and be at . . . . . Ps 55:6
they are soon gone, and we f away . . . . . . Ps 90:10

FOES
Consider how many are my f, and . . . . . . Ps 25:19
it is he who will tread down our f. . . . . . . Ps 60:12

FOLLOW
If the Lord is God, f him; . . . . 1 Kgs 18:21
"F me, and I will make you fishers of . . . . . Mt 4:19
and take up his cross and f me. . . . . Mt 16:24
he goes before them, and the sheep f . . . . Jn 10:4
If anyone serves me, he must f me; . . . . . Jn 12:26
F the pattern of the sound words . . . . . . 2 Tm 1:13
their labors, for their deeds f them!" . . . . Rv 14:13

FOLLOWED
I wholly f the Lord my God. . . . . Jos 14:8
they left their nets and f him. . . . . Mt 4:20
earth marveled as they f the beast. . . . . . . Rv 13:3

FOLLY
O God, you know my f; the wrongs I . . . . . Ps 69:5
of her cubs rather than a fool in his f. . . . Prv 17:12
The devising of f is sin, and the scoffer . . Prv 24:9
word of the cross is f to those who . . . . 1 Cor 1:18
wisdom of this world is f with God. . . . . 1 Cor 3:19
very far, for their f will be plain to all, . . 2 Tm 3:9

FOOD
I have given every green plant for f." . . . . . Gn 1:30
moving thing that lives shall be f for . . . . . Gn 9:3
not defile himself with the king's f, ... Dn 1:8
Is not life more than f, and. . . . . Mt 6:25
"My f is to do the will of him who sent . . . Jn 4:34
Do not work for the f that perishes, ... Jn 6:27
Do not, for the sake of f, destroy the . . Rom 14:20
F will not commend us to God. . . . . 1 Cor 8:8
But if we have f and clothing, with. . . . . . 1 Tm 6:8
is poorly clothed and lacking in daily f, . . Jas 2:15

FOODS
(Thus he declared all f clean.) . . . . Mk 7:19
abstinence from f that God created . . . . . 1 Tm 4:3
to be strengthened by grace, not by f, . . Heb 13:9

FOOL
The f says in his heart, "There is no . . . . Ps 14:1
way of a f is right in his own eyes, ... Prv 12:15
so honor is not fitting for a f. . . . . Prv 26:1
A f gives full vent to his spirit, but . . . . . . Prv 29:11
whoever says, 'You f!' will. . . . . Mt 5:22
But God said to him, 'F! This night . . . . . . Lk 12:20

FOOLISH
my people are f; they know me not; . . . . Jer 4:22
like a f man who built his house . . . . Mt 7:26
But God chose what is f in the world. . . 1 Cor 1:27
Therefore do not be f, but understand . . Eph 5:17
For we ourselves were once f, ... Ti 3:3

FOOLISHNESS
deceit, sensuality, envy, slander, pride, f. . Mk 7:22
For the f of God is wiser than men, ... 1 Cor 1:25

FOOLS
f despise wisdom and instruction. . . . . Prv 1:7
You blind f! For which is greater, the . . . . Mt 23:17
Claiming to be wise, they became f, . . . Rom 1:22
We are f for Christ's sake, but you . . . . . 1 Cor 4:10

FOOT
He will not let your f be moved; . . . . Ps 121:3
And if your f causes you to sin, ... Mk 9:45
lest you strike your f against a stone.'" . . . . Lk 4:11
If the f should say, "Because I am. . . . . 1 Cor 12:15

FOOTSTOOL
is my throne, and the earth is my f; . . . . Is 66:1
until I make your enemies your f.' . . . . . . Lk 20:43
is my throne, and the earth is my f. . . . . Acts 7:49
should be made a f for his feet. . . . . Heb 10:13

FORBEARANCE
In your f take me not away; know that . . Jer 15:15
riches of his kindness and f and . . . . Rom 2:4
because in his divine f he had passed . . Rom 3:25

FORCES
And if anyone f you to go one mile, go . . . Mt 5:41
and everyone f his way into it. . . . . Lk 16:16

FOREFATHERS
turned back to the iniquities of their f, . . Jer 11:10
are beloved for the sake of their f. . . . . Rom 11:28
the futile ways inherited from your f, ... 1 Pt 1:18

FOREHEADS
a mark on the f of the men who sigh. . . . . Ezk 9:4
sealed the servants of our God on their f." . . Rv 7:3
face, and his name will be on their f. . . . . Rv 22:4

FOREIGN
forsake the Lord and serve f . . . . Jos 24:20
you shall not bow down to a f god. . . . . . . Ps 81:9

FOREIGNER
"I am a sojourner and f among you; . . . . . Gn 23:4
and give praise to God except this f?" . . . . Lk 17:18
I will be a f to the speaker . . . . 1 Cor 14:11

FOREKNEW
those whom he f he also predestined . . Rom 8:29
has not rejected his people whom he f. . Rom 11:2

FOREKNOWLEDGE
to the definite plan and f of God, ... Acts 2:23
according to the f of God the Father, ... 1 Pt 1:2

FOREKNOWN
He was f before the foundation of . . . . . . 1 Pt 1:20

FORERUNNER
Jesus has gone as a f on our behalf, . . . Heb 6:20

FORETOLD
had made, as the Lord had f. . . . . 2 Kgs 24:13
But what God f by the mouth of all . . . . Acts 3:18

FOREVER
tree of life and eat, and live f—" . . . . Gn 3:22
This is my name f, and thus I am to . . . . . . Ex 3:15
dwell in the house of the Lord f. . . . . Ps 23:6
his steadfast love endures f, ... Ps 100:5
for riches do not last f; and does a. . . . . Prv 27:24
but the word of our God will stand f. . . . . . Is 40:8
but my salvation will be f, and my . . . . Is 51:6
eats of this bread, he will live f. . . . . Jn 6:51
you another Helper, to be with you f, ... Jn 14:16
another place, "You are a priest f, ... Heb 5:6
word of the Lord remains f." . . . . 1 Pt 1:25
whoever does the will of God abides f. . . 1 Jn 2:17
that abides in us and will be with us f: . . . . 2 Jn 2
Christ, and he shall reign f and ever." . . . . . Rv 11:15

FORFEIT
gain the whole world and f his soul? . . . . Mk 8:36

FORGAVE
servant released him and f him the . . . . . Mt 18:27
one another, as God in Christ f you. . . . . Eph 4:32

FORGET
take care lest you f the Lord, ... Dt 6:12
O my soul, and f not all his benefits, ... Ps 103:2
these may f, yet I will not f you. . . . . Is 49:15

FORGETTING
But one thing I do: f what lies behind . . . Phil 3:13

FORGIVE
But you are a God ready to f, gracious . . Neh 9:17
my trouble, and f all my sins. . . . . Ps 25:18
For I will f their iniquity, ... Jer 31:34
and f us our debts, as we also. . . . . Mt 6:12
Who can f sins but God alone?" . . . . Mk 2:7
who is in heaven may f you your . . . . Mk 11:25
f, and you will be forgiven; . . . . Lk 6:37
And Jesus said, "Father, f them, for . . . . . Lk 23:34
has forgiven you, so you also must f. . . . . Col 3:13
he is faithful and just to f us our sins . . . . . 1 Jn 1:9

FORGIVEN
people of Israel, and they shall be f, ... Nm 15:25
is the one whose transgression is f, ... Ps 32:1
people who dwell there will be f. . . . . Is 33:24
'Your sins are f,' or to say, ... Mt 9:5
word against the Son of Man will be f, . . Mt 12:32
But he who is f little, loves little." . . . . Lk 7:47
alive together with him, having f us . . . . . Col 2:13
if he has committed sins, he will be f. . . . Jas 5:15
because your sins are f for his name's . . . 1 Jn 2:12

FORGIVENESS
the Lord our God belong mercy and f, . . . Dn 9:9
poured out for many for the f of sins. . . Mt 26:28
a baptism of repentance for the f. . . . . Mk 1:4
of Jesus Christ for the f of your sins, . . . Acts 2:38
we have redemption, the f of sins. . . . . Col 1:14
shedding of blood there is no f of sins. . Heb 9:22

FORGIVES
who f all your iniquity, who heals all . . . . Ps 103:3
"Who is this, who even f sins?" . . . . Lk 7:49

FORGIVING
f iniquity and transgression and sin, ... Ex 34:7
you, O Lord, are good and f, ... Ps 86:5

FORGOTTEN
failed me, my close friends have f me. . . . Jb 19:14
God, my rock: "Why have you f me? . . . . . Ps 42:9
former troubles are f and are hidden . . . . . Is 65:16
And not one of them is f before God. . . . . Lk 12:6
having f that he was cleansed from . . . . . . 2 Pt 1:9

FORM
by taking the f of a servant . . . . Phil 2:7
Abstain from every f of evil. . . . . 1 Thes 5:22

FORMED
then the Lord God f the man. . . . . Gn 2:7
For you f my inward parts; . . . . Ps 139:13
"Before I f you in the womb I knew . . . . Jer 1:5
and f the spirit of man within him: . . . . Zec 12:1
of childbirth until Christ is f in you! . . . . . Gal 4:19
and the earth was f out of water and . . . 2 Pt 3:5

FORSAKE
He will not leave you or f you." . . . . Dt 31:6
if you f him, he will f you. . . . . 2 Chr 15:2
For the Lord will not f his. . . . . Ps 94:14
let the wicked f his way, and . . . . Is 55:7

"I will never leave you nor f . . . . Heb 13:5

FORSAKEN
my God, why have you f me? . . . . Ps 22:1
not seen the righteous f or his children. . Ps 37:25
my God, why have you f me?". . . . . Mt 27:46
persecuted, but not f; struck down, ... 2 Cor 4:9

FORSAKING
F the right way, they have gone . . . . 2 Pt 2:15

FORTRESS
is my rock and my f and my deliverer,. 2 Sm 22:2
For you are my rock and my f; . . . . Ps 31:3

FORTY
rain on the earth f days and f . . . . Gn 7:4
people of Israel ate the manna f years, . . Ex 16:35
was on the mountain f days and f . . . . . . Ex 24:18
after fasting f days and f nights, ... Mt 4:2
for f days, being tempted by the devil. . . . . Lk 4:2
appearing to them during f days and . . . Acts 1:3

FOUND
If you seek him, he will be f by you, . . . 2 Chr 15:2
at a time when you may be f; . . . . Ps 32:6
"Seek the LORD while he may be f; . . . . Is 55:6
f by those who did not seek me. . . . . Is 65:1
he was lost, and is f.'" . . . . Lk 15:32
anyone's name was not f written in . . . . . Rv 20:15

FOUNDATION
Of old you laid the f of the earth, ... Ps 102:25
a precious cornerstone, of a sure f: . . . . . . Is 28:16
loved me before the f of the world. . . . . . Jn 17:24
For no one can lay a f other than . . . . . . 1 Cor 3:11
chose us in him before the f of the . . . . . . Eph 1:4
But God's firm f stands, bearing this . . . 2 Tm 2:19
was foreknown before the f of the . . . . . . 1 Pt 1:20
book of life from the f of the world . . . . . . Rv 17:8

FOUNDATIONS
looking forward to the city that has f, . . Heb 11:10
And the wall of the city had twelve f, . . . Rv 21:14

FOUNDER
to glory, should make the f of their . . . . . Heb 2:10
looking to Jesus, the f and perfecter . . . . Heb 12:2

FOUNTAIN
For with you is the f of life; in . . . . Ps 36:9
the f of wisdom is a bubbling brook. . . . . Prv 18:4
forsaken me, the f of living waters, ... Jer 2:13

FRAGRANCE
spreads the f of the knowledge of him . . 2 Cor 2:14

FRAGRANT
anointing oil and for the f incense, ... Ex 25:6
gave himself up for us, a f offering. . . . . . Eph 5:2

FRAME
For he knows our f; he remembers. . . . . Ps 103:14
My f was not hidden from you, ... Ps 139:15

FRANKINCENSE
They shall bring gold and f, and . . . . Is 60:6
him gifts, gold and f and myrrh. . . . . Mt 2:11

FREE
and the truth will set you f." . . . . Jn 8:32
But the f gift is not like the trespass. . . . Rom 5:15
you have been set f from sin . . . . Rom 6:22
Spirit of life has set you f in Christ . . . . . . Rom 8:2
Live as people who are f, not using . . . . . 1 Pt 2:16

FREED
everyone who believes is f from . . . . . . Acts 13:39
To him who loves us and has f us . . . . Rv 1:5

FREEDOM
to corruption and obtain the f of the . . . Rom 8:21
the Spirit of the Lord is, there is f. . . . . . 2 Cor 3:17
For f Christ has set us free; . . . . Gal 5:1
They promise them f, but they . . . . 2 Pt 2:19

FRET
F not yourself because of evildoers;. . . . . . Ps 37:1
F not yourself because of evildoers,. . . . Prv 24:19

FRIEND
face to face, as a man speaks to his f. . . . Ex 33:11
A f loves at all times, and a brother . . . . . Prv 17:17
to ruin, but there is a f who sticks . . . . . Prv 18:24
gracious, will have the king as his f. . . . . . Prv 22:11
Faithful are the wounds of a f;. . . . . Prv 27:6
a f of tax collectors and sinners!' . . . . Mt 11:19

FRIENDS
a whisperer separates close f. . . . . Prv 16:28
make f for yourselves by means of. . . . . . . Lk 16:9
lay down his life for his f. . . . . Jn 15:13

FRIENDSHIP
when the f of God was upon my tent, ... Jb 29:4
The f of the LORD is for those . . . . Ps 25:14
Make no f with a man given to anger, . . Prv 22:24
Do you not know that f with the world . . . Jas 4:4

FRUIT
and f trees bearing f in . . . . Gn 1:11
one wise, she took of its f and ate, ... Gn 3:6
Blessed shall be the f of your womb . . . . . Dt 28:4
of water that yields its f in its season, ... Ps 1:3
The f of the righteous is a tree of life, . . Prv 11:30
salvation and righteousness may bear f; . . Is 45:8
leaves will not wither, nor their f fail, . . . Ezk 47:12
Bear f in keeping with repentance. . . . . Mt 3:8
healthy tree bears good f, ... Mt 7:17
branch that does bear f he prunes, ... Jn 15:2
But the f of the Spirit is love, ... Gal 5:22
(for the f of light is found in . . . . Eph 5:9
filled with the f of righteousness. . . . . Phil 1:11

FRUITFUL
"Be f and multiply and fill the earth. . . . . . Gn 1:28
I will make you exceedingly f, ... Gn 17:6
people of Israel were f and increased . . . . . Ex 1:7
they shall multiply and be f. . . . . Ezk 36:11
you rains from heaven and f seasons, . . Acts 14:17
in the flesh, that means f labor for me. . . Phil 1:22

FULFILL
your heart's desire and f all your plans!. . . Ps 20:4
not come to abolish them but to f . . . . Mt 5:17
This was to f the Scripture which says, . . Jn 19:24
If you really f the royal law according . . . . Jas 2:8

FULFILLED
A desire f is sweet to the soul, but to . . . Prv 13:19
in their case the prophecy of Isaiah is f. . Mt 13:14
Scripture has been f in your hearing." . . . . Lk 4:21
Prophets and the Psalms must be f." . . . Lk 24:44
requirement of the law might be f in us, . . Rom 8:4
one who loves another has f the law. . . . Rom 13:8
For the whole law is f in one word: . . . . , Gal 5:14
angel, the mystery of God would be f, ... Rv 10:7

FULL
earth shall be f of the knowledge. . . . . Is 11:9
Jesus, f of the Holy Spirit, returned . . . . Lk 4:1
"Woe to you who are f now, for you . . . . . Lk 6:25
And Stephen, f of grace and power, ... Acts 6:8

FULLNESS
earth is the LORD's and the f . . . . Ps 24:1
For from his f we have all received, ... Jn 1:16
until the f of the Gentiles has come . . . . Rom 11:25
But when the f of time had come, God . . . Gal 4:4
may be filled with all the f of God. . . . . . Eph 3:19
For in him all the f of God was pleased. . . Col 1:19

FURNACE
be cast into a burning fiery f." . . . . Dn 3:6
throw them into the fiery f. In that. . . . . . Mt 13:42

FURY
in anger and in f and in great wrath. . . . . . Jer 21:5

there will be wrath and f. . . . . Rom 2:8
cup of the wine of the f of his wrath. . . . . Rv 16:19

FUTILE
give thanks to him, but they became f . . Rom 1:21
thoughts of the wise, that they are f." . 1 Cor 3:20
has not been raised, your faith is f . . . . 1 Cor 15:17

FUTILITY
For the creation was subjected to f, ... Rom 8:20
Gentiles do, in the f of their minds. . . . . . Eph 4:17

FUTURE
behold the upright, for there is a f . . . . . . Ps 37:37
not for evil, to give you a f and a hope. . . Jer 29:11
or the present or the f—all are yours,. . 1 Cor 3:22
a good foundation for the f, ... 1 Tm 6:19

GABRIEL
"G, make this man understand the . . . . Dn 8:16
I was speaking in prayer, the man G, ... Dn 9:21
the angel answered him, "I am G. . . . . Lk 1:19

GAD
has come!" so she called his name G. . . . Gn 30:11
LORD came to the prophet G, ... 2 Sm 24:11

GAIN
What does man g by all the toil . . . . Eccl 1:3
does it profit a man to g the whole . . . . . Mk 8:36
but have not love, I g nothing. . . . . 1 Cor 13:3
in order that I may g Christ . . . . Phil 3:8
godliness with contentment is great g, . . 1 Tm 6:6
not for shameful g, but eagerly; . . . . 1 Pt 5:2

GALILEE
beyond the Jordan, G of the nations. . . . . . . Is 9:1
beyond the Jordan, G of the Gentiles— . . . Mt 4:15
I will go before you to G." . . . . Mt 26:32
see that no prophet arises from G." . . . . . . Jn 7:52
"Men of G, why do you stand looking . . . Acts 1:11

GALL
wanderings, the wormwood and the g!. Lam 3:19
wine to drink, mixed with g, ... Mt 27:34

GAMALIEL
a Pharisee in the council named G, ... Acts 5:34

GARDEN
LORD God planted a g in Eden, ... Gn 2:8
and you shall be like a watered g, like . . . . Is 58:11
where he was crucified there was a g, . . . Jn 19:41

GARMENT
they will all wear out like a g. . . . . Ps 102:26
the earth will wear out like a g, ... Is 51:6
piece of unshrunk cloth on an old g, ... Mt 9:16
might only touch the fringe of his g. . . . . Mt 14:36
there a man who had no wedding g. . . . . Mt 22:11
they will all wear out like a g, ... Heb 1:11

GARMENTS
for Adam and for his wife g of skins . . . . . Gn 3:21
they divide my g among them, ... Ps 22:18
clothed me with the g of salvation; . . . . Is 61:10
Jesus, they took his g and divided . . . . . . Jn 19:23
have rotted and your g are moth-eaten. . . Jas 5:2

GATE
of God, and this is the g of heaven." . . . . Gn 28:17
"Enter by the narrow g. For . . . . Mt 7:13
in Jerusalem by the Sheep G a pool, ... Jn 5:2

GATES
Enter his g with thanksgiving, ... Ps 100:4
build my church, and the g of hell . . . . . . Mt 16:18
high wall, with twelve g, and at the . . . . . Rv 21:12
that they may enter the city by the g. . . . Rv 22:14

GATH
Tell it not in G, publish it not in the . . . . 2 Sm 1:20

GATHER
"G to me my faithful ones, who. . . . . Ps 50:5

O Lord our God, and **g** us . . . . Ps 106:47
time is coming to **g** all nations and . . . . . . Is 66:18
Lord, and all nations shall **g** to it, ... Jer 3:17
whoever does not **g** with me scatters. . . . Mt 12:30
"**G** up the leftover fragments, ... Jn 6:12

GATHERED
where two or three are **g** in my name,. . . Mt 18:20
How often would I have **g** your. . . . . Mt 23:37
Before him will be **g** all the nations,. . . . . Mt 25:32
and our being **g** together to him, ... 2 Thes 2:1
the earth and **g** the grape harvest . . . . . . Rv 14:19

GAVE
The Lord **g**, and the Lord. . . . . Jb 1:21
and who **g** you this authority?". . . . . Mt 21:23
those whom you **g** me I have lost not . . . . Jn 18:9
he bowed his head and **g** up his spirit. . . Jn 19:30
For they **g** according to their means,. . . 2 Cor 8:3
g himself for our sins to deliver us . . . . Gal 1:4
as Christ loved us and **g** himself up . . . . . Eph 5:2
who **g** himself as a ransom for all, ... 1 Tm 2:6

GENEALOGIES
to myths and endless **g**, ... 1 Tm 1:4
avoid foolish controversies, **g**, ... Ti 3:9

GENEALOGY
people to be enrolled by **g**. . . . . Neh 7:5
The book of the **g** of Jesus . . . . Mt 1:1
He is without father or mother or **g**, ... Heb 7:3

GENERATION
One **g** shall commend your works to . . . . Ps 145:4
and their children to another **g**.. . . . . Jl 1:3
"But to what shall I compare this **g**? . . . . . Mt 11:16
An evil and adulterous **g** seeks for a . . . . . Mt 16:4
this **g** will not pass away until all these . Mt 24:34
"Why does this **g** seek a sign?. . . . . Mk 8:12
"Save yourselves from this crooked **g**." . Acts 2:40

GENERATIONS
These are the **g** of the heavens and the . . Gn 2:4
have been our dwelling place in all **g**. . . . . Ps 90:1
be forever, and my salvation to all **g**." . . . . . Is 51:8
So all the **g** from Abraham to David. . . . . . Mt 1:17
from now on all **g** will call me blessed; . . . Lk 1:48

GENEROSITY
to me? Or do you begrudge my **g**?'. . . . . Mt 20:15
the one who contributes, in **g**;. . . . . Rom 12:8

GENEROUS
Whoever is of a **g** heart, let him bring. . . . Ex 35:5
but the righteous is **g** and gives;. . . . . Ps 37:21
but blessed is he who is **g** to the poor. . . Prv 14:21
their food with glad and **g** hearts, ... Acts 2:46
enriched in every way to be **g** in every . . 2 Cor 9:11
to be **g** and ready to share, ... 1 Tm 6:18

GENEROUSLY
He is ever lending **g**, and his children . . . Ps 37:26
It is well with the man who deals **g** . . . . . . Ps 112:5
ask God, who gives **g** to all without. . . . . . Jas 1:5

GENTILE
Now the woman was a **G**, a . . . . Mk 7:26
live like a **G** and not like a Jew, ... Gal 2:14

GENTILES
Do not even the **G** do the same? . . . . Mt 5:47
up empty phrases as the **G** do, ... Mt 6:7
For the **G** seek after all these things, ... Mt 6:32
a light for revelation to the **G**, ... Lk 2:32
until the times of the **G** are fulfilled.. . . . . Lk 21:24
the **G** exercise lordship over them, ... Lk 22:25
Spirit was poured out even on the **G**. . Acts 10:45
we are turning to the **G**. . . . . Acts 13:46
opened a door of faith to the **G**. . . . . . . Acts 14:27
From now on I will go to the **G**.". . . . . . . Acts 18:6
Is he not the God of **G** also? Yes, ... Rom 3:29
salvation has come to the **G**, so as to . . Rom 11:11
block to Jews and folly to **G**, ... 1 Cor 1:23
that God would justify the **G** by faith, ... Gal 3:8

you must no longer walk as the **G** do, . . . Eph 4:17
how great among the **G** are the riches . . Col 1:27

GENTLE
learn from me, for I am **g** and lowly in. . . Mt 11:29
imperishable beauty of a **g** and quiet . . . . 1 Pt 3:4

GENTLENESS
by the meekness and **g** of Christ . . . . . . 2 Cor 10:1
g, self-control; against such . . . . Gal 5:23
restore him in a spirit of **g**.. . . . . Gal 6:1
with all humility and **g**, with patience,. . . Eph 4:2
correcting his opponents with **g**. . . . . . . 2 Tm 2:25

GETHSEMANE
went with them to a place called **G**,. . . . Mt 26:36

GHOST
on the sea they thought it was a **g**, ... Mk 6:49

GIANTS
were descended from the **g** in Gath, . . 2 Sm 21:22
was one of the descendants of the **g**, . 1 Chr 20:4

GIBEON
"Sun, stand still at **G**, and moon,. . . . . . . Jos 10:12

GIDEON
"A sword for the Lord and for **G**!". . . . . . . Jgs 7:20
For time would fail me to tell of **G**,. . . . . Heb 11:32

GIFT
A man's **g** makes room for him and . . . . . Prv 18:16
who boasts of a **g** he does not give. . . . . Prv 25:14
pleasure in all his toil—this is God's **g** . . . Eccl 3:13
brother, and then come and offer your **g**. . Mt 5:24
"If you knew the **g** of God, and who . . . . . Jn 4:10
will receive the **g** of the Holy Spirit. . . . . Acts 2:38
God gave the same **g** to them as he . . . Acts 11:17
justified by his grace as a **g**,. . . . . Rom 3:24
sin is death, but the free **g** of God is . . . Rom 6:23
But each has his own **g** from God, ... 1 Cor 7:7
be to God for his inexpressible **g**!. . . . . 2 Cor 9:15
not your own doing; it is the **g** of God, . . Eph 2:8
Do not neglect the **g** you have, which . . 1 Tm 4:14
you to fan into flame the **g** of God, ... 2 Tm 1:6
who have tasted the heavenly **g**, ... Heb 6:4
Every good **g** and every perfect **g** is . . . . . Jas 1:17
each has received a **g**, use it to serve . . . 1 Pt 4:10

GIFTS
your train and receiving **g** among men,. . Ps 68:18
Having **g** that differ according to the. . . Rom 12:6
Now concerning spiritual **g**, ... 1 Cor 12:1
and earnestly desire the spiritual **g**, ... 1 Cor 14:1
host of captives, and he gave **g** to men.". . Eph 4:8
by **g** of the Holy Spirit distributed . . . . . . Heb 2:4

GILEAD
Is there no balm in **G**? Is there no. . . . . . . Jer 8:22
If there is iniquity in **G**, they shall . . . . Hos 12:11

GILGAL
all Israel with him, to the camp at **G**. . . . Jos 10:15
"Come, let us go to **G** . . . . 1 Sm 11:14

GIVE
my glory I **g** to no other, nor my praise. . . Is 42:8
But when you **g** to the needy, do not . . . . . Mt 6:3
G us this day our daily bread, ... Mt 6:11
For what can a man **g** in return for his . . Mk 8:37
g, and it will be given to you. . . . . Lk 6:38
'It is more blessed to **g** than to.. . . . . . . Acts 20:35
So then each of us will **g** an account . . Rom 14:12
If I **g** away all I have, and if . . . . 1 Cor 13:3
Each one must **g** as he has decided. . . . 2 Cor 9:7

GIVEN
"This is my body, which is **g** for you. . . . . Lk 22:19
Holy Spirit who has been **g** to us.. . . . . . . Rom 5:5
the things freely **g** us by God. . . . . 1 Cor 2:12
But grace was **g** to each one of us. . . . . . Eph 4:7

GIVES
One **g** freely, yet grows all the richer; . . . Prv 11:24

Whoever **g** to the poor will not want, . . Prv 28:27
be to God, who **g** us the victory . . . . . . 1 Cor 15:57
letter kills, but the Spirit **g** life. . . . . 2 Cor 3:6
presence of God, who **g** life to all. . . . . . 1 Tm 6:13
on it, for the glory of God **g** it light,. . . . . Rv 21:23

GLAD
Therefore my heart is **g**, and my. . . . . Ps 16:9
I will rejoice and be **g** in your . . . . Ps 31:7
Be **g** in the Lord, and rejoice, ... Ps 32:11
a river whose streams make **g** the city . . . Ps 46:4
I was **g** when they said to me, "Let . . . . . . Ps 122:1
A **g** heart makes a cheerful face, but. . . . Prv 15:13
see my day. He saw it and was **g**." . . . . Jn 8:56

GLADNESS
anointed you with the oil of **g**. . . . . Ps 45:7
Let me hear joy and **g**; let the. . . . . Ps 51:8
Serve the Lord with **g**! Come. . . . . Ps 100:2
ashes, the oil of **g** instead of mourning, . . . Is 61:3
and give them **g** for sorrow.. . . . . Jer 31:13
anointed you with the oil of **g**. . . . . Heb 1:9

GLEAN
go to the field and **g** among the ears of . . . Ru 2:2
"They shall **g** thoroughly as a vine the. . . . Jer 6:9

GLOOM
wrapped in darkness, cloud, and **g**. . . . . Dt 4:11
For them the **g** of utter darkness has. . . . 2 Pt 2:17

GLORIFIED
I will be **g**.'" And Aaron held his peace. . . . Lv 10:3
'Let the Lord be **g**, that we . . . . Is 66:5
Fear seized them all, and they **g** God, ... Lk 7:16
Jesus said, "Now is the Son of Man **g**, ... Jn 13:31
those whom he justified he also **g**. . . . . . Rom 8:30

GLORIFY
heart, and I will **g** your name forever.. . . . Ps 86:12
Father, **g** your name." Then a voice . . . . . Jn 12:28
g your Son that the Son may **g** you, ... Jn 17:1
with a price. So **g** God in your body. . . 1 Cor 6:20
see your good deeds and **g** God. . . . . 1 Pt 2:12
will not fear, O Lord, and **g** your name?. . . Rv 15:4

GLORIOUS
G things of you are spoken, O city of. . . . . Ps 87:3
On the **g** splendor of your majesty, ... Ps 145:5
to the praise of his **g** grace, with which. . . Eph 1:6
lowly body to be like his **g** body, ... Phil 3:21

GLORY
The **g** of the Lord dwelt on . . . . Ex 24:16
Moses said, "Please show me your **g**." . . . Ex 33:18
Ichabod, saying, "The **g** has departed . . 1 Sm 4:21
for the **g** of the Lord filled the . . . . 1 Kgs 8:11
doors, that the King of **g** may come in. . . . Ps 24:7
Declare his **g** among the nations,. . . . . Ps 96:3
Let your **g** be over all the earth! . . . . Ps 108:5
not to us, but to your name give **g**, ... Ps 115:1
It is the **g** of God to conceal things,. . . . . Prv 25:2
the whole earth is full of his **g**!" . . . . Is 6:3
My **g** I will not give to another. . . . . Is 48:11
And behold, the **g** of the God of Israel . . Ezk 43:2
I will change their **g** into shame. . . . . Hos 4:7
"When the Son of Man comes in his **g**, . . Mt 25:31
and the **g** of the Lord shone around . . . . . . Lk 2:9
"**G** to God in the highest, and on earth . . . Lk 2:14
with the **g** that I had with you before . . . . Jn 17:5
not worth comparing with the **g**. . . . . . . Rom 8:18
you do, do all to the **g** of God. . . . . 1 Cor 10:31
since he is the image and **g** of God,. . . . 1 Cor 11:7
eternal weight of **g** beyond all. . . . . 2 Cor 4:17
Christ might be to the praise of his **g**. . . . Eph 1:12
according to his riches in **g** in Christ . . . . Phil 4:19
then you also will appear with him in **g**. . . Col 3:4
on in the world, taken up in **g**.. . . . . 1 Tm 3:16
to shine on it, for the **g** of God gives it . . Rv 21:23

GLUTTON
g will come to poverty, and slumber . . . Prv 23:21
A **g** and a drunkard, a friend of tax . . . . . . Lk 7:34

GLUTTONS
a companion of **g** shames his father. . . . . Prv 28:7
are always liars, evil beasts, lazy **g**.". . . . . . . Ti 1:12

GNASHING
will be weeping and **g** of teeth.". . . . . Mt 8:12

GO
will not let you **g** unless you bless me.". Gn 32:26
the God of Israel, 'Let my people **g**,. . . . . . . Ex 5:1
"If your presence will not **g** with me,. . . . Ex 33:15
your God is with you wherever you **g**." . . . Jos 1:9
For where you **g** I will **g**,. . . . . Ru 1:16
Where shall I **g** from your Spirit? . . . . Ps 139:7
G therefore and make disciples of all. . . . Mt 28:19
But if I **g**, I will send him to you. . . . . Jn 16:7
"that it may **g** well with you and that . . . Eph 6:3
Never shall he **g** out of it, and I will . . . . . . Rv 3:12

GOAT
one male **g** for a sin offering; . . . . Nm 7:16

GOATS
not by means of the blood of **g** . . . . .Heb 9:12
blood of bulls and **g** to take away sins. . Heb 10:4

GOD
G sent him out from the garden of. . . . . . Gn 3:23
the sons of **G** saw that the daughters . . . . Gn 6:2
"For I have seen **G** face to face,. . . . . Gn 32:30
evil against me, but **G** meant it for. . . . . . Gn 50:20
And **G** heard their groaning, and . . . . .Ex 2:24
G called to him out of the bush,. . . . . .Ex 3:4
to be my people, and I will be your **G**,. . . . .Ex 6:7
no one like the LORD our **G**. . . . . .Ex 8:10
do not let **G** speak to us, lest we die.". . .Ex 20:19
serve the LORD, for he is our **G**." . . . . Jos 24:18
defy the armies of the living **G**?" . . . . . 1 Sm 17:26
there is no **G** like you, in heaven . . . . . . 1 Kgs 8:23
G who answers by fire, he is **G**." . . . . . .1 Kgs 18:24
sinned against the LORD their **G**,. . . . . . 2 Kgs 17:7
cherubim, you are the **G**, you alone,. . .2 Kgs 19:15
for our **G** is greater than all gods. . . . . . . 2 Chr 2:5
LORD filled the house of **G**. . . . . 2 Chr 5:14
hearts to seek the LORD **G**. . . . . 2 Chr 11:16
Shall we receive good from **G**, and. . . . . . . Jb 2:10
My **G**, my **G**, why have you. . . . . Ps 22:1
G is our refuge and strength, a very. . . . . . Ps 46:1
"Be still, and know that I am **G**. . . . . .Ps 46:10
Your way, O **G**, is holy. What **g** . . . . Ps 77:13
my fortress, my **G**, in whom I trust.". . . . . . Ps 91:2
Be exalted, O **G**, above the heavens! . . . .Ps 108:5
you are the **G**, you alone, of all the. . . . . . .Is 37:16
I am the last; besides me there is no **g**. . . . Is 44:6
But the LORD is the true **G**;. . . . . .Jer 10:10
And I will be their **G**, and they shall . . . . Jer 31:33
'Ah, Lord **G**! It is you who have made. . . .Jer 32:17
is proud, and you have said, 'I am a **g**,. . .Ezk 28:2
our **G** whom we serve is able to deliver . . Dn 3:17
I am the LORD your **G** and there . . . . Jl 2:27
do this to you, prepare to meet your **G**, . Am 4:12
Who is a **G** like you, pardoning iniquity. . . Mi 7:18
one Father? Has not one **G** created us?. . Mal 2:10
Caesar's, and to **G** the things that are . . . Mt 22:21
that is, "My **G**, my **G**, why. . . . . Mt 27:46
The Lord our **G**, the Lord is one. . . . . .Mk 12:29
But if it is by the finger of **G** that I cast. . Lk 11:20
answered him, "My Lord and my **G**!" . . . .Jn 20:28
G raised him up, loosing the pangs of. . Acts 2:24
For **G** shows no partiality. . . . . .Rom 2:11
"Abraham believed **G**, and it was . . . . . . .Rom 4:3
If **G** is for us, who can be against us?. . . Rom 8:31
do all to the glory of **G**. . . . . .1 Cor 10:31
is not a **G** of confusion but of peace. . .1 Cor 14:33
one **G** and Father of all, who is over. . . . . Eph 4:6
though he was in the form of **G**,. . . . . .Phil 2:6
proclaiming himself to be **G**. . . . . 2 Thes 2:4
to fall into the hands of the living **G**. . . .Heb 10:31
for our **G** is a consuming fire. . . . . .Heb 12:29
"Abraham believed **G**, and it was . . . . Jas 2:23
G is light, and in him is no darkness. . . . . . .1 Jn 1:5
G is love, and whoever abides in love . . .1 Jn 4:16
which he is called is The Word of **G**. . . . . Rv 19:13

GODDESS
after Ashtoreth the **g** of the Sidonians,. .1 Kgs 11:5
temple of the great **g** Artemis may be . .Acts 19:27

GODLINESS
silly myths. Rather train yourself for **g**; . .1 Tm 4:7
g with contentment is great gain,. . . . . . .1 Tm 6:6
the appearance of **g**, but denying. . . . . . .2 Tm 3:5
of the truth, which accords with **g**,. . . . . Ti 1:1
us all things that pertain to life and **g**,. . . .2 Pt 1:3
and steadfastness with **g**,. . . . . .2 Pt 1:6

GODLY
the LORD has set apart the **g** . . . . .Ps 4:3
let everyone who is **g** offer prayer to. . . . .Ps 32:6
a peaceful and quiet life, **g** and. . . . . .1 Tm 2:2
all who desire to live a **g** life in Christ . . 2 Tm 3:12

GODS
"You shall have no other **g** before me. . . . Ex 20:3
Have the **g** of the nations delivered . . . . . . Is 37:12
written in your Law, 'I said, you are **g**'? . . Jn 10:34
g made with hands are not **g**. . . . . Acts 19:26

GOLD
have made for themselves gods of **g**. . . . Ex 32:31
More to be desired are they than **g**,. . . . . Ps 19:10
I love your commandments above **g**,. . . Ps 119:127
which is greater, the **g** or the temple. . . . Mt 23:17
a man wearing a **g** ring and fine. . . . . Jas 2:2
Your **g** and silver have corroded,. . . . . Jas 5:3
more precious than **g** that perishes . . . . . . 1 Pt 1:7
and the street of the city was pure **g**, . . . Rv 21:21

GOLGOTHA
came to a place called **G** . . . . .Mt 27:33
of a Skull, which in Aramaic is called **G**. . .Jn 19:17

GOLIATH
a champion named **G** of Gath,. . . . . 1 Sm 17:4
gave him the sword of **G** . . . . .1 Sm 22:10

GOMORRAH
LORD destroyed Sodom and **G**.). . . . . Gn 13:10
been like Sodom, and become like **G**. . . . . . . Is 1:9
land of Sodom and **G** than for that . . . . . Mt 10:15

GOOD
had made, and behold, it was very **g**. . . . . Gn 1:31
LORD God said, "It is not **g** that. . . . . .Gn 2:18
evil against me, but God meant it for **g**,. . Gn 50:20
there is none who does **g**. . . . . .Ps 14:1
For you, O Lord, are **g** and forgiving,. . . . .Ps 86:5
For it is **g** to sing praises to our God;. . . . .Ps 147:1
Do not withhold **g** from those to . . . . Prv 3:27
G sense makes one slow to anger,. . . . . . Prv 19:11
Woe to those who call evil **g** and . . . . Is 5:20
He has told you, O man, what is **g**;. . . . . Mi 6:8
are evil, know how to give **g** gifts to . . . . . Mt 7:11
"Why do you ask me about what is **g**? . . Mt 19:17
Love your enemies, do **g** to . . . . .Lk 6:27
The **g** person out of the **g** treasure. . . . . . . .Lk 6:45
all things work together for **g**,. . . . . .Rom 8:28
Let no one seek his own **g**, but the . . .1 Cor 10:24
he who began a **g** work in you . . . . Phil 1:6
For everything created by God is **g**,. . . . .1 Tm 4:4
So also **g** works are conspicuous,. . . . . . 1 Tm 5:25
They are to do **g**, to be rich in **g** . . . . 1 Tm 6:18
but he disciplines us for our **g**, ... Heb 12:10
you have tasted that the Lord is **g**. . . . . . . .1 Pt 2:3

GOODNESS
will make all my **g** pass before you . . . . . Ex 33:19
Surely **g** and mercy shall follow . . . . .Ps 23:6
For how great is his **g**, and how great . . . Zec 9:17
But when the **g** and loving kindness . . . . . . Ti 3:4

GOSPEL
and proclaiming the **g** of the kingdom . . .Mt 4:23
the **g** must first be proclaimed to. . . . . . .Mk 13:10
preaching the **g** and healing . . . . .Lk 9:6
there they continued to preach the **g**. . . Acts 14:7
I am eager to preach the **g** to you . . . . . .Rom 1:15
I do it all for the sake of the **g**,. . . . . 1 Cor 9:23
even if our **g** is veiled, it is veiled . . . . . . 2 Cor 4:3
is preaching to you a **g** contrary to . . . . . . Gal 1:9
to proclaim the mystery of the **g**,. . . . . . . .Eph 6:19
before in the word of the truth, the **g**,. . . . Col 1:5
by God to be entrusted with the **g**, . . . 1 Thes 2:4
share in suffering for the **g** by the . . . . . .2 Tm 1:8
this is why the **g** was preached. . . . . .1 Pt 4:6
with an eternal **g** to proclaim. . . . . .Rv 14:6

GOSSIP
g, conceit, and disorder. . . . . 2 Cor 12:20

GOSSIPS
deceit, maliciousness. They are **g**,. . . . . . Rom 1:29
not only idlers, but also **g**. . . . . 1 Tm 5:13

GRACE
listen to my plea for **g**. . . . . .Ps 86:6
found **g** in the wilderness; . . . . .Jer 31:2
top stone amid shouts of '**G**, ...Zec 4:7
from the Father, full of **g** and truth. . . . . . . .Jn 1:14
be saved through the **g** of the Lord . . . . Acts 15:11
obtained access by faith into this **g** . . . . .Rom 5:2
but where sin increased, **g** abounded . .Rom 5:20
you are not under law but under **g**. . . . . Rom 6:14
otherwise **g** would no longer be **g**. . . . . . .Rom 11:6
But by the **g** of God I am what I am, . .1 Cor 15:10
God is able to make all **g** abound to . . . 2 Cor 9:8
"My **g** is sufficient for you, for my. . . . . 2 Cor 12:9
I do not nullify the **g** of God,. . . . . Gal 2:21
by **g** you have been saved— . . . . Eph 2:5
be strengthened by the **g** that is in . . . . . 2 Tm 2:1
For the **g** of God has appeared, ... Ti 2:11
so that being justified by his **g** we . . . . Ti 3:7
draw near to the throne of **g**, ...Heb 4:16
opposes the proud, but gives **g** to the. . . .Jas 4:6
as good stewards of God's varied **g**: . . . .1 Pt 4:10
The **g** of the Lord Jesus be with all. . . . . .Rv 22:21

GRACIOUS
And I will be **g** to whom I will be . . . . . . .Ex 33:19
to shine upon you and be **g** to you;. . . . .Nm 6:25
But the LORD was **g** to them . . . . 2 Kgs 13:23
The LORD is merciful and **g**, ...Ps 103:8
The LORD is **g** and merciful, ...Ps 145:8
G words are like a honeycomb,. . . . . Prv 16:24
the LORD waits to be **g** to you,. . . . . .Is 30:18
God of hosts, will be **g** to the remnant . . Am 5:15
LORD answered **g** and comforting . . . . .Zec 1:13
yes, Father, for such was your **g** will. . . . . Mt 11:26
and marveled at the **g** words that were . . Lk 4:22

GRAFT
for God has the power to **g** them in. . . .Rom 11:23

GRAIN
brothers went down to buy **g** in Egypt. . Gn 42:3
The firstfruits of your **g**, of your wine . . . . Dt 18:4
you provide their **g**, for so . . . . .Ps 65:9
began to pluck heads of **g** and to eat. . . . Mt 12:1
choked it, and it yielded no **g**. . . . . Mk 4:7
I say to you, unless a **g** of wheat falls . . . Jn 12:24

GRANDCHILDREN
G are the crown of the aged, and the . . . Prv 17:6
But if a widow has children or **g**, let. . . . . 1 Tm 5:4

GRANT
May he **g** you your heart's desire . . . . .Ps 20:4
hand and at my left is not mine to **g**,. . . Mt 20:23
who conquers I will **g** to eat of the tree . . .Rv 2:7

GRAPES
a branch with a single cluster of **g**,. . . . . Nm 13:23
it to yield **g**, but it yielded wild **g**. . . . . .Is 5:2
nor are **g** picked from a bramble bush. . . Lk 6:44
the vine of the earth, for its **g** are ripe." . Rv 14:18

GRASS
like **g** that is renewed in the morning: . . . .Ps 90:5
As for man, his days are like **g**;. . . . . Ps 103:15

caught up to the third **h**—whether in. . .2 Cor 12:2
But our citizenship is in **h**, ... Phil 3:20
of the hope laid up for you in **h**. . . . . Col 1:5
and unfading, kept in **h** for you, ... 1 Pt 1:4
Then I saw a new **h** and a new earth,. . . . . Rv 21:1

HEAVENLY

be perfect, as your **h** Father is perfect. . . Mt 5:48
a multitude of the **h** host praising God . . . Lk 2:13
can you believe if I tell you **h** things?. . . . . Jn 3:12
every spiritual blessing in the **h** places,. . . Eph 1:3
bring me safely into his **h** kingdom. . . . .2 Tm 4:18
better country, that is, a **h** one. . . . . Heb 11:16

HEAVENS

God created the **h** and the earth. . . . . Gn 1:1
When I look at your **h**, the work of. . . . . . . .Ps 8:3
The **h** declare the glory of God, ...Ps 19:1
The **h** declare his righteousness,. . . . . .Ps 50:6
and the **h** are the work of your hands. . Ps 102:25
your steadfast love is great above the **h**;. . Ps 108:4
For as the **h** are higher than the earth, . . . Is 55:9
His splendor covered the **h**, and . . . . Hab 3:3
and behold, the **h** were opened to him,. . . Mt 3:16
and the powers of the **h** will be shaken. . Mt 24:29
who also ascended far above all the **h**, . .Eph 4:10
and the **h** are the work of your hands;. . . Heb 1:10
we are waiting for new **h** and a new . . . .2 Pt 3:13

HEAVY

and night your hand was **h** upon me; . . . .Ps 32:4
to me, all who labor and are **h** laden,. . . . Mt 11:28
They tie up **h** burdens, hard to bear, ...Mt 23:4

HEBREW

escaped came and told Abram the **H**, . . . Gn 14:13
he said to them, "I am a **H**, and I fear . . . . Jon 1:9
tribe of Benjamin, a **H** of Hebrews;. . . . . . .Phil 3:5

HEBRON

by the oaks of Mamre, which are at **H**,. . Gn 13:18
David was king in **H** over the house. . . . 2 Sm 2:11

HEEL

your head, and you shall bruise his **h**.". . . .Gn 3:15
my bread has lifted his **h** against me.' . . . .Jn 13:18

HEIGHT

nor **h** nor depth, nor anything else in. . .Rom 8:39
breadth and length and **h** and depth, . . .Eph 3:18

HEIR

your very own son shall be your **h**.". . . . . .Gn 15:4
and if a son, then an **h** through God. . . . . . Gal 4:7
whom he appointed the **h** of all things,. . .Heb 1:2

HEIRS

h of God and fellow **h** . . . . Rom 8:17
are Abraham's offspring, **h** according . . .Gal 3:29
mystery is that the Gentiles are fellow **h**,. . Eph 3:6
by his grace we might become **h** . . . . Ti 3:7

HELL

fool!' will be liable to the **h** of fire. . . . . . . .Mt 5:22
can destroy both soul and body in **h**. . . .Mt 10:28
course of life, and set on fire by **h**. . . . . . . .Jas 3:6
when they sinned, but cast them into **h** . 2 Pt 2:4

HELMET

as a breastplate, and a **h** of salvation. . . . .Is 59:17
and take the **h** of salvation, ...Eph 6:17
faith and love, and for a **h** the hope. . . 1 Thes 5:8

HELP

Lord, there is none like you to **h**, ... 2 Chr 14:11
to my God I cried for **h**. . . . . Ps 18:6
From where does my **h** come? . . . . Ps 121:1
I will strengthen you, I will **h** you,. . . . . Is 41:10
knelt before him, saying, "Lord, **h** me." . . Mt 15:25
"I believe; **h** my unbelief!". . . . . Mk 9:24
the fainthearted, **h** the weak,. . . . . .1 Thes 5:14
tempted, he is able to **h** those. . . . . .Heb 2:18

HELPED

"Till now the Lord has **h** us." . . . . 1 Sm 7:12
because you, Lord, have **h** me. . . . . Ps 86:17
in a day of salvation I have **h** you; . . . . Is 49:8
in a day of salvation I have **h** you.". . . . . 2 Cor 6:2

HELPER

alone; I will make him a **h** fit for him.". . . .Gn 2:18
you have been the **h** of the fatherless. . . . Ps 10:14
Father, and he will give you another **H**, . . Jn 14:16
confidently say, "The Lord is my **h**;. . . . . .Heb 13:6

HEM

You **h** me in, behind and before,. . . . . Ps 139:5
and surround you and **h** you in on . . . . . . Lk 19:43

HERBS

bread and bitter **h** they shall eat. . . . . Ex 12:8
is a dinner of **h** where love is than . . . . . .Prv 15:17

HERESIES

who will secretly bring in destructive **h**, . .2 Pt 2:1

HEROD

of Judea in the days of **H** the king,. . . . . Mt 2:1
For **H** had seized John and bound him . . . Mt 14:3
governor of Judea, and **H** being . . . . Lk 3:1
from here, for **H** wants to kill you.". . . . . . .Lk 13:31
jurisdiction, he sent him over to **H**,. . . . . . .Lk 23:7

HEZEKIAH

fourteenth year of King **H**, ...2 Kgs 18:13
In the fourteenth year of King **H**, ...Is 36:1
Did **H** king of Judah and all Judah put . Jer 26:19

HID

and the man and his wife **h** themselves . . Gn 3:8
I **h** a hundred men of the Lord's . . . . . . 1 Kgs 18:13
in the shadow of his hand he **h** me;. . . . . . Is 49:2
prophet, but the Lord **h** them. . . . . .Jer 36:26
but Jesus **h** himself and went out. . . . . .Jn 8:59

HIDDEN

Declare me innocent from **h** faults. . . . . . . .Ps 19:12
Better is open rebuke than **h** love. . . . . . . Prv 27:5
your sins have **h** his face from you . . . . Is 59:2
he reveals deep and **h** things; he knows . Dn 2:22
For nothing is **h** except to be made . . . . . Mk 4:22
died, and your life is **h** with Christ . . . . Col 3:3

HIDE

h me in the shadow of your wings, ... Ps 17:8
H your face from my sins, and blot out . . . Ps 51:9
H not your face from me, lest I be like. . . Ps 143:7
"Fall on us and **h** us from the face of. . . . .Rv 6:16

HIGH

wine. (He was priest of God Most **H**.) . . . Gn 14:18
people were sacrificing at the **h** places,. . 1 Kgs 3:2
your dwelling place—the Most **H**, ... Ps 91:9
he makes me tread on my **h** places. . . . . .Hab 3:19
led him to Caiaphas the **h** priest, ...Mt 26:57
me, Jesus, Son of the Most **H** God? . . . . . . Mk 5:7
will be called the Son of the Most **H**. . . . . . Lk 1:32

HIGHWAY

The **h** of the upright turns aside from . . .Prv 16:17
And a **h** shall be there, and it shall be . . . . Is 35:8

HILL

A city set on a **h** cannot be hidden. . . . . . . Mt 5:14
brought him to the brow of the **h**. . . . . .Lk 4:29

HIP

Jacob's **h** was put out of joint as he. . . . Gn 32:25

HOLD

and your right hand shall **h** me. . . . . Ps 139:10
who, hearing the word, **h** it fast . . . . Lk 8:15
evil; **h** fast to what is good. . . . . Rom 12:9
H fast what you have, so that no one. . . . . Rv 3:11

HOLINESS

Who is like you, majestic in **h**, ...Ex 15:11
the Lord in the splendor of **h**. . . . . .Ps 29:2
h befits your house, O Lord, ...Ps 93:5
and it shall be called the Way of **H**; . . . . . . Is 35:8
bringing **h** to completion in the fear . . . .2 Cor 7:1
not called us for impurity, but in **h**. . . . . 1 Thes 4:7
they continue in faith and love and **h**, . . 1 Tm 2:15
and for the **h** without which no one. . . . Heb 12:14
ought you to be in lives of **h** and . . . . 2 Pt 3:11

HOLY

blessed the seventh day and made it **h**, . . Gn 2:3
which you are standing is **h** ground.". . . . . .Ex 3:5
a kingdom of priests and a **h** nation. . . . . . Ex 19:6
the Sabbath day, to keep it **h**. . . . . Ex 20:8
be **h**, for I the Lord your God am **h**. . . . . . . Lv 19:2
"There is none **h** like the Lord: . . . . .1 Sm 2:2
And who shall stand in his **h** place? . . . . . .Ps 24:3
H and awesome is his name! . . . . .Ps 111:9
"**H**, **h**, **h** is the Lord. . . . . Is 6:3
conceived in her is from the **H** Spirit. . . . . .Mt 1:20
who you are—the **H** One of God.". . . . . . . .Mk 1:24
blasphemes against the **H** Spirit never. . . Mk 3:29
and the **H** Spirit descended on him in . . . .Lk 3:22
Father give the **H** Spirit to those who . . . . Lk 11:13
But the Helper, the **H** Spirit, whom. . . . . . Jn 14:26
receive power when the **H** Spirit has . . . . Acts 1:8
For God's temple is **h**, and you are. . . . .1 Cor 3:17
in order to present you **h** and blameless . . Col 1:22
upright, **h**, and disciplined. . . . . .Ti 1:8
a high priest, **h**, innocent, unstained, . . . Heb 7:26
"You shall be **h**, for I am **h**." . . . . 1 Pt 1:16
"**H**, **h**, **h**, is the Lord God . . . . Rv 4:8
For you alone are **h**. All nations will. . . . . .Rv 15:4
And I saw the **h** city, new Jerusalem,. . . . .Rv 21:2

HOME

God settles the solitary in a **h**;. . . . . .Ps 68:6
Even the sparrow finds a **h**, ...Ps 84:3
because man is going to his eternal **h**, . .Eccl 12:5
"Return to your **h**, and declare how . . . . . .Lk 8:39
come to him and make our **h** with him. . . Jn 14:23
that while we are at **h** in the body we . . 2 Cor 5:6
self-controlled, pure, working at **h**,. . . . . Ti 2:5

HOMELESS

and bring the **h** poor into your house;. . . . Is 58:7
are poorly dressed and buffeted and **h**, . .1 Cor 4:11

HOMES

"See, we have left our **h** and followed . . . Lk 18:28
and breaking bread in their **h**,. . . . . .Acts 2:46

HOMETOWN

coming to his **h** he taught them in . . . . . .Mt 13:54
you, no prophet is acceptable in his **h**. . . .Lk 4:24

HOMOSEXUALITY

adulterers, nor men who practice **h**,. . . . 1 Cor 6:9
men who practice **h**, enslavers,. . . . . .1 Tm 1:10

HONEST

Whoever gives an **h** answer kisses . . . . .Prv 24:26
hold it fast in an **h** and good heart, ... Lk 8:15
rather let him labor, doing **h** work . . . . . Eph 4:28

HONEY

a land flowing with milk and **h**, ...Ex 3:8
taste of it was like wafers made with **h**. . Ex 16:31
much fine gold; sweeter also than **h**. . . . . Ps 19:10
taste, sweeter than **h** to my mouth! . . . .Ps 119:103
his waist and ate locusts and wild **h**. . . . . . .Mk 1:6

HONEYCOMB

Gracious words are like a **h**, sweetness . Prv 16:24
my spice, I ate my **h** with my honey, ... Sg 5:1

HONOR

"**H** your father and your mother, that. . . . Ex 20:12
those who **h** me I will **h**, ...1 Sm 2:30
H the Lord with your wealth . . . . .Prv 3:9
wisdom, and humility comes before **h**. . Prv 15:33
of hosts, him you shall **h** as holy. . . . . .Is 8:13
For God commanded, '**H** your father . . . . . Mt 15:4
that a prophet has no **h** in his own. . . . . . Jn 4:44

I am the good shepherd. . . . . .Jn 10:11
"I am the resurrection and the life. . . . . . . .Jn 11:25
"I am the way, and the truth, and the . . . . Jn 14:6
"I am the Alpha and the Omega,". . . . . Rv 1:8

IDLE
by no means reduce it, for they are i. . . . . .Ex 5:8
an i person will suffer hunger. . . . . .Prv 19:15
sing i songs to the sound of the harp . . . .Am 6:5
'Why do you stand here i all day?' . . . . . . Mt 20:6
brothers, admonish the i, encourage . . 1 Thes 5:14
condemnation from long ago is not i, . . . 2 Pt 2:3

IDLENESS
does not eat the bread of i. . . . . Prv 31:27
some among you walk in i,. . . . . .2 Thes 3:11

IDOL
An i! A craftsman casts it, and a . . . . Is 40:19
"What profit is an i when its maker . . . . .Hab 2:18
know that "an i has no real existence," . 1 Cor 8:4
is anything, or that an i is anything? . . 1 Cor 10:19

IDOLATER
or greed, or is an i, reviler, ... 1 Cor 5:11
covetous (that is, an i), has no . . . . Eph 5:5

IDOLATERS
or the greedy and swindlers, or i,. . . . . . 1 Cor 5:10
Do not be i as some of them. . . . . 1 Cor 10:7

IDOLATRY
and presumption is as iniquity and i. . . 1 Sm 15:23
bear the penalty for your sinful i, ... Ezk 23:49
Therefore, my beloved, flee from i. . . . . 1 Cor 10:14

IDOLS
Do not turn to i or make for. . . . . Lv 19:4
All who fashion i are nothing, and . . . . Is 44:9
let your collection of i deliver you!. . . . . . .Is 57:13
Their i are like scarecrows in a. . . . . Jer 10:5
abstain from the things polluted by i, . Acts 15:20
as he saw that the city was full of i. . . . .Acts 17:16
You who abhor i, do you rob temples? .Rom 2:22
Now concerning food offered to i: we . . . 1 Cor 8:1
That food offered to i is anything, or . . 1 Cor 10:19
you turned to God from i to serve . . . . . 1 Thes 1:9
Little children, keep yourselves from i. . . 1 Jn 5:21

IGNORANCE
brothers, I know that you acted in i,. . . . Acts 3:17
The times of i God overlooked, but . . . Acts 17:30
the life of God because of the i. . . . . .Eph 4:18
to the passions of your former i,. . . . . 1 Pt 1:14
should put to silence the i of foolish . . . . 1 Pt 2:15

IGNORANT
being i of the righteousness of God, . . . Rom 10:3
Satan; for we are not i of his designs. . . 2 Cor 2:11
deal gently with the i and wayward, ... Heb 5:2
about matters of which they are i, ...2 Pt 2:12

ILL
Simon's mother-in-law lay i with a. . . . . . .Mk 1:30
there was an official whose son was i. . . . .Jn 4:46
is why many of you are weak and i, . . . 1 Cor 11:30

ILLNESS
in his i you restore him to full health. . . . . Ps 41:3
"This i does not lead to death. . . . . .Jn 11:4

IMAGE
"Let us make man in our i,. . . . . .Gn 1:26
be shed, for God made man in his own i. . Gn 9:6
shall not make for yourself a carved i, . . . Ex 20:4
i of jealousy, which provokes to . . . . .Ezk 8:3
Nebuchadnezzar made an i of gold,. . . . . . . Dn 3:1
to be conformed to the i of his Son, . . .Rom 8:29
since he is the i and glory of God, ... 1 Cor 11:7
He is the i of the invisible God,. . . . . .Col 1:15
would not worship the i of the beast. . . . Rv 13:15

IMAGES
All worshipers of i are put to shame,. . . . .Ps 97:7

nothing; their metal i are empty wind. . . . .Is 41:29
of the immortal God for i resembling. . . Rom 1:23

IMITATE
give you in ourselves an example to i. . 2 Thes 3:9
of their way of life, and i their faith. . . . . .Heb 13:7
do not i evil but i good. . . . . .3 Jn 11

IMITATORS
Be i of me, as I am of Christ. . . . . .1 Cor 11:1
Therefore be i of God, as beloved. . . . . Eph 5:1
And you became i of us and . . . . 1 Thes 1:6
became i of the churches of God in . . . 1 Thes 2:14
may not be sluggish, but i . . . . .Heb 6:12

IMMANUEL
bear a son, and shall call his name I. . . . . . .Is 7:14
call his name I" (which means, ... Mt 1:23

IMMORAL
not to associate with sexually i people . 1 Cor 5:9
but the sexually i person sins against . . 1 Cor 6:18
the sexually i, sorcerers, idolaters, ... Rv 21:8

IMMORALITY
wife, except on the ground of sexual i, . . .Mt 5:32
of man, come evil thoughts, sexual i,. . . . .Mk 7:21
not in sexual i and sensuality, ...Rom 13:13
The body is not meant for sexual i, ... 1 Cor 6:13
But sexual i and all impurity . . . . Eph 5:3

IMMORTAL
exchanged the glory of the i God. . . . . . Rom 1:23
To the King of the ages, i, invisible, ... 1 Tm 1:17

IMMORTALITY
seek for glory and honor and i,. . . . . Rom 2:7
and this mortal body must put on i. . . 1 Cor 15:53
who alone has i, who dwells in . . . . 1 Tm 6:16
and brought life and i to light through . 2 Tm 1:10

IMPERISHABLE
perishable body must put on the i,. . . . 1 Cor 15:53
to an inheritance that is i, undefiled, ... 1 Pt 1:4

IMPOSSIBLE
move, and nothing will be i for you." . . . .Mt 17:20
"With man this is i, but with God all . . . .Mt 19:26
in which it is i for God to lie, ...Heb 6:18
And without faith it is i to please him,. . . Heb 11:6

IMPOSTORS
We are treated as i, and yet are true;. . . 2 Cor 6:8
while evil people and i will go on . . . . . . 2 Tm 3:13

IMPRISONMENT
become confident in the Lord by my i, . . Phil 1:14
and flogging, and even chains and i. . . . Heb 11:36

IMPRISONMENTS
beatings, i, riots, labors, sleepless. . . . . . 2 Cor 6:5
with far greater labors, far more i, ... 2 Cor 11:23

IMPURITY
them up in the lusts of their hearts to i,. .Rom 1:24
as slaves to i and to lawlessness. . . . . . . Rom 6:19
have not repented of the i,. . . . . 2 Cor 12:21
sexual immorality, i, sensuality, ... Gal 5:19
For God has not called us for i,. . . . . . . 1 Thes 4:7

INCENSE
the cloud of the i may cover the mercy. . .Lv 16:13
my prayer be counted as i before you, . . .Ps 141:2
enter the temple of the Lord and burn i. . . Lk 1:9
having the golden altar of i and the ark . Heb 9:4
i, which are the prayers of the saints. . . . . .Rv 5:8

INCLINE
and i your heart to the LORD,. . . . . .Jos 24:23
But you did not i your ear or listen . . . . Jer 35:15
O my God, i your ear and hear. Open . . . .Dn 9:18

INCREASE
Of the i of his government and of peace. . . Is 9:7
run to and fro, and knowledge shall i." . . .Dn 12:4

apostles said to the Lord, "I our faith!" . . . Lk 17:5
He must i, but I must decrease.". . . . . .Jn 3:30
And the word of God continued to i,. . . . Acts 6:7
i the harvest of your righteousness. . . . 2 Cor 9:10
may the Lord make you i and abound . . 1 Thes 3:12

INCREASED
And because lawlessness will be i, the . . Mt 24:12
And Jesus i in wisdom and in stature . . . .Lk 2:52
But the word of God i and multiplied. . Acts 12:24
but where sin i, grace abounded all . . . .Rom 5:20

INCREASES
the wicked increase, transgression i, . . . Prv 29:16
to him who has no might he i strength. . Is 40:29

INCURABLE
flee away in a day of grief and i pain. . . . . .Is 17:11
is my pain unceasing, my wound i,. . . . . . .Jer 15:18

INDESTRUCTIBLE
but by the power of an i life. . . . . .Heb 7:16

INDIGNATION
Hot i seizes me because of the wicked,. Ps 119:53
upon me, for you had filled me with i. . . . Jer 15:17
shall prosper till the i is accomplished; . . Dn 11:36
Who can stand before his i? . . . . Na 1:6

INFANTS
Out of the mouth of babies and i, ...Ps 8:2
"'Out of the mouth of i and nursing . . . . . Mt 21:16
they were bringing even i to him that . . . .Lk 18:15
Like newborn i, long for the pure . . . . .1 Pt 2:2

INHABIT
you come into the land you are to i, ... Nm 15:2
For the upright will i the land, and. . . . . . Prv 2:21

INHABITANTS
let all the i of the world stand in awe . . . .Ps 33:8
men of Judah, to the i of Jerusalem, ... Dn 9:7
the i of Jerusalem a spirit of grace. . . . . Zec 12:10

INHERIT
offspring, and they shall i it forever.'". . . . Ex 32:13
The righteous shall i the land. . . . . .Ps 37:29
his own household will i the wind, ...Prv 11:29
LORD will i Judah as his portion. . . . . Zec 2:12
are the meek, for they shall i the earth. . . . .Mt 5:5
what must I do to i eternal life?". . . . . . . .Mk 10:17
unrighteous will not i the kingdom of . . 1 Cor 6:9
flesh and blood cannot i the kingdom. . 1 Cor 15:50
such things will not i the kingdom of. . . . Gal 5:21

INHERITANCE
of Egypt, to be a people of his own i, . . . Dt 4:20
places; indeed, I have a beautiful i. . . . . . . Ps 16:6
A good man leaves an i to his. . . . . Prv 13:22
Wisdom is good with an i, an . . . . Eccl 7:11
"This shall be their i: I am their i: . . . . . Ezk 44:28
tell my brother to divide the i with me." . .Lk 12:13
For if the i comes by the law, it no. . . . . . Gal 3:18
In him we have obtained an i, ...Eph 1:11
you to share in the i of the saints. . . . . . . .Col 1:12
from the Lord you will receive the i . . . . . Col 3:24
may receive the promised eternal i, ...Heb 9:15
to an i that is imperishable, undefiled,. . . . 1 Pt 1:4

INIQUITIES
For my i have gone over my head;. . . . . . .Ps 38:4
my sins, and blot out all my i. . . . . Ps 51:9
nor repay us according to our i. . . . . Ps 103:10
The i of the wicked ensnare him, ...Prv 5:22
he was crushed for our i; upon him . . . . . . Is 53:5
righteous, and he shall bear their i. . . . . . . Is 53:11
but your i have made a separation. . . . . . . Is 59:2
turning from our i and gaining insight. . . .Dn 9:13
on us; he will tread our i underfoot. . . . . . . Mi 7:19
For I will be merciful toward their i, ...Heb 8:12

INIQUITY
A God of faithfulness and without i,. . . . . .Dt 32:4
sin to you, and I did not cover my i;. . . . . .Ps 32:5

Wash me thoroughly from my **i**, ... Ps 51:2
who forgives all your **i**, who heals all .... Ps 103:3
and let no **i** get dominion over me. .... Ps 119:133
the LORD has laid on him the **i** .... Is 53:6
Who is a God like you, pardoning **i** .... Mi 7:18
I have taken your **i** away from you, ... Zec 3:4
the name of the Lord depart from **i**." ... 2 Tm 2:19

INJUSTICE
"You shall do no **i** in court. You shall ..... Lv 19:15
for there is no **i** with the LORD .... 2 Chr 19:7
Whoever sows **i** will reap calamity, ... Prv 22:8
plowed iniquity; you have reaped **i**; .... Hos 10:13
Is there **i** on God's part? By no means! . Rom 9:14

INK
written not with **i** but with the Spirit ... 2 Cor 3:3
I would rather not use paper and **i**. ...... 2 Jn 12

INN
there was no place for them in the **i**. ...... Lk 2:7
brought him to an **i** and took care of .... Lk 10:34

INNOCENT
and do not kill the **i** and righteous, ... Ex 23:7
errors? Declare me **i** from hidden faults ... Ps 19:12
because they have shed **i** blood in their ... Jl 3:19
so be wise as serpents and **i** as doves. .. Mt 10:16
"I am **i** of this man's blood; .... Mt 27:24
"Certainly this man was **i**!" .... Lk 23:47
what is good and **i** as to what is evil... Rom 16:19
such a high priest, holy, **i**, unstained, ... Heb 7:26

INQUIRED
people of Israel **i** of the LORD, ... Jgs 1:1
David **i** of the LORD, "Shall .... 1 Sm 23:2
he **i** of them where the Christ was to ...... Mt 2:4

INSCRIBED
Oh that they were **i** in a book! .... Jb 19:23
tell you what is **i** in the book of truth: ... Dn 10:21
tribes of the sons of Israel were **i**— ..... Rv 21:12

INSIGHT
the knowledge of the Holy One is **i**. ..... Prv 9:10
lavished upon us, in all wisdom and **i**. .... Eph 1:8

INSOLENT
The **i** have dug pitfalls for me; they do . Ps 119:85
slanderers, haters of God, **i**, ... Rom 1:30
persecutor, and **i** opponent. But I .... 1 Tm 1:13

INSTRUCT
I will **i** you and teach you in .... Ps 32:8
knowledge and able to **i** one another. . Rom 15:14
the mind of the Lord so as to **i** him?" .. 1 Cor 2:16
with my mind in order to **i** others, ... 1 Cor 14:19

INSTRUCTED
when a wise man is **i**, he gains .... Prv 21:11
because you are **i** from the law; .... Rom 2:18

INSTRUCTION
which I have written for their **i**." .... Ex 24:12
Whoever heeds **i** is on the path to life, .. Prv 10:17
Whoever ignores **i** despises himself, ... Prv 15:32
in former days was written for our **i**, ... Rom 15:4
but they were written down for our **i**, . 1 Cor 10:11
so that he may be able to give **i** .... Ti 1:9

INSTRUCTS
in the night also my heart **i** me. .... Ps 16:7
therefore he **i** sinners in the way. .... Ps 25:8

INSULT
but the prudent ignores an **i**. .... Prv 12:16
in saying these things you **i** us also." .... Lk 11:45

INSULTS
oppresses a poor man **i** his Maker, ... Prv 14:31
whoever **i** his brother will be liable. ...... Mt 5:22

INTEGRITY
away from evil? He still holds fast his **i**, ... Jb 2:3
till I die I will not put away my **i** .... Jb 27:5

May **i** and uprightness preserve me, ... Ps 25:21
I will walk with **i** of heart .... Ps 101:2
he is a shield to those who walk in **i**, ... Prv 2:7
Whoever walks in **i** walks securely, ... Prv 10:9
works, and in your teaching show **i**, ... Ti 2:7

INTELLIGENT
when he closes his lips, he is deemed **i** .. Prv 17:28
An **i** heart acquires knowledge, and ..... Prv 18:15

INTERCEDES
but the Spirit himself **i** for us .... Rom 8:26

INTERCESSION
the sin of many, and makes **i** for the ..... Is 53:12
he always lives to make **i** for them. .... Heb 7:25

INTEREST
and you shall not exact **i** from him. ..... Ex 22:25
does not put out his money at **i** and ..... Ps 15:5
received what was my own with **i**. ...... Mt 25:27

INTERESTS
and his **i** are divided. And .... 1 Cor 7:34
look not only to his own **i**, ... Phil 2:4

INTERMARRY
You shall not **i** with them, ... Dt 7:3
commandments again and **i** with the .... Ezr 9:14

INTERPRET
You shall not **i** omens or tell fortunes .... Lv 19:26
and understanding to **i** dreams, ... Dn 5:12
Do all speak with tongues? Do all **i**? .. 1 Cor 12:30
But if there is no one to **i**, let .... 1 Cor 14:28

INTERPRETATION
a tongue, or an **i**. Let all things be .... 1 Cor 14:26
from someone's own **i**. .... 2 Pt 1:20

INTERPRETATIONS
"Do not **i** belong to God? .... Gn 40:8
that you can give **i** and solve problems. .. Dn 5:16

INVALID
who had been an **i** for thirty-eight years ... Jn 5:5

INVISIBLE
For his **i** attributes, namely, ... Rom 1:20
in heaven and on earth, visible and **i**, ... Col 1:16
immortal, **i**, the only God, ... 1 Tm 1:17
for he endured as seeing him who is **i**. . Heb 11:27

INVITE
one of you will **i** his neighbor to come .. Zec 3:10
the main roads and **i** to the wedding ..... Mt 22:9
But when you give a feast, **i** the poor, ... Lk 14:13

INWARD
you delight in truth in the **i** being, ... Ps 51:6
the **i** mind and heart of a man are deep .. Ps 64:6
For you formed my **i** parts; .... Ps 139:13

INWARDLY
bless with their mouths, but **i** they curse . Ps 62:4
sheep's clothing but **i** are ravenous ...... Mt 7:15

IOTA
heaven and earth pass away, not an **i**, ... Mt 5:18

IRON
of all instruments of bronze and **i**. ...... Gn 4:22
them with a rod of **i** and dash them in .... Ps 2:9
I sharpens **i**, and one man .... Prv 27:17
and he will rule them with a rod of **i**. .... Rv 19:15

IRREVERENT
Have nothing to do with **i**, silly myths ... 1 Tm 4:7
But avoid **i** babble, for it will lead ...... 2 Tm 2:16

IRREVOCABLE
the gifts and the calling of God are **i**. . Rom 11:29

ISAAC
a son, and you shall call his name **I**. ..... Gn 17:19
for through **I** shall your offspring be .... Gn 21:12

wood in order and bound **I** his son. ..... Gn 22:9
soon as **I** had finished blessing Jacob, . Gn 27:30
God of Abraham, the God of **I**, ... Ex 3:6
children by one man, our forefather **I**, .. Rom 9:10
when he was tested, offered up **I**, ... Heb 11:17
he offered up his son **I** on the altar? .... Jas 2:21

ISAIAH
sackcloth, to the prophet **I** .... 2 Kgs 19:2
I the prophet the son of Amoz wrote .. 2 Chr 26:22
And the LORD said to **I**, "Go out .... Is 7:3
I when he said, "The voice of one .... Mt 3:3
prophet **I**: "He took our illnesses and ..... Mt 8:17
Well did **I** prophesy of you, when he ..... Mt 15:7
and he was reading the prophet **I**. ..... Acts 8:28
I cries out concerning Israel: "Though .. Rom 9:27
Then **I** is so bold as to say, "I have .... Rom 10:20

ISHMAEL
You shall call his name **I**, because .... Gn 16:11
The sons of Abraham: Isaac and **I**. ..... 1 Chr 1:28

ISRAEL
shall no longer be called Jacob, but **I**, .. Gn 32:28
All these are the twelve tribes of **I**. ..... Gn 49:28
Then Moses made **I** set out .... Ex 15:22
"Hear, O **I**: The LORD our God, ... Dt 6:4
"The glory has departed from **I**, ... 1 Sm 4:22
I commanded to shepherd my people **I**, .. 2 Sm 7:7
And he will redeem **I** from all .... Ps 130:8
I was holy to the LORD, ... Jer 2:3
new covenant with the house of **I** and ... Jer 31:31
For **I** has forgotten his Maker and built .. Hos 8:14
When **I** was a child, I loved him, and ..... Hos 11:1
ruler who will shepherd my people **I**.'" ..... Mt 2:6
no one in **I** have I found such faith. ...... Mt 8:10
to the lost sheep of the house of **I**. .... Mt 10:6
Gentiles, and for glory to your people **I**." . Lk 2:32
at this time restore the kingdom to **I**?" .. Acts 1:6
God has brought to **I** a Savior, ... Acts 13:23
not all who are descended from **I** belong .. Rom 9:6
all **I** will be saved, ... Rom 11:26
new covenant with the house of **I** and ... Heb 8:8
tribes of the sons of **I** were inscribed— .. Rv 21:12

ISRAELITE
said of him, "Behold, an **I** indeed, in ...... Jn 1:47
For I myself am an **I**, a descendant of ... Rom 11:1

ISRAELITES
They are **I**, and to them belong the ..... Rom 9:4
such glory that the **I** could not gaze at . 2 Cor 3:7
exodus of the **I** and gave directions .... Heb 11:22

ISSACHAR
husband." So she called his name **I**. ..... Gn 30:18

JACOB
Esau's heel, so his name was called **J** ... Gn 25:26
J said, "Sell me your birthright now." .... Gn 25:31
J said to his father, "I am Esau .... Gn 27:19
Then **J** awoke from his sleep and said, .. Gn 28:16
So **J** served seven years for Rachel, ... Gn 29:20
J was left alone. And a man wrestled .. Gn 32:24
God appeared to **J** again, when he ...... Gn 35:9
Now the sons of **J** were twelve. .... Gn 35:22
Egypt, **J** and all his offspring with him, .. Gn 46:6
"Yet I have loved **J** .... Mal 1:2
As it is written, "**J** I loved, but Esau I ... Rom 9:13
By faith **J**, when dying, blessed each ... Heb 11:21

JAIRUS
the rulers of the synagogue, **J** by name, . Mk 5:22

JAMES
J the son of Zebedee and John. .... Mt 4:21
And are not his brothers **J** and Joseph .. Mt 13:55
Jesus took with him Peter and **J**, and .... Mt 17:1
He killed **J** the brother of John with the .. Acts 12:2
After they finished speaking, **J** replied, .. Acts 15:13
the other apostles except **J** the Lord's .... Gal 1:19

JONATHAN
And Saul and J his son .... 1 Sm 13:16
And J spoke well of David to Saul ..... 1 Sm 19:4
"J lies slain on your high places........2 Sm 1:25

JOPPA
He went down to J and found a ship..... Jon 1:3
Send therefore to J and ask for Simon. . Acts 10:32

JORDAN
of you will pass over the J .... Nm 32:21
that Moses gave you beyond the J, ...Jos 1:14
the nation finished passing over the J. .. Jos 3:17
"Go and wash in the J seven times, ... 2 Kgs 5:10
baptized by him in the river J,............Mt 3:6

JOSEPH
sons of Rachel: J and Benjamin........ Gn 35:24
Now Israel loved J more than .... Gn 37:3
Now J was handsome in form.......... Gn 39:6
And J stored up grain in great .... Gn 41:49
So J went up to bury his father......... Gn 50:7
king over Egypt, who did not know J...... Ex 1:8
Moses took the bones of J with him,..... Ex 13:19
Mary had been betrothed to J,.......... Mt 1:18
Lord appeared in a dream to J in Egypt,. . Mt 2:19
And J took the body and wrapped it... Mt 27:59

JOSHUA
Moses said to J, "Choose for us men,..... Ex 17:9
And J the son of Nun, the assistant of. . Nm 11:28
J the son of Nun, who stands before..... Dt 1:38
J said, "Alas, O Lord GOD,................Jos 7:7
So J made a covenant with the people . . Jos 24:25

JOSIAH
J was eight years old when he began . 2 Kgs 22:1
J put away the mediums ....2 Kgs 23:24
J kept a Passover to the LORD ....2 Chr 35:1
word of the LORD came in the days of J . . . Jer 1:2

JOURNEY
and eat, for the j is too great for you." .1 Kgs 19:7
great city, three days' j in breadth.........Jon 3:3
no bag for your j, or two tunics or...... Mt 10:10
"For it will be like a man going on a j,. . . Mt 25:14
Jesus, wearied as he was from his j,.......Jn 4:6

JOY
the j of the LORD is your strength."......Neh 8:10
You have put more j in my heart..........Ps 4:7
him glad with the j of your presence........ Ps 21:6
but j comes with the morning. ....Ps 30:5
works of your hands I sing for j..........Ps 92:4
"For you shall go out in j and be led .....Is 55:12
take j in the God of my salvation.........Hab 3:18
from the tomb with fear and great j,.....Mt 28:8
I bring you good news of great j......... Lk 2:10
and that your j may be full..............Jn 15:11
and no one will take your j from you. ... Jn 16:22
fill you with all j and peace in ....Rom 15:13
complete my j by being of the same .....Phil 2:2
For you are our glory and j.......... 1 Thes 2:20
Count it all j, my brothers,...............Jas 1:2
things so that our j may be complete.....1 Jn 1:4

JOYFUL
let us make a j noise to the rock of our... Ps 95:1
Make a j noise to the LORD,............ Ps 100:1
A j heart is good medicine, ... Prv 17:22
for them than to be j and to do good . . . Eccl 3:12
make them j in my house of prayer;...... Is 56:7

JUBILEE
That fiftieth year shall be a j for you;.....Lv 25:11
And when the j of the people of Israel . . Nm 36:4

JUDAH
she called his name J.................. Gn 29:35
And J said to Israel his father, "Send.... Gn 43:8
The scepter shall not depart from J, ... Gn 49:10
But the house of J followed David.....2 Sm 2:10
cities of J, "Behold your God!" .... Is 40:9
are too little to be among the clans of J, . . Mi 5:2
"I will strengthen the house of J, and I . . Zec 10:6
no means least among the rulers of J;.....Mt 2:6
that our Lord was descended from J, . . .Heb 7:14
the Lion of the tribe of J, the Root........Rv 5:5

JUDAISM
devout converts to J followed Paul ... Acts 13:43
I was advancing in J beyond many of ....Gal 1:14

JUDAS
and J Iscariot, who betrayed him.........Mt 10:4
already put it into the heart of J Iscariot, . Jn 13:2
dipped the morsel, he gave it to J,...... Jn 13:26

JUDEA
was born in Bethlehem of J.............. Mt 2:1
spread through the whole of J and all.... Lk 7:17
"Men of J and all who dwell in .... Acts 2:14
delivered from the unbelievers in J,....Rom 15:31

JUDGE
Shall not the J of all the earth do what. . Gn 18:25
for he comes to j the earth...........1 Chr 16:33
God is a righteous j, and a God...........Ps 7:11
he will j the peoples with equity."....... Ps 96:10
for there I will sit to j all the.............. Jl 3:12
"J not, that you be not judged............ Mt 7:1
for I did not come to j the world but.... Jn 12:47
a day on which he will j the world .....Acts 17:31
know that the saints will j the world? .. 1 Cor 6:2
who is to j the living and the dead, ...2 Tm 4:1
There is only one lawgiver and j,......... Jas 4:12
behold, the J is standing at the door......Jas 5:9
to him who is ready to j the living and . . .1 Pt 4:5
whom the authority to j was committed. . Rv 20:4

JUDGED
he said to him, "You have j rightly." ......Lk 7:43
under the law will be j by the law...... Rom 2:12
But if we j ourselves truly, we ....1 Cor 11:31
we who teach will be j with greater.........Jas 3:1
And the dead were j by what ....Rv 20:12

JUDGES
"You shall appoint j and officers in all ... Dt 16:18
Then the LORD raised up j, ... Jgs 2:16
surely there is a God who j on earth." . . . .Ps 58:11
God j the secrets of men by Christ..... Rom 2:16
It is the Lord who j me.................. 1 Cor 4:4
call on him as Father who j impartially . . .1 Pt 1:17
in righteousness he j and makes war......Rv 19:11

JUDGMENT
wicked will not stand in the j, nor......... Ps 1:5
but it is God who executes j,.............Ps 75:7
Teach me good j and knowledge,...... Ps 119:66
God will bring every deed into j,....... Eccl 12:14
by fire will the LORD enter into j,..........Is 66:16
on the day of j people will give account. .Mt 12:36
but has given all j to the Son, ...Jn 5:22
concerning sin and righteousness and j: . . Jn 16:8
God's righteous j will be revealed.......Rom 2:5
all stand before the j seat of God; .... Rom 14:10
body eats and drinks j on himself. .... 1 Cor 11:29
Therefore let no one pass j............. Col 2:16
man to die once, and after that comes j, . . Heb 9:27
a fearful expectation of j, and a fury . . Heb 10:27
Mercy triumphs over j.................. Jas 2:13
For it is time for j to begin at ....1 Pt 4:17
day of j and destruction of the ungodly. . 2 Pt 3:7
gloomy darkness until the j .... Jude 6
j has come, and worship him who ....Rv 14:7

JUDGMENTS
our God; his j are in all the earth...... 1 Chr 16:14
your j are like the great deep;...........Ps 36:6
LORD of hosts, Render true j, ...Zec 7:9
the Almighty, true and just are your j!" . . . Rv 16:7

JUST
without iniquity, j and upright is he.......Dt 32:4
works of his hands are faithful and j;..... Ps 111:7
The thoughts of the righteous are j;..... Prv 12:5
and does what is j and right,.......... Ezk 18:27
are right and his ways are j;............ Dn 4:37
sends rain on the j and on the unjust.... Mt 5:45
so that he might be j and the justifier . . Rom 3:26
disobedience received a j retribution, ... Heb 2:2
J and true are your ways, O King .... Rv 15:3

JUSTICE
You shall not pervert j.................. Dt 16:19
j and abundant righteousness ....Jb 37:23
For the LORD loves j; he will............Ps 37:28
I will sing of steadfast love and j; ....Ps 101:1
Blessed are they who observe j, ...Ps 106:3
When j is done, it is a joy to the........Prv 21:15
Evil men do not understand j,..........Prv 28:5
By j a king builds up the land, but he . . .Prv 29:4
do good; seek j, correct oppression; ...... Is 1:17
And I will make j the line,................Is 28:17
For the LORD is a God of j;...............Is 30:18
he will bring forth j to the nations.........Is 42:1
and I will set my j for a light ....Is 51:4
But let j roll down like waters,...........Am 5:24
LORD require of you but to do j, ...Mi 6:8
every morning he shows forth his j;......Zep 3:5
Or by asking, "Where is the God of j?" . . Mal 2:17
and he will proclaim j to the Gentiles.... Mt 12:18
and neglect j and the love of God....... Lk 11:42
And will not God give j to his elect,...... Lk 18:7

JUSTIFICATION
for our trespasses and raised for our j. .Rom 4:25
one act of righteousness leads to j..... Rom 5:18

JUSTIFIED
Yet wisdom is j by her deeds." ....Mt 11:19
for by your words you will be j,......... Mt 12:37
this man went down to his house j, ... Lk 18:14
and are j by his grace as a gift,........Rom 3:24
For we hold that one is j by faith apart . . Rom 3:28
For if Abraham was j by works, he......Rom 4:2
since we have been j by faith,.......... Rom 5:1
whom he called he also j, and those . . .Rom 8:30
with the heart one believes and is j,. . . Rom 10:10
you were j in the name of the Lord .... 1 Cor 6:11
in order to be j by faith in Christ........ Gal 2:16
in order that we might be j by faith. ....Gal 3:24
so that being j by his grace we might..... Ti 3:7
You see that a person is j by works .....Jas 2:24

JUSTIFIER
he might be just and the j of the one . .Rom 3:26

JUSTIFIES
He who j the wicked and he who.......Prv 17:15
work but believes in him who j the......Rom 4:5
against God's elect? It is God who j. . . .Rom 8:33

JUSTIFY
But he, desiring to j himself, said to.....Lk 10:29
who will j the circumcised by faith.....Rom 3:30
foreseeing that God would j the Gentiles . Gal 3:8

JUSTLY
No one enters suit j; no one goes to law. . Is 59:4
entrusting himself to him who judges j.. .1 Pt 2:23

KEEP
garden of Eden to work it and k it.......Gn 2:15
"As for you, you shall k my covenant, ...Gn 17:9
K back your servant also from.......... Ps 19:13
chide, nor will he k his anger forever.....Ps 103:9
k you from all evil; he will k your ....Ps 121:7
K your heart with all vigilance, for ......Prv 4:23
a time to k, and a time to cast away;..... Eccl 3:6
enter life, k the commandments."....... Mt 19:17
who hear the word of God and k it!"..... Lk 11:28
"If you love me, you will k my .... Jn 14:15
Holy Father, k them in your name, ... Jn 17:11
of God, that we k his commandments. . . .1 Jn 5:3
and with those who k the words of this . Rv 22:9

KEEPER

"I do not know; am I my brother's **k**?" . . . . Gn 4:9
The LORD is your **k**; . . . . Ps 121:5
I, the LORD, am its **k**; . . . . Is 27:3

KEEPS

the faithful God who **k** covenant and . . . . . . Dt 7:9
awesome God who **k** covenant and . . . . . . Neh 1:5
he who **k** you will not slumber . . . . Ps 121:3
Does not he who **k** watch over your . . . . Prv 24:12
the law? Yet none of you **k** the law . . . . Jn 7:19
Blessed is the one who **k** the words . . . . . . Rv 22:7

KEPT

and your sins have **k** good from you . . . . . Jer 5:25
"All these I have **k**. What do I still . . . . Mt 19:20
Because you have **k** my word about . . . . . Rv 3:10

KEY

his shoulder the **k** of the house of David . . . Is 22:22
the true one, who has the **k** of David, ... Rv 3:7
in his hand the **k** to the bottomless pit . . . Rv 20:1

KEYS

I will give you the **k** of the kingdom of . . Mt 16:19
and I have the **k** of Death and Hades . . . . . Rv 1:18

KILL

and whoever finds me will **k** me." . . . . Gn 4:14
and they will **k** him, and he will be . . . . . . Mt 17:23
of whom they will **k** and persecute,' . . . . . Lk 11:49
do not fear those who **k** the body, ... Lk 12:4
the law. Why do you seek to **k** me?" . . . . . Jn 7:19

KILLED

up against his brother Abel and **k** him . . . . Gn 4:8
LORD **k** all the firstborn in the . . . . Ex 13:15
and he sent and **k** all the male children . . . Mt 2:16
And when he is **k**, after three days he . . . . Mk 9:31
of the prophets whom your fathers **k** . . . . Lk 11:47
sake we are being **k** all the day long; . . . Rom 8:36
who **k** both the Lord Jesus and the . . . 1 Thes 2:15
they were **k** with the sword . . . . Heb 11:37
Antipas my faithful witness, who was **k** . . . Rv 2:13

KILLS

the city that **k** the prophets and stones. . Mt 23:37
coming when whoever **k** you will think . . . Jn 16:2

KIND

is their seed, each according to its **k**, ... Gn 1:11
all his words and **k** in all his works.] . . . . Ps 145:13
A man who is **k** benefits himself, but . . . . Prv 11:17
for he is **k** to the ungrateful and the evil . . . Lk 6:35
Love is patient and **k**; love does not . . . . 1 Cor 13:4
Be **k** to one another, tenderhearted, ... Eph 4:32
not be quarrelsome but **k** to everyone, . . 2 Tm 2:24
pure, working at home, **k**, and . . . . Ti 2:5

KINDNESS

righteousness and **k** will find life, ... Prv 21:21
I led them with cords of **k**, with the . . . . . Hos 11:4
show **k** and mercy to one another, ... Zec 7:9
but God's **k** to you, provided you . . . . . . Rom 11:22
patience, **k**, the Holy Spirit, genuine . . . . 2 Cor 6:6
of his grace in **k** toward us in Christ . . . . . . Eph 2:7
the goodness and loving **k** of God our . . . . Ti 3:4

KING

"Give us a **k** to judge us." And Samuel . . 1 Sm 8:6
LORD your God was your **k** . . . . 1 Sm 12:12
The LORD is **k** forever and ever; . . . . Ps 10:16
Who is this **K** of glory? . . . . Ps 24:8
For God is the **K** of all the earth; sing . . . . Ps 47:7
for my eyes have seen the **K**, ... Is 6:5
Holy One, the Creator of Israel, your **K**." . . Is 43:15
is the living God and the everlasting **K** . . Jer 10:10
Behold, your **k** is coming to you; . . . . Zec 9:9
he who has been born **k** of the Jews? . . . . . Mt 2:2
'Behold, your **k** is coming to you, ... Mt 21:5
"Are you the **K** of the Jews?" . . . . Mt 27:11
"Blessed is the **K** who comes in . . . . Lk 19:38
Son of God! You are the **K** of Israel!" . . . . . Jn 1:49
"We have no **k** but Caesar." . . . . Jn 19:15
To the **K** of the ages, immortal, invisible, . . 1 Tm 1:17
the **K** of kings and Lord of lords, ... 1 Tm 6:15
for he is Lord of lords and **K** of kings, . . . Rv 17:14
written, **K** of kings and Lord of lords . . . . . Rv 19:16

KINGDOM

and you shall be to me a **k** of priests . . . . . Ex 19:6
establish the throne of his **k** forever . . . 2 Sm 7:13
Yours is the **k**, O LORD, and . . . . 1 Chr 29:11
The scepter of your **k** is a scepter of . . . . . Ps 45:6
in the heavens, and his **k** rules over all . . Ps 103:19
His **k** is an everlasting **k**, ... Dn 4:3
Your **k** come, your will be done, on . . . . . . Mt 6:10
is least in the **k** of heaven is greater . . . . . . Mt 11:11
"The **k** of heaven may be compared to . . Mt 13:24
a rich person to enter the **k** of God." . . . . Mt 19:24
against nation, and **k** against **k**, ... Mt 24:7
'The **k** of God has come near to you.' . . . . . Lk 10:9
"My **k** is not of this world. If my **k** . . . . Jn 18:36
For the **k** of God is not a matter of . . . Rom 14:17
For the **k** of God does not consist . . . . 1 Cor 4:20
blood cannot inherit the **k** of God, ... 1 Cor 15:50
of uprightness is the scepter of your **k** . . . Heb 1:8
"The **k** of the world has become the . . . . . Rv 11:15

KINGS

nations, and **k** shall come from you . . . . . . Gn 17:6
The **k** of the earth set themselves, ... Ps 2:2
By me **k** reign, and rulers decree . . . . Prv 8:15
your God is God of gods and Lord of **k**, . Dn 2:47
out of this kingdom ten **k** shall arise, ... Dn 7:24
before governors and **k** for my sake, ... Mt 10:18
that many prophets and **k** desired . . . . . . Lk 10:24
The **k** of the earth set themselves, and . . Acts 4:26

KISS

K the Son, lest he be angry, and you . . . . . Ps 2:12
righteousness and peace **k** each other . . . Ps 85:10
Let him **k** me with the kisses of his . . . . Sg 1:2
"The one I will **k** is the man; seize . . . . . . Mt 26:48
you betray the Son of Man with a **k**?" . . . Lk 22:48
Greet one another with a holy **k**. . . . . . Rom 16:16

KISSED

her head and **k** his feet and anointed . . . . Lk 7:38
they embraced Paul and **k** him, ... Acts 20:37

KNEE

'To me every **k** shall bow, every tongue . . Is 45:23
the Lord, every **k** shall bow to me, ... Rom 14:11
the name of Jesus every **k** should bow, . . Phil 2:10

KNEES

all the **k** that have not bowed to Baal . . 1 Kgs 19:18
and fell on his **k** before Elijah and . . . . . . 2 Kgs 1:13
and fell upon my **k** and spread out my . . . Ezr 9:5
He got down on his **k** three times a day . . Dn 6:10
For this reason I bow my **k** before the . . . Eph 3:14

KNELT

rest of the people **k** down to drink . . . . Jgs 7:6
he had **k** with hands outstretched . . . . 1 Kgs 8:54
stone's throw, and **k** down and prayed, . . Lk 22:41

KNEW

"Before I formed you in the womb I **k** . . . . . Jer 1:5
for I **k** that you are a gracious God and . . . Jon 4:2
'I never **k** you; depart from me, ... Mt 7:23
demons to speak, because they **k** him . . . . Mk 1:34
But he **k** their thoughts, and he said . . . . . . Lk 6:8
man, for he himself **k** what was in man . . . Jn 2:25

KNIT

and **k** me together with bones and . . . . . . Jb 10:11
nourished and **k** together through its . . . Col 2:19

KNOCK

seek, and you will find; **k**, and it will . . . . . . Mt 7:7
k at the door, saying, 'Lord, open to us,' . Lk 13:25

KNOW

K then in your heart that, as a man . . . . Dt 8:5
you only, **k** the hearts of all the . . . . 1 Kgs 8:39
For I **k** that my Redeemer lives, and . . . . . Jb 19:25
"I **k** that you can do all things, and that . . Jb 42:2
Make me to **k** your ways, O . . . . Ps 25:4
For I **k** my transgressions, and my sin . . . . Ps 51:3
And I applied my heart to **k** wisdom . . . . Eccl 1:17
a heart to **k** that I am the LORD, ... Jer 24:7
saying, '**K** the LORD,' for they . . . . Jer 31:34
him, yet the world did not **k** him . . . . Jn 1:10
I **k** my own and my own **k** me, ... Jn 10:14
life, that they **k** you the only true God, . . . Jn 17:3
"It is not for you to **k** times or seasons . . Acts 1:7
And we **k** that for those who love God . . Rom 8:28
k in part; then I shall **k** fully, ... 1 Cor 13:12
that I may **k** him and the power of his . . . Phil 3:10
'**K** the Lord,' for they shall all **k** me, ... Heb 8:11
Whoever says "I **k** him" but does not . . . . . 1 Jn 2:4
you may **k** that you have eternal life . . . . . 1 Jn 5:13
"'I **k** your works, your toil and your . . . . Rv 2:2
and you will not **k** at what hour I will . . . . . . Rv 3:3

KNOWING

Jesus, **k** their thoughts, said, "Why do . . . . . Mt 9:4
Jesus, **k** all that would happen to him, ... Jn 18:4
surpassing worth of **k** Christ Jesus my . . . Phil 3:8

KNOWLEDGE

and the tree of the **k** of good and evil . . . . Gn 2:9
out speech, and night to night reveals **k**. . Ps 19:2
Such **k** is too wonderful for me; it is . . . . . Ps 139:6
The wise lay up **k**, but the mouth of . . . Prv 10:14
Whoever loves discipline loves **k**, ... Prv 12:1
In everything the prudent acts with **k**, . . Prv 13:16
shall be full of the **k** of the LORD . . . . Is 11:9
My people are destroyed for lack of **k**; . . Hos 4:6
will be filled with the **k** of the glory . . . . . Hab 2:14
to give **k** of salvation to his people in . . . . Lk 1:77
For you have taken away the key of **k** . . . Lk 11:52
filled with all **k** and able to instruct . . . Rom 15:14
This "**k**" puffs up, but love builds up . . . . . 1 Cor 8:1
the love of Christ that surpasses **k**, ... Eph 3:19
all the treasures of wisdom and **k**. . . . . Col 2:3
your faith with virtue, and virtue with **k**, . . 2 Pt 1:5
But grow in the grace and **k** of our . . . . . 2 Pt 3:18

KNOWN

Make them **k** to your children . . . . Dt 4:9
you have searched me and **k** me! . . . . Ps 139:1
a child makes himself **k** by his acts, ... Prv 20:11
bad, for the tree is **k** by its fruit . . . . Mt 12:33
at the Father's side, he has made him **k** . . . Jn 1:18
For what can be **k** about God is plain . . . Rom 1:19
"For who has **k** the mind of the Lord, . . Rom 11:34
if anyone loves God, he is **k** by God. . . . . 1 Cor 8:3
to know God, or rather to be **k** by God, . . Gal 4:9
better for them never to have **k** the way . . 2 Pt 2:21

KNOWS

But he **k** the way that I take; . . . . Jb 23:10
LORD **k** the way of the righteous, ... Ps 1:6
righteous man **k** the rights of the poor; . . Prv 29:7
he **k** what is in the darkness, ... Dn 2:22
he **k** those who take refuge in him. . . . . Na 1:7
your Father **k** what you need before . . . . . . Mt 6:8
that day and hour no one **k**, ... Mt 24:36
k what is the mind of the Spirit, ... Rom 8:27
imagines that he **k** something, he . . . . 1 Cor 8:2
"The Lord **k** those who are his," . . . . 2 Tm 2:19
So whoever **k** the right thing to do and . Jas 4:17
loves has been born of God and **k** God. . . 1 Jn 4:7
stone that no one **k** except the one who . . Rv 2:17

LABAN

had a brother whose name was **L**. . . . . . Gn 24:29
Arise, flee to **L** my brother in Haran . . . . Gn 27:43
Then Jacob said to **L**, "Give me my . . . . . Gn 29:21

LABOR

Six days you shall **l**, and do all your . . . . . Ex 20:9
shall eat the fruit of the **l** of your hands; . . Ps 128:2
your **l** for that which does not satisfy? . . . Is 55:2
Come to me, all who **l** and are heavy . . . . Mt 11:28
you to reap that for which you did not **l** . . Jn 4:38

them, walking and l and praising God. . . Acts 3:8

LEARN
that they may l to fear me all the days . . . Dt 4:10
lest you l his ways and entangle . . . . Prv 22:25
l to do good; seek justice, correct. . . . . Is 1:17
No one could l that song except the . . . . . Rv 14:3

LEARNED
and l from the Father comes to me— . . . .Jn 6:45
for I have l in whatever situation I am . . . Phil 4:11
in what you have l and have firmly. . . . .2 Tm 3:14

LEARNING
saying, "How is it that this man has l, ... Jn 7:15
always l and never able to arrive at . . . . .2 Tm 3:7

LEAST
Yet the one who is l in the kingdom. . . . . . Mt 11:11
it to one of the l of these my brothers, . Mt 25:40
For I am the l of the apostles, ...1 Cor 15:9

LEAVE
'Therefore a man shall l his father and. . . . Mt 19:5
"I will not l you as orphans; I will . . . . Jn 14:18
"Therefore a man shall l his father and . . Eph 5:31

LEAVEN
day you shall remove l out of your. . . . . . Ex 12:15
of heaven is like l that a woman took . . . Mt 13:33
and beware of the l of the Pharisees . . . . . Mt 16:6
know that a little l leavens the whole. . . 1 Cor 5:6
A little l leavens the whole lump. . . . . Gal 5:9

LEAVES
they sewed fig l together and made . . . . . .Gn 3:7
be for food, and their l for healing.". . . . Ezk 47:12
to it and found nothing on it but only l. . Mt 21:19
the wolf coming and l the sheep and. . . . Jn 10:12

LED
I have l you in the paths of uprightness. . .Prv 4:11
like a gentle lamb l to the slaughter. . . . . Jer 11:19
Jesus was l up by the Spirit into the . . . . . . Mt 4:1
For all who are l by the Spirit of God. . . Rom 8:14
But if you are l by the Spirit, you are. . . . Gal 5:18

LEFT
in the field; one will be taken and one l. . .Mt 24:40
on his right, but the goats on the l. . . . . .Mt 25:33

LEGION
He replied, "My name is L, ... Mk 5:9

LEGS
his arms and l like the gleam of . . . . .Dn 10:6
already dead, they did not break his l. . . . Jn 19:33
like the sun, and his l like pillars of fire. . . . Rv 10:1

LEND
"If you l money to any of my people . . . .Ex 22:25
him and l him sufficient for his need,. . . . . Dt 15:8
love your enemies, and do good, and l,. . .Lk 6:35
'Friend, l me three loaves, ...Lk 11:5

LENDS
the man who deals generously and l;. . . . .Ps 112:5
generous to the poor l to the Lord, ...Prv 19:17

LENGTH
gave it to him, l of days forever and. . . . . . Ps 21:4
for l of days and years of life and peace . . Prv 3:2
all the saints what is the breadth and l . . Eph 3:18

LEPER
a mighty man of valor, but he was a l. . . 2 Kgs 5:1
a l came to him and knelt before him,. . . . .Mt 8:2
at Bethany in the house of Simon the l, . Mt 26:6

LEPERS
these l came to the edge of the camp, . 2 Kgs 7:8
Heal the sick, raise the dead, cleanse l, . . . Mt 10:8
And there were many l in Israel in the. . . .Lk 4:27
entered a village, he was met by ten l, . . .Lk 17:12

LEPROSY
Therefore the l of Naaman shall cling . 2 Kgs 5:27
l broke out on his forehead in the. . . . 2 Chr 26:19
And immediately his l was cleansed. . . . . . .Mt 8:3

LEPROUS
it out, behold, his hand was l like snow. . . .Ex 4:6
over the tent, behold, Miriam was l, ... Nm 12:10

LETTER
of the heart, by the Spirit, not by the l. . .Rom 2:29
For the l kills, but the Spirit gives life. . . 2 Cor 3:6
does not obey what we say in this l, . 2 Thes 3:14

LETTERS
For they say, "His l are weighty and. . 2 Cor 10:10
as he does in all his l when he speaks . . .2 Pt 3:16

LEVEL
My foot stands on l ground;. . . . . Ps 26:12
the path of the upright is a l highway. . . .Prv 15:19
The path of the righteous is l; you . . . . Is 26:7

LEVI
Therefore his name was called L. . . . . . . Gn 29:34
all the sons of L gathered around him. . .Ex 32:26
To the tribe of L alone Moses gave no. . .Jos 13:14
he saw L the son of Alphaeus sitting . . . . .Mk 2:14
And L made him a great feast in his . . . . .Lk 5:29

LEVIATHAN
"Can you draw out L with a fishhook. . . . . .Jb 41:1
You crushed the heads of L; you gave. . . . Ps 74:14
sword will punish L the fleeing serpent, . . . Is 27:1

LIAR
love, and a poor man is better than a l. . . Prv 19:22
for he is a l and the father of lies.. . . . . . . .Jn 8:44
God be true though every one were a l, . Rom 3:4
have not sinned, we make him a l, ... 1 Jn 1:10
and hates his brother, he is a l; . . . . 1 Jn 4:20

LIARS
the insincerity of l whose consciences. . . 1 Tm 4:2
immoral, sorcerers, idolaters, and all l, ... Rv 21:8

LIBERTY
For why should my l be determined . .1 Cor 10:29
the law of l, and perseveres, being no . . . Jas 1:25
who are to be judged under the law of l. Jas 2:12

LIE
falsely; you shall not l to one another. . . . . Lv 19:11
God is not man, that he should l, ... Nm 23:19
A faithful witness does not l, ... Prv 14:5
filled your heart to l to the Holy Spirit. . . Acts 5:3
truth about God for a l and worshiped . Rom 1:25
Do not l to one another, seeing. . . . . Col 3:9
it is impossible for God to l, ...Heb 6:18
and because no l is of the truth. . . . . .1 Jn 2:21

LIES
no one who utters l shall continue . . . . . . Ps 101:7
he who breathes out l will not escape. . . Prv 19:5
of eternal life, which God, who never l, ... Ti 1:2

LIFE
require a reckoning for the l of man. . . . . . Gn 9:5
then you shall pay l for l, ... Ex 21:23
Therefore choose l, that you and your . . . Dt 30:19
desires l and loves many days, ... Ps 34:12
the blessing, l forevermore. . . . . Ps 133:3
reproofs of discipline are the way of l, . . . Prv 6:23
not know that it will cost him his l. . . . . . . Prv 7:23
righteousness and kindness will find l, . . . Prv 21:21
you have delivered my l from the pit . . . . .Is 38:17
and to give his l as a ransom for. . . . . . . Mt 20:28
and the l was the light of men. . . . . Jn 1:4
whoever believes has eternal l. . . . . .Jn 6:47
we go? You have the words of eternal l, . .Jn 6:68
And this is eternal l, that they know. . . . . . Jn 17:3
killed the Author of l, whom God raised . . Acts 3:15
who gives l to the dead and calls . . . . . . Rom 4:17
lead the l that the Lord has assigned. . . 1 Cor 7:17
in hope of eternal l, which God, who . . . . . . .Ti 1:2
"Whoever desires to love l and see . . . . . 1 Pt 3:10
we have passed out of death into l, ... 1 Jn 3:14
Whoever has the Son has l; . . . . 1 Jn 5:12
the world in the book of l of the Lamb . . . Rv 13:8
was opened, which is the book of l. . . . . .Rv 20:12

LIFT
To you, O Lord, I l up my soul. . . . . Ps 25:1
Let us l up our hearts and hands to . . . . Lam 3:41
Therefore l your drooping hands and. . . Heb 12:12

LIFTED
he shall be high and l up, and shall be. . . .Is 52:13
so must the Son of Man be l up, ... Jn 3:14
And I, when I am l up from the earth, . . . Jn 12:32

LIGHT
And God said, "Let there be l," . . . . .Gn 1:3
night in a pillar of fire to give them l,. . . . Ex 13:21
Lift up the l of your face upon us, ...Ps 4:6
I may walk before God in the l of life. . . . Ps 56:13
L dawns in the darkness for the upright;. Ps 112:4
a lamp to my feet and a l to my path. . .Ps 119:105
The unfolding of your words gives l; . . .Ps 119:130
let us walk in the l of the Lord. . . . . .Is 2:5
I form l and create darkness, ... Is 45:7
I will make you as a l for the nations,. . . . . Is 49:6
Lord will be your everlasting l, ... Is 60:20
"You are the l of the world. A city . . . . Mt 5:14
The l shines in the darkness, and the. . . . . . Jn 1:5
the l has come into the world,. . . . . Jn 3:19
"I am the l of the world. . . . . Jn 8:12
While you have the l, believe in the . . . . . Jn 12:36
"'I have made you a l for the Gentiles, . . Acts 13:47
of darkness and put on the armor of l. . . Rom 13:12
Walk as children of l . . . . Eph 5:8
who dwells in unapproachable l,. . . . . . . 1 Tm 6:16
loves his brother abides in the l, ...1 Jn 2:10
By its l will the nations walk, ...Rv 21:24
or sun, for the Lord God will be their l, . . .Rv 22:5

LIGHTNING
and the flashes of l and the sound of . . . Ex 20:18
his face like the appearance of l, ...Dn 10:6
For as the l comes from the east . . . . . . .Mt 24:27
His appearance was like l, ...Mt 28:3
"I saw Satan fall like l from heaven. . . . . . Lk 10:18
From the throne came flashes of l, and. . . .Rv 4:5

LIGHTS
"Let there be l in the expanse of the . . . . . Gn 1:14
established the heavenly l and the sun. . . Ps 74:16
whom you shine as l in the world, ... Phil 2:15

LIKENESS
he made him in the l of God. . . . . .Gn 5:1
carved image, or any l of anything. . . . . . Ex 20:4
liken God, or what l compare with him? . Is 40:18
his own Son in the l of sinful flesh . . . . . . .Rom 8:3
created after the l of God in true . . . . . . Eph 4:24
a servant, being born in the l of men. . . . .Phil 2:7
curse people who are made in the l of . . . Jas 3:9

LILIES
Consider the l of the field, how they . . . . Mt 6:28

LILY
brim of a cup, like the flower of a l. . . . 1 Kgs 7:26
I am a rose of Sharon, a l of the valleys. . . . Sg 2:1
to Israel; he shall blossom like the l; . . . . .Hos 14:5

LIMIT
Can you find out the l of the Almighty? . . .Jb 11:7
transgressors have reached their l, ... Dn 8:23

LINEN
She makes l garments and sells them;. . Prv 31:24
wrapped it in a l shroud and laid him . . .Lk 23:53
in, he saw the l cloths by themselves; . . . Lk 24:12
not lying with the l cloths but folded up. .Jn 20:7
the armies of heaven, arrayed in fine l, . . Rv 19:14

But I say to you, **L** your enemies. . . . . Mt 5:44
"You shall **l** the Lord your God with . . . . .Mt 22:37
even sinners **l** those who **l** . . . . .Lk 6:32
Greater **l** has no one than this, ...Jn 15:13
"Simon, son of John, do you **l** me?" . . . . . .Jn 21:16
but God shows his **l** for us in that. . . . . . .Rom 5:8
Let **l** be genuine. Abhor what is evil; . . . Rom 12:9
L does no wrong to a neighbor; . . . . . . Rom 13:10
L is patient and kind;. . . . . .1 Cor 13:4
three; but the greatest of these is **l**. . . . 1 Cor 13:13
Let all that you do be done in **l**. . . . . . . 1 Cor 16:14
For the **l** of Christ controls us,. . . . . 2 Cor 5:14
but only faith working through **l**. . . . . .Gal 5:6
the fruit of the Spirit is **l**, joy, peace,. . . . . Gal 5:22
speaking the truth in **l**, we are to grow . .Eph 4:15
prayer that your **l** may abound more . . . . . Phil 1:9
but of power and **l** and self-control.. . . . . 2 Tm 1:7
how to stir up one another to **l** and . . . Heb 10:24
Let brotherly **l** continue. . . . . Heb 13:1
"You shall **l** your neighbor as yourself," . . . Jas 2:8
since **l** covers a multitude of sins. . . . . .1 Pt 4:8
See what kind of **l** the Father has given . . 1 Jn 3:1
Beloved, let us **l** one another, for **l** . . . . . . .1 Jn 4:7
God is **l**, and whoever abides in **l** . . . . . . .1 Jn 4:16
but perfect **l** casts out fear. . . . . .1 Jn 4:18
keep yourselves in the **l** of God, ...Jude 21
have abandoned the **l** you had at first. . . . .Rv 2:4
Those whom I **l**, I reprove and. . . . . .Rv 3:19

LOVED

because he **l** your fathers and chose . . . . .Dt 4:37
the LORD **l** Israel forever, ... 1 Kgs 10:9
I have **l** you with an everlasting love; . . . . .Jer 31:3
"I have **l** you," says the LORD. . . . . Mal 1:2
"For God so **l** the world, that he gave . . . . Jn 3:16
just as I have **l** you, you also are to . . . . . Jn 13:34
Father has **l** me, so have I **l** . . . . Jn 15:9
because you have **l** me and have . . . . Jn 16:27
conquerors through him who **l** us. . . . . .Rom 8:37
who **l** me and gave himself for me. . . . . .Gal 2:20
of the great love with which he **l** us, ... Eph 2:4
who **l** us and gave us eternal comfort . . 2 Thes 2:16
We love because he first **l** us. . . . . .1 Jn 4:19

LOVER

therefore hear this, you **l** of pleasures,. . . . Is 47:8
but hospitable, a **l** of good, ...Ti 1:8

LOVERS

The Pharisees, who were **l** of money,. . . . Lk 16:14
l of pleasure rather than **l** of God,. . . . . . 2 Tm 3:4

LOVES

the LORD reproves him whom he **l**, ... Prv 3:12
He who **l** money will not be satisfied . . . .Eccl 5:10
Whoever **l** father or mother more than . . Mt 10:37
But he who is forgiven little, **l** little." . . . . .Lk 7:47
And he who **l** me will be loved by my . . . Jn 14:21
But if anyone **l** God, he is known by. . . . .1 Cor 8:3
compulsion, for God **l** a cheerful giver. . 2 Cor 9:7
He who **l** his wife **l** himself.. . . . . Eph 5:28
For the Lord disciplines the one he **l**, ...Heb 12:6
l the world, the love of the Father is not . . 1 Jn 2:15
whoever **l** God must also love his . . . . . . .1 Jn 4:21

LOW

he who remembered us in our **l** estate, . . Ps 136:23
I know how to be brought **l**, and I . . . . . . Phil 4:12

LOWER

made him a little **l** than the heavenly. . . . . .Ps 8:5
also descended into the **l** regions, ... Eph 4:9
him for a little while **l** than the angels; . . Heb 2:7

LOWLY

the LORD is high, he regards the **l**,. . . . . . . Ps 138:6
Better to be **l** and have a servant than . . Prv 12:9
he who is **l** in spirit will obtain honor. . .Prv 29:23
Let the **l** brother boast in his exaltation, . . Jas 1:9

LUKE

L the beloved physician greets you, as . . Col 4:14
L alone is with me. Get Mark and . . . . . . 2 Tm 4:11

LUKEWARM

So, because you are **l**, and neither hot. . . . Rv 3:16

LUST

treacherous are taken captive by their **l**. . .Prv 11:6
not in the passion of **l** like the Gentiles . . 1 Thes 4:5

LUXURY

It is not fitting for a fool to live in **l**, ... Prv 19:10
clothing and live in **l** are in kings' . . . . .Lk 7:25
on the earth in **l** and in self-indulgence. . . Jas 5:5
As she glorified herself and lived in **l**, ... Rv 18:7

LYING

L lips are an abomination to the LORD,. . Prv 12:22
A **l** tongue hates its victims,. . . . . .Prv 26:28
there is swearing, **l**, murder, stealing,. . . . Hos 4:2

MACEDONIA

"Come over to **M** and help us." . . . . Acts 16:9

MADE

In wisdom have you **m** them all; the . . .Ps 104:24
for I am fearfully and wonderfully **m**. . . . Ps 139:14
I found, that God **m** man upright,. . . . . . Eccl 7:29
All these things my hand has **m**, and. . . . . Is 66:2
It is you who have **m** the heavens. . . . . . .Jer 32:17
All things were **m** through him, and. . . . . . . Jn 1:3
Christ Jesus has **m** me his own.. . . . . Phil 3:12

MAGDALENE

Mary **M** went and announced to the. . . . . Jn 20:18

MAGIC

had previously practiced **m** in the city. . . Acts 8:9
who had practiced **m** arts brought. . . . .Acts 19:19

MAGNIFIES

And Mary said, "My soul **m** the Lord, ... Lk 1:46

MAGNIFY

Oh, **m** the LORD with me, and let. . . . . .Ps 34:3
sake, to **m** his law and make it glorious. . .Is 42:21

MAGOG

I will send fire on **M** and on those who . .Ezk 39:6
the four corners of the earth, Gog and **M**,. .Rv 20:8

MAINTAIN

poor and cannot **m** himself with you, . . .Lv 25:35
and their plea, and **m** their cause.. . . . . 1 Kgs 8:45
that the LORD will **m** the cause . . . . Ps 140:12

MAJESTIC

how **m** is your name in all the earth! . . . . . . Ps 8:1
through, I will make you **m** forever, ...Is 60:15
was borne to him by the **M** Glory,. . . . . . . 2 Pt 1:17

MAJESTY

the glory and the victory and the **m**, . . 1 Chr 29:11
On the glorious splendor of your **m**, ... Ps 145:5
he had no form or **m** that we should . . . . . Is 53:2
all were astonished at the **m** of God. . . . . .Lk 9:43
hand of the throne of the **M** in heaven, . . .Heb 8:1
but we were eyewitnesses of his **m**. . . . . . 2 Pt 1:16
be glory, **m**, dominion, and authority,. . . . Jude 25

MAKE

"You shall not **m** for yourself a carved. . . Ex 20:4
how will you **m** it salty again?. . . . . Mk 9:50
and take him by force to **m** him king, ... Jn 6:15
come to him and **m** our home with him. . Jn 14:23

MAKER

Can a man be pure before his **M**?. . . . . Jb 4:17
kneel before the LORD, our **M**! . . . . .Ps 95:6
the LORD is the **m** of them all. . . . . Prv 22:2
say of its **m**, "He did not make me";. . . . . .Is 29:16
forgotten the LORD, your **M**, ... Is 51:13
For your **M** is your husband, ... Is 54:5
has forgotten his **M** and built palaces, . . .Hos 8:14
For its **m** trusts in his own creation . . . . .Hab 2:18

MALE

him; **m** and female he created them. . . . . .Gn 1:27
beginning made them **m** and female, ...Mt 19:4
nor free, there is no **m** and female,. . . . . . Gal 3:28
She gave birth to a **m** child, one who is . . Rv 12:5

MALICE

But Jesus, aware of their **m**, said, "Why . .Mt 22:18
covetousness, **m**. They are full of envy, . Rom 1:29
put away from you, along with all **m**. . . . .Eph 4:31
anger, wrath, **m**, slander, and obscene. . . . Col 3:8
So put away all **m** and all deceit and. . . . . 1 Pt 2:1

MALIGN

much more will they **m** those of his. . . . .Mt 10:25
flood of debauchery, and they **m** you; . . . .1 Pt 4:4

MAN

God said, "Let us make **m** in our image, . .Gn 1:26
because she was taken out of **M**.". . . . . . . Gn 2:23
sought out a **m** after his own heart,. . . 1 Sm 13:14
what is **m** that you are mindful of him, ...Ps 8:4
and he who has a cool spirit is a **m** of. . Prv 17:27
nest is a **m** who strays from his home.. . . Prv 27:8
than that a **m** should rejoice in his work . . Eccl 3:22
heaven there came one like a son of **m**, . .Dn 7:13
for the Son of **M** is coming at an hour . . Mt 24:44
'**M** shall not live by bread alone.'" . . . . .Lk 4:4
and descending on the Son of **M**." . . . . .Jn 1:51
came into the world through one **m**, . . . Rom 5:12
each **m** should have his own wife. . . . . . .1 Cor 7:2
the head of every **m** is Christ, ... 1 Cor 11:3
When I became a **m**, I gave up . . . . .1 Cor 13:11
that the **m** of God may be complete,. . . 2 Tm 3:17
as it is appointed for **m** to die once,. . . . Heb 9:27
I will not fear; what can **m** do to me?". . .Heb 13:6
like a son of **m**, clothed with a long . . . . . . Rv 1:13

MAN'S

the work of a **m** hand comes back to . . .Prv 12:14
When a **m** ways please the LORD, ... Prv 16:7
was preached by me is not **m** gospel. . . . . Gal 1:11

MANAGE

not know how to **m** his own household, . 1 Tm 3:5
bear children, **m** their households, ... 1 Tm 5:14

MANASSEH

the name of the firstborn **M**. . . . . Gn 41:51
Thus he put Ephraim before **M**. . . . . Gn 48:20
"Because **M** king of Judah has. . . . . 2 Kgs 21:11
Then **M** knew that the LORD was . . . . . 2 Chr 33:13

MANGER

in swaddling cloths and laid him in a **m**, . . . Lk 2:7

MANIFEST

is hidden that will not be made **m**,. . . . . . . Lk 8:17
each one's work will become **m**, for. . . . 1 Cor 3:13
but was made **m** in the last times. . . . . . .1 Pt 1:20
life was made **m**, and we have seen. . . . . . 1 Jn 1:2

MANIFESTATION

To each is given the **m** of the Spirit for. .1 Cor 12:7

MANIFESTED

Jesus may also be **m** in our bodies. . . . 2 Cor 4:10
He was **m** in the flesh, vindicated by . . . 1 Tm 3:16
and at the proper time **m** in his word . . . . . .Ti 1:3

MANNA

house of Israel called its name **m**.. . . . . . Ex 16:31
is nothing at all but this **m** to look at." . . .Nm 11:6
Our fathers ate the **m** in the wilderness; . . Jn 6:31
I will give some of the hidden **m**, ...Rv 2:17

MANNER

in an unworthy **m** will be guilty. . . . . . . 1 Cor 11:27
urge you to walk in a **m** worthy of . . . . . . .Eph 4:1
Only let your **m** of life be worthy of. . . . . Phil 1:27
as to walk in a **m** worthy of the Lord, ...Col 1:10
you to walk in a **m** worthy of God,. . . . 1 Thes 2:12

MARAH

the water of **M** because it was bitter;. . . . Ex 15:23

MARK
And the LORD put a **m** on Cain, ... Gn 4:15
but touch no one on whom is the **m**. . . . . Ezk 9:6
of John whose other name was **M**, ... Acts 12:12
Barnabas took **M** with him and . . . . Acts 15:39
Get **M** and bring him with you, for he . . 2 Tm 4:11
greetings, and so does **M**, my son. . . . . . . 1 Pt 5:13
can buy or sell unless he has the **m**,. . . . . Rv 13:17

MARKS
to remove the **m** of circumcision. . . . . . . 1 Cor 7:18
for I bear on my body the **m** of Jesus. . . . Gal 6:17

MARRED
his appearance was so **m**, beyond . . . . Is 52:14

MARRIAGE
they neither marry nor are given in **m**, . Mt 22:30
he who refrains from **m** will do even . . 1 Cor 7:38
Let **m** be held in honor among all, ... Heb 13:4
for the **m** of the Lamb has come, ... Rv 19:7

MARRIED
For a **m** woman is bound by law to . . . . . Rom 7:2
To the **m** I give this charge (not I, but . . 1 Cor 7:10
But the **m** man is anxious about . . . . 1 Cor 7:33

MARRY
with his wife, it is better not to **m**." . . . . . Mt 19:10
resurrection they neither **m** nor are . . . . Mt 22:30
For it is better to **m** than to burn . . . . 1 Cor 7:9
Yet those who **m** will have worldly. . . . 1 Cor 7:28
So I would have younger widows **m**, . . . 1 Tm 5:14

MARRYING
drinking, **m** and giving in marriage, ... Mt 24:38

MARTHA
But **M** was distracted with much. . . . . Lk 10:40
M said to him, "I know that he will rise . . . Jn 11:24
M served, and Lazarus was one of . . . . Jn 12:2

MARTYRS
the saints, the blood of the **m** of Jesus. . . Rv 17:6

MARVEL
Do not **m** at this, for an hour is coming. . . Jn 5:28
"I did one work, and you all **m** at it. . . . . . . Jn 7:21
angel said to me, "Why do you **m**? . . . . . . Rv 17:7

MARVELOUS
a new song, for he has done **m** things! . . . Ps 98:1
with things too great and too **m** for me. . . Ps 131:1
Lord's doing, and it is **m** in our eyes'? . . . Mt 21:42

MARY
they saw the child with **M** his mother, ... Mt 2:11
among whom were **M** Magdalene and . . Mt 27:56
the son of **M** and brother of James and . . Mk 6:3
he appeared first to **M** Magdalene, ... Mk 16:9
And the virgin's name was **M**. . . . . Lk 1:27
M, for you have found favor with God. . . . . Lk 1:30
M said, "My soul magnifies the . . . . Lk 1:46
M treasured up all these things, ... Lk 2:19
M has chosen the good portion, ... Lk 10:42
M therefore took a pound of expensive. . . Jn 12:3
M stood weeping outside the tomb,. . . . . Jn 20:11
M the mother of Jesus, and his brothers. . Acts 1:14
the house of **M**, the mother of John. . . . Acts 12:12

MASTER
M, we are perishing!" And he awoke . . . . . Lk 8:24
"Jesus, **M**, have mercy on us." . . . . Lk 17:13
he who is both their **M** and yours is. . . . . Eph 6:9
you also have a **M** in heaven. . . . . Col 4:1

MASTERS
"No one can serve two **m**, for either . . . . Mt 6:24
M, do the same to them, and stop your. . Eph 6:9
earthly **m**, not by way of eye-service, . . . Col 3:22
be subject to your **m** with all respect, . . . 1 Pt 2:18

MATTHEW
a man called **M** sitting at the tax booth, . . . Mt 9:9
Thomas and **M** the tax collector;. . . . . Mt 10:3
and Thomas, Bartholomew and **M**, ... Acts 1:13

MATURE
Yet among the **m** we do impart . . . . 1 Cor 2:6
in evil, but in your thinking be **m**. . . . . 1 Cor 14:20
to **m** manhood, to the measure of . . . . . . Eph 4:13
Let those of us who are **m** think this . . . . Phil 3:15
we may present everyone **m** in Christ. . . . Col 1:28
But solid food is for the **m**, for those. . . . Heb 5:14

MEASURE
a full and fair **m** you shall have,. . . . . Dt 25:15
what is the **m** of my days; let me know. . . Ps 39:4
power; his understanding is beyond **m**. . . Ps 147:5
and with the **m** you use it will be . . . . Mt 7:2
God, for he gives the Spirit without **m**. . . . Jn 3:34
the **m** of faith that God has assigned. . . Rom 12:3
us according to the **m** of Christ's gift. . . . Eph 4:7
"Rise and **m** the temple of God and the . . . Rv 11:1

MEASURED
Who has **m** the Spirit of the LORD, ... Is 40:13
"If the heavens above can be **m**,. . . . . Jer 31:37

MEAT
"Oh that we had **m** to eat! . . . . Nm 11:4
It is good not to eat **m** or drink wine . . Rom 14:21
brother stumble, I will never eat **m**, ... 1 Cor 8:13
sold in the **m** market without raising . . 1 Cor 10:25

MEDIATES
as the covenant he **m** is better, since it . . Heb 8:6

MEDIATOR
and there is one **m** between God and . . . 1 Tm 2:5
Therefore he is the **m** of a new . . . . Heb 9:15
Jesus, the **m** of a new covenant, ... Heb 12:24

MEDITATE
Isaac went out to **m** in the field toward . . Gn 24:63
but you shall **m** on it day and night,. . . . . . Jos 1:8
I **m** on all that you have done; . . . . Ps 143:5

MEDITATION
of my mouth and the **m** of my heart be . Ps 19:14
May my **m** be pleasing to him, for I . . . . Ps 104:34
I love your law! It is my **m** all the day. . . Ps 119:97

MEDIUM
woman who is a **m** or a necromancer . . . Lv 20:27
"Behold, there is a **m** at En-dor.". . . . . . . 1 Sm 28:7

MEEK
But the **m** shall inherit the land and. . . . . . Ps 37:11
The **m** shall obtain fresh joy in the . . . . Is 29:19
"Blessed are the **m**, for they shall . . . . Mt 5:5

MEEKNESS
kindness, humility, **m**, and patience,. . . . . Col 3:12
and receive with **m** the implanted word, . . Jas 1:21

MEET
the people out of the camp to **m** God, . . Ex 19:17
Steadfast love and faithfulness **m**; . . . . . . Ps 85:10
all the city came out to **m** Jesus, ... Mt 8:34
not neglecting to **m** together, as is the . . Heb 10:25

MEETING
In the tent of **m**, outside the veil that is . . Ex 27:21
at Shiloh and set up the tent of **m** there. . . Jos 18:1
they brought up the ark, the tent of **m**, . . 2 Chr 5:5

MELCHIZEDEK
And **M** king of Salem brought out . . . . . . Gn 14:18
a priest forever after the order of **M**." . . . Ps 110:4
God a high priest after the order of **M**. . . Heb 5:10
For this **M**, king of Salem, priest of the . . . Heb 7:1

MELODY
I will sing and make **m** to the LORD. . . . . . . Ps 27:6
is steadfast! I will sing and make **m**! . . . . . . Ps 57:7
singing and making **m** to the Lord . . . . . . Eph 5:19

MELT
The mountains **m** like wax before the . . . . Ps 97:5
be feeble, and every human heart will **m**. . . Is 13:7
heavenly bodies will **m** as they burn! . . . . 2 Pt 3:12

MEMBERS
Do not present your **m** to sin as . . . . Rom 6:13
For as in one body we have many **m**, . . Rom 12:4
that your bodies are **m** of Christ? . . . . . . 1 Cor 6:15
God arranged the **m** in the body, ... 1 Cor 12:18
for we are **m** one of another. . . . . Eph 4:25

MEMORY
The **m** of the righteous is a blessing, ... Prv 10:7
has done will also be told in **m** of her." . . Mt 26:13

MEN
was life, and the life was the light of **m**. . . . Jn 1:4
"We must obey God rather than **m**. . . . . Acts 5:29
spread to all **m** because all sinned— . . . Rom 5:12
stand firm in the faith, act like **m**, ... 1 Cor 16:13
not as the word of **m** but as what it. . . 1 Thes 2:13
Older **m** are to be sober-minded, ... Ti 2:2
but **m** spoke from God as they were . . . . 2 Pt 1:21

MEPHIBOSHETH
became lame. And his name was **M**.. . . . 2 Sm 4:4
And **M** the son of Jonathan, son of. . . . . 2 Sm 9:6
"Why did you not go with me, **M**?" . . . 2 Sm 19:25

MERCIES
ceases; his **m** never come to an end; . . . Lam 3:22
the Father of **m** and God of all comfort, . 2 Cor 1:3

MERCIFUL
For the LORD your God is a **m** . . . . Dt 4:31
The LORD is **m** and gracious,. . . . . Ps 103:8
your God, for he is gracious and **m**, ... Jl 2:13
that you are a gracious God and **m**, ... Jon 4:2
"Blessed are the **m**, for they shall . . . . Mt 5:7
Be **m**, even as your Father is **m**. . . . . Lk 6:36
For I will be **m** toward their iniquities, . . . Heb 8:12
how the Lord is compassionate and **m**. . . . Jas 5:11

MERCY
"You shall make a **m** seat of pure gold. . . Ex 25:17
Have **m** on me, O God, according to . . . . . . Ps 51:1
and his **m** is over all that he has made. . . Ps 145:9
make it known; in wrath remember **m**. . . Hab 3:2
what this means, 'I desire **m**, and not. . . . . Mt 12:7
because of the tender **m** of our God, ... Lk 1:78
"Jesus, Son of David, have **m** on me!" . . . Lk 18:38
have **m** on whom I have **m**, ... Rom 9:15
But God, being rich in **m**, because . . . . . . Eph 2:4
But I received **m** for this reason, ... 1 Tm 1:16
grant him to find **m** from the Lord on . . 2 Tm 1:18
but according to his own **m**, by the . . . . Ti 3:5
of glory overshadowing the **m** seat. . . . . . Heb 9:5
M triumphs over judgment. . . . . Jas 2:13
According to his great **m**, he has . . . . 1 Pt 1:3
m, but now you have received **m**. . . . . 1 Pt 2:10

MERIBAH
the name of the place Massah and **M**, ... Ex 17:7
They angered him at the waters of **M**, . . Ps 106:32

MESSAGE
entrusting to us the **m** of reconciliation. . 2 Cor 5:19
through me the **m** might be fully . . . . . . 2 Tm 4:17
This is the **m** we have heard from him. . . . 1 Jn 1:5

MESSENGER
servant, or deaf as my **m** whom I send? . . Is 42:19
I send my **m**, and he will prepare the. . . . . Mal 3:1
"'Behold, I send my **m** before your face, . . Mt 11:10

MESSIAH
"We have found the **M**" (which means. . . . . Jn 1:41
"I know that **M** is coming (he who is . . . . . Jn 4:25

METHUSELAH
Thus all the days of **M** were 969 years, . . Gn 5:27

MICHAEL
withstood me twenty-one days, but **M**,.. Dn 10:13
"At that time shall arise **M**, the great ..... Dn 12:1
But when the archangel **M**, contending ... Jude 9
Now war arose in heaven, **M** and his ..... Rv 12:7

MICHAL
Now Saul's daughter **M** loved David. .. 1 Sm 18:20
So **M** let David down through the..... 1 Sm 19:12
And David said to **M**, "It was before.... 2 Sm 6:21

MIDNIGHT
At **m** the LORD struck down .... Ex 12:29
But at **m** there was a cry, 'Here is the .... Mt 25:6
will come, in the evening, or at **m**, ... Mk 13:35
at **m** and say to him, 'Friend, lend .... Lk 11:5
About **m** Paul and Silas were praying . Acts 16:25

MIDST
shall know that I am in the **m** of Israel, ... Jl 2:27
kingdom of God is in the **m** of you." ..... Lk 17:21
that God did through him in your **m**, ... Acts 2:22

MIDWIVES
the king of Egypt said to the Hebrew **m**, .. Ex 1:15

MIGHT
with all your soul and with all your **m**...... Dt 6:5
But I say that wisdom is better than **m**,. .Eccl 9:16
Not by **m**, nor by power, but by my ...... Zec 4:6

MIGHTY
who is **m** as you are, O LORD,............ Ps 89:8
for he who is **m** has done great things ... Lk 1:49
voice for all the **m** works that they...... Lk 19:37
was a prophet **m** in deed and word ..... Lk 24:19

MILE
And if anyone forces you to go one **m**, ... Mt 5:41

MILK
I fed you with **m**, not solid food, for..... 1 Cor 3:2
You need **m**, not solid food,............ Heb 5:12
long for the pure spiritual **m**, that by it ... 1 Pt 2:2

MILL
And he ground at the **m** in the prison... Jgs 16:21
Two women will be grinding at the **m**;... Mt 24:41

MIND
of man, that he should change his **m**. .. Nm 23:19
and try me; test my heart and my **m**. .... Ps 26:2
peace whose **m** is stayed on you,......... Is 26:3
with all your soul and with all your **m**... Mt 22:37
serve the law of God with my **m**, ... Rom 7:25
but to set the **m** on the Spirit is life ..... Rom 8:6
who has known the **m** of the Lord,.... Rom 11:34
transformed by the renewal of your **m**,. Rom 12:2
But we have the **m** of Christ........... 1 Cor 2:16
Have this **m** among yourselves, which .... Phil 2:5
quietly, and to **m** your own affairs,.... 1 Thes 4:11
has sworn and will not change his **m**, ... Heb 7:21

MINDFUL
what is man that you are **m** of him, ... Ps 8:4
their God will be **m** of them and restore .. Zep 2:7
"What is man, that you are **m** of him, ... Heb 2:6

MINDS
he opened their **m** to understand the ... Lk 24:45
set their **m** on the things of the Spirit.... Rom 8:5
has blinded the **m** of the unbelievers, .. 2 Cor 4:4
to be renewed in the spirit of your **m**,.. Eph 4:23
Set your **m** on things that are above,..... Col 3:2
I will put my laws into their **m**, and .... Heb 8:10
preparing your **m** for action, ... 1 Pt 1:13

MINE
I have called you by name, you are **m**..... Is 43:1
"They shall be **m**, says the LORD .... Mal 3:17

MINISTER
or in prison, and did not **m** to you?'.... Mt 25:44
a **m** of Christ Jesus to the Gentiles.... Rom 15:16
I was made a **m** according to the gift .... Eph 3:7
a **m** in the holy places, in the true tent .. Heb 8:2

MINISTERED
And the boy **m** to the LORD .... 1 Sm 2:11
they followed him and **m** to him, ... Mk 15:41
that these hands **m** to my necessities.. Acts 20:34

MINISTERS
were eyewitnesses and **m** of the word..... Lk 1:2
taxes, for the authorities are **m** of God,.. Rom 13:6
angels winds, and his **m** a flame of fire.". .Heb 1:7

MINISTRY
Jesus, when he began his **m**, was........ Lk 3:23
to prayer and to the **m** of the word."....Acts 6:4
and gave us the **m** of reconciliation; .. 2 Cor 5:18
work of an evangelist, fulfill your **m**..... 2 Tm 4:5
Christ has obtained a **m** that is as much.. Heb 8:6

MIRACLES
seeing signs and great **m** performed,... Acts 8:13
was doing extraordinary **m** by the ..... Acts 19:11
to another the working of **m**, to ...... 1 Cor 12:10
to you and works **m** among you do so ... Gal 3:5
wonders and various **m** and by gifts .... Heb 2:4

MIRIAM
M sang to them: "Sing to the LORD, ... Ex 15:21
M and Aaron spoke against Moses .... Nm 12:1
M was shut outside the camp seven..... Nm 12:15
And **M** died there and was buried there... Nm 20:1

MIRROR
For now we see in a **m** dimly, but..... 1 Cor 13:12
looks intently at his natural face in a **m**. . Jas 1:23

MIRTH
the heart of fools is in the house of **m**... Eccl 7:4
The **m** of the tambourines is stilled,...... Is 24:8

MISERIES
weep and howl for the **m** that are .... Jas 5:1

MISERY
and remember their **m** no more......... Prv 31:7
in their paths are ruin and **m**, ... Rom 3:16

MISLEADING
"We found this man **m** our nation and.... Lk 23:2

MISLEADS
"'Cursed be anyone who **m** a blind...... Dt 27:18
Whoever **m** the upright into an evil .... Prv 28:10

MIST
like a cloud and your sins like **m**; .... Is 44:22
For you are a **m** that appears for a little . Jas 4:14

MISTREAT
You shall not **m** any widow or.......... Ex 22:22
rulers, to **m** them and to stone them, .. Acts 14:5

MOAB
bore a son and called his name **M**....... Gn 19:37
went to sojourn in the country of **M**, ... Ru 1:1

MOABITE
"No Ammonite or **M** may enter the ...... Dt 23:3

MOCK
All who see me **m** me; they make........ Ps 22:7
Fools **m** at the guilt offering, but the.... Prv 14:9
And they will **m** him and spit on him, .. Mk 10:34

MOCKED
And at noon Elijah **m** them, saying, ... 1 Kgs 18:27
m him, saying, "Hail, King of the Jews!" . Mt 27:29
Do not be deceived: God is not **m**,....... Gal 6:7

MOCKING
Jesus in custody were **m** him as they.... Lk 22:63
But others **m** said, "They are filled ..... Acts 2:13
Others suffered **m** and flogging, and ... Heb 11:36

MOCKS
Whoever **m** the poor insults his Maker;.. Prv 17:5
The eye that **m** a father and scorns to.. Prv 30:17

MODESTY
parts are treated with greater **m**, ... 1 Cor 12:23
apparel, with **m** and self-control, ... 1 Tm 2:9

MOMENT
anger for a **m** I hid my face from you,.... Is 54:8
a nation be brought forth in one **m**? ..... Is 66:8
kingdoms of the world in a **m** of time,..... Lk 4:5

MONEY
He who loves **m** will not be satisfied .... Eccl 5:10
he who has no **m**, come, buy and eat!..... Is 55:1
You cannot serve God and **m**........... Mt 6:24
in the ground and hid his master's **m**.... Mt 25:18
no staff, nor bag, nor bread, nor **m**;....... Lk 9:3
could obtain the gift of God with **m**! ... Acts 8:20
not quarrelsome, not a lover of **m**....... 1 Tm 3:3
For the love of **m** is a root of all kinds.. 1 Tm 6:10
Keep your life free from love of **m**,...... Heb 13:5

MONEY-CHANGERS
he overturned the tables of the **m** and .. Mt 21:12
and pigeons, and the **m** sitting there. .... Jn 2:14

MONEYBAG
Carry no **m**, no knapsack, no sandals, ... Lk 10:4
now let the one who has a **m** take it,.... Lk 22:36
thought that, because Judas had the **m**, .. Jn 13:29

MOON
He made the **m** to mark the seasons; .. Ps 104:19
the **m** and stars to rule over the night, .. Ps 136:9
turned to darkness, and the **m** to blood,... Jl 2:31
and the **m** will not give its light,....... Mt 24:29
will be signs in sun and **m** and stars,.... Lk 21:25
turned to darkness and the **m** to blood, .. Acts 2:20
the sun, and another glory of the **m**,.. 1 Cor 15:41
the full **m** became like blood, ... Rv 6:12
has no need of sun or **m** to shine on it,.. Rv 21:23

MORALS
"Bad company ruins good **m**."........ 1 Cor 15:33

MORDECAI
in Susa the citadel whose name was **M**, .. Est 2:5
But **M** did not bow down or pay......... Est 3:2
For **M** was great in the king's house,..... Est 9:4

MORNING
when the **m** stars sang together and..... Jb 38:7
O LORD, in the **m** you hear .... Ps 5:3
take the wings of the **m** and dwell in.... Ps 139:9
In the **m** sow your seed, and at evening.. Eccl 11:6
they are new every **m**; great is your.... Lam 3:23
They were at the tomb early in the **m**,... Lk 24:22

MORSEL
Better is a dry **m** with quiet than a....... Prv 17:1
Then after he had taken the **m**, Satan ... Jn 13:27

MORTAL
'Can **m** man be in the right before God?.. Jb 4:17
give life to your **m** bodies through his... Rom 8:11
and the **m** puts on immortality,....... 1 Cor 15:54
so that what is **m** may be swallowed ... 2 Cor 5:4

MOSES
She named him **M**, "Because,"........... Ex 2:10
God said to **M**, "I AM WHO I AM."......... Ex 3:14
So **M** and Aaron went to Pharaoh........ Ex 7:10
Then **M** stretched out his staff toward.... Ex 9:23
M implored the LORD his God........... Ex 32:11
M would put the veil over his face ..... Ex 34:35
M erected the tabernacle. He laid its .... Ex 40:18
Now the man **M** was very meek, more... Nm 12:3
M sent them to spy out the land of ..... Nm 13:17
M and Aaron, "Because you did not.... Nm 20:12
So **M** made a bronze serpent and set it.. Nm 21:9
Then **M** summoned Joshua and said to ... Dt 31:7
M the servant of the LORD died.......... Dt 34:5

NAMES
The man gave **n** to all livestock and to . . Gn 2:20
engrave on them the **n** of the sons of . . . .Ex 28:9
the stars; he gives to all of them their **n**. . . Ps 147:4
but rejoice that your **n** are written in. . . .Lk 10:20
whose **n** are in the book of life. . . . . .Phil 4:3
dwellers on earth whose **n** have not. . . . . . Rv 17:8

NAOMI
Elimelech and the name of his wife **N**,. . . . . Ru 1:2
"A son has been born to **N**.". . . . . .Ru 4:17

NAPHTALI
prevailed." So she called his name **N**.. . . . Gn 30:8
Bilhah, Rachel's servant: Dan and **N**. . . . Gn 35:25
and the land of **N**, but in the latter time . . . . Is 9:1
sea, in the territory of Zebulun and **N**,. . . . Mt 4:13

NARD
alabaster flask of ointment of pure **n**, ...Mk 14:3
expensive ointment made from pure **n**,. . . Jn 12:3

NATHAN
word of the Lord came to **N**,. . . . . 2 Sm 7:4
N said to David, "You are the man!. . . . 2 Sm 12:7
he did not invite **N** the prophet or . . . . .1 Kgs 1:10
in the history of **N** the prophet,. . . . . . . 2 Chr 9:29

NATHANAEL
N said to him, "Can anything good. . . . . . . Jn 1:46
N of Cana in Galilee, the sons of. . . . . Jn 21:2

NATION
I will make of you a great **n**,. . . . . .Gn 12:2
me a kingdom of priests and a holy **n**. . . . Ex 19:6
Blessed is the **n** whose God is the . . . . . . Ps 33:12
Righteousness exalts a **n**, but sin is a. . . Prv 14:34
that the righteous **n** that keeps faith . . . . . Is 26:2
here I am," to a **n** that was not called . . . . .Is 65:1
For **n** will rise against **n**, ...Mt 24:7
for he loves our **n**, and he is the one . . . . . .Lk 7:5
a royal priesthood, a holy **n**,. . . . . .1 Pt 2:9
to every **n** and tribe and language . . . . . . .Rv 14:6

NATIONS
shall be the father of a multitude of **n**. . . .Gn 17:4
Let the **n** be glad and sing for joy, ...Ps 67:4
Declare his glory among the **n**, ...Ps 96:3
Praise the Lord, all **n**! Extol . . . . Ps 117:1
the hills; and all the **n** shall flow to it,. . . . . . .Is 2:2
the **n** are like a drop from a bucket,. . . . . .Is 40:15
praise to sprout up before all the **n**. . . . . . . .Is 61:11
n will know that I am the Lord,. . . . . . . .Ezk 36:23
n, and languages should serve him;. . . . . .Dn 7:14
And many **n** shall join themselves to . . . . .Zec 2:11
Then all **n** will call you blessed, for. . . . . . Mal 3:12
must first be proclaimed to all **n**. . . . . Mk 13:10
By its light will the **n** walk, and the . . . . .Rv 21:24

NATURAL
if God did not spare the **n** branches, . . . Rom 11:21
The **n** person does not accept the . . . . .1 Cor 2:14
If there is a **n** body, there is also a . . . .1 Cor 15:44

NATURE
his eternal power and divine **n**,. . . . . Rom 1:20
mind, and were by **n** children of wrath,. . .Eph 2:3
of God and the exact imprint of his **n**,. . . .Heb 1:3
may become partakers of the divine **n**,. . .2 Pt 1:4

NAZARETH
And he went and lived in a city called **N**, .Mt 2:23
from God to a city of Galilee named **N**,. . . Lk 1:26
good come out of **N**?" Philip said to . . . . . Jn 1:46
It read, "Jesus of **N**, the King of the . . . . . Jn 19:19
In the name of Jesus Christ of **N**, rise . . . Acts 3:6
And he said to me, 'I am Jesus of **N**, . . . Acts 22:8

NAZIRITE
makes a special vow, the vow of a **N**,. . . . .Nm 6:2
for the child shall be a **N** to God from . . . Jgs 13:7

NEAR
a god so **n** to it as the Lord. . . . . .Dt 4:7
Be not far from me, for trouble is **n**,. . . . . .Ps 22:11
Lord is **n** to the brokenhearted . . . . Ps 34:18
Lord is **n** to all who call on him, ... Ps 145:18
I bring **n** my righteousness; it is not far. . .Is 46:13
He who vindicates me is **n**. Who will . . . . . Is 50:8
all these things, you know that he is **n**, . .Mt 24:33
kingdom of God has come **n** to you.'. . . . . Lk 10:9
"The word is **n** you, in your mouth . . . . . Rom 10:8
far off and peace to those who were **n**. . Eph 2:17
what is written in it, for the time is **n**. . . . . . Rv 1:3

NEARER
For salvation is **n** to us now than . . . . . . Rom 13:11

NEBUCHADNEZZAR
In his days, **N** king of Babylon came . . 2 Kgs 24:1
Jerusalem into exile by the hand of **N**. . .1 Chr 6:15
N also carried part of the vessels of. . . 2 Chr 36:7
of the Lord that **N** had carried . . . . .Ezr 1:7
of those exiles whom **N** the king of . . . . . Neh 7:6
whom **N** king of Babylon had carried. . . . . Est 2:6
for **N** king of Babylon is making war . . . . .Jer 21:2
the eunuchs brought them in before **N**.. . . Dn 1:18
Then King **N** fell upon his face and. . . . . . Dn 2:46
Now I, **N**, praise and extol and honor the. . Dn 4:37

NECESSARY
Was it not **n** that the Christ should. . . . . .Lk 24:26
"It was **n** that the word of God be . . . . Acts 13:46
proving that it was **n** for the Christ to . . Acts 17:3

NEED
you a blessing until there is no more **n**. . . Mal 3:10
Father knows what you **n** before you. . . . . .Mt 6:8
'The Lord has **n** of it and will send it . . . . . Mk 11:3
it was distributed to each as any had **n**.. Acts 4:35
will supply every **n** of yours according. . . Phil 4:19
and find grace to help in time of **n**. . . . . .Heb 4:16
world's goods and sees his brother in **n**,. 1 Jn 3:17

NEEDS
Contribute to the **n** of the saints and. . .Rom 12:13
not only supplying the **n** of the saints. 2 Cor 9:12
sent me help for my **n** once and again. . . Phil 4:16

NEEDY
your brother, to the **n** and to the poor, . . . Dt 15:11
I was a father to the **n**, and I searched. . . Jb 29:16
As for me, I am poor and **n**, but the. . . . .Ps 40:17
and reaches out her hands to the **n**.. . . . Prv 31:20
graze, and the **n** lie down in safety; . . . . . .Is 14:30
silver, and the **n** for a pair of sandals— . . .Am 2:6
"Thus, when you give to the **n**, sound . . . . .Mt 6:2
Sell your possessions, and give to the **n**.. Lk 12:33
There was not a **n** person among them,. . Acts 4:34

NEGLECT
We will not **n** the house of our God.". . Neh 10:39
instruction and be wise, and do not **n** it.. Prv 8:33
herb, and **n** justice and the love of God. . Lk 11:42
escape if we **n** such a great salvation?. . . Heb 2:3
Do not **n** to do good and to share . . . . . Heb 13:16

NEHEMIAH
with Zerubbabel, Jeshua, **N**, Seraiah, ... Ezr 2:2
in the days of **N** the governor and . . . . .Neh 12:26

NEIGHBOR
but you shall love your **n** as yourself:. . . . .Lv 19:18
Whoever despises his **n** is a sinner,. . . . . .Prv 14:21
Better is a **n** who is near than a . . . . Prv 27:10
was said, 'You shall love your **n** and. . . . . Mt 5:43
said to Jesus, "And who is my **n**?" . . . . . . Lk 10:29
Love does no wrong to a **n**; . . . . Rom 13:10
his own good, but the good of his **n**. . .1 Cor 10:24
"You shall love your **n** as yourself.". . . . . . Gal 5:14

NESTS
In them the birds build their **n**; the. . . . . Ps 104:17
birds of the air come and make **n**. . . . . Mt 13:32

NET
heaven is like a **n** that was thrown into . . Mt 13:47
of Simon casting a **n** into the sea,. . . . . Mk 1:16
"Cast the **n** on the right side of the boat, . Jn 21:6

NETS
Let the wicked fall into their own **n**,. . . . .Ps 141:10
woman whose heart is snares and **n**,. . . . Eccl 7:26
they left their **n** and followed him. . . . . Mk 1:18
But at your word I will let down the **n**.". . . . Lk 5:5

NEVER
and **n** again shall there be a flood to . . . . . Gn 9:11
love of the Lord **n** ceases; . . . . Lam 3:22
"**N** was anything like this seen in . . . . .Mt 9:33
I will give him will **n** be thirsty again. . . . . . Jn 4:14
whoever comes to me I will **n** cast out. . . .Jn 6:37
them eternal life, and they will **n** perish, . Jn 10:28
I will **n** blot his name out of the book . . . . .Rv 3:5

NEW
Sing to him a **n** song; play skillfully . . . . . . Ps 33:3
Oh sing to the Lord a **n** song; . . . . Ps 96:1
I create **n** heavens and a **n** earth, ...Is 65:17
I will give you a **n** heart, and a **n**. . . . . . Ezk 36:26
Neither is **n** wine put into old wineskins. . Mt 9:17
for you is the **n** covenant in my blood. . .Lk 22:20
A **n** commandment I give to you, that. . . Jn 13:34
create in himself one **n** man in place of. . Eph 2:15
and have put on the **n** self, which is. . . . . Col 3:10
by the **n** and living way that he. . . . . . . Heb 10:20
with a **n** name written on the stone that. . Rv 2:17
they were singing a **n** song before the . . .Rv 14:3
"Behold, I am making all things **n**.". . . . . . . Rv 21:5

NEWS
heart, and good **n** refreshes the bones.. Prv 15:30
who publishes peace, who brings good **n**. .Is 52:7
and the poor have good **n** preached to. . . Mt 11:5
I bring you good **n** of great joy that. . . . . . Lk 2:10
anointed me to proclaim good **n** to the. . . Lk 4:18
preaching good **n** of peace through. . . Acts 10:36
And this word is the good **n** that was . . . 1 Pt 1:25

NICODEMUS
was a man of the Pharisees named **N**,. . . . . Jn 3:1
N, who had gone to him before, and . . . . .Jn 7:50
N also, who earlier had come to Jesus . . Jn 19:39

NIGHT
light Day, and the darkness he called **N**. . . Gn 1:5
the **n** is long, and I am full of tossing. . . . . .Jb 7:4
and on his law he meditates day and **n**. . . . Ps 1:2
love, and at **n** his song is with me, ...Ps 42:8
You will not fear the terror of the **n**,. . . . . . Ps 91:5
the moon and stars to rule over the **n**, . . Ps 136:9
the **n** is bright as the day, for darkness . Ps 139:12
Her lamp does not go out at **n**.. . . . . .Prv 31:18
This **n** your soul is required of you,. . . . . Lk 12:20
This man came to Jesus by **n** and. . . . . .Jn 3:2
n is coming, when no one can work. . . . . . .Jn 9:4
We are not of the **n** or of the darkness. . .1 Thes 5:5
And **n** will be no more. They will. . . . . .Rv 22:5

NILE
I will strike the water that is in the **N**, ... Ex 7:17

NINEVEH
land he went into Assyria and built **N**,. . . Gn 10:11
"Arise, go to **N**, that great city, and call. . . Jon 1:2
An oracle concerning **N**. The book of. . . . . . Na 1:1
became a sign to the people of **N**, ... Lk 11:30

NOAH
But **N** found favor in the eyes of the . . . . . Gn 6:8
They went into the ark with **N**, two . . . . . .Gn 7:15
"This is like the days of **N** to me: as I. . . . . Is 54:9
if these three men, **N**, Daniel, and Job, . Ezk 14:14
until the day when **N** entered the ark,. . Mt 24:38
By faith **N**, being warned by God . . . . Heb 11:7
God's patience waited in the days of **N**, 1 Pt 3:20
the ancient world, but preserved **N**,. . . . . 2 Pt 2:5

NOBLE
Hear, for I will speak **n** things, ...Prv 8:6
he who is **n** plans **n** things,. . . . . Is 32:8

powerful, not many were of **n** birth.... 1 Cor 1:26
office of overseer, he desires a **n** task.... 1 Tm 3:1

NOISE
let us make a joyful **n** to the rock of our.. Ps 95:1
Make a joyful **n** to the LORD,............ Ps 100:1

NONE
may know that there is **n** like me in all ... Ex 9:14
"There is **n** holy like the LORD:..........1 Sm 2:2
For there is **n** like you, and there is no.. 2 Sm 7:22
no other; I am God, and there is **n** like.... Is 46:9
There is **n** like you, O LORD; .... Jer 10:6
written: "**N** is righteous, no, not one; ... Rom 3:10

NORTH
stay not, for I bring disaster from the **n**,.. Jer 4:6
the king of the **n** shall again raise a ......Dn 11:13

NOTHING
and there is **n** hidden from its heat....... Ps 19:6
done, and there is **n** new under the sun...Eccl 1:9
outstretched arm! **N** is too hard for you... Jer 32:17
n is covered that will not be revealed,... Mt 10:26
For **n** will be impossible with God." ...... Lk 1:37
"I can do **n** on my own. As I hear, I.......Jn 5:30
leftover fragments, that **n** may be lost." .. Jn 6:12
fruit, for apart from me you can do **n**..... Jn 15:5
mountains, but have not love, I am **n**...1 Cor 13:2
for we brought **n** into the world,.........1 Tm 6:7
to the defiled and unbelieving, **n** is pure; .. Ti 1:15
be perfect and complete, lacking in **n**..... Jas 1:4
am rich, I have prospered, and I need **n**,.. Rv 3:17

NULLIFY
Does their faithlessness **n** the ....Rom 3:3
I do not **n** the grace of God, for if....... Gal 2:21

NUMBER
"Look toward heaven, and **n** the stars,....Gn 15:5
So teach us to **n** our days that we may.. Ps 90:12
He determines the **n** of the stars; he .... Ps 147:4
Lord added to their **n** day by day those ..Acts 2:47
n of a man, and his **n** is 666............ Rv 13:18

NUMBERED
struck him after he had **n** the people... 2 Sm 24:10
of heaven cannot be **n** and the sands of.. Jer 33:22

OATH
to David a sure **o** from which he will.... Ps 132:11
But I say to you, Do not take an **o** at all,. Mt 5:34
the **o** that he swore to our father .... Lk 1:73
his purpose, he guaranteed it with an **o**,.. Heb 6:17
heaven or by earth or by any other **o**,.... Jas 5:12

OBEDIENCE
to him shall be the **o** of the peoples.... Gn 49:10
to bring about the **o** of faith for the..... Rom 1:5
so by the one man's **o** the many will ... Rom 5:19
when your **o** is complete............. 2 Cor 10:6
he learned **o** through what he suffered. . Heb 5:8
for **o** to Jesus Christ and for sprinkling ... 1 Pt 1:2

OBEDIENT
know whether you are **o** in everything.. 2 Cor 2:9
himself by becoming **o** to the point......Phil 2:8
to rulers and authorities, to be **o**,..........Ti 3:1
As **o** children, do not be conformed..... 1 Pt 1:14

OBEY
"But if you carefully **o** his voice and.....Ex 23:22
Be careful to **o** all these words that I.... Dt 12:28
Behold, to **o** is better than sacrifice,... 1 Sm 15:22
'**O** my voice, and I will be your God,..... Jer 7:23
"We must **o** God rather than men.......Acts 5:29
are self-seeking and do not **o** the truth,. .Rom 2:8
you are slaves of the one whom you **o**,. .Rom 6:16
Children, **o** your parents in everything, ..Col 3:20
those who do not **o** the gospel of our. 2 Thes 1:8
of eternal salvation to all who **o** him,.... Heb 5:9
O your leaders and submit to them,.... Heb 13:17
when we love God and **o** his ....1 Jn 5:2

OBEYED
blessed, because you have **o** my voice." .Gn 22:18
But they have not all **o** the gospel..... Rom 10:16
my beloved, as you have always **o**,...... Phil 2:12
By faith Abraham **o** when he was....... Heb 11:8

OBLIGATION
I am under **o** both to Greeks and to.....Rom 1:14
o to bear with the failings of the weak,. .Rom 15:1

OBSERVE
ruler, **o** carefully what is before you, ... Prv 23:1
You **o** days and months and seasons.... Gal 4:10

OBSOLETE
new covenant, he makes the first one **o**...Heb 8:13

OBSTACLE
rather than put an **o** in the way of .....1 Cor 9:12
We put no **o** in anyone's way, so that .. 2 Cor 6:3

OBSTINATE
hardened his spirit and made his heart **o**,..Dt 2:30
Because I know that you are **o**, and...... Is 48:4

OBTAIN
they shall **o** gladness and joy, ...Is 51:11
but to **o** salvation through our Lord... 1 Thes 5:9
may **o** the salvation that is in Christ....2 Tm 2:10
that no one fails to **o** the grace of God. . Heb 12:15

OBTAINED
Through him we have also **o** access by ..Rom 5:2
Not that I have already **o** this or........ Phil 3:12
But as it is, Christ has **o** a ministry...... Heb 8:6

OFFENDED
A brother **o** is more unyielding than a...Prv 18:19
blessed is the one who is not **o** by me." .. Mt 11:6
the Pharisees were **o** when they heard .. Mt 15:12

OFFENSE
Whoever covers an **o** seeks love, but.... Prv 17:9
sanctuary and a stone of **o** and a.........Is 8:14
And they took **o** at him. But Jesus said.. Mt 13:57
Give no **o** to Jews or to Greeks or to. .1 Cor 10:32
In that case the **o** of the cross has.......Gal 5:11

OFFENSES
stirs up strife, but love covers all **o**..... Prv 10:12
for calmness will lay great **o** to rest..... Eccl 10:4

OFFER
go to my servant Job and **o** up a burnt...Jb 42:8
O right sacrifices, and put your trust......Ps 4:5
continually **o** up a sacrifice of praise ... Heb 13:15

OFFERING
had regard for Abel and his **o**,.......... Gn 4:4
you will not be pleased with a burnt **o**... Ps 51:16
when his soul makes an **o** for guilt, he....Is 53:10
So if you are **o** your gift at the altar......Mt 5:23
rich putting their gifts into the **o** box,.....Lk 21:1
For by a single **o** he has perfected for. . Heb 10:14

OFFERINGS
knowledge of God rather than burnt **o**... Hos 6:6
than all whole burnt **o** and sacrifices."...Mk 12:33
"Sacrifices and **o** you have not desired,. .Heb 10:5

OFFICE
days be few; may another take his **o**!....Ps 109:8
"'Let another take his **o**.'............ Acts 1:20

OFFSPRING
between your **o** and her **o**;.............Gn 3:15
"To your **o** I will give this land."..........Gn 12:7
I will make your **o** as the dust of the .... Gn 13:16
I will pour my Spirit upon your **o**, and.... Is 44:3
an offering for guilt, he shall see his **o**; ...Is 53:10
Godly **o**. So guard yourselves .... Mal 2:15
have said, "'For we are indeed his **o**.'.. Acts 17:28
of the promise are counted as **o**. ....Rom 9:8
are Christ's, then you are Abraham's **o**,. .Gal 3:29

OIL
and the jug of **o** shall not be empty, ... 1 Kgs 17:14
wind or to grasp **o** in one's right hand. . Prv 27:16
wise took flasks of **o** with their lamps.... Mt 25:4
You did not anoint my head with **o**, but . .Lk 7:46
has anointed you with the **o** of gladness. .Heb 1:9
anointing him with **o** in the name of .... Jas 5:14

OINTMENT
In pouring this **o** on my body, she has... Mt 26:12
"Why was the **o** wasted like that? ....Mk 14:4
anointed the Lord with **o** and wiped his ...Jn 11:2

OLD
Remember the days of **o**; consider the ... Dt 32:7
I have been young, and now am **o**, yet I. .Ps 37:25
Do not cast me off in the time of **o** age;.. Ps 71:9
even when he is **o** he will not depart.... Prv 22:6
The **o** has passed away; behold, the....2 Cor 5:17
have put off the **o** self with its practices. . Col 3:9
than the **o** as the covenant he mediates. Heb 8:6

OLDER
the **o** shall serve the younger." .... Gn 25:23
"Now his **o** son was in the field, and .... Lk 15:25
"The **o** will serve the younger." .... Rom 9:12
not rebuke an **o** man but encourage .... 1 Tm 5:1

OLIVE
her mouth was a freshly plucked **o** leaf... Gn 8:11
I am like a green **o** tree in the house of... Ps 52:8
And there are two **o** trees by it, one on. ..Zec 4:3
off, and you, although a wild **o** shoot,. . Rom 11:17
These are the two **o** trees and the two ... Rv 11:4

OLIVES
the Mount of **O** shall be split in two..... Zec 14:4
As he sat on the Mount of **O**, the ....Mt 24:3
hymn, they went out to the Mount of **O**.. Mt 26:30
but Jesus went to the Mount of **O**......... Jn 8:1

OLIVET
out and lodged on the mount called **O**... Lk 21:37
to Jerusalem from the mount called **O**,.. Acts 1:12

ONCE
make atonement for it **o** in the year.....Ex 30:10
death he died he died to sin, **o** for all,.. Rom 6:10
since he did this **o** for all when he ..... Heb 7:27
just as it is appointed for man to die **o**,. Heb 9:27
For Christ also suffered **o** for sins, the... 1 Pt 3:18

ONE
wife, and they shall become **o** flesh. .... Gn 2:24
our God, the LORD is **o**...................Dt 6:4
O thing have I asked of the ....Ps 27:4
Two are better than **o**, because they .... Eccl 4:9
him, "Are you the **o** who is to come, ... Mt 11:3
his wife, and the two shall become **o**.... Mt 19:5
No **o** can come to me unless the Father. . Jn 6:44
I and the Father are **o**."...............Jn 10:30
may be **o** even as we are **o**,............ Jn 17:22
though many, are **o** body in Christ, ... Rom 12:5
that **o** has died for all, therefore all ... 2 Cor 5:14
o Lord, **o** faith, **o** baptism, ... Eph 4:5
You believe that God is **o**; you do well... Jas 2:19

OPEN
O your mouth wide, and I will fill it...... Ps 81:10
You **o** your hand; you satisfy the....... Ps 145:16
Can a demon **o** the eyes of the blind?".. Jn 10:21
you, Corinthians; our heart is wide **o**... 2 Cor 6:11
I have set before you an **o** door,..........Rv 3:8
"Who is worthy to **o** the scroll and........Rv 5:2

OPENED
when you eat of it your eyes will be **o**, ... Gn 3:5
and was praying, the heavens were **o**,.... Lk 3:21
Then he **o** their minds to understand....Lk 24:45
that anyone **o** the eyes of a man born....Jn 9:32
he said, "Behold, I see the heavens **o**,. . Acts 7:56
living way that he **o** for us through ... Heb 10:20

immorality, impurity, **p**, evil desire, ... Col 3:5
lust of defiling **p** and despise authority.. .2 Pt 2:10

PASSIONS
God gave them up to dishonorable **p**... Rom 1:26
we were living in the flesh, our sinful **p**, . . Rom 7:5
the flesh with its **p** and desires.......... Gal 5:24
So flee youthful **p** and pursue .... 2 Tm 2:22
to renounce ungodliness and worldly **p**, . . . Ti 2:12
do not be conformed to the **p** of your... 1 Pt 1:14

PASSOVER
eat it in haste. It is the LORD's **P**.......... Ex 12:11
directed them, and they prepared the **P**.. Mt 26:19
"I have earnestly desired to eat this **P** . . . Lk 22:15
For Christ, our **P** lamb, has been........ 1 Cor 5:7
By faith he kept the **P** and sprinkled . . . Heb 11:28

PASTURE
God, and we are the people of his **p**,..... Ps 95:7
are his people, and the sheep of his **p**. . . Ps 100:3
and on rich **p** they shall feed on the.... Ezk 34:14
saved and will go in and out and find **p**... Jn 10:9

PASTURES
He makes me lie down in green **p**........ Ps 23:2

PATH
You make known to me the **p** of life;..... Ps 16:11
me on a level **p** because of my enemies.. .Ps 27:11
a lamp to my feet and a light to my **p**. .Ps 119:105
But the **p** of the righteous is like the.... Prv 4:18
p of life leads upward for the prudent, . Prv 15:24
he sowed, some seeds fell along the **p**,... Mt 13:4

PATHS
He leads me in **p** of righteousness .... Ps 23:3
O LORD; teach me your **p**................ Ps 25:4
him, and he will make straight your **p**..... Prv 3:6
have made known to me the **p** of life;.. Acts 2:28
and make straight **p** for your feet, so... Heb 12:13

PATIENCE
and good heart, and bear fruit with **p**..... Lk 8:15
to those who by **p** in well-doing seek . . . Rom 2:7
endured with much **p** vessels of wrath . . Rom 9:22
with all humility and gentleness, with **p**, . Eph 4:2
display his perfect **p** as an example..... 1 Tm 1:16
when God's **p** waited in the days of.... 1 Pt 3:20
And count the **p** of our Lord as......... 2 Pt 3:15

PATIENT
Rejoice in hope, be **p** in tribulation, ... Rom 12:12
Love is **p** and kind; love does not envy. . 1 Cor 13:4
help the weak, be **p** with them all..... 1 Thes 5:14
but is **p** toward you, not wishing that . . . 2 Pt 3:9

PATTERN
you make them after the **p** for them,... Ex 25:40
according to the **p** that was shown ..... Heb 8:5

PAUL
who was also called **P**, filled with the . . Acts 13:9
they called Zeus, and **P**, Hermes, ... Acts 14:12
they stoned **P** and dragged him out of . . Acts 14:19
the Jews a favor, Felix left **P** in prison. . . Acts 24:27
then is Apollos? What is **P**? Servants.... 1 Cor 3:5
I, **P**, an old man and now a prisoner...... Phlm 9
as our beloved brother **P** also wrote .... 2 Pt 3:15

PAVEMENT
his feet as it were a **p** of sapphire....... Ex 24:10
seat at a place called The Stone **P**,....... Jn 19:13

PAY
if the thief is found, he shall **p** double..... Ex 22:7
P to all what is owed to them: taxes . . . Rom 13:7

PEACE
I will give **p** in the land, and you shall .... Lv 26:6
countenance upon you and give you **p**.. Nm 6:26
for he will speak **p** to his people, ... Ps 85:8
You keep him in perfect **p** whose mind . . . Is 26:3
the effect of righteousness will be **p**,..... Is 32:17
is no **p**," says my God, "for the wicked." . . Is 57:21
I will extend **p** to her like a river,......... Is 66:12
'**P**, **p**,' when there is no **p**............... Jer 6:14
and he shall speak **p** to the nations;..... Zec 9:10
come to bring **p**, but a sword.......... Mt 10:34
"**P**! Be still!" And the wind ceased,...... Mk 4:39
go in **p**, and be healed of your disease.". Mk 5:34
to God in the highest, and on earth **p** .... Lk 2:14
you enter, first say, '**P** be to this house!' . . Lk 10:5
P I leave with you; my **p** I give .... Jn 14:27
in me you may have **p**. In the world..... Jn 16:33
among them and said, "**P** be with you." Jn 20:26
we have **p** with God through our Lord... Rom 5:1
God has called you to **p**.............. 1 Cor 7:15
is not a God of confusion but of **p**..... 1 Cor 14:33
For he himself is our **p**, who has made . . Eph 2:14
And the **p** of God, which surpasses all.... Phil 4:7
making **p** by the blood of his cross...... Col 1:20
And let the **p** of Christ rule in your...... Col 3:15
Strive for **p** with everyone,............ Heb 12:14
righteousness is sown in **p** by those..... Jas 3:18
do good; let him seek **p** and pursue it. . . .1 Pt 3:11
was permitted to take **p** from the earth, . . Rv 6:4

PEACEABLY
as it depends on you, live **p** with all. . . Rom 12:18

PEACEFUL
My people will abide in a **p** habitation, . . . Is 32:18
that we may lead a **p** and quiet life,..... 1 Tm 2:2
it yields the **p** fruit of righteousness.... Heb 12:11

PEACEMAKERS
"Blessed are the **p**, for they shall be....... Mt 5:9

PEARL
who, on finding one **p** of great value, . . . Mt 13:46
each of the gates made of a single **p**, . . . Rv 21:21

PEARLS
and do not throw your **p** before pigs, ... Mt 7:6

PENALTY
A man of great wrath will pay the **p**,.... Prv 19:19
in themselves the due **p** for their error. . Rom 1:27

PENNY
get out until you have paid the last **p**..... Mt 5:26
Are not two sparrows sold for a **p**? ..... Mt 10:29

PENTECOST
When the day of **P** arrived, they were . . . Acts 2:1

PEOPLE
the God of Israel, 'Let my **p** go,........... Ex 5:1
the burden of all this **p** on me?......... Nm 11:11
God has chosen you to be a **p** for his ..... Dt 7:6
Your **p** shall be my **p**,.................. Ru 1:16
if my **p** who are called by my name... 2 Chr 7:14
God restores the fortunes of his **p**,....... Ps 53:6
blows on it; surely the **p** are grass........ Is 40:7
my **p** shall know my name.............. Is 52:6
But my **p** have forgotten me;........... Jer 18:15
be my **p** and I will be their God,........ Jer 24:7
My **P**, for you are not my **p**,............. Hos 1:9
p honors me with their lips, but their..... Mk 7:6
make ready for the Lord a **p** prepared." . . . Lk 1:17
the earth, will draw all **p** to myself."..... Jn 12:32
has God rejected his **p**? By no means!. . . Rom 11:1
desires all **p** to be saved and to .... 1 Tm 2:4
propitiation for the sins of the **p**. .... Heb 2:17
be mistreated with the **p** of God than . . Heb 11:25
with them, and they will be his **p**,........ Rv 21:3

PEOPLES
kingdom, that all **p**, nations,............ Dn 7:14
above the hills; and **p** shall flow to it,...... Mi 4:1
Gentiles, and let all the **p** extol him." . . . Rom 15:11
from all tribes and **p** and languages, ... Rv 7:9

PERFECT
the flock, to be accepted it must be **p**; . . Lv 22:21
My dove, my **p** one, is the only one,...... Sg 6:9
You therefore must be **p**, as your .... Mt 5:48
but when the **p** comes, the partial .... 1 Cor 13:10
for my power is made **p** in weakness.". . 2 Cor 12:9
of their salvation **p** through suffering. . . . Heb 2:10
that you may be **p** and complete,........ Jas 1:4

PERFECTED
single offering he has **p** for all time .... Heb 10:14
in him truly the love of God is **p**......... 1 Jn 2:5

PERFECTER
Jesus, the founder and **p** of our faith, . . . Heb 12:2

PERFECTION
I have seen a limit to all **p**, but your.... Ps 119:96
Now if **p** had been attainable through... Heb 7:11

PERISH
is against the law, and if I **p**, I **p**." .... Est 4:16
but the way of the wicked will **p**.......... Ps 1:6
take the sword will **p** by the sword..... Mt 26:52
you repent, you will all likewise **p**. .... Lk 13:3
eternal life, and they will never **p**,....... Jn 10:28
they will **p**, but you remain;............. Heb 1:11
not wishing that any should **p**, ... 2 Pt 3:9

PERISHABLE
What is sown is **p**; what is raised is . . . 1 Cor 15:42
not with **p** things such as silver......... 1 Pt 1:18

PERISHED
did not accept discipline; truth has **p**; . . . Jer 7:28
The godly has **p** from the earth, and ...... Mi 7:2
have fallen asleep in Christ have **p**..... 1 Cor 15:18
existed was deluged with water and **p**... 2 Pt 3:6

PERISHING
him, saying, "Save us, Lord; we are **p**." . . . Mt 8:25
of the cross is folly to those who are **p**, . . 1 Cor 1:18
it is veiled to those who are **p**. .... 2 Cor 4:3

PERPLEXED
While they were **p** about this, behold,.... Lk 24:4
crushed; **p**, but not driven to despair; . . 2 Cor 4:8

PERSECUTE
enemies and pray for those who **p** you, . Mt 5:44
persecuted me, they will also **p** you. .... Jn 15:20
Bless those who **p** you; bless and do . . Rom 12:14

PERSECUTED
for so they **p** the prophets............. Mt 5:12
reviled, we bless; when **p**, we endure; . . 1 Cor 4:12
p, but not forsaken; struck down, but . . 2 Cor 4:9
a godly life in Christ Jesus will be **p**, . . . 2 Tm 3:12

PERSECUTING
this was why the Jews were **p** Jesus,..... Jn 5:16
to him, "Saul, Saul, why are you **p** me?" . Acts 9:4

PERSECUTION
when tribulation or **p** arises on .... Mt 13:21
that day a great **p** against the church in. . Acts 8:1
Shall tribulation, or distress, or **p**, or . . . Rom 8:35

PERSECUTIONS
hardships, **p**, and calamities.......... 2 Cor 12:10
faith in all your **p** and in the afflictions . . 2 Thes 1:4
p I endured; yet from them all......... 2 Tm 3:11

PERSECUTOR
as to zeal, a **p** of the church;............ Phil 3:6
though formerly I was a blasphemer, **p**, .1 Tm 1:13

PERSEVERANCE
To that end keep alert with all **p**, ... Eph 6:18

PERSIA
In the first year of Cyrus king of **P**,....... Ezr 1:1
The army of **P** and Media and the......... Est 1:3
these are the kings of Media and **P**...... Dn 8:20

PERSIST
P in this, for by so doing you will...... 1 Tm 4:16
As for those who **p** in sin, rebuke...... 1 Tm 5:20

PERSON
The good **p** out of his good treasure . . . . Mt 12:35
from the heart, and this defiles a **p**. . . . . . Mt 15:18
he will repay each **p** according to what. . Mt 16:27
perhaps for a good **p** one would dare . . . Rom 5:7

PERSUADE
the fear of the Lord, we **p** others. . . . . . . 2 Cor 5:11

PERSUADED
With patience a ruler may be **p**, and a. . Prv 25:15
some of them were **p** and joined Paul . . Acts 17:4

PERSUASIVENESS
and sweetness of speech increases **p**. . . Prv 16:21
speech judicious and adds **p** to his lips. . Prv 16:23

PERVERSE
end will be, for they are a **p** generation,. . Dt 32:20
A **p** heart shall be far from me; I will . . . . Ps 101:4
the mouth of the wicked, what is **p**. . . . Prv 10:32

PERVERT
bribe in secret to **p** the ways of justice.. Prv 17:23
and you **p** the words of the living God,. Jer 23:36
who **p** the grace of our God into . . . . Jude 4

PESTILENCE
LORD sent a **p** on Israel from . . . . .2 Sm 24:15
nor the **p** that stalks in darkness, ... Ps 91:6
with famine and with **p** and by wild. . . . . . Rv 6:8

PETER
Simon (who is called **P**) and Andrew. . . . . Mt 4:18
So **P** got out of the boat and walked. . . . Mt 14:29
And I tell you, you are **P**, and on this. . . . Mt 16:18
days Jesus took with him **P** and James, . . Mt 17:1
Now **P** was sitting outside in the . . . . . . Mt 26:69
But **P** rose and ran to the tomb;. . . . . Lk 24:12
be called Cephas" (which means **P**). . . . . . Jn 1:42
Jesus said to Simon **P**, "Simon,. . . . . .Jn 21:15
But **P**, standing with the eleven, lifted . . Acts 2:14
Then **P**, filled with the Holy Spirit, ... Acts 4:8
P was sleeping between two soldiers, . . Acts 12:6
debate, **P** stood up and said to them, . . Acts 15:7
through **P** for his apostolic ministry to. . . . Gal 2:8

PETITION
of Israel grant your **p** that you have. . . . .1 Sm 1:17
found Daniel making **p** and plea before . . Dn 6:11

PHARAOH
Then Joseph said to **P**, "The dreams of . .Gn 41:25
"Go in, tell **P** king of Egypt to let the. . . . . Ex 6:11
I will get glory over **P** and all his host,. . . Ex 14:17
For the Scripture says to **P**, "For this . . . Rom 9:17

PHARISEE
You blind **P**! First clean the inside. . . . . . Mt 23:26
The **P**, standing by himself, prayed. . . . . . . Lk 18:11
"Brothers, I am a **P**, a son of Pharisees. . .Acts 23:6
Hebrew of Hebrews; as to the law, a **P**;. . .Phil 3:5

PHARISEES
exceeds that of the scribes and **P**, ... Mt 5:20
Then the **P** went and plotted how to . . . . Mt 22:15
"But woe to you, scribes and **P**, ... Mt 23:13
P cleanse the outside of the cup. . . . . Lk 11:39
P, saying, "Is it lawful to heal on the . . . . . Lk 14:3

PHILIP
P and Bartholomew; Thomas and. . . . . Mt 10:3
He found **P** and said to him, "Follow . . . . . Jn 1:43
P said to him, "Lord, show us the. . . . . Jn 14:8
James and Andrew, **P** and Thomas, ... Acts 1:13
So **P** ran to him and heard him . . . . .Acts 8:30

PHILIPPI
came into the district of Caesarea **P**, ... Mt 16:13
and from there to **P**, which is a . . . . .Acts 16:12
and been shamefully treated at **P**, ...1 Thes 2:2

PHILISTINES
to Gerar to Abimelech king of the **P**. . . . . .Gn 26:1
When the **P** captured the ark of God, . . . 1 Sm 5:1
Now the **P** gathered their armies for . . . .1 Sm 17:1
David defeated the **P** and subdued . . . . .2 Sm 8:1
Jeremiah the prophet concerning the **P**, . .Jer 47:1

PHILOSOPHERS
and Stoic **p** also conversed with him. . . .Acts 17:18

PHILOSOPHY
you captive by **p** and empty deceit,. . . . . . Col 2:8

PHINEHAS
daughters of Putiel, and she bore him **P**. .Ex 6:25
When **P** the son of Eleazar, son of . . . . . .Nm 25:7
Gilead, **P** the son of Eleazar the priest, . Jos 22:13
the two sons of Eli, Hophni and **P**, ... 1 Sm 1:3

PHYLACTERIES
For they make their **p** broad and their. . . .Mt 23:5

PHYSICIAN
who are well have no need of a **p**, ... Mt 9:12
to me this proverb, '**P**, heal yourself.' . . . . .Lk 4:23
Luke the beloved **p** greets you,. . . . . Col 4:14

PHYSICIANS
with lies; worthless **p** are you all. . . . . Jb 13:4
though she had spent all her living on **p**, .Lk 8:43

PIECE
No one puts a **p** of unshrunk cloth on . . . . Mt 9:16
They gave him a **p** of broiled fish,. . . . . . .Lk 24:42

PIECES
falls on this stone will be broken to **p**;. . . Mt 21:44
And they paid him thirty **p** of silver.. . . . . Mt 26:15

PIERCED
they have **p** my hands and feet— . . . . Ps 22:16
on me, on him whom they have **p**, ... Zec 12:10
But one of the soldiers **p** his side . . . . Jn 19:34
will look on him whom they have **p**." . . . . Jn 19:37
eye will see him, even those who **p** him, . . . Rv 1:7

PIGS
do not throw your pearls before **p**,. . . . . . . .Mt 7:6
a herd of many **p** was feeding at some . . Mt 8:30
to be fed with the pods that the **p** ate, . . Lk 15:16

PILATE
delivered him over to **P** the governor. . . . .Mt 27:2
Pontius **P** being governor of Judea,. . . . . . . Lk 3:1
And Herod and **P** became friends with . . Lk 23:12
P answered, "What I have written I . . . . . Jn 19:22
over and denied in the presence of **P**, . . Acts 3:13
anointed, both Herod and Pontius **P** . . . Acts 4:27
in his testimony before Pontius **P** . . . . . . 1 Tm 6:13

PILLAR
In the **p** of the cloud he spoke . . . . .Ps 99:7
God, a **p** and buttress of the truth. . . . . . 1 Tm 3:15

PINIONS
catching them, bearing them on its **p**,. . . .Dt 32:11
are they the **p** and plumage of love? . . . . Jb 39:13

PIT
my soul from going down into the **p**,. . . .Jb 33:28
He drew me up from the **p** of . . . . .Ps 40:2
redeems your life from the **p**, ...Ps 103:4
Whoever digs a **p** will fall into it, ...Prv 26:27
they have dug a **p** for my life. . . . . Jer 18:20
lead the blind, both will fall into a **p**." . . . Mt 15:14
and threw him into the **p**, and shut it. . . . Rv 20:3

PITCHED
Now Jacob had **p** his tent in the hill. . . . .Gn 31:25
for the ark of God and **p** a tent for it. . . 1 Chr 15:1
for he had **p** a tent for it in Jerusalem.) . . 2 Chr 1:4

PITIED
we are of all people most to be **p**. . . . . 1 Cor 15:19

PITY
They close their hearts to **p**; with their . . Ps 17:10
I looked for **p**, but there was none,. . . . . Ps 69:20
in his love and in his **p** he redeemed . . . . . Is 63:9
their own shepherds have no **p** on them. . Zec 11:5
And Jesus in **p** touched their eyes, and. .Mt 20:34
Moved with **p**, he stretched out his . . . . . . Mk 1:41

PLACE
"Surely the LORD is in this **p**, ...Gn 28:16
and caused the dawn to know its **p**,. . . . . Jb 38:12
You are a hiding **p** for me; you . . . . .Ps 32:7
How lovely is your dwelling **p**, O. . . . . Ps 84:1
been our dwelling **p** in all generations. . . . Ps 90:1
it is gone, and its **p** knows it no more.. . Ps 103:16
eyes of the LORD are in every **p**, ... Prv 15:3
and his resting **p** shall be glorious. . . . . Is 11:10
that I go to prepare a **p** for you? . . . . Jn 14:2
together into a dwelling **p** for God by . . Eph 2:22
the dwelling **p** of God is with man.. . . . . . . Rv 21:3

PLACES
noticed how they chose the **p** of honor, . . Lk 14:7
he entered once for all into the holy **p**, . .Heb 9:12

PLAGUE
"Yet one **p** more I will bring. . . . . Ex 11:1
to befall you, no **p** come near your tent. . Ps 91:10
strike the earth with every kind of **p**,. . . . . Rv 11:6

PLAGUES
people of diseases and **p** and evil. . . . . Lk 7:21
By these three **p** a third of mankind. . . . . .Rv 9:18
add to him the **p** described in this book,. .Rv 22:18

PLAIN
become level, and the rough places a **p**. . . Is 40:4
can be known about God is **p** to them, . .Rom 1:19

PLAINLY
If you are the Christ, tell us **p**." . . . . Jn 10:24
but will tell you **p** about the Father. . . . . . Jn 16:25

PLAN
us and that God had frustrated their **p**, . Neh 4:15
Do not **p** evil against your neighbor, ...Prv 3:29
but those who **p** peace have joy. . . . . . . Prv 12:20
to the definite **p** and foreknowledge of . .Acts 2:23
as a **p** for the fullness of time, to unite . . Eph 1:10
what is the **p** of the mystery hidden . . . . Eph 3:9

PLANNED
I **p** from days of old what now I . . . . . 2 Kgs 19:25
"As I have **p**, so shall it be, ...Is 14:24

PLANS
heart's desire and fulfill all your **p**! . . . . . . .Ps 20:4
The heart of man **p** his way, but . . . . Prv 16:9
P are established by counsel; by wise . . Prv 20:18
p formed of old, faithful and sure. . . . . Is 25:1
But he who is noble **p** noble things,. . . . . . Is 32:8
For I know the **p** I have for you, ...Jer 29:11

PLANT
given you every **p** yielding seed that . . . . .Gn 1:29
God appointed a **p** and made it . . . . .Jon 4:6
"Every **p** that my heavenly Father has. . . Mt 15:13
of the earth or any green **p** or any tree, . . Rv 9:4

PLANTED
Scarcely are they **p**, scarcely sown, ... Is 40:24
tree, 'Be uprooted and **p** in the sea,' . . . . . Lk 17:6
I **p**, Apollos watered, but God gave . . . . 1 Cor 3:6

PLEA
God responded to the **p** for the land. . 2 Sm 21:14
to my prayer; listen to my **p** for grace. . . .Ps 86:6
my **p** before the LORD . . . . Dn 9:20

PLEAD
to the Lord I **p** for mercy:. . . . . .Ps 30:8
P my cause and redeem me; give. . . . . .Ps 119:154
for the LORD will **p** their cause. . . . . .Prv 22:23

PLEADED
"And I **p** with the LORD at . . . . .Dt 3:23
Three times I **p** with the Lord about. . . 2 Cor 12:8

"Sing **p** to the LORD, for he has . . . . Is 12:5

PRAISING

p and giving thanks to the LORD, ... Ezr 3:11
healed, turned back, **p** God with a loud. . . Lk 17:15
p God and having favor with all . . . . Acts 2:47
walking and leaping and **p** God. . . . . Acts 3:8

PRAY

LORD by ceasing to **p** for you, ... 1 Sm 12:23
P for the peace of Jerusalem! . . . . Ps 122:6
Love your enemies and **p** for . . . . Mt 5:44
P then like this: "Our Father in heaven, ... Mt 6:9
p for those who abuse you. . . . . Lk 6:28
ought always to **p** and not lose heart. . . . . . Lk 18:1
men went up into the temple to **p**, ... Lk 18:10
do not know what to **p** for as we . . . . . . Rom 8:26
For if I **p** in a tongue, my spirit prays. . 1 Cor 14:14
we have not ceased to **p** for you, ... Col 1:9
p without ceasing, ... 1 Thes 5:17
that in every place the men should **p**, . . . 1 Tm 2:8
and **p** for one another, ... Jas 5:16

PRAYED

I **p** to the LORD my God. . . . . Dn 9:4
Jonah **p** to the LORD his God . . . . Jon 2:1
a little farther he fell on his face and **p**,. Mt 26:39
Pharisee, standing by himself, **p** thus: . . . . Lk 18:11
all outside, and knelt down and **p**; . . . . . Acts 9:40

PRAYER

God, hear my **p**; give ear to the words . . . Ps 54:2
be called a house of **p** for all peoples." . . . Is 56:7
seeking him by **p** and pleas for mercy. . . . Dn 9:3
'My house shall be called a house of **p**,'. . Mt 21:13
And whatever you ask in **p**, you will. . . . . Mt 21:22
accord were devoting themselves to **p**, . . Acts 1:14
in tribulation, be constant in **p**. . . . . Rom 12:12
You also must help us by **p**, so . . . . 2 Cor 1:11
Continue steadfastly in **p**, being . . . . Col 4:2
made holy by the word of God and **p**. . . . 1 Tm 4:5
The **p** of a righteous person has great. . . Jas 5:16

PRAYERS

for a pretense make long **p**. . . . . Mk 12:40
granted us through the **p** of many. . . . . . 2 Cor 1:11
for you, remembering you in my **p**, ... Eph 1:16
know that through your **p** and the help. . Phil 1:19
that supplications, **p**, intercessions, ... 1 Tm 2:1
so that your **p** may not be hindered. . . . . . 1 Pt 3:7
incense, which are the **p** of the saints. . . . . . Rv 5:8

PRAYING

And whenever you stand **p**, forgive, ... Mk 11:25
I am **p** for them. I am not **p** . . . . Jn 17:9
Then after fasting and **p** they laid. . . . . . Acts 13:3
and Silas were **p** and singing hymns . . Acts 16:25

PREACH

that time Jesus began to **p**, saying, ... Mt 4:17
For they **p**, but do not practice. . . . . Mt 23:3
commanded us to **p** to the people. . . . Acts 10:42
So I am eager to **p** the gospel to . . . . Rom 1:15
And how are they to **p** unless they. . . . Rom 10:15
folly of what we **p** to save those. . . . . . . 1 Cor 1:21
Woe to me if I do not **p** the gospel! . . . . 1 Cor 9:16
so that we may **p** the gospel in lands. . 2 Cor 10:16
I might **p** him among the Gentiles, ... Gal 1:16
to **p** to the Gentiles the unsearchable . . . Eph 3:8
Some indeed **p** Christ from envy. . . . . Phil 1:15

PREACHED

he **p** good news to the people. . . . . Lk 3:18
And he came and **p** peace to you. . . . . . . Eph 2:17
through those who **p** the good news. . . . . 1 Pt 1:12

PREACHING

John the Baptist came **p** in the. . . . . Mt 3:1
And he was **p** the word to them. . . . . Mk 2:2
not cease teaching and **p** that the . . . . . Acts 5:42
teaching and **p** the word of the Lord, . Acts 15:35
are they to hear without someone **p**? . Rom 10:14
then our **p** is in vain and your faith. . . . 1 Cor 15:14

If anyone is **p** to you a gospel contrary . . . Gal 1:9
persecute us is now **p** the faith he . . . . . . Gal 1:23
those who labor in **p** and teaching. . . . . 1 Tm 5:17

PRECEPT

For it is **p** upon **p**, **p** upon. . . . . Is 28:10

PRECEPTS

the **p** of the LORD are right, ... Ps 19:8
all his **p** are trustworthy; . . . . Ps 111:7
I will meditate on your **p** and fix my . . . . Ps 119:15
I give you good **p**; do not forsake my . . . . Prv 4:2

PRECIOUS

How **p** is your steadfast love, ... Ps 36:7
P in the sight of the LORD is . . . . Ps 116:15
She is far more **p** than jewels. . . . . Prv 31:10
your faith—more **p** than gold that . . . . 1 Pt 1:7
but with the **p** blood of Christ, ... 1 Pt 1:19
a cornerstone chosen and **p**, ... 1 Pt 2:6

PREDESTINED

and your plan had **p** to take place. . . . . . Acts 4:28
he foreknew he also **p** to be conformed. . Rom 8:29
p us for adoption as sons through Jesus. . Eph 1:5
having been **p** according to the . . . . Eph 1:11

PREDICTIONS

remember the **p** of the holy prophets . . . 2 Pt 3:2
the **p** of the apostles of our Lord Jesus. . . Jude 17

PREEMINENT

dead, that in everything he might be **p**. . . Col 1:18

PREPARE

You **p** a table before me in the . . . . Ps 23:5
P your work outside; get everything . . . Prv 24:27
"In the wilderness **p** the way of the . . . . . . Is 40:3
to you, **p** to meet your God, ... Am 4:12
messenger, and he will **p** the way. . . . . Mal 3:1
'**P** the way of the Lord; . . . . Mt 3:3
And if I go and **p** a place for you, I. . . . . . . Jn 14:3

PREPARED

which he has **p** beforehand for glory— . Rom 9:23
what God has **p** for those who love . . . . 1 Cor 2:9
He who has **p** us for this very thing . . . . 2 Cor 5:5
good works, which God **p** beforehand, . . Eph 2:10
always being **p** to make a defense to. . . . 1 Pt 3:15

PRESENCE

themselves from the **p** of the LORD. . . . . . . Gn 3:8
set the bread of the **P** on the table . . . . Ex 25:30
Let us come into his **p** with . . . . Ps 95:2
Come into his **p** with singing! . . . . Ps 100:2
Or where shall I flee from your **p**? . . . . . . Ps 139:7
bring us with you into his **p**. . . . . 2 Cor 4:14
away from the **p** of the Lord and from. . 2 Thes 1:9
now to appear in the **p** of God on . . . . . Heb 9:24

PRESENT

but **p** yourselves to God as those who . Rom 6:13
life or death or the **p** or the future— . . 1 Cor 3:22
absent in body, I am **p** in spirit; . . . . 1 Cor 5:3
so that he might **p** the church to . . . . . . Eph 5:27
in order to **p** you holy and blameless. . . . Col 1:22

PRESERVE

for God sent me before you to **p** life. . . . Gn 45:5
but the lips of the wise will **p** them. . . . . Prv 14:3
Whoever seeks to **p** his life will lose it, . . Lk 17:33
who have faith and **p** their souls. . . . . . Heb 10:39

PRESERVES

The LORD **p** the faithful but. . . . . Ps 31:23
He **p** the lives of his saints; he delivers . . Ps 97:10
The LORD **p** all who love . . . . Ps 145:20
wisdom **p** the life of him who has it. . . . . Eccl 7:12

PRESS

let us **p** on to know the LORD; . . . . Hos 6:3
I **p** on toward the goal for the prize. . . . . Phil 3:14

PRESSED

Good measure, **p** down, shaken . . . . Lk 6:38

I am hard **p** between the two. My desire . . Phil 1:23

PRESSURE

my **p** will not be heavy upon you. . . . . Jb 33:7
there is the daily **p** on me of my. . . . . . 2 Cor 11:28

PREVAIL

for not by might shall a man **p**. . . . . 1 Sm 2:9

PREVAILED

Moses held up his hand, Israel **p**, ... Ex 17:11

PRICE

the **p** of wisdom is above pearls. . . . . Jb 28:18
the **p** of him on whom a **p** had . . . . Mt 27:9
for you were bought with a **p**. . . . . 1 Cor 6:20
You were bought with a **p**; do not . . . . . 1 Cor 7:23
desires take the water of life without **p**. . Rv 22:17

PRIDE

In the **p** of his face the wicked does not . . Ps 10:4
P and arrogance and the way of evil . . . . Prv 8:13
P goes before destruction, ... Prv 16:18
One's **p** will bring him low, ... Prv 29:23
sensuality, envy, slander, **p**, foolishness. . . Mk 7:22
of the eyes and **p** of life— . . . . 1 Jn 2:16

PRIEST

(He was **p** of God Most High.) . . . . Gn 14:18
I will raise up for myself a faithful **p**, . . . 1 Sm 2:35
"You are a **p** forever after the order. . . . . Ps 110:4
the lips of a **p** should guard knowledge, . . Mal 2:7
Judea, there was a **p** named Zechariah, . . . Lk 1:5
For we do not have a high **p** who is. . . . . Heb 4:15
place, "You are a **p** forever, ... Heb 5:6
we have such a high **p**, one who is. . . . . . . Heb 8:1

PRIESTHOOD

And the **p** shall be theirs by a statute . . . . Ex 29:9
but he holds his **p** permanently, ... Heb 7:24
up as a spiritual house, to be a holy **p**, . . . 1 Pt 2:5
a chosen race, a royal **p**, a holy nation, . . . 1 Pt 2:9

PRIESTS

me a kingdom of **p** and a holy nation. . . . . Ex 19:6
p became obedient to the faith. . . . . Acts 6:7
a kingdom and **p** to our God, ... Rv 5:10
but they will be **p** of God and . . . . Rv 20:6

PRINCE

Everlasting Father, **P** of Peace. . . . . Is 9:6
casts out demons by the **p** of demons." . Mt 9:34
following the **p** of the power of the air, . . . Eph 2:2

PRISCA

Greet **P** and Aquila, my fellow workers. . . Rom 16:3
Aquila and **P**, together with the . . . . . . 1 Cor 16:19
Greet **P** and Aquila, and the. . . . . 2 Tm 4:19

PRISCILLA

come from Italy with his wife **P**, ... Acts 18:2
but when **P** and Aquila heard him, ... Acts 18:26

PRISON

keeper of the **p** put Joseph in charge . . Gn 39:22
I was in **p** and you came to me.' . . . . Mt 25:36
Lord opened the **p** doors and brought . Acts 5:19
Lord had brought him out of the **p**. . . . . Acts 12:17
Christ, on account of which I am in **p**— . . . Col 4:3
Remember those who are in **p**, ... Heb 13:3
went and proclaimed to the spirits in **p**, . . 1 Pt 3:19
ended, Satan will be released from his **p**. . Rv 20:7

PRISONER

For this reason I, Paul, a **p** for Christ . . . . . Eph 3:1
about our Lord, nor of me his **p**, ... 2 Tm 1:8

PRISONERS

The LORD sets the **p** free; . . . . Ps 146:7
to bring out the **p** from the dungeon, ... Is 42:7
supposing that the **p** had escaped. . . . Acts 16:27

PRIZE

run, but only one receives the **p**? . . . . . 1 Cor 9:24
for the **p** of the upward call of God in . . . Phil 3:14

hopes in him purifies himself as he is **p**. . .1 Jn 3:3

PURGE
P me with hyssop, and I shall be clean;. . . Ps 51:7
"**P** the evil person from among you.". . .1 Cor 5:13

PURIFIED
may be refined, **p**, and made white,. . . . . Dn 11:35
Having **p** your souls by your obedience. . 1 Pt 1:22

PURIFY
Many shall **p** themselves and make . . . . . Dn 12:10
to **p** for himself a people for his own. . . . . .Ti 2:14
p our conscience from dead works to . . .Heb 9:14

PURITY
He who loves **p** of heart, and whose . . . .Prv 22:11
by **p**, knowledge, patience, kindness,. . . 2 Cor 6:6
younger women as sisters, in all **p**. . . . . . .1 Tm 5:2

PURPLE
the crown of thorns and the **p** robe. . . . . . Jn 19:5
city of Thyatira, a seller of **p** goods,. . . .Acts 16:14

PURPOSE
and that no **p** of yours can be thwarted. . .Jb 42:2
The LORD will fulfill his **p** for me;. . . . . Ps 138:8
LORD has made everything for its **p**,. . . . . Prv 16:4
stand, and I will accomplish all my **p**,' . . . Is 46:10
but it shall accomplish that which I **p**,. . . . Is 55:11
the lawyers rejected the **p** of God for . . . .Lk 7:30
But for this **p** I have come to this hour. . . Jn 12:27
who are called according to his **p**. . . . . .Rom 8:28
mystery of his will, according to his **p**,. . . .Eph 1:9
according to the eternal **p** that he has. . . Eph 3:11
but because of his own **p** and grace,. . . . .2 Tm 1:9
the unchangeable character of his **p**,. . . .Heb 6:17

PURSUE
do good; seek peace and **p** it. . . . . Ps 34:14
So then let us **p** what makes for peace. . Rom 14:19
P love, and earnestly desire the . . . . 1 Cor 14:1
P righteousness, godliness, faith, ...1 Tm 6:11
do good; let him seek peace and **p** it. . . . .1 Pt 3:11

PUT
And I will **p** my Spirit within you, and . .Ezk 36:27
I will **p** my Spirit upon him, and he will . . Mt 12:18
But **p** on the Lord Jesus Christ, and. . . Rom 13:14
P on the whole armor of God, that you. . Eph 6:11
And above all these **p** on love, which. . . . Col 3:14

QUAIL
In the evening **q** came up and covered . . Ex 16:13
and it brought **q** from the sea and let . . . Nm 11:31

QUARREL
so quit before the **q** breaks out. . . . . .Prv 17:14
Whoever meddles in a **q** not his own. . . Prv 26:17
but not to **q** over opinions.. . . . . .Rom 14:1
before God not to **q** about words, ...2 Tm 2:14
and cannot obtain, so you fight and **q**. . . . Jas 4:2

QUARRELED
Therefore the people **q** with Moses . . . . . . Ex 17:2

QUARRELING
where there is no whisperer, **q** ceases.. .Prv 26:20
and sensuality, not in **q** and jealousy. . . .Rom 13:13
lifting holy hands without anger or **q**;. . .1 Tm 2:8
evil of no one, to avoid **q**, to be gentle,. . . . Ti 3:2

QUARRELS
for controversy and for **q** about words,. .1 Tm 6:4
you know that they breed **q**. . . . . 2 Tm 2:23
What causes **q** and what causes fights . . . Jas 4:1

QUARRELSOME
than in a house shared with a **q** wife. . . . Prv 21:9
but gentle, not **q**, not a lover of money. . 1 Tm 3:3
servant must not be **q** but kind to . . . . 2 Tm 2:24

QUEEN
Now when the **q** of Sheba heard of. . . . 1 Kgs 10:1
made her **q** instead of Vashti. . . . . .Est 2:17
make cakes for the **q** of heaven. . . . . .Jer 7:18
since in her heart she says, 'I sit as a **q**,. . . Rv 18:7

QUENCH
Many waters cannot **q** love, neither . . . . . . .Sg 8:7
Do not **q** the Spirit. . . . . .1 Thes 5:19

QUENCHED
shall not die, their fire shall not be **q**,. . . . Is 66:24
worm does not die and the fire is not **q**. . Mk 9:48
q the power of fire, escaped the edge. . Heb 11:34

QUESTIONING
and all were **q** in their hearts. . . . . Lk 3:15

QUESTIONS
And Solomon answered all her **q**. . . . . . . 2 Chr 9:2
anyone dare to ask him any more **q**. . . . Mt 22:46

QUICK
A man of **q** temper acts foolishly,. . . . . . . .Prv 14:17
let every person be **q** to hear, slow to . . . .Jas 1:19

QUIET
with **q** than a house full of feasting . . . . . .Prv 17:1
he will **q** you by his love; . . . . Zep 3:17
beauty of a gentle and **q** spirit,. . . . . .1 Pt 3:4

QUIETLY
spirit, but a wise man **q** holds it back. . . .Prv 29:11
and to aspire to live **q**, and to mind . . . 1 Thes 4:11
Let a woman learn **q** with all . . . . .1 Tm 2:11

QUIETNESS
is a handful of **q** than two hands full . . . . Eccl 4:6
in **q** and in trust shall be your strength.". .Is 30:15
result of righteousness, **q** and trust . . . . . . Is 32:17

QUIVER
is the man who fills his **q** with them!. . . . Ps 127:5
polished arrow; in his **q** he hid me away.. . Is 49:2

RABBI
But you are not to be called **r**, for you. . . .Mt 23:8
"**R**" (which means Teacher),. . . . . Jn 1:38

RACE
the **r** is not to the swift, ... Eccl 9:11
know that in a **r** all the runners run,. . . 1 Cor 9:24
the good fight, I have finished the **r**, . . . 2 Tm 4:7
run with endurance the **r** that is set. . . . . Heb 12:1

RACHEL
So Jacob served seven years for **R**, ... Gn 29:20
Then God remembered **R**, and God . . . . Gn 30:22
R weeping for her children; . . . . Mt 2:18

RADIANCE
He is the **r** of the glory of God . . . . .Heb 1:3
having the glory of God, its **r** like a . . . . . .Rv 21:11

RADIANT
Those who look to him are **r**,. . . . . .Ps 34:5
My beloved is **r** and ruddy,. . . . . .Sg 5:10
Then you shall see and be **r**; . . . . Is 60:5
and his clothes became **r**, intensely . . . . . . Mk 9:3

RAHAB
name was **R** and lodged there. . . . . Jos 2:1
Salmon the father of Boaz by **R**,. . . . . Mt 1:5
By faith **R** the prostitute did not perish. Heb 11:31
was not also **R** the prostitute justified . . . Jas 2:25

RAIN
I will send **r** on the earth forty days and . . Gn 7:4
May my teaching drop as the **r**, my . . . . . .Dt 32:2
shall be neither dew nor **r** these years, . 1 Kgs 17:1
let the clouds **r** down righteousness;. . . . . Is 45:8
and sends **r** on the just and on the. . . . . . Mt 5:45
he prayed fervently that it might not **r**,. . Jas 5:17

RAINBOW
the throne was a **r** that had the . . . . .Rv 4:3
in a cloud, with a **r** over his head,. . . . . Rv 10:1

RAINS
I will give you your **r** in their season,. . . . .Lv 26:4
by giving you **r** from heaven and . . . . . .Acts 14:17
until it receives the early and the late **r**. . . Jas 5:7

RAISE
from these stones to **r** up children for. . . . .Mt 3:9
Heal the sick, **r** the dead, cleanse lepers,. .Mt 10:8
temple, and in three days I will **r** it up.". . . Jn 2:19
and I will **r** him up on the last day." . . . . . Jn 6:40
and will also **r** us up by his power. . . . . .1 Cor 6:14
he who raised the Lord Jesus will **r** us . . 2 Cor 4:14
was able even to **r** him from the dead,. . Heb 11:19
who is sick, and the Lord will **r** him up. . . Jas 5:15

RAISED
Lazarus, whom he had **r** from the dead. . . Jn 12:9
This Jesus God **r** up, and of that we all. . Acts 2:32
trespasses and **r** for our justification. . . .Rom 4:25
he who **r** Christ Jesus from the dead. . . .Rom 8:11
that he was **r** on the third day in. . . . . . .1 Cor 15:4
what is **r** is imperishable. . . . . .1 Cor 15:42
and **r** us up with him and seated us. . . . . Eph 2:6
If then you have been **r** with Christ,. . . . . . . .Col 3:1
who **r** him from the dead and gave him . .1 Pt 1:21

RAM
went and took the **r** and offered it up . . .Gn 22:13
a **r** standing on the bank of the canal. . . . . Dn 8:3

RANSOM
Truly no man can **r** another, or give to. . . .Ps 49:7
But God will **r** my soul from the power . . Ps 49:15
and to give his life as a **r** for many.". . . . Mt 20:28
who gave himself as a **r** for all, ...1 Tm 2:6

RANSOMED
knowing that you were **r** from the futile . 1 Pt 1:18
and by your blood you **r** people for God. . .Rv 5:9

RASH
Be not **r** with your mouth, nor let your . . Eccl 5:2
ought to be quiet and do nothing **r**. . . . Acts 19:36

RAVENS
And the **r** brought him bread and. . . . . .1 Kgs 17:6
Consider the **r**: they neither sow nor . . . . Lk 12:24

READ
the Covenant and **r** it in the hearing . . . . .Ex 24:7
They **r** from the book, from the Law . . . . Neh 8:8
"Have you not **r** what David did when. . . . Mt 12:3
written in the Law? How do you **r** it?". . .Lk 10:26

READY
But you are a God **r** to forgive, gracious . .Neh 9:17
I was **r** to be sought by those who. . . . . . . .Is 65:1
Therefore you also must be **r**, for the. . . Mt 24:44
obedient, to be **r** for every good work, ...Ti 3:1

REAP
sow in tears shall **r** with shouts of joy!. . . Ps 126:5
righteousness; **r** steadfast love;. . . . . Hos 10:12
deposit, and **r** what you did not sow.' . . . Lk 19:21
sows bountifully will also **r** bountifully. . 2 Cor 9:6
will from the Spirit **r** eternal life. . . . . .Gal 6:8
for the hour to **r** has come, ... Rv 14:15

REAPERS
and gleaned in the field after the **r**,. . . . . . .Ru 2:3
end of the age, and the **r** are angels. . . . . .Mt 13:39

REASON
"Come now, let us **r** together, ... Is 1:18
this **r** the Father loves me, because I. . . . Jn 10:17
pure, then peaceable, gentle, open to **r**, . Jas 3:17

REBEKAH
And **R** lifted up her eyes, and when. . . . Gn 24:64
his prayer, and **R** his wife conceived. . . . .Gn 25:21
he ate of his game, but **R** loved Jacob. . Gn 25:28
But Jacob said to **R** his mother, ... Gn 27:11
There they buried Isaac and **R** his wife,. .Gn 49:31

REBEL
obey his voice; do not **r** against him, ... Ex 23:21
those who **r** against the light, ... Jb 24:13

REBELLED
because you **r** against my word in the . . Nm 27:14
But they **r** and grieved his Holy Spirit; . . . . Is 63:10

REBELLION
not come, unless the **r** comes first, ... 2 Thes 2:3
do not harden your hearts as in the **r**, . . . Heb 3:8

REBELLIOUS
but the **r** dwell in a parched land. . . . . Ps 68:6
God has opened my ear, and I was not **r**; . Is 50:5
this people has a stubborn and **r** heart; . . Jer 5:23

REBUILD
and **r** the house of the Lord, ... Ezr 1:3
of God, and to **r** it in three days.'" . . . . . . Mt 26:61
and I will **r** the tent of David that has . . Acts 15:16

REBUKE
Better is open **r** than hidden love. . . . . Prv 27:5
took him aside and began to **r** him, ... Mt 16:22
Do not **r** an older man but encourage . . . 1 Tm 5:1
in sin, **r** them in the presence of all, ... 1 Tm 5:20
exhort and **r** with all authority. . . . . Ti 2:15

REBUKED
Then he rose and **r** the winds and the . . . Mt 8:26
And Jesus **r** the demon, and it came . . . . Mt 17:18
seeing his disciples, he **r** Peter and said, . Mk 8:33
and he **r** them for their unbelief and . . . . Mk 16:14
but was **r** for his own transgression; . . . . . 2 Pt 2:16

RECEIVE
But to all who did **r** him, who believed . . . . Jn 1:12
so that we might **r** the promised Spirit . . Gal 3:14
You ask and do not **r**, because you ask . . . Jas 4:3
God, to **r** glory and honor and power, ... Rv 4:11

RECEIVED
I say to you, they have **r** their reward. . . . . . Mt 6:2
in prayer, believe that you have **r** it, ... Mk 11:24
For I **r** from the Lord what I also. . . . . . 1 Cor 11:23
Therefore, as you **r** Christ Jesus the . . . . . . Col 2:6

RECEIVES
"Whoever **r** you **r** me, and . . . . Mt 10:40
"Whoever **r** one such child in my name . . . Mt 18:5

RECKONING
I will require a **r** for the life of man. . . . . . . Gn 9:5
So now there comes a **r** for his blood.". Gn 42:22

RECOMPENSE
Vengeance is mine, and **r**, for the time . . Dt 32:35
is with him, and his **r** before him. . . . . Is 40:10
coming soon, bringing my **r** with me, . . . Rv 22:12

RECONCILE
and might **r** us both to God in one. . . . . . Eph 2:16
and through him to **r** to himself all. . . . . . Col 1:20

RECONCILED
First be **r** to your brother, and then . . . . . . Mt 5:24
were enemies we were **r** to God by . . . . Rom 5:10
or else be **r** to her husband), ... 1 Cor 7:11
you on behalf of Christ, be **r** to God. . . 2 Cor 5:20

RECONCILIATION
whom we have now received **r**. . . . . Rom 5:11
rejection means the **r** of the world, ... Rom 11:15
himself and gave us the ministry of **r**; . 2 Cor 5:18

RED
made Israel set out from the **R** Sea, ... Ex 15:22
to him who divided the **R** Sea in two, . . Ps 136:13
'It will be fair weather, for the sky is **r**.' . . . Mt 16:2
crossed the **R** Sea as on dry land, but . . Heb 11:29

REDEEM
I will **r** you with an outstretched arm . . . . . . Ex 6:6
R us for the sake of your steadfast love! . . Ps 44:26
Is my hand shortened, that it cannot **r**? . . . Is 50:2
to **r** those who were under the law, so . . . Gal 4:5
gave himself for us to **r** us from all. . . . . Ti 2:14

REDEEMED
Let the **r** of the Lord say so, ... Ps 107:2
and you shall be **r** without money." . . . . . . Is 52:3
for he has visited and **r** his people . . . . Lk 1:68
Christ **r** us from the curse of the law by . Gal 3:13

REDEEMER
For I know that my **R** lives, and at . . . . . . Jb 19:25
for their **R** is strong; he will plead their . . Prv 23:11
R, who formed you from the womb: . . . . Is 44:24
Holy One of Israel is your **R**. . . . . Is 54:5

REDEEMS
Lord **r** the life of his servants; . . . . Ps 34:22
he **r** their life, and precious is their. . . . . . Ps 72:14
who **r** your life from the pit, ... Ps 103:4

REDEMPTION
were waiting for the **r** of Jerusalem. . . . . . . Lk 2:38
heads, because your **r** is drawing near." . Lk 21:28
through the **r** that is in Christ Jesus, . . . Rom 3:24
adoption as sons, the **r** of our bodies. . . Rom 8:23
righteousness and sanctification and **r**, . 1 Cor 1:30
In him we have **r** through his blood, ... Eph 1:7
in whom we have **r**, the forgiveness of . . . Col 1:14
own blood, thus securing an eternal **r**. . . Heb 9:12

REED
a bruised **r** he will not break, and a . . . . . . Is 42:3
to see? A **r** shaken by the wind? . . . . Mt 11:7

REFINED
Behold, I have **r** you, but not as silver; . . . Is 48:10
and make themselves white and be **r**, . . . Dn 12:10
like burnished bronze, **r** in a furnace, ... Rv 1:15

REFUGE
select cities to be cities of **r** for you, ... Nm 35:11
Preserve me, O God, for in you I take **r**. . . . Ps 16:1
God is our **r** and strength, a very . . . . Ps 46:1
the shadow of your wings I will take **r**, . . . Ps 57:1
your heart before him; God is a **r** for us. . . Ps 62:8
my God the rock of my **r**. . . . . Ps 94:22
is a shield to those who take **r** in him. . . . Prv 30:5
to us, for we have made lies our **r**, ... Is 28:15
But the Lord is a **r** to his . . . . Jl 3:16

REFUSE
yet you **r** to come to me that you may . . . Jn 5:40
do not **r** him who is speaking. . . . . Heb 12:25

REFUSED
I have called and you **r** to listen, ... Prv 1:24
them, but they **r** to take correction. . . . . . . Jer 5:3
Our fathers **r** to obey him, but thrust . . . Acts 7:39
because they **r** to love the truth and . . 2 Thes 2:10

REGARD
Whoever is righteous has **r** for the life. . Prv 12:10
So do not let what you **r** as good be . . Rom 14:16
we **r** no one according to the flesh. . . . 2 Cor 5:16
"My son, do not **r** lightly the discipline . . Heb 12:5

REHOBOAM
And **R** his son reigned in his place. . . . . 1 Kgs 11:43
Then King **R** took counsel with . . . . 1 Kgs 12:6

REIGN
The Lord will **r** forever, ... Ps 146:10
Behold, a king will **r** in righteousness, ... Is 32:1
'We do not want this man to **r** over us.'. . Lk 19:14
Let not sin therefore **r** in your mortal. . . Rom 6:12
For he must **r** until he has put all . . . . . 1 Cor 15:25
if we endure, we will also **r** with him; . . . 2 Tm 2:12
Christ, and he shall **r** forever and ever." . . . Rv 11:15
and they will **r** with him for a thousand. . Rv 20:6
light, and they will **r** forever and ever. . . . Rv 22:5

REIGNED
death **r** through that one man, ... Rom 5:17
so that, as sin **r** in death, grace also. . . . Rom 5:21
They came to life and **r** with Christ for . . Rv 20:4

REIGNS
God **r** over the nations; God sits on . . . . . . Ps 47:8
Lord **r**; he is robed in majesty; . . . . Ps 93:1
The Lord **r**, let the earth rejoice; . . . . Ps 97:1
says to Zion, "Your God **r**." . . . . Is 52:7
For the Lord our God the Almighty **r**. . . . . Rv 19:6

REJECT
My God will **r** them because they . . . . Hos 9:17
we escape if we **r** him who warns. . . . . . Heb 12:25
dreams, defile the flesh, **r** authority, ... Jude 8

REJECTED
that the builders **r** has become the . . . . Ps 118:22
Jesus is the stone that was **r** by you, ... Acts 4:11
God has not **r** his people whom he . . . . . Rom 11:2
and nothing is to be **r** if it is received . . . 1 Tm 4:4
a living stone **r** by men but in the sight. . . 1 Pt 2:4

REJECTS
one who **r** me **r** him who sent . . . . Lk 10:16
The one who **r** me and does not receive . . Jn 12:48

REJOICE
those who seek the Lord **r**! . . . . 1 Chr 16:10
But let all who take refuge in you **r**; . . . . Ps 5:11
my heart shall **r** in your salvation. . . . . Ps 13:5
has made; let us **r** and be glad in it. . . . . Ps 118:24
the righteous increase, the people **r**, ... Prv 29:2
the bride, so shall your God **r** over you. . . . Is 62:5
he will **r** over you with gladness; . . . . Zep 3:17
R and be glad, for your reward is great . . . Mt 5:12
but **r** that your names are written in . . . . Lk 10:20
Not only that, but we **r** in our sufferings, . . Rom 5:3
R with those who **r**, weep. . . . . Rom 12:15
R in the Lord always; again I will say, ... Phil 4:4
R always, ... 1 Thes 5:16
In this you **r**, though now for a little. . . . . . 1 Pt 1:6

REJOICED
that same hour he **r** in the Holy Spirit . . . Lk 10:21
and all the people **r** at all the glorious. . . . Lk 13:17
If you loved me, you would have **r**, ... Jn 14:28

REJOICES
my heart is glad, and my whole being **r**; . . Ps 16:9
The light of the eyes **r** the heart, and . . . Prv 15:30
he **r** over it more than over the. . . . . Mt 18:13
and my spirit **r** in God my Savior, ... Lk 1:47

REJOICING
r that they were counted worthy to . . . . Acts 5:41
they began **r** and glorifying the word . . Acts 13:48
as sorrowful, yet always **r**; as poor, yet. . 2 Cor 6:10

RELEASE
them once more, desiring to **r** Jesus, ... Lk 23:20
"**R** the four angels who are bound at. . . . . Rv 9:14

RELEASED
When they were **r**, they went to their . . Acts 4:23
But now we are **r** from the law, ... Rom 7:6

RELENT
God may turn and **r** and turn from his. . . . Jon 3:9

RELIEF
I must speak, that I may find **r**; I must . . Jb 32:20
to send **r** to the brothers living in. . . . . . Acts 11:29
of taking part in the **r** of the saints— . . . 2 Cor 8:4

RELIGION
promoting self-made **r** and asceticism. . . Col 2:23
R that is pure and undefiled before God, . . Jas 1:27

RELY
Lord our God, for we **r** on you, ... 2 Chr 14:11
of the Lord and **r** on his God. . . . . Is 50:10
But that was to make us **r** not on. . . . . . . 2 Cor 1:9
For all who **r** on works of the law are . . . Gal 3:10

REMAIN
Each one should **r** in the condition in. . 1 Cor 7:20
But to **r** in the flesh is more necessary . . Phil 1:24
they will perish, but you **r**; . . . . .Heb 1:11

REMEMBER
I will see it and **r** the everlasting . . . . .Gn 9:16
You shall **r** the LORD your God, ... Dt 8:18
R the wondrous works that he has . . . . 1 Chr 16:12
R not the sins of my youth or my . . . . .Ps 25:7
R how short my time is! . . . . .Ps 89:47
R also your Creator in the days of . . . . . . Eccl 12:1
my own sake, and I will not **r** your sins. . . Is 43:25
and I will **r** their sin no more." . . . . Jer 31:34
"Jesus, **r** me when you come into your . .Lk 23:42
Only, they asked us to **r** the poor, ... Gal 2:10
r that you were at that time separated . . Eph 2:12
R Jesus Christ, risen from the dead, ...2 Tm 2:8
and I will **r** their sins no more." . . . . .Heb 8:12
R those who are in prison, ...Heb 13:3

REMEMBERED
But God **r** Noah and all the beasts and . . . .Gn 8:1
Then God **r** Rachel, and God listened to . .Gn 30:22
I am to be **r** throughout all generations. . . Ex 3:15
Hannah his wife, and the LORD **r** . . . . .1 Sm 1:19
we sat down and wept, when we **r** Zion. . .Ps 137:1
fainting away, I **r** the LORD, ...Jon 2:7
And they **r** his words, ...Lk 24:8
then they **r** that these things had been . . .Jn 12:16

REMEMBERS
our frame; he **r** that we are dust. . . . . . . Ps 103:14
He **r** his covenant forever, the word . . . . . Ps 105:8

REMEMBRANCE
is given for you. Do this in **r** of me." . . . . . Lk 22:19
which is for you. Do this in **r** of me." . . 1 Cor 11:24

REMNANT
you to preserve for you a **r** on earth, ... Gn 45:7
for we are left a **r** that has escaped, ... Ezr 9:15
A **r** will return, the **r** of Jacob, ... Is 10:21
I will gather the **r** of Israel; . . . . Mi 2:12
that the **r** of mankind may seek the . . . .Acts 15:17
only a **r** of them will be saved, ...Rom 9:27
So too at the present time there is a **r**, . .Rom 11:5

REMOVE
And I will **r** the heart of stone from . . . Ezk 36:26
possible for you. **R** this cup from me. . . . Mk 14:36
come to you and **r** your lampstand . . . . . . .Rv 2:5

REND
Oh that you would **r** the heavens and . . . . .Is 64:1
and **r** your hearts and not your . . . . .Jl 2:13

RENDER
What shall I **r** to the LORD. . . . . .Ps 116:12
"Therefore **r** to Caesar the things that . . . Mt 22:21
He will **r** to each one according to his . . .Rom 2:6

RENEW
and **r** a right spirit within me. . . . . Ps 51:10
the LORD shall **r** their strength; . . . . .Is 40:31

RENEWED
so that your youth is **r** like the eagle's. . . Ps 103:5
inner self is being **r** day by day. . . . . 2 Cor 4:16
and to be **r** in the spirit of your minds, . Eph 4:23
which is being **r** in knowledge after . . . . . Col 3:10

RENOUNCE
Why does the wicked **r** God and say in. . Ps 10:13
does not **r** all that he has cannot be my . Lk 14:33

REPAY
nor **r** us according to our iniquities. . . . . Ps 103:10
then he will **r** each person according . . . .Mt 16:27
be blessed, because they cannot **r** you. . . Lk 14:14
R no one evil for evil, but give. . . . . .Rom 12:17
"Vengeance is mine; I will **r**." And . . . . . Heb 10:30
Do not **r** evil for evil or reviling for . . . . . . .1 Pt 3:9
me, to **r** each one for what he has done. . .Rv 22:12

REPENT
despise myself, and **r** in dust and ashes." .Jb 42:6
"**R**, for the kingdom of heaven is at . . . . . . .Mt 3:2
unless you **r**, you will all likewise perish. . . Lk 13:3
Peter said to them, "**R** and be baptized. .Acts 2:38
R therefore, and turn back, that . . . . Acts 3:19
r, and do the works you did at first. . . . . . . .Rv 2:5
They did not **r** and give him glory. . . . . . . .Rv 16:9

REPENTANCE
Bear fruit in keeping with **r**. . . . . .Mt 3:8
"I baptize you with water for **r**, but he. . . . Mt 3:11
a baptism of **r** for the forgiveness. . . . . .Mk 1:4
to call the righteous but sinners to **r**." . . . .Lk 5:32
and that **r** and forgiveness of sins. . . . . . .Lk 24:47
to give **r** to Israel and forgiveness. . . . . . Acts 5:31
kindness is meant to lead you to **r**? . . . . .Rom 2:4
godly grief produces a **r** that leads to . 2 Cor 7:10
of **r** from dead works and of faith. . . . . . . .Heb 6:1

REPROACH
a nation, but sin is a **r** to any people. . . Prv 14:34
blameless and above **r** before him, ... Col 1:22
the camp and bear the **r** he endured. . . Heb 13:13

REPROOF
he who rejects **r** leads others astray. . . . .Prv 10:17
he who listens to **r** gains intelligence. . . Prv 15:32
God and profitable for teaching, for **r**, . .2 Tm 3:16

REPROVE
r a wise man, and he will love you. . . . . . . .Prv 9:8
r, rebuke, and exhort, with complete . . . 2 Tm 4:2
Those whom I love, I **r** and discipline, ... Rv 3:19

REPROVES
the LORD **r** him whom he loves, ... Prv 3:12

REQUESTS
thanksgiving let your **r** be made known . .Phil 4:6
we have the **r** that we have asked . . . . . .1 Jn 5:15

REQUIRE
does the LORD your God **r** of you, ... Dt 10:12
what does the LORD **r** of you . . . . .Mi 6:8

REQUIRED
This night your soul is **r** of you, and. . . . . Lk 12:20
was given, of him much will be **r**, ... Lk 12:48

RESCUE
righteousness deliver me and **r** me; . . . . . . Ps 71:2
other god who is able to **r** in this way.". . Dn 3:29
The Lord will **r** me from every evil . . . . .2 Tm 4:18
Lord knows how to **r** the godly from . . . . 2 Pt 2:9

RESCUED
yet from them all the Lord **r** me. . . . . 2 Tm 3:11

RESIST
say to you, Do not **r** the one who is evil. .Mt 5:39
and ears, you always **r** the Holy Spirit. . . Acts 7:51
R the devil, and he will flee from you. . . . . Jas 4:7
R him, firm in your faith, knowing. . . . . . . .1 Pt 5:9

RESPECT
to them, saying, 'They will **r** my son.' . . . . Mt 21:37
'Though I neither fear God nor **r** man, ... Lk 18:4
r to whom **r** is owed, ... Rom 13:7
brothers, to **r** those who labor among . .1 Thes 5:12
be subject to your masters with all **r**, ... 1 Pt 2:18

REST
seventh day is a Sabbath of solemn **r**, . . . Ex 31:15
not answer, and by night, but I find no **r**. .Ps 22:2
a dove! I would fly away and be at **r**; . . . . .Ps 55:6
my wrath, "They shall not enter my **r**." . . Ps 95:11
a little folding of the hands to **r**, ... Prv 6:10
Spirit of the LORD shall **r** upon . . . . Is 11:2
"In returning and **r** you shall be saved; . . .Is 30:15
walk in it, and find **r** for your souls. . . . . . Jer 6:16
heavy laden, and I will give you **r**. . . . . Mt 11:28
For we who have believed enter that **r**, . . Heb 4:3
up forever and ever, and they have no **r**, .Rv 14:11
"that they may **r** from their labors, ... Rv 14:13

RESTITUTION
he shall make **r** from the best in his own. .Ex 22:5
make full **r** for his wrong, ...Nm 5:7

RESTORATION
the owner of the pit shall make **r**. . . . . Ex 21:34
Aim for **r**, comfort one another, ... 2 Cor 13:11

RESTORE
R to me the joy of your salvation, ...Ps 51:12
I will lead him and **r** comfort to him. . . . . .Is 57:18
For I will **r** health to you, and your . . . . . Jer 30:17
I will **r** to you the years that the . . . . Jl 2:25
"Elijah does come first to **r** all things. . . . .Mk 9:12
anyone of anything, I **r** it fourfold." . . . . Lk 19:8
you at this time **r** the kingdom to. . . . . . . Acts 1:6
are spiritual should **r** him in a spirit . . . . . . Gal 6:1
to **r** them again to repentance, since . . . . Heb 6:6

RESTORES
He **r** my soul. He leads me in paths of . . . .Ps 23:3

RESTS
On God **r** my salvation and my glory; . . . .Ps 62:7
to life, and whoever has it **r** satisfied; . . Prv 19:23
Spirit of glory and of God **r** upon you. . . .1 Pt 4:14

RESURRECTION
came to him, who say that there is no **r**, . .Mt 22:23
For in the **r** they neither marry nor. . . . . Mt 22:30
you will be repaid at the **r** of the just." . . Lk 14:14
are sons of God, being sons of the **r**. . . . Lk 20:36
"I am the **r** and the life. . . . . .Jn 11:25
become with us a witness to his **r**." . . . . Acts 1:22
that there will be a **r** of both the just. . Acts 24:15
be united with him in a **r** like his. . . . . . . .Rom 6:5
So is it with the **r** of the dead. . . . . .1 Cor 15:42
may know him and the power of his **r**, . . Phil 3:10
living hope through the **r** of Jesus . . . . 1 Pt 1:3
years were ended. This is the first **r**. . . . . Rv 20:5

RETURN
you are dust, and to dust you shall **r**." . . . .Gn 3:19
but if you **r** to me and keep my . . . . .Neh 1:9
R, O LORD! How long? . . . . Ps 90:13
my mouth; it shall not **r** to me empty, ... Is 55:11
R, O Israel, to the LORD . . . . Hos 14:1
"**r** to me with all your heart, ...Jl 2:12
R to me, and I will **r** to you, ...Mal 3:7
what shall a man give in **r** for his soul? . . Mt 16:26
good, and lend, expecting nothing in **r**, . . .Lk 6:35

REUBEN
and she called his name **R**, ... Gn 29:32
"**R**, you are my firstborn, my might, ... Gn 49:3

REVEAL
to whom the Son chooses to **r** him. . . . . . Mt 11:27
was pleased to **r** his Son to me, ...Gal 1:16
otherwise, God will **r** that also to you. . . . Phil 3:15

REVEALED
but the things that are **r** belong to us . . .Dt 29:29
the glory of the LORD shall be **r**, ... Is 40:5
nothing is covered that will not be **r**, ...Mt 10:26
flesh and blood has not **r** this to you, . . . Mt 16:17
on the day when the Son of Man is **r**. . . . .Lk 17:30
righteousness of God is **r** from faith for. .Rom 1:17
with the glory that is to be **r** to us. . . . . . Rom 8:18
when the Lord Jesus is **r** from heaven. .2 Thes 1:7
a salvation ready to be **r** in the last time. . 1 Pt 1:5

REVELATION
light for **r** to the Gentiles, and for glory. . .Lk 2:32
according to the **r** of the mystery. . . . . .Rom 16:25
but I received it through a **r** of Jesus. . . . .Gal 1:12
brought to you at the **r** of Jesus Christ. . . .1 Pt 1:13

REVERENCE
to one another out of **r** for Christ. . . . . . .Eph 5:21

ROOSTER
you, this very night, before the r crows,. . Mt 26:34
Peter, the r will not crow this day, ...Lk 22:34
the r will not crow till you have. . . . . Jn 13:38

ROOT
In that day the r of Jesse, who shall. . . . . . Is 11:10
And since they had no r, they withered. . . Mt 13:6
"The r of Jesse will come,. . . . . .Rom 15:12
of the tribe of Judah, the R of David,. . . . . .Rv 5:5
I am the r and the descendant of David, . .Rv 22:16

ROOTED
that you, being r and grounded in love,. .Eph 3:17
r and built up in him and established. . . . . Col 2:7

ROUGH
become level, and the r places a plain. . . . Is 40:4
the r places shall become level ways,. . . . . .Lk 3:5
sea became r because a strong wind. . . . . Jn 6:18

RUIN
A foolish son is r to his father, and a . . . .Prv 19:13
A r, r, r I will make it. . . . . Ezk 21:27
and the r of that house was great." . . . . . .Lk 6:49
in their paths are r and misery, ... Rom 3:16
plunge people into r and destruction. . . .1 Tm 6:9

RUINS
the house of our God, to repair its r, ... Ezr 9:9
how Jerusalem lies in r with its gates . . .Neh 2:17
And your ancient r shall be rebuilt; . . . . . .Is 58:12
all our pleasant places have become r. . . . Is 64:11
I will make Jerusalem a heap of r, ... Jer 9:11
fallen; I will rebuild its r, and I will . . . . .Acts 15:16
does no good, but only r the hearers. . .2 Tm 2:14

RULE
to r over the day and over the night,. . . . . Gn 1:18
desire is for you, but you must r over it." . Gn 4:7
Can you establish their r on the earth? . .Jb 38:33
the sun to r over the day, for his. . . . . Ps 136:8
The hand of the diligent will r, while . . . Prv 12:24
even he who arises to r the Gentiles;. . .Rom 15:12
far above all r and authority and power . Eph 1:21
who is the head of all r and authority. . . . Col 2:10
let the peace of Christ r in your hearts,. . Col 3:15
Let the elders who r well be considered . . 1 Tm 5:17
and he will r them with a rod of iron,. . . . .Rv 2:27

RULER
When you sit down to eat with a r, ... Prv 23:1
A r who lacks understanding is a . . . . . . Prv 28:16
Many seek the face of a r, but it is . . . . .Prv 29:26
shall come a r who will shepherd my. . . . . .Mt 2:6
now will the r of this world be cast . . . . . .Jn 12:31
'Who made you a r and a judge over. . . Acts 7:27

RULERS
a land transgresses, it has many r, ...Prv 28:2
and makes the r of the earth as . . . . Is 40:23
"You know that the r of the Gentiles . . . Mt 20:25
by, watching, but the r scoffed at him, . .Lk 23:35
For r are not a terror to good conduct,. Rom 13:3
None of the r of this age understood. . . .1 Cor 2:8
or dominions or r or authorities— . . . . .Col 1:16

RULES
Lord, and he r over the nations. . . . . .Ps 22:28
heavens, and his kingdom r over all. . . . Ps 103:19
and he who r his spirit than he who. . . . Prv 16:32
know not the r of the Lord. . . . . Jer 8:7
to keep these r without prejudging,. . . . 1 Tm 5:21
unless he competes according to the r. . .2 Tm 2:5

RUN
So r that you may obtain it. . . . . 1 Cor 9:24
So I do not r aimlessly; I do not box as . .1 Cor 9:26
I was not running or had not r in vain. . . . Gal 2:2

RUNNING
pressed down, shaken together, r over,. . .Lk 6:38
You were r well. Who hindered you . . . . . . Gal 5:7

RUTH
and the name of the other R. . . . . .Ru 1:4
Also R the Moabite, the widow . . . . .Ru 4:10
and Boaz the father of Obed by R,. . . . . Mt 1:5

SABBATH
rest, a holy S to the Lord;. . . . . Ex 16:23
"Remember the S day, to keep it holy. . . . Ex 20:8
For the Son of Man is lord of the S." . . . . . Mt 12:8
"Is it lawful on the S to do good or . . . . . . Mk 3:4
to a festival or a new moon or a S.. . . . . . Col 2:16
there remains a S rest for the people. . . . Heb 4:9

SACKCLOTH
his garments and put s on his loins . . . . Gn 37:34
have repented long ago in s and ashes. . . Mt 11:21

SACRIFICE
and Jacob offered a s in the . . . . .Gn 31:54
'It is the s of the Lord's Passover, ... Ex 12:27
to obey is better than s, ... 1 Sm 15:22
In s and offering you have not. . . . . Ps 40:6
Offer to God a s of thanksgiving, ...Ps 50:14
For you will not delight in s, or I would. . Ps 51:16
'I desire mercy, and not s.' For. . . . . Mt 9:13
a fragrant offering and s to God. . . . . Eph 5:2
a s acceptable and pleasing to God. . . . . Phil 4:18
is obligated to offer s for his own sins. . . Heb 5:3
to put away sin by the s of himself. . . . . Heb 9:26

SACRIFICED
on which the Passover lamb had to be s. . Lk 22:7
Christ, our Passover lamb, has been s. . .1 Cor 5:7

SACRIFICES
Offer right s, and put your trust in the. . . . .Ps 4:5
The s of God are a broken spirit;. . . . . .Ps 51:17
yet s to the Lord what is blemished. . . . . .Mal 1:14
than all whole burnt offerings and s." . . .Mk 12:33
to God, to offer gifts and s for sins. . . . . . .Heb 5:1
have, for such s are pleasing to God. . . . Heb 13:16
to offer spiritual s acceptable to God. . . . .1 Pt 2:5

SAD
not eat? And why is your heart s? . . . . . . 1 Sm 1:8
heard these things, he became very s,. . . Lk 18:23
walk?" And they stood still, looking s. . . . Lk 24:17

SADDUCEES
Pharisees and S coming to his baptism, . . .Mt 3:7
of the leaven of the Pharisees and S." . . . . Mt 16:6
The same day S came to him, who say . .Mt 22:23

SAFE
righteous man runs into it and is s. . . . . Prv 18:10
whoever trusts in the Lord is s. . . . . .Prv 29:25
And if in a s land you are so trusting, ...Jer 12:5

SAFETY
enemies around, so that you live in s, . . . Dt 12:10
O Lord, make me dwell in s. . . . . .Ps 4:8
He redeems my soul in s from the battle. .Ps 55:18
an abundance of counselors there is s. . . Prv 11:14

SAINTS
As for the s in the land, they are the . . . . . Ps 16:3
Love the Lord, all you his s! . . . . Ps 31:23
He preserves the lives of his s; . . . . Ps 97:10
Lord is the death of his s.. . . . . Ps 116:15
But the s of the Most High shall receive . . Dn 7:18
And many bodies of the s who had . . . . .Mt 27:52
evil he has done to your s at Jerusalem. . .Acts 9:13
locked up many of the s in prison after. .Acts 26:10
are loved by God and called to be s: . . . . Rom 1:7
intercedes for the s according to the . . .Rom 8:27
Contribute to the needs of the s and. . .Rom 12:13
in the Lord in a way worthy of the s, . . . Rom 16:2
not know that the s will judge the . . . . . 1 Cor 6:2
not only supplying the needs of the s. . 2 Cor 9:12
to equip the s for the work of ministry,. .Eph 4:12
generations but now revealed to his s. . . Col 1:26
on that day to be glorified in his s,. . . .2 Thes 1:10
that was once for all delivered to the s. . . Jude 3
incense, which are the prayers of the s.. . . .Rv 5:8
linen is the righteous deeds of the s. . . . . .Rv 19:8

SAKE
Yet for your s we are killed all the day. . .Ps 44:22
deal on my behalf for your name's s;. . . Ps 109:21
was pleased, for his righteousness' s,. . . . .Is 42:21
Delay not, for your own s, O my God, ...Dn 9:19
For our s he made him to be sin who . 2 Cor 5:21
I counted as loss for the s of Christ. . . . . . .Phil 3:7

SALT
she became a pillar of s. . . . . .Gn 19:26
"You are the s of the earth, but if s . . . . . . Mt 5:13
always be gracious, seasoned with s,. . . . .Col 4:6

SALVATION
S belongs to the Lord; . . . . .Ps 3:8
and exalted be the God of my s— . . . . . .Ps 18:46
Lord is my light and my s; . . . . Ps 27:1
He alone is my rock and my s,. . . . . .Ps 62:2
tell of his s from day to day. . . . . .Ps 96:2
and my song; he has become my s. . . . . .Ps 118:14
my song, and he has become my s." . . . . . .Is 12:2
of the earth shall see the s of our God. . . .Is 52:10
wait quietly for the s of the Lord.. . . . . . Lam 3:26
S belongs to the Lord!". . . . . .Jon 2:9
I will wait for the God of my s; . . . . Mi 7:7
and has raised up a horn of s for us. . . . . . Lk 1:69
for my eyes have seen your s . . . . .Lk 2:30
"Today s has come to this house, ... Lk 19:9
what we know, for s is from the Jews. . . . .Jn 4:22
And there is s in no one else, for . . . . . . Acts 4:12
behold, now is the day of s. . . . . 2 Cor 6:2
work out your own s with fear and. . . . . . Phil 2:12
has appeared, bringing s for all people, . . . Ti 2:11
we escape if we neglect such a great s?. Heb 2:3
Concerning this s, the prophets who . . . . 1 Pt 1:10
count the patience of our Lord as s,. . . . .2 Pt 3:15
"S belongs to our God who sits on. . . . . . .Rv 7:10
S and glory and power belong to our . . . . Rv 19:1

SAMARIA
Now the famine was severe in S.. . . . . . .1 Kgs 18:2
the king of Assyria captured S, ... 2 Kgs 17:6
And he had to pass through S. . . . . .Jn 4:4

SAMARITAN
But a S, as he journeyed, came to . . . . . . Lk 10:33
giving him thanks. Now he was a S. . . . . . .Lk 17:16
The S woman said to him, "How is it . . . . . .Jn 4:9

SAME
If then God gave the s gift to them as. . Acts 11:17
be united in the s mind and the s. . . . . . 1 Cor 1:10
are varieties of gifts, but the s Spirit;. . .1 Cor 12:4
Christ is the s yesterday and today . . . . .Heb 13:8

SAMSON
bore a son and called his name S. . . . . . Jgs 13:24
And S said, "With the jawbone . . . . .Jgs 15:16
And S grasped the two middle pillars . . Jgs 16:29
to tell of Gideon, Barak, S, Jephthah,. . . Heb 11:32

SAMUEL
and she called his name S,. . . . . 1 Sm 1:20
Therefore Eli said to S, "Go, lie down, . . .1 Sm 3:9
When S became old, he made his sons . . 1 Sm 8:1
the Lord had revealed to S:. . . . . 1 Sm 9:15
made seven of his sons pass before S. . 1 Sm 16:10
"Where are S and David?" And one . . . 1 Sm 19:22
with fear because of the words of S. . 1 Sm 28:20
S also was among those who called. . . . . .Ps 99:6
of David and S and the prophets— . . . . . Heb 11:32

SANCTIFICATION
as slaves to righteousness leading to s.. Rom 6:19
the fruit you get leads to s and its end,. .Rom 6:22
righteousness and s and redemption, . .1 Cor 1:30
For this is the will of God, your s:. . . . . 1 Thes 4:3
through s by the Spirit and belief in. . 2 Thes 2:13
of God the Father, in the s of the Spirit, . . 1 Pt 1:2

SANCTIFIED
of Israel, and it shall be s by my glory. . .Ex 29:43
that they also may be s in truth. . . . . .Jn 17:19
inheritance among all those who are s. . Acts 20:32
a place among those who are s . . . . . . Acts 26:18
be acceptable, s by the Holy Spirit. . . . Rom 15:16
in Corinth, to those s in Christ Jesus,. . . . 1 Cor 1:2
But you were washed, you were s,. . . . . 1 Cor 6:11
we have been s through the offering. . .Heb 10:10

SANCTIFIES
I am the LORD who s you. . . . . .Lv 20:8
For he who s and those who are. . . . . Heb 2:11

SANCTIFY
know that I, the LORD, s you. . . . . Ex 31:13
I, the LORD, who s you, am holy. . . . . Lv 21:8
S them in the truth; your word is truth. . . .Jn 17:17
that he might s her, having cleansed . . . Eph 5:26
of peace himself s you completely,. . . 1 Thes 5:23
to s the people through his own blood.. Heb 13:12

SANCTUARY
your abode, the s, O Lord, ... Ex 15:17
And let them make me a s, that I may. . . .Ex 25:8
Arise and build the s of the LORD . . . . .1 Chr 22:19
Praise God in his s; praise him in his . . . . Ps 150:1
yet I have been a s to them for a . . . . . . .Ezk 11:16
to come shall destroy the city and the s. . . Dn 9:26

SAND
of heaven and as the s that is on . . . . . . .Gn 22:17
of Israel shall be like the s of the sea, . . . Hos 1:10
man who built his house on the s. . . . . . . .Mt 7:26
sons of Israel be as the s of the sea, . . .Rom 9:27

SANDALS
not come near; take your s off your feet, . .Ex 3:5
Joshua, "Take off your s from your. . . . . . Jos 5:15
than I, whose s I am not worthy to. . . . . . . Mt 3:11
or two tunics or s or a staff,. . . . . .Mt 10:10

SAPPHIRE
feet as it were a pavement of s stone,. . .Ex 24:10
of a throne, in appearance like s; . . . . Ezk 1:26
The first was jasper, the second s, ... Rv 21:19

SARAH
S, who is ninety years old, bear a. . . . . . . Gn 17:17
So S laughed to herself, saying,. . . . . Gn 18:12
S lived 127 years; these were the . . . . .Gn 23:1
By faith S herself received power to. . . . . .Heb 11:11
as S obeyed Abraham, calling him lord. . .1 Pt 3:6

SAT
he s down at the right hand of God, . . .Heb 10:12
I also conquered and s down with my. . . . Rv 3:21

SATAN
Then S stood against Israel and . . . . 1 Chr 21:1
and S also came among them. . . . . Jb 1:6
And the LORD said to S, "The. . . . . .Zec 3:2
"Be gone, S! For it is written, "'You . . . . . .Mt 4:10
And if S casts out S, he is divided . . . . . .Mt 12:26
to Peter, "Get behind me, S! You are . . . .Mt 16:23
forty days, being tempted by S. . . . . Mk 1:13
"I saw S fall like lightning from . . . . Lk 10:18
Then S entered into Judas called . . . . .Lk 22:3
why has S filled your heart to lie to the. . Acts 5:3
light and from the power of S to God,. Acts 26:18
will soon crush S under your feet. . . . .Rom 16:20
S disguises himself as an angel. . . . . . . 2 Cor 11:14
flesh, a messenger of S to harass me, . .2 Cor 12:7
have handed over to S that they may . . 1 Tm 1:20
serpent, who is called the devil and S,. . . . Rv 12:9
who is the devil and S, and bound him . . Rv 20:2
S will be released from his prison. . . . . . . Rv 20:7

SATISFIED
with treasure; they are s with children,. . Ps 17:14
leads to life, and whoever has it rests s;. . Prv 19:23
Three things are never s; four never. . . . Prv 30:15
anguish of his soul he shall see and be s;. Is 53:11
for righteousness, for they shall be s.. . . . . .Mt 5:6

SATISFIES
who s you with good so that your youth. .Ps 103:5
For he s the longing soul,. . . . . Ps 107:9

SATISFY
S us in the morning with your steadfast . .Ps 90:14
your labor for that which does not s? . . . . Is 55:2
For I will s the weary soul, and every. . . Jer 31:25

SAUL
a son whose name was S,. . . . . .1 Sm 9:2
there they made S king before the. . . . . 1 Sm 11:15
"I regret that I have made S king,. . . . . . 1 Sm 15:11
"S has struck down his thousands,. . . . . 1 Sm 18:7
"Is S also among the prophets?". . . . . . 1 Sm 19:24
And there lay S sleeping within the . . . .1 Sm 26:7
Then S said to his armor-bearer,. . . . . . . 1 Sm 31:4
And S approved of his execution. . . . . Acts 8:1
voice saying to him, "S, S, ...Acts 9:4
But S, who was also called Paul, filled . . Acts 13:9

SAVE
our God, s us, please, from his hand, . .2 Kgs 19:19
O God, s me by your name,. . . . . Ps 54:1
S me according to your steadfast love!. . Ps 109:26
hand is not shortened, that it cannot s,. . . .Is 59:1
I am with you to s you and deliver you, Jer 15:20
for he will s his people from their sins.". . . Mt 1:21
to sink he cried out, "Lord, s me.". . . . . . .Mt 14:30
For whoever would s his life will lose. . . .Mt 16:25
to judge the world but to s the world.. . . Jn 12:47
all people, that by all means I might s . . 1 Cor 9:22
came into the world to s sinners, ...1 Tm 1:15
not have works? Can that faith s him?. . . Jas 2:14

SAVED
I was brought low, he s me. . . . . Ps 116:6
"Turn to me and be s, all the ends of. . . . Is 45:22
name of the LORD shall be s. . . . . Jl 2:32
"Who then can be s?". . . . . .Mt 19:25
"He s others; he cannot save himself.. . . Mt 27:42
to the woman, "Your faith has s you;. . . . .Lk 7:50
that the world might be s through him.. . . Jn 3:17
I say these things so that you may be s. . .Jn 5:34
among men by which we must be s." . . Acts 4:12
what must I do to be s?" . . . . Acts 16:30
on the name of the Lord will be s." . . . Rom 10:13
in this way all Israel will be s, as it . . . . Rom 11:26
to us who are being s it is the power. . . 1 Cor 1:18
loss, though he himself will be s, ... 1 Cor 3:15
For by grace you have been s through . . Eph 2:8
desires all people to be s and to come . . 1 Tm 2:4
he s us, not because of works. . . . . Ti 3:5

SAVES
the LORD s not with sword . . . . 1 Sm 17:47
Now I know that the LORD s. . . . . .Ps 20:6
and s the lives of the needy. . . . . Ps 72:13
to this, now s you, not as a removal of . . 1 Pt 3:21

SAVIOR
my stronghold and my refuge, my s; . . 2 Sm 22:3
O S of those who seek refuge from . . . . . . Ps 17:7
They forgot God, their S, who had . . . . . Ps 106:21
he will send them a s and defender,. . . . . .Is 19:20
and besides me there is no s. . . . . Is 43:11
that I am the LORD your S, ... Is 49:26
I, the LORD, am your S and . . . . Is 60:16
hope of Israel, its s in time of trouble,. . . . Jer 14:8
but me, and besides me there is no s. . . .Hos 13:4
my spirit rejoices in God my S, ... Lk 1:47
born this day in the city of David a S, ...Lk 2:11
that this is indeed the S of the world." . . .Jn 4:42
God has brought to Israel a S,. . . . . Acts 13:23
church, his body, and is himself its S. . . . Eph 5:23
it is pleasing in the sight of God our S,. . 1 Tm 2:3
living God, who is the S of all people, . . 1 Tm 4:10
loving kindness of God our S appeared,. . . . Ti 3:4
the Lord and S through your apostles,. . . 2 Pt 3:2
sent his Son to be the S of the world. . . .1 Jn 4:14
to the only God, our S, through Jesus . . . Jude 25

SCALES
and false s are not good. . . . . .Prv 20:23
the mountains in s and the hills . . . . .Is 40:12
something like s fell from his eyes,. . . . . Acts 9:18
And its rider had a pair of s in his hand. . . .Rv 6:5

SCARLET
though your sins are like s, they shall . . . . . Is 1:18
stripped him and put a s robe on him,. . .Mt 27:28

SCATTER
And I will s you among the nations,. . . . .Lv 26:33
I will s them among the nations whom . . Jer 9:16

SCATTERED
'He who s Israel will gather him,. . . . . . . .Jer 31:10
and the sheep of the flock will be s.' . . . . Mt 26:31
children of God who are s abroad. . . . . . . .Jn 11:52
indeed it has come, when you will be s, . Jn 16:32
who were s went about preaching . . . . . . Acts 8:4

SCEPTER
The s shall not depart from Judah,. . . . . Gn 49:10
Jacob, and a s shall rise out of Israel; . . Nm 24:17
uprightness is the s of your kingdom. . . . .Heb 1:8

SCHEME
as they s together against me, as they . . .Ps 31:13
to seek wisdom and the s of things,. . . . Eccl 7:25

SCOFFER
corrects a s gets himself abuse, ...Prv 9:7
but a s does not listen to rebuke. . . . . .Prv 13:1
"S" is the name of the arrogant,. . . . . . . Prv 21:24
Drive out a s, and strife will go out,. . . . Prv 22:10
the s is an abomination to mankind. . . . .Prv 24:9
shall come to nothing and the s cease, . . Is 29:20

SCOFFERS
way of sinners, nor sits in the seat of s;. . . . .Ps 1:1
S set a city aflame, but the wise turn. . . .Prv 29:8
s will come in the last days . . . . 2 Pt 3:3
"In the last time there will be s,. . . . . .Jude 18

SCORCHING
neither s wind nor sun shall strike . . . . . . Is 49:10
sun rose, God appointed a s east wind,. . .Jon 4:8
the burden of the day and the s heat.'. . .Mt 20:12
shall not strike them, nor any s heat. . . . . .Rv 7:16

SCORN
My friends s me; my eye pours out . . . . .Jb 16:20
LORD is to them an object of s; . . . . Jer 6:10

SCORNED
deed you have utterly s the LORD,. . . . . 2 Sm 12:14
s by mankind and despised by the. . . . . . .Ps 22:6

SCORPION
if he asks for an egg, will give him a s?. . . Lk 11:12
like the torment of a s when it stings. . . . . .Rv 9:5

SCRIBES
righteousness exceeds that of the s. . . . . Mt 5:20
"But woe to you, s and Pharisees, ... Mt 23:13
chief priests with the s mocked him to . . Mk 15:31
s stood by, vehemently accusing him. . . . Lk 23:10
great clamor arose, and some of the s . .Acts 23:9

SCRIPTURE
"Today this S has been fulfilled in your . . . Lk 4:21
S must be fulfilled in me: 'And he was. . .Lk 22:37
Whoever believes in me, as the S has . . . .Jn 7:38
God came—and S cannot be broken—. . . Jn 10:35
S says, "They will look on him whom. . . . Jn 19:37
And the S, foreseeing that God would. . . . Gal 3:8
yourself to the public reading of S, ... 1 Tm 4:13
All S is breathed out by God and . . . . . .2 Tm 3:16
that no prophecy of S comes from. . . . . 2 Pt 1:20

SCRIPTURES
you know neither the S nor the power . .Mt 22:29
he interpreted to them in all the S . . . . . .Lk 24:27

opened their minds to understand the S,. . Lk 24:45
You search the S because you think. . . . . .Jn 5:39
he reasoned with them from the S, ... Acts 17:2
examining the S daily to see if these . . . Acts 17:11
showing by the S that the Christ was . Acts 18:28
through his prophets in the holy S, ... Rom 1:2
encouragement of the S we might. . . . . Rom 15:4
for our sins in accordance with the S, . . 1 Cor 15:3

SCROLL

s was found on which this was written:. . . Ezr 6:2
rot away, and the skies roll up like a s. . . . Is 34:4
eyes and saw, and behold, a flying s!. . . . . Zec 5:1
And he rolled up the s and gave it . . . . . . .Lk 4:20
"Who is worthy to open the s and . . . . .Rv 5:2

SEA

and the LORD drove the s back . . . . Ex 14:21
"Or who shut in the s with doors when. . .Jb 38:8
gathers the waters of the s as a heap;. . . .Ps 33:7
The s is his, for he made it, ...Ps 95:5
dwell in the uttermost parts of the s,. . . . Ps 139:9
when he assigned to the s its limit, so. . .Prv 8:29
And I saw a beast rising out of the s,. . . . . Rv 13:1
beside the s of glass with harps of God . . Rv 15:2
passed away, and the s was no more. . . . . Rv 21:1

SEAL

Set me as a s upon your heart, as a. . . . . . .Sg 8:6
For on him God the Father has set his s." . .Jn 6:27
and who has also put his s on us . . . . . .2 Cor 1:22
When the Lamb opened the seventh s,. . . . Rv 8:1
"Do not s up the words of the prophecy. . Rv 22:10

SEALED

were s with the promised Holy Spirit, . . . Eph 1:13
by whom you were s for the day of. . . . Eph 4:30

SEALS

the Lamb opened one of the seven s, ... Rv 6:1

SEARCH

if you s after him with all your heart . . . . .Dt 4:29
S me, O God, and know my heart! Try. . Ps 139:23
if you seek it like silver and s for it. . . . . . .Prv 2:4
"I the LORD s the heart and test. . . . . .Jer 17:10
You s the Scriptures because you think. . .Jn 5:39

SEARCHED

O LORD, you have s me and . . . . .Ps 139:1
to be yours s and inquired carefully, ... 1 Pt 1:10

SEARCHES

for the LORD s all hearts . . . . 1 Chr 28:9
And he who s hearts knows what is. . . .Rom 8:27
For the Spirit s everything, even. . . . . . .1 Cor 2:10
that I am he who s mind and heart,. . . . . .Rv 2:23

SEASON

For everything there is a s, and a time . . .Eccl 3:1
doing good, for in due s we will reap, ...Gal 6:9
be ready in s and out of s; . . . . 2 Tm 4:2

SEASONS

And let them be for signs and for s,. . . . . . Gn 1:14
He made the moon to mark the s; . . . . . Ps 104:19
He changes times and s; he removes. . . . .Dn 2:21
Now concerning the times and the s,. . . 1 Thes 5:1

SEAT

you love the best s in the synagogues. . . Lk 11:43
down on the judgment s at a place . . . . . .Jn 19:13
stand before the judgment s of God;. . Rom 14:10
before the judgment s of Christ,. . . . . . 2 Cor 5:10

SEATED

LORD our God, who is s on high,. . . . . .Ps 113:5
see the Son of Man s at the right hand. . Mt 26:64
s us with him in the heavenly places . . . . Eph 2:6
Christ is, s at the right hand of God. . . . . . .Col 3:1
high priest, one who is s at the right . . . . .Heb 8:1
God who was s on the throne,. . . . . .Rv 19:4

SECOND

And a s is like it: You shall love your . . . Mt 22:39
appear a s time, not to deal with sin . . . Heb 9:28
Over such the s death has no power,. . . . Rv 20:6

SECRET

"The s things belong to the LORD . . . . . . .Dt 29:29
you teach me wisdom in the s heart. . . . . . Ps 51:6
our s sins in the light of your presence. . . Ps 90:8
from you, when I was being made in s,. Ps 139:15
himself, and do not reveal another's s,. . .Prv 25:9
so that your giving may be in s. . . . . .Mt 6:4
has been given the s of the kingdom of . . Mk 4:11
come together. I have said nothing in s. . Jn 18:20
mystery that was kept s for long ages. . Rom 16:25
But we impart a s and hidden wisdom . .1 Cor 2:7
I have learned the s of facing plenty . . . . Phil 4:12

SECRETS

For he knows the s of the heart. . . . . Ps 44:21
goes about slandering reveals s,. . . . . Prv 11:13
given to know the s of the kingdom . . . . . Lk 8:10
God judges the s of men by Christ. . . . . Rom 2:16
the s of his heart are disclosed, and. . .1 Cor 14:25

SECURE

feet upon a rock, making my steps s.. . . . .Ps 40:2
in a peaceful habitation, in s dwellings,. . .Is 32:18
You felt s in your wickedness,. . . . . .Is 47:10
and made the tomb s by sealing the . . . Mt 27:66

SECURELY

Whoever walks in integrity walks s, ... Prv 10:9
this, you lover of pleasures, who sit s, ... Is 47:8
be saved, and Jerusalem will dwell s.. . . Jer 33:16
against a nation at ease, that dwells s, . Jer 49:31

SECURITY

"There will be peace and s in my days." . . Is 39:8
destruction. Jerusalem shall dwell in s. . .Zec 14:11
"There is peace and s," then sudden . . .1 Thes 5:3

SEE

face, for man shall not s me and live.". . Ex 33:20
yet in my flesh I shall s God, ... Jb 19:26
Come and s what God has done: . . . . .Ps 66:5
lest they s with their eyes, and hear. . . . . . .Is 6:10
and all flesh shall s it together, ... Is 40:5
the pure in heart, for they shall s God. . . . .Mt 5:8
people longed to s what you s,. . . . . Mt 13:17
I say to you, you will s heaven opened,. . . .Jn 1:51
that though I was blind, now I s.". . . . . . . .Jn 9:25
whom no one has ever seen or can s. . . 1 Tm 6:16
without which no one will s the Lord. . . Heb 12:14
because we shall s him as he is. . . . . .1 Jn 3:2
They will s his face, and his name. . . . . . . Rv 22:4

SEED

given you every plant yielding s that. . . . .Gn 1:29
it is felled." The holy s is its stump. . . . . . . .Is 6:13
a man who sowed good s in his field, . . . Mt 13:24
"A sower went out to sow his s. . . . . .Lk 8:5
He who supplies s to the sower . . . . . . 2 Cor 9:10
not of perishable s but of imperishable, . 1 Pt 1:23
sinning, for God's s abides in him, ...1 Jn 3:9

SEEDS

Other s fell on good soil and produced. . . Mt 13:8
It is the smallest of all s, but when it . . . . Mt 13:32

SEEING

The hearing ear and the s eye, the. . . . . Prv 20:12
the lame walking, and the blind s. . . . . . . Mt 15:31
to keep them from s the light of the . . . 2 Cor 4:4

SEEK

If you s him, he will be found by you, . 1 Chr 28:9
"S my face." My heart says to you,. . . . . . .Ps 27:8
With my whole heart I s you;. . . . . .Ps 119:10
and those who s me diligently find me.. . Prv 8:17
"S the LORD while he may be. . . . . Is 55:6
to be found by those who did not s me. . . .Is 65:1
when you s me with all your heart. . . . . Jer 29:13
I will s the lost, and I will bring back . . . Ezk 34:16
s righteousness; s humility; . . . . .Zep 2:3
But s first the kingdom of God . . . . .Mt 6:33
s, and you will find; knock,. . . . . .Mt 7:7
Son of Man came to s and to save . . . . . . Lk 19:10
You will s me and you will not find me. . . .Jn 7:34
found by those who did not s me; . . . .Rom 10:20
with Christ, s the things that are above, . . .Col 3:1
that he rewards those who s him.. . . . . . . Heb 11:6
city, but we s the city that is to come. . . Heb 13:14

SEEKING

s him by prayer and pleas for mercy . . . . . Dn 9:3
kept s from him a sign from heaven. . . . . . Lk 11:16
the Father is s such people to worship . . .Jn 4:23

SEEKS

who has understanding s knowledge, . . .Prv 15:14
asks receives, and the one who s finds,. . . .Mt 7:8
no one understands; no one s for God. . .Rom 3:11

SEEN

"For I have s God face to face, ... Gn 32:30
no eye has s a God besides you,. . . . . Is 64:4
No one has ever s God; the only God,. . . . .Jn 1:18
Whoever has s me has s the Father.. . . . . . Jn 14:9
"I have s the Lord"—and that he had. . . . Jn 20:18
For the things that are s are transient,. . 2 Cor 4:18
for, the conviction of things not s. . . . . . . .Heb 11:1
Though you have not s him, you love . . . . 1 Pt 1:8

SEES

For the LORD s not as man s: . . . . 1 Sm 16:7
heaven; he s all the children of man; . . . . Ps 33:13
And whoever s me s him . . . . Jn 12:45

SELF

We know that our old s was crucified . . .Rom 6:6
Though our outer s is wasting away, . . 2 Cor 4:16
and to put on the new s, created after . Eph 4:24
have put off the old s with its practices . . Col 3:9

SELF-CONTROL

A man without s is like a city broken. . .Prv 25:28
tempt you because of your lack of s. . . . .1 Cor 7:5
Every athlete exercises s in all things. . 1 Cor 9:25
gentleness, s; against such things. . . . . . . Gal 5:23
in faith and love and holiness, with s.. . . 1 Tm 2:15
not of fear but of power and love and s. . .2 Tm 1:7
and knowledge with s, and . . . . .2 Pt 1:6

SELF-CONTROLLED

a lover of good, s, upright, holy,. . . . . Ti 1:8
Likewise, urge the younger men to be s. . . . Ti 2:6
therefore be s and sober-minded . . . . .1 Pt 4:7

SELF-INDULGENCE

but inside they are full of greed and s. . .Mt 23:25
lived on the earth in luxury and in s. . . . . . Jas 5:5

SELF-INDULGENT

but she who is s is dead even while. . . . .1 Tm 5:6

SELFISH

For where jealousy and s ambition. . . . . . Jas 3:16

SELL

Buy truth, and do not s it; buy . . . . .Prv 23:23
because they s the righteous for silver, . . .Am 2:6
s what you possess and give to . . . . Mt 19:21
no one can buy or s unless he has . . . . . . Rv 13:17

SEND

"Oh, my Lord, please s someone else." . . . Ex 4:13
I will s an angel before you, and I will . . . .Ex 33:2
S out your light and your truth; let. . . . . . .Ps 43:3
"Here I am! S me." . . . . Is 6:8
of the harvest to s out laborers into his. . Mt 9:38
But if I go, I will s him to you. . . . . .Jn 16:7

SENDING

"Behold, I am s you out as sheep . . . . Mt 10:16
has sent me, even so I am s you.". . . . . . . .Jn 20:21

SENNACHERIB
S king of Assyria came and invaded. . . .2 Chr 32:1
S king of Assyria came up against . . . . .Is 36:1

SENSUALITY
deceit, s, envy, slander, pride, ... Mk 7:22
not in sexual immorality and s, ...Rom 13:13
impurity, sexual immorality, and s. . . . .2 Cor 12:21
evident: sexual immorality, impurity, s, . . Gal 5:19
given themselves up to s, greedy . . . . . . .Eph 4:19
living in s, passions, drunkenness,. . . . . . . .1 Pt 4:3
And many will follow their s, ... 2 Pt 2:2
pervert the grace of our God into s . . . . . . Jude 4

SENT
receives me receives him who s me. . . . Mt 10:40
believes not in me but in him who s me. . .Jn 12:44
are they to preach unless they are s?. . Rom 10:15
of time had come, God s forth his Son,. . . Gal 4:4

SEPARATE
and let it s the waters from the waters.". . . Gn 1:6
God has joined together, let not man s.". . Mt 19:6
and he will s people one from another . . Mt 25:32
Who shall s us from the love of. . . . . . . .Rom 8:35
and be s from them, says the Lord, . . . 2 Cor 6:17

SEPARATED
God, who has s you from the peoples. . .Lv 20:24
at that time s from Christ, alienated. . . . .Eph 2:12
unstained, s from sinners, and exalted. . Heb 7:26

SEPARATES
he who repeats a matter s close friends. . . Prv 17:9
But if the unbelieving partner s, let it . . 1 Cor 7:15

SEPARATION
iniquities have made a s between you. . . . Is 59:2
to make a s between the holy and the. . Ezk 42:20

SERAPHIM
Above him stood the s. Each had six. . . . . . Is 6:2
Then one of the s flew to me, having. . . . . . Is 6:6

SERPENT
Now the s was more crafty than any . . . . . . Gn 3:1
So Moses made a bronze s and set it. . . . Nm 21:9
if he asks for a fish, will give him a s? . . . . Mt 7:10
And as Moses lifted up the s in the . . . . . . Jn 3:14
And he seized the dragon, that ancient s, . Rv 20:2

SERPENTS
so be wise as s and innocent as doves. . . Mt 10:16
authority to tread on s and scorpions,. . . Lk 10:19

SERVANT
"Speak, for your s hears.". . . . . .1 Sm 3:10
Behold, my s shall act wisely; he. . . . . .Is 52:13
"Behold, my s whom I have chosen,. . . . . Mt 12:18
be great among you must be your s,. . . Mt 20:26
"Who then is the faithful and wise s,. . . Mt 24:45
'Well done, good and faithful s.. . . . . .Mt 25:21
him, 'You wicked and slothful s! . . . . Mt 25:26
"Behold, I am the s of the Lord; . . . . Lk 1:38
No s can serve two masters, ... Lk 16:13
'A s is not greater than his master.'. . . . . . .Jn 15:20
the name of your holy s Jesus." . . . . . . .Acts 4:30
I have made myself a s to all, ...1 Cor 9:19
emptied himself, by taking the form of a s,. .Phil 2:7
s of God and of the Lord Jesus Christ,. . . . .Jas 1:1
I am a fellow s with you and your. . . . . . . Rv 19:10

SERVANTS
persistently sent all my s the prophets . . Jer 7:25
have not listened to your s the prophets,. Dn 9:6
wished to settle accounts with his s. . . . . Mt 18:23
'We are unworthy s; we have only . . . . . . Lk 17:10
Calling ten of his s, he gave them ten . . . Lk 19:13
No longer do I call you s, for the . . . . .Jn 15:15
cover-up for evil, but living as s of God. . 1 Pt 2:16
until we have sealed the s of our God . . . . .Rv 7:3

SERVE
the older shall s the younger.". . . . . Gn 25:23
to s the LORD your God with . . . . Dt 10:12
my house, we will s the LORD." . . . . Jos 24:15
your God and him only shall you s.'" . . . . .Mt 4:10
of Man came not to be served but to s,. .Mt 20:28
You cannot s God and money.". . . . . Lk 16:13
but with my flesh I s the law of sin. . . . .Rom 7:25
"The older will s the younger.". . . . . Rom 9:12
in zeal, be fervent in spirit, s the Lord. . Rom 12:11
but through love s one another. . . . . Gal 5:13
then let them s as deacons if they . . . . . 1 Tm 3:10
rather they must s all the better since . . . 1 Tm 6:2
from dead works to s the living God.. . . .Heb 9:14
received a gift, use it to s one another, . . 1 Pt 4:10

SERVES
If anyone s me, he must follow me; . . . . . Jn 12:26
Whoever thus s Christ is acceptable . . Rom 14:18
as one who s by the strength that God . . 1 Pt 4:11

SERVICE
if s, in our serving; the one. . . . . Rom 12:7
there are varieties of s, but the. . . . . . . .1 Cor 12:5
rendering s with a good will as to the . . . Eph 6:7

SET
I have s the LORD always. . . . . Ps 16:8
but to s the mind on the Spirit is life . . . .Rom 8:6
S your minds on things that are above,. . . Col 3:2

SETH
a son and called his name S, ... Gn 4:25

SEVEN
march around the city s times, ...Jos 6:4
s that are an abomination to him:. . . . . . . Prv 6:16
there shall be s weeks. Then . . . . Dn 9:25
I forgive him? As many as s times?". . . . . Mt 18:21
Then it goes and brings s other spirits . . Lk 11:26
John to the s churches that are in Asia: . . . Rv 1:4
who holds the s stars in his right . . . . Rv 2:1
the Lamb opened one of the s seals,. . . . . . Rv 6:1
s angels s golden bowls full. . . . . Rv 15:7

SEVENTH
And on the s day God finished his . . . . Gn 2:2
but on the s day you shall rest;. . . . . Ex 23:12
God rested on the s day from all his . . . . Heb 4:4

SEVENTY
of Jacob who came into Egypt were s. . Gn 46:27
it kept Sabbath, to fulfill s years.. . . . . 2 Chr 36:21
The years of our life are s, or even by . . .Ps 90:10
Then after s years are completed, I . . . . Jer 25:12
of Jerusalem, namely, s years. . . . . Dn 9:2
"S weeks are decreed about your. . . . . . . Dn 9:24

SEXUAL
Flee from s immorality. Every other . . . .1 Cor 6:18
We must not indulge in s immorality . . .1 Cor 10:8
that you abstain from s immorality; . . . 1 Thes 4:3
to idols and practice s immorality. . . . . . . .Rv 2:14

SHADE
LORD is your s on your right. . . . . .Ps 121:5
birds of the air can make nests in its s." . Mk 4:32

SHADOW
take refuge in the s of your wings. . . . . . .Ps 36:7
shall return and dwell beneath my s; . . . .Hos 14:7
by at least his s might fall on some . . . . Acts 5:15
These are a s of the things to come, ... Col 2:17
law has but a s of the good things to . . . Heb 10:1

SHAKEN
salvation, my fortress; I shall not be s. . . .Ps 62:6
they were gathered together was s,. . . . Acts 4:31
not to be quickly s in mind or . . . . 2 Thes 2:2
receiving a kingdom that cannot be s,. .Heb 12:28

SHALLUM
S the son of Jabesh began to reign in . .2 Kgs 15:13

SHALMANESER
him came up S king of Assyria. . . . . 2 Kgs 17:3
S king of Assyria came up against . . . . 2 Kgs 18:9

SHAME
in you I trust; let me not be put to s;. . . . .Ps 25:2
Then I shall not be put to s, having my . . Ps 119:6
but the wicked brings s and disgrace. . . . Prv 13:5
Instead of your s there shall be a double . . Is 61:7
I will change their glory into s. . . . . Hos 4:7
hope does not put us to s, because . . . . .Rom 5:5
believes in him will not be put to s." . . .Rom 10:11
is foolish in the world to s the wise;. . . .1 Cor 1:27
is their belly, and they glory in their s,. . . Phil 3:19
believes in him will not be put to s." . . . . .1 Pt 2:6
not shrink from him in s at his coming. . .1 Jn 2:28

SHARE
Is it not to s your bread with the hungry . Is 58:7
has two tunics is to s with him who. . . . . . .Lk 3:11
give me the s of property that is . . . . .Lk 15:12
not wash you, you have no s with me.". . . Jn 13:8
now s in the nourishing root of the . . . . Rom 11:17
Let the one who is taught the word s all. . Gal 6:6
something to s with anyone in need. . . . Eph 4:28
to do good and to s what you have, . . . Heb 13:16
But rejoice insofar as you s Christ's . . . . .1 Pt 4:13
God will take away his s in the tree of. . .Rv 22:19

SHARES
for he s his bread with the poor. . . . . .Prv 22:9
to the one who s the faith of Abraham,. .Rom 4:16

SHARON
I am a rose of S, a lily of the valleys. . . . . . . Sg 2:1
S shall become a pasture for flocks,. . . . . .Is 65:10

SHEAVES
shouts of joy, bringing his s with him. . . . Ps 126:6

SHEBA
Now when the queen of S heard of . . . . 1 Kgs 10:1

SHECHEM
them were given S, the city of refuge . . .Jos 21:21

SHED
by man shall his blood be s, for God . . . . . Gn 9:6
and they make haste to s blood. . . . . .Prv 1:16
s from the foundation of the world, ... Lk 11:50
"Their feet are swift to s blood;. . . . . Rom 3:15
For they have s the blood of saints . . . . . .Rv 16:6

SHEDDING
and without the s of blood there is no . Heb 9:22

SHEEP
we are regarded as s to be slaughtered. . . Ps 44:22
his people, and the s of his pasture. . . . . .Ps 100:3
I have gone astray like a lost s; seek . . .Ps 119:176
All we like s have gone astray; we . . . . Is 53:6
"My people have been lost s. . . . . .Jer 50:6
will search for my s and will seek. . . . . . Ezk 34:11
I will set them together like s in a fold, . . . Mi 2:12
like s without a shepherd . . . . Mt 9:36
man has a hundred s, and one of them. . Mt 18:12
shepherd separates the s from the goats. . Mt 25:32
for I have found my s that was lost.' . . . . . Lk 15:6
The s hear his voice, and he calls . . . . Jn 10:3
I lay down my life for the s. . . . . Jn 10:15
My s hear my voice, and I. . . . . .Jn 10:27
"Like a s he was led to the slaughter . . . Acts 8:32
are regarded as s to be slaughtered." . . .Rom 8:36
you were straying like s, but have. . . . . . .1 Pt 2:25

SHELTER
He who dwells in the s of the Most . . . . . . .Ps 91:1
for a refuge and a s from the storm. . . . . . . Is 4:6
throne will s them with his presence.. . . . . Rv 7:15

SHEM
Noah fathered S, Ham, and Japheth. . . . . Gn 5:32
be the LORD, the God of S;. . . . . Gn 9:26

SHEOL
"No, I shall go down to S to my son, . . . Gn 37:35

so he who goes down to S does not . . . . . . Jb 7:9
in S who will give you praise? . . . . Ps 6:5
For you will not abandon my soul to S, . . Ps 16:10
If I make my bed in S, you are there! . . . . Ps 139:8
the rod, you will save his soul from S. . . Prv 23:14
consigned to the gates of S for the rest . . Is 38:10
out of the belly of S I cried, and you . . . . . Jon 2:2
His greed is as wide as S; like death. . . . . Hab 2:5

SHEPHERD

the God who has been my s all my life . . Gn 48:15
'You shall be s of my people Israel, ... 2 Sm 5:2
The LORD is my s; I shall not. . . . . Ps 23:1
Be their s and carry them forever. . . . . Ps 28:9
He will tend his flock like a s; . . . . Is 40:11
will keep him as a s keeps his flock.' . . . . Jer 31:10
As a s seeks out his flock when he. . . . . Ezk 34:12
And he shall stand and s his flock . . . . Mi 5:4
they are afflicted for lack of a s. . . . . Zec 10:2
"Strike the s, and the sheep will . . . . Zec 13:7
helpless, like sheep without a s. . . . . Mt 9:36
For it is written, 'I will strike the s, ... Mt 26:31
I am the good s. The good s lays . . . . Jn 10:11
Lord Jesus, the great s of the sheep, . . Heb 13:20
returned to the S and Overseer of . . . . . . 1 Pt 2:25
And when the chief S appears, you . . . . . . 1 Pt 5:4
of the throne will be their s, and he . . . . . . Rv 7:17

SHEPHERDS

they are s who have no understanding; . . . Is 56:11
"'And I will give you s after my . . . . Jer 3:15
"Woe to the s who destroy and scatter . . . Jer 23:1
region there were s out in the field, ... Lk 2:8
evangelists, the s and teachers, ... Eph 4:11

SHIELD

"Fear not, Abram, I am your s; . . . . Gn 15:1
But you, O LORD, are a s . . . . Ps 3:3
LORD is my strength and my s; . . . . Ps 28:7
the LORD God is a sun and s; . . . . Ps 84:11
take up the s of faith, with which you . . . Eph 6:16

SHINE

LORD make his face to s upon . . . . Nm 6:25
bless us and make his face to s upon us, . Ps 67:1
A man's wisdom makes his face s, and . . . Eccl 8:1
who are wise shall s like the brightness . . . Dn 12:3
let your light s before others, so that. . . . . Mt 5:16
Then the righteous will s like the sun. . . . Mt 13:43
"Let light s out of darkness," . . . . 2 Cor 4:6
the dead, and Christ will s on you." . . . . . Eph 5:14
among whom you s as lights in the . . . . . Phil 2:15

SHINES

which s brighter and brighter until. . . . . . Prv 4:18
The light s in the darkness, and the . . . . Jn 1:5

SHINING

away and the true light is already s. . . . . . 1 Jn 2:8
face was like the sun s in full strength. . . . Rv 1:16

SHONE

of his face s because he had been . . . . . Ex 34:29
his face s like the sun, and his clothes . . . . Mt 17:2
and the glory of the Lord s around . . . . Lk 2:9
out of darkness," has s in our hearts . . . 2 Cor 4:6

SHORT

but the years of the wicked will be s. . . Prv 10:27
of the elect those days will be cut s. . . . Mt 24:22
sinned and fall s of the glory of God, . . . Rom 3:23

SHOUT

people shall s with a great s, ... Jos 6:5
with a great s when they praised . . . . Ezr 3:11
S for joy in the LORD, O you . . . . Ps 33:1
S for joy to God, all the earth; . . . . Ps 66:1

SHOW

Moses said, "Please s me your glory." . . . Ex 33:18
greater works than these will he s him, . . . Jn 5:20
"Lord, s us the Father, and it is enough . . . Jn 14:8
to s perfect courtesy toward all people. . . . Ti 3:2
and I will s you what must take place . . . . . Rv 4:1

SHOWERS

grass, like s that water the earth! . . . . Ps 72:6
season; they shall be s of blessing. . . . . Ezk 34:26

SHREWD

this world are more s in dealing with. . . . . Lk 16:8

SHRINK

not of those who s back and are . . . . . Heb 10:39
have confidence and not s from him . . . . 1 Jn 2:28

SHROUD

body and wrapped it in a clean linen s . Mt 27:59
And Joseph bought a linen s, and . . . . . Mk 15:46

SHUT

He shall open, and none shall s; and . . . . Is 22:22
For you s the kingdom of heaven in. . . . . Mt 23:13
open door, which no one is able to s. . . . . . Rv 3:8

SICK

Hope deferred makes the heart s, ... Prv 13:12
with a word and healed all who were s. . . Mt 8:16
s and in prison and you did not visit . . . Mt 25:43
s man answered him, "Sir, I have no. . . . . . . Jn 5:7
Is anyone among you s? Let him call. . . . Jas 5:14

SICKNESS

I will take s away from among you. . . . . . Ex 23:25
A man's spirit will endure s, but a. . . . . . . Prv 18:14

SIDE

"Who is on the LORD's s? Come to . . . . . . Ex 32:26
The LORD is on my s; I will not. . . . . Ps 118:6
God, who is at the Father's s, he has . . . . . . Jn 1:18
the soldiers pierced his s with a spear, . . Jn 19:34
he showed them his hands and his s. . . . Jn 20:20
striving s by s for the faith. . . . . Phil 1:27

SIFT

to s the nations with the sieve of . . . . Is 30:28
you, that he might s you like wheat, ... Lk 22:31

SIGHT

I sinned and done what is evil in your s, . . Ps 51:4
Precious in the s of the LORD is . . . . Ps 116:15
He said, "Lord, let me recover my s." . . . . Lk 18:41
I went and washed and received my s." . . . Jn 9:11
up, and a cloud took him out of their s. . Acts 1:9
And for three days he was without s, . . . Acts 9:9
and it is pleasing in the s of God our. . . . 1 Tm 2:3
in us that which is pleasing in his s, ... Heb 13:21

SIGN

And God said, "This is the s of the . . . . Gn 9:12
it shall be a s of the covenant between . . . Gn 17:11
The blood shall be a s for you, on the . . . Ex 12:13
and adulterous generation seeks for a s, . . Mt 12:39
generation seeks for a s, but no s. . . . . Mt 16:4
This is a clear s to them of their . . . . Phil 1:28
This is the s of genuineness in every . . 2 Thes 3:17
And a great s appeared in heaven: . . . . Rv 12:1

SIGNS

him for all the s and the wonders that. . . Dt 34:11
he works s and wonders in heaven. . . . . . Dn 6:27
arise and perform great s and wonders, . . Mt 24:24
Now Jesus did many other s in the . . . . Jn 20:30
the heavens above and s on the earth. . Acts 2:19
For Jews demand s and Greeks seek . . . 1 Cor 1:22
while God also bore witness by s and . . . Heb 2:4

SILAS

sent Judas called Barsabbas, and S, . . . Acts 15:22
midnight Paul and S were praying . . . . Acts 16:25
When S and Timothy arrived from . . . . . Acts 18:5

SILENCE

For God alone my soul waits in s; . . . . Ps 62:1
a time to keep s, and a time to speak; . . . Eccl 3:7
let all the earth keep s before him." . . . . Hab 2:20
put to s the ignorance of foolish people. . . 1 Pt 2:15
there was s in heaven for about half an. . . . Rv 8:1

SILENT

For when I kept s, my bones wasted . . . . . Ps 32:3
you have done, and I have been s; . . . . . . Ps 50:21
Even a fool who keeps s is considered . Prv 17:28
Be s before the Lord GOD! . . . . Zep 1:7
But Jesus remained s. And the high. . . . Mt 26:63
like a lamb before its shearer is s, ... Acts 8:32
let each of them keep s in church. . . . . 1 Cor 14:28

SILOAM

tower in S fell and killed them: do you . . . Lk 13:4
wash in the pool of S" (which means. . . . . . Jn 9:7

SILVER

Abram was very rich in livestock, in s, ... Gn 13:2
Your s has become dross, your best. . . . . . . Is 1:22
The s is mine, and the gold is mine, ... Hg 2:8
paid him thirty pieces of s. . . . . Mt 26:15
Peter said, "I have no s and gold, but . . . Acts 3:6
"May your s perish with you, because . . Acts 8:20

SIMEON

And she called his name S. . . . . Gn 29:33
And S blessed them and said to Mary . . . . Lk 2:34
Barnabas, S who was called Niger, ... Acts 13:1

SIMON

"Blessed are you, S Bar-Jonah! For. . . . . . Mt 16:17
found a man of Cyrene, S by name. . . . . . Mt 27:32
S, whom he named Peter, and Andrew . . . Lk 6:14
and S who was called the Zealot, ... Lk 6:15
So S Peter went aboard and hauled. . . . . . Jn 21:11
son of Alphaeus and S the Zealot and. . . Acts 1:13
He is lodging with one S, a tanner, ... Acts 10:6

SIMPLE

LORD is sure, making wise the s; . . . . Ps 19:7
The s believes everything, but the . . . . . . Prv 14:15
and the s will learn prudence; . . . . Prv 19:25

SIN

and be sure your s will find you out. . . . Nm 32:23
Be angry, and do not s; ponder in . . . . Ps 4:4
no health in my bones because of my s . . . Ps 38:3
and my s is ever before me. . . . . Ps 51:3
that I might not s against you. . . . . Ps 119:11
is taken away, and your s atoned for." . . . . . Is 6:7
little ones who believe in me to s, ... Mt 18:6
"Temptations to s are sure to come, ... Lk 17:1
"Let him who is without s among you . . . . . Jn 8:7
made him to be s who knew no s, ... 2 Cor 5:21
As for those who persist in s, rebuke . . . 1 Tm 5:20
been tempted as we are, yet without s. . Heb 4:15
when it has conceived gives birth to s, . . . Jas 1:15
to do and fails to do it, for him it is s. . . . Jas 4:17
He committed no s, neither was deceit . . 1 Pt 2:22
If we say we have no s, we deceive . . . . . . 1 Jn 1:8

SINAI

LORD came down on Mount S, ... Ex 19:20
of the LORD dwelt on Mount S, ... Ex 24:16
spoke to Moses on Mount S, saying, ... Lv 25:1

SINCERE

led astray from a s and pure devotion . . 2 Cor 11:3
with a s heart, as you would Christ, ... Eph 6:5
a good conscience and a s faith. . . . . 1 Tm 1:5
mercy and good fruits, impartial and s. . . Jas 3:17

SINCERITY

serve him in s and in faithfulness. . . . . . . Jos 24:14
godly s, not by earthly wisdom. . . . . 2 Cor 1:12
people-pleasers, but with s of heart, ... Col 3:22

SINFUL

"Depart from me, for I am a s man, ... Lk 5:8
into the hands of s men and be crucified . . Lk 24:7
were living in the flesh, our s passions, . . Rom 7:5
scoffing, following their own s desires. . . 2 Pt 3:3

SING

"I will s to the LORD, ... Ex 15:1
S to him a new song; play skillfully. . . . . . . Ps 33:3

SPENT
physicians, and had **s** all that she had,.. . Mk 5:26
when he had **s** everything, a severe . . . . . Lk 15:14

SPICES
s for the anointing oil and for the. . . . . . . .Ex 25:6
tomb, taking the **s** they had prepared.. . . . Lk 24:1

SPIES
men who had been **s** went in and. . . . . . .Jos 6:23
So they watched him and sent **s**, ... Lk 20:20

SPIRIT
"My **S** shall not abide in man forever,. . . . . Gn 6:3
I have filled him with the **S** of God, ... Ex 31:3
a harmful **s** from God is tormenting . . . 1 Sm 16:15
be a double portion of your **s** on me.". . 2 Kgs 2:9
You gave your good **S** to instruct . . . . . . Neh 9:20
The **S** of God has made me,. . . . . .Jb 33:4
Into your hand I commit my **s**;. . . . . Ps 31:5
Where shall I go from your **S**?. . . . . Ps 139:7
Let your good **S** lead me on level. . . . . . Ps 143:10
but the LORD weighs the **s**. . . . . Prv 16:2
and the **s** returns to God who gave it. . . .Eccl 12:7
I have put my **S** upon him;. . . . . .Is 42:1
that I will pour out my **S** on all flesh;. . . . . Jl 2:28
I will put my **S** upon him, and he will. . . . Mt 12:18
with a loud voice and yielded up his **s**. . Mt 27:50
child grew and became strong in **s**, ... Lk 1:80
"The **S** of the Lord is upon me, ... Lk 4:18
into your hands I commit my **s**!". . . . . . . .Lk 23:46
unless one is born of water and the **S**,. . . . . Jn 3:5
God is **s**, and those who worship him . . . .Jn 4:24
It is the **S** who gives life;. . . . . .Jn 6:63
set their minds on the things of the **S**.. . .Rom 8:5
are varieties of gifts, but the same **S**;. . .1 Cor 12:4
the **S** of the Lord is, there is freedom. . .2 Cor 3:17
But the fruit of the **S** is love, joy,. . . . . Gal 5:22
Do not quench the **S**. . . . . .1 Thes 5:19
I was in the **S** on the Lord's day,. . . . . Rv 1:10

SPIRITS
he cast out the **s** with a word . . . . Mt 8:16
the **s** are subject to you, but rejoice. . . . .Lk 10:20
the evil **s** came out of them. . . . . Acts 19:12
all ministering **s** sent out to serve. . . . . . . Heb 1:14
proclaimed to the **s** in prison, ... 1 Pt 3:19
God of the **s** of the prophets, has sent . . Rv 22:6

SPIRITUAL
s truths to those who are **s**. . . . . .1 Cor 2:13
Now concerning **s** gifts, ... 1 Cor 12:1
a natural body; it is raised a **s** body.. . .1 Cor 15:44
with every **s** blessing in the heavenly. . . . . Eph 1:3
will in all **s** wisdom and understanding,. . . Col 1:9

SPIT
Then they **s** in his face and struck. . . . . . Mt 26:67
and shamefully treated and **s** upon. . . . . . Lk 18:32
nor cold, I will **s** you out of my mouth. . . . Rv 3:16

SPLENDOR
Worship the LORD in the **s** of . . . . .Ps 96:9
You are clothed with **s** and majesty,. . . . . Ps 104:1
present the church to himself in **s**, ... Eph 5:27

SPLIT
under him, and the valleys will **s** open, ... Mi 1:4
of Olives shall be **s** in two from east . . . . Zec 14:4

SPOKE
"No one ever **s** like this man!" . . . . .Jn 7:46
God **s** to our fathers by the prophets, ... Heb 1:1
but men **s** from God as they were . . . . . . 2 Pt 1:21

SPOKEN
Glorious things of you are **s**, O city . . . . . .Ps 87:3
that I have **s** to you are spirit and life. . . . .Jn 6:63

SPOT
without **s** or wrinkle or any such. . . . . . . Eph 5:27
be found by him without **s** or blemish, . .2 Pt 3:14

SPRING
in him a **s** of water welling up to eternal. . Jn 4:14

SPRINKLING
s it over the mercy seat and in front . . . . .Lv 16:15
the **s** of defiled persons with the ashes. .Heb 9:13
Jesus Christ and for **s** with his blood: . . . . 1 Pt 1:2

SPY
"Send men to **s** out the land of Canaan, . Nm 13:2
who slipped in to **s** out our freedom . . . . . Gal 2:4

STAFF
Moses took the **s** of God in his hand. . . . . Ex 4:20
And I took my **s** Favor, and I broke it, . . .Zec 11:10
the manna, and Aaron's **s** that budded,. . Heb 9:4

STAND
said to the people, "Fear not, **s** firm, ... Ex 14:13
"Who is able to **s** before the LORD,. . . . 1 Sm 6:20
the wicked will not **s** in the judgment,. . . . . Ps 1:5
glorify him, and **s** in awe of him,. . . . . . . .Ps 22:23
but the house of the righteous will **s**.. . . . Prv 12:7
the wall and **s** in the breach before . . . Ezk 22:30
by faith into this grace in which we **s**, . . .Rom 5:2
For we will all **s** before the judgment. . Rom 14:10
S therefore, having fastened on the belt . .Eph 6:14
is the true grace of God. **S** firm in it. . . . . 1 Pt 5:12

STANDING
on which you are **s** is holy ground.". . . . . . .Ex 3:5
if you are **s** fast in the Lord. . . . . 1 Thes 3:8
great and small, **s** before the throne,. . . .Rv 20:12

STANDS
to contend; he **s** to judge peoples. . . . . .Is 3:13
thinks that he **s** take heed lest he fall. . 1 Cor 10:12

STAR
a **s** shall come out of Jacob,. . . . . Nm 24:17
When they saw the **s**, they rejoiced . . . . . . Mt 2:10
I saw a **s** fallen from heaven to earth, ... Rv 9:1
of David, the bright morning **s**." . . . . .Rv 22:16

STARS
lesser light to rule the night—and the **s**. . . Gn 1:16
heaven, and number the **s**, if you are. . . . .Gn 15:5
when the morning **s** sang together and. . .Jb 38:7
to righteousness, like the **s** forever. . . . . . .Dn 12:3
as many as the **s** of heaven and as. . . . . Heb 11:12
In his right hand he held seven **s**, from . . . Rv 1:16

STATURE
in wisdom and in **s** and in favor with . . . . .Lk 2:52
he could not, because he was small in **s**.. . Lk 19:3

STATUTES
and his **s** I did not put away from me. . . . Ps 18:22
may be steadfast in keeping your **s**!. . . . . Ps 119:5

STEADFAST
but showing **s** love to thousands . . . . Dt 5:10
but my **s** love will not depart from. . . . .2 Sm 7:15
but **s** love surrounds the one who trusts . . Ps 32:10
O God, according to your **s** love;. . . . . .Ps 51:1
is good, for his **s** love endures forever.. . . Ps 136:1
What is desired in a man is **s** love, ... Prv 19:22
The **s** love of the LORD never . . . . Lam 3:22
be **s**, immovable, always abounding. . .1 Cor 15:58
continue in the faith, stable and **s**, ... Col 1:23
who remains **s** under trial, for when. . . . . . .Jas 1:12

STEADFASTNESS
the love of God and to the **s** of Christ. . .2 Thes 3:5
testing of your faith produces **s**. . . . . .Jas 1:3
and self-control with **s**, and **s**. . . . . .2 Pt 1:6

STEAL
"You shall not **s**. . . . . .Ex 20:15
and where thieves break in and **s**,. . . . . . . .Mt 6:19
preach against stealing, do you **s**? . . . . . Rom 2:21
You shall not murder, You shall not **s**, . . Rom 13:9
Let the thief no longer **s**, but rather. . . . Eph 4:28

STEPHEN
whole gathering, and they chose **S**,. . . . . Acts 6:5
And **S**, full of grace and power, was. . . . . Acts 6:8
And as they were stoning **S**, he called. . Acts 7:59
that arose over **S** traveled as far. . . . . . . Acts 11:19

STEPS
The **s** of a man are established by the. . . Ps 37:23
but the prudent gives thought to his **s**. . .Prv 14:15
so that you might follow in his **s**. . . . . 1 Pt 2:21

STEWARDS
Moreover, it is required of **s** that they . . 1 Cor 4:2
as good **s** of God's varied grace:. . . . . . . .1 Pt 4:10

STEWARDSHIP
I am still entrusted with a **s**. . . . . .1 Cor 9:17
heard of the **s** of God's grace . . . . .Eph 3:2
according to the **s** from God that. . . . . . . Col 1:25
rather than the **s** from God that . . . . 1 Tm 1:4

STIFF-NECKED
and behold, it is a **s** people. . . . . .Ex 32:9
"You **s** people, uncircumcised in heart. . Acts 7:51

STILL
Be **s** before the LORD and wait. . . . . .Ps 37:7
"Be **s**, and know that I am God.. . . . . .Ps 46:10
The sun and moon stood **s** in their. . . . . . Hab 3:11
s do right, and the holy **s** be holy.". . . . . . Rv 22:11

STING
O Sheol, where is your **s**? . . . . Hos 13:14
O death, where is your **s**?" . . . . .1 Cor 15:55
The **s** of death is sin, and the power . .1 Cor 15:56

STONE
this **s** shall be a witness against us, ...Jos 24:27
Philistine with a sling and with a **s**,. . . .1 Sm 17:50
lest you strike your foot against a **s**.. . . . .Ps 91:12
The **s** that the builders rejected has. . . . Ps 118:22
foundation in Zion, a **s**, a tested **s**, ...Is 28:16
I will remove the heart of **s** from. . . . . . . .Ezk 11:19
a **s** was cut out by no human hand,. . . . . Dn 2:34
asks him for bread, will give him a **s**? . . . . .Mt 7:9
"'The **s** that the builders rejected . . . . . . .Mt 21:42
he rolled a great **s** to the entrance of. . . Mt 27:60
command this **s** to become bread." . . . . . . .Lk 4:3
be the first to throw a **s** at her." . . . . .Jn 8:7
This Jesus is the **s** that was rejected by. . . Acts 4:11
I am laying in Zion a **s** of stumbling, . . .Rom 9:33
a living **s** rejected by men but in the . . . . .1 Pt 2:4

STONED
cast him out of the city and **s** him. . . . . . Acts 7:58
I was beaten with rods. Once I was **s**. . .2 Cor 11:25
They were **s**, they were sawn in two, . . . Heb 11:37

STONES
chose five smooth **s** from the brook. . .1 Sm 17:40
God is able from these **s** to raise up. . . . . . .Mt 3:9
were silent, the very **s** would cry out.". . .Lk 19:40

STORM
He made the **s** be still, and the waves . .Ps 107:29
a shelter from the **s** and a shade from. . . . Is 25:4
there arose a great **s** on the sea,. . . . . .Mt 8:24
springs and mists driven by a **s**. . . . . .2 Pt 2:17

STRAIGHT
enemies; make your way **s** before me. . . . . .Ps 5:8
and your gaze be **s** before you. . . . . .Prv 4:25
of the blameless keeps his way **s**,. . . . . . . .Prv 11:5
make **s** in the desert a highway for our. . . . Is 40:3
"Rise and go to the street called **S**, ...Acts 9:11

STRANGE
stirred him to jealousy with **s** gods;. . . . . Dt 32:16
For by people of **s** lips and with. . . . . Is 28:11
For you bring some **s** things to our . . . Acts 17:20

STRANGER
I was a **s** and you welcomed me, ...Mt 25:35
A **s** they will not follow, but they will. . . . . Jn 10:5

STRANGERS
So then you are no longer s and aliens, ... Eph 2:19
they were s and exiles on ... Heb 11:13
Do not neglect to show hospitality to s, ... Heb 13:2

STRAW
longer give the people s to make bricks, ... Ex 5:7
silver, precious stones, wood, hay, s— ... 1 Cor 3:12

STRAY
me, but I do not s from your precepts ... Ps 119:110
to her ways; do not s into her paths, ... Prv 7:25

STREAM
of the nations like an overflowing s; ... Is 66:12
righteousness like an ever-flowing s. ... Am 5:24

STREAMS
He is like a tree planted by s of water ... Ps 1:3
As a deer pants for flowing s, ... Ps 42:1
All s run to the sea, but the sea is not ... Eccl 1:7
the storm, like s of water in a dry place, ... Is 32:2

STREET
Wisdom cries aloud in the s, in the ... Prv 1:20
in the synagogues and at the s corners, ... Mt 6:5
and the s of the city was pure gold, ... Rv 21:21

STRENGTH
equipped me with s for the battle; ... 2 Sm 22:40
Seek the LORD and his s; ... 1 Chr 16:11
joy of the LORD is your s." ... Neh 8:10
LORD is my s and my shield; ... Ps 28:7
but God is the s of my heart and my ... Ps 73:26
Blessed are those whose s is in you, ... Ps 84:5
Seek the LORD and his s; ... Ps 105:4
my Lord, the s of my salvation, ... Ps 140:7
A wise man is full of s, and a man ... Prv 24:5
S and dignity are her clothing, and she ... Prv 31:25
all your mind and with all your s.' ... Mk 12:30
may have s to comprehend with all ... Eph 3:18

STRENGTHEN
s me according to your word! ... Ps 119:28
S the weak hands, and make firm the ... Is 35:3
I will s you, I will help you, I will ... Is 41:10
have turned again, s your brothers." ... Lk 22:32
hands and s your weak knees, ... Heb 12:12

STRENGTHENED
grant you to be s with power through ... Eph 3:16
You then, my child, be s by the grace ... 2 Tm 2:1
Lord stood by me and s me, ... 2 Tm 4:17
it is good for the heart to be s by grace, ... Heb 13:9

STRENGTHENS
do all things through him who s me. ... Phil 4:13

STRETCH
"S out your hand." And the man ... Mt 12:13
you are old, you will s out your hands, ... Jn 21:18
while you s out your hand to heal, and ... Acts 4:30

STRETCHED
created the heavens and s them out, ... Is 42:5
who s out the heavens and founded ... Zec 12:1
Jesus s out his hand and touched ... Mt 8:3

STRIFE
By insolence comes nothing but s, ... Prv 13:10
A hot-tempered man stirs up s, but ... Prv 15:18
Who has sorrow? Who has s? ... Prv 23:29
They are full of envy, murder, s, deceit, ... Rom 1:29
there is jealousy and s among you, ... 1 Cor 3:3

STRIKE
and you shall s the rock, and water ... Ex 17:6
lest you s your foot against a stone. ... Ps 91:12
lest you s your foot against a stone.'" ... Lk 4:11
if what I said is right, why do you s ... Jn 18:23

STRONG
Be s and courageous. Do not fear ... Dt 31:6
Be s and courageous, for you shall ... Jos 1:6

This God is my s refuge ... 2 Sm 22:33
Their Redeemer is s; the LORD ... Jer 50:34
We who are s have an obligation to ... Rom 15:1
is weak in the world to shame the s; ... 1 Cor 1:27
firm in the faith, act like men, be s. ... 1 Cor 16:13
Finally, be s in the Lord ... Eph 6:10
sword, were made s out of weakness, ... Heb 11:34

STRONGHOLD
The LORD is a s for the ... Ps 9:9
he is their s in the time of trouble ... Ps 37:39
LORD, my strength and my s, ... Jer 16:19
The LORD is good, a s in ... Na 1:7

STRUGGLE
how great a s I have for you ... Col 2:1
In your s against sin you have not yet ... Heb 12:4

STUBBORN
righteousness, for you are a s people ... Dt 9:6
So I gave them over to their s hearts, ... Ps 81:12
Like a s heifer, Israel is s; ... Hos 4:16

STUDY
Ezra had set his heart to s the Law of ... Ezr 7:10
and much s is a weariness ... Eccl 12:12

STUMBLE
nothing can make them s. ... Ps 119:165
way securely, and your foot will not s ... Prv 3:23
straight path in which they shall not s, ... Jer 31:9
walks in the day, he does not s, ... Jn 11:9
that causes your brother to s. ... Rom 14:21
eat meat, lest I make my brother s. ... 1 Cor 8:13
For we all s in many ways. And if ... Jas 3:2
They s because they disobey ... 1 Pt 2:8

STUMBLING
and a rock of s to both houses ... Is 8:14
They have stumbled over the s stone, ... Rom 9:32
a s block and a retribution for them; ... Rom 11:9
never to put a s block or hindrance ... Rom 14:13
a s block to Jews and folly to Gentiles, ... 1 Cor 1:23
become a s block to the weak ... 1 Cor 8:9
and in him there is no cause for s. ... 1 Jn 2:10
to keep you from s and to present ... Jude 24

SUBDUE
fill the earth and s it, and have dominion ... Gn 1:28
to s nations before him and to loose ... Is 45:1
No one had the strength to s him ... Mk 5:4

SUBJECT
even the demons are s to us in your ... Lk 10:17
Let every person be s to the governing ... Rom 13:1
enables him even to s all things to ... Phil 3:21
we not much more be s to the Father ... Heb 12:9
Be s for the Lord's sake to every ... 1 Pt 2:13

SUBJECTED
For the creation was s to futility, not ... Rom 8:20
that God s the world to come, ... Heb 2:5
and powers having been s to him ... 1 Pt 3:22

SUBJECTION
Therefore one must be in s, not only ... Rom 13:5
put all things in s under his feet." ... 1 Cor 15:27
putting everything in s under his feet." ... Heb 2:8

SUBMISSION
to speak, but should be in s, as the ... 1 Cor 14:34
because of your s that comes from your ... 2 Cor 9:13

SUBMISSIVE
came to Nazareth and was s to them ... Lk 2:51
with all dignity keeping his children s, ... 1 Tm 3:4
kind, and s to their own husbands, ... Ti 2:5
Remind them to be s to rulers ... Ti 3:1

SUBMIT
to God, for it does not s to God's law; ... Rom 8:7
they did not s to God's righteousness ... Rom 10:3
Wives, s to your own husbands, ... Eph 5:22
Wives, s to your husbands, as is fitting ... Col 3:18

Obey your leaders and s to them, for ... Heb 13:17
S yourselves therefore to God ... Jas 4:7

SUBMITS
Now as the church s to Christ, so also ... Eph 5:24

SUBMITTING
s to one another out of reverence for ... Eph 5:21
by s to their own husbands, ... 1 Pt 3:5

SUCCEED
believe his prophets, and you will s." ... 2 Chr 20:20
fail, but with many advisers they s. ... Prv 15:22
strength, but wisdom helps one to s. ... Eccl 10:10

SUCCESS
that you may have good s wherever ... Jos 1:7
David had s in all his undertakings, ... 1 Sm 18:14
and give s to your servant today, ... Neh 1:11
O LORD, we pray, give us s! ... Ps 118:25

SUFFER
he must go to Jerusalem and s many ... Mt 16:21
of Man will certainly s at their hands." ... Mt 17:12
eat this Passover with you before I s. ... Lk 22:15
the prophets, that his Christ would s, ... Acts 3:18
counted worthy to s dishonor for the ... Acts 5:41
with Christ, provided we s with him in ... Rom 8:17
endure the same sufferings that we s ... 2 Cor 1:6
believe in him but also s for his sake, ... Phil 1:29
that we were to s affliction, ... 1 Thes 3:4
For it is better to s for doing good, if ... 1 Pt 3:17
Do not fear what you are about to s. ... Rv 2:10

SUFFERED
For you s the same things from your ... 1 Thes 2:14
he himself has s when tempted, ... Heb 2:18
learned obedience through what he s ... Heb 5:8
Jesus also s outside the gate in order ... Heb 13:12
because Christ also s for you, ... 1 Pt 2:21
For Christ also s once for sins, the ... 1 Pt 3:18
whoever has s in the flesh has ceased ... 1 Pt 4:1

SUFFERING
for they saw that his s was very great ... Jb 2:13
knowing that s produces endurance, ... Rom 5:3
but share in s for the gospel by the ... 2 Tm 1:8
of their salvation perfect through s ... Heb 2:10
Is anyone among you s? Let him pray ... Jas 5:13
one endures sorrows while s unjustly ... 1 Pt 2:19
s wrong as the wage for their ... 2 Pt 2:13

SUFFERINGS
For I consider that the s of this present ... Rom 8:18
as we share abundantly in Christ's s, ... 2 Cor 1:5
his resurrection, and may share his s, ... Phil 3:10
Now I rejoice in my s for your sake, ... Col 1:24
when he predicted the s of Christ and ... 1 Pt 1:11

SUFFERS
for he is an epileptic and he s terribly ... Mt 17:15
If one member s, all suffer together; ... 1 Cor 12:26
Yet if anyone s as a Christian, let ... 1 Pt 4:16

SUFFICIENCY
from us, but our s is from God, ... 2 Cor 3:5
so that having all s in all things at all ... 2 Cor 9:8

SUFFICIENT
S for the day is its own trouble ... Mt 6:34
"My grace is s for you, for my power ... 2 Cor 12:9

SUN
And the s stood still, and the moon ... Jos 10:13
like the s shining forth on a cloudless ... 2 Sm 23:4
In them he has set a tent for the s, ... Ps 19:4
from the rising of the s to its setting ... Ps 50:1
The s shall not strike you by day, ... Ps 121:6
So the s turned back on the dial the ten ... Is 38:8
The s shall be no more your light by day, ... Is 60:19
The s and the moon are darkened, ... Jl 2:10
For he makes his s rise on the evil and ... Mt 5:45
of those days the s will be darkened, ... Mt 24:29
the s shall be turned to darkness ... Acts 2:20

do not let the **s** go down on your anger, . . Eph 4:26
need no light of lamp or **s**, for. . . . . .Rv 22:5

SUPERIOR
having become as much **s** to angels . . . . .Heb 1:4
that the inferior is blessed by the **s**. . . . . . Heb 7:7

SUPPER
rose from **s**. He laid aside his outer . . . . . . Jn 13:4
it is not the Lord's **s** that you eat. . . . . . 1 Cor 11:20
invited to the marriage **s** of the Lamb." . . . Rv 19:9

SUPPLICATION
making **s** for all the saints, ... Eph 6:18
by prayer and **s** with thanksgiving let . . . . Phil 4:6

SUPPLICATIONS
I urge that **s**, prayers, intercessions, ... 1 Tm 2:1
Jesus offered up prayers and **s**, ... Heb 5:7

SUPPLY
their abundance may **s** your need, ... 2 Cor 8:14
And my God will **s** every need. . . . . .Phil 4:19

SURE
All your commandments are **s**; . . . . Ps 119:86
For I am **s** that neither death nor life, . . Rom 8:38

SURPASSES
because of the glory that **s** it. . . . . 2 Cor 3:10
the love of Christ that **s** knowledge, ... Eph 3:19
of God, which **s** all understanding, ... Phil 4:7

SURPASSING
show that the **s** power belongs to God. . 2 Cor 4:7
because of the **s** grace of God upon . . 2 Cor 9:14

SURROUNDED
Therefore, since we are **s** by so great a . . Heb 12:1
of the earth and **s** the camp of the saints. . Rv 20:9

SURROUNDS
but steadfast love **s** the one who trusts. . Ps 32:10
so the Lord **s** his people, ... Ps 125:2

SUSTAIN
on the Lord, and he will **s** you; . . . . Ps 55:22
who will **s** you to the end, guiltless in . . . 1 Cor 1:8

SWEAR
what is false and does not **s** deceitfully. . . Ps 24:4
to those of old, 'You shall not **s** falsely, . . . Mt 5:33
But above all, my brothers, do not **s**, ... Jas 5:12

SWEAT
By the **s** of your face you shall eat . . . . Gn 3:19
and his **s** became like great drops . . . . . Lk 22:44

SWEET
into the water, and the water became **s**. . Ex 15:25
How **s** are your words to my taste, ... Ps 119:103
lie down, your sleep will be **s**. . . . . Prv 3:24
A desire fulfilled is **s** to the soul, but . . . . Prv 13:19
and it was in my mouth as **s** as honey. . . . Ezk 3:3
It was **s** as honey in my mouth, but . . . . . Rv 10:10

SWORD
a flaming **s** that turned every way to. . . . Gn 3:24
Lord saves not with **s** and spear. . . . . . 1 Sm 17:47
I have not come to bring peace, but a **s**. . . Mt 10:34
For all who take the **s** will perish by. . . . Mt 26:52
for he does not bear the **s** in vain. . . . . . Rom 13:4
of salvation, and the **s** of the Spirit, ... Eph 6:17
active, sharper than any two-edged **s**, . . . Heb 4:12
his mouth came a sharp two-edged **s**, ... Rv 1:16
mouth comes a sharp **s** with which to. . . Rv 19:15

SWORDS
Beat your plowshares into **s**, ... Jl 3:10
they shall beat their **s** into plowshares, ... Mi 4:3
him a great crowd with **s** and clubs, ... Mt 26:47

SYMPATHY
in the Spirit, any affection and **s**, ... Phil 2:1
unity of mind, **s**, brotherly love, ... 1 Pt 3:8

SYNAGOGUE
hometown he taught them in their **s**, ... Mt 13:54
he went to the **s** on the Sabbath day, ... Lk 4:16
named Jairus, who was a ruler of the **s**. . . Lk 8:41
But the ruler of the **s**, indignant . . . . Lk 13:14
that they would not be put out of the **s**; . Jn 12:42

SYNAGOGUES
over to courts and flog you in their **s**, . . . Mt 10:17
at feasts and the best seats in the **s**. . . . . Mt 23:6

SYRIA
So his fame spread throughout all **S**, ... Mt 4:24
when Quirinius was governor of **S**. . . . . Lk 2:2
in Antioch and **S** and Cilicia, ... Acts 15:23
I went into the regions of **S** and Cilicia. . . . Gal 1:21

TABERNACLE
you concerning the pattern of the **t**, ... Ex 25:9
glory of the Lord filled the **t**. . . . . Ex 40:34

TABITHA
turning to the body he said, "**T**, arise." . Acts 9:40

TABLE
"You shall make a **t** of acacia wood. . . . . . Ex 25:23
"Can God spread a **t** in the wilderness?. . Ps 78:19
crumbs that fall from their masters' **t**." . . Mt 15:27
"Let their **t** become a snare and a trap, . . Rom 11:9
cannot partake of the **t** of the Lord . . . 1 Cor 10:21

TABLES
preaching the word of God to serve **t**. . . . Acts 6:2

TABLET
write them on the **t** of your heart. . . . . Prv 7:3
it is engraved on the **t** of their heart, ... Jer 17:1

TABLETS
that I may give you the **t** of stone, ... Ex 24:12
The **t** were the work of God, and the. . . . Ex 32:16
mountain and put the **t** in the ark. . . . . Dt 10:5

TAIL
will make you the head and not the **t**, . . . Dt 28:13
His **t** swept down a third of the stars. . . . . Rv 12:4

TAKE
You shall not add to it or **t** from it. . . . . . . Dt 12:32
Do not **t** to heart all the things that . . . . . Eccl 7:21
"**T**, eat; this is my body." . . . . Mt 26:26
'Rise, **t** up your bed and walk'? . . . . Mk 2:9
deny himself and **t** up his cross. . . . . Mk 8:34
"**T** nothing for your journey, ... Lk 9:3
down my life that I may **t** it up again. . . . Jn 10:17
we cannot **t** anything out of the world. . . 1 Tm 6:7
T hold of the eternal life to which you. . 1 Tm 6:12

TAKEN
and judgment he was **t** away; . . . . Is 53:8
even what he has will be **t** away. . . . . Mt 13:12
t up from you into heaven, will come. . . . Acts 1:11

TAKES
Blessed is the man who **t** refuge in him! . . Ps 34:8
who **t** away the sin of the world! . . . . Jn 1:29
No one **t** it from me, but I lay it down . . . Jn 10:18
and if anyone **t** away from the words . . . Rv 22:19

TALENTS
to him who owed him ten thousand **t**. . . . Mt 18:24
To one he gave five **t**, to another two, . . . Mt 25:15

TALK
and shall **t** of them when you sit in . . . . Dt 6:7
And my tongue will **t** of your righteous. . Ps 71:24
profit, but mere **t** tends only to poverty. . Prv 14:23
I will no longer **t** much with you, for . . . . Jn 14:30
does not consist in **t** but in power. . . . . 1 Cor 4:20
Let no corrupting **t** come out of . . . . Eph 4:29
nor foolish **t** nor crude joking, ... Eph 5:4
and their **t** will spread like gangrene. . . . 2 Tm 2:17

TAMAR
and her name was **T**. Gn 38:6
house of Perez, whom **T** bore to Judah, . . Ru 4:12
a beautiful sister, whose name was **T**. . . 2 Sm 13:1
So **T** lived, a desolate woman, in. . . . . . 2 Sm 13:20
the father of Perez and Zerah by **T**, ... Mt 1:3

TAMBOURINE
sister of Aaron, took a **t** in her hand, ... Ex 15:20
They sing to the **t** and the lyre and . . . . . . Jb 21:12

TARRY
Those who **t** long over wine; . . . . Prv 23:30
who **t** late into the evening as wine . . . . Is 5:11

TARSHISH
a fleet of ships of **T** at sea with the . . 1 Kgs 10:22
to flee to **T** from the presence of the. . . . . Jon 1:3

TARSUS
So Barnabas went to **T** to look for . . . . . Acts 11:25
Paul replied, "I am a Jew, from **T** in . . . Acts 21:39

TASTE
Oh, **t** and see that the Lord is . . . . Ps 34:8
of the earth, but if salt has lost its **t**, ... Mt 5:13
here who will not **t** death until they . . . . . Mt 16:28
keeps my word, he will never **t** death.'. . . . Jn 8:52
Do not handle, Do not **t**, Do not touch . . Col 2:21
of God he might **t** death for everyone. . . Heb 2:9

TASTED
mixed with gall, but when he **t** it, ... Mt 27:34
who have **t** the heavenly gift, and have. . Heb 6:4
if indeed you have **t** that the Lord is . . . . . 1 Pt 2:3

TAUGHT
O God, from my youth you have **t** me, . . . Ps 71:17
Who **t** him the path of justice, and. . . . . . Is 40:14
he **t** them as one who had authority, ... Mk 1:22
'And they will all be **t** by God.'. . . . . Jn 6:45
in words not **t** by human wisdom . . . . . . 1 Cor 2:13
Let the one who is **t** the word share all . . . Gal 6:6
the traditions that you were **t** by us, . 2 Thes 2:15
hold firm to the trustworthy word as **t**, ... Ti 1:9

TAX
Do not even the **t** collectors do the . . . . . Mt 5:46
"Does your teacher not pay the **t**?" . . . . . Mt 17:24
Show me the coin for the **t**." . . . . Mt 22:19
a Pharisee and the other a **t** collector. . . . Lk 18:10

TAXES
Is it lawful to pay **t** to Caesar, or not?" . . Mt 22:17
t to whom **t** are owed, ... Rom 13:7

TEACH
You shall **t** them diligently to your . . . . Dt 6:7
T me your way, O Lord, ... Ps 27:11
he will **t** you all things and bring to . . . . . Jn 14:26
woman to **t** or to exercise authority. . . . 1 Tm 2:12
who will be able to **t** others also. . . . . 2 Tm 2:2
t what accords with sound doctrine. . . . . Ti 2:1
have no need that anyone should **t** you. . 1 Jn 2:27

TEACHER
"A disciple is not above his **t**, nor a . . . . . Mt 10:24
"**T**, what good deed must I do to have . . Mt 19:16
to be called rabbi, for you have one **t**, . . . Mt 23:8
know that you are a **t** come from God, ... Jn 3:2
If I then, your Lord and **T**, have washed . Jn 13:14
preacher and apostle and **t**, ... 2 Tm 1:11

TEACHERS
Are all **t**? Do all work miracles? . . . . 1 Cor 12:29
evangelists, the shepherds and **t**, ... Eph 4:11
accumulate for themselves **t** to suit . . . . 2 Tm 4:3
by this time you ought to be **t**, ... Heb 5:12
Not many of you should become **t**, ... Jas 3:1
just as there will be false **t** among you, . . . 2 Pt 2:1

TEACHES
whoever does them and **t** them will be . . . Mt 5:19
the one who **t**, in his teaching; . . . . Rom 12:7
all good things with the one who **t**. . . . . . . Gal 6:6
If anyone **t** a different doctrine and . . . . . 1 Tm 6:3

TEACHING
forsake not your mother's **t**,. . . . . Prv 1:8
the **t** of kindness is on her tongue. . . . . . Prv 31:26
"What is this? A new **t** with authority! . . . Mk 1:27
he will know whether the **t** is from God . . Jn 7:17
t and admonishing one another in all . . . Col 3:16
of Scripture, to exhortation, to **t**. . . . . 1 Tm 4:13
and in your **t** show integrity, dignity, ... Ti 2:7
Whoever abides in the **t** has both the . . . . . 2 Jn 9

TEACHINGS
according to human precepts and **t**? . . . . Col 2:22
be led away by diverse and strange **t**, . . . Heb 13:9

TEAR
a time to **t**, and a time to sew; . . . . Eccl 3:7
He will wipe away every **t** from their . . . . . Rv 21:4

TEARS
heard your prayer; I have seen your **t**. . 2 Kgs 20:5
every night I flood my bed with **t**; . . . . Ps 6:6
My **t** have been my food day and night, . . Ps 42:3
put my **t** in your bottle. . . . . Ps 56:8
but folly with her own hands **t** it down. . . Prv 14:1
God will wipe away **t** from . . . . Is 25:8
cover the Lord's altar with **t**, ... Mal 2:13
his feet with her **t** and wiped them . . . . . . Lk 7:38
anguish of heart and with many **t**, ... 2 Cor 2:4
told you and now tell you even with **t**, . . Phil 3:18
I remember your **t**, I long to see you, ... 2 Tm 1:4

TEETH
I have escaped by the skin of my **t**. . . . . . Jb 19:20
Like vinegar to the **t** and smoke to. . . . . Prv 10:26
sour grapes, his **t** shall be set on edge. . Jer 31:30
gave you cleanness of **t** in all your . . . . Am 4:6
will be weeping and gnashing of **t**." . . . . . . Mt 8:12
and they ground their **t** at him. . . . . Acts 7:54

TELL
t of his salvation from day to day. . . . . Ps 96:2
t of all his wondrous works! . . . . Ps 105:2
charged the disciples to **t** no one that . . . Mt 16:20
against you, go and **t** him his fault, ... Mt 18:15
When he comes, he will **t** us all things." . . Jn 4:25
If you are the Christ, **t** us plainly." . . . . Jn 10:24

TEMPER
A man of quick **t** acts foolishly, ... Prv 14:17
but he who has a hasty **t** exalts folly. . . . Prv 14:29

TEMPEST
a shelter from the raging wind and **t**." . . . . Ps 55:8
many days, and no small **t** lay on us, . . Acts 27:20

TEMPLE
Solomon purposed to build a **t** for the . . 2 Chr 2:1
The Lord is in his holy **t**; . . . . Ps 11:4
the Lord and to inquire in his **t**. . . . . Ps 27:4
But the Lord is in his holy **t**; . . . . Hab 2:20
city and set him on the pinnacle of the **t** . . Mt 4:5
something greater than the **t** is here. . . . . . Mt 12:6
Day after day I sat in the **t** teaching, . . . Mt 26:55
After three days they found him in the **t**, . Lk 2:46
Jesus answered them, "Destroy this **t**, ... Jn 2:19
attending the **t** together and breaking . . Acts 2:46
that you are God's **t** and that God's . . . . 1 Cor 3:16
that your body is a **t** of the Holy Spirit. . 1 Cor 6:19
grows into a holy **t** in the Lord. . . . . Eph 2:21
that he takes his seat in the **t** of God, . 2 Thes 2:4
Then God's **t** in heaven was opened, ... Rv 11:19
for its **t** is the Lord God the Almighty . . . Rv 21:22

TEMPLES
does not live in **t** made by man, ... Acts 17:24

TEMPTATION
And lead us not into **t**, but deliver us. . . . Mt 6:13
pray that you may not enter into **t**. . . . . . Mt 26:41
And when the devil had ended every **t**, . . Lk 4:13
No **t** has overtaken you that is not . . . . 1 Cor 10:13
those who desire to be rich fall into **t**, . . 1 Tm 6:9

TEMPTATIONS
For it is necessary that **t** come, but . . . . . . Mt 18:7
"**T** to sin are sure to come, but woe . . . . Lk 17:1

TEMPTED
into the wilderness to be **t** by the devil. . . . Mt 4:1
watch on yourself, lest you too be **t**. . . . . . Gal 6:1
he is able to help those who are being **t**. . Heb 2:18
in every respect has been **t** as we are, . . . Heb 4:15
But each person is **t** when he is lured . . . . Jas 1:14

TEMPTER
t came and said to him, "If you are the . . . . Mt 4:3
that somehow the **t** had tempted you . . 1 Thes 3:5

TEN
the covenant, the **T** Commandments. . . Ex 34:28
heaven will be like **t** virgins who took . . . . Mt 25:1
and give it to him who has the **t** talents. . Mt 25:28
Jesus answered, "Were not **t** cleansed? . . Lk 17:17
And the **t** horns that you saw are **t**. . . . . . Rv 17:12

TENDER
your heart was **t** and you humbled . . . 2 Chr 34:27
my compassion grows warm and **t**. . . . . . Hos 11:8
because of the **t** mercy of our God, ... Lk 1:78
sympathy, brotherly love, a **t** heart, ... 1 Pt 3:8

TENDERHEARTED
Be kind to one another, **t**, forgiving . . . . Eph 4:32

TENDS
Whoever **t** a fig tree will eat its fruit, . . . Prv 27:18
Or who **t** a flock without getting some . . 1 Cor 9:7

TENT
In the **t** of meeting, outside the veil . . . . . Ex 27:21
moving about in a **t** for my dwelling. . . . 2 Sm 7:6
"Enlarge the place of your **t**, and let . . . . . Is 54:2
My **t** is destroyed, and all my cords . . . . Jer 10:20
For we know that if the **t** that is our . . . . 2 Cor 5:1
and more perfect **t** (not made with . . . . . Heb 9:11
and the sanctuary of the **t** of witness in . . Rv 15:5

TENTH
Abram gave him a **t** of everything. . . . . . Gn 14:20
Abraham apportioned a **t** part of . . . . Heb 7:2

TENTMAKERS
for they were **t** by trade. . . . . Acts 18:3

TENTS
Jacob was a quiet man, dwelling in **t**. . . Gn 25:27
shall pitch their **t** by their companies, . . . Nm 1:52
in the twilight and abandoned their **t**, . . 2 Kgs 7:7
If you wish, I will make three **t** here, ... Mt 17:4

TERRIFIED
him walking on the sea, they were **t**, ... Mt 14:26
this, they fell on their faces and were **t**. . . Mt 17:6
hear of wars and tumults, do not be **t**, . . . Lk 21:9
and the rest were **t** and gave glory to . . . . Rv 11:13

TERROR
I will send my **t** before you and will . . . . . Ex 23:27
whispering of many—**t** on every side! . . . . Ps 31:13
You will not fear the **t** of the night, ... Ps 91:5

TEST
Do not fear, for God has come to **t** you . . Ex 20:20
put the Lord your God to the **t**, ... Dt 6:16
try me; **t** my heart and my mind. . . . . Ps 26:2
Let us **t** and examine our ways, ... Lam 3:40
they put God to the **t** and they escape.' . Mal 3:15
not put the Lord your God to the **t**.'" . . . . . . Mt 4:7
"Why put me to the **t**, you hypocrites? . . Mt 22:18
have agreed together to **t** the Spirit of . . Acts 5:9
We must not put Christ to the **t**, ... 1 Cor 10:9
But let each one **t** his own work, ... Gal 6:4
but **t** everything; hold fast what is . . . . 1 Thes 5:21
trial when it comes upon you to **t** you, . . 1 Pt 4:12
but **t** the spirits to see whether they . . . . . 1 Jn 4:1

TESTED
After these things God **t** Abraham . . . . Gn 22:1
For you, O God, have **t** us; . . . . Ps 66:10
for gold, and a man is **t** by his praise. . . Prv 27:21
t first; then let them serve as deacons. . 1 Tm 3:10
By faith Abraham, when he was **t**, ... Heb 11:17

TESTIFIED
(For Jesus himself had **t** that a prophet . Jn 4:44
Jesus was troubled in his spirit, and **t**, . . . Jn 13:21
because we **t** about God that he. . . . . . 1 Cor 15:15

TESTIFIES
that the Holy Spirit **t** to me in every . . . Acts 20:23
And the Spirit is the one who **t**, ... 1 Jn 5:6

TESTIFY
"Though our iniquities **t** against us, act, . Jer 14:7
it hates me because I **t** about it that its. . . . Jn 7:7
And we have seen and **t** that the Father . 1 Jn 4:14

TESTIFYING
t both to Jews and to Greeks of . . . . . . Acts 20:21
t to the kingdom of God and trying . . . Acts 28:23

TESTIMONY
on Mount Sinai, the two tablets of the **t** . Ex 31:18
world as a **t** to all nations, and then. . . . . Mt 24:14
even about this their **t** did not agree. . . Mk 14:59
dust from your feet as a **t** against them." . . Lk 9:5
in him because of the woman's **t**, ... Jn 4:39
and we know that his **t** is true. . . . . Jn 21:24
were giving their **t** to the resurrection . . Acts 4:33
not be ashamed of the **t** about our Lord. . . 2 Tm 1:8
This **t** is true. Therefore rebuke them . . . . . . Ti 1:13
And this is the **t**, that God gave us. . . . . . 1 Jn 5:11
of the word of God and the **t** of Jesus. . . . . Rv 1:9
of the Lamb and by the word of their **t**, . . Rv 12:11

TESTING
For the Lord your God is **t** you, ... Dt 13:3
for a while, and in time of **t** fall away. . . . . Lk 8:13
for you know that the **t** of your faith . . . . . . Jas 1:3

TESTS
The Lord **t** the righteous, ... Ps 11:5
for gold, and the Lord **t** hearts. . . . . Prv 17:3
but to please God who **t** our hearts. . . 1 Thes 2:4

THANK
And now we **t** you, our God, and . . . . . 1 Chr 29:13
Let them **t** the Lord for his. . . . . Ps 107:8
Jesus declared, "I **t** you, Father, ... Mt 11:25
'God, I **t** you that I am not like other . . . . . Lk 18:11
I **t** my God in all my remembrance . . . . Phil 1:3
We always **t** God, the Father of our . . . . Col 1:3

THANKS
his saints, and give **t** to his holy name. . . Ps 30:4
Oh give **t** to the Lord, for he . . . . Ps 118:1
All your works shall give **t** to you, ... Ps 145:10
and when he had given **t** he gave it to . Mt 26:27
on his face at Jesus' feet, giving him **t**. . . Lk 17:16
the loaves, and when he had given **t**, ... Jn 6:11
not honor him as God or give **t** to him, . . Rom 1:21
But **t** be to God, who gives us the . . . . 1 Cor 15:57
But **t** be to God, who in Christ always. . 2 Cor 2:14
T be to God for his inexpressible gift! . . 2 Cor 9:15
giving **t** always and for everything to. . . Eph 5:20
give **t** in all circumstances; for this . . . . 1 Thes 5:18
give glory and honor and **t** to him . . . . Rv 4:9

THANKSGIVING
I will magnify him with **t**. . . . . Ps 69:30
Sing to the Lord with **t**; . . . . Ps 147:7
through us will produce **t** to God. . . . . . . 2 Cor 9:11
but instead let there be **t**. . . . . Eph 5:4
as you were taught, abounding in **t**. . . . . . . Col 2:7
For what **t** can we return to God for . . 1 Thes 3:9
received with **t** by those who believe. . . . 1 Tm 4:3
glory and wisdom and **t** and honor and . . Rv 7:12

Mary Magdalene came to the **t** early,..... Jn 20:1

TOMBS
For you are like whitewashed **t**, which... Mt 23:27
The **t** also were opened. And many ..... Mt 27:52
met him out of the **t** a man with an...... Mk 5:2
all who are in the **t** will hear his voice .... Jn 5:28

TOMORROW
Do not boast about **t**, for you do not.... Prv 27:1
"Let us eat and drink, for **t** we die."...... Is 22:13
"Therefore do not be anxious about **t**,... Mt 6:34
"Let us eat and drink, for **t** we die."... 1 Cor 15:32
yet you do not know what **t** will bring... Jas 4:14

TONGUE
"Every one who laps the water with his **t**,.. Jgs 7:5
Keep your **t** from evil and your lips ..... Ps 34:13
but the **t** of the wise brings healing. .... Prv 12:18
Death and life are in the power of the **t**,.. Prv 18:21
and the **t** of the mute sing for joy. .... Is 35:6
bow, every **t** shall swear allegiance.'..... Is 45:23
ears were opened, his **t** was released,... Mk 7:35
me, and every **t** shall confess to God.".. Rom 14:11
For one who speaks in a **t** speaks not.. 1 Cor 14:2
than ten thousand words in a **t**. ...... 1 Cor 14:19
and every **t** confess that Jesus Christ is.. Phil 2:11
does not bridle his **t** but deceives his ... Jas 1:26
but no human being can tame the **t**...... Jas 3:8
let him keep his **t** from evil and his ..... 1 Pt 3:10

TONGUES
and arrows, whose **t** are sharp swords.... Ps 57:4
speak in other **t** as the Spirit gave ...... Acts 2:4
telling in our own **t** the mighty works ... Acts 2:11
them speaking in **t** and extolling God.. Acts 10:46
began speaking in **t** and prophesying... Acts 19:6
Do all speak with **t**? Do all interpret?.. 1 Cor 12:30
If I speak in the **t** of men and of....... 1 Cor 13:1
Now I want you all to speak in **t**, but... 1 Cor 14:5
Thus **t** are a sign not for believers .... 1 Cor 14:22
and do not forbid speaking in **t**....... 1 Cor 14:39

TOOTH
eye for eye, **t** for **t**, hand............... Ex 21:24
trouble is like a bad **t** or a foot that.... Prv 25:19

TORCH
and a flaming **t** passed between these .. Gn 15:17

TORCHES
and empty jars, with **t** inside the jars.... Jgs 7:16
the throne were burning seven **t** of fire, ... Rv 4:5

TORMENT
you come here to **t** us before the time?". Mt 8:29
High God? I beg you, do not **t** me."...... Lk 8:28
lest they also come into this place of **t**.' . Lk 16:28
t was like the **t** of a scorpion............ Rv 9:5

TORMENTED
harmful spirit from the LORD **t**........ 1 Sm 16:14
they will be **t** day and night forever..... Rv 20:10

TORN
for the LORD has **t** the kingdom....... 1 Sm 28:17
for he has **t** us, that he may heal us; ..... Hos 6:1
the curtain of the temple was **t** in two,.. Mt 27:51
there were so many, the net was not **t**.... Jn 21:11

TORTURED
Some were **t**, refusing to accept .... Heb 11:35

TOUCH
to herself, "If I only **t** his garment, ... Mt 9:21
diseases pressed around him to **t** him..... Mk 3:10
a blind man and begged him to **t** him. .. Mk 8:22
children to him that he might **t** them, ... Mk 10:13
T me, and see. For a spirit does not..... Lk 24:39
the Lord, and **t** no unclean thing; ..... 2 Cor 6:17
and the evil one does not **t** him......... 1 Jn 5:18

TOUCHED
Jesus stretched out his hand and **t** him, ... Mt 8:3
He **t** her hand, and the fever left her,..... Mt 8:15
t their eyes, saying, "According to your.. Mt 9:29
And as many as **t** it were made well..... Mt 14:36
"Who was it that **t** me?" When all .... Lk 8:45
you have not come to what may be **t**,.. Heb 12:18
looked upon and have **t** with our hands,.. 1 Jn 1:1

TOWER
ourselves a city and a **t** with its top...... Gn 11:4
refuge, a strong **t** against the enemy...... Ps 61:3
name of the LORD is a strong **t**; .... Prv 18:10
eighteen on whom the **t** in Siloam fell.... Lk 13:4
For which of you, desiring to build a **t**,.. Lk 14:28

TRADITION
your disciples break the **t** of the elders?.. Mt 15:2
So for the sake of your **t** you have .... Mt 15:6
empty deceit, according to human **t**,..... Col 2:8
in accord with the **t** that you received .. 2 Thes 3:6

TRADITIONS
there are many other **t** that they observe,.. Mk 7:4
maintain the **t** even as I delivered...... 1 Cor 11:2
zealous was I for the **t** of my fathers..... Gal 1:14
hold to the **t** that you were taught... 2 Thes 2:15

TRAIN
T up a child in the way he should go; ... Prv 22:6
Rather **t** yourself for godliness;......... 1 Tm 4:7

TRAINED
he is fully **t** will be like his teacher....... Lk 6:40
being **t** in the words of the faith and.... 1 Tm 4:6
of discernment **t** by constant practice... Heb 5:14
to those who have been **t** by it. .... Heb 12:11

TRAINING
for while bodily **t** is of some value,...... 1 Tm 4:8
t us to renounce ungodliness and......... Ti 2:12

TRANCE
they were preparing it, he fell into a **t**.. Acts 10:10
praying in the temple, I fell into a **t** ... Acts 22:17

TRANSFIGURED
And he was **t** before them, and his face .. Mt 17:2

TRANSFORM
who will **t** our lowly body............. Phil 3:21

TRANSFORMED
but be **t** by the renewal of your mind,.. Rom 12:2
are being **t** into the same image from.. 2 Cor 3:18

TRANSGRESS
purposed that my mouth will not **t**....... Ps 17:3
the waters might not **t** his command, ... Prv 8:29
that no one **t** and wrong his brother .. 1 Thes 4:6

TRANSGRESSED
for we have greatly **t** in this matter...... Ezr 10:13
the shepherds **t** against me;............. Jer 2:8
All Israel has **t** your law and turned ...... Dn 9:11
But like Adam they **t** the covenant; ...... Hos 6:7

TRANSGRESSION
Make me know my **t** and my sin......... Jb 13:23
Blessed is the one whose **t** is forgiven, ... Ps 32:1
Whoever loves **t** loves strife; he who .... Prv 17:19
stricken for the **t** of my people? .... Is 53:8
but where there is no law there is no **t**... Rom 4:15

TRANSGRESSIONS
For I know my **t**, and my sin is ever...... Ps 51:3
so far does he remove our **t** from us.... Ps 103:12
Whoever conceals his **t** will not........ Prv 28:13
who blots out your **t** for my own sake,.. Is 43:25
But he was pierced for our **t**;............ Is 53:5
It was added because of **t**, until the..... Gal 3:19

TRANSGRESSORS
to death and was numbered with the **t**; .. Is 53:12
'And he was numbered with the **t**.'...... Lk 22:37
sin and are convicted by the law as **t**..... Jas 2:9

TRAP
Keep me from the **t** that they have laid.. Ps 141:9
of the Herodians, to **t** him in his talk..... Mk 12:13
day come upon you suddenly like a **t**.... Lk 21:34

TREAD
it is he who will **t** down our foes........ Ps 60:12
he will **t** our iniquities underfoot. .... Mi 7:19
He will **t** the winepress of the fury of.... Rv 19:15

TREASURE
You fill their womb with **t**; .... Ps 17:14
house of the righteous there is much **t**,.. Prv 15:6
than great **t** and trouble with it......... Prv 15:16
fear of the LORD is Zion's **t**.............. Is 33:6
For where your **t** is, there your heart..... Mt 6:21
out of his good **t** brings forth good,..... Mt 12:35
poor, and you will have **t** in heaven;..... Mt 19:21
But we have this **t** in jars of clay, ... 2 Cor 4:7
thus storing up **t** for themselves as .... 1 Tm 6:19
You have laid up **t** in the last days........ Jas 5:3

TREASURED
to be a people for his **t** possession, ... Dt 7:6
But Mary **t** up all these things,........... Lk 2:19

TREASURES
T gained by wickedness do not profit,... Prv 10:2
but lay up for yourselves **t** in heaven, ... Mt 6:20
in whom are hidden all the **t** of wisdom .. Col 2:3

TREASURY
open to you his good **t**, the heavens,.... Dt 28:12
"It is not lawful to put them into the **t**, ... Mt 27:6
These words he spoke in the **t**, as he..... Jn 8:20

TREE
The **t** of life was in the midst of the...... Gn 2:9
but of the **t** of the knowledge of good ... Gn 2:17
shall not remain all night on the **t**, ... Dt 21:23
He is like a **t** planted by streams of .... Ps 1:3
The fruit of the righteous is a **t** of life,.. Prv 11:30
Every **t** therefore that does not bear ..... Mt 3:10
for the **t** is known by its fruit. .... Mt 12:33
bore our sins in his body on the **t**, ... 1 Pt 2:24
I will grant to eat of the **t** of life,.......... Rv 2:7
have the right to the **t** of life and .... Rv 22:14

TREES
shall not destroy its **t** by wielding an.... Dt 20:19
Then shall all the **t** of the forest sing .... Ps 96:12
The **t** of the LORD are watered......... Ps 104:16
"Look at the fig tree, and all the **t**....... Lk 21:29
fruitless **t** in late autumn, twice dead, ... Jude 12

TREMBLE
The LORD reigns; let the peoples **t**!....... Ps 99:1
T, O earth, at the presence of the Lord,.. Ps 114:7
they do not **t** as they blaspheme the.... 2 Pt 2:10

TREMBLED
smoking, the people were afraid and **t**,.. Ex 20:18
for his heart **t** for the ark of God....... 1 Sm 4:13
of him the guards **t** and became like .... Mt 28:4

TREMBLES
and contrite in spirit and **t** at my word.... Is 66:2

TREMBLING
came in fear and **t** and fell down before.. Mk 5:33
how you received him with fear and **t**... 2 Cor 7:15

TRESPASS
But the free gift is not like the **t**. For if .. Rom 5:15
For if, because of one man's **t**, death... Rom 5:17
Rather through their **t** salvation has.... Rom 11:11

TRESPASSES
For if you forgive others their **t**, your..... Mt 6:14
neither will your Father forgive your **t**. ... Mt 6:15
delivered up for our **t** and raised for ... Rom 4:25
following many **t** brought justification. . Rom 5:16
not counting their **t** against them, ... 2 Cor 5:19
we were dead in our **t**, made us alive ... Eph 2:5

who, on finding one pearl of great **v**, . . . Mt 13:46

VANISH
So he made their days **v** like a breath,. . . Ps 78:33
for the heavens **v** like smoke, the earth. . . . Is 51:6

VANISHED
And he **v** from their sight. . . . . Lk 24:31
The sky **v** like a scroll that is being. . . . . . . Rv 6:14

VANITY
V of vanities, says the Preacher, ... Eccl 1:2
all is **v** and a striving after wind. . . . . Eccl 1:14

VASHTI
But Queen **V** refused to come at the . . . . . Est 1:12

VEGETABLES
let us be given **v** to eat and water to. . . . . Dn 1:12
while the weak person eats only **v**. . . . . Rom 14:2

VEIL
And the **v** shall separate for you the . . . . Ex 26:33
with them, he put a **v** over his face. . . . . Ex 34:33
turns to the Lord, the **v** is removed. . . . 2 Cor 3:16

VENGEANCE
V is mine, and recompense, for. . . . . Dt 32:35
O God of **v**, shine forth! . . . . Ps 94:1
For the LORD has a day of **v**, ... Is 34:8
for these are days of **v**, to fulfill all. . . . . . Lk 21:22
"**V** is mine, I will repay, ... Rom 12:19
in flaming fire, inflicting **v** on those . . . 2 Thes 1:8
"**V** is mine; I will repay." . . . . Heb 10:30

VESSEL
the same lump one **v** for honorable use . . Rom 9:21
he will be a **v** for honorable use,. . . . . . . 2 Tm 2:21

VEXATION
The **v** of a fool is known at once, but. . . . Prv 12:16
Remove **v** from your heart, and put . . . . Eccl 11:10

VICTORY
but the **v** belongs to the LORD. . . . . Prv 21:31
quench, until he brings justice to **v**; . . . . . Mt 12:20
"Death is swallowed up in **v**.". . . . . 1 Cor 15:54
thanks be to God, who gives us the **v** . . 1 Cor 15:57
the **v** that has overcome the world. . . . . . . 1 Jn 5:4

VINDICATE
V me, O LORD, for I have. . . . . Ps 26:1
For the LORD will **v** his people . . . . Ps 135:14

VINE
Yet I planted you a choice **v**, wholly. . . . . . Jer 2:21
they shall blossom like the **v**;. . . . . Hos 14:7
of this fruit of the **v** until that day . . . . . Mt 26:29
"I am the true **v**, and my Father is . . . . Jn 15:1
the clusters from the **v** of the earth,. . . . . Rv 14:18

VINEYARD
Naboth the Jezreelite had a **v** in. . . . . . . 1 Kgs 21:1
My beloved had a **v** on a very fertile . . . . Is 5:1
Many shepherds have destroyed my **v**; . . Jer 12:10
in the morning to hire laborers for his **v**. . Mt 20:1
said, 'Son, go and work in the **v** today.' . . Mt 21:28
Who plants a **v** without eating any of . . . 1 Cor 9:7

VIOLENCE
sight, and the earth was filled with **v**. . . . . Gn 6:11
in his death, although he had done no **v**, . Is 53:9
V shall no more be heard in your land, . . Is 60:18
Put away **v** and oppression,. . . . . Ezk 45:9
the blood of man and **v** to the earth,. . . . Hab 2:17

VIPER
a **v** came out because of the heat and . . Acts 28:3

VIPERS
he said to them, "You brood of **v**!. . . . . Mt 3:7
You serpents, you brood of **v**, how. . . . . . Mt 23:33

VIRGIN
Behold, the **v** shall conceive and bear . . . . . Is 7:14
"Behold, the **v** shall conceive and bear . . . Mt 1:23
"How will this be, since I am a **v**?" . . . . Lk 1:34
to present you as a pure **v** to Christ. . . . 2 Cor 11:2

VIRGINS
will be like ten **v** who took their lamps . . . Mt 25:1

VISIBLE
is exposed by the light, it becomes **v**, . . . Eph 5:13
was not made out of things that are **v**. . . Heb 11:3

VISION
Abram in a **v**: "Fear not, Abram, I am . . . . Gn 15:1
Where there is no prophetic **v**. . . . . Prv 29:18
The oracle concerning the valley of **v**. . . . . . Is 22:1
has been told is true, but seal up the **v**, . Dn 8:26
commanded them, "Tell no one the **v**, ... Mt 17:9
that they had even seen a **v** of angels, . . Lk 24:23
praying, and in a trance I saw a **v**, ... Acts 11:5
And a **v** appeared to Paul in the night: . Acts 16:9
was not disobedient to the heavenly **v**, . Acts 26:19

VISIONS
were opened, and I saw **v** of God. . . . . Ezk 1:1
had understanding in all **v** and dreams.. . . Dn 1:17
and your young men shall see **v**,. . . . . . . Acts 2:17
I will go on to **v** and revelations of the . . 2 Cor 12:1

VISIT
see you sick or in prison and **v** you?' . . . Mt 25:39
to **v** orphans and widows in their . . . . Jas 1:27

VISITATION
you did not know the time of your **v**." . . . Lk 19:44

VISITED
for he has **v** and redeemed his people. . . . Lk 1:68
"God has **v** his people!" . . . . Lk 7:16
related how God first **v** the Gentiles, . . . Acts 15:14

VOICE
there came a **v** to him and said, ... 1 Kgs 19:13
in the morning you hear my **v**; . . . . Ps 5:3
for a bird of the air will carry your **v**,. . Eccl 10:20
thresholds shook at the **v** of him who . . . . . Is 6:4
who is of the truth listens to my **v**." . . . . . Jn 18:37
Spirit says, "Today, if you hear his **v**, ... Heb 3:7

VOID
The earth was without form and **v**,. . . . . Gn 1:2
tradition you have made **v** the word . . . . . Mt 15:6
for one dot of the Law to become **v** . . . . . Lk 16:17
faith is null and the promise is **v**. . . . . . . Rom 4:14
by God, so as to make the promise **v**. . . . Gal 3:17

VOW
If a man vows a **v** to the LORD, ... Nm 30:2
When you **v** a **v** to God, do not. . . . . Eccl 5:4

VOWS
my **v** I will perform before those who . . . Ps 22:25

WAGE
The **w** of the righteous leads to life . . . . Prv 10:16
wrong as the **w** for their wrongdoing. . . . 2 Pt 2:13

WAGES
who oppress the hired worker in his **w**,. . . Mal 3:5
'Call the laborers and pay them their **w**, . Mt 20:8
and be content with your **w**." . . . . Lk 3:14
For the **w** of sin is death, but the free . . Rom 6:23
"The laborer deserves his **w**.". . . . . 1 Tm 5:18

WAIT
W for the LORD; be strong,. . . . . Ps 27:14
W for the LORD and keep his way,. . . . . . . Ps 37:34
God alone, O my soul, **w** in silence, ... Ps 62:5
but they who **w** for the LORD . . . . Is 40:31
one should **w** quietly for the salvation. . Lam 3:26
If it seems slow, **w** for it; it will surely . . . Hab 2:3
but to **w** for the promise of the Father,. . Acts 1:4
groan inwardly as we **w** eagerly for. . . . Rom 8:23
as you **w** for the revealing of our Lord. . . 1 Cor 1:7
we ourselves eagerly **w** for the hope. . . . . Gal 5:5
and to **w** for his Son from heaven, ... 1 Thes 1:10

WAITED
I **w** patiently for the LORD; . . . . Ps 40:1
this is our God; we have **w** for him, ... Is 25:9

WAITING
w for our blessed hope, the appearing . . . . Ti 2:13
but to save those who are eagerly **w**. . . Heb 9:28
w for and hastening the coming of the . . 2 Pt 3:12

WAITS
For God alone my soul **w** in silence;. . . . . . Ps 62:1
Blessed is he who **w** and arrives at the . . Dn 12:12
For the creation **w** with eager longing. . Rom 8:19

WALK
w before me, and be blameless, ... Gn 17:1
God, to **w** in all his ways, to love him, . . . Dt 10:12
I will **w** before the LORD in . . . . Ps 116:9
"This is the way, **w** in it,". . . . . Is 30:21
'We will not **w** in it.'. . . . . Jer 6:16
are forgiven,' or to say, 'Rise and **w**'? . . . . . Mt 9:5
W while you have the light, lest . . . . Jn 12:35
Christ of Nazareth, rise up and **w**!" . . . . . . Acts 3:6
we too might **w** in newness of life. . . . . . . Rom 6:4
who **w** not according to the flesh but . . . Rom 8:4
for we **w** by faith, not by sight. . . . . 2 Cor 5:7
But I say, **w** by the Spirit, and you . . . . . . Gal 5:16
W as children of light . . . . Eph 5:8
But if we **w** in the light, as he is in . . . . 1 Jn 1:7
And this is love, that we **w** according . . . . . 2 Jn 6
By its light will the nations **w**, and . . . . . . Rv 21:24

WALKED
Enoch **w** with God, and he was not,. . . . . Gn 5:24
Noah **w** with God. . . . . Gn 6:9
The people who **w** in darkness have . . . . . . Is 9:2
healed, and he took up his bed and **w**. . . . . Jn 5:9
in which you once **w**, following the . . . . . . Eph 2:2

WALKING
the LORD God **w** in the garden. . . . . Gn 3:8
night he came to them, **w** on the sea. . . . Mt 14:25
before God, **w** blamelessly in all the. . . . . . Lk 1:6
you eat, you are no longer **w** in love. . . Rom 14:15

WALKS
He who **w** blamelessly and does what. . . . Ps 15:2
Whoever **w** in uprightness fears the. . . . . Prv 14:2
The one who **w** in the darkness does. . . . Jn 12:35
and **w** in the darkness, and does not . . . . 1 Jn 2:11

WALL
great shout, and the **w** fell down flat, . . . Jos 6:20
his face to the **w** and prayed to the . . . 2 Kgs 20:2
Come, let us build the **w** of Jerusalem, . . Neh 2:17
a man to batter him, like a leaning **w**, ... Ps 62:3
down through an opening in the **w**,. . . . Acts 9:25
in his flesh the dividing **w** of hostility . . . Eph 2:14
It had a great, high **w**, with twelve . . . . . . Rv 21:12

WANDER
and he made them **w** in the wilderness. . Nm 32:13
I would **w** far away; I would lodge . . . . . . Ps 55:7
her ways **w**, and she does not know it. . . . Prv 5:6
Therefore the people **w** like sheep;. . . . . . Zec 10:2

WANDERING
was not worthy—**w** about in deserts . . . Heb 11:38
a sinner from his **w** will save his soul. . . . Jas 5:20

WANT
is my shepherd; I shall not **w**. . . . . Ps 23:1
Whoever gives to the poor will not **w**,. . Prv 28:27
"What do you **w** me to do for you?" . . . Mt 20:32
Twelve, "Do you **w** to go away as well?". . Jn 6:67
For I do not do what I **w**, but I do . . . . . Rom 7:15

WAR
"There is a noise of **w** in the camp.". . . . . Ex 32:17
though **w** arise against me, yet I will . . . . Ps 27:3
by counsel; by wise guidance wage **w**. . Prv 20:18
a time for **w**, and a time for peace. . . . . . Eccl 3:8
Wisdom is better than weapons of **w**, . . Eccl 9:18

neither shall they learn **w** anymore........ Is 2:4
this horn made **w** with the saints and .... Dn 7:21
out to encounter another king in **w**,..... Lk 14:31
another law waging **w** against the law.. Rom 7:23
we are not waging **w** according to.... 2 Cor 10:3
flesh, which wage **w** against your soul....1 Pt 2:11
Now **w** arose in heaven, Michael and..... Rv 12:7
They will make **w** on the Lamb, and..... Rv 17:14
righteousness he judges and makes **w**....Rv 19:11

WARFARE
and cry to her that her **w** is ended,...... Is 40:2
For the weapons of our **w** are not .... 2 Cor 10:4
by them you may wage the good **w**,....1 Tm 1:18

WARM
him, the flesh of the child became **w**. .2 Kgs 4:34
Again, if two lie together, they keep **w**,.. Eccl 4:11

WARN
I will **w** you whom to fear: fear him ...... Lk 12:5
five brothers—so that he may **w** them, .. Lk 16:28
an enemy, but **w** him as a brother.... 2 Thes 3:15

WARNED
Moreover, by them is your servant **w**; .... Ps 19:11
And being **w** in a dream not to return.... Mt 2:12
Who **w** you to flee from the wrath to .....Mt 3:7
refused him who **w** them on earth,.....Heb 12:25

WARS
He makes **w** cease to the end of the .....Ps 46:9
And you will hear of **w** and rumors ..... Mt 24:6

WASH
w me, and I shall be whiter than snow.... Ps 51:7
W yourselves; make yourselves clean;..... Is 1:16
O Jerusalem, **w** your heart from evil,.... Jer 4:14
to him, "Go, **w** in the pool of Siloam"......Jn 9:7
and began to **w** the disciples' feet .... Jn 13:5
be baptized and **w** away your sins,.... Acts 22:16

WASHED
But you were **w**, you were sanctified, .. 1 Cor 6:11
They have **w** their robes and made ...... Rv 7:14

WASHING
cleansed her by the **w** of water with ... Eph 5:26
by the **w** of regeneration and renewal..... Ti 3:5

WATCH
keeping **w** on the evil and the good..... Prv 15:3
W therefore, for you know neither the... Mt 25:13
W and pray that you may not enter.....Mt 26:41
keeping **w** over their flock by night........Lk 2:8
Keep a close **w** on yourself and on..... 1 Tm 4:16
they are keeping **w** over your souls,.... Heb 13:17

WATCHED
as in the days when God **w** over me,.....Jb 29:2
for the high official is **w** by a higher,..... Eccl 5:8
And they **w** Jesus, to see whether he .... Mk 3:2

WATCHES
Unless the LORD **w** over the city,.........Ps 127:1
The LORD **w** over the sojourners;........Ps 146:9

WATCHFUL
Be **w**, stand firm in the faith, act like .. 1 Cor 16:13
prayer, being **w** in it with thanksgiving.... Col 4:2

WATCHMAN
the Lord said to me: "Go, set a **w**; ....Is 21:6
I have made you a **w** for the house of... Ezk 3:17
The prophet is the **w** of Ephraim with ... Hos 9:8

WATER
but there was no **w** for the people........Ex 17:1
I am poured out like **w**, and all my...... Ps 22:14
lofty abode you **w** the mountains;..... Ps 104:13
if he is thirsty, give him **w** to drink,..... Prv 25:21
He is like a tree planted by **w**, that........Jer 17:8
the feast tasted the **w** now become wine, .Jn 2:9
unless one is born of **w** and the Spirit, ...Jn 3:5
he would have given you living **w**." ......Jn 4:10
his heart will flow rivers of living **w**.'".....Jn 7:38
persons, were brought safely through **w**. .1 Pt 3:20
he who came by **w** and blood—Jesus ....1 Jn 5:6
will guide them to springs of living **w**,.... Rv 7:17
showed me the river of the **w** of life,..... Rv 22:1

WATERED
I planted, Apollos **w**, but God gave .... 1 Cor 3:6

WATERS
was hovering over the face of the **w**.......Gn 1:2
the flood of **w** came upon the earth...... Gn 7:6
sea dry land, and the **w** were divided.... Ex 14:21
He leads me beside still **w**...............Ps 23:2
words of a man's mouth are deep **w**;.... Prv 18:4
Many **w** cannot quench love, neither ......Sg 8:7
When you pass through the **w**, I will ..... Is 43:2
spring of water, whose **w** do not fail...... Is 58:11
forsaken me, the fountain of living **w**, ...Jer 2:13
glory of the LORD as the **w** cover ....Hab 2:14
On that day living **w** shall flow out...... Zec 14:8
who plants nor he who **w** is anything,...1 Cor 3:7

WAX
are out of joint; my heart is like **w**;...... Ps 22:14
as **w** melts before fire, so the wicked.....Ps 68:2

WAY
But he knows the **w** that I take; ....Jb 23:10
Commit your **w** to the LORD; ....Ps 37:5
Keep your **w** far from her, and do not .... Prv 5:8
There is a **w** that seems right to a man,. .Prv 16:25
the **w** of an eagle in the sky, the **w**..... Prv 30:19
the **w** the spirit comes to the bones in .. Eccl 11:5
"This is the **w**, walk in it," ....Is 30:21
"My **w** is hidden from the LORD,......... Is 40:27
Jesus said to him, "I am the **w**, and ...... Jn 14:6
if he found any belonging to the **W**, ... Acts 9:2
new and living **w** that he opened for .. Heb 10:20

WAYS
please show me now your **w**, that I ..... Ex 33:13
work is perfect, for all his **w** are justice... Dt 32:4
Make me to know your **w**, ...Ps 25:4
I will teach transgressors your **w**, ...Ps 51:13
In all your **w** acknowledge him,.......... Prv 3:6
neither are your **w** my **w**, ... Is 55:8
the **w** of the LORD are right, ...Hos 14:9
man, unstable in all his **w**. .... Jas 1:8

WEAK
For while we were still **w**, at the right ...Rom 5:6
As for the one who is **w** in faith,........Rom 14:1
to bear with the failings of the **w**,.......Rom 15:1
God chose what is **w** in the world to ...1 Cor 1:27
become a stumbling block to the **w**.... 1 Cor 8:9
To the **w** I became **w**, that I.......... 1 Cor 9:22
For when I am **w**, then I am strong....2 Cor 12:10
hands and strengthen your **w** knees,... Heb 12:12

WEAKER
that seem to be **w** are indispensable,. .1 Cor 12:22

WEAKNESS
Likewise the Spirit helps us in our **w**....Rom 8:26
the **w** of God is stronger than men.....1 Cor 1:25
It is sown in **w**; it is raised in power....1 Cor 15:43
for my power is made perfect in **w**." .. 2 Cor 12:9
For he was crucified in **w**, but lives ... 2 Cor 13:4
since he himself is beset with **w**........ Heb 5:2

WEAKNESSES
I will not boast, except of my **w**—..... 2 Cor 12:5
to sympathize with our **w**, but one who. .Heb 4:15

WEALTH
have not asked for possessions, **w**, honor, . 2 Chr 1:11
must perish and leave their **w** to others...Ps 49:10
Honor the LORD with your **w** ....Prv 3:9
W gained hastily will dwindle,.......... Prv 13:11
may bring to you the **w** of the nations,... Is 60:11
have **w** to enter the kingdom of God!" . Mk 10:23
to receive power and **w** and wisdom..... Rv 5:12

WEAPONS
Wisdom is better than **w** of war, but ....Eccl 9:18
with the **w** of righteousness for the.... 2 Cor 6:7
For the **w** of our warfare are not of ... 2 Cor 10:4

WEAR
the earth will **w** out like a garment,.......Is 51:6
or 'What shall we **w**?' ....Mt 6:31

WEARINESS
and much study is a **w** of the flesh..... Eccl 12:12
But you say, 'What a **w** this is,' ....Mal 1:13

WEARY
in a dry and **w** land where there is no.... Ps 63:1
I am **w** with my crying out; my throat....Ps 69:3
And let us not grow **w** of doing good,....Gal 6:9
do not grow **w** in doing good........ 2 Thes 3:13
you may not grow **w** or fainthearted.....Heb 12:3

WEDDING
"Can the **w** guests mourn as long as.....Mt 9:15
a man who had no **w** garment.......... Mt 22:11
day there was a **w** at Cana in Galilee, ... Jn 2:1

WEEK
the dawn of the first day of the **w**,....... Mt 28:1
On the first day of every **w**, each of....1 Cor 16:2

WEEP
a time to **w**, and a time to laugh;....... Eccl 3:4
in Jerusalem; you shall **w** no more........Is 30:19
"Blessed are you who **w** now, for .... Lk 6:21
on her and said to her, "Do not **w**." ...... Lk 7:13
of Jerusalem, do not **w** for me,.........Lk 23:28
w with those who **w**..................Rom 12:15

WEEPING
W may tarry for the night, but joy ....Ps 30:5
He who goes out **w**, bearing the seed... Ps 126:6
In that place there will be **w** and......... Mt 8:12
w, she began to wet his feet with her ....Lk 7:38
And all were **w** and mourning for her,....Lk 8:52
But Mary stood **w** outside the tomb,..... Jn 20:11

WEIGHED
knowledge, and by him actions are **w**....1 Sm 2:3
"Oh that my vexation were **w**, and all .....Jb 6:2
in a measure and **w** the mountains in ....Is 40:12
you have been **w** in the balances and ... Dn 5:27
your hearts be **w** down with dissipation. . Lk 21:34

WEIGHT
for us an eternal **w** of glory beyond... 2 Cor 4:17
let us also lay aside every **w**,........... Heb 12:1

WELCOME
did we see you a stranger and **w** you,.. Mt 25:38
the one who is weak in faith, **w** him, ...Rom 14:1
Therefore **w** one another as Christ has . Rom 15:7

WELCOMED
when Jesus returned, the crowd **w** him, . Lk 8:40
he came to Galilee, the Galileans **w** ......Jn 4:45

WELL
that it may go **w** with you and with..... Dt 4:40
flowing water from your own **w**......... Prv 5:15
When it goes **w** with the righteous,.....Prv 11:10
righteous that it shall be **w** with them, ...Is 3:10
"Those who are **w** have no need of a.....Mt 9:12
His master said to him, '**W** done, good .. Mt 25:21
"Daughter, your faith has made you **w**; .. Mk 5:34
Jacob's **w** was there; so Jesus, wearied....Jn 4:6

WEPT
times." And he went out and **w** bitterly...Mt 26:75
Jesus **w**...............................Jn 11:35

WEST
as far as the east is from the **w**, so far.. Ps 103:12
come from east and **w** and recline at..... Mt 8:11

WHEAT
weeds among the **w** and went away..... Mt 13:25

WITHER

Their leaves will not **w**, nor their fruit . . Ezk 47:12
"How did the fig tree **w** at once?" . . . . . . Mt 21:20

WITHERS

renewed; in the evening it fades and **w**. . Ps 90:6
The grass **w**, the flower fades when . . . . . . Is 40:7
The grass **w**, and the flower falls, ... 1 Pt 1:24

WITHHOLD

No good thing does he **w** from those . . . Ps 84:11
Do not **w** good from those to whom it . . Prv 3:27
if you **w** forgiveness from any, it is . . . . . . Jn 20:23

WITNESS

"You shall not bear false **w** against. . . . . . Ex 20:16
"A single **w** shall not suffice against. . . . . Dt 19:15
A truthful **w** saves lives, but one. . . . . . . Prv 14:25
You shall not bear false **w**, ... Mt 19:18
but came to bear **w** about the light. . . . . . . Jn 1:8
If I alone bear **w** about myself, my . . . . Jn 5:31
while their conscience also bears **w**, . . . Rom 2:15
The Spirit himself bears **w** with our . . . . Rom 8:16
Holy Spirit also bears **w** to us;. . . . . Heb 10:15
word of God and for the **w** they had . . . . . Rv 6:9

WITNESSES

by the evidence of two or three **w**.. . . . . . Mt 18:16
though many false **w** came forward. . . . Mt 26:60
you will be my **w** in Jerusalem and in . . . Acts 1:8
on the evidence of two or three **w**. . . . . 1 Tm 5:19
I will grant authority to my two **w**, ... Rv 11:3

WIVES

And his **w** turned away his heart. . . . . . . 1 Kgs 11:3
W, submit to your own husbands, ... Eph 5:22
Husbands, love your **w**, as Christ . . . . . . Eph 5:25
Their **w** likewise must be dignified,. . . . . . 1 Tm 3:11
Likewise, **w**, be subject to your own. . . . . . 1 Pt 3:1

WOE

W to those who join house to house,. . . . . . Is 5:8
W to those who call evil good and. . . . . . . Is 5:20
"**W** to you, Chorazin! . . . . Mt 11:21
"**W** to the world for temptations to sin!. . . Mt 18:7
but **w** to the one by whom the . . . . Mt 18:7
"But **w** to you, scribes and Pharisees, . . . Mt 23:13
W to them! For they walked in the way . . Jude 11
"**W**, **w**, **w** to those . . . . Rv 8:13

WOMAN

made into a **w** and brought her to . . . . . . Gn 2:22
"A **w** shall not wear a man's garment, ... Dt 22:5
He gives the barren **w** a home, ... Ps 113:9
A gracious **w** gets honor, and . . . . Prv 11:16
but a **w** who fears the LORD . . . . Prv 31:30
who looks at a **w** with lustful intent . . . . . . Mt 5:28
And instantly the **w** was made well. . . . . . . Mt 9:22
and what sort of **w** this is who is . . . . Lk 7:39
"**W**, you are freed from your . . . . Lk 13:12
A **w** from Samaria came to draw water. . . . Jn 4:7
Pharisees brought a **w** who had been . . . . . Jn 8:3
"**W**, why are you weeping?". . . . . Jn 20:13
For a married **w** is bound by law . . . . Rom 7:2
of God, but **w** is the glory of man. . . . . . 1 Cor 11:7
in the Lord **w** is not independent of. . . . 1 Cor 11:11
God sent forth his Son, born of **w**, ... Gal 4:4
Let a **w** learn quietly with all . . . . 1 Tm 2:11
I do not permit a **w** to teach or to . . . . . 1 Tm 2:12
showing honor to the **w** as the weaker . . . 1 Pt 3:7

WOMB

and from my mother's **w** you have. . . . . . Ps 22:10
the fruit of the **w** a reward. . . . . Ps 127:3
knitted me together in my mother's **w**. . Ps 139:13
The LORD called me from the **w**, ... Is 49:1
"Before I formed you in the **w** I knew . . . . . Jer 1:5
Holy Spirit, even from his mother's **w**. . . . . . Lk 1:15
the baby in my **w** leaped for joy.. . . . . Lk 1:44
him, "Blessed is the **w** that bore you,. . . . . Lk 11:27
into his mother's **w** and be born?" . . . . Jn 3:4

WOMEN

The wisest of **w** builds her house,. . . . . Prv 14:1
Rise up, you **w** who are at ease, hear. . . . . Is 32:9
Two **w** will be grinding at the mill; one . . Mt 24:41
"Blessed are you among **w**, and . . . . Lk 1:42
w should keep silent in the churches. . 1 Cor 14:34
likewise also that **w** should adorn. . . . . . . 1 Tm 2:9
Older **w** likewise are to be reverent . . . . Ti 2:3
For this is how the holy **w** who hoped. . . . 1 Pt 3:5

WONDERFUL

Your testimonies are **w**; therefore. . . . . . Ps 119:129
Such knowledge is too **w** for me; . . . . Ps 139:6
W are your works; my soul knows it . . . Ps 139:14
name shall be called **W** Counselor, ... Is 9:6
name, for you have done **w** things,. . . . . Is 25:1
he is **w** in counsel and excellent in . . . . . . Is 28:29
the scribes saw the **w** things that he . . . . Mt 21:15

WONDERS

awesome in glorious deeds, doing **w**? . . . . Ex 15:11
I will remember your **w** of old. . . . . Ps 77:11
despite his **w**, they did not believe. . . . . . Ps 78:32
to him who alone does great **w**, ... Ps 136:4
his signs, how mighty his **w**! . . . . Dn 4:3
"And I will show **w** in the heavens . . . . Jl 2:30
see signs and **w** you will not believe." . . . . Jn 4:48
And I will show **w** in the heavens . . . . . . Acts 2:19
with all power and false signs and **w**, . 2 Thes 2:9
by signs and **w** and various miracles . . . . Heb 2:4

WONDROUS

stop and consider the **w** works of God. . . Jb 37:14
your **w** deeds and your thoughts toward. . Ps 40:5
on your **w** works, I will meditate. . . . . Ps 145:5

WOOD

Shall I fall down before a block of **w**?" . . . Is 44:19
precious stones, **w**, hay, straw— . . . . 1 Cor 3:12

WORD

w of the LORD came to Abram. . . . . Gn 15:1
but man lives by every **w** that comes . . . . . Dt 8:3
the **w** of the LORD was rare. . . . . 1 Sm 3:1
the **w** of the LORD is upright, ... Ps 33:4
you mighty ones who do his **w**, ... Ps 103:20
I have stored up your **w** in my heart, ... Ps 119:11
but a good **w** makes him glad. . . . . Prv 12:25
Every **w** of God proves true; he is. . . . . . . Prv 30:5
so shall my **w** be that goes out from . . . . . Is 55:11
he who executes his **w** is powerful. . . . . Jl 2:11
alone, but by every **w** that comes from. . . Mt 4:4
The sower sows the **w**. . . . . Mk 4:14
In the beginning was the **W**, and the. . . . . . . Jn 1:1
And the **W** became flesh and dwelt. . . . . . . Jn 1:14
if you hold fast to the **w** I preached . . . . 1 Cor 15:2
of the Spirit, which is the **w** of God,. . . . . Eph 6:17
holding fast to the **w** of life, so that. . . . . Phil 2:16
Let the **w** of Christ dwell in you richly,. . . Col 3:16
whatever you do, in **w** or deed, ... Col 3:17
For the **w** of God is living and active, . . . Heb 4:12
the living and abiding **w** of God;. . . . . 1 Pt 1:23
but the **w** of the Lord remains forever.". . 1 Pt 1:25
and the **w** of God abides in you, ... 1 Jn 2:14
who bore witness to the **w** of God . . . . Rv 1:2

WORDS

The **w** of the LORD are pure . . . . Ps 12:6
There is no speech, nor are there **w**, ... Ps 19:3
Let the **w** of my mouth and the . . . . Ps 19:14
LORD is faithful in all his **w** . . . . Ps 145:13
When **w** are many, transgression is not . . Prv 10:19
Gracious **w** are like a honeycomb,. . . . . . Prv 16:24
Whoever restrains his **w** has knowledge,. . Prv 17:27
And I have put my **w** in your mouth. . . . . . Is 51:16
Take with you **w** and return to the . . . . . . Hos 14:2
but my **w** will not pass away.. . . . . Mt 24:35
the disciples were amazed at his **w**. . . . . Mk 10:24
at the gracious **w** that were coming. . . . . . Lk 4:22
we go? You have the **w** of eternal life, ... Jn 6:68
we impart this in **w** not taught by . . . . . 1 Cor 2:13
I would rather speak five **w** with my . . 1 Cor 14:19
the pattern of the sound **w** that you . . . 2 Tm 1:13
Blessed is the one who keeps the **w** . . . . . Rv 22:7
if anyone takes away from the **w** of. . . . . Rv 22:19

WORK

God finished his **w** that he had done, ... Gn 2:2
shall bring us relief from our **w** . . . . Gn 5:29
"Six days you shall do your **w**, but . . . . . . Ex 23:12
height, for the people had a mind to **w**. . Neh 4:6
at your heavens, the **w** of your fingers, ... Ps 8:3
the heavens are the **w** of your hands. . . Ps 102:25
Do not forsake the **w** of your hands. . . . . Ps 138:8
Commit your **w** to the LORD, ... Prv 16:3
Do you see a man skillful in his **w**?. . . . . Prv 22:29
w of the LORD with slackness, ... Jer 48:10
And he could do no mighty **w** there, ... Mk 6:5
"This is the **w** of God, that you believe . . . Jn 6:29
all things **w** together for good, ... Rom 8:28
what sort of **w** each one has done. . . . . 1 Cor 3:13
abounding in the **w** of the Lord, ... 1 Cor 15:58
according to the power at **w** within us,. Eph 3:20
w out your own salvation with fear . . . . . Phil 2:12
Whatever you do, **w** heartily, as for . . . . . Col 3:23
in every good **w** and word. . . . . 2 Thes 2:17
If anyone is not willing to **w**, let him . 2 Thes 3:10
as to overlook your **w** and the love . . . . Heb 6:10

WORKER

What gain has the **w** from his toil?. . . . . . Eccl 3:9
to give to this last **w** as I give to you. . . . Mt 20:14
a **w** who has no need to be ashamed, . . 2 Tm 2:15

WORKERS

For we are God's fellow **w**. . . . . 1 Cor 3:9
that we may be fellow **w** for the truth. . . . . 3 Jn 8

WORKING

"My Father is **w** until now, and I am. . . . . . Jn 5:17
but only faith **w** through love. . . . . Gal 5:6
according to the **w** of his great might . . . Eph 1:19
was given me by the **w** of his power. . . . . . Eph 3:7

WORKMANSHIP

Are not you my **w** in the Lord? . . . . 1 Cor 9:1
For we are his **w**, created in Christ . . . . . . Eph 2:10

WORKS

at the **w** of your hands I sing for joy. . . . . . Ps 92:4
The LORD **w** righteousness . . . . Ps 103:6
and let her **w** praise her in the gates. . . . . Prv 31:31
may see your good **w** and give glory to . . Mt 5:16
may be clearly seen that his **w** have . . . . . Jn 3:21
was full of good **w** and acts of charity. . Acts 9:36
not because of **w** but because of him . . . Rom 9:11
grace, it is no longer on the basis of **w**;. . Rom 11:6
not justified by **w** of the law but. . . . . Gal 2:16
not a result of **w**, so that no one may . . . Eph 2:9
for it is God who **w** in you, both to. . . . . . Phil 2:13
So also good **w** are conspicuous, ... 1 Tm 5:25
not because of our **w** but because . . . . . . 2 Tm 1:9
up one another to love and good **w**, . . Heb 10:24
Show me your faith apart from your **w**,. . Jas 2:18
so also faith apart from **w** is dead. . . . . . . Jas 2:26

WORLD

yes, the **w** is established; . . . . 1 Chr 16:30
for the **w** and its fullness are mine.. . . . . . Ps 50:12
will judge the **w** with righteousness, ... Ps 98:9
gains the whole **w** and forfeits . . . . Mt 16:26
throughout the whole **w** as a testimony . Mt 24:14
God did not send his Son into the **w** to. . . Jn 3:17
this is indeed the Savior of the **w**.". . . . . . . Jn 4:42
I have come into the **w** as light, so. . . . . . Jn 12:46
but because you are not of the **w**, ... Jn 15:19
But take heart; I have overcome the **w**." . Jn 16:33
As you sent me into the **w**, so I have. . . . . Jn 17:18
"My kingdom is not of this **w**. . . . . Jn 18:36
your faith is proclaimed in all the **w**. . . . . Rom 1:8
the whole **w** may be held accountable . . Rom 3:19
w did not know God through wisdom, . . 1 Cor 1:21
no hope and without God in the **w**. . . . . . Eph 2:12
Jesus came into the **w** to save sinners, . . 1 Tm 1:15

Daily Bible Reading Plan

This plan for reading the Bible each day is designed to take you straight through the Bible, cover to cover, in one year. Each day you will read a portion of the biblical text, perhaps three chapters on average. As you follow this reading schedule, then, you encounter the Word of God as it has been given to us.

We encourage you to use this reading plan specifically for the *Gospel Transformation Bible* because this will be the clearest way to get a rich sense of the unfolding plan of redemption that runs right through the Bible from Genesis to Revelation. It would be especially useful to build into your daily reading, along with the biblical text, the study notes of the *Gospel Transformation Bible*. These notes illuminate the gospel passage by passage and also give pointers as to how the gospel in any given text transforms the human heart. This strategy of reading straight through the Bible along with the accompanying notes will expand and deepen your understanding of how the whole Bible fits together and ultimately culminates in Jesus Christ.

This is just one of many good schedules for reading through the Bible. This plan and a number of others are available for free at www.esv.org. What matters supremely, of course, is not which reading plan you use, but that you are nourishing your soul regularly on the Word of God—God's message of grace to his people, mediated through his Spirit, testifying to the person and work of his own dear Son.

January 1	Genesis 1–3
January 2	Genesis 4–7
January 3	Genesis 8–11
January 4	Genesis 12–15
January 5	Genesis 16–18
January 6	Genesis 19–21
January 7	Genesis 22–24
January 8	Genesis 25–26
January 9	Genesis 27–29
January 10	Genesis 30–31
January 11	Genesis 32–34
January 12	Genesis 35–37
January 13	Genesis 38–40
January 14	Genesis 41–42
January 15	Genesis 43–45
January 16	Genesis 46–47
January 17	Genesis 48–50
January 18	Exodus 1–3
January 19	Exodus 4–6
January 20	Exodus 7–9
January 21	Exodus 10–12
January 22	Exodus 13–15
January 23	Exodus 16–18
January 24	Exodus 19–21
January 25	Exodus 22–24
January 26	Exodus 25–27
January 27	Exodus 28–29
January 28	Exodus 30–32
January 29	Exodus 33–35
January 30	Exodus 36–38
January 31	Exodus 39–40
February 1	Leviticus 1–4
February 2	Leviticus 5–7
February 3	Leviticus 8–10
February 4	Leviticus 11–13
February 5	Leviticus 14–15
February 6	Leviticus 16–18
February 7	Leviticus 19–21
February 8	Leviticus 22–23
February 9	Leviticus 24–25
February 10	Leviticus 26–27
February 11	Numbers 1–2
February 12	Numbers 3–4
February 13	Numbers 5–6
February 14	Numbers 7–8
February 15	Numbers 9–10
February 16	Numbers 11–13
February 17	Numbers 14–15
February 18	Numbers 16–17
February 19	Numbers 18–20
February 20	Numbers 21–22
February 21	Numbers 23–25
February 22	Numbers 26–27
February 23	Numbers 28–30
February 24	Numbers 31–32
February 25	Numbers 33–34
February 26	Numbers 35–36
February 27	Deuteronomy 1–2
February 28	Deuteronomy 3–4
March 1	Deuteronomy 5–7
March 2	Deuteronomy 8–10
March 3	Deuteronomy 11–13
March 4	Deuteronomy 14–16
March 5	Deuteronomy 17–20
March 6	Deuteronomy 21–23
March 7	Deuteronomy 24–27
March 8	Deuteronomy 28–29
March 9	Deuteronomy 30–31
March 10	Deuteronomy 32–34
March 11	Joshua 1–4
March 12	Joshua 5–8
March 13	Joshua 9–11
March 14	Joshua 12–15
March 15	Joshua 16–18
March 16	Joshua 19–21
March 17	Joshua 22–24
March 18	Judges 1–2
March 19	Judges 3–5
March 20	Judges 6–7
March 21	Judges 8–9
March 22	Judges 10–12
March 23	Judges 13–15
March 24	Judges 16–18
March 25	Judges 19–21
March 26	Ruth
March 27	1 Samuel 1–3
March 28	1 Samuel 4–8
March 29	1 Samuel 9–12
March 30	1 Samuel 13–14
March 31	1 Samuel 15–17
April 1	1 Samuel 18–20
April 2	1 Samuel 21–24

April 3 .... 1 Samuel 25–27
April 4 .... 1 Samuel 28–31
April 5 .... 2 Samuel 1–3
April 6 .... 2 Samuel 4–7
April 7 .... 2 Samuel 8–11
April 8 .... 2 Samuel 12–15
April 9 .... 2 Samuel 16–18
April 10 .... 2 Samuel 19–21
April 11 .... 2 Samuel 22–24
April 12 .... 1 Kings 1–2
April 13 .... 1 Kings 3–5
April 14 .... 1 Kings 6–7
April 15 .... 1 Kings 8–9
April 16 .... 1 Kings 10–11
April 17 .... 1 Kings 12–14
April 18 .... 1 Kings 15–17
April 19 .... 1 Kings 18–20
April 20 .... 1 Kings 21–22
April 21 .... 2 Kings 1–3
April 22 .... 2 Kings 4–5
April 23 .... 2 Kings 6–8
April 24 .... 2 Kings 9–11
April 25 .... 2 Kings 12–14
April 26 .... 2 Kings 15–17
April 27 .... 2 Kings 18–19
April 28 .... 2 Kings 20–22
April 29 .... 2 Kings 23–25
April 30 .... 1 Chronicles 1–2
May 1 .... 1 Chronicles 3–4
May 2 .... 1 Chronicles 5–6
May 3 .... 1 Chronicles 7–8
May 4 .... 1 Chronicles 9–11
May 5 .... 1 Chronicles 12–14
May 6 .... 1 Chronicles 15–17
May 7 .... 1 Chronicles 18–21
May 8 .... 1 Chronicles 22–24
May 9 .... 1 Chronicles 25–27
May 10 .... 1 Chronicles 28–29
May 11 .... 2 Chronicles 1–4
May 12 .... 2 Chronicles 5–8
May 13 .... 2 Chronicles 9–12
May 14 .... 2 Chronicles 13–16
May 15 .... 2 Chronicles 17–20
May 16 .... 2 Chronicles 21–24
May 17 .... 2 Chronicles 25–27
May 18 .... 2 Chronicles 28–31
May 19 .... 2 Chronicles 32–34
May 20 .... 2 Chronicles 35–36
May 21 .... Ezra 1–3
May 22 .... Ezra 4–7
May 23 .... Ezra 8–10
May 24 .... Nehemiah 1–3
May 25 .... Nehemiah 4–5
May 26 .... Nehemiah 6–7
May 27 .... Nehemiah 8–9
May 28 .... Nehemiah 10–11
May 29 .... Nehemiah 12–13
May 30 .... Esther 1–5
May 31 .... Esther 6–10
June 1 .... Job 1–3
June 2 .... Job 4–7
June 3 .... Job 8–10
June 4 .... Job 11–13
June 5 .... Job 14–16
June 6 .... Job 17–20
June 7 .... Job 21–23
June 8 .... Job 24–28
June 9 .... Job 29–31
June 10 .... Job 32–34
June 11 .... Job 35–37
June 12 .... Job 38–39
June 13 .... Job 40–42
June 14 .... Psalms 1–8
June 15 .... Psalms 9–16
June 16 .... Psalms 17–20
June 17 .... Psalms 21–25
June 18 .... Psalms 26–31
June 19 .... Psalms 32–35
June 20 .... Psalms 36–39
June 21 .... Psalms 40–45
June 22 .... Psalms 46–50
June 23 .... Psalms 51–57
June 24 .... Psalms 58–65
June 25 .... Psalms 66–69
June 26 .... Psalms 70–73
June 27 .... Psalms 74–77
June 28 .... Psalms 78–79
June 29 .... Psalms 80–85
June 30 .... Psalms 86–89
July 1 .... Psalms 90–95
July 2 .... Psalms 96–102
July 3 .... Psalms 103–105

July 4	Psalms 106–107
July 5	Psalms 108–114
July 6	Psalms 115–118
July 7	Psalms 119:1–88
July 8	Psalms 119:89–176
July 9	Psalms 120–132
July 10	Psalms 133–139
July 11	Psalms 140–145
July 12	Psalms 146–150
July 13	Proverbs 1–4
July 14	Proverbs 5–9
July 15	Proverbs 10–11
July 16	Proverbs 12–13
July 17	Proverbs 14–15
July 18	Proverbs 16–18
July 19	Proverbs 19–21
July 20	Proverbs 22–23
July 21	Proverbs 24–26
July 22	Proverbs 27–29
July 23	Proverbs 30–31
July 24	Ecclesiastes 1–4
July 25	Ecclesiastes 5–8
July 26	Ecclesiastes 9–12
July 27	Song of Solomon
July 28	Isaiah 1–4
July 29	Isaiah 5–8
July 30	Isaiah 9–12
July 31	Isaiah 13–17
August 1	Isaiah 18–22
August 2	Isaiah 23–27
August 3	Isaiah 28–30
August 4	Isaiah 31–35
August 5	Isaiah 36–39
August 6	Isaiah 40–43
August 7	Isaiah 44–48
August 8	Isaiah 49–53
August 9	Isaiah 54–58
August 10	Isaiah 59–62
August 11	Isaiah 63–66
August 12	Jeremiah 1–3
August 13	Jeremiah 4–6
August 14	Jeremiah 7–9
August 15	Jeremiah 10–13
August 16	Jeremiah 14–17
August 17	Jeremiah 18–22
August 18	Jeremiah 23–25
August 19	Jeremiah 26–29
August 20	Jeremiah 30–31
August 21	Jeremiah 32–34
August 22	Jeremiah 35–37
August 23	Jeremiah 38–41
August 24	Jeremiah 42–45
August 25	Jeremiah 46–48
August 26	Jeremiah 49–50
August 27	Jeremiah 51–52
August 28	Lamentations 1–2
August 29	Lamentations 3–5
August 30	Ezekiel 1–4
August 31	Ezekiel 5–8
September 1	Ezekiel 9–12
September 2	Ezekiel 13–15
September 3	Ezekiel 16–17
September 4	Ezekiel 18–20
September 5	Ezekiel 21–22
September 6	Ezekiel 23–24
September 7	Ezekiel 25–27
September 8	Ezekiel 28–30
September 9	Ezekiel 31–33
September 10	Ezekiel 34–36
September 11	Ezekiel 37–39
September 12	Ezekiel 40–42
September 13	Ezekiel 43–45
September 14	Ezekiel 46–48
September 15	Daniel 1–3
September 16	Daniel 4–6
September 17	Daniel 7–9
September 18	Daniel 10–12
September 19	Hosea 1–7
September 20	Hosea 8–14
September 21	Joel
September 22	Amos 1–5
September 23	Amos 6–9
September 24	Obadiah–Jonah
September 25	Micah
September 26	Nahum
September 27	Habakkuk
September 28	Zephaniah–Haggai
September 29	Zechariah 1–7
September 30	Zechariah 8–14
October 1	Malachi
October 2	Matthew 1–2
October 3	Matthew 3–4

October 4	Matthew 5–7
October 5	Matthew 8–10
October 6	Matthew 11–12
October 7	Matthew 13–14
October 8	Matthew 15–17
October 9	Matthew 18–19
October 10	Matthew 20–21
October 11	Matthew 22–23
October 12	Matthew 24–25
October 13	Matthew 26
October 14	Matthew 27–28
October 15	Mark 1–3
October 16	Mark 4–5
October 17	Mark 6–7
October 18	Mark 8–9
October 19	Mark 10–11
October 20	Mark 12–13
October 21	Mark 14
October 22	Mark 15–16
October 23	Luke 1
October 24	Luke 2–3
October 25	Luke 4–5
October 26	Luke 6–7
October 27	Luke 8–9
October 28	Luke 10–11
October 29	Luke 12–13
October 30	Luke 14–15
October 31	Luke 16–18
November 1	Luke 19–20
November 2	Luke 21–22
November 3	Luke 23–24
November 4	John 1–2
November 5	John 3–4
November 6	John 5–6
November 7	John 7–8
November 8	John 9–10
November 9	John 11–13
November 10	John 14–16
November 11	John 17–19
November 12	John 20–21
November 13	Acts 1–3
November 14	Acts 4–6
November 15	Acts 7–9
November 16	Acts 10–12
November 17	Acts 13–15
November 18	Acts 16–18
November 19	Acts 19–21
November 20	Acts 22–25
November 21	Acts 26–28
November 22	Romans 1–2
November 23	Romans 3–4
November 24	Romans 5–6
November 25	Romans 7–8
November 26	Romans 9–11
November 27	Romans 12–13
November 28	Romans 14–16
November 29	1 Corinthians 1–4
November 30	1 Corinthians 5–8
December 1	1 Corinthians 9–11
December 2	1 Corinthians 12–14
December 3	1 Corinthians 15–16
December 4	2 Corinthians 1–4
December 5	2 Corinthians 5–9
December 6	2 Corinthians 10–13
December 7	Galatians 1–3
December 8	Galatians 4–6
December 9	Ephesians 1–3
December 10	Ephesians 4–6
December 11	Philippians
December 12	Colossians
December 13	1 Thessalonians
December 14	2 Thessalonians
December 15	1 Timothy
December 16	2 Timothy
December 17	Titus–Philemon
December 18	Hebrews 1–6
December 19	Hebrews 7–10
December 20	Hebrews 11–13
December 21	James
December 22	1 Peter
December 23	2 Peter
December 24	1 John
December 25	2 John–Jude
December 26	Revelation 1–3
December 27	Revelation 4–7
December 28	Revelation 8–12
December 29	Revelation 13–16
December 30	Revelation 17–19
December 31	Revelation 20–22

Colophon

The Crossway *ESV Gospel Transformation Bible* Publishing Team

EDITORIAL TEAM

Lane T. Dennis .... *Executive Editor*
Dane Ortlund .... *Managing Editor*
Bill Deckard .... *Senior Project Editor*

PROOFREADING AND EDITORIAL ASSISTANCE

Timothy Gulsvig .... *Bible Proofreader*
Peachtree Editorial and Proofreading Services
Valerie Martin

INTERIOR DESIGN

Erik Maldre .... *Senior Designer*

COVER DESIGN

Matthew Wahl

TYPESETTING

A.J. Penney .... *Bible Typesetter*
Abigail Heidorn .... *Bible Typesetter*

PRODUCTION

Dallas Richards .... *Bible Production Director*
Brian Martin .... *Bible Production Assistant*
Christine Guthrie .... *Bible Production Coordinator*
Donald Jones .... *Bible Project Manager*

INDEX

Jeremey Houlton

MANAGEMENT LEADERS

Lane T. Dennis .... *President and Publisher*
Geoffrey L. Dennis .... *Chief Operating Officer, Executive Vice President*
Dane Ortlund .... *Vice President for Bible Publishing*
Josh Dennis .... *Senior Vice President, Design*
M. Ebeth Dennis .... *Senior Vice President, Publishing Ministry*
Randall D. Jahns .... *Senior Vice President, Sales, Marketing, and Bible Production*
Paul K. Thomas .... *Senior Vice President, Finance*
Justin Taylor .... *Vice President, Book Publishing*
Daniel J. Kok .... *Senior Vice President, Operations*

ESV GOSPEL TRANSFORMATION BIBLE SPECIFICATIONS AND PRODUCTION

Typefaces .... *Bible text, Lexicon; Study Notes, Gotham*
Text paper .... *Thincoat Plus (36 gsm), delfortgroup, Tervakoski, Finland. Programme for the Endorsement of Forest Certification (PEFC), certificate number 5039 02*
Binding type .... *Smyth sewn*
Printing and binding .... *R. R. Donnelley & Sons*

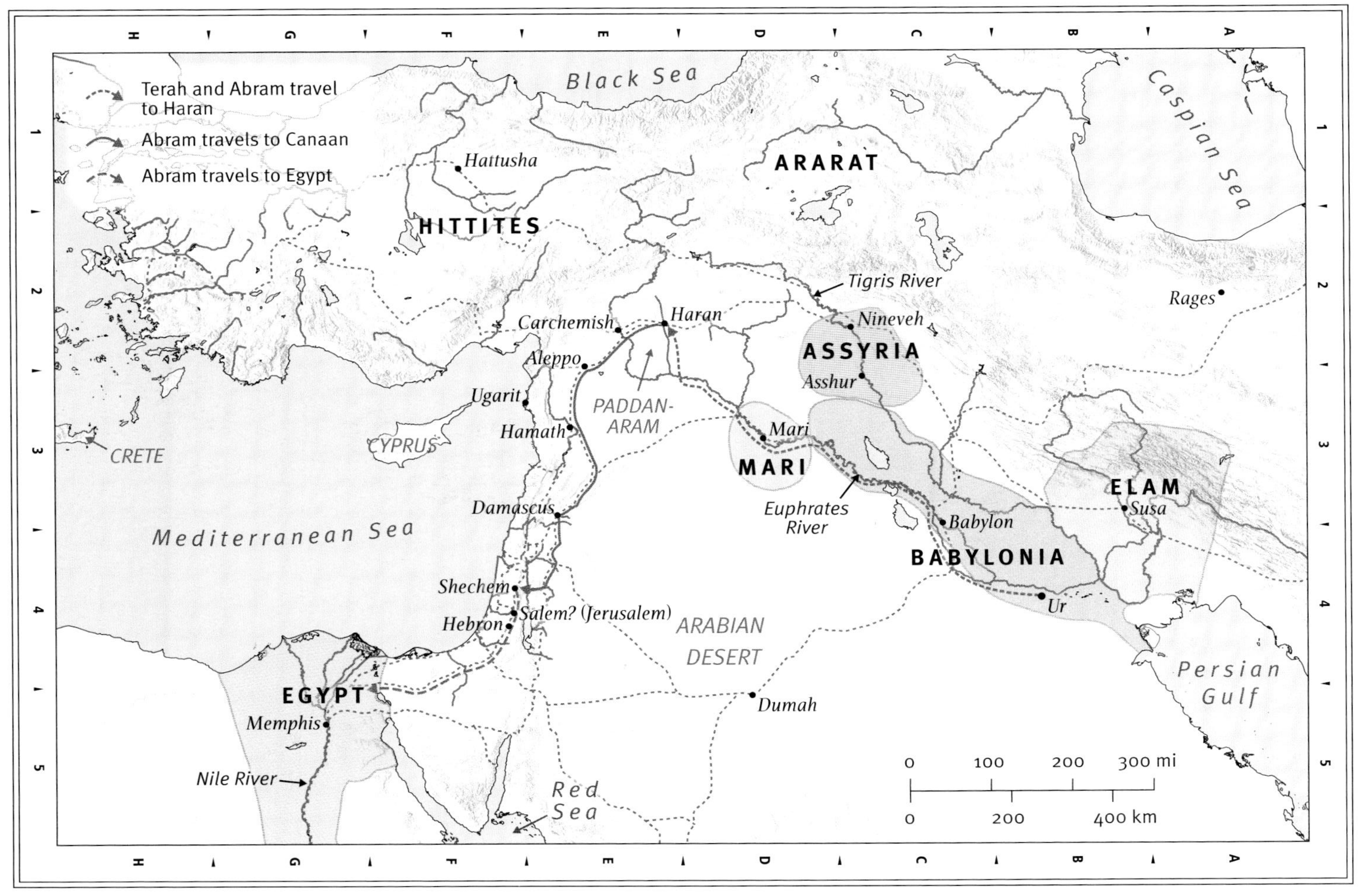
Terah and Abram travel to Haran
Abram travels to Canaan
Abram travels to Egypt
Black Sea
Caspian Sea
Hattusha
ARARAT
HITTITES
Tigris River
Rages
Carchemish
Haran
Nineveh
ASSYRIA
Aleppo
Asshur
Ugarit
PADDAN-ARAM
Hamath
Mari
CYPRUS
CRETE
MARI
ELAM
Damascus
Euphrates River
Susa
Babylon
Mediterranean Sea
BABYLONIA
Shechem
Ur
Salem? (Jerusalem)
Hebron
ARABIAN DESERT
Persian Gulf
EGYPT
Dumah
Memphis
Nile River
Red Sea
0 100 200 300 mi
0 200 400 km

THE EXODUS FROM EGYPT

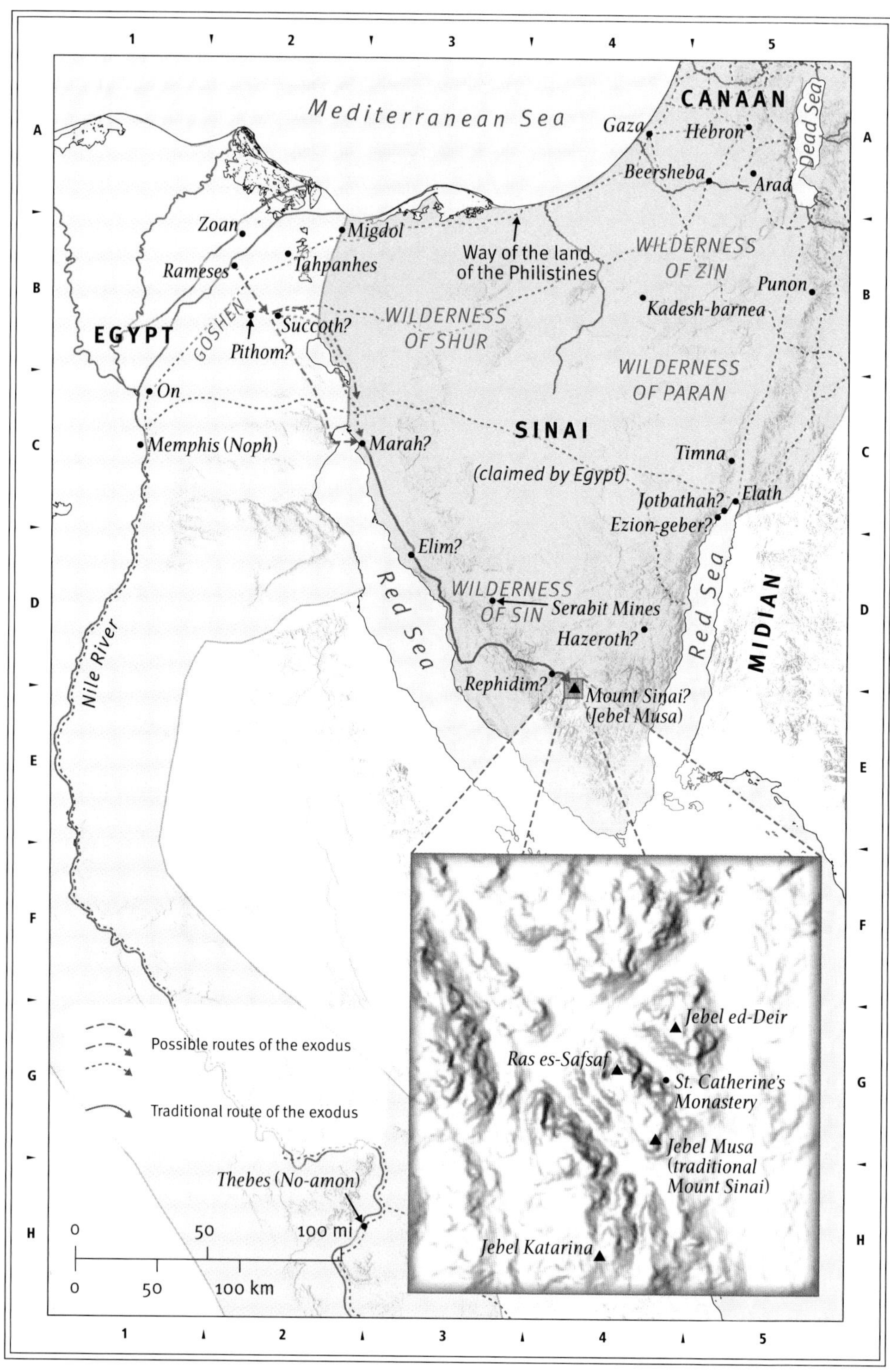

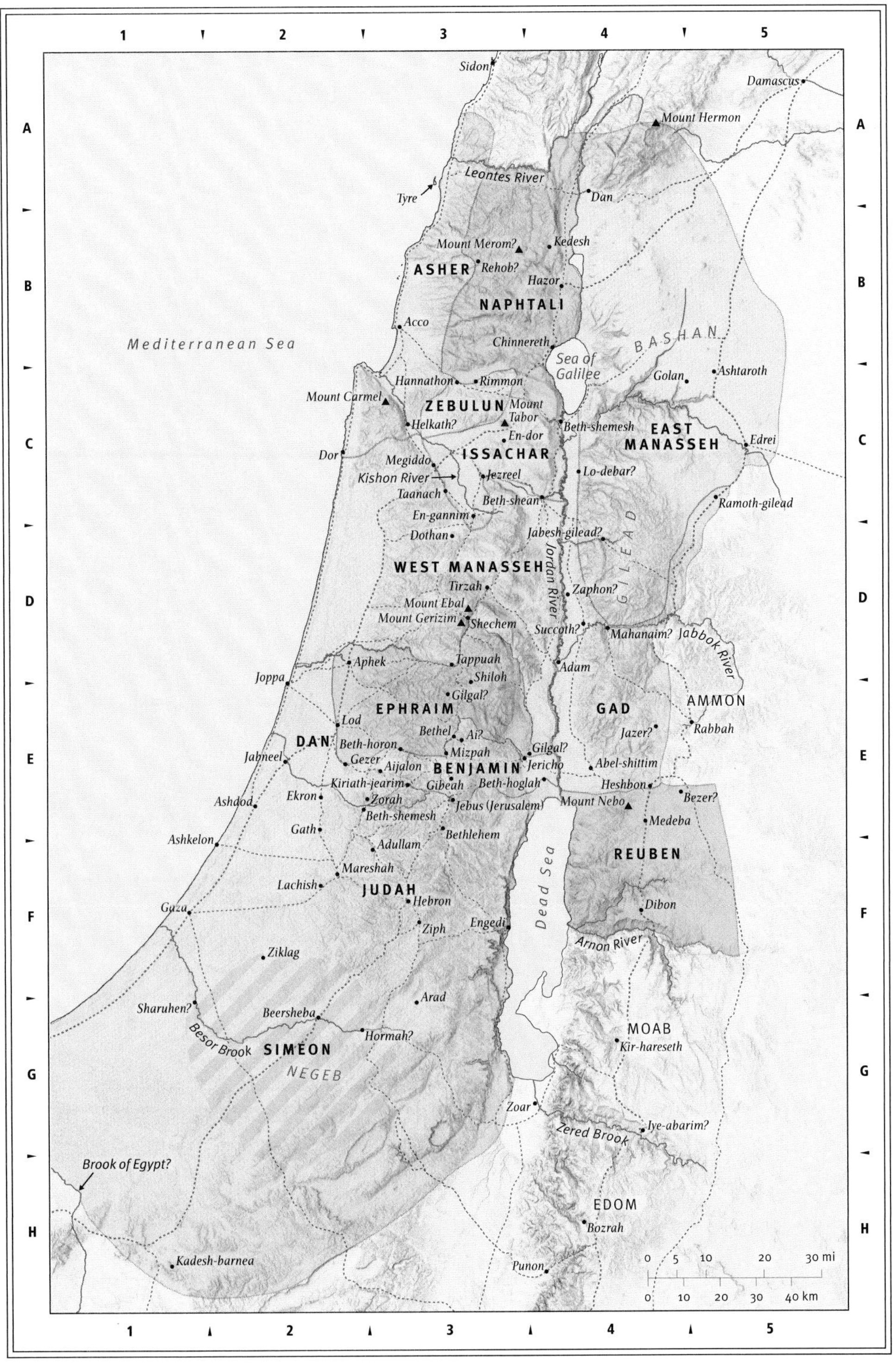
Sidon
Damascus
Mount Hermon
Leontes River
Tyre
Dan
Mount Merom?
Kedesh
ASHER
Rehob?
Hazor
NAPHTALI
Acco
Mediterranean Sea
Chinnereth
Sea of Galilee
BASHAN
Golan
Ashtaroth
Hannathon
Rimmon
Mount Carmel
ZEBULUN
Mount Tabor
Helkath?
En-dor
Beth-shemesh
EAST MANASSEH
Edrei
Dor
ISSACHAR
Megiddo
Kishon River
Jezreel
Lo-debar?
Taanach
Beth-shean
Ramoth-gilead
En-gannim
Dothan
Jabesh-gilead?
GILEAD
WEST MANASSEH
Jordan River
Tirzah
Zaphon?
Mount Ebal
Mount Gerizim
Shechem
Succoth?
Mahanaim?
Jabbok River
Aphek
Tappuah
Adam
Joppa
Shiloh
Gilgal?
AMMON
EPHRAIM
GAD
Lod
Bethel
Ai?
Jazer?
Rabbah
DAN
Beth-horon
Mizpah
Gilgal?
Jabneel
Gezer
Aijalon
BENJAMIN
Jericho
Abel-shittim
Kiriath-jearim
Gibeah
Beth-hoglah
Heshbon
Ashdod
Ekron
Zorah
Jebus (Jerusalem)
Mount Nebo
Bezer?
Beth-shemesh
Medeba
Gath
Ashkelon
Adullam
Bethlehem
Dead Sea
REUBEN
Mareshah
Lachish
JUDAH
Hebron
Gaza
Dibon
Ziph
Engedi
Arnon River
Ziklag
Arad
Sharuhen?
Beersheba
Hormah?
MOAB
Kir-hareseth
Besor Brook
SIMEON
NEGEB
Zoar
Iye-abarim?
Zered Brook
Brook of Egypt?
EDOM
Bozrah
Kadesh-barnea
Punon
0 5 10 20 30 mi
0 10 20 30 40 km
1 2 3 4 5
A B C D E F G H

ISRAEL UNDER SAUL, DAVID, AND SOLOMON

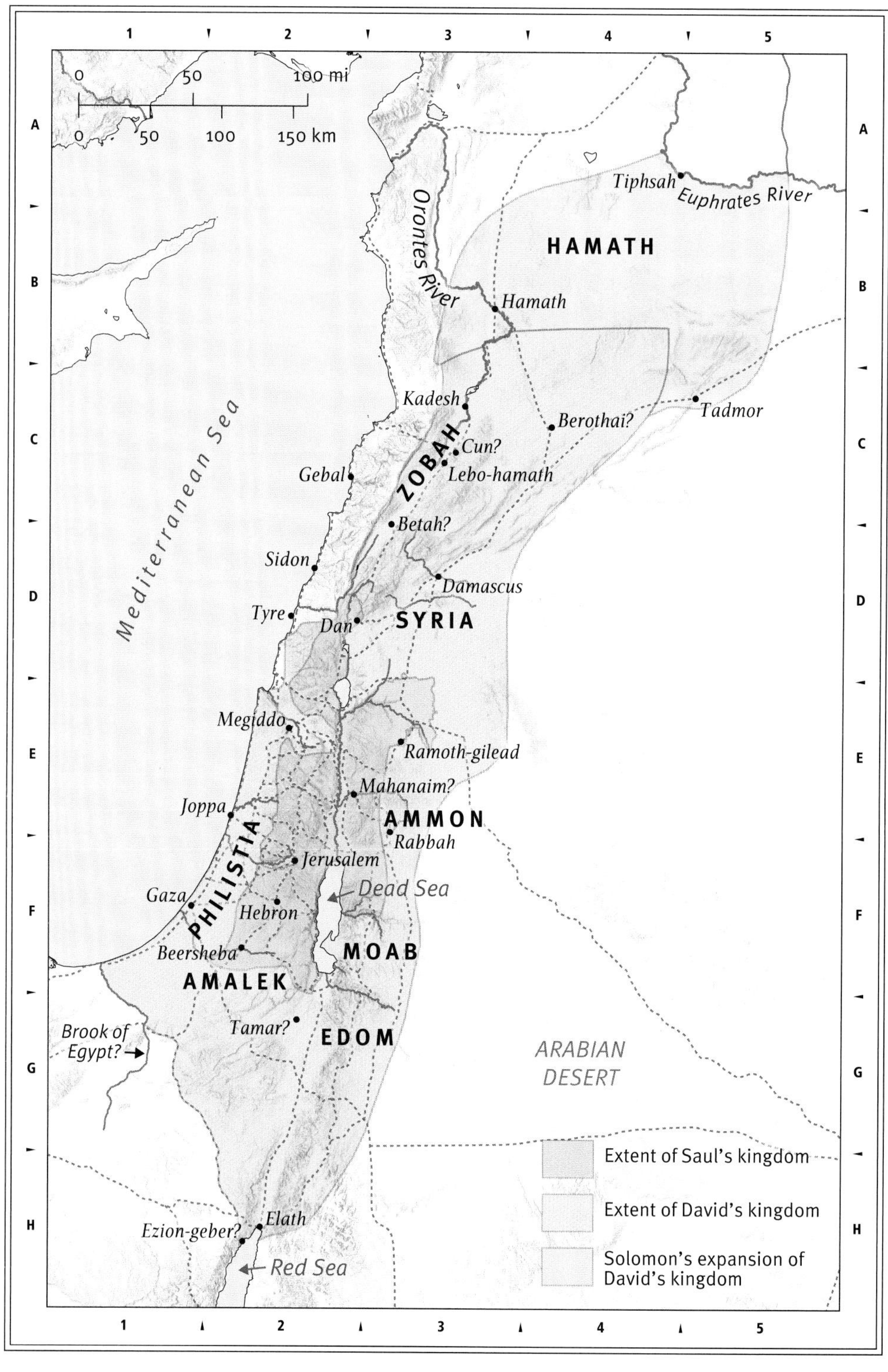

1 The **Gate of the Essenes** allowed the Essenes to access latrines outside the city walls in accordance with their strict laws of hygiene.

2 **Herod's Palace** was the Jerusalem home of Herod the Great from 23 to 4 B.C. Pilate, who normally resided in Caesarea Maritima, resided in this palace during his visits to Jerusalem, including his visit for the Passover preceding Christ's crucifixion.

3 The **Praetorium** was in Herod's Palace (Matt. 27:27; Mark 15:16), which served as Pilate's official headquarters and as a fortress. A raised stone pavement, used for official judgments, stood outside the palace and was the site of Jesus' condemnation under Pilate (John 19:13).

4 Herod the Great fortified three towers to protect his palace: from west to east there was the **Tower**
5 **of Hippicus** (155 feet/47 m tall), the **Tower of**
6 **Phasael** (138 feet/42 m tall), and the **Tower of Mariamne** (95 feet/29 m tall).

7 The two-level **Palatial Mansion** (6,500 sq. feet/604 sq. m) may have been the Palace of Annas, who served as high priest from A.D. 6 to 15. Annas's son-in-law Caiaphas held this office from A.D. 18 to 36 and presided at the trial of Jesus (Matt. 26:57).

8 This is often considered the most likely location of **Golgotha**, the place of Jesus' death. It was on a hill overlooking a quarry, outside the Second Wall of the city and near the Gennath (Garden) Gate.

9 Herod the Great lived in the luxurious **Hasmonean Palace** from the mid-30s to 23 B.C. while awaiting the building of his own new palace. Herod Antipas ("Herod the Tetrarch") lived in this palace during his reign, 4 B.C.–A.D. 39. Jesus appeared before him here in either A.D. 30 or 33.

10 The **Archives** building contained the public registers (including genealogies) as well as bonds taken by money-lenders, which allowed the recovery of debts.

11 The **Xystus**, built on the site of the former Greek Gymnasium, was a place of mass assembly.

12 The **Council House** was a public building, perhaps functioning as a municipal office.

13 **The Temple** was reconstructed by Herod the Great, beginning in 20/19 B.C.

14 The **Bethesda Pools** (see John 5:2) were twin pools, each measuring c. 312 by 164–196 feet (95 by 50–60 m), and c. 50 feet (15 m) deep. A small Roman temple dedicated to Aesculapius stood to the east of the pools.

15 The **Garden of Gethsemane** was located approximately 300 yards (274 m) from Jerusalem and the Temple Mount. The Mount of Olives was "a Sabbath day's journey away" from Jerusalem (Acts 1:12), approximately 1,100 yards, or 3/5 of a mile.

16 The ravine of the **Kidron Valley** has always served as Jerusalem's eastern boundary.

17 The **Pool of Siloam** (cf. John 9:7), a focal point of Jerusalem, adjoined a large dam and reservoir, and received water from the Gihon Spring.

18 The **Hinnom Valley** was to the south of the hill that was the original city of David.

19 The **Upper City** housed luxurious villas of wealthy residents in the Herodian period.

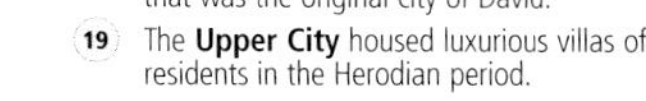

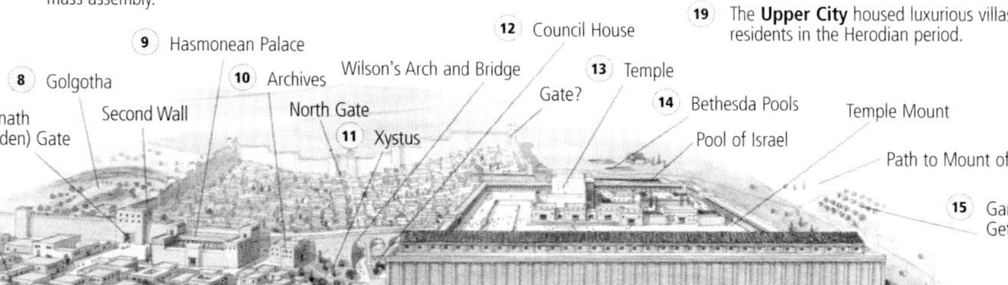

JERUSALEM IN THE TIME OF JESUS

The heavily fortified city of Jerusalem lay atop adjacent hills in the mountainous region of Judea. It therefore proved difficult even for the Romans to recapture during the Jewish revolt, although they eventually did so after a bitter siege in A.D. 70. The oldest portion of Jerusalem, called "the city of David" and "Mount Zion," lay to the south of the temple, but the city walls in the first century also encompassed the newer Upper City to the west of the temple. To the east, across the Kidron Valley (John 18:1), stood the Mount of Olives (Mark 13:3). To the south of Zion lay the Hinnom Valley. The reconstruction above depicts Jerusalem around A.D. 30, and the general direction of the drawing is looking north.

PALESTINE IN THE TIME OF JESUS

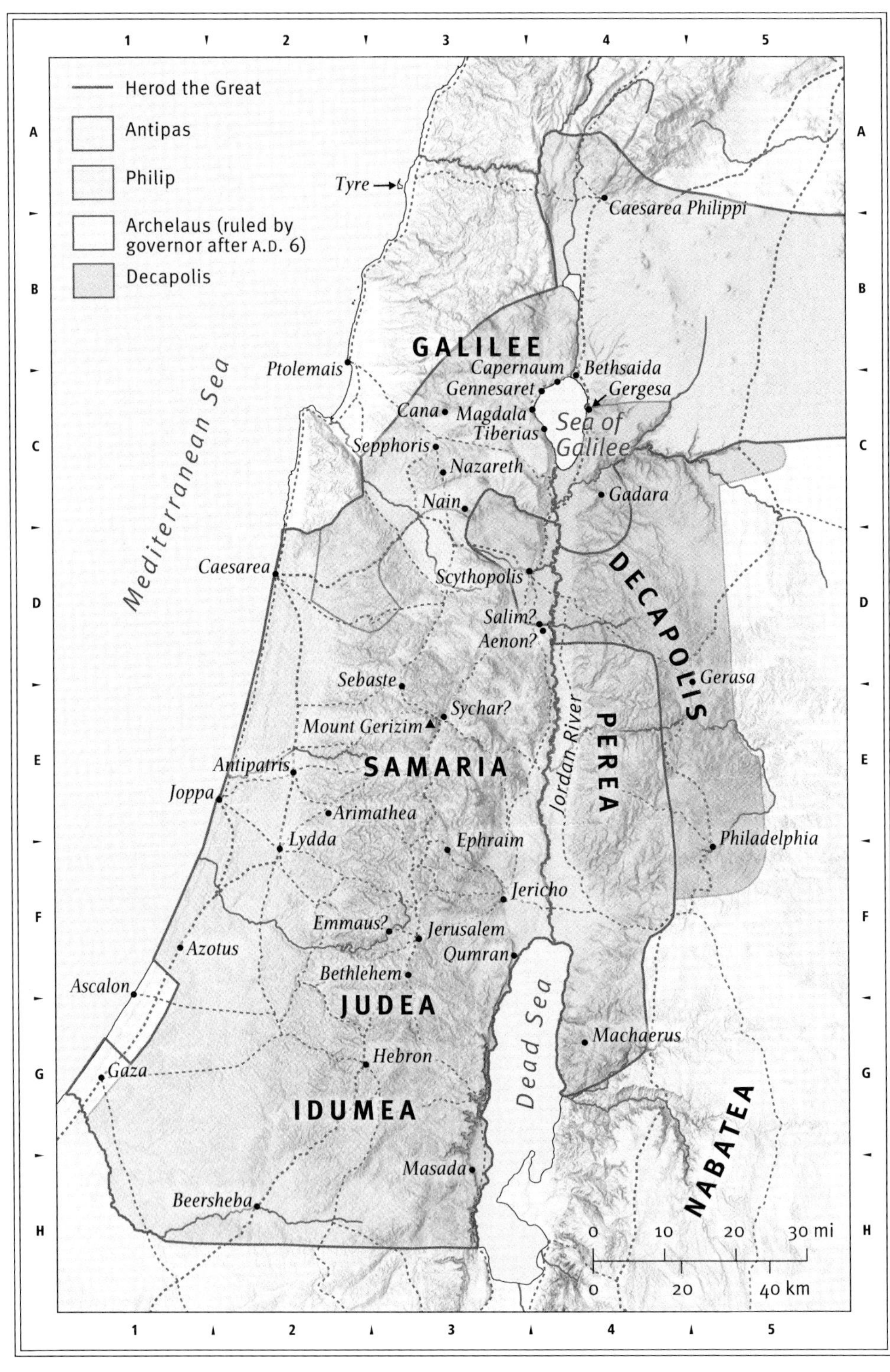

Herod the Great
Antipas
Philip
Archelaus (ruled by governor after A.D. 6)
Decapolis
GALILEE
SAMARIA
JUDEA
IDUMEA
DECAPOLIS
PEREA
NABATEA
Mediterranean Sea
Sea of Galilee
Dead Sea
Jordan River
Tyre
Caesarea Philippi
Ptolemais
Capernaum
Bethsaida
Gennesaret
Gergesa
Cana
Magdala
Tiberias
Sepphoris
Nazareth
Nain
Gadara
Caesarea
Scythopolis
Salim?
Aenon?
Sebaste
Gerasa
Sychar?
Mount Gerizim
Antipatris
Joppa
Arimathea
Lydda
Ephraim
Philadelphia
Jericho
Emmaus?
Jerusalem
Azotus
Qumran
Bethlehem
Ascalon
Machaerus
Hebron
Gaza
Masada
Beersheba
0 10 20 30 mi
0 20 40 km

PAUL'S FIRST AND SECOND MISSIONARY JOURNEYS

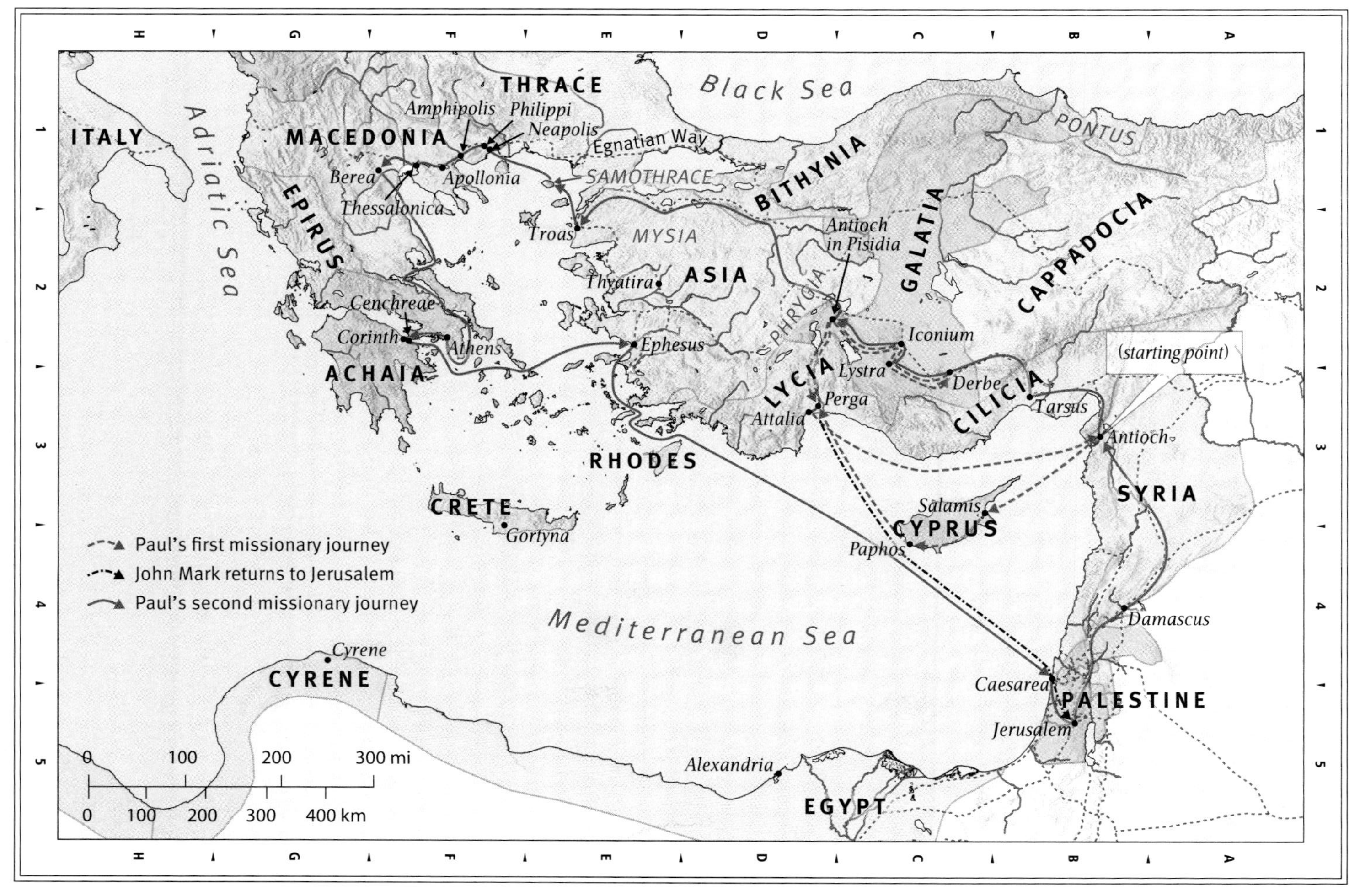

Black Sea
PONTUS
CAPPADOCIA
GALATIA
BITHYNIA
ASIA
MYSIA
PHRYGIA
LYCIA
CILICIA
SYRIA
PALESTINE
CYPRUS
RHODES
CRETE
THRACE
MACEDONIA
EPIRUS
ACHAIA
ITALY
EGYPT
CYRENE
SAMOTHRACE
Egnatian Way
Adriatic Sea
Mediterranean Sea
(starting point)
Antioch
Tarsus
Derbe
Iconium
Lystra
Antioch in Pisidia
Perga
Attalia
Salamis
Paphos
Damascus
Caesarea
Jerusalem
Alexandria
Cyrene
Gortyna
Ephesus
Thyatira
Troas
Neapolis
Philippi
Amphipolis
Apollonia
Thessalonica
Berea
Athens
Cenchreae
Corinth
Paul's first missionary journey
John Mark returns to Jerusalem
Paul's second missionary journey
0 100 200 300 mi
0 100 200 300 400 km
A B C D E F G H
1 2 3 4 5

PAUL'S THIRD MISSIONARY JOURNEY AND HIS VOYAGE TO ROME

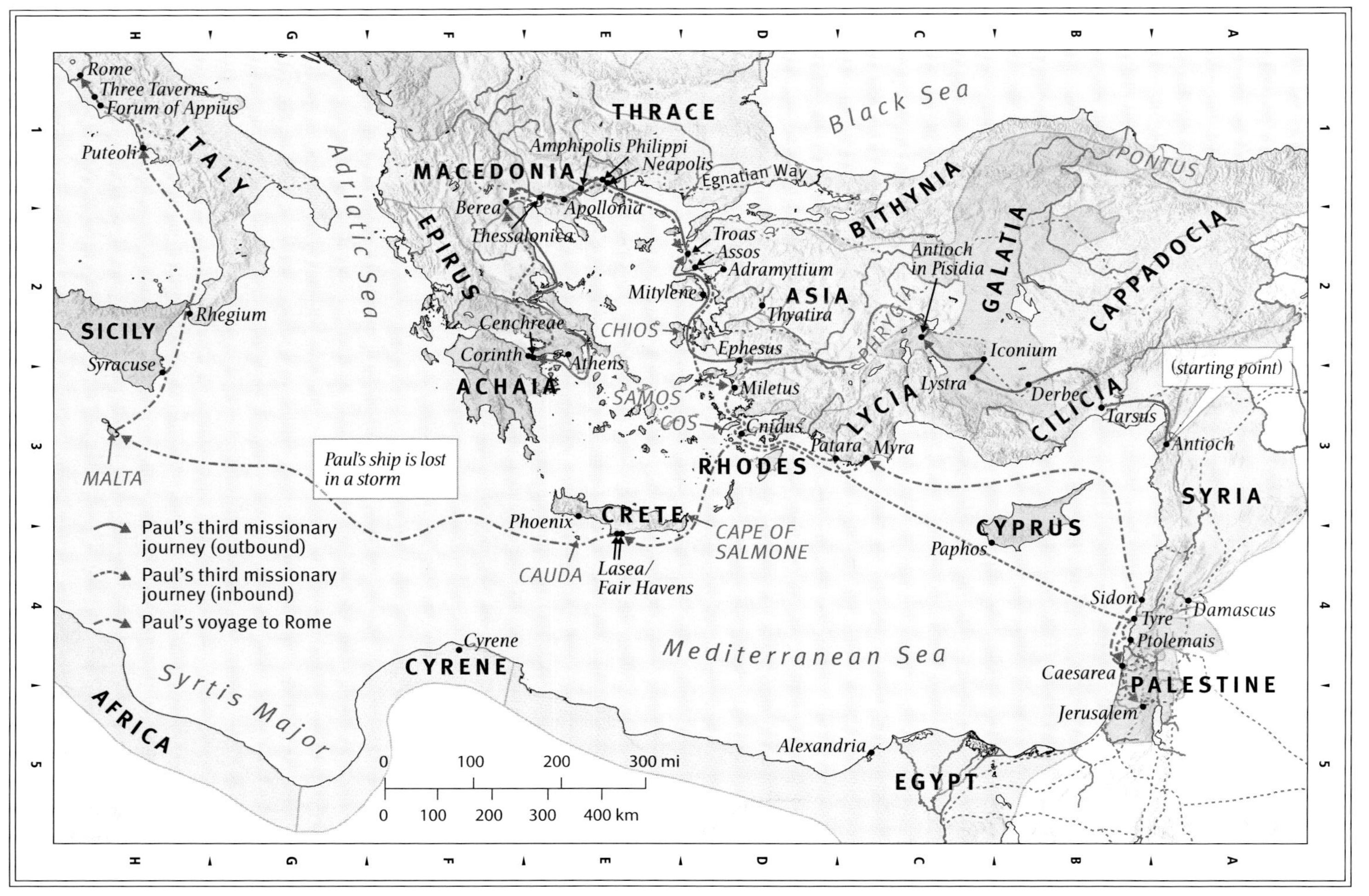